LAROUSSE

CONCISE
DICTIONARY
PORTUGUESE
ENGLISH

ENGLISH
PORTUGUESE

LAROUSSE

CONTENTS
ÍNDICE

© Larousse/VUEF, 2003

Larousse/VUEF, Paris
www.larousse-bilingues.com

ISBN 85-08-080503-6
Sales/Distribuição: Editora Ática
ISBN 203-542001-6
Sales/Distribuição: Houghton Mifflin Company, Boston.

LAROUSSE

DICIONÁRIO AVANÇADO

PORTUGUÊS INGLÊS

INGLÊS PORTUGUÊS

LAROUSSE

Project Management
Direção da obra

Luzia Araújo   Valerie Grundy

Editors
Redação

Alison Aiken	Maria Inês Alves
Laura Bocco	Shirley Brotherton-Pinniger
Salete Cechin	Karoll Ferreira
José A. Gálvez	Daniel Grassi
Mike Harland	Bill Martin
Viviane Possamai	Julia Rice
Christine Robinson	Sergio Tellaroli

Publishing Manager
Direção Geral

Janice McNeillie

Prepress
Diagramação

David Reid   Sharon McTeir

PREFACE

This CONCISE dictionary is a reliable and user-friendly tool for use in all language situations. It provides accurate and up-to-date information on written and spoken Portuguese and English as they are used today.

Its 90,000 words and phrases and 120,000 translations give you access to Portuguese texts of all types. The dictionary aims to be as comprehensive as possible in a book of this size, and includes many proper names and abbreviations, as well as a selection of the most common terms from computing, business and currents affairs.

Carefully construced entries and a clear page design help you to find the translation that you are looking for fast. Examples (from basic constructions and common phrases to idioms) have been included to help put a word in context and give a clear picture of how it is used.

The dictionary provides extra help for students of Portuguese with the inclusion of boxes on life and culture in Brazil that appear within the dictionary text itself, and a central section which gives fuller background details on political and cultural life in Brazil, as well as a useful communication guide.

A NOSSOS LEITORES

Este Dicionário AVANÇADO é a ferramenta de consulta ideal para toda uma gama de situações que vão da aprendizagem de uma língua estrangeira, em casa ou na escola, até as necessidades cotidianas no trabalho.

O Dicionário AVANÇADO Inglês-Português foi desenvolvido para responder com rapidez e eficiência às dificuldades com que nos defrontamos na leitura do inglês contemporâneo, bem como na redação de trabalhos escolares, cartas e relatórios.

Com suas mais de 90 mil palavras e expressões – e um número de traduções superior a 120 mil –, este dicionário permitirá ao leitor compreender com clareza toda uma variedade de textos, desde obras literárias e artigos jornalísticos até documentos comerciais, folhetos e manuais, possibilitando a realização de resumos e traduções com eficácia e apuro.

A atualidade das siglas e abreviações, bem como dos termos comerciais e de informática aqui incluídos, é outro fator a atestar a abrangência e contemporaneidade deste dicionário.

Valendo-se do tratamento claro e detalhado dado aqui ao vocabulário básico, dos muitos exemplos de construções gramaticais e de uso mais atualizado da língua, bem como dos indicadores de contexto a conduzir à tradução mais adequada, o usuário deste Dicionário AVANÇADO poderá expressar-se em inglês com precisão e segurança.

Especial atenção foi dedicada também à apresentação de cada entrada, tanto do ponto de vista de sua estrutura quanto da tipologia empregada, visando a facilitar a consulta e o entendimento.

Aliando precisão e praticidade, profundidade de conteúdo e facilidade de consulta, o Dicionário AVANÇADO é a obra ideal para todos aqueles que já superaram os níveis iniciais de aprendizagem da língua inglesa, demandando para o seu cotidiano – na escola, em casa ou no trabalho – um dicionário prático, mas abrangente.

ABREVIATURAS		ABBREVIATIONS
abreviatura	*abrev/abbr*	abbreviation
adjetivo	*adj*	adjective
advérbio	*adv*	adverb
antes de substantivo	*antes de subst*	before noun
artigo	*art*	article
auxiliar	*aux*	auxiliary
comparativo	*compar*	comparative
conjunção	*conj*	conjuction
contínuo	*cont*	continuous
definido	*def*	definite
demonstrativo	*dem/demos*	demonstrative
especialmente	*esp*	especially
interjeição	*excl*	exclamation
substantivo feminino	*f*	feminine noun
familiar	*fam*	informal
figurado	*fig*	figurative
formal	*fml*	formal
inseparável	*fus*	inseparable
geralmente	*ger/gen*	generally
humorístico	*hum*	humorous
indefinido	*indef*	indefinite
familiar	*inf*	informal
interjeição	*interj*	exclamation
invariável	*inv*	invariable
irônico	*irôn/iro*	ironic
literal	*lit*	literal
locução	*loc*	phrase
substantivo masculino	*m*	masculine noun
substantivo	*n*	noun
numeral	*num*	numeral
	o.s.	oneself
pejorativo	*pej*	pejorative
pessoal	*pess/pers*	personal
plural	*pl*	plural
possessivo	*poss*	possessive
particípio passado	*pp*	past participle
preposição	*prep*	preposition
pronome	*pron*	pronoun
passado	*pt*	past tense
marca registrada	®	registered trademark
relativo	*relat*	relative
substantivo	*s*	noun
	sb	someone, somebody
separável	*sep*	separable
singular	*sg*	singular
gíria	*sl*	slang
	sthg	something
sujeito	*suj/subj*	subject
superlativo	*superl*	superlative
substantivo incontável	*U*	uncountable noun

ABREVIATURAS

inglês britânico	*UK*
inglês americano	*US*
verbo	*v/vb*
verbo intransitivo	*vi*
verbo impessoal	*v impess/impers*
verbo pronominal	*vpr*
verbo transitivo	*vt*
vulgar	*vulg*
equivalente cultural	≃

ABBREVIATIONS

| British English |
| American English |
| verb |
| intransitive verb |
| impersonal verb |
| pronominal verb |
| transitive verb |
| vulgar |
| cultural equivalent |

CAMPOS SEMÂNTICOS

	FIELD LABELS	
administração	**ADMIN**	administration
aeronáutica	**AERON**	aeronautics
agricultura	**AGR**	agriculture
anatomia	**ANAT**	anatomy
arqueologia	**ARCHEOL**	archeology
arquitetura	**ARQUIT/ARCHIT**	architecture
astrologia	**ASTROL**	astrology
astronomia	**ASTRON**	astronomy
automóveis	**AUT(O)**	automobiles, cars
biologia	**BIOL**	biology
botânica	**BOT**	botany
química	**CHEM**	chemistry
ciências	**CIÊN/SCIENCE**	science
cinema	**CINE(MA)**	cinema
comércio	**COM(M)**	commerce
informática	**COMPUT**	information technology
construção	**CONSTR**	construction, building
costura	**COST**	sewing
culinária	**CULIN**	culinary, cooking
ecologia	**ECOLOG**	ecology
economia	**ECON**	economy
educação, escola	**EDUC**	education, school
eletricidade, eletrônica	**ELETR/ELEC**	electricity, electronics
esporte	**ESP**	sport
farmacologia	**FARM**	pharmacology
finanças	**FIN**	finance
física	**FÍS**	physics
fotografia	**FOTO**	photography
geografia	**GEOGR**	geography
geologia	**GEOL**	geology
geometria	**GEOM**	geometry
gramática	**GRAM(M)**	grammar
história	**HIST**	history
indústria	**IND**	industry
jornalismo	**JORN**	journalism
jurídico	**JUR**	juridical, legal
lingüística	**LING**	linguistics
literatura	**LITER**	literature
matemática	**MAT(H)**	mathematics
mecânica	**MEC**	mechanical engineering
medicina	**MED**	medicine
metalurgia	**METAL**	metallurgy
meteorologia	**METEOR**	meteorology
militar	**MIL**	military
mineralogia	**MIN**	mineralogy
mitologia	**MITOL/MYTH**	mythology
música	**MÚS/MUS**	music
náutica	**NAUT**	nautical
farmacologia	**PHARM**	pharmacology
fotografia	**PHOT**	photography
física	**PHYS**	physics
política	**POL(ÍT)**	politics
psicologia	**PSICOL/PSYCH**	psychology
química	**QUÍM**	chemistry
ferrovia	**RAIL**	railways
religião	**RELIG**	religion
escola	**SCH**	school
sociologia	**SOCIOL**	sociology

CAMPOS SEMÂNTICOS		FIELD LABELS
bolsa de valores	**ST EX**	stock exchange
teatro	**TEATR/THEAT**	theatre
técnico, tecnologia	**TEC/TECH**	technical, technology
telecomunicações	**TELEC**	telecommunications
tipografia	**TIP/TYP**	printing, typography
televisão	**TV**	television
universidade	**UNIV**	university
veterinária	**VETER**	veterinary science
zoologia	**ZOOL**	zoology

FONÉTICA

Vogais portuguesas
[a] pá cada
[ɛ] sé, seta, hera
[e] ler mês
[i] ir, sino, nave
[ɔ] nota, pó
[o] corvo, avô
[u] azul, tribo

Ditongos portugueses
[aj] faixa, mais
[ej] leite, rei
[ɛj] hotéis, pastéis
[ɔj] herói, bóia
[oj] coisa, noite
[uj] azuis, fui
[aw] nau, jaula
[ɛw] céu, véu
[ew] deus, seu
[iw] riu, viu

Vogais nasais
[ã] maçã, santo
[ẽ] lençol, sempre
[ĩ] fim, patim
[õ] onde, com, honra
[ũ] jejum, nunca

Ditongos nasais
[ãj] cãibra, mãe
[ãw] camarão, cão
[ẽj] bem, quem
[õj] cordões, leões

Semivogais portuguesas
[j] eleito, maio
[w] luar, quadro

Consoantes
[b] beijo, abrir
[d] dama, prenda

PHONETICS

English vowels
[ɪ] pit, big, rid
[e] pet, tend
[æ] pat, bag, mad
[ʌ] run, cut
[ɒ] pot, log
[ʊ] put, full
[ə] mother, suppose
[iː] bean, weed
[aː] barn, car
[ɔː] born, lawn
[uː] loop, loose
[ɜː] burn, learn, bird

English dipthongs
[eɪ] bay, late, great
[aɪ] buy, light, aisle
[ɔɪ] boy, foil
[əʊ] no, road, blow
[aʊ] now, shout, town
[ɪə] peer, fierce, idea
[eə] pair, bear, share
[ʊə] sure, tour

English semi-vowels
[j] you, spaniel
[w] wet, why, twin

English consonants
[p] pop, people
[b] bottle, bib

[dʒ]	dia, bonde	[t]	train, tip
[f]	faca, afinal	[d]	dog, did
[g]	grande, agora	[k]	come, kitchen
[ʒ]	gelo, cisne, anjo	[g]	gag, great
[l]	lata, feliz, cola	[tʃ]	chain, wretched
[ʎ]	malha, telha	[dʒ]	jet, fridge
[m]	mesa, cama	[f]	fib, physical
[n]	nada, banana	[v]	vine, live
[ɲ]	linha, sonho	[θ]	think, fifth
[ŋ]	anca, inglês	[ð]	this, with
[p]	pão, gripe	[s]	seal, peace
[s]	cima, desse, caça	[z]	zip, his
[ʃ]	noz, bis, caixa, chá	[ʃ]	sheep, machine
[t]	tema, lata, porta	[ʒ]	usual, measure
[tʃ]	tio, infantil	[h]	how, perhaps
[v]	vela, ave	[m]	metal, comb
[x]	rádio, terra	[n]	night, dinner
[z]	zelo, brisa	[ŋ]	sung, parking
		[l]	little, help
		[r]	right, carry

O símbolo fonético [(x)] em português indica que o 'r' final da palavra é apenas levemente pronunciado, exceto quando seguido de uma vogal: nesse caso, pronuncia-se [r].

O símbolo ['] indica que a sílaba subseqüente é a tônica, sobre a qual recai o acento principal; [ˌ] indica que a sílaba subseqüente é a subtônica, sobre a qual recai o acento secundário.

As regras de pronúncia aplicadas ao português refletem a língua falada no Rio de Janeiro.

The symbol [(x)] in Portuguese phonetics indicates that final 'r' is often barely sounded unless it is followed by a word beginning with a vowel, in which case it is pronounced [r].

The symbol ['] indicates that the following syllable carries primary stress and [ˌ] that the following syllable carries secondary stress.

Portuguese phonetics reflect the language as spoken in Rio de Janeiro.

COMO UTILIZAR ESTE DICIONÁRIO

Como encontrar a palavra ou expressão que procuramos?

A primeira coisa a fazer é perguntar:

Trata-se de uma palavra ou de uma abreviatura?
Seria um substantivo composto?
Uma expressão ou locução?
Trata-se de um verbo pronominal ou *phrasal verb*?

Palavras e abreviaturas

Em geral, encontraremos a palavra que procuramos no lugar que lhe corresponde na ordem alfabética. Se desejamos a tradução para o português de uma palavra inglesa, consultamos a parte inglês-português do dicionário; se desconhecemos o sentido de uma palavra do português, procuraremos por sua tradução na parte português-inglês. A palavra em **negrito**, que aparece no início de cada verbete do dicionário, chama-se "entrada".

Se duas palavras são escritas de forma idêntica, mas uma delas começa com **maiúscula**, a palavra em maiúscula aparecerá depois daquela que começa com letra minúscula.

ad (*abbr of* **advertisement**) *n fam* **-1.** [in newspaper] anúncio *m*. **- 2.** [on TV] propaganda *f.*
AD (*abbr of* **Anno Domini**) d.C.

Palavras contendo **hífen**, **apóstrofe** ou **ponto** aparecem depois daquelas de mesma grafia, mas que não apresentam esses sinais gráficos.

its [ɪts] *poss adj* o seu (a sua), dele (dela).
it's [ɪts] = **it is**, **it has**.

Da mesma forma, uma palavra com **acento** figurará depois de outra de mesma grafia, mas sem acento.

do [du] = **de + o**.
dó [ˈdɔ] *m* **-1.** [piedade] pity; **ter ~ de alguém** to take pity on sb. **- 2.** *MÚS* doh.

Em alguns casos, as entradas são seguidas de um pequeno **número sobrescrito**. Isso quer dizer que, imediatamente antes ou após, haverá outra entrada idêntica, também seguida de um número, mas com significado ou pronúncia diferente. São os chamados homógrafos. Atenção: certifique-se de não estar consultando a entrada errada! É necessário prestar muita atenção à categoria gramatical.

bow¹ [baʊ] ◇ *n* **-1.** [act of bowing] reverência *f* **- 2.** [of ship] proa *f.* ◇ *vt* [lower] inclinar. ◇ *vi* **-1.** [make a bow] inclinar-se **- 2.** [defer]: **to ~ to sthg** submeter-se a algo.
➠ **bow down** *vi* [give in]: **to ~ down (to sb)** render-se(a alguém).
➠ **bow out** *vi* afastar-se.
bow² [bəʊ] *n* **-1.** [gen & *MUS*] arco *m* **- 2.** [knot] laço *m*.

Às vezes, vamos encontrar palavras precedidas de um losango negro (➠), chamadas "sub-entradas". Um exemplo disso são os verbos pronominais do português ou os *phrasal verbs* ingleses. Além disso, se buscamos uma palavra que possui duas formas, maiúscula e minúscula, com significados diferentes, nós encontraremos a forma em maiúscula como sub-entrada daquela em minúscula, precedida de um losango negro.

beneficiar [16] [benefiˈsja(x)] *vt* **-1.** [favorecer] to benefit. **- 2.** [processar] to process. **- 3.** [melhorar] to improve.
➠ **beneficiar-se** *vp* [favorecer-se] to profit.

ascension [əˈsenʃn] *n* [to throne] ascensão *f.*
➠ **Ascension** *n RELIG* Ascensão *f.*

Da mesma forma, se procuramos um substantivo cuja forma plural possui um significado distinto do singular (como **glass/glasses** em inglês; ou **bem/bens**, em português), encontraremos a palavra no plural como sub-entrada da forma singular, precedida do símbolo (➡).

> **glass** [glɑːs] ◇ n **-1.** (U) [material] vidro m **-2.** [for drinking] copo m **-3.** (U) [glassware] objetos mpl de cristal. ◇ comp de vidro.
> ➡ **glasses** npl [spectacles] óculos m inv; [binoculars] binóculos mpl.

Alguns substantivos aparecem como entradas já no plural, seja porque não existem no singular ou porque a forma singular é pouco freqüente. É o caso, por exemplo, de **scissors**, em inglês, ou **juros**, em português.

Substantivos compostos

O substantivo composto é uma expressão que, como tal, possui um significado próprio, mas que se compõe de mais de uma palavra (**virtual reality**, por exemplo, ou **café com leite**). Os substantivos compostos poderão ser encontrados na entrada correspondente a seu primeiro elemento. Assim sendo, **café com leite** aparecerá em **café**. Os demais compostos com o substantivo **café** como primeiro elemento - **café expresso**, **café pingado** - figuram em ordem alfabética.

> **café** [ka'fɛ] m **-1.** [ger] coffee; ~ **(preto)** black coffee; ~ **com leite** white coffee UK, coffee with cream US; ~ **expresso** espresso; ~ **pingado** coffee with a tiny drop of milk; **ser** ~ **pequeno** fam [tarefa] to be small beer; [pessoa] to be small fry. **-2.** [desjejum]: ~ **(da manhã)** breakfast. **-3.** [estabelecimento] café.

No caso dos substantivos compostos do inglês, é característica deste dicionário listá-los como entradas, em ordem alfabética. Assim, **blood donor** aparecerá depois de **blood-curdling**, que, por sua vez, sucede a **blood count**.

> **blood count** n contagem f de glóbulos sangüíneos.
> **blood-curdling** adj de gelar o sangue.
> **blood donor** n doador m, -ra f de sangue.

Se o composto, seja em inglês ou português, se tornou uma unidade autônoma - isto é, se seu significado conjunto já se destacou da soma de seus elementos -, ele é tratado à parte, sendo precedido de um losango negro.

Expressões e locuções

Expressões e locuções devem ser localizadas a partir do primeiro substantivo que as forma. Se a expressão não possui um substantivo, deve-se procurá-la pelo adjetivo ou, na ausência deste, pelo verbo. No interior de cada verbete, as expressões aparecem em **negrito**, com o símbolo ~ representando a entrada correspondente.

Algumas expressões de significado e valor gramatical próprio (as chamadas locuções), como **in spite of** (inglês) ou **atrás de** (português), figuram vinculadas a seu primeiro elemento importante, precedidas do símbolo (➡).

Isso possibilita destacar a diferença de sentido e função gramatical entre a locução em si e a entrada à qual ela está vinculada.

> **time** [taɪm] ◇ n **-1.** (U) [general measurement, spell] tempo m; **to get the** ~ **to do sthg** ter tempo para fazer algo; **to take** ~ levar tempo; **to take** ~ **out to do sthg** tirar tempo para fazer algo; **it's high** ~ ... já é hora de ...; **to get** ~ **and a half** receber o pagamento combinado mais a metade; **to have no** ~ **for sb/sthg** não ter tempo a perder com alguém/algo; **to make good** ~ fazer uma boa média (de tempo); **to pass the** ~ passar o tempo; **to play for** ~ tentar ganhar tempo; **to take one's** ~ **(doing sthg)** dar-se seu tempo(para fazer algo)...

> **spite** [spaɪt] ◇ n (U) rancor m; **to do sthg out of** OR **from** ~ fazer algo por maldade. ◇ vt magoar.
> ➡ **in spite of** prep apesar de; **to do sthg in** ~ **of o.s.** [unintentionally] fazer algo a contragosto.

> **atrás** [a'trajʃ] adv **-1.** [posição] behind; **lá** ~ back there. **-2.** [no tempo] ago. **-3.** [em classificação]: **estar/ficar** ~ **(de)** to be ranked behind; **não ficar** ~ fam fig not to be far behind.
> ➡ **atrás de** loc prep **-1.** [posição] behind. **-2.** [em seguimento a] after; **logo** ~ **de** right behind. **-3.** [em busca de - pessoa] after; [- objeto, explicação] looking for.

Verbos pronominais e *phrasal verbs*

A maioria dos verbos pronominais e *phrasal verbs* apresenta-se na entrada correspondente ao verbo em questão, precedida do símbolo (✦).

---

aclarar [4] [akla'ra(x)] *vt* [questão, mistério] to clarify.
✦ **aclarar-se** *vp* to become clear.

Informações culturais

Para entender e falar melhor uma língua estrangeira, é necessário algum conhecimento acerca das especificidades culturais do(s) país(es) onde ela é falada. Contudo, uma entrada de dicionário não é o local apropriado para esse tipo de informação. Assim sendo, na parte inglês-português deste dicionário, o leitor de língua portuguesa encontrará **boxes** informativos dedicados a particularidades culturais dos países de língua inglesa.

GUY FAWKES NIGHT

Festividade britânica celebrada na noite de 5 de novembro, em comemoração ao complô católico encabeçado por Guy Fawkes, em 1605, que tinha por objetivo explodir as casas do Parlamento. Nessa noite, os britânicos acendem fogueiras, nas quais queimam uma efígie de Guy Fawkes, e soltam fogos de artifício, razão pela qual a noite é também conhecida como *Fireworks Night* ou *Bonfire Night*.

O box **Guy Fawkes' Night**, por exemplo, nos informa sobre uma peculiaridade histórico-cultural britânica para a qual não há equivalente no Brasil.

HOW TO USE THE DICTIONARY

How to find the word or expression you are looking for:

First ask yourself some basic questions:

Is it a single word, a hyphenated word or an abbreviation?
Is it a compound noun?
Is it a phrase?
Is it a reflexive verb?

Single words, hyphenated words and abbreviations

As a rule, you can find the word you are looking for in its alphabetical order. If you want to translate an English word into Portuguese, you should look on the English–Portuguese side of the dictionary, and if you want to know what a Portuguese term means, you should look on the Portuguese–English side. The word in **bold** at the start of each entry is called the 'headword'.

Entries beginning with a **capital** appear after those spelled the same way but with a small letter.

> **ad** (*abbr of* **advertisement**) *n fam* **-1.** [in newspaper] anúncio *m.* **-2.** [onTV] propaganda *f.*
> **AD** (*abbr of* **Anno Domini**) d.C.

Words with a **hyphen**, a **full stop** or an **apostrophe** come after those spelled the same way but without any of these punctuation marks.

> **its** [ɪts] *poss adj* o seu (a sua), dele (dela).
> **it's** [ɪts] = **it is**, **it has**.

In some cases, the entry is followed by a number in **superscript**. This means that just before or just after there is another entry, also followed by a number, which is written the same way but which has a completely different meaning or pronunciation. You must take care not to choose the wrong entry.

> **bow¹** [baʊ] ⟨ *n* **-1.** [act of bowing] reverência *f.* **-2.** [of ship] proa *f.* ⟨ *vt* [lower] inclinar. ⟨ *vi* **-1.** [make a bow] inclinar-se **-2.** [defer]: **to ~ to sthg** submeter-se a algo.
> ◆ **bow down** *vi* [give in]: **to ~ down (to sb)** render-se(a alguém).
> ◆ **bow out** *vi* afastar-se.
> **bow²** [bəʊ] *n* **-1.** [gen & *MUS*] arco *m* **-2.** [knot] laço *m.*

You will sometimes see words followed by a grey lozenge, called sub-entries. English phrasal verbs and Portuguese pronominal verbs fall into this category.

> **beneficiar** [16] [benefi'sja(x)] *vt* **-1.** [favorecer] to benefit. **-2.** [processar] to process. **-3.** [melhorar] to improve.
> ◆ **beneficiar-se** *vp* [favorecer-se] to profit.

If you are looking up a noun which has a form with an initial capital which has a different meaning from the form without a capital, you should look at the form without a capital.

> **ascension** [ə'senʃn] *n* [to throne] ascensão *f.*
> ◆ **Ascension** *n RELIG* Ascensão *f.*

If you are looking up a noun which, in the plural, has a different meaning from the noun in its singular form (like **glass/glasses** in English), you will find it under the singular form; the plural form will be there as a sub-entry, indicated by the symbol ➡.

> **glass** [glɑ:s] ◇ n **-1.** (U) [material] vidro m **-2.** [for drinking] copo m **-3.** (U) [glassware] objetos mpl de cristal. ◇ comp de vidro.
> ➡ **glasses** npl [spectacles] óculos m inv; [binoculars] binóculos mpl.

Some plural nouns appear as headwords in their own right when they are never or rarely used in the singular (e.g. **juros** in Portuguese, **scissors** in English).

Compound nouns

A compound is a word or expression which has a single meaning but is made up of more than one word, e.g. **point of order, kiss of life, virtual reality, International Monetary Fund**.

It is a feature of this dictionary that English compounds appear in the A–Z list in strict alphabetical order. The compound **blood donor** will therefore come after **blood-curdling** which itself follows **blood count**.

> **blood count** n contagem f de glóbulos sangüíneos.
> **blood-curdling** adj de gelar o sangue.
> **blood donor** n doador m, -ra f de sangue.

On the Portuguese-English side however you should look under the first element of the compound. So, for example, you will find **café com leite** at the entry **café**. If there is more than one compound within an entry they will appear in their alphabetical order within the entry, regardless of any preposition between the two parts of the compound. So at **café** you will find **café pingado** after **café expresso**.

Phrases

If looking for a phrase, you should look first under the noun that is used in the phrase. If there is no noun, then you should look under the adjective, and if there is no adjective, under the verb. Phrases appear in entries in bold, the symbol ~ standing for the headword.

> **time** [taɪm] ◇ n **-1.** (U) [general measurement, spell] tempo m; **to get the ~ to do sthg** ter tempo para fazer algo; **to take ~** levar tempo; **to take ~ out to do sthg** tirar tempo para fazer algo; **it's high ~ ...** já é hora de ...; **to get ~ and a half** receber o pagamento combinado mais a metade; **to have no ~ for sb/sthg** não ter tempo a perder com alguém/algo; **to make good ~** fazer uma boa média (de tempo); **to pass the ~** passar o tempo; **to play for ~** tentar ganhar tempo; **to take one's ~ (doing sthg)** dar-se seu tempo(para fazer algo)...

Some very fixed phrases like **in spite of** in English or **atrás de** in Portuguese are entered under the first important element and preceded by ➡.

> **spite** [spaɪt] ◇ n (U) rancor m; **to do sthg out of OR from ~** fazer algo por maldade. ◇ vt magoar.
> ➡ **in spite of** prep apesar de; **to do sthg in ~ of o.s.** [unintentionally] fazer algo a contragosto.

> **atrás** [a'trajʃ] adv **-1.** [posição] behind; **lá ~** back there. **-2.** [no tempo] ago. **-3.** [em classificação]: **estar/ficar ~ (de)** to be ranked behind; **não ficar ~** fam fig not to be far behind.
> ➡ **atrás de** loc prep **-1.** [posição] behind. **-2.** [em seguimento a] after; **logo ~ de** right behind. **-3.** [em busca de - pessoa] after; [- objeto, explicação] looking for.

Reflexive verbs

Portuguese reflexive verbs are entered under the main form, after the symbol ➡.

> **aclarar** [4] [akla'ra(x)] *vt* [questão, mistério] to clarify.
> ➡ **aclarar-se** *vp* to become clear.

Cultural information

An appreciation of the culture of a foreign country is key to being able to understand and speak its language well. Cultural information on Brazil is provided in this dictionary in boxes on the Portuguese–English side of the dictionary.

> **BOSSA NOVA**
> Musical movement born in Rio de Janeiro in the late 50s; the bossa nova revolutionized the samba, condensing its rhythmic wealth into a syncopated beat with polished jazz chords for piano and guitar. The bossa nova's delicate melody and subtle song were to have a great influence on western popular music through two of the art form's greatest exponents, Tom Jobim and João Gilberto.

TRADEMARKS

Words considered to be trademarks are marked with the symbol ®. However, neither the presence nor the absence of such designation should be regarded as affecting the legal status of any trademark.

MARCAS REGISTRADAS

O símbolo ® indica que a palavra em questão é uma marca registrada. Este símbolo, ou a sua eventual ausência, não afeta, no entanto, a situação legal da marca.

PORTUGUESE VERBS

Portuguese verbs have a number, which refers to the conjugation table given at the back of the dictionary. This number is not repeated for reflexive verbs when they are sub-entries.

VERBOS PORTUGUESES

Os verbos portugueses são seguidos de um número que remete à tabela de conjugação, ao final do dicionário. Esse número não se repete nos verbos pronominais tratados como sub-entrada.

LIST OF BRAZILIAN CULTURAL BOXES
LISTA DE BOXES CULTURAIS BRASILEIROS

AFOXÉS
AMAZÔNIA
BAHIA
BIODIVERSIDADE
BOSSA NOVA
BRASÍLIA
CACHAÇA
CAFÉ
CAIPIRINHA
CANDOMBLÉ
CAPOEIRA
CARNAVAL
CATARATAS DO IGUAÇU
CHORO
CORDEL
DITADURA MILITAR

ESPORTES
FAVELAS
FEIJOADA
FERNANDO DE NORONHA
FESTAS JUNINAS
FUTEBOL
GENOMA
GUARANÁ
ILHAS
JEITINHO BRASILEIRO
LÍNGUA PORTUGUESA
LITERATURA BRASILEIRA
MERCOSUL
MISTURA DE RAÇAS
MOEDA
MÚSICA

OURO PRETO
PANTANAL
PATRIMÔNIOS CULTURAIS
PAU-BRASIL
POROROCA
RIO DE JANEIRO
SAMBA
SANTOS-DUMONT
SÃO FRANCISCO
SECA
TELENOVELAS
TROPICALISMO
TUPI
VESTIBULAR

LISTA DE BOXES CULTURAIS INGLESES
LIST OF ENGLISH CULTURAL BOXES

A-LEVEL
APRIL FOOL'S DAY
BILL OF RIGHTS
BROADSHEET/BROADSIDE
BUILDING SOCIETY
CHURCH OF ENGLAND
THE CITY
CONGRESS
CONSTITUTION
DOWNING STREET
ELECTION
ENGLISH BREAKFAST
FLEET STREET
FOURTH OF JULY
FRATERNITY
-GATE

GREEN CARD
GUY FAWKES' NIGHT
HALLOWEEN
HOUSE OF COMMONS
HOUSE OF LORDS
HOUSE OF REPRESENTIVES
L
LABOR DAY
LICENSING HOURS
MEDICARE/MEDICAID
NATIVE AMERICAN
OXBRIDGE
PENTAGON
PILGRIM FATHERS
POPPY DAY
PRIMARIES

PUB
PUBLIC SCHOOL
SAINT PATRICK'S DAY
SAT
SENATE
SUPREME COURT
TABLOID
THANKSGIVING
WALL STREET
WESTMINSTER
WHITEHALL
WHITE HOUSE
WORLD SERIES
YANKEE

PORTUGUÊS - INGLÊS
PORTUGUESE-ENGLISH

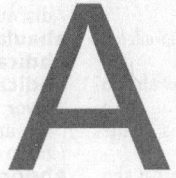

a¹, A [a] *m* [letra] a, A.

a² [a] ◇ *artigo definido* ▷ **o**. ◇ *prep* **-1.** [introduz um complemento indireto] to; **mostrar algo a alguém** to show sthg to sb, to show sb sthg; **diga ao Zé para vir** tell Zé to come; **peça o chapéu ao Paulo** ask Paulo for the hat. **-2.** [relativo a direção] to; **fomos à praia** we went to the beach; **vamos ao cinema** we're going to the movies; **cheguei a Salvador ontem** I arrived in Salvador yesterday; **ele percorreu o país de norte a sul** he travelled the country from north to south. **-3.** [relativo a posição, lugar, distância]: **é à esquerda/direita** it's on the left/right; **fica na saída do teatro** it's on the way out of the theatre. **-4.** [introduz um complemento direto]: **amar a Deus** to love God; **ele criou o menino como a um filho** he raised the boy like his own son. **-5.** [relativo a quantidade, medida, preço]: **aos centos/às dezenas** by the hundred/dozen; **a quanto estão as pêras?** how much are the pears?; **a quilo/metro** by the kilo/metre. **-6.** [indica modo, maneira]: **feito à mão** handmade; **bater à máquina** to type; **ir a pé/cavalo** to go on foot/horseback; **viajar a trabalho/passeio** to go on a business/pleasure trip; **à moda da casa** house style; **sal a gosto** salt to taste; **pagar à vista/a prazo** to pay cash/on time; **a olho nu** with the naked eye. **-7.** [relativo a velocidade]: **dirigir a 60 km/h** to drive at 60 kph; **ela ia a 100km/h** she was doing 100 kph. **-8.** [indica freqüência]: **três vezes ao dia** three times a day; **estou lá às terças e quintas** I'm there on Tuesdays and Thursdays. **-9.** [introduz complemento de tempo]: **as lojas abrem às nove horas** the shops open at nine (o'clock); **eles chegam daqui a 2 horas** they're arriving in two hours' time; **fica a dez minutos daqui** it's ten minutes from here; **à noite** at night. **-10.** [indica série]: **de ... a** from ... to; **façam os exercícios de um a dez** do the exercises one to ten. **-11.** [seguido de infinitivo para exprimir momento]: **ele começou a falar** he started speaking; **ele tropeçou ao subir no** ônibus he tripped as he was getting on the bus. **-12.** [seguido de infinitivo indicando duas ações]: **ela saiu a cantar** she went out singing; **ele nunca aprendeu a assobiar** he never learned to whistle; **começou a chover** it started to rain. **-13.** [em locuções]: **a não ser que** unless; **à exceção de** except for; **a partir de** from; **a respeito de** regarding.

à [a] = **a + a**.

AA (*abrev de* **Alcoólicos Anônimos**) *m* AA.

AACC (*abrev de* **Associação de Assistência à Criança com Câncer**) *f Brazilian association for assistance to children with cancer.*

AACD (*abrev de* **Associação de Assistência à Criança Defeituosa**) *f Brazilian association for assistance to disabled children.*

aba ['aba] *f* **-1.** [de chapéu] brim. **-2.** [de casaca] tail.

abacate [aba'katʃi] *m* avocado.

abacateiro [abaka'tejru] *m* avocado tree.

abacaxi [abaka'ʃi] *m* **-1.** [fruta] pineapple. **-2.** *fam* [problema, dificuldade] difficulty; **ter ~s para resolver** to have some difficulties to sort out; **descascar um ~** to get out of a fix.

abade, dessa [a'badʒi, desa] *m, f* abbot (*f* abbess).

abadia [aba'dʒial] *f* abbey.

abafado, da [aba'fadu, da] *adj* **-1.** [ar, sala] stuffy. **-2.** [pessoa - sem ar] suffocated. **-3.** [som] muffled.

abafador [abafa'do(x)] *m* **-1.** [de bule de chá] tea cosy. **-2.** [de instrumento] mute.

abafamento [abafa'mẽntu] *m* **-1.** [sufoco] suffocation. **-2.** [de som] muffling.

abafar [4] [aba'fa(x)] ◇ *vt* **-1.** [sufocar] to suffocate. **-2.** [cobrir] to cover. **-3.** [apagar] to smother. **-4.** [amortecer] to muffle. **-5.** [ocultar] to cover up. ◇ *vi* **-1.** [sufocar] to suffocate. **-2.** *fam* [fazer sucesso] to steal the show.

abagunçado, da [abagũn'sadu, da] *adj* messed-up.

abagunçar [abagũn'sa(x)] *vt* to mess sthg up.

abaixado, da [abaj'ʃadu, da] <> *pp* ▷ **abaixar.**
<> *adj* **-1.** [pessoa] stooped. **-2.** [persiana] lowered.
abaixar [4] [abaj'ʃa(x)] *vt* to lower; ~ **o volume** to
turn down the volume.
➡ **abaixar-se** *vp* [curvar-se] to crouch down.
abaixo [a'bajʃul] <> *adv* **-1.** [posição] down; **mais**
~ lower down. **-2.** [direção] further down; **escada**
~ downstairs; **ladeira** ~ downhill; **rio** ~ downstream. **-3.** [em texto] below. <> *interj* down with;
~ **a opressão!** down with oppression!
➡ **abaixo de** *loc prep* **-1.** [em posição inferior]
below. **-2.** [em número inferior etc] under.
abaixo-assinado [a,bajʃuasi'nadu] (*pl* **abaixo-
assinados)** *m* petition.
abajur [aba'ʒu(x)l (*pl* -es) *m* **-1.** [pantalha] shade.
-2. [lâmpada] table lamp.
abalado, da [aba'ladu, da] *adj* **-1.** [pessoa] shaken. **-2.** [saúde] impaired.
abalar [4] [aba'la(x)] *vt* **-1.** [prédio, fundações] to
rock. **-2.** [pessoa] to shake. **-3.** [saúde] to impair.
➡ **abalar-se** *vp* [comover-se] to be moved.
abalizado, da [abali'zadu, da] *adj* **-1.** [profissional]
skilled. **-2.** [opinião] expert.
abalo [a'balul] *m* **-1.** [tremor] tremor; ~ **sísmico**
earth tremor. **-2.** [efeito ruim] setback. **-3.** *fig* [co-
moção] uproar.
abalroar [20] [abawro'a(x)] *vt* to collide with.
abanar [4] [aba'na(x)] *vt* **-1.** [com leque, jornal] to
fan. **-2.** [com mão, lenço] to wave. **-3.** [rabo] to wag.
-4. [cabeça] to shake.
➡ **abanar-se** *vp* [ventilar-se] to fan o.s.
abandonado, da [abãndo'nadu, da] *adj* **-1.** [de-
samparado] abandoned. **-2.** [descuidado] neglected.
abandonar [4] [abãndo'na(x)] *vt* **-1.** [desamparar]
to abandon. **-2.** [negligenciar] to neglect. **-3.** [deixar
- estudos, profissão] to give up; [- cônjuge] to leave.
-4. [renegar] to reject.
➡ **abandonar-se** *vp* **-1.** [desleixar-se] to let o.s.
go. **-2.** [entregar-se]: ~**-se a algo** to surrender o.s.
to sthg.
abandono [abãn'donul *m* **-1.** [ato] abandonment.
-2. [estado] neglect. **-3.** [relaxamento] shabbiness.
-4. [entrega] surrender.
abarcar [12] [abax'ka(x)] *vt* **-1.** [abranger] to comprise. **-2.** [alcançar] to cover. **-3.** [monopolizar] to
monopolize.
abarrotado, da [abaxo'tadu, da] *adj:* ~ **(de)**
packed (with).
abarrotar [4] [abaxo'ta(x)] *vt:* ~ **algo (de)** to pack
sthg (with).
abastado, da [abaʃ'tadu, da] *adj* well-off.
abastardar [4] [abaʃtax'da(x)] *vt* to bastardize.
abastecer [25] [abaʃte'se(x)] *vt:* ~ **algo (de)** to
supply sthg (with).
➡ **abastecer-se** *vp:* ~**-se (de algo)** to stock up
(with sthg).
abastecimento [abaʃtesi'mẽntul *m* supply.
abate [a'batʃil *m* slaughter.
abatedouro [abate'dorul *m* [matadouro] slaughterhouse.
abater [5] [aba'te(x)] *vt* **-1.** [matar - animais] to

slaughter; [- pessoa] to kill. **-2.** [diminuir] to
reduce. **-3.** [enfraquecer] to weaken. **-4.** [desanimar]
to shatter.
abatido, da [aba'tʃidu, da] *adj* **-1.** [pálido] drawn.
-2. [enfraquecido] weakened. **-3.** [desanimado]
downcast.
abatimento [abatʃi'mẽntul *m* **-1.** [palidez] paleness. **-2.** [fraqueza] weakness. **-3.** [desânimo] dejection. **-4.** [redução] reduction; **fazer um** ~ to give a
discount.
abaulado, da [abaw'ladu, da] *adj* convex.
abdicação [abdʒika'sãwl (*pl* -ões) *f* abdication.
abdicar [12] [abdʒi'ka(x)] <> *vt:* ~ **o trono (em
favor de alguém)** to abdicate the throne (in
favour of sb). <> *vi* to abdicate; ~ **de algo** *fig* to
forgo sthg.
abdominal [abdomi'nawl (*pl* -ais) *adj* abdominal.
➡ **abdominais** *mpl* sit-ups.
abecê [abe'sel *m* **-1.** [alfabeto] ABC. **-2.** *fig* [rudimen-
tos] fundamentals (*pl*).
abecedário [abese'darjul *m* alphabet.
abeirar [4] [abej'ra(x)] *vt* to bring near.
➡ **abeirar-se** *vp:* ~**-se de** to draw near to.
abelha [a'beʎal *f* bee.
abelha-mestra [a,eʎa'meʃtral (*pl* **abelhas-
mestras)** *f* queen bee.
abelhudo, da [abe'ʎudu, da] *adj* nosy.
abençoado, da [abẽ'swadu, da] *adj* **-1.** [bento]
blessed. **-2.** [bem-sucedido] successful.
abençoar [20] [abẽ'swa(x)] *vt* to bless; **(que)**
Deus te abençoe! God bless you!
aberração [abexa'sãwl (*pl* -ões) *f* aberration.
aberrante [abe'xãntʃil *adj* incongruous.
aberto, ta [a'bɛxtu, ta] <> *pp* ▷ **abrir.** <> *adj*
-1. [ger] open. **-2.** [registro, torneira] turned on. **-3.**
[sem cobertura - terraço] open-air; [- carro] convertible. **-4.** [céu] clear. **-5.** [embrulho, pacote etc]
unwrapped. **-6.** [camisa etc] undone. **-7.** [sincero]
frank. **-8.** [liberal] open-minded.
➡ **aberto** *m* ESP open.
abertura [abex'tural *f* **-1.** [ger] opening; **cerimônia de** ~ opening ceremony. **-2.** [orifício] gap. **-3.**
[início] start. **-4.** [de golfo, enseada] width. **-5.** [em
roupa] neckline. **-6.** [em idéias] openness. **-7.** FOT
aperture. **-8.** MÚS overture. **-9.** [POL - democrática]
liberalization; [- de aeroporto, porto] deregulation.
abestalhado, da [abeʃta'ʎadu, da] *adj* moronic.
ABF (*abrev de* **Associação Brasileira de Franchising)** *f* Brazilian franchising association.
ABI (*abrev de* **Associação Brasileira de Imprensa)** *f*
Brazilian press association.
abilolado, da [abilo'ladu, da] *adj* *fam* potty,
loony.
abismado, da [abiʒ'madu, da] *adj* dismayed.
abismo [a'biʒmul *m* **-1.** [precipício] abyss. **-2.** *fig*
[grande diferença] chasm. **-3.** *fig* [situação difícil]: **estar à beira de um** ~ to be on the brink.
abissal [abi'sawl (*pl* -ais) *adj* [região] deep.
abjeto, ta [ab'ʒɛtu, ta] *adj* abject.
ABL (*abrev de* **Academia Brasileira de Letras)** *f*

Brazilian academy of arts.

abnegação [abnega'sãw] *f* self-sacrifice.

abnegado, da [abne'gadu, dal] *adj* self-sacrificing.

abnegar [14] [abne'ga(x)] *vi* [renunciar]: ~ **de algo** to renounce sthg.

   ⇒ **abnegar-se** *vp* [sacrificar-se] to sacrifice o.s.

ABNT (*abrev de* **Associação Brasileira de Normas Técnicas**) *f Brazilian body overseeing technical standards*, ≃ BSI *UK*, ≃ ANSI *US*.

abóbada [a'bɔbadal *f* vault.

abóbora [a'bɔboral *f* pumpkin.

abobrinha [abo'briɲal *f* courgette *UK*, zucchini *US*.

abocanhar [4] [aboka'ɲa(x)] *vt* - 1. [morder] to bite. - 2. *fig* [apoderar-se de] to seize.

aboletar-se [abole'ta(x)sil *vp* to install o.s.

abolição [abolisãw] *f* abolition.

abolir [79] [abo'li(x)] *vt* to abolish.

abominação [abomina'sãw] (*pl* -ões) *f* abomination.

abominar [4] [abomi'na(x)] *vt* to loathe.

abominável [abomi'navewl] (*pl* -eis) *adj* abominable.

abonado, da [abo'nadu, dal] <> *adj* [rico] well-off. <> *m, f*[rico] well-off person; **os** ~**s** the well-off.

abonar [4] [abo'na(x)] *vt* - 1. [gen] to back up. - 2. [afiançar] to guarantee. - 3. [aprovar] to approve. - 4. [dar] to grant. - 5. [adiantar] to advance. - 6. [relevar] to excuse.

abono [a'bonul *m* - 1. [aprovação] approval. - 2. [fiança] collateral. - 3. [pagamento extra] bonus; ~ **de Natal** Christmas bonus. - 4. [relevação] pardon.

abordagem [abox'daʒẽl (*pl* -ns) *f* approach.

abordar [4] [abox'da(x)] *vt* - 1. [ir a bordo de] to board. - 2. [pessoa] to approach. - 3. [assunto] to broach.

aborígine [abo'riʒenil *adj* - 1. [indígena] native. - 2. [da Austrália] aboriginal.

   ⇒ **aborígines** *mpl* & *fpl* - 1. [população indígena] natives. - 2. [da Austrália] Aborigines.

aborrecer [25] [aboxe'se(x)] *vt* - 1. [amolar] to annoy. - 2. [entediar] to bore.

   ⇒ **aborrecer-se** *vp* - 1. [amolar-se]: ~**-se com alguém** to get annoyed with sb. - 2. [entediar-se]: ~**-se (com alguém/algo)** to get bored (with sb/sthg).

aborrecido, da [aboxe'sidu, dal] *adj* - 1. [amolado] annoyed. - 2. [enfadonho] boring.

aborrecimento [aboxesi'mẽntul *m* [amolação] annoyance.

abortar [4] [abox'ta(x)] <> *vi* [MED - espontaneamente] to have a miscarriage; [- intencionalmente] to have an abortion. <> *vt* [plano, greve, etc] to abort.

aborto [a'boxtul *m* [MED - espontâneo] miscarriage; [- intencional] abortion.

abotoadura [abotwa'dural *f* cuff-link.

abotoar [20] [abo'twa(x)] *vt* [roupa] to button.

abr. (*abrev de* **abril**) Apr.

abraçar [13] [abra'sa(x)] *vt* - 1. [com os braços] to hug. - 2. *fig* [seguir] to embrace.

   ⇒ **abraçar-se** *vp* to hug each other.

abraço [a'brasul *m* hug; **dar um** ~ **em alguém** to give sb a hug; **um** ~ [em cartas] best wishes.

abrandar [4] [abrãn'da(x)] <> *vt* - 1. [dor] to ease. - 2. [lei, palavreado] to moderate. <> *vi* - 1. [ger] to soften. - 2. [dor, ira, calor, vento] to die down.

abrangente [abrãn'ʒẽntʃil *adj* all-embracing.

abranger [26] [abrãn'ʒe(x)] *vt* - 1. [incluir] to include. - 2. [entender] to grasp. - 3. [conter em sua área] to comprise.

abrasar [4] [abra'za(x)] *vt* - 1. [incendiar] to set alight. - 2. [esquentar muito] to scorch.

abrasileirar [4] [abrazilej'ra(x)] *vt* to Brazilianize.

   ⇒ **abrasileirar-se** *vp* [pessoa] to become Brazilianized.

abrasivo, va [abra'zivu, val *adj* abrasive.

abreugrafia [abrewgra'fial *f* X-ray.

abreviação [abrevja'sãw] (*pl* -ões) *f* - 1. [de palavra] abbreviation. - 2. [resumo] abridgemeht. - 3. [diminuição] curtailment.

abreviar [16] [abre'vja(x)] *vt* - 1. [pôr em abreviatura] to abbreviate. - 2. [resumir] to abridge. - 3. [tornar breve] to shorten.

abreviatura [abrevja'tural *f* abbreviation.

abridor [abri'do(x)] (*pl* -es) *m*: ~ **de garrafa** bottle opener; ~ **de lata** can opener.

abrigar [14] [abri'ga(x)] *vt* - 1. [albergar] to shelter. - 2. [proteger]: ~ **alguém de algo** to protect sb from sthg.

   ⇒ **abrigar-se** *vp* [albergar-se] to take shelter.

abrigo [a'brigul *m* - 1. [refúgio] shelter; ~ **anti-aéreo** bomb shelter. - 2. [cobertura] cover. - 3. [asilo] home.

abril [a'briwl *m* April; **primeiro de** ~ April Fool's Day; *veja também* **setembro**.

abrilhantar [4] [abriʎãn'ta(x)] *vt fig* enhance.

abrir [6] [a'bri(x)] <> *vt* - 1. [ger] to open. - 2. [pernas, braços] to stretch out. - 3. [camisa etc] to undo. - 4. [mapa] to open out. - 5. [registro, torneira, água] to turn on. - 6. [túnel] to bore. - 7. [estrada] to make. - 8. [exceção, precedente] to create. - 9. [apetite] to whet. <> *vi* - 1. [ger] to open. - 2. [sinal de tráfego] to turn green. - 3. [tempo] to clear up.

   ⇒ **abrir-se** *vp* [confidenciar]: ~**-se com alguém** to confide in sb.

ab-rogação [abxoga'sãw] (*pl* -ões) *f* - 1. [de lei] repeal. - 2. [de uso, costume] discontinuation.

ab-rogar [14] [abxo'ga(x)] *vt* - 1. [lei] to repeal. - 2. [uso, costume] to discontinue.

abrolho [a'broʎul *m* thorn.

abrupto, ta [a'bruptu, tal *adj* - 1. [súbito] sudden. - 2. [áspero] abrupt.

abrutalhado, da [abruta'ʎadu, dal *adj* brusque.

ABS (*abrev de* **antilock braking system**) *m* ABS; **freios** ~ ABS brakes.

absenteísmo [absẽnte'iʒmul *m* absenteeism.

absolutamente [absoˌluta'mẽntʃil *adv* - 1. [completamente] absolutely. - 2. [de modo nenhum] absolutely not.

absoluto, ta [abso'lutu, ta] *adj* absolute; **em ~** not at all.

absolver [5] [absow've(x)] *vt*: **~ alguém (de algo)** JUR to acquit sb (of sthg); RELIG to absolve sb (of sthg); [inocentar] to clear sb (of sthg).

absolvição [absowvi'sãw] *f* **-1.** JUR acquittal. **-2.** RELIG absolution.

absorção [absox'sãw] *f* **-1.** [de água, vapores, gases] absorption. **-2.** [de valores, cultura] absorption.

absorto, ta [ab'soxtu, ta] *adj* [concentrado] absorbed.

absorvente [absox'vẽntʃi] *adj* **-1.** [substância] absorbent. **-2.** [pessoa, leitura, trabalho] absorbing.

~ absorvente *m*: **~ higiênico** sanitary towel.

absorver [5] [absoxve(x)] *vt* to absorb; **~ energia** to use up energy; **~ tempo** to take up time.

~ absorver-se *vp* [concentrar-se]: **~-se em algo** to absorb o.s. in sthg.

abstêmio, mia [abʃ'temju, mja] <> *adj* abstemious. <> *m, f* teetotaller.

abstenção [abʃtẽn'sãw] *f* **-1.** [de prazeres, de fumo] abstinence. **-2.** [do voto] abstention.

abster-se [1] [abʃ'texsil] *vp*: **~ (de algo/de fazer algo)** to abstain (from sthg/from doing sthg).

abstinência [abʃtʃi'nẽnsja] *f* abstinence.

abstração [abʃtra'sãw] *f* **-1.** [alheamento] abstraction. **-2.** [isolamento] isolation. **-3.** [concentração] concentration.

abstrair [68] [abʃtra'i(x)] *vt* **-1.** [afastar] to keep away from. **-2.** [isolar] to separate out.

~ abstrair-se *vp* **-1.** [alhear-se]: **~-se de** to distance o.s. from. **-2.** [concentrar-se]: **~-se em** to absorb o.s. in. **-3.** [abster-se]: **~-se de** to abstain from.

abstrato, ta [abʃ'tratu, ta] *adj* abstract.

absurdo, da [ab'suxdu, da] *adj* absurd.

~ absurdo *m* absurdity.

abulia [abu'abu'dabil] *f* apathy.

abundância [abũn'dãnsja] *f* **-1.** [grande quantidade] abundance; **em ~** in abundance. **-2.** [riqueza]: **ele vive com ~** he is a man of means.

abundante [abũn'dãntʃi] *adj*: **~ (em/de)** abundant (in/with).

abundar [4] [abũn'da(x)] *vi* to abound; **~ em** ou **de** to abound in ou with.

aburguesado, da [abuxge'zadu, da] *adj* bourgeois.

aburguesar [4] [abuxge'za(x)] *vt* to gentrify.

~ aburguesar-se *vp* **-1.** [pessoa] to become bourgeois. **-2.** [área] to become gentrified.

abusado, da [abu'zadu, da] *adj* forward.

abusar [4] [abu'za(x)] *vi* **-1.** [aproveitar-se, exceder-se] to go too far. **-2.** [praticar excessos]: **~ de algo** to abuse sthg. **-3.** [aproveitar-se]: **~ de alguém/algo** to take advantage of sb/sthg. **-4.** [sexualmente]: **~ de alguém** to abuse sb.

abusivo, va [abu'zivu, va] *adj* **-1.** [tratamento] abusive. **-2.** [preço] excessive.

abuso [a'buzu] *m*: **~ (de)** abuse (of); **~ de confiança** breach of trust; **~ sexual** sexual abuse.

abutre [a'butri] *m* vulture.

AC (*abrev de* **Estado do Acre**) *m State of Acre*.

a.C. (*abrev de* **antes de Cristo**) *adj* BC.

acabado, da [aka'badu, da] *adj* **-1.** [terminado] finished. **-2.** [móvel, roupa etc]: **bem/mal ~** well/badly finished. **-3.** [gasto] worn. **-4.** [abatido, exausto] exhausted. **-5.** [envelhecido] aged.

acabamento [akaba'mẽntul] *m* finish.

acabar [4] [aka'ba(x)] <> *vt* **-1.** [terminar] to finish. **-2.** [rematar] to finish off. <> *vi* **-1.** [terminar] to finish, to end; **~ bem/mal** to end well/badly; **~ de fazer algo** to finish doing sthg; [há pouco] to have just done sthg. **-2.** [terminar por]: **~ fazendo algo** to end up doing sthg. **-3.** [ter como conseqüência]: **~ em algo** to end up in sthg. **-4.** [ter como limite]: **~ em algo** to end in sthg. **-5.** [abolir]: **~ com algo** to put an end to sthg. **-6.** [destruir]: **~ com algo** to destroy sthg. **-7.** [tornar-se] to end up.

~ acabar-se *vp* **-1.** [terminar] to finish, to end. **-2.** [desgastar-se] to wear o.s. out.

acabrunhado, da [akabru'nadu, da] *adj* **-1.** [desanimado] disheartened. **-2.** [envergonhado] embarrassed.

acabrunhar [4] [akabru'na(x)] *vt* **-1.** [desanimar] to dishearten. **-2.** [envergonhar] to embarrass.

acácia [a'kasja] *f* acacia.

academia [akade'mial] *f* **-1.** [escola] school. **-2.** [sociedade] academy; **Academia Brasileira de Letras** *Brazilian Academy of language and literature*. **-3.** ESP school; **~ de ginástica** gym.

acadêmico, ca [aka'demiku, ka] <> *adj* academic. <> *m, f* academic.

açafrão [asa'frãw] *m* saffron.

acalanto [aka'lãntu] *m* lullaby.

acalentar [4] [akalẽn'ta(x)] *vt* **-1.** [ninar] to lull. **-2.** *fig* [nutrir] to cherish. **-3.** [aconchegar] to cuddle.

acalmar [4] [akaw'ma(x)] <> *vt* [pessoa, ânimos] to calm. <> *vi* **-1.** [pessoa] to calm down. **-2.** [ventania] to abate. **-3.** [mar] to become calm.

~ acalmar-se *vp* [pessoa, ânimos] to calm down.

acalorado, da [akalo'radu, da] *adj* [discussão etc] heated.

acamado, da [aka'madu, da] *adj* bedridden.

açambarcar [12] [asãnbax'ka(x)] *vt* **-1.** [apropriar-se de] to appropriate. **-2.** [monopolizar] to corner.

acampamento [akãnpa'mẽntul] *m* **-1.** [atividade] camping; [lugar] campsite. **-2.** MIL encampment.

acampar [4] [akãn'pa(x)] <> *vt* to encamp. <> *vi* to camp.

acanhado, da [aka'nadu, da] *adj* shy.

acanhamento [akana'mẽntul] *m* shyness.

acanhar-se [4] [aka'naxsil] *vp*: **~ (de fazer algo)** to be shy (about doing sthg).

ação [a'sãw] (*pl* -ões) *f* **-1.** [atuação] action. **-2.** [feito] act; **~ de graças** thanksgiving. **-3.** [capacidade de agir]: **sem ~** helpless. **-4.** [efeito] effect. **-5.** [enredo] plot; **filme de ~** action movie. **-6.** JUR legal action; **mover uma ~ contra alguém** to bring a legal action against sb; **~ judicial** lawsuit. **-7.** FIN share; **~ ordinária** ordinary share; **~ preferencial** preference share. **-8.** MIL action.

acarajé [akara'ʒɛ] *m bean fritter*.

acareação [akarja'sãw] (pl-ões) f confrontation.
acarear [15] [aka'rja(x)] vt to confront.
acariciar [16] [akari'sja(x)] vt to caress.
acarinhar [4] [akari'ɲa(x)] vt to caress.
acarretar [4] [akaxe'ta(x)] vt to cause.
acasalamento [akazala'mẽntul m mating.
acasalar [4] [akaza'la(x)] vt to mate.
acaso [a'kazul m chance; **essa descoberta foi um** ~ it was a chance discovery.
→ **ao acaso** loc adv at random.
→ **por acaso** loc adv by chance.
acastanhado, da [akaʃta'ɲadu, da] adj brown.
acatamento [akata'mẽntul m -1. [respeito]: ~ (a) respect (for). -2. [cumprimento]: ~ (a ou de) deference (to).
acatar [4] [aka'ta(x)] vt -1. [respeitar] to respect. -2. [cumprir] to obey.
acautelar [4] [akawte'la(x)] vt to caution.
→ **acautelar-se** vp: ~-se (contra) to guard (against).
acebolado, da [asebo'ladu, da] adj cooked with onions.
aceder [5] [ase'de(x)] vi: ~ a algo to accede to sthg; ~ em fazer algo to agree to do sthg.
aceitação [asejta'sãw] f-1. [anuência] acceptance. -2. [admissão, aprovação] approval. -3. [receptividade] acceptability.
aceitar [4] [asej'ta(x)] vt -1. [anuir a] to accept. -2. [admitir, aprovar] to approve.
aceitável [asej'tavew] (pl-eis) adj acceptable.
aceito, ta [a'sejtu, ta] <> pp ▷ aceitar. <> adj -1. [pessoa, produto] well-received. -2. [proposta, solução] accepted.
aceleração [aselera'sãw] f-1. FíS acceleration. -2. [de processo etc] progress.
acelerado, da [asele'radu, da] adj quick.
acelerador [aselera'do(x)] (pl-es) m accelerator.
acelerar [4] [asele'ra(x)] <> vt -1. AUTO to accelerate. -2. [apressar] to hurry. <> vi AUTO to accelerate.
acelga [a'sewga] f chard.
acenar [4] [ase'na(x)] <> vt -1. [sinalizar] to indicate. -2. [fazer movimento com - cabeça] to nod; [- mãos] to wave. <> vi -1. [sinalizar - com cabeça] to nod; [- com mãos,lenço] to wave. -2. [prometer]: ~ algo (a alguém) to offer (sb) sthg.
acendedor [asẽnde'do(x)] m [de bico de gás] lighter.
acender [5] [asẽn'de(x)] <> vt -1. [cigarro, fósforo] to light. -2. [lâmpada, luz] to switch on. -3. fig [ânimo] to excite. <> vp [lâmpada, luz] to be turned on.
aceno [a'senu] m -1. [gesto] gesture. -2. [com a cabeça] nod. -3. [com a mão] wave.
acento [a'sẽntul m -1. [gráfico] accent; ~ agudo/ circunflexo acute/circumflex accent. -2. [intensidade] stress.
acentuação [asẽntwa'sãw] f accentuation.
acentuado, da [asẽn'twadu, da] adj -1. [palavra, vogal] accented. -2. [sílaba] stressed. -3. [proeminente] accentuated. -4. [marcante] marked.

acentuar [4] [asẽn'twa(x)] vt -1. [palavra, vogal] to stress. -2. [enfatizar] to emphasize. -3. [realçar] to accentuate.
acepção [asep'sãw] (pl-ões) f sense.
acerca [a'sexka] → **acerca de** loc adv about, concerning.
acercar-se [12] [asex'kaxsi] vp: ~ de [ir] to go towards; [vir] to draw near to.
acerola [ase'rɔla] f fruit similar to Barbados Cherry, commonly drunk as a fruit juice, rich in vitamins and minerals.
acertado, da [asex'tadu, da] adj -1. [relógio] correct. -2. [medida, decisão] sensible. -3. [combinado] arranged.
acertar [4] [asex'ta(x)] <> vt -1. [relógio] to set. -2. [combinar] to arrange. -3. [contas] to settle. -4. [igualar] to even up. -5. [endireitar] to put right. -6. [encontrar] to find. -7. [fazer atingir]: ~ algo em algo to land sthg on sthg. -8. [aplicar] to strike. <> vi -1. [em adivinhação, jogo] to guess correctly. -2. [atingir]: ~ em algo/alguém to hit sthg/sb.
acerto [a'sextul m -1. [em decisão, escolha] right decision. -2. [acordo] agreement. -3. [de contas] settling. -4. [sensatez]: com ~ with sensitivity.
acervo [a'sexvul m [patrimônio] collection.
aceso, sa [a'sezu, za] <> pp ▷ acender. <> adj -1. [cigarro, fósforo] lit. -2. [lâmpada, luz] on. -3. fig [pessoa] excited.
acessar [4] [ase'sa(x)] vt COMPUT to access.
acessível [ase'sivɛw] (pl-eis) adj -1. [de acesso fácil] accessible. -2. [que se pode obter] available. -3. [tratável] approachable. -4. [inteligível] comprehensible. -5. [módico] affordable.
acesso [a'sesul m -1. [ger] access. -2. [aproximação] approach; de fácil ~ accessible; de difícil ~ inaccessible. -3. [trato]: de fácil ~ approachable. -4. [ímpeto] fit. -5. MED attack. -6. COMPUT access; ~ discado dial-up access.
acessório, ria [ase'sɔrjul adj accessory.
→ **acessório** m accessory.
acetinado, da [aseti'nadu, da] adj satiny.
acetona [ase'tona] f [removedor de esmalte] nail polish remover.
achacar [12] [aʃa'ka(x)] vt-1. [tachar]: ~ alguém de algo to accuse sb of sthg. -2. fam [extorquir dinheiro de] to extort money from.
achado [a'ʃadul m -1. [coisa encontrada] find. -2. [descoberta] discovery. -3. [pechincha] bargain. -4. [coisa providencial] godsend. -5. loc: não se dar por ~ to play dumb.
achaque [a'ʃakil m ailment.
achar [4] [a'ʃa(x)] <> vt-1. [encontrar - procurando] to find; [- por acaso] to come across. -2. [descobrir, encontrar] to find. -3.: ~ graça em algo to find sthg amusing. -4. [supor, opinar] to think; ~ que ... to think that ...; acho que sim I think so. <> vi [decidir]: ~ de fazer algo to decide to do sthg.
→ **achar-se** vp -1. [estar] to be. -2. [considerar-se] to consider o.s.
achatar [4] [aʃa'ta(x)] vt -1. [aplanar] to flatten. -2. [rebaixar] to lower.

achegar-se [14] [aʃe'gaxsil *vp*: ~ **(a/de)** to get closer (to).

acidentado, da [asidẽn'tadu, da] <> *adj* -**1.** [terreno] rough. -**2.** [viagem, vida] turbulent. -**3.** [pessoa] injured. <> *m, f* [pessoa] injured person.

acidental [asidẽn'taw] (*pl* -**ais**) *adj* -**1.** [fortuito] accidental. -**2.** [secundário] incidental.

acidentar-se [asidẽn'tarsil *vp* -**1.** [sofrer acidente] to have an accident. -**2.** [vitimar-se] to be injured.

acidente [asi'dẽntʃil *m* -**1.** [desastre] accident; ~ **de carro** car accident. -**2.** [eventualidade] circumstance; **por** ~ by chance. ~ **geográfico** geographic accident. ~ **de trabalho** accident at work, industrial accident. ~ **vascular cerebral** *MED* stroke.

acidez [asi'deʒl *f* acidity.

ácido, da ['asidu, da] *adj* -**1.** *QUÍM* acid. -**2.** [bebida, fruta, sabor] acidic.
◆ **ácido** *m* -**1.** *QUÍM* acid; ~ **úrico** uric acid. -**2.** *fam* [droga] acid.

acima [a'simal *adj* -**1.** [ger] above; **mais** ~ higher up. -**2.** [em direção à parte superior]: **morro** *ou* **ladeira** ~ uphill.
◆ **acima de** *loc prep* -**1.** [em posição superior] above. -**2.** [quantia, quantidade] more than.

acinte [a'sĩntʃil *m* provocation.

acintosamente [asĩntoza'mẽntʃil *adv* deliberately.

acintoso, osa [asĩn'tozu, ozal *adj* provocative.

acinzentado, da [da, asĩzẽ'tadul *adj* greyish.

acionar [4] [asjo'na(x)l *vt* -**1.** [mecanismo, medidas] to set in motion. -**2.** *JUR* to sue.

acionista [asjo'niʃtal *mf* shareholder; ~ **majoritário/minoritário** majority/minority shareholder.

acirrado, da [asi'xadu, da] *adj* -**1.** [luta, discussão, ânimo] tough. -**2.** [ódio] bitter.

acirrar [4] [asi'xa(x)l *vt* -**1.** [instigar]: ~ **alguém contra algo/alguém** to incite sb against sthg/sb. -**2.** [exacerbar] to stir up.

aclamação [aklama'sãwl *f* -**1.** [ovação] ovation; **por** ~ by acclamation. -**2.** [proclamação] proclamation.

aclamar [4] [akla'ma(x)l *vt* -**1.** [ovacionar] to applaud. -**2.** [proclamar] to proclaim.

aclarado, da [akla'radu, da] *adj* [questão, mistério] clarified.

aclarar [4] [akla'ra(x)l *vt* [questão, mistério] to clarify.
◆ **aclarar-se** *vp* to become clear.

aclimatação [aklimata'sãwl *f* acclimatization.

aclimatar [4] [aklima'ta(x)l *vt*: ~ **algo/alguém a algo** to acclimatize sth/sb to sthg.
◆ **aclimatar-se** *vp*: ~-**se (a algo)** to acclimatize o.s. (to sthg).

aclive [a'klivil *m* slope; **um caminho em** ~ an uphill slope.

ACM (*abrev de* **Associação Cristã de Moços**) *f* ≃ YMCA.

acne ['aknil *f* acne.

aço ['asul *m* steel; ~ **inoxidável** stainless steel.

acocorado, da [akoko'radu, da] *adj* squatting.

acocorar-se [4] [akoko'raxsil *vp* to squat down.

ações [a'sõjʃl *pl* ⊳ **ação**.

açoitar [4] [asoj'ta(x)l *vt* -**1.** [com açoite] to whip. -**2.** [suj: vento, temporal] to lash.

açoite [a'sojtʃil *m* whip.

acolá [ako'lal *adv* over there.

acolchoado, da [akow'ʃwadu, da] *adj* [forrado] quilted.
◆ **acolchoado** *m* quilt.

acolchoar [20] [akow'ʃwa(x)l *vt* [forrar] to quilt.

acolhedor, ra [akoʎe'do(x), ral *adj* welcoming.

acolher [5] [ako'ʎe(x)l *vt* -**1.** [ger] to welcome. -**2.** [hospedar] to put sb up. -**3.** [admitir] to receive.

acolhida [ako'ʎidal *f* -**1.** [hospedagem] hospitality. -**2.** [recepção] welcome.

acometer [5] [akome'te(x)l *vt* -**1.** [atacar] to attack. -**2.** [suj: doença, desejo, sentimento] to strike.

acomodação [akomoda'sãwl (*pl* -**ões**) *f* -**1.** [alojamento] accommodation. -**2.** [aposento, instalação] room. -**3.** [arranjo, arrumação] layout. -**4.** [adaptação] adaptation.

acomodado, da [akomo'dadu, da] *adj* -**1.** [alojado, instalado] settled. -**2.** [conformado] reconciled.

acomodar [4] [akomo'da(x)l *vt* -**1.** [alojar, instalar] to accommodate. -**2.** [adaptar]: ~ **algo a** *ou* **com algo** to adapt sthg to sthg.
◆ **acomodar-se** *vp* -**1.** [alojar-se, instalar-se] to settle o.s. -**2.** [conformar-se] to reconcile o.s.

acompanhado, da [akõnpa'ɲadu, da] *adj* accompanied.

acompanhamento [akõnpaɲa'mẽntul *m* -**1.** [de processo, doença] monitoring. -**2.** *MÚS* accompaniment. -**3.** *CULIN* side order, side dish.

acompanhante [akõnpa'ɲãntʃil *mf* companion.

acompanhar [4] [akõnpa'ɲa(x)l <> *vt* -**1.** [ger] to accompany. -**2.** [processo, doença] to monitor. -**3.** [suj: problema, preocupações] to stay with. -**4.** [margear] to run parallel to. -**5.** [compreender] to keep up with. -**6.** [combinar]: ~ **algo com algo** to accompany sthg with sthg. -**7.** *CULIN* to go with. <> *vi MÚS* to accompany.

Aconcágua [akon'kagwal *n*: **o (Monte)** ~ (Mount) Aconcagua.

aconchegado, da [akõnʃe'gadu, da] *adj* snug, cosy.

aconchegante [akõnʃe'gãntʃil *adj* cosy.

aconchegar [14] [akõnʃe'ga(x)l *vt* -**1.** [nos braços] to cuddle. -**2.** [na cama, nas cobertas] to tuck up *ou* in.
◆ **aconchegar-se** *vp* -**1.** [nos braços] to snuggle. -**2.** [na cama, nas cobertas] to tuck o.s. up *ou* in.

aconchego [akõn'ʃegul *m* warmth.

acondicionamento [akõndʒisjona'mẽntul *m* packaging.

acondicionar [4] [akõndʒisjo'na(x)l *vt* -**1.** [embrulhar] to wrap. -**2.** [embalar] to package.

aconselhar [4] [akõnse'ʎa(x)l *vt* -**1.** [dar conselho a]: ~ **alguém (a fazer algo** *ou* **a que faça algo)** to advise sb (to do sthg). -**2.** [recomendar] to recommend.
◆ **aconselhar-se** *vp* to seek advice; ~-**se com**

alguém to seek the advice of sb.

aconselhável [akõnse'ʎavɛw] (pl-eis) adj advisable.

acontecer [25] [akõnte'se(x)] vi to happen.

acontecimento [akõntesi'mẽntu] m event.

acoplado, da [ako'pladu, da] adj [conectado - peças] connected; [- naves espaciais] docked.

acoplar [4] [ako'pla(x)] vt to couple.

acordado, da [akox'dadu, da] adj -1. [desperto] awake; **sonhar** ~ to daydream. -2. [combinado] agreed.

acordar [4] [akox'da(x)] <> vt -1. [despertar] to wake. -2. [combinar]: ~ **algo/fazer algo** to arrange sthg/to do sthg; ~ **que** to agree that. <> vi -1. [despertar] to wake. -2. [concordar]: ~ **em algo/fazer algo** to agree to sthg/to do sthg.

acorde [a'kɔxdʒil] m MÚS chord.

acordeão [akox'dʒjãw] (pl-ões) m accordion.

acordeonista [akoxdʒjo'niʃta] mf accordionist.

acordo [a'koxdu] m agreement; **chegar a um** ~ to arrive at an agreement; **de** ~ agreed; **de** ~ **com** [conforme] according to; **estar de** ~ **(com alguém/em fazer algo)** to be in agreement (with sb/to do sthg); **de comum** ~ by common accord.

Açores [a'soriʃ] npl: **os** ~ the Azores.

acorrentar [4] [akoxẽn'ta(x)] vt to chain.

acossado, da [ako'sadu, da] <> adj [perseguido] persecuted, hounded. <> m, f victim.

acossar [4] [ako'sa(x)] vt -1. [perseguir] to pursue. -2. [acuar] to corner.

acostamento [akoʃta'mẽntu] m hard shoulder.

acostumado, da [akoʃtu'madu, da] adj -1. [habitual] usual. -2. [habituado]: **estar** ~ **a** ou **com algo** to be used to sthg; **estar** ~ **a fazer algo** to be in the habit of doing sthg.

acostumar [4] [akoʃtu'ma(x)] <> vt: ~ **alguém/algo a algo** to accustom sb/sthg to sthg; ~ **alguém a fazer algo** to accustom sb to doing sthg. <> vi: ~ **com algo** to get used to sthg.

➡ **acostumar-se** vp to accustom o.s.; ~**-se a algo/a fazer algo** to accustom o.s. to sthg/to doing sthg.

acotovelar [4] [akotove'la(x)] vt -1. [para chamar a atenção] to nudge. -2. [empurrar] to elbow.

➡ **acotovelar-se** vp [empurrar-se] to elbow one's way.

açougue [a'sogil] m butcher's.

açougueiro, ra [aso'gejru, ra] m butcher.

acovardado, da [akovax'dadu, da] adj intimidated.

acovardar [4] [akovax'da(x)] vt [amedrontar] to intimidate.

➡ **acovardar-se** vp -1. [amedrontar-se] to be intimidated. -2. [perder o ânimo] to become disheartened.

acre ['akri] adj -1. [ácido, amargo] acrid. -2. fig [áspero] harsh.

Acre ['akri] n Acre.

acreditar [4] [akredʒi'ta(x)] <> vt -1. [crer] to believe. -2. [abonar] to confirm. <> vi -1. [crer]: ~

em algo/alguém to believe in sthg/sb. -2. [confiar]: ~ **em algo/alguém** to have confidence in sthg/sb.

acrescentar [4] [akresẽn'ta(x)] vt to add.

acrescer [25] [akre'se(x)] <> vt [adicionar]: ~ **algo (a algo)** to add sthg (to sthg). <> vi: **acresce que** ... in addition to which ...

acréscimo [a'krɛsimul] m -1. [adição] addition. -2. [aumento] increase.

acrílico [a'krilikul] m acrylic.

acrimônia [akri'monja] f acrimony.

acrobacia [akroba'sial] f acrobatics (pl).

acrobata [akro'batal] mf acrobat.

acuado, da [a'kuadu, da] adj [acossado] cornered.

acuar [4] [a'kwa(x)] <> vt to corner. <> vi to retreat.

açúcar [a'suka(x)] m sugar; ~ **mascavo** brown sugar.

açucarado, da [asuka'radu, da] adj sugary.

açucareiro [asuka'rejru] m sugar bowl.

açude [a'sudʒil] m dam.

acudir [61] [aku'dʒi(x)] <> vt to run to help. <> vi to rush to sb's aid.

acuidade [akwi'dadʒil] f sharpness.

acumulação [akumula'sãw] (pl-ões) f accumulation.

acumulado, da [akumu'ladu, da] adj -1. [juros] accrued. -2. [prêmio] rollover.

acumular [4] [akumu'la(x)] vt -1. [ajuntar] to accrue. -2. [amontoar] to accumulate. -3. [reunir] to collate. -4. [cargos] to combine.

acúmulo [a'kumulul] m accumulation.

acupuntura [akupũn'tural] f acupuncture.

acupunturista [akupũntu'riʃtal] mf acupuncturist.

acusação [akuza'sãw] (pl-ões) f -1. [incriminação] accusation. -2. [promotoria]: **a** ~ the prosecution.

acusado, da [aku'zadu, da] m, f [réu] defendant.

acusar [4] [aku'za(x)] vt -1. [gen]: ~ **alguém (de algo)** to accuse sb (of sthg). -2. JUR: ~ **alguém de algo** to charge sb with sthg. -3. [recebimento] to acknowledge. -4. [mostrar] to reveal.

acústico, ca [a'kuʃtʃiku, ka] adj acoustic.

➡ **acústica** f FÍS acoustics.

AD (abrev de **Anno Domini**) AD.

adaga [a'daga] f dagger.

adágio [a'daʒul] m -1. MÚS adagio. -2. [provérbio] adage.

adaptação [adapta'sãw] (pl-ões) f adaptation.

adaptado, da [adap'tadu, da] adj adapted.

adaptador [adapta'do(x)] (pl-res) m: ~ **de rede** COMPUT network adaptor.

adaptar [4] [adap'ta(x)] vt -1. [fixar] to fit. -2. [peça teatral, música, linguagem] to adapt.

➡ **adaptar-se** vp [ambientar-se] to adapt o.s.

adega [a'dɛga] f cellar.

ademais [adʒi'majʃ] adv [além disso] moreover.

adendo [a'dẽndul] m addendum.

adentro [a'dẽntrul] adv: **casa/noite** ~ into the house/night; **mar** ~ out to sea.

adepto, ta [a'dɛptu, ta] m, f: ~ **(de)** follower (of).

adequadamente [adekwada'mẽntʃil *adv* adequately.

adequado, da [ade'kwadu, dal *adj* appropriate.

adequar [23] [ade'kwa(x)l *vt*: ~ **algo a algo** to adapt sthg to sthg.

adereço [ade'resul *m* -**1.** [enfeite] decoration. -**2.** [jóia] adornment.

aderência [ade'rẽnsjal *f* -**1.** [de cola] adherence. -**2.** [a partido, campanha etc] support.

aderente [ade'rẽntʃil <> *adj* [substância] adhesive. <> *mf* [adepto] adherent.

aderir [57] [ade'ri(x)l *vi* -**1.** [colar-se] to stick. -**2.** [a partido, campanha] to adhere. -**3.** [a moda, estilo de vida] to follow.

adesão [ade'zãwl (*pl* -ões) *f* [a partido, campanha] adhesion; **jantar de** ~ fund-raising dinner; **documento de** ~ petition.

adesivo, va [ade'zivu, val *adj* adhesive.
  ➡ adesivo *m* Sellotape® *UK*, Scotch tape® *US*.

adestrador, ra [adeʃ'trado(x), ral *m, f* [de animais] trainer.

adestramento [adeʃtra'mẽntul *m* training.

adestrar [4] [adeʃ'tra(x)l *vt* to train.

adeus [a'dewʃl <> *m* farewell. <> *interj* goodbye!

adiamento [adʒja'mẽntul *m* [prorrogação] postponement.

adiantado, da [adʒjãn'tadu, dal *adj* -**1.** [trabalho] ahead of schedule. -**2.** [relógio] fast. -**3.** [pagamento] advance *(antes de subst)*. -**4.** [aluno, povo] advanced.
  ➡ adiantado *adv*: **pagar** ~ to pay in advance; **cheguei** ~ **ao encontro** I arrived early for the meeting.

adiantamento [adʒjãnta'mẽntul *m* -**1.** [progresso] progress. -**2.** [de quantia, salário] advance.

adiantar [4] [adʒjãn'ta(x)l <> *vt* -**1.** [trabalho] to get ahead with. -**2.** [relógio] to put forward. -**3.** [quantia, salário] to advance. -**4.** [dizer antecipadamente] to anticipate. <> *vi* -**1.** [relógio] to be fast. -**2.** [trazer benefício]: ~ **fazer algo** to be worth doing sthg.
  ➡ adiantar-se *vp* -**1.** [em trabalho, estudos] to get ahead. -**2.** [avançar]: ~-**se para** to go towards. -**3.** [sobrepujar]: ~-**se a alguém** to surpass sb.

adiante [a'dʒjãntʃil *adv* -**1.** [na frente] ahead; **mais** ~ [no espaço] further on; [no tempo] later on; **logo** ~ just ahead. -**2.** [em explicação, narração]: **ir** ~ to go ahead. -**3.**: **levar algo** ~ [obra, plano] to go ahead with sthg.

adiar [16] [a'dʒja(x)l *vt* to postpone.

adição [adʒi'sãwl (*pl* -ões) *f* -**1.** [acréscimo] addition. -**2.** *MAT* sum.

adicionar [4] [adʒisjo'na(x)l *vt* -**1.** [acrescentar] to add. -**2.** *MAT* to add up.

adido, da [a'dʒidu, dal *m,f* [em embaixada] attaché.

adiposo, osa [adʒi'pozu, ɔzal *adj* adipose.

aditivo [adʒi'tʃivul *m* additive.

adivinhação [adʒiviɲa'sãwl *f* -**1.** [previsão] prediction. -**2.** [conjetura] guess. -**3.** [decifração] solution.

adivinhar [4] [adʒivi'ɲa(x)l *vt* -**1.** [presente, futuro] to predict. -**2.** [resposta, causa, intenção] to guess. -**3.** [enigma, mistério] to solve.

adivinho, nha [adʒi'viɲu, ɲal *m,f* fortune-teller.
  ➡ adivinha *f* [adivinhação] riddle.

adjacências [adʒa'sẽnsjaʃl *fpl* neighbourhood.

adjacente [adʒa'sẽntʃil *adj* adjacent.

adjetivo [adʒɛ'tʃivul *m* adjective.

adjudicação [adʒudʒika'sãwl (*pl* -ões) *f* *JUR* adjudication.

adjudicar [12] [adʒudʒi'ka(x)l *vt JUR*: ~ **algo a alguém** to adjudicate sthg for sb.

adjunto, ta [ad'ʒũntu, tal <> *adj* [assistente] assistant. <> *m, f* -**1.** [assistente] assistant. -**2.** *GRAM* adjunct.

administração [adʒiminiʃtra'sãwl (*pl* -ões) *f* -**1.** [ger] administration; ~ **de empresas** [curso] business studies; ~ **pública** public administration. -**2.** [pessoal] management.
  ➡ Administração *f* [governo] Administration.

administrador, ra [adʒiminiʃtra'do(x), ral (*mpl* -es, *fpl* -s) *m, f* administrator.

administrar [4] [adʒiminiʃ'tra(x)l *vt* -**1.** [gerir] to manage. -**2.** [dar] to administer.

administrativo, va [adʒiminiʃtra'tʃivu, val *adj* administrative.

admiração [adʒimira'sãwl *f* -**1.** [respeito] admiration. -**2.** [surpresa] surprise.

admirado, da [adʒimi'radu, dal *adj* -**1.** [respeitado] admired. -**2.** [surpreso]: ~ **(de)** astonished (at).

admirador, ra [adʒimira'do(x), ral *m, f* admirer.

admirar [4] [adʒimi'ra(x)l <> *vt* -**1.** [respeitar, contemplar] to admire. -**2.** [surpreender] to surprise. <> *vi* [surpreender] to be astounding; **não é de** ~ **(que ...)** it's no wonder (that ...).
  ➡ admirar-se *vp* -**1.** [mutuamente] to admire each other. -**2.** [surpreender-se]: ~-**se (de algo)** to be surprised (at sthg); **não me admiro!** I'm not surprised!

admirável [adʒimi'ravɛwl (*pl* -eis) *adj* -**1.** [excelente] admirable. -**2.** [assombroso] amazing.

admissão [adʒimi'sãwl (*pl* -ões) *f* -**1.** [ger] admission. -**2.** [contratação] employment.

admissível [adʒimi'sivewl (*pl* -eis) *adj* acceptable.

admitir [6] [adʒimi'tʃi(x)l *vt* -**1.** [ger] to admit. -**2.** [aceitar] to tolerate. -**3.** [consentir em] to permit. -**4.** [contratar] to take on. -**5.** [comportar] to allow.

admoestação [adʒmweʃta'sãwl (*pl* -ões) *f* -**1.** [advertência] warning. -**2.** [reprimenda] reprimand.

admoestar [4] [adʒmweʃ'ta(x)l *vt* -**1.** [advertir]: ~ **alguém de** *ou* **sobre** to warn sb of *ou* about. -**2.** [repreender]: ~ **alguém (de)** to reprimand sb (for).

ADN (*abrev de* ácido desoxirribonucleico) *m* DNA.

adoçante [ado'sãntʃil *m* sweetener.

adoção [ado'sãwl (*pl* -ões) [-õjʃl *f* adoption.

adoçar [13] [ado'sa(x)l *vt* -**1.** [café, chá] to sweeten. -**2.** *fig* [velhice, vida] to ease.

adocicado, da [adosi'kadu, dal *adj* slightly sweet.

adoecer [25] [adwe'se(x)l <> *vi*: ~ **(de)** to fall ill

(with). <> *vt* to make ill.
adoentado, da [adwĕn'tadu, da] *adj* ill.
adoidado, da [adoj'dadu, da] <> *adj* [amalucado] mad. <> *adv fam* [muito] madly.
adolescência [adole'sĕnsja] *f* adolescence.
adolescente [adole'sĕntʃi] <> *adj* adolescent. <> *mf* adolescent.
adoração [adora'sãw] *f* adoration.
adorar [4] [ado'ra(x)] *vt* -1. [divindade] to adore. -2. [gostar muito de] to love.
adorável [ado'ravɛw] (*pl* -eis) *adj* lovely.
adormecer [25] [adoxme'se(x)] <> *vi* -1. [dormir] to fall asleep. -2. [ficar dormente] to go numb. <> *vt* [causar sono a] to make sleepy.
adormecido, da [adoxme'sidu, da] *adj* -1. [que está dormindo] asleep. -2. [dormente] numb.
adornar [4] [adox'na(x)] *vt* to adorn.
adorno [a'doxnu] *m* adornment; **de** ~ decorative.
adotar [4] [ado'ta(x)] *vt* to adopt.
adotivo, va [ado'tʃivu, va] *adj* adoptive.
adquirir [6] [adʒiki'ri(x)] *vt* -1. [comprar] to buy. -2. [conseguir] to acquire.
adrede [a'dredʒi] *adv* on purpose.
adrenalina [adrena'lina] *f* adrenalin.
Adriático [a'drjatʃikul *n*: **o (mar)** ~ the Adriatic (Sea).
adro ['adrul *m* churchyard.
adstringente [adʒiʃtrĩn'ʒĕntʃi] <> *adj* astringent. <> *m* astringent lotion.
aduana [a'dwana] *f* customs (*pl*).
aduaneiro, ra [adwa'nejru, ra] *adj* customs (*pl*).
adubar [4] [adu'ba(x)] *vt* to fertilize.
adubo [a'dubu] *m* [fertilizante] fertilizer; ~ orgânico/químico organic/chemical fertilizer.
adulação [adula'sãw] *f* flattery.
adulador, ra [adula'do(x), ra] <> *adj* flattering. <> *m*, *f* flatterer.
adular [4] [adu'la(x)] *vt* to flatter.
adulteração [aduwtera'sãw] (*pl* -ões) *f* -1. [de texto] falsification. -2. [de alimento, medicamento] adulteration.
adulterar [4] [aduwte'ra(x)] *vt* -1. [texto] to falsify. -2. [alimento, medicamento] to adulterate.
adultério [aduw'tɛrjul *m* adultery.
adúltero, ra [a'duwteru, ra] <> *adj* adulterous. <> *m*, *f* adulterer (*f* adulteress).
adulto, ta [a'duwtu, ta] <> *adj* adult. <> *m*, *f* adult.
adunco [a'dũnkul *adj* [nariz] hooked.
adventício, cia [adʒvĕn'tʃisju, sja] <> *adj* -1. [forasteiro] alien. -2. [casual] chance. <> *m*, *f* [forasteiro] outsider.
advento [adʒ'vĕntul *m* advent.
advérbio [adʒ'vɛxbjul *m* adverb.
adversário, ria [adʒivex'sarju, rja] *m*, *f* adversary.
adversidade [adʒivexsi'dadʒi] *f* adversity.
adverso, sa [adʒi'vexsu, sa] *adj* -1. [difícil] adverse. -2. [desfavorável]: ~ **a algo** unfavourable to sthg. -3. [contrário]: ~ **a algo** opposed to sthg.

advertência [adʒivex'tĕnsja] *f* -1. [aviso] warning. -2. [repreensão] reprimand.
advertir [54] [adʒivex'tʃi(x)] *vt* -1. [prevenir, avisar] to warn. -2. [repreender] to reprimand.
advindo, da [ad'vĩndu, da] *adj*: ~ **de** resulting from.
advir [67] [adʒ'vi(x)] *vi* -1. [resultar]: ~ **de** to result from. -2. [suceder]: ~ **(a)** to happen to.
advocacia [adʒivoka'sia] *f* advocacy.
advogado, da [adʒivo'gadu, da] *m*, *f* lawyer; ~ **do diabo** devil's advocate.
advogar [14] [adʒivo'ga(x)] <> *vt* -1. JUR to advocate. -2. *fig* [defender] to defend. <> *vi* -1. [exercer a profissão de advogado] to practise law. -2. [interceder]: ~ **por algo/alguém** to represent sthg/sb.
aéreo, rea [a'ɛrju, rja] *adj* -1. AERON air (*antes de subst*). -2. [pessoa] absent-minded.
aerobarco [aɛro'baxkul *m* hovercraft.
aeróbico, ca [ae'rɔbiku, ka] *adj* aerobic.
➡ **aeróbica** *f* aerobics (*sg*).
aeroclube [aɛro'klubil *m* flying club.
aerodinâmico, ca [aɛrodʒi'nãmiku, ka] *adj* aerodynamic.
➡ **aerodinâmica** *f* aerodynamics (*pl*).
aeródromo [aɛ'rɔdromul *m* airfield.
aeroespacial [aɛroʃpa'sjawl (*pl* -ais) *adj* aerospace (*antes de subst*).
aerofoto [aɛro'fɔtul *f* aerial photograph.
aerograma [aɛro'gramal *m* aerogramme UK, aerogram US.
aeromoça [aɛro'mosal *f* air stewardess, flight attendant.
aeromodelismo [a,ɛromode'liʒmul *m* -1. [técnica] model aeroplane making. -2. ESP model aeroplane flying.
aeronauta [aɛro'nawtal *m*, *f* airline pilot.
aeronáutica [aɛro'nawtʃikal *f* -1. [ciência] aeronautics (*sg*). -2. MIL air force.
aeronave [aɛro'navil *f* aircraft.
aeroporto [aɛro'poxtul *m* airport.
aerossol [aɛro'sowl (*pl* -óis) *m* aerosol.
afã [a'fãl *m* -1. [ânsia - por sucesso] longing; [- de agradar] eagerness; [- para fazer algo] urge. -2. [entusiasmo, vontade] enthusiasm.
afabilidade [afabili'dadʒil *f* affability.
afagar [14] [afa'ga(x)] *vt* -1. [person] to caress. -2. [animal, hair] to stroke.
afago [a'fagul *m* stroke, caress.
afamado, da [afa'madu, dal *adj* famous.
afanar [4] [afa'na(x)] *vt fam* [roubar] to nick, to steal.
afasia [afa'zial *f* aphasia.
afastado, da [afaʃ'tadu, da] *adj* -1. [praia, terras] remote. -2. [casa] isolated. -3. [parente] distant. -4. [pernas] apart.
afastamento [afaʃta'mĕntul *m* -1. [distanciamento] withdrawal. -2. [de cargo] removal.
afastar [4] [afaʃ'ta(x)] *vt* -1. [tirar do caminho] to push out of the way. -2. [apartar] to put aside. -3. [pôr de lado] to part. -4. [distanciar] to keep away

(sep). **-5.** [de cargo] to remove. **-6.** [frustrar] to thwart.

➡ **afastar-se** *vp* **-1.** [distanciar-se - no espaço] to move aside *(sep)*; [- de amigos etc] to part. **-2.** [sair] to leave. **-3.** [de cargo] to take leave from.

afável [a'favɛwl] *(pl* **-eis)** *adj* affable.

afazeres [afa'zeriʃ] *mpl* affairs; ~ **domésticos** housework *(sg)*.

Afeganistão [afeganiʃ'tãwl *n* Afghanistan.

afegão, gã [afegiãw, ga] <> *adj* Afghan. <> *m, f* Afghan.

afeição [afej'sãwl *f* affection; **sentir** ~ **por alguém/algo** to feel affection for sb/sthg.

afeiçoado, da [afej'swadu, da] *adj* attached.

afeiçoar-se [20] [afej'swaxsil *vp*: ~ **a alguém/algo** to become attached to sb/sthg.

afeito, ta [a'fejtu, ta] *adj*: ~ **a** accustomed to.

aferidor [aferi'do(x)l *m* [instrumento] meter.

aferir [57] [afe'ri(x)l *vt* **-1.** [conferir] to check. **-2.** [avaliar] to estimate. **-3.** [cotejar]: ~ **algo/alguém por algo** to judge sthg/sb by sthg.

aferrado, da [afe'xadu, da] *adj* [apegado] attached.

aferrar-se [4] [afe'xaxsil *vp* [apegar-se]: ~ **a algo** to cling to sthg.

aferrolhar [4] [afexo'ʎa(x)l *vt* **-1.** [com ferrolho] to bolt. **-2.** *fig* [aprisionar] to lock up *(sep)*.

aferventar [4] [afexvẽn'ta(x)l *vt* to boil.

afetação [afeta'sãwl *f* affectation.

afetado, da [afe'tadu, da] *adj* affected.

afetar [4] [afe'ta(x)l *vt* to affect.

afetividade [afetʃivi'dadʒil *f* **-1.** affection. **-2.** PSIC affectivity.

afetivo, va [afe'tʃivu, va] *adj* **-1.** affectionate, kind. **-2.** PSIC affective.

afeto [a'fɛtul *m* **-1.** affection. **-2.** PSIC affect.

afetuoso, osa [afe'tuozu, ɔza] *adj* affectionate.

afiado, da [a'fjadu, da] *adj* sharp.

afiançar [13] [afjãn'sa(x)l *vt* **-1.** [réu] to bail out. **-2.** [dívida, empréstimo] to guarantee.

afiar [16] [a'fja(x)l *vt* [faca, tesoura] to sharpen.

aficionado, da [afisjo'nadu, da] *m, f* enthusiast.

afigurar-se [4] [afigu'raxsil *vp* to seem, to appear.

afilado, da [afi'ladu, da] *adj* fine.

afilhado, da [afi'ʎadu, da] *m, f* godchild.

afiliação [afilja'sãwl *f* affiliation.

afiliado, da [afi'ljadu, da] *m, f* affiliate.

afiliar [16] [afi'lja(x)l *vt* to affiliate.

➡ **afiliar-se** *vp*: ~**-se a algo** to join sthg.

afim [a'fĩl *(pl* **-ns)** *adj* **-1.** [objetivos] similar. **-2.** [almas] kindred.

afinação [afina'sãwl *(pl* **-ões)** [sõjʃl *f* MÚS tuning.

afinado, da [afi'nadu, da] *adj* **-1.** [instrumento] tuned. **-2.** [pessoa]: ~ **com** attuned to.

afinal [afi'nawl *adv* **-1.** [por fim] finally, in the end; ~ **, ele vem ou não vem?** so is he coming or not?; ~ **(de contas)** in the end. **-2.** [pensando bem] all things considered.

afinar [4] [afi'na(x)l <> *vt* **-1.** [voz, instrumento] to tune. **-2.** [idéias, sentimentos]: ~ **algo com algo** to

attune sthg to sthg. **-3.** [estilo, modos] to refine. <> *vi* **-1.** [emagrecer] to slim down. **-2.** [concordar]: ~ **com alguém em algo** to see eye to eye with sb over sthg. **-3.** [dar-se bem]: ~ **com alguém** to get on with sb.

afinco [a'fĩŋkul *m* perseverance; **com** ~ assiduously.

afinidade [afini'dadʒil *f* **-1.** [semelhança] affinity. **-2.** [parentesco]: **são primas por** ~ they look on each other as cousins.

afins [a'fĩʃl *pl* ➡ **afim**.

afirmação [afixma'sãwl *(pl* **-ões)** *f* **-1.** [declaração] assertion. **-2.** [auto-afirmação] self-assertion.

afirmar [4] [afix'ma(x)l *vt* **-1.** [declarar] to declare. **-2.** [confirmar] to assert.

➡ **afirmar-se** *vp* **-1.** [estabelecer-se] to establish o.s. **-2.** [sentir-se seguro] to assert o.s.

afirmativamente [afixmatʃiva'mẽntʃil *adv*: **responder** ~ to reply in the affirmative.

afirmativo, va [afixma'tʃivu, va] *adj* affirmative.

➡ **afirmativa** *f* assertion.

afivelar [4] [afive'la(x)l *vt* to buckle.

afixar [4] [afik'sa(x)l *vt* [aviso, cartaz] to affix.

aflição [afli'sãwl *(pl* **-ões)** *f* **-1.** [sofrimento] distress *(U)*. **-2.** [ansiedade] anxiety. **-3.** [desconforto]: **dar** ~ **a alguém** to unsettle sb.

afligir [52] [afli'ʒi(x)l *vt* **-1.** [fazer sofrer] to distress. **-2.** [causar ansiedade a] to trouble. **-3.** [suj: mal] to torment.

➡ **afligir-se** *vp*: ~**-se (com)** to worry (about).

aflitivo, va [afli'tʃivu, va] *adj* distressing.

aflito, ta [a'flitu, ta] *adj* distressed; **estar** ~ **com algo/para fazer algo** to be desperate about sthg/to do sthg.

aflorar [4] [aflo'ra(x)l *vi* **-1.** [vir à tona] to come to the surface. **-2.** [surgir] to surface.

afluência [aflu'ẽnsjal *f* **-1.** [de líquido] flow. **-2.** [de pessoas] flood. **-3.** [riqueza] affluence.

afluente [aflu'ẽntʃil <> *adj* [rico] affluent. <> *m* [curso de rio] tributary.

afluir [74] [a'flwi(x)l *vt*: ~ **a** *ou* **para/de** to flow into *ou* towards/from; [pessoas] to flock to *ou* towards/from.

afobação [afoba'sãwl *f* **-1.** [agitação, atrapalhação] turmoil. **-2.** [pressa] haste. **-3.** [ansiedade] anxiety.

afobado, da [afo'badu, da] *adj* **-1.** [ger] flustered. **-2.** [ansioso] upset.

afobamento [afoba'mẽntul *m* = **afobação**.

afobar [4] [afo'ba(x)l *vt* **-1.** [ger] to fluster. **-2.** [deixar ansioso] to perturb.

➡ **afobar-se** *vp* **-1.** [ficar agitado] to get flustered. **-2.** [apressar-se] to fret. **-3.** [ficar ansioso] to worry.

afofar [4] [afo'fa(x)l *vt* **-1.** [almofada] to fluff up. **-2.** [terra] to loosen.

afogado, da [afo'gadu, da] *adj* **-1.** [pessoa] drowned. **-2.** [motor] flooded. **-3.** [em dívidas] weighed down. **-4.** [em trabalho] swamped.

afogador [afoga'do(x)l *(pl* **-es)** *m* AUTO choke.

afogamento [afoga'mẽntul *m* drowning.

afogar [14] [afo'ga(x)l <> *vt* **-1.** [pessoa] to drown.

- **2.** [motor] to flood. - **3.** [pensamentos, sentimento] to quell. ◇ *vi* - **1.** [pessoa] to drown. - **2.** [motor] to flood.

➡ **afogar-se** *vp* [pessoa] to drown o.s.

afoito, ta [aˈfojtu, ta] *adj* in a hurry *(depois de subst/de verbo)*.

afonia [afoˈnia] *f* aphonia.

afônico, ca [aˈfoniku, ka] *adj* silent.

afora [aˈfɔra] ◇ *adv*: **pelo mundo** ~ throughout the world; **mar** ~ across the sea; **pela vida** ~ throughout life; **sair** *ou* **ir por aí** ~ to go off; **porta** ~ out the door. ◇ *prep* apart from.

aforismo [afoˈriʒmul] *m* aphorism.

afortunado, da [afoxtuˈnadu, da] *adj* fortunate.

Afoxés [aˈfoʃɛʃ] *mpl traditional groups who parade through the streets during Carnival.*

AFOXÉS

Religious procession related to *candomblé*; *afoxés* were made up of groups of black people, who took to the streets and sang to the sound of percussion instruments such as *atabaques* and *agogôs*. Nowadays, *afoxés* are carnival displays typical of Bahia. The most popular one is known as *Filhos de Gandhi* ('Sons of Gandhi').

afrescalhado, da [afreʃkaˈʎadu, da] *adj fam* camp.

afresco [aˈfreʃku] *m* fresco.

África [ˈafrika] *n* Africa.

africano, na [afriˈkãnu, na] ◇ *adj* African. ◇ *m, f* African.

afro-americano, na [afrwameriˈkãnu, na] ◇ *adj* Afro-American. ◇ *m, f* Afro-American.

afro-brasileiro, ra [afrobraziˈlejru, ra] *adj* Afro-Brazilian.

afrodisíaco, ca [afrodʒiˈziaku, ka] *adj* aphrodisiac.

➡ **afrodisíaco** *m* aphrodisiac.

afronta [aˈfrõtal] *f* affront.

afrontado, da [afrõˈtadu, da] *adj* [ultrajado] outraged.

afrontar [4] [afrõˈta(x)] *vt* - **1.** [ultrajar] to outrage. - **2.** [atacar] to confront.

afrouxar [4] [afroˈʃa(x)] ◇ *vt* - **1.** [soltar] to loosen. - **2.** [relaxar] to relax. ◇ *vi* - **1.** [soltar-se] to come undone. - **2.** [pessoa] to give up.

afta [ˈafta] *f* mouth ulcer.

afugentar [4] [afuʒẽˈta(x)] *vt* to chase away.

afundar [4] [afũˈda(x)] ◇ *vt* - **1.** [fazer ir ao fundo - pessoa] to force to the ground; [- âncora] to drop. - **2.** [aprofundar] to deepen. ◇ *vi* to sink.

➡ **afundar-se** *vp* - **1.** *fam* [em exame] to fail. - **2.** [embranhar-se - em afazeres] to become engulfed; [- no matagal] to go deep. - **3.** [imergir] to sink. - **4.** [perder-se] to lose o.s.

afunilar [4] [afuniˈla(x)] *vt* - **1.** [dar forma de funil] to shape into a funnel. - **2.** [estreitar] to narrow.

➡ **afunilar-se** *vp* [estreitar-se - rio] to narrow; [- análise] to be narrowed down.

agá [aˈga] *m* aitch.

agachado, da [agaˈʃadu, da] *adj* squat.

agachar-se [7] [agaˈʃaxsi] *vp* - **1.** [acocorar-se] to squat. - **2.** *fig* [aviltar-se] to grovel.

agarrado, da [agaˈxadu, da] *adj* - **1.** [preso com força]: ~ **a** *ou* **em algo** clinging to *ou* onto sthg. - **2.** [apegado]: ~ **a** *ou* **com alguém** clinging to *ou* onto sb.

agarramento [agaxaˈmẽtul] *m* [entre namorados] clinch; **ser pego de** ~ **com alguém** to be caught in a clinch with sb.

agarrar [4] [agaˈxa(x)] ◇ *vt* - **1.** [segurar com força] to grasp. - **2.** [capturar] to catch. ◇ *vi* - **1.** [segurar com força]: ~ **em** to hold on to. - **2.** [goleiro] to defend.

➡ **agarrar-se** *vp* - **1.** [segurar com força]: ~**-se a** *ou* **em** to hold on to. - **2.** [abraçar-se fortemente] to cling to each other.

agasalhado, da [agazaˈʎadu, da] *adj* warmly wrapped.

agasalhar [4] [agazaˈʎa(x)] *vt* to wrap up warmly.

➡ **agasalhar-se** *vp* to wrap o.s. up warmly.

agasalho [agaˈzaʎul] *m* - **1.** [casaco, manta] warm clothing. - **2.** [suéter] jumper.

ágeis [ˈaʒejʃ] *pl* ▷ **ágil**.

agência [aˈʒẽsjal] *f* - **1.** [empresa] agency; ~ **de notícias** news agency; ~ **de viagens** travel agency. - **2.** [sucursal] branch; ~ **de correios** post-office branch.

agenciamento [aʒẽsjamẽtul] *m* - **1.** [negociação] negotiation. - **2.** [representação] representation. - **3.** [obtenção, busca] recruitment.

agenciar [16] [aˈʒẽsja(x)] *vt* - **1.** [ger] to manage. - **2.** [servir de agente a] to act as agent for.

agenda [aˈʒẽda] *f* - **1.** [de compromissos] diary; ~ **eletrônica** electronic organizer. - **2.** [programação - de reunião] agenda; [- de semana] schedule.

agendar [4] [aʒẽˈda(x)] *vt* to schedule.

agente [aˈʒẽtʃi] ◇ *m, f* [pessoa] agent; ~ **secreto** secret agent; ~ **de viagens** travel agent. ◇ *m* - **1.** [ger] agent. - **2.** *GRAM* subject.

agigantado, da [aʒigãˈtadu, da] *adj* gigantic.

agigantar [4] [aʒigãˈta(x)] *vt* to magnify; **o vento agigantou as ondas** the wind swelled the waves.

ágil [ˈaʒiw] *(pl* **ágeis)** *adj* agile.

agilidade [aʒiliˈdadʒi] *f* agility.

agilizar [4] [aʒiliˈza(x)] *vt* to activate.

ágio [ˈaʒju] *m* interest.

agiota [aˈʒjɔta] *m, f* [usurário] usurer.

agir [52] [aˈʒi(x)] *vi* to act; ~ **bem/mal** to act properly/wrongly.

agitação [aʒitaˈsãw] *(pl* -**ões)** *f* - **1.** [movimento - de garrafa] shaking; [- de líquido] stirring; [- de braços] waving. - **2.** *PSIC* [excitação] agitation. - **3.** [inquietação] restlessness. - **4.** [rebuliço] agitation. - **5.** [política, social] unrest.

agitado, da [aʒiˈtadu, da] *adj* - **1.** [excitado] agitated. - **2.** [inquieto] disturbed. - **3.** [tumultuado] unsettled. - **4.** [mar] rough.

agitador, ra [aʒitaˈdo(x), ra] *m, f* agitator.

agitar [4] [aʒiˈta(x)] *vt* - **1.** [movimentar - garrafa etc] to shake; [- líquido] to stir; [- braços] to wave.

- 2. [excitar] to unnerve. **- 3.** [inquietar] to worry. **- 4.** [sublevar] to agitate. **- 5.** *fam* [fazer, organizar] to organize. ◇ *vi*[movimentar]: **'agite antes de usar'** 'shake before use'.

◆ **agitar-se** *vp* **- 1.** [inquietar-se] to become agitated. **- 2.** [movimentar-se - na cama] to be restless; [- na rua, no trabalho etc] to run around.

agito [a'ʒitu] *m fam* excitement.

aglomeração [aglomera'sãw] (*pl* -ões) *f* **- 1.** [de coisas] stack. **- 2.** [de pessoas] mass; ~ **urbana** built-up area.

aglomerado [aglome'radu] *m* **- 1.** [de coisas] pile. **- 2.** [de pessoas] mass.

aglomerar [4] [aglome'ra(x)] *vt* to mass.

◆ **aglomerar-se** *vp*[pessoas] to swarm.

aglutinação [aglutʃina'sãw] *f* **- 1.** [fusão] agglutination. **- 2.** [combinação] almagamation.

aglutinar [4] [aglutʃi'na(x)] *vt* **- 1.** [com cola] to glue. **- 2.** [palavras, sufixo] to agglutinate.

ago. (*abrev de* **agosto**) Aug.

agonia [ago'nia] *f* **- 1.** [ger] agony; **que** ~**!** *fig* what a pain! **- 2.** [de moribundo] death throes *(pl)*. **- 3.** *fig* [declínio] decline.

agoniado, da [ago'njadu, da] *adj* **- 1.** [aflito] distressed. **- 2.** [irritado] irritated.

agoniar [16] [ago'nja(x)] *vt* **- 1.** [afligir] to distress. **- 2.** [irritar] to irritate.

agonizante [agoni'zãntʃi] *adj* dying.

agonizar [4] [agoni'za(x)] *vi* to be dying.

agora [a'gɔra] ◇ *adv* **- 1.** [neste momento] now; **e** ~**?** now what?; ~ **mesmo** right now; [há pouco] just now; **até** ~ until now; **de** ~ **em diante** from now on. **- 2.** [atualmente] nowadays. **- 3.** [doravante] from now on. ◇ *conj* [mas] now.

agorafobia [ˌagorafo'bia] *f* agoraphobia.

agorinha [ago'riɲa] *adv* just now.

agosto [a'goʃtu] *m* August; *veja também* **setembro**.

agourar [4] [ago'ra(x)] ◇ *vt* [pressagiar] to portend. ◇ *vi* [fazer mau agouro] to bode ill.

agourento, ta [ago'rẽntu, ta] *adj* **- 1.** [supersticioso] superstitious. **- 2.** [que anuncia desgraças] ominous; **que mulher mais agourenta!** what a prophet of doom that woman is!

agouro [a'goru] *m* omen; **mau** ~ bad omen.

agraciar [16] [agra'sja(x)] *vt* **- 1.** [condecorar] to decorate. **- 2.** [preso, exilado] to pardon.

agradabilíssimo, ma [agradabi'lisimu, ma] *adj* = *superl de* **agradável**.

agradar [4] [agra'da(x)] ◇ *vt* [causar prazer a] to please. ◇ *vi* **- 1.** [satisfazer]: ~ **(a) alguém** to please sb. **- 2.** [aprazer]: ~ **a** to delight. **- 3.** [ser agradável] to please, to be pleasing.

agradável [agra'davɛw] (*pl* -eis) *adj* pleasant.

agradecer [25] [agrade'se(x)] ◇ *vt*: ~ **algo** to say thank you for sthg. ◇ *vi* **- 1.** [dizer obrigado] to say thank you; ~ **a alguém por algo** to thank sb for sthg. **- 2.** [ficar grato] to be grateful.

agradecido, da [agrade'sidu, da] *adj* grateful.

agradecimento [agradesi'mẽntu] *m* [gratidão] thanks *(pl)*, thank you; **carta de** ~ thank-you letter.

◆ **agradecimentos** *mpl* thanks.

agrado [a'gradu] *m*: **fazer um** ~ **a alguém** [presentear] to give sb a present; [acariciar] to be affectionate with sb.

agrário, ria [a'grarju, rja] *adj* agrarian.

agravamento [agrava'mẽntu] *m* worsening.

agravante [agra'vãntʃi] ◇ *adj* aggravating. ◇ *m* [o que piora a situação]: **o agravante é que ...** the annoying thing is that ...

agravar [4] [agra'va(x)] ◇ *vt* [piorar] to worsen. ◇ *vi JUR*: ~ **de algo** to appeal against sthg.

◆ **agravar-se** *vp*[piorar] to worsen.

agravo [a'gravu] *m JUR* appeal.

agredir [58] [agre'dʒi(x)] *vt* **- 1.** [atacar] to attack. **- 2.** [insultar] to insult. **- 3.** *fig* [afetar] to offend.

agregado, da [agre'gadu, da] ◇ *adj* attached. ◇ *m*, *f* [hóspede] guest.

◆ **agregado** *m CONSTR* aggregate.

agregar [4] [agre'ga(x)] *vt* to add; ~ **algo a algo** to add sthg to sthg.

◆ **agregar-se** *vp* [associar-se]: ~**-se a algo** to join sthg.

agressão [agre'sãw] (*pl* -ões) *f* aggression.

agressividade [agresivi'dadʒi] *f* aggressiveness.

agressivo, va [agre'sivu, va] *adj* aggressive.

agressor, ra [agre'so(x), ra] *m*, *f* aggressor.

agreste [a'grɛʃtʃi] ◇ *adj* rural. ◇ *m* stony, *unfertile area of north-eastern Brazil*.

agrião [agri'ãw] (*pl* -ões) *m* watercress.

agrícola [a'grikola] *adj* agricultural.

agricultor, ra [agrikuw'to(x), ra] *m*, *f* farmer.

agricultura [agrikuw'tura] *f* agriculture.

agridoce [agri'dosi] *adj* **- 1.** [comida] sweet and sour. **- 2.** [emoções] bitter-sweet.

agroindústria [agrwĩn'duʃtrja] *f* agro-industry.

agronomia [agrono'mia] *f* agronomy.

agrônomo, ma [a'gronomu, ma] *m*, *f* agronomist.

agropecuário, ria [agrope'kwarju, rja] *adj* mixed-farming *(antes de subst)*.

◆ **agropecuária** *f* mixed farming.

agrotóxico [agro'tɔksiku] *m* pesticide.

agrupamento [agrupa'mẽntu] *m* collection.

agrupar [4] [agru'pa(x)] *vt* to collect.

◆ **agrupar-se** *vp* to be grouped together.

agrura [a'grura] *f* scourge.

água [ˈagwa] *f* **- 1.** water; ~ **benta** holy water; ~ **boricada** boric acid; ~ **corrente** running water; ~ **doce/salgada** fresh/salt water; **peixe de** ~ **doce** freshwater fish; ~ **mineral/gasosa/sem gás** mineral/sparkling/still water; ~ **oxigenada** hydrogen peroxide; ~ **potável** drinking water; ~ **de rosas** rose water; ~ **sanitária** chemically purified water; **claro como** ~ crystal-clear; **com** ~ **na boca** watering at the mouth; **ir nas** ~**s de alguém** to go with sb's wishes. **- 2.** *fig* [plano]: **ir por** ~ **abaixo** to go down the drain.

◆ **águas** *fpl* **- 1.** [chuvas] rainwater *(sg)*. **- 2.** [minerais, termais] waters, thermal springs.

aguaceiro [agwa'sejru] *m* downpour.

água-com-açúcar [͵agwakwa'suka(x)] *adj (inv)* sentimental.

água-de-coco [͵agwadʒi'kokul] *f* coconut milk.

água-de-colônia [͵agwadʒiko'lonjal] (*pl* **águas-de-colônia**) *f* eau-de-Cologne.

aguado, da [a'gwadu, da] *adj* watered-down.

água-furtada [͵agwafux'tada] (*pl* **águas-furta-das**) *f* garret.

água-marinha [͵agwama'riɲa] (*pl* **águas-mari-nhas**) *f* aquamarine.

aguar [22] [a'gwa(x)] *vt* **-1.** [diluir] to water down. **-2.** [regar] to water.

aguardar [4] [agwax'da(x)] <> *vt* to await. <> *vi* to wait; ~ **por** to wait for.

aguardente [agwax'dẽntʃi] *f* brandy; ~ **de cana** cachaça.

aguarrás [agwa'xaʃ] *f* turpentine.

água-viva [͵agwa'viva] (*pl* **águas-vivas**) *f* jelly-fish.

aguçado, da [agu'sadu, da] *adj* **-1.** [ger] sharp. **-2.** [apetite] keen; [interesse] lively.

aguçar [13] [agu'sa(x)] *vt* **-1.** [ger] to sharpen. **-2.** [estimular] to stimulate.

agudeza [agu'deza] *f* sharpness.

agudo, da [a'gudu, da] *adj* **-1.** [ger] acute. **-2.** [pe-netrante] sharp. **-3.** [nota, voz] shrill.

agüentar [4] [agwẽn'ta(x)] <> *vt* **-1.** [ger] to bear; ~ **fazer algo** to be able to bear to do sthg. **-2.** [tolerar] to put up with. <> *vi* **-1.** [resistir] to support; **não** ~ **de algo** to be unable to bear sthg. **-2.** *loc:* ~ **a mão** *fam* [esperar] to hold on; [re-sistir a situação difícil] to hang on.

➡ **agüentar-se** *vp* [permanecer] to remain.

aguerrido, da [age'xidu, da] *adj* **-1.** [afeito à guer-ra] warlike. **-2.** [combativo] bellicose.

águia [agja] *f* **-1.** [ave] eagle. **-2.** *fig* [pessoa] talented person.

agulha [a'guʎa] *f* needle.

ah [a] *interj* ah!

ai [͵aj] <> *interj* **-1.** [de dor] ouch! **-2.** [de cócegas] eek! **-3.** [suspiro] oh! **-4.** [lamento] oh dear! **-5.** [ge-mido] oh no! <> *m* [de dor] groan.

➡ **ai de** *loc adj* damn.

aí [a'i] <> *adv* **-1.** [ger] there; **espera** ~! wait there! **-2.** [em lugar indeterminado]: **por** ~ around. **-3.** [para lugar indeterminado]: **sair por** ~ **(afora)** to go off somewhere. **-4.** [junto, em anexo] herewith. **-5.** [nesse caso, então] then. **-6.** [aproximadamente]: **por** ~ around. **-7.** [em data, período]: ~ **pelos anos 60** around the 60s. **-8.** [e assim por diante] : **e por** ~ **afora** and so on and so forth. **-9.** *fam* [saudando]: **e** ~! hi! <> *interj* **-1.** [animando] go on! **-2.** [malician-do]: ~ ... **hein?** well, now ...

aiatolá [ajato'la] *m* ayatollah.

aidético, ca [aj'dɛtʃiku, ka] <> *adj* suffering from AIDS. <> *m, f* AIDS sufferer, person with AIDS.

AIDS (*abrev de* **Acquired Immunodeficiency Syn-drome**) *f* AIDS.

ainda [a'ĩnda] *adv* **-1.** [ger] still; ~ **não** not yet; ~ (assim) still. **-2.** [um dia] one day. **-3.** [ao menos]: **se** ~ ... if at least.

➡ **ainda agora** *loc adv* just now.

➡ **ainda bem** *loc adv* just as well.

➡ **ainda por cima** *loc adv* still; **ele não ajuda, e** ~ **por cima reclama** he's not helping, and on top of that he's complaining.

➡ **ainda que** *loc conj* even if.

aipim [aj'pĩ] (*pl* **-ns**) *m* cassava.

aipo ['ajpu] *m* celery.

airoso, osa [aj'rozu, ɔza] *adj* elegant.

ajardinado, da [aʒaxdʒi'nadu, da] *adj* with gar-den.

ajardinar [4] [aʒaxdʒi'na(x)] *vt* to turn into a garden.

ajeitar [4] [aʒej'ta(x)] *vt* **-1.** [endireitar] to straight-en. **-2.** [arrumar] to tidy up. **-3.** [acomodar] to tuck up.

➡ **ajeitar-se** *vp* **-1.** [arrumar-se] to tidy o.s. up. **-2.** [a emprego] to adapt. **-3.** [acomodar-se] to settle down. **-4.** [adaptar-se]: ~**-se com algo** to get used to sthg.

ajoelhado, da [aʒwe'ʎadu, da] *adj* kneeling.

ajoelhar [4] [aʒwe'ʎa(x)] *vi* to kneel.

➡ **ajoelhar-se** *vp* to kneel down.

ajuda [a'ʒuda] *f* **-1.** [auxílio] help; **dar** ~ **a alguém (em algo)** to help sb (with sthg); **sem** ~ without help; **vir em** ~ **de alguém** to come to sb's aid. **-2.** *ECON & POL* aid; ~ **de custo** financial assistance.

ajudante [aʒu'dãntʃi] *mf* assistant.

ajudar [4] [aʒu'da(x)] <> *vt* **-1.** [auxiliar]: ~ **alguém (em algo)** to help sb (with sthg); ~ **alguém a fa-zer algo** to help sb do sthg. **-2.** [facilitar] to help. **-3.** [missa] to serve at. <> *vi* **-1.** [auxiliar] to help; ~ **a alguém** to help sb; ~ **em algo** to help with sthg. **-2.** [facilitar] to help.

➡ **ajudar-se** *vp* to help each other.

ajuizado, da [aʒwi'zadu, da] *adj* sensible.

ajuizar [4] [aʒwi'za(x)] *vt* **-1.** *JUR* [levar a juízo] to bring before a court. **-2.** [formar juízo sobre] to form an opinion on.

ajuntamento [aʒũnta'mẽntu] *m* **-1.** [de pessoas] gathering. **-2.** [de objetos] pile.

ajuntar [4] [aʒũn'ta(x)] *vt* **-1.** [reunir] to assemble. **-2.** [amontoar] to pile up. **-3.** [acrescentar] to add.

ajustar [4] [aʒuʃ'ta(x)] *vt* **-1.** [regular] to adjust. **-2.** [adaptar]: ~ **algo a algo** [idéias, procedimento] to adapt sthg to sthg; ~ **algo em algo** [peça] to fit sthg into sthg. **-3.** [apertar] to tighten. **-4.** [acertar] to agree; ~ **contas** to settle accounts.

➡ **ajustar-se** *vp* [adaptar-se] to adapt.

ajustável [aʒuʃ'tavew] (*pl* **-eis**) *adj* adjustable.

ajuste [a'ʒuʃtʃi] *m* **-1.** [acordo] agreement. **-2.** [de peça - encaixe] fitting; [- aperto] tightening. **-3.** [re-gulagem] adjustment. **-4.** [acerto]: ~ **de contas** settlement of accounts, *fig* settling of scores.

AL (*abrev de* **Estado de Alagoas**) *n* State of Alagoas.

ala ['ala] *f* **-1.** [ger] wing. **-2.** [de escola de samba] group; **a** ~ **das baianas** *the section of the carnival parade made up of women wearing typical Bahia costumes.*

Alá [a'la] *m* Allah.

alagadiço, ça [alaga'dʒisu, sa] *adj* subject to flooding *(depois de verbo)*.

alagado, da [ala'gadu, da] *adj* flooded.

alagamento [alaga'mẽntul *m* flooding.

alagar [14] [ala'ga(x)] *vt* to flood.

Alagoas [ala'goaʃ] *n* Alagoas.

ALALC (*abrev de* **Associação Latino-Americana de Livre Comércio**) *f Latin-American free trade association.*

alambique [alãn'bikí] *m* still *(for making alcohol).*

alameda [ala'meda] *f* avenue.

alaranjado, da [alarãn'ʒadu, da] *adj* orange-coloured.

alarde [a'laxdʒi] *m* - **1.** [ostentação] ostentation; **fazer ~ de algo** to show off sthg. - **2.** [bazófia] boastfulness; **fazer ~ de algo** to brag about sthg.

alardear [15] [alax'dʒja(x)] *vt* - **1.** [ostentar] to parade. - **2.** [gabar-se de] to brag about.

alargamento [alaxga'mẽntu] *m* [de estrada] widening.

alargar [14] [alax'ga(x)] *vt* - **1.** [estrada] to widen. - **2.** [roupa] to let out.

alarido [ala'ridu] *m* [gritaria, algazarra] uproar.

alarmante [alax'mãntʃi] *adj* alarming.

alarmar [4] [alax'ma(x)] *vt* to alarm.

  ⬥ **alarmar-se** *vp* to become alarmed.

alarme [a'laxmi] *m* alarm; **campainha de ~** alarm bell; **dar o ~** to sound the alarm.

alarmista [alax'miʃta] *adj* alarmist.

Alasca [a'laʃka] *n* Alaska.

alastrar [4] [alaʃ'tra(x)] *vt* [propagar, espalhar] to spread.

  ⬥ **alastrar-se** *vp* to spread.

alavanca [ala'vãŋka] *f* - **1.** [peça] lever; **~ de mudanças** AUTO gear lever. - **2.** *fig* [meio de ação] lever.

alavancagem [alavãŋ'kaʒẽl *f* ECON leverage.

alavancar [alavaŋ'ka(x)] *vt* [promover] to launch; ECON to leverage.

albanês, esa [awbã'neʃl ⬦ *adj* Albanian. ⬦ *m, f* Albanian.

  ⬥ **albanês** *m* [língua] Albanian.

Albânia [aw'bãnja] *n* Albania.

albergue [aw'bɛxgil *m* - **1.** [hospedaria] hostel; [para jovens] youth hostel. - **2.** [asilo] refuge.

albino, na [aw'binu, na] ⬦ *adj* albino. ⬦ *m, f* albino.

álbum ['awbũl (*pl* **-ns**) *m* album.

albumina [awbu'mina] *f* albumin.

ALCA (*abrev de* **Área de Livre Comércio das Américas**) *f* FTAA.

alça ['awsa] *f* - **1.** [de mala, vestido] strap. - **2.** [em arma]: **~ de mira** sights *(pl).*

alcachofra [awka'ʃofra] *f* artichoke.

alcaçuz [awka'suʒ] *m* liquorice plant.

alçada [aw'sada] *f* - **1.** [competência] competence; **ser da ~ de alguém** to be sb's responsibility. - **2.** JUR jurisdiction.

álcali ['awkalil *m* alkali.

alcalino, na [awka'linu, na] *adj* alkaline.

alcançar [13] [awkãn'sa(x)] *vt* - **1.** [ger] to reach. - **2.** [pegar] to catch. - **3.** [entender] to grasp. - **4.** [conseguir] to attain.

alcançável [awkãn'savewl (*pl* **-eis**) *adj* attainable.

alcance [aw'kãnsil *m* - **1.** [de arma, míssil] range. - **2.** [de pessoa]: **ao meu/ao teu ~** within my/your reach; **ao ~ da vista** within sight; **fora do ~ de** [objeto, pessoa] out of reach of; [entendimento] beyond the grasp of. - **3.** [importância]: **de pequeno/grande ~** of minor/major importance.

alçapão [awsa'pãw] (*pl* **-ões**) *m* - **1.** [portinhola] trapdoor. - **2.** [armadilha] trap.

alcaparra [awka'paxa] *f* caper.

alçar [13] [aw'sa(x)] *vt* - **1.** [levantar - carga, viga] to lift; [- braço] to raise. - **2.** [voz] to raise. - **3.** [vôo] to rise.

  ⬥ **alçar-se** *vp* [a cargo] to rise.

alcatéia [awka'tɛja] *f* [de lobos] pack.

alcatra [aw'katra] *f* rump steak.

alcatrão [awka'trãw] *m* tar.

álcool ['awkow] (*pl* **-óis**) *m* alcohol.

alcoólatra [aw'kɔlatra] ⬦ *adj* alcoholic. ⬦ *mf* alcoholic.

alcoólico, ca [aw'kwɔliku, ka] *adj* alcoholic.

alcoolismo [awko'liʒmul *m* alcoholism.

alcoolizado, da [awkoli'zadu, da] *adj* [pessoa] drunk.

Alcorão [awko'rãw] *m* Koran.

alcova [aw'koval *f* dressing room.

alcoviteiro, ra [awkovi'tejru, ra] *m, f* gossip.

alcunha [aw'kuɲa] *f* nickname.

aldeão, deã [aw'dʒjãw, dja] (*mpl* **-ões**, **-ãos**, *fpl* **-s**) *m, f* villager.

aldeia [aw'deja] *f* village; **~ de pescadores** fishing village.

aldraba [aw'draba] *f* [de bater] door-knocker.

aleatório, ria [alea'tɔrju, rja] *adj* random.

alecrim [ale'krĩ] *m* rosemary.

alegação [alega'sãwl (*pl* **-ões**) *f* allegation.

alegado, da [ale'gadu, da] *adj* alleged.

  ⬥ **alegado** *m* JUR allegation.

alegar [14] [ale'ga(x)] *vt* to allege; **~ que** to allege that; JUR to allege that.

alegoria [alego'ria] *f* allegory.

alegórico, ca [ale'gɔrikul *adj* allegorical; ▷ **carro**.

alegrar [4] [ale'gra(x)] *vt* to cheer up.

  ⬥ **alegrar-se** *vp* to be happy; **alegre-se!** cheer up!

alegre [a'lɛgril *adj* - **1.** [pessoa] cheerful. - **2.** [festa, bar, voz] lively. - **3.** [cor] bright. - **4.** [embriagado] merry.

alegria [ale'gria] *f* - **1.** [qualidade] cheerfulness. - **2.** [satisfação] contentment. - **3.** [júbilo] joy.

aléia [a'lɛja] *f* - **1.** [alameda] alley. - **2.** [passagem] alley.

aleijado, da [alej'ʒadu, da] ⬦ *adj* crippled. ⬦ *m, f* cripple.

aleijar [4] [alej'ʒa(x)] *vt* to cripple.

aleitamento [alejtamẽntul *m* breastfeeding.

além [a'lẽj] ⬦ *m* [o outro mundo]: **o ~** the beyond. ⬦ *adv* - **1.** [em lugar afastado] over there. - **2.** [mais

adiante] further on; **mais** ~ further.
⬥ **além de** *loc prep* **-1.** [mais adiante de] beyond. **-2.** [do outro lado de, acima de] beyond. **-3.** [afora] apart from.
⬥ **além disso** *loc conj* besides.
⬥ **além do mais** *loc conj* furthermore.
Alemanha [ale'mãɲal *n* Germany.
alemão, mã [ale'mãw, mãl ◇ *adj* German. ◇ *m, f* German.
⬥ **alemão** *m* [língua] German.
alentado, da [alẽ'tadu, dal *adj* **-1.** [animoso] brave. **-2.** [volumoso] bulky. **-3.** [corpulento] stout.
alentar [4] [alẽta(x)] *vt* to comfort.
alento [a'lẽtul *m* **-1.** [ânimo] courage. **-2.** [fôlego] breath.
alergia [alex'ʒial *f* **-1.** *MED* allergy; **ter** ~ **a algo** to be allergic to sthg. **-2.** *fig* [aversão] allergy; **ter** ~ **a algo/alguém** to be allergic to sthg/sb.
alérgico, ca [a'lɛxʒiku, kal *adj* **-1.** *MED* : ~ **(a)** allergic (to). **-2.** *fig* [averso]: ~ **a** allergic to.
alerta [a'lɛxtal ◇ *adj* alert. ◇ *adv* alert. ◇ *m* warning.
alertar [4] [alex'ta(x)] *vt* : ~ **alguém (de/sobre algo)** to alert sb (to sthg).
alfabético, ca [awfa'bɛtʃiku, kal *adj* alphabetical.
alfabetização [awfabetʃiza'sãw] *f* **-1.** [ato] teaching to read and write. **-2.** [estado] literacy.
alfabetizado, da [awfabetʃi'zadu, dal *adj* literate.
alfabetizar [4] [awfabetʃi'za(x)] *vt* to teach to read and write.
alfabeto [awfa'bɛtul *m* alphabet.
alface [aw'fasil *f* lettuce.
alfafa [aw'fafal *f* alfalfa.
alfaiataria [awfajata'rial *f* tailor's shop.
alfaiate [awfa'jatʃil *m* tailor.
alfândega [aw'fãndegal *f* **-1.** [administração] customs (*pl*). **-2.** [local] customs house.
alfandegário, ria [awfãnde'garju, rjal *adj* customs (*antes de subst*).
alfazema [awfa'zemal *f* lavender.
alfinetada [awfine'tadal *f* **-1.** [picada de alfinete] pin-prick. **-2.** [dor] sharp pain. **-3.** *fig* [dito] stinging remark; **dar uma** ~ **em alguém** to make a stinging remark to sb.
alfinetar [4] [awfine'ta(x)] *vt* **-1.** *COST* to pin. **-2.** *fig* [criticar] to criticize.
alfinete [awfi'netʃil *m* **-1.** *COST* pin. **-2.** [prendedor]: ~ **de fralda** nappy pin; ~ **de segurança** safety pin. **-3.** [jóia] pin.
alfineteira [awfine'tejral *f* **-1.** [caixa] pin box. **-2.** [almofadinha] pincushion.
alforje [aw'fɔxʒil *m* saddlebag.
alga [ˈawgal *f* seaweed.
algarismo [awga'riʒmul *m* number.
algazarra [awga'zaxal *f* shouting; **fazer** ~ to make a racket.
álgebra [ˈawʒebral *f* algebra.
algébrico, ca [aw'ʒɛbriku, kal *adj* *MAT* algebraic.
algemar [4] [awʒe'ma(x)] *vt* to handcuff.

algemas [aw'ʒemaʃl *fpl* handcuffs.
algo [ˈawgul ◇ *pron* **-1.** *(em frases afirmativas)* something. **-2.** *(em frases interrogativas)* anything. ◇ *adv* somewhat.
algodão [awgo'dãwl *m* cotton; ~ **(hidrófilo)** cotton wool; **uma camisa de** ~ a cotton shirt.
algodão-doce [awgo͵dãw'dosil *(pl* **algodões-doces)** *m* candyfloss.
algodoeiro [awgo'dwejrul *m* cotton plant.
algoritmo [awgo'xitʃimul *m* algorithm.
algoz [aw'gɔʒl *m* **-1.** [carrasco] executioner. **-2.** [pessoa cruel] cruel person.
alguém [aw'gẽjl ◇ *pron indef* **-1.** [alguma pessoa] someone; ~ **quebrou este vaso** someone broke this vase; **tem** ~ **lá embaixo** there's someone downstairs **-2.** [em frases interrogativas] anybody, anyone; ~ **me telefonou?** did anybody phone me?; ~ **quer mais café?** does anybody want more coffee?; **tem** ~ **aí?** is anybody there?; ~ **mais** anybody else. **-3.** [determinada pessoa] somebody; **ele sabia que haveria** ~ **à sua espera** he knew there would be somebody waiting for him; **você é** ~ **que admiro muito** you are somebody I admire greatly. **- 4.** *fig* [pessoa importante] somebody; **se um dia eu me tornar** ~, **lembrarei dos velhos amigos** if one day I become somebody, I'll remember my old friends; **ele é** ~ **na empresa?** is he somebody in the company?; **ser** ~ **(na vida)** to be somebody in life. ◇ *m* [uma pessoa]: **esse** ~ that person; **um** ~ a person.
algum, ma [aw'gũ, mal *(mpl* **-ns**, *fpl* **-s)** ◇ *adj* **-1.** [indeterminado] some; **ela morou** ~ **tempo em Londres** she lived for some time in London; **me dê** ~ **dinheiro** give me some money; ~ **dia vamos te visitar** some day we'll come and see you **-2.** [em interrogativas, negativas] any; ~ **problema?** any problems?; **de jeito** *ou* **modo** ~ in no way; **não há problema** ~ there's no problem, there aren't any problems; **em parte alguma do país** nowhere in the country; **coisa alguma** nothing; **não há melhora alguma** there is no improvement, there isn't any improvement. ◇ *pron* **-1.** [indicando pessoa] somebody; **alguns preferem cinema, outros, teatro** some people prefer the cinema, others the theatre **-2.** [indicando coisa] one; **abra a caixa de bombons e prove alguns** open the box of sweets and try some **-3.** [em interrogativas: pessoa] anybody **-4.** [em interrogativas: coisa] any; ~ **dia** *ou* some day; **alguma coisa** something, anything; **alguma vez** sometime.
⬥ **alguns** *pron pl* some.
⬥ **alguma** *f* [evento, feito]: **deve ter lhe acontecido alguma** something must have happened to him; **esse menino aprontou alguma** that boy has been up to something.
alheamento [aʎea'mẽntul *m* [indiferença] indifference.
alhear [15] [aʎeia(x)] *vt* **-1.** [desviar] to turn. **-2.** [bens] to separate.
⬥ **alhear-se** *vp* [distanciar-se] to distance o.s.
alheio, alheia [a'ʎeju, a'ʎejal *adj* **-1.** [de outra

pessoa]: **um problema** ~ somebody else's problem. **- 2.** [irrelevante]: ~ **a irrelevant to. - 3.** [afastado, abstraído]: ~ **(a)** unaware (of).

→ **alheios** *mpl* [estranhos] outsiders.

alho [ˈaʎu] *m* garlic; **confundir** ~**s com bugalhos** to confuse two different things.

alho-poró [aˌʎupoˈrɔl] (*pl* **alhos-porós**) *m* leek.

alhures [aˈʎuriʃl] *adv* elsewhere.

ali [aˈlil] *adv* **- 1.** [naquele lugar] there; ~ **dentro/fora** in/out there; **logo** ~ right there; **por** ~ around there. **- 2.** [naquele momento] then.

aliado, da [aˈljadu, da] ⬦ *adj* allied. ⬦ *m, f* ally.

→ **Aliados** *mpl*: **os Aliados** the Allies.

aliança [aˈljãnsal] *f* **- 1.** [pacto] alliance. **- 2.** [anel] wedding ring.

aliar [16] [aˈlja(x)] *vt* [qualidades] to combine.

→ **aliar-se** *vp* [nações] to become allied.

aliás [aˈljajʃl] *adv* **- 1.** [a propósito] as a matter of fact. **- 2.** [diga-se de passagem] incidentally. **- 3.** [ou por outra] or rather.

álibi [ˈalibil] *m* alibi.

alicate [aliˈkatʃil] *m* pliers *(pl)*; ~ **de unhas** nail clippers *(pl)*.

alicerçado, da [alisexˈsadu, da] *adj* based.

alicerce [aliˈsɛxsil] *m* CONSTR foundation.

aliciamento [alisiaˈmẽntul] *m* [sedução] seduction.

aliciar [16] [aliˈsja(x)l] *vt* **- 1.** [atrair, seduzir] to entice. **- 2.** [convocar] to recruit. **- 3.** [subornar] to bribe.

alienação [aljenaˈsãwl] *f* **- 1.** [falta de consciência, participação] lack of awareness. **- 2.** PSIC : ~ **mental** mental illness. **- 3.** [de bens] assignment.

alienado, da [aljeˈnadu, da] *adj* **- 1.** [não participante] alienated. **- 2.** [louco] insane. **- 3.** [bens] assigned.

alienar [4] [aljeˈna(x)l] *vt* **- 1.** [tornar não participante] to alienate. **- 2.** [afastar] to drive away. **- 3.** [bens] to assign.

→ **alienar-se** *vp* [afastar-se] to withdraw.

alienígena [aljeˈniʒenal] *mf* alien.

alijar [4] [aliˈʒa(x)l] *vt* **- 1.** [carga] to jettison. **- 2.** [isentar]: ~ **alguém de algo** to free sb of sth.

→ **alijar-se** *vp* [isentar-se]: ~**-se de algo** to be released from sthg.

alimentação [alimẽntaˈsãwl] *f* **- 1.** [ato] feeding. **- 2.** [dieta] diet. **- 3.** [de máquina, impressora] feeding. **- 4.** ELETR supply.

alimentador [alimẽntaˈdo(x)l] *m*: ~ **de papel** paper feed.

alimentar [4] [alimẽnˈta(x)l] (*pl* **-es**) ⬦ *adj* alimentary. ⬦ *vt* **- 1.** [ger] to feed. **- 2.** [nutrir] to feed. **- 3.** [esperança] to feed. ⬦ *vi* [nutrir] to provide nourishment.

→ **alimentar-se** *vp* to feed o.s.; ~**-se de algo** to live on sthg.

alimentício, cia [alimẽnˈtʃisju, sjal] *adj* **- 1.** [qualidades] nutritious; **gêneros** ~**s** foodstuffs. **- 2.** [pensão] maintenance.

alimento [aliˈmẽntul] *m* **- 1.** [comida] food. **- 2.** [nutrição] nourishment.

alínea [aˈlinjal] *f* indent.

alinhado, da [aliˈɲadu, dal] *adj* **- 1.** [posto em linha reta] in a row. **- 2.** [elegante] elegant. **- 3.** [correto] correct.

alinhamento [aliɲaˈmẽntul] *m* **- 1.** [enfileiramento] row. **- 2.** [de estrada] direction. **- 3.** TIP justifying.

alinhar [4] [aliˈɲa(x)l] *vt* **- 1.** [enfileirar] to line up. **- 2.** [estrada] to straighten. **- 3.** TIP to justify.

alinhavar [4] [aliɲaˈva(x)l] *vt* COST to tack UK, to baste.

alinhavo [aliˈɲavul] *m* tacking UK, basting.

alíquota [aˈlikwotal] *f* tax rate.

alisar [4] [aliˈza(x)l] *vt* **- 1.** [tornar liso - cama, cabelo] to smooth; [- tábua] to plane. **- 2.** [acariciar] to caress.

alistamento [aliʃtaˈmẽntul] *m* **- 1.** [em partido] enrolment. **- 2.** MIL enlistment.

alistar [4] [aliʃˈta(x)l] *vt* **- 1.** [em partido] to enrol. **- 2.** MIL to enlist.

→ **alistar-se** *vp* **- 1.** [em partido] to enrol. **- 2.** MIL to enlist.

aliteração [aliteraˈsãwl] *f* alliteration.

aliviado, da [aliˈvjadu, dal] *adj* **- 1.** [pessoa - tranqüilizado] relieved; [- folgado] slackened. **- 2.** [consciência] relieved. **- 3.** [embarcação] lightened.

aliviar [16] [aliˈvja(x)l] ⬦ *vt* **- 1.** [gen] to relieve. **- 2.** [folgar] to slacken. **- 3.** [desafogar]: ~ **alguém de algo** to unburden sb of sthg. **- 4.** [embarcação] to lighten. ⬦ *vi* **- 1.** [diminuir] to ease. **- 2.** [confortar] to comfort.

→ **aliviar-se** *vp* to be relieved; ~**-se de algo** to be relieved of sthg.

alívio [aˈlivjul] *m* relief; **que** ~**!** what a relief!

alma [ˈawmal] *f* **- 1.** [essência humana] soul. **- 2.** [espírito desencarnado] spirit; ~ **do outro mundo** ghost. **- 3.** [pessoa]: **não ver viva** ~ not to see a living soul. **- 4.** [caráter] heart; ~ **gêmea** soulmate. **- 5.** [entusiasmo] heart and soul; **com** ~ with enthusiasm. **- 6.** [bondade]: **pessoa sem** ~ heartless person. **- 7.** *fig* [de negócio, empresa, partido] essence.

almaço [awˈmasul] *adj* [papel] foolscap.

almanaque [awmaˈnakil] *m* almanac.

almejar [4] [awmeˈʒa(x)l] ⬦ *vt* to long for; ~ **fazer algo** to long to do sthg. ⬦ *vi*: ~ **por algo** to long for sthg.

almirantado [awmirãnˈtadul] *m* **- 1.** [corporação] admiralty. **- 2.** [posto] admiralship.

almirante [awmiˈrãntʃil] *m* admiral.

almoçar [13] [awmoˈsa(x)l] ⬦ *vt* to have for lunch. ⬦ *vi* to have lunch.

almoço [awˈmosul] *m* lunch; **na hora do** ~ at lunchtime; ~ **americano** buffet lunch; ~ **de negócios** business lunch.

almofada [awmoˈfadal] *f* cushion.

almofadinha [awmofaˈdʒiɲal] *f* [para alfinetes] pincushion.

almôndega [awˈmõndegal] *f* meatball.

almoxarifado [awmoʃariˈfadul] *m* warehouse.

almoxarife [awmoʃaˈrifil] *mf* warehouseperson.

alô [aˈlol] ⬦ *interj* [ao telefone] hello! ⬦ *m* hello.

alocação [alokaˈsãwl] (*pl* **-ões**) *f* allocation.

alocar [12] [aloˈka(x)l] *vt* to allocate.

aloirado, da [aloj'radu, da] *adj* fair-haired.
alojamento [aloʒa'mẽntu] *m* **-1.** [ger] accommodation. **-2.** MIL billet.
alojar [4] [alo'ʒa(x)] *vt* **-1.** [hospedar] to accommodate. **-2.** MIL to billet. **-3.** [armazenar] to store.
  ➡ **alojar-se** *vp* **-1.** [hospedar-se] to stay. **-2.** [acampar] to camp.
alongamento [alõŋga'mẽntu] *m* **-1.** [ger] lengthening. **-2.** [de prazo] extension. **-3.** [ginástica] stretching.
alongar [14] [alõŋ'ga(x)] *vt* **-1.** [ger] to lengthen. **-2.** [perna, braço] to stretch. **-3.** [conversa] to prolong.
  ➡ **alongar-se** *vp* **-1.** [corpo] to stretch. **-2.** [conversa] to prolong. **-3.** [sobre assunto] to expand.
alopata [alo'pata] *mf* allopath.
alopatia [alopa'tʃia] *f* allopathy.
aloprado, da [alo'pradu, da] *adj fam* crazy.
alourado, da [alow'radu, da], **aloirado, da** [aloj'radu, da] *adj* fair-haired.
alpaca [aw'paka] *f* alpaca.
alpargata [aw'paxgata] *f* espadrille.
alpendre [aw'pẽndri] *m* [telheiro] porch.
alpercata [awpex'kata] = **alpargata**.
Alpes ['awpiʃ] *npl*: **os** ~ the Alps.
alpinismo [awpi'niʒmu] *m* mountaineering.
alpinista [awpi'niʃta] *mf* mountaineer.
alpino, na [aw'pinu, na] *adj* Alpine.
alpiste [aw'piʃtʃi] *m* [planta] canary grass.
alqueire [aw'kejri] *m measure for land area = 4.84 hectares in Rio de Janeiro, Minas Gerais e Goiás and 2.42 hectares in São Paulo.*
alquimia [awki'mia] *f* alchemy.
alquimista [awki'miʃta] *mf* alchemist.
alta ['awta] *f* ⊳ **alto**.
alta-fidelidade [ˌawtafideli'dadʒi] *f* hi-fi.
altaneiro, ra [awta'nejru, ra] *adj* haughty.
altar [aw'ta(x)] (*pl* **-es**) *m* altar.
altar-mor [awˌta(x)'mɔ(x)] (*pl* **altares-mores**) *m* high altar.
alta-roda [ˌawta'xɔda] (*pl* **altas-rodas**) *f* high society.
alta-tensão [ˌawtatẽnsãw] (*pl* **altas-tensões**) *f* high voltage.
altear [15] [awte'a(x)] *vt* **-1.** [construção] to build. **-2.** [preço, voz] to raise. **-3.** [posição]: ~ **sua posição numa firma** to move up within a company.
alteração [awtera'sãw] (*pl* **-ões**) *f* **-1.** [modificação - em gosto, clima, programação] change; [- de texto, roupa] alteration. **-2.** [perturbação] worry. **-3.** [tumulto] commotion.
alterado, da [awte'radu, da] *adj* **-1.** [modificado - gosto, clima, programação] changed; [- texto, roupa] altered. **-2.** [perturbado] worried.
alterar [4] [awte'ra(x)] *vt* **-1.** [modificar] to change. **-2.** [perturbar] to worry.
  ➡ **alterar-se** *vp* [perturbar-se] to be worried.
altercar [12] [awtex'ka(x)] *vi*: ~ **(com)** to quarrel (with).
alternado, da [awtex'nadu, da] *adj* alternated.
alternância [awtex'nãnsja] *f* alternation.

alternar [4] [awtex'na(x)] ⟨⟩ *vt*: ~ **algo (com)** to alternate sthg (with). ⟨⟩ *vi*: ~ **com** to alternate with.
  ➡ **alternar-se** *vp* [revezar-se] to alternate; [pessoas] to take turns.
alternativo, va [awtexna'tʃivu, va] *adj* alternative.
  ➡ **alternativa** *f* alternative.
alteza [aw'teza] *f*: **Sua Alteza** Your Highness.
altissonante [awtʃiso'nãntʃil *adj* **-1.** [voz] booming. **-2.** [orquestra] majestic.
altitude [awtʃi'tudʒil *f* altitude.
altivez [awtʃi'veʒ] *f* **-1.** [arrogância] presumption. **-2.** [dignidade] dignity.
altivo, va [aw'tʃivu, va] *adj* **-1.** [arrogante] presumptuous. **-2.** [digno] dignified.
alto, ta ['awtu, ta] *adj* **-1.** [ger] high; [forte] loud; **ler em voz** ~ to read aloud. **-2.** [em estatura] tall. **-3.** *(antes de subst)* [superior] high; **de** ~ **luxo** of great luxury. **-4.** *(antes de subst)* [importante - cargo] top; [- negócio] big. **-5.** [avançado]: **altas horas (da noite)** late; **altas horas da madrugada** early hours of the morning. **-6.** *(antes de subst)* [grave - risco] high; [- perigo] grave; **alta traição** high treason. **-7.** GEOGR upper. **-8.** HIST high; **alta Antigüidade** early antiquity. **-9.** [MÚS - tom, nota] high; [- voz, saxofone] alto. **-10.** *fam* [embriagado] high.
  ➡ **alto** ⟨⟩ *m* **-1.** [topo] top. **-2.** MÚS [saxofone] alto. **-3.** [mando, poder]: **do** ~ from above. ⟨⟩ *adv* **-1.** [falar] aloud. **-2.** [voar] high. ⟨⟩ *interj*: **alto!** stop!
  ➡ **alta** *f* **-1.** MED discharge; **dar/receber** ~ to discharge/to be discharged. **-2.** [de preços] rise. **-3.** [de cotação] rise; **estar em** ~ [cotação] to be rising; *fam* [reputação] to be in favour; *fam* [moda] to be highly fashionable.
  ➡ **por alto** *loc adv* roughly.
alto-astral [ˌawtwaʃ'trawl (*pl* **-ais**) *fam* ⟨⟩ *m* cool; **estar de** ~ to be cool. ⟨⟩ *adj* cool.
alto-falante ['awtufa'lãntʃil (*pl* **-s**) *m* loudspeaker.
alto-mar [ˌawtu'ma(x)] (*pl* **altos-mares**) *m* open sea.
alto-relevo [ˌawture'levul (*pl* **altos-relevos**) *m* high relief; **em** ~ in relief.
altruísmo [awtru'iʒmu] *m* altruism.
altruísta [awtru'iʃta] ⟨⟩ *adj* altruistic. ⟨⟩ *mf* [pessoa] altruist.
altruístico, ca [awtru'iʃtʃiku, ka] *adj* altruistic.
altura [aw'tura] *f* **-1.** [ger] height; **a dez mil metros de** ~ at an altitude of ten thousand metres. **-2.** [de som, volume] level. **-3.** [momento] time; **nessa** ~ **do campeonato** *fam fig* at this stage. **-4.** [localização]: **na** ~ **de** close to; **a loja fica na avenida principal, mas em que** ~**?** the shop is on the main road, but how far up? **-5.** [nível]: **à** ~ **de** equal to.
  ➡ **alturas** *fpl* RELIG [céu]: **as** ~**s** the heavens; **pôr algo/alguém nas** ~**s** *fig* to praise sthg/sb highly.
aluado, da [alu'adu, da] *adj* crazy, lunatic.
alucinação [alusina'sãw] (*pl* **-ões**) *f* hallucination.
alucinado, da [alusi'nadu, da] ⟨⟩ *adj* **-1.** PSIC

hallucinated. -2. *fig* [apaixonado]: ~ **por** crazy about. **-3.** *fig* [desvairado] frantic. <> *m, f PSIC* lunatic.

alucinante [alusi'nãntʃil] *adj fam* **-1.** [enlouquecedor] maddening. **-2.** [ótimo, incrível] amazing.

alucinar [4] [alusi'na(x)] <> *vt* **-1.** [enlouquecer] to drive crazy. **-2.** [apaixonar] to drive wild. **-3.** *PSIC* to cause to hallucinate. <> *vi PSIC* to be hallucinogenic.

alucinógeno, na [alusi'nɔʒɛnu, na] *adj* hallucinogenic.

➨ **alucinógeno** *m* hallucinogen.

aludir [6] [alu'dʒi(x)] *vi*: ~ **a** to allude to.

alugar [14] [alu'ga(x)] *vt* **-1.** [tomar de aluguel - carro, traje] to hire; [- apartamento] to rent. **-2.** [dar em aluguel - carro, traje] to hire out; [- apartamento] to rent out. **-3.** *fam* [incomodar] to annoy.

aluguel [alu'gɛwl] (*pl* **-eis**) *m* **-1.** [ato - carro] rental; [- apartamento] renting. **-2.** [pagamento] rent.

alumínio [alu'minju] *m* aluminium *UK*, aluminum *US*.

alunissagem [aluni'saʒẽ] (*pl* **-ns**) *f* lunar landing.

alunissar [4] [aluni'sa(x)] *vi* to land on the moon.

aluno, na [a'lunu, na] *m, f* pupil; ~ **externo** day pupil; ~ **interno** boarder.

alusão [alu'zãw] (*pl* **-ões**) *f* allusion; **fazer uma** ~ **a** to allude to, to make a reference to.

alusivo, va [alu'zivu, va] *adj* allusive.

alvará [awva'ra] *m* permit.

alvejante [awve'ʒãntʃi] <> *adj* bleaching. <> *m* bleach.

alvejar [4] [awve'ʒa(x)] *vt* **-1.** [mirar em] to aim at. **-2.** [branquear] to bleach, to whiten.

alvenaria [awvena'ria] *f* masonry; **de** ~ stonework.

alvéolo [al'vɛwlul] *f* **-1.** [cavidade] cavity. **-2.** [*ANAT* - do pulmão]: ~ **pulmonar** alveolus; [- de dente] cavity.

alvo, va [ˈawvu, ˈval] *adj* white.

➨ **alvo** *m* **-1.** [mira] target; **acertar no** ~ to hit the target. **-2.** *fig* [objeto]: **ser** ~ **de** to be the target of.

alvorada [awvo'rada] *f* dawn.

alvorecer [25] [awvore'se(x)] <> *m* [alvorada] daybreak. <> *vi* [amanhecer] to dawn.

alvoroçar [13] [awvoro'sa(x)] *vt* **-1.** [agitar] to stir up. **-2.** [entusiasmar] to excite.

➨ **alvoroçar-se** *vp* **-1.** [agitar-se] to be startled. **-2.** [entusiasmar-se] to get excited.

alvoroço [awvo'rosu] *m* [agitação] commotion; **fazer** ~ to cause a commotion.

alvura [aw'vural] *f* **-1.** [branqueza] whiteness. **-2.** [pureza] innocence.

AM <> *f* (*abrev de* **Amplitude Modulation**) AM. <> *m* (*abrev de* **Estado do Amazonas**) *State of Amazon*.

ama ['amal] *f* ▷ **amo**.

amabilidade [amabili'dadʒil] *f* **-1.** [delicadeza, cortesia] courtesy. **-2.** [de gesto, palavra] kindness.

amabilíssimo, ma [amabi'lisimu, ma] *superl* ▷ amável.

amaciante [ama'sjãntʃil] *m*: ~ **de roupas** fabric conditioner.

amaciar [16] [ama'sja(x)] <> *vt* **-1.** [tornar macio] to soften. **-2.** [bife] to tenderize. **-3.** [motor] to run in. <> *vi* [motor] to run in.

ama-de-leite [ˌãmadʒi'lejtʃil] (*pl* **amas-de-leite**) *f* wet nurse.

amado, da [a'madu, da] <> *adj* **-1.** [ger] favourite. **-2.** [person] beloved. <> *m, f* beloved, love.

amador, ra [ama'do(x)] (*mpl* **-es**, *fpl* **-s**) <> *adj* amateur. <> *m, f* amateur.

amadorismo [amado'riʒmul] *m* **-1.** [diletantismo] dilettantism. **-2.** *pej* [antiprofissionalismo] amateurism.

amadorístico, ca [amado'riʃtʃiku, ka] *adj* amateurish.

amadurecer [25] [amadure'se(x)] <> *vt* **-1.** [frutar] to ripen. **-2.** *fig* [pessoa] to mature. <> *vi* **-1.** [fruta] to ripen. **-2.** *fig* [pessoa] to mature. **-3.** *fig* [idéia, projeto] to come to fruition.

âmago ['ãmagul] *m* **-1.** [cerne - de madeira] heart; [- de questão] heart. **-2.** [essência] essence. **-3.** [alma, interior] heart.

amainar [4] [amaj'na(x)] *vi* **-1.** [tormenta, tempestade] to die down. **-2.** [ira] to subside. **-3.** [distúrbio, bombardeio] to ease off.

amaldiçoar [20] [amawdi'swa(x)] *vt* to curse.

amálgama [a'mawgama] *m* amalgam.

amalgamar [4] [amawga'ma(x)] *vt* to amalgamate.

amalucado, da [amalu'kadu, da] *adj* crazy.

amamentação [amamẽta'sãw] (*pl* **-ões**) *f* breastfeeding.

amamentar [4] [amamẽ'ta(x)] *vt & vi* to breastfeed.

amanhã [amã'ɲã] <> *adv* tomorrow; ~ **de manhã** tomorrow morning; ~ **à noite** tomorrow night; ~ **de tarde** tomorrow afternoon/evening; **depois de** ~ the day after tomorrow. <> *m* tomorrow.

amanhecer [25] [amãɲe'se(x)] <> *m* dawn; **ao** ~ at dawn. <> *vi* **-1.** [dia] to dawn. **-2.** [pessoa]: **hoje amanheci com dor de cabeça** today I woke up with a headache.

amansar [4] [amã'sa(x)] <> *vt* **-1.** [animal] to break in. **-2.** *fig* [pessoa etc] to calm down. <> *vi* **-1.** [animal] to become tame. **-2.** *fig* [pessoa etc] to relent.

amante [a'mãntʃil] *mf* lover.

amanteigado, da [amãntej'gadu, da] *adj* **-1.** [torrada, pão] buttered. **-2.** [biscoito] buttery.

Amapá [ama'pa] *n* Amapá.

amar [4] [a'ma(x)] <> *vt* **-1.** [sentir amor por] to love. **-2.** [fazer amor com] to make love to. <> *vi* [sentir amor] to be in love.

➨ **amar-se** *vp* **-1.** [mutuamente] to love each other. **-2.** [fazer amor] to make love.

amarelado, da [amare'ladu, da] *adj* yellowish.

amarelar [4] [amare'la(x)] <> *vt* [tornar amarelado]

to turn yellow. <> *vi fam* [acovardar-se] to pale.

amarelinha [amarɛ'liɲa] *f* hopscotch.

amarelo, la [ama'rɛlu, la] *adj* yellow.
➤ **amarelo** *m* yellow.

amarfanhar [4] [amaxfa'ɲa(x)] *vt* to crumple.

amargar [14] [amax'ga(x)] <> *vt* **-1.** [tornar amargo] to make bitter. **-2.** *fig* [fazer sofrer] to embitter. <> *vi* **-1.** [tornar-se amargo] to go bitter. **-2.** *loc*: **ser de ~** to be the last straw.

amargo, ga [a'maxgu, ga] *adj* bitter.

amargor [amax'go(x)] *m* **-1.** [sabor amargo] bitter taste. **-2.** [sensação de desgosto] bitterness.

amargura [amax'gura] *f* **-1.** [ger] bitterness. **-2.** *fig* [sofrimento] bitterness.

amargurado, da [amaxgu'radu, da] *adj* **-1.** [pessoa] bitter. **-2.** [expressão, texto] acrimonious.

amargurar [4] [amaxgu'ra(x)] *vt* **-1.** [afligir] to make bitter. **-2.** [tornar sofrido] to sour.

amarra [a'maxa] *f* **-1.** [corrente, cabo - de âncora] moorings *(pl)*; [- de vela] sheet. **-2.** [grilhão] shackle.

amarrado, da [ama'xadu, da] *adj* **-1.** [atado] tied up. **-2.** *fig* [cara] glowering. **-3.** *fam fig* [comprometido] committed.

amarrar [4] [ama'xa(x)] *vt* **-1.** [atar] to tie. **-2.** *NÁUT* to moor. **-3.** *fig*: **~ a cara** to glower.
➤ **amarrar-se** *vp fam* **-1.** [apaixonar-se]: **~-se em alguém** to become attached to sb. **-2.** [gostar muito]: **~-se em algo** to be keen on sthg.

amarronzado, da [amaxõn'zadu, da] *adj* brownish.

amarrotar [4] [amaxo'ta(x)] <> *vt* to crumple. <> *vi* to be crumpled.

ama-seca [ˌama'sɛka] *(pl* amas-secas*) f* nanny.

amasiar-se [7] [amazi'axsi] *vp dated* to live together; **~ com alguém** to live with sb.

amassado, da [ama'sadu, da] *adj* [tecido, roupa, papel] crumpled; [carro] smashed up.

amassar [4] [ama'sa(x)] *vt* **-1.** [massa] to knead; [bolo, pão] to mix. **-2.** [roupa] to crease. **-3.** [papel] to crumple. **-4.** [carro] to smash up.

amável [a'mavɛw] *(pl* -eis*) adj* friendly.

amazona [ama'zona] *f* **-1.** [mulher que anda a cavalo] horsewoman. **-2.** [mulher guerreira] Amazon.

Amazonas [ama'zonaʃ] *n* **-1.** [rio]: **o ~** the Amazon. **-2.** [estado] Amazonas.

Amazônia [ama'zonja] *n* Amazonia.

AMAZÔNIA

The area of *Amazônia* exceeds 7 million km², over half of which is in Brazilian territory. The Amazon basin has the most extensive river network and the greatest flow of freshwater in the world; it is also home to the world's largest tropical forest. Its enormous biodiversity includes over 60,000 species of trees, some of which can reach a height of 100m or more.

---

amazônico, ca [ama'zoniku, ka] *adj* Amazonian.

Amã [a'mã] *n* Amman.

âmbar [ˈãnba(x)] *m* amber.

AmBev (*abrev de* **American Beverage Company**) *f* ≃ AmBev, *Brazilian drinks manufacturer*.

ambição [ãnbi'sãw] *(pl* -ões*) f* ambition.

ambicionar [4] [ãnbisjo'na(x)] *vt* to set one's sights on.

ambicioso, osa [ãnbi'sjozu, ɔza] <> *adj* ambitious. <> *m, f* go-getter.

ambidestro, tra [ãnbi'deʃtru, tra] *adj* ambidextrous.

ambiental [ãnbjěn'taw] *(pl* -ais*) adj* environmental.

ambientalista [ãnbjěnta'liʃta] <> *adj* environmental. <> *mf* environmentalist.

ambientar [4] [ãnbjěn'tar] *vt* **-1.** [filme, enredo] to set. **-2.** [adaptar] to acclimatize.
➤ **ambientar-se** *vp* [adaptar-se] to mingle.

ambiente [ãn'bjěntʃi] <> *adj* ambient. <> *m* **-1.** [gen & *COMPUT*] environment. **-2.** [em sala, boate] area. **-3.** *fig* [atmosfera] atmosphere.

ambigüidade [ãnbigwi'dadʒi] *f* ambiguity.

ambíguo, gua [ãn'bigwu, gwa] *adj* ambiguous.

âmbito [ˈãnbitu] *m* [campo de ação] field.

ambivalência [ãnbiva'lěnsja] *f* ambivalence.

ambivalente [ãnbiva'lěntʃi] *adj* ambivalent.

ambos, bas [ˈãnbuʃ, baʃ] <> *adj* both. <> *pron* both.

ambrosia [ãnbro'zia] *f a sweet dish of eggs and milk*.

ambulância [ãnbu'lãnsja] *f* ambulance.

ambulante [ãnbu'lãntʃi] <> *adj* **-1.** [vendedor, pipoqueiro - na calçada] street *(antes de subst)*; [- de porta em porta] door-to-door *(antes de subst)*. **-2.** [biblioteca, posto médico] mobile. **-3.** *fam fig*: **ele é uma enciclopédia ~** he's a walking encyclopedia. <> *mf* [vendedor ambulante] street vendor.

ambulatório [ãnbula'tɔrju] *m* outpatient department.

ameaça [a'mjasa] *f* threat; **~ de bomba** bomb scare; **~ de enfarte** risk of heart attack; **~ de morte** death threat.

ameaçador, ra [amjasa'do(x), ra] *adj* threatening, menacing.

ameaçar [13] [amja'sa(x)] *vt* to threaten; **~ fazer algo** to threaten to do sthg; **~ alguém de morte** to threaten sb with death.

amealhar [4] [amja'ʎa(x)] <> *vt* [juntar] to amass. <> *vi* [poupar] to save up.

ameba [a'mɛba] *f* amoeba *UK*, ameba *US*.

amedrontador, ra [amedrõnta'do(x), ra] *adj* frightening.

amedrontar [4] [amedrõn'ta(x)] *vt* to frighten.
➤ **amedrontar-se** *vp* to feel afraid.

ameia [a'meja] *f* battlement.

ameixa [a'mejʃa] *f* **-1.** [fresca] plum. **-2.** [seca] prune.

amém [a'mě] <> *interj* amen! <> *m fig*: **dizer ~ a** to give in to.

amêndoa [a'měndwa] *f* almond.

amendoado, da [amě'dwadu, da] *adj* [olhos] almond-shaped.

amendoeira [amě'dwejra] *f* almond tree.

amendoim [amẽn'dwĩ] (pl -ns) m peanut; ~ **torrado** roasted peanut.

amenidade [ameni'dadʒi] f -1. [suavidade] mildness. -2. [delicadeza] gentleness.

➡ **amenidades** fpl [futilidades] trivialities.

amenizar [4] [ameni'za(x)] vt -1. [abrandar] to reduce. -2. [tornar agradável] to make pleasant. -3. [briga, conflito] to settle. -4. [facilitar] to lighten.

ameno, na [a'menu, na] adj -1. [brando - sabor] mild; [- repreensão] quiet; [- pena] light. -2. [agradável] pleasant.

América [a'mɛrika] n America; ~ **Central** Central American; ~ **do Norte** North America; ~ **do Sul** South America; ~ **Hispânica** Spanish America; ~ **Latina** Latin America.

americanizado, da [amerikãni'zadu, da] adj Americanized.

americanizar [amerikãni'za(x)] vt to Americanize.

americano, na [ameri'kãnu, na] <> adj American. <> m, f American.

ameríndio, dia [ame'rĩndʒu, dʒa] <> adj Amerindian. <> m, f Amerindian.

amesquinhar [4] [ameʃki'ɲa(x)] vt [tornar mesquinho] to demean.

➡ **amesquinhar-se** vp -1. [tornar-se avaro] to become mean. -2. [humilhar-se] to demean o.s.

ametista [ame'tʃiʃta] f amethyst.

amianto [a'mjãntu] m asbestos.

amicíssimo, ma [ami'sisimu, ma] superl ▷ **amigo**.

amido [a'midu] m starch.

amigar-se [14] [ami'gaxsi] vp [amancebar-se] to live together; ~ **com alguém** to live with sb.

amigável [ami'gavɛw] (pl -eis) adj friendly.

amígdala [a'migdala] f tonsil.

amigdalite [amigda'litʃi] f tonsillitis.

amigo, ga [a'migu, ga] <> adj friendly. <> m, f friend; ~ **do peito** bosom buddy; ~ **secreto** ou **oculto** [jogo] a game of present swapping in which you draw a person's name from a hat and then anonymously give them a present after a certain period of time; [pessoa] the person to whom the present is given in this game.

amigo-da-onça, amiga-da-onça [ˌamigu-da'õsa, ˌamigada'õsa] m, f fam false friend.

amistoso, osa [amiʃ'tozu, ɔza] adj friendly.

➡ **amistoso** m ESP friendly.

amiúde [a'mjudʒi] adv often.

amizade [ami'zadʒi] f -1. [relação] friendship; **fazer** ~ **(com alguém)** to make friends (with sb); ~ **colorida** fam casual relationship. -2. [estima] friendliness; **ela o tratou com** ~ she treated him in a friendly manner.

amnésia [am'nɛzja] f amnesia.

amo, ma ['amo, ma] m, f master (f mistress).

➡ **ama** f [governanta] nanny.

amolação [amola'sãw] (pl -ões) f [incômodo, aborrecimento] hassle.

amolado, da [amo'ladu, da] adj -1. [afiado] sharp. -2. [aborrecido] annoyed.

amolador [amola'do(x)] m [de facas] knife sharpener.

amolar [4] [amo'la(x)] <> vt -1. [faca] to sharpen. -2. [incomodar, aborrecer] to annoy. <> vi [causar incômodo] to be annoying.

➡ **amolar-se** vp [aborrecer-se] to get annoyed.

amoldar [4] [amow'da(x)] vt [adaptar, ajustar]: ~ **algo (a)** to adapt sthg (to).

➡ **amoldar-se** vp [adaptar-se, ajustar-se]: ~-se **(a)** to adapt (to).

amolecer [25] [amole'se(x)] <> vt -1. [tornar mole] to soften. -2. fig [abrandar] to mollify. <> vi -1. [tornar-se mole] to soften. -2. fig [tornar-se brando] to relent.

amônia [a'monja] f ammonia.

amoníaco [amo'niaku] m ammonia.

amontoado [amõn'twadu] m pile.

amontoar [20] [amõn'twa(x)] vt to pile up.

➡ **amontoar-se** vp to pile up.

amor [a'mo(x)] (pl -es) m love; ~ **livre** free love; **fazer** ~ to make love; **pelo** ~ **de Deus!** for God's sake!; **ser um** ~ **(de pessoa)** to be a gem (of a person).

amora [a'mɔra] f mulberry.

amoral [amo'raw] (pl -ais) <> adj amoral. <> mf unscrupulous person.

amora-preta [aˌmɔra'preta] (pl amoras-pretas) f mulberry.

amordaçar [13] [amoxda'sa(x)] vt to gag.

amoreco [amo'rɛku] m: **um** ~ a darling.

amorenado, da [amore'nadu, da] adj swarthy.

amorfo, fa [a'mɔxfu, fa] adj -1. [sem forma] amorphous. -2. fig [pessoa] dreary.

amornar [4] [amox'na(x)] <> vt to warm up. <> vi to cool down.

amoroso, osa [amo'rozu, ɔza] adj [pessoa] loving; **um caso** ~ a love affair.

amor-perfeito [aˌmoxpex'fejtu] (pl amores-perfeitos) m heartsease.

amor-próprio [aˌmox'prɔprju] (pl amores-próprios) m -1. [auto-estima] self-esteem. -2. [orgulho] conceitedness.

amortecedor [amoxtese'do(x)] (pl -es) m shock absorber.

amortização [amoxtiza'sãw] (pl -ões) f -1. [pagamento parcial] part payment. -2. FIN [de ações] amortization.

amortizar [4] [amoxti'za(x)] vt -1. [pagar parte de] to repay (in part). -2. FIN [ações] to amortize.

amostra [a'mɔʃtra] f sample; ~ **grátis** free sample.

amostragem [amoʃ'traʒẽ] (pl -ns) f -1. [coleta, seleção] sampling. -2. [amostra] selection. -3. [em estatística] cross sample.

amotinado, da [amotʃi'nadu, da] adj mutinous.

amotinar [4] [amotʃi'na(x)] vt to lead into mutiny.

➡ **amotinar-se** vp to mutiny.

amparar [4] [ãnpa'ra(x)] vt -1. [escorar, segurar] to hold. -2. [ajudar] to support.

➡ **amparar-se** vp [escorar-se, segurar-se]: ~-se

(contra/em) to lean (against/on).

amparo [ãn'paru] *m* **-1.** [apoio] hold. **-2.** [ajuda] support.

amperagem [ãnpe'raʒẽ] *f* [eletr] amperage.

ampère [ãn'pɛril *m* amp, ampere.

ampliação [ãnplia'sãw] (*pl* **-ões**) *f* **-1.** [aumento - de forma, imagem] enlargement; [- de ângulo] widening. **-2.** [extensão] extension. **-3.** [desenvolvimento - de estudos] broadening; [- de negócio] expansion. **-4.** [FOT - processo] blow-up; [- exemplar] enlargement.

ampliar [16] [ãnpli'a(x)] *vt* **-1.** [aumentar- forma, imagem] to enlarge; [- ângulo] to widen. **-2.** [estender] to extend. **-3.** [desenvolver- estudos] to broaden; [- negócio] to expand.

amplificação [anplifika'sãw] (*pl* **-ões**) *f* **-1.** [aumento - de forma, imagem] enlargement; [- de ângulo] widening. **-2.** [de som] amplification.

amplificador [ãnplifika'do(x)l (*pl* **-es**) *m* [de som] amplifier.

amplificar [12] [ãnplifi'ka(x)l *vt* **-1.** [aumentar- forma, imagem] to enlarge; [- ângulo] to widen. **-2.** [som] to amplify.

amplitude [ãnpli'tudʒil *f* **-1.** [espaço] spaciousness. **-2.** *fig* [abrangência] scope. **-3.** TEC amplitude.

amplo, pla ['ãnplu, 'plal *adj* **-1.** [espaçoso] spacious. **-2.** [abrangente] broad. **-3.** [lato]: **no sentido mais ~ da palavra** in the broadest sense of the word. **-4.** *(antes de subst)* [ilimitado] ample.

ampola [ãn'polal *f* ampoule *UK*, ampule *US*.

ampulheta [ãnpu'ʎetal *f* hour-glass.

amputação [ãnputa'sãw] (*pl* **-ões**) *f* amputation.

amputar [4] [ãnpu'ta(x)l *vt* to amputate.

Amsterdã [amiʃtex'dãl *n* Amsterdam.

amuado, da [a'mwadu, dal *adj* [aborrecido] sulking.

amuar [4] [a'mwa(x)l *vt* [aborrecer] to annoy.
➜ **amuar-se** *vp* [aborrecer-se]: **~-se (com** *ou* **contra)** to get annoyed (with).

amulatado, da [amula'tadu, dal *adj* mulattolooking.

amuleto [amu'letul *m* amulet.

anã [a'nãl *f* ➭ **anão**.

anacrônico, ca [ana'kroniku, kal *adj* anachronistic.

anacronismo [anakro'niʒmul *m* anachronism.

anafilático, ca [anafi'latiku, kal *adj* ➭ **choque**.

anagrama [ana'grãmal *m* anagram.

anágua [a'nagwal *f* petticoat.

anais [a'najʃl *mpl* annals.

anal [a'nawl (*pl* **-ais**) *adj* anal.

analfabetismo [anawfabe'tʃiʒmul *m* illiteracy.

analfabeto, ta [anawfa'bɛtu, tal <> *adj* illiterate. <> *m, f* illiterate.

analgésico, ca [anaw'ʒɛziku, kal *adj* analgesic.
➜ **analgésico** *m* [remédio] painkiller, analgesic.

analisar [4] [anali'za(x)l *vt* **-1.** [examinar, avaliar] to analyse. **-2.** PSIC to put through analysis.

análise [a'nalizil *f* [ger & PSIC] analysis; **~s clínicas** clinical tests.

analista [ana'liʃtal *mf* **-1.** [ger & PSIC] analyst; **~ de sistemas** systems analyst.

analítico, ca [ana'litʃiku, kal *adj* analytical.

analogia [analo'ʒial *f* analogy; **por ~** by analogy.

análogo, ga [a'nalogu, gal *adj* analogous.

ananás [ana'naʃl (*pl* **-ases**) *m* pineapple.

anão, ã [a'nãw, ãl (*mpl* **-ões**, *fpl* **-s**) *m, f* dwarf.

anarquia [anax'kial *f* **-1.** [ausência de governo] anarchy. **-2.** *fig* [bagunça] shambles.

anárquico, ca [a'naxkiku, kal *adj* **-1.** [sistema, sociedade] anarchic. **-2.** *fig* [caótico] chaotic.

anarquismo [anax'kizmul *m* anarchism.

anarquista [anax'kiʃtal <> *adj* [partido, sociedade] anarchist. <> *mf* **-1.** [militante] anarchist. **-2.** *fig* [bagunceiro, agitador] agitator.

anarquizar [4] [anaxki'za(x)l *vt* *fig* **-1.** [tornar anárquico] to reduce to anarchy. **-2.** [incitar à desordem] to incite to riot. **-3.** [abagunçar] to make a mess of. **-4.** [desmoralizar, ridicularizar] to satirize.

ANATEL (*abrev de* **Agência Nacional de Telecomunicações**) *f* Brazilian state telecommunications regulator, ≃ Oftel *UK*, ≃ ODTR *US*.

anátema [a'natemal *m* [maldição, estigma] anathema.

anatomia [anato'mial *f* anatomy.

anatômico, ca [ana'tomiku, kal *adj* anatomical.

anca ['ãŋkal *f* **-1.** [de pessoa] hip. **-2.** [de animal] haunch.

ancestral [ãn'seʃtrawl (*pl* **-ais**) <> *adj* ancestral, age-old. <> *mf* ancestor.
➜ **ancestrais** *mpl* ancestors.

anchova [ãn'ʃoval *f* anchovy.

ancião, ciã [ã'sjãw, sjãl (*mpl* **-ões**, *fpl* **-s**) <> *adj* aged. <> *m, f* venerable person.

ancinho [ãn'siɲul *m* rake.

anciões [ã'sjõjʃl *pl* ➭ **ancião**.

âncora ['ãŋkoral *f* ECON: **~ cambial** exchange rate pegging.

ancoradouro [ãŋkora'dorul *m* anchorage.

ancorar [4] [ãŋko'ra(x)l <> *vt* **-1.** [fundear] to anchor. **-2.** *fig* [basear] to base. <> *vi* [fundear] to base.
➜ **ancorar-se** *vp* *fig* [basear-se] to be based.

andada [ãn'dadal *f* walk; **dar uma ~** to take a walk.

andaime [ãn'dãjmil *m* scaffolding.

andamento [ãnda'mẽntul *m* **-1.** [prosseguimento] progress; **dar ~ a algo** to set in motion; **estar em ~** to be under way. **-2.** [direção] direction. **-3.** MÚS tempo.

andança [ãn'dãnsaʃl *f* [viagem] travel.

andar [4] [ãn'da(x)l (*pl* **-es**) <> *m* **-1.** [jeito de caminhar] walk. **-2.** [pavimento] storey *UK*, story *US*. <> *vi* **-1.** [caminhar] to walk. **-2.** [usar como transporte]: **~ de bicicleta/a cavalo** to ride a bicycle/horse; **~ de avião/carro/trem** to go by plane/car/train. **-3.** [movimentar-se] to go. **-4.** [errar] to wander. **-5.** [progredir, funcionar] to go. **-6.** [passar] to go, to pass. **-7.** [conviver]: **~ com alguém** to get along with sb. **-8.** [ter caso amoroso]: **~ com alguém** to be going out with sb. **-9.** [estar] to be; **~ em** *ou* **por** to be travelling in; ~ **fazendo algo** to be doing sthg. **-10.**: ~ **por** to be around. **-11.** [ir-se]: **ir andando** to be on one's way. **-12.** [apressar-se]: **anda (com isso)!** get a move on! ⋄ *vt* [percorrer] to do; **andamos 50 quilômetros em um dia** we did 50 kms in one day.

andarilho, lha [ãnda'riʎu, ʎa] *m, f* walker.

Andes ['ãndiʃ] *npl*: **os** ~ the Andes.

andino, na [ãn'dinu, na] ⋄ *adj* Andean. ⋄ *m, f* Andean.

andorinha [ãndo'riɲa] *f* swallow.

Andorra [ãn'dɔxa] *n*: **(o principado de)** ~ (the principality of) Andorra.

andrógino, na [ãn'drɔʒinu, na] *adj* androgynous.

anedota [ane'dɔta] *f* joke.

anel [a'nɛw] (*pl -éis*) *m* **-1.** [ger] ring. **-2.** [de corrente] circuit. **-3.** [de cabelo] lock.

anelado, da [ane'ladu, da] *adj* curly.

anemia [ane'mia] *f* anaemia *UK*, anemia *US*.

anêmico, ca [a'nemiku, ka] *adj* anaemic *UK*, anemic *US*.

anestesia [aneʃte'zial *f* **-1.** [efeito] anaesthesia *UK*, anesthesia *US*. **-2.** [anestésico] anaesthetic *UK*, anesthetic *US*; **tomar** ~ to have an anaesthetic; ~ **geral/local** general/local anaesthetic.

anestesiado, da [aneʃte'zjadu, da] *adj* [paciente] anaesthetized.

anestesiar [16] [aneʃte'zja(x)] *vt* **-1.** [entorpecer] to anaesthetize *UK*, anesthetize *US*. **-2.** [aplicar anestesia] to give an anaesthetic to *UK*, to give an anesthetic to *US*.

anestésico, ca [aneʃ'teziku, ka] *adj* anaesthetizing *UK*, anesthetizing *US*.
➡ **anestésico** *m* anaesthetic *UK*, anesthetic *US*.

anexação [aneksa'sãw] (*pl -ões*) *f* **-1.** [de cláusulas, documentos] attachment. **-2.** [de terras, país] annexation.

anexado, da [ane'ksadu, da] *adj COMPUT* attached.

anexar [4] [anek'sa(x)] *vt COMPUT*: ~ **um arquivo** to attach a file.

anexo [a'nɛksul *m COMPUT* attachment.

ANFAVEA (*abrev de* **Associação Nacional dos Fabricantes de Veículos Automotores**) *f Brazilian association of automobile manufacturers*.

anfetamina [ãnfeta'minal *f* amphetamine.

anfíbio, bia [ãn'fibju, bja] *adj* amphibious.
➡ **anfíbio** *m* amphibian.

anfiteatro [ãnfi'tʃjatru] *m* amphitheatre *UK*, amphitheater *US*.

anfitrião, triã [ãnfi'trjãw, trjã] (*mpl -ões*, *fpl -s*) *m, f* host (*f* hostess).

angariar [16] [ãnga'rja(x)] *vt* to attract.

angelical [ãnʒeli'kawl (*pl -ais*) *adj* angelic.

angina [ãn'ʒinal *f*: ~ **(do peito)** angina (pectoris).

anglicano, na [ãngli'kanu, na] ⋄ *adj* Anglican. ⋄ *m, f* Anglican.

anglicismo [ãngli'siʒmul *m* Anglicism.

anglófono, na [ãŋ'glɔfonu, na] ⋄ *adj* English-speaking. ⋄ *m, f* English speaker.

anglo-saxão, xã [ˌãŋglosak'sãw, sã] (*mpl -ões*, *fpl -ãs*) ⋄ *adj* Anglo-Saxon. ⋄ *m, f* Anglo-Saxon.

anglo-saxônico, ca [ˌãŋglosak'soniku, ka] (*mpl -s*, *fpl -s*) *adj* Anglo-Saxon.

Angola [ãŋ'gɔla] *n* Angola.

angolano, na [ãŋgo'lãnu, na] ⋄ *adj* Angolan. ⋄ *m, f* Angolan.

angorá [ãŋgo'ra] ⋄ *adj* angora. ⋄ *m* [tecido] angora. ⋄ *mf* [gato] angora.

angra ['ãŋgra] *f* bay.

angu [ãŋ'gu] *m* **-1.** [ger] ≃ porridge. **-2.** *fam fig* [confusão, problema]: **um ~-de-caroço** a tough nut to crack.

angular [ãŋgu'la(x)] *adj* angular.

ângulo ['ãŋgulul *m* **-1.** [ger] angle; ~ **agudo/obtuso/reto** acute/obtuse/right angle. **-2.** [canto] corner. **-3.** [de mira] angle (of vision).

anguloso, sa [ãŋgu'lozu, lɔza] *adj* angled.

angústia [ãŋ'guʃtʃja] *f* anguish.

angustiado, da [ãŋguʃ'tʃjadu, da] *adj* anguished.

angustiante [ãŋguʃ'tʃjãntʃil *adj* harrowing.

angustiar [16] [ãŋguʃ'tʃja(x)] *vt* to cause anguish to.
➡ **angustiar-se** *vp* to become distressed; ~ **-se com algo** to be distressed by sthg; ~ **-se de** *ou* **por** to be distressed about.

anil [a'niw] *m* [cor] blue.

animação [anima'sãw] *f* **-1.** [entusiasmo] enthusiasm. **-2.** [alegria] jollity. **-3.** [movimento] hustle and bustle. **-4.** *CINE* animation.

animado, da [ani'madu, da] *adj* **-1.** [entusiasmado] spirited. **-2.** [alegre, movimentado] lively.

animador, ra [anima'do(x), ra] (*mpl -es*, *fpl -s*) ⋄ *adj* encouraging. ⋄ *m, f* animator.

animal [ani'maw] (*pl -ais*) ⋄ *adj* **-1.** [ger] animal. **-2.** *fam pej* [pessoa] brutal. ⋄ *mf fam pej* [pessoa - bruto] brute; [- ignorante] ass. ⋄ *m ZOOL* animal; ~ **doméstico** [de estimação] domestic animal; [de criação] livestock.

animalesco, ca [anima'leʃku, ka] *adj* animal.

animar [4] [ani'ma(x)] *vt* **-1.** [ger] to liven up. **-2.** [encorajar]: ~ **alguém (a fazer algo)** to encourage sb (to do sthg). **-3.** [entusiasmar] to enthuse. **-4.** [fomentar, estimular] to stimulate. **-5.** [dar animação] to animate. **-6.** *RELIG* [dar vida a] to bring to life.
➡ **animar-se** *vp* **-1.** [tomar coragem]: ~ **-se (a fazer algo)** to resolve (to do sthg). **-2.** [entusiasmar-se] to become enthusiastic. **-3.** [debate, conversa, festa] to liven up. **-4.** [alegrar-se] to cheer up. **-5.** *RELIG* [ganhar vida] to come to life.

ânimo ['ãnimul ⋄ *m* **-1.** [coragem] courage. **-2.** [entusiasmo] enthusiasm; **perder o** ~ to lose courage; **recobrar o** ~ to regain one's resolve. **-3.** [estímulo] life; **representar um novo** ~ **para** to give a new lease of life to. ⋄ *interj*: ~! come on!

animosidade [animozi'dadʒil *f* animosity.

aninhar [4] [ani'ɲa(x)] ◇ *vt* -**1.** [acolher, aconchegar] to cuddle. -**2.** [abrigar] to shelter. ◇ *vi* [fazer ninho] to nest.

➡ **aninhar-se** *vp* -**1.** [aconchegar-se] to nestle. -**2.** [fazer ninho] to nest.

aniquilação [anikila'sãw] *f* -**1.** [anulação] rescission. -**2.** [esgotamento] exhaustion. -**3.** [destruição] annihilation; ~ **moral** moral decay. -**4.** *fig* [ruína] ruin.

aniquilar [4] [aniki'la(x)] *vt* -**1.** [anular] to rescind. -**2.** [esgotar] to exhaust. -**3.** [destruir] to annihilate. -**4.** *fig* [arruinar] to ruin.

➡ **aniquilar-se** *vp* -**1.** [esgotar-se] to be exhausted. -**2.** *fig* [moralmente] to destroy o.s.

anis [a'niʃ] (*pl* -**es**) *m* aniseed; **licor de** ~ anisette.

anistia [aniʃ'tʃia] *f* amnesty.

anistiado, da [aniʃ'tʃiadu, da] ◇ *adj* amnestied. ◇ *m, f* person granted amnesty.

aniversariante [anivexsa'rjãntʃi] ◇ *adj*: **a cidade** ~ the city that is celebrating its anniversary. ◇ *mf* [pessoa] birthday boy (*f* birthday girl).

aniversariar [16] [anivexsa'rja(x)] *vi* -**1.** [pessoa] *to celebrate one's birthday/anniversary.* -**2.** [cidade] *to celebrate its anniversary.*

aniversário [anivex'sarju] *m* -**1.** [de acontecimento] anniversary. -**2.** [de nascimento] birthday. -**3.** [festa] birthday party.

anjo ['ãnʒu] *m* angel; ~ **da guarda** guardian angel.

Ankara [ãŋ'karal *n* Ankara.

ano ['ãnul *m* [período] year; **no** ~ **de 1969, o homem foi à Lua** in 1969, man went to the moon; **os** ~**s 70** the 1970s; ~ **bissexto** leap year; ~ **civil** calendar year; ~ **corrente** current year; ~ **financeiro** financial year; ~ **fiscal** tax year; ~ **letivo** academic year; **este** ~ this year; **há** ~**s** *ou* **faz** ~ **s que** it's years since; **faz** ~**s que não o vejo** it's years since I saw him, I haven't seen him for years; **(no)** ~ **passado** last year; **(no)** ~ **que vem** next year; **por** ~ a year, per year.

➡ **anos** *mpl* [idade]: **tenho vinte** ~ **(de idade)** I'm twenty (years old); **quantos** ~**s você tem?** how old are you?; **ela faz nove** ~**s em outubro** she'll be nine in October.

ano-bom [ˌãnu'bõl (*pl* **anos-bons**) *m* [festa] New Year.

anões [a'nõjʃl *pl* ➣ **anão**.

anoitecer [25] [anojte'se(x)] ◇ *m* nightfall; **ao** ~ at nightfall. ◇ *vi* -**1.** [cair a noite]: **quando anoiteceu, acendemos as luzes** when it got dark we turned on the lights. -**2.** [estar em algum lugar ao anoitecer] to be somewhere when night falls; **anoitecemos na estrada** night fell while we were on the road.

ano-luz [ˌãnu'luʃ] (*pl* **anos-luz**) *m* light year.

anomalia [anoma'lial *f* abnormality.

anômalo, la [a'nomalu, lal *adj* abnormal.

anonimato [anoni'matul *m* anonymity; **ficar no** ~ to remain in anonymity; **viver no** ~ to live in anonymity.

anônimo, ma [a'nonimu, mal *adj* anonymous.

ano-novo [ˌãnu'novul (*pl* **anos-novos**) *m* -**1.** [período] new year. -**2.** [festa] New Year.

anoraque [ano'rakil *m* anorak.

anorexia [anorek'sial *f* anorexia.

anoréxico, ca [ano'reksiku, kal ◇ *adj* anorexic. ◇ *m, f* anorexic.

anormal [anox'mawl (*pl* -**ais**) ◇ *adj* -**1.** [ger] abnormal. -**2.** [incomum] unusual. -**3.** [extraordinário] extraordinary. -**4.** [deficiente] retarded. ◇ *m* -**1.** [pessoa excepcional] abnormal person. -**2.** *fam pej* [idiota] cretin.

anormalidade [anoxmali'dadʒil *f* -**1.** [anomalia] abnormality. -**2.** [situação] abnormal situation.

anotação [anota'sãwl (*pl* -**ões**) *f* note.

anotar [4] [ano'ta(x)] *vt* -**1.** [tomar nota de] to note down. -**2.** [apor observações a] to annotate.

anseio [ãn'sejul *m* desire; **no** ~ **de fazer algo** in one's eagerness to do sthg.

ânsia ['ãnsjal *f* -**1.** [desejo]: **ter** ~ **(por algo/de fazer algo)** to be longing for sthg/to do sthg; ~**s de vômito** nausea. -**2.** [ansiedade] anxiety.

ansiar [17] [ãn'sja(x)] *vi*: ~ **por algo/por fazer algo** to long for sthg/to do sthg.

ansiedade [ãnsje'dadʒil *f* -**1.** [ger] anxiety; **com** ~ anxiously. -**2.** [desejo] longing.

ansioso, osa [ãn'sjozu, ɔzal *adj* [angustiado, desejoso] anxious; **o presidente aguarda** ~ **o resultado das eleições** the president is anxiously awaiting the election results.

anta ['ãntal *f* -**1.** *ZOOL* tapir. -**2.** *fam pej* [idiota]: **ser uma** ~ to be an ass.

antagônico, ca [ãnta'goniku, kal *adj* [contrário] antagonistic; **opiniões antagônicas** conflicting opinions.

antagonismo [ãntago'niʒmul *m* -**1.** [oposição] antagonism; ~ **de idéias** conflict of ideas. -**2.** [rivalidade] competition.

antagonista [ãntago'niʃtal ◇ *adj* -**1.** [candidato, partido] opposing. -**2.** [opinião, idéia] conflicting. ◇ *mf* [rival] opponent.

antártico, ca [ãn'taxtʃiku, kal *adj* Antarctic.

➡ **Antártico** *n*: **o (oceano)** ~ the Antarctic (Ocean).

Antártida [ãn'taxtʃidal *n*: **a** ~ Antarctica.

ante ['ãntʃil *prep* -**1.** [diante de] before; **jurar** ~ **a Bíblia** to swear on the Bible; **jurar** ~ **o juiz** to swear before the judge. -**2.** [em consequência de] as a result of.

ante- ['ãntʃi-] *prefixo* ante-.

antebraço [ãntʃi'brasul *m* forearm.

antecedência [ãntese'dẽnsjal *f*: **com** ~ in advance; **com uma semana de** ~ a week in advance.

antecedente [ãntese'dẽntʃil ◇ *adj* [precedente] preceding. ◇ *m* -**1.** [precedente] predecessor. -**2.** *GRAM, MAT* antecedent.

➡ **antecedentes** *mpl* [pessoais] track record *(sg)*; **ter bons** ~**s** to have a clean record; ~**s criminais** criminal record *(sg)*.

anteceder [5] [ãntese'de(x)] ◇ *vt* [preceder, chegar antes de] to precede. ◇ *vi* [preceder]: ~ **a** to precede.

◆ **anteceder-se** *vp* [antecipar-se]: ~ (a) to be ahead (of).

antecessor, ra [ãntese'so(x), ra] ◇ *adj* preceding. ◇ *m, f* predecessor.

antecipação [ãntesipa'sãwl (*pl* -ões) *f* - **1.** [adiantamento]: a ~ **de metas** the early achievement of goals; a ~ **do comunicado provocou uma crise** the bringing forward of the announcement caused a crisis. - **2.** [salarial] advance. - **3.** [antecedência]: **com** ~ in advance; **com uma semana/ um mês de** ~ a week/month in advance.

antecipadamente [ãntesi,pada'mẽntʃi] *adv* in advance.

antecipado, da [ãntesi'padu, da] *adj* - **1.** [pagamento] advance *(antes de subst)*. - **2.** [eleições] early.

antecipar [4] [ãntesi'pa(x)] *vt* - **1.** [fazer ocorrer mais cedo] to bring forward. - **2.** [adiantar-se a] to anticipate.

◆ **antecipar-se** *vp* [adiantar-se]: ~-se a algo/alguém to pre-empt sthg/sb; ~-se a alguém em algo to steal a march on sb in sthg.

antegozar [4] [ãntego'za(x)] *vt* to have a foretaste of.

antemão [ãnte'mãw] ◆ **de antemão** *loc adv* beforehand.

antena [ãn'tena] *f* - **1.** [ger] antenna; **de** ~**s ligadas** with one's antennae out. - **2.** *RÁDIO, TV* aerial; ~ **parabólica** satellite dish.

anteontem [ãntʃi'õntẽ] *adv* the day before yesterday.

anteparo [ãnte'parul *m* [proteção] screen.

antepassado, da [ãntepa'sadu, da] *m, f* ancestor.

antepenúltimo, ma [ãntepe'nuwtʃimu, ma] *adj* last but two, antepenultimate.

antepor [45] [ãnteẽpo(x)l *vt* - **1.** [contrapor]: ~ **algo a algo** to respond to sthg with sthg. - **2.** [preferir]: ~ **algo a algo** to prefer sthg to sthg.

◆ **antepor-se** *vp* [contrapor-se]: ~-se a algo to place o.s. in front of sthg.

anterior [ãnte'rjo(x)l (*pl* -es) *adj* - **1.** [prévio]: ~ (a) before. - **2.** [antigo]: ~ (a) previous (to). - **3.** [em posição] front; **membro** ~ forelimb; **músculo** ~ anterior muscle.

anteriormente [ãnterioxẽmẽntʃi] *adv* [previamente] previously; ~ **a algo** prior to sthg.

antes ['ãnʃiʃl *adv* - **1.** [previamente] beforehand; **o quanto** ~ ás soon as possible; **pouco** ~ a little before. - **2.** [antigamente] in the past; **como** ~ as ever; **de** *ou* **que** ~ as before. - **3.** [de preferência] rather. - **4.** [ao contrário] on the contrary.

◆ **antes de** *loc prep* before; ~ **de fazer algo** before doing sthg; ~ **da hora/do tempo** early; ~ **de tudo** above all.

◆ **antes que** *loc conj* before; **fui embora** ~ **que chovesse** I left before it rained.

ante-sala [,ãnte'sala] (*pl* -s) *f* antechamber.

antever [40] [ãnte've(x)l *vt* to foresee.

antevéspera [,ãnte'vɛʃperal *f:* **(na)** ~ the day before yesterday.

antevisão [,ãnte'vizãwl *f* - **1.** [visão antecipada]: **ter uma** ~ **de** to foresee. - **2.** [pressentimento] premonition.

anti- ['ãntʃi-] *prefixo* anti-, non-.

antiácido, da [ãn'tʃjasidu, da] *adj* antacid.
◆ **antiácido** *m* antacid.

antiaderente [ãntʃjade'rẽntʃil (*pl* -s) ◇ *adj* non-stick. ◇ *m* non-stick surface.

antiaéreo, rea [ãntʃja'ɛrju, rjal *adj* anti-aircraft; **abrigo** ~ bomb shelter.

antialérgico, ca [ãntʃja'lexʒiku, kal *adj* hypo-allergenic.
◆ **antialérgico** *m* antihistamine.

antiamericano, na [ãntʃjameri'kãnu, nal *adj* anti-American.

antibiótico, ca [ãntʃi'bjotʃiku, kal *adj* antibiotic.
◆ **antibiótico** *m* antibiotic.

anticaspa [ãntʃi'kaʃpal *adj* anti-dandruff.

anticlímax [ãntʃi'klimãksl *m inv* anticlimax.

anticoagulante [ãntʃikwagu'lãntʃil ◇ *adj* anti-coagulant. ◇ *m* anticoagulant.

anticomunista [ãntʃikomu'niʃtal ◇ *adj* anti-communist. ◇ *mf* [pessoa] anti-communist.

anticoncepcional [ãntʃikõnsepsjo'nawl (*pl* -ais) ◇ *adj* contraceptive. ◇ *m* [pílula, dispositivo] contraceptive.

anticongelante [ãntʃikõnʒe'lãntʃil ◇ *adj* anti-freeze. ◇ *m* antifreeze.

anticorpo [ãntʃi'koxpul *m* antibody.

anticorrosivo [ãntʃikoxo'zivul *adj* - **1.** non-corrosive. - **2.** [proteção] anti-corrosive.

antidemocrático, ca [ãntʃidemo'kratʃiku, kal *adj* anti-democratic.

antidepressivo, va [ãntʃidepre'sivu, val *adj* antidepressant.
◆ **antidepressivo** *m* antidepressant.

antiderrapante [ãntʃidexa'pãntʃil *adj* non-skid.

antídoto [ãn'tʃidotul *m* antidote.

antiestético, ca [ãntʃjeʃ'tɛtʃiku, kal *adj* tasteless.

antiético, ca [ãn'tʃjɛtʃiku, kal *adj* unethical.

antigamente [ãntʃiga'mẽntʃil *adv* in the past; **de** ~ old-fashioned.

antigo, ga [ãn'tʃigu, gal *adj* - **1.** [ger] old. - **2.** [antiquado, remoto] old-fashioned. - **3.** *(antes de subst)* [anterior] former, previous. - **4.** *(antes de subst)* [veterano] longstanding; **ser** ~ **no clube** to be a longstanding member of the club; **ser** ~ **na empresa** to be a longstanding member of staff; **ser** ~ **no cargo** to be an old hand at the job. - **5.** *HIST* [da Antigüidade] ancient.
◆ **antigos** *mpl HIST* [homens] ancients.

antigüidade [ãntʃigwi'dadʒil *f* - **1.** [idade] age. - **2.** [em cargo, função] seniority. - **3.** [peça, monumento] antique.
◆ **Antigüidade** *f* [época] antiquity.
◆ **antigüidades** *fpl* - **1.** [peças] antiques; **loja de** ~**s** antique shop. - **2.** [monumentos] ancient monuments.

anti-higiênico, ca [ãntʃi'ʒjeniku, kal (*mpl* -s, *fpl* -s) *adj* unhygienic.

anti-histamínico, ca [ãntʃji'iʃta'miniku, ka] *adj* antihistamine.

➡ **anti-histamínico** *m* antihistamine.

anti-horário [ãntʃjo'rarju] *adj*: **sentido/movimento ~** anticlockwise direction/movement.

antiinflacionário, ria [ãntʃiflasjo'narju, rja] *adj* anti-inflationary.

antiinflamatório, ria [ãntʃjĩnflama'tɔriu, rja] <> *adj* anti-inflammatory. <> *m* anti-inflammatory.

antilhano, na [ãntʃi'ʎanu, na] <> *adj* West Indian. <> *m, f* West Indian.

Antilhas [ãn'tʃiʎas] *npl*: **as ~** the West Indies.

antílope [ãn'tʃilopi] *m* antelope.

antinatural [ãntʃinatu'raw] (*pl* -ais) *adj* unnatural.

antinuclear [ãntʃinukle'a(x)] *adj* anti-nuclear.

antipático, ca [ãntʃi'patʃiku, ka] *adj* unpleasant.

antipatizar [4] [ãntʃipatʃi'za(x)] *vi*: **~ com alguém** to dislike sb.

antipatriótico, ca [ãntʃipa'trjɔtʃiku, ka] *adj* unpatriotic.

antiperspirante [ãntʃipexʃpi'rantʃil] <> *adj* antiperspirant. <> *mf* antiperspirant.

antipoluente [ãntʃipo'lwẽntʃil] <> *adj* **-1.** [sistema, proteção] anti-pollution. **-2.** [material] non-polluting. <> *m* anti-pollution agent.

antiquado, da [ãntʃi'kwadu, da] *adj* antiquated.

antiquário, ria [ãntʃi'kwarju, rja] *m, f* [comerciante] antique dealer.

➡ **antiquário** *m* [loja] antique shop.

antiqüíssimo, ma [ãntʃi'kisimu, ma] *superl* ▷ antigo.

anti-semita [ãntʃise'mita] (*pl* -s) <> *adj* anti-Semitic. <> *mf* [pessoa] anti-Semite.

anti-séptico, ca [antʃi'sɛptʃiku, ka] *adj* antiseptic.

➡ **anti-séptico, antisséptico** *m* [desinfetante] antiseptic.

anti-social [ãntʃiso'sjaw] (*pl* -ais) *adj* antisocial.

antisséptico [ˌãntʃi'sɛptʃiku] = **anti-séptico**.

antitabagismo [ãntʃitaba'ʒizmu] *m* anti-smoking.

antitabagista [ãntʃitaba'ʒista] <> *adj* anti-smoking. <> *mf* anti-smoker.

antitérmico, ca [ãntʃi'tɛxmiku, ka] *adj* antipyretic.

➡ **antitérmico** *m* [comprimido] antipyretic.

antiterrorismo [ãntʃitexo'riʒmu] *m* anti-terrorism.

antiterrorista [ãntʃitexo'riʃta] <> *adj* anti-terrorist. <> *mf* anti-terrorist.

antítese [ãn'tʃitezi] *f* antithesis.

antivírus [ãntʃi'viruʃ] *m inv* **-1.** BIOL antivirus. **-2.** COMPUT antivirus program.

antolhos [ã'tɔʎuʃ] *mpl* blinkers.

antologia [ãntolo'ʒia] *f* anthology.

antológico, ca [ãnto'lɔʒiko, ka] *adj* outstanding.

antônimo [ãn'tonimu] *m* antonym.

antro ['ãntru] *m* **-1.** [caverna] cave. **-2.** [de animal] lair. **-3.** [de bandidos etc] den.

antropofagia [ãntropofa'ʒia] *f* cannibalism.

antropófago, ga [ãntro'pɔfagu, ga] <> *adj* cannibalistic. <> *m, f* cannibal.

antropologia [ãntropolo'ʒia] *f* anthropology.

antropólogo, ga [ãntro'pɔlogu, ga] *m, f* anthropologist.

anual [a'nwaw] (*pl* -ais) *adj* annual, yearly.

anuário [a'nwarju] *m* yearbook.

anuidade [anwi'dadʒi] *f* annuity.

anuir [74] [a'nwi(x)] *vi* to agree; **~ a** *ou* **em algo** to agree to *ou* on sthg; **~ a** *ou* **em fazer algo** to agree to do sthg.

anulação [anula'sãw] (*pl* -ões) *f* **-1.** [cancelamento, invalidação] cancellation. **-2.** [casamento] annulment. **-3.** [pena] revocation. **-4.** [gol] disallowance.

anular [4] [anu'la(x)] <> *vt* **-1.** [cancelar, invalidar] to cancel. **-2.** [casamento] to annul. **-3.** [pena] to revoke. **-4.** [gol] to disallow. **-5.** [sobrepujar] to cancel out. <> *adj* **-1.** [forma] circular. **-2.** [dedo] ring. <> *m* [dedo] ring finger.

anunciante [anũn'sjãntʃil] *m* COM advertiser.

anunciar [16] [anũn'sja(x)] *vt* **-1.** [ger] to announce. **-2.** COM [produto] to advertise.

anúncio [a'nũnsjul] *m* **-1.** [comunicado] announcement. **-2.** [cartaz, aviso] notice. **-3.** [publicitário] advertisement; **~s classificados** classifieds.

ânus ['ãnuʃ] *m inv* anus.

anuviar [16] [anuvi'a(x)] *vt* to cloud.

➡ **anuviar-se** *vp* **-1.** [o céu] to become cloudy. **-2.** *fig* [rosto] to cloud.

anverso [ãn'vɛxsul] *m* obverse.

anzol [ãn'zɔwl] (*pl* -óis) *m* hook.

ao [aw] = **a + o**.

aonde [a'õndʒil] *adv* where; **~ quer que ...** wherever ...

aos [awʃ] = **a + os**.

AP (*abrev de* **Estado do Amapá**) *n* State of Amapá.

apadrinhar [4] [apadri'ɲa(x)] *vt* **-1.** [criança] to be godfather to. **-2.** [noivo] to be best man to. **-3.** *fig* [proteger] to take under one's wing. **-4.** *fig* [patrocinar] to sponsor.

APAE (*abrev de* **Associação de Pais e Amigos dos Excepcionais**) *f* Brazilian association of parents and friends of the disabled.

apagado, da [apa'gadu, da] *adj* **-1.** [fogo] extinguished. **-2.** [desligado] out (*depois de verbo*). **-3.** [com borracha] rubbed out *UK*, erased *US*. **-4.** [desvanecido] faded. **-5.** *fig* [sem brilho] lacklustre. **-6.** *fig* [pessoa] dull.

apagador [apaga'do(x)] *m* board eraser.

apagão [apa'gãwl] (*pl* -ões) *m* [blecaute] power cut.

apagar [14] [apa'ga(x)] <> *vt* **-1.** [fogo] to put out. **-2.** [vela] to blow out. **-3.** [luz, lanterna] to turn out. **-4.** [lustre] to dim. **-5.** [com borracha, apagador] to rub out. **-6.** [fazer desvanecer-se] to fade. **-7.** [abrandar] to dull. **-8.** COMPUT [eliminar] to delete. **-9.** *fam fig* [matar] to wipe out. <> *vi fam fig* [adormecer] to crash out.

➡ **apagar-se** *vp* **-1.** [extingüir-se] to die out. **-2.** [desligar-se] to go out. **-3.** [desvanecer-se] to fade. **-4.** [abrandar-se] to dull.

apaixonado, da [apajʃo'nadu, da] *adj* -**1.** [enamorado] in love; **estar ~ (por alguém)** to be in love (with sb). -**2.** [exaltado] impassioned. -**3.** [aficcionado]: **ser ~ (por algo)** to be passionate about sthg.

apaixonante [apajʃo'nãntʃil *adj* exciting.

apaixonar-se [4] [apajʃo'naxsil *vp* -**1.** [enamorarse]: **~ (por alguém)** to fall in love (with sb). -**2.** [aficcionar-se]: **~ (por algo)** to become passionate (about sthg).

apalermado, da [apalex'madu, da] *adj* idiotic.

apalpar [4] [apaw'pa(x)] *vt* to feel.

➡ **apalpar-se** *vp* [examinar-se] to examine o.s.

apanhado [apã'nadul *m* -**1.** [resumo] summary. -**2.** [de flores] bunch.

apanhar [4] [apã'ɲa(x)] <> *vt* -**1.** [ger] to catch. -**2.** [pegar] to pick out. -**3.** [alcançar] to get. -**4.** [pegar do chão] to pick up. -**5.** [agarrar] to grab. -**6.** [colher] to pick. -**7.** [ir buscar] to fetch. -**8.** [tomar condução] to take. <> *vi* -**1.** [ser espancado] to be beaten; **~ de alguém** to take a beating from sb; **~ de algo** to be beaten with sthg. -**2.** *ESP* [perder] to lose. -**3.** *fig* [ter dificuldades] to go through a lot.

apara [a'para] *f* -**1.** [madeira] shaving. -**2.** [papel] shred.

aparador [apara'do(x)] (*pl* -es) *m* [móvel] sideboard.

aparafusar [4] [aparafu'za(x)] *vt* -**1.** [parafuso] to screw in. -**2.** [prender] to screw.

aparar [4] [apa'ra(x)] *vt* -**1.** [cabelo, barba, unhas] to trim. -**2.** [unhas] to clip. -**3.** [golpe] to fend off. -**4.** [tábua, folhas] to smooth out.

aparato [apa'ratul *m* -**1.** [pompa] ceremony. -**2.** [conjunto - de ferramentas] collection; [- de armas] apparatus. -**3.** *fig* [de conceitos, análises] structure.

aparecer [25] [apare'se(x)] *vt* -**1.** [ger] to appear. -**2.** [ser perceptível] to be apparent. -**3.** [comparecer] to turn up; *fam* [fazer visita] to drop in. -**4.** *fam pej* [exibir-se] to show off.

aparecimento [aparesi'mẽntul *m* appearance.

aparelhado, da [apare'ʎadu, da] *adj* -**1.** [preparado] prepared. -**2.** [madeira] planed.

aparelhagem [apare'ʎaʒẽl (*pl* -ns) *f* -**1.** [equipamento] equipment; [de som] sound system. -**2.** [da madeira] planing. -**3.** *NÁUT* rigging.

aparelhar [4] [apare'ʎa(x)] *vt* -**1.** [preparar] to equip. -**2.** *NÁUT* to rig.

➡ **aparelhar-se** *vp* [preparar-se] to equip o.s.

aparelho [apa'reʎul *m* -**1.** [conjunto] set; **~ de chá** tea set; **~ de jantar** dinner service. -**2.** [equipamento] equipment; **~ de som** sound system. -**3.** [máquina] machine; **~ de barbear** shaving equipment; **~ de rádio/TV** radio/television set; **~ eletrodoméstico** domestic appliance. -**4.** *PESCA* tackle. -**5.** *POL* hideout. -**6.** *ANAT* system; **~ digestivo** digestive system; **~ fonador** voice box.

aparência [apa'rẽnsja] *f* -**1.** [aspecto] appearance; **sob a ~ de** in the guise of; **na ~** by all appearances. -**2.** [ilusão] show.

➡ **aparências** *fpl* [exterioridades] appearances; **as ~s enganam** *prov* one shouldn't judge by appearances; **manter as ~s** to keep up appearances; **salvar as ~s** to save appearances.

aparentado, da [aparẽn'tadu, da] *adj* -**1.** [que tem parentesco] related; **ser ~ de alguém** to be related to sb; **bem ~** well connected. -**2.** [que tem boa aparência]: **bem ~** smart.

aparentar [4] [aparẽn'ta(x)] *vt* -**1.** [parecer] to seem. -**2.** [fingir] to pretend.

aparente [apa'rẽntʃil *adj* -**1.** [falso] feigned. -**2.** [visível] visible.

aparição [apari'sãwl (*pl* -ões) *f* apparition.

apartamento [apaxta'mẽntul *m* -**1.** [residência] apartment, flat *UK*. -**2.** [de hotel] hotel suite.

apartar [4] [apax'ta(x)] *vt* -**1.** [separar] to split. -**2.** [briga] to break up.

➡ **apartar-se** *vp* [afastar-se] to split from.

aparte [a'paxtʃil *m* [observação] aside; **fazer um ~** to make an aside.

apartheid [apax'tajdʒil *m* apartheid.

apartidário, ria [apartʃi'darju, rjal *adj* non-partisan.

aparvalhado, da [apaxva'ʎadu, da] *adj* -**1.** [idiota] idiotic. -**2.** [sem reação]: **ficar ~** to be stunned.

apatetado, da [apate'tadu, da] *adj* [trapalhão] foolish.

apatia [apa'tʃial *f* indifference.

apático, ca [a'patʃiku, kal *adj* indifferent.

apátrida [a'patridal *mf* stateless person.

apavorado, da [apavo'radu, da] *adj* terrified.

apavoramento [apavora'mẽntul *m* panic, terror.

apavorante [apavo'rãntʃil *adj* terrifying.

apavorar [4] [apavo'ra(x)] <> *vt* to terrify. <> *vi* to be terrifying.

➡ **apavorar-se** *vp* to become terrified.

apaziguar [21] [apazi'gwa(x)] *vt* to calm.

➡ **apaziguar-se** *vp* -**1.** to calm down. -**2.** [inimigos] to make peace.

apear [a'pja(x)] *vi* to dismount.

apedrejar [4] [apedre'ʒa(x)] *vt* to stone.

apegado, da [ape'gadu, da] *adj* [afeiçoado]: **~ (a)** attached (to).

apegar-se [14] [ape'gaxsil *vp* [afeiçoar-se]: **~ a algo/alguém** to become attached to sthg/sb.

apego [a'pegul *m* [afeição] attachment; **ter ~ por** to be attached to.

apelação [apela'sãwl (*pl* -ões) *f* -**1.** [apelo] appeal. -**2.** *JUR* appeal. -**3.** *fam* [vulgarização] solicitation.

apelante [ape'lãntʃil *mf* appellant.

apelar [4] [ape'la(x)] *vi* -**1.** [recorrer]: **~ a** to appeal to; **~ (para a violência)** to turn nasty. -**2.** [invocar]: **~ a** [compreensão, amizade] to call upon. -**3.** *JUR*: **~ (de)** to appeal (against). -**4.** [vulgarmente] to turn nasty.

apelidar [4] [apeli'da(x)] *vt*: **~ alguém de algo** to nickname sb sthg.

apelido [ape'lidul *m* [alcunha] nickname; **chato é ~! ele é insuportável!** *fam* boring's an understatement! he's odious!

apelo [a'pelul *m* appeal; **~ a alguém/algo** appeal to sb/sthg.

apenas [a'penaʃ] ⟨⟩ *adv* [só] only. ⟨⟩ *conj* [logo que] as soon as.

apêndice [a'pēndʒisil] *m* appendix.

apendicite [apēndʒi'sitʃil] *f* appendicitis.

Apeninos [ape'ninuʃ] *npl*: **os** ~ the Apennines.

apequenar [4] [apeke'na(x)] *vt* **- 1.** [tornar pequeno] to lessen. **- 2.** *fig* [rebaixar, humilhar] to belittle.

➡ **apequenar-se** *vp fig* [rebaixar-se, humilhar-se] to belittle o.s.

aperceber-se [5] [apexse'bexsil *vp*: ~ **de** to realise.

aperfeiçoamento [apexfejswa'mẽntul] *m* [aprimoramento] improvement.

aperfeiçoar [20] [apexfej'swa(x)l *vt* to improve.

➡ **aperfeiçoar-se** *vp* [aprimorar-se] to improve; ~**-se em algo** to improve in *ou* at sthg.

aperitivo, va [aperi'tʃivu, val *adj* appetizing.

➡ **aperitivo** *m* **- 1.** [bebida] aperitif. **- 2.** [petisco] appetizer.

aperreação [apexja'sãwl (*pl* **-ões**) *f* **- 1.** [aborrecimento] vexation. **- 2.** [situação difícil] hardship.

aperreado, da [ape'xjadu, dal *adj* **- 1.** [aborrecido] vexed. **- 2.** [em situação difícil] troubled.

aperrear [15] [ape'xja(x)l *vt* **- 1.** [aborrecer] to annoy. **- 2.** [afligir] to vex.

➡ **aperrear-se** *vp* **- 1.** [aborrecer-se] to become vexed. **- 2.** [afligir-se] to be anxious.

apertado, da [apex'tadu, dal ⟨⟩ *adj* **- 1.** [ger] tight. **- 2.** [passagem] narrow. **- 3.** [poltrona, sala, teatro] cramped. **- 4.** [difícil] hard. **- 5.** [sem tempo] pressed. **- 6.** [sem dinheiro] strapped for cash; **orçamento** ~ tight budget. **- 7.** *fam* [para ir ao banheiro]: **estar** ~ to be desperate to go to the bathroom. **- 8.** [coração]: **estar com o coração** ~ to be anguished. ⟨⟩ *adv* [com dificuldade] only just.

apertar [4] [apex'ta(x)l ⟨⟩ *vt* **- 1.** [cingir]: ~ **algo (contra/entre)** to clasp sthg (against/between); ~ **alguém (contra/entre)** to clasp sb (against/between); ~ **a mão de alguém** [cumprimentar] to shake sb's hand. **- 2.** [espremer] to squeeze. **- 3.** [incomodar por ser justo] to constrict. **- 4.** [tornar mais justo] to tighten. **- 5.** [pressionar - botão] to do up; [- gatilho] to squeeze. **- 6.** *fig* [intensificar] to tighten up on. **- 7.** [passo, ritmo] to speed up. **- 8.** [cortar] to cut. **- 9.** [coração] to wring. **-10.** *fig* [pessoa] to put pressure on. ⟨⟩ *vi* **- 1.** [roupa, sapato] to be tight. **- 2.** [chuva, frio, fome] to intensify. **- 3.** [prazo] to run out. **- 4.** [estrada, rio] to narrow.

➡ **apertar-se** *vp* **- 1.** [cortar gastos] to tighten one's belt. **- 2.** [ficar sem dinheiro] to be pressed for cash. **- 3.** [com a roupa] to squeeze o.s. into.

aperto [a'pextul *m* **- 1.** [em cumprimento]: ~ **de mãos** handshake. **- 2.** *fig* [apuro] problem; **passar um** ~ to have a rough time. **- 3.** *fig* [financeiro] hardship.

apesar [ape'za(x)l *prep*: ~ **de** in spite of; ~ **de que** even though; ~ **disso** in spite of this.

apetecer [25] [apete'se(x)l *vi* to be appetizing; ~ **a alguém** to appeal to sb.

apetecível [apete'sivewl (*pl* **-eis**) *adj* **- 1.** [prato, receita] appetizing. **- 2.** *fig* [idéia proposta] attractive.

apetite [ape'tʃitʃil *m* appetite; **abrir o** ~ to whet the appetite; **bom** ~! enjoy your meal!; **ter um** ~ **de sucesso/riqueza/poder** to have an appetite for success/wealth/power.

apetitoso, osa [apetʃi'tozu, ɔzal *adj* tasty.

apetrechar [4] [apetre'ʃa(x)l *vt*: ~ **alguém (com/para algo)** to equip sb (with/for sthg).

➡ **apetrechar-se** *vp*: ~**-se (com/para algo)** to equip o.s. (with/for sthg).

apetrechos [ape'treʃuʃ] *mpl* **- 1.** [de guerra] equipment (*U*). **- 2.** [de pesca] tackle (*U*).

ápice ['apisil *m* **- 1.** [cimo] top, summit. **- 2.** *fig* [apogeu] peak.

apicultura [apikuw'tural *f* bee-keeping.

apiedar-se [4] [apje'daxsil *vp*: ~ **(de alguém/algo)** to feel sorry (for sb/sthg).

apimentado, da [apimẽn'tadu, dal *adj* **- 1.** [com muita pimenta] peppery. **- 2.** *fig* [sensual] spicy.

apimentar [4] [apimẽn'ta(x)l *vt* to pepper.

apinhado, da [api'nadu, dal *adj* crowded; ~ **de gente** crowded with people.

apinhar [4] [api'na(x)l *vt* [lotar] to crowd.

➡ **apinhar-se** *vp* **- 1.** [aglomerar-se] to crowd. **- 2.** [lotar]: ~**-se (de gente)** to be crowded (with people).

apitar [4] [api'ta(x)l ⟨⟩ *vi* **- 1.** [com apito] to whistle. **- 2.** *fam fig* [ter autoridade] to know a lot; **ele apita muito em medicina** he knows a lot about medicine; **ele não apita nada em casa** he's not the one who wears the trousers. ⟨⟩ *vt* [*ESP* - arbitrar] to referee; [- falta, pênalti] to whistle.

apito [a'pitul *m* [instrumento, silvo] whistle.

aplacar [12] [apla'ka(x)l ⟨⟩ *vt* **- 1.** [serenar] to subdue. **- 2.** [abrandar] to assuage. ⟨⟩ *vi* **- 1.** [serenar-se] to die down. **- 2.** [abrandar-se] to calm down.

➡ **aplacar-se** *vp* to calm down.

aplainar [4] [aplaj'na(x)l *vt* **- 1.** [madeira] to plane. **- 2.** [nivelar] to level out.

aplanar [4] [apla'na(x)l *vt* **- 1.** [nivelar] to level out. **- 2.** [alisar] to smooth. **- 3.** *fig* [obstáculos] to smooth out.

aplaudir [6] [aplaw'di(x)l ⟨⟩ *vt* to applaud; ~ **alguém/algo de pé** to give sb/sthg a standing ovation. ⟨⟩ *vi* to clap, to applaud.

aplauso [a'plawzul *m* **- 1.** [ger] applause; **o filme recebeu o** ~ **da crítica** the film received critical acclaim. **- 2.** *fig* [aprovação] approval; **as medidas contra o crime contam com meu** ~ I applaud the measures against crime.

aplicação [aplika'sãwl (*pl* **-ões**) *f* **- 1.** [ger] application. **- 2.** [ornato] adornment.

aplicado, da [apli'kadu, dal *adj* **- 1.** [esforçado] hard-working. **- 2.** [prático] applied.

aplicar [12] [apli'ka(x)l ⟨⟩ *vt* **- 1.** [ger] to apply. **- 2.** [injeção] to give. **- 3.** *FIN* to invest. ⟨⟩ *vi FIN* to invest.

➡ **aplicar-se** *vp* **- 1.** [esforçar-se]: ~**-se em/para algo** to work hard at/for sthg. **- 2.** [adequar-se]: ~**-se a algo** to apply to sthg.

aplicativo, va [aplika'tʃivu, val *adj COMPUT*: **programa** ~ application.

➡ **aplicativo** *m COMPUT* application.

aplicável [apli'kavew] (*pl* -eis) *adj* -1. [ger] applicable. -2. [apropriado] appropriate.

aplique [a'plikil *m* -1. [de luz] wall light. -2. [peruca] hairpiece.

APM (*abrev de* Associação de Pais e Mestres) *f* ≃ PTA.

apocalipse [apoka'lipsil *m* apocalypse.

apocalíptico, ca [apoka'liptʃiku, kal *adj* -1. [do Apocalipse] apocalyptic. -2. [terrível] terrifying. -3. [difícil de entender] enigmatic.

apócrifo, fa [a'pɔkrifu, fal *adj* apocryphal.
➡ **apócrifo** *m* [texto] apocrypha *(pl)*.

apoderar-se [4] [apode'raxsil *vp*: ~ **de algo** to take over sthg.

apodrecer [25] [apodre'se(x)l ⬦ *vi* -1. [comida] to go off. -2. [dente] to rot. -3. *fam* [pessoa]: ~ **em** to rot in. ⬦ *vt* [tornar podre] to rot.

apodrecimento [apodresi'mẽntul *m* rot.

apogeu [apo'ʒew] *m* -1. [de império, carreira, romance] crowning point. -2. *ASTRON* apogee.

apoiar [16] [apo'ja(x)] *vt* -1. [ger] to support. -2. [firmar]: ~ **algo em** *ou* **sobre algo** to rest sthg on sthg. -3. [fundamentar]: ~ **algo em** *ou* **sobre algo** to base sthg on sthg.
➡ **apoiar-se** *vp* -1. [amparar-se mutuamente] to support one another. -2. [firmar-se] to lean. -3. [fundamentar-se] to be based on.

apoio [a'pojul *m* -1. [ger] support; ~ **moral** moral support. -2. [patrocínio] sponsorship; ~ **cultural** cultural sponsorship. -3. [alicerce] foundations *(pl)*. -4. *fig* [fundamento] basis.

apólice [a'pɔlisil *f* policy; ~ **de seguro** insurance policy.

apolítico, ca [apo'litʃiku, kal *adj* apolitical.

apologia [apolo'ʒial *f* defence.

apologista [apolo'ʒiʃtal *mf* apologist.

apontador [apõnta'do(x)l (*pl* -es) *m* -1. [de lápis] pencil sharpener. -2. [de jogo] marker.

apontamento [apõnta'mẽntul *m* [anotação] notes *(pl)*.

apontar [4] [apõn'ta(x)l ⬦ *vt* -1. [ger] to point out. -2. [arma] to aim. -3. [citar] to name. -4. [notas] to make notes. -5. [jogo] to mark. -6. [lápis] to sharpen. ⬦ *vi* -1. [com arma]: ~ **para** to aim at; **apontar!** aim! -2. [com o dedo]: ~ **para** to point at. -3. [aparecer] to appear.

apoplético, ca [apo'plɛtʃiku, kal *adj* apoplectic.

apoquentar [4] [apokẽnta(x)l *vt* to annoy.
➡ **apoquentar-se** *vp* to get annoyed.

aporrinhação [apoxiɲa'sãwl (*pl* -ões) *f mfam* annoyance.

aporrinhar [4] [apoxi'ɲa(x)l *vt mfam* to annoy.

aportar [4] [apox'ta(x)l *vi* [desembarcar, ancorar]: ~ **em** to dock in.

aportuguesar [4] [apoxtuge'za(x)l *vt* to make Portuguese.
➡ **aportuguesar-se** *vp* to become Portuguese.

após [a'pojʃl *prep* after.

aposentado, da [apozẽn'tadu, dal ⬦ *adj* -1.

[pessoa] retired. -2. [sapato] discarded. -3. [carro, máquina] disused. ⬦ *m, f* retired person.

aposentadoria [apozẽntado'rial *f* -1. [condição] retirement. -2. [vencimentos] pension.

aposentar [4] [apozẽn'ta(x)l *vt* -1. [pessoa] to pension off. -2. [máquina] to discard.
➡ **aposentar-se** *vp* to retire.

aposento [apo'zẽntul *m* bedroom.

apossar-se [4] [apo'saxsil *vp*: ~ **de algo** to take possession of sthg.

aposta [a'pɔʃtal *f* bet.

apostar [4] [apoʃ'ta(x)l ⬦ *vt* to bet; ~ **que** to bet that. ⬦ *vi*: ~ **em** to bet on.

apostila [apoʃ'tʃilal *f* -1. [nota marginal] marginal note. -2. [matéria de aula] handout.

apóstolo [a'pɔʃtulul *m* apostle.

apóstrofo [a'pɔʃtroful *m* apostrophe.

apoteose [apote'ɔzil *f* apotheosis.

aprazer [32] [apra'ze(x)l *vi*: ~ **a alguém** to please sb.

aprazível [apra'zivɛwl (*pl* -eis) *adj* pleasant.

apreçar [13] [apre'sa(x)l *vt* [dar valor a] to value.

apreciação [apresja'sãwl (*pl* -ões) *f* -1. [análise] consideration. -2. [julgamento] assessment.

apreciador, ra [apresja'do(x), ral *m, f* aficionado.

apreciar [16] [apre'sja(x)l *vt* -1. [ger] to appreciate. -2. [gostar de] to enjoy.

apreciativo, va [apresja'tʃivu, val *adj* appreciative.

apreciável [apre'sjavewl (*pl* -eis) *adj* -1. [estimável] considerable. -2. [significativo] notable.

apreço [a'presul *m* [estima, consideração] consideration.

apreender [5] [aprjẽn'de(x)l *vt* -1. [tomar] to seize; ~ **algo a alguém** to seize sthg from sb. -2. [compreender] to understand, to comprehend.

apreensão [aprjẽn'sãwl (*pl* -ões) *f* -1. [tomada] seizure. -2. [percepção] understanding, comprehension. -3. [preocupação] apprehension.

apreensivo, va [aprjẽn'sivu, val *adj* apprehensive.

apregoar [20] [apre'gwa(x)l *vt* to proclaim.

aprender [5] [aprẽn'de(x)l ⬦ *vt* to learn. ⬦ *vi* to learn; ~ **a fazer algo** to learn to do sthg; ~ **de cor** to learn by heart.

aprendiz [aprẽn'dʒiʒl (*pl* -es) *mf* learner.

aprendizado [aprẽndʒi'zadul (*pl* -es) *m*, **aprendizagem** *f* [aprẽndʒi'zaʒẽl learning.

apresentação [aprezẽnta'sãwl (*pl* -ões) *f* [ger] presentation.

apresentador, ra [aprezẽnta'do(x), ral *m, f* -1. [de seminário, painel] speaker. -2. *RÁDIO, TV* presenter.

apresentar [4] [aprezẽn'ta(x)l *vt* -1. [ger] to present; ~ **uma comunicação** to give a talk. -2. [fazer] to make. -3. [moção, recurso] to introduce.
➡ **apresentar-se** *vp* -1. [dar-se a conhecer] to introduce o.s. -2. [comparecer] to present o.s. -3. [manifestar-se] to arise. -4. [candidatar-se] to put o.s. forward.

apresentável [aprezẽn'tavewl (*pl* -eis) *adj* presentable.

apressado, da [apre'sadu, da] *adj* hurried; **estar** ~ to be in a hurry.

apressar [4] [apre'sa(x)] *vt* to hurry.

➡ **apressar-se** *vp* to hurry.

aprimorado, da [aprimo'radu, da] *adj* improved.

aprimoramento [aprimora'mēntu] *m* improvement.

aprimorar [4] [aprimo'ra(x)] *vt* to improve.

➡ **aprimorar-se** *vp*: ~-se (em algo) to try hard (at sthg).

aprisionamento [aprizjona'mēntu] *m* -1. [de pessoa] imprisonment. -2. [de passarinho] captivity.

aprisionar [4] [aprizjo'na(x)] *vt* -1. [prender] to imprison. -2. [meter em prisão] to put in prison. -3. [capturar] to keep in captivity.

aprofundamento [aprofūnda'mēntu] *m* in-depth examination.

aprofundar [4] [aprofūn'da(x)] *vt* -1. [ger] to deepen. -2. [investigação] to intensify. -3. [conhecimentos] to improve. -4. [divergências] to increase.

➡ **aprofundar-se** *vp* -1. [no solo, no mar] to go down. -2. [em investigações, análise] to intensify. -3. [em área de conhecimento] to immerse o.s. -4. [em selva, mato] to penetrate deeper.

aprontar [4] [aprōnta(x)] ⬦ *vt* -1. [preparar] to prepare. -2. [terminar] to complete. -3. *fam* [briga, confusão] to cause. ⬦ *vi fam* [criar confusão] to play up.

➡ **aprontar-se** *vp* -1. [vestir-se, arrumar-se] to get ready. -2. [preparar-se] to prepare o.s.

apropriação [aproprja'sãw] (*pl* -ões) *f* -1. [assenhoramento] takeover. -2. [tomada] seizure. -3. COM [adequação]: ~ de custos cost adjustment.

apropriado, da [apro'prjadu, da] *adj* -1. [adequado] appropriate. -2. [tomado] seized.

apropriar [16] [apro'prja(x)] *vt* [adequar] to adapt.

➡ **apropriar-se** *vp*: ~-se de algo to take possession of sthg.

aprovação [aprova'sãw] (*pl* -ões) *f* -1. [ger] approval. -2. [em exame] pass.

aprovar [4] [apro'va(x)] *vt* -1. [apoiar] to approve. -2. [sancionar] to approve. -3. [em exame] to pass.

aproveitador, ra [aprovejta'do(x), ra] (*mpl* -es, *fpl* -s) ⬦ *adj* opportunistic. ⬦ *m,f* opportunist.

aproveitamento [aprovejta'mēntu] *m* -1. [uso] good use. -2. [nos estudos] improvement; **ter um bom** ~ to do well.

aproveitar [4] [aprovej'ta(x)] ⬦ *vt* -1. [tirar proveito de]: **aproveitei que chovia para descansar** I took advantage of the rainy weather to have a rest. -2. [não desperdiçar] to make the most of, to put to good use. -3. [usar] to use. ⬦ *vi* [tirar proveito]: ~ **para fazer algo** to take opportunity to do sthg; **aproveite!** make the most of it!; **aproveite enquanto é tempo!** make the most of it while you can!, make hay while the sun shines!

➡ **aproveitar-se** *vp*: ~-se de algo/alguém to take advantage of sthg/sb.

aproveitável [aprovej'tavew] (*pl* -eis) *adj* reusable.

aprovisionamento [aprovizjona'mēntu] *m* supply.

aprovisionar [4] [aprovizjo'na(x)] *vt* [abastecer] to supply.

aprox. (*abrev de* **aproximadamente**) *adv* approx.

aproximação [aprosima'sãw] (*pl* -ões) *f* -1. [chegada] approach. -2. [estimativa] approximation. -3. [de países] coming together. -4. [de pontos de vista] similarity.

aproximado, da [aprosi'madu, da] *adj* approximate.

aproximar [4] [aprosi'ma(x)] *vt* -1. [precipitar] to bring forward. -2. [cálculo] to approximate. -3. [pessoas, países] to bring together. -4. [levar para perto] to draw up. -5. [fazer parecer perto] to bring closer.

➡ **aproximar-se** *vp* -1. [achegar-se] to approach. -2. [pessoas, países] to draw closer. -3. [assemelhar-se] to be similar.

aprumado, da [apru'madu, da] *adj* -1. [vertical] straight. -2. *fig* [altivo] upright. -3. [elegante] elegant.

aprumo [a'prumu] *m* -1. [posição vertical] straightness. -2. [altivez] rectitude. -3. [elegância] elegance.

aptidão [aptʃi'dãw] (*pl* -ões) *f* -1. [ger] aptitude. -2. [jeito]: **ter** ~ **para** to have an aptitude for.

apto, ta ['aptu, ta] *adj* suitable; ~ **para** fit for.

Apto. (*abrev de* **apartamento**) *m* Flat no. *UK*, Apt. *US*.

apunhalar [4] [apuɲa'la(x)] *vt* -1. [esfaquear] to stab. -2. *fig* [trair] to stab in the back.

apuração [apura'sãw] (*pl* -ões) *f* -1. [de votos] counting. -2. [de fatos, informações] examination. -3. [de conta] checking.

apurado, da [apu'radu, da] *adj* -1. [ger] refined. -2. [aguçado] sharp.

apurar [4] [apu'ra(x)] *vt* -1. [tornar puro] to purify. -2. [refinar] to refine. -3. [aprimorar] to perfect. -4. [aguçar] to sharpen. -5. [averiguar] to verify. -6. [votos] to count. -7. [conta] to check.

➡ **apurar-se** *vp* -1. [tornar-se puro] to become pure. -2. [no trajar] to smarten o.s. up. -3. [aprimorar-se] to become perfect.

apuro [a'purul] *m* -1. [esmero] care. -2. [dificuldade] fix; **estar em** ~**s** to be in a fix. -3. [aperto financeiro] hardship.

aquarela [akwa'rɛla] *f* water colour.

aquariano, na [akwa'rjãnu, na] *m, f ASTROL* Aquarian.

aquário [a'kwarju] *m* [para peixes] aquarium.

➡ **Aquário** *m ASTROL* Aquarius.

aquático, ca [a'kwatʃiku, ka] *adj* aquatic; **pólo/ massagem** ~ water polo/massage; **ginástica** ~ aquarobics; **esportes** ~**s** aquatics.

aquecedor [akese'do(x)] (*pl* -es) *adj* heating.

➡ **aquecedor** *m* heater.

aquecer [25] [ake'se(x)] ⬦ *vt* -1. [ger] to warm up. -2. [esquentar] to heat. ⬦ *vi* -1. [esquentar] to become hot. -2. [dar calor] to give warmth.

➡ **aquecer-se** *vp* -1. [ger] to warm up. -2.

[esquentar-se] to warm o.s. **-3.** *fig* [debate] to become heated.

aquecimento [akesi'mẽntul *m* **-1.** [ger] heating; ~ **central** central heating. **-2.** [econômico] warming. **-3.** *ESP* [muscular] warm up; **ir para o** ~ to go for a warm-up.

àquela [a'kɛlal = **a + aquela**.

aquele, aquela [a'keli, a'kɛlal ◇ *adj* that, those *pl.*◇ *pron* that one; ~ **ali** that one there; ~ **que** [relativo a pessoa] the one who, those who *pl*; [relativo a objeto] the one which; **peça àquele homem/àquela mulher** ask that man/woman.

àquele [a'kelil = **a + aquele**.

aquém [a'kẽj] *adv* **-1.** [deste lado] this side; ~ **de** on this side of. **-2.** [abaixo]: ~ **de** below.

aqui [a'kil *adv* **-1.** [neste lugar] here; ~ **dentro/fora** in/out here; ~ **e agora** here and now; ~ **mesmo** right here; **eis** ~ here is; **por** ~ round here; **estar por** ~ **(com algo/alguém)** to be up to here (with sthg/sb). **-2.** [neste momento] at that point; **até** ~ up to now. **-3.** [nisto] on this point.

aquiescência [akje'sẽnsjal *f* acquiescence.

aquiescer [25] [akje'se(x)] *vi*: ~ **a** to accede to; ~ **em** to agree to.

aquietar [4] [akje'ta(x)] *vt* to quieten.

➡ **aquietar-se** *vp* to quieten down.

aquilatar [4] [akila'ta(x)] *vt* **-1.** [metais] to assay. **-2.** [estimar] to weigh up.

aquilino, na [aki'linu, nal *adj* [nariz] aquiline.

aquilo [a'kilul *pron* that; **você chama aquilo de carro!** you call that a car!

àquilo [a'kilul = **a + aquilo**.

aquinhoar [20] [akiɲo'a(x)] *vt* to endow.

aquisição [akizi'sãwl (*pl*-ões) *f* acquisition.

aquisitivo, va [akizi'tʃivu, val *adj* [poder] acquisitive.

ar [a(x)l (*pl*-ares) *m* **-1.** [ger] air; **o avião está no** ~ the plane is in the sky; **ao** ~ **livre** in the open air; **tomar** ~ **(fresco)** to get some (fresh) air; ~ **condicionado** [atmosfera] air conditioning; **ir pelos ares** to be blown sky-high; **corrente de** ~ draught. **-2.** *RÁDIO,TV*: **no** ~ on the air; **ir ao** ~ to be broadcast, to go on the air; **sair do** ~ to come off the air. **-3.** *fig* [aspecto] appearance. **-4.** *loc*: **apanhar as coisas no** ~ to pick things up quickly; **dar o** ~ **de sua** *ou* **da graça** to show up; **estar no** ~ to be up in the air; **ficar no** ~ to be confused.

➡ **ares** *mpl* **-1.** [clima] air; **mudar de ares** to get a change of air. **-2.** [pose] airs (*pl*).

árabe ['arabil ◇ *adj* Arab. ◇ *m, f* Arab. ◇ *m* [língua] Arabic.

arabesco [ara'beʃkul *m* arabesque.

Arábia Saudita [a,rabjasaw'dʒital *n* Saudi Arabia.

arábico, ca [a'rabiku, kal *adj* **-1.** [da Arábia] Arabian. **-2.** [algarismo] Arabic. **-3.** [goma]: **goma arábica** gum arabic.

Aracajú [araka'ʒul *n* Aracajú.

arado [a'radul *m* plough.

aragem [a'raʒẽl (*pl*-ns [a'raʒẽʃl) *f* breeze.

Aral [a'rawl *n*: **o mar de** ~ the Aral Sea.

aramado, da [ara'madu, dal *adj* [estádio] fenced in.

➡ **aramado** *m* **-1.** [cerca] wire fencing. **-2.** [porta-objetos] wire basket/rack.

arame [a'rãmil *m* [cabo] wire; ~ **farpado** barbed wire.

aranha [a'rãɲal *f* spider.

aranha-caranguejeira [a,rãɲakarãɲge'ʒejral (*pl* aranhas-caranguejeiras) *f* bird-eating spider.

arapuca [ara'pukal *f* **-1.** [armadilha, cilada] trap; **cair numa** ~ to fall into a trap. **-2.** *fam fig* [estabelecimento] shady company.

araque [a'rakil *m*: **de** ~ *fam* rubbish.

arar [4] [a'ra(x)l *vt* to plough.

arara [a'raral *f* macaw; **estar/ficar uma** ~ to be hopping mad.

araruta [ara'rutal *f* arrowroot.

arbitragem [axbi'traʒẽl (*pl*-ns) *f* **-1.** [julgamento] arbitration. **-2.** [*ESP* - ato] adjudication; [- decisão] decision; [- os juízes] referees (*pl*).

arbitrar [4] [axbi'tra(x)l *vt* **-1.** [questão, litígio] to arbitrate. **-2.** *ESP* [partida, campeonato] to referee. **-3.** [adjudicar]: ~ **algo a alguém** to award sb sthg.

arbitrariedade [axbitrarje'dadʒil *f* arbitrariness.

arbitrário, ria [axbi'trarju, rjal *adj* arbitrary.

arbítrio [ax'bitrjul *m* **-1.** [resolução] judgment; **deixar algo ao** ~ **de alguém** to leave sthg to the discretion of sb. **-2.** [faculdade] free will.

árbitro ['axbitrul *m* **-1.** [de questão, litígio] mediator. **-2.** [juiz] judge. **-3.** [*ESP* - em futebol, box] referee; [- em tênis] umpire.

arborizado, da [axbori'zadu, dal *adj* **-1.** [bairro, terreno] wooded. **-2.** [rua] tree-lined.

arborizar [4] [axbori'za(x)l *vt* to plant with trees.

arbusto [ax'buʃtul *m* bush.

arca ['axkal *f* **-1.** [caixa] chest. **-2.** [barca]: **Arca de Noé** Noah's Ark.

arcabouço [axka'bosul *m* **-1.** [linhas gerais] outline. **-2.** *ARQUIT* [estrutura] framework.

arcada [ax'kadal *f* **-1.** [de arcos] arcade; ~ **dentária** dental arch. **-2.** [arco] arch.

arcaico, ca [ax'kajku, kal *adj* **-1.** [antigo] archaic. **-2.** [antiquado] antiquated.

arcaizante [axkaj'zãntʃil *adj* archaic.

arcanjo [ax'kãnʒul *m* archangel.

arcar [12] [ax'ka(x)l *vi*: ~ **com algo** to take responsibility for sthg.

arcebispo [axse'biʃpul *m* archbishop.

arco ['axkul *m* **-1.** [ger] arch; **em** ~ arched. **-2.** [arma, instrumento musical] bow; ~**-e-flecha** *ESP* archery. **-3.** *GEOM*, *ELETR & MAT* arc. **-4.** [de barril] hoop.

arco-da-velha [,axkuda'veʎal *m*: **coisas do** ~ fantastic things; **história do** ~ tall story.

arco-e-flecha [axkuifleʃal (*pl* arcos-e-flechas) *m* **-1.** *ESP* archery. **-2.** [arma] bow and arrow.

arco-íris [ax'kwiriʃl (*pl* arcos-íris) *m inv* rainbow.

ar-condicionado [,a(x)kõndʒisjo'nadul (*pl* ares-condicionados) *m* [aparelho] air conditioning.

ardência [ax'dẽnsjal *f* burning.

ardente [axˈdẽntʃil] *adj* burning.

arder [5] [axˈde(x)] *vi* **-1.** [ger] to burn; ~ **em chamas** to be in flames; ~ **em febre** [pessoa] to have a burning fever. **-2.** [ferimento] to sting.

ardido, da [axˈdʒidu, da] *adj* **-1.** [costas, olhos] stinging. **-2.** [pimenta, comida] hot.

ardil [axˈdʒiw] (*pl* **-is**) *m* cunning.

ardiloso, losa [axdʒiˈlozu, lɔza] *adj* [pessoa] cunning.

ardor [axˈdo(x)] (*pl* **-es**) *m* [paixão] ardour.

ardoroso, rosa [axdoˈrozu, rɔza] *adj* amorous.

ardósia [axˈdɔzja] *f* slate.

árduo, dua [ˈaxdwu, dwa] *adj* **-1.** [escarpado] arduous. **-2.** [difícil] hard. **-3.** [sofrimento] painful.

área [ˈarja] *f* **-1.** [ger] area; ~ **interditada** forbidden territory; ~ **de serviço** service point. **-2.** [de conhecimento etc] field.

areal [aˈrejw] (*pl* **-ais**) *m* sandy area.

arear [15] [aˈrja(x)] *vt* [polir] to polish.

areia [aˈreja] *f* sand; ~ **movediça** quicksand; **ser muita** ~ **para o caminhão de alguém** to be too hot for sb to handle.

arejado, da [areˈʒadu, da] *adj* **-1.** [ventilado] airy. **-2.** [fig] [pessoa, cabeça] open-minded.

arena [aˈrena] *f* **-1.** [ger] arena. **-2.** [de circo] ring. **-3.** [de teatro] amphitheatre.

arenito [areˈnitu] *m* sandstone.

arenoso, osa [areˈnozu, ɔza] *adj* sandy.

arenque [aˈrẽŋki] *m* herring.

ares [ˈariʃ] ⊳ **ar**.

aresta [aˈrɛʃta] *f* [quina] edge.

arfar [4] [axˈfa(x)] *vi* **-1.** [ofegar] to pant. **-2.** NÁUT to pitch.

argamassa [axgaˈmasa] *f* mortar.

Argel [axˈʒɛw] *n* Algeria.

Argélia [axˈʒɛlja] *n* Algeria.

argelino, na [axʒeˈlinu, na] ⟨⟩ *adj* Algerian. ⟨⟩ *m, f* Algerian.

Argentina [axʒẽnˈtʃina] *n*: **(a)** ~ Argentina.

argentino, na [axʒẽnˈtʃinu, na] ⟨⟩ *adj* Argentinian. ⟨⟩ *m, f* Argentinian.

argila [axˈʒila] *f* clay.

argiloso, losa [axʒiˈlozu, lɔza] *adj* [terreno] clay.

argola [axˈgɔla] *f* **-1.** [aro] ring. **-2.** [de porta] knocker.

argúcia [axˈgusja] *f* **-1.** [agudeza] shrewdness. **-2.** [sutileza] subtlety.

argüição [axgwiˈsãw] (*pl* **-ões**) *f* oral exam.

argüir [75] [axˈgwi(x)] *vt* [alunos, candidatos] to examine.

argumentação [axgumẽntaˈsãw] (*pl* **-ões**) *f* argument, reasoning.

argumentar [4] [axgumẽnˈta(x)] ⟨⟩ *vt* [alegar] to argue. ⟨⟩ *vi* [expor argumentos] to argue one's case.

argumento [axguˈmẽntu] *m* **-1.** [em teoria, debate] argument. **-2.** [de filme, TV, romance] theme, plot.

arguto, ta [axˈgutu, ta] *adj* **-1.** [agudo] shrewd. **-2.** [sutil] subtle.

ária [ˈarja] *f* MÚS aria.

ariano, na [aˈrjãnu, na] ⟨⟩ *adj* Aryan. ⟨⟩ *m, f*

-1. [pessoa] Aryan. **-2.** ASTROL Arian.

aridez [ariˈdeʒ] *f* **-1.** [de clima, estação] dryness. **-2.** [de terra, região] aridity. **-3.** *fig* [de teoria, pensamento] barrenness.

árido, da [ˈaridu, da] *adj* **-1.** [clima, estação] dry. **-2.** [terra, região] arid. **-3.** *fig* [teoria, pensamento] barren.

arisco, ca [aˈriʃku, ka] *adj* **-1.** [insociável] antisocial. **-2.** [animal] untameable.

aristocracia [ariʃtokraˈsia] *f* aristocracy.

aristocrata [ariʃtoˈkrata] *mf* aristocrat.

aristocrático, ca [ariʃtoˈkratʃiku, ka] *adj* aristocratic.

aritmético, ca [aritʃˈmɛtʃiku, ka] *adj* arithmetic.
    aritmética *f* arithmetic.

arma [ˈaxma] *f* **-1.** [ger] weapon; **depor as** ~**s** to lay down arms; ~ **biológica/química** biological/ chemical weapon; ~ **branca** knife (or other weapon with a blade); ~ **de fogo** firearm; ~ **nuclear** nuclear weapon. **-2.** MIL [do Exército] force.
    armas *fpl* **-1.** [forças armadas] forces. **-2.** [brasão] arms.

armação [axmaˈsãw] (*pl* **-ões**) *f* **-1.** [de barraca, estrutura, peças] framework. **-2.** [estrutura] frame. **-3.** [de óculos] frames (*pl*). **-4.** [de onda] point near a shoreline where the waves start to break. **-5.** [de tempestade] gathering. **-6.** *fam* [golpe] con. **-7.** *fam* [programa, aventura] move.

armada [axˈmada] ⟨⟩ **Armada** *f* navy.

armadilha [axmaˈdiʎa] *f* trap; **cair numa** ~ to fall into a trap.

armador, ra [axmaˈdo(x), ra] *m, f* **-1.** [NÁUT - dono] shipowner; [- firma] ship chandler's. **-2.** [operário] ship chandler.

armadura [axmaˈdura] *f* **-1.** [de cavaleiro] armour. **-2.** [de ouriço, besouro] shell. **-3.** ELETR armature. **-4.** CONSTR framework.

armamentista [axmamẽnˈtʃiʃta] *adj* ⊳ **corrida**.

armamento [axmaˈmẽntu] *m* **-1.** [armas] armament. **-2.** NÁUT fitting out.

armar [4] [axˈma(x)] ⟨⟩ *vt* **-1.** [com arma] to arm. **-2.** [carregar] to load. **-3.** [gatilho] to cock. **-4.** [montar] to assemble. **-5.** [preparar] to set up. **-6.** [saia etc] to give body to. **-7.** *fam* [planejar - golpe] to plot; [- programa, aventura] to plan. **-8.** *fam* [provocar] to cause. **-9.** NÁUT to fit out. ⟨⟩ *vi fam* [urdir trama] to scheme; ~ **contra** to plot against.
    armar-se *vp* **-1.** [com armas] to arm o.s. **-2.** *fig* [munir-se]: ~**-se de** to arm o.s with.

armarinho [axmaˈriɲu] *m* haberdasher's UK, notions store US.

armário [axˈmarju] *m* **-1.** [de roupa] wardrobe; ~ **embutido** fitted wardrobe. **-2.** [de cozinha etc] cupboard.

armazém [axmaˈzẽ] (*pl* **-ns**) *m* **-1.** [depósito] warehouse. **-2.** [loja] store.

armazenagem [axmazeˈnaʒẽ] *f*, **armazenamento** *m* [axmazenaˈmẽntu] storage.

armazenar [4] [axmazeˈna(x)] *vt* to store.

Armênia [axˈmenja] *n* Armenia.

armênio, nia [axˈmenju, nja] ⟨⟩ *adj* Armenian. ⟨⟩ *m, f* Armenian.

armênio m [língua] Armenian.
arminho [ax'miɲul] m ermine.
armistício [axmiʃ'tʃisju] m armistice.
aro ['arul m -1. [ger] rim. -2. [argola] ring. -3. [de porta] frame.
aroma [a'romal m -1. [de perfume] scent. -2. [de café, comida] aroma.
aromático, ca [aro'matʃiku, ka] adj -1. [essência, erva] aromatic. -2. [tempero, comida] spicy.
arpão [ax'pãw] (pl -ões) m harpoon.
arpejo [ax'peʒu] m arpeggio.
arpoar [20] [ax'pwa(x)] vt to harpoon.
arpões [ax'põjʃ] pl ⊳ arpão.
arqueado, da [ax'kjadu, da] adj -1. [pernas] bandy. -2. [sobrancelhas] arched.
arquear [16] [ax'kja(x)] vt to arch.
◆ **arquear-se** vp to bend.
arqueiro, ra [ax'kejru, ra] m, f -1. [atirador] archer. -2. [goleiro] goalkeeper.
arqueologia [axkjolo'ʒia] f archaeology.
arqueológico, ca [axkjo'lɔʒiku, ka] adj archaeological.
arqueólogo, ga [ax'kjɔlogu, ga] m, f archaeologist.
arquétipo [ax'kɛtʃipu] m archetype.
arquibancada [axkibãŋ'kada] f -1. [local] terrace; **ir de** ~ to sit on the terraces. -2. [público] terraces (pl).
arquimilionário, ria [axkimiljo'narju, rja] ◇ adj multimillionaire. ◇ m, f [pessoa] multimillionaire.
arquipélago [axki'pɛlagu] m archipelago.
arquitetar [4] [axkite'ta(x)] vt to design.
arquiteto, ta [axki'tɛtu, ta] m, f architect.
arquitetônico, ca [axkite'toniku, ka] adj architectural.
arquitetura [axkite'tural f architecture.
arquivamento [axkiva'mẽntul m -1. [de documentos, fichas etc] filing. -2. [de projeto, processo] shelving.
arquivar [4] [axki'va(x)] vt -1. [ger] to file. -2. [projeto, processo] to shelve.
arquivista [axki'viʃta] mf archivist.
arquivo [ax'kivul m -1. [ger] file; ~ **morto** dead file; **abrir/fechar um** ~ to open/close a file. -2. [local] archive. -3. [móvel] filing cabinet. -4. [de instituição] file.
arraia [a'xaja] f [peixe] ray.
arraial [axa'jaw] (pl -ais) m [povoado] village.
arraia-miúda [a,xajami'uda] f hoi polloi (pl).
arraigado, da [axaj'gadu, da] adj -1. [costume, idéia, mentalidade] deep-rooted. -2. fig [defensor, admirador] staunch.
arraigar [14] [axaj'ga(x)] vi [criar raízes] to put down roots.
◆ **arraigar-se** vp -1. [ger] to take root. -2. [pessoa] to settle down.
arrancada [axãŋ'kada] f -1. [puxão] tug. -2. [partida] start. -3. [em competição, disputa] spurt; **dar uma** ~ to jump ahead.
arrancar [12] [axãŋ'ka(x)] ◇ vt -1. [tirar]: ~ **algo**

de alguém to pull sthg off sb; ~ **algo (de algo)** [pétala, botão] to pull sthg (off sthg); [folha] to tear sthg (out of sthg); [raiz] to pull sthg up (out of sthg). -2. [conseguir]: ~ **algo de alguém** to draw sthg from sb. -3. [fazer sair]: ~ **alguém de algum lugar** to turf sb out of somewhere. ◇ vi -1. [dar partida] to start off. -2. [em competição] to put on a spurt.
◆ **arrancar-se** vt fam [fugir]: ~-**se (de)** to scarper (from).
arranco [a'xãŋko] m [puxão] tug.
arranha-céu [a,xãɲa'sɛw] (pl **arranha-céus**) m skyscraper.
arranhão [axã'ɲãw] (pl -ões) m scratch; **ele saiu sem muitos arranhões dessa situação** he came out of that situation relatively unscathed.
arranhar [4] [axa'ɲa(x)] ◇ vt -1. [ger] to scratch. -2. fig [tocar mal] to bash away at. -3. fig [idioma] to scratch by. ◇ vi [provocar arranhão] to scratch.
◆ **arranhar-se** vp to scratch o.s.
arranjador, ra [axãnʒa'dor, ra] m, f MÚS arranger.
arranjar [4] [axãn'ʒa(x)] vt -1. [ger] to arrange. -2. [resolver] to sort out. -3. [conseguir] to obtain. -4. [contrair] to catch. -5. [encontrar] to find.
◆ **arranjar-se** vp [virar-se] to get by.
arranjo [a'xãnʒul m -1. [ger] arrangement. -2. [acordo] deal. -3. [mamata] scam.
arranque [a'xãŋki] m ⊳ motor.
arrasado, da [axa'zadu, da] adj -1. [devastado] razed, devastated. -2. [arruinado] ruined. -3. [deprimido] devastated. -4. [muito cansado] worn out.
arrasador, ra [axaza'do(x), ra] adj -1. [devastador] crippling. -2. [notícia, crítica] devastating. -3. [vitória] overwhelming.
arrasar [4] [axa'za(x)] vt -1. [devastar] to raze. -2. [arruinar] to destroy. -3. [com críticas] to demolish.
◆ **arrasar-se** vp -1. [ser devastado] to be devastated. -2. [destruir-se] to be destroyed. -3. [arruinar-se] to collapse in ruins. -4. [em exame, competição] to flop.
arrastado, da [axaʃ'tadu, da] adj -1. [demorado] sluggish. -2. [lento] slow.
arrastão [axaʃ'tãw] (pl -tões) m -1. [PESCA - rede] dragnet; [- ato] haul. -2. [puxão] tug. -3. fig [assalto] mobbing.
arrasta-pé [a,xaʃta'pɛ] (pl **arrasta-pés**) m fam shindig.
arrastar [4] [axaʃ'ta(x)] ◇ vt -1. [ger] to drag. -2. fig [impelir]: ~ **alguém a algo** to lead sb into sthg. ◇ vi [roçar] to drag.
◆ **arrastar-se** vp -1. [rastejar] to crawl. -2. [andar com dificuldade] to drag o.s. -3. [decorrer lentamente] to drag on.
arrasto [a'xaʃtul m -1. [ato] dragging. -2. [rede] trawl. -3. PÍS [força] drag.
arrazoado, da [axa'zwadu, da] adj [discurso, argumento] reasoned.
◆ **arrazoado** m [defesa] defence.
arrazoar [20] [axa'zwa(x)] vi [argumentar] to argue.
arrear [15] [a'xja(x)] vt [montaria] to harness.

arrebanhar [4] [axeba'ɲa(x)] *vt* -**1.** [gado] to herd. -**2.** *fig* [reunir] to gather.

arrebatado, da [axeba'tadu, da] *adj* -**1.** [impetuoso] impetuous. -**2.** [exaltado] fiery.

arrebatador, ra [axebata'do(x), ra] *adj* fiery.

arrebatamento [axebata'mẽntul *m* -**1.** [impetuosidade] impetuousness. -**2.** [exaltação] fervour.

arrebatar [4] [axeba'ta(x)] *vt* -**1.** [arrancar]: ∼ **algo de algo/alguém** to grab sthg from sthg/sb. -**2.** [carregar] to drag off. -**3.** *fig* [aplausos] to draw. -**4.** *fig* [coração] to break.

 ➡ **arrebatar-se** *vp* -**1.** [exaltar-se] to get carried away. -**2.** [maravilhar-se] to be entranced.

arrebentação [axebẽnta'sãwl *f* [local] *point close to a shoreline at which the waves break*.

arrebentado, da [axebẽn'tadu, da] *adj* -**1.** [em mau estado] broken. -**2.** [ferido] battered. -**3.** [muito cansado] worn out.

arrebentar [4] [axebẽn'ta(x)l ◇ *vt* -**1.** [quebrar, romper] to break. -**2.** [estragar] to wreck. -**3.** [ferir] to smash; ∼ **alguém** [surrar] to give sb a bashing; ∼ **a cara de alguém** to smash sb's face in. ◇ *vi* -**1.** [quebrar-se, romper-se] to snap. -**2.** [bomba] to explode. -**3.** *fig* [guerra, revolução] to break out. -**4.** *fam fig* [fazer sucesso]: ∼ **(em algo)** to have a smashing win (at sthg).

 ➡ **arrebentar-se** *vp* [ferir-se] to smash o.s.up.

arrebitado, da [axebi'tadu, da] *adj* -**1.** [para cima] turned up. -**2.** [bumbum, nariz] pert.

arrebitar [4] [axebi'ta(x)] *vt* to turn up.

arrecadação [axekada'sãwl (*pl* -**ões**) *f* -**1.** [coleta] collection. -**2.** [receita] revenue.

arrecadar [4] [axeka'da(x)] *vt* to collect.

arrecife [axe'sifil *m* reef.

arredar [4] [axe'da(x)] *vt* [retirar] to remove; ∼ **(o) pé (de)** [de lugar] to budge from; [de intenção, princípios] to budge (from).

 ➡ **arredar-se** *vp* [retirar-se] to withdraw.

arredio, dia [axe'dʒiu, dʒial *adj* [pessoa] withdrawn.

arredondado, da [axedõn'dadu, da] *adj* round.

arredondar [4] [axedõn'da(x)] *vt* -**1.** [formato] to round off. -**2.** [conta] to round up.

arredores [axe'dɔriʃ *mpl* -**1.** [cercanias] neighbourhood. -**2.** [periferia] outskirts.

arrefecer [25] [axefe'se(x)l ◇ *vt* -**1.** [tornar frio] to cool. -**2.** [febre] to lower. -**3.** *fig* [desanimar] to cool. ◇ *vi* -**1.** [tornar-se frio] to cool down. -**2.** [ger] to subside.

ar-refrigerado [ˌa(x)xefriʒe'radul (*pl* **ares-refrigerados**) *m* -**1.** [aparelho] air-conditioner. -**2.** [sistema] air-conditioning.

arregaçar [13] [axega'sa(x)] *vt* to roll up.

arregalado, da [axega'ladu, da] *adj* staring.

arregalar [4] [axega'la(x)] *vt* to open wide.

arreganhado, da [axega'ɲadu, da] *adj* gaping.

arreganhar [4] [axega'ɲa(x)] *vt* -**1.** [gola de blusa] to open. -**2.** [boca] to open in a grin.

arregimentar [4] [axeʒimẽn'ta(x)] *vt* to drum up.

arreio [a'xeju] *m* [cavalo] harness.

arrematar [4] [axema'ta(x)] *vt* -**1.** [ger] to finish off. -**2.** [dizer concluindo] to conclude. -**3.** [em leilão - comprar] to bid successfully for; [- vender] to auction off.

arremate [axe'matʃil *m* -**1.** [ger] finishing off. -**2.** [conclusão] finish.

arremessar [4] [axeme'sa(x)] *vt* to throw.

 ➡ **arremessar-se** *vp* to throw o.s.

arremesso [axe'mesul *m* [lançamento] throw; ∼ **de peso** *ESP* shot-put.

arremeter [5] [axeme'te(x)] *vi* to charge; ∼ **contra** to attack.

arremetida [axeme'tʃidal *f* attack.

arrendamento [axẽnda'mẽntul *m* leasing, hiring, rental.

arrendar [4] [axẽn'da(x)] *vt* -**1.** [dar] to let, to lease. -**2.** [tomar] to rent, to take a lease on.

arrepender-se [5] [axepẽn'dexsil *vp* to repent; ∼ **de algo/de fazer algo** to regret sthg/doing sthg.

arrependido, da [axepẽn'dʒidu, da] *adj* repentent, sorry.

arrependimento [axepẽndʒi'mẽntul *m* -**1.** [remorso] regret. -**2.** [de crime] remorse. -**3.** *RELIG* repentance.

arrepiado, da [axe'pjadu, da] *adj* -**1.** [eriçado - cabelo] standing on end *(depois de subst/verbo)*; [- pele] goose-pimpled. -**2.** *fig* [assustado] terrified.

arrepiar [16] [axe'pja(x)] *vt* -**1.** [eriçar - cabelo] to cause to stand on end; [- pele] to give goose pimples. -**2.** [fig] [assustar] to terrify; **(ser) de** ∼ **os cabelos** to be enough to make your hair stand on end.

 ➡ **arrepiar-se** *vp* [ficar eriçado - cabelo] to stand on end; [- pessoa] to shiver.

arrepio [axe'piwl *m* shiver; **dar** ∼**s (a alguém)** *fig* to send shivers up sb's spine.

arresto [a'xɛʃtul *m JUR* confiscation.

arrevesado, da [axeve'zadu, da] *adj* -**1.** [obscuro] obscure. -**2.** [confuso] complicated.

arriado, da [a'xjadu, da] *adj* -**1.** [muito cansado] dead beat. -**2.** [devido a doença] drained.

arriar [16] [a'xja(x)l ◇ *vt* -**1.** [abaixar - cortina, calça] to lower; [- pneu] to let down. -**2.** [cansar muito] to exhaust. -**3.** [pôr de cama] to lay up. ◇ *vi* -**1.** [pneu, bateria] to go flat. -**2.** [vergar] to sag. -**3.** [desanimar] to lose heart.

arrimo [a'ximul *m* support; ∼ **de família** family support.

arriscado, da [axiʃ'kadu, da] *adj* -**1.** [perigoso] hazardous, risky. -**2.** [audacioso] daring.

arriscar [12] [axiʃ'ka(x)l ◇ *vt* -**1.** [pôr em perigo] to put at risk. -**2.** [palpite] to risk. ◇ *vi* [tentar] to take the risk; **quem não arrisca não petisca** *prov* nothing ventured nothing gained.

 ➡ **arriscar-se** *vp* [pôr-se em perigo] to take a risk; ∼**-se a fazer algo** to risk doing sthg.

arritmia [axitʃ'mial *f* arrhythmia.

arrivista [axi'viʃtal ◇ *adj* opportunistic. ◇ *mf* opportunist.

arroba [a'xobal *f COMPUT* at.

arrochado, da [axo'ʃadu, da] *adj* -**1.** [apertado] tight. -**2.** [difícil] tricky.

arrochar [4] [axoˈʃa(x)] *vt* **-1.** [apertar] to squeeze. **-2.** *fig* [diminuir] to shrink. **-3.** *fam fig* [pressionar] to grill.

arrocho [aˈxoʃul] *m* **-1.** [diminuição] lessening; ~ **salarial** wage squeeze. **-2.** [dificuldade financeira] hardship. **-3.** *fam fig* [pressão] grilling; **dar um** ~ **em alguém** to give sb a grilling.

arrogância [axoˈgãnsja] *f* arrogance.

arrogante [axoˈgãntʃi] *adj* arrogant.

arrogar-se [14] [axoˈgaxsi] *vp* to claim.

arroio [aˈxoju] *m* stream.

arrojado, da [axoˈʒadu, da] *adj* **-1.** [ger] bold. **-2.** [ousado] daring. **-3.** [temerário] rash.

arrojar [4] [axoˈʒa(x)] *vt* [atirar]: ~ **algo (em/contra algo)** to hurl sthg (at/against sthg).

arrolamento [axolaˈmẽntul] *m* **-1.** [levantamento] register. **-2.** [lista] list.

arrolar [4] [axoˈla(x)] *vt* [listar] to list.

arrolhar [4] [axoˈʎa(x)] *vt* [garrafa] to cork.

arromba [aˈxõnba] ➡ **de arromba** *loc adj fam* fantastic.

arrombamento [axõnbaˈmẽntul] *m* [abertura forçada]: **foi necessário o** ~ **da porta** it was necessary to break down the door.

arrombar [4] [axõnˈba(x)] *vt* **-1.** [ger] to break into. **-2.** [porta] to break down.

arrotar [4] [axoˈta(x)] ⟨⟩ *vi* [dar arroto] to belch. ⟨⟩ *vt* **-1.** [cheiro] to burp. **-2.** *fam fig* [alardear] to boast about.

arroto [aˈxotul] *m* burp; **dar** *ou* **soltar um** ~ to let out a burp.

arroubo [aˈxobul] *m* [enlevo] moment of ecstasy; ~ **de algo** outpouring of sthg.

arroz [aˈxoʒ] *m* rice; ~ **à grega** Greek risotto, *rice with ham, smoked bacon, sweet peppers, onion and peas*; ~ **doce** rice pudding.

arrozal [axoˈzaw] (*pl* **-ais**) *m* paddy field.

arroz-doce [axoʒˈdosil *m* CULIN *rice pudding sprinkled with cinnamon and cloves*.

arruaça [aˈxwasal] *f* riot; **fazer** ~ to run riot.

arruaceiro, ra [axwaˈsejru, ra] ⟨⟩ *adj* rowdy. ⟨⟩ *m, f* rioter.

arruela [aˈxwɛla] *f* washer.

arruinado, da [axwiˈnadu, da] *adj* ruined.

arruinar [4] [axwiˈna(x)] *vt* **-1.** [arrasar] to demolish. **-2.** [destruir] to destroy. **-3.** [causar falência] to ruin. ➡ **arruinar-se** *vp* [ruir] to be ruined.

arrulhar [4] [axuˈʎa(x)] *vi* **-1.** [pombo] to coo. **-2.** *fig* [namorados] to bill and coo.

arrulho [aˈxuʎul] *m* **-1.** [de pombo] cooing. **-2.** [de namorados] wooing.

arrumação [axumaˈsãw] *f* **-1.** [arranjo] arrangement. **-2.** [de quarto, armário] tidying; **fazer uma** ~ **em algo** to tidy sthg up. **-3.** [de malas, bagagem] packing.

arrumadeira [axumaˈdejral] *f* [criada] maid.

arrumar [4] [axuˈma(x)] *vt* **-1.** [pôr em ordem] to arrange; ~ **a vida** *fam fig* to set one's life in order. **-2.** [quarto, armário] to tidy. **-3.** [malas, bagagem] to pack. **-4.** [vestir, aprontar] to straighten up. **-5.** [conseguir] to get.

arrumar-se *vp* **-1.** [vestir-se, aprontar-se] to get ready. **-2.** [na vida] to set o.s. up. **-3.** [virar-se] to fend for o.s. **-4.** *fam* [na vida amorosa]: ~**-se (com alguém)** to hitch up (with sb).

arsenal [axseˈnawl (*pl* **-ais**) *m* arsenal.

arsênico [axˈsenikul *m* arsenic.

arsênio [axˈsenjul *m* arsenic.

arte [ˈaxtʃil *f* **-1.** [ger] art; ~ **abstrata/figurativa** abstract/figurative art; ~ **dramática** theatre; ~ **moderna** modern art. **-2.** [arte-final] artwork. **-3.** [ofício] art. **-4.** [técnica] art; ~ **culinária** cuisine; ~ **marcial** martial art; ~**s e ofícios** arts and crafts. **-5.** [primor]: **com** ~ skilfully. **-6.** [astúcia] cunning. **-7.** *fam* [travessura] mischief; **fazer** ~ to get up to mischief.

➡ **artes** *fpl* **-1.** [visuais] arts; ~**s gráficas** graphic arts; ~**s plásticas** plastic arts. **-2.** [curso]: **(belas)** ~**s** fine arts. **-3.** [artifício]: **por** ~**s de** through the artful wiles of.

artefato [axteˈfatul *m* **-1.** [instrumento] artefact. **-2.** [produto] goods (*pl*); ~**s de madeira/couro** wooden/leather goods.

arteiro, ra [axˈtejru, ra] *adj* mischievous.

artéria [axˈtɛrjal *f* artery.

arterial [axteˈrjawl (*pl* **-ais**) *adj* arterial.

arteriosclerose [axterjoʃkleˈrɔzil *f* arteriosclerosis.

artesã [axteˈzãl *f* ⊳ **artesão**.

artesanal [axtezaˈnawl (*pl* **-ais**) *adj* craftwork.

artesanato [axtezaˈnatul *m* craftwork.

artesão, sã [axteˈzãw, zãl (*mpl* **-ãos**, *fpl* **-s**) *m, f* craftsman (*f* craftswoman).

ártico, ca [ˈaxtʃikul *adj* Arctic.

➡ **Ártico** *n*: **o Ártico** the Arctic; **o Oceano Glacial Ártico** the Arctic Ocean.

articulação [axtʃikulaˈsãwl (*pl* **-ões**) *f* **-1.** [ligação] connection. **-2.** ANAT joint. **-3.** POL link.

articulado, da [axtʃikuˈladu, da] *adj* **-1.** [membro, boneco] articulated. **-2.** [pessoa - ao falar] articulate; [- bem relacionado] well connected.

articular [4] [axtʃikuˈla(x)] *vt* **-1.** [ligar] to link. **-2.** [pronunciar] to articulate. **-3.** [organizar] to put together.

➡ **articular-se** *vp* **-1.** [ligar-se] to be joined. **-2.** [organizar-se] to organize o.s.; ~**-se em** to be organised in.

articulista [axtʃikuˈliʃtal *mf* JORN article writer.

artífice [axˈtʃifisil *mf* **-1.** [artesão] craftsman (*f* craftswoman). **-2.** [criador, mentor] author.

artificial [axtʃifiˈsjawl (*pl* **-ais**) *adj* **-1.** [ger] artificial. **-2.** [dissimulado] false.

artificialidade [axtʃifisjaliˈdadʒil *f* artificiality.

artifício [axtʃiˈfisjul *m* **-1.** [processo] artifice. **-2.** [subterfúgio] trick. **-3.** [dissimulação] pretence.

artigo [axˈtʃigul *m* article; ~ **de luxo** luxury item; ~**s esportivos** sports goods; ~**s de toucador** toiletries; ~ **de fundo** editorial.

artilharia [axtʃiʎaˈrial *f* artillery.

artilheiro, ra [axtʃiˈʎejru, ra] *m, f* **-1.** [atirador] gunner. **-2.** FUT striker.

artimanha [axtʃiˈmãŋal *m* **-1.** [estratagema]

stratagem. **-2.** [astúcia] cunning.
artista [axˈtʃiʃta] *mf* **-1.** [ger] artist. **-2.** [ator] actor (*f* actress). **-3.** [pessoa manhosa] crafty person.
artístico, ca [axˈtʃiʃtʃiku, ka] *adj* artistic.
artrite [axˈtritʃi] *f* arthritis.
artrose [axˈtrɔzi] *f* arthrosis.
arvorar [4] [axvoˈra(x)] *vt* **-1.** [cruz, bandeira] to hoist. **-2.** [elevar]: ~ **alguém em algo** to hold sb up as sthg.
   arvorar-se *vp* [elevar-se]: ~**-se em algo** to claim to be sthg.
árvore [ˈaxvoriʟ *f* **-1.** [vegetal] tree; ~ **genealógica** family tree; ~ **de Natal** Christmas tree. **-2.** *TEC* shaft.
arvoredo [axvoˈreduʟ *m* grove.
as [aʃ] ⊳ **a**.
ás, ases [ˈajʃ, ˈazeʃ] <> *mf* [pessoa exímia]: ~ **de algo** ace at sthg. <> *m* [carta] ace.
às [ajʃ] = **a + as**.
asa [ˈazaʟ *f* **-1.** [de pássaro, avião, inseto] wing; **dar** ~**s à imaginação** to give free rein to one's imagination. **-2.** [de xícara] handle.
asa-delta [ˌazaʒˈdɛwtaʟ (*pl* **asas-delta**) *f* **-1.** [veículo] hang-glider. **-2.** [esporte] hang-gliding.
ascendência [asẽˈdẽsjaʟ *f* **-1.** [antepassados] descent. **-2.** [influência, domínio] influence; **ter** ~ **sobre** to hold sway over.
ascendente [asẽˈdẽntʃi] <> *adj* rising. <> *m, f* [antepassado] ancestor.
ascender [5] [asẽˈde(x)] *vi* to rise.
ascensão [asẽˈsãw] (*pl* **-ões**) *f* **-1.** [ger] rise. **-2.** [subida] climb.
ascensorista [asẽnsoˈriʃtaʟ *mf* lift operator.
asceta [aˈsɛtaʟ *mf* ascetic.
ASCII (*abrev de* **American Standard Code for Information Interchange**) *m* ASCII.
asco [ˈaʃkuʟ *m* disgust; **dar** ~ **a alguém** to make sb sick; **ser um** ~ to be a disgrace; **ter** ~ **de** to detest.
asfaltado, da [aʃfawˈtadu, daʟ *adj* asphalted.
asfaltar [4] [aʃfawˈta(x)] *vt* to asphalt.
asfalto [aʃˈfawtuʟ *m* asphalt.
asfixia [aʃfikˈsiaʟ *f* asphyxia.
asfixiante [aʃfikˈsjãntʃi] *adj* **-1.** [substância, ambiente] asphyxiating. **-2.** *fig* [calor] suffocating. **-3.** *fig* [regime, disciplina] oppressive.
asfixiar [16] [aʃfikˈsja(x)] *vt* **-1.** [matar por asfixia] to asphyxiate. **-2.** [sufocar] to be suffocating. **-3.** *fig* [oprimir] to suppress.
   asfixiar-se *vp* **-1.** [morrer por asfixia] to be asphyxiated. **-2.** [sufocar-se] to gasp for breath.
Ásia [ˈazjaʟ *n* Asia; ~ **Central** Central Asia.
asiático, ca [aˈzjatʃiku, kaʟ <> *adj* Asian. <> *m, f* Asian.
asilo [aˈziluʟ *m* **-1.** [para orfãos, anciãos] home. **-2.** [refúgio] refuge. **-3.** *POL* asylum; ~ **político** political asylum.
asma [ˈaʒmaʟ *f* asthma.
asmático, ca [aʒˈmatʃiku, kaʟ <> *adj* asthmatic. <> *m, f* [pessoa] asthmatic.

asneira [aʒˈnejraʟ *f* **-1.** [ação] blunder; **dizer/fazer uma** ~ to say/do something stupid. **-2.** [condição] stupidity.
asno [ˈaʒnuʟ *m* **-1.** [animal] ass, donkey. **-2.** *fam fig* & *pej* [idiota] silly ass.
aspargo [aʃˈpaxguʟ *m* asparagus.
aspas [ˈaʃpaʃ] *fpl* quotation marks; **entre** ~ in inverted commas.
aspecto [aʃˈpɛktuʟ *m* **-1.** [aparência] look; **ter bom/ mau** ~ [pessoa] to look right/dodgy; [coisa] to look good/bad. **-2.** [faceta] aspect; **em todos os** ~**s** in every way. **-3.** [ângulo] angle; **sob este** ~ from this angle. **-4.** [visão, detalhe] view.
aspereza [aʃpeˈrezaʟ *f* **-1.** [no tato] roughness. **-2.** *fig* [severidade, rispidez] harshness.
aspergir [64] [aʃpexˈʒi(x)] *vt* to sprinkle.
áspero, ra [ˈaʃperu, raʟ *adj* **-1.** [ao tato] rough. **-2.** *fig* [severo, ríspido] harsh.
asperso, sa [aʃˈpɛxsu, saʟ *pp* ⊳ **aspergir**.
aspiração [aʃpiraˈsãw] (*pl* **-ões**) *f* **-1.** [de ar - por pessoa] inhalation; [- por máquina] suction. **-2.** *LING* aspiration. **-3.** [desejo]: **ter** ~ **a algo** to aspire to sthg.
aspirador [aʃpiraˈdo(x)] (*pl* **-es**) *m*: ~ **(de pó)** vacuum cleaner; **passar o** ~ **(em)** to vacuum, to hoover.
aspirante [aʃpiˈrãntʃi] *mf* **-1.** [candidato]: **ser** ~ **(a algo)** to be a candidate (for sthg). **-2.** *MIL* & *NÁUT* cadet.
aspirar [4] [aʃpiˈra(x)] <> *vt* **-1.** [sugar] to aspirate, to suck in. **-2.** [ar - pessoa] to inhale; [- máquina] to suction. **-3.** *LING* to aspirate. <> *vi* **-1.** [desejar]: ~ **a algo** to aspire to sthg. **-2.** [respirar] to breathe. **-3.** [soprar brisa] to blow.
aspirina® [aʃpiˈrinaʟ *f* aspirin®.
asqueroso, osa [aʃkeˈrozu, ɔzaʟ *adj* disgusting.
assadeira [asaˈdejraʟ *f* roasting dish.
assado, da [aˈsadu, daʟ *adj* roast.
   assado *m* roast.
assadura [asaˈduraʟ *f* **-1.** [em bebê] nappy rash. **-2.** [em adulto] rash.
assalariado, da [asalaˈrjadu, daʟ <> *adj* wage-earning. <> *m, f* wage earner.
assaltante [asawˈtãntʃi] *mf* **-1.** [na rua] mugger. **-2.** [de banco] robber. **-3.** [de casa] burglar.
assaltar [4] [asawˈta(x)] *vt* **-1.** [atacar] to attack. **-2.** [roubar - na rua] to mug; [- banco] to rob; [- casa] to break into. **-3.** *fig* [acometer] to assail.
assalto [aˈsawtuʟ *m* **-1.** [ataque] attack. **-2.** [na rua] mugging. **-3.** [a banco] robbery. **-4.** [a casa] burglary.
assanhado, da [asaˈnadu, daʟ *adj* **-1.** [excitado, irrequieto] excited. **-2.** [criança] excitable. **-3.** [desavergonhado] brazen. **-4.** [namorador] passionate.
assanhar [4] [asaˈna(x)] *vt* **-1.** [excitar, agitar] to excite. **-2.** [sensualmente] to arouse.
   assanhar-se *vp* **-1.** [excitar-se, agitar-se] to become excited. **-2.** [sensualmente] to become aroused.
assar [4] [aˈsa(x)] <> *vt* **-1.** [no forno] to roast. **-2.** [na grelha] to grill. <> *vi* to roast.

assassinar [4] [asasi'na(x)] *vt* -**1.** [matar] to murder. -**2.** *POL* to assassinate.

assassinato [asasi'natu], **assassínio** [asa'sinju] *m* -**1.** [de pessoa comum] murder. -**2.** *POL* assassination.

assassino, na [asa'sinu, na] <> *adj* deadly. <> *m, f* -**1.** [de pessoa comum] killer, murderer. -**2.** *POL* assassin.

assaz [a'saʒ] *adv* quite.

asseado, da [a'sjadu, da] *adj* clean, neat.

assediar [16] [ase'dʒja(x)] *vt* -**1.** [sitiar] to besiege. -**2.** [perseguir] to hound. -**3.** [importunar]: ~ **alguém (com)** to pester sb (with). -**4.** [sexualmente] to harass.

assédio [a'sɛdʒjul *m* -**1.** [cerco] siege. -**2.** [insistência] hounding; **ele se acostumou com o ~ dos repórteres** he became used to being hounded by reporters; ~ **sexual** sexual harassment.

assegurar [4] [asegu'ra(x)] *vt* -**1.** [garantir] to ensure; ~ **alguém de algo** to assure sb of sthg; ~ **algo a alguém** to assure sb sthg; ~ **alguém de que** to assure sb that. -**2.** [afirmar] to give an assurance.
➡ **assegurar-se** *vp*: ~-**se de fazer algo** to make sure of doing sthg.

asseio [a'sejul *m* cleanliness, neatness.

assembléia [asẽn'blɛjal *f* -**1.** [reunião] meeting; ~ **geral** annual general meeting. -**2.** [órgão] assembly; **Assembléia Legislativa** Legislative Assembly.

assemelhar [4] [aseme'ʎa(x)] *vt* [tornar semelhante] to liken.
➡ **assemelhar-se** *vp* [ser parecido] to look alike; ~-**se a algo/alguém** to look like sthg/sb.

assenhorear-se [15] [aseɲo'rjaxsil *vp*: ~ **de** to take possession of.

assentado, da [asẽn'tadu, da] *adj* -**1.** [firme] secure. -**2.** [combinado] arranged. -**3.** [ajuizado] sound. -**4.** [em terras] landed.

assentamento [asẽnta'mẽntul *m* -**1.** [registro] registration. -**2.** [nota] entry. -**3.** [em terras] settling.

assentar [4] [asẽn'ta(x)] <> *vt* -**1.** [firmar] to set. -**2.** [colocar] to place. -**3.** [tijolos] to lay. -**4.** [em terras] to settle. -**5.** *fig* [basear] to base. -**6.** [anotar, registrar] to note down. -**7.** [estabelecer] to establish. -**8.** [determinar] to agree. -**9.** [decidir] to resolve. <> *vi* -**1.** [ger] to settle. -**2.** *fig* [cair]: ~ **a ou em alguém** to suit sb.
➡ **assentar-se** *vp* -**1.** [firmar-se] to be founded. -**2.** *fig* [basear-se] to be based. -**3.** *fig* [ajuizar-se] to settle down.

assente [a'sẽntʃil <> *pp* ▷ **assentar**. <> *adj* [combinado, fixo] agreed.

assentir [56] [asẽn'tʃi(x)] *vi* -**1.** [concordar]: ~ **(em)** to agree (to). -**2.** [aceder]: ~ **(a)** to accede (to).

assento [a'sẽntul *m* -**1.** [para sentar] seat. -**2.** *fig* [base]: **ter ~ to** to be based on.

assepsia [asep'sial *f MED* asepsis.

asséptico, ca [a'sɛptʃiku, ka] *adj* aseptic.

assertiva [asex'tʃival *f* assertion.

assessor, ra [ase'so(x), ral *m, f* -**1.** [consultor] consultant. -**2.** [assistente] adviser; ~ **de comunicação** public relations, PR; ~ **de imprensa** press adviser. -**3.** *POL* aide.

assessoramento [asesora'mẽntul *m* assistance.

assessorar [4] [aseso'ra(x)] *vt* -**1.** [prestar consultoria]: ~ **alguém (em algo)** to advise sb (on sthg). -**2.** [assistir] to assist.

assessoria [aseso'rial *f* -**1.** [consultoria] consultancy. -**2.** [assistência] assistance. -**3.** [setor, órgão, conselho] advisors *(pl)*; ~ **de comunicação** public relations, PR; ~ **de imprensa** press advisors *(pl)*.

asseveração [asevera'sãwl *(pl* -ões) *f* -**1.** [afirmação] assertion. -**2.** [garantia] affirmation.

asseverar [4] [aseve'ra(x)] *vt* -**1.** [afirmar] to assert. -**2.** [garantir] to affirm.

assexuado, da [asek'swadu, da] *adj* asexual.

assiduidade [asidwi'dadʒi] *f* -**1.** [a aulas, trabalho] regular attendance. -**2.** [diligência] diligence; **com ~** diligently.

assíduo, dua [a'sidwu, dwa] *adj* -**1.** [a aulas, trabalho] regularly attending. -**2.** [diligente] diligent.

assim [a'sĩ] <> *adv* -**1.** [deste modo] just like that; ~ **sendo** that being the case; **como ~?** how do you mean? -**2.** [igualmente] the same; **algo ~** [algo parecido] something similar; **e ~ por diante** and so on; ~ **como** [tal como] just like; [também] as well as. -**3.** [deste tamanho]: **ser grande ~** to be this big. <> *conj* [então] so; ~ **mesmo, mesmo ~** even so.
➡ **assim que** *loc conj* as soon as.

assimétrico, ca [asi'mɛtriku, ka] *adj* -**1.** [ger] asymmetrical. -**2.** *ESP* asymmetric.

assimilação [asimila'sãwl *(pl* -ões) *f* -**1.** [ger] assimilation. -**2.** [de alimento] absorbtion.

assimilar [4] [asimi'la(x)] *vt* -**1.** [ger] to assimilate. -**2.** [apropriar-se de] to absorb. -**3.** [comparar]: ~ **algo (a algo)** to compare sthg (to sthg).

assinalado, da [asina'ladu, da] *adj* -**1.** [marcado] marked. -**2.** [eminente] distinguished. -**3.** [notável] outstanding.

assinalar [4] [asina'la(x)] *vt* -**1.** [marcar] to mark. -**2.** [distinguir] to indicate. -**3.** [especificar] to specify. -**4.** [observar] to point out. -**5.** [celebrizar] to distinguish.

assinante [asi'nãntʃil *mf* subscriber.

assinar [4] [asi'na(x)] <> *vt* -**1.** [firmar] to sign. -**2.** [ser assinante de] to subscribe to. <> *vi* [firmar] to sign.

assinatura [asina'tural *f* -**1.** [firma] signature. -**2.** [subscrição] subscription.

assistência [asiʃ'tẽnsjal *f* -**1.** [ger] assistance, aid; ~ **jurídica** legal aid; ~ **médica** medical aid; ~ **técnica** technical assistance; ~ **social** social work. -**2.** [presença] attendance. -**3.** [espectadores] audience. -**4.** [ambulância] emergency assistance.

assistente [asiʃ'tẽntʃil <> *adj* [auxiliar] assistant. <> *mf* -**1.** [auxiliar] assistant; ~ **social** social worker. -**2.** [espectador - em jogo] spectator; [- em teatro, cinema] member of the audience.

assistir [6] [asiʃ'tʃi(x)] ◇ *vt* -**1.** [socorrer] to assist. -**2.** [auxiliar] to assist. -**3.** [fazer companhia a] to attend. ◇ *vi* -**1.** [estar presente]: ~ **a** [ver] to watch; [testemunhar] to witness; [comparecer a] to attend. -**2.** [caber]: ~ **a alguém** to pertain to sb.

assoalho [a'swaʎu] *m* floor.

assoar [20] [a'swa(x)] *vt* to blow *(one's nose)*.

assoberbado, da [asobex'badu, da] *adj* [de trabalho] snowed under.

assoberbar [4] [asobex'ba(x)] *vt*: ~ **alguém (de trabalho)** to overload sb (with work).

assobiar [aso'bja(x)] *m* = **assoviar**.

assobio [aso'biw] *m* = **assovio**.

associação [asosja'sãw] (*pl* -**ões**) *f* -**1.** [ger] association; ~ **de moradores** residents' association. -**2.** [parceria, aliança] partnership.

associado, da [aso'sjadu, da] ◇ *adj* -**1.** [relacionado] associated. -**2.** [sócio] associate. -**3.** [médico, advogado etc] associate. ◇ *m, f* [sócio] associate, partner.

associar [16] [aso'sja(x)] *vt* relacionar; ~ **algo a algo** to associate sthg with sthg.
➡ **associar-se** *vp* -**1.** COM [formar associação] to form a partnership. -**2.** [entrar de sócio]: ~**-se a** to become a member of.

assolar [4] [aso'la(x)] *vt* to devastate.

assomar [4] [aso'ma(x)] *vi* -**1.** [aparecer]: ~ **(a)** to appear (at). -**2.** [subir]: ~ **a** to climb.

assombração [asõnbra'sãw] (*pl* -**ões**) *f* ghost.

assombrar [4] [asõn'bra(x)] *vt* -**1.** [assustar] to frighten. -**2.** [rondar] to haunt. -**3.** [impressionar] to amaze.

assombro [a'sõnbru] *m* -**1.** [admiração] astonishment. -**2.** [espanto, maravilha]: **ser um** ~ to be amazing.

assombroso, osa [asõn'brozu, rɔza] *adj* amazing.

assoprar [4] [aso'pra(x)] ◇ *vt* -**1.** [vela] to blow out. -**2.** [vidro] to blow. -**3.** *fam* [resposta, palpite] to whisper. ◇ *vi* [brisa, vento] to blow.

assoviar [16] [aso'vja(x)], **assobiar** [aso'bja(x)] *vi* & *vt* to whistle.

assovio [aso'viw], **assobio** [aso'bju] *m* whistling, whistle; **dar um** ~ to whistle.

assumido, da [asu'midu, da] *adj fam* -**1.** [declarado] acknowledged. -**2.** [homossexual]: **ser um gay** ~ to be openly gay.

assumir [6] [asu'mi(x)] ◇ *vt* -**1.** [chamar a si] to assume. -**2.** [reconhecer - filho] to recognize; [- erro] to admit. -**3.** [tomar posse de] to take up. -**4.** [adotar, adquirir] to take on. -**5.** [homossexualidade] to come out. ◇ *vi* [tomar posse] to take office.

Assunção [asũn'sãw] *n* [cidade] Asunción.

assuntar [4] [asũn'ta(x)] ◇ *vt* -**1.** [prestar atenção a] to notice. -**2.** [verificar] to find out about. ◇ *vi* [meditar]: ~ **(em)** to reflect (on).

assunto [a'sũntu] *m* [tema] subject; ~ **urgente** urgent business; **não ter** ~ *fig* to have nothing to talk about.

assustadiço, ça [asuʃta'dʒisu, sa] *adj* nervous.

assustador, ra [asuʃta'do(x), ra] (*mpl* -**es**, *fpl* -**s**) *adj* -**1.** [amedrontador] terrifying. -**2.** [alarmante] alarming.

assustar [4] [asuʃ'ta(x)] ◇ *vt* -**1.** [amedrontar] to frighten. -**2.** [alarmar] to alarm. ◇ *vi* -**1.** [amedrontar] to be terrifying. -**2.** [alarmar] to be alarming.
➡ **assustar-se** *vp*: ~**-se (com)** [amedrontar-se] to be terrified (by); [alarmar-se] to be alarmed (by).

asteca [aʃ'tɛka] ◇ *adj* Aztec. ◇ *mf* Aztec.

asterisco [aʃte'riʃku] *m* asterisk.

astigmatismo [aʃtʃigma'tʃiʒmu] *m* astigmatism.

astral [aʃ'trawl] (*pl* -**ais**) ◇ *adj* ASTRO astrological. ◇ *m* [humor, ambiente] mood.

astrologia [aʃtrolo'ʒial] *f* astrology.

astrólogo, ga [aʃ'trɔlogu, ga] *m, f* astrologist.

astronauta [aʃtro'nawta] *mf* astronaut.

astronáutica [aʃtro'nawtʃika] *f* astronautics *(sg)*.

astronave [aʃtro'navi] *f* spaceship.

astronomia [aʃtrono'mia] *f* astronomy.

astronômico, ca [aʃtro'nomiku, ka] *adj* astronomical.

astúcia [aʃ'tusja] *f* -**1.** [esperteza] shrewdness. -**2.** [ardil] ruse.

astuto, ta [aʃ'tutu, ta] *adj* -**1.** [esperto] shrewd. -**2.** [ardiloso] cunning.

at. (*abrev de* **atenção a**) attn.

ata [l'ata] *f* [de reunião] minutes *(pl)*.

atacadista [ataka'dʒiʃta] ◇ *adj* COM [comércio, mercado, vendedor] wholesale. ◇ *mf* [vendedor] wholesaler.

atacado, da [ata'kadu, da] *adj fam* [pessoa]: **estar** *ou* **andar** ~ to be in a foul mood.
➡ **atacado** *m* COM : **no/por** ~ wholesale.

atacante [ata'kãntʃi] ◇ *adj* attacking. ◇ *mf* attacker.

atacar [12] [ata'ka(x)] ◇ *vt* -**1.** [lançar ataque contra] to attack. -**2.** [acometer] to strike at. -**3.** *fig* [combater] to tackle. -**4.** *fig* [criticar] to hit out at. ◇ *vi* -**1.** [lançar ataque] to attack. -**2.** [vírus] to strike. -**3.** ESP [time, jogador] to go on the attack. ◇ *interj*: **atacar!** charge!

atado, da [a'tadu, da] *adj* -**1.** [desajeitado] clumsy. -**2.** [confuso, perplexo] bewildered.

atadura [ata'dura] *f* bandage.

atalho [a'taʎu] *m* COMPUT shortcut.

atapetar [4] [atape'ta(x)] *vt* to carpet.

ataque [a'taki] *m* -**1.** [ger] attack; ~ **aéreo** air strike; ~ **cardíaco** heart attack; ~ **epilético** epileptic fit; ~ **histérico** fit of hysteria; ~ **de nervos** attack of nerves; ~ **de riso** fit of laughter; **ter um** ~ **(de raiva)** *fam* to have a fit (of rage). -**2.** [FUT - de time] attack; [- campo, ação]: **no** ~ on the attack.

atar [4] [a'ta(x)] *vt* to tie; **não** ~ **nem desatar** [pessoa] to shilly-shally; [negócio, namoro] to be getting nowhere.

atarantado, da [atarãn'tadu, da] *adj* -**1.** [dia] hectic. -**2.** [pessoa] flustered.

atarantar [4] [atarãn'ta(x)] *vt* to fluster.

atarefado, da [ˌatare'fadu, da] *adj* busy.

atarracado, da [ataxa'kadu, da] *adj* -**1.** [pessoa]

thickset. - **2.** [pescoço, perna] thick.

atarraxar [4] [ataxa'ʃa(x)] *vt* to screw.

ataúde [ata'udʒi] *m* coffin.

atávico, ca [a'taviku, ka] *adj* atavistic.

atazanar [4] [ataza'na(x)] *vt* to taunt.

até [a'tɛ] ⬦ *prep* - **1.** [no espaço] as far as, up to; **de ... > ... from ... to ... - 2.** [no tempo] until, till; ~ **que enfim!** at long last!; **ir** ~ **o fim com algo** to see sthg through; ~ **agora** so far, up until now. - **3.** [prazo - antes de] before; [- extensão] until. - **4.** [despedida]: **até!** see you!; ~ **amanhã** until tomorrow; ~ **já** see you soon; ~ **logo** bye for now; ~ **a vista** until next time. - **5.** [com quantidades] up to. ⬦ *adv* [mesmo, inclusive] even.
➡ **até que** *loc conj* - **1.** [até quando] until. - **2.** [bem que]: ~ **que** admittedly.

atear [15] [ate'a(x)] *vt* - **1.** [fogo]: ~ **fogo a algo** to set fire to sthg. - **2.** *fig* [espalhar] to inflame.

atéia [a'tɛja] *f* ▷ **ateu.**

ateliê [ate'lje] *m* studio.

atemorizado, da [atemori'zadu, da] *adj* frightened.

atemorizador, ra [atemoriza'do(x), ra] *adj* alarming.

atemorizante [atemori'zãntʃi] *adj* frightening.

atemorizar [4] [atemori'za(x)] *vt* - **1.** [assustar] to frighten. - **2.** [intimidar] to alarm.

Atenas [a'tenaʃ] *n* Athens.

atenção [atẽ'sãw] (*pl* -ões) ⬦ *f* - **1.** [interesse] attention; **chamar a** ~ **(de)** [atrair] to catch the eye (of); **chamar a** ~ **de alguém** [advertir] to warn sb; **prestar** ~ **(a)** to pay attention (to). - **2.** [cuidado] care. - **3.** [cortesia] consideration (U). ⬦ *interj*: ~! [cuidado] beware!; [exigindo concentração] pay attention!; [em aeroporto, conferência] your attention please!

atencioso, osa [atẽ'sjozu, ɔza] *adj* - **1.** [que presta atenção] attentive. - **2.** [polido, cortês] considerate.

atendente [atẽ'dẽntʃi] *mf* auxiliary.

atender [5] [atẽ'de(x)] ⬦ *vt* - **1.** [satisfazer] to attend to. - **2.** [deferir] to grant. - **3.** [receber] to receive. - **4.** [responder] to answer. - **5.** [em loja] to serve. - **6.** [cuidar de - convidado, hóspede] to look after; [- paciente, ferido] to tend. ⬦ *vi* - **1.** [satisfazer]: ~ **a** to attend to. - **2.** [responder]: ~ **(a)** to answer; ~ **por** [por nome, apelido] to answer to. - **3.** [loja, vendedor] to serve; ~ **bem/mal** to give good/bad service. - **4.** [dar atenção]: ~ **a** to heed.

atendimento [atẽdʒi'mẽntu] *m* - **1.** [serviço] service; ~ **médico** medical care; **horário de** ~ opening times. - **2.** [recepção]: **tivemos pronto** ~ **no ministério** we were dealt with swiftly at the ministry.

ateniense [ate'njẽsil] ⬦ *adj* Athenian. ⬦ *m, f* Athenian.

atentado [atẽ'tadu] *m* - **1.** [ataque] attack; ~ **a bomba/tiros** bomb/gun attack; ~ **terrorista** terrorist attack. - **2.** [contra pessoa] attempt on one's life. - **3.** [contra edifício, monumento]: ~ **(a/contra)** attack (on/against). - **4.** [crime, ofensa]: ~

(a algo) attack (on sthg); ~ **ao pudor** indecent exposure.

atentar [4] [atẽ'ta(x)] *vi* - **1.** [prestar atenção]: ~ **para** *ou* **a** to pay attention to. - **2.** [cometer atentado]: ~ **contra (a vida de) alguém** to make an attempt on sb's life; ~ **contra algo** [violar, ofender] to offend against sthg.

atento, ta [a'tẽntu, ta] *adj* - **1.** [interessado, concentrado] attentive. - **2.** [cuidadoso] painstaking.

atenuação [atenwa'sãw] (*pl* -ões) *f* - **1.** [de pressão, pena] reduction. - **2.** [de combate] subduing. - **3.** [de dor] easing.

atenuante [ate'nwãntʃil] ⬦ *adj* extenuating. ⬦ *m* JUR extenuating circumstance.

atenuar [4] [ate'nwa(x)] *vt* - **1.** [pressão, pena] to reduce. - **2.** [combate] to die down. - **3.** [dor] to ease.

aterrador, ra [atexa'do(x), ra] *adj* terrifying.

aterragem [ate'xaʒẽjl] (*pl* -ns) *f* = aterrissagem.

aterrar [4] [ate'xar] *vt* [cobrir com terra] to level.

aterrissagem [atexi'saʒẽjl] (*pl* -ns) *f* landing.

aterrissar [atexi'sa(x)], **aterrizar** [atexi'za(x)] [4] *vi* to land.

aterro [a'texul] *m* [área aterrada] levelling.

aterrorizado, da [atexori'zadu, da] *adj* terrified.

aterrorizante [atexori'zãntʃil] *adj* terrifying.

aterrorizar [4] [atexori'za(x)] *vt* to terrorize.

ater-se [1] [a'texsil] *vp* - **1.** [limitar-se]: ~ **a** to keep to. - **2.** [fiar-se por] to rely on.

atestado, da [ateʃ'tadu, da] *adj* certified.
➡ **atestado** *m* - **1.** [certificado] certificate; ~ **médico** medical certificate; ~ **de óbito** death certificate; **passar um** ~ to issue a certificate. - **2.** *fig* [prova] confirmation. - **3.** JUR testimony.

atestar [4] [ateʃ'ta(x)] *vt* - **1.** [certificar] to certify. - **2.** [provar] to confirm. - **3.** [testemunhar] to vouch for.

ateu, atéia [a'tew, a'tɛjal] ⬦ *adj* atheist. ⬦ *m, f* atheist.

atinado, da [atʃi'nadu, da] *adj* [sensato] sensible.

atinar [4] [atʃi'na(x)] ⬦ *vt* - **1.** [descobrir, acertar] to work out. - **2.** [perceber] to realize. ⬦ *vi* - **1.** [encontrar]: ~ **com** to come up with. - **2.** [ter consciência de]: ~ **em** to be aware of.

atingir [52] [atʃĩn'ʒi(x)] *vt* - **1.** [ger] to reach. - **2.** [acertar] to hit. - **3.** [objetivo] to achieve. - **4.** *fig* [ferir] to wound. - **5.** [afetar] to affect. - **6.** [compreender] to grasp.

atingível [atʃĩn'ʒivewl] (*pl* -eis) *adj* achievable, attainable.

atípico, ca [a'tʃipiku, ka] *adj* untypical, atypical.

atirado, da [atʃi'radu, da] *adj fam* [pessoa] forward.

atirador, ra [atʃira'do(x), ra] *m, f* shot, shooter.

atirar [4] [atʃi'ra(x)] ⬦ *vt* - **1.** [lançar]: ~ **algo (em)** to throw sthg (into); ~ **algo (por)** to throw sthg (through). - **2.** [fig] [olhares, beijos] to cast. ⬦ *vi* [dar disparo]: ~ **(em)** to fire (at).
➡ **atirar-se** *vp* - **1.** [lançar-se]: ~-**se (a/em)** to throw o.s. (at); *fig* [dedicar-se] to throw o.s. into; ~-**se contra** to throw onself against. - **2.** *fam* [insinuar-se amorosamente] to come on to.

atitude [atʃi'tudʒi] f - **1.** [modo de agir] response; **tomar uma** ~ [reagir, tomar uma providência] to take a stance. - **2.** [postura] attitude.

ativa [a'tʃiva] f ⊳ **ativo**.

ativação [ativa'sãw] (pl -**ões**) f [aceleração, intensificação] acceleration.

ativar [4] [atʃi'va(x)] vt - **1.** [acionar] to turn on. - **2.** [bomba] to activate. - **3.** [estimular] to stimulate.

atividade [atʃivi'dadʒi] f - **1.** [ger] activity; ~ **extracurricular** extracurricular activity; **entrar em** ~ to be put into action; **em** ~ [aparelho] functioning; [pessoa] on the go. - **2.** [ocupação] pursuit. - **3.** [movimento intenso] bustle.

ativo, va [a'tivu, va] adj - **1.** [ger] active. - **2.** [que trabalha] working. - **3.** [ágil, movimentado] lively.
    ◆ **ativo** m COM assets (pl).
    ◆ **ativa** f MIL: **estar na** ~ to be in active service; **da** ~ staff (antes de subst).

atlântico, ca [at'lãntʃiku, ka] adj Atlantic.
    ◆ **Atlântico** n: **o (oceano) Atlântico** the Atlantic Ocean.

atlas ['atlaʃ] m inv atlas.

Atlas ['atlaʃ] n: **o** ~ the Atlas Mountains.

atleta [a'tlɛta] mf athlete.

atlético, ca [a'tlɛtʃiku, ka] adj athletic.

atletismo [atle'tʃiʒmu] m athletics (sg).

atmosfera [atmoʃ'fɛra] f - . GEOGR atmosphere. - **2.** fig [ambiente] mood.

atmosférico, ca [atmoʃ'fɛriku, ka] adj atmospheric.

ato ['atu] m - **1.** [ger] act; ~ **sexual** sexual act; ~ **falho** Freudian slip; **em** ~ **contínuo** straight away; **no** ~ [imediatamente] on the spot. - **2.** [cerimônia] action; ~ **público** public ceremony. - **3.** POL [decreto]: ~ **(institucional)** act, law.

à-toa [a'toa] adj - **1.** [sem importância] insignificant. - **2.** [simples] simple.

atoalhado, da [atwa'ʎadu, da] adj towelling.

atolado, da [ato'ladu, da] adj - **1.** [carro, rua] muddy. - **2.** fig [pessoa]: ~ **(de coisas para fazer)** snowed under (with things to do).

atolar [4] [ato'la(x)] vt to get bogged down.
    ◆ **atolar-se** vp fig [pessoa] to be snowed under.

atoleiro [ato'lejru] m - **1.** [de lama] quagmire. - **2.** fig [situação] morass.

atômico, ca [a'tomiku, ka] adj atomic.

atomizador [atomiza'do(x)] m atomizer, spray.

átomo ['atomu] m atom.

atonal, nais [a'tonaw, aiʃ] adj MÚS atonal.

atônito, ta [a'tonitu, ta] adj astonished.

ator, atriz [a'to(x), a'triʒ] (mpl -**res**, fpl -**zes**) m, f actor, actress.

atordoado, da [atox'dwadu, da] adj dazed.

atordoamento [atoxdwa'mẽntul m bewilderment.

atordoante [atox'dwãntʃi] adj deafening.

atordoar [20] [atox'dwa(x)] vt to daze.

atormentado, da [atoxmẽn'tadu, da] adj tormented.

atormentar [4] [atoxmẽn'ta(x)] vt to torment.

atóxico, ca [a'tɔksiku, ka] adj non-toxic.

ATP (abrev de **Associação dos Tenistas Profissionais**) f ATP.

atração [atra'sãw] (pl -**ões**) f - **1.** FÍS attraction. - **2.** [de cinema, teatro] main attraction. - **3.** [propensão] pull. - **4.** [sexual] attraction.

atracar [12] [atra'ka(x)] vt & vi NÁUT to moor.
    ◆ **atracar-se** vp - **1.** fig [em briga] to come to blows. - **2.** fam fig [amorosamente] to clinch.

atraente [atra'ẽntʃil adj - **1.** [objeto, efeito] eye-catching. - **2.** [proposta, vantagem] appealing. - **3.** [pessoa] attractive.

atraiçoar [20] [atraj'swa(x)] vt to betray.

atrair [68] [atra'i(x)] vt - **1.** [fascinar] to attract. - **2.** [chamar a si] to bring. - **3.** [aliciar] to entice.

atrapalhação [atrapa⌐a'sãw] (pl -**ões**) f [confusão] muddle.

atrapalhar [4] [atrapa'⌐a(x)] ◇ vt - **1.** [confundir] to muddle. - **2.** [perturbar] to upset. - **3.** [dificultar] to confound. ◇ vi [perturbar] to be disturbing.
    ◆ **atrapalhar-se** vp [confundir-se] to get into a muddle.

atrás [a'trajʃ] adv - **1.** [posição] behind; **lá** ~ **back** there. - **2.** [no tempo] ago. - **3.** [em classificação]: **estar/ficar** ~ **(de)** to be ranked behind; **não ficar** ~ fam fig not to be far behind.
    ◆ **atrás de** loc prep - **1.** [posição] behind. - **2.** [em seguimento a] after; **logo** ~ **de** right behind. - **3.** [em busca de - pessoa] after; [- objeto, explicação] looking for.

atrasado, da [atra'zadu, da] adj - **1.** [ger] slow. - **2.** [tardio] late. - **3.** [país, povo, costume] backward. - **4.** [pagamento, conta] overdue. - **5.** [número, edição] back.
    ◆ **atrasados** mpl arrears.

atrasar [4] [atra'za(x)] ◇ vt - **1.** [fazer demorar] to delay. - **2.** [retardar] to hold back. - **3.** [relógio] to put back. - **4.** [pagamento] to be late with. ◇ vi - **1.** [demorar] to be delayed. - **2.** [publicação] to be late. - **3.** [relógio] to be slow. - **4.** [pagamento] to arrive late. - **5.** [em trabalho, encomenda] to fail to keep up.
    ◆ **atrasar-se** vp [pessoa]: ~-**se (para)** to be late (for).

atraso [a'trazu] m - **1.** [demora] delay; **chegar com** ~ to arrive late; **um** ~ **de vida** a drag. - **2.** [de pagamento] late payment. - **3.** [de país, povo, costumes] backwardness.

atrativo, va [atra'tʃivu, va] adj attractive.
    ◆ **atrativo** m attraction.

atravancar [12] [atravãŋ'ka(x)] vt - **1.** [bloquear] to block. - **2.** [lotar] to clutter.

através [atra'vɛʃ] adv [de lado a lado] through.
    ◆ **através de** loc adv - **1.** [por entre] amongst. - **2.** [pelo centro de] through. - **3.** [no decorrer de] through. - **4.** [por meio de] by means of. - **5.** [por via de] through.

atravessado, da [atrave'sadu, da] adj - **1.** [de través] askew; ~ **sobre** (lying) across. - **2.** [cruzado] crossed. - **3.** [passado de lado a lado] (stuck) across. - **4.** fig [irritado] irritated; **estar com alguém** ~ **na garganta** to be fed up with sb.

atravessar [4] [atrave'sa(x)] vt - **1.** [ger] to cross.

- 2. [pôr de través] to place across. **- 3.** [transpassar] to pierce. **- 4.** *fig* [passar por] to go through.

atrelar [4] [atre'la(x)] *vt* **- 1.** [prender] to tie up, to tether. **- 2.** [ligar] to attach; ~ **algo a algo** to attach sthg to sthg.

atrever-se [5] [atre'vexsi] *vp*: ~ **(a fazer algo)** to dare (to do sthg).

atrevido, da [atre'vidu, da] *adj* **- 1.** [petulante] impertinent. **- 2.** [ousado] bold.

atrevimento [atrevi'mẽntul] *m* **- 1.** [petulância] insolence. **- 2.** [ousadia - condição] boldness; [- ato] effrontery.

atribuição [atribwi'sãw] (*pl* **-ões**) *f* **- 1.** [ato] attribution. **- 2.** [prerrogativa] prerogative.

➡ **atribuições** *fpl* [poderes] powers.

atribuir [74] [atri'bwi(x)] *vt* **- 1.** [imputar]: ~ **algo a alguém/algo** to attribute sthg to sb/sthg. **- 2.** [conceder]: ~ **algo a alguém** to award sb sthg.

atribulação [atribula'sãw] (*pl* **-ões**) *f* adversity.

atribulado, da [atribu'ladu, da] *adj* wretched.

atribular [4] [atribu'la(x)] *vt* to afflict.

➡ **atribular-se** *vp* to be distressed.

atributo [atri'butu] *m* attribute.

átrio ['atriu] *m* **- 1.** [vestíbulo] hallway. **- 2.** [pátio] courtyard.

atritar [atri'ta(x)] *vt* to rub.

atrito [a'tritu] *m* **- 1.** [fricção] friction. **- 2.** *fig* [conflito] conflict; **entrar em** ~ to have a misunderstanding.

atriz [a'triʒ] *f* ➪ **ator**.

atrocidade [atrosi'dadʒi] *f* atrocity.

atrofia [atro'fia] *f* atrophy.

atrofiado, da [atro'fjadu, da] *adj* atrophied.

atrofiar [16] [atro'fja(x)] <> *vt* to cripple. <> *vi* to atrophy.

➡ **atrofiar-se** *vp* to become atrophied.

atropeladamente [atropelada'mẽntʃi] *adv* [atabalhoadamente] chaotically.

atropelamento [atropela'mẽntul] *m* [de pedestre] running over.

atropelar [4] [atrope'la(x)] *vt* **- 1.** [pedestre] to run over. **- 2.** [esbarrar em, empurrar] to crash into. **- 3.** *fig* [precipitar]: ~ **as coisas** to rush things.

atropelo [atro'pelu] *m* **- 1.** [confusão] turmoil. **- 2.** [dificuldade, aflição] headache, problem.

atroz [a'trɔʒ] *adj* **- 1.** [cruel] atrocious. **- 2.** [terrível] terrible.

atuação [atwa'sãw] (*pl* **-ões**) [-õjʃ] *f* **- 1.** [ger] performance. **- 2.** [participação] role.

atual [a'twaw] (*pl* **-ais**) *adj* **- 1.** [corrente] present. **- 2.** [moderno] current.

atualidade [atwali'dadʒi] *f* **- 1.** [período atual] present time. **- 2.** [modernidade] modernity.

➡ **atualidades** *fpl* [JORN] news *(sg)*.

atualização [atwaliza'sãw] (*pl* **-ões**) *f* updating.

atualizado, da [atwali'zadu, da] *adj* up-to-date.

atualizar [4] [atwali'za(x)] *vt* to update.

➡ **atualizar-se** *vp* [pessoa] to bring o.s. up to date.

atualmente [atwaw'mẽntʃi] *adv* **- 1.** [no momento] currently. **- 2.** [hoje em dia] nowadays.

atuante [a'twãntʃi] *adj* active.

atuar [4] [a'twa(x)] *vi* **- 1.** [ger] to act. **- 2.** [participar de]: ~ **em** to act on/in. **- 3.** [contribuir para]: ~ **para** *ou* **por** to work for *ou* towards. **- 4.** [influenciar]: ~ **sobre** to influence.

atum [a'tũ] (*pl* **-ns**) *m* tuna.

aturar [4] [atu'ra(x)] *vt* to endure, to put up with.

aturdido, da [atur'dʒidu, da] *adj* stunned.

aturdir [6] [atux'dʒi(x)] <> *vt* to stun. <> *vi* to deafen.

audácia [aw'dasja] *f* **- 1.** [intrepidez] boldness. **- 2.** [insolência] audacity; **que** ~! what a cheek!

audacioso, sa [awda'sjozu, ɔza] *adj* **- 1.** [pessoa] intrepid. **- 2.** [ato] gallant. **- 3.** [decisão] bold.

audaz [aw'daʒ] (*pl* **-es**) *adj* [intrépido] audacious.

audição [awdʒi'sãw] (*pl* **-ões**) *f* **- 1.** [ger] hearing. **- 2.** [concerto] audition.

audiência [aw'dʒjẽnsjal *f* **- 1.** [ger] audience; **dar uma** ~ to grant an audience. **- 2.** [mídia - *RÁDIO*] listeners *(pl)*; [- *TV*] viewers *(pl)*; **índices de** ~ ratings *(pl)*. **- 3.** *JUR* hearing.

áudio [l'awdʒul *m* audio.

audiovisual [ˌawdʒuvi'zwawl (*pl* **-ais**) <> *adj* audiovisual. <> *m* projector.

auditar [4] [awdʒi'ta(x)] *vt* *FIN* to audit.

auditivo, va [awdʒi'tʃivu, val *adj* auditory.

auditor, ra [awdʒi'to(x), ral *m, f* **- 1.** *FIN* auditor. **- 2.** [juiz] judge, magistrate. **- 3.** [ouvinte] listener.

auditoria [awdʒito'rial *f* **- 1.** [serviço] audit; **fazer a** ~ **de** to carry out an audit of. **- 2.** [empresa] firm of accountants.

auditório [awdʒi'tɔrjul *m* **- 1.** [recinto] courtroom. **- 2.** [platéia] auditorium.

audível [aw'dʒivewl (*pl* **-eis**) *adj* audible.

auê [aw'el *m fam* [confusão] uproar; **fazer um** ~ to create an uproar.

auferir [57] [awfe'ri(x)] *vt* to obtain.

auge [l'awʒil *m* height.

augurar [4] [awgu'ra(x)] *vt* **- 1.** [prognosticar] to foretell. **- 2.** [indicar] to augur. **- 3.** [desejar] to wish.

augúrio [aw'gurjul *m* **- 1.** [prognóstico] prophecy. **- 2.** [sinal] indication.

aula [l'awla] *f* [escola] **- 1.** lesson; **dar** ~ to teach. **- 2.** [universidade] lecture; ~ **inaugural** introductory lecture.

aumentar [4] [awmẽn'ta(x)] <> *vt* **- 1.** [ger] to increase. **- 2.** [adicionar]: ~ **algo (a)** to add sthg (to/onto). <> *vi* **- 1.** [ger] to increase. **- 2.** [crescer] to grow.

aumento [aw'mẽntul *m* **- 1.** [ger] price increase. **- 2.** [de salário] rise *UK*, raise *US*. **- 3.** [crescimento] increase. **- 4.** [ampliação] magnification.

aura [l'awral *f* **- 1.** [halo] halo. **- 2.** *fig* [ar] aura.

áureo, rea [l'awrju, rjal *adj* golden.

auréola [aw'rɛwlal *f* halo.

aurora [aw'rɔral *f* dawn.

auscultar [4] [auʃ'kuw'ta(x)] *vt* **- 1.** *MED* to sound, to auscultate. **- 2.** *fig* [sondar] to sound (out).

ausência [aw'zẽnsjal *f* **- 1.** [falta de presença] absence. **- 2.** *fig* [inexistência] lack.

ausentar-se [7] [awzẽn'taxsil *vp* to absent o.s.

ausente [awˈzẽntʃi] ⬦ *adj* **-1.** [não-presente] absent. **-2.** [omisso] neglectful. ⬦ *mf* [não-presente] absent.

auspiciar [16] [awʃpiˈsja(x)] *vt* [prenunciar] to augur.

auspício [awʃˈpisju] *m* **-1.** [prenúncio] sign. **-2.** [patrocínio]: **sob os ~s de** under the auspices of.

auspicioso, osa [awʃpiˈʃjozu, ɔza] *adj* auspicious.

austeridade [awʃteriˈdadʒi] *f* **-1.** [severidade, seriedade] severity. **-2.** [em gastos] austerity.

austero, ra [awʃˈtɛru, ra] *adj* **-1.** [severo] strict. **-2.** [em gastos] austere.

austral [awʃˈtraw] (*pl* **-ais**) *adj* southern.

Austrália [awʃˈtralja] *n* Australia.

australiano, na [awʃtraˈljãnu, na] ⬦ *adj* Australian. ⬦ *m, f* Australian.

Áustria [ˈawʃtria] *n* Austria.

austríaco, ca [awʃˈtriaku, ka] ⬦ *adj* Austrian. ⬦ *m, f* Austrian.

autarquia [awtaxˈkia] *f* autocracy.

autárquico, ca [awˈtaxkiku, ka] *adj* autocratic.

autenticação [awtẽntʃiˈkasãw] (*pl* **-ões**) *f* COMPUT verification.

autenticar [12] [awtẽntʃiˈka(x)] *vt* to authenticate.

autenticidade [awtẽntʃisiˈdadʒi] *f* [genuinidade] authenticity.

autêntico, ca [awˈtẽntʃiku, ka] *adj* **-1.** [genuíno] authentic. **-2.** [original] original. **-3.** *(antes de subst) pej* [verdadeiro] real.

autismo [awˈtʃiʒmu] *m* autism.

autista [awˈtʃiʃta] ⬦ *adj* autistic. ⬦ *mf* autistic.

auto [ˈawtu] *m* **-1.** JUR (legal) brief. **-2.** TEATRO medieval allegorical play.
  ➡ **autos** *mpl* JUR legal papers.

auto-adesivo, va [ˌawtwadeˈzivu, va] (*mpl* **-s**, *fpl* **-s**) ⬦ *adj* self-adhesive. ⬦ *m* sticker.

auto-afirmação [ˌawtwafixmaˈsãw] *f* self-assertion.

autobiografia [awtobjograˈfia] *f* autobiography.

autobiográfico, ca [awtubjoˈgrafiku, ka] *adj* autobiographical.

autoconfiança [awtukõˈfjãnsa] *f* self-confidence.

autoconhecimento [awtukoɲesiˈmẽntu] *m* self-knowledge.

autocontrole [awtukõˈtroli] *m* self-control.

autocrata [awtoˈkrata] ⬦ *adj* autocratic. ⬦ *mf* autocrat.

autocrítica [awtoˈkritika] *f* self-criticism; **fazer uma ~** to admit to one's faults.

autóctone [awˈtɔktoni] ⬦ *adj* native. ⬦ *mf* [nativo] native.

autodefesa [awtudeˈfeza] *f* self-defence.

autodenominar-se [7] [awtudenomiˈnaxsi] *vp* to call o.s.

autodestruição [awtudeʃtrujˈsãw] *f* self-destruction.

autodeterminação [awtudetexminaˈsãw] *f* self-determination.

autodidata [awtodʒiˈdata] ⬦ *adj* self-taught. ⬦ *mf* self-taught person.

autodisciplina [awtudʒisiˈplina] *f* self-discipline.

autodomínio [ˌawtodoˈminju] *m* self-control.

autódromo [awˈtɔdromu] *m* racetrack.

auto-escola [ˌawtwiʃˈkɔla] (*pl* **auto-escolas**) *f* driving school.

auto-estima [ˌawtwiʃˈtʃima] *f* self-esteem.

auto-estrada [ˌawtwiʃˈtrada] (*pl* **auto-estradas**) *f* motorway UK, freeway US.

autografar [4] [awtograˈfa(x)] *vt* to sign.

autógrafo [awˈtografu] *m* autograph.

automação [awtomaˈsãw] *f* = **automatização**.

automático, ca [awtoˈmatʃiku, ka] *adj* automatic.

automatização [awtomatʃizaˈsãw] (*pl* **-ões**) *f* automation.

automatizar [4] [awtomatʃiˈza(x)] *vt* to automate.

autômato [awˈtomatu] *m* **-1.** [aparelho] robot. **-2.** *fig* [pessoa] automaton.

automedicar-se [7] [awtumedʒiˈkaxsi] *vp* to self-medicate.

automobilismo [awtomobiˈliʒmu] *m* motor racing.

automobilista [awtomobiˈliʃta] *mf* ESP racing driver.

automóvel [awtoˈmɔvɛw] (*pl* **-eis**) *m* car.

autonomia [awtonoˈmia] *f* **-1.** [independência] autonomy. **-2.** [de veículo] range; **~ de vôo** flight range.

autônomo, ma [awˈtonomu, ma] ⬦ *adj* **-1.** [independente] autonomous. **-2.** [trabalhador] autonomist. ⬦ *m, f* [trabalhador] autonomist.

autopeça [awtoˈpɛsa] *f* spare part *(for car)*.

autópsia [awˈtɔpsja] *f* autopsy.

autor, ra [awˈto(x), ra] (*mpl* **-es**, *fpl* **-s**) *m, f* author.

autoral [awtoˈraw] (*pl* **-ais**) *adj* authorial.

auto-retrato [ˌawtoxeˈtratu] (*pl* **auto-retratos**) *m* self-portrait.

autoria [awtoˈria] *f* **-1.** LITER authorship; **ser de ~ de alguém** to be written by sb. **-2.** [de crime] perpetration.

autoridade [awtoriˈdadʒi] *f* **-1.** [ger] authority; **ter/não ter ~** to have/not to have authority. **-2.** [perito]: **ser uma ~ em algo** to be an authority on sthg.

autoritário, ria [awtoriˈtarju, ja] *adj* authoritarian.

autoritarismo [awtoritaˈriʒmu] *m* authoritarianism.

autorização [awtorizaˈsãw] (*pl* **-ões**) *f* permission; **dar ~ a alguém (para algo/para fazer algo)** to give sb permission (for sthg/to do sthg).

autorizar [4] [awtoriˈza(x)] *vt* **-1.** [permitir] to authorize. **-2.** [capacitar] to enable.

auto-serviço [ˌawtusexˈvisu] (*pl* **auto-serviços**) *m* self-service.

auto-suficiente [ˌawtusufiˈsjẽntʃi] (*pl* **-s**) *adj*

self-sufficient; **ser** ~ **em algo** to be self-sufficient in sthg.

auto-sugestão [ˌawtusuʒeʃ'tãw] (*pl*-ões) *f* auto-suggestion.

autuar [4] [aw'twa(x)] *vt* to report; ~ **alguém em flagrante** to catch sb red-handed.

auxiliar [16] [awsi'lja(x)] (*pl*-es) <> *adj*-**1.** [ger] assistant. -**2.** [enfermeiro] auxiliary. <> *mf* assistant; ~ **administrativo** administrative assistant. <> *vt* to assist.

auxílio [aw'silju] *m* assistance; **prestar** ~ **a** to give assistance to.

auxílio-desemprego [awˌsiljudʒiʒĩn'pregu] (*pl* auxílios-desemprego) *m* unemployment benefit.

auxílio-doença [awˌsilju'dwẽnsa] (*pl* auxílios-doença) *m* sickness benefit.

auxílio-natalidade [awˌsiljunatali'dadʒi] (*pl* auxílios-natalidade) *m* maternity grant.

av. (*abrev de* avenida) *f* Av.

avacalhado, da [avaka'ʎadu, da] *adj*-**1.** [camisa, cabelo] dishevelled. -**2.** [trabalho] slipshod.

avacalhar [ava'kaʎa(x)] *vt*-**1.** [pôr em ridículo] *fam* to make a travesty of. -**2.** [executar com desleixo] *fam* to make a mess of.

aval [a'vaw] (*pl*-ais) *m*-**1.** [ger] backing.-**2.** [garantia] warranty.

avalanche [ava'lãnʃi], **avalancha** *f* avalanche.

avaliação [avalja'sãw] (*pl*-ões) *f*-**1.** [de preço, prejuízos] estimate.-**2.** [de qualidade, vantagens] appraisal. -**3.** [opinião] opinion. -**4.** *EDUC* assessment.

avaliar [16] [ava'lja(x)] *vt*-**1.** [preço, prejuízo] to estimate. -**2.** [imóvel] to value. -**3.** [qualidade, vantagens, idéia] to evaluate. -**4.** *EDUC* to assess.

avalista [ava'liʃta] *mf* backer.

avançado, da [avãn'sadu, da] *adj*-**1.** [adiantado] jutting out. -**2.** [hora] late. -**3.** [nível] advanced. -**4.** [idéia, pessoa] progressive.

avançar [13] [avã'sa(x)] <> *vi*-**1.** [adiantar-se] to move forward.-**2.** [estender-se] to spread. -**3.** [atacar, investir] to advance. -**4.** [atirar-se]: ~ **em algo** to throw o.s. upon sthg. <> *vt* [adiantar] to advance.

avanço [a'vãsu] *m*-**1.** [de tropa] advance. -**2.** [adiantamento] headway. -**3.** [melhora] step in the right direction. -**4.** [progresso] progress.

avantajado, da [avãnta'ʒadu, da] *adj* imposing.

avante [a'vãntʃi] <> *adv*-**1.** [adiante] ahead. -**2.** [para diante] onward. <> *interj* forward!

avarento, ta [ava'rẽntu, ta] <> *adj* miserly. <> *m, f* miser.

avareza [ava'reza] *f* avarice.

avaria [ava'ria] *f*-**1.** [de veículo, máquina] breakdown. -**2.** [de carga, casco] damage.

avariado, da [ava'rjadu, da] *adj*-**1.** [veículo, máquina] broken down. -**2.** [carga, casco] damaged.

avariar [16] [ava'rja(x)] <> *vt* to break down. <> *vi*-**1.** to spoil. -**2.** [casco] to be damaged.

avaro, ra [a'varu, ra] <> *adj* avaricious. <> *m, f* miser.

ave ['avi] *f* bird; ~ **de rapina** bird of prey.

aveia [a'veja] *f* oat.

avelã [ave'lã] *f* hazelnut.

aveludado, da [avelu'dadu, da] *adj* velvety.

avenida [ave'nida] *f* avenue.

avental [avẽn'taw] (*pl*-ais) *m*-**1.** [proteção] apron. -**2.** [vestido] pinafore dress.

aventar [4] [avẽn'ta(x)] *vt* to air.

aventura [avẽn'tura] *f*-**1.** [experiência] adventure. -**2.** [amorosa] love affair.

aventurar [4] [avẽntu'ra(x)] *vt* to risk.
- **aventurar-se** *vp* to venture (forth); ~-**se a fazer algo** to dare to do sthg.

aventureiro, ra [avẽntu'rejru, ra] <> *adj* adventurous. <> *m, f* adventurer (*f* adventuress).

averiguação [averigwa'sãw] (*pl*-ões) *f*-**1.** [investigação] investigation. -**2.** [verificação] check.

averiguar [21] [averi'gwa(x)] *vt*-**1.** [investigar] to investigate. -**2.** [verificar] to check.

avermelhado, da [avexme'ʎadu, da] *adj* reddish.

aversão [avex'sãw] (*pl*-ões) *f* aversion; **ter** ~ **a algo** to have an aversion to sthg.

avesso, ssa [a'vesu] *adj* [lado] wrong.
- **avesso** *m* [lado] underside; **virar pelo** ~ [blusa etc] to turn inside out; *fig* [revirar] to turn upside down.
- **às avessas** *loc adj* [oposto]: **ser um santo às avessas** to be anything but a saint.

avestruz [aveʃ'truʃ] (*pl*-es) *f* ostrich.

aviação [avja'sãw] *f*-**1.** [sistema] aviation. -**2.** [força aérea] air force.

aviador, ra [avja'do(x), ra] *m, f* pilot, aviator.

aviamento [avja'mẽntu] *m*-**1.** *COST* trimmings (*pl*). -**2.** [de receita médica] preparation.

avião [a'vjãw] (*pl*-ões) *m*-**1.** [veículo] aeroplane; ~ **a jato** jet plane; **ir de** ~ to fly. -**2.** *fam* [mulher] stunner. -**3.** *gír* [droga] drug pedlar.

aviar [16] [a'vja(x)] *vt* [receita médica] to make up.

avicultor, ra [avikuw'to(x), ra] *m, f* poultry breeder.

avicultura [avikuw'tura] *f* poultry breeding.

avidez [avi'deʒ] *f*-**1.** [desejo] eagerness; **com** ~ eagerly. -**2.** [cobiça] greed.

ávido, da ['avidu, da] *adj*-**1.** [desejoso] eager. -**2.** [cobiçoso] greedy.

aviltamento [aviwta'mẽntu] *m* [degradação] degradation.

aviltar [4] [aviw'ta(x)] *vt* [degradar] to weaken.
- **aviltar-se** *vp* [degradar-se] to degenerate.

avinagrado, da [avina'gradu, da] *adj* sour.

avisar [4] [avi'za(x)] <> *vt*-**1.** [informar] to warn; ~ **alguém de algo** to inform sb of sthg. -**2.** [advertir]: ~ **alguém de algo** to warn sb about/of sthg. <> *vi*-**1.** [informar] to give warning. -**2.** [advertir] to give fair warning; **estou avisando ...** I'm warning you ...

aviso [a'vizu] *m*-**1.** [placa] notice. -**2.** [notificação] notification; ~ **de crédito** credit note. -**3.** [informação] sign. -**4.** [advertência] warning sign; ~ **prévio** [notificação, período] notice.

avistar [4] [aviʃ'ta(x)] *vt* to catch sight of.
- **avistar-se** *vp* [ter entrevista] to meet; ~-**se**

com alguém to have a meeting with sb.
avivar [4] [avi'va(x)] vt -**1.** [ger] to revive. -**2.** [memória] to rekindle.
avizinhar-se [4] [avizi'naxsil vp [aproximar-se] to draw near.
avo ['avul m [fração] fractional part.
avô [a'vol, **avó** [a'vɔl m, f grandfather (f grandmother).
   → **avós** pl grandparents.
avoado, da [avo'adu, dal adj scatty.
avolumar [4] [avolu'ma(x)] vt [aumentar - em volume] to swell; [- em quantidade] to increase.
   → **avolumar-se** vp -**1.** [em volume] to rise. -**2.** [em quantidade] to increase.
avós [a'vɔʃ] pl ⊳ avô.
avulso, sa [a'vuwsu, sal adj loose.
   → **avulso** m flyer.
avultado, da [avuw'tadu, dal adj large.
avultar [4] [avuw'ta(x)] <> vt [fazer crescer] to increase. <> vi -**1.** [sobressair] to tower above. -**2.** [crescer] to grow.
axila [ak'sila] f armpit.
axioma [ak'sjoma] m axiom.
axiomático, ca [aksio'matʃiku, kal adj axiomatic.
azaléia [aza'lɛja] f azalea.
azar [a'za(x)] (pl -**es**) m bad luck; ∼! tough!; que ∼! damn!; ∼ o seu! your loss!; dar ∼ to bring bad luck; estar com ∼ to be down on one's luck.
azaração [azara'sãw] (pl -ões) f fam flirtation.
azarado, da [aza'radu, dal adj jinxed.
azarar [4] [aza'ra(x)] fam <> vt to woo. <> vi to pull.
azedar [4] [aze'da(x)] <> vt -**1.** [comida, leite] to cause to go sour. -**2.** fig [pessoa] to irritate. <> vi [leite, vinho] to go sour.
azedo, da [a'zedu, dal adj -**1.** [sabor] sour. -**2.** fig [pessoa] bitter.
azedume [aze'dumil m -**1.** [em sabor] bitterness. -**2.** fig [em pessoa] bitterness.
azeite [a'zejtʃil m: ∼ (de oliva) (olive) oil.
azeitona [azej'tonal f olive.
Azerbaijão [azexbaj'ʒãw] n Azerbaijan.
azerbaijano, na [azexbaj'ʒãnu, nal <> adj Azerbaijani. <> m, f Azerbaijani.
azeviche [aze'viʃil m [cor] jet black.
azia [a'zial f heartburn.
aziago, ga [azi'agu, gal adj ill-omened.
azucrinar [4] [azukri'na(x)] vt to annoy.
azul [a'zuwl (pl azuis) <> adj blue; está tudo ∼ fig everything is rosy. <> m blue.
azulado, da [azu'ladu, dal adj bluish.
azul-claro, ra [a'zuwklaru, ral <> adj light blue. <> m light blue.
azulejado, da [azule'ʒadu, dal adj tiled.
azulejar [4] [azule'leʒa(x)] vt to tile.
azulejo [azu'leʒul m [ornamental] tile.
azul-escuro, ra [a'zuwiʃkuru, ral <> adj dark blue. <> m dark blue.
azul-marinho [a,zuwma'riɲul <> adj inv ultramarine. <> m ultramarine.

azul-turquesa [a,zuwtux'kezal <> adj inv turquoise. <> m turquoise.

b, B [bel m [letra] b, B.
BA (abrev de Estado da Bahia) n State of Bahia.
B2B (abrev de business-to-business) m B2B.
baba ['babal f dribble.
babá [ba'bal f nursemaid.
babaca [ba'bakal mfam adj stupid.
baba-de-moça [,babadʒi'mosal (pl babas-de-moça) m, f CULIN egg and coconut pudding.
babado, da [ba'badu, dal adj [molhado de baba] dribbly.
   → **babado** m -**1.** [em roupa etc] frill. -**2.** fam [caso] gossip.
babador [baba'do(x)] m bib.
babaquice [baba'kisil f fam [estupidez] stupidity.
babar [4] [ba'ba(x)] <> vt to dribble on. <> vi -**1.** [deitar baba] to dribble. -**2.** fam [ficar impressionado] to drool.
   → **babar-se** vp -**1.** [deitar baba em si] to dribble. -**2.** fig [gostar muito de]: ∼-se por to drool over.
babosa [ba'bɔsal f aloe.
baboseira [babo'zejral f [tolice, bobagem] nonsense.
baby-sitter [,bejbi'site(x)] (pl baby-sitters) mf baby-sitter.
bacalhau [baka'ʎawl m cod.
bacalhoada [bakaʎo'adal f a dish made with salt cod boiled with potatoes, cabbage, whole onions and other vegetables, mixed with hardboiled eggs and olives and seasoned with vinegar and olive oil.
bacana [ba'kãnal <> adj cool. <> mf fam [pessoa] toff.
bacanal [baka'nawl (pl -ais) f bacchanal.
BACEN (abrev de Banco Central do Brasil) m central bank of Brazil.
bacharel [baʃa'rɛwl (pl -éis) mf: ∼ em Artes/Direito/Economia Arts/Law/Economics graduate.
bacharelado [baʃare'ladul m -**1.** [grau] degree. -**2.** [curso] undergraduate course.
bacharelar-se [4] [baʃare'laxsil vp: ∼ (em algo) to obtain a degree (in sthg).
bacia [ba'sial f -**1.** [ger] basin. -**2.** [sanitária] lavatory. -**3.** ANAT pelvis.
bacilo [ba'silul m bacillus.

➡ **bacilos** *mpl* bacilli.
backbone [bak'bonil (*pl* **backbones**) *m* backbone.
background [bɛk'grawndʒil (*pl* **-s**) *m* background.
backup [bɛ'kapil (*pl* **-s**) *m* backup.
baço, ça ['basu, 'sal ◇ *adj* **-1.** [pele] dull. **-2.** [metal] tarnished. ◇ *m* ANAT spleen.
bacon ['bejkõl *m* bacon.
bactéria [bak'tɛrjal *f* bacterium.
➡ **bactérias** *fpl* bacteria.
badalação [badala'sãwl (*pl* **-ões**) *f* *fam* [movimento, diversão] movement.
badalado, da [bada'ladu, dal *fam* *adj* **-1.** [movimentado, divertido] swinging. **-2.** [famoso, falado] much talked about.
➡ **badalada** *f* [de sino] peal.
badalar [4] [bada'la(x)] ◇ *vt* [tocar] to ring. ◇ *vi* **-1.** [tocar] to peal. **-2.** *fam* [sair, divertir-se] to go out and enjoy o.s.
badalo [ba'dalul *m* **-1.** [de sino] peal. **-2.** *fam* [diversão] fun.
badejo [ba'deʒul *m* serran.
baderna [ba'dɛxnal *f* **-1.** [bagunça] mess. **-2.** [tumulto] revelry.
badulaque [badu'lakil *m* trinket.
➡ **badulaques** *mpl* odds and ends.
bafafá [bafa'fal *m* *fam* [tumulto] hoo-ha.
bafo ['baful *m* breath; **~-de-onça** *fam* bad breath.
bafômetro [ba'fometrul *m* breathalyzer.
baforada [bafo'radal *f* [fumaça] blast.
bagaço [ba'gasul *m* [de fruta] remains of fruit (*once juice has been extracted*); **estar/ficar um ~** *fig* to be drained, to be exhausted.
bagageiro [baga'ʒejrul *m* AUTO luggage rack.
bagagem [ba'gaʒẽl (*pl* **-ns**) *f* **-1.** [equipagem] luggage. **-2.** *fig* [conhecimentos, experiência] experience.
bagatela [baga'tɛlal *f* *fig* [ninharia] next to nothing.
Bagdá [bag'dal *n* Baghdad.
bago ['bagul *m* **-1.** [fruto] berry. **-2.** [uva] grape. **-3.** [de chumbo] shot. **-4.** *vulg* [testículo] ball.
baguete [ba'gɛtʃil *f* baguette.
bagulho [ba'guʎul *m* **-1.** [objeto] trinket. **-2.** *fig* & *pej* [pessoa]: **ser um ~** to be ugly.
bagunça [ba'gũnsal *f* mess.
bagunçado, da [bagũn'sadu, dal *adj* cluttered.
bagunçar [bagũn'sa(x)l, *vt* **-1.** [fazer confusão em] to clutter. **-2.** *fig* [atrapalhar, tumultuar] to upset.
bagunceiro, ra [bagũn'sejru, ral *adj* [pessoa - desordeiro] disorderly; [- relaxado] untidy.
Bahamas [ba'amaʃl *npl*: **as** ~ the Bahamas.
Bahia [ba'ial *n* Bahia.

BAHIA

Important state in north-east Brazil; Bahia was the main centre for the slave trade during colonial times. Founded in 1549, the city of Salvador was the capital of Brazil until the mid-eighteenth century. The decisive contribution of the Negroes endowed Bahia with an immense cultural wealth, as much in its many syncretic cults and African-inspired rhythms, as in the fundamental influence of Bahians in Brazilian art, from literature to popular music. Salvador is now one of the main tourist centres of the country, famous mainly for its churches and its carnival.

baia ['bajal *f* stall.
baía [ba'ial *f* bay.
baiana [ba'jãnal *f*: **rodar a** ~ to make a fuss.
baiano, na [baj'ãnu, nal ◇ *adj* Bahian. ◇ *m, f* Bahian.
baião [baj'ãwl (*pl* **-ões**) *m* [ritmo, dança] baião, *popular music from north-eastern Brazil*.
baila ['bajlal *f*: **trazer à** ~ to raise (the issue); **vir à** ~ to come to light.
bailado [baj'ladul *m* dance.
bailar [4] [baj'la(x)] *vt* & *vi* to dance.
bailarino, na [bajla'rinu, nal *m, f* dancer.
baile ['bajlil *m* ball; ~ **de carnaval** carnival ball; ~ **à fantasia** fancy-dress party; ~ **funk** funk party; **dar um** ~ **em** *fig* [superar] to crush.
bainha [ba'iɲal *f* **-1.** [de arma] sheath. **-2.** COST hem.
baioneta [bajo'netal *f* bayonet; ~ **calada** bayoneted rifle.
bairrista [baj'xiʃtal ◇ *adj* **-1.** [que defende interesse do bairro] community-based. **-2.** [muito patriota] regionalistic. ◇ *mf* **-1.** [do local] local. **-2.** [patriota] regionalist.
bairro ['bajxul *m* neighbourhood.
baita ['bajtal *adj* (*antes de subst*) **-1.** [soco, sucesso] tremendous. **-2.** [gripe, resfriado] terrible. **-3.** [abraço] huge.
baixa ['bajʃal *adj* ➪ **baixo**.
baixada [baj'ʃadal *f* GEOGR valley.
baixa-mar [ˌbajʃa'ma(x)l (*pl* **baixa-mares**) *f* low tide.
baixar [4] [baj'ʃa(x)l *vt* COMPUT [fazer download]: ~ **um arquivo** to download a file.
baixaria [bajʃa'rial *f* **-1.** [ger] depravity. **-2.** [escândalo] disgrace.
baixela [baj'ʃɛlal *f* dinner service.
baixeza [baj'ʃezal *f* low-mindedness.
baixio [baj'ʃiul *m* sandbank.
baixista [baj'ʃiʃtal *mf* bass player.
baixo, xa ['bajʃu, ʃal *adj* **-1.** [ger] low. **-2.** [pessoa] short. **-3.** [cabeça, olhar] lowered. **-4.** [bairro, cidade] lower. **-5.** [metal] base. **-6.** (*antes de subst*) [rio] downriver. **-7.** (*antes de subst*) [época] late. **-8.** (*antes de subst*) [vil, grosseiro] base; ~ **nível** *fam* [baixaria] disgrace; **palavrão de** ~ **nível** swear word.
➡ **baixo** ◇ *m* **-1.** [MÚS - instrumento] bass; [- cantor] bass player. **-2.** *fam* [bairro] lower town. ◇ *adv* **-1.** [a pouca altura] low. **-2.** *fig* [em posição inferior]: **estar/ficar por** ~ to be/become disheartened. **-3.** [falar] softly.
➡ **baixa** *f* **-1.** [ger] drop; **em baixa** falling. **-2.** [de serviço] sick-leave; **dar** *ou* **ter baixa (de)** to go on *ou* take sick-leave (from). **-3.** MIL loss.
➡ **para baixo** *loc adv* downwards.
➡ **por baixo (de)** *loc adv* underneath.

baixo-astral [ˌbajʃwaʃ'trawl] *m fam* glumness; **estar/ficar de** ~ to be/become glum.

baixote, ta [baj'ʃɔtʃi, ta] <> *adj* shortish. <> *m, f* shortish person.

bajulação [baʒula'sãw] (*pl* -ões) *f* adulation.

bajulador, ra [baʒula'do(x), ra] <> *adj* adulatory. <> *m, f* adulator.

bajular [4] [baʒu'la(x)] *vt* to adulate.

bala ['bala] *f* -**1.** [munição] bullet; ~ **de festim** blank cartridge. -**2.** [doce] boiled sweet. -**3.** *loc*: **estar/ficar uma** ~ *fam* to be/go ballistic.

balada [ba'lada] *f* ballad.

balaio [ba'laju] *m* basket.

balança [ba'lãnsa] *f* scales (*pl*); ~ **comercial** balance of trade.

➤ **Balança** *f ASTRO* Libra.

balançar [13] [balãn'sa(x)] <> *vt* -**1.** [fazer oscilar - bebê, navio] to rock; [- quadril] to wiggle; [- galho, carro, avião] to shake. -**2.** [compensar] to counterbalance. <> *vi* -**1.** [oscilar] to shake. -**2.** [em balanço, cadeira] to rock.

➤ **balançar-se** *vp* [sacudir-se] to sway.

balancear [15] [balãn'sja(x)] *vt* -**1.** *AUTO* to balance (*wheels*). -**2.** [compensar] to counterbalance.

balancete [balãn'setʃi] *m COM* balance.

balanço [ba'lãnsu] *m* -**1.** [de criança] swing. -**2.** [ação] swinging. -**3.** *ECON* : ~ **de pagamentos** balance of payments.

balangandã [balãngãn'dã] *m* amulet.

balão [ba'lãw] (*pl* -ões) *m* -**1.** [dirigível] airship. -**2.** [de brinquedo] balloon; **soltar um** ~ to release a balloon. -**3.** [sonda] probe; ~ **meteorológico** metereological balloon. -**4.** [tanque]: ~ **de oxigênio** oxygen cylinder. -**5.** [em estrada etc] *place for doing U-turns*. -**6.** [em história em quadrinhos] bubble.

balão-de-ensaio [baˌlãwdʒĩn'saju] (*pl* balões-de-ensaio) *m* -**1.** [instrumento] pilot balloon. -**2.** *fig* [boato]: **soltar um** ~ to spread a rumour.

balão-sonda [baˌlãw'sõnda] (*pl* balões-sondas) *m* pilot balloon.

balaustrada [balawʃ'trada] *f* balustrade.

balaústre [bala'uʃtri] *m* baluster.

balbuciar [16] [bawbu'sja(x)] <> *vt* to stammer. <> *vi* to babble.

balbúrdia [baw'buxdʒja] *f* hustle and bustle.

balcão [baw'kãw] (*pl* -ões) *m* -**1.** [sacada] balcony. -**2.** [de loja] counter. -**3.** *DE TEATRO* dress circle; ~ **nobre** balcony; ~ **simples** upper circle.

Balcãs ['bawkãʃ] *npl*: **os** ~ the Balkans.

balcânico, ca [baw'kãniku, ka] <> *adj* Balkan. <> *m, f* Balkan.

balconista [bawko'niʃta] *mf* shop assistant.

balde ['bawdʒi] *m* bucket.

baldeação [bawdʒja'sãw] (*pl* -ões) *f* transfer; **fazer** ~ to change.

baldio, dia [baw'dʒiu, dʒia] *adj* gone to wasteland.

balé [ba'lɛ] *m* ballet.

baleeira [bale'ejra] *f* whaler.

baleia [ba'leja] *f* -**1.** *ZOOL* whale. -**2.** *fam fig & pej*

[pessoa]: **ser uma** ~ to look like a beached whale.

baleiro, ra [ba'lejru, ra] <> *m, f* [vendedor] sweet seller. <> *m* [pote] sweet jar.

Bali ['bali] *n* Bali.

balido [ba'lidu] *m* bleating.

balística [ba'liʃtʃika] *f* ballistics *(sg)*.

baliza [ba'liza] *f* -**1.** [estaca] goalpost. -**2.** [bóia] buoy. -**3.** [luminosa] beacon. -**4.** *ESP* goal.

balizamento [baliza'mẽntu] *m* beaconing, signposting.

balneário [baw'njarju] *m* baths (*pl*).

balões [ba'lõjʃ] *pl* ➤ **balão**.

balofo, fa [ba'lofu, fa] <> *adj* puffy. <> *m, f* puffed-up person.

balsa ['bawsa] *f* -**1.** [jangada] raft. -**2.** [barca] catamaran. -**3.** [salva-vidas] lifeboat.

bálsamo ['bawsamu] *m* balsam.

Báltico ['bawtʃiku] *n*: **o (mar)** ~ the Baltic (Sea).

baluarte [ba'lwaxtʃi] *m* stronghold.

balzaquiana [bawza'kjana] *f* *woman in her late twenties or early thirties*.

bamba ['bãnba] *fam* <> *adj* [perito] expert. <> *mf* [perito] expert.

bambear [15] [bãn'bja(x)] <> *vt* [afrouxar] to loosen. <> *vi* -**1.** [tornar-se frouxo] to work itself loose. -**2.** *fig* [hesitar] to falter.

bambo, ba ['bãnbu, ba] *adj* -**1.** [corda, laço, parafuso] loose. -**2.** [perna] faltering.

bambolê [bãnbo'le] *m* hula hoop.

bamboleante [bãnbo'ljãntʃi] *adj* -**1.** [que balança] swaying. -**2.** [sem firmeza - parafuso, cordo] loose; [- estaca] wobbly.

bambolear [15] [bãnbo'lja(x)] <> *vt* [balançar] to sway. <> *vi* to sway.

bambu [bãn'bu] *m* -**1.** [planta] bamboo. -**2.** [vara] bamboo-stick.

bambuzal [bãnbu'zawl] (*pl* -ais) *m* bamboo thicket.

banal [ba'nawl] (*pl* -ais) *adj* mundane.

banalidade [banali'dadʒi] *f* simplicity.

banalizar [4] [banali'za(x)] *vt* to make commonplace.

banana [ba'nãna] <> *f* [fruta] banana; **dar uma** ~ **(para alguém)** *vulg fig* to say 'up yours!' (to sb). <> *mf fam fig & pej* [bobo, idiota] fool.

bananada [bana'nada] *f* banana sweetmeat.

bananal [bana'nawl] (*pl* -ais) *m* banana plantation.

bananeira [bana'nejra] *f* banana tree; **plantar** ~ *fig* to do a handstand.

banca ['bãnka] *f* -**1.** [de jogo] game of chance. -**2.** [estande]: ~ **(de jornal)** newspaper stand. -**3.** [comissão]: ~ **(examinadora)** (examination) board. -**4.** [escritório] desk. -**5.** [mesa de trabalho] worktop; **botar** ~ to boss about.

bancada [bãŋ'kada] *f* -**1.** [banco] bench. -**2.** [*POL* - de partido] bench; [- de estado] representatives (*pl*). -**3.** [mesa de trabalho] workbench.

bancar [12] [bãŋ'ka(x)] *vt* -**1.** [financiar] to back. -**2.** [comportar-se como] to play.

bancário, ria [bãŋ'karju, rja] ◇ *adj* bank. ◇ *m, f* [empregado] bank employee.

bancarrota [bãŋka'xota] *f* bankruptcy; **ir à** ~ to go bankrupt.

banco ['bãŋku] *m* -**1.** [ger] bank; ~ **24 horas** 24-hour bank; ~ **de sangue** blood bank. -**2.** [assento] bench; ~ **dos réus** prisoners' dock. -**3.** *COMPUT* : ~ **de dados** databank. -**4.** *GEOL* : ~ **de areia** sandbank.

banda ['bãnda] *f*: *COMPUT* ~ **larga** broadband.

bandagem [bãda'ʒẽ] (*pl* -**ns**) *f* bandage.

Band-aid® [bãn'dejdʒ] *m* Band-Aid®.

bandalheira [bãnda'ʎejra] *f* roguery.

bandear-se [15] [bãn'dʒjaxsi] *vp*: ~ **para** *ou* **a** to side with.

bandeira [bãn'dejra, ra] *f* -**1.** [ger] flag; ~ **branca** white flag; ~ **a meio pau** flag at half-mast; **jurar a** ~ to swear to the flag; ~ **dois** taxi night-rate. -**2.** [estandarte] standard. -**3.** [de porta] fanlight. -**4.** *loc*: **dar** ~ **de que** to let it be known that.

bandeirante [bãndej'rãntʃi] ◇ *m* [explorador] expedition member. ◇ *f* [moça] Girl Guide.

bandeirinha [bãn'dejriɲa] *m ESP* linesman.

bandeirola [bãndej'rɔla] *f* banderole.

bandeja [bãn'deʒa] *f* tray; **dar de** ~ to proffer.

bandejão [bãnde'ʒãw] (*pl* -**ões**) *m* [*UNIV* - refeição] meal on a tray; [- refeitório] canteen.

bandido, da [bãn'dʒidu, da] ◇ *m, f* -**1.** [marginal] bandit. -**2.** [mau-caráter] rogue. ◇ *adj fam fig* [malvado, ruim] cruel.

banditismo [bãdʒi'tʃiʒmu] *m* banditry.

bando ['bãndu] *m* -**1.** [de pessoas, animais] flock; **em** ~ in flocks. -**2.** [quadrilha] gang. -**3.** [facção] group. -**4.** [monte] stack.

bandô [bãn'do] *m* pelmet.

bandoleiro, ra [bãndo'lejru, ra] *m, f* bandit.

bandolim [bãndo'lĩ] (*pl* -**ns**) *m* mandolin.

bandolinista [bãndoli'niʃta] *mf* mandolin player.

bangalô [bãŋga'lo] *m* bungalow.

Bangkok [bãŋ'kɔk] *n* Bangkok.

bangue-bangue [bãŋgi'bãŋgi] *m*: **(filme de)** ~ Western (movie).

banguela [bãŋ'gɛla] *adj* toothless.

banha ['bãɲa] *f* -**1.** [no homem] fat. -**2.** [de porco] lard.

banhar [4] [bã'ɲa(x)] *vt* -**1.** [dar banho em] to bathe. -**2.** [mergulhar]: ~ **algo (em)** to dip sthg (into). -**3.** [molhar]: ~ **algo (com/em)** to bathe sthg (with/in). -**4.** [rio, mar] to wash.

➡ **banhar-se** *vp* -**1.** [tomar banho] to bathe. -**2.** [molhar-se]: ~-**se em algo** to become bathed in sthg.

banheira [bã'ɲejra] *f* -**1.** [para banho] bathtub. -**2.** *fam fig* [carro] charabanc.

banheiro [bã'ɲejru] *m* toilet; ~ **feminino/masculino** ladies'/men's toilet.

banhista [bã'ɲiʃta] *mf* bather.

banho ['bãɲu] *m* -**1.** [ger] immersion; **tomar um** ~ **de algo** to immerse o.s. in sthg. -**2.** [de entusiasmo] wave. -**3.** [para asseio]: ~ **(de chuveiro)** shower;

tomar ~ to have a shower; **tomar** ~ **(de banheira)** to take a bath; ~ **de assento** hip bath; ~ **de espuma** foam bath. -**4.** [na praia, em clube etc]: **tomar um** ~ **de mar/piscina** to swim in the sea/pool; **tomar um** ~ **de sol** to sunbathe. -**5.** *fam fig* [surra]: **dar um** ~ **em alguém** to wipe sb out. -**6.** *loc*: **dar um** ~ **de algo em alguém** [derramar] to drench sb in sthg; **vai tomar** ~! *fam* get away!

banho-maria [ˌbãɲuma'ria] (*pl* **banhos-marias**, **banhos-maria**) *m CULIN* double boiler, bain-marie.

banimento [bani'mẽtu] *m* banishment.

banir [79] [ba'ni(x)] *vt* to banish.

banjo ['bãʒu] *m* banjo.

banner ['banex] (*pl* **banners**) *m COMPUT* banner.

banqueiro, ra [bãŋ'kejru, ra] *m, f* banker.

banqueta [bãŋ'keta] *f* banquette.

banquete [bãŋ'ketʃi] *m* banquet.

banquetear [15] [bãŋke'tʃja(x)] *vt* [festejar] to give a banquet in honour of.

➡ **banquetear-se** *vp* [participar de banquete] to treat o.s. to a wonderful meal.

baque ['baki] *m* -**1.** [choque] shock; **levar um** ~ to be given a shock; **ele levou um baque com a notícia** the news gave him a shock. -**2.** [ruído] thud. -**3.** [queda] fall.

baquear [15] [ba'kja(x)] *vi* -**1.** [cair] to fall. -**2.** *fig* [abalar-se] to be shaken.

bar [ba(x)] (*pl* -**es**) *m* bar.

baralho [ba'raʎu] *m* pack.

barão [ba'rãw] (*pl* -**ões**) *m, f* baron.

barata [ba'rata] *f* cockroach; **estar entregue às** ~**s** [pessoa] to let o.s. go; [projeto, construção] to fall into a state of neglect.

baratear [15] [bara'tʃja(x)] *vt* to mark down.

barateiro, ra [bara'tejru, ra] *adj* cut-price.

baratinado, da [baratʃi'nadu, da] *adj* -**1.** [sobrecarregado, apressado] stressed. -**2.** [transtornado - pessoa] upset; [- idéia, atitude] disturbed.

baratinar [4] [baratʃi'na(x)] *vt* -**1.** [atrapalhar, assoberbar] to stress. -**2.** [transtornar] to upset.

barato, ta [ba'ratu, ta] ◇ *adj* -**1.** [produto, serviço, preço] cheap. -**2.** [barateiro] cut-price. -**3.** *fam* [ordinário] common or garden. ◇ *adv* [cobrar etc] cheaply. ◇ *m* -**1.** *gír droga* high. -**2.** *fam* [legal]: **que** ~! how cool!; **ser um** ~ to be cool.

barba ['baxba] *f* -**1.** [de homem] beard; **fazer a** ~ to shave; **fazer algo nas** ~**s de alguém** *fig* to do sthg under sb's nose; **pôr as** ~**s de molho** *fig* to lie low. -**2.** [de animal] whiskers.

barbada [bax'bada] *f* -**1.** *fam* [facilidade]: **ser uma** ~ to be a piece of cake. -**2.** *gír turfe* [palpite] dead cert.

barbado, da [bax'badu, da] *adj* bearded.

Barbados [bax'baduʃ] *n* Barbados.

barbante [bax'bãntʃi] *m* string.

barbaramente [baxbara'mẽtʃi] *adv* -**1.** [cruelmente] brutally. -**2.** [demasiadamente] atrociously.

barbaridade [baxbari'dadʒi] *f* -**1.** [crueldade] barbarity. -**2.** [expressando espanto]: **que** ~! great! -**3.** [tolice] absurdity.

barbárie [bax'barje] *f* barbarity.

barbarismo [baxba'riʒmu] *m* barbarism.

bárbaro, ra [ˈbaxbaru, ra] *adj* **-1.** [terrível] barbaric. **-2.** [ótimo] great.

barbatana [baxba'tãna] *f* fin.

barbeador [barbja'do(x)] (*pl* -es) *m* razor.

barbear [15] [bax'bja(x)] *vt* to shave.

➡ **barbear-se** *vp* to shave.

barbearia [baxbja'ria] *f* barbershop.

barbeiragem [baxbej'raʒẽ] *f* *fam* [no trânsito] bad driving; **fazer uma** ~ to drive badly.

barbeiro, ra [bax'bejru, ra] <> *adj fam* [motorista] careless. <> *m* **-1.** [quem corta cabelos, barba] barber. **-2.** [barbearia] barbershop. **-3.** [inseto] kissing bug.

barbicha [bax'biʃa] *fam* <> *f* [cavanhaque] goatee. <> *m* [pessoa de cavanhaque] man with a goatee.

barbitúrico [baxbi'turiku] *m* barbiturate.

barbudo, da [bax'budu, da] <> *adj* bearded. <> *m* bearded man.

barca [ˈbaxka] *f* ship.

barcaça [bax'kasa] *f* barge.

barco [ˈbaxku] *m* boat; ~ **a motor** motor boat; ~ **a remo** rowing boat; ~ **a vela** sailing boat; **deixar o** ~ **correr** *fig* to let matters run their course; **estar no mesmo** ~ *fig* to be in the same boat; **tocar o** ~ **para frente** *fig* to carry on with one's life.

barganha [bax'gãɲa] *f* bargain.

barganhar [4] [baxgã'ɲa(x)] *vt & vi* to bargain.

barítono, na [ba'ritonu, na] <> *adj* baritone. <> *m* baritone.

barlavento [baxla'vẽntu] *m NÁUT* windward; **a** ~ to windward.

barman [ˈbaxmɛ] (*pl* -s) *m* barman.

barões [ba'rõjʃ] *pl* ➡ **barão**.

barômetro [ba'rometru] *m* barometer.

baronesa [baro'neza] *f* ➡ **barão**.

barqueiro, ra [bax'kejru, ra] *m*, *f* boatman.

barra [ˈbaxa] *f* **-1.** [ger] bar; ~ **de chocolate** chocolate bar; ~**s paralelas** parallel bars. **-2.** [de metal] ingot; ~ **de direção** tiller. **-3.** [de madeira] pole. **-4.** [de balé] barre. **-5.** [traço] score. **-6.** [acabamento] trimming. **-7.** [faixa] strip. **-8.** *GEOGR* sandbar. **-9.** *loc*: **agüentar a** ~ *fam* to stick it out; **forçar a** ~ to make things difficult; **ser uma** ~ *fam* [ser difícil] to be a pain.

barraca [ba'xaka] *f* **-1.** [ger] tent. **-2.** [em feira] stall. **-3.** [de madeira] hut.

barracão [baxa'kãw] (*pl* -ões) *m* **-1.** [telheiro] shed. **-2.** [habitação] big house.

barraco [ba'xaku] *m* shack.

barragem [ba'xaʒẽ] (*pl* -ns) *f* **-1.** [represa] dam. **-2.** [barreira] barrage.

barranco [ba'xãŋku] *m* **-1.** [ribanceira] ravine. **-2.** [escarpa] escarpment. **-3.** [precipício] precipice.

barra-pesada [ˌbaxape'zada] (*pl* barras-pesadas) *fam adj* **-1.** [violento] threatening. **-2.** [difícil] tough.

barrar [4] [ba'xa(x)] *vt* **-1.** [obstruir] to block. **-2.** [excluir] to bar.

barreira [ba'xejra] *f* **-1.** [escarpa] embankment. **-2.** *fig* [dificuldade] barrier. **-3.** [fronteira] roadblock. **-4.** *ESP* hurdle.

barrento, ta [ba'xẽntu, ta] *adj* clayey.

barrete [ba'xetʃi] *m* [gorro] (woolly) hat.

barrica [ba'xika] *f* barrel.

barricada [baxi'kada] *f* barricade.

barriga [ba'xiga] *f* **-1.** *ANAT* belly. **-2.** [saliência] bulge. **-3.** *loc*: **chorar de** ~ **cheia** to complain for no reason; **tirar a** ~ **da miséria** to get one's fill.

barrigudo, da [baxi'gudu, da] *adj* pot-bellied.

barril [ba'xiw] (*pl* -is) *m* cask.

barro [ˈbaxu] *m* clay.

barroco, ca [ba'xoku, ka] *adj* baroque.

barrote [ba'xɔtʃi] *m* beam.

barulheira [baru'ʎejra] *f* din.

barulhento, ta [baru'ʎẽntu, ta] *adj* noisy.

barulho [ba'ruʎu] *m* **-1.** [ruído] noise. **-2.** *fig* [confusão] fuss.

basco, ca [ˈbaʃku, ka] <> *adj* Basque. <> *m, f* Basque.

➡ **basco** *m* [língua] Basque.

basculante [baʃku'lãntʃi] *m* swivel window.

base [ˈbazi] *f* **-1.** [ger] base; ~ **monetária** monetary base. **-2.** [camada] base coat. **-3.** *fig* [fundamento] basis; **com** ~ **em** based on; **na** ~ **de** with the support of.

baseado, da [ba'zjadu, da] *adj* [fundamentado] based.

➡ **baseado** *m fam* [droga] spliff.

basear [15] [ba'zja(x)] *vt*: ~ **algo em algo** to base sthg on sthg.

➡ **basear-se** *vp*: ~**-se em algo** to base o.s. on sthg.

básico, ca [ˈbaziku, ka] *adj* basic.

basílica [ba'zilika] *f* basilica.

basquete [baʃ'kɛtʃi], **basquetebol** [baʃketʃi'bɔw] *m* basketball.

basta [ˈbaʃta] <> *m*: **dar um** ~ **em** to stop. <> *interj* that's enough!

bastante [baʃ'tãntʃi] <> *adj* **-1.** [suficiente] enough. **-2.** [numeroso] many. <> *adv* enough.

bastão [baʃ'tãw] (*pl* -ões) *m* stick.

bastar [4] [baʃ'ta(x)] *vi* [ser suficiente] to be enough.

➡ **bastar-se** *vp* [ser auto-suficiente]: ~**-se a si próprio** to be self-sufficient.

bastardo, da [baʃ'taxdu, da] *adj* bastard.

bastião [baʃtʃi'ãw] (*pl* -ões) *m* **-1.** [fortificação] bastion. **-2.** *fig* [sustentáculo] bastion.

bastidor [baʃtʃi'do(x)] *m* [moldura] frame.

➡ **bastidores** *mpl* **-1.** *TEATRO* wings. **-2.** [lado secreto] shadowy side.

bastões [baʃ'tõjʃ] *pl* ➡ **bastão**.

bata [ˈbata] *f* **-1.** [blusa] blouse. **-2.** [jaleco] white coat, overall.

batalha [ba'taʎa] *f* **-1.** [ger] battle. **-2.** *fig* [esforço] struggle.

batalhador, ra [bataʎa'do(x), ra] *adj* hardworking.

batalhão [bata'ʎãw] (pl -ões) m -1. MIL battallion. -2. [multidão] crowd.

batalhar [4] [bata'ʎa(x)] vi -1. [combater] to battle. -2. fig [lutar] to fight.

batata [ba'tata] f potato; ~ frita chips UK, fries US; ~ da perna calf (of the leg).

batata-doce [ba,tata'dosi] (pl batatas-doces) f sweet potato.

bate-boca [,batʃi'boka] (pl bate-bocas) m quarrel.

bate-bola [,batʃi'bɔla] (pl bate-bolas) m warm-up.

batedeira [bate'dejra] f -1. [para fazer bolos etc] whisk. -2. [para fazer manteiga] churn.

batedor [bate'do(x)] m -1. [polícia] escort. -2.: ~ de carteiras [ladrão] bag-snatcher.

batelada [bate'lada] f -1. [carregamento] boat-load. -2. fig [granda quantidade]: uma ~ de a large number of.

batente [ba'tẽntʃi] m -1. [ombreira] doorpost. -2. fam [trabalho] work; pegar firme no ~ to toil away.

bate-papo [,batʃi'papu] (pl bate-papos) m fam chat.

bater [5] [ba'te(x)] ◇ vt -1. [ger] to beat; ~ o pé to stamp one's foot. -2. [datilografar]: ~ algo (à máquina) to type sthg out. -3. [fechar com força] to slam. -4. [foto] to take. -5. [usar todo dia] to wear every day. -6. fam [furtar]: ~ carteira to pickpocket. ◇ vi -1. [dar pancadas]: ~ em alguém/algo to hit sb/sthg. -2. [colidir]: ~ em algo to collide with sthg. -3. [horas, sino] to strike. -4. [coração] to beat. -5. loc: não ~ bem fam [ser meio doido] to be off one's rocker.
➤ **bater-se** vp: ~-se por to fight for.

bateria [bate'ria] f -1. [de cozinha] set of kitchen utensils. -2. [MÚS - instrumentos de percussão] percussion; [- conjunto de pratos, caixa e bombo] drum kit. -3. ELETR battery.

baterista [bate'riʃta] mf [MÚS - percussionista] percussionist; [- que toca bateria] drummer.

batido, da [ba'tʃidu, da] ◇ adj -1. [ger] beaten. -2. [comum demais] worn out. ◇ adv [às pressas] in a hurry.
➤ **batida** f -1. [ger] beat. -2. [de relógio, sino] strike. -3. [à porta] knock. -4. AUTO collision. -5. [bebida] crush.

batina [ba'tʃina] f RELIG cassock.

batismal [batʃiʒ'maw] (pl -ais) adj baptismal.

batismo [ba'tʃiʒmu] m baptism.

batistério [batʃiʃ'tɛrju] m baptistery.

batizado, da [batʃi'zadu, da] ◇ adj baptized. ◇ m baptism.

batizar [4] [batʃi'za(x)] vt -1. [ger] to baptize. -2. [apelidar] to nickname.

batom [ba'tõ] (pl -ns) m lipstick.

batucada [batu'kada] f street gathering for samba music and expression.

batucar [12] [batu'ka(x)] vi -1. MÚS to dance and sing the batuque. -2. [martelar] to hammer.

batuque [ba'tuki] m Afro-Brazilian dance.

batuta [ba'tuta] ◇ f [de maestro] baton. ◇ adj

fam [exímio]: ser ~ em algo to be a maestro in sthg.

baú [ba'u] m trunk.

baunilha [baw'niʎa] f vanilla.

bazar [ba'za(x)] (pl -es) m -1. [ger] bazaar. -2. [loja] bazaar.

bazuca [ba'zuka] f bazooka.

BB (abrev de Banco do Brasil) m Brazilian state-owned bank.

BC (abrev de Banco Central do Brasil) m central bank of Brazil.

bê-á-bá [bea'ba] m -1. [abecedário] alphabet. -2. fig [noções básicas] ABC.

beatitude [beatʃi'tudʒi] f beatitude.

beato, ta [be'atu, ta] ◇ adj -1. [beatificado] blessed. -2. [fanático religioso] churchy. ◇ m -1. [quem foi beatificado] beatified person. -2. [devoto] worshipper.

bêbado, da ['bebadu, da] ◇ adj drunk. ◇ m, f -1. [que bebe regularmente] drunkard. -2. [que bebeu demais] drunk.

bebê [be'be] m baby.

bebedeira [bebe'dejra] f -1. [estado do bêbado] drunkenness; tomar uma ~ to get drunk. -2. [ato de se embebedar] drinking bout.

bêbedo ['bebedu] adj ⊳ bêbado.

bebedouro [bebe'doru] m -1. [aparelho] drinking fountain. -2. [para animais] drinking trough.

beber [5] [be'be(x)] ◇ vt -1. [tomar líquido] to drink. -2. [absorver] to soak up. ◇ vi -1. [tomar bebida alcoólica] to have a drink. -2. [embriagar-se] to get drunk.

bebericar [12] [beberi'ka(x)] ◇ vt [beber degustando] to sip. ◇ vi [beber pouco] to sip.

beberrão, rrona [bebe'xãw, xona] ◇ adj [que bebe muito] heavy drinking. ◇ m [ébrio] heavy drinker.

bebida [be'bida] f -1. [líquido potável] drink. -2. [alcoólica] (alcoholic) drink.

bebível [be'bivew] (pl -eis) adj [tolerável] drinkable.

beca ['bɛka] f -1. [toga] robe. -2. fig [magistratura] magistrature.

beça ['bɛsa] f: à ~ [em grande quantidade] in large numbers; [ao extremo] gostei à ~ da nova revista I enjoyed the new magazine very much.

beco ['bɛku] m alley; estar num ~ sem saída to be in a catch-22 situation.

bedelho [be'deʎu] m latch; meter o ~ em [intrometer-se] to stick one's oar in.

beduíno, na [be'dwinu, na] ◇ adj Bedouin. ◇ m, f Bedouin.

bege ['bɛʒi] ◇ adj inv beige. ◇ m beige.

begônia [be'gonja] f begonia.

beiço ['bejsu] m lip.

beiçudo, da [bej'sudu, da] adj pouting.

beija-flor [,bejʒa'flo(x)] (pl beija-flores) m hummingbird.

beijar [4] [bej'ʒa(x)] vt to kiss.
➤ **beijar-se** vp to kiss.

beijo ['bejʒu] m kiss; dar um ~ em alguém to give sb a kiss.

beijoca [bej'ʒɔka] *f fam* smackeroo.

beira ['bejra] *f* edge; **à ~ de** [na borda] on the edge of; *fig* on the brink of.

beirada [bej'rada] *f* -1. [beira] side. -2. [bocado] slither.

beira-mar [ˌbejra'ma(x)] *f*: **à ~** by the sea.

beirar [4] [bej'ra(x)] *vt* -1. [caminhar à beira de] to walk alongside. -2. [estar à beira de] to be on the edge of. -3. [estar próximo de] to be close to.

Beirute [bej'rutʃi] *n* Beirut.

beisebol [bejze'bɔw] *m* baseball.

belas-artes [ˌbɛla'zaxtʃiʃ] *fpl* fine arts.

beldade [bew'dadʒi] *f* -1. [beleza] beauty. -2. [mulher bonita] beautiful woman.

beleléu [bele'lɛw] *loc adv fam*: **ir para o ~** [morrer] to die; [desaparecer] to disappear; [fracassar] to fail.

Belém [be'lẽj] *n* -1. [no Brasil] Belém. -2. [na Palestina] Bethlehem.

beleza [be'leza] *f* -1. [de lugar etc] beauty. -2. [mulher bela] beautiful woman; **ser uma ~** [pessoa, lugar] to be beautiful.

belga ['bɛwga] <> *adj* Belgian. <> *m, f* Belgian.

Bélgica ['bɛwʒika] *n* Belgium.

Belgrado [bew'gradu] *n* Belgrade.

beliche [be'liʃi] *m* bunk bed.

bélico, ca ['bɛliku, ka] *adj* war *(antes de subst)*.

belicoso, cosa [beli'kozu, kɔza] *adj* -1. [aguerrido] quarrelsome. -2. [pronto para a guerra] bellicose. -3. [que incita à guerra] war-mongering.

beligerante [beliʒe'rãntʃi] *adj* belligerent.

beliscão [beliʃ'kãw] *(pl* -ões) *m* pinch; **dar um ~ alguém** to pinch sb.

beliscar [12] [beliʃ'ka(x)] <> *vt* -1. [pessoa] to pinch. -2. *fig* [comida] to pick at *(food)*. <> *vi fig* [comer] to pick at one's food.

beliscões [beliʃ'kõjʃ] *pl* ⊳ **beliscão**.

Belize [be'lizi] *n* Belize.

belo, la ['bɛlu, la] <> *adj* -1. [perfeito] lovely. -2. [sublime] wonderful. -3. *(antes de subst)* [considerável] fine. -4. *(antes de subst)* [gratificante] excellent. -5. [indefinido]: **um ~ dia ...** one fine day ... <> *m* [estética] beauty.

Belo Horizonte [ˌbɛlori'zõntʃi] *n* Belo Horizonte.

bel-prazer [ˌbɛwpra'ze(x)] *m*: **ao seu ~** to one's heart's content.

beltrano [bew'trãnu] *m* so-and-so.

bem ['bẽj] <> *adv* -1. [ger] well. -2. [muito, bastante] very. -3. [exatamente] exactly; **~ ali** right there. -4. [de bom grado]: **~ que eu gostaria de ajudar, mas não posso** I'd very much like to help, but I can't. -5. [expressando opinião]: **estar ~** [de saúde] to be well; [de aspecto] to look good; [financeiramente] to be well-off; **cair ~** [comida] to go down well; **fazer ~ a alguém** [suj: exercício etc] to be good for sb; **ficar** *ou* **cair ~** [atitude] to be suitable; **ficar ~ em alguém** [roupa] to suit sb well. -6. [saudando]: **tudo ~?** *fam* how are you?; **tudo ~** [em resposta] fine. -7. [concordando]: **tá ~** all right. -8. [em conclusão, introdução] well now. -9. [em congratulação]: **muito ~!** well done! <> *m* -1. [ger] good. -2. [pessoa amada] loved one. -3. *fam* [forma de tratamento]: **meu ~** my darling. -4. [patrimônio] assets *(pl)*.

➡ **bens** *mpl* -1. [patrimônio] assets. -2. [produtos]: **~ de consumo** consumer goods.

➡ **bem como** *loc adv* as well as.

➡ **nem bem** *loc adv* scarcely.

➡ **se bem que** *loc conj* even though.

bem-acabado, da [bẽjaka'badu, da] *(mpl* -s, *fpl* -s) *adj* well-finished.

bem-agradecido, da [bẽjagrade'sidu, da] *(mpl* -s, *fpl* -s) *adj* grateful.

bem-apessoado, da [bẽjape'swadu, da] *(mpl* -s, *fpl* -s) *adj* presentable.

bem-arrumado, da [bẽjaxu'madu, da] *(mpl* -s, *fpl* -s) *adj* -1. [pessoa] well dressed. -2. [casa] well appointed.

bem-casado, da [bẽjka'zadu, da] *(mpl* -s, *fpl* -s) *adj* happily married.

bem-comportado, da [bẽjkõnpox'tadu, da] *(mpl* -s [-ʃ], *fpl* -s [-ʃ]) *adj* well behaved.

bem-conceituado, da [bẽjkõnsej'twadu, da] *(mpl* -s [-ʃ], *fpl* -s [-ʃ]) *adj* well respected.

bem-disposto, ta [bẽjdʒiʃ'poʃtu, ta] *adj* good-humoured.

bem-educado, da [bẽjedu'kadu, da] *(mpl* -s, *fpl* -s) *adj* well bred.

bem-estar [bẽjʃ'ta(x)] *m* well-being.

bem-feito, ta [bẽj'fejtu, ta] *(mpl* -s, *fpl* -s) *adj* -1. [bem-acabado] well made. -2. [de belas formas] elegant. -3. [quando algo ruim ocorre]: **~ serves you right!**

bem-humorado, da [bẽjumo'radu, da] *(mpl* -s, *fpl* -s) *adj* good-humoured.

bem-intencionado, da [bẽjĩntẽnsjo'nadu, da] *(mpl* -s, *fpl* -s) *adj* well meaning.

bem-me-quer [bẽjmi'kɛ(x)] *m* daisy.

bem-nascido, da [bẽjna'sidu, da] *(mpl* -s, *fpl* -s) *adj* well born.

bem-passado, da [bẽjpa'sadu, da] *(mpl* -s, *fpl* -s) *adj* [carne] well cooked.

bem-sucedido, da [bẽjsuse'dʒidu, da] *(mpl* -s, *fpl* -s) *adj* successful.

bem-te-vi [bẽjtʃi'vi] *(pl* bem-te-vis) *m* great kiskadee.

bem-vindo, da [bẽj'vĩndu, da] *adj* welcome.

bem-visto, ta [bẽj'viʃtu, ta] *(mpl* -s, *fpl* -s) *adj* respected.

benchmarking [bɛnʃmarkiŋ] *m* ECON benchmarking.

benção [bẽnsãw] *(pl* -ções) *f* blessing.

bendito, ta [bẽn'dʒitu, ta] *adj* [abençoado] blessed.

bendizer [29] [bẽndʒi'ze(x)] *vt* -1. [falar bem de] to praise. -2. [abençoar] to bless.

beneficência [benefi'sẽnsja] *f* -1. [bondade] kindness. -2. [caridade] charity.

beneficente [benefi'sẽntʃi] *adj* -1. [bondoso] kind. -2. [caridoso] charitable.

beneficiado, da [benefi'sjadu, da] <> *adj* [que se beneficiou] benefitting. <> *m* [beneficiário] beneficiary.

beneficiar [16] [benefi'sja(x)] *vt* **-1.** [favorecer] to benefit. **-2.** [processar] to process. **-3.** [melhorar] to improve.

➥ **beneficiar-se** *vp* [favorecer-se] to profit.

beneficiário, ria [benefi'sjarju, rja] <> *adj* favoured. <> *m* [herdeiro beneficiado] beneficiary.

benefício [bene'fisju] *m* benefit.

benéfico, ca [be'nɛfiku, ka] *adj* **-1.** [ger] beneficial. **-2.** [favorável] favourable.

benemérito, ta [bene'mɛritu, ta] <> *adj* **-1.** [que merece o bem] deserving. **-2.** [digno de honras] praiseworthy. **-3.** [ilustre] renowned. <> *m* worthy person.

beneplácito [bene'plasitu] *m* [aprovação] approval.

benevolência [benevo'lẽnsja] *f* **-1.** [boa-vontade] benevolence. **-2.** [complacência] friendliness. **-3.** [afeto] kindness.

benevolente [benevo'lẽntʃi] *adj* **-1.** [bondoso] kindly. **-2.** [complacente] friendly.

benévolo, la [benɛ'volu, la] *adj* **-1.** [benevolente] benevolent. **-2.** [tolerante] tolerant.

benfazejo, ja [bẽnfa'zeʒu, ʒal *adj* [benéfico] beneficial.

benfeitor, ra [bẽnfej'to(x), ra] <> *adj* [benévolo] benevolent. <> *m* [aquele que faz benfeitoria] benefactor.

benfeitoria [bẽnfejto'rial *f* **-1.** [obra de melhoria] improvement. **-2.** [benefício] benefit.

bengala [bẽŋ'galal *f* walking stick.

benigno, na [be'nignu, nal *adj* **-1.** [benévolo] gentle. **-2.** [complacente] friendly. **-3.** *MED* benign.

benjamim [bẽnʒa'mĩl (*pl* **-ns**) *m* ELETR adaptor.

benquisto, ta [bẽn'kiʃtu, tal *adj* **-1.** [querido] loved. **-2.** [bem-aceito] welcomed.

bens ['bẽjʃl *pl* ➪ **bem**.

bento, ta ['bẽntu, tal <> *pp* ➪ **benzer**. <> *adj* holy.

benzedeira [bẽnze'dejral *f* healer.

benzer [5] [bẽn'ze(x)] *vt* [abençoar] to bless.

➥ **benzer-se** *vp* [fazer o sinal-da-cruz] to make the sign of the cross.

benzina [bẽn'zinal *f* benzine.

berbere [bex'bɛril, **berber** [bex'bɛ(x)l <> *adj* Berber. <> *mf* Berber.

➥ **berbere** *m* [língua] Berber.

berçário [bex'sarjul *m* nursery.

berço ['bexsul *rm* **-1.** cradle. **-2.** *loc*: **nascer em** ~ **de ouro** to be born with a silver spoon in one's mouth.

Berlim [bex'lĩl *n* Berlin.

berimbau [berĩn'bawl *m* MÚS berimbau, *small Brazilian percussion instrument*.

berinjela [berĩn'ʒɛlal *f* aubergine *UK*, eggplant *US*.

berlinda [bex'lĩndal *f*: **estar na** ~ to be the butt of jokes.

berloque [bex'lɔkil *m* trinket.

bermuda [bex'mudal *f* Bermuda shorts (*pl*).

berrante [bex'ãntʃil *adj* gaudy.

barrar [4] [ba'xa(x)l *vt* to bar.

berreiro [be'xejrul *m* **-1.** [gritaria] shouting. **-2.** [choradeira] wailing.

berro ['bɛxul *m* bellow; **estar aos** ~**s** to be bellowing; **falar aos** ~**s** to talk too loud.

besouro [be'zorul *m* beetle.

besta ['beʃtal *fam* <> *adj* **-1.** [pedante] pedantic. **-2.** [idiota] idiotic; **fazer alguém de** ~ to make a fool of sb. **-3.** [surpreso]: **ficar** ~ to be dumbfounded. **-4.** [insignificante] insignificant. <> *f* **-1.** [animal] beast. **-2.** *fam* [pessoa pedante] pedant. **-3.** *fam* [pessoa idiota] fool.

bestalhão, lhona [beʃta'ʎãw, ʎonal (*mpl* **-lhões**, *fpl* **-s**) <> *adj* **-1.** [pateta] idiotic. **-2.** [ignorante] ignorant. <> *m* **-1.** [paspalhão] simpleton. **-2.** [ignorante] ignoramus.

bestial [beʃ'tjawl (*pl* **-ais**) *adj* **-1.** [brutal] bestial. **-2.** [repugnante] depraved.

bestialidade [beʃtʃjali'dadʒil *f* bestiality.

bestificar [12] [beʃtʃifi'ka(x)l *vt* **-1.** [bestializar] to bestialize. **-2.** [assombrar] to dumbfound. **-3.** [imbecilizar] to stupefy.

best-seller [ˌbɛʃt'sɛle(x)l (*pl* **-s**) *m* best-seller.

besuntar [4] [bezũn'ta(x)l *vt* **-1.** [untar]: ~ **de** *ou* **com** to grease with. **-2.** [lambuzar]: ~ **de** *ou* **com** to smear.

beterraba [bete'xabal *f* beetroot.

betoneira [beto'nejral *f* cement mixer.

betume [be'tumil *m* bitumen.

bexiga [be'ʃigal *f* ANAT bladder.

bezerro, rra [be'zexu, xal *m,f* calf; **pensar na morte da bezerra** to daydream.

bibelô [bibe'lol *m* [objeto decorativo] knick-knack.

bíblia ['bibljal *f* bible.

➥ **Bíblia** *f* Bible.

bíblico, ca ['bibliku, kal *adj* biblical.

bibliografia [bibljogra'fial *f* bibliography.

biblioteca [bibljo'tɛkal *f* library.

bibliotecário, ria [bibljote'karju, rjal *m, f* librarian.

biblioteconomia [bibljotekono'mial *f* librarianship.

biboca [bi'bɔkal *f* **-1.** [casebre] hut. **-2.** [venda] small shop.

bica ['bikal *f* water outlet; **suar em** ~**s** to be streaming with perspiration.

bicada [bi'kadal *f* peck.

bicama [bi'kãmal *f* sofa bed.

bicampeão, peã [bikãnpjãw, pjal (*mpl* **-peões**, *fpl* **-s**) <> *adj* twice champion. <> *m* twice champion.

bicar [12] [bi'ka(x)l *vt* **-1.** [dar bicadas] to peck. **-2.** [bebericar] to sip.

bicarbonato [bikaxbo'natul *m* bicarbonate.

bicentenário, ria [bisẽnte'narju, rjal <> *adj* bicentennial. <> *m* bicentenary.

bíceps ['bisepsl *m* (*inv*) biceps.

bicha ['biʃal *f* **-1.** [lombriga] earthworm. **-2.** *fam pej* [efeminado] fairy.

bichado, da [bi'ʃadu, dal *adj* worm-eaten.

bicheiro [bi'ʃejrul *m* [em jogo do bicho] bookie (*collecting money for illegal lottery bets*).

bicho ['biʃu] m -**1.** [animal] animal. -**2.** [inseto, piolho] insect. -**3.** fam [pessoa feia]: **ser um** ~ to be enough to scare one's own mother. -**4.** fam [sujeito] mate. -**5.** [loc]: **ver que** ~ **dá** to see what will come of it; **virar** ~ fig to turn nasty.

bicho-da-seda [ˌbiʃuda'sedal (pl **bichos-da-seda**) m silkworm.

bicho-de-sete-cabeças (pl **bichos-de-sete-cabeças**) fam m -**1.** [coisa difícil]: **ser um** ~ to be hideous; **fazer um** ~ **de algo** to make a mountain out of a molehill. -**2.** [coisa que amedronta]: **ser um** ~ to be a hideous thing.

bicho-do-mato [ˌbiʃudu'matu] (pl **bichos-do-mato**) m fig [pessoa] loner.

bicho-papão [ˌbiʃopa'pãw] (pl **bichos-papões**) m -**1.** [imagem] bogeyman. -**2.** fig [coisa ou pessoa que amedronta]: **o diretor é severo mas não é nenhum** ~ the manager is strict but he won't eat you; **a idéia do fim do mundo é um** ~ the idea of the end of the world is a terrifying prospect.

bicicleta [besi'klɛta] f bicycle; ~ **ergométrica** ergonometric bicycle; **andar de** ~ to ride a bike.

bicicletário [bisikle'tarju] m cycle rack.

bico ['biku] m -**1.** [de ave] beak. -**2.** [ponta] tip. -**3.** fam [boca] mouth; **abrir o** ~ to pipe up; **calar o** ~ to pipe down. -**4.** [chupeta] teat. -**5.** fam [biscate] odd job. -**6.** ANAT: ~ **do peito** nipple. -**7.** [de gás] burner.

bico-de-papagaio [ˌbikudʒipapa'gaju] (pl **bicos-de-papagaio**) m -**1.** [doença] osteophyte on the spinal column. -**2.** [nariz adunco] hooked nose.

bicolor [biko'lo(x)] adj bicoloured.

bicudo, da [bi'kudu, da] <> adj -**1.** [que tem bico] beaked. -**2.** [pontiagudo] pointed. -**3.** fam [difícil] painful. <> m [peixe] boulengerella.

BID (abrev de **Banco Interamericano de Desenvolvimento**) m IDB.

bidê [bi'de] m bidet.

bidimensional [bidʒimẽsjo'naw] (pl **-ais**) adj two-dimensional.

Bielo-Rússia [bjɛlo'xusja] n Belarus.

bielo-russo, sa, bielorusso, sa [bjɛlo'xusu, ˌsal <> adj Belorussian. <> m, f Belorussian.

bienal [bje'naw] (pl **-ais**) <> adj biennial. <> f biennial.

biênio ['bjenju] m two years.

bife ['bifi] m -**1.** CULIN steak; ~ **a cavalo** steak with a fried egg; ~ **à milanesa** steak milanese. -**2.** [pele humana]: **tirar um** ~ to nick one's skin.

bifocal [bifo'kaw] (pl **-ais**) adj bifocal.

bifurcado, da [bifux'kadu, da] adj forked.

bifurcar [12] [bifux'ka(x)] vi to fork.

➡ **bifurcar-se** vp to fork.

bigamia [biga'mia] f bigamy.

bígamo, ma ['bigamu, ma] <> adj bigamous. <> m, f bigamist.

bigode [bi'gɔdʒi] m moustache.

bigodudo, da [bigo'dudu, da] adj moustached.

bigorna [bi'gɔxna] f anvil.

bijuteria [biʒute'ria] f piece of jewellery.

bilateral [bilate'raw] (pl **-ais**) adj bilateral.

bilhão [bi'ʎãw] (pl **-ões**) num billion.

bilhar [bi'ʎa(x)] (pl **-es**) m -**1.** [jogo] billiards (sg). -**2.** [estabelecimento] billiard hall.

bilhete [bi'ʎetʃi] m -**1.** [ger] ticket; ~ **de ida** one-way ticket; ~ **de ida e volta** return ticket. -**2.** [mensagem] note; **dar o** ~ **azul** to sack; **receber o** ~ **azul** to be given the sack.

bilheteiro, ra [biʎe'tejru, ra] m, f ticket clerk.

bilheteria [biʎete'ria] f ticket office.

bilhões [bi'ʎõjʃ] pl ⊳ **bilhão**.

biliar [bili'a(x)] adj bilious; **vesícula** ~ gall bladder.

bilíngüe [bi'lĩgwi] adj bilingual.

bilionário, ria [biljo'narju, rja] <> adj billionaire. <> m, f billionaire.

bílis ['biliʃ] f (inv) bile.

bimensal [bimẽ'saw] (pl **-ais**) adj fortnightly, twice-monthly.

bimestral [bimeʃ'traw] (pl **-ais**) adj two-monthly.

bimestre [bi'meʃtri] m two-month period.

bimotor [bimo'to(x)] <> adj twin-engined. <> m twin-engined plane.

binário, ria [bi'narju, rja] adj binary.

bingo ['bĩgu] m bingo.

binóculo [bi'nɔkulu] m binoculars (pl).

binômio [bi'nomju] m MAT binomial.

biodegradável [bjwdegra'davew] (pl **-eis**) adj biodegradable.

biodiversidade [bjwdʒivexsi'dadʒi] f biodiversity.

BIODIVERSIDADE

Over 20% of the world's existing plants can be found in Brazil; the country's animal biodiversity is equally rich: Brazilian fauna includes not only 10% of all amphibians and mammals in the world, but also 17% of the planet's existing birds.

---

bioengenharia [biowẽʒeɲa'ria] f bioengineering.

biofísica [bjo'fizika] f biophysics (sg).

biografia [bjogra'fia] f biography.

biográfico, ca [bjo'grafiku, ka] adj biographical.

biógrafo, fa ['bjɔgrafu, fa] m, f biographer.

biologia [bjolo'ʒia] f biology.

biológico, ca [bjo'lɔʒiku, ka] adj biological.

biólogo, ga ['bjɔlogu, ga] m, f biologist.

biombo ['bjõbu] m screen.

biônico, ca ['bjoniku, ka] adj -**1.** [relativo à biônica] bionic. -**2.** irôn & POL undemocratically appointed politician.

biópsia [bjɔp'sia] f biopsy.

bioquímica [bjo'kimika] f biochemistry.

biorritmo [bjo'xitʃmu] m biorhythm.

BIOS (abrev de **Basic Input/Output System**) m BIOS.

biosfera [bjos'fɛra] f biosphere.

bipartidário, ria [bipaxtʃi'darju, rja] adj bipartisan.

bipartidarismo [bipaxtʃida'riʒmu] *m* biparti-sanship.

bípede ['bipedʒil *adj* biped.

biqueira [bi'kejra] *f* -**1.** [ger] tip. -**2.** [calha] gutter.

biquíni [bi'kini] *m* bikini.

BIRD (*abrev de* Banco Internacional de Reconstru-ção e Desenvolvimento) *m* IBRD.

birita [bi'rita] *f fam* (alcoholic) drink.

Birmânia [bix'mãnja] *n* Burma.

birmanês, esa [bixma'neʃ, ezal ◇ *adj* Bur-mese. ◇ *m, f* Burmese.
➡ **birmanês** *m* [língua] Burmese.

birosca [bi'rɔʃka] *f* -**1.** [pequena mercearia] small shop. -**2.** [botequim] snack bar.

birra ['bixal *f* -**1.** [teimosia] temper; **fazer** ~ to throw a tantrum. -**2.** [irritação, zanga]: **ficar de** ~ **com alguém** to be at loggerheads with sb.

birrento, ta [bi'xẽntu, tal *adj* wilful.

biruta [bi'ruta] ◇ *adj* [pessoa] mad. ◇ *m* [pes-soa] madman. ◇ *f* [dispositivo] windsock.

bis ['biʃ] ◇ *m* encore; **pedir um** ~ to demand an encore; **fazer** *ou* **dar um** ~ to give an encore. ◇ *interj* encore!

bisar [4] [bi'za(x)] *vt* -**1.** [pedir repetição de] to demand an encore. -**2.** [repetir] to give an encore.

bisavô, vó [biza'vo, vɔl *m, f* great-grandfather (*f* great-grandmother).
➡ **bisavós** *mpl* great-grandparents.

bisbilhotar [4] [biʒbiʎo'ta(x)] ◇ *vt* [examinar] to pry. ◇ *vi fam* [fazer mexericos] to gossip.

bisbilhoteiro, ra [biʒbiʎo'tejru, ral ◇ *adj* -**1.** [curioso] nosy. -**2.** [mexeriqueiro] gossipy. ◇ *m, f* -**1.** [pessoa curiosa] nosy parker. -**2.** [pessoa mexeri-queria] gossip.

bisbilhotice [biʒ'biʎo'tʃisi] *f* -**1.** [curiosidade] med-dling. -**2.** [mexerico] gossip.

biscate [biʃ'katʃil *m fam* odd job.

biscateiro, ra [biʃka'tejru, ral *m, f* odd-job man.

biscoito [biʃ'kojtul *m* biscuit; ~ **amanteigado** buttery biscuit.

bisnaga [biʒ'nagal *f* -**1.** [pão] baguette. -**2.** [tubo] tube.

bisneto, ta [biʒ'nɛtu, tal *m, f* great-grandchild.

bisonho, nha [bi'zoɲu, ɲal *adj* -**1.** [inexperiente] inexperienced. -**2.** [novato] novice.

bispado [biʃ'padul *m* -**1.** [diocese] diocese. -**2.** [dignidade episcopal] episcopate.

bispo ['biʃpul *m* bishop.

bissexto, ta [bi'sejʃtu, tal *adj*: **ano** ~ leap year.
➡ **bissexto** *m* 29 February.

bissexual [bisek'swawl (*pl* -ais) ◇ *adj* bisexual. ◇ *m* bisexual.

bisturi [biʃtu'ril *m* scalpel.

bit ['bitʃil *m COMPUT* bit.

bitmap ['bitimapil *m COMPUT* bitmap.

bitola [bi'tolal *f* gauge.

bizarro, a [bi'zaxu, xal *adj* bizarre.

blablablá [blabla'blal *m fam* chatter.

black-tie [blɛk'tajl *m* black tie, dinner jacket.

blasé [bla'zel *adj* blasé.

blasfemar [4] [blaʃfe'ma(x)] ◇ *vt RELIG* to take in vain. ◇ *vi* -**1.** *RELIG* to swear. -**2.** [praguejar]: ~ **contra** to defame.

blasfêmia [blaʃ'femjal *f* -**1.** *RELIG* blasphemy. -**2.** [ultraje] defamation.

blasfemo, ma [blaʃ'femu, mal *adj* [palavras] blas-phemous.
➡ **blasfemo** *m* [pessoa] blasphemer.

blazer ['blejzɛ(x)l (*pl* -es) *m* blazer.

blecaute [ble'kawtʃil *m* blackout.

blefar [4] [ble'fa(x)l ◇ *vi* -**1.** [em jogo] to bluff. -**2.** [tapear] to deceive. ◇ *vt* [tapear] to trick.

blefe ['blɛfil *m* -**1.** [truque] trick. -**2.** [no jogo] bluff.

blindado, da [blĩ'dadu, dal *adj* armoured.

blindagem [blĩ'daʒẽl *f* armour.

blitz ['blitiʃl (*pl* blitze) *f* blitz.

bloco ['blɔkul *m* -**1.** [ger] block. -**2.** [papel] pad. -**3.** [grupo]: ~ **de Carnaval** group of carnival revellers.
➡ **em bloco** *loc adv* en bloc.

bloquear [15] [blo'kja(x)] *vt* -**1.** [cercar] to sur-round. -**2.** [impedir] to block off. -**3.** *PSIC* to block.

bloqueio [blo'kejul *m* -**1.** [cerco] blockade. -**2.** [obstrução] obstacle; *MED, PSIC* blockage. -**3.** *ECON*: ~ **econômico** economic blockade.

blue chip [bluw'ʃipil (*pl* blue chips) *f ECON* blue chip.

blues ['bluwʃl *m* (*inv*) *MÚS* blues.

blusa ['bluzal *f* blouse.

BM (*abrev de* Banco Mundial) *m* World Bank.

BM & F (*abrev de* Bolsa de Mercadorias e Futuros) *f Brazilian commodities and futures market.*

BNDES (*abrev de* Banco Nacional de Desenvolvi-mento Econômico e Social) *m Brazilian bank for financing economic and social develop-ment.*

BNH (*abrev de* Banco Nacional da Habitação) *m national bank for financing low-paid workers to buy their own homes.*

BO (*abrev de* Boletim de Ocorrência) *m Brazilian crime report.*

boa ['boal *f* ⊳ **bom**.

boa-fé [ˌboa'fɛl *f* -**1.** [ger] good faith; **agir de** ~ to act in good faith. -**2.** [ingenuidade] naivety.

boa-gente [ˌboa'ʒẽntʃil *adj* (*inv*) trustworthy.

boa-noite [ˌboa'nojtʃil (*pl* boas-noites) *f* good night.

boa-pinta [ˌboa'pĩntal (*pl* boas-pintas) *fam* ◇ *adj* good-looking. ◇ *m* looker.

boa-praça [ˌboa'prasal (*pl* boas-praças) *UK fam adj* kind-hearted.

boas-festas [ˌboaʒ'fɛʃtaʃl *fpl inv* [felicitações - no Natal] Happy Christmas; [- no Ano-Novo] Happy New Year.

boas-vindas [ˌboaʒ'vĩndaʃl *fpl inv* welcome.

boa-tarde [ˌboa'taxdʒil (*pl* boas-tardes) *f* good afternoon.

boataria [bwata'rial *f* rumour.

boate ['bwatʃil *f* nightclub.

boateiro, ra [bwa'tejru, ral ◇ *adj* gossipy. ◇ *m, f* rumour-monger.

boato ['bwatu] *m* rumour.

boa-vida [ˌboa'vidal (*pl* **boas-vidas**) *m* bon vivant.

Boa Vista [ˌboa'viʃta] *n* Boa Vista.

bobagem [bo'baʒẽ] (*pl* **-ns**) ◇ *f* **-1.** [coisa supérflua] frippery. **-2.** [dito] rubbish. **-3.** [fato sem importância] trifle. ◇ *adj* [desaconselhável]: **ser ~ fazer algo** to be foolish to do sthg.

bobalhão, lhona [boba'ʎaw, ʎona] (*mpl* **-lhões**, *fpl* **-s**) *m, f* fool.

bobeada [bo'bjada] *f fam* foolishness; **dar uma ~** to be a fool.

bobear [15] [bo'bja(x)] *vi* **-1.** [fazer besteira] to make a mistake. **-2.** [deixar-se enganar] to be tricked. **-3.** [descuidar-se] to be careless. **-4.** [perder uma chance] to blow it.

bobeira [bo'bejra] *f* mistake; **marcar ~** *fam* [ser enganado] to be a fool; [perder uma chance] to blow it.

bobina [bo'bina] *f* bobbin.

bobo, ba ['bobu, ba] ◇ *adj* foolish. ◇ *m, f* fool.
➡ **bobo** *m*: **~ da corte** court jester.

bobó [bo'bɔ] *m CULIN* : **~ (de camarão)** *shrimp bobó*.

boboca [bo'bɔka] ◇ *mf* idiot. ◇ *adj* idiotic.

boca ['boka] *f* **-1.** [ger] mouth; **~ do estômago** *MED* cardia; **~ da noite** nightfall; **cala a ~!** *fam* shut up! **-2.** [de calça] top. **-3.** *fam* [emprego] opening. **-4.** *fam* [pessoa para alimentar] mouth to feed. **-5.** *POL*: **~ de urna** ballot-box slit. **-6.** *loc*: **bater ~** to argue; **botar a ~ no trombone** *fam* [denunciar] to complain loudly; **falar da ~ para fora** not to mean what one is saying.
➡ **de boca** *loc adv* unwritten.

boca-a-boca [ˌboka'boka] ◇ *m MED* mouth-to-mouth resuscitation. ◇ *adj*: **respiração ~** kiss of life.

boca-de-fumo [ˌbokadʒi'fumu] (*pl* **bocas-de-fumo**) *f fam* drug-dealing patch.

boca-de-sino [ˌbokadʒi'sinu] *adj inv* flared, bell-bottomed.

bocadinho [boka'dʒiɲu] *m* **-1.** [pequena quantidade]: **um ~ (de)** a little bit (of). **-2.** [tempo curto]: **um ~** a little bit.

bocado [bo'kadu] *m* **-1.** [grande quantidade]: **um ~ de** quite a lot of. **-2.** [pedaço, porção]: **um ~ (de)** a bit (of). **-3.** [mordida] mouthful.
➡ **um bocado** *loc adv* [bastante] quite.

bocal [bo'kaw] (*pl* **-ais**) *m* **-1.** [ger] mouth. **-2.** *MÚS* mouthpiece.

boçal [bo'saw] (*pl* **-ais**) *adj* **-1.** [ignorante] stupid. **-2.** [grosseiro] rude.

boçalidade [bosali'dadʒi] *f* **-1.** [ignorância] stupidity. **-2.** [grosseria] rudeness.

boca-livre [ˌboka'livri] (*pl* **bocas-livres**) *f* **-1.** [em evento] free meal. **-2.** [em serviços públicos] gravy train, *a place where a blind eye is turned to the misappropriation of public funds.*

bocejar [4] [bose'ʒa(x)] *vi* to yawn.

bocejo [bo'seʒu] *m* yawn.

boceta [bu'seta] *f vulg* [vulva] cunt.

bochecha [bu'ʃeʃa] *f* cheek.

bochechar [4] [boʃe'ʃa(x)] ◇ *vt* to rinse one's mouth with. ◇ *vi* to rinse one's mouth.

bochecho [bo'ʃeʃu] *m* mouthwash.

bochechudo, da [boʃe'ʃudu, da] *adj* chubby-cheeked.

bocó [bo'kɔ] *adj* **-1.** [infantil] childish. **-2.** [tolo] silly.

bodas ['bodaʃ] *fpl* wedding anniversary *(sg)*; **~ de ouro** golden wedding *(sg)*; **~ de prata** silver wedding *(sg)*.

bode ['bɔdʒi] *m* **-1.** *ZOOL* billy goat; **~ expiatório** *fig* scapegoat. **-2.** *fam* [problema]: **dar ~** to be hell to pay.

bodega [bo'dɛga] *f* **-1.** *fam* [coisa sem valor] rubbish. **-2.** [taberna] tavern.

boêmia [bo'emja] *f* bohemian lifestyle.

Boêmia [bo'emja] *n* Bohemia.

boêmio, mia [bo'emju, mja] ◇ *adj* **-1.** [vida etc] bohemian. **-2.** [da Boêmia] Bohemian. ◇ *m, f* **-1.** [pessoa boêmia] bohemian. **-2.** [da Boêmia] Bohemian.

bofe ['bɔfi] *m fam* **-1.** [pulmão] lungs *(pl)*. **-2.** *fam* [pessoa feia] monster.

bofetada [bofe'tada] *f* slap in the face.

bofetão [bofe'tãw] (*pl* **-ões**) *m* hard slap on the face.

Bogotá [bogo'ta] *n* Bogotá.

boi ['boj] *m* ox.

bói ['bɛj] *m* office boy.

bóia ['bɔja] *f* **-1.** *NÁUT* buoy; **~ salva-vidas** lifebuoy. **-2.** *fam* [comida] grub.

boiada [bo'jada] *f* drove of oxen.

bóia-fria [ˌbɔja'fria] (*pl* **bóias-frias**) *m* agricultural dayworker.

boiar [4] [bo'ja(x)] *vi* **-1.** [flutuar] to float. **-2.** *fam* [não entender]: **estar/ficar boiando** to be thrown by.

boicotar [4] [bojko'ta(x)] *vt* to boycott.

boicote [boj'kɔtʃi] *m* boycott.

boiler ['bɔjle(x)] (*pl* **-s**) *m* boiler.

boina ['bojna] *f* cap.

bojo ['boʒu] *m* **-1.** [saliência] bulge. **-2.** [de navio] belly.

bojudo, da [bo'ʒudu, da] *adj* rounded.

bola ['bɔla] *f* **-1.** [objeto] ball; **ser bom de ~** to play football very well; **~ de futebol** football; **~ de gude** marble; **~ de neve** snowball; *fig* [situação] snowball. **-2.** *ESP* [jogada] shot. **-3.** *fam fig* [cabeça]: **não ser bom da ~** to be not right in the head. **-4.** *fam fig* [pessoa engraçada]: **ser uma ~** to be a good laugh. **-5.** *loc*: **dar ~ para alguém** [flertar] to flirt with sb; **dar ~ para algo** [dar importância a] to care about sthg; **não dar ~ (para)** [ignorar] to ignore; **não dar ~ para algo** [não dar importância a] to ignore sthg; **pisar na ~** *fig* to make a mistake; **trocar as ~s** to get mixed up.

bolacha [bo'laʃa] *f* **-1.** [biscoito] biscuit; **~ d'água** water biscuit. **-2.** *fam* [bofetada]: **dar uma ~ em alguém** to slap sb; **levar uma ~ de alguém** to be slapped by sb. **-3.** [em bares, restaurantes] coaster.

bolada [bo'lada] *f* -**1.** [pancada] hit *(with a ball)*. -**2.** [vez]: **de uma** ~ **só** in one go. -**3.** [de dinheiro] jackpot.

bolar [4] [bo'la(x)] ⬦ *vt* to devise. ⬦ *vi* to be successful.

boléia [bo'lɛja] *f* lorry driver's seat.

boletim [bole'tʃĩ] *(pl* -ns) *m* -**1.** [publicação] bulletin. -**2.** *EDUC* school report. -**3.** [nota] memo; ~ **médico** medical report.

boleto [bo'letu] *m* requisition.

bolha ['boʎa] ⬦ *f* -**1.** [em líquido, material] bubble. -**2.** [na pele] blister. ⬦ *mf* *fam* [pessoa] bore.

boliche [bo'liʃi] *m* -**1.** [jogo] pool. -**2.** [estabelecimento] pool room.

bolinagem [bolina'ʒẽ] *(pl* -ns) *f* *fam* touching up.

bolinar [4] [boli'na(x)] *vt* *fam* to touch up.

bolinho [bo'liɲu] *m* croquette; ~ **de bacalhau** salt cod croquette.

Bolívia [bo'livja] *n* Bolivia.

boliviano, na [boli'vjãnu, na] ⬦ *adj* Bolivian. ⬦ *m, f* Bolivian.

bolo ['bolu] *m* -**1.** *CULIN* cake. -**2.** [quantidade]: **um** ~ **de** a load of. -**3.** *fam* [confusão] commotion; **dar o maior** ~ to cause a commotion; **deu o maior** ~ **quando ...** there was a great to-do when ... -**4.** [em jogo etc] stake. -**5.** *loc*: **dar o** ~ **em alguém** to stand sb up.

bolor [bo'lo(x)] *m* mould.

bolorento, ta [bolo'rẽntu, ta] *adj* mouldy.

bolota [bo'lɔta] *f* -**1.** [fruto do carvalho] acorn. -**2.** [caroço] lump.

bolsa ['bowsa] *f* -**1.** [acessório] purse. -**2.** *EDUC*: ~ **(de estudos)** bursary. -**3.** *FIN*: ~ **(de valores)** stock market. -**4.** *MED*: ~ **d'água** amniotic sac.

bolsista [bow'siʃta] *EDUC* ⬦ *adj* scholarship *(antes de subst)*. ⬦ *mf* scholarship holder.

bolso ['bowsu] *m* pocket; **de** ~ pocket *(antes de subst)*.

bom, boa ['bõ, 'boa] *(mpl* bons, *fpl* boas) *adj* -**1.** [ger] good; **ser** ~ **em algo** to be good at sthg; **ficar** ~ to be well made/done. -**2.** [curado] well. -**3.** [seguro] safe. -**4.** [amplo, confortável] spacious. -**5.** [em saudação]: **tudo** ~? how are you? -**6.** [pedindo opinião, permissão]: **está** ~? all right?
➡ **bom** ⬦ *interj*: **que** ~! how great! ⬦ *m*: **o** ~ **é que ...** the good thing is that ...
➡ **bons** *mpl* [pessoas honradas]: **os bons** the great.
➡ **boa** *fam* ⬦ *adj f* [boazuda] sexy. ⬦ *f irôn* [situação difícil]: **meter-se numa boa** to put o.s. in a tight spot; **livrar-se de uma boa** to get out of a tight spot.
➡ **às boas** *loc adv*: **viver às boas com alguém** to get on well with sb; **voltar às boas (com alguém)** to make up (with sb).

bomba ['bõmba] *f* -**1.** [explosivo] bomb; ~ **atômica** atomic bomb; ~ **de hidrogênio** hydrogen bomb. -**2.** [fogo de artifício] rocket. -**3.** [máquina, aparelho] pump; ~ **d'água** water pump; ~ **de ar** air pump; ~ **de gasolina** petrol pump; ~

de incêndio fire extinguisher. -**4.** *fig* [acontecimento] shock. -**5.** *fig* [coisa ruim]: **ser uma** ~ to be a flop. -**6.** *EDUC*: **levar** ~ **(em algo)** to fail at sthg. -**7.** [trabalho mal-acabado]: **estar/ficar uma** ~ to be/end up shoddy. -**8.** [doce] bombe.

bombachas [bõn'baʃaʃ] *fpl* gaucho pants.

bombardear [15] [bõnbax'dʒja(x)] *vt* to bombard.

bombardeio [bõnbax'deju] *m* bombardment.

bomba-relógio [ˌbõnbaxe'lɔʒju] *(pl* bombas-relógios, bombas-relógio) *f* time bomb.

bombástico, ca [bõn'baʃtʃiku, ka] *adj* -**1.** [estrondoso] deafening. -**2.** *fig* [empolado] bombastic.

bombear [15] [bõn'bja(x)] *vt & vi* to pump.

bombeiro [bõn'bejru] *m* -**1.** [de incêndios] firefighter. -**2.** [encanador] plumber.

bombom [bõn'bõ] *(pl* -ns) *m* sweetie.

bombordo [bõn'bɔxdu] *m* *NÁUT* port.

bom-tom [bõn'tõ] *m* good manners; **ser de** ~ to be socially acceptable.

bonachão, ona [bona'ʃãw, ɔna] *(mpl* -ões, *fpl* -s) *adj* kind-hearted.

bonaerense [bonaj'rẽnsi] ⬦ *adj* Buenos Aires *(antes de subst)*. ⬦ *mf* person from Buenos Aires.

bonança [bo'nãnsa] *f* -**1.** *NÁUT* calm. -**2.** *fig* [tranqüilidade] calm.

bondade [bõn'dadʒi] *f* -**1.** [qualidade] kindness. -**2.** [benevolência] goodness; **ter a** ~ **de fazer algo** to be kind enough to do sthg.

bonde ['bõndʒi] *m* -**1.** [veículo] tram; **pegar o** ~ **andando** *fig* to come in (a conversation) half way. -**2.** *fam* [mulher feia] ugly woman.

bondoso, sa [bõn'dozu, ɔza] *adj* kind.

boné [bo'nɛ] *m* cap.

boneca [bo'nɛka] *f* -**1.** [ger] doll; ~ **de pano** rag doll. -**2.** *fam* [homosexual] queen.

boneco [bo'nɛku] *m* -**1.** [ger] stencil. -**2.** [brinquedo] doll. -**3.** *fig* [fantoche] puppet.

bonificação [bonifika'sãw] *(pl* -ões) *f* -**1.** [gratificação] bonus. -**2.** [desconto] discount.

boníssimo, ma [bo'nisimu, ma] *superl* ⬦ **bom.**

bonitão, tona [boni'tãw, tona] *(mpl* -ões, *fpl* -s) *adj* handsome.

bonito, ta [bo'nitu, ta] *adj* -**1.** [ger] beautiful. -**2.** *iron* [lamentável] lovely.
➡ **bonito** *adv* [bem] well.

bonitona [boni'tona] *f* ⬦ **bonitão.**

bons ['bõjʃ] *pl* ⬦ **bom.**

bônus ['bonuʃ] *m (inv)* -**1.** [prêmio] prize. -**2.** [debênture] share.

boot ['buti] *(pl* boots) *m* *COMPUT* [inicialização] boot-up; **dar** ~ to reboot.

boquiaberto, ta [bokja'bɛxtu, ta] *adj* gaping.

boquinha [bo'kiɲa] *f* -**1.** [boca pequena] small mouth. -**2.** *fig* [refeição]: **fazer uma** ~ snack.

borboleta [boxbo'leta] *f* -**1.** *ZOOL* butterfly. -**2.** [roleta] turnstile.

borboletear [15] [boxbole'tʃja(x)] *vi* -**1.** [vaguear] to flutter. -**2.** *fig* [devanear] to daydream.

borbotão [boxbo'tãw] (*pl* -ões) *m*: **aos borbotões** in spurts.
borbulhante [boxbu'ʎãntʃi] *adj* fizzy.
borbulhar [4] [boxbu'ʎa(x)] *vi* to bubble.
borda ['bɔxda] *f* -1. edge. -2. [lençol] hem. -3. [jardim] border. -4. [rio] bank. -5. [piscina] side.
bordadeira [boxda'dejra] *f* embroiderer.
bordado, da [box'dadu, da] *adj* embroidered.
→ **bordado** *m* embroidery.
bordão [box'dãw] (*pl* -ões) *m* -1. [cajado] crook. -2. *fig* [arrimo] prop. -3. [MÚS - corda] bass string; [- nota] lowest note. -4. [frase] slogan.
bordar [4] [box'da(x)] *vt & vi* to embroider.
Bordeaux [box'do] *n* Bordeaux.
bordejar [4] [boxde'ʒa(x)] *vi* NÁUT to tack.
bordel [box'dɛw] (*pl* -eis) *m* brothel.
bordo ['bɔxdu] *m* -1. [de navio] board; **a ~ on board**. -2. [ao bordejar] tack.
bordô [box'do] ⇔ *adj* burgundy. ⇔ *n* Bordeaux.
bordoada [box'dwada] *f* beating.
bordões [box'dõjʃ] *pl* ⊳ **bordão**.
boreste [bo'rɛʃtʃi] *m* NÁUT starboard; **a ~ to starboard**.
boricado, da [bori'kadu, da] *adj* boric.
borla ['bɔxla] *f* -1. [pendão] tassel. -2. [pompom] pompom.
borocoxô [boroko'ʃo] *adj* feeble.
borra ['boxa] *f* -1. [de café] grounds *(pl)*. -2. [de vinho] dregs *(pl)*.
borra-botas [ˌboxa'bɔtaʃ] *mf inv* good-for-nothing.
borracha [bo'xaʃa] *f* -1. [ger] rubber. -2. [para apagar] rubber, eraser. -3. [mangueira] hosepipe.
borrachudo [boxa'ʃudu] *m* black fly.
borracheiro [boxa'ʃejru] *m* -1. [pessoa] tyre fitter. -2. [oficina] tyre-fitting workshop.
borrado, da [bo'xadu, da] *adj* -1. [manchado] stained. -2. *fam* [de fezes] foul.
borrão [bo'xãw] (*pl* -ões) *m* stain.
borrar [4] [bo'xa(x)] *vt* -1. [manchar] to stain. -2. [riscar] to cross out. -3. [pintar] to smear. -4. *fam* [de fezes] to foul.
→ **borrar-se** *vp vulg* [de fezes] to shit o.s.; **~-se (de medo)** *fig* to be shitting o.s.
borrasca [bo'xaʃka] *f* -1. [tempestade] thunderstorm. -2. [em alto mar] squall.
borrifar [4] [boxi'fa(x)] *vt* to spray.
borrifo [bo'xifu] *m* spray.
borrões [bo'xõjʃ] *pl* ⊳ **borrão**.
Bósnia-Herzegovina [ˌbɔʒnjexzego'vina] *n* Bosnia-Herzegovina.
bósnio, nia ['bɔʒnju, nja], **bosniano, na** [boʒni'ãnu, na] ⇔ *adj* Bosnian. ⇔ *m, f* Bosnian.
bosque ['bɔʃki] *m* wood.
bossa ['bɔsa] *f* -1. [ger] bump. -2. *fam* [charme] appeal; **ter ~ to be appealing**. -3. *fam* [aptidão]: **ter ~ (para algo)** to have an aptitude (for sthg). -4. *MÚS*: **~ nova** bossa nova.

BOSSA NOVA

Musical movement born in Rio de Janeiro in the late 50s; the bossa nova revolutionized the samba, condensing its rhythmic wealth into a syncopated beat with polished jazz chords for piano and guitar. The bossa nova's delicate melody and subtle song were to have a great influence on western popular music through two of the art form's greatest exponents, Tom Jobim and João Gilberto.

bosta ['bɔʃta] *f* -1. [de animal] dung. -2. [de ser humano] excrement.
bota ['bɔta] *f* boot; **~s de borracha** wellington boots, rubber boots; **bater as ~s** [morrer] to kick the bucket; **onde Judas perdeu as ~s** Godforsaken place.
bota-fora [ˌbɔta'fɔra] (*pl* bota-foras) *m* [despedida] send-off.
botânico, ca [bo'taniku, ka] ⇔ *adj* botanic. ⇔ *m, f* botanist.
→ **botânica** *f* botany.
botão [bo'tãw] (*pl* -ões) *m* -1. [ger] button; **falar/pensar com os seus botões** to think to o.s. -2. [de jogo] counter. -3. [de flor] bud.
botar [4] [bo'ta(x)] ⇔ *vt* -1. [ger] to put; **~ algo em dia** to bring sthg up to date; **~ fora** to throw away. -2. [roupa, sapatos] to put on. -3. [defeito] to point out. ⇔ *vi loc*: **~ para quebrar** [empreender mudanças] to make sweeping changes; [fazer sucesso] to be a huge hit.
bote ['bɔtʃi] *m* -1. [barco] boat; **~ inflável** inflatable boat; **~ salva-vidas** lifeboat. -2. [golpe - com arma] thrust; [- salto] leap; [- de cobra] lunge; **dar o ~** to lunge.
boteco [bo'tɛku] (*pl* -s), **botequim** [bote'kĩ] (*pl* -ns) *m* tavern.
boticário, ria [botʃi'karju, rja] *m, f* dispensing chemist.
botijão [botʃi'ʒãw] (*pl* -ões) *m* cylinder.
botina [bo'tʃina] *f* ankle-boot.
botões [bo'tõjʃ] *pl* ⊳ **botão**.
Bovespa (*abrev de* **Bolsa de Valores do Estado de São Paulo**) *f São Paulo stock exchange*.
bovino, na [bo'vinu, na] *adj* bovine.
boxe ['bɔksi] *m* -1. *ESP* boxing. -2. [em banheiro] shower cubicle.
boxeador [boksja'do(x)] *m* boxer.
boy ['bɔj] *m* = **bói**.
bps [bepe'esil (*abrev de* **bit por segundo**) COMPUT bps.
BR *abrev de* Brasil.
braça ['brasa] *f* NÁUT fathom.
braçada [bra'sada] *f* -1. [de flores] armful. -2. [em natação] stroke.
braçadeira [brasa'dejra] *f* -1. [para o braço] armband. -2. [de cortina] tie-back. -3. [metálica] clasp. -4. *ESP* [correia] wristband.
braçal [bra'saw] (*pl* -ais) *adj* physical; **trabalho ~** physical work.
bracelete [brase'letʃi] *m* bracelet.
braço ['brasu] *m* -1. [ger] arm; **cruzar os ~s** to fold

one's arms; *fig* [ficar impassível] to do nothing; *fig* [fazer greve] to go on strike; **de ~s cruzados** with arms folded; *fig* [impassível] impassively; **dar o ~ a alguém** to give one's arm to sb; **de ~ dado** arm in arm; **no ~** [à força] by force; **~ direito** *fig* right arm. **-2.** [de toca-discos] arm. **-3.** [de balança] pointer. **-4.** [trabalhador] hand. **-5.** [ramo] limb. **-6.** *loc:* **meter o ~ em alguém** to beat sb up; **não dar o ~ a torcer** to stick to one's guns; **receber (alguém) de ~s abertos** to welcome (sb) with open arms.

bradar [4] [bra'da(x)]l ◇ *vt* to proclaim. ◇ *vi* to shout.

Bradesco (*abrev de* **Banco Brasileiro de Descontos**) *m largest private Brazilian bank.*

brado ['bradul *m* shout.

braguilha [bra'giʎal *f* flies *UK (pl),* fly *US.*

braile ['brajlil *m* Braille.

bramido [bra'midul *m* **-1.** [ger] roar. **-2.** [grito] scream.

bramir [79] [bra'mi(x)] *vi* **-1.** [ger] to roar. **-2.** [gritar] to scream.

branco, ca ['brãŋku, kal ◇ *adj* **-1.** [ger] white; **arma ~** weapon with a blade. **-2.** [versos] blank. ◇ *m, f* [pessoa] White.
→ **branco** *m* **-1.** [cor] white; **~ do olho** white of the eye. **-2.** [espaço] blank space. **-3.** [esquecimento] blank; **me deu um ~** my mind went blank.
→ **em branco** ◇ *loc adj* [espaço] blank. ◇ *loc adv* **-1.** [sem preencher]: **deixar algo em ~** to leave sthg blank. **-2.** [sem dormir]: **passar a noite em ~** to have a sleepless night. **-3.** [sem comemorar]: **passar uma data em ~** not to celebrate an important date.

brancura [brãŋ'kural *f* whiteness.

brandir [79] [brãn'dʒi(x)] *vt* to brandish.

brando, da ['brãndu, dal *adj* **-1.** [ger] mild. **-2.** [fraco - ação] weak; [- febre] mild. **-3.** [fogo, forno] warm.

brandura [brãn'dural *f* mildness.

branquear [15] [brãŋ'kja(x)] *vt & vi* to whiten.

brasa ['brazal *f* **-1.** [de carvão] embers *(pl);* **na ~** in the embers. **-2.** [incandescência] heat; **em ~** red-hot. **-3.** *loc:* **mandar ~** *fam* to get cracking; **puxar a ~ para a sua sardinha** *fam* to look after number one.

brasão [bra'zãwl *(pl* -ões) *m* coat of arms.

braseiro [bra'zejrul *m* brazier.

Brasil [bra'ziwl *n:* **(o) ~** Brazil.

brasileiro, ra [brazi'lejru, ral ◇ *adj* Brazilian. ◇ *m, f* Brazilian.

Brasília [bra'ziljal *n* Brasilia.

brasões [bra'zõjʃl *pl* ⊳ **brasão.**

Bratislava [bratʃiʒ'laval *n* Bratislava.

bravata [bra'vatal *f* bravado.

bravio, via [bra'viw, vial *adj* **-1.** [selvagem] wild. **-2.** [feroz] fierce.

bravo, va ['bravu, val ◇ *adj* **-1.** [corajoso] brave. **-2.** [animal] wild. **-3.** [mar] rough. ◇ *m, f* [pessoa] intrepid person.
→ **bravo** *interj* bravo!

bravura [bra'vural *f* **-1.** [coragem] courage. **-2.** [de animal] wildness.

brecar [12] [bre'ka(x)] ◇ *vt* **-1.** [frear] to brake. **-2.** [conter] to curb. ◇ *vi* [frear] to brake.

brecha ['brɛʃal *f* **-1.** [ger] gap. **-2.** [fenda, abertura] opening. **-3.** [prejuízo] hole. **-4.** *fam* [oportunidade] break.

brechó [bre'ʃɔl *m* second-hand shop.

brega ['brɛgal *adj fam* [cafona] tacky.

brejo ['brɛʒul *m* swamp; **ir para o ~** *fam* to go out the window.

brenha ['breɲal *f* thicket.

breu ['brewl *m* **-1.** pitch; **escuro como ~** pitch black. **-2.** [escuridão] darkness.

breve ['brɛvil ◇ *adj* **-1.** [ger] short. **-2.** [rápido] fleeting. **-3.** [conciso] brief; **ser ~** to be brief. **-4.** *MÚS* [nota] short. ◇ *adv* [dentro de pouco tempo] soon; **até ~** see you soon; **(dentro) em ~** soon. ◇ *m RELIG* [escapulário] scapular. ◇ *f MÚS* breve.

brevê [bre'vel *m* diploma.

brevemente [ˌbrɛvi'mẽntʃil *adv* **-1.** [dentro de pouco tempo] shortly. **-2.** [de modo conciso] concisely.

brevidade [brevi'dadʒil *f* **-1.** [curteza] shortness. **-2.** [rapidez] brevity. **-3.** *CULIN* cassava-flour cake.

bricabraque [brika'brakil *m* **-1.** [conjunto] bric-a-brac. **-2.** [loja] junk shop.

bridge ['bridʒil *m* bridge.

briga ['brigal *f* **-1.** [luta] brawl; **partir para a ~** to roll up one's sleeves; **~ de foice** long, drawn-out brawl; **~ de galo** cockfight. **-2.** [desavença] dispute. **-3.** [rixa] fight.

brigada [bri'gadal *f* brigade.

brigadeiro [briga'dejrul *m* **-1.** *MIL* brigadier. **-2.** *CULIN confectionery made with condensed milk and chocolate, very common at birthday parties.*

brigão, gona [bri'gãw, gonal *(mpl* -ões, *fpl* -s) ◇ *adj* brawling. ◇ *m, f* brawler.

brigar [4] [bri'ga(x)] *vi* **-1.** [ger] to fight; **~ por algo** to fight for sthg. **-2.** [desavir-se] to fall out.

brilhante [bri'ʎãntʃil ◇ *adj* **-1.** [que reluz] sparkling. **-2.** *fig* [notável] brilliant. ◇ *m* [diamante] sparkler.

brilhar [4] [bri'ʎa(x)] *vi* **-1.** [reluzir] to shine. **-2.** *fig* [distinguir-se] to excel.

brilho ['briʎul *m* **-1.** [luz] shine. **-2.** [de cor] brightness. **-3.** [de metal etc] gleam. **-4.** *fig* [distinção] excellence; **dar ~ a** to make sthg shine; **com ~** brilliantly. **-5.** *fig* [esplendor] splendour. **-6.** *gír* [droga] [cocaína] coke.

brim [brĩl *m* coarse cloth.

brincadeira [brĩŋka'dejral *f* **-1.** [divertimento] play. **-2.** [jogo] game. **-3.** [gracejo] joke; **de ~** as a joke;

~ **de mau gosto** joke in bad taste; **deixe de** ~! stop kidding!; **fora de** ~ seriously. -**4.** *fam* [coisa fácil] child's play; **não ser** ~ to be no joke.

brincalhão, ona [brĩŋka'ʎãw, ɔna] (*mpl* -**ões**, *fpl* -**s**) *adj* playful.

brincar [12] [brĩŋ'ka(x)] <> *vi* -**1.** [divertir-se] to play; ~ **de algo/de fazer algo** to play with/at doing sthg; ~ **de esconder** to play hide-and-seek. -**2.** [gracejar]: ~ **com alguém** to joke with sb; **está brincando?** are you kidding?; **estar (só) brincando** to be (only) joking. -**3.** [no Carnaval] to party. <> *vt* [Carnaval] to celebrate.

brinco ['brĩŋku] *m* -**1.** [adorno] earring. -**2.** *fig* [primor]: **estar/ficar um** ~ to be shiny.

brindar [4] [brĩn'da(x)] <> *vt* -**1.** [no ato de beber] to toast. -**2.** [presentear]: ~ **alguém (com algo)** to make sb a present (of sthg). -**3.** [conceder]: ~ **alguém com algo** to reward sb with sthg. <> *vi* [no ato de beber]: ~ **a algo** to drink a toast to sthg.

brinde ['brĩndʒi] *m* -**1.** [no ato de beber] toast; **erguer um** ~ **(a)** to raise one's glass (to). -**2.** [presente] free gift.

brinquedo [brĩŋ'kedu] *m* toy.

brio ['briw] *m* -**1.** [honra, dignidade] honour; **mexer com os** ~**s de alguém** to attack sb's honour. -**2.** [galhardia] dignity.

brioche [bri'ɔʃi] *m* brioche.

brioso, osa ['brjozu, ɔza] *adj* noble.

brisa ['briza] *f* breeze.

brita ['brita] *f* CONSTR gravel.

britadeira [brita'dejra] *f* pneumatic drill.

britânico, ca [bri'tãniku, ka] <> *adj* British. <> *m, f* British person, Briton.

broa ['broa] *f* cornflour bread; ~ **de milho** maize-flour bread.

broca ['brɔka] *f* drill.

brocado [bro'kadu] *m* brocade.

broche ['brɔʃi] *m* brooch.

brochura [bro'ʃura] *f* -**1.** [livro] binding; **em** ~ in paperback. -**2.** [folheto] brochure.

brócolis ['brɔkoliʃ] *mpl* broccoli (*sg*).

bronco, ca ['brõŋku, ka] *adj* -**1.** [rude] ill-mannered. -**2.** [burro] slow-witted.

➡ **bronca** *f fam* [repreensão] telling-off; **dar uma** ~ **em alguém** to give sb a telling-off; **levar uma** ~ **(de alguém)** to be given a telling-off (by sb).

bronquear [15] [brõŋ'kja(x)] *vi fam* to get furious; ~ **com alguém** to tell sb off.

brônquio ['broŋkju] *m* bronchus.

bronquite [brõŋ'kitʃi] *f* bronchitis.

bronze ['brõzi] *m* bronze.

bronzeado, da [brõ'zeadu, da] *adj* tanned.

➡ **bronzeado** *m* tan; **pegar um** ~ to get a suntan.

bronzeador [brõzea'do(x)] (*pl* -**es**) *adj* suntan (*antes de subst*).

➡ **bronzeador** *m* suntan lotion.

bronzear [15] [brõ'zja(x)] *vt* to tan.

➡ **bronzear-se** *vp* to sunbathe.

brotar [4] [bro'ta(x)] *vi* -**1.** [germinar, desabrochar - planta] to sprout; [- muda] to begin; [- flor] to

blossom. -**2.** [manar] to flow; ~ **de** to spurt from. -**3.** *fig* [esperança, suspeita, paixão] to grow.

broto ['brotul *m* -**1.** [de vegetal] sprout; ~ **de bambu** bamboo shoot; ~ **de feijão** bean sprout. -**2.** [de flor] shoot. -**3.** [jovem] sapling.

brotoeja [bro'tweʒa] *f* rash.

broxa [brɔ'ʃa] <> *f* [pincel] brush. <> *m vulg* [homem impotente] dickless guy. <> *adj vulg* [impotente] dickless.

bruços ['brusuʃ] *mpl*: **de** ~ lying face down.

bruma ['bruma] *f* mist.

brumoso, osa [bru'mozu, ɔza] *adj* misty.

brusco, ca ['bruʃku, ka] *adj* -**1.** [repentino] sudden. -**2.** [tosco, grosseiro] coarse.

brutal [bru'taw] (*pl* -**ais**) *adj* -**1.** [violento, bárbaro] brutal. -**2.** [tremendo, grande] tremendous.

brutalidade [brutali'dadʒi] *f* brutality.

brutamontes [bruta'mõntʃiʃ] *m inv* [homem corpulento] hulk.

bruto, ta ['brutu, ta] *adj* -**1.** [rude, grosseiro] brutish. -**2.** [tosco] coarse. -**3.** (*antes de subst)* [tremendo, grande] tremendous. -**4.** [violento] brutal. -**5.** [produto] raw; **em** ~ raw. -**6.** [sem decréscimo] gross.

bruxa ['bruʃa] *f* -**1.** [feiticeira] witch. -**2.** [mariposa] moth. -**3.** *fam pej* [mulher má] bad woman. -**4.** *fam pej* [mulher feia] hag.

bruxaria [bruʃa'ria] *f* witchcraft.

Bruxelas [bru'ʃɛlaʃ] *n* Brussels.

bruxo ['bruʃu] *m* sorcerer.

Bucareste [buka'rɛʃtʃi] *n* Bucharest.

bucha ['buʃa] *f* -**1.** [de parafuso] Rawlplug®. -**2.** [para buracos] lid. -**3.** [de arma] wad. -**4.** [de balão] wick.

➡ **na bucha** *loc adv fam* [sem demora] promptly.

bucho ['buʃu] *m* -**1.** [de boi] maw. -**2.** *fam* [pessoa feia]: **ser um** ~ to look gross.

buço ['busu] *m* down.

bucólico, ca [bu'kɔliku, ka] *adj* bucolic.

Budapeste [buda'peʃtʃi] *n* Budapest.

budismo [bu'dʒiʒmu] *m* Buddhism.

budista [bu'dʒiʃta] <> *adj* Buddhist. <> *mf* Buddhist.

bueiro [bu'ejru] *m* gutter.

Buenos Aires [bwenu'zajriʃ] *n* Buenos Aires.

búfalo ['bufalu] *m* buffalo.

bufante [bu'fãntʃi] *adj* bouffant.

bufar [4] [bu'fa(x)] *vi* -**1.** [ofegar] to pant. -**2.** [de raiva] to fume.

bufê, buffet [bu'fe] *m* buffet.

bug ['bugi] (*pl* **bugs**) *m* COMPUT bug.

bugiganga [buʒĩ'gãŋga] *f* piece of junk.

bujão [bu'ʒãw] (*pl* -**ões**) *m* cylinder; ~ **de gás** gas cylinder.

bula ['bula] *f* -**1.** MED information leaflet. -**2.** RELIG: ~ **(papal)** papal bull.

bulbo ['buwbu] *m* bulb.

buldôzer [buw'doze(x)] (*pl* -**es**) *m* bulldozer.

bule ['buli] *m* pot.

Bulgária [buw'garja] *n* Bulgaria.

búlgaro, ra ['buwgaru, ra] <> *adj* Bulgarian. <> *m, f* Bulgarian.

búlgaro m [língua] Bulgarian.

bulhufas [bu'ʎufaʃ] pron fam [coisa nenhuma]: **não entender/ouvir** ~ to understand/hear nothing.

buliçoso, osa [buli'sozu, ɔza] adj **-1.** [agitado] turbulent. **-2.** [vivo] lively.

bulimia [buli'mia] f bulimia.

bulir [61] [bu'li(x)] <> vt [mover] to ruffle. <> vi **-1.** [mover-se] to sway. **-2.** [tocar, mexer]: ~ **em** to fiddle with sthg. **-3.** [provocar]: ~ **com alguém** to taunt sb.

bumbum [bũn'bũ] (pl **-ns**) m fam bottom, bum.

bunda ['bũnda] (pl **-ns**) f fam bottom, bum.

bunda-mole [ˌbũnda'mɔli] (pl **bundas-moles**) mf fam wimp.

buquê [bu'ke] m bouquet; ~ **de flores** bouquet of flowers.

buraco [bu'raku] m **-1.** [ger] hole; ~ **da fechadura** keyhole. **-2.** [de agulha] eye. **-3.** [jogo] rummy.

burburinho [buxbu'riɲu] m **-1.** [agitação] clamour. **-2.** [rumor] murmur.

burguês, guesa [bux'geʃ, gezal] <> adj bourgeois. <> m, f [pessoa] bourgeois.

burguesia [buxge'zia] f bourgeoisie; **alta** ~ upper middle class.

burilar [4] [buri'la(x)] vt **-1.** [lavrar] to engrave. **-2.** fig [aprimorar] to perfect.

burla ['buxla] f **-1.** [fraude] double-dealing. **-2.** [zombaria] jeering.

burlar [4] [bux'la(x)] vt **-1.** [fraudar, lesar] to cheat. **-2.** [enganar] to deceive. **-3.** [lei] to defraud.

burlesco, ca [bux'leʃku, ka] adj burlesque.

burocracia [burokra'sia] f bureaucracy.

burocrata [buro'krata] m f bureaucrat.

burocrático, ca [buro'kratʃiku, ka] adj bureaucratic.

burocratizar [4] [burokratʃi'za(x)] vt to bureaucratize.

burrice [bu'xisi] f **-1.** [estupidez] stupidity. **-2.** [ato, dito] something stupid; **foi** ~ **minha ter aceitado a proposta** it was silly of me to accept that offer.

burro, a ['buxu, xa] <> adj stupid. <> m, f [pessoa imbecil] ass.

➡ **burro** m ZOOL donkey; ~ **de carga** beast of burden; fig workhorse; **dar com os** ~ **s n'água** to lose out.

➡ **pra burro** fam loc adv: **ele pinta mal pra** ~ he paints terribly; **a mulher do hotel era feia pra** ~ the woman in the hotel was terribly ugly.

bursite [bux'sitʃi] f bursitis.

busca ['buʃka] f search; **em** ~ **de** in search of; **dar** ~ **a** to search for.

buscador [buʃka'do(x)] m COMPUT search engine.

busca-pé [buʃka'pɛ] (pl **-s**) m firecracker.

buscar [12] [buʃ'ka(x)] vt **-1.** [procurar] to search for. **-2.** [tratar de obter] to seek. **-3.** [pegar, trazer] to fetch; **ir** ~ to go and fetch; **mandar** ~ to send for. **-4.** [esforçar-se por]: ~ **fazer algo** to try to do sthg. **-5.** COMPUT to search.

bússola ['busola] f compass.

bustiê [buʃ'tʃje] m bustier.

busto ['buʃtu] m **-1.** [ger] bust; **ela tem 85 cm de** ~ her bust size is 85 cm. **-2.** [torso] torso.

butique [bu'tʃiki] f boutique.

buzina [bu'zina] f horn, hooter.

buzinada [buzi'nada] f honk; **dar uma** ~ to honk.

buzinar [4] [buzi'na(x)] <> vt **-1.** AUTO to honk. **-2.** fig [dizer com insistência] to harp on; ~ **algo nos ouvidos de alguém** to harp on about sthg to sb. <> vi AUTO to honk.

búzio ['buzju] m [concha] conch; **jogar** ~ **s** [espírit] to cast shells (in fortune telling).

byte ['bajtʃi] m COMPUT byte.

c, C ['se] m [letra] c, C.
➡ **C** abrev de **celsius**.

cá ['ka] adv **-1.** [lugar] here; **vem** ~! come here!; **de** ~ **para lá** from here to there; **do lado de** ~ this side; **mais para** ~ closer. **-2.** [tempo]: **de uma semana para** ~ for the past week; **de uns tempos para** ~ recently; **de lá para** ~ since then. **-3.** [na intimidade]: ~ **comigo** to myself; ~ **entre nós** just between ourselves.

CA (abrev de **Centro Acadêmico**) m centre in a Brazilian university where students meet to discuss problems concerning their course etc.

caatinga [ka'tʃĩga] f caatinga.

cabal [ka'baw] (pl **-ais**) adj **-1.** [pleno, completo] utter. **-2.** [exato] complete. **-3.** [prova] ultimate.

cabala [ka'bala] f **-1.** [doutrina] cabbala. **-2.** fig [maquinação] cabal.

cabalístico, ca [kaba'liʃtʃiku, ka] adj cabalistic.

cabana [ka'bãna] f hut.

cabaré [kaba'rɛ] m cabaret.

cabeça [ka'besa] <> f **-1.** [ger] head; **de** ~ [calcular] in one's head; **de** ~ head first; **de** ~ **erguida** fig with one's head held high; **por** ~ per head; **só faz o que lhe dá na** ~ he only does what he has a mind to; **meter na** ~ to get into one's head; **não bater bem da** ~ to be off one's rocker; **não estar com** ~ **para fazer algo** not to be in the mood to do sthg; **passar pela** ~ to cross one's mind; **subir à** ~ [suj: sucesso, dinheiro] to go to one's head; **ter a** ~ **no lugar** [ser ajuizado] to be level-headed; ~ **fria** fig cool-headed; **com a** ~ **no ar** with one's head in the clouds; ~ **a** ~ neck and neck. **-2.** [inteligência] mind; **usar a** ~ to use one's head. **-3.** [pessoa inteligente] brains. **-4.** [topo, parte de cima]: **de** ~ **para baixo** upside down. **-5.**

[de lista] top. **- 6.** *fam* [de glande] glans. **- 7.** [loc]: **fazer a ~ de alguém** to influence sb's thinking; **levar na ~** *fam* to take a hard knock; **não esquentar a ~** *fam* not to get hot and bothered; **perder a ~** to lose one's head; **quebrar a ~** to rack one's brains. <> *mf* head.

cabeçada [kabe'sada] *f* **-1.** [pancada] headbutt; **dar uma ~ em alguém** to headbutt sb; **dar uma ~ em algo** to bang one's head on sthg; **dar uma ~** *fig* to take a knock. **- 2.** *FUT* header.

cabeça-de-vento [ka,besad3i'vẽntul (*pl* **cabeças-de-vento**) *mf* scatterbrain.

cabeça-dura [ka,besa'dura] (*pl* **cabeças-duras**) <> *adj* [teimoso] headstrong. <> *mf* headstrong person.

cabeça-feita [ka,besa'fejta] (*pl* **cabeças-feitas**) *adj fam* [pessoa responsável] level-headed.

cabeçalho [kabe'saʎu] *m* **-1.** [de livro] title. **- 2.** [de página, capítulo] heading.

cabecear [15] [kabe'sja(x)] *FUT vt* [bola] to head.

cabeceira [kabe'sejra] *f* head; **livro de ~** bedside book.

cabeçudo, da [kabe'sudu, da] *adj* **-1.** [de cabeça grande] big-headed. **- 2.** *fam* [teimoso] pig-headed.

cabedal [kabe'daw] (*pl* **-ais**) *m* wealth.

cabeleira [kabe'lejra] *f* **-1.** [natural] head of hair. **- 2.** [peruca] wig.

cabeleireiro, ra [kabelej'rejru, ra] *m, f* [profissional] hairdresser.

➥ **cabeleireiro** *m* [salão] hairdressing salon.

cabelo [ka'belu] *m* [ger] hair; **~ liso/crespo/pixaim** straight/curly/woolly hair; **de arrepiar os ~s** *fig* hair-raising.

cabeludo, da [kabe'ludu, da] *adj* **-1.** hairy. **- 2.** *fam fig* [complicado, obsceno] hairy.

➥ **cabeludo** *m fam* [homem] hairy man.

caber [34] [ka'be(x)] *vi* **-1.** [ger] to fit; **não ~ em si de** *fam fig* to be overwhelmed with; **~ (em)** to fit (in); **~ por** to fit through; **~ fazer algo** to have to do sthg. **- 2.** [ser oportuno] to be time to. **- 3.** [ser compatível]: **~ em algo** to be compatible with sthg. **- 4.** [competir]: **~ a alguém fazer algo** to be the responsibility of sb to so sthg. **- 5.** [partilha]: **~ a alguém** to be allocated to sb.

cabide [ka'bidʒi] *m* [de armário] clothes hanger; [de pé] coat hanger; [de parede] coat hook; **~ de empregos** *fig* [pessoa] Jack-of-all-trades (but master of none); *fig* [empresa estatal] jobs-for-the-boys organisation.

cabideiro [kabi'dejru] *m* **-1.** [de pé] coat hanger. **- 2.** [de parede] coat hook.

cabimento [kabi'mẽntu] *m* [adequação] sense; **ter/não ter ~** to make/not to make sense.

cabine [ka'binil] *f* **-1.** [ger] cabin. **- 2.** [telefônica] phone box *UK*, phone booth *US*. **- 3.** [guarita] sentry box. **- 4.** *FERRO* [compartimento] carriage, compartment. **- 5.** *AERON* [de comando] cockpit. **- 6.** [vestuário] changing room.

cabisbaixo, xa [kabiʒ'bajʃu, ʃa] *adj* crestfallen.

cabível [ka'bivew] (*pl* **-eis**) *adj* fitting.

cabo [ˈkabu] *m* **-1.** [de panela, faca, vassoura] handle.

- 2. [fim] end. **- 3.** *CORDA* : **~ de aço** iron cable. **- 4.** *ELETR* cable. **- 5.** *GEOGR* cape. **- 6.** *MIL* corporal. **- 7.** *POL* : **~ eleitoral** electoral canvasser. **- 8.** [fim]: **dar ~ de** [pessoa] to kill; [problema] to put an end to; [tarefa] to finish; **levar algo a ~** [tarefa, projeto] to see sthg through; **ao ~ de** by the end of; **de ~ a rabo** [de uma extremidade a outra] from one end to the other; [do início ao fim] from the beginning to the end.

caboclo, cla [ka'boklu, cla] <> *adj* **-1.** [pele] copper-coloured. **- 2.** [pessoa] bumpkinish. <> *m, f* **-1.** [mestiço de banco com índio] caboclo. **- 2.** [pessoa da roça] bumpkin.

cabotino, na [kabo'tʃinu, na] <> *adj* theatrical. <> *m, f* show-off.

Cabo Verde [,kabu'vexd3il *n* Cape Verde.

cabra [ˈkabra] <> *f* [animal] goat. <> *m fam* **-1.** [homem] guy. **- 2.** [capanga] gunman.

cabra-cega [,kabra'sega] (*pl* **cabras-cegas**) *f* blind man's buff.

cabra-macho [,kabra'maʃul (*pl* **cabras-machos**) *m* tough guy.

cabreiro, ra [ka'brejru, ra] *adj fam* [desconfiado] suspicious.

cabresto [ka'breʃtu] *m* [para cavalos] halter.

cabrito [ka'britul *m* kid.

caça [ˈkasal <> *f* **-1.** [ato] hunt; **~ às bruxas** witch-hunt; **à ~ de** in pursuit of. **- 2.** [animal - caçado por homem] game; [- caçado por outro animal] prey; game. **- 3.** [passatempo] hunting. <> *m AERON* fighter.

caçada [ka'sadal *f* [jornada] hunting trip.

caçador, ra [kasa'do(x), ra] (*mpl* **-es**, *fpl* **-s**) *m, f* hunter.

caça-minas [,kasa'minaʃ] *m inv* minesweeper.

caça-níqueis [,kasa'nikejʃ] *m inv* **-1.** [máquina] slot-machine. **- 2.** *fam* [empresa, loja] cowboy outfit.

cação [ka'sãw] (*pl* **-ões**) *m* dogfish.

caçapa [ka'sapal *f* pocket (*on billiard table*).

caçar [13] [ka'sa(x)] <> *vt* **-1.** [animais] to hunt. **- 2.** [a tiro] to shoot. **- 3.** [buscar - documentos, prova, tesouro] to search for; [- recompensa] to seek. **- 4.** [perseguir] to hunt down. **- 5.** *fam* [marido] to hunt for. <> *vi* [andar à caça] to hunt.

cacareco [kaka'rɛkul *m* piece of junk.

➥ **cacarecos** *mpl* junk (*sg*).

cacarejar [4] [kakare'ʒa(x)] *vi* to cluck.

cacarejo [kaka'reʒu] *m* clucking.

caçarola [kasa'rɔla] *f* casserole.

cacau [ka'kaw] *m* **-1.** [fruto] cacao. **- 2.** [semente] cocoa bean. **- 3.** [pó] cocoa.

cacetada [kase'tada] *f* whack; **dar uma ~ (em algo/alguém)** to whack (sthg/sb).

cacete [ka'setʃil <> *adj* [tedioso] tedious. <> *m* **-1.** [porrete] truncheon. **- 2.** *vulg* [pênis] rod.

➥ **pra cacete** *mfam* <> *loc pron*: **gente pra ~** shitloads of people. <> *loc adv* : **chato/bom/forte pra cacete** bloody boring/good/strong.

cachaça [ka'ʃasa] *f* sugar-cane brandy.

CACHAÇA

Cachaça is the most popular alcoholic drink in Brazil; it is a fermented drink, obtained from the distillation of sugar-cane sap, and it is very high in alcohol. Its popularity can be measured by the many names that Brazilians give this drink, such as *pinga*, *caninha*, *branquinha*, *mel*, among many others.

cachaceiro, ra [kaʃa'sejru, ra] ⟨⟩ *adj* drunken. ⟨⟩ *m, f* drunkard.

cache [ka'ʃe] *m* COMPUT cache.

cachê [ka'ʃe] *m* fee *(for performance)*.

cacheado, da [ka'ʃjadu, da] *adj* curly.

cachecol [kaʃe'kɔw] *(pl* -óis*)* *m* scarf.

cachimbo [ka'ʃĩbu] *m* pipe.

cacho ['kaʃu] *m* -**1**. [ger] bunch. -**2**. [de cabelos - anel] lock; [- mecha] strand.

cachoeira [ka'ʃwejra] *f* waterfall.

cachorra [ka'ʃoxa] *f* ⊳ **cachorro**.

cachorrada [kaʃo'xada] *f* -**1**. [matilha] pack of dogs. -**2**. *fam fig* [canalhice] scam; **fazer uma ~ com alguém** to scam sb.

cachorrinho, nha [kaʃo'xiɲu, ɲa] *m, f* [filhote] puppy.
    ◆ **cachorrinho** *m* [nado] doggy-paddle.

cachorro, rra [ka'ʃoxu, ra] *m, f* -**1**. [cão] dog; **soltar os ~s (em cima de alguém)** *fig* to lash out (at sb); **estar matando ~ a grito** to be scraping the barrel. -**2**. *fam pej* [patife] bastard.
    ◆ **cachorra** *f*: **estar com a ~** *fig* to be in a bad mood.

cachorro-quente [ka,ʃoxu'kẽtʃil *(pl* cachorros-quentes*)* *m* hot dog.

cacife [ka'sifi] *m* stake; **ter ~ para** *fig* [ter dinheiro para] to be able to afford; [ter condições de] to have what it takes.

cacique [ka'sikil *m* -**1**. [indígena] cacique, tribal chief. -**2**. *fig* [chefão] boss.

caco ['kaku] *m* -**1**. [de vidro etc] shard. -**2**. *fam* [pessoa]: **estar um ~** [estar velho] to be a wreck; [estar desgastado] to be a wreck; [estar exausto] to be wiped out.

caçoar [20] [ka'swa(x)] *vi* to mock; **~ de algo/alguém** to make fun of sthg/sb.

cações [ka'sõjʃ] *pl* ⊳ **cação**.

cacoete [ka'kwetʃi] *m* tic.

cacto ['kaktu] *m* cactus.

caçula [ka'sula] ⟨⟩ *adj* youngest. ⟨⟩ *mf* youngest child.

CAD *(abrev de* **Computer Aided Design***)* *m* CAD.

cada ['kada] *adj (inv)* -**1**. [valor de unidade] each; **uma coisa de ~ vez** one thing at a time; **~ (um)** [em preço] each; **~ qual, ~ um** each one. -**2**. [todo] every; **a ~** every; **aumentar a ~ dia** to increase from day to day; **em ~ dez pessoas, uma sofre de ...** one out of ten people suffers from ... -**3**. [valor progressivo]: **~ vez** more and more. -**4**. [valor intensivo] such; **me acontece ~ uma!** would you believe it!

cadafalso [kada'fawsu] *m* gallows *(pl)*.

cadarço [ka'daxsu] *m* shoelace.

cadastramento [kadaʃtra'mẽtul *m* registration.

cadastrar [4] [kadaʃ'tra(x)] *vt* -**1**. [registrar] to register. -**2**. COMPUT [dados] to record.
    ◆ **cadastrar-se** *vp* [inscrever-se] to register o.s.

cadastro [ka'daʃtru] *m* -**1**. [registro] register. -**2**. [ato] registration. -**3**. [ficha de criminoso] criminal record. -**4**. [de banco, clientes] records *(pl)*. -**5**. [de imóveis] land registry. -**6**. COMPUT [de dados] data record.

cadáver [ka'davɛ(x)] *(pl* -es*)* *m* corpse.

cadavérico, ca [kada'vɛriku, ka] *adj* -**1**. [exame] post-mortem *(antes de subst)*. -**2**. [pessoa, palidez, rosto] cadaverous.

cadê [ka'de] *adv fam* where is/are.

cadeado [ka'dʒjadul *m* padlock.

cadeia [ka'deja] *f* -**1**. [ger] chain. -**2**. [prisão] prison. -**3**. [série, seqüência] series *(inv)*; **~ de montanhas** mountain range. -**4**. [de emissoras de TV] network.

cadeira [ka'dejra] *f* -**1**. [ger] chair; **~ de balanço** rocking chair; **~ de rodas** wheelchair; **~ cativa** [em estádio] reserved place; **falar de ~** to speak with authority. -**2**. [disciplina] subject. -**3**. [em teatro] seat.
    ◆ **cadeiras** *fpl* ANAT hips.

cadela [ka'dɛla] *f* [cão] bitch ⊳ **cão**.

cadência [ka'dẽsja] *f* -**1**. [ritmo] rhythm. -**2**. [de estilo, fala] cadence.

cadenciado, da [kadẽ'sjadu, da] *adj* -**1**. [ritmado] rhythmic. -**2**. [pausado] measured.

cadente [ka'dẽtʃi] *adj* [estrela] falling.

caderneta [kadex'netal *f* -**1**. [livrete] note pad. -**2**. [escolar] mark sheet. -**3**. FIN: **~ de poupança** savings account.

caderno [ka'dɛxrnul *m* -**1**. [de notas] notebook. -**2**. [de jornal] section.

cadete [ka'detʃil *m* cadet.

cadinho [ka'dʒiɲul *m* -**1**. [recipiente] crucible. -**2**. *fig* [local] melting pot.

caducar [12] [kadu'ka(x)] *vi* -**1**. [prazo, documento, lei] to expire. -**2**. [pessoa] to become senile.

caduco, ca [ka'duku, ka] *adj* -**1**. [prazo, documento, lei] expired. -**2**. [pessoa] senile. -**3**. BOT deciduous.

caduquice [kadu'kisil *f* [senilidade] senility.

cães ['kãjʃ] *pl* ⊳ **cão**.

cafajestada [kafaʒeʃ'tadal *f* *fam* con; **fazer uma ~ com alguém** to pull a fast one on sb.

cafajeste [kafa'ʒɛʃtʃi] *fam* ⟨⟩ *adj* -**1**. [canalha] crooked. -**2**. [vulgar] vulgar. ⟨⟩ *mf* [pessoa canalha] con man.

café [ka'fɛl *m* -**1**. [ger] coffee; **~ (preto)** black coffee; **~ com leite** white coffee *UK*, coffee with cream *US*; **~ expresso** espresso; **~ pingado** *coffee with a tiny drop of milk*; **ser ~ pequeno** *fam* [tarefa] to be small beer; [pessoa] to be small fry. -**2**. [desjejum]: **~ (da manhã)** breakfast. -**3**. [estabelecimento] café.

CAFÉ

The *cafézinho*, so greatly enjoyed by the Brazilians, played a decisive role in the country's history. Coffee was the main export at the end of the nineteenth century; it propelled Brazilian industrialisation, bringing about the opening of roads and railways throughout the central south of the country. Coffee was a determining factor in the development of São Paulo as the industrial and financial centre of Brazil.

café-com-leite [ˌkafɛkõn'lejtʃi] *adj inv* [cor] coffee-coloured.

cafeeiro, ra [kafe'ejru, ra] ⬦ *adj* [setor, indústria] coffee *(antes de subst)*. ⬦ *m* coffee bush.

cafeicultor, ra [kafejkuw'to(x), ra] *m, f* coffee planter.

cafeína [kafe'ina] *f* caffeine.

cafetã [kafe'tã] *f* kaftan.

cafetão, tina [kafe'tãw, tʃina] *(mpl -ões, fpl -s) m, f* pimp.

cafeteira [kafe'tejra] *f* coffee pot.

cafetina [kafe'tʃina] *f* ⊳ **cafetão.**

cafezal [kafe'zaw] *(pl -ais) m* coffee plantation.

cafezinho [kafɛ'ziɲu] *m fam* small black coffee.

cafona [ka'fona] ⬦ *adj* [pessoa, roupa, música] tacky. ⬦ *mf* [pessoa] tacky person.

cafonice [kafo'nisi] *f* tackiness.

cafundó-do-judas [kafũnˌdɔdu'ʒudaʃ] *m*: **no ~** out in the sticks.

cafuné [kafu'nɛ] *m*: **fazer ~ em alguém: fazer ~ em alguém** to scratch sb's head gently.

cagada [ka'gada] *f vulg* crap.

cágado [ka'gadu] *m* terrapin.

caganeira [kaga'nejra] *f vulg* runs *(pl)*.

cagão, gona [ka'gãw, gona] *(mpl -ões, fpl -s) m, f fam* [medroso, tímido] wimp.

cagar [14] [ka'ga(x)] *vulg* ⬦ *vi* **- 1.** [defecar] to have a crap. **- 2.** *fig* [menosprezar]: **~ para alguém/algo** not to give a shit about sb/sthg. ⬦ *vt fig* [impôr]: **~ regras** to be full of shit.

➡ **cagar-se** *vp* [defecar nas calças] to shit o.s.; **~ -se de medo** *fig* to be shit scared.

caiado, da [ka'jadu, da] *adj* ≃ whitewashed.

caiaque [ka'jakil *m* kayak.

caiar [16] [ka'ja(x)] *vt* to whitewash.

caibro [ˈkajbru] *m* joist.

caído, da [ka'idu, da] *adj* **- 1.** [derrubado] fallen. **- 2.** [pendente] droopy. **- 3.** *fig* [abatido] depressed. **- 4.** *fig* [apaixonado]: **estar ~ por alguém** to be in love with sb. **- 5.** *fig* [desanimado] subdued. **- 6.** *fig* [feio] saggy.

➡ **caída** *f* [queda] fall.

caimento [kaj'mẽntu] *m* [de roupa] hang.

caipira [kaj'pira] *fam* ⬦ *adj* provincial. ⬦ *mf* [pessoa - do interior] country bumpkin; [- sem traquejo social] boor.

caipirinha [kajpi'riɲa] *f* caipirinha, *cocktail made with sugar-cane brandy and lime juice.*

CAIPIRINHA

One of the most typical alcoholic beverages of Brazil; *caipirinha* is prepared with slices or chunks of lemon, *cachaça*, ice and sugar. It is an essential accompaniment to Brazilian *feijoadas* and barbecues, and probably originates from the interior of the state of São Paulo, which would explain its name: *caipira* is the name given to those who were born there. Variations of *caipirinha* include *caipirosca* (made with vodka instead of *cachaça*) and *caipiríssima* (made with rum).

cair [68] [ka'i(x)] *vi* **- 1.** [ger] to fall; **~ de joelhos** to fall to one's knees; **~ de quatro** to fall on all fours; *fig* [surpreender-se] to fall over backward; **estar caindo de sono** *fig* to be dropping with tiredness; **~ em** to fall into; **~ nas garras de alguém** *fig* to fall into sb's clutches. **- 2.** [desabar] to collapse. **- 3.** [desprender-se - dente, cabelo, folha] to fall out; [- botão] to fall off. **- 4.** [deixar-se enganar] to fall for. **- 5.** [entregar-se a]: **~ em** [na farra] to join in. **- 6.** EDUC [em prova] to crop up. **- 7.** *loc*: **~ bem/mal** [penteado, roupa, cor] to suit/not to suit; [frase, atitude] to go down well/badly; [comida, bebida] to agree/not to agree with; **estar caindo aos pedaços** to be falling to pieces; **~ em si** [reconhecer o erro] to accept one's mistake; [voltar à realidade] to come down to earth; **não ter onde ~ morto** to have nothing to one's name.

cais [ˈkajʃ] *m inv* quay.

Cairo [ˈkajru] *n* Cairo.

caixa [ˈkajʃa] ⬦ *f* **- 1.** [ger] box; **~ acústica** loudspeaker; **~ de fósforos** matchbox. **- 2.** [para correspondência]: **~ de correio** postbox *UK*, mailbox *US*; **~ postal** *ou* **de coleta** postal box. **- 3.** [mecanismo]: **~ de chave** console; **~ de luz** fuse-box; **~ de marchas** *ou* **de mudanças** gearbox. **- 4.** [máquina]: **~ registradora** cash till. **- 5.** [seção] till. **- 6.** [banco] savings bank; **~ dois** undeclared assets; **~ econômica** national savings bank. **- 7.** ANAT: **~ craniana** cranium; **~ torácica** thorax. **- 8.** TIP : **~ alta/baixa** upper/lower case. ⬦ *m* **- 1.** [máquina]: **~ eletrônico** cashpoint. **- 2.** [livro] ledger; **~ dois** fraudulent books *(pl)*. ⬦ *mf* [funcionário] cashier.

caixa-d'água [ˈkajʃa'dagwa] *(pl* **caixas-d'água***) f* water tank.

caixa-de-fósforos [ˈkajʃadʒi'ʃɔʃforuʃ] *f fam* [habitação, carro] matchbox.

caixa-forte [ˈkajʃa'fɔxtʃi] *(pl* **caixas-fortes***) f* safe.

caixão [kaj'ʃãw] *(pl -ões) m* [ataúde] coffin.

caixa-preta [ˈkajʃa'preta] *(pl* **caixas-pretas***) f* AERON black box.

caixeiro, ra [kaj'ʃejru, ra] *m, f* **- 1.** [balconista] sales assistant. **- 2.** [entregador] delivery person.

caixeiro-viajante, caixeira-viajante [kajˌʃejruvja'ʒãntʃi, kajˌʃejravja'ʒãntʃil *m, f* commercial traveller.

caixilho [kaj'ʃiʎu] *m* [moldura] frame.

caixões [kaj'ʃõjʃ] *pl* ⊳ **caixão.**

caixote [kajˈʃɔtʃi] m crate.

caju [kaˈʒu] m cashew.

cajueiro [kaˈʒwejru] m cashew tree.

cal [ˈkaw] f - **1.** [substância] lime, quicklime. - **2.** [extinta] slaked lime. - **3.** [para caiar] whitewash.

calabouço [kalaˈbosu] m dungeon.

calada [kaˈlada] f: **na ~ da noite** in the dead of night.

calado, da [kaˈladu, da] adj quiet.

calafetagem [kalafeˈtaʒẽ] (pl -ns) f caulking.

calafetar [4] [kalafeˈta(x)] vt to stop up.

calafrio [kalaˈfriw] m shiver; **ter ~s** to have the shivers.

calamar [kalaˈma(x)] m squid.

calamidade [kalamiˈdadʒi] f calamity.

calamitoso, tosa [kalamiˈtozu, tɔza] adj calamitous.

calão [kaˈlãw] m: **(baixo) ~** foul language.

calar [4] [kaˈla(x)] <> vt - **1.** [ocultar] to keep quiet about. - **2.** [silenciar] to silence; **cala a boca!** shut up! - **3.** [conter] to ignore. - **4.** euf [armas, canhões] to silence. <> vi - **1.** [manter-se em silêncio] to keep quiet. - **2.** [repercutir]: **~ em** to reverberate through.
  ➤ calar-se vp [parar de falar] to go quiet, to stop talking.

calça [ˈkawsa] f trousers UK (pl), pants US (pl).

calçada [kawˈsada] f pavement UK, sidewalk US.

calçadão [kawsaˈdãw] (pl -ões) m pavement.

calçadeira [kawsaˈdejra] f shoehorn.

calçado, da [kawˈsadu, da] adj - **1.** [caminho, rua] paved. - **2.** [pessoa, pé] with shoes on (depois de subst).
  ➤ calçado m [sapato, tênis] footwear.

calçamento [kawsaˈmẽntu] m paving.

calcanhar [kawkaˈɲa(x)] (pl -es) m heel.

calcanhar-de-aquiles [kawka̠naxdʒiaˈkiliʃ] (pl calcanhares-de-aquiles) m Achilles' heel.

calção [kawˈsãw] (pl -ões) m shorts (pl); **~ de banho** swim shorts (pl).

calcar [12] [kawˈka(x)] vt - **1.** [pisar] to tread on. - **2.** [comprimir]: **~ algo em** to press sthg into. - **3.** fig [basear]: **~ algo em** to base sthg on.

calçar [13] [kawˈsa(x)] vt - **1.** [sapatos, luvas] to put on; [tamanho] to take a size. - **2.** [pavimentar] to pave. - **3.** [pôr calço em] to wedge.
  ➤ calçar-se vp [pôr sapatos] to put one's shoes on.

calcário, ria [kawˈkarju, rja] adj - **1.** [substância, pedra] chalky, calcareous. - **2.** [água] hard.
  ➤ calcário m [rocha] limestone.

calcificação [kawsifikaˈsãw] f calcification.

calcificar [12] [kawsifiˈka(x)] vt to calcify.
  ➤ calcificar-se vp to calcify.

calcinha [kawˈsiɲa] f panties (pl).

cálcio [ˈkawsju] m calcium.

calço [ˈkawsu] m [cunha] wedge.

calções [kalˈsõiʃ] pl ➤ **calção**.

calculadora [kawkulaˈdora] f calculator.

calcular [4] [kawkuˈla(x)] <> vt - **1.** [fazer a conta de] to calculate. - **2.** [avaliar, estimar] to estimate. - **3.** [imaginar] to imagine. - **4.** [supor, prever]: **~ que** to guess that. <> vi [fazer contas] to calculate.

calculável [kawkuˈlavew] (pl -eis) adj calculable.

calculista [kawkuˈliʃta] <> adj calculating. <> mf opportunist.

cálculo [ˈkawkulu] m - **1.** [conta] calculation. - **2.** [estimativa] estimate. - **3.** MAT calculus. - **4.** MED stone; **~ renal** kidney stone.

calda [ˈkawda] f syrup.

caldeira [kawˈdejra] f TEC boiler.

caldeirão [kawdejˈrãw] (pl -ões) m cauldron.

caldo [ˈkawdu] m - **1.** [sopa] broth; **~ verde** green vegetable and potato soup. - **2.** [sumo] juice; **~ de cana** sugar-cane juice. - **3.** [tempero]: **~ de carne/galinha** beef/chicken stock. - **4.** fig [mistura]: **~ de cultura** melting pot of cultures. - **5.** fam [mergulho]: **dar um ~ em alguém** to duck sb.

calefação [kalefaˈsãw] f heating.

caleidoscópio [kalejdoʃˈkɔpju] m kaleidoscope.

calejado [kaleˈʒadu] adj - **1.** [mão, pé] calloused. - **2.** fig [vivido] experienced. - **3.** fig [endurecido] hardened.

calejar [4] [kaleˈʒa(x)] vt - **1.** [mãos, pés] to cause to become calloused. - **2.** fig [endurecer] to harden.

calendário [kalẽnˈdarju] m calendar.

calha [kaˈʎa] f - **1.** [sulco] channel. - **2.** [para a chuva] gutter.

calhamaço [kaʎaˈmasu] m tome.

calhambeque [kaʎãnˈbɛki] m fam jalopy.

calhar [4] [kaˈʎa(x)] vi - **1.** [acontecer]: **~ que** to happen that. - **2.** [concidir] to happen that; **calhou de elas usarem vestidos iguais** they happened to be wearing the same dress. - **3.** [convir]: **vir a ~ to come at just the right time.

calhau [kaˈʎaw] m pebble.

calibrado, da [kaliˈbradu, da] adj - **1.** [pneu] balanced. - **2.** fam [meio embriagado] tipsy.

calibragem [kaliˈbraʒẽ] (pl -ns) f calibration.

calibrar [4] [kaliˈbra(x)] vt - **1.** [pneu] to balance. - **2.** [instrumento] to calibrate.

calibre [kaˈlibri] m [de cano] calibre.

cálice [ˈkalisi] m - **1.** [taça] liqueur glass. - **2.** RELIG chalice.

cálido, da [ˈkalidu, da] adj warm.

caligrafia [kaligraˈfia] f - **1.** [arte] calligraphy. - **2.** [letra] handwriting.

calista [kaˈliʃta] mf chiropodist UK, podiatrist US.

calma [ˈkawma] f ➤ **calmo**.

calmante [kawˈmãntʃi] <> adj calming. <> m tranquillizer.

calmaria [kawmaˈria] f lull.

calmo, ma [ˈkawmu, ma] adj [ger] calm.
  ➤ calma f - **1.** [quietude] tranquillity. - **2.** [serenidade] serenity; **calma!** just a moment!; **manter/perder a ~** to keep/lose one's composure.

calo [ˈkalu] m [endurecimento da pele] callus; [no pé] corn; **pisar nos ~s de alguém** fig to hit a raw nerve.

calombo [kaˈlõnbu] m - **1.** [ger] lump. - **2.** [em estrada] bump.

calor [kaˈlo(x)] m - **1.** [ger] heat; **estar com ~** , sentir ~ to be/feel hot; **fazer** ~ to be hot. -**2.** [quentura] warmth.

calorão [kalo'rãw] *m* [tempo] heatwave.

calorento, ta [kalo'rẽntu, ta] *adj* -**1.** [pessoa] sensitive to heat. -**2.** [local] hot.

caloria [kalo'ria] *f* calorie.

caloroso, osa [kalo'rozu, ɔza] *adj* -**1.** [ger] warm. -**2.** [manifestação, protesto] fervent.

calota [ka'lɔta] *f* AUTO hubcap.

calote [ka'lɔtʃi] *m fam* [de dívida] bad debt; **dar o** ~ **em alguém** to welsh on sb.

caloteiro, ra [kalo'tejru, ra] <> *adj* unreliable. <> *m, f* bad payer.

calouro, ra [ka'loru, ra] *m, f* -**1.** EDUC fresher *UK*, freshman *US*. -**2.** [novato] novice.

calúnia [ka'lunja] *f* calumny.

caluniador, ra [kalunja'do(x), ra] <> *adj* slanderous. <> *m, f* slanderer.

caluniar [16] [kalu'nja(x)] *vt* to slander.

calunioso, niosa [kalu'njozu, njɔza] *adj* slanderous.

calvário [kaw'varju] *m* -**1.** [via crucis] way of the cross. -**2.** *fig* [sofrimento] bitter trial.

calvície [kaw'visi] *f* baldness.

calvo, va ['kawvu, va] *adj* bald.

cama ['kãma] *f* bed; ~ **de casal** double bed; ~ **de solteiro** single bed; **estar de** ~ [estar doente] to be bedridden.

camada [ka'mada] *f* -**1.** [ger] layer. -**2.** [de tinta] coat.

camafeu [kama'few] *m* cameo.

câmara ['kãmara] *f* -**1.** [ger] chamber; ~ **de gás** gas chamber; ~ **mortuária** burial chamber; ~ **alta/baixa** upper/lower house; ~ **de comércio** chamber of commerce; **Câmara dos Deputados** House of Representatives; ~ **municipal** town council. -**2.** CINE & FOTO camera; ~ **escura** darkroom. -**3.** TV television camera; **em** ~ **lenta** in slow motion. -**4.** [de pneu]: ~ **(de ar)** inner tube.
◆ **câmara** *mf* [cinegrafista] cameraman.
◆ **de câmara** *loc adj* MÚS chamber.

câmara-ardente [ˌkãmaraax'dẽntʃi] (*pl* **câmaras-ardentes**) *f*: **estar exposto em** ~ to lie in wake.

camarada [kama'rada] *adj* -**1.** [amigável] friendly. -**2.** [preço] good.

camaradagem [kamara'daʒẽ] (*pl* -**ns**) *f* -**1.** [convivência] companionship. -**2.** [procedimento] good turn; **por** ~ out of friendship.

câmara-de-ar [ˌkãmara'dʒja(x)] (*pl* **câmaras-de-ar**) *f* inner tube.

camarão [kama'rãw] (*pl* -**ões**) *m* -**1.** [comum] shrimp. -**2.** [graúdo] prawn.

camareiro, ra [kama'rejru, ra] *m, f* -**1.** [in hotel] chambermaid, room cleaner. -**2.** [on boat] cabin cleaner.

camarilha [kama'riʎa] *f* clique.

camarim [kama'rĩ] (*pl* -**ns**) *m* dressing room.

Camarões [kama'rõjʃ] *n* Cameroon.

camaronês, esa [kamaro'nejʃ, ɛza] <> *adj* Cameroonian. <> *m, f* Cameroonian.

camarote [kama'rɔtʃi] *m* -**1.** NÁUT cabin. -**2.** TEATRO box.

cambada [kãn'bada] *f* -**1.** [porção] load. -**2.** [súcia] bunch.

cambalacho [kãnba'laʃu] *m* scam.

cambaleante [kãnba'ljãntʃi] *adj* unsteady.

cambalear [15] [kãnba'lja(x)] *vi* to stagger.

cambalhota [kãnba'ʎɔta] *f* somersault; **dar uma** ~ to somersault.

cambial [kãn'bjaw] (*pl* -**ais**) *adj* exchange.

cambiar [4] [kãn'bja(x)] <> *vt* -**1.** [moeda] to exchange. -**2.** [transformar]: ~ **algo em** to change sthg into. <> *vi* [trocar]: ~ **de** to change.

câmbio ['kãnbju] *m* -**1.** [ger] exchange; ~ **livre** free trade; ~ **negro** black economy; ~ **oficial/paralelo** official/parallel exchange; [taxa] exchange rate. -**2.** AUTO [mudança] gear stick.

cambista [kãn'biʃta] *mf* -**1.** [de moeda] money changer. -**2.** [de ingressos] (ticket) tout.

Camboja [kãn'bɔʒa] *n* Cambodia.

cambojano, na [kãnbo'ʒãnu, na] <> *adj* Cambodian. <> *m, f* Cambodian.

camburão [kãnbu'rãw] (*pl* -**ões**) *m* police van.

camélia [ka'mɛlja] *f* camellia.

camelo [ka'melu] *m* -**1.** [animal] camel. -**2.** *fig* [pessoa burra] idiot.

camelô [kame'lo] *m* pedlar.

câmera ['kãmera] <> *f* camera. <> *mf* [operador] camera operator.

cameraman [ˌkãmera'mẽj] (*pl* **cameramen**) *m* TV & CINE camera operator.

caminhada [kami'ɲada] *f* -**1.** [passeio] walk. -**2.** [extensão] trek.

caminhão [kami'ɲãw] (*pl* -**ões**) *m* lorry *UK*, truck *US*.

caminhar [kami'ɲa(x)] *vi* -**1.** [andar] to walk. -**2.** [progredir] *fig* to progress; ~ **para** to lead to.

caminho [ka'miɲu] *m* -**1.** [via, estrada] road. -**2.** [extensão, direção] way; **havia um obstáculo no meio do** ~ there was an obstruction in the way; **cortar** ~ to take a short cut; **ser meio** ~ **andado** *fig* to be half way there. -**3.** *fig* [meio] way. -**4.** *fig* [rumo] route.

caminhoneiro, ra [kamiɲo'nejru, ra] *m, f* lorry driver *UK*, truck driver *US*.

caminhonete [kamiɲo'nɛtʃi], **camioneta** [kamio'nɛta] *f* van.

camisa [ka'miza] *f* shirt; ~ **esporte** sports shirt; ~ **pólo** polo shirt; ~ **social** dress shirt; **mudar de** ~ *ESP* & *fig* to change sides.

camisa-de-força [kaˌmizadʒi'foxsa] (*pl* **camisas-de-força**) *f* straitjacket.

camisa-de-vênus [kaˌmizadʒi'venuʃ] = **camisinha**.

camisão [kami'sãw] (*pl* -**ões**) *m* smock.

camiseta [kami'zeta] *f* T-shirt.

camisinha [kami'ziɲa] *f* condom.

camisola [kami'zɔla] *f* nightdress.

camomila [kamo'mila] *f* camomile; **de** ~ camomile.

campainha [kãmpa'iɲa] *f* bell.

campal [kãn'pawl] (pl -ais) adj -1. [relativo ao campo] rural. -2. [ao ar livre]: **missa** ~ open-air mass.

campanário [kãnpa'narju] m bell tower.

campanha [kãn'pãɲa] f -1. [ger] campaign; **fazer** ~ **(de/contra)** to campaign for/against. -2. [planície] plain.

campeão, ã [kãn'pjãw, ã] (mpl -ões, fpl -s) <> adj [time etc] champion. <> m, f champion.

campeonato [kãnpjo'natu] m championship.

campestre [kãn'pɛʃtri] adj rural.

campina [kãn'pina] f -1. [prado] meadow. -2. [planície] plain.

camping [kãn'pĩŋ] m -1. [atividade] camping. -2. [lugar] campsite.

campismo [kãn'piʒmu] m camping.

campista [kãn'piʃta] mf camper.

campo ['kãnpul m -1. [ger] field. -2. [zona rural] countryside; **casa de** ~ country house. -3. [área] camp; ~ **de aviação** airfield; ~ **de concentração** concentration camp. -4. ESP: ~ **de futebol** football pitch; ~ **de golfe** golf course; ~ **de tênis** tennis court. -5. fig [âmbito] field; ~ **de ação** field of action. -6. fig [ocasião] scope. -7. loc: **embolar o meio de** ~ to mess it all up.
➡ **de campo** loc adj [pesquisa] field.

Campo Grande [ˌkãnpu'grãndʒi] n Campo Grande.

camponês, esa ['kãnpo'neʃ, eza] (mpl -eses, fpl -s) <> adj rural. <> m, f countryman (f countrywoman).

campus ['kãnpuʃ] m inv campus.

camuflado, da [kamu'fladu, da] adj camouflaged.

camuflagem [kamu'flaʒẽ] (pl ns) f camouflage.

camuflar [4] [kamu'fla(x)] vt -1. [dissimular] to camouflage. -2. fig [disfarçar] to disguise.

camundongo [kamũn'dõŋgu] m mouse.

camurça [ka'muxsa] f suede; **de** ~ suede.

cana ['kãna] f -1. [ger] cane. -2. fam [cachaça] gutrot, cachaça, sugar-cane brandy. -3. fam [cadeia] jail; **ir em** ~ to be locked up.

Canadá [kana'da] n: **(o)** ~ Canada.

cana-de-açúcar [ˌkãnadʒja'suka(x)] (pl canas-de-açúcar) f sugar cane.

canadense [kana'dẽsi] <> adj Canadian. <> mf Canadian.

canal [ka'naw] (pl -ais) m -1. [ger] canal; **canais competentes** proper channels. -2. GEOGR,TV channel. -3. [conduto] pipe. -4. fig [meio, via] channel.

canalha [ka'naʎa] <> adj despicable. <> mf rotter.

canalização [kanaliza'sãw] (pl -ões) f -1. [ato] piping. -2. [tubulação] plumbing.

canalizar [4] [kanali'za(x)] vt -1. [rios] to channel. -2. [pôr canos de esgotos] to lay with pipes. -3. [abrir canais] to canalize. -4. fig [dirigir] to channel.

canapé [kana'pɛ] m couch.

canapê [kana'pe] m canapé.

Canárias [ka'narjaʃ] npl: **as (Ilhas)** ~ the Canary Islands, the Canaries.

canário [ka'narju] m canary.

canastra [ka'naʃtra] f -1. [cesto] large basket. -2. [jogo] canasta.

canastrão, trona [kanaʃ'trãw, trona] (mpl -ões, fpl -s) m, f TEATRO ham actor.

canavial [kana'vjaw] (pl -ais) m cane field.

canavieiro, ra [kana'vjejru, ra] adj cane-growing.

Canberra [kãn'bɛxa] n Canberra.

canção [kãn'sãw] (pl -ões) f song.

cancela [kãn'sɛla] f gate.

cancelamento [kãnsela'mẽntu] m -1. [passagem] cancellation. -2. [processo] overruling.

cancelar [4] [kãnse'la(x)] vt -1. [anular] to cancel. -2. [riscar] to cross out. -3. [desistir de] to call off. -4. [suprimir - atividade, pagamento] to cancel; [- regalia] to revoke.

câncer ['kãse(x)] (pl -es) m MED cancer; ~ **de mama** breast cancer.
➡ **Câncer** m ASTRO Cancer; **ser** ~ to be a Cancer; **Trópico de** ~ Tropic of Cancer.

canceriano, na [kãse'rjãnu, na] <> adj ASTRO Cancerian. <> m, f Cancerian.

cancerígeno, na [kãse'riʒenu, na] adj MED carcinogenic.

cancerologista [kãserolo'ʒiʃta] mf cancer specialist.

canceroso, rosa [kãse'rozu, rɔza] <> adj cancerous. <> m, f cancer patient.

cancha ['kãnʃa] f -1. [raia] track. -2. fig [experiência] track record.

canções [kãn'sõjʃ] pl ▷ canção.

candeeiro [kãn'djejru] m lamp.

candelabro [kãnde'labru] m -1. [castiçal] candlestick. -2. [lustre] chandelier.

candente [kãn'dẽntʃi] adj -1. [ardente] red-hot. -2. fig [inflamado] inflamed.

candidatar-se [7] [kãndʒida'taxsi] vp -1. [à presidência da república] to stand for. -2. [à vaga] to apply for.

candidato, ta [kãndʒi'datu, ta] m -1. POL candidate. -2. [pretendente - a vaga] applicant; [- a exame] candidate.

candidatura [kãndʒida'tura] f -1. [ger] candidature. -2. [proposta] application.

cândido, da ['kãndʒidu, da] adj -1. [imaculado] candid. -2. fig [inocente] naive.

candomblé [kãndõn'blɛ] m -1. [religião] Yoruba religious tradition in Bahia and its ceremony. -2. [local] Candomblé shrine.

CANDOMBLÉ

Afro-Brazilian religion that worships West-African gods, known as *orixás*. The temples where *candomblé* ceremonies take place are called *terreiros* and the celebrations are held to the sound of percussion instruments, such as *atabaques*. One of the better known celebrations is the feast of Iemanjá, the queen of the oceans and seas, celebrated on 31st December in Rio de Janeiro and on 2nd February in Bahia, when devotees throw offerings into the sea.

candura [kãn'dura] f **-1.** [alvura] candour. **-2.** fig [inocência] naivety.

caneca [ka'nɛka] f mug.

caneco [ka'nɛku] m tankard.

canela [ka'nɛla] f **-1.** [especiaria] cinnamon. **-2.** ANAT shin.

canelada [kane'lada] f kick in the shins.

caneta [ka'neta] f pen; ~ **esferográfica** ballpoint pen; ~ **marca-texto** highlighter; ~ **pilot** felt-tip pen.

caneta-tinteiro [ka,netatʃĩn'tejru] (pl canetas-tinteiros) f fountain pen.

canga ['kãŋga] f [de praia] beach wrap.

cangaceiro [kãŋga'sejru] m bandit.

cangote [kãn'gɔtʃi] m (back of the) neck.

canguru [kãŋgu'ru] m kangaroo.

cânhamo ['kãɲamul m hemp.

canhão [ka'ɲãw] (pl -ões) m **-1.** MIL cannon. **-2.** fam fig [mulher feia] hag.

canhestro, tra [ka'ɲeʃtru, tra] adj **-1.** [desajeitado] clumsy. **-2.** [acanhado] awkward.

canhões [ka'ɲõjʃ] pl ⊳ **canhão**.

canhoto, ta [ka'ɲotu, ta] <> adj left-handed. <> m, f left-handed person.

➡ **canhoto** m [em talão] stub.

canibal [kani'baw] (pl -ais) <> adj cannibalistic. <> m, f cannibal.

canibalismo [kaniba'liʒmu] m cannibalism.

caniço [ka'nisu] m **-1.** PESCA rod. **-2.** fam [perna fina] pin.

canil [ka'niw] (pl -is) m kennel.

caninha [ka'niɲa] f sugar-cane alcohol.

canino, na [ka'ninu, na] adj **-1.** [ger] canine. **-2.** [fome] ravenous.

➡ **canino** m [dente] canine.

canivete [kani'vetʃi] m penknife.

canja ['kãʒa] f **-1.** CULIN thin broth of rice and chicken. **-2.** fig [coisa fácil]: **ser** ~ to be a cinch. **-3.** MÚS: **dar uma** ~ to do a turn.

canjica [kãn'ʒika] f a sweet dish of maize, coconut milk and cinnamon.

cano ['kãnu] m **-1.** [tubo] pipe; ~ **de esgoto** sewer pipe. **-2.** [de arma] barrel. **-3.** [de bota] leg. **-4.** [trambique] swindle. **-5.** loc: **entrar pelo** ~ to come a cropper.

canoa [ka'noa] f canoe.

canoagem [ka'nwaʒẽ] f canoeing.

canoeiro, ra [ka'nwejru, ra] m, f canoeist.

canonização [kanoniza'sãw] (pl -ões) f canonization.

canonizar [4] [kanoni'za(x)] vt **-1.** [santificar] to canonize. **-2.** [consagrar] to endorse.

cansaço [kãn'sasu] m weariness.

cansado, da [kãn'sadu, da] adj **-1.** [fatigado] tired. **-2.** [enfastiado] weary.

cansar [4] [kãn'sa(x)] <> vt **-1.** [fatigar] to tire. **-2.** [entediar] to bore. **-3.** [aborrecer] to annoy. <> vi **-1.** [ficar cansado] to get tired; ~ **de algo/alguém** to get tired of sthg/sb; ~ **de fazer algo** to be tired of doing sthg. **-2.** [fazer ficar cansado] to be tiring. **-3.** [aborrecer] to be boring. **-4.** [desistir]: ~ **de**

fazer algo to weary of doing sthg.

➡ **cansar-se** vp **-1.** [fatigar-se] to get tired. **-2.** [entediar-se]: ~**-se de algo** to get bored with sthg. **-3.** [aborrecer-se]: ~**-se de algo** to become weary of sthg.

cansativo, va [kãnsa'tʃivu, va] adj **-1.** [fatigante] tiring. **-2.** [enfadonho] boring.

canseira [kãn'sejra] f **-1.** [cansaço] weariness. **-2.** fam [esforço] hassle.

cantada [kãn'tada] f smooth talk.

cantado, da [kãn'tadu, da] adj sung.

cantar [4] [kãn'ta(x)] <> vt **-1.** [ger] to sing. **-2.** [dizer em voz alta] to sing out. **-3.** fam [tentar seduzir] to sweet talk. <> vi MÚS to sing.

cântaro ['kãntaru] m pitcher.

cantarolar [4] [kãntaro'la(x)] vt & vi to hum.

canteiro [kãn'tejru] m **-1.** [jardim]: ~ **de flores** flower bed. **-2.** [construção]: ~ **de obras** work site. **-3.** [operário] stone mason.

cantiga [kãn'tʃiga] f ballad.

cantil [kãn'tʃiw] (pl -is) m **-1.** [frasco] flask. **-2.** [ferramenta] plane.

cantina [kãn'tʃina] f canteen.

canto ['kãntu] m **-1.** [ger] corner. **-2.** [de triângulo] angle. **-3.** [lugar retirado] quiet corner. **-4.** [MÚS - som musical] song; ~ **gregoriano** Gregorian chant; [- arte] singing.

cantoneira [kãnto'nejra] f **-1.** [como reforço] angle iron. **-2.** [como enfeite] corner plate. **-3.** [para fotos] corner slot. **-4.** [prateleira] corner shelf.

cantor, ra [kãn'to(x), ra] (mpl -es, fpl -s) m, f singer.

cantoria [kãnto'ria] f singing.

canudo [ka'nudul m **-1.** [tubo] tube. **-2.** [para beber] straw. **-3.** fam [diploma] certificate.

cão ['kãw] (pl cães) mf **-1.** ZOOL dog; ~ **de caça** hound; ~ **de guarda** guard dog. **-2.** loc: **quem não tem** ~ **caça com gato** there is more than one way to skin a cat.

➡ **de cão** loc adj [dia, férias etc] dreadful.

caolho, lha [ka'oʎu, ʎa] <> adj **-1.** [zarolho] one-eyed. **-2.** [estrábico] cross-eyed. <> m, f **-1.** [pessoa zarolha] one-eyed person; **ele é um** ~ he only has one eye. **-2.** [pessoa estrábica] cross-eyed person.

caos ['kawʃ] m inv chaos.

caótico, ca [ka'ɔtʃiku, ka] adj chaotic.

capa ['kapa] f **-1.** [ger] cover; ~ **dura** hard cover; **de** ~ **dura** hardback. **-2.** [roupa] cape; ~ **(de chuva)** rain cape. **-3.** fig [aparência] cloak.

capacete [kapa'setʃi] m helmet.

capacho [ka'paʃu] m **-1.** [tapete] door mat. **-2.** fig [pessoa servil] toady.

capacidade [kapasi'dadʒi] f **-1.** [ger] capacity. **-2.** [habilidade] ability. **-3.** fig [sumidade] genius.

capacitar [4] [kapasi'ta(x)] vt **-1.** [habilitar]: ~ **alguém a fazer algo** to prepare sb to do sthg. **-2.** [convencer]: ~ **alguém de algo** to convince sb of sthg.

➡ **capacitar-se** vp [convencer-se]: ~**-se de algo** to become convinced of sthg.

capado, da [ka'padu, da] <> adj [castrado]

castrated. <> *m* gelded pig.
capar [4] [ka'pa(x)] *vt* to castrate.
capataz [kapa'taʒ] *m* foreman.
capaz [ka'paʃ] (*pl* -es) *adj* -**1.** [competente] competent. -**2.** [apropriado] capable. -**3.** [provável]: **é ~ de nevar** it might snow. -**4.**: **ser ~ de fazer algo** [dispor-se a, ter coragem de] to be capable of doing sthg.
capcioso, osa [kap'sjozu, ɔza] *adj* [pergunta] trick.
capela [ka'pɛla] *f* chapel.
capelão [kape'lãw] (*pl* -ães) *m* chaplain.
capenga [ka'pẽga] <> *adj* lame. <> *mf* cripple.
capengar [14] [kapẽŋ'ga(x)] *vi* to limp.
CAPES (*abrev de* **Coordenação de Aperfeiçoamento de Pessoal de Nível Superior**) *f Brazilian educational body that finances postgraduate studies.*
capeta [ka'peta] *m* -**1.** [diabo] devil. -**2.** *fam* [traquinas] troublemaker.
capilar [kapi'la(x)] *adj* -**1.** [do cabelo] hair (*antes de subst*). -**2.** [vaso] capillary.
capim [ka'pĩ] *m* grass.
capinar [4] [kapi'na(x)] *vt* [limpar] to weed.
capita ['kapita] ** per capita** *loc adj* per capita.
capital [kapi'taw] (*pl* -ais) <> *adj* -**1.** [essencial] major. -**2.** [pena] capital. <> *m ECON* capital; **~ de giro** working capital; **~ de risco** venture capital. <> *f* [cidade] capital.
capitalismo [kapita'liʒmu] *m* capitalism.
capitalista [kapita'liʃta] <> *adj* capitalist. <> *mf* capitalist.
capitalização [kapitaliza'sãw] *f ECON* capitalization.
capitalizar [4] [kapitali'za(x)] *vt* -**1.** *ECON* to capitalize. -**2.** *fig* [tirar proveito de] to capitalize on.
capitanear [15] [kapita'nja(x)] *vt* -**1.** *MIL* to command. -**2.** [dirigir] to head.
capitania [kapitã'nia] ** capitania do porto** *f* port authority.
capitão, ã [kapi'tãw, ã] (*mpl* -ães, *fpl* -s) *m, f* -**1.** [ger] captain. -**2.** [chefe] leader.
capitulação [kapitula'sãw] (*pl* -ões) *f* [rendição] surrender.
capitular [kapitu'la(x)] <> *vi* to capitulate. <> *adj* capitular. <> *f* [letra] capital.
capítulo [ka'pitulu] *m* chapter.
capô [ka'po] *m AUTO* bonnet *UK*, hood *US*.
capoeira [ka'pwejra] *f* [dança] capoeira, *acrobatic game in dance form that is very popular in north-eastern Brazil.*

capoeirista [kapwej'riʃta] *mf person who does capoeira dancing.*
capota [ka'pɔta] *f AUTO* hood.
capotar [4] [kapo'ta(x)] *vi* to overturn.
caprichar [4] [kapri'ʃa(x)] *vi*: **~ (em)** to take delight in.
capricho [ka'priʃu] *m* -**1.** [esmero] care. -**2.** [vontade] whim. -**3.** [teimosia] obstinacy.
caprichoso, osa [kapri'ʃozu, ɔza] *adj* -**1.** [cuidadoso] meticulous. -**2.** [voluntarioso] capricious. -**3.** [teimoso] obstinate.
capricorniano, na [kaprikox'njãnu, na] <> *adj* Capricorn. <> *m, f* Capricorn.
Capricórnio [kapri'kɔxnjul *m ASTRO* Capricorn; **ser de ~** to be a Capricorn; **Trópico de ~** Tropic of Capricorn.
cápsula ['kapsula] *f* capsule.
captação [kapta'sãw] (*pl* -ões) *f ECON*: **~ de recursos** fund-raising.
captar [4] [kap'ta(x)] *vt* -**1.** [atrair] to win. -**2.** [sintonizar] to pick up. -**3.** [água] to collect. -**4.** [compreender] to catch.
captura [kap'tura] *f* capture.
capturar [kaptu'ra(x)] *vt* to capture.
capuz [ka'puʃ] (*pl* -es) *m* hood.
caquético, ca [ka'kɛtʃiku, ka] *adj* doddering.
caqui [ka'ki] *m inv* kaki fruit.
cáqui ['kaki] <> *adj inv* khaki. <> *m* drill.
cara ['kara] <> *f* -**1.** [rosto] face; **~ a ~** face to face; **ser a ~ de alguém** to be the image of sb. -**2.** [aspecto] look; **estar com uma ~ boa** [pessoa] to look well; [comida] to look good; **ficar com ~ de tacho** to be dumbfounded. -**3.** [de moeda] side. -**4.** *fam* [coragem] nerve. <> *m* -**1.** *fam* [sujeito] guy. -**2.** *loc*: **amarrar a ~** to sulk; **dar as ~ s (em)** to show up for; **dar de ~ com alguém** to bump into sb; **encher a ~** *fam* to have a skinful; **estar com ~ de que** [parecer que] to look like; **estar na ~** to be staring one in the face; **meter a ~ em algo** *fig* to put one's back into sthg; **não ir com a ~ de alguém** not to be keen on sb.
carabina [kara'bina] *f* rifle.
Caracas [ka'rakaʃ] *n* Caracas.
caracol [kara'kɔw] (*pl* -óis) *m* -**1.** [molusco] snail. -**2.** [de cabelo] curl.
** de caracol** *loc adj* [escada] spiral.
caractere [karak'tɛril *m* character.
caracteres [karak'tɛriʃ] *pl* ⊳ **caráter**.
** caracteres** *mpl* -**1.** [características individuais] characteristics. -**2.** [legendas, créditos] credits.
característico, ca [karakte'riʃtʃiku, ka] *adj* characteristic.
** característica** *f* characteristic.
caracterização [karakteriza'sãw] (*pl* -ões) *f* -**1.** [descrição] characterization. -**2.** [TEATRO - maquilagem] make-up; [- indumentária] wardrobe.
caracterizar [4] [karakteri'za(x)] *vt* -**1.** [descrever] characterize. -**2.** [TEATRO - maquilagem] to make up; [- indumentária] to dress.
** caracterizar-se** *vp* [distinguir-se]: **~-se por** to be characterized by.

cara-de-pau [ˌkaradʒi'pawl] fam ⟨⟩ adj shameless. ⟨⟩ mf shameless person.

caralho [kara'ʎul] vulg ⟨⟩ interj fuck!, fuck me! ⟨⟩ m [pênis] dick, cock.

caramanchão [karamãn'ʃãwl] (pl -ões) m pergola.

caramba [ka'rãnbal] interj my goodness! UK, gee! US; está frio/quente pra ~ it's incredibly cold/hot.

carambola [karãm'bɔlal] f star fruit.

caramelado, da [karame'ladu, dal] adj caramelized.

caramelo [kara'mɛlul] m -1. [calda] caramel. -2. [bala] toffee.

cara-metade [ˌkarame'tadʒil] (pl caras-metades) f better half.

caramujo [kara'muʒul] m shellfish.

caranguejo [karãŋ'geʒul] m crab.

carão [ka'rãwl] (pl -ões) m ticking off; passar um ~ em alguém to tick sb off.

carapaça [kara'pasal] f carapace.

carapuça [kara'pusal] f -1. [gorro] cap. -2. [indireta]: enfiar a ~ to take it personally.

caraquenho, nha [kara'kẽɲu, ɲãl] ⟨⟩ adj Caracas (antes de subst). ⟨⟩ m, f person from Caracas.

caratê [kara'tel] m karate.

caráter [ka'rate(x)] (pl -es) m [índole, natureza, cunho] character; uma pessoa de ~ /sem ~ a person of good moral fibre/with no moral fibre.

 ⟶ a caráter loc adv [vestir-se] in character.

caravana [kara'vãnal] f caravan.

carboidrato [kaxbwi'dratul] m carbohydrate.

carbônico, ca [kax'boniku, kal] adj carbonic.

carbonizar [4] [kaxboni'za(x)] vt to carbonize.

carbono [kax'bonul] m QUÍM carbon; de ~ carbon (antes de subst).

carburador [kaxbura'do(x)] (pl -es) m carburettor UK, carburator US.

carcaça [kax'kasal] f -1. [esqueleto] carcass. -2. [armação] frame. -3. [de navio] hull.

cárcere ['kaxseril] m jail.

carcereiro, ra [kaxse'rejru, ral] m jailer.

carcomer [kaxko'me(x)] vt [roer] to eat into.

carcomido, da [kaxko'midu, dal] adj -1. [roído] worm-eaten. -2. [gasto] frayed. -3. fig [rosto] pockmarked.

cardápio [kax'dapjul] m menu.

cardeal [kax'dʒjawl] (pl -ais) ⟨⟩ m RELIG cardinal. ⟨⟩ adj [ponto] cardinal.

cardíaco, ca [kax'dʒiaku, kal] ⟨⟩ adj cardiac, heart; ataque ~ heart attack; ser ~ to have heart trouble. ⟨⟩ m, f heart patient, person with heart problems.

cardigã [kaxdʒi'gãl] m cardigan.

cardinal [kaxdʒi'nawl] (pl -ais) adj cardinal.

cardiologista [kaxdʒolo'ʒiʃtal] mf cardiologist.

cardiovascular [ˌkaxdʒjovaʃku'la(x)] (pl -es) adj cardiovascular.

cardume [kax'dumil] m shoal.

careca [ka'rɛkal] ⟨⟩ adj bald; estar ~ de saber algo to know sthg full well. ⟨⟩ m bald man. ⟨⟩ f bald patch.

carecer [25] [kare'se(x)] vt -1. [não ter]: ~ de to lack. -2. [precisar]: ~ de to need.

careiro, ra [ka'rejru, ral] adj pricey.

carência [ka'rẽnsjal] f -1. [falta]: ~ de lack of. -2. [falta de afeto]: ~ afetiva lack of care. -3. [em seguro, financiamento]: período de ~ moratorium.

carente [ka'rẽntʃil] adj -1. [desprovido] lacking. -2. [pobre] needy.

carestia [kareʃ'tʃial] f -1. [custo alto] high cost. -2. [escassez] scarcity.

careta [ka'retal] ⟨⟩ adj -1. fam [conservador - pessoa] fuddy-duddy; [- roupa, festa] dated. -2. fam [que não usa drogas] clean. ⟨⟩ f [com o rosto] grimace; fazer ~ to pull faces.

caretice [kare'tʃisil] f fam [convencionalismo]: meu pai é a ~ em pessoa my father is as old-fashioned as they come.

carga [ˈkaxgal] f -1. [ato] loading. -2. [carregamento] cargo; ~ aérea air freight. -3. [fardo] load. -4. [de arma de fogo] charge. -5. [de caneta] cartridge. -6. ELETR: ~ elétrica electric charge. -7. fig [peso] burden. -8. fig [responsabilidade] load; ~ horária working hours.

carga-d'água [ˌkaxga'dagwal] (pl cargas-d'água) f [chuva] downpour.

 ⟶ **cargas-d'água** fpl [motivo]: por que cargas-d'água ...? why on earth ...?

cargo [ˈkaxgul] m -1. [função] post. -2. [responsabilidade] responsibility.

cargueiro, ra [kax'gejru, ral] adj cargo.

 ⟶ **cargueiro** m cargo ship.

cariado, da [ka'riadu, dal] adj [dente] decayed.

cariar [16] [ka'rja(x)] ⟨⟩ vt to rot. ⟨⟩ vi to decay.

Caribe [ka'ribil] n: o (mar do) ~ the Caribbean (Sea).

caribenho, nha [kari'bẽɲu, ɲal] ⟨⟩ adj Caribbean. ⟨⟩ m, f Caribbean.

caricatura [karika'tural] f -1. [desenho] caricature. -2. fig [reprodução mal-feita] distortion.

caricatural [karikatu'rawl] (pl -ais) adj grotesque.

caricaturista [karikatu'riʃtal] mf caricaturist.

carícia [ka'risjal] f caress.

caridade [kari'dadʒil] f -1. [benevolência] charity. -2. [esmola] alms (pl).

caridoso, osa [kari'dozu, ɔzal] adj charitable.

cárie ['karil] f caries.

carimbar [4] [karĩn'ba(x)] vt to stamp.

carimbo [ka'rĩnbul] m stamp.

carinho [ka'riɲul] m -1. [afago] caress. -2. [cuidado] care.

carinhosamente [kariɲoza'mẽntʃil] adv -1. [afetuosamente] affectionately. -2. [cuidadosamente] carefully.

carinhoso, osa [kari'ɲozu, ɔzal] adj affectionate.

carioca [ka'rjɔkal] ⟨⟩ adj carioca. ⟨⟩ mf carioca.

carisma [ka'riʒmal] m charisma.

carismático, ca [kariʒ'matʃiku, ka] adj charismatic.

caritativo, va [karita'tʃivu, va] adj charitable.

carnal [kax'naw] (pl -ais) adj -1. [da carne, do corpo] carnal. -2. [consanguíneo] blood- (antes de subst).

carnaval [kaxna'vaw] (pl -ais) m -1. [festa popular] carnival. -2. fig [desordem] mess. -3. fig [estardalhaço] racket.

CARNAVAL

The greatest of all Brazilian festivals; carnaval officially lasts for four days, from Saturday until Shrove Tuesday. Although its most famous display is the parade of the Samba Schools of Rio de Janeiro, broadcast throughout the entire country, carnaval is celebrated in different ways in the various Brazilian states. In Salvador (BA), it is characterized by the parade of the afoxés and the trios-elétricos, drawing behind them vast numbers of revellers. Recife and Olinda (PE) celebrate carnaval with a parade of revellers partying to the sound of the frevo.

carnavalesco, ca [kaxnava'leʃku, ka] adj -1. [relativo ao carnaval] carnival. -2. [extravagante] over the top.
➡ **carnavalesco** m -1. [folião] reveller. -2. [organizador] carnival planner.

carne ['kaxni] f -1. [ger] flesh; **em ~ e osso** in the flesh; **em ~ viva** raw; **ser de ~ e osso** fig to be only human, after all. -2. CULIN meat; **~ assada** roast meat. -3. [parentesco] flesh and blood.

carnê [kax'ne] m [de pagamento] slate.

carne-de-sol [ˌkaxnidʒi'sɔw] (pl carnes-de-sol) f CULIN lightly dried meat.

carneiro [kax'nejru] m lamb.

carne-seca [ˌkaxni'seka] (pl carnes-secas) f CULIN dried meat.

carniça [kax'nisa] f carrion; **pular ~** to play leapfrog.

carnificina [kaxnifi'sina] f carnage.

carnívoro, ra [kax'nivoru, ra] adj carnivorous.
➡ **carnívoro** m carnivore.

carnoso, osa [kax'nozu, ɔza] adj -1. [semelhante à carne] meaty. -2. [fruto] fleshy. -3. [folha] pulpy.

carnudo, da [kax'nudu, da] adj -1. [lábios] full. -2. [fruta, perna] plump.

caro, ra ['karu, ra] adj -1. [ger] expensive. -2. [querido, custoso] dear.
➡ **caro** adv -1. [por alto preço] for a high price. -2. fig [com alto custo] dear.

carochinha [karo'ʃina] f ⊳ **história**.

caroço [ka'rosu] m stone.

carola [ka'rɔla] ⟨⟩ adj pious. ⟨⟩ mf pious person.

carona [ka'rona] f lift; **dar/pegar ~** to give/hitch a lift; **ir/viajar de ~** to hitchhike.

Cárpatos ['kaxpatuʃ] npl: **os ~** the Carpathians.

carpete [kax'pɛtʃi] m fitted carpet.

carpintaria [kaxpĩta'ria] f -1. [ofício] carpentry. -2. [oficina] carpenter's shop.

carpinteiro, ra [kaxpĩ'tejru] m, f carpenter.

carranca [ka'xãŋka] f -1. fam [cara fechada] sour face. -2. [em embarcação] figurehead.

carrancudo, da [kaxãŋ'kudu, da] adj surly.

carrapato [kaxa'patu] m -1. [inseto] tick. -2. fam [pessoa dependente] hanger-on.

carrapicho [kaxa'piʃu] m -1. [arbusto] burr. -2. [carapinha] Afro hairstyle.

carrasco [ka'xaʃku] m -1. [algoz] executioner. -2. fig [tirano] tyrant.

carreata [ka'xjata] f motorcade.

carregado, da [kaxe'gadu, da] adj -1. [caminhão etc]: **~ (de)** laden with. -2. [fisionomia] sullen. -3. [ambiente] dismal. -4. [estilo] dark. -5. [céu] threatening.

carregador [kaxega'do(x)] (pl -es) m, f -1. [de bagagem] porter. -2. [transportador] carrier.

carregamento [kaxega'mẽntu] m -1. [ato] loading. -2. [carga] load.

carregar [14] [kaxe'ga(x)] ⟨⟩ vt -1. [ger] to load. -2. [levar] to transport. -3. fig [sentimento etc] to carry. -4. [bateria] to charge. -5. [impregnar] to fill. ⟨⟩ vi -1. [pôr em demasia]: **~ em** to overdo. -2. [exagerar]: **~ em** to overstate.

carreira [ka'xejra] f -1. [correria] run. -2. [profissão] career. -3. [fileira]: **~ de algo** row of sthg. -4. NÁUT slipway. -5. [turfe] racecourse. -6. [trilha] track.

carreirista [kaxej'riʃta] mf careerist.

carreta [ka'xeta] f -1. [caminhão] truck. -2. [carroça] cart.

carretel [kaxe'tɛw] (pl -éis) m -1. [cilindro] reel. -2. [molinete] fishing reel.

carretilha [kaxe'tʃiʎa] f -1. [roldana] pulley. -2. [cortadeira] pastry cutter.

carrilhão [kaxi'ʎãw] (pl -ões) m -1. [sinos] carillon. -2. [relógio] chime.

carrinho [ka'xiɲu] m -1. [para transportar criança] pushchair UK, stroller US. -2. [para transportar comida etc] trolley; **~ de chá** tea trolley UK, tea cart US; **~ de feira** shopping trolley; **~ de mão** handcart.

carro ['kaxu] m -1. [veículo] car; **~ alegórico** float; **~ de bombeiro** fire engine; **~ de passeio** car; **~ de praça** taxi. -2. [vagão] waggon. -3. [de ônibus] bus. -4. [de máquina de escrever] carriage. -5. loc: **pôr o ~ adiante dos bois** to put the cart before the horse.

carro-bomba [ˌkaxu'bõnba] (pl carros-bombas, carros-bomba) m car bomb.

carroça [ka'xɔsa] f -1. [de tração animal] cart. -2. [calhambeque] trap.

carroceria [kaxose'ria] f car body.

carro-chefe [ˌkaxũ'ʃefi] (pl carros-chefes) m leading float.

carrocinha [kaxɔ'siɲa] f dog wagon.

carro-forte [ˌkaxu'fɔxtʃi] (pl carros-fortes) m armoured car.

carrossel [kaxɔ'sɛw] (pl -éis) m roundabout UK, merry-go-round US.

carruagem [ka'xwaʒẽ] (pl -ns) f carriage.

carta ['kaxta] f -1. [missiva] letter; **~ registrada** registered letter. -2. [de baralho] playing card;

dar as ~**s** to deal the cards. - **3**. [mapa] map. - **4**. [constituição]: ~ **magna** charter.

→ **carta branca** f: dar/ter ~ **branca** to give/have carte blanche.

carta-bomba [ˌkaxta'bõnba] (pl **cartas-bombas**, **cartas-bomba**) f letter bomb.

cartada [kax'tada] f - **1**. [em jogo] card play. - **2**. fig [ato arriscado] risk; **jogar a última** ~ to play one's last card.

cartão [kax'tãw] (pl -ões) m card; ~ **de crédito** credit card; ~ **de telefone** phone card; ~ **de embarque** boarding card; ~ **de visita** business card.

cartão-postal [kaxˌtãwpoʃtaw] (pl **cartões-postais**) m postcard.

cartaz [kax'taʃ] (pl -es) m - **1**. [anúncio] poster. - **2**. [popularidade]: **ter** ~ to be popular. - **3**. CINE & TEATRO : **estar em** ~ to be showing.

carteado [kax'tʃjadu] m card game.

carteira [kax'tejra] f - **1**. [para dinheiro]: ~ **(de notas)** wallet. - **2**. [mesa] desk. - **3**. [documento]: ~ **de identidade** identity card; ~ **de estudante** student card; ~ **de investimentos** ECON investment portfolio; ~ **de sócio** membership card; ~ **de motorista** driving licence UK, driver's license US; ~ **profissional** ou **de trabalho** employment contract. - **4**. [de cigarros] pack. - **5**. [de títulos, ações] portfolio.

carteiro, ra [kax'tejru, ra] m, f postman (f postwoman).

cartel [kax'tɛw] (pl -éis) m COM cartel.

cartela [kax'tɛla] f [mostruário] card.

cartilagem [kaxtʃi'laʒẽ] (pl -ns) f ANAT cartilage.

cartões [kax'tõjʃ] mpl ▷ **cartão**.

cartografia [kaxtogra'fia] f cartography.

cartola [kax'tɔla] ◇ f [chapéu] top hat. ◇ m - **1**. fam [pessoa importante] snob. - **2**. pej & FUT club manager who abuses his position.

cartolina [kaxto'lina] f card.

cartomante [kaxto'mãntʃi] mf card reader.

cartório [kax'tɔrju] m - **1**. [arquivo] archive. - **2**. [de registro civil] registry office. - **3**. [de registro de imóveis] Land Registry.

cartucho [kax'tuʃu] m - **1**. [de arma] cartridge. - **2**. [invólucro] tube; **queimar o último** ~ fig to play one's last card.

cartum [kax'tũ] (pl -ns) m cartoon.

cartunista [kaxtu'niʃta] mf cartoonist.

caruncho [ka'rũʃu] m woodworm.

carvalho [kax'vaʎu] m oak.

carvão [kax'vãw] (pl -ões) m - **1**. [combustível] coal; ~ **vegetal** charcoal. - **2**. [tição] cinder.

casa ['kaza] f - **1**. [ger] house; ~ **de campo** country house; ~ **popular** council house; ~ **geminada** semi-detached house. - **2**. [lar] home; **em** ~ at home; **ir para** ~ to go home; **você é da** ~ [convidado, hóspede] make yourself at home. - **3**. [estabelecimento] building; ~ **de câmbio** bureau de change; **Casa da Moeda** Mint; ~ **noturna** nightclub; ~ **de saúde** hospital. - **4**. [de botões] buttonhole. - **5**. MAT place. - **6**. [instalação]:

~ **de máquinas** engine housing.

casaca [ka'zaka] f cloak; **virar a** ~ to be a turncoat.

casacão [kaza'kãw] (pl -ões) m overcoat.

casaco [ka'zaku] m coat; ~ **de pele** fur coat.

casa-grande [ˌkaza'grãndʒi] (pl **casas-grandes**) f main house.

casal [ka'zaw] (pl -ais) m - **1**. [homem e mulher] couple. - **2**. [de filhos] pair.

casamenteiro, ra [kazamẽn'tejru, ra] adj matchmaking; **Santo Antônio, o santo** ~ St Anthony the matchmaker.

casamento [kaza'mẽntu] m - **1**. [ger] marriage. - **2**. [cerimônia] wedding; ~ **civil/religioso** civil/religious wedding.

casar [4] [ka'za(x)] ◇ vt - **1**. [ger] to marry. - **2**. [emparelhar] to pair. ◇ vi [em matrimônio]: ~ **(com alguém)** to marry (sb); ~ **no civil/no religioso** to have a civil/religious wedding.

→ **casar-se** vp - **1**. [em matrimônio] to marry. - **2**. [combinar-se] to go.

casarão [kaza'rãw] (pl -ões) m large house.

casca ['kaʃka] f - **1**. [de pão] crust. - **2**. [de ferida] scab. - **3**. [de ovo] shell. - **4**. [de fruta] peel. - **5**. fig [aparência] sullenness.

casca-grossa [ˌkaʃka'grɔsa] (pl **cascas-grossas**) mf uncouth person.

cascalho [kaʃ'kaʎu] m gravel.

cascão [kaʃ'kãw] (pl -ões) m - **1**. [crosta] hard crust. - **2**. [de sujeira] grime.

cascata [kaʃ'kata] f - **1**. [queda d'água] waterfall. - **2**. fam [mentira] fib. - **3**. fam [bazófia] bragging.

cascateiro, ra [kaʃka'tejru, ra] fam ◇ adj bullshit. ◇ m, f bullshitter.

cascavel [kaʃka'vɛw] (pl -éis) ◇ m ZOOL rattlesnake. ◇ f fig [mulher] cow.

casco ['kaʃku] m - **1**. [de navio] hull. - **2**. [de tartaruga] shell. - **3**. [garrafa] cask. - **4**. [crânio] scalp.

cascudo, da [kaʃ'kudu, da] adj [de casca dura] crusty.

→ **cascudo** m - **1**. [inseto] horn-shelled insect. - **2**. [pancada] rap on the head; **dar um** ~ **em alguém** to rap sb on the head.

casebre [ka'zɛbri] m hovel.

caseiro, ra [ka'zejru, ra] ◇ adj - **1**. [produto] home-made. - **2**. [trabalho] home- (antes de subst). - **3**. [roupa] homespun. - **4**. [pessoa] family man. ◇ m, f [empregado] caretaker.

caserna [ka'zexna] f MIL barracks (pl).

casmurro, rra [kaʒ'muxu, xa] adj - **1**. [teimoso] stubborn. - **2**. [sorumbático] gloomy.

caso ['kazu] ◇ m - **1**. [fato] matter; **o** ~ **é que ...** the fact is that ... - **2**. [circunstância]: **em todo** ~ anyway; **neste** ~ in that case; **no** ~ **de** should there be; ~ **de emergência** emergency. - **3**. [história] story. - **4**. [amoroso] affair. - **5**. [problema]: **criar** ~ to cause a problem. - **6**. MED, GRAM case. - **7**. loc: **fazer pouco** ~ **de** to take little account of; **não vem ao** ~ it's not relevant; **ser um** ~ **perdido** to be a lost cause. ◇ conj if.

casório [ka'zɔrju] m fam splicing.

caspa [ˈkaʃpal f dandruff.

Cáspio [ˈkaʃpjul n: o (mar) ~ the Caspian (Sea).

casquinha [kaʃˈkiɲal f -1. [de sorvete] cone. -2. [de pele] scab.

cassado, da [kaˈsadu, dal m, f person deprived of his/her civil rights.

cassar [4] [kaˈsa(x)] vt -1. POL to annul. -2. [licença, direitos] to quash.

cassete [kaˈsɛtʃil <> adj inv [fita, gravador] tape- (antes de subst). <> m [gravador] tape.

cassetete [kaseˈtɛtʃil m truncheon.

cassino [kaˈsinul m casino.

casta [ˈkaʃtal f -1. [camada social] caste. -2. fig [raça] race.

castanha [kaʃˈtãɲal f ⊳ castanho.

castanha-do-pará [kaʃˌtãɲadupaˈral (pl casta-nhas-do-pará) m Brazil nut.

castanheiro [kaʃtãˈɲejrul m chestnut tree.

castanho, nha [kaʃˈtãɲu, ɲal adj [olhos etc] brown.

⬧ **castanha** f [fruto] chestnut; ~ de caju cashew.

castanholas [kaʃtãˈɲɔlaʃ] fpl castanets.

castelo [kaʃˈtɛlul m castle.

castiçal [kaʃtʃiˈsawl (pl -ais) m candlestick.

castiço, ça [kaʃˈtʃisu, sal adj -1. [puro] top-breed. -2. [de boa casta] well-bred. -3. fig [vernáculo] vernacular.

castidade [kaʃtʃiˈdaʒil f chastity.

castigar [14] [kaʃtʃiˈga(x)] vt -1. [punir] to punish. -2. fam [tocar] to bash out.

⬧ **castigar-se** vp [penitenciar-se] to do penance.

castigo [kaʃˈtʃigul m -1. [punição] punishment; estar/ficar de ~ to be being punished. -2. fig [mortificação] torture; ser um ~ to be torture.

casto, ta [ˈkaʃtu, tal adj chaste.

castrado, da [kaʃˈtradu, dal adj castrated.

castrar [4] [kaʃˈtra(x)] vt -1. [capar] to castrate. -2. fig [impedir] to muzzle. -3. fig [personalidade] to castrate.

casual [kaˈzwawl (pl -ais) adj chance (antes de subst).

casualidade [kazwaliˈdaʒil f chance; por ~ by chance.

casulo [kaˈzulul m -1. [de insetos] cocoon. -2. [de sementes] boll.

cata [ˈkatal f: à ~ de algo/alguém in search of sthg/sb.

cataclismo [kataˈkliʒmul m -1. [dilúvio] flood. -2. GEOL cataclysm. -3. fig [desastre] cataclysm. -4. fig [convulsão social] revolt.

catacumbas [kataˈkũbaʃl fpl catacombs.

catalão, lã [kataˈlãw, lãl <> adj Catalan. <> m, f Catalan.

⬧ **catalão** m [língua] Catalan.

catalisador, ra [katalizaˈdo(x), ral adj catalytic.

⬧ **catalisador** m catalyst.

catalogar [14] [kataloˈga(x)] vt to catalogue.

catálogo [kaˈtalogul m catalogue; ~ (de telefo-nes) telephone directory.

Catalunha [kataˈlũɲal n Catalonia.

catapora [kataˈpɔral f chickenpox.

catar [4] [kaˈta(x)] vt -1. [procurar] to search for. -2. [pegar, recolher] to pick up. -3. [tirar, limpar de] to pick out; ~ piolhos to delouse. -4. [escolher] to pick over; ~ feijão/arroz to pick over beans/ rice.

catarata [kataˈratal f -1. [queda d'água] waterfall. -2. MED cataract.

CATARATAS DO IGUAÇU

Situated in the interior of the National Park of Iguaçu (PR), on the border between Brazil and Argentina, the Iguaçu falls pour out 13 million litres of water per second from an altitude that varies between 40 and 90 metres. Its 275 waterfalls are spread, on the Brazilian side, over a width of 800 metres. The almost 90m high *Garganta do Diabo* is its most famous fall.

catarro [kaˈtaxul m catarrh.

catarse [kaˈtaxsil f catharsis.

catástrofe [kaˈtaʃtrɔfil f catastrophe.

catastrófico, ca [kataʃˈtrɔfiku, kal adj cata-strophic.

catatau [kataˈtawl (pl -ais) m fam: um ~ de a pile of.

cata-vento [kataˈvẽtul (pl cata-ventos) m weathervane.

catecismo [kateˈsiʒmul m catechism.

cátedra [ˈkatedral f -1. UNIV chair. -2. RELIG throne.

catedral [kateˈdrawl (pl -ais) f cathedral.

catedrático, ca [kateˈdratʃiku, kal <> m, f chair. <> adj chair.

categoria [kategoˈrial f -1. [grupo] category. -2. [qualidade] quality; de (alta) ~ high quality. -3. [social] standing. -4. [cargo] position.

categórico, ca [kateˈgɔriku, kal adj categoric.

categorização [kategorizaˈsãwl (pl -ões) f cate-gorization.

categorizar [4] [kategoriˈza(x)] vt to classify.

catequese [kateˈkɛzil f religious instruction.

catequizar [4] [katekiˈza(x)] vt -1. RELIG to teach doctrine to. -2. fig [doutrinar] to indoctrinate.

cateter [kateˈtɛ(x)] m MED catheter.

cateterismo [kateteˈriʒmul m MED catheteriza-tion.

catinga [kaˈtʃĩgal f [mau-cheiro] stench.

cativante [katʃiˈvãtʃil adj entrancing.

cativar [4] [katʃiˈva(x)] vt -1. [escravizar] to capture. -2. [seduzir] to captivate.

cativeiro [katʃiˈvejrul m -1. [escravidão] slavery. -2. [prisão] captivity.

cativo, va [kaˈtʃivu, val <> adj -1. [preso] captive. -2. [sujeito]: ~ a attracted by. -3. [cadeira] exclusive. <> m, f -1. [escravo] slave. -2. [prisionei-ro] prisoner.

catolicismo [katoliˈsiʒmul m Catholicism.

católico, ca [kaˈtɔliku, kal adj -1. RELIG Catholic. -2. fig [correto, tradicional]: não ser muito ~ to be unconventional. -3. fig [bem, de bom humor]: ele não está muito ~ he's not in a good mood.

catorze [kaˈtoxzil num fourteen; veja também seis.

catucar [12] [katu'ka(x)] vt = cutucar.

caução [kaw'sãw] (pl -ões) f -1. [cautela] care. -2. [garantia] pledge. -3. JUR bail.

Cáucaso ['kawkazu] n Caucasus.

caucionar [4] [kawsjo'na(x)] vt -1. [garantir] to pledge. -2. JUR to stand bail for.

cauções [kaw'sõjʃ] fpl ⊳ caução.

cauda ['kawda] f -1. [de animal] tail. -2. [de vestido] train.

caudaloso, osa [kawda'lozu, ɔza] adj torrential.

caudilho [kaw'dʒiʎu] m military commander.

caule ['kawli] m stem.

causa ['kawza] f -1. [ger] cause. -2. [motivo] reason; por ~ de because of.

causador, ra [kawza'do(x), ra] ⬦ adj causal. ⬦ m, f cause.

causar [4] [kaw'za(x)] vt to cause.

cáustico, ca ['kawʃtʃiku, ka] adj caustic.

cautela [kaw'tɛla] f -1. [precaução] precaution; com ~ with care. -2. [título] share certificate. -3. [de penhor] pawn ticket.

cautelar [kawte'la(x)] adj precautionary.

cauteloso, osa [kawte'lozu, ɔza] adj cautious.

cauterizar [4] [kawteri'za(x)] vt to cauterize.

cava ['kava] f ⊳ cavo.

cavaco [ka'vaku] m: ~s do ofício part of the job.

cavala [ka'vala] f [peixe] mackerel.

cavalar [kava'la(x)] adj excessive.

cavalaria [kavala'ria] f -1. MIL cavalry. -2. [cavalos] herd of horses. -3. [ordem] chivalry.

cavalariça [kavala'risa] f [estrebaria] stable.

cavalariço [kavala'risu] m [estribeiro] groom UK, stableman US.

cavaleiro, ra [kava'lejru] m, f [quem monta] horseman (f horsewoman).
➤ **cavaleiro** m [medieval] knight.

cavalete [kava'letʃi] m -1. [de pintor] easel. -2. [de mesa] trestle. -3. [para instrumento] bridge.

cavalgar [14] [kavaw'ga(x)] vt & vi to ride.

cavalheiresco, ca [kavaʎej'reʃku, ka] adj noble.

cavalheiro [kava'ʎejru] ⬦ m gentleman. ⬦ adj [educado] well-bred.

cavalo [ka'valu] m -1. ZOOL horse; a ~ on horseback. -2. [em xadrez] knight. -3. fig [pessoa agressiva] pig; ele agiu como um ~ he behaved like a pig. -4. [cavalo-vapor] horsepower. -5. loc: fazer um ~ de batalha to make a fuss about nothing; pode tirar o ~ da chuva que ela não vai aceitar sua proposta you can forget that, as she's not going to accept your proposal.

cavalo-de-pau [kavaludʒi'paw] (pl cavalos-de-pau)m wheel spin.

cavalo-de-Tróia [ka'valudʒitrɔja] (pl cavalos-de-Tróia) m COMPUT Trojan horse.

cavalo-marinho [ka,valuma'riɲu] (pl cavalos-marinhos) m sea-horse.

cavanhaque [kava'ɲaki] m goatee.

cavaquinho [kava'kiɲu] m small guitar.

cavar [4] [ka'va(x)] ⬦ vt -1. [ger] to dig. -2. [emprego] to search long and hard. ⬦ vi [escavar] to dig.

cave ['kavi] f cellar.

caveira [ka'vejra] f -1. [crânio] skull. -2. fig [rosto macilento] cavernous face. -3. loc: fazer a ~ de alguém to run sb down.

caverna [ka'vɛxna] f cavern.

cavernoso, osa [kavex'nozu, ɔza] adj cavernous.

caviar [ka'vja(x)] m caviar.

cavidade [kavi'dadʒi] f cavity.

cavilha [ka'viʎa] f peg.

cavo, va ['kavu, va] adj [côncavo] hollow.
➤ **cava** f [de manga] armhole.

caxias [ka'ʃiaʃ] ⬦ adj (inv) scrupulous. ⬦ mf (inv) hard taskmaster.

caxumba [ka'ʃũba] f mumps (sg).

CBF (abrev de Confederação Brasileira de Futebol) f Brazilian football federation.

c/c (abrev de conta corrente) f c/a.

CD [se'de] (abrev de Compact Disc) m CD.

CDB (abrev de Certificado de Depósito Bancário) m type of investment offered by Brazilian banks.

CDC (abrev de Código de Defesa do Consumidor) m Brazilian consumer protection legislation.

CD-i (abrev de Compact Disc-Interativo) m CD-I.

CD-ROM (abrev de Compact Disc-Read Only Memory) m CD-ROM.

CE ⬦ f (abrev de Comunidade Européia) EC. ⬦ m (abrev de Estado do Ceará) State of Ceará.

cear [15] ['sja(x)] ⬦ vt to have for supper. ⬦ vi to have supper.

Ceará [sja'ra] n Ceará.

CEASA (abrev de Companhia de Entrepostos e Armazéns S.A) m Brazilian company of fruit and vegetable wholesalers.

cebola [se'bola] f onion.

cebolinha [sebo'liɲa] f chive.

CEBRAP (abrev de Centro Brasileiro de Análise e Planejamento) m independent research centre for the study of Brazilian society.

cê-cedilha [,sese'dʒiʎa] (pl cês-cedilhas) m c-cedilla.

cê-dê-efe [sede'ɛfi] (pl cê-dê-efes) mf fam -1. [com o trabalho] workaholic. -2. [com os estudos] swot.

cedente [se'dẽtʃi] mf transferor.

ceder [5] [se'de(x)] ⬦ vt -1. [dar] to hand over. -2. [emprestar] to loan. ⬦ vi -1. [aquiescer]: ~ a algo to give in to sthg. -2. [diminuir] to fall. -3. [afrouxar-se] to loosen. -4. [curvar-se ao peso] to give way. -5. [sucumbir]: ~ a algo to give way to sthg. -6. [transigir] to give in.

cedilha [se'diʎa] f cedilla.

cedo ['sedu] adv [de manhãzinha] early; mais ~ ou mais tarde sooner or later; o mais ~ possível as soon as possible; quanto mais ~ melhor the sooner the better.

cedro ['sɛdru] m cedar.

cédula ['sɛdula] f -1. [dinheiro] banknote. -2. [em votação]: ~ eleitoral ballot paper.

CEF (abrev de Caixa Econômica Federal) f Brazilian state-owned bank financing loans for house purchase.

cefaléia [sefa'lɛja] f headache.

cegar [14] [se'ga(x)] *vt* **-1.** [ger] to blind. **-2.** [suj: paixão, raiva] to make blind. **-3.** [tesoura etc] to blunt.

cego, ga ['sɛgu, ga] <> *adj* **-1.** [ger] blind. **-2.** [tesoura] blunt. <> *m, f* blind person.

➡ **às cegas** *loc adv* **-1.** [sem ver] blindly. **-2.** [sem saber] in the dark.

cegonha [se'goɲa] *f* [ave] stork; **esperar a chegada da** ~ *fam* to be pregnant.

cegueira [se'gejra] *f* blindness.

ceia ['seja] *f* supper; **a última** ~ *RELIG* the Last Supper; ~ **de Natal** Christmas Eve midnight supper.

ceifa ['sejfa] *f* **-1.** [ato] harvest. **-2.** [época] harvest-time. **-3.** *fig* [destruição, mortandade] death-toll.

ceifar [4] [sej'fa(x)] <> *vt* **-1.** [trigo, espigas] to harvest. **-2.** *fig* [vidas] to take. <> *vi* [colher] to harvest.

Ceilão [sej'lãw] *n* Ceylon.

cela ['sɛla] *f* cell.

celebração [selebra'sãw] (*pl* -ões) *f* **-1.** [realização] celebration. **-2.** [comemoração] commemoration.

celebrado, da [sele'bradu, da] *adj* [afamado] celebrated.

celebrar [4] [sele'bra(x)] *vt* **-1.** [ger] to celebrate. **-2.** [exaltar] to glorify.

célebre ['sɛlebri] *adj* famous.

celebridade [selebri'dadʒi] *mf* celebrity.

celebrizar [4] [selebri'za(x)] *vt* [conferir fama a] to make famous.

➡ **celebrizar-se** *vp* to become famous.

celeiro [se'lejru] *m* **-1.** [para cereais] granary. **-2.** [depósito] store.

célere ['sɛleri] *adj* quick.

celeste [se'lɛʃtʃi] *adj* heavenly.

celestial [seleʃ'tʃjaw] (*pl* -ais) *adj* celestial.

celeuma [se'lewma] *f* hubbub.

celibatário, ria [seliba'tarju, rja] <> *adj* celibate. <> *m, f* unmarried person.

celibato [seli'batu] *m* celibacy.

celofane [selo'fãni] <> *adj* [papel] cellophane. <> *m* cellophane.

celsius [sew'siuʃ] *adj* Celsius.

celta ['sɛwta] <> *adj* Celtic. <> *mf* [pessoa] Celt. <> *m* [língua] Celtic.

célula ['sɛlula] *f* cell; ~ **fotoelétrica** photo-electric cell.

celular [selu'la(x)] <> *adj* cellular. <> *m* *TELEC* cellular phone.

celulite [selu'litʃi] *f* cellulite.

celulose [selu'lɔzi] *f* cellulose.

cem ['sẽ] *num* **-1.** [cardinal] one/a hundred; ~ **por cento** one/a hundred per cent; *veja também* **seis**. **-2.** [muitos]: ~ **vezes** hundreds of times.

➡ **cem por cento** <> *loc adj*: ser ~ **por cento** to be one hundred per cent. <> *loc adv* [totalmente] completely.

cemitério [semi'tɛrju] *m* cemetery.

cena ['sena] *f* **-1.** [de peça, filme, novela] scene; ~ **s externas** outdoor scenes. **-2.** [palco] stage; **levar à** ~ to stage; **em** ~ on stage. **-3.** [acontecimento]

spectacle. **-4.** [escândalo]: **fazer uma** ~ to make a scene.

cenário [se'narju] *m* **-1.** [ger] scene. **-2.** [em teatro, cinema, TV] scenery. **-3.** [panorama] sight.

cenho ['seɲu] *m* frown.

cênico, ca ['seniku, ka] *adj* TEATRO stage *(antes de subst)*; **artes cênicas** performing arts.

cenografia [senogra'fia] *f* scenography.

cenógrafo, fa [se'nɔgrafu, fa] *m, f* scenographer.

cenoura [se'noura] *f* carrot.

censo ['sẽsu] *m* census.

censor, ra [sẽso(x), ra] *m, f* censor.

censura [sẽ'sura] *f* **-1.** [crítica] criticism. **-2.** [repreensão] reprimand. **-3.** [condenação] condemnation. **-4.** [prática] censure. **-5.** [organismo] board of censors. **-6.** [proibição] censorship. **-7.** [corte] cut.

censurado, da [sẽsu'radu, da] *adj* [proibido] censored.

censurar [4] [sẽsu'ra(x)] *vt* **-1.** [criticar] to criticise. **-2.** [repreender] to reprove. **-3.** [condenar] to condemn. **-4.** [examinar] to censor. **-5.** [proibir] to ban. **-6.** [cortar] to cut.

censurável [sẽsu'ravew] (*pl* -eis) *adj* [decisão, comportamento] open to criticism.

centavo [sẽ'tavu] *m* cent; **estar sem um** ~ to be penniless.

centeio [sẽ'teju] *m* rye.

centelha [sẽ'teʎa] *f* spark.

centena [sẽ'tena] *f* hundred; **às** ~ **s** in their hundreds; **uma** ~ **de vezes** a hundred times.

centenário, ria [sẽte'narju, rja] <> *adj*: **um homem** ~ a hundred-year-old man; **ele é** ~ he is a hundred years old. <> *m, f* [pessoa] centenarian.

➡ **centenário** *m* [comemoração] centenary.

centésimo, ma [sẽ'tɛzimu, ma] <> *num* hundredth. <> *m, f* [pessoa] hundredth.

➡ **centésimo** *m* hundredth.

centígrado, da [sẽ'tʃigradu] *adj* centigrade *(depois de subst)*.

➡ **centígrado** *m* centigrade.

centilitro [sẽtʃi'litru] *m* centilitre.

centímetro [sẽ'tʃimetru] *m* centimetre.

cento ['sẽtu] *num*: ~ **e dez** one/a hundred and ten; **por** ~ per cent; *veja também* **seis**.

centopéia [sẽto'pɛja] *f* centipede.

central [sẽ'traw] (*pl* -ais) <> *adj* **-1.** [ger] central. **-2.** *fig* [problema, ponto, argumento] central. <> *f* **-1.** [agência, delegacia]: ~ **de polícia** police station; ~ **de atendimento** call centre; ~ **de correios** post office; ~ **telefônica** telephone exchange. **-2.** [usina]: ~ **elétrica** power station; ~ **nuclear** nuclear power station.

centralização [sẽtraliza'sãw] *f* centralization.

centralizar [4] [sẽtrali'za(x)] *vt* to centralize.

centrar [4] [sẽ'tra(x)] <> *vt* **-1.** [ger] to centre. **-2.** *FUT* [bola, passe]: ~ to kick into the centre. <> *vi* *FUT* to shoot.

centrífuga [sẽtri'fuga], **centrifugadora** [sẽtrifuga'dora] *f* centrifuge.

centro ['sẽtru] *m* **-1.** [ger] centre; ~ **de gravidade** centre of gravity; ~ **da Terra** centre of the

Earth; ~ **de mesa** centrepiece; **ser o ~ das atenções** to be the centre of attention; ~ **comercial** shopping centre *UK*, shopping mall *US*; ~ **cultural** cultural centre; ~ **espírita** spiritualist centre; ~ **financeiro** financial centre; ~ **industrial** industrial centre; ~ **produtor** manufacturing centre; ~ **de atendimento** service centre; ~ **de processamento de dados** data processing centre. **- 2.** [de cidade] (city) centre; **ir ao ~** to go downtown. **- 3.** [metrópole] metropolis.

centroavante [ˌsẽntrw'vãntʃi] *m* centre forward.

CEP (*abrev de* **Código de Endereçamento Postal**) *m* ≃ post code *UK*, ≃ zip code *US*.

CEPAL (*abrev de* **Comissão Econômica para a América Latina**) *f* ECLAC.

cepo ['sepu] *m* **- 1.** [toro] log. **- 2.** [para decapitação] block.

cera ['sera] *f* **- 1.** [ger] wax. **- 2.** [para polir] wax polish. **- 3.** *fam fig* [manha] sham; **fazer ~** to sham.

cerâmica [se'rãmika] *f* **- 1.** [ger] ceramics. **- 2.** [fábrica] pottery. **- 3.** [argila cozida] ceramic.

ceramista [sera'miʃta] *mf* potter, ceramicist.

cerca ['sexka] *f* [de arame, madeira, ferro] fence; ~ **viva** hedge.

• cerca de *loc prep* around.

cercado, da [sex'kadu, da] *adj* fenced.

• cercado *m* **- 1.** [terreno] enclosure. **- 2.** [para animais] pen. **- 3.** [para crianças] playground.

cercanias [sexka'niaʃ] *fpl* **- 1.** [arredores] outskirts. **- 2.** [vizinhança] neighbourhood.

cercar [12] [sex'ka(x)] *vt* **- 1.** [ger] to surround. **- 2.** [pôr cerca em] to fence.

• cercar-se *vp* [rodear-se]: ~**-se de** to surround o.s. with.

cercear [15] [sex'sja(x)] *vt* [liberdade, privilégios] to restrict.

cerco ['sexku] *m* [assédio] siege; **fechar o ~ a** to close in on, to clamp down on; **pôr ~ a** to lay siege to.

cerda ['sexda] *f* [de escova de dentes] bristle.

cereal [se'rjal] (*pl* -ais) *m* cereal.

cerebral [sere'braw] (*pl* -ais) *adj* **- 1.** *ANAT* cerebral. **- 2.** [intelectual] intellectual.

cérebro ['serebru] *m* **- 1.** *ANAT* brain. **- 2.** *fig* [líder, mentor]: **o ~** the brains (*sg*).

cereja [se'reʒa] *f* cherry.

cerejeira [sere'ʒejra] *f* **- 1.** [árvore] cherry tree. **- 2.** [madeira] cherry wood.

cerimônia [seri'monja] *f* **- 1.** [solenidade] ceremony; ~ **de posse** investiture. **- 2.** [formalidade] formality; **fazer ~** to stand on ceremony; **sirva-se sem ~!** just help yourself!

cerimonial [serimo'njaw] (*pl* -ais) *m* [protocolo] ceremonial.

cerimonioso, osa [serimo'njozu, ɔza] *adj* ceremonious.

cerne ['sexni] *m* **- 1.** [de madeira] heartwood. **- 2.** *fig* [de questão] heart.

ceroulas [se'rolaʃ] *fpl* long johns.

cerração [sexa'sãw] *f* [neblina] fog.

cerrado, da [se'xadu, da] *adj* **- 1.** [fechado - porta, olhos] closed; [- punhos, dentes] clenched. **- 2.** [intenso] [bombardeio] heavy. **- 3.** [denso, espesso] thick.

• cerrado *m* [vegetação] *dense, low vegetation found in northern and central Brazil*.

cerrar [4] [se'xa(x)] *vt* [fechar - porta, olhos] to close; [-punhos, centes] to clench.

• cerrar-se *vp* **- 1.** [fechar-se] to close; ~**-se em** to shut oneself in. **- 2.** [céu] to become dark.

certa ['sexta] *f* ⊳ **certo**.

certame [sex'tãmi] *m* [concurso, competição] contest.

certeiro, ra [sex'tejru, ra] *adj* accurate.

certeza [sex'teza] *f* certainty; **tem ~?** are you sure?; **ter ~ de algo** to be sure about sthg; **ter ~ de que** to be sure that; **com ~** definitely.

certidão [sextʃi'dãw] (*pl* -ões) *f* certificate; ~ **de casamento** marriage certificate; ~ **de nascimento** birth certificate.

certificação [sextʃifika'sãw] (*pl* -ões) *f* certification.

certificado [sextʃifi'kadu] *m* certificate.

certificar [12] [sextʃifi'ka(x)] *vt* **- 1.** [assegurar]: **alguém de algo/de que** to assure sb of sthg/that. **- 2.** [atestar] to affirm.

• certificar-se *vp*: ~**-se de que/de algo** to make sure that/of sthg.

certo, ta ['sextu, ta] ⟨⟩ *adj* **- 1.** [ger] right. **- 2.** [correto, certeiro] correct. **- 3.** [sensato, acertado] sensible. **- 4.** [infalível, seguro] certain; **ser ~ que** to be certain that. **- 5.** [com razão]: **estar ~** to be right. **- 6.** [com certeza]: **estar ~ de que/de algo** to be sure that/of sthg. ⟨⟩ *pron* **- 1.** (*antes de subst*) [um, algum] right; **certa vez** once. **- 2.** *loc*: **dar ~** to work; **está ~** [está bem] all right.

• certo ⟨⟩ *m* **- 1.** [correto] (what is) right; **ele não sabe distinguir entre o ~ e o errado** he doesn't know the difference between right and wrong. **- 2.** [verdade] truth. ⟨⟩ *adv* **- 1.** [certamente] certainly. **- 2.** [corretamente] correctly.

• certa f: na certa definitely.

• ao certo *loc adv* for sure.

• por certo *loc adv* definitely.

cerveja [sex'veʒa] *f* [bebida] beer.

cervejaria [sexveʒa'ria] *f* **- 1.** [fábrica] brewery. **- 2.** [estabelecimento] *beer bar, usually serving food if wanted*.

cervical [sexvi'kaw] (*pl* -ais) *adj* cervical.

cerzir [58] [sex'zi(x)] ⟨⟩ *vt* to darn. ⟨⟩ *vi* to do invisible mending.

cesariana [seza'rjãna], **cesárea** [se'zarja] *f* Caesarean.

cessação [sesa'sãw] *f* ending.

cessão [se'sãw] (*pl* -ões) *f* **- 1.** [cedência] assignment. **- 2.** [transferência] transfer.

cessar [4] [se'sa(x)] ⟨⟩ *vi* to come to an end; ~ **com algo/de fazer algo** to stop sthg/doing sthg; **sem ~** non-stop. ⟨⟩ *vt* **- 1.** [fogo] to cease. **- 2.** [trabalho] to stop.

cessar-fogo [se̩sax'fogu] *m* (*inv*) ceasefire.

cessões [se'sõjʃ] *pl* ⊳ **cessão**.

cesta ['seʃta] *f* **- 1.** [ger] basket; ~ **básica** basic *monthly supplies that the average lower-middle-class family needs in order to survive.* - **2.** [conteúdo] basketful. - **3.** [ESP - aro] basket; [- ponto] stitch.

cesto ['seʃtu] *m* basket; ~ **de roupa suja** laundry basket.

CETESB (*abrev de* Companhia Estadual de Tecnologia de Saneamento Básico e Defesa do Meio Ambiente) *f São Paulo environment agency.*

ceticismo [setʃi'siʒmul *m* scepticism.

cético, ca ['sɛtʃiku, ka] <> *adj* sceptical. <> *m, f* sceptic.

cetim [se'tʃĩl *m* satin.

cetro ['sɛtrul *m* sceptre.

céu ['sɛwl *m* - **1.** [firmamento] sky; **a** ~ **aberto** [ao ar livre] in the open; [mineração] open-cast; **cair do** ~ **fig** to be heaven-sent; **mover** ~ **s e terra** *fig* to move heaven and earth. - **2.** RELIG heaven. - **3.** ANAT : ~ **da boca** roof of the mouth.

cevada [se'vadal *f* barley.

cevar [4] [se'va(x)] *vt* - **1.** [alimentar] to feed. - **2.** [fazer engordar] to fatten.

CFC (*abrev de* clorofluorocarboneto) *m* CFC.

chá ['ʃal *m* - **1.** [ger] tea; ~ **completo** afternoon tea; ~ **de camomila/menta** camomile/mint tea; ~ **preto** black tea. - **2.** [reunião] tea party; ~ **beneficente** fund-raising tea; ~ **dançante** tea dance. - **3.** *loc*: **depois de aparecer vários dias seguidos, ele tomou um** ~ **de sumiço** having turned up several days in a row he's gone missing; **tomar** ~ **de cadeira** to be a wallflower; **levei o maior** ~ **de cadeira no consultório ontem** I waited for ages at the doctor's yesterday.

chã ['ʃãl *f* plain.

chacal [ʃa'kawl (*pl* -ais) *m* jackal.

chácara ['ʃakaral *f* - **1.** [no campo] smallholding. - **2.** [na cidade] large town house. - **3.** [casa de campo] country house.

chacina [ʃa'sinal *f* slaughter.

chacinar [4] [ʃasi'na(x)] *vt* to slaughter.

chacoalhar [4] [ʃakwa'ʎa(x)] <> *vt* [agitar] to shake. <> *vi* [sacudir] to shake.

chacota [ʃa'kɔtal *f* - **1.** [deboche] ridicule. - **2.** [objeto de deboche] butt of ridicule.

chacrinha [ʃa'kriɲal *fam f* - **1.** [reunião] meeting. - **2.** *pej* [bagunça] mess.

chá-de-panela [,ʃadʒipa'nɛlal (*pl* chás-de-panela) *m* (bridal) shower *US*, party at which presents are given to a bride-to-be.

chafariz [ʃafa'riʃl (*pl* -es) *m* fountain.

chafurdar [4] [ʃafux'da(x)] *vi*: ~ **em** [lama etc] to wallow in; *fig* [vícios etc] to become involved in.

chaga ['ʃagal *f* - **1.** [ferida] wound. - **2.** *fig* [mal] scourge.

chalé [ʃa'lɛl *m* cottage.

chaleira [ʃa'lejral *f* kettle.

chama ['ʃamal *f* flame; **em** ~ **s** in flames.

chamada [ʃa'madal *f* - **1.** [telefônica] call; **fazer uma** ~ **a cobrar** to make a reverse charge call *UK*, to call collect *US*. - **2.** [verificação de presença] roll call. - **3.** JORN headline. - **4.** [repreensão]: **dar**

uma ~ **em alguém** to reprimand sb.

chamar [4] [ʃa'ma(x)] <> *vt* - **1.** [ger] to call; **ela decidiu chamá-la de Júlia** she decided to call her 'Júlia'. - **2.** [com gesto] to hail. - **3.** [convocar] to summon; [para função]: ~ **alguém para algo** to call sb for sthg. - **4.** [convidar] to invite; ~ **a atenção** [suj: pessoa, roupa] to attract attention; [para aspecto etc] to draw attention; ~ **a atenção de alguém** [repreender] to reprimand sb. - **5.** [acordar] to wake. - **6.** [qualificar]: ~ **algo/alguém de algo** to call sthg/sb sthg. <> *vi* - **1.** [dar sinal para vir] to call over; **chamei, mas ela não quis vir** I called her over but she didn't want to come. - **2.** [para acudir]: ~ **por alguém** to call out for sb; ~ **por socorro** to call for help. - **3.** [telefone] to ring.

➤ **chamar-se** *vp* [ter por nome] to be called; **como você se chama?** what's your name?

chamariz [ʃama'riʒl *m* - **1.** [isca] bait. - **2.** [seta, anúncio] advert. - **3.** *fig* [engodo] illusion.

chamativo, va [ʃama'tʃivu, val *adj* flashy.

chamego [ʃa'megul *m* state of excitement; **estar/ficar de** ~ **com alguém** to caress sb.

chaminé [ʃami'nɛl *f* chimney.

champanha [ʃãm'pãɲal, **champanhe** [ʃãm'paɲil *m ou f* champagne.

chamuscar [12] [ʃamuʃ'ka(x)] *vt* - **1.** [roupa] to scorch. - **2.** [cabelo] to singe. - **3.** [pessoa, braço] to burn.

➤ **chamuscar-se** *vp* to burn o.s.

chance ['ʃãnsil *f* chance; **dar uma** ~ **a** *ou* **para alguém/algo** to give sb/sthg a chance; **ele tem boas** ~ **s de ganhar** he has a good chance of winning.

chancela [ʃãn'sɛlal *f* seal.

chancelaria [ʃãnsela'rial *f* - **1.** [repartição] chancery. - **2.** [ministério do exterior] foreign ministry.

chanceler [ʃãnse'lɛ(x)] *mf* - **1.** [ministro] minister. - **2.** [chefe de governo] head of government.

chanchada [ʃãn'ʃadal *f* - **1.** CINE blue movie. - **2.** TEATRO pornographic play.

chantagear [15] [ʃãnta'ʒja(x)] *vt* to blackmail.

chantagem [ʃãn'taʒẽl (*pl* -ns) *f* blackmail.

chantagista [ʃãnta'ʒiʃtal *mf* blackmailer.

chão ['ʃãwl *m* - **1.** [piso] floor. - **2.** [solo] ground.

chapa ['ʃapal <> *f* - **1.** [folha] sheet; ~ **de metal/aço** metal/steel sheet. - **2.** [para grelhar] hotplate; **bife na** ~ steak on the griddle. - **3.** AUTO [placa] number plate *UK*, license plate *US*; ~ **fria** false number plate *UK*, false license plate *US*. - **4.** [de impressão] plate. - **5.** FOT shot. - **6.** [radiografia] X-ray. - **7.** POL [eleitoral] roll. <> *mf* [camarada] mate.

chapelaria [ʃapela'rial *f* - **1.** [loja] hat shop. - **2.** [fábrica] millinery factory.

chapeleiro, ra [ʃape'lejru, ral *m, f* milliner.

chapéu [ʃa'pɛwl *m* hat; **de tirar o** ~ fantastic.

chapéu-coco [ʃa,pɛw'kokul (*pl* chapéus-cocos) *m* bowler hat.

chapinha [ʃa'piɲal *f* [de garrafa] stopper.

charada [ʃa'radal *f* [enigma] puzzle; **matar uma** ~ to solve a problem.

charco ['ʃaxkul *m* puddle.

charge [ˈʃaxʒi] *f* cartoon.

chargista [ʃaxˈʒiʃta] *mf* cartoonist.

charlatão, tã [ʃaxlaˈtãw, tã] (*mpl* **-ães**, *fpl* **-s**) <> *adj* charlatan. <> *m, f* impostor.

charme [ˈʃaxmi] *m* charm; **fazer** ~ to play it cool.

charmoso, osa [ʃaxˈmozu, ɔza] *adj* charming.

charrete [ʃaˈxetʃi] *f* chariot.

charter [ˈʃarte(x)] <> *adj inv* charter. <> *m* charter plane.

charuto [ʃaˈrutu] *m* cigar.

chassi [ʃaˈsi] *m* **-1.** [ger] chassis. **-2.** ARTE [de tela] stretcher.

chateação [ʃatʃiaˈsãw] (*pl* **-ões**) *f* **-1.** [aborrecimento] boredom. **-2.** [maçada] bore.

chatear [15] [ʃaˈtʃja(x)] <> *vt* **-1.** [aborrecer] to annoy. **-2.** [incomodar] to bother. **-3.** [enfadar] to irritate. **-4.** [implicar com] to tease. <> *vi* **-1.** [aborrecer] to be boring. **-2.** [incomodar] to be annoying.

  ➥ **chatear-se** *vp* [aborrecer-se] to become bored.

chatice [ʃaˈtʃisi] *f* boredom.

chato, ta [ˈʃatu, ta] <> *adj* **-1.** [superfície, forma] flat; **ele tem pés** ~**s** he's got flat feet. **-2.** [filme, música] boring. **-3.** [desagradável] unwelcome. **-4.** [embaraçoso] tricky. <> *m, f* bore; **um** ~ **de galochas** a drag.

  ➥ **chato** *m* [coisa desagradável]: **o** ~ **é que vamos passar o final de semana trabalhando** the annoying thing is we're going to spend the weekend working.

  ➥ **chata** *f* [embarcação] boat.

chatura [ʃaˈtura] *f fam* drag.

chauvinismo [ʃawviˈniʒmu] *m* chauvinism.

chauvinista [ʃoviˈniʃta] *mf* chauvinist.

chavão [ʃaˈvãw] (*pl* **-ões**) *m* hackneyed phrase.

chave [ˈʃavi] *f* **-1.** [de fechadura] key; ~ **mestra** master key. **-2.** [ferramenta] spanner; ~ **de fenda** *ou* **para fusos** screwdriver; ~ **de porcas** wrench; ~ **inglesa** adjustable spanner *UK*, monkey wrench *US*. **-3.** ELETR switch. **-4.** [golpe] blow; ~ **de braço** armlock. **-5.** [sinal gráfico] curly bracket. **-6.** *fig* [de problema] key.

-chave [ˈʃliavi] *sufixo* key- (*prefixo*).

chaveiro [ʃaˈvejru] *m* **-1.** [utensílio] key-rack. **-2.** [profissional] locksmith.

chavões [ʃaˈvõjʃ] *pl* ⊳ chavão.

checar [12] [ʃeˈka(x);] *vt* to check.

check-up [ʃeˈkapi] (*pl* **check-ups**) *m* check-up.

chefe [ˈʃɛfi] *mf* **-1.** [superior] head; ~ **de estado** head of state; ~ **de família** head of the family; ~ **de turma** shift supervisor. **-2.** *fam* [garçom] waiter. **-3.** *fam* [freguês] mate.

chefia [ʃeˈfia] *f* **-1.** [direção] management. **-2.** [repartição, sala] management office.

chefiar [16] [ʃeˈfja(x)] *vt* to lead.

chega [ˈʃega] *m fam* [repreensão]: **dar um** ~ **(para lá) em alguém** to tear a strip off sb.

chegada [ʃeˈgada] *f* **-1.** [vinda, regresso] arrival. **-2.** [aproximação] approach. **-3.** ESP finishing line.

chegado, da [ʃeˈgadu, da] *adj* **-1.** [ger] close. **-2.** [propenso]: **ser** ~ **a** to be very fond of.

chegar [14] [ʃeˈga(x)] <> *vi* **-1.** [a um lugar]: ~ **em** to arrive at; ~ **em casa** to arrive home; ~ **de** to arrive from. **-2.** [aproximar-se] to approach; **chega aqui** *fam* come here; **chega para cá** move over here. **-3.** [afastar-se]: **chega para lá** [ir embora] go away; [deslocar-se] move over. **-4.** [verão, noite, hora] to arrive. **-5.** [bastar] to be enough; **chegar!** that's enough! **-6.** [alcançar] to reach; **não** ~ **aos pés de** [não ser comparável a] to come nowhere near. **-7.** [conseguir]: ~ **a (ser) algo** to succeed in becoming sthg; ~ **a fazer algo** to manage to do sthg. **-8.** [ir ao extremo]: ~ **a fazer algo** to reach the point of doing sthg. **-9.** *fam* [partir]: **vou chegando** I'm pushing off. <> *vt* **-1.** [aproximar]: ~ **algo para cá** to bring sthg over here. **-2.** [afastar]: ~ **algo para lá/para o lado** to move sthg over there/to one side.

  ➥ **chegar-se** *vp* [aproximar-se] to come closer.

cheio, cheia [ˈʃeju, ˈʃeja] *adj* **-1.** [ger] full; ~ **de** full of; ~ **de manchas** covered in stains; ~ **de dedos** *fam fig* [receoso] full of apprehension; [tímido] timid; ~ **de frescura** *fam fig* finicky; ~ **da nota** *fam* [rico] loaded; ~ **de si** [orgulhoso] proud; [arrogante] full of o.s. **-2.** [gordo] plump. **-3.** *fam* [farto]: **estar** ~ **(de alguém/algo)** to be fed up with sb/sthg.

  ➥ **cheia** *f* **-1.** [de rio] flood. **-2.** [época] flood season.

  ➥ **em cheio** *loc adv*: **acertar em** ~ to hit the mark.

cheirar [4] [ʃejˈra(x)] <> *vt* **-1.** [flor, perfume, comida] to smell. **-2.** [cocaína] to snort. <> *vi* **-1.** [flor, perfume, comida] to smell; ~ **a** [ter cheiro de] to smell of; *fig* [parecer] to smack (of); ~ **bem/mal** to smell nice/bad; **isto não me cheira bem** it makes me feel uncomfortable. **-2.** [cocaína]: **passou a noite cheirando** he spent the whole night snorting (coke).

cheiroso, osa [ʃejˈrosu, ɔza] *adj* scented; **estar** ~ to be scented.

cheiro-verde [ˌʃejuˈvexdʒi] (*pl* **cheiros-verdes**) *m* parsley and spring onion.

cheque [ˈʃɛki] *m* cheque; ~ **em branco** blank cheque; ~ **compensado** cleared cheque; ~ **cruzado** crossed cheque; ~ **especial** guaranteed cheque; ~ **nominal** nominative cheque; ~ **ao portador** bearer cheque; ~ **pré-datado** predated cheque; ~ **voador** *ou* **sem fundos** bounced cheque.

chiado [ˈʃjadu] *m* **-1.** [de roda, porta] squeak. **-2.** [de passarinho] chirp.

chiar [16] [ˈʃja(x)] *vi* **-1.** [emitir chio - pessoa, respiração] to wheeze; [- vento] whistle. **-2.** *fam* [reclamar] to kick up a stink.

chibata [ʃiˈbata] *f* [vara] stick.

chiclete [ʃiˈklɛtʃi] *m* chewing gum; ~ **de bola** bubble gum.

chicória [ʃiˈkɔrja] *f* chicory.

chicote [ʃiˈkɔtʃi] *m* whip.

chicotear [15] [ʃikoˈtʃja(x)] *vt* to whip.

chifrada [ʃiˈfrada] *f* horn thrust.

chifrar [4] [ʃi'fra(x)] vt -**1.** [toureiro, tronco] to gore. - **2.** fam fig [marido, namorada] to two-time.

chifre [ʃifri] m [de animal] horn; **pôr** ~**s em** fam fig [em marido, namorada] to two-time.

chifrudo, da [ʃi'frudu, da] adj -**1.** [animal] large-horned. - **2.** fam fig [marido, namorada] two-timed.

Chile ['ʃilil n Chile.

chileno, na [ʃi'lenu, na] <> adj Chilean. <> m, f Chilean.

chilique [ʃi'liki] m fam faint; **ter um** ~ to have a fit.

chilrear [15] [ʃiw'xja(x)] vi to chirp.

chilreio [ʃiw'xeju] m chirping.

chimarrão [ʃima'xãw] (pl -ões) m herbal tea.

chimpanzé [ʃĩnpãn'zɛ] m chimpanzee.

China ['ʃina] n: (a) ~ China.

chinelo [ʃi'nɛlu] m slipper; **botar no** ~ fam [superar] to outdo.

chinês, esa [ʃi'neʃ, eza] (pl -eses, fpl -s) <> adj Chinese. <> m, f [da China] Chinese.

chinfrim [ʃĩn'frĩ] (pl -ns) adj worthless.

chip ['ʃipi] m COMPUT microchip.

Chipre ['ʃipri] n Cyprus.

chique ['ʃiki] adj chic.

chiqueiro [ʃi'kejru] m -**1.** [de porcos] pigsty. - **2.** fam fig [bagunça] pigsty.

chispa ['ʃiʃpa] f [faísca] spark.

chispar [4] [ʃiʃ'pa(x)] vi [correr] to race.

chita ['ʃita] f printed cotton.

choça ['ʃɔsa] f hut.

chocalhar [4] [ʃoka'ʎa(x)] <> vt to rattle. <> vi [soar] to rattle.

chocalho [ʃo'kaʎu] m -**1.** MÚS maraca. - **2.** [brinquedo] rattle. - **3.** [de gado, cavalo] bell.

chocante [ʃo'kãntʃi] adj -**1.** [assustador, ofensivo] shocking. - **2.** fam [ótimo] wicked.

chocar [12] [ʃo'ka(x)] <> vt -**1.** [assustar, ofender] to shock. - **2.** ZOOL to hatch. <> vi -**1.** [causar espanto, ofensa] to shock. - **2.** ZOOL to brood.
    ➡ **chocar-se** vp -**1.** [colidir]: ~-**se (contra)** to collide (with). - **2.** [assustar-se]: ~-**se (com)** to be shocked (by). - **3.** [discordar]: ~-**se em relação a** to clash over.

chocho, cha ['ʃoʃu, ʃa] adj -**1.** [sem graça] dull. - **2.** [fruta, ovo] rotten.

choco, ca ['ʃoku, ka] adj -**1.** [ave] sitting. - **2.** [ovo - fertilizado] fertilized; [- estragado] addled.

chocolate [ʃoko'latʃil m chocolate.

chofer [ʃo'fɛ(x)] (pl -es) mf driver.

chofre ['ʃofril ➡ de chofre loc adv [subitamente] suddenly.

chopada [ʃo'pada] f fam beer-drinking session.

chope ['ʃopil m beer.

choque ['ʃɔki] m -**1.** [ger] shock; **estado de** ~ state of shock; **dar um** ~ **(em alguém)** to give (sb) a shock; **levar** ou **tomar um** ~ to get a shock. - **2.** [colisão] crash. - **3.** [conflito, confronto] clash.

choradeira [ʃora'dejra] f -**1.** [choro] crying. - **2.** [lamúria] grumbling. - **3.** [pedido] complaining.

choramingar [ʃoramĩn'ga(x)] vi to whine.

choramingas [14] [ʃora'mĩngaʃ] mf crybaby.

choramingo [ʃora'mĩngul m whine.

chorão, ona [ʃo'rãw, ona] (mpl -ões, fpl -onas) <> adj moaning. <> m, f [pessoa] crybaby.
    ➡ **chorão** m BOT weeping willow.

chorar [4] [ʃo'ra(x)] <> vi -**1.** [verter lágrimas] to cry. - **2.** fig [barganhar] to haggle. <> vt -**1.** [lágrima] to cry; ~ **a morte de alguém** to mourn the death of sb. - **2.** fig [barganhar] to haggle. - **3.** loc: ~ **as mágoas** to pour out; ~ **miséria** to moan about poverty.

chorinho [ʃo'riɲu] m MÚS = choro.

choro ['ʃorul m -**1.** [pranto] crying. - **2.** MÚS a type of traditional Brazilian music started at the end of the nineteenth century.

CHORO

One of the more polished expressions of Brazilian music, the choro, or chorinho, is an instrumental musical genre characterized by virtuosity and improvisation. Choro originated in Rio de Janeiro towards the end of the nineteenth century and is derived from the polka and the maxixe, a precursor of the samba. It is generally performed to the accompaniment of percussion instruments, guitars, a cavaquinho (small four-stringed guitar), a mandolin and certain wind instruments such as the flute or the clarinet.

---

chorona [ʃo'ronal f ➡ chorão.

choroso, osa [ʃo'rozu, ɔza] adj tearful.

choupana [ʃo'pãnal f hut.

chouriço [ʃo'risul m chorizo.

chove-não-molha [ˌʃovinãw'moʎal m inv fam shilly-shallying.

chover [47] [ʃo've(x)] v impess -**1.** METEOR to rain; ~ **a cântaros** to pour down with rain; **nem que chova canivete** fig come what may. - **2.** fig [cair do alto] to shower. - **3.** fig [sobrevir em demasia] to pour in.

chuchu [ʃu'ʃul m fruit-bearing climbing plant; **está frio pra** ~ fam it's bloody cold; **tinha comida pra** ~ fam there was loads of food at the party.

chucrute [ʃu'krutʃil m choucroute, sauerkraut.

chulé [ʃu'lɛl m smell of feet.

chulear [15] [ʃu'lja(x)] vt to hem.

chulo, lo ['ʃulu, lal adj vulgar.

chumaço [ʃu'masul m -**1.** [enchimento] padding. - **2.** [de algodão, gaze] wadding.

chumbado, da [ʃũn'badu, dal adj fam worn out.

chumbar [4] [ʃũn'ba(x)] vt -**1.** [soldar] to solder. - **2.** [grade, portão] to secure. - **3.** [rede, anzol] to drop.

chumbo ['ʃũnbul m lead.

chupado, da [ʃu'padu, dal adj fam [magro] skinny.
    ➡ **chupada** f [chupadela] suck.

chupão [ʃu'pãwl (pl -ões) fam m -**1.** [beijo] slurpy kiss. - **2.** [marca] love bite.

chupar [4] [ʃu'pa(x)] vt to suck.

chupeta [ʃu'petal f -**1.** [de criança] dummy UK, comforter US. - **2.** fam AUTO : **fazer uma** ~ to use jump-leads.

churrascaria [ʃuxaʃka'rial f restaurant specializing in grilled and spit-roasted meat; ~

rodízio restaurant where diners may pick and choose from food offered.

churrasco [ʃu'xaʃku] *m* -**1**. [carne] barbecued meat. -**2**. [refeição] barbecue.

churrasqueira [ʃuxaʃ'kejral *f* rotisserie.

churrasquinho [ʃuxaʃ'kiɲu] *m* kebab.

chutar [4] [ʃu'ta(x)] ⟷ *vt* -**1**. [objeto, pessoa] to kick. -**2**. *fam* [resposta] to take a stab at. -**3**. *fam* [funcionário, namorado]: ~ **alguém** to give sb the push. ⟷ *vi* -**1**. [dar chute] to kick. -**2**. *fam* [em prova] to take a pot shot. -**3**. *loc*: ~ **alto** to tell tall stories.

chute ['ʃutʃil *m* -**1**. [pontapé] kick. -**2**. *fam* [mentira] bullshit. -**3**. *fam* [dispensa] push; **dar um** ~ **em alguém** to give sb the push.

chuteira [ʃu'tejral *f* football boot; **pendurar as** ~**s** [aposentar-se] to hang up one's boots.

chuva ['ʃuval *f* -**1**. METEOR rain; ~ **ácida** acid rain; ~ **fina** drizzle; ~ **de granizo** *ou* **pedra** hail; **tomar** ~ to get wet in the rain; **estar na** ~ *fig* to be drunk. -**2**. *fig* [de papel picado etc] shower.

chuvarada [ʃuva'radal *f* downpour.

chuveirada [ʃuvej'radal *f* shower.

chuveiro [ʃu'vejrul *m* shower.

chuviscar [12] [ʃuviʃ'ka(x)] *vi* to drizzle.

chuvisco [ʃu'viʃkul *m* -**1**. [chuva] drizzle. -**2**. CULIN confection made of egg-yolk and sugar.

chuvoso, osa [ʃu'vozu, ɔzal *adj* rainy.

Cia (*abrev de* **Companhia**) *f* Co.

cianeto [sja'netul *m* cyanide.

cibercafé [sibex'kafel *m* cybercafé.

ciberespaço [sibereʃ'pasul *m* cyberspace.

cibernética [sibex'nɛtʃikal *f* cybernetics (*sg*).

cibernético, ca [sibex'netʃiku, kal *adj* cybernetic.

➥ **cibernética** *f* cybernetics.

ciberpunk [sibex'pũŋkil *mf* net hacker.

CIC (*abrev de* **Cartão de Identificação do Contribuinte**) *m Brazilian tax-payer's identity card for individual contributions.*

cicatriz [sika'triʃl (*pl* -**es**) *f* scar.

cicatrização [sikatriza'sãwl *f* healing.

cicatrizar [4] [sikatri'za(x)] ⟷ *vt* -**1**. [fechar] to heal. -**2**. [cobrir de cicatrizes] to scar. ⟷ *vi* [fechar-se] to heal.

cicerone [sise'ronil *mf* guide.

ciceronear [sise'ronja(x)] *vt* to act as a guide for.

ciciar [16] [si'sja(x)] *vi* to whisper.

cíclico, ca ['sikliku, kal *adj* cyclic.

ciclismo [si'kliʒmul *m* cycling.

ciclista [si'kliʃtal *mf* cyclist.

ciclo ['siklul *m* cycle; ~ **básico** UNIV foundation course.

ciclone [si'klonil *m* cyclone.

ciclotimia [siclotʃi'mial *f* PSIC cyclothymia.

ciclotímico, ca [siklo'tʃimiku, kal ⟷ *adj* cyclothymic. ⟷ *m*, *f* cyclothymic.

ciclovia [siklo'vial *f* bicycle lane.

cidadã [sida'dãl *f* ▷ **cidadão**.

cidadania [sidada'nial *f* citizenship.

cidadão, dã [sida'dãw, dal (*pl* -**ãos**, *fpl* -**s**) *m*, *f* citizen.

cidade [si'dadʒil *f* -**1**. [centro urbano] city; [pequena] small town; ~ **satélite** satellite town. -**2**. [bairro central] town. -**3**. *fig* [população] city.

Cidade do Cabo [si,dadʒidu'kabul *n* Cape Town.

Cidade do México [si,dadʒidu'mɛʃikul *n* Mexico City.

cidadela [sida'dɛlal *f* citadel.

cidra ['sidral *f* citron.

ciência ['sjẽnsjal *f* -**1**. [saber] science; ~**s econômicas** economics; ~**s humanas** humanities; ~**s ocultas** occultism (*sg*); ~**s sociais** social science (*sg*). -**2**. [da vida, do amor] art. -**3**. [conhecimento] knowledge; **dar** ~ **de algo (a alguém)** to tell sb sthg; **tome** ~ take this on board.

ciente ['sjẽntʃil *adj* learned; **estar** ~ **(de algo)** to be aware of sthg.

cientificismo [sjẽntʃifi'siʒmul *m scientific spirit.*

científico, ca [sjẽn'tʃifiku, kal *adj* scientific.

cientista [sjẽn'tʃiʃtal *mf* scientist.

cifra ['sifral *f* -**1**. [ger] cipher. -**2**. [soma, quantia] sum. -**3**. MÚS figure.

cifrão [si'frãwl (*pl* -**ões**) *m* dollar sign.

cifrar [si'fra(x)] *vt* to write in code.

cigano, na [si'gãnu, nal ⟷ *adj* gipsy. ⟷ *m*, *f* gipsy.

cigarra [si'gaxal *f* -**1**. ZOOL cicada. -**2**. [campainha] buzzer.

cigarreira [siga'xejral *f* [estojo] cigarette case.

cigarrilha [siga'xiʎal *f* cheroot.

cigarro [si'gaxul *m* cigarette.

cilada [si'ladal *f* -**1**. [ger] trap. -**2**. [emboscada] ambush.

cilindrada [silĩ'dradal *f* cubic capacity.

cilíndrico, ca [si'lĩdriku, kal *adj* cylindrical.

cilindro [si'lĩdrul *m* GEOM, AUTO cylinder.

cílio ['siljul *m* eyelash.

cima ['simal *f*: **lá em** ~ [no topo, no alto] up there; [em andar superior] upstairs; **andar de** ~ upstairs; **ainda por** ~ on top of that; **de** ~ from the top; **de** ~ **de** from the top of; **de** ~ **para baixo** from top to bottom; **em** ~ **de** on top of; **em** ~ **da mesa** on the table; **para** ~ upwards; **por** ~ **de** over; **dar em** ~ **de alguém** to chat sb up; **estar por** ~ to be quids in; **tudo em** ~? *fam* everything all right?

cimentado, da [simẽn'tadu, dal *adj* -**1**. CONSTR cemented. -**2**. [consolidado] sealed.

cimentar [4] [simẽn'ta(x)] *vt* to cement.

cimento [si'mẽntul *m* cement; ~ **armado** reinforced concrete.

cimo [si'mul *m* top.

cinco ['sĩŋkul *num* five; *veja também* **seis**.

cindir [6] [sĩn'dʒi(x)] *vt* -**1**. [separar] to separate. -**2**. [cortar] to cut through.

cineasta [si'njaʃtal *mf* cinematographer.

cinéfilo, la [si'nɛfilu, lal *m*, *f* film enthusiast.

cinegrafista [sinegra'fiʃtal *mf* cameraman (*f* camerawoman).

cinema [si'nemal *m* cinema; ~ **mudo** silent film.

cinematografia [sinematogra'fia] f cinematography.

cinematográfico, ca [sinemato'grafiku, ka] adj cinematographic.

Cingapura [sĩŋga'pural n Singapore.

cingir [52] [sĩn'ʒi(x)] vt -1. [ger] to encircle. -2. [pôr à cintura] to gird.

cínico, ca ['siniku, ka] <> adj shameless. <> m, f immoral person.

cinismo [si'niʒmu] m impudence.

cinqüenta [sĩŋ'kwẽnta] num fifty; veja também seis.

cinqüentão, tona [sĩŋkwẽn'tãw, tona] (mpl -ões, fpl -s) <> adj quinquagenarian. <> m, f quinquagenarian.

cinta ['sĩnta] f -1. [faixa] belt. -2. [feminina] girdle.

cinta-liga [‚sĩnta'liga] (pl cintas-ligas) f suspender belt.

cintilante [sĩntʃi'lãntʃil adj scintillating.

cintilar [4] [sĩntʃi'la(x)] vi to scintillate.

cinto ['sĩntul m belt; ~ de segurança safety belt.

cintura [sĩn'tural f waist.

cinturão [sĩntu'rãw] (pl -ões) m belt; ~ verde green belt.

cinza ['sĩnzal <> adj inv [cor] grey. <> m [cor] grey. <> f [de combustão] ash.

➭ **cinzas** fpl ashes.

cinzeiro [sĩn'zejrul m ashtray.

cinzel [sĩn'zɛwl (pl -éis) m chisel.

cinzelar [4] [sĩnze'la(x)] vt -1. [lavrar] to chisel. -2. [gravar] to engrave. -3. fig [frase, verso] to polish.

cinzento, ta [sĩn'zẽntu, ta] adj grey.

cio ['siwl m rut; estar no ~ to be in a rut.

cioso, ciosa ['sjozu, 'sjoza] adj jealous.

CIPA (abrev de Comissão Interna de Prevenção de Acidentes) f Brazilian commission for prevention of accidents at work, ≃ HSE UK, ≃ OHSA US.

cipreste [si'prɛʃtʃil m cypress.

cipriota [sipri'ota] <> adj Cypriot. <> m, f Cypriot.

circense [six'sẽnsil adj circus (antes de subst).

circo ['sixkul m circus.

circuito [six'kujtul m circuit.

circulação [sixkula'sãwl f circulation.

circulante [sirku'lãntʃil adj -1. [itinerante] itinerant. -2. ECON: capital ~ ready capital.

circular [4] [sixku'la(x)] (pl -es) <> adj [formato] circular. <> m [ônibus] shuttle. <> f [carta, ofício] circular. <> vt -1. [rodear] to circle. -2. [dar voltas por] to surround. <> vi -1. [ger] to circulate. -2. [percorrer] to wander.

círculo ['sixkulul m -1. GEOM circle; ~ vicioso vicious circle. -2. fig [meio, grupo] circle.

circunavegação [sixkŭnavega'sãwl f circumnavigation.

circunavegar [14] [sixkŭnave'ga(x)] vt to circumnavigate.

circuncidado [sixkŭnsi'dadul adj circumcised.

circuncidar [4] [sixkŭnsi'da(x)] vt to circumcise.

circuncisão [sixkŭnsi'zãw] f circumcision.

circundante [sixkŭn'dãntʃil adj surrounding.

circundar [4] [sixkŭn'da(x)] vt to surround.

circunferência [sixkŭnfe'rẽnsjal f circumference.

circunflexo [sixkŭn'flɛksul GRAM <> adj circumflex. <> m circumflex.

circunscrever [6] [sixkŭnʃkre've(x)] vt -1. [ger] to contain. -2. [inscrever] to circumscribe. -3. [restringir] to restrict.

➭ **circunscrever-se** vp [restringir-se] to be restricted.

circunscrição [sixkŭnʃkri'sãw] (pl -ões) f [repartição] division; ~ eleitoral electoral constituency.

circunscrito, ta [sixkŭnʃ'kritu, ta] <> pp ▷ circunscrever. <> adj circumscribed.

circunspe(c)ção [sixkŭnʃpe(k)sãw] (pl -ões) f circumspection.

circunspecto, ta [sixkŭnʃ'pɛktu, ta] adj circumspect.

circunstância [sixkŭnʃ'tãnsjal f -1. [ger] circumstance. -2. JUR: ~s atenuantes/agravantes attenuating/aggravating circumstances. -3. [caso] event.

circunstanciado, da [sixkŭnʃtãn'sjadu, da] adj detailed.

circunstantes [sixkŭnʃ'tãntʃiʃl mpl onlookers.

cirrose [si'xɔzil f cirrhosis.

cirurgia [sirux'ʒial f surgery; ~ plástica plastic surgery; ~ estética aesthetic surgery UK, esthetic surgery US; ~ reconstrutora ou reparadora reconstructive surgery.

cirurgião, ã [sirux'ʒjãw‚ʒjã, al (pl -ões, fpl -s) m, f surgeon.

cirurgião-dentista, cirurgiã-dentista [sirux‚ʒjãwdẽn'tʃiʃta, sirux‚ʒjãdẽntʃiʃtal (mpl cirurgiões-dentistas, fpl cirurgiãs-dentistas) m, f dental surgeon.

cirúrgico, ca [si'ruxʒiku, ka] adj surgical; ataque ou bombardeio ~ fig surgical strike.

cisão [si'zãw] (pl -ões) f -1. [divisão] split. -2. [discordância] division.

cisco ['siʃkul m dust.

cisma ['siʒmal <> m schism. <> f [mania] crazy idea.

cismado, da [siʒ'madu, da] adj wary.

cismar [4] [siʒ'ma(x)] <> vt [convencer-se de]: ~ que to be convinced that. <> vi -1. [decidir]: ~ de ou em fazer algo to determine upon doing sthg. -2. [implicar]: ~ com to clash with. -3. [insistir]: ~ em to insist on.

cisne ['siʒnil m swan.

cisões [si'zõjʃl pl ▷ cisão.

cisterna [siʃ'tɛxnal f cistern.

cistite [siʃ'tʃitʃil f cystitis.

citação [sita'sãwl (pl -ões) f -1. [de trecho, autor] quotation. -2. JUR citation.

citadino, na [sita'dʒinu, nal adj citizen.

citar [4] [si'ta(x)] vt -1. [trecho, autor] to quote. -2. JUR to summons.

cítrico, ca ['sitriku, ka] adj -1. [fruta] citrus. -2. [ácido] citric.

ciúme ['sjumi] *m* jealousy; **ficar com** ~ *ou* ~**s** to become jealous; **ter** ~ *ou* ~**s de alguém** to be jealous of sb.

ciumeira [sju'mejra] *f* jealousy.

ciumento, ta [sju'mẽntu, ta] *adj* jealous.

cívico, ca ['siviku, ka] *adj* civic.

civil [si'viw] (*pl* **-is**) ⋄ *adj* **-1.** [direito, tribunal] civil. **-2.** [vida, traje] civilian. ⋄ *mf* [pessoa] civilian. ⋄ *m* [casamento civil]: **casar-se no** ~ to have a civil wedding.

civilidade [sivili'dadʒil] *f* courtesy.

civilização [siviliza'sãw] (*pl* **-ões**) *f* civilization.

civilizadamente [civilizada'mẽntʃil] *adv* **-1.** [com educação] politely. **-2.** [com ordem] in a civilized manner.

civilizador, ra [siviliza'do(x), ra] *adj* civilizing.

civilizar [4] [sivili'za(x)] *vt* to civilize.
➡ **civilizar-se** *vp* to become civilized.

civismo [si'viʒmu] *m* public spirit.

cl. (*abrev de* **centilitro**) *m* cl.

clã ['klã] (*pl* **clãs**) *m* clan.

clamar [4] [kla'ma(x)] ⋄ *vt* to clamour. ⋄ *vi*: ~ **por/contra algo** to clamour for/to protest against sthg.

clamor [kla'mo(x)] (*pl* **-es**) *m* clamour *UK*, clamor *US*.

clamoroso, osa [klamo'rozu, ɔza] *adj* clamorous.

clandestino, na [klãndeʃ'tʃinu, na] *adj* clandestine.

claque ['klaki] *f* **-1.** *TEATRO* paid participating audience. **-2.** [de fãs, seguidores] group of fans.

clara ['klara] *f* ⊳ **claro**.

clarabóia [klara'bɔja] *f* skylight.

clarão [kla'rãw] (*pl* **-ões**) *m* **-1.** [de raio, flash] flash. **-2.** [claridade] brightness.

clarear [15] [kla'rja(x)] ⋄ *vt* **-1.** [iluminar] to light up. **-2.** [dia, céu] to brighten. ⋄ *vi* **-1.** [amanhecer] to get light. **-2.** [dia, céu] to brighten.

clareira [kla'rejra] *f* [em floresta] glade, clearing.

clareza [kla'reza] *f* clarity; **com** ~ clearly.

claridade [klari'dadʒil] *f* [luz] clarity.

clarim [kla'rĩ] (*pl* **-ns**) *m* bugle.

clarinete [klari'netʃil] *m* clarinet.

clarividência [klarivi'dẽnsja] *f* far-sightedness.

clarinetista [klarine'tʃiʃta] *mf* clarinettist *UK*, clarinetist *US*.

clarividente [klarivi'dẽntʃil] ⋄ *adj* **-1.** [sagaz] wise. **-2.** [prudente] cautious. **-3.** [vidente] clairvoyant. ⋄ *mf* [vidente] clairvoyant.

claro, ra ['klaru, ra] *adj* **-1.** [ger] bright; **dia** ~ daylight. **-2.** [límpido, nítido, explícito] clear; **deixar** ~ **que** to make explicit; **estar** ~ **(que/por que)** to be obvious (that/why); **ser** ~ **(que)** to be obvious (that); **ser** ~ **como água** to be crystal clear.
➡ **claro** ⋄ *adv* [evidentemente]: **claro!** of course!; ~ **que sim!/que não!** of course!/of course not! ⋄ *m* **-1.** [em escrita] space. **-2.** [em pintura] highlight.
➡ **clara** *f*: ~ **(de ovo)** egg white.

➡ **às claras** *loc adv* in broad daylight.
➡ **em claro** *loc adv*: **passar a noite em** ~ to have a sleepless night.

clarões [kla'rõjʃ] ⊳ **clarão**.

classe ['klasi] *f* **-1.** [ger] class; ~ **média** middle class; ~ **trabalhadora** *ou* **operária** working class; ~ **executiva** business class; ~ **turística** tourist class; **primeira** ~ first class. **-2.** [categoria]: **de primeira** ~ first class; **ela tem** ~ she's got class; **com** ~ charmingly; **de** ~ classy.

clássico, ca ['klasiku, ka] *adj* **-1.** [ger] classic; **música** ~ classical music. **-2.** [da Antiguidade] classical.
➡ **clássico** *m* [obra-prima] classic.

classificação [klasifika'sãw] (*pl* **-ões**) *f* **-1.** [ger] classification. **-2.** [qualificação] label. **-3.** [para cinema e TV] rating.

classificado, da [klasifi'kadu, da] ⋄ *adj* classified. ⋄ *m, f* [em concurso, competição] classified entrant.
➡ **classificado** *m* [anúncio] classified advertisement, classified ad.
➡ **classificados** *mpl JORN* [seção] classifieds.

classificar [12] [klasifi'ka(x)] *vt* to classify.
➡ **classificar-se** *vp* **-1.** [ser aprovado] to pass. **-2.** [obter posição de]: ~**-se em primeiro lugar** to be first.

classificatório, ria [klasifika'tɔrju, rja] *adj* classifying.

classudo, da [kla'sudu, da] *adj fam* classy.

claudicante [klawdʒi'kãntʃi] *adj* [capengante] hobbling.

claudicar [12] [klawdʒi'ka(x)] *vi* **-1.** [mancar] to limp. **-2.** *fig* [ir mal] to limp along.

claustro ['klawʃtru] *m* cloister.

claustrofobia [klawʃtrofo'bia] *f* claustrophobia.

claustrofóbico, ca [klawʃtro'fɔbiku, ka] *adj* claustrophobic.

cláusula ['klawzula] *f* clause.

clausura [klaw'zura] *f* **-1.** [recinto] enclosure. **-2.** [vida] seclusion.

clave ['klavi] *f MÚS* clef.

clavícula [kla'vikula] *f* clavicle, collarbone.

clemência [kle'mẽnsja] *f* **-1.** [qualidade] leniency. **-2.** [perdão] clemency.

clemente [kle'mẽntʃi] *adj* clement.

cleptomaníaco, ca [klɛptoma'niaku, ka] *m, f* kleptomaniac.

clérigo ['klɛrigu] *m* clergyman.

clero ['klɛru] *m* clergy.

clicar [12] [kli'ka(x)] *vi* to click.

clichê [kli'ʃe] *m* **-1.** *FOT* proof. **-2.** [chavão] cliché. **-3.** [tipográfico] type. **-4.** *JORN* edition; **segundo** ~ second edition.

cliente [kli'ẽntʃi] *m COMPUT* client.

clientela [kliẽn'tɛla] *f* **-1.** clientele. **-2.** [de médico] patients (*pl*).

clientelismo [kliẽnte'liʒmu] *m POL* political patronage.

clima ['klima] *m* **-1.** *METEOR* climate. **-2.** *fam fig* [atmosfera] atmosphere.

climático, ca [kli'matʃiku, ka] *adj* climatic.

clímax ['klimaks] *m inv* **-1.** [ger] climax. **-2.** [auge] peak.

clinicar [12] [klini'ka(x)] *vi* to be in clinical practice.

clínico, ca ['kliniku, ka] <> *adj* clinical. <> *m, f* [médico] doctor; ~ **geral** general practitioner, GP.
→ **clínica** *f*-**1.** [local] clinic. **-2.** [prática] medicine; **clínica geral** general practice.

clipe ['klipi] *m* **-1.** [videoclipe] clip. **-2.** [para papéis] paper clip.

clitóris [kli'tɔriʃ] *m inv* clitoris.

clonagem [klo'naʒẽ] (*pl* -**ns**) *f* BIOL cloning.

clonar [klo'na(x)] *vt* BIOL to clone.

clone ['kloni] *m* clone.

cloro ['klɔru] *m* chlorine.

clorofila [kloro'fila] *f* chlorophyll.

clorofórmio [kloro'fɔxmju] *m* chloroform.

close ['klɔzi] *m* close-up; **dar um** ~ **(em)** to take a close-up (of).

CLT (*abrev de* **Consolidação das Leis do Trabalho**) *f* Brazilian legislation regulating the rights and responsibilities of workers.

clube ['klubi] *m* club.

cm (*abrev de* **centímetro**) *m* cm.

CNH (*abrev de* **Carteira Nacional de Habilitação**) *f* driving licence *UK*, driver's license *US*.

coabitar [4] [koabi'ta(x)] *vi*: ~ **(com alguém)** to live (with sb).

coação [koa'sãw] *f* force.

coadjuvante [kwadʒu'vãntʃi] <> *adj* back-up; **ator** ~ supporting actor; **criminoso** ~ accomplice. <> *mf*-**1.** CINE, TEATRO, TV supporting role. **-2.** [cúmplice] accomplice.

coadjuvar [4] [kwadʒu'va(x)] *vt* **-1.** [ajudar] to collaborate in. **-2.** CINE, TEATRO, TV to support.

coador [kwa'do(x)] (*pl* -**es**) *m* **-1.** [crivo] sieve. **-2.** [de café] filter. **-3.** [para legumes] colander.

coadunar [4] [koadu'na(x)] *vt* **-1.** [idéias, propostas] to combine. **-2.** [pessoas] to unite.
→ **coadunar-se** *vp* [combinar-se] to be combined; ~-**se com** to tie in with.

coagir [52] [kwa'ʒi(x)] *vt*: ~ **alguém (a fazer algo)** to coerce sb (into doing sthg).

coagulação [kwagula'sãw] (*pl* -**ões**) *f* [do sangue] clotting.

coagular [4] [kwagu'la(x)] <> *vt* [solidificar] to clot. <> *vi* -**1.** [sangue] to clot. **-2.** [leite] to curdle.
→ **coagular-se** *vp* -**1.** [sangue] to clot. **-2.** [leite] to curdle.

coágulo ['kwagulu] *m* [de sangue] clot.

coalhado, da [kwa'ʎadu, da] *adj* [leite] curdled.
→ **coalhada** *f* curdled milk.

coalhar [4] [kwa'ʎa(x)] *vt & vi* to curdle.
→ **coalhar-se** *vp* to curdle.

coalho [ko'aʎu] *m* clot.

coalizão [kwali'zãw] (*pl* -**ões**) *f* coalition.

coar [20] ['kwa(x)] *vt*-**1.** [líquido] to filter. **-2.** [café] to percolate.

co-autor, ra [ˌkoaw'to(x), ra] (*mpl* -**res**, *fpl* -**ras**) *m, f* co-author.

co-autoria [ˌkoawto'ria] (*pl* -**s**) *f* co-authorship.

coaxar [4] [kwa'ʃa(x)] <> *m* [de sapo] croak. <> *vi* [sapo] to croak.

cobaia [ko'baja] *f* guinea pig.

cobalto [ko'bawtu] *m* cobalt.

coberto, ta [ko'bɛxtu, ta] <> *pp* ⊳ **cobrir**. <> *adj* covered.
→ **coberta** *f*-**1.** [colcha, cobertor] bed cover. **-2.** [cobertura] covering. **-3.** [telhado] roofing.

cobertor [kobex'to(x)] (*pl* -**es**) *m* [de lã] blanket; *fam* ~ **de orelha** lover.

cobertura [kobex'tura] *f*-**1.** [ger] cover; **dar** ~ **a** to cover up. **-2.** [apartamento] penthouse. **-3.** [calda] topping. **-4.** JORN coverage.

cobiça [ko'bisa] *f* greed.

cobiçar [13] [kobi'sa(x)] *vt* to covet.

cobiçoso, osa [kobi'sozu, ɔza] *adj* -**1.** [pessoa] greedy. **-2.** [olhar, interesse] avid.

cobra ['kɔbra] <> *adj fam* [perito] ace. <> *f*-**1.** ZOOL snake. **-2.** *pej* [mau-caráter] snake. <> *mf fam* [perito] ace.

cobrador, ra [kobra'do(x), ra] (*mpl* -**es**, *fpl* -**s**) *m, f* **-1.** [recebedor, caixa] debt collector; ~ **de impostos** tax collector. **-2.** [de ônibus] conductor.

cobrança [ko'brãsa] *f* -**1.** [de taxa, passagem, ingresso] fee. **-2.** *fig* [exigência] demands (*pl*). **-3.** ESP penalty; ~ **de pênalti** FUT penalty kick.

cobrar [4] [ko'bra(x)] *vt* -**1.** [taxa, passagem, ingresso] to collect. **-2.** [preço] to charge. **-3.** *fig* [promessa, favor] to exact. **-4.** ESP to take a penalty; ~ **um pênalti** FUT to take a penalty.

cobre ['kɔbri] *m* -**1.** [metal] copper. **-2.** [dinheiro, moeda] coin.

cobrir [59] [ko'bri(x)] *vt* -**1.** [ger] to cover. **-2.** [ocultar] to conceal. **-3.** [envolver] to wrap up. **-4.** [exceder] to exceed. **-5.** [encher]: ~ **algo/alguém de algo** to cover sthg/sb with sthg. **-6.** ZOOL [fêmea] to breed.
→ **cobrir-se** *vp* -**1.** [ocultar-se, resguardar-se] to hide o.s. **-2.** [com cobertor] to cover o.s. **-3.** [encher-se]: ~-**se de** to cover o.s with.

coca ['kɔka] *f* coca.

cocada [ko'kada] *f* coconut ice *UK*, coconut candy *US*.

cocaína [koka'ina] *f* cocaine.

coçar [13] [ko'sa(x)] <> *vt* to scratch. <> *vi* to itch.
→ **coçar-se** *vp* to scratch o.s; **não tenho tempo nem para me** ~ I haven't got time to blink.

cocar [ko'ka(x)] *m* crest.

cóccix ['kɔksis] *m inv* coccyx.

cócegas ['kɔsigaʃ] *fpl*: **fazer** ~ **em alguém** to tickle sb; **sentir** ~ to feel itchy.

coceguento, ta [kose'gẽtu, ta] *adj* ticklish.

coceira [ko'sejra] *f* [sensação] itch.

cocheira [ko'ʃejra] *f* stable; **informação de** ~ *fam* inside information.

cocheiro [ko'ʃejru] *m* coachman.

cochichar [4] [koʃi'ʃa(x)] *vi* to whisper.

cochicho [ko'ʃiʃu] *m* whisper.

cochilar [4] [koʃi'la(x)] *vi* -**1.** [dormir um pouco] to

take a nap. **-2.** [dormitar] to doze off.
cochilo [ko'ʃilu] *m* nap; **tirar um** ~ to take a nap.
coco ['koku] *m* **-1.** [fruta] coconut. **-2. fam fig** [cabeça] nut.
cocô [ko'ko] *m fam* poo; **fazer** ~ to have a poo.
cócoras ['kɔkoraʃ] ◆ **de cócoras** *loc adv* squatting.
cocoricar [12] [kokori'ka(x)] *vi* to crow.
cocuruto [koku'rutu] *m* **-1.** [de morro] top. **-2.** [no chão] mound. **-3.** [da cabeça] crown.
codificação [kodʒiʃika'sãw] (*pl* **-ões**) *f* COMPUT coding.
codificador [kodʒifika'do(x)] *m* COMPUT encoder.
codificar [12] [kodʒifi'ka(x)] *vt* **-1.** [ger] to encode. **-2.** [direito, leis] to codify.
código ['kɔdʒigu] *m* [ger] code; ~ **de barras** bar code; ~ **civil** civil code; ~ **de ética profissional** code of professional ethics.
código-fonte ['kɔdigu'fõntʃi] (*pl* **códigos-fonte**) *m* COMPUT source code.
codinome [kodʒi'nɔmi] *m* code name.
codorna [ko'dɔxna] *f* quail.
co-editar [4] [koedʒi'ta(x)] *vt* to co-edit.
co-editor, ra [koedʒi'to(x), ra] (*mpl* **-res**, *fpl* **-ras**) *m, f* co-editor.
coeficiente [koefi'sjẽntʃi] *m* **-1.** MAT coefficient. **-2. fig** [fator] factor.
coelho ['kweʎu] *m* rabbit; **matar dois** ~**s de uma cajadada só** to kill two birds with one stone.
coentro ['kwẽntru] *m* coriander.
coerção [koex'sãw] *f* coercion.
coercivo, va [koex'sivu, va], **coercitivo, va** [koexsi'tʃivu, va] *adj* coercive.
coerência [koe'rẽnsja] *f* coherence.
coerente [koe'rẽntʃi] *adj* coherent.
coesão [koe'zãw] *f* cohesion.
coeso, sa ['kwɛzu, za] *adj* **-1.** [unido, ligado] united. **-2.** [coerente] coherent.
coexistência [koezi'ʃtẽnsja] *f* coexistence.
coexistir [6] [koeziʃ'tʃi(x)] *vi* to coexist.
COFINS (*abrev de* **Contribuição para o Financiamento da Seguridade Social**) *m Brazilian employer's social security contributions, based on profits.*
cofre ['kɔfri] *m* safe; **os** ~**s públicos** the public coffers.
cofre-forte [ˌkofri'fɔxtʃi] (*pl* **cofres-fortes**) *m* strongroom.
cogitar [4] [koʒi'ta(x)] ◇ *vt* **-1.** [considerar] to consider. **-2.** [planejar]: ~ **fazer algo** to consider doing sthg. ◇ *vi* [refletir] to deliberate; ~ **sobre algo** to think about sthg.
cognato [kog'natu] *m* cognate; **falso** ~ false cognate.
cognome [kog'nɔmi] *m* nickname.
cognominar [4] [kognomi'na(x)] *vt*: ~ **alguém** to give a cognomen to sb.
cogumelo [kogu'mɛlu] *m* **-1.** [comestível] mushroom. **-2.** [venenoso] toadstool.
COI (*abrev de* **Comitê Olímpico Internacional**) *m* IOC.

coibição [kojbi'sãw] (*pl* **-ões**) *f* restraint.
coibir [77] [koj'bi(x)] *vt* to restrain; ~ **alguém de fazer algo** to restrain sb from doing sthg.
coice ['kojsil *m* **-1.** [de animal] backward kick; **dar um** ~ **em fig** to give sb a kick in the teeth. **-2.** [de arma] butt.
coifa ['kojfa] *f* [para fogão] extractor hood.
coincidência [koĩsi'dẽnsja] *f* coincidence; **que** ~! what a coincidence!; **ser uma** ~ to be a coincidence.
coincidente [koĩsi'dẽntʃi] *adj* coincidental.
coincidentemente [koĩsidẽntʃi'mẽntʃil *adv* coincidentally.
coincidir [6] [koĩsi'di(x)] *vi* **-1.** [eventos, datas] to coincide. **-2.** [concordar]: ~ **(em)** to agree (upon).
coisa ['kojzal *f* **-1.** [ger] thing. **-2.** [assunto] topic. **-3.** *loc*: ~ **do arco da velha** [feito] incredible thing; **deu uma** ~ **nele fam** sthg came over him; **ele não diz** ~ **com** ~ he talks absolute rubbish; **que** ~! goodness me!; **a festa foi uma** ~ [ser ótimo] the party was amazing; **ser uma** ~ [ser terrível] to be dreadful.
◆ **coisa de** *loc adv* roughly.
◆ **coisas** *fpl fam* [genitais] private parts.
coisíssima [koj'zisimal *f*: **ele não é corrupto** ~ **nenhuma** [de modo algum] no way is he corrupt; **ele não sabia** ~ **nenhuma** he knew absolutely nothing.
coitado, da [koj'tadu, dal ◇ *adj* [pessoa] wretched; **coitado!** poor thing!; **coitado do povo que ...** poor people who ... ◇ *m, f* poor wretch.
coito ['kojtul *m* sex; ~ **anal** anal sex.
cola ['kɔla] *f* **-1.** [adesivo] glue. **-2. fam** EDUC [ato] cribbing. **-3. fam** EDUC [objeto] crib.
colaboração [kolabora'sãw] (*pl* **-ões**) *f* **-1.** [ajuda] cooperation. **-2.** [em jornal etc] freelance work.
colaborador, ra [kolabora'do(x), ra] *m, f* **-1.** [ajudante] collaborator. **-2.** [de jornal etc] freelance.
colaborar [4] [kolabo'ra(x)] *vi* **-1.** [ajudar] to cooperate; ~ **em algo/com alguém** to cooperate on sthg with sb. **-2.** [em jornal etc]: ~ **em algo** to freelance on sthg.
colação [kola'sãw] (*pl* **-ões**) *f* [concessão] bestowal; ~ **de grau** conferment of a degree.
colagem [ko'laʒẽ] (*pl* **-ns**) *f* **-1.** [ato] glueing. **-2.** ARTE collage.
colante [ko'lãntʃi] *adj* [roupa] clinging.
colapso [ko'lapsul *f* collapse; **entrar em** ~ to collapse; ~ **cardíaco** heart failure; ~ **nervoso** nervous breakdown.
colar [4] [ko'la(x)] (*pl* **-es**) *vt* COMPUT to paste.
colarinho [kola'riɲu] *m* **-1.** [de camisa] collar. **-2.** *fam* [de cerveja] head; **com/sem** ~ with/without a head.
colarinho-branco [kolaˌriɲu'brãɲkul (*pl* **colarinhos-brancos**) *m* white-collar worker; **crime do** ~ white-collar crime.
colateral [kolate'raw] (*pl* **-ais**) *adj* collateral.
colcha ['kowʃa] *f* bedspread; ~ **de retalhos fig** mishmash.
colchão [kow'ʃãw] (*pl* **-ões**) *m* mattress.

colcheia [kow'ʃeja] f *MÚS* quaver *UK*, eighth note *US*.

colchete [kow'ʃetʃi] m **-1.** [de roupa] hook; ~ **de gancho** hook and eye; ~ **de pressão** press stud. **-2.** [sinal] bracket.

colchões [kow'ʃõjʃ] pl ⊳ **colchão**.

colchonete [kowʃo'netʃi] m bolster.

coleção [kole'sãw] (pl **-ões**) f collection.

colecionador, ra [kolesjona'do(x), ra] (mpl **-res**, fpl **-s**) m, f collector.

colecionar [4] [kolesjo'na(x)] vt to collect.

colega [ko'lɛga] mf **-1.** [amigo] friend. **-2.** [de escola] schoolfriend. **-3.** [de trabalho] colleague.

colegial [kole'ʒjaw] (pl **-ais**) ◇ adj school (antes de subst). ◇ mf schoolboy (f schoolgirl).

colégio [ko'lɛʒju] m **-1.** [escola] school. **-2.** [de intelectuais] college. **-3.** [de clérigos] chapter. **-4.** [de eleitores]: ~ **eleitoral** electoral college.

coleguismo [kole'giʒmu] m esprit de corps.

coleira [ko'lejra] f dog collar.

cólera ['kɔleral] ◇ f [ira] anger. ◇ m *MED* cholera.

colérico, ca [ko'lɛriku, ka] ◇ adj [irado] angry. ◇ m, f *MED* cholera victim.

colesterol [koleʃte'rɔw] m cholesterol.

coleta [ko'lɛta] f collection; ~ **de dados** fact-gathering.

coletânea [kole'tãnja] f collectanea.

coletar [4] [kole'ta(x)] vt to collect.

colete [ko'letʃi] m waistcoat *UK*, vest *US*; ~ **salva-vidas** life jacket.

coletividade [koletʃivi'dadʒi] f community.

coletivo, va [kole'tʃivu, va] adj **-1.** [de muitos] collective. **-2.** [transporte, banheiro] public.

➡ **coletivo** m **-1.** [ônibus] public transport. **-2.** [futebol] trials. **-3.** [ling] collective noun.

coletor, ra [kole'to(x), ra] m, f [de impostos] collector.

colheita [ko'ʎejta] f **-1.** [ger] harvest. **-2.** [produto] crop.

colher [5] [ko'ʎɛ(x)] (pl **-es** [ko'ʎɛriʃ]) ◇ f **-1.** [talher] spoon; ~ **de chá** teaspoon; ~ **de sobremesa** dessertspoon; ~ **de sopa** tablespoon; **dar uma** ~ **de chá a alguém** fig to do sb a favour. **-2.** [ferramenta]: ~ **de pedreiro** trowel. ◇ vt **-1.** [fruta, verdura, safra] to pick. **-2.** [dados] to gather.

colherada [koʎe'rada] f spoonful.

colibri [koli'bri] m hummingbird.

cólica ['kɔlika] f colic; ~ **menstrual** period pains (pl).

colidir [6] [koli'dʒi(x)] vi [chocar-se] to collide; ~ **com/contra** to collide with/against.

coligação [koliga'sãw] (pl **-ões**) f coalition; ~ **partidária** ou **eleitoral** political coalition.

coligar [14] [koli'ga(x)] vt to bind together.

➡ **coligar-se** vp to unite; ~**-se com** to align o.s with.

coligir [52] [koli'ʒi(x)] vt to compile.

colina [ko'lina] f hill.

colírio [ko'lirju] m eyewash; **ser um** ~ **para os olhos de alguém** fam to be a sight for sore eyes.

colisão [koli'zãw] (pl **-ões**) f collision.

colite [ko'litʃi] f colitis.

collant [ko'lã] m tights (pl).

colméia [kow'mɛja] f beehive.

colo ['kɔlu] m **-1.** [ger] neck. **-2.** [regaço] lap; **no** ~ on one's lap.

colocação [koloka'sãw] (pl **-ões**) f **-1.** [ato] fitting. **-2.** [posição, emprego] position. **-3.** [em concurso, competição] place. **-4.** [observação] observation.

colocar [12] [kolo'ka(x)] vt **-1.** [ger] to place. **-2.** [dar emprego a] to employ. **-3.** [situar - no espaço] to site. **-4.** [instalar - ar-condicionado] to install; [- pneu] to fit; [- carpete] to lay; [- cortina] to hang. **-5.** [levantar] to raise.

➡ **colocar-se** vp **-1.** [pôr-se] to position o.s. **-2.** [em concurso, competição] to be placed. **-3.** [imaginar-se]: **coloque-se no meu lugar** put yourself in my place.

Colômbia [ko'lõnbja] n Colombia.

colombiano, na [kolõn'bjãnu, na] ◇ adj Colombian. ◇ m, f Colombian.

cólon ['kɔlõ] m *ANAT* colon.

colônia [ko'lonja] f **-1.** [ger] colony; **Brasil** ~ colonial Brazil. **-2.** [para crianças]: ~ **de férias** summer camp. **-3.** [perfume] cologne; **água de** ~ eau de cologne.

colonial [kolo'njaw] (pl **-ais**) adj colonial.

colonialismo [kolonja'liʒmu] m colonialism.

colonização [koloniza'sãw] f colonization.

colonizador, ra [koloniza'do(x), ra] ◇ adj [nação, esforço] colonizing. ◇ m, f [pessoa] settler.

colonizar [4] [koloni'za(x)] vt to colonize.

colono, na [ko'lɔnu, na] m, f **-1.** [povoador] colonist. **-2.** [cultivador] smallholder.

coloquial [kolo'kjaw] (pl **-ais**) adj colloquial.

coloquialismo [kolokja'liʒmu] m familiar tone.

colóquio [ko'lɔkju] m **-1.** [congresso] symposium. **-2.** ant [conversa] conversation.

coloração [kolora'sãw] (pl **-ões**) f colouration.

colorido, da [kolo'ridu, da] adj multi-coloured *UK*, multi-colored *US*.

➡ **colorido** m colour *UK*, color *US*.

colorir [79] [kolo'ri(x)] vt **-1.** [dar cor a] to colour *UK*, to color *US*. **-2.** fig [avivar] to brighten.

colossal [kolo'saw] (pl **-ais**) adj colossal.

colosso [ko'losu] m [ger] colossus.

coluna [ko'luna] f **-1.** [ger] column; ~ **social** society column. **-2.** [pilar] pillar. **-3.** *ANAT*: ~ **vertebral** spinal column.

colunável [kolu'navew] (pl **-eis**) ◇ adj [pessoa, festa] glamorous. ◇ mf [celebridade] celebrity.

colunista [kolu'niʃta] mf columnist; ~ **social** society columnist.

com [kõ] prep **-1.** with; **ela mora** ~ **um amigo** she lives with a friend; ~ **quem você vai?** who are you going with? **-2.** [relativo a modo] with; ~ **cuidado** with care; [relativo a instrumento] with; **ela escreve** ~ **a mão direita** she writes with her right hand; ~ **o tempo, a mulher conseguiu superar o trauma** with time, the woman managed to overcome the trauma **-3.** [indica causa] with, because of; **só** ~ **muito esforço é que ele conseguiu** only with a lot of effort did he manage to do it; **estar** ~ **dor de cabeça** to have a headache; **estar** ~ **fome** to be hungry; **estar** ~ **pressa** to be in a hurry. - **4.** [apesar de] in spite of; ~ **todo esse trabalho ele ainda encontra tempo para estudar** in spite of all that work, he still finds time to study; **você vai jogar bola** ~ **chuva?** are you going to play football in the rain?; ~ **86 anos, ele continua cheio de energia** at 86, he is still full of energy. - **5.** *(em loc prep)* with; ~ **relação a** in relation to; ~ **vistas a** with an aim to; **de acordo** ~ in accordance with; **em parceria** ~ in partnership with.

coma [ˈkoma] *m MED* coma; **estado de** ~ comatose state; **em** ~ in a coma.

comadre [koˈmadri] *f* - **1.** [madrinha] *a godmother in relation to her godchild's parents; a child's mother in relation to its godparents.* - **2.** [amiga] friend. - **3.** [urinol] bedpan.

comandante [komãnˈdãntʃi] *mf* - **1.** *MIL, NÁUT* commander. - **2.** [dirigente] leader.

comandar [4] [komãnˈda(x)] *vt* - **1.** *MIL, NÁUT* to command. - **2.** [dirigir] to head.

comando [koˈmãndu] *m* [ger] command.

comarca [koˈmaxka] *f* area of jurisdiction.

combalido, da [kõbaˈlidu, da] *adj* enfeebled.

combate [kõˈbatʃi] *m* - **1.** [luta, oposição] fight. - **2.** [bélico] skirmish; **fora de** ~ *fig* flat on one's back.

combatente [kõbaˈtẽntʃi] *mf* combatant.

combater [5] [kõbaˈte(x)] <> *vt* [lutar contra, opor-se a] to struggle. <> *vi* [belicamente] to fight.

combinação [kõbinaˈsãw] *(pl* -ões) *f* - **1.** [ger] combination. - **2.** *QUÍM* compound. - **3.** [acordo, plano] agreement. - **4.** [peça de roupa] slip.

combinar [4] [kõbiˈna(x)] <> *vt* - **1.** [associar, reunir] to combine. - **2.** [encontro, jantar] to fix; **combinado!** agreed! - **3.** [plano, fuga] to plan. <> *vi* - **1.** [planejar]: **combinamos de ir ao cinema** we fixed up to go to the cinema. - **2.** [cores, roupas] to match; ~ **com algo** to go with sthg.

comboio [kõˈboju] *m* - **1.** [ger] convoy. - **2.** *FERRO* train.

combustão [kõbuʃˈtãw] *(pl* -ões) *f* combustion.

combustível [kõbuʃˈtʃivɛw] *(pl* -eis) <> *adj* combustible. <> *m* fuel.

começar [13] [komeˈsa(x)] <> *vt* to start. <> *vi* to begin, to start; ~ **a fazer algo** to start doing sthg, to start to do sthg; ~ **por** to begin with; **para** ~ [em primeiro lugar] first of all.

começo [koˈmesu] *m* beginning.

comédia [koˈmɛdʒja] *f* comedy.

comediante [komeˈdʒjãntʃi] *mf* comedian.

comedido, da [komeˈdʒidu, da] *adj* - **1.** [moderado] moderate. - **2.** [prudente] prudent.

comedimento [komedʒiˈmẽntu] *m* [moderação] moderation.

comedir-se [70] [komeˈdʒixsi] *vp* [conter-se] to restrain o.s.

comemoração [komemoraˈsãw] *(pl* -ões) *f* celebration.

comemorar [4] [komemoˈra(x)] *vt* to celebrate.

comemorativo, va [komemoraˈtʃivu, val] *adj* commemorative.

comensal [komẽˈsãw] *(pl* -ais) *mf* dinner guest.

comentar [4] [komẽnˈta(x)] *vt* - **1.** [fato, festa, incidente] to comment on. - **2.** [observar]: ~ **que** to remark that. - **3.** *ESP* [partida] to commentate.

comentário [komẽnˈtarjul] *m* commentary; **fazer um** ~ to do a commentary; **sem** ~s no comment; ~ **esportivo** sports commentary; ~ **político** political commentary.

comentarista [komẽntaˈriʃtal] *mf* commentator; ~ **esportivo** sports commentator; ~ **político** political commentator.

comer [5] [koˈme(x)] *(pl* -es) <> *vt* - **1.** [alimentar-se de] to eat. - **2.** *fig* [suprimir] to swallow. - **3.** *fig* [corroer] to corrode. - **4.** *fig* [consumir] to devour. - **5.** [em damas, xadrez] to take. - **6.** *vulg fig* [sexualmente] to fuck. <> *vi* [alimentar-se] to eat; **dar de** ~ **a alguém** to feed sb; ~ **por quatro** [comer demais] to stuff o.s.

➡ **comer-se** *vp*: ~-**se de raiva/vontade** to be consumed with anger/desire.

comercial [komexˈsjawl] *(pl* -ais) <> *adj* commercial. <> *m* [anúncio] advertisement, commercial.

comercialização [komexsjalizaˈsãw] *(pl* -ões) *f* commercialization.

comercializar [4] [komexsjaliˈza(x)] *vt* to market.

comercializável [komexsjaliˈzavewl] *(pl* -eis) *adj* marketable.

comerciante [komexˈsjãntʃi] *mf* businessman (*f* businesswoman).

comerciar [18] [komexˈsja(x)] *vi* to trade; ~ **com** to trade with.

comerciário, ria [komexˈsjarju, rjal] *m, f* trader.

comércio [koˈmɛxsjul] *m* - **1.** [compra e venda] trade. - **2.** [tráfico] trafficking. - **3.** [estabelecimento] premises. - **4.** [mercado comercial] business. - **5.** *fig* [troca de idéias, influências] exchange.

comes [ˈkɔmiʃ] *mpl fam*: ~ **e bebes** food and drink.

comestíveis [komeʃˈtʃiveiʃl] *mpl* comestibles.

comestível [komeʃˈtʃivɛwl] *(pl* -eis) *adj* edible.

cometa [koˈmetal] *m* comet.

cometer [5] [komeˈte(x)] *vt* to commit.

cometimento [kometʃiˈmẽntul] *m* - **1.** [de crime, pecado, infração] committing. - **2.** [empreendimento] undertaking.

comichão [komiˈʃãwl] *(pl* -ões) *f* itch; **ter** *ou* **sentir** ~ to have/feel an itch.

comicidade [komisiˈdadʒil] *f* comedy.

comício [koˈmisjul] *m* rally; ~ **relâmpago** short public rally.

cômico, co [ˈkomiku, kal] <> *adj* comical. <> *m, f* [comediante] comedian.

comida [koˈmidal] *f* - **1.** [alimento] food. - **2.** [refeição] meal; ~ **caseira** home cooking.

comigo [koˈmigul] *pron*: **ela não fala** ~ she won't speak to me; **o livro dele está** ~ I've got his book; **matemática é** ~ **mesmo** maths is my thing; **ela acenou, mas pensei que não era** ~ she nodded, but I thought that she didn't agree with me; **isto não é justo, pensei** ~ that isn't fair, I thought to myself; **deixa** ~! leave it with me!

comilança [komiˈlãnsal] f spread, blowout.

comilão, lona [komiˈlãw, lonal] (mpl -ões, fpl -s) ◇ adj gluttonous. ◇ m, f glutton.

cominho [koˈmiɲul] m cumin.

comiserar-se [4] [komizeˈraxsil] vp to feel pity; ~ (de) to feel pity for.

comissão [komiˈsãw] (pl -ões) f -1. [comitê] committee; **Comissão Parlamentar de Inquérito** Parliamentary Investigative Committee. -2. [gratificação] commission.

comissário, ria [komiˈsarju, rjal] m, f agent; ~ **de bordo** air steward (f air stewardess).

comissionar [4] [komisjoˈna(x)] vt -1. [encarregar] to commission. -2. [confiar] to entrust.

comitê [komiˈtel] m committee; ~ **executivo** executive committee.

comitiva [komiˈtʃival] f retinue.

commodity [comɔˈdʒitʃil] (pl commodities) f ECON commodity.

como [ˈkomul] ◇ adv -1. [ger] as. -2. [de que modo] how; ~? [o que você disse?] I'm sorry?; ~ **assim?** how do you mean? -3. [comparativo]: **ser** ~ **algo/alguém** to be like sthg/sb. -4. [exclamativo]: **como!** what!; **e** ~! fam and how!; ~ **não!** [pois não] of course! ◇ conj -1. [porque] because. -2. [conforme] as.

➡ **como que** loc adv: ~ **que por um golpe de mágica, tudo desapareceu** as if by magic, everything disappeared.

➡ **como quer que** loc conj however.

➡ **como quiser** loc adv as; **fazer algo** ~ **quiser** to do as one wishes.

➡ **como se** loc conj as if.

comoção [komoˈsãw] (pl -ões) f -1. [abalo] shock. -2. [revolta] unrest.

cômoda [ˈkomodal] f chest of drawers.

comodidade [komodʒiˈdadʒil] f -1. [conforto] comfort. -2. [conveniência] convenience.

comodismo [komoˈdʒiʒmul] m indolence.

comodista [komoˈdʒiʃtal] ◇ adj passive. ◇ mf passive person.

cômodo, da [ˈkomodu, dal] adj -1. [confortável] comfortable. -2. [conveniente] appropriate.

➡ **cômodo** m [aposento] room.

comovente [komoˈvẽntʃil], **comovedor, ra** [komoveˈdo(x), ral] adj moving.

comover [5] [komoˈve(x)] ◇ vt to move. ◇ vi to be moving.

➡ **comover-se** vp to be moved.

comovido, da [komoˈvidul] adj moved.

compactador [kõmpakˈtado(x)] m COMPUT (file) compressor.

compactar [kõmpzkˈta(x)] vt COMPUT: ~ **arquivos** to compress files.

compacto, ta [kõmˈpaktu, tal] adj -1. [pequeno] compact. -2. [denso, comprimido] dense.

➡ **compacto** m [disco] compact disc, CD.

compadecer-se [25] [kõnpadeˈsexsil] vp: ~ **de** to take pity on.

compadecido, da [kõnpadeˈsidu, dal] adj compassionate.

compadecimento [kõnpadesiˈmẽntul] m [piedade] compassion.

compadre [kõnˈpadril] m -1. [padrinho do filho] a godfather in relation to his godchild's parents ou a child's father in relation to its godparents. -2. fam [companheiro] companion; **meu** ~ my friend.

compaixão [kõnpajˈʃãw] f -1. [piedade] compassion. -2. [misericórdia] mercy.

companheirismo [kõnpaɲeiˈriʒmul] m companionship.

companheiro, ra [kõnpaˈɲejru, ral] m, f -1. [que acompanha] companion; ~ **de viagem** travelling companion. -2. [colega] colleague. -3. [marido, namorado] partner. -4. fam [amigo] mate.

companhia [kõnpaˈɲial] f [ger] company; **em** ~ **de** in the company of; **fazer** ~ **a alguém** to keep sb company.

comparação [kõnparaˈsãw] (pl -ões) f comparison.

comparar [4] [kõnpaˈra(x)] vt: ~ **algo/alguém (com)** to compare sthg/sb (with).

➡ **comparar-se** vp: ~-**se com** to compare o.s. to; **isto não se compara com ...** this does not bear comparison with ...

comparável [kõnpaˈravewl] (pl -eis) adj comparable.

comparecer [25] [kõnpareˈse(x)] vi: ~ (a) to appear (at).

comparecimento [kõnparesiˈmẽntul] m presence; ~ **às urnas** turnout at the ballot-boxes.

comparsa [kõnˈpaxsal] mf -1. [cúmplice] accomplice. -2. TEATRO extra.

compartilhar [4] [kõmpaxtʃiˈʎa(x)] ◇ vt [partilhar] to share. ◇ vi [participar]: ~ **de** to share in.

compartimentar [4] [kõnpaxtʃimẽnˈta(x)] vt to split (into separate rooms, parts etc).

compartimento [kõnpaxtʃiˈmẽntul] m -1. [divisão] compartment; ~ **de carga** cargo bay. -2. [aposento] room.

compartir [6] [kõnpaxˈtʃi(x)] vt & vi = **compartilhar**.

compassado, da [kõnpaˈsadu, dal] adj -1. [pausado] measured. -2. [cadenciado] rhythmic. -3. [comedido] moderate.

compassivo, va [kõnpaˈsivu, val] adj compassionate.

compasso [kõnˈpasul] m -1. [instrumento] pair of compasses. -2. MÚS beat. -3. [ritmo] time; **dentro/fora do** ~ in/out of time.

compatibilidade [kõnpatʃibiliˈdadʒil] f compatibility.

compatível [kõnpaˈtʃivewl] (pl -eis) adj compatible.

compatriota [kõnpatriˈɔtal] mf compatriot.

compelir [57] [kõnpeˈli(x)] vt: ~ **alguém a**

fazer algo to force sb to do sthg.
compêndio [kõn'pẽndʒiu] *m* **-1.** [livro] textbook. **-2.** [síntese] summary.
compenetração [kõnpenetra'sãw] *f* **-1.** [concentração] concentration. **-2.** [convicção] conviction.
compenetrado, da [kõnpene'tradu, da] *adj* **-1.** [concentrado] concentrated. **-2.** [convicto] convinced.
compenetrar [4] [kõnpene'tra(x)] *vt* [convencer] to convince.
 ➡ **compenetrar-se** *vp* **-1.** [convencer-se]: ~**-se de** to become convinced of. **-2.** [concentrar-se] to concentrate.
compensação [kõnpẽnsa'sãw] (*pl* -ões) *f* **-1.** [reparação] compensation; **em** ~ to make up for it. **-2.** [equilíbrio] balance. **-3.** [de cheque] clearance.
compensado [kõnpẽn'sadu] *m* [madeira] plywood.
compensador, ra [kõnpẽnsa'do(x), ra] *adj* compensatory.
compensar [4] [kõnpẽn'sa(x)] ◇ *vt* **-1.** [dar reparo a] to make up for. **-2.** [equilibrar] to compensate for. **-3.** [cheque] to clear. ◇ *vi* [valer a pena] to pay.
competência [kõnpe'tẽnsja] *f* **-1.** [habilidade] competence. **-2.** [responsabilidade] responsibility; **ser da** ~ **de alguém** to be the responsibility of sb.
competente [kõnpe'tẽntʃi] *adj* **-1.** [hábil] competent. **-2.** [responsável] responsible.
competição [kõnpetʃi'sãw] (*pl* -ões) *f* **-1.** [disputa, concorrência] competition. **-2.** *ESP* [prova] contest.
competidor, ra [kõnpetʃi'do(x), ra] *m, f ESP* competitor.
competir [57] [kõnpe'tʃi(x)] *vi* to compete; ~ **com** to compete with.
competitividade [kõnpetʃitʃivi'dadʒi] *f* competitiveness.
competitivo, va [kõnpetʃi'tʃivu, va] *adj* competitive.
compilação [kõnpila'sãw] *f* compilation.
compilar [4] [kõnpi'la(x)] *vt* to compile.
complacência [kõnpla'sẽnsja] *f* complacency.
complacente [kõnpla'sẽntʃi] *adj* complacent.
compleição [kõnplej'sãw] (*pl* -ões) *f* build.
complementar [4] [kõnplemẽn'ta(x)] (*pl* -es) ◇ *adj* additional. ◇ *vt* to complement.
complemento [kõnple'mẽntu] *m* **-1.** [acréscimo] addition; ~ **alimentar** food supplement; ~ **salarial** additional wages. **-2.** *GRAM* object.
completamente [kõm,pleta'mẽntʃi] *adv* completely.
completar [4] [kõnple'ta(x)] *vt* **-1.** [terminar] to complete. **-2.** [idade] to reach. **-3.** [com gasolina *etc*] to fill up.
completo, ta [kõn'plɛtu, ta] *adj* **-1.** [trabalho] finished. **-2.** [idade]: **ele tem 16 anos** ~**s** he is 16 years old. **-3.** [tanque] full.
 ➡ **por completo** *loc adv* [inteiramente] completely.
complexado, da [kõnplek'sadu, da] *adj* hung-up; **estar/ficar** ~ to have a complex.
complexidade [kõnpleksi'dadʒi] *f* complexity.

complexo, xa [kõm'plɛksu, sa] *adj* complex.
 ➡ **complexo** *m* complex; ~ **de Édipo** Oedipus complex; ~ **de inferioridade** inferiority complex.
complicação [kõnplika'sãw] (*pl* -ões) *f* **-1.** [ger] complexity. **-2.** *MED* complication.
complicado, da [kõnpli'kadu, da] *adj* complicated; **ser** ~ to be complicated.
complicar [12] [kõnpli'ka(x)] *vt* [tornar complexo] to complicate.
 ➡ **complicar-se** *vp* to worsen.
complô [kõn'plo] *m* conspiracy.
componente [kõnpo'nẽntʃi] *m* component.
compor [45] [kõn'po(x)] ◇ *vt* **-1.** [formar, integrar] to comprise. **-2.** [música, versos] to compose. **-3.** [discurso, livro] to write. **-4.** [enfeitar] to arrange. **-5.** *POL* [aliança, acordo] to constitute. **-6.** *TIP* to typeset. ◇ *vi* **-1.** [música] to compose. **-2.** *TIP* to typeset.
 ➡ **compor-se** *vp* **-1.** [ser integrado por]: ~**-se de** to consist of. **-2.** [controlar-se] to compose o.s.
comporta [kõn'pɔxta] *f* floodgate.
comportamento [kõnpoxta'mẽntu] *m* **-1.** [de pessoa] behaviour; **bom/mau** ~ good/bad behaviour. **-2.** [reação] reaction.
comportar [4] [kõnpox'ta(x)] *vt* **-1.** [suportar] to hold. **-2.** [conter] to contain.
 ➡ **comportar-se** *vp* **-1.** [pessoa] to behave; ~ **se bem/mal** to behave well/badly. **-2.** [reagir] to behave.
composição [kõnpozi'sãw] (*pl* -ões) *f* **-1.** [ger] composition. **-2.** [de trem, metrô] formation. **-3.** *TIP* typesetting.
compositor, ra [kõnpozi'to(x), ra] (*mpl* -es, *fpl* -s) *m, f* **-1.** *MÚS* composer. **-2.** *TIP* typesetter; ~ **tipográfico** typesetter.
composto, ta [kõn'poʃtu, ta] ◇ *pp* ▷ **compor**. ◇ *adj* composed.
 ➡ **composto** *m QUÍM* compound.
compostura [kõnpoʃ'tura] *f* composure; **perder a** ~ to lose one's composure.
compota [kõn'pɔta] *f* stewed fruit, fruit compote.
compra ['kõnpra] *f* **-1.** [ato] purchase; **fazer** ~**s** to shop; **ir às** ~**s** to go shopping. **-2.** [coisa comprada] shopping.
comprador, ra [kõnpra'do(x), ra] *m, f* purchaser, buyer.
comprar [4] [kõn'pra(x)] *vt* **-1.** [adquirir] to buy. **-2.** *fig* [subornar] to bribe. **-3.** *loc*: ~ **briga** to pick a fight; ~ **a briga de alguém** to take up sb's cause.
comprazer-se [32] [kõnpra'zexsi] *vp*: ~ **com** *ou* **em fazer algo** to take pleasure in doing sthg.
compreender [5] [kõnprjẽn'de(x)] *vt* **-1.** [entender] to understand. **-2.** [abranger] to comprise.
compreensão [kõnprjẽ'sãw] *f* **-1.** [entendimento intelectual] comprehension. **-2.** [aceitação] understanding. **-3.** [percepção] realization.
compreensível [kõnprjẽ'sivew] (*pl* -eis) *adj* understandable.
compreensivo, va [kõnprjẽ'sivu, va] *adj* **-1.**

[pessoa, atitude] understanding. **-2.** [medida] comprehensive.

compressa [kõn'prɛsa] *f* compress.

compressão [kõnpre'sãw] (*pl* **-ões**) *f* compression.

compressor, ra [kõnpre'so(x), ra] *adj* ▷ **rolo**.

comprido, da [kõn'pridu, da] *adj* **-1.** [longo] long. **-2.** [alto] tall.

comprimento [kõnpri'mẽntu] *m* length; **três metros de** ~ three metres in length, three metres long.

comprimido, da [kõnpri'midu, da] *adj* compressed.
➡ **comprimido** *m* tablet.

comprimir [6] [kõnpri'mi(x)] *vt* **-1.** [reduzir sob pressão - ar, volume] to compress; [- barriga] to pull in. **-2.** [apertar] to squeeze.

comprometedor, ra [kõnpromete'do(x), ra] *adj* compromising.

comprometer [5] [kõnprome'te(x)] *vt* **-1.** [ger] to compromise. **-2.** [empenhar] to commit.
➡ **comprometer-se** *vp* **-1.** [assumir compromisso]: ~**-se (com)** to make a commitment (to). **-2.** [ser envolvido]: ~**-se (em)** to become involved (in).

comprometido, da [kõnprome'tʃidu, da] *adj* **-1.** [ocupado] busy. **-2.** [amorosamente] engaged.

compromisso [kõnpro'misu] *m* **-1.** [encontro *etc*] appointment. **-2.** [promessa] promise; **assumir um** ~ to undertake. **-3.** [obrigação] obligation; **sem** ~ under no obligation. **-4.** [acordo] agreement; **solução de** ~ compromise solution. **-5.** [namoro, noivado] engagement.

comprovação [kõnprova'sãw] (*pl* **-ões**) *f* **-1.** [prova] proof. **-2.** ADMIN [de gastos] evidence.

comprovante [kõnpro'vantʃil] ⟨⟩ *adj* confirming. ⟨⟩ *m* receipt.

comprovar [4] [kõnpro'va(x)] *vt* to confirm.

compulsão [kõnpuw'sãw] (*pl* **-ões**) *f* compulsion; **ter** ~ **por** to have a compulsion for.

compulsivo, va [kõnpuw'sivu, va] *adj* compulsive.

compulsório, ria [kõnpuw'sɔrju, rja] *adj* compulsory.

compunção [kõnpũn'sãw] *f* compunction.

compungir [52] [kõnpũn'ʒi(x)] ⟨⟩ *vt* to move. ⟨⟩ *vi* to be moving.

computação [kõnputa'sãw] *f* **-1.** [ato] computation. **-2.** [ciência, curso] computing.

computador [kõnputa'do(x)] (*pl* **-es**) *m* computer.

computadorizar [4] [kõnputadori'za(x)] *vt* to computerize.

computadorizado, da [kõmputa'dori'zadu, da] *adj* computerized.

computar [4] [kõnpu'ta(x)] *vt* **-1.** [contar] to count. **-2.** [calcular] to compute, to calculate. **-3.** [incluir] to include.

cômputo ['kõnputu] *m* **-1.** [contagem] counting. **-2.** [cálculo] estimate.

comum [ko'mũ] (*pl* **-ns**) ⟨⟩ *adj* **-1.** [ordinário] ordinary. **-2.** [mútuo] mutual; **ter algo em** ~ to

have sthg in common. **-3.** [usual] common. ⟨⟩ *m* [usual] usual thing; **o** ~ **é ficarmos em casa aos domingos** we usually stay at home on Sundays; **fora do** ~ [extraordinário] out of the ordinary.

comuna [ko'muna] *mf fam* [comunista] Commie.
➡ **comuna** *f* ADMIN commune.

comungar [14] [komũn'ga(x)] *vi* **-1.** RELIG to receive Communion. **-2.** *fig* [partilhar]: ~ **de algo** to share sthg.

comunhão [komu'ɲãw] (*pl* **-ões**) *f* **-1.** [união] unity; ~ **de bens** [em matrimônio] joint ownership of property. **-2.** RELIG Communion.

comunicação [komunika'sãw] (*pl* **-ões**) *f* **-1.** [ato] communication. **-2.** [ciência] communications *(sg)*; ~ **de massa** mass media; ~ **social** the media. **-3.** [mensagem] message. **-4.** [em congresso, simpósio] speech. **-5.** [ligação] link.

comunicador, ra [komunika'do(x), ra] *m, f* communicator.

comunicar [12] [komuni'ka(x)] ⟨⟩ *vt* **-1.** [informar sobre]: ~ **algo a alguém** to inform sb of sthg. **-2.** [ligar] to link. ⟨⟩ *vi* [ligar-se]: ~ **com** to be connected to.
➡ **comunicar-se** *vp* **-1.** [dialogar, entender-se] to communicate. **-2.** [entrar em contato]: ~**-se com** to contact.

comunicativo, va [komunika'tʃivu, va] *adj* communicative.

comunidade [komuni'dadʒil] *f* community; **Comunidade Européia** European Community.

comunismo [komu'niʒmul] *m* communism.

comunista [komu'niʃtal] ⟨⟩ *adj* communist. ⟨⟩ *mf* communist.

comunitário, ria [komuni'tarju, rja] *adj* community.

comutador [komuta'do(x)] *m* switch.

comutar [4] [komu'ta(x)] *vt* **-1.** JUR to commute. **-2.** [trocar] to exchange.

concatenação [kõnkatena'sãw] (*pl* **-ões**) *f* [encadeamento] (close) linkage.

concatenar [4] [kõnkate'na(x)] *vt* to link together.

côncavo, va ['kõnkavu, va] *adj* concave.
➡ **côncavo** *m* hollow.

conceber [5] [kõnse'be(x)] ⟨⟩ *vt* [gerar] to conceive. ⟨⟩ *vi* [engravidar] to conceive.

concebível [kõnse'bivew] (*pl* **-eis**) *adj* [imaginável] conceivable.

conceder [5] [kõnse'de(x)] *vt* **-1.** [dar, outorgar] to concede. **-2.** [permitir]: ~ **que alguém faça algo** to allow sb to do sthg. **-3.** [admitir]: ~ **que** to admit that.

conceito [kõn'sejtul] *m* **-1.** [idéia] concept. **-2.** [opinião] opinion. **-3.** [reputação] reputation. **-4.** EDUC [nota] grade.

conceituação [kõnsejtua'sãw] (*pl* **-ões**) *f* **-1.** [definição] conceptualization. **-2.** [avaliação] rating.

conceituado, da [kõsej'twadu, da] *adj* respected.

conceituar [4] [kõnsej'twa(x)] *vt* **-1.** [formular conceito de] to conceptualize. **-2.** [avaliar] to assess.

concentração [kõnsẽntra'sãw] (*pl* -ões) *f* - **1.** [ger] concentration. - **2.** *ESP* athletic briefing and training usually the day before an important event.

concentrado, da [kõsẽn'tradu, da] adj - **1.** [ger] concentrated. - **2.** [centralizado] centralized. - **3.** [aglomerado] gathered together.

➡ **concentrado** *m* [substância] concentrate.

concentrar [4] [kõnsẽn'tra(x)] *vt* - **1.** [ger] to concentrate. - **2.** [centralizar] to centralize. - **3.** [aglomerar] to bring together, to mass.

➡ **concentrar-se** *vp* - **1.** [aglomerar-se] to mass. - **2.** [pessoa, atenção, esforço]: ~-**se (em algo)** to concentrate (on sthg).

concepção [kõnsep'sãw] (*pl* -ões) *f* - **1.** [geração] conception. - **2.** [conceito] concept. - **3.** [opinião] opinion.

concernente [kõnsex'nẽntʃi] *adj*: ~ **a** concerning.

concernir [54] [kõnsex'ni(x)] *vi*: ~ **a** to concern; **no que me concerne, ...** as far as I'm concerned, ...

concerto [kõn'sextu] *m* *MÚS* concert.

concessão [kõnse'sãw] (*pl* -ões) *f* - **1.** [ger] concession; **fazer uma** ~ **a** to make a concession to. - **2.** [entrega - de empréstimo, licença *etc*] granting; [- de prêmio] awarding. - **3.** [permissão] permission.

concessionário, ria [kõnsesjo'narju, rja] *m, f* concessionaire.

➡ **concessionária** *f* [empresa] agency.

concha ['kõnʃa] *f* - **1.** [de molusco] shell. - **2.** [para líquidos] ladle.

conchavo [kõn'ʃavu] *m* conspiracy; **fazer um** ~ to form a conspiracy.

conciliação [kõnsilja'sãw] (*pl* -ões) *f* reconciliation.

conciliador, ra [kõnsilja'do(x), ra] ⟨⟩ *adj* conciliatory. ⟨⟩ *m, f* [pessoa] conciliator.

conciliar [16] [kõnsi'lja(x)] *vt* to reconcile.

conciliatório, ria [kõnsilja'tɔrju, rja] *adj* conciliatory.

conciliável [kõnsi'ljavew] (*pl* -eis) *adj* reconcilable.

concílio [kõn'silju] *m* *RELIG* council.

concisão [kõnsi'sãw] *f* concision.

conciso, sa [kõn'sizu, za] *adj* concise.

conclamar [4] [kõnkla'ma(x)] *vt* - **1.** [bradar] to shout. - **2.** [aclamar] to acclaim. - **3.** [convocar]: ~ **alguém a fazer algo** to incite sb to do sthg; ~ **alguém para algo** to call on sb for sthg.

conclave [kõn'klavi] *m* conclave.

concludente [kõnklu'dẽntʃi] *adj* conclusive.

concluir [74] [kõnklu'i(x)] *vt* - **1.** [terminar] to conclude. - **2.** [deduzir] to deduce.

conclusão [kõnklu'zãw] (*pl* -ões) *f* [ger] conclusion; **chegar a uma** ~ [chegar a uma dedução] to reach a conclusion; [chegar a um acordo] to come to an agreement; ~: *fam* [resultado] upshot.

conclusivo, va [kõnklu'zivu, va] *adj* conclusive.

concomitante [kõnkomi'tãntʃi] *adj* concomitant; ~ **a** simultaneous with.

concordância [kõŋkox'dãnsja] *f* agreement.

concordante [kõŋkox'dãntʃi] *adj* corroborating.

concordar [4] [kõŋkox'da(x)] ⟨⟩ *vt*: ~ **que** to agree that. ⟨⟩ *vi* to agree; ~ **com algo/alguém** to agree with sthg/sb; ~ **em fazer algo** to agree to do sthg; **não concordo!** I disagree!

concordata [kõŋkox'data] *f* - **1.** *FIN* composition; **entrar em** ~ to make a composition; **pedir a** ~ to seek a composition. - **2.** *RELIG* concordat.

concórdia [kõŋ'kɔxdʒja] *f* - **1.** [harmonia] concord. - **2.** [paz] peace.

concorrência [kõŋko'xẽnsja] *f* - **1.** [ger] competition. - **2.** *fig* [licitação] tender; **abrir uma** ~ to call to tender.

concorrente [kõŋko'xẽntʃi] *adj* - **1.** [competidor] competitor. - **2.** [candidato] candidate.

concorrer [5] [kõŋko'xe(x)] *vi* - **1.** [ger] to compete; ~ **com alguém** to compete with sb; ~ **a algo** [ger] to apply for sthg; *POL* to be running for sthg. - **2.** [contribuir]: ~ **para algo** to contribute to sthg.

concorrido, da [kõŋko'xidu, da] *adj* - **1.** [disputado] disputed. - **2.** *fam* [festa, bar *etc*] popular.

concretamente [kõnkreta'mẽntʃi] *adv* [em termos reais] really, actually.

concretização [kõnkretʃiza'sãw] (*pl* -ões) *f* realization.

concretizar [4] [kõŋkreti'za(x)] *vt* to realize.

➡ **concretizar-se** *vp* [sonho, projeto, anseio] to be realized.

concreto, ta [kõŋ'kretu, ta] *adj* [sólido] concrete.

➡ **concreto** *m* concrete; ~ **armado** reinforced concrete.

concretude [kõnkre'tudʒi] *f* concrete nature.

concunhado, da [kõnku'ɲadu, da] *m, f* the brother-in-law or sister-in-law of one's husband or wife.

concupiscência [kõnkupi'sẽnsja] *f* - **1.** [ambição] ambition. - **2.** [lascívia] lust.

concupiscente [kõɲkupis'sẽntʃi] *adj* materialistic.

concursado, da [kõɲkux'sadu, da] ⟨⟩ *adj* referring to a person who has been successful in a competitive examination giving access to a position, particularly in public office.

concurso [kõŋ'kuxsu] *m* - **1.** [exame] competitive examination; ~ **público** public competitive examination. - **2.** [sorteio] lottery.

concussão [kõɲku'sãw] (*pl* -ões) *f* - **1.** *MED* concussion. - **2.** *fig* [desfalque] embezzlement.

condado [kõn'dadu] *m* county.

condão [kõn'dãw] *m* ▷ **varinha**.

conde, dessa ['kõndʒi, dʒesa] *m, f* count (*f* countess).

condecoração [kõndekora'sãw] (*pl* -ões) *f* - **1.** [cerimônia] investiture. - **2.** [insígnia] decoration.

condecorar [4] [kõndeko'ra(x)] *vt* to decorate.

condenação [kõndena'sãw] (*pl* -ões) *f* - **1.** *JUR* conviction. - **2.** [reprovação] condemnation.

condenar [4] [kõnde'na(x)] *vt* - **1.** [ger] to condemn; ~ **alguém a algo** to sentence sb to sthg. - **2.** *JUR* [declarar culpado] to find guilty. - **3.** *fig* [interditar] to condemn. **- 4.** *fig* [desenganar] to disillusion; ~ **um paciente** to give up hope of saving a patient.

condenável [kõnde'navew] (*pl* -**eis**) *adj* [reprovável] reprehensible.

condensação [kõdẽnsa'sãw] (*pl* -**ões**) *f* condensation.

condensar [4] [kõndẽn'sa(x)] *vt* to condense.

➡ **condensar-se** *vp* to condense.

condescendência [kõndesẽn'dẽnsja] *f* condescension.

condescendente [kõndesẽn'dẽntʃi] *adj* condescending.

condescender [5] [kõndesẽn'de(x)] *vi* to acquiesce; ~ **a** *ou* **em** to agree to.

condessa [kõn'desa] *f* ▷ **conde**.

condição [kõndʒi'sãw] (*pl* -**ões**) *f* - **1.** [ger] position; **de** ~ **humilde** of humble position; **de** ~ [rico] wealthy; **na** ~ **de** in the capacity of. **- 2.** [exigência] condition; **com a** ~ **de que** on condition that. **- 3.** [natureza] nature; ~ **humana** human condition.

➡ **condições** *fpl* **- 1.** [ger] conditions; **condições atmosféricas** atmospheric conditions; **condições próprias/impróprias de banho** [praia] suitable/unsuitable conditions for swimming; **condições de vida** living conditions; **condições de trabalho** working conditions. **- 2.** [estado] condition (*sg*); **em boas condições (de uso)** in good (working) order; **sem condições** [em mau estado] in poor condition. **- 3.** [capacidade] requirement; **estar em condições de fazer algo** to be able do sthg; **ter condições de fazer algo** to be able to do sthg. **- 4.** [meios] means.

condicionado, da [kõndʒisjo'nadu, da] *adj* conditioned; **estímulo/reflexo** ~ conditioned stimulation/reflex; **venda** ~ conditional sale.

condicionamento [kõndʒisjona'mẽntu] *m* conditioning; ~ **físico** physical condition.

condigno, na [kõn'dʒignu, na] *adj* **- 1.** [adequado] adequate. **- 2.** [merecido] worthy.

condimentar [4] [kõndʒimẽn'ta(x)] *vt* to season.

condimento [kõndʒi'mẽntu] *m* condiment.

condizente [kõndʒi'zẽntʃi] *adj*: ~ **com** appropriate for.

condizer [29] [kõndʒi'ze(x)] *vi*: ~ **com** to match.

condoer-se [28] [kõndo'exsi] *vp*: ~ **de** to be sorry for.

condolência [kõndo'lẽnsja] *f* sympathy.

➡ **condolências** *fpl* condolences.

condomínio [kõndo'minju] *m* **- 1.** [conjunto de casas, apartamentos] condominium. **- 2.** [pagamento] service charge.

condômino, na [kõn'dominu, na] *m, f* [co-proprietário] *person living in a condominium.*

condução [kõndu'sãw] (*pl* -**ões**) *f* **- 1.** [ato] transportation. **- 2.** [transporte] transport. **- 3.** [ônibus] bus. **- 4.** *FÍSICA* conduction.

conducente [kõndu'sẽntʃi] *adj*: ~ **a** conducive to.

conduta [kõn'duta] *f* conduct, behaviour; **má** ~ bad behaviour.

conduto [kõn'dutu] *m* **- 1.** [tubo] tube. **- 2.** [cano] pipe. **- 3.** [canal] channel.

condutor, ra [kõndu'to(x), ra] (*mpl* -**es**, *fpl* -**s**) ◇ *adj* [de eletricidade] conductor. ◇ *m, f* [de veículo] driver.

➡ **condutor** *m ELETR* conductor.

conduzir [72] [kõndu'zi(x)] ◇ *vt* -**1.** [levar]: ~ **algo/alguém (a)** to transport sthg/sb (to). **- 2.** [empresa, equipe] to lead. **- 3.** *ELETR* to conduct. ◇ *vi* [levar]: ~ **a** to lead to.

➡ **conduzir-se** *vp* [portar-se] to behave.

cone ['koni] *m* cone.

conectar [4] [konek'ta(x)] *vt* to connect.

➡ **conectar-se** *vp* to connect; ~ **à internet** to connect to the Internet.

conectividade [konektʃivi'dadʒi] *f* connectivity.

cônego ['konegu] *m* canon.

conexão [konek'sãw] (*pl* -**ões**) *f* **- 1.** [ger & *COMPUT*] connection; ~ **discada** *ou* **dial-up** dial-up connection; ~ **a cabo** cable connection. **- 2.** [nexo] link. **- 3.** [relação] relationship.

conexo, xa [ko'nɛksu, sa] *adj* connected.

confabulação [kõnfabula'sãw] (*pl* -**ões**) *f* **- 1.** [conspiração] conspiracy. **- 2.** [conversa] chat.

confabular [4] [kõnfabu'la(x)] *vi* **- 1.** [conspirar] to conspire. **- 2.** [conversar] to chat; ~ **com** to chat with.

confecção [kõnfek'sãw] (*pl* -**ões**) *f* **- 1.** [ger] making. **- 2.** [fábrica de roupas] clothing factory.

confeccionar [4] [kõnfeksjo'na(x)] *vt* [fabricar, fazer] to make.

confederação [kõnfedera'sãw] (*pl* -**ões**) *f* confederation.

confeitar [4] [kõnfej'ta(x)] *vt* [bolo] to sugar-coat.

confeitaria [kõnfejta'ria] *f* cake shop.

confeiteiro, ra [kõnfej'tejru, ra] *m, f* confectioner.

conferência [kõnfe'rẽsja] *f* **- 1.** [verificação] check. **- 2.** [palestra] lecture; **fazer uma** ~ to give a lecture.

conferencista [kõnferẽn'siʃta] *m f* [palestrante] speaker.

conferente [kõnfe'rẽntʃi] *mf* [em uma verificação] checker, controller.

conferir [57] [kõnfe'ri(x)] ◇ *vt* **- 1.** [verificar] to check. **- 2.** [cotejar, comparar] to compare. **- 3.** [dar]: ~ **algo a alguém/algo** to invest sb/sthg with sthg. **- 4.** [título, encargo] to confer. ◇ *vi* **- 1.** [estar correto]: ~ **(com)** to agree (with). **- 2.** [garantir] to make sure.

confessar [4] [kõnfe'sa(x)] ◇ *vt* **- 1.** [fazer confissão de] to confess. **- 2.** *RELIG* [ouvir confissão de] to hear confession. ◇ *vi* **- 1.** [fazer confissão] to make a confession. **- 2.** *RELIG* to confess.

➡ **confessar-se** *vp* **- 1.** *RELIG* to confess. **- 2.** [admitir ser] to confess to being; ~ **-se culpado** *JUR* to plead guilty.

confessionário [kõnfesjo'narju] *m* confessional.

confesso, sa [kõn'fesu, sa] *adj* confessed.

confessor [kõnfe'so(x)] *m RELIG* confessor.

confete [kõn'fɛtʃil *m* confetti; **jogar** ~ *fam* [bajular] to please sb.

confiabilidade [kõnfjabili'dadʒi] *f* [credibilidade] reliability.

confiado, da [kõn'fjadu, da] *adj* [atrevido] cheeky.

confiança [kõn'fjãnsa] *f* -**1.** [segurança] confidence. -**2.** [fé] trust; **digno de** ~ worthy of trust; **ter** ~ **em alguém** to have confidence in sb; **de** ~ trustworthy. -**3.** *fam* [intimidade] familiarity; **dar** ~ **a alguém** to allow sb to treat one in a familiar way.

confiante [kõn'fjãntʃi] *adj* -**1.** [seguro] confident. -**2.** [esperançoso]: ~ **(em)** trusting (in).

confiar [16] [kõn'fja(x)] ⟨⟩ *vi*: ~ **em** to trust in. ⟨⟩ *vt* -**1.** [entregar]: ~ **algo a alguém** to entrust sthg to sb. -**2.** [contar]: ~ **algo a alguém** to confide in sb about sthg.

confiável [kõn'fjavew] (*pl* -**eis**) *adj* reliable.

confidência [kõnfi'dẽnsja] *f* confidence; **em** ~ in confidence.

confidencial [kõnfidẽn'sjaw] (*pl* -**ais**) *adj* confidential.

confidenciar [16] [kõnfidẽn'sja(x)] *vt*: ~ **algo a alguém** to confide sthg to sb.

confidente [kõnfi'dẽntʃi] *m f* confidant (*f* confidante).

configuração [kõnfigura'sãw] (*pl* -**ões**) *f* -**1.** [disposição - de objetos, peças] arrangement; [- de astros] configuration. -**2.** [forma] shape. -**3.** *COMPUT* configuration.

configurar [4] [kõnfigu'ra(x)] *vt* to represent.

confinamento [kõnfina'mẽntu] *m* confinement.

confinar [4] [kõnfi'na(x)] ⟨⟩ *vt* [isolar, enclausurar]: ~ **alguém/algo em** to confine sb/sthg to/in. ⟨⟩ *vi* ◆ **confinar-se** *vp* [isolar-se, enclausurar-se] to isolate o.s.

confins [kõn'fĩʃ] *mpl* [limite extremo] ends; **nos** ~ **de Judas** *fam* in the back of beyond.

confirmação [kõnfixma'sãw] (*pl* -**ões**) *f* confirmation.

confirmar [4] [kõnfix'ma(x)] *vt* [comprovar] to confirm.
◆ **confirmar-se** *vp* -**1.** [cumprir-se] to be confirmed. -**2.** [justificar-se] to be justified.

confiscar [12] [kõnfiʃ'ka(x)] *vt* to confiscate.

confisco [kõn'fiʃku] *m* confiscation.

confissão [kõnfi'sãw] (*pl* -**ões**) *f* [de falta, crime] confession.

conflagração [kõnflagra'sãw] (*pl* -**ões**) *f* -**1.** [guerra] war. -**2.** [revolução] revolution.

conflagrar [4] [kõnfla'gra(x)] *vt* [levar à guerra] to convulse.

conflitante [kõnfli'tãntʃi] *adj* conflicting.

conflito [kõn'flitu] *m* [ger] conflict; ~ **de gerações** generation gap; **entrar em** ~ **(com)** to clash (with).

confluência [kõn'flwẽnsia] *f* -**1.** [de rios] confluence. -**2.** [de estradas, ruas] junction.

confluente [kõn'flwẽntʃi] *adj* -**1.** [rio] confluent. -**2.** [estrada, rua] merging.

confluir [kõn'flui(x)] *vi* to merge.

conformação [kõnfoxma'sãw] (*pl* -**ões**) *f* -**1.** [resignação] resignation. -**2.** [forma] shape.

conformado, da [kõnfox'madu, da] *adj* [resignado] resigned.

conformar [4] [kõnfox'ma(x)] *vt* [formar] to shape.
◆ **conformar-se** *vp* -**1.** [resignar-se]: ~**-se com** to resign o.s. to. -**2.** [acomodar-se]: ~**-se a** *ou* **com** to conform to *ou* with.

conforme [kõn'fɔxmi] ⟨⟩ *prep* [de acordo com, segundo] in accordance with. ⟨⟩ *conj* -**1.** [ger] as. -**2.** [de acordo com] according to. -**3.** [dependendo de] depending on.
◆ **conformes** *mpl*: **dentro dos** ~**s** *fam* in accordance with the requirements.

conformidade [kõnfoxmi'dadʒi] *f* [acordo] agreement; **em** ~ **com** in accordance with.

conformismo [kõnfox'miʒmul *m* conformity.

conformista [kõnfox'miʃta] *mf* conformist.

confortante [kõnfox'tãntʃi] *adj* comforting.

confortar [4] [kõnfox'ta(x)] *vt* [consolar] to comfort.

confortável [kõnfox'tavɛw] (*pl* -**eis**) *adj* comfortable.

conforto [kõn'foxtu] *m* comfort.

confraria [kõnfra'ria] *f* fraternity.

confraternização [kõnfratexniza'sãw] (*pl* -**ões**) *f* fraternization.

confraternizar [4] [kõnfratexni'za(x)] ⟨⟩ *vt* -**1.** [reunir, ligar] to socialize. -**2.** [reconciliar] to reconcile. ⟨⟩ *vi* -**1.** [reunir-se, ligar-se] to unite. -**2.** [comemorar] to celebrate.

confrontação [kõnfrõnta'sãw] (*pl* -**ões**) *f* -**1.** [comparação] comparison. -**2.** [acareação] confrontation.

confrontar [4] [kõnfrõn'ta(x)] *vt* -**1.** [comparar] to compare. -**2.** [acarear] to confront.
◆ **confrontar-se** *vp* [defrontar-se] to face each other.

confronto [kõn'frõntu] *m* -**1.** [comparação] comparison. -**2.** [choque] confrontation.

confundir [6] [kõnfũn'di(x)] *vt* -**1.** [ger] to confuse; ~ **algo com** to confuse sthg with. -**2.** [misturar] to muddle. -**3.** [trocar] to mix up.
◆ **confundir-se** *vp* to become confused; ~**-se com** to become confused with.

confusão [kõnfu'zãw] (*pl* -**ões**) *f* -**1.** [mistura] muddle. -**2.** [troca] mixing up; **fazer** ~ [confundir-se] to become confused. -**3.** [indistinção] confusion. -**4.** [caos] mess. -**5.** [problema] hassle; **dar** ~ to cause a hassle. -**6.** [tumulto] melee.

confuso, sa [kõn'fuzu, za] *adj* -**1.** [obscuro] obscure. -**2.** [misturado] muddled. -**3.** [indistinto] hazy. -**4.** [atrapalhado] confused.

congelado, da [kõnʒe'ladu, da] *adj* frozen.
◆ **congelado** *m* frozen food *(inv)*.

congelador [kõnʒela'do(x)] (*pl* -**es**) *m* freezer.

congelamento [kõnʒela'mẽntu] *m* -**1.** [de água, alimento *etc*] freezing. -**2.** *ECON* [de preços, salários] freeze.

congelar [4] [kõnʒe'la(x)] ⟨⟩ *vt* [água, rio, alimento] to freeze. ⟨⟩ *vi* -**1.** [ficar congelado] to freeze. -**2.**

[sentir frio] to be freezing.

➤ **congelar-se** *vp* [ficar congelado] to freeze.

congênere [kõnˈʒeniɾ] *adj* similar.

congênito, ta [kõnˈʒenitu, ta] *adj* congenital.

congestão [kõnʒeʃˈtãw] (*pl* -ões) *f* congestion; ~ **nasal** nasal congestion.

congestionado, da [kõnʒeʃtjoˈnadu, da] *adj* -**1**. [trânsito] congested. -**2**. [nariz, artéria] blocked.

congestionamento [kõnʒeʃtjonaˈmẽntu] *m* -**1**. [engarrafamento] congestion; ~ **de tráfego** traffic congestion. -**2**. [de nariz, artéria] blockage.

congestionar [4] [kõnʒeʃtʃjoˈna(x)] *vt* -**1**. [trânsito]: ~ **o trânsito** to cause traffic congestion. -**2**. [nariz, artéria] to block.

➤ **congestionar-se** *vp* -**1**. [trânsito] to become congested. -**2**. [nariz, artéria] to become blocked.

conglomeração [kõŋglomeraˈsãw] (*pl* -ões) *f* conglomeration.

conglomerado [kõŋglomeˈradu] *m* conglomerate.

conglomerar [4] [kõŋglomeˈra(x)] *vt* -**1**. [reunir] to conglomerate. -**2**. [empresas] to merge.

Congo [ˈkõŋgu] *n*: **o** ~ the Congo.

congolês, esa [kõŋgoˈleʃ, eza] <> *adj* Congolese. <> *m, f* Congolese.

congratular [4] [kõŋgratuˈla(x)] *vt*: ~ **alguém (por algo)** to congratulate sb (on sthg).

congregação [kõŋgregaˈsãw] (*pl* -ões) *f* -**1**. RELIG congregation. -**2**. [reunião] coming together.

congregar [14] [kõŋgreˈga(x)] *vt* [reunir] to bring together.

➤ **congregar-se** *vp* [reunir-se] to congregate.

congressista [kõŋgreˈsiʃta] *m f* -**1**. [participante] delegate (*at a conference*). -**2**. POL congressman (*f* congresswoman).

congresso [kõŋˈgrɛsul] *m* -**1**. [conferência] conference. -**2**. POL: **o Congresso** Congress.

conhaque [koˈnaki] *m* cognac.

conhecedor, ra [koɲeseˈdo(x), ra] (*mpl* -es, *fpl* -s) <> *adj* [ciente]: ~ **(de)** aware (of). <> *m, f* [especialista]: ~ **(de)** specialist (in).

conhecer [25] [koɲeˈse(x)] *vt* -**1**. [ger] to know. -**2**. [entender de] to understand. -**3**. [pessoa pela primeira vez] to meet; ~ **alguém de nome/de vista** to know sb by name/sight. -**4**. [loja, casa *etc*] to see. -**5**. [país] to visit. -**6**. [reconhecer]: ~ **algo/alguém (por)** to recognize sthg/sb (by).

➤ **conhecer-se** *vp* -**1**. [a si próprio] to know o.s. -**2**. [pessoas] to know one another; [pela primeira vez] to meet.

conhecido, da [koɲeˈsidu, da] <> *adj* -**1**. [famoso] well-known; ~ **por** known for. -**2**. [sabido] wise. -**3**. [notório] notorious. <> *m, f* [pessoa] acquaintance.

conhecimento [koɲesiˈmẽntul] *m* -**1**. [saber] knowledge; ~ **de causa** due knowledge; **levar algo ao** ~ **de alguém** to bring sthg to the attention of sb; **não tomar** ~ **de** [não dar importância a] not to attach importance to; **ser de** ~ **geral que** to be general knowledge that; **ter** ~ **de** to be aware of; **tomar** ~ **de** to find out about. -**2**.

[conhecido] acquaintance. -**3**. COM: ~ **aéreo** air waybill.

➤ **conhecimentos** *mpl* -**1**. [noções] knowledge (*sg*). -**2**. [relações, conhecidos] friends.

cônico, ca [ˈkoniku, ka] *adj* conical.

conivência [koniˈvẽnsja] *f* connivance.

conivente [koniˈvẽntʃi] *adj* conniving; **ser** ~ **com** to connive in.

conjetura [kõnʒeˈtural] *f* conjecture; **fazer** ~**s (sobre)** to make conjectures (about).

conjeturar [4] [kõnʒetuˈra(x)] *vt* to conjecture.

conjugação [kõnʒugaˈsãw] (*pl* -ões) *f* -**1**. [união] union. -**2**. GRAM conjugation.

conjugado, da [kõnʒuˈgadu, da] *adj* -**1**. [apartamento, sala] adjoining. -**2**. GRAM conjugated.

➤ **conjugado** *m* [apartamento] adjoining apartment.

conjugal [kõnʒuˈgaw] (*pl* -ais) *adj* marital; **vida** ~ married life.

conjugar [14] [kõnʒuˈga(x)] *vt* -**1**. [unir] to combine. -**2**. GRAM to conjugate.

➤ **conjugar-se** *vp* [unir-se] to be connected.

cônjuge [ˈkõnʒuʒil] *m* spouse.

conjunção [kõnʒũnˈsãw] (*pl* -ões) *f* -**1**. [união] combination. -**2**. GRAM conjunction.

conjuntivite [kõnʒũntʃiˈvitʃil] *f* conjunctivitis.

conjunto, ta [kõnˈʒũntu, ta] *adj* combined, joint.

➤ **conjunto** *m* -**1**. [grupo] combination. -**2**. [totalidade]: **o** ~ **de** the whole of; **em** ~ together. -**3**. MÚS group. -**4**. [residencial] complex; ~ **habitacional** housing complex. -**5**. [traje] suit. -**6**. MAT set.

conjuntura [kõnʒũnˈtural] *f* conjuncture.

conluio [kõnˈlujul] *m* collusion.

conosco [koˈnoʃkul] *pron pess* with us.

conotação [konotaˈsãw] (*pl* -ões) *f* connotation.

conotar [4] [konoˈta(x)] *vt* to connote.

conquanto [kõnˈkwãntul] *conj* although.

conquista [kõnˈkiʃta] *f* conquest.

conquistador, ra [kõnkiʃtaˈdo(x), ra] <> *adj* -**1**. [exército, país] conquering. -**2**. [sedutor] seductive. <> *m, f* -**1**. [de terras, país] conqueror. -**2**. [sedutor-homem] lady-killer; [- mulher] femme fatale.

conquistar [4] [kõnkiʃˈta(x)] *vt* -**1**. [subjugar] to conquer. -**2**. [alcançar] to achieve. -**3**. [ganhar] to win. -**4**. [seduzir] to seduce.

consagração [kõnsagraˈsãw] (*pl* -ões) *f* -**1**. [aclamação] acclaim. -**2**. [exaltação] acclamation; **fazer a** ~ **de** to be an acclamation of. -**3**. [dedicação] dedication. -**4**. [aceitação] acceptance. -**5**. RELIG consecration.

consagrar [4] [kõnsaˈgra(x)] *vt* -**1**. [levar à aclamação] to lead to the acclamation of. -**2**. [exaltar] to glorify. -**3**. [dedicar] to dedicate. -**4**. [tornar aceito] to become accepted. -**5**. RELIG to consecrate.

➤ **consagrar-se** *vi* -**1**. [atingir a aclamação] to achieve acclaim. -**2**. [dedicar-se]: ~**se a algo** to dedicate oneself to sthg.

consangüíneo, nea [kõnsãŋˈgwinju, nja] <> *adj* related by blood. <> *m, f* [parente] blood relation.

consorte

consciência [kõn'sjẽnsja] *f* -**1**. [conhecimento] awareness; ~ **de classe** class-consciousness; ~ **política** political awareness; **ter/tomar** ~ **de** to be/become aware of. -**2**. [sentidos]: **perder a** ~ to lose consciousness. -**3**. [moral] conscience; **estar com a** ~ **limpa/pesada** to have a clear/guilty conscience. -**4**. [cuidado, responsabilidade] care.

consciencioso, osa [kõnsjẽn'sjozu, oza] *adj* conscientious.

consciente [kõnʃ'sjẽntʃi] <> *adj* conscious. <> *m* PSIC consciousness.

conscientemente [kõnsjẽntʃi'mẽntʃi] *adv* consciously.

conscientizar [4] [kõnsjẽntʃi'za(x)] *vt* [dar conhecimento a]: ~ **alguém (de algo)** to raise sb's awareness (of something).
~ **conscientizar-se** *vp* [tomar consciência de]: ~ **-se (de algo)** to become aware (of sthg).

cônscio, cia ['kõnsju, sja] *adj* lucid.

consecução [kõnseku'sãw] *f* attainment.

consecutivo, va [kõnseku'tʃivu, va] *adj* consecutive.

conseguinte [kõnse'gĩntʃi] ~ **por conseguinte** *loc conj* consequently.

conseguir [55] [kõnse'gi(x)] *vt* -**1**. [obter] to obtain. -**2**. [alcançar] to achieve; ~ **fazer algo** to manage to do sthg.

conselheiro, ra [kõnse'ʎejru, ra] *m, f* -**1**. [ger] adviser. -**2**. [membro de conselho] councillor.

conselho [kõ'seʎu] *m* -**1**. [advertência] advice; **dar um** ~ **a alguém** to give sb a piece of advice. -**2**. [órgão] council; ~ **administrativo** board of directors; ~ **de Estado** Council of State; ~ **de ministros** Cabinet; ~ **de guerra** council of war.

consenso [kõ'sẽnsu] *m* consensus.

consensual [kõnsẽn'swaw] (*pl* -**ais**) *adj* consensual.

consentimento [kõnsẽntʃi'mẽntu] *m* consent.

consentir [56] [kõnsẽn'tʃi(x)] <> *vt* -**1**. [permitir] to grant. -**2**. [aprovar] to approve. <> *vi* [concordar, anuir]: ~ **em algo** to consent to sthg; ~ **em fazer algo** to agree to do sthg.

conseqüência [kõnse'kwẽnsja] *f* [resultado] consequence; **em** ~ **de** because of, owing to; **por** ~ consequently.

conseqüente [kõnse'kwẽntʃi] *adj* -**1**. [resultante] consequent. -**2**. [coerente] coherent.

consertar [4] [kõnsex'ta(x)] *vt* -**1**. [reparar] to repair. -**2**. [remediar] to rectify.

conserto [kõn'sextu] *m* repair.

conserva [kõn'sɛrva] *f* preserve; **em** ~ preserved.

conservação [kõnsexva'sãw] *f* -**1**. [ger] conservation. -**2**. [preservação] preservation.

conservacionista [kõnsexvasjo'niʃta] <> *adj* conservationist. <> *mf* conservationist.

conservado, da [kõnsex'vadu, da] *adj* -**1**. [carro, casa] well kept. -**2**. [pessoa] well preserved.

conservador, ra [kõnsexva'do(x), ra] <> *adj* conservative. <> *m, f* conservative.

conservadorismo [kõnsexvado'riʒmu] *m* conservatism.

conservante [kõnser'vãntʃi] *m* preservative.

conservar [4] [kõnsex'va(x)] *vt* -**1**. [preservar] to preserve. -**2**. [sabor, qualidade *etc*] to conserve. -**3**. [manter] to maintain.
~ **conservar-se** *vp* -**1**. [pessoa] to be well preserved. -**2**. [permanecer] to remain.

conservatório [kõnsexva'tɔrju] *m* conservatoire.

consideração [kõnsidera'sãw] (*pl* -**ões**) *f* -**1**. [ger] consideration; **levar em** ~ to take into consideration; **falta de** ~ **(com alguém)** lack of consideration (towards sb). -**2**. [pensamento] thought.

considerado, da [kõnside'radu, da] *adj* respected.

considerar [4] [kõnside'ra(x)] *vt* -**1**. [ger] to consider. -**2**. [respeitar, estimar]: ~ **muito alguém/algo** to have a high regard for sb/sthg.
~ **considerar-se** *vp* [julgar-se] to consider o.s.

considerável [kõnside'ravɛw] (*pl* -**eis**) *adj* considerable.

consignação [kõnsigna'sãw] (*pl* -**ões**) *f* -**1**. [registro] report. -**2**. COM consignment; **venda por** ~ sale on consignment; **em** ~ on consignment. -**3**. [de verbas] allocation.

consignar [4] [kõnsig'na(x)] *vt* -**1**. [produtos] to consign. -**2**. [registrar] to record. -**3**. [verbas] to allocate.

consigo [kõn'sigu] *pron pess* with him/her/you/it.

consistência [kõnsiʃ'tẽnsja] *f* consistency; **ganhar** ~ to thicken.

consistente [kõnsiʃ'tẽntʃi] *adj* -**1**. [sólido] solid. -**2**. [espesso] thick. -**3**. [coerente, sólido] consistent.

consistir [6] [kõnsiʃ'tʃi(x)] *vi* [constituir-se]: ~ **em** to consist of; ~ **em fazer algo** to consist in doing sthg.

consoante [kõn'swãntʃi] <> *adj* LING consonant. <> *f* LING consonant. <> *prep* [de acordo com] according to.

consolação [kõnsola'sãw] (*pl* -**ões**) *f* comfort.

consolador, ra [kõnsola'do(x), ra] *adj* comforting.

consolar [4] [kõnso'la(x)] *vt* to comfort.
~ **consolar-se** *vp*: ~ **-se (com)** to console o.s. (with).

console [kõn'sɔli] *m* console.

consolidação [kõnsolida'sãw] (*pl* -**ões**) *f* [estabilização] consolidation.

consolidar [4] [kõnsoli'da(x)] <> *vt* -**1**. [estabilizar, ratificar] to consolidate. -**2**. [fratura] to calcify. <> *vi* [tornar-se sólido] to solidify.

consolo [kõn'solu] *m* -**1**. [consolação] comfort. -**2**. *vulg* [consolo-de-viúva] dildo.

consomê [kõnso'me] *m* consommé.

consonância [kõnso'nãnsja] *f* consonance; **em** ~ **com** in accordance with.

consórcio [kõn'sɔxsju] *m* -**1**. [união] partnership. -**2**. [de interesses, necessidades] uniting. -**3**. COM consortium.

consorte [kõn'sɔxtʃi] *m, f* consort.

conspícuo, cua [kõnʃ'pikwu, kwa] *adj* -**1**. [evidente] conspicuous. -**2**. [ilustre] remarkable.

conspiração [kõnʃpira'sãw] (*pl* -ões) *f* conspiracy.

conspirador, ra [kõnʃpira'do(x), ra] *m*, *f* conspirator.

conspirar [4] [kõnʃpi'ra(x)] <> *vi*: ~ **(contra)** to conspire (against). <> *vt* to plot.

conspiratório, ria [kõʃpira'tɔrju, rja] *adj* conspiratorial.

constância [kõnʃ'tãnsja] *f* -**1**. [de ruído, incômodo] persistence. -**2**. [no amor] constancy. -**3**. [perseverança] perseverance. -**4**. [de idéias, opiniões] constancy.

constante [kõnʃ'tãntʃi] *adj* -**1**. [ger] constant. -**2**. [pessoa, amor] faithful. -**3**. [que consta]: ~ **de** pertaining to.

constar [4] [kõnʃ'ta(x)] *vi* -**1**. [informação]: ~ **(em** *ou* **de)** to appear (in). -**2**. [ser assegurado]: ~ **que** to be said that. -**3**. [ser do conhecimento de]: **não lhe constava que o preço tivesse subido** he was not aware that the price had risen. -**4**. [constituir-se]: ~ **de** to consist of.

constatação [kõnʃtata'sãw] (*pl* -ões) *f* -**1**. [observação] observation. -**2**. [comprovação] confirmation.

constatar [4] [kõnʃta'ta(x)] *vt* -**1**. [observar] to notice. -**2**. [comprovar] to prove.

constelação [kõnʃtela'sãw] (*pl* -ões) *f* constellation.

consternação [kõnʃtexna'sãw] (*pl* -ões) *f* [desalento, desolação] dismay.

consternado, da [kõnʃter'nadu, da] *adj* dismayed.

consternar [4] [kõnʃtex'na(x)] *vt* to discourage.

constipação [kõnʃtʃipa'sãw] (*pl* -ões) *f* -**1**. [prisão de ventre] constipation. -**2**. [resfriado] cold.

constipado, da [kõnʃtʃi'padu, da] *adj* -**1**. [resfriado]: **estar** ~ to have a cold. -**2**. [com prisão de ventre] constipated.

constitucional [kõnʃtʃitusjo'naw] (*pl* -ais) *adj* constitutional.

constitucionalidade [kõnʃtʃitusionali'dadʒi] *f* constitutionality.

constituição [kõnʃtʃitwi'sãw] (*pl* -ões) *f* -**1**. [formação] make-up. -**2**. [consistência] composition. -**3**. *POL* [carta] constitution.

constituinte [kõnʃtʃi'twĩntʃi] <> *adj* -**1**. [componente] constituent. -**2**. *POL* representative. <> *mf* *POL* [deputado] deputy.

▸ **Constituinte** *f* *POL* [assembléia]: **a Constituinte** the Constituent Assembly.

constituir [74] [kõnʃtʃi'twi(x)] *vt* -**1**. [compor, ser] to constitute. -**2**. [criar, estabelecer] to establish.

▸ **constituir-se** *vp* -**1**. [estabelecer-se como]: ~-**se em algo** to establish o.s. as sthg. -**2**. [ser]: ~-**se em algo** to be sthg, to constitute sthg.

constitutivo, va [kõnʃtʃitu'tʃivu, va] *adj* -**1**. [formador] constituent. -**2**. [indispensável] essential. -**3**. [característico] characteristic.

constrangedor, ra [kõnʃtrãnʒe'do(x), ra] *adj* -**1**. [embaraçador] embarrassing. -**2**. [repressivo] repressive.

constranger [26] [kõnʃtrãn'ʒe(x)] *vt* -**1**. [embaraçar] to embarrass. -**2**. [reprimir, refrear] to curb. -**3**. [coagir]: ~ **alguém a fazer algo** to force sb to do sthg.

▸ **constranger-se** *vp* [ficar embaraçado] to be embarrassed.

constrangimento [kõnʃtrãnʒi'mẽntu] *m* -**1**. [embaraço] embarrassment. -**2**. [repressão] restriction.

construção [kõnʃtru'sãw] (*pl* -ões) *f* -**1**. [edifício] building; **em** ~ under construction (*depois de verbo*). -**2**. [intelectual, imaginária] feat.

construir [73] [kõnʃtru'i(x)] *vt* to build.

construtivo, va [kõnʃtru'tʃivu, va] *adj* constructive.

construtor, ra [kõnʃtru'to(x), ra] (*mpl* -es, *fpl* -s) <> *adj* building (*antes de subst*). <> *m*, *f* builder.

▸ **construtora** *f* [empresa] building company.

cônsul ['kõnsuw] (*pl* -es) *m* consul.

consulado [kõnsu'ladu] *m* consulate.

consulente [kõnsu'lẽntʃi] *mf* advice seeker.

cônsules ['kõnsuliʃ] *pl* ⤏ **cônsul**.

consulesa [kõnsu'leza] *f* -**1**. [diplomata] consul. -**2**. [esposa] consul's wife.

consulta [kõn'suwta] *f* -**1**. [sobre problema, dúvida] query; **fazer uma** ~ **a alguém** to consult sb. -**2**. *MED* consultation; **horário de** ~ surgery hours; **ter uma** ~ **(com)** to have an appointment (with).

consultar [4] [kõnsuw'ta(x)] *vt* to consult; ~ **alguém sobre algo** to consult sb about sthg.

consultivo, va [kõnsuw'tʃivu, va] *adj* consultative.

consultor, ra [kõnsuw'to(x), ra] *m*, *f* consultant.

consultoria [kõnsuwto'ria] *f* [serviço] consultancy; **empresa de** ~ consultancy.

consultório [kõnsuw'tɔrju] *m* -**1**. *MED* consulting room. -**2**. *JORN*: ~ **sentimental** agony column.

consumação [kõnsuma'sãw] (*pl* -ões) *f* -**1**. [realização] realization, carrying out. -**2**. [completude] completion. -**3**. [de casamento] consummation. -**4**. [em restaurante, bar]: ~ **mínima** minimum order.

consumado, da [kõnsu'madu, da] *adj* -**1**. [realizado] realized, carried out. -**2**. [completado] completed. -**3**. [casamento] consummated.

consumar [4] [kõnsu'ma(x)] *vt* -**1**. [realizar] to realize, to carry out. -**2**. [completar] to complete. -**3**. [casamento] to consummate.

▸ **consumar-se** *vp* -**1**. [realizar-se] to be realized, to be carried out. -**2**. [completar-se] to be completed. -**3**. [casamento] to be consummated. -**4**. [profecia] to come true.

consumidor, ra [kõsumi'do(x), ra] (*mpl* -es, *fpl* -s) <> *adj* consumer. <> *m*, *f* consumer.

consumir [6] [kõnsu'mi(x)] <> *vt* -**1**. [ger] to consume. -**2**. [comprar] to purchase. -**3**. [corroer, devorar] to corrode. -**4**. *fig* [desgastar] to consume. <> *vi* [comprar] to consume.

▸ **consumir-se** *vp* -**1**. [combustível, fogo] to burn itself out. **-2.** *fig* [pessoa] to wear o.s. out.

consumismo [kõnsu'miʒmu] *m* consumerism.

consumista [kõnsu'miʃta] *adj* consumerist.

consumo [kõn'sumu] *m* **-1.** [ger] consumption. **-2.** [compra] sale; **bens de** ~ consumer goods; **sociedade de** ~ consumer society. **-3.** [de drogas] use.

conta ['kõnta] *f* **-1.** [ger] account; **pôr na** ~ to charge to one's account; **abrir uma** ~ to open an account; ~ **conjunta** joint account; ~ **corrente** current account; ~ **negativa** overdrawn account; ~ **de poupança** savings account. **-2.** [cálculo] counting; **acertar** *ou* **ajustar contas com alguém** *fig* to settle a score with sb; **demais da** ~ *fig* in excess; **fazer** ~**s** to make calculations; **pedir as** ~**s** *fig* [demitir-se] to resign; **perder a** ~ **de algo** to lose count of sthg; **ser a** ~ **certa** to be the correct amount; **afinal de** ~**s** after all. **-3.** [em restaurante] bill; **a** ~**, por favor!** the bill, please!; **pedir a** ~ to ask for the bill. **-4.** [fatura] invoice; ~ **de gás/luz/telefone** gas/electricity/telephone bill. **-5.** [consideração]: **levar algo em** ~ to take sthg into account; **dar(-se)** ~ **de** to realize. **-6.** [justificação, razão]: **à** ~ **de** on account of; **por** ~ **de** because of. **-7.** [informação, satisfação] account; **dar** ~ to give an account of; **prestar** ~**s de** to account for. **-8.** [responsabilidade, capacidade]: **dar** ~ **de** to manage; **deixar por** ~ **de alguém** to leave to sb; **não ser da** ~ **de alguém** to be nobody's business; **tomar** ~ **de alguém/algo** [cuidar, encarregar-se de] to look after sb/sthg; **tomar** ~ **de** [difundir-se por] to take over. **-9.** [de colar] bead. **-10.** *loc:* **dar** ~ **do recado** to do well; **fazer de** ~ **que** [imaginar] to pretend; [fingir] to pretend; **ficar por** ~ to get angry; **ter alguém em alta** ~ to hold sb in high esteem.

➡ **por conta própria** *loc adv* on one's own account; **trabalhar por** ~ **própria** to be self-employed.

contábil [kõn'tabiw] *(pl* **-eis)** *adj* accountancy *(antes de subst).*

contabilidade [kõntabili'dadʒi] *f* **-1.** [ofício] accountancy; ~ **de custos** cost accounting. **-2.** [setor] accounts department.

contabilista [kõntabi'liʃta] *m f* accountant.

contabilizar [4] [kõntabili'za(x)] *vt* **-1.** [registrar] to keep accounts. **-2.** [calcular] to count.

contado, da [kõn'tadu, da] *adj* accounted for; **estar com o dinheiro** ~ to have every penny accounted for; **ele está com seus dias** ~**s** his days are numbered.

contador [kõnta'do(x)] *(pl* **-es)** *m, f* **-1.** COM accountant. **-2.** [narrador]: ~ **de histórias** storyteller.

➡ **contador** *m* TEC meter.

contadoria [kõntado'ria] *f* accounts department.

contagem [kõn'taʒẽ] *(pl* **-ns)** *f* **-1.** [ato] counting; ~ **regressiva** countdown. **-2.** [escore] score.

contagiante [kõnta'ʒjãntʃi] *adj* contagious.

contagiar [16] [kõnta'ʒja(x)] *vt* **-1.** [infectar] to infect. **-2.** *fig* [influenciar] to affect.

➡ **contagiar-se** *vp* **-1.** [infectar-se] to become infected. **-2.** *fig* [influenciar-se] to be affected.

contágio [kõn'taʒju] *m* contagion.

contagioso, osa [kõnta'ʒjozu, za] *adj* contagious.

conta-gotas [ˌkõnta'gotaʃ] *m inv* dropper.

contaminação [kõntamina'sãw] *(pl* **-ões)** *f* contamination.

contaminado, da [kõntami'nadu, da] *adj* **-1.** [infectado, poluído] contaminated. **-2.** [por doença] infected.

contaminar [4] [kõntami'na(x)] ⬦ *vt* [contagiar] to contaminate. ⬦ *vi fig* [corromper] to corrupt.

contanto [kõn'tãntu] ➡ **contanto que** *loc adv* provided that.

contar [4] [kõn'ta(x)] ⬦ *vt* **-1.** [enumerar] to count. **-2.** [narrar] to tell. **-3.** [supor]: ~ **que** to expect. ⬦ *vi* **-1.** [fazer contas] to count. **-2.** [importar] to matter. **-3.:** ~ **com** [ger] to count on; [dispor] to have. **-4.** [pretender]: ~ **(em) fazer algo** to intend to do sthg. **-5.** [incluir]: ~ **algo/alguém entre algo** to count sthg/sb as (being) sthg.

contatar [4] [kõnta'ta(x)] *vt* to contact.

contato [kõn'tatu] *m* contact.

contêiner [kõn'tejne(x)] *m* container.

contemplação [kõntẽnpla'sãw] *m* contemplation.

contemplar [4] [kõntẽn'pla(x)] *vt* **-1.** [olhar] to contemplate. **-2.** [premiar] to reward.

➡ **contemplar-se** *vp* [olhar-se] to look at o.s.

contemplativo, va [kõntẽnpla'tʃivu, va] *adj* contemplative.

contemporaneidade [kõntẽnporãnej'dadʒi] *f* contemporary nature.

contemporâneo, nea [kõntẽmpo'ranju, nja] ⬦ *adj* contemporary. ⬦ *m, f* contemporary.

contemporizar [4] [kõntẽnpori'za(x)] ⬦ *vt* [acalmar] to calm. ⬦ *vi* [transigir]: ~ **(com)** to compromise (with).

contenção [kõntẽn'sãw] *f* **-1.** [diminuição - de despesas] cutback; [- de gestos, palavras] restraint. **-2.** [interrupção de fluxo] containment.

contencioso, osa [kõntẽn'sjozu, ɔza] *adj* contentious.

contenda [kõn'tẽnda] *f* dispute.

contentamento [kõntẽnta'mẽntu] *m* **-1.** [alegria] happiness. **-2.** [satisfação] contentment.

contentar [4] [kõntẽn'ta(x)] *vt* **-1.** [satisfazer] to content. **-2.** [agradar] to please.

➡ **contentar-se** *vp* [satisfazer-se]: ~**-se com** to be satisfied with.

contente [kõn'tẽntʃi] *adj* happy.

contento [kõn'tẽntu] ➡ **a contento** *loc adv* satisfactorily.

conter [1] [kõn'te(x)] *vt* **-1.** [controlar] to control. **-2.** [ter] to contain.

➡ **conter-se** *vp* [controlar-se] to restrain o.s.

conterrâneo, nea [kõnte'xãnju, nja] ⬦ *adj* fellow *(antes de subst);* **é um amigo** ~ he is a friend who comes from the same place as me. ⬦ *m, f* compatriot.

contestação [kõnteʃta'sãw] (pl -ões) f -1. [negação] dispute. -2. [impugnação] challenge. -3. [oposição] opposition. -4. [réplica] reply.

contestar [4] [kõnteʃ'ta(x)] ⬦ vt -1. [negar] to dispute. -2. [impugnar] to challenge. ⬦ vi -1. [opor-se] to oppose. -2. [responder]: ~ (a) to reply (to).

contestatório, ria [kõnteʃta'tɔrju, rja] adj contentious; **movimento** ~ protest movement.

contestável [kõnteʃ'tavew] (pl -eis) adj questionable.

conteúdo [kõn'tjudu] m contents (pl).

contexto [kõn'teʃtu] m context.

contextualização [kõnteʃtwaliza'sãw] (pl -ões) f contextualization.

contextualizar [kõnteʃtwali'za(x)] vt to put into context.

contido [kõn'tʃidu] adj -1. [encerrado] contained. -2. [reprimido] repressed.

contigo [kõn'tʃigu] pron pess with you.

contíguo, gua [kõn'tʃigwu, gwa] adj adjacent; ~ a next to.

continência [kõntʃi'nẽnsja] f MIL salute; **fazer** ou **bater** ~ (a alguém) to salute (sb).

continental [kõntʃinẽn'taw] (pl -ais) adj continental.

continente [kõntʃi'nẽntʃi] m continent.

contingência [kõntʃĩn'ʒẽnsja] f contingency.

contingente [kõntʃĩn'ʒẽntʃi] ⬦ adj contingent. ⬦ m contingent.

continuação [kõntʃinwa'sãw] (pl -ões) f continuation.

continuar [4] [kõntʃi'nwa(x)] ⬦ vt [prosseguir] to continue. ⬦ vi -1. [perdurar] to continue. -2. [prolongar-se] to go on. -3. [prosseguir]: ~ em algo to continue with sthg; ~ fazendo algo ou a fazer algo to continue doing sthg/to do sthg. ⬦ v de ligação (antes de adjetivo) [expressa qualidade, estado]: a cidade continua bonita the city is still beautiful.

continuidade [kõntʃinwi'dadʒi] f continuity.

contínuo, nua [kõn'tʃinwu, nwa] ⬦ adj -1. [sem interrupção] continuous. -2. [constante] constant. ⬦ m [pessoa] office junior.

contista [kõn'tʃiʃta] mf story writer.

conto ['kõntu] m story; ~ de fadas ou da carochinha fairy tale.

conto-do-vigário ['kõntuduvi'garju] (pl contos-do-vigário) m confidence trick; **cair no** ~ to be tricked; **passar o** ~ **em alguém** to try to con sb.

contorção [kõntox'sãw] (pl -ões) f contortion.

contorcer [25] [kõntox'se(x)] vt to warp.
➡ **contorcer-se** vp to writhe.

contornar [4] [kõntox'na(x)] vt -1. [rodear] to go around. -2. fig [resolver] to get around.

contornável [kõntox'navew] (pl -eis) adj surmountable.

contorno [kõn'toxnu] m outline.

contra ['kõntra] ⬦ prep [ger] against. ⬦ adv against. ⬦ m -1. [dificuldade] hard knock. -2. [contestação] objection; **dar o** ~ to object; **pesar os prós e os** ~s to weigh up the pros and the cons; **ser do** ~ to object on principle.

contra-almirante [ˌkõntraawmi'rãntʃi] (pl contra-almirantes) m rear admiral.

contra-argumento [ˌkõntraaxgu'mẽntu] (pl contra-angumentos) m counter-argument.

contra-atacar [12] [ˌkõntraata'ka(x)] vt to counter-attack.

contra-ataque [ˌkõntra'taki] (pl contra-ataques) m counter-attack.

contrabaixista [ˌkõntra'bajʃiʃta] mf double-bass player.

contrabaixo [ˌkõntra'bajʃu] m -1. [instrumento] double bass. -2. [músico] bassist.

contrabalançar [13] [ˌkõntrabalãn'sa(x)] vt to counterbalance; ~ **algo com algo** to compensate sthg with sthg.

contrabandear [15] [ˌkõntrabãn'dʒja(x)] vt to smuggle.

contrabandista [ˌkõntrabãn'dʒiʃta] mf smuggler.

contrabando [ˌkõntra'bãndu] m -1. [ato] smuggling. -2. [mercadoria] contraband; **fazer** ~ to smuggle.

contração [kõntra'sãw] (pl -ões) f contraction.

contracapa [ˌkõntra'kapa] f inside cover.

contracenar [4] [ˌkõntrase'na(x)] vi: ~ (com) to perform (with).

contracepção [ˌkõntrasep'sãw] (pl -ões) f contraception.

contraceptivo, va [ˌkõntrasep'tʃivu, va] m contraceptive.

contracheque [ˌkõntra'ʃɛki] m payslip.

contradição [ˌkõntradʒi'sãw] (pl -ões) f contradiction; **entrar** ou **cair em** ~ to contradict o.s.

contraditório, ria [ˌkõntradʒi'tɔrju, rja] adj contradictory.

contradizer [29] [ˌkõntradʒi'ze(x)] vt to contradict.
➡ **contradizer-se** vp to contradict o.s.

contrafeito, ta [ˌkõntra'fejtu, ta] adj constrained.

contrafilé [ˌkõntrafi'lɛ] m rump steak.

contragosto [kõntra'goʃtu] ➡ **a contragosto** loc adv unwillingly.

contraído, da [kõntra'idu, da] adj -1. [tenso] tense. -2. [assumido] agreed. -3. [adquirido] contracted.

contra-indicação [ˌkõntraĩndʒika'sãw] (pl contra-indicações) f [de remédio] contraindication.

contra-indicado [ˌkõntraĩndʒi'kadu] (pl contra-indicados) adj -1. [remédio] contraindicated. -2. [medida, solução] inadvisable.

contra-indicar [12] [ˌkõntraĩndʒi'ka(x)] vt to contraindicate.

contrair [68] [kõntra'i(x)] vt -1. [ger] to contract. -2. [assumir]: ~ **matrimônio** to get married; ~ **dívidas** to run up debts; ~ **compromisso** to take on responsibilities. -3. [adquirir - doenças] to catch; [- hábitos] to acquire.
➡ **contrair-se** vp [encolher-se] to contract.

contralto [kõn'trawtu] *m* **-1.** [voz] contralto. **-2.** [tom de instrumento] alto. **-3.** [cantora] contralto.

contramão [ˌkõntra'mãw] <> *adj* **-1.** [em sentido contrário] one-way. **-2.** [inconveniente] out of one's way. <> *f*: **na** ~ on the wrong side of the road.

contramestre [ˌkõntra'mɛʃtril *m* **-1.** [em fábrica *etc*] foreman. **-2.** [náut] first mate.

contra-ofensiva [ˌkõntraofẽn'sival (*pl* **contra-ofensivas**) *f* counteroffensive.

contra-oferta [ˌkõntrao'fɛxta] (*pl* **contra-ofertas**) *f* counteroffer.

contraparente [ˌkõntrapa'rẽntʃil *m* **-1.** [distante] distant relative. **-2.** [afim] in-law.

contrapartida [ˌkõntrapar'tʃida] *f* **-1.** [oposto] opposite. **-2.** [compensação]: **em** ~ in compensation.

contrapeso [ˌkõntra'pezul *m* counterbalance.

contrapor [45] [ˌkõntra'po(x)] *vt* [confrontar] to confront; ~ **algo a algo** to set sthg against sthg. ➡ **contrapor-se** *vp* [opor-se]: ~**-se a algo** to be opposed to sthg.

contraproducente [ˌkõntraprodu'sẽntʃil *adj* counterproductive.

contra-regra [ˌkõntra'xɛgra] (*pl* **contra-regras**) *mf* stage manager.

contra-revolução [ˌkõntraxevolu'sãw] (*pl* **contra-revoluções**) *f* counter-revolution.

contrariado, da [kõntra'rjadu, da] *adj* annoyed.

contrariar [16] [kõntra'rja(x)] *vt* **-1.** [vontade, interesse] to thwart. **-2.** [declaração, informação] to contradict. **-3.** [desobedecer - ordem, instrução] to disobey; [- lei] to break. **-4.** [descontentar] to annoy. ➡ **contrariar-se** *vp* **-1.** [descontentar-se] to get annoyed. **-2.** [contradizer-se] to contradict o.s.

contrariedade [kõntrarje'dadʒil *f* nuisance.

contrário, ria [kõn'trarju, rja] *adj* **-1.** [lado] opposite. **-2.** [ponto de vista, decisão] opposing; **ser** ~ **a algo** to be against sthg; **caso** ~ otherwise. ➡ **contrário** *m* opposite; **do** ~ otherwise; **pelo** *ou* **ao** ~ on the contrary; **ao** ~ [de outra maneira] the other way round; [roupa] back to front.

contra-senso [ˌkõntra'sẽnsul (*pl* **contra-sensos**) *m* nonsense (*inv*).

contrastante [kõntraʃ'tãntʃil *adj* contrasting.

contrastar [4] [kõntraʃ'ta(x)] <> *vt*: ~ **algo com algo** to contrast sthg with sthg. <> *vi* to contrast; ~ **em algo** to contrast in sthg.

contraste [kõn'traʃtʃil *m* contrast.

contratação [kõntrata'sãw] (*pl* **-ões**) *f* recruitment.

contratante [kõntra'tãntʃil <> *adj* contracting. <> *mf* contractor.

contratar [4] [kõntra'ta(x)] *vt* to recruit.

contratempo [ˌkõntra'tẽmpul *m* **-1.** [imprevisto] setback. **-2.** [dificuldade] hurdle. **-3.** [aborrecimento] upset.

contrato [kõn'tratul *m* **-1.** [documento] contract. **-2.** [acordo] agreement.

contratual [kõntra'twawl (*pl* **-ais**) *adj* contractual.

contravenção [ˌkõntravẽn'sãw] (*pl* **-ões**) *f* contravention.

contraventor, ra [ˌkõntravẽn'to(x), ral *m*, *f* offender.

contribuição [kõntribwi'sãw] (*pl* **-ões**) *f* **-1.** [ger] contribution. **-2.** [tributo - sindical] dues (*pl*); [- fiscal] tax.

contribuinte [kõntri'bwĩntʃil *m f* **-1.** [colaborador] contributor. **-2.** [aquele que paga imposto] taxpayer.

contribuir [74] [kõntri'bwi(x)] *vi* **-1.** [ger] to contribute; ~ **com algo (para algo)** [fornecer, colaborar] to contribute sthg (for/to sthg). **-2.** [ter parte em um resultado]: ~ **para algo** to contribute to sthg.

contrição [kõntri'sãw] *f* contrition.

contrito, ta [kõn'tritu, tal *adj* contrite.

controlar [4] [kõntro'la(x)] *vt* to control. ➡ **controlar-se** *vp* [dominar-se] to control o.s.

controlável [kõntro'lavewl (*pl* **-eis**) *adj* controllable.

controle [kõn'trolil *m* control; ~ **remoto** remote control.

controvérsia [kõntro'vɛrsjal *f* controversy; **em** ~ controversial.

controverso, sa [kõntro'vɛrsu, sal *adj* controversial.

contudo [kõn'tudul *conj* however.

contumácia [kõntu'masjal *f* **-1.** obstinacy. **-2.** *JUR* contempt of court.

contumaz [kõntu'majʒl *adj* obstinate.

contundente [kõntũn'dẽntʃil *adj* **-1.**: **por instrumento** ~ with a blunt instrument. **-2.** *fig* [decisivo] decisive.

contundir [5] [kõntũn'dʒi(x)] *vt* to bruise. ➡ **contundir-se** *vp* to bruise o.s.

conturbação [kõntuxba'sãw] (*pl* **-ões**) *f* **-1.** [perturbação] commotion. **-2.** [motim] riot.

conturbar [4] [kõntux'ba(x)] *vt* **-1.** [perturbar] to disturb. **-2.** [amotinar] to stir up. ➡ **conturbar-se** *vp* **-1.** [perturbar-se] to become troubled. **-2.** [amotinar-se] to rebel.

contusão [kõntu'zãwl (*pl* **-ões**) *f* bruise.

conúbio [kõ'nubjul *m* [aliança] alliance.

convalescença [kõnvaleʃ'sẽnsal *f* convalescence.

convalescente [kõnvale'sẽntʃil <> *adj* convalescent. <> *mf* convalescent patient.

convalescer [25] [kõnvale'se(x)] *vi* to convalesce.

convenção [kõnvẽn'sãw] (*pl* **-ões**) *f* convention; ~ **social** social convention.

convencer [25] [kõnvẽn'se(x)] <> *vt* [persuadir]: ~ **alguém (de algo)** to convince sb (of sthg); ~ **alguém a fazer algo** to persuade sb to do sthg. <> *vi fig* [agradar] to impress. ➡ **convencer-se** *vp* [persuadir-se]: ~**-se de algo** to convince o.s. of sthg.

convencido, da [kõnvẽn'sidu, dal *adj* **-1.** [convicto] convinced. **-2.** *fig* [presunçoso] conceited.

convencimento [kõnvẽnsi'mẽntul *m* **-1.** [convicção] conviction. **-2.** *fig* [presunção] conceit.

convencional [kõvẽnsjo'naw] (*pl* -**ais**) *adj* -**1.** [ger] conventional. -**2.** *pej* [comum] commonplace.

convencionar [4] [kõvẽnsjo'na(x)] *vt* to agree on.

conveniado, da [kõnve'njadu, da] <> *adj* associated. <> *m, f* associate.

conveniência [kõnve'njẽnsja] *f* convenience; **ser da ~ de alguém** to be suitable for sb.
➡ **conveniências** *fpl* [regras sociais] decorum; **loja de ~s** convenience store.

conveniente [kõnve'njẽntʃil] *adj* -**1.** [ger] convenient. -**2.** [oportuno] opportune.

convênio [kõ'venju] *m* -**1.** [acordo] agreement. -**2.** [entre instituições] accord.

convento [kõ'vẽntu] *m* convent.

convergência [kõnver'gẽnsja] *f* convergence.

convergente [kõnver'ʒẽntʃil] *adj* convergent.

convergir [64] [kõnvex'ʒi(x)] *vi* -**1.** [mesma direção]: **~ para** to converge on. -**2.** [ter a mesma tendência]: **~ (para)** to aim (at). -**3.** [afluir]: **~ (de/para)** to converge (from/towards).

conversa [kõn'vexsa] *f* -**1.** [diálogo] chat; **~ fiada** *ou* **mole** chit-chat. -**2.** [mentira]: **~ (fiada)** nonsense (*inv*). -**3.** *loc*: **passar uma ~ em alguém** to soft-soap sb; **ir na ~ de alguém** to be taken in by sb.

conversação [kõnvexsa'sãw] (*pl*-**ões**) *f* conversation.

conversador, deira [kõnvexsa'do(x), dejra] *adj* chatty.

conversado [kõnvex'sadu] *adj* [problema, assunto] discussed; **estamos ~s** there is nothing more to be said.

conversa-fiada [kõn‚vexsa'fjada] (*pl* **conversas-fiadas**) *mf* [pessoa] loudmouth.

conversão [kõnvex'sãw] (*pl*-**ões**) *f* conversion.

conversar [4] [kõnvex'sa(x)] *vi* to talk, to hold a conversation.

conversibilidade [kõnvexsibili'dadʒil] *f* convertibility.

conversível [kõnvex'sivew] (*pl*-**eis**) <> *adj* convertible. <> *m AUTO* convertible.

conversor [kõnvex'so(x)] *m* -**1.** [dispositivo] transformer. -**2.** *COMPUT* converter.

converter [5] [kõnvex'te(x)] *vt* -**1.** [transformar]: **~ algo/alguém em algo** to convert sthg/sb into sthg. -**2.** [trocar]: **~ algo em algo** to change sthg into sthg. -**3.** *POL & RELIG*: **~ alguém a** to convert sb to.
➡ **converter-se** *vp POL & RELIG*: **~-se (a)** to convert (to).

convertido, da [kõnvex'tʃidu, da] <> *adj* converted. <> *m, f POL & RELIG* convert.

convés [kõn'vɛʃl] (*pl*-**veses**) *m* deck.

convexo, xa [kõn'vɛksu, sa] *adj* convex.

convicção [kõnvik'sãw] (*pl*-**ões**) *f* conviction; **ter ~ de que** to be convinced that.

convicto, ta [kõn'viktu, ta] <> *adj* -**1.** [convencido] convinced. -**2.** [réu] convicted. <> *m, f* [presidiário] convict.

convidado, da [kõnvi'dadu, da] *m, f* guest.

convidar [4] [kõnvi'da(x)] <> *vt* -**1.** [ger] to invite. -**2.** *fig* [induzir]: **~ alguém a** to invite sb to. <> *vi fig* [induzir]: **~ a** to be conducive to.
➡ **convidar-se** *vp* -**1.** [invitar-se] to invite o.s. -**2.** [oferecer-se] to put o.s. forward.

convidativo, va [kõnvida'tʃivu, va] *adj* inviting.

convincente [kõnvĩ'sẽntʃil] *m* convincing.

convir [67] [kõn'vi(x)] *vi* -**1.** [concordar]: **~ (com alguém) em algo** to agree (with sb) about sthg; **você há de ~ que** you have to agree that. -**2.** [ser conveniente, proveitoso]: **~ a alguém** to be convenient for sb. -**3.** [condizer]: **~ a alguém** to be appropriate for sb.

convite [kõn'vitʃil] *m* invitation.

conviva [kõn'viva] *m f* guest.

convivência [kõnvi'vẽnsja] *f* -**1.** [convívio] closeness. -**2.** [familiaridade] familiarity.

conviver [5] [kõnvi've(x)] *vi* -**1.** [coexistir] to coexist. -**2.** [lidar]: **~ com** to cope with.

convívio [kõn'vivju] *m* [convivência] closeness.

convocação [kõnvoka'sãw] (*pl*-**ões**) *f* [chamamento] summons.

convocar [12] [kõnvo'ka(x)] *vt* -**1.** [chamar] to summon. -**2.** [reunir] to convene. -**3.** *MIL* to call up.

convosco [kõn'voʃku] *pron pess* with you.

convulsão [kõnvuw'sãw] (*pl* -**ões**) *f* -**1.** *MED* convulsion. -**2.** *fig* upheaval.

convulsionar [4] [kõnvuwsjo'na(x)] *vt* -**1.** [pôr em convulsão] to convulse. -**2.** *fig* [povo, país] to agitate.

convulsivo, va [kõnvuw'sivu, va] *adj* convulsive.

cookie [ˈkokil] (*pl* **cookies**) *m COMPUT* cookie.

cooper [ˈkupe(x)] *m* jogging; **fazer ~** to go jogging.

cooperação [kwopera'sãw] (*pl* -**ões**) *f* cooperation.

cooperante [kwope'rãntʃil] *adj* cooperative.

cooperar [4] [kwope'ra(x)] *vi*: **~ (com)** to cooperate (with).

cooperativo, va [kwopera'tʃivu, va] *adj* cooperative.
➡ **cooperativa** *f* cooperative.

coordenação [kooxdena'sãw] *f* [ato] coordination.

coordenada [kooxde'nadal] *f* -**1.** *fam* [orientação] instructions. -**2.** *GEOM* coordinate.

coordenar [koorde'na(x)] *m* to coordinate.

copa [ˈkɔpa] *f* -**1.** [cômodo] pantry. -**2.** [parte superior] crown. -**3.** *ESP* cup.
➡ **copas** *fpl* [naipe] hearts.

copeiro, ra [ko'pejro, ra] *m, f* domestic servant (*who waits at table*).

Copenhague [kõpe'nagil] *n* Copenhagen.

cópia [ˈkɔpja] *f* -**1.** [ger] copy. -**2.** [fotocópia] photocopy.

copiadora [kopja'doral] *f* -**1.** [loja] print shop. -**2.** [máquina] photocopier.

copiar [16] [ko'pja(x)] *vt* to copy.

copidescar [kopi'deʃka(x)] *vt* [revisar] to copy edit.

copidesque [kopi'dɛʃki] <> *m* [redação final] copy-editing. <> *mf* [redator] copy editor.

co-piloto, ta [kopi'lotu, ta] (*mpl* **co-pilotos**, *fpl* **co-pilotas**) *m, f* copilot.

copioso, piosa [ko'pjozu, pjɔzal *adj* -**1.** [ger] copious. -**2.** [refeição] copious.

copista [ko'piʃta] *mf* [copiador] copyist.

copo ['kɔpu] *m* -**1.** [recipiente] glass. -**2.** [conteúdo] glassful. -**3.** *loc*: **ser um bom** ~ to be a heavy drinker.

COPOM (*abrev de* **Comitê de Política Monetária**) [ko'põ] *m* [econ] Monetary Policy Committee.

cópula *f* [coito] copulation.

copular [ko'pula(x)] *vi* to copulate.

copyright [kopi'xajtʃil, **copirraite** [kopi'xajtʃil *m* copyright.

coque ['kɔki] *m* bun.

coqueiro [ko'kejru] *m* coconut palm.

coqueluche [koke'luʃil *f* -**1.** [doença] whooping cough. -**2.** *fig* [moda]: **o bambolê foi** ~ **nos anos setenta** the hula hoop was all the rage in the seventies.

coquete [ko'kɛtʃil *adj* coquettish.

coquetel [koke'tɛwl (*pl* -**éis**) *m* -**1.** [drinque] cocktail. -**2.** [festa] cocktail party.

coqueteleira [kokete'lejral *f* cocktail shaker.

cor ['ko(x)l (*pl* -**es**) *f* -**1.** [tom] colour; ~ **de burro quando foge** *hum* undefinable color. -**2.** [de pele] complexion; **ficar sem** ~ to go pale. -**3.** *fig* [feição] tone.
    ➡ **de cor** *loc adv* by heart.

coração [kora'sãw] (*pl* -**ões**) *m* [ger] heart; **abrir o** ~ [confidenciar] to open one's heart; **ter um** ~ **de ouro** [ser bondoso] to have a good heart.

corado, da [ko'radu, da] *adj* -**1.** [na face] ruddy. -**2.** [avermelhado] reddish. -**3.** *fig* [envergonhado] shamefaced. -**4.** *CULIN* sautéed.

coragem [ko'raʒẽl *f* courage.

corajoso, osa [kora'ʒozu, ɔza] *adj* courageous.

coral [ko'rawl (*pl* -**ais**) <> *m* -**1.** [ger] coral. -**2.** *MÚS* choir. <> *f* [cobra] coral snake. <> *adj* coral.

corante [ko'rãntʃil <> *adj* colouring. <> *m* dye.

corar [4] [ko'ra(x)l <> *vt CULIN* to brown. <> *vi* [enrubescer] to blush.

corcova [kox'kɔval *f* hump.

corcunda [kox'kũndal <> *adj* hunchbacked. <> *mf* hunchback.

corda ['kɔrdal *f* -**1.** [ger] spring; **dar** ~ **em** to wind up. -**2.** [fio] rope; **pular** ~ skipping. -**3.** [varal] clothesline. -**4.** *loc*: **dar** ~ **para alguém** *fig* [alimentar a conversa] to get sb going; [flertar] to flirt with sb; **estar com a** ~ **toda** *fig* to be really wound up.
    ➡ **cordas** *fpl* -**1.** *ANAT*: ~**s vocais** vocal cords. -**2.** *MÚS*: **quarteto de** ~**s** string quartet.

cordão [kor'dãwl (*pl* -**ões**) *m* -**1.** [corda fina] twine. -**2.** [jóia] chain. -**3.** [cadarço] shoelace. -**4.** [bloco carnavalesco] carnival block. -**5.** *ANAT*: ~ **umbilical** umbilical cord.

cordato, ta [kox'datu, ta] *adj* sensible.

cordeiro [kor'dejru] *m* lamb.
    ➡ **cordeiros** *mpl fig* [seguidores] disciples.

cordel [kor'dɛwl (*pl* -**éis**) *m* -**1.** [barbante] string. -**2.** *LITER*: **(literatura de)** ~ popular Brazilian literature.

> **CORDEL**
>
> A popular form of literature, typical of the north-east of Brazil; the *cordel* ('string') consists of a small booklet, made up usually of a single sheet of paper folded over three times, to make eight pages. The *cordel* tells stories, in verse, of the people of the north-east. In order to sell these booklets in the street or at fairs, it is customary to hang them up with pieces of twine, hence the name *cordel*.

cor-de-rosa [ˌkordʒi'xɔzal <> *adj* -**1.** [cor] pink. -**2.** *fig* [feliz] rose-tinted. <> *m* [cor] pink.

cordial [kor'dʒjawl (*pl* -**ais**) *adj* -**1.** [gentil] cordial. -**2.** [afetuoso] warm.

cordialidade [koxdʒjali'dadʒil *f* -**1.** [gentileza] cordiality. -**2.** [afeição] warmth.

cordilheira [koxdʒi'ʎejral *f* mountain range.

cordões *pl* ➡ **cordão**.

coreano, na [ko'rjãnu, nal <> *adj* Korean. <> *m, f* Korean.

Coréia *n* Korea; ~ **do Norte** North Korea; ~ **do Sul** South Korea.

coreografia [korjogra'fial *f* choreography.

coreógrafo, fa [ko'rjɔgrafu, fal *m, f* choreographer.

coreto [ko'retul *m* bandstand.

corisco [ko'riʃkul *m* -**1.** [ger] flash. -**2.** *fig* bright spark.

corista [ko'riʃta] *m, f* -**1.** [em coro] chorister. -**2.** [vedete] chorus girl.

coriza [ko'rizal *f* runny nose.

corja ['kɔxʒal *f* gang.

córnea [ko'xnjal *f* cornea.

cornear [15] [kox'nja(x)l *vt* -**1.** [com os chifres] to gore. -**2.** *fam* [trair] to two-time.

córner ['kɔxne(x)l *m* corner (kick).

corneta [kox'netal *f* cornet.

corneteiro, ra [koxne'tejru, ral *m, f* bugler.

cornija [kox'niʒal *f* [em parede] cornice.

corno ['kɔxnul *m* -**1.** [de animal] horn. -**2.** *vulg* [pessoa] cuckold.

cornudo, da [kox'nudu, dal <> *adj* [animal] horned.
    ➡ **cornudo** *m vulg* [pessoa] cuckold.

coro ['korul *m* -**1.** [ger] chorus; **em** ~ in chorus. -**2.** [cantores] choir. -**3.** [balcão] organ loft.

coroa [ko'roal <> *f* -**1.** [ger] crown. -**2.** [de flores] garland. -**3.** [calvície] bald spot. <> *mf* [pessoa] *fam* old fogey.

coroação [korwa'sãwl (*pl* -**ões**) *f* coronation.

coroar [20] [koro'a(x)l *vt* -**1.** [ger] to crown. -**2.** [premiar] to reward.

coroinha *m* altar server.

corolário [koro'larjul *m* corollary.

coronário, ria [koro'narju, rjal *adj* coronary.

coronel [koro'nɛwl (*pl* -**éis**) *m* -**1.** *MIL* colonel. -**2.** *POL* political baron.

coronha [ko'roɲa] *f* butt.

coronhada [koro'ɲada] *f* blow with a rifle butt.

corpete [kox'petʃi] *m* bodice.

corpo ['koxpu] *m* -1. [ger] body; ~ **de baile** dance group; ~ **de bombeiros** fire department; ~ **diplomático** diplomatic corps; ~ **docente** faculty; [tronco] trunk; [carne] flesh; [formas] body. -2. [cadáver] corpse, body. -3. [consistência]: **tomar** ~ to thicken. -4. *JUR*: ~ **de delito** material fact. -5. *MED*: ~ **estranho** foreign body. -6. *loc*: **fazer** ~ **mole** to skulk; **tirar o** ~ **fora** to duck out.

corporação [koxpora'sãw] (*pl* -ões) *f* corporation.

corporal [koxpo'raw] (*pl* -ais) *adj* corporal.

corporativismo [koxporatʃi'viʒmu] *m* corporatism.

corporativista [koxporatʃi'viʃta] <> *adj* [relativo ao corporativismo] corporate. <> *mf* [partidário] corporatist.

corporativo, va [koxpo'ratʃivu, va] *adj* corporative.

corpulência [koxpu'lẽnsja] *f* corpulence.

corpulento, ta [koxpu'lẽntu, ta] *adj* corpulent.

correção [koxe'sãw] (*pl* -ões) *f* -1. [ato] marking; ~ **monetária** inflationary adjustment. -2. [qualidade] exactness.

corre-corre [kɔxi'kɔxi] *m* mad rush.

corredor, ra [koxe'do(x), ra] (*mpl* -es, *fpl* -s) *m, f* [atleta] runner.
 ◆ **corredor** *m* [passagem - em casa] corridor; [- em avião, etc] aisle.

córrego ['kɔxegu] *m* brook.

correia [ko'xeja] *f* -1. [tira] strap. -2. [em máquina] belt. -3. [em carro] fan belt.

correio [ko'xeju] *m* -1. [serviço] mail. -2. [correspondência] post; **agência dos** ~**s** post office. -3. *fig* [carteiro] postman *UK*, mailman *US*. -4. *COMPUT*: ~ **eletrônico** email.

correlação [koxela'sãw] (*pl* -ões) *f* correlation.

correlacionar [koxelasjo'na(x)] *vt* to correlate.
 ◆ **correlacionar-se** *vp* to correlate.

correligionário, ria [koxeliʒjo'narju, rja] <> *adj* partisan. <> *m, f* -1. *POL* fellow party member. -2. *RELIG* coreligionist.

corrente [ko'xẽntʃi] <> *adj* -1. [atual] current. -2. [comum] common. -3. [fluente - língua] fluent; [- estilo] flowing. -4. [água] running. <> *f* -1. [ger] current; ~ **marítima** marine current; **remar contra a** ~ *fig* to swim against the tide. -2. [corrente] chain. -3. [vento]: ~ **de ar** draught.

correnteza [koxẽn'teza] *f* current.

correntista [koxẽn'tʃiʃta] *mf* account holder.

correr [5] [ko'xe(x)] <> *vi* -1. [ger] to run. -2. [passar] to fly past. -3. [circular] to circulate. -4. [espalhar-se] to spread. -5. [despesas]: ~ **por conta de alguém** to go on sb's tab. <> *vt* -1. [percorrer]: ~ **a fazenda** to go all over sthg. -2. [passar de leve] to run. -3. [olhar rapidamente]: **corri os olhos pela revista** I ran my eyes over the magazine. -4. [estar exposto a]: ~ **o risco de algo** to run the risk of sthg.

correria [koxe'ria] *f* rushing about.

correspondência [koxeʃpõn'dẽnsja] *f* correspondence.

correspondente [koxeʃpõn'dẽntʃil] <> *adj* corresponding. <> *mf* correspondent; ~ **de guerra** war correspondent.

corresponder [5] [koxeʃpõn'de(x)] *vi* -1. [ger]: ~ **a** to correspond to. -2. [retribuir]: ~ **a** to reciprocate.
 ◆ **corresponder-se** *vp* to correspond with.

corretagem [koxe'taʒẽ] *f* -1. [atividade] brokerage. -2. [remuneração] commission.

corretamente [ko,xeta'mẽntʃi] *adv* correctly.

corretivo, va [koxe'tʃivu, va] *adj* [que corrige] corrective.
 ◆ **corretivo** *m* [castigo] punishment.

correto, ta [ko'xɛtu, ta] *adj* -1. [ger] correct. -2. [íntegro] honest.

corretor, ra [koxe'to(x), ra] (*mpl* -es, *fpl* -s) *m, f* [agente] broker; ~ **de imóveis** estate agent *UK*, realtor *US*; ~ **de Bolsa** stockbroker.
 ◆ **corretora** *f* [instituição] agency.

corrida [ko'xida] *f* -1. [ato] running. -2. *ESP* racing. -3. [de táxi] fare.

corrido, da [ko'xidu, da] *adj* [rápido] rushed.

corrigir [52] [koxi'ʒi(x)] *vt* -1. [retificar] to correct. -2. [eliminar] to repair. -3. [repreender] to tell off. -4. [atenuar] to attenuate.
 ◆ **corrigir-se** *vp* [emendar-se] to correct o.s.

corrimão [koxi'mãw] (*pl* -ãos, -ões) *m* handrail.

corrimento [koxi'mẽntu] *m* discharge.

corriqueiro, ra [koxi'kejru, ra] *adj* everyday.

corroborar [4] [koxobo'ra(x)] *vt* to corroborate.

corroer [28] [koxo'e(x)] *vt* -1. [carcomer] to eat away. -2. [danificar] to corrode. -3. *fig* [depravar] to undermine.

corromper [5] [koxõn'pe(x)] *vt* -1. [perverter] to pervert. -2. [subornar] to corrupt. -3. [adulterar] to tamper with.
 ◆ **corromper-se** *vp* [perverter-se] to become corrupt.

corrompido, da [koxõn'pidu, da] *adj* [pervertido] corrupted; **arquivo** ~ *COMPUT* corrupted file.

corrosão [koxo'sãw] (*pl* -ões) *f* -1. [de metais] corrosion. -2. *GEOL* erosion.

corrosivo, va [koxo'zivu, va] *adj* corrosive.

corrupção [koxup'sãw] (*pl* -ões) *f* -1. [perversão] pervertion. -2. [suborno] corruption.

corrupto, ta [ko'xuptu, ta] *adj* corrupt.

Córsega ['kɔxsega] *n* Corsica.

cortada [kox'tada] *f* *ESP* smash; **dar uma** ~ to smash the ball; **dar uma** ~ **em alguém** *fig* to cut sb short.

cortado, da [kox'tadu, da] *adj* -1. [ger] cut. -2. [relações] severed. -3. *fig* [coração] broken.
 ◆ **cortado** *m* *fig* [apuro] struggle.

cortador [koxta'do(x)] *m* cutter.

cortante [kox'tãntʃil] *adj* -1. [ger] cutting. -2. [que corta] sharp.

cortar [4] [kox'ta(x)] <> *vt* -1. [ger] to cut. -2. [árvore] to cut down. -3. [suprimir] to cut out. -4. *AUTO* to stall. **-5.** [interromper] to interrupt. **-6.** [pôr fim a] to end. **-7.** [encurtar]: ~ **caminho** to take a short cut. ◇ *vi* **-1.** [ter bom gume] to cut. **-2.** *ESP* to smash the ball.

➤ **cortar-se** *vp* [ferir-se] to cut o.s.

corte¹ ['kɔxtʃi] *m* **-1.** [ger] cut. **-2.** [gume] cutting edge; **ter bom** ~ to be sharp; **estar sem** ~ to be blunt. **-3.** [porção de tecido]: ~ **de algo** length of sthg. **-4.** *ELETR*: ~ **de luz** power cut.

corte² ['kɔxtʃi] *f* **-1.** [ger] court. **-2.** *fig* [de admiradores *etc*] entourage. **-3.** [cortejar]: **fazer a** ~ **a alguém** to court sb.

cortejar [4] [koxte'ʒa(x)] *vt* to court.

cortejo [kox'teʒu] *m* **-1.** [séquito] cortege. **-2.** [procissão] procession.

cortês [kox'teʃ] *adj* polite.

cortesão, sã [koxte'zãw, zã] (*mpl* **-ãos, -ões**, *fpl* **-s**) ◇ *adj* courtly. ◇ *m, f* courtier. ◇ *f* courtesan.

cortesia [koxte'zia] *f* **-1.** [delicadeza] courtesy. **-2.** [presente] complimentary gift. **-3.** [mesura] bow.

cortiça [kox'tʃisa] *f* cork.

cortiço [kox'tʃisu] *m* **-1.** [para abelhas] beehive. **-2.** [habitação] slum dwelling.

cortina [kox'tʃina] *f* **-1.** [peça] curtain. **-2.** *fig* [nuvem] screen.

cortisona [koxtʃi'zona] *f* cortisone.

coruja [ko'ruʒa] ◇ *f* *ZOOL* owl. ◇ *adj* [pai, mãe] doting.

corvo ['koxvu] *m* crow.

cós ['kɔʃ] *m inv* **-1.** [tira de pano] waistband. **-2.** [cintura] waist.

coser [5] [ko'ze(x)] ◇ *vt* to stitch. ◇ *vi* to sew.

cosmético, ca [koʒ'mɛtʃiku, ka] *adj* cosmetic.

➤ **cosmético** *m* cosmetic.

cósmico, ca ['kɔʒmiku, ka] *adj* cosmic.

cosmo ['kɔʒmu] *m* cosmos.

cosmonauta [koʒmo'nawta] *mf* cosmonaut.

cosmopolita [koʒmopo'lita] ◇ *adj* cosmopolitan. ◇ *mf* [pessoa] cosmopolitan person.

costa ['kɔʃta] *f* [litoral] coast.

costado [koʃ'tadu] *m NÁUT* [forro] hull cladding.

Costa do Marfim [ˌkɔʃtadumax'fĩ] *n* Ivory Coast.

Costa Rica [ˌkɔʃta'xika] *n* Costa Rica.

costa-riquense [ˌkɔʃtaxi'kẽnsi], **costarriquenho, nha** [ˌkɔʃtaxi'kẽɲu, ɲa] ◇ *adj* Costa Rican. ◇ *m, f* Costa Rican.

costas ['kɔʃtaʃ] *fpl* **-1.** [ger] back. **-2.** [encosto] backrest. **-3.** *loc*: **carregar nas** ~ *fig* to shoulder the burden; **ter** ~ **quentes** *fig* to be under sb's wing.

costela [koʃ'tɛla] *f* rib.

costeleta [koʃte'leta] *f* **-1.** *CULIN* chop. **-2.** [suíças] sideburns.

costumar [4] [koʃtu'ma(x)] *vt* **-1.** [ter o hábito de]: ~ **fazer algo** to be in the habit of doing sthg; **costumo correr todas as manhãs** I usually go running every morning. **-2.** [habituar] to accustom.

costume [koʃ'tumi] *m* **-1.** [hábito] habit; **ter o** ~ **de**

fazer algo to be in the habit of doing sthg; **como de** ~ as usual. **-2.** [roupa] costume.

➤ **costumes** *mpl* [de um povo] customs.

costumeiro, ra [koʃtu'mejru, ra] *adj* usual, customary.

costura [koʃ'tura] *f* **-1.** [ger] sewing; **alta** ~ haute couture. **-2.** [linha de junção] seam.

costurar [4] [koʃtu'ra(x)] ◇ *vt* **-1.** *COST* to stitch. **-2.** *fig* [texto] to tidy up. ◇ *vi* **-1.** *COST* to sew. **-2.** *fam AUTO* to weave in and out.

costureira [koʃtu'rejra] *f* seamstress.

costureiro [koʃtu'rejru] *m* [estilista] couturier.

cota ['kɔta] *f* **-1.** [quinhão] quota. **-2.** [prestação, parcela] instalment.

cotação [kota'sãw] (*pl* **-ões**) *f* **-1.** [ato] quoting. **-2.** [preço] quote. **-3.** *fig* [possibilidade de êxito] chance. **-4.** *fig* [conceito] reputation.

cotado, da [ko'tadu, da] *adj* **-1.** [com bom preço] well priced. **-2.** *fig* [favorito] favourite. **-3.** *fig* [conceituado] respected. **-4.** [avaliado] valued.

cotar [4] [ko'ta(x)] *vt* **-1.** [ger] to quote. **-2.** [avaliar]: ~ **algo/alguém em** to value sthg/sb at.

cotejar [4] [kote'ʒa(x)] *vt* to compare.

cotejo [ko'teʒu] *m* comparison.

cotidiano, na [kotʃi'dʒianu, na] *adj* everyday.

➤ **cotidiano** *m* routine.

cotizar [4] [kotʃi'za(x)] *vt* **-1.** [distribuir por cotas] to allocate. **-2.** [cotar] to value, to assess.

➤ **cotizar-se** *vp* to club together.

coto *m* **-1.** [mus] koto. **-2.** [zool] feather follicle.

cotonete [koto'nɛʃi] *m* cotton bud.

cotovelada [kotove'lada] *f* **-1.** [batida] hefty nudge. **-2.** [cutucada] nudge.

cotovelo [koto'velu] *m* **-1.** *ANAT* elbow; **falar pelos** ~**s** *fig* to talk non-stop. **-2.** [de estrada *etc*] bend.

couraça [ko'rasa] *f* **-1.** [armadura] breastplate. **-2.** [de animal] plating. **-3.** *NÁUT* armour plate.

couraçado, da [kora'sadu, da] *adj* [que tem couraça] armoured.

➤ **couraçado** *m NÁUT* battleship.

couro ['koru] *m* **-1.** [de animal] hide; [curtido] leather; ~ **cru** rawhide; **de** ~ leather. **-2.** [humano]: ~ **cabeludo** scalp. **-3.** *loc*: **não dar no** ~ to underperform.

couve ['kovi] *f* spring greens.

couve-de-bruxelas [ˌkovidʒibru'ʃɛlaʃ] (*pl* **couves-de-bruxelas**) *f* Brussels sprout.

couve-flor [ˌkovi'flo(x)] (*pl* **couves-flores**) *f* cauliflower.

couvert [ko'vɛ(x)] *m* cover charge.

cova ['kɔva] *f* **-1.** [sepultura] grave. **-2.** [caverna] cavern. **-3.** [buraco] hole.

covarde [ko'vaxdʒi] ◇ *adj* cowardly. ◇ *mf* coward.

covardia [kovax'dʒia] *f* cowardice.

coveiro [ko'vejru] *m* gravedigger.

covil [ko'viw] (*pl* **-is**) *m* **-1.** [ger] den. **-2.** *fig* [casebre] hovel.

covinha [ko'viɲa] *f* dimple.

coxa ['koʃa] *f ANAT* thigh; ~ **de galinha** *CULIN*

chicken drumstick; **fazer (algo) nas** ~s *vulg* to do it any old how.

coxear [15] [ko'ʃja(x)] *vi* to limp.

coxia [ko'ʃial] *f* aisle.

coxo, xa ['koʃu, ʃal *adj* -1. [ger] lame. -2. [móvel] wobbly *(on account of having one leg shorter than the others)*.

cozer [5] [ko'ze(x)] *vt* to cook.

cozido, da [ko'zidu, dal *adj* cooked.

➡ **cozido** *m* stew.

cozinha [ko'ziɲal *f* -1. [cômodo] kitchen. -2. [arte] cookery; ~ **brasileira** Brazilian cuisine; **aula/livro de** ~ cookery class/book.

cozinhar [4] [kozi'ɲa(x)] <> *vt* -1. [cozer] to cook. -2. *fig* [adiar] to put off. <> *vi* to cook.

cozinheiro, ra [kozi'ɲejru, ral *m, f* cook.

CPD (*abrev de* **Centro de Processamento de Dados**) *m* data-processing department.

CPF (*abrev de* **Cadastro de Pessoa Física**) *m Brazilian tax-payer's identity card for individual contributions*, ≃ NI number *UK*, ≃ social security number *US*.

CPMF (*abrev de* **Contribuição Provisória sobre Movimentação Financeira**) *f Brazilian tax on bank transactions*.

crachá [kra'ʃal *m* badge.

crack[1] ['krakil *m* crack (cocaine).

crack[2] ['krakil (*pl* **cracks**) *m COMPUT* hack.

cracker (*pl* **crackers**) *m COMPUT* hacker.

crânio ['krãnjul *m* -1. *ANAT* skull. -2. *fam* [gênio]: **ser um** ~ to be a brainbox.

crápula ['krapulal *mf* villain.

craque ['krakil <> *mf* [pessoa exímia]: **ser um** ~ **em algo** to be an expert in sthg. <> *m FUT* football star *UK*, soccer star *US*.

crase ['krazil *f LING* crasis.

crasso, ssa ['krasu, sal *adj* -1. [grosseiro] crass. -2. [espesso] viscous.

cratera [kra'tɛral *f* crater.

cravar [4] [kra'va(x)] *vt* -1. [fazer penetrar] to drive in. -2. [engastar] to set. -3. *fig* [fixar]: ~ **os olhos em alguém** to stare at sb.

cravejar [4] [krave'ʒa(x)] *vt* -1. [com cravos] to nail. -2. [com pedras preciosas] to set.

cravo ['kravul *m* -1. [flor] carnation. -2. [prego] nail. -3. *MÚS* harpsichord. -4. [especiaria] clove. -5. [na pele] blackhead.

crawl ['krɔwl *m ESP* crawl.

creche ['krɛʃil *f* crèche.

credenciais [kredẽnsi'ajʃl *fpl* [qualificações] credentials.

credenciamento [kredẽnsia'mẽntul *m* accreditation.

credenciar [16] [kredẽn'sja(x)] *vt* -1. [dar credenciais a] to accredit. -2. [habilitar] to qualify.

➡ **credenciar-se** *vp JORN* to be accredited.

crediário [kre'dʒjarjul *m* hire purchase.

credibilidade [kredʒibili'dadʒil *f* credibility.

creditar [4] [kredʒi'ta(x)] *vt* -1. [depositar] to deposit. -2. [inscrever como credor]: ~ **alguém em** to credit sb with. -3. [atribuir]: ~ **algo a algo/**

alguém to put sthg down to sb/sthg.

crédito ['krɛdʒitul *m* -1. [ger] credit; **digno de** ~ creditworthy. -2. *FIN* credit; **venda a** ~ sale on credit. -3. [boa reputação] credibility.

credo ['krɛdul *m* -1. [crença] belief. -2. [reza]: **o Credo** the Creed.

credor, ra [kre'do(x), ral (*mpl* -es, *fpl* -s) <> *adj* -1. *FIN* credit (*antes de subst*). -2. [merecedor] deserving. <> *m, f FIN* creditor.

credulidade [kreduli'dadʒil *f* credulity.

crédulo, ula ['krɛdulu, lal <> *adj* gullible. <> *m, f* gullible person.

cremação [krema'sãwl (*pl* -ões) *f* cremation.

cremar [4] [kre'ma(x)] *vt* to cremate.

crematório [krema'tɔrjul *m* crematorium.

creme ['kremil <> *adj inv* [cor] cream. <> *m* -1. [ger] cream; ~ **de leite** dairy cream; ~ **chantilly** whipped cream. -2. [cosmético] face cream. -3. [pasta]: ~ **dental** toothpaste. -4. [flavour]: **sorvete de** ~ vanilla ice cream.

cremoso, osa [kre'mozu, ɔzal *adj* creamy.

crença ['krẽnsal *f* -1. *RELIG* belief. -2. [convicção] conviction.

crendice [krẽn'dʒiʃil *f* superstition.

crente ['krẽntʃil <> *adj* -1. [que tem fé] believing. -2. [protestante] Protestant. -3. [convencido]: **estar** ~ **que** to be sure that. <> *mf* -1. [quem tem fé] believer. -2. [protestante] Protestant.

crepitação [krepita'sãwl (*pl* -ões) *f* crackling.

crepitante [krepi'tãntʃil *adj* crackling.

crepitar [4] [krepi'ta(x)] *vi* to crackle.

crepom [kre'põl <> *adj* [papel] crêpe. <> *m* [tecido] crêpe.

crepuscular [krepuʃku'la(x)] *adj* twilight.

crepúsculo [kre'puʃkulul *m* -1. [ao amanhecer] dawn. -2. [ao anoitecer] dusk. -3. *fig* [declínio] twilight.

crer [37] ['kre(x)] <> *vt* [ger] to believe. <> *vi* [acreditar]: ~ **em** to believe in.

crescendo [kre'sẽndul *m* crescendo.

crescente [kre'sẽntʃil <> *adj* -1. [tamanho] growing. -2. [formato] crescent. <> *m* [fase da lua] crescent moon.

crescer [4] [kre'se(x)] *vi* -1. [aumentar] to grow. -2. *CULIN* to rise.

crescido, da [kre'sidu, dal *adj* grown-up.

crescimento [kresi'mẽntul *m* growth.

crespo, pa ['kreʃpu, pal *adj* -1. [anelado] curly. -2. [áspero] rough.

Creta ['krɛtal *n* Crete.

cretinice [kretʃi'nisil *f* stupidity.

cretino, na [kre'tʃinu, nal <> *adj* cretinous. <> *m, f* cretin.

cria ['krial *f* offspring (*inv*).

criação [krja'sãwl (*pl* -ões) *f* -1. [ger] creation. -2. [de animais] raising. -3. [de filhos] upbringing.

➡ **de criação** *loc adj* adopted.

criado-mudo [ˌkrjadu'mudul (*pl* **criados-mudos**) *m* bedside table.

criador, ra [kria'do(x), ral (*mpl* -es, *fpl* -s) <> *adj* creative. <> *m, f* -1. [autor] creator. -2. [de animais] breeder.

➡ **Criador** m [Deus]**: o Criador** the Creator.
criança [kri'ãnsa] f **-1.** [infante] child. **-2.** [pessoa infantil] child.
criançada [krjãn'sada] f: **a** ~ the kids (pl).
criancice [krjãn'sisi] f childishness.
criar [16] [kri'a(x)] vt **-1.** [produzir] to create. **-2.** [fundar] to found. **-3.** [educar] to bring up. **-4.** [animais] to raise. **-5.** [plantas] to cultivate.
➡ **criar-se** vp [educar-se] to grow up.
criatividade [kriatʃivi'dadʒi] f creativity.
criativo, va [kria'tʃivu, va] adj creative.
criatura [kria'tura] f creature.
crime ['krimi] m crime.
criminal [krimi'naw] (pl -ais) adj criminal.
criminalidade [kriminali'dadʒi] f criminality.
criminalista [krimina'liʃta] m f criminologist.
criminoso, osa [krimi'nozu, ɔza] <> adj criminal. <> m, f criminal.
crina ['krina] f mane.
crioulo, la ['krjolu, la] <> adj **-1.** [comida, dialeto] Creole. **-2.** [negro] black. <> m, f [pessoa negra] black person.
cripta ['kripta] f crypt.
criptografar [kriptogra'fa(x)] vt COMPUT to encrypt.
criptografia [kriptogra'fia] f COMPUT cryptography.
críquete ['kriketʃi] m cricket.
crisântemo [kri'zãntemu] m chrysanthemum.
crise ['krizi] f **-1.** MED attack. **-2.** [escassez] shortage. **-3.** [fase difícil] crisis. **-4.** fig [acesso] fit; **ter uma** ~ to have a fit.
crisma ['kriʒma] f confirmation.
crismar [kriʒ'ma(x)] vt REL to confirm.
crista ['kriʃta] f **-1.** [de galo] comb. **-2.** [cume] crest.
cristal [kriʃ'taw] (pl -ais) m crystal.
cristaleira [kriʃta'lejra] f display cabinet.
cristalino, na [kriʃta'linu, na] adj crystalline.
cristalização [kriʃtaliza'sãw] (pl -ões) f crystallization.
cristalizar [4] [kriʃtali'za(x)] <> vt [tornar cristalino] to crystallize. <> vi [tornar-se cristalino] to crystallize.
➡ **cristalizar-se** vp [consolidar-se] to crystallize.
cristandade [kriʃtãn'dadʒi] f Christianity.
cristão, ã [kriʃ'tãw, ã] <> adj Christian. <> mf Christian.
cristianismo [kriʃtjã'niʒmu] m Christianity.
cristo ['kriʃtu] m fig [vítima] victim.
Cristo ['kriʃtu] m Christ.
critério [kri'tɛrju] m criterion.
criterioso, osa [krite'rjozu, ɔza] adj selective.
criticar [12] [kritʃi'ka(x)] vt **-1.** [censurar] to criticize. **-2.** [analisar] to review.
crítico, ca ['kritʃiku, ka] <> adj critical. <> m, f [pessoa] critic.
➡ **crítica** f **-1.** [censura] criticism (inv); **ser alvo de** ~s to be criticized. **-2.** [análise] review. **-3.** [os críticos]: **a** ~ critics (pl).
crivar [4] [kri'va(x)] vt **-1.** [com balas, facadas] to

riddle. **-2.** [fig] [com perguntas] to bombard.
crível ['krivew] (pl -eis) adj believable.
crivo ['krivu] m **-1.** [peneira] sieve. **-2.** fig [escrutínio] scrutiny.
Croácia [kro'asja] n Croatia.
croata [kro'ata] <> adj Croat. <> mf Croat.
crocante [kro'kãntʃi] adj crunchy.
crochê [kro'ʃe] m crochet.
crocodilo [kroko'dʒilu] m crocodile.
cromado, da [kro'madu, da] adj chromium-plated.
cromo ['kromu] m chrome.
cromossomo [kromo'somu] m [genética] chromosome.
cromoterapia [ˌkromotera'pia] f colour therapy.
crônica ['kronika] f **-1.** HIST & LITER chronicle. **-2.** JORN column.
crônico, ca ['kroniku, ka] adj **-1.** [ger] chronic. **-2.** [inveterado] inveterate.
cronista [kro'niʃta] m f **-1.** HIST & LITER chronicler. **-2.** JORN columnist.
cronograma [krono'grãma] m schedule.
cronologia [kronolo'ʒia] f chronology.
cronológico, ca [krono'lɔʒiku, ka] adj chronological.
cronometrar [4] [kronome'tra(x)] vt to time.
cronômetro [kro'nometru] m stopwatch.
croquete [kro'kɛtʃi] m croquette.
croqui [kro'ki] m sketch.
crosta ['kroʃta] f **-1.** [de pão, terra] crust. **-2.** [de ferida] scab.
cru, crua ['kru, 'krua] adj **-1.** [não cozido] raw. **-2.** [não refinado] crude. **-3.** fig [duro] harsh.
crucial [kru'sjaw] (pl -ais) adj **-1.** [ger] crucial. **-2.** [difícil] important.
crucificação [krusifika'sãw] (pl -ões) f RELIG: **a** ~ the Crucifixion.
crucificar [12] [krusifi'ka(x)] vt to crucify.
crucifixo [krusi'fiksu] m crucifix.
cruel [kru'ɛw] (pl -éis) adj **-1.** [perverso] cruel. **-2.** [doloroso] cruel. **-3.** [violento] violent.
crueldade [kruew'dadʒi] f cruelty.
cruento, ta [kru'ẽntu, ta] adj bloody.
crustáceos [kruʃ'tasjuʃ] mpl crustacea (pl).
cruz ['kruʃ] (pl -es ['kruziʃ]) f cross.
➡ **Cruz Vermelha** f Red Cross.
cruzada [kru'zada] f crusade.
cruzado, da [kru'zadu, da] adj crossed.
➡ **cruzado** m [moeda] cruzado (former Brazilian currency).
cruzador [kruza'do(x)] m NÁUT cruiser.
cruzamento [kruza'mẽntu] m **-1.** [de estradas] junction. **-2.** [de raças] crossbreeding.
cruzar [4] [kru'za(x)] <> vt **-1.** [ger] to cross. **-2.** [animais] to crossbreed. <> vi **-1.** [rua]: ~ **com** to intersect. **-2.** [navio] to cruise. **-3.** fig [encontrar]: ~ **com alguém** to bump into sb.
➡ **cruzar-se** vp [encontrar-se] to bump into each other.
cruzeiro [kru'zejru] m **-1.** NÁUT cruise. **-2.** [moeda]

cruzeiro *(former Brazilian currency)*.

CTI *(abrev de* **Centro de Terapia Intensiva)** *m* ICU.

cu ['ku] *m vulg* arse; **fazer ~-doce** to act cool; **~ -do-mundo** arsehole.

cuba ['kuba] *f* vat.

Cuba ['kuba] *n* Cuba.

cubano, na ['kubãnu, na] <> *adj* Cuban. <> *m,* *f* Cuban.

cúbico, ca ['kubiku, ka] *adj* cubic.

cubículo [ku'bikulu] *m* cubicle.

cubismo [ku'biʒmu] *m* cubism.

cubista [ku'biʃta] <> *adj* cubist. <> *mf* cubist.

cubo ['kubu] *m* **-1.** [ger] cube. **-2.** GEOM hexahedron. **-3.** MAT cube. **-4.** AUTO: **~ de roda** wheel hub.

cuca ['kuka] *fam f* **-1.** [cabeça] head. **-2.** [mente] intellect; **fundir a ~** [baratinar] to do one's head in; [confundir] to addle one's brain. **-3.** CULIN sponge cake.

cuca-fresca [ˌkuka'freʃka] *(pl* **cucas-frescas)** *mf fam* cool person.

cuco ['kuku] *m* **-1.** [ave] cuckoo. **-2.** [relógio] cuckoo clock.

cucuia [ku'kuja] *f fam*: **ir para a ~** to go out the window.

cu-de-ferro [ˌkudʒi'fɛxu] *(pl* **cus-de-ferro)** *fam* <> *adj* anal-retentive. <> *mf* anal-retentive.

cueca ['kwɛka] *f* underpants *(pl)*.

cueiro [ku'ejru] *m* nappy *UK*, diaper *US*.

Cuiabá [kuja'ba] *n* Cuiabá.

cuíca ['kwika] *f* cuíca, *an instrument resembling a drum whose sound is produced by vibrating a cord on the inside.*

cuidado, da [kwi'dadu, da] *adj* [tratado]: **bem/mal ~** well/badly cared for.

➤ **cuidado** *m* **-1.** [ger] care; **~!** careful! **-2.** [encargo]: **sob os ~s de** in the care of.

cuidadoso, osa [kwida'dozu, ɔza] *adj* careful.

cuidar [4] [kwi'da(x)] *vi* [tratar]: **~ de alguém/algo** to take care of sb/sthg.

➤ **cuidar-se** *vp* **-1.** [tratar-se] to take care of o.s. **-2.** [prevenir-se] to be careful.

cujo, ja ['kuʒu, ʒa] *pron rel* **-1.** [de quem] whose. **-2.** [de que] whose.

culatra [ku'latra] *f* gun breech.

culinário, ria [kuli'narju, rja] *adj* culinary.

➤ **culinária** *f* cookery.

culminante [kuwmi'nãntʃi] *adj* culminating.

culminar [4] [kuwmi'na(x)] *vi*: **~ com algo** to culminate with sthg.

culote [ku'lɔtʃi] *m* **-1.** [calça] jodphurs *(pl)*. **-2.** [nas coxas] big thighs *(pl)*.

culpa ['kuwpa] *f* **-1.** [falta] fault; **pôr a ~ em** to blame; **ter ~ de** to be to blame for. **-2.** JUR guilt.

culpabilidade [kuwpabili'dadʒil] *f* guilt.

culpado, da [kuw'padu, da] <> *adj* guilty. <> *m,* *f* criminal.

culpar [4] [kuw'pa(x)] *vt*: **~ alguém (de)** [atribuir a culpa] to blame sb (for); [acusar] to accuse sb (of).

➤ **culpar-se** *vp* to take the blame o.s.

cultivar [4] [kuwtʃi'va(x)] *vt* to cultivate.

➤ **cultivar-se** *vp* [instruir-se] to cultivate one's mind.

cultivável [kuwtʃi'vavewl] *(pl* **-eis)** *adj* arable.

cultivo [kuw'tʃivul] *m* cultivation.

culto, ta ['kuwtu, ta] *adj* **-1.** [instruído] well educated. **-2.** [civilizado] civilized.

➤ **culto** *m* **-1.** RELIG ritual. **-2.** [veneração] worship.

cultura [kuw'tural] *f* **-1.** [conhecimento] culture. **-2.** [civilização] civilization. **-3.** [cultivo] culture. **-4.** [criação - de animais] breeding; [- de germes, bactérias] culture.

cultural [kuwtu'raw] *(pl* **-ais)** *adj* cultural.

cumbuca [kũn'buka] *f* gourd.

cume ['kumi] *m* **-1.** [topo] summit. **-2.** *fig* [apogeu] apex.

cúmplice ['kũnplisi] *mf* **-1.** [co-autor] accomplice. **-2.** *fig* [parceiro] partner.

cumplicidade [kũnplisi'dadʒil] *f* complicity.

cumpridor, ra [kũnpri'do(x), ra] *adj* [responsável]: **é ~ da sua palavra** he keeps his word.

cumprimentar [4] [kũnprimẽn'ta(x)] *vt* **-1.** [saudar] to greet. **-2.** [elogiar] to compliment.

➤ **cumprimentar-se** *vp* [saudar-se] to greet one another.

cumprimento [kũnpri'mẽntul] *m* **-1.** [saudação] congratulation. **-2.** [elogio] compliment. **-3.** [realização] fulfilment.

cumprir [6] [kũn'pri(x)] <> *vt* **-1.** [dever, obrigação] to fulfill. **-2.** [lei] to obey. **-3.** [promessa] to keep. **-4.** [caber] to be sb's responsibility. <> *vi* [convir] to be necessary, to be convenient.

➤ **cumprir-se** *vp* [concretizar-se] to come true.

cumulativo, va [kumula'tʃivu, va] *adj* cumulative.

cúmulo ['kumulul] *m* height.

cunha ['kuɲa] *f* wedge.

cunhado, da [ku'ɲadu, da] *m, f* brother-in-law, sister-in-law.

cunhar [4] [ku'ɲa(x)] *vt* **-1.** [moedas] to mint. **-2.** [palavras] to create.

cunho ['kuɲul] *m* **-1.** [marca] mark. **-2.** *fig* [selo] stamp. **-3.** *fig* [caráter] nature.

cunilíngua [kuni'lĩŋwa] *f* cunnilingus.

cupê [ku'pel] *m* coupé.

cupido [ku'pidul] *m* cupid.

cupim [ku'pĩl] *(pl* **-ns)** *m* termite.

cupincha [ku'pĩʃal] *m f* mate.

cupom [ku'põl] *(pl* **-ns)** *m* coupon.

cúpula ['kupula] *f* **-1.** [abóbada] dome. **-2.** [chefia] leadership.

cura ['kura] <> *f* **-1.** [ger] cure; **não ter ~** *fig* to be incurable. **-2.** [recuperação] recovery. <> *m* [pároco] curate.

curado, da [ku'radu, da] *adj* **-1.** [pessoa, doença] cured. **-2.** [ferimento] healed. **-3.** [carne, queijo] cured.

curador, ra [kura'do(x), ra] *m, f* **-1.** JUR [de menores] guardian. **-2.** [de instituições] caretaker. **-3.** [de arte] curator.

curandeiro, ra [kurãn'dejru, ra] *m* healer.

curar [4] [ku'ra(x)] <> *vt* **-1.** [pessoa, doença] to cure; ~ **alguém de algo** to cure sb of sthg. **-2.** [ferimento] to heal. <> *vi* [sarar] to heal.
➡ **curar-se** *vp* **-1.** [sarar] to heal. **-2.** [emendar-se] to mend one's ways.

curativo [kura't∫ivul] *m* dressing.

curável [ku'ravew] (*pl* **-eis**) *adj* curable.

Curdistão [kuxdʒi∫'tãw] *n* Kurdistan.

curdo, da ['kurdu, da] <> *adj* Kurdish. <> *m, f* [pessoa] Kurd.
➡ **curdo** *m* [língua] Kurdish.

curetagem [kure'taʒẽ] (*pl* **-ns**) *f* curettage.

curinga [ku'rĩga] *m* **-1.** [ger] joker.- **2.** COMPUT: (caractere) ~ wild card.

curiosidade [kurjozi'dadʒi] *f* curiosity.

curioso, osa [ku'rjozu, ɔza] <> *adj* **-1.** [ger] curious. **-2.** [bisbilhoteiro] nosy. **-3.** [interessante] interesting. <> *m, f* **-1.** [pessoa interessada] bystander. **-2.** [amador] amateur.
➡ **curioso** *m* [coisa singular]: **o** ~ **é ...** the strange thing is ...
➡ **curiosos** *mpl* [espectadores] onlookers.

Curitiba [kuri't∫iba] *n* Curitiba.

curral [ku'xaw] (*pl* **-ais**) *m* corral.

currar [4] [ku'xa(x)] *vt fam* to rape.

currículo [ku'xikulu] *m* **-1.** [histórico] curriculum vitae UK, resume US. **-2.** [matérias] curriculum.

curriculum vitae [ku,xiculũ'vitaj] *m (inv)* curriculum vitae UK, resume US.

cursar [4] [kux'sa(x)] *vt* **-1.** [curso] to study. **-2.** [escola] to attend.

cursinho [kur'siɲu] *m* [pré-vestibular] *preparatory course for university entry.*

cursivo, va [kux'sivu, va] *adj* [letra] cursive.

curso ['kursu] *m* **-1.** [ger] flow. **-2.** [rumo] course. **-3.** [andamento]: **em** ~ current. **-4.** [EDUC- nível] key stage UK, grade US; [- estabelecimento] school; ~ **de férias** summer school; ~ **normal** teacher training course *(for primary school)*; ~ **de primeiro grau** primary school UK, grade school US; ~ **de segundo grau** secondary school UK, high school US; ~ **superior** degree course; ~ **supletivo** supplementary course.

cursor [kux'so(x)] (*pl* **-es**) *m* COMPUT cursor.

curta-metragem [,kuxtame'traʒẽ] (*pl* **curtas-metragens**) *m* short film.

curtição [kuxt∫i'sãw] *f* **-1.** [de couro] tanning. **-2.** *fam* [prazer] fun.

curtido, da [kux't∫idu, da] *adj* **-1.** [couro] tanned. **-2.** *fig* [sofrido] fed up. **-3.** *fig* [endurecido] hard-boiled.

curtir [6] [kux't∫i(x)] *vt* **-1.** [couro] to tan. **-2.** [sofrer] to suffer. **-3.** *fam* [desfrutar de] to enjoy.
➡ **curtir-se** *vp fam*: eles se curtem muito they really hit it off.

curto, ta ['kuxtu, ta] <> *adj* **-1.** [com pouco comprimento] short. **-2.** [breve] brief. **-3.** [limitado] intellectually limited. <> *m* ELETR = **curto-circuito.**

curto-circuito [,kuxtusix'kujtu] (*pl* **curtos-circuitos**) *m* ELETR short circuit.

curva ['kuxva] *f* **-1.** [de rua *etc*] bend; ~ **fechada** sharp bend, hairpin bend. **-2.** [arqueamento] curve. **-3.** GEOM arc. **-4.** [em gráfico] curve.
➡ **curvas** *fpl* [de mulher] curves.

curvado, da [kux'vadu, da] *adj* curved, bent.

curvar [4] [kux'va(x)] <> *vt* **-1.** [arquear] to arch. **-2.** *fig* [dominar] to subdue. <> *vi* [envergar] to stoop.
➡ **curvar-se** *vp* **-1.** [envergar-se] to bend down. **-2.** [prostrar-se] to bow. **-3.** *fig* [submeter-se]: ~**-se a** to give in to.

curvatura [kuxva'tura] *f* curvature.

curvilíneo, nea [kuxvi'linju, nja] *adj* [forma, objeto, linha] curvilinear.

curvo, va ['kuxvu, va] *adj* **-1.** [arqueado] curved. **-2.** [sinuoso - estrada, caminho] bendy; [- rio] meandering.

cuscuz [ku∫'ku∫] *m* couscous.

cusparada [ku∫pa'rada] *f* gob of spittle.

cuspe ['ku∫pi] *m* spittle.

cuspida [ku∫'pida] *f fam*: **dar** ~**s em** to spit on *ou* at.

cuspido, da [ku∫'pidu, da] *adj* **-1.** [telefone] crackling. **-2.** [pessoa] affronted.

cuspir [61] [ku∫'pi(x)] <> *vt* to spit. <> *vi* to spit; ~ **no prato em que comeu** *fig* to bite the hand that feeds you.

custa ['ku∫ta] *f*: **à** ~ **de** at the expense of.
➡ **custas** *fpl* JUR costs.

custar [4] [ku∫'ta(x)] <> *vt* **-1.** [preço] to cost; **custe o que** ~ whatever the cost; *fig* ~ **os olhos da cara** to cost an arm and a leg. **-2.** *fig* [acarretar] to cause; **não** ~ **nada fazer algo** not to cost anything to do sthg. <> *vi* **-1.** [produto, serviço]: ~ **barato/caro** to be cheap/expensive. **-2.** [ser difícil, penoso]: **não custava você ter ajudado ...** it wouldn't have hurt you to help me ...; ~ **caro** to cost a great deal. **-3.** [ter dificuldade]: ~ **a fazer algo** to find sthg hard to do. **-4.** [demorar] to be late; ~ **a fazer algo** to take a lot of doing.

custear [15] [ku∫'tja(x)] *vt* to defray.

custeio [ku∫'teju] *m* defrayal.

custo ['ku∫tu] *m* **-1.** [preço] cost; ~ **de vida** cost of living. **-2.** *fig* [dificuldade]: **ser um** ~ **fazer algo** to be difficult to do sthg; **a todo** ~ at all costs.

custódia [ku∫'tɔdʒia] *f* custody.

CUT (*abrev de* **Central Única dos Trabalhadores**) *f* *central trade union body,* ≃ TUC UK.

cutelaria [kutela'ria] *f* cutlery.

cutelo [ku'tɛlu] *m* cutlass.

cutia [ku't∫ia] *f* agouti.

cutícula [ku't∫ikula] *f* cuticle.

cútis ['kut∫i∫] *f inv* cutis.

cutucada [kutu'kada] *f* **-1.** [com o cotovelo] nudge. **-2.** [como o dedo] poke.

cutucar [12] [kutu'ka(x)], **catucar** [katu'ka(x)] *vt* **-1.** [com o cotovelo] to nudge. **-2.** [com o dedo] to poke.

C.V. (*abrev de* **curriculum vitae**) *m* CV.

CVM (*abrev de* **Comissão de Valores Mobiliários**) *f* *regulatory body overseeing the sale of shares,* ≃ FSA *UK*.

czar, ina [ˈkza(x), ina] *m, f* czar (*f* czarina).

d, D [de] *m* [letra] d, D.
da [da] = de + a.
DAC (Departamento de Aviação Civil) *m civil aviation department,* ≃ CAA.
dadaísmo [dadaˈiʒmu] *m* dadaism.
dadaísta [dadaˈiʃta] <> *adj* Dadaist. <> *mf* Dadaist.
dádiva [ˈdadiva] *f* **-1.** [donativo] donation. **-2.** [dom] gift.
dadivoso, osa [dadʒiˈvozu, ɔza] *adj* generous.
dado, da [ˈdadu, da] *adj* **-1.** [ger] given. **-2.** [presenteado] presented. **-3.** [afável] friendly. **-4.** [afeito]: **ser ~ a algo** to be fond of sthg.
 ◆ **dado** *m* **-1.** [em jogo] dice. **-2.** [informação] data.
 ◆ **dados** *mpl* COMPUT data.
 ◆ **dado que** *loc conj* given that.
daí [daˈi] = de + aí.
Dakar [daˈka(x)] *n* Dakar.
dali [daˈli] = de + ali.
dália [ˈdalja] *f* dahlia.
dálmata [ˈdawmata] *m* Dalmatian.
daltônico, ca [dawˈtoniku, ka] <> *adj* colour-blind. <> *m, f* colour-blind person.
dama [ˈdama] *f* **-1.** [mulher] lady; **~ de companhia** companion; **~ de honra** bridesmaid. **-2.** POL: **primeira-~** first lady. **-3.** [em uma área específica] grande dame. **-4.** [em xadrez, baralho] queen.
 ◆ **damas** *fpl* [jogo] checkers.
damasco [daˈmaʃku] *m* **-1.** [fruta] apricot. **-2.** [tecido] damask.
Damasco [daˈmaʃku] *n* Damascus.
danação [danaˈsãw] *f* **-1.** [maldição] damnation. **-2.** *fam* [travessura] mischief.
danado, da [daˈnadu, da] <> *adj* **-1.** [amaldiçoado] damned. **-2.** [zangado] annoyed. **-3.** [travesso] mischievous. **-4.** [incrível] unbelievable. **-5.** [hábil]: **ser ~ para algo** to be incredibly good at sthg. <> *m* **-1.** [pessoa amaldiçoada] cursed person. **-2.** *fam* [esperto] joker.
danar-se [4] [dãˈnaxsi] *vp* [zangar-se] to become furious; **dane-se!** *fam* to hell with it!
dança [ˈdãsa] *f* dance; **~ folclórica** folkdance; **~ de salão** ballroom dance; **~ do ventre** belly dance.

dançante [dãnˈsãntʃi] *adj* dancing; **chá ~** tea dance.
dançar [13] [dãnˈsa(x)] <> *vi* **-1.** [bailar] to dance. **-2.** *fam* [sair-se mal] to flop. **-3.** *fam* [deixar de acontecer] to fall through. <> *vt* [bailar] to dance.
dançarino, na [dãnsaˈrinu, na] *m, f* ballet dancer.
danceteria [dãnseteˈria] *f* dancehall.
danificar [12] [danifiˈka(x)] *vt* to damage.
 ◆ **danificar-se** *vp* to get damaged.
daninho, nha [daˈninu, ɲal] *adj* harmful; **erva daninha** weed.
dano [ˈdãnu] *m* damage.
danoso, osa [daˈnozu, ɔza] *adj* [nocivo]: **~ a** damaging to.
Danúbio [daˈnubju] *n*: **o ~** the Danube.
daquela [daˈkɛla] = de + aquela ⊳ aquele.
daquele [daˈkeli] = de + aquele ⊳ aquele.
daqui [daˈki] = de + aqui ⊳ aqui.
daquilo [daˈkilu] = de + aquilo ⊳ aquilo.
dardo [ˈdaxdu] *m* **-1.** [seta] dart. **-2.** ESP javelin.
dar [11] [ˈda(x)] <> *vt* **-1.** [entregar, presentear] to give; **~ algo a alguém** to give sb sthg, to give sthg to sb. **-2.** [produzir] to yield. **-3.** [causar, provocar] to give; **isto me dá sono/pena** this makes me sleepy/sad; **isto vai ~ muito que fazer** this is going to be a lot of work; **o amor só dá problemas** love is nothing but trouble. **-4.** [filme, programa]: **deu no noticiário hoje** it was on the news today. **-5.** [exprime ação] to give; **~ um berro** to cry out; **~ um pontapé em alguém** to kick sb; **~ um passeio** to go for a walk. **-6.** [festa, concerto] to have, to hold; **vão ~ uma festa** they're going to have *ou* throw a party. **-7.** [dizer] to say; **ele me deu boa-noite** he said good night to me. **-8.** [ensinar] to teach; **o que é que você está dando nas suas aulas?** what do you teach in your class?; **ela dá aula numa escola** she teaches at a school; **eu gostaria de ~ aulas de inglês** I would like to teach English. **-9.** [aprender, estudar] to do; **o que é que estão dando em Inglês?** what are you doing in English at the moment?; **estamos dando o verbo "to be"** we're doing the verb "to be". <> *vi* **-1.** [horas]: **já deram cinco horas** it's just gone five o'clock. **-2.** [condizer]: **~ com** to go with; **as cores não dão umas com as outras** the colours clash. **-3.** [proporcionar]: **~ de beber a alguém** to give sb sthg to drink; **~ de comer a alguém** to feed sb. **-4.** [em locuções]: **dá igual/no mesmo** it doesn't matter; **~ ares de** to look like; **~ à luz** to give birth; **~ de si** to give of o.s.
 ◆ **dar com** *v + prep* [encontrar, descobrir] to meet; **dei com ele no cinema** I met him at the movies.
 ◆ **dar em** *v + prep* [resultar]: **a discussão não vai ~ em nada** the discussion will come to nothing.
 ◆ **dar para** *v + prep* [servir para, ser útil para] to be good for; [suj: varanda, janela] to look onto; [suj: porta] to lead to; [ser suficiente para] to be enough for; [ser possível] to be possible; **dá para você fazer isso hoje?** could you do it today?; **dá para ir a pé?** is it

within walking distance?; **não vai ~ para eu chegar na hora** I won't be able to get there on time.

→ **dar por** *v + prep* [aperceber-se de] to notice.

→ **dar-se** *vp*: **~-se bem/mal com alguém** to get on well/badly with sb; **o professor deu-se mal com a brincadeira** the teacher did not appreciate the joke; **~-se por vencido** to give up.

das [daʃ] = **de + as.**

DAT (*abrev de* **digital audio tape**) *f* DAT.

data [ˈdata] *f* **-1.** [em carta *etc*] date; **~ de nascimento** date of birth. **-2.** [época] time; **de longa ~** of long standing.

data-base [ˌdataˈbazi] (*pl* **datas-bases**) *f* baseline date.

datação [dataˈsãw] (*pl* **-ões**) *f* dating.

data-limite [ˌdataliˈmitʃi] (*pl* **datas-limites**) *f* deadline.

datar [4] [daˈta(x)] ⬦ *vt* **-1.** [pôr data em] to date. **-2.** [considerar que existe]: **~ algo de** to date sthg at. ⬦ *vi* [existir]: **~ de** to date from.

datilografar [4] [datʃilograˈfa(x)] *vt* to type.

datilografia [datʃilograˈfia] *f* typing.

datilógrafo, fa [datʃiˈlografu, fal *m, f* typist.

dativo [daˈtʃivul *m* GRAM dative.

DC (*abrev de* **Depois de Cristo**) AD.

DDT (*abrev de* **Dicloro-Difenil-Tricloretana**) *m* DDT.

de [dʒi] *prep* **-1.** [indica posse] of; **o lápis do Mário** Mário's pencil; **o carro daquele homem** that man's car; **a recepção do hotel** the hotel reception; **a casa é dela** it's her house, the house is hers; **as fases da lua** the phases of the moon. **-2.** [indica matéria] (made) of; **um bolo ~ chocolate** a chocolate cake; **um relógio ~ ouro** a gold watch. **-3.** [indica conteúdo] of; **um copo d'água** a glass of water. **-4.** [usado em descrições, determinações]: **uma camiseta ~ manga curta** a short-sleeved T-shirt; **uma nota ~ 50 reais** a 50-real note; **o senhor ~ preto** the man in black. **-5.** [indica assunto] about; **fale da viagem** tell me about the trip; **um livro ~ informática** a book about *ou* on computers; **um livro ~ geografia** a geography book. **-6.** [indica origem] from; **sou ~ Salvador** I'm from Salvador; **os habitantes do bairro** the locals; **um produto do Brasil** a Brazilian product. **-7.** [indica tempo]: **o jornal das nove** the nine o'clock news; **partimos às três da tarde** we left at three in the afternoon; **trabalho das nove às cinco** I work from nine to five. **-8.** [indica uso]: **a sala ~ espera** the waiting room; **uma máquina ~ calcular** a calculator; **a porta ~ entrada** the front door. **-9.** [usado em denominações, nomes] of. **-10.** [indica causa, modo]: **chorar ~ alegria** to cry with joy; **está tudo ~ pernas para o ar** everything is upside down; **morrer ~ frio** to freeze to death; **ele viajou ~ carro** he travelled by car. **-11.** [indica autor] by; **um filme ~ Glauber Rocha** a film by Glauber Rocha; **o último livro ~ Ferreira Gullar** Ferreira Gullar's latest book. **-12.** [introduz um complemento]: **cheio ~ gente** full of people, crowded; **desconfiar ~ alguém** to distrust sb;

difícil ~ esquecer hard to forget; **gostar ~ algo/alguém** to like sthg/sb. **-13.** [em comparações]: **do que** than; **teu carro é mais rápido do que este** your car is faster than this one. **-14.** [em superlativos] of; **o melhor ~ todos** the best of all. **-15.** [dentre] of; **uma daquelas cadeiras** one of those chairs; **um dia destes** one of these days; **um desses hotéis serve** one of those hotels will do. **-16.** [indica série]: **~ dois em dois dias** every two days; **~ quinze em quinze minutos** every fifteen minutes; **~ três em três metros** every three metres.

deão [dʒiˈãwl (*pl* **deãos, deães**) *m* dean.

debaixo [deˈbajʃul *adv* underneath.

→ **debaixo de** *loc prep* under.

debalde [deˈbawdʒil *adv* in vain.

debandada [debãnˈdadal *f* **-1.** [fuga] stampede. **-2.** [confusão]: **em ~** in disarray.

debandar [4] [debãnˈda(x)l ⬦ *vt* [dispersar] to break up. ⬦ *vi* [pôr-se em fuga] to scatter.

→ **debandar-se** *vp* [dispersar-se] to break up.

debate [deˈbatʃil *m* **-1.** [discussão] debate. **-2.** [disputa] discussion.

debatedor, ra [debateˈdo(x), ral *m, f* debater.

debater [5] [debaˈte(x)l ⬦ *vt* **-1.** [discutir] to debate. **-2.** [questionar] to dispute. ⬦ *vi* [discutir] to discuss.

→ **debater-se** *vp* [agitar-se] to struggle.

débeis [ˈdɛbejʃl *pl* ⮕ **débil**.

debelar [4] [debeˈla(x)l *vt* **-1.** [ger] to overcome. **-2.** [dominar] to defeat.

debênture [deˈbẽnturil *f* COM debenture.

débil [ˈdɛbiwl (*pl* **-eis**) ⬦ *adj* **-1.** [fraco] weak. **-2.** PSIC retarded. ⬦ *mf* PSIC: **~ mental** mentally retarded person; *fam* [idiota] fool.

debilidade [debiliˈdadʒil *f* **-1.** [fraqueza] weakness. **-2.** PSIC: **~ mental** mental retardation.

debilitação [debilitaˈsãwl *f* [enfraquecimento] debilitation.

debilitante [debiliˈtãntʃil *adj* debilitating.

debilitar [4] [debiliˈta(x)l *vt* to debilitate.

→ **debilitar-se** *vp* to weaken.

debilóide [debiˈlɔjdʒil *fam* ⬦ *adj* stupid. ⬦ *mf* dunderhead.

debitar [4] [debiˈta(x)l *vt* to debit.

débito [ˈdɛbitul *m* debit.

debochado, da [deboˈʃadu, dal *adj* scornful.

debochar [4] [deboˈʃa(x)l *vi*: **~ de algo/alguém** to scorn sb/sthg.

deboche [deˈbɔʃil *m* scorn.

debruçar [13] [debruˈsa(x)l *vt* to lean.

→ **debruçar-se** *vp* to lean over.

debulhar [4] [debuˈʎa(x)l *vt* **-1.** [grãos] to thresh. **-2.** [casca] to shell.

→ **debulhar-se** *vp* **~-se em lágrimas** *fig* to dissolve into tears.

debutante [debuˈtãntʃil *f* debutante.

debutar [4] [debuˈta(x)l *vi* to make one's debut.

década [ˈdɛkadal *f* decade.

decadência [dekaˈdẽnsjal *f* decadence.

decadente [deka'dẽntʃi] adj decadent.
decair [68] [deka'i(x)] vi -1. [deteriorar] to deteriorate. -2. [pender] to wither. -3. [diminuir] to diminish.
decalcar [12] [dekaw'ka(x)] vt to trace.
decalque [de'kawkil m tracing.
decano [de'kãnul m -1. [membro mais antigo] oldest member. -2. [de universidade] dean.
decantar [4] [dekãn'ta(x)] vt -1. [líquido] to decant. -2. [exaltar] to sing the praises of.
decapitar [4] [dekapi'ta(x)] vt to decapitate.
decatleta [deka'tlɛta] mf ESP decathlete.
decatlo [de'katlu] m decathlon.
decência [de'sẽnsja] f decency.
decênio [de'senju] m decade.
decente [de'sẽntʃi] adj -1. [digno] decent. -2. [decoroso] demure. -3. [apropriado, asseado - roupa] decent; [- restaurante, casa] clean. -4. [bem-feito] well done.
decentemente [desẽntʃi'mẽntʃi] adv -1. [dignamente, com decoro] decently. -2. [adequadamente] satisfactorily.
decepar [4] [dese'pa(x)] vt to cut off.
decepção [desep'sãw] (pl -ões) f -1. [desapontamento] disappointment. -2. [desilusão] disillusion.
decepcionado, da [desepsjo'nadu, da] adj -1. [desapontado] disappointed. -2. [desiludido] disillusioned.
decepcionar [4] [desepsjo'na(x)] vt -1. [desapontar] to disappoint. -2. [desiludir] to disillusion.
 ➡ **decepcionar-se** vp [desapontar-se]: ~-se com algo/alguém to be disappointed with sthg/sb.
decerto [dʒi'sextu] adv surely.
decibel [desi'bɛwl (pl -éis) m decibel.
decididamente [desidʒida'mẽntʃil adv -1. [com certeza] certainly. -2. [resolutamente] decidedly.
decidido, da [desi'dʒidu, da] adj -1. [resolvido] resolved. -2. [resoluto] resolute.
decidir [6] [desi'dʒi(x)] <> vt -1. [resolver] to resolve. -2. [deliberar] to decide; ~ que to decide that; ~ fazer algo to decide to do sthg. -3. [concluir] to decide. <> vi -1. [tomar decisão]: ~ (sobre algo) to make a decision (about sthg). -2. [optar]: ~ entre to decide between.
 ➡ **decidir-se** vp -1. [tomar decisão] to make a decision; ~-se a fazer algo to decide to do sthg. -2. [optar]: ~-se por to opt for.
decifrar [4] [desi'fra(x)] vt -1. [ler, interpretar] to decipher. -2. [entender] to unravel.
decifrável [desi'fravewl (pl -eis) adj decipherable.
décima l'dɛsimal ⊳ **décimo**.
decimal [desi'mawl (pl -ais [dɛsi'majʃl) <> adj decimal. <> m decimal.
décimo, ma l'dɛsimu, mal num tenth.
 ➡ **décimo** m tenth part; veja também sexto.
decisão [desi'zãw] (pl -ões) f -1. [deliberação] decision; tomar uma ~ to make a decision. -2. [qualidade] decisiveness.
decisivo, va [desi'zivu, val adj -1. [deliberativo, crítico] decisive. -2. [terminante] deciding.

declamação [deklama'sãw] f recitation, declamation.
declamar [4] [dekla'ma(x)] <> vt [recitar] to recite. <> vi -1. [recitar] to declaim. -2. pej [falar com afetação] to posture.
declaração [deklara'sãw] (pl -ões) f -1. [documento] written declaration. -2. [depoimento] testimony; ~ de amor declaration of love; fazer uma ~ to make a declaration. -3. [inventário] statement; ~ de imposto de renda income tax declaration.
declarado, da [dekla'radu, dal adj -1. [patenteado] declared. -2. [confessado] self-declared.
declarante [dekla'rãntʃil mf JUR declarant.
declarar [4] [dekla'ra(x)] vt -1. [ger] to declare; ~ que to declare that. -2. [confessar] to confess.
 ➡ **declarar-se** vp -1. [manifestar-se]: ~-se a favor de/contra to declare o.s for/against. -2. [confessar-se] to confess o.s. to be. -3. [designar-se] to declare o.s.
declinação [deklina'sãw] (pl -ões) f -1. GRAM declension. -2. [diminuição] reduction. -3. [declive] slope.
declinar [4] [dekli'na(x)] <> vt -1. [ger] to decline. -2. [revelar] to disclose. <> vi -1. [astro] to set. -2. [mesa, terreno] to slope. -3. [dia, tarde] to draw to a close.
declínio [de'klinjul m decline.
declive [de'klivil m [de terreno] slope.
decô [de'kol adj decor.
decodificador [dekodʒifika'do(x)] m COMPUT & TV decoder.
decodificar [12] [dekodʒifi'ka(x)] vt COMPUT & TV to decode.
decolagem [deko'laʒẽl (pl -ns) f take-off.
decolar [4] [deko'la(x)] vi to take off.
decompor [45] [dekõn'po(x)] vt -1. [separar elementos de] to break down. -2. [dividir em partes] to dissect. -3. [estragar] to rot. -4. [alterar] to change.
 ➡ **decompor-se** vp -1. [estragar-se] to rot. -2. [alterar-se] to change o.s.
decomposição [dekõnpozi'sãw] (pl -ões) f -1. [apodrecimento] rotting. -2. [divisão em partes] dissection. -3. [separação de elementos] breakdown. -4. [alteração] change. -5. [desorganização] break-up.
decomposto, ta [dekõn'poʃtu, tal <> pp ⊳ **decompor**. <> adj -1. [putrefato] rotten. -2. [dividido] dissected.
decoração [dekora'sãw] (pl -ões) f decoration.
decorador, ra [dekora'do(x), ral m, f [profissional] decorator.
decorar [4] [deko'ra(x)] vt -1. [memorizar] to learn by heart. -2. [ornamentar] to decorate.
decorativo, va [dekora'tʃivu, val adj decorative.
decoro [de'korul m -1. [decência] decency; com ~ properly. -2. [dignidade] dignity.
decoroso, osa [deko'rozu, ɔzal adj decent.
decorrência [deko'xẽnsjal f consequence; em ~ de as a consequence of.

decorrente [deko'xẽntʃi] *adj:* ~ **de** resulting from.

decorrer [5] [deko'xe(x)] <> *m* [decurso]: **no** ~ **de** in the course of, during. <> *vi* -**1.** [derivar]: ~ **de** to stem from. -**2.** [passar] to pass.

decorrido, da [deko'xidu, da] *adj* [terminado]: **decorrida a votação, ...** once the voting was over, ...

decotado, da [deko'tadu, da] *adj* low-cut.

decotar [4] [deko'ta(x)] *vt* to cut a low neckline in.

decote [de'kɔtʃi] *m* décolletage.

decrépito, ta [de'krɛpitu, ta] *adj* decrepit.

decrepitude [dekrepi'tudʒi] *f* [caducidade] decrepitude.

decrescente [dekre'sẽntʃi] *adj* falling.

decrescer [25] [dekre'se(x)] *vi* to decrease.

decréscimo [de'krɛsimu] *m* decrease.

decretação [dekreta'sãw] (*pl* -**ões**) *f* decreeing.

decretar [4] [dekre'ta(x)] <> *vt* -**1.** [ordenar] to decree. -**2.** [determinar] to determine. <> *vi* [ordenar] to decree.

decreto [de'krɛtu] *m* -**1.** [ordem] decree; [judicial] fiat. -**2.** *loc:* **nem por** ~ not for all the tea in China.

decreto-lei [de͵krɛtu'lej] (*pl* **decretos-lei**) *m* law by decree.

decúbito [de'kubitu] *m:* **em** ~ **dorsal/lateral** lying on one's back/side.

decurso [de'kuxsu] *m* course; **no** ~ **de** in the course of.

dedal [de'daw] (*pl* -**ais**) *m* thimble.

dedão [de'dãw] (*pl* -**ões**) *m* -**1.** [polegar] thumb. -**2.** [do pé] big toe.

dedetização [dedetʃiza'sãw] (*pl* -**ões**) *f* fumigation.

dedetizar [4] [dedetʃi'za(x)] *vt* to fumigate.

dedicação [dedʒika'sãw] (*pl* -**ões**) *f* -**1.** [devotamento] dedication. -**2.** [amor] devotion.

dedicado, da [dedʒi'kadu, da] *adj* dedicated.

dedicar [12] [dedʒi'ka(x)] *vt* [devotar]: ~ **algo a alguém** to devote sthg to sb; [oferecer] to dedicate.
➤ **dedicar-se** *vp* [devotar-se]: ~**-se a algo/alguém** to devote o.s to sthg/sb; ~**-se a fazer algo** to devote o.s to doing sthg.

dedicatória [dedʒika'tɔrja] *f* dedication.

dedilhar [4] [dedʒi'ʎa(x)] <> *vt* [cordas, música] to strum. <> *vi* [tamborilar] to drum one's fingers.

dedo ['dedu] *m* -**1.** [da mão] finger; ~ **anular** ring finger; ~ **indicador** forefinger; ~ **mindinho** *ou* **mínimo** little finger; ~ **polegar** thumb. -**2.** [do pé] toe. -**3.** [quantidade]: **um** ~ **de algo** a finger of sthg. -**4.** *loc:* **cheio de** ~**s** finicky; **não levantar um** ~ not to lift a finger.
➤ **a dedo** *loc adv* [escolher] with care.

dedo-duro [͵dedu'duru] (*pl* **dedos-duros**) *mf* -**1.** [POL, crime] squealer. -**2.** [criança] tell-tale.

dedões [de'dõjʃ] *pl* ⊳ **dedão**.

dedução [dedu'sãw] (*pl* -**ões**) *f* deduction.

dedurar [4] [dedu'ra(x)] *fam vt* -**1.** [crime] to squeal. -**2.** [criança] to tell tales.

dedutível [dedu'tʃivew] (*pl* -**eis**) *adj* deductible.

dedutivo, va [dedu'tʃivu, va] *adj* deductive.

deduzir [72] [dedu'zi(x)] <> *vt* -**1.** [subtrair] to subtract. -**2.** [concluir] to deduce. <> *vi* [tirar dedução] to deduce.

defasado, da [defa'zadu, da] *adj* out of phase.

defasagem [defa'zaʒẽ] (*pl* -**ns**) *f* [discrepância] gap.

defecar [12] [defe'ka(x)] *vi* to defecate.

defecção [defek'sãw] (*pl* -**ões**) *f* defection.

defectivo, va [defek'tʃivu, va] *adj* defective.

defeito [de'fejtu] *m* -**1.** [físico] defect. -**2.** [moral] flaw. -**3.** [falha] fault; **com** ~ out of order; **pôr** ~ **em algo** [criticar] to find fault with sthg.

defeituoso, osa [defej'twozu, ɔza] *adj* -**1.** [com falha] faulty. -**2.** [físico] defective.

defender [5] [defẽn'de(x)] *vt* -**1.** [proteger]: ~ **algo/alguém (contra** *ou* **de)** to defend sthg/sb (against). -**2.** [sustentar] to stand up for.
➤ **defender-se** *vp* [proteger-se]: ~**-se (contra** *ou* **de)** to defend o.s (against).

defensável [defẽn'savew] (*pl* -**eis**) *adj* defensible.

defensivo, va [defẽn'sivu, va] *adj* defensive.
➤ **defensiva** *f* -**1.** [meios de defesa] defences *UK*, defenses *US*. -**2.** [atitude]: **estar/ficar na** ~ to be/stay on the defensive.

defensor, ra [defẽn'so(x), ra] (*mpl* -**es**, *fpl* -**s**) *m*, *f* -**1.** [de causa *etc*] defender. -**2.** *JUR* defendant.

deferência [defe'rẽnsja] *f* -**1.** [respeito] deference. -**2.** [condescendência] acquiescence.

deferente [defe'rẽntʃi] *adj* -**1.** [atencioso] deferential. -**2.** [condescendente] acquiescent.

deferir [57] [defe'ri(x)] <> *vt* -**1.** [atender] to grant. -**2.** [conceder]: ~ **algo a alguém** to award sthg to sb. <> *vi* -**1.** [atender]: ~ **a algo** to yield to sthg. -**2.** [acatar]: ~ **a algo** to respect sthg.

defesa [de'feza] *f* -**1.** [proteção] defence. -**2.** *JUR* defence lawyer. -**3.** *FUT* defence. -**4.** *UNIV:* ~ **de tese** viva.

defeso, sa [de'fezu, za] *adj* [proibido] forbidden.

deficiência [defi'sjẽnsja] *f* -**1.** [carência] deficiency. -**2.** *MED:* ~ **física/mental** physical/mental disability.

deficiente [defi'sjẽntʃi] <> *adj* deficient. <> *mf* *MED:* ~ **(físico/mental)** physically/mentally disabled.

déficit ['dɛfisitʃ] *m* *ECON:* ~ **público** public deficit.

deficitário, ria [defisi'tarju, rja] *adj* [orçamento, saldo] negative; [empresa] loss-making.

definhamento [defiɲa'mẽntu] *m* [debilitação] debilitation, wasting away.

definhar [4] [defi'ɲa(x)] <> *vt* to drain. <> *vi* to waste away.

definição [defini'sãw] (*pl* -**ões**) *f* -**1.** [explicação] explanation. -**2.** [decisão] decision. -**3.** [de imagem] definition.

definido, da [defi'nidu, da] *adj* -**1.** [exato, claro] defined. -**2.** *GRAM* definite.

definir [6] [defi'ni(x)] *vt* -**1.** [fixar, explicar] to define. -**2.** [decidir] to determine.
➤ **definir-se** *vp* -**1.** [pronunciar-se]: ~**-se sobre/contra/a favor de** to come out for/against/in favour of. -**2.** [decidir-se] to make up one's mind.

- **3.** [descrever-se]: ~-se como to describe o.s. as.

definitivamente [defini̯tʃiva'mẽntʃil *adv* **-1.** [para sempre] definitively. **-2.** [decididamente] definitely.

definitivo, va [defini'tʃivu, val *adj* **-1.** [final] definitive. **-2.** [permanente] permanent; **em caráter** ~ definitively.

deflagrar [4] [defla'gra(x)] <> *vt* **-1.** [causar a explosão] to ignite. **-2.** *fig* [provocar] to inflame. <> *vi* **-1.** [explodir] to explode. **-2.** *fig* [irromper] to erupt.

deflorar [4] [deflo'ra(x)] *vt* [mulher] to deflower.

deformação [defoxma'sãwl (*pl*-ões) *f* distortion.

deformar [4] [defox'ma(x)] *vt* **-1.** [tornar disforme] to deform. **-2.** [deturpar] to distort.

→ **deformar-se** *vp* [tornar-se disforme] to become deformed.

deformidade [defoxmi'dadʒil *f* deformity.

defraudar [4] [defraw'da(x)] *vt* to defraud.

defrontar [4] [defrõn'ta(x)] <> *vi* **-1.** [estar]: ~ com to face onto. **-2.** [deparar]: ~ com to come upon. <> *vt* **-1.** [encarar] to face. **-2.** [confrontar] to compare.

→ **defrontar-se** *vp* [deparar-se]: ~-se com to come face to face with.

defronte [de'frõntʃil <> *adv* [em frente] opposite. <> *prep*: ~ a/de in front of.

defumado, da [defu'madu, dal *adj* smoked.

defumador [defuma'do(x)] *m* **-1.** [recipiente] burner. **-2.** [substância] *substance used in burners for its smell*.

defumar [4] [defu'ma(x)] *vt* **-1.** [curar] to cure. **-2.** [perfumar] to perfume.

defunto, ta [de'fũntu, tal <> *adj* [morto] dead. <> *m, f* [cadáver] corpse.

degelar [4] [deʒe'la(x)] <> *vt* [descongelar] to defrost. <> *vi* [derreter-se] to melt.

degelo [de'ʒelul *m* thaw.

degeneração [deʒenera'sãwl *f* **-1.** [ger] degeneration. **-2.** [depravação] corruption.

degenerado, da [deʒene'radu, dal *adj* degenerate.

degenerar [4] [deʒene'ra(x)] *vi* **-1.** [ger] to degenerate. **-2.** [depravar-se] to become depraved.

→ **degenerar-se** *vp* [depravar-se] to be led astray.

degenerativo, va [deʒenera'tʃivu, val *adj* degenerative.

deglutição [deglutʃi'sãwl (*pl*-ões) *f* swallowing.

deglutir [6] [deglu'tʃi(x)] <> *vt & vi* to swallow.

degola [de'gɔlal *f* **-1.** [decapitação] decapitation. **-2.** [demissão] large-scale redundancy. **-3.** *ESP* sacking.

degolar [4] [dego'la(x)] *vt* to behead.

degradação [degrada'sãwl *f* degradation.

degradante [degra'dãntʃil *adj* [aviltante] demeaning.

degradar [4] [degra'da(x)] *vt* **-1.** [privar] to strip. **-2.** [aviltar] to demean.

→ **degradar-se** *vp* [aviltar-se] to demean o.s.

dégradé [degra'del *adj* gradational.

degrau [de'grawl *m* **-1.** [de escada] step. **-2.** *fig* [meio] means.

degredar [degre'da(x)] *vt* to exile.

degredo [de'gredul *m* **-1.** [pena] exile. **-2.** [lugar] place of exile.

degringolar [4] [degrĩngo'la(x)] *vi* **-1.** [cair] to fall down. **-2.** *fig* [deteriorar-se] to go off the rails. **-3.** *fig* [desordenar-se - esquema] to get in a mess; [- fila, jogo] to become disorderly. **-4.** [arruinar-se] to go bankrupt.

degustação [deguʃta'sãwl (*pl*-ões) *f* tasting.

degustar [4] [deguʃ'ta(x)] *vt* **-1.** [provar] to taste. **-2.** [saborear] to savour.

deificar [12] [dejfi'ka(x)] *vt* to deify.

deitada [dej'tadal *f fam*: dar uma ~ to have a lie-down.

deitado, da [dej'tadu, dal *adj* **-1.** [pessoa] lying down (*depois de verbo*). **-2.** [objeto] set down (*depois de verbo*).

deitar [4] [dej'ta(x)] <> *vt* **-1.** [pessoa] to lay down. **-2.** [objeto] to set down. <> *vi* [pessoa] to lie down; ~ **e rolar** *fig* to call the shots.

→ **deitar-se** *vp* [pessoa] to go to bed.

deixa ['dejʃal *f* **-1.** [dica] hint. **-2.** *TEATRO* cue. **-3.** [chance] opportunity.

deixar [4] [dej'ʃa(x)] <> *vt* **-1.** [ger] to leave. **-2.** [abandonar] to abandon. **-3.** [demitir-se de] to resign. **-4.** [consentir]: ~ **alguém fazer/que alguém faça algo** to allow sb to do sthg; ~ **passar algo** to overlook sthg. **-5.** [tornar possível]: **não** ~ **alguém fazer algo** not to allow sb to do sthg. **-6.** [esperar] to let. **-7.** [ignorar]: ~ **algo/alguém pra lá** to let sthg/sb be. **-8.** [não considerar, esquecer] to forget; **me deixa (em paz)!** leave me alone! <> *vi* **-1.** [parar]: ~ **de fazer algo** to stop doing sthg. **-2.** [não se preocupar]: **pode** ~ it's fine; **deixa pra lá!** forget it! **-3.** [expressando pedido]: **não deixe de ir no concerto!** make sure you go to the concert! **-4.** *loc*: ~ **(muito) a desejar** to leave much to be desired.

→ **deixar-se** *vp* [permitir-se]: ~-se **fazer algo** to allow o.s. to do sthg.

dejeto [de'ʒɛtul *m* dejection.

dela ['delal = de + ella.

delação [dela'sãwl (*pl*-ões) *f* **-1.** [denúncia] accusation. **-2.** [acusação] charge.

delas ['dɛlaʃ] = de + ellas.

delatar [4] [dela'ta(x)] *vt* **-1.** [denunciar] to denounce. **-2.** [acusar] to accuse. **-3.** [informar] to inform.

→ **delatar-se** *vp* [denunciar-se] to betray o.s.

delator, ra [dela'to(x), ral *m, f* informer.

délavé [dela'vel *adj* faded.

dele ['delil = de + ele.

delegação [delega'sãwl (*pl*-ões) *f* delegation; ~ **de poderes** transfer of powers.

delegacia [delega'sial *f* police station; ~ **de polícia** police station.

delegado, da [dele'gadu, dal *m, f* delegate; ~ **de polícia** chief of police.

delegar [14] [dele'ga(x)] *vt* -**1.** [dar]: ~ algo a alguém to delegate sthg to sb. -**2.** [enviar] to send sb as a delegate.

deleitar [4] [delej'ta(x)] *vt* to delight.
◆ **deleitar-se** *vp*: ~-se com to rejoice in.

deleite [de'lejtʃi] *m* delight.

deleitoso, osa [delej'tozu, ɔza] *adj* delightful.

deles ['delif] = de + eles.

deletar [4] [dele'ta(x)] *vt COMPUT* to delete.

deletério, ria [dele'tɛrju, rja] *adj* harmful.

delgado, da [dew'gadu, da] *adj* -**1.** [fino] slim. -**2.** [esbelto] slender.

deliberação [delibera'sãw] (*pl* -ões) *f* -**1.** [discussão] discussion; em ~ under discussion. -**2.** [decisão] decision.

deliberadamente [deliberada'mẽntʃi] *adj* [propositalmente] deliberately.

deliberado, da [delibe'radu, da] *adj* -**1.** [decidido] wilful. -**2.** [propositado] deliberate.

deliberar [4] [delibe'ra(x)] <> *vt* [decidir] to decide. <> *vi* [refletir sobre]: ~ **sobre** to ponder upon.

deliberativo, va [delibera'tʃivu, va] *adj* deliberative.

delicadeza [delika'deza] *f* -**1.** [ger] delicacy. -**2.** [leveza] fineness. -**3.** [fragilidade] fragility. -**4.** [apuro]: ~ **de detalhes** attentiveness to detail. -**5.** [cortesia] politeness.

delicado, da [deli'kadu, da] *adj* -**1.** [ger] delicate. -**2.** [sensível] urbane. -**3.** [cortês] polite.

delícia [de'lisja] *f* -**1.** [deleite] delight. -**2.** [coisa saborosa]: **ser/estar uma** ~ to be delicious. -**3.** [pessoa encantadora]: **ser uma** ~ to be a delight.

deliciar [16] [deli'sja(x)] *vt* to delight.
◆ **deliciar-se** *vp*: ~-se com algo to be delighted with sthg.

delicioso, osa [deli'sjozu, ɔza] *adj* -**1.** [vinho, doce] delicious. -**2.** [passeio] delightful.

delimitação [delimita'sãw] (*pl* -ões) *f* demarcation.

delimitar [4] [delimi'ta(x)] *vt* -**1.** [demarcar] to mark the limits of. -**2.** [restringir] to outline.

delineador [delinja'do(x)] *m* eyeliner.

delinear [15] [deli'nja(x)] *vt* to outline.

delinqüência [delĩŋ'kwẽnsja] *f* delinquency.

delinqüente [delĩŋ'kwẽntʃi] <> *adj* delinquent. <> *mf* delinquent.

delirante [deli'rãntʃi] *adj* -**1.** *PSIC* delirious. -**2.** [extravagante, aloucado] wild. -**3.** [maravilhoso] wonderful.

delirar [4] [deli'ra(x)] *vi* -**1.** *PSIC* to be delirious. -**2.** [sentir intensamente]: ~ **de algo** to be overcome with sthg.

delírio [de'lirju] *m* -**1.** *PSIC* delirium. -**2.** [excitação] excitement. -**3.** [êxtase] ecstasy.

delirium tremens [de'lirjũ 'trɛmẽns] *m* delirium tremens.

delito [de'litul] *m* -**1.** [falta] sin. -**2.** [crime] crime.

delonga [de'lõŋga] *f* delay; sem mais ~ without further delay.

delongar [14] [de'lõŋ'ga(x)] *vt* [retardar] to postpone.
◆ **delongar-se** *vp* -**1.** [demorar-se] to delay. -**2.** [prolongar-se] to prolong.

delta ['dɛwta] *m* delta.

demagogia [demago'ʒia] *f* demagogy.

demagógico, ca [dema'gɔʒiku, ka] *adj* demagogic.

demagogo, ga [dema'gogu, ga] *m, f* demagogue.

demais [de'majf] <> *adv* -**1.** [em demasia, muitíssimo] too much. -**2.** *fam* [ótimo]: **estar/ser** ~ to be amazing. <> *pron* [outros]: **os/as** ~ the others.

demanda [de'mãnda] *f* -**1.** *ECON* demand. -**2.** *JUR* lawsuit. -**3.** [disputa] dispute. -**4.** [pedido] request.

demandar [4] [demãn'da(x)] *vt* -**1.** *JUR* to sue. -**2.** [exigir] to demand. -**3.** [pedir] to request.

demão [de'mãw] (*pl* -s) *f* coat.

demarcação [demaxka'sãw] (*pl* -ões) *f* -**1.** [delimitação] demarcation. -**2.** [separação] boundary.

demarcado, da [demax'kadu, da] *adj* -**1.** [delimitado] demarcated. -**2.** [separado] set apart.

demarcar [12] [demax'ka(x)] *vt* -**1.** [delimitar] to demarcate. -**2.** [fixar] to define. -**3.** [separar] to distinguish between.

demarcatório, ria [demaxka'tɔrju, rja] *adj* boundary (*antes de subst*).

demasia [dema'zia] *f* excess; em ~ in excess.

demasiadamente [demazjada'mẽntʃi] *adv* -**1.** [demais] excessively. -**2.** [muito] too.

demasiado, da [dema'zjadu, da] <> *adj* excessive. <> *adv* too much; por ~ too.

demência [de'mẽnsja] *f* -**1.** *MED* dementia. -**2.** [loucura] insanity.

demente [de'mẽntʃi] *adj* -**1.** *MED* demented. -**2.** [louco] insane.

demérito, ta [de'mɛritu, ta] *adj* unworthy.
◆ **demérito** *m* [desmérito] unworthiness.

demissão [demi'sãw] (*pl* -ões) *f* -**1.** [solicitado pelo empregador] dismissal. -**2.** [solicitado pelo empregado] resignation; pedir ~ to tender one's resignation.

demissionário, ria [demisjo'narju, rja] *adj* resigning.

demitir [6] [demi'tʃi(x)] *vt* to dismiss.
◆ **demitir-se** *vp* to resign.

democracia [demokra'sia] *f* democracy.

democrata [demo'krata] *mf* democrat.

democrático, ca [demo'kratʃiku, ka] *adj* -**1.** [relativo a democracia] democratic. -**2.** [indiferente às classes sociais] egalitarian.

democratização [demokratʃiza'sãw] *f* democratization.

democratizar [4] [demokratʃi'za(x)] *f* -**1.** [tornar democrático] to democratize. -**2.** [popularizar] to make accessible.
◆ **democratizar-se** *vp* [tornar-se democrático] to become democratic.

démodé [demo'de] *adj* outmoded.

demografia [demogra'fia] *f* demography.

demográfico, ca [demo'grafiku, ka] *adj* demographic.

demolição [demoli'sãw] (*pl* -ões) *f* -1. demolition. -2. *fig* [ger] de reputação] destruction; [- de obstáculo] elimination.

demolidor, ra [demo'lido(x), ra] <> *adj* demolition (*antes de subst*). <> *m,f* demolition expert.

demolir [79] [demo'li(x)] *vt* -1. [destruir] to demolish. -2. *fig* [- reputação] to destroy; [- obstáculo] to overcome.

demoníaco, ca [demo'niaku, ka] *adj* demonic.

demônio [de'monju] *m* demon.

demonstração [demõnʃtra'sãw] (*pl* -ões) *f* -1. [ger] demonstration. -2. [apresentação] display.

demonstrar [4] [demõnʃ'tra(x)] *vt* -1. [ger] to demonstrate. -2. [afeto, antipatia *etc*] to show. -3. [habilidades, talentos] to display.

➡ **demonstrar-se** *vp* [revelar-se] to show o.s.

demonstrativo, va [demõnʃtra'tʃivu, va] *adj* demonstrative.

demonstrável [demõnʃ'travew] (*pl* -eis) *adj* demonstrable.

demora [de'mɔra] *f* [atraso] delay; **sem ~** without delay.

demorado, da [demo'radu, da] *adj* delayed.

demorar [4] [demo'ra(x)] <> *vt* [retardar] to delay. <> *vi* -1. [tardar] to be late; **~ a fazer algo** to take a long time to do sthg. -2. [permanecer] to stay.

➡ **demorar-se** *vp* -1. [tardar] to be late; **~-se a fazer algo** to take a long time to do sthg. -2. [permanecer] to remain.

demover [5] [demo've(x)] *vt* -1. [dissuadir]: **~ alguém de algo/fazer algo** to dissuade sb from sthg/doing sthg. -2. [remover] to move.

➡ **demover-se** *vp* [dissuadir-se]: **~-se de algo** to dissuade o.s. from sthg.

DENARC (*abrev de* **Departamento de Investigações sobre Narcóticos**) *m Brazilian police narcotics department.*

DENATRAN (*abrev de* **Departamento Nacional de Trânsito**) *m Brazilian national department responsible for transport law.*

dendê [dẽn'de] *m* -1. *BOT* palm. -2. [azeite] palm oil.

denegrir [58] [dene'gri(x)] *vt* [escurecer] to blacken.

dengo ['dẽngu] *m* -1. [faceirice] foppery. -2. [manha] affectation.

dengoso, osa [dẽn'gozu, ɔza] *adj* whining.

dengue ['dẽngi] *f MED* dengue.

denodado, da [deno'dadu, da] *adj* -1. [ousado] daring. -2. [impetuoso] impetuous.

denominação [denomina'sãw] (*pl* -ões) *f* -1. [nomeação] name. -2. [designação] designation. -3. *REL* denomination.

denominador, ra [denomina'do(x), ra] *adj* designatory.

➡ **denominador** *m MAT* denominator; **~ comum** common denominator.

denominar [4] [denomi'na(x)] *vt* -1. [nomear] to name. -2. [designar] to designate.

➡ **denominar-se** *vp* to be called.

denotar [4] [deno'ta(x)] *vt* -1. [indicar] to indicate. -2. [significar] to denote.

densidade [dẽnsi'dadʒi] *f* density; **de alta/dupla ~** high/double density.

denso, sa ['dẽnsu, sa] *adj* -1. [ger] dense. -2. [espesso] thick.

dentada [dẽn'tada] *f* bite.

dentado, da [dẽn'tadu, da] *adj* serrated.

dentadura [dẽnta'dura] *f* -1. [natural] set of teeth. -2. [postiça] denture.

dental [dẽn'taw] (*pl* -ais) *adj* dental; **pasta ~** toothpaste.

dentário, ria [dẽn'tarju, rja] *adj* dental.

dente ['dẽntʃi] *m* -1. [ger] tooth; **~ de leite** milk tooth; **~ de siso** wisdom tooth; **falar entre os ~s** to mutter. -2. [de elefante] tusk. -3. [alho] clove.

dente-de-leão [dẽntʃidʒi'lãw] (*pl* **dentes-de-leão**) *m* dandelion.

dentição [dẽntʃi'sãw] *f* -1. [processo] dentition. -2. [as dentes] teething; **primeira/segunda ~** milk/second teeth.

dentifrício, cia [dẽntʃi'frisju, sja] *adj* dental.

➡ **dentifrício** *m* toothpaste.

dentista [dẽn'tʃiʃta] *mf* dentist.

dentre ['dẽntri] *prep* among.

dentro ['dẽntru] <> *adv* in; **aí/lá ~** in there. <> *prep* -1.: **~ de** [no interior de] inside; [no tempo] within; **por ~** [na parte interna] inside. -2. *loc*: **estar por ~ (de algo)** *fam* to be in touch (with sthg); **não dei uma ~** *fam* I didn't get a single thing right.

dentuço, ça [dẽn'tusu, sa] <> *adj* buck-toothed. <> *m, f* [pessoa] buck-toothed person.

➡ **dentuça** *f* [arcada] buck-teeth.

denúncia [de'nũnsja] *f* -1. [acusação] accusation. -2. [à polícia] report. -3. [*JUR* - de pessoa, crime] condemnation; [- de contrato] termination; **~ vazia** unfettered right to forfeiture.

denunciar [16] [denũn'sja(x)] *vt* -1. [acusar] to denounce. -2. [divulgar] to expose. -3. [*JUR* - pessoa, crime] to condemn; [- contrato] to terminate. -4. [evidenciar] to reveal.

➡ **denunciar-se** *vp* -1. [delatar-se] to confess. -2. [trair-se] to betray o.s.

deparar [4] [depa'ra(x)] *vi*: **~ com** to come across.

departamental [depaxtamẽn'taw] (*pl* -ais) *adj* departmental.

departamento [departa'mẽntul] *m* department.

depauperado, da [depawpe'radu, da] *adj* -1. [empobrecido] impoverished. -2. [enfraquecido] exhausted.

depauperar [4] [depawpe'ra(x)] *vt* -1. [empobrecer] to impoverish. -2. [debilitar] to weaken.

➡ **depauperar-se** *vp* [debilitar-se] to become weak.

depenar [4] [depe'na(x)] *vt* -1. [ave] to pluck. -2. [pessoa] to lift. -3. [casa] to clean out.

dependência [depẽn'dẽnsja] *f* -1. [ger] dependency. -2. [cômodo] room.

dependente [depẽn'dẽntʃil] <> *adj* [subordinado]

dependent. <> *mf* dependant.
depender [5] [depẽn'de(x)] *vi* -**1.** [ger]: ~ **de** to depend upon. -**2.** [financeiramente]: ~ **de** to be dependent upon. -**3.** [de droga]: ~ **de** to be dependent on.
dependurar [4] [depẽndu'ra(x)] *vt* [pendurar]: ~ algo (em algo) to hang sthg (on sthg).
➨ **dependurar-se** *vp*: ~-se em algo to hang from sthg.
depilação [depila'sãw] (*pl* -ões) *f* depilation.
depilador, ra [depila'do(x), ra] *m, f beautician who does hair-removal.*
depilar [4] [depi'la(x)] *vt* to remove hair from.
➨ **depilar-se** *vp* -**1.** [com cera - na estética] to have a wax; [- em casa] to wax. -**2.** [com lâmina] to shave.
depilatório, ria [depila'tɔrju, rja] *adj* hair-removing.
➨ **depilatório** *m* hair removal cream/wax.
deplorar [4] [deplo'ra(x)] *vt* to lament.
deplorável [deplo'ravew] (*pl* -eis) *adj* -**1.** [lamentável] lamentable. -**2.** [detestável] deplorable.
depoente [depo'ẽntʃi] *m JUR* witness.
depoimento [depoj'mẽntu] *m* -**1.** [ger] statement. -**2.** [ato] testimony.
depois [de'pojʃ] <> *adv* -**1.** [posteriormente] after; logo ~ straight after. -**2.** [além disso] besides. <> *prep*: ~ **de fazer algo** after doing sthg.
➨ **depois que** *loc conj* after.
depor [45] [de'po(x)] <> *vt* -**1.** [colocar] to put down. -**2.** [destituir] to depose. -**3.** *JUR*: ~ **que** to testify that. -**4.** [expressar] to express. <> *vi JUR*: ~ **(a favor/contra)** to testify (for/against).
➨ **depor-se** *vp* [depositar-se] to settle.
deportação [depoxta'sãw] (*pl* -ões) *f* deportation.
deportar [4] [depox'ta(x)] *vt* to deport.
deposição [depozi'sãw] (*pl* -ões) *f* [destituição] deposition.
depositante [depozi'tãntʃi] *mf* depositor.
depositar [4] [depozi'ta(x)] *vt* to deposit.
➨ **depositar-se** *vp* [assentar] to settle.
depositário, ria [depozi'tarju, rja] *m, f* -**1.** [quem recebe em depósito] depositary. -**2.** *fig* [confidente] confidant.
depósito [de'pɔzitu] *m* -**1.** [ger] deposit. -**2.** [reservatório] depository.
depravação [deprava'sãw] (*pl* -ões) *f* -**1.** [perversão] perversion. -**2.** [degeneração] degeneration.
depravado, da [depra'vadu, da] <> *adj* depraved. <> *m, f* depraved person.
depravar [4] [depra'va(x)] *vt* -**1.** [corromper] to corrupt. -**2.** [estragar] to ruin.
➨ **depravar-se** *vp* [corromper-se] to become corrupted.
depreciação [depresja'sãw] (*pl* -ões) *f* [desvalorização] depreciation.
depreciar [16] [depre'sja(x)] *vt* -**1.** [desvalorizar] to devalue. -**2.** [subestimar] to undervalue.
➨ **depreciar-se** *vp* -**1.** [desvalorizar-se] to fall in value. -**2.** [subestimar-se] to underestimate o.s.
depredação [depreda'sãw] (*pl* -ões) *f* -**1.** [destruição] destruction. -**2.** [pilhagem] robbery.

depredador, ra [depreda'do(x), ra] <> *adj* harmful, damaging. <> *m, f* damaging person.
depredar [4] [depre'da(x)] *vt* -**1.** [destruir] to destroy. -**2.** [saquear] to loot.
depreender [5] [depreẽn'de(x)] *vt* -**1.** [compreender] to conclude. -**2.** [deduzir] to deduce.
depressa [de'prɛsa] *adv* quickly.
depressão [depre'sãw] (*pl* -ões) *f* -**1.** *PSIC* depression. -**2.** [en terreno, superfície] dip. -**3.** *fig* [abatimento] despondency.
depressivo, va [depre'sivu, va] *adj* depressive.
deprimente [depri'mẽntʃi] *adj* depressing.
deprimido, da [depri'midu, da] *adj* depressed.
deprimir [6] [depri'mi(x)] *vt* to depress.
➨ **deprimir-se** *vp* to become depressed.
depto (*abrev de* **departamento**) *m* dept.
depuração [depura'sãw] (*pl* -ões) *f* purification.
depurar [4] [depu'ra(x)] *vt* to purify.
➨ **depurar-se** *vp* to become purified.
deputado, da [depu'tadu, da] *m, f* -**1.** *POL* deputy. -**2.** [delegado] representative.
deque ['dɛkil] *m* decking.
DER (*abrev de* **Departamento de Estradas de Rodagem**) *m Brazilian highways department.*
deriva [de'riva] *f* drift; à ~ drifting; ir à ~ to drift.
derivação [deriva'sãw] (*pl* -ões) *f* -**1.** *GRAM* derivation. -**2.** *fig* [origem] origin.
derivado, da [deri'vadu, da] *adj* [proveniente]: ~ **de** derived from.
➨ **derivado** *m* derivative.
➨ **derivada** *f MAT* derivative.
derivar [4] [deri'va(x)] *vi* -**1.** [resultar]: ~ **de** to derive from. -**2.** [ficar à deriva] to drift. -**3.** *GRAM*: ~ **de** to stem from.
derivativo, va [deriva'tʃivu, va] *adj* derivative.
➨ **derivativo** *m* [distração] distraction.
dermatologia [dexmatolo'ʒial] *f* dermatology.
dermatológico, ca [dexmato'lɔgiku, ka] *adj* dermatological.
dermatologista [dexmatolo'ʒiʃta] *mf* dermatologist.
derradeiro, ra [dexa'dejru, ra] *adj* final.
derramamento [dexama'mẽntul] *m* -**1.** [de água, leite] spillage. -**2.** [de lágrimas] flow; ~ **de sangre** bloodshed.
derramar [4] [dexa'ma(x)] *vt* -**1.** [ger] to spill -**2.** [espalhar] to strew.
➨ **derramar-se** *vp* [verter] to spill.
derrame [de'xãmil] *m* -**1.** [de líquido] spillage. -**2.** [de lágrimas, sangue] flow. -**3.** *MED* haemorrhage; ~ **cerebral** brain haemorrhage.
derrapagem [dexa'paʒẽl] (*pl* -ns) *f* skid.
derrapar [4] [dexa'pa(x)] *vi* to skid.
derredor [dexe'do(x)l] *adv fml*: em ~ **(de)** around.
derreter [5] [dexe'te(x)] <> *vt* to melt. <> *vi* [liquefazer-se] to melt.
➨ **derreter-se** *vp* -**1.** *fig* [comover-se]: ~ **(com algo)** to be moved (by sthg). -**2.** *fig* [apaixonar-se]: ~-se todo (por alguém) to fall completely (for sb).
derretido, da [dexe'tʃidu, da] *adj* -**1.** [liquefeito]

melted. **-2.** *fig* [comovido] moved. **-3.** *fig* [apaixonado] besotted.

derrocada [dexoˈkadal *f* **-1.** [desmoronamento] destruction. **-2.** [ruína] ruin.

derrota [deˈxɔta] *f* **-1.** [fracasso] defeat. **-2.** NÁUT course.

derrotado, da [dexoˈtadu, da] *adj* defeated.

derrotar [4] [dexoˈta(x)] *vt* to defeat.

derrotista [dexoˈtʃiʃta] ◇ *adj* defeatist. ◇ *mf* defeatist.

derrubar [4] [dexuˈba(x)] *vt* **-1.** [fazer cair] to knock down. **-2.** [vencer] to overcome. **-3.** [destituir] to overthrow. **-4.** [destruir] to defame. **-5.** [prostrar] to lay low. **-6.** *fam* [prejudicar] to knock.

desabafar [4] [dʒizabaˈfa(x)] ◇ *vt*: ~ algo (com alguém) to share sthg (with sb). ◇ *vi*: ~ (com alguém) to open up (to sb).

➡ **desabafar-se** *vp*: ~-se (com alguém) to open up (to sb).

desabafo [dʒizaˈbaful *m* outpouring.

desabalado, da [dʒizabaˈladu, da] *adj* **-1.** [excessivo] enormous. **-2.** [espavorido]: **sair/correr** ~ to go/run headlong.

desabamento [dʒizabaˈmẽntul *m* collapse.

desabar [4] [dʒizaˈba(x)] *vi* **-1.** [ruir] to tumble down. **-2.** [cair com força] to fall heavily.

desabitado, da [dʒizabiˈtadu, da] *adj* unoccupied.

desabituar [4] [dʒizabiˈtwa(x)] *vt*: ~ alguém de algo/de fazer algo to wean sb off sthg/doing sthg.

➡ **desabituar-se** *vp*: ~-se de algo/de fazer algo to wean o.s. off sthg/doing sthg.

desabonar [4] [dʒizaboˈna(x)] *vt* to discredit.

desabotoar [20] [dʒizaboˈtwa(x)] *vt* to unbutton.

➡ **desabotoar-se** *vp* to open up.

desabrigado, da [dʒizabriˈgadu, da] ◇ *adj* **-1.** [sem casa] homeless. **-2.** [exposto] unsheltered. ◇ *m, f* [pessoa] homeless person; os ~s the homeless.

desabrigar [dʒizaˈbriga(x)] *vt* [tirar do abrigo] to leave without shelter.

desabrigo [dʒizaˈbrigul *m* **-1.** [falta de abrigo] lack of shelter. **-2.** *fig* [abandono] lack of protection.

desabrochar [4] [dʒizabroˈʃa(x)] *vi* **-1.** [flor] to bloom. **-2.** *fig* [pessoa] to blossom.

desacatar [4] [dʒizakaˈta(x)] ◇ *vt* **-1.** [afrontar] to disrespect. **-2.** [desprezar] to disregard. ◇ *vi* *fam* [causar espanto] to stun.

desacato [dʒizaˈkatul *m* **-1.** [afronta] disrespect. **-2.** [desprezo] disregard. **-3.** *fam* [pessoa]: **ser um** ~ to be a show-off.

desaceleração [dʒizaseleraˈsãwl *f* deceleration.

desacelerar [4] [dʒizaseleˈra(x)] *vt* to slow down.

desacerto [dʒizaˈsextul *m* **-1.** [erro] mistake. **-2.** [tolice] blunder.

desacomodar [4] [dʒizakomoˈda(x)] *vt* **-1.** [desorganizar] to disarrange. **-2.** [desalojar] to ask to leave.

desacompanhado, da [dʒizakõnpaˈɲadu, da] *adj* unaccompanied.

desaconselhar [4] [dʒizakõnseˈʎa(x)] *vt*: ~ algo (a alguém) to warn (sb) against sthg.

desaconselhável [dʒizakõnseˈʎavɛwl (*pl* -eis) *adj* not recommended *(depois de verbo)*.

desacordado, da [dʒizakoxˈdadu, da] *adj* senseless.

desacordo [dʒizaˈkoxdul *m* **-1.** [falta de acordo] disagreement. **-2.** [desarmonia] disharmony.

desacostumado, da [dʒizakoʃtuˈmadu, da] *adj*: ~ (a) unaccustomed (to).

desacostumar [4] [dʒizakoʃtuˈma(x)] *vt*: ~ alguém de algo to wean sb off sthg.

➡ **desacostumar-se** *vp* [desabituar-se]: ~-se de algo/de fazer algo to wean o.s. off sthg/doing sthg.

desacreditado, da [dʒizakredʒiˈtadu, da] *adj* discredited.

desacreditar [4] [dʒizakrediˈta(x)] *vt* to discredit.

➡ **desacreditar-se** *vp* [perder o crédito] to become discredited.

desafeto [dʒizaˈfɛtul *m* opponent.

desafiador, ra [dʒizafjaˈdo(x), ral ◇ *adj* challenging. ◇ *m, f* challenger.

desafiar [16] [dʒizaˈfja(x)] *vt* **-1.** [propor luta] to challenge. **-2.** [afrontar] to defy.

desafinação [dʒizafinaˈsãwl (*pl* -ões) *f* disharmony.

desafinado, da [dʒizafiˈnadu, da] *adj* out of tune.

desafinar [4] [dʒizafiˈna(x)] ◇ *vt*: ~ un instrumento to put an instrument out of tune. ◇ *vi* to be out of tune.

desafio [dʒizaˈfiwl *m* **-1.** [provocação] challenge. **-2.** LITER & MÚS *literary/musical competition between two people*.

desafivelar [4] [dʒizafiveˈla(x)] *vt* to unclasp.

desafogado, da [dʒizafoˈgadu, da] *adj* **-1.** [pessoa - de preocupações, de opressão] relieved; [- de trabalho] unencumbered. **-2.** [trânsito] clear.

desafogar [14] [dʒizafoˈga(x)] ◇ *vt* **-1.** [desoprimir - garganta] to clear; [- espírito] to free. **-2.** [desabafar] to relieve. **-3.** [aliviar]: ~ alguém (de algo) to relieve sb (of sthg). ◇ *vi* [desabafar-se]: ~ (com alguém) to open up (to sb).

➡ **desafogar-se** *vp* [desabafar-se] to unburden o.s.

desafogo [dʒizaˈfogul *m* **-1.** [alívio] relief; **dar** ~ a algo to relieve sthg. **-2.** [de trabalho] break.

desaforado, da [dʒizafoˈradu, da] *adj* insulting.

desaforo [dʒizaˈforul *m* insult; **eu não levo** ~ **para casa** I'm not going to take it lying down.

desafortunado, da [dʒizafoxtuˈnadu, da] *adj* unfortunate.

desagasalhado, da [dʒizagazaˈʎadu, da] *adj* unsheltered.

deságio [deˈzaʒjul *m* ECON discount.

desagradar [4] [dʒizagraˈda(x)] ◇ *vt* to displease. ◇ *vi*: ~ a alguém to displease sb.

➡ **desagradar-se** *vp* to be displeased.

desagradável [dʒizagraˈdavewl (*pl* -eis) *adj* unpleasant.

desagrado [dʒiza'gradu] *m* displeasure.

desagravo [dʒiza'gravu] *m* **-1.** [reparação de agravo] recompense; **de ~** to make amends. **-2.** *JUR* reparation.

desagregação [dʒizagrega'sãw] (*pl* **-ões**) *f* **-1.** [dissolução] break-up. **-2.** [separação] division.

desagregar [14] [dʒizagre'ga(x)] *vt*-**1.** [dissolver] to dissolve. **-2.** [separar] to split.

➡ **desagregar-se** *vp* [dissociar-se] to split.

desaguar [22] [dʒiza'gwa(x)] <> *vi* [vazar-se]: **~ em** to flow into. <> *vt* [drenar] to drain.

desajeitado, da [dʒizaʒej'tadu, da] *adj* clumsy.

desajuizado, da [dʒizaʒwi'zadu, -da] *adj* senseless.

desajustado, da [dʒizaʒuʃ'tadu, da] <> *adj* **-1.** *PSIC* maladjusted. **-2.** [desajuntado] in need of adjustment. <> *m, f PSIC* maladjusted person.

desajustamento [dʒizaʒuʃta'mẽntu] *m PSIC* maladjustment.

desajustar [4] [dʒizaʒuʃ'ta(x)] *vt* **-1.** *PSIC* to disturb. **-2.** [desajuntar] to undo.

desajuste [dʒiza'ʒuʃtʃi] *m* **-1.** *PSIC* maladjustment. **-2.** [de peças, máquina] loosening.

desalentado, da [dʒizalẽn'tadu, da] *adj* discouraged.

desalentar [4] [dʒizalẽn'ta(x)] <> *vt* to discourage. <> *vi* to lose heart.

➡ **desalentar-se** *vp* to become discouraged.

desalento [dʒiza'lẽntu] *m* discouragement.

desalinhado, da [dʒizali'ɲadu, da] *adj* dishevelled.

desalinhar [dʒiza'liɲa(x)] *vt*-**1.** [tirar do alinhamento] to break up. **-2.** [desarrumar] to mess up.

desalinho [dʒiza'liɲu] *m* dishevelment.

desalmado, da [dʒizaw'madu, da] *adj* soulless.

desalojar [4] [dʒizalo'ʒa(x)] <> *vt*: **~ alguém de** to remove sb from. <> *vi* to quit.

desamarrar [4] [dʒizama'xa(x)] <> *vt* [desfazer] to untie. <> *vi NÁUT* to lift anchor.

desamarrotar [4] [dʒizamaxo'ta(x)] *vt* to smooth.

desamassar [4] [dʒizama'sa(x)] *vt* to straighten out.

desambientado, da [dʒizãnbjẽn'tadu, da] *adj* disorientated.

desamor [dʒiza'mo(x)] *m* antipathy.

desamparado, da [dʒizãnpa'radu, da] *adj* **-1.** [pessoa - abandonado] abandoned; [- sem ajuda] unassisted. **-2.** [lugar] abandoned.

desamparar [4] [dʒizãnpa'ra(x)] *vt* [abandonar] to abandon.

desamparo [dʒizãn'parul] *m* **-1.** [abandono] abandonment. **-2.** [falta de ajuda] helplessness.

desandar [4] [dʒizãn'da(x)] *vi* **-1.** *fam* [clara, maionese] to separate. **-2.** [começar]: **~ a rir** to burst out laughing; **~ a chorar** to burst into tears; **~ a correr** to break into a run; **~ a falar** to start speaking.

desanimação [dʒizanima'sãw] *f* dejection.

desanimado, da [dʒizani'madu, da] *adj* despondent.

desanimador, ra [dʒizanima'do(x), ra] *adj* disheartening.

desanimar [4] [dʒizani'ma(x)] <> *vt* **-1.** [fazer perder o ânimo]: **~ alguém** to dishearten sb. **-2.** [desencorajar]: **~ alguém de fazer algo** to discourage sb from doing sthg. <> *vi* -**1.** [perder o ânimo] to become disheartened; **~ de fazer algo** to become disheartened about doing sthg. **-2.** [ser desencorajador] to be discouraging.

desânimo [dʒi'zãnimul *m* despondency.

desanuviar [16] [dʒizanu'vja(x)] *vt* **-1.** [céu] to clear. **-2.** *fig* [pessoa, mente] to calm.

➡ **desanuviar-se** *vp* **-1.** [céu] to clear. **-2.** *fig* [pessoa, mente] to become calm.

desaparafusar [4] [dʒizaparafu'za(x)] *vt* to unscrew.

desaparecer [25] [dʒizapare'se(x)] *vi* to disappear.

desaparecido, da [dʒizapare'sidu, da] <> *adj* missing. <> *m, f* [pessoa] missing person.

desaparecimento [dʒizaparesi'mẽntu] *m* **-1.** [sumiço] disappearance. **-2.** [falecimento] loss.

desapegado, da [dʒizape'gadu, da] *adj* detached.

desapegar [14] [dʒizape'ga(x)] *vt* : **~ alguém de algo/alguém** to detach sb from sthg/sb.

➡ **desapegar-se** *vp*: **~-se de algo/alguém** to detach o.s. from sthg/sb.

desapego [dʒiza'pegul *m* **-1.** [desamor] lack of love. **-2.** [indiferença] indifference.

desapertar [4] [dʒizapex'ta(x)] *vt* to loosen.

desapiedado, da [dʒizapje'dadu, da] *adj* ruthless.

desapontador, ra [dʒizapõnta'do(x), ra] *adj* disappointing.

desapontamento [dʒizapõnta'mẽntul *m* disappointment.

desapontar [4] [dʒizapõn'ta(x)] *vt* to disappoint.

➡ **desapontar-se** *vp* to be disappointed.

desapossar [4] [dʒizapo'sa(x)] *vt*: **~ alguém de algo** to deprive sb of sthg.

➡ **desapossar-se** *vp*: **~-se de algo** to deprive o.s. of sthg.

desapreço [dʒiza'presul *m* discontent.

desaprender [5] [dʒizaprẽn'de(x)] <> *vt* to forget. <> *vi*: **~ a fazer algo** to forget how to do sthg.

desapropriação [dʒizaproprja'sãw] (*pl* **-ões**) *f* dispossession.

desapropriar [16] [dʒizapro'prja(x)] *vt*-**1.** [desapossar]: **~ alguém de algo** to deprive sb of sthg. **-2.** [expropriar]: **~ algo (de alguém)** to expropriate sthg (from sb).

desaprovação [dʒizaprova'sãw] (*pl* **-ões**) *f* disapproval.

desaprovar [4] [dʒizapro'va(x)] *vt*-**1.** [reprovar] to disapprove. **-2.** [censurar] to censure.

desarmado, da [dʒizax'madu, da] *adj* **-1.** [ger] disarmed. **-2.** [sem arma] unarmed.

desarmamento [dʒizaxma'mẽntul *m* disarmament.

desarmar [4] [dʒizax'ma(x)] *vt* -**1.** [ger] to disarm. -**2.** [barraca, brinqueda] to take down. -**3.** [arma] to disable.

→ **desarmar-se** *vp* [criminoso] to hand over one's arms.

desarmonia [dʒizaxmo'nia] *f* -**1.** [falta de harmonia] disharmony. -**2.** *fig* [divergência] discord.

desarraigar [14] [dʒizaxaj'ga(x)] *vt* -**1.** [arrancar] to uproot. -**2.** [extinguir] to stamp out.

desarranjado, da [dʒizaxãn'ʒadu, da] *adj* -**1.** [desarrumado] untidy. -**2.** *MED*: estar ∼ to be queasy.

desarranjar [4] [dʒizaxãn'ʒa(x)] *vt* [desarrumar] to make untidy.

desarranjo [dʒiza'xãnʒu] *m* disorder.

desarregaçar [dʒizaxega'sa(x)] *vt* [mangas] to roll down.

desarrumado, da [dʒizaxu'madu, da] *adj* untidy.

desarrumar [4] [dʒizaxu'ma(x)] *vt* -**1.** [ger] to make untidy. -**2.** [mala] to unpack.

desarticulado, da [dʒizaxtʃiku'ladu, da] *adj* -**1.** [deslocado] dislocated. -**2.** [desfeito] broken up.

desarticular [4] [dʒizaxtʃiku'la(x)] *vt* to dislocate.

desarvorado, da [dʒizaxvo'radu, da] *adj* disorientated.

desassociar [16] [dʒizaso'sja(x)] *vt*: ∼ algo/alguém (de) to dissociate sthg/sb (from).

→ **desassociar-se** *vp*: ∼-se (de) to dissociate o.s. (from).

desassossego [dʒizaso'segu] *m* uneasiness.

desastrado, da [dʒiza'ʃtradu, da] *adj* clumsy.

desastre [dʒi'zaʃtri] *m* -**1.** [acidente] accident. -**2.** *fig* [fracasso]: ser um ∼ to be a disaster.

desastroso, osa [dʒizaʃ'trozu, ɔza] *adj* disastrous.

desatar [4] [dʒiza'ta(x)] ◇ *vt* -**1.** [desfazer] to undo. -**2.** [desprender] to loosen. ◇ *vi* [começar]: ∼ a fazer algo to start to do sthg suddenly.

desatarraxar [4] [dʒizataxa'ʃa(x)] *vt* to undo.

desatenção [dʒizatẽn'sãw] *f* -**1.** [distração] lack of attention. -**2.** [descortesia] lack of courtesy.

desatento, ta [dʒiza'tẽntu, ta] *adj* inattentive.

desatinado, da [dʒizatʃi'nadu, da] ◇ *adj* mad. ◇ *m, f* mad person.

desatinar [4] [dʒizatʃi'na(x)] ◇ *vt* to drive mad. ◇ *vi* to go mad.

desatino [dʒiza'tʃinu] *m* idiocy.

desativar [4] [dʒizatʃi'va(x)] *vt* -**1.** [tornar inativo] to close down. -**2.** [desmontar] to deactivate.

desatolar [4] [dʒizato'la(x)] *vt* to pull out of the mud.

desatrelar [4] [dʒizatre'la(x)] *vt* -**1.** [cão] to unleash. -**2.** [cavalo] to unharness.

desatualizado, da [dʒizatwali'zadu, da] *adj* out-of-date.

desautorizar [4] [dʒizawtori'za(x)] *vt* -**1.** [não permitir] to disallow. -**2.** [fazer perder a autoridade] to discredit.

desavença [dʒiza'vẽnsa] *f* -**1.** [briga] enmity. -**2.** [dissensão] dissent.

desavergonhado, da [dʒizavexgo'ɲadu, da] *adj* unashamed.

desavisado, da [dʒizavi'zadu, da] *adj* not made aware.

desbancar [12] [dʒiʒbãŋ'ka(x)] *vt*: ∼ alguém (em algo) to outdo sb (at sthg).

desbaratar [4] [dʒiʒbara'ta(x)] *vt* -**1.** [dissipar]: ∼ algo (em algo) to squander sthg (on sthg). -**2.** [arruinar] to destroy. -**3.** [vencer] to defeat.

desbastar [4] [dʒiʒbaʃ'ta(x)] *vt* to thin (out).

desbocado, da [dʒiʒbo'kadu, da] *adj fig* lewd.

desbotado, da [dʒiʒbo'tadu, da] *adj* faded.

desbotar [4] [dʒiʒbo'ta(x)] *vt* to fade.

desbragadamente [dʒiʒbragada'mẽntʃil] *adv* shamelessly.

desbravador, ra [dʒiʒbrava'do(x), ral] *m, f* -**1.** [de terra, mata] explorer. -**2.** [de animais] tamer.

desbravar [4] [dʒiʒbra'va(x)] *vt* -**1.** [terras, matas] to explore. -**2.** [animais selvagens] to tame. -**3.** [cavalo] to break in.

desbundante [dʒiʒbũn'dãntʃil] *adj fam* amazing.

desbundar [4] [dʒiʒbũn'da(x)] *vi fam* [perder compostura] to freak out.

desbunde [dʒiʒ'bũndʒil] *m fam* sensation.

desburocratizar [4] [dʒiʒburokratʃi'za(x)] *vt* to get rid of bureaucracy from.

descabelado, da [dʒiʃkabe'ladu, da] *adj* with untidy hair *(depois de subst)*.

descabelar [4] [dʒiʃkabe'la(x)] *vt fam* to ruffle the hair of.

→ **descabelar-se** *vp fam* to ruffle one's hair.

descabido, da [dʒiʃka'bidu, da] *adj* -**1.** [absurdo] ridiculous. -**2.** [impróprio] inappropriate.

descadeirado, da [dʒiʃkadej'radu, da] *adj* -**1.** [com dor nas cadeiras]: estar ∼ to have painful hips. -**2.** [exausto] exhausted.

descalabro [dʒiʃka'labrul] *m* disaster, ruin.

descalçar [13] [dʒiʃkaw'sa(x)] *vt* to take off.

→ **descalçar-se** *vp* to take off one's shoes/gloves.

descalço, ça [dʒiʃ'kawsu, sal] *adj* barefoot.

descambar [4] [dʒiʃkãn'ba(x)] *vi* -**1.** [para o lado]: ∼ para to topple towards. -**2.** [degenerar]: ∼ em to degenerate into.

descampado, da [dʒiʃkãn'padu, da] *adj* uninhabited.

→ **descampado** *m* open country.

descansado, da [dʒiʃkãn'sadu, da] *adj* -**1.** [tranqüilo] calm. -**2.** [lento] slow.

descansar [4] [dʒiʃkãn'sa(x)] ◇ *vt* -**1.** [ger] to rest. -**2.** *fig* [tranqüilizar] to calm. ◇ *vi* -**1.** [repousar] to rest. -**2.** *fig* [tranqüilizar-se] to calm down. -**3.** *ant* & *fig* [morrer] to be at rest.

descanso [dʒiʃ'kãnsul] *m* -**1.** [repouso] rest. -**2.** [folga] break. -**3.** [para travessa *etc*] trivet.

descaracterizar [4] [dʒiʃkara(k)teri'za(x)] *vt* to destroy the character of.

descarado, da [dʒiʃka'radu, da] ◇ *adj* shameless. ◇ *m, f* shameless person.

descaramento [dʒiʃkara'mẽntu] *m* shamelessness.

descarga [dʒiʃ'kaxga] *f* -**1.** [ato] unloading. -**2.** [vaso sanitário] flush; **dar a** ~ to flush. -**3.** [de arma] fire. -**4.** ELETR: ~ **elétrica** electrical discharge.

descarregar [14] [dʒiʃkaxe'ga(x)] <> *vt* -**1.** [carga] to unload. -**2.** [arma] to fire. -**3.** ELETR to discharge. -**4.** [desabafar] to give vent to. <> *vi* [bateria] to go flat.

descarrilamento [dʒiʃkaxila'mẽntu] *m* derailment.

descarrilar [4] [dʒiʃkaxi'la(x)] *vt & vi* to derail.

descartar [4] [dʒiʃkax'ta(x)] *vt* to discard.
➤ **descartar-se** *vp*: ~**-se de** [de carta, pessoa] to get rid of; [de compromisso] to free o.s. of.

descartável [dʒiʃkax'tavɛw] (*pl* -**eis**) *adj* disposable.

descascador [dʒiʃkaʃka'do(x)] *m* peeler.

descascar [12] [dʒiʃkaʃ'ka(x)] <> *vt* to peel. <> *vi* -**1.** [perder a casca] to lose its shell. -**2.** [perder a pele] to peel; **com tanto sol, estou descascando todo** with all this sun, I'm peeling all over.

descaso [dʒiʃ'kasu] *m* negligence.

descendência [desẽ'dẽnsja] *f* descendancy.

descendente [desẽ'dẽntʃi] <> *adj* descendent; **ser** ~ **de** to be a descendant of. <> *mf* [pessoa] descendant.

descender [5] [desẽn'de(x)] *vi* -**1.** [pessoa]: ~ **de** to be descended from. -**2.** [palavra]: ~ **de** to stem from.

descentralização [dʒisẽntraliza'sãw] *f* decentralization.

descentralizar [4] [dʒiʃsẽntrali'za(x)] *vt* to decentralize.

descer [25] [de'se(x)] <> *vt* -**1.** [escada] to go down. -**2.** [carga] to take down. <> *vi* -**1.** [ger] to go down. -**2.** [de ônibus] to get off.

descida [de'sida] *f* [declive] descent.

desclassificação [dʒiʃklasifika'sãw] (*pl* -**ões**) *f* disqualification.

desclassificar [12] [dʒiʃklasifi'ka(x)] *vt* -**1.** [eliminar] to disqualify. -**2.** [desmoralizar] to disgrace.

descoberto, ta [dʒiʃko'bɛxtu, ta] <> *pp* ▷ **descobrir.** <> *adj* -**1.** [ger] discovered. -**2.** [exposto] uncovered. -**3.** BANCO [conta] overdrawn.
➤ **descoberta** *f* discovery.
➤ **a descoberto** *loc adv* FIN [saque] overdrawn, in the red.

descobridor, ra [dʒiʃkobri'do(x), ra] *m, f* discoverer.

descobrimento [dʒiʃkobri'mẽntu] *m* [de continentes] discovery.

descobrir [59] [dʒiʃko'bri(x)] *vt* -**1.** [ger] to discover. -**2.** [tirar a proteção de] to uncover. -**3.** [estátua] to unveil.
➤ **descobrir-se** *vp* [tirar a coberta] to appear.

descolado, da [dʒiʃko'ladu, da] *adj fam* trendy, cool.

descolar [4] [deʃko'lar] <> *vt* -**1.** [desgrudar]: ~ **algo (de)** to detach sthg (from). -**2.** *fam* [conseguir]

to fix up. <> *vi* [afastar-se]: ~ **de alguém** to move away from sb.

descolorir [79] [dʒiʃkolo'ri(x)] <> *vt* [tirar a cor] to discolour. <> *vi* [perder a cor] to fade.

descomedido, da [dʒiʃkome'dʒidu, da] *adj* immoderate.

descompassado, da [dʒiʃkõnpa'sadu, da] *adj* -**1.** [ritmo] out of time. -**2.** [desmedido] excessive. -**3.** [desordenado] untidy.

descompor [45] [dʒiʃkõn'po(x)] *vt* [desordenar] to muddle.

descomposto, osta [dʒiʃkõn'poʃtu, ɔʃta] <> *pp* ▷ **descompor.** <> *adj* -**1.** [desalinhado] confused. -**2.** [desfeito] disordered. -**3.** [desfigurado] upset.

descompostura [dʒiʃkõnpoʃ'tura] *f* -**1.** [repreensão] reprimand; **passar uma** ~ **em alguém** to reprimand sb. -**2.** [insulto] affront.

descompressão [dʒiʃkõnpre'sãw] (*pl* -**ões**) *f* decompression.

descomprometido, da [dʒiʃkõnprome'tʃidu, da] *adj* no longer compromised *(depois de verbo)*.

descomunal [dʒiʃkomu'naw] (*pl* -**ais**) *adj* -**1.** [gigantesco] huge. -**2.** [fora do comum] unusual.

desconcentrar [4] [dʒiʃkõnsẽn'tra(x)] *vt* to distract.
➤ **desconcentrar-se** *vp* to lose concentration.

desconcentrado, da [dʒiʃkõnsex'tadu, da] *adj* lacking concentration.

desconcertado, da [dʒiʃkõnsex'tadu, da] *adj* -**1.** [confuso] confused. -**2.** [frustrado] upset.

desconcertante [dʒiʃkõnsex'tãntʃil] *adj* -**1.** [desorientador] confusing. -**2.** [frustrante] upsetting.

desconcertar [dʒiʃkõnsex'ta(x)] *vt* -**1.** [desorientar] to confuse. -**2.** [frustrar] to upset.
➤ **desconcertar-se** *vp* -**1.** [desarranjar-se] to break down. -**2.** [perturbar-se] to become bewildered. -**3.** [frustrar-se] to be upset.

desconectar [4] [dʒiʃkonek'ta(x)] *vt* to disconnect.
➤ **desconectar-se** *vp* [comput] to be disconnected.

desconexo, xa [dʒiʃko'nɛksu, ksa] *adj* -**1.** [incoerente] incoherent. -**2.** [desunido] disconnected.

desconfiado, da [dʒiʃkõn'fjadu, da] *adj* distrustful.

desconfiança [dʒiʃkõn'fjãnsa] *f* distrust.

desconfiar [16] [dʒiʃkõn'fja(x)] <> *vt* [conjeturar]: ~ **que** to fear that. <> *vi* -**1.** [ficar suspeitoso] to suspect. -**2.** [não confiar em]: ~ **de** to be distrustful of. -**3.** [suspeitar de]: ~ **de** to be suspicious of.

desconfortável [dʒiʃkõnfor'tavɛw] (*pl* -**eis**) *adj* uncomfortable.

desconforto [dʒiʃkõn'foxtu] *m* discomfort.

descongelar [4] [dʒiʃkõnʒe'la(x)] *vt* to defrost.

descongestionante [dʒiʃkõnʒeʃtʃjo'nãntʃi] <> *adj* decongestant. <> *m* decongestant.

descongestionar [4] [dʒiʃkõnʒeʃtʃjo'na(x)] *vt* -**1.** to decongest. -**2.** *fig* [trânsito, rua] to clear.

desconhecer [25] [dʒiʃkoɲe'se(x)] *vt* -**1.** [ignorar]

not to know. **-2.** [estranhar] not to recognize. **-3.** [ser ingrato a] to be ungrateful for.

desconhecido, da [dʒiʃkoɲeˈsidu, da] <> *adj* [incógnito] unknown. <> *m, f* [pessoa] unknown person.

desconhecimento [dʒiʃkoɲesiˈmẽntul] *m* ignorance.

desconjuntado, da [dʒiʃkõnʒũnˈtadu, da] *adj* dislocated.

desconjuntar [4] [dʒiʃkõnʒũnˈta(x)] *vt* to dislocate.

desconsideração [dʒiʃkõnsideraˈsãwl] (*pl* -ões) *f* **-1.** [desrespeito] disrespect. **-2.** [ofensa] insult.

desconsiderar [4] [dʒiʃkõnsideˈra(x)] *vt* to overlook.

desconsolado, da [dʒiʃkõnsoˈladu, da] *adj* disconsolate.

desconsolar [4] [dʒiʃkõnsoˈla(x)] <> *vt* to sadden. <> *vi* to become saddened.

➡ **desconsolar-se** *vp* to become dispirited.

descontar [4] [dʒiʃkõnˈta(x)] *vt* **-1.** [deduzir]: ~ algo (de) to deduct sthg (from). **-2.** [título de crédito - pagar] to pay off; [- receber] to receive. **-3.** *fam* [revidar]: ~ algo (em alguém) to pay sthg back (to sb). **-4.** *fig* [não fazer caso de] to take no notice of.

descontentamento [dʒiʃkõntẽntaˈmẽntul] *m* **-1.** [desprazer] displeasure. **-2.** [insatisfação] dissatisfaction.

descontentar [4] [dʒiʃkõntẽnˈta(x)] *vt* to displease.

➡ **descontentar-se** *vp* to be displeased.

descontente [dʒiʃkõnˈtẽntʃi] *adj* displeased.

descontínuo, nua [dʒiʃkõnˈtʃinwu, nwal] *adj* discontinued.

desconto [dʒiʃˈkõntul] *m* discount; com ~ at a discount; dar um ~ *fig* to make allowances.

descontração [dʒiʃkõntraˈsãwl] *f* relaxation.

descontraído, da [dʒiʃkõntraˈidu, da] *adj* relaxed.

descontrair [68] [dʒiʃkõntraˈi(x)] *vt* to relax.

➡ **descontrair-se** *vp* to relax.

descontrolado, da [dʒiʃkõntroˈladu, da] *adj* uncontrolled.

descontrolar [4] [dʒiʃkõntroˈla(x)] *vt* to lose control of.

➡ **descontrolar-se** *vp* **-1.** [pessoa] to lose control of o.s. **-2.** [situação] to get out of control.

descontrole [dʒiʃkõnˈtrolil] *m* lack of control.

desconversar [4] [dʒiʃkõnvexˈsa(x)] *vi* to change the subject.

descorar [4] [dʒikoˈra(x)] <> *vt* [desbotar] to discolour. <> *vi* [empalidecer] to turn pale.

descortês, tesa [dʒiʃkoxˈteʃ, tezal] *adj* discourteous.

descortesia [dʒiʃkoxteˈzial] *f* discourtesy.

descortinar [4] [dʒiʃkoxtʃiˈna(x)] *vt* **-1.** [avistar] to reveal. **-2.** [correndo a cortina] to unveil. **-3.** [revelar]: ~ algo a alguém to reveal sthg to sb.

descoser [5] [dʒiʃkoˈze(x)], **descosturar** [dʒiʃkoʃtuˈra(x)] <> *vt* to unstitch. <> *vi* to come unstiched.

descrédito [dʒiʃˈkrɛdʒitul] *m* discredit.

descrença [dʒiʃˈkrẽnsal] *f* disbelief.

descrente [dʒiʃˈkrẽntʃil] *adj* disbelieving.

descrer [37] [dʒiʃˈkre(x)] *vi* to disbelieve: ~ de algo/alguém not to believe in sthg/sb.

descrever [5] [dʒiʃkreˈve(x)] *vt* **-1.** [expor] to describe. **-2.** [traçar] to trace.

descrição [dʒiʃkriˈsãwl] (*pl* -ões) *f* description.

descritivo, va [dʒiʃkriˈtʃivu, val] *adj* descriptive.

descuidado, da [dʒiʃkujˈdadu, da] *adj* **-1.** [desleixado] uncared-for. **-2.** [irrefletido] careless.

descuidar [4] [dʒiʃkujˈda(x)] *vi*: ~ de algo to neglect sthg.

➡ **descuidar-se** *vp*: ~-se de algo to become careless about sthg.

descuido [dʒiʃˈkujdul] *m* **-1.** [ger] carelessness. **-2.** [erro] error.

desculpa [dʒiʃˈkuwpal] *f* **-1.** [ger] excuse. **-2.** [perdão] forgiveness; pedir ~s a alguém por algo to ask sb forgiveness for sthg.

desculpar [4] [dʒiʃkuwˈpa(x)] *vt* **-1.** [perdoar]: ~ alguém (por algo) to forgive sb (for sthg). **-2.** [justificar] to give as an excuse.

➡ **desculpar-se** *vp* [justificar-se]: ~-se (com alguém) por algo to apologize (to sb) for sthg.

desculpável [dʒiʃkuwˈpavewl] (*pl* -eis) *adj* forgiveable.

descumprir [6] [dʒiʃkũnˈpri(x)] *vt* to disobey.

desde [ˈdeʒdʒil] *prep* **-1.** [tempo] since; ~ então from then on; ~ já straight away. **-2.** [espaço] from.

➡ **desde que** *loc conj* **-1.** [tempo] since. **-2.** [visto que] as. **-3.** [contanto que] as long as.

desdém [deʒˈdẽl] *m* disdain.

desdenhar [4] [deʒdeˈɲa(x)] *vt* **-1.** [desprezar] to despise. **-2.** [escarnecer] to scorn.

desdenhoso, osa [deʒdeˈɲozu, ɔzal] *adj* disdainful.

desdentado, da [dʒiʒdẽnˈtadu, da] *adj* toothless.

desdita [dʒiʒˈdʒital] *f* bad luck.

desdizer [29] [dʒiʒdʒiˈze(x)] *vt* **-1.** [negar] to deny. **-2.** [desmentir] to contradict.

➡ **desdizer-se** *vp* [negar o que havia dito] to retract.

desdobramento [dʒiʒdobraˈmẽntul] *m* unfolding, development.

desdobrar [4] [dʒiʒdoˈbra(x)] *vt* **-1.** [abrir] to unfold. **-2.** [dividir]: ~ algo em algo to divide sthg into sthg. **-3.** [aumentar] to develop.

➡ **desdobrar-se** *vp* **-1.** to unfold. **-2.** [empenhar-se]: ~-se (em algo) *fig* to make an effort (at sthg).

deseducar [12] [dʒizeduˈka(x)] *vt* **-1.** [educar mal] to educate poorly. **-2.** [estragar] to spoil.

desejar [4] [dezeˈʒa(x)] <> *vt* **-1.** [querer] to wish; ~ que to hope that; ~ fazer algo to want to do sthg. **-2.** [ambicionar]: ~ algo to wish for sthg; ~ fazer algo to wish to do sthg. **-3.** [formulando votos]: ~ algo a alguém to wish sb sthg. **-4.** [sexualmente] to desire. <> *vi*: deixar a ~ to leave sthg to be desired.

desejável [dese'ʒavewl (*pl* **-eis**) *adj* desirable.

desejo [de'ʒeʒu] *m* **-1.** [ger] desire. **-2.** [ambição] wish. **-3.** [de grávida] craving.

desejoso, osa [dese'ʒosu, ɔsal *adj*: ~ **de algo/de fazer algo** keen for sthg/to do sthg.

deselegância [dʒizele'gãnsjal *f* inelegance.

deselegante [dʒizele'gãntʃil *adj* inelegant.

desembaçar [13] [dʒizĩnba'sa(x)] *vt* to wipe the steam of.

desembainhar [4] [dʒizẽmbaj'ɲa(x)] *vt* to unsheathe; [sword] to draw.

desembalar [4] [dʒizĩnba'la(x)] *vt* to unwrap.

desembaraçado, da [dʒizẽmbara'sadu, dal *adj* **-1.** [desinibido] uninhibited. **-2.** [livre] free. **-3.** [expedito] prompt. **-4.** [cabelo, novelo] loose.

desembaraçar [13] [dʒizĩnbara'sa(x)] *vt* **-1.** [livrar] to free. **-2.** [desemaranhar] to loosen. **-3.** [liberar] to unencumber.

→ **desembaraçar-se** *vp* **-1.** [desinibir-se] to open up. **-2.** [livrar-se]: ~**-se de algo/alguém** to free o.s. of sthg/sb.

desembaraço [dʒizĩnba'rasul *m* **-1.** [desinibição] ease. **-2.** [agilidade] agility.

desembarcar [12] [dʒizĩnbax'ka(x)] <> *vt* **-1.** [carga] to unload. **-2.** [passageiros] to disembark. <> *vi* [descer de transporte] to disembark.

desembargador, ra [dʒizẽmbaxga'do(x), ral *m, f* high court judge.

desembarque [dʒizĩn'baxkil *m* disembarcation.

desembestar [dʒizĩnbeʃ'ta(x)] *vi* [disparar] to bolt.

desembocadura [dʒizĩnboka'dural *f* discharge.

desembocar [12] [dʒizĩnbo'ka(x)] *vi* [rio, rua]: ~ **em** to discharge into.

desembolsar [4] [dʒizĩnbow'sa(x)] *vt* [gastar] to spend.

desembolso [dʒizĩn'bowsul *m* [gasto] expenditure.

desembrulhar [4] [dʒizĩnbru'ʎa(x)] *vt* to unwrap.

desembuchar [4] [dʒizĩnbu'ʃa(x)] *fam* <> *vt* [confessar] to get off one's chest. <> *vi* to open up.

desempacotar [4] [dʒizĩnpako'ta(x)] *vt* to unpack.

desempatar [4] [dezĩnpa'ta(x)] <> *vt ESP*: ~ **a partida** to score a deciding point or goal in a match. <> *vi* to decide; **a eleição só desempatou no final** the election was only decided at the finish.

desempate [dʒizĩn'patʃil *m ESP* decision.

desempenhar [4] [dʒizĩnpe'ɲa(x)] *vt* **-1.** [ger] to perform. **-2.** [cumprir] to carry out.

desempenho [dʒizĩn'peɲul *m* performance.

desempregado, da [dʒizĩnpre'gadu, dal <> *adj* unemployed. <> *m, f* unemployed person.

desempregar [14] [dʒizĩnpre'ga(x)] *vt* to sack, to lay off.

→ **desempregar-se** *vp* to lose one's job.

desemprego [dʒizĩn'pregul *m* unemployment.

desencadear [15] [dʒizĩŋka'dʒja(x)] *vt* [provocar] to unleash.

→ **desencadear-se** *vp* [irromper] to break out.

desencaixar [4] [dʒizĩŋkaj'ʃa(x)] *vt* to dislocate.

→ **desencaixar-se** *vp* to become dislocated.

desencaixotar [4] [dʒizĩŋkajʃo'ta(x)] *vt* to take out of a box.

desencalhar [4] [dʒizĩŋka'ʎa(x)] <> *vt NÁUT* to set loose. <> *vi* **-1.** *NÁUT* to free itself. **-2.** *fam* [pessoa] to get hitched.

desencaminhar [4] [dʒizĩŋkami'ɲa(x)] *vt* to lead astray.

→ **desencaminhar-se** *vp* to go astray.

desencantar [4] [dʒizĩŋkãn'ta(x)] *vt* **-1.** [desiludir] to disillusion. **-2.** [de feitiço *etc*] to free from a spell. **-3.** [encontrar] to unearth.

→ **desencantar-se** *vp* [desiludir-se] to become disenchanted.

desencanto [dʒizĩŋ'kãntul *m* [desilusão] disenchantment.

desencardir [6] [dʒizĩŋkax'di(x)] *vt* to clean.

desencargo [dʒizĩŋ'kaxgul *m* [cumprimento] carrying out; **por** ~ **de consciência** to clear one's conscience.

desencarregar-se [14] [dʒizĩŋkaxe'gaxsil *vp* [desobrigar-se]: ~ **de algo** to unburden o.s. of sthg.

desencavar [4] [dʒizĩŋka'va(x)] *vt* to dig up.

desencontrado, da [dʒizĩŋkõn'tradu, dal *adj* **-1.** [contrário] contrary. **-2.** [desalinhado] out of step.

desencontrar [4] [dʒizĩŋkõn'tra(x)] *vt* [fazer que não se encontrem] to send in different directions.

→ **desencontrar-se** *vp* **-1.** [não se encontrar]: ~**-se (de)** to diverge (from). **-2.** [perder-se um do outro] to fail to meet one another.

desencontro [dʒizĩŋ'kõntrul *m* **-1.** [falta de encontro] failure to meet. **-2.** [divergência] difference.

desencorajar [4] [dʒizĩŋkora'ʒa(x)] *vt* to discourage.

desencostar [4] [dʒizĩŋkoʃ'ta(x)] *vt*: ~ **algo/alguém (de)** to move sthg/sb away (from).

→ **desencostar-se** *vp*: ~**-se de algo** to stop leaning against sthg.

desenferrujar [4] [dʒizĩfexu'ʒa(x)] *vt* **-1.** [metal] to remove rust from. **-2.** *fig* [pernas] to stretch; [língua] to polish, brush up.

desenfreado, da [dʒizẽnfre'adu, dal *adj* wild.

desenganado, da [dʒizẽŋga'nadu, dal *adj* [sem cura] incurable; [desiludido] disenchanted.

desenganar [4] [dʒizẽŋga'na(x)] *vt* **-1.** [doente] to give up hope for. **-2.** [desiludir] to disillusion.

→ **desenganar-se** *vp* [desiludir-se]: ~**-se de algo/alguém** to have no illusions about sthg/sb.

desengano [dʒizĩŋ'gãnul *m* [desilusão] disillusionment.

desengarrafar [4] [dʒizĩŋgaxa'fa(x)] *vt* **-1.** [líquido] to pour from a bottle. **-2.** *fig* [trânsito] to clear.

desengatar [4] [dʒizĩŋga'ta(x)] *vt* to uncouple.

desengonçado, da [dʒizẽŋgõ'sadu, dal *adj* **-1.** [desconjuntado] disjointed. **-2.** [desajeitado] clumsy.

desengrenado, da [dʒiziŋgre'nadu, da] *adj* AUTO in neutral.

desengrenar [4] [dʒiziŋgre'na(x)] *vt* AUTO to put into neutral.

desenhar [4] [deze'ɲa(x)] ⬦ *vt* -1. [traçar] to outline. -2. TEC to design. -3. ARTE to draw. ⬦ *vi* [traçar desenhos] to draw up.
➡ **desenhar-se** *vp* [figurar-se] to take shape.

desenhista [deze'niʃtal *m, f* designer.

desenho [de'zeɲul *m* -1. [expressão de formas] drawing. -2. ARTE & TEC design; ~ **industrial** technical drawing. -3. CINE: ~ **animado** (animated) cartoon.

desenlace [dʒizẽn'lasil *m* unfolding, development.

desenredar [4] [dʒizẽnxe'da(x)] *vt* -1. [desembaraçar]: ~ **alguém de** to extricate sb from. -2. [resolver] to resolve. -3. [descobrir] to unravel.
➡ **desenredar-se** *vp* [desembaraçar-se]: ~-se de to extricate o.s. from.

desenrolar [4] [dʒizẽnxo'la(x)] ⬦ *m* to progress. ⬦ *vt* -1. [estender] to unroll. -2. [expor] to unfold.
➡ **desenrolar-se** *vp* -1. [desenroscar-se] to uncurl o.s. -2. [mostrar-se] to open out.

desentender-se [5] [dʒizẽntẽn'dexsil *vp*: ~ **(com)** to disagree (with).

desentendido, da [dʒizẽntẽn'dʒidu, da] *adj*: fazer-se de ~ to pretend not to understand.
➡ **desentendido** *m* person who does not understand.

desentendimento [dʒizẽntẽndʒi'mẽntul *m* misunderstanding.

desenterrar [4] [dʒizẽnte'xa(x)] *vt* -1. [ger] to dig up. -2. [exumar] to exhume. -3. [descobrir] to unearth.

desentortar [4] [dʒizẽntox'ta(x)] *vt* to straighten.

desentrosado, da [dʒizẽntro'zadu, da] *adj* out of line.

desentupir [61] [dʒizẽntu'pi(x)] *vt* to unblock.

desenvolto, ta [dʒizẽn'vowtu, ta] *adj* wanton.

desenvoltura [dʒizĩnvow'tural *f* lack of inhibition.

desenvolver [5] [dʒizĩnvow've(x)] *vt* -1. [ger] to develop. -2. [melhorar] to improve. -3. [teorizar sobre] to expand on. -4. [correr] to run.
➡ **desenvolver-se** *vp* -1. [crescer] to develop. -2. [progredir] to progress.

desenvolvido, da [dʒizẽvow'vidu, da] ⬦ *pp* ⊳ **desenvolver**. ⬦ *adj* -1. [concebido] conceived. -2. [adiantado] advanced. -3. [crescido] developed.

desenvolvimento [dʒizĩnvowvi'mẽntul *m* -1. [crescimento] development. -2. [concepção] conception.

desequilibrado, da [dʒizekili'bradu, da] ⬦ *adj* -1. [sem equilíbrio] unbalanced. -2. PSIC unstable. ⬦ *m, f* PSIC unstable person.

desequilibrar [4] [dʒizekili'bra(x)] *vt* -1. [fazer perder o equilíbrio] to unbalance.
➡ **desequilibrar-se** *vp* -1. PSIC to become

unstable. -2. *fig* [descontrolar] to get out of control.

desequilíbrio [dʒizeki'librjul *m* -1. [falta de equilíbrio] lack of balance. -2. PSIC instability.

deserção [dezex'sãwl (*pl* -ões) *f* desertion.

deserdar [4] [dezex'da(x)] *vt* to disinherit.

desertar [4] [dezex'ta(x)] ⬦ *vt* [abandonar] to abandon. ⬦ *vi* -1. MIL to desert. -2. [abandonar]: ~ **de algo** to abandon sthg. -3. [bandear]: ~ **para algo** to go over to sthg.

deserto, ta [de'zɛxtu, ta] *adj* deserted.
➡ **deserto** *m* desert.

desertor, ra [dezex'to(x), ra] *m, f* deserter.

desesperado, da [dʒiziʃpe'radu, da] *adj* -1. [sem esperança] desperate. -2. [irritado] irritated. -3. [intenso - briga, competição] fierce; [- amor] intense.

desesperador, ra [dʒiziʃpera'do(x), ra] *adj* -1. [sem esperança] hopeless. -2. [irritante] irritating.

desesperança [dʒiziʃpe'rãnsal *f* despair.

desesperar [4] [dʒizeʃpe'ra(x)] ⬦ *vt* -1. [arrasar] to dishearten. -2. [irritar] to drive mad. ⬦ *vi* [perder a esperança] to give up hope.
➡ **desesperar-se** *vp* -1. [perder a esperança] to give up hope. -2. [afligir-se] to get upset.

desespero [dʒiziʃ'perul *m* -1. [desesperança] despair. -2. [aflição] despondency; **levar alguém ao** ~ to lead sb to despair.

desestabilizar [4] [dʒiziʃtabili'za(x)] *vt* to destabilize.
➡ **desestabilizar-se** *vp* to become destabilized.

desestimulante [dʒiziʃtʃimulãntʃil *adj* discouraging.

desestimular [4] [dʒiziʃtʃimu'la(x)] *vt* to discourage.

desfaçatez [dʒiʃfasa'teʃl *f* effrontery.

desfalcar [12] [dʒiʃfaw'ka(x)] *vt* -1. [reduzir] to reduce. -2. [privar] to deprive. -3. [defraudar] to defraud.

desfalecer [25] [dʒiʃfale'se(x)] *vi* -1. [desmaiar] to faint. -2. [esmorecer] to lose heart.

desfalque [dʒiʃ'fawkil *m* -1. [redução] reduction. -2. [privação] loss. -3. [fraude] fraud.

desfavorável [dʒiʃfavo'ravɛwl (*pl* -eis) *adj* -1. [desvantajoso] unfavourable. -2. [oposto] adverse.

desfazer [31] [dʒiʃfa'ze(x)] ⬦ *vt* -1. [desmanchar] to undo. -2. [dispersar] to disperse. -3. [acabar com] to put an end to. -4. [anular] to annul. ⬦ *vi* ~ **de** *ou* **em** [desdenhar] to despise.
➡ **desfazer-se** *vp* -1. [desmanchar-se] to come undone. -2. [dispersar-se] to disperse. -3. [acabar-se] to end. -4. [desembaraçar-se]: ~-se de algo to get rid of sthg. -5. [despojar-se]: ~-se de algo to be stripped of sthg. -6. *fig* [desmanchar-se]: ~-se em lágrimas to burst into tears; ~-se em sorrisos to break into smiles; ~-se em gentilezas to be desperate to please.

desfechar [4] [dʒiʃfe'ʃa(x)] *vt* -1. [disparar] to fire. -2. [insultos] to loose off.

desfecho [dʒiʃ'feʃul *m* ending.

desfeita [dʒiʃ'fejtal *f* insult.

desfeito, ta [dʒʃ'fejtu, ta] ⬦ *pp* ⊳ **desfazer**.

◇ **adj -1.** [desmanchado] undone. **-2.** [acabado] ended. **-3.** [desarrumada] untidy. **-4.** [anulado] annulled.

desferir [57] [dʒiʃfe'ri(x)] vt [aplicar] to direct.

desfiado, da [dʒiʃ'fjadu, da] adj **-1.** [meia, tecido] frayed. **-2.** fig [assunto, tema] well-worn.

desfiar [16] [dʒiʃ'fja(x)] ◇ vt **-1.** [tecido etc] to unravel. **-2.** [terço] to unthread. **-3.** [galinha] to cut up. ◇ vi [tecido etc] to unravel.

desfigurar [4] [dʒiʃfigu'ra(x)] vt **-1.** [transformar] to disfigure. **-2.** fig [adulterar] to adulterate.

➡ **desfigurar-se** vp [transformar-se] to alter.

desfiladeiro [dʒiʃfila'dejru] m ravine.

desfilar [4] [dʒiʃfi'la(x)] ◇ vt [exibir] to parade. ◇ vi [passar em desfile - soldado] to march past; [- manequim, escola de samba] to parade.

desfile [dʒiʃ'fili] m [passar em desfile - soldado] march past; [- manequim, escola de samba] parade.

desforra [dʒiʃ'fɔxa] f revenge.

desfraldar [4] [dʒiʃfraw'da(x)] vt to unfurl.

desfrutar [4] [dʒiʃfru'ta(x)] ◇ vt to enjoy. ◇ vi: ~ **de algo** to enjoy sthg.

desfrute [dʒiʃ'frutʃi] m [prazer] enjoyment.

desgarrado, da [dʒiʒga'xadu, da] adj [perdido] lost.

desgarrar-se [4] [dʒiʒga'xaxsi] vp [perder-se]: ~ **de algo** to lose sight of sthg; ~ **(do caminho)** to lose one's way.

desgastante [dʒiʒgaʃ'tãntʃi] adj **-1.** [estressante] stressful. **-2.** [cansativo] tiring. **-3.** [desprestigiante] damaging.

desgastar [4] [dʒiʒgaʃ'ta(x)] vt **-1.** [ger] to wear out. **-2.** [gastar] to wear away. **-3.** [desprestigiar] to damage.

desgaste [dʒiʒ'gaʃtʃi] m **-1.** [deterioração] deterioration. **-2.** [dano] harm.

desgostar [4] [dʒiʒgoʃ'ta(x)] ◇ vt [contrariar] to displease. ◇ vi [não gostar]: ~ **de algo** to dislike sthg.

➡ **desgostar-se** vp [deixar de gostar]: ~-**se de algo/de fazer algo** to no longer enjoy sthg/doing sthg.

desgosto [dʒiʒ'goʃtu] m **-1.** [desprazer] displeasure. **-2.** [pesar] regret.

desgostoso, osa [dʒiʒgoʃ'tozu, ɔza] adj **-1.** [triste] sad. **-2.** [contrariado] displeased.

desgovernado, da [dʒiʒgovex'nadu, da] adj **-1.** [país] misruled. **-2.** [veículo, animal] out of control.

desgraça [dʒiʒ'grasa] f **-1.** [infortúnio] misfortune. **-2.** [miséria] penury. **-3.** fig [pessoa inábil]: **ser uma** ~ to be a disgrace. **-4.** loc: **cair em** ~ [perder o prestígio] to fall from grace.

desgraçado, da [dʒiʒgra'sadu, da] ◇ adj **-1.** [desafortunado] unfortunate. **-2.** [miserável] wretched. **-3.** [vil] vile. **-4.** m fam [grande] hellish. ◇ m, f **-1.** [desafortunado] unfortunate. **-2.** [pessoa vil] beggar.

desgraçar [13] [dʒiʒgra'sa(x)] vt to disgrace.

desgravar [4] [dʒiʒgra'va(x)] vt to wipe.

desgrenhado, da [dʒiʒgre'nadu, da] adj **-1.** [despenteado] tousled. **-2.** [desarrumado] untidy.

desgrenhar [4] [dʒiʒgre'ɲa(x)] vt [despentear] to tousle.

desgrudar [4] [dʒiʒgru'da(x)] vt **-1.** [descolar]: ~ **algo de algo** to unstick sthg from sthg. **-2.** [afastar]: ~ **alguém de alguém/algo** fig to drag sb away from sb/sthg.

➡ **desgrudar-se** vp [afastar-se] to break away.

desguarnecer [25] [dʒiʒgwaxne'se(x)] vt **-1.** MIL to unman. **-2.** [despojar]: ~ **algo/alguém de algo** to take sthg/sb away from sthg.

desidratação [dezidrata'sãw] (pl -ões) f dehydration.

desidratante [dʒizidra'tãntʃi] adj dehydrating.

desidratar [4] [dʒizidra'ta(x)] vt to dehydrate.

➡ **desidratar-se** vp to become dehydrated.

design [dʒi'zajni] (pl -s) m design.

designação [dezigna'sãw] (pl -ões) f **-1.** [nome] designation. **-2.** [escolha] appointment.

designar [4] [dezig'na(x)] vt **-1.** [denominar] to designate. **-2.** [simbolizar] to symbolize. **-3.** [determinar] to award. **-4.** [escolher]: ~ **alguém para algo** to appoint sb as sthg.

designer [dʒi'zajnɛ(x)] (pl -s) mf designer.

desígnio [de'zignju] m design.

desigual [dezi'gwaw] (pl -ais) adj **-1.** [diferente] different. **-2.** [irregular] irregular. **-3.** [injusto] unfair.

desigualdade [dʒizigwaw'dadʒi] f **-1.** [diferença] difference. **-2.** [injustiça] inequality.

desiludir [6] [dʒizilu'dʒi(x)] vt: ~ **alguém (de algo /de fazer algo)** to dissuade sb (from sthg/from doing sthg); ~ **alguém (com algo)** to disappoint sb) with sthg).

➡ **desiludir-se** vp: ~-**se (com algo)** to be disappointed (by sthg).

desilusão [dʒizilu'zãw] (pl -ões) f disappointment.

desimpedido, da [dʒizĩmpe'dʒidu, da] adj **-1.** [desatravancado] clear. **-2.** [livre de compromisso] unencumbered.

desimpedir [70] [dʒizĩnpe'dʒi(x)] vt to clear.

desinchar [4] [dʒizĩn'ʃa(x)] vt to reduce.

desincompatibilizar [4] [dʒizĩnkõmpatʃibili'za(x)] vt to get rid of incompatibility between.

➡ **desincompatibilizar-se** vp to cease to be incompatible.

desincumbir-se [6] [dʒizĩnkũn'bixsi] vp: ~ **de algo** to be released from sthg.

desinência f GRAM ending.

desinfetante [dʒizĩnfe'tãntʃi] ◇ adj disinfectant. ◇ m disinfectant.

desinfetar [4] [dʒizĩnfe'ta(x)] vt MED to disinfect.

desinflamar [4] [dʒizĩnfla'ma(x)] ◇ vt to reduce inflammation in/on. ◇ vi to become less inflamed.

desinibido, da [dʒizini'bidu, da] adj uninhibited.

desinibir [6] [dʒizini'bi(x)] vt to make less inhibited.

➡ **desinibir-se** vp to lose one's inhibitions, to come out of o.s.

desintegração [dʒizĩntegra'sãw] f disintegration.
desintegrar [4] [dʒizĩnte'gra(x)] vt to cause to
disintegrate.
➧ **desintegrar-se** vp to disintegrate.
desinteressado, da [dʒizĩntere'sadu, da] adj
- **1.** [sem interesse] disinterested. - **2.** [despreendido]
detached.
desinteressar [4] [dʒizĩntere'sa(x)] vt: ~ alguém
de algo to destroy sb's interest in sthg.
➧ **desinteressar-se** vp: ~-se de algo to lose
interest in sthg.
desinteresse [dʒizĩnte'resi] m - **1.** [falta de interes-
se] lack of interest. - **2.** [despreendimento] detachment.
desintoxicação [dʒizĩntoksika'sãw] (pl -ões) f
detoxification.
desintoxicar [12] [dʒizĩntoksi'ka(x)] vt to detox-
ify.
desistência [dezi∫'tẽnsja] f withdrawal.
desistir [6] [dezi∫'t∫i(x)] vi to give up; ~ **de algo**
/de fazer algo to give up sthg/doing sthg.
desjejum [dʒiʒe'ʒũ] (pl -ns) m breakfast.
deslanchar [4] [dʒiʒlãn'sa(x)] vi - **1.** [dar partida] to
set off. - **2.** [progredir rápido] to take off.
deslavado, da [dʒiʒla'vadu, da] adj brazen.
desleal [dʒiʒ'ljaw] (pl -ais) adj disloyal.
deslealdade [dʒiʒleaw'dadʒi] f disloyalty.
desleixado, da [dʒiʒlej'∫adu, da] adj messy.
desleixo [dʒiʒ'lej∫u] m mess.
desligado, da [dʒiʒli'gadu, da] adj - **1.**
ELETR switched off. - **2.** [desconectado] disconnected. - **3.** [afastado]: ~ **de** detached from. - **4.** fig
[despreendido] indifferent. - **5.** fig [distraído] absent-minded.
desligar [14] [dʒiʒli'ga(x)] ◇ vt ELETR to switch off;
~ **o carro** to switch off the engine. ◇ vi fam
[despreocupar-se] to switch off.
➧ **desligar-se** vp - **1.** [afastar-se]: ~-se de to
switch off from. - **2.** fig [despreender-se]: ~-se de
to abandon. - **3.** fig [distrair-se] to switch off.
deslizamento [dʒiʒliza'mẽntu] m slip; ~ **de terra**
landslide.
deslizante [dʒiʒli'zãnt∫i] adj slippery.
deslizar [4] [dʒiʒli'za(x)] vi - **1.** [movimentar-se - cis-
nes, dançarino] to glide; [- terra, encosta] to slide.
- **2.** [escorregar] to slip. - **3.** fig [falhar] to make a
slip.
deslize [dʒiʒ'lizil] m - **1.** [escorregão] slip. - **2.** fig [fa-
lha] blunder. - **3.** fig [engano] slip.
deslocado, da [dʒiʒlo'kadu, da] adj - **1.** MED
dislocated. - **2.** [transferido] transferred. - **3.** fig
[desambientado] out of place.
deslocamento [dʒiʒloka'mẽntu] m - **1.** MED
dislocation. - **2.** [movimentação] movement.
deslocar [12] [dʒiʒlo'ka(x)] vt - **1.** MED to dislocate.
- **2.** [transferir] to transfer. - **3.** [mover] to move.
➧ **deslocar-se** vp [mover-se] to move around.
deslumbrado, da [dʒiʒlũn'bradu, da] adj
dazzled.
deslumbramento [dʒiʒlũnbra'mẽntu] m dazzle.

deslumbrante [dʒiʒlũn'brãnt∫i] adj dazzling.
deslumbrar [4] [dʒiʒlũn'bra(x)] ◇ vt to dazzle.
◇ vi to be dazzling.
➧ **deslumbrar-se** vp to be dazzled.
desmaiado, da [dʒiʒma'jadu, da] adj - **1.** MED
unconscious. - **2.** [pálido] pale.
desmaiar [4] [dʒiʒmaj'a(x)] vi to faint.
desmaio [dʒiʒ'majul] m faint.
desmamar [4] [dʒiʒma'ma(x)] ◇ vt to wean. ◇
vi to be weaned.
desmancha-prazeres [dʒiʒ,mãn∫apra'zeri∫l] mf
inv killjoy.
desmanchar [4] [dʒiʒmãn'∫a(x)] vt - **1.** [desfazer] to
undo. - **2.** [acabar com] to break off.
➧ **desmanchar-se** vp - **1.** [dissolver-se] to come
undone. - **2.** fig [expandir-se]: ~-se em algo to be
lavish with sthg.
desmantelar [4] [dʒiʒmãnte'la(x)] vt - **1.** [desmon-
tar] to dismantle. - **2.** [desmoronar] to demolish.
➧ **desmantelar-se** vp - **1.** [desmontar-se] to fall
apart. - **2.** [desmoronar-se] to collapse.
desmarcar [12] [dʒiʒmax'ka(x)] vt - **1.** [tirar as marcas
de] to remove markings from. - **2.** [adiar] to
postpone.
desmascaramento [dʒiʒma∫kara'mẽntu] m un-
masking.
desmascarar [4] [dʒiʒma∫ka'ra(x)] vt - **1.** [revelar]
to reveal. - **2.** [desmoralizar] to demoralize.
desmatamento [dʒiʒmata'mẽntu] m deforestation.
desmatar [4] [dʒiʒma'ta(x)] vt to deforest.
desmazelado, da [dʒiʒmaze'ladu, da] adj slovenly.
desmazelar-se [7] [dʒiʒmaze'laxsil] vp to become
slovenly.
desmazelo [dʒiʒma'zelul] m slovenliness.
desmedido, da [dʒiʒme'dʒidu, da] adj immense.
desmembramento [dʒiʒmẽnbra'mẽntu] m dis-
membering.
desmembrar [4] [dʒiʒmẽn'bra(x)] vt to divide up.
➧ **desmembrar-se** vp to divide.
desmemoriado, da [dʒiʒmemo'rjadu, da] adj
forgetful.
desmentido [dʒiʒmẽn't∫idul] m contradiction.
desmentir [56] [dʒiʒmẽn't∫i(x)] vt - **1.** [negar] to
deny. - **2.** [discrepar de] to disagree with. - **3.** [con-
tradizer] to contradict.
➧ **desmentir-se** vp [contradizer-se] to contradict o.s.
desmerecer [25] [dʒiʒmere'se(x)] vt - **1.** [menospre-
zar] to despise. - **2.** [não merecer] not to deserve.
desmesurado, da [dʒiʒmezu'radu, da] adj excessive.
desmiolado, da [dʒiʒmjo'ladu, da] adj - **1.** [sem
juízo] brainless. - **2.** [esquecido] forgetful.
desmistificação [dʒiʒmit∫ifica'sãw] (pl -ões) f
demystification.
desmistificar [12] [dʒiʒmi∫t∫ifi'ka(x)] vt to demystify.
desmitificar [dʒiʒmit∫ifi'ka(x)] vt to dispel the
myth about.

desmontar [4] [dʒiʒmõn'ta(x)] <> *vt* -**1.** [separar as partes de] to dismantle. -**2.** *fig* [destruir] to destroy. <> *vi* [apear]: ~ **(de algo)** to dismount (from sthg).

desmontável [dʒiʒmõn'tavew] (*pl* -**eis**) *adj* that can be taken apart, knockdown *US*.

desmoralização [dʒiʒmoraliza'sãw] *f* demoralization.

desmoralizante [dʒiʒmorali'zãntʃi], **desmoralizador, ra** [dʒiʒmoraliza'do(x), ra] *adj* demoralizing.

desmoralizar [4] [dʒiʒmorali'za(x)] *vt* to demoralize.

➡ **desmoralizar-se** *vp* to be demoralized.

desmoronamento [dʒiʒmorona'mẽntu] *m* landslide.

desmoronar [4] [dʒiʒmoro'na(x)] <> *vt* to knock down. <> *vi* to collapse.

desmotivado, da [dʒiʒmotʃi'vadu, da] *adj* demotivated.

desmunhecar [12] [dʒiʒmuɲe'ka(x)] *vi fam* to be camp.

desnatado, da [dʒiʒna'tadu, da] *adj* skimmed.

desnecessário, ria [dʒiʒnese'sarju, rja] *adj* unnecessary.

desnível [dʒiʒ'nivεw] (*pl* -**eis**) *m* unevenness.

desnivelar [4] [dʒiʒnive'la(x)] *vt* to make uneven.

desnorteado, da [dʒiʒnox'tʃjadu, da] *adj* [perturbado] bewildered.

desnorteante [dʒiʒnox'tʃjãntʃi] *adj* bewildering.

desnortear [15] [dʒiʒnox'tʃja(x)] *vt* -**1.** [desorientar] to disorientate. -**2.** *fig* [perturbar] to confuse.

➡ **desnortear-se** *vp* -**1.** [perder-se] to get lost. -**2.** *fig* [perturbar-se] to become confused.

desnudar [4] [dʒiʒnu'da(x)] *vt* -**1.** [despir] to undress. -**2.** *fig* [revelar] to reveal.

➡ **desnudar-se** *vp* [despir-se] to undress.

desnutrição [dʒiʒnutri'sãw] *f* malnutrition.

desnutrido, da [dʒiʒnu'tridu, da] *adj* malnourished.

desobedecer [25] [dʒizobede'se(x)] *vi*: ~ **(a)** to disobey.

desobediência [dʒizobe'dʒjẽnsja] *f* disobedience.

desobediente [dʒizobe'dʒjẽntʃi] *adj* disobedient.

desobrigar [14] [dʒizobri'ga(x)] *vt*: ~ **alguém de algo/de fazer algo** to release sb from sthg/doing sthg.

desobstruir [74] [dʒizobʃtru'i(x)] *vt* to clear.

desocupação [dʒizokupa'sãw] *f* emptiness.

desocupado, da [dʒizoku'padu, da] <> *adj* -**1.** [ocioso] idle. -**2.** [disponível] available. -**3.** [vazio] empty. <> *m, f* -**1.** [desempregado] unemployed person. -**2.** [vagabundo] layabout.

desocupar [4] [dʒizoku'pa(x)] *vt* -**1.** [deixar livre] to leave free. -**2.** [esvaziar] to empty.

desodorante [dʒizodo'rãntʃi] *m* deodorant.

desodorizar [4] [dʒizodori'za(x)] *vt* to deodorize.

desolação [dezola'sãw] *f* -**1.** [tristeza] sadness.

-**2.** [devastação] devastation.

desolado, da [dezo'ladu, da] *adj* -**1.** [triste] sad. -**2.** [devastado] devasted.

desolador, ra [dezola'do(x), ra] *adj* [entristecedor] devastating.

desolar [4] [dezo'la(x)] *vt* to devastate.

desonestidade [dʒizoneʃtʃi'dadʒi] *f* dishonesty.

desonesto, ta [dʒizo'nɛʃtu, ta] <> *adj* -**1.** [indigno] contemptible. -**2.** [mentiroso] dishonest. <> *m, f* [pessoa indigna] despicable person.

desonra [dʒi'zõnxa] *f* dishonour.

desonrar [4] [dʒizõn'xa(x)] *vt* to dishonour.

➡ **desonrar-se** *vp* to disgrace o.s.

desonroso, osa [dʒizõn'xozu, ɔza] *adj* dishonourable.

desopilar [4] [dʒizopi'la(x)] *vt* -**1.** *MED* to clear an obstruction from. -**2.** [mente] to relieve.

desoprimir [6] [dʒizopri'mi(x)] *vt* to free from oppression.

desordeiro, ra [dʒizox'dejru, ra] <> *adj* rowdy. <> *m, f* rowdy person.

desordem [dʒi'zɔxdẽ] (*pl* -**ns**) *f* -**1.** [bagunça] mess. -**2.** [tumulto] commotion.

desordenar [4] [dʒizoxde'na(x)] *vt* to upset.

desorganização [dʒizoxganiza'sãw] *f* confusion.

desorganizar [4] [dʒizoxgani'za(x)] *vt* to throw into confusion.

➡ **desorganizar-se** *vp* to be disorganized.

desorientação [dʒizorjẽnta'sãw] *f* disorientation.

desorientar [4] [dʒizorjẽn'ta(x)] *vt* -**1.** [desnortear] to disorientate. -**2.** [perturbar] to bewilder. -**3.** *PSIC* to disturb.

➡ **desorientar-se** *vp* -**1.** [desnortear-se] to become disorientated. -**2.** [perturbar-se] to become disconcerted.

desossar [4] [dʒizo'sa(x)] *vt* to bone.

desovar [4] [dʒizo'va(x)] <> *vi* [pôr ovos] to lay eggs. <> *vt fig* [livrar-se de] to get rid of.

despachado, da [dʒiʃpa'ʃadu, da] *adj* -**1.** [enviado] dispatched. -**2.** [eficiente] efficient.

despachante [dʒiʃpa'ʃãntʃi] *mf* forwarding agent.

despachar [4] [dʒiʃpa'ʃa(x)] *vt* -**1.** [enviar] to send. -**2.** [resolver] to dispatch. -**3.** [atender] to attend to. -**4.** [mandar embora] to get rid of.

despacho [dʒiʃ'paʃul *m* -**1.** [resolução] determination. -**2.** *ESPIRIT* religious offering.

despedaçar [13] [dʒiʃpeda'sa(x)] *vt* -**1.** [quebrar em pedaços] to smash. -**2.** *fig* [magoar]: ~ **o coração de alguém** to break sb's heart.

➡ **despedaçar-se** *vp* [quebrar-se em pedaços] to smash.

despedida [dʒiʃpe'dʒida] *f* [ato] farewell.

despedir [70] [dʒiʃpe'dʒi(x)] *vt* [demitir] to dismiss.

➡ **despedir-se** *vp* [dizer adeus]: ~**-se (de alguém)** to say goodbye (to sb).

despeitado, da [dʒiʃpej'tadu, da] *adj* -**1.** [invejoso] envious. -**2.** *fam* [que tem o peito magro] flat.

despeito [dʒiʃ'pejtu] *m* [inveja] spite.

➤ **a despeito de** *loc conj* [apesar de] despite.

despejar [4] [dʒiʃpe'ʒa(x)] *vt* - **1.** [inquilino] to evict. - **2.** [entornar] to pour.

despejo [dʒiʃ'peʒu] *m* [de inquilino] eviction.

despencar [12] [dʒiʃpēŋ'ka(x)] *vi* [cair]: ~ **de algo** to fall from sthg.

despender [5] [dʒiʃpēn'de(x)] *vt* to spend.

despenhadeiro [dʒiʃpeɲa'dejrul *m* precipice.

despensa [dʒiʃ'pēnsal *f* pantry.

despentear [15] [dʒiʃpēn'tʒja(x)] *vt* to tousle.

➤ **despentear-se** *vp fig* to let one's hair down.

despercebido, da [dʒiʃpexse'bidu, dal *adj* unnoticed.

desperdiçar [13] [dʒiʃpexdʒi'sa(x)] *vt* to waste.

desperdício [dʒiʃpex'dʒisjul *m* waste.

despersonalizar [4] [dʒiʃpexsonali'za(x)] *vt* to depersonalize.

despertador [dʒiʃpexta'do(x)] (*pl* -**es**) *m* alarm clock.

despertar [4] [dʒiʃpex'ta(x)] ◇ *m* awakening. ◇ *vt* - **1.** [acordar] to wake. - **2.** [provocar] to awaken. - **3.** *fig* [tirar]: ~ **alguém de algo** to rouse sb from sthg. ◇ *vi* - **1.** [ger] to wake up. - **2.** *fig* [sair]: ~ **de algo** to rouse o.s. from sthg.

desperto, ta [dʒiʃ'pɛxtu, tal *adj* awake.

despesa [dʒiʃ'pezal *f* expense.

despido, da [dʒiʃ'pidu, dal *adj* - **1.** [nu] naked. - **2.** *fig* [desprovido]: ~ **de algo** lacking sthg.

despir [57] [dʒiʃ'pi(x)] *vt* [roupa, pessoa] to undress.

➤ **despir-se** *vp* - **1.** [tirar a roupa] to get undressed. - **2.** *fig* [despojar-se]: ~-**se de algo** to abandon sthg.

despistar [4] [dʒiʃpiʃ'ta(x)] *vt* to mislead.

desplante [dʒiʃ'plãntʃil *m fig* cheek.

despojado, da [dʒiʃpo'ʒadu, dal *adj* - **1.** [privado]: ~ **de algo** stripped of sthg. - **2.** [desprendido] generous. - **3.** [sem enfeite] unadorned.

despojamento [dʒiʃpoʒa'mēntul *m* [privação, abandono] shedding.

despojar [4] [dʒiʃpo'ʒa(x)] *vt* - **1.** [roubar] to rob. - **2.** [espoliar] to clean out.

➤ **despojar-se** *vp* [privar-se]: ~-**se de algo** to renounce sthg.

despojos [dʒiʃ'poʒoʃl *mpl* remains; ~ **mortais** mortal remains.

despoluir [74] [dʒiʃpo'lwi(x)] *vt* to clean up.

despontar [4] [dʒiʃpõn'ta(x)] *vi* to rise.

desportista [dʒiʃpox'tʃiʃtal ◇ *adj* sporty. ◇ *mf* sportsman (*f* sportswoman).

desporto [dʒiʃ'poxtul *m* sport.

déspota ['dɛʃpotal ◇ *adj* despotic. ◇ *mf* despot.

despotismo [deʃpo'tʃiʒmul *m* despotism.

despovoado, da [dʒiʃpo'vwadu, dal *adj* uninhabited.

desprazer [dʒiʃpra'ze(x)] *m* displeasure.

despregado, da [dʒiʃpre'gadu, dal *adj* loose.

despregar [14] [dʒiʃpre'ga(x)] ◇ *vt*: ~ **algo (de)** to unfasten sthg (from); **não despregou os olhos de mim** *fig* he didn't take his eyes off me. ◇ *vi* to come undone.

➤ **despregar-se** *vp* [soltar-se] to come loose.

desprender [5] [dʒiʃprēn'de(x)] *vt* - **1.** [soltar]: ~ **alguém/algo (de algo)** to untie sthg (from sthg). - **2.** [escalar] to release.

➤ **desprender-se** *vp* - **1.** [soltar-se]: ~-**se (de algo)** to get free (from sthg). - **2.** [exalar]: ~-**se de algo** to extricate o.s. from sthg.

desprendido, da [dʒiʃprēn'dʒidu, dal *adj* detached.

desprendimento [dʒiʃprēndʒi'mēntul *m* [desapego] detachment.

despreocupado, da [dʒiʃpreoku'padu, dal *adj* carefree.

despreparado, da [dʒiʃprepa'radu, dal *adj* unprepared.

despreparo [dʒiʃpre'parul *m* lack of preparation.

desprestigiar [16] [dʒiʃpreʃtʃi'ʒja(x)] *vt* to discredit.

despretensioso, osa [dʒiʃpretēn'sjozu, ɔzal *adj* unpretentious.

desprevenido, da [dʒiʃpreve'nidu, dal *adj* [distraído] unaware; **ser pego** ~ to be taken by surprise.

desprezar [4] [dʒiʃpre'za(x)] *vt* - **1.** [menosprezar] to despise. - **2.** [não dar importância] to scorn. - **3.** [não considerar] to disregard.

desprezível [dʒiʃpre'zivewl (*pl* -**eis**) *adj* - **1.** [vil] despicable. - **2.** [ínfimo] least.

desprezo [dʒiʃ'prezul *m* - **1.** [desdém] disdain. - **2.** [repulsa] revulsion.

desproporção [dʒiʃpropox'sãwl (*pl* -**ões**) *f* inequality.

desproporcional [dʒiʃpropoxsjo'nawl (*pl* -**ais**) *adj*: ~ **(a)** disproportionate (to).

despropositado, da [dʒiʃpropozi'tadu, dal *adj* unreasonable.

despropósito [dʒiʃpro'pɔzitul *m* - **1.** [disparate] absurdity. - **2.** *fig* [excesso]: **un** ~ more than enough.

desproteger [26] [dʒiʃprote'ʒe(x)] *vt* to abandon.

desprotegido, da [dʒiʃprote'gidu, dal *adj* [desamparado] vulnerable.

desprover [41] [dʒiʃpro've(x)] *vt*: ~ **alguém (de algo)** to deprive sb (of sthg).

➤ **desprover-se** *vp*: ~-**se de algo** to strip o.s. of sthg.

desprovido, da [dʒiʃpro'vidu, dal *adj*: ~ **de algo** lacking sthg.

despudor [dʒiʃpu'do(x)] *m* shamelessness.

despudorado, da [dʒiʃpudo'radu, dal *adj* shameless.

desqualificar [12] [dʒiʃkwalifi'ka(x)] *vt* - **1.** [tornar indigno] to render unfit. - **2.** [inabilitar] to disqualify; ~ **alguém (para)** to disqualify sb (from).

➤ **desqualificar-se** *vp* [inabilitar-se]: ~-**se (para)** to be eliminated (from).

desquitar-se [4] [dʒiʃki'taxsil *vp* to get divorced.

desquite [dʒiʃ'kitʃil *m* divorce.

desratização [dʒiʒxatiza'sãwl *f* extermination of rats and mice.

desratizar [4] [dʒiʒxati'za(x)] *vt* to exterminate rats and mice.

desregrado, da [dʒiʒxe'gradu, da] <> *adj* -**1.** [desordenado] disorderly. -**2.** [devasso] dissolute. <> *m, f* [devasso] debauched person.

desregulado, da [dʒiʃregu'ladu, da] *adj* [motor, aparelho] poorly adjusted.

desregular [4] [dʒiʒxegu'la(x)] *vt* irregular.

desrespeitar [4] [dʒiʒxeʃpej'ta(x)] *vt* -**1.** [desacatar] to disregard. -**2.** [desobedecera] to disobey.

desrespeito [dʒiʒxeʃ'pejtu] *m*: ~ **(a)** disrespect (for).

desrespeitoso, osa [dʒiʒxeʃpej'tozu, ɔza] *adj* disrespectful.

dessa ['dɛsa] = de + esse.

desse ['desi] = de + esse.

destacado, da [dʒiʃta'kadu, da] *adj* -**1.** [separado] detached. -**2.** [proeminente] eminent.

destacamento [dʒiʃtaka'mẽntu] *m* detachment.

destacar [12] [dʒiʃta'ka(x)] *vt* -**1.** [ger] to detach. -**2.** [fazer sobressair] to highlight.

➡ **destacar-se** *vp* [fazer-se notar] to be outstanding.

destacável [dʒiʃta'kavɛw] (*pl* -**eis**) *adj* detachable.

destampado, da [dʒiʃtãn'padu, da] *adj* uncovered.

destampar [4] [dʒiʃtãn'pa(x)] *vt* to remove the lid from.

destapar [4] [dʒiʃta'pa(x)] *vt* to uncover.

destaque [dʒiʃ'taki] *m* -**1.** [realce] prominence. -**2.** [pessoa ou assunto relevante] highlight.

desta ['dɛʃta] = de + esta.

deste ['deʃtʃi] = de + este.

destemido, da [dʒiʃte'midu, da] *adj* fearless.

destempero [dʒiʃtẽn'peru] *m* -**1.** [disparate] blunder. -**2.** *fam* [diarréia] diarrhoea. -**3.** *fam* [grande quantidade] mountain.

desterrar [4] [dʒiʃte'xa(x)] *vt* to exile.

desterro [dʒiʃ'texu] *m* exile.

destilação [deʃtʃila'sãw] *f* distillation.

destilar [4] [deʃtʃi'la(x)] *vt* to distil.

destilaria [deʃtʃila'rial] *f* distillery.

destinação [deʃtʃina'sãw] (*pl* -**oes**) *f* destination.

destinar [4] [deʃtʃi'na(x)] *vt* -**1.** [reservar] to put aside. -**2.** [aplicar] to allocate.

➡ **destinar-se** *vp* -**1.** [ser designado]: ~-**se a** to be intended for. -**2.** [dedicar-se] to dedicate oneslf.

destinatário, ria [deʃtʃina'tarju, rja] *m, f* addressee.

destino [deʃ'tʃinu] *m* -**1.** [direção] destination. -**2.** [aplicação] purpose. -**3.** [futuro] destiny.

destituição [deʃtʃitwi'sãw] *f* destitution.

destituir [74] [deʃtʃi'twi(x)] *vt* -**1.** [privar]: ~ **alguém de algo** to deprive sb of sthg. -**2.** [demitir]: ~ **alguém (de algo)** to deprive sb (of sthg).

destoante [dʒiʃto'ãntʃi] *adj* -**1.** [desafinado] discordant. -**2.** [divergente] divergent.

destoar [20] [dʒiʃto'a(x)] *vi* -**1.** [desafinar] to be out of tune. -**2.** [divergir]: ~ **de algo** to diverge from

sthg. -**3.** [não condizer]: ~ **de algo** to clash with sthg.

destorcer [25] [dʒiʃtox'se(x)] *vt* [endireitar] to straighten.

destorcido, da [dʒiʃtox'sidu, da] *adj* untwisted.

destrambelhado, da [dʒiʃtrãnbe'ʎadu, da] *adj* -**1.** [aloprado] foolish. -**2.** [desajeitado] awkward. -**3.** [sem propósito] hair-brained.

destrancar [12] [dʒiʃtrãn'ka(x)] *vt* to unlock.

destratar [4] [dʒiʃtra'ta(x)] *vt* to offend.

destravar [4] [dʒiʃtra'va(x)] *vt* -**1.** [porta] to unlock. -**2.** [língua] to loosen.

destreza [deʃ'treza] *f* skill.

destrinchar [4] [dʒiʃtrĩn'ʃa(x)] *vt* -**1.** [resolver] to unravel. -**2.** [detalhar] to detail.

destro, tra ['dɛʃtru, tra] *adj* dexterous.

destroçar [13] [dʒiʃtro'sa(x)] *vt* -**1.** [ger] to destroy. -**2.** [despedaçar] to pull to pieces.

destroços [dʒiʃ'trɔsuʃ] *mpl* wreckage *(sg)*.

destróier [dʒiʃ'trɔje(x)] *m* destroyer.

destronar [4] [dʒiʃtro'na(x)] *vt* to dethrone.

destroncar [12] [dʒiʃtrõŋ'ka(x)] *vt* -**1.** [deslocar] to dislocate. -**2.** [decepar] to cut off.

destruição [dʒiʃtruj'sãw] *f* destruction.

destruidor, ra [dʒiʃtruj'do(x), ra] <> *adj* destructive. <> *m, f* destroyer.

destruir [74] [dʒiʃtru'i(x)] <> *vt* -**1.** [ger] to destroy. -**2.** [aniquilar] to annihilate. <> *vi* [ter efeito negativo] to be destroying.

➡ **destruir-se** *vp* -**1.** [a si próprio] to destroy o.s. -**2.** [um ao outro] to destroy one another.

destrutivo, va [dʒiʃtru'tʃivu, va] *adj* destructive.

desumano, na [dʒizu'mãnu, na] *adj* inhuman.

desunião [dʒiʒun'jãw] *f* -**1.** [separação] separation. -**2.** [discórdia] discord.

desunir [6] [dʒizu'ni(x)] *vt* [separar] to separate.

desusado, da [dʒizu'zadu, da] *adj* out of date.

desvairado, da [dʒiʒvaj'radu, da] <> *adj* -**1.** [louco] crazy. -**2.** [descontrolado] uncontrolled. <> *m, f* -**1.** [pessoa louca] crazy person. -**2.** [pessoa descontrolada] person who is quite out of control.

desvalido, da [dʒiʒva'lidu, da] *adj* -**1.** [desamparado] destitute. -**2.** [miserável] wretched.

desvalorização [dʒiʒvaloriza'sãw] (*pl* -**ões**) *f* devaluation.

desvalorizar [4] [dʒiʃvalori'za(x)] *vt* & *vi* to devalue.

➡ **desvalorizar-se** *vp* to undervalue o.s.

desvanecer [25] [dʒiʒvane'se(x)] *vt* [dissipar] to dispel.

➡ **desvanecer-se** *vp* -**1.** [dissipar-se] to disappear. -**2.** [desbotar-se] to fade.

desvanecido, da [dʒiʒvane'sidu, da] *adj* -**1.** [dissipado] dispelled. -**2.** [desbotado] faded.

desvantagem [dʒiʒvãn'taʒẽl] (*pl* -**ns**) *f* disadvantage; **em** ~ at a disadvantage.

desvantajoso, osa [dʒiʒvãnta'ʒozu, ɔza] *adj* disadvantageous.

desvão [dʒiʒ'vãw] *m* loft.

desvario [dʒiʒva'riw] *m* madness.

desvelar [4] [dʒiʒve'la(x)] *vt* -**1.** [provocar vigília] to keep awake. -**2.** [descobrir] to uncover; ~ **uma estátua** to unveil a statue. -**3.** [aclarar] to clear up.
➡ **desvelar-se** *vp* to stay awake.

desvelo [dʒiʒ'velu] *m* [zelo] zeal.

desvencilhar [4] [dʒiʒvẽnsi'ʎa(x)] *vt* [soltar]: ~ **algo/alguém (de algo)** to save sthg/sb (from sthg).
➡ **desvencilhar-se** *vp* -**1.** [soltar-se]: ~-**se (de algo)** to free o.s. (from sthg). -**2.** *fig* [livrar-se]: ~ **de alguém/algo** to get rid of sb/sthg.

desvendar [4] [dʒiʒvẽn'da(x)] *vt* -**1.** [tirar a venda de] to remove the blindfold from. -**2.** [revelar] to reveal.

desventura [dʒiʒvẽn'tural] *f* misfortune.

desviar [16] [dʒiʒ'vja(x)] *vt* -**1.** [mudar a direção de] to deviate. -**2.** *fig* [roubar] to misappropriate.
➡ **desviar-se** *vp* [mudar a direção] to deviate.

desvincular [4] [dʒiʒvĩŋku'la(x)] *vt* : ~ **algo de algo** to dissociate sthg from sthg.
➡ **desvincular-se** *vp*: ~-**se de algo/alguém** to break ties with sthg/sb.

desvio [dʒiʒ'viw] *m* -**1.** [mudança de direção] diversion. -**2.** [da coluna vertebral] curvature. -**3.** *fig* deviation. -**4.** [roubo] misappropriation.

desvirar [4] [dʒiʒvi'ra(x)] *vt* to turn back to the normal position.

desvirginar [4] [dʒiʒvixʒi'na(x)] *vt* to deflower.

desvirtuar [4] [dʒiʒvix'twa(x)] *vt* to misconstrue.

detalhadamente [detaʎada'mẽntʃil] *adv* in detail.

detalhado, da [deta'ʎadu, da] *adj* detailed.

detalhar [4] [deta'ʎa(x)] *vt* to detail.

detalhe [de'taʎil] *m* detail; **entrar em** ~**s** to go into detail.

detalhista [deta'ʎiʃta] *adj* meticulous.

detecção [detek'sãw] *f* detection.

detectar [4] [detek'ta(x)] *vt* to detect.

detector [detek'to(x)] (*pl* -**es**) *m* detector.

detenção [detẽn'sãw] (*pl* -**ões**) *f* detention.

détente [de'tãntʃi] *f* POL détente.

detento, ta [de'tẽntu, ta] *m, f* prisoner.

detentor, ra [detẽn'to(x), ra] *m, f* holder.

deter [1] [de'te(x)] *vt* -**1.** [parar] to stop. -**2.** [prender] to detain. -**3.** [manter, reter] to keep. -**4.** [reprimir] to hold back. -**5.** [ter em seu poder] to retain.
➡ **deter-se** *vp* -**1.** [parar] to stop. -**2.** [ficar] to remain. -**3.** [reprimir-se] to hold back. -**4.** [ocupar-se]: ~-**se em algo** to dwell on sthg.

detergente [detex'ʒẽntʃil] <> *adj* cleansing. <> *m* detergent.

deterioração [deterjora'sãwl *f* deterioration.

deteriorar [4] [deterjo'ra(x)] <> *vt* -**1.** [estragar] to spoil. -**2.** [piorar] to damage. <> *vi* [piorar] to worsen.
➡ **deteriorar-se** *vp* -**1.** [estragar] to become spoiled. -**2.** *fig* [piorar] to deteriorate.

determinação [detexmina'sãwl (*pl* -**ões**) *f* -**1.** [empenho] determination. -**2.** [ordem] order.

determinado, da [detexmi'nadu, da] *adj* -**1.** [resoluto] determined. -**2.** [estabelecido] fixed. -**3.**

(antes de subst) [certo] certain; **em** ~ **momento ...** at a certain moment.

determinante [detexmi'nãntʃil] <> *adj* determining. <> *m* MAT determinant.

determinar [4] [detexmi'na(x)] *vt* -**1.** [ger] to determine. -**2.** [precisar] to state.
➡ **determinar-se** *vp* [decidir-se]: ~-**se a fazer algo** to decide to do sthg.

detestar [4] [deteʃ'ta(x)] *vt* to detest.
➡ **detestar-se** *vp* to detest o.s.

detestável [deteʃ'tavewl (*pl* -**eis**) *adj* detestable.

detetive [dete'tʃivil] *mf* detective.

detidamente [detʃida'mẽntʃil] *adv* minutely.

detido, da [de'tʃidu, da] *adj* -**1.** [retido] retained. -**2.** [preso] detained.

detonação [detona'sãwl (*pl* -**ões**) *f* detonation.

detonar [4] [deto'na(x)] <> *vt* [arma, bomba] to detonate. <> *vi* -**1.** [arma, bomba] to detonate. -**2.** [trovão] to thunder.

DETRAN (*abrev de* **Departamento Estadual de Trânsito**) *m Brazilian state department responsible for licensing of drivers and vehicles,* ≃ DVLA.

detrás [de'trajʃl *adv* behind.
➡ **detrás de** *loc prep* behind.
➡ **por detrás** *loc adv* from behind.

detrimento [detri'mẽntul *m*: **em** ~ **de** to the detriment of.

detrito [de'tritul *m* detritus.

deturpação [detuxpa'sãwl (*pl* -**ões**) *f* corruption.

deturpar [4] [detux'pa(x)] *vt* -**1.** [adulterar] to distort. -**2.** [corromper] to corrupt.

deus, sa ['dewʃ, sal (*mpl* -**ses**, *fpl* -**sas**) *m, f* god.
➡ **Deus** *m* God; **Deus e o mundo** [todo o mundo] the world and his wife; **graças a Deus!** thank God!; **meu Deus do céu!** my goodness!

deus-dará [,dewʃda'ral *m* -**1.**: **ficar ao** ~ [à ventura] to be left unattended. -**2.**: **viver ao** ~ [a esmo] to have no aims in one's life.

deus-nos-acuda [,dewʃnuʃa'kudal *m* commotion.

devagar [dʒiva'ga(x)] <> *adv* slowly. <> *adj inv fam* -**1.** [lento] slow. -**2.** [sem graça] boring; **ser** ~ **quase parando** to go at a snail's pace.

devagarinho [dʒivaga'riɲul *adv* nice and slowly.

devanear [15] [deva'nja(x)] *vi* to muse.

devaneio [deva'nejul *m* reverie.

devassa [de'vasal *f* official inquiry.

devassado, da [deva'sadu, da] *adj* open.

devassidão [devasi'dãwl *f* licentiousness.

devasso, ssa [de'vasu, sal <> *adj* debauched. <> *m, f* debauched person.

devastar [4] [devaʃ'ta(x)] *vt* -**1.** [assolar] to devastate. -**2.** [despovoar] to drive people out of.

deve ['dɛvil *m* COM debit.

devedor, ra [deve'do(x), ral <> *adj* [firma, pessoa] in debt. <> *m, f* debtor.

dever [5] [de've(x)] (*pl* -**es**) <> *m* -**1.** [obrigação] duty; **cumprir seu** ~ to do one's duty. -**2.** EDUC: ~ **(de casa)** homework; **fazer o** ~ **(de casa)** to do one's homework. <> *vt* -**1.** [dinheiro, favores]: ~

algo (a alguém) to owe sthg (to sb). **-2.** [expressando probabilidade]: **deve fazer sol amanhã** it ought to be sunny tomorrow; **deve ser meia-noite** it must be midnight; **ela deve chegar à noite** she should arrive in the evening; **deve ter acontecido alguma coisa** something must have happened. **-3.** [expressando sugestão]: **você deve sair cedo** you ought to go out early. **-4.** [expressando necessidade]: **devo praticar mais esportes** I should do more sport. **-5.** [expressando obrigação]: **você deve ser pontual sempre** you must always be on time. ⬦ *vi* [ter dívida]: **ele deve muito na praça** she owes a lot at the market; **ela deve a todos os amigos** she owes a lot to all her friends, she's in debt to all her friends.

➡ **dever-se a** *vp* [ser consequência de] to be due to.

deveras [de'vɛraʃ] *adv* really.

devidamente [de͵vida'mẽntʃil *adv* duly.

devido, da [de'vidu, da] *adj* due; **no ~ tempo** in due course.

➡ **devido a** *loc adv* due to.

devoção [devo'sãw] *f* **-1.** RELIG devotion. **-2.** [dedicação] dedication.

devolução [devolu'sãw] (*pl* -ões) *f* return.

devoluto, ta [devo'lutu, ta] *adj* **-1.** [vago, vazio] vacant. **-2.** [jur] repossessed.

devolver [5] [devow've(x)] *vt* **-1.** [restituir] to return. **-2.** [replicar] to respond to. **-3.** [vomitar] to throw up.

devorar [4] [devo'ra(x)] *vt* **-1.** [ger] to consume. **-2.** [comida] to devour. **-3.** *fig* [livro] to read voraciously.

devotar [4] [devo'ta(x)] *vt*: **~ algo a algo/alguém** to devote sthg to sthg/sb.

➡ **devotar-se** *vp*: **~-se a algo/alguém** to devote o.s. to sthg/sb.

devoto, ta [de'votu, ta] ⬦ *adj* devout. ⬦ *m, f* devotee.

dez ['dɛʒ] *num* ten; *veja também* **seis**.

dez. (*abrev de* **dezembro**) Dec.

dezembro [de'zẽbru] *m* December; *veja também* **setembro**.

dezena [de'zena] *f* **-1.** [ger] ten. **-2.** [em jogo]: **ganhei na ~** I got ten numbers right.

dezenove [deze'nɔvi] *num* nineteen; *veja também* **seis**.

dezesseis [deze'sejʃ] *num* sixteen; *veja também* **seis**.

dezessete [deze'sɛtʃi] *num* seventeen; *veja também* **seis**.

dezoito [de'zoitu] *num* eighteen; *veja também* **seis**.

DF (*abrev de* **Distrito Federal**) *m* Federal District.

dia ['dʒia] *m* **-1.** [gen] day; **bom ~!** good morning!; **de um ~ para outro** from one day to the next; **no ~ anterior/seguinte** the previous/next day; **mais ~, menos dia** sooner or later; **o ~ todo** all day long; **todo ~, todos os ~s** all day, every day; **todo santo ~** every single day. **~ cheio** busy day; **um ~ daqueles** one of those days. **-2.** [data] date; **no ~ dez** on the tenth; **~ de Reis** Twelfth

Night; **~ santo** feast day. **-3.** [luz do sol]: **de ~** in the daytime. **-4.** [atualidade]: **em ~** up-to-date; **hoje em ~** nowadays. **-5.** [horário de trabalho]: **~ de folga** day off; **~ útil** working day.

➡ **dias** *mpl* **-1.** [época]: **nos meus ~s** in my day. **-2.** [vida]: **ele está com seus ~s contados** his days are numbered.

dia-a-dia *m* daily routine.

diabetes [dʒia'bɛtʃiʃ] *m ou f* diabetes.

diabético, ca [dʒia'bɛtʃiku, ka] ⬦ *adj* diabetic. ⬦ *m, f* diabetic.

diabo ['dʒiabul] ⬦ *m* devil; **aconteceu o ~** it all happened; **comer o pão que o ~ amassou** to go through hell; **dizer** *ou* **falar o ~ de alguém** to bad-mouth sb; **estar com o ~ no corpo** to be restless; **fazer o ~** to run riot. ⬦ *adj fam*: **o ~ de carro parou** the damned car has stopped. ⬦ *interj* damn!

➡ **como o diabo** *loc adv fam*: **é feia como o ~!** she's as ugly as sin!

diabólico, ca [dʒia'bɔliku, ka] *adj* diabolical.

diabrura [dʒia'brura] *f* devilish trick.

diacho ['dʒiaʃul *interj fam* what the devil!

diácono ['dʒiakonul *m* deacon.

diadema [dʒia'demal *m* diadem.

diáfano, na ['dʒiafãnu, nal *adj* diaphanous.

diafragma [dʒia'fragmal *m* diaphragm.

diagnosticar [12] [dʒiagnoʃtʃi'ka(x)] *vt* diagnose.

diagnóstico [dʒiag'nɔʃtʃikul *m* diagnosis.

diagonal [dʒiago'nawl (*pl* -ais) ⬦ *adj* diagonal. ⬦ *f* diagonal.

diagrama [dʒia'grãmal *m* diagram.

diagramador, ra [dʒiagrama'do(x), ral *m, f* typesetter.

diagramar [4] [dʒiagra'ma(x)] *vt* to work as a typesetter.

dialética [dʒia'lɛtʃikal *f* dialectic.

dialeto [dʒia'lɛtul *m* dialect.

diálise [dʒiálizil *f* dialysis.

dialogar [14] [dʒialo'ga(x)] *vi* **-1.** [conversar]: **~ (com)** to talk (to). **-2.** [negociar]: **~ (com)** to negotiate (with).

diálogo ['dʒialogul *m* dialogue.

dial-up *m COMPUT* dial-up.

diamante [dʒia'mãntʃil *m* diamond.

diâmetro ['dʒiãmetrul *m* diameter.

diante ➡ **por diante** *loc adv*: **e assim ~** and so on.

➡ **diante de** *loc adv* in the face of; **~ de algo /alguém** in front of sthg/sb.

➡ **daqui por diante** *loc adv* from now on.

dianteira [dʒiãn'tejral *f* lead; **na ~** ahead.

dianteiro, ra [dʒiãn'tejru, ral *adj* front.

diapasão [dʒiapa'zãwl *m* tuning fork.

diapositivo [dʒiapozi'tʃivul *m* slide.

diário, ria [dʒ'iarju, rjal *adj* daily.

➡ **diário** *m* **-1.** [caderno] diary; **~ de bordo** logbook. **-2.** [para viagem] journal. **-3.** [jornal] daily paper. **-4.** *COM* ledger.

➡ **diária** *f* [de hotel] daily rate.

➡ **Diário Oficial** *m* official gazette.

diarista [dʒja'riʃta] *m f* diarist.
diarréia [dʒja'xɛja] *f* diarrhoea.
dica ['dʒikal *f fam* hint.
dicção [dʒik'sãw] *f* diction.
dicionário [dʒisjo'narjul *m* dictionary.
dicionarista [dʒisjona'riʃtal *mf* lexicographer.
dicotomia [dʒikoto'mial *f* dichotomy.
didata [dʒi'datal *mf* teacher.
didático, ca [dʒi'datʃiku, kal *adj* **-1.** [pessoa] didactic. **-2.** [explicação] instructive.
➡ **didática** *f* didactics.
DIEESE (*abrev de* **Departamento Intersindical de Estatísticas e Estudos Sócio-Econômicos**) *m trade union body for the support of workers in São Paulo.*
diesel ['dʒizɛwl *m* diesel; **motor (a)** ~ diesel engine.
dieta ['dʒjɛtal *f* diet; **fazer** ~ to diet.
dietético, ca [dʒje'tɛtʃiku, kal *adj* dietary; **chocolate** ~ diet chocolate; **bebida** ~ diet drink.
dietista [dʒje'tʃiʃtal *mf* dietician.
difamação [dʒifama'sãw] (*pl* **-ões**) *f* slander.
difamador, ra [dʒifama'do(x), ral ◇ *adj* slanderous. ◇ *m, f* slanderer.
difamar [4] [dʒifa'ma(x)l *vt* to slander.
difamatório, ria [dʒifama'tɔrju, rjal *adj* defamatory.
diferença [dʒife'rẽnsal *f* **-1.** [desigualdade] difference. **-2.** [distinção]: **fazer** ~ **entre** to distinguish between; **fazer** ~ to make a difference. **-3.** [prejuízo]: **fazer** ~ **para alguém** to matter to sb. **-4.** [discordância]: **ter** ~**(s) com alguém** to have one's differences with sb. **-5.** MAT remainder.
diferenciação [dʒiferẽnsja'sãw] *f*: **fazer** ~ **entre** to differentiate between.
diferencial [dʒiferẽn'sjawl (*pl* **-ais**) ◇ *adj* differential. ◇ *m* AUTO differential. ◇ *f* MAT differential.
diferenciar [16] [dʒiferẽn'sja(x)l *vt*: ~ **algo/alguém (de)** to distinguish sthg/sb (from).
➡ **diferenciar-se** *vp* to differ.
diferente [dʒife'rẽntʃil ◇ *adj* different; ~ **de** different from *UK*, different than *US*. ◇ *adv* differently.
diferir [57] [dʒife'ri(x)l *vi*: ~ **(em algo)** to differ (on sthg); ~ **de algo/alguém** to differ from sthg/sb.
difícil [dʒi'fisiwl (*pl* **-eis**) ◇ *adj* **-1.** [ger] difficult, hard. **-2.** [delicado] tricky. **-3.** [improvável]: **acho muito** ~ **ele vir hoje** I think it is very unlikely he will come today. ◇ *adv*: **falar /escrever** ~ to use fancy words. ◇ *m*: **o** ~ **é** the trouble is.
dificílimo, ma [dʒifi'silimu, mal *superl* extremely difficult.
dificilmente [dʒifisiw'mẽntʃil *adv*: ~ **voltarei a falar com ele** it will be hard for me ever to speak to him again.
dificuldade [dʒifikuw'dadʒil *f* **-1.** [ger] problem; **pôr** ~ **em algo/em fazer algo** to object to sthg/to doing sthg; **ter** ~**s com algo** to have problems with sthg; **ter** ~ **em fazer algo** to have difficulty in doing sthg. **-2.** [qualidade de difícil] difficulty. **-3.** [impedimento] snag. **-4.** [relutância]: **ter** ~ **em fazer algo** to be loath to do sthg. **-5.** [situação crítica] trouble; **em** ~**(s)** in trouble; **meter-se em** ~**s** to get into trouble; **passar** ~**(s)** to have a hard time.
dificultar [4] [dʒifikuw'ta(x)l *vt* to complicate.
difteria [dʒifte'rial *f* diphtheria.
difundir [6] [dʒifũn'di(x)l *vt* to spread.
difusão [dʒifu'zãwl *f* transmission.
difuso, sa [dʒi'fuzu, zal *adj* diffuse.
digerir [57] [dʒiʒe'ri(x)l *vt* to digest.
digestão [dʒiʒeʃ'tãwl *f* digestion.
digestivo, va [dʒiʒeʃ'tʃivu, val *adj* digestive.
digitação [dʒiʒita'sãwl (*pl* **-ões**) *f* COMPUT keying-in.
digitador, ra [dʒiʒita'do(x), ral *m, f* keyboarder.
digital [dʒiʒi'tawl (*pl* **-ais**) *adj* **-1.** [ger] digital. **-2.** [dos dedos] finger.
digitalizado, da [dʒiʒitali'zadu, dal *adj* COMPUT digitized.
digitalizar [4] [dʒiʒitali'za(x)l *vt* COMPUT to digitize.
digitar [4] [dʒiʒi'ta(x)l *vt* COMPUT to key in.
dígito ['dʒiʒitul *m* digit.
digladiar-se [16] [dʒigla'dʒjaxsil *vp* **-1.** [com espada] to fight with a sword. **-2.** *fig* [lutar] to battle it out.
dignamente [dʒigna'mẽntʃil *adv* with dignity.
dignar-se [7] [dʒig'naxsil *vp*: ~**-se a fazer algo** to deign to do sthg.
dignidade [dʒigni'dadʒil *f* **-1.** [cargo] office. **-2.** [decência, honra] dignity; **com** ~ with dignity.
dignificar [12] [dʒignifi'ka(x)l *vt* to dignify.
dignitário, ria [dʒigni'tarju, rjal *m, f* dignitary.
digno, na ['dʒignu, nal *adj* worthy; **ser** ~ **de algo /de fazer algo** to be worthy of sthg/doing sthg.
digressão [dʒigre'sãwl (*pl* **-ões**) *f* digression.
dilaceração [dʒilasera'sãwl *f* laceration.
dilacerante [dʒilase'rãntʃil *adj* agonizing.
dilacerar [4] [dʒilase'ra(x)l *vt* [despedaçar] to tear to pieces.
➡ **dilacerar-se** *vp* [afligir-se] to be torn apart.
dilapidação [dʒilapida'sãwl *f* **-1.** [destruição] dilapidation. **-2.** [esbanjamento] squandering.
dilapidar [4] [dʒilapi'da(x)l *vt* **-1.** [derrubar] to reduce to rubble. **-2.** [esbanjar] to squander.
dilatação [dʒilata'sãwl *f* dilation.
dilatador, ra [dʒilata'do(x), ral ◇ *adj* MED dilator. ◇ *m* MED dilator.
dilatar [4] [dʒila'ta(x)l *vt* **-1.** [ampliar] to dilate. **-2.** [adiar] to delay.
dilema [dʒi'lemal *m* dilemma.
diletante [dʒile'tãntʃil ◇ *adj* dilettantish. ◇ *mf* dilettante.
diletantismo [dʒiletãn'tʃiʒmul *m* dilettantism.
diligência [dʒili'ʒẽnsjal *f* **-1.** [cuidado] diligence. **-2.** [presteza] promptness. **-3.** [pesquisa] enquiry. **-4.** [veículo] stagecoach. **-5.** JUR formality.
diligenciar [16] [dʒiliʒẽn'sja(x)l *vt* to strive for.
diligente [dʒili'ʒẽntʃil *adj* diligent.

diluente [dʒil'wentʃil] <> *adj* diluent. <> *m* diluent.

diluição [dʒilwi'sãw] *f* dilution.

diluir [74] [dʒi'lwi(x)] *vt*: ~ **algo (em algo)** to dilute sthg (in sthg).

dilúvio [dʒi'luviw] *m* flood.

dimensão [dʒimẽn'sãw] (*pl* **-ões**) *f* **-1.** [ger] dimension. **-2.** [tamanho] size.

dimensionar [4] [dʒimẽnsjo'na(x)] *vt* to dimension.

diminuição [dʒiminwi'sãw] *f* reduction.

diminuir [74] [dʒimi'nwi(x)] <> *vt* **-1.** [reduzir] to reduce. **-2.** [subtrair]: ~ **algo de** *ou* **em algo** to deduct sthg from sthg. <> *vi* [reduzir-se] to lessen; ~ **de peso/largura** to decrease in weight/width.

diminutivo [dʒiminu'tʃivul] *m* GRAM diminutive.

diminuto, ta [dʒimi'nutu, ta] *adj* minute.

dinâmico, ca [dʒi'nãmiku, ka] *adj* dynamic.
* **dinâmica** *f* **-1.** MEC dynamics (*pl*). **-2.** *fig* [atividade] dynamic; ~ **de grupo** teamwork.

dinamismo [dʒina'miʒmu] *m* dynamism.

dinamitar [4] [dʒinami'ta(x)] *vt* to dynamite.

dinamite [dʒina'mitʃi] *f* dynamite.

dinamizar [4] [dʒinami'za(x)] *vt* to motivate.

Dinamarca [dʒina'marka] *n* Denmark.

dinamarquês, esa [dʒinamax'keʃ, eza] <> *adj* Danish. <> *m, f* Dane.
* **dinamarquês** *m* [língua] Danish.

dínamo ['dʒinamul] *m* dynamo.

dinastia [dʒinaʃ'tʃia] *f* dynasty.

dinheirão [dʒinej'rãw] *m fam*: **um** ~ a mint.

dinheiro [dʒi'nejrul] *m* money; ~ **vivo** hard cash.

dinossauro [dʒino'sawrul] *m* dinosaur.

diocese [dʒjo'sezil] *f* diocese.

dióxido ['dʒjɔksidul] *m* QUÍM dioxide; ~ **de carbono** carbon dioxide.

diploma [dʒi'ploma] *m* diploma.

diplomacia [dʒiploma'sia] *f* **-1.** [ciência] diplomacy. **-2.** [representantes] diplomatic corps. **-3.** *fig* [tato] tact; **com** ~ tactfully.

diplomado, da [dʒiploma'du, da] <> *adj* [formado] graduated. <> *m,f* graduate.

diplomar [4] [dʒiplo'ma(x)] *vt* to graduate.
* **diplomar-se** *vp*: ~-**se (em algo)** to get a diploma/degree (in sthg).

diplomata [dʒiplo'mata] *mf* **-1.** [representante] diplomat. **-2.** *fig* [negociador hábil] mediator.

diplomático, ca [dʒiplo'matʃiku, ka] *adj* diplomatic.

dique ['dʒikil] *m* dyke.

direção [dʒire'sãw] (*pl* **-ões**) *f* **-1.** [rumo, sentido] direction; **em** ~ **a** towards, headed for. **-2.** [de empresa] management. **-3.** [de partido] leadership. **-4.** [de filme, peça de teatro] direction. **-5.** [de jornal] editors. **-6.** [diretores] board of directors. **-7.** AUTO steering.

direcionamento [dʒiresiona'mẽntul] *m* COMPUT forwarding.

direcionar [4] *vt* to channel.

direita [dʒi'rejta] *f* ▷ **direito**.

direitinho [dʒirej'tʃiɲul] *adv* just right.

direitista [dʒirej'tʃiʃta] *mf* right-winger.

direito, ta [dʒi'rejtu, ta] *adj* **-1.** [lado] right-hand. **-2.** [destro] right. **-3.** [digno] honest. **-4.** [arrumado] straight.
* **direito** <> *m* **-1.** JUR law; ~ **civil** civil law. **-2.** [prerrogativa] right. **-3.** [lado] right side. <> *adv* properly.
* **direita** *f* **-1.** [lado direito] right-hand side; **à** ~ on *ou* to the right. **-2.** POL right; **ser de** ~ to be right-wing.
* **direitos** *mpl*: ~ **autorais** copyright *(sg)*; ~ **humanos** human rights.

diretamente [dʒirɛta'mẽntʃil] *adv* straight.

diretas [dʒi'rɛtaʃ] *fpl* POL direct elections.

direto, ta [dʒi'rɛtu, ta] *adj* **-1.** [ger] direct. **-2.** TV [transmissão] live.
* **direto** *adv* straight.

diretor, ra [dʒire'to(x), ra] (*mpl* **-res**, *fpl* **-ras**) *m, f* **-1.** [de escola] head. **-2.** [de empresa, teatro, cinema] director. **-3.** [de jornal] editor.

diretoria [dʒireto'ria] *f* **-1.** [de escola] headship. **-2.** [de empresa] directorship.

diretório [dʒire'tɔriw] *m* **-1.** [conselho] board; ~ **acadêmico** students' union. **-2.** COMPUT directory; ~ **raiz** root directory.

diretriz [dʒire'triʒ] *f* directive.

DIRF (*abrev de* **Declaração de Imposto de Renda na Fonte**) *f* Brazilian *declaration of income tax at source.*

dirigente [dʒiri'ʒẽntʃil] *mf* leader.

dirigir [52] [dʒiri'ʒi(x)] <> *vt* **-1.** [administrar - empresa, hotel] to manage; [- filme, peça de teatro] to direct. **-2.** AUTO to drive. **-3.** [bicicleta] to ride. **-4.** [atenção, esforços]: ~ **esforços para algo** to direct one's energy towards sthg. **-5.** [enviar] to address. <> *vi* AUTO to drive.
* **dirigir-se** *vp* **-1.** [encaminhar-se]: ~-**se a** to go to. **-2.** [falar com]: ~-**se a alguém** to speak to sb.

dirimir [6] [dʒiri'mi(x)] *vt* to settle.

discagem [dʒiʃ'kaʒẽl] *f* dialling; ~ **direta** direct dialling.

discar [12] [dʒiʃ'ka(x)] *vt* to dial.

discente [dʒi'sẽntʃil] *adj* student.

discernimento [dʒisexni'mẽntul] *m* discernment.

discernir [54] [dʒisex'ni(x)] *vt* **-1.** [perceber] to recognize. **-2.** [distinguir]: ~ **entre algo e algo** to distinguish between sthg and sthg.

discernível [dʒisex'nivew] (*pl* **-eis**) *adj* perceptible.

disciplina [dʒisi'plina] *f* discipline.

disciplinador, ra [dʒisiplina'do(x), ra] *adj* disciplinary.

disciplinar [4] [dʒisipli'na(x)] <> *adj* disciplinary. <> *vt* to discipline.
* **disciplinar-se** *vp* to discipline o.s.

discípulo, la [dʒi'sipulu, la] *m, f* disciple.

disc-jóquei [dʒisk'ʒɔkej] (*pl* **disc-jóqueis**) *mf* disc jockey.

disco ['dʒiʃku] *m* **-1.** [ger] disc; ~ **voador** flying saucer. **-2.** *MÚS* record; ~ **laser** compact disc; **mudar o** ~ *fig* to stop banging on; **não mudar o** ~ to keep banging on. **-3.** [de telefone] dial. **-4.** *COMPUT* disk; ~ **flexível/rígido** floppy/hard disk; ~ **de sistema** system disk.

discordância [dʒiʃkox'dãnsja] *f* **-1.** [ger] disagreement. **-2.** [resultados, opinião, gosto] difference.

discordante [dʒiʃkox'dãntʃi] *adj* at variance.

discordar [4] [dʒiʃkox'da(x)] *vi*: ~ **(de algo/alguém)** to disagree (with sthg/sb).

discórdia [dʒiʃ'kɔrdʒja] *f* discord.

discorrer [5] [dʒiʃko'xe(x)] *vi*: ~ **sobre algo** to talk about sthg (at length).

discoteca [dʒiʃko'tɛka] *f* **-1.** [boate] discotheque. **-2.** [coleção de discos] record collection.

discotecário, ria [dʒiʃkote'kariw, rial] *m, f* disc jockey.

discrepância [dʒiʃkre'pãnsja] *f* discrepancy.

discrepante [dʒiʃkre'pãntʃi] *adj* differing.

discrepar [4] [dʒiʃkre'pa(x)] *vi*: ~ **de algo/alguém** to differ from sthg/sb.

discretamente [dʒiʃkreta'mẽntʃi] *adv* discreetly.

discreto, ta [dʒiʃ'krɛtu, ta] *adj* **-1.** [roupa] modest. **-2.** [pessoa] discreet.

discrição [dʒiʃkri'sãw] *f* discretion.

discriminação [dʒiʃkrimina'sãw] *f* **-1.** [diferenciação] differentiation. **-2.** [segregação] discrimination.

discriminador, ra [dʒiʃkrimina'do(x), ral] *adj* biased.

discriminar [4] [dʒiʃkrimi'na(x)] *vt* **-1.** [listar] to itemize. **-2.** [segregar] to isolate.

discriminatório, ria [dʒiʃkrimina'tɔrju, rjal] *adj* **-1.** [lista] itemized. **-2.** [medida] discriminatory.

discursar [4] [dʒiʃkux'sa(x)] *vi*: ~ **(sobre)** to make a speech (about).

discurso [dʒiʃ'kuxsu] *m* speech.

discussão [dʒiʃku'sãw] (*pl* **-ões**) *f* **-1.** [debate] discussion. **-2.** [briga] argument.

discutido, da [dʒiʃku'tʃidu, dal] <> *pp* ▷ **discutir**. <> *adj* much-discussed.

discutir [6] [dʒiʃku'tʃi(x)] <> *vt* [debater]: ~ **algo (com alguém)** to discuss sthg (with sb). <> *vi* [brigar]: ~ **(com alguém)** to argue (with sb).

discutível [dʒiʃku'tʃivew] (*pl* **-eis**) *adj* arguable.

disenteria [dʒizẽnte'rial] *f* dysentery.

disfarçado, da [dʒiʃfax'sadu, dal] *adj* disguised.
➡ **disfarçada** *f*: **dar uma** ~ **(em algo)** to mask (sthg).

disfarçar [13] [dʒiʃfax'sa(x)] *vt* [dissimular] to disguise.
➡ **disfarçar-se** *vp* [fantasiando-se]: ~**-se de algo** to disguise o.s. as sthg.

disfarce [dʒiʃ'faxsil] *m* disguise.

disfasia [dʒiʃfa'zial] *f MED* dysphasia.

disforme [dʒiʃ'fɔxmil] *adj* [horrendo] deformed.

disfunção [dʒiʃfũn'sãw] (*pl* **-ões**) *f* dysfunction.

dislexia [dʒiʒlek'sial] *f* dyslexia.

disléxico, ca [dʒiʒ'lɛksiku, kal] *adj* dyslexic.

díspar ['dʒiʃpa(x)] *adj* disparate.

disparado, da [dʒiʃpa'radu, dal] *adj* [lançado - tiro, flecha] fired; [- pedra] hurled.
➡ **disparado** *adv* **-1.** [a toda velocidade] at full speed. **-2.** [com grande superioridade] by far.
➡ **disparada** *f*: **em** ~ like a shot.

disparar [4] [dʒiʃpa'ra(x)] <> *vt* [desfechar, lançar - tiro, flecha] to fire; [- pedra] to hurl. <> *vi* **-1.** [descarregar-se] to fire. **-2.** [correr] to shoot off.

disparatado, da [dʒiʃpara'tadu, dal] *adj* absurd.

disparate [dʒiʃpa'ratʃi] *m* nonsense.

disparidade [dʒiʃpari'dadʒil] *f* disparity.

disparo [dʒiʃ'parul] *m* shot.

dispêndio [dʒiʃ'pẽndʒul] *m* expense.

dispendioso, osa [dʒiʃpẽn'djozu, ɔzal] *adj* costly.

dispensa [dʒiʃ'pẽnsal] *f* dispensation.

dispensar [4] [dʒiʃpẽn'sa(x)] *vt* **-1.** [prescindir] to do without. **-2.** [conceder]: ~ **algo a alguém** to grant sthg to sb. **-3.** [eximir]: ~ **alguém (de algo)** to excuse sb (from sthg).

dispensável [dʒiʃpẽn'savew] (*pl* **-eis**) *adj* expendable.

dispepsia [dʒiʃpep'sial] *f* dyspepsia.

dispersão [dʒiʃpex'sãw] *f* dispersal.

dispersar [4] [dʒiʃpex'sa(x)] *vt* to disperse.
➡ **dispersar-se** *vp* to disperse.

dispersivo, va [dʒiʃpex'sivu, val] *adj* **-1.** [pessoa] easily distracted. **-2.** [barulho] distracting.

display *m* display.

displicência [dʒiʃpli'sẽnsjal] *f* carelessness.

displicente [dʒiʃpli'sẽntʃil] *adj* careless.

disponibilidade [dʒiʃponibili'dadʒil] *f* availability; **em** ~ openly available.

disponível [dʒiʃpo'nivɛwl] (*pl* **-eis**) *adj* available.

dispor [45] [dʒiʃ'po(x)] <> *m*: **ao** ~ **de alguém** at sb's disposal. <> *vt* **-1.** [arrumar] to arrange. **-2.** [determinar] to decide. <> *vi* **-1.** [usar]: ~ **de** to have at one's disposal; **disponha!** go ahead! **-2.** [ter]: ~ **de** to have available.
➡ **dispor-se** *vp* **-1.** [decidir-se] to decide. **-2.** [propor-se] to be prepared.

disposição [dʒiʃpozi'sãw] *m* **-1.** [arrumação] arrangement. **-2.** [ânimo, vontade]: **minha** ~ **para trabalhar hoje é pouca** I don't feel much like working today. **-3.** [subordinação]: **à** ~ **de** available to.

dispositivo [dʒiʃpozi'tʃivul] *m* **-1.** [mecanismo] mechanism, device; ~ **intra-uterino** intrauterine device. **-2.** *JUR* provision. **-3.** *fig* [meio] measures (*pl*).

disposto, ta [dʒiʃ'poʃtu, tal] *adj* **-1.** [arrumado] arranged. **-2.** [animado] in a good mood; ~ **a algo/a fazer algo** willing for sthg/to do sthg.

disputa [dʒiʃ'putal] *f* **-1.** [briga] dispute. **-2.** [competição] contest.

disputar [4] [dʒiʃpu'ta(x)] <> *vt* **-1.** [concorrer a] to enter. **-2.** [competir por] to compete for. <> *vi* [rivalizar]: ~ **com algo/alguém** to rival sthg/sb.

disquete [dʒiʃ'kɛtʃil] *m COMPUT* floppy disk.

dissabor [dʒisa'bo(x)] *m* annoyance.

dissecar [12] [dʒise'ka(x)] *vt* **-1.** [corpo] to dissect.
-2. *fig* [analisar] to examine in detail.
disse-me-disse ['dʒisimi'dʒisi] *m inv* gossip.
disseminação [dʒisemina'sãw] *f* spread.
disseminar [4] [dʒisemi'na(x)] *vt* to spread.
➤ **disseminar-se** *vp* to spread.
dissensão [dʒisẽn'sãw] (*pl* **-ões**) *f* dissension.
dissentir [56] [dʒisẽn'tʃi(x)] *vi* **-1.** [discordar]: ~ **de**
algo/alguém to disagree with sthg/sb. **-2.** [dis-
crepar]: ~ **de algo** to be at odds with sthg.
dissertação [dʒisexta'sõw] (*pl* **-ões**) *f* **-1.** [tratado]
dissertation. **-2.** [discurso] lecture.
dissertar [4] [dʒisex'ta(x)] *vi*: ~ **(sobre algo)** to
lecture (on sthg).
dissidência [dʒisi'dẽnsja] *f* **-1.** [divergência] difference of opinion. **-2.** [cisão] breakaway. **-3.** [dissi-
dentes] dissidents *(pl)*.
dissidente [dʒisi'dẽntʃi] <> *adj* dissident. <>
mf dissident.
dissídio [dʒi'sidʒu] *m* dispute; ~ **coletivo** collective dispute.
dissimilar [4] [dʒisimi'la(x)] *vt* to dissimilate.
dissimulação [dʒisimula'sãw] *f* **-1.** [fingimento]
pretence *UK*, pretense *US*. **-2.** [disfarce] disguise.
dissimular [4] [dʒisimu'la(x)] <> *vt* **-1.** [disfarçar]
to disguise. **-2.** [fingir] to feign. <> *vi* [disfarçar] to
dissimulate.
dissipação [dʒisipa'sãw] *f* dissipation.
dissipar [4] [dʒisi'pa(x)] *vt* **-1.** [dispersar] to
disperse. **-2.** [esbanjar] to squander.
➤ **dissipar-se** *vp* to vanish.
disso ['dʒisu] = **de + isso.**
dissociação [dʒisosia'sãw] (*pl* **-ões**) *f* dissocia-
tion.
dissociar [16] [dʒiso'sja(x)] *vt*: ~ **algo de algo** to
dissociate sthg from sthg.
dissolução [dʒisolu'sãw] *f* dissolution.
dissoluto, ta [dʒiso'lutu, ta] *adj* dissolute.
dissolver [5] [dʒisow've(x)] *vt* to dissolve.
➤ **dissolver-se** *vp* **-1.** [extinguir-se] to break up.
-2. [desmanchar-se] to dissolve.
dissonância [dʒiso'nãnsja] *f* **-1.** *MÚS* discord. **-2.**
[som desagradável] cacophony. **-3.** *fig* [desarmonia]
incongruity.
dissonante [dʒiso'nãntʃi] *adj* **-1.** *MÚS* discordant.
-2. [sons] jarring. **-3.** *fig* [desarmônico] incongruous.
dissuadir [6] [dʒiswa'di(x)] *vt*: ~ **alguém (de al-**
go/de fazer algo) to dissuade sb (from
sthg/doing sthg).
dissuasão [dʒiswa'zãw] *f* dissuasion.
dissuasivo, va [dʒiswa'zivu, va] *adj* dissuasive.
distância [dʒiʃ'tãnsja] *f* **-1.** [espaço] distance;
manter-se à ~ **de** to keep at a distance from.
-2. *fig* [intervalo] gap. **-3.** [diferença] difference.
distanciamento [dʒiʃtãnsja'mẽntu] *m* separation.
distanciar [16] [dʒiʃtãn'sja(x)] *vt* to separate.
➤ **distanciar-se** *vp* to move away.
distante [dʒiʃ'tãntʃi] *adj* **-1.** [longe] distant. **-2.** *fig*
[alheado] aloof.

distar [4] [dʒiʃ'ta(x)] *vi*: **a cidade não dista muito,**
estamos chegando lá the city isn't very far, we're
nearly there; *fig* **os poetas distam muito dos es-**
critores de prosa poets are very different from
prose writers; **o Rio dista 420 km de São Paulo**
Rio is 420 km from São Paulo.
distender [5] [dʒiʃtẽn'de(x)] *vt* [ger] to stretch;
[músculo] to pull.
distensão [dʒiʃtẽn'sãw] (*pl* **-ões**) *f* **-1.** *MED*
relaxation. **-2.** *POL* calm.
distinção [dʒiʃtĩn'sãw] (*pl* **-ões**) *f* [ger] distinction;
[honraria] honour.
distinguir [53] [dʒiʃtĩŋ'gi(x)] *vt* **-1.** [caracterizar] to
typify. **-2.** [discernir] to distinguish. **-3.** [separar] to
differentiate. **-4.** [perceber] to make out. **-5.**
[premiar] to decorate.
➤ **distinguir-se** *vp* [sobressair-se] to stand
out.
distintivo, va [dʒiʃtʃĩn'tʃivu, va] *adj* distinctive.
➤ **distintivo** *m* badge.
distinto, ta [dʒiʃ'tʃintu, ta] *adj* **-1.** [diferente]
different. **-2.** [perceptível] distinct. **-3.** [ilustre]
distinguished. **-4.** [elegante - pessoa] refined; [-
roupa] elegant; [- postura] distinguished.
disto ['dʒiʃtu] = **de + isto.**
distorção [dʒiʃtox'sãw] (*pl* **-ões**) *f* distortion.
distorcer [25] [dʒiʃtox'se(x)] *vt* to distort.
distração [dʒiʃtra'sãw] (*pl* **-ões**) *f* **-1.** [descuido]
carelessness. **-2.** [diversão] distraction.
distraído, da [dʒiʃtra'idu, da] *adj* **-1.** [desatento]
inattentive. **-2.** [alheio] absent-minded.
distrair [68] [dʒiʃtra'i(x)] *vt* **-1.** [divertir] to amuse.
-2. [entreter] to entertain. **-3.** [desviar a atenção]: ~
alguém (de) to distract sb (from).
➤ **distrair-se** *vp* **-1.** [divertir-se] to amuse o.s.
-2. [alhear-se] to lose concentration.
distribuição [dʒiʃtribwi'sãw] (*pl* **-ões**) *f* distribution.
distribuidor, ra [dʒiʃtribwi'do(x), ra] (*mpl* **-es**, *fpl*
-s) *m, f* [pessoa] distributor.
➤ **distribuidor** *m AUTO* distributor.
➤ **distribuidora** *f FIN* broker.
distribuir [74] [dʒiʃtri'bwi(x)] *vt* **-1.** [repartir] to
distribute. **-2.** [atribuir] to allocate. **-3.** [entregar]
to deliver. **-4.** [dispor] to arrange. **-5.** [levar] to
supply. **-6.** [dirigir] to bestow.
distrito [dʒiʃ'tritu] *m* **-1.** [divisão administrativa]
district; ~ **eleitoral** electoral constituency. **-2.**
[policial] *administrative area of a town or city in*
which there is at least one police station, police
district *US*.
➤ **Distrito Federal** *m* [no Brasil] Brasilia.
distúrbio [dʒiʃ'tuxbju] *m* **-1.** [agitação]
disturbance. **-2.** [sublevação] riot. **-3.** *MED & PSIC*
problem.
ditado [dʒi'tadu] *m* **-1.** [exercício escolar] dictation.
-2. [provérbio] saying.
ditador, ra [dʒita'do(x), ra] (*mpl* **-es**, *fpl* **-s**) *m, f* **-1.**
POL dictator. **-2.** *fig* [pessoa autoritária] despot.
ditadura [dʒita'dura] *f* dictatorship.

DITADURA MILITAR

In Brazil, in 1964, as happened in many South American countries throughout the 60s and 70s, a military coup deposed the country's president. The hardening of the military regime, especially from 1968 onwards, curtailed the civil liberties of the Brazilian people for two decades, stopping them from electing their rulers by direct vote until 1989. The growing protests of the civilian population, expressed through widespread popular demonstrations from the end of the 70s onwards, gradually restored the democratic freedoms of the country. The military government brought about some economic growth, but deepened foreign debt, increased the inequality of national income distribution and reinforced social inequality, evils which beset Brazil to this day.

ditame [dʒi'tãmi] *m* [preceito] rule.
ditar [4] [dʒi'ta(x)] *vt* **-1.** [texto] to dictate. **-2.** [impor] to impose.
ditatorial [dʒitato'rjaw] (*pl* -**ais**) *adj* [autoritário] dictatorial.
dito, ta ['dʒitu, ta] <> *pp* ⊳ **dizer.** <> *adj* aforementioned.
➤ **dito** *m* [provérbio] saying.
dito-cujo, dita-cuja [ˌdʒitu'kuʒu, ˌdʒita'kuʒa] (*mpl* **ditos-cujos**, *fpl* **ditas-cujas**) *m, f fam*: o ~ the said person.
ditongo [dʒi'tõŋgu] *m* diphthong.
ditoso, osa [dʒi'tozu, ɔza] *adj* [venturoso] fortunate.
DIU (*abrev de* **Dispositivo Intra-Uterino**) *m* IUD.
diurético, ca [dʒju'rɛtʃiku, ka] *adj* diuretic.
➤ **diurético** *m* diuretic.
diurno, na ['dʒjuxnu, na] *adj* daytime.
divã [dʒi'vã] *m* couch.
divagação [dʒivaga'sãw] (*pl* -**ões**) *f* **-1.** [devaneio] daydream. **-2.** [digressão] digression.
divagar [14] [dʒiva'ga(x)] *vi* **-1.** [vaguear]: ~ **por** to wander about. **-2.** [devanear] to daydream. **-3.** [desviar-se do assunto] to digress.
divergência [dʒivex'ʒẽnsja] *f* **-1.** [discordância] divergence. **-2.** [desacordo] disagreement.
divergente [dʒivex'ʒẽntʃi] *adj* divergent.
divergir [64] [dʒivex'ʒi(x)] *vi* **-1.** [afastar-se] to branch off. **-2.** [discordar]: ~ **(de alguém)** to disagree (with sb).
diversão [dʒivex'sãw] (*pl* -**ões**) *f* **-1.** [entretenimento] entertainment, amusement. **-2.** [passatempo] pastime.
diversidade [dʒivexsi'dadʒi] *f* **-1.** [variedade] diversity. **-2.** [divergência] difference.
diversificação [dʒivexsifika'sãw] (*pl* -**ões**) *f* diversification.
diversificar [12] [dʒivexsifi'ka(x)] <> *vt* [tornar diverso] to diversify. <> *vi* [variar] to vary.
diverso, sa [dʒi'vɛxsu, sa] *adj* [diferente] different.
➤ **diversos** *adj pl* [vários] various.
divertido, da [dʒivex'tʃidu, da] *adj* entertaining, amusing.
divertimento [dʒivextʃi'mẽntu] *m* entertainment, amusement.

divertir [54] [dʒivex'tʃi(x)] *vt* to entertain, to amuse.
➤ **divertir-se** *vp* to have a good time.
dívida ['dʒividal *f* debt; ~ **pública** national debt; ~ **externa** foreign debt.
dividendo [dʒivi'dẽndu] *m* dividend.
dividido, da [dʒivi'dʒidu, da] *adj* [em sentimento] divided.
dividir [6] [dʒivi'dʒi(x)] <> *vt* **-1.** [ger] to divide. **-2.** [repartir] to share. **-3.** [separar] to split. **-4.** [demarcar] to mark out. <> *vi MAT* to divide.
➤ **dividir-se** *vp* **-1.** [separar-se] to split up. **-2.** [divergir] to be divided.
divindade [dʒivĩn'dadʒil *f* divinity.
divisa [dʒi'vizal *f* **-1.** [fronteira] border. **-2.** [insígnia] emblem. **-3.** [slogan] slogan.
➤ **divisas** *fpl FIN* foreign exchange *(sg)*.
divisão [dʒivi'zãw] (*pl* -**ões**) *f* **-1.** [partilha] sharing. **-2.** *MAT* division. **-3.** [discórdia] disagreement. **-4.** [compartimento] compartment.
divisar [4] [dʒivi'za(x)] *vt* **-1.** [avistar] to make out. **-2.** [marcar] to delimit.
divisível [dʒivi'zivew] (*pl* -**eis**) *adj* divisible.
divisor, ra [dʒivi'zo(x), ral <> *adj* [separador] separating. <> *m MAT* divisor.
divisório, ria [dʒivi'zɔrju, rja] *adj* dividing.
➤ **divisória** *f* partition.
divorciado, da [dʒivox'sjadu, da] <> *adj* divorced. <> *m, f* divorcé (*f* divorcée).
divorciar [16] [dʒivox'sja(x)] *vt* **-1.** [cônjuge] to divorce. **-2.** [separar] to separate.
➤ **divorciar-se** *vp* **-1.** [cônjuges]: ~-**se (de)** to get divorced (from). **-2.** *fig* [afastar-se] to cut o.s. off.
divórcio [dʒi'vɔxsju] *m* divorce.
divulgação [dʒivuwga'sãw] *f* **-1.** [de notícias] publication. **-2.** [de doutrina, conhecimento, cultura] spread. **-3.** [de segredo] disclosure. **-4.** [de produto] marketing.
divulgador, ra [dʒivuwga'do(x), ral *m, f* discloser.
divulgar [14] [dʒivuw'ga(x)] *vt* **-1.** [notícias] to publicize. **-2.** [doutrina, conhecimento, cultura] to spread. **-3.** [segredo] to disclose. **-4.** [produto] to market.
dizer [29] [dʒi'ze(x)] <> *vt* **-1.** [ger] to tell. **-2.** [falar] to say; ~ **que** to say that; ~ **que sim/não** to say yes/no; ~ **algo (a alguém)** to tell (sb) sthg; ~ **uma prece** to say a prayer. **-3.** [aconselhar, pensar, opinar] to say. **-4.** [significar] to mean; **esse título não me diz nada** the title means nothing to me; **querer** ~ to mean; **quer** ~, ... that is to say, ... **-5.** [atrair] to appeal. <> *vi* [falar]: **tive uma idéia! - diga!** I've had an idea! - tell me!; **dito e feito** no sooner said than done. <> *v impess* [afirmar]: **dizem que** it is said that; **a bem** ~ [na verdade] in fact; **que dirá** [quanto mais] let alone; [muito menos] even less.
➤ **dizer-se** *vp* [afirmar de si mesmo] to claim to be.
➤ **dizeres** *mpl* [dito] sayings.
➤ **até dizer chega** *loc adv* beyond belief.

➡ **por assim dizer** *loc adv* so to speak.
dizimar [4] [dʒizi'ma(x)] *vt* **-1.** [destruir em parte] to decimate. **-2.** *fig* [dissipar] to squander.
dízimo ['dizimu] *m* RELIG tithe.
DJ [di'ʒej] (*abrev de* **Disc jockey**) *m* DJ.
dl (*abrev de* **decilitro**) *m* dl.
DLL (*abrev de* **Dynamic Link Library**) *f* DLL.
dm (*abrev de* **decímetro**) *m* dm.
DNA (*abrev de* **ácido desoxirribonucleico**) *m* DNA.
do [du] **= de + o.**
dó ['dɔ] *m* **-1.** [piedade] pity; **ter ~ de alguém** to take pity on sb. **-2.** MÚS doh.
doação [dwa'sãw] (*pl* **-ões**) *f* donation.
doador, ra [dwa'do(x), ra] *m, f* donor.
doar [20] ['dwa(x)] *vt*: **~ algo (a alguém/algo)** to donate sthg (to sb/sthg).
dobra ['dɔbra] *f* **-1.** [parte voltada] fold. **-2.** [prega] pleat. **-3.** [vinco] crease.
dobradiça [dobra'disal] *f* hinge.
dobradinha [dobra'diɲal] *f* **-1.** CULIN tripe dish. **-2.** *fam* [dupla] pair.
dobrado, da [do'bradu, da] *adj* **-1.** [com dobras] folded. **-2.** [flexionado] bent. **-3.** [duplicado] doubled.
dobrar [4] [do'bra(x)] <> *vt* **-1.** [fazer dobras em] to fold. **-2.** [flexionar] to bend. **-3.** [duplicar] to double. **-4.** [circundar] to turn. **-5.** *fig* [fazer ceder] to win sb over. <> *vi* **-1.** [duplicar-se] to double. **-2.** [sino] to toll. **-3.** [envergar] to bend.
➡ **dobrar-se** *vp* **-1.** [curvar-se] to stoop. **-2.** *fig* [ceder] to give in.
dobro ['dobru] *m* double.
DOC (*abrev de* **Documento de Operação de Crédito**) *m* Brazilian *certificate of credit transfer between accounts*.
doca ['dɔka] *f* dock.
doce ['dosi] <> *adj* **-1.** [no sabor] sweet. **-2.** [terno] gentle. **-3.** [água] fresh. <> *m* **-1.** CULIN dessert, pudding. **-2.** [loc]: **fazer ~ fam** to play hard to get; **ser um ~ (de pessoa)** to be a sweetie.
doce-de-coco [,dosidʒi'koku] (*pl* **doces-de-coco**) *m* [pessoa]: **ser um ~** to be a sweetie.
doceiro, ra [do'sejru, ra] *m, f* confectioner.
docemente [dosi'mẽntʃil] *adv* gently.
docência [do'sẽnsja] *f* teaching.
docente [do'sẽntʃil] <> *adj* teaching. <> *mf* teacher.
dócil ['dɔsiw] (*pl* **-eis**) *adj* docile.
docilidade [dosili'dadʒi] *f* docility.
documentação [dokumẽnta'sãw] *f* **-1.** [em arquivos] documentation. **-2.** [pessoal] papers.
documental [dokumẽn'taw] (*pl* **-ais**) *adj* documentary.
documentar [4] [dokumẽn'ta(x)] *vt* to document.
documentário [dokumẽn'tarju] *m* documentary.
documento [doku'mẽntu] *m* document.
doçura [do'sural] *f* **-1.** [gosto doce] sweetness. **-2.** [suavidade] gentleness.
doença ['dwẽnsal] *f* **-1.** MED illness. **-2.** *fig* [mania] obsession.

doente ['dwẽntʃil] <> *adj* **-1.** MED sick, ill. **-2.** *fam* [fanático] obsessed. <> *mf* [pessoa] patient.
doentio, tia [dwẽn'tʃiw, tʃial *adj* **-1.** [débil] sickly. **-2.** [mórbido] unhealthy.
doer [48] ['dwe(x)] *vi* **-1.** [fisicamente] to hurt. **-2.** [causar pena, dó]: **~ (a alguém)** to distress (sb).
dogma ['dɔgmal] *m* **-1.** RELIG doctrine. **-2.** [opinião] dogma.
dogmático, ca [dog'matʃiku, ka] *adj* dogmatic.
doidão, dona [doj'dãw, dɔnal (*mpl* **-ões**, *fpl* **-s**) *fam adj* **-1.** [maluco] crazy. **-2.** [sob efeito de droga]: **estar ~** to be high.
doideira [doj'dejra], **doidice** [doj'dʒise] *f* **-1.** [ato de maluco] madness. **-2.** [imprudência] foolishness. **-3.** [exagero]: **ser uma ~** to be crazy.
doidivanas [dojdʒi'vãnaʃl *mf inv fam* tearaway.
doido, da ['dojdu, dal <> *adj* **-1.** [maluco] mad. **-2.** [imprudente, insensato] foolish. **-3.** [excêntrico] crazy. **-4.** [exagerado] insane. **-5.** [apaixonado]: **ser ~ por** to be mad about. **-6.** [encantado] thrilled. <> *m, f* [pessoa] madman (*f* mad woman).
doído, da [do'idu, dal *adj* **-1.** [dolorido] sore. **-2.** [doloroso] painful. **-3.** [magoado] pained.
doidona [doj'donal *adj f* ⮕ **doidão**.
dois, duas ['doiʃ, 'duaʃl *num* two; *veja também* **seis**.
dois-pontos [,dojʃ'põntuʃl *m inv* colon (*punctuation mark*).
dólar ['dɔla(x)l (*pl* **-es**) *m* dollar.
dolarização [dolariza'sãwl *f* dollarization.
dolarizar [dolari'za(x)l *vt* to base on the dollar.
doleiro, ra [do'lejru, ral *m, f* dollar dealer.
dolo ['dɔlul *m* fraud.
dolorido, da [dolo'ridu, dal *adj* sore.
doloroso, osa [dolo'rozu, ɔzal *adj* painful.
➡ **dolorosa** *f fam* [conta] tab.
doloso, osa [do'lozu, ɔzal *adj* premeditated; **crime ~** premeditated crime.
dom ['dõ] (*pl* **-ns**) *m* **-1.** [dádiva] gift. **-2.** [aptidão] knack. **-3.** [virtude] talent.
dom. (*abrev de* **domingo**) *f* Sun.
domador, ra [doma'do(x), ral (*mpl* **-es**, *fpl* **-s**) *m, f* tamer.
domar [4] [do'ma(x)] *vt* **-1.** [animal] to tame. **-2.** [subjugar] to subdue. **-3.** [reprimir] to repress.
doméstica [do'mɛʃtʃikal *f* ⮕ **doméstico**.
domesticado, da [domeʃtʃi'kadu, dal *adj* domesticated.
domesticar [12] [domeʃtʃi'ka(x)l *vt* to domesticate.
doméstico, ca [do'mɛʃtʃiku, kal *adj* domestic.
➡ **doméstica** *f* maid.
domiciliar [domisi'lja(x)l *adj* home; **prisão ~** house arrest.
domicílio [domi'siljul *m* residence; **entrega a ~** home delivery.
dominação [domina'sãwl *f* domination.
dominador, ra [domina'do(x), ral <> *adj* domineering. <> *m, f* [pessoa] ruler.
dominante [domi'nãntʃil *adj* dominant.

dominar [4] [domi'na(x)] <> vt -**1.** [controlar] to dominate. -**2.** [conhecer] to master. -**3.** [abranger] to overlook. <> vi-**1.** [ter influência]: ~ **em** to hold sway over. -**2.** [predominar]: ~ **em** to stand out in.
→ **dominar-se** vp [controlar-se] to control o.s.

domingo [do'mĩŋgul] m Sunday; ~ **de Páscoa** Easter Sunday; ~ **de Ramos** Palm Sunday; veja também **sexta-feira.**

domingueiro, ra [domĩŋ'gejru, ra] adj Sunday.

dominical [domini'kawl] (pl -ais) adj -**1.** RELIG dominical. -**2.** [relativo a domingo] Sunday (antes de subst).

dominicano, na [domini'kãnu, na] <> adj Dominican. <> m, f Dominican.

domínio [do'minju] m -**1.** [dominação]: ~ **(sobre)** control (over). -**2.** [posse] power. -**3.** [território] domain. -**4.** [controle] command. -**5.** [conhecimento] mastery. -**6.** COMPUT domain.

dom-juan (pl dom-juans) m Don Juan.

domo ['domul m dome.

dona ['donal f ▷ **dono.**

donatário, ria [dona'tarju, rjal m, f recipient.

donde ['dõndel = de + onde.

dondoca [dõn'dɔkal f fam socialite.

dono, na ['donu, na] m, f [proprietário, senhor] owner; ~ **da bola** fam big boss; ~ **da verdade** know-all UK, know-it-all US; ser ~ **de seu nariz** to lead one's own life.
→ **dona** f -**1.** [título - de casada] Mrs, Ms; [- de solteira] Miss, Ms. -**2.** fam [mulher] madam.
→ **dona de casa** f housewife.

dons pl ▷ **dom.**

donzela [dõn'zɛlal f virgin.

dopado, da [do'padu, da] adj -**1.** [pessoa] drugged. -**2.** [cavalo] doped.

dopar [4] [do'pa(x)] vt -**1.** [pessoa] to drug. -**2.** [cavalo] to dope.
→ **dopar-se** vp to take drugs.

doping m ESP doping.

dor ['do(x)] (pl -es) f -**1.** [física] pain. -**2.** [pesar] grief.

doravante [dora'vãntʃil adv from now on.

dor-de-cotovelo [ˌdoxdʒikoto'velul (pl dores-de-cotovelo) f fam jealousy.

dor-d'olhos ['do(x)dɔʎuʃl (pl dores-d'olhos) f fam eye infection.

dormência [dox'mẽnsjal f numbness.

dormente [dor'mẽntʃil adj numb.
→ **dormente** m [ferro] sleeper.

dormida [dox'midal f [sono] sleep; **dar uma** ~ to have a sleep.

dormideira [doxmi'dejral f -**1.** [sonolência] drowsiness. -**2.** BOT poppy.

dormido, da [dox'midu, dal adj fam [da véspera] yesterday's.

dorminhoco, ca [doxmi'ɲoku, kal <> adj sleepy. <> m, f sleepyhead.

dormir [59] [dor'mi(x)] <> vi -**1.** [cair no sono] to sleep. -**2.** [ter relações sexuais]: ~ **com alguém** to sleep with sb. <> vt -**1.** [sesta, noite]: **dormi uma deliciosa noite** I had a wonderful night's sleep;

dormimos uma sesta ótima esta tarde we had a really good nap this afternoon. -**2.** loc: ~ **como uma pedra** to sleep like a log; fig ~ **no ponto** [bobear] to miss the boat.

dormitar [4] [doxmi'ta(x)] vi to doze.

dormitório [dormi'tɔrjul m -**1.** [coletivo] dormitory. -**2.** [quarto] bedroom.

dorsal [dox'sawl (pl -ais) adj dorsal; **coluna** ~ spine, spinal column.

dorso l'doxsul m back.

dos [duʃl = de + os.

DOS (abrev de Disc Operating System) m DOS.

dosagem [do'zaʒẽl (pl -ns) f dosage.

dosar [4] [do'za(x)] vt -**1.** [regular - medicamento, drinque] to measure out; [- palavras] to measure. -**2.** [misturar] to mix.

dose ['dɔzil f -**1.** [remédio] dose. -**2.** [bebida] measure; ~ **cavalar** massive dose; **ser** ~ **para leão** fam to be too much.

dossiê [do'sjel m dossier.

dotação [dota'sãwl (pl -ões) f allocation.

dotado, da [do'tadu, dal adj -**1.** [que tem dote] gifted. -**2.** [possuidor]: ~ **de** endowed with.

dotar [4] [do'ta(x)] vt -**1.** [em casamento]: ~ **alguém de algo** to give sthg to sb as a dowry. -**2.** [favorecer]: ~ **alguém/algo de algo** to endow sb/sthg with sthg. -**3.** [prover]: ~ **algo de algo** to provide sthg with sthg.

dote ['dɔtʃil m -**1.** [bens] dowry. -**2.** fig [dom natural] gift.

DOU (abrev de Diário Oficial da União) m official Brazilian government publication, ≃ Weekly Information Bulletin UK, ≃ Federal Register US.

dourado, da [do'radu, dal adj golden; **peixinho** ~ goldfish.
→ **dourado** m -**1.** [cor] golden colour. -**2.** [peixe] gilthead.

dourar [4] [do'ra(x)] vt to gild; ~ **a pílula** to sugar the pill.

douto, ta ['dotu, tal adj: ~ **(em)** learned (in).

doutor, ra [do'to(x), ral (mpl -es, fpl -s) m, f -**1.** MED doctor. -**2.** UNIV: ~ **(em)** doctor (of). -**3.** [conhecedor]: ~ **em** expert on.

doutorado [doto'radul m doctorate.

doutorando, da [doto'rãndu, dal m candidate for doctorate.

doutrina [do'trinal f doctrine.

doutrinar [dotri'na(x)] <> vt -**1.** [ensinar] to teach. -**2.** [convencer] to indoctrinate. <> vi to give instruction.

download [do'lodil (pl downloads) m COMPUT download; **fazer (um)** ~ to download.

doze l'dozil num twelve; veja também **seis.**

DP (abrev de Distrito Policial) m police district.

Dr. (abrev de Doutor) m Dr.

Dra. (abrev de Doutora) f Dr.

draga l'dragal f dredger.

dragagem [dra'gaʒẽl (pl -ns) f dredging.

dragão [dra'gãwl (pl -ões) m dragon.

drama l'drãmal m -**1.** TEATRO play. -**2.** fig [catástrofe] tragedy. **-3. loc: fazer** ~ to make a scene; **ser um** ~ to be a nightmare.

dramalhão [drama'ʎãw] (pl -ões) m pej melodrama.

dramático, ca [dra'matʃiku, ka] adj dramatic.

dramatização [dramatʃiza'sãw] (pl -ões) f TEATRO dramatization.

dramatizar [4] [dramatʃi'za(x)] ◇ vt to dramatize. ◇ vi fig [ser dramático] to exaggerate.

dramaturgia [dramatux'ʒia] f play-writing.

dramaturgo, ga [drama'turgu, ga] m, f dramatist, playwright.

drapeado, da [dra'pjadu, da] adj draped.
◆ **drapeado** m [caimento] hang.

drástico, ca [ˈdraʃtʃiku, ka] adj drastic.

drenagem [dre'naʒẽl (pl -ns) f drainage.

drenar [4] [dre'na(x)] vt to drain.

dreno ['drenu] m **-1.** [tubo] drainpipe. **-2.** MED drain, drainage tube.

driblar [4] [dri'bla(x)] vt **-1.** FUT to dribble. **-2.** fig [enganar] to dodge.

drible ['dribli] m FUT dribble.

drinque ['driŋki] m drink.

drive ['drajvi] (pl drives) m COMPUT disk drive.

driver ['drive(x)] (pl drivers) m COMPUT driver; ~ de vídeo video driver; ~ de impressora printer driver.

droga ['drɔga] ◇ f **-1.** [medicamento, entorpecente] drug. **-2.** fam fig [coisa ruim]: **ser uma** ~ to be a disaster. ◇ interj fam damn!

drogado, da [dro'gadu, da] ◇ adj drugged. ◇ m, f [pessoa] drug addict.

drogar [4] [dro'ga(x)] vt to drug.
◆ **drogar-se** vp to take drugs.

drogaria [droga'ria] f chemist's (shop) UK, drugstore US.

dromedário [drome'darju] m dromedary.

dropes ['drɔpiʃ] m inv drop (sweet).

dualidade [ˌdwali'dadʒi] f duality.

duas ['duaʃ] num ▷ dois.

duas-peças [ˌduaʃ'pɛsaʃ] mpl two-piece.

dubiedade [dubje'dadʒi] f [ambiguidade] dubiousness.

dúbio, bia ['dubju, bja] adj dubious.

dublado, da [du'bladu, da] adj CINE dubbed.

dublador, ra [dubla'do(x), ra] m,f CINE dubber.

dublagem [du'blaʒẽl (pl -ns) f CINE dubbing.

dublar [4] [du'blax] vt CINE to dub.

dublê [du'ble] mf double.

Dublin n Dublin.

dublinense [dubli'nẽsi] ◇ adj Dublin (antes de subst). ◇ mf Dubliner.

ducado [du'kadu] m duchy.

ducentésimo, ma [dusẽn'tɛzimu, ma] num twohundredth.

ducha ['duʃa] f **-1.** [jorro de água] shower; **tomar uma** ~ to take a shower. **-2.** [boxe] shower (cubicle).

duelar [dwe'la(x)] vi **-1.** [combater] to fight a duel. **-2.** fig [confrontar] to confront each other.

duelo ['dwɛlu] m duel.

duende ['dwẽdʒi] m goblin.

dueto ['dwetu] m duet.

dulcíssimo, ma [duw'sisimu, ma] adj very sweet.

dumping ['dãnpĩŋ] m COM dumping.

duo ['duw] m [dueto] duo.

duodeno [dwo'denu] m duodenum.

dupla ['dupla] f ▷ duplo.

duplex m duplex.

duplicação [duplika'sãw] (pl -ões) f [de receita etc] doubling.

duplicar [12] [dupli'ka(x)] ◇ vt **-1.** [dobrar] to double. **-2.** [aumentar] to redouble. ◇ vi [dobrar] to double.

duplicata [dupli'kata] f **-1.** [título] trade note. **-2.** [cópia] duplicate.

duplicidade [duplisi'dadʒi] f fig [falsidade] duplicity.

duplo, pla ['duplu, pla] adj double; **dupla cidadania** dual nationality.

duque, duquesa ['duki, du'keza] m, f duke (f duchess).

durabilidade [durabili'dadʒi] f durability.

duração [dura'sãw] f duration.

duradouro, ra [dura'doru, ra] adj lasting.

duramente [dura'mẽntʃi] adv **-1.** [severamente] strongly. **-2.** [cruelmente] harshly.

durante [du'rãntʃi] prep during.

durão, rona [du'rãw, rɔna] (mpl -ões, fpl -s) adj strict.

durar [4] [du'ra(x)] vi to last.

durável [du'ravew] (pl -eis) adj lasting, durable.

durex® [du'rɛkiʃ] m [fita adesiva] Sellotape® UK, Scotch tape® US.

dureza [du'reza] f **-1.** [rijeza] hardness. **-2.** [rigor] harshness. **-3.** [crueldade] callousness. **-4.** fam [dificuldade]: **ser uma** ~ to be a hardship. **-5.** fam [falta de dinheiro]: **estar na maior** ~ to be hard up.

duro, ra ['duru, ra] adj **-1.** [ger] harsh. **-2.** [carne, material, água] hard. **-3.** [vida, trabalho, tarefa] tough. **-4.** fam [sem dinheiro]: **estar** ~ to be hard up. **-5.** loc: **dar** ~ (para algo/ fazer algo) to work flat out (for sthg/to do sthg).

durona [du'rona] f ▷ durão.

dúvida ['duvida] f doubt; **sem** ~ without a doubt.

duvidar [4] [duvi'da(x)] ◇ vt: ~ **que** to doubt that. ◇ vi: ~ **de alguém/algo** to doubt sb/sthg.

duvidoso, osa [duvi'dozu, ɔza] adj **-1.** [incerto] doubtful. **-2.** [suspeito] dubious.

duzentos, tas [du'zẽntuʃ, taʃ] num two hundred; veja também **seis**.

dúzia ['duzja] f dozen; **meia** ~ half a dozen.

DVD (abrev de Digital Video Disk) m DVD.

e, E [ɛl *m* [letra] e, E.
ébano [ˈɛbanu] *m* ebony.
ébrio, ébria [ˈɛbrju, ˈɛbrja] <> *adj* drunk. <> *m, f* drunkard.
EBTU (*abrev de* **Empresa Brasileira de Transportes Urbanos**) *f Brazilian company for urban transport planning.*
ebulição [ibuliˈsãw] *f* -**1.** [de líquido] boiling. -**2.** *fig* [agitação] excitement.
e-business [ɛbusiˈnɛɛsil] *m* ECON e-business.
eclampsia *f* eclampsia.
eclesiástico, ca [eklɛˈzjastʃiku, ka] *adj* ecclesiastical.
   ➡ **eclesiástico** *m* [membro do clero] clergyman.
eclético, ca [eˈklɛtʃiku, ka] *adj* eclectic.
eclipsar [4] [eklipˈsa(x)] *vt* to eclipse.
eclipse [eˈklipsi] *m* eclipse.
eclodir [6] [ekloˈdʒi(x)] *vi* -**1.** [surgir] to emerge. -**2.** [estourar] to break out.
eclosão [ekloˈzãw] (*pl* -**ões**) *f* -**1.** [aparecimento] emergence. -**2.** [desenvolvimento] development. -**3.** [de flor] blooming.
eclusa [eˈkluzal] *f* lock (*on waterway*).
eco [ˈɛkul] *m* echo.
ecoar [20] [eˈkwa(x)] *vt & vi* to echo.
ecologia [ekoloˈʒial] *f* ecology.
ecológico, ca [ekoˈlɔʒiku, ka] *adj* ecological.
ecólogo, ga [eˈkɔlogu, ga] *m, f* ecologist.
e-commerce [ɛkoˈmɛxsil] *m* ECON e-commerce.
economia [ekonoˈmia] *f* -**1.** [ger] economy; ~ **doméstica** domestic economy; ~ **dirigida** managed economy; ~ **de mercado** market economy; ~ **mista** mixed economy; **fazer** ~ to economize. -**2.** [estudo] economics; ~ **política** political economy.
   ➡ **economias** *fpl* [poupança] savings.
econômico, ca [ekoˈnomiku, ka] *adj* -**1.** [ger] economical. -**2.** [relativo à economia] economic.
economista [ekonoˈmiʃtal] *mf* economist.
economizar [4] [ekonomiˈza(x)] <> *vt* -**1.** [gastar, usar com moderação] to economize on. -**2.** [acumular] to save. <> *vi* [fazer economia] to economize.
ecossistema [ˌɛkosiʃˈtemal] *m* ecosystem.
ECT (*abrev de* **Empresa Brasileira de Correios e Telégrafos**) *f Brazilian postal service,* ≃ The Post Office *UK,* ≃ USPS *US.*
ecumênico, ca [ekuˈmeniku, ka] *adj* ecumenical.
eczema [ekˈzemal] *m* eczema.
ed. (*abrev de* **edifício**) *m* building.
edema [eˈdemal] *m* oedema *UK,* edema *US.*
éden [ˈɛdẽn] *m* Eden.
edição [edʒiˈsãw] (*pl* -**ões**) *f* -**1.** [ger] edition; ~ **atualizada** revised edition; ~ **pirata** pirate copy. -**2.** [publicação] publication; -**3.** [seleção] editing.
edificação [edʒifikaˈsãw] (*pl* -**ões**) *f* -**1.** [ger] building. -**2.** *fig* [moral, religiosa] edification. -**3.** *fig* [instrução] instruction.
edificante [edʒifiˈkãntʃi] *adj* -**1.** [moralizante] edifying. -**2.** [instrutivo] instructive.
edificar [12] [edʒifiˈka(x)] <> *vt* -**1.** [construir] to build. -**2.** *fig* [moralmente] to edify. <> *vi fig* [moralmente] to inspire.
edifício [edʒiˈfisjul] *m* building.
Édipo [ˈɛdʒipul] *m* ▷ **complexo.**
edital [edʒiˈtawl] (*pl* -**ais**) *m* proclamation.
editar [4] [edʒiˈta(x)] *vt* -**1.** [ger] to produce. -**2.** [livro, revista] to publish. -**3.** [preparar texto] to edit.
edito [eˈdʒitul] *m* edict.
editor, ra [edʒiˈto(x), ra] <> *adj* [casa] publishing. <> *m, f* -**1.** [ger] editor. -**2.** [dono de editora] publisher. -**3.** RÁDIO & TV producer; ~ **de imagem** *ou* **de VT** video editor. -**4.** COMPUT: ~ **de texto** text editor.
   ➡ **editora** *f* [estabelecimento] publisher.
editoração [edʒitoraˈsãw] *f* editing; ~ **eletrônica** electronic publishing.
editorar [4] [edʒitoˈra(x)] *vt* [editar] to edit.
editoria [edʒitoˈrial] *f* section.
editorial [edʒitorˈjawl] (*pl* -**ais**) <> *adj* editorial. <> *m* editorial.
editorialista [edʒitorjaˈliʃtal] *mf* editorial writer.
edredom [edreˈdõl] (*pl* -**ns**) *m* eiderdown.
educação [edukaˈsãw] *f* -**1.** [ensino] education; ~ **física/sexual** physical/sex education. -**2.** [criação] upbringing. -**3.** [polidez] manners; **falta de** ~ bad manners.
educacional [edukasjoˈnaw] (*pl* -**ais**) *adj* educational.
educado, da [eduˈkadu, dal] *adj* [polido] well-mannered.
educador, ra [edukaˈdo(x), ral] *m, f* instructor.
educandário [edukãnˈdarjul] *m* educational establishment.
educar [12] [eduˈka(x)] *vt* -**1.** [instruir] to educate. -**2.** [criar] to bring up. -**3.** [adestrar] to instruct.
   ➡ **educar-se** *vp* [instruir-se] to teach o.s.
educativo, va [edukaˈtʃivu, val] *adj* educational.
EEUU (*abrev de* **Estados Unidos da América do Norte**) *mpl* USA.
efeito [eˈfejtul] *m* effect; **fazer** ~ to have an effect; **levar a** ~ to put into effect; **para todos os** ~**s** to all intents and purposes; **sob o** ~ **de** as a result of; ~ **colateral** side effect; ~**s especiais** CINE special effects; ~ **estufa** greenhouse effect.

efemérides [efe'mɛridʒiz] *fpl* **-1.** [notícia diária] daily news. **-2.** [registro] *section of a newspaper listing events that happened in the past on the day of issue*.

efêmero, ra [e'femeru, ra] *adj* [passageiro] ephemeral.

efervescência [efexve'sēnsja] *f* **-1.** [de líquido] effervescence. **-2.** *fig* [agitação] excitement.

efervescente [eferve'sēntʃi] *adj* **-1.** [líquido, comprimido] effervescent. **-2.** *fig* [agitado] excited.

efervescer [25] [efexve'se(x)] *vi* **-1.** [líquido] to effervesce. **-2.** *fig* [agitar-se] to become excited.

efetivamente [efɛ‚tʃiva'mēntʃi] *adv* **-1.** [permanentemente] permanently. **-2.** [realmente] actually.

efetivar [4] [efetʃi'va(x)] *vt* **-1.** [realizar] to carry out. **-2.** [admitir] to employ.

efetividade [efetʃivi'dadʒi] *f* effectiveness.

efetivo, va [efe'tʃivu, va] *adj* **-1.** [positivo] effective. **-2.** [permanente] permanent. **-3.** [seguro] certain.
- **efetivo** *m* **-1.** MIL military strength. **-2.** COM liquid assets.

efetuar [4] [efe'twa(x)] *vt* to carry out.

eficácia [efi'kasja] *f* **-1.** [de pessoa] efficiency. **-2.** [de medida, tratamento] effectiveness.

eficaz [efi'kaʃ] (*pl* **-es**) *adj* **-1.** [pessoa] efficient. **-2.** [medida, tratamento] effective.

eficiência [efi'sjēnsja] *f* efficiency.

eficiente [efi'sjēntʃi] *adj* efficient.

efígie [e'fiʒi] *f* effigy.

efusão [efu'zãw] (*pl* **-ões**) *f* **-1.** [de líquido, gás] spillage. **-2.** *fig* [demonstração] outburst.

efusivo, va [efu'zivu, va] *adj fig* [expansivo] effusive.

e.g. (*abrev de* **exempli gratia**) e.g.

Egeu [e'gewl] *n*: **o (mar)** ~ the Aegean (Sea).

égide ['ɛʒidʒi] *f fig* [proteção]: **sob a** ~ **de** under the aegis of.

egípcio, cia [e'ʒipsju, ja] <> *adj* Egyptian. <> *m*, *f* Egyptian.

Egito [e'ʒitu] *n* Egypt.

ego ['ɛgu] *m* ego.

egocêntrico, ca [ego'sēntriku, ka] <> *adj* egocentric. <> *m*, *f* egocentric person.

egocentrismo [egosēn'triʒmu] *m* egocentricity.

egoísmo [e'gwiʒmu] *m* egoism.

egoísta [e'gwiʃta] <> *adj* egotistic. <> *mf* [pessoa] egotist.

egrégio, gia [e'greʒju, ʒja] *adj (antes de subst)* [ilustre] distinguished.

egresso, ssa [e'grɛsu, sa] *adj* graduate.
- **egresso** *m* **-1.** [ex-detento] ex-prisoner. **-2.** [ex-frade] former monk.

égua ['ɛgwal] *f* mare.

ei [ej] *interj* hey!

ei-lo ['ejlu] = **eis + o**.

eira ['ejra] *f*: **sem** ~ **nem beira** without a penny to one's name.

eis ['ejʃ] *adv* here is/are.

eixo ['ejʃu] *m* **-1.** [de rodas] axle. **-2.** [de máquina] shaft. **-3.** MAT axis. **-4.** [trecho] area *(between two points)*. **-5.** *loc*: **entrar nos** ~**s** to be on the

right track; **sair dos** ~**s** to lose control.

ejaculação [eʒakula'sãwl] (*pl* **-ões**) *f* ejaculation.

ejacular [4] [eʒaku'la(x)] *vt* & *vi* to ejaculate.

ejetar [4] [eʒe'ta(x)] *vt* to eject.

ela ['ɛla] ⊳ **ele**.

elã [e'lã] *m* enthusiasm.

elaboração [elabora'sãwl] (*pl* **-ões**) *f* preparation.

elaborador, ra [elabora'do(x), ra] *m*, *f* maker.

elaborar [4] [elabo'ra(x)] *vt* to prepare.

elasticidade [elaʃtʃisi'dadʒi] *f* elasticity.

elástico, ca [e'laʃtʃiku, ka] *adj* **-1.** [tecido etc] elastic. **-2.** *fig* [flexível] adaptable.
- **elástico** *m* **-1.** [para prender notas *etc*] rubber band. **-2.** [para roupa] elastic. **-3.** [para cabelo] elastic band.

ele, ela ['eli, 'ɛla] (*mpl* **eles**, *fpl* **elas**) *pron pess (de + ele = dele; de + ela = dela; em + ele = nele; em + ela = nela)* **-1.** [pessoa] he (*f* she); ~ **é médico** he is a doctor; **ela foi embora** she has gone away; **elas viajaram** they travelled; **eles têm uma filha** they have one daughter; **que só** ~ as only he can be/do; ~ **mesmo** *ou* **próprio** him himself. **-2.** [animal, coisa] it; **o cachorro?** ~ **uivou a noite inteira** the dog? it howled all night long; **ela dá flor em novembro** it flowers in November; **o relatório? aqui está** ~ the report? here it is; **eles já foram vendidos** they have already been sold; ~ **mesmo** itself. **-3.** *(depois de prep)* [pessoa] him, her, it; **este livro pertence a** ~ this book belongs to him; **jantei com** ~ I had dinner with them; **todos olharam para eles** ~ everybody looked at them; **sou mais velho que** ~ I am older than him; **decidimos ir sem ela** we decided to go without her; **deram um tiro nele** they shot him; **aquele é o carro dele** that's his car; **os jornais só falam dela** the newspapers talk about nothing but her. **-4.** *loc*: **agora é que são elas** there's the rub; **ser elas por elas** to be tit for tat.

elefante [ele'fãntʃi] *m* elephant; ~ **branco** *fig* white elephant.

elefantíase [elefãn'tʃiazi] *f* elephantiasis.

elefantino, na [elefãn'tʃinu, na] *adj* elephantine.

elegância [ele'gãnsja] *f* elegance; **com** ~ elegantly.

elegante [ele'gãntʃi] *adj* elegant.

eleger [26] [ele'ʒe(x)] *vt* **-1.** [por meio de votos] to elect. **-2.** [escolher] to select.

elegia [ele'ʒia] *f* elegy.

elegível [ele'ʒivewl] (*pl* **-eis**) *adj* eligible.

eleição [elej'sãwl] (*pl* **-ões**) *f* **-1.** [por meio de votos] election. **-2.** [escolha] selection.

eleito, ta [e'lejtu, ta] <> *pp* ⊳ **eleger**. <> *adj* **-1.** [por votos] elected. **-2.** [escolhido] selected.

eleitor, ra [elej'to(x), ra] (*mpl* **-es**, *fpl* **-s**) *m*, *f* voter.

eleitorado [elejto'radul *m* electorate; **conhecer o seu** ~ *fam fig* to know who one is dealing with.

eleitoral [elejto'rawl] (*pl* **-ais**) *adj* electoral.

eleitoreiro, ra [elejto'rejru, ra] *adj pej* vote-catching.

elementar [elemēn'ta(x)] (*pl* **-es**) *adj* **-1.** [rudimentar] elementary. **-2.** [fundamental] fundamental.

elemento [ele'mẽntul] *m* **-1.** [ger] element; **estar no seu ~** to be in one's element. **-2.** [indivíduo] individual; **bom/mau ~** good/bad lot.

➤ **elementos** *mpl* **-1.** [ger] elements. **-2.** [dados] facts.

elencar [elẽn'ka(x)] *vt* [listar] to list.

elenco le'lẽnkul *m* **-1.** *TEATRO* cast list. **-2.** [rol] list.

elepê [eli'pel *m* LP.

eletivo, va [ele'tʃivu, val *adj* elective.

eletricidade [eletrisi'dadʒil *f* electricity.

eletricista [eletri'siʃta] *mf* electrician.

elétrico, ca le'lɛtriku, kal *adj* **-1.** *ELÉTR* electric. **-2.** *fig* [agitado] excited.

eletrificar [4] [eletrifi'ka(x)] *vt* to electrify.

eletrizante [eletri'zãntʃil *adj fig* electrifying.

eletrizar [4] [eletri'za(x)] *vt* **-1.** *ELÉTR* to electrify. **-2.** *fig* [arrebatar] to thrill.

Eletrobras (*abrev de* Centrais Elétricas Brasileiras S/A) *f* Brazilian electricity company.

eletrocardiograma [e͵lɛtrokaxdʒo'grãma] *m* *MED* electrocardiogram.

eletrochoque [elɛtro'ʃɔki] *m* electroconvulsive therapy.

eletrocutar [4] [eletroku'ta(x)] *vt* to electrocute.

eletrodinâmica [elɛtrodʒi'nãmika] *f* *FÍS* electrodynamics (*sg*).

eletrodo [ele'trodul *m* electrode.

eletrodomésticos [eletrodo'mɛʃtʃikuʃ] *mpl* domestic appliances.

eletroeletrônico, ra [elɛktro'eletroniko, kal ⋄ *adj* electronics. ⋄ *m, f* electronic device.

eletroencefalograma [e͵lɛtrwẽnsɛfalo'grãma] *m* electroencephalogram.

eletromagnético, ca [elɛtromag'nɛtʃiku, kal *adj* electromagnetic.

elétron *m* electron.

eletrônica [ele'tronikal *f* electronics (*sg*).

eletrônico, ca [ele'troniku, kal *adj* electronic.

elevação [eleva'sãwl (*pl* -ões) *f* - **1.** [ger] elevation. - **2.** [aumento] rise.

elevado, da [ele'vadu, dal *adj* - **1.** [alto] high. - **2.** [nobre] noble.

➤ **elevado** *m* [via] flyover.

elevador [eleva'do(x)l (*pl* -es) *m* lift *UK*, elevator *US*.

elevar [4] [ele'va(x)] *vt* - **1.** [erguer] to lift up. - **2.** [aumentar] to raise. - **3.** [exaltar] to acclaim.

➤ **elevar-se** *vp* to rise.

eliminação [elimina'sãwl (*pl* -ões) *f* elimination.

eliminar [4] [elimi'na(x)] *vt* - **1.** [ger] to eliminate. - **2.** [descartar] to exclude.

eliminatório, ria [elimina'tɔrju, rjal *adj* eliminatory.

➤ **eliminatória** *f* - **1.** *ESP* heat. - **2.** *EDUC* test.

elipse le'lipsil *f* ellipsis.

elite [e'litʃil *f* elite.

elitismo [eli'tʃiʒmul *m* elitism.

elitista [eli'tʃiʃta] *adj* elitist.

elitizar [4] [elitʃi'za(x)] *vt* to class among the elite.

elixir [eli'ʃi(x)l *m* elixir.

elo l'ɛlul *m* link.

elocução [eloku'sãwl *f* elocution.

elogiar [16] [elo'ʒjarl *vt* to praise.

elogio [elo'ʒiul *m* praise.

elogioso, osa [elo'ʒozu, ɔzal *adj* flattering.

El Salvador *n* El Salvador.

elucidação [elusida'sãwl (*pl* -ões) *f* clarification.

elucidar [4] [elusi'da(x)] *vt* to explain.

elucidativo, va [elusida'tʃivu, val *adj* explanatory.

elucubração [elukubra'sãwl (*pl* -ões) *f* meditation.

elucubrar [4] [eluku'bra(x)] ⋄ *vt* [intelectualmente] to dream up. ⋄ *vi* [refletir, pensar] to muse.

em [ẽl *prep* (*em + o = no; em + a = na*) **-1.** [lugar - dentro de] in; **no bolso/estojo/quarto** in the pocket/case/bedroom; **na bolsa/caixa/sala** in the purse/box/living room; [- num certo ponto de] at; **~ casa** at home; **no trabalho** at work; **nas ruas** on the streets; **moramos na capital** we live in the capital; **depositei o dinheiro no banco** I deposited the money in the bank; [- sobre] on; **o bife mal cabia no prato** the steak hardly fitted on the plate; **havia um vaso de flores na mesa** there was a vase of flowers on the table; [- cidade, país] in; **~ Londres/São Paulo** in London/São Paulo; **no Porto/Rio de Janeiro** in Oporto/Rio de Janeiro; **~ Portugal** in Portugal; **no Brasil** in Brazil; **na França** in France; **nos Estados Unidos** in the United States. **-2.** [tempo] in; **inaugurado ~ 1967** officially opened in 1967; **ele tirou férias ~ maio** he took his holidays in May; **~ 7 de setembro de 1622** on 7th September 1622; **comemoram a liberdade no 25 de abril** freedom is celebrated on 25th April; **no Natal** at Christmas; **na Semana Santa** during Holy Week; **ela fez tudo ~ uma semana** she did everything in one week; **o serviço ficará pronto ~ dois dias** the work will be ready in two days' time; **naquela época** at that time in those days; **~ breve** soon. **-3.** [introduzindo o objeto indireto] in; **enfiar/esquecer/guardar algo ~** to slip/forget/keep sthg in; **acreditar ~** to believe in; **pensar ~** to think of; **ele caiu num buraco** he fell in a hole; **ela caiu/no chão** she fell on the floor; **ela entrou na sala** she entered the room; **vou no jornaleiro e já volto** I am going to the newsagent's and I'll be right back. **-4.** [assunto] in; **doutorado ~ sociologia** graduated in sociology; **ele é perito ~ balística** he is an expert in ballistics. **-5.** [modo] in; **ele falou ~ voz baixa** he spoke in a low voice; **ela falou ~ português** she spoke in Portuguese; **ele dirige ~ alta velocidade** he drives fast; **ela pagou ~ libras/reais** she paid in pounds sterling/reals; **o preço aumentou ~ 10%** the price has gone up by 10%; **ele gasta tudo o que ganha ~ livros** he spends all he earns on books; **bife na chapa** grilled steak. **-6.** [estado]: **a multidão ~ euforia** the rejoicing crowd; **ela ainda está ~ convalescença** she is still convalescing; **um carro usado ~ boas condições** a well-kept second-hand car; **países ~ guerra** countries at war. **-7.** [material]: **estátua ~ bronze**

bronze statue; **camisa ~ viscose** rayon shirt. **- 8.** *(em loc adv, loc prep)* on; **com base ~** based on/in; **de tempos ~ tempos** from time to time; **~ busca de** in search of; **~ caso de** in case of; **~ geral** in general; **~ meio a** in the middle of; **na verdade** in truth; **no mínimo/máximo** at least/the most.

emagrecer [25] [emagre'se(x)] <> *vt* [causar perda de peso] to cause to lose weight. <> *vi* **-1.** [perder peso] to lose weight. **-2.** [definhar] to slim down.

emagrecimento [emagresi'mẽntul] *m* slimming.

e-mail *m* e-mail.

emanar [4] [ema'na(x)] *vi* **-1.** [exalar-se]: **~ de** to emanate from. **-2.** [originar-se]: **~ de** to stem from.

emancipação [emãnsipa'sãw] *(pl* -ões) *f* **-1.** [de mulheres, escravos] emancipation. **-2.** [de menor] coming of age. **-3.** [de país] liberation.

emancipado, da [emãnsi'padu, da] *adj* liberated.

emancipar [4] [emãnsi'pa(x)] *vt* **-1.** [ger] to emancipate. **-2.** [país] to liberate.
↠ **emancipar-se** *vp* **-1.** [mulheres] to become emancipated. **-2.** [menor] to come of age. **-3.** [país] to become free.

emaranhado, da [emarã'ɲadu, da] *adj* [embaraçado] tangled.
↠ **emaranhado** *m* [confusão] confusion.

emaranhar [4] [emarã'ɲa(x)] *vt* **-1.** [enredar] to tangle. **-2.** *fig* [complicar] to confuse.
↠ **emaranhar-se** *vp* [enredar-se] to become entangled.

embaçado, da [ẽba'sadu, da] *adj* **-1.** [vidro] misted up. **-2.** [olhos] misty.

embaçar [13] [ẽba'sa(x)] *vt* **-1.** [vidro] to mist up. **-2.** [olhos] to mist.

embaciado, da [ẽba'sjadu, da] *adj* **-1.** [metal] tarnished. **-2.** [vidro] misted up. **-3.** [olhos] misty.

embaciar [16] [ẽba'sja(x)] <> *vt* **-1.** [vidro] to mist up. **-2.** [olhos] to mist. <> *vi* **-1.** [metal] to tarnish. **-2.** [vidro, olhos] to cloud.

embainhar [4] [ẽbaj'ɲa(x)] *vt* **-1.** [espada] to sheathe. **-2.** [roupa] to hem.

embaixada [ẽbaj'ʃada] *f* **-1.** [local] embassy. **-2.** [cargo] ambassadorial duties. **-3.** [funcionários] embassy staff.

embaixador, ra [ẽbajʃa'do(x), ra] *(mpl* -es, *fpl* -s) *m, f* ambassador.

embaixatriz [ẽbajʃa'triʃ] *f* [esposa do embaixador] ambassadress.

embaixo [ẽ'bajʃu] *adv* **-1.:** **~ de** underneath. **-2.: aí ~** down there. **-3.: lá ~** downstairs.
↠ **embaixo de** *loc prep* under.

embalado, da [ẽba'ladu, da] <> *adj* **-1.** [empacotado] wrapped, packed. **-2.** [acelerado] fast. **-3.** [drogado] high. <> *adv* [aceleradamente] more quickly.

embalagem [ẽba'laʒẽ] *(pl* -ns) *f* **-1.** [ato] wrapping, packing. **-2.** [invólucro] package.

embalar [4] [ẽba'la(x)] *vt* **-1.** [acondicionar] to wrap. **-2.** [berço] to rock. **-3.** [balanço] to swing.
↠ **embalar-se** *vp* [balançar-se] to rock o.s.

embalo [ẽ'balu] *m* **-1.** [balanço] rocking. **-2.** [impulso] push. **-3.** [euforia causada por droga] high. **-4.** *fam* [festa]: **festa de ~** swinging party.

embalsamado, da [ẽbawsa'madu, da] *adj* **-1.** [cadáver] embalmed. **-2.** [perfumado] scented.

embalsamar [4] [ẽbaws'ma(x)] *vt* **-1.** [cadáver] to embalm. **-2.** [perfumar] to perfume.

embananado, da [ẽbana'nadu, da] *fam adj* **-1.** [situação] snarled up. **-2.** [pessoa] in a hole, in trouble.

embananar [4] [ẽbana'na(x)] *vt* [situação] to complicate.
↠ **embananar-se** *vp* *fam* [pessoa] to be in a hole, to be in trouble.

embaraçar [13] [ẽbara'sa(x)] *vt* **-1.** [obstruir] to block. **-2.** [acanhar] to embarrass. **-3.** [cabelos] to tangle. **-4.** [dificultar] to complicate.
↠ **embaraçar-se** *vp* [embaralhar-se] to become embroiled.

embaraço [ẽba'rasu] *m* **-1.** [obstáculo] obstacle. **-2.** [acanhamento] embarrassment. **-3.** [dificuldade] difficult situation.

embaraçoso, osa [ẽbara'sozu, ɔza] *adj* embarrassing.

embaralhar [4] [ẽbara'ʎa(x)] *vt* **-1.** [cartas] to shuffle. **-2.** [confundir] to jumble.
↠ **embaralhar-se** *vp* [confundir-se] to become confused.

embarcação [ẽbaxka'sãw] *(pl* -ões) *f* vessel.

embarcadouro [ẽbaxka'doru] *m* quay.

embarcar [12] [ẽbax'ka(x)] <> *vt* **-1.** [pessoa] to board. **-2.** [carga] to load. <> *vi* **-1.:** **~ (em)** [subir a bordo] to board; [viajar] to travel. **-2.** *fam* [cair na conversa]: **~ em algo** to fall for sthg.

embargado, da [ẽbax'gadu, da] *adj* **-1.** [impedido] blocked. **-2.** [contido] carefully controlled.

embargar [14] [ẽbax'ga(x)] *vt* **-1.** [JUR - apreender] to seize; [- impedir] to block. **-2.** [conter] to control.

embargo [ẽ'baxgul] *m* **-1.** JUR seizure. **-2.** [obstáculo] impediment.

embarque [ẽ'baxki] *m* **-1.** [de pessoa] boarding. **-2.** [de carga] loading.

embasamento [ẽbaza'mẽntul] *m* **-1.** [base] foundation. **-2.** *fig* [fundamento] basis.

embasar [ẽba'za(x)] *vt* **-1.** [alicerçar] to lay the foundations of. **-2.** [fundamentar] to base.

embasbacado, da [ẽbaʒba'kadu, da] *adj* astounded.

embasbacar [12] [ẽbaʒba'ka(x)] *vt* to astound.
↠ **embasbacar-se** *vp* to be astounded.

embate [ẽ'batʃil] *m* **-1.** [colisão] crash. **-2.** [choque] shock. **-3.** [resistência] resistance.

embebedar [4] [ẽbebe'da(x)] *vt & vi* to intoxicate.
↠ **embebedar-se** *vp* to become intoxicated.

embeber [5] [ẽbe'be(x)] *vt* **-1.** [ensopar]: **~ algo em algo** to soak sthg in sthg. **-2.** [absorver] to soak up.
↠ **embeber-se** *vp* [absorver-se]: **~-se em** to be absorbed in.

embelezador, ra [ēnbeleza'do(x), ra] *adj* beautifying.
embelezar [4] [ēnbele'za(x)] *vt* [tornar belo] to beautify.
➡ **embelezar-se** *vp* [enfeitar-se] to make o.s. beautiful.
embevecer [25] [ēnbeve'se(x)] *vt* to delight.
➡ **embevecer-se** *vp* to be delighted.
embevecido, da [ēnbeve'sidu, da] *adj* delighted.
embicar [12] [ēnbi'ka(x)] <> *vt* [tornar bicudo] to sharpen. <> *vi* -**1.** [esbarrar] to meet. -**2.** [implicar]: ~ **com algo/alguém** to become entangled with sthg/sb. -**3.** [dirigir-se]: ~ **para** to head towards.
embirrar [4] [ēnbi'xa(x)] *vi* -**1.** [teimar]: ~ **em** to insist upon. -**2.** [antipatizar]: ~ **com** to take a disliking to. -**3.** [ficar birrento] to be obstinate.
embocadura [ēnboka'dura] *f* -**1.** [de rio] mouth. -**2.** [de instrumento] mouthpiece.
embolar [4] [ēnbo'la(x)] <> *vt* [emaranhar] to entangle. <> *vi* -**1.** [engalfinhar-se]: ~ **com alguém** to grapple with sb. -**2.** [encaroçar] to make lumpy.
➡ **embolar-se** *vp* [engalfinhar-se]: ~-**se (com alguém)** to become locked in battle (with sb).
embolia [ēnbo'lia] *f* embolism.
êmbolo ['ēnbolu] *m* -**1.** [bomba] piston. -**2.** [seringa] plunger. -**3.** *MED* embolism.
embolorado, da [ēnbolo'radu, da] *adj* [mofado - pão, fruta] mouldy; [- roupa, casa] musty.
embolorar [4] [ēnbolo'ra(x)] *vi* to become mouldy.
embolsar [4] [ēnbow'sa(x)] *vt* -**1.** [receber] to pocket. -**2.** [pagar] to pay.
embonecar [12] [ēnbone'ka(x)] *vt* to doll up.
➡ **embonecar-se** *vp* to doll o.s. up.
embora [ēn'bora] <> *conj* although. <> *adv* : **ir** ~ to go; **vá-se** ~! go away!
emborcar [12] [ēnbox'ka(x)] *vt* -**1.** [canoa] to overturn. -**2.** [vasilha] to turn upside down.
emboscada [ēnboʃ'kada] *f* ambush.
embotado, da [ēnbo'tadu, da] *adj* -**1.** [enfraquecido] weakened. -**2.** [insensível] numb.
embotar [4] [ēnbo'ta(x)] *vt* to blunt.
Embraer (*abrev de* **Empresa Brasileira de Aeronáutica**) *f Brazilian aeronautical company.*
embranquecer [25] [ēnbrāŋke'se(x)] <> *vt* to whiten. <> *vi* to turn white.
Embratel (*abrev de* **Empresa Brasileira de Telecomunicações S/A**) *f Brazilian telecommunications company.*
embravecer [25] [ēnbrave'se(x)] <> *vt* to make wild. <> *vi* to become furious.
➡ **embravecer-se** *vp* to become furious.
embreagem [ēnbre'aʒẽ] (*pl* -**ns**) *f* clutch.
embrear [15] [ēm'brja(x)] <> *vt* to engage (the clutch). <> *vi* to engage the clutch.
embrenhar-se [15] [ēnbre'ɲaxsi] *vp*: ~-**se em/ por** to conceal o.s. in.
embriagado, da [ēnbrja'gadu, da] <> *adj* -**1.** [bêbado] drunk. -**2.** *fig* [enlevado] intoxicated. <> *m, f* [pessoa bêbada] drunk.

embriagante [ēnbrja'gãntʃi] *adj* intoxicating.
embriagar [14] [ēnbrja'ga(x)] <> *vt* to intoxicate. <> *vi* [embebedar] to intoxicate.
➡ **embriagar-se** *vp* [enlevar-se] to become intoxicated.
embriaguez [ēnbrja'geʒ] *f* -**1.** [ebriedade] drunkenness. -**2.** *fig* [enlevo] intoxication.
embrião [ēn'brjãw] (*pl* -**ões**) *m* embryo.
embrionário, ria [ēnbrjo'narju, ja] *adj* [relativo a embrião] embryonic.
embromação [ēnbroma'sãw] (*pl* -**ões**) *f* -**1.** [embuste] deception. -**2.** [protelação] delaying tactic.
embromador, ra [ēmbroma'do(x), ra] *fam* <> *adj* -**1.** [enrolador] dishonest. -**2.** [trapaceiro] fraudulent. <> *m, f* -**1.** [pessoa enroladora] cheat. -**2.** [pessoa trapaceira] fraud.
embromar [4] [ēnbro'ma(x)] <> *vt* -**1.** [enrolar] to fool. -**2.** [enganar] to bamboozle. <> *vi* -**1.** [protelar] to procrastinate. -**2.** [fazer rodeios] to beat about the bush.
embrulhada [ēnbru'ʎada] *f fam* [confusão] muddle.
embrulhar [4] [ēnbru'ʎa(x)] *vt* -**1.** [empacotar] to wrap. -**2.** *fig* [estômago] to upset. -**3.** [confundir] to screw up. -**4.** [enganar] to trick.
➡ **embrulhar-se** *vp* [enrolar-se] to get into a muddle.
embrulho [ēn'bruʎu] *m* -**1.** [pacote] package. -**2.** [confusão] confusion.
embrutecer [25] [ēnbrute'se(x)] <> *vt* to make brutal. <> *vi* to brutalize.
➡ **embrutecer-se** *vp* to become brutalized.
emburrado, da [ēnbu'xadu, da] *adj* [aborrecido] sulky.
emburrar-se [4] [ēnbu'xaxsi] *vp* [aborrecer-se] to sulk.
embuste [ēn'buʃtʃi] *m* -**1.** [mentira] deception. -**2.** [armadilha] trick.
embusteiro, ra [ēnbuʃ'tejru, ra] <> *adj* deceitful. <> *m, f* [pessoa] trickster.
embutido, da [ēnbu'tʃidu, da] *adj* [armário, estante] built-in.
embutir [6] [ēnbu'tʃi(x)] *vt* -**1.** [armário] to build in. -**2.** [pedra, marfim] to inlay.
emenda [e'mēnda] *f* -**1.** [correção] correction. -**2.** *JUR* amendment. -**3.** *COST* repair. -**4.** [ligação] join.
emendar [4] [emēn'da(x)] *vt* -**1.** [corrigir] to correct. -**2.** *JUR* to amend. -**3.** [reparar] to redress. -**4.** [ligar] to join.
➡ **emendar-se** *vp* [corrigir-se] to mend one's ways.
emergência [emex'ʒēnsja] *f* -**1.** [ger] emergency. -**2.** [surgimento] emergence.
emergente [emex'ʒēntʃi] *adj* emerging.
emergir [78] [emex'ʒi(x)] *vi* to emerge.
emérito, ta [e'mɛritu, ta] *adj* emeritus.
emigração [emigra'sãw] (*pl* -**ões**) *f* -**1.** [de pessoas] emigration. -**2.** [de aves] migration.
emigrado, da [emi'gradu, da] <> *adj* emigrant. <> *m, f* emigré.

emigrante [emi'grãntʃi] <> adj emigrant. <> mf emigré.

emigrar [4] [emi'gra(x)] vi -1. [pessoa] to emigrate. -2. [ave] to migrate.

eminência [emi'nẽnsja] f -1. [ger] eminence. -2. [título, tratamento] Eminence. -3. [pessoa importante] important person; ~ **parda** eminence grise.

eminente [emi'nẽntʃi] adj -1. [ilustre] eminent. -2. [elevado] high.

emir [e'mi(x)] m emir.

emirado [emi'radu] m emirate.

Emirados Árabes Unidos n: os ~ the United Arab Emirates.

emissão [emi'sãw] (pl -ões) f -1. [ger] emission. -2. [de moeda, títulos, passagens aéreas] issue. -3. RÁDIO & TV transmission.

emissário, ria [emi'sarju, rja] m, f [mensageiro] emissary.
➡ **emissário** m [esgoto] outlet.

emissor, ra [emi'so(x), ra] (mpl -es, fpl -s) adj FIN issuing.
➡ **emissor** m [transmissor] transmitter.
➡ **emissora** f transmitter.

emitente [emi'tẽntʃi] <> adj FIN issuing. <> mf FIN issuer.

emitir [6] [emi'tʃi(x)] <> vt -1. [ger] to issue. -2. [sons, raios] to emit. -3. [opinião, idéias] to transmit. <> vi FIN to issue money.

emoção [emo'sãw] (pl -ões) f emotion.

emocional [emosjo'naw] (pl -ais) adj emotional.

emocionante [emosjo'nãntʃi] adj -1. [comovente] moving. -2. [empolgante] gripping.

emocionar [4] [emosjo'na(x)] <> vt -1. [comover] to move. -2. [excitar] to thrill. <> vi [provocar emoção] to thrill.
➡ **emocionar-se** vp [comover-se]: ~-se com algo/alguém to get emotional about sthg/sb.

emoldurar [4] [emowdu'ra(x)] vt to frame.

emoticom [ɛmo'tikõ] (pl -ns) m COMPUTE emoticon.

emotividade [emotʃivi'dadʒi] f emotiveness.

emotivo, va [emo'tʃivu, va] adj emotional.

empacar [12] [ẽnpa'ka(x)] vi -1. [recusar-se a andar] to stand stock still. -2. [não progredir] to stand still. -3. [parar] to dry up; ~ **em algo** to get bogged down in sthg.

empacotar [4] [ẽnpako'ta(x)] <> vt [embalar] to wrap up. <> vi fam [morrer] to snuff it.

empada [ẽn'pada] f CULIN pie.

empadão [ẽnpa'dãw] (pl -ões) m pie.

empalhar [4] [ẽnpa'ʎa(x)] vt -1. [animal] to stuff. -2. [cadeira, garrafa] to cover in wickerwork.

empalidecer [25] [ẽnpalide'se(x)] <> vt [tornar pálido] to cause to turn pale. <> vi [perder a cor] to turn pale.

empanada [ẽnpa'nada] f CULIN large pie.

empanturrado, da [ẽnpãntu'xadu, da] adj stuffed full.

empanturrar [4] [ẽnpãntu'xa(x)] vt: ~ **alguém de algo** to stuff sb with sthg.
➡ **empanturrar-se** vp: ~-se **de algo** to stuff o.s with sthg.

empapar [4] [ẽnpa'pa(x)] <> vt [ensopar] to drench. <> vi [fazer papo] to soak through.
➡ **empapar-se** vp [ensopar-se] to get drenched.

empapuçado, da [ẽnpapu'sadu, da] adj [olhos] puffy; [roupa] puffed.

empapuçar [ẽnpapu'sa(x)] vt [inchar] to stuff.

emparedar [4] [ẽnpare'da(x)] vt [enclausurar] to shut away.
➡ **emparedar-se** vp [isolar-se] to shut o.s. away.

emparelhado, da [ẽnpare'ʎadu, da] adj [lado a lado] paired.

emparelhar [4] [ẽnpare'ʎa(x)] <> vt [por em pares] to pair up. <> vi -1. [equivaler]: ~ **(em algo)** to be equal (in sthg). -2. [equiparar-se]: ~ **com** to be equal to. -3. [correr parelhas]: ~ **(com alguém)** to draw alongside.
➡ **emparelhar-se** vp [empatar] to become equal.

empastar [4] [ẽnpaʃ'ta(x)] vt -1. [ger] to plaster. -2. [tornar pastoso] to make a paste of.

empatar [4] [ẽnpa'ta(x)] <> vi [em jogo]: ~ **com** to draw with. <> vt -1. [impedir] to hinder. -2. [ocupar] to take up. -3. [aplicar] to tie up.

empate [ẽn'patʃi] m [jogo, votação] tie; **dar** ~ to end in a draw.

empatia [ẽnpa'tʃia] f empathy.

empecilho [ẽnpe'siʎu] m obstacle.

empedernido, da [ẽnpedex'nidu, da] adj harsh.

empedrar [4] [ẽnpe'dra(x)] vt [cobrir com pedras] to pave.

empenado, da [ẽnpe'nadu, da] adj -1. [deformado] warped. -2. [fora de prumo] leaning.

empenar [4] [ẽnpe'na(x)] <> vt [entortar] to warp. <> vi [entortar-se] to warp.

empenhado, da [ẽnpe'ɲadu, da] adj -1. [disposto] determined. -2. [penhorado] pawned.

empenhar [4] [ẽnpe'ɲa(x)] vt -1. [dar em penhor] to pawn. -2. [aplicar] to apply. -3. [comprometer] to pledge.
➡ **empenhar-se** vp [aplicar-se]: ~-se **(para fazer algo)** to commit o.s. (to do do sthg); ~-se **em algo** to get into debt over sthg.

empenho [ẽn'peɲu] m -1. [diligência] commitment; **pôr todo o** ~ **em algo** to put all one's effort into sthg. -2. [compromisso] commitment. -3. [penhor] pledge.

emperiquitado, da [ẽnperiki'tadu, da] adj flashy.

emperiquitar-se [7] [ẽnperiki'taxsi] vp to get dolled up.

emperrado, da [ẽnpe'xadu, da] adj -1. [entravado] jammed. -2. [teimoso] stubborn.

emperrar [4] [ẽnpe'xa(x)] <> vi [tornar-se imóvel] to stick. <> vt -1. [entravar] to cause to stick. -2. [dificultar] to bog down.

empertigado, da [ẽnpextʃi'gadu, da] adj upright.

empertigar-se [14] [ẽnpextʃi'gaxsi] vp to stand up straight.

empestar [15] [ẽnpeʃ'ta(x)] vt -1. [contaminar] to infest. -2. [infectar com mau cheiro]: ~ **algo (com**

algo) to stink out sthg (with sthg).

empilhadeira [ẽnpiʎa'dejra] f fork-lift truck.

empilhar [4] [ẽnpi'ʎa(x)] vt [amontoar] to stack.

empinado, da [ẽnpi'nadu, da] adj straight.

empinar [4] [ẽnpi'na(x)] <> vt -1. [peito, corpo, nariz] to thrust out. -2. [pipa] to empty. <> vi [cavalo] to rear.

empipocado, da [ẽnpipo'kadu, da] adj spotty.

empipocar [12] [ẽnpipo'ka(x)] vi [corpo, superfície, massa] to come out in spots.

empírico, ca [ẽn'piriku, ka] adj empirical.

emplacar [12] [ẽnpla'ka(x)] vt -1. [veículo] to put a number plate on. -2. fam fig [idade] to make it to.

emplastrar [4] [ẽnplaʃ'tra(x)] vt to put in plaster.

emplastro [ẽn'plaʃtru] m [medicamento] plaster.

empobrecer [25] [ẽnpobre'se(x)] <> vt -1. [tornar pobre] to impoverish. -2. [o solo] to deplete. <> vi [tornar-se pobre] to become poor.

empobrecimento [ẽnpobresi'mẽntu] m -1. [ger] impoverishment. -2. [do solo] depletion.

empoeirado, da [ẽnpoej'radu, da] adj dusty.

empoeirar [4] [ẽnpoej'ra(x)] vt to cover in dust.

empolado, da [ẽnpo'ladu, da] adj -1. [pele] blistered. -2. fig [linguagem, estilo] pompous.

empolar [4] [ẽnpo'la(x)] <> vt [pele] to cause to swell. <> vi [pele] to blister.

➠ **empolar-se** vp -1. [pele] to become blistered. -2. [tornar-se soberbo] to become puffed up.

empolgação [ẽnpowga'sãw] f enthusiasm; **com** ~ with enthusiasm.

empolgante [ẽnpow'gãntʃi] adj thrilling.

empolgar [14] [ẽnpow'ga(x)] vt to fill with enthusiasm.

➠ **empolgar-se** vp [entusiasmar-se] to become enthusiastic.

emporcalhar [4] [ẽnpoxka'ʎa(x)] vt to dirty.

➠ **emporcalhar-se** vp [pessoa] to get dirty.

empório [ẽn'pɔrjul m -1. [mercado] market. -2. [armazém] department store.

empossado, da [ẽmpo'sadu, da] adj newly appointed.

empossar [4] [ẽnpo'sa(x)] vt [dar posse a] to install in office.

empreendedor, ra [ẽnprjẽnde'do(x), ra] <> adj [ativo] enterprising. <> m, f [pessoa] entrepreneur.

empreender [5] [ẽnprjẽn'de(x)] vt to undertake.

empreendimento [ẽnprjẽndʒi'mẽntu] m undertaking.

empregado, da [ẽnpre'gadu, da] m, f [funcionário] employee.

➠ **empregada** f [em casa de família]: **empregada (doméstica)** maid.

empregador, ra [ẽnprega'do(x), ra] m, f employer.

empregar [14] [ẽnpre'ga(x)] vt -1. [ger] to use. -2. [dar emprego a] to employ. -3. [ocupar] to put to use.

➠ **empregar-se** vp [obter trabalho] to get a job.

empregatício, cia [ẽnprega'tʃisju, sja] adj employment.

emprego [ẽn'pregu] m -1. [trabalho] job. -2. [local de trabalho] work. -3. [uso] use.

empreguismo [ẽnpre'giʒmu] m nepotism.

empreitada [ẽnprej'tada] f -1. [trabalho, empresa] contract. -2. [tarefa] venture. -3. [empresa] undertaking.

empreiteira [ẽnprej'tejra] f contracting company.

empreiteiro [ẽnprej'tejru] m contractor.

empresa [ẽn'preza] f -1. [firma] company; ~ estatal/privada state-owned/privately-owned company. -2. [empreendimento] enterprise.

empresariado [ẽnpreza'rjadu] m employers (pl).

empresarial [ẽnpreza'rjaw] (pl -ais) adj company.

empresário, ria [ẽnpre'zarju, rja] m, f -1. [dono de empresa] employer. -2. [de artista, jogador] agent.

emprestado, da [ẽnpreʃ'tadu, da] adj loaned; **pedir algo** ~ to borrow sthg.

emprestar [4] [ẽnpreʃ'ta(x)] vt to lend.

empréstimo [ẽn'prɛʃtʃimul m [de dinheiro] loan.

emproado, da [ẽnpro'adu, da] adj arrogant.

empulhação [ẽnpuʎa'sãw] (pl -ões) f [logro] hoax.

empurra-empurra [ẽnpuˌxẽn'puxal (pl empurras-empurras ou empurra-empurras) m pushing and shoving.

empurrão [ẽnpu'xãw] (pl -ões) m shove; **dar um** ~ to give a shove; **levar um** ~ to be shoved.

empurrar [4] [ẽnpu'xa(x)] vt -1. [impelir com força] to shove; **'empurre'** [aviso] 'push' -2. [impingir] to palm off.

emudecer [25] [emude'se(x)] <> vt [fazer calar] to silence. <> vi [calar-se] to go quiet.

emulação [emula'sãw] f -1. [competição] rivalry. -2. [estímulo] ambition.

emular [4] [emu'la(x)] <> vt -1. [rivalizar com] to compete with. -2. [imitar] to emulate. <> vi [competir]: ~ **com** to compete with.

emulsão [emuw'zãw] (pl -ões) f QUÍM emulsion; ~ **fotográfica** photographic emulsion.

enaltecer [25] [enawte'se(x)] vt to honour.

enamorado, da [enamo'radu, da] adj in love.

enamorar-se [4] [enamo'raxsi] vp: ~-**se de** ou **por alguém** to fall in love with sb.

encabeçar [4] [ẽŋkabe'sa(x)] vt -1. [vir à frente de] to head. -2. [chefiar] to lead.

encabulação [ẽŋkabula'sãw] f -1. [acanhamento] embarrassment. -2. [constrangimento] constraint.

encabulado, da [ẽŋkabu'ladu, da] adj -1. [acanhado] embarrassed. -2. [envergonhado] ashamed.

encabular [4] [ẽŋkabu'la(x)] <> vt [envergonhar] to embarrass. <> vi [acanhar-se] to be embarrassed.

➠ **encabular-se** vp -1. [acanhar-se] to be embarrassed. -2. [envergonhar-se] to be ashamed.

encaçapar [4] [ẽŋkasa'pa(x)] vt -1. [bola] to pocket. -2. fam [surrar] to spank.

encadeamento [ẽŋkadʒia'mẽntu] m chain.

encadear [15] [ẽŋka'dʒja(x)] *vt* [concatenar] to link.
➤ **encadear-se** *vp* [concatenar-se] to become linked.

encadernação [ẽŋkadexna'sãw] (*pl* -ões) *f* bookbinding.

encadernado, da [ẽŋkadex'nadu, da] *adj* bound.

encadernar [4] [ẽŋkadex'na(x)] *vt* to bind.

encaixar [4] [ẽŋkaj'ʃa(x)] <> *vt* -1. [inserir]: ~ algo (em algo) to fit sthg (into sthg). -2. [encaixotar] to box. <> *vi* [entrar no encaixe] to fit.
➤ **encaixar-se** *vp* to fit.

encaixe [ẽŋ'kajʃi] *m* -1. [ato] entrance. -2. [cavidade] groove. -3. [junção] joint.

encaixotar [4] [ẽŋkajʃo'ta(x)] *vt* to box.

encalacrado, da [ẽŋkala'kradu, da] *adj* in trouble.

encalacrar [4] [ẽŋkala'kra(x)] *vt* to lead into difficulties.
➤ **encalacrar-se** *vp* to get into difficulties.

encalço [ẽŋ'kawsu] *m*: **estar no ~ de algo/alguém** to be in pursuit of sthg/sb.

encalhado, da [ẽŋka'ʎadu, da] *adj* -1. [embarcação] aground. -2. [mercadoria] unsaleable. -3. *fam* [pessoa solteira] on the shelf.

encalhar [4] [ẽŋka'ʎa(x)] *vi* -1. [embarcação] to run aground. -2. [mercadoria] to remain unsold. -3. [processo] to grind to a halt. -4. *fam* [pessoa solteira] to be left on the shelf.

encaminhar [4] [ẽŋkami'ɲa(x)] *vt* -1. [dirigir] to direct. -2. [orientar] to guide. -3. [dar andamento] to get going.
➤ **encaminhar-se** *vp* [dirigir-se]: ~-se para/a to set out for/to.

encampar [4] [ẽŋkãm'pa(x)] *vt* -1. JUR to rescind. -2. [empresa] to take into administration.

encanador, ra [ẽŋkana'dox, ra] (*mpl* -es, *fpl* -s) *m*, *f* plumber.

encanamento [ẽŋkana'mẽntu] *m* [sistema] plumbing.

encanar [4] [ẽŋka'na(x)] *vt* -1. [canalizar] to channel. -2. *fam* [prender] to lock up.

encantado, da [ẽŋkãn'tadu, da] (*mpl* -es, *fpl* -s) *adj* [ger] enchanted.

encantador, ra [ẽŋkãnta'do(x), ra] (*mpl* -es, *fpl* -s) *adj* -1. [fascinante] charming. -2. [deslumbrante] fantastic.

encantamento [ẽŋkãnta'mẽntu] *m* -1. [magia] enchantment. -2. [deslumbramento] fascination.

encantar [4] [ẽŋkãn'ta(x)] *vt* -1. [enfeitiçar] to bewitch. -2. [fascinar] to charm. -3. [deslumbrar] to fascinate.
➤ **encantar-se** *vp*: ~-se com algo to be enchanted by sthg.

encanto [ẽŋ'kãntu] *m* -1. [ger] charm. -2. *fam* [pessoa]: **ser um ~** to be a charming person.

encapado, da [ẽŋka'padu, da] *adj* covered.

encapar [4] [ẽŋka'pa(x)] *vt* to cover.

encapetado, da [ẽŋkape'tadu, da] *adj* [criança] mischievous.

encapetar-se [ẽŋkape'ta(x)si] *vp* [endiabrar-se] to go into a tantrum.

encapotar [4] [ẽŋkapo'ta(x)] *vt* [cobrir] to wrap.
➤ **encapotar-se** *vp* [cobrir-se] to wrap o.s. up.

encaracolado, da [ẽŋkaraco'ladu, da] *adj* curly.

encaracolar [4] [ẽŋkarako'la(x)] <> *vt* [cabelo] to curl. <> *vi* [cabelo] to curl.

encarar [4] [ẽŋka'ra(x)] *vt* -1. [fitar] to stare at. -2. [enfrentar] to face up to. -3. [considerar] to consider.

encarcerar [4] [ẽŋkaxse'ra(x)] *vt* [prender] to incarcerate.

encardido, da [ẽŋkar'dʒidu, da] *adj* -1. [roupa] soiled. -2. [pele] grimy.

encardir [6] [ẽŋkax'dʒi(x)] <> *vt* -1. [roupa] to soil. -2. [pele] to make grimy. <> *vi* [ficar mal lavado] to be badly washed.

encarecer [25] [ẽŋkare'se(x)] <> *vt* -1. [tornar mais caro] to make more expensive. -2. [elogiar] to praise. <> *vi* [ficar mais caro] to go up in price.

encarecidamente [ẽŋkaresida'mẽntʃil] *adv* [insistentemente]: **pedir ~** to ask insistently.

encarecimento [ẽŋkaresi'mẽntu] *m* increase in price; **~ da vida** rise in the cost of living.

encargo [ẽŋ'kaxgu] *m* -1. [ger] duty. -2. [responsabilidade] responsibility.

encarnação [ẽŋkaxna'sãw] (*pl* -ões) *f* -1. [ger] incarnation. -2. [personificação]: **ser a ~ de algo** to be the embodiment of sthg. -3. *fam* [implicância] teasing.

encarnado, da [ẽŋkax'nadu, da] *adj* [vermelho] red.

encarnar [4] [ẽŋkax'na(x)] <> *vi* -1. [alma, espirito] to represent. -2. [implicar] *fam*: ~ **em alguém** to tease sb. <> *vt* -1. [personificar] to personify. -2. TEATRO to play.

encaroçar [13] [ẽŋkaro'sa(x)] *vi* -1. [pele] to come up in bumps. -2. [molho, massa] to be lumpy.

encarregado, da [ẽŋkaxe'gadu, da] <> *adj*: ~ **de algo/fazer algo** in charge of sthg/with doing sthg. <> *m*, *f* person in charge; ~ **de negócios** chargé d'affaires.

encarregar [14] [ẽŋkaxe'ga(x)] *vt*: ~ **alguém de algo** to put sb in charge of sthg.
➤ **encarregar-se** *vp*: ~-se **de algo/fazer algo** to take charge of sthg/doing sthg.

encartar [4] [ẽŋkax'ta(x)] *vt* to insert.

encarte [ẽŋ'kaxtʃi] *m* -1. [em publicação] insertion. -2. [de disco, CD] insert.

encasquetar [4] [ẽŋkaʃke'ta(x)] *vt*: ~ **que** to be convinced that; ~ **uma idéia** to be obsessed with an idea.

encefalograma [ẽnsɛfalo'grãmal] *m* encephalogram.

encenação [ẽnsena'sãw] *f* -1. TEATRO staging. -2. [produção] production. -3. *fig* [fingimento] play-acting.

encenar [4] [ẽnse'na(x)] *vt* -1. TEATRO to stage. -2. [produzir] to produce. -3. *fig* [fingir] to play-act.

enceradeira [ẽnsera'dejral] *f* floor-polisher.

encerado, da [ẽnse'radu, da] *adj* waxed.
➤ **encerado** *m* [oleado] tarpaulin.

encerar [4] [ẽnse'ra(x)] *vt* to polish.

encerramento [ẽnsexa'mẽntul *m* closure.

encerrar [4] [ẽnse'xa(x)] *vt* -**1.** [acabar]: ~ **algo (com algo)** to close sthg (with sthg). -**2.** [confinar] to shut. -**3.** [conter] to contain.

➡ **encerrar-se** *vp* [enclausurar-se]: ~**-se (em)** to shut o.s. up (in).

encestar [4] [ẽnseʃ'ta(x)] *ESP* [basquete] *vt* & *vi* to score.

encetar [4] [ẽnse'ta(x)] *vt* [começar] to start.

encharcado, da [ẽnʃax'kadu, da] *adj* -**1.** [alagado] flooded. -**2.** [ensopado] soaking wet.

encharcar [12] [ẽnʃar'ka(x)] *vt* -**1.** [alagar] to flood. -**2.** [ensopar] to drench.

➡ **encharcar-se** *vp* [ensopar-se] to become soaked.

enchente [ẽn'ʃẽntʃil *f* flood.

encher [5] [ẽn'ʃe(x)] ◇ *vt* -**1.** [ger] to fill; ~ **o saco (de alguém)** *m fam* to piss sb off. -**2.** [fartar]: ~ **algo (de)** to saturate sthg (with). -**3.** [balão, bola, pneu] to inflate. ◇ *vi* [tornar-se cheio] to become full.

➡ **encher-se** *vp* -**1.** [tornar-se cheio] to become full. -**2.** [fartar-se]: ~**-se de** to have too much of. -**3.** [aborrecer-se] to become fed up.

enchimento [ẽnʃi'mẽntul *m* -**1.** [ato] filling. -**2.** [coisa com que se enche] stuffing.

enchova [ẽn'ʃoval *f* anchovy.

encíclica [ẽn'siklikal *f RELIG* encyclical.

enciclopédia [ẽnsiklo'pɛdʒjal *f* -**1.** [obra] encyclopedia. -**2.** *fam* [pessoa sábia] walking encyclopedia.

enciclopédico, ca [ẽnsiklo'pɛdʒiku, kal *adj* encyclopedic.

enciumar-se [4] [ẽnsju'maxsil *vp* to be jealous.

enclausurar [4] [ẽŋklawzu'ra(x)l *vt* to shut away.

➡ **enclausurar-se** *vp* to shut o.s. away.

encoberto, ta [ẽŋko'bɛxtu, tal ◇ *pp* ⊳ **encobrir.** ◇ *adj* -**1.** [céu, tempo] overcast. -**2.** [escondido] hidden. -**3.** [disfarçado] concealed.

encobrir [59] [ẽŋko'bri(x)l *vt* -**1.** [ger] to conceal. -**2.** [esconder] to hide.

➡ **encobrir-se** *vp* -**1.** [esconder-se] to hide. -**2.** [disfarçar-se] to disguise o.s. -**3.** [céu, sol] to become overcast.

encolerizar [4] [ẽŋkoleri'za(x)l *vt* [pessoa] to enrage.

➡ **encolerizar-se** *vp* [pessoa] to get angry.

encolher [5] [ẽŋko'ʎe(x)l ◇ *vt* -**1.** [contrair] to tuck in; ~ **os ombros** to shrug one's shoulders. -**2.** [diminuir o tamanho de] to shrink. ◇ *vi* [roupa] to shrink.

➡ **encolher-se** *vp* -**1.** [espremer-se] to squeeze up. -**2.** [de frio] to shrivel.

encomenda [ẽŋko'mẽndal *f* -**1.** [mercadoria] order; **fazer uma** ~ to order; **feito sob** ~ made to order. -**2.** [pacote] parcel.

encomendar [4] [ẽŋkomẽn'da(x)l *vt* -**1.** [obra, compra]: ~ **algo a alguém** to order sthg from sb. -**2.** *RELIG* to commend.

encompridar [4] [ẽŋkõnpri'da(x)l *vt* to lengthen.

encontrão [ẽŋkõn'trãwl (*pl* -**ões**) *m* -**1.** [esbarrão]

bump; **dar um** ~ to shove. -**2.** [empurrão] shove.

encontrar [4] [ẽŋkõn'tra(x)l ◇ *vt* -**1.** [pessoa - por acaso] to meet; [- em certa condição] to find. -**2.** [coisa perdida, procurada] to find. -**3.** [dificuldades] to come up against. -**4.** [solução, erro] to discover. ◇ *vi*: ~ **com alguém** [por acerto] to meet up with sb; [por acaso] to meet sb.

➡ **encontrar-se** *vp* -**1.**: ~**-se (com alguém)** [por acerto] to have a meeting (with sb); [por acaso] to meet (sb). -**2.** [estar] to be. -**3.** [colidir] to collide. -**4.** *PSIC* to find o.s.

encontro [ẽŋ'kõntrul *m* meeting; **ir ao** ~ **de** to go to meet; **de** ~ **a** [contra] against; **o carro foi de** ~ **ao muro** the car crashed into the wall; [em contradição a] in contrast with.

encorajamento [ẽŋkoraʒa'mẽntul *m* encouragement.

encorajar [4] [ẽŋkora'ʒa(x)l *vt* to encourage.

encorpado, da [ẽŋkor'padu, dal *adj* -**1.** [forte] corpulent. -**2.** [espesso - tecido] thick; [- vinho] full-bodied.

encorpar [4] [ẽŋkox'pa(x)l *vt* -**1.** [fazer crescer] to make grow. -**2.** [engrossar] to thicken.

encosta [ẽŋ'kɔʃtal *f* hillside.

encostar [4] [ẽŋkoʃ'ta(x)l ◇ *vt* -**1.** [aproximar] to put against. -**2.** [quase fechar] to leave ajar. -**3.** [estacionar] to pull up. -**4.** [deitar] to rest. -**5.** *fig* [pôr de lado] to put aside. ◇ *vi* -**1.** [tocar]: ~ **em algo/alguém** to lean against sthg/sb. -**2.** [bater]: ~ **a mão em alguém** to hit sb with one's hand.

➡ **encostar-se** *vp* -**1.** [deitar-se] to recline. -**2.** [apoiar-se] to lean. -**3.** *fig* [aproveitar-se de]: ~**-se em alguém** to lean on sb. -**4.** *fig* [fugir de trabalho] to lie back.

encosto [ẽŋ'koʃtul *m* [espaldar] back.

encouraçado, da [ẽŋkora'sadu, dal *adj* ironclad.

➡ **encouraçado** *m NÁUT* battleship.

encravado, da [ẽŋkra'vadu, dal *adj* -**1.** [unha] ingrown. -**2.** [pêlo] ingrowing.

encravar [4] [ẽŋkra'va(x)l *vt*: ~ **algo (em algo)** to imbed sthg in sthg).

encrenca [ẽ'ŋkrẽnkal *f* -**1.** [problema] tight spot. -**2.** [briga] fight; **meter-se numa** ~ to get caught up in a fight.

encrencar [12] [ẽŋkrẽn'ka(x)l ◇ *vt* [meter em complicação] to embarrass. ◇ *vi* -**1.** [quebrar - carro] to break down; [- computador] to go down. -**2.** [complicar-se] to become complicated. -**3.** *fam* [implicar]: ~ **com alguém/algo** to take issue with sb/sthg.

encrenqueiro, ra [ẽŋkrẽn'kejru, ral *adj* troublemaking.

encrespado, da [ẽŋkreʃ'padu, dal *adj* -**1.** [cabelo] tightly-curled. -**2.** [mar] choppy.

encrespar [4] [ẽŋkreʃ'pa(x)l *vt* -**1.** [cabelo] to curl. -**2.** [mar] to ripple.

➡ **encrespar-se** *vp* -**1.** [mar] to become choppy, to get choppy. -**2.** *fig* [irritar-se] to become angry, to get angry.

encruar [4] [ẽŋkru'a(x)l *vi* to harden.

encruzilhada [ẽŋkruzi'ʎadal f crossroads *(sg).*
encucado, da [ẽŋku'kadu, dal *adj* perturbed.
encucar [12] [ẽŋku'ka(x)l *vi* to become confused.
encurralado, da [ẽŋkuxa'ladu, dal *adj* [cercado] cornered.
encurralar [4] [ẽŋkuxa'la(x)l *vt* to herd.
encurtar [4] [ẽŋkux'ta(x)l *vt* to shorten.
end. (*abrev de* endereço) *m* add.
endêmico, ca [ẽn'demiku, kal *adj* endemic.
endemoninhado, da [ẽdemoni'ɲadu, dal *adj*
- 1. [pessoa - possuído] possessed; [- levado] mischievous. **- 2.** [expressão, olhar] diabolical.
endereçamento [ẽnderesa'mẽntul *m* **-1.** [ger] address. **- 2.** *COMPUT* addressing.
endereçar [13] [ẽndere'sa(x)l *vt* **-1.** [sobrescrever] to address. **-2.** [enviar] to send.
endereço [ẽnde'resul *m* address; ~ **eletrônico** e-mail address.
endeusar [4] [ẽndew'za(x)l *vt* to deify.
endiabrado, da [ẽndʒia'bradu, dal *adj* mischievous.
endinheirado, da [ẽndʒiɲej'radu, dal *adj* well-off.
endireitar [4] [ẽndʒirej'ta(x)l *vt* **-1.** [descurvar] to straighten. **-2.** [arrumar] to tidy.
➠ **endireitar-se** *vp* [corrigir-se] to go straight.
endividado, da [ẽndʒivi'dadu, dal *adj* in debt.
endividamento [ẽndʒivida'mẽntul *m* state of being in debt.
endividar-se [4] [ẽndʒivi'daxsil *vp* to fall into debt.
endócrino, na [ẽn'dɔkrinu, nal *adj* endocrine.
endocrinologia [ẽn,dokrinolo'ʒial f endocrinology.
endocrinologista [ẽn,dokrinolo'ʒiʃtal *mf* endocrinologist.
endoidar [4] [ẽndoj'da(x)l *vi* to go mad; **meu relógio endoidou** my watch has gone haywire.
endoidecer [25] [ẽndojde'se(x)l <> *vt* to drive mad. <> *vi* to go mad.
endoscopia [ẽndoʃko'pial f endoscopy.
endossar [4] [ẽndo'sa(x)l *vt* to endorse.
endosso [ẽn'dosul *m* endorsement.
endurecer [25] [ẽndure'se(x)l <> *vt* to harden. <> *vi* -**1.** [ficar duro] to go hard. - **2.** [ficar difícil] to be hard. - **3.** *fig* [tornar-se frio]: ~ **(com alguém)** to harden (towards sb).
endurecimento [ẽnduresi'mẽntul *m* hardening.
enegrecer [25] [enegre'se(x)l *vt & vi* to darken.
ENEM (*abrev de* **Exame Nacional do Ensino Médio**) *m exam taken at the end of middle education in Brazil.*
enema [e'nemal *m* enema.
energético, ca [enex'ʒɛtʃiku, kal *adj* energizing.
➠ **energética** f energy.
energia [enex'ʒial f energy; ~ **atômica/nuclear/ solar** atomic/nuclear/solar energy.
enérgico, ca [e'nɛxʒiku, kal *adj* energetic.
energizante [enexʒi'zãntʃil *adj* energizing.
energizar [4] [enexʒi'za(x)l *vt* to energize.
enervante [enex'vãntʃil *adj* annoying.

enervar [4] [enex'va(x)l *vt* to annoy.
➠ **enervar-se** *vp* to get annoyed.
enevoado, da [ene'vwadu, dal *adj* misty.
enfadar [4] [ẽnfa'da(x)l *vt* to bore.
➠ **enfadar-se** *vp* to get bored.
enfado [ẽn'fadul *m* boredom.
enfadonho, nha [ẽnfa'doɲu, ɲal *adj* boring.
enfaixar [4] [ẽnfaj'ʃa(x)l *vt* to bandage.
enfartar [4] [ẽnfax'ta(x)l *vi* to have a clot.
enfarte [ẽn'faxtʃil *m* MED clot.
ênfase ['ẽnfazil f emphasis; **dar** ~ **a** to emphasize.
enfastiado, da [ẽnfaʃ'tʃjadu, dal *adj* bored.
enfastiar [16] [ẽnfaʃ'tʃja(x)l *vt* to bore.
➠ **enfastiar-se** *vp* to get bored.
enfático, ca [ẽn'fatʃiku, kal *adj* emphatic.
enfatizar [4] [ẽnfatʃi'za(x)l *vt* to emphasize.
enfear [15] [ẽnfe'a(x)l <> *vt* to make ugly. <> *vi* to become ugly.
enfeitar [4] [ẽnfej'ta(x)l *vt* to decorate.
➠ **enfeitar-se** *vp* to dress up.
enfeite [ẽn'fejtʃil *m* decoration.
enfeitiçar [13] [ẽnfejtʃi'sa(x)l *vt* **-1.** [lançar feitiço] to bewitch. **- 2.** *fig* [fascinar] to charm.
enfermagem [ẽnfex'maʒẽl f nursing.
enfermaria [ẽnfexma'rial f sickroom.
enfermeiro, ra [ẽnfex'mejru, ral *m*, f nurse.
enfermidade [ẽnfexmi'dadʒil f illness.
enfermo, ma [ẽn'fexmu, mal <> *adj* sick. <> *m*, f sick person.
enferrujado, da [ẽnfexu'ʒadu, dal *adj* [oxidado] rusty.
enferrujar [4] [ẽnfexu'ʒa(x)l <> *vt* to rust. <> *vi* to go rusty.
enfezado, da [ẽnfe'zadu, dal *adj* annoyed.
enfezar [4] [ẽnfe'za(x)l *vt* to annoy.
➠ **enfezar-se** *vp* to get annoyed.
enfiar [16] [ẽn'fja(x)l *vt* **-1.** [introduzir]: ~ **algo (em algo)** to thread sthg (onto sthg). **-2.** [vestir] to slip on. **-3.** [pôr] to put.
➠ **enfiar-se** *vp* [meter-se]: ~**-se em algo** to slip into sthg.
enfileirar [4] [ẽnfilej'ra(x)l *vt* to put in line.
➠ **enfileirar-se** *vp* to get in line.
enfim [ẽn'fĩl *adv* finally; **até que** ~ finally; ~ **sós!** alone at last!
enfisema [ẽnfi'zemal f emphysema.
enfocar [12] [ẽnfo'ka(x)l *vt* to focus.
enfoque [ẽn'fɔkil *m* focus.
enforcamento [ẽnfoxka'mẽntul *m* [de pessoa] hanging.
enforcar [ẽfox'ka(x)l *vt* **-1.** [pessoa] to hang. **-2.** *fam fig* [dia de trabalho, aula] to skip.
➠ **enforcar-se** *vp* [pessoa] to hang o.s.
enfraquecer [25] [ẽnfrake'se(x)l <> *vt* to weaken. <> *vi* to grow weak.
➠ **enfraquecer-se** *vp* to weaken o.s.
enfraquecido, da [ẽnfrake'sidu, dal *adj* weakened.
enfraquecimento [ẽnfrakesi'mẽntul *m* weakening.

enfrentamento [ẽnfrẽnta'mẽntul *m* clash, confrontation.

enfrentar [4] [ẽnfrẽn'ta(x)] *vt* to face.

enfronhado, da [ẽnfro'ɲadu, da] *adj*: **bem ~ em algo** well-versed in sthg.

enfronhar [4] [ẽnfro'ɲa(x)] *vt*: **~ alguém em algo** to instruct sb in sthg.

➡ **enfronhar-se** *vp*: **~-se em algo** to become knowledgeable about sthg.

enfumaçado, da [ẽnfuma'sadu, da] *adj* smoky.

enfumaçar [13] [ẽnfuma'sa(x)] *vt* to make smoky.

enfurecer [25] [ẽnfure'se(x)] *vt* to infuriate.

➡ **enfurecer-se** *vp* to get infuriated.

enfurecido, da [ẽnfure'sidu, da] *adj* infuriated.

enfurnar-se [4] [ẽnfux'naxsi] *vp*: **~-se em** to hide o.s. in.

engaiolar [4] [ẽŋgajo'la(x)] *vt* to put in a cage.

engajado, da [ẽŋga'ʒadu, da] *adj* engaged.

engajamento [ẽŋgaʒa'mẽntul *m* -**1.** [ger] engagement. -**2.** [de trabalhadores] taking on.

engajar [4] [ẽŋga'ʒa(x)] *vt* [trabalhadores] to take on.

➡ **engajar-se** *vp* -**1.** *POL*: **~-se (em)** to engage o.s. (in). -**2.** *MIL*: **~-se (em)** to become engaged (in). -**3.** [em campanha, luta]: **~-se em** to get involved (in). -**4.** [trabalhador]: **~-se (em)** to be engaged (in).

engalfinhar-se [4] [ẽŋgawfi'naxsi] *vp* to get entangled.

engambelar [4] [ẽŋgãnbe'la(x)] *vt* to deceive.

enganação [ẽŋgana'sãw] *f* deception.

enganador, ra [ẽŋgana'do(x), ra] *adj* deceptive.

enganar [4] [ẽŋga'na(x)] *vt* -**1.** [iludir] to deceive. -**2.** [trair] to cheat.

➡ **enganar-se** *vp* -**1.** [iludir-se] to fool o.s. -**2.** [cometer um erro] to make a mistake.

enganchar [4] [ẽŋgãn'ʃa(x)] ◇ *vt*: **~ algo (em algo)** to hook sthg up (to sthg). ◇ *vi*: **~ (em algo)** to catch (in sthg).

engano [ẽŋ'gãnul *m* [equívoco] error; [em telefonema]: **ser ~ to** be a wrong number.

engarrafado, da [ẽŋgaxa'fadu, da] *adj* -**1.** [bebida] bottled. -**2.** [rua, trânsito] blocked.

engarrafamento [ẽŋgaxafa'mẽntul *m* -**1.** [de bebida] bottling. -**2.** [no trânsito] traffic jam.

engarrafar [4] [ẽŋgaxa'fa(x)] *vt* -**1.** [bebida] to bottle. -**2.** [rua, trânsito] to block.

engasgar [14] [ẽŋgaʒ'ga(x)] ◇ *vt* [na garganta] to choke. ◇ *vi* to choke.

➡ **engasgar-se** *vp* [na garganta] to choke o.s.

engasgo [ẽŋ'gaʒgul *m* [na garganta] choking.

engastar [4] [ẽŋgaʃ'ta(x)] *vt* to set.

engaste [ẽŋ'gaʃtʃil *m* [stone] setting.

engatar [4] [ẽŋga'ta(x)] *vt* -**1.** [atrelar]: **~ algo (em algo)** to couple sthg (with sthg). -**2.** [engrenar] to get into gear. -**3.** [iniciar] to start.

engate [ẽŋ'gatʃil *m* connection.

engatilhar [4] [ẽŋgatʃi'ʎa(x)] *vt* -**1.** [arma] to cock. -**2.** *fig* [resposta *etc*] to prepare.

engatinhar [4] [ẽŋgatʃi'ɲa(x)] *vi* -**1.** [bebê] to crawl. -**2.** *fig* [ser principiante]: **~ em algo** to feel one's way in sthg.

engavetamento [ẽŋgaveta'mẽntul *m* -**1.** [de carros] smash. -**2.** [de papéis] putting into a drawer. -**3.** [de projeto, processo] *fig* shelving.

engavetar [4] [ẽŋgave'ta(x)] ◇ *vt* -**1.** [papéis *etc*] to put into a drawer. -**2.** *fig* [processo, projeto] to shelve. ◇ *vi* [carros] to concertina.

➡ **engavetar-se** *vp* [carros] to concertina.

engendrar [4] [ẽnʒẽn'dra(x)] *vt* to create.

engenharia [ẽnʒeɲa'rial *f* engineering; **~ genética** genetic engineering.

engenheiro, ra [ẽnʒe'ɲejru, ra] *m, f* engineer.

engenho [ẽn'ʒeɲul *m* -**1.** [habilidade] inventiveness. -**2.** [máquina] engine. -**3.** [moenda] mill. -**4.** [fazenda de cana de açúcar] sugar plant.

engenhoca [ẽnʒe'ɲokal *f pej* [aparelho] Heath-Robinson device.

engenhoso, osa [ẽnʒe'ɲozu, ɔza] *adj* ingenious.

engessado, da [ẽne'sadu, da] *adj* plastered.

engessar [4] [ẽnʒe'sa(x)] *vt* to put in plaster.

englobar [4] [ẽŋglo'ba(x)] *vt* to encompass.

engodo [ẽŋ'godul *m* -**1.** [isca] bait. -**2.** [farsa] flattery.

engolir [59] [ẽŋgo'li(x)] *vt* -**1.** [ger] to swallow. -**2.** *fig* [sobrepujar]: **~ alguém** to eclipse sb.

engomado, da [ẽŋgo'madu, da] *adj* starched.

engomar [4] [ẽŋgo'ma(x)] *vt* to starch.

engordar [4] [ẽŋgox'da(x)] ◇ *vt* to fatten. ◇ *vi* to put on weight; **açúcar engorda** sugar is fattening.

engordurado, da [ẽŋgoxdu'radu, da] *adj* greasy.

engordurar [4] [ẽŋgoxdu'ra(x)] *vt* to grease.

engraçadinho, nha [ẽŋgrasa'dʒiɲu, ɲal ◇ *adj* [pequeno, gracioso] cute. ◇ *m, f pej* clown.

engraçado, da [ẽŋgra'sadu, da] *adj* amusing.

engraçar-se [13] [ẽŋgra'saxsil *vp*: **~ para o lado de alguém** to take advantage of sb.

engradado [ẽŋgra'dadul *m* crate.

engrandecer [25] [ẽŋgrãnde'se(x)] *vt* to elevate.

➡ **engrandecer-se** *vp* to elevate o.s.

engravidar [4] [ẽŋgravi'da(x)] ◇ *vt* to make pregnant. ◇ *vi* to become pregnant.

engraxar [4] [ẽŋgra'ʃa(x)] *vt* to polish.

engraxate [ẽŋgra'ʃatʃil *mf* shoe shiner.

engrenagem [ẽŋgre'naʒẽl (*pl* -**ns**) *f* -**1.** *AUTO* gear. -**2.** *fig* [política, social] mechanism.

engrenar [4] [ẽŋgre'na(x)] *vt* -**1.** *AUTO* to put in gear. -**2.** [iniciar] to start.

engrossar [4] [ẽŋgro'sa(x)] ◇ *vt* -**1.** [aumentar] to enlarge. -**2.** [encorpar] to thicken. -**3.** [tornar grave] to deepen. ◇ *vi fig* [ser grosseiro]: **~ (com alguém)** to be rough (with sb).

enguia [ẽŋ'gial *f* eel.

enguiçado, da [ẽŋgi'sadu, da] *adj* -**1.** [com defeito] broken down. -**2.** [emperrado] bogged down.

enguiçar [13] [ẽŋgi'sa(x)] *vi* -**1.** [carro] to break down. -**2.** [relógio] to stop.

enguiço [ẽŋ'gisul *m* breakdown.

engulho [ẽŋ'guʎul *m* nausea.

enigma [e'nigmal *m* enigma.

enigmático, ca [enigi'matʃiku, ka] *adj* enigmatic.
enjaular [19] [ēnʒaw'la(x)] *vt* to put in a cage.
enjeitado, da [ēnʒej'tadu, da] *adj* rejected.
enjeitar [4] [ēnʒej'ta(x)] *vt* **- 1.** [rejeitar] to reject. **- 2.** [abandonar] to abandon.
enjoado, da [ēn'ʒwadu, da] *adj* **- 1.** [nauseado] nauseous. **- 2.** *fig* [cansado]: ~ de algo /de fazer algo fed up with sthg/with doing sthg. **- 3.** *fig* [chato] boring.
enjoar [20] [ēn'ʒwa(x)] <> *vt* **- 1.** [nausear] to make nauseous. **- 2.** *fig* [cansar] to bore. <> *vi* **- 1.** [nausear-se] to feel sick. **- 2.** *fig* [cansar-se]: ~ de algo /de fazer algo to become bored with sthg/with doing sthg.
enjoativo, va [ēnʒwa'tʃivu, va] *adj* nauseating.
enjôo [ēn'ʒoul *m* **- 1.** [náusea] sickness; ~ de gravidez morning sickness. **- 2.** *fig* [aborrecimento]: ser um ~ to be a bore.
enlaçar [13] [ēnla'sa(x)] *vt* **- 1.** [prender com laço] to tie up. **- 2.** [envolver] to bog down.
enlace [ēn'lasil *m* **- 1.** [união] union. **- 2.** [casamento] marriage.
enlameado, da [ēnla'mjadu, da] *adj* **- 1.** [com lama] muddy. **- 2.** *fig* [vilipendiado] muddied.
enlamear [15] [ēnla'mja(x)] *vt* to muddy.
enlatado, da [ēnla'tadu, da] *adj* canned.
 ➡ **enlatado** *m* **- 1.** [comida em lata] canned food. **- 2.** *pej* [série de TV] trash TV.
enlatar [15] [ēnla'ta(x)] *vt* to can.
enlevar [4] [ēnle'va(x)] *vt* to entrance.
 ➡ **enlevar-se** *vp* **- 1.** [extasiar-se] to become entranced. **- 2.** [absorver-se]: ~-se em to become absorbed in.
enlevo [ēn'levul *m* enchantment.
enlouquecer [25] [ēnloke'se(x)] <> *vt* to drive mad. <> *vi* to go mad.
enlouquecido, da [ēnloke'sidu, da] *adj* crazed.
enlouquecimento [ēnlokesi'mēntul *m* (growing) insanity.
enluarado, da [ēnlwa'radu, da] *adj* moonlit.
enobrecer [25] [enobre'se(x)] *vt* to ennoble.
 ➡ **enobrecer-se** *vp* to glorify o.s.
enojado, da [eno'ʒadu, da] *adj* disgusted.
enojar [4] [eno'ʒa(x)] *vt* to disgust.
 ➡ **enojar-se** *vp* [sentir nojo]: enojava-se com o cheiro de frango the smell of chicken made him/her sick.
enorme [e'nɔxmil *adj* enormous.
enormidade [enoxmi'dadʒil *f* enormity; uma ~ de a vast quantity of.
enquadramento [ēŋkwadra'mēntul *m* CINE & FOTO frame.
enquadrar [4] [ēŋkwa'dra(x)] <> *vt* **- 1.** [ajustar]: ~ algo em algo to frame sthg in sthg. **- 2.** [autuar] to charge. <> *vi* [combinar]: ~ com to fit in with.
 ➡ **enquadrar-se** *vp* [ajustar-se]: ~-se (em algo) to fit in (with sthg).
enquanto [ēŋ'kwãntul *conj* **- 1.** [ger] while. **- 2.** [considerado como]: isso é interessante ~ experiência it's interesting as an experience; ~ isso meanwhile.

 ➡ **por enquanto** *loc adv* for the time being.
enquete [ēn'kɛtʃil *f* survey.
enraivecer [25] [ēnxajve'se(x)] *vt* to anger.
 ➡ **enraivecer-se** *vp* to become angry.
enraizar [4] [ēnxaj'za(x)] *vt* to root.
 ➡ **enraizar-se** *vp* to take root.
enrascada [ēnxaʃ'kadal *f* tight spot; meter-se numa ~ to get into a tight spot.
enrascado, da [ēnxaʃ'kadu, da] *adj* in a fix (depois de verbo).
enrascar-se [12] [ēnxaʃ'kaxsil *vp* to get in a fix.
enredar [4] [ēnre'da(x)] *vt* **- 1.** [emaranhar] to twist. **- 2.** *fig* [enganar] to deceive.
 ➡ **enredar-se** *vp* **- 1.** [pessoa] to become entangled. **- 2.** [peixe] to fall into a net.
enredo [ēn'xedul *m* plot.
enrijecer [25] [ēnxiʒe'se(x)] *vt* to stiffen.
 ➡ **enrijecer-se** *vp* to become stiff.
enriquecer [25] [ēnxike'se(x)] <> *vt* to enrich. <> *vi* to become rich.
 ➡ **enriquecer-se** *vp*: ~-se com algo to become rich in sthg.
enriquecimento [ēnxikesi'mēntul *m* **- 1.** [financeiro] increase in wealth. **- 2.** [cultural] enrichment.
enrolado, da [ēnxo'ladu, da] *adj* **- 1.** [embrulhado]: ~ em algo rolled up in sthg. **- 2.** [cabelo] coiled. **- 3.** *fam* [confuso] screwed up.
enrolar [4] [ēnxo'la(x)] <> *vt* **- 1.** [dar forma de rolo] to roll. **- 2.** [embrulhar]: ~ algo /alguém em algo to wrap sthg/sb up in sthg. **- 3.** *fam* [complicar] to screw up. **- 4.** *fam* [enganar] to take in. <> *vi fam* [protelar] to put things off.
 ➡ **enrolar-se** *vp* **- 1.** [agasalhar-se]: ~-se em algo to wrap o.s. up in sthg. **- 2.** *fam* [confundir-se] to screw things up.
enroscar [4] [ēnxoʃ'ka(x)] *vt*: ~ algo em to entwine sthg in.
 ➡ **enroscar-se** *vp* **- 1.** [encolher-se de frio] to curl up. **- 2.** [embolar-se] to become entangled.
enrouquecer [25] [ēnxoke'se(x)] <> *vt* to make hoarse. <> *vi* to become hoarse.
enrubescer [25] [ēnxube'se(x)] <> *vt* to redden. <> *vi* to blush, go red.
enrugado, da [ēnxu'gadu, da] *adj* wrinkled.
enrugar [14] [ēnxu'ga(x)] *vt & vi* to wrinkle.
enrustido [ēnxuʃ'tʃidul *m* [homossexual] closet gay.
ensaboar [20] [ēnsa'bwa(x)] *vt* to wash with soap.
 ➡ **ensaboar-se** *vp* to soap o.s.
ensaiar [4] [ēnsa'ja(x)] *vt* to practise UK, to practice US.
ensaio [ēn'sajul *m* **- 1.** [experiência] trial. **- 2.** TEATRO rehearsal. **- 3.** LITER essay.
ensaísta [ēnsa'iʃtal *mf* essayist.
ensangüentado, da [ēnsãngwēn'tadu, da] *adj* blood-stained.
ensangüentar [4] [ēnsãngwēn'ta(x)] *vt* to stain with blood.
enseada [ēn'sjadal *f* inlet.
ensebado, da [ēnse'badu, da] *adj* greasy.

ensebar [4] [ẽnse'ba(x)] *vt* to grease.
ensejar [4] [ẽnse'ʒa(x)] *vt* : ~ **algo a alguém** to offer the opportunity of sthg to sb.
ensejo [ẽn'seʒu] *m* opportunity.
ensimesmado, da [ẽnsimeʒ'madu, da] *adj* introverted.
ensinamento [ẽnsina'mẽntu] *m* instruction.
ensinar [4] [ẽnsi'na(x)] *vt* : ~ **alguém a fazer algo** to teach sb how to do sthg; ~ **algo a alguém** to teach sthg to sb.
ensino [ẽn'sinu] *m* **-1.** [transmissão de conhecimento] teaching. **-2.** [educação] education; ~ **fundamental/medio** primary/secondary education; ~ **superior** higher education; ~ **supletivo** *speeded-up education programme for adults who missed out on a full schooling.*
ensolarado, da [ẽnsola'radu, da] *adj* sunny.
ensombrecido, da [ẽnsõnbre'sidu, da] *adj* gloomy.
ensopado, da [ẽnso'padu, da] *adj* **-1.** CULIN stewed. **-2.** *fig* [encharcado] soaking.
◆ **ensopado** *m* CULIN stew.
ensopar [4] [ẽnso'pa(x)] *vt* to soak.
ensurdecedor, ra [ẽnsuxdese'dox, ra] (*mpl* -**es**, *fpl* -**s**) *adj* deafening.
ensurdecer [25] [ẽnsuxde'se(x)] *vt* to deafen.
entabular [4] [ẽntabu'la(x)] *vt* to open.
entalado, da [ẽnta'ladu, da] *adj* stuck.
entalar [4] [ẽnta'la(x)] ◇ *vt* [apertar] to squeeze. ◇ *vi* [encravar] to stick.
entalhador, ra [ẽntaʎa'do(x), ra] *m, f* woodcarver.
entalhar [4] [ẽnta'ʎa(x)] *vt* to carve.
entalhe [ẽn'taʎi] *m* groove.
entanto [ẽn'tãntu] ◆ **no entanto** *loc adv* however.
então [ẽn'tãw] *adv* then; **até** ~ up until then; **desde** ~ since then; **e** ~? well then?; **para** ~ so that; **pois** ~ then.
entardecer [25] [ẽntaxde'se(x)] ◇ *vi* to get late. ◇ *m* sunset.
ente ['ẽntʃi] *m* **-1.** [ser] being. **-2.** [corporação, órgão] entity.
enteado, da [ẽn'tʒjadu, da] *m, f* stepchild, stepson (*f* stepdaughter).
entediante [ẽnte'dʒjãntʃi] *adj* boring.
entediar [16] [ẽnte'dʒa(x)] *vt* to bore.
◆ **entediar-se** *vp* to get bored.
entendedor, ra [ẽntẽnde'do(x), ra] ◇ *adj* knowledgeable. ◇ *m, f* expert; **a bom** ~ **meia palavra basta** a word is sufficient to the wise.
entender [5] [ẽntẽn'de(x)] ◇ *vt* **-1.** [compreender] to understand; **dar a** ~ to give the impression. **-2.** [ouvir] to hear. **-3.** [interpretar] to perceive. **-4.** [deduzir]: ~ **que** to see (that). ◇ *vi* **-1.** [inferir]: **o que você** ~ **por isso?** what do you deduce from it? **-2.** [conhecer]: ~ **de** to know about. ◇ *m*: **no** ~ **de alguém** in the opinion of sb.
◆ **entender-se** *vp* **-1.** [comunicar-se] to get along. **-2.** [chegar a um acordo]: ~**se (com alguém)** to see eye to eye (with sb). **-3.** [ter o uso da razão]:

desde que me entendo por gente, gosto de música for as long as I can remember, I've liked music.
entendido, da [ẽntẽn'dʒidu, da] ◇ *adj* **-1.** [perito] expert; ~ **em algo** expert in sthg. **-2.** *fam* [homossexual] gay. ◇ *m, f* **-1.** [perito] expert. **-2.** *fam* [homossexual] gay.
◆ **bem entendido** *loc adv* understood.
entendimento [ẽntẽndʒi'mẽntu] *m* **-1.** [compreensão] understanding. **-2.** [juízo] perception. **-3.** [acordo] agreement.
enternecer [25] [ẽntexne'se(x)] *vt* to touch.
◆ **enternecer-se** *vp* to be touched.
enterrar [4] [ẽnte'xa(x)] *vt* **-1.** to bury. **-2.** *fig* [encerrar] to close. **-3.** *fig* [arruinar] to ruin. **-4.** [enfiar]: enterrou a estaca no coração do vampiro he rammed the stake into the vampire's heart; enterrou o chapéu na cabeça he rammed his hat on his head.
◆ **enterrar-se** *vp* **-1.** [isolar-se] to hide o.s. away. **-2.** [arruinar-se] to ruin o.s.
enterro [ẽn'texu] *m* **-1.** [sepultamento] burial. **-2.** [funeral] funeral.
entidade [ẽntʃi'dadʒi] *f* entity.
entoação [ẽntwa'sãw] *f* chanting.
entoar [20] [ẽn'twa(x)] *vt* to chant.
entonação [ẽntona'sãw] *f* intonation.
entornar [4] [ẽntox'na(x)] ◇ *vt* **-1.** [derramar] to spill. **-2.** [despejar] to pour. ◇ *vi fig* [embriagar-se] to drink heavily.
entorpecente [ẽntoxpe'sẽntʃi] *m* narcotic.
entorpecer [25] [ẽntoxpe'se(x)] *vt* **-1.** [causar torpor] to stupefy. **-2.** *fig* [insensibilizar] to numb.
entorpecido, da [ẽntoxpe'sidu, da] *adj* numb.
entorpecimento [ẽntoxpesi'mẽntu] *m* **-1.** [paralisia] stupor. **-2.** *fig* [estagnação] numbness.
entorse [ẽn'toxsi] *f* sprain.
entortar [4] [ẽntox'ta(x)] ◇ *vt* **-1.** [curvar] to bend. **-2.** [empenar] to jam. ◇ *vi* [empenar - porta] to warp; [- roda] to buckle.
entourage [ãntu'xaʒi] *m* entourage.
entrada [ẽn'trada] *f* **-1.** [ger] entry; 'proibida a ~' 'no entry'. **-2.** [lugar] entrance; ~ **de serviço** service entrance. **-3.** [admissão] admission. **-4.** [porta] doorway. **-5.** [corredor] hallway. **-6.** CULIN starter. **-7.** [calvície] receding hairline. **-8.** [pagamento inicial] down payment. **-9.** [ingresso] ticket; ~ **gratuita** *ou* **franca** free admission; **meia** ~ half price. **-10.** [abertura] opening. **-11.** TEC inlet. **-12.** COMPUT input. **-13.** [início]: **dar** ~ **em algo** to institute sthg.
entra-e-sai [ˌẽntri'saj] *m inv* coming and going.
entranhado, da [ẽntra'ɲadu, da] *adj* deepseated.
entranhar [4] [ẽntra'ɲa(x)] *vi*: ~ **(em algo)** to penetrate (sthg).
entranhas [ẽn'traɲaʃ] *fpl* **-1.** [vísceras] bowels. **-2.** *fig* [profundeza] depths.
entrar [4] [ẽn'tra(x)] *vi* **-1.** [adentrar]: ~ **(em)** to go/come (into). **-2.** [penetrar] to enter. **-3.** [começar a trabalhar] to begin. **-4.** [contribuir]: ~ **com algo** to

contribute sthg. **-5.** [começar]: ~ **de férias** to go on vacation. **-6.** [aprofundar-se]: ~ **em algo** to go into sthg. **-7.** [entabular]: ~ **em algo** to enter into sthg. **-8.** [envolver-se]: ~ **em algo** to become involved in sthg. **-9.** [caber]: ~ **em algo** to fit into sthg. **-10.** [ser componente]: ~ **em algo** to be part of sthg. **-11.** [ingressar]: ~ **para algo** [universidade] to go to sthg; [clube] to join sthg. **-12.** *COMPUT*: ~ **com algo** to enter sthg. **-13.** *loc*: ~ **bem** *fam* to get one's fingers burnt.

entrave [ẽn'travi] *m* obstacle.

entre ['ẽntri] *prep* between; **os dois dividiram o bolo** ~ **eles** the two shared the cake between them; **os alunos sempre conversavam** ~ **si** the schoolchildren always talked among themselves; **cá** ~ **nós** [confidencialmente] between you and me.

entreaberto, ta [ˌẽntrja'bɛxtu, ta] *adj* **-1.** [porta] ajar. **-2.** [olho] half-open.

entreabrir [6] [ẽntrja'bri(x)] *vt* to half-open.
➡ **entreabrir-se** *vp* to open up.

entrecortado, da [ẽntrekox'tadu, da] *adj* intermittent.

entrecortar [ẽntre'koxta(x)] *vt* **-1.** [cortar] to cut off. **-2.** [interromper] to interrupt.

entrega [ẽn'trɛga] *f* **-1.** [de carta, prêmio] delivery; ~ **em domicílio** home delivery; **pronta** ~ speedy delivery. **-2.** [dedicação]: ~ **a algo/alguém** dedication to sthg/sb. **-3.** [rendição] surrender.

entregador, ra [ẽntrega'do(x), ra] *m, f* [funcionário] delivery person.

entregar [14] [ẽntre'ga(x)] *vt* **-1.** [passar às mãos de - mercadoria, carta] to deliver; [- presente] to give; [- prêmio] to award. **-2.** [delatar] to inform on. **-3.** [devolver] to return. **-4.** [confiar]: ~ **algo/alguém a alguém** to entrust sthg/sb to sb.
➡ **entregar-se** *vp* **-1.** [render-se - inimigo] to surrender; [- à dor *etc*]: ~**-se a algo** to surrender to sthg. **-2.** [dedicar-se]: ~**-se a algo** to dedicate o.s. to sthg. **-3.** [deixar-se seduzir]: ~**-se a alguém** to give o.s. to sb. **-4.** *loc*: ~ **os pontos** to give up.

entregue [ẽn'trɛgi] *pp* ⊳ **entregar**.

entreguismo [ẽntre'giʒmu] *m* selling-out, *policy of allowing exploitation of the country's natural resources by foreign entities.*

entreguista [ẽntre'giʃta] *adj supportive or typical of selling-out.*

entrelaçamento [ẽntrelasa'mẽntu] *m* [união] interlinking.

entrelaçar [13] [ẽntrela'sa(x)] *vt* to entwine.

entrelinha [ẽntre'liɲa] *f* [espaço] line space.
➡ **entrelinhas** *fpl*: **nas** ~**s** *fig* [subentendido] between the lines.

entremear [15] [ẽntre'mja(x)] *vt*: ~ **algo com algo** to mix sthg with sthg.

entreolhar-se [7] [ẽntrjo'ʎaxsi] *vp* to exchange glances.

entrepor [45] [ẽntre'po(x)] *vt* to insert.
➡ **entrepor-se** *vp*: ~**-se entre** to come between.

entreposto, ta [ẽntre'poʃtu, ta] *pp* ⊳ **entrepor**.
➡ **entreposto** *m* warehouse.

entressafra [ẽntri'safra] *f* period between harvests.

entretanto [ẽntri'tãntu] *conj* however.

entretenimento [ẽntriteni'mẽntu] *m* **-1.** [passatempo] pastime. **-2.** [diversão] entertainment.

entreter [1] [ẽntre'te(x)] *vt* **-1.** [ger] to entertain. **-2.** [ocupar] to occupy.
➡ **entreter-se** *vp* **-1.** [divertir-se] to amuse o.s. **-2.** [ocupar-se] to occupy o.s.

entretido, da [ẽntre'tʃidu, da] *adj* **-1.** [distraído] entertained. **-2.** [ocupado] occupied.

entrevar [4] [ẽntre'va(x)] *vt* to cripple.

entrever [40] [ẽntre've(x)] *vt* **-1.** [ver] to glimpse. **-2.** [prever] to foresee.

entrevero [ẽntre'verol] *m* mêlée *UK*, melee *US*.

entrevista [ẽntre'viʃta] *f* interview; ~ **coletiva** press conference.

entrevistado, da [ẽntre'viʃtadu, da] *m, f* interviewee.

entrevistador, ra [ẽntre'viʃtado(x), ra] (*mpl* **-es**, *fpl* **-s**) *m, f* interviewer.

entrevistar [4] [ẽntre'viʃta(x)] *vt* to interview.

entristecedor, ra [ẽntriʃtese'do(x), ra] *adj* saddening.

entristecer [25] [ẽntriʃte'se(x)] ⟨⟩ *vt* to sadden. ⟨⟩ *vi* to become sad.
➡ **entristecer-se** *vp* to become sad.

entroncamento [ẽntrõŋka'mẽntu] *m* junction.

entrosado, da [ẽntro'zadu, da] *adj* [ambientado] integrated.

entrosamento [ẽntroza'mẽntu] *m* integration.

entrosar [4] [ẽntro'za(x)] *vt* **-1.** [endentar] to mesh. **-2.** [ambientar]: ~ **alguém com alguém** to integrate sb with sb.
➡ **entrosar-se** *vp* [entender-se]: ~**-se (com alguém)** to get along (with sb).

entulhar [4] [ẽntu'ʎa(x)] *vt*: ~ **algo (de** *ou* **com)** to cram sthg with.

entulho [ẽn'tuʎul] *m* debris.

entupido, da [ẽntu'pidu, da] *adj* **-1.** [pia, nariz, ouvido] blocked. **-2.** [de comida] stuffed. **-3.** [de gente] packed.

entupimento [ẽntupi'mẽntu] *m* blockage.

entupir [60,61] [ẽntu'pi(x)] *vt* to block.
➡ **entupir-se** *vp*: ~**-se de comida** to stuff o.s. with food; ~**-se de bebida** to pump o.s. full of drink.

enturmar-se [7] [ẽntux'maxsil] *vp*: ~**-se (com)** to make friends (with).

entusiasmado, da [ẽntuzjaʒ'madu, da] *adj* enthusiastic.

entusiasmar [4] [ẽntuzjaʒ'ma(x)] *vt* to fill with enthusiasm.
➡ **entusiasmar-se** *vp* to get enthusiastic.

entusiasmo [ẽntu'zjaʒmul] *m* enthusiasm.

entusiasta [ẽntu'zjaʃta] ⟨⟩ *adj* enthusiastic. ⟨⟩ *mf* enthusiast.

entusiástico, ca [ẽntu'zjaʃtʃiku, ka] *adj* enthusiastic.

enumeração [enumera'sãwl] (*pl* **-ões**) *f* enumeration.

enumerar [4] [enume'ra(x)] *vt* to enumerate.
enunciado, da [enũ'sjadu, da] <> *adj* stated. <> *m* statement.
enunciar [16] [enũ'sja(x)] *vt* to state.
envaidecer [25] [ẽnvajde'se(x)] *vt* to flatter.
➡ **envaidecer-se** *vp* to feel flattered.
envelhecer [25] [ẽnveʎe'se(x)] <> *vt* -**1.** [tornar velho] to age. -**2.** [fazer parecer velho]: ~ alguém to make sb look older. <> *vi* -**1.** [ficar velho] to grow old. -**2.** [fazer parecer velho] to age.
envelhecido, da [ẽnveʎe'sidu, da] *adj* aged.
envelhecimento [ẽnveʎesi'mẽntu] *m* ageing.
envelopar [ẽnve'lopa(x)] *vt* to put in an envelope.
envelope [ẽnve'lɔpi] *m* envelope.
envenenado, da [ẽnvene'nadu, da] *adj* -**1.** [ger] poisoned. -**2.** *fam fig* [carro] souped up.
envenenamento [ẽnvenena'mẽntu] *m* poisoning.
envenenar [4] [ẽnvene'na(x)] *vt* -**1.** [intoxicar] to poison. -**2.** [corromper] to corrupt. -**3.** *AUTO* to soup up.
➡ **envenenar-se** *vp* [intoxicar-se] to poison o.s.
enveredar [4] [ẽnvere'da(x)] *vi* to make one's way; ~ por/para to head for.
envergadura [ẽnvexga'dura] *f* -**1.** [dimensão] wingspan. -**2.** *fig* [importância] scope. -**3.** *fig* [capacidade]: é um poeta de pouca ~ he's a poet of little talent.
envergar [14] [ẽnvex'ga(x)] <> *vt* -**1.** [entortar] to bend. -**2.** [vestir] to wear. <> *vi* [arquear] to warp.
envergonhado, da [ẽnvexgo'ɲadu, da] *adj* -**1.** [tímido] shy. -**2.** [por má ação] ashamed.
envergonhar [4] [ẽnvexgo'ɲa(x)] *vt* -**1.** [acanhar] to embarrass. -**2.** [com má ação] to disgrace.
➡ **envergonhar-se** *vp* -**1.** [acanhar-se] to be embarrassed. -**2.** [por má ação] to be ashamed.
envernizado, da [ẽnvexni'zadu, da] *adj* [com verniz] varnished.
envernizar [4] [ẽnvexni'za(x)] *vt* to varnish.
enviado, da [ẽn'vjadu, da] *m, f* envoy.
enviar [16] [ẽn'vja(x)] *vt* : ~ algo a *ou* para alguém to send sthg to sb.
envidar [4] [ẽnvi'da(x)] *vt* to endeavour *UK*, to endeavor *US*.
envidraçado, da [ẽnvidra'sadu, da] *adj* glazed.
envidraçar [13] [ẽnvidra'sa(x)] *vt* to glaze.
enviesado, da [ẽnvje'zadu, da] *adj* slanting.
enviesar [ẽnvje'za(x)] *vt* -**1.** [pôr obliquamente] to put at an angle. -**2.** [envesgar] to cross.
envio [ẽn'viu] *m* dispatch.
enviuvar [4] [ẽnvju'va(x)] *vi* to be widowed.
envolto, ta [ẽn'vowtu, ta] <> *pp* > **envolver**. <> *adj* wrapped.
envoltório [ẽnvow'tɔrju] *m* wrapping.
envolvente [ẽnvow'vẽntʃi] *adj* compelling.
envolver [5] [ẽnvow've(x)] *vt* -**1.** [cobrir]: ~ algo/alguém (em) to wrap sthg/sb (in). -**2.** [comprometer]: ~ alguém (em) to involve sb (in). -**3.** [acarretar] to involve. -**4.** [abraçar] to embrace.
➡ **envolver-se** *vp* -**1.** [comprometer-se]: ~-se em

ou com to get involved in *ou* with. -**2.** [intrometer-se]: ~-se em to get involved in.
envolvimento [ẽnvowvi'mẽntu] *m* involvement.
enxada [ẽn'ʃada] *f* hoe.
enxadrista [ẽnʃa'driʃta] *mf* chess player.
enxaguada [ẽnʃa'gwada] *f* rinse.
enxaguar [22] [ẽnʃa'gwa(x)] *vt* to rinse.
enxágüe *m* = enxaguada.
enxame [ẽn'ʃami] *m* swarm.
enxaqueca [ẽnʃa'keka] *f* migraine.
enxergar [14] [ẽnʃex'ga(x)] <> *vt* -**1.** [ver] to catch sight of. -**2.** *fig* [perceber] to make out. <> *vi* [ver] to see.
➡ **enxergar-se** *vp*: ele não se enxerga he doesn't know his limitations.
enxerido, da [ẽnʃe'ridu, da] *adj* nosy.
enxertar [4] [ẽnʃex'ta(x)] *vt* -**1.** [planta] to graft. -**2.** *fig* [inserir] to insert.
enxerto [ẽn'ʃextu] *m* -**1.** [de planta] grafting. -**2.** *MED* graft. -**3.** *fig* [inserção] insertion.
enxofre [ẽn'ʃofril] *m* sulphur *UK*, sulfur *US*.
enxotar [4] [ẽnʃo'ta(x)] *vt* to drive away.
enxoval [ẽnʃo'vawl] (*pl* -ais) *m* [de noiva] trousseau.
enxugador [ẽnʃuga'do(x)] *m* clothes dryer.
enxugar [14] [ẽnʃu'ga(x)] *vt* -**1.** [secar] to dry. -**2.** *fig* [diminuir] to rationalize.
enxurrada [ẽnʃu'xada] *f* -**1.** [torrente] torrent. -**2.** *fig* [amontoado] flood.
enxuto, ta [ẽn'ʃutu, ta] *adj* -**1.** [seco] dry. -**2.** *fig* [bonito] good-looking.
enzima [ẽn'zima] *f* enzyme.
epicentro [epi'sẽntru] *m* epicentre *UK*, epicenter *US*.
épico, ca ['ɛpiku, ka] *adj* epic.
➡ **épico** *m LITER* epic.
epidemia [epide'mia] *f* -**1.** *MED* epidemic. -**2.** *fig* [modismo] mania.
epidêmico, ca [epi'demiku, ka] *adj MED* epidemic.
epiderme [epi'dexmi] *f* epidermis.
epidural [epidu'rawl] *adj* epidural.
epifania [epifa'nia] *f* Epiphany.
epígrafe [e'pigrafi] *f* epigraph; em ~ in epigraph.
epigrama [epi'grama] *f* epigram.
epilepsia [epilep'sia] *f* epilepsy.
epiléptico, ca [epi'lɛptʃiku, ka] <> *adj* epileptic. <> *m, f* epileptic.
epílogo [e'pilugu] *m* epilogue.
episcopado [epiʃko'padu] *m* bishopric.
episcopal [epiʃko'pawl] (*pl* -ais) *adj* episcopal.
episódico, ca [epi'zɔdiku, ka] *adj* episodic.
episódio [epi'zɔdjul] *m* episode.
epistemologia *f* epistemology.
epístola [e'piʃtola] *f* -**1.** [bíblia] Epistle. -**2.** [carta] letter.
epistolar [epiʃto'la(x)] *adj* epistolary.
epistolário [epiʃto'lariwl] *m* collection of letters.
epitáfio [epi'tafju] *m* epitaph.
época ['ɛpoka] *f* -**1.** [período] age; filme de ~ period movie; naquela ~ at that time; fazer ~

to be epoch-making. **-2.** [estação] season.

epopéia [epo'pɛja] f epic.

equação [ekwa'sãw] (pl -ões) f equation.

equacionamento [ekwasiona'mẽntu] m rationalizing.

equacionar [4] [ekwasjo'na(x)] vt to set out.

equador [ekwa'do(x)] m equator.

Equador [ekwa'do(x)] n Ecuador.

equânime [e'kwãnimi] adj unbiased.

equatorial [ekwato'rjaw] (pl -ais) adj equatorial.

equatoriano, na <> adj Ecuadorean. <> m, f Ecuadorean.

eqüestre [e'kwɛʃtri] adj equestrian.

eqüidade [ekwi'dadʒi] f equity.

eqüidistante [ekwidʒiʃ'tãntʃi] adj equidistant.

eqüilátero, ra [ekwi'lateru, ra] adj equilateral.

equilibrado, da [ekili'bradu, da] adj balanced.

equilibrar [4] [ekili'bra(x)] vt to balance.

➡ **equilibrar-se** vp to balance.

equilíbrio [eki'libriw] m equilibrium.

equilibrista [ekili'briʃta] mf trapeze artist.

eqüino, na [e'kwinu, na] adj equine.

equinócio [eki'nɔsju] m equinox.

equipagem [ekipa'ʒẽ] f crew.

equipamento [ekipa'mẽntu] m equipment.

equipar [4] [eki'pa(x)] vt: ~ algo/alguém (de) to equip sthg/sb (with).

➡ **equipar-se** vp: ~-se (de) to equip o.s. (with).

equiparação [ekipara'sãw] m parity.

equiparar [4] [ekipa'ra(x)] vt: ~ algo (a ou com algo) to compare sthg (against sthg).

➡ **equiparar-se** vp -1. [igualar-se]: ~-se (a ou com algo) to compare o.s. (with sthg). -2. [comparar-se]: ~-se (a ou com alguém) to compare o.s. (with sb).

equiparável [ekipa'ravew] (pl -eis) adj comparable.

equipe [e'kipi] f team; ~ de socorros rescue team.

equitação [ekita'sãw] f horse-riding.

eqüitativamente [ekwitatʃiva'mẽntʃi] adv equitably.

eqüitativo, va [ekwita'tʃivu, va] adj equitable.

equivalência [ekiva'lẽnsja] f equivalence.

equivalente [ekiva'lẽntʃi] adj equivalent.

equivaler [43] [ekiva'le(x)] vi: ~ a to be equivalent to.

➡ **equivaler-se** vp to be equal.

equivocado, da [ekivo'kadu, da] adj mistaken.

equivocar-se [12] [ekivo'kaxsi] vp to make a mistake.

equívoco [e'kivoku] m mistake.

era ['ɛra] f era.

erário [e'rarju] m exchequer.

ereção [ere'sãw] (pl -ões) f erection.

eremita [ere'mita] mf hermit.

ereto, ta [e'rɛtu, ta] adj erect.

erguer [27] [ex'ge(x)] vt -1. [levantar] to raise. -2. [construir] to erect.

➡ **erguer-se** vp [levantar-se] to get up.

eriçado, da [eri'saɗu, da] adj standing on end.

eriçar [13] [eri'sa(x)] vt to make stand on end.

erigir [52] [eri'ʒi(x)] vt to erect.

ermo, ma ['exmu, ma] adj deserted.

erodir [6] [ero'dʒi(x)] vt to erode.

erógeno, na [e'rɔʒenu, na] adj erogenous.

erosão [ero'zãw] f erosion.

erótico, ca [e'rɔtʃiku, ka] adj erotic.

erotismo [ero'tʃiʒmu] m eroticism.

erradicação [exadʒika'sãw] f eradication.

erradicar [12] [exadʒi'ka(x)] vt to eradicate.

errado, da [e'xadu, da] adj -1. [incorreto] wrong. -2. [inadequado] inappropriate. -3. loc: dar ~ to go wrong.

errante [e'xãntʃi] adj wandering.

errar [4] [e'xa(x)] <> vt [não acertar - alvo] to miss; [- conta, resposta] to get wrong. <> vi -1. [enganar-se]: ~ (em algo) to be wrong (in sthg). -2. [proceder mal] to go wrong. -3. [vagar] to wander.

errata [e'xata] f erratum.

erro ['exu] m [ger] error; ~ de impressão printing error; ~ de pronúncia mispronunciation.

errôneo, nea [e'xonju, nja] adj erroneous.

erudição [erudʒi'sãw] f erudition.

erudito, ta [eru'dʒitu, ita] <> adj erudite. <> m, f scholar.

erupção [erup'sãw] (pl -ões) f eruption.

erva ['ɛxva] f -1. BOT herb; ~ daninha weed. -2. fam [maconha] grass.

erva-cidreira [ˌɛxva'sidrejra] (pl ervas-cidreiras) f lemon verbena.

erva-doce [ˌɛxva'dosil] (pl ervas-doces) f fennel.

erva-mate [ˌɛxva'matʃi] (pl ervas-mates) f matte.

ervilha [ex'viʎa] f pea.

ES (abrev de Estado do Espírito Santo) m state of Espírito Santo.

esbaforido, da [iʒbafo'ridu, da] adj breathless.

esbaldar-se [4] [iʒbaw'daxsi] vp to have great fun.

esbanjador, ra [iʒbãnʒa'do(x), ra] adj spendthrift.

esbanjamento [iʒbãnʒa'mẽntu] m [de dinheiro] squandering.

esbanjar [4] [iʒbãn'ʒa(x)] vt -1. [dinheiro] to squander. -2. [saúde] to be bursting with.

esbarrão [iʒba'xãw] m bump.

esbarrar [4] [iʒba'xa(x)] vi: ~ em algo/alguém to bump into sthg/sb.

esbelto, ta [iʒ'bɛwtu, ta] adj svelte.

esboçar [13] [iʒbo'sa(x)] vt -1. [ger] to sketch. -2. [sorriso] to trace.

esboço [iʒ'bosu] m -1. [desenho] sketch. -2. [primeira versão] draft. -3. [tentativa] hint. -4. [resumo] outline.

esbodegado, da [ˌiʒbode'gadul] adj -1. [estragado] worn out. -2. [exausto] exhausted.

esbodegar [iʒbode'ga(x)] ➡ **esbodegar-se** vp fam [descuidar-se] to let o.s. go.

esbofetear [15] [iʒbofe'tʃja(x)] vt to slap.

esbórnia [iʒ'bɔxnja] f wild party.

esborrachar-se [4] [iʒboxa'ʃaxsil] *vp* **-1.** [arrebentar-se] to burst. **-2.** [cair] to fall sprawling.

esbranquiçado, da [iʒbrãnki'sadu, da] *adj* whitish.

esbravejar [4] [iʒbrave'ʒa(x)] *vi:* ~ **(com alguém)** to shout (at sb).

esbugalhado, da [iʒbuga'ʎadu, da] *adj* bulging.

esbugalhar [4] [iʒbuga'ʎa(x)] *vt* to bulge.

esburacado, da [iʒbura'kadu, da] *adj* **-1.** [rua, jardim] potholed. **-2.** [rosto] pitted.

esburacar [12] [iʒbura'ka(x)] *vt* to make holes in.

escabeche [iʃka'bɛʃi] *m* marinade.

escabroso, sa [iʃka'brozu, zal] *adj* **-1.** [difícil] tough. **-2.** [imoral] immoral.

escada [iʃ'kadal] *f* **-1.** [interna] stairs (*pl*), staircase. **-2.** [externa] steps (*pl*); ~ **de caracol** spiral staircase; ~ **de incêndio** fire escape; ~ **rolante** escalator. **-3.** *fig* [meio] ladder.

escadaria [iʃkada'rial] *f* staircase.

escafandrista [iʃkafãn'driʃtal] *mf* deep-sea diver.

escafandro [iʃka'fãndrul] *m* diving suit.

escafeder-se [5] [iʃkafe'dexsil] *vp* to slip off.

escala [iʃ'kalal] *f* **-1.** [ger] scale; **em grande** ~ on a grand scale. **-2.** [parada] stopover; **sem** ~ nonstop. **-3.** [turno] turn.

escalação [iʃkala'sãw] *f* [designação] selection.

escalada [iʃka'ladal] *f* climbing.

escalão [iʃka'lãw] (*pl* **-ões**) *m* level; **o alto** ~ **do governo** the upper echelon of government.

escalar [4] [iʃka'la(x)] *vt* **-1.** [subir] to climb. **-2.** [designar] to select.

escaldado, da [iʃkaw'dadu, da] *adj* **-1.** [fervido] scalded. **-2.** *fig* [experiente] wary.

escaldar [4] [iʃkaw'da(x)] *vt* to scald.

escaler [iʃka'lɛ(x)] *m* launch.

escalonamento [iʃkalona'mẽntul] *m* scheduling.

escalonar [4] [iʃkalo'na(x)] *vt* to schedule.

escalope [iʃka'lɔpil] *m* escalope.

escalpelar [iʃkawpe'la(x)] *vt* [escalpar] to scalp.

escalpelo [iʃkaw'pelul] *m* scalpel.

escama [iʃ'kãmal] *f* scale.

escamar [4] [iʃka'ma(x)] ◇ *vt* [peixe] to scale. ◇ *vi* [pele] to flake.

escamotear [15] [iʃkamo'tʃja(x)] *vt* to filch.

escancarado, da [iʃkãŋka'radu, da] *adj* **-1.** [aberto] wide open. **-2.** [evidente] brazen. **-3.** [franco] open.

escancarar [4] [iʃkãŋka'ra(x)] *vt* **-1.** [abrir] to open wide. **-2.** [exibir] to display openly.

escandalizar [4] [iʃkãndali'za(x)] *vt* to scandalize.

➡ **escandalizar-se** *vp* to be shocked.

escândalo [iʃ'kãndalul] *m* **-1.** [fato] scandal. **-2.** [indignação] outrage. **-3.** [alvoroço]: **fazer** *ou* **dar um** ~ to make a scene.

escandaloso, sa [iʃkãnda'lozu, ɔzal] *adj* **-1.** [chocante] shocking. **-2.** [chamativo] outrageous.

Escandinávia [iʃkãndʒi'navjal] *n* Scandinavia.

escandinavo, va [iʃkãndʒi'navu, val] ◇ *adj* Scandinavian. ◇ *m, f* Scandinavian.

escanear [15] [iʃkã'nea(x)] *vt* COMPUT to scan.

escangalhar [4] [iʃkãŋga'ʎa(x)] *vt* **-1.** [ger] to break. **-2.** [sapatos] to fall apart.

escaninho [iʃka'niɲul] *m* pigeon-hole.

escanteio [iʃkãn'tejul] *m* corner.

escapada [iʃka'padal] *f* **-1.** [fuga] escape. **-2.** [ato leviano] escapade; **no meio da reunião, ele deu uma** ~ **para comprar flores para a mulher** in the middle of the meeting, he slipped out to buy flowers for his wife; **ele vive dando** ~**s com outras mulheres** he is always having affairs with other women; **a mulher sabe que ele dá umas** ~**s do casamento** his wife knows he has affairs outside marriage, his wife knows that he strays.

escapamento [iʃkapa'mẽntul] *m* **-1.** [de gás] leak. **-2.** [de veículo] exhaust.

escapar [4] [iʃka'pa(x)] *vi* **-1.** [sobreviver]: ~ **(de algo)** to escape (from sthg). **-2.:** ~ **a alguém** to escape (from) sb. **-3.** [fugir] to escape from. **-4.** [esquivar-se] to avoid; ~ **de fazer algo** to get out of doing sthg. **-5.** [soltar-se, cair]: ~ **de algo** to run away from sthg. **-6.** *loc:* ~ **de boa** to have a close shave; **deixar** ~ [não aproveitar] to miss; [revelar por descuido] to let drop.

escapatória [iʃkapa'tɔrjal] *f* **-1.** [saída] way out. **-2.** [desculpa] excuse.

escape [iʃ'kapil] *m* [de veículo] exhaust pipe; **válvula de** ~ escape valve; **minha válvula de** ~ **é dançar todos os dias** *fig* my outlet is to dance every day.

escapismo [iʃka'piʒmul] *m* escapism.

escapulida [iʃkapu'lidal] *f* [saída] outing; **dar uma** ~ to slip away.

escapulir [61] [iʃkapu'li(x)] *vi:* ~ **(de algo)** to escape (from sthg).

escarafunchar [4] [iʃkarafũn'ʃa(x)] *vt* to rummage in.

escaramuça [iʃkara'musal] *f* skirmish.

escaravelho [iʃkara'veʎul] *m* beetle.

escarcéu [iʃkax'sɛw] *m*: **fazer um** ~ to throw a fit.

escarlate [iʃkax'latʃil] *adj* scarlet.

escarlatina [iʃkaxla'tʃinal] *f* scarlet fever.

escarnecer [25] [iʃkaxne'se(x)] *vi:* ~ **de algo/alguém** to mock sthg/sb, to make fun of sthg/sb.

escárnio [iʃ'karnjul] *m* **-1.** [desdém] scorn. **-2.** [zombaria] mockery.

escarpa [iʃ'kaxpal] *f* escarpment.

escarpado, da [iʃkar'padu, da] *adj* steep.

escarrado, da [iʃka'xadu, da] *adj*: **o menino é o avô** ~ the boy is the spitting image of his grandfather.

escarrapachar-se [4] [iʃkaxapa'ʃaxsil] *vp* to sprawl.

escarrar [4] [iʃka'xa(x)] ◇ *vt* to spit. ◇ *vi* to hawk.

escarro [iʃ'kaxul] *m* phlegm.

escasseamento [iʃkasja'mẽntul] *m* shortage.

escassear [15] [iʃka'sja(x)] *vi* to become scarce.

escassez [iʃka'seʒl] *f* shortage.

escasso, a [iʃ'kasu, sa] *adj* scarce.

escavação [iʃkava'sãw] (*pl* -ões) *f* excavation.

escavadeira [iʃkava'dejra] *f* digger.

escavar [12] [iʃka'va(x)] *vt* to dig.

esclarecedor, ra [iʃklarese'do(x), ra] *adj* illuminating.

esclarecer [25] [iʃklare'se(x)] *vt* **-1.** [explicar] to clarify. **-2.** [elucidar] to explain. **-3.** [informar] to inform.

→ **esclarecer-se** *vp* [informar-se] to find out.

esclarecido, da [iʃklare'sidu, da] *adj* **-1.** [resolvido] solved. **-2.** [informado] well informed.

esclarecimento [iʃklaresi'mẽntu] *m* **-1.** [explicação] explanation. **-2.** [informação] (piece of) information.

esclerosado, da [iʃklero'zadu, da] *adj* senile.

esclerose [iʃkle'rɔzi] *f* sclerosis; ~ **múltipla** multiple sclerosis.

esclerótica [iʃkle'rɔtʃika] *f* white of the eye, sclera.

escoadouro [iʃkoa'doru] *m* drain.

escoar [20] [iʃ'kwa(x)] *vi*: ~ **(por)** to drain (through).

escocês, esa [iʃko'seʒ, eza] ◇ *adj* Scottish. ◇ *m, f* Scot.

→ **escocês** *m* [língua] Gaelic.

Escócia [iʃ'kɔsja] *n* Scotland.

escoicear [15] [iʃkoj'sja(x)] *vt & vi* to kick.

escola [iʃ'kɔla] *f* [ger] school; ~ **particular/pública** private/public school *US*, private/state school *UK*; ~ **naval** naval college; ~ **de samba** *group of musicians and samba dancers who perform in street parades during carnival celebrations in Brazil.*

escolado, da [iʃko'ladu, da] *adj* experienced.

escola-modelo [iʃ,kɔlamo'delu] (*pl* escolas-modelo) *f* model school.

escolar [iʃko'la(x)] (*pl* -es) *adj* school (*antes de subst*).

escolaridade [iʃkolari'dadʒi] *f* schooling.

escolarização [iʃkolariza'sãw] *f* school education.

escolarizar [4] [iʃkolari'za(x)] *vt* to educate.

escolha [iʃ'koʎa] *f* choice.

escolher [5] [iʃko'ʎe(x)] *vt* to choose.

escolhido, da [iʃko'ʎidu, da] *adj* selected, chosen.

escoliose [iʃkoli'ɔzi] *f* MED curvature of the spine.

escolta [iʃkowta] *f* escort.

escoltar [4] [iʃkow'ta(x)] *vt* to escort.

escombros [iʃ'kõnbruʃ] *mpl* ruins.

esconder [5] [iʃkõn'de(x)] *vt* to hide.

→ **esconder-se** *vp* to hide.

esconderijo [iʃkõnde'riʒu] *m* hiding place.

escondidas [iʃkõn'dʒidaʃ] → **às escondidas** *loc adv* secretly.

esconjurar [4] [iʃkõnʒu'ra(x)] *vt* **-1.** [juramento] to swear. **-2.** [maldição] to curse.

escopeta [iʃko'peta] *f* shotgun.

escopo [iʃ'kopu] *m* purpose.

escora [iʃ'kɔra] *f* prop.

escorar [4] [iʃko'ra(x)] *vt* [pôr escoras] to support, to prop up.

→ **escorar-se** *vp* **-1.** [encostar-se]: ~-**se (em)** to lean (on). **-2.** [fundamentar-se]: ~-**se em** to go by. **-3.** [amparar-se]: ~-**se em** to rely on.

escorbuto [iʃkox'butu] *m* scurvy.

escória [iʃ'kɔrja] *f* **-1.** [resíduo] slag. **-2.** *fig* [ralé] scum.

escoriação [iʃkorja'sãw] (*pl* -ões) *f* abrasion.

escorpiano, na [iʃkox'pãjanu, na] ◇ *adj* Scorpio. ◇ *m, f* Scorpio.

escorpião [iʃkox'pjãw] (*pl* -ões) *m* ZOOL scorpion.

→ **Escorpião** *m* ASTRO Scorpio.

escorraçar [13] [iʃkoxa'sa(x)] *vt* to throw out.

escorredor [iʃkoxe'do(x)] *m* [para alimentos] colander; ~ **de pratos** dish drainer, draining board.

escorregadiço, dia [iʃkoxega'dʒisu, dʒia], **escorregadio, dia** [iʃkoxega'dʒiu, dʒia] *adj* slippery.

escorregador [iʃkoxega'do(x)] *m* slide.

escorregão [iʃkoxe'gãw] (*pl* -ões) *m* **-1.** [queda] slip. **-2.** *fig* [deslize] slip-up.

escorregar [14] [iʃkoxe'ga(x)] *vi* **-1.** [deslizar] to slip. **-2.** *fig* [errar]: ~ **em algo** to slip up on sthg.

escorrer [5] [iʃko'xe(x)] ◇ *vt* [tirar líquido de] to drain. ◇ *vi* [verter] to drip.

escorrido, da [iʃko'xidu, da] *adj* **-1.** [enxuto] dry. **-2.** [liso] straight, smooth.

escoteiro, ra [iʃko'tejru, ra] *m* scout.

escotilha [iʃko'tiʎa] *f* hatch, hatchway.

escova [iʃ'koval *f* **-1.** [utensílio] brush; ~ **de dentes** toothbrush; ~ **de cabelo** hair brush. **-2.** [penteado]: **fazer uma** ~ [em si mesmo] to style one's hair.

escovar [4] [iʃko'va(x)] *vt* to brush.

escrachado, da [iʃkra'ʃadu, da] *adj fam* scruffy.

escrachar [iʃkra'ʃa(x)] *vt fam* **-1.** [desmascarar] to unmask. **-2.** [repreender] to tick off.

escracho [iʃ'kraʃul *m fam* [bagunça] shambles.

escravatura [iʃkrava'tural *f* slavery.

escravidão [iʃkravi'dãwl *f* slavery.

escravização [iʃkraviza'sãw] *f* enslavement.

escravizar [4] [iʃkravi'za(x)] *vt* **-1.** [tornar escravo] to enslave. **-2.** *fig* [subjugar] to dominate.

escravo, va [iʃ'kravu, va] ◇ *adj* **-1.** [ger] slave. **-2.** *fig* [dominado]: **ser** ~ **de alguém/algo** to be sb/sthg's slave. ◇ *m, f* slave.

escravocrata [iʃkravo'krata] ◇ *adj* slave-owning. ◇ *mf* slave-owner.

escrevente [iʃkre'vẽntʃil *mf* clerk.

escrever [5] [iʃkre've(x)] *vt & vi* to write.

→ **escrever-se** *vp* **-1.** [pessoas] to correspond. **-2.** [palavras] to spell; **esta palavra se escreve com x** this word is spelt with an 'x'.

escrevinhador, ra [iʃkreviɲa'do(x), ra] *m, f* hack (writer).

escrevinhar [4] [iʃkrevi'ɲa(x)] *vt* to scribble.

escrita [iʃ'krital *f* **-1.** [letra] handwriting. **-2.** [tradição] tradition.

escrito, ta [iʃ'kritu, ta] ◇ *pp* ▷ **escrever**. ◇ *adj* written; **por** ~ in writing; **ser algo/alguém**

~ to be the spitting image of sthg/sb.
- **escrito** m text.
- **escritos** mpl [obra literária] manuscripts.

escritor, ra [iʃkri'to(x), ra] (mpl -es, fpl -s) m, f writer.

escritório [iʃkri'tɔrju] m -1. COM office. -2. [em casa] study.

escritura [iʃkri'tura] f -1. JUR deed. -2. [na compra de imóvel] exchange of contracts.

escritura [iʃkri'tura] ➡ **Escrituras** fpl: as ~ the Scriptures.

escriturar [4] [iʃkri'tura(x)] vt to draw up.

escriturário, ria [iʃkritu'rarju, rja] m, f clerk.

escrivã [iʃkri'vã] f ▷ **escrivão**.

escrivaninha [iʃkriva'niɲa] f desk.

escrivão, vã [iʃkri'vãw, vã] (mpl -ões, fpl -s) m, f registrar.

escroto, ta [iʃ'krotu, ta] adj vulg [ordinário] shitty.
- **escroto** m ANAT scrotum.

escrúpulo [iʃ'krupulu] m -1. [ger] scruple; **sem** ~**s** unscrupulous. -2. [cuidado] care.

escrupuloso, osa [iʃkrupu'lozu, ɔza] adj scrupulous.

escrutinar [4] [iʃkrutʃi'na(x)] vt to scrutinize.

escrutínio [iʃkru'tʃinju] m scrutiny.

escudar [4] [iʃku'da(x)] vt [proteger] to shield.
- **escudar-se** vp -1. [proteger-se] to shield o.s. -2. fig [amparar-se]: ~**-se em algo/alguém** to shield o.s. with sthg/sb.

escudeiro [iʃku'dejru] m squire.

escudo [iʃkudu] m -1. [proteção] shield. -2. [moeda] escudo.

esculachado, da [iʃkula'ʃadu, da] adj fam messed up.

esculachar [4] [iʃkula'ʃa(x)] fam vt -1. [avacalhar] to mess up. -2. [repreender] to tell off.

esculacho [iʃku'laʃu] m fam [repreensão] telling-off.

esculhambado, da [iʃkuʎãn'badu, da] adj messed up.

esculhambar [4] [iʃkuʎãn'ba(x)] fam vt -1. [repreender] to tell off. -2. [avacalhar] to trash. -3. [desarrumar] to mess up. -4. [quebrar] to screw up.

esculpir [6] [iʃkuw'pi(x)] vt to sculpt.

escultor, ra [iʃkuw'to(x), ra] (mpl -es, fpl -s) m, f sculptor.

escultura [iʃkuw'tura] f sculpture.

escultural [iʃkuwtu'rawl] (pl -ais) adj statuesque.

escumadeira [iʃkuma'dejra] f skimmer.

escuna [iʃ'kuna] f schooner.

escuras [iʃ'kuraʃ] fpl ▷ **escuro**.

escurecer [25] [iʃkure'se(x)] <> vt [tornar escuro] to darken. <> vi -1. [anoitecer] to go dark. -2. [ficar escuro] to get dark.

escuridão [iʃkuri'dãw] f darkness.

escuro, ra [iʃ'kuru, ra] adj -1. [ger] dark. -2. [pessoa] dark-skinned.
- **escuro** m [escuridão] darkness; **fazer algo no** ~ fig to do sthg in the dark.
- **às escuras** loc adv -1. [sem luz] in the dark.

-2. fig [às escondidas] on the quiet.

escusa [iʃ'kuza] f excuse.

escusado, da [iʃku'zadu, da] adj unnecessary.

escusar [4] [iʃku'za(x)] vt -1. [desculpar]: ~ **alguém (de)** to excuse sb (for). -2. [dispensar]: ~ **alguém de** to excuse sb from.
- **escusar-se** vp -1. [desculpar-se]: ~**-se (de)** to excuse o.s. (for). -2. [dispensar-se]: ~**-se de** to be excused from.

escusável [iʃku'zavewl] (pl -eis) adj excusable.

escuso, sa [iʃ'kuzu, za] adj underhand.

escuta [iʃ'kuta] f listening; ~ **telefônica** phone tap.
- **à escuta** loc adv listening.

escutar [4] [iʃku'ta(x)] <> vt -1. [ouvir] to hear; [prestar atenção] to listen to. -2. [dar ouvidos a] to hear out. -3. [atender a] to heed. <> vi [ouvir] to hear; [prestar atenção] to listen.

esdrúxulo, la [iʒ'druʃulu, la] adj weird.

esfacelar [4] [iʃfase'la(x)] vt to destroy.
- **esfacelar-se** vp to destroy o.s.

esfaimado, da [iʃfaj'madu, da] adj famished.

esfaltar-se [4] [iʃfaw'taxsil] vp to tire o.s. out.

esfaquear [15] [iʃfa'kja(x)] vt to stab.

esfarelar [4] [iʃfare'la(x)] vt to crumble.
- **esfarelar-se** vp to crumble.

esfarrapado, da [iʃfaxa'padu, da] adj -1. [roto] scruffy. -2. [não-convincente] unconvincing.

esfarrapar [4] [iʃfaxa'pa(x)] vt to tear up.

esfera [iʃ'fɛra] f -1. [ger] sphere. -2. [globo] globe.

esférico, ca [iʃ'fɛriku, ka] adj spherical.

esferográfica [iʃfero'grafika] f ballpoint pen.

esfiapar [4] [iʃfja'pa(x)] vt & vi to fray.

esfinge [iʃ'fĩʒil] f sphinx.

esfolar [4] [iʃfo'la(x)] vt -1. [tirar a pele] to skin. -2. [arranhar] to graze. -3. [cobrar caro] to rip off.
- **esfolar-se** vp to graze o.s.

esfomeado, da [iʃfo'mjadu, da] adj starving.

esforçado, da [iʃfox'sadu, da] adj committed.

esforçar-se [13] [iʃfox'saxsil] vp to make an effort.

esforço [iʃ'foxsul] m effort.

esfregação [iʃfrega'sãw] f -1. [fricção] rubbing. -2. fam [bolinagem]: **estar na** ~ to pet.

esfregão [iʃfre'gãwl] (pl -ões) m mop.

esfregar [14] [iʃfre'ga(x)] vt -1. [friccionar] to scrub. -2. [lavar] to scrub.
- **esfregar-se** vp -1. [friccionar-se] to rub o.s. -2. [lavar-se] to scrub o.s. -3. fam [bolinar-se] to fondle each other.

esfriamento [iʃfrja'mẽntul] m cooling.

esfriar [16] [iʃfri'a(x)] <> vt to cool. <> vi -1. [perder o calor] to get cold. -2. fig [arrefecer] to cool.

esfumaçado, da [iʃfuma'sadu, da] adj smoky.

esfumaçar [13] [iʃfuma'sa(x)] vt to smoke out.

esfuziante [iʃfu'zjãntʃil] adj [alegre] effusive.

esganar [4] [iʒga'na(x)] vt to strangle.

esganiçado, da [iʒgani'sadu, da] adj shrill.

esgarçar [13] [iʒgax'sa(x)] <> vt to tear. <> vi to wear thin.

esgoelar [4] [iʒgwe'la(x)] vt [esganar] to strangle.
- **esgoelar-se** vp [gritar] to yell.

esgotado, da [iʒgo'tadu, da] *adj* -**1.** [exausto] exhausted. -**2.** [acabado - paciência, crédito] exhausted; [- reservas naturais] depleted; [- prazo] finished. -**3.** *fig* [esquadrinhado] scrutinized. -**4.** [totalmente vendido] sold out.

esgotamento [iʒgota'mẽntul] *m* [exaustão] exhaustion; ~ **nervoso** nervous breakdown.

esgotante [iʒgo'tãntʃi] *adj* exhausting.

esgotar [4] [iʒgo'ta(x)] *vt* -**1.** [ger] to exhaust. -**2.** [esquadrinhar] to scrutinize. -**3.** [esvaziar, secar] to drain.

➡ **esgotar-se** *vp* -**1.** [ger] to be exhausted. -**2.** [ser vendido totalmente] to be sold out.

esgoto [iʒ'gotul] *m* drain.

esgrima [iʒ'grima] *f* fencing.

esgrimir [6] [iʒgri'mi(x)] *vi* to fence.

esgueirar-se [4] [iʒgej'raxsil] *vp* to slip away.

esguelha [iʒ'geʎa] *f* slant.

➡ **de esguelha** *loc adv* obliquely; **olhar de esguelha** to cast a sidelong glance.

esguichar [4] [iʒgi'ʃa(x)] <> *vt* to squirt. <> *vi* to gush.

esguicho [iʒ'giʃul] *m* squirt.

esguio, guia [iʒ'giu, gia] *adj* willowy.

eslavo, va [iʒ'lavu, va] <> *adj* Slav. <> *m, f* Slav.

➡ **eslavo** *m* [língua] Slavic.

eslovaco, ca [iʒlo'vaku, ka] <> *adj* Slovakian. <> *m, f* Slovak.

➡ **eslovaco** *m* [língua] Slovak.

Eslováquia [iʒlo'vakja] *n* Slovakia.

Eslovênia [iʒlo'venja] *n* Slovenia.

esloveno, na [iʒlo'venu, na] <> *adj* Slovene. <> *m, f* Slovene.

➡ **esloveno** *m* [língua] Slovene.

esmagador, ra [iʒmaga'do(x), ral] (*mpl* -es, *fpl* -s) *adj fig* overwhelming.

esmagar [14] [iʒma'ga(x)] *vt* -**1.** [esmigalhar] to crush. -**2.** *fig* [vencer] to overpower.

esmaltado, da [iʒmaw'tadu, da] *adj* enamelled.

esmaltar [4] [iʒmaw'ta(x)] *vt* to enamel.

esmalte [iʒ'mawtʃil] *m* enamel; ~ **de unha** nail polish *UK*, nail enamel *US*.

esmerado, da [iʒme'radu, da] *adj* -**1.** [cuidadoso] meticulous. -**2.** [bem acabado - produção] accomplished; [- trabalho] well finished.

esmeralda [iʒme'rawda] *f* emerald.

esmerar-se [4] [iʒme'raxsil] *vp*: ~**-se em algo/em fazer algo** to be meticulous about sthg/about doing sthg.

esmero ['iʒmerul] *m* meticulousness.

esmigalhar [4] [iʒmiga'ʎa(x)] *vt* -**1.** [fazer em migalhas] to crumble. -**2.** [despedaçar] to shatter. -**3.** [esmagar] to crush.

➡ **esmigalhar-se** *vp* -**1.** [fazer-se em migalhas] to crumble. -**2.** [despedaçar-se] to shatter.

esmiuçar [13] [iʒmju'sa(x)] *vt* -**1.** [explicar] to explain in great detail. -**2.** [investigar] to scrutinize.

esmo ['eʒmul] ➡ **a esmo** *loc adv* at random.

esmola [iʒ'mɔla] *f* alms *(pl)*.

esmolar [4] [iʒmo'la(x)] <> *vt* to beg for. <> *vi* to beg.

esmorecer [25] [iʒmore'se(x)l] <> *vt* [pessoa] to discourage. <> *vi* -**1.** [pessoa] to lose heart. -**2.** [luz] to diminish.

esmorecimento [iʒmoresi'mẽntul] *m* discouragement.

esmurrar [4] [iʒmu'xa(x)] *vt* to punch.

esnobação [iʒnoba'sãwl] *f* snobbery.

esnobar [4] [iʒno'ba(x)l] <> *vt* to be snobbish towards. <> *vi* to be snobbish.

esnobe [iʒ'nɔbil] <> *adj* snobbish. <> *mf* snob.

esnobismo [iʒno'biʒmul] *m* snobbishness.

esôfago [e'zofagul] *m* oesophagus *UK*, esophagus *US*.

esotérico, ca [ezo'tɛriku, ka] *adj* esoteric.

esoterismo [ezote'riʃmul] *m* esotericism.

espaçado, da [iʃpa'sadu, da] *adj* -**1.** [com intervalos] spaced out. -**2.** [esparso] scattered.

espaçar [13] [iʃpa'sa(x)] *vt* to space out.

espacial [iʃpa'sjawl] (*pl* -ais) *adj* space *(antes do subst)*.

espaço [iʃ'pasul] *m* -**1.** [ger] space; ~ **aéreo** air space. -**2.** [o universo] outer space. -**3.** [de tempo] space.

espaçoso, osa [iʃpa'sozu, ɔza] *adj* spacious.

espada [iʃ'pada] *f* [arma] sword.

➡ **espadas** *fpl* [naipe] spades.

espadachim [iʃpada'ʃĩ] (*pl* -ns) *m* swordsman.

espádua [iʃ'padwal] *f* shoulder blade.

espaguete [iʃpa'gɛtʃil] *m* spaghetti.

espairecer [25] [iʃpajre'se(x)l] *vt & vi* to relax.

espairecimento [iʃpajresi'mẽntul] *m* relaxation.

espaldar [4] [iʃpaw'da(x)l] *m* [de cadeira, sofá] back.

espalhafato [iʃpaʎa'fatul] *m* commotion.

espalhafatoso, osa [iʃpaʎafa'tozu, ɔza] *adj* -**1.** [roupa] gaudy. -**2.** [pessoa, jeito] loud.

espalhar [4] [iʃpa'ʎa(x)] *vt* -**1.** [ger] to spread. -**2.** [dispersar - semente] to scatter; [- fumaça, odor] to spread. -**3.** [difundir] to diffuse.

➡ **espalhar-se** *vp* -**1.** [dissipar-se] to dissipate. -**2.** [propagar-se] to be spread.

espalmado, da [iʃpaw'madu, da] *adj* splayed.

espalmar [4] [iʃpaw'ma(x)] *vt* -**1.** [abrir] to splay. -**2.** [desviar] to deflect.

espanador [iʃpana'do(x)l] (*pl* -es) *m* duster.

espanar [4] [iʃpa'na(x)] *vt* to dust.

espancamento [iʃpãŋka'mẽntul] *m* beating.

espancar [12] [iʃpãŋ'ka(x)] *vt* to beat.

Espanha [iʃ'pãɲa] *n* Spain.

espanhol, la [iʃpã'ɲɔw, la] (*mpl* -óis, *fpl* -s) <> *adj* Spanish. <> *m, f* Spaniard.

➡ **espanhol** *m* [língua] Spanish.

espantado, da [iʃpãn'tadu, da] *adj* -**1.** [assustado] startled. -**2.** [surpreso] astonished.

espantalho [iʃpãn'taʎul] *m* [boneco] scarecrow.

espantar [4] [iʃpãn'ta(x)l] *vt* -**1.** [assustar] to frighten. -**2.** [afugentar] to frighten (away). -**3.** [surpreender] to amaze. <> *vi* [surpreender] to be amazing.

➡ **espantar-se** *vp* -**1.** [assustar-se] to be frightened. -**2.** [surpreender-se] to be amazed.

espanto [iʃ'pãntul] *m* -**1.** [susto] fright. -**2.** [assombro] amazement.

espantoso, osa [iʃpãn'tozu, ɔza] *adj* -1. [surpreendente] startling. -2. [admirável] astounding.

esparadrapo [iʃpara'drapul] *m* sticking plaster *UK*, Band-Aid® *US*.

espargir [52] [iʃpax'ʒi(x)] *vt* to spray.

esparramado, da [iʃpaxa'madu, da] *adj* -1. [espalhado] scattered. -2. [derramado] splashed. -3. [refastelado] sprawled.

esparramar [4] [iʃpaxa'ma(x)] *vt* -1. [espalhar] to scatter. -2. [derramar] to splash.
➡ **esparramar-se** *vp* [refastelar-se] to sprawl.

esparramo [iʃpa'xamul] *m* scattering.

esparso, sa [iʃ'paxsu, sa] *adj* -1. [espalhado] sparse. -2. [raro] scarce.

espartano, na [iʃpax'tãnu, na] *adj* spartan.

espartilho [iʃpax'tiʎul] *m* corset.

espasmo [iʃ'paʒmul] *m* spasm.

espasmódico, ca [iʃpaʒ'mɔdʒiku, ka] *adj* spasmodic.

espatifar [4] [iʃpatʃi'fa(x)] *vt & vi* to smash.
➡ **espatifar-se** *vp* to shatter.

espátula [iʃ'patula] *f* spatula.

espavento [iʃpa'vẽntu] *m* fright.

espavorido, da [iʃpavo'ridu, da] *adj* terrified.

especial [iʃpe'sjawl] (*pl* -ais) *adj* special; em ~ in particular.

especialidade [iʃpesjali'dadʒi] *f* speciality.

especialista [iʃpesja'liʃta] <> *adj* [perito]: ~ em expert in. <> *mf* -1. [profissional] expert. -2. [perito]: ~ em specialist in.

especialização [iʃpesjaliza'sãwl] (*pl* -ões) *f* specialization.

especializado, da [iʃpesjali'zadu, da] *adj* -1. [treinado]: ~ (em) specialized (in). -2. [específico] specialized.

especializar-se [4] [iʃpesjali'zaxsi] *vp*: ~ (em) to specialize (in).

especiaria [iʃpesja'rial] *f* spice.

espécie [iʃ'pɛsjil] *f* -1. BIOL species. -2. [tipo] kind.
➡ **em espécie** *loc adv* FIN (in) cash.

especificação [iʃpesifika'sãwl] (*pl* -ões) *f* specification.

especificar [12] [iʃpesifi'ka(x)] *vt* to specify.

específico, ca [iʃpe'sifiku, ka] *adj* specific.

espécime [iʃ'pɛsimil] (*pl* -es), **espécimen** (*pl* -ns) *m* specimen.

espectador, ra [iʃpekta'do(x), ral (*mpl* -res, *fpl* -ras) *m, f* -1. [testemunha] witness. -2. [de espetáculo *etc*] spectator.
➡ **espectadores** *mpl* viewers.

espectro [iʃ'pɛktrul] *m* -1. [fantasma] ghost. -2. FÍSICA spectrum. -3. *fig* [pessoa esquálida] wretch.

especulação [iʃpekula'sãwl] (*pl* -ões) *f* speculation.

especulador, ra [iʃpekula'do(x), ral <> *adj* speculative. <> *m, f* BOLSA & COM speculator.

especular [4] [iʃpeku'la(x)] <> *vt* [averiguar] to speculate upon. <> *vi* -1. [informar-se]: ~ sobre algo to speculate about sthg. -2. [teorizar]: ~ (sobre algo) to speculate (about sthg). -3. BOLSA & COM: ~ (em) to speculate (in).

especulativo, va [iʃpekula'tʃivu, val *adj* speculative.

espelhar [4] [iʃpe'ʎa(x)] *vt* [mostrar] to reflect.
➡ **espelhar-se** *vp* -1. [refletir-se] to be reflected. -2. [mirar-se] to reflect.

espelho [iʃ'peʎul] *m* mirror; ~ retrovisor rearview mirror.

espelunca [iʃpe'lũŋka] *f* dump.

espera [iʃ'pɛral] *f* -1. [ato] wait; à ~ de waiting for. -2. [tempo] delay. -3. [tocaia] ambush.

esperado, da [iʃpe'radu, da] *adj* -1. [aguardado] awaited. -2. [previsto] expected.

esperança [iʃpe'rãsal] *f* -1. [expectativa] expectation. -2. [confiança] hope.

esperançoso, osa [iʃperãn'sozu, ɔza] *adj* hopeful.

esperanto [iʃpe'rãntul] *m* Esperanto.

esperar [13] [iʃpe'ra(x)] <> *vt* -1. [aguardar] to wait for. -2. [bebê] to expect. -3. [desejar]: ~ que to hope that; ~ fazer algo to hope to do sthg. -4. [supor] to expect. -5. [estar destinado a] to await. -6. [contar obter] to expect. <> *vi* [aguardar]: to hope; fazer alguém ~ to make sb wait; espera (aí)! wait (a moment)!
➡ **esperar-se** *vp*: como era de se ~ as was to be expected.

esperável [iʃpe'ravewl] (*pl* -eis) *adj* probable.

esperma [iʃ'pɛxmal] *m* sperm.

espermatozóide *m* spermatozoon, spermatozoa (*pl*).

espermicida [iʃpexmi'sidal] <> *adj* spermicidal. <> *m* spermicide.

espernear [15] [iʃpex'nja(x)] *vi* -1. [sacudir as pernas] to kick one's legs. -2. *fig* [protestar] to (put up a) protest.

espertalhão, ona [iʃpexta'ʎãw, onal (*mpl* -ões, *fpl* -s) <> *adj* crafty. <> *m, f* smart operator.

esperteza [iʃpex'tezal *f* -1. [inteligência] intelligence. -2. [astúcia] shrewdness; foi muita ~ dele fazer isso it was very shrewd of him to do that.

esperto, ta [iʃ'pɛxtu, tal *adj* -1. [inteligente] smart. -2. [ativo] lively. -3. [espertalhão] clever. -4. *fam* [bacana] groovy.

espesso, a [iʃ'pesu, sal *adj* thick.

espessura [iʃpe'sural *f* thickness.

espetacular [iʃpetaku'la(x)l (*pl* -es) *adj* amazing.

espetáculo [iʃpe'takulul *m* -1. [show] show. -2. [maravilha]: ser um ~ to be amazing. -3. [cena ridícula] spectacle; ele deu o maior ~ aqui por causa da bebedeira he made a spectacle of himself here being so drunk.

espetada [iʃpe'tadal *f* -1. [furada] prick. -2. [cul] kebab. -3. *fig* [implicância]: dar ~ em alguém to needle sb.

espetar [4] [iʃpe'ta(x)l *vt* to impale.
➡ **espetar-se** *vp* to prick o.s.

espeto [iʃ'petul *m* -1. [utensílio de churrasco] (roasting) spit. -2. *fig* [pessoa magra] beanpole. -3. *fig* [situação difícil]: ser um ~ to be difficult.

espevitado, da [iʃpevi'tadu, dal *adj* lively.

espevitar [iʃpevi'ta(x)] ➡ **espevitar-se** *vp* **-1.** [mostrar-se afetado] to show off. **-2.** [irritar-se] to fly off the handle.

espezinhar [4] [iʃpɛzi'ɲa(x)] *vt* **-1.** [implicar com] to put down. **-2.** [humilhar] to trample (on).

espiada [iʃ'pjada] *f* peep; **dar uma** ~ to have a peep, to have a look-see.

espião, pia [iʃ'pjãw, pia] (*mpl* **-ões,** *fpl* **-s**) *m, f* spy.

espiar [16] [iʃ'pja(x)] <> *vt* **-1.** [olhar] to watch. **-2.** [espionar] to spy on. <> *vi* **-1.** [olhar]: ~ **(por)** [pela fechadura] to look (through); [pelo canto do olho] to glance. **-2.** [espionar] to spy.

espicaçar [13] [iʃpika'sa(x)] *vt* *fig* [torturar] to torment.

espichado, da [iʃpi'ʃadu, da] *adj* **-1.** [pessoa] stretched out. **-2.** [corda] tight.

espichar [4] [iʃpi'ʃa(x)] <> *vt* [esticar] to stretch out. <> *vi* [crescer] to shoot up.
➡ **espichar-se** *vp* [espreguiçar-se] to stretch (out).

espiga [iʃ'piga] *f* ear.

espigão [iʃpi'gãw] (*pl* **-ões**) *m* **-1.** [pua] spike. **-2.** [pico] peak.

espinafrar [4] [iʃpina'fra(x)] *vt* **-1.** [repreender] to reprimand. **-2.** [criticar] to lambaste.

espinafre [iʃpi'nafri] *m* spinach.

espingarda [iʃpĩŋ'gaxda] *f* shotgun.

espinha [iʃ'piɲa] *f* **-1.** [na pele] pimple. **-2.** [de peixe] bone. **-3.** *ANAT* spine.

espinhento, ta [iʃpi'ɲẽntu, ta] *adj* **-1.** [planta] thorny. **-2.** [peixe] bony.

espinho [iʃ'piɲu] *m* **-1.** [de planta] thorn. **-2.** [de porco-espinho] quill. **-3.** [de ouriço] spine. **-4.** *fig* [dificuldade] snag.

espinhoso, osa [iʃpi'ɲozu, ɔza] *adj* thorny.

espionagem [iʃpio'naʒẽ] *f* espionage.

espionar [4] [iʃpio'na(x)] <> *vt* to spy on. <> *vi* to snoop.

espiral [iʃpi'raw] (*pl* **-ais**) <> *adj* spiral. <> *f* spiral; **em** ~ in a spiral; **escada em** ~ spiral staircase.

espírita [iʃ'pirita] <> *adj* spiritualistic. <> *mf* spiritualist.

espiritismo [iʃpiri'tʃiʒmul] *m* spiritualism.

espírito [iʃ'piritu] *m* **-1.** [ger] spirit. **-2.** [temperamento]: ~ **esportivo** competitive spirit; **ter** ~ **forte/fraco** to be strong/weak willed; **ser** ~ **de porco** to be a busybody.
➡ **Espírito Santo** *m* Holy Spirit.

espiritual [iʃpiri'twaw] (*pl* **-ais**) *adj* spiritual.

espiritualidade [iʃpiritwali'dadʒi] *f* spirituality.

espirituoso, osa [iʃpiri'twozu, ɔza] *adj* witty.

espirrar [4] [iʃpi'xa(x)] <> *vi* **-1.** [dar espirro] to sneeze. **-2.** [jorrar] to squirt out. <> *vt* [jorrar] to squirt.

espirro [iʃ'pixul] *m* sneeze.

esplanada [iʃpla'nada] *f* esplanade.

esplêndido, da [iʃ'plẽndʒidu, da] *adj* splendid.

esplendor [iʃplẽn'do(x)] *m* splendour *UK*, splendor *US*.

espocar [12] [iʃpo'ka(x)] *vi* to explode.

espoleta [iʃpo'leta] *f* detonator.

espoliar [16] [iʃpo'lja(x)] *vt* to plunder.

espólio [iʃ'pɔlju] *m* **-1.** [herança] inheritance. **-2.** [restos] remains *(pl)*.

esponja [iʃ'põʒa] *f* **-1.** [ger] sponge. **-2.** *fig* [beberrão] soak.

esponjoso, osa [iʃpõn'ʒozu, ɔza] *adj* spongy.

espontaneidade [iʃpõntanej'dadʒi] *f* spontaneity.

espontâneo, nea [iʃpõn'tãnju, nja] *adj* spontaneous.

espora [iʃ'pɔra] *f* spur.

esporádico, ca [iʃpo'radʒiku, ka] *adj* sporadic.

esporão [iʃpo'rãw] (*pl* **-ões**) *m* spur.

esporro [iʃ'poxul] *m* *vulg* **-1.** [barulho] racket. **-2.** [repreensão] tongue-lashing.

esporte [iʃ'pɔxtʃi] *m* sport.

ESPORTES

Although football is the absolute favourite sport of the Brazilian people, Brazil has excelled in other sports as well, including basketball, volleyball, sailing, swimming, judo, tennis and motor racing. Three Brazilian drivers have been Formula 1 world champions more than once: Emerson Fittipaldi ('72 and '74), Nelson Piquet ('81, '83 and '87) and Ayrton Senna ('88, '90 and '91).

esportista [iʃpox'tʃiʃta] <> *adj* sporty. <> *mf* sportsman (*f* sportswoman).

esportividade [iʃpoxtʃivi'dadʒi] *f* sportsmanship.

esportivo, va [iʃpox'tʃivu, va] *adj* sports (*antes de subst*).
➡ **esportiva** *f* (sense of) fair play.

esposa [iʃpo'zal] *f* wife.

esposar [4] [iʃ'poza(x)] *vt* to marry.

esposo [iʃ'pozul] *m* husband.

espraiar [4] [iʃpraj'a(x)] <> *vt* to spread. <> *vi* to sprawl, to wash ashore.

espreguiçadeira [iʃpregisa'dejra] *f* deckchair.

espreguiçar-se [13] [iʃpregi'saxsi] *vp* to stretch.

espreita [iʃ'prejta] *loc*: **à** ~ **(de)** on the lookout (for).

espreitar [4] [iʃprej'ta(x)] *vt* to peep at, to have a peep at.

espremedor [iʃpreme'do(x)] (*pl* **-es**) *m* masher; ~ **de laranja** orange squeezer.

espremer [5] [iʃpre'me(x)] *vt* **-1.** [apertar] to squeeze. **-2.** [comprimir - fruta] to squeeze; [- toalha molhada] to wring out.
➡ **espremer-se** *vp* [apertar-se] to press together.

espuma [iʃ'pumal] *f* foam.

espumante [iʃpu'mãntʃi] *adj* sparkling.

espumar [4] [iʃpu'ma(x)] *vi* to foam.

espumoso, osa [iʃpu'mozu, ɔza] *adj* foamy.

espúrio, ria [iʃ'purju, rja] *adj* spurious.

esquadra [iʃ'kwadra] *f* **-1.** *NÁUT* fleet. **-2.** *MIL* squadron.

esquadrão [iʃkwa'drãw] (*pl* **-ões**) *m* squadron.

esquadria [iʃkwa'dria] f frame.

esquadrilha [iʃkwa'driʎa] f flotilla.

esquadrinhar [4] [iʃkwadri'ɲa(x)] vt -1. [procurar] to search. -2. [analisar] to examine.

esquadro [iʃ'kwadru] m set square.

esqualidez [iʃkwali'deʃ] f squalour.

esquálido, da [iʃ'kwalidu, da] adj squalid.

esquartejar [4] [iʃkwaxte'ʒa(x)] vt to quarter.

esquecer [25] [iʃke'se(x)] <> vt to forget; ~ que to forget that. <> vi: ~ (de algo/alguém) to forget (sthg/sb); ~ de fazer algo to forget to do sthg.
 esquecer-se vp: ~-se (de algo) to forget (about sthg); ~-se de fazer algo to forget to do sthg.

esquecido, da [iʃke'sidu, da] adj -1. [não lembrado] forgotten. -2. [distraído] forgetful.

esquecimento [iʃkesi'mẽntu] m forgetfulness; cair no ~ to become a thing of the past.

esqueitista [iʃkej'tʃiʃta] mf skateboarder.

esquelético, ca [iʃke'lɛtʃiku, ka] adj skeletal.

esqueleto [iʃke'letu] m -1. [ossatura] skeleton. -2. [estrutura] skeleton. -3. [esboço] rough draft. -4. fig [pessoa magra] bag of bones, skeleton.

esquema [iʃ'kema] m -1. [gráfico] diagram. -2. [plano] plan; ~ de segurança security plan. -3. [resumo] schema.

esquemático, ca [iʃke'matʃiku, ka] adj schematic.

esquematização [iʃkematʃiza'sãwl] (pl -ões) f schematization.

esquematizar [4] [iʃkematʃi'za(x)] vt -1. [representar em desenho] to sketch. -2. [planejar] to plan. -3. [sintetizar] to plan.

esquentado, da [iʃkẽn'tadu, da] adj -1. [aquecido] heated. -2. fig [exaltado] irritable.

esquentar [4] [iʃkẽn'ta(x)] <> vt [aquecer] to heat up. <> vi -1. [aquecer] to get hot. -2. fig [exaltar-se] to become irritable.
 esquentar-se vp -1. [aquecer-se] to warm o.s. up. -2. fig [exaltar-se] to get annoyed.

esquerdista [iʃkex'dʒiʃta] <> adj leftist. <> mf leftist.

esquerdo, da [iʃ'kexdu, da] adj left.
 esquerda f -1. [lado] left; à ~ on the left. -2. POL left wing.

esquete [iʃ'kɛtʃi] m sketch.

esqui [iʃ'ki] m -1. [patim] ski. -2. [esporte] skiing; ~ aquático water-skiing.

esquiador, ra [iʃkja'do(x), ra] m, f skier.

esquiar [16] [iʃ'kja(x)] vi to ski.

esquife [iʃ'kifi] m coffin.

esquilo [iʃ'kilu] m squirrel.

esquimó [iʃki'mɔ] <> adj Eskimo. <> mf Eskimo.
 esquimó m [língua] Eskimo.

esquina [iʃ'kina] f corner; dobrar a ~ to turn the corner; minha rua faz ~ com a avenida principal my street goes off the main street.

esquisitice [iʃkizi'tʃisil] f -1. [qualidade] eccentricity. -2. [ato, dito] incongruity.

esquisito, ta [iʃki'zitu, ta] adj -1. [incomum] strange. -2. [pessoa] strange.

esquivar-se [4] [iʃki'vaxsi] vp: ~-se de algo to dodge sthg.

esquivo, va [iʃ'kivu, va] adj aloof.
 esquiva f dodge.

esquizofrenia [iʃkizofre'nia] f schizophrenia.

esquizofrênico, ca [iʃkizo'freniku, ka] <> adj schizophrenic. <> m, f schizophrenic.

esse, essa ['esi, 'ɛsa] <> adj that, those (pl). <> pron that (one), those (ones) (pl).

essência [e'sẽnsja] f essence.

essencial [esẽn'sjawl] (pl -ais) <> adj -1. [ger] essential. -2. [preocupação, benefício, trecho] main. <> m: o ~ [o mais importante] the main thing.

essencialmente [esẽnsjaw'mẽntʃil] adv -1. [substancialmente] essentially. -2. [basicamente] essentially.

esta ['eʃta] > este.

estabanado, da [iʃtaba'nadu, da] adj careless.

estabelecer [25] [iʃtabele'se(x)] vt -1. [ger] to establish. -2. [instalar] to set up.
 estabelecer-se vp -1. [firmar-se] to establish o.s. -2. [instalar-se] to be established. -3. [em negócio] to become established. -4. [determinar-se]: ~-se (que) to be established (that).

estabelecimento [iʃtabelesi'mẽntul] m establishment.

estabilidade [iʃtabili'dadʒil] f stability; ~ financeira financial stability.

estabilização [iʃtabiliza'sãwl] f stabilization.

estabilizador [iʃtabiliza'do(x)] (pl -es) m COMPUT transformer.

estabilizar [4] [iʃtabili'za(x)] vt to stabilize.
 estabilizar-se vp to become stable.

estábulo [iʃ'tabulul] m stable.

estaca [iʃ'takal] f -1. [para cravar] stake. -2. [de construção] support. -3. [de barraca] post. -4. loc: voltar à ~ zero to go back to square one.

estacada [iʃta'kadal] f -1. [de proteção] stockade. -2. [fileira] fence.

estação [iʃta'sãwl] (pl -ões) f -1. [de trem, metrô, ônibus] station. -2. [período]: ~ (do ano) season (of the year); ~ de chuvas rainy season; [de colheita]: frutas da ~ fruits of the season. -3. [estância]: ~ de águas spa. -4. [para fins científicos] station. -5. RÁDIO & TV station.

estacar [12] [iʃta'ka(x)] vi to stop short.

estacionamento [iʃtasjona'mẽntul] m -1. [ato] parking. -2. [lugar] car park.

estacionar [4] [iʃtasjo'na(x)] <> vt AUTO to park. <> vi -1. AUTO to park. -2. [não evoluir] to remain stationary.

estacionário, ria [iʃtasjo'narju, rja] adj -1. [parado] stationary. -2. ECON [estagnado] stagnant.

estada [iʃ'tadal], **estadia** [iʃ'tadʒal] f stay.

estádio [iʃ'tadʒjul] m stadium.

estadista [iʃta'dʒiʃtal] mf statesman.

estado [iʃ'tadul] m -1. [ger] state; em bom/mau ~ in good/bad condition; ~ civil marital status; ~ de coisas state of affairs; ~ de espírito state of

mind; ~ **de saúde** (state of) health; **em** ~ **interessante** in an interesting condition, pregnant; ~ **de sítio** state of siege; **em** ~ **de** in a state of; ~ **gasosa/líquido/sólido** gaseous/liquid/solid state. **-2.** *POL* state.
➤ **Estado** *m* [país] state.
estado-maior [iʃˌtadumaˈjɔ(x)] (*pl* **estados-maiores**) *m MIL* general staff *UK*, army/air staff *US*.
Estados Unidos da América *n*: **os** ~ the United States of America.
estadual [iʃtaˈdwaw] (*pl* **-ais**) *adj* [receita, constituição] state (*antes de subst*).
estadunidense [iʃtaduniˈdẽnsil] <> *adj* American. <> *mf* American.
estafa [iʃˈtafa] *f* **-1.** [esgotamento] exhaustion; **ter uma** ~ to be exhausted. **-2.** [fadiga] exhaustion.
estafado, da [iʃtaˈfadu, da] *adj* exhausted.
estafante [iʃtaˈfãntʃil] *adj* exhausting.
estafar [4] [iʃtaˈfa(x)] *vt* to exhaust.
estafeta [iʃtaˈfetal] *m* courier.
estagflação [iʃtagˈflasãw] *f ECON* stagflation.
estagiar [16] [iʃtaˈʒja(x)] *vi*: ~ **(em)** to train (in).
estagiário, ria [iʃtaˈʒjarju, rjal] *m*, *f* trainee.
estágio [iʃˈtaʒul] *m* **-1.** [fase] stage. **-2.** [treinamento] training period.
estagnação [iʃtagnaˈsãw] *f* stagnation.
estagnado, da [iʃtagˈnadu, da] *adj* stagnant.
estagnar [4] [iʃtagˈna(x)] <> *vt* to make stagnant. <> *vi* to stagnate.
➤ **estagnar-se** *vp* to be stagnant.
estalagem [iʃtaˈlaʒẽl] (*pl* **-ns**) *f* inn.
estalar [4] [iʃtaˈla(x)] <> *vt* **-1.** [dedos] to snap. **-2.** [nozes, ovos] to crack. <> *vi* **-1.** [rachar] to crack. **-2.** [crepitar] to crackle.
estaleiro [iʃtaˈlejrul] *m* shipyard.
estalido [iʃtaˈlidul] *m* **-1.** [de dedos] snapping. **-2.** [de chicote, fogos] cracking.
estalo [iʃˈtalul] *m* [de dedos] snap; [de chicote] crack; [de trovão] crash; [de foguete] bang; **dar um** ~ to crack; **me deu um** ~ *fig* I had a flash of inspiration; **de** ~ [de repente] suddenly.
estampa [iʃˈtãnpal] *f* **-1.** [ger] print. **-2.** [aparência] appearance.
estampado, da [iʃtãnˈpadu, da] *adj* **-1.** [tecido] printed. **-2.** *fig* [evidente] etched.
➤ **estampado** *m* **-1.** [tecido] printed cloth. **-2.** [padrão impresso] print.
estampar [4] [iʃtãnˈpa(x)] *vt* **-1.** [imprimir] to print. **-2.** [marcar] to imprint. **-3.** *fig* [mostrar]: **a mulher estampava no rosto seu desespero** the woman's despair was etched on her face.
estamparia [iʃtãnpaˈrial] *f* **-1.** [oficina] print shop, room. **-2.** [tecido] printed material.
estampido [iʃtãnˈpidul] *m* bang.
estancar [12] [iʃtãŋˈka(x)] *vt & vi* to stem *UK*, to staunch *US*.
estância [iʃˈtãnsjal] *f* **-1.** [fazenda] estate. **-2.** [estação]: ~ **hidromineral** spa. **-3.** [estrofe] strophe, stanza.
estandarte [iʃtãnˈdaxtʃil] *m* standard.
estande [iʃˈtãndʒil] *m* stand.

estanho [iʃˈtãɲul] *m* tin.
estanque [iʃˈtãŋkil] *adj* **-1.** [estancado] tight, watertight **-2.** [vedado]: **compartimento** ~ airtight compartment.
estante [iʃˈtãntʃil] *f* **-1.** [móvel] bookcase. **-2.** [suporte] stand.
estapafúrdio, dia [iʃtapaˈfurdʒju, dʒjal] *adj* outlandish.
estar [10] [iʃˈta(x)] *vi* **-1.** [com lugar] to be; [em casa] to be at home, to be in; **ela estará lá à hora certa** she'll be there on time; **estarei no emprego às dez** I'll be at work at ten. **-2.** [exprime estado] to be; **está quebrado** it's out of order; ~ **bem/mal de saúde** to be well/unwell; **está muito calor/frio** it's very hot/cold. **-3.** [manter-se] to be; **estive em casa toda a tarde** I was at home all afternoon; **estive esperando** I was waiting; **estive fora três anos** I lived abroad for three years; **deixe** ~ ... let it be ... **-4.** [em locuções]: **está bem** *ou* **certo!** OK!, all right!
➤ **estar a** *v* + *prep* [relativo a preço] to cost, to be; **o camarão está a 25 reais o quilo** shrimp cost *ou* are 25 reals a kilo.
➤ **estar de** *v* + *prep*: ~ **de baixa/férias** to be on sick leave/vacation; ~ **de saia** to be wearing a skirt; ~ **de vigia** to keep watch.
➤ **estar para** *v* + *prep*: ~ **para fazer algo** to be about to do sthg; **estou para sair** I'm about to go out, I'm on my way out; **ele está para chegar** he'll be here any minute now; **não estou para brincadeiras** I'm not in the mood for silly games.
➤ **estar perante** *v* + *prep* [frente a] to be facing; **você está perante um gênio** you're in the presence of a genius.
➤ **estar por** *v* + *prep* [apoiar] to support; [por realizar]: **a cama está por fazer** the bed hasn't been made yet; **a limpeza está por fazer** the cleaning hasn't been done yet.
➤ **estar sem** *v* + *prep*: **estou sem tempo** I don't have time; **estou sem dinheiro** I don't have any cash; **ele está sem comer há dois dias** he hasn't eaten for two days.
estardalhaço [iʃtaxdaˈʎasul] *m* **-1.** [bulha] racket. **-2.** [ostentação] flamboyance.
estarrecer [25] [iʃtaxeˈse(x)] <> *vt* to appal *UK*, to appall *US*. <> *vi* to be appalled.
estarrecido, da [iʃtaxeˈsidu, da] *adj* shaken.
estatal [iʃtaˈtaw] (*pl* **-ais**) <> *adj* state (*antes de subst*). <> *f* [empresa] state-owned company.
estatelado, da [iʃtateˈladu, da] *adj* [no chão] sprawled.
estatelar-se [4] [iʃtateˈlaxsil] *vp* [cair]: ~**-se (em)** to fall flat (on).
estática [iʃˈtatikal] *f FÍS* static.
estático, ca [iʃˈtatʃiku, kal] *adj* **-1.** [imóvel] still. **-2.** *FÍS* static.
estatístico, ca [iʃtaˈtʃiʃtʃiku, kal] <> *adj* statistical. <> *m*, *f* [profissional] statistician.
➤ **estatística** *f* statistics.
estatização [iʃtatʃizaˈsãw] (*pl* **-ões**) *f* nationalization.

estatizar [4] [iʃtatʃi'za(x)] *vt* to nationalize.
estátua [iʃ'tatwal *f* statue.
estatueta [iʃta'twetal *f* statuette.
estatura [iʃta'tural *f* - **1.** [física] stature; ~ **alta /baixa/mediana** tall/short/medium stature. - **2.** [intelectual, moral] standing.
estatutário, ria [iʃtatu'tarju, rjal *adj* - **1.** [norma] statutory. - **2.** [funcionário]: **funcionário** ~ civil servant.
estatuto [iʃta'tutul *m* statute.
estável [iʃ'tavewl (*pl* -**eis**) *adj* - **1.** [ger] stable. - **2.** [cotação] fixed.
este¹ [ˈeʃtʃil *m* east
este², esta [ˈeʃtʃil <> *adj* this, these (*pl*). <> *pron* this (one), these ones (*pl*).
esteio [iʃ'tejul *m* - **1.** [escora] prop. - **2.** NÁUT chock. - **3.** *fig* [amparo] breadwinner.
esteira [iʃ'tejral *f* - **1.** [tecido] woven mat. - **2.** [usada na praia] reed mat. - **3.** [rolante] moving carpet. - **4.** *fig* [caminho] path; **na** ~ **de** in the course of.
estelionatário, ria [iʃteljona'tarju, rjal *m*, *f* swindler.
estelionato [iʃteljo'natul *m* swindle.
estêncil [iʃ'tẽsiwl (*pl* -**eis**) *m* stencil.
estender [5] [iʃtẽn'de(x)] *vt* - **1.** [ger] to spread. - **2.** [roupa] to hang out. - **3.** [corda, fio] to stretch out. - **4.** [massa] to roll out. - **5.** [pernas, braços, mãos] to stretch out. - **6.** [limites] to extend. - **7.** [oferecer]: ~ **algo para alguém** to give sthg to sb. - **8.** [prolongar] to prolong. - **9.** [fazer abranger]: ~ **algo a alguém/algo** to extend sthg to (include) sb/sthg.
➤ **estender-se** *vp* - **1.** [ocupar]: ~**-se por** to spread out over. - **2.** [durar]: ~**-se (por)** to last (for). - **3.** [alastrar-se]: ~**-se (por)** to spread (throughout). - **4.** [deitar-se]: ~**-se (em)** to lie down (on). - **5.** [falar, escrever muito]: ~**-se (sobre)** to enlarge (upon). - **6.** [abranger]: ~**-se a** to include.
estenodatilografia [iʃtenodatʃiloɡra'fial *f* shorthand typing.
estenodatilógrafo, fa [iʃtenodatʃi'loɡrafu, fal *m*, *f* shorthand typist *UK*, stenographer *US*.
estenografar [4] [iʃtenogra'fa(x)] *vt* to write in shorthand.
estenografia [iʃtenogra'fial *f* shorthand *UK*, stenography *US*.
estenógrafo, fa [iʃte'nɔgrafu, fal *m*, *f* shorthand typist *UK*, stenographer *US*.
estepe [iʃ'tɛpil <> *m* [pneu] spare wheel. <> *f* [vegetação] steppe.
esterco [iʃ'texkul *m* manure.
estéreo [iʃ'tɛrjul *adj* stereo.
estereofônico, ca [iʃterjo'foniku, kal *adj* stereophonic.
estereotipado, da [iʃterjotʃi'padu, dal *adj* stereotypical.
estereotipar [4] [iʃterjotʃi'pa(x)] *vt* to stereotype.
estereótipo [iʃte'rjɔtʃipul *m* stereotype.
estéril [iʃ'tɛriwl (*pl* -**eis**) *adj* - **1.** [ger] sterile. - **2.** [terreno] barren. - **3.** *fig* [inútil, infrutífero] pointless.
esterilidade [iʃterili'dadʒil *f* - **1.** [infertilidade]

sterility. - **2.** [da terra] barrenness. - **3.** [escassez] dearth.
esterilização [iʃteriliza'sãwl (*pl* -**ões**) *f* sterilization.
esterilizado, da [iʃterili'zadu, dal *adj* sterilized.
esterilizador [iʃteriliza'do(x)] *m* sterilizer.
esterilizar [4] [iʃterili'za(x)] *vt* to sterilize.
esterlino, na [iʃtex'linu, nal <> *adj*: **libra** ~ pound sterling. <> *m* sterling.
esteróide [iʃte'rɔjdʒil *m* steroid.
esteta [iʃ'tɛtal *mf* aesthete *UK*, esthete *US*.
esteticista [iʃtetʃi'siʃtal *mf* beautician.
estético, ca [iʃ'tɛtʃiku, kal *adj* - **1.** [artístico] aesthetic *UK*, esthetic *US*. - **2.** [harmonioso] tasteful.
➤ **estética** *f* - **1.** FILOSOFIA aestheticism *UK*, estheticism *US*. - **2.** [beleza] beauty; [do corpo] physical beauty.
estetoscópio [iʃtetoʃ'kɔpjul *m* stethoscope.
estiagem [iʃ'tʃjaʒẽl (*pl* -**ns**) *f* - **1.** [período seco] dry spell. - **2.** [de rio, fonte] drying out.
estiar [16] [iʃ'tʃja(x)l *vi* - **1.** [parar de chover] to stop raining. - **2.** [faltar chuva] to be dry.
estibordo [iʃtʃi'bɔxdul *m* starboard; **a** ~ to starboard.
esticada [iʃtʃi'kadal <> *f*: **dar uma** ~ [espichar-se] to have a stretch. <> *f*: **dar uma** ~ **em** *fam* to procede to.
esticar [12] [iʃtʃi'ka(x)l <> *vt* to stretch. <> *vi* - **1.** [distender-se] to stretch. - **2.** *fam* [prolongar saída]: ~ **(em)** to go on (to).
➤ **esticar-se** *vp* [pessoa] to stretch.
estigma [iʃ'tʃigmal *m* - **1.** [ger] stigma. - **2.** [ferrete] mark; **a Inquisição o condenou a usar o** ~ **de cristão-novo** the Inquisition branded him a neo-Christian.
estigmatizar [4] [iʃtʃigmatʃi'za(x)l *vt* - **1.** [com infâmia] to stigmatize; **eles o estigmatizaram de traidor** they branded him a traitor. - **2.** [com preconceito] to revile.
estilete *m* [punhal] stiletto.
estilhaçar [13] [iʃtʃiʎa'sa(x)l *vt* to shatter.
➤ **estilhaçar-se** *vp* to be shattered.
estilhaço [iʃtʃi'ʎasul *m* - **1.** [de plástico, granada] splinter. - **2.** [de vidro] shard.
estilista [iʃtʃi'liʃtal *mf* - **1.** [escritor] stylist. - **2.** [de moda] fashion designer.
estilístico, ca [iʃtʃi'liʃtʃiku, kal *adj* - **1.** [talento, característica] stylish. - **2.** [análise] stylistic.
estilização [iʃtʃiliza'sãwl (*pl* -**ões**) *f* stylization.
estilizar [4] [iʃtʃili'za(x)l *vt* to stylize.
estilo [iʃ'tʃilul *m* style; ~ **de época** style of the period; **ter** ~ *fig* [ser autêntico] to have real style; **de** ~ [de época] fashionable; ~ **de vida** way of life; **em grande** ~ [com pompa] in grande style.
estima [iʃ'tʃimal *f* - **1.** [apreço] esteem. - **2.** [afeição] affection.
estimação [iʃtʃima'sãwl *f*: **de** ~ prized; **minha caneta de** ~ my favourite pen; **animal de** ~ (family) pet.
estimado, da [iʃtʃi'madu, dal *adj* - **1.** [avaliado] estimated. - **2.** [querido] esteemed.

estimar [4] [iʃtʃi'ma(x)] *vt* **-1.** [ger] to prize. **-2.** [avaliar]: ~ **algo (em)** to estimate sthg (at). **-3.** [desejar]: ~ **as melhoras de alguém** to hope sb gets better; ~ **que** to hope that.

estimativa [iʃtʃima'tʃival *f* estimation; ~ **de custo** estimate; **fazer uma** ~ **de algo** to make an appraisal of sthg.

estimável [iʃtʃi'mavew] (*pl* -**eis**) *adj* **-1.** [avaliável]: ~ **em** reckoned at. **-2.** [digno de respeito] respectable.

estimulação [iʃtʃimula'sãw] *f* stimulation.

estimulante [iʃtʃimu'lãntʃi] <> *adj* stimulating. <> *m* stimulant.

estimular [4] [iʃtʃimu'la(x)] *vt* **-1.** [excitar, ativar] to stimulate. **-2.** [instigar] to incite. **-3.** [incentivar]: ~ **alguém (a fazer algo)** to encourage sb (to do sthg).

estímulo [iʃ'tʃimulu] *m* **-1.** [ger] stimulus. **-2.** [excitação] stimulant. **-3.** [incentivo] motivation.

estio [iʃ'tʃiu] *m* summer.

estipêndio [iʃtʃi'pẽndʒu] *m* stipend.

estipular [4] [iʃtipu'la(x)] *vt* to stipulate.

estiramento [iʃtʃira'mẽntu] *m* MED [distensão] strain.

estirar [4] [iʃtʃi'ra(x)] *vt* **-1.** [alongar] to stretch. **-2.** [estender ao comprido] to stretch out.

➡ **estirar-se** *vp* [deitar-se] to stretch o.s out.

estirpe [iʃ'tʃixpi] *f* lineage.

estiva [iʃ'tʃiva] *f* NÁUT stowage.

estivador, ra [iʃtʃiva'do(x), ra] (*mpl* -**es**, *fpl* -**s**) *m, f* stevedore.

estocada [iʃto'kada] *f* stab.

estocagem [iʃto'kaʒẽ] *f* [provisão] stock.

estocar [12] [iʃto'ka(x)] *vt* **-1.** [armazenar] to stock. **-2.** [dar estocada em] to stab.

Estocolmo [iʃto'kowmu] *n* Stockholm.

estofado, da [iʃto'fadu, da] <> *adj* **-1.** [forrado] upholstered. **-2.** [acolchoado] padded. <> *m* suite.

estofador, ra [iʃtofa'do(x), ra] *m, f* upholsterer.

estofar [4] [iʃto'fa(x)] *vt* **-1.** [revestir] to upholster. **-2.** [acolchoar] to stuff.

estofo [iʃ'toful] *m* **-1.** [revestimento] reupholstery. **-2.** [acolchoamento] stuffing.

estoicismo [iʃtoj'siʒmul] *m* stoicism.

estóico, ca [iʃ'tɔjku, ka] <> *adj* **-1.** FILOSOFIA stoical, stoic. **-2.** *fig* [austero] stoical. <> *m, f fig* [pessoa austera] stoic.

➡ **estóica** *f* FILOSOFIA stoicism.

estojo [iʃ'toʒul] *m* case; ~ **de unhas** manicure set.

estola [iʃ'tɔla] *f* stole.

estomacal [iʃtoma'kaw] (*pl* -**ais**) *adj* stomach (*antes de subst*).

estômago [iʃ'tomagul] *m* **-1.** ANAT stomach; **estar com o** ~ **embrulhado** to have an upset stomach; **forrar o** ~ to have a bite to eat. **-2.** *fig* [paciência]: **ter** ~ **para (fazer) algo** to have the stomach for (doing) sthg.

Estônia [iʃ'tonjal] *n* Estonia.

estoniano, na [iʃto'njãnu, na] <> *adj* Estonian. <> *m, f* Estonian.

➡ **estoniano** *m* [língua] Estonian.

estonteante [iʃtõn'tʃãntʃi] *adj* stunning.

estopa [iʃ'tɔpal *f* tow.

estopim (*pl* -**ns**) *m* **-1.** [de bomba] fuse. **-2.** *fig* [de crise, revolta] trigger.

estoque [iʃ'tɔkil *m* **-1.** [provisão] stock; **em** ~ in stock. **-2.** [local] store.

estória [iʃ'tɔrjal *f* story.

estorricar [12] [iʃtoxi'ka(x)] *vt & vi* to scorch.

estorvar [4] [iʃtox'va(x)] *vt* **-1.** [obstruir] to obstruct. **-2.** [importunar] to disturb.

estorvo [iʃ'toxvul *m* **-1.** [obstáculo] obstacle; [pessoa] hindrance. **-2.** [incômodo] disturbance.

estourado, da [iʃto'radu, da] *adj* **-1.** [temperamental] boisterous. **-2.** *fam* [fatigado] knackered.

estourar [4] [iʃto'ra(x)] <> *vi* **-1.** [bomba] to explode. **-2.** [pneu] to blow up. **-3.** [guerra, revolução] to break out. **-4.** [escândalo] to become public. **-5.** *fig* [rebentar] to burst; **estar estourando de raiva/alegria** to be bursting with rage/joy. **-6.** [ralhar]: ~ **(com alguém)** to explode (at sb). **-7.** [no mais tardar]: **estourando cinco e meia** no later than five-thirty. <> *vt* **-1.** [bomba] to explode. **-2.** [boca-de-fumo] to bust up.

estouro [iʃ'torul *m* **-1.** [ger] explosion. **-2.** *fam*: **ser um** ~ [filme, pessoa] to be a hit; [notícia, carro] to be a sensation.

estouvado, da [iʃto'vadu, da] *adj* [desajuizado] foolhardy.

estrábico, ca [iʃ'trabiku, ka] *adj* cross-eyed.

estrabismo [iʃtra'biʒmul *m* squint, strabismus.

estraçalhar [4] [iʃtrasa'ʎa(x)] *vt* **-1.** [livro, objeto] to tear to shreds. **-2.** [pessoa] to kill.

➡ **estraçalhar-se** *vp* **-1.** [objeto] to smash. **-2.** [pessoa] to smash one another.

estrada [iʃ'trada] *m* **-1.** road; ~ **principal** main road UK, highway US; ~ **secundária** secondary road, B road; ~ **de ferro** railway track UK, railroad US; ~ **de rodagem** public road; ~ **vicinal** link road. **-2.** *fig* [carreira] work; **estar na** ~ to be in the field.

estrado [iʃ'tradul *m* **-1.** [de cama] frame. **-2.** [tablado] platform.

estragado, da [iʃtra'gadu, da] *adj* **-1.** [podre] rotten. **-2.** [danificado] damaged. **-3.** [mimado] spoilt.

estragão [iʃtra'gãw] *m* tarragon.

estraga-prazeres [iʃ,tragapra'zeriʃ] *mf inv* killjoy, spoilsport.

estragar [14] [iʃtra'ga(x)] <> *vt* **-1.** [ger] to spoil. **-2.** [danificar] to damage. <> *vi* [apodrecer] to go off.

➡ **estragar-se** *vp* **-1.** [deteriorar-se] to be ruined. **-2.** [avariar-se] to go wrong. **-3.** [apodrecer] to go rotten.

estrago [iʃ'tragul *m* **-1.** [dano] damage; **fazer um** ~ **em algo** to cause damage to sthg. **-2.** [desperdício] disaster.

estrangeiro, ra [iʃträn'ʒejru, ra] <> *adj* foreign. <> *m, f* [pessoa] foreigner.

➡ **estrangeiro** *m*: **no** ~ abroad.

estrangulador, ra [iʃträngula'do(x), ra] *m, f* strangler.

estrangulamento [iʃtrãŋgula'mẽntul] *m* **-1.** [de pessoa] strangulation. **-2.** [obstrução] blocking.

estrangular [4] [liʃtrãŋgu'la(x)] *vt* to strangle.

estranhamento [iʃtrãɲa'mentul] *m* [espanto] surprise.

estranhar [4] [liʃtrã'ɲa(x)] <> *vt* **-1.** [achar fora do comum] to find strange. **-2.** [surpreender-se com] to be surprised by. **-3.** [não se habituar a] to be unaccustomed to. **-4.** [retrair-se diante de] to feel ill at ease with. **-5.** [hostilizar] to harass. <> *vi* [causar estranheza] to be strange.

➡ **estranhar-se** *vp* [hostilizar-se] to fall out with each other.

estranho, nha [iʃ'trãɲu, ɲal *adj* **-1.** [diferente, estrangeiro] foreign. **-2.** [incomum, desconhecido] strange; **não ser ~ para alguém** to be familiar to sb.

estratagema [iʃtrata'ʒemal *m* stratagem.

estratégia [iʃtra'tɛʒjal *f* strategy.

estratégico, ca [iʃtra'tɛʒiku, kal *adj* strategic.

estrategista [iʃtrate'ʒiʃtal *mf* strategist.

estratificar-se [12] [iʃtratʃifi'kaxsil *vp* **-1.** [em camadas] to be stratified. **-2.** *fig* [cristalizar-se] to take shape.

estrato [iʃ'tratul *m* stratum.

estratosfera [iʃtratoʃ'fɛral *f* stratosphere.

estreante [iʃ'trjãntʃil *adj* debut (*antes de subst*).

estrear [15] [iʃtre'a(x)] <> *vt* **-1.** [roupa, carro] to try out for the first time. **-2.** [filme, show] to premiere. **-3.** [carreira] to start. <> *vi* **-1.** [filme, show] to premiere. **-2.** [artista, jogador] to debut.

estrebaria [iʃtreba'rial *f* stable.

estrebuchar [4] [liʃtrebu'ʃa(x)] *vi* [em agonia] to writhe.

estréia [iʃ'trɛjal *f* **-1.** [de filme, show] premiere. **-2.** [de artista, jogador] debut. **-3.** [de roupa, carro] first time out.

estreitamento [iʃtrejta'mẽntul *m* **-1.** [ger] narrowing. **-2.** [diminuição] shrinking. **-3.** [de relações] strengthening.

estreitar [4] [liʃtrej'ta(x)] <> *vt* **-1.** [diminuir] to shrink. **-2.** [apertar] to narrow. **-3.** [roupa] to constrict. **-4.** [relações, laços] to strengthen. **-5.** [tornar mais rigoroso] to tighten up. <> *vi* [estrada] to narrow.

➡ **estreitar-se** *vp* **-1.** [largura] to narrow. **-2.** [amizade, união] to strengthen.

estreiteza [iʃtrej'tezal *f* narrowness.

estreito, ta [iʃ'trejtu, tal *adj* **-1.** [apertado] narrow. **-2.** [vestido, saia] straight. **-3.** [relação, amizade] strong.

➡ **estreito** *m GEOGR* strait.

estrela [iʃ'trelal *f* **-1.** [ger] star; **~ de cinema** film star *UK*, movie star *US*; **~ cadente** shooting star. **-2.** [sorte] lucky star; **ter boa/má ~** to have good/bad luck.

estrela-de-davi [iʃ'treladzidavil (*pl* estrelas-de-davi) *f* Star of David.

estrelado, da [iʃtre'ladu, dal *adj* **-1.** [céu, noite] starry. **-2.** [ovo] fried.

estrela-do-mar [iʃtreladu'ma(x)] (*pl* estrelas-do-mar) *f* starfish.

estrelar [4] [liʃtre'la(x)] *vt* **-1.** [filme, peça] to star. **-2.** [ovos] to fry.

estrelato [iʃtre'latul *m*: **o ~** stardom.

estrelinha [iʃtre'liɲal *f* [fogo de artifício] sparkler.

estrelismo [iʃtre'liʒmul *m prima donna-ish behaviour*.

estremecer [25] [liʃtreme'se(x)] <> *vt* to shake. <> *vi* **-1.** [tremer de espanto] to shiver. **-2.** [sacudir] to shudder. **-3.** [sofrer abalo] to be shaken.

estremecido, da [iʃtreme'sidu, dal *adj* [amizade, união] shaken.

estremecimento [iʃtremesi'mẽntul *m* shaking.

estrepar-se [4] [iʃtre'paxsil *vp* to come unstuck.

estrépito [iʃ'trɛpitul *m* racket; **fazer ~** to make a racket; **com ~** noisily.

estrepitoso, osa [iʃtrepi'tozu, ɔzal *adj* **-1.** [ruidoso] noisy. **-2.** *fig* [sensacional] resounding.

estressado, da [iʃtre'sadu, dal *adj* stressed (out).

estressante [iʃtre'sãntʃil *adj* stressful.

estressar [iʃtre'sa(x)] *vt* to cause stress to.

➡ **estressar-se** *vp* to become stressed.

estresse [iʃ'trɛʃil *m* stress.

estria [iʃ'trial *f* **-1.** [sulco] groove. **-2.** [na pele] stretch mark.

estribeira [iʃtri'bejral *f*: **perder as ~s** *fam* to lose one's head.

estribilho [iʃtri'biʎul *m MÚS* chorus.

estribo [iʃ'tribul *m* **-1.** [de cavalo] stirrup. **-2.** [degrau] step.

estricnina [iʃtrik'ninal *f* strychnine.

estridente [iʃtri'dẽntʃil *adj* strident.

estrilar [4] [liʃtri'la(x)] *vi fam* **-1.** [vociferar] to make a shrill noise. **-2.** [reclamar] to clamour.

estrilo [iʃ'trilul *m fam*: **dar um ~** to fly off the handle.

estripulia [iʃtripu'lial *f* mischief.

estritamente [iʃtrita'mẽntʃil *adv* [à risca] to the letter.

estrito, ta [iʃ'tritu, tal *adj* **-1.** [rigoroso] strict. **-2.** [exato] precise; **no sentido ~ da palavra** in the strict sense of the word.

estrofe [iʃ'trɔfil *f* stanza.

estrogênio [iʃtro'ʒenjul *m* oestrogen.

estrogonofe [iʃtrogo'nɔfil *m CULIN* stroganoff.

estrondo [iʃ'trõndul *m* rumble.

estrondoso, osa [iʃtrõn'dozu, ɔzal *adj* **-1.** [ruidoso] roaring. **-2.** [espetacular] spectacular.

estropiado, da [iʃtro'pjadu, dal *adj* **-1.** [aleijado] crippled. **-2.** [exausto] worn out.

estropiar [16] [iʃtro'pja(x)] *vt* **-1.** [aleijar] to cripple. **-2.** [cansar] to tire out. **-3.** *fig* [mutilar] to mutilate. **-4.** *fig* [pronunciar mal] to mispronounce.

estrume [iʃ'trumil *m* manure.

estrupício *m fam pej* [pessoa estúpida]: **ser um ~** to be an idiot.

estrutura [iʃtru'tural *f* **-1.** *CONST* structure. **-2.** [armação] frame.

estruturação [iʃtrutura'sãw] (*pl* -ões) *f* structuring.

estrutural [iʃtrutu'rawl (*pl* -ais) *adj* structural.

estruturalismo [iʃtrutura'liʒmul] *m* structuralism.

estruturalista [iʃtrutura'liʃtal] *adj* structuralist.

estruturar [4] [iʃtrutu'ra(x)] *vt* to structure.

estuário [iʃ'twarjul] *m* estuary.

estudado, da [iʃtu'dadu, dal] *adj* studied.

estudante [iʃtu'dãntʃi] *mf* student.

estudantil [iʃtudãn'tʃiw] (*pl* -**is**) *adj* student *(antes de subst).*

estudar [4] [iʃtu'da(x)] *vt* & *vi* to study.

estúdio [iʃ'tudʒjul] *m* studio.

estudioso, osa [iʃtu'dʒjozu, ɔzal] <> *adj* studious. <> *m, f* expert.

estudo [iʃ'tudul] *m* study; **ter muito** ~ to be very learned; ~ **de caso** case study; ~ **de viabilidade** feasibility study.

> **estudos** *mpl* [formação escolar] studies.

estufa [iʃ'tufal] *f* -**1.** [para plantas] greenhouse. -**2.** [aquecedor] stove.

estufar [4] [iʃtu'fa(x)] *vt* -**1.** [aquecer em estufa] to heat in the oven. -**2.** [encher] to stuff; **ele estufou o peito de orgulho** *fig* he puffed (his chest out) with pride; **o dinheiro estufava sua carteira** his wallet was stuffed with money. -**3.** *CULIN* [carne] to stew.

estupefação [iʃtupefa'sãwl] *f* [espanto] amazement.

estupefato, ta [iʃtupe'fatu, tal] *adj* [espantado] amazed.

estupendo, da [iʃtu'pẽndu, dal] *adj* -**1.** [maravilhoso] wonderful. -**2.** [espantoso] amazing.

estupidamente [iʃtupida'mẽntʃil] *adv* -**1.** [de maneira absurda] stupidly. -**2.** [extremamente] extremely; **uma cerveja estupidamente gelada, por favor** an extremely cold beer, please.

estupidez [iʃtupi'deʃl] *f* -**1.** [condição] stupidity. -**2.** [ato] stupid thing. -**3.** *fam* [grosseria]: **não é a primeira vez que ela me faz uma** ~ it is not the first time he's been rude to me.

estúpido, da [iʃ'tupidu, dal] <> *adj* -**1.** [burro] stupid. -**2.** [grosseiro] rude; **um calor** ~ *fig* an unbearable heat. <> *m, f* -**1.** [pessoa burra] stupid person. -**2.** [pessoa grosseira] rude person.

estupor [iʃtu'po(x)] *m* -**1.** [estado] stupor. -**2.** [estarrecimento] amazement.

estuporado, da [iʃtupo'radu, dal] *adj* -**1.** [paralisado] stupefied. -**2.** [estarrecido] stunned. -**3.** *fam* [estragado] messed up. -**4.** *fam* [cansado] wiped out. -**5.** *fam* [ferido] messed up.

estuporar [iʃtupo'ra(x)] *vt* -**1.** [cair em estupor] to paralise. -**2.** [assustar] to shock. -**3.** [arruinar] to smash.

estuprador [iʃtupra'do(x)] *m* rapist.

estuprar [4] [iʃtu'pra(x)] *vt* to rape.

estupro [iʃ'tuprul] *m* rape.

estuque [iʃ'tukil] *m* stucco.

esturricado, da [iʃtuxi'kadu, dal] *adj* dry.

esturricar [12] [iʃtuxi'ka(x)] <> *vt* to dry. <> *vi* to become dry.

esvair-se [68] [iʒva'ixsil] *vp* -**1.** [desaparecer] to disappear. -**2.** [desmaiar] to faint. -**3.** *loc:* ~ **em sangue** to bleed copiously; ~ **em lágrimas** to dissolve into tears.

esvaziamento [iʒvazja'mẽntul] *m* -**1.** [desocupação] emptying. -**2.** [evacuação] evacuation. -**3.** [perda de importância] nullification.

esvaziar [16] [iʒva'zja(x)] *vt* -**1.** [desocupar] to empty. -**2.** [beber de uma só vez] to drain. -**3.** [tirar a importância de] to nullify.

> **esvaziar-se** *vp* [tornar-se vazio] to empty.

esverdeado, da [iʒvex'dʒadu, dal] *adj* greenish.

esvoaçante [iʒvwa'sãntʃil] *adj* fluttering.

esvoaçar [13] [iʒvwa'sa(x)] *vi* to flutter.

ET (*abrev de* **Extra Terrestre**) *m* ET.

eta [ˈetal] *interj* blast; ~ **ferro!** gee whiz!

ETA (*abrev de* **Euskadi Ta Askatasuna**) *m* ETA.

etapa [eˈtapal] *f* stage; **por** ~**s** in stages.

etário, ria [eˈtarju, rjal] *adj* aged.

etc. (*abrev de* **et cetera**) etc.

éter [ˈɛte(x)] *m* ether.

etéreo, rea [eˈtɛrju, rjal] *adj* ethereal.

eternidade [etexniˈdadʒil] *f* eternity.

eternizar [4] [etexniˈza(x)] *vt* -**1.** [tornar eterno] to eternalize. -**2.** [imortalizar] to immortalize. -**3.** *fam* [prolongar] to drag out.

> **eternizar-se** *vp* -**1.** [tornar-se eterno] to become eternal. -**2.** [imortalizar-se] to become immortal. -**3.** *fam* [prolongar-se] to drag on.

eterno, na [eˈtɛxnu, nal] *adj* eternal.

Ethernet [etexˈnetil] *f* *COMPUT* Ethernet®.

ético, ca [ˈɛtʃiku, kal] *adj* ethical.

> **ética** *f* ethics *(pl).*

etimologia [etʃimoloˈʒial] *f* etymology.

etíope [eˈtʃiopil] <> *adj* Ethiopian. <> *mf* Ethiopian.

Etiópia [eˈtʃiˈɔpjal] *n* Ethiopia.

etiqueta [etʃiˈketal] *f* -**1.** [ger] label; ~ **adesiva** sticky label. -**2.** [boas maneiras] etiquette. -**3.** [de preço] ticket; [de roupa] label.

etiquetar [4] [etʃikeˈta(x)] *vt* to label.

etnia [etʃˈnial] *f* ethnic group.

étnico, ca [ˈɛtʃniku, kal] *adj* ethnic.

etnocentrismo [etʃnosẽnˈtriʒmul] *m* ethnocentrism.

etnografia [etʃnograˈfial] *f* ethnography.

etnologia [etʃnoloˈʒial] *f* ethnology.

etos [ˈɛtuʃl] *m* *inv* ethos.

eu [ˈewl] *pron* I; **e** ~ **?** what about me?; **sou** ~ it's me; ~ **mesmo** *ou* **próprio** (I) myself.

EUA (*abrev de* **Estados Unidos da América**) *n* USA.

eucalipto [ewkaˈliptul] *m* eucalyptus.

eucaristia [ewkariʃˈtʃial] *f* Eucharist.

eufemismo [ewfeˈmiʒmul] *m* euphemism.

eufonia [ewfoˈnial] *f* euphony.

euforia [ewfoˈrial] *f* euphoria.

eufórico, ca [ewˈfɔriku, kal] *adj* euphoric.

eunuco [ewˈnukul] *m* eunuch.

euro [ˈewrul] *m* [moeda] euro.

eurodólar [ewroˈdɔla(x)] *m* Eurodollar.

Europa [ewˈrɔpal] *n* Europe.

europeizar [4.19] [ewropejiˈza(x)] *vt* to Europeanize.

➡ **europeizar-se** *vp* to become Europeanized.

europeu, péia [ewro'pew, pɛja] ◇ *adj* European. ◇ *m, f* European.

eutanásia [ewta'nazja] *f* euthanasia.

evacuação [evakwa'sãw] (*pl* -ões) *f* evacuation.

evacuar [4] [eva'kwa(x)] ◇ *vt* -**1.** [desocupar] to evacuate. -**2.** [expelir]: ~ **sangue** to bleed; ~ **fezes** to defecate. ◇ *vi* [defecar] to evacuate.

evadir [6] [eva'dʒi(x)] *vt* -**1.** [evitar] to avoid. -**2.** [eludir] to evade.

➡ **evadir-se** *vp* [escapar] to escape.

evanescente [evane'sẽntʃi] *adj* evanescent.

evangelho [evãn'ʒɛʌu] *m* Gospel; **o** ~ **segundo Mateus** the Gospel according to Matthew.

evangélico, ca [evãn'ʒɛliku, ka] ◇ *adj* evangelical. ◇ *m, f* [pessoa] evangelist.

evangelização [evãnʒeliza'sãw] (*pl* -ões) *f* conversion (to Christianity).

evangelizar [evãnʒeli'za(x)] *vt* to convert (to Christianity).

evaporação [evapora'sãw] (*pl* -ões) *f* evaporation.

evaporar [4] [evapo'ra(x)] ◇ *vt* [vaporizar] to evaporate. ◇ *vi* to evaporate.

➡ **evaporar-se** *vp* to evaporate.

evasão [eva'zãw] (*pl* -ões) *f* -**1.** [fuga] escape. -**2.** *fig* [evasiva] evasion.

evasivo, va [eva'zivu, va] *adj* evasive.

➡ **evasiva** *f* evasion.

evento [e'vẽntu] *m* event.

eventual [evẽn'twaw] (*pl* -ais) *adj* chance (*antes de subst*).

eventualidade [evẽntwali'dadʒi] *f* eventuality.

eventualmente [evẽntwal'mẽntʃi] *adv* [às vezes] occasionally.

Everest [eve'rɛʃtʃi] *n* : **o** ~ (Mount) Everest.

evidência [evi'dẽnsja] *f* evidence; **em** ~ [destacado] obvious.

evidenciar [16] [evidẽn'sja(x)] *vt* -**1.** [comprovar] to prove. -**2.** [mostrar] to be evidence of. -**3.** [destacar] to show clearly.

➡ **evidenciar-se** *vp* -**1.** [comprovar-se] to be proven. -**2.** [destacar-se] to be shown clearly.

evidente [evi'dẽntʃi] *adj* obvious.

evidentemente [evidẽntʃi'mẽntʃi] *adv* clearly.

evitar [4] [evi'ta(x)] *vt* -**1.** [fugir a] to avoid; ~ **fazer algo** to avoid doing sthg. -**2.** [impedir] to prevent.

evitável [evi'tavew] (*pl* -eis) *adj* avoidable.

evocação [evoka'sãw] (*pl* -ões) *f* recollection.

evocar [12] [evo'ka(x)] *vt* [trazer à lembrança] to bring to mind.

evolução [evolu'sãw] (*pl* -ões) *f* -**1.** BIOL evolution. -**2.** [desenrolar] development. -**3.** [movimento] expansion. -**4.** MIL exercise.

evoluído, da [evo'lwidu, da] *adj* -**1.** [adiantado] advanced. -**2.** [aberto] open.

evoluir [74] [evo'lwi(x)] *vi* -**1.** [espécie] to evolve. -**2.** [adiantar-se] to progress.

ex. (*abrev de* **exemplo**) e.g.

exacerbação [ezaseba'sãw] *f* -**1.** [ger] exacerbation. -**2.** [irritação] provocation.

exacerbante [ezasex'bãntʃi] *adj* [intensificador] exacerbating.

exacerbar [4] [ezasex'ba(x)] *vt* -**1.** [intensificar] to exacerbate. -**2.** [irritar] to provoke.

➡ **exacerbar-se** *vp* -**1.** [intensificar-se] to be exacerbated. -**2.** [irritar-se] to be provoked.

exagerado, da [ezaʒe'radu, da] ◇ *adj* exaggerated. ◇ *m, f*: **o que ele diz é típico de um** ~ what he says is typical of an exaggerator.

exagerar [4] [ezaʒe'ra(x)] *vt* & *vi* to exaggerate.

exagero [eza'ʒeru] *m* exaggeration.

exalação [ezala'sãw] (*pl* -ões) *f* exhalation.

exalar [4] [eza'la(x)] *vt* to exhale.

exaltação [ezawta'sãw] *f* -**1.** [engrandecimento] exaltation. -**2.** [irritação] irritation. -**3.** [excitação] excitement.

exaltado, da [ezaw'tadu, da] *adj* -**1.** [facilmente irritável] irritable. -**2.** [fanático] fanatical. -**3.** [exacerbado] irritated.

exaltar [4] [ezaw'ta(x)] *vt* -**1.** [engrandecer] to exalt. -**2.** [irritar] to irritate. -**3.** [excitar] to excite.

➡ **exaltar-se** *vp* [irritar-se] to become irritated.

exame [e'zãmi] *m* -**1.** [ger] examination; **fazer um** ~ to have an examination; ~ **de sangue** blood test. -**2.** EDUC [teste] examination, exam; **fazer um** ~ to sit an examination; ~ **de direção** driving test. -**3.** [inspeção] inspection.

examinador, ra [ezamina'do(x), ra] ◇ *adj* examining. ◇ *m, f* examiner.

examinar [4] [ezami'na(x)] *vt* -**1.** [ger] to examine. -**2.** [inspecionar] to inspect.

exasperação [ezaʃpera'sãw] *f* exasperation.

exasperado, da [ezaʃpe'radu, da] *adj* exasperated.

exasperador, ra [ezaʃpera'do(x), ra] *adj* exasperating.

exasperante [ezaʃpe'rãntʃi] *adj* exasperating.

exasperar [4] [ezaʃpe'ra(x)] *vt* to exasperate.

➡ **exasperar-se** *vp* to become exasperated.

exatamente [ezata'mẽntʃi] *adv* exactly.

exatidão [ezatʃi'dãw] *f* -**1.** [precisão] accuracy. -**2.** [perfeição] perfection.

exato, ta [e'zatu, ta] *adj* -**1.** [preciso] exact. -**2.** [correto] correct, right.

exaurir [6] [ezaw'ri(x)] *vt* [esgotar] to exhaust.

➡ **exaurir-se** *vp* to be exhausted.

exaustão [ezawʃ'tãw] *f* exhaustion.

exaustivo, va [ezawʃ'tʃivu, va] *adj* -**1.** [esgotante] exhausting. -**2.** [completo] exhaustive.

exausto, ta [e'zawʃtu, ta] ◇ *pp* ▷ **exaurir**. ◇ *adj* exhausted.

exaustor [ezawʃ'to(x)] (*pl* -es) *m* extractor fan.

exceção [ese'sãw] (*pl* -ões) *f*: **com** ~ **de** except for, with the exception of.

excedente [ese'dẽntʃi] ◇ *adj* excess (*antes de subst*). ◇ *m* -**1.** COM surplus. -**2.** [aluno] student on waiting list.

exceder [5] [ese'de(x)] *vt* exceed.

➡ **exceder-se** *vp* [cometer excessos] to go too far.

excelência [ese'lẽnsja] f -1. [primazia] excellence; **por ~ par** excellence. -2. [tratamento]: **(Vossa) Excelência** Your Excellency.

excelente [ese'lẽntʃi] adj excellent.

excelentíssimo, ma [eselẽn'tʃisimu, ma] adj superl [tratamento] most excellent; **~ Senhor** Your Excellence; **o ~ senhor presidente da república** His Excellency, the president of the republic.

excelso, sa [e'sɛwsu, sa] adj -1. [sublime] sublime. -2. [excelente] excellent.

excentricidade [esẽntrisi'dadʒi] f eccentricity.

excêntrico, ca le'sẽntriku, ka] <> adj eccentric. <> m, f eccentric.

excepcional [esepsjo'naw] (pl -ais) <> adj -1. [extraordinário, excelente] exceptional. -2. MED disabled. <> mf MED [pessoa] person with special needs.

excepcionalidade [esepsjonali'dadʒi] f -1. [condição de extraordinário] exceptional nature. -2. [excelência] exceptional quality.

excepcionalmente [esepsjonaw'mẽntʃil adv exceptionally.

excerto [e'sɛxtul m excerpt.

excessivamente [esesiva'mẽntʃi] adv excessively.

excessivo, va [ese'sivu, va] adj excessive.

excesso [e'sɛsul m -1. [ger] excess; **~ de peso** [obesidade] excess weight; [em bagagem] excess baggage; **~ de velocidade** excessive speed. -2. COM surplus. -3. [desmando]: **cometer ~s** to go too far.

exceto [e'sɛtul prep except.

excetuar [4] [ese'twa(x)] vt to except.

excitação [esita'sãwl f -1. [agitação] excitement. -2. [sexual] arousal.

excitamento [esita'mẽntul m [agitação] excitement.

excitado, da [esi'tadu, da] adj -1. [agitado] excited. -2. [sexualmente] aroused.

excitante [esi'tãntʃi] adj -1. [ger] stimulating; **uma droga ~** a stimulant. -2. [filme] exciting.

excitar [4] [esi'ta(x)] vt -1. [agitar] to excite. -2. [sexualmente] to arouse. -3. [incitar] to incite.

  ➡ excitar-se vp -1. [agitar-se] to become excited. -2. [sexualmente] to become aroused.

exclamação [iʃklama'sãwl (pl -ões) f exclamation.

exclamar [4] [iʃkla'ma(x)] vi to exclaim.

exclamativo, va [iʃklama'tʃivu, va] adj exclamatory; **ponto de ~** exclamation mark.

excluir [74] [iʃklu'i(x)] vt -1. [eliminar] to exclude. -2. [omitir]: **~ algo/alguém de** to exclude sthg/sb from. -3. [privar]: **~ algo/alguém de** to leave sthg/sb out of. -4. [por incompatibilidade] to preclude.

exclusão [iʃklu'zãwl (pl -ões) f exclusion.

exclusividade [iʃkluzivi'dadʒi] f -1. [uso, posse] exclusivity. -2. COM [direito] sole rights.

exclusivista [iʃkluzi'viʃta] <> adj [individualista] self-centred. <> mf self-centred person.

exclusivo, va [iʃklu'zivu, va] adj exclusive.

excomungado, da [iʃkomũŋ'gadu, da] <> adj RELIG excommunicated. <> m, f excommunicated person.

excomungar [14] [iʃkomũŋ'ga(x)] vt to excommunicate.

excreção [iʃkre'sãwl (pl -ões) f -1. BIOL excretion. -2. [substância excretada] excreta.

excremento [iʃkre'mẽntul m excrement.

excretar [iʃkre'ta(x)] vt [expelir] to excrete.

excruciante [iʃkru'sjãntʃil adj excruciating.

excursão [iʃkux'sãwl (pl -ões) f -1. [ger] excursion. -2. [em caminhada] walk, ramble.

excursionar [4] [iʃkuxsjo'na(x)] vi: **~ (por)** to tour.

excursionista [iʃkuxsjo'niʃtal mf [turista] tourist; [por um dia] day-tripper; [em caminhada] walker, rambler.

execrar [4] [eze'kra(x)] vt to execrate.

execrável [eze'kravewl (pl -eis) adj execrable.

execução [ezeku'sãwl (pl -ões) f -1. [ger] execution. -2. [de peça musical] performance.

executante [ezeku'tãntʃil <> adj [de peça musical] performing. <> mf -1. [músico] performer. -2. [jur] executor.

executar [4] [ezeku'ta(x)] vt -1. [ger] to execute. -2. [peça musical] to perform.' -3. [cumprir] to carry out.

executivo, va [ezeku'tʃivu, va] <> adj executive. <> m, f executive.

executor, ra [ezeku'to(x), ral m, f executor.

exemplar [ezẽn'pla(x)] (pl -es) <> adj [modelar] exemplary. <> m -1. [de livro, jornal] copy. -2. [peça] example. -3. [modelo] model. -4. BIOL [espécie] specimen.

exemplificação [ezẽnplifika'sãwl (pl -ões) f exemplification.

exemplificar [ezẽnplifi'ka(x)] vt to exemplify.

exemplo [e'zẽnplul m -1. [ger] example; **por ~** for example; **bom/mau ~** good/bad example; **dar o ~** to set an example; **seguir o ~ de** to follow the example of; **ser um ~ de algo** to be a model of sthg; **a ~ de** just like. -2. [lição]: **servir de ~ a alguém** to serve as a warning to sb.

exéquias [ẽ'zɛkjaʃl fpl funeral rites.

exeqüível [ezeẽkwivewl (pl -eis) adj feasible.

exercer [25] [ezex'se(x)] vt -1. [desempenhar] to carry out; [profissão] to practise UK, to practice US. -2. [fazer sentir]: **~ algo (sobre)** to exert sthg (on).

exercício [ezex'sisjul m -1. [ger] exercise; **fazer ~** to exercise; **em ~** [presidente, diretor] in office; [professor] in service; [de profissão] practising; [de direitos] excercising; **em pleno ~ de suas faculdades mentais** in full command of one's mental faculties. -2. EDUC exercise. -3. COM: **~ anterior /corrente** previous/current financial year.

exercitar [4] [ezexsi'ta(x)] vt -1. [ger] to exercise. -2. [praticar, treinar] to practise UK, to practise US.

  ➡ exercitar-se vp [adestrar-se] to take exercise.

exército [e'zɛxsitul m army.

exibição [ezibi'sãw] (*pl* **-ões**) *f* **-1.** [demonstração] exhibition; **ser pura** ~ [ser falso] to be just for show. **-2.** [do corpo] exhibition. **-3.** [de filme, obra de arte] exhibition.

exibicionismo [ezibisjo'niʒmu] *m* **-1.** [ostentação] ostentation. **-2.** *PSIC* exhibitionism.

exibicionista [ezibisjo'niʃta] <> *adj* [ostentativo] ostentatious. <> *mf*-**1.** [pessoa] show-off. **-2.** *PSIC* exhibitionist.

exibido, da [ezi'bidu, da] *fam* <> *adj* [exibicionista] flamboyant. <> *m, f* [pessoa] exhibitionist.

exibidor, ra [ezibi'do(x), ra] <> *adj* [que exibe] exhibiting. <> *mf* [dono de cinema] cinema owner.

exibir [6] [ezi'bi(x)] *vt* **-1.** [ger] to show. **-2.** [ostentar] to exhibit. **-3.** [expor] [obra de arte] to exhibit.
  ➡ **exibir-se** *vp* **-1.** [mostrar-se] to show off. **-2.** [indecentemente] to expose o.s.

exigência [ezi'ʒẽnsja] *f* **-1.** [imposição] demand. **-2.** [requisito] requirement. **-3.** [rigor] urgent request.

exigente [ezi'ʒẽntʃi] *adj* [rigoroso] demanding.

exigir [52] [ezi'ʒi(x)] *vt* **-1.** [reclamar] to demand; ~ **que alguém faça algo** to demand that sb do sthg. **-2.** [requerer] to require.

exíguo, gua [e'zigwu, gwa] *adj* **-1.** [diminuto] tiny. **-2.** [minguado] meagre.

exilado, da [ezi'ladu, da] <> *adj* [pessoa] exiled. <> *m, f* [pessoa] exile.

exilar [4] [ezi'la(x)] *vt* to exile.
  ➡ **exilar-se** *vp* to be exiled.

exílio [e'zilju] *m* **-1.** [ger] exile. **-2.** [expatriação] deportation.

exímio, mia [e'zimju, mja] *adj* [excelente] excellent.

eximir [6] [ezi'mi(x)] *vt* : ~ **alguém de algo** to exempt sb from sthg.
  ➡ **eximir-se** *vp*: ~**-se de algo** to excuse o.s. from sthg.

existência [eziʃ'tẽnsja] *f* existence.

existencial [eziʃtẽn'sjaw] (*pl* **-ais**) *adj* existential.

existencialismo [eziʃtẽnsja'liʒmu] *m* existentialism.

existente [eziʃ'tẽntʃi] *adj* **-1.** [que existe] existing. **-2.** [vivente] living.

existir [6] [eziʃ'tʃi(x)] *vi* **-1.** [haver] to be. **-2.** [viver] to exist. **-3.** *loc* [ser fantástico]: **não** ~ *fam* to be incredible; **este sorvete não existe!** this ice cream is incredible!

êxito [e'zitu] *m* **-1.** [sucesso] success; **ter/não ter** ~ **(em)** to be successful/unsuccessful (in). **-2.** [filme, música]: **ser um** ~ to be a success, to be a hit.

êxodo [e'zodu] *m* exodus; ~ **rural** rural exodus.

exoneração [ezonera'sãw] (*pl* **-ões**) *f* exoneration.

exonerar [4] [ezone'ra(x)] *vt* **-1.** [demitir]: ~ **alguém de algo** to exonerate sb from sthg. **-2.** [desobrigar]: ~ **alguém de algo** to exonerate sb from sthg.
  ➡ **exonerar-se** *vp* **-1.** [demitir-se]: ~**-se de algo** to exonerate o.s. from sthg. **-2.** [desobrigar-se]: ~**-se de algo** to release o.s. from sthg.

exorbitância [ezoxbi'tãnsja] *f* **-1.** [excesso] excess. **-2.** *fam* [preço excessivo] extortionate price.

exorcismo [ezox'siʒmu] *m* exorcism.

exorcista [ezox'siʃta] *mf* exorcist.

exorcizar [4] [ezoxsi'za(x)] *vt* to exorcize.

exortar [4] [ezox'ta(x)] *vt*: ~ **alguém a fazer algo** to exhort sb to do sthg.

exótico, ca [e'zotʃiku, ka] *adj* exotic.

exotismo [ezo'tʃiʒmu] *m* exoticism.

expandir [6] [iʃpãn'dʒi(x)] *vt* [ger] to spread.
  ➡ **expandir-se** *vp* **-1.** [dilatar-se] to spread, to be spread. **-2.** [ser expansivo] to be expansive.

expansão [iʃpãn'sãw] (*pl* **-ões**) *f* **-1.** [ato] expansion. **-2.** [efusão] outpouring.

expansionista [iʃpãsjo'niʃta] <> *adj* expansionist. <> *mf* expansionist.

expansividade [iʃpãnsivi'dadʒi] *f* expansiveness.

expansivo, va [iʃpã'sivu, va] *adj* expansive.

expatriação [iʃpatrja'sãw] (*pl* **-ões**) *f* expatriation.

expatriado, da [iʃpa'trjadu, da] <> *adj* [pessoa] expatriated. <> *m, f* [pessoa] expatriate.

expatriar [16] [iʃpa'trja(x)] *vt* to expatriate.

expectativa [iʃpekta'tʃiva] *f* expectation; **na** ~ **de** in the expectation of; ~ **de vida** life expectancy.

expectorante [iʃpekto'rãntʃi] <> *adj* expectorant. <> *m* expectorant.

expectorar [4] [iʃpekto'ra(x)] *vt & vi* to expectorate.

expedição [iʃpedʒi'sãw] (*pl* **-ões**) *f* **-1.** [de mercadorias] dispatch. **-2.** [por navio] shipment. **-3.** [por correio] dispatch. **-4.** [viagem] expedition. **-5.** [de documento] issue.

expedidor, ra [iʃpedʒi'do(x), ra] *adj* forwarding.

expediência [iʃpe'dʒjẽnsja] *f* [desembaraço, diligência] efficiency.

expediente [iʃpe'dʒjẽntʃi] <> *adj* [desembaraçado, diligente] efficient; **ser** ~ to be efficient. <> *m* **-1.** [horário] office hours; **durante o** ~ during office hours; **fora do** ~ out of office hours; ~ **administrativo/bancário** banking/business hours; **meio** ~ part-time. **-2.** [pessoal] resourceful. **-3.** [desembaraço, diligência]: **ter** ~ to be resourceful. **-4.** [meios, recursos] expedient. **-5.** [correspondência] correspondence.

expedir [70] [iʃpe'dʒi(x)] *vt* **-1.** [carta, mercadoria] to send. **-2.** [documento etc] to issue.

expedito, ta [iʃpe'dʒitu, ta] *adj* **-1.** [pessoa] efficient. **-2.** [trabalho, solução] expeditious.

expelir [57] [iʃpe'li(x)] *vt* to expel.

experiência [iʃpe'rjẽnsja] *f* experience; **em** ~ on trial.

experienciar [16] [iʃperjẽn'sja(x)] *vt* to experience.

experiente [iʃpe'rjẽntʃi] *adj* experienced.

experimentação [iʃperimẽnta'sãw] (*pl* **-ões**) *f* experimentation.

experimentado, da [iʃperimẽn'tadu, da] *adj* **-1.**

[experimento] experienced. **-2.** [testado] tested. **-3.** [provado] tried.

experimental [iʃperimĕn'tawl] *(pl -ais) adj* experimental.

experimentar [4] [iʃperimĕn'ta(x)] *vt* **-1.** [testar] to test. **-2.** [provar- comida, bebida] to try; [- roupa] to try on. **-3.** [sofrer] to go through. **-4.** [sentir] to experience.

experimento [iʃperi'mĕntul] *m* experiment.

expiação [iʃpja'sãwl] *(pl -ões) f*: ~ **(de algo)** atonement (for sthg).

expiar [16] [iʃ'pja(x)] *vt* to atone for.

expiatório, ria [iʃpja'tɔrju, rjal *adj* ▷ **bode.**

expiração [iʃpira'sãwl] *(pl -ões) f* **-1.** [de ar] exhalation. **-2.** [fim de prazo] expiry.

expirar [4] [iʃpi'ra(x)] <> *vt* [ar] to exhale. <> *vi* **-1.** [encerrar] to expire. **-2.** [morrer] to die.

explanação [iʃplana'sãwl *(pl-ões) f* explanation.

explanar [4] [iʃpla'na(x)] *vt* to explain.

explicação [iʃplika'sãwl *(pl-ões) f* explanation.

explicar [12] [iʃpli'ka(x)] *vt* & *vi* to explain.
  ⏺ **explicar-se** *vp* [justificar-se] to explain o.s.

explicativo, va [iʃplika'tʃivu, val *adj* explanatory.

explicável [iʃpli'kavewl *(pl -eis) adj* [justificável] explainable.

explicitar [4] [iʃplisi'ta(x)] *vt* to make explicit.

explícito, ta [iʃ'plisitu, tal *adj* explicit.

explodir [6] [iʃplo'di(x)] <> *vi* **-1.** [bomba, avião, carro] to explode. **-2.** *fig* [não se conter] to burst; ~ **de** to be bursting with; ~ **em** to burst into. <> *vt* **-1.** [bomba] to detonate. **-2.** [edifício, avião] to blow up.

exploração [iʃplora'sãwl *(pl -ões) f* **-1.** [ger] exploration. **-2.** [emprego] use. **-3.** [de negócio] running. **-4.** [agrícola] cultivation, growing. **-5.** [abuso] exploitation. **-6.** [exorbitância]: **ser uma** ~ to be exorbitant.

explorador, ra [iʃplora'do(x), ral <> *adj* **-1.** [pessoa, companhia] exploring, exploratory. **-2.** [aproveitador] exploitative. <> *m, f* **-1.** [desbravador] explorer. **-2.** [aproveitador] exploiter.

explorar [4] [iʃplo'ra(x)] *vt* **-1.** [ger] to exploit. **-2.** [empregar] to use. **-3.** [negócio] to run. **-4.** [desbravar] to explore.

exploratório, ria [iʃplora'tɔriu, rial *adj* exploratory.

explosão [iʃplo'zãwl *(pl-ões) f* explosion.

explosivo, va [iʃplo'zivu, val *adj* explosive.
  ⏺ **explosivo** *m* [material] explosive.

EXPO *(abrev de* **Exposição)** *f* exhibition.

expoente [iʃ'pwĕntʃil <> *mf* [figura ilustre] exponent. <> *m* MAT exponent.

expor [45] [iʃ'po(x)] *vt* **-1.** [mostrar] to display. **-2.** [explicar] to explain. **-3.** [exibir] to exhibit. **-4.** [revelar] to reveal. **-5.** [submeter]: ~ **algo (a algo)** to expose sthg (to sthg).
  ⏺ **expor-se** *vp* **-1.** [submeter-se]: ~**-se a algo** to expose o.s. to sthg. **-2.** [exibir-se] to expose o.s.

exportação [iʃpoxta'sãwl *(pl -ões) f* **-1.** [ato] export. **-2.** [produtos] exports *(pl).*

exportador, ra [iʃpoxta'do(x), ral <> *adj* **-1.** [país, companhia] exporting. **-2.** [política] export *(antes de subst).* <> *m, f* exporter.

exportar [4] [iʃpox'ta(x)] *vt* to export.

exposição [iʃpozi'sãwl *(pl -ões) f* **-1.** [mostra] display. **-2.** [explicação] explanation. **-3.** [narração] narrative. **-4.** FOTO exposure.

expositor, ra [iʃpozi'to(x), ral *m, f* exhibitor.

exposto, osta [iʃ'poʃtu, oʃtal <> *pp* ▷ **expor.** <> *adj* [à vista - mercadoria] on show; [- corpo] exposed; [- fratura] compound.

expressão [iʃpre'sãwl *(pl-ões) f* **-1.** [ger] expression; ~ **escrita/oral** written/oral expression; ~ **artística** artistic expression; ~ **corporal** self-expression though movement. **-2.** [manifestação]: ~ **(de algo)** expression (of sthg). **-3.** [vivacidade] expressiveness.

expressar [4] [iʃpre'sa(x)] *vt* to express.
  ⏺ **expressar-se** *vp* to express o.s.

expressionismo [iʃpresjo'niʒmul *m* expressionism.

expressionista [iʃpresjo'niʃtal <> *adj* expressionist. <> *mf* expressionist.

expressividade [iʃpresivi'dadʒil *f* expressiveness.

expressivo, va [iʃpre'sivu, val *adj* expressive.

expresso, sa [iʃ'prɛsu, sal <> *pp* ▷ **expressar.** <> *adj* express.
  ⏺ **expresso** *m* express.

exprimir [6] [iʃpri'mi(x)] *vt* to express.
  ⏺ **exprimir-se** *vp* to express o.s.

expropriação [iʃproprja'sãwl *(pl -ões) f* JUR expropriation.

expropriar [16] [iʃpropri'a(x)] *vt* JUR to expropriate.

expugnar [4] [iʃpugi'na(x)] *vt* to storm.

expulsão [iʃpuw'sãwl *(pl-ões) f* **-1.** [saída forçada] expulsion. **-2.** ESP sending-off.

expulsar [4] [iʃpuw'sa(x)] *vt* **-1.** [ger] to expel. **-2.** [inimigo] to drive out. **-3.** [deportar] to deport. **-4.** ESP to send off.

expulso, sa [iʃ'puwsu, sal <> *pp* ▷ **expulsar.** <> *adj* expelled.

expurgar [14] [iʃpux'ga(x)] *vt* **-1.** [limpar] to clean. **-2.** [corrigir] to expurgate. **-3.** [livrar]: ~ **algo (de)** to purge sthg (of).

expurgo [iʃ'puxgul *m* purge.

êxtase ['eʃtazil *m* **-1.** [enlevo] ecstasy. **-2.** [transe]: **estar em** ~ to be in ecstasy.

extasiado, da [iʃta'zjadu, dal *adj* **-1.** [enlevado] ecstatic. **-2.** [pasmado] astounded.

extasiar [16] [iʃta'zja(x)] *vt* to enrapture.
  ⏺ **extasiar-se** *vp* to be entranced.

extemporâneo, nea [iʃtĕnpo'rãnju, jal *adj* extemporary, extemporaneous.

extensão [iʃtĕn'sãwl *(pl -ões) f* **-1.** [ger] extent; **em toda a** ~ **da palavra** in the full meaning of the word. **-2.** [dimensão, área] area. **-3.** [comprimento] length; **a vegetação cobria toda a** ~ **da praia** the vegetation covered the whole length and breadth of the beach. **-4.** [duração] duration. **- 5.** [ampliação] scope. **- 6.** [ramal telefônico, fio elétrico] extension.

extensivo, va [iʃtẽn'sivu, va] *adj* **-1.** [extensível] extending. **-2.** [amplo] extensive.

extenso, sa [iʃ'tẽnsu, sa] *adj* **-1.** [ger] long. **-2.** [amplo, abrangente] extensive. **-3.** *loc:* **por** ~ **in** full.

extenuado, da [iʃte'nwadu, da] *adj* worn out.

extenuante [iʃte'nwãntʃi] *adj* **-1.** [cansativo] exhausting. **-2.** [debilitante] debilitating.

extenuar [4] [iʃtẽ'nwa(x)] *vt* **-1.** [cansar] to wear out. **-2.** [debilitar] to debilitate.

➡ **extenuar-se** *vp* **-1.** [cansar-se] to wear o.s. out. **-2.** [debilitar-se] to be debilitated.

exterior [iʃte'rjo(x)] (*pl* **-es**) ◇ *adj* **-1.** [externo] outer. **-2.** [com outros países] external. **-3.** [aparência] external. **-4.** [o estrangeiro]: **o** ~ abroad; **estar no** ~ to be abroad; **ser do** ~ to be a foreigner. ◇ *m* [aparência] appearance.

exterioridade [iʃterjori'dadʒi] *f* external nature; [aparências] (outward) appearances.

exteriorização [iʃterjoriza'sãw] (*pl* **-ões**) *f* manifestation.

exteriorizar [4] [iʃterjori'za(x)] *vt* to externalize.

exteriormente [iʃterjox'mẽntʃi] *adv* from the outside.

exterminação [iʃtexmina'sãw] (*pl* **-ões**) *f* extermination.

exterminar [4] [iʃtexmi'na(x)] *vt* **-1.** [aniquilar] to exterminate. **-2.** [erradicar] to eradicate.

extermínio [iʃtex'minju] *m* extermination.

externa [iʃ'tɛxna] *f* ▷ **externo**.

externato [iʃtɛx'natu] *m* day school.

externo, na [iʃtɛxnu, na] *adj* **-1.** [exterior - parede] exterior; [- lado] external. **-2.** [aparente] exterior. **-3.** [medicamento]: **uso** ~ external use.

extinção [iʃtʃĩn'sãw] *f* extinction; **em** ~ endangered.

extinguir [53] [iʃtʃĩŋ'gi(x)] *vt* **-1.** [fogo] to extinguish. **-2.** [exterminar] to exterminate. **-3.** [dissolver] to dissolve. **-4.** ECOL to endanger.

➡ **extinguir-se** *vp* **-1.** [fogo] to go out. **-2.** [desaparecer] to disappear. **-3.** ECOL to become extinct.

extinto, ta [iʃ'tʃĩntu, ta] *adj* **-1.** [ger] extinct. **-2.** [fogo] extinguished. **-3.** [associação] defunct.

extintor [iʃtʃĩn'to(x)] (*pl* **-res**) *m*: ~ (**de incêndio**) (fire) extinguisher.

extirpar [4] [iʃtix'pa(x)] *vt* **-1.** [arrancar] to pull out. **-2.** [extrair - dente] to extract; [- tumor] to remove. **-3.** [erradicar] to eradicate.

extorquir [79] [iʃtox'ki(x)] *vt*: ~ **algo (de alguém)** to extort sthg (from sb).

extorsão [iʃtox'sãw] (*pl* **-ões**) *f* extortion.

extorsivo, va [iʃtox'sivu, va] *adj* extortionate.

extra ['ɛʃtra] ◇ *adj* [extraordinário] extra. ◇ *mf* extra.

extração [iʃtra'sãw] (*pl* **-ões**) *f* **-1.** [ger] extraction. **-2.** [sorteio] draw.

extraconjugal [ɛʃtrakõnʒu'gaw] (*pl* **-ais**) *adj* extramarital.

extracurricular [ɛʃtrakuxiku'la(x)] *adj* extracurricular.

extradição [eʃtradʒi'sãw] (*pl* **-ões**) *f* extradition.

extraditar [4] [iʃtradʒi'ta(x)] *vt* to extradite.

extrair [68] [iʃtra'i(x)] *vt* [tirar]: ~ **algo (de)** to extract sthg (from).

extrajudicial [ɛʃtraʒudʒi'sjaw] (*pl* **-ais**) *adj* extrajudicial.

extranet [ejʃtra'netil] *f* COMPUT extranet.

extra-oficial [ɛʃtraofi'sjaw] (*pl* **-ais**) *adj* unofficial.

extraordinário, ria [iʃtraordʒi'narju, rja] *adj* extraordinary.

extrapolação [eʃtrapola'sãw] (*pl* **-ões**) *f* extrapolation.

extrapolar [4] [iʃtrapo'la(x)] *vt* to go beyond.

extraterreno, na [iʃtra'texenu, na] *adj* extraterrestrial.

extraterrestre [eʃtrate'xeʃtri] ◇ *adj* extraterrestrial. ◇ *mf* extraterrestrial.

extrato [iʃ'tratul] *m* **-1.** [ger] extract; ~ **de tomate** tomato puree. **-2.** [resumo] excerpt; ~ **bancário** bank statement.

extravagância [iʃtrava'gãnsja] *f* extravagance; **fazer uma** ~ to be extravagant.

extravagante [iʃtrava'gãntʃi] ◇ *adj* [excêntrico] eccentric.

extravasar [4] [iʃtrava'sa(x)] ◇ *vt* [exteriorizar - sentimento, alegria] to show; [- raiva] to give vent to. ◇ *vi* **-1.** [expandir-se] to burst out. **-2.** [transbordar] to spill over.

extraviado, da [iʃtra'vjadu, da] *adj* missing.

extraviar [16] [iʃtra'vja(x)] *vt* **-1.** [perder] to lose. **-2.** [dinheiro] to embezzle. **-3.** *fig* [perverter] to lead astray.

➡ **extraviar-se** *vp* **-1.** [carta] to go astray; [processo] to get lost. **-2.** [pessoa - perder-se] to get lost; *fig* [perverter-se] to be led astray.

extravio [iʃtra'viw] *m* **-1.** [perda]: ~ (**de algo**) loss (of sthg). **-2.** [roubo] embezzlement.

extremado, da [iʃtre'madu, da] *adj* extreme.

extremar-se [4] [iʃtre'maxsil] *vp*: ~ **em esforços** to do one's utmost.

extrema-unção [iʃtremaũn'sãw] (*pl* **extrema-unções**) *f* extreme unction, sacrament of the sick.

extremidade [iʃtremi'dadʒil] *f* **-1.** [fim, limite] end. **-2.** [ponta] tip. **-3.** [beira] edge.

➡ **extremidades** *fpl* ANAT extremities.

extremista [iʃtre'miʃta] ◇ *adj* extremist. ◇ *mf* extremist.

extremo, ma [iʃ'tremu, ma] *adj* (*antes de subst*) **-1.** [ger] extreme; **o Extremo Oriente** the Far East. **-2.** [derradeiro, exagerado] extreme.

➡ **extremo** *m* **-1.** [limite, ponta] extreme; **de um** ~ **ao outro** from one extreme to another. **-2.** [máximo] utmost; **ao** ~ to the utmost.

➡ **extremos** *mpl* [exagero] extremes.

extroversão [iʃtrovex'sãw] *f* extroversion.

extroverter-se [5] [iʃtrovex'texsil] *vp* to become (more) outgoing.

extrovertido, da [iʃtrɔvexˈtʃidu, da] <> *adj* extrovert. <> *m, f* extrovert.
exu [eˈʃu] *m* devil *(in voodoo rituals)*.
exuberância [ezubeˈrãnsja] *f* exuberance.
exuberante [ezubeˈrãntʃi] *adj* exuberant.
exultação [ezuwtaˈsãw] *f* exultation.
exultante [ezuwˈtãntʃi] *adj* exultant.
exultar [4] [ezuwˈta(x)] *vi:* ~ **(de)** to exult (in).
exumação [ezuˈmasãw] *(pl* **-ões)** *f* exhumation.
exumar [4] [ezuˈma(x)] *vt* **-1.** [corpo] to exhume.
   -2. *fig* [lembranças] to dig up.
ex-voto [ɛksˈvɔtu] *(pl* **ex-votos)** *m* icon.

f, F [ˈɛfi] *m* [letra] f, F.
fá [fa] *m* MÚS F, fa(h).
fã [fã] *(pl* **fãs)** *mf* fan.
FAB *(abrev de* **Força Aérea Brasileira)** *m* Brazilian Air Force.
fábrica [ˈfabrika] *f* factory.
fabricação [fabrikaˈsãw] *(pl* **-ões)** *f* manufacture; **de** ~ **caseira** home-made.
fabricante [fabriˈkãntʃi] *mf* manufacturer.
fabricar [12] [fabriˈka(x)] *vt* **-1.** [manufaturar] to manufacture. **-2.** [inventar] to fabricate.
fabril [faˈbriw] *(pl* **-is)** *adj* manufacturing.
fábula [ˈfabula] *f* **-1.** [conto] fable. **-2.** *fam* [fortuna] fortune.
fabuloso, osa [fabuˈlozu, ɔza] *adj* [ger] fabulous.
faca [ˈfaka] *f* knife; **entrar na** ~ *fam* to go under the knife; **estar com a** ~ **e o queijo na mão** *fam* to have things in hand; **ser uma** ~ **de dois gumes** *fam* to be a double-edged sword.
facada [faˈkada] *f* **-1.** [golpe] stab; **ser uma** ~ **pelas costas** *fig* to be a stab in the back. **-2.** *fam* cut; **dar uma** ~ **em alguém** [pedir dinheiro a alguém] to cadge money off sb.
façanha [faˈsãɲa] *f* exploit.
facão [faˈkãw] *(pl* **-ões)** *m* carving knife.
facção [fakˈsãw] *(pl* **-ões)** *f* faction.
faccioso, sa [fakˈsjozu, ɔza] *adj* factional.
face [ˈfasi] *f* **-1.** [ger] face; **fazer** ~ **a** *fig* [enfrentar] to face up to; [custear] to take on board; ~ **a** ~ **face to face. -2.** [lado] side. **-3.** [superfície]: **a** ~ **das águas** the surface of the water; **a** ~ **da terra** the face of the earth. **-4.** [aspecto] facet.
   ◆ **em face de** *loc prep* [diante de] faced with.
faceiro, ra [faˈsejru, ra] *adj* **-1.** [alegre - pessoa, sorriso] cheerful; [- dança] merry. **-2.** [elegante] smart.

fáceis [ˈfasejʃ] *pl* ▷ **fácil**.
faceta [faˈseta] *f* [aspecto] facet.
facetado, da [faseˈtadu, da] *adj* [pedra] faceted.
fachada [faˈʃada] *f* **-1.** [de prédio] façade. **-2.** *fig fam* [aparência] mug; **ser só** ~ to be merely a façade.
facho [ˈfaʃu] *m* beam.
facial [faˈsjaw] *(pl* **-ais)** *adj* facial.
fácil [ˈfasiw] *(pl* **-eis)** *adj* **-1.** [simples] easy. **-2.** [dócil] easy(-going). **-3.** *pej* [mulher] easy.
   ◆ **fácil** *adv* easily.
facilidade [fasiliˈdadʒi] *f* **-1.** [ausência de dificuldade] ease; **com** ~ easily. **-2.** [aptidão]: **ter** ~ **(para algo)** to have an aptitude (for sthg).
   ◆ **facilidades** *fpl* [meios] facilities.
facílimo, ma [faˈsilimu, ma] *adj superl* ▷ **fácil**.
facilitação [fasilitaˈsãw] *f* **-1.** [ato] facilitation. **-2.** [fornecimento] provision.
facilitar [4] [fasiliˈta(x)] <> *vt* **-1.** [tornar fácil] to make easy. **-2.** [facultar] to facilitate. <> *vi* [descuidar-se] to be careless.
facínora [faˈsinora] *m* criminal.
fã-clube [fãˈklubi] *(pl* **fãs-clubes)** *m* fan club.
facões [faˈkõjʃ] *pl* ▷ **facão**.
fac-símile [fakˈsimili] *(pl* **fac-símiles)** *m* **-1.** [cópia] facsimile. **-2.** [máquina] fax machine.
factível [fakˈtʃivew] *(pl* **-eis)** *adj* feasible.
factótum [fakˈtɔtu] *m* factotum.
faculdade [fakuwˈdadʒi] *f* **-1.** [capacidade] faculty. **-2.** [propriedade] property. **-3.** [escola superior] faculty.
facultar [4] [fakuwˈta(x)] *vt* **-1.** [conceder] to grant. **-2.** [permitir] to permit.
facultativo, va [fakuwtaˈtʃivu, va] <> *adj* optional. <> *m, f* (medical) doctor.
fada [ˈfada] *f* fairy.
fadado, da [faˈdadu, da] *adj:* **estar** ~ **a algo** to be fated to sthg.
fada-madrinha [ˌfadamaˈdriɲa] *(pl* **fadas-madrinhas)** *f* fairy godmother.
fadiga [faˈdʒiga] *f* fatigue.
fado [ˈfadu] *m* **-1.** [destino] fate. **-2.** MÚS fado, *type of Portuguese folk song.*
fagueiro, ra [faˈgejru, ra] *adj* **-1.** [meigo] sweet. **-2.** [agradável] pleasant. **-3.** [contente] happy.
fagulha [faˈguʎa] *f* spark.
fahrenheit [fareˈnajtʃi] *adj* Fahrenheit.
faia [ˈfaja] *f* beech tree.
fair-play [fɛxˈplej] *m* fair play.
faisão [fajˈzãw] *(pl* **-ões)** *m* pheasant.
faísca [faˈiʃka] *f* spark.
faiscante [fajʃˈkãntʃi] *adj* **-1.** [fogo] flickering. **-2.** [olhos] sparkling.
faiscar [12] [fajʃˈka(x)] *vi* **-1.** [fogo] to flicker. **-2.** [olhos] to flash.
faixa [ˈfajʃa] *f* **-1.** [tira] strip. **-2.** [para a cintura] belt. **-3.** [para o peito] sash; ~ **de campeão/miss** champion's/beauty queen's sash; ~ **presidencial** presidential sash. **-4.** [para pedestres]: ~ **(de pedestres)** (pedestrian) crossing. **-5.** [pista] lane. **-6.** [atadura] bandage. **-7.** [de terra] strip.

-8. [para mensagem] banner. **-9.** [intervalo] interval; ~ **etária** age group; ~ **salarial** salary band. **-10.** [de disco] track.

faixa-título [ˌfajʃaˈtʃitulu] (*pl* **faixas-título**) *f* [de disco] title track.

fajuto, ta [faˈʒutu, ta] *adj fam* **-1.** [de má qualidade - tecido, equipamento] shoddy; [- político] second-rate. **-2.** [dinheiro] counterfeit.

fala [ˈfala] *f* **-1.** [ger] speech; **perder a** ~ to be struck dumb. **-2.** [parte de diálogo] words *(pl)*.

falação [falaˈsãw] (*pl* **-ões**) *f fam* **-1.** [ato] talk. **-2.** [discurso] speech.

falácia [faˈlasja] *f* fallacy.

faladeira [falaˈdejra] *adj* & *f* ▷ **falador.**

falado, da [faˈladu, da] *adj* **-1.** [comentado] much talked about. **-2.** [famoso] well-known. **-3.** *fam* [de má fama] notorious.

falador, deira [falaˈdo(x), dejra] (*mpl* **-es**, *fpl* **-s**) ◇ *adj* [pessoa] talkative. ◇ *m,f* [pessoa] chatterbox.

falange [faˈlãʒi] *f* phalanx.

falante [faˈlãtʃi] *adj* talking.

falar [4] [faˈla(x)] ◇ *vi* **-1.** [verbalmente] to speak; ~ **de** *ou* **em algo** to talk about sthg; ~ **com alguém** to speak to sb; ~ **alto/baixo** to speak loudly/softly; ~ **alto com alguém** *fig* to give sb a good talking-to; ~ **da boca para fora** *fam* not to mean a word one is saying; ~ **em inglês/espanhol** to speak in English/Spanish; ~ **mais alto** *fig* to win the day; ~ **para dentro** to mumble; ~ **pelos cotovelos** [falar muito] to talk one's head off; ~ **por alguém** to speak on behalf of sb; ~ **por** ~ to talk for the sake of talking; ~ **sozinho/dormindo** to talk to o.s./in one's sleep; **por** ~ **em ...** speaking *ou* talking of ...; **sem** ~ **de** *ou* **em ...** not to mention ...; **agora, falando sério, ...** but seriously, ...; **falou, está falado!** *fam* [OK] OK! **-2.** [discursar] to make a speech. **-3.** [tratar]: ~ **de** *ou* **sobre algo** to talk about sthg. **-4.** [confessar] to talk. ◇ *vt* **-1.** [idioma]: ~ **inglês/espanhol** to speak English/Spanish. **-2.** [dizer] to say; ~ **que** to say that; ~ **bem/mal de** to speak well/ill of; ~ **bobagem** to talk nonsense. **-3.** [contar]: ~ **algo (a alguém)** to tell (sb) sthg **-4.** *loc*: **dar o que** ~ [ser muito comentado] to cause a stir.

▶ **falar-se** *vp* **-1.** [dialogar] to talk. **-2.** [estar em boas relações] to be talking to one another; **não se** ~ to not be talking to one another.

falatório [falaˈtɔrju] *m* **-1.** [ruído] voices *(pl)*. **-2.** [discurso] diatribe. **-3.** [maledicência] slander.

falcão [fawˈkãw] (*pl* **-ões**) *m* falcon.

falcatrua [fawkaˈtrua] *f* fraud.

falecer [25] [faleˈse(x)] *vi* to pass away.

falecido, da [faleˈsidu, da] ◇ *adj* [pessoa] deceased. ◇ *m, f* [pessoa] deceased.

falecimento [falesiˈmẽtu] *m* decease.

falência [faˈlẽsja] *f* bankruptcy; **abrir** ~ to declare o.s. bankrupt; **ir à** ~ to go bankrupt; **levar à** ~ to bankrupt.

falésia [faˈlɛzja] *f* cliff.

falha [ˈfaʎa] *f* **-1.** [fenda] fault. **-2.** [defeito] defect. **-3.** [omissão] omission.

falhar [4] [faˈʎa(x)] ◇ *vt* **-1.** [errar] to fail. **-2.** [faltar com - promessa] to break; [- obrigação] to fail. ◇ *vi* **-1.** [não funcionar, fracassar] to fail. **-2.** [não acertar] to miss.

falho, lha [ˈfaʎu, ʎa] *adj* **-1.** [defeituoso] faulty. **-2.** [deficiente] flawed.

fálico, ca [ˈfaliku, ka] *adj* phallic.

falido, da [faˈlidu, da] ◇ *adj* bankrupt. ◇ *m, f* bankrupt.

falir [79] [faˈli(x)] *vi* **-1.** [abrir falência] to go bankrupt. **-2.** [fracassar] to fail.

falível [faˈlivew] (*pl* **-eis**) *adj* fallible.

falo [ˈfalu] *m* phallus.

falsário, ria [fawˈsarju, rja] *m* **-1.** [falsificador] forger. **-2.** [perjuro] perjurer.

falsear [15] [fawˈsja(x)] ◇ *vt* [falsificar] to falsify. ◇ *vi* [pisar em falso] to miss one's step.

falsete [fawˈsetʃi] *m MÚS* falsetto.

falsidade [fawsiˈdadʒi] *f* **-1.** [fingimento] hypocrisy. **-2.** [mentira] lie; ~ **ideológica** false declaration.

falsificação [fawsifikaˈsãw] (*pl* **-ões**) *f* forgery.

falsificador, ra [fawsifikaˈdo(x), ra] *m, f* [pessoa] forger.

falsificar [12] [fawsifiˈka(x)] *vt* **-1.** [ger] to forge. **-2.** [adulterar - alimento, remédio] to adulterate; [- documento] to falsify. **-3.** [desvirtuar] to misrepresent.

falso, sa [ˈfawsu, sa] *adj* **-1.** [ger] false. **-2.** [falsificado] forged. **-3.** [fingido] deceitful. **-4.** [errôneo] erroneous. **-5.** *loc*: **pisar em** ~ to miss one's step.

falso-testemunho [ˌfawsoteʃteˈmuɲul] (*pl* **falsos-testemunhos**) *m* false witness.

falta [ˈfawta] *f* **-1.** [carência] lack; **ter** ~ **de** to be in need of; ~ **de água** water shortage; ~ **de ar** airlessness; ~ **de respeito** lack of respect; ~ **de responsabilidade** lack of responsibility. **-2.** [ausência] absence; **sentir** ~ **de algo/alguém** to miss sthg/sb; **na** ~ **de** for lack of; **sem** ~ without fail. **-3.** [erro, pecado] fault. **-4.** *ESP* foul; **cobrar/-cometer uma** ~ to commit a foul.

faltar [4] [fawˈta(x)] *vi* **-1.** [não haver]: **falta água/luz/comida** there's no water/electricity/food; **falta honestidade** there's a lack of honesty; ~ **sal/tempero** to need salt/seasoning. **-2.** [estar ausente] to be absent; **ontem faltaram cinco alunos** yesterday five students were absent; **falta o Hélio** Hélio's not here, Hélio's missing. **-3.** [ser escasso]: **falta-lhe dinheiro** he hasn't got enough money; **falta-lhe saúde** he's not too healthy; **faltou-lhe força de vontade** he lacked the willpower; **nada nos falta** we have everything we need, we want for nothing. **-4.** [restar - por fazer]: **só falta fazermos o bolo** all that's left for us to do is make the cake; **falta pintarmos a casa** we've still got to paint the house; [- por acontecer]: **só me faltava essa!** *fam* that's all I needed!; [- por decorrer]: **faltam dois meses para o**

festival there are two months to go before the festival; **falta uma semana para irmos embora** it's a week until we go. **-5.** [omitir-se]: **nunca faltou quando a família precisava** he was always there when the family needed him. **-6.** [morrer] to die.

falto, ta [ˈfawtu, ta] *adj*: ~ **de** lacking in.

faltoso, osa [faw'tozu, ɔza] *adj* **-1.** [culpado] guilty. **-2.** [que falta muito] frequently absent.

fama [ˈfãma] *f* **-1.** [celebridade] fame. **-2.** [reputação] reputation; **de** ~ by reputation; **de má** ~ of ill repute.

famigerado, da [famiʒe'radu, da] *adj* [célebre] famous.

família [faˈmilja] <> *f* family; **de boa** ~ from a good family; **estar em** ~ to be one of the family; **ser de** ~ to run in the family. <> *adj fam* [decente]: **ser** ~ to be respectable.

familiar [famiˈlja(x)] (*pl* **-es**) <> *adj* **-1.** [relativo à família] family *(antes de subst)*. **-2.** [conhecido] familiar. <> *mf* [pessoa da família]: **um** ~ a family member; **os** ~ **es** the family *(sg)*.

familiaridade [familjari'dadʒi] *f* **-1.** [intimidade] familiarity. **-2.** [informalidade] informality.

familiarização [familjariza'sãw] *f* familiarization.

familiarizar [4] [familjari'za(x)] *vt* to familiarize.
→ **familiarizar-se** *vp*: ~**-se com algo/alguém** to familiarize o.s. with sthg/sb.

faminto, ta [faˈmĩtu, ta] *adj* famished.

famoso, osa [faˈmozu, ɔza] *adj* famous.

fanático, ca [faˈnatʃiku, ka] <> *adj* **-1.** POL & RELIG fanatical. **-2.** [apaixonado]: ~ **(por)** crazy (about). <> *m, f* [pessoa] fanatic.

fanatismo [fanaˈtʃiʒmu] *m* fanaticism.

fanfarrão, ona [fãfa'xãw, ɔna] <> *adj* (*mpl* **-ões**, *fpl* **-s**) <> *adj* boastful. <> *m, f* braggart.

fanfarronice [fãnwfaxo'nisi] *f* [gabarolice] boasting.

fanho, nha [ˈfaɲu, ɲa], **fanhoso, sa** [fãˈɲozu, za] *adj* **-1.** [voz] nasal. **-2.** [pessoa] *with a nasal-sounding voice.*

faniquito [faniˈkitu] *m fam* strop; **dar um** ~ to get into a strop.

fantasia [fãnta'zia] *f* **-1.** [coisa imaginada] fantasy; **jóia de** ~ [bijuteria] costume jewellery. **-2.** [imaginação] fancy. **-3.** [capricho] whim. **-4.** [traje] fancy dress; ~ **de Carnaval** fancy dress; ~ **de árabe/pirata** Arab/pirate costume. **-5.** MÚS fantasia.

fantasiar [16] [fãnta'zja(x)] *vt* **-1.** [imaginar] to imagine. **-2.** [pôr fantasia]: ~ **alguém de algo** to dress sb up as sthg. **-3.** [devanear] to daydream.
→ **fantasiar-se** *vp*: ~**-se (de)** to dress up (as).

fantasioso, osa [fãta'zjozu, ɔza] *adj* fanciful.

fantasista [fãta'ziʃta] <> *adj* fanciful. <> *mf* whimsical person.

fantasma [fãn'taʒma] *m* **-1.** [espectro] ghost. **-2.** [alucinação] phantom. **-3.** *fig* [coisa terrível] spectre.

fantasmagórico, ca [fãtazma'gɔriku, ka] *adj* phantasmagorical.

fantástico, ca [fãn'taʃtʃiku, ka] *adj* **-1.** [ger] fantastic. **-2.** *fam* [ótimo] fantastic.
→ **fantástico** *m* [fantasia]: **o** ~ the fantastic.

fantoche [fãn'tɔʃi] *m* puppet.

fanzoca [fãn'zɔka] *mf mfam* junkie.

FAQs (*abrev de* **Frequently Asked Questions**) *fpl* FAQs.

faqueiro [faˈkejru] *m* **-1.** [jogo de talheres] cutlery set. **-2.** [pessoa] cutler.

faquir [faˈki(x)] *m* fakir.

faraó [faraˈɔ] *m* pharaoh.

faraônico, ca [faraˈoniku, ka] *adj* **-1.** [relativo aos faraós] pharaonic. **-2.** *fig* [grandioso] grandiose.

FARC (*abrev de* **Forças Armadas Revolucionárias da Colômbia**) *f* FARC.

farda [ˈfaxda] *f* [uniforme] uniform.

fardar [4] [fax'da(x)] *vt* to put in uniform.

fardo [ˈfaxdu] *m* **-1.** [carga] load. **-2.** *fig* [peso] burden.

farejar [4] [fare'ʒa(x)] <> *vt* to sniff. <> *vi* [tomar o faro] to pick up the scent.

farelento, ta [fare'lẽtu, ta] *adj* crumbly.

farelo [faˈrɛlu] *m* **-1.** [de pão] crumb. **-2.** [de cereal] husk; ~ **de trigo** wheat bran.

farfalhante [faxfa'ʎãntʃi] *adj* rustling.

farfalhar [4] [faxfa'ʎa(x)] *vi* to rustle.

farináceo, cea [fari'nasju, sja] *adj* farinaceous.
→ **farináceos** *mpl* [alimentos] starchy foods.

faringe [faˈrĩʒi] *f* pharynx.

faringite [farĩ'ʒiti] *f* pharyngitis.

farinha [faˈriɲa] *f*: ~ **(de mesa ou de mandioca)** cassava flour; ~ **de rosca** toasted breadcrumbs; ~ **de trigo** wheat flour.

farinhento, ta [fariˈɲẽtu, ta] *adj* [que se esfarinha] floury.

farmacêutico, ca [farma'sewtiku, ka] <> *adj* pharmaceutical. <> *m, f* pharmacist.

farmácia [fax'masja] *f* **-1.** [ger] pharmacy. **-2.** [coleção de medicamentos] first-aid box *ou* cabinet.

farmacologia [faxmakolo'ʒia] *f* pharmacology.

farnel [fax'nɛw] (*pl* **-éis**) *m* **-1.** [provisões] packed meal. **-2.** [saco] lunch box.

faro [ˈfaru] *m* **-1.** [olfato] sense of smell. **-2.** *fig* [intuição] nose.

faroeste [faˈrwɛʃtʃi] *m* **-1.** [filme] western. **-2.** [região] far west.

farofa [faˈrɔfa] *f* CULIN fried manioc flour

farofeiro, ra [faro'fejru, ra] *m, f fam* [de praia] beach bum.

farol [faˈrɔw] (*pl* **-óis**) *m* **-1.** [para navegantes] lighthouse. **-2.** AUTO headlight; ~ **alto/baixo** full/low beam.

faroleiro [faro'lejru] *m* lighthouse keeper.

farolete [farɔ'letʃi] *m* AUTO indicator; ~ **dianteiro** sidelight; ~ **traseiro** rear light.

farpa [ˈfaxpa] *f* **-1.** [de madeira] splinter. **-2.** [metálica] shard. **-3.** *fam* [crítica] barb.

farpado, da [fax'padu, da] *adj* ▷ **arame**.

farra [ˈfaxa] *f* binge; **cair na** ~ to paint the town red; **fazer algo de** *ou* **por** ~ to do sthg as a joke.

farrapo [faˈxapu] *m* [trapo] rag; **estar um** ~ *fig*

[coisa] to be ragged; [pessoa] to be in rags; ~ **humano** failure.

farrear [15] [faˈxja(x)] *vi* to rave.

farrista [faˈxiʃta] <> *adj* fun-loving. <> *mf* raver.

farsa [ˈfaxsa] *f* -**1.** TEATRO farce. -**2.** *fig* [fraude] sham; **ser uma** ~ to be a sham.

farsante [faxˈsãntʃi] *mf* -**1.** [pessoa sem palavra] fraud. -**2.** [pessoa brincalhona] buffoon.

farsesco, ca [faxˈseʃku, ka] *adj* farsical.

fartar [4] [faxˈta(x)] *vt* -**1.** [saciar] to satiate; ~ **alguém com** to stuff sb with. -**2.** [cansar]: ~ **alguém (com)** to wear sb out (with).

➥ **fartar-se** *vp* -**1.** [saciar-se]: ~**-se (de algo)** to gorge (on sthg). -**2.** [cansar-se]: ~**-se (de algo/alguém)** to have had enough of sthg/sb.

farto, ta [ˈfaxtu, ta] *adj* -**1.** [saciado] replete. -**2.** [abundante] lavish. -**3.** [cansado]: **estar** ~ **(de algo/ alguém)** to be fed up (with sthg/sb).

fartura [faxˈtura] *f* [abundância] abundance; ~ **de algo** abundance of sthg.

fascículo [faˈsikulu] *m* [de publicação] fascicle.

fascinação [fasinaˈsãw] *f* -**1.** [atração] fascination; **ter** ~ **por algo/alguém** to be fascinated by sthg/sb. -**2.** [deslumbramento] delight.

fascinante [fasiˈnãntʃi] *adj* -**1.** [cativante] fascinating. -**2.** [deslumbrante] amazing.

fascinar [4] [fasiˈna(x)] <> *vt* [cativar] to fascinate. <> *vi* [deslumbrar] to delight.

fascínio [faˈsinju] *m* [atração] fascination.

fascismo [faˈsiʒmu] *m* fascism.

fascista [faˈsiʃta] <> *adj* fascist. <> *mf* fascist.

fase [ˈfazi] *f* -**1.** [ger] phase; **ser só** ~ to be a passing phase. -**2.** ASTRON: **as** ~**s da Lua** the phases of the moon.

fastidioso, osa [faʃtʃiˈdʒjozu, ɔza] *adj* fastidious.

fastígio [faʃˈtʃiʒu] *m* apex.

fastio [faʃˈtʃiu] *m* -**1.** [falta de apetite] lack of appetite. -**2.** [tédio] boredom.

FAT (*abrev de* **Fundo de Amparo ao Trabalhador**) *m* Brazilan fund for the support of workers.

fatal [faˈtaw] (*pl* -**ais**) *adj* -**1.** [mortal] fatal. -**2.** [inevitável] inevitable.

fatalidade [fataliˈdadʒi] *f* -**1.** [destino] fate. -**2.** [desgraça] misfortune.

fatalista [fataˈliʃta] <> *adj* fatalistic. <> *mf* fatalist.

fatalmente [fatawˈmẽntʃi] *adv* -**1.** [mortalmente] fatally. -**2.** [certamente] surely. -**3.** [inevitavelmente] inevitably.

fatia [faˈtʃia] *f* slice.

fatiado, da [faˈtʃiadu, da] *adj* sliced.

fatiar [4] [faˈtʃja(x)] *vt* to slice.

fatídico, ca [faˈtʃidʒiku, ka] *adj* fateful.

fatigante [fatiˈgãntʃi] *adj* -**1.** [cansativo] tiresome. -**2.** [enfadonho] tedious.

fatigar [14] [fatiˈga(x)] *vt* -**1.** [cansar] to tire. -**2.** [enfadar] to bore.

➥ **fatigar-se** *vp* -**1.** [cansar-se] to tire. -**2.** [enfadar-se] to become bored.

fato [ˈfatu] *m* [ger] fact; ~ **consumado** fait accompli; **ser (um)** ~ to be a fact.

➥ **de fato** *loc adv* in fact.

fator [faˈto(x)] (*mpl* -**res**) *m* factor; ~ **Rh** rhesus factor.

fátuo, tua [ˈfatwu, twa] *adj* [vão] fatuous.

fatura [faˈtura] *f* invoice.

faturamento [faturaˈmẽntul] *m* -**1.** COM turnover. -**2.** [fatura] invoicing.

faturar [4] [fatuˈra(x)] <> *vt* -**1.** [mercadorias]: ~ **algo a alguém** to invoice sb for sthg. -**2.** [dinheiro]: **faturou um bom dinheiro** he got a good price. -**3.** *fam* [obter] to land. <> *vi fam* [ganhar dinheiro] to rake it in; ~ **alto** to make loads of dosh.

fauna [ˈfawna] *f* fauna.

fausto, ta [ˈfawʃtu, ta] *adj* fortunate.

➥ **fausto** *m* luxury.

faustoso, sa [fawˈʃtozu, ɔza] *adj* [luxuoso] sumptuous.

fava [ˈfava] *f*: **ser** ~**s contadas** to be a sure thing; **mandar alguém às** ~**s** to send sb on their way.

favela [faˈvɛla] *f* slum.

FAVELAS

Urban phenomenon common to all large cities of Brazil, *favelas* are nuclei of crude, improvised dwellings, found inside built-up areas or on the outskirts of the cities. Devoid of basic public amenities, such as water and sewerage, *favelas* are generally made up of conglomerations of dwellings known as *barracos*, built of various materials such as pieces of wood and pasteboard. In some cases, however, the houses can be made of masonry.

---

favelado, da [favɛˈladu, da] *m, f* slum dweller.

favo [ˈfavu] *m* honeycomb.

favor [faˈvo(x)] (*pl* -**es**) *m* -**1.** [ger] favour *UK*, favor *US*; **fazer um** ~ **para alguém** to do sb a favour *UK*, to do sb a favor *US*; **pedir um** ~ **a alguém** to ask a favour of sb *UK*, to ask a favor of sb *US*; **por** ~ please; **por** ~**, que horas são?** excuse me, what time is it?; **fam** [em reprimenda] do me a favour!; **quer fazer o** ~ **de se calar?** would you kindly shut up! -**2.** [benefício]: **a** ~ **de** in favour of *UK*, in favor of *US*; **em** ~ **de** for; **ter algo a seu** ~ to have sthg in one's favour *UK* ou favor *US*.

favorável [favoˈravɛw] (*pl* -**eis**) *adj*: ~ **(a algo/a fazer algo)** favourable (to sthg/to doing sthg).

favorecer [25] [favoreˈse(x)] *vt* -**1.** [ger] to favour *UK*, to favor *US*. -**2.** [melhorar] to improve.

➥ **favorecer-se** *vp* [beneficiar-se] to take advantage of.

favorecido, da [favoreˈsidu, da] <> *adj* [protegido] favourite. <> *m, f* [beneficiário] beneficiary.

favoritismo [favoriˈtʃiʒmul] *m* favouritism *UK*, favoritism *US*.

favorito, ta [favoˈritu, ta] <> *adj* favourite *UK*, favorite *US*. <> *m, f* favourite *UK*, favorite *US*.

faxina [faˈʃina] *f* bundle of twigs; **fazer uma** ~ to have a spring clean.

faxineiro, ra [faʃiˈnejru, ra] *m, f* cleaner.

fax-modem (pl -dens) m fax-modem.
faz-de-conta [ˌfajʒdʒiˈkõnta] m make-believe.
fazenda [faˈzẽnda] f -1. [propriedade rural] fazenda. -2. [de gado] cattle ranch. -3. [de café, cacau] plantation. -4. [tecido] cloth. -5. ECON revenue.
fazenda-modelo [faˌzẽndamoˈdelu] (pl fazendas-modelos, fazendas-modelo) f model ranch.
fazendeiro, ra [fazẽnˈdejru, ra] m, f -1. [dono de fazenda] rancher. -2. [de café, cacau] planter. -3. [de gado] cattle rancher.
fazer [31] [faˈze(x)] ⟷ vt -1. [produzir] to make; ~ muito barulho to make a lot of noise; ~ planos/um vestido to make plans/a dress; ~ uma pergunta to ask a question. -2. [comida] to cook. -3. [gerar] to produce. -4. [realizar]: **estou fazendo um curso de computadores** I'm taking a computer course; **vamos** ~ **uma festa** let's have a party. -5. [praticar] to do; **você devia** ~ **mais exercício** you should exercise more; **faço jogging todas as manhãs** I go jogging every morning. -6. [cama] to make; ~ **a cama** to make the bed. -7. [transformar] to make; ~ **alguém feliz** to make sb happy. -8. [anos]: **faço anos amanhã** it's my birthday tomorrow; **fazemos cinco anos de casados** we've been married (for) five years. -9. [obrigar] to make; ~ **alguém fazer algo** to make sb do sthg; ~ **alguém rir/chorar** to make sb laugh/cry. -10. [cálculo, conta] to do; **faz a conta para ver quanto é** work out the check to see what it comes to. ⟷ vi -1. [causar]: ~ **bem/mal a algo** to be good/bad for sthg; ~ **bem/mal a alguém** [coisa] to be good/bad for sb; ~ **mal a alguém** [pessoa] to hurt sb. -2. [obrigar]: **faça (com) que ele venha** make him come; [imaginar]: ~ **de conta que ...** to pretend that ... ⟷ v impess -1.: **faz frio/calor** it's cold/hot. -2. [tempo]: **faz um ano que não o vejo** it's been a year since I last saw him; **faz tempo que estou à espera** I've been waiting for a while; **o Sérgio partiu faz três meses** Sérgio left three months ago. -3. [importar]: **não faz mal se está quebrado** it doesn't matter if it's broken; **tanto faz** it doesn't matter.
➤ **fazer-se** vp [preparar-se] to be made; [ser correto]: **é assim que se faz** that's the way to do it; ~-**se com** [ser preparado com] to be made with.
➤ **fazer-se de** vp + prep [pretender ser]: **ele gosta de** ~-**se de importante** he likes to act important; ~-**se de tolo** to act stupid; ~-**se de desentendido** to feign ignorance.
faz-tudo [fajʒˈtudul] mf inv handyman.
FBI (abrev de Federal Bureau of Investigation) m FBI.
fé [ˈfɛ] f [ger] faith; **de boa** ~ in good faith; **de má** ~ dishonestly; **fazer** ~ **em** to have faith in.
fealdade [feawˈdadʒi] f ugliness.
FEBEM (abrev de Fundação Estadual do Bem-Estar do Menor) f organization set up by individual states in Brazil for the rehabilitation of young offenders.
Febraban (abrev de Federação Brasileira de

Associações de Bancos) f Brazilian banking representative body.
febrão [feˈbrãw] (pl -ões) m acute fever.
febre [ˈfɛbri] f -1. MED fever; ~ **amarela** yellow fever; ~ **do feno** hayfever. -2. fig [desejo]: ~ **de fortuna/poder** longing for fortune/power. -3. fig [mania] mania.
febril [feˈbriw] (pl -is) adj feverish.
fecal [feˈkaw] (pl -ais) adj faecal.
fechado, da [feˈʃadu, da] adj -1. [ger] closed. -2. [pessoa] reticent. -3. AUTO [sinal] red light. -4. [tempo, céu] overcast. -5. [mato] dense. -6. [expressão] blank.
➤ **fechada** f AUTO: **dar uma** ~ **em alguém** to cut in front of sb; **levei uma** ~ **de ele** he cut in front of me.
fechadura [feʃaˈdura] f lock.
fechamento [feʃaˈmẽntu] m closure.
fechar [4] [feˈfa(x)] ⟷ vt -1. [ger] to close. -2. AUTO to cut in front of. ⟷ vi -1. [cicatrizar-se] to close. -2. [tempo] to turn close. -3. [sinal de trânsito] to turn red. -4. [parar de funcionar] to close down.
➤ **fechar-se** vp -1. [encerrar-se] to close o.s. off. -2. [retrair-se] to shut o.s. off.
fecho [ˈfeʃu] m -1. [de roupa] fastening; ~ **ecler** zip. -2. [de porta, bolsa] catch. -3. [término] end.
fécula [ˈfɛkula] f starch.
fecundação [fekũndaˈsãw] (pl -ões) f fertilization.
fecundar [4] [fekũnˈda(x)] vt to fertilize.
fecundidade [fekũndʒiˈdadʒi] vt fertility.
fecundo, da [feˈkũndu, da] adj -1. [ger] fertile. -2. fig [criador] creative.
fedelho, lha [feˈdeʎu, ʎa] m, f fam brat.
fedentina [fedẽnˈtʃina] f stench.
feder [5] [feˈde(x)] vi to stink; **não** ~ **nem cheirar** to be wishy-washy.
federação [federaˈsãw] (pl -ões) f federation.
federal [fedeˈraw] (pl -ais) adj -1. [da Federação] federal. -2. fam [enorme] huge.
federalismo [federaˈliʒmu] m federalism.
federalizar [4] [federaliˈza(x)] vt to federalize.
federativo, va [federaˈtʃivu, va] adj federalist.
fedido, da [feˈʒidu, da] adj stinking.
fedor [feˈdo(x)] m stench.
fedorento, ta [fedoˈrẽntu, ta] adj stinking.
feedback [ˌfidʒiˈbɛkil] m feedback.
feição [fejˈsãw] (pl -ões) f -1. [forma] shape. -2. [natureza] character **à** ~ **de** [ao jeito de] in the manner of.
➤ **feições** fpl [face] features.
feijão [fejˈʒãw] (pl -ões) m bean.
feijão-fradinho [fejʒãwfraˈdʒiɲul] (pl feijões-fradinhos) m black-eyed bean.
feijão-mulatinho [fejʒãwmulaˈtʃiɲul] (pl feijões-mulatinhos) m kidney bean.
feijão-preto [fejʒãwˈpretul] (pl feijões-pretos) m black bean.
feijão-tropeiro [fejʒãwtroˈpejrul] (pl feijões-tropeiros) m bean casserole.

feijoada [fej'ʒwada] f typical Brazilian dish made with black beans, pork, sausage and vegetables.

> **FEIJOADA**
>
> A typical Brazilian dish, feijoada consists of black beans stewed with pork (dried meat, rib, loin, tail, trotter, ear). It is generally served with chopped cabbage, farofa and orange. It is said that the feijoada was created by black slaves, who used up those parts of the pig disdained by their masters.

feijoeiro [fej'ʒwejru] m bean.

feio, feia ['fejo, 'feja] adj -**1.** [ger] ugly. -**2.** [tempo] nasty.
 ◆ **feio** adv: **fazer** ~ [dar vexame] to behave badly; **ficar** ~ [dar má impressão] to be rude; **perder** ~ ESP to lose badly.

feioso, osa [fe'jozu, ɔza] adj plain.

feira ['fejra] f [ger] fair; ~ **livre** vegetable market.

feirante [fej'rãntʃi] mf stallholder.

feita ['fejta] f: **certa** ~ once; **de uma** ~ once and for all.

feitiçaria [fejtʃisa'ria] f witchcraft.

feiticeiro, ra [fejtʃi'sejru, ra] <> adj [encantador] bewitching. <> m, f [pessoa] sorcerer (f witch).

feitiço [fej'tʃisu] m spell; **voltar-se o** ~ **contra o feiticeiro** to be hoist by one's own petard.

feitio [fej'tʃiw] m -**1.** [forma] shape. -**2.** [natureza] make-up. -**3.** [de roupa] cut.

feito, ta ['fejtu, ta] <> pp ▷ **fazer**. <> adj -**1.** [concluído, pronto] finished. -**2.** [adulto]: **homem** ~/**mulher feita** grown man/woman.
 ◆ **feito** <> m [façanha] deed. <> conj [tal qual] just like.

feitor, ra [fej'to(x), ra] m, f -**1.** [administrador] manager. -**2.** [capataz] steward.

feitura [fej'tura] f make-up.

feiúra [fej'ura] f ugliness.

feixe ['fejʃi] m -**1.** [molho] bunch. -**2.** [de luz] beam.

fel ['fɛw] m -**1.** [ger] bitterness. -**2.** [bílis] bile.

felação [fela'sãw] (pl -ões) f fellatio.

felicidade [felisi'dadʒi] f -**1.** [ventura] happiness. -**2.** [êxito] success. -**3.** [boa sorte] good luck.
 ◆ **felicidades** fpl congratulations.

felicíssimo, ma [feli'sisimu, ma] superl ▷ **feliz**.

felicitação [felisita'sãw] (pl -ões) f praise.
 ◆ **felicitações** fpl congratulations.

felicitar [4] [felisi'ta(x)] vt: ~ **alguém (por algo)** to congratulate sb (on sthg).

felino, na [fe'linu, na] <> adj -**1.** [ger] feline. -**2.** fig [traiçoeiro] sly. <> m [animal] feline; **os** ~**s** the cat family (sg).

feliz [fe'liʒ] (pl -es) adj -**1.** [ger] happy; **ser** ~ **(em algo)** to be lucky (in sthg); **estar/ficar** ~ to be happy; ~ **aniversário** happy birthday; **Feliz Ano-Novo** happy new year; **Feliz Natal** happy Christmas UK, merry Christmas US; **ser** ~ to be happy. -**2.** [oportuno] good. -**3.** [bem-sucedido] successful.

felizardo, da [feli'zaxdu, da] m, f very lucky person.

felizmente [feliʒ'mẽntʃi] adv -**1.** [por felicidade] luckily. -**2.** [de modo feliz] happily.

felonia [felo'nia] f felony.

felpa ['fewpa] f -**1.** [de tecido] nap. -**2.** [de animal] down.

felpudo, da [few'pudu, da] adj downy.

feltro ['fewtru] m felt.

fêmea ['femja] f female.

feminilidade [feminili'dadʒi] f femininity.

feminino, na [femi'ninu, na] adj feminine.
 ◆ **feminino** m GRAM feminine.

feminismo [femi'niʒmu] m feminism.

feminista [femi'niʃta] <> adj feminist. <> mf feminist.

fêmur ['femu(x)] m femur.

fenda ['fẽnda] f -**1.** [rachadura] crack. -**2.** GEOL crevice.

fender [5] [fẽn'de(x)] vt to split.
 ◆ **fender-se** vp to split.

fenecer [25] [fene'se(x)] vi -**1.** [extingüir-se] to die out. -**2.** [morrer] to die. -**3.** [murchar] to wilt.

feno ['fenu] m hay.

fenomenal [fenome'naw] (pl -ais) adj -**1.** [maravilhoso] wonderful. -**2.** [surpreendente] phenomenal.

fenômeno [fe'nomenu] m phenomenon.

fenomenologia [fenomenolo'ʒial f phenomenology.

fera ['fɛra] f -**1.** fig [ger] brute. -**2.** [animal] wild animal; **ficar uma** ~ **(com)** to be very angry (with). -**3.** fam fig [pessoa perita] ace; **ser (uma)** ~ **em algo** fam fig to be an ace at sthg.

féretro ['fɛretru] m coffin.

feriado [fe'rjadu] m (public) holiday; ~ **bancário** bank holiday UK.

férias ['fɛrjaʃ] fpl holidays UK, vacation (sg) US; **de** ~ on holiday UK, on vacation US; **entrar/sair de** ~ to go on holiday UK, to go on vacation US; **passar as** ~ **em** to spend one's holiday in UK, to spend one's vacation in US; **tirar** ~ to take one's holidays UK, to take one's vacation US.

ferida [fe'rida] f wound; **tocar na** ~ fig to re-open the wound.

ferido, da [fe'ridu, da] <> adj -**1.** [machucado] wounded. -**2.** [magoado] wounded. <> m, f [pessoa] injured person; **os** ~**s** the injured.

ferimento [feri'mẽntu] m injury.

ferino, na [fe'rinu, na] adj -**1.** [cruel] cruel. -**2.** fig [mordaz] biting.

ferir [57] [fe'ri(x)] vt -**1.** [machucar] to wound. -**2.** fig [magoar] to wound.
 ◆ **ferir-se** vp -**1.** [machucar-se] to hurt o.s. -**2.** fig [magoar-se]: ~-**se com** to be wounded by.

fermentação [fexmẽnta'sãw] (pl -ões) f fermentation.

fermentar [4] [fexmẽn'ta(x)] <> vt to ferment. <> vi to ferment.

fermento [fex'mẽntu] m yeast; ~ **em pó** powdered yeast.

Fernando de Noronha *m National Marine Park situated off the coast of Rio Grande do Norte in Brazil.*

FERNANDO DE NORONHA

The archipelago Fernando de Noronha (PE) comprises 19 islands situated 345 km off the coast of Rio Grande do Norte, and totalling 26 km². The largest of these islands is the only inhabited one, and is also called Fernando de Noronha. Here is to be found the only urban centre of the islands, Vila dos Remédios. Because of its crystal-clear waters, dolphins, sharks and fifteen species of coral, Fernando de Noronha has been made into a National Marine Park.

ferocidade [ferosi'dadʒi] *f* ferocity.

ferocíssimo, ma [fero'sisimu, ma] *superl* ➣ **feroz**.

feroz [fe'rɔʃ] (*pl* -es) *adj* fierce.

ferrado, da [fe'xadu, da] *adj* -1. [cavalo] shod. -2. *fam fig* [em mau estado] falling apart.

ferradura [fexa'dura] *f* horseshoe.

ferragem [fe'xaʒẽ] (*pl* -ns) *f* -1. [peças] hardware. -2. [guarnição] ironwork.

ferramenta [fexa'mẽnta] *f* tool.

ferramental [fexa'mẽntaw] (*pl* -ais) *m* tool kit.

ferrão [fe'xãw] (*pl* -ões) *m* -1. [de inseto] sting. -2. [aguilhão] barb.

ferrar [4] [fe'xa(x)] *vt* -1. [ornar de ferro] to decorate with ironwork. -2. [cavalgadura] to shoe. -3. [marcar a ferro] to brand. -4. *fam fig* [prejudicar] to damage.

➣ **ferrar-se** *vp* [sair-se mal] to do badly.

ferreiro [fe'xejru] *m* blacksmith.

ferrenho, nha [fe'xeɲu, ɲal] *adj* -1. [inflexível] iron. -2. [obstinado] passionate.

férreo, rrea ['fexju, xja] *adj* iron.

ferrete [fe'xetʃi] *m* branding iron.

ferro ['fexu] *m* -1. [material] iron; **a ~ e fogo** *fig* by hook or by crook; **de ~** *fig* [vontade, punhos] of iron; [pessoa] made of iron; **~ batido** wrought iron; **~ fundido** cast iron; **~ ondulado** corrugated iron; **~ velho** [sucata] scrap metal. -2. [aparelho]: **~ (de passar)** iron; **passar a ~** to iron. -3. *loc*: **levar ~** to fail.

➣ **ferros** *mpl* [grilhões] chains.

ferroada [fe'xwada] *f* sting.

ferroar [20] [fe'xwa(x)] ◇ *vt* -1. [picar] to sting. -2. [criticar] to criticize. ◇ *vi* -1. [picar] to sting. -2. [latejar, doer] to really hurt.

ferrões [fe'xõjʃ] *pl* ➣ **ferrão**.

ferrolho [fe'xoʎu] *m* bolt.

ferroso, sa [fe'xozu, ɔza] *adj* [ferruginoso] rust coloured.

ferro-velho [ˌfexu'veʎu] (*pl* ferros-velhos) *m* -1. [estabelecimento] scrapyard. -2. [sucata] scrap metal.

ferrovia [fexo'via] *f* railway *UK*, railroad *US*.

ferroviário, ria [fexo'vjarju, ja] ◇ *adj* railway *UK*, railroad *US*. ◇ *m, f* railway employee *UK*, railroad employee *US*.

ferrugem [fe'xuʒẽ] *f* rust.

fértil ['fɛxtiw] (*pl* -eis) *adj* -1. [terreno, período] fertile. -2. [pessoa] productive.

fertilidade [fextʃili'dadʒi] *f* -1. [de terra, pessoa] fertility. -2. [abundância] abundance.

fertilização [fextʃiliza'sãw] (*pl* -ões) *f* fertilization.

fertilizante [fextʃili'zãntʃi] ◇ *adj* fertilizing; **método ~** method of fertilization. ◇ *m* fertilizer.

fertilizar [4] [fextʃili'za(x)] *vt* to fertilize.

fervente [fex'vẽntʃi] *adj* boiling.

ferver [5] [fex've(x)] ◇ *vt* to boil; **~ algo em fogo baixo** to simmer on a low heat. ◇ *vi* to become excited; **~ de raiva** *fig* to be steaming with anger.

fervilhar [4] [fexvi'ʎa(x)] *vi* -1. [ferver] to boil. -2. *fig* [pulular]: **~ (de)** to swarm (with). -3. *fig* [de excitação] to bubble.

fervor [fex'vo(x)] *m* fervour *UK*, fervor *US*.

fervoroso, osa [fexvo'rozu, ɔza] *adj* -1. [ardoroso] fervent. -2. [dedicado] devoted.

fervura [fex'vura] *f* -1. [ebulição] boiling. -2. *fig* [efervescência] fervour *UK*, fervor *US*.

festa ['fɛʃta] *f* -1. [reunião] party; **~ de arromba** thrash. -2. [comemoração]: **~ da Independência** Independence Day party; **~s juninas** *traditional celebrations held in Brazil in June*. -3. [alegria] thrill. -4. [carinho]: **fazer ~ (s) (em)** to cuddle up to. -5. *loc*: **fazer a ~** to have a field day.

➣ **festas** *fpl* [Natal e Ano-Novo] festive season (*sg*).

FESTAS JUNINAS

Popular religious festivals during the month of June; these festivals of ancient origin came over with the Portuguese, and mostly celebrate the feast days of St Anthony (13th), St John (24th) and St Peter (29th). They are celebrated with music, typical drinks and dishes, always including fires and bonfires. Nowadays these festivities are held mainly in the north and northeast of the country.

festança [feʃ'tãnsa] *fam* thrash.

festeiro, ra [feʃ'tejru, ra] *adj* party-going.

festejar [4] [feʃte'ʒa(x)] *vt* to celebrate.

festejo [feʃ'teʒu] *m* celebration.

festim [feʃ'tʃĩ] (*pl* -ns) *m* -1. [festa] feast. -2. [cartucho sem bala]: **tiro de ~** blank shot.

festival [feʃtʃi'vaw] (*pl* -ais) *m* -1. [festa] festival. -2. *fig* [grande quantidade] load.

festividade [feʃtʃivi'dadʒi] *f* festivity.

festivo, va [feʃ'tʃivu, va] *adj* festive.

fetal [fe'taw] (*pl* -ais) *adj* foetal *UK*, fetal *US*.

fetiche [fe'tʃiʃi] *m* fetish.

fetichismo [fetʃi'ʃiʒmu] *m* fetishism.

fetichista [fetʃi'ʃiʃta] ◇ *adj* fetishistic. ◇ *m, f* fetishist.

fétido, da ['fɛtʃidu, da] *adj* fetid.

feto ['fɛtu] *m* foetus *UK*, fetus *US*.

feudal [few'daw] (*pl* -ais) *adj* feudal.

feudalismo [fewda'liʒmu] *m* feudalism.
fev. (*abrev de* **fevereiro**) Feb.
fevereiro [feve'rejru] *m* February; *veja também* **setembro.**
fezes ['fɛziʃ] *fpl* faeces *UK*, feces *US*.
FGTS (*abrev de* **Fundo de Garantia por Tempo de Serviço**) *m* *monthly contribution towards the support of sacked and unemployed workers in Brazil.*
FGV (*abrev de* **Fundação Getúlio Vargas**) *f* *Brazilian private educational organization for improvement in public administration.*
FIA (*abrev de* **Federação Internacional de Automobilismo**) *f* FIA.
fiação [fja'sãw] (*pl* -ões) *f* -**1.** ELETR wiring; **fazer a ~ (de)** to wire (sthg). -**2.** [fábrica] spinning mill.
fiado, da ['fjadu, da] *adj* -**1.** [vendido a crédito] sold on credit (*depois do subst*). -**2.** [conversa]: **isso é conversa fiada** that's far-fetched.
➡ **fiado** *adv* [a crédito] on credit.
fiador, ra [fja'do(x), ra] *m, f* guarantor.
fiambre ['fjãnbri] *m* ham.
fiança ['fjãnsa] *f* -**1.** [garantia] guarantee. -**2.** JUR bail; **sob ~** on bail; **pagar ~** to post bail.
fiapo ['fjapu] *m* thread.
fiar [16] ['fja(x)] *vt* [reduzer a fio] to spin.
➡ **fiar-se** *vp* [confiar em]: **~-se em alguém/algo** to trust sb/sthg.
fiasco ['fjaʃku] *m* fiasco.
fibra ['fibra] *f* [ger] fibre *UK*, fiber *US*; **mulher de ~** gutsy woman; **~ óptica** fibre optics (*pl*) *UK*, fiber optics (*pl*) *US*; **~ de vidro** fibreglass *UK*, fiberglass *US*.
fibroma [fi'broma] *m* fibroma.
fibroso, sa [fi'brozu, ɔza] *adj* fibrous.
ficar [12] [fi'ka(x)] *vi* -**1.** [ger] to remain; **só ficaram duas garrafas de refrigerante** there are only two bottles of soda left. -**2.** [permanecer] to stay; **~ sentado/de pé** to remain seated/standing; **~ por isso mesmo** to remain the same; **~ sem** not to have. -**3.** [estar situado] to be. -**4.** [tornar-se] to become; **~ com frio** to be cold; **~ feliz com algo** to be happy about sthg; **~ de bem/de mal (com alguém)** to get on well/badly (with sb); **~ bom** [de doença] to recover; [pintura etc] to be good. -**5.** [ser adiado]: **~ para** to leave until. -**6.** [combinar]: **~ de fazer algo** to agree to do sthg. -**7.** [persistir]: **~ fazendo algo** to go on doing sthg. -**8.** [prometer]: **~ de fazer algo** to promise to do sthg. -**9.** [custar]: **~ em** to come to. -**10.** [comprar]: **fico com a verde** I'll take the green. -**11.** [manter sob posse, tutela]: **~ com** to be left with. -**12.** [assumir função]: **~ de** to work as. -**13.** [ser]: **não fica bem** it's not right. -**14.** [assentar a]: **~ bem em** *ou* **para alguém** to look good on sb; **~ bem de algo** to look good in sthg. -**15.** [vir a]: **~ sabendo de algo** to get to know sthg. -**16.** *loc*: **~ atrás** [ser inferior] to be behind; **~ sobrando** [ser relegado] to be left out; **~ sujo** [no conceito alheio] to get a bad name.
ficção [fik'sãw] (*pl* -ões) *f* fiction.

ficcional [fik'sionaw] (*pl* -ais) *adj* LITER fictional.
ficcionista [fiksjo'niʃta] *mf* fiction writer.
ficha ['fiʃa] *f* -**1.** [ger] file; **ter ~ na polícia** to have a police record. -**2.** [de telefone] plug. -**3.** [de jogo] token. -**4.** *fam* [informação]: **dar a ~ de** to give information on; **ter ~ limpa** to have a clean record.
fichado, da [fi'ʃadu, da] *adj*: **ser ~ (na polícia)** to have a police record.
fichar [4] [fi'ʃa(x)] *vt* to file.
fichário [fi'ʃarju] *m* -**1.** [ger] file. -**2.** [móvel] filing cabinet.
fichinha [fi'ʃiɲa] *f fam* cinch.
fictício, cia [fik'tʃisju, sja] *adj* fictitious.
fidalgo, ga [fi'dawgu, ga] *m, f* noble.
fidalguia [fidaw'gia] *f* nobility.
fidedigno, na [fide'dʒignu, na] *adj* trustworthy.
fidelidade [fideli'dadʒi] *f* -**1.** [lealdade] faithfulness. -**2.** [conjugal] fidelity. -**3.** [precisão] precision; **com ~** faithfully.
fiduciário, ria [fidu'sjarju, rja] *adj* fiduciary.
➡ **fiduciário** *m* JUR trustee.
fiel ['fjɛw] (*pl* -éis) *adj* -**1.** [ger] faithful. -**2.** [constante] loyal.
➡ **fiéis** *mpl* RELIG: **os fiéis** the faithful (*pl inv*).
fielmente [fjew'mẽntʃi] *adv* faithfully.
FIFA (*abrev de* **Féderation Internationale de Football Association**) *f* FIFA.
figa ['figa] *f* charm.
➡ **de uma figa** *loc adj fam* effing.
fígado ['figadu] *m* liver; **desopilar o ~** *fig* to make one feel good.
figo ['figu] *m* fig.
figueira [fi'gejra] *f* fig tree.
figura [fi'gura] *f* -**1.** [ger] figure; **ser uma ~** *fam* to be a character; **mudar de ~** to change. -**2.** [em carta] picture card, court card. -**3.** GRAM: **~ de linguagem** figure of speech.
figura-chave [fi.gura'ʃavi] (*pl* **figuras-chave**) *f* key figure.
figurado, da [figu'radu, da] *adj* figurative.
figurante [figu'rãntʃi] *mf* extra.
figurão [figu'rãw] (*pl* -ões) *m* bigwig.
figurar [4] [figu'ra(x)] ⟨⟩ *vt* -**1.** [representar] to represent. -**2.** [ter a forma de] to look like. -**3.** [aparentar] to look. ⟨⟩ *vi* -**1.** [atuar]: **~ em** to act in. -**2.** [fazer parte]: **~ em/entre** to appear on/among.
figurinha [figu'riɲa] *f* -**1.** [cromo] sticker; **trocar ~s (com alguém)** *fig* to swap notes (with sb). -**2.** [pessoa]: **ele é uma ~ difícil** he's jumped up.
figurinista [figuri'niʃta] *mf* clothes designer.
figurino [figu'rinu] *m* -**1.** [molde] pattern. -**2.** [revista] fashion magazine. -**3.** CINE, TEATRO & TV [exemplo] model. -**4.** *fig*: **como manda o ~** as it should be.
Fiji ['fiʒi] *n* Fiji.
fila ['fila] *f* [fileira - de pessoas] queue *UK*, line *US*; [- de cadeiras] row; **em ~** in line; **fazer ~** to queue *UK*, to form a line *US*; **~ indiana** single file.

filamento [fila'mẽntu] *m* filament.
filantropia [filãntro'pial *f* philanthropy.
filantrópico, ca [filãn'tropiku, ka] *adj* philanthropic.
filantropo, opa [filãn'tropu, ɔpa] *m, f* philanthropist.
filão [fi'lãw] (*pl* -ões) *m fig* [oportunidade] opportunity.
filar [16] [fi'la(x)] *vt fam* to cadge.
filarmônico, ca [filax'moniku, ka] *adj* philharmonic.
➡ **filarmônica** *f* philharmonic.
filatelia [filate'lia] *f* philately, stamp collecting.
filé [fi'lɛ] *m* fillet; ~ **mignon** filet mignon.
fileira [fi'lejra] *f* row.
➡ **fileiras** *fpl* MIL ranks.
filete [fi'lete] *m* fillet.
filha ['fiʎa] *f* ▷ **filho**.
filharada [fiʎa'rada] *f* many sons and daughters.
filhinho, nha [fi'ʎiɲu, ɲa] *m, f* young son; ~ **da mamãe** mummy's boy; ~ **de papai** spoilt brat.
filho, lha ['fiʎu, 'fiʎa] *m, f*-**1.** [descendente] son; ~ **adotivo** adopted son; ~ **de criação** adopted son; ~ **único** only son; ~ **da mãe** *vulg* bastard; ~ **da puta** *vulg* son of a bitch. -**2.** *loc:* **ter um** ~ *fig* to have a turn, to have a fainting fit; **ser** ~ **único de mãe solteira** *fig* to be unique.
filhote [fi'ʎɔtʃi] *m* -**1.** [de animal - de leão, urso] cub; [- de cachorro] puppy. -**2.** [filho] young son.
filiação [filja'sãw] (*pl* -ões) *f*-**1.** [pais] filiation. -**2.** [admissão] affiliation.
filial [fi'ljaw] (*pl* -ais) <> *adj* [amor] filial. <> *f* [sucursal] branch.
filiar [16] [fi'ʎa(x)] *vt:* ~ **alguém a algo** to sign sb up to sthg.
➡ **filiar-se** *vp:* ~-**se a algo** to sign o.s. up to sthg.
filigrana [fili'grãna] *f* filigree.
Filipinas [fili'pinaʃ] *npl:* (as) ~ the Philippines.
filipino, na [fili'pinu, na] <> *adj* Filipino. <> *m, f* Filipino.
➡ **filipino** *m* [língua] Filipino.
filmadora [fiwma'dora] *f* movie camera.
filmagem [fiw'maʒẽ] (*pl* -ns) *f* filming.
filmar [4] [fiw'ma(x)] <> *vt* to film. <> *vi* to film.
filme ['fiwmi] *m* -**1.** [obra cinematográfica] film *UK*, movie *US*; ~ **de bangue-bangue** Western; ~ **de época** period film *UK*, period movie *US*; ~ **mudo** silent film *UK*, silent movie *US*; ~ **de suspense** thriller. -**2.** *loc:* **queimar o** ~ to ruin one's image.
filmografia [fiwmogra'fia] *f* filmography.
filmoteca [fiwmo'tɛka] *f* film library.
filó [fi'lɔ] *m* voile.
filões [fi'lõjʃ] *mpl* ▷ **filão**.
filologia [filolo'ʒia] *f* philology.
filólogo, ga [fi'lɔlogu, ga] *m, f* philologist.
filosofar [4] [filozo'fa(x)] *vi* to philosophize.
filosofia [filozo'fia] *f* philosophy.
filosófico, ca [filo'zofiku, ka] *adj* philosophical.
filósofo, fa [fi'lɔzofu, fi'lɔzofa] *m, f* philosopher.
filtragem [fiwtra'ʒẽ] (*pl* -ns) *f* [filtração] filtration.

filtrar [4] [fiw'tra(x)] *vt* -**1.** [purificar] to filter. -**2.** [selecionar] to select.
filtro ['fiwtru] *m* filter; ~ **de ar** air filter.
fim ['fĩ] (*pl* -ns) *m* [ger] end; ~ **de semana** weekend; ~ **de mundo, do mundo** [cafundó] middle of nowhere; **no** ~ **das contas** after all; **ser o** ~ **(da picada)** to be the last straw; **por** ~ finally.
➡ **a fim de** *loc prep* in order to; **estar a** ~ **de fazer algo** to be planning on doing sthg; **estar a** ~ **de alguém** to be attracted to sb.
fimose [fi'mɔzi] *f* phimosis.
finado, da [fi'nadu, da] <> *adj* dead. <> *m, f* dead person.
➡ **finados** *mpl* RELIG: **os** ~**s** All Souls.
final [fi'naw] (*pl* -ais) <> *adj* final; **minuto** ~ last minute; **ponto** ~ full stop. <> *m* end; ~ **feliz** happy ending. <> *f* ESP final.
finalidade [finali'dadʒi] *f* end.
finalista [fina'liʃta] *mf* finalist.
finalização [finaliza'sãw] (*pl* -ões) *f* conclusion.
finalizar [4] [finali'za(x)] <> *vt* [concluir] to conclude. <> *vi* FUT [fazer gol] to score.
finanças [fi'nãnsaʃ] *fpl* -**1.** [ciência] finance *(sg)*. -**2.** [situação financeira] finances.
financeiro, ra [finãn'sejru, ra] *adj* financial.
➡ **financeira** *f* [firma] finance company.
financiamento [finãnsja'mẽntu] *m* financing.
financiar [16] [finãn'sja(x)] *vt* to finance.
financista [finãn'siʃta] *mf* financier.
fincar [12] [fĩŋ'ka(x)] *vt* [cravar] to stick.
findar [4] [fĩn'da(x)] *vt & vi* to end.
➡ **findar-se** *vp* to end.
findo, da [fĩndu, da] *adj* finished.
fineza [fi'neza] *f*-**1.** [espessura] fineness. -**2.** [gentileza] politeness.
fingido, da [fĩn'ʒidu, da] <> *adj* fake. <> *m, f* dissembler.
fingimento [fĩnʒi'mẽntu] *m* pretence *UK*, pretense *US*.
fingir [52] [fĩ'ʒi(x)] <> *vt* to fake. <> *vi* to pretend.
➡ **fingir-se** *vp:* ~-**se de algo** to pretend to be sthg.
finito, ta [fi'nitu, ta] *adj* finite.
finitude [fini'tudʒi] *f* [limitação] finite nature.
finlandês, esa [fĩnlãn'dejʃ, eza] <> *adj* Finnish. <> *m, f* Finnish person, Finn.
➡ **finlandês** *m* [língua] Finnish.
Finlândia [fĩn'lãndʒja] *n* Finland.
fino, na ['finu, na] *adj* -**1.** [ger] fine. -**2.** [agudo] shrill. -**3.** [refinado] elegant. -**4.** *loc:* **ser o** ~ to be the best; **tirar um** ~ **de** to come within a hair's breadth of.
fins [fĩʃ] *mpl* ▷ **fim**.
finura [fi'nura] *f* -**1.** [espessura] fineness. -**2.** [refinamento] refinement.
fio ['fiw] *m* -**1.** [ger] thread. -**2.** ELETR wire. -**3.** [gume] blade. -**4.** [filete] trickle. -**5.** *loc:* **bater um** ~ *fam* to have a phone conversation.
➡ **a fio** *loc adj:* **dias/horas a** ~ days/hours on end.

por um fio *loc adv*: **o emprego dele está por um ~** his job hangs by a thread; **escapou da morte por um ~** he escaped death by a hair's breadth.

fiorde [ˈfjoxdʒil] *m* fjord.

firma [ˈfixmal] *f* -1. COM firm. -2. [assinatura] signature.

firmamento [fixmaˈmẽntul] *m* firmament.

firmar [4] [fixˈma(x)] ◇ *vt* -1. [fixar] to steady. -2. [assinar] to sign. -3. [estabelecer] to establish. -4. [basear]: **~ algo em algo** to base sthg on sthg. ◇ *vi* [estabilizar-se] to settle.
◆ **firmar-se** *vp* to settle.

firme [ˈfixmi] *adj* -1. [ger] firm. -2. [fixo] steady, stable. -3. [constante] settled. -4. [estável] stable.

firmeza [fixˈmeza] *f* -1. [ger] firmness. -2. [estabilidade] steadiness, stability. -3. [segurança] soundness.

fiscal [fiʃˈkaw] (*pl* -ais) ◇ *adj* [relativo ao fisco] fiscal. ◇ *mf* -1. [aduaneiro] customs officer. -2. [supervisor - de impostos] inspector; [- de prova] invigilator.

fiscalização [fiʃkalizaˈsãw] (*pl* -ões) *f* overseeing.

fiscalizar [4] [fiʃkaliˈza(x)] *vt* -1. [estabelecimento, obras] to oversee. -2. [prova] to invigilate.

fisco [ˈfiʃku] *m*: **o ~** the public purse.

fisgada [fiʒˈgada] *f* stabbing pain.

fisgar [14] [fiʒˈga(x)] *vt* -1. [peixe] to harpoon. -2. [pessoa] to understand.

físico, ca [ˈfiziku, ka] ◇ *adj* [ger] physical; **educação física** physical education. ◇ *m, f* FÍSICA physicist.
◆ **físico** *m* [corpo] physique.
◆ **física** *f* [ciência] physics (*sg*).

fisiologia [fizjoloˈʒial] *f* physiology.

fisiológico, ca [fizjoˈlɔʒiku, ka] *adj* -1. MED physiological. -2. POL self-serving.

fisiologismo [fizjoloˈʒiʒmul] *m* POL self-interest.

fisionomia [fizjonoˈmial] *f* features (*pl*), appearance; **ela está com boa ~** she's looking well.

fisionomista [fizjonoˈmiʃta] *mf* person who is good at remembering faces.

fisioterapeuta [fizjoteraˈpewtal] *mf* physiotherapist.

fisioterapia [fizjoteraˈpial] *f* physiotherapy.

fissura [fiˈsural] *f* -1. GEOL fissure. -2. *fam* [gana] hankering.

fissurado, da [fisuˈradu, dal] *adj* -1. [rachado] cracked. -2. *fam* [maluco por]: **~ em** mad about.

fissurar [4] [fisuˈra(x)] *vt* to crack.

fístula [ˈfiʃtula] *f* fistula.

fita [ˈfital] *f* -1. [tira] ribbon; **~ crepe** crêpe bandage; **~ durex**® *ou* **colante** Sellotape® *UK;* Scotch tape® *US;* **~ de impressora** typewriter ribbon; **~ isolante** insulating tape; **~ magnética** magnetic tape; **~ métrica** tape measure, measuring tape. -2. [filme] tape. -3. [cassete]: **~ de vídeo** videotape; **~ virgem** blank tape. -4. [manha] play-acting.

fitar [4] [fiˈta(x)] *vt* to stare.
◆ **fitar-se** *vp* to stare at one another.

fiteiro, ra [fiˈtejru, ral] *adj* play-acting.

fito [ˈfitul] *m* target.

fivela [fiˈvɛla] *f* -1. [fecho] buckle. -2. [de cabelo] hair clip.

fixação [fiksaˈsãw] (*pl* -ões) *f* fixation.

fixador [fiksaˈdo(x)] (*pl* -es) *m* -1. [de cabelo] hairspray. -2. [de essência] fixing agent.

fixar [4] [fikˈsa(x)] *vt* -1. [prender] to fix. -2. [apreender] to make stick. -3. [estabelecer] to set.
◆ **fixar-se** *vp* -1. [estabilizar-se] to be fixed. -2. [estabelecer residência] to settle. -3. [fitar]: **~ em** to stare at.

fixo, xa [ˈfiksu, ksal] *adj* fixed.

flacidez [flasiˈdejʒl] *f* flaccidity.

flácido, da [ˈflasidu, dal] *adj* flaccid.

flagelado, da [flaʒeˈladu, dal] *adj* flogged.

flagelante [flaʒeˈlãntʃil] *adj* -1. [chicote] searing. -2. [isolamento] punishing.

flagelo [flaˈʒelul] *m* scourge.

flagrante [flaˈgrãntʃil] ◇ *adj* flagrant. ◇ *m*: **pegar em ~ (de algo)** to catch in the act (of sthg); **em ~** red-handed, in flagrante.

flagrar [4] [flaˈgra(x)] *vt* to catch in the act.

flama [ˈflãmal] *f* flame.

flambar [4] [flãˈba(x)] *vt* to flambé.

flamejante [flameˈʒãntʃil] *adj* flaming.

flamejar [4] [flameˈʒa(x)] *vi* to flame.

flamenco, ca [flaˈmẽŋku, kal] ◇ *adj* flamenco.
◆ **flamenco** *m* flamenco.

flamengo, ga [flaˈmẽŋgu, gal] *adj* Flemish.
◆ **flamengo** *m* [língua] Flemish.

flamingo [flaˈmĩŋgul] *m* flamingo.

flâmula [ˈflãmulal] *f* pennant.

flanco [ˈflãŋkul] *m* flank.

flanela [flaˈnɛlal] *f* flannel.

flanelinha [flaneˈliɲal] *mf fam* unofficial car-park attendant.

flanquear [15] [flãŋˈkja(x)] *vt* -1. [atacar de flanco] to attack in the flank. -2. [ladear] to flank.

flash [ˈflɛʃil] (*pl* -es) *m* flash.

flash-back [flaʃˈbakil] (*pl* **flash-backs**) *m* flashback.

flatulência [flatuˈlẽnsjal] *f* flatulence.

flauta [ˈflawtal] *f* flute; **~ doce** tin whistle; **~ transversa** transverse flute; **levar algo na ~** to take sthg lightly.

flautim [flawˈtʃil] (*pl* -ns) *m* piccolo.

flautista [flawˈtʃiʃtal] *mf* flautist.

flebite [fleˈbitʃil] *f* phlebitis.

flecha [ˈflɛʃal] *f* arrow.

flechada [fleˈʃadal] *f* -1. [arremesso] arrow shot. -2. [ferimento] arrow wound.

flertar [4] [flexˈta(x)] *vi*: **~ (com alguém)** to flirt (with sb).

flerte [ˈflextʃil] *m* flirt.

fleuma [ˈflewmal] *f* phlegm.

fleumático, ca [flewˈmatʃiku, kal] *adj* phlegmatic.

flexão [flekˈsãwl] (*pl* -ões) *f* -1. [movimento] flexing. -2. GRAM inflexion.

flexibilidade [fleksibiliˈdadʒil] *f* flexibility.

flexibilização [fleksibiliza'sãw] (pl -ões) f relaxation.

flexibilizar [fleksibili'za(x)] vt to relax.

flexionado, da [fleksio'nadu, da] adj LING inflected.

flexionar [4] [fleksjo'na(x)] <> vt -1. [joelho etc] to flex. -2. GRAM to inflect. <> vi GRAM to inflect.

flexível [flek'sivɛw] (pl -eis) adj flexible.

flexões [flek'sõjʃ] fpl ▷ flexão.

fliperama [flipe'rãma] m -1. [máquina] pinball machine. -2. [estabelecimento] amusement arcade.

floco ['flɔkul] m flake; ~ de milho cornflake; ~ de neve snowflake.
  ▸ **flocos** mpl: sorvete de ~s chocolate chip ice-cream.

flor ['flo(x)] (pl -es) f -1. BOT flower. -2. [pessoa boa]: ser uma ~ to be a gem. -3. loc: a fina ~ de the flower of; na ~ da idade in the prime of life; não ser ~ que se cheire not to be trusted.

flora ['flɔral] f flora.

floral [flo'raw] (pl -ais) <> adj floral. <> m floral infusion; **florais de Bach** Bach flower remedies.

floreado, da [flo'rjadu, da] adj flowery.

florear [15] [flo'rja(x)] vt [rebuscar] to embellish.

floreio [flo'reju] m flourish.

Florença [flo'rẽsa] n Florence.

florescente [flore'sẽtʃi] adj -1. [BOT - árvore] blossoming; [- planta] flowering. -2. fig [próspero] flowering.

florescer [25] [flore'se(x)] vi -1. [BOT - árvore] to blossom; [- planta] to flower. -2. fig [prosperar] to flower.

floresta [flo'rɛʃta] f forest.

florestal [floreʃ'taw] (pl -ais) adj forest (antes de subst).

Florianópolis [florja'nɔpoliʃ] n Florianópolis.

floricultor, ra [florikuw'to(x), ra] m, f floriculturist.

floricultura [florikuw'tura] f floriculture.

florido, da [flo'ridu, da] adj flower-filled.

florir [79] [flo'ri(x)] vi -1. [árvore] to blossom. -2. [planta] to flower.

florista [flo'riʃta] mf florist.

flotilha [flo'tiʎa] f flotilla.

fluência [flu'ẽsja] f fluency.

fluente [flu'ẽtʃi] adj fluent.

fluidez [fluj'deʒ] f fluidity.

fluido, da [flu'idu, ida] adj -1. [substância] fluid. -2. fig [fácil] flowing; **tráfego** ~ smooth-flowing traffic.
  ▸ **fluido** m fluid.

fluir [74] [flwi(x)] vi -1. [ger] to flow. -2. [derivar]: ~ de to derive from.

flúor ['fluo(x)] m fluoride.

fluorescente [flworeʃ'sẽtʃi] adj fluorescent.

flutuação [flutwa'sãw] (pl -ões) f fluctuation.

flutuante [flu'twãtʃi] adj -1. [boiante] floating. -2. [oscilante] fluctuating.

flutuar [4] [flu'twa(x)] vi -1. [ger] to float. -2. [variar] to fluctuate.

fluvial [flu'vjaw] (pl -ais) adj river (antes de subst).

fluxo ['fluksu] m -1. [ger] flow. -2. COM: ~ de caixa cash flow. -3. MED: ~ menstrual menstrual flow. -4. FÍSICA: ~ de massa flow rate.

fluxograma [flukso'grama] m flow chart.

FM (abrev de freqüencia modulada) m FM.

FMI (abrev de Fundo Monetário Internacional) m IMF.

fobia [fo'bia] f phobia.

foca ['fɔka] <> f ZOOL seal. <> mf [jornalista] cub reporter.

focal [fo'kaw] (pl -ais) adj focal.

focalização [fokaliza'sãw] f focusing.

focalizar [4] [fokali'za(x)], **focar** [4] [fo'ka(x)] vt to focus.

focinho [fo'siɲu] m -1. [de suíno] snout. -2. [de cão] muzzle.

foco ['fɔkul] m focus.

foder [5] ['fode(x)] vulg <> vt [copular com] to fuck. <> vi [copular] to fuck.
  ▸ **foder-se** vp vulg [dar-se mal] to fuck up.

fodido, da [fo'dʒidu, da] vulg adj -1. [ferrado] fucked; ~ e mal pago up shit creek without a paddle. -2. [pobre] loser.

fofo, fa ['fofu, fa] adj -1. [macio] soft. -2. [gracioso] cute.

fofoca [fo'fɔka] f gossip; **fazer** ~ to spread gossip.

fofocar [12] [fofo'ka(x)] vi to gossip.

fofoqueiro, ra [fofo'kejru, ra] <> adj gossipy. <> m, f gossip.

fofura [fo'fura] f cuteness; **ser uma** ~ to be cute.

fogão [fo'gãw] (pl -ões) m stove, cooker.

fogareiro [foga'rejru] m (paraffin) cooker, coal pot.

fogaréu [foga'rɛw] m torch.

fogo ['fogul] (pl fogos) m -1. [ger] fire; **pegar** ~ to catch fire; **brincar com** ~ fig to play with fire; **ser** ~ **(na roupa)** to mean trouble. -2. [excitação] flame; ~ **de palha** hot air. -3. [desejo sexual] sex drive. -4. [disparo]: **abrir** ~ to open fire; **fogo!** fire!; **poder de** ~ firepower. -5. [pirotecnia]: ~(s) **de artifício** fireworks. -6. loc: **estar de** ~ [estar embriagado] to be plastered.

fogões [fo'gõjʃ] mpl ▷ fogão.

fogo-fátuo [ˌfogu'fatwul] (pl fogos-fátuos) m will-o'-the-wisp.

fogoso, osa [fo'gozu, ɔza] adj -1. [arrebatado] fiery. -2. [sexualmente] aroused.

fogueira [fo'gejra] f bonfire.

foguete [fo'getʃi] m rocket; **soltar** ~s **antes da hora** fig to count one's chickens before they're hatched.

fogueteiro, ra [foge'tejru, ra] m, f pyrotechnist.

foguetório [foge'tɔrju] m noise of fireworks.

foice ['fojsi] f scythe.

folclore [fow'klɔri] m folklore.

folclórico, ca [fow'klɔriku, ka] adj folk.

fole ['fɔli] m bellows (pl).

fôlego ['folegu] m -1. [respiração] breath; **perder o** ~ to lose one's breath; **tomar** ~ to take a breath. **-2.** *fig* [ânimo]: **recuperar o** ~ to recover one's breath.

folga ['fɔwga] *f* **-1.** [descanso] break; **dia de** ~ day off. **-2.** [abuso]: **que** ~**!** what a cheek! **-3.** [sobra de espaço] space. **-4.** [sobra de tempo] gap.

folgado, da [fow'gadu, da] *adj* **-1.** [largo] loose. **-2.** [abusado] cocky. **-3.** [despreocupado] easy.

◆ **folgado** *adv* easily.

folgazão, zona [fowga'zãw, zɔna] (*mpl* -ões, *fpl* -s) *adj* idler.

folha ['foʎa] *f* **-1.** *BOT* leaf. **-2.** [página] page; ~ **de rosto** title page; ~ **de pagamento** pay sheet. **-3.** [chapa] plate. **-4.** [jornal] newspaper. **-5.** [lâmina] blade. **-6.** [pedaço de papel] sheet.

◆ **em folha** *loc adv*: **novo em** ~ brand new.

folhagem [fo'ʎaʒẽ] (*pl* -ns) *f* foliage.

folha-seca [ˌfoʎa'seka] (*pl* **folhas-secas**) *f* *FUT* lob.

folheado, da [fo'ʎadu, da] *adj* **-1.** [revestido]: ~ **a ouro/prata** gold-/silver-plated. **-2.** *CULIN*: **massa folheada** puff pastry.

folhear [15] [fo'ʎja(x)] *vt* to leaf through.

folhetim [foʎe'tʃĩ] (*pl* -ns) *m* serialization.

folhetinesco, ca [foʎetʃi'neʃku, ka] *adj* [de folhetim] *published daily in a newspaper or magazine.*

folheto [fo'ʎetu] *m* pamphlet.

folhinha [fo'ʎiɲa] *f* [calendário] calendar.

folia [fo'lia] *f* revelry.

folião, ona [fo'ljãw, ɔna] (*mpl* -ões, *fpl* -s) *m, f* reveller.

folículo [fo'likulu] *m* follicle.

foliona [fo'ljona] *f* ⊳ **folião**.

fome ['fɔmi] *f* [ger] hunger; **estar com** ~ to be hungry; **passar** ~ to go hungry.

fomentar [4] [fomẽ'ta(x)] *vt* to foment.

fomento [fo'mẽtu] *m* **-1.** *MED* poultice. **-2.** [estímulo] fomentation.

fominha [fo'miɲa] *adj* mean.

fonador, ra [fona'do(x), ra] *adj* phonic; **aparelho** ~ speech apparatus.

fone ['fɔni] (*abrev de* **telefone**) *m* phone.

fonema [fo'nema] *m* phoneme.

fonético, ca [fo'nɛtʃiku, ka] *adj* phonetic.

◆ **fonética** *f* phonetics *(sg)*.

fônico, ca ['foniku, ka] *adj* phonic.

fonoaudiologia [fonawdʒiolo'gia] *f* speech therapy.

fonoaudiólogo, ga [ˌfonaw'dʒjɔlogu, ga] *m, f* speech therapist.

fonologia [fonolo'ʒia] *f* phonology.

fonte ['fõtʃi] ⟨⟩ *f* **-1.** [ger] source; **de** ~ **limpa** from a reliable source; **imposto retido na** ~ taxed at source. **-2.** [chafariz] fountain. **-3.** *COMPUT* [tipo de caractere] font. ⟨⟩ *m* *COMPUT* source code.

fora ['fɔra] ⟨⟩ *m* **-1.** [gafe] gaffe; **dar um** ~ to commit a gaffe. **-2.** *fig* [dispensa]: **dar um** ~ **em alguém** to rebuff sb; **levar um** ~ **de alguém** to be rebuffed by sb; **fora!** get out! **-3.** *loc*: **dar o** ~ [partir] to skedaddle. ⟨⟩ *adv* **-1.** [na parte exterior]: **do lado de** ~ on the outside; **por** ~ outside. **-2.**

[ao ar livre]: **lá** ~ outside. **-3.** [em outro lugar] away, out; **fui para** ~ **a semana** I went away last week; **jantei** ~ **ontem** I went out to dinner yesterday; **a família está** ~ **no momento** the family is out *ou* away at the moment; [no estrangeiro] abroad. **-4.** *fig* [distanciado]: ~ **de** out of; **estar** ~ **de si** to be beside o.s. ⟨⟩ *prep* [exceto] except for, apart from.

◆ **de fora** *loc adv* **-1.** [nu] exposed; **ficar com as pernas de** ~ to have one's legs exposed. **-2.** [sem participar]: **ficar de** ~ to be left out.

◆ **para fora** *loc adv*: **ela costura para** ~ she takes sewing in.

◆ **por fora** *loc adv* **-1.** [cobrar, pagar]: **cobrar por** ~ to receive on the side; **pagar por** ~ to pay on the side. **-2.** [ignorante]: **estar por** ~ **(de)** to be unaware (of).

◆ **fora de série** *loc adj* [excepcional] exceptional.

fora-da-lei [ˌfɔrada'lej] *mf inv* outlaw.

fora-de-estrada ['fɔradʒiʃ'trada] ⟨⟩ *adj* off-road. ⟨⟩ *m* all-terrain vehicle.

foragido, da [fora'ʒidu, da] ⟨⟩ *adj* fugitive. ⟨⟩ *m, f* fugitive.

foragir-se [52] [fora'ʒixsi] *vp* to flee.

forasteiro, ra [foraʃ'tejru, ra] *m, f* foreigner.

forca ['foxka] *f* gallows *(sg)*.

força ['foxsa] *f* **-1.** [ger] power. **-2.** [energia física, moral] strength; **ter** ~ **para fazer algo** to have (the) strength to do sthg; ~ **de vontade** will power. **-3.** [violência] force; **à** ~ by force; **com** ~ violently. **-4.** [esforço]: **fazer** ~ to try hard. **-5.** *MIL* force; ~**s armadas** armed forces. **-6.** [causa]: **motivo de** ~ **maior** due to unavoidable circumstances; **por** ~ **de** by force of. **-7.** [ânimo, apoio]: **dar** ~ **a alguém** to give support to sb.

◆ **força de expressão** *f* understatement.

forcado [fox'kadu] *m* pitchfork.

forçado, da [fox'sadu, da] *adj* **-1.** [ger] forced. **-2.** [interpretação] far-fetched.

forçar [13] [fur'sar] *vt* **-1.** [obrigar]: ~ **alguém (a algo/a fazer algo)** to force sb (to sthg/to do sthg). **-2.** [arrombar] to force. **-3.** [obter por força] to (obtain by) force. **-4.** [vista, voz] to strain. **-5.** [desvirtuar] to misinterpret. **-6.** *loc*: ~ **a barra** [insistir, pressionar] to force sb's hand.

◆ **forçar-se** *vp*: ~**-se a fazer algo** to force o.s. to do sthg, to make o.s. do sthg.

força-tarefa [ˌfoxsata'rɛfa] (*pl* **forças-tarefa**) *f* task force.

fórceps ['fɔxsepiʃ] *m inv* forceps *(pl)*.

forçosamente [foxsoza'mẽtʃi] *adv* necessarily.

forçoso, osa [fox'sozu, ɔza] *adj* necessary.

forense [fo'rẽsi] *adj* judicial.

forja ['fɔxʒa] *f* forge.

forjado, da [fox'ʃadu, da] *adj* **-1.** [utensílio, metal] forged. **-2.** [notícia] fabricated.

forjar [4] [fox'sa(x)] *vt* to forge.

forma ['foxma] *f* **-1.** [ger] form; **desta** ~ in this way, thus. **-2.** [estado físico, feitio] shape; **em** ~ **de** in the shape of; **estar em** ~ to be in shape; **estar**

fora de ~ to be out of shape. **-3.** [fila]: **entrar em** ~ to fall into line.

➤ **formas** *fpl* [silhueta] figure *(sg).*

➤ **de forma que** *loc conj* so that.

➤ **da mesma forma** *loc adv* similarly.

➤ **de forma alguma** *loc adv* in no way.

➤ **de qualquer forma** *loc adv* all the same.

➤ **de tal forma** *loc adv* in such a way.

fôrma ['fɔxma] *f* **-1.** CULIN mould. **-2.** [molde] mould, cast. **-3.** [de sapato] last.

formação [foxma'sãw] *(pl* **-ões)** *f* **-1.** [ger] formation. **-2.** [educação] upbringing.

formado, da [fox'madu, da] *adj* **-1.** [constituído]: ~ **por** made up of. **-2.** [graduado]: **ser** ~ **por** to be educated by.

formador, ra [foxma'do(x), ra] *adj*: ~ **de vício** habit-forming, addictive; ~ **de opinião** opinion-making.

formal [fox'maw] *(pl* **-ais)** *adj* formal.

formalidade [foxmali'dadʒi] *f* formality; **com** ~ formally.

formalismo [foxma'liʒmu] *m* **-1.** [convencionalismo] formality. **-2.** ARTE formalism.

formalizar [4] [foxmali'za(x)] *vt* **-1.** [ger] to formalize. **-2.** [estruturar] to formulate.

formando, da [fox'mãndu, da] *m, f* finalist.

formão [fox'mãw] *(pl* **-ões)** *m* chisel.

formar [4] [fox'ma(x)] <> *vt* **-1.** [ger] to form. **-2.** [educar] to educate. <> *vi* MIL [entrar em fila] to fall in.

➤ **formar-se** *vp* **-1.** [constituir-se] to form. **-2.** [graduar-se] to graduate.

formatar [4] [foxma'ta(x)] *vt* COMPUT to format.

formativo, va [foxma'tʃivu, va] *adj* formative.

formato [fox'matu] *m* **-1.** [forma] shape. **-2.** [modelo] format.

formatura [foxma'tura] *f* EDUC graduation.

fórmica ['fɔxmika] *f* formica®.

formidável [foxmi'davɛw] *(pl* **-eis)** *adj* **-1.** [fantástico] fantastic. **-2.** [imenso] formidable.

formiga [fox'miga] *f* ant.

formigamento [foxmiga'mẽntu] *m* pins and needles.

formigar [14] [foxmi'ga(x)] *vi* **-1.** [coçar] to have pins and needles. **-2.** *fig* [abundar]: ~ **de** to swarm with.

formigueiro [foxmi'gejru] *m* **-1.** [de formigas] anthill. **-2.** *fig* [multidão] swarm.

formol [fox'mɔw] *(pl* **-óis)** *m* formaldehyde.

formoso, osa [fox'mozu, ɔza] *adj* beautiful.

formosura [foxmo'zura] *f* beauty.

fórmula ['fɔxmula] *f* **-1.** [ger] formula. **-2.** [modo] (polite) phrase, (politeness) formula. **-3.** AUTO: ~ **um** Formula One.

formulação [foxmula'sãw] *(pl* **-ões)** *f* formulation.

formular [4] [foxmu'la(x)] *vt* to formulate.

formulário [foxmu'larju] *m* form; ~ **contínuo** COMPUT continuous stationery.

fornalha [fox'naʎa] *f* furnace.

fornecedor, ra [foxnese'do(x), ra] *(mpl* **-es,** *fpl* **-s)**

<> *adj* supplying. <> *m, f* supplier.

fornecer [25] [foxne'se(x)] *vt* to supply.

fornecimento [foxnesi'mẽntu] *m* supply.

fornicar [12] [foxni'ka(x)] *vi* to fornicate.

forno ['foxnu] *m* **-1.** CULIN oven; ~ **de microondas** microwave (oven). **-2.** [fornalha] kiln. **-3.** *fig* [lugar quente]: **ser/estar um** ~ to be like an oven.

foro ['foru] *m* forum.

forquilha [fox'kiʎa] *f* pitchfork.

forra ['fɔxa] *f*: **ir à** ~ to take one's revenge.

forração [foxa'sãw] *(pl* **-ões)** *f* filling.

forragem [fo'xagẽ] *(pl* **-ns)** *f* forage.

forrar [4] [fo'xa(x)] *vt* **-1.** [ger] to line. **-2.** [sofá, chão] to cover. **-3.** [parede] to paper.

forro ['foxu] *m* **-1.** [interno] lining. **-2.** [externo] cover.

forró [fo'xɔ] *m typical Brazilian dance of the north-east.*

fortalecer [25] [foxtale'se(x)] *vt* to strengthen.

fortalecimento [foxtalesi'mẽntu] *m* strengthening.

fortaleza [foxta'leza] *f* **-1.** [forte] fortress. **-2.** *fig* [bastião] fortress.

Fortaleza [foxta'leza] *n* Fortaleza.

forte ['fɔxtʃi] <> *adj* **-1.** [ger] strong. **-2.** [piada, palavra, filme] crude. **-3.** [poderoso] powerful. **-4.** [versado]: **ser** ~ **em algo** to be strong at sthg. **-5.** [intenso - emoção, calor, dor] intense; [- chuva] heavy. **-6.** [violento] violent. <> *m* **-1.** [fortaleza] stronghold. **-2.** *fig* [ponto forte] strength. <> *adv* heavily.

fortificação [foxtʃifika'sãw] *(pl* **-ões)** *f* fortification.

fortificante [foxtʃifi'kãntʃi] <> *adj* fortifying. <> *m* fortifier.

fortificar [12] [foxtʃifi'ka(x)] *vt* to fortify.

➤ **fortificar-se** *vp* to fortify o.s.

fortuitamente [foxtwita'mẽntʃi] *adv* fortuitously.

fortuito, ta [fox'twitu, ta] *adj* fortuitous.

fortuna [fox'tuna] *f* fortune.

fosco, ca ['foʃku, ka] *adj* tarnished.

fosfato [foʃ'fatu] *m* phosphate.

fosforescente [foʃfore'sẽntʃi] *adj* phosphorescent.

fosforescer [25] [foʃfore'se(x)] *vi* to phosphoresce.

fósforo ['fɔʃfuru] *m* **-1.** QUÍM phosphor. **-2.** [palito] matchstick.

fossa ['fɔsa] *f* **-1.** [buraco] hole; ~ **nasal** nostril; ~ **das Marianas** Mariana Trench. **-2.** [esgoto] ditch. **-3.** *fig* [depressão] slump; **estar/entrarna** ~ to be down in the dumps.

fóssil ['fɔsiw] *(pl* **-eis)** *m* fossil.

fosso ['fosu] *m* ditch.

foto ['fɔtu] *f* photo.

fotocomposição [fotokõmpozi'sãw] *(pl* **-ões)** *f* photocomposition, filmsetting.

fotocópia [foto'kɔpja] *f* photocopy.

fotocopiar [16] [fotoko'pja(x)] *vt* to photocopy.

fotofobia [fotofo'bia] *f* photophobia.

fotofóbico, ca [foto'fɔbiku, ka] *adj* photophobic.

fotogênico, ca [foto'ʒeniku, ka] *adj* photogenic.

fotografar [4] [fotogra'fa(x)] *vt* to photograph.

fotografia [fotogra'fia] *f* **-1.** [técnica] photography. **-2.** [foto] photograph.

fotográfico, ca [foto'grafiku, ka] *adj* photographic.

fotógrafo, fa [fo'tɔgrafu, fa] *m, f* photographer.

fotolito [foto'litu] *m* plate.

fotômetro [fo'tometru] *m* light meter.

fotomontagem [foto'mõtaʒẽ] *(pl* **-ns)** *f* photomontage.

fóton ['fɔtõ] *(pl* **-tons, -nes)** *m* [fís] photon.

fotonovela [fotono'vɛla] *f* photo-strip story.

fotossíntese [foto'sĩtezi] *f* photosynthesis.

fototerapia [fototera'pia] *f* phototherapy.

foxtrote [fɔks'trɔtʃi] *m* foxtrot.

foyer [fwa'je] *m* foyer.

foz ['fɔʃ] *f* estuary.

fração [fra'sãw] *(pl* **-ões)** *f* **-1.** [pedaço] bit. **-2.** MAT fraction.

fracassar [4] [fraka'sa(x)] *vi* to fail.

fracasso [fra'kasu] *m* failure.

fracionar [4] [frasjo'na(x)] *vt* to fragment.

fracionário, ria [frasiona'riu, ria] *adj* MAT fractional.

fraco, ca ['fraku, ka] *adj* **-1.** [ger] weak. **-2.** [medíocre]: ~ **(em)** weak (at). **-3.** [não ativo - bebida] weak; [- cigarro] mild; [- perfume] delicate.
◆ **fraco** ◇ *adv* weakly. ◇ *m* **-1.** [ponto fraco] weak point. **-2.** [inclinação] weakness.

frade ['fradʒi] *m* friar.

fragata [fra'gata] *f* frigate.

frágil ['fraʒiw] *(pl* **-eis)** *adj* fragile.

fragilidade [fraʒili'dadʒi] *f* fragility.

fragilizar [4] [fraʒili'za(x)] *vt* to make vulnerable.

fragmentação [fragmẽta'sãw] *(pl* **-ões)** *f* fragmentation.

fragmentar [4] [fragmẽ'ta(x)] *vt* to fragment.
◆ **fragmentar-se** *vp* to fragment.

fragmento [frag'mẽtu] *m* fragment.

fragrância [fra'grãsja] *f* fragrance.

fragrante [fra'grãtʃi] *adj* fragrant.

fralda ['frawda] *f* **-1.** [cueiro] nappy *UK*, diaper *US*. **-2.** [de camisa] shirt tail.

framboesa [frãm'bweza] *f* raspberry.

frame ['frejmi] *m* COMPUT frame.

França ['frãsa] *n* France.

francamente [ˌfrãŋka'mẽtʃi] *adv* frankly.

francês, esa [frã'seʃ, eza] *(mpl* **-eses,** *fpl* **-s)** ◇ *adj* French. ◇ *m, f* Frenchman (*f* Frenchwoman).
◆ **francês** *m* [língua] French.

franco, ca ['frãŋku, ka] *adj* **-1.** [ger] free. **-2.** [sincero] frank. **-3.** [clara] candid.
◆ **franco** *m* [moeda] franc.

franco-atirador, ra ['frãŋkuatriʃirado(x), ra] *m, f* sniper.

franco-brasileiro, ra [ˌfrãŋkobrazi'lejru, ra] *(mpl* **franco-brasileiros,** *fpl* **franco-brasileiras)** *adj* Franco-Brazilian.

francófono, na [frã'kɔfonu, na] ◇ *adj* French-speaking. ◇ *m, f* French speaker.

franga ['frãŋga] *f* pullet.

frangalho [frãŋ'gaʎu] *m* [farrapo] tatter; **em** ~ **s** *fig* in tatters.

frango ['frãŋgu] ◇ *m* ZOOL chicken. ◇ *m* FUT easy goal.

franja ['frãʒa] *f* fringe.

franjado, da [frã'ʒadu, da] *adj* **-1.** [cabelo, xale] fringed. **-2.** [rebuscado] recherché.

franqueado, da [frã'keadu, da] *m* franchise.

franquear [15] [frãŋ'kja(x)] *vt* **-1.** [liberar]: **a entrada foi franqueada, vamos à festa!** they've opened the doors, let's party! **-2.** [isentar de imposto] to exempt (from). **-3.** [pagar o transporte] to pay transport costs (for). **-4.** [ceder franquia] to franchise.

franqueza [frã'keza] *f* frankness.

franquia [frã'kia] *f* **-1.** COM franchise. **-2.** [isenção] exemption; ~ **de bagagem** baggage allowance; ~ **postal** postage.

franzido, da [frã'zidu, da] *adj* **-1.** [saia] gathered, pleated. **-2.** [pele] wrinkled.

franzino, na [frã'zinu, na] *adj* delicate.

franzir [6] [frã'zi(x)] *vt* **-1.** [preguear] to pleat. **-2.** [enrugar] to wrinkle; ~ **a sobrancelha** to frown.

fraque ['fraki] *m* frock coat.

fraquejar [4] [frake'ʒa(x)] *vi* to weaken.

fraqueza [fra'keza] *f* weakness.

frasco ['fraʃku] *m* flask.

frase ['frazi] *f* **-1.** [oração] sentence; ~ **feita** aphorism. **-2.** MÚS phrase.

fraseado [fra'zjadu] *m* phrasing.

fraseologia [frazjolo'gia] *f* phraseology.

frasqueira [fraʃ'kejra] *f* bottle rack.

fraternal [fratex'naw] *(pl* **-ais)** *adj* fraternal, brotherly.

fraternidade [fratexni'dadʒi] *f* fraternity.

fraterno, na [fra'tɛxnu, na] *adj* fraternal, brotherly.

fratricida [fratri'sida] *mf* fratricide.

fratura [fra'tura] *f* fracture.

fraturar [4] [fratu'ra(x)] *vt* to fracture.

fraudar [4] [fraw'da(x)] *vt* to defraud.

fraude ['frawdʒi] *f* fraud.

fraudulento, ta [frawdu'lẽtu, ta] *adj* fraudulent.

freada [fre'ada] *f* braking; **dar uma** ~ to brake.

frear [15] [fre'a(x)] ◇ *vt* **-1.** AUTO to brake. **-2.** *fig* [controlar] to curb. ◇ *vi* AUTO to brake.

freático, ca ['freatʃiku, ka] *adj*: **lençol** ~ water table; **camada freática** aquifer.

freelance [fri'lãsi] ◇ *adj* freelance. ◇ *mf* freelance, freelancer.

freeware [fri'wari] *(pl* **freewares)** *m* COMPUT freeware.

freezer ['frizɛx] *(pl* **-res)** *m* freezer.

frege ['freʒi] *m* quarrel.

freguês, esa [frɛ'geʃ, ezа] *(mpl* **-eses,** *fpl* **-s)** *m, f* **-1.** [cliente] customer. **-2.** [paroquiano] parishioner.

freguesia [frege'zia] f -1. [clientela] clientele. -2. [paroquia] parish.

frei [frej] m friar.

freio ['freju] m -1. [cavalo] rein. -2. [carro] brake; ~ **de mão** handbrake; ~ **de pé** footbrake.

freira ['frejra] f nun.

freixo ['frejʃu] m ash.

fremir [6] [fre'mi(x)] vi -1. [rugir] to roar. -2. [tremer] to tremble.

frêmito ['fremitu] m shiver.

frenesi [frene'zi] m frenzy.

freneticamente [frenɛtʃika'mẽntʃi] adv frenetically.

frenético, ca [fre'nɛtʃiku, ka] adj frenetic.

frente ['frẽntʃi] f -1. [lado dianteiro]: **na ~ (de)** in front (of); **estar à ~ de** fig to be ahead of. -2. [avante]: **em ~** ahead; **ir para a ~** to move on; **levar algo à ~** to make sthg succeed. -3. [resistência] front; ~ **de combate** frontline. -4. [presença] in front of; ~ **a ~** face to face. -5. METEOR: ~ **fria/quente** cold/warm front.

frentista [frẽn'tʃiʃta] mf forecourt attendant.

freqüência [fre'kwẽnsja] f -1. [ger] frequency; **com ~** frequently. -2. [pessoas] attendance.

freqüentador, ra [frekwẽnta'do(x), ra] m, f regular.

freqüentar [4] [frekwẽn'ta(x)] vt -1. [visitar] to frequent. -2. [cursar] to attend.

freqüente [fre'kwẽntʃi] adj recurrent.

freqüentemente [frekwẽntʃi'mẽntʃi] adv frequently.

fresa ['freza] f MEC milling cutter, drill.

fresca ['freʃka] f ⊳ **fresco**.

frescão [freʃ'kãw] (pl -ões) m de luxe coach.

fresco, ca ['freʃku, ka] adj -1. [ger] fresh. -2. [ameno] cool. -3. fam [luxento] posh. -4. fam [homossexual] camp.
    ➡ **fresca** f [aragem] breeze.

frescobol [freʃko'bɔw] (pl -óis) m beach tennis.

frescões [freʃ'kõjʃ] mpl ⊳ **frescão**.

frescor [freʃ'ko(x)] m [viço, vigor] freshness.

frescura [freʃ'kura] f -1. [frescor] freshness. -2. [afetação] affectation. -3. [formalidade] convention.

fresta ['frɛʃta] f slit.

fretado, da [fre'tadu, da] adj -1. [navio, caminhão] chartered. -2. [carro] hired.

fretar [4] [fre'ta(x)] vt to hire UK, to rent US.

frete ['frɛtʃi] m freight; **fazer ~** to freight.

freudiano, na [frɔj'dʒanu, na] adj Freudian.

frevo ['frevu] m Brazilian carnival street-dance, where dancers improvise their own dances.

fria ['fria] f fam [apuros] fix; **entrar numa ~** to be in a fix.

friagem ['frjaʒẽ] f cold.

fricção [frik'sãw] f friction.

friccionar [4] [friksjo'na(x)] vt to rub.

fricote [fri'kɔtʃi] m: **fazer ~s** to put on airs.

fricoteiro, ra [friko'tejru, ra] ⟨⟩ adj vain. ⟨⟩ m, f show-off.

frieira [fri'ejra] f chilblain.

frieza ['frjeza] f -1. [insensibilidade] cold-heartedness. -2. [desinteresse] off-handedness.

frigideira [friʒi'dejra] f frying pan.

frigidez [friʒi'deʒ] f frigidity.

frígido, da [friʒidu, da] adj frigid.

frigir [63] [fri'ʒi(x)] vt to fry.

frigorífico [frigo'rifikul] m -1. [loja] cold store. -2. [aparelho] fridge, refrigerator.

frila ['frila] mf fam freelance.

frio, fria ['friu, 'fria] adj -1. [sem calor] cold. -2. [insensível] cold. -3. [falso] fake. -4. [cor] cold. -5. [luz] cold.
    ➡ **frio** m [baixa temperatura] cold; **estar com ~** to be cold; **fazer ~** to be cold.
    ➡ **frios** mpl [carne] cold meats.

friorento, ta [frjo'rẽntu, ta] adj chilly.

frisa ['friza] f TEATRO box.

frisar [4] [fri'za(x)] vt -1. [salientar] to highlight. -2. [enrolar] to curl.

friso ['frizu] m -1. [borda] border. -2. ARQUIT frieze.

fritada [fri'tada] f fried food.

fritar [4] [fri'ta(x)] vt to fry.

frito, ta ['fritu, ta] adj -1. CULIN fried. -2. fam [em apuros]: **estar ~** to be in hot water.
    ➡ **fritas** fpl chips UK, (French) fries US.

fritura [fri'tural] f fried food, fry-up UK.

frivolidade [frivoli'dadʒi] f frivolity.

frívolo, la ['frivolu, la] adj frivolous.

frondoso, osa [frõn'dozu, ɔza] adj leafy.

fronha ['froɲa] f pillowcase.

front [frõ] m MIL front.

frontal [frõn'taw] (pl -ais) adj frontal.

fronte ['frõntʃi] f forehead.

fronteira [frõn'tejra] f ⊳ **fronteiro**.

fronteiriço, ça [frõntej'risu, sa] adj border (antes de subst).

fronteiro, ra [frõn'tejru, ra] adj facing.
    ➡ **fronteira** f -1. [extremidade] border. -2. fig [limite] border.

frontispício [frõntʃiʃ'pisju] m frontispiece.

frota ['frɔta] f fleet.

frouxo, xa ['froʃu, ʃa] adj -1. [folgado] loose. -2. [fraco, ineficiente] weak. -3. [condescendente]: **ser ~ com alguém** to be weak with sb. -4. [covarde] feeble.

frufru [fru'fru] m frill, frou-frou.

frugal [fru'gaw] (pl -ais) adj frugal.

frugalidade [frugali'dadʒi] f frugality.

fruição [frwi'sãw] f fruition.

fruir [74] [frwi(x)] vi: ~ **de algo** to enjoy sthg.

frustração [fruʃtra'sãw] (pl -ões) f -1. [malogro] frustration. -2. [decepção] frustration.

frustrado, da [fruʃ'tradu, da] adj -1. [malogrado] frustrated. -2. [decepcionado] disappointed.

frustrante [fruʃ'trãntʃi] adj frustrating.

frustrar [4] [fruʃ'tra(x)] vt -1. [malograr] to frustrate. -2. [decepcionar] to cheat. -3. [privar]: ~ **alguém de algo** to deprive sb of sthg.
    ➡ **frustrar-se** vp -1. [malograr-se] to be frustrated. -2. [decepcionar-se] to be disappointed.

fruta l'frutal ffruit.

fruta-de-conde [ˌfrutadʒi'kõndʒi] (pl **frutas-de-conde**) f custard apple.

fruta-pão [ˌfruta'pãw] (pl **frutas-pães, frutas-pão**) f breadfruit.

fruteiro, ra lfru'tejru, ral adj fruit-loving.
➡ **fruteira** ffruit tree.

frutífero, ra lfru'tʃiferu, ral adj -**1**. [árvore] fruit-bearing. -**2**. [proveitoso] fruitful.

fruto l'frutul m -**1**. [fruta] fruit. -**2**. fig [resultado] fruit.

FTP (abrev de File Transfer Protocol) m FTP.

fubá lfu'bal m -**1**. [de milho] maize flour. -**2**. [de arroz] rice flour.

fuça l'fusal f fam [focinho] conk, nose; **nas ∼s de** under the nose of.

fuçar [13] lfu'sa(x)l fam ⟨⟩ vt to meddle in. ⟨⟩ vi to meddle.

fuga l'fugal f -**1**. [escapada] escape. -**2**. fig [alívio] escape. -**3**. MÚS fugue.

fugaz lfu'gaʒl adj fleeting.

fugida lfu'ʒidal f escape; **dar uma ∼** to make one's escape.

fugidio, dia lfu'ʒidio, dial adj -**1**. [animal] skittish. -**2**. [pessoa, personalidade] retiring.

fugir [62] lfu'ʒi(x)l vi -**1**. [escapar]: **∼ (de)** to escape (from). -**2**. [evitar]: **∼ de algo/alguém** to avoid sthg/sb.

fugitivo, va lfuʒi'tʃivu, val ⟨⟩ adj fugitive. ⟨⟩ m, f fugitive.

fulano, na lfu'lanu, nal m, f so-and-so; **∼ de tal** some so-and-so; **∼, beltrano e sicrano** Tom, Dick or Harry.

fuleiro, ra lfu'lejru, ral adj shabby.

fúlgido, da l'fuwʒidu, dal adj dazzling.

fulgir [78] lfuw'ʒi(x)l vi to dazzle.

fulgor lfuw'go(x)l m brilliance.

fulgurante lfuwgu'rãntʃil adj shining.

fuligem lfu'liʒēl f soot.

fulminante lfuwmi'nãntʃil adj -**1**. [mortal] deadly. -**2**. fig [irado] vicious.

fulminar [4] lfuwmi'na(x)l vt -**1**. [matar] to kill. -**2**. [aniquilar] to annihilate.

fulo, la l'fulu, lal adj: **estar** ou **ficar ∼ da vida** to be totally fed up.

fumaça lfu'masal f smoke; **e lá vai ∼** something or other.

fumaceira lfuma'sejral f (cloud of) smoke.

fumante lfu'mãntʃil mf smoker; **não ∼** non-smoker.

fumar [4] lfu'ma(x)l ⟨⟩ vt to smoke. ⟨⟩ vi to smoke.

fumê lfu'mel adj inv smoky.

fumegante lfume'gãntʃil adj steaming.

fumegar [4] lfume'ga(x)l vi -**1**. [fumaçar] to smoke. -**2**. fig [enfurecer-se] to blow up.

fumo l'fumul m -**1**. [tabaco] tobacco. -**2**. [maconha] dope; **puxar ∼** to draw (on a spliff). -**3**. [vício] smoking.

fumódromo lfu'mɔdromul m fam smoking area.

FUNAI (abrev de Fundação Nacional do Índio) f Brazilian government organization for the protection of the indigenous population.

FUNARTE (abrev de **Fundação Nacional de Arte**) f Brazilian government organization for the promotion of artistic activities.

FUNASA (abrev de **Fundação Nacional de Saúde**) f Brazilian government organization for health education and prevention of disease among indigenous peoples.

função lfũn'sãwl (pl -**ões**) f -**1**. [cargo] function. -**2**. [responsabilidade] function. -**3**. [utilidade] role. -**4**. [espetáculo] performance. -**5**. [papel] function. -**6**. [atribuição] function. -**7**. GRAM function. -**8**. MAT function.
➡ **em função de** loc prep due to.

funcional lfũnsjo'nawl (pl -**ais**) adj -**1**. [ger] functional. -**2**. [público] civil-service. -**3**. [de carreira] service-related.

funcionalidade lfũnsjonali'dadʒil f functionality.

funcionalismo lfũnsjona'liʒmul m -**1**. [praticidade] practicality. -**2**. [servidores]: **∼ público** civil service.

funcionamento lfũnsjona'mēntul m functioning; **horário de ∼** opening hours, working hours.

funcionar [4] lfũsjo'na(x)l vi -**1**. [máquina etc] to work; **pôr algo para ∼** to switch sthg on. -**2**. [loja etc] to be open. -**3**. [exercer função]: **∼ como algo** to work as sthg. -**4**. [dar certo] to work.

funcionário, ria lfũsjo'narju, rjal m, f employee; **∼ público** civil servant.

funções lfũn'sõjʃl fpl ➡ **função**.

fundação lfũnda'sãwl (pl -**ões**) f -**1**. [alicerce] foundation. -**2**. [instituição] foundation. -**3**. [criação] founding.

fundador, ra lfũnda'do(x), ral ⟨⟩ adj founding. ⟨⟩ m, f founder.

fundamentação lfũndamēnta'sãwl (pl -**ões**) f foundation.

fundamental lfũndamēn'tawl (pl -**ais**) adj fundamental.

fundamentalismo lfũndamēnta'liʒmul m RELIG fundamentalism.

fundamentalista lfũndamēnta'liʃtal ⟨⟩ adj fundamentalist. ⟨⟩ mf fundamentalist.

fundamentar [4] lfũndamēn'ta(x)l vt -**1**. [basear]: **∼ algo em algo** to base sthg on sthg. -**2**. [justificar] to found.
➡ **fundamentar-se** vp [basear-se]: **∼-se em algo** to be based on sthg.

fundamento lfũnda'mēntul m fundament; **sem ∼** unfounded.

FUNDAP (abrev de **Fundação do Desenvolvimento Administrativo**) f Brazilian organization for the coordination of training and educational programmes.

fundar [4] lfũn'da(x)l vt -**1**. [instituir] to found. -**2**. [criar] to establish.

fundear [15] lfũn'dʒja(x)l vi to drop anchor.

fundição lfũdʒi'sãwl (pl -**ões**) f melting down.

fundilho [fũn'dʒiʎu] *m* seat, bottom.

fundir [6] [fũn'dʒi(x)] *vt* -**1.** [derreter] to melt. -**2.** [moldar] to cast. -**3.** [incorporar] to merge. -**4.** *fam* [perturbar]: ~ **a cuca de alguém** to do sb's head in.

➡ **fundir-se** *vp* -**1.** [derreter-se] to melt. -**2.** [incorporar-se] to merge.

fundo, da ['fũndu, da] *adj* -**1.** [profundo] deep. -**2.** [reentrante] sunken. -**3.** *fam* [despreparado]: ~ **(em algo)** weak (at sthg).

➡ **fundo** ◇ *m* -**1.** [base] bottom. -**2.** [de local] rear. -**3.** [segundo plano] background; **ao** ~ **in the** distance. -**4.** [de tecido, papel] background. -**5.** *MÚS*: ~ **musical** background music. -**6.** [íntimo]: **eu o perdoei do** ~ **da alma** I forgave him from the bottom of my heart. -**7.** *fig* [teor] element. -**8.** *FIN* fund; ~ **de garantia** security; ~ **de investimento** investment fund; **emprestei-lhe dinheiro a** ~ **perdidos** I lent him some money without expecting repayment. -**9.** *MED*: ~ **do olho** back of the eye. ◇ *adv* [profundamente] deeply; **a** ~ **in depth**.

➡ **fundos** *mpl* -**1.** [de casa] funds. -**2.** [capital] capital; **cheque sem** ~ unsecured cheque.

➡ **no fundo** *loc adv* [intrinsecamente] basically.

fundura [fũn'dura] *f* depth.

fúnebre ['funebri] *adj* funereal.

funeral [fune'raw] (*pl* -**ais**) *m* funeral.

funerário, ria [fune'rarju, rja] *adj* funeral *(antes de subst)*.

➡ **funerária** *f* funeral parlour.

funesto, ta [fu'nɛʃtu, ta] *adj* dire.

fungar [14] [fũŋ'ga(x)] *vi* to sniff.

fungicida [fũnʒi'sida] *m* fungicide.

fungo ['fũŋgu] *m* fungus.

funicular [funiku'la(x)] ◇ *adj* funicular. ◇ *m* -**1.** [sistema] funicular. -**2.** [veículo] cable car.

funil [fu'niw] (*pl* -**is**) *m* funnel.

funilaria [funi'laria] *f* panel beating.

funileiro [funi'lejru] *f* panel beater.

FUNRURAL (*de abrev* **Fundo de Assistência e Previdência ao Trabalhador Rural**) *m Brazilian fund for the assistance and support of rural workers.*

furacão [fura'kãw] (*pl* -**ões**) *m* -**1.** [ciclone] cyclone. -**2.** *fig* [turbilhão] maelstrom; **como um** ~ like a whirlwind.

furadeira [fura'dejra] *f* drill.

furado, da [fu'radu, da] *adj* -**1.** [pneu] punctured. -**2.** [orelha] pierced. -**3.** [sapato] holey. -**4.** *fam* [infrutífero] unsuccessful.

fura-greve ['furagrevi] *mf* blackleg.

furão, rona [fu'rãw, rona] (*mpl* -**ões**, *fpl* -**s**) *adj* [cavador] unreliable.

furar [4] [fu'ra(x)] ◇ *vt* -**1.** [pneu] to puncture. -**2.** [orelha] to pierce. -**3.** [sapato] to make a hole in. -**4.** [frustrar] to fail. -**5.** [não aderir a] to leave. ◇ *vi* -**1.** [perfurar] to puncture. -**2.** [sapato] to get a hole. -**3.** [malograr] to fail.

furgão [fux'gãw] (*pl* -**ões**) *m* van.

fúria ['furja] *f* fury; **estar/ficar uma** ~ to be in a fury.

furibundo, da [furi'bũndu, da] *adj* livid, incensed.

furioso, osa [fu'rjozu, ɔza] *adj* -**1.** [raivoso] furious. -**2.** [violento] furious.

furo ['furu] *m* -**1.** [buraco] puncture. -**2.** [orelha] hole. -**3.** [sapato] hole. -**4.** *fig* [falha] mistake; **dar um** ~ to put one's foot in it. -**5.** *JORN*: ~ **(de reportagem)** scoop.

furões [fu'rõjʃ] *mpl* ➡ **furão**.

furona [fu'ronal *f* ➡ **furão**.

furor [fu'ro(x)] *m* -**1.** [fúria] fury. -**2.** [arrebatamento]: **fazer algo com** ~ to do sthg furiously. -**3.** *loc*: **causar** ~ to cause fury.

furreca [fu'xɛka] *adj fam* mean.

furta-cor [ˌfuxta'ko(x)] (*pl* **furta-cores**) *adj* iridescent.

furtar [4] [fux'ta(x)] ◇ *vt* [roubar] to steal. ◇ *vi* [roubar] to steal.

➡ **furtar-se** *vp* [esquivar-se]: ~-**se a algo** to dodge sthg.

furtivo, va [fux'tʃivu, va] *adj* -**1.** [às ocultas] furtive. -**2.** [dissimulado] furtive.

furto ['fuxtu] *m* theft.

furúnculo [fu'rũŋkulu] *m* boil.

fusão [fu'zãw] (*pl* -**ões**) *f* -**1.** [ger] fusion. -**2.** *COM* amalgamation. -**3.** [liga] amalgam.

fuseau [fu'zo] *m* leggings (*pl*).

fuselagem [fuze'laʒẽ] (*pl* -**ns**) *f* fuselage.

fusível [fu'zivew] (*pl* -**eis**) *m* fuse.

fuso ['fuzu] *m* [peça] screw.

➡ **fuso horário** *m* time zone.

fusões [fu'zõjʃ] *fpl* ➡ **fusão**.

fustigar [14] [fuʃtʃi'ga(x)] *vt* to whip.

futebol [futʃi'bɔw] *m* football; ~ **de salão** five-a-side football.

FUTEBOL

Football is one of the great passions of the Brazilian people, who have made an art form of their most popular sport. Five times World Cup champions ('58, '62, '70, '94 and 2002), the Brazilians export their star players throughout the world, especially to Spain and Italy. The pride of the nation, Pelé, is considered the greatest football player of all time.

---

futebolismo [futʃibo'liʒmu] *m* [paixão] football mania.

futebolista [futʃibo'liʃta] *mf* -**1.** [jogador] footballer. -**2.** [fã] football fan. -**3.** [conhecedor] football expert.

futebolístico, ca [futʃibo'liʃtʃiku, ka] *adj* football *(antes de subst)*.

futevôlei [futʃi'volej] *m ESP* sport practised on the beach and following the rules of volleyball but in which the hands are not allowed to touch the ball.

fútil ['futʃiw] (*pl* -**eis**) *adj* -**1.** [leviano] frivolous. -**2.** [insignificante] trivial.

futilidade [futʃili'dadʒi] *f* -**1.** [leviandade] frivolity. -**2.** [insignificância] triviality. -**3.** [coisa fútil] triviality.

futrica [fu'trikɐ] *f* rag; **correr ~s (com)** to rag.
futurista [futu'riʃtɐ] *adj* futuristic.
futuro, ra [fu'turu, ɐ] *adj* future.
 ➡ **futuro** *m* **-1.** [tempo] future. **-2.** [destino] future. **-3.** GRAM future.
FUVEST (*abrev de* Fundação do Vestibular do Estado de São Paulo) *f organization regulating entrance examinations at some universities in São Paulo.*
fuxicar [12] [fuʃi'ka(x)] *vt* to gossip.
fuxico [fu'ʃiku] *m* gossip.
fuxiqueiro, ra [fuʃi'kejru, ɐ] <> *adj* gossipy. <> *m, f* gossip.
fuzil [fu'ziw] (*pl* -is) *m* rifle.
fuzilamento [fuzila'mẽtu] *m* shooting.
fuzilante [fuzi'lãtʃi] *adj* **-1.** [ameaçador] threatening. **-2.** [fatal] fatal.
fuzilar [4] [fuzi'la(x)] <> *vt* **-1.** [atirar] to shoot. **-2.** *fig* [ameaçar]: **~ alguém com os olhos** to look daggers at sb. <> *vi fig*: **~ (de ódio)** [pessoa] to radiate hatred; [olhos] to flash.
fuzileiro [fuzi'lejru] *m* rifleman; **~ naval** marine.
fuzuê [fu'zwe] *m* party.

G

g¹, G [ʒe] *m* [letra] g, G.
g² (*abrev de* grama) *m* g.
gabar-se [4] [gabax'si] *vp*: **~-se (de)** to boast (about).
gabardine [gabax'dʒini] *m* gaberdine.
gabaritado, da [gabari'tadu, ɐ] *adj* high-calibre.
gabaritar [4] [gabari'ta(x)] *vt* to enable.
 ➡ **gabaritar-se** *vp* to be able.
gabarito [gaba'ritu] *m* **-1.** [qualidade] high calibre. **-2.** [respostas] results (*pl*). **-3.** [limite] maximum size.
gabinete [gabi'netʃi] *m* **-1.** [escritório] study. **-2.** POL cabinet.
gado ['gadu] *m* cattle.
gaélico, ca [ga'ɛliku, ɐ] *adj* Gaelic.
 ➡ **gaélico** *m* [língua] Gaelic.
gafanhoto [gafã'ɲotu] *m* grasshopper.
gafe ['gafi] *f* gaffe.
gafieira [ga'fjejrɐ] *f* **-1.** [baile] ball. **-2.** [dança] dance.
gagá [ga'ga] *adj* gaga.
gago, ga ['gagu, ɐ] <> *adj* stammering. <> *m, f* stammerer.

gagueira [ga'gejrɐ] *f* stammer.
gaguejar [4] [gage'ʒa(x)] *vt & vi* to stammer.
gaiato, ta [ga'jatu, ɐ] *adj* mischievous.
gaiola [ga'jɔlɐ] <> *f* **-1.** [clausura] cage. **-2.** *fam* [prisão] jail. <> *m* [vapor] steamboat.
gaita ['gajtɐ] *f* **-1.** MÚS mouth organ; **~ de foles** bagpipe. **-2.** *fam fig* [dinheiro] dosh.
gaivota [gaj'vɔtɐ] *f* seagull.
gala ['galɐ] *f*: **de ~** gala; **uniforme de ~** dress uniform.
galã [ga'lã] *m* **-1.** [ator] lead. **-2.** [sedutor] playboy.
galáctico, ca [ga'laktʃiku, ɐ] *adj* galactic.
galante [ga'lãtʃi] *adj* gallant.
galanteador [galãtʃja'do(x)] *adj* gallant.
galantear [15] [galãn'tʃja(x)] *vt* to play the gallant.
galanteio [galãn'teju] *m* gallantry.
galão [ga'lãw] (*pl* -ões) *m* **-1.** MIL stripe. **-2.** [enfeite] braid. **-3.** [medida] gallon.
Galápagos [ga'lapaguʃ] *npl*: **as (ilhas) ~** the Galapagos (Islands).
galardão [galax'dãw] (*pl* -ões) *m* reward.
galáxia [ga'laksjɐ] *f* galaxy.
galé [ga'lɛ] *f* galley.
galera [ga'lɛrɐ] *f* **-1.** NÁUT galley. **-2.** *fam* [grupo] crowd.
galeria [gale'riɐ] *f* **-1.** TEATRO circle. **-2.** [coleção] collection. **-3.** [canalização] drainage. **-4.** [loja de arte] gallery. **-5.** [centro comercial] shopping centre.
Gales ['galiʃ] *n*: **País de ~** Wales.
galês, esa [ga'leʃ, ezɐ] <> *adj* Welsh. <> *m, f* Welshman (*f* Welshwoman).
 ➡ **galês** *m* [língua] Welsh.
galeto [ga'letu] *m* roast poussin.
galgar [14] [gaw'ga(x)] *vt* **-1.** [saltar] to jump across. **-2.** [subir] to climb. **-3.** *fig* [ascender] to move up.
galhardia [gaʎax'dʒiɐ] *f* **-1.** [elegância] smartness. **-2.** [bravura] bravery.
galhardo, da [ga'ʎaxdu, ɐ] *adj* **-1.** [elegante] smart. **-2.** [bravo] gallant.
galheta [ga'ʎetɐ] *f* cruet.
galheteiro [gaʎe'tejru] *m* cruet-stand.
galho ['gaʎu] *m* **-1.** BOT branch. **-2.** *fam* [problema] pickle; **dar ~** to cause a pickle; **quebrar um ~** to get out of a pickle.
Galícia [ga'lisjɐ] *n* Galicia.
galicismo [gali'siʒmu] *m* Gallicism.
galináceos [gali'nasjuʃ] *mpl* Galliformes.
galinha [ga'liɲɐ] <> *f* **-1.** [ave] hen. **-2.** CULIN chicken. **-3.** *fam* [namorador] easy lay. **-4.** *loc*: **a ~ do vizinho é sempre mais gorda** the grass is always greener on the other side of the fence. <> *m, f fam* [covarde] chicken.
galinha-d'angola [ga,liɲadãŋ'gɔla] (*pl* galinhas-d'angola) *f* guinea-fowl.
galinhagem [gali'naʒẽ] *f fam* [bolinação] touching up.
galinha-morta [ga,liɲa'mɔxta] (*pl* galinhas-mortas) *mf* [covarde] chicken.

galinheiro [gali'ɲejru] *m* poulterer.

galo [ˈgalu] *m* -**1.** [ave] cockerel, rooster; ~ **de briga** *ou* **de rinha** fighting cock. -**2.** [inchaço] bump.

galocha [gaˈlɔʃa] *f* galosh; **chato de** ~ drag.

galopante [galoˈpãntʃi] *adj fig* galloping.

galopar [4] [galoˈpa(x)] *vi* to gallop.

galope [gaˈlɔpi] *m* gallop.

galpão [gawˈpãw] (*pl* -**ões**) *m* hangar.

galvanizado, da [gawvaniˈzadu, da] *adj* [ferro, chapa] galvanized.

galvanizar [4] [gawvaniˈza(x)] *vt* to galvanize.

gama [ˈgãma] *f* -**1.** *MÚS* scale. -**2.** *fig* [série] range.

gamado, da [gaˈmadu, da] *adj*: **ser/estar** ~ **por alguém** to be hooked on sb.

gamão [gaˈmãw] *m* backgammon.

gamar [4] [gaˈma(x)] *vi* to be hooked; ~ **por alguém** to fall for sthg/sb.

gambá [gãnˈba] *m ZOOL* opossum; **bêbado como um** ~ *fam* drunk as a skunk.

Gâmbia [ˈgãnbja] *n* Gambia.

gambito [gãnˈbitu] *m* [xadrez] gambit.

gamela [gaˈmɛla] *f* trough.

gana [ˈgãna] *f* -**1.** [desejo]: ~ **de algo/de fazer algo** desire for sthg/to do sthg. -**2.** [raiva]: **ter** ~ **de alguém** to be furious with sb.

Gana [ˈgãna] *n* Ghana.

ganância [gaˈnãnsja] *f* greed.

ganancioso, osa [ganãˈsjozu, ɔza] *adj* greedy.

gancho [ˈgãnʃu] *m* -**1.** [peça] hook. -**2.** *COST* hook. -**3.** *fig* [recurso] bait.

gandaia [gãnˈdaja] *f fig* dissipation; **ele passou a noite na** ~ he spent the night in dissipation; **ontem fomos para a** ~ yesterday we went on a binge, self-indulgence; **cair na** ~ to descend into a life of dissipation.

gandaiar [gãndaˈja(x)] *vi* -**1.** [farrear] to live it up, to party. -**2.** [vadiar] to idle about.

gânglio [ˈgãŋglju] *m* ganglion.

gangorra [gãŋˈgoxa] *f* seesaw.

gangrena [gãŋˈgrena] *f* gangrene.

gangrenar [4] [gãŋgreˈna(x)] *vi* to become gangrenous.

gângster [ˈgãŋgiʃte(x)] *m* gangster.

gangue [ˈgãŋgi] *f* gang.

ganhador, ra [gaɲaˈdo(x), ra] <> *adj* winning. <> *m, f* winner.

ganha-pão [ˌgãɲaˈpãw] (*pl* **ganha-pães**) *m* -**1.** [trabalho] living, livelihood. -**2.** [objeto de trabalho] livelihood.

ganhar [4] [gaˈɲa(x)] <> *vt* -**1.** [ger] to win. -**2.** [receber] to get. -**3.** [salário] to earn. -**4.** [lucrar] to gain; ~ **tempo** to gain time; **ganhou o dia quando recebeu a notícia** it made his day when he got the news. -**5.** [atingir] to reach. <> *vi* -**1.** [vencer]: ~ **de alguém** to beat sb; ~ **de alguém em algo** to outdo sb at sthg. -**2.** [como remuneração] to earn. -**3.** [lucrar]: ~ **(com)** to profit (from); **sair ganhando** to come out on top.

ganho [ˈgãɲu] <> *pp* >> **ganhar**. <> *m* -**1.** [salário] earnings *(pl)*. -**2.** [lucro] profit. -**3.** *COM*: ~ **de**

capital capital gain. -**4.** *JUR*: ~ **de causa** successful lawsuit.

ganido [gaˈnidu] *m* whine.

ganir [6] [gaˈni(x)] *vi* to whine.

ganso [ˈgãnsul] *m* goose.

GAPA (*abrev de* **Grupo de Apoio à Prevenção à Aids**) *m* Brazilian non-governmental organization working in AIDS prevention.

garagem [gaˈraʒẽ] (*pl* -**ns**) *f* garage.

garagista [garaˈʒiʃta] *mf* -**1.** [manobrista] car jockey. -**2.** [proprietário] garage owner.

garanhão [garaˈɲãw] (*pl* -**ões**) *m* -**1.** [cavalo] stallion. -**2.** *fig* [homem] stud.

garantia [garãnˈtʃia] *f* -**1.** [ger] guarantee. -**2.** [de dívida] collateral.

garantir [6] [garãnˈtʃi(x)] *vt* -**1.** [assegurar]: ~ **algo a alguém** to assure sb of sthg; ~ **que** to guarantee that. -**2.** [prometer]: ~ **algo a alguém** to promise sb sthg. -**3.** [asseverar] to guarantee.

   >> **garantir-se** *vp* [defender-se]: ~**-se contra algo** to protect o.s. against sthg.

garatuja [garaˈtuʒa] *f* scribble.

garbo [ˈgaxbu] *m* -**1.** [elegância] elegance. -**2.** [distinção] distinction.

garboso, osa [gaxˈbozu, ɔza] *adj* -**1.** [elegante] elegant. -**2.** [distinto] distinguished.

garça [ˈgaxsa] *f* heron.

garçom [gaxˈsõ] (*pl* -**ns**) *m* waiter.

garçonete [garsoˈnɛtʃi] *f* waitress.

garçonnière [gaxsoˈnjɛ(x)] *f* love nest.

garfada [gaxˈfada] *f* forkful.

garfo [ˈgaxful] *m* fork; **ser um bom** ~ *fig* to be a gourmet.

gargalhada [gaxgaˈʎada] *f* burst of laughter; **cair na** ~ to fall about laughing; **dar** *ou* **soltar uma** ~ to burst out laughing.

gargalhar [gaxgaˈʎa(x)] *vi* to roar with laughter.

gargalo [gaxˈgalu] *m* -**1.** [de garrafa] neck. -**2.** [obstáculo] *fig* bottleneck.

garganta [gaxˈgãnta] *f* -**1.** *ANAT* throat; **molhar a** ~ *fam* [beber] to wet one's whistle; **não passar pela** ~ to stick in one's throat; **ter boa** ~ [ter boa voz] to have a good voice. -**2.** [desfiladeiro] mountain pass.

gargantilha [gaxgãnˈtʃiʎa] *f* choker.

gargarejar [4] [gaxgareˈʒa(x)] *vi* to gargle.

gargarejo [gaxgaˈreʒu] *m* -**1.** [ato] gargling. -**2.** [líquido] gargle.

gari [gaˈri] *mf* roadsweeper.

garimpar [4] [garĩˈpa(x)] *vi* to prospect *(for precious metals or stones)*.

garimpeiro, ra [garĩˈpejru, ra] *m, f* prospector.

garimpo [gaˈrĩpul] *m* [mina] mining deposit.

garoa [gaˈroa] *f* drizzle.

garoar [20] [garˈrwa(x)] *vi* to drizzle.

garota [gaˈrota] *f* >> **garoto**.

garotada [garoˈtada] *f*: **a** ~ the kids *(pl)*.

garoto, ta [gaˈrotu, ta] *m, f* -**1.** [menino] boy, kid. -**2.** [prostituto]: ~ **de programa** prostitute.

   >> **garoto** *m* [chope] small glass of draught beer.

   >> **garota** *f* [namorada] girlfriend.

garoto-propaganda, garota-propaganda [gar͵rotupropa'gãnda, gar͵rotapropa'gãnda] (*mpl* **garotos-propaganda**, *fpl* **garotas-propaganda**) *m* cover-boy (*f* cover-girl).

garoupa [ga'ropal *f* grouper.

garra ['gaxal *f* -**1.** [de animal] claw. -**2.** *fig* [entusiasmo] enthusiasm; **ter** ~ to be enthusiastic.

garrafa [ga'xafal *f* bottle; ~ **térmica** Thermos flask® *UK*, Thermos bottle® *US*.

garrafada [gaxa'fadal *f* [pancada]: **dar uma** ~ **em alguém** to hit sb with a bottle.

garrafal [gaxa'fawl (*pl* -**ais**) *adj fig* [imenso - letra] large; [- aviso] severe.

garrafão [gaxa'fãw] *m* flagon.

garrancho [ga'xãnʃul *m* scrawl.

garrote [ga'xɔtʃil *m* -**1.** [de tortura] garrotte *UK*, garrote *US*. -**2.** [torniquete] tourniquet.

garupa [ga'rupal *f* -**1.** [de cavalo] hindquarters, rump. -**2.** [de bicicleta, moto] pillion; **andar na** ~ to ride pillion.

gás ['gajʃ] (*pl* **gases**) *m* -**1.** [fluido] gas; ~ **encanado** piped gas; ~ **natural** natural gas; ~ **carbônico** carbon dioxide; ~ **lacrimogêneo** tear gas. -**2.** [do intestino] wind, flatulence. -**3.** *fam fig* [entusiasmo] go.

gaseificar [12] [gazejfi'ka(x)l *vt* to gasify.
➡ **gaseificar-se** *vp* to be gasified.

gasoduto [gazo'dutul *m* gas pipeline.

gasóleo [ga'zɔljul *m* diesel.

gasolina [gazo'linal *f* petrol *UK*, gasoline *US*.

gasômetro [ga'zometrul *m* gasometer.

gasoso, osa [ga'zozu, ɔzal *adj* fizzy.
➡ **gasosa** *f* fizzy drink *UK*, soda *US*.

gastador, ra [gaʃta'do(x), ral ⬦ *adj* wasteful. ⬦ *m, f* wasteful person.

gastar [4] [gaʃ'ta(x)l ⬦ *vt* -**1.** [despender] to spend. -**2.** [consumir - energia, gasolina] to consume; [- tempo] to take up. -**3.** [usar - roupa, sapato] to wear; [- cosmético, produto] to use. -**4.** [desperdiçar] to waste. -**5.** [desgastar] to wear out. ⬦ *vi* -**1.** [despender dinheiro] to spend money. -**2.** [desgastar-se] to wear out.
➡ **gastar-se** *vp* [desgastar-se] to wear out.

gasto, ta ['gaʃtu, tal ⬦ *pp* ⬦ **gastar**. ⬦ *adj* -**1.** [ger] worn out. -**2.** [consumido - tempo] spent; [- energia] used up; [- electricidade] consumed. -**3.** [despendido] spent. -**4.** [produto, cosmético] used up. -**5.** [desperdiçado] wasted. -**6.** [envelhecido] worn.
➡ **gasto** *m* [despesa] expense.
➡ **gastos** *mpl* [despesas] expenses; ~**s públicos** public expenditure *(sg)*.

gástrico, ca ['gaʃtriku, kal *adj* gastric.

gastrite [gaʃ'tritʃil *f* gastritis *(inv)*.

gastroenterite [gaʃtrẽnte'ritʃil *f* gastroenteritis *(inv)*.

gastronomia [gaʃtrono'mial *f* gastronomy.

gastronômico, ca [gaʃtro'nomiku, kal *adj* gastronomic.

gastrônomo, ma [gaʃ'tronomu, mal *m, f* gastronome.

gata ['gatal *f* ⬦ **gato**.

gateway [gejtʃi'wejl (*pl* **gateways**) *m* COMPUT gateway.

gatilho [ga'tʃiʎul *m* trigger.

gatinhas [ga'tʃiɲaʃl *fpl*: **andar de** ~ to go on all fours, to crawl.

gato, ta ['gatu, tal *m, f* -**1.** [animal] cat; ~ **montês** wild cat; ~ **escaldado tem medo de água fria** *prov* once bitten, twice shy; **vender** ~ **por lebre** to sell a pig in a poke. -**2.** *fam* [pessoa] sexy person.
➡ **gato** *m* ELETR illegal electrical connection; **fazer um** ~ to make an illegal electrical connection.

gato-pingado [͵gatupĩ'gadul (*pl* **gatos-pingados**) *m*: **havia apenas uns gatos-pingados no cinema** there was hardly a soul in the cinema.

gato-sapato [͵gatusa'patul (*pl* **gatos-sapatos**) *m*: **fazer** ~ **de alguém** to treat sb like a doormat.

gatuno, na [ga'tunu, nal ⬦ *adj* thieving. ⬦ *m, f* thief.

gaúcho, cha [ga'uʃu, ʃal ⬦ *adj* Rio Grande do Sul *(antes de subst)*. ⬦ *m, f* person from Rio Grande do Sul.

gaveta [ga'vetal *f* drawer.

gavetão [gave'tãwl (*pl* -**ões**) *m* large drawer.

gaveteiro [gave'tejrul *m* drawer-runner.

gavião [ga'vjãwl (*pl* -**ões**) *m* hawk.

gaze ['gazil *f* -**1.** [tecido] gauze. -**2.** [para curativo] antiseptic gauze.

gazela [ga'zelal *f* gazelle.

gazeta [ga'zetal *f* -**1.** [jornal] gazette. -**2.** [vadiação]: **fazer** ~ to play truant.

gazua [ga'zual *f* skeleton key.

GB *(abrev de Great Britain)* *n* GB.

geada ['ʒjadal *f* frost.

gear [ʒia(x)l *vi* to freeze.

gel [ʒɛl *f* gel.

geladeira [ʒela'dejral *f* refrigerator, fridge.

gelado, da [ʒe'ladu, dal *adj* -**1.** [comida] frozen. -**2.** [bebida] chilled. -**3.** [mar, vento] icy.

gelar [4] [ʒe'la(x)l ⬦ *vt* -**1.** [comida] to freeze. -**2.** [bebida] to chill. ⬦ *vi* to be freezing.

gelatina [ʒela'tʃinal *f* -**1.** [gel] gelatine. -**2.** [sobremesa] jelly *UK*, Jell-O® *US*.

gelatinoso, osa [ʒelatʃi'nozu, ɔzal *adj* gelatinous.

geléia [ʒe'lɛjal *f* jam *UK*, jelly *US*.

geleira [ʒe'lejral *f* glacier.

gélido, da ['ʒɛlidu, dal *adj* -**1.** [gelado] icy. -**2.** *fig* [imóvel] frozen.

gelo ['ʒelul ⬦ *adj inv* light grey *UK*, light gray *US*. ⬦ *m* -**1.** [água solidificada] ice. -**2.** [cor] light grey *UK*, light gray *US*. -**3.** *fig* [indiferença]: **dar um** ~ **em alguém** to give sb the cold shoulder; **quebrar o** ~ to break the ice. -**4.** *loc*: **estar um** ~ to be freezing cold.

gelo-seco [͵ʒelu'sekul (*pl* **gelos-secos**) *m* dry ice.

gema ['ʒemal *f* -**1.** [do ovo] yolk. -**2.** [pedra preciosa] gem.

da gema *loc adv* [autêntico]: **ela é carioca da ~** she is a true carioca.
gemada [ʒe'mada] *f* eggnog.
gêmeo, mea ['ʒemju, mja] ⇔ *adj* twin. ⇔ *m, f* twin.
 Gêmeos *mpl* ASTRO Gemini; **ser Gêmeos** to be Gemini.
gemer [5] [ʒe'me(x)] *vi* **-1.** [de dor] to groan. **-2.** [lastimar-se] to moan. **-3.** [ranger] to wail. **-4.** *fig* [vento] to howl.
gemido [ʒe'midu] *m* **-1.** [de dor] groan. **-2.** [de animal] howl. **-3.** [lamento] wail.
geminiano, na [ʒemi'nanu, na] ⇔ *adj* Gemini *(antes de subst).* ⇔ *m, f* Gemini.
gene ['ʒeni] *m* gene.
genealogia [ʒenjalo'ʒia] *f* genealogy.
genealógico, ca [ʒenja'lɔʒiku, ka] *adj* genealogical; **árvore genelógica** family tree.
Genebra [ʒe'nɛbra] *n* Geneva.
general [gene'raw] *(pl* **-ais)** *m* general.
generalidade [ʒenerali'dadʒi] *f* **-1.** [totalidade] generality. **-2.** [maioria] majority.
 generalidades *fpl* [assuntos gerais] general matters.
generalização [ʒeneraliza'sãw] *(pl* **-ões)** *f* generalization.
generalizar [4] [generali'za(x)] ⇔ *vi* [fazer generalizações] to generalize. ⇔ *vt* [difundir] to spread.
 generalizar-se *vp* [difundir-se] to spread.
genérico, ca [ʒe'nɛriku, ka] *adj* generic.
gênero ['ʒenerul] *m* **-1.** [ger] gender; **estudos de ~** gender studies. **-2.** [tipo] kind. **-3.** [estilo] style. **-4.** BIO genus. **-5.** *loc:* **fazer ~** to play up.
 gêneros *mpl* [mercadorias] goods; **~s alimentícios** foodstuffs; **~s de primeira necessidade** essentials.
generosidade [ʒenerozi'dadʒi] *f* generosity.
generoso, osa [ʒene'rozu, ɔza] *adj* generous.
gênese ['ʒenezi] *f* genesis *(inv).*
genética [ʒe'nɛtʃika] *f* genetics *(sg).*
genético, ca [ʒe'nɛtʃiku, ka] *adj* genetic.
gengibre [ʒẽn'ʒibril] *m* ginger.
gengiva [ʒẽn'ʒiva] *f* gum.
gengivite [ʒẽnʒi'vitʃi] *f* gingivitis.
genial [ʒe'njaw] *(pl* **-ais)** *adj* **-1.** [extraordinário] inspired. **-2.** *fam* [formidável] terrific.
genialidade [ʒenjali'dadʒi] *f* genius.
gênio ['ʒenjul] *m* **-1.** [ger] genius; **ser um ~ (em algo)** to be a genius (at sthg). **-2.** [temperamento] nature; **~ bom/ruim** good-/bad-tempered. **-3.** MITOL genie.
genioso, osa [ʒe'njozu, ɔza] *adj* ill-natured.
genital [ʒeni'taw] *(pl* **-ais)** *adj* genital.
genitália [ʒeni'talja] *f* genitalia.
genitivo, va [ʒeni'tʃivu] *m* LING genitive.
genitor, ra [ʒeni'to(x), ra] *m, f* progenitor.
genocídio [ʒeno'sidʒjul] *m* genocide.
genoma [geno'ma] *m* genome.

GENOMA

Brazil has played a significant part in 'Projeto Genoma', dedicated to the genetic sequencing of the DNA of living beings. The success of Brazilian researchers has contributed greatly towards the scientific recognition of the country in the field of biotechnology.

Gênova ['ʒenova] *n* Genoa.
genro ['ʒẽnxul] *m* son-in-law.
gentalha [ʒẽn'taʎa], **gentinha** [ʒẽn'tʃina] *f* pleb.
gente ['ʒẽntʃi] ⇔ *f* **-1.** [pessoas] people; **~ bem** upper classes; **~ grande** grown-ups; **minha ~** my family; **toda a ~** everybody; *fam* [amigos, colegas] folks; **oi/tchau, ~** hi/bye, folks. **-2.** [alguém] somebody, someone. **-3.** *fam* [nós]: **a ~ vai viajar** we're going travelling; **você quer ir com a ~?** do you want to come with us?; **o carro da ~ está enguiçado** our car has broken down. ⇔ *interj* [exprimindo espanto] gosh!
gentil [ʒẽn'tʃiw] *(pl* **-is)** *adj* kind.
gentileza [ʒẽntʃi'leza] *f* kindness; **por ~ poderia me ajudar?** would you be so kind as to help me?
gentinha [ʒẽn'tʃina] *f* = **gentalha.**
genuíno, na [ʒe'nwinu, na] *adj* genuine.
geofísica [ʒew'fizika] *f* geophysics *(sg).*
geografia [ʒjogra'fia] *f* geography.
geográfico, ca [ʒeo'grafiku, ka] *adj* geographical.
geógrafo, fa [ʒe'ɔgrafu, fa] *m, f* geographer.
geologia [ʒjolo'ʒia] *f* geology.
geológico, ca [geo'lɔgiku, ka] *adj* geological.
geólogo, ga [ʒe'ɔlogu, gal] *m, f* geologist.
geometria [ʒjome'tria] *f* geometry.
geométrico, ca [ʒeo'mɛtriku, ka] *adj* geometric.
geopolítica [geo'politika] *f* geopolitics.
geopolítico, ca [ʒeopo'litʃiku, ka] *adj* geopolitical.
geração [ʒera'sãw] *(pl* **-ões)** *f* generation; **~ espontânea** [biol] spontaneous generation; **de última ~** COMPUT & TEC latest generation.
gerador [ʒera'do(x)] *(pl* **-res)** *adj:* **empresa ~ a de empregos** job-creating company; **grupo ~ de problemas** problem-causing group.
 gerador *m* TEC generator.
geral [ʒe'raw] *(pl* **-ais)** ⇔ *adj* [genérico] general; **de um modo ~** on the whole. ⇔ *m* [o normal] normal thing. ⇔ *f* **-1.** FUT & TEATRO gallery. **-2.** [revisão, arrumação] spring clean; **dar uma ~ em algo** to have a blitz on sthg.
 em geral *loc adv* in general.
geralmente [ʒeraw'mẽntʃi] *adv* generally.
gerânio [ʒe'rãnju] *m* geranium.
gerar [4] [ʒe'ra(x)] *vt* **-1.** [ger] to generate. **-2.** [ter filhos] to beget. **-3.** [causar] to breed.
gerativo, va [ʒera'tʃivu, va] *adj* generative.
gerência [ʒe'rẽnsja] *f* management.
gerenciador [ʒerẽnsja'do(x)] *m* COMPUT manager.
gerencial [ʒerẽn'sjaw] *(pl* **-ais)** *adj* management *(antes do subst).*

gerenciamento [ʒerēnsja'mēntul] *m* management.

gerenciar [16] [ʒerēn'sja(x)] ⟨⟩ *vt* to manage. ⟨⟩ *vi* to manage.

gerente [ʒe'rēntʃil] *mf* manager; ~ **de vendas** sales manager.

gergelim [ʒexʒe'lĩl] *m* sesame.

geriatra [ʒe'rjatra] *mf* geriatrician.

geriatria [ʒerja'tria] *f* geriatrics *(sg).*

geriátrico, ca [ʒe'rjatriku, ka] *adj* geriatric.

geringonça [ʒerĩn'gõnsa] *f* contraption.

gerir [57] [ʒe'ri(x)] *vt* to manage.

germânico, ca [ʒex'maniku, ka] *adj* Germanic.

germanófono, na [gexma'nɔfonu, na] ⟨⟩ *adj* German-speaking. ⟨⟩ *m,f* German speaker.

germe ['ʒɛxmi] *m* germ; **ser o** ~ **de uma idéia** to be the germ of an idea.

germicida [ʒexmi'sida] *m* germicide.

germinação [ʒexmina'sãw] (*pl* -ões) *f* germination.

germinar [4] [ʒexmi'na(x)] *vi* to germinate.

gerúndio [ʒe'rũndʒiu] *m* gerund.

gesso ['ʒesu] *m* -1. [nas artes plásticas] plaster of Paris. -2. [em parede] cast.

gestação [ʒeʃta'sãw] (*pl* -ões) *f* gestation.

gestante [ʒeʃ'tãntʃi] *f* pregnant woman.

gestão [ʒeʃ'tãw] (*pl* -ões) *f* -1. [administração] administration. -2. [gerência] management.

gesticulação [ʒeʃtʃikula'sãw] (*pl* -ões) *f* gesticulation.

gesticular [4] [ʒeʃtʃiku'la(x)] *vi* to gesticulate.

gesto ['ʒɛʃtu] *m* gesture; **fazer um** ~ to make a gesture.

gestual [ʒeʃ'tuaw] (*pl* -ais) *adj* gestural.

gibi [ʒi'bi] *m* comic; **não estar no** ~ *fam* to be no joke.

Gibraltar [ʒibraw'ta(x)] *n* Gibraltar.

GIF (*abrev de* Graphics Interchange Format) *m* GIF.

gigabyte [giga'baijtʃi] (*pl* gigabytes) *m* COMPUT gigabyte.

gigante [ʒi'gãntʃi] ⟨⟩ *adj* gigantic. ⟨⟩ *m* giant.

gigantesco, ca [ʒigãn'teʃku, ka] *adj* gigantic.

gigolô [ʒigo'lo] *m* gigolo.

gilete® [ʒi'lɛtʃi] ⟨⟩ *f* [lâmina] razor blade. ⟨⟩ *m* *vulg* [bissexual] AC/DC.

gim ['ʒĩ] (*pl* -ns) *m* gin.

ginasial [ʒina'ziaw] (*pl* -ais) ⟨⟩ *adj* [relativo a ginásio] secondary school *UK*, high school *US*. ⟨⟩ *m* [curso] *dated* primary education.

ginásio [ʒi'nazju] *m* -1. EDUC secondary school. -2. [para esportes] gymnasium.

ginasta [ʒi'naʃta] *mf* gymnast.

ginástica [ʒi'naʃtʃika] *f* -1. [esporte] gymnastics *(sg).* -2. [aeróbica, corretiva] exercises *(pl).*

gincana [ʒĩŋ'kãna] *f* gymkhana.

ginecologia [ˌʒinɛkolo'ʒia] *f* gynaecology.

ginecológico, ca [ʒineko'loʒiku, ka] *adj* gynaecological.

ginecologista [ˌʒinɛkolo'ʒiʃta] *mf* gynaecologist.

ginete [ʒi'netʃil] *m* thoroughbred.

ginga ['ʒĩŋgal *f* -1. [remo] oar. -2. [movimento]: **ter** ~ **to be nimble**.

gingar [14] [ʒĩn'ga(x)] *vi* to sway.

girafa [ʒi'rafal *f* giraffe.

girar [4] [ʒi'ra(x)] ⟨⟩ *vi* -1. [rodar] to rotate. -2. *fig* [funcionar]: ~ **em torno de** to revolve around. ⟨⟩ *vt* [fazer rodar] to turn.

girassol [ˌʒira'sɔwl (*pl* -óis) *m* sunflower.

giratório, ria [ʒira'tɔrju, rjal *adj* revolving; **cadeira giratória** swivel chair; **ponte giratória** swing bridge.

gíria ['ʒirjal *f* -1. [calão] slang. -2. [jargão] jargon.

giro, ra ['ʒiru, ral *m* -1. [volta] rotation. -2. *fam* [passeio] stroll; **dar um** ~ to take a stroll.

giz [ʒiʒ] *m* chalk.

glacê [gla'sel *m* icing.

glaciação [glasia'sãwl (*pl* -ões) *f* [período geológico] glaciation.

glacial [gla'sjawl (*pl* -ais) *adj* glacial.

gladiador [gladʒia'do(x)] *m* gladiator.

glamour [gla'mu(x)] *m* glamour *UK*, glamor *US*.

glamouroso, osa [glamu'rozu, ɔzal *adj* glamorous.

glande ['glãndʒi] *f* -1. [do carvalho] acorn. -2. ANAT glans.

glândula ['glãndulal *f* gland.

glandular [glãndu'la(x)] *adj* glandular.

glaucoma [glaw'komal *m* glaucoma.

gleba ['glɛbal *f* field.

glicerina [glise'rinal *f* glycerine.

glicose [gli'kɔzil *f* glucose.

global [glo'bawl (*pl* -ais) *adj* -1. [total] total. -2. [relativo ao globo] global.

globalização [globaliza'sãwl (*pl* -ões) *f* globalization.

globalizado, da [globali'zadu, dal *adj* globalized.

globalizante [globali'zãntʃil *adj* globalizing.

globalizar [globa'liza(x)] *vt* to globalize.

➤ **globalizar-se** *vp* to become globalized.

globo ['globul *m* globe; ~ **ocular** eyeball; ~ **terrestre** terrestrial globe.

globular [globu'la(x)] *adj* globular.

glóbulo ['glɔbulul *m* globule; ~**s brancos/vermelhos** white/red blood corpuscles.

glória ['glɔrjal *f* glory.

glorificação [glorifika'sãwl (*pl* -ões) *f* glorification,

glorificar [12] [glorifi'ka(x)] *vt* -1. [honrar] to glorify. -2. [canonizar] to canonize.

glorioso, osa [glo'rjozu, ɔzal *adj* glorious.

glosa ['glɔzal *f* gloss.

glosar [4] [glo'za(x)] *vt* -1. [comentar] to gloss. -2. [conta] to scrap.

glossário [glo'sarjul *m* glossary.

glote ['glɔtʃil *f* ANAT glottis.

GLP (*abrev de* Gás Liquefeito de Petróleo) *m* LPG.

glucose [glu'kɔzil *f* glucose.

glutão, ona [glu'tãw, ɔnal (*mpl* -ões, *fpl* -s) ⟨⟩ *adj* [pessoa] greedy. ⟨⟩ *m, f* [pessoa] glutton.

glúten ['glutēl (*pl* -s) *m* gluten.

glúteo, tea [ˈglutew, tʃia] ◇ *adj* ANAT gluteal. ◇ *m* gluteus.

glutões [gluˈtõjʃ] *pl* ⊳ **glutão**.

glutona [gluˈtona] *f* ⊳ **glutão**.

gnomo [ˈgnomu] *m* gnome.

GO (*abrev de* **Estado de Goiás**) *n* State of Goiás.

Gobi [ˈgɔbil] *m*: **o deserto de** ~ the Gobi Desert.

godê [goˈde] *adj* flared.

goela [ˈgwɛla] *f* throat.

gogó [goˈgɔ] *m fam* [pomo-de-adão] Adam's apple.

goiaba [goˈjaba] *f* guava.

goiabada [gojaˈbada] *f* guava jelly.

goiabeira [gojaˈbejra] *f* guava tree.

Goiânia [goˈjãnja] *n* Goiânia.

Goiás [goˈjaʃ] *n* Goiás.

gol [ˈgowl] (*pl* **-es**) *m* goal; **marcar um** ~ to score a goal.

gola [ˈgɔla] *f* collar; ~ **rulê** polo neck.

golaço [goˈlasu] *m fam* FUT great goal.

gole [ˈgɔli] *m* gulp; **de um** ~ **só** in one gulp; **tomar um** ~ to take a sip.

goleada [goˈljada] *f* FUT hammering.

golear [15] [goˈlja(x)] *vt* FUT to thrash.

goleiro [goˈlejru] *m* goalkeeper.

golfada [gowˈfada] *f* [jorro] spurt.

golfar [4] [gowˈfa(x)] ◇ *vt* **-1.** [vomitar] to cough up. **-2.** [expelir] to spurt out. ◇ *vi* [sair em golfadas] to spurt out.

golfe [ˈgowfi] *m* golf.

golfinho [gowˈfiɲu] *m* dolphin.

golfista [gowˈfiʃta] *mf* golfer.

golfo [ˈgowfu] *m* gulf.

Golfo Pérsico [ˌgowfuˈpɛxsiku] *n* Persian Gulf.

golinho [goˈliɲu] *m* sip; **aos** ~**s** in sips.

golpe [ˈgowpi] *m* **-1.** [ger] stroke; ~ **de sorte** stroke of luck; ~ **de vista** [olhar] glance; [no trânsito] knock; ~ **de mestre** master stroke; **dar o** ~ **do baú** to marry for money. **-2.** [pancada, abalo moral] blow; [soco] punch; [de faca] slash; [de chicote] lash; **dar um** ~ **em alguém** to hit sb; ~ **baixo** *fam fig* dirty trick; ~ **mortal** mortal blow; ~ **de vento** gust of wind. **-3.** POL coup; ~ **de Estado** coup d'état.

golpear [15] [gowˈpja(x)] *vt* **-1.** [dar pancada em] to hit; [com soco] to punch; [com chicote] to lash; [com faca] to slash. **-2.** [moralmente] to wound.

golpista [gowˈpiʃta] ◇ *adj* [pessoa] tricky. ◇ *mf* [pessoa] trickster.

goma [ˈgoma] *f* gum, glue; ~ **de mascar** chewing gum.

gomo [ˈgomu] *m* slice.

gôndola [ˈgõndula] *f* gondola.

gondoleiro [gõndoˈlejru] *m* gondolier.

gongo [ˈgõgu] *m* **-1.** MÚS gong. **-2.** [sino] bell.

gonorréia [gonoˈxɛja] *f* gonorrhoea UK, gonorrhea US.

gorar [4] [goˈra(x)] ◇ *vt* [fracassar] to thwart. ◇ *vi* [fracassar] to fail.

gordo, da [ˈgordu, da] ◇ *adj* **-1.** [pessoa] fat; **nunca ter visto alguém mais** ~ [não conhecer] not have seen sb before. **-2.** [carne] fatty. **-3.** *fig* [quantia] considerable. ◇ *m*, *f* fat person.

gorducho, cha [goxˈduʃu, ʃa] ◇ *adj* plump. ◇ *m*, *f* plump person.

gordura [goxˈdura] *f* **-1.** [banha] fat. **-2.** [líquida] grease. **-3.** [obesidade] fatness.

gordurento, ta [goxduˈrẽntu, ta] *adj* **-1.** [gordo] fatty. **-2.** [ensebado] greasy.

gorduroso, osa [goxduˈrozu, ɔza] *adj* **-1.** [ger] greasy. **-2.** [comida] fatty.

gorila [goˈrila] *m* gorilla.

gorjear [15] [goxˈʒja(x)] *vi* to chirp.

gorjeio [goxˈʒeju] *m* chirp.

gorjeta [goxˈʒeta] *f* tip.

gororoba [goroˈrɔba] *f fam* [comida] grub, nosh; [comida ruim] muck.

gorro [ˈgoxu] *m* cap.

gosma [ˈgɔʒma] *f* spittle.

gosmento, ta [goʒˈmẽntu, ta] *adj* slimy.

gostar [4] [goʃˈta(x)] *vi* **-1.** [ter prazer, gosto]: ~ **de** to enjoy; ~ **de fazer algo** to enjoy doing sthg; **eu** ~ **ia de ir** I would like to go; **gostei de vê-lo feliz** it was good to see him happy; ~ **mais de algo do que de** to prefer sthg to; ~ **de alguém** [simpatizar com] to like sb; [sentir afeição por] to be fond of sb. **-2.** [aproveitar]: ~ **de** to enjoy. **-3.** [ter costume]: ~ **de fazer algo** to like doing sthg. **-4.** [aprovar]: ~ **de** to like.

➡ **gostar-se** *vp* [mutuamente] to be fond of each other *ou* one another.

gosto [ˈgoʃtu] *m* **-1.** [ger] taste; **ter** ~ **de** to taste of; **de bom/mau** ~ in good/bad taste; **a seu** ~ to one's taste; **com** ~ tastefully; **falta de** ~ lack of taste; **para o meu** ~ for my liking. **-2.** [prazer] pleasure; **ter** ~ **em fazer algo** to enjoy doing sthg; **tomar** ~ **por algo** to take a liking to sthg.

gostoso, osa [goʃˈtozu, ɔza] *adj* **-1.** [comida, bebida] tasty. **-2.** [cheiro] lovely. **-3.** [ambiente, música] pleasant. **-4.** [cama, cadeira] comfortable. **-5.** [risada] hearty. **-6.** *fam* [sensual, bonito] gorgeous.

gostosura [goʃtoˈzural] *f fam*: **ser uma** ~ to be lovely.

gota [ˈgotal] *f* **-1.** [ger] drop; **ser a** ~ **d'água** to be the last straw; **ser uma** ~ **de água no oceano** to be a drop in the ocean. **-2.** [de suor] bead. **-3.** MED gout.

goteira [goˈtejra] *f* [buraco no telhado] leak.

gotejante [goteˈʒãntʃi] *adj* dripping.

gotejar [4] [goteˈʒa(x)] *vt* & *vi* to drip.

gótico, ca [ˈgɛtʃiku, ka] *adj* Gothic.

➡ **gótico** *m*: **o** ~ the Gothic style.

gotícula [goˈtʃikula] *f* droplet.

gourmet [guxˈme] (*pl* **-s**) *mf* gourmet.

governabilidade [govexnabiliˈdadʒi] *f* governability.

governador, ra [govexnaˈdo(x), ra] *m*, *f* governor.

governamental [govexnamẽnˈtaw] (*pl* **-ais**) *adj* government (antes de subst), governmental.

governanta [govexˈnãnta] *f* **-1.** [de criança] governess. **-2.** [de casa] housekeeper.

governante [govexˈnãntʃi] ◇ *adj* [que governa] governing. ◇ *mf* [quem governa] governor.

governar [4] [govex'na(x)] <> vt **-1.** POL to govern. **-2.** [embarcação] to steer. **-3.** [dominar] to dominate. <> vi POL to govern.

governista [govex'niʃtal <> adj pro-government. <> mf government supporter.

governo [go'vexnul m **-1.** POL government. **-2.** [controle]: **o carro estava sem** ~ the car was out of control. **-3.** NÁUT steering. **-4.** loc: **para seu** ~ for your information.

gozação [goza'sâwl (pl -ões) f teasing; **fazer uma** ~ **(com alguém)** to tease (sb).

gozado, da [go'zadu, dal adj **-1.** [engraçado] funny. **-2.** [estranho] strange.

➤ **gozada** f fam: **dar uma** ~ **em alguém** to pull sb's leg.

gozador, ra [goza'do(x), ral <> adj comical. <> m, f joker.

gozar [4] [go'za(x)] <> vt **-1.** [desfrutar] to enjoy. **-2.** fam [troçar de] to make fun of. <> vi **-1.** [desfrutar]: ~ **de** to enjoy. **-2.** fam [troçar] to mock; ~ **da cara de alguém** to mock sb. **-3.** fam [ter orgasmo] to come.

gozo ['gozul m **-1.** [prazer] pleasure. **-2.** [graça]: **ser um** ~ to be a laugh. **-3.** [uso]: ~ **de algo** use of sthg; **estar em pleno** ~ **das faculdades mentais** to be in full possession of one's mental faculties. **-4.** [orgasmo] orgasm.

GP (abrev de **Grande Prêmio**) m grand prix.

GPS (abrev de **Global Positioning System**) m GPS.

Grã-Bretanha [ˌgrãnbre'tãɲal n: **(a)** ~ Great Britain.

graça ['grasal f **-1.** [ger] grace. **-2.** [humor] wit; **achar** ~ **de** OU **em algo** to find sthg funny; **fazer** ~ [gracejar] to joke; **ter** ~ to be funny. **-3.** [encanto] charm; **cheio de** ~ full of charm; **não ter** ~ **nenhuma** [ser chato] to be boring; [estar errado] to be wrong; **sem** ~ dull; **ver** ~ **em alguém/algo** to see sthg funny in sb/sthg; **não sei que** ~ **ela vê nele** I don't know what she sees in him. **-4.** [favor, proteção] favour; **cair nas** ~s **de** to be in favour with. **-5.** [nome] name. **-6.** loc: **ficar sem** ~ to be embarrassed.

➤ **graças a** loc prep **-1.** [devido a] due to, thanks to. **-2.** [agradecimento]: **dar** ~ **s a** to give thanks to; ~**s a Deus!** thank goodness!

➤ **de graça** loc adj **-1.** [grátis] free. **-2.** [muito barato] given away.

gracejar [4] [grase'ʒa(x)] vi to joke.

gracejo [gra'seʒul m joke.

gracinha [gra'siɲal f: **ser uma** ~ [criança, rosto] to be sweet; [cidade, desenho] to be attractive; **que** ~**!** how sweet!

gracioso, osa [gra'sjozu, ɔzal adj gracious.

gradação [grada'sâwl (pl -ões) f gradient.

gradativo, va [grada'tʃivu, val adj gradual.

grade ['gradʒil f **-1.** [em janela] grille. **-2.** [no chão] grating. **-3.** loc: **atrás das** ~s fam [na cadeia] behind bars.

gradeado, da [gra'dʒiadu, dal adj [com grades - jardim] fenced; [- janela] with a grating (antes de subst).

➤ **gradeado** m [gradeamento] fencing.

gradear [15] [gra'dʒja(x)] vt **-1.** [janela] to put bars on. **-2.** [área] to fence off.

grado ['gradul m [vontade]: **de bom/mau** ~ willingly/unwillingly.

graduação [gradwa'sâwl (pl -ões) f **-1.** [classificação] grading. **-2.** MIL rank. **-3.** [EDUC - colação] graduation; [- curso]: **curso de** ~ degree course.

graduado, da [gra'dwadu, dal adj **-1.** [dividido em graus] graduated. **-2.** [diplomado] graduate. **-3.** [conceituado] graded. **-4.** MIL ranked.

gradual [gra'dwawl (pl -ais) adj gradual.

graduar [4] [gra'dwa(x)] vt **-1.** [regular] to regulate. **-2.** [classificar]: ~ **em** to classify according to. **-3.** [marcar os graus] to graduate. **-4.** EDUC: ~ **alguém em algo** to confer a degree on sb in sthg. **-5.** MIL: ~ **alguém em general/ coronel** to promote sb to general/colonel.

➤ **graduar-se** vp EDUC: ~**-se em algo** to graduate in sthg.

graduável [gra'dwavewl (pl -eis) adj adjustable.

grafar [4] [gra'fa(x)] vt [escrever] to write.

grafia [gra'fial f **-1.** [escrita] writing. **-2.** [ortografia] spelling.

gráfico, ca ['grafiku, kal <> adj **-1.** [visual] graphic. **-2.** [tipográfico] typographic. <> m, f [profissional] typesetter.

➤ **gráfico** m **-1.** [diagrama] diagram; ~ **de barras** bar chart. **-2.** MAT graph.

➤ **gráfica** f [estabelecimento] graphics studio.

➤ **gráficos** mpl COMPUT graphics.

grã-finagem [grãnfi'naʒêl (pl grã-finagens) f [classe]: **a** ~ the upper class.

grã-fino, na [grãn'finu, nal (mpl grã-finos, fpl grã-finas) <> adj posh. <> m, f toff.

grafite [gra'fitʃil f **-1.** [material] graphite. **-2.** [de lápis] lead. **-3.** [pichação] graffiti.

grafologia [grafolo'ʒial f graphology.

grama ['grãmal <> f [relva] grass. <> m [medida] gramme.

gramado [gra'madul m **-1.** [de parque, jardim] lawn. **-2.** FUT pitch.

gramar [4] [gra'ma(x)] vt to sow with grass.

gramática [gra'matʃikal f ▷ **gramático**.

gramatical [gramatʃi'kâwl (pl -ais) adj grammatical.

gramático, ca [gra'matʃiku, kal <> adj grammatical. <> m, f grammarian.

➤ **gramática** f **-1.** [disciplina] grammar. **-2.** [livro] grammar book.

gramofone [gramo'fonil m gramophone.

grampeador [grãnpja'do(x)] (pl -es) m stapler.

grampear [15] [grãm'pja(x)] vt **-1.** [prender com grampos] to staple. **-2.** [telefone] to tap.

grampo ['grãnpul m **-1.** [para papel] staple. **-2.** [para cabelos] hairgrip. **-3.** [de chapéu] hatpin. **-4.** [de carpinteiro] clamp. **-5.** [de telefone] tap.

grana ['grãnal f fam dosh.

granada [gra'nadal f **-1.** [arma] projectile; ~ **de mão** hand grenade. **-2.** [pedra] garnet.

Granada [gra'nada] *n* **-1.** [na Espanha] Granada. **-2.** [nas Antilhas] Grenada.

grandalhão, lhona [grãnda'ʎãw, ʎɔna] (*mpl* -lhões, *fpl* -s) *adj* large.

grandão, dona [grãn'dãw, dɔna] (*mpl* -ões, *fpl* -s) *adj* huge.

grande ['grãndʒi] *adj* **-1.** [em tamanho] large; **o Grande São Paulo** Greater São Paulo. **-2.** [em altura] tall. **-3.** [crescido] grown-up. **-4.** *(antes de subst)* [intenso] great. **-5.** *(antes de subst)* [excessivo] grand. **-6.** *(antes de subst)* [notável] great. **-7.** *(antes de subst)* [excepcional] great. **-8.** *(antes de subst)* [generoso] generous.

➤ **grandes** *mpl*: **os ~ s** [os poderosos] the great.

grandeza [grãn'deza] *f* **-1.** [ger] greatness. **-2.** [ostentação] grandeur.

grandiloqüência [grãndʒilo'kwẽnsja] *f* grandiloquence.

grandiloqüente [grãndʒilo'kwẽntʃi] *adj* grandiloquent.

grandiosidade [grãndʒjozi'dadʒi] *f* magnificence.

grandioso, osa [grãn'dʒjozu, ɔza] *adj* grandiose.

granel [gra'nɛw] *m*: **a ~** in bulk; **comprar/vender a ~** to buy/sell in bulk.

granito [gra'nitu] *m* granite.

granizo [gra'nizu] *m* hailstone; **chover ~** to hail; **chuva de ~** hail.

granja ['grãnʒa] *f* farm.

granulado, da [granu'ladu, da] *adj* granulated.

grânulo ['grãnulu] *m* granule.

grão ['grãw] (*pl* grãos) *m* **-1.** [semente] seed; [de café] bean. **-2.** [de areia] grain.

➤ **grãos** *mpl* [cereais] cereal.

grão-de-bico [,grãwdʒi'biku] (*pl* grãos-de-bico) *m* chick pea **UK**, garbanzo bean **US**.

grapefruit [,greip'frutʃi] *m* grapefruit.

grasnar [4] [graʒ'na(x)] *vi* **-1.** [corvo] to caw. **-2.** [pato] to quack. **-3.** *fig* [gritar] to shout.

gratidão [gratʃi'dãw] *f* gratitude.

gratificação [gratʃifika'sãw] (*pl* -ões) *f* **-1.** [bônus] bonus. **-2.** [recompensa] reward. **-3.** [gorjeta] tip.

gratificante [gratʃifi'kãntʃi] *adj* gratifying.

gratificar [12] [gratʃifi'ka(x)] *vt* **-1.** [dar bônus] to give a bonus. **-2.** [dar gorjeta a] to tip. **-3.** [recompensar] to reward; **esse trabalho gratifica muito** this work is very rewarding.

gratinado, da [gratʃi'nadu, da] *adj* au gratin, gratiné.

➤ **gratinado** *m* **-1.** [prato] gratin. **-2.** [crosta] crust.

grátis ['gratʃiʃ] *adj* free.

grato, ta ['gratu, ta] *adj* **-1.** [agradecido]: **ficar ~ a alguém por algo/por fazer algo** to be grateful to sb for sthg/doing sthg. **-2.** *(antes de subst)* [agradável] pleasant.

gratuidade [gratwi'dadʒi] *f* gratuity.

gratuito, ta [gra'twitu, ta] *adj* **-1.** [grátis] free. **-2.** [sem fundamento] gratuitous.

grau ['graw] *m* **-1.** [ger] degree. **-2.** [nível, gradação] level.

graúdo, da [gra'udu, da] <> *adj* **-1.** [grande] large. **-2.** [influente] important. <> *m, f* [pessoa poderosa] bigwig.

gravação [grava'sãw] (*pl* -ões) *f* **-1.** [em fita, disco, telefone] recording. **-2.** [em madeira] carving.

gravador, ra [grava'do(x), ra] (*pl* -es) *m, f* [quem faz gravuras] engraver.

➤ **gravador** *m* [aparelho] tape recorder.

➤ **gravadora** *f* [empresa] record company.

gravar [4] [gra'va(x)] *vt* **-1.** [ger] to record. **-2.** [em pedra, metal, madeira] to carve. **-3.** [na memória] to memorize.

gravata [gra'vata] *f* **-1.** [adereço] tie. **-2.** [golpe] stranglehold; **dar uma ~ em alguém** to get sb in a stranglehold.

gravata-borboleta [gra,vataboxbo'leta] (*pl* gravatas-borboletas, gravatas-borboleta) *f* bow tie.

grave ['gravi] *adj* **-1.** [profundo] serious. **-2.** [sério] grave. **-3.** [rígido] grave. **-4.** *MÚS* deep. **-5.** *LING* [acento] grave.

gravemente [grave'mẽntʃi] *adv* seriously.

graveto [gra'vetu] *m* piece of kindling.

grávida ['gravida] *adj* pregnant.

gravidade [gravi'dadʒi] *f* gravity; **centro de ~** centre of gravity.

gravidez [gravi'deʒ] *f* pregnancy; **~ tubária** ectopic pregancy.

graviola [gra'vjɔla] *f* sweetsop.

gravitar [4] [gravi'ta(x)] *vi* **-1.** [orbitar] to gravitate. **-2.** *fig* [seguir]: **~ em torno de** to gravitate around.

gravura [gra'vura] *f* **-1.** [estampa] print. **-2.** [em madeira, metal] engraving.

graxa ['graʃa] *f* **-1.** [para couro] polish; **~ de sapatos** shoe polish. **-2.** [lubrificante] grease.

Grécia ['grɛsja] *f* Greece.

gregário, ria [gre'garju, rja] *adj* gregarious.

grego, ga ['gregu, 'ga] <> *adj* **-1.** [relativo à grécia] Greek. **-2.** *fig* [obscuro]: **isso para mim é ~** that's Greek to me. <> *m, f* [pessoa] Greek.

➤ **grego** *m* *LING* Greek; **falar ~** *fam* to speak a foreign language.

gregoriano, na [grego'rjanu, na] *adj* Gregorian.

grelha ['greʎa] *f* grill; **na ~** cooked on the grill.

grelhado, da [gre'ʎadu, da] *adj* grilled.

➤ **grelhado** *m* grilled food.

grelhar [4] [gre'ʎa(x)] *vt* to grill.

grêmio ['gremju] *m* **-1.** [associação] guild. **-2.** [clube] club.

grená [gre'na] <> *adj* dark red. <> *m* dark red.

greta ['greta] *f* crack.

greve ['grɛvi] *f* strike; **fazer ~** to strike; **~ de fome** hunger strike.

grevista [gre'viʃta] *mf* striker.

grifado, da [gri'fadu, da] *adj* italicized.

grifar [4] [gri'fa(x)] *vt* **-1.** [compor em grifo] to italicize. **-2.** [sublinhar] to underline. **-3.** *fig* [enfatizar] to emphasize.

grife ['grifi] *f* label.

grifo ['grifu] *m* italics.

grilado, da [gri'ladu, da] *adj fam*: estar/ficar ~
(com) to be/get worked up (about).

grilagem [grila'ʒẽ] (*pl* **-ns**) *f falsification of
property deeds.*

grilar [4] [gri'la(x)] <> *vt fam* [preocupar] to worry.
<> *vi fam* [chatear-se] to get annoyed.

➧ **grilar-se** *vp fam*: ~-se por *ou* com to get
worked up about.

grileiro, ra [gri'lejru, ra] *m, f forger of property
deeds.*

grilhão [gri'ʎãw] (*pl* **-ões**) *m* chain.

grilo [ˈgrilu] *m* **-1.** [inseto] cricket. **-2.** *fam* [proble-
ma] hiccup; **dar** ~ to cause a hiccup.

grinalda [gri'nawda] *f* garland.

gringo, ga [ˈgrĩŋgu, ga] *m, f fam pej* foreigner.

gripado, da [gri'padu, da] *adj*: estar/ficar ~ to
have/get flu.

gripar-se [4] [gri'paxsil] *vp* to catch flu.

gripe [ˈgripi] *f* flu; **pegar uma** ~ to go down with
flu.

grisalho, lha [gri'zaʎu, ʎa] *adj* greying *UK*,
graying *US*.

gritante [gri'tãntʃi] *adj* **-1.** [evidente] glaring. **-2.**
[de cor viva] dazzling.

gritar [4] [gri'ta(x)] *vt & vi* to shout; ~ com alguém
to shout at sb.

gritaria [grita'ria] *f* shouting.

grito [ˈgritu] *m* **-1.** [brado] shout; **falar aos** ~s to
shout; **protestar aos** ~s to shout protests; **chegar aos** ~s to reach screaming point; **dar um**
~ to give a shout. **-2.** [de animal] scream. **-3.** [de
dor] scream. **-4.** [de pavor] scream.

➧ **no grito** *loc adv fam* by force.

Groenlândia [groẽn'lãndʒia] *n* Greenland.

grogue [ˈgrɔgi] *adj* [pessoa] groggy.

grosa [ˈgrɔza] *f* [doze dúzias] gross.

grosar [gro'za(x)] *vt* [limar, debastar] to file.

groselha [gro'zeʎa] *f* redcurrant.

grosseiro, ra [gro'sejru, ra] *adj* **-1.** [rude] rude.
-2. [chulo] vulgar. **-3.** [ordinário] coarse.

grosseria [grose'ria] *f* rudeness; **dizer/fazer uma**
~ to say/do something rude.

grosso, ssa [ˈgrosu, sa] *adj* **-1.** [ger] thick. **-2.**
[áspero] rough. **-3.** [rude] rude. **-4.** *fam* [abundan-
te]: **dinheiro** ~ a considerable sum of money.

➧ **grosso** *adv*: falar ~ com alguém to get
tough with sb.

➧ **grosso modo** *loc adv* roughly.

grossura [gro'sura] *f* **-1.** [espessura] thickness.
-2. *fam* [grosseria] rudeness.

grotão [gro'tãw] (*pl* **-ões**) *m* gorge.

grotesco, ca [gro'teʃku, ka] *adj* grotesque.

➧ **grotesco** *m*: o ~ the grotesque.

grua [ˈgrua] *f* crane.

grudado, da [gru'dadu, da] *adj fig*: ser ~ com alguém to be very attached to sb.

grudar [4] [gru'da(x)] <> *vt*: ~ algo em algo to
stick sthg on sthg. <> *vi* to stick.

grude [ˈgrudʒi] *m* **-1.** [cola] glue. **-2.** *fam* [comida
ruim] muck.

grudento, ta [gru'dẽntu, ta] *adj* sticky.

grumete [gru'mɛtʃi] *m* cabin boy.

grunhido [gru'ɲidu] *m* grunt.

grunhir [6] [gru'ɲi(x)] *vi* **-1.** [porco] to grunt. **-2.**
fig [resmungar] to grumble.

grupo [ˈgrupul *m* group; ~ étnico ethnic group;
~ sanguíneo blood group; ~ de discussão *COMPUT*
newsgroup.

gruta [ˈgruta] *f* cave, grotto.

guache [ˈgwaʃi] *m* gouache.

guaraná [gwara'na] *m* guarana; ~ em pó powdered guarana; ~ natural natural guarana.

GUARANÁ

A small fruit borne by a very common bush in Amazonas
and Pará; it is used to make one of the most popular
national drinks, *guaraná*. High in caffeine, it is
considered by alternative medicine as an excellent
source of energy. It is sold as a soft drink and can also
be obtained in the form of a powder.

---

guarani [gwara'ni] (*pl* **guaranis**) <> *adj* Guarani
(*antes de subst*). <> *m, f* Guarani. <> *m* **-1.** [língua]
Guarani. **-2.** [moeda] guarani.

guarda [ˈgwaxda] <> *f* **-1.** [proteção] care; **ficar
de** ~ to stand guard. **-2.** *MIL* guard. <> *mf* [poli-
cial] police officer.

guarda-chuva [ˌgwaxda'ʃuva] (*pl* **guarda-
chuvas**) *m* umbrella.

guarda-costas [ˌgwaxda'kɔʃtaʃ] *mf inv* **-1.** *NÁUT*
coastguard. **-2.** *fig* [para defesa] bodyguard.

guardador, ra [gwaxda'do(x), ra] *m, f*: ~ (de automóveis) (car) attendant.

guardados [gwax'daduʃ] *mpl* bits and pieces.

guarda-florestal [ˌgwaxdaflore'ʃtaw] (*pl*
guardas-florestais) *mf* forest ranger.

guarda-louça [ˌgwaxda'losa] (*pl* **guarda-louças**)
m dresser.

guarda-mor [ˌgwaxda'mɔ(x)] (*pl* **guardas-mores**)
m head customs-officer.

guarda-móveis [ˌgwaxda'mɔvejʃ] *m* (*inv*) furniture warehouse.

guardanapo [ˌgwaxda'napu] *m* (table) napkin.

guarda-noturno [ˌgwaxdano'tuxnu] (*pl*
guardas-noturnos) *mf* nightwatchman.

guardar [4] [gwax'da(x)] *vt* **-1.** [ger] to keep; ~
segredo sobre algo to keep quiet about sthg; ~
silêncio to keep silent. **-2.** [pôr no lugar]: ~ algo
(em) to put sthg away (in). **-3.** [reservar]: ~ algo
(para) to keep sthg (for); ~ lugar para alguém
[em teatro, ônibus] to keep a seat for sb. **-4.** [gravar
na memória] to remember. **-5.** [vigiar] to guard.
-6. [cuidar de] to look after. **-7.** [observar] to keep;
guardadas as (devidas) proporções to a certain
extent.

➧ **guardar-se** *vp* **-1.** [proteger-se]: ~-se de to
steer clear of. **-2.** [prevenir-se]: ~-se de to watch
out for.

guarda-roupa [ˌgwaxda'xopa] (*pl* **guarda-
roupas**) *m* wardrobe.

guarda-sol [ˌgwaxda'sɔw] (*pl* **guarda-sóis**) *m*
parasol.

guarda-volumes [ˌgwaxdavoˈlumiʃ] *m (inv)* left-luggage office.

guardião, diã [gwaxˈdʒjãw, dʒjã] *(mpl* -ães, -ões, *fpl* -s) *m*, *f* guardian.

guarida [gwaˈrida] *f* -**1.** [refúgio] den. -**2.** [proteção]: **dar ~ a alguém** to harbour sb.

guarita [gwaˈrita] *f* -**1.** [torre] watchtower. -**2.** [casinha] sentry box.

guarnecer [25] [gwaxneˈse(x)] *vt* -**1.** [abastecer] to supply; **~ alguém de algo** to supply sb with sthg. -**2.** MIL to occupy. -**3.** NÁUT to crew.

guarnição [gwaxniˈsãw] *(pl* -ões) *f* -**1.** [ger] garnish. -**2.** MIL garrison. -**3.** NAUT crew.

Guatemala [gwateˈmala] *n* Guatemala.

guatemalteco, ca [gwatemawˈtɛku, ka] <> *adj* Guatemalan. <> *m*, *f* Guatemalan.

gude [ˈgudʒi] *m* ⊳ **bola**.

gueixa [ˈgejʃa] *f* geisha.

guelra [ˈgɛwxa] *f* gill.

guerra [ˈgɛxa] *f* -**1.** [ger] war; **declarar ~ a** to declare war on; **em ~** at war; **estar em pé de ~ (com)** to be ready for war (with); **~ civil** civil war; **~ fria** cold war; **~ mundial** world war; **~ nuclear** ou **atômica** nuclear war; **~ química** chemical warfare; **~ santa** holy war; **fazer ~ a** to do battle with; **~ de nervos** war of nerves. -**2.** *fig* [disputa] battle.

guerra-relâmpago [ˌgɛxaˈxelãmpagu] *(pl* -**guerras-relâmpago)** *f* blitzkrieg.

guerrear [15] [geˈxja(x)] *vi*: **~ (com/contra)** to be at war (with/against).

guerreiro, ra [geˈxejru, ra] <> *adj* -**1.** [belicoso] warlike. -**2.** [espírito, índole] fighting. <> *m*, *f* [pessoa] warrior.

guerrilha [geˈxiʎa] *f* guerrilla warfare.

guerrilhar [4] [gexiˈʎa(x)] *vi* to engage in guerrilla warfare.

guerrilheiro, ra [gexiˈʎejru, ra] <> *adj* guerrilla *(antes de subst).* <> *m*, *f* guerrilla.

gueto [ˈgetu] *m* ghetto.

guia [ˈgia] <> *f* guide. <> *m* [manual - turístico, cultural] guide; [- de instruções] manual. <> *mf* [pessoa] guide; **~ turístico** tourist guide.

Guiana [gwiˈjãna] *n* Guyana.

guianense [gwijaˈnẽnsi] <> *adj* Guyanese. <> *mf* Guyanese.

guiar [16] [ˈgja(x)] <> *vt* -**1.** [orientar] to guide. -**2.** [proteger] to watch over. -**3.** AUTO [dirigir] to drive. <> *vi* AUTO to drive.

➡ **guiar-se** *vp* [orientar-se] to orientate o.s.

guichê [giˈʃe] *m* -**1.** [no cinema, teatro] ticket office. -**2.** [em banco] counter.

guidom [giˈdõ] *(pl* -ns) *m* handlebars *(pl).*

guilhotina [giʎoˈtʃina] *f* guillotine.

guilhotinar [4] [giʎotʃiˈna(x)] *vt* to guillotine.

guimba [ˈgĩba] *f* *fam* [ponta de cigarro] stub.

guinada [giˈnada] *f* -**1.** NÁUT yaw. -**2.** AUTO veer; **dar uma ~** to veer. -**3.** *fig* [virada] change of direction; **dar uma ~** to change direction.

guinchar [4] [gĩˈʃa(x)] <> *vt* [carro] to tow. <> *vi* [chiar] to squeal.

guincho [ˈgĩʃu] *m* -**1.** [reboque] tow. -**2.** [chiado] squeal.

guindar [4] [gĩˈda(x)] *vt* -**1.** [levantar] to raise. -**2.** *fig* [promover] to promote; **~ alguém a algo** to promote sb to sthg.

guindaste [gĩˈdaʃtʃi] *m* crane.

guineano, na [gineˈãnu, na] <> *adj* Guinean. <> *m*, *f* Guinean.

Guiné-Bissau [giˌnɛbiˈsaw] *n* Guinea-Bissau.

Guiné Equatorial [giˌnɛkwatoˈrjaw] *n* Equatorial Guinea.

guirlanda [gixˈlãda] *f* garland.

guisa [ˈgiza] *f*: **à ~ de** in the manner of.

guisado, da [giˈzadu, da] *m* CULIN stew.

guisar [4] [giˈza(x)] *vt* to stew.

guitarra [giˈtaxa] *f*: **~ (elétrica)** electric guitar.

guitarrista [gitaˈxiʃta] *mf* guitarist.

guizo [ˈgizu] *m* bell.

gula [ˈgula] *f* gluttony.

gulodice [guloˈdʒisi] *f* greediness.

guloseima [guloˈzejma] *f* titbit.

guloso, osa [guˈlozu, ɔza] *adj* greedy.

gume [ˈgumi] *m* blade.

guri, ria [guˈri, ria] *m* kid.

gurizada [guriˈzada] *f* [criançada] kids *(pl).*

guru [guˈru] *m* guru.

gutural [gutuˈraw] *(pl* -ais) *adj* guttural.

h¹, H [ˈaˈga] *m* [letra] h, H.

h² *(abrev de* **hora)** *f* hr., h.

ha *(abrev de* **hectare)** *m* ha.

hã [ã] *interj* -**1.** [reflexão]: **hã!** ah! -**2.** [pergunta]: **hã?** sorry?

habeas-corpus [ˌabjasˈkɔxpuʃ] *m inv* habeas corpus.

hábil [ˈabiw] *(pl* -eis) *adj* -**1.** [ger] skilful. -**2.** [sutil] subtle. -**3.** *loc*: **em tempo ~** in due course.

habilidade [abiliˈdadʒi] *f* -**1.** [aptidão] ability. -**2.** [competência] talent. -**3.** [astúcia] skill. -**4.** [sutileza] subtlety.

habilidoso, osa [abiliˈdozu, ɔza] *adj* skilful *UK*, skillful *US*.

habilitação [abilitaˈsãw] *(pl* -ões) *f* -**1.** [aptidão] aptitude. -**2.** [conhecimento formal] qualification. -**3.** JUR [documento] validation.

➡ **habilitações** *fpl* [qualificações] qualifications.

habilitado, da [abiliˈtadu, da] *adj* -**1.** [profissional liberal] qualified. -**2.** [operário] skilled.

habilitar [4] [abili'ta(x)] *vt* **-1.** [capacitar] to enable. **-2.** [preparar] to prepare. **-3.** [dar direito a] to entitle to.
➡ **habilitar-se** *vp* [capacitar-se] to prepare o.s.
habitação [abita'sãw] (*pl* -**ões**) *f* **-1.** [casa] house. **- 2.** POL [moradia] housing.
habitacional [abitasjo'naw] (*pl* -**ais**) *adj* housing (*antes de subst*).
habitante [abi'tãntʃi] *mf* inhabitant.
habitar [4] [abi'ta(x)] ◇ *vt* **-1.** [morar em] to live in. **- 2.** [povoar] to inhabit. ◇ *vi* [viver] to live.
hábitat ['abitatʃ] *m* habitat; ~ **natural** natural habitat.
habitável [abi'tavew] (*pl* -**eis**) *adj* inhabitable.
hábito ['abitul *m* habit; **ter o** ~ **de fazer algo** to be used to doing sthg; **por força do** ~ through force of habit.
habituado, da [abi'twadu, da] *adj*; ~ **(a algo)** used (to sthg); ~ **a fazer algo** used to doing sthg.
habitual [abi'twaw] (*pl* -**ais**) *adj* habitual.
habituar [4] [abi'twa(x)] *vt* to accustom to; ~ **alguém a algo/a fazer algo** to get sb used to sthg/to doing sthg.
➡ **habituar-se** *vp*: ~-**se a (fazer) algo** to get used to (doing) sthg.
habitué [abi'twe] *m* habitué.
hacker [xake(x)ʃ] (*pl* **hackers**) *m* COMPUT hacker.
hadoque [a'dɔki] *m* haddock.
Haia ['aja] *n* The Hague.
Haiti [aj'tʃi] *n* Haiti.
hálito ['alitul *m* breath; **mau** ~ bad breath.
hall ['ɔw] *m* hall; ~ **de entrada** entrance hall.
halo ['alul *m* halo.
haltere [aw'tɛri] *m* dumb-bell.
halterofilismo [awterofi'liʒmul *m* weightlifting.
halterofilista [awterofi'liʃta] *mf* weight lifter.
hambúrguer [ãn'buxge(x)] (*pl* -**es**) *m* hamburger.
handicap [ãndʒi'kapil *m* handicap.
hangar [ãŋ'ga(x)] (*pl* -**es**) *m* hangar.
Hanói [a'nɔj] *n* Hanoi.
Harare [a'raril *n* Harare.
haras ['araʃ] *m* *inv* stud (*for racehorses*).
hardware [ax'dwɛ(x)] *m* COMPUT hardware.
harém [a'rẽ] (*pl* -**ns**) *m* harem.
harmonia [axmo'nial *f* harmony.
harmônico, ca [ax'moniku, ka] *adj* harmonic.
➡ **harmônica** *f* harmonica, mouth organ.
harmonioso, osa [axmo'njozu, ɔza] *adj* harmonious.
harmonizar [4] [axmoni'za(x)] *vt* **-1.** MÚS to harmonize. **-2.** [conciliar]: ~ **algo com algo** to reconcile sthg with sthg.
➡ **harmonizar-se** *vp*: ~-**se (com algo)** to be in harmony (with sthg).
harpa ['axpal *f* harp.
harpista [ax'piʃta] *mf* harpist.
haste ['aʃtʃi] *f* **-1.** [de bandeira] pole. **-2.** [caule] stalk.

hasteamento [aʃtʃja'mẽntul *m* hoisting.
hastear [15] [aʃ'tʃja(x)] *vt* to raise.
Havaí [ava'i] *n* Hawaii.
havaiano, na [ava'jãnu, nal ◇ *adj* Hawaiian. ◇ *m*, *f* Hawaiian.
havana [a'vãnal ◇ *adj* [cor] beige. ◇ *m* [charuto] Havana cigar.
Havana [a'vãnal *n* Havana.
havanês, esa [ava'neʃ, ezal ◇ *adj* Havana (*antes de subst*). ◇ *m*, *f* person from Havana.
haver [2] [a've(x)] *v impess* **-1.** [existir, estar, ter lugar]: **há** there is, there are *pl*; **havia** there was, there were *pl*; **há um café muito bom ao fim da rua** there's a very good café at the end of the street; **não há nada aqui** there's nothing here; **não há correio amanhã** there's no mail tomorrow. **-2.** [exprime tempo]: **estou esperando há dez minutos** I've been waiting for ten minutes; **há séculos que não vou lá** I haven't been there for ages; **há três dias que não o vejo** I haven't seen him for three days. **-3.** [exprime obrigação]: **há que esperar três dias** you'll have to wait three days. **- 4.** [em locuções]: **haja o que houver** come what may; **não há de quê!** don't mention it! ◇ *v aux* [em tempos compostos] to have; **ele havia chegado há pouco** he had just arrived; **como não havia comido estava com fome** I was hungry because I hadn't eaten; **havíamos reservado com antecedência** we'd reserved in advance.
➡ **haver de** *v* + *prep* [dever] to have; [exprime intenção]: **hei de ir** I'll go.
➡ **haver-se com** *vp* + *prep*: ~-**se com alguém** [prestar contas a] to answer to sb.
➡ **haveres** *mpl* [pertences] belongings; [bens] assets.
haxixe [a'ʃiʃil *m* hashish.
HC (*abrev de* **Hospital das Clínicas**) *m* *famous teaching hospital in São Paulo*.
HD (*abrev de* **Hard Disk**) *m* HD.
hectare [ek'taril *m* hectare.
hectograma [ekto'grãmal *m* hectogram, hectogramme.
hectolitro [ekto'litrul *m* hectolitre.
hedge [ɛdjil *m* ECON [proteção cambial] hedge.
hediondo, da [e'dʒõndu, dal *adj* hideous.
hedonista [edo'niʃta] ◇ *adj* hedonistic. ◇ *mf* hedonist.
hegemonia [eʒemo'nial *f* hegemony.
hegemônico, ca [ege'moniku, kal *adj* hegemonic.
hein [ẽj] *interj*: ~**?** what?; **aí,** ~**?** *fam* [muito bem] not bad, eh?
hélice ['ɛlisil *f* propeller.
helicóptero [eli'kɔpterul *m* helicopter.
heliporto [eli'poxtul *m* heliport.
Helsinki [ɛw'sĩŋkil *n* Helsinki.
hematologia [ematolo'ʒial *f* haematology UK, hematology US.
hematoma [ema'tomal *f* bruise, haematoma UK, hematoma US.

hemisférico, ca [emiʃˈferiku, ka] *adj* hemispherical.

hemisfério [emiʃˈfɛrju] *m* hemisphere.

hemodiálise [emoˈdʒjalizi] *f* dialysis.

hemofilia [emofiˈlia] *f* haemophilia *UK*, hemophilia *US*.

hemofílico, ca [ɛmoˈfiliku, ka] <> *adj* haemophilic *UK*, hemophilic *US*. <> *m, f* haemophiliac *UK*, hemophiliac *US*.

hemoglobina [emogloˈbina] *f* haemoglobin *UK*, hemoglobin *US*.

hemograma [emoˈgrãma] *m* full blood count.

hemorragia [emoxaˈʒia] *f* haemorrhage *UK*, hemorrhage *US*.

hemorrágico, ca [emoˈxagiku, ka] *adj* haemorrhagic.

hemorróidas [emoˈxɔjdaʃ] *fpl* haemorrhoid *UK*, hemorrhoid *US*.

henê [eˈne], **hena** [ˈɛna] *f* henna.

hepatite [epaˈtʃitʃi] *f* hepatitis.

heptágono [epˈtagonul] *m* heptagon.

hera [ˈɛra] *f* ivy.

heráldica [eˈrawdʒika] *f* heraldry.

herança [eˈrãnsa] *f* inheritance.

herbáceo, cea [ex'basju, sja] *adj* herbaceous.

herbanário [exba'narju] *m* herbarium.

herbicida [exbiˈsida] *m* herbicide.

herbívoro, ra [ex'bivoru, ra] <> *adj* herbivorous. <> *m, f* herbivore.

hercúleo, lea [ex'kulju, lja] *adj fig* [muito forte] Herculean.

herdar [4] [ex'da(x)] *vt* -**1.** [ger]: ~ algo de alguém to inherit sthg from sb. -**2.** [legar]: ~ algo a alguém to pass sthg on to sb.

herdeiro, ra [ex'dejru, ra] *m, f* heir.

hereditariedade [eredʒitarje'dadʒi] *f* heredity.

hereditário, ria [eredʒi'tarju, rja] *adj* hereditary.

herege [eˈrɛʒil] *mf* heretic.

heresia [ere'zia] *f* heresy.

herético, ca [eˈrɛtʃiku, ka] <> *adj* heretical. <> *m, f* heretic.

hermafrodita [exmafroˈdʒita] <> *adj* hermaphrodite, hermaphroditic. <> *mf* hermaphrodite.

hermético, ca [exˈmɛtʃiku, ka] *adj* -**1.** [bem fechado] hermetic, airtight. -**2.** *fig* [obscuro] hermetic.

hérnia [ˈɛxnja] *f* hernia; ~ de disco slipped disc.

herói [eˈrɔj] *m* hero.

heróico, ca [eˈrɔjku, ka] *adj* heroic.

heroína [eˈrwina] *f* heroine.

heroísmo [eˈrwiʒmul] *m* heroism.

herpes [ˈɛxpiʃ] *m* herpes; ~ genital genital herpes.

hertz [ˈɛxts] *m* hertz.

hesitação [eziˈtasãw] (*pl* -ões) *f* hesitation.

hesitante [eziˈtãntʃil] *adj* hesitant.

hesitar [4] [eziˈta(x)] *vi*: ~ em fazer algo to hesitate to do sthg.

heterodoxo, xa [eteroˈdɔksu, ksa] *adj* heterodox.

heterogêneo, nea [eteroˈʒenju, nja] *adj* heterogeneous.

heterônimo [eteˈronimul] *m* pen-name, nom de plume.

heterossexual [eterosekˈswawl] (*pl* -ais) <> *adj* heterosexual. <> *mf* heterosexual.

hexagonal [ezagoˈnawl] (*pl* -ais) *adj* hexagonal.

hexágono [eˈzagonul] *m* hexagon.

hiato [ˈjatul] *m* hiatus.

hibernação [ibexnaˈsãw] (*pl* -ões) *f* hibernation.

hibernar [4] [ibexˈna(x)] *vi* to hibernate.

hibisco [iˈbiʃku] *m* hibiscus.

híbrido, da [ˈibridu, da] *adj* [mesclado] hybrid.
➡ **híbrido** *m* [animal ou vegetal]: ser um ~ (de) to be a hybrid (of).

hidramático, ca [idra'matʃiku, ka] *adj* Hydra-Matic®.

hidratante [idraˈtãntʃil] <> *adj* moisturizing. <> *m* moisturizer.

hidratar [4] [idraˈta(x)] *vt* -**1.** [pele] to moisturize. -**2.** *MED* to hydrate.

hidrato [iˈdratul] *m*: ~ de carbono carbohydrate.

hidráulico, ca [iˈdrawliku, ka] *adj* hydraulic.
➡ **hidráulica** *f* hydraulics (*sg*).

hidrelétrica [idreˈlɛtrikal] *f* -**1.** [usina] hydroelectric power station. -**2.** [empresa] hydroelectric company.

hidrelétrico, ca [idreˈlɛtriku, ka] *adj* hydroelectric.

hidroavião [ˌidrwaˈvjãwl] (*pl* -ões) *m* seaplane.

hidrocarboneto [idrokaxboˈnetul] *m* hydrocarbon.

hidrodinâmica [idrodʒiˈnãmikal] *f* hydrodynamics (*sg*).

hidrófilo, la [iˈdrɔfilu, la] *adj* absorbent.

hidrofobia [idrofoˈbial] *f* hydrophobia, rabies.

hidrófobo, ba [iˈdrɔfobu, ba] <> *adj* hydrophobic. <> *m, f* hydrophobic person.

hidrogênio [idroˈʒenjul] *m* hydrogen.

hidrografia [idrograˈfial] *f* hydrography.

hidromassagem [idrumaˈsaʒẽl] (*pl* -ns) *f* hydromassage.

hidroplano [idroˈplãnul] *m* hydroplane.

hidroterapia [idroteraˈpial] *f* hydrotherapy.

hidrovia [idroˈvial] *f* waterway.

hiena [ˈjenal] *f* hyena.

hierarquia [jerarˈkial] *f* hierarchy.

hierárquico, ca [jeˈraxkiku, ka] *adj* hierarchical.

hierarquizar [4] [jeraxkiˈza(x)] *vt* to organize into a hierarchy.

hieróglifo [jeˈrɔgliful] *m* hieroglyph.

hífen [ˈifẽl] (*pl* -es) *m* hyphen.

hifenizar [4] [lifeniˈza(x)] *vt* hyphenate.

Hi-Fi (*abrev de* High Fidelity) *m* hi-fi.

higiene [iˈʒjenil] *f* hygiene.

higiênico, ca [iˈʒjeniku, ka] *adj* hygienic; **papel** ~ toilet paper.

higienizar [4] [ʒjeniˈza(x)] *vt* to sterilize.

hilariante [ilaˈrjãntʃil] *adj* hilarious.

hilário, ria [iˈlarju, rja] *adj* [hilariante] hilarious.

Himalaia [imaˈlajal *n*: **o** ~ the Himalayas (*pl*).
hímen [ˈimɛl (*pl* -**ns**) *m* ANAT hymen.
hindi [ˈĩndʒil *m* Hindi.
hindu [ĩnˈdul (*pl* **hindus**) ⬦ *adj* -**1**. [da índia] Indian. -**2**. RELIG Hindu. ⬦ *m*, *f* -**1**. [da índia] Indian. -**2**. RELIG Hindu.
hinduísmo [ĩnˈdwiʒmul *m* Hinduism.
hino [ˈinul *m* hymn; ~ **nacional** national anthem.
hiper [ˈipe(x)l *prefixo* -**1**. [extremo, grande] hyper-. -**2**. *fam* [super] hyper-.
hipérbole [iˈpɛxbolil *f* -**1**. MAT hyperbola. -**2**. [exagero] hyperbole.
hiperinflação [iperĩnflaˈsãwl (*pl* -**ões**) *f* hyperinflation.
hiperlink [iperˈlinkil *m* COMPUT hyperlink.
hipermercado [ˌipexmexˈkadul *m* hypermarket.
hipermetropia [ipexmetroˈpial *f* hypermetropia, long-sightedness.
hipersensível [ipexsẽnˈsivewl (*pl* -**eis**) *adj* hypersensitive.
hipertensão [ˌipextẽnˈsãwl (*pl* -**ões**) *f* high blood pressure, hypertension.
hipertenso, sa [ipexˈtẽsu, sal *adj* with high blood-pressure; **ser** ~ to have high blood pressure.
hipertexto [ipexˈtejʃtul *m* COMPUT hypertext.
hipertrofia [ipextroˈfial *f* -**1**. MED hypertrophy. -**2**. [fig] excessive increase.
hipertrofiar [ipextroˈfja(x)l *vt* to overstretch.
➥ **hipertrofiar-se** *vp* to become overdeveloped.
hípico, ca [ˈipiku, kal *adj* -**1**. [clube, competição] riding. -**2**. [sociedade] equestrian.
hipismo [iˈpiʒmul *m* horse riding, equestrianism.
hipnose [ipˈnɔzil *f* hypnosis.
hipnótico, ca [ipˈnɔtʃiku, kal *adj* hypnotic.
➥ **hipnótico** *m* [substância] hypnotic.
hipnotizado, da [ipnotʃiˈzadu, dal *adj* hypnotized.
hipnotizador, ra [ipnotʃizaˈdo(x), ral ⬦ *adj* hypnotizing. ⬦ *m*, *f* hypnotist.
hipnotizar [4] [ipnotʃiˈza(x)l *vt* to hypnotize.
hipocondria [ipokõnˈdrial *f* hypochondria.
hipocondríaco, ca [ˌipokõnˈdriaku, kal ⬦ *adj* hypochondriac. ⬦ *m*, *f* hypochondriac.
hipocrisia [ipokriˈzial *f* hypocrisy.
hipócrita [iˈpɔkrital ⬦ *adj* hypocritical. ⬦ *mf* hypocrite.
hipodérmico, ca [ipoˈdɛxmiku, kal *adj* hypodermic.
hipódromo [iˈpɔdrumul *m* racecourse.
hipófise [iˈpɔfizil *f* ANAT pituitary.
hipoglicemia [ipogliseˈmial *f* hypoglycaemia *UK*, hypoglycemia *US*.
hipopótamo [ipoˈpɔtamul *m* hippopotamus.
hipoteca [ipoˈtɛkal *f* mortgage.
hipotecar [12] [ipoteˈka(x)l *vt* to mortgage.
hipotecário, ria [ipoteˈkarju, rjal *adj* mortgage (*antes de subst*).

hipotenusa [ipoteˈnuzal *f* hypotenuse.
hipotermia [ipotexˈmial *f* hypothermia.
hipótese [iˈpɔtezil *f* -**1**. [conjectura] hypothesis. -**2**. [possibilidade] eventuality; **não abandonaria meus filhos em** ~ **alguma** I wouldn't abandon my children under any circumstances, under no circumstance would I abandon my children; **na melhor/pior das** ~**s** at best/worst.
hipotético, ca [ipoˈtɛtʃiku, kal *adj* hypothetical.
hirsuto, ta [ixˈsutu, tal *adj* hairy.
hispânico, ca [iʃˈpaniku, kal ⬦ *adj* Hispanic. ⬦ *m*, *f* Hispanic.
hispano, na [iʃˈpãnu, nal ⬦ *adj* Hispanic. ⬦ *m*, *f* Hispanic.
hispano-americano, na [iʃˌpãnwameriˈkãnu, nal ⬦ *adj* Spanish-American. ⬦ *m*, *f* Spanish American.
histerectomia [iʃterektoˈmial *f* hysterectomy.
histeria [iʃteˈrial *f* hysteria.
histérico, ca [iʃˈtɛriku, kal *adj* hysterical.
histerismo [iʃteˈriʒmul *m* MED hysteria.
histologia [iʃtoloˈʒial *f* histology.
história [iʃˈtɔrjal *f* -**1**. [ger] history; ~ **antiga** ancient history; ~ **do Brasil** Brazilian history; ~ **natural** natural history. -**2**. [narração] story; ~ **do arco-da-velha** tall story; ~ **da carochinha** fairy tale; ~ **em quadrinhos** comic strip. -**3**. [lorota] nonsense; ~ **para boi dormir** empty talk. -**4**. [recato]: **deixa de** ~! come off it! -**5**. [explicação] excuse. -**6**. [idéia, proposta] suggestion. -**7**. [acontecimento] event; [caso amoroso] love affair. -**8**. [enredo] storyline. -**9**. [boato] rumour. -**10**. [tradição] tradition. -**11**. [problema] problem. -**12**. *fam* [abuso]: **que** ~ **é essa de ...?** what's the idea of ...?
historiador, ra [iʃtorjaˈdo(x), ral *m*, *f* historian.
historiar [16] [iʃtoˈrja(x)l *vt* to narrate.
historicidade [iʃtorisiˈdadʒil *f* historicity, historical authenticity.
histórico, ca [iʃˈtɔriku, kal *adj* -**1**. [ger] historical. -**2**. [importante] historic.
➥ **histórico** *m* history.
historieta [iʃtoˈrjetal *f* short story.
histrião [iʃtriˈãwl (*pl* -**ões**) *m* [comediante] comic.
histriônico, ca [iʃtriˈoniku, kal *adj* histrionic.
histrionismo [iʃrjoˈniʒmul *m* histrionics (*pl*).
hit [ˈitil *m* COMPUT hit.
HIV (*abrev de* **Human Immunodeficiency Virus**) *m* HIV.
hobby [ˈɔbil *m* hobby.
hoje [ˈoʒil *adv* today; **ainda** ~ before the end of the day; **de** ~ **em diante** from today onwards, from this day forth; ~ **noite** tonight; ~ **em dia** nowadays; ~ **faz um mês** a month ago today.
Holanda [oˈlãndal *f* Holland, The Netherlands.
holandês, esa [olãˈdeʃ, ezal (*mpl* -**eses** *fpl* -**s**) ⬦ *adj* Dutch. ⬦ *m*, *f* Dutchman (*f* Dutchwoman).
➥ **holandês** *m* [língua] Dutch.
holding [ˈxowdiŋl *f* holdings (*pl*).
holocausto [oloˈkawʃtul *m* holocaust.
holofote [oloˈfotʃil *m* searchlight.

holograma [olo'grãma] *m* hologram.
hombridade [õnbri'dadʒi] *f* decency.
home banking ['xomibãnkĩn] *m* COMPUT home banking.
homem ['ɔmẽ] (*pl* -ns) *m* -1. [ger] man; ~ de negócios businessman; ~ do povo man of the people. -2. [humanidade]: o ~ mankind. -3. [chefe]: ser o ~ da casa to be the man of the house.
homem-feito [ˌomẽn'fejtu] (*pl* homens-feitos) *m* grown man.
homem-rã [ˌomẽn'xã] (*pl* homens-rãs) *m* frogman.
homenageado, da [omena'ʒjadu, da] <> *adj* venerated. <> *m, f*: o ~ da festa é ... this party is being held in homage to ...
homenagear [15] [omena'ʒja(x)] *vt* to pay homage to.
homenagem [ome'naʒẽ] (*pl* -ns) *f* homage; em ~ a algo/alguém in homage to sthg/sb.
homenzarrão [omẽnza'xãw] (*pl* -ões) *m* strapping man.
homeopata [omjo'pata] <> *adj* homeopathic. <> *mf* homeopath.
homeopatia [omjopa'tʃia] *f* homeopathy.
homeopático, ca [omjo'patʃiku, ka] *adj* homeopathic.
homérico, ca [o'mɛriku, ka] *adj fig* [extraordinário] epic.
homicida [omi'sida] <> *adj* homicidal. <> *mf* murderer.
homicídio [omi'sidʒju] *m* homicide; ~ culposo manslaughter.
homogeneidade [omoʒenej'dadʒi] *f* homogeneity.
homogeneizado, da [omoʒenej'zadu, da] *adj* homogenized.
homogêneo, nea [omo'ʒenju, nja] *adj* homogeneous.
homologação [omologa'sãw] (*pl* -ões) *f* ratification.
homologar [14] [omolo'ga(x)] *vt* -1. [lei, casamento] to ratify. -2. [sociedade] to grant official recognition to.
homólogo, ga [o'mɔlogu, ga] <> *adj* -1. [ger] homologous. -2. [correspondente] equivalent. <> *m, f* [pessoa] counterpart, opposite number.
homônimo, ma [o'monimu, ma] *adj* homonymous.
➡ **homônimo** *m* -1. [pessoa] namesake. -2. GRAM homonym.
homossexual [omosek'swaw] (*pl* -ais) <> *adj* homosexual. <> *m, f* homosexual.
homossexualidade [omosekswali'dadʒi] *f* homosexuality.
homossexualismo [omosekswa'liʒmu] *m* homosexuality.
Honduras [õn'duraʃ] *n* Honduras.
hondurenho, nha [õndu'reɲu, ɲa] <> *adj* Honduran. <> *m, f* Honduran.
honestamente [oneʃta'mẽntʃi] *adv* honestly.

honestidade [oneʃtʃi'dadʒi] *f* honesty; com ~ honestly.
honesto, ta [o'nɛʃtu, ta] *adj* honest.
Honolulu [onolu'lu] *n* Honolulu.
honorário, ria [ono'rarju, rja] *adj* honorary.
honorários [ono'rarjuʃ] *mpl* fee *(sg)*.
honorífico, ca [ono'rifiku, ka] *adj* honorific.
honra ['õnxa] *f* -1. [ger] honour UK, honor US; em ~ de alguém in honour of sb UK, in honor of sb US. -2. [motivo de orgulho] credit.
➡ **honras** *fpl* honours UK, honors US; ~ militares military honours UK, military honors US; fazer as ~ da casa to do the honours UK, to do the honors US.
honradez [õnxa'deʒ] *f* honesty.
honrado, da [õ'xadu, da] *adj* -1. [digno] worthy. -2. [respeitado] respectable.
honrar [4] [õ'xa(x)] *vt* [respeitar] to honour UK, to honor US.
➡ **honrar-se** *vp* [lisonjear-se]: ~-se com algo/em fazer algo to be honoured in sthg/to do sthg UK, to be honored in sthg/to do sthg US.
honraria [õnxa'ria] *f* honour UK, honor US.
honroso, osa [õ'xozu, ɔza] *adj* honourable UK, honorable US.
hóquei ['ɔkej] *m* hockey; ~ sobre gelo ice hockey.
hora ['ɔra] *f* -1. [do dia] hour; de ~ em ~ every hour. -2. [ger] time; altas ~s very late at night; dar as ~s to tell the time; ~ legal official time; que ~s são? what time is it?; ~ extra extra time; ~s vagas spare time; chegar a ~ to arrive on time; fazer algo fora de ~ to do sthg at the wrong time; em boa ~ opportunely; em má ~ inopportunely; estar na ~ de fazer algo to be time to do sthg; na ~ H on the dot; de última ~ last minute *(antes de subst)*; na última ~ at the last minute; não vejo a ~ de ir embora I can't wait for the time to leave; na ~ on time; em cima da ~ dead on time; perder a ~ to be late. -3. [compromisso]: marcar ~ com alguém to make an appointment with sb. -4. [brincadeira]: fazer ~ com alguém to play with sb. -5. loc: estar pela ~ da morte to cost the earth; fazer ~ to waste time.
horário, ria [o'rarju, rja] *adj* hourly.
➡ **horário** *m* -1. [tabela] timetable. -2. [hora prefixada] time; ~ nobre prime time; ~ de verão summer time.
horda ['ɔxda] *f* horde.
horista [o'riʃta] <> *adj* paid by the hour *(depois de subst)*. <> *mf* employee paid by the hour.
horizontal [orizõn'taw] (*pl* -ais) <> *adj* horizontal. <> *f* [linha] horizontal.
horizonte [ori'zõntʃi] *m* horizon.
hormonal [oxmo'naw] (*pl* -ais) *adj* hormonal.
hormônio [ox'monju] *m* hormone.
horóscopo [o'rɔʃkopu] *m* horoscope.
horrendo, da [o'xẽndu, da] *adj* -1. [atemorizante] frightful. -2. [feio] horrendous.
horripilante [oxipi'lãntʃi] *adj* horrifying.

horripilar [4] [oxipi'la(x)] *vt* to horrify.
→ **horripilar-se** *vp* to be horrified.
horrível [o'xivɛw] (*pl* -eis) *adj* -1. [ger] terrible.
-2. [feio] horrible.
horror [o'xo(x)] (*pl*-es) *m* -1. [medo]: **ter** ~ **(de** *ou*
a algo) to have a horror (of sthg). -2. [repulsa]:
ter ~ **a algo/a fazer algo** to have a horror of
sthg/doing sthg. -3. [coisa feia]: **fiquei um** ~ **com**
essa roupa I looked a fright in those clothes. -4.
[atrocidade]: **que** ~! how awful! -5. [ruim]: **ser um**
~ to be terrible.
→ **horrores** *mpl* -1. [palavras injuriosas]: **dizer** ~
de algo/alguém to say horrible things about
sthg/sb. -2. [ações terríveis]: **fazer** ~ to do
horrible things. -3. [quantia vultuosa]: **ele está fa-**
turando ~ **es** he is raking it in. -4. [grande quan-
tidade]: ~ **de algo** vast amounts of sthg.
horrorizar [4] [oxori'za(x)] *vt* to terrify.
→ **horrorizar-se** *vp* to be terrified.
horroroso, osa [oxo'rozu, ɔzal *adj* -1. [ger]
terrible. -2. [feio] frightful.
horta ['ɔxta] *f* vegetable garden.
hortaliças [oxta'lisaʃ] *fpl* vegetables.
hortelã [oxte'lã] *f* mint.
hortelã-pimenta [oxte,lãpi'mẽnta] (*pl* **hortelãs-**
pimenta) *f* peppermint.
hortênsia [ox'tẽnsja] *f* hydrangea.
horticultor, ra [oxtʃikuw'to(x), ra] (*mpl* -es, *fpl* -s)
m, f horticulturist.
horticultura [oxtʃikuw'tura] *f* horticulture.
hortifrutigranjeiro, ra [oxtʃiʃrutʃigrãn'ʒejru,
ra] *adj relating to fruit, vegetable and small
farm production.*
→ **hortifrutigranjeiro** *m* smallholder *(producing fruit and vegetables).*
hortigranjeiros [oxtʃigrãn'ʒeiruʃ] *mpl* farm
produce.
horto ['ɔxtul *m* allotment.
hospedagem [oʃpe'daʒẽl (*pl* -ns) *f* -1. [acomoda-
ção] accommodation. -2. [diária] board and
lodging. -3. [pensão] inn.
hospedar [4] [oʃpe'da(x)] *vt* to lodge.
→ **hospedar-se** *vp* to lodge.
hospedaria [oʃpeda'ria] *f* guest house.
hóspede ['ɔʃpedʒil *mf* guest.
hospedeiro, ra [oʃpe'dejru, ra] *m, f* host.
hospício [oʃ'pisjul *m* hospice.
hospital [oʃpi'taw] (*pl* -ais) *m* hospital.
hospitalar [oʃpita'la(x)] *adj* hospital *(antes de
subst).*
hospitaleiro, ra [oʃpita'lejru, ra] *adj* hospitable.
hospital-escola [oʃpi,tawiʃ'kɔla] (*pl* **hospitais-**
escola, hospitais-escolas) *m* teaching hospital.
hospitalidade [oʃpitali'dadʒil *f* hospitality.
hospitalização [oʃpitaliza'sãw] *f* hospitaliza-
tion.
hospitalizar [4] [oʃpitali'za(x)] *vt* to hospitalize.
host ['xoʃtʃil *m* COMPUT host.
hostess ['ɔʃtes] *f* hostess.
hóstia ['ɔʃtʃial *f* Host.
hostil [oʃ'tiwl (*pl* -is) *adj* -1. [contrário]: ~ **a algo/**

alguém hostile to sthg/sb. -2. [agressivo] hostile.
hostilidade [oʃtʃili'dadʒil *f* [sentimento] hostility.
→ **hostilidades** *fpl* MIL hostilities.
hostilizar [4] [oʃtili'za(x)] *vt* to be hostile towards.
hotel [o'tɛwl (*pl* -éis) *m* hotel; ~ **de alta rotativi-**
dade hotel of ill repute.
hotelaria [otela'ria] *f* -1. COM hotel management.
-2. [conjunto de hotéis] hotels *(pl).*
hoteleiro, ra [ote'lejru, ra] ◇ *adj* hotel; **rede**
hoteleira chain of hotels. ◇ *m, f* hotelier.
hp *(abrev de* **horsepower**) *m* hp.
HTML *(abrev de* **Hypertext Markup Language**) *m*
HTML.
HTTP *(abrev de* **Hypertext Transfer Protocol**) *m*
HTTP.
hum [ũl *interj* hum!
humanamente [umãna'mẽntʃil *adv* humanly; ~
impossível humanly impossible.
humanidade [umani'dadʒil *f* humanity.
humanismo [uma'niʒmul *m* humanism.
humanista [uma'niʃtal ◇ *adj* humanistic. ◇
mf humanist.
humanitário, ria [umani'tarju, rjal *adj* humanitarian.
humanizar [4] [umani'za(x)] *vt* to humanize.
→ **humanizar-se** *vp* to become humanized.
humano, na [u'manu, nal *adj* -1. [da humanidade]
human; **ser** ~ human being. -2. [bondoso]
human, understanding.
humanóide [uma'nɔjdʒil ◇ *adj* humanoid. ◇
mf humanoid.
humanos [u'mãnuʃl *mpl* humans.
humildade [umiw'dadʒil *f* -1. [pobreza]
humbleness. -2. [modéstia] humility. -3. [submis-
são] humility; **com** ~ humbly.
humilde [u'miwdʒil *adj* humble; **os** ~**s** the poor
(pl).
humildemente [umiwdʒi'mẽntʃil *adv* humbly.
humilhação [umiʎa'sãwl (*pl* -ões) *f* humiliation.
humilhante [umi'ʎãntʃil *adj* humiliating.
humilhar [4] [umi'ʎa(x)] *vt* to humiliate.
→ **humilhar-se** *vp* to humble o.s.
humor [u'mo(x)] *m* -1. [ger] humour UK, humor
US; **de** ~ humorous; ~ **negro** black humour. -2.
[ânimo] mood; **estar de bom/mau** ~ to be good-/
bad-tempered; **estar com** ~ **de cão** to be in a
foul mood. -3. [senso de humor] sense of humour
UK, sense of humor US.
humorismo [umo'riʒmul *m* humour UK, humor
US.
humorista [umo'riʃtal *mf* comedian.
humorístico, ca [umo'riʃtʃiku, kal *adj* comedy
(antes de subst).
húmus ['umuʃl *m inv* humus.
húngaro, ra ['ũŋgaru, ral ◇ *adj* Hungarian. ◇
m, f Hungarian.
→ **húngaro** *m* [língua] Hungarian.
Hungria [ũŋ'gria] *n* Hungary.
hurra ['uxal *interj* hooray, hurrah.
Hz *(abrev de* **hertz**) *m* Hz.

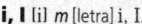

i, I [i] *m* [letra] i, I.

ianque [ˈjãŋki] <> *adj* Yankee. <> *m, f* Yank.

iate [ˈjatʃi] *m* yacht.

iatismo [jaˈtʃiʒmu] *m* yachting, sailing.

iatista [jaˈtʃiʃta] *mf* yachtsman (*f* yachtswoman).

IBAMA (*abrev de* Instituto Brasileiro do Meio Ambiente e dos Recursos Naturais Renováveis) *m Brazilian organization responsible for preserving the country's natural environment.*

Ibase (*abrev de* Instituto Brasileiro de Análises Sociais e Econômicas) *m Brazilian institute for social and economic analysis.*

IBDF (*abrev de* Instituto Brasileiro de Desenvolvimento Florestal) *m Brazilian institute for forestry development.*

IBGE (*abrev de* Instituto Brasileiro de Geografia e Estatística) *m Brazilian institute of geography and statistics.*

ibidem [iˈbidɛ] *adv* ibid., ibidem.

Ibope (*abrev de* Instituto Brasileiro de Opinião Pública e Estatística) *m Brazilian opinion poll institute.*

IBP (*abrev de* Instituto Brasileiro de Petróleo) *m Brazilian petroleum institute.*

içar [13] [iˈsa(x)] *vt* to hoist.

iceberg [ajsˈbɛxgil *m* iceberg.

ICMS (*abrev de* Imposto sobre a Circulação de Mercadorias e Serviços) *m government tax on goods and services,* ≃ VAT *UK.*

ícone [ˈikoni] *m* icon.

iconoclasta [ikonoˈklaʃta] <> *adj* iconoclastic. <> *mf* iconoclast.

iconografia [ikonograˈfial *f* iconography.

icterícia [ikteˈrisja] *f* jaundice.

ida [ˈidal *f* **-1.** [ato de ir] going; **~ s e vindas** comings and goings. **-2.** [partida] departure. **-3.** [viagem] journey; **na ~** on the outward journet; **(bilhete de) ~ e volta** return ticket. **-4.** [bilhete]: **só comprei a ~** I only bought a single (ticket).

idade [iˈdadʒil *f* [ger] age; **de ~** [idoso] elderly; **ser menor/maior de ~** to be under/of age; **pessoa da terceira ~** senior citizen; **estar na ~ de fazer algo** to be of an age to do sthg; **~ adulta** adulthood; **~ escolar** school age; **Idade Média**

Middle Ages *(pl)*; **~ da pedra** Stone Age.

ideação [ideaˈsãw] *f* ideation.

ideal [iˈdeawl (*pl* **-ais**) <> *adj* ideal. <> *m* **-1.** [valores] ideal. **-2.** [perfeição] ideal thing.

idealismo [ideaˈliʒmul *m* idealism.

idealista [ideaˈliʃta] <> *adj* idealistic. <> *mf* idealist.

idealização [idealizaˈsãw] (*pl* **-ões**) *f* **-1.** [endeusamento] idealization. **-2.** [planejamento] planning.

idealizador [idealizaˈdo(x)] *m, f* planner.

idealizar [4] [idealiˈza(x)] *vt* **-1.** [endeusar] to idealize. **-2.** [planejar] to plan.

idear [4] [iˈdea(x)] *vt* [planejar] to plan.

ideário [ideˈarjul *m* ideas *(pl).*

idéia [iˈdɛja] *f* **-1.** [ger] idea; **~ de jerico** stupid idea; **estar com ~ de** to be thinking of; **~ fixa** idée fixe, fixed idea; **fazer uma ~ errada de alguém** to misjudge sb; **ter uma ~ errada de algo** to have the wrong idea about sthg; **fazer ou ter ~ de algo** to have an idea of sthg. **-2.** [mente, opinião] mind; **mudar de ~** to change one's mind.
➡ **idéias** *fpl* [concepções] ideas; **trocar ~** to exchange ideas.

idem [ˈidɛ] *pron* idem.

idêntico, ca [iˈdʒẽntʃiku, ka] *adj* identical.

identidade [idẽntʃiˈdadʒi] *f* identity; **(carteira de) ~** identity card.

identificação [idẽntʃifikaˈsãw] (*pl* **-ões**) *f* identification.

identificar [12] [idʒẽntʃifiˈka(x)] *vt* to identify.
➡ **identificar-se** *vp* **-1.** [revelar-se] to identify o.s. **-2.** [espelhar-se]: **~-se com algo/alguém** to identify o.s. with sthg/sb.

ideologia [ideoloˈʒial *f* ideology.

ideológico, ca [ideoˈlɔʒiku, ka] *adj* ideological.

ídiche [ˈidiʃil *m* = iídiche.

idílico, ca [iˈdʒiliku, ka] *adj* idyllic.

idílio [iˈdʒiljul *m* idyll.

idioma [iˈdʒjomal *m* language.

idiomático, ca [idʒoˈmatʃiku, ka] *adj* idiomatic; **expressão idiomática** idiomatic expression.

idiossincrasia [idʒjosĩŋkraˈzial *f* idiosyncrasy.

idiota [iˈdʒjɔta] <> *adj* idiotic. <> *mf* idiot.

idiotia [idʒjoˈtʃial *f* idiocy.

idiotice [idʒoˈtʃisil *f* idiocy.

ido, ida [ˈidu, ˈidal *adj* past.

idólatra [iˈdɔlatral <> *adj* idolatrous. <> *mf* [de ídolos] idol worshipper.

idolatrar [4] [idolaˈtra(x)] *vt* to idolize.

idolatria [idolaˈtrial *f* idolatry.

ídolo [ˈidulul *m* idol.

idoneidade [idonejˈdadʒil *f* fitness.

idôneo, nea [iˈdonju, njal *adj* **-1.** [pessoa, julgamento] fitting. **-2.** [empresa] suitable.

idos [ˈiduʃl *mpl* bygone times.

idoso, osa [iˈdozu, ɔzal *adj* aged.

Iemanjá [jemãˈʒal *f goddess of the sea and water, in Afro-Brazilian lore.*

iene [ˈjenil *m* yen.

Ierevan [jereˈval *n* Yerevan.

iglu [iˈglul *m* igloo.

ignaro, ra [igi'naru, ra] *adj* ignorant.

ignição [igni'sãw] *f* ignition.

ignóbil [ig'nɔbiw] (*pl* **-eis**) *adj* ignoble.

ignomínia [igno'minja] *f* ignominy.

ignominoso, osa [ignomi'nozu, ɔza] *adj* ignominious.

ignorado, da [igno'radu, da] *adj* unknown.

ignorância [igno'rãnsja] *f* **-1.** [desconhecimento]
ignorance. **-2.** [grosseria] rudeness; **com** ~
rudely. **-3.** [violência]: **apelar para a** ~ to resort
to violence.

ignorante [igno'rãntʃi] <> *adj* **-1.** [leigo]: ~ **(em)**
ignorant (of). **-2.** [grosseiro] rude. <> *mf* **-1.** [lei-
go] lay person. **-2.** [grosseiro] rude person.

ignorar [4] [igno'ra(x)] *vt* **-1.** [desconhecer] not to
know. **-2.** [desprezar] to ignore.

ignoto, ta [ig'nɔtu, ta] *adj* unknown.

IGP (*abrev de* **Índice Geral de Preços**) *m general
price index.*

IGP-M (*abrev de* **Índice Geral de Preços de Mercado**) *m general index of market prices.*

igreja [i'greʒa] *f* church.

Iguaçu [igwa'su] *n*: **as cataratas do** ~ the Iguaçu
Falls.

igual [i'gwaw] (*pl* **-ais**) <> *adj* **-1.** [idêntico] equal.
-2. [uniforme] the same. <> *mf* equal; **de** ~
para ~ as equals; **por** ~ evenly. <> *adv* the
same as.

igualar [4] [igwa'la(x)] *vt* **-1.** [tornar igual] to make
equal. **-2.** [nivelar] to level.

◆ **igualar-se** *vp* **-1.** [tornar-se igual]: ~**-se a al-
go/alguém** to equal sthg/sb. **-2.** [nivelar-se]: ~**-
se com algo** to equal sthg. **-3.** [comparar-se]: ~**-
se a algo/alguém** to bear comparison with
sthg/sb.

igualdade [igwaw'dadʒi] *f* **-1.** [ger] equality. **-2.**
[constância] regularity.

igualitário, ria [igwali'tarju, rja] *adj* egalitarian.

igualmente [igwaw'mẽntʃi] *adv* equally.

iguana [i'gwãnal *m* iguana.

iguaria [igwa'ria] *f* delicacy.

ih [i] *interj* eek!

iídiche ['jidiʃi], **ídiche** ['idiʃi] *m* Yiddish.

ilação [ila'sãw] (*pl* **-ões**) *f* inference.

ilegal [ile'gaw] (*pl* **-ais**) *adj* illegal.

ilegalidade [ilegali'dadʒi] *f* illegality.

ilegítimo, ma [ile'ʒitʃimu, ma] *adj* illegitimate.

ilegível [ile'ʒivɛw] (*pl* **-eis**) *adj* illegible.

ileso, sa [i'lezu, za] *adj* unharmed.

iletrado, da [ile'tradu, da] *adj* **-1.** [inculto]
unlettered. **-2.** [analfabeto] illiterate.

ilha ['iʎa] *f* island.

largest fluvial island in the world, with an area of 20,000
km²: the island of Bananal. Its fauna is extremely
abundant and the island of Bananal is home to the
National Park of Araguaia and two indigenous
reserves: Carajás and Javaés.

ilhar [4] [i'ʎa(x)] *vt* to isolate.

ilharga [i'ʎaxga] *f* ANAT flank.

ilhéu, ilhoa [i'ʎɛw, i'ʎoa] *m*, *f* islander.

ilhós [i'ʎɔʃ] (*pl* **ilhoses**) *m* eyelet.

ilhota [i'ʎɔta] *f* islet.

ilícito, ta [i'lisitu, ta] *adj* illicit.

ilimitado, da [ilimi'tadu, da] *adj* unlimited.

ilógico, ca [i'lɔʒiku, ka] *adj* illogical.

iludir [6] [ilu'di(x)] *vt* to delude.

◆ **iludir-se** *vp* to delude o.s.

iluminação [ilumina'sãw] (*pl* **-ões**) *f* **-1.** [luzes]
lighting. **-2.** *fig* [insight] inspiration.

iluminado, da [ilumi'nadu, da] *adj* **-1.** [que recebe luz - sala] lit; [- palco, estádio] floodlit. **-2.** *fig*
[esclarecido] enlightened.

iluminante [ilumi'nãntʃi] *adj* illuminating.

iluminar [4] [ilumi'na(x)] *vt* **-1.** [alumiar] to light
up. **-2.** *fig* [esclarecer] to enlighten.

◆ **iluminar-se** *vp* to light up.

Iluminismo [ilumi'niʒmu] *m* Enlightenment.

iluminista [ilumi'niʃta] <> *adj* Enlightenment
(*antes de subst*). <> *mf* member or follower of the
Enlightenment.

ilusão [ilu'zãw] (*pl* **-ões**) *f* illusion; ~ **de ótica**
optical illusion; **viver de ilusões** to delude o.s.

ilusionista [iluzjo'niʃta] *mf* illusionist.

ilusório, ria [ilu'zɔrju, rja] *adj* illusory.

ilustração [iluʃtra'sãw] (*pl* **-ões**) *f* illustration.

ilustrado, da [iluʃ'tradu, da] *adj* **-1.** [com figuras]
illustrated. **-2.** [instruído] learned.

ilustrador, ra [iluʃtra'do(x), ra] <> *adj* illustrative. <> *m*, *f* illustrator.

ilustrar [4] [iluʃ'tra(x)] *vt* **-1.** [ger] to illustrate. **-2.**
[instruir] to enlighten.

◆ **ilustrar-se** *vp* [instruir-se] to enlighten o.s.

ilustrativo, va [iluʃtra'tʃivu, va] *adj* illustrative.

ilustre [i'luʃtri] *adj* illustrious, distinguished; **um**
~ **desconhecido** a complete unknown.

ilustríssimo, ma [iluʃ'trisimu, ma] *superl* ▷
ilustre; ~ **senhor** honourable gentleman *UK*,
honorable gentleman *US*.

ímã ['imã] *m* magnet.

imaculado, da [imaku'ladu, da] *adj* immaculate.

imagem [i'maʒẽ] (*pl* **-ns**) *f* **-1.** [gen] image. **-2.**
[TV] picture.

imagético, ca [ima'getiku, ka] *adj* fully illustrated.

imaginação [imaʒina'sãw] *f* imagination.

imaginar [4] [imaʒi'na(x)] <> *vt* **-1.** [fantasiar] to
imagine. **-2.** [supor]: ~ **que** to imagine that. <>
vi to daydream; **imagina!** just imagine!

◆ **imaginar-se** *vp* [supor-se] to imagine o.s.

imaginário, ria [imaʒi'narju, rja] *adj* imaginary.

imaginativo, va [imaʒina'tʃivu, va] *adj* imaginative.

imaginável [imaʒi'navew] (*pl* -eis) *adj* imaginable.

imaginoso, osa [imaʒi'nozu, ɔza] *adj* fanciful.

imantar [4] [imãn'ta(x)] *vt* to magnetize.

imaturidade [imaturi'dadʒi] *f* immaturity.

imaturo, ra [ima'turu, ra] *adj* immature.

imbatível [ĩnba'tʃivɛw] (*pl* -eis) *adj* unbeatable.

imbecil [ĩnbe'siw] (*pl* -is) <> *adj* stupid, idiotic. <> *mf* imbecile.

imbecilidade [ĩnbesili'dadʒi] *f* stupidity.

imberbe [ĩn'bɛxbi] *adj* -1. [sem barba] beardless. -2. [juvenil] youthful.

imbricar [12] [ĩmbri'ka(x)] *vt* to overlap.
➡ **imbricar-se** *vp* to overlap.

imbuído, da [ĩmbu'idu, da] *adj* imbued.

imbuir [74] [ĩm'bwi(x)] *vt*: ~ algo de algo to impregnate sthg with sthg; ~ alguém de algo to instil sthg in sb.

imediações [imedʒja'sõiʃ] *fpl* vicinity *(sg)*; nas ~ de near, in the vicinity of.

imediatamente [ime,dʒjata'mẽntʃi] *adv* immediately.

imediatismo [imedʒja'tʃiʒmu] *m* immediacy.

imediatista [imedʒja'tʃiʃta] *adj* immediate.

imediato, ta [ime'dʒjatu, ta] *adj* immediate.
➡ **imediato** *m* second in command.
➡ **de imediato** *loc adv* at once.

imemorial [imemo'rjaw] (*pl* -ais) *adj* immemorial.

imensidão [imẽnsi'dãw], **imensidade** [imẽnsi'dadʒi] *f* immensity.

imenso, sa [i'mẽsu, sa] *adj* immense; sinto uma saudade imensa dele I miss him immensely.

imensurável [imẽnsu'ravew] (*pl* -eis) *adj* immeasurable.

imerecido, da [imere'sidu, da] *adj* undeserved.

imergir [78] [imex'ʒi(x)] <> *vt* to immerse. <> *vi* -1. [afundar] to sink. -2. *fig* [entrar]: ~ em algo to sink into sthg.

imersão [imex'sãw] (*pl* -ões) *f* immersion.

imerso, sa [i'mɛxsu, sa] *adj* immersed.

imigração [imigra'sãw] (*pl* -ões) *f* immigration.

imigrante [imi'grãntʃi] <> *adj* immigrant. <> *mf* immigrant.

imigrar [4] [imi'gra(x)] *vi* to immigrate.

iminência [imi'nẽnsja] *f* imminence; em ~ imminent; na ~ de fazer algo on the point of doing sthg.

iminente [imi'nẽntʃi] *adj* imminent.

imiscuir-se [74] [imiʃ'kwixsil] *vp* to become involved.

imitação [imita'sãw] (*pl* -ões) *f* imitation.

imitador, ra [imita'do(x), ra] <> *adj* imitation *(antes de subst)*. <> *m, f* imitator.

imitar [4] [imi'ta(x)] *vt* -1. [arremedar] to imitate. -2. [falsificar] to forge.

imitativo, va [imita'tʃivu, va] *adj* imitative.

IML *(abrev de* Instituto Médico Legal) *m Brazilian institute of forensic medicine.*

imobiliário, ria [imobi'larju, rja] *adj* property *(antes de subst).*

➡ **imobiliária** *f* estate agency.

imobilidade [imobili'dadʒi] *f* immobility.

imobilizar [4] [imobili'za(x)] *vt* to immobilize.

imoderação [imodera'sãw] *f* immoderation.

imoderado, da [imode'radu, da] *adj* immoderate.

imodéstia [imo'dɛʃtʃja] *f* immodesty.

imodesto, ta [imo'dɛʃtu, ta] *adj* immodest.

imolar [4] [imo'la(x)] *vt* -1. [sacrificar] to immolate. -2. [prejudicar] to damage.

imoral [imo'raw] (*pl* -ais) *adj* immoral.

imoralidade [imorali'dadʒi] *f* immorality.

imortal [imox'taw] (*pl* -ais) <> *adj* immortal. <> *mf member of the Academia Brasileira de Letras.*

imortalidade [imoxtali'dadʒi] *f* immortality.

imortalizar [4] [imoxtali'za(x)] *vt* to immortalize.

imóvel [i'mɔvɛw] (*pl* -eis) <> *adj* -1. [pessoa] immobile. -2. [olho, bem] fixed; bens imóveis real estate *(U).* <> *m* property.

impaciência [ĩnpa'sjẽnsja] *f* impatience.

impacientar [4] [ĩmpasjẽn'ta(x)] *vt* to be impatient.
➡ **impacientar-se** *vp* to become impatient.

impaciente [ĩnpa'sjẽntʃi] *adj* -1. [sem paciência] impatient. -2. [ansioso] anxious.

impactante [ĩnpak'tãntʃi] *adj* [chocante] shattering.

impactar [4] [ĩnpak'ta(x)] <> *vt* -1. [impressionar, abalar] to shatter. -2. [colidir contra] to crash into. <> *vi* to have an impact.

impacto [ĩn'paktu] *m* impact.

impagável [ĩmpa'gavew] (*pl* -eis) *adj* priceless.

ímpar ['ĩnpa(x)] (*pl* -es) *adj* -1. [número] odd. -2. [único] peerless; ele é um amigo ~ he's a friend in a million.

imparcial [ĩnpax'sjaw] (*pl* -ais) *adj* impartial.

imparcialidade [ĩnpaxsjali'dadʒi] *f* impartiality.

impasse [ĩn'pasi] *m* deadlock, impasse.

impassível [ĩnpa'sivew] (*pl* -eis) *adj* impassive.

impávido, da [ĩm'pavidu, da] *adj* undaunted.

impeachment [ĩnpit'ʃimẽnt] *m* impeachment.

impecável [ĩnpe'kavew] (*pl* -eis) *adj* impeccable.

impedido, da [ĩmpe'dʒidu, da] *adj* -1. [bloqueado] blocked. -2. *FUT* off-side. -3. [impossibilitado]: ~ de fazer algo prevented from doing sthg.

impedimento [ĩnpedʒi'mẽntul] *m* -1. *FUT* off-side. -2. *fig* [obstáculo] impediment. -3. *POL* impeachment.

impedir [70] [ĩmpe'dʒi(x)] *v* -1. [obstruir] to obstruct. -2. [coibir] to prevent; ~ alguém de fazer algo to prevent sb from doing sthg.

impelir [57] [ĩmpe'li(x)] *vt* -1. [empurrar] to thrust. -2. [instigar]: ~ alguém a algo to drive sb to sthg; ~ alguém a fazer algo to impel sb to do sthg.

impenetrável [ĩnpene'travew] (*pl* -eis) *adj* impenetrable.

impenitente [ĩnpeni'tẽntʃi] *adj* unrepentant.

impensado, da [ĩnpẽn'sadu, da] *adj* -1. [não-pensado] thoughtless. -2. [imprevisto] unthought of.

impensável [ĩpẽn'savɛw] (*pl* -eis) *adj* unthinkable.

imperador [ĩpera'do(x)] (*mpl* -es) *m* emperor (*f* empress).

imperar [4] [ĩmpe'ra(x)] *vi* -1. [reinar] to rule. -2. [prevalecer] to prevail.

imperativo, va [ĩmpera't∫ivu, va] *adj* -1. [urgente] imperative. -2. [autoritário] imperious.
➡ **imperativo** *m* imperative.

imperatriz [ĩmpera'tri∫] (*mpl* -zes) *f* ➣ **imperador**.

imperceptível [ĩmpexsep't∫ivew] (*pl* -eis) *adj* imperceptible.

imperdível [ĩmpex'dʒivew] (*pl* -eis) *adj* -1. [show, filme, aula] unmissable. -2. [jogo, eleição, questão] impossible to lose *(depois de verbo)*.

imperdoável [ĩmpex'dwavɛw] (*pl* -eis) *adj* unforgivable.

imperecível [ĩmpere'sivew] (*pl* -eis) *adj* imperishable.

imperfeição [ĩmpexfej'sãw] (*pl* -ões) *f* [defeito] imperfection.

imperfeito, ta [ĩmpex'fejtu, ta] *adj* imperfect.
➡ **imperfeito** *m* GRAM imperfect.

imperial [ĩmpe'rjaw] (*pl* -ais) *adj* imperial.

imperialismo [ĩmperja'liʒmu] *m* imperialism.

imperialista [ĩmperja'li∫ta] <> *adj* imperialist. <> *mf* imperialist.

imperícia [ĩmpe'risja] *f* -1. [inabilidade] incompetence. -2. [inexperiência] inexperience.

império [ĩ'perju] *m* empire.

imperioso, osa [ĩmpe'rjozu, ɔza] *adj* -1. [ger] imperious. -2. [urgente] imperative.

impermeabilizante [ĩmpexmjabili'zãnt∫i] <> *adj* waterproofing. <> *m* waterproofer.

impermeabilizar [4] [ĩmpexmjabili'za(x)] *vt* to waterproof.

impermeável [ĩmpex'mjavɛw] (*pl* -eis) <> *adj* impermeable, waterproof. <> *m* [capa de chuva] raincoat.

impertinência [ĩmpext∫i'nẽnsja] *f* impertinence.

impertinente [ĩmpext∫i'nẽnt∫i] *adj* impertinent.

imperturbável [ĩmpextux'bavɛw] (*pl* -eis) *adj* imperturbable.

impessoal [ĩmpe'swaw] (*pl* -ais) *adj* -1. [objetivo] objective. -2. GRAM impersonal.

impessoalidade [ĩmpeswali'dadʒi] *f* [impessonalidade] impersonal nature.

ímpeto ['ĩmpetu] *m* -1. [movimento brusco] sudden movement; **ele se levantou num ~** he stood up with a start. -2. [impulso] urge, impulse; **sentir um ~ de fazer algo** to feel an urge to do sthg.

impetrar [4] [ĩmpe'tra(x)] *vt* JUR: **~ algo** to petition for sthg.

impetuosidade [ĩmpetwozi'dadʒi] *f* impetuosity.

impetuoso, osa [ĩmpe'twozu, ɔza] *adj* -1. [pessoa] impetuous. -2. [chuva] driving. -3. [rio] fast-flowing.

impiedade [ĩmpje'dadʒi] *f* [crueldade] cruelty.

impiedoso, osa [ĩmpje'dozu, ɔza] *adj* merciless.

impingir [52] [ĩmpĩn'ʒi(x)] *vt*: **~ algo a alguém** to fob sthg off on sb.

ímpio, pia [ĩ'ĩmpiu, pia] <> *adj* pitiless. <> *m,f* pitiless person.

implacável [ĩmpla'kavɛw] (*pl* -eis) *adj* -1. [impiedoso] implacable. -2. [inexorável] unrelenting.

implantação [ĩmplãnta'sãw] *f* -1. [introdução] establishing. -2. [implementação] implementation. -3. MED implant.

implantar [4] [ĩmplãn'ta(x)] *vt* -1. [introduzir] to establish. -2. [implementar] to implement. -3. MED to implant.

implante [ĩ'plãnt∫i] *m* MED implant.

implementação [ĩmplemẽnta'sãw] *f* implementation.

implementar [4] [ĩmplemẽn'ta(x)] *vt* to implement.

implemento [ĩmple'mẽntu] *m* implement.

implicação [ĩmplika'sãw] (*pl* -ões) *f* -1. [conseqüência] implication. -2. [envolvimento] involvement.

implicância [ĩmpli'kãnsja] *f* -1. [provocação] provoking; **meus filhos passam o dia inteiro de ~ um com o outro** my children spend the whole day provoking each other. -2. [antipatia]: **ter uma ~ com alguém** to dislike sb.

implicante [ĩmpli'kãnt∫i] *adj* provocative.

implicar [12] [ĩmpli'ka(x)] <> *vt* [envolver]: **~ alguém em algo** to involve sb in sthg. <> *vi* -1. [pressupor]: **~ em algo** to involve sthg. -2. [acarretar]: **~ em algo** to result in sthg. -3. [provocar]: **~ com alguém** to torment sb.

implícito, ta [ĩ'plisitu, ta] *adj* implicit.

implodir [78] [ĩmplo'dʒi(x)] <> *vt* to implode. <> *vi* to implode.

implorar [4] [ĩmplo'ra(x)] *vt*: **~ algo (a alguém)** to beg (sb) for sthg.

implosão [ĩmplo'zãw] (*pl* -ões) *f* implosion.

impoluto, ta [ĩmpo'lutu, ta] *adj* unpolluted.

imponderado, da [ĩmpõnde'radu, da] *adj* rash.

imponderável [ĩmpõnde'ravew] (*pl* -eis) *adj* imponderable.

imponência [ĩmpo'nẽnsja] *f* impressiveness.

imponente [ĩmpo'nẽnt∫i] *adj* impressive, imposing.

impontual [ĩmpõn'twaw] (*pl* -ais) *adj* unpunctual.

impopular [ĩmpopu'la(x)] (*pl* -es) *adj* unpopular.

impopularidade [ĩmpopulari'dadʒi] *f* unpopularity.

impor [45] [ĩm'po(x)] *vt* to impose; **~ algo a alguém** to impose sthg on sb.
➡ **impor-se** *vp* [afirmar-se] to establish o.s.

importação [ĩmpoxta'sãw] (*pl* -ões) *f* -1. [ato] importation. -2. [produtos] imports (*pl*).

importador, ra [ĩmpoxta'do(x), ra] <> *adj* importing (*antes de subst*). <> *m, f* importer.
➡ **importadora** *f* -1. [companhia] importer. -2. [loja] *shop selling imported goods*.

importância [ĩmpox'tãnsja] *f* -1. [mérito] importance; **não dar ~ a alguém/algo** to not care about sb/sthg; **ela não dá ~ ao que ele disse** she doesn't care about what he said; **isso não tem ~** that doesn't matter. **-2.** [quantia] sum.

importante [ĩnpox'tãntʃi] *adj* important.

importar [4] [ĩmpox'ta(x)] ⬦ *vt COM* to import. ⬦ *vi* **-1.** [ser importante] to matter. **-2.** [resultar]: **~ em** to result in. **-3.** [atingir]: **~ em** to add up to.
➡ **importar-se** *vp* [fazer caso]: **não ~-se (com algo/de fazer algo)** not to mind sthg/about doing sthg.

importe [ĩn'pɔxtʃi] *m* **-1.** [soma] amount. **-2.** [preço] cost.

importunação [ĩnpoxtuna'sãw] *f* annoyance.

importunar [4] [ĩmpoxtu'na(x)] *vt* to annoy.

importuno, na [ĩnpox'tunu, na] *adj* annoying.

imposição [ĩnpozi'sãw] (*pl* **-ões**) *f* imposition.

impossibilidade [ĩnposibili'dadʒi] *f* impossibility.

impossibilitado, da [ĩnposibili'tadu, da] *adj*: **~ de fazer algo** unable to do sthg.

impossibilitar [4] [ĩmposi'bili'ta(x)] *vt*: **~ algo** to make sthg impossible; **~ alguém de fazer algo** to prevent sb from doing sthg.

impossível [ĩnpo'sivɛw] (*pl* **-eis**) *adj* impossible.

impostação [ĩnpoʃta'sãw] *f* diction.

imposto, osta [ĩm'poʃtu, ɔsta] *pp* ➤ **impor**.
➡ **imposto** *m* tax; **~ sobre Circulação de Mercadorias e Serviços** ≃ value added tax *UK*, ≃ sales tax *US*; **~ predial** ≃ council tax *UK*; **~ de renda** income tax.

impostor, ra [ĩnpoʃ'to(x), ra] (*mpl* **-es**, *fpl* **-s**) *m* impostor.

impostura [ĩnpoʃ'tura] *f* fraud.

impotência [ĩnpo'tẽnsja] *f* impotence.

impotente [ĩnpo'tẽntʃi] *adj* impotent.

impraticável [ĩnpratʃi'kavɛw] (*pl* **-eis**) *adj* **-1.** [impossível] impossible. **-2.** [inexequível] unworkable. **-3.** [intransitável] impassable.

imprecar [12] [ĩmpre'ka(x)] ⬦ *vt* to curse. ⬦ *vi* to curse.

imprecisão [ĩnpresi'zãw] (*pl* **-ões**) *f* imprecision.

impreciso, sa [ĩnpre'sizu, za] *adj* imprecise.

impregnar [4] [ĩmpreg'na(x)] ⬦ *vt* to impregnate; **~ algo de algo** to impregnate sthg with sthg. ⬦ *vi*: **~ en** to pervade.

imprensa [ĩn'prẽnsa] *f* **-1.** [ger] press; **~ marrom** gutter press. **-2.** [tipografia] printing press.

imprensar [ĩmprẽn'sa(x)] *vt* **-1.** [espremer] to crush. **-2.** [pressionar] to press.

imprescindível [ĩnpresĩn'dʒivɛw] (*pl* **-eis**) *adj* indispensable.

impressão [ĩnpre'sãw] (*pl* **-ões**) *f* **-1.** [marca] imprint; **~ digital** fingerprint. **-2.** [reprodução] printing. **-3.** [sensação] feeling; **ter boa/má impressão de alguém/algo** to have a good/bad impression of sb/sthg.

impressionante [ĩnpresjo'nãntʃi] *adj* impressive.

impressionar [ĩmpresju'na(x)] ⬦ *vt* to impress. ⬦ *vi* to impress.
➡ **impressionar-se** *vp*: **-se com alguém/algo** [comover-se] to be moved by sb/sthg.

impressionável [ĩnpresjo'navɛw] (*pl* **-eis**) *adj* impressionable.

impressionismo [ĩnpresjo'niʒmu] *m* Impressionism.

impressionista [ĩnpresjo'niʃta] ⬦ *adj* Impressionist. ⬦ *m, f* Impressionist.

impresso, a [ĩn'prɛsu, sa] ⬦ *pp* ➤ **imprimir**. ⬦ *adj* printed.
➡ **impresso** *m* printed matter *(sg)*.

impressora [ĩnpre'soral] *f* printer; **~ laser** laser printer; **~ a jato de tinta** ink-jet printer; **~ matricial** dot matrix printer.

imprestável [ĩnpreʃ'tavɛw] (*pl* **-eis**) *adj* **-1.** [inútil] unhelpful. **-2.** [estragado] useless.

impreterível [ĩnprete'rivɛw] (*pl* **-eis**) *adj* unavoidable.

imprevidente [ĩnprevi'dẽntʃi] *adj* **-1.** [imprudente] imprudent. **-2.** [que não soube prever] improvident.

imprevisão [ĩnprevi'zãw] *f* **-1.** [desleixo] carelessness. **-2.** [falta de previsão] improvidence.

imprevisível [ĩnprevi'zivɛw] (*pl* **-eis**) *adj* unforeseeable.

imprevisto, ta [ĩnpre'viʃtu, ta] *adj* unexpected.
➡ **imprevisto** *m*: **surgiu um ~ nos nossos planos** something unforeseen cropped up in our plans.

imprimir [ĩmpri'mi(x)] ⬦ *vt* to print. ⬦ *vi COMPUT* to print.

improbabilidade [ĩnprobabili'dadʒi] *f* improbability.

ímprobo, ba [ˈĩmprobu, ba] *adj* dishonest.

improcedente [ĩnprose'dẽntʃi] *adj* unjustified.

improdutivo, va [ĩnprodu'tʃivu, va] *adj* unproductive.

improfícuo, cua [ĩnpro'fikwu, kwa] *adj* useless.

impropério [ĩnpro'pɛrju] *m* insult.

impróprio, pria [ĩn'prɔprju, prja] *adj* inappropriate.

improrrogável [ĩnproxo'gavɛw] (*pl* **-eis**) *adj* nonpostponable.

improvável [ĩnpro'vavɛw] (*pl* **-eis**) *adj* improbable.

improvisação [ĩnproviza'sãw] *f* improvisation.

improvisado, da [ĩnprovi'zadu, da] *adj* improvised.

improvisar [4] [ĩmprovi'za(x)] ⬦ *vt* to improvise. ⬦ *vi* **-1.** to improvise. **-2.** *TEATRO* to ad-lib.

improviso [ĩnpro'vizu] *m* **-1.** [repente]: **de ~** [de repente] suddenly; [sem preparação] off the cuff; **falar de ~** to speak off the cuff. **-2.** *TEATRO* improvisation.

imprudência [ĩnpru'dẽnsja] *f* [descuido] carelessness.

imprudente [ĩnpru'dẽntʃi] *adj* careless.

impudico, ca [ĩnpu'dʒiku, ka] *adj* shameless.

impugnação [ĩnpugna'sãw] (*pl* **-ões**) *f* [contestação] challenge.

impugnar [4] [ĩmpug'na(x)] *vt* **-1.** [refutar] to refute. **-2.** [opor-se a] to oppose.

impulsionar [4] [ĩmpuwsju'na(x)] *vt* **-1.** [impelir] to propel. **-2.** [estimular] to speed up.

impulsividade [ĩnpuwsivi'dadʒil] *f* impulsiveness.

impulsivo, va [ĩnpuw'sivu, val *adj* impulsive.

impulso [ĩn'puwsul *m* **-1.** [ger] impulse, urge; **dar um novo ~ a** to give a new impetus to; **tomar ~** to gain strength; **por ~** on impulse. **-2.** [força] thrust; **tomar ~** to take a run.

impune [ĩn'puni] *adj* unpunished.

impunemente [ĩmpune'mẽntʃil *adv* with impunity.

impunidade [ĩnpuni'dadʒil *f* impunity.

impureza [ĩnpu'rezal *f* impurity.

impuro, ra [ĩm'puru, ĩm'pural *adj* impure.

imputação [ĩmputa'sãwl (*pl* **-ões**) *f* [acusação] accusation.

imputar [4] [ĩmpu'ta(x)] *vt*: **~ algo a alguém** to attribute sthg to sb.

imundície [ĩmũn̪dʒisjil, **imundícia** [ĩmun'dʒis-jal *f* [falta de asseio] filthiness.

imundo, da [i'mũndo, dal *adj* filthy.

imune [i'munil *adj*: **~ (a)** immune to.

imunidade [imuni'dadʒil *f* immunity.

imunização [imuniza'sãwl *f* immunization.

imunizar [4] [imuni'za(x)] *vt* to immunize.

imunologia [imunolo'ʒial *f* immunology.

imutável [imu'tavewl (*pl*-eis) *adj* immutable.

inabalável [inaba'lavewl (*pl* **-eis**) *adj* unshakeable.

inábil [i'nabiwl (*pl*-eis) *adj* **-1.** [desajeitado] clumsy. **- 2.** [incapaz] incapable.

inabilidade [inabili'dadʒil *f* inability.

inabilidoso, osa [inabili'dozu, ozal *adj* inept.

inabilitar [4] [inabili'ta(x)] *vt* **-1.** [incapacitar] to disable. **-2.** [reprovar] to disqualify.

➠ **inabilitar-se** *vp* [reprovar-se] to fail.

inabitado, da [inabi'tadu, dal *adj* uninhabited.

inabitável [inabi'tavewl (*pl* **-eis**) *adj* uninhabitable.

inacabado, da [inaka'badu, dal *adj* unfinished.

inacabável [inaka'bavewl (*pl*-eis) *adj* unending.

inação [ina'sãwl *f* **-1.** [inércia] inaction. **-2.** [indecisão] indecision.

inaceitável [inasej'tavewl (*pl* **-eis**) *adj* unacceptable.

inacessível [inase'sivewl (*pl* **-eis**) *adj* inaccessible.

inacreditável [inakredʒi'tavewl (*pl* **-eis**) *adj* unbelievable.

inadaptado, da [inadap'tadu, dal *adj* maladjusted.

inadiável [ina'dʒavewl (*pl*-eis) *adj* pressing.

inadimplência [inadʒĩn'plẽnsjal *f* JUR noncompliance.

inadimplente [inadʒĩn'plẽntʃil *adj* noncompliant.

inadmissível [inadʒimi'sivewl (*pl* **-eis**) *adj* unacceptable.

inadvertência [inadʒivex'tẽnsjal *f* inadvertence; **por ~** inadvertently.

inadvertidamente [inadʒivertʃida'mẽntʃil *adv* inadvertently.

inadvertido, da [inadver'tʃidu, dal *adj* inadvertent.

inalação [inala'sãwl (*pl*-ões) *f* inhalation.

inalar [4] [ina'la(x)] *vt* to inhale.

inalcançável [inawkãn'savɛwl (*pl* **-eis**) *adj* inaccessible.

inalterado, da [inawte'radu, dal *adj* **-1.** [imudado] unaltered. **- 2.** [calmo] composed.

inalterável [inawte'ravewl (*pl*-eis) *adj* **-1.** [imudável] immutable. **- 2.** [impertubável] imperturbable.

inanição [inani'sãwl *f* starvation.

inanimado, da [inani'madu, dal *adj* inanimate.

inapetência [inape'tẽnsjal *f* loss of appetite.

inapetente [inape'tẽntʃil *adj* lacking appetite (*depois de verbo*).

inaplicável [inapli'kavewl (*pl* **-eis**) *adj* inapplicable.

inaproveitável [inaprovej'tavewl (*pl* **-eis**) *adj* useless.

inaptidão [inaptʃi'dãwl *f* inabilty.

inapto, ta [i'naptu, tal *adj* unsuitable.

inatacável [inata'kavewl (*pl* **-eis**) *adj* unassailable.

inatenção [inatẽn'sãwl *f* inattention.

inatingível [inatʃĩn'ʒivewl (*pl* **-eis**) *adj* unattainable.

inatividade [inatʃivi'dadʒil *f* **-1.** [ger] retirement. **- 2.** [inércia] inactivity. **-3.** [desemprego] inactivity.

inativo, va [ina'tʃivu, val *adj* **-1.** [ger] retired. **- 2.** [parado] idle.

inato, ta ['inatu, tal *adj* innate.

inaudito, ta [inaw'dʒitu, tal *adj* unheard of.

inaudível [inaw'dʒivewl (*pl*-eis) *adj* inaudible.

inauguração [inawgura'sãwl (*pl*-ões) *f* inauguration.

inaugural [inawgu'rawl (*pl*-ais) *adj* inaugural.

inaugurar [4] [inawgu'ra(x)] *vt* to open.

inca ['ĩŋkal ⬦ *adj* Inca. ⬦ *mf* Inca.

incalculável [ĩŋkawku'lavewl (*pl*-eis) *adj* incalculable.

incandescente [ĩŋkãnde'sẽntʃil *adj* incandescent.

incansável [ĩŋkãn'savewl (*pl*-eis) *adj* tireless.

incapacidade [ĩŋkapasi'dadʒil *f* **-1.** [deficiência] incapacity. **- 2.** [incompetência] incompetence.

incapacitado, da [ĩŋkapasi'tadu, dal ⬦ *adj* **-1.** [inválido] disabled. **- 2.** [impedido] unable; **estar ~ de fazer algo** to be unable to do sthg. ⬦ *m, f* disabled person.

incapacitar [4] [ĩŋkapasi'ta(x)] *vt* to incapacitate.

incapaz [ĩŋka'paʃl (*pl*-es) *adj* **-1.** [incompetente]: **~ (para)** incompetent (for). **- 2.** JUR incompetent. **- 3.** [imprestativo]: **ser ~ de fazer algo** [não se dignar al] to be incapable of doing sthg.

incauto, ta [ĩŋ'kawtu, tal *adj* **-1.** [imprudente] reckless. **- 2.** [ingênuo] naive.

incendiar [17] [ĩsẽn'dʒja(x)] *vt* to set fire to.

➠ **incendiar-se** *vp* to catch fire.

incendiário, ria [ĩnsĕn'dʒjarju, rja] ◇ *adj* [bomba etc] incendiary. ◇ *m, f* arsonist.

incêndio [ĩn'sĕndʒju] *m* fire; ~ **provocado** *ou* **criminoso** arson.

incenso [ĩn'sĕnsu] *m* incense.

incentivador, ra [ĩnsĕntʃiva'do(x), ra] *adj* -**1.** [olhar, atitude] motivating. -**2.** [consumo, negócio] stimulating.

incentivar [4] [ĩsĕntʒi'va(x)] *vt* to stimulate.

incentivo [ĩnsĕn'tʃivu] *m* incentive.

incerteza [ĩnsex'tezal *f* uncertainty.

incerto, ta [ĩ'sɛxtu, ta] *adj* uncertain.

incessante [ĩnse'sãntʃi] *adj* incessant.

incesto [ĩn'sɛʃtu] *m* incest.

incestuoso, osa [ĩnseʃ'twozu, ɔza] *adj* incestuous.

inchação [ĩnʃa'sãw] *f* swelling.

inchaço [ĩn'ʃasu] *m fam* swelling.

inchado, da [ĩ'ʃadu, da] *adj* swollen.

inchar [4] [ĩ'sa(x)] ◇ *vt* to swell. ◇ *vi* to swell.

◆ **inchar-se** *vp* [envaidecer-se] to be puffed up (with pride).

incidência [ĩnsi'dĕnsja] *f* incidence.

incidente [ĩnsi'dĕntʃi] *m* incident.

incidir [6] [ĩnsi'dʒi(x)] *vi* -**1.** [refletir]: ~ **em** *ou* **sobre** to reflect in. -**2.** [recair]: ~ **em** *ou* **sobre** to be placed on. -**3.** [incorrer]: ~ **em** to fall into.

incinerador, ra [ĩnsine'rado(x), ra] ◇ *adj* incineration (*antes de subst*). ◇ *m* incinerator.

incinerar [4] [ĩnsine'ra(x)] *vt* to incinerate.

incipiente [ĩnsi'pjĕntʃi] *adj* incipient.

incisão [insi'zãw] (*pl*-ões) *f* -**1.** [corte] cut. -**2.** MED incision.

incisivo, va [ĩsi'zivu, va] *adj* -**1.** [cortante] cutting. -**2.** [direto] incisive.

incitação [ĩnsita'sãw] (*pl*-ões) *f* incitement.

incitamento [ĩnsita'mĕntu] *m* incitement.

incitar [4] [ĩsi'ta(x)] *vt* -**1.** [instigar]: ~ **alguém a algo** to incite sb to sthg; ~ **alguém a fazer algo** to incite sb to do sthg. -**2.** [suj: ambição *etc*]: ~ **alguém (a algo/a fazer algo)** to drive sb to sthg/to do sthg. -**3.** [animal] to urge on.

incivil [ĩnsi'viw] (*pl*-is) *adj* discourteous.

incivilidade [ĩnsivili'dadʒi] *f* discourtesy.

inclemência [ĩŋkle'mĕnsja] *f* -**1.** [impiedade] ruthlessness. -**2.** *fig* [rigor] mercilessness.

inclemente [ĩŋkle'mĕntʃi] *adj* -**1.** [impiedoso] ruthless. -**2.** *fig* [rigoroso] merciless.

inclinação [ĩŋklina'sãw] (*pl*-ões) *f* -**1.** [queda] inclination. -**2.** *fig* [propensão]: ~ **para** inclination towards. -**3.** [atração]: ~ **por** attraction towards.

inclinado, da [ĩŋkli'nadu, da] *adj* -**1.** [oblíquo] inclined. -**2.** *fig* [propenso]: **estar** ~ **a algo/a fazer algo** to be inclined towards sthg/to do sthg.

inclinar [4] [ĩŋkli'na(x)] *vt* -**1.** [fazer pender] to tilt. -**2.** [curvar] to bend.

◆ **inclinar-se** *vp* -**1.** [curvar-se] to bow. -**2.** [tender a]: ~-**se a** to tend towards.

incluir [74] [ĩŋklu'i(x)] *vt* -**1.** [abranger] to include. -**2.** [inserir]: ~ **algo em algo** to insert sthg in sthg.

◆ **incluir-se** *vp* to include o.s.

inclusão [ĩŋklu'zãw] *f* inclusion.

inclusive [ĩŋklu'zivi] *adv* -**1.** [com inclusão de] including; **de segunda a sábado** ~ from Monday to Saturday inclusive. -**2.** [até mesmo] even.

incluso, sa [ĩŋ'kluzo, za] *adj* included.

incoercível [ĩŋkwex'sivew] (*pl*-eis) *adj* uncontrollable.

incoerência [ĩŋkwe'rĕnsja] *f* -**1.** [ilogicidade] incoherence. -**2.** [discordância]: **ser uma** ~ **com algo** to conflict with sthg.

incoerente [ĩŋkwe'rĕntʃi] *adj* -**1.** [ilógico] illogical. -**2.** [discordante] conflicting. -**3.** [incompreensível] incoherent.

incógnito, ta [ĩŋ'kɔgnitu, ta] *adj* incognito (*depois de verbo*).

◆ **incógnita** *f* -**1.** MAT unknown quantity. -**2.** [mistério]: **ser uma** ~ to be a mystery.

◆ **incógnito** *adv* incognito.

incolor [ĩŋko'lo(x)] (*pl*-es) *adj* colourless.

incólume [ĩŋ'kɔlumi] *adj* safe and sound.

incomensurável [ĩŋkomĕnsu'ravew] (*pl*-eis) *adj* unmeasurable.

incomodado, da [ĩŋkomo'dadu, da] *adj* [importunado] annoyed.

◆ **incomodada** *adj & f* [menstruada] having one's period.

incomodar [4] [ĩŋkomo'da(x)] ◇ *vt* to annoy. ◇ *vi* [irritar]: ~ **a** to annoy.

◆ **incomodar-se** *vp* -**1.** [irritar-se] to become annoyed. -**2.** [importar-se] to mind; **você se incomoda se eu fechar a porta?** would you mind if I closed the door?

incômodo, da [ĩŋ'komodu, da] *adj* -**1.** [ger] uncomfortable. -**2.** [enfadonho] boring.

◆ **incômodo** *m* -**1.** [embaraço] problem. -**2.** [menstruação] period, time of the month.

incomparável [ĩŋkõnpa'ravew] (*pl*-eis) *adj* incomparable.

incompatibilidade [ĩŋkonpatʃibili'dadʒi] *f* incompatibility.

incompatibilizar [4] [ĩnkõmpatʃibili'za(x)] *vt*: ~ **alguém com alguém** to put sb in sb's bad books.

◆ **incompatibilizar-se** *vp*: ~-**se (com)** to clash (with).

incompatível [ĩŋkõnpa'tʃivew] (*pl*-eis) *adj* incompatible.

incompetência [ĩŋkõnpe'tĕnsja] *f* incompetence.

incompetente [ĩŋkõnpe'tĕntʃi] ◇ *adj* incompetent. ◇ *mf* incompetent.

incompleto, ta [ĩŋkõn'plɛtu, ta] *adj* incomplete, unfinished.

incompreendido, da [ĩŋkõnprjĕn'dʒidu, da] *adj* misunderstood.

incompreensão [ĩŋkõnprjĕn'sãw] *f* incomprehension.

incompreensível [ĩŋkõnprjĕn'sivew] (*pl*-eis) *adj* incomprehensible.

incompreensivo, va [ĩŋkõnprjĕn'sivu, va] *adj* uncomprehending.

incomum [ĩŋko'mũ] (*pl* **-ns**) *adj* uncommon.
incomunicável [ĩŋkomuni'kavɛwl] (*pl* **-eis**) *adj* **-1.** [sem comunicação] cut off. **-2.** [que não deve se comunicar] incommunicado. **-3.** *fig* [insociável] uncommunicative.
inconcebível [ĩŋkõnse'bivɛwl] (*pl* **-eis**) *adj* inconceivable.
inconciliável [ĩŋkõnsi'ljavɛwl] (*pl* **-eis**) *adj* irreconcilable.
inconcludente [ĩŋkõŋklu'dẽntʃil] *adj* inconclusive.
inconcluso, sa [ĩŋkõŋ'kluzu, za] *adj* unfinished.
incondicional [ĩŋkõndʒisjo'nawl] (*pl* **-ais**) *adj* **-1.** [total] unconditional. **-2.** [fiel] loyal.
inconfessável [ĩŋkõnfe'savewl] (*pl* **-eis**) *adj* unconfessable.
inconfesso, ssa [ĩŋkõn'fɛsu, sa] *adj* unconfessed.
inconfidência [ĩŋkõnfi'dẽnsjal] *f* disloyalty.
inconfidente [ĩŋkõnfi'dẽntʃil] <> *adj* disloyal. <> *mf* untrustworthy person.
inconformado, da [ĩŋkõnfox'madu, da] *adj*: **ela está ~** she has not come to terms with it.
inconfundível [ĩŋkõnfũn'dʒivɛwl] (*pl* **-eis**) *adj* unmistakable.
incongruência [ĩŋkõŋ'grwẽnsjal] *f* incongruity.
incongruente [ĩŋkõŋ'grwẽntʃil, **incôngruo, grua** [ĩn'kõŋgrwu, grwal *adj* incongruous.
inconsciência [ĩŋkõn'sjẽnsjal] *f* **-1.** MED unconsciousness. **-2.** [leviandade] lack of awareness.
inconsciente [ĩŋkõn'sjẽntʃil] <> *adj* **-1.** [ger] unconscious. **-2.** [leviano] thoughtless. <> *m* PSIC: **o ~** the unconscious.
inconscientemente [ĩŋkõnsjẽntʃi'mẽntʃil] *adv* unconsciously.
inconseqüência [ĩŋkõnse'kwẽnsjal] *f* **-1.** [incoerência] inconsistency. **-2.** [irresponsabilidade] irresponsibility.
inconseqüente [ĩŋkõnse'kwẽntʃil] <> *adj* **-1.** [incoerente] inconsistent. **-2.** [irresponsável] irresponsible. <> *mf* irresponsible person.
inconsistência [ĩŋkõnsiʃ'tẽnsjal] *f* **-1.** [fraqueza] inconsistency. **-2.** [fluidez] weakness.
inconsistente [ĩŋkõnsiʃ'tẽntʃil] *adj* **-1.** [fraco] inconsistent. **-2.** [fluido] runny.
inconsolável [ĩŋkõnso'lavewl] (*pl* **-eis**) *adj* inconsolable.
inconstância [ĩŋkõnʃ'tãnsjal] *f* inconstancy.
inconstante [ĩŋkõnʃ'tãntʃil] *adj* **-1.** [instável] unstable. **-2.** [volúvel] inconstant.
inconstitucional [ĩŋkõnʃtʃitusjo'nawl] (*pl* **-ais**) *adj* unconstitutional.
inconstitucionalidade [ĩŋkõnʃtʃitusjonali'dadʒil] *f* unconstitutionality.
incontável [ĩŋkõn'tavewl] (*pl* **-eis**) *adj* countless.
incontestável [ĩŋkõnteʃ'tavɛwl] (*pl* **-eis**) *adj* incontestable.
inconteste [ĩŋkõn'tɛʃtʃil] *adj* undisputed.
incontinência [ĩŋkõntʃi'nẽnsjal] *f* MED incontinence.

incontinente [ĩŋkõntʃi'nẽntʃil] *adj* MED incontinent.
incontinênti [ĩŋkõutʃi'nẽntʃil] *adv* at once.
incontrolável [ĩŋkõntro'lavewl] (*pl* **-eis**) *adj* uncontrollable.
incontroverso, sa [ĩŋkõntro'vɛxsu, sal *adj* incontrovertible.
inconveniência [ĩŋkõnve'njẽnsjal] *f* **-1.** [falta de conveniência] inconvenience. **-2.** [grosseria] rudeness.
inconveniente [ĩŋkõnve'njẽntʃil] <> *adj* **-1.** [inoportuno] inconvenient. **-2.** [inadequado] unsuitable. **-3.** [incômodo] annoying. <> *m* **-1.** [desvantagem] disadvantage. **-2.** [obstáculo] obstacle.
INCOR (*abrev de* **Instituto do Coração do Hospital das Clínicas**) *m* *institute of coronary diseases at the Hospital das Clínicas in São Paulo.*
incorporação [ĩŋkoxpora'sãwl] (*pl* **-ões**) *f* **-1.** COM incorporation. **-2.** [espirit] possession. **-3.** [inclusão] inclusion.
incorporado, da [ĩŋkoxpo'radu, da] *adj* **-1.** COM incorporated. **-2.** [espirit] possessed. **-3.** [embutido] incorporated.
incorporar [4] [ĩŋkoxpo'ra(x)] <> *vt* **-1.** COM to incorporate. **-2.** [espirit] to become possessed by. **-3.** [juntar]: **~ algo a algo** to include sthg in sthg. <> *vi* [espirit] to take possession of.
➡ **incorporar-se** *vp* [juntar-se] to join.
incorreção [ĩŋkoxe'sãwl] (*pl* **-ões**) *f* inaccuracy.
incorrer [5] [ĩŋko'xe(x)] *vi*: **~ em algo** to fall into sthg.
incorreto, ta [ĩŋko'xɛtu, ta] *adj* incorrect.
incorrigível [ĩŋkoxi'ʒivɛwl] (*pl* **-eis**) *adj* incorrigible.
incorruptível [ĩŋkoxup'tʃivewl] (*pl* **-eis**) *adj* incorruptible.
INCRA (*abrev de* **Instituto Nacional de Colonização e Reforma Agrária**) *m* Brazilian *land reform institute.*
incredulidade [ĩŋkreduli'dadʒil] *f* incredulity.
incrédulo, la [ĩŋ'krɛdulu, la] *adj* incredulous.
incrementado, da [ĩŋkremẽn'tadu, da] *adj* **-1.** *fam* [melhorado - carro, computador] jazzed up; [- bebida, comida] fancy. **-2.** *fam* [moderno] trendy.
incrementar [4] [ĩŋkremẽn'ta(x)] *vt* **-1.** [aumentar] to increase. **-2.** [desenvolver] to develop. **-3.** *fam* [melhorar] to jazz up.
incremento [ĩŋkre'mẽntul] *m* **-1.** [aumento] increment. **-2.** [desenvolvimento] development.
incriminar [4] [ĩŋkrimi'na(x)] *vt* to incriminate.
incrível [ĩŋ'krivɛwl] (*pl* **-eis**) *adj* **-1.** [inacreditável] incredible. **-2.** *fam* [maravilhoso] incredible.
incrustação [ĩŋkruʃta'sãwl] (*pl* **-ões**) *f* inlay.
incrustar [4] [ĩŋkruʃ'ta(x)] *vt* to inlay.
incubação [ĩŋkuba'sãwl] *f* incubation.
incubadora [ĩŋkuba'doral *f* incubator.
incubar [4] [ĩŋku'ba(x)] *vt* & *vi* to incubate.
inculcar [12] [ĩŋkuw'ka(x)] *vt* to inculcate.
inculto, ta [ĩŋ'kuwtu, tal *adj* **-1.** [terreno] uncultivated. **-2.** [pessoa] coarse.

incumbência [ĩŋkũn'bẽnsja] f incumbency.
incumbir [6] [ĩŋkũm'bi(x)] <> vt: ~ **alguém de algo** to put sb in charge of sthg. <> vi: ~ **a alguém fazer algo** to be sb's responsibility to do sthg.
  ➡ **incumbir-se** vp: ~-se **de algo** to take charge of sthg.
incurável [ĩŋku'ravɛw] (pl -eis) adj incurable.
incursão [ĩŋkux'sãw] (pl -ões) f incursion.
incutir [6] [ĩŋku'tʃi(x)] vt: ~ **algo** (a ou em alguém) to inspire sthg (in sb).
indagação [ĩndaga'sãw] f inquiry.
indagar [14] [ĩnda'ga(x)] <> vt to ask for. <> vi to make inquiries.
indébito, ta [ĩn'dɛbitu, ta] adj unreasonable.
indecência [ĩnde'sẽnsja] f **-1.** [indecoro] indecency. **-2.** [obscenidade] obscenity.
indecente [ĩnde'sẽntʃi] adj **-1.** [obsceno] indecent. **-2.** [imoral] unscrupulous.
indecifrável [ĩndesi'fravɛw] (pl -eis) adj indecipherable.
indecisão [ĩndesi'zãw] (pl -ões) f indecision.
indeciso, sa [ĩnde'sizu, za] adj indecisive.
indeclinável [ĩndekli'navew] (pl -eis) adj that cannot be refused (depois de subst).
indecoroso, osa [ĩndeko'rozo, ɔza] adj indecent.
indefectível [ĩndefek'tʃivew] (pl -eis) adj that cannot fail (depois de subst).
indefensável [ĩndefẽn'savew] (pl -eis) adj indefensible; **um pênalti** ~ an unstoppable penalty.
indeferido, da [ĩndefe'ridu, da] adj rejected.
indeferir [57] [ĩndefe'ri(x)] vt to reject.
indefeso, sa [ĩnde'fezu, za] adj defenceless.
indefinição [ĩndefini'sãw] (pl -ões) f indecision.
indefinido, da [ĩndefi'nidu, da] adj **-1.** [ger] indefinite. **-2.** [vago] vague.
indefinível [ĩndefi'nivew] (pl -eis) adj indefinable.
indelével [ĩnde'lɛvew] (pl -eis) adj indelible.
indelicadeza [ĩndelika'deza] f **-1.** [grosseria] rudeness. **-2.** [desfeita] bad manners (pl).
indelicado, da [ĩndeli'kadu, da] adj indelicate.
indenização [ĩndeniza'sãw] (pl -ões) f indemnity, compensation.
indenizar [4] [ĩndeni'za(x)] vt: ~ **alguém (por algo)** to indemnify sb (for sthg), to compensate sb (for sthg).
independência [ĩndepẽn'dẽnsja] f independence.
independente [ĩndepẽn'dẽntʃi] adj **-1.** [ger] independent. **-2.** [separado, de livre acesso] separate. **-3.** [auto-suficiente] independent. **-4.** [financeiramente] of independent means, financially independent.
independer [5] [ĩndepẽn'de(x)] vi: ~ **de algo** to be independent of sthg.
indescritível [ĩndeʃkri'tʃivɛw] (pl -eis) adj indescribable.
indesculpável [ĩndʒiʃkuw'pavewl] (pl -eis) adj unforgivable.

indesejável [ĩndeze'ʒavɛwl] (pl -eis) adj undesirable.
indestrutível [ĩndeʃtru'tʃivɛwl] (pl -eis) adj **-1.** [não destrutível] indestructible. **-2.** fig [inabalável] enduring.
indeterminado, da [ĩndetexmi'nadu, da] adj **-1.** [não fixado] indeterminate; **por tempo** ~ for an indefinite length of time. **-2.** [impreciso] imprecise.
indevassável [ĩndeva'savewl] (pl -eis) adj impenetrable.
indevido, da [ĩnde'vidu, da] adj **-1.** [imerecido] undeserved. **-2.** [impróprio] inappropriate.
índex ['ĩndeks] m index.
indexação [ĩndeksa'sãw] (pl -ões) f **-1.** ECON & COM index-linking. **-2.** COMPUT index.
indexar [4] [ĩndek'sa(x)] vt **-1.** [ger] to index. **-2.** ECON & COM to index-link.
Índia ['ĩndʒja] n India.
indiano, na [ĩn'dʒjanu, na] <> adj [da Índia] Indian. <> m, f [habitante da Índia] Indian.
indicação [ĩndʒika'sãw] (pl -ões) f **-1.** [denotação] sign. **-2.** [de caminho etc] sign. **-3.** [recomendação] recommendation; ~ **de uso** instructions for use. **-4.** [menção] indication.
indicado, da [ĩndʒi'kadu, da] adj **-1.** [recomendado] recommended. **-2.** [apropriado] appropriate.
indicador, ra [ĩndʒika'do(x), ra] (pl -es, fpl -s) adj [que indica]: ~ **de** indicator of.
  ➡ **indicador** m **-1.** [ger] indicator. **-2.** [dedo] index finger.
indicar [4] [ĩndʒi'ka(x)] vt **-1.** [ger] to indicate. **-2.** [apontar]: ~ **algo com o dedo** to point to sthg. **-3.** [recomendar] to recommend. **-4.** [mencionar] to indicate. **-5.** [designar] to name.
indicativo, va [ĩndʒika'tʃivu, va] adj **-1.** [que indica] indicative. **-2.** GRAM indicative.
  ➡ **indicativo** m GRAM indicative.
índice ['ĩndʒisi] m **-1.** [lista] index; ~ **remissivo** subject index; ~ **onomástico** name index. **-2.** [medida] level; ~ **de audiência** ratings; ~ **do custo de vida** cost of living index. **-3.** [dedo] index finger.
indiciado, da [ĩndʒi'sjadu, da] m, f accused, defendant.
indiciar [16] [ĩndʒi'sja(x)] vt **-1.** [acusar] to accuse. **-2.** [submeter a inquérito] to investigate.
indício [in'dʒisju] m **-1.** [vestígio] sign. **-2.** JUR [prova] evidence (inv).
Índico n: o (Oceano) ~ the Indian Ocean.
indiferença [ĩndʒife'rẽnsa] f indifference.
indiferente [ĩndʒife'rẽntʃi] adj: ~ (a algo) indifferent (to sthg).
indígena [ĩn'dʒiʒena] <> adj indigenous. <> mf native.
indigência [ĩndʒi'ʒẽnsja] f **-1.** [miséria] poverty. **-2.** [indigentes]: a ~ **do país** the indigence of the country. **-3.** [falta] lack.
indigente [ĩndʒi'ʒẽntʃi] <> adj poverty-stricken. <> mf poor person.
indigestão [ĩndʒiʒeʃ'tãw] (pl -ões) f indigestion.

indigesto, ta [ĩndʒi'ʒɛʃtu, ta] *adj* indigestible.
indignação [ĩndʒigna'sãw] (*pl* -ões) *f* indignation.
indignado, da [ĩndʒig'nadu, da] *adj* indignant; **ficar ~ (com)** to be indignant (at).
indignar [4] [ĩndʒig'na(x)] *vt* to anger.
➡ **indignar-se** *vp*: **~-se (com)** to be indignant (about).
indignidade [ĩndʒigni'dadʒi] *f* -1. [falta de dignidade] indignity. -2. [ultraje] outrage.
indigno, gna [ĩn'dʒignu, gna] *adj* -1. [não merecedor]: **~ de algo** unworthy of sthg. -2. [vil] despicable.
índio, dia ['ĩndʒju, dʒja] ◇ *adj* Indian. ◇ *m,f* Indian; **programa de ~** *fig* boring programme.
indireto, ta [ĩndʒi'rɛtu, ta] *adj* indirect.
➡ **indireta** *f* hint; **dar uma ~** to make a hint.
indisciplina [ĩndʒisi'plina] *f* indiscipline.
indisciplinado, da [ĩndʒisipli'nadu, da] *adj* undisciplined.
indiscreto, ta [ĩndʒiʃ'krɛtu, ta] *adj* indiscreet.
indiscrição [ĩndʒiʃkri'sãw] (*pl* -ões) *f* indiscretion.
indiscriminado, da [ĩndʒiʃkrimi'nadu, da] *adj* indiscriminate.
indiscutível [ĩndʒiʃku'tʃivɛw] (*pl* -eis) *adj* incontestable.
indispensável [ĩndʒiʃpẽn'savɛw] (*pl* -eis) ◇ *adj* indispensable, essential. ◇ *m*: **o ~** the essentials.
indisponível [ĩndʒiʃpo'nivɛw] (*pl* -eis) *adj* unavailable.
indispor [45] [ĩndʒiʃ'po(x)] *vt* -1. [adoecer] to make ill, to upset. -2. [inimizar] to set at odds.
➡ **indispor-se** *vp* [inimizar-se]: **~-se com alguém** to fall out with sb.
indisposição [ĩndʒiʃpozi'sãw] (*pl* -ões) *f* [mal-estar] illness.
indisposto, osta [ĩndʒiʃ'poʃtu, ɔʃta] ◇ *pp* ▷ indispor. ◇ *adj* unwell.
indissolúvel [ĩndʒiso'luvɛw] (*pl* -eis) *adj* -1. [irrevogável] indissoluble. -2. [insolúvel] insoluble.
indistinguível [ĩndʒiʃtʃĩŋ'givɛw] (*pl* -eis) *adj* indistinguishable.
indistintamente [ĩndʒiʃtʃĩnta'mẽntʃi] *adv* -1. [vagamente] indistinctly. -2. [indiferentemente] without distinction.
indistinto, ta [ĩndʒiʃ'tʃĩntu, ta] *adj* indistinct.
individual [ĩndʒivi'dwaw] (*pl* -ais) *adj* individual.
individualidade [ĩndʒividwali'dadʒi] *f* individuality.
individualismo [ĩndʒividwa'liʒmul *m* individualism.
individualista [ĩndʒividwa'liʃta] ◇ *adj* individualistic. ◇ *mf* individualist.
indivíduo [ĩndʒi'vidwu] *m* -1. [pessoa] individual. -2. *fam* [cara] person.
indivisível [ĩndʒivi'sivɛw] (*pl* -eis) *adj* indivisible.
indiviso, sa [ĩndʒi'vizu, za] *adj* undivided.
indizível [ĩndʒi'zivɛw] (*pl* -eis) *adj* -1. [inexprimível] inexpressible. -2. [extraordinário] extraordinary.

indócil [ĩn'dɔsiw] (*pl* -eis) *adj* -1. [rebelde] wayward. -2. [impaciente] restless.
indo-europeu, éia [ĩndwewro'pew, pɛja] *adj* Indo-European.
➡ **indo-europeu** *m* [língua] Indo-European.
índole ['ĩndoli] *f* -1. [temperamento] temperament. -2. [tipo] character.
indolência [ĩndo'lẽnsja] *f* indolence.
indolente [ĩndo'lẽntʃi] *adj* indolent.
indolor [ĩndo'lo(x)] (*pl* -es) *adj* painless.
indomável [ĩndo'mavew] (*pl* -eis) *adj* indomitable.
indômito, ta [ĩn'domitu, ta] *adj* indomitable, untamed.
Indonésia [ĩndo'nɛzja] *n* Indonesia.
indonésio, sia [ĩndo'nɛzju, zja] ◇ *adj* Indonesian. ◇ *m, f* Indonesian.
➡ **indonésio** *m* [língua] Indonesian.
indoor [ĩn'dɔ(x)] *adj inv* *ESP* indoor.
indubitável [ĩndubi'tavew] (*pl* -eis) *adj* indubitable; **é ~ que ...** it is beyond doubt that ...
indução [ĩndu'sãw] (*pl* -ões) *f* -1. [lógica] induction; **por ~** by induction. -2. [persuasão] persuasion.
indulgência [ĩnduw'ʒẽnsja] *f* -1. [tolerância] leniency. -2. [perdão] indulgence. -3. *JUR* clemency.
indulgente [ĩnduw'ʒẽntʃi] *adj* lenient.
indultar [4] [ĩnduw'ta(x)] *vt* *JUR* to reprieve.
indulto [ĩn'duwtul *m* *JUR* reprieve.
indumentária [ĩndumẽn'tarja] *f* attire.
indústria [ĩn'duʃtria] *f* industry; **~ automobilística** car industry *UK*, automobile industry *US*; **~ fabril** manufacturing industry; **~ leve** *ou* **de consumo** light industry; **~ pesada** heavy industry; **~ brasileira** made in Brazil.
industrial [ĩnduʃ'trjaw] (*pl* -ais) ◇ *adj* industrial. ◇ *mf* industrialist.
industrialização [ĩnduʃtrjaliza'sãw] *f* industrialization.
industrializado, da [ĩnduʃtrjali'zadu, da] *adj* industrialized; **produto ~** manufactured product.
industrializar [4] [ĩnduʃtrjali'za(x)] *vt* -1. [ger] to industrialize. -2. [produto] to manufacture. -3. [usar na indústria] to put to industrial use.
➡ **industrializar-se** *vp* to become industrialized.
industrioso, osa [ĩnduʃ'trjozu, ɔza] *adj* -1. [habilidoso] clever. -2. [diligente] industrious.
induzir [72] [ĩndu'zi(x)] *vt* -1. [levar]: **~ alguém a algo** to lead sb to sthg; **~ alguém a fazer algo** to persuade sb to do sthg. -2. [deduzir]: **~ algo de algo** to deduce sthg from sthg.
inebriante [ine'brjãntʃi] *adj* intoxicating.
inebriado, da [inebri'adu, da] *adj* [extasiado] intoxicated.
inebriar [16] [ine'brja(x)] *vt* to intoxicate.
➡ **inebriar-se** *vp* to be intoxicated.
ineditismo [inedʒi'tʃiʒmul *m*: **o ~ dos contos** the fact that the stories are unpublished.

inédito, ta [i'nɛdʒitu, ta] *adj* **-1.** [não publicado] unpublished. **-2.** [novo] novel.

inefável [ine'favɛw] (*pl* **-eis**) *adj* ineffable.

ineficácia [inefi'kasja] *f* **-1.** [ger] ineffectiveness. **-2.** [de pessoa] inefficience.

ineficaz [inefi'kaʃ] (*pl* **-es**) *adj* **-1.** [ger] ineffective. **-2.** [pessoa] inefficient.

ineficiência [inefi'sjẽnsja] *f* inefficiency.

ineficiente [inefi'sjẽntʃil] *adj* inefficient.

inegável [ine'gavɛw] (*pl* **-eis**) *adj* undeniable.

inegociável [inego'sjavew] (*pl* **-eis**) *adj* non-negotiable.

inelegível [inele'givew] (*pl* **-eis**) *adj* unelectable.

inenarrável [inena'xavew] (*pl* **-eis**) *adj* inexpressible.

inépcia [i'nɛpsja] *f* ineptitude.

inepto, ta [i'nɛptu, ta] *adj* inept.

inequívoco, ca [ine'kivoku, ka] *adj* unmistakable.

inércia [i'nɛxsja] *f* inertia.

inerente [ine'rẽntʃil] *adj* inherent.

inerte [i'nɛxtʃil] *adj* inert.

inescrupuloso, osa [ineʃkrupu'lozu, ɔza] *adj* unscrupulous.

inescrutável [ineʃkru'tavew] (*pl* **-eis**) *adj* inscrutable.

inesgotável [inezgo'tavew] (*pl* **-eis**) *adj* **-1.** [inacabável] inexhaustible. **-2.** [copioso] profuse.

inesperado, da [ineʃpe'radu, da] *adj* unexpected.

➥ **inesperado** *m* surprise.

inesquecível [ineʃke'sivɛw] (*pl* **-eis**) *adj* unforgettable.

inestimável [ineʃtʃi'mavɛw] (*pl* **-eis**) *adj* **-1.** [ger] priceless. **-2.** [prejuízo] incalculable.

inevitabilidade [inevitabili'dadʒil] *f* inevitability.

inevitável [inevi'tavɛw] (*pl* **-eis**) ⬦ *adj* inevitable. ⬦ *m*: **o ~** the inevitable.

inexatidão [ineza'tjidãw] (*pl* **-ões**) *f* inexactitude.

inexato, ta [ine'zatu, ta] *adj* inaccurate.

inexaurível [inezauw'rivew] (*pl* **-eis**) *adj* inexhaustible.

inexcedível [inese'dʒivew] (*pl* **-eis**) *adj* unsurpassable.

inexequível [ineze'kwivɛw] (*pl* **-eis**) *adj* unfeasible.

inexistência [in*eziʃ*'tẽnsja] *f* **-1.** [não existência] absence. **-2.** [carência] lack.

inexistente [ineziʃ'tẽntʃil] *adj* non-existent.

inexistir [6] [ineziʃ'ti(x)] *vi* not to exist.

inexorável [inezo'ravew] (*pl* **-eis**) *adj* inexorable.

inexperiência [ineʃpe'rjẽnsja] *f* inexperience.

inexperiente [ineʃpe'rjẽntʃil] *adj* inexperienced.

inexplicável [ineʃpli'kavew] (*pl* **-eis**) *adj* inexplicable.

inexplorado, da [ineʃplo'radu, da] *adj* unexplored.

inexpressivo, va [ineʃpre'sivu, va] *adj* **-1.** [rosto] expressionless. **-2.** [diferença] inexpressible.

inexpugnável [ineʃpug'navew] (*pl* **-eis**) *adj* **-1.**

[invencível] insuperable. **-2.** *fig* [firme] unassailable.

infalível [ĩnfa'livɛw] (*pl* **-eis**) *adj* infallible.

infame [ĩn'fãmi] *adj* **-1.** [vil] shameful. **-2.** [péssimo] dreadful.

infâmia [ĩn'fãmja] *f* **-1.** [calúnia] slander. **-2.** [desonra] discredit. **-3.** [vilania] infamy.

infância [ĩn'fãnsja] *f* childhood; **primeira ~** early childhood, infancy.

infantaria [ĩnfãnta'ria] *f* infantry.

infante, ta [ĩ'fãntʃi, tʃa] *m*, *f* **-1.** [príncipe] infante (*f* infanta), prince (*f* princess). **-2.** [criança] infant.

➥ **infante** *m* [soldado] infantryman.

infanticida [ĩnfãntʃi'sida] ⬦ *adj* infanticide. ⬦ *m*, *f* infanticide, child-killer.

infantil [ĩnfãn'tiw] (*pl* **-is**) *adj* **-1.** [próprio da infância] childhood (*antes de subst*). **-2.** [para criança] children's (*antes de subst*). **-3.** *fig* [imaturo] childish.

infantilidade [ĩnfãntʃili'dadʒi] *f* childishness.

infanto-juvenil [ĩn,fãntuʒuve'niw] (*pl* **infanto-juvenis**) *adj* children's (*antes de subst*).

infarto [ĩn'faxtu] *m* = **enfarte**.

infatigável [ĩnfatʒi'gavew] (*pl* **-eis**) *adj* **-1.** [incansável] tireless. **-2.** [zeloso] untiring.

infecção [ĩnfek'sãw] (*pl* **-ões**) *f* infection.

infeccionar [4] [ĩfeksjo'na(x)] ⬦ *vt* to infect. ⬦ *vi* to become infected.

infeccioso, osa [ĩnfek'sjozu, ɔza] *adj* infectious.

infecto, ta [ĩ'fɛktu, ta] *adj* **-1.** [ger] contaminated. **-2.** *fig* [vil] sick.

infelicidade [ĩnfelisi'dadʒil] *f* **-1.** [tristeza] unhappiness. **-2.** [desgraça] misfortune. **-3.** [azar] bad luck; **por ~** unfortunately.

infeliz [ĩnfe'liʒ] (*pl* **-es**) ⬦ *adj* **-1.** [ger] unfortunate. **-2.** [triste] unhappy. **-3.** [desafortunado] wretched. ⬦ *mf* **-1.** [triste] unfortunate person. **-2.** [desgraçado] wretch; **como um ~** *fig* desperately.

infelizmente [ĩnfeliʒ'mẽntʃil] *adv* unfortunately.

infenso, sa [ĩ'fẽnsu, sa] *adj* adverse.

inferior [ĩnfe'rjo(x)] (*pl* **-es**) ⬦ *adj* **-1.** [ger]: **~** inferior to. **-2.** [que está mais baixo] lower. **-3.** [em valor]: **~ (a)** lower (than). **-4.** [em quantidade]: **~ (a)** fewer (than). **-5.** [em altura]: **~ a** shorter (than). **-6.** [em qualidade]: **~ (a)** inferior (to). ⬦ *mf* [subalterno] inferior.

inferioridade [ĩnferjori'dadʒil] *f* **-1.** [condição, posição] inferiority. **-2.** *PSIC*: **complexo de ~** inferiority complex.

inferiorizar-se [4] [ĩferjori'zaxsil] *vp* to degrade o.s.

inferir [57] [ĩfe'ri(x)] *vt*: **~ algo (de)** to infer sthg (from).

infernal [ĩnfex'naw] (*pl* **-ais**) *adj* *fig* infernal.

inferninho [ĩnfex'niɲul] *m* dive.

infernizar [4] [ĩfexni'za(x)] *vt* to render hellish; **~ a vida de alguém** to make sb's life hell.

inferno [ĩn'fɛxnul] *m* hell; **vá para o ~!** go to hell!

infértil [ĩ'fɛxtiw] *adj* infertile.

infertilidade [ĩnfextʃili'dadʒil] f infertility.
infestado, da [ĩnfeʃ'tadu, da] adj infested.
infestar [4] [ĩnfeʃ'ta(x)] vt to infest.
infidelidade [ĩnfideli'dadʒil] f infedility.
infiel [ĩn'fjɛw] (pl -éis) <> adj -1. [desleal] unfaithful. -2. [inexato] inaccurate. <> mf RELIG non-believer.
infiltração [ĩnfiwtra'sãw] (pl -ões) f infiltration.
infiltrar [4] [ĩfiw'tra(x)] vt [parede] to penetrate.
◆ **infiltrar-se** vp to infiltrate; ~-se em algo to filter (into) sthg.
ínfimo, ma ['ĩfimu, ma] adj insignificant; preço ~ rock-bottom price.
infindável [ĩnfĩn'davɛw] (pl -eis) adj -1. [inacabável] interminable. -2. [permanente] unending. -3. [energia] boundless.
infinidade [ĩnfini'dadʒil] f: uma ~ de vezes/roupas countless times/clothes.
infinitamente [ĩnfinita'mẽntʃil] adv infinitely.
infinitesimal [ĩnfinitezi'maw] (pl -ais) adj infinitesimal.
infinitivo, va [ĩnfini'tʃivu, va] GRAM adj infinitive.
◆ **infinitivo** m infinitive.
infinito, ta [ĩnfi'nitu, ta] adj -1. [ger] infinite. -2. [inumerável] countless.
◆ **infinito** m LING infinitive.
inflação [ĩnfla'sãw] f ECON inflation.
inflacionar [4] [ĩnflasjo'na(x)] vt ECON to inflate.
inflacionário, ria [ĩnflasjo'narju, rja] adj ECON inflationary.
inflamação [ĩnflama'sãw] (pl -ões) f MED inflammation.
inflamado, da [ĩnfla'madu, da] adj -1. MED inflamed. -2. fig [exaltado] heated.
inflamar [4] [ĩfla'ma(x)] <> vt to inflame. <> vi MED to become inflamed.
inflamatório, ria [ĩnflama'tɔrju, rja] adj inflammatory.
inflamável [ĩnfla'mavɛw] (pl -eis) adj inflammable.
inflar [4] [ĩ'fla(x)] vt -1. [balão, bóia] to inflate. -2. [vela] to fill. -3. [peito] to puff out.
inflexível [ĩnflek'sivɛw] (pl -eis) adj -1. [invergável] stiff. -2. fig [implacável] inflexible.
infligir [52] [ĩfli'ʒi(x)] vt: ~ algo (a alguém) to inflict sthg (on sb).
influência [ĩnflu'ẽnsja] f influence.
influenciar [16] [ĩflwẽn'sja(x)] <> vt to influence. <> vi: ~ em algo to influence sthg.
◆ **influenciar-se** vp: ~-se (com algo) to be influenced by sthg; ~-se (por alguém/algo) to be influenced (by sb/sthg).
influenciável [ĩnflwẽn'sjavew] (pl -eis) adj easily influenced.
influente [ĩnflu'ẽntʃil] adj influential.
influir [74] [ĩnflu'i(x)] vi -1. [importar] to matter, to be important. -2. [atuar] ~ em algo to interfere in sthg. -3. [influenciar]: ~ para algo to play a role in sthg.
influxo [ĩn'fluksu] m -1. [convergência] influx. -2. [maré alta] high tide.

infográfico, ca [ĩnfo'grafiku, ka] adj computer graphic (antes de subst).
◆ **infográfico** m computer graphics designer.
informação [ĩnfoxma'sãw] (pl -ões) f -1. [ger] information. -2. [notícia] news. -3. MIL intelligence. -4. COMPUT data (inv).
informado, da [ĩnfox'madu, da] adj -1. [esclarecido] well-informed. -2. [notificado]: ~ de algo informed of sthg.
informal [ĩnfox'maw] (pl -ais) adj informal.
informalidade [ĩnfoxmali'dadʒil] f informality.
informante [ĩnfox'mãntʃil] mf informant.
informar [4] [ĩfox'ma(x)] <> vt -1. [esclarecer] to inform. -2. [notificar]: ~ alguém de algo to notify sb of sthg. <> vi [ser informativo] to inform.
◆ **informar-se** vp -1. [atualizar-se] to keep o.s. up to date. -2. [esclarecer-se]: ~-se sobre algo to make inquiries about sthg, to inquire about sthg.
informático, ca [ĩnfox'matʃiku, ka] <> adj computer (antes de subst). <> m, f [pessoa] IT specialist.
◆ **informática** f -1. [ciência] computer science. -2. [atividade] computing.
informativo, va [ĩnfoxma'tʃivu, va] adj informative.
informatização [ĩnfoxmatʃiza'sãw] f COMPUT computerization.
informatizar [4] [ĩnfurmati'za(x)] vt to computerize.
informe [ĩn'fɔxmi] <> adj shapeless. <> m -1. [informações] information. -2. MIL (piece of) intelligence.
infortúnio [ĩnfox'tunju] m misfortune.
infração [ĩnfra'sãw] (pl -ões) f -1. [de lei etc] infringement; ~ de trânsito driving offence UK, driving offense US. -2. ESP foul.
Infraero (abrev de Empresa Brasileira de Infra-Estrutura Aeroportuária) f Brazilian company responsible for airport insfrastructure, ≃ BAA UK.
infra-estrutura [,ĩnfraʃtru'tural] (pl infra-estruturas) f infrastructure.
infrator, ra [ĩnfra'to(x), ra] (mpl -es, fpl -s) <> adj law-breaking. <> m, f infringer.
infravermelho, lha [ĩnfravex'meʎu, ʎa] adj infrared.
infreqüente [ĩnfre'kwẽntʃil] adj infrequent.
infringir [52] [ĩnfrĩ'ʒi(x)] vt to infringe.
infrutífero, ra [ĩnfru'tʃiferu, ra] adj fruitless.
infundado, da [ĩnfũn'dadu, da] adj unfounded, groundless.
infundir [6] [ĩnfũn'dʒi(x)] vt -1. [inspirar] to inspire. -2. [incutir] to instill.
infusão [ĩnfu'zãw] (pl -ões) f infusion.
ingenuidade [ĩnʒenwi'dadʒil] f ingenuousness, naivety.
ingênuo, nua [ĩn'ʒenwu, nwa] <> adj ingenuous, naive. <> m, f ingenuous person, naive person.
ingerência [ĩnʒe'rẽnsja] f intervention.

ingerir [57] [ĩnʒeˈri(x)] *vt* to ingest.
ingestão [ĩnʒeʃˈtãw] *f* ingestion.
Inglaterra [ĩnglaˈtɛxa] *n* England.
inglês, esa [ĩnˈgleʃ, eza] (*mpl* -**eses**, *fpl* -**s**) ◇ *adj* English. ◇ *mf* Englishman (*f* Englishwoman).
➡ **inglês** *m* [língua] English.
inglório, ria [ĩnˈglɔrju, rja] *adj* inglorious.
ingovernabilidade [ĩngovexnabiliˈdadʒi] *f* ungovernability.
ingovernável [ĩngovexˈnavew] (*pl* -**eis**) *adj* -**1**. [rebelde] unruly. -**2**. [fora de controle] ungovernable.
ingratidão [ĩngratʃiˈdãw] *f* ingratitude.
ingrato, ta [ĩnˈgratu, ta] *adj* -**1**. [sem gratidão] ungrateful. -**2**. [ruim] disagreeable.
ingrediente [ĩngreˈdjẽntʃi] *m* ingredient.
íngreme [ˈĩngremi] *adj* steep.
ingressar [ĩngreˈsa(x)] *vi*: ~ **em algo** to enter sthg.
ingresso [ĩnˈgrɛsu] *m* -**1**. [bilhete] (entrance) ticket. -**2**. [entrada] entry. -**3**. [admissão] entrance.
íngua [ˈĩngwa] *f* bubo, *a swollen lymph node in the groin.*
inhame [iˈɲãmi] *m* yam.
inibição [inibiˈsãw] (*pl* -**ões**) *f* inhibition.
inibido, da [iniˈbidu, iniˈbida] *adj* inhibited.
inibidor, ra [inibiˈdo(x), ra] *adj* inhibiting.
inibir [iniˈbi(x)] *vt* -**1**. [embaraçar] to embarrass. -**2**. [dificultar] to inhibit. -**3**. [impedir]: ~ **alguém (de fazer algo)** to prevent sb (from doing sthg).
➡ **inibir-se** *vp* [ficar inibido] to become inhibited.
iniciação [inisjaˈsãw] (*pl* -**ões**) *f* initiation.
iniciado, da [iniˈsjadu, da] ◇ *adj* [pessoa] initiated. ◇ *m, f* [pessoa] initiate.
inicial [iniˈsjaw] (*pl* -**ais**) ◇ *adj* initial. ◇ *f* [letra] initial.
➡ **iniciais** *fpl* initials.
iniciante [iniˈsjãntʃi] ◇ *adj* [pessoa] beginning. ◇ *mf* [pessoa] beginner.
iniciar [iniˈsja(x)] *vt* -**1**. [começar] to initiate, to begin. -**2**. [introduzir]: ~ **alguém em algo** to introduce sb to sthg.
➡ **iniciar-se** *vp* [introduzir-se]: ~-**se em algo** to get into sthg.
iniciativa [inisjaˈtʃiva] *f* initiative; **não ter** ~ to have no initiative; **por** ~ **própria** on one's own initiative; **tomar a** ~ to take the initiative; ~ **privada** private initiative.
início [iˈnisju] *m* beginning; **desde o** ~ from the outset; **no** ~ in the beginning.
inigualável [inigwaˈlavew] (*pl* -**eis**) *adj* unequalled.
inimaginável [inimaʒiˈnavew] (*pl* -**eis**) *adj* unimaginable.
inimigo, ga [iniˈmigu, ga] ◇ *adj* enemy *(antes de subst).* ◇ *m, f* enemy.
inimizade [inimiˈzadʒi] *f* enmity.
ininteligível [inĩnteliˈgivew] (*pl* -**eis**) *adj* unintelligible.
ininterrupto, ta [inĩnteˈxuptu, ta] *adj* uninterrupted.

iniqüidade [inikwiˈdadʒi] *f* iniquity.
iníquo, qua [iˈnikwu, kwa] *adj* iniquitous.
injeção [ĩnʒeˈsãw] (*pl* -**ões**) *f* injection.
injetado, da [iʒeˈtadu, da] *adj* -**1**. [fluido] injected. -**2**. [corado de sangue]: **olhos** ~**s** bloodshot eyes.
injetar [4] [iʒeˈta(x)] *vt* to inject.
injunção [ĩnʒũnˈsãw] (*pl* -**ões**) *f* -**1**. [ordem] injunction. -**2**. [pressão] pressure.
injúria [ĩnˈʒurja] *f* insult.
injuriado, da [ĩnʒuˈrjadu, da] *adj* [pessoa] insulted.
injuriar [16] [iʒuˈrja(x)] *vt* [insultar] to insult.
➡ **injuriar-se** *vp fam* [zangar-se] to get angry.
injurioso, osa [ĩnʒuˈrjozu, ɔza] *adj* insulting.
injustiça [ĩnʒuʃˈtʃisa] *f* injustice.
injustiçado, da [ĩnʒuʃtʃiˈsadu, da] ◇ *adj* unjustly treated. ◇ *m, f* victim of injustice.
injustificável [ĩnʒuʃtʃifiˈkavew] (*pl* -**eis**) *adj* unjustifiable.
injusto, ta [iˈʒuʃtu, ta] *adj* unfair.
INL (*abrev de* **Instituto Nacional do Livro**) *m Brazilian national book institute.*
INMETRO (*abrev de* **Instituto Nacional de Metrologia, Normalização e Qualidade Industrial**) *m Brazilian national institute of industrial standards,* ≃ TSI *UK*, ≃ NIST *US*.
inobservado, da [inobizexˈvadu, da] *adj* unobserved.
inobservância [inobisexˈvãnsja] *f* [violação] nonobservance.
inobservante [inobisexˈvãntʃi] *adj* unobservant.
inocência [inoˈsẽnsja] *f* innocence; **perder a** ~ to lose one's innocence.
inocentar [4] [inosẽnˈta(x)] *vt*: ~ **alguém de algo** to clear sb of sthg.
➡ **inocentar-se** *vp*: **inocentou-se por sua sinceridade** his sincerity showed that he was innocent.
inocente [inoˈsẽntʃi] ◇ *adj* innocent. ◇ *mf* innocent person.
inoculação [inokulaˈsãw] (*pl* -**ões**) *f* innoculation.
inocular [4] [inokuˈla(x)] *vt* to innoculate.
inócuo, cua [iˈnɔkwu, kwa] *adj* innocuous.
inodoro, ra [inoˈdɔru, ra] *adj* odourless.
inofensivo, va [inofẽˈsivu, va] *adj* inoffensive.
inolvidável [inowviˈdavew] (*pl* -**eis**) *adj* unforgettable.
inominável [inomiˈnavew] (*pl* -**eis**) *adj fig* [vil] intolerable.
inoperante [inopeˈrãntʃi] *adj* inoperative.
inopinado, da [inopiˈnadu, da] *adj* -**1**. [imprevisto] unexpected. -**2**. [extraordinário] extraordinary.
inoportuno, na [inopoxˈtunu, na] *adj* inopportune.
inorgânico, ca [inoxˈganiku, ka] *adj* inorganic.
inóspito, ta [iˈnɔʃpitu, ta] *adj* inhospitable.
inovação [inovaˈsãw] (*pl* -**ões**) *f* innovation.

inovador, ra [inova'do(x), ra] ⬦ *adj* innovative. ⬦ *m, f* innovator.

inovar [4] [ino'va(x)] *vt* to innovate.

inoxidável [inoksi'davɛw] (*pl* -eis) *adj* ▷ aço.

INPC (*abrev de* Índice Nacional de Preços ao Consumidor) *m national index of retail prices,* ≃ RPI *UK*.

inqualificável [ĩŋkwalifi'kavew] (*pl* -eis) *adj* indescribable.

inquebrantável [ĩŋkebrãn'tavew] (*pl* -eis) *adj* unbreakable.

inquérito [ĩŋ'kɛritul *m* enquiry.

inquestionável [ĩŋkeʃtʃjo'navew] (*pl* -eis) *adj* unquestionable.

inquietação [ĩŋkjeta'sãw] (*pl* -ões) *f* anxiety.

inquietante [ĩŋkje'tãntʃil, **inquietador, ra** [ĩŋkjeta'do(x), ra] *adj* worrying.

inquietar [4] [ĩŋkje'ta(x)] *vt* to worry.
➡ **inquietar-se** *vp* to worry.

inquieto, ta [ĩŋ'kjɛtu, ta] *adj* **-1.** [apreensivo] worried. **- 2.** [agitado] restless.

inquietude [ĩŋkje'tudʒi] *f* **-1.** [apreensão] worry. **- 2.** [agitação] restlessness.

inquilino, na [ĩŋki'linu, na] *m, f* tenant.

inquirição [ĩŋkiri'sãw] (*pl* -ões) *f* inquiry.

inquirir [6] [ĩŋki'ri(x)] ⬦ *vt* **- 1.** [investigar] to enquire. **- 2.** [interrogar] to question. **- 3.** JUR to examine. ⬦ *vi* [indagar] to investigate.

Inquisição [ĩŋkizi'sãw] *f:* a ~ the Inquisition.

inquisitivo, va [ĩŋkizi'tʃivu, va] *adj* inquisitive.

insaciável [ĩnsa'sjavɛw] (*pl* -eis) *adj* insatiable.

insalubre [ĩnsa'lubril *adj* **- 1.** [local, clima] unhealthy. **- 2.** [trabalho] damaging to the health. **- 3.** [água] unfit for drinking.

insanidade [ĩnsani'dadʒi] *f* insanity.

insano, na [ĩ'sanu, na] ⬦ *adj* **- 1.** [demente] insane. **- 2.** *fig* [incansável] relentless. ⬦ *m, f* madman (madwoman).

insaciabilidade [ĩnsasjabili'dadʒi] *f* insatiable appetite.

insatisfação [ĩnsatʃiʃfa'sãw] (*pl* -ões) *f* dissatisfaction.

insatisfatório, ria [ĩnsatʃiʃfa'tɔrju, rja] *adj* unsatisfactory.

insatisfeito, ta [ĩnsatʃiʃ'fejtu, ta] *adj* dissatisfied.

inscrever [5] [ĩʃkre've(x)] *vt* **- 1.** [gravar] to inscribe. **- 2.** [pessoa]: ~ alguém (em algo) to register sb (for sthg).
➡ **inscrever-se** *vp* [pessoa]: ~-se (em algo) to register (for sthg).

inscrição [ĩʃkri'sãw] (*pl* -ões) *f* **- 1.** [mensagem] inscription. **- 2.** [matrícula, assentamento] registration; **número de** ~ registration number.

inscrito, ta [ĩ'ʃkritu, ta] ⬦ *pp* ▷ inscrever. ⬦ *adj* **- 1.** [mensagem] inscribed. **- 2.** [pessoa] registered.

insegurança [ĩnsegu'rãnsa] *f* **- 1.** [falta de segurança] lack of safety. **- 2.** [de pessoa] insecurity.

inseguro, ra [ĩnse'guru, ra] *adj* **- 1.** [perigoso] unsafe. **- 2.** [pessoa] insecure.

inseminação [ĩnsemina'sãw] (*pl* -ões) *f* insemination; ~ **artificial** artificial insemination.

inseminar [4] [ĩsemi'na(x)] *vt* to inseminate.

insensatez [ĩnsẽnsa'teʒl *f* foolishness.

insensato, ta [ĩnsẽn'satu, ta] *adj* foolish.

insensibilidade [ĩnsẽnsibili'dadʒil *f* insensitivity.

insensibilizar [4] [ĩsẽsibili'ta(x)] *vt* [tornar insensível] to desensitize.
➡ **insensibilizar-se** *vp* [emocionalmente] to harden o.s.

insensível [ĩnsẽn'sivɛw] (*pl* -eis) *adj* **- 1.** [sem sensibilidade] numb. **- 2.** [impassível] insensitive.

inseparável [ĩnsepa'ravɛw] (*pl* -eis) *adj* inseparable.

inserção [ĩnsex'sãw] (*pl* -ões) *f* **- 1.** [introdução]: ~ **(de algo em algo)** insertion (of sthg into sthg). **- 2.** COMPUT insertion.

inserir [57] [ĩse'ri(x)] *vt* **- 1.:** ~ **algo em algo** to insert sthg into sthg. **- 2.** COMPUT to insert.
➡ **inserir-se** *vp*: ~ -em algo to fit into sthg.

inseticida [ĩnsetʃi'sidal *m* insecticide.

inseto [ĩn'sɛtul *m* insect.

insídia [ĩn'sidʒjal *f* ambush.

insidioso, osa [ĩnsi'dʒjozu, ɔzal *adj* insidious.

insight [ĩn'sajtʃil *m* insight; **ter um** ~ to have insight.

insigne [ĩn'signil *adj* celebrated.

insígnia [ĩn'signjal *f* insignia.

insignificância [ĩnsignifi'kãnsjal *f* insignificance.

insignificante [ĩnsignifi'kãntʃil *adj* insignificant.

insincero, ra [ĩnsĩ'sɛru, ra] *adj* insincere.

insinuação [ĩnsinwa'sãw] (*pl* -ões) *f* **- 1.** [indireta, sugestão] insinuation. **- 2.** [amorosa] advance.

insinuante [ĩnsi'nwãntʃil *adj* [que se insinua] insinuating.

insinuar [4] [ĩnsi'nwa(x)] *vt* **- 1.** [afirmar indiretamente] to hint at; ~ **que** to insinuate that. **- 2.** [sugerir]: ~ **que** to suggest that.
➡ **insinuar-se** *vp* **- 1.** [passar]: ~-se por *ou* entre to insinuate o.s. in *ou* among. **- 2.** [amorosamente]: ~-se (para alguém) to make advances (to sb).

insípido, da [ĩn'sipidu, da] *adj* **- 1.** [sem sabor] insipid. **- 2.** *fig* [sem graça] insipid.

insistência [ĩnsiʃ'tẽnsja] *f* insistence.

insistente [ĩnsiʃ'tẽntʃil *adj* insistent.

insistir [6] [ĩnsiʃ'ti(x)] *vi* [perseverar]: ~ **em (fazer algo)** to insist on (doing sthg); ~ **para alguém fazer algo** to insist that sb do sthg.

insociável [ĩnso'sjavɛw] (*pl* -eis) *adj* antisocial.

insolação [ĩnsola'sãw] (*pl* -ões) *f* sunstroke; **ter uma** ~ to have sunstroke.

insolência [ĩnso'lẽnsjal *f* insolence.

insolente [ĩnso'lẽntʃil ⬦ *adj* insolent. ⬦ *mf* insolent person.

insólito, ta [ĩn'sɔlitu, ta] *adj* unusual.

insolúvel [ĩnso'luvɛw] (*pl* -eis) *adj* insoluble.

insolvência [ĩnsow'vẽnsjal *f* insolvency.

insolvente [ĩnsow'vẽntʃil] *adj* insolvent.
insondável [ĩnsõn'davew] (*pl* -**eis**) *adj* unfathomable.
insone [ĩn'soni] *adj* -**1.** [pessoa] insomniac. -**2.** [noite] sleepless.
insônia [ĩn'sonja] *f* insomnia.
insosso, ssa [ĩn'sosu, sa] *adj* -**1.** [sem sal] unsalted. -**2.** [sem sabor] tasteless. -**3.** *fig* [sem graça] dull.
inspeção [ĩnʃpe'sãw] (*pl* -**ões**) *f* inspection.
inspecionar [4] [ĩʃpɛsjo'na(x)] *vt* to inspect.
inspetor, ra [ĩnʃpe'to(x), ra] (*mpl* -**es**, *fpl* -**s**) *m, f* inspector; ~ **da alfândega** customs officer.
inspetoria [ĩnʃpeto'ria] *f* inspectorate.
inspiração [ĩnʃpira'sãw] (*pl* -**ões**) *f* -**1.** [estímulo] inspiration. -**2.** [na respiração] breathing in.
inspirador, ra [ĩnʃpira'do(x), ra] (*mpl* -**es**, *fpl* -**s**) *adj* inspiring.
inspirar [4] [ĩʃpi'ra(x)] *vt* -**1.** [estimular] to inspire. -**2.** [ar] to breathe in.
→ **inspirar-se** *vp* [obter estímulo] to be inspired.
instabilidade [ĩnʃtabili'dadʒi] *f* instability.
instalação [ĩnʃtala'sãw] (*pl* -**ões**) *f* -**1.** [ger] installation. -**2.** [sistema]: ~ **elétrica/hidráulica** electric/hydraulic plant.
→ **instalações** *fpl* -**1.** [para esporte, lazer] facilities. -**2.** [de indústria] plant.
instalador, ra [ĩʃtala'do(x), ra] *m, f* fitter.
instalar [4] [ĩʃta'la(x)] *vt* -**1.** [ger] to install. -**2.** [estabelecer] to establish. -**3.** [num cargo]: ~ **alguém em** to install sb in.
→ **instalar-se** *vp* -**1.** [alojar-se] to install o.s. -**2.** [em um cargo] to install o.s.
instância [ĩʃ'tãnsja] *f* -**1.** [solicitação] demand; **em última** ~ as a last resort. -**2.** [jurisdição] jurisdiction. -**3.** *JUR* stages of a law suit; **tribunal de segunda** ~ court of second instance.
instantâneo, nea [ĩnʃtãn'tãnju, nja] *adj* instant.
→ **instantâneo** *m* *FOT* snap, snapshot.
instante [ĩnʃ'tãntʃi] <> *m* moment; **a cada** ~ at any moment; **nesse** ~ at that moment; **num** ~ in a moment. <> *adj* -**1.** [iminente] imminent. -**2.** [urgente] urgent.
instar [4] [ĩ'ta(x)] <> *vt* [pedir]: ~ **que alguém faça algo** to request that sb do sthg. <> *vi* [insistir]: ~ **com alguém para que faça algo** to urge sb to do sthg; ~ **por algo** to insist on sthg.
instauração [ĩnʃtawra'sãw] (*pl* -**ões**) *f* establishment.
instaurar [4] [ĩʃtaw'ra(x)] *vt* -**1.** [estabelecer] to establish. -**2.** [criar] to set up.
instável [ĩnʃ'tavew] (*pl* -**eis**) *adj* -**1.** [ger] unstable. -**2.** [sem equilíbrio] wobbly.
instigação [ĩʃtʃiga'sãw] (*pl* -**ões**) *f* instigation.
instigar [14] [ĩʃtʃi'ga(x)] *vt* -**1.** [incitar]: ~ **alguém a fazer algo** to encourage sb to do sthg. -**2.** [provocar]: ~ **alguém contra alguém** to rouse sb against sb.
instilar [4] [ĩʃtʃi'la(x)] *vt* to instil.
→ **instilar-se** *vp* [infiltrar-se]: ~-**se em** to insinuate o.s. in.

instintivo, va [ĩnʃtʃĩn'tʃivu, va] *adj* instinctive.
instinto [ĩnʃ'tʃĩntu] *m* instinct; ~ **de sobrevivência** survival instinct.
institucional [ĩnʃtʃitusjo'naw] (*pl* -**ais**) *adj* institutional.
instituição [ĩnʃtʃitwi'sãw] (*pl* -**ões**) *f* institution; ~ **de caridade** charity, charitable institution.
instituir [74] [ĩʃtʃi'twi(x)] *vt* -**1.** [estabelecer] to institute. -**2.** [marcar] to set. -**3.** [nomear] to name.
instituto [ĩnʃtʃi'tutu] *m* institute; ~ **de beleza** beauty parlour.
instrução [ĩnʃtru'sãw] (*pl* -**ões**) *f* -**1.** [educação] education; **ter/não ter** ~ to be/not to be educated. -**2.** [ordem] instruction.
→ **instruções** *fpl* instructions.
instruído, da [ĩʃ'trwidu, da] *adj* educated.
instruir [74] [ĩʃtru'i(x)] *vt* -**1.** [ger] to instruct. -**2.** [educar] to educate. -**3.** [informar]: ~ **alguém sobre algo** to instruct sb on sthg. -**4.** [adestrar] to train.
→ **instruir-se** *vp* [educar-se] to become educated; ~-**se em algo** to train in sthg.
instrumentação [ĩnʃtrumẽnta'sãw] (*pl* -**ões**) *f* *MÚS* instrumentation.
instrumentador, ra [ĩnʃtrumẽnta'do(x), ra] *m, f* -**1.** *MÚS* score writer. -**2.** [em uma cirurgia] theatre nurse.
instrumental [ĩnʃtrumẽn'taw] (*pl* -**ais**) <> *adj* *MÚS* instrumental. <> *m* [equipamento] instrument; ~ **cirúrgico** surgical instrument.
instrumentar [47] [ĩnʃtrumẽn'ta(x)] *vt* *MÚS* to write scores.
instrumentista [ĩnʃtrumẽn'tʃiʃta] *mf* instrumentalist.
instrumento [ĩnʃtru'mẽntul] *m* -**1.** [ger] instrument; ~ **de sopro** wind instrument. -**2.** [ferramenta] tool; ~ **de trabalho** work tool.
instrutivo, va [ĩnʃtru'tʃivu, va] *adj* educational.
instrutor, ra [ĩnʃtru'to(x), ra] (*mpl* -**es**, *fpl* -**s**) *m, f* instructor.
insubordinação [ĩnsuboxdʒina'sãw] (*pl* -**ões**) *f* insubordination.
insubordinado, da [ĩnsuboxdʒi'nadu, da] *adj* insubordinate.
insubordinar-se [4] [ĩnsuboxdʒi'naxsi] *vp* to rebel.
insubstituível [ĩnsubʃtʃi'twivɛw] (*pl* -**eis**) *adj* irreplaceable.
insucesso [ĩnsu'sɛsu] *m* failure.
insuficiência [ĩnsufi'sjẽnsja] *f* -**1.** [carência] lack. -**2.** *MED* insufficiency.
insuficiente [ĩnsufi'sjẽntʃi] <> *adj* -**1.** [não-suficiente] insufficient. -**2.** [incompetente] inadequate. <> *m* [nota escolar] fail; **tirar** ~ to fail.
insuflar [4] [ĩsu'fla(x)] *vt* -**1.** [soprar] to blow into. -**2.** *fig* [incutir]: ~ **algo em alguém** to provoke sthg in sb.
insular [4] [ĩsu'la(x)] <> *adj* insular. <> *vt* to isolate.
insulina [ĩnsu'lina] *f* insulin.

insultar [4] [isuw'ta(x)] *vt* to insult.

insulto [ĩn'suwtu] *m* insult.

insultuoso, osa [ĩn'suw'twozu, ɔza] *adj* insulting.

insumo [ĩn'sumu] *m* input.

insuperável [ĩnsupe'ravɛw] (*pl* -eis) *adj* -1. [invencível] insuperable. -2. [imbatível] unsurpassable.

insuportável [ĩnsupox'tavɛw] (*pl* -eis) *adj* unbearable.

insurgente [ĩnsux'ʒẽntʃi] <> *adj* insurgent. <> *mf* insurgent.

insurgir-se [52] [ĩsux'ʒixsi] *vp* to revolt.

insurreição [ĩnsuxej'sãw] (*pl* -ões) *f* insurrection.

insurreto, ta [ĩnsu'xɛtu, ta] <> *adj* insurgent. <> *m, f* insurgent.

insuspeito, ta [ĩnsuʃ'pejtu, ta] *adj* -1. [inocente] beyond suspicion. -2. [imparcial] impartial.

insustentável [ĩnsuʃtẽn'tavew] (*pl* -eis) *adj* untenable.

intacto, ta [ĩn'ta(k)tu, ta] *adj* = intato.

intangibilidade [ĩntãnʒibili'dadʒil *f* intangibility.

intangível [ĩntãn'ʒivew] (*pl* -eis) *adj* -1. [impalpável] intangible. -2. *fig* [intocável] irreproachable.

intato, ta [ĩn'tatu, ta] *adj* -1. [ileso] intact. -2. *fig* [puro] inviolate.

íntegra ['ĩntegral *f* entirety; **na** ~ in entirety.

integração [ĩntegra'sãw] (*pl* -ões) *f* integration.

integral [ĩnte'grawl (*pl* -ais) *adj* [total] whole; **leite** ~ full-cream milk; **cereal** ~ wholegrain cereal; **arroz** ~ brown rice; **pão** ~ wholemeal bread; **trigo** ~ wholewheat.

integralismo [ĩntegra'liʒmul *m* Integralism, *Brazilian political movement of the 1930s*.

integralmente [ĩntegraw'mẽntʃil *adv* fully.

integrante [ĩnte'grãntʃil <> *adj* component. <> *mf* -1. [membro] constituent. -2. [parte] component. -3. *GRAM* conjunction.

integrar [4] [ĩnte'gra(x)l *vt* -1. [unir] to integrate. -2. [formar] to comprise. -3. [fazer parte] to be a member.

 ➡ **integrar-se** *vp* -1. [inteirar-se] to combine. -2. [juntar-se]: ~-se em *ou* a algo to join sthg.

integridade [ĩntegri'dadʒil *f* integrity.

íntegro, gra ['ĩntegru, gral *adj* -1. [inteiro] entire. -2. [honesto] honest.

inteiramente [ĩn̩tejra'mẽntʃil *adv* entirely.

inteirar [4] [ĩntej'ra(x)l *vt* -1. [completar] to make up. -2. [informar]: ~ alguém de algo to inform sb of sthg.

 ➡ **inteirar-se** *vp* [informar-se]: ~-se de algo to find out about sthg.

inteireza [ĩntej'rezal *f* -1. [totalidade] entirety. -2. *fig* [retidão] integrity.

inteiriço, ça [ĩntej'risu, sal *adj* all-in-one.

inteiro, ra [ĩn'tejru, ral *adj* -1. [todo] whole. -2. [intacto] intact. -3. [completo] entire. -4. [ileso] in one piece *(depois de verbo)*. -5. [inteiriço] all-in-one *(antes de subst)*; [total] complete. -6. *fam* [conservado] in good shape.

intelecto [ĩnte'lɛktul *m* intellect.

intelectual [ĩntelɛ'twawl (*pl* -ais) <> *adj* intellectual. <> *mf* intellectual.

intelectualidade [ĩntelɛktwali'dadʒil *f* -1. [qualidade] intellect. -2. [o meio intelectual]: **a** ~ the intelligentsia.

inteligência [ĩnteli'ʒẽnsjal *f* -1. [destreza mental] intelligence. -2. [entendimento] comprehension. -3. [pessoa] brain. -4. *COMP*: ~ artificial artificial intelligence.

inteligente [ĩnteli'ʒẽntʃil *adj* intelligent.

inteligível [ĩnteli'ʒivewl (*pl* -eis) *adj* intelligible.

intemperança [ĩntẽmpe'rãnsal *f* intemperance.

intempérie [ĩntẽn'pɛril *f* bad weather.

intempestivo, va [ĩntẽmpeʃ'tʃivu, val *adj* untimely.

intenção [ĩntẽn'sãwl (*pl* -ões) *f* intention; **com boa** ~ with good intentions, well meaning; **com má** ~ with bad intentions; **segundas intenções** ulterior motives; **ter a** ~ de fazer algo to intend to do sthg, to have the intention of doing sthg.

intencional [ĩntẽnsjo'nawl (*pl* -ais) *adj* intentional.

intencionar [4] [ĩntẽsjo'na(x)l *vt* to intend.

intendente [ĩntẽn'dẽntʃil *mf* -1. [administrador] administrator. -2. *MIL* quartermaster.

intensidade [ĩntẽnsi'dadʒil *f* intensity.

intensificação [ĩntẽsifika'sãwl *f* intensification.

intensificar [12] [ĩntẽsifi'ka(x)l *vt* to intensify.

 ➡ **intensificar-se** *vp* to intensify.

intensivo, va [ĩntẽ'sivu, val *adj* intensive.

intenso, sa [ĩn'tẽsu, sal *adj* intense.

intentar [4] [ĩntẽn'ta(x)l *vt* -1. [tentar] to attempt. -2. [projetar] to plan. -3. [cometer] to commit. -4. *JUR*: ~ uma ação contra alguém to take sb to court.

intento [ĩn'tẽntul *m* intent.

interação [ĩntera'sãwl (*pl* -ões) *f* interaction.

interagir [52] [ĩntera'ʒi(x)l *vi*: ~ com algo/alguém to interact with sthg/sb.

interatividade [ĩnteratʃivi'dadʒil *f* COMPUT interactivity.

interativo, va [ĩntera'tʃivu, val *adj* COMPUT interactive.

intercalar [4] [ĩntex'kala(x)l *vt* -1. [interpor]: ~ algo em *ou* entre to place sthg in *ou* between. -2. [inserir]: ~ algo em to insert sthg in(to).

 ➡ **intercalar-se** *vp* [interpor-se]: ~-se em *ou* entre to intervene in/between.

intercambiar [4] [ĩnterkãn'bia(x)l *vt* to interchange.

intercambiável [ĩnterkãn'bjavɛwl (*pl* -eis) *adj* interchangeable.

intercâmbio [ĩnter'kãnbjul *m* exchange.

interceder [5] [ĩntexse'de(x)l *vi*: ~ por alguém to intercede on behalf of sb.

interceptar [4] [ĩntexsep'ta(x)l *vt* -1. [ger] to cut off. -2. [fazer parar] to stop. -3. [apoderar-se de] to intercept.

intercessão [ĩntexse'sãwl (*pl* -ões) *f* intercession.

interconexão [ĩntexkonek'sãw] (*pl* -ões) *f* interconnection.

intercontinental [ĩntexkõntʃinẽn'taw] (*pl* -ais) *adj* intercontinental.

interdependente [ĩntexdepẽn'dẽntʃi] *adj* interdependent.

interdição [ĩntexdʒi'sãw] (*pl* -ões) *f* -1. [proibição] ban. -2. [bloqueio] closure. -3. *JUR* injunction.

interdisciplinar [ĩntexdʒisipli'na(x)] *adj* interdisciplinary.

interdisciplinaridade [ĩntexdʒisiplinari'dadʒi] *f* interdisciplinary nature.

interditado, da [ĩntexdʒi'tadu, da] *adj* -1. [proibido] banned. -2. [bloqueado] closed.

interditar [4] [ĩntexdʒi'ta(x)] *vt* -1. [proibir] to ban. -2. [bloquear] to close. -3. *JUR* to interdict.

interessado, da [ĩntere'sadu, da] <> *adj* interested. <> *m, f* interested party.

interessante [ĩntere'sãntʃi] *adj* interesting.

interessar [4] [ĩntere'sa(x)] <> *vt* to interest. <> *vi* [despertar interesse] to be of interest; **a quem possa** ~ *fml* to whom it may concern.
➡ **interessar-se** *vp* [ter interesse]: ~**-se em** *ou* **por** to take an interest in.

interesse [ĩnte'resi] *m* -1. [ger] interest. -2. [vantagem] benefit; **no** ~ **de** in the interest of; **por** ~ **próprio** out of self-interest.

interesseiro, ra [ĩntere'sejru, ra] <> *adj* self-seeking. <> *m, f* egotist.

interestadual [ĩntereʃta'dwaw] (*pl* -ais) *adj* interstate.

interface [ˌĩntex'fasi] *f* COMPUT interface.

interferência [ĩntexfe'rẽnsja] *f* interference.

interferir [57] [ĩntexfe'ri(x)] *vi* -1. [intervir]: ~ **em algo** to interfere in sthg. -2. [em rádio, televisão] to cause interference.

interfonar [4] [ĩntexfo'na(x)] *vi*: ~ **a alguém** to call sb on the internal phone.

interfone [ˌĩntex'foni] *m* intercom.

ínterim ['ĩnterĩ] *m* interim; **nesse** ~ meanwhile.

interior [ĩnte'rjo(x)] (*pl* -es) <> *adj* inner. <> *m* interior.

interiorano, na [ĩnterjo'rãnu, na] <> *adj* country (*antes de subst*). <> *m,f* country dweller.

interiorizar [ĩnterjori'za(x)] *vt* to internalize.

interjeição [ĩntexʒej'sãw] (*pl* -ões) *f* exclamation.

interligação [ĩntexliga'sãw] (*pl* -ões) *f* interconnection.

interligar [14] [ĩntexli'ga(x)] *vt* to interconnect.
➡ **interligar-se** *vp* to be interconnected.

interlocutor, ra [ĩntexloku'to(x), ra] (*pl* -es, *fpl* -s) *m, f* interlocutor.

interlúdio [ĩntex'ludʒju] *m* interlude.

intermediar [17] [ĩntexme'dʒja(x)] *vt* -1. [servir como mediador] to mediate; ~ **um debate entre** to chair a debate between. -2. [entremear, intercalar] to mix.

intermediário, ria [ĩntexme'dʒjarju, rja] <> *adj* intermediate. <> *m, f* -1. [mediador] mediator. -2. COM intermediary.

intermédio [ĩnter'mɛdʒu] *m*: **por** ~ **de** through.

interminável [ĩntexmi'navɛw] (*pl* -eis) *adj* endless.

intermitente [ĩntexmi'tẽntʃi] *adj* intermittent.

internação [ĩntexna'sãw] (*pl* -ões) *f* -1. [de doente] admission. -2. [de aluno] boarding.

internacional [ĩntexnasjo'naw] (*pl* -ais) *adj* international.

internacionalizar [4] [ĩntexnasjonali'za(x)] *vt* to internationalize.
➡ **internacionalizar-se** *vp* to become international.

internamento [ĩntexna'mẽntu] *m* admission.

internar [4] [ĩntex'na(x)] *vt* -1. MED to admit. -2. [aluno] to board. -3. POL to intern.

internato [ĩntex'natu] *m* EDUC boarding school.

internauta [ĩntex'nawta] *mf* COMPUT Internet user *ou* surfer.

Internet [ĩntex'nɛtʃi] *f*: **a** ~ the Internet.

interno, na [ĩn'texnu, na] <> *adj* -1. [interior] inside; **de uso** ~ for internal use. -2. POL internal. -3. [aluno] boarding. <> *m, f* -1. MED houseman *UK*, intern *US*. -2. [aluno] boarder.

interpelação [ĩntexpela'sãw] (*pl* -ões) *f* -1. [indagação] questioning. -2. *JUR* summons (*sg*).

interpelar [4] [ĩntexpe'la(x)] *vt* -1. [indagar]: ~ **alguém sobre algo** to question sb about sthg. -2. [pedir explicações] to question. -3. *JUR* to summons.

interplanetário, ria [ĩntexplane'tarju, rja] *adj* interplanetary.

Interpol (*abrev de* International Criminal Police Organization) *f* Interpol.

interpolação [ĩntexpola'sãw] (*pl* -ões) *f* [inserção] insertion.

interpolar [4] [ĩntexpo'la(x)] *vt* -1. [texto, narrativa] to insert. -2. [intercalar] to interpolate.

interpor [45] [ĩntex'po(x)] *vt* -1. [entremeter] to put in. -2. [fazer intervir] to intervene with.
➡ **interpor-se** *vp* -1. [pôr-se entre, mediar]: ~**-se entre** to intervene between. -2. [contrapor-se]: ~**-se a algo/alguém** to oppose sthg/sb.

interposto, ta [ĩntex'poʃtu, ta] <> *pp* ▷ **interpor**. <> *adj* interposing.

interpretação [ĩntexpreta'sãw] (*pl* -ões) *f* -1. [ger] interpretation. -2. [tradução] interpreting.

interpretar [4] [ĩntexpre'ta(x)] *vt* -1. [ger] to interpret. -2. [traduzir] to interpret.

interpretativo, va [ĩntexpreta'tʃivu, va] *adj* interpretative.

intérprete [ĩn'tɛxpretʃi] *mf* -1. LING interpreter. -2. CINE, TEATRO & TV performer.

interregno [ĩnte'xɛgnu] *m* [intervalo] interlude.

inter-racial [ĩntexa'sjaw] (*pl* -ais) *adj* interracial.

inter-relacionado, da [ĩntexelasjo'nadu, da] *adj* interrelated.

inter-relacionar [4] [ĩntexelasjo'na(x)] *vt* to interrelate.

interrogação [ĩntexoga'sãw] (*pl* -ões) *f* interrogation; **ponto de** ~ question mark.

interrogador, ra [ĩntexoga'do(x), ra] *m, f* interrogator.

interrogar [14] [ĩntexu'ga(x)] *vt* -1. [indagar]: ~

alguém (sobre algo) to interrogate sb (about sthg). **-2.** *JUR* to put questions to.

interrogativo, va [ĩntexoga'tʃivu, va] *adj* **-1.** [indagativo] questioning. **-2.** *GRAM* interrogative.

interrogatório [ĩntexoga'tɔrjul] *m* interrogation.

interromper [5] [ĩntexõm'pe(x)] *vt* to interrupt.

interrompido, da [ĩntexõn'pidu, da] *adj* interrupted.

interrupção [ĩntexup'sãw] (*pl* -ões) *f* interruption.

interruptor [ĩntexup'to(x)] (*pl* -es) *m* switch.

interseção [ĩntexse'sãw] (*pl* -ões) *f* intersection.

interstício [ĩntexʃ'tʃisju] *m* interstice.

interurbano, na [ĩnterux'bãnu, na] *adj* **-1.** intercity *UK*, inter-urban *US*. **-2.** [telefonema] long distance.

➡ **interurbano** *m* [telefonema] long distance call.

intervalo [ĩntex'valu] *m* **-1.** [ger] interval; **a** ~ **s** at intervals; ~ **comercial** commercial break. **-2.** [no espaço] distance.

intervenção [ĩntexvẽn'sãw] (*pl* -ões) *f* **-1.** [interferência] intervention; ~ **cirúrgica** operation, surgical intervention. **-2.** *JUR* mediation.

intervencionismo [ĩntexvẽnsjo'niʒmu] *m* interventionism.

intervencionista [ĩntexvẽnsjo'niʃta] <> *adj* interventionist. <> *mf* interventionist.

interventor, ra [ĩntexvẽn'to(x), ra] *m, f* interim governor.

intervir [67] [ĩntex'vi(x)] *vi* to intervene.

intestinal [ĩnteʃtʃi'naw] (*pl* -ais) *adj* intestinal.

intestino [ĩnteʃ'tʃinu] *m* intestine; ~ **delgado** small intestine; ~ **grosso** large intestine.

intimação [ĩntʃima'sãw] (*pl* -ões) *f* **-1.** [ordem] order. **-2.** *JUR* summons (*sg*).

intimar [4] [ĩntʃi'ma(x)] *vt* **-1.** [ordenar]: ~ **alguém (a fazer algo)** to order sb (to do sthg). **-2.** *JUR* to summons.

intimidação [ĩntʃimida'sãw] (*pl* -ões) *f* intimidation.

intimidade [ĩntʃimi'dadʒi] *f* **-1.** [vida íntima] privacy. **-2.** [familiaridade] intimacy; **ter** ~ **com alguém** to be close to sb.

intimidar [4] [ĩntʃimi'da(x)] *vt* to intimidate.

➡ **intimidar-se** *vp* to be intimidated.

íntimo, ma ['ĩntʃimu, ma] <> *adj* **-1.** [interior e profundo] intimate. **-2.** [privado] private. <> *m* **-1.** [âmago]: **no** ~, **ela sabia que estava errada** deep down, she knew that she was wrong. **-2.** [amigo] close friend.

intitular [4] [ĩntʃitu'la(x)] *vt* **-1.** [dar título a] to title; ~ **algo de algo** to call sth sthg. **-2.** [chamar]: ~ **alguém de algo** to call sb sthg.

➡ **intitular-se** *vp* [denominar-se] to call o.s.

intocável [ĩnto'kavew] (*pl* -eis) *adj* untouchable.

intolerância [ĩntole'rãnsja] *f* intolerance.

intolerante [ĩntole'rãntʃi] *adj* intolerant.

intolerável [ĩntole'ravew] (*pl* -eis) *adj* intolerable.

intoxicação [ĩntoksika'sãw] (*pl* -ões) *f* poisoning;

~ **alimentar** food poisoning.

intoxicar [12] [ĩntoksi'ka(x)] *vt* to poison.

➡ **intoxicar-se** *vp* to poison o.s.

intraduzível [ĩntradu'zivew] (*pl* -eis) *adj* **-1.** [que não tem tradução] untranslatable. **-2.** [inexprimível] inexpressible.

intragável [ĩntra'gavew] (*pl* -eis) *adj* unpalatable.

intranet l'ĩntranetʃi] *f* *COMPUT* intranet.

intranqüilidade [ĩntrãŋkwili'dadʒi] *f* disquiet.

intranqüilo [ĩntrãn'kwilu] *adj* restless.

intransferível [ĩntrãnʃfe'rivew] (*pl* -eis) *adj* **-1.** [bilhete, documento] non-transferable. **-2.** [inadiável] non-postponable.

intransigência [ĩntrãnzi'ʒẽnsja] *f* intransigence.

intransigente [ĩntrãnzi'ʒẽntʃi] *adj* **-1.** [intolerante] intransigent. **-2.** *fig* [austero] uncompromising.

intransitável [ĩntrãnzi'tavew] (*pl* -eis) *adj* impassable.

intransitivo, va [ĩntrãnzi'tʃivu, va] *adj* intransitive.

intransponível [ĩntrãnʃpo'nivew] (*pl* -eis) *adj* **-1.** [rio, barreira] impassable. **-2.** [problema, obstáculo] insurmountable.

intratável [ĩntra'tavew] (*pl* -eis) *adj* [insociável] intractable.

intra-uterino, intra-uterina [ĩntrawte'rinu, na] (*mpl* intra-uterinos, *fpl* intra-uterinas) *adj* intrauterine.

intravenoso, osa [ĩntrave'nozu, ɔza] *adj* intravenous.

intrépido, da [ĩn'trɛpidu, da] *adj* intrepid.

intricado, da [ĩntri'kadu, da] *adj* **-1.** [emaranhado] tangled. **-2.** [confuso] intricate.

intriga [ĩn'triga] *f* **-1.** [trama] intrigue. **-2.** [cilada] conspiracy. **-3.** [enredo] plot.

➡ **intrigas** *fpl* [fofoca] gossip (*sg*).

intrigante [ĩntri'gãntʃi] *adj* intriguing.

intrigar [14] [ĩntri'ga(x)] <> *vt* [despertar curiosidade de] to intrigue. <> *vi* [excitar a curiosidade] to intrigue.

intrínseco, ca [ĩn'trĩnseku, ka] *adj* intrinsic.

introdução [ĩntrodu'sãw] (*pl* -ões) *f* introduction.

introdutório, ria [ĩntrodu'tɔrju, rja] *adj* introductory.

introduzir [72] [ĩntrodu'zi(x)] *vt* **-1.** [inserir]: ~ **algo (em)** to introduce sthg (into). **-2.** [fazer adotar] to introduce.

➡ **introduzir-se** *vp*: ~ **(em)** to find one's way (into).

intróito [ĩn'trɔjtu] *m* **-1.** [início] beginning. **-2.** *REL* introit.

intrometer-se [5] [ĩntrome'texsi] *vp*: ~**-se em algo** to meddle in sthg.

intrometido, da [ĩntrome'tʃidu, da] <> *adj* meddlesome, interfering. <> *m, f* meddler.

intromissão [ĩntromi'sãw] (*pl* -ões) *f* meddling.

introspecção [ĩntroʃpek'sãw] *f* introspection.

introspectivo, va [ĩntroʃpek'tʃivu, va] *adj* introspective.

introversão [ĩntrovex'sãw] *f* introversion.
introvertido, da [ĩntrovex't∫idu, da] <> *adj*
introverted. <> *m, f* introvert.
intruso, sa [ĩn'truzu, za] *m, f* intruder.
intuição [ĩntwi'sãw] (*pl* -ões) *f* intuition.
intuir [74] [ĩn'twi(x)] <> *vt* to intuit. <> *vi* to be
intuitive.
intuitivo, va [ĩntwi't∫ivu, va] *adj* intuitive.
intuito [ĩn'twitu] *m* -1. [objetivo] purpose. -2. [in-
tento] intention.
intumescência [ĩntume'sẽnsja] *f* swelling.
intumescer-se [25] [ĩntume'sɛxsi] *vp* to swell
(up).
intumescido, da [ĩntume'sidu, da] *adj* swollen.
inumano, na [inu'manu, na] *adj* inhuman.
inúmeros, ras [i'numeru∫, ra∫] *adj pl* [antes de
subst] innumerable.
inundação [inũnda'sãw] (*pl* -ões) *f* flood.
inundado, da [inũn'dadu, da] *adj* -1. [de água]
flooded. -2. *fig* covered.
inundar [4] [inũn'da(x)] <> *vt* [alagar] to flood. <>
vt fig [encher] to swamp. <> *vi* [transbordar] to
flood.
   ➡ **inundar-se** *vp* [alagar-se] to become flooded.
inusitado, da [inuzi'tadu, da] *adj* unusual.
inútil [i'nut∫iw] (*pl* -eis) *adj* -1. [imprestável]
useless. -2. [desnecessário] needless. -3. [vão]
pointless; **ser** ~ **fazer algo** to be pointless to
do sthg.
inutilidade [inut∫ili'dadʒi] *f* uselessness.
inutilizar [4] [inut∫ili'za(x)] *vt* -1. [tornar inútil] to
render useless. -2. [danificar] to ruin. -3. [frus-
trar] to thwart.
inutilizável [inut∫ili'zavew] (*pl* -eis) *adj* [não-
utilizável] unusable.
inutilmente [i‚nut∫iwmẽnt∫i] *adv* uselessly.
invadir [6] [ĩnva'di(x)] *vt* -1. [ger] to invade. -2.
fig [dominar] to overwhelm.
invalidar [4] [ĩnvali'da(x)] *vt* -1. [anular] to
invalidate. -2. [pessoa] to disable.
invalidez [ĩnvali'deʒ] *f* disability.
inválido, da [ĩnvalidu, da] <> *adj* -1. [nulo]
invalid. -2. [pessoa] invalid, disabled. <> *m, f*
[pessoa] invalid.
invariável [ĩnva'rjavew] (*pl* -eis) *adj* invariable.
invasão [ĩnva'zãw] (*pl* -ões) *f* invasion.
invasivo, va [ĩnva'zivu, va] *adj* -1. [agressivo]
invasion *(antes de subst)*. -2. *MED* invasive.
invasor, ra [ĩva'zo(x), ra] <> *adj* invading. <> *m,*
f invader.
inveja [ĩn'veʒa] *f* envy.
invejar [4] [ĩnvɛ'ʒa(x)] <> *vt* -1. [ter inveja de] to
envy. -2. [cobiçar] to covet. <> *vi* [ter inveja] to be
envious.
invejável [ĩnve'ʒavew] (*pl* -eis) *adj* enviable.
invejoso, osa [ĩnve'ʒozu, ɔza] <> *adj* [pessoa]
envious. <> *m, f* [pessoa] envious person.
invenção [ĩnvẽn'sãw] (*pl* -ões) *f* -1. [ger]
invention. -2. *fig* [mentira] fabrication.
invencibilidade [ĩnvẽnsibili'dadʒi] *f* invincibili-
ty.

invencionice [ĩnvẽnsjo'nisi] *f* [mentira, embuste]
fabrication.
invencível [ĩnvẽn'sivew] (*pl* -eis) *adj* invincible.
inventar [4] [ĩnvẽn'ta(x)] <> *vt* to invent. <> *vi*
[cismar]: ~ **de fazer algo** to get it into one's head
to do sthg.
inventariar [16] [ĩnvẽnta'rja(x)] *vt* to inventory.
inventário [ĩnvẽn'tarju] *m* inventory.
inventivo, va [ĩnvẽn't∫ivu, va] *adj* inventive.
inventor, ra [ĩnvẽn'to(x), ra] (*mpl* -es, *fpl* -s) *m, f*
inventor.
inverdade [ĩnvex'dadʒi] *f* untruth.
invernada [ĩnvex'nada] *f* winter pasture.
invernal [ĩnvex'naw] (*pl* -ais) *adj* wintry.
inverno [ĩn'vɛxnu] *m* winter.
inverossímil [ĩnvero'simiw] (*pl* -eis) *adj* implausible.
inversão [ĩnvex'sãw] (*pl* -ões) *f* inversion.
inverso, sa [ĩn'vɛxsu, sa] *adj* -1. [invertido]
inverse. -2. [oposto] opposite.
   ➡ **inverso** *m* [contrário] opposite.
invertebrado, da [ĩnvexte'bradu, da] <> *adj*
[animal] invertebrate. <> *m* [animal] invertebrate.
inverter [5] [ĩnvex'te(x)] *vt* -1. [virar ao contrário] to
reverse. -2. [trocar a ordem de] to invert. -3. [mu-
dar] to alter.
invés [ĩn'vɛ∫] *m* inside out.
   ➡ **ao invés de** *loc prep* instead of.
investida [ĩnve∫'t∫ida] *f* -1. [ataque] attack. -2.
fig [tentativa] attempt.
investidor, ra [ĩve∫t∫i'do(x), ra] *m, f* investor.
investidura [ĩnve∫t∫i'dura] *f* investiture.
investigação [ĩnve∫t∫iga'sãw] (*pl* -ões) *f* -1. [in-
quérito] investigation; ~ **policial** police
investigation. -2. [pesquisa] inquiry; ~ **científica**
scientific investigation.
investigador, ra [ĩnve∫t∫iga'do(x), ra] *m, f* [agen-
te policial] detective.
investigar [14] [ĩnve∫t∫i'ga(x)] *vt* -1. [inquirir] to
investigate. -2. [pesquisar] to research.
investimento [ĩnve∫t∫i'mẽntu] *m* investment.
investir [54] [ĩve∫'t∫i(x)] <> *vt* -1. [dinheiro, verba]
to invest. -2. [empossar]: ~ **alguém diretor da em-**
presa to install sb as director of a company. <>
vi -1. [aplicar dinheiro, verba]: ~ **(em algo)** to invest
(in sthg). -2. [atacar]: ~ **contra algo** to storm
sthg. -3. [atirar-se]: ~ **para algo** to rush to sthg.
inveterado, da [ĩnvete'radu, da] *adj* [muito antigo]
inveterate.
inviabilidade [ĩnvjabili'dadʒi] *f* impracticabili-
ty.
inviabilizar [4] [ĩvjabili'za(x)] *vt* to make unviable.
   ➡ **inviabilizar-se** *vp* to become unviable.
inviável [ĩn'vjavɛw] (*pl* -eis) *adj* unviable.
invicto, ta [ĩn'viktu, ta] *adj* unbeaten.
inviolabilidade [ĩnviolabili'dadʒi] *f* inviolabili-
ty.
inviolável [ĩnvjo'lavew] (*pl* -eis) *adj* inviolable.
invisível [ĩnvi'zivew] (*pl* -eis) *adj* invisible.
in vitro [‚in'vitru] *loc adj* in vitro.

invocação [ĩvo'kasãw] (*pl* -ões) *f* invocation.

invocado, da [ĩvo'kadu, dal *adj fam* -**1.** [irritado] annoyed. -**2.** [cismado] preoccupied. -**3.** [incomum] bizarre. -**4.** [inconstante] inconsistent.

invocar [12] [ĩvo'ka(x)l <> *vt* -**1.** [chamar] to invoke. -**2.** *fam* [irritar] to wind up, to annoy. <> *vi fam* [antipatizar]: ~ **com alguém** to dislike sb.

invólucro [ĩn'vɔlukrul *m* -**1.** [envoltório] envelope. -**2.** [membrana] membrane. -**3.** [caixa] casing.

involuntário, ria [ĩnvolũn'tarju, rjal *adj* involuntary.

invulnerável [ĩvuwne'ravewl (*pl* -eis) *adj* invulnerable.

iodo [ˈjodul *m* iodine.

IOF (*abrev de* Imposto sobre Operações Financeiras) *m Brazilian tax on financial transactions.*

ioga [ˈjɔgal *f* yoga.

iogue [ˈjɔgil <> *adj* yoga (*antes de subst*). <> *mf* yogi.

iogurte [ju'guxtʃil *m* yoghurt.

ioiô [jo'jol *m* yo-yo.

íon [ˈiõl (*pl* íons) *m* ion.

ionizar [joni'za(x)l *vt* to ionize.

IPC (*abrev de* Índice de Preços ao Consumidor) *m* consumer price index.

IPEM (*abrev de* Instituto de Pesos e Medidas) *m Brazilian institute of weights and measures.*

IPTU (*abrev de* Imposto Predial e Territorial Urbano) *m annual tax based on the value of a house.*

IPVA (*abrev de* Imposto sobre Propriedade de Veículos Automotores) *m tax paid annually on the value of a car*, ≃ road tax UK.

ir [66] [ˈi(x)l *vi* -**1.** [deslocar-se] to go; **fomos de ônibus** we went by bus; **iremos a pé** we'll go on foot, we'll walk; **vamos?** shall we go? -**2.** [assistir, freqüentar] to go; **ele nunca vai às reuniões** he never goes to the meetings; **você não vai à aula?** aren't you going to your class?; **vou ao cinema muitas vezes** I often go to the cinema. -**3.** [estender-se] to go; **o caminho vai até ao lago** the path leads to the lake. -**4.** [desenrolar-se] to go; **isto não vai nada bem** this isn't going at all well; **como vai você?** how are you?; **como vão as coisas?** how are things?; **os negócios vão mal** business is bad. -**5.** [exprime duração gradual]: ~ **fazendo algo** to continue doing sthg; **vá tentando!** keep trying! -**6.** [seguido de infinitivo]: **vou falar com ele** I'll speak to him; **você vai gostar** you'll like it; **não vou fazer nada** I'm not going to do anything. -**7.** [seguido de gerúndio]: **eu ia caindo** I almost fell. -**8.** [em locuções]: ~ **dar em** [desembocar] to lead to; ~ **ter com** [encontrar] to go and meet up with.

◆ **ir de** *v* + *prep* [ir disfarçado] to go as; [escolher]: **eu vou de filé com fritas, e você?** I'll have the steak and fries, what about you?

◆ **ir por** *v* + *prep* [auto-estrada, escadas] to take; ~ **pela esquerda/direita** to go (on the) left/right; ~ **pelo jardim** to go through the garden.

◆ **ir-se** *vp* [partir] to go; **ele já se foi** he's already left; ~**-se embora** to leave; **vai-te embora!** go away!

IR (*abrev de* Imposto de Renda) *m* income tax.

ira [ˈiral *f* anger.

Irã [iˈrãl *m*: (o) ~ Iran.

irado, da [iˈradu, dal *adj* angry.

iraniano, na [iraˈnjãnu, nal <> *adj* Iranian. <> *m, f* Iranian.

Iraque [iˈrakil *n*: (o) ~ Iraq.

iraquiano, na [iraˈkjanu, nal <> *adj* Iraqi. <> *m, f* Iraqi.

irascível [iraˈsivewl (*pl* -eis) *adj* irascible.

ir-e-vir [iriˈvi(x)l (*pl* ires-e-vires) *m* coming and going.

iridescente [irideˈsẽntʃil *adj* iridescent.

íris [ˈiriʃl *f inv* iris.

Irlanda [ixˈlãndal *n* Ireland; ~ **do Norte** Northern Ireland.

irlandês, esa [ixlãnˈdeʃ, ezal (*mpl* -eses, *fpl* -s) <> *adj* Irish. <> *m, f* Irishman (*f* Irishwoman).

◆ **irlandês** *m* [língua] Irish.

irmã [ixˈmãl *f* ▷ **irmão**.

irmanar [4] [ixmaˈna(x)l *vt* to unite (as brothers).

◆ **irmanar-se** *vp*: ~**-se com algo/alguém** to join with sthg/sb.

irmandade [ixmãnˈdaʒil *f* -**1.** [RELIG - de irmãos] brotherhood; [- de irmãs] sisterhood. -**2.** [confraternidade] fraternity.

irmão, mã [ixˈmãw, mãl *m, f* -**1.** [parente] brother (sister); ~ **de criação** stepbrother; ~ **gêmeo** twin brother; **irmãos siameses** siamese twins. -**2.** [afim] twin.

ironia [iroˈnial *f* irony.

irônico, ca [iˈroniku, kal *adj* ironic.

ironizar [4] [ironiˈza(x)l *vt* & *vi* to mock.

IRPF (*abrev de* Imposto de Renda de Pessoa Física) *m income tax paid by individuals.*

IRPJ (*abrev de* Imposto de Renda de Pessoa Jurídica) *m corporation tax.*

irracional [ixasjoˈnawl (*pl* -ais) *adj* irrational.

irracionalidade [ixasjonaliˈdaʒil *f* irrationality.

irradiação [ixadʒjaˈsãwl (*pl* -ões) *f* -**1.** [transmissão] broadcast. -**2.** [propagação] diffusion. -**3.** MED irradiation.

irradiar [16] [ixaˈdʒja(x)l *vt* -**1.** [transmitir] to broadcast. -**2.** [propagar] to spread. -**3.** *fig* [externar] to radiate.

◆ **irradiar-se** *vp* -**1.** [difundir-se] to be spread about. -**2.** [transmitir-se] to be broadcast.

irreal [iˈxjawl (*pl* -ais) *adj* unreal.

irrealizado, da [ixealiˈzadu, dal *adj* unrealized.

irrealizável [ixealiˈzavewl (*pl* -eis) *adj* unachievable.

irreconciliável [ixekõnsiˈljavɛwl (*pl* -eis) *adj* irreconcilable.

irreconhecível [ixekoɲeˈsivewl (*pl* -eis) *adj* unrecognizable.

irrecorrível [ixekoˈxivewl (*pl* -eis) *adj* [sentença] unappealable.

irrecuperável [ixekupeˈravɛw] (pl -eis) adj irrecoverable.

irrecusável [ixekuˈzavew] (pl -eis) adj which cannot be refused.

irredutível [ixeduˈtʃivew] (pl -eis) adj indomitable.

irrefletido, da [ixefleˈtʃidu, da] adj rash.

irrefreável [ixefreˈavew] (pl -eis) adj irrepressible.

irrefutável [ixefuˈtavew] (pl-eis) adj irrefutable.

irregular [ixeguˈla(x)] (pl -es) adj -**1.** [desigual] irregular. -**2.** [pouco convencional] unorthodox. -**3.** [irrecuperável] incurable.

irregularidade [ixegulariˈdaʒi] f -**1.** [inconstância] unreliability. -**2.** [procedimento irregular] irregularity.

irrelevância [ixeleˈvãnsja] f irrelevance.

irrelevante [ixeleˈvãntʃi] adj irrelevant.

irremediável [ixemeˈdʒjavɛw] (pl -eis) adj irreparable.

irremediavelmente [ixemedjavewˈmẽntʃi] adv irremediably.

irremovível [ixemoˈvivew] (pl -eis) adj immovable; **ser/estar** ~ **em algo** to be immovable in sthg.

irreparável [ixepaˈravew] (pl -eis) adj irreparable.

irrepreensível [ixeprjẽnˈsivew] (pl -eis) adj irreproachable.

irreprimível [ixepriˈmivɛw] (pl-eis) adj irrepressible.

irrequietação [ixikjetaˈsãw] f restlessness.

irrequieto, ta [ixeˈkjɛtu, ta] adj [desassossegado] restless.

irresistível [ixeziʃˈtʃivew] (pl-eis) adj irresistible.

irresoluto, ta [ixezoˈlutu, ta] adj irresolute.

irresponsabilidade [ixeʃpõsabiliˈdaʒil f irresponsibility.

irresponsável [ixeʃpõnˈsavɛw] (pl -eis) <> adj irresponsible. <> mf irresponsible person.

irrestrito, ta [ixeʃˈtritu, ta] adj unlimited, limitless.

irreverência [ixeveˈrẽnsja] f irreverence.

irreverente [ixeveˈrẽntʃi] adj irreverent.

irreversível [ixevexˈsivew] (pl -eis) adj irreversible.

irrevogável [ixevoˈgavew] (pl -eis) adj irrevocable.

irrigação [ixigaˈsãw] (pl-ões) f irrigation.

irrigar [14] [ixiˈga(x)] vt to irrigate.

irrisório, ria [ixiˈzɔrju, rja] adj -**1.** [de zombaria] derisory. -**2.** fig [ínfimo] derisory.

irritabilidade [ixitabiliˈdaʒil f irritability.

irritação [ixitaˈsãw] (pl-ões) f irritation.

irritadiço, ça [ixitaˈdʒisu, sa] adj irritable.

irritante [ixiˈtãntʃi] adj irritating.

irritar [4] [ixiˈta(x)] vt to irritate.
  ➡ **irritar-se** vp [exasperar-se] to become irritated.

irritável [ixiˈtavew] (pl-eis) adj irritable.

irromper [5] [ixõmˈpe(x)] vi -**1.** [entrar]: ~ **em** to burst into. -**2.** [surgir]: ~ **de** to surge from; ~ **em** to break out.

isca [ˈiʃka] f-**1.** [ger] bait. -**2.** CULIN morsel.

isenção [izẽnˈsãw] (pl -ões) f -**1.** [dispensa] exemption. -**2.** [livramento] release. -**3.** [imparcialidade] impartiality.

isentar [4] [izẽnˈta(x)] vt -**1.** [dispensar]: ~ **alguém de algo/de fazer algo** to exempt sb from sthg/from doing sthg. -**2.** [livrar]: ~ **alguém de algo/fazer algo** to let sb off from sthg/from doing sthg.
  ➡ **isentar-se** vp to free o.s.

isento, ta [iˈzẽntu, ta] adj -**1.** [dispensado] exempt. -**2.** [livre] free. -**3.** [imparcial] unbiased.

Islã [izˈlã] m Islam.

Islamabad [izlamaˈbadʒil n Islamabad.

islâmico, ca [izˈlamiku, ka] adj Islamic.

islamismo [izlaˈmiʒmul m Islam.

islamita [izlaˈmita] <> adj Islamic. <> mf Islamist.

islandês, esa [izlãnˈdeʃ, eza] <> adj Icelandic. <> m, f Icelander.
  ➡ **islandês** m [língua] Icelandic.

Islândia [izˈlãndʒja] f Iceland.

ISO (abrev de **International Standards Organization**) f ISO.

isolacionismo [izolasjoˈniʒmul m isolationism.

isolado, da [izoˈladu, da] adj -**1.** [separado] isolated. -**2.** [só] lone. -**3.** [afastado] remote. -**4.** ELETR insulated.

isolamento [izolaˈmẽntul m -**1.** [ger] isolation. -**2.** ELETR insulation.

isolante [izoˈlãntʃil <> adj ELETR insulating. <> m insulator.

isolar [4] [izoˈla(x)] <> vt -**1.** [ger] to isolate; ~ **algo de algo** to isolate sthg from sthg. -**2.** ELETR to insulate. <> vi [afastar mau agouro]: **isola!** touch wood!
  ➡ **isolar-se** vp [afastar-se]: ~-**se de alguém/algo** to isolate o.s from sb/sthg.

isonomia [izonoˈmia] f equality.

isopor [izoˈpox] m polystyrene.

isqueiro [iʃˈkejrul m lighter.

Israel [iʒxaˈɛw] n Israel.

israelense [iʒxaeˈlẽnsil, **israelita** [iʒxaeˈlita] <> adj Israeli. <> mf Israeli.

isso [ˈisul <> pron that; **é isso aí!** that's right!; **foi por isso que ele não veio** that's why he didn't come; **é por isso mesmo que en não vou!** that is exactly why I'm not going!; **isso não!** no way!; **não gosto disso** I don't like that; **não mexa nisso!** leave that alone!
  ➡ **por isso** loc adv therefore; **mem por** ~ not really.

Istambul [iʃtãnˈbuwl n Istanbul.

istmo [ˈiʃtʃimul m isthmus.

isto [ˈiʃtul pron this; **disto eu não quero** I don't want any of this; **escreva nisto** write on this; **isto é** [quer dizer] that is (to say); **isto é que é vida!** this is the life!

Itália [iˈtalja] n Italy.

italiano, na [ita'ljanu, na] ◇ *adj* Italian. ◇ *m, f* Italian.
➡ **italiano** *m* [língua] Italian.
itálico, ca [i'taliku, ka] *adj TIPO* italic.
➡ **itálico** *m TIPO* italic.
Itamarati [itamara'tʃi] *m* Brazilian foreign ministry.
item ['itɛ] (*pl* **itens**) *m* -**1**. [ger] item. -**2**. *JUR* [artigo] point.
itinerante [itʃine'rãntʃi] ◇ *adj* itinerant. ◇ *mf* itinerant.
itinerário [itʃine'rarju] *m* -**1**. [roteiro] route. -**2**. [caminho] itinerary.
Iugoslávia [iwgo'ʒlavja] *f* Yugoslavia; **a ex-~** the ex-Yugoslavia.
iugoslavo, va [iwgoʒ'lavu, va] ◇ *adj* Yugoslav. ◇ *m, f* Yugoslav.

j, J ['ʒɔta] *m* [letra] j, J.
já ['ʒa] ◇ *adv* -**1**. [ger] already. -**2**. [agora] now. -**3**. [sem demora] just; **~ vou** just coming. -**4**. [até mesmo] even. -**5**. [daqui a pouco] soon; **até ~** see you soon. -**6**. [alguma vez] ever. ◇ *conj* however. ◇ *loc*: **~ era!** *fam* that's history!
➡ **desde já** *loc prep* from now on.
➡ **já que** *loc conj* since.
jabuti [ʒabu'tʃi] *m* jabuti, *indigenous Brazilian tortoise.*
jabuticaba [ʒabutʃi'kaba] *f* jaboticaba, *Brazilian evergreen tree or the fruit of this tree.*
jaca ['ʒaka] *f* jack fruit.
jacarandá [ʒakarãn'da] *f* jacaranda.
jacaré [ʒaka'rɛ] *m* -**1**. *ZOOL* Yacare caiman. -**2**. [surfe]: **pegar ~** to surf.
Jacarta [ʒa'kaxta] *n* Djakarta, Jakarta.
jacinto [ʒa'sĩntu] *m* hyacinth.
jactância [ʒak'tãnsja] *f* -**1**. [vaidade] boasting. -**2**. [arrogância] arrogance.
jactar-se [7] [ʒak'taxsi] *vp*: **~-se (de)** to boast (about).
jade ['ʒadʒi] *m* jade.
jaguar [ʒa'gwa(x)] (*pl* **-es**) *m* jaguar.
jaguatirica [ʒagwatʃi'rika] *f* leopard.
jagunço [ʒa'gũsu] *m* bodyguard.
jaleco [ʒa'lɛku] *m* coat.
Jamaica [ʒa'majka] *f* Jamaica.
jamais [ʒa'majʃ] *adv* never; *(com palavra negativa)* ever.

jamanta [ʒa'mãnta] *f* [caminhão] articulated truck.
jan. (*abrev de* **janeiro**) Jan.
janeiro [ʒa'nejru] *m* January; *veja também* **setembro**.
janela [ʒa'nɛla] *f* window.
janelão [ʒane'lãw] (*pl* **-ões**) *m* picture window.
jangada [ʒãŋ'gada] *f* raft.
jangadeiro, ra [ʒãŋga'dejru, ra] *m, f* raft owner.
janta ['ʒãnta] *f* dinner.
jantar [4] [ʒãn'ta(x)] (*pl* **-es**) ◇ *vt* to have for dinner. ◇ *vi* to have dinner. ◇ *m* dinner; **~ americano** buffet dinner.
Japão [ʒa'pãw] *n*: **(o) ~** Japan.
japona [ʒa'pona] *f* jacket.
japonês, esa [ʒapo'neʃ, eza] (*mpl* **-eses**, *fpl* **-s**) ◇ *adj* Japanese. ◇ *m, f* Japanese person.
➡ **japonês** *m* [língua] Japanese.
jaqueta [ʒa'keta] *f* jacket.
jaquetão [ʒake'tãw] (*pl* **-ões**) *m* double-breasted jacket.
jararaca [ʒara'raka] *f* -**1**. [cobra] viper. -**2**. *fig* [pessoa] harridan.
jarda ['ʒaxda] *f* yard.
jardim [ʒax'dʒĩ] (*pl* **-ns**) *m* garden; **~ botânico** botanical garden; **~ zoológico** zoo.
jardim-de-infância [ʒaxdʒĩndʒĩfãnsja] (*pl* **jardins-de-infância**) *m* kindergarten.
jardim-de-inverno [ʒaxdʒĩndʒĩvexnu] (*pl* **jardins-de-inverno**) *m* conservatory.
jardinagem [ʒaxdʒi'naʒẽ] *f* gardening.
jardineiro, ra [ʒaxdʒi'nejru, ra] *m, f* [pessoa] gardener.
➡ **jardineira** *f* -**1**. [móvel] jardinière. -**2**. [em parapeito] window box. -**3**. [roupa] overalls *(pl)*.
jargão [ʒax'gãw] (*pl* **-ões**) *m* jargon.
jarra ['ʒaxa] *f* [pote] carafe; [vaso] vase.
jarro ['ʒaxu] *m* jug.
jasmim [ʒaʒ'mĩ] (*pl* **-ns**) *m* jasmine.
jato ['ʒatu] *m* -**1**. [raio] beam. -**2**. [avião] jet. -**3**. [propulsão]: **a ~** jet propelled. -**4**. [jorro] stream.
jaula ['ʒawla] *f* cage.
Java ['ʒava] *n* Java.
javali [ʒava'li] *m* wild boar.
jazer [33] [ʒa'ze(x)] *vi* -**1**. [estar sepultado] to lie. -**2**. [estar deitado] to be lying.
jazida [ʒa'zida] *f* seam.
jazigo [ʒa'zigu] *m* grave.
jazz ['ʒajʃ] *m* jazz.
jazzista [ʒa'ziʃta] *mf* jazz artist.
JC (*abrev de* **Jesus Cristo**) *m* JC.
jeans ['ʒĩʃ] *m inv* jeans *(pl)*.
jeca ['ʒɛka] *adj* rustic.
jeca-tatu ['ʒɛkatatu] (*pl* **-tus**) *m character from children's literature representing the village people of the Brazilian interior.*
jegue ['ʒɛgi] *m* ass.
jeitinho [ʒej'tʃiɲu] *m* touch; **dar um ~** to get something done one way or another.

JEITINHO BRASILEIRO

One of the more striking characteristics of the Brazilian people is their ability to rise to any occasion. Brazilians' adaptability to challenges and new situations is a cultural trait expressed in the famous *jeitinho brasileiro*, the belief that they will always have a special knack (*jeitinho*) for getting out of a tricky situation.

jeito ['ʒejtu] *m* **-1.** [modo] way; **ao ~ de** in the manner of; **de ~ algum!** no way!; **de qualquer ~** anyway; [sem cuidado] any old how. **-2.** [aspecto] air. **-3.** [índole] disposition. **-4.** [torção]: **dar um mau ~ em** to sprain. **-5.** [propensão]: **ter** *ou* **levar ~ para (fazer) algo** to be good at (doing) sthg. **-6.** [habilidade] aptitude; **falta de ~** clumsiness; **ter falta de ~ para (fazer) algo** to be bad at (doing) sthg. **-7.** [diplomacia] tact; **fazer algo com ~** to do sthg carefully. **-8.** [graça]: **ficar sem ~** to feel embarrassed. **-9.** [arrumação] clean up; **dar um ~ em algo** to tidy up. **-10.** [solução] solution; **dar um ~ em algo** to do something about sthg. **-11.** [corretivo]: **dar um ~ em alguém** to set sb straight. **-12.** [juízo]: **tomar ~** to grow up.

jeitoso, osa [ʒej'tozu, ɔza] *adj* **-1.** [habilidoso] dexterous. **-2.** [funcional] practical. **-3.** [diplomático] tactful.

jejuar [4] [ʒe'ʒwa(x)] *vi* to fast.

jejum [ʒe'ʒũl (*pl* -ns) *m* fast; **em ~** fasting.

Jeová [ʒeo'val *m*: **testemunha de ~** Jehovah's Witness.

jerico [ʒe'riku] *m* donkey; **idéia de ~** stupid idea.

jérsei ['ʒɛxsej] *m* jersey.

Jerusalém [ʒeruza'lẽ] *n* Jerusalem.

jesuíta [ʒe'zwita] <> *adj* Jesuit. <> *m* Jesuit.

jesuítico, ca [ʒezu'itʃiku, ka] *adj* [período, missão] Jesuitical.

jesus [ʒe'zuʃ] *interj* (good) heavens!

jetom [ʒe'tõl (*pl* -ns) *m* **-1.** [remuneração] payment. **-2.** [ficha] jetton.

jet set [ʒɛt'sɛtʃil *m* jet set.

jet ski [ʒɛtʃiʃ'kil (*pl* jet skis) *m* jet ski.

jibóia [ʒi'bɔja] *f* [cobra] boa.

jiboiar [4] [ʒibo'ja(x)] *vi* to rest and digest after a big meal.

jiló [ʒi'lɔ] *m* type of Brazilian vegetable.

jingle ['ʒĩngow] *m* jingle.

jipe ['ʒipil *m* jeep.

jiu-jitsu [ʒu'ʒitsu] *m* jiu-jitsu.

joalheiro, ra [ʒoa'ʎejru, ra] *m, f* jeweller *UK*, jeweler *US*.

joalheria [ʒwaʎe'ria] *f* jewellers *UK*, jewelers *US*.

joanete [ʒwa'netʃil *m* bunion.

joaninha [ʒwa'niɲa] *f* **-1.** [inseto] ladybird. **-2.** [carro de polícia] patrol car.

joão-ninguém [ʒuãwnĩ'gẽl (*pl* joões-ninguém) *m*: **um ~** a nobody, a nonentity.

joça ['ʒɔsal *f fam* mess.

jocoso, sa [ʒoko'zu, za] *adj* [divertido, cômico] jocular.

joelheira [ʒwe'ʎeira] *f ESP* knee-pad.

joelho ['ʒweʎul *m* knee; **de ~s** kneeling, on one's knees; **ficar de ~s** to kneel down.

jogada [ʒo'gadal *f* **-1.** [*ESP* - tática] strategy; [- lance] shot. **-2.** *fam* [esquema] scam. **-3.** *fam* [intenção] intention. **-4.** *loc*: **tirar alguém da ~** to eliminate sb from the equation.

jogado, da [ʒo'gadu, da] *adj* thrown.

jogador, ra [ʒoga'do(x), ra] *m, f* **-1.** [atleta] player; **~ de futebol** football player. **-2.** [apostador] gambler.

jogar [14] [ʒo'ga(x)] <> *vt* **-1.** [tomar parte em jogo de] to play. **-2.** [atirar] to throw. **-3.** [apostar]: **~ algo em algo** to gamble sthg on sthg. **-4.** [desfazer-se de]: **~ algo fora** to throw sthg out. **-5.** [desperdiçar]: **~ algo fora** to throw around. <> *vi* **-1.** [divertir-se num jogo] to play. **-2.** [apostar]: **~ em algo** to bet on sthg. **-3.** [na Bolsa]: **~ em** to speculate on. **-4.** [manipular]: **~ com algo** to play around with sthg. **-5.** [balançar] to toss.

➡ **jogar-se** *vp* **-1.** [lançar-se] to throw o.s. **-2.** [paquerar]: **~-se para cima de alguém** to be all over sb.

jogatina [ʒoga'tʃina] *f* gambling.

jogging ['ʒɔgĩ] *m* **-1.** [corrida] jogging; **fazer ~ to** go jogging. **-2.** [roupa] tracksuit.

jogo ['ʒogul (*pl* jogos) *m* **-1.** [ger] game; **~ limpo** clean game; **~ de azar** game of chance. **-2.** [partida] match. **-3.** [vício de jogar] gambling. **-4.** [conjunto] collection. **-5.** [aposta] bet. **-6.** *MEC* set. **-7.** *fig* [ardil] ruse. **-8.** [manipulação] play. **-9.** [movimentação] movement. **-10.** [balanço] tossing. **-11.** *AUTO* running. **-12.** *fam* [intenção] game. **-13.** *loc*: **abrir o ~** to lay one's cards on the table; **esconder o ~** to have a card up one's sleeve; **ter ~ de cintura para algo** to be quite capable of getting out of sthg.

jogo-da-velha [ˌʒoguda'vɛʎal (*pl* jogos-da-velha) *m* noughts and crosses *UK*, tic-tac-toe *US*.

joguete [ʒo'getʃil *m* plaything; **fazer alguém de ~** to make a laughing stock of sb.

jóia ['ʒɔjal <> *adj fam* delightful. <> *f* **-1.** [enfeite] jewel. **-2.** [taxa] fee.

joio ['ʒojul *m* darnel; **separar o ~ do trigo** to separate the wheat from the chaff.

jojoba [ʒo'ʒɔbal *f* jojoba.

jóquei ['ʒɔkej], **jóquei-clube** *m* Jockey Club.

jornada [ʒox'nadal *f* **-1.** [ger] journey. **-2.** [período] duration; **~ de trabalho** working day.

jornal [ʒox'naw] (*pl* -ais) *m* **-1.** [gazeta] newspaper. **-2.** [noticiário] news.

jornaleiro, ra [ʒoxna'lejru, ra] *m, f* [pessoa] newspaper vendor.

➡ **jornaleiro** *m* [banca] news-stand.

jornalista [ʒoxna'liʃtal *mf* journalist.

jornalístico, ca [ʒoxna'liʃtʃiku, ka] *adj* journalistic.

jorrar [4] [ʒo'xa(x)] <> *vt* to spurt. <> *vi* to gush.

jorro ['ʒoxul *m* torrent.

jovem ['ʒɔvẽl (*pl* -ns) <> *adj* **-1.** [juvenil] youthful. **-2.** [para jovens] young. <> *mf* young person.

jovial [ʒo'vjawl (*pl* -ais) *adj* jovial.

jovialidade [ʒovjali'dadʒil *f* joviality.

joystick [ʒɔj'ʃtʃik] (*pl* **joysticks**) *m* *COMPUT* joystick.

juazeiro [ʒwa'zejrul *m* jujube.

juba ['ʒubal *f* mane.

jubilação [ʒubila'sãw] (*pl* -ões) *UNIV f* **-1.** [aposentadoria] retirement. **-2.** [desligamento] suspension.

jubilado, da [ʒubi'ladu, da] *adj* [aluno] barred (*from a course for not having fulfilled the formal requirements*).

jubilar [4] [ʒubi'la(x)] *UNIV vt* **-1.** [aposentar] to retire. **-2.** [desligar] to suspend.

jubileu [ʒubi'lew] *m* jubilee; ~ **de prata** silver jubilee.

júbilo ['ʒubilul *m* elation.

jubiloso, osa [ʒubi'lozu, zal *adj* elated.

judaico, ca [ʒu'dajku, kal *adj* Jewish.

judaísmo [ʒuda'iʒmul *m* Judaism.

judas ['ʒudaʃl *m* Judas, traitor.

judeu, dia [ʒu'dew, dʒial <> *adj* Jewish. <> *m, f* Jewish person, Jew.

judiação [ʒudʒja'sãw] (*pl* -ões) *f* abuse, ill-treatment.

judiar [16] [ʒu'dʒja(x)] *vi:* ~ **de alguém** to abuse sb, to ill-treat sb.

judicial [ʒudʒi'sjaw] (*pl* -ais) *adj* judicial.

judiciário, ria [ʒudʒi'sjarju, rjal *adj* judicial.
Judiciário *m:* o ~ the judiciary.

judicioso, osa [ʒudʒi'sjozu, ɔzal *adj* judicious.

judô [ʒu'dol *m* judo.

judoca [ʒu'dɔkal *mf* judoka.

jugo ['ʒugul *m:* **sob o** ~ **de** under the yoke of.

juiz, íza ['ʒwiʃ, izal (*mpl* -es, *fpl* -s) *m, f* -**1.** *JUR* judge; ~ **de direito** district judge; ~ **de menores** judge in a juvenile court; ~ **de paz** justice of the peace. **-2.** *ESP* referee.

juizado [ʒuj'zadu, dal *m* court; ~ **de menores** juvenile court; ~ **de pequenas causas** small claims court.

juízo ['ʒwizul *m* -**1.** [julgamento] judgement. **-2.** [conceito] opinion. **-3.** [sensatez] prudence; **perder o** ~ to lose one's mind. **-4.** *JUR* [foro] tribunal.

Juízo Final [,ʒwizufi'nawl *m:* o ~ Judgement Day.

jujuba [ʒu'ʒubal *f* -**1.** *BOT* jujube. **-2.** [bala] *jujube-flavoured boiled sweet.*

jul. (*abrev de* **julho**) Jul.

julgador, ra [ʒuwga'do(x), ral <> *adj* judging. <> *m, f* judge.

julgamento [ʒuwga'mẽntul *m* **-1.** [juízo] judgement. **-2.** [audiência] hearing. **-3.** [sentença] sentence.

julgar [14] [ʒuw'ga(x)] *vt* **-1.** [sentenciar sobre] to judge. **-2.** [avaliar]: ~ **algo/alguém por algo** to judge sthg/sb by sthg. **-3.** [supor] to think; ~ **que** to think that.
julgar-se *vp* [supor-se] to consider o.s.

julho ['ʒuʎul *m* July; *veja também* **setembro**.

jumento [ʒu'mẽntul *m* donkey.

jun. (*abrev de* **junho**) Jun.

junção [ʒũn'sãwl (*pl* -ões) *f* -**1.** [união] union. **-2.** [ponto] junction.

junco [ʒũŋkul *m* reed.

junho ['ʒuɲul *m* June; *veja também* **setembro**.

junino, na [ʒu'ninu, nal *adj* ➢ **festa**.

júnior ['ʒunjo(x)] (*pl* **juniores**) <> *adj* junior. <> *mf* *ESP* junior.

junta [ʒũntal *f* -**1.** [comissão] council. **-2.** *POL* junta. **-3.** [articulação] joint. **-4.** [órgão]: ~ **comercial** chamber of commerce. **-5.** [parelha]: ~ **de bois** yoke of oxen.

juntamente [ʒũnta'mẽntʃil *adv:* ~ **com** together with.

juntar [4] [ʒũn'ta(x)] <> *vt* **-1.** [unir]: ~ **algo (a algo)** to mix sthg (with sthg). **-2.** [aproximar]: ~ **alguém (a alguém)** to unite sb (with sb). **-3.** [colocar junto] to mix (together). **-4.** [aglomerar] to assemble. **-5.** [recolher] to collect. <> *vi* [aglomerar-se] to cluster. <> *vi* [economizar]: ~ **(para)** to save (for).
juntar-se *vp* [associar-se]: ~**-se a** to mix with; ~**-se com** to unite o.s with.

junto, ta ['ʒũntu, tal <> *adj* together. <> *adv* at the same time; ~ **de** next to.
junto a, junto de *loc prep* next to.
junto com *loc prep* together.

jura ['ʒural *f* vow.

jurado, da [ʒu'radu, dal <> *adj* sworn. <> *m, f* juror.

juramentado, da [ʒuramẽn'tadu, dal *adj* under oath.

juramento [ʒura'mẽntul *m* oath; **fazer** ~ **a** to swear an oath to; **sob** ~ under oath.

jurar [4] [ʒu'ra(x)] <> *vt* -**1.** [prometer] to swear; ~ **fazer algo** to swear to do sthg; ~ **que** to swear that. **-2.** [sob juramento]: ~ **fazer algo** to take an oath to do sthg. <> *vi* [prestar juramento]: ~ **(por/sobre)** to swear (by/on).

júri ['ʒuril *m* jury.

jurídico, ca [ʒu'ridʒiku, kal *adj* legal.

jurisconsulto, ta [ʒurʃkõn'suwtu, tal *m, f* legal expert *UK*, jurist *US*.

jurisdição [ʒuriʒdʒi'sãwl *f* jurisdiction.

jurisprudência [ʒuriʃpru'dẽnsjal *f* jurisprudence.

jurista [ʒu'riʃtal *mf* legal expert *UK*, jurist *US*.

juros ['ʒuruʃl *mpl* interest (*sg*); **empréstimo a** ~/**sem** ~**s** loan with/without interest; ~ **acumulados** accumulated interest; ~ **fixos/variáveis** fixed/variable interest.

jururu [ʒuru'rul *adj* gloomy.

jus [ʒuʃl *m:* **fazer** ~ **a algo** to do justice to sthg.

jusante [ʒu'zãntʃil *f:* **a** ~ **de** downstream of.

justamente [ʒuʃta'mẽntʃil *adv* **-1.** [com justiça] rightly. **-2.** [precisamente] precisely.

justapor [45] [ʒuʃta'po(x)] *vt:* ~ **algo (a algo)** to juxtapose sthg (with sthg).
justapor-se *vp* to be juxtaposed.

justaposição [ʒuʃtapozi'sãwl (*pl* -ões) *f* juxtaposition.

justaposto, osta [ʒuʃta'poʃtu, ɔʃtal *pp* ➢ **justapor**.

justeza [ʒuʃ'teza] *f* precision.

justiça [ʒuʃ'tʃisa] *f* -**1.** [virtude] fairness; **com ~** justly; **fazer ~ a alguém/algo** to do justice to sb/sthg. -**2.** [eqüidade] equality; **~ social** social justice. -**3.** [tribunal] justice; **ir à ~** to go to court; **Justiça do Trabalho** Industrial Tribunal. -**4.** [poder judiciário]: **a Justiça** the judiciary.

justiceiro, ra [ʒuʃtʃi'sejru, ra] *adj* just.

justificação [ʒuʃtʃifika'sãw] (*pl* -ões) *f* justification.

justificar [12] [ʒuʃtʃifi'ka(x)] *vt* to justify.

➡ **justificar-se** *vp* [explicar-se]: **~-se por algo** to excuse o.s for sthg.

justificativa [ʒuʃtʃifika'tʃiva] *f* justification.

justificável [ʒuʃtʃifi'kavew] (*pl* -eis) *adj* justifiable.

justo, ta ['ʒuʃtu, ta] <> *adj* -**1.** [ger] fair. -**2.** [apertado] tight. -**3.** [exato] precise. -**4.** [merecido] just. <> *adv* just.

juta ['ʒutal *f* jute.

juvenil [ʒuve'niw] (*pl* -is) <> *adj* -**1.** [de jovens] youth, teenage. -**2.** *ESP* junior. <> *m ESP* [campeonato] junior.

juventude [ʒuvẽn'tudʒi] *f* youth.

k, K [ka] *m* [letra] k, K.

kafkiano, na [kaf'kianu, na] *adj* Kafkaesque.

Kalahari [kala'xari] *n*: **o deserto de ~** the Kalahari Desert.

Kampala [kãn'pala] *n* Kampala.

karaokê [karaw'ke] *m* -**1.** [atividade] karaoke. -**2.** [casa noturna] karaoke bar.

kardecismo [kaxde'siʒmu] *m religious doctrine of the Frenchman Allan Kardec.*

kart ['kaxtʃi] *m* go-cart.

kartódromo [kax'tɔdromu] *m* go-kart track.

Katmandu [katʃimãn'du] *n* Kathmandu.

Kb (*abrev de* **kilobyte**) *m* Kb.

kg (*abrev de* **quilograma**) *m* kg.

ketchup [kɛ'tʃupi] *m* (tomato) ketchup.

Khartum [kax'tũ] *n* Khartoum.

Kíev ['kjɛvi] *n* Kiev.

Kingston ['kiŋgiʃtõ] *n* Kingston.

Kinshasa [kin'ʃaza] *n* Kinshasa.

kit ['kitʃi] *m* kit.

kitchenette [kitʃi'nɛtʃi] *f* kitchenette.

kitsch [kitʃi] *adj inv* kitsch.

kiwi ['kiwi] *m* [fruta] kiwi fruit.

kl (*abrev de* **quilolitro**) *m* kl.

km (*abrev de* **quilômetro**) *m* km.

km/h (*abrev de* **quilômetro por hora**) *m* km/h.

know-how [now'haw] *m* know-how.

Kuala Lumpur [kwalalãn'pu(x)] *n* Kuala Lumpur.

Kuwait [ku'ajtʃi] *n* Kuwait.

kW (*abrev de* **kilowatt**) *m* kW.

l, L ['ɛli] *m* [letra] l, L.

-la [la] *pron* -**1.** [pessoa] her; -**2.** [coisa] it; -**3.** [você] you.

lá ['la] *adv* there; **quero lá saber!** what do I care!; **sei lá!** how should I know; **para lá de** beyond.

lã ['lã] *f* wool; **calça de ~** woollen trousers; **de pura ~** pure wool; **~ de camelo** camel hair.

labareda [laba'reda] *f* flame.

lábia ['labja] *f* [conversa] smooth talk; **ter ~** to have the gift of the gab.

labial [la'bjaw] (*pl* -ais) *adj* labial.

lábio ['labju] *m* [ANAT- beiço] lip; [- genital] labium; **~ leporino** harelip, cleft lip.

labirinto [labi'rĩntu] *m* labyrinth.

laborar [4] [labo'ra(x)] *vi*: **~ em erro** to make a mistake.

laboratorial [laborato'riaw] (*pl* -ais) *adj* laboratory *(antes de subst)*.

laboratório [labora'tɔrju] *m* laboratory; **~ de línguas** language laboratory.

laborioso, osa [labo'rjozu, ɔza] *adj* -**1.** [trabalhador] hard-working. -**2.** [trabalhoso] laborious.

labuta [la'buta] *f* toil.

labutar [4] [labu'ta(x)] *vi* to toil.

laca ['laka] *f* lacquer; **de ~** lacquered.

laçar [13] [la'sa(x)] *vt* [animal] to lasso.

laçarote [lasa'rɔtʃi] *m* large bow.

laço ['lasu] *m* -**1.** [nó] bow; **dar um ~ em algo** to tie a bow in sthg. -**2.** [para laçar animais] lasso. -**3.** *fig* [vínculo] tie; **~s de família** family ties.

lacônico, ca [la'kɔniku, ka] *adj* laconic.

lacraia [la'kraja] *f* centipede.

lacrar [4] [la'kra(x)] *vt* to seal.

lacre ['lakri] *m* sealing wax.

lacrimal [lakri'maw] (*pl* -ais) *adj* lachrymal.

lacrimejante [lakrime'ʒãntʃi] *adj* tearful.

lacrimejar [4] [lakrime'ʒa(x)] *vi* -**1.** [olhos] to water. -**2.** [pessoa] to weep.

lacrimogêneo, nea [lakrimo'ʒenju, njal *adj* ▷ gás.

lacrimoso, osa [lakri'mozu, ɔzal *adj* [olhos] tearful.

lactação [lakta'sãwl (*pl* -ões) *f* [amamentação] lactation.

lactante [lak'tãntʃil ◇ *adj* lactating. ◇ *f* nursing woman.

lácteo, tea ['laktju, tjal *adj* -1. [produto] milky. -2. ▷ via.

lactose [lak'tɔzil *f* lactose.

lacuna [la'kunal *f* -1. [vão] gap. -2. [espaço em branco] blank. -3. [omissão] omission.

ladainha [lada'iɲal *f* -1. [oração] litany. -2. *fig* [lengalenga] rigmarole.

ladear [15] [la'dʒa(x)l *vt* -1. [ger] to flank. -2. [correr paralelo a] to run alongside. -3. *fig* [contornar] to skirt.

ladeira [la'dejral *f* -1. [rampa] slope. -2. [rua íngreme] steep road.

ladino, na [la'dʒinu, nal *adj* [esperto] sharp.

lado ['ladul *m* -1. [ger] side; **do ~ avesso** inside out; **estar do ~ de alguém** to be on sb's side; **por um ~ ... por outro ~** on the one hand ... on the other hand. -2. [direção, local] direction; **de todos os ~ s** everywhere; **de um ~ para outro** from one side to the other; **do ~ de fora** outside.
➡ **ao lado** *loc adv* -1. [na casa adjacente] next door. -2. [próximo] close by.
➡ **ao lado de** *loc prep* next to.
➡ **de lado** *loc adv* [sentar, andar] on the side; **deixar algo de ~** [pôr de reserva] to put sthg aside; [desconsiderar] to drop sthg; **deixar alguém de ~** [ignorar] to ignore sb; **olhar alguém de ~** [desdenhar] to look down on sb.

ladrão, ladra [la'drãw, 'ladral (*mpl* -ões, *fpl* -s) ◇ *adj* thieving. ◇ *m*, *f* thief; **~ de loja** shoplifter.
➡ **ladrão** *m* [tubo] overflow pipe.

ladrar [4] [la'dra(x)l *vi* to bark.

ladrilhar [4] [ladri'ɲa(x)l *vt* to tile.

ladrilheiro, ra [ladri'ɲejru, ral *m*, *f* tiler.

ladrilho [la'driʎul *m* tile.

ladroagem [la'drwaʒẽl (*pl* -ns), **ladroeira** [la'drwejral *f* theft, robbery.

ladrões [la'drõjʃl *pl* ▷ ladrão.

lagarta [la'gaxtal *f* ZOOL caterpillar.

lagartixa [lagax'tʃiʃal *f* (small) lizard.

lagarto [la'gaxtul *m* ZOOL lizard.

lago ['lagul *m* -1. GEOGR lake. -2. [de jardim] pond. -3. *fig* [poça] puddle; **a cozinha está um ~** the kitchen is flooded.

lagoa [la'goal flake.

lagosta [la'goʃtal *f* lobster.

lagostim [lagoʃ'tʃil (*pl* -ns) *m* crayfish.

lágrima ['lagrimal *f* tear; **derramar ~s** to cry.

laguna [la'gunal *f* lagoon.

laia ['lajal *f* kind, type.

laico, ca ['lajku, kal *adj* -1. [pessoa] lay. -2. [ensino] secular.

laje ['laʒil *f* -1. [pedra] flagstone. -2. CONSTR concrete flooring.

lajear [15] [la'ʒja(x)l *vt* to pave.

lajota [la'ʒɔtal *f* small flagstone.

lama ['lãmal *f* -1. [ger] mud. -2. *fig* [má situação]: **tirar alguém da ~** to help s.o. out of trouble.

lamaçal [lama'sawl (*pl* -ais), **lamaceiro** [lama'sejrul *m* muddy place.

lamacento, ta [lama'sẽtu, tal *adj* muddy.

lambada [lãn'badal *f* -1. [golpe] blow. -2. *fig* [descompostura] telling-off. -3. [dança] lambada.

lambança [lãn'bãnsal *f* mess.

lamber [5] [lãm'be(x)l *vt* to lick.

lambida [lãn'bidal *f* lick; **dar uma ~ em algo** to have a lick of sthg, to lick sthg.

lambido, da [lãm'bidu, dal *adj* -1. [cara] clean. -2. [cabelo] straight.

lambiscar [12] [lãmbiʃ'ka(x)l ◇ *vt* to nibble. ◇ *vi* to pick.

lambreta® [lãn'bretal *f* motor scooter.

lambri [lãn'bril (*pl* -bris) *m* panelling.

lambuja [lãn'buʒal *f* [vantagem] advantage.

lambuzar [4] [lãmbu'za(x)l *vt*: **~ alguém/algo (de com algo)** to cover sb/sthg (in sthg).

lambuzeira [lãnbu'zejral *f* mess.

lamentação [lamẽta'sãwl (*pl* -ões) *f* complaint.

lamentar [4] [lamẽn'ta(x)l *vt* to regret; **lamento muito, mas ...** I am very sorry, but ...; **lamentamos comunicar-lhe ...** we regret to inform you ...
➡ **lamentar-se** *vp*: **~-se (de algo)** [lastimar-se] to feel sorry (about sthg).

lamentável [lamẽn'tavɛwl (*pl* -eis) *adj* -1. [lastimável] regrettable. -2. [deplorável] deplorable.

lamentavelmente [lamẽntavew'mẽntʃil *adv* unfortunately.

lamento [la'mẽntul *m* lament.

lâmina ['lãminal *f* -1. [ger] blade; **~ de barbear** razor blade. -2. [de vidro] slide.

laminado, da [lami'nadu, dal *adj* laminated.
➡ **laminado** *m* laminate.

laminar [4] [lami'na(x)l *vt* [reduzir a lâminas] to shave.

lâmpada ['lãnpadal *f* -1. [bulbo] light; **~ (elétrica)** (light) bulb; **~ fluorescente** fluorescent light bulb; **~ neon** neon light. -2. [aparelho] lamp; **~ de mesa** table lamp.

lamparina [lãnpa'rinal *f* [aparelho] blowlamp.

lampejar [4] [lãmpe'ʒa(x)l *vi* to flash.

lampejo [lãn'peʒul *m* flash.

lampião [lãn'pjãwl (*pl* -ões) *m* street light.

lamúria [la'murjal *f* lamentation.

lamuriante [lamu'rjãntʃil *adj* whining.

lamuriar-se [16] [lamu'rjaxsil *vp*: **~ (de algo)** to moan (about sthg).

LAN (*abrev de* **Local Area Network**) *f* LAN.

lança ['lãnsal *f* spear.

lançador, ra [lãnsa'do(x), ral *m*, *f* -1. ESP thrower. -2. [em leilão] bidder. -3. COM promoter.

lançamento [lãnsa'mẽntul *m* -1. [arremesso] throw. -2. ESP: **~ de dardos** to play darts; **~ de disco** discus throwing. -3. [ger] launch; **novo ~** [livro] new title. -4. [escrituração] entry. -5. [de impostos] rate.

lança-perfume [ˌlãnsapex'fumil (*pl*lança-perfumes) *m canister of perfumed ethyl chloride used during carnival.*

lançar [13] [lã'sa(x)] *vt* -**1.** [ger] to launch. -**2.** [atirar] to throw. -**3.** [pôr em voga] to start. -**4.** [escriturar] to enter. -**5.** [impostos] to set. -**6.** [dirigir] to cast.

➡ **lançar-se** *vp* -**1.** [atirar-se] to throw o.s. -**2.** [iniciar-se]: ~-**se em algo** to take up sthg; ~-**se como algo** to set o.s.up as sthg.

lance ['lãnsil] *m* -**1.** [episódio, passagem] moment. -**2.** [fato] incident. -**3.** [em leilão] bid. -**4.** [no jogo - aposta] bet; [- jogada] play. -**5.** [de escada] staircase. -**6.** [de casas] terrace. -**7.** [rasgo] surge.

lancha ['lãnʃal *f* -**1.** NÁUT launch; ~ **salva-vidas** lifeboat. -**2.** *fam* [pé] large foot. -**3.** *fam* [calçado] large shoe; **este sapato está uma** ~ this shoe is like a boat.

lanchar [4] [lã'ʃa(x)] ◇ *vt* to snack on. ◇ *vi* to have tea.

lanche ['lãnʃil *m* [refeição ligeira] snack (*in the afternoon).*

lancheira [lãn'ʃejral *f* lunch box.

lanchonete [lãnʃo'nɛtʃil *f* snack bar.

lancinante [lãnsi'nãntʃil *adj* piercing.

languidez [lãngi'deʒl *f* [debilitação] langour.

lânguido, da ['lãngidu, dal *adj* languid.

lanhar [4] [la'ɲa(x)] *vt* [ferir] to scratch.

➡ **lanhar-se** *vp* [ferir-se] to scratch o.s.

lanho ['lãɲul *m* scratch.

lanígero, ra [la'niʒeru, ral *adj* [animal] woolly.

lanolina [lãno'linal *f* lanolin.

lantejoula [lãnte'ʒolal *f* sequin.

lanterna [lãn'tɛxnal *f* -**1.** [aparelho] lantern; ~ **elétrica** torch *UK*, flashlight *US*. -**2.** AUTO light.

lanterninha [lãntex'niɲal *mf* usher.

laparoscopia [laparoʃko'pial *f* laparoscopy.

La Paz [la'paʃl *n* La Paz.

lapela [la'pɛlal *f* lapel.

lapidar [4] [lapi'da(x)] *vt* to polish.

lápide ['lapidʒil *f* -**1.** [comemorativa] plaque. -**2.** [tumular] tombstone.

lápis ['lapiʃl *m inv* pencil; ~ **de cera** wax crayon; ~ **de cor** colouring pencil; ~ **de olho** eye pencil.

lapiseira [lapi'zejral *f* pencil case.

lápis-lazúli [ˌlapiʃla'zulil (*pl* lápis-lazúlis) *m* lapis-lazuli.

Lapônia [la'ponjal *f* Lapland.

lapso ['lapsul *m* -**1.** [falta] mistake. -**2.** [espaço de tempo] lapse.

laptop ['lapitopil (*pl* laptops) *m* COMPUT laptop.

laquê [la'kel *m* hairspray.

laqueadura [lakja'dural *f* MED tubal ligation.

laquear [15] [la'kja(x)] *vt* -**1.** [com laca] to gloss. -**2.** MED to ligate.

lar ['la(x)] (*pl* -es) *m* home.

laranja [la'rãnʒal ◇ *f* [fruta] orange. ◇ *m* -**1.** [cor] orange. -**2.** *fam* [testa-de-ferro] scapegoat. ◇ *adj (inv)* [cor] orange.

laranjada [larãn'ʒadal *f* orangeade.

laranjal [larãn'ʒawl (*pl* -ais) *m* orange grove.

laranjeira [larãn'ʒejral *f* orange tree.

larápio [la'rapjul *m* thief.

lareira [la'rejral *f* fireplace.

larga ['laxgal *f* ⊳ **largo**.

largada [lax'gadal *f* [em corrida] start; **dar a** ~ to start.

largado, da [lax'gadu, dal *adj* neglected.

largar [14] [lax'ga(x)] ◇ *vt* -**1.** [ger] to leave. -**2.** [soltar] to loosen. -**3.** [deixar cair] to drop. -**4.** [pôr em liberdade] to release. -**5.** [deixar em paz] to leave alone. -**6.** *fam* [dar] to give; ~ **a mão em alguém** to slap sb. ◇ *vi* -**1.** [deixar]: ~ **de algo/de ser algo** to stop doing sthg/being sthg. -**2.** NÁUT to set sail.

➡ **largar-se** *vp* -**1.** [desprender-se] to untie o.s. from. -**2.** [ir] to go.

largo, ga ['laxgu, gal *adj* -**1.** [grande de lado a lado] wide. -**2.** [folgado] loose. -**3.** (*antes de subst*) [extenso] great, large. -**4.** (*antes de subst*) [prolongado] long. -**5.** (*antes de subst*) [abundante] abundant.

➡ **largo** *m* [praça] square.

➡ **larga** *f*: **viver à larga** to live lavishly.

➡ **largas** *fpl*: **dar largas a algo** to give free rein to sthg.

➡ **ao largo** *loc adv*: **passar ao** ~ (**de**) to give a wide berth (to); **avistar algo ao** ~ to make something out in the distance; **ao** ~ **da costa brasileira** off the Brazilian coast; **fazer-se ao** ~ to head for the open sea.

largueza [lax'gezal *f* largesse; **com** ~ with largesse.

largura [lax'gural *f* width; **tem 3 metros de** ~ it is 3 metres wide; ~ **de banda** COMPUT bandwidth.

larica [la'rikal *f fam* [fome] hunger.

laringe [la'rĩʒil *f* larynx.

laringite [larĩ'ʒitʃil *f* laryngitis.

larva ['laxval *f* larva.

lasanha [la'zãɲal *f* lasagne.

lasca ['laʃkal *f* sliver.

lascado, da [laʃ'kadu, dal *adj* [rachado] cracked.

➡ **lascado** *adv fam* [a toda] full speed.

lascar [12] [laʃ'ka(x)] ◇ *vt* -**1.** [rachar] to break. -**2.** *fam* [dar]: ~ **algo em alguém** suddenly to do sthg to sb. -**3.** *fam* [lançar]: ~ **algo em algo/alguém** to throw sthg at sthg/sb. ◇ *vi* [rachar] to crack.

➡ **de lascar** *loc adj fam* [terrível]: **ser/estar de** ~ to be nasty.

lascívia [la'sivjal *f* lasciviousness.

lascivo, va [la'sivu, val *adj* lascivious.

laser ['lejze(x)] (*pl* -es) ◇ *adj (inv)* ⊳ **raio**. ◇ *m (inv)* laser.

lassidão [lasi'dãwl, **lassitude** [lasi'tudʒil *f* [fadiga] lassitude.

lasso, ssa ['lasu, sal *adj* -**1.** [fatigado] weary. -**2.** [bambo] weak.

lástima ['laʃtʃimal *f* -**1.** [pessoa]: **ser/estar uma** ~ to be pathetic; [coisa] to be a disgrace. -**2.** [pena]: **é uma** ~ (**que**) it is a pity (that); **que** ~! what a pity!

lastimar [4] [laʃtʃi'ma(x)] *vt* -**1.** [lamentar] to

regret. **-2.** [ter pena de] to pity.

▶ lastimar-se vp [lamentar-se]: ~-**se (de algo)** to moan (about sthg).

lastimável [laʃtʃi'mavɛwl (pl -**eis**) adj -**1.** [lamentável] regrettable. -**2.** [deplorável] disgraceful.

lastimoso, osa [laʃtʃi'mozu, ɔzal adj pitiful.

lastro ['laʃtrul m -**1.** NÁUTballast. -**2.** FINguaranty. -**3.** fig [base] grounding.

lastro ['laʃtrol m ECONstandard.

lata ['latal f-**1.** [material] tin. -**2.** [recipiente] can; ~ **de conserva** tin; ~ **de lixo** rubbish bin -**3.** fam na ~ straight.

latada [la'tadal f [treliça] lattice.

latão [la'tãwl (pl -**ões**) m [material] brass.

lataria [lata'rial f -**1.** AUTO bodywork. -**2.** [latas] large quantity of tins.

latejante [late'ʒãntʃil adjthrobbing.

latejar [4] [late'ʒa(x)l vito throb.

latejo [la'teʒul m throb.

latente [la'tẽntʃil adj latent.

lateral [late'rawl (pl -**ais**) ◇ adjlateral. ◇ m FUT outfielder. ◇ f ESP [linha] sideline.

látex ['latɛksl m inv latex.

laticínio [latʃi'sinjul m dairy produce.

latido [la'tʃidul m bark.

latifundiário, ria [latʃifũn'dʒjarju, rjal ◇ adj landed. ◇ m, flandowner.

latifúndio [latʃi'fũndʒjul m large property.

latim [la'tʃil m Latin; **gastar o seu** ~ to waste one's breath.

latino, na [la'tʃinu, nal ◇ adj Latin. ◇ m, f Latin.

latino-americano, latino-americana [la,tʃinwameri'kanu, la,tʃinwameri'kanal ◇ adj Latin American. ◇ m, fLatin American.

latir [6] [la'tʃi(x)l vito bark.

latitude [latʃi'tudʒil f-**1.** [ger] latitude. -**2.** [amplitude] capacity.

▶ latitudes fpl [região] latitudes.

lato, ta ['latu, tal adjbroad.

latrina [la'trinal flatrine.

latrocínio [latro'sinjul m larceny.

lauda ['lawdal fpage.

laudatório, ria [lawda'tɔrju, rjal adj laudatory.

laudo ['lawdul m -**1.** [parecer] verdict. -**2.** [documento] written verdict.

laureado, da [law'rjadu, dal adjlaureate.

laurel [law'rɛwl (pl -**éis**) m award, prize.

lauto, ta ['lawtu, tal adj [farto] sumptuous.

lava ['laval flava.

lavabo [la'vabul m -**1.** [pia] washbasin. -**2.** [local] bathroom.

lavadeira [lava'dejral f -**1.** [trabalhadora] washerwoman. -**2.** [libélula] dragonfly.

lavadora [lava'doral fwashing machine.

lavagem [la'vaʒɛl (pl -**ns**) f-**1.** [limpeza] washing; ~ **a seco** dry-cleaning. -**2.** MEDwashout. -**3.** PSIC: ~ **cerebral** brainwashing. -**4.** FIN: ~ **de dinheiro** money laundering. -**5.** fam ESP: **dar uma** ~ **num time** to wipe out a team. -**6.** [comida de porcos] swill.

La Valetta [lava'letal n Valletta.

lavanda [la'vãndal f-**1.** BOTlavender. -**2.** [colônia] lavender water. -**3.** [recipiente com água] finger bowl.

lavanderia [lavãnde'rial flaundry.

lavar [4] [la'va(x)l vt to wash; ~ **a seco** to dry-clean.

▶ lavar-se vp to wash o.s.

lavatório [lava'tɔrjul m -**1.** [pia] washbasin. -**2.** [toalete] cloakroom.

lavoura [la'voral fcultivation.

lavrador, ra [lavra'do(x), ral (mpl -**es**, fpl -**s**) m, f ploughman.

lavrar [4] [la'vra(x)l ◇ vt-**1.** [terra] to plough. -**2.** [sentença, escritura, contrato] to draw up. -**3.** [madeira] to plane. ◇ vi [alastrar-se] to rage.

laxante [la'ʃãntʃil adjlaxative.

lazer [la'ze(x)l m -**1.** [descanso] pleasure. -**2.** [tempo de folga] leisure.

LBV (abrev de **Legião da Boa Vontade**) f Brazilian charitable organization for support of the needy.

leal [le'awl (pl -**ais**) adjloyal.

lealdade [leaw'dadʒil floyalty.

leão [le'ãwl (pl -**ões**) m, flion.

▶ Leão m -**1.** ASTRO Leo. -**2.** fig [fisco]: **o Leão** the taxman.

leão-de-chácara [leãwdʒi'ʃakaral (pl leões-de-chácara) m fam bouncer.

leão-marinho [le,ãwma'riɲul (pl leões-marinhos) m sea lion.

leasing ['lisĩɳl m ECONleasing.

lebre ['lɛbril fhare.

lecionar [4] [lesjo'na(x)l ◇ vtto teach. ◇ vito teach.

legado [le'gadul m -**1.** [herança] legacy. -**2.** [enviado] envoy.

legal [le'gawl (pl -**ais**) ◇ adj-**1.** JURlegal. -**2.** fam [bom, bonito] cool. -**3.** [hora] official time. ◇ adv fam [bem] well.

legalidade [legali'dadʒil flegality.

legalização [legaliza'sãwl (pl -**ões**) flegalization.

legalizar [4] [legali'za(x)l vtto legalize.

legar [14] [le'ga(x)l vt -**1.** JUR to bequeath. -**2.** [transmitir] to pass on.

legenda [le'ʒẽndal f -**1.** [em foto, desenho etc] caption. -**2.** CINE subtitle. -**3.** POL number identifying political party on ballot sheet; **votar na** ~ to vote for the party.

legendado, da [leʒẽn'dadu, dal adj -**1.** [filme] subtitled. -**2.** [fotos] captioned.

legendar [le'ʒẽnda(x)l vt -**1.** [filme] to subtitle. -**2.** [fotos] to caption.

legendário, ria [leʒẽn'darju, rjal adjlegendary.

legião [le'ʒjãwl (pl -**ões**) f [de fãs, leitores] legion.

legislação [leʒiʒla'sãwl (pl -**ões**) flegislation.

legislador, ra [leʒiʒla'do(x), ral m, flegislator.

legislar [4] [leʒiʒ'la(x)l ◇ vito legislate. ◇ vtto legislate.

legislativo, va [leʒiʒla'tʃivu, val adjlegislative.

▶ Legislativo m: **o Legislativo** the legislature. ~

legislatura [leʒiʒla'tural *f* **-1.** [corpo] legislature. **-2.** [período] term.

legista [le'ʒiʃta] *mf* **-1.** [jurista] legal expert. **-2.** [médico] forensic scientist.

legitimar [4] [leʒitʃi'ma(x)] *vt* [legalizar] to legitimize.

legitimidade [leʒitʃimi'dadʒi] *f* legitimacy.

legítimo, ma [le'ʒitʃimu, ma] *adj* **-1.** [ger] legitimate; **em legítima defesa** in legitimate defense. **-2.** [autêntico] authentic.

legível [le'ʒivɛwl] (*pl* **-eis**) *adj* **-1.** [nítido] legible. **-2.** [agradável de ler] readable.

légua ['lɛgwa] *f* [medida] league.

➡ **léguas** *fpl fig* [grande distância] miles.

legume [le'gume] *m* vegetable.

leguminosa [legumi'nɔza] *f* BOT leguminous plant.

➡ **leguminosas** *fpl* BOT leguminosae.

lei ['lej] *f* **-1.** [ger] law; **ditar a** ~ to lay down the law; **promulgar a** ~ to uphold the law; **violar a** ~ to break the law; ~ **marcial** martial law; ~ **trabalhista** industrial law; ~ **da oferta e da procura** the laws of supply and demand. **-2.** [de um metal]: **prata de** ~ hallmarked silver.

leiaute [lej'awtʃil *m* layout.

leigo, ga ['lejgu, ga] <> *adj* **-1.** RELIG secular. **-2.** *fig* [imperito]: **ser** ~ **em algo** to be a layperson in sthg. <> *m, f* [pessoa imperita] layperson.

leilão [lej'lãwl (*pl* **-ões**) *m* auction.

leiloar [20] [lej'lwa(x)] *vt* to auction.

leiloeiro, ra [lej'lwejru, ra] *m, f* auctioneer.

leitão, toa [lej'tãw, toa] (*pl* **-ões**) *m, f* suckling pig.

leite ['lejtʃi] *m* milk; ~ **em pó** powdered milk; ~ **de côco** coconut milk; ~ **condensado** condensed milk; ~ **desnatado** ou **magro** skimmed milk; ~ **integral** full-cream milk; ~ **de magnésia** Milk of Magnesia; ~ **de soja** soya milk.

leiteiro, ra [lej'tejru, ra] <> *adj* [que produz leite] dairy. <> *m, f* [pessoa] milkman (*f* milkwoman).

➡ **leiteira** *f* **-1.** [para ferver leite] milk pan. **-2.** [para servir leite] milk jug.

leiteria [lejte'ria] *f* **-1.** [em fazenda] dairy. **-2.** [lanchonete] milk bar.

leito ['lejtu] *m* bed.

leitor, ra [lej'to(x), ra] (*mpl* **-es**, *fpl* **-s**) *m, f* **-1.** [quem lê] reader. **-2.** UNIV visiting lecturer.

leitoso, osa [lej'tozu, ɔza] *adj* milky.

leitura [lej'tural *f* reading; **ter muita** ~ to be well-read; ~ **dinâmica** speed reading.

lelé [le'lɛl *adj fam*: ~ **(da cuca)** bonkers.

lema ['lema] *m* **-1.** [norma] maxim. **-2.** [político] motto.

lembrança [lẽn'brãnsal *f* **-1.** [recordação] souvenir. **-2.** [presente] gift.

➡ **lembranças** *fpl* [cumprimentos]: **(dê)** ~s **minhas à sua família** (give) my regards to your family.

lembrar [4] [lẽm'bra(x)] <> *vt* **-1.** [recordar] to remember. **-2.** [parecer] to look like. **-3.** [trazer à memória]: ~ **algo a alguém** to remind sb of sthg.

<> *vi* **-1.** [recordar]: ~ **(de alguém/algo)** to remember (sb/sthg). **-2.** [advertir]: ~ **a alguém de algo/de fazer algo** to remind sb of sthg/to do sthg; ~ **a alguém (de) que** to remind sb that.

➡ **lembrar-se** *vp*: ~-**se (de alguém/algo)** to remember (sb/sthg); ~-**se (de) que** to remember that.

lembrete [lẽn'bretʃil *m* memo.

leme ['lemil *m* **-1.** [ger] helm. **-2.** [dispositivo] rudder.

lenço ['lẽnsul *m* **-1.** [para limpar] handkerchief; ~ **de papel** paper handkerchief, tissue. **-2.** [de cabeça] headscarf. **-3.** [de pescoço] neckerchief.

lençol [lẽn'sɔwl (*pl* **-óis**) *m* sheet; ~ **d'água** water table; **estar em maus lençóis** *fig* to be in a fine mess.

lenda ['lẽndal *f* **-1.** [história] legend. **-2.** *fig* [mentira] tall story.

lendário, ria [lẽn'darju, rjal *adj* legendary.

lêndea ['lẽndʒjal *f* nit.

lengalenga [lẽŋga'lẽŋgal *f* rigmarole.

lenha ['leɲa] *f* [para queimar] firewood; **botar** ~ **na fogueira** *fig* to add fuel to the fire; **fazer uma** ~ [criar caso] to make a fuss.

lenhador [leɲa'do(x)l *m* woodcutter.

lenho ['leɲul *m* **-1.** [tora] log. **-2.** [madeira] timber.

leninismo [leni'niʒmul *m* Leninism.

leninista [leni'niʃtal <> *adj* Leninist. <> *mf* Leninist.

lenitivo, va [leni'tʃivu, val *adj* [remédio, terapia] soothing.

➡ **lenitivo** *m* relief.

lenocínio [leno'sinjul *m* procuring.

lente ['lẽntʃil *f* lens; ~ **de aumento** magnifying glass; ~**s de contato** contact lenses.

lentidão [lẽntʃi'dãwl *f* slowness.

lentilha [lẽn'tʃiʎal *f* lentil.

lento, ta ['lẽntu, tal *adj* slow.

leoa [le'oal *f* ➡ **leão**.

leões [le'õjʃl *pl* ➡ **leão**.

leonino, na [leo'ninu, nal <> *adj* **-1.** [caráter] leonine; [contrato] fraudulent. **-2.** ASTRO Leo. <> *m, f* ASTRO Leo.

leopardo [ljo'paxdul *m* leopard.

lépido, da ['lɛpidu, dal *adj* **-1.** [ágil] nimble. **-2.** [contente] happy.

leporino, na [lepo'rinu, nal *adj* ➡ **lábio**.

lepra ['lɛpral *f* leprosy.

leprosário [lepro'zarjul *m* leper colony.

leproso, osa [le'prozu, ɔzal <> *adj* leprous. <> *m, f* [pessoa] leper.

leque ['lɛkil *m* **-1.** [abano] fan. **-2.** *fig* [conjunto]: **um** ~ **de** a range of.

ler [42] ['le(x)l <> *vt* to read. <> *vi* to read.

lerdeza [lex'dezal *f* sluggishness.

lerdo, da ['lɛxdu, dal *adj* **-1.** [vagaroso] sluggish. **-2.** [idiota] slow.

lero-lero [lɛru'lɛrul *m* chit-chat.

lesado, da [le'zadu, dal *adj* [ferido] injured.

lesão [le'zãwl (*pl* **-ões**) *f* **-1.** MED lesion; ~ **corporal** grievous bodily harm. **-2.** JUR [violação] violation.

lesar [4] [le'za(x)] *vt* **-1.** *fig* [prejudicar, enganar] to cheat. **-2.** *JUR* [violar] to violate.

lésbico, ca ['lɛʒbiku, ka] *adj* lesbian.

➡ **lésbica** *f* lesbian.

lesionar [4] [lezjo'na(x)] *vt* to injure.

lesivo, va [le'zivu, va] *adj* [prejudicial] harmful.

lesma ['leʒma] *f* **-1.** [animal] slug. **-2.** *fig* [pessoa] sluggard.

leso, sa [le'zu, za] *adj* [contundido] injured.

leste ['lɛʃtʃi] ⬦ *m (inv)* [ger] east; **a ~ (de)** to the east (of); **para ~** eastward. ⬦ *adj (inv)* easterly.

letal [le'taw] *(pl* -ais) *adj* lethal.

letão, tã [le'tãw, tã] ⬦ *adj* Latvian. ⬦ *m, f* Latvian.

➡ **letão** *m* [língua] Latvian.

letargia [letax'ʒia] *f* lethargy.

letárgico, ca [le'taxʒiku, ka] *adj* lethargic.

letivo, va [le'tʃivu, va] *adj* school *(antes de subst)*; **ano ~** academic year, school year.

Letônia [le'tonja] *n* Latvia.

letra ['letra] *f* **-1.** [caractere] letter; **~ de fôrma** block capital *(pl)*; **~ de imprensa** print; **~ maiúscula/minúscula** capital/small letter; **com todas as ~ s** [explicitamente] in detail. **-2.** [caligrafia] handwriting; **~ de mão** handwriting; **~ de médico** *fig* scrawl. **-3.** [de música] lyrics *(pl)*. **-4.** *COM:* **~ de câmbio** bill of exchange.

➡ **letras** *fpl* **-1.** [curso] arts. **-2.** [literatura] literature.

➡ **à letra, ao pé da letra** *loc adv* **-1.** [literalmente] literally. **-2.** [rigorosamente] to the letter.

➡ **de letra** *loc adv*: **tirar algo de ~** to do sthg with one's eyes closed.

letrado, da [le'tradu, da] *adj* **-1.** [culto] lettered. **-2.** [versado em literatura] well read.

letreiro [le'trejru] *m* notice; **~ luminoso** neon sign.

léu ['lɛw] ➡ **ao léu** *loc adv* **-1.** [à toa] aimlessly. **-2.** [à mostra] uncovered.

leucemia [lewse'mia] *f* leukaemia *UK*, leukemia *US*.

leva ['lɛva] *f* [conjunto] batch.

levadiço [leva'dʒisu] *adj* ➡ **ponte**.

levado, da [le'vadu, da] *adj*: **~ (da breca)** unruly.

leva-e-traz [,levi'traʃ] ⬦ *mf (inv)* [pessoa] gossip. ⬦ *m (inv)* [fofoca] gossip.

levantador, ra [levãnta'do(x), ra] *m, f* *ESP:* **~ de pesos** weightlifter.

levantamento [levãnta'mẽntu] *m* **-1.** [pesquisa] survey. **-2.** [inventário] inventory. **-3.** *ESP:* **~ de pesos** weightlifting.

levantar [4] [levãn'ta(x)] ⬦ *vt* **-1.** [ger] to raise; **~ os olhos** to look up. **-2.** [do chão] to lift; **~ vôo** to take off. **-3.** [tornar mais alto] to lift up. **-4.** [coletar] to collect. **-5.** [inventariar] to count. ⬦ *vi* **-1.** [ficar de pé] to stand. **-2.** [sair da cama] to get up. **-3.** [avivar] to cheer.

➡ **levantar-se** *vp* **-1.** [ficar de pé] to stand up. **-2.** [sair da cama] to get up.

levante [le'vãntʃi] *m* **-1.** [revolta] uprising. **-2.** [leste] east.

levar [4] [le'va(x)] *vt* **-1.** [ger] to take; **isso leva algum tempo** that will take some time; **~ adiante** to carry on; **~ a cabo** to carry out. **-2.** [carregar] to carry. **-3.** [induzir] to lead; **~ alguém a algo/a fazer algo** to bring sb to sthg/to do sthg; **deixar-se ~ por algo** to let o.s. be led by sthg. **-4.** [retirar] to take away. **-5.** [lidar com] to deal with. **-6.** [vida]: **ele leva uma vida dura** he has a hard life; **~ a vida na flauta** to take life as it comes. **-7.** [susto, surra]: **~ um susto** to get a fright; **~ uma surra** to take a beating. **-8.** [ganhar] to win.

leve ['lɛvi] *adj* light; **de ~** lightly.

levedo [le'vedu] *m*, **levedura** *f* [leve'dura] yeast.

levemente [levi'mẽntʃi] *adv* lightly.

leveza [le'veza] *f* lightness.

leviandade [levjãn'dadʒi] *f* **-1.** [imprudência] rashness. **-2.** [falta de seriedade] frivolity.

leviano, na [le'vjanu, na] *adj* **-1.** [imprudente] rash. **-2.** [sem seriedade] frivolous.

levitar [4] [levi'ta(x)] *vi* to levitate.

lexical [leksi'kaw] *(pl* -ais) *adj* [função, unidade] lexical.

léxico, ca ['lɛksiku, ka] *adj* [análise, família] lexical.

➡ **léxico** *m* [vocabulário] lexicon.

lexicografia [leksikogra'fia] *f* lexicography.

lexicógrafo, fa [leksi'kografu, fa] *m* lexicographer.

lexicologia [leksikolo'ʒia] *f* lexicology.

lexicólogo, ga [leksi'kɔlogu, ga] *m* lexicologist.

lhama ['ʎama] *mf* llama.

lhe [ʎe] *(pl* lhes) *pron pess* **-1.** [a ele, ela] (to) him/her/it; **dei-~ um presente** I gave him/her a present; **Maria ~ contou um segredo** Maria told him/her a secret; **acertaram-~ um tiro** they shot him/her; **isto lhes custou caro** this cost them a lot of money **-2.** [a você] (to) you; **telefonei-~ ontem** I phoned you yesterday; **o que ~ aconteceu?** what's happened to you?; **ouçam bem o que lhes digo!** listen carefully to what I say! **-3.** [indicando posse - dele, dela] his *(f* her); **roubaram-~ o carro** they stole his/her car; **ardia-lhes a vista** their eyes were stinging; **[- de você]** your; **beijei-~ as faces** I kissed your cheeks; **não lhes pesa a consciência?** doesn't your conscience trouble you? **-4.** [para enfatizar - a ele, ela] his *(f* her); **não sei como ele agüenta as confusões que sua namorada ~ a pronta** I don't know how he puts up with his girlfriend's nonsense; **[- a você]** you; **não sei como você agüenta as confusões que sua namorada ~ apronta** I don't know how you put up with your girlfriend's nonsense.

lhufas ['ʎufaʃ] *pron indef fam* zilch.

lia ['lia] *f* sediment.

liame ['ʎjãmi] *m* tie.

libanês, esa [liba'neʃ, eza] ⬦ *adj* Lebanese. ⬦ *m, f* Lebanese.

Líbano ['libanu] *n*: **o ~** Lebanon.

libelo [li'bɛlu] *m* **-1.** [ger] lampoon. **-2.** *JUR* indictment.

libélula [li'bɛlula] *f* dragonfly.

liberação [libera'sãw] f -**1.** [ger] release. -**2.** [libertação] liberation. -**3.** [de preços, câmbio] freedom from controls. -**4.** [de cheque] clearing. -**5.** [do aborto] legalization.

liberal [libe'raw] (pl -**ais**) <> adj liberal. <> mf POL liberal.

liberalidade [liberali'dadʒi] f [generosidade] liberality.

liberalismo [libera'liʒmu] m liberalism.

liberalização [liberaliza'sãw] f freedom from controls.

liberalizar [4] [liberali'za(x)] vt [preços, mercado] to liberalize.

liberar [4] [libe'ra(x)] vt -**1.** [ger] to release; ~ **alguém de algo** to release sb from sthg. -**2.** [libertar] to release. -**3.** [preço, câmbio] to free from controls. -**4.** [cheque] to clear. -**5.** [aborto] to legalize.

liberdade [libex'dadʒi] f freedom; **dar ~ a alguém (para fazer algo)** to give sb the freedom (to do sthg); **estar em** ~ to be free; **pôr em** ~ to set free; **ter** ~ **para fazer algo** to be at liberty to do sthg; **tomar a** ~ **de fazer algo** to take the liberty of doing sthg; **estar em** ~ **condicional** to be on parole; ~ **de expressão** freedom of speech; ~ **de imprensa** freedom of press; ~ **de opinião** freedom of thought; ~ **sob fiança** release on bail.

➨ **liberdades** fpl liberties; **tomar** ~ **com alguém** to take liberties with sb.

Libéria [li'bɛrja] n Liberia.

líbero ['liberu] m FUT sweeper.

libertação [libex'tasãw] (pl -**ões**) f liberation.

libertador, ra [libexta'do(x), ra] <> adj liberating. <> m, f liberator.

libertar [4] [libex'ta(x)] vt [tornar livre] to liberate.

libertinagem [libextʃi'naʒẽ] f loose living.

libertino, na [libex'tʃinu, na] <> adj libertine. <> m, f libertine.

liberto, ta [li'bextu, ta] <> adj -**1.** [escravo] liberated. -**2.** [salvo] free. <> m,f [escravo] freedman / freedwoman).

Líbia ['libja] n Libya.

libidinoso, osa [libidʒi'nozu, ɔza] adj libidinous.

libido [li'bidu] f libido.

líbio, bia ['libju, bja] <> adj Libyan. <> m, f Libyan.

libra ['libra] f pound; ~ **(esterlina)** pound (sterling).

➨ **Libra** m ASTRO Libra; **ser Libra** to be a Libran.

libreto [li'bretu] m libretto.

Libreville [ˌlibre'vili] n Libreville.

libriano, na [li'brjanu, na] <> adj Libran. <> m, f Libran.

lição [li'sãw] (pl -**ões**) f -**1.** EDUC lesson. -**2.** fig [ensinamento] lesson; **dar uma** ~ **a alguém** to teach sb a lesson; **servir de** ~ **a alguém** to be a lesson to sb. -**3.** fig [repreensão]: **dar uma** ~ **em alguém** to teach sb a lesson.

licença [li'sẽsa] f -**1.** [permissão] permission; **dar**

~ **a alguém (para fazer algo)** to give sb permission (to do sthg); **com** ~ excuse me; ~ **poética** poetic licence. -**2.** [de trabalho] permit; **estar de** ~ to be on leave; **tirar** ~ to go on leave. -**3.** [documento] licence UK, license US.

licença-maternidade [li'sẽsa'matexni'dadʒil] (pl **licenças-maternidade**) f maternity leave.

licença-prêmio [liˌsẽsa'premju] (pl **licenças-prêmio**) f six-months' leave from work, awarded every five years.

licenciado, da [lisẽ'sjadu, da] <> adj -**1.** UNIV graduated. -**2.** [do trabalho] on leave. <> m, f UNIV graduate.

licenciar [16] [lisẽ'sja(x)] vt [do trabalho] to allow time off work.

➨ **licenciar-se** vp -**1.** UNIV: ~-se **(em algo)** to obtain a degree (in sthg). -**2.** [do trabalho] to go on leave.

licenciatura [lisẽsja'tura] f -**1.** [grau] degree. -**2.** [curso] degree course.

licencioso, osa [lisẽ'sjozu, ɔza] adj [obsceno] licentious.

licitação [lisita'sãw] (pl -**ões**) f -**1.** [em leilão] bid. -**2.** [concorrência] tender; **abrir uma** ~ to put a project out to tender; **vencer uma** ~ to win a tender.

licitante [lisi'tãntʃi] mf bidder.

lícito, ta ['lisitu, ta] adj -**1.** [legal] lawful. -**2.** [correto] licit.

lições [li'sõiʃ] pl ▷ **lição**.

licor [li'ko(x)] (pl -**es**) m liqueur.

licoroso, osa [liko'rozu, ɔza] adj sweet and strong.

lida ['lida] f -**1.** [trabalho] toil. -**2.** [leitura] read; **dar uma** ~ **em algo** to have a read of sthg.

lidar [4] [li'da(x)] vi: ~ **com alguém/algo** [conviver com] to deal with sb/sthg; [tratar] to deal with sb/sthg; [trabalhar com] to deal with sb/sthg.

lide ['lidʒi] f -**1.** [combate] battle. -**2.** JUR case.

líder ['lide(x)] (pl -**es**) mf leader.

liderança [lide'rãsa] f leadership.

liderar [4] [lide'ra(x)] vt to lead.

lido, da ['lidu, da] <> pp ▷ **ler**. <> adj: **muito** ~ [culto] well read; [autor, obra] much read.

lifting ['liftĩŋ] m facelift.

liga ['liga] f -**1.** [associação] league. -**2.** [de meias] garter. -**3.** [de metais] alloy.

ligação [liga'sãw] (pl -**ões**) f -**1.** [ger] connection; **fazer a** ~ **entre algo e algo** to connect sthg with sthg. -**2.** TELEC (telephone) call; **a** ~ **caiu** we have been cut off; **completar a** ~ to get through (on the phone); **fazer uma** ~ **(para alguém)** to make a call (to sb). -**3.** [relacionamento - amoroso] liaison; [- profissional] relationship.

ligado, da [li'gadu, da] adj -**1.** [ger] connected. -**2.** [absorto] immersed; **ser** ~ **em algo** to be knowledgeable in sthg. -**3.** [afeiçoado] attached.

➨ **ligada** f TELEC phonecall; **dar uma** ~ **para alguém** to call sb.

ligadura [liga'dura] f -**1.** [atadura] bandage. -**2.** MÚS ligature.

ligamento [liga'mẽntu] *m* -**1.** ANAT ligament. -**2.** MED: ~ **de trompas** tubal ligation.

ligar [14] [li'ga(x)] ⬦ *vt* -**1.** [ger] to connect. -**2.** [unir] to connect, to join. -**3.** [criar vínculos] to tie. -**4.** [dar importância a]: **não ~ a mínima (para alguém/algo)** to not pay the least bit of attention to sb/sthg. ⬦ *vi* -**1.** [telefonar] to call; ~ **para alguém/algum lugar** to call sb/somewhere (on the phone). -**2.** [dar importância] to care; ~ **para alguém/algo** to care about sb/sthg. -**3.** [dar atenção] to notice; ~ **para alguém/algo** to notice sb/sthg.
➥ **ligar-se** *vp* -**1.** [unir-se] to unite; ~**-se a alguém/algo** to unite o.s. to sb/sthg. -**2.** [relacionar-se]: ~**-se a algo** to be connected to sthg. -**3.** [afeiçoar-se] to become attached.

ligeireza [liʒej'reza] *f* -**1.** [rapidez] lightness. -**2.** [agilidade] agility.

ligeiro, ra [li'ʒejru, ra] *adj* -**1.** [rápido] light. -**2.** [ágil] agile. -**3.** *(antes de subst)* *fig* [sutil] slight.
➥ **ligeiro** *adv* -**1.** [rapidamente] swiftly. -**2.** [com agilidade] nimbly.

lilás [li'laʃ] *(pl* **lilases)** ⬦ *adj* [cor] lilac. ⬦ *m* lilac.

lima ['lima] *f* -**1.** [fruta] lime. -**2.** [ferramenta] file.

Lima ['lima] *n* Lima.

limão [li'mãw] *(pl* **-ões)** *m* lemon.

limbo ['lĩbu] *m*: **estar no ~** *fig* to be in limbo.

limenho, nha [li'mẽɲu, ɲa] ⬦ *adj* Lima *(antes de subst).* ⬦ *m, f* *person from Lima.*

limiar [li'mja(x)] *m* threshold.

liminar [4] [li'mi'na(x)] *f* JUR preliminary verdict.

limitação [limita'sãw] *(pl* **-ões)** *f* limitation.

limitado, da [limi'tadu, da] *adj* limited.

limitar [4] [limi'ta(x)] *vt* [restringir] to limit.
➥ **limitar-se** *vp* -**1.** [restringir-se]: ~**-se a fazer algo** to limit o.s. to doing sthg. -**2.** [confinar-se]: ~**-se com algo** to border on sthg.

limite [li'mitʃi] *m* [ger] limit; ~ **de idade** age limit; **passar dos ~s** to go too far.

limítrofe [li'mitrofi] *adj* bordering.

limo ['limu] *m* BOT slime.

limoeiro [li'mwejru] *m* lemon tree.

limões [li'mõiʃ] *pl* ➞ **limão**.

limonada [limo'nada] *f* lemonade *UK*, lemon soda *US*.

limpador [lĩpa'do(x)] *(pl* **-es)** *m* cleaner; ~ **de chaminé** chimney sweep; ~ **de pára-brisas** windscreen wiper *UK*, windshield wiper *US*.

limpa-pés [ˌlĩpa'pɛʃ] *m inv* boot scraper.

limpar [4] [lĩ'pa(x)] *vt* -**1.** [ger] to clean. -**2.** *fig* [elevar]: ~ **a imagem de alguém/algo** to clean up sb's/sthg's image. -**3.** [enxugar] to dry. -**4.** [esvaziar] to clean. -**5.** [roubar] to clean out. -**6.** *fig* [livrar] to rid.
➥ **limpar-se** *vp* -**1.** [assear-se] to wash o.s. -**2.** [moralmente] to make a clean start.

limpeza [lĩ'peza] *f* -**1.** [estado] cleanliness. -**2.** [ato] cleaning; **fazer uma ~ em algo** [livrar de excessos] to clear sthg out; [livrar de mass elemento] to clean sthg up; [roubar] to clean sthg out; ~ **de pele** skin cleansing; ~ **pública** refuse

collection. -**3.** [esmero] neatness.

límpido, da ['lĩpidu, da] *adj* -**1.** [translúcido] limpid. -**2.** [nítido] clear.

limpo, pa ['lĩpu, pa] ⬦ *pp* ➞ **limpar**. ⬦ *adj* -**1.** [asseado] clean. -**2.** [esmerado] neat; **passar a ~** to make a clean copy. -**3.** *fig* [honrado] blameless. -**4.** [desanuviado] clear. -**5.** [sem dinheiro] broke. -**6.** [sem descontos]: **recebi 100 mil ~s** I received 100,000 clear. -**7.** *loc*: **tirar a ~** to get to the bottom of.
➥ **limpa** *f* -**1.** [limpeza]: **dar uma ~ em algo** to have a clean in sthg. -**2.** *fam fig* [roubo]: **fazer uma ~ (em algo)** to clean (sthg) out.

limusine [limu'zini] *f* limousine.

lince ['lĩsi] *m* lynx; **ter olhos de ~** to have eyes like a hawk.

linchamento [lĩʃa'mẽntu] *m* lynching.

linchar [4] [lĩ'ʃa(x)] *vt* to lynch.

lindeza [lĩ'deza] *f* beauty.

lindo, da ['lĩdu, da] *adj* beautiful; **ser ~ de morrer** *fam* to be a knockout.

linear [li'nja(x)] *adj* linear.

linearidade [linja'ridaʒi] *f* linearity.

linfático, ca [lĩ'fatʃiku, ka] *adj* lymphatic.

lingerie [lãʒe'xi] *f* lingerie.

lingote [lĩ'gotʃi] *m* ingot.

língua [li'ŋgwa] *f* -**1.** [órgão] tongue; **ter ~ presa** to be tongue-tied; **dar com a ~ nos dentes** to spill the beans; **ficar de ~ de fora** to be exhausted; **pagar pela ~** to pay dearly; **estar na ponta da ~** to be on the tip of one's tongue; **ter uma ~ comprida** to be a gossip; **dobrar a ~** to mind what one says. -**2.** [idioma] language; ~ **materna** mother tongue; ~ **morta** dead language.

LÍNGUA PORTUGUESA

The Portuguese language is spoken in Europe (Portugal), South America (Brazil), Africa (Cape Verde, São Tomé and Príncipe, Angola, Mozambique, Guinea-Bissau) and Asia (East Timor, Goa, and Macao). It is the sixth most spoken language in the world, mostly through the 200 million speakers of Portuguese in Brazil. Brazilian Portuguese has acquired specific characteristics through the incorporation of many words mainly of African and indigenous origin. It has, therefore, many differences in pronunciation, spelling, vocabulary and even grammar, in relation to the Portuguese spoken in other parts of the world, although it remains essentially the same language.

---

linguado [lĩ'gwadu] *m* [peixe] (Brazilian) flounder.

linguagem [lĩ'gwaʒẽ] *(pl* **-ns)** *f* language; ~ **de máquina** machine language; ~ **de programação** programming language.

linguajar [lĩgwa'ʒa(x)] *m* language.

linguarudo, da [lĩgwa'rudu, da] ⬦ *adj* gossipy. ⬦ *m, f* gossip.

lingüeta [lĩ'gwetal] *f* -**1.** [de fechadura] catch. -**2.** [balança] pointer.

lingüiça [liɲ'gwisa] f chorizo; **encher** ~ *fam* to waffle.

lingüista [liɲ'gwiʃta] *mf* linguist.

lingüístico, ca [liɲ'gwiʃtʃiku, ka] *adj* linguistic.
  ➡ **lingüística** f linguistics *(pl)*.

linha ['liɲal f **-1.** [ger] line; **as** ~**s gerais de algo** the general outlines of sthg; **em** ~**s gerais** in general terms; ~ **de mira** line of sight; ~ **de saque** service line; ~ **de crédito** credit line; ~**s inimigas** enemy lines; ~ **de fogo** firing line; ~ **de montagem** assembly line; ~ **cruzada** crossed line; **não dar** ~ to be dead; ~ **de conduta** code of conduct; **andar na** ~ *fig* to toe the line; **sair da** ~ *fig* to be out of line. **-2.** [fio de costura] thread. **-3.** [via] route; ~ **aérea** airline; ~ **férrea** railway line *UK*, railroad *US*. **-4.** [elegância] flair; **é um homem de** ~ he has a flair for things; **portar-se/vestir-se com muita** ~ to behave/dress o.s. with a lot of flair; **perder a** ~ to lose face. **-5.** *COMPUT*: ~ **de comando** command line; ~ **dedicada** dedicated line; ~ **discada** dial-up line.

linhaça [li'ɲasa] f linseed.

linha-dura [ˌliɲa'dura] *(pl* **linhas-duras)** ⋄ *mf* hardliner. ⋄ *adj (inv)* hard-line.

linhagem [li'ɲaʒẽ] f lineage.

linho ['liɲu] *m* **-1.** [tecido] linen. **-2.** [planta] flax.

link ['liɲnki] *(pl* **links)** *m COMPUT* link.

linóleo [li'nɔlju] *m* linoleum.

lipoaspiração [lipu'aʃpirasãw] *(pl* **-ões)** f liposuction.

liquefazer [31] [likefa'ze(x)] *vt* **-1.** [ger] to melt. **-2.** [tornar líquido] to liquefy.
  ➡ **liquefazer-se** *vp* to melt.

liquefeito, ta [like'fejtu, ta] ⋄ *pp* ▷ **liquefazer**. ⋄ *adj* molten.

líquen ['likẽ] *m BOT* lichen.

liquidação [likida'sãw] *(pl* **-ões)** f **-1.** [dissolução] settlement. **-2.** *FIN* liquidation. **-3.** *COM* clearance sale; **(estar) em** ~ (to be) in liquidation. **-4.** [destruição] elimination.

liquidar [4] [liki'da(x)] ⋄ *vt* **-1.** [ger] to liquidate. **-2.** [dissolver] to settle. **-3.** [destruir] to eliminate. ⋄ *vi* **-1.** *COM* to hold a clearance sale. **-2.**: ~ **com alguém/algo** [destruir] to destroy sb/sthg.

liquidez [liki'dejʃ] f *ECON* liquidity.

liqüidificador [likwidʒifika'do(x)] *m* liquidizer.

liqüidificar [likwidʒifi'ka(x)] *vt* to liquidize.

líquido, da ['likidu, 'likida] *adj* **-1.** [estado] liquid. **-2.** [valor] net; **peso** ~ *COM* net weight.
  ➡ **líquido** *m* [fluido] liquid.

lira ['lira] f **-1.** [instrumento] lyre. **-2.** *fig* [poesia] lyric poem. **-3.** [moeda] lira.

lírico, ca ['liriku, ka] *adj* **-1.** [gênero] lyrical. **-2.** *fig* [romântico] romantic.
  ➡ **lírica** f [coleção de poesia] lyrical poetry.

lírio ['lirju] *m* lily.

lírio-do-vale [ˌlirjudu'vali] *(pl* **lírios-do-vale)** *m* lily of the valley.

lirismo [li'riʒmu] *m* **-1.** [em poesia] lyricism. **-2.** *fig* [romantismo] romance.

Lisboa [liʒ'boa] *n* Lisbon.

lisboeta [liʒ'bweta] ⋄ *adj* Lisbon *(antes de subst)*. ⋄ *mf* person from Lisbon.

liso, sa ['lizu, 'liza] *adj* **-1.** [superfície] smooth. **-2.** [cabelo] straight. **-3.** [tecido] plain. **-4.** *fam* [sem dinheiro] broke.

lisonja [li'zõʒa] f flattery.

lisonjeador, ra [lisõʒja'do(x), ra] ⋄ *adj* flattering. ⋄ *m, f* flatterer.

lisonjear [15] [lizõ'ʒja(x)] *vt* to flatter.

lisonjeiro, ra [lizõ'ʒejru, ra] *adj* flattering.

lista ['liʃta] f **-1.** [relação] list; ~ **civil** civil list; ~ **negra** black list; ~ **de discussão** newsgroup; ~ **telefônica** telephone directory. **-2.** [listra] stripe.

listagem [liʃ'taʒẽ] *(pl* **-ns)** f listing.

listar [4] [liʃ'ta(x)] *vt COMPUT* to list.

listra ['liʃtra] f stripe.

listrado, da [liʃ'tradu, da], **listado, da** [liʃ'tadu, da] *adj* striped.

lisura [li'zura] f [de superfície] smoothness.

literal [lite'raw] *(pl* **-ais)** *adj* literal.

literalmente [literaw'mẽtʃi] *adv* literally.

literário, ria [lite'rarju, lite'rarja] *adj* literary.

literato, ta [lite'ratu, ta] *m* writer.

literatura [litera'tura] f literature; ~ **comparada** comparative literature; ~ **de cordel** *popular fairground novelettes*; ~ **de ficção** fiction writing; ~ **de vanguarda** avant-garde writing.

LITERATURA BRASILEIRA

Although not very widespread because of language difficulties, Brazilian literature has a wealth of good writers and poets. The great names of modern Brazilian poetry include Carlos Drummond de Andrade (1902-1987) from Minas Gerais and João Cabral de Melo Neto (1920-1999) from Pernambuco. Within prose writing, foremost are the novels of Machado de Assis (1839-1908) from Rio de Janeiro, the leading exponent of nineteenth century realism, those of Gumarães Rosa (1908-1967) from Minas Gerais, and those of Jorge Amado (1912-2001) from Bahia, the best known and most widely translated Brazilian author.

litigar [14] [litʃi'ga(x)] ⋄ *vt* [pleitear] to litigate. ⋄ *vi* [abrir processo] to litigate.

litígio [li'tʃiʒju] *m* **-1.** *JUR* [questão] litigation. **-2.** *fig* [disputa] quarrel.

litigioso, osa [litʃi'ʒozu, ɔza] *adj JUR* contentious.

litografia [litogra'fia] f **-1.** [técnica] lithography. **-2.** [gravura] lithograph.

litogravura [ˌlitogra'vura] f [gravura] lithograph.

litoral [lito'raw] *(pl* **-ais)** ⋄ *adj* [costeiro] coastal. ⋄ *m* [beira-mar] coast.

litorâneo, nea [lito'ranju, nja] *adj* coastal.

litro ['litru] *m* [medida] litre *UK*, liter *US*.

Lituânia [li'twãnja] f Lithuania.

lituano, na [li'twãnu, na] ⋄ *adj* Lithuanian. ⋄ *mf* Lithuanian.
  ➡ **lituano** *m* [língua] Lithuanian.

liturgia [litux'ʒia] f liturgy.

lívido, da ['lividu, da] *adj* pallid.

livrar [4] [li'vra(x)] *vt* - **1.** [libertar] to free. - **2.** [salvar]: ~ **alguém/algo de algo** to save sb/sthg from sthg.

➤ **livrar-se** *vp* - **1.** [libertar-se]: ~ **-se (de alguém/algo)** to free o.s. (from sb/sthg). - **2.** : ~ **-se de algo** [salvar-se] to escape from sthg; [evitar] to avoid sthg.

livraria [livra'ria] *f* bookshop *UK*, bookstore *US*.

livre ['livri] *adj* - **1.** [ger] free. - **2.** [independente] independent; **de** ~ **e espontânea vontade of** one's own free will. - **3.** [permitido] free. - **4.** [solto] free. - **5.** [isento]: ~ **de algo** free of sthg; ~ **de impostos** tax-free.

livre-arbítrio [ˌlivrjax'bitrju] (*pl* **livres-arbítrios**) *m* free will.

livre-docência [ˌlivrido'sẽnsja] (*pl* **livres-docências**) *f* [título universitário] *entitlement to teach and examine university lecturers.*

livre-docente ['livri'do'sẽntʃi] (*pl* -**s**) *mf* ≃ research professor. ⬦ *m* [título] ≃ research professor.

livre-iniciativa ['livri'inisja'tʃiva] (*pl* -**s**) *m ECON* free enterprise.

livreiro, ra [liv'rejru, ra] *m,f* bookseller.

livre-pensador, ra [ˌlivripẽnsa'do(x), ra] (*pl* **livres-pensadores** *m* freethinker.

livresco, ca [li'vreʃku, ka] *adj* book *(antes de subst).*

livro ['livru] *m* - **1.** [ger] book; ~ **de bolso** pocketbook; ~ **brochado** paperback; ~ **de capa dura** hardback; ~ **de cozinha** cookery book; ~ **didático** text book; ~ **de cabeceira** favourite reading. - **2.** *loc*: **ser um** ~ **aberto** to be an open book.

livro-caixa [ˌlivro'kajʃa] (*pl* **livros-caixas**) *m* cash book.

lixa ['liʃa] *f* - **1.** [papel] sandpaper. - **2.** [de ferro] file; ~ **de unhas** nail file.

lixadeira [liʃa'dejra] *f* sander.

lixar [4] [li'ʃa(x)] *vt* - **1.** [madeira] to sand. - **2.** [unhas] to file.

➤ **lixar-se** *vp fam* [não se incomodar]: **ele está se lixando com a demissão** he couldn't care less about the resignation.

lixeira [li'ʃejra] *f* - **1.** [em prédio] rubbish chute *UK*, garbage chute *US*. - **2.** [local] rubbish dump *UK*, garbage dump *US*.

lixeiro [li'ʃejru] *m* refuse collector *UK*, dustman *UK*, garbage collector *US*.

lixo ['liʃu] *m* - **1.** [restos] rubbish *UK*, garbage *US*; ~ **atômico** nuclear waste. - **2.** [coisa sem valor] rubbish *UK*, garbage *US*; **estar um** ~ [estar ruim, feio] to be rubbish.

-lo [lu] *pron* [pessoa] him; [coisa] it; [você] you.

lobby ['lɔbi] (*pl* **lobbies**) *m POL* lobby.

lobinho [lo'biɲu] *m* [aprendiz de escoteiro] cub scout.

lobisomem [lobi'zɔmẽ] (*pl* -**ns**) *m* werewolf.

lobista [lo'biʃta] *mf* lobbyist.

lobo ['lobu] *m* wolf.

lobo-do-mar [ˌlobudu'ma(x)] (*pl* **lobos-do-mar**) *m* sea dog, old salt.

lobotomia [loboto'mia] *f* lobotomy.

lóbulo ['lɔbulu] *m* lobe; ~ **de orelha** ear lobe.

locação [loka'sãw] (*pl* -**ões**) *f* - **1.** [de carro, vídeo] hire, rental. - **2.** [de telefone, imóvel] rental. - **3.** *CINE* location.

locador, ra [loka'do(x), ra] *m* - **1.** [de imóvel] landlord. - **2.** [de carro] lessor.

➤ **locadora** *f* [agência] hire *ou* rental company; ~ **de vídeo** video hire *ou* rental shop.

local [lo'kaw] (*pl* -**ais**) ⬦ *adj* local. ⬦ *m* place.

localidade [lokali'dadʒi] *f* - **1.** [lugar] locality. - **2.** [povoado] town.

localização [lokaliza'sãw] (*pl* -**ões**) *f* - **1.** [ato] tracking down, localization. - **2.** [lugar] positioning.

localizar [4] [lokali'za(x)] *vt* - **1.** [encontrar] to find. - **2.** [limitar a certo local] to site.

➤ **localizar-se** *vp* [situar-se] to be sited.

loção [lo'sãw] (*pl* -**ões**) *f* lotion; ~ **após-barba** aftershave.

locatário, ria [loka'tarju, rja] *m* - **1.** [carro] lessee. - **2.** [imóvel] tenant.

locomoção [lokomo'sãw] (*pl* -**ões**) *f* locomotion.

locomotiva [lokomo'tʃiva] *f* locomotive.

locomover-se [5] [lokomo'vexsi] *vp* to move.

locução [loku'sãw] (*pl* -**ões**) *f* - **1.** [expressão] expression. - **2.** [dicção] diction. - **3.** *GRAM* phrase.

locutor, ra [loku'to(x), ra] (*mpl* -**es**, *fpl* -**s**) *m,f* [profissional] presenter.

lodaçal [loda'saw] (*pl* -**ais**) *m* [lamaçal] mud.

lodacento, ta [loda'sẽntu, ta] *adj* muddy.

lodo ['lodu] *m* mud.

lodoso, osa [lo'dozu, ɔza] *adj* = **lodacento**.

logaritmo [loga'ritʃimu] *m* logarithm.

lógico, ca ['lɔʒiku, ka] *adj* logical; **(é)** ~ **!** of course!

➤ **lógica** *f* - **1.** [ger] logic. - **2.** [raciocínio] reasoning.

log-in (*pl* **logins**) *m COMPUT* login.

logística [lo'ʒiʃtʃika] *f* logistics (*pl*).

logo ['lɔgu] ⬦ *adv* - **1.** [sem demora] at once; ~ **de saída** *ou* **de cara** straight away; **vem** ~ **!** come at once! - **2.** [em breve] soon; **até** ~ **!** see you later!; ~ **mais** in a while. - **3.** [exatamente]: ~ **agora** right now; ~ **ali** right there. - **4.** [pouco]: ~ **antes/ depois** just before/after. ⬦ *conj* [portanto] therefore.

➤ **logo que** *loc adv* as soon as.

➤ **tão logo** *loc adv* as soon as.

logomarca [logo'maxka] *f* logo.

logotipo [logo'tʃipu] *m* logo.

logradouro [logra'doru] *m* public area.

lograr [4] [lo'gra(x)] *vt* - **1.** [conseguir] to achieve; ~ **fazer algo** to manage to do sthg. - **2.** [empulhar] to trick.

logro ['logru] *m* fraud.

loiro, ra [lo'jru, ra] *adj* = **louro**.

loja ['lɔʒa] *f* - **1.** *COM* shop *UK*, store *US*; ~ **de antiguidades** antique shop; ~ **de brinquedos** toy shop; ~ **de departamentos** department store; ~

de ferragens ironmonger's *UK*, hardware store *US*; ~ **de produtos naturais** health food store. - **2.** [maçônica] lodge.

lojista [lo'ʒiʃta] *mf* shopkeeper.

lombada [lõn'bada] *f* - **1.** [de livro] spine. - **2.** [de boi] fillet. - **3.** [no solo] ridge.

lombalgia [lõnbaw'ʒia] *f* backache.

lombar [lõn'ba(x)] *adj* lumbar.

lombinho [lõn'biɲul] *m* [carne de porco] pork fillet.

lombo ['lõnbu] *m* - **1.** [dorso] lower back. - **2.** [carne] loin. - **3.** [elevação] ridge.

lombriga [lõn'briga] *f* roundworm.

lona ['lona] *f* - **1.** [tecido] canvas. - **2.** [cobertura] tarpaulin. - **3.** [de pneu] layer. - **4.** *loc*: **estar na** ~ *fam* to be wiped out.

Londres ['lõndriʃ] *n* London.

londrino, na [lõn'drinu, na] <> *adj* London (antes de subst). <> *m, f* Londoner.

longamente [lõŋga'mẽntʃil] *adv* - **1.** [em grande extensão] for a long way. - **2.** [por muito tempo] for a long time.

longa-metragem [ˌlõŋgame'traʒẽl] (*pl* **longas-metragens**) *m*: **(filme de)** ~ feature-length film.

longe ['lõnʒil] <> *adv* far (away); **é** ~ **?** is it far?; **ir** ~ **demais** *fig* [exceder-se] to go too far; **ver** ~ *fig* [ter visão] to look far ahead. <> *adj* remote.

➡ **ao longe** *loc adv* - **1.** [no espaço] in the distance. - **2.** [no tempo] a long way.

➡ **de longe** *loc adv* - **1.** [no espaço] from far away. - **2.** [no tempo]: **vir de** ~ to be longstanding. - **3.** [sem comparação] by far.

➡ **longe de** <> *loc conj* far from; ~ **disso** far from it. <> *loc prep* far from.

longevidade [lõnʒevi'dadʒi] *f* longevity.

longevo, va [lõnʒe'vu, va] *adj* - **1.** [muito idoso] elderly. - **2.** [duradouro] long-lived.

longínquo, qua [lõ'ʒĩŋkwu, kwa] *adj* - **1.** [no espaço] distant, remote. - **2.** [no tempo] distant.

longitude [lõnʒi'tudʒi] *f GEOGR* longitude.

longitudinal [lõnʒitudʒi'naw] (*pl* **-ais**) *adj* longitudinal.

longo, ga ['lõŋgu, ga] *adj* - **1.** [ger] long. - **2.** *(antes de subst)* [duradouro] lasting.

➡ **longo** *m* [vestido] long dress.

➡ **ao longo de** *loc prep* - **1.** [no sentido longitudinal] along. - **2.** [à beira de] alongside. - **3.** [no tempo]: **ao** ~ **dos anos** over the years.

lontra ['lõntra] *f* otter.

loquacidade [lokwasi'dadʒi] *m* loquaciousness.

loquaz [lo'kwaʒ] *adj* - **1.** [falador] talkative. - **2.** [eloqüente] eloquent.

lorde ['lɔxdʒil] *m* - **1.** [título] Lord. - **2.** *fig* [homem refinado] refined gentleman.

lordose [lox'dɔzil] *f MED* lordosis, curvature of the spine.

lorota [lo'rɔta] *f fam* fib.

losango [lo'zãŋgul] *m* diamond, lozenge.

lotação [lota'sãw] (*pl* **-ões**) *f* - **1.** [capacidade] capacity; ~ **esgotada** [cinema, teatro] sold out, full house. - **2.** [quadro de pessoal] number of personnel. - **3.** [veículo] minibus.

lotado, da [lo'tadu, da] *adj* [cheio] full, crowded.

lotar [4] [lo'ta(x)] <> *vt* [encher] to fill. <> *vi* [encher]: ~ **(de)** to fill (with).

lote ['lɔtʃil] *m* - **1.** [parte] parcel. - **2.** [conjunto] set. - **3.** [terreno] plot.

loteamento [lotʃja'mẽntul] *m* division into plots.

lotear [15] [lo'tʃja(x)] *vt* to divide into plots.

loteca [lo'tɛkal] *f fam* football pools *UK*, lottery *US*.

loteria [lote'ria] *f* lottery; **ganhar na** ~ to win the lottery; **jogar na** ~ to play the lottery; ~ **esportiva** (football) pools *UK*, lottery *US*.

loto ['lɔtul] *m* lottery.

louça ['losa] *f* china; **de** ~ china *(antes de subst)*; **lavar/secar a** ~ to wash/dry the dishes; ~ **de cerâmica** ceramics; ~ **de jantar** dinner service.

louco, ca ['loku, ka] <> *adj* - **1.** [ger] crazy. - **2.** [insano] mad. - **3.** [transtornado] crazed; **deixar alguém** ~ to drive sb mad; **ficar** ~ **com algo** to go mad with sthg; ~ **de fome** crazed with hunger. - **4.** [furioso]: ~ **(da vida com)** spitting mad (at). - **5.** [apaixonado]: **ser** ~ **por alguém/algo** to be crazy about sb/sthg. - **6.** [excêntrico] weird. - **7.** [intenso] extreme. - **8.** [extraordinário] unbelievable. <> *m, f* [insano] lunatic; ~ **varrido** *ou* **de pedra** *fam* stark raving mad.

➡ **louca** *f*: **dar a louca em alguém** to go mad.

loucura [lo'kura] *f* - **1.** [insanidade] insanity. - **2.** [imprudência] lunacy, madness; **ser (uma)** ~ **fazer algo** to be madness to do sthg. - **3.** [extravagância] antics *(pl)*; **fazer** ~ **s** to get up to antics. - **4.** [paixão] passion; **ter** ~ **por alguém/algo** to be mad about sb/sthg.

louro, ra ['loru, ra] <> *adj* [cabelo, pessoa] fair. <> *m, f* [pessoa] fair-haired person.

➡ **louro** *m* - **1.** [cor] fair, blond. - **2.** [árvore] laurel. - **3.** *CULIN* bay leaf. - **4.** [papagaio] polly parrot.

➡ **louros** *mpl fig* [glórias] laurels.

lousa ['loza] *f* - **1.** [quadro-negro] blackboard. - **2.** [pedra] slate; ~ **tumular** tombstone.

louva-a-deus [ˌlova'dewʃ] *m inv* praying mantis.

louvação [lova'sãw] (*pl* **-ões**) *f* - **1.** [louvor] praise. - **2.** *LITER* popular poetry written for a special occasion, sometimes set to music.

louvar [4] [lo'va(x)] <> *vt* - **1.** [elogiar] to praise. - **2.** [glorificar] to exalt. <> *vi*: ~ **a Deus** to praise God.

louvável [lo'vavɛwl] (*pl* **-eis**) *adj* praiseworthy.

louvor [lo'vo(x)] *m*: ~ **a alguém/algo** [elogio] praise for sb/sthg; [glorificação] glorification of sb/sthg.

Ltda (*abrev de* **Limitada**) *f* Ltd.

lua ['lua] *f* moon; ~ **cheia/nova** full/new moon; **estar no mundo da** ~ to be daydreaming; **ser de** ~ to have mood swings.

lua-de-mel [ˌluadʒi'mɛwl] (*pl* **luas-de-mel**) *f* honeymoon.

Luanda ['lwãndal] *n* Luanda.

luar ['lwa(x)] *m* moonlight.

lubrificação [lubrifika'sãw] (pl -ões) f lubrication.
lubrificante [lubrifi'kãntʃi] <> adj lubricating. <> m lubricant.
lubrificar [12] [lubrifi'ka(x)] vt to lubricate.
lucidez [lusi'deʃ] f lucidity.
lúcido, da ['lusidu, da] adj lucid.
lucrar [4] [lu'kra(x)] <> vt : ~ algo com ou em algo [financeiramente] to make a profit of sthg from sthg; [tirar vantagem de] to enjoy sthg through sthg; ~ algo em fazer algo to gain sthg by doing sthg. <> vi [financeiramente] to make a profit; ~ com algo [tirar vantagem de] to benefit from sthg.
lucratividade [lukratʃivi'dadʒi] f profitability.
lucrativo, va [lukra'tʃivu, va] adj -1. [financeiramente] lucrative, profitable; com/sem fins ~s profit/non-profit-making. -2. [proveitoso] useful.
lucro ['lukru] m -1. [financeiro] profit; ter ~ to make a profit; ~ bruto gross profit; ~ líquido net profit; participação nos ~s profit-sharing. -2. [proveito] gain.
ludibriar [16] [ludʒi'brja(x)] vt to swindle.
lúdico, da ['ludʒiku, ka] adj play (antes de subst).
lufada [lu'fada] f gust.
lugar [lu'ga(x)] (pl -es) m -1. [ger] place; em algum ~ somewhere; em ~ nenhum nowhere; em outro ~ somewhere else; ~ de nascimento place of birth; em primeiro ~ [em competição] in first place; [em argumentação] in the first place; tirar o primeiro/segundo ~ to come first/second. -2. [espaço] room. -3. [assento] seat. -4. [função, ocupação] position; colocar-se no ~ de alguém to put o.s. in sb else's shoes. -5. [situação]: no seu ~ eu faria o mesmo if I were you, I would do the same. -6. loc: dar ~ a to give rise to; ter ~ to take place.
◆ em lugar de loc prep instead of; vá em meu ~ go instead of me.
lugar-comum [lu,gaxku'mũ] (pl lugares-comuns) m commonplace.
lugarejo [luga'reʒu] m small village.
lugar-tenente [lu,ga(x)te'nẽntʃi] m deputy.
lúgubre ['lugubri] adj gloomy.
lula ['lula] f squid.
lumbago [lũn'bagu] m lumbago.
lume ['lumi] m -1. ant [fogo] fire. -2. [luz] light.
luminária [lumi'narja] f lamp.
luminosidade [luminozi'dadʒi] f brightness.
luminoso, osa [lumi'nozu, ɔza] adj -1. [que emite luz] luminous. -2. fig [raciocínio, idéia, talento] brilliant.
lunar [lu'na(x)] (pl -es) adj lunar.
lunático, ca [lu'natʃiku, ka] adj lunatic.
luneta [lu'neta] f telescope.
lupa ['lupa] f magnifying glass.
lúpulo ['lupulu] m BOT hop.
Lusaka [lu'zaka] n Lusaka.
lusco-fusco [,luʃku'fuʃku] m twilight.
lusitano, na [luzi'tanu, na] <> adj Lusitanian. <> m, f Lusitanian.

luso, sa [za, 'luzu] <> adj Portuguese. <> m, f Portuguese person.
luso-brasileiro, ra ['luzubrazi'lejru, ra] (mpl -ros, fpl -ras) <> adj Luso-Brazilian. <> m, f Luso-Brazilian.
lusófono, na [na, lu'zɔfonu, na] <> adj Portuguese-speaking. <> m, f Portuguese speaker.
lustra-móveis [,luʃtra'mɔvejʃ] m inv furniture polish.
lustrar [4] [luʃ'tra(x)] vt [móvel] to polish.
lustre ['luʃtri] m -1. [polimento] polish; dar um ~ em algo to give sthg a polish. -2. [luminária] chandelier.
lustroso, osa [luʃ'trozu, ɔza] adj shiny.
luta ['luta] f -1. [ger] struggle; ~ de classes class war; ser uma ~ (fazer algo) to be a struggle (to do sthg); ir à ~ to fight for it. -2. [combate] fight; ~ armada armed battle. -3. ESP: ~ de boxe boxing; ~ livre wrestling.
lutador, ra [luta'do(x), ra] <> adj [esforçado] tough. <> m, f -1. [ger] fighter. -2. BOXE boxer.
lutar [4] [lu'ta(x)] <> vi -1. [combater]: ~ (com/contra alguém) to fight with/against sb; ~ por algo to fight for sthg. -2. fig [combater]: ~ por/contra algo to fight for/against sthg; ~ com algo [enfrentar] to battle with sthg. -3. [empenhar-se] to use all one's forces; ~ (por algo/para fazer algo) to fight (for sthg/to do sthg). -4. [resistir] to fight; ~ contra algo to fight against sthg. <> vt [judô, caratê, capoeira, luta livre] to fight.
luterano, na [lute'ranu, na] <> adj [pessoa, igreja, doutrina] Lutheran. <> m, f [crente] Lutheran.
luto ['lutu] m mourning; estar de ~ (por algo) to be in mourning (over sthg); estar de ~ to be in mourning; tirar o ~ to come out of mourning; pôr ~ to go into mourning.
luva ['luva] f glove; cair como uma ~ to fit like a glove.
◆ luvas fpl [pagamento] payment.
luxação [luʃa'sãw] (pl -ões) f dislocation.
luxar [4] [lu'ʃa(x)] vt [deslocar] to dislocate.
Luxemburgo [luʃẽn'buxgu] n Luxemburg.
luxemburguês, esa [luʃẽnbux'geʃ, eza] <> adj Luxemburg (antes de subst). <> m, f person from Luxemburg.
luxo ['luʃu] m -1. [pompa] ostentation; de ~ luxury (antes de subst). -2. [extravagância] luxury; dar-se ao ~ de algo to treat o.s. to sthg. -3. [afetação, cerimônia] ceremony; cheio de ~ full of airs and graces; fazer ~ to play hard to get.
luxuosidade [luʃwozi'dadʒi] f luxuriousness.
luxuoso, osa [lu'ʃwozu, ɔza] adj luxurious.
luxúria [lu'ʃurja] f [lascívia] lust.
luxuriante [luʃu'rjãntʃi] adj [vegetação] luxuriant.
luxurioso, osa [luʃu'rjozu, ɔza] adj = luxuriante.
luz ['luʃ] (pl -es) f -1. [claridade, fonte de luz] light; acender a ~ to turn on the light; apagar a ~ to turn off the light; ~ do dia daylight; ~ (elétrica) electric light; ~ de freio brake light; ~ natural natural light; à ~ de vela by candlelight. -2. [eletricidade] electricity; corte de ~ power cut;

falta ~ **todos os dias aqui** the electricity gets cut off here every day. **- 3.** *fig* [discernimento]: **ter uma ~ to see the light. - 4.** *loc*: **dar à ~** to give birth.
luzidio, dia [luzi'dʒiu, dʒia] *adj* gleaming.
luzir [72] [lu'zi(x)] *vi* to shine.
Lycra® ['lajkra] *f* Lycra®; **de ~** Lycra®.

m, M ['emi] *m* [letra] m, M.
má [ma] ▷ **mau**.
MA (*abrev de* **Estado do Maranhão**) *m State of Maranhão*.
maca ['maka] *f* MED trolley.
maçã [ma'sã] *f* apple; **~ ácida** cooking apple; **~ do rosto** cheek; **~ do amor** toffee apple.
macabro, bra [ma'kabru, ma'kabra] *adj* macabre.
macacão [maka'kãw] (*pl* -ões) *m* overalls (*pl*) *UK*, coveralls (*pl*) *US*.
macaco, ca [ma'kaku, ka] *m* [animal] monkey; **~ velho** *fig* [pessoa experiente] old hand.
➡ **macaco** *m* AUTO jack.
➡ **macaca** f: **estar/acordar com a macaca** *fam* to be/wake up in a foul mood.
maçada [ma'sada] *f* [situação enfadonha] bore.
macadame [maka'dãmi] *m inv* tarmac.
macambúzio, zia [makãm'buzju, zja] *adj* sullen.
maçaneta [masa'neta] *f* handle.
maçante [ma'sãntʃi] *adj* boring.
Macapá [maka'pa] *n* Macapá.
macaquear [15] [maka'kja(x)] ⬦ *vt* [imitar] to ape, to imitate. ⬦ *vi* to monkey about.
macaquice [maka'kisi] f: **fazer ~s** to monkey around.
maçarico [masa'riku] *m* blow torch.
maçaroca [masa'rɔka] *f* **- 1.** [emaranhado] tangle. **- 2.** [mixórdia] mess.
macarrão [maka'xãw] *m* **- 1.** [massa] pasta. **- 2.** [em tiras] spaghetti.
macarrônico, ca [maka'xoniku, ka] *adj fam* [idioma] broken.
Maceió [masej'ɔ] *n* Maceió.
macerado, da [mase'radu, da] *adj* **- 1.** [esmagado] crushed. **- 2.** [impregnado] marinated. **- 3.** *fig* [macilento] emaciated.
macerar [4] [mase'ra(x)] *vt* **- 1.** [esmagar] to crush. **- 2.** [impregnar]: **~ algo em algo** to marinate sthg in sthg. **- 3.** *fig* [mortificar] to torment.

macete [ma'setʃi] *m* **- 1.** [instrumento] mallet. **- 2.** *fam* [truque] trick; **cheio de ~s** [sofisticado] full of gadgets.
machadada [ma'ʃadu] *f* axe blow.
machadinha [maʃa'dʒiɲa] *f* cleaver.
machado [ma'ʃadu] *m* axe.
machão, ona [ma'ʃãw, ɔna] (*mpl* -ões, *fpl* -s) *adj* **- 1.** *pej* [ger] macho. **- 2.** [corajoso] brave.
➡ **machão** *m* macho man.
➡ **machona** *f vulg* [lésbica] dyke.'
machete [ma'ʃetʃi] *m* machete.
machismo [ma'ʃiʒmu] *m* machismo.
machista [ma'ʃiʃta] ⬦ *adj* macho. ⬦ *m* male chauvinist.
macho ['maʃu] ⬦ *adj* **- 1.** [ger] manly. **- 2.** [gênero] male. ⬦ *m* **- 1.** [animal] male. **- 2.** TEC tap. **- 3.** [prega] box pleat.
machões [ma'ʃõjʃ] *pl* ▷ **machão**.
machona [ma'ʃona] *f* ▷ **machão**.
machucado, da [maʃu'kadu, da] *adj* **- 1.** [ferido] hurt. **- 2.** [contundido] injured. **- 3.** [esmagado] bruised. **- 4.** [lascado] scratched. **- 5.** [magoado] hurt.
➡ **machucado** *m* [ferida] wound.
machucar [12] [maʃu'kax] ⬦ *vt* **- 1.** [ferir] to hurt. **- 2.** [contundir] to injure. **- 3.** [esmagar] to bruise. **- 4.** [lascar] to scratch. **- 5.** [magoar] to hurt. ⬦ *vi* to hurt.
➡ **machucar-se** *vp* **- 1.** [ferir-se] to injure o.s. **- 2.** [contundir-se] to hurt o.s. **- 3.** *fam* [sair-se mal]: **~se (com algo)** to get o.s. hurt (by sthg).
maciço, ça [ma'sisu, sa] *adj* **- 1.** [sólido] massive. **- 2.** [em quantidade] massive. **- 3.** *fig* [sólido] solid.
➡ **maciço** *m* [cadeia montanhosa] massif.
macieira [ma'sjejra] *f* apple tree.
maciez [ma'sjeʒ] *f* softness.
macilento, ta [masi'lẽntu, ta] *adj* **- 1.** [pálido] pale. **- 2.** [sem brilho] dull.
macio, cia [ma'siu, sia] *adj* **- 1.** [ger] smooth. **- 2.** [fofo] soft.
maciota [ma'sjɔta] f: **na ~** effortlessly.
maço ['masu] *m* **- 1.** [de notas, folhas] bundle. **- 2.** [de cartas] pack. **- 3.** [de cigarros] packet.
maçom [ma'sõ] (*pl* -ns) *m* [membro da maçonaria] Freemason.
maçonaria [masona'ria] *f* freemasonary.
maconha [ma'koɲa] *f* **- 1.** BOT hemp. **- 2.** [droga] cannabis, to marijuana; **cigarro de ~** spliff.
maconhado, da [mako'ɲadu, da] *adj* high (*on drugs*).
maconheiro, ra [mako'ɲejru, ra] ⬦ *adj* [viciado] addicted. ⬦ *m, f* **- 1.** [viciado] addict. **- 2.** [vendedor] pusher.
maçônico, ca [ma'soniku, ka] *adj* Masonic.
má-criação [,makrja'sãw] *f* = **malcriação**.
macro ['makru] *f* COMPUT macro.
macrobiótico, ca [makro'bjɔtʃiku, ka] *adj* macrobiotic.
➡ **macrobiótica** *f* **- 1.** [doutrina] macrobiotics. **- 2.** [dieta] macrobiotic diet.
macrocosmo [makro'kɔʒmu] *m* macrocosm.

macroeconomia [makrwekono'mia] *f* macro-economics.

mácula ['makula] *f fig* [desonra, mancha] stain; **sem** ~ untarnished.

maculado, da [maku'ladu, da] *adj* **-1.** [manchado] stained. **-2.** [desonrado] tarnished.

macumba [ma'kũba] *f* [espirit- religião] macumba, *Afro-Brazilian religion;* [- despacho] sacrificial offering; **fazer uma** ~ **contra alguém** to put a macumba curse on sb.

macumbeiro, ra [makũm'bejru, ra] <> *adj* [relativo à macumba] macumba *(antes de subst).* <> *m, f* [adepto] macumba initiate.

Madagascar [madagaʃ'ka(x)] *n* Madagascar.

madame [ma'dãmi], **madama** [ma'dama] *f* **-1.** [senhora] Madam. **-2.** *irôn* [mulher rica] lady. **-3.** *irôn* [esposa] ladyship. **-4.** [cafetina] madam.

madeira [ma'dejrã] *f* wood; ~ **de lei** hardwood; **de** ~ wooden; **bater na** ~ to touch wood.

Madeira [ma'dejra] <> *n* Madeira <> *m* [vinho] Madeira (wine).

madeira-branca [ma͵dejra'brãŋka] *(pl* **madeiras-brancas)** *f* softwood.

madeiramento [madejra'mẽntu] *m* [de casa, telhado] timber.

madeireiro, ra [madej'rejru, ra] <> *adj* timber *(antes de subst).* <> *m, f* timber merchant.

➡ **madeireira** *f* [empresa] timber merchant's.

madeixa [ma'dejʃa] *f* [mecha] lock.

madona [ma'dona] *f* Madonna.

madrasta [ma'draʃta] *f* **-1.** [esposa do pai] stepmother. **-2.** *fig* [mãe má] unfit mother.

madre ['madri] *f* **-1.** [religiosa] nun. **-2.** [título] Mother; ~ **superiora** Mother Superior, Reverend Mother.

madrepérola [͵madre'pɛrula] *f* mother-of-pearl.

madressilva [͵madre'siwva] *f BOT* honeysuckle.

Madri [ma'dri] *n* Madrid.

madrileno, na [madri'lenu, na] <> *adj* Madrid *(antes de subst).* <> *m & f* person from Madrid.

madrinha [ma'driɲa] *f* **-1.** [RELIG - de batismo] godmother; [- de crisma] sponsor; [- de casamento] chief bridesmaid. **-2.** *fig* [protetora, patrocinadora] patroness.

madrugada [madru'gada] *f* early morning; **às três da** ~ at three in the morning; **de** ~ in the early hours.

madrugador, ra [madruga'do(x), ra] <> *adj* early rising. <> *m, f* early riser.

madrugar [14] [madru'ga(x)] *vi* **-1.** [acordar cedo] to wake up early. **-2.** [chegar cedo] to get in early.

maduro, ra [ma'duru, ra] *adj* **-1.** [fruto] ripe. **-2.** [pessoa, atitude, decisão] mature.

mãe ['mãj] *f* **-1.** [ger] mother; ~ **adotiva** adoptive mother; ~ **de criação** foster mother; ~ **de família** wife and mother; ~ **solteira** single mother. **-2.** [como forma de tratamento] mother. **-3.** [pessoa dedicada]: **ser uma** ~ **para alguém** to be a mother to sb.

mãe-benta [͵mãj'bẽnta] *(pl* **mães-bentas)** *f CULIN* small rice-flour cake.

mãe-de-santo [͵mãjʃdʒi'sãntu] *(pl* **mães-de-santo)** *f* [espirit] *high priestess in Afro-Brazilian religion.*

maestria [majʃ'tria] *f* mastery; **com** ~ masterfully.

maestro, trina [ma'ɛʃtru, trina] *m, f* maestro.

má-fé [͵ma'fɛ] *f inv* bad faith; **agir de** ~ to act in bad faith.

máfia ['mafja] *f* **-1.** [bando do crime organizado] Mafia. **-2.** [grupo de corruptos] mafia.

mafioso, osa [ma'fjozu, ɔza] <> *adj* **-1.** [pessoa] Mafioso. **-2.** [ação] of the Mafia. <> *m, f* [membro da máfia] Mafioso.

má-formação [͵mafoxma'sãw] *f* = **malformação**.

mafuá [ma'fwa] *m fam fig* [bagunça] shambles *(sg).*

magazine [maga'zini] *m* **-1.** [loja] boutique. **-2.** [revista] magazine.

magérrimo, ma [ma'ʒɛximu, ma] *adj* [superl de magro] terribly thin, thinnest.

magia [ma'ʒia] *f* magic; ~ **negra** black magic.

mágico, ca [ma'ʒiku, ka] <> *adj* magic. <> *m, f* [prestidigitador] magician.

➡ **mágica** *f* **-1.** [prestidigitação] magic. **-2.** [truque] trick; **fazer mágica** to perform magic; *fig* to work miracles.

magistério [maʒiʃ'tɛrju] *m* **-1.** [profissão] teaching. **-2.** [classe dos professores] teaching profession. **-3.** [ensino] teaching.

magistrado, da [maʒiʃ'tradu, da] *m* magistrate.

magistral [maʒiʃ'traw] *(pl* **-ais)** *adj* [exemplar] masterly.

magistralmente [maʒiʃtraw'mẽntʃi] *adv* [com maestria] masterfully.

magistratura [maʒiʃtra'tura] *f* [os magistrados] magistracy.

magnanimidade [magnãnimi'dadʒi] *f* magnanimity.

magnânimo, ma [mag'nanimu, ma] *adj* magnanimous.

magnata [mag'nata] *m* magnate.

magnésia [mag'nɛzja] *f* magnesia.

magnésio [mag'nɛzju] *m* magnesium.

magnético, ca [mag'nɛtʃiku, ka] *adj* magnetic.

magnetismo [magne'tʃiʒmu] *m* magnetism.

magnetizar [4] [magnetʃi'za(x)] *vt* **-1.** [imantar] to magnetize. **-2.** *fig* [atrair] to fascinate.

magnificência [magnifi'sẽnsja] *f* [suntuosidade] magnificence.

magnífico, ca [mag'nifiku, ka] *adj* magnificent.

magnitude [magni'tudʒi] *f* [dimensão] magnitude.

magnólia [mag'nɔlja] *f* magnolia.

mago, ga ['magu, ga] <> *m, f* wizard *(f* witch). <> *adj*: **os reis** ~**s** the Three Kings.

mágoa [ma'gwal] *f* **-1.** [ressentimento] grief. **-2.** [tristeza] sorrow.

magoado, da [ma'gwadu, da] *adj*: **estar/ficar** ~ **(com algo)** [ressentido] to be/feel offended (by sthg); [triste] to be hurt (by sthg).

magoar [20] [ma'gwa(x)] <> *vt* [ferir] to hurt. <> *vi* [ferir] to hurt.

magrela [ma'grɛla] adj skinny.

magreza [ma'greza] f thinness.

magricela [magri'sɛla] adj = magrela.

magro, gra ['magru, ra] adj -1. [franzino] slim. -2. [sem gordura - carne, presunto] lean; [- leite] skimmed. -3. (antes de subst) fig [parco] meagre UK, meager US.

mai. (abrev de maio) May.

mail [mejo] (pl mails) m COMPUT e-mail.

mainframe [mɛjn'frejmi] m COMPUT mainframe.

maio ['maju] m May; veja também setembro.

maiô [ma'jo] m swimming costume UK, swimsuit US.

maionese [majo'nɛzi] f mayonnaise.

maior [ma'jɔ(x)] (pl -es) <> adj -1. [comparativo]: ~ (do) que [de tamanho] bigger than; [de importância] more important than; [de número] larger than. -2. [superlativo]: o/a ~ ... [de tamanho] the biggest ...; [de importância] the highest ...; [de número] the largest ...; ser o ~ barato [pessoa] to be really cool; [coisa] to be really great. -3. [adulto]: ser ~ (de idade) to be of age; ser de 21 anos to be over 21. -4. MÚS: em dó ~ in C major. <> mf -1. [de tamanho]: o/a ~ the largest. -2. fam [superior]: ser o/a ~ to be the best. -3. [adulto] adult; ser de ~ to be an adult; ser ~ e vacinado fam to be grown up. <> f [notícia]: você já soube da ~? have you heard the latest?; tenho ~ para contar have I got sthg to tell you!

maioral [majo'raw] (pl -ais) mf: o ~ the boss; ele se acha o ~ he thinks he's the greatest.

maioria [majo'ria] f majority; a ~ de the majority of; ~ absoluta absolute majority; a ~ das pessoas acha ... the majority think ...

maioridade [majori'dadʒi] f age of majority; atingir a ~ to come of age.

mais ['majʃ] <> adv -1. [em comparações] more: a Ana é ~ alta/inteligente Ana is taller/more intelligent; ~ do que more than; ~ ... do que ... more ... than ...; bebeu um copo a ~! he's had one too many!; deram-me dinheiro a ~ they gave me too much money; é ~ alta do que eu she's taller than me. -2. [como superlativo]:o/a ~ ... the most ...; o ~ engraçado/inteligente the funniest/most intelligent. -3. [indica adição] any more; não necessito de ~ trabalho I don't need any more work; não necessito de ~ ninguém I don't need anyone else. -4. [indica intensidade]: que dia ~ feliz! what a great day!; que casa ~ feia! what a horrible house! -5. [indica preferência]: vale ~ a pena ficar em casa it would be better to stay at home; gosto ~ de comida chinesa I prefer Chinese food. -6. [em locuções]: de ~ a ~ [ainda por cima] what's more; ~ ou menos more or less; por ~ que se esforce however hard he tries; sem ~ nem menos for no apparent reason; uma vez ~, ~ uma vez once ou yet again.<> adj inv -1. [em comparações] more; eles têm ~ dinheiro they have more money; está ~ calor hoje it's hotter today; ~ ... do que more ... than. -2. [como superlativo] (the)

most; a pessoa que ~ discos vendeu the person who sold (the) most records; os que ~ dinheiro têm those who have (the) most money. -3. [indica adição] more; ~ água, por favor I'd like some more water, please; ~ alguma coisa? anything else?; tenho ~ três dias de férias I have another three days of vacation left. <> conj and; quero uma sopa ~ pão com manteiga I'd like some soup and some bread and butter. <> prep [indica soma]plus; dois ~ dois são quatro two plus two is four.

maisena [maj'zena] f: de ~ cornflour UK, cornstarch US.

mais-valia [,majʃva'lia] (pl mais-valias) f ECON surplus value.

maître ['mɛtri] m head waiter.

maiúsculo, la [ma'juʃkulu, la] adj: letra maiúscula capitals (pl).

➡ **maiúscula** f capital letter.

majestade [maʒeʃ'tadʒi] f majesty.

➡ **Majestade** f: Sua Majestade Your Majesty, His Majesty, Her Majesty.

majestoso, osa [maʒeʃ'tozu, ɔza] adj [grandioso] majestic.

major [ma'ʒɔ(x)] (pl -res) m MIL major.

majoração [maʒora'sãw] f increase.

majorar [4] [maʒo'ra(x)] vt to increase.

majoritário, ria [maʒori'tarju, rja] adj majority (antes de subst); a opinião majoritária é que ... the majority opinion is that ...

mal ['maw] (pl -es) m -1. [ger] evil; cortar o ~ pela raiz to stop things going from bad to worse; a luta entre o bem e o ~ the fight between good and evil. -2. [dano] damage; fazer ~ (a) [à saúde] to damage; o cigarro faz ~ à saúde smoking damages your health; fazer ~ a alguém [afetar] to upset sb; [deflorar] to deflower sb; você fez ~ em se divorciar you did the wrong thing in getting divorced; não faz ~ it doesn't matter; querer ~ a alguém to wish sb ill. -3. [doença] illness. -4. [sofrimento] stress. -5. [inconveniente]: o ~ é que ... the problem is that ... -6. [opinião desfavorável]: falar ~ de alguém/algo to speak ill of sb/sthg.

➡ **mal** <> adv -1. [ger] badly; dar-se ~ (em algo) to do badly (in sthg); de ~ a pior from bad to worse; ~ e porcamente lousily. -2. [quase não]: ele ~ consegue dormir he barely manages to sleep. -3. [injustamente] wrongly. -4. [rudemente] rudely. -5. [de maneira desfavorável] unfavourably; levar alguém/algo a ~ to take sb/sthg badly; não me leve a ~, mas ... don't get me wrong, but ... -6. PSIC [doente] down; estar ~ to feel down; passar ~ to feel sick. <> conj just; ~ cheguei, ele saiu just as I arrived, he left.

mala ['mala] f -1. [recipiente] suitcase; fazer as ~s to pack one's bags; ~ de mão hand luggage. -2. AUTO boot UK, trunk US. -3. COM: ~ direta mail order. -4. [serviço]: ~ aérea air mail; ~ postal mail. -5. fam pej [pessoa chata]: ser uma ~ to be a pain.

malabarismo [malaba'riʒmu] *m* -**1.** [arte] juggling. -**2.** *fig* [habilidade] deftness; **fazer** ~**s** to juggle.

malabarista [malaba'riʃta] *mf* juggler.

mal-acabado, da [mawaka'badu] *adj* -**1.** [construção, móvel] poorly finished. -**2.** [corpo] in poor shape.

mala-direta [maladʒi'rɛta] (*pl* **malas diretas**) *f* [marketing] direct marketing.

mal-afamado, da [mawafa'madu, da] *adj* notorious.

mal-agradecido, da [mawagrade'sidu, da] (*pl* -**s**) ◇ *adj* ungrateful. ◇ *m, f*: **o** ~ **nem sequer me agradeceu** he's so ungrateful he didn't even thank me.

malagueta [mala'geta] *m* chilli pepper.

malaio, ia [ma'laju, ja] ◇ *adj* Malay. ◇ *m, f* Malay.
➤ **malaio** *m* [língua] Malay.

mal-ajambrado, da [mawaʒãm'bradu, da] (*pl* -**s**) *adj* scruffy.

malandragem [malãn'draʒẽ] (*pl* -**ns**), **malandrice** [malãn'drisi] *f* -**1.** [patifaria] doubledealing. -**2.** [astúcia] cunning. -**3.** [vadiagem] vagrancy. -**4.** [preguiça] laziness.

malandro, dra [ma'lãndru, dra] ◇ *adj* -**1.** [patife] crooked. -**2.** [astuto] sharp. -**3.** [vadio] vagrant. -**4.** [preguiçoso] idle. ◇ *m, f* -**1.** [patife] crook. -**2.** [astuto] swindler. -**3.** [vadio] vagrant. -**4.** [preguiçoso] layabout.

mal-apanhado, da [mawapa'ɲadu, da] (*pl* -**s**) *adj* = **mal-apessoado.**

mal-apessoado, da [mawape'swadu, da] (*pl* -**s**) *adj* unpleasant-looking.

malária [ma'larja] *f* malaria.

mal-arrumado, da [mawaxu'madu, da] (*pl* -**s**) *adj* untidy.

mala-sem-alça ['malasẽ'sãw] (*pl* **malas-sem-alça**) *mf fam* bore.

Malásia [ma'lazja] *n* Malaysia.

mal-assombrado, da [mawasõm'bradu, da] (*pl* -**s**) *adj* haunted.

malbaratar [4] [mawbara'ta(x)] *vt* to squander.

malcheiroso, osa [mawʃej'rozu, ɔza] *adj* foul-smelling.

malcomportado, da [mawkõmpox'tadu, da] *adj* badly behaved.

malconceituado, da [mawkõnsej'twadu, da] *adj* badly thought of.

malcriação [mawkrja'sãw] (*pl* -**ões**), **má-criação** [makrja'sãw] (*pl* -**ões**) *f* bad manners; **respondeu com** ~ he replied rudely; **fazer** ~ to behave badly.

malcriado, da [mawkri'adu, da] ◇ *adj* ill-mannered. ◇ *m, f* yob.

maldade [maw'dadʒi] *f* -**1.** [ger] cruelty; **bater em criança é uma** ~ it's cruel to hit children; **ser uma** ~ to be cruel. -**2.** [malícia] malice.

maldição [mawdi'sãw] (*pl* -**ões**) *f* curse.

maldito, ta [maw'dʒitu, ta] ◇ *pp* ▷ **maldizer.** ◇ *adj* -**1.** [amaldiçoado] damned. -**2.** [funesto]

tragic. -**3.** [cruel] cruel. -**4.** *(antes de subst) fam* [para enfatizar]: **essa chuva maldita** this bloody rain.

maldizer [29] [mawdʒi'ze(x)] ◇ *vt* to curse. ◇ *vi*: ~ **de algo** to curse sthg.

maldoso, osa [maw'dozu, ɔza] *adj* -**1.** [malvado] nasty. -**2.** *fig* [mordaz] vicious.

maleável [ma'ljavew] (*pl* -**eis**) *adj* malleable.

maledicência [malidʒi'sẽnsja] *f* -**1.** [ação] slander. -**2.** [difamação] defamation.

maledicente [malidʒi'sẽntʃi] ◇ *adj* slanderous. ◇ *m, f* slanderer.

mal-educado, da [maledu'kadu, da] ◇ *adj* rude. ◇ *m, f*: **o** ~ the rude man; **a malcriada** the rude woman.

malefício [male'fisju] *m* -**1.** [ação] wrong. -**2.** [dano] harm.

maléfico, ca [ma'lɛfiku, ka] *adj* harmful.

mal-e-mal ['mawimaw] *adv* extremely poorly.

mal-encarado, da [malẽŋka'radu, da] (*pl* -**s**) *adj* shady.

mal-entendido [mawẽntẽn'dʒidu] (*pl* **mal-entendidos**) ◇ *adj* [mal interpretado] misunderstood. ◇ *m* misunderstanding.

males ['maliʃ] *pl* ▷ **mal.**

mal-estar [maweʃ'ta(x)] (*pl* **mal-estares**) *m* -**1.** [indisposição] upset. -**2.** *fig* [embaraço] uneasiness.

maleta [ma'leta] *f* small suitcase.

malevolência [malevo'lẽnsja] *f* malevolence.

malevolente *adj* [malevo'lẽntʃi] malevolent.

malévolo, la [ma'lɛvolu, la] *adj* malevolent.

malfadado, da [mawfa'dadu, da] *adj* unlucky.

malfeito, ta [maw'fejtu, ta] *adj* -**1.** [mal-acabado] sloppy. -**2.** [deforme] misshapen. -**3.** *fig* [injusto] unjust.

malfeitor, ra [mawfej'to(x), ra] (*mpl* -**es**, *fpl* -**s**) *m* -**1.** [quem comete delito] wrongdoer. -**2.** [bandido] criminal.

malformação [mawfoxma'sãw] (*pl* -**ões**) *f* malformation.

malgrado [maw'gradu] *prep* despite.

malha ['maʎa] *f* -**1.** [tecido] jersey; **de** ~ jersey; **roupas de** ~ knitwear. -**2.** [de rede, tecido] mesh. -**3.** [de balé] leotard. -**4.** [suéter] sweatshirt.

mal-habituado, da [malabi'twadu, da] (*pl* -**s**) *adj* poorly trained.

malhação [maʎa'sãw] (*pl* -**ões**) *f fam* [crítica violenta] panning.

malhado, da [ma'ʎadu, ada] *adj* [animal] mottled.

malhar [4] [ma'ʎa(x)] ◇ *vt* -**1.** [ger] to beat. -**2.** [criticar] to knock. ◇ *vi* [fazer ginástica] *fam* to work out.

malharia [maʎa'ria] *f* -**1.** [loja] knitwear shop. -**2.** [fábrica] textile mill. -**3.** [artigos] knitted goods.

malho ['maʎu] *m* mallet.

mal-humorado, da [mawumo'radu, da] *adj* -**1.** [que tem mau humor] sullen. -**2.** [ranzinza] grumpy.

malícia [ma'lisja] *f* -**1.** [intenção maldosa] malice. -**2.** [intenção licenciosa] licentiousness; **pôr** ~ **em**

algo to misinterpret sthg. **-3.** [manha, marotice] cunning.

malicioso, osa [mali'sjozu, ɔza] adj **-1.** [maldoso] malicious. **-2.** [que vê licenciosidade] licentious. **-3.** [manhoso] sly.

malignidade [maligni'dadʒi] f **-1.** MED malignancy. **-2.** [ação] malice.

maligno, gna [ma'lignu, gna] adj **-1.** [mau] malicious. **-2.** [nocivo] harmful. **-3.** MED malignant.

má-língua [,ma'lĩŋgwa] (pl **más-língua**) f scandalmonger; **dizem as más-línguas que ...** the scandalmongers are saying that ...

mal-intencionado, da [,mawĩntẽnsjo'nadu, da] (pl **-s**) adj malicious.

malmequer [mawmi'kɛ(x)] (pl **-es**) m marigold.

malnutrido, da [mawnu'tridu, da] adj malnourished.

maloca [ma'lɔka] f **-1.** [cabana] teepee. **-2.** [aldeia] encampment. **-3.** [esconderijo] hideout.

malogrado, da [malo'gradu, da] adj thwarted.

malograr [4] [malo'gra(x)] <> vt to thwart. <> vi to fall through.

malogro [ma'logru] m failure.

malote [ma'lɔtʃi] m **-1.** [bolsa] pouch. **-2.** [correspondência] mail. **-3.** [serviço] courier.

malpassado, da [mawpa'sadu, da] adj rare.

malproporcionado, da [mawpropoxsjo'nadu, da] adj out of proportion.

malquisto, ta [maw'kiʃtu, ta] adj disliked.

malsucedido, da [mawsuse'dʒidu, da] adj unsuccessful.

Malta ['mawta] n Malta.

malte ['mawtʃi] m malt.

maltês, esa [maw'teʃ, eza] <> adj Maltese. <> m, f Maltese.

maltrapilho, lha [mawtra'piʎu, ʎa] <> adj ragged. <> m, f **-1.** [mendigo] beggar. **-2.** [criança] urchin.

maltratar [4] [mawtra'ta(x)] vt **-1.** [fisicamente] to mistreat. **-2.** [verbalmente] to abuse. **-3.** [tratar com desleixo] to mishandle.

maluco, ca [ma'luku, ka] <> adj **-1.** PSIC crazy. **-2.** [adoidado] nuts. **-3.** [absurdo] mad. **-4.** [aficionado]: **ser ~ por algo** to be crazy about sthg. <> m, f PSIC insane.

maluquice [malu'kisi] f **-1.** PSIC madness. **-2.** [excentricidade]: **ser uma ~** to be madness.

malvadeza [mawva'deza], **malvadez** [mawva'deʒ] f wickedness.

malvado, da [maw'vadu, da] <> adj wicked. <> m, f thug.

malversação [mawvexsa'sãw] (pl **-ões**) f **-1.** [desvio]: **~ (de algo)** embezzlement (of sthg). **-2.** [mau gerenciamento] mismanagement.

Malvinas [maw'vinaʃ] npl: **as (ilhas) ~** the Falkland Islands, the Falklands.

malvisto, ta [maw'viʃtu, ta] adj **-1.** [malconceituado] badly thought of. **-2.** [antipatizado] disliked.

mama ['mãma] f breast.

mamadeira [mama'dejra] f baby's bottle.

mamãe [mã'mãj] f mummy, mum.

mamão [ma'mãw] (pl **-ões**) m papaya.

mamar [4] [ma'ma(x)] <> vt [sugar] to suck. <> vi **-1.** [alimentar-se] to feed; **dar de ~ a alguém** to breastfeed sb. **-2.** fig [tirar lucros ilícitos]: **ele está mamando nas tetas do governo** he's milking the government dry.

mamário, ria [ma'marju, rja] adj mammary.

mamata [ma'mata] f **-1.** fam [proveito ilícito] racket. **-2.** [facilidade] breeze; **ser uma ~** to be a piece of cake.

mambembe [mãn'bẽnbi] <> adj [circo, teatro] second-rate. <> m [grupo teatral ambulante] travelling theatre.

mameluco, ca [mame'luku, ka] m mixed race person of native Indian and European extraction.

mamífero, ra [ma'miferu, ra] adj mammalian.
↠ **mamífero** m mammal.

mamilo [ma'milu] m nipple.

maminha [ma'miɲa] f [carne] rump steak.

mamoeiro [ma'mwejru] m papaya tree.

mamões [ma'mõjʃ] pl ↣ **mamão**.

mamografia [mãmogra'fia] f mammography.

manada [ma'nada] f herd.

Manágua [ma'nagwa] n Managua.

manancial [manãn'sjaw] (pl **-ais**) m **-1.** [fonte] spring. **-2.** fig [origem] source.

Manaus [ma'nawʃ] n Manaus.

mancada [mãn'kada] f **-1.** [erro] mistake. **-2.** [gafe] gaffe; **dar uma ~** to make a gaffe.

mancar [12] [mãŋ'ka(x)] vi [coxear] to limp.
↠ **mancar-se** vp fam [desconfiar] to take a hint.

mancha ['mãnʃa] f **-1.** [ger] stain. **-2.** [em pintura] blotch. **-3.** [marca] mark.

manchado, da [mã'ʃadu, da] adj **-1.** [com manchas] stained. **-2.** [pintura] blotched. **-3.** [malhado] mottled.

manchar [4] [mã'ʃa(x)] vt **-1.** [ger] to stain. **-2.** [deixar marca] to mark.

manchete [mãn'ʃɛtʃi] f headline; **o acidente virou ~ em todo o país** the accident hit the headlines nationwide.

manco, ca ['mãŋku, ka] <> adj lame. <> m, f disabled person.

mancomunado, da [mãŋkomu'nadu, da] adj hand in glove.

mancomunar [4] [mãŋkomu'na(x)] vt: **~ algo (com alguém)** to collude in sthg (with sb).
↠ **mancomunar-se** vp: **~-se (com alguém)** to collude (with sb).

mandachuva [mãnda'ʃuva] mf **-1.** [pessoa poderosa] boss. **-2.** [chefe, líder] chief.

mandado [mãn'dadu] m **-1.** [autorização] order. **-2.** JUR injunction; **~ de despejo** eviction order; **~ de prisão** arrest warrant; **~ de segurança** injunction.

mandamento [mãnda'mẽntu] m **-1.** [preceito] order. **-2.** RELIG commandment.

mandante [mãn'dãntʃi] mf **-1.** JUR person who grants a mandate. **-2.** [instigador] instigator.

mandão, ona [mãn'dãw, ɔnal (*mpl* -ões) *adj fam* [autoritário] bossy.

mandar [4] [mãn'da(x)] ◇ *vt* -**1.**: ~ alguém fazer *ou* que alguém faça algo [ordenar] to tell sb to do sthg; [recomendar] to order sb to do sthg; ~ chamar alguém to send for sb; ~ dizer que to send word that; ~ embora to send away. -**2.** [enviar] to send. ◇ *vi* -**1.** [chefiar, dominar]: ~ (em alguém/algo) to order (sb/sthg) around; no escritório, é ele quem manda he's the one who gives the orders in the office. -**2.** *fam* [noticiar]: o que é que você manda? what can I do for you?
➡ **mandar-se** *vp* -**1.** *fam* [ir-se embora] to get going. -**2.** [fugir] to take off.

mandarim [mãnda'rĩ] (*pl* -**ns**) *m* -**1.** [título] mandarin. -**2.** [dialeto] Mandarin.

mandatário, ria [mãnda'tarju, rja] *m* -**1.** [representante] deputy, representative. -**2.** [procurador] defence lawyer *UK*, defense lawyer *US*, counsel for the defence *UK*, defense attorney *US*.

mandato [mãn'datu] *m* -**1.** [procuração] mandate. -**2.** [missão] duty. -**3.** [ordem] order. -**4.** *POL* term of office.

mandíbula [mãn'dʒibula] *f* jaw.

mandinga [mãn'dʒĩga] *f* witchcraft.

mandioca [mãn'dʒjɔka] *f* cassava, manioc.

mando ['mãndu] *m* -**1.** [autoridade] authority. -**2.** [ordem] order; a ~ de at the orders of.

mandões [mãn'dõjʃ] *mpl* ▷ **mandão**.

mandona [mãn'dona] *f* ▷ **mandão**.

maneira [4] [ma'nejra] *f* manner; à ~ (de) like; de ~ nenhuma *ou* alguma no way; não volto àquele clube de ~ alguma! no way am I going back to that club!; de ~ que so that; de qualquer ~ [sem cuidado] anyhow; [a qualquer preço] at whatever cost; [de todo modo] whatever; de qualquer ~ será útil it'll be useful, whatever.
➡ **maneiras** *fpl* manners; boas ~s good manners; ter boas ~s to have good manners.

maneirar [4] [manej'ra(x)] ◇ *vt* -**1.** *fam* [contornar] to sort out. -**2.** [controlar] to control. ◇ *vi* -**1.** [acomodar as coisas] to get sorted. -**2.** [controlar-se] to control o.s.

maneiro, ra [ma'nejru, ra] *adj* -**1.** [de fácil uso] simple. -**2.** [fácil] easy. -**3.** *fam* [legal] great.

manejar [4] [mane'ʒa(x)] *vt* -**1.** [ger] to control. -**2.** [manusear] to handle. -**3.** [administrar] to manage.

manejável [mane'ʒavɛw] (*pl* -**eis**) *adj* -**1.** [fácil de usar] simple. -**2.** [controlável] controllable.

manejo [ma'neʒu] *m* -**1.** [manuseio] handling. -**2.** [uso] use. -**3.** [administração] management.

manequim [mane'kĩ] (*pl* -**ns**) ◇ *m* [boneco] dummy. ◇ *mf* [pessoa] model.

maneta [ma'neta] *adj* one-handed.

manga ['mãga] *f* -**1.** [de roupa] sleeve; em ~s de camisa in shirt-sleeves. -**2.** [fruto] mango. -**3.** [filtro] filter. -**4.** *loc*: pôr as ~s de fora to show one's true self; arregaçar as ~s to roll up one's sleeves.

manganês [mãga'neʃ] *m* manganese.

mangue ['mãgil *m* -**1.** [terreno] mangrove swamp. -**2.** [planta] mangrove.

mangueira [mãn'gejra] *f* -**1.** *BOT* mango tree. -**2.** [cano] hose.

manha ['maɲa] *f* -**1.** [habilidade] skill. -**2.** [esperteza] shrewdness. -**3.** *fam* [choro, birra] tantrum; fazer ~ to throw a tantrum.

manhã [ma'ɲã] (*pl* -**s**) *f* morning; amanhã de ~ tomorrow morning; de ~ cedo in the early morning; de *ou* pela ~ in the morning; hoje de ~ this morning; seis horas da ~ six o'clock in the morning.

manhãzinha [maɲã'ziɲa] *f*: de ~ early in the morning.

manhoso, osa [ma'ɲozu, ɔza] *adj* -**1.** [esperto] sly. -**2.** [chorão, birrento] whingeing.

mania [ma'nia] *f* -**1.** *PSIC* mania; ~ de perseguição persecution complex. -**2.** [gosto exagerado] obsession; ~ de algo obsession with sthg. -**3.** [hábito] habit; ter ~ de fazer algo to have a habit of doing sthg. -**4.** [mau hábito] bad habit. -**5.** [peculiaridade, excentricidade] quirk.

maníaco, ca [ma'niaku, ka] ◇ *adj* -**1.** *PSIC* maniacal. -**2.** [fanático]: ser ~ por algo to be manic about sthg. ◇ *m, f PSIC* maniac; ~ sexual sex maniac.

maníaco-depressivo, maníaca-depressiva [ma,niakudepre'sivu, ma,niakadepre'siva] ◇ *adj* manic-depressive. ◇ *m, f* manic-depressive.

manicômio [mani'komju] *m* lunatic asylum.

manicuro, ra [mani'kuru, ra] *m, f* manicurist.

manicure [mani'kuri] *f* manicure.

manifestação [manifeʃta'sãw] (*pl* -**ões**) *f* -**1.** [ger] manifestation. -**2.** [expressão] display.

manifestadamente [manifeʃtada'mẽntʃi] *adv* quite clearly.

manifestante [manifeʃ'tãntʃi] *mf* demonstrator.

manifestar [4] [manifeʃ'ta(x)] *vt* -**1.** [exprimir] to express. -**2.** [revelar] to display.
➡ **manifestar-se** *vp* -**1.** [revelar-se] to reveal o.s. -**2.** [pronunciar-se]: ~-se (sobre/a favor de/contra algo) to express an opinion (on/in favour of/against sthg).

manifesto, ta [mani'fɛʃtu, ta] *adj* manifest.
➡ **manifesto** *m* manifesto.

Manila [ma'nila] *n* Manila.

manilha [ma'niʎa] *f* [tubo] pipe.

manipulação [manipula'sãw] *f* -**1.** [com as mãos] handling. -**2.** [ger] manipulation. -**3.** *FARM* preparation.

manipulador, ra [manipula'do(x), ra] *adj* manipulative.

manipular [manipu'la(x)] *vt* -**1.** [ger] to manipulate. -**2.** [com as mãos] to handle. -**3.** *FARM* to prepare.

maniqueísmo [manike'iʒmul *m* Manicheism.

maniqueísta [manike'iʃta] ◇ *adj* seeing things in black and white. ◇ *mf* Manichaean.

manivela [mani'vɛla] *f* crank.

manjado, da [mã'ʒadu, da] *adj fam* well-known.

manjar [4] [mã'ʒa(x)] ⬦ *m* [iguaria] delicacy. ⬦ *vt fam* -**1.** [compreender] to grasp. -**2.** [observar] to watch. ⬦ *vi* [conhecer]: ~ **de algo** to know about sthg.

manjar-branco [mãn,ʒax'brãŋku] (*pl* **manjares-brancos**) *m* blancmange.

manjedoura [mãnʒe'dora] *f* manger.

manjericão [mãnʒeri'kãw] *m* basil.

manjerona [mãnʒe'rona] *f* marjoram.

mano, na [ˈmanu, na] *m,f fam* -**1.** [irmão] brother (sister). -**2.** *fam* [camarada, amigo] buddy.

manobra [ma'nɔbra] *f* -**1.** [ger] manoeuvre *UK*, maneuver *US*. -**2.** *fig* [manipulação] manipulation.
➥ **manobras** *fpl* MIL manoeuvres *UK*, maneuvers *US*.

manobrar [mano'bra(x)] ⬦ *vt* -**1.** [manejar] to manoeuvre *UK*, to maneuver *US*. -**2.** [dirigir] to direct. -**3.** *fig* [manipular] to manipulate. ⬦ *vi* MIL to manoeuvre *UK*, to maneuver *US*.

manobrista [mano'briʃta] *mf* -**1.** [de carro] valet *UK*, car jockey *US*. -**2.** [de trem] shunter.

mansão [mãn'sãw] (*pl* -**ões**) *f* mansion.

mansidão [mãnsi'dãw] *f* -**1.** [brandura] gentleness; **ele falava com** ~ he spoke gently. -**2.** [tranqüilidade] calmness.

mansinho, nha [mã'siɲu, ɲa] *adj* [diminutivo de manso] gentle.
➥ **de mansinho** *loc adv* -**1.** [de leve] gently. -**2.** [sorrateiramente]: **entrar/sair de** ~ to creep in/out.

manso, sa [ˈmãsu, sa] *adj* -**1.** [brando] gentle. -**2.** [tranqüilo] calm. -**3.** [domesticado] tame.

mansões [man'sõjʃ] *pl* ⯈ **mansão**.

manta [ˈmãnta] *f* -**1.** [cobertor] blanket. -**2.** [xale] shawl. -**3.** [de carne seca] cut.

manteiga [mãn'tejga] *f* butter; **passar** ~ **em algo** to spread butter on sthg; ~ **de cacau** cocoa butter; ~ **derretida** *fam fig* cry baby.

manteigueira [mãntej'gejra] *f* butter dish.

mantenedor, ra [mãntene'do(x), ra] *m, f* -**1.** [de filho, casa] supporter. -**2.** [de máquina] service engineer.

manter [4] [mãn'te(x)] *vt* -**1.** [ger] to keep. -**2.** [em bom estado - máquina] to service; [- casa, saúde] to keep. -**3.** [família] to support. -**4.** [opinião, posição] to hold. -**5.** [relações] to maintain; ~ **boas relações com alguém** to maintain a good relationship with sb.
➥ **manter-se** *vp* -**1.** [sustentar-se] to support o.s. -**2.** [permanecer] to remain; ~**-se a par de algo** to keep abreast of sthg.

mantilha [mãn'tʃiʎa] *f* -**1.** [véu] veil. -**2.** [manta] shawl.

mantimentos [mãntʃi'mẽntuʃ] *m* provisions (*pl*).

manto [ˈmãntu] *m* -**1.** [vestimenta] cloak. -**2.** [de reis] robe. -**3.** *fig* [simulação] smokescreen.

mantô [mãn'to] *m* coat.

manual [ma'nwaw] (*pl* -**ais**) ⬦ *adj* manual; **ter habilidade** ~ to be good with one's hands. ⬦ *m* manual.

manufatura [manufa'tura] *f* [fabricação] manufacture.

manufaturado, da [manufatu'radu, da] *adj* manufactured.

manufaturar [manufatu'ra(x)] *vt* to manufacture.

manuscrito, ta [manuʃ'kritu] *adj* handwritten.
➥ **manuscrito** *m* manuscript.

manusear [manu'zea(x)] *vt* -**1.** [manejar] to handle. -**2.** [folhear] to thumb.

manuseio [manu'zeju] *m* handling.

manutenção [manutẽn'sãw] *f* -**1.** [ger] maintenance. -**2.** [da casa] upkeep. -**3.** [da família] support.

mão [ˈmãw] (*pl* **mãos**) *f* -**1.** [ger] hand; **à** ~ [perto] at hand; [com a mão] by hand; **feito à** ~ handmade; **à** ~ **armada** armed; **dar a** ~ **a alguém** to hold sb's hand; **de** ~**s dadas** hand in hand; **de primeira** ~ firsthand; **de segunda** ~ second-hand; **entregar algo em** ~**s** to deliver sthg by hand; ~**s ao alto!** hands up!; ~**s à obra!** let's get to work!; **pôr a** ~ **em algo** to lay one's hands on sthg; **ter a** ~ **pesada** to be clumsy; **ter algo em** ~ to have sthg to hand. -**2.** [no trânsito]: **esta rua dá** ~ **para a praia** this street takes you to the beach; **fora de** ~ out of the way; ~ **dupla** two-way; ~ **única** one-way; **uma rua de** ~ **dupla/única** a two-way/one-way street. -**3.** [de tinta] coat. -**4.** [habilidade]: **com** ~ **de mestre** with a master touch; **ter uma** ~ **boa para algo** to be good at sthg. -**5.** [poder, controle]: **estar nas** ~**s de alguém** to be in sb's hands; **estar em boas** ~**s** to be in good hands. -**6.** *loc*: **abrir** ~ **de algo** to give sthg up; **agüentar a** ~ *fam* [suportar] to hold out; [aguardar] to hang on; **dar a** ~ **à palmatória** to admit one's mistake; **ficar na** ~ to be duped; **forçar a** ~ to get nasty; **lançar** ~ **de algo** to make use of sthg; **largar a** ~ **em alguém** to hit sb; **largar alguém/algode** ~ to wash one's hands of sb/sthg; **pedir a** ~ **de alguém (em casamento)** to ask for sb's hand (in marriage); **passar a** ~ **em algo** [roubar] to nick sthg; **pôr a** ~ **no fogo por alguém** to stand up for sb; **ser uma** ~ **na roda** to be a great help; **de** ~ **beijada** bucksheet; **dar uma** ~ **a alguém** to give sb a hand; **preciso de uma** ~ I need a hand.

mão-aberta [,mãwa'bɛxta] (*pl* **mãos-abertas**) *adj* generous.

mão-boba [mãw'bɔba] (*pl* -**s**) ⬦ *f fam* [com propósito libidinoso]: **passar a** ~ **em alguém** to touch sb up. ⬦ *m* perv.

mão-cheia [,mãw'ʃeja] *f*: **de** ~ first-rate.

mão-de-obra [mãw'dʒɔbra] (*pl* **mãos-de-obra**) *f* -**1.** [trabalho, custo] labour *UK*, labor *US*; **ser uma** ~ *fig* to be hard work. -**2.** [trabalhadores] workforce; ~ **especializada** skilled labour.

mão-de-vaca [mãwdʒi'vaka] (*pl* -**s**) *f fam* [avaro] skinflint.

mão-leve [,mãw'lɛvil] (*pl* **mãos-leves**) *mf* pilferer.

maoísta [maw'iʃta] ⬦ *adj* Maoist. ⬦ *mf* Maoist.

mapa [ˈmapa] *m* map; **sumir do** ~ *fam fig* to disappear off the face of the earth.

mapa-múndi [ˌmapaˈmũndʒil] (*pl* **mapas-múndi**) *m* world map.

Maputo [maˈputu] *n* Maputo.

maquete [maˈkɛtʃil] *f* model.

maquiado, da [maˈkjadu, da] *adj* [com maquiagem] made-up.

maquiador, ra [makjaˈdo(x), ra], **maquilador, ra** [makilaˈdo(x), ra] *m, f* make-up artist.

maquiagem [maˈkjaʒẽl] (*pl* -ns) *f* -1. [ger] make-up; **ele se encarregou da** ~ he was in charge of make-up. -2. [disfarce]: ~ **financeira** financial cover-up.

maquiar [16] [maˈkjax] *vt* -1. [pintar] to make up. -2. *fig* [mascarar] to cover up.

➡ **maquiar-se** *vp* [pintar-se] to put on one's make-up.

maquiavélico, ca [makjaˈvɛliku, ka] *adj* Machiavellian.

maquilador, ra [makilaˈdo(x), ra] *m, f* = **maquiador**.

maquilagem [makiˈlaʒẽl] *f* = **maquiagem**.

maquilar [4] [makiˈla(x)l *vt* [pintar] to make up.

➡ **maquilar-se** *vp* [pintar-se] to put on one's make-up.

máquina [ˈmakina] *f* -1. [ger] machine; **bater** *ou* **escrever à** ~ to type; **costurar à** ~ to machine-sew; **escrito à** ~ typewritten; **feito à** ~ machine-made; ~ **de calcular** calculator; ~ **de costura** sewing machine; ~ **de escrever** typewriter; ~ **fotográfica** camera; ~ **de lavar (roupa)** washing machine. -2. [locomotora] engine; ~ **a vapor** steam engine. -3. *fig* [de estado, partido *etc*] machinery.

➡ **máquinas** *fpl* machinery.

maquinação [makinaˈsãw] (*pl* -ões) *f* machination.

maquinar [4] [makiˈna(x)l ⬦ *vt* to plot. ⬦ *vi*: ~ **contra alguém/algo** to plot against sb/sthg.

maquinária [makiˈnarja], **maquinaria** [makinaˈria] *f* [máquinas] machinery.

maquinário [makiˈnarju] *m* = **maquinária**.

maquinista [makiˈniʃta] *mf* -1. FERRO engine driver. -2. TEATRO stagehand.

mar [ˈma(x)l (*pl* -es) *m* sea; **em pleno** ~ on the high seas; **fazer-se ao** ~ to set sail; ~ **aberto** open sea; **por** ~ by sea; ~ **Morto** Dead Sea; ~ **Negro** Black Sea; ~ **do Norte** North Sea; ~ **de rosas** [mar calmo] calm sea; *fig* bed of roses; **nem tanto ao** ~ **nem tanto à terra** neither one way nor the other.

mar. (*abrev de* março) Mar.

maraca [maˈraka] *f* maracas (*pl*).

maracujá [marakuˈʒa] *m* passion fruit.

maracujazeiro [marakuʒaˈzejru] *m* passion fruit plant.

maracutaia [marakuˈtaja] *f* dirty trick.

marajá [maraˈʒa] *m* -1. [título] maharaja. -2. *fig* [servidor] a person who has uses their position, not necessarily honestly, in order to become very rich.

Maranhão [maraˈpãw] *n* Maranhão.

marasmo [maˈraʒmu] *m* -1. [desânimo] lethargy. -2. [estagnação] stagnation.

maratona [maraˈtona] *m* marathon.

maratonista [maratoˈniʃta] *mf* marathon runner.

maravilha [maraˈviʎa] *f* wonder; **às mil** ~**s** wonderfully; **ser uma** ~ to be wonderful.

maravilhado, da [maraviˈʎadu, da] *adj*: ~ **(com)** amazed (at).

maravilhar [4] [maraviˈʎa(x)l *vt* to astonish.

➡ **maravilhar-se** *vp*: ~-**se (de algo)** to be amazed (at sthg).

maravilhoso, osa [maraviˈʎozu, ɔza] *adj* wonderful.

marca [ˈmaxka] *f* -1. [ger] mark. -2. [COM- de carro] make; [- de café, queijo] brand; ~ **comercial** *ou* **de fábrica** trademark; ~ **registrada** registered trademark. -3. [de prata] hallmark.

➡ **de marca maior** *loc adj pej* of the first order.

marcação [maxkaˈsãw] (*pl* -ões) *f* -1. [ato de marcar - enxoval] marking; [- gado] branding. -2. *ESP* marking. -3. [perseguição, vigilância] scrutiny; **estar de** ~ **com alguém** to pick on sb.

marcado, da [maxˈkadu, da] *adj* -1. [assinalado - roupa, texto] marked; [- gado] branded. -2. [reservado] booked. -3. [com marca, mancha] marked. -4. [pessoa - traumatizada] marked; [- em evidência] watched.

marcador [maxkaˈdo(x)l *m* -1. [de livro] bookmark. -2. [ESP- quadro] scoreboard; [- jogador] scorer.

marcante [maxˈkãtʃil *adj* marked.

marcapasso [maxkaˈpasul *m* MED pacemaker.

marcar [12] [maxˈka(x)l *vt* -1. [ger] to mark; ~ **época** to make history. -2. [pôr marca em - livro, roupa] to mark; [- animal] to brand. -3. [data, hora, prazo] to fix; ~ **o tempo de algo** to time sthg. -4. [almoço, encontro] to arrange; ~ **uma consulta** to make an appointment. -5. [ESP - jogador] to mark; [- gol] to score. -6. [suj: relógio] to say. -7. [suj: termômetro] to show. -8. [demarcar] to demarcate.

marcenaria [maxsenaˈria] *f* -1. [arte] marquetry. -2. [trabalho] cabinet-making. -3. [oficina] cabinet-maker's workshop.

marceneiro, ra [maxseˈnejru, ra] *m, f* cabinet-maker.

marcha [ˈmaxʃa] *f* -1. [ato] marching; **pôr-se em** ~ to set off. -2. [passo] pace. -3. [ger] march. -4. AUTO gear; **dar** ~ **à ré** to reverse; ~ **à ré** reverse. -5. [MÚS - tradicional] march; ~ **fúnebre** funeral march; [- popular] festive march. -6. *fig* [progressão] course.

marchar [4] [maxˈʃa(x)l *vi* -1. MIL to march; ~ **sobre** [avançar] to march into. -2. [ir]: ~ **para** to go to.

marchetar [4] [maxʃeˈta(x)l *vt* [incrustar]: ~ **algo (de algo)** to inlay sthg (with sthg).

marchinha [maxˈʃiɲal *f* MÚS *a satirical song in double time, in the main performed during carnival.*

marcial [max'sjaw] (pl -ais) adj martial; **corte ~** court martial.

marciano, na [max'sjanu, na] <> adj Martian. <> m, f Martian.

marco ['maxku] m **-1.** [ger] landmark. **-2.** [moeda] mark. **-3.** [da janela] frame.

março ['marsu] m March; *veja também* **setembro.**

maré [ma'rε] f **-1.** [do mar] tide; **~ alta/baixa** high/low tide; **remar contra a ~ fig** to swim against the tide. **-2. fig** [ocasião] spell; **aproveitar a ~** to make the most of one's luck. **-3. fig** [tendência] tendency. **-4. fig** [humor]: **estar de ~ alta** to be in high spirits. **-5. fig** [multidão] sea.

mareado, da [ma'rjadu, da] adj **-1.** [enjoado] seasick. **-2.** [oxidado] tarnished.

marear [15] [ma'rja(x)] <> vt **-1.** [enjoar] to make seasick. **-2.** [oxidar] to tarnish. <> vi [enjoar] to be seasick.

marechal [mare'ʃaw] (pl -ais) m marshal.

maré-cheia [ma,rε'ʃeja] (pl **marés-cheias**) f high tide.

marejar [4] [mare'ʒa(x)] <> vt to shed. <> vi to flow.

~ marejar-se vp: **~-se de lágrimas** to well up with tears.

maremoto [mare'mɔtu] m tidal wave.

maresia [mare'zia] f sea air.

marfim [max'fĩ] m ivory; **de ~** ivory *(antes de subst)*.

margarida [maxga'rida] f BOT daisy.

margarina [maxga'rina] f margarine.

margear [15] [max'ʒja(x)] vt **-1.** [seguir pela margem de] to follow. **-2.** [estar à margem de] to border.

margem ['maxʒẽ] (pl -ns) f **-1.** [ger] margin; **~ de lucro** profit margin. **-2.** [beira - de estrada, lago] edge; **à ~ de** alongside; [- de rio] bank; [- litoral] shore. **-3.** [latitude] room; **~ de erro** margin of error; **~ de segurança** safety margin. **-4.** [limites] edge; **à ~ da sociedade/lei** on the fringes of society/the law; **manter-se à ~ de algo** to remain distant from sthg. **-5.** [ocasião]: **dar ~ a alguém para fazer algo** to give sb the chance to do sthg.

marginal [maxʒi'naw] (pl -ais) <> adj **-1.** [pessoa] delinquent. **-2.** [nota] marginal. <> mf [pessoa] delinquent.

marginalidade [maxʒinali'dadʒi] f delinquency.

marginalizar [4] [maxʒinali'za(x)] vt [excluir] to marginalize.

~ marginalizar-se vp [tornar-se fora-da-lei] to marginalize o.s.

maria-fumaça [ma,riafu'masa] (pl **marias-fuma-ças**) m & f steam train.

maria-mijona [ma,riami'ʒona] adj inv unfashionably long.

maria-mole [ma,ria'mɔli] (pl -s) f CULIN marshmallow dessert covered with coconut.

maria-sem-vergonha [ma,riasẽvex'goɲa] (pl **marias-sem-vergonha**) f BOT busy lizzie.

maria-vai-com-as-outras [ma,riavajkwa'd zowtraʃ] mf inv sheep.

maricas [ma'rikaʃ] **fam** <> adj inv [medroso] chicken. <> m inv [efeminado] pretty boy.

marido [ma'ridu] m husband.

marimbondo [marĩ'bõdu] m hornet.

marina [ma'rina] f marina.

marinar [4] [mari'nax] vt to marinate.

marinha [ma'riɲa] f ⊳ **marinho.**

marinheiro, ra [mari'ɲejru, ra] <> adj sailor's *(antes de subst).* <> m, f sailor; **~ de primeira viagem fig** greenhorn.

marinho, nha [ma'riɲu, ɲa] adj [do mar] marine.

~ marinho <> adj inv [cor] navy. <> m [cor] navy blue.

~ marinha f **-1.** [força] navy; **marinha (de guerra)** navy; **marinha mercante** merchant navy. **-2.** [pintura] seascape.

marionete [marjo'nεtʃi] f puppet.

mariposa [mari'poza] f moth.

marisco [ma'riʃku] m shellfish.

marital [mari'taw] (pl -ais) adj marital.

maritalmente [maritaw'mẽtʃi] adv: **viver ~ (com alguém)** to live together (with sb).

marítimo, ma [ma'ritʃimu, ma] adj maritime.

marketing ['maxketʃĩŋ] m marketing.

marmanjo [max'mãʒu] m grown man.

marmelada [maxme'lada] f **-1.** [doce] quince jam. **-2. fam** [mamata] racket.

marmelo [max'mεlu] m quince.

marmita [max'mita] f **-1.** [recipiente] casserole. **-2.** [refeição] packed lunch.

mármore ['maxmori] m marble; **de ~** marble *(antes de subst).*

marmóreo, rea [max'mɔriu, ria] adj marble.

marola [ma'rɔla] f small wave.

maroto, ta [ma'rotu, ta] adj **-1.** [esperto] crafty. **-2.** [malicioso] malicious.

marquês, quesa [max'keʃ, eza] (mpl -eses, fpl -esas) m, f marquis (f marchioness).

marquise [max'kizi] f canopy.

marra ['maxa] f: **obedeceu na ~** he obeyed under pressure; **invadiram ~** they invaded in strength.

marreco [ma'xεku] m wigeon.

Marrocos [ma'xɔkuʃ] n Morocco.

marrom [ma'xõ] (pl -ns) <> adj brown. <> m brown.

marrom-glacê [ma'xõ'gla'se] (pl -s) m marron glacé.

marroquino, na [maxo'kinu, na] <> adj Moroccan. <> m, f Morrocan.

Marte ['maxtʃi] m Mars.

martelada [maxte'lada] f **-1.** [pancada] blow. **-2.** [ruído] bang.

martelar [maxte'la(x)] <> vt **-1.** [com martelo] to hammer. **-2.** [afligir] to bother. **-3.** [repetir] to repeat. <> vi **-1.** [dar marteladas] to hammer. **-2.** [insistir]: **~ em algo** to keep on about sthg.

martelo [max'tεlu] m hammer.

mártir ['maxti(x)] (pl -es) mf martyr.

martírio [max'tʃirju] m **-1.** [suplício] martyrdom.

-2. *fig* [tormento] torment; **ser um** ~ to be a torment.

martirizante [maxtʃiri'zãntʃil *adj* agonizing.

martirizar [4] [maxtʃiri'za(x)] *vt* **-1.** [torturar] to torture. **-2.** *fig* [atormentar] to torment.

➡ **martirizar-se** *vp* [atormentar-se] to agonize.

marujo [ma'ruʒul *m* sailor.

marulhar [4] [maru'ʎa(x)] *vi* **-1.** [mar] to surge. **-2.** [ondas] to lap. **-3.** [barulho das ondas] to crash.

marulho [ma'ruʎul *m* **-1.** [do mar] surge. **-2.** [das ondas] lapping.

marxismo [max'ksiʒmul *m* Marxism.

marxista [max'ksiʃtal <> *adj* Marxist. <> *mf* Marxist.

marzipã [maxzi'pãl *m* marzipan.

mas [ma(j)ʃl <> *conj* but; ~ **que decepção!** how disappointing! <> *cont* = **me + as**.

➡ **mas também** *loc conj* but also; **não só ... ~ também** not only ... but also.

mascar [12] [maʃ'ka(x)] <> *vt* to chew. <> *vi* to chew.

máscara ['maʃkaral *f* **-1.** [ger] mask; **baile de** ~**s** masked ball; ~ **de oxigênio** oxygen mask; ~ **(de beleza)** face mask. **-2.** [fachada] disguise; **tirar a** ~ **de alguém** to unmask sb.

mascarado, da [maʃka'radu, dal *adj* **-1.** [fantasiado] masked. **-2.** *fig* [disfarçado]: ~ **de mendigo** disguised as a beggar.

mascarar [4] [maʃka'ra(x)] *vt* to mask.

mascate [maʃ'katʃil *m* hawker.

Mascate [maʃ'katʃil *n* Muscat.

mascavo [maʃ'kavul *adj* ➾ **açúcar**.

mascote [maʃ'kɔtʃil *f* mascot.

masculinidade [maʃkulini'dadʒil *f* masculinity.

masculinizado, da [maʃkulini'zadu, dal *adj* [mulher] masculine.

masculinizar [maʃkulini'za(x)] *vt* to masculinize.

masculino, na [maʃku'linu, nal *adj* **-1.** [sexo, população] male. **-2.** [modos, voz]: **esta foi uma reação tipicamente masculina** that was a typically male response. **-3.** *GRAM* masculine.

➡ **masculino** *m* *GRAM* masculine.

másculo, la ['maʃkulu, lal *adj* [viril] manly.

masmorra [maʒ'moxal *f* **-1.** [calabouço] dungeon. **-2.** *fig* [aposento] hole.

masoquismo [mazo'kiʒmul *m* masochism.

masoquista [mazo'kiʃtal <> *adj* masochistic. <> *mf* masochist.

massa ['masal *f* **-1.** [ger] mass. **-2.** [culinária - de pão] dough; [- de bolo] mixture; [- de torta, empada] pastry; [- de tomate] paste. **-3.** [macarrão] pasta. **-4.** [grande quantidade]: **uma** ~ **de** a mass of. **-5.** *CONSTR:* ~ **de vidraceiro** putty. **-6.** [maioria]: **a** ~ **de** the majority of.

➡ **massas** *fpl*: **as** ~**s** the masses.

➡ **em massa** *loc adv* en masse.

massa-corrida ['masako'xidal (*pl* **-s**) *f* plaster skim applied before painting.

massacrante [masa'krãntʃil *adj* annoying.

massacrar [4] [masa'kra(x)] *vt* **-1.** [ger] to

massacre. -2. [oprimir] to oppress. **-3.** *fig* [torturar] to torture.

massacre [ma'sakril *m* massacre.

massagear [15] [masa'ʒea(x)] <> *vt* to massage. <> *vi* to do massage.

massagem [ma'saʒēl (*pl* **-ns**) *f* massage; ~ **facial** facial.

massagista [masa'ʒiʃtal *mf* masseur (masseuse).

massificação [masifika'sãwl (*pl* **-ões**) *f* popularization.

massificado, da [masifika'du, dal *adj* popular (*antes de subst*).

massificar [12] [masifi'ka(x)] *vt* **-1.** [ensino universitário] to popularize. **-2.** [povo] to sell to the masses.

massinha [ma'siɲal *f* **-1.** [para modelar] Plasticine®. **-2.** [comestível]: **sopa de** ~ minestrone.

massudo, da [ma'sudu, dal *adj* **-1.** [pão, torta] heavy. **-2.** [documentação, livro] bulky.

mastectomia [maʃtekto'mial *f* mastectomy.

mastigado, da [maʃtʃi'gadu, dal *adj* **-1.** [triturado] chewed. **-2.** [facilitado] well-explained.

mastigar [14] [maʃtʃi'ga(x)] <> *vt* [triturar] to chew. <> *vi* [triturar] to chew.

mastim [maʃ'tʃĩl (*pl* **-ns**) *m* mastiff.

mastite [mas'tʃitʃil *f* mastitis.

mastodonte [maʃto'dõntʃil *m* **-1.** [mamífero] mammoth. **-2.** *fam* [pessoa] hulk.

mastro ['maʃtrul *m* **-1.** *NÁUT* mast. **-2.** [para bandeira] flagpole.

masturbação [maʃtuxba'sãwl *f* masturbation.

masturbar [4] [maʃtux'ba(x)] *vt* to masturbate.

➡ **masturbar-se** *vp* to masturbate.

mata ['matal *f* forest; ~ **virgem** virgin forest.

mata-baratas [mataba'rataʃl *mpl* [inseticida] cockroach killer.

mata-borrão [,matabo'xãwl (*pl* **mata-borrões**) *m* **-1.** [papel] blotting paper. **-2.** [artefato] blotter.

matacão [mata'kãwl (*pl* **-ões**) *f*: **uma** ~ **de algo** a big lump of sthg.

matado, da [ma'tadu, dal *adj* [serviço] lousy.

matador, ra [mata'do(x), ral *m*, *f* killer.

➡ **matador** *m* [tourada] matador.

matadouro [mata'dorul *m* slaughterhouse.

matagal [mata'gawl (*pl* **-ais**) *m* **-1.** [terreno] bush. **-2.** [mata espessa] thicket.

mata-moscas [,mata'moʃkaʃl *m* (*inv*) fly-swat.

mata-mosquito [,matamoʃ'kitul (*pl* **mata-mosquitos**) *m* mosquito spray.

matança [ma'tãnsal *f* **-1.** [de pessoas] massacre. **-2.** [de animais] slaughter.

matar [4] [ma'ta(x)] <> *vt* **-1.** [ger] to kill. **-2.** [saciar - fome] to satisfy; [- sede] to quench; [- curiosidade] to quell. **-3.** [gazetear] to skip. **-4.** [executar mal] to do badly. **-5.** [decifrar] to guess. **-6.** [fazer desaparecer] to crush. <> *vi* [causar morte] to kill.

➡ **matar-se** *vp* **-1.** [suicidar-se] to kill o.s. **-2.** [cansar-se]: ~**-se de algo/fazer algo** to kill o.s. with sthg/doing sthg.

de matar *loc adj fig* [terrível] terrible; **dor de** ~ excruciating pain; **ser de** ~ to be terrible.

mata-rato [ˌmata'xatu] (*pl* **mata-ratos**) *m* **-1.** [veneno] rat poison. **-2.** *fam* [cigarro] cancer stick.

mate ['matʃil] *m* [bebida] maté.

matelassê [matela'se] *adj* quilted.

matemático, ca [mate'matʃiku, ka] <> *adj* mathematical. <> *m, f* mathematician.

matemática *f* [ciência] mathematics *(sg).*

matéria [ma'tɛrja] *f* **-1.** [ger] matter; ~ **plástica** plastic. **-2.** [assunto] subject; **em** ~ **de política/esporte** in the area of politics/sports. **-3.** *EDUC* subject. **-4.** *JORN* article.

material [mate'rjaw] (*pl* **-ais**) <> *adj* material. <> *m* **-1.** [substância] material. **-2.** [utensílios] materials *(pl);* ~ **de escritório** office stationery; ~ **de limpeza** cleaning products *(pl).* **-3.** [bélico] armaments *(pl).* **-4.** [informativo, didático] teaching material.

materialismo [materja'liʒmu] *m* materialism.

materialista [materja'liʃta] <> *adj* materialistic. <> *mf* materialist.

materializar [4] [materjali'za(x)] *vt* to materialize.

materializar-se *vp* to materialize.

matéria-prima [maˌtɛrja'prima] (*pl* **matérias-primas**) *f* raw material.

maternal [matex'naw] (*pl* **-ais**) <> *adj* maternal. <> *m* *EDUC* nursery school.

maternidade [matexni'dadʒi] *f* **-1.** [qualidade] motherhood. **-2.** [hospital] maternity hospital.

materno, na [ma'tɛxnu, na] *adj* **-1.** [ger] maternal. **-2.** [língua]: **língua** ~ mother tongue.

matilha [ma'tʃiʎa] *f* [cães] pack.

matina [ma'tʃina] *f fam* morning.

matinal [matʃi'naw] (*pl* **-ais**) *adj* morning *(antes de subst).*

matinê [matʃi'ne] *f* matinée.

matiz [ma'tʃiʒ] *m* **-1.** [tom] shade. **-2.** *fig* [traço] tinge.

matizar [4] [matʃi'za(x)] *vt* **-1.** [dar nuances a] to tinge. **-2.** [colorir] to colour *UK,* to color *US.*

mato ['matu] *m* **-1.** [área] scrubland. **-2.** [plantas] weeds *(pl).* **-3.** [roça] countryside. **-4.** *loc:* **estar num** ~ **sem cachorro** *fam* to be up the creek without a paddle; **ser** ~ *fam* to be thick on the ground.

Mato Grosso do Sul [matuˌgrosudu'suw] *n* Mato Grosso do Sul.

matraca [ma'traka] *f* **-1.** [instrumento] rattle; **falar como uma** ~ to talk the hind legs off a donkey. **-2.** *fig* [pessoa] chatterbox.

matraquear [15] [matra'kja(x)] *vi* [tagarelar] to chatter.

matreiro, ra [ma'trejru, ra] *adj fam* [astuto, ardiloso] crafty.

matriarca [ma'trjaxka] *f* matriarch.

matriarcal [matrjax'kaw] (*pl* **-ais**) *adj* matriarchal.

matrícula [ma'trikula] *f* **-1.** [inscrição] enrolment *UK,* enrollment *US;* **fazer (a)** ~ to enrol *UK,* to

enroll *US;* **qual é o seu número de** ~ what's your registration number? **-2.** [taxa] fee.

matricular [4] [matriku'la(x)] *vt:* ~ **alguém (em algo)** to enrol sb (in sthg) *UK,* to enroll sb (in sthg) *US.*

matricular-se *vp:* ~**-se (em algo)** to enrol (in sthg) *UK,* to enroll (in sthg) *US.*

matrimonial [matrimo'njaw] (*pl* **-ais**) *adj* matrimonial.

matrimônio [matri'monju] *m* marriage; **contrair** ~ **(com alguém)** to be joined in marriage (to sb).

matriz [ma'triʃ] (*pl* **-es**) <> *adj* **-1.** [igreja, língua] mother *(antes de subst).* **-2.** [idéia] original. <> *f* **-1.** [de empresa] head office. **-2.** [de igreja] mother church. **-3.** [molde] mould *UK,* mold *US.* **-4.** *MAT* matrix.

matrona [ma'trona] *f pej* matron; **estar uma** ~ to look like an old cow.

maturação [matura'sãw] (*pl* **-ões**) *f* **-1.** [de fruta] ripening. **-2.** *fig* [amadurecimento] maturation.

maturar [4] [matu'ra(x)] <> *vt* to mature. <> *vi* to mature.

maturidade [maturi'dadʒi] *f* maturity.

matusquela [matuʃ'kɛla] *mf fam* lunatic.

matutar [4] [matu'ta(x)] <> *vt* [planejar] to plan. <> *vi* [refletir] to think about; ~ **sobre algo** to turn sthg over in one's mind.

matutino, na [matu'tʃinu, na] *adj* morning.

matutino *m* morning newspaper.

matuto, ta [ma'tutu, ta] <> *adj* **-1.** [da roça] country *(antes de subst).* **-2.** *fam* [sabido] shrewd. <> *m, f* **-1.** [pessoa da roça] country bumpkin. **-2.** [pessoa rude] peasant.

mau, má ['maw, 'ma] <> *adj* **-1.** *(antes de subst)* [ger] bad. **-2.** *(antes de subst)* [incapaz] poor. <> *m, f* **-1.** [pessoa] bad person. **-2.** [em filme etc] baddy.

mau-caráter [ˌmawka'ratex] (*pl* **maus-caráteres**) <> *adj* disreputable. <> *mf* bad character.

mau-olhado [ˌmawo'ʎadu] (*pl* **maus-olhados**) *m* evil eye.

mauricinho [mawri'siɲu] *m fam* posh kid.

Maurício [maw'risju] *n* Mauritius.

máuser® ['mawze(x)] *m* mauser.

mausoléu [mawzo'lɛu] *m* mausoleum.

maus-tratos [mawʃ'tratuʃ] *mpl* abuse.

mavioso, osa [ma'vjozu, ɔza] *adj* affectionate.

maxidesvalorização [maksidʒiʒvaloriza'sãw] (*pl* **-ões**) *f* steep devaluation.

maxilar [maksi'la(x)] (*pl* **-es**) <> *m* jaw. <> *adj* maxillary.

máxima ['masima] *f* ⊳ **máximo**.

maximizar [4] [masimi'za(x)] *vt* **-1.** [aumentar ao máximo] to maximize. **-2.** *MAT* to round up.

máximo, ma ['masimu, ma] *adj* **-1.** [o maior possível] maximum. **-2.** [supremo] highest.

máximo *m* [o mais alto grau] maximum; **ao** ~ to the maximum; **chegar ao** ~ to reach the peak; **no** ~ at most; **ser o** ~ [ser maravilhoso] to be the best.

máxima f -1. [temperatura] maximum. -2. [sentença, princípio] maxim.

maxixe [ma'ʃiʃi] m -1. [legume] gourd. -2. [dança] *Brazilian dance, precursor of the samba.*

mazela [ma'zɛla] f -1. *fam* [doença]: **ela gosta de falar de suas** ~s she likes to talk about her aches and pains. -2. [infortúnio] misfortune.

MB (abrev de **Megabyte**) m MB.

MBA (abrev de **Master of Business Administration**) m MBA.

me [mi] *pron* [complemento direto] me; [complemento indireto] (to) me; [reflexo] myself; **eu nunca** ~ **engano** I'm never wrong; **eu** ~ **machuquei** I've hurt myself; **você já** ~ **contou essa história** you've already told me that story.

meado ['mjadu] m: **no** ~ **de** in the middle of; **em** ~**s de setembro** in mid-September.

meandro ['mjãdru] m meander.

➡ **meandros** *mpl* meanderings.

MEC (abrev de **Ministério da Educação e Cultura**) m Brazilian ministry of education and culture.

Meca ['mɛka] n Mecca.

mecânico, ca [me'kãniku, ka] ◇ *adj* mechanical. ◇ m, f [profissional] mechanic.

➡ **mecânica** f -1. [ger] mechanics (pl). -2. *fig* [mecanismo] workings (pl).

mecanismo [meka'niʒmu] m mechanism; ~ **de defesa** defence mechanism; ~ **de busca** *COMPUT* search engine.

mecanização [mekaniza'sãw] f mechanization.

mecanizar [4] [mekani'za(x)] *vt* to mechanize.

mecenas [me'senaʃ] m *inv* patron.

mecha ['mɛʃa] f -1. [de vela] wick. -2. [de explosivo] fuse. -3. [de cabelo] strand. -4. [cabelo tingido] streak; **fazer** ~ **(no cabelo)** to have one's hair streaked. -5. [em ferimento] wick.

medalha [me'daʎa] f medal.

medalhão [meda'ʎãw] (pl -ões) m -1. [jóia] medallion. -2. *fig* [figurão] high-flyer, big shot.

média ['mɛdʒja] f ➡ **médio**.

mediação [medʒja'sãw] f mediation; **por** ~ **de** through the mediation of.

mediador, ra [medʒja'do(x), ra] m, f mediator.

mediano, na [me'dʒjãnu, na] *adj* -1. [ger] average. -2. [linha] median.

➡ **mediana** f *GEOM* median.

mediante [me'dʒjãntʃi] *prep* -1. [por meio de] through; ~ **ajuda de** with the help of; ~ **a graça de Deus** by the grace of God. -2. [a troco de] in exchange for.

mediar [17] [me'dʒja(x)] ◇ *vt* [intervir em] to mediate; ~ **um debate** to chair a debate. ◇ *vi* [intervir] to mediate; ~ **entre/a favor de** to mediate between/in favour of.

medicação [medʒika'sãw] (pl -ões) f medication.

medicamento [medʒika'mẽntu] m medicine.

medição [medʒi'sãw] (pl -ões) f measurement.

medicar [12] [medʒi'ka(x)] ◇ *vt* to medicate. ◇ *vi* to practise medicine *UK*, to practice medicine *US*.

➡ **medicar-se** *vp* to take medicine.

medicina [medʒi'sina] f medicine; ~ **alternativa** alternative medicine; ~ **legal** forensic medicine.

medicinal [medʒisi'naw] (pl -ais) *adj* medicinal.

médico, ca ['mɛdʒiku, ka] ◇ *adj* medical. ◇ m, f doctor; ~ **de família** family doctor, GP, general expert.

médico-hospitalar [ˌmɛdʒikwoʃpita'la(x)] (pl **médico-hospitalares**) *adj* hospital and medical (antes de subst).

médico-legal [ˌmɛdʒikule'gaw] (pl **médico-legais**) *adj* forensic.

médico-legista, médica-legista [ˌmɛdʒikule'ʒiʃta] (mpl **médicos-legistas**, fpl **médicas-legistas**) m, f forensic expert.

medida [me'dʒida] f -1. [ger] measurement; ~ **de capacidade** measure of capacity. -2. [tamanho] size; **feito sob** ~ made to measure; **tomar as** ~**s de alguém/algo** to take the measurements of sb/sthg. -3. [grau] degree; **na** ~ **do possível** as far as possible. -4. [providência] measure; **tomar** ~**s** to take measures; ~ **provisória** *JUR* emergency measure; ~ **de segurança** safety measure. -5. [limite]: **passar das** ~**s** to go beyond the limits.

➡ **à medida que** *loc conj* as.

➡ **na medida em que** *loc conj* in so far as.

medidor [medʒi'do(x)] m meter; ~ **de pressão** pressure gauge.

medieval [medʒje'vaw] (pl -ais) *adj* medieval.

médio, dia ['mɛdʒju, dja] *adj* -1. [entre dois pontos - ger] middle; [- tamanho] medium. -2. [resultado de cálculo] average. -3. [ensino] secondary.

➡ **média** f -1. *MAT* average; **em** ~ on average. -2. *EDUC* secondary school. -3. [café com leite] white coffee. -4. *loc*: **fazer** ~ **com** to fawn over.

medíocre [me'dʒiwkri] ◇ *adj* mediocre. ◇ *mf* mediocrity.

mediocridade [medʒiwkri'dadʒi] f mediocrity.

medir [70] [me'dʒi(x)] *vt* -1. [ger] to measure; ~ **alguém/algo por algo** to measure sb/sthg against sthg; ~ **alguém/algo por alguém** to measure sb/sthg against sb. -2. [considerar, avaliar] to evaluate. -3. [moderar] to measure; **meça suas palavras!** watch what you say! -4. [olhar com desdém]: ~ **alguém de alto a baixo** to look down on sb.

➡ **medir-se** *vp* -1. [tomar as medidas] to measure o.s. -2. [igualar-se]: ~**-se com alguém em algo** to equal sb at sthg.

meditação [medʒita'sãw] (pl -ões) f meditation.

meditar [4] [medʒi'ta(x)] *vi* to meditate; ~ **sobre algo** to meditate on sthg.

meditativo, va [medʒita'tʃivu, va] *adj* meditative.

mediterrâneo, nea [medʒite'xãnju, nja] *adj* Mediterranean.

➡ **Mediterrâneo** n: **o** (mar) ~ the Mediterranean (Sea).

médium ['mɛdʒjũ] (pl -ns) [espirit] mf medium.

mediúnico, ca [me'dʒuniku, ka] *adj* of a medium *(depois de subst)*.

mediunidade [medʒjuni'dadʒil *f* spiritualism.

medo ['medul *m* -**1.** [pavor] fear; **dar** ~ to frighten; **me dá** ~ **fazer algo** I am frightened of doing sthg; **estar com** *ou***ter** ~ **(de)** to be afraid (of); **estar com** *ou***ter** ~ **de fazer algo** to be afraid of doing sthg; **estar se cagando de** ~ *vulg* to be shitting o.s. with fear; **feio de meter** ~ as ugly as sin; **morrer de** ~ to be frightened to death. -**2.** [receio]: **com** ~ **de/que** for fear of/that; **estar com** *ou***ter** ~ **de** to be afraid of.

medonho, nha [me'doɲu, ɲal *adj* -**1.** [assustador] terrifying. -**2.** [horrível] horrendous.

medrar [4] [me'dra(x)] *vi* -**1.** [planta] to grow. -**2.** *fam* [ficar com medo] to get scared.

medroso, osa [medrozu, ɔzal ◇ *adj* [temeroso] scared. ◇ *m, f* coward.

medula [me'dulal *f* ANAT marrow, medulla; ~ **óssea** bone marrow.

megabyte [mega'bajtʃil *m* COMPUT megabyte.

megaevento [mɛgae'vẽntul *m* huge event.

megafone [mɛga'fonil *m* megaphone.

megahertz [mɛga'xɛxtʃiʃl *m (inv)* megahertz.

megalomania [megaloma'nial *f* megalomania.

megalomaníaco, ca [megaloma'njaku, ka] ◇ *adj* megalomaniac. ◇ *m, f* megalomaniac.

megalópole [mɛga'lɔpolil *f* super-city.

megaton [mega'tõl *m* megaton.

megera [me'ʒeral *f* shrew.

meia ['mejal *f* ⊳ **meio**.

meia-calça [ˌmeja'kawsal *(pl* **meias-calças)** *f* tights *(pl)* UK, pantyhose *(pl)* US.

meia-direita [ˌmejadʒi'rejtal *(pl* **meias-direitas)** FUT ◇ *f* inside right. ◇ *m* inside right.

meia-entrada [ˌmejaẽn'tradal *(pl* **meias-entradas)** *f* half-price ticket.

meia-esquerda [ˌmejaʃ'kexdal *(pl* **meias-esquerdas)** FUT ◇ *f* inside left. ◇ *m* inside left.

meia-estação [ˌmejaiʃta'sãwl *(pl* **meias-estações)** *f* mid-season.

meia-idade [ˌmejej'dadʒil *(pl* **meias-idades)** *f* middle age; **mulher de** ~ middle-aged woman.

meia-lua [ˌmeja'lual *f* -**1.** ASTRO half moon. -**2.** [semicírculo] semicircle.

meia-luz [ˌmeja'luʃl *(pl* **meias-luzes)** *f* half light; **à** ~ in the gloom.

meia-noite [ˌmeja'nojtʃil *(pl* **meias-noites)** *f* midnight; **à** ~ at midnight.

meia-volta [ˌmeja'vɔwtal *(pl* **meias-voltas)** *f* -**1.** [movimento] half turn. -**2.** MIL about-turn UK, about-face US; **fazer** ~ to make an about-turn UK, to make an about-face US.

meigo, ga ['mejgu, gal *adj* gentle.

meiguice [mej'gisil *f* gentleness.

meio, meia ['meju, 'mejal *adj* half; **a** ~ **caminho** halfway; **meia dúzia** half a dozen; **meia hora** half an hour; ~ **quilo** half a kilo; **são três e meia** it's half past three; **um quilo e** ~ a kilo and a half.

➡ **meio** ◇ *adv* half-; ~ **cansado** rather tired.

◇ *m* -**1.** [metade] half; ~ **a** ~ fifty-fifty; **veio** ~ **mundo à festa** *fig* half the world came to the party; **partir ao** ~ to split *ou* break in half; **pelo** ~ [inacabado] halfway through. -**2.** [centro] middle; **o filho do** ~ the middle son; **no** ~ **(de)** in the middle (of). -**3.** [ambiente - social, profissional] circle; [- físico] milieu; ~ **ambiente** environment. -**4.** [modo] way; **por** ~ **de** through, by means of; **por todos os** ~**s** in every way.

➡ **meios** *mpl* [recursos] means; **os** ~**s de comunicação** the media; ~**s de transporte** means of transport.

➡ **meia** ◇ *num* six. ◇ *f* -**1.** [meia - de seda] stocking; [- soquete] sock. -**2.** [entrada] half-price ticket. -**3.** [ponto]: **ponto de meia** stocking stitch.

meio-campo [meju'kãmpul *(pl* **meios-campo)** *m* -**1.** FUT [centro-médio] midfield player. -**2.** [zona] midfield.

meio-dia [ˌmeju'dʒial *(pl* **meios-dias)** *m* midday; **ao** ~ at midday.

meio-fio [ˌmejo'fiwl *(pl* **meios-fios)** *m* kerb UK, curb US.

meio-tempo [ˌmeju'tẽnpul *(pl* **meios-tempos)** *m* -**1.** [ínterim]: **nesse** ~ meanwhile. -**2.** ESP [período] half-time.

meio-termo [ˌmeju'texmul *(pl* **meios-termos)** *m* -**1.** [posição]: ~ **(entre)** mid point (between). -**2.** *fig* [consenso] compromise.

meio-tom [ˌmeju'tõl *(pl* **meios-tons)** *m* -**1.** MÚS semitone. -**2.** [de cor] half-tone.

mel ['mɛwl *m* honey.

melado, da [me'ladu, dal *adj* [pegajoso] sticky.

➡ **melado** *m* [doce] molasses.

melancia [melãn'sial *f* watermelon.

melancolia [melãŋko'lial *f* melancholy.

melancólico, ca [melãŋ'kɔliku, kal *adj* melancholic.

melão [me'lãwl *(pl* -**ões)** *m* melon.

melar [4] [me'la(x)] ◇ *vt* [sujar] to get sticky. ◇ *vi fig* [falhar] to flop.

➡ **melar-se** *vp* [sujar-se] to get sticky.

Melbourne [ˌmɛw'buxnil *n* Melbourne.

meleca [me'lɛkal *f* -**1.** *fam* [secreção] bogey; **ele está tirando** ~ **do nariz** he's picking his nose. -**2.** [coisa ruim]: **ser/ficar uma** ~ to be rubbish. -**3.** *(enfático)*: **essa** ~ **dessa chuva** that dammed rain.

melhor [me'ʎɔ(x)] *(pl* -**es)** ◇ *adj* -**1.** *(comparativo de bom)*: ~ **(do que)** better (than); **bem/muito** ~ much better; **é** ~ **você ...** you had better ...; **quanto mais** ~ the more the better. -**2.** *(superlativo de bom)*: **o/a** ~ the best. ◇ *adv* -**1.** *(comparativo de bom)*: ~ **(do que)** better (than); **estar** ~ to be better; **estar** ~ **de vida** to be better off. -**2.** *(superlativo de bem)* best. ◇ *m, f*: **o/a** ~ the best; **o** ~ **de todas** the best of all; **o** ~ **foi que ...** the best thing was that ...; **levar a** ~ to come off best.

➡ **ou melhor** *loc adv* or rather.

➡ **tanto melhor** *loc adv* so much the better.

melhora [me'ʎoral *f* improvement; **estimo suas**

~s I hope you get better soon.
melhorada [meʎoˈrada] *f fam*: **dar uma ~** to get better.
melhoramento [meʎoraˈmẽntu] *m* improvement.
melhorar [4] [meʎoˈra(x)] <> *vt* to improve. <> *vi* to improve; **~ de algo** to improve in sthg; **~ de vida** to get on in life.
melhoria [meʎoˈria] *f* improvement; **fazer ~s (em algo)** to make improvements (in sthg).
meliante [meˈljãntʃi] *mf* **-1.** [marginal] vagabond. **-2.** [ladrão] thief. **-3.** [patife] scoundrel.
melífluo, flua [meˈliflwu, flwa] *adj fig* [suave] mellifluous.
Melilha [meˈliʎa] *n* Melilla.
melindrar [4] [melĩˈdra(x)] *vt* to offend.
~ melindrar-se *vp* to feel hurt.
melindre [meˈlĩdri] *m* affection.
~ melindres *mpl* [suscetibilidade] oversensitivity.
melindroso, osa [melĩˈdrɔza, ozu] *adj* **-1.** [suscetível, frágil] sensitive. **-2.** [difícil, arriscado] tricky.
~ melindrosa *f* [dos anos vinte] flapper dress.
melodia [meloˈdʒia] *f* melody.
melódico, ca [meˈlɔdʒiku, ka] *adj* melodic.
melodrama [meloˈdrama] *m* melodrama.
melodramático, ca [melodraˈmatʃiku, ka] *adj* melodramatic.
melões [meˈlõjʃ] *pl* ⊳ **melão**.
meloso, osa [meˈlozu, ɔza] *adj* **-1.** *fig* [pessoa] sentimental. **-2.** [voz] honeyed.
melro [ˈmɛwxul] *m* blackbird.
membrana [mẽˈbrãna] *f* membrane.
membro [ˈmẽbru] *m* **-1.** [ANAT - braços, pernas] limb; [- pênis] (male) member, penis. **-2.** [parte] member.
memorando [memoˈrãndu] *m* **-1.** [comunicação] memo. **-2.** [nota diplomática] memorandum.
memorável [memoˈravew] (*pl* **-eis**) *adj* memorable.
memória [meˈmɔrja] *f* **-1.** [ger] memory; **de ~** by heart; **~ de elefante** *fig* memory like an elephant; **~ visual** visual memory; **ter ~ fraca** to have a poor memory; **vir à ~** to come to mind; **~ RAM/ROM** RAM/ROM memory. **-2.** [recordação] recollection; **em ~ de** in memory of.
~ memórias *fpl* memoirs.
memorial [memoˈrjaw] (*pl* **-ais**) *m* memorial.
memorização [ˈmemoriˈzasãw] (*pl* **-ões**) *f* memorizing.
memorizar [4] [memoriˈza(x)] *vt* to memorize.
menção [mẽˈsãw] (*pl* **-ões**) *f* **-1.** [referência] mention; **fazer ~ a algo** to make mention of sthg; **digno de ~** worthy of mention. **-2.** [intento]: **fazer ~ de se levantar** to make as if to get up. **-3.** [distinção]: **~ honrosa** distinction.
mencionar [4] [mẽsjoˈna(x)] *vt* to mention; **(isso) sem mencionar ...** not to mention ...
mendicância [mẽndʒiˈkãnsja] *f* begging.
mendicante [mẽndʒiˈkãntʃi] <> *adj* begging. <> *mf* beggar.

mendigar [14] [mẽndʒiˈga(x)] <> *vt* **-1.** [esmola] to beg for. **-2.** [ajuda, favor] to beg. <> *vi* [pedir esmola] to beg.
mendigo, ga [mẽˈdʒigu, ga] *m, f* beggar.
menear [15] [meˈnja(x)] *vt* to shake.
menina [meˈnina] *f* ⊳ **menino**.
meninada [meniˈnada] *f* kids (*pl*).
meningite [menĩˈʒitʃi] *f* meningitis.
meninice [meniˈnisi] *f* **-1.** [período] childhood. **-2.** [criancice] childishness.
menino, na [meˈninu, na] <> *adj* young. <> *m, f* **-1.** [criança] child; **nasceu um ~** a boy was born; **os ~s** the children; **~ de rua** street child. **-2.** [jovem] youngster. **-3.** [como forma de tratamento] boy.
~ menina *f*: **ser a menina dos olhos de alguém** to be the apple of sb's eye.
menopausa [menoˈpawza] *f* menopause.
menor [meˈnɔ(x)] (*pl* **-es**) <> *adj* **-1.** (*comparativo*): **~ (do que)** [de tamanho] smaller (than); [de idade] younger (than); [de importância, número] less (than); **meu irmão ~** my younger brother. **-2.** (*superlativo*): **o/a ~ ...** [ger] the least; [de tamanho] the smallest. **-3.** [jovem]: **ser ~ (de idade)** [para dirigir, votar] to be under age; *JUR* to be a minor, to be under age. **-4.** (*antes de subst*) [noção, paciência] slightest. **-5.** *MÚS*: **em dó ~** in C minor. <> *mf* **-1.** (*superlativo*): **o/a ~** [de tamanho] the smallest; [de idade] the youngest; **proibido para ~ es** prohibited to under 18s; **um ~ de 15 anos** a youth of 15. **-2.** [jovem] young person. **-3.** *JUR* minor.
menoridade [menoriˈdadʒi] *f* minority.
menos [ˈmenuʃ] <> *adv* **-1.** [em comparações] less; **a Ana é ~ inteligente** Ana is less intelligent; **~ do que** less than; **~ ... do que ...** less ...than ...; **tenho ~ trabalho do que ele** I have less work than him; **tenho um livro a ~** I'm one book short; **deram-me 5 reais a ~** they gave me 5 reais too little, they short-changed me by 5 reais. **-2.** [como superlativo]: **o/a ~ ...** the least ...; **o ~ caro/interessante** the least expensive/interesting. **-3.** [em locuções]: **a ~ que** unless; **ao ~, pelo ~** at least; **isso é o de ~** that's the least of it; **pouco ~ de** just under. <> *adj inv* **-1.** [em comparações] less, fewer *pl*; **como ~ carne** I eat less meat; **eles têm ~ posses** they have fewer possessions; **está ~ frio do que ontem** it's less cold than it was yesterday; **~ ... do que** less ... than, fewer ... than *pl*. **-2.** [como superlativo] (the) least, (the) fewest *pl*; **as que ~ bolos comeram** those who ate (the) fewest cakes; **os que ~ dinheiro têm** those who have (the) least money. <> *prep* **-1.** [exceto] except (for); **todos gostaram ~ ele** they all liked it except (for) him; **tudo isso** anything but that. **-2.** [indica subtração] minus; **três ~ dois é igual a um** three minus two equals one.
menosprezado, da [menoʃpreˈzadu, da] *adj* underestimated.
menosprezar [4] [menoʃpreˈza(x)] *vt* to disdain.

menosprezo [menoʃ'prezu] *m*: ~ **(por)** disdain (for).

mensageiro, ra [mẽsa'ʒejru, ra] *m, f* messenger.

mensagem [mẽsa'ʒẽ] (*pl* -ns) *f* message.

mensal [mẽn'saw] (*pl* -ais) *adj* monthly; **ganho 1.000 reais mensais** I earn 1,000 reals a month.

mensalidade [mẽnsali'dadʒi] *f* monthly payment.

mensalmente [mẽnsaw'mẽntʃi] *adv* monthly.

menstruação [mẽnʃtrwa'sãw] (*pl* -ões) *f* menstruation.

menstruada [mẽnʃ'trwada] *adj f*: **estar/ficar** ~ to be menstruating.

menstrual [mẽnʃ'trwaw] (*pl* -ais) *adj* menstrual.

menstruar [4] [mẽnʃ'trwa(x)] *vi* to menstruate.

mensurável [mẽnsu'ravew] (*pl* -eis) *adj* measurable.

menta ['mẽntal *f* mint; **de** ~ mint *(antes de subst)*.

mental [mẽn'taw] (*pl* -ais) *adj* mental.

mentalidade [mẽntali'dadʒi] *f* mentality.

mentalizar [4] [mẽntali'za(x)] *vt* -**1.** [pensar em] to think. -**2.** [conceber] to imagine.

mente ['mẽntʃi] *f* mind; **ter algo em** ~ to have sthg in mind; **ter em** ~ **fazer algo** to have it in mind to do sthg; **vir à** ~ to come to mind.

mentecapto, ta [mẽnte'kaptu, ta] *m, f* insane, foolish.

mentir [56] [mẽn'tʃi(x)] <> *vt*: ~ **que ...** to lie about ... <> *vi* to lie; ~ **a** *ou* **para alguém** to lie to sb.

mentira [mẽn'tʃira] *f* -**1.** [falsidade] lie; **de** ~ [como brincadeira] as a joke; [falso] fake; **embora pareça** ~ although it seems unlikely; ~ **deslavada** downright lie; ~**!** [mostrando surpresa] you don't say!; **parece** ~ **que ...** it seems unbelievable that ... -**2.** [ato, hábito] lying.

mentiroso, osa [mẽntʃi'rozu, ɔza] <> *adj* -**1.** [ger] untruthful. -**2.** [jornalista, artigo] lying. <> *m, f* [pessoa] liar.

mentol [mẽn'ɔw] *m* menthol.

mentolado, da [mẽnto'ladu, da] *adj* mentholated.

mentor, ra [mẽn'to(x), ra] *m, f* -**1.** [orientador] mentor. -**2.** [autor intelectual]: **o/a** ~ the brains.

menu [me'nul *m* menu.

meramente [mɛra'mẽntʃi] *adv* merely.

mercadinho [mexka'dʒiɲu] *m* local shop *UK*, local store *US*.

mercado [mex'kadu] *m* market; ~ **de capitais** investment market; ~ **financeiro** financial market; ~ **negro** black market; ~ **de trabalho** job market; ~ **das pulgas** flea market.

  ➥ Mercado Comum *m* Common Market.

mercadologia [mexkadolo'ʒia] *f* marketing.

mercadológico, ca [mexkado'lɔʒiku, ka] *adj* marketing *(antes de subst)*.

mercador [mexka'do(x)] *m* merchant.

mercadoria [mexkado'ria] *f* commodity.

  ➥ mercadorias *fpl* merchandise, goods *(pl)*.

mercante [mex'kãntʃi] *adj* merchant *(antes de subst)*.

mercantil [mexkãn'tʃiw] (*pl* -is) *adj* mercantile.

mercantilismo [mexkãntʃi'liʒmu] *m* mercantilism.

mercantilista [mexkãntʃi'liʃta] *adj* mercantilist.

mercê [mex'se] *f*: **estar/ficar à** ~ **de alguém/algo** to be at the mercy of sb/sthg.

mercearia [mexsja'ria] *f* grocery shop.

mercenário, ria [mexse'narju, rja] <> *adj* mercenary. <> *m, f* mercenary.

Mercosul [mexko'suw] (*abrev de* **Mercado do Cone Sul**) *m South American common market*.

mercúrio [mex'kurju] *m* mercury; ~ **cromo** merbromin, Mercurochrome®.

Mercúrio [mex'kurju] *m* Mercury.

merda ['mexda] *mfam* <> *f* -**1.** [ger] crap, shit; **essa** ~ **de ...** this crappy ...; **ser/estar uma** ~ to be crap; **mandar alguém à** ~ to tell sb to bugger off. -**2.** [excremento] shit. <> *mf* [pessoa] shit. <> *interj*: **(que)** ~**!** what crap!

  ➥ de merda *loc adj mfam*: **esta viagem de** ~ this shitty journey.

merecedor, ra [merese'do(x), ra] *adj*: ~ **de** deserving of.

merecer [25] [mere'se(x)] <> *vt* to deserve. <> *vi*: **ele ganhou o prêmio, mas não merecia** he won the prize but he didn't deserve to.

merecido, da [mere'sidu, da] *adj* deserved; **foi um castigo bem** ~ it was a well deserved punishment.

merecimento [meresi'mẽntu] *m* [mérito, valor] merit.

merenda [me'rẽnda] *f* snack; ~ **escolar** free school meal.

merendeira [merẽn'dejra] *f* [lancheira] snack box.

merengue [me'rẽŋgi] *m* meringue.

meretrício [mere'trisjul *m* prostitution.

meretriz [mere'triʒ] *f* prostitute.

mergulhador, ra [mexguʎa'do(x), ra] (*mpl* -es, *fpl* -s) <> *adj* diving. <> *m, f* diver.

mergulhar [4] [mexgu'ʎa(x)] <> *vt* [afundar]: ~ **algo (em algo)** to dip sthg (in sthg). <> *vi* -**1.**: ~ **(em algo)** [afundar] to dive (into sthg); [saltar] to spring (from sthg). -**2.**: ~ **em algo** [penetrar] to plunge into sthg; *fig* [concentrar-se] to plunge o.s. in sthg.

mergulho [mex'guʎu] *m* -**1.** [ger] dive; **dar um** ~ [na praia] to take a dip; [de trampolim] to spring. -**2.** *ESP* diving.

meridiano, na [meri'dʒjãnu, na] *adj* meridian.

  ➥ meridiano *m GEOGR* meridian.

meridional [meridʒio'nawl] (*pl* **-ais**) *adj* southern.

meritíssimo, ma [meri'tʃisimu, ma] *adj* highly deserving.

mérito ['mɛritu] *m* merit; **julgar alguém por seus ~s** to judge sb by their merits.

meritório, ria [meri'tɔrju, rja] *adj* meritorious, deserving.

merluza [mex'luza] *f* hake.

mero, ra ['mɛru, ra] *adj* mere.

merreca [me'xɛka] *f*: **uma ~** a trifle; **custar/pagar uma ~** to cost/pay a trifle; **ser uma ~** [muito pequeno] to be a mere trifle.

mertiolate [mextʃjo'latʃi] *m* Merthiolate®, thiomersal.

mês ['meʃ] (*pl* **meses**) *m*: **de ~ em ~** monthly; **durante todo o ~ de setembro** throughout September; **no ~ que vem** next month; **recebo por ~** I am paid monthly; **uma vez por ~** once a month.

mesa ['meza] *f* **-1.** [móvel] table; **pôr/tirar a ~** to lay/clear the table; **~ de centro** centre table; **~ de jantar** dining table; **~ telefônica** switchboard. **-2.** [de uma assembléia etc] board; **~ eleitoral** polling station officials. **-3.** [apostas] **ganhar toda a ~** to sweep the table. **-4.** *loc*: **virar a ~** to turn the tables.

mesada [me'zada] *f* **-1.** [pagamento] monthly payment. **-2.** [de criança] pocket money *UK*, allowance *US*.

mesa-de-cabeceira [ˌmezadʒikabi'sejra] (*pl* **mesas-de-cabeceira**) *f* bedside table.

mesa-redonda [ˌmezaxe'dõnda] (*pl* **mesas-redondas**) *f* round table.

mesário, ria [me'zarju, rja] *m, f* **-1.** [de mesa eleitoral] polling officer. **-2.** [de associação etc] committee member.

mescla ['mɛʃkla] <> *adj (inv)* [tecido, paletó] blend. <> *f* **-1.** [mistura] mixture. **-2.** [tecido] blend.

mesclar [4] [meʃ'kla(x)] *vt* **-1.** [misturar]: **~ algo (com algo)** to mix sthg (with sthg). **-2.** [incorporar]: **~ algo a algo** to combine sthg with sthg.

mesmice [meʒ'misil *f* sameness.

mesmo, ma ['meʒmu, ma] <> *adj* **-1.** [ger] same; **o ~ batom** the same lipstick; **na mesma hora** [imediatamente] at once. **-2.** [próprio]: **eu ~ fiz isso** I made that myself; **ele ~** himself; **ela mesma** herself; **eles mesmos** themselves. **-3.** [para enfatizar] very. <> *pron*: **o ~/a mesma** the same. ◆ **mesma** <> *f*: **continuar na mesma** [não mudar] to be exactly the same; **ficar na mesma** [não entender] to be none the wiser. <> *m* [a mesma coisa]: **o mesma** the same; **dá no mesma** it's all the same. ◆ **mesmo** *adv* **-1.** [precisamente]: **agora/aqui ~** right now/here; **é assim ~** that's just the way it is; **hoje/ontem ~** just today/yesterday; **por isso ~** for that very reason. **-2.** [realmente] really; **é ~?** really?; **só ~ você consegue fazer isso** only you can do it. **-3.** [até, ainda] even; **~ assim, assim ~** even so; **nem ~** not even.

◆ **mesmo que** *loc conj* even though.

Mesopotâmia [mezopo'tãmja] *n* Mesopotamia.

mesquinharia [meʃkiɲa'ria] *f* meanness.

mesquinhez [meʃki'ɲeʃ] *f* [] meanness.

mesquinho, nha [meʃ'kiɲu, ɲa] *adj* mean.

mesquita [meʃ'kita] *f* mosque.

messias [me'siaʃ] *m fig* messiah.
◆ **Messias** *m*: **o Messias** the Messiah.

mestiçagem [meʃtʃi'saʒẽ] (*pl* **-ns**) *f* **-1.** [cruzamento] cross-breeding. **-2.** [miscigenação] miscegenation.

mestiço, ça [meʃ'tʃisu, sa] <> *adj* mestizo. <> *m, f* mestizo.

mestra ['mɛʃtra] *f* ⊳ **mestre**.

mestrado [meʃ'tradu] *m* **-1.** [grau] masters (degree). **-2.** [curso] masters; **fazer ~** to study for a masters.

mestrando, da [meʃ'trãndu, da] *m* student about to complete a master's degree.

mestre, tra ['mɛʃtri, tra] <> *adj* **-1.** [extraordinário] fantastic. **-2.** [principal] master. <> *m, f* **-1.** [ger] master; **ser ~ em fazer algo** *irôn* to be a past master at doing sthg. **-2.** [fonte de ensinamento] teacher. **-3.** [músico] maestro.

mestre-cuca [ˌmɛʃtri'kuka] (*pl* **mestres-cucas**) *m fam* chef.

mestre-de-cerimônias [ˌmɛʃtridʒiseri'monjaʃl] (*pl* **mestres-de-cerimônias**) *m* master of ceremonies.

mestre-de-obras [ˌmɛʃtri'dʒjɔbraʃ] (*pl* **mestres de-obras**) *m* foreman.

mestre-sala [ˌmɛʃtri'sala] (*pl* **mestres-sala**) *m* [em escola de samba] leader of samba group display during carnival.

mestria [meʃ'tria] *f* = **maestria**.

mesura [me'zura] *f* reverence; **cheio de ~s** kowtowing.

meta ['mɛta] *f* **-1.** [objetivo] aim, goal. **-2.** [gol] goal. **-3.** [na corrida] finishing line.

metabolismo [metabo'liʒmu] *m* metabolism.

metade [me'tadʒi] *f* half; **~ das pessoas** half the people; **cortar pela ~** to cut in half; **deixar pela ~** to leave halfway through; **na ~ do caminho** halfway; **na ~ do filme** halfway through the film; **pela ~ do preço** at half price.

metafísico, ca [meta'fiziku, ka] <> *adj* metaphysical. <> *m, f* [filósofo] metaphysicist.
◆ **metafísica** *f* [disciplina] metaphysics (*pl*).

metáfora [me'tafora] *f* metaphor.

metafórico, ca [meta'fɔriku, ka] *adj* metaphorical.

metal [me'tawl] (*pl* **-ais**) *m* metal.
◆ **metais** *mpl* *MÚS* brass instruments.

metálico, ca [me'taliku, ka] *adj* metallic.

metalinguagem [metaliŋ'gwaʒẽ] (*pl* **-ns**) *f* metalanguage.

metalurgia [metalux'ʒia] *f* metallurgy.

metalúrgico, ca [meta'luxʒiku, ka] <> *adj* metallurgic. <> *m, f* [operário] metallurgist.
◆ **metalúrgica** *f* [oficina] foundry.

metamorfose [metamox'fɔzi] *f* metamorphosis.

metamorfosear [15] [metamoxfo'zja(x)] *vt*: ~ alguém/algo (em) to change sb/sthg (into).

➤ **metamorfosear-se** *vp* -**1.** *BIOL* to metamorphose. -**2.** *fig* [mudar]: ~-se (em) to metamorphose (into).

metano [me'tãnu] *m* methane.

metástase [me'taʃtazi] *f MED* metastasis.

meteórico, ca [mete'ɔriku, ka] *adj* meteoric.

meteorito [metʃju'ritu] *m* meteorite.

meteoro [me'tjoru] *m* meteor.

meteorologia [metʃjorolo'ʒia] *f* meteorology.

meteorológico, ca [metʃjoro'lɔʒiku, ka] *adj* meteorological.

meteorologista [metʃjorolo'ʒiʃta] *mf* -**1.** [especialista] meteorologist. -**2.** *RADIO* & *TV* weather forecaster.

meter [5] [me'te(x)] *vt* -**1.** [ger] to put. -**2.** [enfiar]: ~ algo em *ou* dentro de algo to put sthg in/inside sthg. -**3.** [inspirar]: ele me mete pena he makes me feel sorry for him; ele é feio de ~ medo he's so ugly it's frightening. -**4.** [envolver]: ~ alguém em algo to involve sb in sthg.

➤ **meter-se** *vp* -**1.** [ir, esconder-se] to hide. -**2.** [recolher-se]: ~-se em algum lugar to shut o.s. in somewhere. -**3.** [intrometer-se]: ~-se (em algo) to stick one's nose (in sthg); não se meta! don't interfere! -**4.** [desafiar]: ~-se com alguém to provoke sb. -**5.** [associar-se]: ~-se com alguém to get mixed up with sb. -**6.** [fazer-se de]: ~-se a algo to play at being sthg; ~-se a valente to pretend to be brave. -**7.** [aventurar-se]: ~-se a fazer algo to start doing sthg. -**8.** [envolver-se]: ~-se em algo to get involved in sthg.

meticulosidade [metʃikulozi'dadʒi] *f* meticulousness.

meticuloso, osa [metʃiku'lozu, ɔza] *adj* meticulous.

metido, da [me'tʃidu, da] *adj* -**1.** [abelhudo] meddlesome, nosy. -**2.** [presumido]: ~ (a besta) full of o.s. -**3.** [cheio de intimidades] inquisitive. -**4.** [envolvido]: ~ com alguém involved with sb; ~ em algo involved in sthg. -**5.** [em roupa] dressed.

metódico, ca [me'tɔdʒiku, ka] *adj* methodical.

metodismo [meto'dʒiʒmu] *m* -**1.** *RELIG* Methodism. -**2.** [procedimento] method.

metodista [meto'dʒiʃta] *RELIG* <> *adj* Methodist. <> *mf* Methodist.

método ['mɛtodu] *m* method.

metodologia [metodolo'ʒia] *f* methodology.

metodológico, ca [metodo'lɔʒiku, ka] *adj* methodological.

metonímia [meto'nimja] *f* metonymy.

metragem [me'traʒẽ] *f* -**1.** [medida] length in metres *UK ou* meters *US*. -**2.** *CINE*: filme de curta/longa ~ short/feature-length film.

metralhadora [metraʎa'dora] *f* machine gun.

metralhar [4] [metra'ʎa(x)] *vt* -**1.** [atirar em] to machine-gun. -**2.** *fig* [bombardear]: ~ alguém de perguntas to fire questions at sb.

métrico, ca ['mɛtriku, ka] *adj* -**1.** [do metro] metric; fita métrica tape measure. -**2.** *LITER* metrical.

➤ **métrica** *f LITER* metre *UK*, meter *US*.

metro ['mɛtru] *m* metre *UK*, meter *US*; ~ cúbico cubic metre; ~ quadrado square metre.

metrô [me'tro] *m* underground *UK*, subway *US*.

metrópole [me'trɔpoli] *f* -**1.** [cidade principal] capital. -**2.** [cidade grande] metropolis. -**3.** [nação] mother country.

metropolitano, na [metropoli'tãnu, na] *adj* metropolitan.

metroviário, ria [metro'vjarju, rja] <> *adj* underground *UK (antes de subst)*, subway *US (antes de subst)*. <> *m, f* [funcionário] underground worker *UK*, subway worker *US*.

meu, minha ['mew, 'miɲa] <> *adj* -**1.** [ger] my; este é o ~ carro this is my car; ~ Deus! my God!; minha nossa! oh me, oh my!, gosh! -**2.** [caro a mim] my; como vai, ~ caro Affonso? how are you, my dear Affonso?; ~ irmão *fam* [tratamento] my friend. <> *pron*: o ~ /a minha mine; um amigo ~ a friend of mine; os ~s [a minha família] my family; este jeito de andar é bem ~ this manner of walking is quite me.

mexer [5] [me'ʃe(x)] <> *vt* -**1.** [ger] to move. -**2.** [misturar] to mix. <> *vi* -**1.** [mover] to move. -**2.**: ~ em alguém/algo [tocar] to touch sb/sthg; [mudar de posição, remexer] to fiddle with sb/sthg. -**3.**: ~ com alguém [caçoar] to tease sb; [provocar] to provoke sb; [afetar] to affect sb. -**4.** [trabalhar]: ~ com algo to work with sthg.

➤ **mexer-se** *vp* -**1.** [mover-se] to move. -**2.** [apressar-se] to hurry; mexam-se! get a move on! -**3.** [agir] to move.

mexerica [meʃe'rika] *f* tangerine.

mexericar [12] [meʃeri'ka(x)] *vi* to gossip.

mexerico [meʃe'riku] *m* -**1.** [ato] gossip. -**2.** [intriga] intrigue.

mexeriqueiro, ra [meʃeri'kejru, ra] <> *adj* gossipy. <> *m, f* busybody, gossip.

mexicano, na [meʃi'kãnu, na] <> *adj* Mexican. <> *m, f* Mexican.

México ['mɛʃiku] *n* Mexico.

mexido, da [me'ʃidu, da] *adj* -**1.** [papéis] muddled. -**2.** [ovos] scrambled.

mexilhão [meʃi'ʎãw] *(pl -ões) m* mussel.

mezanino [meza'ninu] *m* mezzanine.

mg *(abrev de* miligrama*) m* mg.

MG *(abrev de* Estado de Minas Gerais*) n* State of Minas Gerais.

mi [mi] *m MÚS* E, mi.

miado ['mjadu] *m* miaow.

miar [16] ['mja(x)] *vi* to mew.

miasma ['mjaʒma] *m* -**1.** [emanação] miasma. -**2.** *fig*: ~ social social miasma.

miau ['mjaw] *m* miaow.

miçanga [mi'sãŋga] *f* -**1.** [conta] glass bead. -**2.** [ornato] beads *(pl)*.

micção [mik'sãw] *(pl -ões) f* urination.

mico ['miku] *m ZOOL* capuchin monkey.

mico-leão [miku'ljãw] (*pl* **micos-leão**) *m* ZOOL golden lion tamarin.

micose [mi'kɔzi] *f* fungal infection, mycosis.

micro ['mikru] *m* COMPUT computer, PC.

micro- [mikru-] *prefixo* micro-.

micróbio [mi'krɔbju] *m* microbe.

microbiologia [mikrobjolo'ʒia] *f* microbiology.

microcirurgia [mikrosirux'ʒia] *f* microsurgery.

microcomputador [mikrokõnputa'do(x)] *m* microcomputer.

microcosmo [mikro'kɔʒmu] *m* microcosm.

microempresa [mikrowẽn'preza] *f* small business.

microempresário, ria [mikrwẽnpre'zarju, ria] *m* small-business owner.

microfilme [mikro'fiwmi] *m* microfilm.

microfone [mikro'foni] *m* microphone.

microfonia [mikro'fonia] *f* ELETRON *vibrations in a sound system*.

microinformática [mikrwĩnfox'matʃika] *f* microcomputing.

microonda [mikro'õnda] *f* microwave.

➡ **microondas** *mpl* [forno] microwave oven *(sg)*.

microônibus [mikro'onibuʃ] *m inv* minibus.

microorganismo [mikrwoxga'niʒmu] *m* microorganism.

microprocessador [mikruprosesa'do(x)] *m* microprocessor.

microscópico, ca [mikroʃ'kɔpiku, ka] *adj* microscopic.

microscópio [mikroʃ'kɔpju] *m* microscope.

mictório [mik'tɔrju] *m* urinal.

mídia ['midʒja] *f* media.

migalha [mi'gaʎa] *f* [de pão, bolo] crumb.

➡ **migalhas** *fpl* [sobras] leftovers.

migração [migra'sãw] (*pl* **-ões**) *f* migration.

migrante [mi'grãntʃi] ◇ *adj* **-1.** [pássaro] migratory. **- 2.** [população] migrant. ◇ *mf* migrant.

migrar [4] [mi'gra(x)] *vi* to migrate.

migratório, ria [migra'tɔrju, ria] *adj* migratory.

mijada [mi'ʒada] *f fam* pee; **dar uma** ~ to have a pee.

mijar [4] [mi'ʒa(x)] *vi fam* to pee.

➡ **mijar-se** *vp mfam* to piss o.s.; ~**-se de rir** to wet *ou* piss o.s. laughing.

mijo ['miʒu] *m fam* pee.

mil ['miw] *num* **-1.** [número] thousand; **três** ~ three thousand. **- 2.** [grande número] a thousand. **- 3.** *loc*: **estar a** ~ *fam* to be working flat out; **seis**

milagre [mi'lagri] *m* miracle; **por** ~ miraculously.

milagroso, osa [mila'grozu, ɔza] *adj* miraculous.

milanesa [mila'neza] *f*: **à** ~ in breadcrumbs.

milenar [mile'na(x)] *adj* **-1.** [que tem um milênio] millenary. **- 2.** *fig* [antigo] age-old.

milênio [mi'lenju] *m* millennium.

milésimo, ma [mi'lɛzimu, ma] *num* thousandth; **a milésima parte** the thousandth part.

mil-folhas [miw'foʎaʃ] *f inv* millefeuille.

milha ['miʎa] *f* mile; ~ **marítima** nautical mile.

milhão [mi'ʎãw] (*pl* **-ões**) *num* million; **três milhões** three million.

milhar [mi'ʎa(x)] (*pl* **-es**) *m* thousand.

➡ **milhares** *mpl*: ~ **es de pessoas** thousands of people.

milharal [miʎa'raw] (*pl* **-ais**) *m* maize field UK, corn field US.

milho ['miʎu] *m* **-1.** [planta] maize UK, corn US. **- 2.** [grão] corn; ~ **de pipoca** popcorn. **- 3.** *loc*: **catar** ~ to type very slowly.

milhões [mi'ʎõjʃ] *pl* ▷ **milhão**.

miliardário, ria [miljax'darju, ria] ◇ *adj* multimillionaire. ◇ *m, f* multimillionaire.

milícia [mi'lisja] *f* militia.

milico [mi'liku] *m fam pej* military type; **os** ~**s** the military.

miligrama [mili'grãma] *m* milligram.

mililitro [mili'litru] *m* millilitre UK, milliliter US.

milímetro [mi'limetru] *m* millimetre UK, millimeter US.

milionário, ria [miljo'narju, ria] ◇ *adj* millionaire. ◇ *m, f* millionaire.

milionésimo, ma [miljo'nɛzimu, ma] *num* millionth; **a milionésima parte** the millionth part.

militância [mili'tãnsja] *f* militancy.

militante [mili'tãntʃi] ◇ *adj* militant. ◇ *mf* militant.

militar [4] [mili'ta(x)] ◇ *adj* military. ◇ *mf* career soldier; **os** ~ **es** the military *(inv)*. ◇ *vi* **-1.** [lutar]: ~ **(por/contra)** to fight for/against. **- 2.**: ~ **em** MIL to serve in; POL to be active in.

militarismo [milita'riʒmu] *m* militarism.

militarista [milita'riʃta] ◇ *adj* militaristic. ◇ *mf* militarist.

militarizar [4] [militari'za(x)] *vt* to militarize.

mil-réis [miw'xɛj] *m inv early Brazilian and Portuguese monetary unit*.

mim ['mĩ] *pron* **-1.** [com preposição: complemento indireto] me; **ela comprou um presente para** ~ she bought a present for me, she bought me a present; **ele fez o serviço por** ~ he did the work for me; **a** ~ **ele não faria isto** he wouldn't do that to me; **falaram mal de** ~ they spoke ill of me; **o que você tem contra** ~**?** what have you got against me?; **eles foram embora sem** ~ they left without me; **para** ~**, este é o melhor quadro** [para expressar opinião] for me, this is the best painting; **por** ~**, você pode ficar aqui** [de minha parte] as far as I'm concerned, you can stay here. **- 2.** [com preposição: reflexo] myself; **a** ~**, você não engana** you don't fool me; **comprei-o para** ~ **(mesmo** *ou* **próprio)** I bought it for myself; **preciso cuidar mais de** ~ I need to look after myself a bit better; **de** ~ **para** ~ [comigo mesmo] to myself.

mimado, da [mi'madu, da] *adj* spoiled.

mimar [4] [mi'ma(x)] *vt* **-1.** [fazer todas as vontades de] to spoil. **- 2.** [tratar com carinho] to pamper.

mimeografar [4] [mimjogra'fa(x)] *vt* to mimeograph.

mimeógrafo [mi'mjɔgrafu] *m* mimeograph.

mímico, ca ['mimiku, ka] <> *adj* imitative. <> *m, f* **-1.** [pessoa] mimic. **-2.** [ator] mime artist. ➡ **mímica** *f* mime; **fazer mímica** to mimic; **por mímica** in mime.

mimo ['mimu] *m* **-1.** [carinho] affection; **fazer ~s a alguém** to be affectionate towards sb. **-2.** [pessoa ou coisa graciosa]: **ser um ~** to be a delight.

mimoso, osa [mi'mozu, ɔza] *adj* **-1.** [carinhoso] affectionate. **-2.** [gracioso] delightful. **-3.** [delicado] delicate.

mina ['mina] *f* **-1.** [ger] mine; **~ de carvão/ouro** coal/gold mine. **-2.** *fig*: **ser uma ~** [de lucros] to be a goldmine; [preciosidade] to be precious; **ser uma ~ de informações** to be a mine of information. **-3.** *fam* [garota] girl.

minar [4] [mi'na(x)] <> *vt* **-1.** [pôr minas em] to mine. **-2.** [deteriorar, prejudicar] to undermine. <> *vi* [água]: **~ (de)** to stream (from).

minarete [mina'retʃi] *m* minaret.

Minas Gerais [,minaʒe'rajʃ] *n* Minas Gerais.

mindinho [mĩn'dʒinu] *m fam* pinky.

mineiro, ra [mi'nejru, ra] <> *adj* **-1.** [relativo a mina] mining. **-2.** [de Minas Gerais] from Minas Gerais. <> *m, f* **-1.** [operário] miner. **-2.** [de Minas Gerais] *person from Minas Gerais.*

mineração [minera'sãw] *f* **-1.** [exploração] mining. **-2.** [depuração] purifying.

minerador, ra [minera'do(x),ra] <> *adj* mining *(antes de subst).* <> *m, f* miner. ➡ **mineradora** *f* mining company.

mineral [mine'raw] *(pl* **-ais)** <> *adj* mineral. <> *m* mineral.

mineralogia [mineralo'ʒia] *f* mineralogy.

minério [mi'nɛrju] *m* ore; **~ de ferro** iron ore.

mingau [mĩŋ'gaw] *m* **-1.** [papa] porridge. **-2.** *fig* [coisa mole] mush.

míngua ['mĩŋgwa] *f* lack; **estar à ~ de algo** to be short of sthg; **viver à ~ de algo** to live with a shortage of sthg.

minguado, da [mĩŋ'gwadu, da] *adj* **-1.** [escasso] scarce; **~ de algo** lacking sthg. **-2.** [pouco desenvolvido] flat.

minguante [mĩŋ'gwãntʃi] *m* ASTRON [moon] waning, last quarter.

minguar [4] [mĩŋ'gwa(x)] <> *vt* [reduzir] to reduce. <> *vi* [escassear] to dwindle.

minha ['miɲa] ▷ **meu.**

minhoca [mi'ɲɔka] *f* earthworm; **com ~s na cabeça** with strange ideas.

míni ['mini] <> *adj inv* mini. <> *m* [vestido] minidress. <> *f* [saia] miniskirt.

miniatura [minja'tura] *f* miniature; **em ~** in miniature.

mínima ['minima] *f* ▷ **mínimo.**

minimalista [minima'liʃta] *adj* minimalist.

minimizar [4] [minimi'za(x)] *vt* **-1.** [tornar mínimo] to minimize. **-2.** [subestimar] to underestimate. **-3.** [fazer pouco caso de] to play down.

mínimo, ma ['minimu, ma] *adj* **-1.** [ger] minimal. **-2.** [muito pequeno] tiny. **-3.** [o menor possível] smallest. **-4.** *(antes de subst)* [nenhum] slightest.

➡ **mínimo** *m* [limite] least; **o ~ que posso fazer** the least I can do; **no ~** at least.

➡ **mínima** *f* **-1.** METEOR minimum (temperature). **-2.** MÚS minim. **-3.** *loc*: **não dar a mínima (para alguém/algo)** not to have the least concern (for sb/sthg).

minissaia [,mini'saja] *f* miniskirt.

minissérie [,mini'sɛri] *f* miniseries.

ministerial [miniʃte'rjaw] *(pl* **-ais)** *adj* ministerial.

ministeriável [miniʃterj'avɛw] *(pl* **-eis)** *mf* ministerial candidate.

ministério [miniʃ'tɛrju] *m* **-1.** [ger] ministry; **Ministério da Fazenda** ≃ HM Treasury *UK,* ≃ the Treasury *US*; **Ministério do Interior** Home Office *UK,* Department of the Interior *US*; **Ministério Público** public prosecution; **Ministério das Relações Exteriores** ≃ Foreign (and Commonwealth) Office *UK,* ≃ State Department *US*; **Ministério do Trabalho** ≃ Department of Employment *UK,* ≃ Department of Labor *US*; **Ministério da Educação e Cultura** ≃ Department of Education; **Ministério dos Transportes** ≃ Department of Transport. **-2.** [gabinete] cabinet.

ministra [mi'niʃtra] *f* ▷ **ministro.**

ministrar [4] [miniʃ'tra(x)] *vt* to administer.

ministro, tra [mi'niʃtru, tra] *m, f* minister; **~ sem pasta** minister without portfolio; **~ da Fazenda** ≃ Chancellor of the Exchequer *UK,* ≃ Secretary of the Treasury *US*; **~ do Interior** ≃ Home Secretary *UK,* ≃ Secretary of the Interior *US*; **~ das Relações Exteriores** ≃ Foreign Secretary *UK,* ≃ Secretary of State *US*; **~ da Educação e Cultura** ≃ Secretary for Education; **~ dos Transportes** ≃ Secretary for Transport.

minorar [4] [mino'ra(x)] *vt* to diminish.

minoria [mino'ria] *f* minority.

minoritário, ria [minori'tarju, rja] *adj* minority *(antes de subst).*

minúcia [mi'nusja] *f* **-1.** [detalhe] detail. **-2.** [coisa sem importância] minutiae *(pl).*

minuciosidade [minusjozi'dadʒi] *f* meticulousness.

minucioso, osa [minu'sjozu, ɔza] *adj* meticulous.

minúsculo, la [mi'nuʃkulu, la] *adj* **-1.** [tamanho] minuscule. **-2.** [letra] lower case *(antes de subst).* ➡ **minúscula** *f* [letra] lower case.

minuta [mi'nuta] *f* **-1.** [rascunho] draft. **-2.** [prato] cooked to order.

minuteria [minute'ria] *f* timing device.

minuto [mi'nutu] *m* minute; **num ~** *fig* [rapidamente] in a minute; **um ~!** one minute!

miolo ['mjolu] *m* **-1.** [pão] crumb. **-2.** [fruta] pulp. ➡ **miolos** *mpl* **-1.** CULIN brains. **-2.** *fam* [cérebro] brains.

mioma ['mjoma] *m* myoma.

míope ['mjupi] <> *adj* short-sighted, myopic. <> *mf* short-sighted person, myope.

miopia [mju'pia] *f* myopia.

miosótis [mjo'zɔtʃiʃ] *m inv BOT* forget-me-not.
mira ['mira] *f* -**1.** [ger] aim. -**2.** [de arma] sight.
mirabolante [mirabo'lãntʃi] *adj* -**1.** [surpreendente] incredible. -**2.** [espalhafatoso] gaudy.
miraculoso, osa [miraku'lozu, ɔza] *adj* [espantoso] miraculous.
mirada [mi'rada] *f* look.
miragem [mi'raʒẽ] (*pl* -**ns**) *f* -**1.** [efeito ótico] mirage. -**2.** *fig* [ilusão] illusion.
miramar [mira'ma(x)] *m* sea-view belvedere.
mirante [mi'rãntʃi] *m* belvedere.
mirar [4] [mi'ra(x)] <> *vt* -**1.** [fitar] to stare at. -**2.** [apontar para] to aim at. -**3.** [observar] to watch. <> *vi* [apontar]: ~ **(em algo)** to aim (at sthg).
➡ **mirar-se** *vp* -**1.** [olhar-se]: ~**-se (em algo)** to look at o.s. (in sthg). -**2.** [seguir o exemplo de]: ~ **se em alguém** to follow the example of sb.
miríade [mi'riadʒi] *f fig* myriad.
mirim [mi'rĩ] (*pl* -**ns**) *adj* little.
misantropo, pa [mizãn'tropu, pa] *m, f* misanthrope.
miscelânea [mise'lãnja] *f* -**1.** [coletânea] miscellany. -**2.** *fig* [mistura] assortment.
miscigenação [misiʒena'sãw] *f* interbreeding.
mise-en-plis [mizãn'pli] *m inv* shampoo and set.
miserável [mize'ravɛw] (*pl* -**eis**) <> *adj* -**1.** [ger] miserable. -**2.** [sovina] miserly. -**3.** [vil] despicable. -**4.** [terrível] dreadful. <> *mf* -**1.** [infeliz] miserable person. -**2.** [pessoa pobre] poor wretch. -**3.** [pessoa vil] despicable person.
miseravelmente [mizeravew'mẽntʃi] *adv* -**1.** [desgraçadamente] wretchedly. -**2.** [pobremente] in misery.
miséria [mi'zɛrja] *f* -**1.** [desgraça] misery. -**2.** [pobreza] poverty; **chorar** ~ to whinge. -**3.** [sovinice] meanness. -**4.** [ninharia]: **custar/ganha-ruma** ~ to cost/to earn a pittance.
➡ **misérias** *fpl*: **fazer** ~**s** to do wonders; **fazer** ~**s com alguém** to cause sb misery.
misericórdia [mizeri'kɔrdʒja] *f*: ~ **(de/com)** mercy (on/for).
misericordioso, osa [mizerikox'dʒjozu, ɔza] *adj* compassionate.
mísero, ra ['mizeru, ra] *adj fig* [escasso] miserly.
misoginia [mizoʒi'nia] *f* misogyny.
misógino, na [mi'zɔʒinu, na] <> *adj* misogynous. <> *m, f* mysoginist.
missa ['misa] *f* -**1.** *RELIG* mass; ~ **do galo** midnight mass. -**2.** *loc*: **não saber da** ~ **a metade** *fam* to not know the half of it.
missal [mi'saw] (*pl* -**ais**) *m* missal.
missão [mi'sãw] (*pl* -**ões**) *f* mission.
misse ['misi] *f* beauty queen.
míssil ['misiw] (*pl* -**eis**) *m* missile; ~ **de curto/médio/longo alcance** short-/medium-/long-range missile.
missionário, ria [misjo'narju, rja] <> *adj* missionary. <> *m, f* missionary.
Mississippi [misi'sipi] *n*: **o** ~ the Mississippi.

missiva [mi'siva] *f* missive.
missões [mi'sõjʃ] *pl* ▷ **missão**.
Missouri [mi'zuri] *n*: **o** ~ the Missouri.
mister [miʃ'te(x)] *m* -**1.** [ofício] office. -**2.** [necessidade] need; **ser** ~ **fazer algo** to be necessary to do sthg.
mistério [miʃ'tɛrju] *m* -**1.** [ger] mystery; **não ter** ~ to be straightforward. -**2.** [segredo] secret; **fazer** ~ to make a mystery.
misterioso, osa [miʃte'rjozu, ɔza] *adj* mysterious.
misticismo [miʃtʃi'siʒmu] *m* mysticism.
místico, ca ['miʃtʃiku, ka] <> *adj* mystic. <> *m, f* [pessoa] mystic.
mistificador, ra [miʃtʃifika'do(x), ra] <> *adj* mystifying *(antes de subst)*. <> *m, f* deceiver.
mistificar [12] [miʃtʃifi'ka(x)] *vt* to mystify.
misto, ta ['miʃtu, ta] *adj* mixed.
➡ **misto** *m* mixture.
misto-quente [ˌmiʃtu'kẽntʃi] (*pl* **mistos-quentes**) *m toasted cheese and ham sandwich.*
mistura [miʃ'tura] *f* mixture.

MISTURA DE RAÇAS

A large part of Brazil's cultural wealth is due to the many races that make up the Brazilian people. The Indians, Portuguese and Negroes of the colonial period were joined, from the mid-nineteenth century onwards, by millions of immigrants from, amongst many others, Italy, Germany, Spain, Syria, Lebanon and Japan.

misturar [4] [miʃtu'ra(x)] *vt* -**1.** [combinar, juntar] to mix. -**2.** [confundir] to mix up.
➡ **misturar-se** *vp* [socialmente]: ~**-se com alguém** to mix with sb.
mistureba [miʃtu'rɛba] *f fam* hotchpotch.
mítico, ca ['mitʃiku, ka] *adj* mythical.
mitificar [12] [mitʃifi'ka(x)] *vt* to mythicize.
mitigar [14] [mitʃi'ga(x)] *vt* to mitigate.
mito ['mitu] *m* -**1.** [ger] myth. -**2.** [pessoa] legend.
mitologia [mitolo'ʒia] *f* mythology.
mitológico, ca [mito'lɔʒiku, ka] *adj* mythological.
miudeza [mju'deza] *f* -**1.** [pormenor] detail. -**2.** [insignificância] trifle.
miudezas [mju'dezaʃ] *fpl* -**1.** [objetos pequenos] odds and ends. -**2.** [quinquilharia] trinkets.
miúdo, da ['mjudu, da] *adj* [pequeno] small.
➡ **miúdos** *mpl* -**1.** [dinheiro] small change. -**2.** [de animal] giblets. -**3.** *loc*: **trocar em** ~**s** to put it simply.
mixagem [mik'saʒẽ] *f CINE & RÁDIO* mixing.
mixar¹ [4] [mi'ʃa(x)] *vi fam* [gorar] to go down the drain.
mixar² [4] [mi'ʃa(x)] *vt CINE & RÁDIO* to mix.
mixaria [miʃa'ria] *f* -**1.** *fam* [soma insignificante]: **uma** ~ peanuts. -**2.** [coisa sem valor] rubbish.
mixórdia [mi'ʃɔxdʒja] *f* mess.
mixuruca [miʃu'ruka] *adj* -**1.** [presente] worthless. -**2.** [festa] lifeless.
ml (*abrev de* **mililitro**) *m* ml.

mm (*abrev de* **milímetro**) *m* mm.

mnemônico, ca [mne'moniku, ka] *adj* mnemonic.

mó ['mɔ] *f* -**1.** [de moinho] millstone. -**2.** [de afiar] whetstone.

moagem ['mwaʒẽ] *f* grinding.

móbile ['mɔbili] *m* mobile.

mobília [mo'bilja] *f* furniture; **sem** ~ unfurnished.

mobiliar [16] [mobi'lja(x)] *vt* to furnish.

mobiliário [mobi'ljarju] *m* furniture.

mobilidade [mobili'dadʒi] *f* mobility; ~ **social** social mobility.

mobilização [mobiliza'sãw] *f* mobilization.

mobilizar [14] [mobili'za(x)] *vt* to mobilize.

moça ['mosa] *f*▷ **moço.**

moçada [mo'sada] *f fam group of young people.*

Moçambique [mosãn'biki] *n* Mozambique.

moção [mo'sãw] *f* motion.

mocassim [moka'sĩ] (*pl* **-ns**) *m* moccasin.

mochila [mo'ʃila] *f* rucksack.

mocidade [mosi'dadʒi] *f* -**1.** [período] youth. -**2.** [os jovens]: **a** ~ the young.

mocinho, nha [mo'siɲu, ɲa] *m, f* -**1.** [jovem] boy. -**2.** [herói] hero.

moço, ça ['mosu, sa] ◇ *adj* [pessoa] young. ◇ *m, f* -**1.** [jovem] young person. -**2.** [adulto] young boy (young girl). -**3.** [como forma de tratamento]: **ei,** ~! hey, man!

moções [mo'sõjʃ] *pl*▷ **moção.**

moda ['mɔda] *f* -**1.** [ger] fashion; **cair** *ou* **sair de** ~ to fall out of fashion; **estar na** ~ to be in fashion, to be fashionable; **fora de** ~ out of fashion; **lançar uma** ~ to start a fashion. -**2.** [coqueluche] craze. -**3.** [maneira] way; **faço tudo à minha** ~ I do everything my way; **à** ~ **portuguesa** Portuguese-style. -**4.** *loc*: **inventar** ~ to create a new fad.

modalidade [modali'dadʒi] *f* -**1.** [tipo] mode. -**2.** *ESP* event.

modelador [modela'do(x)] *m* [cinta] girdle.

modelagem [mode'laʒẽ] (*pl* **-ns**) *f* -**1.** [ato] modelling. -**2.** [produto] moulding *UK*, molding *US*. -**3.** [do corpo] shape.

modelar [4] [mode'la(x)] *vt* -**1.** [ger] to mould *UK*, to mold *US*. -**2.** *fig* [moldar]: ~ **algo por algo** to model sthg on sthg.

modelista [mode'liʃta] *mf* designer.

modelo [mo'delu] ◇ *m* model; ~ **econômico** economic model. ◇ *mf* model; ~ **vivo** live model.

modem ['modẽ] (*pl* **-ns**) *m COMPUT* modem.

moderação [modera'sãw] *f* moderation.

moderado, da [mode'radu, da] *adj* moderate.

moderar [4] [mode'ra(x)] *vt* to moderate.

➡ **moderar-se** *vp* [comedir-se] to control o.s.

modernidade [modexni'dadʒi] *f* modernity.

modernismo [modex'niʒmu] *m* modernism.

modernização [modexniza'sãw] *f* modernization.

modernizar [4] [modexni'za(x)] *vt* to modernize.

➡ **modernizar-se** *vp* to keep o.s. up to date.

moderno, na [mo'dɛxnu, na] *adj* modern.

modernoso, osa [modex'nozu, ɔza] *adj* newfangled.

modess® ['mɔdeʃ] *m inv* sanitary towel *UK*, sanitary napkin *US*.

modestamente [modeʃta'mẽntʃi] *adv* -**1.** [ger] modestly. -**2.** [sem pretensão] with modesty.

modéstia [mo'dɛʃtja] *f* modesty.

modesto, ta [mo'dɛʃtu, ta] *adj* modest.

módico, ca ['mɔdʒiku, ka] *adj* -**1.** [barato, parco] modest. -**2.** [moderado] moderate.

modificação [modʒifika'sãw] (*pl* **-ões**) *f* -**1.** [alteração] modification. -**2.** [transformação] transformation.

modificar [12] [modʒifi'ka(x)] *vt* -**1.** [ger] to modify. -**2.** [transformar] to change.

➡ **modificar-se** *vp* to alter.

modinha [mo'dʒiɲa] *f popular Brazilian song.*

modismo [mo'dʒiʒmu] *m* -**1.** [tendência] trend. -**2.** [moda] fashion.

modista [mo'dʒiʃta] *mf* dressmaker.

modo ['mɔdu] *m* -**1.** [ger] way; **de** ~ **algum** in no way; **desse** ~ that way; **de um** ~ **geral** in general; ~ **de usar** directions for use. -**2.** [jeito] manner; ~ **de andar** gait. -**3.** *GRAM* mood.

➡ **modos** *mpl* manners.

➡ **de modo que** *loc conj* -**1.** [de maneira que] so (that). -**2.** [assim sendo] so that.

modorra [mo'doxa] *f* -**1.** [moleza] lethargy. -**2.** [sonolência] drowsiness.

modulação [modula'sãw] (*pl* **-ões**) *f* modulation; ~ **de freqüência** frequency modulation.

modulado, da [modu'ladu, da] *adj* modular.

modular [4] [modu'la(x)] ◇ *adj* modular. ◇ *vt* to modulate.

módulo ['mɔdulu] *m* -**1.** [unidade] module. -**2.** [veículo]: ~ **lunar** lunar module.

moeda ['mwɛda] *f* -**1.** [peça] coin; **uma** ~ **de 10 centavos** a 10 cent coin; **uma** ~ **falsa** a counterfeit coin. -**2.** [dinheiro] money; ~ **forte** hard currency; **pagar na mesma** ~ to pay sb back in their own coin; ▷ **casa.**

MOEDA ▮

The monetary unit in Brazil has undergone many changes throughout history, due to the various periods of high inflation that the country has gone through. In the post-war period, Brazil has adopted, successively, the cruzeiro, the cruzeiro novo, the cruzado, the cruzado novo and the cruzado real. Since 1994, with the relative economic stability of the country, the real has become the Brazilian monetary unit.

moedor [mwe'do(x)] *m* -**1.** [de café, pimenta] mill. -**2.** [de carne] mincer *UK*, grinder *US*.

moenda [mo'wẽnda] *f* sugar mill.

moer [28] [mwe'(x)] ◇ *vt* -**1.** [café, pimenta] to grind. -**2.** [carne] to mince *UK*, to grind *US*. -**3.** [para extrair suco] to mill. ◇ *vi* [moinho] to grind.

mofado, da [mo'fadu, da] *adj* mouldy *UK*, moldy *US*.

mofar [4] [mo'fa(x)l] <> *vt* [cobrir de mofo] to cover in mould *UK ou* mold *US*. <> *vi* -1. [criar mofo] to go mouldy *UK ou* moldy *US*. -2. *fig*: ~ **(em)** [ficar esperando] to kick one's heels (in); [permanecer] to gather moss (in).

mofo ['moful *m* mould *UK*, mold *US*; **criar** ~ to go mouldy *UK ou* moldy *US*; **o pão está cheio de** ~ the bread is all mouldy *UK ou* moldy *US*; **esta camisa está com cheiro de** ~ this shirt smells musty.

Mogadício [moga'disju] *n* Mogadishu.

mogno ['mɔgnul *m* mahogany.

moído, da ['mwidu, da] *adj* -1. [café, pimenta] ground. -2. [carne] minced *UK*, ground *US*. -3. *fig* [doído]: ~ **de algo** hurting from sthg; ~ **de cansaço** shattered, tired out.

moinho ['mwiɲul *m* mill; ~ **de vento** windmill.

moisés [moj'zɛʃl *m inv* carrycot.

moita ['mojtal *f* thicket.
➡ **na moita** *loc adv* [às escondidas] in secret; **ficar na** ~ [fazer segredo] to keep quiet.

mola ['mɔlal *f* -1. [dispositivo] spring. -2. *fig* [impulsionador]: ~ **(mestra)** driving force.

molambento, ta [molãn'bɛntu, ta] *adj* ragged.

molambo [mo'lãnbu] *m* [roupa em mau estado] rags *(inv)*.

molar [mo'la(x)] *(pl -es)* <> *adj* [dente] molar. <> *m* molar.

moldar [4] [mow'da(x)] *vt* -1. [fazer o molde de] to make a mould *UK ou* mold *US* of. -2. [modelar] to mould *UK*, to mold *US*. -3. *fig* [dar forma a] to shape.
➡ **moldar-se** *vp fig* [orientar-se]: ~**-se por algo** to mould *UK ou* mold *US* o.s. on sthg.

Moldávia [mow'davja] *n* Moldova, Moldavia.

moldávio, via [mow'davju, vja] <> *adj* Moldovan, Moldavian. <> *m, f* Moldovan, Moldavian.

molde ['mɔwdʒi] *m* mould *UK*, mold *US*; ~ **(de vestido)** (dress) pattern.

moldura [mow'dural *f* -1. [de quadro, espelho] frame. -2. *ARQUIT* moulding *UK*, molding *US*.

mole ['mɔli] <> *adj* -1. [ger] soft. -2. [flácido] flabby. -3. [lento] languid. -4. [fraco] limp. -5. [indolente] lazy. -6. [condescendente]: **ser** ~ **com alguém** to be lenient with sb. -7. *fam* [fácil] a piece of cake. <> *adv* -1. [lentamente]: **falar** ~ to speak languidly. -2. [facilmente] easily.

moleca [mo'lɛka] *f* ➡ moleque.

molecada [mole'kada] *f* bunch of kids.

molecagem [mole'kaʒẽ] *(pl -ns)* *f* -1. [travessura] prank. -2. [brincadeira] trick. -3. [patifaria]: **fazer uma** ~ **com alguém** to trick sb.

molécula [mo'lɛkula] *f* molecule.

molecular [moleku'la(x)] *adj* molecular.

moleira [mo'lejra] *f ANAT* fontanelle *UK*, fontanel *US*.

molejo [mo'leʒu] *m* -1. [de veículo] suspension. -2. *fam* [de pessoa, corpo] wiggle.

molenga [mo'lẽŋga] *adj* lazy.

moleque, leca [mo'lɛki, lɛka] <> *adj* -1. [travesso] wild. -2. [brincalhão] mischievous. <> *m, f* -1. [criança] youngster; ~ **(de rua)** (street) urchin. -2. [criança travessa] rascal. -3. [patife] scoundrel.

molestador [moleʃta'do(x)] *m* molester.

molestar [4] [moleʃ'ta(x)] *vt* -1. [importunar] to annoy. -2. [ofender] to offend. -3. [sexualmente] to molest.

moléstia [mo'lɛʃtʃja] *f* ailment.

moletom [mole'tõ] *m* brushed cotton; **de** ~ flannel *(antes de subst)*.

moleza [mo'leza] *f* -1. [maciez] softness. -2. [lentidão] slowness. -3. [fraqueza, falta de energia] limpness; **sentir** ~ to feel limp. -4. *fam* [coisa fácil]: **ser uma** ~ to be a piece of cake.

molhado, da [mo'ʎadu, da] *adj* wet.
➡ **molhado** *m* wet area.
➡ **molhada** *f*: **dar uma molhada em algo** to wet sthg.

molhar [4] [mo'ʎa(x)] *vt* -1. [banhar] to wet; ~ **algo em algo** to dip *ou* dunk sthg in sthg. -2. [umedecer] to dampen. -3. [regar] to water. -4. *fam* [urinar] to wet.
➡ **molhar-se** *vp* -1. [cobrir-se de líquido] to wet o.s. -2. *fam* [urinar] to get wet.

molhe ['mɔʎi] *m* -1. [de defesa] breakwater. -2. [de atracação] jetty.

molheira [mo'ʎejra] *f* sauce boat.

molho¹ ['mɔʎu] *m* sauce; ~ **de salada** salad dressing; ~ **branco** white sauce; ~ **inglês** Worcestershire sauce; ~ **pardo** *gravy made with chicken blood and vinegar*.
➡ **de molho** <> *loc adv*: **pôr/deixar de** ~ [roupa, feijão] to put/leave to soak. <> *loc adj*: **ficar de** ~ *fig* [pessoa] to stay in bed.

molho² ['mɔʎu] *m* bunch.

molinete [moli'netʃi] *m PESCA* fishing reel.

molusco [mo'luʃku] *m* mollusc.

momentaneamente [momẽntãnja'mẽntʃi] *adv* momentarily.

momentâneo, nea [momẽn'tãnju, nja] *adj* momentary.

momento [mo'mẽntu] *m* -1. moment; **de um** ~ **para outro** from one moment to the next; **neste** ~ [agora mesmo] just now; **a qualquer** ~ any moment now; **(no)** ~ **oportuno** (at the) right moment. -2. [tempo presente]: **do** ~ of the moment; **no** ~ at the moment.

Mônaco ['monaku] *n*: **(o principado de)** ~ (the principality of) Monaco.

monarca [mo'naxka] *mf* monarch.

monarquia [monax'kia] *f* monarchy.

monarquista [monax'kiʃta] <> *adj* monarchic. <> *mf* monarchist.

monastério [monaʃ'tɛrju] *m* monastery.

monástico, ca [mo'naʃtʃiku, ka] *adj* monastic.

monção [mõn'sãw] *(pl -ões)* *f* [vento] monsoon.

monetário, ria [mone'tarju, rja] *adj* monetary; ➡ **correção.**

monetarismo [moneta'riʒmu] *m* monetarism.
monetarista [moneta'riʃta] <> *adj* monetarist.
<> *mf* [partidário] monetarist.
monge, ja ['mõʒi, ʒa] *m, f* [monje] monk; [monja] nun.
mongol [mõŋ'gɔw] <> *adj* Mongol. <> *m* Mongol.
Mongólia [mõŋ'gɔlja] *n* Mongolia.
mongolismo [mõŋgo'liʒmu] *m* MED Down's syndrome.
mongolóide [mõŋgo'lɔjdʒi] MED <> *adj* Down's syndrome *(antes de subst).* <> *mf* (person with) Down's syndrome.
monitor, ra [moni'to(x), ra] *(mpl* **-es**, *fpl* **-s**) *m, f* EDUC monitor.
→ **monitor** *m* **-1.** [ger] monitor. **-2.** TV screen.
monitorar [4] [monito'ra(x)] *vt* to monitor.
monja ['mõʒa] *f* ⊳ **monge**.
monocromático, ca [monokro'matʃiku, ka] *adj* monochromatic.
monóculo [mo'nɔkulu] *m* monocle.
monocultura [monokuw'tura] *f* monoculture.
monogamia [monoga'mia] *f* monogamy.
monógamo, ma [mo'nɔgamu, ma] *adj* monogamous.
monografia [monogra'fia] *f* monograph.
monograma [mono'grãma] *m* monogram.
monolítico, ca [mono'litʃiku, ka] *adj* monolithic.
monologar [14] [monolo'ga(x)] *vi* **-1.** [falar consigo mesmo] to talk to o.s. **-2.** TEATRO to give a monologue.
monólogo [mo'nɔlogu] *m* monologue.
mononucleose [ˌmononukle'ɔzi] *f* mononucleosis.
monopólio [mono'pɔlju] *m* monopoly.
monopolista [monopo'liʃta] <> *adj* monopolistic. <> *mf* monopolist.
monopolizar [4] [monopoli'za(x)] *vt* to monopolize.
monossílabo, ba [mono'silabu, ba] *adj* monosyllabic.
→ **monossílabos** *mpl* monosyllables.
monotonia [monoto'nia] *f* monotony.
monótono, na [mo'nɔtonu, na] *adj* monotonous.
monóxido [mo'nɔksidu] *m* monoxide; **~ de carbono** carbon monoxide.
monsenhor [mõnse'ɲo(x)] *m* Monsignor.
monstrengo, ga [mõnʃ'treŋgu, ga] *m, f* [pessoa, coisa] monstrosity.
monstro ['mõnʃtru] <> *adj inv* [enorme] huge. <> *m* [criatura disforme] monster; **ser um ~** [ser um prodígio] to be a wizard; [ser cruel, enorme, horrendo] to be monstrous.
monstruosidade [mõnʃtrwozi'dadʒi] *f* monstrosity.
monstruoso, osa [mõnʃ'trwozu, ɔza] *adj* **-1.** [com conformação de monstro] deformed. **-2.** [enorme] enormous. **-3.** [horrendo] monstrous.
monta ['mõnta] *f*: **de pouca ~** of little importance.

montador, ra [mõnta'do(x), ra] *m, f* CINE (film) editor.
montagem [mõn'taʒẽ] *(pl* **-ns**) *f* **-1.** [de equipamento, casa] assembly. **-2.** CINE (film) editing. **-3.** TEATRO (theatre) production.
montanha [mõn'tãɲa] *f* mountain.
montanha-russa [mõnˌtãɲa'rusa] *(pl* **montanhas-russas**) *f* roller coaster.
Montanhas Rochosas [mõnˌtãɲaʃxo'ʃozaʃ] *n*: **as ~** the Rocky Mountains, the Rockies.
montanhês, esa [mõnta'ɲeʃ, ezal *(pl* **-eses**) <> *adj* mountain *(antes de subst).* <> *m, f* highlander.
montanhismo [mõnta'ɲiʒmu] *m* mountaineering.
montanhista [mõnta'ɲiʃta] <> *adj* mountaineering. <> *mf* mountaineer.
montanhoso, osa [mõntã'ɲozu, ɔza] *adj* mountainous.
montante [mõn'tãntʃi] *m* **-1.** [soma] amount, sum. **-2.** [direção]: **a ~ de** upstream of.
montão [mõn'tãw] *(pl* **-ões**) *m* pile.
montar [4] [mõn'ta(x)] <> *vt* **-1.** [armar] to prime. **-2.** [instalar] to ready. **-3.** [pôr sobre]: **~ alguém em algo** to mount sb on sthg. **-4.** CINE to edit. **-5.** TEATRO to produce. <> *vi* **-1.** [cavalgar]: **~ (a cavalo)** to ride (horseback). **-2.** [pôr-se sobre]: **~ em algo** to mount sthg. **-3.** [atingir]: **~ a** *ou* **em algo** to amount to sthg.
montaria [mõnta'ria] *f* [cavalo] mount.
monte ['mõntʃi] *m* **-1.** [elevação] hill. **-2.** [pilha] pile. **-3.** *fig* [grande quantidade]: **um ~ de** a load of; **comida aos ~s** loads of food.
montepio [mõntʃi'piw] *m* trust fund.
montês [mõn'teʃ] *adj* mountain *(antes de subst)*; **cabra ~** mountain goat.
Montevidéu [mõntevi'dɛw] *n* Montevideo.
montoeira [mõn'twjra] *f*: **uma ~ de** a heap of.
montões [mõn'tõjʃ] *pl* ⊳ **montão**.
monumental [monumẽn'taw] *(pl* **-ais**) *adj* **-1.** [enorme] monumental. **-2.** [magnífico] magnificent.
monumento [monu'mẽntu] *m* monument.
moqueca [mo'kɛka] *f* Brazilian fish *or* chicken stew made with coconut milk, onions and palm oil.
moradia [mora'dʒia], **morada** [mo'rada] *f* dwelling.
morador, ra [mora'do(x), ra] *(mpl* **-es**, *fpl* **-s**) *m, f* resident.
moral [mo'raw] *(pl* **-ais**) <> *adj* moral. <> *m* [estado de espírito] morale; **levantar o ~ (de alguém)** to raise the morale (of sb). <> *f* **-1.** [ética] morals *(pl).* **-2.** [de história, fato] moral. **-3.** [estado de espírito]: **estar de ~ baixa** to be demoralized.
moralidade [morali'dadʒi] *f* morality.
moralismo [mora'liʒmu] *m* moralism.
moralista [mora'liʃta] <> *adj* moralistic. <> *mf* moralist.
moralização [morali'zasãw] *(pl* **-ões**) *f* moralization.
moralizar [4] [morali'za(x)] <> *vt* [tornar mais

moral] to moralize. <> *vi* [pregar moral]: ~ **(sobre)** to moralize (on).

morango [mo'rãŋgu] *m* strawberry.

morar [4] [mo'ra(x)] *vi* -**1.** [habitar]: ~ **(em)** to live (in). -**2.** *fam* [entender] to catch on; **morou?** got it?

moratória [mora'tɔrja] *f* moratorium.

morbidez [moxbi'deʒ] *f* morbidity.

mórbido, da ['mɔxbidu, da] *adj* morbid.

morcego [mox'segu] *m* bat.

mordaça [mox'dasa] *f* -**1.** [de animal] muzzle. -**2.** *fig* [pano] gag.

mordaz [mox'daʒ] *adj* biting.

morder [5] [mox'de(x)] <> *vt* & *vi* to bite.

mordida [mox'dʒida] *f* bite; **dar uma** ~ **(em)** to bite (into).

mordomia [moxdo'mia] *f* -**1.** [num emprego] perks *(pl)*. -**2.** [conforto, luxo] comfort.

mordomo [mox'domu] *m* butler.

morena [mo'rena] *f* ⊳ **moreno**.

morenaço, ça [more'nasu, sa] *m, f* dark-haired beauty.

moreno, na [mo'renu, na] <> *adj* -**1.** [tipo - de pele] dark-skinned; [- de cabelo] dark-haired. -**2.** [bronzeado] tanned; **ficar** ~ to tan; **estar** ~ to be tanned. <> *m, f* -**1.** [de pele] dark-skinned person. -**2.** [de cabelo] dark-haired person. -**3.** [cor] tan.

morfina [mox'fina] *f* morphine.

morfologia [moxfolo'ʒia] *f* GRAM morphology.

moribundo, da [mori'bũndu, da] *adj* dying.

moringa [mo'rĩŋga] *f* water-cooler.

mormacento, ta [moxma'sẽntu, ta] *adj* sultry.

mormaço [mox'masu] *m* sultry weather.

mormente [mɔx'mẽntʃi] *adv* especially.

mórmon ['mɔxmõ] *mf* Mormon.

morno, na ['mɔxnu, na] *adj* lukewarm.

morosidade [morozi'dadʒi] *f* slowness.

moroso, osa [mo'rozu, ɔza] *adj* slow.

morrer [5] [mo'xe(x)] *vi* -**1.** [ger] to die; ~ **afogado** to drown; **ele morreu atropelado** he was knocked down and killed. -**2.** [cair no esquecimento] to be dead. -**3.** *AUTO* to die. -**4.** *fig* [sentir intensamente]: **estou morrendo de calor/fome/frio** I'm dying of heat/hunger/cold; **morro de vontade de viajar** I'm dying to travel; **morri de medo** I was scared to death; **morri de rir** I died laughing. -**5.** *fam* [desembolsar]: ~ **em** to cough up.

morro ['moxu] *m* -**1.** [monte] hill. -**2.** [favela] slum.

mortadela [moxta'dɛla] *f salami-type sausage.*

mortal [mox'taw] *(pl* -**ais)** <> *adj* -**1.** [ger] mortal. -**2.** [terrível - dor] dreadful; [- pecado] deadly. <> *mf* mortal.

mortalha [mox'taʎa] *f* shroud.

mortalidade [moxtali'dadʒi] *f* mortality.

mortandade [moxtãn'dadʒi] *f* slaughter.

morte ['mɔxtʃi] *f* -**1.** [ger] death. -**2.** [fim] ending. -**3.** *fig*: **ser uma** ~ [ser muito penoso] to be the end for sb. -**4.** *loc*: **pensar na** ~ **da bezerra** *fig* to daydream; **ser de** ~ *fam* to be impossible.

morteiro [mox'tejru] *m* mortar.

mortífero, ra [mox'tʃiferu, ra] *adj* lethal.

mortificar [12] [moxtʃifi'ka(x)] *vt* -**1.** [torturar] to torture. -**2.** [atormentar] to torment.

morto, ta ['moxtu, 'mɔxta] <> *pp* ⊳ **matar**. <> *adj* -**1.** [ger] dead; **nem** ~ no way; **não ter onde cair** ~ to have nowhere to lay one's head. -**2.** [sem atividades] deadly. -**3.** [desbotado] faded. -**4.** [sentindo intensamente]: ~ **de fome** dying of hunger; ~ **de raiva** seething with rage. <> *m, f* [falecido] deceased.

➡ **morto** *m* [biriba] *pile of overturned playing cards.*

mosaico [mo'zajku] *m* mosaic.

mosca ['moʃka] *f* fly; **acertar na** ~ to hit the jackpot; **estar/viver às** ~**s** to be empty.

moscovita [moʃko'vita] <> *adj* Muscovite. <> *m, f* Muscovite.

Moscou [moʃ'kow] *n* Moscow.

mosquiteiro [moʃki'tejru] *m* mosquito net.

mosquito [moʃ'kitu] *m* mosquito.

mostarda [moʃ'taxda] *f* mustard.

mosteiro [moʃ'tejru] *m* [de monges] monastery; [de monjas] convent.

mostra ['mɔʃtra] *f* -**1.** [exposição] display. -**2.** [manifestação] sign; **dar** ~**s de algo** to show signs of sthg.

mostrador [moʃtra'do(x)] *(pl* -**es)** *m* dial.

mostrar [4] [moʃ'tra(x)] *vt* -**1.** [ger] to show. -**2.** [apontar] to point out.

➡ **mostrar-se** *vp* -**1.** [revelar-se] to show o.s. to be. -**2.** [exibir-se] to show off.

mostruário [moʃ'trwarju] *m* display case.

mote ['mɔtʃi] *m LITER* [tema] theme.

motel [mo'tɛw] *(pl* -**éis)** *m* motel.

motim [mo'tʃĩ] *(pl* -**ns)** *m* -**1.** [do povo] riot. -**2.** [de tropas] mutiny.

motivação [motʃiva'sãw] *(pl* -**ões)** *f* motivation.

motivado, da [motʃiva'du, da] *adj* [incentivado] motivated.

motivar [4] [motʃi'va(x)] *vt* -**1.** [estimular] to motivate. -**2.** [provocar] to provoke. -**3.** [induzir]: ~ **alguém a fazer algo** to motivate sb to do sthg.

motivo [mo'tʃivu] *m* -**1.** [causa]: ~ **(de/para)** cause (of/for); **dar** ~ **a** to give rise to; **por** ~**s de força maior** for reasons beyond our control; **sem** ~ without reason; **ser** ~ **de** to be a cause for; **(não) ter** ~ **para** to have (no) reason to. -**2.** [justificativa] reason. -**3.** *ARTE, MÚS* motif.

moto¹ ['mɔtu] *m* [lema] motto.

➡ **de moto próprio** *loc adv* of one's own accord.

moto² ['mɔtu] *f* [motocicleta] motorbike.

motoca [mo'tɔka] *f fam* (motor)bike.

motocicleta [ˌmotosi'klɛta] *f* motorcycle, motorbike.

motociclismo [motosi'kliʒmu] *m* motorcycling.

motociclista [motosi'kliʃta] *mf* motorcyclist, biker.

motoneta [moto'neta] *f* motor scooter.

motoqueiro, ra [moto'kejru, ra] *m, f* -**1.** *fam*

[motociclista] biker. **-2.** [entregador] deliveryman *(on a bike)*.

motor [mo'to(x)] *(pl* **-es)** <> *adj* **-1.** *TEC* driving. **-2.** *ANAT* motor. <> *m* engine; ~ **de arranque** starter (motor); ~ **diesel** diesel engine; ~ **de explosão** internal combustion engine; ~ **de popa** outboard motor.

motorista [moto'riʃta] *mf* driver.

motorizado, da [motori'zadu, da] *adj* motorized.

motorizar [4] [motori'za(x)] *vt* to motorize.
➡ **motorizar-se** *vp* [pessoa] to get one's own car.

motorneiro, ra [motox'nejru, ra] *m, f* tram driver *UK*, streetcar driver *US*.

motosserra [moto'sɛxa] *f* chainsaw.

motriz [mo'triʒ] *adj f* ⊳ **motor**.

mouco, ca ['moku, ka] *adj ant* deaf.

mountain bike [ˌmawntẽn'bajki] *f* mountain bike.

mourisco, ca [mo'riʃku, ka] *adj* Moorish.

mouro, ra ['moru, ra] <> *adj* Moorish. <> *m, f* Moor.

mouse [ˌmawzi] *m COMPUT* mouse.

movediço, ça [move'dʒisu, sa] *adj TEC* moving; **areia movediça** quicksand.

móvel ['mɔvɛw] *(pl* **-eis)** <> *adj* movable. <> *m* piece of furniture.
➡ **móveis** *mpl* furniture *(sg)*.

mover [5] [mo've(x)] *vt* **-1.** [ger] to move. **-2.** [começar] to set in motion.
➡ **mover-se** *vp* to move.

movido, da [mo'vidu, da] *adj* **-1.** [impelido]: ~ **a algo/a fazer algo** moved to sthg/ to do sthg; ~ **por algo** moved by sthg. **-2.** [promovido]: ~ **contra alguém/algo** started against sb/sthg. **-3.** [acionado]: ~ **a álcool/vapor** ethanol/steam-driven.

movimentação [movimẽnta'sãw] *(pl* **-ões)** *f* [ato] movement.

movimentado, da [movimẽn'tadu, da] *adj* **-1.** [bairro, loja, dia] busy. **-2.** [música, peça, show] lively.

movimentar [4] [movimẽn'ta(x)] *vt* **-1.** [ger] to move. **-2.** *fig* [animar] to liven up.

movimento [movi'mẽntu] *m* **-1.** [ger] movement. **-2.** [animação] bustle.

MP <> *m (abrev de* **Ministério Público)** *Brazilian state government.* <> *f (abrev de* **Medida Provisória)** *emergency law.*

MPB *(abrev de* **Música Popular Brasileira)** *f generic term for all popular Brazilian music.*

MS *(abrev de* **Estado do Mato Grosso do Sul)** *m State of Mato Grosso do Sul.*

MS-DOS *(abrev de* **Microsoft Disk Operating System)** *m* MS-DOS.

MST *(abrev de* **Movimento dos Trabalhadores Sem-Terra)** *m Brazilian movement for landless workers.*

MT *(abrev de* **Estado do Mato Grosso)** *m State of Mato Grosso.*

muamba ['mwãnba] *f* **-1.** *fam* [mercadoria contrabandeada] contraband. **-2.** [mercadoria roubada] loot.

muambeiro, ra [mwãn'bejru, ra] *m, f* **-1.** [contrabandista] smuggler. **-2.** [vendedor de objetos roubados] fence.

muco ['muku] *m* mucus.

mucosa [mu'kɔza] *f* mucous membrane.

muçulmano, na [musuw'mãnu, na] <> *adj* Muslim. <> *m, f* Muslim.

muda ['muda] *f* **-1.** *BOT* seedling. **-2.** *ZOOL* moult; **estar na** ~ to be moulting *UK*, to be molting *US*. **-3.** [vestuário]: ~ **(de roupa)** change (of clothes).

mudança [mu'dãnsa] *f* **-1.** [ger] move; **fazer a** ~ to move (house). **-2.** [modificação] change. **-3.** *AUTO* gear.

mudar [4] [mu'da(x)] <> *vt* to change. <> *vi* [modificar] to change; ~ **de algo** to change sthg; ~ **de casa** to move house; ~ **de roupa** to change clothes.

mudez [mu'deʒ] *f* muteness.

mudo, da ['mudu, da] <> *adj* **-1.** [ger] silent. **-2.** *MED* mute. **-3.** [telefone] dead. <> *m, f* mute.

mugido [mu'ʒidu] *m* moo.

mugir [52] [mu'ʒi(x)] *vi* [vaca] to moo.

muito, ta ['muĩntu, ta] <> *adj* **-1.** [grande quantidade - no sg] a lot of; ~ **problema** a lot of problems *(pl)*; **levou** ~ **tempo** it took a long time; **sinto muita fome** I'm very hungry; [- no pl] many; ~ **s dias** many days; [- em frases interrogativas e negativas] much, many; **não tenho** ~ **tempo/**~**s alunos** I haven't much time/many pupils. **-2.** *(no sg)* [demais] too much; ~ **calor** too hot; **muita gente** too many people. <> *pron (no sg)* much; *(no pl)* a lot; **tenho** ~ **que fazer** I've got a lot to do; ~**s concordam comigo** many agree with me.
➡ **muito** *adv* **-1.** [intensamente] a lot; **gostei** ~ **de ir ao cinema** I enjoyed going to the cinema very much; **não gosto** ~ I don't like it very much; ~ **feliz** very happy; ~ **mais** much more; **sinto** ~, **mas não posso** I'm very sorry, but I can't. **-2.** [muito tempo] a long time; ~ **antes/depois** a long time before/afterwards; ~ **mais tarde** much later. **-3.** [freqüentemente] often; **ela faz** ~ **isso** she often does that; **você vem** ~ **aqui?** do you come here often? **-4.** *loc:* **quando** ~ at most.
➡ **por muito que** *loc conj* however much.

mula ['mula] *f* mule.

mulato, ta [mu'latu, ta] <> *adj* mulatto. <> *m, f* mulatto.

muleta [mu'leta] *f* **-1.** [para andar] crutch. **-2.** *fig* [apoio] support.

mulher [mu'ʎɛ(x)] *(pl* **-es)** *f* **-1.** [ser] woman; ~ **fatal** femme fatale; ~ **de negócios** businesswoman; ~ **da vida** prostitute. **-2.** [esposa] wife.

mulheraço [muʎe'rasu] *(pl* **-s)** **mulherão** [muʎe'rãw] *(pl* **-ões)** *f* fantastic woman.

mulherengo [muʎe'rẽŋgu] <> *adj* womanizing. <> *m* womanizer.

mulher-feita [mu‚ʎɛx'fejta] (pl **mulheres-feitas**) f grown woman.

mulherio [muʎe'riw] m -1. [grupo de mulheres] group of women. -2. [as mulheres] women.

mulher-objeto [muɲe(x)'obʒetu] (pl **mulheres-objeto**) f female sex object.

multa ['muwta] f fine; **levar uma** ~ to get fined; **dar uma** ~ to fine.

multar [4] [muw'ta(x)] vt: ~ **alguém (em R$ 100)** to fine sb (100 R$).

multicolor [muwtʃico'lo(x)] adj multicoloured UK, multicolored US.

multicultural [muwti'kuwturãw] (pl -ais) adj multicultural.

multidão [muwtʃi'dãw] (pl -ões) f -1. [de pessoas] crowd. -2. [grande quantidade] multitude; **uma** ~ **de** fig lots of.

multifacetado, da [muwtʃi'fasetadu, da] adj [personalidade, talento] multifaceted.

multiforme [muwtʃi'fɔxmil] adj multiform.

multilateral [muwtʃilate'raw] (pl -ais) adj multilateral.

multimilionário, ria [muwtʃimiljo'narju, rja] <> adj multimillionaire (antes de subst). <> m, f multimillionaire.

multinacional [‚muwtʃinasjo'naw] (pl -ais) <> adj multinational. <> f multinational.

multiplicação [muwtʃiplika'sãw] (pl -ões) f -1. [ger] multiplication. -2. [aumento] increase.

multiplicar [12] [muwtʃipli'ka(x)] <> vt -1. MAT to multiply; **x multiplicado por y é igual a z** x times y equals z. -2. [aumentar] to increase. <> vi MAT to multiply.
▸ **multiplicar-se** vp -1. [aumentar] to increase. -2. BIOL to multiply.

multiplicidade [muwtʃiplisi'dadʒi] f multiplicity.

múltiplo, pla ['muwtʃiplu, pla] adj multiple.
▸ **múltiplo** m multiple.

multiprocessamento [muwtʃiprosesa'mẽntul] m COMPUT multiprocessing.

multirracial [muwtʃixa'sjaw] (pl -ais) adj multiracial.

multiuso [muwtʃi'uzul] adj inv multipurpose.

multiusuário, ria [muwtʃiuz'arju, rja] adj COMPUT multiuser.

múmia ['mumja] f -1. [cadáver] mummy. -2. fig [pessoa] moron.

mundano, na [mũn'dãnu, na] adj mundane.

mundial [mũn'dʒjaw] (pl -ais) <> adj -1. [política, guerra] world (antes de subst). -2. [organização, fama] worldwide. <> m [campeonato] world championship; [de futebol] World Cup.

mundo ['mũndul] m -1. [ger] world; **o outro** ~ the next world; **vir ao** ~ to come into the world. -2. [pessoas]: **todo o** ~ everyone; **veio meio** ~ loads of people came. -3. [quantidade]: **um** ~ **de** loads of. -4. loc: **abarcar o** ~ **com as pernas** to take on too much; **estar no** ~ **da lua** to be miles away; **prometer** ~ **s e fundos** to promise the world; **como este** ~ **é pequeno** what a small world;

desde que o ~ é ~ since time immemorial.
▸ **Mundo** m: **Novo Mundo** New World; **Terceiro Mundo** Third World.

munguzá [mũŋgu'za] m corn meal.

munheca [mu'ɲɛka] f -1. fam [mão] hand. -2. [pulso] wrist.

munição [muni'sãw] (pl -ões) f ammunition.

municipal [munisi'paw] (pl -ais) adj municipal.

municipalidade [munisipali'dadʒil] f local authority.

municipalizar [munisipali'za(x)] vt [instituições, serviços] to municipalize.

município [muni'sipju] m -1. [divisão administrativa] local authority. -2. [território] town.

Munique [mu'nikil n Munich.

munir [6] [mu'ni(x)] vt: ~ **alguém de algo** to equip sb with sthg.
▸ **munir-se** vp: ~**-se de algo** to equip o.s. with sthg; ~**-se de coragem** to arm o.s. with courage; ~**-se de paciência** to arm o.s. with patience.

muque ['mukil] m brute force.

mural [mu'raw] (pl -ais) <> adj wall (antes de subst). <> m [pintura] mural.

muralha [mu'raʎa] f wall.

murchar [4] [mux'ʃa(x)] <> vt -1. [planta] to wither. -2. [sentimento] to fade. -3. fig [retrair] to shrink. <> vi -1. [planta] to wilt. -2. fig [pessoa] to droop.

murcho, cha ['muxʃu, ʃa] adj -1. [planta] wilting. -2. [bola] soft. -3. [pessoa - sem energia] languid; [- triste] droopy.

murmurante [muxmu'rãntʃil] adj murmuring.

murmurar [4] [muxmu'ra(x)] <> vt [sussurar] to whisper. <> vi -1. [sussurar] to murmur. -2. [falar mal]: ~ **a respeito de alguém** to complain about sb; ~ **contra alguém** to speak ill of sb.

murmurinho [muxmu'riɲul m -1. [de vozes] murmuring. -2. [de folhas] rustling. -3. [som confuso] murmur.

murmúrio [mux'murjul m -1. [de vozes] murmuring. -2. [de folhas] rustling. -3. [de água] trickling.

muro ['murul m wall.

murro ['muxul m punch; **dar um** ~ **em alguém/ algo** to punch sb/sthg; **dar** ~ **em ponta de faca** fig to bang one's head against a brick wall.

musa ['muza] f muse.

musculação [muʃkula'sãw] f bodybuilding.

muscular [muʃku'la(x)] adj muscular.

musculatura [muʃkula'tura] f musculature.

músculo ['muʃkulu] m -1. ANAT muscle. -2. CULIN sinewy meat.

musculoso, osa [muʃku'lozu, ɔza] adj -1. [cheio de músculo - costas, pernas] muscular; [- carne de comer] tough. -2. fig [forte] tough.

museu [mu'zewl m museum; ~ **de arte** art gallery.

musgo ['muʒgul m moss.

musgoso, osa [muʒ'gozu, ɔza] adj mossy.

música ['muzika] f &rhd; **músico**.

MÚSICA

The samba is, without doubt, the best known expression of Brazilian music. Yet it is far from being the only one. The size of a continent and with strong regional culture, Brazil has a huge variety of rhythms and dances, from the *baião* and *frevo* in the northeast to the gaucho *milonga*. Such a wealth of rhythms gives Brazil a prominent position in the international musical world, to which Brazil has contributed names that range from Heitor Villa-Lobos, in classical music, to Gilberto Gil and Milton Nascimento, in popular music, including famous musicians such as Egberto Gismonti, Toninho Horta and Naná Vasconcelos.

N

musicado, da [muzi'kadu, da] *adj* set to music.

musical [muzi'kaw] (*pl* -ais) <> *adj* musical. <> *m* musical.

musicalidade [muzikali'dadʒi] *f* musicality.

musicar [muzi'ka(x)] *vt* to set to music.

musicista [muzi'siʃta] *mf* -1. [músico] musician. -2. [especialista] musicologist.

músico, ca ['muziku, ka] <> *adj* [profissional] musical. <> *m, f* musician.

➡ **música** *f* -1. [ger] music; ~ **de câmara** chamber music; ~ **clássica** classical music; ~ **folclórica** folk music. -2. [canção] song.

musicologia [muzikolo'ʒia] *f* musicology.

musicólogo, ga [muzi'kɔlogu, ga] *m* musicologist.

musse ['musi] *f CULIN* mousse.

musselina [muse'lina] *f* muslin.

mutabilidade [mutabili'dadʒi] *f* mutability.

mutação [muta'sãw] (*pl* -ões) *f* -1. *BIOL* mutation. -2. *fig* [transformação] change.

mutável [mu'tavew] (*pl* -eis) *adj* changeable.

mutilação [mutila'sãw] (*pl* -ões) *f* -1. [orgânico] mutilation. -2. [de texto] cutting.

mutilado, da [mutʃi'ladu, da] <> *adj* mutilated. <> *m, f* cripple.

mutilar [4] [mutʃi'la(x)] *vt* -1. [pessoa] to mutilate. -2. [texto] to cut.

mutirão [mutʃi'rãw] (*pl* -ões) *m* joint effort.

mutreta [mu'treta] *f fam* cheating; **fazer (uma)** ~ to cheat.

mutuamente [mutwa'mẽntʃi] *adv* mutually.

mútuo, tua ['mutwu, twa] *adj* mutual.

muxoxo [mu'ʃoʃu] *m* tutting; **fazer** ~ to tut.

n, N ['eni] *m* -1. [letra] n, N. -2. [quantidade indeterminada] n; **contamos** ~ **vezes a mesma história** we told the story for the nth time.

na [na] = **em + a**.

-na [na] *pron* [pessoa] her; [coisa] it; [você] you.

nabo ['nabu] *m* turnip.

nação [na'sãw] (*pl* -ões) *f* nation.

nacional [nasjo'naw] (*pl* -ais) *adj* national.

nacionalidade [nasjonali'dadʒi] *f* nationality.

nacionalismo [nasjona'liʒmu] *m* nationalism.

nacionalista [nasjona'liʃta] <> *adj* nationalist. <> *mf* nationalist.

nacionalização [nasjonaliza'sãw] (*pl* -ões) *f* nationalization.

nacionalizar [4] [nasjonali'za(x)] *vt* -1. [estatizar] to nationalize. -2. [naturalizar] to naturalize.

naco ['naku] *m* [pedaço]: **um** ~ **(de)** a piece (of).

nações [na'sõjʃ] *fpl* ▷ **nação**.

➡ **Nações Unidas** *fpl* United Nations.

nada ['nada] <> *pron indef* [coisa alguma] nothing; **não li** ~ **desse autor** I haven't read anything by this author; **ele fez a barba? – fez** ~! has he had a shave? – no, he hasn't!; **antes de mais** ~ first of all; **de** ~! [resposta a obrigado] not at all!, you're welcome!; **como se** ~ **tivesse acontecido** as if nothing had happened; **isso não é** ~! that's nothing!; ~ **disso!** not at all!; ~ **feito** nothing doing; ~ **de novo** nothing new; ~ **mais** nothing more; **não quero** ~ **mais com ele** I don't want anything more to do with him; ~ **mau** not bad; **não dizer** ~ to say nothing, not to say anything; **não foi** ~ [resposta a desculpa!] don't mention it; **por** ~ **neste mundo** for love nor money; **quase** ~ hardly anything, next to nothing; **que** ~! nonsense! <> *adv* [de modo algum] not at all; **não gostei** ~ **do filme** I didn't enjoy the film at all; ~ **menos do que** nothing less than; **não é** ~ **difícil** it isn't at all difficult. <> *m* -1. [vazio]: **o** ~ the void. -2. [ninharia]: **um** ~ a trifle, nothing.

nada-consta [ˌnada'kõnʃta] *m inv* deed of indemnity.

nadadeira [nada'dejra] *f* -1. [de animal] fin. -2. [de mergulhador] flipper.

nadador, ra [nada'do(x), ra] (*mpl* -es, *fpl* -s) <> *adj* swimming. <> *m, f* swimmer.
nadar [4] [na'da(x)] *vi* -**1.** [em piscina, mar, rio] to swim. -**2.** [estar imerso] to be swimming; ~ **em dinheiro** *fig* to be rolling in money; **ficar nadando** *fig* to be out of one's depth.
nádegas ['nadegaʃ] *fpl* buttocks.
nado ['nadu] *m* swimming; **atravessar algo a** ~ to swim across sthg; ~ **borboleta** butterfly (stroke); ~ **cachorrinho** doggy paddle; ~ **de costas** backstroke; ~ **de peito** breaststroke; ~ **livre** freestyle.
NAFTA (*abrev de* **North American Free Trade Agreement**) *f* NAFTA.
naftalina [nafta'lina] *f* naphthaline.
háilon ['najlõ] *m* nylon.
naipe ['najpi] *m* -**1.** [cartas] suit. -**2.** *fig* [qualidade]: **de bom** ~ first class.
Nairóbi [naj'rɔbi] *n* Nairobi.
namoradeira [namora'dejra] *adj* flirtatious.
namorado, da [namo'radu, da] <> *adj* enamoured. <> *m, f* boyfriend (*f* girlfriend).
namorador, ra [namora'do(x), ra] *adj* flirtatious.
namorar [4] [namo'ra(x)] <> *vt* -**1.** [manter namoro] to be going out with. -**2.** [cobiçar] to covet. -**3.** [fitar] to stare longingly at. <> *vi* -**1.** [manter namoro] to be going out together. -**2.** [trocar carícias] to flirt.
namorico [namo'riku] *m* flirtation.
namoro [na'moru] *m* relationship.
nanico, ca [na'niku, ka] *adj* tiny.
nanquim [nãŋ'kĩ] *m* Indian ink.
não [nãw] <> *adv* -**1.** [resposta] no. -**2.** [negação] not; **ela** ~ **é fácil** she's not easy; **ela é médica,** ~ **é?** she's a doctor, isn't she?; **eu** ~ **tenho dinheiro** I haven't got any money; **agora** ~ not now; **como** ~? why not?; ~ **muito** not much; ~ **sei** I don't know; ~ **tem de quê** [resposta a obrigado] not at all, you're welcome; **pois** ~! [como interj] of course! <> *m* [recusa] refusal.
não-agressão [ˌnãwagre'sãw] *f*: **pacto de** ~ non-aggression pact.
não-alinhado, da [ˌnãwali'nadu, da] (*mpl* -s, *fpl* -s) *adj* non-aligned.
não-conformista [ˌnãwkõfox'miʃta] (*pl* -s) <> *adj* non-conformist. <> *mf* non-conformist.
não-governamental [nãwgovexnemẽn'taw] (*pl* -ais) *adj* non-governmental.
não-intervenção [ˌnãwĩntexvẽn'sãw] *f JUR* non-intervention.
napa ['napa] *f* nappa leather.
naquela [na'kɛla] = **em + aquela**.
naquele [na'keli] = **em + aquele**.
naquilo [na'kilu] = **em + aquilo**.
narcisismo [naxsi'ziʒmul] *m* narcissism.
narcisista [naxsi'ziʃta] *adj* narcissistic.
narciso [nax'sizu] *m* -**1.** *BOT* narcissus. -**2.** [pessoa] narcissist.
narcótico, ca [nax'kɔtʃiku, ka] *adj* narcotic.
➤ **narcótico** *m* narcotic.
narcotizar [4] [naxkotʃi'za(x)] *vt* to drug.

narcotráfico [naxko'trafiku] *m* drug traffic.
narigudo, da [nari'gudu, da] <> *adj* with a large nose; **ser** ~ to have a large nose. <> *m, f* large-nosed person.
narina [na'rina] *f* nostril.
nariz [na'riʃ] (*pl* -es) (*pl* -es [na'riziʃ]) *m* -**1.** [ger] nose. -**2.** *loc*: **dar com o** ~ **na porta** to find the doors closed; **meter o** ~ **em** to stick one's nose into; **torcer o** ~ **(para alguém/algo)** to turn up one's nose at sb/sthg; **sou dono do meu** ~ I know my own mind.
narração [naxa'sãw] (*pl* -ões) *f* -**1.** [conto] story. -**2.** [relato] narrative.
narrador, ra [naxa'do(x), ra] *m, f* narrator.
narrar [4] [na'xa(x)] *vt* -**1.** [contar] to describe. -**2.** [relatar] to recount.
narrativo, va [naxa'tʃivu, va] *adj* narrative.
➤ **narrativa** *f* = **narração**.
nas [naʃ] = **em + as**.
-nas [naʃ] *pron pl* [elas] them; [vocês] you.
NASA (*abrev de* **National Aeronautics and Space Administration**) *f* NASA.
nasal [na'zaw] (*pl* -ais) *adj* nasal.
nasalado, da [naza'ladu, da] *adj* nasal.
nascença [na'sẽsa] *f* [nascimento] birth; **de** ~ from birth; **ela é surda de** ~ she has been deaf from birth; **marca de** ~ birthmark.
nascente [na'sẽtʃi] <> *adj* -**1.** [interesse, povo] emerging. -**2.** [planta] sprouting. <> *m* -**1.** [fonte] spring. -**2.** [nascer do sol] sunrise. -**3.** [leste] east.
nascer [25] [na'se(x)] *vi* -**1.** [vir ao mundo] to be born. -**2.** [brotar] to sprout. -**3.** [originar-se] to originate. -**4.** [surgir - sol, lua] to rise; [- dia] to dawn. -**5.** [formar-se] to be born. -**6.** [descender]: ~ **de** to be born into. -**7.** [ter aptidão]: **ele nasceu para o comércio** he is a born businessman. -**8.** [aparecer] to appear. -**9.** *loc*: ~ **em berço de ouro** to be born with a silver spoon in one's mouth; ~ **de novo** to take on a new lease of life; **eu não nasci ontem** I wasn't born yesterday.
nascido, da [na'sidu, da] *adj* [pessoa] born; **bem** ~ from a good family.
nascimento [nasi'mẽntul] *m* -**1.** [nascença] birth; **de** ~ since birth. -**2.** *fig* [origem] origin.
NASDAQ (*abrev de* **National Association of Securities Dealers Automated Quotation**) *f* NASDAQ.
Nassau [na'sawl] *n* Nassau.
nata ['nata] *f* cream.
natação [nata'sãw] *f* swimming.
natal [na'tawl] (*pl* -ais) *adj* native; **terra** ~ birthplace.
➤ **Natal** *m* Christmas; **Feliz Natal!** happy Christmas!, merry Christmas!
natalício, cia [nata'lisju, sja] *adj*: **aniversário** ~ birthday.
➤ **natalício** *m* birthday.
natalidade [natali'dadʒi] *f* birth rate; **índice de** ~ birth rate.
natalino, na [nata'linu, na] *adj* Christmas (*antes de subst*); **festas natalinas** Christmas celebrations.

natimorto, ta [natʃi'moxtu, ta] *m, f* stillborn baby.

natividade [natʃivi'dadʒi] *f* nativity.

nativo, va [na'tʃivu, va] ◇ *adj* native. ◇ *m, f* native.

nato, ta ['natu, ta] *adj*: ele é um escritor ~ he is a born writer.

natural [natu'raw] (*pl* -ais) ◇ *adj* -1. [ger] natural; ao ~ *CULIN* uncooked; de tamanho ~ life-size. -2. [nascido]: ser ~ de to be a native of. ◇ *mf* [nativo] native.

naturalidade [naturali'dadʒi] *f* -1. [espontaneidade] spontaneity; agir com ~ to act naturally; falar com ~ to speak naturally; admiro sua ~ I admire your naturalness. -2. [local de nascimento]: ele é de ~ brasileira he is Brazilian by birth.

naturalismo [natura'liʒmu] *m ARTE* naturalism.

naturalista [natura'liʃta] *mf* naturalist.

naturalização [naturaliza'sãw] *f* naturalization.

naturalizado, da [naturali'zadu, da] ◇ *adj* naturalized. ◇ *m, f* naturalized citizen.

naturalizar-se [4] [naturali'zaxsi] *vp* to become naturalized.

naturalmente [naturaw'mẽtʃi] ◇ *adv* [evidentemente] naturally. ◇ *interj* of course!

natureba [natu'rɛba] *mf* health freak.

natureza [natu'reza] *f* -1. [ger] nature. -2. [espécie] kind.

natureza-morta [natuˌreza'moxta] (*pl* naturezas-mortas) *f* still life.

nau ['naw] *f LITER* ship.

naufragar [4] [nawfra'ga(x)] *vi* -1. [embarcação] to be wrecked. -2. [pessoa] to be shipwrecked. -3. *fig* [fracassar] to fail.

naufrágio [naw'fraʒju] *m* -1. [de embarcação, pessoa] shipwreck. -2. *fig* [fracasso] failure.

náufrago, ga [ga, 'nawfragu] *m* (shipwreck) survivor, castaway.

náusea ['nawzja] *f* nausea; dar ~s a alguém to make sb sick; sentir ~s to feel sick.

nauseabundo, da [nawzja'bũndu, da], **nauseante** [naw'zjãntʃi] *adj* -1. [que produz náuseas] nauseating. -2. *fig* [nojento] sickening.

nauseado, da [naw'zjadu, da] *adj* [indisposto] nauseous.

nauseante [naw'zjãntʃi] *adj* = **nauseabundo**.

nausear [15] [naw'zja(x)] ◇ *vt* -1. [enjoar] to make sick. -2. [repugnar] to nauseate. ◇ *vi* [sentir náusea] to feel sick.

náutico, ca ['nawtʃiku, ka] *adj* nautical.
➡ **náutica** *f ESP* seamanship.

naval [na'vaw] (*pl* -ais) *adj* naval; construção ~ shipbuilding.

navalha [na'vaʎa] *f* -1. [de barba] razor blade. -2. [faca] blade.

navalhada [nava'ʎada] *f* stab.

nave ['navi] *f* -1. [de igreja] nave. -2. *LITER* [embarcação] ship; ~ espacial spaceship.

navegação [navega'sãw] (*pl* -ões) *f* voyage; companhia de ~ shipping line; ~ costeira coastal

shipping; ~ fluvial river navigation.

navegador, ra [navega'do(x), ra] *m, f* -1. [ger] navigator. -2. *COMPUT* surfer.

navegante [nave'gãntʃi] *mf* navigator.

navegar [14] [nave'ga(x)] ◇ *vt* to pilot. ◇ *vi* -1. [seguir viagem] to sail. -2. *COMPUT* to surf; ~ na Internet to surf the net.

navegável [nave'gavew] (*pl* -eis) *adj* navigable.

navio [na'viw] *m* ship; ~ cargueiro cargo vessel; ~ de guerra warship; ~ mercante merchant ship; ficar a ver ~s to be left high and dry.

navio-petroleiro [naˌviwpetro'lejru] (*pl* navios-petroleiros) *m* oil tanker.

navio-tanque [naˌviw'tãŋki] (*pl* navios-tanques) *m* tanker.

nazismo [na'ziʒmu] *m* Nazism.

nazista [na'ziʃta] ◇ *adj* Nazi. ◇ *mf* Nazi.

NBA (*abrev de* National Basketball Association) *f* NBA.

NE (*abrev de* Nordeste) *m* NE.

neblina [ne'blina] *f* mist.

nebulizador [nebuliza'do(x)] *m* nebulizer.

nebulosa [nebu'lɔza] *f* ⊳ **nebuloso**.

nebulosidade [nebulozi'dadʒi] *f* cloudiness.

nebuloso, osa [nebu'lozu, ɔza] *adj* -1. [ger] cloudy. -2. *fig* [sombrio] dark. -3. *fig* [indefinido] nebulous. -4. *fig* [obscuro] nebulous.
➡ **nebulosa** *f ASTRON* nebula.

nécessaire [nese'sɛ(x)] *f* sponge bag.

necessariamente [nesesarja'mẽtʃi] *adv* necessarily.

necessário, ria [nese'sarju, rja] ◇ *adj* necessary; ser ~ fazer algo to be necessary to do sthg; se for ~ if necessary. ◇ *m* necessities (*pl*); o ~ the necessities.

necessidade [nesesi'dadʒi] *f* [o que se necessita] necessity; gêneros de primeira ~ staple foods; em caso de ~ in case of necessity, if need be; não há ~ (de algo/fazer algo) there is no need (for sthg/to do sthg).
➡ **necessidades** *fpl* -1. [privação] need (*sg*); passar por muitas ~ to suffer many hardships. -2.: fazer suas ~ *fam* [defecar, urinar] to spend a penny.

necessitado, da [nesesi'tadu, da] *adj*: ~ (de) in need (of).
➡ **necessitados** *mpl*: os ~ [miseráveis] the needy.

necessitar [4] [nesesi'ta(x)] ◇ *vt* to need. ◇ *vi* to be in need; ~ de to need.

necrológio [nekro'lɔʒu] *m* obituary.

necrópole [ne'krɔpoli] *f* cemetery.

necrotério [nekro'tɛrju] *m* mortuary *UK*, morgue *US*.

néctar ['nɛkta(x)] (*pl* -es) *m* nectar.

nectarina [nekta'rina] *f* nectarine.

nefando, da [ne'fãndu, da] *adj* -1. [abominável] nefarious. -2. [sacrílego] iniquitous. -3. [malvado] wicked.

nefasto, ta [ne'faʃtu, ta] *adj* -1. [agourento] ominous. -2. [trágico] tragic. -3. [nocivo] harmful.

negação [nega'sãw] (pl -ões) f -1. [recusa] refusal. -2. [inaptidão]: **ser uma ~ em algo** to be hopeless at sthg. -3. [desmentido] denial.

negacear [15] [nega'sja(x)] vt -1. [menear] to shake. -2. [seduzir] to deceive. -3. [recusar] to refuse.

negar [14] [ne'ga(x)] vt -1. [ger] to deny. -2. [recusar, não permitir] to refuse.
➡ **negar-se** vp [recusar-se] to refuse.

negativo, va [nega'tʃivu, va] ◇ adj negative.
◇ adv: **negativo!** nope!
➡ **negativo** m FOT negative.
➡ **negativa** f [recusa] refusal.

negligé [negli'ge] m negligee.

negligência [negli'ʒẽnsja] f negligence.

negligenciar [16] [negli'ʒẽnsja(x)] vt to neglect.

negligente [negli'ʒẽntʃil] adj negligent.

nego, ga ['negu, ga] m, f -1. fam [negro] black. -2. [colega] mate.

negociação [negosja'sãw] (pl -ões) f -1. [transação] transaction. -2. [entendimento] negotiation.

negociador, ra [negosja'do(x), ra] ◇ adj negotiating. ◇ m, f negotiator.

negociante [nego'sjãntʃil] mf businessman (f businesswoman).

negociar [16] [nego'sja(x)] ◇ vi -1. COMM: **~ (com algo)** to trade (in sthg); **~ com alguém/algo** to negotiate with sb/sthg. -2. [discutir] to negotiate. ◇ vt -1. [combinar] to negotiate. -2. COM to trade.

negociata [nego'sjata] f crooked deal.

negociável [nego'sjavew] (pl -eis) adj inv negotiable.

negócio [ne'gɔsju] m -1. COM business; **homem de ~s** businessman; **o mundo dos ~s** the business world. -2. [transação] deal; **fazer um bom ~** to get a good deal; **fechar um ~** to make a deal; **~ da China** very profitable deal; **~ fechado!** it's a deal! -3. [caso] matter; **aconteceu um ~ estranho** something strange happened; **o ~ é o seguinte** the deal is as follows. -4. fam [coisa] thing; **o barco é um ~!** the boat is amazing!; **que ~ é esse?** what's the big idea?

negra ['negra] f ▷ **negro**.

negrito [ne'gritu] m bold type.

negritude [negri'tudʒi] f black awareness.

negro, gra ['negru, gra] ◇ adj black. ◇ m, f black.
➡ **negra** f ESP: **jogar a negra** to play a decider.

negrume [ne'grumi] m darkness.

negrura [ne'grura] f blackness.

nela ['nɛla] = **em + ela**.

nele ['neli] = **em + ele**.

nem [nẽl] conj nor; **nem ... nem ...** neither ... nor ...; **eles ~ (sequer) me convidaram** they didn't even invite me; **~ bem ela tinha saído, ele chegou** hardly had I left than someone else took my place; **~ eu!** nor was I!; **ele foi agressivo mas ~ por isso você deveria ter retrucado** he was aggressive but that was no reason for you to retaliate; **~ sempre** not always; **~ tanto** not so much; **~ todos** not all; **eles saíam sem ~ avisar** they would go out even without warning.
➡ **nem que** loc conj even if.

nenê [ne'ne] m [bebê] baby.

nenhum, ma [ne'ɲũ, ma] (mpl -ns, fpl -s) ◇ adj no; **ele não tomou nenhuma decisão** he has made no decision; **em ~ momento** at no time.
◇ pron none; **não comprei livro ~** I didn't buy a single book; **não comprei ~** I didn't buy any; **não quero nenhuma bebida** I don't want anything to drink; **não tive problema ~** I didn't have a single problem; **~ professor é perfeito** no teacher is perfect; **todos os professores são pessoas, ~ é perfeito** all teachers are human; none is/are perfect; **~ de** none of, not one of; **~ dos dois** neither of them, neither of the two; **~ dos cinco** none of the five, not one of the five.

neoclássico, ca [nɛw'klasiku, ka] adj neoclassical.
➡ **Neoclássico** m neoclassical period.

neofascismo [nɛwfa'siʒmul] m neo-fascism.

neofascista [nɛwfa'siʃta] ◇ adj neo-fascist.
◇ mf neo-fascist.

neófito, ta [ne'ɔfitu, ta] adj [principiante] beginner.

neolatino, na [nɛwla'tʃinu, na] adj Romance.

neoliberal [neo'liberaw] (pl -ais) ◇ adj neoliberal. ◇ mf neoliberal.

neoliberalismo [nɛw'liberaliʒmul] m neoliberalism.

neolítico, ca [neo'litʃiku, ka] adj neolithic.

neologismo [nɛwlo'giʒmul] m neologism.

néon ['nɛõl], **neônio** [ne'onju] m neon.

neonazismo [nɛw'naziʒmul] m neo-Nazism.

neonazista [nɛw'naziʃta] ◇ adj neo-Nazi. ◇ mf neo-Nazi.

neo-realismo [ˌnɛwxea'liʒmul] m neo-realism.

neozelandês, esa [ˌnɛwzelãn'deʃ, eza] ◇ adj New Zealand (antes de subst). ◇ m, f New Zealander.

Nepal [ne'pawl] n Nepal.

nepalês, esa [nepa'leʃ, eza] ◇ adj Nepalese, Nepali. ◇ m, f Nepalese, Nepali.
➡ **nepalês** m [língua] Nepalese, Nepali.

nepotismo [nepo'tʃiʒmul] m nepotism.

nervo [ne'xvul m -1. ANAT nerve; **estar uma pilha de ~s** to be a bag of nerves; **ter ~s de aço** to have nerves of steel. -2. [na carne] sinew. -3. fig [força] driving force.

nervosismo [nexvo'ziʒmul m -1. [ger] nervousness. -2. [irritabilidade] irritability.

nervoso, osa [nex'vozu, ɔza] adj -1. [ger] nervous. -2. [irritado] irritable; **isso me deixa ~!** that gets on my nerves!

nervura [nex'vura] f -1. [prega] rib. -2. BOT vein.

néscio, cia ['nɛʃju, ʃja] adj -1. [estúpido] stupid. -2. [insensato] foolish.

nesga ['neʒga] f [pedaço, tira]: **uma ~ (de)** a piece (of).

nessa ['nɛsa] = **em + essa**.

nessas ['nɛsaʃ] = **em + essas**.

nesse ['nesi] = em + esse.
nesses ['nesiʃ] = em + esses.
nesta ['nɛʃta] = em + esta.
nestas ['nɛstaʃ] = em + estas.
neste ['neʃtʃi] = em + este.
nestes ['nestʃiʃ] = em + estes.
net ['netʃi] *f COMPUT* net.
netiqueta [netʃi'keta] *f COMPUT* netiquette.
neto, ta ['nɛtu, ta] *m, f* grandson (*f* grand-daughter).
➦ **netos** *mpl* grandchildren.
Netuno [ne'tunu] *n* Neptune.
neurastenia [newraʃte'nja] *f* -**1.** *PSIC* neurasthenia. -**2.** *fig* [mau humor] irritability.
neurastênico, ca [newraʃ'teniku, ka] ⬦ *adj* -**1.** *PSIC* neurasthenic. -**2.** *fig* [irritado] irritated. ⬦ *m, f* [pessoa irritadiça] irritable person.
neurocirurgião, giã [newrosirux'ʒjãw, ʒjã] (*mpl* -iões, *fpl* -s) *m, f* neurosurgeon.
neurolingüística [ˌnewroliŋ'gwiʃtʃika] *f* neurolinguistics.
neurologia [newrolo'ʒia] *f* neurology.
neurologista [newrolo'ʒiʃta] *mf* neurologist.
neurose [new'rɔzi] *f* neurosis.
neurótico, ca [new'rɔtʃiku, ka] ⬦ *adj* neurotic. ⬦ *m, f* neurotic.
neurovegetativo, va [newroveʒeta'tʃivu, va] *adj* neurovegetative.
neutralidade [newtrali'dadʒil] *f* neutrality.
neutralização [newtraliza'sãw] *f* neutralization.
neutralizar [4] ['newtrali'za(x)] *vt* to neutralize.
neutro, tra ['newtru, tra] *adj* neutral.
nêutron ['newtrõl] *m* neutron.
nevada [ne'vada] *f* snowfall.
nevado, da [ne'vadu, da] *adj* -**1.** [coberto de neve] snow-covered. -**2.** [branco] snow-white.
nevar [4] [ne'va(x)] *vi* to snow.
nevasca [ne'vaʃka] *f* snowstorm.
neve ['nɛvil] *f* snow; **branco feito** ~ as white as snow.
névoa ['nɛvwa] *f* fog.
nevoeiro [ne'vwejru] *m* thick fog.
nevoento, ta [ne'vwẽtu, ta] *adj* foggy.
nevralgia [nevraw'ʒia] *f* neuralgia.
nevrálgico, ca [ne'vrawʒiku, ka] *adj* neuralgic.
newsgroup [neuʃ'grupil] (*pl* -s) *m COMPUT* newsgroup.
nexo ['nɛksul] *m* -**1.** [ligação] connection. -**2.** [coêrencia] coherence; **sem** ~ incoherent.
nhenhenhém [nɛɲe'ɲẽj] *m* -**1.** [resmungo] grumbling; **deixe de** ~! stop whining! -**2.** [conversa] chattering.
nhoque ['nɔki] *m CULIN* gnocchi.
Niágara ['njagara] *n*: **as cataratas do** ~ the Niagara Falls.
Niamey [nja'mej] *n* Niamey.
Nicarágua [nika'ragwa] *n* Nicaragua.
nicaragüense [nikara'gwẽsi] ⬦ *adj* Nicaraguan. ⬦ *mf* Nicaraguan.
nicho ['niʃul] *m* niche.

nick (*abrev de* **nickname**) ['niki] *m COMPUT* nickname.
Nicósia [ni'kɔzja] *n* Nicosia.
nicotina [niko'tʃina] *f* nicotine.
Níger ['niʒe(x)] *n* Niger.
Nigéria [ni'ʒɛrja] *n* Nigeria.
niilista [nij'liʃta] ⬦ *adj* nihilistic. ⬦ *m,f* nihilist.
Nilo ['nilu] *n*: **o** ~ the Nile.
nimbo ['nĩbu] *m* -**1.** *METEOR* nimbus. -**2.** *fig* [auréola] halo.
ninar [4] [ni'na(x)] ⬦ *vt* to sing to sleep. ⬦ *vi* to fall asleep.
ninfeta [nĩ'feta] *f* nymphette.
ninfomaníaca [nĩʃoma'njaka] *f* nymphomaniac.
ninguém [nĩ'gẽj] ⬦ *pron indef* -**1.** [nenhuma pessoa] nobody; ~ **vai descobrir** nobody will find out; **não conte a** ~! don't tell anybody!, tell nobody!; ~ **respeita mais** ~ nobody respects anybody any more; ~ **mais** nobody else. -**2.** *fig* [pessoa desimportante]: **ser** ~ to be nobody. ⬦ *m fig* [pessoa desimportante]: **esse (zé)** ~ that nobody.
ninhada [ni'nada] *f* brood.
ninharia [nina'ria] *f* trifle.
ninho ['ninu] *m* nest; ~ **de rato** *fam* [bagunça] mess.
nipônico, ca [ni'poniku, ka] ⬦ *adj* Nipponese. ⬦ *m, f* Nipponese.
níquel ['nikew] (*pl* -eis) *m* nickel; **estar sem um** ~ to be penniless.
niquelar [nike'la(x)] *vt* to nickel-plate.
nirvana [nix'vãna] *m inv* nirvana.
nissei [ni'sej] *mf child of Japanese parents born in Brazil.*
nisso ['nisu] = en + isso.
nisto ['niʃtu] = em + isto.
nitidez [nitʃi'deʃ] *f* -**1.** [precisão] sharpness. -**2.** [clareza] clarity. -**3.** [brilho] brightness.
nítido, da ['nitʃidu, da] *adj* -**1.** [preciso] distinct. -**2.** [claro] clear. -**3.** [brilhante] bright.
nitrato [ni'tratul] *m* nitrate.
nítrico, ca ['nitriku, ka] *adj* nitric.
nitrogênio [nitro'ʒenjul] *m* nitrogen.
nitroglicerina [nitroglise'rinal] *f* nitroglycerine.
nível ['nivɛw] (*pl* -eis) *m* -**1.** [ger] level; **em** ~ **de** level with; ~ **superior** *UNIV* higher education. -**2.** [condicões] standard; **alto/baixo** ~ high/low standard; ~ **de vida** standard of living. -**3.** [ferramenta] spirit level.
nivelamento [nivela'mẽtul] *m* -**1.** [aplanamento] levelling *UK*, leveling *US*. -**2.** [equiparação] comparison.
nivelar [4] [nive'la(x)] ⬦ *vt* -**1.** [aplanar] to level. -**2.** [equiparar] to compare; ~ **algo a** *ou* **por** *ou* **com algo** to put sthg on the same level as sthg. -**3.** [medir] to equal. ⬦ *vi* [em altura]: ~ **com algo** to be level with sthg.
➦ **nivelar-se** *vp* [equiparar-se]: ~-**se a** *ou* **por** *ou* **com alguém** to measure up to sb; ~-**se a** *ou*

por *ou* **com algo** to measure up to sthg.

no [nu] = **em** + **o**.

NO (*abrev de* **Noroeste**) *m* NW.

nó ['nɔ] *m* **-1.** [laço] knot; **dar um** ~ to tie a knot; ~ **cego** fast knot; ~ **do dedo** knuckle; **ter um** ~ **na garganta** to have a lump in one's throat. **-2.** *fig* [dificuldade] knotty situation. **-3.** [ponto crucial] nub.

-no [nu] *pron* [pessoa] him; [coisa] it; [você] you.

nobilíssimo, ma [nobi'lisimu, ma] *adj* [superl de nobre] most noble.

nobilitar [4] [nobili'ta(x)] *vt* [dignificar] to ennoble.

nobre ['nɔbri] <> *adj* **-1.** [ger] noble; **bairro** ~ smart area. **-2.** (*antes de subst*) [ilustre] honourable. **-3.** ➭ **horário**. <> *m, f* nobleman (*f* noblewoman).

nobreza [no'breza] *f* nobility.

noção [no'sãw] (*pl* **-ões**) *f* notion; **não ter a menor** ~ **de algo** not to have the slightest idea about sthg.

➭ **noções** *fpl* [rudimentos] basics.

nocaute [no'kawtʃi] *m* **-1.** BOXE knockout; **levar alguém a** ~ **/pôr alguém em** ~ BOXE to knock sb out; *fig* [prostrar] to lay sb out; **perder/vencer por** ~ to lose/win by a knockout. **-2.** [soco] punch.

nocautear [15] [nokaw'tʃja(x)] *vt* to knock out.

nocivo, va [no'sivu, va] *adj* harmful.

noções [no'sõjʃ] *pl* ➭ **noção**.

noctívago [nok'tʃivagu] *adj* & *n* = **notívago**.

nódoa ['nɔdwa] *f* stain.

nódulo ['nɔdulu] *m* ANAT nodule.

nogueira [no'gejra] *f* walnut tree.

noitada [noj'tada] *f* **-1.** [período] night. **-2.** [de diversão] night out. **-3.**: ~ **(de trabalho)** evening's work; **fazer uma** ~ to work at night. **-4.** [de insônia] sleepless night.

noite ['nojtʃi] *f* **-1.** [período] night; **à** *ou* **de** ~ at night; **a** ~ **passada** last night; **boa** ~! [cumprimento] good evening!; [despedida] good night!; **da** ~ **para o dia** from one day to the next, overnight; **esta** ~ [a noite passada] last night; [a próxima noite] this evening, tonight; **ontem/hoje/amanhã a** ~ yesterday/this/tomorrow evening; **passar a** ~ **em claro** to have a sleepless night; **tarde da** ~ late at night; ~ **de Natal** Christmas eve; **ao cair a** ~ at nightfall. **-2.** [vida noturna] nightlife.

noitinha [noj'tʃiɲa] *f*: **à** *ou* **de** ~ at dusk.

noivado [noj'vadu] *m* **-1.** [ger] engagement. **-2.** [festa] engagement party.

noivar [4] [noj'va(x)] *vi* **-1.** [comprometer-se] to become engaged; ~ **com** to become engaged to. **-2.** [manter compromisso] to be engaged.

noivo, va ['nojvu, va] <> *adj* engaged. <> *m, f* **-1.** [comprometido]: **estar/ser** ~ **de alguém** to be sb's fiancé (*f* fiancée), to be engaged to sb. **-2.** [no altar] groom (*f* bride).

➭ **noivos** *mpl*: **os** ~**s** [no altar] the bride and groom; [na lua-de-mel] newly-weds.

nojeira [no'ʒejra] *f* filth; **estar/ficar uma** ~ [coisa]

to be/turn out foul; [serviço] to be/turn out appalling.

nojento, ta [no'ʒẽntu, ta] *adj* **-1.** [que enoja] disgusting. **-2.** [antipático] loathsome.

nojo ['noʒul] *m* **-1.** [náusea] nausea. **-2.** [repulsa] disgust; **estar um** ~ [estar sujo, ruim] to be filthy; **ser um** ~ [ser antipático] to be loathsome.

nômade ['nomadʒi] <> *adj* nomadic. <> *mf* nomad.

nome ['nomi] *m* **-1.** [designação] name; ~ **de batismo** Christian name; ~ **de família** surname; ~ **feio** swearword; ~ **de guerra** pseudonym; **de** ~ [renome] of renown; [reputação] well known. **-2.** [autoridade]: **em** ~ **de algo** in the name of sthg; **em** ~ **de alguém** on behalf of sb. **-3.** *loc*: **dar** ~ **aos bois** to name the culprit.

nomeação [nomja'sãw] (*pl* **-ões**) *f* **-1.** [denominação] naming. **-2.** [para cargo] nomination.

nomeadamente [no,mjada'mẽntʃi] *adv* namely.

nomeado, da [nomea'du, da] *adj* nominated.

nomear [15] [no'mja(x)] *vt* **-1.** [proferir o nome, conferir o nome a] to name. **-2.** [conferir cargo a] to appoint.

nomenclatura [nomẽ̃kla'tural] *f* nomenclature.

nominal [nomi'naw] (*pl* **-ais**) *adj* nominal.

nonagésimo, ma [nona'ʒɛzimu, ma] *num* ninetieth; *veja também* **sexto**.

nono, na ['nonu, na] *num* ninth; *veja também* **sexto**.

nora ['nɔra] *f* daughter-in-law.

nordeste [nox'dɛʃtʃi] <> *adj* north-east. <> *m* northeast.

➭ **Nordeste** *m* north-east region of Brazil.

nordestino, na [na, noxdɛʃ'tʃinu, na] <> *adj* **-1.** northeastern. **-2.** *of north-eastern Brazil (depois de subst)*. <> **-1.** Northeasterner *m, f* **-2.** *person from north-eastern Brazil*.

nórdico, ca ['nɔxdʒiku, ka] <> *adj* Nordic. <> *m, f* Nordic.

norma ['nɔxma] *f* **-1.** [padrão] norm. **-2.** [regra] rule; **ter como** ~ to have as a norm.

normal [nox'maw] (*pl* **-ais**) *adj* **-1.** [ger] normal. **-2.** [no ensino]: **curso/escola** ~ teacher-training course/college *UK*, normal school *US*.

normalidade [noxmali'dadʒi] *f* normality.

normalização [noxmaliza'sãw] *f* normalization.

normalizar [4] [noxmali'za(x)] *vt* to bring back to normal; ~ **relações** to normalize relations.

➭ **normalizar-se** *vp* to return to normal.

normalmente [noxmaw'mẽntʃi] *adv* **-1.** [regularmente] as expected. **-2.** [geralmente] usually.

normativo, va [noxma'tʃivu, va] *adj* normative.

noroeste [no'rwɛʃtʃi] <> *adj* [relativo ao noroeste] north-west. <> *m* northwest.

norte ['nɔxtʃi] <> *adj* [relativo ao norte] north. <>

m **-1.** [direção] north; **ao ~ de** to the north of. **-2.** [região] North. **-3.** [guia] guide.

norte-americano, na [ˌnɔxtʃjameriˈkãnu, nal ◇ *adj* North American. ◇ *m* & *f* North American.

nortear [15] [noxˈtʃja(x)] *vt* **-1.** [guiar] to guide. **-2.** *fig* [orientar] to guide.

   ◆ **nortear-se** *vp:* ~**-se para** [dirigir-se] to head towards; ~**-se por** *fig* [orientar-se] to be guided by.

nortista [noxˈtʃiʃta] ◇ *adj* [do norte] northern. ◇ *mf* [pessoa] northerner.

Noruega [noˈrwɛgal *n* Norway.

norueguês, esa [norweˈgeʃ, ezal ◇ *adj* Norwegian. ◇ *m, f* Norwegian.

   ◆ **norueguês** *m* [língua] Norwegian.

nos¹ [noʃl = **em + os.**

nos² [noʃl *pron pess* **-1.** *(objeto direto)* us; **convidaram-~ para a festa** they invited us to the party. **-2.** *(objeto indireto)* us; **ele ~ deu um presente** he gave us a present; **isto ~ saiu caro** that cost us a lot of money; [para enfatizar] us; **não ~ faça mais isto!** don't do that to us again! **-3.** *(reflexivo)* ourselves; **ontem ~ matriculamos na Universidade** yesterday we registered at University. **-4.** [reciprocamente] each other; **olhamo-~ com ternura** we looked lovingly at each other. **-5.** [indicando posse] us; **ela ~ beijou as faces** she kissed us on the cheeks; **ardia-~ a vista** our eyes were stinging. **-6.** [ao autor] us; **parece-~ ...** it seems to us ...; **neste caso, o que ~ chama a atenção é ...** in this case, what draws our attention is ...

nós [noʃl *pron pess (com + nós = conosco)* **-1.** [sujeito] we; **~ somos casados** we are married; **~, brasileiros/estudantes, somos ...** we Brazilians/students, are ...; **~, que gostamos de música, ...** we, who love music, ...; **não pude ver o jogo; ~ vencemos?** I couldn't watch the match; did we win?; **~ dois/quatro** the two/four of us, we two/four; **só ~ dois** just the two of us; **~ todos** all of us; **~ mesmos** *ou* **próprios ...** ourselves; **~ mesmos pintaremos a casa** we shall paint the house ourselves. **-2.** *(depois de prep)* us; **chegou un convite para ~** an invitation arrived for us, we received an invitation; **o que ele tem contra ~?** what does he have against us?; **você fica para jantar conosco?** are you staying with us for dinner?; **alguns de ~ serão premiados** some of us will be rewarded; **entre ~** [duas pessoas] between the two of us, between you and me; [mais de duas pessoas] among us. **-3.** [o autor] we; **neste capítulo, o que ~ pretendemos é ...** in this chapter, what we are attempting to do is ... **-4.** *loc:* **cá entre ~** between ourselves.

-nos [noʃl *pron pl* [eles] them; [vocês] you ▷ **nos².**

nosso, a [ˈnosu, al ◇ *adj* our; **Nossa Senhora** Our Lady; **nossas coisas/brigas** our things/arguments; **um amigo ~** a friend of ours; **este iate é ~** this yacht is ours. ◇ *pron:* **o ~ /a nossa** ours; **um amigo ~** a friend of ours; **a nossa é maior** ours is bigger; **os ~s** [a nossa família] our family; [do nosso time] ours; **ser um dos ~s** *fam* [estar do nosso lado] to be one of ours; **à nossa!** here's to us!

   ◆ **nossa** *interj* [exprimindo espanto] God; ~ **mãe!**, ~ **senhora!** God!, Holy Mary!

nostalgia [noʃtawˈʒial *f* **-1.** [melancolia] nostalgia. **-2.** [da pátria] homesickness.

nostálgico, ca [noʃˈtawʒiku, kal *adj* nostalgic.

nota [ˈnɔtal *f* **-1.** [ger] note; **digno de ~** noteworthy; **tomar ~** to take note; ~ **de rodapé** footnote; **cheio da ~** loaded; **uma ~ (preta)** a fortune. **-2.** COM bill; ~ **fiscal** invoice; ~ **promissória** promissory note, IOU. **-3.** EDUC mark. **-4.** [comunicado] notice; ~ **oficial** official statement.

notabilizar [4] [notabiliˈza(x)] *vt* to distinguish.

   ◆ **notabilizar-se** *vp:* ~**-se (em/por)** to distinguish o.s. in/through.

notação [notaˈsãwl *(pl* -ões) *f* [sistema] notation; ~ **musical** (scale of) notation.

notadamente [notadaˈmẽntʃil *adv* [em particular] in particular.

notar [4] [noˈta(x)] *vt* [reparar] to note; **fazer ~** to indicate.

   ◆ **notar-se** *vp:* **nota-se que ...** it is clear that ...; **é de se ~ que ...** it is noticeable that ...

notável [noˈtavɛwl *(pl* -eis) *adj* notable.

notebook [ˈnotʃibukil *(pl* -s) *m* COMPUT notebook.

notícia [noˈtʃisjal *f* news *(sg)*; **uma ~** a piece of news; **ter ~s** to have news; **ter ~s de alguém/algo** to have news of sb/sthg, to hear from sb/about sthg.

noticiar [16] [notʃiˈsja(x)] *vt:* ~ **algo a alguém** to inform sb of sthg; ~ **algo** to report sthg; ~ **a alguém que** to inform sb that.

noticiário [notʃiˈsjarjul *m* **-1.** [de jornal] news section. **-2.** [rádio, tv] news bulletin. **-3.** [cinema] newsreel.

noticioso, osa [notʃiˈsjozu, ɔzal *adj* news *(antes de subst)*.

notificação [notʃifikaˈsãwl *(pl* -ões) *f* **-1.** [comunicado] notification. **-2.** JUR instruction.

notificar [12] [notʃifiˈka(x)] *vt* **-1.** [comunicar]: ~ **algo a alguém** to notify sb of sthg. **-2.** JUR to instruct.

notívago, ga [noˈtʃivagu, gal ◇ *adj* nocturnal. ◇ *m, f* [pessoa] sleepwalker.

notoriedade [notorjeˈdadʒil *f* **-1.** [fama] fame. **-2.** [evidência] blatancy.

notório, ria [noˈtɔrju, rjal *adj* **-1.** [famoso] famous, well-known. **-2.** [evidente] blatant; **é público e ~ que ...** it is public knowledge and blatantly clear that ...

noturno, na [noˈtuxnu, nal *adj* **-1.** [trem, aula] night *(antes de subst)*; **vôo ~** night flight. **-2.** [animais, plantas] nocturnal.

   ◆ **noturno** *m* **-1.** MÚS nocturne. **-2.** [trem] night train.

noutro [ˈnotrul = **em + outro.**

nov. *(abrev de* **novembro)** Nov.

nova [ˈnɔval *f* ▷ **novo.**

Nova Déli [ˌnɔva'dɛli] *n* New Delhi.

nova-iorquino, na [ˌnovajox'kinu, na] ◇ *adj* New York *(antes de subst.)*. ◇ *m, f* New Yorker.

novamente [ˌnɔva'mẽntʃi] *adv* -**1.** [outra vez] once again. -**2.** [recentemente] recently.

novato, ta [no'vatu, ta] ◇ *adj* inexperienced. ◇ *m, f* novice.

Nova York [ˌnɔva'jɔxki] *n* New York.

Nova Zelândia [ˌnɔvaze'lãndʒia] *n* New Zealand.

nove ['nɔvi] *num* nine; *veja também* **seis**.

novecentos, tas [nɔve'sẽntuʃ, taʃ] *num* nine hundred; *veja também* **seiscentos**.

nove-horas [nɔ'vjɔraʃ] *fpl* **fam: cheio de** ~ [complicado] fussy; [sofisticado] fancy.

novela [no'vɛla] *f* -**1.** *RÁDIO* & *TV* soap opera. -**2.** *LITER* story.

novelesco, ca [nove'lɛsku, ka] *adj pej* soppy.

novelista [nove'liʃta] *mf* -**1.** [roteirista] script writer. -**2.** [escritor] novelist.

novelo [no'velu] *m* ball of yarn.

novembro [no'vẽnbru] *m* November; *veja também* **setembro**.

novena [no'vena] *f RELIG* novena.

noventa [no'vẽnta] *num* ninety; *veja também* **sessenta**.

noviciado [novi'sjadu] *m RELIG* novitiate.

noviço, ça [no'visu, sa] *m, f RELIG* novice.

novidade [novi'dadʒi] *f* -**1.** [ger] novelty. -**2.** [notícia] news *(sg)*.

novilho, lha [no'viʎu, ʎa] *m, f* calf.

novinho, nha [no'viɲu, ɲa] *adj* -**1.** [pessoa] young. -**2.** [objeto] new.

novo, nova ['novu, 'nɔva] ◇ *adj* -**1.** [ger] new; ~ **em folha** brand new; **o que há de** ~? what's new? -**2.** [jovem] young. -**3.** [outro] different. ◇ *m, f*: **a nova/o novo** the new one.
    ◆ **de novo** *loc adv* again.
    ◆ **novo** *m* unknown.
    ◆ **nova** *f*: **boa nova** good news; **nova economia** new economy.

novo-rico [novu'xiku] *(pl* **novos-ricos)** *m,f* nouveau riche.

noz ['nɔʃ] *(pl* **-es)** *f* nut.

noz-moscada [ˌnɔʒmoʃ'kada] *(pl* **nozes-moscadas)** *f* nutmeg.

nu, nua ['nu, 'nua] *adj* -**1.** [ger] bare. -**2.** [sem roupa] naked; ~ **em pêlo** stark naked. -**3.** [sem rodeios]: **a verdade nua e crua** the naked truth; **a realidade nua e crua** the stark reality. -**4.** *loc*: **pôr algo a** ~ *fig* to bring sthg out into the open.
    ◆ **nu** *m ARTE* nude.

nuança [nu'ãnsa], **nuance** [nu'ãsi] *f* nuance.

nublado, da [nu'bladu, da] *adj* cloudy.

nublar [4] [nu'bla(x)] *vt* to cloud.
    ◆ **nublar-se** *vp* to become cloudy.

nuca ['nuka] *f* nape.

nuclear [nukle'a(x)] *(pl* **-es)** *adj* -**1.** *TEC* nuclear. -**2.** *fig* [central] central.

núcleo ['nukliu] *m* nucleus.

nudez [nu'deʃ] *f* -**1.** [de pessoa] nudity. -**2.** [de coisas] bareness.

nudismo [nu'dʒiʒmu] *m* nudism.

nudista [nu'dʒiʃta] ◇ *adj* nudist. ◇ *mf* nudist.

nulidade [nuli'dadʒi] *f* insignificance; **ser uma** ~ [coisa] to amount to nothing; [pessoa] to be a nonentity.

nulo, la ['nulu, la] *adj* -**1.** [sem valor] invalid. -**2.** [nenhum] non-existent. -**3.** [inepto] useless; **ser** ~ **em algo** to be useless at sthg.

num [nũ] = **em** + **um**.

núm. *(abrev de* **número)** *m* no.

numa ['numa] *cont* = **em** + **uma**.

numeração [numera'sãw] *(pl* **-ões)** *f* -**1.** [ato] numbering. -**2.** [sistema] numbers; ~ **arábica/decimal** Arabic/decimal figures; ~ **romana** Roman numerals. -**3.** [de calçados, roupas] size.

numerado, da [nume'radu, da] *adj* numbered.

numeral [nume'raw] *(pl* **-ais)** *m GRAM* numeral.

numerar [4] [nume'ra(x)] *vt* -**1.** [pôr número em] to number. -**2.** [pôr em ordem numérica] to place in numerical order.

numerário [nume'rarju] *m* cash.

numérico, ca [nu'mɛriku, ka] *adj* numerical.

número ['numeru] *m* -**1.** [ger] number; ~ **cardinal/ordinal** cardinal/ordinal number; ~ **par/ímpar** even/odd number; ~ **primo** prime number; **sem-**~ countless; **um sem-**~ **de vezes** countless times; ~ **de telefone/fax** telephone/fax number. -**2.** [tamanho]: **que** ~ **você calça?** what size shoe do you wear? -**3.** [edição] issue; ~ **atrasado** back number. -**4.** [categoria]: **ser o** ~ **um** to be number one. -**5.** [quadro] act.

numeroso, osa [nume'rozu, ɔza] *adj* numerous.

nunca ['nũŋka] *adv* -**1.** [sentido negativo] never; ~ **mais** never again; **ele quase** ~ **sorri** he hardly ever smiles. -**2.** [sentido afirmativo]: **como** ~ as never before; **mais do que** ~ more than ever.

núncio ['nũnsju] *m* nuncio.

nuns [nũʃ] = **em** + **ums**.

nupcial [nup'sjaw] *(pl* **-ais)** *adj* wedding *(antes de subst)*.

núpcias ['nupsjaʃ] *fpl* wedding.

nutrição [nutri'sãw] *f* nutrition.

nutricionista [nutrisjo'niʃta] *mf* nutritionist.

nutrido, da [nu'tridu, da] *adj* -**1.** [bem alimentado] well-fed. -**2.** [robusto] fit.

nutriente [nu'trjẽntʃi] ◇ *adj* nutritional. ◇ *m* nutrient.

nutrir [6] [nu'tri(x)] ◇ *vt* -**1.** [alimentar]: ~ **(com/de)** to nourish (with). -**2.** *fig* [acalentar]: ~ **algo por** to nurture sthg for. -**3.** *fig* [fornecer]: ~ **algo de** to provide sthg with. ◇ *vi* to be nourishing; ~ **de** to provide with.
    ◆ **nutrir-se** *vp* -**1.** [alimentar-se]: ~**-se de** to obtain nourishment from; ~**-se com** to feed on. -**2.** [prover-se] *fig*: ~**-se de algo** to supply o.s. with.

nutritivo, va [nutri'tʃivu, va] *adj* nourishing; **valor** ~ nutritional value.

nuvem ['nuvẽ] *(pl* **-ns)** *f* -**1.** [do céu] cloud. -**2.** *fig* [aglomeração - de pessoas] swarm; [- de insetos, gases, fumaça] cloud. **-3.** *loc:* **cair das nuvens** to come down to earth; **estar nas nuvens** to daydream; **passar em brancas nuvens** [data] to pass by unnoticed; **pôr nas nuvens** to praise to the skies.

O

o¹, O [ɔ] *m* [letra] o, O.

o², a [u, a] (*mpl* **os**, *fpl* **as**) ⬦ *artigo definido* **-1.** [com substantivo genérico] the; **a casa** the house; **o hotel** the hotel; **os alunos** the students; **os noivos** the bride and groom. **-2.** [com substantivo abstrato]: **a vida** life; **o amor** love. **-3.** [com adjetivo substantivado]: **o melhor/pior** the best/worst; **vou fazer o possível** I'll do what I can. **-4.** [com nomes geográficos]: **a Inglaterra** England; **o Amazonas** the Amazon; **o Brasil** Brazil; **os Estados Unidos** the United States; **os Pirineus** the Pyrenees. **-5.** [indicando posse]: **quebrei o nariz** I broke my nose; **estou com os pés frios** my feet are cold. **-6.** [enfaticamente]: **ele pensa que é O gênio** he thinks he is THE genius; **ela é A supermãe** she is THE supermother; **Tentação, O perfume** Tentação, THE perfume. **-7.** [com nome de pessoa]: **o Alexandre** Alexandre; **a Helena** Helena; **o Sr. Mendes** Mr. Mendes. **-8.** [por cada] a, per; **3 reais a dúzia** 3 reals a dozen; **o linho é 5 reais o metro** linen is 5 reals per metre. **-9.** [em datas, períodos] the; **o dois de Abril** the second of April *UK*, April second *US*; **o pós-guerra** the post-war years. **-10.** [em títulos] the; **Alexandre o Grande** Alexander the Great; **D. Maria a louca** Queen Mary the madwoman. ⬦ *pron pess* **-1.** [pessoa] him (*f* her), them *pl*; **eu a deixei ali** I left her there; **ela o amava muito** she loved him very much; **não os vi** I didn't see them. **-2.** [você, vocês] you; **eu o chamei, Dirceu, mas você não ouviu** I called you, Dirceu, but you didn't hear; **prazer em conhecê-los, meus senhores** pleased to meet you, gentlemen. **-3.** [coisa] it, them *pl*; **onde estão as chaves? não consigo achá-los** where are the keys? I can't find them; **este paletó é novo, comprei-o no mês passado** this jacket is new, I bought it last month. **-4.** [em locuções]: **o/a da esquerda** the one on the left; **os que desejarem vir terão de pagar** those who wish to come will have to pay; **o que (é que) ...?** what (is) ...?; **o que (é que) está acontecendo?** what's going on?; **era**

o que eu pensava it's just as I thought; **o quê?** what? ⬦ *pron dem* **-1.** [especificativo - com substantivo] the one; **feche a porta da frente e a dos fundos** close the front door and the one at the back; **compre o que for mais barato** buy the one that's cheapest; **2.** [- com adjetivo] the; **destas balas, adoro as vermelhas** out of these sweets, I prefer the red ones **3.** [indicando posse] one; **minha casa e a de Teresa** my house and Teresa's, mine and Teresa's house; **minha casa é grande e a de Teresa é pequena** my house is big and Teresa's one is small.

ó [ɔ] *interj* oh!

ô [o] *interj* oh!

OAB (*abrev de* **Ordem dos Advogados do Brasil**) *f* *Brazilian law society.*

oásis [ɔ'aziʃ] *m inv* oasis.

oba ['oba] *interj* **-1.** [de alegria] great! **-2.** [cumprimento] hi!

obcecado, da [obise'kadu, da] *adj* obsessive.

obcecar [12] [obise'ka(x)] *vt* to obsess.

➡ **obcecar-se** *vp:* ~ **(por/com)** to become obsessed by/with.

obedecer [25] [obede'se(x)] ⬦ *vt* to obey. ⬦ *vi:* ~ **a (alguém/algo)** to obey (sb/sthg).

obediência [obe'dʒjẽnsja] *f* obedience.

obediente [obe'dʒjẽntʃi] *adj* obedient.

obelisco [obe'liʃku] *m* obelisk.

obesidade [obezi'dadʒi] *f* obesity.

obeso, sa [o'bezu, za] ⬦ *adj* obese. ⬦ *m, f* obese person.

óbice ['ɔbisi] *m* obstacle.

óbito ['ɔbitu] *m* death.

obituário [obi'twarju] *m* obituary.

objeção [obʒe'sãw] (*pl* **-ões**) *f* **-1.** [contestação] objection. **-2.** [obstáculo] obstacle; **fazer** *ou* **pôr** ~ **a** to make an objection to.

objetar [4] [obʒe'ta(x)] ⬦ *vt:* ~ **que** to contest (that). ⬦ *vi:* ~ **(a)** to object (to).

objetiva [obʒe'tʃiva] *f* *FOT* lens.

objetivar [4] [obʒetʃi'va(x)] *vt* [visar a] to have as one's objective.

objetividade [obʒetʃivi'dadʒi] *f* objectivity.

objetivo, va [obʒe'tʃivu, va] *adj* objective.

➡ **objetivo** *m* objective, aim.

objeto [ob'ʒetu] *m* **-1.** [coisa] object. **-2.** [de estudo] subject.

oblíquo, qua [o'blikwu, kwa] *adj* **-1.** [diagonal - luz, chuva, traço] slanting; [- terreno, reta] sloping; [- ângulo] oblique. **-2.** *fig* [dissimulado] devious.

obliterar [4] [oblite'ra(x)] *vt* **-1.** [apagar] to obliterate. **-2.** *MED* to block.

oblongo, ga [ob'lõŋgu, ga] *adj* oblong.

oboé [o'bwɛ] *m* oboe.

oboísta [o'bwiʃta] *mf* oboist.

óbolo ['ɔbulu] *m* [esmola] alms (*pl*).

obra ['ɔbra] *f* **-1.** [trabalho] work; ~ **de arte** work of art; ~ **de caridade** charitable work; **ser** ~ **de alguém** *fig* to be the work of sb. **-2.** *CONSTR* works (*pl*); **em** ~**s** under repair.

obra-prima [ˌɔbra'prima] (*pl* **obras-primas**) *f* **-1.**

obrar

[melhor obra] masterpiece. -**2.** [perfeição]: **ser/estar uma** ~ to be a work of art.

obrar [4] lo'bra(x)] <> *vt* [fazer] to perform. <> *vi* -**1.** [influir]: ~ **sobre** to work on. -**2.** [trabalhar]: ~ **(contra/a favor de)** to work (against/for).

obreiro, ra [o'brejru, ra] *m, f* worker.

obrigação [obriga'sãw] (*pl* -ões) *f* -**1.** [dever] obligation; **cumprir (com) suas** ~**s** to fulfil one's obligations *UK*, to fulfill one's obligations *US*. -**2.** *COM* bond.

obrigado, da [obri'gadu, da] *interj* [agradecimento]: **(muito)** ~ **(por)** thank you (very much) (for).

obrigar [14] [obri'ga(x)] *vt*: ~ **alguém a fazer algo** [forçar] to force sb to do sthg; [impor] to require sb to do sthg; [induzir] to compel sb to do sthg.

➡ **obrigar-se** *vp* to take it upon o.s.

obrigatoriedade [obrigatorje'dadʒi] *f* obligatory nature.

obrigatório, ria [obriga'tɔrju, rja] *adj* obligatory.

obscenidade [obiseni'dadʒi] *f* obscenity; **ser uma** ~ to be a disgrace.

obsceno, na [obi'senu, na] *adj* obscene.

obscurecer [25] [obiʃkure'se(x)] *vt* -**1.** [escurecer] to darken. -**2.** *fig* [entristecer] to trouble. -**3.** *fig* [prejudicar] to damage; *fig* [perturbar] to unsettle.

➡ **obscurecer-se** *vp* to become dark.

obscuridade [obiʃkuri'dadʒi] *f* -**1.** [escuridão] darkness. -**2.** [anonimato] obscurity. -**3.** *fig* [esquecimento] obscurity.

obscuro, ra [obi'ʃkuru, ra] *adj* -**1.** [escuro] dark. -**2.** *fig* [desconhecido, confuso] obscure.

obsequiar [16] [obize'kja(x)] *vt* -**1.** [fazer agrados a] to please. -**2.** [presentear]: ~ **alguém (com algo)** to make a present (of sthg) to sb.

obséquio [obi'zɛkju] *m* favour *UK*, favor *US*; **por** ~ **please**; **quer fazer o** ~ **de ...?** *irôn* would you kindly ...?

obsequioso, osa [obize'kjozu, ɔza] *adj* -**1.** [prestativo] obliging. -**2.** [respeitoso] respectful.

observação [obizexva'sãw] (*pl* -ões) *f* -**1.** [ato] observation. -**2.** [comentário] remark. -**3.** [cumprimento] observance.

observador, ra [obisexva'do(x), ra] (*pl* -es, *fpl* -s) <> *adj* [perspicaz] observant. <> *m, f* observer.

observância [obisex'vãnsja] *f* observance.

observar [4] [obisex'va(x)] *vt* -**1.** [ger] to observe. -**2.** [contemplar] to look at. -**3.**: ~ **que** [notar] to notice that; [comentar] to remark that.

observatório [obisexva'tɔrju] *m* observatory.

observável [obisex'vavew] (*pl* -eis) *adj* observable.

obsessão [obse'sãw] (*pl* -ões) *f* obsession.

obsessivo, va [obse'sivu, va] *adj* obsessive.

obsoleto, ta [obso'letu, ta] *adj* obsolete.

obstáculo [obiʃ'takulu] *m* obstacle; **corrida de** ~**s** *ESP* obstacle race.

obstante [obiʃ'tãntʃi] ➡ **não obstante** <> *loc conj* nevertheless. <> *loc prep* in spite of.

obstar [4] [obiʃi'ta(x)] *vi*: **nada obsta a que ele viaje**

there is nothing to prevent him from travelling.

obstetra [obiʃ'tɛtral] *mf* obstetrician.

obstetrícia [obiʃte'trisjal] *f* obstetrics *(sg)*.

obstinação [obiʃtʃina'sãw] (*pl* -ões) *f* obstinacy.

obstinado, da [obiʃtʃi'nadu, da] *adj* -**1.** [perseverante] obdurate. -**2.** [teimoso] obstinate.

obstinar-se [4] [obiʃtʃi'naxsil] *vp*: ~ **em algo** to persist in sthg.

obstrução [obiʃtru'sãw] (*pl* -ões) *f* -**1.** [entupimento] blockage. -**2.** [impedimento] obstruction.

obstruir [74] [obiʃ'trwi(x)] *vt* -**1.** [entupir] to block. -**2.** [impedir] to obstruct.

obtenção [obitẽn'sãw] (*pl* -ões) *f* -**1.** [aquisição] acquisition. -**2.** [consecução] achievement.

obtenível [obiteẽ'nivewl] (*pl* -eis) *adj* achievable.

obter [1] [obi'te(x)] *vt* -**1.** [diploma, verbas, absolvição] to obtain. -**2.** [desempenho, sucesso] to achieve.

obturação [obtura'sãw] (*pl* -ões) *f* [de dente] filling.

obturador [obtura'do(x)] (*pl* -es) *m* *FOT* shutter.

obturar [4] [obtu'ra(x)] *vt* [dente] to fill.

obtuso, sa [obi'tuzu, za] *adj* -**1.** [arredondado] blunt. -**2.** [bronco] obtuse. -**3.** [obscuro] obscure.

obviedade [ob'vjedadʒil] *f*: **dizer** ~**s** to state the obvious.

óbvio, via l'ɔbvju, vjal *adj* obvious; **é** ~ **que ...** it's obvious that ...; **é** ~**!** of course!

➡ **óbvio** *m*: **o óbvio** the obvious; **ser o** ~ **ululante** to be blatantly obvious.

ocasião [oka'zjãwl (*pl* -ões) *f* -**1.** [ger] time; **em certas ocasiões** sometimes; **em duas ocasiões** twice; **certa** ~ ... once. -**2.** [oportunidade]: **aproveitar a** ~ to seize the moment; **ter** ~ **de fazer algo** to have the opportunity to do sthg.

ocasional [okazjo'nawl (*pl* -ais) *adj* chance *(antes de subst)*.

ocasionar [4] [okazjo'na(x)] *vt* -**1.** [causar] to cause, to bring about. -**2.** [proporcionar]: ~ **algo a alguém** to afford sb sthg.

ocaso lo'kazul *m* -**1.** [do sol] sunset. -**2.** *fig* [fim] end. -**3.** *fig* [decadência] decline.

Oceania [osjã'nial *n* Oceania.

oceânico, ca lo'sjãniku, kal *adj* oceanic.

oceano lo'sjãnul *m* [mar] ocean; ~ **Antártico** Antarctic Ocean; ~ **Atlântico** Atlantic Ocean; ~ **Ártico** Arctic Ocean; ~ **Índico** Indian Ocean; ~ **Pacífico** Pacific Ocean.

oceanografia losjanogra'fial *f* oceanography.

ocidental [osidẽn'tawl (*pl* -ais) <> *adj* western. <> *m, f* westerner.

ocidentalizar [osidẽntali'za(x)] *vt* to westernize.

➡ **ocidentalizar-se** *vp* to become westernized.

ocidente losi'dẽntʃil *m* west.

➡ **Ocidente** *m*: **o Ocidente** the West.

ócio l'ɔsjul *m* -**1.** [tempo livre] free time. -**2.** [desocupação]: **estar no** ~ to be unoccupied. -**3.** [indolência] idleness.

ociosidade losjozi'dadʒil *f* -**1.** [desocupação]

estar na ~ to be unoccupied. **- 2.** [indolência] idleness.

ocioso, sa [o'sjozu, za] *adj* **- 1.** [desocupado] unoccupied. **- 2.** [improdutivo] unproductive. **- 3.** [indolente] idle. **- 4.** [inútil] useless.

oco, oca ['oku, 'oka] *adj* **- 1.** [vazio] hollow. **- 2.** *fig* [fútil] empty.

ocorrência [oko'xẽnsja] *f* **- 1.** [acontecimento] event; ~ **policial** police matter. **- 2.** [circunstância] circumstance.

ocorrer [5] [oko'xe(x)] *vi* **- 1.** [acontecer] to occur. **- 2.** [vir à memória]: ~ **a alguém** to occur to sb.

ocre ['ɔkri] <> *adj* ochre *UK (antes de subst)*, ocher *US (antes de subst)*. <> *m* ochre.

octaedro [ˌokta'ɛdru] *m* octahedron.

octogenário, ria [oktoʒe'narju, rja] <> *adj* octogenarian. <> *m, f* octogenarian.

octogonal [oktogo'naw] *(pl* -ais) *adj* octagonal.

octógono [ok'tɔgonu] *m* octagon.

ocular [oku'la(x)] *adj* ocular.

oculista [oku'liʃta] *mf* oculist, ophthalmologist.

óculo ['ɔkulu] *m* **- 1.** [de navio] porthole. **- 2.** ARQUIT oculus.

óculos *mpl* glasses *(pl)*; ~ **s escuros** sunglasses; ~ **s de natação** goggles.

ocultar [4] [okuw'ta(x)] *vt* to conceal.

ocultar-se *vp* to hide.

ocultas [o'kuwtaʃ] **às ocultas** *loc adv* secretly.

ocultismo [okuw'tʃiȝmu] *m* occultism.

oculto, ta [o'kuwtu, ta] *adj* **- 1.** [secreto, desconhecido] hidden. **- 2.** [sobrenatural] occult.

ocupação [okupa'sãw] *(pl* -ões) *f* **- 1.** [ger] occupation. **- 2.** [de um espaço] occupancy.

ocupacional [okupasjo'naw] *(pl* -ais) *adj* occupational.

ocupado, da [oku'padu, da] *adj* **- 1.** [ger] occupied. **- 2.** [atarefado] busy. **- 3.** TELEC engaged *UK*, busy *US*; **dar (sinal de)** ~ to give the engaged tone *UK*, to give the busy signal *US*.

ocupante [oku'pãntʃi] *mf* occupant.

ocupar [4] [oku'pa(x)] *vt* **- 1.** [ger] to occupy. **- 2.** [atrair] to attract.

ocupar-se *vp* **- 1.** [preencher tempo] to keep o.s. occupied. **- 2.** [cuidar de]: ~ -**se com alguém/ algo** to look after sb/sthg.

odalisca [oda'liʃka] *f* odalisque.

ode ['ɔdȝi] *f* ode.

odiar [17] [o'dȝja(x)] <> *vt* to hate. <> *vi* to hate.

odiar-se *vp* **- 1.** [a si mesmo] to hate o.s. **- 2.** [um ao outro] to hate one another.

odiento, ta [o'dȝjẽntu, ta] *adj* hateful.

ódio ['ɔdȝju] *m* hatred, hate; **ter** ~ **a/de alguém** to hate sb; **ter** ~ **a/de algo** to hate sthg.

odioso, osa [o'dȝjozu, ɔza] *adj* odious.

odisséia [odȝi'sɛja] *f* odyssey.

odontologia [odõntolo'ȝia] *f* odontology, dentistry.

odontologista [odõntolo'ȝiʃta] *mf* odontologist, dentist.

odor [o'do(x)] *(pl* -es) *m* odour.

OEA *(abrev de* **Organização dos Estados Americanos)** *f* OAS.

oeste ['wɛʃtʃil] <> *adj inv* west. <> *m*: **a** ~ **de** west of; **em direção ao** ~ westwards.

ofegante [ofe'gãntʃi] *adj* **- 1.** [arquejante] panting. **- 2.** [cansado] breathless.

ofegar [12] [ofe'ga(x)] *vi* to pant.

ofender [5] [ofẽn'de(x)] *vt* to offend.

ofender-se *vp* [sentir-se insultado] to be offended.

ofensa [o'fẽnsa] *f* **- 1.** [insulto] insult. **- 2.** [desrespeito] offence *UK*, offense *US*.

ofensivo, va [ofẽn'sivu, va] *adj* offensive; ~ **à moral** morally offensive.

ofensiva *f* offensive; **estar/ficar na** ~ to be/get on the offensive; **tomar a** ~ MIL to take the offensive.

oferecer [25] [ofere'se(x)] *vt* to offer.

oferecer-se *vp* [propor seus serviços] to offer o.s.; ~ -**se para fazer algo** to offer to do sthg.

oferecido, da [ofere'sidu, da] *adj pej* easy.

oferecimento [oferesi'mẽntu] *m* offer.

oferenda [ofe'rẽnda] *f* RELIG offering.

oferta [o'fɛxta] *f* **- 1.** [ger] offer; **em** ~ on offer. **- 2.** ECON supply; **a** ~ **e a demanda** supply and demand.

ofertar [4] [ofex'ta(x)] *vt* to offer.

off-line ['ɔflajni] *adv* COMPUT off-line.

off-set [ˌɔfi'sɛtʃi] *m* offset printing.

oficial [ofi'sjaw] *(pl* -ais) <> *adj* official. <> *mf* **- 1.** MIL officer. **- 2.** [funcionário] official; ~ **de justiça** JUR bailiff.

oficializar [4] [ofisjali'za(x)] *vt* to officialize.

oficiar [16] [ofi'sja(x)] <> *vt* [endereçar ofício] to send officially; ~ **algo a alguém** to address sthg officially to sb. <> *vi* RELIG to officiate.

oficina [ofi'sina] *f* workshop; ~ **mecânica** garage.

ofício [o'fisju] *m* **- 1.** [profissão] profession. **- 2.** [incumbência] job. **- 3.** RELIG office. **- 4.** [correspondência] official letter. **- 5.** [cartório]: ~ **de notas** notary public.

oficioso, osa [ofi'sjozu, ɔza] *adj* [não-oficial] unofficial; **de caráter** ~ unofficially.

oftalmologia [oftawmolo'ȝia] *f* ophthalmology.

oftalmológico, ca [oftawmo'lɔȝiku, ka] *adj* ophthalmological.

oftalmologista [oftawmolo'ȝiʃta] *mf* ophthalmologist.

ofuscante [ofuʃkãntʃi] *adj* dazzling.

ofuscar [12] [ofuʃ'ka(x)] <> *vt* **- 1.** [encobrir] to conceal. **- 2.** [suplantar em brilho] to outshine. **- 3.** [olhos] to dazzle. **- 4.** *fig* [apagar] to overshadow. <> *vi* [turvar a vista] to dazzle.

ogro ['ɔgru] *m* ogre.

ogum [o'gũ] *m god of war in Afro-Brazilian cults.*

oh [ɔ] *interj* oh!

oi ['oj] *interj* **- 1.** [como saudação] hi! **- 2.** [como resposta indagativa] mm?

oitava-de-final [oiˌtavadȝifi'naw] *(pl* **oitavas-de-final)** *f* ESP *round prior to quarter finals.*

oitavo, va [oj'tavu, va] <> *num* eighth; **a oitava parte** the eighth part. <> *m* eighth; *veja também* **sexto**.

oitenta [ōj'tēnta] *num* eighty; *veja também* **sessenta**.

oito ['ojtu] *num* eight; *veja também* **seis**; **ou ~ ou oitenta** all or nothing.

oitocentos, tas [ojtu'sēntuʃ] *num* eight hundred; *veja também* **seiscentos**.

ojeriza [oʒe'riza] *f* loathing; **ter ~ a alguém/algo** to have a loathing for sb/sthg.

ola ['ola] *f ESP* Mexican wave.

olá [o'la] *interj* hello.

olaria [ola'ria] *f* [fábrica] pottery.

oleado [o'ljadu] *m* tarpaulin.

oleiro, ra [o'lejru, ra] *m, f* potter.

óleo ['ɔlju] *m* oil; **~ de bronzear** sun-tan oil; **~ de cozinha** cooking oil; **~ diesel** diesel oil; **~ de fígado de bacalhau** cod liver oil; **~ de rícino** castor oil.

oleoduto [oljo'dutu] *m* pipeline.

oleosidade [oljozi'dadʒi] *f* greasiness.

oleoso, osa [o'ljozu, ɔza] *adj* greasy.

olfato [ow'fatu] *m* smell.

olhada [o'ʎada] *f* look; **dar uma ~ (em)** to take a look (at).

olhadela [oʎa'dɛla] *f* glance.

olhar [4] [o'ʎa(x)] <> *vt* **-1.** [ger] to look at. **-2.** [cuidar de] to keep an eye on. **-3.** [ponderar] to look at. <> *vi* [ver] to look; **olha!** look!; **~ para alguém/algo** to look at sb/sthg; **~ por** [cuidar de] to keep an eye on. <> *m* look.
   ➤ olhar-se *vp* **-1.** [ver-se] to look at o.s. **-2.** [entreolhar-se] to look at each other.

olheiras [o'ʎejraʃ] *fpl* shadows under the eyes.

olho [o'ʎu] (*pl* olhos) *m* **-1.** [ger] eye; **a ~ nu** to the naked eye; **de ~** [medir] by eye; **~ grande** *fig* envy; **pôr ~ grande em algo** to have one's eye on sthg; **~ de sogra** *CULIN* Brazilian plum pudding *with caramelized topping*; **ter ~ de peixe morto** to be glassy-eyed; **estar de ~ em alguém/algo** to have one's eye on sb/sthg. **-2.** [vista] glance; **dirigiu os ~s para todos durante o show** she cast her eyes over everyone during the show; **a ~s vistos** in front of one's very eyes; **passar os ~s por algo** to run one's eyes over sthg; **longe dos ~s, longe do coração** out of sight, out of mind. **-3.** [de queijo] hole. **-4.** [de agulha] eye; **~ mágico** magic eye. **-5.** *loc:* **abrir os ~s** to open one's eyes; **abrir os ~s de alguém** to open sb's eyes; **custar/pagar os ~s da cara** to cost/pay an arm and a leg; **não pregar o ~** not to sleep a wink; **não ver com bons ~s** to take a dim view of; **pôr alguém no ~ da rua** to fire sb; **ter o ~ maior do que a barriga** to have eyes bigger than one's stomach.

olho-de-gato [oʎudʒi'gatu] (*pl* olhos-de-gato) *m* reflector.

oligarquia [oligax'kia] *f* oligarchy.

oligárquico, ca [oli'gaxkiku, ka] *adj* oligarchical.

oligopólio [oligo'pɔljul] *m* oligopoly.

olimpíada [olĩ'piada] *f* Olympiad; **as ~s** the Olympics.

olímpico, ca [o'lĩmpiku, ka] *adj* Olympic.

olmo ['owmu] *m* elm.

OLP (**Organização para Libertação da Palestina**) *f* PLO.

olvidar [4] [owvi'da(x)] *vt* to forget.
   ➤ olvidar-se *vp:* **~-se (de)** to forget.

Omã [o'mã] *n* Oman.

ombreira [ōn'brejra] *f* **-1.** [de roupa] shoulder pad. **-2.** [de porta] doorpost.

ombro ['ōnbru] *m ANAT* shoulder; **~ a ~** shoulder to shoulder; **encolher os ~s** to shrug.

OMC (*abrev de* **Organização Mundial de Comércio**) *f* WTO.

omelete [ome'lɛtʃi] *f* omelette *UK*, omelet *US*.

omissão [omi'sãw] (*pl* -ões) *f* omission.

omisso, ssa [o'misu, sa] *adj* **-1.** [negligente, ausente] negligent. **-2.** [faltando] omitted.

omitir [6] [omi'tʃi(x)] *vt* to omit.
   ➤ omitir-se *vp:* **~-se de algo** to refrain from sthg.

omoplata [omo'plata] *f* shoulder blade, scapula.

OMS (*abrev de* **Organização Mundial de Saúde**) *f* WHO.

onanismo [ona'niʒmu] *m* onanism.

onça ['õnsa] *f* **-1.** [animal] jaguar; **estar/ficar uma ~** to be wild. **-2.** [peso] ounce.

onça-parda [ˌõnsa'paxda] (*pl* onças-pardas) *f ZOOL* puma.

onça-pintada [o'õnsapĩntada] (*pl* -s) *f ZOOL* jaguar.

oncologia [õŋkolo'ʒia] *f* oncology.

oncologista [õŋkolo'ʒiʃta] *mf* oncologist.

onda ['õnda] *f* **-1.** [ger] wave; **pegar ~** [surfar] to surf. **-2.** [moda] vogue; **estar na ~** to be in vogue. **-3.** *fam* [fingimento] lie. **-4.** *FÍSICA:* **~ curta/média/longa** short/medium/long wave; **~ sonora** sound wave. **-5.** *loc:* **deixar de ~** to stop messing about; **fazer ~** to make a fuss; **ir na ~ de alguém** to be taken in by sb.

onde ['õndʒi] (*a + onde = aonde*) <> *adv (interrogativo)* **-1.** where; **~ fica o museu?** where is the museum?; **não sei ~ deixei meus óculos** I don't know where I've left my glasses; **aonde vamos esta noite?** where are we going tonight?; **por ~ vieram?** which way did you come?; **~ quer que** wherever; **carregue sua carteira por ~ você** for keep your wallet with you wherever you go. **-2.** *loc:* **fazer por ~** to do what's necessary. <> *pron* **-1.** *(relativo)* where; **a casa ~ moro** the house where I live; **o vale por ~ passa o rio** the valley where the river flows. **-2.** *(indefinido)* where; **eles não têm ~ morar** they have nowhere to live, they don't have anywhere to live; **pretendo voltar ~ estivemos ontem** I intend to go back to where we were yesterday; **até ~ eu sei** as far as I know.

ondeado, da [õn'dʒjadu, da] *adj* **-1.** [saia, desenho] flowing. **-2.** [cabelo] wavy.

ondear [15] [õn'dʒja(x)] *vi* to ripple.
ondulação [õndula'sãw] (*pl*-**ões**) *f* undulation.
ondulado, da [õndu'ladu, da] *adj* -**1.** [cabelo] wavy. -**2.** [folha] curled.
ondulante [õndu'lãntʃi] *adj* wavy.
onerar [4] [one'ra(x)] *vt* -**1.** [impor ônus a] to burden. -**2.** [sobrecarregar] to put a burden upon.
oneroso, osa [one'rozu, ɔza] *adj* -**1.** [dispendioso] costly. -**2.** [pesado] burdensome.
ONG (*abrev de* **Organização Não-Governamental**) *f* NGO.
ônibus ['onibuʃ] *m inv* bus.
onipotência [onipo'tẽsja] *f* omnipotence.
onipotente [ˌonipo'tẽntʃi] *adj* omnipotent.
onipresença [oni'prezẽnsa] *f* omnipresence.
onipresente [onipre'zẽntʃi] *adj* omnipresent.
onírico, ca [o'niriku, ka] *adj* dreamlike.
onisciência [oni'sjẽsja] *f* omniscience.
onisciente [oni'sjẽntʃi] *adj* omniscient.
onívoro, ra [o'nivuru, ra] *adj* omnivorous.
ônix ['oniks] *m (inv)* onyx.
on-line ['õlajni] *adv* COMPUT on-line.
onomástico, ca [ono'maʃtʃiku, ka] *adj* onomastic.
onomatopéia [onomato'pɛja] *f* onomatopoeia.
ontem ['õntẽ] *adv* yesterday; ~ **de manhã** yesterday morning; ~ **à noite/à tarde** yesterday evening/afternoon.
ONU ['onu] (*abrev de* **Organização das Nações Unidas**) *f* UN.
ônus ['onuʃ] *m* -**1.** *(inv)* [peso] excess weight. -**2.** *fig* [encargo] obligation. -**3.** [imposto pesado] heavy tax.
onze ['õzi] *num* eleven; *veja também* **seis**.
opa ['opa] *interj* [de admiração] wow!; [de saudação] hi!
opacidade [opasi'dadʒi] *f* opacity.
opaco, ca [o'paku, ka] *adj* opaque.
opala [o'pala] *f* -**1.** [mineral] opal. -**2.** [tecido] *fine cotton material.*
opção [op'sãw] (*pl*-**ões**) *f* -**1.** [escolha] choice. -**2.** [preferência] preference.
opcional [opsjo'naw] (*pl*-**ais**) *adj* optional.
open market ['opẽn'maxkitʃ] *m* open market.
OPEP (*abrev de* **Organização dos Países Exportadores de Petróleo**) *f* OPEC.
ópera ['ɔpera] *f* opera.
operação [opera'sãw] (*pl*-**ões**) *f* operation.
operacional [operasjo'naw] (*pl*-**ais**) *adj* operational.
operacionalidade [operasjionali'dadʒi] *f* operating efficiency.
operado, da [ope'radu, da] <> *adj* operated. <> *m, f person or animal having had an operation.*
operador, ra [opera'do(x), ra] (*mpl*-**es**, *fpl*-**s**) *m, f* operator.
operante [ope'rãntʃi] *adj* operative.
operar [4] [ope'ra(x)] <> *vt* -**1.** [fazer funcionar] to operate. -**2.** MED to operate on. -**3.** [realizar] to perform. <> *vi* -**1.** [ger] to operate. -**2.** MED to

operate. -**3.** [trabalhar]: ~ **com algo** to work with sthg.
➡ **operar-se** *vp* [ocorrer] to take place.
operária [ope'rarjal *f* ⊳ **operário**.
operariado [opera'rjadu] *m*: **o** ~ the working class.
operário, ria [ope'rarju, rja] <> *adj* -**1.** [greve] workers' *(antes de subst).* -**2.** [classe] working. -**3.** [abelha] worker *(antes de subst).*<> *m, f* [trabalhador] worker.
opereta [ope'reta] *m* operetta.
opinar [4] [opi'na(x)] <> *vi* [emitir opinião]: ~ **(sobre alguém/algo)** to give one's opinion (on sb/sthg); ~ **a favor de/contra algo** to make a statement in favour of/against sthg. <> *vt*: ~ **que** to declare that.
opinião [opi'njãw] (*pl*-**ões**) *f* opinion; **a** ~ **pública** public opinion; **dar uma** ~ to give an opinion; **mudar de** ~ to change one's mind; **ser de** ~ **que** to be of the opinion that.
ópio ['ɔpju] *m* opium.
oponente [opo'nẽntʃi] <> *adj* opposing. <> *mf* opponent.
opor [45] [o'po(x)] *vt* -**1.** [resistência, objeção] to oppose. -**2.** [argumento, razão] to set.
➡ **opor-se** *vp* -**1.** [ser contrário]: ~**-se (a algo)** to be opposed (to sthg). -**2.** [contradizer]: ~**-se a algo** to be in opposition to sthg.
oportunamente [opoxtuna'mẽntʃi] *adv* opportunely.
oportunidade [opoxtuni'dadʒi] *f* opportunity; **aproveitar a** ~ to seize the opportunity; **na primeira** ~ at the first opportunity.
oportunismo [opoxtu'niʒmul *m* opportunism.
oportunista [opoxtu'niʃta] <> *adj* opportunistic. <> *mf* opportunist.
oportuno, na [opox'tunu, na] *adj* opportune; **momento** ~ opportune moment.
oposição [opozi'sãw] (*pl*-**ões**) *f* -**1.** [objeção] opposition; **fazer** ~ **a** to oppose; **em** ~ **a** against. -**2.** POL: **a** ~ the opposition.
oposicionista [opozisjo'niʃta] <> *adj* opposition *(antes de subst).*<> *mf* member of the opposition.
oposto, ta [o'poʃtu, o'pɔʃta] *adj* -**1.** [contrário] opposite. -**2.** [em frente a] opposite.
➡ **oposto** *m* [inverso] opposite.
opressão [opre'sãw] (*pl*-**ões**) *f* -**1.** [ger] oppression. -**2.** [sufocação - no peito] tightness; [- no coração] oppression.
opressivo, va [opre'sivu, va] *adj* oppressive.
opressor, ra [opre'so(x), ra] *m, f* oppressor.
oprimido, da [opri'midu, da] *adj* oppressed.
oprimir [6] [opri'mi(x)] *vt* -**1.** [ger] to oppress. -**2.** [comprimir] to crush.
optar [4] [op'ta(x)] *vi*: ~ **(por/entre)** to opt (for/between); ~ **por fazer algo** to opt to do sthg, to choose to do sthg.
optativo, va [opta'tʃivu, va] *adj* optional.
óptico, ca ['ɔptʃiku, ka] <> *adj* optical. <> *mf* optician.

óptica f -1. FÍS optics (sg). -2. [loja] optician's. -3. [ponto de vista] point of view.

opulência [opu'lēnsja] f opulence.

opulento, ta [opu'lēntu, ta] adj opulent.

opúsculo [o'puʃkulu] m -1. [livreto] booklet. -2. [folheto] pamphlet.

ora ['ɔra] <> adv [agora] now; **ela ~ quer uma coisa, ~ quer outra** first she wants one thing, then she wants another; **por ~** for now. <> conj now. <> interj: **~ bolas!** oh hell!; **~ viva!** hi there!

oração [ora'sãw] (pl -ões) f -1. [reza] prayer; **fazer uma ~** to say a prayer. -2. GRAM clause.

oráculo [o'rakulu] m oracle.

orador, ra [ora'do(x), ra] (mpl -es, fpl -s) m, f orator.

oral [o'raw] (pl -ais) <> adj oral. <> f oral (exam).

orangotango [orãŋgu'tãŋgu] m orang-utan.

orar [4] [o'ra(x)] vi: **~ (a/por)** to pray (to/for).

oratório, ria [ora'tɔrju, rja] <> adj oratorial. <> m -1. RELIG oratory. -2. MÚS oratorio.

◆ **oratória** f [arte de falar] oratory.

orbe ['ɔxbi] m orb.

órbita ['ɔxbita] f -1. ASTRON orbit; **a lua está em ~ da Terra** the moon orbits the Earth; **o satélite entrou em ~** the satellite entered into orbit; **entrar em ~** fam fig to be spaced out; **estar fora de ~** fam fig to be out of one's mind. -2. [de olho] socket. -3. fig [área] orbit.

orbitar [oxbi'ta(x)] vi -1. [descrever órbita] to orbit. -2. fig [em torno de alguém] to revolve around.

orçamentário, ria [oxsamēn'tarju, rja] adj budget (antes de subst).

orçamento [oxsa'mēntu] m -1. [de família, governo] budget. -2. [de obra] estimate; **~ sem compromisso** estimate without obligation, free estimate.

orçar [13] [ox'sa(x)] <> vt [calcular] to estimate. <> vi [avaliar] to make an estimate; **~ em** to estimate at.

ordeiro, ra [ox'dejru, ra] adj orderly.

ordem ['ɔxdẽ] (pl -ns) f -1. [ger] order; **dar uma ~ em algo** to tidy sthg up; **estar em ~** to be tidy; **~ do dia** agenda; **manter a ~** to maintain order; **tudo em ~?** everything OK?; **~ pública/social** public/social order; **às suas ordens** at your service; **até nova ~** until further notice; **dar ~ a alguém para fazer algo** to tell sb to do sthg; **~ de pagamento** money order; **~ de prisão** prison order. -2. [categoria]: **foi um prejuízo da ~ de bilhões** there was damage in the order of billions; **de primeira/segunda ~** first/second rate; **~ dos Advogados** Law Society; **~ de grandeza** MAT order of magnitude.

ordenação [oxdena'sãw] (pl -ões) f -1. RELIG ordination. -2. [ordem] ordering.

ordenado, da [oxde'nadu, da] adj -1. [organizado] organized. -2. RELIG ordained.

◆ **ordenado** m [salário] salary, wages (pl).

ordenança [oxde'nãnsa] <> mf [soldado]

orderly. <> f MIL [regulamento] ordinance.

ordenar [4] [oxde'na(x)] vt to order.

◆ **ordenar-se** vp -1. RELIG to be ordained. -2. [organizar-se] to organize o.s.

ordenhar [4] [oxde'na(x)] vt to milk.

ordinal [oxdʒi'naw] (pl -ais) adj ordinal.

ordinariamente [oxdʒinarja'mēntʃi] adv usually.

ordinário, ria [oxdʒi'narju, rja] adj -1. [ger] ordinary. -2. [de má qualidade] poor. -3. [comum, freqüente] usual.

orégano [o'rɛganu] m oregano.

orelha [o'reʎa] f -1. ANAT ear; **estar de ~ em pé** fam fig to have one's wits about one; **~s de abano** protruding ears; **estar até as ~s com algo** to be up to one's ears in sthg. -2. [aba] flap.

orelhada [ore'ʎada] f: **de ~** by ear.

orelhão [ore'ʎãw] (pl -ões) m [cabine de telefone público] open telephone booth.

orelhudo, da [ore'ʎudu, da] adj -1. [de orelhas grandes] big-eared. -2. [estúpido] asinine. -3. [teimoso] stubborn.

orfanato [oxfa'natu] m orphanage.

orfandade [oxfãn'dadʒi] f orphanhood.

órfão, ã ['ɔxfãw, fã] <> adj orphaned; **~ de pai/mãe** fatherless/motherless. <> m, f orphan.

orfeão [ox'fjãw] (pl -ões) m choir.

organdi [oxgãn'dʒi] m organdie UK, organdy US.

orgânico, ca [ox'gãniku, ka] adj organic.

organismo [oxga'niʒmu] m -1. [ger] organism. -2. fig [instituição] organization.

organista [oxga'niʃta] mf organist.

organização [oxganiza'sãw] (pl -ões) f organization.

organizacional [oxganiza'sionaw] (pl -ais) adj organizational.

organizador, ra [oxganiza'do(x), ra] m, f organizer.

organizar [4] [oxgani'za(x)] vt to organize.

◆ **organizar-se** vp to get organized.

organograma [oxgano'grãmal] m organization chart, organigram.

órgão ['ɔxgãw] (pl -s) m -1. [ger] organ. -2. [instituição] body; **~ de imprensa** news publication.

orgasmo [ox'gaʒmu] m orgasm.

orgia [ox'ʒia] f orgy.

orgulhar [4] [oxgu'ʎa(x)] vt to make proud.

◆ **orgulhar-se** vp: **~-se de** to pride o.s. on.

orgulho [ox'guʎu] m -1. [ger] pride. -2. [arrogância] arrogance.

orgulhoso, osa [oxgu'ʎozu, ɔza] adj -1. [brioso] self-satisfied. -2. [satisfeito] proud. -3. [arrogante] arrogant.

orientação [orjẽnta'sãw] (pl -ões) f -1. [ger] direction; **~ profissional** careers guidance. -2. [supervisão] supervision. -3. fig [linha, tendência] orientation.

orientador, ra [orjẽnta'do(x), ra] <> adj supervisory. <> m, f -1. [guia] adviser; **~ profissional** careers counsellor. -2. [supervisor] supervisor.

oriental [orjēn'taw] (*pl* -**ais**) <> *adj* oriental. <> *mf* oriental.

orientar [4] [orjēn'ta(x)] *vt* - **1.** [situar] to orient. - **2.** [nortear] to put in the right direction. - **3.** [supervisionar] to supervise. - **4.** *fig* [aconselhar] to advise.

• **orientar-se** *vp* - **1.** [nortear-se] to orient o.s.; ~-**se por algo** to be guided by sthg. - **2.** [aconselhar-se, informar-se] to take advice.

oriente [o'rjēntʃi] *m* east.

• **Oriente** *m*: **o Oriente** the East; **Extremo Oriente** Far East; **Oriente Médio** Middle East.

orifício [ori'fisju] *m* orifice.

origem [o'riʒē] (*pl* -**ns**) *f* - **1.** [início] origin; **ter ~ em** to originate from. - **2.** [ascendência] origin; **de ~ brasileira** of Brazilian descent; **país de ~** country of origin. - **3.** [causa] cause; **dar ~ a** to give rise to.

original [oriʒi'naw] (*pl* -**ais**) <> *adj* original. <> *m* [obra] original.

originalidade [oriʒinali'dadʒi] *f* - **1.** [origem] origin. - **2.** [excentricidade] originality.

originalmente [oriʒinaw'mēntʃi] *adv* originally.

originário, ria [oriʒi'narju, rja] *adj* [proveniente]: ~ **de** native of.

Orinoco [ori'noku] *n*: **o ~** the Orinoco.

oriundo, da [o'rjūndu, da] *adj*: ~ **de** from.

orixá [ori'ʃa] *m* Orisha, *a Yoruba divinity that symbolizes the forces of nature and acts as an intermediary between worshippers and the highest divinity.*

orla ['ɔxla] *f* [faixa] edge; ~ **marítima** coastline.

ornamentação [oxnamēnta'saw] (*pl* -**ões**) *f* decoration.

ornamental [oxnamēn'taw] (*pl* -**ais**) *adj* ornamental.

ornamento [oxna'mēntu] *m* ornament.

ornar [4] [ox'na(x)] *vt* to decorate.

ornato [ox'natu] *m* ornament.

ornitologia [oxnitolo'ʒia] *f* ornithology.

orquestra [ox'kɛʃtra] *f* orchestra; ~ **de câmara** chamber orchestra; ~ **sinfônica** symphony orchestra.

orquestração [oxkeʃtra'saw] (*pl* -**ões**) *f* orchestration.

orquestrar [4] [oxkeʃ'tra(x)] *vt* to orchestrate.

orquídea [ox'kidʒja] *f* orchid.

ortodontista [oxtodõn'tʃiʃta] *mf* orthodontist.

ortodoxia [oxtodok'sia] *f* orthodoxy.

ortodoxo, xa [oxto'dɔksu, ksa] <> *adj* orthodox. <> *m*, *f* RELIG orthodox person.

ortografia [oxtogra'fia] *f* orthography, spelling.

ortográfico, ca [oxto'grafiku, ka] *adj* orthographic, spelling.

ortopedia [oxtope'dʒia] *f* orthopaedics *(pl)* UK, orthopedics *(pl)* US.

ortopédico, ca [oxto'pɛdʒiku, ka] *adj* orthopaedic UK, orthopedic US.

ortopedista [oxtope'dʒiʃta] *mf* orthopaedist UK, orthopedic US.

orvalhar [4] [oxva'ʎa(x)] *vi*: **orvalhou a noite inteira** the dew fell all night.

orvalho [ox'vaʎu] *m* dew.

os [uʃ] ▷ **o**.

oscilação [osila'saw] (*pl* -**ões**) *f* - **1.** [movimento] swinging. - **2.** [variação] swing. - **3.** *fig* [hesitação] hesitation.

oscilante [osi'lãntʃi] *adj* - **1.** *inv* [movimento] swinging. - **2.** [variável] variable. - **3.** *fig* [hesitante] hesitant.

oscilar [4] [osi'la(x)] *vi* - **1.** [ger] to swing. - **2.** *fig* [hesitar] to hesitate.

oscilatório, ria [osila'tɔrju, rja] *adj* swinging.

Oslo ['oʒlu] *n* Oslo.

osmose [oʒ'mɔzi] *f* osmosis.

ossatura [osa'tura] *f* - **1.** [esqueleto] skeletal structure. - **2.** [estrutura] framework.

ósseo, óssea ['ɔsju, 'ɔsja] *adj* bone *(antes de subst)*.

ossificação [osifika'saw] *f* ossification.

osso ['osu] (*pl* **ossos**) *m* - **1.** ANAT bone. - **2.** *fig* [dificuldade]: ~**s do ofício** occupational hazards; **ser um ~ duro de roer** to be a tough nut to crack.

ostensivo, va [oʃtēn'sivu, va] *adj* - **1.** [pessoa, luxo] ostentatious. - **2.** [policiamento] overt.

ostentação [oʃtēnta'saw] (*pl* -**ões**) *f* ostentation.

ostentar [4] [oʃtēn'ta(x)] *vt* - **1.** [exibir] to show off. - **2.** [alardear] to display.

ostentoso, osa [oʃtēntozu, ɔza] *adj* ostentatious.

osteopata [oʃtʃjo'pata] *mf* osteopath.

osteoporose [oʃtʃjopo'rɔzi] *f* osteoporosis.

ostra ['oʃtra] *f* oyster.

ostracismo [oʃtra'siʒmu] *m* ostracism.

OTAN [o'tã] (*abrev de* **Organização do Tratado do Atlântico Norte**) *f* NATO.

otário, ria [o'tarju, rja] *m*, *f* sucker.

ótico, ca ['ɔtʃiku, ka] <> *adj* optic, optical. <> *m*, *f* [especialista] optician.

• **ótica** *f* - **1.** [loja] optician's. - **2.** *fig* [ponto de vista] viewpoint. - **3.** FÍSICA optics *(sg)*.

otimismo [otʃi'miʒmu] *m* optimism.

otimista [otʃi'miʃta] <> *adj* optimistic. <> *mf* optimist.

otimização [otʃimiza'saw] (*pl* -**ões**) *f* optimization.

otimizar [otʃimi'za(x)] *vt* to optimize.

ótimo, ma ['ɔtʃimu, ma] <> *adj* (*superl de* **bom**) best. <> *interj* great!

otite [o'tʃitʃi] *f* otitis.

otorrinolaringologista [otoxinularĩngolo'ʒiʃta] *mf* ear, nose and throat specialist.

Ottawa [o'tawa] *n* Ottawa.

ou [ow] *conj* or; ~ ..., ~ ... either ..., or ...; ~ **seja** in other words.

ouriçado, da [ori'sadu, da] *adj fam* prickly.

ouriçar [13] [ori'sa(x)] *vt* [pessoa] to bristle.

• **ouriçar-se** *vp* to become more excited.

ouriço [o'risu] *m* - **1.** [casca espinhosa] burr. - **2.** ZOOL hedgehog.

ouriço-do-mar [o,risudu'ma(x)] (*pl* **ouriços-do-mar**) *m* sea urchin.

ourives [o'riviʃ] *mf inv* goldsmith.
ourivesaria [oriveza'rial *f* - **1.** [arte] goldworking.
 - **2.** [oficina, loja] goldsmith's.
ouro ['orul *m* - **1.** [metal] gold; **de ~** *lit* gold; *fig*
 [coração] of gold; **~ branco** white gold; **valer
 ~ fig** to be invaluable. - **2.** *fig* [dinheiro] money.
 ◆ **ouros** *mpl* [naipe] diamonds.

OURO PRETO

Ouro Preto is considered nowadays as a World Heritage
Site; throughout the nineteenth century, it was the
state capital of Minas Gerais. The city houses the
masterpiece of Brazilian baroque: the church of St
Francis of Assisi, created by Antônio Francisco Lisboa,
the *Aleijadinho* (Cripple), who was also renowned for
his soapstone sculptures.

ousadia [oza'dʒial *f* daring; **ter a ~ de fazer algo**
 to have the audacity to do sthg.
ousado, da [o'zadu, dal *adj* - **1.** [audacioso] audacious. - **2.** [corajoso] daring.
ousar [4] [o'za(x)] ◇ *vt* to dare. ◇ *vi* to be
 daring.
out. (*abrev de* **outubro**) Oct.
outdoor [awtʃi'dɔrl *m* billboard, hoarding.
outeiro [o'tejrul *m* small hill.
outonal [oto'nawl (*pl* -**ais**) *adj* autumnal.
outono [o'tonul *m* autumn.
outorgante [otox'gãntʃil ◇ *adj* granting. ◇
 mf grantor.
outorgar [14] [otox'ga(x)] *vt*: **~ algo a alguém** to
 grant sthg to sb, to grant sb sthg.
outorgado, da [owtox'gadu, dal *adj* granted.
outra ['otral *f* ▷ **outro**.
outrem [o'trẽl *pron* - **1.** *inv (pl)* other people. - **2.**
 (sg) someone else.
outro, outra ['otru, 'otral ◇ *adj* - **1.** [ger] other;
 ~ dia the other day. - **2.** [diferente] another; **de ~
 modo** in another way; **em ~ lugar** somewhere
 else; **entre outras coisas** among other things;
 outra coisa something else; **~s tipos** other
 sorts. - **3.** [novo, adicional] another; **no ~ dia** the
 next day; **outra vez** again. ◇ *pron* another; **o
 ~** the other; **de um momento para o ~** from
 one moment to the next; **tanto um quanto o ~**
 both of them; **(um) ~** another; **nem um, nem ~**
 neither one nor the other, neither of them; **os
 ~s** [pessoas] others; [objetos] the others; **dos ~s**
 [pessoas] other people's.
 ◆ **outra** *f*: **a outra** [amante] the other woman;
 estar em outra *fam* to be into something else; **...
 e não deu outra** *fam* ... and that's precisely what
 happened.
outrora [o'trɔral *adv* in the past.
outrossim [otro'sĩl *adv* likewise.
outubro [o'tubrul *m* October; *veja também* setembro.

ouvido [o'vidul *m* - **1.** *ANAT* ear; **entrar por um ~ e
 sair pelo outro** to go in one ear and out the
 other. - **2.** [audição] hearing; **dar ~s a algo/
 alguém** to listen to sthg/sb; **de ~** by ear; **ser
 todo ~s** to be all ears; **ter bom ~ para algo** to
 have a good ear for sthg.
ouvinte [o'vĩntʃil *mf* - **1.** *RÁDIO* listener. - **2.** *UNIV*
 auditor.
ouvir [71] [o'vi(x)] ◇ *vt* - **1.** [pela audição] to hear.
 - **2.** [atentamente] to listen to. ◇ *vi* - **1.** [pela audição]
 to hear; **~ dizer que** to hear that; **~ falar de
 algo/alguém** to hear of sthg/sb. - **2.**
 [atentamente] to listen. - **3.** [ser repreendido] to get
 a telling off.
ova ['ɔval *f* roe; **uma ~!** *fam* no way!
ovação [ova'sãwl (*pl* -ões) *f* ovation.
ovacionar [4] [ovasjo'na(x)] *vt* to applaud.
oval [o'vawl (*pl* -ais) *adj* oval.
ovalado, da [ova'ladu, dal *adj* oval.
ovariano, na [ova'rjãnu, nal *adj* ovarian.
ovário [o'varjul *m* ovary.
ovelha [o'veʎal *f* sheep; **~ negra** *fig* black
 sheep.
overdose [,ovex'dɔzil *f* overdose.
ovni ['ɔvnil *m* (*abrev de* **Objeto Voador Não-
 Identificado**) UFO.
ovo ['ovul (*pl* **ovos**) *m* *ANAT* egg; **~ de codorna**
 quail egg; **~ cozido** hard-boiled egg; **~ estala-
 do** *ou* **frito** fried egg; **~ de granja** free-range
 egg; **~ mexido** scrambled egg; **~ de Páscoa**
 Easter egg; **~ quente** boiled egg; **acordar/estar
 de ~ virado** *fam* to get out of bed on the wrong
 side; **pisar em ~s** to tread on egg shells; **ser um
 ~** [quarto, apartamento] to be tiny.
ovóide [o'vɔjdʒil *adj* ovoid.
ovulação [ovula'sãwl *f* ovulation.
ovular [ovu'la(x)] ◇ *adj* oval. ◇ *vi* to ovulate.
óvulo ['ɔvulul *m* ovum.
oxalá [oʃa'lal ◇ *interj* let's hope. ◇ *m* *RELIG*
 highest *Yoruba divinity in Afro-Brazilian
 cults.*
oxidação [oksida'sãwl (*pl* -ões) *f* - **1.** *QUÍM* oxida-
 tion. - **2.** [ferrugem] rust.
oxidar [4] [oksi'da(x)] *vt* - **1.** *QUÍM* to oxidize. - **2.**
 [enferrujar] to rust.
 ◆ **oxidar-se** *vp* [enferrujar] to rust.
óxido ['ɔksidul *m* oxide; **~ de carbono** carbon
 monoxide.
oxigenado, da [oksiʒe'nadu, dal *adj* - **1.** [cabelo]
 bleached. - **2.** *QUÍM*: **água oxigenada** (hydrogen)
 peroxide.
oxigenar [4] [oksiʒe'na(x)] *vt* - **1.** [ger] to oxygenate. - **2.** [cabelo] to bleach.
oxum [o'ʃũl *m Yoruba water goddess worshipped
 in Afro-Brazilian cults.*
ozônio [o'zonjul *m* ozone.
ozonizar [4] [ozoni'za(x)] *vt* to ozonize.

P

p, P [pe] *m* [letra] p, P.
pá ['pa] *f* **-1.** spade; ~ **de lixo** dustpan; ~ **mecânica** mechanical digger; ~ **para torta** cake slice. **-2.** [de hélice] blade. **-3.** *fam* [quantidade]: **uma** ~ **de** a mass of. **-4.** *loc*: **ser da** ~ **virada** to be of dubious character.
PA (*abrev de* **Estado do Pará**) *m State of Pará*.
PABX (*abrev de* **Private Automatic Branch Exchange**) *m* PABX.
paca ['paka] <> *mf ZOOL* paca. <> *adv fam* bloody; **isso está bom** ~ this is bloody good.
pacatez [paka'teʒ] *f* quietness.
pacato, ta [pa'katu, ta] *adj* quiet.
pachorra [pa'ʃoxa] *f* slowness.
pachorrento, ta [paʃo'xẽntu, ta] *adj* lumbering.
paciência [pa'sjẽnsja] *f* patience; **perder a** ~ to lose patience; **ter** ~ to be patient.
paciente [pa'sjẽntʃi] <> *adj* patient. <> *mf MED* patient.
pacificação [pasifika'sãw] *f* pacification.
pacificador, ra [pasifika'do(x), ra] <> *adj* pacifying. <> *m, f* peacemaker.
pacificar [12] [pasifi'ka(x)] *vt* to pacify.
pacífico, ca [pa'sifiku, ka] *adj* **-1.** [tranqüilo] tranquil. **-2.** [indiscutível] indisputable.
Pacífico [pa'sifiku] *n*: **o (oceano)** ~ the Pacific (Ocean).
pacifismo [pasi'fiʒmu] *m* pacifism.
pacifista [pasi'fiʃta] <> *adj* pacifist. <> *mf* pacifist.
paço ['pasu] *m* [palácio] palace.
paçoca [pa'sɔka] *f* **-1.** [doce] sweet made with peanuts and brown sugar. **-2.** *fig* [coisa amassada]: **estar uma** ~ to be all crumpled up.
pacote [pa'kɔtʃi] *m* **-1.** [embrulho] packet. **-2.** *ECON* package. **-3.** [turismo]: ~ **de viagem** package holiday.
pacto ['paktu] *m* [acordo] pact; ~ **social** social pact.
pactuante [pak'twãntʃi] *adj* cooperating.
pactuar [21] [pak'twa(x)] <> *vt* [combinar] to agree. <> *vi*: ~ **com alguém** to be in league with sb.
padaria [pada'ria] *f* bakery.

padecer [25] [pade'se(x)] <> *vt* to suffer. <> *vi*: ~ **de algo** to suffer from sthg.
padecimento [padesi'mẽntu] *m* suffering.
padeiro, ra [pa'dejru, ra] *m* baker.
padiola [pa'dʒjɔla] *f* stretcher.
padrão [pa'drãw] (*pl* **-ões**) <> *adj* [tamanho] standard. <> *m* **-1.** [ger] standard; ~ **de vida** standard of living. **-2.** [desenho] pattern.
padrasto [pa'draʃtu] *m* stepfather.
padre ['padri] *m* **-1.** [sacerdote] priest. **-2.** [como título] father.
    Santo Padre *m* Holy Father.
padrinho [pa'driɲu] *m* **-1.** [testemunha] godfather. **-2.** [paraninfo] guest of honour. **-3.** [protetor] protector.
    padrinhos *mpl* [padrinho e madrinha] godparents.
padroeiro, ra [pa'drwejru, ra] *m, f* patron saint.
padrões [pa'drõjʃ] *pl* **padrão**.
padronização [padroniza'sãw] (*pl* **-ões**) *f* standardization.
padronizado, da [padroni'zadu, da] *adj* [estandardizado] standardized.
padronizar [4] [padroni'za(x)] *vt* to standardize.
pães ['pãjʃ] *pl* **pão**.
paetê [pae'te] *m* sequin.
pág. (*abrev de* **página**) *f* p.
pagã [pa'gã] *f* **pagão**.
pagador, ra [paga'do(x), ra] <> *adj* paying. <> *m, f* payer; **ser bom/mau** ~ to be a good/bad payer.
pagamento [paga'mẽntu] *m* **-1.** [ger] payment. **-2.** [salário]: **dia de** ~ pay day. **-3.** *COM* [prestação, de dívida] repayment; ~ **contra entrega** cash on delivery; ~ **à vista** cash payment.
pagão, gã [pa'gãw, gã] (*mpl* **-s**, *fpl* **-s**) <> *adj* pagan. <> *m, f* pagan.
pagar [4] [pa'ga(x)] <> *vt* **-1.** [ger] to pay. **-2.** [compensar, reembolsar] to repay. <> *vi*: ~ **(a alguém)** to pay (sb); ~ **por algo** [desembolsar] to pay for sthg; *fig* [crime, pecado] to pay; **você me paga!** *fig* you'll pay for this!; ~ **caro** *fig* to pay dearly; ~ **para ver** *fig* to demand proof.
página ['paʒina] *f* page; ~ **de rosto** facing page.
paginação [paʒina'sãw] (*pl* **-ões**) *f* pagination.
paginar [4] [paʒi'na(x)] *vt* to paginate.
pago, ga ['pagu, ga] <> *pp* **pagar**. <> *adj* paid.
pagode [pa'gɔdʒi] *m* **-1.** [templo] pagoda. **-2.** *MÚS* type of samba. **-3.** [festa] party where pagode is danced.
pagodeiro, ra [pago'dejru, ra] [ra] *m* pagode singer.
págs. (*abrev de* **páginas**) *fpl* pp.
pai ['paj] *m* **-1.** [ger] father; ~ **adotivo** adoptive father; ~ **de criação** foster father; ~ **de família** paterfamilias. **-2.** [protetor] protector.
    pais *mpl* [pai e mãe] parents.
pai-de-santo [ˌpajdʒi'sãntu] (*pl* **pais-de-santo**) *m religious and spiritual candomblé leader*.

pai-dos-burros [ˌpajduʃˈbuxuʃ] (pl **pais-dos-burros**) m fam wordbook.

painel [pajˈnɛwl (pl **-éis**) m -**1.** [ger] panel. -**2.** [quadro, panorama] picture. -**3.** ARQUIT frame.

pai-nosso [ˌpajˈnɔsul (pl **pais-nossos**) m Our Father, the Lord's Prayer.

paio [ˈpajul m salami-like pork sausage.

paiol [paˈjɔwl (pl **-óis**) m -**1.** [celeiro] store. -**2.** [depósito] arsenal; ~ **de pólvora** fig powder keg.

pairar [4] [pajˈra(x)] vi -**1.** [sustentar-se]: ~ **em/sobre** to hover in/over. -**2.** [ameaçar]: ~ **sobre** to hang over.

país [paˈiʃl (pl **-es**) m country.

paisagem [pajˈzaʒěl (pl **-ns**) f -**1.** [vista] view. -**2.** [pintura] landscape.

paisagista [pajzaˈʒiʃtal <> adj landscape (antes de subst).<> mf -**1.** ARQUIT landscape architect. -**2.** ARTE landscape painter.

paisano, na [pajˈzãnu, nal m, f [civil] civilian.
➡ **à paisana** loc adv in mufti.

País Basco [paˌiʃˈbaʃkul n: **o** ~ the Basque Country.

Países Baixos [paˌiziʃˈbajʃuʃl n: **os** ~ the Netherlands.

paixão [pajˈʃãwl (pl **-ões**) f passion.

paixonite [pajʃoˈnitʃil f fam: **ter** ~ **aguda** to be madly in love.

pajé [paˈʒɛl m Amerindian priest and medicine man.

pajear [15] [paˈʒja(x)] vt [tomar conta de] to look after.

pajem [ˈpaʒěl (pl **-ns**) <> m page. <> f nanny.

PAL (abrev de Phase Alternate Line) m PAL.

pala [ˈpalal f -**1.** [de roupa] yoke. -**2.** [de boné] peak. -**3.** [de sapato] tongue. -**4.** AUTO sun visor. -**5.** fam [dica] tip.

palacete [palaˈsetʃil m stately home.

palácio [paˈlasjul m -**1.** [residência] palace. -**2.** [sede] headquarters (pl).

paladar [palaˈda(x)l (pl **-es**) m -**1.** [ger] taste. -**2.** ANAT palate.

palafita [palaˈfital f -**1.** [habitação] house built on stilts. -**2.** [estacas] stilts (pl).

palanque [paˈlãŋkil m -**1.** [de comício] seating. -**2.** [para espectadores] stand.

palato [paˈlatul m ANAT palate.

palavra [paˈlavral f -**1.** [ger] word; ~**s cruzadas** crossword (puzzle) (sg); **medir as** ~**s** fig to measure one's words; **não dar uma** ~ not to say a word; ~ **de ordem** watchword; **pessoa sem** ~ person who cannot be trusted; **ter** ~ to keep one's word; ~ **de honra** word of honour. -**2.** [fala] speaking. -**3.** [direito de falar] right to speak; **dar a** ~ **a alguém** to hand the floor to sb; **pedir a** ~ to ask permission to speak.

palavra-chave [paˌlavraˈʃavil (pl **palavras-chaves, palavras-chave**) f keyword.

palavrão [palaˈvrãwl (pl **-ões**) m swear word.

palavreado [palaˈvrjadul m chatter, gabble.

palco [ˈpawkul m -**1.** TEATRO stage. -**2.** fig [cenário] scene.

paleolítico, ca [paljoˈlitʃiku, kal adj paleolithic.

paleontologia [paljõntoloˈʒial f paleontology.

palerma [paˈlɛxmal <> adj foolish. <> mf fool.

Palestina [paleʃˈtʃinal n Palestine.

palestino, na [paleʃˈtʃinu, nal <> adj Palestinian. <> m, f Palestinian.

palestra [paˈlɛʃtral f [conferência] lecture, talk.

palestrante [paleʃˈträntʃil mf speaker (at conference).

palestrar [4] [paleʃˈtra(x)l vi to give a talk.

paleta [paˈletal f palette.

paletó [paleˈtɔl m overcoat.

palha [ˈpaʎal f straw; ~ **de aço** wire wool; **não mexer uma** ~ fam fig not to lift a finger.

palhaçada [paʎaˈsadal f -**1.** [brincadeira] clowning; **fazer** ~**s** to clown around. -**2.** [cena ridícula] ridiculous sight.

palhaço, ça [paˈʎasu, sal m, f -**1.** [artista] clown. -**2.** fam [bobo] clown.

palheiro [paˈʎejrul m [celeiro] hayloft.

palheta [paˈʎetal f -**1.** ARTE palette. -**2.** [lâmina - de veneziana] slat; [- de ventilador] blade. -**3.** [MÚS - para dedilhar] plectrum; [- embocadura] reed.

palhoça [paˈʎɔsal f straw hut.

paliativo, va [paljaˈtʃivu, val <> adj palliative. <> m palliative.

paliçada [paliˈsadal f -**1.** [tapume] palisade. -**2.** MIL stockade.

palidez [paliˈdeʒl f -**1.** [de cor] paleness. -**2.** [de pessoa, rosto] pallor.

pálido, da [ˈpalidu, dal adj pale.

palitar [4] [paliˈta(x)l vt: ~ **os dentes** to pick one's teeth.

paliteiro [paliˈtejrul m toothpick holder.

palito [paˈlitul m -**1.** [para os dentes] toothpick. -**2.** [biscoito] straw. -**3.** [fósforo] matchstick. -**4.** [pessoa magra] matchstick.

PAL-M (abrev de Phase Alternate Line-Modified) m PAL-M.

palma [ˈpawmal f palm.
➡ **palmas** fpl [aplauso]: **bater** ~ to clap.

palmada [pawˈmadal f smack; **dar/levar umas** ~**s** to smack/be smacked.

Palmas [ˈpawmaʃl n Palmas.

palmatória [pawmaˈtɔrjal f ferule; ~ **do mundo** better than everyone else; **dar a mão à** ~ to climb down.

palmeira [pawˈmejral f palm tree.

palmilha [pawˈmiʎal f inner sole.

palmito [pawˈmitul m Assai palm.

palmo [ˈpawmul m handspan; **não enxergar um** ~ **adiante do nariz** not to be able to see past the end of one's nose; ~ **a** ~ inch by inch.

palmtop [ˈpawmtɔpil (pl **palmtops**) m COMPUT palmtop.

palpável [pawˈpavɛwl (pl **-eis**) adj [tangível] palpable.

pálpebra [ˈpawpebral f eyelid.

palpitação [pawpitaˈsãwl (pl **-ões**) f throbbing.
➡ **palpitações** fpl palpitations.

palpitar [4] [pawpiˈta(x)l vi -**1.** [pulsar] to throb. -**2.**

[agitar-se] to quiver. - **3.** [opinar] to speculate.

palpite [paw'pitʃil *m* - **1.** [opinião] speculation. - **2.** [intuição]: **ter um** ~ to have a hunch. - **3.** [turfe] tip.

palpiteiro, ra [pawpi'tejru, ra] <> *adj* opinionated. <> *m, f* opinionated person.

paludismo [palu'dʒizmul *m* malaria.

pamonha [pa'moɲal <> *adj* sluggish, dull. <> *mf* sluggard, dullard.

pampa ['pãnpal *m* - **1.** GEOGR pampas. - **2.**: **às** ~**s** [com substantivo] loads of; [com adjetivo] extremely; [com advérbio] really.

panaca [pa'nakal <> *adj* dim-witted. <> *mf* dimwit.

panacéia [pana'sɛjal *f* panacea.

Panamá [pana'mal *n* Panama.

panamenho, nha [pana'meɲu, ɲal <> *adj* Panamanian. <> *m, f* Panamanian.

pan-americano, na [,pãnameri'kãnu, nal *adj* pan-American.

pança ['pãnsal *f fam* paunch.

pancada [pãŋ'kadal <> *adj fam* nuts. <> *f* - **1.** [golpe] blow; **dar uma** ~ **em alguém** to hit sb; **levar uma** ~ **de alguém** to be hit by sb. - **2.** [batida] hit. - **3.** [chuva]: ~ **d'água** downpour.

pancadaria [pãŋkada'rial *f* brawl.

pâncreas ['pãŋkrjaʃl *m* pancreas.

pançudo, da [pãn'sudu, dal *adj* paunchy.

panda ['pãndal *m* ZOOL panda.

pandarecos [pãnda'rɛkuʃl *mpl fam*: **em** ~ [exausto] shattered; [destruído] in pieces; [moralmente] thoroughly dejected.

pândego, ga ['pãndegu, gal *adj* - **1.** [engraçado] funny. - **2.** [folião] reveller.

➡ **pândega** *f* [folia] revelry.

pandeiro [pãn'dejrul *m* MÚS tambourine.

pandemônio [pãnde'monjul *m* pandemonium.

pane ['pãnil *f* breakdown.

panegírico [pane'ʒirikul *m* panegyric.

panela [pa'nɛlal *f* - **1.** [recipiente] saucepan; ~ **de pressão** pressure cooker. - **2.** *fig* [conteúdo] saucepanful.

panelaço [pane'lasul *m banging of pots and pans as a form of protest.*

panelinha [panɛ'liɲal *f* clique.

panfletar [4] [pãnfle'ta(x)l *vi* to hand out pamphlets.

panfleto [pãn'fletul *m* pamphlet.

pangaré [pãŋga'rɛl *m* nag.

pânico ['pãnikul *m* panic; **estar/entrar em** ~ to panic.

panificação [panifika'sãwl *f* - **1.** [padaria] bakery. - **2.** [fabrico] bread making.

pano ['pãnul *m* - **1.** [tecido] cloth; ~ **de chão** floor cloth; ~ **de pó** duster; ~ **de prato** tea towel; **por baixo/debaixo do** ~ *fig* on the quiet; **dar** ~ **para mangas** *fig* to get people talking; **pôr** ~**s quentes em algo** *fig* to calm sthg down. - **2.** TEATRO curtain; ~ **de fundo** backdrop.

panorama [pano'rãmal *m* panorama.

panorâmico, ca [pano'rãmiku, kal *adj* panoramic.

➡ **panorâmica** *f* [exposição] panorama.

panqueca [pãŋ'kɛkal *f* pancake.

pantalonas [pãnta'lonaʃl *fpl* - **1.** [calças] pantaloons. - **2.** [de bailarino] leggings.

pantanal [pãnta'nawl *(pl* -ais) *m* large swamp.

PANTANAL

The *pantanal* (swamp) of Mato Grosso extends over the south-west of Mato Grosso, the west of Mato Grosso do Sul and part of Paraguay. The swamp is periodically flooded by the many lakes and gullies that crisscross it; it is the largest flood plain in the world and one of Brazil's finest natural features. Within it can be found 650 species of birds, 60 species of mammals, 260 species of fish and 50 species of reptiles.

---

pântano ['pãntanul *m* swamp.

pantanoso, osa [pãnta'nozu, ɔzal *adj* swampy.

panteão [pãn'tʃjãwl *(pl* -ões) *m* pantheon.

pantera [pãn'tɛral *f* ZOOL panther.

pantomima [pãnto'mimal *f* TEATRO pantomime.

pantufa [pãn'tufal *f* slipper.

pão ['pãwl *(pl* pães) *m* - **1.** [alimento] bread; ~ **de carne** meat loaf; ~ **de centeio** rye bread; ~ **de fôrma** tin loaf; ~ **de mel** honey bread; ~ **dormido** stale bread; ~ **francês** small baguette; ~ **integral** wholemeal bread; **comer o** ~ **que o diabo amassou** to go through a bad patch; **com ele é** ~, ~, **queijo, queijo** you know where you stand with him. - **2.** [sustento] daily bread; **ganhar o** ~ to earn a crust. - **3.** RELIG Eucharist.

pão-de-ló [,pãwdʒi'lɔl *(pl* pães-de-ló) *m* sponge cake.

pão-durismo [,pãwdu'riʒmul *m inv* stinginess.

pão-duro [,pãw'durul *(pl* pães-duros) <> *adj* miserly. <> *m, f* miser.

pãozinho [pãw'ziɲul *m* roll.

papa ['papal *f* - **1.** [mingau] pap. - **2.** [pasta] mush; **não ter** ~**s na língua** to be outspoken.

➡ **Papa** *m* RELIG Pope.

papada [pa'padal *f* ANAT double chin.

papagaiada [papaga'jadal *f fam* farce.

papagaio [papa'gajul <> *m* - **1.** ZOOL parrot. - **2.** [pipa]: **soltar** ~ to fly a kite. - **3.** COM promissory note. - **4.** AUTO provisional licence. <> *interj fam*: ~ **(s)!** golly!

papaguear [papa'gja(x)l <> *vt* [repetir] to parrot. <> *vi* [tagarelar] to chatter away.

papai [pa'pajl *m* daddy; **o** ~ **aqui** *fam* [eu] yours truly.

➡ **Papai Noel** *m*: **o Papai Noel** Father Christmas.

papaia [pa'pajal *m* papaya, pawpaw.

papal [pa'pawl *(pl* -ais) *adj* RELIG papal.

papar [4] [pa'pa(x)l *fam* <> *vt* - **1.** [comer] to gobble. - **2.** [conseguir] to win. <> *vi* to eat.

paparicar [12] [papari'ka(x)l *vt* to mollycoddle.

paparicos [papa'rikuʃl *mpl* smotherings.

papear [15] [pa'pja(x)l *vi*: ~ **(com/sobre)** to chat (with/about).

papel [pa'pɛwl *(pl* -éis) *m* - **1.** [ger] role; **fazer o** ~

de to play the part of; **fazer ~ de bobo** *fig* to look like a fool. **-2.** [folha] paper; **~ crepon** crepe paper; **~ de carta** notepaper; **~ de embrulho** wrapping paper; **~ de seda** tissue paper; **~ higiênico** toilet paper; **~ laminado** *ou* **de alumínio** aluminium foil; **~ machê** papier mâché; **~ ofício** headed paper; **~ pardo** brown wrapping paper; **ficar no ~** to remain on the drawing board. **-3.** [documento] paper; **de ~ passado** officially. **- 4.** *FIN* paper money. **- 5.** *gír droga* twist.

papelada [pape'ladа] *f* **-1.** [papéis] pile of paper. **- 2.** [documentos] stack of papers.

papelão [pape'lãw] *m* **-1.** [papel] cardboard. **- 2.** *fig* [fiasco] fiasco; **que ~!** what a fiasco!

papelaria [papela'riа] *f* stationer.

papel-bíblia [pa'pewbiblia] (*pl* **papéis-bíblia**) *m* India paper.

papel-carbono [pa,pεwkax'bonul] (*pl* **papéis-carbono**) *m* carbon paper.

papel-manteiga [pa'pεwmãntejga] (*pl* **papéis-manteiga**) *m* tracing paper.

papel-moeda [pa,pεw'mwεda] (*pl* **papéis-moeda**) *m* paper money.

papelote [pape'lɔtʃi] *m gír droga* twist.
➡ **papelotes** *mpl* [para o cabelo] curling paper.

papel-pergaminho [pa,pεwpexga'miɲu] (*pl* **papéis-pergaminho**) *m* parchment.

papiro [pa'piru] *m* papyrus.

papo ['papu] *m* **-1.** [de ave] crop. **- 2.** *fam* [de pessoa] double chin; **estar no ~** to be in the bag; **ficar de ~ para o ar** *fig* to sit on one's hands. **-3.** *fam* [conversa] chat; **ser bom ~** to be good company; **~ furado** [mentira] hot air; **ficar de ~ furado** [conversa] to stay and have a chat; **bater (um) ~** to (have a) natter.

papo-de-anjo [,papu'dʒjãnʒul] (*pl* **papos-de-anjo**) *m CULIN* baked egg sweet.

papo-furado [,papufu'radu] (*pl* **papos-furados**) ◇, *adj* full of hot air. ◇ *mf:* **ser um ~** to be full of hot air.

papoula [pa'pola] *f* poppy.

páprica ['paprika] *f* paprika.

Papua-Nova Guiné [pa,puanɔvagi'ne] *n* Papua New Guinea.

papudo, da [pa'pudu, da] *adj* double-chinned.

paquera [pa'kera] ◇ *f fam* [paqueração] casual affair. ◇ *mf* pick-up.

paquerar [4] [pake'ra(x)] *fam* ◇ *vt* to flirt with. ◇ *vi* to pull.

paquete [pa'ketʃi] *m ant & NÁUT* steamship.

Paquistão [pakiʃ'tãw] *n* Pakistan.

paquistanês, esa [pakiʃta'neʃ, eza] ◇ *adj* Pakistani. ◇ *m, f* Pakistani.

par ['pa(x)] (*pl* **-es**) ◇ *adj* **-1.** *MAT* even. **- 2.** [parelho] paired. ◇ *m* **-1.** [dupla] pair; **de ~ em ~** wide (open); **~ a ~** side by side; **sem ~** peerless. **- 2.** [casal] couple. **- 3.** [em dança] partner. ◇ *f TELEC:* **~ trançado** twisted pair.
➡ **a par** *loc adj:* **estar a ~ de algo** to be well informed about sth.

para ['para] *prep* **-1.** [exprime finalidade, destinação] for; **um telefonema ~ o senhor** a phone call for the gentleman; **esta água não é boa ~ beber** this water is not good for drinking; **eu queria algo ~ comer** I would like something to eat; **~ que serve isto?** what's this for? **-2.** [indica motivo, objetivo] (in order) to; **cheguei mais cedo ~ arranjar lugar** I arrived early (in order) to get a seat; **era só ~ lhe agradar** it was only to please you. **-3.** [indica direção] towards; **ela apontou ~ cima/ baixo** she pointed upwards/downwards; **olhei ~ ela** I looked at her; **ele seguiu ~ o aeroporto** he headed for the airport; **vá ~ casa!** go home! **-4.** [relativo a tempo]: **de uma hora ~ a outra** from one hour to the next; **quero isso pronto ~ amanhã** I want it done by tomorrow; **estará pronto ~ a semana/o ano** it'll be ready next week/ year; **são quinze ~ as três** it's a quarter of three *US*, it's a quarter to three *UK*. **- 5.** [em comparações]: **é caro demais ~ as minhas posses** it's too expensive for my budget; **~ o que come, está magro** he's thin, considering how much he eats. **- 6.** [relativo a opinião, sentimento]: **~ mim** as far as I'm concerned; **~ ele, você está errado** as far as he's concerned, you are wrong. **- 7.** [exprime iminência]: **estar ~ fazer algo** to be about to do sthg; **o ônibus está ~ sair** the bus is about to leave; **ele está ~ chegar** he'll be here any minute now. **- 8.** [em locuções]: **~ com** towards; **~ mais de** well over; **~ que** so that; **é ~ já!** coming up!

Pará [pa'ra] *n* Pará.

parabenizar [4] [parabeni'za(x)] *vt:* **~ alguém por algo** to congratulate sb on sthg.

parabéns [para'bẽnʃ] *mpl* **-1.** [congratulações] congratulations; **dar ~ a alguém** to congratulate sb; **estar de ~ (por algo)** to be congratulated (on sthg); **meus ~!** congratulations! **- 2.** [por aniversário] congratulations; **cantar ~** to sing 'Happy Birthday'.

parábola [pa'rabola] *f* **-1.** [narrativa] parable. **- 2.** *MAT* parabola.

pára-brisa [,para'briza] (*pl* **pára-brisas**) *m* windscreen *UK*, windshield *US*.

pára-choque [,para'ʃɔki] (*pl* **pára-choques**) *m AUTO* bumper.

paradeiro [para'dejru] *m* whereabouts.

paradigma [para'dʒigma] *m* paradigm.

paradisíaco, ca [paradʒi'ziaku, ka] *adj fig* idyllic.

parado, da [pa'radu, da] *adj* **-1.** [imóvel] motionless. **- 2.** [sem vida] dull. **- 3.** [desativado] stopped. **- 4.** [abandonado] axed. **- 5.** [em greve] on strike. **- 6.** [sem trabalhar] unemployed.
➡ **parada** *f* **-1.** [de ônibus, trem] stop. **- 2.** [pausa] break; **dar uma ~ (em algo)** to have a break (from sthg); **~ cardíaca** cardiac arrest. **- 3.** [desfile] parade. **- 4.** *MÚS:* **~ de sucessos** hit parade. **- 5.** *fam* [dificuldade] obstacle; **agüentar a ~** to take it. **- 6.** *loc:* **ser uma ~** *fam* [ser difícil] to be difficult; [ser bonito] *fam* to be a knockout; **topar qualquer ~** to be ready for anything.

paradoxal [paradok'sawl] (*pl* **-ais**) *adj* paradoxical.

paradoxo [para'dɔksu] *m* paradox.

paraestatal [paraiʃta'tawl] (*pl* **-ais**) <> *adj* public. <> *f* public organization.

parafernália [parafɛx'nalja] *f* **-1.** [tralha] paraphernalia. **-2.** [equipamento] equipment.

parafina [para'fina] *f* paraffin.

paráfrase [pa'rafrazi] *f* paraphrase.

parafrasear [15] [parafra'zja(x)] *vt* to paraphrase.

parafusar [4] [parafu'za(x)] *vt* to screw.

parafuso [para'fuzu] *m* screw; **entrar em** ~ *fam* to be thrown off track; **ter um** ~ **de menos** *fam* to have a screw loose.

paragem [pa'raʒẽ] (*pl* **-ns**) *f*[local] stop; **em outras paragens** elsewhere.

parágrafo [pa'ragraful] *m* paragraph.

Paraguai [para'gwajl] *n:* **(o)** ~ Paraguay.

paraguaio, ia [para'gwaju, ja] <> *adj* Paraguayan. <> *m, f* Paraguayan.

Paraíba [para'iba] *n* Paraíba.

paraíso [para'izu] *m* paradise; ~ **fiscal** *ECON fam* tax haven.

pára-lama [ˌpara'lãma] (*pl* **pára-lamas**) *m* mudguard.

paralela [para'lɛla] *f* ⊳ **paralelo**.

paralelamente [paralela'mẽntʃil] *adv* **-1.** [em paralelo] in parallel. **-2.** [simultaneamente] as well as.

paralelepípedo [paralele'pipedul] *m* paving stone.

paralelo, la [para'lɛlu, la] *adj* parallel.
◆ **paralelo** *m* parallel; **traçar um** ~ to draw a parallel.
◆ **paralela** *f MAT* parallel (line).

paralisação [paraliza'sãwl] (*pl* **-ões**) *f* **-1.** [interrupção] stoppage. **-2.** [greve] strike.

paralisar [4] [parali'za(x)] *vt* [fazer parar] to paralyse.
◆ **paralisar-se** *vp*[obra] to be paralysed.

paralisia [parali'zia] *f* paralysis.

paralítico, ca [para'litʃiku, ka] <> *adj* paralytic. <> *m, f* paralytic.

Paramaribo [parama'ribu] *n* Paramaribo.

paramédico, ca [para'mɛdʒiku, ka] *adj* paramedic.

paramentado, da [paramẽn'tadu, da] *adj* dressed up.

paramentar [4] [paramẽn'ta(x)] *vt* [adornar] to decorate.
◆ **paramentar-se** *vp* [adornar-se] to dress o.s up.

paramento [para'mẽntu] *m* ornament.
◆ **paramentos** *mpl RELIG* vestments.

parâmetro [pa'rãmetru] *m* parameter.

paramilitar [paramili'ta(x)] *adj* paramilitary.

Paraná [para'na] *n* Paraná.

paraninfo [para'nĩnful] *m* sponsor.

paranóia [para'nɔja] *f* **-1.** *PSIC* paranoia. **-2.** *fig* [coletiva] fear.

paranóico, ca [para'nɔiku, ka] *adj* paranoid.

paranormal [paranox'mawl] (*pl* **-ais**) <> *adj* paranormal. <> *mf* psychic.

paranormalidade [paranoxmali'dadʒi] *f* paranormal nature.

parapeito [para'pejtu] *m* **-1.** [de janela] window sill. **-2.** [muro] parapet.

parapente [para'pẽntʃil] *m ESP* paragliding.

paraplégico, ca [para'plɛʒiku, ka] <> *adj* paraplegic. <> *m, f* paraplegic.

pára-quedas [ˌpara'kɛdaʃ] *m inv* parachute; **saltar de** ~ to parachute.

pára-quedista [ˌparake'dʒiʃtal] (*pl* **pára-quedistas**) *mf* **-1.** [quem salta] parachutist. **-2.** *MIL* paratrooper.

parar [4] [pa'ra(x)] <> *vi* **-1.** [deter-se] to stop; ~ **de fazer algo** to stop doing sthg; **sem** ~ nonstop. **-2.** [permanecer] to stay. **-3.** [acabar]: **ir** ~ to end up. **-4.** [interromper-se] to stop. <> *vt* **-1.** [deter] to stop. **-2.** [paralisar] to bring to a standstill.

pára-raios [ˌpara'xajuʃ] *m inv* lightning conductor *UK*, lightning rod *US*.

parasita [para'zita] <> *adj* parasitic. <> *mf* parasite.

parceiro, ra [pax'sejru, ra] *m, f* partner.

parcela [pax'sɛla] *f* **-1.** [parte] portion. **-2.** [de pagamento] instalment. **-3.** [de terreno] plot. **-4.** [do eleitorado] section. **-5.** *MAT* factor.

parcelado, da [paxse'ladu, da] *adj*[pagamento] in instalments.

parcelamento [paxsela'mẽntul] *m* **-1.** [de pagamento] payment by instalments. **-2.** [de terra] distribution.

parcelar [4] [paxse'la(x)] *vt* to divide into instalments.

parceria [paxse'ria] *f* partnership; **fazer algo em** ~ to do sthg in partnership.

parcial [pax'sjaw] (*pl* **-ais**) *adj* **-1.** [incompleto] partial. **-2.** [não-isento] biased.

parcialidade [paxsjali'dadʒi] *f* bias.

parcimônia [parsi'monja] *f* [moderação] parsimony; **com** ~ frugally.

parcimonioso, osa [paxsimo'njozu, ɔza] *adj* parsimonious.

parco, ca [ˈpaxku, ka] *adj*[escasso] scanty; ~ **de algo** lacking in sthg.

pardacento, ta [paxda'sẽntu, ta] *adj* brownish.

pardal [pax'daw] (*pl* **-ais**) *m* sparrow.

pardieiro [pax'dʒejrul] *m* ruin.

pardo, da [ˈpaxdu, da] *adj* **-1.** [escuro] dark. **-2.** [mulato] coloured.

parecer [25] [pare'se(x)] <> *m* judgement, opinion. <> *vi* **-1.** [ger] to seem; ~ **a alguém** to seem to sb; ~ **a alguém que** to think that; ~ **(com) algo/alguém** to resemble sthg/sb. **-2.** [ser possível]: ~ **que** to look like. **-3.** [aparentar]: **ao que parece** apparently.
◆ **parecer-se** *vp* [assemelhar-se] to resemble one another; ~**-se com algo/alguém** to resemble sthg/sb.

parecido, da [pareˈsidu, da] *adj*: **ser ~ (com alguém/algo)** to be similar (to sb/sthg).

paredão [pareˈdãw] (*pl*-**ões**) *m* -**1.** [encosta] steep face. -**2.** [muro] high wall.

parede [paˈredʒi] *f* wall; **~ divisória** dividing wall; **subir pelas ~s** to go up the wall.

parelha [paˈreʎa] *f* -**1.** [de cavalos] team. -**2.** [par] pair.

parente, ta [paˈrẽtʃi, ta] <> *m, f* relative. <> *adj*: **ser ~ de alguém** to be related to sb.

parentela [parẽˈtɛla] *f* relatives *(pl)*.

parentesco [parẽˈteʃku] *m* kinship.

parêntese [paˈrẽtezi] *m* -**1.** [sinal] parenthesis; **abrir/fechar ~s** to open/close brackets. -**2.** [digressão] digression; **abrir um ~** to go off at a tangent.

páreo [ˈparju] *m* -**1.** [turfe] race. -**2.** [disputa] competition; **estar no ~** *fig* to be in the race; **um ~ duro** *fig* a hard nut to crack.

pária [ˈparja] *m* pariah.

paridade [pariˈdadʒi] *f* parity; **abaixo/acima da ~** below/above par.

parir [6] [paˈri(x)] <> *vt* to give birth to. <> *vi* to give birth.

Paris [paˈriʃ] *n* Paris.

parlamentar [4] [paxlamẽˈta(x)] <> *adj* parliamentary. <> *mf* member of parliament. <> *vi* to discuss.

parlamentarismo [paxlamẽtaˈriʒmu] *m* parliamentarianism.

parlamentarista [paxlamẽtaˈriʃta] <> *adj* parliamentarian. <> *mf* parliamentarian.

parlamento [paxlaˈmẽtu] *m POL* parliament.

parmegiana [parmeˈʒjãna] *f CULIN*: **à ~** cooked in the oven with a filling of tomato sauce and mozzarella cheese.

parmesão [paxmeˈzãw] *adj* parmesan.

pároco [ˈparoku] *m RELIG* parish priest.

paródia [paˈrɔdʒja] *f* parody.

parodiar [16] [paroˈdʒja(x)] *vt* to parody.

paróquia [paˈrɔkja] *f* -**1.** *RELIG* parish. -**2.** *fig* [vizinhança] neighbourhood.

paroquial [paroˈkjaw] (*pl*-**ais**) *adj RELIG* parochial, parish *(antes de subst)*.

paroquiano, na [paroˈkjãnu, na] *m, f* parishioner.

paroxismo [parokˈsiʒmu] *m* -**1.** *MED* paroxysm. -**2.** *fig* [culminância] brink.

parque [ˈpaxki] *m* park; **~ de diversões** amusement park; **~ industrial** industrial park; **~ nacional** national park.

parquímetro [paxˈkimetru] *m* parking meter.

parreira [paˈxejra] *f* grapevine.

parricida [paxiˈsida] <> *adj* parricidal. <> *mf* parricide.

parrudo, da [paˈxudu, da] *adj* squat.

parte [ˈpaxtʃi] *f* -**1.** [fração] part; **a maior ~ de** the majority of, most; **em grande ~** largely; **em ~** in parts; **fazer ~ de algo** to belong to sthg; **por ~s** in sections; **tomar ~ em** to take part in. -**2.** [lado] side; **~ interna** inside; **à ~** [separadamente]

separately; **à ~ de** [além de] apart from; **de ~ a ~** each other; **em alguma/qualquer ~** somewhere; **em ~ alguma** anywhere; **por toda (a) ~** everywhere. -**3.** [quinhão] share; **a ~ do leão** the lion's share. -**4.** *JUR* party. -**5.** [denúncia]: **dar ~ de algo/alguém** to report sthg/sb.
◆ **da parte de** *loc prep* from.

parteira [paxˈtejra] *f* midwife.

partição [paxtʃiˈsãw] *f COMPUT* partition.

participação [paxtʃisipaˈsãw] (*pl*-**ões**) *f* -**1.** [atuação]: **~ em algo** participation in sthg. -**2.** [comunicação]: **fazer uma ~ (a alguém)sobre algo** to make a statement (to sb) about sthg. -**3.** *COM* share.

participante [paxtʃisiˈpãtʃi] <> *adj* participating. <> *mf* participant.

participar [4] [paxtʃisiˈpa(x)] <> *vi* -**1.** [tomar parte]: **~ de algo** to take part in sthg. -**2.** [compartilhar]: **~ de algo** to share in sthg. <> *vt* [anunciar]: **~ algo (a alguém)** to announce sthg (to sb).

participativo, va [paxtʃisipaˈtʃivu, va] *adj* participatory; **orçamento ~** a public-spending budget agreed upon after organized public discussion with the local electorate.

particípio [paxtʃiˈsipju] *m* participle; **~ passado/presente** past/present participle.

partícula [paxˈtʃikula] *f* particle.

particular [paxtʃikuˈla(x)] (*pl*-**es**) <> *adj* -**1.** [privado] private. -**2.** [especial] particular. <> *m* -**1.** [singularidade] detail. -**2.** *fam* [conversa] private talk.
◆ **em particular** *loc adv* in private.
◆ **particulares** *mpl fam* [detalhes íntimos] personal details.

particularidade [paxtʃikulariˈdadʒi] *f* detail.

particularizar [4] [paxtʃikulariˈza(x)] *vt* -**1.** [especificar] to specify. -**2.** [detalhar] to go into the details of.

particularmente [paxtʃikulaxˈmẽtʃi] *adv* [especialmente] particularly.

partida [paxˈtʃida] *f* -**1.** [saída] departure. -**2.** [*ESP* - largada] start; **dar a ~** to give the off; [- jogo] game. -**3.** [*COM* - quantidade] shipment; [- remessa] consignment. -**4.** *AUTO*: **dar ~** to start.

partidário, ria [paxtʃiˈdarju, rja] *adj* -**1.** [de partido] party *(antes de subst)*. -**2.** [seguidor] follower.

partido, da [paxˈtʃidu, da] *adj* [quebrado] broken.
◆ **partido** *m* -**1.** [político] party; **Partido dos Trabalhadores** Workers' Party. -**2.** [defesa]: **tomar o ~ de alguém** to take sb's side; **tomar ~ em algo** to take part in sthg. -**3.** [vantagem]: **tirar ~ de algo** to make the most of sthg. -**4.** [pretendente] catch.

partilha [paxˈtʃiʎa] *f* sharing.

partilhar [4] [paxtʃiˈʎa(x)] <> *vt* -**1.** [dividir] to share. -**2.** [distribuir] to share out. <> *vi* [compartilhar]: **~ de algo** to share in sthg.

partir [6] [paxˈtʃi(x)] <> *vt* to break. <> *vi* -**1.** [ir embora] to leave. -**2.**: **~ de** [originar-se em] to start from; [basear-se em] to take as one's starting point. **-3.** *fam* [recorrer]: ~ **para** to resort to; ~ **para outra** to change tack.

➤ **a partir de** *loc prep* **-1.** [desde] from. **-2.** [dali em diante]: **a** ~ **daquele momento** from that moment on; **a** ~ **de agora** from now on.

➤ **partir-se** *vp* to break.

partitura [paxtʃi'tural *f* score.

parto ['paxtul *m* childbirth; **estar em trabalho de** ~ to be in labour *UK*, to be in labor *US*; **ser um** ~ *fig* [ser difícil] to be heavy going; ~ **prematuro** premature birth.

parturiente [paxtu'rjẽntʃi] *f* woman giving birth, parturient.

parvo, va ['paxvu, va] ◇ *adj* stupid. ◇ *m, f* fool.

Páscoa ['paʃkwa] *f* **-1.** *RELIG* Easter. **-2.** *GEOG*: **a ilha de** ~ Easter Island.

pasmaceira [paʒma'sejra] *f* apathy.

pasmado, da [paʒ'madu, da] *adj* amazed.

pasmar [4] [paʒ'ma(x)] ◇ *vt* to amaze. ◇ *vi* to be amazed.

➤ **pasmar-se** *vp* to be surprised.

pasmo, ma ['paʒmu, ma] *adj* amazed.

➤ **pasmo** *m* amazement.

paspalhão, lhona [paʃpa'ʎãw, ʎona] (*mpl* -ões, *fpl* -s) ◇ *adj* simple. ◇ *m, f* simpleton.

paspalho [paʃ'paʎu] *m* fool.

pasquim [paʃ'kĩ] (*pl* -ns) *m* [jornal] lampoon.

passa ['pasa] *f* raisin.

passada [pa'sada] *f* [passo] step; **dar uma** ~ **em** to drop by.

passadeira [pasa'dejra] *f* **-1.** [tapete] stair carpet. **-2.** [mulher] ironing woman.

passadiço [pasa'dʒisu] *m* *NÁUT* bridge.

passado, da [pa'sadu, da] *adj* **-1.** [que passou - tempo] past; [- semana, ano] last. **-2.** [ultrapassado]: **meio** ~ dated. **-3.** [fruta] overripe. **-4.** [carne]: **bem** ~ well done; **mal** ~ rare. **-5.** [vexado] infuriated.

➤ **passado** *m* past.

passageiro, ra [pasa'ʒejru, ra] ◇ *adj* passing. ◇ *m, f* passenger.

passagem [pa'saʒẽ] (*pl* -ns) *f* **-1.** [caminho] way; ~ **de nível** level crossing; ~ **de pedestres** pedestrian crossing; ~ **subterrânea** underpass. **-2.** [condução - preço] fare; [- bilhete] ticket; ~ **de ida** one-way ticket; ~ **de ida e volta** return ticket. **-3.** [trecho] passage. **-4.** [transição] transition.

➤ **de passagem** *loc adv* in passing; **diga-se de** ~ ... I have to say ...; **estar de** ~ to be passing through.

passamento [pasa'mẽntu] *m* passing.

passaporte [pasa'pɔxtʃi] *m* passport.

passar [4] [pa'sa(x)] ◇ *vt* **-1.** [transpor] to cross. **-2.** [ultrapassar] to overtake; ~ **a frente de alguém** to get in front of sb; ~ **alguém para trás** *fig* [enganar] to dupe sb; [trair] to deceive sb. **-3.** [padecer] to endure. **-4.** [tarefa escolar] to set. **-5.** [reprimenda] to tell off. **-6.** [expedir] to send. **-7.** [entregar] to pass. **-8.** [deslizar]: ~ **algo em/por**

to run sth over/through. **-9.** [tempo] to spend. **-10.** [espalhar] to spread. **-11.** [coar] to sieve. **-12.** [grelhar] to grill. **-13.** [a ferro] to iron. ◇ *vi* **-1.** [ger] to pass; ~ **por algo** to pass o.s. off as sth ou as being sth; ~ **(de ano)** to go up (a year); ~ **raspando** to scrape through. **-2.** [ir] to go past; ~ **em/por** to go in/through; ~ **pela cabeça de alguém** *fig* to cross one's mind; ~ **por cima de alguém** *fig* to go over sb's head. **-3.** [cruzar]: ~ **por alguém/algo** to go by sb/sthg. **-4.** [sentir-se] to feel; **como está passando?** [cumprimentando] how do you do? **-5.** [viver]: ~ **sem algo** to do without. **-6.** [sofrer]: ~ **por algo** to go through sthg. **-7.** [trocar de lado] to cross over. **-8.** [ser mais tarde que] to be past. **-9.** [ter mais dias] to be over; **ela já passou dos 40** she's over 40 now; **aos cinco anos, o menino não passara dos 18 quilos** at five years of age, the boy still didn't weigh more than 18kg. **-10.** [ser apenas]: **não** ~ **de** *pej* to be no more than. **-11.** [ser aceitável] to be passable.

➤ **passar-se** *vp* **-1.** [suceder-se] to happen. **-2.** [transcorrer] to go by.

passarela [pasa'rɛla] *f* **-1.** [para pedestre] footbridge. **-2.** [para manequim] catwalk.

passarinho [pasa'riɲu] *m* birdie.

pássaro ['pasaru] *m* bird.

passatempo [,pasa'tẽnpu] *m* hobby; **como** ~ as a hobby.

passável [pa'savew] (*pl* -eis) *adj* passable.

passe ['pasi] *m* **-1.** [licença] permit. **-2.** [*ESP* - de bola] pass; [- de jogador] transfer. **-3.** [lance]: ~ **de mágica** sleight of hand. **-4.** *REL* laying on of hands.

passear [15] [pa'sja(x)] *vi* **-1.** [ger] to go for a walk; **mandar alguém ir** ~ *fig* to send sb packing. **-2.** [cavalo, carro] to ride.

passeata [pa'sjata] *f* [protesto] demonstration.

passeio [pa'seju] *m* **-1.** [a pé] walk; **dar** ou **fazer um** ~ to go for a walk. **-2.** [a cavalo, de carro] ride; **fazer um** ~ to go for a ride. **-3.** [calçada] pavement *UK*, sidewalk *US*; ~ **público** public footpath.

passional [pasjo'naw] (*pl* -ais) *adj* **-1.** [discurso, atitude, artista] passionate. **-2.** [crime] of passion.

passista [pa'siʃta] *mf* samba dancer.

passível [pa'sivew] (*pl* -eis) *adj*: ~ **de algo** liable to sthg.

passividade [pasivi'dadʒi] *f* [condição] passivity.

passivo, va [pa'sivu, va] *adj* passive.

➤ **passivo** *m* *COM* liabilities (*pl*).

passo ['pasu] *m* **-1.** [ger] step; **seguir os** ~**s de alguém** *fig* to follow in sb's footsteps; **dar um mau** ~ to go astray. **-2.** [medida]: **a uns seis** ~**s (de distância)** a short distance away; **a um** ~ **de** *fig* on the verge of. **-3.** [ruído de passos] footsteps. **-4.** [pegada] footprint. **-5.** [marcha] step; **apertar o** ~ to quicken one's step; **a** ~ **de tartaruga** at a snail's pace. **-6.** [modo de andar] walk.

➤ **ao passo que** *loc adv* **-1.** [enquanto] whilst. **-2.** [contudo] whereas.

pasta l'paʃtal *f-***1.** [creme] paste; ~ **de atum** tuna paste; ~ **de dentes** toothpaste. - **2.** *CULIN:* ~ **de atum/ricota** tuna/ricotta cheese spread. - **3.** [de couro] briefcase. - **4.** [de cartolina] folder. - **5.** *POL* portfolio.

pastagem [paʃ'taʒẽl (*pl -***ns**) *f* pasture.

pastar [4] [paʃ'ta(x)] *vi* to graze; **vá** ~! *fig* & *pej* get lost!

pastel [paʃ'tɛwl (*pl -***éis**) <> *adj* [cor] pastel. <> *m* - **1.** [ger] pastel. - **2.** [comida] pastie.

pastelão [paʃte'lãwl (*pl -***ões**) *m* - **1.** *CULIN* [empadão] pie. - **2.** *CINE* slapstick.

pastelaria [paʃtela'rial *f* cake shop.

pasteurizado, da [paʃtewri'zadu, dal *adj* pasteurized.

pasteurizar [4] [paʃtewri'za(x)l *vt* to pasteurize.

pastiche [paʃ'tʃiʃil *m* pastiche.

pastilha [paʃ'tʃiʎal *f-***1.** [bala] pastille. - **2.** *MED* pill; ~ **de garganta** throat lozenge. - **3.** *COMPUT* chip. - **4.** *CONSTR* mosaic piece.

pasto l'paʃtul *m* - **1.** [erva] grass. - **2.** [pastagem] pasture.

pastor, ra [paʃ'to(x), ral (*mpl -***es**, *fpl -***s**) *m, f AGR* shepherd (*f* shepherdess).
 ➡ **pastor** *m RELIG* pastor.

pastoral [paʃto'rawl (*pl -***ais**) *RELIG* <> *adj* pastoral. <> *f church body providing care and support in the community.*

pastorear [15] [paʃto'rja(x)] <> *vt* to tend. <> *vi* to take animals to pasture.

pastoril [paʃto'riwl (*pl -***is**) *adj* pastoral.

pastoso, osa [paʃ'tozu, ɔzal *adj* pasty.

pata l'patal *f-***1.** [de animal - de cão, gato] paw; [- de cavalo] foot. - **2.** [ave] (female) duck.

patada [pa'tadal *f* kick; **dar/levar uma** ~ [de animal] to kick/to be kicked; *fig* [pessoa] to assault/be assaulted.

Patagônia [pata'gonjal *n*: **a** ~ Patagonia.

patamar [pata'ma(x)] (*pl -***es**) *m* - **1.** [de escada] landing. - **2.** *fig* [nível] level.

patavina [pata'vinal *pron* nothing; **não entender/saber** ~ not to understand/know anything.

patê [pa'tel *m* pâté.

patente [pa'tẽtʃil <> *adj* obvious. <> *f-***1.** *COM* patent. - **2.** *MIL* rank; **altas/baixas** ~**s** high/low ranks.

patentear [15] [patẽn'tʃja(x)] *vt COM* to patent.

paternal [patex'nawl (*pl -***ais**) *adj* paternal, fatherly.

paternalista [patexna'liʃtal *adj* paternalistic.

paternidade [patexni'dadʒil *f* paternity.

paterno, na [pa'tɛxnu, nal *adj* paternal, father's (*antes de subst*).

pateta [pa'tɛtal <> *adj* foolish. <> *mf* fool.

patetice [pate'tʃisil *f* foolishness.

patético, ca [pa'tɛtʃiku, kal *adj* pathetic.

patíbulo [pa'tʃibulul *m* gallows (*pl*).

patifaria [patʃifa'rial *f*[ato] underhand trick.

patife [pa'tʃifil <> *adj* roguish. <> *m* scoundrel.

patim [pa'tĩl (*pl -***ns**) *m* skate; **patins de rodas** roller skates.

patinação [patʃina'sãwl *f* skating; ~ **artística** figure skating; ~ **no gelo** ice skating.

patinador, ra [patʃina'do(x), ral *m, f* skater.

patinar [4] [patʃi'na(x)] *vi* - **1.** [de patins] to skate. - **2.** [carro] to skid.

patinete [patʃi'nɛtʃil *f* skateboard.

patinhar [4] [patʃi'ɲa(x)] *vi* [chafundar] to slosh about.

patinho [pa'tʃiɲul *m* - **1.** *ZOOL* duckling. - **2.** [carne] leg of beef. - **3.** [urinol] bedpan.

pátio l'patʃjul *m* patio.

pato l'patul *m* - **1.** *ZOOL* duck. - **2.** *fam* [otário] sucker; **cair como um** ~ to be a laughing stock. - **3.** *loc*: **pagar o** ~ to carry the can.

patologia [patolo'ʒial *f* pathology.

patológico, ca [pato'lɔʒiku, kal *adj* pathological.

patologista [patolo'ʒiʃtal *mf* pathologist.

patota [pa'tɔtal *f fam* gang.

patrão, roa [pa'trãw, roal (*mpl -***õe**, *fpl -***oas**) *m, f* - **1.** [empregador] boss. - **2.** [de criados] master. - **3.** [como forma de tratamento] sir.
 ➡ **patroa** *f-***1.** [mulher do patrão] master's/boss's wife. - **2.** *fam* [esposa] missus.

pátria l'patrjal *f* fatherland; **salvar a** ~ *fig* to save the day.

patriarca [pa'trjaxkal *m* patriarch.

patriarcal [patrjax'kawl (*pl -***ais**) *adj* patriarchal.

patricinha [patri'siɲal *f pej* posh girl.

patrício, cia [pa'trisju, sjal *m, f* compatriot.

patrimonial [patrimo'njawl (*pl -***ais**) *adj* patrimonial.

patrimônio [patri'monjul *m* - **1.** [bens] patrimony. - **2.** [herança] inheritance; ~ **histórico** historical heritage.

PATRIMÔNIOS CULTURAIS

Apart from historical centres such as Salvador (BA), Olinda (PE), São Luís (MA), Goiás (GO), Ouro Preto and Diamantina (MG), Brazil has at least another ten localities recognized by UNESCO as World Heritage Sites. In Piauí, for example, the National Park of Serra da Capivara contains one of the most important archaeological sites in the world, with around 30,000 cave paintings.

---

patriota [pa'trjɔtal *mf* patriot.

patriótico, ca [pa'trjɔtʃiku, kal *adj* patriotic.

patriotismo [patrjo'tʃiʒmul *m* patriotism.

patroa [pa'troal *f* ➡ **patrão.**

patrocinador, ra [patrosina'do(x), ral (*mpl -***es**, *fpl -***s**) <> *adj* sponsoring. <> *m, f* sponsor.

patrocinar [4] [patrosi'na(x)] *vt* - **1.** [ger] to support. - **2.** [financiar] to sponsor.

patrocínio [patro'sinjul *m* - **1.** [financiamento] sponsorship. - **2.** [apoio] support.

patrões [pa'trõjʃl *pl* ➡ **patrão.**

patrono [pa'tronul *m* patron.

patrulha [pa'truʎal *f* - **1.** [ronda] patrol. - **2.** [censura] censorship.

patrulhamento [patruʎa'mẽntu] *m* patrolling.
patrulhar [4] [patru'ʎa(x)] *vt* **-1.** [vigiar] to patrol.
- 2. [censurar] to censure.
patrulheiro [patru'ʎejru] *m* [navio] patrol boat.
pau ['paw] *m* **-1.** [bastão] stick. **- 2.** [madeira]: **de ~**
wooden. **- 3.** [de bandeira] pole; **a meio ~** at half
mast. **- 4.** *fam* [briga] brawl; **o ~ comeu** all hell
broke loose; **sair no ~** to start fighting. **- 5.** *fam*
[moeda] *slang for Brazilian currency*. **- 6.** **mfam**
[pênis] cock. **-7.** *loc fam*: **a dar com um ~** tons,
loads; **meter o ~ em** [surrar] to beat up; [criticar]
to run down; **ser ~ para toda obra** to be up for
anything.
 ◆ paus *mpl* [naipe] clubs; **de ~s** of clubs.
 ◆ pau a pau *loc adj* on an equal footing.
pau-a-pique [ˌpawa'piki] *m*: **de ~** of wattle and
daub.
pau-brasil [ˌpawbra'ziw] *m* Brazil wood.

PAU-BRASIL

Pau-brasil was a very common tree on the Brazilian
shoreline, from Rio de Janeiro to Rio Grande do Norte.
Much sought after during colonial times, it was through
constant reference to the name of this red-wooded
tree that the Portuguese named the country Brazil.

pau-d'água [ˌpaw'dagwa] (*pl* **paus-d'água**) *m*
[beberrão] soak.
pau-de-arara [ˌpawdʒia'rara] (*pl* **paus-de-arara**)
mf [retirante do Nordeste] *migrant from north-
eastern Brazil*.
 ◆ pau-de-arara *m* [tortura] *form of torture
where victim is suspended face down from a pole*.
pau-de-sebo [ˌpawdʒi'sebu] (*pl* **paus-de-sebo**)
m [mastro de cocanha] greasy pole.
paulada [paw'lada] *f* blow (with a stick); **dar/le-
var uma ~** to hit/be hit with a stick.
paulatinamente [pawlatʃina'mẽntʃi] *adv* gradually.
paulatino, na [pawla'tʃinu, na] *adj* gradual.
Paulicéia [pawli'sɛja] *n* São Paulo.
paulista [paw'liʃta] ◇ *adj* São Paulo *(antes de
subst)*. ◇ *mf person from São Paulo*.
paupérrimo, ma [paw'pɛximu, ma] *adj* extremely poor.
pausa ['pawza] *f* **-1.** [interrupção, intervalo] break.
- 2. [descanso] rest.
pausadamente [pawzada'mẽntʃi] *adv* slowly
and surely.
pausado, da [paw'zadu, da] *adj* **-1.** [lento] leisurely. **- 2.** [cadenciado] rythmic.
 ◆ pausado *adv* unhurriedly.
pauta ['pawta] *f* **-1.** [linha] guideline; **sem ~**
unruled. **- 2.** [folha com linhas] ruled sheet. **- 3.**
[lista] list. **- 4.** [ordem do dia] agenda; **em ~** on
the agenda. **- 5.** *MÚS* stave. **- 6.** *JORN* issue, topic.
pautado, da [paw'tadu, da] *adj* ruled.
pautar [4] [paw'ta(x)] *vt* **-1.** [assuntos] to list. **- 2.** *fig*
[orientar]: **~ algo por algo** to guide sthg by sthg.
 ◆ pautar-se *vp fig* [orientar-se]: **~-se por algo**
to guide o.s by sthg.

pauzinho [paw'ziɲu] *m fam*: **mexer os ~s** to pull
strings.
pavão [pa'vãw] (*pl* **-ões**) *mf* peacock.
pavê [pa've] *m CULIN cream cake made of sponge
soaked in liqueur*.
pavilhão [pavi'ʎãw] (*pl* **-ões**) *m* **-1.** [prédio] annex.
- 2. [de exposições] stand. **- 3.** [tenda, abrigo] tent. **- 4.**
fig [bandeira] banner.
pavimentação [pavimẽnta'sãw] *f* paving.
pavimentar [4] [pavimẽn'ta(x)] *vt* to pave.
pavimento [pavi'mẽntu] *m* **-1.** [andar] storey *UK*,
story *US*. **- 2.** [chão] floor. **- 3.** [de rua] pavement.
pavio [pa'viw] *m* wick; **ter o ~ curto** [ser de briga]
to have a short fuse.
pavões [pa'võjʃ] *pl* ⊳ **pavão**.
pavonear [15] [pavo'nja(x)] ◇ *vt pej* [ostentar] to
show off. ◇ *vi pej* [desfilar] to strut.
 ◆ pavonear-se *vp* **-1.** [assoberbar-se] to parade.
- 2. [enfeitar-se] to dress up.
pavor [pa'vo(x)] *m* fear; **ter ~ de alguém/algo** to
dread sb/sthg.
pavoroso, osa [pavo'rozu, ɔza] *adj* **-1.** [repulsivo]
appalling. **- 2.** [muito ruim, feio] dreadful.
paz ['paʃ] (*pl* **-es**) *f* peace; **acordo de ~** peace
treaty; **assinar a ~** to sign a peace treaty; **deixar alguém em ~** to leave sb in peace; **fazer as
pazes** to make up; **~ de espírito** peace of mind.
PB (*abrev de* **Estado da Paraíba**) *n State of Paraíba*.
PBX (*abrev de* **Private Branch Exchange**) PBX.
PC (*abrev de* **Personal Computer**) *m* PC.
Pça. (*abrev de* **Praça**) *f* Sq.
PC do B (*abrev de* **Partido Comunista do Brasil**) *m
Brazilian communist party*.
PCI (*abrev de* **Placa de Circuito Interno**) *f internal
circuit board*.
PDT (*abrev de* **Partido Democrático Trabalhista**) *m*
Democratic Labour Party, *the second largest
left-wing party in Brazil*.
PDV (*abrev de* **Programa de Demissão Voluntária**)
m Brazilian voluntary redundancy scheme.
pé ['pɛ] *m* **-1.** [ger] foot; **não arredar o ~** not to
budge; **~ chato** flat foot; **a ~** on foot; **com um ~
nas costas** with the greatest of ease; **em *ou*de ~**
standing; **~ ante ~** on tiptoe; **acordar com o ~
direito/esquerdo** to wake up in a good/bad
mood; **dar no ~** *fam* [fugir] to do a runner; **cuidado que aquela parte da piscina não dá ~** be
careful because you will be out of your depth in
that part of the pool; *fig* [ser possível] to be viable;
estar de ~ *fam* to still be on; **ficar com o ~ atrás**
to be on one's guard; **meter os ~s pelas mãos** to
go haywire; **não chegar aos ~s de ~** to be
nowhere near as good as; **não largar do ~ de
alguém** to stick like glue to sb; **não ter ~ nem
cabeça** not to make any sense; **pegar no ~ de
alguém** *fig* [implicar] to leave sb alone; [brincar] to
pull sb's leg; **ser ~ no chão** to have one's feet
firmly on the ground. **- 2.** [base - de monumento,
morro] foot; **ao ~ de** at the foot of; **ao ~ do
ouvido** in secret; [- de mesa] leg; [- de copo]
stem. **- 3.** *BOT* plant. **- 4.** [de calçado, meia] sole. **- 5.**

[situação] state of affairs; **em que** ~ **estão as coisas?** what's the state of play?; **em** ~ **de guerra/igualdade** on a war/equal footing.

➡ **ao pé da letra** *loc adv* to the letter.

PE (*abrev de* **Estado de Pernambuco**) *n State of Pernambuco.*

peão [ˈpjãw] (*pl* -ões) *m* -**1.** [trabalhador] labourer *UK*, laborer *US*. -**2.** [xadrez] pawn.

peça [ˈpɛsal] *f* -**1.** [ger] piece; ~ **fundamental** *fig* vital part; *MÚS* ~ **de resistência** pièce de résistance; [o forte de alguém] strong point. -**2.** *MEC* part; ~ **de reposição** *ou* ~ **sobressalente** replacement *ou* spare part. -**3.** [cômodo] room. -**4.** [brincadeira]: **pregar uma** ~ **em alguém** to play a practical joke on sb. -**5.** *TEATRO* play. -**6.** *JUR* document.

pecado [peˈkadul] *m* -**1.** *RELIG* sin; ~ **capital** cardinal sin; ~ **mortal** mortal sin; ~ **original** original sin; **pagar os seus** ~**s** to pay for one's sins. -**2.** [pena]: **que** ~**!** what a sin!

pecador, ra [pekaˈdo(x), ral] *m, f* sinner.

pecaminoso, osa [pekamiˈnozu, ɔzal] *adj* sinful.

pecar [12] [peˈka(x)] *vi* -**1.** *RELIG* to sin. -**2.** [errar]: ~ **por algo** to err on the side of sthg.

pechincha [peˈʃĩʃal] *f* bargain; **ser uma** ~ to be a bargain.

pechinchar [4] [peˈʃĩʃa(x)l] *vi* to haggle.

peçonha [peˈsoɲal] *f* poison.

pecuário, ria [peˈkwarju, rjal] *adj* cattle.

➡ **pecuária** *f* [criação] cattle-raising.

pecuarista [pekwaˈriʃtal] *mf* cattle dealer.

peculiar [pekuˈlja(x)l] (*pl* -es) *adj* -**1.** [característico] particular. -**2.** [curioso] peculiar.

peculiaridade [pekuljariˈdaʒil] *f* peculiarity.

pecúlio [peˈkuljul] *m* -**1.** [economias] nest egg. -**2.** [bens] belongings (*pl*).

pedaço [peˈdasul] *m* -**1.** [parte] piece; **aos** ~**s** in pieces; **estar caindo aos** ~**s** to be falling to pieces. -**2.** [trecho] piece. -**3.** [lugar] area. -**4.** *fam* [beleza]: **ser um** ~ **(de mau caminho)** to be a bit of all right.

pedágio [peˈdaʒjul] *m* toll.

pedagogia [pedagoˈʒial] *f* -**1.** [prática] teaching method. -**2.** [curso] education.

pedagógico, ca [pedaˈgɔʒiku, kal] *adj* teaching (*antes de subst*).

pedagogo, ga [pedaˈgogu, gal] *m, f* educationalist.

pé-d'água [ˌpɛˈdagwal] (*pl* pés-d'água) *m* deluge.

pedal [peˈdawl] (*pl* -ais) *m* pedal.

pedalada [pedaˈladal] *f* pedalling; **dar uma** ~ to go for a bike ride.

pedalar [4] [pedaˈla(x)l] *vt* to pedal. *vi* to pedal.

pedalinho [pedaˈliɲul] *m* pedalo.

pedante [peˈdãntʃil] *adj* pedantic. *m, f* pedant.

pedantismo [pedãnˈtʃiʒmul] *m* pedantry.

pé-de-atleta [ˌpɛdʒjaˈtlɛtal] *m* athlete's foot.

pé-de-cabra [pɛdʒiˈkabral] (*pl* pés-de-cabra) *m* -**1.** [alavanca] crowbar. -**2.** *fam* [diabo] devil.

pé-de-galinha [ˌpɛdʒigaˈliɲal] (*pl* pés-de-galinha) *m* crow's foot.

pé-de-meia [ˌpɛdʒiˈmejal] (*pl* pés-de-meia) *m* nest egg; **fazer um** ~ to get some savings together.

pé-de-moleque [ˌpɛdʒimuˈlɛkil] (*pl* pés-de-moleque) *m* -**1.** [doce] peanut brittle. -**2.** [calçamento] crazy paving.

pé-de-ouvido [ˌpɛdʒioˈvidul] (*pl* pés-de-ouvido) *m* [tapa] clip round the ear.

pé-de-pato [ˌpɛdʒiˈpatul] (*pl* pés-de-pato) *m* -**1.** [nadadeira] flipper. -**2.** *fam* [diabo] Satan.

pedestal [pedeʃˈtawl] *m* pedestal.

pedestre [peˈdɛʃtril] *mf* pedestrian.

pé-de-valsa [ˌpɛdʒiˈvawsal] (*pl* pés-de-valsas) *m* expert dancer.

pé-de-vento [ˌpɛdʒiˈvẽntul] (*pl* pés-de-vento) *m* squall.

pediatra [peˈdʒjatral] *mf* paediatrician *UK*, pediatrician *US*.

pediatria [pedʒjaˈtrial] *f* paediatrics *UK*, pediatrics *US*.

pedicuro, re [pedʒiˈkuru, ril] *m, f* pedicure.

pedido [peˈdʒidul] *m* -**1.** [ger] order. -**2.** [solicitação] request; **a** ~ to an encore; **a** ~ **de alguém** at sb's request; ~ **de casamento** marriage proposal; ~ **de demissão** resignation; ~ **de divórcio** divorce petition.

➡ **pedida** *f fam* suggestion; **ser uma boa pedida** to be a good idea.

pedigree [pedʒiˈgril] *m* pedigree.

pedinte [peˈdʒĩntʃil] *mf* beggar.

pedir [70] [peˈdʒi(x)l] *vt* -**1.** [solicitar] to ask for; ~ **algo a alguém** to ask sb for sthg; ~ **a alguém que faça algo** to ask sb to do sthg; ~ **algo emprestado** to borrow sthg; ~ **alguém em casamento** to ask for sb's hand in marriage; ~ **desculpas** *ou* **perdão (por algo)** to apologize (for sthg). -**2.** [cobrar] to charge. -**3.** [necessitar] to call for. -**4.** [encomendar] to order. -**5.** [exigir, requerer] to demand; ~ **satisfações (a alguém)** to demand an apology (from sb). *vi* [fazer pedidos] to make demands; ~ **por alguém** to pray for sb.

pé-direito [ˌpɛdʒiˈrejtul] (*pl* pés-direitos) *m* height of a room.

pedra [ˈpɛdral] *f* -**1.** [ger] stone. -**2.** [fragmento] pebble; ~ **de amolar** grindstone; ~ **de gelo** ice cube; ~ **de toque** *fig* touchstone; ~ **preciosa** precious stone; **dormir como uma** ~ to sleep like a log; **pôr uma** ~ **em cima de** *fig* to bury; **ser de** ~ to be made of stone; **vir com quatro** ~**s na mão** to jump down sb's throat. -**3.** [de açúcar] sugar lump.

pedrada [peˈdradal] *f* -**1.** [com pedra] blow (with a stone). -**2.** *fig* [golpe] blow.

pedra-pomes [ˌpɛdraˈpomiʃl] (*pl* pedras-pomes) *f* pumice stone.

pedra-sabão [ˌpɛdrasaˈbãwl] (*pl* pedras-sabão) *f* soapstone.

pedregoso, osa [pedreˈgozu, ɔzal] *adj* stony.

pedregulho [pedre'guʎu] *m* boulder.
pedreira [pe'drejra] *f* stone quarry.
pedreiro [pe'drejru] *m* CONSTR mason.
pé-frio [ˌpɛ'friw] (*pl* **pés-frios**) *m*: **ser um ~** to be jinxed.
pega ['pɛga] *m* -**1.** [briga] quarrel. -**2.** *fam* [corrida] illegal street race.
pegada [pe'gada] *f* footprint.
pegado, da [pe'gadu, da] *adj* -**1.** [contíguo] next door. -**2.** [unido] close.
pegajoso, osa [pega'ʒozu, ɔza] *adj* sticky.
pega-ladrão [ˌpɛgala'drãw] (*pl* **pega-ladrões**) *m* safety catch/switch.
pegar [14] [pe'ga(x)] <> *vt* -**1.** [ger] to pick up. -**2.** [surpreender] to catch. -**3.** [embarcar em] to catch. -**4.** [seguir por] to take. -**5.** [compreender] to take in. -**6.** [vivenciar] to experience. -**7.** [aceitar fazer] to take on. <> *vi* -**1.** [segurar] to catch; **~ em algo** to hold on to sthg. -**2.** [grudar]: **~ em algo** to stick to sthg. -**3.** [difundir-se - moda, mania] to catch on; [- doença] to be catching. -**4.** [fogo]: **a fogueira pega mais rápido com álcool** the fire lights quicker with alcohol; **ele pegou fogo na casa** he set fire to the house. -**5.** [planta] to take root. -**6.** *RÁDIO &* *TV*: **~ (bem/mal)** to have good/poor reception. -**7.** [motor] to start. -**8.** [iniciar]: **~ em algo** to start sthg. -**9.** [atitude]: **~ bem/mal** to go down well/badly; **não pega bem** it doesn't do. -**10.** [decidir-se]: **~ a fazer algo** to make up one's mind and do sthg.
➤ pegar-se *vp* [brigar]: **~-se (com)** to come to blows (with).
pega-rapaz [ˌpɛgaxa'paʒ] (*pl* **pega-rapazes**) *m* kiss-curl.
peia ['peja] *f ant &* *fig* [estorvo] hindrance.
peidar [4] [pej'da(x)] *vi mfam* to fart.
peido ['pejdu] *m mfam* fart.
peitar [4] [pej'ta(x)] *vt* -**1.** [enfrentar] to face. -**2.** [subornar] to bribe.
peitilho [pej'tʃiʎu] *m* shirt front.
peito ['pejtu] *m* -**1.** ANAT chest; **~ do pé** instep; **meter o ~** *fam* to put one's heart into it. -**2.** [de mulher, ave] breast; **dar o ~** to breastfeed. -**3.** *fig* [coragem] courage; **no ~ (e na raça)** fearlessly.
peitoril [pejto'riw] (*pl* -**is**) *m* windowsill.
peitudo, da [pej'tudu, da] *adj* -**1.** [de peito grande] big-chested. -**2.** [valente] plucky.
peixada [pej'ʃada] *f* fish stew.
peixaria [pejʃa'ria] *f* fishmonger.
peixe ['pejʃi] *m* ZOOL fish; **não ter nada com o ~** *fam* to have nothing to do with it; **vender o seu ~** [tratar de seus interesses] to look out for one's own interests; [opinar] to have one's say.
peixeira [pej'ʃejra] *f* [facão] *small, sharp knife*.
peixeiro, ra [pej'ʃejru, ra] *m, f* [vendedor] fishmonger.
Peixes ['pejʃiʃ] *mpl* [zodíaco] Pisces; **ser de ~** to be Pisces.
pejorativo, va [peʒora'tʃivu, va] *adj* pejorative.
pela ['pela] = **por** + **a**.

pelada [pe'lada] *FUT f* -**1.** [jogo informal] (friendly) match. -**2.** [jogo ruim] wasted game.
pelado, da [pe'ladu, da] *adj* -**1.** [nu] naked. -**2.** [sem pêlos] shorn.
pelanca [pe'lãŋka] *f* -**1.** [em pessoa] flabby skin. -**2.** [de carne] poor quality meat.
pelancudo, da [pelãŋ'kudu, da] *adj* -**1.** [pessoa, braço] flabby. -**2.** [carne] flaccid.
pelar [4] [pe'la(x)] <> *vt* -**1.** [animal] to skin. -**2.** [cabeça] to shave. <> *vi*: **estar pelando** [estar quentíssimo] to be scalding.
➤ pelar-se *vp fam*: **~-se de medo** to be scared stiff.
pelas ['pelaʃ] = **por** + **as**.
pele ['pɛli] *f* -**1.** [de pessoa] skin; **~ e osso** skin and bone; **cair na ~ de** *fig fam* to pester; **salvar a ~ de alguém** *fig fam* to save sb's skin; **sentir algo na ~** *fig* to experience sthg first hand. -**2.** [animal] hide; **de ~** hide. -**3.** [couro] leather; **de ~** leather. -**4.** [agasalho] fur. -**5.** [de fruta, legume] skin, peel.
peleja [pe'leʒa] *f* battle.
pelejar [4] [pele'ʒa(x)] *vi* -**1.** [combater] to fight. -**2.** *fig* [lutar]: **~ (por/para algo)** to fight (for sthg).
pelerine [pele'rini] *f* cape.
pelica [pe'lika] *f* kid leather.
pelicano [peli'kãnu] *m* ZOOL pelican.
película [pe'likula] *f* -**1.** CINE film. -**2.** [de pele] membrane. -**3.** [camada fina] layer.
pelo ['pelu] = **por** + **o**.
pêlo ['pelu] *m* -**1.** [em pessoa] hair; **nu em ~** stark naked. -**2.** [de animal] fur.
pelos ['peluʃ] = **por** + **os**.
pelota [pe'lɔta] *f* -**1.** [bola] ball; **dar ~ a alguém/algo** *fig* to pay attention to sb/sthg. -**2.** [em molho, creme] lump. -**3.** [na pele] spot.
pelotão [pelo'tãw] (*pl* -**ões**) *m* platoon; **~ de fuzilamento** firing squad.
pelúcia [pe'lusja] *f* plush.
peludo, da [pe'ludu, da] *adj* hairy.
pélvico, ca ['pɛwviku, ka] *adj* pelvic.
pélvis ['pɛwviʃ] *f (inv)* ANAT pelvis.
pena ['pena] *f* -**1.** [de ave] feather. -**2.** [pesar] sorrow; **que ~!** what a pity!; **ser uma ~** to be a pity; **valer a ~** *fig* [compensar] to be worthwhile; **a duras ~s** with great difficulty. -**3.** JUR punishment; **~ capital** *ou* **de morte** capital punishment *ou* death penalty; **cumprir ~** to serve a sentence; **sob ~ de** *fig* under penalty of. -**4.** [piedade] pity; **dar ~** to arouse pity; **ter ~ de** to be sorry for. -**5.** *ant* [caneta] pen.
penacho [pe'naʃu] *m* -**1.** [de plumas] plume. -**2.** [crista] crest.
penal [pe'naw] (*pl* -**ais**) *adj* JUR penal.
penalidade [penali'dadʒi] *f* -**1.** JUR penalty. -**2.** [castigo] punishment. -**3.** *FUT*: **~ máxima** penalty (kick).
penalizar [4] [penali'za(x)] *vt* -**1.** [dar pena a] to distress. -**2.** [castigar] to punish.
pênalti [pe'nawtʃi] *m FUT* penalty.

penar [4] [pe'na(x)] <> m [sofrimento] suffering. <> vt [sofrer] to hurt, to distress. <> vi [sofrer] to suffer.

penca ['pĕnka] f bunch; **uma ~ de algo** fig [quantidade] a bunch of sthg; **em ~** fig [quantidade] loads of.

pendão [pĕn'dãw] (pl -ões) m -**1.** [estandarte] pennant. -**2.** [bandeira] flag. -**3.** [de milho] tassel.

pendência [pĕn'dĕnsja] f -**1.** [contenda] dispute. -**2.** [algo por decidir] pending matter.

pendente [pĕn'dĕntʃi] <> adj -**1.** [ger] hanging. -**2.** [por decidir] pending. <> m [de jóia] pendant.

pender [5] [pĕn'de(x)] vi -**1.** [estar pendurado] to hang. -**2.** [inclinar-se]: **~ para/sobre** to hang towards/over. -**3.** [tender] to have a leaning; **o jovem pende para as letras** the young man has a leaning towards literature.

pendões [pĕn'dõjʃ] pl ⊳ **pendão**.

pendor [pĕn'do(x)] m tendency.

pêndulo ['pĕndulu] m pendulum.

pendurado, da [pĕndu'radu, da] adj -**1.** [pendente]: **~ (em)** hanging (on). -**2.** fig [conta] on tick.

pendurar [4] [pĕndu'ra(x)] vt -**1.** [colocar] to hang. -**2.** fig [conta] to pay on tick.
 ➧ **pendurar-se** vp [pessoa] to hang.

penduricalho [pĕnduri'kaʎu], **penduruca-lho** [pĕnduru'kaʎu] m trinket.

penedo [pe'nedu] m boulder.

peneira [pe'nejra] f -**1.** [para peneirar] sieve. -**2.** fig [seleção]: **passar na** ou **pela ~** to pass the selection.

peneirar [4] [penej'ra(x)] <> vt [na peneira] to sieve. <> vi fig [chuviscar] to drizzle.

penetra [pe'nɛtra] mf fam gatecrasher; **entrar de ~** to gatecrash.

penetração [penetra'sãw] (pl -ões) f -**1.** [ger] penetration. -**2.** fig [difusão] circulation.

penetrante [pene'trãntʃi] adj penetrating.

penetrar [4] [pene'tra(x)] <> vt to penetrate. <> vi -**1.** [entrar, infiltrar-se]: **~ em/por/entre** to penetrate. -**2.** fam [em festa] to gatecrash.

penhasco [pe'ɲaʃku] m cliff.

penhoar [pe'ɲwa(x)] m dressing gown.

penhor [pe'ɲo(x)] m pawn; **fazer o ~ de algo** to pawn ou hock sthg, to leave sthg in pawn ou hock; **casa de ~ es** pawnshop; **dar em ~** to pawn, to hock.

penhora [pe'ɲɔra] f JUR confiscation.

penhorado, da [peɲo'radu, da] adj pawned, hocked.

penhorar [4] [peɲo'ra(x)] vt to pawn, to hock.

penicilina [penisi'lina] f penicillin.

penico [pe'niku] m chamber pot, potty; **pedir ~** fam fig to eat humble pie.

península [pe'nĩnsula] f peninsula.

peninsular [penĩsu'la(x)] adj peninsular.

pênis ['peniʃ] m inv penis.

penitência [peni'tĕnsja] f RELIG -**1.** [contrição] contrition. -**2.** [expiação] penance; **fazer ~ to do penance.**

penitenciar [16] [penitĕn'sja(x)] vt RELIG -**1.** [impor

penitência a] to give a penance to; **o arrependi-mento penitencia meu coração** my heart is mortified with remorse. -**2.** [expiar] to do penance.
 ➧ **penitenciar-se** vp: **~-se de/por** to punish o.s. for.

penitenciário, ria [penitĕn'sjarju, rja] <> adj penitentiary. <> m, f prisoner.
 ➧ **penitenciária** f penitentiary.

penitente [peni'tĕntʃi] <> adj penitent. <> inf penitent.

penoso, osa [pe'nozu, ɔza] adj -**1.** [assunto, traba-lho] hard. -**2.** [tratamento, correção] harsh.

pensado, da [pĕn'sadu, da] adj considered; **de caso ~** on purpose.

pensador, ra [pĕnsa'do(x), ra] m, f thinker.

pensamento [pĕnsa'mĕntu] m -**1.** [ger] thought; **~ positivo** positive thinking; **fazer ~ positivo** to think positively. -**2.** [mente, opinião] mind. -**3.** [doutrina] thinking. -**4.** [idéia] idea.

pensante [pĕn'sãntʃi] adj thinking.

pensão [pĕn'sãw] (pl -ões) f -**1.** [pequeno hotel] boarding house. -**2.** [renda] pension; **~ alimentí-cia** maintenance allowance. -**3.** [restaurante] boarding house. -**4.** [refeição]: **dar ~** [hotel] to provide board; [cozinhar para fora] to provide meals; **~ completa** full board.

pensar [4] [pĕn'sa(x)] <> vt to think. <> vi -**1.** [ger] to think; **~ em/sobre algo** to think about sthg. -**2.** [tencionar] to intend.

pensativo, va [pĕnsa'tʃivu, va] adj thoughtful.

pênsil ['pĕnsiw] (pl -seis) adj [suspenso] hanging.

pensionato [pĕnsjo'natu] m hostel.

pensionista [pĕnsjo'niʃta] mf -**1.** [beneficiário] pensioner. -**2.** [morador] boarder.

penso, sa ['pĕnsu] adj hanging.

pentacampeão [ˌpĕntakãn'pjãw] (pl -ões) m five-times champion.

pentágono [pĕn'tagunu] m GEOM pentagon.

pentatlo [pĕn'tatlu] m pentathlon.

pente ['pĕntʃi] m -**1.** [de cabelo] comb. -**2.** [de pis-tola] cartridge.

penteadeira [pĕntʃja'dejra] f dressing table.

penteado, da [pĕn'tʃjadu] adj well groomed.
 ➧ **penteado** m hairstyle.

pentear [15] [pĕn'tʃja(x)] vt -**1.** [cabelo] to comb. -**2.** [fazer penteado] to style.
 ➧ **pentear-se** vp [pessoa] to do one's hair.

Pentecostes [pĕnte'kɔʃtʃiʃ] m RELIG Pentecost.

pente-fino [pĕntʃi'finu] (pl pentes-finos) m -**1.** [pente] fine-tooth comb. -**2.** fam fig [crivo] close scrutiny; **passar algo pelo ~** to go through sthg with a fine-tooth comb.

pentelhação [pĕnteʎa'sãw] (pl -ões) f [chateação] fam aggro, hassle.

pentelhar [4] [pĕnte'ʎa(x)] vt fam to aggravate.

pentelho, lha [pĕn'teʎu, ʎa] fam <> adj [chato] aggravating. <> m, f [pessoa chata] pain in the neck.
 ➧ **pentelho** m fam [pêlo] pubic hair.

penugem [pe'nuʒẽ] (pl -ns) f down.

penúltimo, ma [pe'nuwtʃimu, ma] *adj* penultimate, last but one.

penumbra [pe'nũnbra] *f* -**1**. [meia-luz] half-light. -**2**. *fig* [obscuridade] obscurity.

penúria [pe'nurja] *f* penury; ~ **de algo** lack of sthg.

peões ['pjõjʃ] *pl* ▷ **peão.**

pepino [pe'pinu] *m* -**1**. [fruto] cucumber. -**2**. *fig* [problema] bit of a problem.

pepita [pe'pital *f* [de ouro] nugget.

pequena [pe'kena] *f* ▷ **pequeno.**

pequenez [peke'neʒ] *f* -**1**. [de tamanho] smallness. - **2**. *fig* [mesquinhez] meanness.

pequenininho, nha [pekeni'ninu, ɲa] *adj* tiny.

pequenino, na [peke'ninu, na] <> *adj* very small. <> *m, f* [criança] child.

➡ **pequeninos** *mpl*: **os** ~**s** [as crianças] the children; [os humildes] the little people.

pequeno, na [pe'kenu, na] <> *adj* -**1**. [tamanho] small. -**2**. [mesquinho] mean. <> *m, f* [criança] child.

➡ **pequena** *f* [namorada] girlfriend.

pequeno-burguês, pequeno-burguesa [pe͵kenubux'geʃ, pe͵kenabux'geza] (*pl* **peguenos-burgueses**) <> *adj* petit bourgeois. <> *m, f* petit bourgeois.

Pequim [pe'kĩ] *n* Beijing.

pequinês [peki'neʃ] *m* [cão] Pekinese.

pêra ['pera] (*pl* **pêras**) *f* pear.

peralta [pe'rawta] <> *adj* mischievous. <> *m, f* mischief-maker.

perambular [4] [perãnbu'la(x)] *vi*: ~ **(por)** to wander (through).

perante [pe'rãntʃi] *prep* -**1**. [no espaço] before; **jurar** ~ **a Bíblia** to swear on the Bible. -**2**. [no sentido] faced with.

pé-rapado, da [͵pɛxa'padu, da] (*mpl* **pés-rapados**, *fpl* **pés-rapadas**) *m, f* loser.

percalço [pex'kawsu] *m* pitfall.

per capita [pex'kapita] *loc adj* per capita.

perceber [5] [pexse'be(x)] *vt* -**1**. [através dos sentidos] to perceive. -**2**. [compreender] to realize. -**3**. [notar] to notice.

percentagem [pexsẽn'taʒẽ] (*pl* **-ns**) *f* percentage.

percentual [pexsẽn'twaw] (*pl* **-ais**) <> *adj* percentage. <> *m* [percentagem] percentage.

percepção [pexsep'sãw] *f* [dos sentidos] perception.

perceptível [pexsep'tʃivew] (*pl* **-eis**) *adj* perceptible.

perceptivo, va [pexsep'tʃivu, va] *adj* perceptive.

percevejo [pexse'veʒu] *m* -**1**. *ZOOL* bedbug. -**2**. [prego] drawing pin.

percorrer [5] [pexko'xe(x)] *vt* -**1**. [viajar] to travel through. -**2**. [passar por] to pass through. -**3**. [esquadrinhar] to search. -**4**. [consultar] to search through.

percurso [pex'kuxsu] *m* route.

percussão [pexku'sãw] (*pl* **-ões**) *f* percussion.

percussionista [pexkusjo'niʃta] *mf* drummer.

percutir [6] [pexku'tʃi(x)] *vt* to hit.

perda ['pexda] *f* -**1**. [ger] loss. -**2**. [desperdício]: ~ **de tempo** waste of time. -**3**. [prejuízo] damage; ~**s e danos** damages.

perdão [pex'dãw] (*pl* **-dões**) *m* [escusa] pardon; **pedir** ~ **a alguém** to apologize to sb; **perdão!** sorry!

perdedor, ra [pexde'do(x), ra] <> *adj* losing. <> *m, f* [de competição] loser.

perder [44] [pex'de(x)] <> *vt* -**1**. [ger] to lose. -**2**. [não chegar a tempo, não comparecer] to miss. -**3**. [desperdiçar] to waste; **pôr tudo a** ~ to ruin everything. <> *vi* [ser vencido] to lose; ~ **de** *ou* **para alguém** to lose to *ou* against sb; **saber** ~ to be a good loser.

➡ **perder-se** *vp* -**1**. [extraviar-se] to get lost; ~ **-se de alguém** to wander away from sb. -**2**. [arruinar-se] to waste one's life. -**3**. *ant* [mulher] to lose one's virginity. -**4**. [atrapalhar-se] to get bogged down. -**5**. [absorver-se] to lose o.s.

perdição [pexdʒi'sãw] *f* -**1**. [ruína] decay. -**2**. [mau caminho] evil; **ser uma** ~ *fig irôn* to be irresistible. -**3**. [desonra] fall from grace.

perdidamente [pexdʒida'mẽntʃi] *adv* desperately.

perdido, da [pex'dʒidu, da] <> *adj* -**1**. [ger] lost. -**2**. [amorosamente]: ~ **(de amor) por alguém** desperately in love with sb. -**3**. [arruinado]: **nem tudo está** ~ all is not lost; **meu pai descobriu que fui reprovado, estou** ~! my father's found out I've failed, I'm done for! <> *m, f* [pervertido] pervert.

perdigão [pexdʒi'gãw] (*pl* **-ões**) *m* [macho] male partridge.

perdigueiro [pexdʒi'gejru] *m* [cão] pointer.

perdiz [pex'dʒiʃ] (*pl* **-es**) *f* [fêmea] female partridge.

perdoar [20] [pex'dwa(x)] <> *vt* -**1**. [desculpar] to forgive; ~ **algo (a alguém)** to forgive (sb for) sthg. -**2**. [eximir de] to pardon. -**3**. *fig* [desperdiçar]: **não** ~ to make the most of. <> *vi* [desculpar] to forgive.

perdoável [pex'dwavew] (*pl* **-eis**) *adj* forgivable.

perdulário, ria [pexdu'larju, rja] *adj* wasteful.

perdurar [4] [pexdu'ra(x)] *vi* -**1**. [durar muito]: ~ **(por/através de)** to last (for/throughout). -**2**. [permanecer] to carry on.

pereba [pe'reba] *f* sore.

perebento, ta [pere'bẽntu, ta] *adj* covered in sores.

perecer [25] [pere'se(x)] *vi* -**1**. [extingüir-se] to perish. -**2**. [morrer] to die. -**3**. *ant* [frustrar-se] to come to nothing.

perecível [pere'sivew] (*pl* **-eis**) *adj* perishable.

peregrinação [peregrina'sãw] (*pl* **-ões**) *f* -**1**. [viagem] journey. -**2**. *RELIG* pilgrimage.

peregrinar [4] [peregri'na(x)] *vi* -**1**. [viajar] to travel. -**2**. *RELIG* to go on a pilgrimage.

peregrino, na [pere'grinu, na] *m, f* -**1**. [viajante] traveller. -**2**. *RELIG* pilgrim.

pereira [pe'rejra] *f* pear tree.

peremptório, ria [perẽnp'tɔrju, rja] *adj* -**1**. [final]

decisive. - **2.** [taxativo] peremptory.

perene [pe'renil *adj* -**1.** [eterno] eternal. -**2.** [incessante] unceasing. -**3.** *BOT* perennial.

perereca [pere'rɛka] *f* -**1.** *ZOOL* tree frog. -**2.** *mfam* [vulva] pussy.

perfazer [31] [pexfa'ze(x)] *vt* -**1.** [total] to reach. -**2.** [ação] to complete.

perfeccionismo [pexfeksjo'niʒmu] *m* perfectionism.

perfeccionista [pexfeksjo'niʃta] <> *adj* perfectionist. <> *mf* perfectionist.

perfeição [pexfej'sãw] *f* perfection; **ser uma ~** to be perfect; **à ~** to perfection.

perfeitamente [pex,fejta'mẽntʃi] <> *adv* perfectly. <> *interj* [de acordo] of course!

perfeito, ta [pex'fejtu, ta] *adj* -**1.** [ger] perfect. -**2.** *(antes de subst)* [completo] perfect.
◆ **perfeito** *m GRAM* perfect.

perfídia [pex'fidʒja] *f* [traição] treachery.

pérfido, da [ˈpɛxfidu, da] *adj* treacherous.

perfil [pex'fiw] *(pl* -**is**) *m* -**1.** [ger] profile; **de ~** in profile. -**2.** *fig* [retrato] outline. -**3.** [caráter] personality.

perfilar [4] [pexfi'la(x)] *vt* -**1.** [alinhar] to line up. -**2.** [aprumar] to straighten up.
◆ **perfilar-se** *vp* -**1.** [alinhar-se] to line up. -**2.** [aprumar-se] to stand to attention.

performance [pex'fɔxmãnsi] *f* performance.

perfumado, da [pexfu'madu, da] *adj* perfumed.

perfumar [4] [pexfu'ma(x)] *vt* to perfume.
◆ **perfumar-se** *vp* to put perfume on.

perfumaria [pexfuma'ria] *f* -**1.** [loja] perfume shop. -**2.** *fig & pej* [bobagem] nonsense.

perfume [pex'fumi] *m* perfume.

perfurado, da [pexfu'radu, da] *adj* perforated.

perfurar [4] [pexfu'ra(x)] *vt* to perforate.

perfuratriz [pexfura'triʒ] *f* drill.

pergaminho [pexga'miɲu] *m* [documento] parchment.

pérgula [ˈpɛxgula] *f* pergola.

pergunta [pex'gũnta] *f* question; **fazer uma ~ a alguém** to ask sb a question; **~ capciosa** trick question.

perguntador, ra [pexgũnta'do(x), ra] *adj pej* nosy.

perguntar [4] [pexgũn'ta(x)] <> *vt* -**1.** [indagar] to ask; **~ algo a alguém** to ask sb sthg. -**2.** [interrogar] to question. <> *vi* [indagar] to ask questions; **~ por alguém** to ask after sb.
◆ **perguntar-se** *vp* to wonder.

perícia [pe'risja] *f* -**1.** [ger] expertise. -**2.** [policial] investigation. -**3.** [examinadores] investigators.

pericial [peri'sjaw] *(pl* -**ais**) *adj* expert.

periclitante [perikli'tãntʃi] *adj* perilous.

periclitar [4] [perikli'ta(x)] *vi* to be in peril.

periculosidade [perikulozi'dadʒi] *f* peril; **de alta ~** highly perilous.

peridural [peridu'raw] *(pl* -**ais**) <> *adj* epidural. <> *f* epidural.

periferia [perife'ria] *f* -**1.** [contorno] periphery. -**2.** *GEOM* circumference. -**3.** [subúrbio] outskirts *(pl)*.

periférico, ca [peri'fɛriku, ka] *adj* -**1.** [que contorna] peripheral. -**2.** *fig* [marginal] superficial.
◆ **periférico** *m COMPUT* peripheral.

perigar [14] [peri'ga(x)] *vi* to be in danger; **~ com** to be endangered by; **periga ele ser morto** he may be dead; **~ chover** to look like it's going to rain.

perigo [pe'rigu] *m* danger; **correr ~** to be in danger; **estar a ~** *fam fig* [dinheiro] to be broke; **fig** [em dificuldade] to be in trouble; **estar em ~** to be in danger; **pôr em ~** to endanger; **fora de ~** out of danger; **ser um ~** [ser perigoso] to be dangerous; *fam fig* [ser uma tentação] to be tantalizing.

perigoso, osa [peri'gozu, ɔza] *adj* dangerous.

perímetro [pe'rimetru] *m* perimeter; **~ urbano** city limits *(pl)*.

periodicamente [perjɔdʒika'mẽntʃi] *adv* periodically.

periódico, ca [pe'rjɔdʒiku, ka] *adj* periodic.
◆ **periódico** *m* -**1.** [jornal] periodical (newspaper). -**2.** [revista] periodical (magazine).

período [pe'riwdu] *m* -**1.** [ger] period; **~ de carência** term. -**2.** *UNIV* semester; **~ letivo** school term.

peripécia [peri'pɛsja] *f* -**1.** [aventura] adventure. -**2.** [incidente] incident.

periquito [peri'kitu] *m* budgerigar.

periscópio [peris'kɔpju] *m* periscope.

perito, ta [pe'ritu, ta] <> *adj* [experiente, especialista] expert; **~ em algo** expert in sthg. <> *m, f* -**1.** [especialista] expert. -**2.** [quem faz perícia] investigator.

peritonite [perito'nitʃi] *f* peritonitis.

perjúrio [pex'ʒurju] *m* perjury.

permanecer [25] [pexmane'se(x)] *vi* to remain.

permanência [pexma'nẽnsja] *f* -**1.** [continuação, constância] endurance. -**2.** [estada] stay.

permanente [pexma'nẽntʃi] <> *adj* permanent. <> *m* [cartão] pass. <> *f* [penteado] perm; **fazer uma ~** to have a perm.

permeável [pex'mjavew] *(pl* -**eis**) *adj* permeable; **~ a algo** permeable to sthg.

permeio [pex'meju] *adv*: **de ~** in between.

permissão [pexmi'sãw] *(pl* -**ões**) *f* permission; **ter ~ (para fazer algo)** to have permission (to do sthg).

permissível [pexmi'sivew] *(pl* -**eis**) *adj* permissible.

permissivo, va [pexmi'sivu, va] *adj* permissive.

permitir [6] [pexmi'tʃi(x)] *vt* -**1.** [admitir] to allow; **~ a alguém fazer algo** to allow sb to do sthg. -**2.** [conceder]: **~ algo a alguém** to grant sb sthg.
◆ **permitir-se** *vp* [tomar a liberdade de] to allow o.s.

permuta [pex'muta] *f* exchange.

permutação [pexmuta'sãw] *(pl* -**ões**) *f* -**1.** *MAT* permutation. -**2.** [troca] exchange.

permutar [4] [pexmu'ta(x)] *vt*: **~ algo (por algo)** to exchange sthg (for sthg).

perna [ˈpɛxna] *f* leg; **~ de pau** wooden leg; **bater**

~ *fig* to wander; **passar a ~ em alguém** *fig* [enganar] to con sb; [trair] to cheat on sb; **trocar as ~s** *fam* [cambalear] to trip over one's feet.

perna-de-pau [ˌpɛxnadʒi'paw] (*pl* **pernas-depau**) *mf* **-1.** *fam pej* [perneta] one-legged man. **-2.** *FUT* & *pej*: **aquele jogador é um ~!** that player has two left feet!

Pernambuco [pexnãn'buku] *n* Pernambuco.

perneta [pex'neta] *fam pej* <> *adj* one-legged. <> *mf* one-legged person.

pernicioso, osa [pexni'sjozu, ɔza] *adj* **-1.** [nocivo] destructive. **-2.** *MED* pernicious.

pernil [pex'niw] (*pl* **-is**) *m* *CULIN* hock.

pernilongo [pexni'lõŋgul] *m* stilt.

pernoitar [4] [pexnoj'ta(x)] *vi* to spend the night.

pernoite [per'nojtʃi] *m*: **após um ~ na minha casa** after spending the night at my house.

pernóstico, ca [pex'nɔstʃiku, ka] <> *adj* pretentious. <> *mf* pretentious person.

pérola ['pɛrola] *f* **-1.** [de ostra] pearl. **-2.** *fig* [pessoa, peça rara] gem.

perpassar [4] [pexpa'sa(x)] *vt* *fig* [atravessar] to imbue.

perpendicular [pexpẽndʒiku'la(x)] (*pl* **-es**) <> *adj* perpendicular; **ser ~ a algo** to be at right angles to sthg. <> *f* perpendicular.

perpetrar [4] [pexpe'tra(x)] *vt* to perpetrate.

perpetuar [4] [pexpe'twa(x)] *vt* to prolong.

➤ **perpetuar-se** *vp* to survive.

perpétuo, tua [pex'pɛtwu, twa] *adj* **-1.** [eterno] eternal. **-2.** [vitalício] permanent. **-3.** *JUR*: **prisão perpétua** life imprisonment. **-4.** *(antes de subst)* [freqüente] on-going.

perplexidade [pexpleksi'dadʒi] *f* perplexity.

perplexo, xa [pex'plɛksu, sa] *adj* perplexed; **estar/ficar ~** to be perplexed.

perscrutar [4] [pexʃkru'ta(x)] *vt* [investigar] to scrutinize.

perseguição [pexsegi'sãw] (*pl* **-ões**) *f* **-1.** [ger] persecution. **-2.** *fig* [de um objetivo] pursuit.

perseguidor, ra [pexsegi'do(x), ra] *m*, *f* **-1.** [que acossa] pursuer. **-2.** *fig* [de um objetivo] seeker.

perseguir [55] [pexse'gi(x)] *vt* **-1.** [ger] to pursue. **-2.** *POL* & *RELIG* to persecute.

perseverança [pexseve'rãnsa] *f* perseverance.

perseverante [pexseve'rãntʃi] *adj* persevering.

perseverar [4] [pexseve'ra(x)] *vi* **-1.** [persistir]: **~ (em)** to persevere (with). **-2.** [permanecer] to last.

Pérsia ['pɛxsja] *n* Persia.

persiana [pex'sjana] *f* blind.

persignar-se [7] [pexsig'naxsi] *vp* to cross o.s.

persistência [pexsiʃ'tẽnsja] *f* persistence.

persistente [pexsiʃ'tẽntʃi] *adj* persistent.

persistir [6] [pexsiʃ'tʃi(x)] *vi* [insistir]: **~ (em algo)** to persist (in sthg).

personagem [pexso'naʒẽ] (*pl* **-ns**) *m*, *f* **-1.** *CINE, LITER* & *TEATRO* character. **-2.** [celebridade] celebrity.

personalidade [pexsonali'dadʒi] *f* personality; **dupla ~** split personality.

personalizado, da [pexsonali'zadu, da] *adj* personalized.

personalizar [412] [pexsonali'za(x)] *vt* [tonar pessoal] to personalize.

personificação [pexsonifika'sãw] (*pl* **-ões**) *f* personification.

personificar [12] [pexsonifi'ka(x)] *vt* personify.

perspectiva [pexʃpek'tʃiva] *f* **-1.** [ger] perspective. **-2.** [probabilidade] prospect; **em ~** [em vista] in prospect; [a distância] in perspective.

perspicácia [pexʃpi'kasja] *f* insight.

perspicaz [pexʃpi'kaʃ] (*pl* **-es**) *adj* insightful.

perspirar [4] [pexʃpi'ra(x)] *vi* to perspire, to sweat.

persuadir [6] [pexswa'dʒi(x)] <> *vt* **-1.** [convencer]: **~ alguém (a fazer algo)** to persuade sb (to do sthg); **persuadiu a mulher de que tinha razão** he persuaded his wife that he was right. **-2.** [induzir]: **~ alguém a fazer algo** to persuade sb to do sthg. <> *vi* [induzir] to persuade.

➤ **persuadir-se** *vp* **-1.** [convencer-se]: **~-se (de algo)** to be persuaded (of sthg). **-2.** [resolver-se]: **~-se (a fazer algo)** to make up one's mind (to do sthg).

persuasão [pexswa'zãw] *f* persuasion.

persuasivo, va [pexswa'zivu, va] *adj* persuasive.

pertencente [pextẽn'sẽntʃi] *adj*: **~ a algo/alguém** belonging to sthg/sb.

pertencer [25] [pextẽn'se(x)] *vi*: **~ a** [ger] to belong to; [concernir] to refer to.

pertences [pex'tẽnsiʃ] *mpl* [objetos pessoais] belongings.

pertinácia [pextʃi'nasja] *f* persistence.

pertinaz [pextʃi'najʒ] *adj* persistent.

pertinência [pextʃi'nẽnsja] *f* pertinence.

pertinente [pextʃi'nẽntʃi] *adj* **-1.** [ger] pertinent. **-2.** [importante] relevant.

perto ['pɛxtu] <> *adj* nearby. <> *adv* near; **de ~** [a pouca distância] closely; *fig* [intimamente] first--hand; **~ de** [ger] close to; [em comparação] next to.

perturbação [pextuxba'sãw] (*pl* **-ões**) *f* **-1.** [ger] disturbance; **~ da ordem** breach of the peace. **-2.** [transtorno] perturbation. **-3.** *MED* trouble.

perturbado, da [pextux'badu, da] *adj* **-1.** [transtornado]: **~ (com algo)** perturbed (by sthg). **-2.** [desorientado] disorientated; **ser ~ (das idéias)** *irôn* to be addled.

perturbador, ra [pextuxba'do(x), ra] *adj* disturbing.

perturbar [4] [pextux'ba(x)] <> *vt* **-1.** [ger] to perturb. **-2.** [atrapalhar] to disturb. **-3.** [envergonhar] to embarass. <> *vi* [atordoar] to pester.

➤ **perturbar-se** *vp* **-1.** [atrapalhar-se] to be worried. **-2.** [incomodar-se] to worry. **-3.** [envergonhar-se] to be embarrassed.

peru, rua [pe'ru, rua] *m*, *f* [ave] turkey.

➤ **peru** *n* *mfam* [pênis] cock.

➤ **perua** *f* **-1.** [caminhonete] estate car *UK*, station wagon *US*. **-2.** *fam pej* [mulher] hussy.

Peru [pe'ru] *n*: **(o) ~** Peru.

peruada [pe'rwada] *f* **-1.** [palpite] tip. **-2.** [espiada] look-see.

peruano, na [pe'rwãnu, na] ◇ *adj* Peruvian. ◇ *m, f* Peruvian.

peruar [4] [pe'rwa(x)] *vi* **-1.** [palpitar] to speculate. **-2.** [espiar] to size up.

peruca [pe'ruka] *f* wig.

perueiro, ra [pe'ruejru, ra] *m* [motorista de perua] minibus driver.

perversão [pexvex'sãw] (*pl* -ões) *f* **-1.** [depravação] perversion. **-2.** [alteração] alteration.

perversidade [pexvexsi'dadʒi] *f* perversity.

perverso, sa [pex'vɛxsu, sa] *adj* perverse.

perverter [5] [pexvex'te(x)] *vt* **-1.** [corromper] to pervert. **-2.** [alterar] to alter. **-3.** [deturpar] to distort.

➡ **perverter-se** *vp* [corromper-se] to become depraved.

pervertido, da [pexvex'tʃidu, da] ◇ *adj* [corrompido] depraved. ◇ *m, f* pervert.

pesadelo [peza'delu] *m* nightmare.

pesado, da [pe'zadu, da] *adj* **-1.** [ger] heavy. **-2.** [tenso] tense. **-3.** [grosseiro] coarse.

➡ **pesado** *m*: **pegar no** ~ to do hard work.

pesagem [pe'zaʒẽ] *f* weighing.

pêsames ['pezamiʃ] *mpl* condolences; **dar os** ~ **(a alguém)** to offer one's condolences (to sb).

pesar [4] [pe'za(x)] ◇ *m* sadness; **apesar dos** ~ **es** in spite of everything. ◇ *vt* to weigh. ◇ *vi* **-1.** [ger] to weigh. **-2.** [recair]: ~ **sobre alguém** to fall on sb. **-3.** [onerar] to be burdensome. **-4.** [influenciar]: ~ **em algo** to influence sthg. **-5.** [causar tristeza]: ~ **a alguém** to grieve sb. **-6.** [causar remorso] to weigh sb down.

➡ **pesar-se** *vp* [verificar o peso] to weigh o.s.

pesaroso, osa [peza'rozu, ɔza] *adj* **-1.** [triste] sorrowful. **-2.** [arrependido] sorry.

pesca ['pɛʃka] *f* **-1.** [ato] fishing; **ir à** ~ to go fishing; ~ **submarina** skin diving. **-2.** [o que se pescou] catch.

pescada [peʃ'kada] *f* whiting.

pescado [peʃ'kadu] *m* catch (*of fish*).

pescador, ra [peʃka'do(x), ra] (*mpl* -es, *fpl* -s) *m, f* fisherman (*f* fisherwoman).

pescar [12] [peʃ'ka(x)] ◇ *vt* **-1.** [apanhar] to fish. **-2.** *fig* [conseguir] to get. **-3.** *fig* [conquistar] to catch. ◇ *vi fam* [entender]: ~ **(de algo)** to catch on (to sthg).

pescoção [peʃko'sãw] (*pl* -ões) *m* **-1.** [pescoçada] blow on the neck; **levar um** ~ **de alguém** to be given a blow on the neck by sb. **-2.** [pescoço grande] large neck.

pescoço [peʃ'kosu] *m* neck; **até o** ~ *fig* up to one's neck; **torcer o** ~ **de alguém** *fig* to wring sb's neck.

pescoçudo, da [peʃko'sudu, da] *adj* thick-necked.

peso ['pezu] *m* **-1.** [ger] weight; ~ **bruto/líquido** gross/net weight; ~ **pesado** heavyweight; **ter dois** ~**s e duas medidas** *fig* to have double standards; **ele é um intelectual de** ~ he is a weighty intellectual. **-2.** [para papéis] paperweight. **-3.** [em atletismo] weights (*pl*). **-4.** [moeda]

peso. **-5.** *fig* [carga] burden.

➡ **em peso** *loc adj* en masse.

pespontar [4] [peʃpõ'ta(x)] *vt COST* to backstitch.

pesponto [peʃ'põntu] *m* backstitch.

pesqueiro, ra [peʃ'kejru, ra] *adj* fishing (*antes de subst*).

pesquisa [peʃ'kiza] *f* **-1.** [investigação] search. **-2.**: ~ **de mercado** market research; ~ **de opinião** opinion poll. **-3.** [estudo] research; ~ **de campo** field research; ~ **e desenvolvimento** research and development.

pesquisador, ra [peʃkiza'do(x), ra] ◇ *adj* research (*antes de subst*). ◇ *m, f* researcher.

pesquisar [4] [peʃki'za(x)] ◇ *vt* **-1.** [investigar] to investigate. **-2.** [estudar] to research. ◇ *vi* [estudar] to do research.

pêssego ['pesegu] *m* peach.

pessegueiro [pese'gejru] *m* peach tree.

pessimismo [pesi'miʒmu] *m* pessimism.

pessimista [pesi'miʃta] ◇ *adj* pessimistic. ◇ *mf* pessimist.

péssimo, ma ['pɛsimu, ma] *adj* (*superl de mau*) terrible; **ficou** ~ **com a notícia** the news made him feel terrible.

pessoa [pe'soal] *f* [ger] person; **em** ~ personally; ~ **física** *JUR* private individual; ~ **jurídica** *JUR* legal entity.

pessoal [pe'swaw] (*pl* -ais) ◇ *adj* personal. ◇ *m* **-1.** [empregados] personnel (*pl*), staff. **-2.** [grupo] people (*pl*).

pessoalmente [peswaw'mẽntʃi] *adv* personally.

pestana [peʃ'tãna] *f* **-1.** [cílio] eyelash; **queimar as** ~**s** *fig* [estudar] to swot; **tirar uma** ~ *fig* [dormir] to catch forty winks. **-2.** *COST* flap. **-3.** *MÚS* barré.

pestanejar [4] [peʃtane'ʒa(x)] *vi* to blink; **sem** ~ *fig* without batting an eyelid.

peste ['pɛʃtʃi] *f* **-1.** [ger] plague. **-2.** *fig* [pessoa] pest. **-3.** *fig* [coisa perniciosa] scourge.

pesticida [peʃtʃi'sida] *f* pesticide.

pestilência [peʃtʃi'lẽnsja] *f* [fedor] stench.

pestilento, ta [peʃtʃi'lẽntu, ta] *adj* **-1.** [fedorento] stinking. **-2.** [infectado] pestilent.

pétala ['pɛtala] *f* petal.

petardo [pe'taxdu] *m FUT* powerful kick.

peteca [pe'tɛka] *f* [brinquedo] shuttlecock; **não deixar a** ~ **cair** *fam fig* to keep the ball rolling.

peteleco [pete'lɛku] *m* flick.

petição [petʃi'sãw] (*pl* -ões) *f* **-1.** [requerimento] petition. **-2.** [súplica] plea. **-3.** [estado]: **em** ~ **de miséria** in a pitiful state.

peticionário, ria [petʃisjo'narju, rja] *m, f JUR* petitioner.

petiscar [12] [petʃiʃ'ka(x)] ◇ *vt* to pick at. ◇ *vi* to snack; **quem não arrisca não petisca** he who dares wins.

petisco [pe'tʃiʃku] *m* titbit *UK*, tidbit *US*.

petit-pois [petʃi'pwa] *m inv* pea.

petrechos [pe'treʃuʃ] *mpl* **-1.** *MIL* munitions. **-2.** [utensílios] utensils.

petrificado, da [petrifi'kadu, da] *adj* petrified.

petrificar [12] [petrifi'ka(x)] *vt* **-1.** [tornar em pedra] to harden. **-2.** [insensibilizar] to numb. **-3.** [aterrorizar] to petrify.

Petrobras (*abrev de* **Petróleo Brasileiro S/A**) *f Brazilian state-owned petroleum company.*

petrodólar [petro'dɔla(x)] *m* petrodollar.

petroleiro, ra [petro'lejru] ⬦ *adj:* **navio-** ~ (oil) tanker. ⬦ *m, f* [pessoa] oilman.

petróleo [pe'trɔlju] *m* petroleum, oil; ~ **bruto** crude oil.

petrolífero, ra [petro'liferu, ra] *adj* oil.

petroquímico, ca [petro'kimiku, ka] ⬦ *adj* petrochemical. ⬦ *m, f* petroleum chemist.

➤ **petroquímica** *f* [indústria] petrochemicals (*pl*).

petulância [petu'lãnsja] *f* petulance.

petulante [petu'lãntʃi] *adj* petulant.

petúnia [pe'tunja] *f* petunia.

PFL (*abrev de* **Partido da Frente Liberal**) *m* Party of the Liberal Front, *the largest, very right-wing party in Brazil.*

Phnom Penh [fnõn'pẽ] *n* Phnom Penh.

pia [ˈpia] *f* sink, washbasin; ~ **batismal** baptismal font.

piaçaba [pia'saba] *f BOT* palm *native to Brazil up to 15 meters in height producing a fibre used in the manufacture of brushes.*

piada [ˈpjada] *f* joke.

piadista [pja'dʒiʃta] *mf* joker.

piamente [pja'mẽntʃi] *adv* earnestly.

pianista [pja'niʃta] *mf* pianist.

piano [ˈpjãnu] *m* piano; ~ **de cauda** grand piano.

pianola [pja'nɔla] *f* pianola.

pião [ˈpjãw] (*pl* **-ões**) *m* spinning top.

piar [16] [ˈpja(x)] *vi* **-1.** [ave - pinto] to cheep; [- passarinho] to chirp; [- coruja] to hoot. **-2.** *fam* [falar]: **não** ~ not to make a peep.

PIB (*abrev de* **Produto Interno Bruto**) *m* GDP.

picada [piˈkada] *f* ⬥ **picado.**

picadeiro [pika'dejru] *m* (circus) ring.

picadinho [pika'dʒiɲu] *m CULIN* **-1.** [de carne] minced meat. **-2.** [de legumes] vegetable stew.

picado, da [piˈkadu, da] *adj* **-1.** [ger] stung; **ser** ~ **por algo** to be bitten by sthg. **-2.** [em pedaços] chopped up. **-3.** [mar] choppy. **-4.** [vôo] nose-diving.

➤ **picada** *f* **-1.** [espetada] prick. **-2.** [mordida] bite. **-3.** [caminho] trail.

picanha [piˈkãɲa] *f* [carne bovina] rump.

picante [piˈkãntʃi] *adj* spicy.

pica-pau [ˌpikaˈpaw] (*pl* **pica-paus**) *m* woodpecker.

picar [12] [piˈka(x)] *vt* **-1.** [espetar] to prick. **-2.** [morder] to bite. **-3.** [cortar em pedaços] to chop. **-4.** [lascar] to splinter. **-5.** [bicar] to peck.

➤ **picar-se** *vp* **-1.** [espetar-se] to prick o.s. **-2.** [com droga] to inject o.s.

picardia [pikax'dʒia] *f* **-1.** [implicância] spitefulness. **-2.** [maldade] spite.

picaresco, ca [pika'reʃku, ka] *adj* [burlesco] burlesque.

picareta [pika'reta] ⬦ *f* [instrumento] pickaxe

UK, pickax *US.* ⬦ *mf* [mau-caráter] con artist.

picaretagem [pikare'taʒẽ] (*pl* **-ns**) *f* con.

pichação [piʃa'sãw] (*pl* **-ões**) *f* **-1.** [grafite] graffiti. **-2.** *fam* [crítica] smear.

pichar [4] [piˈʃa(x)] *vt* **-1.** [grafitar] to graffitti. **-2.** *fam* [criticar] to smear. **-3.** [aplicar piche em] to pitch.

piche [ˈpiʃi] *m* pitch.

picles [ˈpikleʃ] *mpl* pickles.

pico [ˈpiku] *m* **-1.** [cume] summit. **-2.** [de faca etc] point. **-3.** *fam* [de droga] shot.

picolé [piko'lɛ] *m* ice lolly.

picotar [4] [piko'ta(x)] *vt* to perforate.

picote [piˈkɔtʃi] *m* [perfuração] perforation.

pictórico, ca [pik'tɔriku, ka] *adj* pictorial.

picuinha [piˈkwiɲa] *f* [implicância] dispute; **estar de** ~ **com alguém** to be at odds with sb.

piedade [pje'dadʒi] *f* **-1.** [compaixão] pity; **ter** ~ **de alguém** to have pity on sb. **-2.** [religiosidade] piety.

piedoso, osa [pje'dozu, ɔza] *adj* pious.

piegas [ˈpjɛgaʃ] *adj inv* soppy.

pieguice [pje'gisi] *f* soppiness.

píer [ˈpie(x)] *m* pier.

pifado, da [piˈfadu, da] *fam adj* [enguiçado] broken down.

pifão [piˈfãw] (*pl* **-ões**) *m fam* drunk; **tomar um** ~ to have a skinful.

pifar [4] [piˈfa(x)] *vi fam* **-1.** [enguiçar] to break down. **-2.** [gorar] to fall through.

pigarrear [15] [piga'xja(x)] *vi* to hawk.

pigarro [piˈgaxu] *m* phlegm.

pigméia [pigˈmɛja] *f* ⬥ **pigmeu.**

pigmentação [pigmẽnˈtaˈsãw] *f* pigmentation.

pigmento [pigˈmẽntu] *m* pigment.

pigmeu, méia [pigˈmew, mɛja] ⬦ *adj* [pequeno] pygmy. ⬦ *m, f* pygmy.

pijama [piˈʒama] *m* pyjamas (*pl*) *UK*, pajamas (*pl*) *US.*

pilantra [piˈlãntra] *mf* rogue.

pilantragem [pilãn'traʒẽ] (*pl* **-ns**) *f* roguishness.

pilão [piˈlãw] (*pl* **-ões**) *m* pestle.

pilar [4] [piˈla(x)] (*pl* **-es**) ⬦ *m* [coluna] pillar. ⬦ *vt* to grind.

pilastra [piˈlaʃtra] *f* pilaster.

pileque [piˈlɛki] *m* skinful; **estar de** ~ to be smashed; **tomar um** ~ to have a skinful.

pilha [ˈpiʎa] *f* **-1.** [monte] pile. **-2.** *ELETR* battery. **-3.** [pessoa]: **estar/ser uma** ~ **(de nervos)** to be a bundle of nerves. **-4.** *COMPUT* stack.

pilhagem [piˈʎaʒẽ] (*pl* **-ns**) *f* **-1.** [saque] pillage. **-2.** [objetos] booty.

pilhar [4] [piˈʎa(x)] *vt* **-1.** [saquear] to pillage. **-2.** [roubar] to rob.

pilhéria [piˈʎɛrja] *f* jest.

pilheriar [16] [piʎeˈrja(x)] *vi* to jest.

pilões [piˈlõjʃ] *pl* ⬥ **pilão.**

pilotagem [piloˈtaʒẽ] *f* flying.

pilotar [4] [piloˈta(x)] ⬦ *vt* to steer. ⬦ *vi* to steer.

pilotis [piloˈtʃiʃ] *mpl ARQUIT* stilts.

piloto [piˈlotu] ⬦ *adj* [modelo] pilot. ⬦ *m* **-1.** [ger] pilot; ~ **automático** automatic pilot. **-2.**

[de corrida] driver; ~ **de prova** racing driver. - **3.** [bico de gás] pilot light.

pílula [ˈpilula] f pill; ~ **anticoncepcional** contraceptive pill.

pimenta [piˈmẽnta] f - **1.** CULIN pepper. - **2.** fig [malícia] spite.

pimenta-do-reino [piˌmẽntaduˈxejnu] (pl pimentas-do-reino) f black pepper.

pimenta-malagueta [piˌmẽntamalaˈgeta] (pl pimentas-malaguetas) f chilli pepper UK, chili pepper US.

pimentão [pimẽnˈtãw] (pl -ões) m: ~ **verde/vermelho** green/red pepper; **estar/ficar um** ~ fig to be/go as red as a beetroot.

pimenteira [pimẽnˈtejra] f - **1.** BOT pepper tree. - **2.** [recipiente] pepper pot.

pimpolho [pĩnˈpoʎu] m [criança] kid.

pinacoteca [pinakoˈtɛka] f - **1.** [coleção] art collection. - **2.** [museu] art gallery.

pináculo [piˈnakulu] m pinnacle.

pinça [ˈpĩnsa] f - **1.** MED forceps (pl). - **2.** [de sobrancelha] tweezers (pl).

pinçar [13] [pĩnˈsa(x)] vt - **1.** [segurar] to grip (with pincers). - **2.** [sobrancelhas] to pluck. - **3.** fig [selecionar] to select.

píncaro [ˈpĩŋkaru] m - **1.** [cume] peak. - **2.** fig [apogeu] height.

pincel [pĩnˈsɛw] (pl -éis) m brush; ~ **de barba** shaving brush.

pincelada [pĩnseˈlada] f (brush) stroke.

pincelar [4] [pĩnseˈla(x)] vt to paint.

pincenê [pĩnseˈne] m pince-nez.

pindaíba [pĩndaˈiba] f: **estar na** ~ fam to be skint.

pinel [piˈnew] (pl -éis) adj fam crazy; **ficar** ~ to be driven crazy.

pinga [ˈpĩŋga] f fam [cachaça] booze.

pingado, da [pĩŋˈgadu, da] <> adj - **1.** [cheio de pingos]: ~ **de algo** splashed with sthg. - **2.** [leite] with a drop of milk; [café] with a drop of milk. <> m [café] coffee with a drop of milk.

pingar [14] [pĩŋˈga(x)] <> vi - **1.** [gotejar] to drip. - **2.** [chover] to spit. - **3.** [render] to trickle in. <> vt - **1.** [respingar] to spill. - **2.** [gotejar] to allow to drip through.

pingente [pĩnˈʒẽntʃi] m [objeto] pendant.

pingo [ˈpĩŋgu] m - **1.** [gota] drop. - **2.** [pequena quantidade]: **um** ~ **de** a little; ~ **de gente** [criança] little person. - **3.** [sinal ortográfico] dot; **pôr os** ~**s nos is** fig to dot the i's and cross the t's.

pingue-pongue [ˌpĩŋgiˈpõŋgi] (pl pinguepongues) m ping-pong, table tennis.

pingüim [pĩŋˈgwĩ] (pl -ns) m penguin.

pinguinho [pĩŋˈgiɲu] m - **1.** [pingo] droplet. - **2.** [pouquinho]: **um** ~ **(de)** a tiny bit (of).

pinha [ˈpiɲa] f - **1.** [fruto do pinheiro] pine cone. - **2.** [fruta] pine nut.

pinhão [piˈɲãw] (pl -ões) m pine nut.

pinheiral [piɲejˈraw] (pl -ais) m pine forest.

pinheiro [piˈɲejru] m pine tree.

pinho [ˈpiɲu] m - **1.** BOT pine (tree). - **2.** [madeira]

pine wood. - **3.** fam [violão] fiddle.

pinicada [piniˈkada] f - **1.** [de ave] peck. - **2.** [de agulha, espinho] stab.

pinicar [12] [piniˈka(x)] vt - **1.** [comichar] to be itchy. - **2.** [bicar] to peck. - **3.** [cutucar] to jab.

pinimba [piˈnĩnba] f fam argument; **estar de** ~ **com alguém** to be at loggerheads with sb.

pino [ˈpinu] m - **1.** [peça] peg. - **2.** [AUTO - em motor] crankpin; [- tranca] lock; **bater** ~ to rattle; fam fig [estar mal] to fall apart. - **3.** [cume]: **a** ~ **at the** zenith; **sol a** ~ midday sun.

pinóia [piˈnɔja] fam f - **1.** [chatice]: **ser uma** ~ to be boring; **que** ~! what a bore! - **2.** [porcaria] junk. - **3.** [mentira]: **uma** ~! my foot!

pinote [piˈnɔtʃi] m buck; **dar** ~**s** to buck.

pinotear [15] [pinoˈtʃja(x)] vi to leap.

pinta [ˈpĩnta] f - **1.** [sinal] mole. - **2.** fam [aparência]: **o rapaz é boa** ~ the boy is looking good; **essa comida está com boa** ~ that food looks good; **ter** ~ **de algo** to look like sthg. - **3.** fam [indício]: **estar com** ~ **de (ser) difícil** to look (like being) difficult; **ela deu na** ~ **que ia nos assaltar** [demonstrar] she looked like she was going to attack us.

pinta-brava [pĩntaˈbrava] (pl pintas-bravas) mf [mau elemento] shady character.

pintado, da [pĩnˈtadu, da] adj - **1.** [colorido - papel] coloured; [- parede, olhos, unhas] painted; [- face] painted, made-up; [- cabelo] dyed. - **2.** [sardento] freckled. - **3.** [idêntico]: **ser alguém** ~ to be the spitting image of sb.

pintar [4] [pĩnˈta(x)] <> vt - **1.** [ger] to paint. - **2.** [com tinta - ger] to paint; [- cabelo] to dye. - **3.** fig [conceber] to paint as. <> vi - **1.** ARTE to paint. - **2.** fam [aparecer] to turn up. - **3.** [exceder-se] to get overexcited; ~ **e bordar** fig to have a great time.

➡ **pintar-se** vp [maquilar-se] to make o.s. up.

pinto, ta [ˈpĩntu, ta] m, f - **1.** ZOOL chick; **ficar (molhado) como um** ~ to get soaked to the bone. - **2.** mfam [pênis] cock. - **3.** [coisa fácil]: **ser** ~ to be a pushover.

pintor, ra [pĩnˈto(x), ra] (mpl -es, fpl -s) m, f painter.

pintura [pĩnˈtura] f - **1.** ARTE painting; ~ **a óleo** oil painting. - **2.** [de casa etc] paintwork. - **3.** [maquiagem] make-up.

pio, pia [ˈpiw, ˈpia] adj - **1.** [devota] pious. - **2.** [caridoso] charitable.

➡ **pio** m [de ave] peep; **não dê um** ~, **senão atiro** not a peep, or else I'll shoot.

piões [ˈpjõjʃ] pl ▷ **pião**.

piolho [ˈpjoʎu] m louse.

pioneirismo [pjonejˈriʒmu] m pioneering nature.

pioneiro, ra [pjoˈnejru, ra] <> adj pioneering. <> m, f pioneer.

pior [ˈpjɔ(x)] (pl -es) <> adj - **1.** [comparativo]: ~ **(do que)** worse (than). - **2.** [superlativo]: **o/a** ~ ... the worst ... <> m: **o** ~ **(de)** [inferior] the worst (of); **o** ~ **é que** ... the worst of it is that ... <> f: **o/a** ~ **(de)** the worst (of); **estar na** ~ to be in a jam;

levar a ~ to lose. <> *adv* [comparativo]: ~ **(do que)** worse (than); **ela está** ~ **de saúde** her health is worse.

piora [ˈpjɔral] *f* deterioration.

piorar [4] [pjoˈra(x)] *vi* to deteriorate.

pipa [ˈpipa] *f* -**1.** [vasilhame] barrel. -**2.** [de papel] kite; **soltar** ~ to fly a kite.

piparote [pipaˈrɔtʃil] *m* flick.

pipi [piˈpil] *m fam* wee-wee *UK*, pee-pee *US*; **fazer** ~ to wee *UK*, to go pee-pee *US*.

pipilar [16] [pipiˈla(x)] *vi* to chirp.

pipoca [piˈpɔka] *f* -**1.** [de milho] popcorn. -**2.** [em pele] blister.

pipocar [12] [pipoˈka(x)] *vi* -**1.** [estourar] to burst out. -**2.** [espocar] to crackle. -**3.** [surgir] to sprout up.

pipoqueiro, ra [pipoˈkeiru, ral] *m, f* [vendedor] popcorn seller.

➡ **pipoqueira** *f* [panela] popcorn-making pan.

pique [ˈpikil] *m* -**1.** [brincadeira] catch. -**2.** [disposição] enthusiasm; **perder o** ~ to lose one's momentum; **ter** ~ to have what it takes. -**3.** [corte] notch. -**4.** *NÁUT:* **ir a** ~ to sink.

piquenique [ˌpikiˈnikil] *m* picnic.

piquete [piˈketʃil] *m* -**1.** [de greve] picket. -**2.** *MIL* squad.

pira [ˈpiral] *f fam:* **dar o** ~ [ir-se embora] to scarper; [fugir] to abscond.

piração [piraˈsãwl] (*pl* -ões) *f fam* -**1.** [doidice] madness. -**2.** [ser excelente]: **aquele filme é uma** ~ that film is really great.

pirado, da [piˈradu, dal] *adj* crazy.

pirâmide [piˈramidʒil] *f* pyramid.

piranha [piˈrãɲal] *f* -**1.** [peixe] piranha. -**2.** *mfam pej* [mulher] hussy. -**3.** [prendedor de cabelo] hair clasp.

pirão [piˈrãwl] (*pl* -ões) *m CULIN* cassava porridge.

pirar [4] [piˈra(x)] *vi* -**1.** [endoidar] to go insane. -**2.** [fugir] to scarper.

pirata [piˈratal] <> *adj* pirate. <> *mf* pirate.

pirataria [pirataˈrial] *f* [roubo] piracy.

piratear [pir200ˈtea(x)] *vt:* ~ **um programa** to pirate a program.

Pireneus [pireˈnewʃl] *n:* **os** ~ the Pyrenees.

pires [ˈpiriʃl] *m inv* saucer.

pirilampo [piriˈlãnpul] *m* glow-worm.

pirotecnia [pirotekˈnial] *f* -**1.** [arte] pyrotechnics *(sg).* -**2.** [fabricação] fireworks manufacturing.

pirotécnico, ca [piroˈtɛkniku, kal] <> *adj* [com fogos de artifício] firework *(antes de subst).* <> *m, f* [fabricante] firework manufacturer.

pirraça [piˈxasal] *f:* **fazer algo por** ~ to do sthg out of spite; **fazer** ~ **a alguém** [fazer desfeita] to spite sb.

pirracento, ta [pixaˈsẽntu, tal] *adj* spiteful.

pirralho, lha [piˈxaʎu, ʎal] *m, f* child.

pirueta [piˈrwetal] *f* pirouette.

pirulito [piruˈlitul] *m* -**1.** [bala] lollipop. -**2.** *fam* [pênis] willy.

pisada [piˈzadal] *f* -**1.** [passo] footstep; **dar uma** ~ **em algo/alguém** to tread on sthg/sb. -**2.** [pegada] footprint.

pisão [piˈsãwl] (*pl* -ões) *m* [pisadela]: **dar um** ~ **no pé de alguém** to tread on sb's toes.

pisar [4] [piˈza(x)] <> *vt* -**1.** to tread on. -**2.** [esmagar] to crush. -**3.** [percorrer] to set foot on. <> *vi* -**1.** [andar]: ~ **(em)** to walk *ou* tread (on); **saber onde** ~ *fig* to know what one is getting into. -**2.**: ~ **em** [tocar com os pés] to step on; [ir, vir] to set foot in; [humilhar] to crush; ▷ **bola, ovos.**

piscadela [piʃkaˈdɛlal] *f* -**1.** [ato reflexo] blink. -**2.** [sinal] wink; **dar uma** ~ to give a wink.

pisca-pisca [ˌpiʃkaˈpiʃkal] (*pl* **pisca-piscas**) *m AUTO* indicator.

piscar [12] [piʃˈka(x)] <> *vt* [olho] to blink; ~ **o olho para alguém** [dar sinal] to wink at sb. <> *vi* -**1.** [pessoa, olho] to wink. -**2.** [trocar sinais]: ~ **para alguém** to wink at sb. -**3.** [tremeluzir] to twinkle. <> *m* twinkling; **num** ~ **de olhos** in a twinkling of an eye.

pisciano, na [piˈsjãnu, nal] <> *adj:* **ser** ~ to be a Piscean. <> *m, f* Piscean.

piscicultura [pisikuwˈtural] *f* fish farming, pisciculture.

piscina [piˈsinal] *f* swimming pool.

piso [ˈpizul *m* -**1.** [ger] floor. -**2.** [revestimento] flooring. -**3.** [salário]: ~ **(salarial)** minimum (professional) wage.

pisotear [15] [pizoˈtʃja(x)] *vt* -**1.** [pisar] to trample (on). -**2.** [humilhar] to trample over.

píssico, ca [ˈpisiku, kal] <> *adj* crazy. <> *m, f* lunatic.

pista [ˈpiʃtal] *f* -**1.** [vestígio] trace. -**2.** [encalço]: **na** ~ **de** in pursuit of, on the trail of. -**3.** *fig* [informação] clue. -**4.** [de rua, estrada] track. -**5.** *AERON* runway. -**6.** [*ESP*- de automobilismo, atletismo] track; [- de esqui] piste; [- de equitação] ring; [- de tênis] court. -**7.** [de dança] floor.

pistache [piʃˈtaʃil, **pistacho** [piʃˈtaʃul *m* pistachio.

pistola [piʃˈtɔlal] *f* -**1.** [arma] pistol. -**2.** [para pintar] (spray) gun.

pistolão [piʃtoˈlãwl] (*pl* -ões) *m* -**1.** [pessoa] connection. -**2.** [recomendação] recommendation.

pistoleiro, ra [piʃtoˈlejru, ral] *m, f* [criminoso] gunman.

➡ **pistoleira** *f mfam* [vagabunda] tart.

pistom [piʃˈtõl] (*pl* -ns) *m* -**1.** [instrumento] trumpet. -**2.** [de motor] piston.

pitada [piˈtadal] *f* pinch.

pitanga [piˈtãŋgal] *f* (red Brazil) cherry.

pitar [4] [piˈta(x)] <> *vi* to smoke. <> *vt* to smoke.

piteira [piˈtejral] *f* cigarette-holder.

pito [ˈpitul *m* -**1.** [cachimbo] pipe. -**2.** *fam* [repreensão] talking-to; **dar um** ~ **em alguém** to tell sb off; **levar um** ~ **de alguém** to be told off by sb. -**3.** *loc:* **sossegar o** ~ *fam* to calm down.

pitonisa [pitoˈnizal] *f* fortune teller.

pitoresco, ca [pitoˈreʃku, kal] <> *adj* picturesque. <> *m* attraction.

pituitária [pitujˈtarial] *f ANAT* pituitary.

pivete [pi'vɛtʃi] *m* child thief.
pivô [pi'vo] *m* -**1**. [de dente] pivot. -**2**. *fig* [suporte] pivot. -**3**. *fig* [agente principal] central figure. -**4**. [jogador] centre.
pixaim [piʃa'ĩ] (*pl* -**ns**) <> *adj* frizzy. <> *m* frizzy hair.
pixote [pi'ʃɔtʃi] *m* small child.
pizza ['pitsa] *f* pizza.
pizzaria [pitsa'rial *f* pizzeria.
plá [pla] *m*: **ter** *ou* **bater um** ~ **com alguém** to have a chat with sb.
placa ['plaka] *f* -**1**. [ger] plaque. -**2**. [lâmina] sheet. -**3**. [aviso] sign; ~ **de sinalização** road sign. -**4**. AUTO number plate *UK*, license plate *US*; ~ **fria** false number plate. -**5**. COMPUT & ELECTRON board; ~ **de vídeo** video card. -**6**. [na pele] blotch.
placa-mãe ['plakamãjl] (*pl* **placas-mãe** *ou* **placas-mães**) *f* COMPUT motherboard.
placar [pla'ka(x)] *m* -**1**. [escore] score. -**2**. [marcador] scoreboard.
placebo [pla'sebul] *m* placebo.
placenta [pla'sẽnta] *f* ANAT placenta.
placidez [plasi'deʒl] *f* quietness.
plácido, da ['plasidu, dal] *adj* -**1**. [pessoa, olhar, semblante] placid. -**2**. [lugar, dia, vida] quiet.
plagiador, ra [plaʒja'do(x), ral] *m, f* plagiarist.
plagiar [16] [pla'ʒia(x)] *vt* to plagiarize.
plagiário, ria [ju, pla'ʒjarju, rjal] *m, f* plagiarist.
plágio ['plaʒjul] *m* plagiarism.
plaina ['plãjna] *f* [ferramenta] plane.
planador [plana'do(x)] (*pl* -**es**) *m* glider.
planalto [pla'nawtul] *m* plateau.
● **Planalto** *m* [palácio presidencial] president's office.
planar [4] [pla'na(x)] *vi* to glide.
planejador, ra [planeʒa'do(x), ral] *m, f* planner.
planejamento [planeʒa'mẽntul] *m* planning; ~ **familiar** family planning.
planejar [4] [plane'ʒa(x)] *vt* -**1**. [ger] to plan. -**2**. ARQUIT to design.
planeta [pla'netal] *m* planet.
planetário, a [plane'tarjul] *adj* planetary.
● **planetário** *m* planetarium.
plangente [plãn'ʒẽntʃil] *adj* plaintive.
planície [pla'nisjil] *f* plain.
planificar [12] [planifi'ka(x)] *vt* -**1**. [ger] to plan out. -**2**. [tornar plano] to level.
planilha [pla'niʎal] *f* -**1**. [formulário] table. -**2**. COMPUT spreadsheet.
plano, na ['plãnu, nal] <> *adj* -**1**. [superfície] flat. -**2**. [liso] smooth. <> *m* -**1**. [ger] plan; ~ **piloto** outline plan. -**2**. [superfície plana] level surface. -**3**. [posição]: **em primeiro/segundo** ~ in the foregound/background; **para ela isso fica em segundo** ~ *fig* for her this takes second place. -**4**. [nível] level. -**5**. [seguro]: ~ **de saúde** health plan. -**6**. GEOM plane.
planta ['plãntal] *f* -**1**. BIOL plant. -**2**. ANAT: ~ **do pé** sole of the foot. -**3**. ARQUIT plan.
plantação [plãnta'sãwl] *m* -**1**. [ato] planting. -**2**. [terreno] plantation. -**3**. [produtos] crops (*pl*).

plantado, da [plãn'tadu, dal] *adj* planted; **deixar alguém** ~ **em algum lugar** to leave sb standing somewhere.
plantão [plãn'tãwl] (*pl* -**ões**) *m* -**1**. [serviço - diurno] duty; [- noturno] night duty; **estar de** ~ to be on duty; **médico de** ~ duty doctor. -**2**. [plantonista] person on duty.
plantar [4] [plãn'ta(x)] *vt* -**1**. [planta, árvore] to plant. -**2**. [semear] to sow. -**3**. [fincar] to drive in. -**4**. *fig* [estabelecer] to establish. -**5**. [incutir] to inspire. -**6**. [pôr] to set up.
● **plantar-se** *vp* [pôr-se] to remain.
plantões [plãn'tõjʃ] *pl* ▷ **plantão**.
plantonista [plãnto'niʃta] *mf* person on duty.
plaqueta [pla'ketal] *f* -**1**. [placa pequena] small plaque, plaquette. -**2**. AUTO licensing badge. -**3**. COMPUT chip.
plasma ['plaʒmal] *m* plasma.
plasmar [4] [plaʒ'ma(x)] *vt* to shape.
plástico, ca ['plaʃtʃiku, kal] *adj* plastic.
● **plástico** *m* [matéria] plastic; **de** ~ plastic.
● **plástica** *f* -**1**. [cirurgia] plastic surgery; **fazer plástica** to have plastic surgery. -**2**. [corpo] build.
plastificado, da [plaʃtʃifi'kadu, dal] *adj* laminated.
plastificar [12] [plaʃtʃifi'ka(x)] *vt* to laminate.
plataforma [plata'fɔxmal] *f* -**1**. [ger] platform; ~ **de exploração de petróleo** oil rig; ~ **de lançamento** launch pad. -**2**. GEOGR shelf.
platéia [pla'tɛjal] *f* -**1**. [espaço] stalls (*pl*) *UK*, orchestra *US*. -**2**. [público] audience.
platina [pla'tʃinal] *f* [metal] platinum.
platinado, da [platʃi'nadu, dal] *adj* platinum blond (*antes de subst*).
● **platinado** *m* AUTO contact point.
platô [pla'tol] *m* plateau.
platônico, ca [pla'toniku, kal] *adj* platonic.
plausível [plaw'zivɛwl] (*pl* -**eis**) *adj* [aceitável] plausible.
playback [plej'bɛkil] *m* MÚS playback.
playboy [plej'bɔjl] *m* playboy.
playground [plej'grawndʒil] *m* playground.
plebe ['plɛbil] *f* common people.
plebeu, béia [ple'bew, bɛjal] <> *adj* plebeian. <> *m, f* plebeian.
plebiscito [plebi'situl] *m* plebiscite.
plêiade ['plejadʒil] *f* [reunião] soirée.
pleitear [15] [plej't∫ja(x)] *vt* -**1**. [diligenciar] to strive for. -**2**. JUR to contest. -**3**. [concorrer a] to compete for.
pleito ['plejtul] *m* -**1**. JUR legal dispute, lawsuit. -**2**. [eleição]: ~ (**eleitoral**) election.
plenamente [,plena'mẽntʃil] *adv* fully.
plenária [ple'narial] *f* plenary (session).
plenário [ple'narjul] *m* -**1**. [assembléia] plenary session. -**2**. [local] chamber.
plenipotenciário, ria [plenipotẽn'sjarju, rjal] <> *adj* plenipotentiary. <> *m, f* plenipotentiary.
plenitude [pleni'tudʒil] *f* fulfilment.
pleno, na ['plɛnu, nal] *adj* -**1**. [cheio]: ~ **de** full of.

-2. [total] complete; **em plena luz do dia** in broad daylight; **em plena rua** smack in the middle of the street; **em plena forma** on top form; **em ~ verão** in high summer; **~s poderes** full powers.

pleonasmo [pljo'naʒmu] *m* pleonasm.

pletora [ple'tora] *f* fig plethora.

pleurisia [plewri'zia] *f* pleurisy.

plissado, da [pli'sadu, da] *adj* pleated.

plugado, da [plu'gadu, da] *adj* **-1.** [aparelho] plugged. **-2.** [pessoa]: **passar o dia ~ no computador** to spend the day glued to the computer.

plugar [plu'ga(x)] *vt* to plug.

plug-in ['plugĩn] *m* COMPUT plug-in.

plugue ['plugi] *m* plug.

pluma ['pluma] *f* **-1.** [de ave] feather. **-2.** [para escrever] quill. **-3.** [adorno] plume.

plumagem [plu'maʒẽ] *f* plumage.

plural [plu'raw] (*pl* **-ais**) <> *adj* plural. <> *m* plural.

pluralidade [plurali'dadʒi] *f* **-1.** [diversidade] diversity. **-2.** [maioria] majority.

pluralismo [plura'liʒmu] *m* **-1.** [diversidade] diversity. **-2.** POL pluralism.

pluralista [plura'liʃta] *adj* **-1.** [diverso] diverse. **-2.** POL pluralist.

Plutão [plu'tãw] *n* Pluto.

plutocracia [plutokra'sia] *f* plutocracy.

plutocrata [pluto'krata] *mf* plutocrat.

plutônio [plu'tonju] *m* plutonium.

pluvial [plu'vjaw] (*pl* **-ais**) *adj* pluvial, rain (*antes de subst*).

pluviométrico, ca [pluvjo'mɛtriku, ka] *adj* rainfall (*antes de subst*).

PM (*abrev de* **Polícia Militar**) *f* military police.

PMDB (*abrev de* **Partido do Movimento Democrático Brasileiro**) *m* Brazilian Party for Democratic Movement, *the largest party of the centre*.

PNB (*abrev de* **Produto Nacional Bruto**) *m* GNP.

pneu [pi'new] *m* **-1.** AUTO tyre *UK*, tire *US*; **~ sobressalente** spare tyre *UK*, spare tire *US*. **-2.** *fam* [gordura] spare tyre *UK*, spare tire *US*.

pneumático, ca [pinew'matʃiku, ka] *adj* pneumatic.

◆ **pneumático** *m* [pneu] tyre *UK*, tire *US*.

pneumonia [pinewmu'nia] *f* pneumonia.

pó ['pɔ] *m* **-1.** [poeira] dust; **tirar o ~ de algo** to dust sthg. **-2.** [substância pulverizada] powder; **em ~** powdered. **-3.** [pó-de-arroz] face powder. **-4.** *fam* [cocaína] snow.

pô [po] *interj* **-1.** *fam* [mostrando irritação] damn it! **-2.** [mostrando surpresa] blimey! *UK*, gee whiz! *US*.

pobre ['pɔbri] <> *adj* **-1.** [ger] poor. **-2.** [escasso]: **~ de/em algo** lacking in sthg. **-3.** (*antes do subst*) [digno de pena] poor. <> *m* [pessoa] poor person; **os ~s** the poor.

pobre-diabo [ˌpɔbri'dʒjabu] (*pl* **pobres-diabos**) *m* poor devil.

pobretão, tona [pobre'tãw, tona] (*mpl* **-ões**, *fpl* **-s**) *m, f* **-1.** [pessoa muito pobre] pauper. **-2.** *euf* poor thing.

pobreza [po'breza] *m* **-1.** [miséria] poverty. **-2.** [escassez]: **~ de** ou **em algo** lack of sthg; **~ de espírito** simplicity.

poça ['pɔsa] *f*: **~ (d'água)** puddle; **~ de sangue** pool of blood.

poção [po'sãw] (*pl* **-ões**) *f* potion.

pocilga [po'siwga] *f* **-1.** [chiqueiro] pigsty. **-2.** *fig* [lugar imundo] hovel.

poço ['posu] *f* **-1.** [cavidade] well; **~ de petróleo** oil well; **ir ao fundo do ~** *fig* to sink to the depths of despair. **-2.** [qualidade]: **ser um ~ de algo** *fig* to be a fount of sthg.

poda ['pɔda] *f* **-1.** [ato] pruning. **-2.** [época] pruning season.

podadeira [poda'dejra] *f* pruning knife.

podar [4] [po'da(x)] *vt* to prune.

pó-de-arroz [ˌpɔdʒja'xoʃ] (*pl* **pós-de-arroz**) *m* face powder.

poder [36] [po'de(x)] <> *m* **-1.** [político, influência] power; **estar no ~** to be in power; **~ de compra** purchasing power; **não tenho ~ nenhum** I'm powerless. **-2.** [possessão] power; **estar em ~ de alguém** to be in sb's power; **ter em seu ~ algo** to have sthg within one's power. <> *v aux* **-1.** [ser capaz de]: **~ fazer algo** to be able to do sthg; **posso fazê-lo** I can do it; **posso ajudar?** can I help?, may I help?; **você podia tê-lo feito antes** you could have done it earlier; **não posso mais!** [em relação a cansaço] I've had enough!; [em relação a comida] I'm full! **-2.** [estar autorizado para]: **~ fazer algo** to be allowed to do sthg; **posso fumar?** may I smoke?; **você não pode estacionar aqui** you can't park here; **não pude sair ontem** I wasn't allowed (to go) out yesterday. **-3.** [ser capaz moralmente] can; **não podemos magoar o gato** we can't hurt the cat. **-4.** [exprime possibilidade]: **você podia ter vindo de ônibus** you could have come by bus; **cuidado que você pode se machucar!** be careful, you might hurt yourself! **-5.** [exprime indignação, queixa]: **não pode ser!** this is outrageous!; **você podia ter nos avisado** you could have warned us!; **pudera!** I wish! <> *v impess* [ser possível]: **pode não ser verdade** it might not be true; **pode acontecer a qualquer um** it could happen to anybody; **pode ser que chova** it might rain.

◆ **poder com** *v + prep* **-1.** [suportar] to bear; **não posso com mentirosos** I cannot bear liars. **-2.** [rival, adversário] to bear. **-3.** [peso] to carry; **você não pode com tanto peso** you can't carry all that weight.

poderio [pode'riw] *m* power.

poderoso, sa [pode'rozu, sa] *adj* **-1.** [influente] powerful. **-2.** [eficaz] powerful.

◆ **poderosos** *mpl*: **os ~** the powers that be.

pódio ['pɔdʒju] *m* podium.

podre ['podri] <> *adj* **-1.** [ger] rotten. **-2.** *fig* [corrupto] corrupt. **-3.** *fig* [cheio]: **estou ~ (de cansaço)** I am dog-tired; **~ de gripe** full of flu; **~ de rico** filthy rich. <> *m* **-1.** [parte]: **o ~ da maçã** the bad part of the apple. **-2.** *fig* [defeito] dark secret.

podridão [podri'dãw] (pl -ões) f -1. [estado de podre] decay. -2. fig [corrupção] corruption.

poeira ['pwejra] f dust; ~ **radioativa** fallout.

poeirento, ta [pwej'rẽntu, ta] adj dusty.

poema ['pwema] m poem.

poente ['pwẽntʃi] <> adj [sol] setting. <> m -1. [ocidente] west. -2. [do sol] sunset.

poesia [pwi'zia] f -1. [arte] poetry. -2. [poema] poem. -3. [encanto] charm.

poeta, tisa ['pwɛta, tʃiza] m, f poet.

poético, ca ['pwɛtʃiku, ka] adj poetic.

➡ **poética** f ARTE poetics (sg).

poetizar [4] [pwetʃi'za(x)] <> vi [fazer versos] to write poetry. <> vt [tornar poético] to poeticize.

pogrom [po'grõ] m pogrom.

pois ['pojʃ] conj -1. [portanto] therefore. -2. [mas] well. -3. [porque] as.

➡ **pois bem** loc adv well then.

➡ **pois então** loc adv well then.

➡ **pois é** loc adv indeed.

➡ **pois não** <> loc adv [em loja, restaurante]: ~ não? can I help you? <> interj of course!

➡ **pois sim** interj: ~ sim! certainly not!, yeah right!

polaco, ca [po'laku, ka] <> adj Polish. <> m, f Pole.

➡ **polaco** m [língua] Polish.

polainas [po'lãjnaʃ] fpl gaiters.

polar [po'la(x)] adj polar.

polaridade [polari'dadʒi] f polarity.

polarizar [4] [polari'za(x)] vt to polarize.

polca ['powka] f polka.

polegada [pole'gada] f inch.

polegar [pole'ga(x)] (pl -es) m thumb.

poleiro [po'lejru] m perch.

polêmico, ca [po'lemiku, ka] adj controversial.

➡ **polêmica** f controversy.

polemista [pole'miʃta] adj argumentative.

polemizar [4] [polemi'za(x)] vi: ~ **sobre algo** to debate on sthg.

pólen ['pɔlẽ] m pollen.

polenta [po'lẽnta] f polenta.

polia [po'lia] f pulley.

poliamida [polja'mida] f polyamide.

polichinelo [poliʃi'nɛlu] m Mr Punch.

polícia [po'lisja] <> f [corporação] police, police force; ~ **de choque** riot police; ~ **federal** federal police; ~ **militar** state police (force); ~ **rodoviária** traffic police. <> mf [policial] police officer.

policial [poli'sjaw] (pl -ais) <> adj police (antes de subst). <> mf police officer.

policiamento [polisja'mẽntu] m policing.

policiar [16] [poli'sja(x)] vt -1. [vigiar] to police. -2. [controlar] to control.

➡ **policiar-se** vp [controlar-se] to control o.s.

policlínica [poli'klinika] f general hospital.

policultura [polikuw'tura] f mixed farming.

polidez [poli'deʒ] f [cortesia] politeness.

polido, da [po'lidu, da] adj -1. [cortês] polite. -2. [liso] polished. -3. [lustroso] shiny.

poliéster [po'ljɛʃte(x)] m polyester.

poliestireno [poljeʃtʃi'renu] m polystyrene.

polietileno [poljetʃi'lenu] m polythene.

poligamia [poli'gamia] f polygamy.

polígamo, ma [po'ligamu, ma] adj polygamous.

poliglota [poli'glɔta] <> adj polyglot. <> m polyglot.

polígono [po'ligonu] m GEOM polygon.

polimento [poli'mẽntu] m -1. [lustração] polishing. -2. fig [finura] refinement.

polinização [poliniza'sãw] (pl -ões) f pollination.

polinizar [4] [polini'za(x)] <> vt to pollinate. <> vi to pollinate.

polinômio [poli'nomju] m MAT polynomial.

poliomielite [poljo'mjelitʃi] f MED polio(myelitis).

pólipo ['polipu] m MED polyp.

polir [60] [po'li(x)] vt -1. [ger] to polish. -2. fig [aprimorar- pessoa] to refine; [- linguagem] to polish up.

polissílabo [poli'silabu] (f -ba) [ba] adj polysyllabic.

➡ **polissílabo** m polysyllable.

politécnica [pɔli'tɛknika] f polytechnic.

política [po'litʃika] f ⊳ **político**.

politicagem [politʃi'kaʒẽ] f politicking.

político, ca [po'litʃiku, ka] adj -1. POL political. -2. fig [hábil] astute.

➡ **político** m politician.

➡ **política** f -1. [ciência] politics (pl). -2. [programa] policy; **política econômica** economic policy; **política de boa vizinhança** good neighbour policy UK, good neighbor policy US. -3. fig [habilidade] astuteness.

politiqueiro, ra [politʃi'kejru, ra] <> pej <> adj politicking. <> m, f political wheeler-dealer.

politização [politʃiza'sãw] (pl -ões) f politicization.

politizar [4] [politʃi'za(x)] vt to politicize.

➡ **politizar-se** vp to become politically aware.

polivalente [poliva'lẽntʃi] adj -1. [versátil] versatile. -2. MED polyvalent.

pólo ['pɔlu] m -1. [ger] pole. -2. fig [extremo] side. -3. ASTRON: ~ **magnético** magnetic pole. -4. [concentração] hub; ~ **petroquímico** petrochemicals complex. -5. ESP polo; ~ **aquático** water polo.

Polônia [po'lonja] n Poland.

polpa ['powpa] f pulp.

polpudo, da [pow'pudu, da] adj -1. [fruta] fleshy. -2. [vultuoso] sizeable.

poltrão, ona [pow'trãw, ɔna] (mpl -ões, fpl -s) m, f coward.

poltrona [pow'trona] f armchair.

poluente [po'lwẽntʃi] <> adj pollutant. <> m pollutant.

poluição [poluj'sãw] f pollution.

poluidor, ra [poluj'do(x), ra] adj polluting.

poluir [74] [po'lwi(x)] vt -1. [sujar] to pollute. -2. fig [corromper] to corrupt.

polvilhar [4] [powvi'ʎa(x)] vt -1. [cobrir de pó] to powder. -2. [salpicar] to sprinkle.

polvilho [pow'viʎu] m -1. [pó] powder. -2. [farinha] manioc flour.

polvo [ˈpowvul] *m* octopus.

pólvora [ˈpɔwvora] *f* gunpowder; **descobrir a ~ fig** *irôn* to do sthg highly original.

polvorosa [powvoˈrɔza] *f*: **em ~** [agitado] in a flap; [desarrumado] in a mess.

pomada [poˈmada] *f* ointment.

pomar [poˈma(x)] (*pl* -es) *m* orchard.

pombo, ba [ˈpõbu, ba] *m, f* dove, pigeon.

➡ **pomba** *interj* for heaven's sake!

pombo-correio [ˌpõbukoˈxeju] (*pl* **pombos-correios**) *m* -**1.** [ave] carrier pigeon. -**2.** *fig* [pessoa] go-between.

pomo [ˈpomu] *m* pome; **~ de discórdia** bone of contention.

pomo-de-Adão [ˌpomudʒjaˈdãw] (*pl* **pomos-de-Adão**) *m* Adam's apple.

pompa [ˈpõpa] *f* splendour.

pomposo, osa [põˈpozu, ɔza] *adj* ostentatious.

ponche [ˈpõʃi] *m* punch.

poncheira [põˈʃejra] *f* punchbowl.

poncho [ˈpõʃu] *m* poncho.

ponderação [põderaˈsãw] *f* -**1.** [reflexão] reflection. -**2.** [prudência] care.

ponderado, da [põdeˈradu, da] *adj* cautious.

ponderar [4] [põdeˈra(x)] ⟨⟩ *vi* -**1.** [refletir] to reflect. -**2.** [argumentar] to hold forth. ⟨⟩ *vt* -**1.** [avaliar] to weigh up. -**2.** [considerar] to consider.

pônei [ˈponej] *m* pony.

ponta [ˈpõta] *f* -**1.** [extremidade] end; **na ~ do pé** on tiptoe; **na ~ do dedo** at one's fingertips. -**2.** [bico] point. -**3.** [canto] corner. -**4.** [vértice] apex. -**5.** *fig* [quantidade]: **estou com uma ~ de fome** I'm a touch hungry. -**6.** [de cigarro] cigarette end. -**7.** *CINE* & *TEATRO*: **fazer uma ~** to have a walk-on part. -**8.** *COM*: **~ de estoque** excess stock. -**9.** *GEOGR*: **~ de terra** point. -**10.** *loc*: **saber na ~ da língua** to have on the tip of one's tongue.

ponta-cabeça [ˌpõtakaˈbesa] *f*: **de ~** head first.

pontada [põˈtada] *f* -**1.** [dor] twinge. -**2.** [ferroada] sting.

ponta-de-lança [ˌpõtadʒiˈlãnsa] (*pl* **pontas-de-lança**) *mf* *FUT* attacker.

ponta-direita [ˌpõtadʒiˈrejta] (*pl* **pontas-direitas**) *mf* *FUT* right-winger.

ponta-esquerda [ˌpõtajʃˈkexda] (*pl* **pontas-esquerdas**) *mf* *FUT* left-winger.

pontal [põˈtaw] (*pl* -ais) *m* [de terra] promontory.

pontão [põˈtãw] (*pl* -ões) *m* [plataforma] pontoon.

pontapé [põtaˈpɛ] *m* -**1.** [chute] kick; **dar um ~ em alguém** to kick sb. -**2.** *fig* [rejeição]: **ele levou um ~ da namorada** his girlfriend kicked him out.

pontaria [põtaˈria] *f* aim.

ponte [ˈpõtʃi] *f* -**1.** [ger] bridge; **~ levadiça** drawbridge; **~ suspensa** *ou* **pênsil** suspension bridge. -**2.** *AERON*: **~ aérea** air lift. -**3.** *MED*: **~ de safena** (heart) bypass operation.

pontear [15] [põˈtʃja(x)] *vt* -**1.** [pontilhar] to dot. -**2.** [dar pontos] to sew.

ponteira [põˈtejra] *f* tip.

ponteiro [põˈtejru] *m* -**1.** [de velocímetro] pointer. -**2.** [de bússola] needle. -**3.** [de relógio] hand.

pontiagudo, da [põtʃjaˈgudu, da] *adj* pointed.

pontificar [12] [põtʃifiˈka(x)] *vi* to pontificate.

pontífice [põˈtʃifisi] *m* pope.

pontilhado, da [põtʃiˈʎadu, da] ⟨⟩ *adj* dotted. ⟨⟩ *m* [conjunto de pontos] dotted line.

pontilhar [4] [põtʃiˈʎa(x)] *vt* to dot.

pontinha [põˈtʃiɲa] *f*: **estar/ficar com uma ~ de inveja de algo/alguém** to feel a little envious of sthg/sb.

ponto [ˈpõtu] *m* -**1.** [ger] point; **~ final** terminus; **~ de ônibus** bus stop; **~ de táxi** taxi rank; **~ pacífico** established fact. -**2.** [costura, operação] stitch; **~ de meia** stocking stitch; **~ de tricô** garter stitch; **dar ~s** to put in stitches. -**3.** [sinal] spot. -**4.** [pontuação]: **~ (final)** full stop *UK*, period *US*; **dois ~s** colon; **~ de interrogação/exclamação** question/exclamation mark. -**5.** [mancha] mark. -**6.** [livro de presença] register; **assinar o ~** to sign in; **~ facultativo** optional day off. -**7.** [de calda] consistency. -**8.** [matéria escolar] topic. -**9.** *fig* [fim]: **pôr um ~ final em algo** to put and end to sthg. -**10.** *MÚS* (religious) chant. -**11.** *GEOGR*: **~ cardeal** cardinal point. -**12.** *AUTO*: **~ morto** neutral. -**13.** [espírit] spirit. -**14.** [boca-de-fumo] drugs den. -**15.** [traço]: **~ fraco** weak point. -**16.** *loc*: **dormir no ~** to miss the boat; **entregar os ~s** to give up; **não dar ~ sem nó** to look after number one.

➡ **a ponto de** *loc adv* on the point of.

pontocom [põtuˈkɔ] *adj* *ECON*: **empresa ~** dotcom company.

ponto-de-venda [ˌpõtudʒiˈvenda] (*pl* **pontos-de-venda**) *m* *COM* outlet.

pontões [põˈtõjʃ] *pl* ➡ **pontão**.

ponto-e-vírgula [ˌpontwiˈvixgula] (*pl* **ponto-e-vírgulas**) *m* semicolon.

pontuação [põtwaˈsãw] (*pl* -ões) *f* punctuation.

pontual [põˈtwaw] (*pl* -ais) *adj* punctual.

pontualidade [põtwaliˈdadʒi] *f* punctuality.

pontuar [4] [põˈtwa(x)] ⟨⟩ *vi* to punctuate. ⟨⟩ *vt* to punctuate.

pontudo, da [põˈtudu, da] *adj* pointed.

poodle [ˈpudow] *m* poodle.

pool [puw] *m* pool.

POP (*abrev de* **Post Office Protocol**) *m* POP.

popa [ˈpopa] *f* stern.

população [populaˈsãw] (*pl* -ões) *f* population; **~ operária** working population; **~ escolar** school population.

populacional [populasjoˈnaw] (*pl* -ais) *adj* population (*antes de subst*).

popular [popuˈla(x)] (*pl* -es) ⟨⟩ *adj* popular. ⟨⟩ *m* [homem da rua] ordinary person.

popularidade [populariˈdadʒi] *f* popularity.

popularizar [4] [populariˈza(x)] *vt* to popularize.

➡ **popularizar-se** *vp* to become popular.

populismo [popuˈliʒmu] *m* *POL* populism.

populista [popuˈliʃta] *adj* populist.

populoso, osa [popuˈlozu, ɔza] *adj* populous.

pôquer ['poke(x)] *m* poker.

por [po(x)] *prep* **-1.** [indica causa] because of, due to; **foi ~ sua causa** it was your fault; **~ falta de fundos** due to lack of funds; **~ hábito** through force of habit. **-2.** [indica objetivo] for; **lutar ~ algo** to fight for sthg. **-3.** [indica meio, modo, agente] by; **foi escrito pela Cristina** it was written by Cristina; **~ correio/fax** by post/fax; **~ escrito** in writing; **~ avião** [carta] (by) air mail. **-4.** [relativo a tempo] for; **ele partiu ~ duas semanas** he went away for two weeks. **-5.** [relativo a lugar] through; **entramos no Brasil pelo Paraguai** we crossed into Brazil via Paraguay; **está ~ aí** it's around there somewhere; **~ onde você vai?** which way are you going?; **vamos ~ aqui** we're going this way. **-6.** [relativo a troca, preço] for; **paguei apenas 20 reais ~ este casaco** I only paid 20 reals for this coat; **troquei o carro velho ~ um novo** I exchanged my old car for a new one. **-7.** [indica distribuição] per; **25 ~ cento** 25 per cent; **são 100 reais ~ dia/mês** it's 100 reals per day/month. **-8.** [em locuções]: **~ que** why; **~ que (é que) ...?** why (is it that) ...?; **~ mim tudo bem!** that's fine by me!

pôr [45] ['po(x)] *vt* **-1.** [ger] to put; **~ a mesa** to set the table; **~ a roupa** to put on clothes; **~ defeito em tudo** to find fault with everything; **~ a culpa em alguém** to put the blame on sb; **~ o dedo na ferida** *fig* to touch a raw nerve. **-2.** [incutir]: **não lhe ponha medo!** don't frighten him! **-3.** [guardar] to keep. **-4.** [desovar] to lay.
➤ **pôr-se** *vp* **-1.** [colocar-se] to stand; **~-se de pé** to stand up. **-2.** [sol] to set. **-3.** [começar]: **~-se a fazer algo** to start doing sthg; **~-se a caminho** to set off.

porão [po'rãw] (*pl* -ões) *f* **-1.** [de navio] hold. **-2.** [de casa] basement.

porca ['pɔxka] *f* **-1.** *ZOOL* sow. **-2.** [parafuso] nut.

porcalhão, lhona [poxka'ʎãw, ʎona] (*mpl* -ões, *fpl* -s) ◇ *adj* **-1.** [imundo] filthy. **-2.** [que faz sujeira] messy. **-3.** [que trabalha mal] bungling. ◇ *m, f* **-1.** [imundo] filthy person. **-2.** [quem faz sujeira] messy person. **-3.** [quem trabalha mal] bungler.

porção [pox'sãw] (*pl* -ões) *f* [parte] portion; **uma ~ de** a portion of; [grande quantidade] a lot of.

porcaria [poxka'ria] ◇ *adj* [sem valor] rubbishy. ◇ *f* **-1.** [imundície] filth. **-2.** *fig* [coisa malfeita] piece of junk. **-3.** *fig* [coisa sem valor] rubbish.

porcelana [poxse'lãna] *f* porcelain.

porcentagem [poxsẽn'taʒẽ] (*pl* -ns) *f* percentage.

porco, ca ['poxku, ka] ◇ *adj* **-1.** [suja] dirty. **-2.** [grosseiro] coarse. **-3.** [malfeito] shoddy. ◇ *m, f* **-1.** *ZOOL* pig. **-2.** *CULIN* pork. **-3.** [pessoa] *fam* pig.

porções [pox'sõjʃ] *pl* ▷ **porção**.

pôr-do-sol [ˌpoxdu'sɔw] (*pl* pores-do-sol) *m* sunset.

porco-espinho [ˌpoxkwiʃ'piɲu] (*pl* porcos-espinhos) *m* porcupine.

porém [po'rẽj] ◇ *conj* [contudo] but, however. ◇ *m* [obstáculo] snag.

pormenor [poxme'nɔ(x)] (*pl* -es) *m* detail.

pormenorizar [4] [poxmenori'za(x)] *vt* to detail.

pornô [pox'no] ◇ *adj inv fam* porn. ◇ *m* *CINE* porn film.

pornochanchada [poxnoʃãn'ʃada] *m* *CINE* soft porn film *UK*, soft porn movie *US*.

pornografia [poxnogra'fia] *f* pornography.

pornográfico, ca [poxno'grafiku, ka] *adj* pornographic.

poro ['pɔru] *m* pore.

porões [po'rõjʃ] *pl* ▷ **porão**.

pororoca [poro'rɔka] *f* [onda] bore.

POROROCA

Word of Tupi origin, meaning 'thundering crash'; it describes the encounter of the waters of the Amazon with the Atlantic Ocean. Creating waves over 5m high and destroying everything in its passage, this phenomenon occurs mainly in March and is one of the main tourist attractions in Amazonia.

---

poroso, osa [po'rozu, ɔza] *adj* porous.

porquanto [pox'kwãntu] *conj* since.

porque [pux'ke] *conj* because; **ela trabalha ~ precisa** she works because she needs to; **~ sim** just because.

porquê [pux'ke] *m*: **o ~** the reason (for); **não entendo o ~ dessa atitude** I don't understand the reason for that attitude.

porquinho-da-Índia [pox,kiɲuda'ĩndʒja] (*pl* porquinhos-da-Índia) *m* guinea pig.

porra ['pɔxa] ◇ *f vulg* [esperma] spunk. ◇ *interj vulg* [exprime irritação] fucking hell!; **mas que ~!** fuck!

porrada [po'xada] *mfam* *f* **-1.** [pancada]: **ele deu uma ~ com o carro no muro** he smashed the car into the wall; **o garçom levou uma ~ do bêbado** the waiter took one hell of a beating from the drunkard. **-2.** [quantidade]: **uma ~ de** loads of. **-3.** *fig* [revés] fuck-up.

porra-louca [ˌpoxa'loka] (*pl* porras-loucas) *fam* ◇ *adj* crazy. ◇ *mf* nutter.

porre ['pɔxi] *fam* *m* **-1.** [bebedeira] booze-up; **estar/ficar de ~** to be plastered; **tomar um ~** to get a skinful. **-2.**: **ser um ~** [pessoa, festa] to be a drag.

porretada [poxe'tada] *m* beating.

porrete [po'xetʃi] *m* club.

porta ['pɔxta] *m* **-1.** [peça] door; **~ corrediça** sliding door; **~ dos fundos** back door; **~ da frente/da rua** front/street door; **~ giratória** revolving door. **-2.** *fig* [possibilidade, saída] opportunity. **-3.** *COMPUT*: **~ paralela** parallel port; **~ serial** serial port.

porta-aviões [ˌpɔxta'vjõjʃ] *m inv* aircraft carrier.

porta-bandeira [ˌpɔxtabãn'dejra] (*pl* porta-bandeiras) *mf* standard-bearer.

portador, ra [poxta'do(x), ra] (*mpl* -es, *fpl* -s) ◇ *adj* **-1.** [de vírus, doença] carrying. **-2.** [de notícias] bearing. ◇ *m, f* **-1.** [de bagagem, AIDS] carrier.

- **2.** [de títulos, letras de câmbio, notícias] bearer; **ao ~** [cheque, ação] to the bearer.

porta-estandarte [ˌpɔxtiʃtãnˈdaxtʃi] (*pl* **porta-estandartes**) *mf* standard-bearer.

porta-guardanapos [ˌpɔxtagwaxdaˈnapuʃ] *m inv* napkin holder.

porta-jóias [ˌpɔxtaˈʒɔjaʃ] *m inv* jewellery box.

portal [poxˈtaw] (*pl* **-ais**) *m* **-1.** [pórtico] doorway. **- 2.** *COMPUT* portal.

porta-luvas [ˌpɔxtaˈluvaʃ] *m inv AUTO* glove compartment.

porta-malas [ˌpɔxtaˈmalaʃ] *m inv AUTO* boot *UK*, trunk *US*.

porta-moedas [ˌpɔxtaˈmwɛdaʃ] *m inv* [porta-níqueis] purse.

portanto [poxˈtãntu] *conj* therefore.

portão [poxˈtãw] (*pl* **-ões**) *m* gate.

portar [4] [poxˈta(x)] *vt* [carregar] to carry.

➡ portar-se *vp* [comportar-se] to behave.

porta-retratos [ˌpɔxtaxeˈtratuʃ] *m (inv)* photo frame.

porta-revistas [ˌpɔxtaxeˈviʃtaʃ] *m (inv)* magazine rack.

portaria [poxtaˈria] *f* **-1.** [de edifício] entrance hall. **- 2.** [documento oficial] order; **baixar uma ~** to issue a decree.

portátil [poxˈtatʃiw] (*pl* **-eis**) *adj* portable.

porta-voz [ˌpɔxtaˈvɔjʃ] (*pl* **porta-vozes**) *mf* spokesperson.

porte [ˈpɔxtʃi] *m* **-1.** [transporte] carriage. **- 2.** [preço] charge; **~ pago** post paid. **- 3.** [postura] bearing. **- 4.** [tamanho] scale; **de grande/médio/ pequeno ~** large/medium/small-sized. **- 5.** [importância] stature; **de grande ~** of great stature. **- 6.** [licença]: **~ de arma** gun permit.

porteiro, ra [poxˈtejru, ra] *m, f* [de edifício] caretaker *UK*, janitor *US*; **~ eletrônico** entryphone.

➡ porteira *f* [cancela] gate.

portento [poxˈtẽntu] *m* marvel.

portentoso, osa [poxtẽnˈtozu, ɔza] *adj* marvellous.

portfolio [portˈfɔlju] *m* portfolio.

pórtico [ˈpɔxtʃiku] *m* portico.

portinhola [poxtʃiˈɲɔla] *f* **-1.** [pequena porta] small door, trapdoor. **- 2.** [postigo] window.

Port Louis [ˌpɔxtʃˈlujʃ] *n* Port Louis.

Port Moresby [ˌpɔxtʃˈmɔreʒbil *n* Port Moresby.

porto [ˈpoxtul *m* port; **~ de escala** port of call; **~ livre** freeport.

Porto Alegre [ˌpoxtwaˈlɛgril *n* Porto Alegre.

portões [poxˈtõjʃ] *pl* ⊳ **portão**.

Porto Príncipe [ˌpoxtuˈprĩnsipil *n* Port-au-Prince.

Porto Rico [ˌpoxtuˈxikul *n* Puerto Rico.

Porto Velho [ˌpoxtuˈvɛʎul *n* Porto Velho.

portuário, ria [poxˈtwarju, rja] *adj* port (*antes de subst*).◇ *m, f* [funcionário] port official.

Portugal [poxtuˈgaw] *n* Portugal.

português, esa [poxtuˈgeʃ, eza] (*mpl* **-eses**, *fpl* **-s**) ◇ *adj* Portuguese. ◇ *m, f* Portuguese person.

➡ português *m* [língua] Portuguese.

portunhol [poxtuˈɲɔw] *m* mixture of Portuguese and Spanish.

porventura [poxvẽnˈtural *adv* by chance; **se ~ você ...** if you happen to ...

porvir [poxˈvi(x)] *m* future.

posar [4] [poˈza(x)] *vi* **-1.** [fazer pose] to pose. **- 2.** [bancar]: **~ de** to pose as.

pós-datado, da [ˌpɔjʃdaˈtadu, da] (*mpl* **-s**, *fpl* **-s**) *adj* post-dated.

pós-datar [ˌpɔjʃdaˈta(x)] *vt* to postdate.

pose [ˈpɔzil *f* **-1.** [de modelo etc] pose. **- 2.** *pej* [afetação] affectedness; **ela está com muita ~ desde sua promoção** she's full of airs and graces since being promoted; **fazer ~ de** to pretend to be.

pós-escrito [ˌpɔjʃiʃˈkritul (*pl* **pós-escritos**) *m* postscript, PS.

pós-graduação [ˌpɔjʃgradwaˈsãwl (*pl* **pós-graduações**) *f* qualifying for a degree as a postgraduate *UK* or graduate *US* student.

pós-graduado, pós-graduada [ˌpɔjʃgraˈdwadu, da] (*mpl* **pós-graduados**, *fpl* **pós-graduadas**) ◇ *adj* postgraduate *UK*, graduate student *US*. ◇ *m, f* postgraduate *UK*, graduate *US*.

pós-guerra [ˌpɔjʃˈgɛxal (*pl* **pós-guerras**) *m* postwar (*antes de sust*).

posição [poziˈsãwl (*pl* **-ões**) *f* **-1.** [ger] position; **tomar uma ~** to take a stand. **- 2.** [arranjo] positioning.

posicionamento [pozisjonaˈmẽntul *m* **-1.** [maneira de colocar] positioning. **- 2.** [opinião] position.

posicionar [4] [pozisjoˈna(x)] *vt* **-1.** [ger] to position. **- 2.** [funcionário] to place.

➡ posicionar-se *vp* **-1.** [ger] to take up position. **- 2.** [opinar] to take a stand. **- 3.** [tomar atitude] to make a stand.

positivista [pozitʃiˈviʃtal ◇ *adj* positivist. ◇ *mf* positivist.

positivo, va [poziˈtʃivu, val *adj* positive.

➡ positivo ◇ *m FOT* positive. ◇ *interj fam* [sim] affirmative.

posologia [pozoloˈʒial *f* dosage.

pós-operatório, a [ˌpɔjʃopeʰaˈtɔrju, rja] (*mpl* **-s**, *fpl* **-s**) ◇ *adj* post-operative. ◇ *m* postoperative period.

pós-parto [ˌpɔjʃˈpaxtul (*pl* **pós-partos**) *m* postnatal period.

pospor [45] [poʃˈpo(x)] *vt* **-1.** [pôr depois] to put after. **- 2.** [adiar] to postpone.

posposto, ta [poʃˈpoʃtu, tal *adj* **-1.** [posto depois] put after. **- 2.** [adiado] postponed.

possante [poˈsãntʃil *adj* powerful.

posse [ˈpɔsil *f* **-1.** [de bens] ownership; **pessoa de ~s** person of means. **- 2.** [ocupação] possession; **tomar ~ de** to take possession of. **- 3.** [investidura] swearing-in; **cerimônia de ~** swearing-in ceremony; **tomar ~** to take office.

➡ posses *fpl* [bens] possessions.

posseiro, ra [poˈsejru, ral *m, f* leaseholder.

possessão [poseˈsãwl (*pl* **-ões**) *f* possession.

possessivo, va [pose'sivu, va] *adj* possessive.
→ **possessivo** *m GRAM* possessive.
possesso, sa [po'sesu, sa] ◇ *adj* [furioso] enraged. ◇ *m, f* possessed person.
possibilidade [posibili'dadʒi] *f* **-1.** [gen] possibility. **-2.** [oportunidade] opportunity.
possibilitar [4] [posibili'ta(x)] *vt* to make possible.
possível [po'sivɛw] (*pl* **-eis**) ◇ *adj* possible. ◇ *m*: **o ~** what is possible; **fazer o ~** to do one's best.
possivelmente [posivew'mẽntʃi] *adv* possibly.
possuidor, ra [poswi'do(x), ra] *adj*: **ser ~ de** to be the owner of.
possuir [74] [po'swi(x)] *vt* [ter] to have.
posta [ˈpɔʃta] *f* [pedaço] piece; **~ de peixe** piece of fish.
postal [poʃ'taw] (*pl* **-ais**) ◇ *adj* post, postage. ◇ *m* postcard.
postar [4] [poʃ'ta(x)] *vt* to post.
→ **postar-se** *vp* to position o.s.
posta-restante [ˌpɔʃtaxeʃ'tãntʃi] (*pl* **postas-restantes**) *f* poste restante.
poste [ˈpɔʃtʃi] *m* **-1.** [haste] post. **-2.** *ELECTR:* **~ de iluminação** lamp post; **~ telegráfico** telegraph pole.
pôster [ˈpoʃte(x)] (*pl* **-es**) *m* poster.
postergar [14] [poʃtex'ga(x)] *fml vt* **-1.** [adiar] to postpone. **-2.** [desprezar] to set aside.
posteridade [poʃteri'dadʒi] *f* posterity.
posterior [poʃte'rjo(x)] (*pl* **-es**) *adj* **-1.** [no tempo] later. **-2.** [traseiro] rear.
postiço, ça [poʃ'tʃisu, sa] *adj* false.
postigo [poʃ'tʃigu] *m* small door.
posto, ta [ˈpoʃtu, ˈpɔʃta] *pp* ▷ **pôr**.
→ **posto** *m* **-1.** [ger] post; **~ de gasolina** petrol station *UK*, gas station *US*; **~ de salvamento** first-aid post; **~ de saúde** health centre *UK*, health center *US*. **-2.** [de polícia] station. **-3.** [diplomático] posting.
→ **a postos** *loc adv* at the ready.
→ **posto que** *loc conj* since.
posto-chave [ˌpoʃtu'ʃavi] (*pl* **postos-chave**) *m* key position.
postulado [poʃtu'ladu] *m* assumption.
postulante [poʃtu'lãntʃi] ◇ *adj* candidate. ◇ *mf* applicant, candidate.
postular [4] [poʃtu'la(x)] *vt* **-1.** [pedir] to request. **-2.** [teorizar] to postulate. **-3.** *JUR* to apply for.
póstumo, ma [ˈpɔʃtumu, ma] *adj* posthumous.
postura [poʃ'tura] *m* **-1.** [ger] posture. **-2.** [municipal] position. **-3.** *fig* [atitude] point of view.
posudo, da [po'zudu, da] *adj* affected.
potássio [po'tasju] *m* potassium.
potável [po'tavɛw] (*pl* **-eis**) *adj*: **água ~** drinking water.
pote [ˈpɔtʃi] *m* pot, jar.
potência [po'tẽnsja] *m* **-1.** [ger] power. **-2.** [sexual] potency.
potenciação [potẽnsia'sãw] (*pl* **-ões**) *f* [mat] exponentiation.

potencial [potẽn'sjaw] (*pl* **-ais**) ◇ *adj* potential. ◇ *m* potential; **o poder econômico em ~ do país é enorme** the country's potential economic power is great.
potencialidade [potẽnsjali'dadʒi] *f* [capacidade de realização] potencial.
potentado [potẽn'tadu] *m* potentate.
potente [po'tẽntʃi] *adj* powerful.
pot-pourri [pupu'xi] *m* pot-pourri.
potro [ˈpotru] *m* colt.
pouca-vergonha [ˌpokavex'goɲa] (*pl* **poucas-vergonhas**) *f* **-1.** [ato] disgrace. **-2.** [falta de vergonha] shamelessness.
pouco, ca [ˈpoku, ka] ◇ *adj* little; **de pouca importância** of little importance; **faz ~ tempo, tempo (atrás)** a short time ago; (*pl*) few; **poucas pessoas** few people. ◇ *pron* little; (*pl*) few; **muito ~s** very few; **~s** [pessoas] few; **dizer/ouvir poucas e boas** to tell/hear some home truths.
→ **pouco** *m*: **um ~** a little; **um ~ de** a little; **nem um ~ (de)** not at all; **aos ~s** gradually.
→ **pouco** *adv* little; **dormi ~** I hardly slept; **isso é ~ comum** that's uncommon, that's rare; **há ~** a short time ago; **daqui a ~, dentro em ~** shortly; **por ~ o carro não me atropelou** the car nearly ran me over; **~ a ~** little by little; **fazer ~ de** [zombar] to make fun of; [menosprezar] to belittle.
pouco-caso [ˌpoku'kazu] *m* contempt; **ele fez ~ da minha história** he treated my story with contempt.
poupador, ra [popa'do(x), ra] *adj* thrifty.
poupança [po'pãnsa] *f* **-1.** [economia] saving. **-2.** [fundo]: **(caderneta de) ~** savings account (book).
poupar [4] [po'pa(x)] ◇ *vt* **-1.** [economizar] to save. **-2.** [resguardar]: **~ alguém (de algo)** to spare sb (from sthg). **-3.** [respeitar] to spare. ◇ *vi* [economizar] to save.
→ **poupar-se** *vp* [eximir-se] to spare o.s.
pouquinho [po'kiɲu] *m*: **um ~ (de algo)** a little (sthg).
pouquíssimo, ma [po'kisimu, ma] *superl* ▷ **pouco**.
pousada [po'zada] *f* **-1.** [hospedaria] inn. **-2.** [hospedagem] lodging.
pousar [4] [po'za(x)] ◇ *vi* **-1.** [aterrissar] to land. **-2.** [baixar] to settle. **-3.** [pernoitar] to spend the night. **-4.** [assentar] to rest. ◇ *vt* to put.
pouso [ˈpozu] *m* **-1.** [aterrissagem] landing; **~ de emergência** emergency landing. **-2.** [lugar de descanso] bolt-hole.
povão [po'vãw] *m* hoi polloi (*pl*).
povaréu [pova'rɛw] *m* [multidão] crowd.
povo [ˈpovu] *m* **-1.** [habitantes] people. **-2.** [multidão] crowd. **-3.** [família, amigos] family.
povoação [povwa'sãw] (*pl* **-ões**) *f* **-1.** settlement. **-2.** [aldeia] village. **-3.** [habitantes] population.
povoado, da [po'vwadu, da] ◇ *adj* populated. ◇ *m* [aldeia] village.
povoamento [povwa'mẽntu] *m* settlement.

povoar [20] [po'vwa(x)] *vt* to populate.

poxa ['poʃa] *interj* gosh!

PPB (*abrev de* **Partido Progressista Brasileiro**) *m* Brazilian Progressive Party, *a right-wing party*.

PPS (*abrev de* **Partido Popular Socialista**) *m* Popular Socialist Party, *a centre-right party*.

PR (*abrev de* **Estado do Paraná**) *m State of Paraná*.

pra ['pra] *fam* = **para**, **para a**.

praça ['prasa] <> *f* **-1.** [largo] square. **-2.** [mercado financeiro] market. **-3.** MIL: ~ **de guerra** fortress. **-4.** [de touros] bull ring. <> *m* MIL [soldado] private (soldier).

pracinha [pra'siɲa] *m Brazilian soldier in World War II*.

prado ['pradu] *m* **-1.** [campo] meadow. **-2.** [hipódromo] racecourse.

pra-frente [,pra'frẽntʃi] *adj inv fam* trendy.

praga ['praga] *f* **-1.** [ger] curse; **rogar uma** ~ **a alguém** to curse sb. **-2.** [doença] scourge. **-3.** ZOOL plague. **-4.** [pessoa chata] pest.

Praga ['praga] *n* Prague.

pragmático, ca [prag'matʃiku, ka] *adj* pragmatic.

pragmatismo [pragma'tʃiʒmu] *m* pragmatism.

praguejar [4] [prage'ʒa(x)] *vi:* ~ **(contra)** to curse (at).

praia ['praja] *f* beach.

prancha ['prãnʃa] *f* **-1.** [tábua] plank. **-2.** [de surfe] board. **-3.** NÁUT gangplank. **-4.** FERRO open wagon.

prancheta [prãn'ʃeta] *f* **-1.** [mesa de desenho] drawing board. **-2.** [suporte para escrever] board.

pranto ['prãntu] *m* weeping.

prata ['prata] *f* **-1.** [metal] silver; **de** ~ silver *(antes de subst)*; ~ **de lei** sterling silver. **-2.** *fam* [dinheiro] pennies *(pl)*.

prataria [prata'ria] *f* **-1.** [objetos de prata] silverware. **-2.** [pratos] crockery.

prateado, da [pra'tʃjadu, da] <> *adj* **-1.** [cor] silver *(antes de subst)*. **-2.** *fig* [brilhante] silvery. <> *m* silver.

pratear [15] [pra'tʃja(x)] *vt* [com prata] to silver.

prateleira [prate'lejra] *f* shelf.

prática ['pratʃika] *f* ▷ **prático**.

praticamente [pratʃika'mẽntʃi] *adv* practically.

praticante [pratʃi'kãntʃi] <> *adj* practising UK, practicing US. <> *mf* practitioner.

praticar [12] [pratʃi'ka(x)] <> *vt* **-1.** [cometer] to commit. **-2.** [exercer] to practise UK, to practice US. <> *vi* [exercitar] to practise US, to practice US.

praticável [pratʃi'kavɛw] (*pl* **-eis**) *adj* **-1.** [realizável] feasible. **-2.** [transitável] passable.

prático, ca ['pratʃiku, ka] <> *adj* practical. <> *m, f* NÁUT pilot.

➡ **prática** *f* practice; **na** ~ in practice; **pôr em** ~ to put into practice.

prato ['pratu] *m* **-1.** [louça] plate; ~ **fundo** soup plate; ~ **raso** dinner plate; ~ **de sobremesa** dessert plate. **-2.** [comida] dish; ~ **do dia** dish of the day; ~ **principal/segundo** ~ main/second course; ~ **de resistência** *fig* pièce de résistance.

- 3. MÚS cymbal. **- 4.** [de toca-disco] turntable. **- 5.** [de balança] scale pan. **- 6.** *loc:* **cuspir no** ~ **em que comeu** to bite the hand that feeds one; **vamos pôr isso em** ~s **limpos!** let's clear this up!; **ser um** ~ **cheio** to be manna from heaven.

praxe ['praʃi] *f* habit; **ter como** ~ to be in the habit of; **ser de** ~ to be customary.

prazenteiro, ra [prazẽn'tejru, ra] *adj* cheerful.

prazer [pra'ze(x)] (*pl* **-es**) *m* **-1.** pleasure. **-2.** [em apresentação]: **muito** ~ **(em conhecê-lo)** delighted (to meet you).

prazeroso, sa [prazeˈrozu, ɔza] *adj* pleasant.

prazo ['prazu] *m* **-1.** [tempo] period; **tenho um** ~ **de trinta dias para pagá-lo** I have thirty days in which to pay him, I have to pay him within thirty days; **a** ~ on credit; **a curto/médio/longo** ~ in the short/medium/long term. **-2.** [vencimento] deadline; ~ **final** final deadline.

preamar [prea'ma(x)] *f* high tide.

preâmbulo [pre'ãnbulu] *m* **-1.** [prefácio] foreword. **-2.** [introdução] preamble.

preaquecer [25] [prjake'se(x)] *vt* to preheat.

pré-aviso [prea'vizu] (*pl* **pré-avisos**) *m* (advance) notice.

precariedade [prekarje'dadʒi] *m* precariousness.

precário, ria [pre'karju, rja] *adj* **-1.** [ger] precarious. **-2.** [escasso] scarce.

precatória [preka'torja] *f* JUR writ.

precaução [prekaw'sãw] (*pl* **-ões**) *f* caution.

precaver-se [50] [preka'vexsi] *vp* **-1.** [prevenir-se]: ~ **de** *ou* **contra algo** to be forearmed against sthg. **-2.** [preparar-se]: ~ **para algo** to prepare o.s. for sthg.

precavido, da [preka'vidu, da] *adj* cautious.

prece ['prɛsi] *f* **-1.** [oração] prayer. **-2.** [súplica] supplication.

precedência [presen'dẽsja] *f* precedence; **ter** ~ **sobre** to take precedence over.

precedente [prese'dẽntʃi] <> *adj* precedent. <> *m* precedent; **sem** ~s unprecedented.

preceder [5] [prese'de(x)] <> *vt* to precede; ~ **algo de** to precede sthg with. <> *vi:* ~ **a** to precede.

preceito [pre'sejtu] *m* precept.

preceptor [presep'to(x)] *m* tutor.

precificação [presifika'sãw] (*pl* **-ões**) *f* pricing policy.

precificar [presifi'ka(x)] *vt* to price.

preciosidade [presjozi'dadʒi] *f* gem.

preciosismo [presjo'ziʒmu] *m* preciosity.

precioso, osa [pre'sjozu, ɔza] *adj* **-1.** [ger] precious. **-2.** [importante] important. **-3.** [fino, rico] fine.

precipício [presi'pisju] *m* **-1.** [abismo] precipice. **- 2.** *fig* [desgraça] hole.

precipitação [presipita'sãw] (*pl* **-ões**) *f* **-1.** [ger] haste. **- 2.** METEOR precipitation.

precipitado, da [presipi'tadu, da] *adj* hasty.

precipitar [4] [presipi'ta(x)] <> *vt* [antecipar] to precipitate. <> *vi* QUÍM to precipitate.

precipitar-se *vp* -**1.** [ger] to rush. -**2.** [apressar-se] to hurry. -**3.** [despenhar-se] to drop.

precisado, da [presi'zadu, da] *adj*: ~ **de** in need of.

precisamente [pre,siza'mēntʃil] *adv* precisely.

precisão [presi'zāw] *f* -**1.** [exatidão] precision, accuracy. -**2.** [necessidade]: **ter** ~ **de** to be in need of.

precisar [4] [presi'za(x)] <> *vt* -**1.** [ger] to need; ~ **fazer algo** to need to do sthg; **preciso que me ajudem** I need you to help me. -**2.** [indicar] to specify. <> *vi* -**1.** [necessitar] to be in need; ~ **de alguém/algo** to be in need of sb/sthg. -**2.** [ser necessário]: **não precisa** there is no need; **fiz isso sem precisar** I did this when there was no need; '**precisam-se vendedores**' 'salespersons required'; **você precisa da chave para abrir a porta** you need a key to open the door.

preciso, sa [pre'sizu, za] *adj* -**1.** [ger] precise. -**2.** [necessário] necessary.

preço ['presu] *m* -**1.** [ger] price; ~ **de custo** cost price; ~ **à vista** [no comércio] cash price; [na bolsa] spot price; **vou comprar uma Ferrari por qualquer** ~ I am going to buy a Ferrari whatever the cost; **a** ~ **de banana** for peanuts; **não ter** ~ *fig* to be beyond price. -**2.** [importância] value.

precoce [pre'kɔsi] *adj* -**1.** [pessoa] precocious. -**2.** [fruto] early. -**3.** [calvície] premature.

precocidade [prekosi'dadʒi] *f* precociousness.

preconcebido, da [prɛkõnse'bidu, da] *adj* preconceived.

preconceito [prekõn'sejtu] *m* prejudice.

preconizar [4] [prekoni'za(x)] *vt* -**1.** [anunciar] to proclaim. -**2.** [propagar] to spread. -**3.** [elogiar] to praise.

precursor, ra [prekux'so(x), ra] (*mpl* -**es**, *fpl* -**s**) *m, f* precursor.

predador, ra [preda'do(x), ra] (*mpl* -**es**, *fpl* -**s**) <> *adj* predatory. <> *m, f* predator.

pré-datado, da [,prɛda'tadu, da] (*pl* -**s**) *adj* predated.

pré-datar [,prɛda'ta(x)] *vt* to predate.

predatório, ria [preda'tɔrju, rja] *adj* predatory.

predecessor, ra [predese'so(x), ra] (*mpl* -**es**, *fpl* -**s**) *m* predecessor.

predestinado, da [predeʃtʃi'nadu, da] *adj* predestined.

predestinar [4] [predeʃtʃi'na(x)] *vt* to predestine.

predeterminado, da [predetermi'nadu, da] *adj* predetermined.

predeterminar [predetermi'na(x)] *vt* to predetermine.

predial [pre'dʒjaw] (*pl* -**ais**) *adj* ⊳ **imposto**.

predicado [predʒi'kadu] *m* -**1.** [qualidade] quality. -**2.** GRAM predicate.

predição [predʒi'sãw] (*pl* -**ões**) *f* prediction.

predileção [predʒile'sãw] (*pl* -**ões**) *f*: ~ **(por)** predilection (for).

predileto, ta [predʒi'lɛtu, ta] <> *adj* favourite *UK*, favorite *US*. <> *m, f* favourite *UK*, favorite *US*.

prédio ['prɛdʒju] *m* building; ~ **de apartamentos** block of flats *UK*, apartment house *US*; ~ **comercial** commercial building.

predispor [45] [predʒiʃ'po(x)] <> *vt* to predispose. <> *vi*: ~ **a** to predispose to.

predispor-se *vp*: ~**-se a fazer algo** to be predisposed to do sthg.

predisposição [predʒiʃpozi'sãw] *f* predisposition.

predisposto, osta [predʒiʃ'poʃtu, ɔʃta] *adj* -**1.** [ger] predisposed. -**2.** [à doença] prone.

predizer [29] [predʒi'ze(x)] <> *vt* to predict, to forecast. <> *vi* [profetizar] to make predictions.

predominância [predomi'nãnsja] *f* predominance.

predominante [predomi'nãntʃil] *adj* predominant.

predominar [4] [predomi'na(x)] *vi* to predominate.

predomínio [predo'minju] *m* -**1.** [supremacia] supremacy. -**2.** [influência] predominance.

pré-eleitoral [,prɛelejto'raw] (*pl* -**ais**) *adj* pre-election (*antes de subst*).

preeminência [preemi'nẽnsja] *f* pre-eminence.

preeminente [preemi'nẽntʃil] *adj* pre-eminent.

preencher [5] [preẽn'ʃe(x)] *vt* -**1.** [completar - formulário, lacunas] to fill in; [- buracos] to fill. -**2.** [ocupar- tempo, férias] to spend; [- cargo, vaga] to fill. -**3.** [satisfazer] to fulfil *UK*, to fulfill *US*.

preenchimento [preẽnʃi'mẽntul *m* -**1.** [de formulário, espaço em branco] filling in. -**2.** [de cargo, vaga, buraco] filling. -**3.** [de requisitos] fulfilment.

pré-escolar [,prɛiʃko'la(x)] (*pl* **pré-escolares**) *adj* pre-school (*antes de subst*).

preestabelecer [25] [,preeʃtabele'se(x)] *vt* to pre-establish.

pré-estréia [,prɛiʃ'trɛja] (*pl* -**s**) *f* preview.

preexistente [preeziʃ'tẽntʃil] *m* pre-existing.

preexistir [6] [preeziʃ'tʃi(x)] *vi* to pre-exist; ~ **a algo** to pre-exist sthg.

pré-fabricado, da [,prɛfabri'kadu, da] *adj* prefabricated.

prefaciar [16] [prefa'sja(x)] *vt* to preface.

prefácio [pre'fasju] *m* preface.

prefeito, ta [pre'fejtu, ta] *m, f* mayor.

prefeitura [prefej'tural *f* town hall.

preferência [prefe'rẽnsja] *f* -**1.** [precedência] priority; **dar** ~ **a** to give preference to. -**2.** AUTO: **ter** ~ to have priority. -**3.** [predileção] preference; **de** ~ preferably; **ter** ~ **por** to have a preference for.

preferencial [preferẽn'sjaw] (*pl* -**ais**) <> *adj* priority (*antes de subst*). <> *f* main road.

preferido, da [prefe'ridu, da] *adj* favourite *UK*, favorite *US*.

preferir [57] [prefe'ri(x)] *vt*: ~ **algo (a algo)** to prefer sthg (to sthg); **prefiro que você fique** I would prefer you to stay.

preferível [prefe'rivew] (*pl* -**eis**) *adj*: ~ **(a)** preferable (to).

prefigurar [4] [prefigu'ra(x)] *vt* to prefigure.

prefixo [pre'fiksu] *m* prefix.

prega ['prɛga] *f* - **1.** [dobra - em papel, pano] fold; [- na saia] pleat. - **2.** [ruga] wrinkle.

pregado, da [pre'gadu, da] *adj* - **1.** [fixado] nailed. - **2.** [olhos] glued. - **3.** [cansado] exhausted.

pregador [prega'do(x)] *m* - **1.** [orador] preacher. - **2.** [utensílio]: ~ **de roupa** clothes peg.

pregão [pre'gãw] (*pl* -ões) *m* - **1.** [proclamação] cry. - **2.** *BOLSA* trading. - **3.** [em leilão] bidding.

pregar [14] [pre'ga(x)] <> *vt* - **1.** [ger] to fix; ~ **os olhos em alguém/algo** to stare at sb/sthg; **não preguei os olhos a noite toda** I didn't sleep a wink all night. - **2.** [com prego] to nail. - **3.** [infligir]: ~ **algo em alguém** to inflict sthg on sb; ~ **um susto em alguém** to give sb a fright; ~ **uma mentira em alguém** to tell sb a lie; ~ **uma peça em alguém** to play a trick on sb. - **4.** *RELIG* [louvar] to preach. <> *vi* - **1.** [pronunciar sermão] to preach. - **2.** [clamar]: ~ **por/contra algo** to preach for/against sthg. - **3.** [cansar-se] to collapse.

prego ['prɛgu] *m* - **1.** [peça] nail. - **2.** [casa de penhor] pawn shop; **pôr algo no** ~ to pawn sthg. - **3.** [cansaço] exhaustion; **dar o** ~ to collapse.

pregões [pre'gõjʃ] *pl* > **pregão.**

pré-gravado, da [ˌprɛgra'vadu, da] (*pl* -s) *adj* pre-recorded.

pregresso, sa [pre'grɛsu, sa] *adj* earlier.

preguear [15] [pre'gja(x)] *vt* - **1.** [saia] to pleat. - **2.** [calça] to put a crease in.

preguiça [pre'gisa] *f* - **1.** [indolência] laziness; **estar com** ~ **(de fazer algo)** to be too lazy (to do sthg). - **2.** [animal] sloth.

preguiçoso, osa [pregi'sozu, ɔza] <> *adj* lazy. <> *m, f* lazy person.

pré-história [ˌprɛiʃ'tɔrja] *f* prehistory.

pré-histórico, ca [prɛiʃ'tɔriku, ka] *adj* prehistoric.

preia ['prɛja] *f* prey.

preia-mar [ˌprɛja'ma(x)] (*pl* preia-mares) *f* high tide.

prejudicar [12] [preʒudʒi'ka(x)] *vt* - **1.** [afetar] to damage. - **2.** [transtornar] to disrupt. - **3.** [depreciar] to impair.

prejudicial [preʒudʒi'sjaw] (*pl* -ais) *adj* harmful.

prejuízo [pre'ʒwizu] *m* - **1.** [dano] damage. - **2.** [financeiro] loss.

prejulgar [14] [preʒuw'ga(x)] *vt* to prejudge.

prelado [pre'ladu] *m* prelate.

preleção [prele'sãw] (*pl* -ões) *f* lecture.

preliminar [prelimi'na(x)] <> *adj* preliminary. <> *f* [partida] preliminary.

prelo ['prɛlu] *m* [printing] press; **no** ~ in print.

prelúdio [pre'ludʒju] *m* prelude.

prematuro, ra [prema'turu, ra] *adj* - **1.** [bebê] premature. - **2.** [colheita, fruta] early.

pré-medicação [ˌprɛmed3ika'sãw] (*pl* -ões) *f* pre-medication.

premeditado, da [premed3i'tadu, da] *adj* premeditated.

premeditar [4] [premed3i'ta(x)] *vt* to premeditate.

premência [pre'mẽnsja] *f* urgency.

pré-menstrual [ˌprɛmẽnʃ'trwaw] (*pl* -ais) *adj* premenstrual.

premente [pre'mẽntʃil] *adj* urgent.

premiado, da [pre'mjadu, da] <> *adj* prizewinning. <> *m, f* prizewinner.

premiar [16] [pre'mja(x)] *vt* - **1.** [dar prêmio] to award a prize to. - **2.** [recompensar] to reward.

premiê [pre'mje] , **premier** [pre'mje] *m* premier.

prêmio ['premju] *m* - **1.** [em concurso, jogo] prize; ~ **de consolação** consolation prize. - **2.** [recompensa] reward. - **3.** [seguro] premium. - **4.** *ESP*: **Grande Prêmio** [de turfe, automobilismo] Grand Prix.

premissa [pre'misa] *f* premise.

pré-moldado, da [ˌprɛmow'dadu, da] (*pl* -s) *adj* precast.

➡ **pré-moldado** *m* [bloco] breeze block *UK*, cinder block *US*.

premonição [premuni'sãw] (*pl* -ões) *f* premonition.

premonitório, ria [premuni'tɔrju, rja] *adj* premonitory.

pré-natal [ˌprɛna'taw] (*pl* pré-natais) *adj* antenatal *UK*, prenatal *US*.

prenda ['prẽda] *f* - **1.** [presente] present. - **2.** [em jogo] forfeit.

➡ **prendas** *fpl*: ~ **s domésticas** housework (*inv*).

prendado, da [prẽ'dadu, da] *adj* gifted.

prendedor [prẽde'do(x)] *m* peg; ~ **de papel** paper clip; ~ **de cabelo** hairgrip; ~ **de gravata** tie clip.

prender [5] [prẽ'de(x)] <> *vt* - **1.** [pregar] to fasten. - **2.** [amarrar] to tie. - **3.** [reter] to keep. - **4.** [capturar] to arrest. - **5.** [atrair] to capture. - **6.** [afetivamente] to unite. - **7.** [impedir] to restrict. <> *vi* [ficar preso]: ~ **em algo** to catch on sthg.

➡ **prender-se** *vp* - **1.**: ~ -**se a alguém** [afeiçoar-se] to grow attached to sb; [em relacionamento] to tie o.s. down to sb. - **2.** [preocupar-se]: ~ -**se a algo** to get caught up in sthg.

prenhe ['prɛɲil] *adj* pregnant.

prenome [pre'nɔmil] *m* forename.

prensa ['prẽsa] *f* - **1.** [ger] press. - **2.** *fam*: **dar uma** ~ **em alguém** to tighten the screws on sb.

prensar [4] [prẽ'sa(x)] *vt* - **1.** [na prensa] to compress. - **2.** [fruta] to squeeze. - **3.** [pessoa]: ~ **alguém contra algo** to press sb against sthg.

prenunciar [16] [prenũ'sja(x)] *vt* to forewarn.

prenúncio [pre'nũsjo] *m* harbinger; **essas nuvens são um** ~ **de chuva** clouds are a sign of rain.

preocupação [preokupa'sãw] (*pl* -ões) *f* concern.

preocupante [preoku'pãntʃil] *adj* worrying.

preocupar [4] [preoku'pa(x)] *vt* [inquietar] to worry.

➡ **preocupar-se** *vp*: ~ -**se (com algo/alguém)** to worry (about sthg/sb).

preparação [prepara'sãw] (*pl* -ões) *f* [preparo] preparation.

preparado, da [prepa'radu, da] *adj* - **1.** [disposto] ready. - **2.** [instruído] well prepared.

➡ **preparado** *m* *FARM* preparation.

preparar [4] [prepa'ra(x)] *vt* to prepare.
➤ **preparar-se** *vp* -**1.** [aprontar-se] to get ready.
-**2.** [instruir-se]: ∼-**se para algo** to train for sthg.
preparativos [prepara'tʃivuʃ] *mpl* preparations,
arrangements.
preparo [pre'paru] *m* -**1.** [preparação] preparation. -**2.** [condição]: ∼ **físico** physical fitness.
preponderância [prepõnde'rãnsja] *f* preponderance.
preponderante [prepõnde'rãntʃi] *adj* prepon-
derant, predominant.
preponderar [4] [prepõnde'ra(x)] *vi* to prepon-
derate; ∼ **sobre algo** to prevail over sthg.
preposição [prepozi'sãw] (*pl* -**ões**) *f* preposition.
preposto, ta [pre'poʃtu, ta] *m, f* [representante]
representative.
prepotência [prepo'tẽnsja] *f* -**1.** [grande poder]
forcefulness. -**2.** [despotismo] tyranny.
prepotente [prepo'tẽntʃi] *adj* -**1.** [poderoso]
forceful. -**2.** [despótico] overbearing.
prepúcio [pre'pusju] *m* prepuce.
prerrogativa [prexoga'tʃiva] *f* prerogative.
presa ['preza] *f* -**1.** [na guerra] spoils (*pl*). -**2.** [preia]
prey. -**3.** [dente] fang. -**4.** [garra] talon. -**5.** [vítima]
slave. -**6.** [mulher encarcerada] (female) prisoner.
presbiteriano, na [preʒbite'rjãnu, na] ⬦ *adj*
Presbyterian. ⬦ *m, f* Presbyterian.
presbítero [preʃ'biʃteru] *m* [padre] priest.
presciência [pre'sjẽnsja] *f* [previsão] prescience.
presciente [pre'sjẽntʃi] *adj* prescient.
prescindir [6] [presĩn'dʒi(x)] *vi*: ∼ **de algo** [dispen-
sar] to do without sthg; [abstrair] to disregard
sthg.
prescindível [presĩn'dʒivew] (*pl* -**eis**) *adj* dispensable.
prescrever [5] [preʃkre've(x)] ⬦ *vt* -**1.** [ger] to
prescribe. -**2.** [determinar] to decide. ⬦ *vi* -**1.** [ca-
ir em desuso] to fall into disuse. -**2.** JUR to lapse.
prescrição [preʃkri'sãw] (*pl* -**ões**) *f* -**1.** [ordem]
order. -**2.** MED prescription. -**3.** JUR lapse.
presença [pre'zẽnsa] *f* -**1.** [ger] presence; ∼ **de
espírito** presence of mind; **marcar** ∼ to be
present; **ter boa** ∼ to be well turned out. -**2.**
[em curso etc] attendance.
presenciar [16] [prezẽn'sja(x)] *vt* to witness.
presente [pre'zẽntʃi] ⬦ *adj* -**1.** [ger] present. -**2.**
[evidente] obvious. -**3.** [interessado] concerned. ⬦
m -**1.** [ger] present. -**2.** [pessoa]: **(entre) os** ∼ **s**
(among) those present. -**3.** [regalo] present, gift;
de ∼ as a present; ∼ **de grego** *fig* unwelcome
gift.
presentear [15] [prezẽn'tʃja(x)] *vt*: ∼ **alguém (com
algo)** to give sb (sthg as) a present.
presentemente [prezẽntʃi'mẽntʃil] *adv* at present.
presepada [preze'pada] *f* nonsense.
presépio [pre'zɛpju] *m* crib, Nativity scene.
preservação [prezexva'sãw] (*pl* -**ões**) *f* preservation.
preservar [4] [prezex'va(x)] *vt* to preserve.
➤ **preservar-se** *vp* to protect o.s.

preservativo [prezexva'tʃivu] *m* -**1.** [substância]
preservative. -**2.** [camisinha] condom.
presidência [prezi'dẽnsja] *f* -**1.** [de país] presidency; **assumir a** ∼ to assume the presidency.
-**2.** [de assembléia] chairmanship; **assumir a** ∼ to
take the chair. -**3.** [tempo em excercício] time in
office.
presidencial [prezidẽn'sjaw] (*pl* -**ais**) *adj* presidential.
presidencialismo [prezidẽnsja'liʒmu] *m* presi-
dentialism.
presidenciável [prezidẽn'sjavew] (*pl* -**eis**) ⬦ *adj*
eligible to be president. ⬦ *mf* presidential
candidate.
presidente, ta [prezi'dẽntʃi, ta] *m, f* -**1.** [de país]
president. -**2.** [de assembléia, empresa] chairman.
➤ **Presidente da República** *m* President of
the Republic.
presidiário, ria [prezi'dʒjarju, rja] ⬦ *adj* prison
(*antes de subst*). ⬦ *m, f* convict.
presídio [pre'zidʒju] *m* prison.
presidir [6] [prezi'dʒi(x)] ⬦ *vt* -**1.** [dirigir] to lead.
-**2.** [reger] to rule. ⬦ *vi*: ∼ **a algo** [dirigir] to
preside over sthg; [reger] to rule sthg.
presilha [pre'ziʎa] *f* -**1.** [de suspensório, sapato]
strap. -**2.** [de cabelo] hairslide.
preso, sa ['prezu, za] ⬦ *adj* -**1.** [encarcerado]
imprisoned. -**2.** [detido] detained, under arrest.
-**3.** [atado] tied. -**4.** *fig* [em engarrafamento, casa]
stuck. -**5.** *fig* [ligado]: **ficar** ∼ **a detalhes** to get
bogged down in detail. -**6.** *fig* [casado] spoken
for. -**7.** *fig* [língua, voz] tongue-tied; **ele está com a
voz presa** he has a catch in his voice. ⬦ *m, f*
[prisioneiro] prisoner.
pressa ['prɛsa] *f* -**1.** [velocidade] speed; **às** ∼**s**
quickly; **com** ∼ in a hurry; **sem** ∼ unhurriedly;
vir sem ∼ to take one's time. -**2.** [urgência] rush;
não ter ∼ not to be urgent; **ter** ∼ **de algo/de fazer algo** to be in a hurry for sthg/to do sthg. -**3.**
[precipitação] hastiness.
pressagiar [16] [presa'ʒja(x)] *vt* to foretell.
presságio [pre'saʒju] *m* -**1.** [indício] sign. -**2.** [pres-
sentimento] premonition.
pressão [pre'sãw] (*pl* -**ões**) *f* -**1.** [ger] pressure;
fazer ∼ **sobre alguém** to put pressure on sb;
contra algo pressure against sthg. -**2.** [colchete]
press stud. -**3.** MED: ∼ **alta/baixa** high/low
(blood) pressure; ∼ **arterial** blood pressure.
-**4.** FÍSICA: ∼ **atmosférica** atmospheric pressure.
pressentimento [presẽntʃi'mẽntul] *m* premonition.
pressentir [56] [presẽn'tʃi(x)] *vt* -**1.** [pressagiar] to
foresee. -**2.** [suspeitar] to suspect. -**3.** [perceber] to
sense.
pressionar [4] [presjo'na(x)] *vt* -**1.** [apertar] to
press. -**2.** *fig* [coagir]: ∼ **alguém (a fazer algo)** to
pressurize sb (into doing sthg).
pressões [pre'sõjʃ] *pl* ➭ **pressão**.
pressupor [45] [presu'po(x)] *vt* to assume.
pressuposto, osta [presu'poʃtu, ɔʃta] *pp* ➭
pressupor.

➤ **pressuposto** *m*: partir de um ~ to assume.
pressurização [presuriza'sãw] *f* pressurization.
pressurizado, da [presuri'zadu, da] *adj* pressurized.
prestação [preʃta'sãw] (*pl* -**ões**) *f* -**1.** [ger] instalment *UK*, installment *US*; **ele só compra à** ~ he only buys on hire purchase. -**2.** [acerto]: ~ **de conta** accounts rendered. -**3.** [trabalho]: ~ **de serviço** services rendered.
prestamista [preʃta'miʃta] *mf* moneylender.
prestar [4] [preʃ'ta(x)] <> *vt* -**1.** [conceder]: ~ **algo (a alguém)** [favores] to grant sthg (to sb); [informações] to provide (sb with) sthg. -**2.** [dispensar]: ~ **algo (a alguém)** to provide (sb with) sthg. -**3.** [apresentar]: ~ **algo (a alguém)** to present sthg (to sb). -**4.** [fazer]: ~ **algo (a alguém/algo)** to provide sthg (to sb/sthg); ~ **atenção** to pay attention. -**5.** [dedicar]: ~ **algo a alguém** to pay sthg to sb. <> *vi* -**1.** [ser útil]: **essa caneta não presta** this pen isn't any good. -**2.** [ter bom caráter]: **ele não presta!** he's no good!
➤ **prestar-se** *vp* -**1.** [dispor-se]: ~-**se a algo** to accept sthg. -**2.** [servir]: ~-**se a algo** to be fit for sthg.
prestativo, va [preʃta'tʃivu, va] *adj* obliging.
prestes ['prɛʃtʃiʃ] *adj inv*: **estar** ~ **a fazer algo** to be about to do sthg.
presteza [preʃ'teza] *f* -**1.** [prontidão] promptness; **com** ~ promptly. -**2.** [agilidade] agility.
prestidigitação [preʃtʃidʒiʒita'sãw] *f* conjuring.
prestidigitador, ra [preʃtʃidʒiʒita'do(x), ra] (*mpl* -**es**, *fpl* -**s**) *m, f* conjurer.
prestigiar [16] [preʃtʃi'ʒja(x)] *vt* to honour *UK*, to honor *US*.
prestígio [preʃ'tʃiʒju] *m* prestige; **é um escritor de** ~ he is an eminent writer.
prestigioso, osa [preʃtʃi'ʒjozu, ɔza] *adj* prestigious.
préstimo ['prɛʃtʃimu] *m* [utilidade] use.
➤ **préstimos** *mpl* [favores]: **oferecer** ~**s a alguém** to offer one's services to sb.
presumido, da [prezu'midu, da] *adj* [presunçoso] presumptuous.
presumir [6] [prezu'mi(x)] *vt* [supor] to presume.
presunção [prezũ'sãw] (*pl* -**ões**) *f* presumption; **ter a** ~ **de ser algo** to believe o.s. to be sthg.
presunçoso, osa [prezũ'sozu, ɔza] *adj* presumptuous.
presunto [pre'zũntu] *m* -**1.** [de porco] ham. -**2.** *gír crime* [defunto] stiff.
prêt-à-porter [prɛtapox'te] *adj inv* ready-to-wear.
pretendente [pretẽn'dẽntʃi] <> *mf* [candidato]: ~ **a algo** applicant for sthg. <> *m* [de uma mulher] suitor.
pretender [5] [pretẽn'de(x)] *vt* -**1.** [desejar]: ~ **fazer algo** to want to do sthg. -**2.** [ter a intenção de]: ~ **fazer algo** to intend to do sthg; ~ **que** to intend (that).
pretensamente [pretẽnsa'mẽntʃi] *adv* supposedly.

pretensão [pretẽn'sãw] (*pl* -**ões**) *f* -**1.** [aspiração] pretension; ~ **salarial** proposed salary. -**2.** [arrogância] pretentions (*pl*). -**3.** [intenção] aim.
pretensioso, osa [pretẽn'sjozu, ɔza] *adj* pretentious.
pretenso, sa [pre'tẽsu, sa] *adj* [suposto] alleged.
preterir [prete'ri(x)] *vt* -**1.** [desprezar] to scorn. -**2.** [omitir] to omit. -**3.** [deixar de promover] to pass over. -**4.** [substituir] to replace.
pretérito, ta [pre'tɛritu] *adj* past.
➤ **pretérito** *m* GRAM preterite.
pretexto [pre'teʃtu] *m* [desculpa] pretext; **a** ~ **de** under the pretext of.
preto, ta ['pretu, ta] <> *adj* [cor] black; **estar/andar** ~ *fig* to be/look gloomy; **ver as coisas pretas** to look on the dark side. <> *m, f* [pessoa] black (person).
➤ **preto** *m* [cor] black.
preto-e-branco [ˌpretwi'brãŋku] *adj inv* black and white.
pretume [pre'tumi] *m* blackness.
prevalecente [prevale'sẽntʃi] *adj* prevailing.
prevalecer [25] [prevale'se(x)] *vi* -**1.** [predominar] to prevail. -**2.** [ter primazia]: ~ (**a/sobre**) to prevail (over).
➤ **prevalecer-se** *vp*: ~-**se de algo** [aproveitar-se] to avail o.s. of sthg.
prevaricação [prevarika'sãw] (*pl* -**ões**) *f* JUR prevarication.
prevaricar [12] [prevari'ka(x)] *vi* -**1.** [faltar ao dever] to fail to do one's duty. -**2.** [proceder mal] to do wrong. -**3.** [cometer adultério] to stray.
prevenção [prevẽn'sãw] (*pl* -**ões**) *f* -**1.** [precaução]: ~ (**a/contra/de**) prevention (against/of). -**2.** [implicância]: **estar de** ~ **contra** *ou* **com alguém** to pick on sb.
prevenido, da [previ'nidu, da] *adj* -**1.** [precavido] precautious. -**2.** [com dinheiro]: **estar** ~ to be in pocket.
prevenir [58] [previ'ni(x)] *vt* -**1.** [avisar] to warn. -**2.** [evitar] to avoid. -**3.** [proibir] to prohibit.
➤ **prevenir-se** *vp* -**1.** [precaver-se]: ~-**se contra alguém/algo** to protect o.s. against sb/sthg. -**2.** [equipar-se] ~-**se de** to equip o.s. with.
preventivo, va [prevẽn'tʃivu, va] *adj* preventive.
➤ **preventivo** *m* [teste]: (**fazer um**) ~ to have a check-up.
prever [40] [pre've(x)] *vt* -**1.** [conjeturar] to foresee; ~ **que** to foresee (that). -**2.** [profetizar] to predict.
pré-vestibular [ˌprɛveʃtʃibu'la(x)] (*pl* pré-vestibulares) <> *adj preparing for university entrance exam.* <> *m* [curso] *university entrance-exam preparatory course.*
prévia ['prɛvja] *f* ➤ **prévio**.
previamente [ˌprɛvja'mẽntʃi] *adv* previously.
previdência [previ'dẽnsja] *f* precaution; ~ **social** social security.
previdente [previ'dẽntʃi] *adj* -**1.** [que prevê] provident. -**2.** [cauteloso] cautious.
prévio, via ['prɛvju, vja] *adj* -**1.** [anterior] previous. -**2.** [preliminar] preliminary.

prévia f - **1.** [pesquisa eleitoral] opinion poll. - **2.** [eleição interna de um partido] leadership elections.

previsão [previ'zãw] (pl -ões) f prediction; ~ do tempo weather forecast.

previsível [previ'zivɛw] (pl -eis) adj predictable.

previsto, ta [pre'viʃtu, ta] <> pp ▷ **prever.** <> adj - **1.** [prognosticado] foreseen. - **2.** [calculado] predicted. - **3.** [em lei] prescribed.

prezado, da [pre'zadu, da] adj - **1.** [estimado] prized. - **2.** [em carta]: **Prezado Senhor** Dear Sir.

prezar [4] [pre'za(x)] vt - **1.** [gostar muito] to cherish. - **2.** [respeitar] to respect.

▶ **prezar-se** vp [respeitar-se] to have self-respect.

primado [pri'madu] m [primazia] primacy.

prima-dona [,prima'dona] (pl prima-donas) f prima donna.

primar [4] [pri'ma(x)] vi - **1.** [destacar-se] to excel. - **2.** [esmerar-se]: ~ **em** to excel in.

primário, ria [pri'marju, rja] adj - **1.** [ger] primary. - **2.** [primitivo] primitive.

▶ **primário** m [curso] primary education UK, elementary education US.

primata [pri'mata] m primate.

primavera [prima'vɛra] f - **1.** [estação] spring. - **2.** BOT primrose.

primaveril [primave'riw] (pl -is) adj spring (antes de subst).

primaz [pri'majʒ] m primate.

primazia [prima'zia] f - **1.** [prioridade] priority. - **2.** [superioridade] primacy.

primeira [pri'mejra] f ▷ **primeiro.**

primeira-dama [pri,mejra'dãma] (pl primeiras-damas) f first lady.

primeiranista [primejra'niʃta] mf first-year student.

primeiro, ra [pri'mejru, ra] <> num first. <> adj [inicial] first; ~ **grau** EDUC middle school; ~ **s socorros** first aid; **à primeira vista** at first sight. <> m, f - **1.** [em ordem]: **ela foi o ~ a chegar** she was the first to arrive. - **2.** [o melhor]: **é o ~ na turma** he is the top of the class.

▶ **primeiro** <> adv [em primeiro lugar] first. <> m [andar] first.

▶ **primeira** f AUTO first; **passar a primeira** to get into first.

▶ **de primeira** <> loc adj - **1.** [hotel, restaurante] first-class. - **2.** [carne] prime. <> loc adv [viajar] first class.

primeiro-de-abril [pri,mejrudʒja'briw] (pl primeiros-de-abril) m April fool.

primeiro-ministro, primeira-ministra [pri,mejrumi'niʃtru, pri,mejrami'niʃtra] (mpl primeiros-ministros, fpl primeiras-ministras) m, f prime minister.

primeiro time [pri,mejro'tʃimi] adj inv: **de** ~ tip-top.

primitivo, va [primi'tʃivu, va] adj primitive.

primo, ma ['primu, ma] <> adj [número] prime. <> m, f [parente] cousin; ~ **em segundo grau** second cousin.

primogênito, ta [primo'ʒenitu, ta] <> adj firstborn. <> m, f firstborn.

primo-irmão, prima-irmã [,primwix'mãw, ,primajx'mã] (mpl primos-irmãos, fpl primas-irmãs) m, f first cousin.

primor [pri'mo(x)] m - **1.** [excelência] excellence. - **2.** [beleza] beauty. - **3.** [esmero]: **com** ~ thoroughly.

primordial [primox'dʒjaw] (pl -ais) adj - **1.** [primitivo] primordial. - **2.** [fundamental] fundamental.

primórdio [pri'mɔrdʒju] m [origem] origin.

primoroso, osa [primo'rozu, ɔza] adj perfect.

princesa [prĩ'seza] f princess.

principado [prĩsi'padu] m principality.

principal [prĩsi'paw] (pl -ais) <> adj - **1.** [mais importante - ator] principal; [- rua, praça, entrada] main. - **2.** [fundamental] main. <> m principal.

principalmente [prĩsipaw'mẽtʃi] adv principally.

príncipe ['prĩsipi] m prince.

principesco, ca [prĩsi'peʃku, ka] adj princely.

principiante [prĩsi'pjãntʃi] <> adj budding. <> mf beginner.

principiar [16] [prĩsi'pja(x)] <> vt to begin. <> vi to begin.

princípio [prĩ'sipju] m - **1.** [ger] beginning; **a** ~ at first; **desde o** ~ from the start; **do** ~ **ao fim** from beginning to end. - **2.** [lei, norma, elemento] principle. - **3.** [premissa]: **partir do** ~ to assume.

▶ **princípios** mpl [morais] principles.

▶ **em princípio** loc adv in principle.

prior ['prio(x)] m prior.

prioridade [prjori'dadʒi] f [primazia] priority; **ter** ~ **sobre alguém/algo** to have priority over sb/sthg.

prioritário, ria [prjori'tarju, rja] adj priority (antes de subst).

priorizar [prjori'za(x)] vt [dar prioridade a] to prioritize.

prisão [pri'zãw] (pl -ões) f - **1.** [captura] arrest. - **2.** [encarceramento] imprisonment; ~ **perpétua** life imprisonment; ~ **preventiva** protective custody. - **3.** [cadeia] prison. - **4.** fig [sufoco] (holy) deadlock. - **5.** MED: ~ **de ventre** constipation.

prisioneiro, ra [prizjo'nejru, ra] m, f prisoner.

prisma ['priʒma] m - **1.** [ger] prism. - **2.** fig [perspectiva]: **sob esse** ~ from that angle.

prisões [pri'zõjʃ] pl ▷ **prisão.**

privação [priva'sãw] (pl -ões) f privation.

▶ **privações** fpl [penúria] hardship.

privacidade [privasi'dadʒi] f privacy.

privada [pri'vada] f toilet.

privado, da [pri'vadu, da] adj - **1.** [particular] private. - **2.** [desprovido] deprived.

privar [4] [pri'va(x)] vt: ~ **alguém de algo** to deprive sb of sthg.

▶ **privar-se** vp: ~-**se de algo** to go without sthg.

privativo, va [priva'tʃivu, va] adj [exclusivo] private.

privatização [privatʃiza'sãw] (pl -ões) f privatization.

privatizar [4] [privatʃi'za(x)] *vt* to privatize.

privilegiado, da [privile'ʒjadu, da] *adj* **-1.** [favorecido] privileged. **-2.** [excepcional] exceptional.

privilegiar [16] [privile'ʒja(x)] *vt* to favour *UK*, to favor *US*.

privilégio [privi'lɛʒju] *m* privilege.

pro [pru] = **para + o.**

pró [prɔ] ⟨⟩ *prep* [a favor de] pro. ⟨⟩ *m* [vantagem] pro; **os ∼s e os contras** the pros and cons.

pró- [prɔ] *prefixo* pro-.

proa ['proa] *f* bow.

probabilidade [probabili'dadʒil] *f* probability, likelihood.

problema [pro'blema] *m* problem.

problemático, ca [proble'matʃiku, ka] *adj* problematic.
   ➡ **problemática** *f* problematic.

problematizar [problematʃi'za(x)] *vt* **-1.** [colocar em dúvida] to cast doubt on. **-2.** [dar forma de problema a] to find problems in. **-3.** [tornar difícil] to complicate.

probo, ba ['probu, ba] *adj* honest.

procedência [prose'dẽsja] *f* **-1.** [origem] origin. **-2.** [lugar de saída] point of departure. **-3.** [fundamento]: **não ter ∼** to be unfounded.

procedente [prose'dẽtʃi] *adj* **-1.** [oriundo] originating. **-2.** [lógico] logical.

proceder [5] [prose'de(x)] *vi* **-1.** [ger] to proceed. **-2.** [prosseguir] to continue. **-3.** [comportar-se] to behave; **∼ mal/bem** to behave badly/well. **-4.** [ter fundamento] to have foundation.

procedimento [prosedʒi'mẽtul] *m* **-1.** [comportamento] behaviour *UK*, behavior *US*. **-2.** [método] method. **-3.** *JUR* proceedings *(pl)*.

processador [prosesa'do(x)] *(pl* **-es)** *m COMPUT* processor; **∼ de texto** word processor.

processamento [prosesa'mẽtul] *m* processing; **∼ de dados** data processing; **∼ de texto** text processing.

processar [4] [prose'sa(x)] *vt* **-1.** *JUR* to sue, to prosecute. **-2.** *COMPUT* to process.

processo [pro'sɛsul] *m* **-1.** [*JUR* - ação] legal proceedings *(pl)*, lawsuit; **abrir** *ou* **mover um ∼ contra** to instigate legal proceedings against, to file a lawsuit against; [- documentação] evidence. **-2.** [método] process. **-3.** [estágio] course.

procissão [prosi'sãw] *(pl* **-ões)** *f* procession.

proclamação [proklama'sãw] *(pl* **-ões)** *f* proclamation.

proclamar [4] [prokla'ma(x)] *vt* to proclaim.

Procon (*abrev de* **Fundação de Proteção e Defesa do Consumidor**) *m Brazilian organization for the protection of consumers' rights.*

procrastinar [4] [prokraʃtʃi'na(x)] ⟨⟩ *vt* to put off. ⟨⟩ *vi* to procrastinate.

procriação [prokrja'sãw] *f* procreation.

procriar [16] [pro'krja(x)] ⟨⟩ *vt* [gerar] to engender. ⟨⟩ *vi* [multiplicar] to procreate.

proctologia [proktolo'ʒial *f* proctology.

procura [pro'kura] *f* **-1.** [busca] search; **estar à ∼**

de to be searching for. **-2.** *COM* demand; **a ∼ e a oferta** supply and demand.

procuração [prokura'sãw] *(pl* **-ões)** *f* power of attorney.

procurado, da [proku'radu, da] *adj* sought after; **ser ∼ pela polícia** to be wanted by the police.

procurador, ra [prokura'do(x), ra] *(mpl* **-es,** *fpl* **-s)** *m, f*: **Procurador Geral da República** ≃ state prosecutor.

procurar [4] [proku'ra(x)] ⟨⟩ *vt* **-1.** [buscar - objeto, pessoa] to look for; [- verdade] to seek. **-2.** [requerer] to look for. **-3.** [esforçar-se por]: **∼ fazer algo** to try to do sthg. **-4.** [contatar] to call on. ⟨⟩ *vi* [buscar]: **∼ (por)** to search (for).

prodigalidade [prodʒigali'dadʒil *f* **-1.** [abundância] abundance. **-2.** [generosidade] generosity.

prodígio [pro'dʒiʒjul *m* **-1.** [pessoa] prodigy. **-2.** [maravilha] feat.

prodigioso, osa [prodʒi'ʒozu, ɔza] *adj* prodigious.

pródigo, ga ['prɔdʒigu, ga] *adj* prodigal.

produção [produ'sãw] *(pl* **-ões)** *f* **-1.** [ger] production. **-2.** [volume, obra] output; **∼ em massa** *ou* **em série** mass production.

produtividade [produtʃivi'dadʒil *f* productivity.

produtivo, va [produ'tʃivu, va] *adj* **-1.** [fértil] productive. **-2.** [rendoso] profitable.

produto [pro'dutul *m* **-1.** [ger] product. **-2.** *AGR* produce. **-3.** *ECON*: **∼ interno bruto** gross domestic product. **-4.** *fig* [consequência]: **ser ∼ de** to be the product of.

produtor, ra [produ'to(x), ra] *(mpl* **-es,** *fpl* **-s)** ⟨⟩ *adj* producing; **país ∼ de petróleo** oil-producing country. ⟨⟩ *m, f* producer.
   ➡ **produtora** *f* [empresa] production company.

produzido, da [produ'zidu, da] *adj* [esmerado] trendy.

proeminência [projmi'nẽsjal *f* prominence.

proeminente [projmi'nẽtʃil *adj* prominent.

proeza [pro'ezal *f* feat.

profanação [profana'sãw] *(pl* **-ões)** *f* profanity.

profanar [4] [profa'na(x)] *vt* to desecrate.

profano, na [pro'fãnu, na] *adj* profane.

profecia [profe'sial *f* prophecy.

proferir [57] [profe'ri(x)] *vt* **-1.** [dizer] to utter. **-2.** [decretar] to pronounce.

professar [4] [profe'sa(x)] ⟨⟩ *vt* **-1.** [exercer profissão] to practise *UK*, to practice *US*. **-2.** [propagar] to profess. ⟨⟩ *vi RELIG* to take holy orders.

professo, ssa [pro'fɛsu, sa] *adj* **-1.** *RELIG* avowed. **-2.** *fig* [perito] seasoned.

professor, ra [profe'so(x), ra] *(mpl* **-es,** *fpl* **-s)** *m, f* teacher; **∼ titular** *ou* **catedrático** university professor.

professorado [profeso'radul *m* **-1.** [magistério] professorship. **-2.** [conjunto de professores] teaching profession.

profeta, tisa [pro'fɛta, tʃiza] *m, f* prophet.

profético, ca [pro'fɛtʃiku, ka] *adj* prophetic.

profetisa [profe'tʃizal *f* ⊳ **profeta.**

profetizar [4] [profetʃi'za(x)] ⟨⟩ *vt* to prophesy.

vi to predict the future.

proficiência [profi'sjẽnsja] *f* proficiency.
proficiente [profi'sjẽntʃi] *adj* [capaz] proficient.
profícuo, a [pro'fikwu, kwa] *adj* useful.
profissão [profi'sãw] (*pl* -ões) *f* -1. [ofício] profession. -2. [carreira] professional life. -3. [declaração] statement; ~ **de fé** RELIG profession of faith.
profissional [profisjo'naw] (*pl* -ais) <> *adj* professional. <> *mf* professional; ~ **liberal** *person in a liberal profession.*
profissionalizante [profisjonali'zãntʃi] *adj* [ensino] vocational.
profissionalizar [4] [profisjonali'za(x)] *vt* to professionalize.
➤ **profissionalizar-se** *vp* -1. [pessoa] to turn professional. -2. [atividade] to become professional.
profundamente [profũda'mẽntʃi] *adv* deeply.
profundezas [profũ'dezaʃ] *fpl* depths.
profundidade [profũdʒi'dadʒi] *f* depth; **o mar aqui tem 20 metros de** ~ here the sea is 20 metres deep.
profundo, da [pro'fũndu, da] *adj* -1. [ger] deep. -2. *fig* [intenso - sono, respeito, amor] deep; [- dor] intense; [- ódio] profound.
profusão [profu'zãw] *f* profusion.
profuso, sa [pro'fuzu, za] *adj* profuse.
progenitor, ra [proʒeni'to(x), ra] *m, f* progenitor.
➤ **progenitores** *mpl* parents.
prognosticar [12] [prognoʃtʃi'ka(x)] <> *vt* [predizer] to forecast. <> *vi* MED to make a prognosis.
prognóstico [prog'nɔʃtʃikul *m* -1. [predição] prediction. -2. MED prognosis.
programa [pro'grãma] *m* -1. [plano] programme UK, program US; **fazer um** ~ to go out; ~ **de índio** *fam fig* boring activity. -2. COMPUT program.
programação [programa'sãw] (*pl*-ões) *f* -1. [ger] programming; ~ **orientada a objetos** object-orientated programming; ~ **visual** graphic design. -2. [organização] planning.
programador, ra [programa'do(x), ra] *m, f* -1. [de rádio, empresa] programme planner. -2. COMPUT programmer; ~ **visual** graphic designer.
programar [4] [progra'ma(x)] *vt* -1. [planejar] to plan. -2. COMPUT to program.
programável [progra'mavew] (*pl* -eis) *adj* programmable.
progredir [58] [progre'dʒi(x)] *vi* -1. [prosperar]: ~ **(em algo)** to progress (in sthg). -2. [agravar-se] to progress.
progressão [progre'sãw] (*pl*-ões) *f* progression.
progressista [progre'siʃta] <> *adj* progressive. <> *mf* progressive.
progressivo, va [progre'sivu, va] *adj* progressive.
progresso [pro'grɛsul *m* progress; **fazer** ~**s em algo** to make progress in sthg.
proibição [projbi'sãw] (*pl*-ões) *f.* prohibition.
proibir [77] [proj'bi(x)] *vt* -1. [impedir]: ~ **alguém (de fazer algo)** to prohibit sb (from doing sthg).

-2. [interdizer] to ban. -3. [vedar] to prevent.
proibitivo, va [projbi'tʃivu, va] *adj* prohibitive.
projeção [proʒe'sãw] (*pl* -ões) *f* -1. [ger] projection; **tempo de** ~ running time. -2. *fig* [notoriedade] prominence.
projetar [4] [proʒe'ta(x)] *vt* -1. [ger] to project. -2. [planejar] to plan. -3. ARQUIT to design.
➤ **projetar-se** *vp* -1. [arremessar-se] to throw o.s. -2. [sombra] to be projected. -3. *fig* [ganhar notoriedade] to project o.s.
projétil [pro'ʒɛtʃiw] (*pl*-teis) *m* projectile.
projetista [proʒe'tʃiʃta] <> *adj* planning, design *(antes de subst)*. <> *mf* planner, designer.
projeto [pro'ʒɛtu] *m* -1. [ger] plan. -2. [empreendimento] project. -3. [esboço de texto] draft; ~ **de lei** bill.
projetor [proʒe'to(x)] (*pl*-es) *m* -1. [ger] projector. -2. [holofote] searchlight.
prol [prɔw] *m*: **em** ~ **de** in favour of.
pró-labore [ˌprɔla'bori] (*pl* pró-labores) *m* remuneration.
prolapso [pro'lapsul *m* MED prolapse.
prole ['prɔli] *f* [filhos] offspring.
proletariado [proleta'rjadul *m* proletariat.
proletário, ria [prole'tarju, rja] <> *adj* proletarian. <> *m, f* proletarian.
proliferação [prolifera'sãw] (*pl*-ões) *f* proliferation.
proliferar [4] [prolife'ra(x)] *vi* to proliferate.
prolífico, ca [pro'lifiku, ka] *adj* prolific.
prolixo, xa [pro'liksu, ksa] *adj* -1. [verboso] long-winded. -2. [muito longo] lengthy.
prólogo ['prɔlogul *m* prologue.
prolongado, da [prolõ'gadu, da] *adj* prolonged.
prolongamento [prolõga'mẽntul *m* extension.
prolongar [14] [prolõ'ga(x)] *vt* -1. [duração] to prolong. -2. [extensão] to extend. -3. [adiar] to put off.
➤ **prolongar-se** *vp* -1. [estender-se] to stretch. -2. [durar] to last.
promessa [pro'mɛsal *f* promise.
prometer [5] [prome'te(x)] <> *vt* -1. [ger] to promise. -2. [comprometer-se]: ~ **algo a alguém** to promise sb sthg; ~ **fazer algo** to promise to do sthg. -3. [assegurar]: ~ **algo a alguém** to promise sb sthg. <> *vi* -1. [fazer promessa] to promise. -2. [ter potencial] to be promising.
prometido, da [prome'tʃidu, da] *adj* promised.
➤ **prometido** *m*: **aqui está o** ~ here's what was promised; **cumprir o** ~ to keep one's promise.
promiscuidade [promiʃkwi'dadʒi] *f* promiscuity.
promiscuir-se [74] [promiʃ'kwixsil *vp* [misturar-se]: ~ **(com)** to mix (with).
promíscuo, cua [pro'miʃkwu, kwa] *adj* -1. [sem ordem] disorderly. -2. [sexualmente] promiscuous.
promissor, ra [promi'so(x), ra] (*mpl*-es, *fpl*-s) *adj* promising.
promissória [promi'sɔrja] *f* [nota] promissory note.

promoção [promo'sãw] (*pl* -ões) *f* promotion; **em** ~ on special offer.

promocional [promo'sjonaw] (*pl* -ais) *adj* promotional.

promontório [promõn'tɔrju] *m* promontory.

promotor, ra [promo'to(x), ra] <> *adj* promoting. <> *m, f* promoter; ~ **público** public prosecutor.

promotoria [promoto'ria] *f* [Ministério Público] state prosecutor's office.

promover [5] [promo've(x)] *vt* - **1.** [ger] to promote. - **2.** [funcionário]: ~ **alguém (a)** to promote sb (to).
➡ **promover-se** *vp* [favorecer-se] to make o.s. look good.

promulgação [promuwga'sãw] *f* promulgation.

promulgar [14] [promuw'ga(x)] *vt* to promulgate.

pronome [pro'nɔmi] *m* pronoun; ~ **oblíquo** objective pronoun; ~ **pessoal** personal pronoun.

pronta-entrega [,prõntaẽn'trɛga] (*pl* **pronta-entregas**) *f* [departamento] immediate delivery department; **vocês têm** ~ **do** you do immediate delivery?, do you have an immediate delivery department?

prontidão [prõntʃi'dãw] *f* - **1.** [alerta] readiness; **estar de** ~ to be on the alert. - **2.** [rapidez] promptness.

prontificar-se [12] [prõntʃifi'kaxsi] *vp*: ~ **para algo/a fazer algo** to volunteer for sthg/to do sthg.

pronto, ta ['prõntu, ta] *adj* - **1.** [concluído, preparado] ready. - **2.** (*antes de subst*) [imediato] prompt. - **3.** [rápido] prompt. - **4.** [disposto]: ~ **a fazer algo** ready to do sthg. - **5.** *fam* [sem recursos] broke.
➡ **pronto** *adv* promptly; **de** ~ promptly.

pronto-socorro [,prõntuso'koxu] (*pl* **prontos-socorros**) *m* [hospital] casualty unit *UK*, emergency unit *US*.

prontuário [prõn'twarju] *m* - **1.** [ficha] file. - **2.** [manual] handbook.

pronúncia [pro'nũnsja] *f* - **1.** LING pronunciation. - **2.** JUR pronouncement.

pronunciamento [pronũnsja'mẽntul] *m* - **1.** [declaração] pronouncement. - **2.** JUR judgment.

pronunciar [16] [pronũn'sja(x)] *vt* to pronounce.
➡ **pronunciar-se** *vp* [emitir juizo]: ~-**se sobre/a favor de** to express an opinion about/in favour of.

propagação [propaga'sãw] (*pl* -ões) *f* - **1.** [ger] propagation. - **2.** [disseminação] spread.

propaganda [propa'gãnda] *f* - **1.** [COM - publicidade] advertising; [- anúncio] advert, advertisement; **fazer** ~ **de algo** to advertise sthg. - **2.** POL propaganda. - **3.** [divulgação] spreading.

propagar [14] [propa'ga(x)] *vt* - **1.** [disseminar] to spread. - **2.** BIOL to propagate.
➡ **propagar-se** *vp* - **1.** [ger] to propagate. - **2.** [disseminar-se] to spread.

propalado, da [propa'ladu, da] *adj* (*antes de subst*) known.

propalar [4] [propa'la(x)] *vt* to divulge.

propender [5] [propẽn'de(x)] *vi*: ~ **para** OU **a** to lean towards.

propensão [propẽn'sãw] (*pl* -ões) *f* inclination.

propenso, sa [pro'pẽnsu, sa] *adj*: ~ **a algo/a fazer algo** inclined to sthg/doing sthg.

propiciar [16] [propi'sja(x)] *vt* - **1.** [permitir, favorecer] to favour *UK*, to favor *US*. - **2.** [proporcionar]: ~ **algo a alguém** to allow sb sthg.

propício, cia [pro'pisju, sja] *adj* - **1.** [favorável]: ~ **a algo** propitious for sthg. - **2.** [oportuno] propitious.

propina [pro'pinaʃ] *f* - **1.** [gratificação] tip. - **2.** [ilegal] bribe.

propor [45] [pro'po(x)] *vt* - **1.** [ger] to propose; ~ **(a alguém) que** to propose (to sb) that. - **2.** JUR [ação] to move.
➡ **propor-se** *vp*: ~-**se a fazer algo** [visar] to aim to do sthg; [dispor-se] to offer to do sthg.

proporção [propox'sãw] (*pl* -ões) *f* proportion.
➡ **proporções** *fpl* - **1.** [tamanho] dimensions. - **2.** [importância] proportions.
➡ **à proporção que** *loc adv* as.

proporcionado, da [propoxsjo'nadu, da] *adj* proportionate.

proporcional [propoxsjo'naw] (*pl* -ais) *adj* proportional; ~ **a algo** proportional to sthg.

proporcionar [4] [propoxsjo'na(x)] *vt* - **1.** [propiciar] to provide. - **2.** [harmonizar]: ~ **algo com algo** to adjust sthg to sthg.

proporções [propox'sõjʃ] *pl* ➪ **proporção**.

proposição [propozi'sãw] (*pl* -ões) *f* - **1.** [proposta] proposal. - **2.** [enunciado] proposition.

propositadamente [propozitada'mẽntʃi] *adv* on purpose.

propositado, da [propozi'tadu, da] *adj* intentional.

proposital [propozi'taw] (*pl* -ais) *adj* intentional.

propósito [pro'pɔzitul] *m* intention; **de** ~ on purpose.
➡ **a propósito** *loc adv* [aliás] by the way.
➡ **a propósito de** *loc prep* concerning.
➡ **fora de propósito** *loc adj* unreasonable.

proposto, osta [pro'poʃtu, ɔʃta] <> *pp* ➪ **propor**. <> *adj* proposed.
➡ **proposta** *f* - **1.** [proposição] proposition. - **2.** [oferta] proposal.

propriamente [prɔprja'mẽntʃi] *adv* - **1.** [exatamente] exactly; ~ **dito** per se; **o Estado** ~ **dito** the actual State. - **2.** [adequadamente] suitably.

propriedade [proprje'dadʒi] *f* - **1.** [ger] property; ~ **pública** public property; ~ **privada** private property. - **2.** [direito de propriedade] ownership.

proprietário, ria [proprje'tarju, rja] *m, f* - **1.** [dono] owner. - **2.** [de imóvel de aluguel] landlord.

próprio, pria ['prɔprju, prja] *adj* - **1.** [ger] proper. - **2.** [particular] own; **meu** ~ **apartamento/carro** my own flat/car. - **3.** [apropriado]: ~ **(para)** suitable (for). - **4.** [peculiar] characteristic. - **5.** [mesmo] -self; **o** ~ **cliente do banco** the customer of the bank himself; **falei com o** ~ **presidente** I spoke to the president himself; **eu** ~ I myself; **é o** ~ [ser ele mesmo] speaking.

propulsão [propuw'sãw] *f* propulsion.

propulsor, ra [propuw'so(x), ra] *adj* propelling. ► **propulsor** *m* propellor.

prorrogação [proxoga'sãw] (*pl* -ões) *f* -1. [prolongação] deferment. -2. *FUT* extra time.

prorrogar [14] [proxo'ga(x)] *vt* to defer, to postpone.

prorrogável [proxo'gavew] (*pl* -eis) *adj* deferrable.

prorromper [5] [proxõn'pe(x)] *vi*: ~ **(de)** to burst (out of); ~ **em** to burst into.

prosa ['prɔza] <> *adj* [cheio de si] puffed up. <> *f* -1. *LITER* prose. -2. [conversa] chat. -3. [conversa fiada] chit-chat.

prosador, ra [proza'do(x), ra] *m, f* prose writer.

prosaico, ca [pro'zajku, ka] *adj* prosaic.

proscênio [pro'senju] *m* proscenium.

proscrever [5] [proʃkre've(x)] *vt* -1. [desterrar] to exile. -2. [expulsar] to ban. -3. [proibir] to prohibit. -4. [abolir] to do away with.

proscrito, ta [proʃ'kritu, ta] <> *pp* ▷ **proscrever**. <> *adj* -1. [desterrado] banished. -2. [expulso] outlawed. -3. [proibido] forbidden. <> *m, f* [exilado] exile.

prosear [15] [pro'zja(x)] *vi* to chat.

prosódia [pro'zɔdʒja] *f GRAM* prosody.

prosopopéia [prozopo'pɛjal *f* -1. [em retórica] prosopopoeia. -2. *fig & pej* [discurso] diatribe. -3. *fig & pej* [pose] airs and graces.

prospecção [proʃpek'sãw] (*pl* -ões) *f GEOL* prospecting; ~ **de petróleo** oil exploration.

prospecto [proʃ'pɛktul *m* leaflet.

prospector, ra [proʃpek'to(x), ra] *m, f GEOL* prospector.

prosperar [4] [proʃpe'ra(x)] *vi* -1. [progredir]: ~ **(em algo)** [melhorar] to prosper (in sthg); [ter sucesso] to thrive (in sthg). -2. [enriquecer] to prosper.

prosperidade [proʃperi'dadʒi] *f* -1. [progresso] prosperity. -2. [sucesso] success.

próspero, ra ['prɔʃperu, ra] *adj* -1. [que progride] thriving. -2. [bem-sucedido] prosperous.

prosseguimento [prosegi'mẽntul *m* continuation; **dar** ~ **a** to continue with.

prosseguir [55] [prose'gi(x)] <> *vt* to continue. <> *vi*: ~ **(em algo)** to continue (in sthg); ~ **fazendo algo** to continue doing sthg.

próstata ['prɔʃtatal *f ANAT* prostate.

prostíbulo [proʃ'tʃibulul *m* brothel.

prostituição [proʃtʃitwi'sãw] *f* prostitution.

prostituir [74] [proʃtʃi'twi(x)] *vt* to prostitute. ► **prostituir-se** *vp* -1. [tornar-se prostituta] to turn to prostitution. -2. [ser prostituta] to be a prostitute. -3. *fig* [corromper-se] to prostitute o.s.

prostituta [proʃtʃi'tutal *f* prostitute.

prostração [proʃtra'sãw] *f* prostration.

prostrado, da [proʃ'tradu, da] *adj* prostrate.

prostrar [4] [proʃ'tra(x)] *vt* -1. [ger] to prostrate. -2. [derrubar] to floor.

► **prostrar-se** *vp* [com reverência] to prostrate o.s.

protagonista [protago'niʃtal *mf* protagonist.

protagonizar [4] [protagoni'za(x)] *vt* -1. *CINE* & *TEATRO* to feature in. -2. [acontecimento] to be at the centre of *UK*, to be at the center of *US*.

proteção [prote'sãw] (*pl* -ões) *f* -1. [resguardo] protection. -2. [favorecimento] favour *UK*, favor *US*. -3. [dispositivo] defence *UK*, defense *US*.

protecionismo [protesjo'niʒmul *m* [econômico] protectionism.

proteger [26] [prote'ʒe(x)] *vt* to protect; ~ **alguém de/contra algo** to protect sb from/against sthg.

► **proteger-se** *vp* [resguardar-se] to protect o.s.

protegido, da [prote'ʒidu, dal <> *adj* [resguardado] protected. <> *m, f* [favorito] protégé (*f* protégée).

proteína [prote'inal *f* protein.

protelar [4] [prote'la(x)] *vt* to postpone.

prótese ['prɔtezil *f MED* prosthesis.

protestante [proteʃ'tãntʃil <> *adj* Protestant. <> *mf* Protestant.

protestantismo [proteʃtãn'tʃiʒmul *m* Protestantism.

protestar [4] [proteʃ'ta(x)] <> *vt* -1. [título, promissória] to contest. -2. [declarar] to profess. <> *vi* -1. [reclamar]: ~ **(contra/em favor de algo)** to protest (against/in favour of sthg); **protesto!** *JUR* I protest! -2. [clamar]: ~ **por algo** to call for sthg.

protesto [pro'tɛʃtul *m* -1. [ger] protest. -2. *fml* [declaração] declaration.

protetor, ra [prote'to(x), ra] (*mpl* -es, *fpl* -s) <> *adj* protective. <> *m, f* protector.

protocolar [4] [protoko'la(x)] <> *adj* formal. <> *vt* to register.

protocolo [proto'kɔlul *m* -1. [ger] protocol; **quebrar o** ~ to break with protocol. -2. [registro] registration. -3. [recibo] record. -4. [setor] registry.

protocolo [proto'kɔlul *m COMPUT* protocol.

protótipo [pro'tɔtʃipul *m* -1. [modelo] prototype. -2. *fig* [exemplo]: **ser o** ~ **de algo** to be the epitome of sthg.

protuberância [protube'rãnsjal *f* protuberance.

protuberante [protube'rãntʃil *adj* protuberant.

prova ['prɔval *f* -1. [ger] proof; **tirar a** ~ **dos noves** to cast out 9s. -2. *EDUC* exam. -3. [teste] test; **à** ~ **de água** waterproof; **à** ~ **de bala** bulletproof; **à** ~ **de fogo** fireproof; **pôr algo à** ~ to put sthg to the test. -4. *ESP* event. -5. *COST* fitting. -6. [de comida, bebida] taster.

provação [prova'sãw] (*pl* -ões) *f* ordeal.

provado, da [pro'vadu, dal *adj* -1. [ger] proven. -2. [experimentado] tried.

provador [prova'do(x)] *m* -1. [em loja] fitting room. -2. [de café, vinho] taster.

provar [4] [pro'va(x)] <> *vt* -1. [demonstrar] to prove; ~ **algo por A mais B** to demonstrate sthg step by step. -2. [testar] to test. -3. [roupa] to try on. -4. [comida, bebida] to taste. <> *vi*: ~ **(de algo)**

[comida, bebida] to have a taste (of sthg).

provável [pro'vavɛwl (*pl* **-eis**) *adj* [possível] probable; **é ~ que chova** it looks like rain; **é ~ que ela não chegue hoje** she's not likely to come today.

provavelmente [provavew'mẽntʃil *adv* probably.

provedor, ra [prove'do(x), ral *m, f* provider; **~ de acesso** Internet service provider.

proveito [pro'vejtul *m* advantage; **em ~ de** in favour of; **tirar ~ de algo** to benefit from sthg.

proveitoso, osa [provej'tozu, ɔzal *adj* **- 1.** [vantajoso] advantageous. **- 2.** [lucrativo] profitable. **- 3.** [útil] useful.

proveniência [prove'njẽnsjal *f* origin.

proveniente [prove'njẽntʃil *adj*: **~ de** [originário] originating from; [resultante] arising from; **esta uva é ~ da Itália** these grapes come from Italy.

proventos [pro'vẽntuʃl *mpl* proceeds.

prover [41] [pro've(x)l ◇ *vt* **- 1.** [ger]: **~ algo/alguém de algo** to provide sthg/sb with sthg. **- 2.** [providenciar] to provide. **- 3.** [vaga, cargo] to fill. ◇ *vi* [atender]: **~ a algo** to take care of sthg.

◆ **prover-se** *vp* [abastecer-se]: **~-se de algo** to provide o.s. with sthg.

proverbial [provex'bjawl *adj* proverbial.

provérbio [pro'vɛrbjul *m* proverb.

proveta [pro'vetal *f* test tube; **bebê de ~** test-tube baby.

providência [provi'dẽnsjal *f* [medida] measure; **tomar ~ s** to take measures.

◆ **Providência** *f*: **Divina Providência** (divine) Providence.

providencial [providẽn'sjawl (*pl* **-ais**) *adj* providential.

providenciar [16] [providẽn'sja(x)l ◇ *vt* **- 1.** [prover] to provide. **- 2.** [tomar providências para] to set into motion. ◇ *vi* **- 1.** [cuidar]: **vamos ~ para que tudo dê certo** let's see to it that all works out. **- 2.** [tomar providências]: **~ contra/para algo** to take measures against/for sthg.

provido, da [pro'vidu, dal *adj* [abastecido]: **~ de algo** supplied with sthg; **bem ~** well stocked; **uma conta bancária bem provida** a fat bank account.

provimento [provi'mẽntul *m* **- 1.** [provisão] stocking up. **- 2.** *JUR* granting; **dar ~** to grant a petition.

província [pro'vĩnsjal *f* **- 1.** [divisão administrativa] province. **- 2.** [interior] provinces (*pl*).

provincianismo [provĩnsja'niʒmul *m* provincialism.

provinciano, na [provĩn'sjãnu, nal *adj pej* provincial.

provindo, da [pro'vĩndu, dal ◇ *pp* ▷ **provir**. ◇ *adj*: **~ de** (coming) from.

provir [67] [pro'vi(x)l *vi*: **~ de** to come from.

provisão [provi'zãwl (*pl* **-ões**) *f* supply.

◆ **provisões** *fpl* supplies.

provisoriamente [provizɔrja'mẽntʃil *adv* provisionally.

provisório, ria [provi'zɔrju, rjal *adj* provisional.

provocação [provoka'sãwl (*pl* **-ões**) *f* **- 1.** [implicância] provocation. **- 2.** [sensual] attraction.

provocador, ra [provoka'do(x), ral (*mpl* **-es**, *fpl* **-s**) ◇ *adj* provocative. ◇ *m, f* provoker.

provocante [provo'kãntʃil *adj* [sensualmente] provocative.

provocar [12] [provo'ka(x)l *vt* **- 1.** [ger] to provoke. **- 2.** [incitar]: **~ alguém (a fazer algo)** to provoke sb (into doing sthg). **- 3.** [chamar a atenção, atrair sensualmente] to arouse. **- 4.** [promover] to cause.

provocativo, va [provoka'tʃivu, val *adj* provocative.

proximidade [prosimi'dadʒil *f* **- 1.** [ger] proximity. **- 2.** [afinidade] closeness.

◆ **proximidades** *fpl* [arredores] proximity (*sg*).

próximo, ma ['prɔsimu, mal ◇ *adj* **- 1.** [no espaço]: **~ (a** *ou* **de)** close (to). **- 2.** [no tempo] recent; **futuro ~** near future. **- 3.** (*antes de subst*) [seguinte] next. **- 4.** [chegado] close. ◇ *m, f* [em fila] next (one).

◆ **próximo** ◇ *m*: **o ~** [o semelhante] neighbour *UK*, neighbor *US*. ◇ *adv* close.

◆ **próxima** *f* [a próxima vez]: **até a próxima!** [em despedida] see you soon!; **fica para a próxima** until some other time.

proxy ['prɔʃil (*pl* **proxies**) *m COMPUT* proxy.

prudência [pru'dẽnsjal *f* caution, prudence; **com ~** carefully.

prudente [pru'dẽntʃil *adj* **- 1.** [comedido] prudent. **- 2.** [cauteloso] cautious.

prumo ['prumul *m* **- 1.** [instrumento] plumb line. **- 2.** *NÁUT* lead.

prurido [pru'ridul *m* **- 1.** [comichão] itch. **- 2.** *fig* [desejo] urge.

PS *m* **- 1.** (*abrev de* Post Scriptum) PS. **- 2.** (*abrev de* Pronto Socorro) first aid.

PSB (*abrev de* Partido Socialista Brasileiro) *m* Brazilian socialist party.

PSDB (*abrev de* Partido da Social Democracia Brasileira) *m* Brazilian social democratic party, the second largest right-wing party in Brazil.

pseudônimo [psew'donimul *m* pseudonym.

psicanálise [psika'nalizil *f* psychoanalysis.

psicanalista [psikana'liʃtal *mf* psychoanalyst.

psicanalítico, ca [psikana'litʃiku, kal *adj* psychoanalitical.

psicodélico, ca [psiko'dɛliku, kal *adj* psychedelic.

psicodrama [psiko'drãmal *m* psychodrama.

psicolingüístico, ca [ˌpsikoliŋ'gwiʃtʃiku, kal *adj* psycholinguistic.

◆ **psicolingüística** *f* psycholinguistics (*sg*).

psicologia [psikolo'ʒial *f* psychology.

psicológico, ca [psiko'lɔʒiku, kal *adj* psychological.

psicólogo, ga [psi'kɔlogu, gal *m, f* psychologist.

psicopata [psiko'patal *mf* psychopath.

psicose [psi'kɔzil *f* **- 1.** *MED* psychosis. **- 2.** *fig* [obsessão]: **~ de algo** obsession with sthg.

psicossomático, ca [psikoso'matʃiku, kal *adj* psychosomatic.

psicotécnico, ca [psiko'tɛkniku, ka] *adj* response *(antes de subst)*.
➤ **psicotécnico** *m* [exame] response test.
psicoterapeuta [psikotera'pewta] *mf* psychotherapist.
psicoterapia [psikotera'pia] *f* psychotherapy.
psicótico, ca [psi'kɔtʃiku, ka] *adj* psychotic.
psique ['psiki] *f* psyche.
psiquiatra [psi'kjatra] *mf* psychiatrist.
psiquiatria [psikja'tria] *f* psychiatry.
psiquiátrico, ca [psi'kjatriku, ka] *adj* psychiatric.
psíquico, ca ['psikiku, ka] *adj* psychic.
psiu [psiw] *interj* **-1.** [para chamar] hey! **-2.** [para calar] hush!
psoríase [pso'rjazi] *f* psoriasis.
PT *(abrev de* **Partido dos Trabalhadores)** *m* Brazilian workers' party, the largest left-wing party in Brazil.
PTB *(abrev de* **Partido Trabalhista Brasileiro)** *m* Brazilian Workers' Party, *a* large party of the centre.
pua ['pua] *f* [de broca] bit; **sentar a ~ em alguém** *fig* to put the pressure on sb.
puberdade [puber'dadʒi] *f* puberty.
púbere ['puberi] *adj* pubescent.
púbico, ca ['pubiku, ka] *adj* pubic.
púbis ['pubiʃ] *m inv* pubis.
publicação [publika'sãw] *(pl* **-ões)** *f* publication.
publicar [12] [publi'ka(x)] *vt* **-1.** [ger] to publish. **-2.** [divulgar] to broadcast.
publicidade [publisi'dadʒi] *f* **-1.** [divulgação] publicity; **dar ~ a algo/alguém** to publicize sthg/sb. **-2.** COM advertising.
publicitário, ria [publisi'tarju, rja] <> *adj* advertising *(antes de subst).* <> *m, f* advertiser.
público, ca ['publiku, ka] *adj* public.
➤ **público** *m* **-1.** [o povo] public. **-2.** [platéia] audience; **o grande ~** general public; **em ~** in public.
PUC *(abrev de* **Pontifícia Universidade Católica)** *f* Pontifical Catholic university.
pudico, ca [pu'dʒiku, ka] *adj* **-1.** [recatado] bashful. **-2.** *pej* prudish.
pudim [pu'dʒĩ] *(pl* **-ns)** *m* pudding; **~ de leite** milk pudding; **~ de pão** bread pudding.
pudor [pu'do(x)] *m* **-1.** [recato] modesty; **ter ~ de** [ter vergonha] to be ashamed of. **-2.** [decoro] decency; **atentado ao ~** indecent assault.
puericultura [pwerikuw'tura] *f* childcare.
pueril [pwe'riw] *(pl* **-is)** *adj* childish, puerile.
puerilidade [pwerili'dadʒi] *f* **-1.** [infantilidade] childishness, puerility. **-2.** *fig* [banalidade] foolish action.
pufe ['pufi] *m* pouffe.
pugilismo [puʒi'liʒmu] *m* boxing.
pugilista [puʒi'liʃta] *m* boxer.
pugnaz [pug'najʃ] *adj* pugnacious.
puído, da ['pwidu, da] *adj* frayed.
puir [74] [pwi(x)] *vt* to fray.
pujança [pu'ʒãsa] *f* **-1.** [força, poderio] power. **-2.** [da vegetação] vitality.

pujante [pu'ʒãntʃi] *adj* powerful.
pula-pula [ˌpula'pula] *(pl* **pula-pulas)** *m* **-1.** [brinquedo] pogo (stick). **-2.** [cama elástica] bouncy castle. **-3.** [ave] golden-crowned warbler.
pular [4] [pu'la(x)] <> *vt* **-1.** [saltar] to jump (over); **~ corda** to skip; **~ a cerca** *fig* [trair] to be unfaithful. **-2.** [páginas, trechos] to skip. **-3.: ~ Carnaval** to celebrate carnival. <> *vi* **-1.** [saltar] to jump; **~ de alegria** to jump for joy. **-2.** [palpitar] to skip a beat.
pulga ['puwga] *f* flea; **estar/ficar com a ~ atrás da orelha** to smell a rat.
pulgão [puw'gãw] *(pl* **-ões)** *m* aphid.
pulgueiro [puw'gejru] *m* [cinema] fleapit.
pulha ['puʎa] *m* creep.
pulmão [puw'mãw] *(pl* **-ões)** *m* lung.
pulmonar [puwmo'na(x)] *adj* pulmonary.
pulo ['pulu] *m* leap; **a um ~ de** [perto de] just a hop away from; **dar um ~ em** *fig* [ir] to stop off at.
pulôver [pu'love(x)] *(pl* **-es)** *m* pullover.
púlpito ['puwpitu] *m* pulpit.
pulsação [puwsa'sãw] *(pl* **-ões)** *f* **-1.** [batimento] pulsation. **-2.** MED [pulso] pulse; **medir as pulsações (cardíacas)** to take the pulse.
pulsar [4] [puw'sa(x)] *vi* [palpitar] to beat, to throb.
pulular [4] [pulu'la(x)] *vi* **-1.** [multiplicar-se] to proliferate. **-2.** [abundar]: **~ de** to swarm with, to teem with.
pulverizador [puwveriza'do(x)] *m* [para líquidos] spray.
pulverizar [4] [puwveri'za(x)] *vt* **-1.** [ger] to spray. **-2.** [reduzir a pó] [destruir] to pulverize.
pum [pũ] *(pl* **puns)** <> *m mfam* [peido] fart; **soltar um ~** to pass wind. <> *interj* bang!
pumba ['pũba] *interj* [para ação rápida] whoosh!
punção [pũ'sãw] *(pl* **-ões)** <> *f* MED puncture. <> *m* [instrumento] stylus.
pungente [pũ'ʒẽntʃi] *adj* poignant.
pungir [78] [pũ'ʒi(x)] *vt* ant & *fig* [afligir] to afflict.
punguista [pũ'giʃta] *m* pickpocket.
punhado [pu'ɲadu] *m*: **um ~ de** a handful of.
punhal [pu'ɲaw] *(pl* **-ais)** *m* dagger.
punhalada [puɲa'lada] *f* stab.
punheta [pu'ɲeta] *f vulg* [masturbação] jacking off, wanking *UK*; **bater** *ou* **tocar ~** to jack off, to wank *UK*.
punho ['puɲu] *m* **-1.** ANAT fist; **de próprio ~** in one's own handwriting. **-2.** [de manga] cuff. **-3.** [de espada, punhal] hilt.
punição [puni'sãw] *(pl* **-ões)** *f* punishment.
punir [6] [pu'ni(x)] *vt* to punish.
punitivo, va [puni'tʃivu, va] *adj* punitive.
puns [pũʃ] *mpl* ⊳ **pum**.
pupila [pu'pila] *f* ANAT pupil.
pupilo, la [pu'pilu, la] *m, f* **-1.** [aluno] pupil. **-2.** [tutelado] ward.
purê [pu're] *m* purée, mash; **~ de batatas** mashed potato.
pureza [pu'reza] *f* purity.
purgação [puxga'sãw] *(pl* **-ões)** *f* **-1.** [expiação]

purge. **-2.** [de ferida] cleansing. **-3.** [purificação] purification.

purgante [pux'gãntʃi] *m* **-1.** [remédio] purgative. **-2.** *fam* [pessoa, trabalho] pain in the neck.

purgar [14] [pux'ga(x)] *vt* **-1.** [expiar] to purge. **-2.** [purificar]: ~ **algo (de algo)** to purge sthg (of sthg).

   ➤ **purgar-se** *vp*: ~-**se (de algo)** to purge o.s. (of sthg).

purgativo, va [puxga'tʃivu, va] *adj* purgative.

   ➤ **purgativo** *m* [remédio] purgative.

purgatório [puxga'tɔrju] *m RELIG* purgatory.

purificação [purifika'sãw] (*pl* -ões) *f* **-1.** [depuração] purification. **-2.** *RELIG* [ritual] cleansing.

purificar [12] [purifi'ka(x)] *vt*: ~ **algo (de algo)** [depurar] to cleanse sthg (of sthg).

   ➤ **purificar-se** *vp* to cleanse o.s.

purista [pu'riʃta] *mf* purist.

puritanismo [puritã'niʒmu] *m* puritanism.

puritano, na [puri'tãnu, na] <> *adj* puritanical. <> *m, f* puritan.

puro, ra [‘puru, ra] *adj* **-1.** [ger] pure. **-2.** *(antes de subst)* [mero] pure. **-3.** *(antes de subst)* [absoluto] plain.

puro-sangue [,puru'sãŋgi] (*pl* **puros-sangues**) *mf* thoroughbred.

púrpura [‘puxpura] *f* [cor] purple.

purpúreo, rea [pux'purju, rja] *adj* crimson.

purpurina [puxpu'rina] *f* purpurin.

purulento, ta [puru'lẽntu, ta] *adj* purulent.

pus [‘puʃ] *m inv* pus.

pusilânime [puzi'lãnimi] *adj* pusillanimous.

pústula [‘puʃtula] *f* **-1.** [vesícula] pustule. **-2.** *fig* & *pej* [pessoa] rat.

puta [‘puta] *f* ⊳ **puto.**

putaria [puta'ria] *f vulg* [prostíbulo] knocking shop.

putativo, va [puta'tʃivu, va] *adj* putative.

puto, ta [‘putu, ta] *vulg adj* **-1.** [devasso] rotten; **o** ~ **de ...** *fam* the bloody ... **-2.** [zangado] mad; **estar/ficar** ~ **(da vida)** to be/get furious.

   ➤ **puto** <> *m vulg* [dinheiro] penny *UK*, dime *US* <> *adj* [extraordinário]: **um** ~ **(de um) ...** a brilliant/hell of a ....

   ➤ **puta** *vulg f* [prostituta] whore; **filho da puta** *fig* son of a bitch; **puta que pariu!** fucking hell!; **mandar alguém para a puta que pariu** to tell sb to fuck off.

putrefação [putrefa'sãw] *f* putrefaction.

putrefato, ta [putre'fatu, ta] *adj* rotten.

putrefazer [31] [putrefa'ze(x)] *vt* to putrefy.

   ➤ **putrefazer-se** *vp* to rot.

pútrido, da [‘putridu, da] *adj* rotten.

puxa [‘puʃa] *interj*: ~ **(vida)!** goodness (me)!, gosh.

puxado, da [pu'ʃadu, da] *adj* **-1.** [cansativo] exhausting. **-2.** [difícil] testing. **-3.** [caro] steep. **-4.** [amendoado] almond-shaped.

   ➤ **puxada** *f* **-1.** [puxão] tug. **-2.** [esforço]: **dar uma puxada** [em corrida] to put on a spurt; [nos estudos] to make an effort.

puxador [puʃa'do(x)] (*pl* -es) *mf* **-1.** [de samba] *the leading singer in an 'escola de samba', a group of musicians and samba dancers who perform in street parades during carnival celebrations in Brazil*. **-2.** [de fumo] (marijuana) smoker. **-3.** [ladrão] thief. <> *m* handle.

puxão [pu'ʃãw] (*pl* -ões) *m* tug; **dar um** ~ **em alguém** to pull s.b.

puxa-puxa [,puʃa'puʃa] (*pl* **puxa-puxas**) <> *adj* toffee *(antes de subst)*. <> *m* toffee.

puxar [4] [pu'ʃa(x)] <> *vt* **-1.** [ger] to pull. **-2.** [arrancar, sacar] to pull out. **-3.** [iniciar - conversa] to start (up); [- briga] to break into; [- samba] to start (up), to break into; ~ **assunto** to bring up a subject. **-4.** [desencadear] to bring about; **uma coisa puxa a outra** one thing leads to another. **-5.** [adular]: ~ **o saco de alguém** *fam fig* to suck up to sb. **-6.** *gír droga* [fumo] to smoke. **-7.** *gír crime* [automóvel] to steal. <> *vi* **-1.** [impor esforço a]: ~ **por** to strain. **-2.** [ser parecido com]: ~ **a alguém** to take after sb. **-3.** [mancar]: ~ **de uma perna** to limp.

puxa-saco [,puʃa'saku] (*pl* **puxa-sacos**) *fam* <> *adj* crawling. <> *mf* crawler.

puxões [pu'ʃõjʃ] *pl* ⊳ **puxão.**

PV (*abrev de* **Partido Verde**) *m Brazilian green party.*

PVC (*abrev de* **Polyvinyl Chloride**) *m* PVC.

q, Q [ke] *m* [letra] q, Q.

Qatar [ka'ta(x)] *n* Qatar.

QG (*abrev de* **Quartel General**) *m* HQ.

QI (*abrev de* **Quociente de Inteligência**) *m* IQ.

QT (*abrev de* **Qualidade Total**) *f* TQM.

qua. (*abrev de* **quarta-feira**) *f* Wed.

quadra [‘kwadra] *f* **-1.** [quarteirão] block; ~ **da praia** beachfront block. **-2.** [esportiva] court. **-3.** [em jogos] four. **-4.** [estrofe] quatrain. **-5.** *AGR* [medida] *area of* 48,400m².

quadrado, da [kwa'dradu, da] *m*: **dois ao** ~ two squared.

quadragésimo, ma [kwadra'ʒɛzimu, ma] *num* fortieth; *veja também* **sexto.**

quadrangular [kwadrãŋgu'la(x)] *adj GEOM* quadrangular.

quadrângulo [kwa'drãŋgulu] *m* quadrangle.

quadriculado, da [kwadriku'ladu, da] *adj* **-1.** [camisa, padrão] checked. **-2.** [papel] squared.

quadril [kwa'driwl (*pl* -**is**) *m* hip.

quadrilátero, ra [kwadri'lateru, ra] *adj* quadrilateral.

→ **quadrilátero** *m* quadrilateral.

quadrilha [kwa'driʎa] *f* -**1.** [de ladrões etc] gang. -**2.** [dança] quadrille.

quadrimestral [kwadrimeʃ'trawl (*pl* -**ais**) *adj* quarterly.

quadrimotor [kwadrimo'to(x)l ◇ *adj* four-engined. ◇ *m* [avião] four-engined plane.

quadrinho [kwa'driɲu] *m* [das tiras] (cartoon) drawing.

→ **quadrinhos** *mpl*: (**história em**) ∼**s** cartoon strip.

quadro ['kwadru] *m* -**1.** [ger] frame. -**2.** [pintura] painting. -**3.** [quadro-negro] blackboard. -**4.** [mural] board; ∼ **de avisos** noticeboard. -**5.** [gráfico] chart. -**6.** *TEC* [painel] panel; ∼ **de luz** light panel. -**7.** *TEATRO* & *TV* scene. -**8.** [situação] picture; ∼ **clínico** clinical picture. -**9.** [de empresa, partido] staff. -**10.** *ESP* [equipe] team.

quadro-negro [ˌkwadru'negru] (*pl* **quadros-negros**) *m* blackboard.

quadrúpede [kwa'drupedʒil ◇ *adj* [animal] quadrupedal, four-footed. ◇ *mf* -**1.** [animal] quadruped. -**2.** *mfam* [estúpido] clot *UK*, dumbhead *US*.

quadruplicar [12] [kwadrupli'ka(x)l ◇ *vt* to quadruple. ◇ *vi* to quadruple.

quádruplo, pla ['kwadruplu, pla] ◇ *adj* quadruple. ◇ *m, f* [quadrigêmeo] quad, quadruplet.

→ **quádruplo** *m* quadruple.

quaisquer ▷ **qualquer**.

qual [kwaw] (*pl* **quais**) ◇ *adj* which; ∼ **perfume você prefere?** which perfume do you prefer?; **não sei** ∼ **caminho devo seguir** I don't know which road I should follow. ◇ *conj fml* [como] like; (**tal**) ∼ exactly like. ◇ *interj* what!; ∼! [exprimindo espanto] what!; [exprimindo negação] no; ∼ **nada!**, ∼ **o quê!** yeah right! ◇ *pron* -**1.** [em interrogativa] what; ∼ **é o seu nome?** what's your name?; ∼ **a cor dos seus cabelos?** what is the colour of your hair?; **quais são suas intenções?** what are your intentions? -**2.** [especificando] which (one); **perguntei** ∼ **seria a melhor opção** I asked which (one) would be the better option; **o/a** ∼ [suj: pessoa] who; [complemento: pessoa] whom; [suj, complemento: coisa] which; **ela teve três filhos, o mais velho dos quais tornou-se médico** she had three sons, the eldest of whom became a doctor; **este é o livro sobre o** ∼ **lhe escrevi** this is the book (which/that) I wrote to you about; **cada** ∼ each and every one; ∼ **deles ...?** which one (of them) ...?

qualidade [kwali'dadʒil *f* -**1.** [ger] quality; ∼ **de vida** quality of life; **de** ∼ good quality. -**2.** [tipo] grade. -**3.** *pej* [baixo nível] ilk. -**4.** [condição]: **na** ∼ **de** in the capacity of.

qualificação [kwalifika'sãwl (*pl* -**ões**) *f* [avaliação] classification.

→ **qualificações** *fpl* [formação, preparo] qualifications.

qualificado, da [kwalifi'kadu, da] *adj* -**1.** [preparado] qualified; **não** ∼ unqualified. -**2.** *JUR* [caracterizado] aggravated.

qualificar [12] [kwalifi'ka(x)l *vt* -**1.** [classificar] to qualify. -**2.** [avaliar] to describe.

→ **qualificar-se** *vp* [classificar-se] to qualify.

qualificativo, va [kwalifika'tʃivu, va] *adj* qualifying.

→ **qualificativo** *m* label.

qualitativo, va [kwalita'tʃivu, va] *adj* qualitative.

qualquer [kwaw'kɛ(x)l (*pl* **quaisquer**) ◇ *adj* -**1.** [algum]: **traga uma bebida** ∼ bring me any old drink; **comprei um jornal** ∼ I bought any old newspaper; **havia** ∼ **coisa de errado** there was something wrong; **num ponto** ∼ **da Sibéria** somewhere or other in Siberia; ∼ **dia venha me visitar** come and see me some day; **a** ∼ **momento** any minute now; **um outro** ∼ [coisa] any other one; [pessoa] some; **ser** ∼ **coisa** [ser ótimo, extraordinário] to be something else. -**2.** (*antes de subst*) [todo] any; **ele enfrenta quaisquer perigos** he braves all dangers; ∼ **pessoa sabe fazer arroz** anybody can cook rice; ∼ **que seja** whatever; ∼ **um** anybody; **todo e** ∼ each and every; **de** ∼ **maneira** *ou* **jeito** [seja como for] somehow or other; [a todo custo] come what may. -**3.** *pej* [ordinário, sem importância]: **ele se contenta com** ∼ **coisa** he's happy with any old thing; **de** ∼ **maneira** *ou* **jeito** [sem cuidado] any (old) how. ◇ *pron* -**1.** [algum]: ∼ (**de**) any (of); **como não posso ter todas, terei de escolher** ∼ as I can't have them all, I'll have to chose any one; **prove quaisquer destas balas** try any one of these sweets; **um** ∼ *pej* [pessoa] a nobody. -**2.** [todo - coisa]: ∼ (**de**) any (of); ∼ **destas substâncias é perigosa** any of these substances is dangerous; [- pessoa] anyone; ∼ **de nós faria o mesmo** anyone of us would do the same.

quando ['kwãndul ◇ *adv* when. ◇ *conj* when; [ao passo que] while; **de** ∼ **em** ∼ from time to time; **de vez em** ∼ from time to time; **desde** ∼ how long; ∼ **mais não seja** at least, if only; ∼ **muito** at (the) most; ∼ **quer que** whenever.

quanta ▷ **quanto**.

quantia [kwãn'tʃial *f* sum.

quantidade [kwãntʃi'dadʒil *f* -**1.** [medida] amount. -**2.** [número] number. -**3.** [abundância]: **uma** ∼ **de** a number of; **em** ∼ in large quantity.

quantificar [12] [kwãntʃifi'ka(x)l *vt* to quantify.

quantitativo, va [kwãntʃita'tʃivu, va] *adj* quantitative.

quanto, ta ['kwãntu, ta] ◇ *adj* -**1.** (*interrogativo*) how; **quantas maçãs você quer?** how many apples do you want?; **há** ∼ **tempo você está esperando?** how long have you been waiting? -**2.** (*exclamativo*) how; **quantos livros!** how many books!, so many books!; **quanta gente!** how many people!, so many people! ◇ *pron* -**1.** (*interrogativo*) how; **quantos fugiram?** how many got away? -**2.** (*exclamativo*) how; **quantos não morrem antes de chegar à idade adulta!** how many died before reaching adulthood! **-3.** *(relativo)*: **tantos ... quantos ...** as many ... as ...; **faça tantas alterações quantas forem necessárias** make as many changes as necessary; **gosto de tudo ~é verdura** I like all green vegetables; **tudo ~é tipo de penteado** all kinds of hairstyles.

quanto ◇ *pron (interrogativo)* [quantia, preço] how; **~ custa este casaco?** how much does this coat cost?; **a ~ está o dólar?** how much is the dollar?; [quantidade]: **~ de maionese devo acrescentar?** how much mayonnaise should I add?; **~ de combustível ainda temos?** how much fuel do we still have? ◇ *adv* [indicando intensidade, proporção] much; **esforcei-me o ~ pude** I tried as much/hard as I could; **sei o ~ o voce me ama** I know how much you love me; **um tanto ~** [meio] somewhat; **tanto ~** as much as; **tanto um quanto o outro são incompetentes** [ambos] both are equally incompetent; **tão ... ~ ... as ... as ...;** **mais tem, mais quer** the more he has, the more he wants; **~ mais rápido, melhor** the faster, the better; **~ mais** [especialmente] especially; [muito menos] especially not.

quanto a *loc prep* [com relação] as for, as far as; **~ a mim** as for me, as far as I'm concerned.

quanto antes *loc adv*: **o ~ antes** as soon as possible.

quantos *pron pl fam*: **um certo Carlos não sei dos quantos** a certain Carlos something or other.

quantas *pron pl fam*: **a quantas** [em que situação] at what stage; **não sei a quantas anda esse processo** I don't know what stage the trial is at.

quão [kwãw] *adv* how.

quarenta [kwa'rēnta] *num* forty; *veja também* **sessenta**.

quarentão, tona [kwarēn'tãw, tona] *(mpl -ões, fpl -s)* ◇ *adj* in one's forties. ◇ *m, f* person in their forties.

quarentena [kwarēn'tena] *f* quarantine.

quarentona [kwarēn'tona] *f* ▷ **quarentão**.

quaresma [kwa'rɛʒma] *f* **-1.** *RELIG* Lent. **-2.** [flor] glory bush.

quarta ['kwaxta] *f* [quarta-feira] Wednesday; *veja também* **sábado**.

quarta-de-final [,kwaxtadʒifi'naw] *(pl quartas-de-final)* *f* quarter final.

quarta-feira [,kwaxta'fejra] *(pl quartas-feiras)* *f* Wednesday; **~ de cinzas** Ash Wednesday; *veja também* **sábado**.

quarteirão [kwaxtej'rãw] *(pl -ões)* *m* block.

quartel [kwax'tɛw] *(pl -éis)* *m* MIL barracks *(pl)*.

quartel-general [kwax,tɛwʒene'raw] *(pl quartéis-generais)* *m* general headquarters *(pl)*.

quarteto [kwax'tetu] *m* **-1.** MÚS quartet; **~ de cordas** string quartet. **-2.** LITER [em poesia] quatrain.

quarto, ta ['kwaxtu, ta] *num* fourth; **a quarta parte** a quarter; *veja também* **sexto**.

quarto *m* **-1.** [a quarta parte] quarter; **passar um mau ~ de hora** *fig* to have a tough time (of it). **-2.** [aposento] bedroom; **~ de casal** double room;

~ de banho bathroom; **~ de despejo** store cupboard; **~ de solteiro** single room. **-3.** MIL [plantão] watch; **estar/ficar de ~** to be/remain on duty. **-4.** [de boi] haunch. **-5.** ASTRON [da lua]: **~ crescente/minguante** first/last quarter.

quarta *f* **-1.** [marcha] fourth; **passar a quarta** to shift into fourth. **-2.** MÚS perfect fourth. **-3.** [medida] quart.

quarto-e-sala [,kwaxtwi'sala] *(pl quarto-e-salas)* *m* studio apartment.

quarto-zagueiro [,kwaxtuza'gejru] *(pl -ros)* *m* FUT fullback.

quartzo ['kwaxtsu] *m* quartz.

quase ['kwazi] *adv* **-1.** [ger] nearly; **estou ~, perdendo a paciência** I am on the verge of losing my temper; **tropecei e ~ caí** I tripped and almost fell. **-2.** [pouco mais, ou menos] almost, nearly; **ela tem ~ dez anos** she is almost ou nearly ten years old; **~ não trabalhei hoje** I hardly worked today; **~ nada/tudo** nothing/everything; **~ nunca** almost never, hardly ever; **~ sempre** nearly always.

quatro ['kwatru] *num* four; **de ~** on all fours; **estar/ficar de ~** [surpreso] to be astounded; **estar de ~ por alguém** [apaixonado] to be head over heels over sb; *veja também* **seis**.

quatrocentos, tas [,kwatru'sẽntuʃ, taʃ] *num* four hundred; *veja também* **seis**.

que [ki] ◇ *adj inv* **-1.** [em interrogativas] what, which; **~ livros você quer?** which books do you want?; **~ dia é hoje?** what day is it today?; **~ horas são?** what time is it? **-2.** [em exclamações]: **mas ~ belo dia!** what a beautiful day!; **~ fome!** I'm starving!; **~ maravilha!** how wonderful! ◇ *pron* **-1.** [em interrogativas] what; **~ é isso?** what's that?; **o ~ você quer?** what do you want?; **o ~ você vai comer?** what are you going to eat? **-2.** [uso relativo: sujeito-pessoa] who; **o homem ~ está correndo** the man who's running; [-coisa] which, that; **a guerra ~ começou em 1939** the war that started in 1939. **-3.** [uso relativo: complemento-pessoa] whom, that; **o homem ~ conheci** the man (whom) I met; [-coisa] which, that; **o bolo ~ comi era ótimo** the cake (that) I ate was great. ◇ *conj* **-1.** [com complemento direto] that; **ele disse-me ~ ia de férias** he told me (that) he was going on holiday. **-2.** [em comparações]: **(do) ~** than; **é mais caro (do) ~ o outro** it's more expensive than the other. **-3.** [exprime causa]: **leva o guarda-chuva ~ está chovendo** take an umbrella because it's raining; **vai depressa ~ você está atrasado** you'd better hurry because you're late. **-4.** [exprime conseqüência] that; **pediu-me tanto ~ acabei por lhe dar** he asked me for it so much that I ended up giving it to him. **-5.** [exprime tempo]: **há horas ~ estou à espera** I've been waiting for hours; **há muito ~ não voulá** I haven't been there for ages. **-6.** [indica desejo] that; **espero ~ você se divirta** I hope (that) you have fun; **quero ~ você o faça** I want you to do it; **~ você seja feliz!** may you be happy! **-7.** [em locuções]: **~ nem** like; **ele chorou**

~ **nem um bebê** he cried like a baby; **ele é feio** ~ **nem o irmão** he's as ugly as his brother.

quê [ˈkel◇ *m* [algo]: **um** ~ something; **um** ~ **de** [toque] a touch of; [sabor] slightly; **um não sei** ~ a je ne sais quoi; **sem** ~ **nem por** ~ [sem motivo] without rhyme or reason. ◇ *interj* [exprimindo espanto] what! ◇ *pron* ▷ **que.**

Quebec [keˈbɛkil *n*: (o) ~ Quebec.

quebra [ˈkɛbra] *f* -**1.** [ger] break. -**2.** [despedaçamento] breakage. -**3.** [falência] bankruptcy. -**4.** COMPUT: ~ **de página** page break.
  ◆ **de quebra** *loc adv* what's more.

quebra-cabeça [ˌkɛbrakaˈbesa] (*pl* **quebra-cabeças**) *m* -**1.** [jogo] puzzle. -**2.** *fig* [problema] dilemma.

quebradiço, ça [kebraˈdʒisu, sa] *adj* fragile.

quebrado, da [keˈbradu, da] *adj* -**1.** [vaso, vidro, braço] broken. -**2.** [enguiçado - carro, máquina] broken down; [- telefone] out of order. -**3.** [cansado] worn out. -**4.** [falido] bankrupt. -**5.** *fam* [sem dinheiro] broke.
  ◆ **quebrados** *mpl* [trocados] change (*sg*).

quebra-galho [ˌkɛbraˈgaʎu] (*pl* **quebra-galhos**) *m* -**1.** [pessoa] Mr Fixit. -**2.** [objeto] contrivance.

quebra-gelos [ˌkɛbraˈʒeluʃ] *m inv* NÁUT icebreaker.

quebra-mar [ˌkɛbraˈma(x)] (*pl* **quebra-mares**) *m* breakwater.

quebra-molas [ˌkɛbraˈmɔlaʃ] *m inv* speed bump *ou* hump, sleeping policeman.

quebra-nozes [ˌkɛbraˈnɔziʃ] *m inv* nutcracker.

quebranto [keˈbrãntu] *m* -**1.** [mau- olhado] evil eye. -**2.** [abatimento] run-down state.

quebra-pau [ˌkɛbraˈpaw] (*pl* **quebra-paus**) *m fam* fisticuffs (*pl*).

quebra-quebra [ˌkɛbraˈkɛbra] (*pl* **quebra-quebras**) *m* riot.

quebrar [4] [keˈbra(x)] ◇ *vt* -**1.** [ger] to break; ~ **algo ao meio** to split sthg in half. -**2.** [espancar] to beat up. -**3.** [enfraquecer] to weaken. -**4.** [interromper] to halt. -**5.** [desviar] to deflect. ◇ *vi* -**1.** [despedaçar-se] to break. -**2.** [enguiçar] to break down. -**3.** [falir] to go bankrupt. -**4.** *fam* [ficar sem dinheiro] to be broke.
  ◆ **quebrar-se** *vp* -**1.** [despedaçar-se] to break. -**2.** [desfazer-se] to be broken.

quebra-vento [ˌkɛbraˈvẽntu] (*pl* **quebra-ventos**) *m* AUTO fanlight.

queda [ˈkɛda] *f* -**1.** [ger] fall; ~ **livre** free fall; ~ **de barreira** landslide; **em** ~ falling. -**2.** [declínio] fall; **estar em** ~ to be falling. -**3.** *fig* [inclinação]: **ter uma** ~ **para algo** to have a flair for sthg; **ter uma** ~ **por alguém** to have a soft spot for sb.

queda-d'água [ˌkɛdaˈdagwal] (*pl* **quedas-d'água**) *f* waterfall.

queda-de-braço [kɛdadʒibrasul] (*pl* **quedas-de-braço** [kɛdaʃibrasul]) *f* -**1.** [jogo] arm-wrestling. -**2.** *fig* [disputa] dispute.

queijada [kejˈʒada] *f* cheesecake.

queijadinha [kejʒaˈdʒiɲal] *f* coconut ice.

queijeira [kejˈʒejra] *f* cheese cover.

queijo [ˈkejʒul] *m* cheese; ~ **prato** (form of) processed cheese; ~ **ralado** grated cheese.

queima [ˈkejma] *f* -**1.** [queimada] burning fire; ~ **de fogos** fireworks display. -**2.** COM & *fig* [liquidação] clearance sale.

queimado, da [kejˈmadu, da] *adj* -**1.** [ger] burnt. -**2.** [de sol - bronzeado] tanned; [- ferido] sunburnt. -**3.** [plantas] scorched. -**4.** *fam fig* [malquisto] ruined.
  ◆ **queimado** *m* [coisa queimada]: **cheiro/gosto de** ~ smell of burning/taste burnt.
  ◆ **queimada** *f* slash-and-burn.

queimadura [kejmaˈdura] *f* -**1.** [com fogo] burn; ~ **de primeiro/segundo grau** first-/second-degree burn. -**2.** [de sol] sunburn.

queimar [4] [kejˈma(x)] ◇ *vt* -**1.** [ger] to burn. -**2.** [atear fogo a] to set on fire. -**3.** [abrasar, ferir - fogo, choque, sol] to burn; [- líquido] to scald. -**4.** [bronzear] to tan. -**5.** COM & *fig* [liquidar] to liquidate. -**6.** *fam fig* [tornar malquisto] to ruin. -**7.** *fig* [dinheiro] to blow. ◇ *vi* -**1.** [abrasar] to be burning hot. -**2.** [arder em febre] to burn (up). -**3.** [lâmpada, fusível] to blow. -**4.** ESP to hit the net. -**5.** [comida] to burn.
  ◆ **queimar-se** *vp* -**1.** [ferir-se - ger] to burn o.s.; [- com líquido fervente] to scald o.s. -**2.** [bronzear-se] to sunbathe. -**3.** *fam fig* [enfezar-se] to take offence. -**4.** *fam fig* [tornar-se malquisto] to blow it.

queima-roupa [ˌkejmaˈxopa] *f*: **à** ~ [disparo] at point-blank range; *fig* [sem rodeios] point-blank.

queixa [ˈkejʃa] *f* -**1.** [reclamação] complaint; **dar** ~ **de algo/alguém** to complain about sthg/sb; **ter** ~ **de algo/alguém** to have a complaint against sthg/sb. -**2.** [lamento] grievance.

queixa-crime [ˌkejʃaˈkrimil] (*pl* **queixas-crime(s)**) *f* JUR citation.

queixada [kejˈʃada] *f* -**1.** [de animal] jaw. -**2.** [queixo grande] prominent jaw.

queixar-se [7] [kejˈʃaxsil] *vp* -**1.** [reclamar]: ~-**se (de algo/alguém)** to complain (about sthg/sb). -**2.** [lamentar-se] to moan.

queixo [ˈkejʃul] *m* chin; **estava com tanto frio que chegava a bater o** ~ [de frio] I was so cold my teeth started chattering; **ele ficou de** ~ **caído** [ficar admirado] his jaw dropped in amazement.

queixoso, osa [kejˈʃozu, ɔza] *adj* -**1.** [agravado] querulous. -**2.** [magoado] aggrieved.

queixudo, da [kejˈʃudu, da] *adj* big-jawed.

queixume [kejˈʃumil] *m* [lamentação] complaint.

quem [ˈkẽj] *pron* [interrogativo: sujeito] who; [interrogativo: complemento] who, whom; [indefinido] whoever; ~ **diria!** who would have thought it!; ~ **é?** [na porta] who's there?; ~ **fala?** [no telefone] who's calling?, who's speaking?; ~ **me dera ser rico!** if only I were rich!; ~ **quer que** whoever; **seja** ~ **for** no matter who it is, whoever it is it is.

quentão [kẽnˈtãw] *m* mulled wine.

quente [ˈkẽntʃil] ◇ *adj* -**1.** [ger] hot. -**2.** [roupa] warm. -**3.** [animado] vibrant. -**4.** *gír* [jornalismo] [notícia] reliable. ◇ *m* [moda]: **o** ~ **agora é usar cabelo comprido** the in thing now is to wear one's hair long.

quentinha [kẽn'tʃiɲa] *f* - **1.** [embalagem] *insulated carton for food.* - **2.** [refeição] snack.

quentura [kẽn'tura] *f* warmth.

quepe ['kɛpi] *m* kepi.

quer [kɛ(x)] ⬦ *conj:* ~ ..., ~ ... whether ... or ...; ~ **você queira,** ~ **não** whether you want to or not. ⬦ *v* ⊳ **querer.**

➡ **onde quer que** *loc pron* wherever.

➡ **o que quer que** *loc pron* whatever.

➡ **quem quer que** *loc pron* whoever.

querela [ke'rɛla] *f* - **1.** [contenda] quarrel. - **2.** JUR charge.

querelar [4] [kere'la(x)] ⬦ *vt* JUR to sue. ⬦ *vi* [queixar-se]: ~ **(contra/de)** to quarrel (with/about).

querer [38] [ke're(x)] ⬦ *m* - **1.** [vontade] wanting. - **2.** [amor] love. ⬦ *vt* - **1.** [ger] to want; **como queira/quiser** as you wish; **como quem não quer nada** casually; **estar querendo fazer algo** [estar na iminência de] to be about to do sthg; **não** ~ **nada com** to want nothing to do with; ~ **dizer** to mean; **quer dizer** [em outras palavras] that is to say; **quer dizer que ...** [então] so that means ... - **2.** [ter a bondade de]: **queiram apertar seus cintos de segurança** please fasten your seatbelts; **quer me passar o vinho, por favor?** would you kindly pass me the wine, please? - **3.** [cobrar]: **quero dois mil pelo carro** I want two thousand for the car. - **4.** [ter afeição por] to love. - **5.** [conseguir]: **não** ~ **fazer algo** not to want to do sthg. ⬦ *vi* - **1.** [desejar, ter vontade]: **não vou porque não quero** I am not going because I don't want to; ~ **é poder** *prov* where there's a will, there's a way; **por** ~ on purpose; **sem** ~ unintentionally. - **2.** [amar] to love; ~ **bem a alguém** to care about sb; ~ **mal a alguém** to wish sb ill.

➡ **querer-se** *vp* [amar-se] to love one another.

querido, da [ke'ridu, da] ⬦ *adj* - **1.** [caro] dear; **ele é muito** ~ **na cidade** he is much liked in town. - **2.** [em carta]: **Querido ...** Dear ... ⬦ *m, f* - **1.** [preferido] favourite *UK*, favorite *US*. - **2.** [como forma de tratamento] darling.

quermesse [kex'mɛsi] *f* fête *UK*, kermis *US*.

querosene [kero'zeni] *m* kerosene.

querubim [keru'bĩ] (*pl* -ns) *m* cherub.

quesito [ke'zitu] *m* - **1.** [ponto, questão] question. - **2.** [requisito] requirement.

questão [keʃ'tãw] (*pl* -ões) *f* - **1.** [ger] question; **isso ocorreu há** ~ **de cinco meses** that happened some five months ago; ~ **de honra** question of honour; ~ **de tempo** question of time; ~ **de vida ou morte** matter of life or death; **em** ~ in question; **fazer** ~ **(de algo)** *fig* [insistir em] to insist (on sthg). - **2.** JUR case.

questionamento [keʃtʃjona'mẽntu] *m* [pôr em dúvida] questioning.

questionar [4] [keʃtʃjo'na(x)] *vt* - **1.** [debater] to dispute. - **2.** [fazer perguntas] to question.

questionário [keʃtʃjo'narju] *m* questionnaire.

questionável [keʃtʃjo'navew] (*pl* -eis) *adj* questionable.

questões [keʃ'tõjʃ] *pl* ⊳ **questão.**

qui. (*abrev de* quinta-feira) *f* Thur.

quiabo ['kjabu] *m* okra.

quibe ['kibi] *m* deep-fried meat dish with mint and other spices.

quibebe [ki'bɛbi] *m* pumpkin purée.

quicar [12] [ki'ka(x)] ⬦ *vt* [bola] to bounce. ⬦ *vi* [bola] to bounce.

quiche ['kiʃi] *f* quiche.

quíchua ['kiʃwa] ⬦ *adj* Quechuan. ⬦ *m, f* Quechuan.

➡ **quíchua** *m* [língua] Quechuan.

quieto, ta ['kjɛtu, ta] *adj* - **1.** [em silêncio] quiet. - **2.** [tranqüilo] calm. - **3.** [imóvel] still.

quietude [kje'tudʒi] *f* tranquillity.

quilate [ki'latʃi] *m* - **1.** [de ouro] carat. - **2.** *fig* [excelência] calibre *UK*, caliber *US*.

quilha ['kiʎa] *f* keel.

quilo ['kilu] *m* kilo; **a** ~ by the kilo.

quilobyte [kilo'bajtʃi] *m* COMPUT kilobyte.

quilohertz [kilo'hɛxtʃis] *m* kilohertz.

quilombo [ki'lõmbu] *m* fortified village where runaway slaves lived.

quilometragem [kilome'traʒẽ] (*pl* -ns) *f* - **1.** [distância percorrida] distance in kilometres *UK ou* kilometers *US*, ≃ mileage. - **2.** [distância entre dois pontos] distance in kilometres *UK ou* kilometers *US*.

quilometrar [4] [kilome'tra(x)] *vt* to measure in kilometres *UK ou* kilometers *US*.

quilométrico, ca [kilo'mɛtriku, ka] *adj fig* [longo] mile (*antes de subst*).

quilômetro [ki'lometru] *m* kilometre *UK*, kilometer *US*.

quilowatt [kilo'vatʃi] *m* kilowatt.

quilowatt-hora [kilo,vatʃi'ɔra] (*pl* -ras) *m* ELETR kilowatt-hour.

quimbanda [kĩ'bãnda] *m* - **1.** [ritual] macumba ritual. - **2.** [feiticeiro] priest of macumba. - **3.** [terreiro] place where macumba is practised.

quimera [ki'mɛra] *f* [fantasia, ilusão] chimera.

químico, ca ['kimiku, ka] ⬦ *adj* chemical. ⬦ *m, f* [profissional] chemist.

➡ **química** *f* - **1.** [ger] chemistry. - **2.** [substância] chemical. - **3.** *fig* [segredo] secret.

quimioterapia [kimjotera'pia] *f* chemotherapy.

quimono [ki'monu] *m* kimono.

quina ['kina] *f* - **1.** [canto] corner; **de** ~ side on. - **2.** [de jogo] jackpot.

quindim [kĩ'dʒĩ] (*pl* -ns) *m* sweet made of egg, sugar and coconut.

quinhão [ki'ɲãw] (*pl* -ões) *m* share.

quinhentista [kiɲẽn'tʃiʃta] *adj* sixteenth century (*antes de subst*).

quinhentos, tas [ki'ɲẽntuʃ, taʃ] *num* five hundred; **ser outros** ~ to be a different kettle of fish; *veja também* **seis.**

quinhões [ki'ɲõjʃ] *pl* ⊳ **quinhão.**

quinina [ki'nina] *f* quinine.

qüinquagésimo, ma [kwiŋkwa'ʒɛzimu, ma] *num* fiftieth; *veja também* **sexto.**

qüinqüênio [kwĩŋ'kwenju] *m* quinquennium.
quinquilharia [kĩŋkiʎa'ria] *f* **-1.** [bugiganga] junk. **-2.** [ninharia] trinket.
➥ **quinquilharias** *fpl* [miudezas] odds and ends.
quinta ['kĩnta] *f* **-1.** [quinta-feira] Thursday. **-2.** [sítio] estate; *veja também* **sábado**.
quinta-essência [ˌkĩntae'sẽnsja] *f* **-1.** [essência] quintessence. **-2.** [plenitude] epitome.
quinta-feira [ˌkĩnta'fejra] (*pl* **quintas-feiras**) *f* Thursday; *veja também* **sábado**.
quintal [kĩn'taw] (*pl* **-ais**) *m* [de casa] backyard.
quinteto [kĩn'tetu] *m* MÚS quintet.
quinto, ta ['kĩntu, ta] *num* fifth; *veja também* **sexto**.
quintuplicar [kĩntupli'ka(x)] *vt*: quintuplicou o número de desempregados the number of unemployed has multiplied by five.
quíntuplo, pla ['kĩntuplu, pla] *adj* quintuple.
➥ **quíntuplo** *m* quintuple.
➥ **quíntuplos** *mpl* [gêmeos] quins, quintuplets.
quinze ['kĩzil] *num* fifteen; *veja também* **seis**.
quinzena [kĩ'zena] *f* **-1.** [tempo] fortnight. **-2.** [salário] fortnight's wages.
quinzenal [kĩze'naw] (*pl* **-ais**) *adj* fortnightly.
quinzenalmente [kĩzenaw'mẽntʃi] *adv* fortnightly.
quiosque ['kjɔʃki] *m* **-1.** [de jardim] gazebo. **-2.** [banca] kiosk.
qüiprocó [kwipro'kɔ] *m* [confusão] mix-up.
quiromancia [kiromãn'sia] *f* palmistry, chiromancy.
quiromante [kiro'mãntʃi] *mf* palm reader.
quisto ['kiʃtu] *m* cyst.
quitação [kita'saw] (*pl* **-ões**) *f* **-1.** [remissão] discharge. **-2.** [pagamento] settlement. **-3.** [recibo] receipt.
quitanda [ki'tãnda] *f* grocer's shop *UK*, grocery store *US*.
quitandeiro, ra [kitãn'dejru, ra] *m, f* greengrocer.
quitar [4] [ki'ta(x)] *vt* **-1.** [pagar] to settle. **-2.** [perdoar] to cancel. **-3.** [devedor] to release.
quite ['kitʃi] *adj* **-1.** [com credor]: estar/ficar ~ (com alguém) to be quits (with sb). **-2.** [livre]: ~ de algo free of sthg. **-3.** [igualado] even.
quitenho, nha [ki'teɲu, ɲal ◇ *adj* Quito (*antes de subst*). ◇ *m, f* person from Quito.
Quito ['kitu] *n* Quito.
quitute [ki'tutʃi] *m* titbit *UK*, tidbit *US*.
quizumba [ki'zũba] *f fam* brawl.
quociente [kwo'sjẽntʃi] *m* MAT quotient; ~ de inteligência intelligence quotient, IQ.

r, R ['ɛxil] *m* [letra] r, R.
rã ['xã] *f* frog.
rabada [xa'bada] *f* **-1.** [rabo] tail. **-2.** CULIN oxtail stew. **-3.** *fam* [de corrida]: ele chegou na ~ he arrived at the tail end.
rabanada [xaba'nada] *f* **-1.** CULIN French toast. **-2.** [golpe com rabo] whack with the tail.
rabanete [xaba'netʃil *m* radish.
Rabat [xa'batʃ] *n* Rabat.
rabeca [xa'bɛka] *f* MÚS fiddle.
rabecão [xabe'kãw] (*pl* **-ões**) *m* [carro fúnebre] hearse.
rabicho [xa'biʃu] *m* **-1.** [trança] pigtail. **-2.** *fam* [caso amoroso] passion.
rabino, na [xa'binu, na] *m* rabbi.
rabiscar [12] [xabiʃ'ka(x)] ◇ *vt* **-1.** [encher com rabiscos] to scribble over. **-2.** [riscos] to scribble. **-3.** [escrever às pressas] to scrawl. **-4.** [desenhar] to sketch. ◇ *vi* [fazer rabiscos] to doodle.
rabisco [xa'biʃku] *m* **-1.** [risco] scribble. **-2.** [esboço] sketch.
➥ **rabiscos** *mpl* [caligrafia ruim] scrawl (*sg*).
rabo ['xabu] *m* **-1.** [cauda] tail; ~ de foguete *fig* can of worms; com o ~ do olho out of the corner of one's eye; meter o ~ entre as pernas *fig* to be left with one's tail between one's legs. **-2.** *vulg* [nádegas] bum.
rabo-de-cavalo [ˌxabudʒika'valu] (*pl* **rabos-de-cavalo**) *m* ponytail.
rabo-de-saia [ˌxabudʒi'saja] (*pl* **rabos-de-saia**) *m fam* piece of skirt.
rabudo, da [xa'budu, da] *adj* [sortudo] lucky.
➥ **rabudo** *m fam* [diabo] devil.
rabugento, ta [xabu'ʒẽntu, ta] *adj* grumpy.
rabugice [xabu'ʒisi] *f* grumpiness.
raça ['xasa] *f* **-1.** [etnia] race. **-2.** [estirpe] lineage. **-3.** *pej* [laia] breed; acabar com a ~ de alguém [matar] to do away with sb. **-4.** *fig* [coragem, determinação] guts; (no peito e) na ~ by sheer guts; ter ~ (para algo) to have the guts (for sthg). **-5.** [de animal] breed; cão/cavalo de ~ pedigree dog/thoroughbred horse.
ração [xa'sãw] (*pl* **-ões**) *f* **-1.** [de alimento] ration. **-2.** [para animal - para cão, gato] food; ~ para cachorro

puppy food; [- para gado, cavalo] feed; ~ **para cavalo** horse feed.

racha [ˈxaʃal] *m* -**1**. *fam* [discórdia] split. -**2**. [em parede etc] crack.

rachadura [xaʃaˈdura] *f* crack.

rachar [4] [xaˈʃa(x)] <> *vt* -**1**. [fender] to crack; **frio de** ~ bitterly cold; **ou vai ou racha** do or die; **sol de** ~ scorching sun. -**2**. [dividir]: ~ **algo (com alguém)** to split sthg (with sb). -**3**. *fig* [dividir] to split. -**4**. [cortar] to split. <> *vi* [fender-se] to crack.

racial [xaˈsjaw] (*pl* -**ais**) *adj* racial.

raciocinar [4] [xasjosiˈna(x)] *vi* to reason.

raciocínio [xasjoˈsinju] *m* reasoning.

racional [xasjoˈnaw] (*pl* -**ais**) *adj* rational.

racionalidade [xasjonaliˈdadʒi] *f* racionality.

racionalização [xasjonalizaˈsãw] *f* rationalization.

racionalizar [4] [xasjonaliˈza(x)] *vt* to rationalize.

racionalmente [xasjonawˈmẽntʃi] *adv* rationally, sensibly.

racionamento [xasjonaˈmẽntu] *m* rationing.

racionar [4] [xasjoˈna(x)] *vt* to ration.

racismo [xaˈsiʒmu] *m* racism.

racista [xaˈsiʃta] <> *adj* racist. <> *mf* racist.

rack [xɛk] *m* rack.

rações [xaˈsõjʃ] *pl* ⇨ **ração**.

radar [xaˈda(x)] (*pl* -**es**) *m* radar.

radiação [xadʒjaˈsãw] (*pl* -**ões**) *f* radiation.

radiador [xadʒjaˈdo(x)] (*pl* -**es**) *m* AUTO radiator.

radialista [xadʒjaˈliʃta] *mf* -**1**. [apresentador] (radio) announcer. -**2**. [da produção] (radio) producer.

radiante [xaˈdʒjãntʃi] *adj* -**1**. [objeto] radiant. -**2**. [de alegria] ecstatic.

radical [xadʒiˈkaw] (*pl* -**ais**) <> *adj* radical. <> *mf* -**1**. [ger] root. -**2**. POL & QUÍM radical; ~ **livre** free radical.

radicalismo [xadʒikaˈliʒmu] *m* radicalism.

radicalizar [4] [xadʒikaliˈza(x)] <> *vt* [aprofundar] to radicalize. <> *vi* [tornar-se radical] to become radical.

➡ **radicalizar-se** *vp* [tornar-se radical] to become radical.

radicar-se [12] [xadʒiˈkaxsi] *vp* to settle.

rádio [ˈxadʒju] <> *m* -**1**. [aparelho] radio. -**2**. QUÍM radium. -**3**. ANAT [osso] radius. <> *f* [emissora] radio station.

radioamador, ra [xadʒjwamaˈdo(x), da] *m, f* radio ham.

radioatividade [xadʒwatʃiviˈdadʒi] *f* radioactivity.

radioativo, va [ˌxadʒwaˈtʃivu, va] *adj* radioactive.

radiodifusão [xadʒodʒifuˈzãw] *f* broadcasting.

radiodifusora [xadʒodʒifuˈzora] *f* broadcasting station.

radioemissora [xadʒwemiˈsora] *f* radio station.

radiografar [4] [xadʒograˈfa(x)] <> *vt* -**1**. MED to X-ray. -**2**. [notícia] to radio. <> *vi* [fazer contato] to radio.

radiografia [ˌxadʒjograˈfia] *f* -**1**. MED X-ray. -**2**. *fig* [análise] in-depth analysis.

radiograma [xadʒjoˈgrama] *m* cablegram.

radiogravador [xadʒjugravaˈdo(x)] *m* radio-cassette player.

radiojornal [xadʒjuʒoxˈnaw] (*pl* -**ais**) *m* radio news *(sg)*.

radiologia [xadʒjoloˈʒial] *f* radiology.

radiologista [xadʒjoloˈʒiʃta] *mf* radiologist.

radionovela [xadʒjunoˈvɛla] *f* radio soap.

radiooperador, ra [xadʒjooperaˈdo(x), ra] *m, f* radio operator.

radiopatrulha [xadʒjupaˈtruʎa] *f* -**1**. [serviço] radio patrol. -**2**. [viatura] patrol car.

radiorepórter [ˌxadʒjuxeˈpɔxte(x)] *mf* radio reporter.

radioso, osa [xaˈdʒjozu, ɔza] *adj* radiant.

radiotáxi [ˌxadʒjoˈtaksil] *m* radio cab.

radioterapia [xadʒjoteraˈpia] *f* radiotherapy.

radiouvinte [xadʒjoˈvĩntʃil] *mf* (radio) listener.

ráfia [ˈxafja] *f* raffia.

ragu [xaˈgu] *m* ragout.

raia [ˈxaja] *f* -**1**. [linha] line. -**2**. [limite] boundary; **às** ~**s de algo** to the limits of sthg. -**3**. [pista - de piscina] (lane) marker; [- de tiro] firing range. -**4**. [peixe] ray. -**5**. *loc*: **fugir da** ~ to cut and run.

raiado, da [xaˈjadu, da] *adj* -**1**. [pista] marked. -**2**. [cano] rifled. -**3**. [piscina] divided into lanes. -**4**. [bandeira] striped.

raiar [4] [xaˈja(x)] <> *vi* -**1**. [brilhar] to shine. -**2**. [despontar] to dawn. <> *vt* [com raias - pista] to mark; [- cano] to rifle; [- piscina] to lane off; [- pintar] to mark with stripes.

rainha [xaˈiɲa] *f* queen.

rainha-mãe [xaˌiɲaˈmãj] (*pl* **rainhas-mães**) *f* queen mother.

raio [ˈxaju] *m* -**1**. [ger] ray; ~ **laser** laser beam; ~ **X** X-ray. -**2**. [de luz] beam. -**3**. METEOR bolt of lightening. -**4**. *fam* [como ênfase]: **perdi o** ~ **da carteira** I lost my blasted wallet. -**5**. GEOM radius. -**6**.: ~ **de ação** [alcance] range; *fig* [área de atuação] range.

raiva [ˈxajva] *f* -**1**. [fúria] rage; **com** ~ **(de)** angry (at); **dar** ~ to drive mad; **morto de** ~ absolutely furious; **ter/tomar** ~ **de** to hate. -**2**. [doença] rabies *(sg)*.

raivoso, osa [xajˈvozu, ɔza] *adj* -**1**. [furioso] furious. -**2**. [doente] rabid.

raiz [xaˈiʒ] (*pl* -**es**) *f* -**1**. [ger] root; **cortar o mal pela** ~ *fig* to root it out; **criar raízes** *fig* to put down roots; ~ **quadrada** square root. -**2**. [origem] roots *(pl)*.

rajada [xaˈʒada] *f* -**1**. [de vento] gust. -**2**. [de tiros] volley.

ralado, da [xaˈladu, da] *adj* -**1**. [moído] grated. -**2**. [esfolado] grazed.

ralador [xalaˈdo(x)] (*pl* -**es**) *m* grater.

ralar [4] [xaˈla(x)] *vt* -**1**. [com ralador] to grate. -**2**. [esfolar] to graze.

ralé [xaˈlɛ] *f* [escória] riff-raff.

ralhar [4] [xaˈʎa(x)] *vi*: ~ **(com alguém)** to tell (sb) off.

rali [xaˈli] *m* rally.

ralo, la [ˈxalu, la] *adj* -**1.** [cabelo, café, sopa] thin. -**2.** [vegetação] sparse.
  ➡ **ralo** *m* drainpipe.

Ram. (*abrev de* ramal) *m* ext.

RAM (*abrev de* **Random Access Memory**) *f* RAM.

rama [ˈxãma] *f* foliage; **em** ~ raw; **pela** ~ *fig* [superficialmente] superficially.

ramadã [xamaˈdã] *m* Ramadan, Ramadhan.

ramagem [xaˈmaʒẽ] *f* BOT branches (*pl*).

ramal [xaˈmaw] (*pl* -**ais**) *m* -**1.** [de telefone] extension. -**2.** FERRO branch line. -**3.** [rodoviário] branch road.

ramalhete [xamaˈʎetʃi] *m* [buquê] bunch.

rameira [xaˈmejra] *f vulg* [prostituta] prostitute.

ramerrão [xameˈxãw] *m* [rotina] grind.

ramificação [xamifikaˈsãw] (*pl* -**ões**) *f* [subdivisão] branch.

ramificar-se [12] [xamifiˈkaxsi] *vp* -**1.** [subdividirse] to be sub-divided. -**2.** [espalhar-se] to branch out.

ramo [ˈxãmu] *m* -**1.** [ger] branch. -**2.** [de flores] bouquet. -**3.** [área] field.

rampa [ˈxãpa] *f* ramp.

rancheiro, ra [xãˈʃejru, ra] *m, f* -**1.** [morador] farmer. -**2.** [zelador] tenant farmer. -**3.** [cozinheiro] cook.

rancho [ˈxãʃu] *m* -**1.** [sítio] smallholding, farm. -**2.** [cabana] hut. -**3.** [refeição] mess. -**4.** MÚS [ritmo] carnival music.

ranço [ˈxãsu] *m* -**1.** [sabor] rancid taste. -**2.** [cheiro] rank smell. -**3.** *fig* [atraso] age-old habit.

rancor [xãŋˈko(x)] *m* -**1.** [ressentimento] resentment; **guardar** ~ **(de)** to be resentful (about). -**2.** [ódio] hatred.

rancoroso, osa [xãŋkoˈrozu, ɔza] *adj* resentful.

rançoso, osa [xãˈsozu, ɔza] *adj* rancid.

ranger [26] [xãˈʒe(x)] <> *m* [ruído - de porta] creaking; [- de dentes] grinding. <> *vt* [os dentes] to grind. <> *vi* to creak.

rangido [xãˈʒidu] *m* -**1.** [de porta] creak. -**2.** [de dente] grinding.

rango [ˈxãŋgu] *m fam* grub.

Rangun [xãŋˈgũ] *n* Rangoon.

ranheta [xãˈŋeta] *adj* surly.

ranhura [xãˈŋura] *f* -**1.** [entalhe] groove. -**2.** [canaleta] keyway. -**3.** [para moeda] slot.

ranzinza [xãˈzĩza] *adj* bolshy.

rapa [ˈxapa] *m* -**1.** [de comida] scrap. -**2.** *fam* [fiscal] *policeman dealing with illegal street traders*. -**3.** *fam* [carro] *police patrol on the look-out for illegal street traders*.

rapadura [xapaˈdura] *f* raw cane sugar.

rapagão, gona [xapaˈgãw, gona] (*mpl* -**ões**, *fpl* -**onas**) *m, f* burly person.

rapapé [xapaˈpɛ] *m* [bajulação] fawning; **fazer** ~ **s a alguém** to kowtow to sb.

rapar [4] [xaˈpa(x)] <> *vt* -**1.** [pelar] to shave. -**2.** *fam* [roubar] to nick. <> *vi fam* [ir embora] to scarper.

rapaz [xaˈpaʒ] (*pl* -**es**) *m* -**1.** [jovem] boy. -**2.** *fam* [cara] man.

rapaziada [xapaˈzjada] *f* [rapazes] lads (*pl*).

rapé [xaˈpɛ] *m* snuff.

rapidamente [xapidaˈmẽtʃi] *adv* rapidly.

rapidez [xapiˈdeʃ] *f* speed; **com** ~ quickly, at speed.

rápido, da [ˈxapidu, da] *adj* -**1.** [veloz] fast, quick. -**2.** [breve] brief.
  ➡ **rápido** <> *m* [trem] express. <> *adv* [ligeiro] quickly.

rapina [xaˈpina] *f* violent robbery; ▷ **ave**.

raposa [xaˈpoza] *f* -**1.** ZOOL vixen (*f* vixen). -**2.** *fig* [pessoa astuta] sly old fox.

rapsódia [xapˈzɔdʒja] *f* rhapsody.

raptado, da [xapˈtadu, da] <> *adj* kidnapped. <> *m, f* kidnap victim.

raptar [4] [xapˈta(x)] *vt* to kidnap.

rapto [ˈxaptu] *m* kidnapping.

raptor, ra [xapˈto(x), ra] *m, f* kidnapper.

raquete [xaˈkɛtʃi] *f* -**1.** [de tênis, squash] racket. -**2.** [de pingue-pongue] bat.

raquidiana [xaki͵dʒjãna] *f* [anestesia] epidural.

raquítico, ca [xaˈkitʃiku, ka] *adj* -**1.** MED rachitic. -**2.** [magro] scrawny. -**3.** [escasso] sparse.

raquitismo [xakiˈtʃiʒmu] *m* MED rickets (*sg or pl*).

raramente [͵xaraˈmẽtʃi] *adv* rarely, seldom.

rarear [15] [xaˈrja(x)] *vi* -**1.** [tornar-se raro] to become scarce. -**2.** [cabelos] to thin. -**3.** [vegetação, população] to thin out.

rarefazer [31] [xarefaˈze(x)] *vt* [tornar menos denso] to make thinner.
  ➡ **rarefazer-se** *vp* -**1.** [tornar-se menos denso] to get thinner. -**2.** [multidão] to disperse.

rarefeito, ta [xareˈfejtu, ta] *adj* -**1.** [pouco denso] rarefied. -**2.** [disperso] dispersed.

raridade [xariˈdadʒi] *f* -**1.** [qualidade] rareness. -**2.** [peça] rarity.

raro, ra [ˈxaru, ra] *adj* rare.
  ➡ **raro** *adv* [raramente] rarely; **não** ~ often.

rasante [xaˈzãtʃi] <> *adj* low-flying. <> *adv*: **o avião passou** ~ the plane flew low.

rascunhar [4] [xaʃkuˈŋa(x)] *vt* to draft.

rascunho [xaʃˈkuŋul *m* draft.

rasgado, da [xaʒˈgadu, da] *adj* -**1.** [tecido, papel] torn. -**2.** *fig* [elogio, gesto] generous. -**3.** *fig* [ritmo, dança] flourishing.

rasgão [xaʒˈgãw] (*pl* -**ões**) *m* tear.

rasgar [14] [xaʒˈga(x)] <> *vt* -**1.** [romper] to tear. -**2.** *fig* [elogios] to heap. <> *vi* [romper-se] to tear.
  ➡ **rasgar-se** *vp* -**1.** [romper-se] to be torn. -**2.** [pessoa] to be consumed.

rasgo [ˈxaʒgu] *m* -**1.** [rasgão] tear. -**2.** [traço] line. -**3.** *fig* [ação, ímpeto] burst.

rasgões [xaʒˈgõjʃ] *pl* ▷ **rasgão**.

raso, sa [ˈxazu, za] *adj* -**1.** [pouco fundo] shallow. -**2.** [colher etc] level. -**3.** [liso] even. -**4.** [rente] close-cropped. -**5.** [sapato] flat. -**6.** [soldado] private.
  ➡ **raso** *m* shallow end.

raspa ['xaʃpa] *f* -**1.** [lasca] shavings *(pl)*. -**2.** [de panela] scrapings *(pl)*.

raspadeira [xaʃpa'dejra] *f* scraper.

raspadinha [xaʃpa'dʒiɲa] *f* scratch card.

raspão [xaʃ'pãw] *(pl* -ões) *m* scratch; **o tiro pegou de ~ no braço** the shot grazed his arm.

raspar [4] [xaʃ'pa(x)] <> *vt* -**1.** [alisar] to smooth down. -**2.** [pêlos] to shave. -**3.** [limpar] to scrape; **~ o tacho** *fig* [as economias] to scrape the bottom of the barrel. -**4.** [arranhar] to scratch. -**5.** [de raspão] to graze. <> *vi* [de raspão]: **~ em** to strike a glancing blow at.

raspões [xaʃ'põjʃ] *pl* ▷ raspão.

rasteiro, ra [xaʃ'tejru, ra] *adj* -**1.** [vegetação] lowlying. -**2.** [vôo] low. -**3.** [que se arrasta] crawling. -**4.** *fig* [superficial] superficial.

➠ **rasteira** *f* trip; **dar uma ~ em alguém** [com pernada] to trip sb up; *fig* [trair] to double-cross sb.

rastejante [xaʃte'ʒãntʃil *adj* -**1.** [que se arrasta - animal] crawling; [- planta] creeping. -**2.** *fig* [submisso] crawling.

rastejar [4] [xaʃte'ʒa(x)] <> *vi* -**1.** [arrastar-se - planta] to creep; [- animal] to crawl; [- cobra] to slide. -**2.** [andar de rastos] to crawl. -**3.** *fig* [rebaixar-se] to grovel. <> *vt* [rastrear] to track.

rastilho [xaʃ'tʃiʎu] *m* [de pólvora] fuse.

rasto ['xaʃtu] *m* -**1.** [pegada] track. -**2.** [de veículo] trail. -**3.** *fig* [vestígios] tracks *(pl)*.

➠ **rastos** *mpl*: **de rastos** on all fours.

rastrear [15] [xaʃ'trja(x)] <> *vt* -**1.** [seguir o rasto de] to track. -**2.** [investigar] to search for. <> *vi* [seguir o rasto] to track.

rastro ['xaʃtru] *m* = rasto.

rasura [xa'zura] *f* crossing out.

rasurar [4] [xazu'ra(x)] <> *vt* to cross out. <> *vi* to cross out.

rata ['xata] *f* *fam* [mancada] blunder; **dar uma ~** to make a stupid mistake; **rato**.

ratazana [xata'zãna] *f* Norway rat.

ratear [15] [xa'tʃja(x)] <> *vt* [dividir] to share out. <> *vi* [motor] to stall.

rateio [xa'teju] *m* -**1.** [divisão] sharing. -**2.** [turfe] [quantia] payout.

ratificação [xatʃifika'sãw] *(pl* -ões) *f* -**1.** [confirmação] ratification. -**2.** [comprovação] confirmation.

ratificar [12] [xatʃifi'ka(x)] *vt* -**1.** [confirmar] to ratify. -**2.** [comprovar] to confirm.

rato, ta ['xatu, ta] *m, f* rat; **~ de biblioteca** *fig* bookworm; **~ de praia** *fig* thief (on the beach).

ratoeira [xa'twejra] *f* -**1.** [para ratos] mousetrap. -**2.** *fig* [armadilha] trap.

ravina [xa'vina] *f* ravine.

ravióli [xa'vjɔli] *m* ravioli.

razão [xa'zãw] *(pl* -ões) <> *f* -**1.** [faculdade] reason; **~ de ser** raison d'être; **de viver** reason for living; **~ de Estado** reasons of state; **em ~ de** on account of. -**2.** [bom senso] (common) sense. -**3.** [justiça]: **dar ~ a alguém** to side with sb; **estar coberto de ~** to be absolutely right; **perder a ~** to lose one's mind; **ter/não ter ~ (de)**

to be right/wrong (to); **com ~** with good reason; **sem ~** for no reason. -**4.** [MAT- proporção] ratio; [- quociente, fração] quotient; **à ~ de** at the rate of. -**5.** FIN account. <> *m* COM ledger.

➠ **razão social** *f* COM trade name.

razoável [xa'zwavew] *(pl* -eis) *adj* -**1.** [ger] reasonable. -**2.** [significativo] significant.

razoavelmente [xazwavew'mẽntʃil *adv* reasonably.

ré ['xɛ] *f* AUTO reverse; **dar uma ~, dar marcha à ~** to reverse, to back up; ▷ réu.

reabastecer [25] [xejabaʃte'se(x)] *vt* -**1.** [tanque, carro, avião] to refuel. -**2.** [despensa, cozinha] to restock. -**3.** [energias] to rebuild.

➠ **reabastecer-se** *vp*: **~-se de algo** to replenish one's supply of sthg.

reabastecimento [xeabaʃtesi'mẽntu] *m* -**1.** [carro] refuelling. -**2.** [cidade] resupplying. -**3.** [despensa] restocking. -**4.** [energias] rebuilding.

reabertura [xeabex'tura] *f* reopening.

reabilitação [xeabilita'sãw] *(pl* -ões) *f* -**1.** [regeneração] rehabilitation. -**2.** [recuperação] rehabilitation; **~ motora** physiotherapy; [da forma física] recovery.

reabilitar [4] [xeabili'ta(x)] *vt* -**1.** [regenerar] to rehabilitate. -**2.** [recuperar] to recover.

➠ **reabilitar-se** *vp* -**1.** [regenerar-se] to be rehabilitated. -**2.** [recuperar-se] to recover.

reabrir [6] [xea'bri(x)] <> *vt* to reopen. <> *vi* to reopen.

reabsorver [5] [xeabsox've(x)] *vt* to reabsorb.

reaça *fam* [xe'asa] <> *adj* reactionary. <> *mf* [pessoa] reactionary.

reação [xea'sãw] *(pl* -ões) *f* -**1.** [ger] reaction; **~ em cadeia** chain reaction. -**2.** [recuperação] recovery.

reacender [5] [xeasẽn'de(x)] *vt* -**1.** [fogo, forno] to relight. -**2.** *fig* [ânimo, nacionalismo] to rekindle.

reacionário, ria [xeasjo'narju, rja] <> *adj* reactionary. <> *m, f* [pessoa] reactionary.

readaptação [xeadapta'sãw] *(pl* -ões) *f* readjustment.

readaptar [4] [xeadap'ta(x)] *vt* to readapt.

➠ **readaptar-se** *vp* to readapt.

readmissão [xeadʒimi'sãw] *f* readmission.

readmitir [6] [xeadʒimi'tʃi(x)] *vt* to readmit.

readquirir [6] [xeadʒiki'ri(x)] *vt* to regain. ·

reafirmar [4] [xeafix'ma(x)] *vt* to reaffirm.

reagir [52] [xea'ʒi(x)] *vi* -**1.** [responder]: **~ (a)** to react (to). -**2.** [protestar, resistir]: **~ (a** *OU* **contra)** to resist. -**3.** [recuperar-se] to rally. -**4.** QUÍM: **~ com** to react with.

reajustar [4] [xeaʒuʃ'ta(x)] *vt*: **~ algo (a algo)** to readjust sthg (to sthg).

➠ **reajustar-se** *vp*: **~-se a algo** to readjust to sthg.

reajuste [xea'ʒuʃtʃil *m* adjustment; **~ salarial** wage adjustment.

real [xe'aw] *(pl* -ais) <> *adj* -**1.** [verdadeiro] true. -**2.** [régio] royal. <> *m* [realidade] reality.

realçar [13] [xeaw'sa(x)] *vt* to highlight.

realce [xe'awsi] *m* **-1.** [destaque] emphasis; **dar ~ a** to emphasize. **-2.** [brilho] highlight.

realejo [xea'leʒu] *m* barrel organ.

realeza [xea'leza] *f* **-1.** [dignidade de rei] royalty. **-2.** [grandeza] *fig* grandeur.

realidade [xeali'dadʒi] *f* reality; **na ~** actually.

realismo [xea'liʒmu] *m* realism.

realista [xea'liʃta] ⬦ *adj* realistic. ⬦ *mf* **-1.** [pessoa] realist. **-2.** [adepto] royalist.

realização [xealiza'sãw] (*pl* **-ões**) *f* **-1.** [ger] realization. **-2.** [execução - de projeto, negócios] realization; [- de congresso, espetáculo] holding; [- de reforma] enactment. **-3.** [pessoal] fulfilment *UK*, fulfillment *US*.

realizado, da [xeali'zadu, da] *adj* **-1.** [pessoa] fulfilled. **-2.** [obra] carried out. **-3.** [sonho] realized.

realizador, ra [xealiza'do(x), ral (*mpl* **-es**, *fpl* **-s**) ⬦ *adj* enterprising. ⬦ *m, f* [pessoa] producer.

realizar [4] [xeali'za(x)] *vt* **-1.** [ger] to realize. **-2.** [executar] to carry out; **ser realizado** [conferência, festa] to take place.

➡ **realizar-se** *vp* **-1.** [concretizar-se] to be realized. **-2.** [ocorrer] to be carried out. **-3.** [alcançar seu ideal] to be fulfilled.

realizável [xeali'zavew] (*pl* **-eis**) *adj* achievable.

realmente [xeaw'mẽntʃi] ⬦ *adv* **-1.** [de fato] in fact. **-2.** [muito] really. ⬦ *interj* [expressando indignação] really!

reanimar [4] [xeani'ma(x)] *vt* **-1.** [fisicamente] to revive. **-2.** [moralmente] to cheer up. **-3.** *MED* to resuscitate.

➡ **reanimar-se** *vp* **-1.** [fisicamente] to come to. **-2.** [moralmente] to rally.

reaparecer [25] [xeapare'se(x)] *vi* to reappear.

reaparecimento [xeaparesi'mẽntu] *m* [ressurgimento] reappearance.

reaprender [5] [xeaprẽn'de(x)] ⬦ *vt* to relearn. ⬦ *vi*: **~ a fazer algo** to learn to do sthg again.

reapresentar [4] [xeaprezẽn'ta(x)] *vt* to represent.

➡ **reapresentar-se** *vp* to reappear.

reaproximação [xeaprosima'sãw] (*pl* **-ões**) *f* rapprochement.

reaproximar [4] [xeaprosi'ma(x)] *vt* to bring together again.

➡ **reaproximar-se** *vp* to grow closer again.

reaquecer [25] [xeake'se(x)] *vt* **-1.** [sopa, café] to reheat. **-2.** [relações] to re-establish.

reaquecimento [xeakesi'mẽntu] *m* **-1.** reheating. **-2.** *ECON* revival.

reassumir [6] [xeasu'mi(x)] ⬦ *vt* to regain. ⬦ *vi* to take over again.

reatar [4] [xea'ta(x)] *vt* **-1.** [nó] to retie. **-2.** [amizade, conversa, negócios] to resume.

reativar [4] [xeatʃi'va(x)] *vt* to revive.

reator [xea'to(x)] *m* reactor; **~ nuclear** nuclear reactor.

reavaliação [xeavalja'sãw] *f* **-1.** [ger] re-evaluation. **-2.** [de jóia] revaluation.

reavaliar [xeava'lja(x)] *vt* to reappraise.

reaver [51] [xea've(x)] *vt* to recover.

reavivar [4] [xeavi'va(x)] *vt* **-1.** [cor] to revive. **-2.** [passado] to reawaken.

rebaixado, da [xebaj'ʃadu, da] *adj* **-1.** [teto, terreno] lowered. **-2.** [preço] cut. **-3.** *fig* [pessoa] discredited. **-4.** *FUT* relegated.

rebaixar [4] [xebaj'ʃa(x)] *vt* **-1.** [teto, terreno] to lower. **-2.** [preço] to cut. **-3.** [pessoa] to discredit. **-4.** *FUT* to relegate.

➡ **rebaixar-se** *vp* [pessoa] to lower o.s.

rebanho [xe'bãɲu] *m* **-1.** [de bois, cabras] herd. **-2.** [de ovelhas] flock. **-3.** *fig* [de fiéis] flock.

rebater [5] [xeba'te(x)] ⬦ *vt* **-1.** [bola] to kick back. **-2.** [golpe] to counter. **-3.** [argumentos, acusações] to rebut. **-4.** [à máquina] to retype. ⬦ *vi* [chutar] to kick back.

rebelar-se [4] [xebe'laxsi] *vp*: **~-se (contra)** to rebel (against).

rebelde [xe'bɛwdʒi] ⬦ *adj* rebellious. ⬦ *mf* rebel.

rebeldia [xebew'dʒia] *f* **-1.** [qualidade] rebelliousness. **-2.** *fig* [oposição] defiance. **-3.** *fig* [obstinação] stubbornness.

rebelião [xebe'ljãw] (*pl* **-ões**) *f* [sublevação] rebellion.

rebentar [4] [xebẽn'ta(x)] ⬦ *vi* **-1.** [ger] to break. **-2.** [não se conter]: **~ de** to burst with; **~ em** to burst into. **-3.** [surgir]: **~ (de/em)** to gush out (from/onto). **-4.** [guerra] to break out. ⬦ *vt* **-1.** [romper] to tear. **-2.** [vidraça, louça] to smash.

rebento [xe'bẽntu] *m* [filho] offspring.

rebite [xe'bitʃi] *m TEC* rivet.

rebobinar [4] [xebobi'na(x)] *vt* [vídeo] to rewind.

rebocador [xeboka'do(x)] (*pl* **-es**) *m NÁUT* tug(-boat).

rebocar [12] [xebo'ka(x)] *vt* **-1.** [barco, carro] to tow. **-2.** [carro mal estacionado] to tow away. **-3.** *CONSTR* to plaster.

reboco [xe'boku] *m CONSTR* plaster.

rebolado [xebo'ladu] *m* swing of the hips.

rebolar [4] [xebo'la(x)] ⬦ *vt* [corpo, quadris] to swing. ⬦ *vi* **-1.** [pessoa, corpo] to sway. **-2.** *fam fig* [empenhar-se] to fight hard.

reboque [xe'bɔki] *m* **-1.** [ger] tow; **a ~** in tow. **-2.** [carro-guincho] towtruck.

rebordosa [xebox'dɔza] *f* **-1.** [situação difícil] tough situation. **-2.** [reincidência de doença] recurrence (*of an illness*).

rebu [xe'bu] *m fam* rumpus.

rebuliço [xebu'lisu] *m* commotion.

rebuscado, da [xebuʃ'kadu, da] *adj* affected.

recado [xe'kadu] *m* message; **dar conta do ~** *fig* to deliver the goods.

recaída [xeka'ida] *f* relapse.

recair [68] [xeka'i(x)] *vi* **-1.** [tornar a fazer]: **~ em erro** to make the same mistake again. **-2.** [culpa, responsabilidade, suspeita]: **~ em ou sobre alguém** to fall (up)on sb. **-3.** [cair outra vez] to fall back.

recalcado, da [xekaw'kadu, da] *PSIC* ⬦ *adj* repressed. ⬦ *m, f* repressed person.

recalcar [12] [xekaw'ka(x)] *vt* **-1.** [comprimir] to

tread upon. **-2.** [reprimir] to repress. **-3.** *PSIC* to inhibit.

recalcitrante [xekawsi'trãntʃil] *adj* recalcitrant.

recalque [xe'kawki] *m PSIC* inhibition.

recanto [xe'kãntu] *m* nook.

recapitulação [xekapitula'sãw] *f* **-1.** [resumo] recapitulation. **-2.** [lembrança] recollection.

recapitular [4] [xekapitu'la(x)] *vt* **-1.** [resumir] to recap. **-2.** [relembrar] to recall.

recatado, da [xeka'tadu, da] *adj* **-1.** [pudico] modest. **-2.** [prudente] restrained.

recato [xe'katu] *m* **-1.** [pudor] modesty. **-2.** [prudência] restraint.

recauchutado, da [xekawʃu'tadu, da] *adj* [pneu] remoulded *UK*, remolded *US*.

recauchutagem [xekawʃu'taʒẽ] (*pl* **-ns**) *f* **-1.** [de pneu] remoulding *UK*, remolding *US*. **-2.** *fig* [em pessoa] plastic surgery; **~ no rosto** facelift.

recauchutar [4] [xekawʃu'ta(x)] *vt* [pneu] to retread.

recear [15] [xe'sja(x)] <> *vt* **-1.** [temer] to fear; **~ fazer algo** to be afraid to do sthg. **-2.** [preocupar-se com]: **~ que** to be worried that. <> *vi* [preocupar-se]: **~ por algo** to worry about sthg.

receber [5] [xese'be(x)] <> *vt* **-1.** [ger] to receive. **-2.** [recepcionar] to entertain. <> *vi* **-1.** [ser pago] to be paid; **a ~** owing. **-2.** [recepcionar] to entertain.

recebimento [xesebi'mẽntu] *m* receipt; **acusar o ~ de** to acknowledge receipt of.

receio [xe'seju] *m* **-1.** [medo] fear. **-2.** [apreensão] concern; **ter ~ (de) que** to be afraid that.

receita [xe'sejta] *f* **-1.** [renda - pessoal] income; [- do Estado] tax revenue; **~ pública** tax revenue. **-2.** *FIN* income. **-3.** *MED*: **~ (médica)** prescription. **-4.** *CULIN* recipe. **-5.** *fig* [fórmula] way.

➡ Receita *f*: **a Receita (federal)** *Brazilian tax office,* ≃ Inland Revenue *UK,* ≃ Internal Revenue Service *US*.

receitar [4] [xesej'ta(x)] <> *vt* to prescribe. <> *vi* to issue prescriptions.

receituário [xesej'twarju] *m* prescription pad.

recém- [xesẽ] *prefixo* newly.

recém-casado, da [xe,sẽka'zadu, da] <> *adj* newly-wed. <> *m, f* newly-wed; **os ~s** the newly-weds.

recém-chegado, da [xe,sẽʃe'gadu, da] <> *adj* recently arrived. <> *m, f* newcomer.

recém-formado, da [xe,sẽfox'madu, da] (*pl* **-s**) <> *adj* newly qualified. <> *m,f* newly qualified person.

recém-nascido, da [xe,sẽna'sidu, da] <> *adj* newborn. <> *m, f* newborn child.

recém-publicado, da [xe,sẽpubli'kadu, da] (*pl* **-s**) *adj* recently published.

recender [5] [xesẽn'de(x)] *vi*: **~ a algo** to smell of sthg.

recenseamento [xesẽnsja'mẽntu] *m* census.

recensear [15] [xesẽn'sja(x)] *vt* to take a census of.

recente [xe'sẽntʃi] <> *adj* **-1.** [tempo] recent. **-2.** [novo] new; **este é o meu mais ~ hobby** this is my latest hobby. <> *adv* recently.

recentemente [xesẽntʃi'mẽntʃil] *adv* recently.

receoso, osa [xe'sjozu, ɔza] *adj* **-1.** [medroso] afraid. **-2.** [apreensivo] apprehensive; **estar ~ de algo/de fazer algo** to be worried about sthg/about doing sthg; **estar ~ de que** to be worried that.

recepção [xesep'sãw] (*pl* **-ões**) *f* reception.

recepcionar [4] [xesepsjo'na(x)] *vt* to entertain.

recepcionista [xesepsjo'niʃta] *mf* receptionist.

receptáculo [xesep'takulu] *m* receptacle.

receptador, ra [xesepta'do(x), ra] *m, f* fence.

receptar [4] [xesep'ta(x)] *vt* to fence.

receptividade [xeseptʃivi'dadʒil] *f* reception.

receptivo, va [xesep'tʃivu, va] *adj* receptive.

receptor [xesep'to(x)] (*pl* **-res**) *m* [aparelho] receiver.

recessão [xese'sãw] (*pl* **-ões**) *f* recession.

recesso [xe'sɛsul] *m* **-1.** [férias] recess. **-2.** [recanto] nook.

rechaçar [13] [xeʃa'sa(x)] *vt* **-1.** [opor-se a] to reject. **-2.** [repelir] to repel. **-3.** [negar] to decline.

recheado, da [xe'ʃjadu, da] *adj* **-1.** [comida]: **~ (com** *ou* **de)** filled (with). **-2.** [repleto]: **~ de algo** stuffed with sthg.

rechear [15] [xe'ʃja(x)] *vt* **-1.** [comida] to fill. **-2.** [encher muito]: **~ algo de algo** to fill sthg with sthg.

recheio [xe'ʃeju] *m* **-1.** [de comida - de carne] stuffing; [- de bolo, pastel] filling. **-2.** *fig* [num texto] padding.

rechonchudo, da [xeʃõn'ʃudu, da] *adj* chubby.

recibo [xe'sibu] *m* receipt.

reciclagem [xesi'klaʒẽ] *f* **-1.** [de material] recycling. **-2.** [de pessoa] retraining.

reciclar [4] [xesi'kla(x)] *vt* **-1.** [material] to recycle. **-2.** [pessoa] to retrain.

recife [xe'sifi] *m* reef.

Recife [xe'sifi] *n* Recife.

recinto [xe'sĩntu] *m* area.

recipiente [xesi'pjẽntʃi] *m* recipient.

recíproca [xe'siproka] *f* ➡ **recíproco**.

reciprocar [12] [xesipro'ka(x)] *vt* to reciprocate.

reciprocidade [xesiprosi'dadʒil] *f* reciprocity.

recíproco, ca [xe'siproku, ka] *adj* reciprocal.

➡ recíproca *f*: **a recíproca** the reverse.

récita [ˈxsita] *f* performance.

recital [xesi'taw] (*pl* **-ais**) *m* recital.

recitar [4] [xesi'ta(x)] *vt* [declamar] to recite.

reclamação [xeklama'sãw] (*pl* **-ões**) *f* **-1.** [queixa] complaint. **-2.** *JUR* [petição] claim.

reclamante [xekla'mãntʃil] *mf JUR* claimant.

reclamar [4] [xekla'ma(x)] <> *vt* [exigir] to demand. <> *vi* **-1.** [protestar]: **~ (de/contra)** to complain (about/against). **-2.** [exigir]: **~ por** to demand.

reclame [xeklãmil] *m* advertisement.

reclinado, da [xekli'nadu, da] *adj* **-1.** [inclinado] bending over. **-2.** [recostado] lying back.

reclinar [4] [xekli'na(x)] *vt* [inclinar]: **~ algo (em** *ou* **sobre)** to rest sthg (against *ou* on).

➡ reclinar-se *vp* [recostar-se] to lie back.

reclinável [xekli'navew] (*pl* **-eis**) *adj* reclining.

reclusão [xeklu'zãw] f -**1**. [isolamento] seclusion. -**2**. [em prisão] imprisonment. -**3**. [pena] solitary confinement.

recluso, sa [xe'kluzu, za] <> adj -**1**. [isolado] reclusive. -**2**. [preso] shut up. <> m, f -**1**. [pessoa que se isola] recluse. -**2**. [prisioneiro] prisoner.

recobrar [4] [xeko'bra(x)] vt to recover.

◆ **recobrar-se** vp: ~-**se de algo** to recover from sthg.

recolher [5] [xeko'ʎe(x)] vt -**1**. [ger] to collect. -**2**. [do chão] to pick up. -**3**. [juntar] to gather (together). -**4**. [pôr ao abrigo] to bring in. -**5**. [levar] to gather. -**6**. [tirar de circulação] to withdraw. -**7**. [coligir] to gather. -**8**. [encolher] to pull back.

◆ **recolher-se** vp -**1**. [ger] to retire. -**2**. [ir para casa] to go home. -**3**. [absorver-se] to become absorbed.

recolhido, da [xeko'ʎidu, da] adj -**1**. [lugar] secluded. -**2**. [absorvido] absorbed. -**3**. [dentro de casa] housebound.

recolhimento [xekoʎi'mẽntu] m -**1**. [ato de levar] reception. -**2**. [arrecadação] collection. -**3**. [de circulação] withdrawal. -**4**. [coleta] gathering. -**5**. [devido a doença] confinement. -**6**. [refúgio] refuge. -**7**. [retraimento] seclusion.

recomeçar [13] [xekome'sa(x)] <> vt to restart. <> vi to start again; ~ **a fazer algo** to start doing sthg again.

recomeço [xeko'mesu] m restart.

recomendação [xekomẽnda'sãw] (pl -ões) f [ger] recommendation; **por** ~ **de** on the recommendation of.

◆ **recomendações** fpl [saudações] regards.

recomendar [4] [xekomẽn'da(x)] vt -**1**. [ger] to recommend; **recomenda-se o uso de produtos naturais** the use of natural products is recommended. -**2**. [pedir] to ask. -**3**. [pedir proteção, favor]: ~ **alguém a alguém** to recommend sb to sb. -**4**. [enviar cumprimentos] to send one's regards.

recomendável [xekomẽn'davɛw] (pl -eis) adj advisable; **é** ~ **que ...** it's advisable that ...

recompensa [xekõn'pẽnsa] f reward.

recompensador, ra [xekõnpẽnsa'do(x), ra] adj rewarding.

recompensar [4] [xekõnpẽn'sa(x)] vt -**1**. [premiar] to reward. -**2**. [remunerar]: ~ **alguém de algo** to compensate sb for sthg.

recompor [45] [xekõn'po(x)] vt -**1**. [restabelecer] to reorganise. -**2**. [reordenar] to rearrange.

recôncavo [xe'kõŋkavu] m wide bay.

reconciliação [xekõnsilja'sãw] (pl -ões) f reconciliation.

reconciliar [16] [xekõnsi'lja(x)] vt to reconcile.

◆ **reconciliar-se** vp: ~-**se com** [pessoa] to be reconciled with; [situação] to become reconciled to.

recondicionado, da [xekõdisio'nadu, da] adj reconditioned.

recondicionar [4] [xekõndʒisjo'na(x)] vt to recondition.

recôndito, ta [xe'kõndʒitu, ta] adj -**1**. [retirado] secluded. -**2**. [íntimo] innermost.

◆ **recôndito** m fig [âmago]: **no** ~ **da alma** in one's heart of hearts.

reconfortante [xekõnfox'tãntʃi] adj relaxing.

reconfortar [4] [xekõnfox'ta(x)] vt to comfort.

reconhecer [25] [xekoɲe'se(x)] vt -**1**. [ger] to recognize. -**2**. [mostrar-se agradecido por] [admitir] to acknowledge. -**3**. [constatar] to accept. -**4**. [autenticar] to authenticate; ~ **firma num documento** to authenticate officially the signature on a document. -**5**. [explorar] to reconnoitre UK, to reconnoiter US.

reconhecido, da [xekoɲe'sidu, da] adj -**1**. [grato] thankful. -**2**. [firma] authenticated.

reconhecimento [xekoɲesi'mẽntu] m -**1**. [ger] recognition. -**2**. [admissão] acknowledgement. -**3**. [autenticação] authentication. -**4**. [gratidão] gratitude. -**5**. [exploração] reconnaissance.

reconhecível [xekoɲe'sivew] (pl -eis) adj recognizable.

reconquista [xekõŋ'kiʃta] f reconquest.

reconquistar [4] [xekõŋkiʃ'ta(x)] vt -**1**. [território] to reconquer. -**2**. [pessoa, confiança] to regain.

reconsiderar [4] [xekõnside'ra(x)] vt to reconsider.

reconstituição [xekõnʃtʃitwi'sãw] (pl -ões) f reconstruction.

reconstituir [74] [xekõnʃtʃi'twi(r)] vt -**1**. [regime, grupo] to reconstitute. -**2**. [enfermo] to revive. -**3**. [crime] to reconstruct.

reconstrução [xekõnʃtru'sãw] f rebuilding, reconstruction.

reconstruir [xekõnʃ'trwi(x)] vt to rebuild, to reconstruct.

recontar [4] [xekõn'ta(x)] vt to recount.

recordação [xekoxda'sãw] (pl -ões) f -**1**. [ato, lembrança] memory. -**2**. [objeto] souvenir.

recordar [4] [xekox'da(x)] vt -**1**. [lembrar] to remember. -**2**. [por semelhança]: ~ **algo/alguém a alguém** to remind sb of sthg/sb. -**3**. [recapitular] to revise.

◆ **recordar-se** vp [lembrar]: ~-**se de alguém/algo** to remember sb/sthg; ~-**se (de) que** to remember that.

recorde [xe'kɔxdʒi] <> adj inv record (antes de subst); **em tempo** ~ in record time. <> m record; **bater/deter um** ~ to break/hold a record.

recordista [xekox'dʒiʃta] <> adj recordbreaking. <> mf -**1**. [quem detém um recorde] record-holder. -**2**. [quem bate um recorde] recordbreaker.

recorrente [xeko'xẽntʃi] <> adj [que se repete] recurring. <> mf JUR appellant.

recorrer [5] [xeko'xe(x)] vi -**1**.: ~ **a** to resort to. -**2**. JUR to appeal; ~ **de algo** to appeal against sthg.

recortado, da [xekox'tadu, da] adj -**1**. [papel, desenho] cut out. -**2**. [borda, litoral] ragged.

recortar [4] [xekox'ta(x)] vt to cut out.

recorte [xe'kɔxtʃi] m [de jornal etc] cutting.

recostar [4] [xekoʃ'ta(x)] vt -**1**. [encostar] to rest. -**2**. [pôr meio deitado] to recline.

recostar-se vp -**1.** [encostar-se] to lean against. -**2.** [pôr-se meio deitado] to lie back.

recreação [xekrja'sãw] f recreation.

recreativo, va [xekrja'tʃivu, va] adj recreational.

recreio [xe'kreju] m -**1.** [entretenimento] entertainment. -**2.** EDUC playtime UK, recess US; **hora do** ~ breaktime.

recriação [xekrja'sãw] (pl -ões) f -**1.** [de história, mito] re-creation. -**2.** [de peça, ópera] new production. -**3.** [de filme] remake.

recriar [16] [xekri'a(x)] vt to recreate.

recriminação [xekrimina'sãw] (pl -ões) f recrimination.

recriminador, ra [xekrimina'do(x), ra] adj reproachful.

recriminar [4] [xekrimi'na(x)] vt to reproach.

recrudescer [25] [xekrude'se(x)] vi to intensify.

recrudescimento [xekrudesi'mẽntul m intensification.

recruta [xe'kruta] mf recruit.

recrutamento [xekruta'mẽntul m recruitment.

recrutar [4] [xekru'ta(x)] vt to recruit.

recuado, da [xe'kwadu, da] adj [edifício] set back.

recuar [4] [xe'kwa(x)] <> vi -**1.** [andar para trás] to step back. -**2.** [retirar-se] to retreat. -**3.** [voltar atrás - em intenção, decisão] to back out of; [- no tempo] to go back. -**4.** [canhão] to recoil. <> vt [mover para trás] to move back.

recuo [xe'kuw] m -**1.** [afastamento]: **com o ~, evitou ser atropelada** by stepping backwards, she avoided being run over; **o ~ do móvel, deu mais espaço na sala** moving this piece of furniture back has given the room more space. -**2.** [retirada] retreat. -**3.** [reconsideração - em intenção, decisão] reassessment; [- no tempo] going back. -**4.** [de canhão] recoil. -**5.** [em rua, terreno] setting back.

recuperação [xekupera'sãw] f -**1.** [reaquisição] recovery. -**2.** [restabelecimento] recuperation. -**3.** [reabilitação] rehabilitation. -**4.** [indenização] compensation.

recuperar [4] [xekupe'ra(x)] vt -**1.** [readquirir] to recover. -**2.** [restabelecer] to regain. -**3.** [reabilitar] to rehabilitate.

➡ **recuperar-se** vp [restabelecer-se] to recuperate.

recurso [xe'kuxsu] m -**1.** [ato]: **o ~ a algo** resorting to sthg. -**2.** [meio] recourse; **como** ou **em último ~** as a last resort. -**3.** [solução]: ~ **contra algo** answer to sthg.

➡ **recursos** mpl [dinheiro] means.

recusa [xe'kuza] f: ~ **(a/de algo)** refusal (to/ of sthg); ~ **a** ou **em fazer algo** refusal to do sthg.

recusar [4] [xeku'za(x)] vt -**1.** [não aceitar] to refuse. -**2.** [não conceder]: ~ **algo (a alguém)** to deny (sb) sthg. -**3.** [negar-se a]: ~ **fazer algo** to refuse to do sthg.

➡ **recusar-se** vp [negar-se a]: ~-**se (a fazer algo)** to refuse (to do sthg).

redação [xeda'sãw] (pl -ões) f -**1.** [ato] writing. -**2.** [modo de redigir] composition. -**3.** EDUC essay. -**4.** [redatores] editorial staff. -**5.** [seção] editorial office.

redargüir [xedax'gwi(x)] <> vt: ~ **que** to retort that. <> vi to retort; ~ **a alguém/algo** to respond to sb/sthg.

redator, ra [xeda'to(x), ra] (mpl -**es**, fpl -**s**) m, f -**1.** JORN writer. -**2.** [de obra de referência] editor, compiler.

redator-chefe, redatora-chefe [xedatoxʃɛfi, xedatoraʃɛfil (mpl redatores-chefes, fpl redatoras-chefes) m, f editor in chief.

rede ['xedʒil f -**1.** [ger] network; **comunicar-se em** ~ to network. -**2.** [para pesca, caça & ESP] net. -**3.** [para cabelo] hairnet. -**4.** [leito] hammock.

rédea ['xɛdʒja] f -**1.** [correia] rein. -**2.** fig [direção]: **tomar as** ~**s de algo** to take the reins of sthg. -**3.** loc: **dar** ~ **larga a algo** to give free rein to sthg.

redemoinho [xedʒi'mwiɲul m -**1.** [de água] whirlpool. -**2.** [de vento] whirlwind.

redenção [xedẽn'sãw] f redemption.

redentor, ra [xedẽn'to(x), ra] m, f [pessoa] redeemer.

➡ **Redentor** m: **o Redentor** RELIG the Redeemer.

redescobrir [59] [xedʒiʃko'bri(x)] vt to rediscover.

redigir [52] [xedʒi'ʒi(x)] <> vt to write. <> vi to write.

redimir [6] [xedʒi'mi(x)] vt -**1.** [RELIG - salvar] to redeem; [- expiar] to atone for. -**2.** [libertar] to set free.

➡ **redimir-se** vp: ~-**se do castigo** to escape punishment; **redimiu-se dos seus erros da juventude** he made up for the errors of his youth.

redobrar [4] [xedo'bra(x)] <> vt -**1.** [dobrar de novo] to fold again. -**2.** [reduplicar, intensificar] to redouble. <> vi to intensify.

redoma [xe'doma] f bell jar.

redondamente [xe,dõnda'mẽntʃi] adv [totalmente]: **me enganei** ~ I was utterly wrong.

redondeza [xedõn'deza] f [qualidade] roundness.

➡ **redondezas** fpl [arredores] surroundings.

redondo, da [xe'dõndu, da] adj -**1.** [circular] round. -**2.** [rechonchudo] plump.

redor [xe'do(x)] m: **ao** ~ **de** around.

redução [xedu'sãw] (pl -ões) f -**1.** [ger] reduction. -**2.** [conversão] conversion.

redundância [xedũn'dãnsja] f redundancy.

redundante [xedũn'dãntʃi] adj redundant.

redundar [4] [xedũn'da(x)] vi [resultar]: ~ **em algo** to result in sthg.

reduto [xe'dutul m -**1.** [fortificação] fort. -**2.** fig [abrigo] shelter. -**3.** fig [lugar de reunião] meeting place.

reduzido, da [xedu'zidu, da] adj -**1.** [diminuído] reduced. -**2.** [pequeno] limited.

reduzir [72] [xedu'zi(x)] vt -**1.** [ger] to reduce. -**2.** [transformar]: ~ **alguém/algo a algo** to reduce sb/ sthg to sthg. -**3.** [converter]: ~ **algo a algo** to convert sthg to sthg. -**4.** [levar]: ~ **alguém a algo** to reduce sb to sthg.

reduzir-se *vp*: ~-se a algo [resumir-se] to be reduced to sthg.

reedição [xeedʒi'sãw] (*pl* -ões) *f* -1. [de obra] reprint. -2. [de medida] reissue.

reeditar [4] [xeedʒi'ta(x)] *vt* to republish.

reeducar [12] [xeedu'ca(x)] *vt* to re-educate.

reeleger [26] [xeele'ʒe(x)] *vt* to re-elect.

reeleger-se *vp* to be re-elected.

reeleição [xeelej'sãw] *f* re-election.

reembolsar [4] [xeẽbow'sa(x)] *vt* -1. [reaver] to recover. -2. [restituir]: ~ alguém (de algo) to refund sb (sthg). -3. [indenizar]: ~ algo a alguém, ~ alguém de algo to reimburse sthg to sb, to reimburse sb for sthg.

reembolso [xeẽbowsul] *m* -1. [recuperação] recovery. -2. [restituição] refund. -3. [indenização] reimbursement.

reencarnação [xeẽkaxna'sãw] *f* reincarnation.

reencarnar [4] [xeẽkax'na(x)] *vi*: ~ (em) to reincarnate (as).

reencarnar-se *vp*: ~-se (em) to be reincarnated (as).

reencontrar [4] [xeẽkõn'tra(x)] *vt* to meet again.

reencontrar-se *vp*: ~-se (com alguém) to meet (sb) again.

reencontro [xeẽŋ'kõntrul] *m* reunion.

reentrância [xeẽn'trãnsjal] *f* recess.

reescalonamento [xeeʃkalona'mẽntul] *m* [of a debt] rescheduling.

reescalonar [4] [xeeʃkalo'na(x)] *vt* [dívida] to reschedule.

reescrever [5] [xeeʃkre've(x)] *vt* to rewrite.

reexaminar [4] [xeezami'na(x)] *vt* to re-examine.

refazer [31] [xefa'ze(x)] *vt* -1. [fazer de novo] to redo. -2. [reconstruir] to rebuild. -3. [recuperar] to recover.

refazer-se *vp* -1. [recuperar-se]: ~-se (de algo) to recover (from sthg). -2. [indenizar-se]: ~-se de algo to be compensated for sthg.

refeição [xefej'sãw] (*pl* -ões) *f* meal; fazer uma ~ to have a meal.

refeito, ta [ta, xe'fejtul] <> *pp* |> **refazer**. <> *adj* -1. [feito de novo] redone. -2. [reconstruído] rebuilt. -3. [recuperado] recovered.

refeitório [xefej'tɔrjul] *m* dining hall.

refém [xe'fɛl] (*pl* -ns) *mf* hostage.

referência [xefe'rẽnsjal] *f* reference; fazer ~ a to refer to.

referências *fpl* [informação] references.

referencial [xefe'rẽnsjaw] (*pl* -ais) *adj* reference (*antes de subst*).

referencial *m* [exemplo, modelo] yardstick.

referendar [457] [xeferẽn'da(x)] *vt* -1. [assinar] to countersign. -2. [validar] to endorse.

referendum [xefe'rẽndũl] *m* POL referendum.

referente [xefe'rẽntʃil] *adj*: ~ a concerning.

referido, da [xefe'ridu, da] *adj* -1. [mencionado] (afore)mentioned. -2. [referente]: ~ a in regard to.

referir [xefe'ri(x)] *vt* [narrar]: ~ algo a alguém to tell sb sthg.

referir-se *vp*: ~-se a [aludir] to allude to; [dizer respeito] to refer to.

refestelado, da [xefeʃte'ladu, da] *adj* [estendido] sprawling.

refestelar-se [7] [xefeʃte'laxsi] *vp* [estender-se] to sprawl.

refil [xe'fiwl] (*pl* -is) *m* refill.

refinado, da [xefi'nadu, da] *adj* refined.

refinamento [xefina'mẽntul] *m* -1. [ato] refining. -2. [requinte] refinement.

refinar [4] [xefi'na(x)] *vt* to refine.

refinaria [xefina'rial] *f* refinery.

refletido, da [xefle'tʃidu, da] *adj* -1. [espelhado] reflected. -2. [ponderado] considered.

refletir [65] [xefle'tʃi(x)] <> *vt* to reflect. <> *vi* -1. [luz]: ~ de to reflect off. -2. [pensar]: ~ (em/sobre) to reflect on/about. -3. [repercutir]: ~ em to reflect on.

refletir-se *vp* -1. [espelhar-se] to be reflected. -2. [repercutir] to reflect on.

refletor [xe'fle'to(x)] (*pl* -es) *m* reflector.

reflexão [xeflek'sãw] (*pl* -ões) *f* reflection.

reflexivo, va [xeflek'sivu, va] *adj* reflective.

reflexo, xa [xe'flɛksu, sa] *adj* -1. [luz] reflected. -2. [movimento] reflex.

reflexo *m* -1. [ger] reflection. -2. ANAT reflex.

reflexos *mpl* [no cabelo] highlights.

reflorestamento [xefloreʃta'mẽntul] *m* reforestation.

reflorestar [4] [xefloreʃ'ta(x)] *vt* to reforest.

refluxo [xe'fluksul] *m* ebb.

refogado, da [xefo'gada, xefo'gadul] *adj* sautéed.

refogado *m* -1. [molho] gravy. -2. [prato] stew.

refogar [14] [xefo'ga(x)] *vt* to sauté.

reforçado, da [xefox'sadu, da] *adj* -1. [ger] reinforced. -2. [refeição] hearty.

reforçar [13] [xefox'sa(x)] *vt* -1. [ger] to reinforce. -2. [ânimo] to invigorate.

reforço [xe'foxsul] *m* -1. [ger] reinforcement. -2. [a tropa, equipe] reinforcements (*pl*). -3. [de vacina] booster.

reforma [xe'fɔxmal] *f* -1. [modificação] reform; ~ ministerial ministerial reshuffle; ~ agrária land reform. -2. ARQUIT renovation; estar em ~ to be under repair. -3. MIL regrouping.

Reforma *f*: a Reforma RELIG the Reformation.

reformado, da [xefox'madu, da] *adj* -1. [modificado - ensino, instituição] reformed; [- leis] amended; [- sofá] repaired. -2. ARQUIT renovated. -3. MIL regrouped.

reformar [4] [xefox'ma(x)] *vt* -1. [modificar - ensino, constituição] to reform; [- sofá] to repair; [- lei] to amend; [- empresa] to restructure. -2. ARQUIT to renovate. -3. MIL to regroup. -4. JUR to amend.

reformar-se *vp* -1. MIL to retire. -2. [regenerar-se] to be reformed.

reformatar [4] [xefoxma'ta(x)] *vt* COMPUT to reformat.

reformatório [xefoxma'tɔrjul] *m* young offender institution *UK*, reformatory *US*.

refrão [xe'frãw] (*pl*-ões) *m* -1. [estribilho] chorus. -2. [provérbio] saying.

refratário, ria [xefra'tarju, rja] *adj* -1. [material] heat-resistant. -2. [rebelde]: **ser ~ a algo** to be impervious to sthg; [imune] to be immune to sthg.

refrear [15] [xefri'a(x)] *vt* [reprimir] to suppress.
➡ **refrear-se** *vp* [conter-se] to contain o.s.

refrega [xe'frɛga] *f* [briga] fight.

refrescante [xefreʃ'kãntʃi] *adj* refreshing.

refrescar [12] [xefreʃ'ka(x)] <> *vt*-1. [tornar menos quente] to cool. -2. [avivar] to refresh. -3. [tranqüilizar] to refresh. <> *vi* [tempo] to cool down.
➡ **refrescar-se** *vp* [pessoa] to refresh o.s.

refresco [xe'freʃku] *m* fruit squash.

refrigeração [xefriʒera'sãw] *m* [de alimentos] refrigeration; [de ambiente] air conditioning.

refrigerado, da [xefriʒe'radu, da] *adj* [alimento] chilled; [ambiente] air conditioned.

refrigerador [xefriʒera'do(x)] *m* -1. [de alimentos] refrigerator. -2. [de máquina] cooler.

refrigerante [xefriʒe'rãntʃi] *m* soft drink.

refrigerar [4] [xefriʒe'ra(x)] *vt*-1. [bebidas, alimentos] to chill. -2. [ambiente] to cool. -3. [máquina] to refrigerate.

refugar [14] [xefu'ga(x)] <> *vt* -1. [recusar] to refuse. -2. [menosprezar] to reject. <> *vi* [recusar-se] to refuse.

refugiado, da [xefu'ʒjadu, da] <> *adj* refugee. <> *m*, *f* refugee.

refugiar-se [16] [xefu'ʒjaxsi] *vp* [abrigar-se] to take refuge; **~ em** [abrigar-se] to take cover in; [asilar-se] to take refuge in; *fig* [amparar-se] to seek solace in.

refúgio [xe'fuʒju] *m* -1. [local] hideaway. -2. *fig* [apoio] refuge.

refugo [xe'fugu] *m* -1. [resto] waste. -2. [mercadoria] rubbish *UK*, garbage *US*.

refulgir [52] [xefuw'ʒi(x)] *vi* -1. [resplandecer] to shine. -2. *fig* [destacar-se] to stand out.

refutação [xefuta'sãw] (*pl*-ões) *f* -1. [desmentido] refutation. -2. [contestação] denial.

refutar [4] [xefu'ta(x)] *vt* to refute.

regaço [xe'gasu] *m* [colo] lap.

regador [xega'do(x)] (*pl*-es) *m* watering can.

regalia [xega'lia] *f* privilege.

regalo [xe'galu] *m* -1. [presente] gift. -2. [prazer]: **ser um ~** to be a pleasure.

regar [14] [xe'ga(x)] *vt*-1. [aguar] to water. -2. [banhar] to wash. -3. [acompanhar] to wash down.

regata [xe'gata] *f* regatta.

regatear [15] [xega'tʃja(x)] <> *vt* to haggle over. <> *vi* to haggle.

regato [xe'gatu] *m* stream.

regência [xe'ʒẽnsja] *f* -1. *MÚS* conducting. -2. *GRAM* government. -3. [administração] rule.

regeneração [xeʒenera'sãw] *f* -1. [recomposição] regeneration. -2. [moral] reform.

regenerar [4] [xeʒene'ra(x)] *vt* -1. [recompor] to regenerate. -2. [moralmente] to reform.
➡ **regenerar-se** *vp* -1. [recompor-se] to be

regenerated. -2. [moralmente] to be reformed.

regente [xe'ʒẽntʃi] *m* -1. *POL* regent. -2. *MÚS* conductor. -3. *UNIV* vice chancellor *UK*, president *US*.

reger [26] [xe'ʒe(x)] <> *vt*-1. [governar] to govern. -2. [regular] to rule. -3. *MÚS* to conduct. -4. *UNIV* to occupy. -5. *GRAM* to govern. <> *vi*-1. [governar] to rule. -2. *MÚS* to conduct.

região [xe'ʒjãw] (*pl*-ões) *f* -1. [território] region. -2. [de cidade, corpo] area.

regime [xe'ʒimil] *m* -1. [ger] system. -2. [dieta] diet; **estar de ~** to be on a diet; **fazer ~** to diet. -3. [regras] rules (*pl*); **~ de vida** way of life.

regimento [xeʒi'mẽntul] *m* -1. [ger] regiment. -2. [normas] rules (*pl*); **~ interno** [de escola] school rules; [de empresa] company rules.

regiões [xe'ʒjõjʃ] *mpl* ▷ **região**.

regional [xeʒjo'naw] (*pl*-ais) *adj* regional.

regionalismo [xeʒjona'liʒmu] *m* regionalism.

regionalizar [xeʒjonali'za(x)] *vt* to regionalize.

registradora [xeʒiʃtra'dora] *f* [caixa] cash register.

registrar [4] [xeʒiʃ'tra(x)] *vt* -1. [ger] to register. -2. [anotar] to record. -3. [memorizar] to remember.

registro [xe'ʒiʃtru] *m* -1. [ger & *LING*] register. -2. [postal] registration. -3. [órgão]: **~ civil** registry office. -4. [torneira] tap *UK*, faucet *US*. -5. [relógio] meter. -6. *MÚS* range.

rego ['xegu] *m* -1. [valão] ditch. -2. [de arado] furrow. -3. *mfam ANAT* bum crack.

regozijar-se [4] [xegozi'ʒaxsi] *vp*: **~ com algo/por fazer algo** to be delighted with sthg/to do sthg.

regozijo [xego'ziʒu] *m* delight.

regra ['xɛgra] *f* -1. [norma] rule; **por via de ~** as a rule. -2. [rotina] routine; **sair da ~** to change one's routine. -3. [prudência]: **com ~** in moderation.

regrado, da [xe'gradu, da] *adj* sensible.

regrar [4] [xe'gra(x)] *vt* to regulate.
➡ **regrar-se** *vp*: **~-se por algo** to be guided by sthg.

regredir [57] [xegre'dʒi(x)] *vi*: **~ (a algo)** to regress (to sthg).

regressão [xegre'sãw] *f* -1. [retrocesso] regression. -2. *PSIC* relapse.

regressar [4] [xegre'sa(x)] *vi*: **~ (de/a)** to return from/to.

regressivo, va [xegre'sivu, va] *adj* regressive.

regresso [xe'grɛsul] *m* return.

régua ['xɛgwa] *f* ruler; **~ de cálculo** slide rule.

régua-tê [ˌxɛgwa'te] (*pl* **réguas-tê**) *f* *ARQUIT* T-square.

regulador, ra [xegula'do(x), ra] *adj* [força] regulating.
➡ **regulador** *m* [medicamento] regulator.

regulagem [xegu'laʒẽl] (*pl*-ns) *f* tuning.

regulamentação [xegulamẽnta'sãw] *f* -1. [ato] regulation. -2. [regras] regulations (*pl*).

regulamentar [4] [xegula'mẽnta(x)] <> *adj* standardizing. <> *vt* to regulate.

regulamento [xegula'mẽntu] *m* rules *(pl)*.
regular [4] [xegu'la(x)] *(pl* -es) ⟨⟩ *adj* -1. [ger]
regular. -2. [legal] legal. -3. [tamanho] medium.
-4. [razoável] reasonable. ⟨⟩ *vt* -1. [ger] to
regulate. -2. [ajustar] to adjust. -3. [conformar]:
~ algo por algo to check sthg against sthg. ⟨⟩
vi -1. [maquina]: ~ **bem/mal** to be well/badly
adjusted. -2. [pessoa]: **não ~ (bem)** to not be
quite right in the head. -3. [ter]: **ele ~ pelos 50**
he's about 50. -4. [aproximar-se]: **meu filho regula
em idade com o seu** my son is about the same
age as yours.
➤ **regular-se por** *vp* [orientar-se] to be guided
by.
regularidade [xegulari'dadʒi] *f* regularity.
regularizar [4] [xegulari'za(x)] *vt* -1. [legalizar] to
legalize. -2. [normalizar] to regularize.
➤ **regularizar-se** *vp* [normalizar-se] to return to
normal.
regurgitar [4] [xeguxʒi'ta(x)] *vt & vi* to regurgitate.
rei ['xej] *m* -1. [ger] king; **ser o ~ de algo** *fig* [da
música, do crime] to be the king of sthg; [da bagun-
ça] to be the world's worst for sthg. -2. *loc*: **ter o
~ na barriga** to be full of o.s.
Reikjavik [xejkʒa'viki] *n* Reykjavik.
reimpressão [xẽjnpre'sãw] *(pl* -ões) *f* reprint.
reimprimir [6] [xẽjnpri'mi(x)] *vt* to reprint.
reinado [xej'nadu] *m* reign.
reinante [xej'nãntʃi] *adj* prevailing.
reinar [4] [xej'na(x)] *vi* -1. [governar] to reign. -2.
fig [dominar] to dominate.
reincidência [xẽjnsi'dẽnsja] *f* -1. [de doença]
relapse. -2. [de crime] recidivism. -3. [de erro]
repetition. -4. [na bebida] backsliding.
reincidente [xẽjnsi'dẽntʃi] ⟨⟩ *adj*: ~ **em algo**
drawn back into sthg; **jamais perdoaremos os erros ~s** we shall never forgive repeated mistakes. ⟨⟩ *mf* reoffender.
reincidir [6] [xẽjnsi'dʒi(x)] *vi* to recur; ~ **em algo**
to commit sthg again.
reingressar [4] [xẽjngre'sa(x)] *vt*: ~ **em** to re-
enter.
reiniciar [16] [xejni'sja(x)] *vt* to restart.
reino ['xejnu] *m* -1. [ger] kingdom. -2. *fig* [âmbito]
realm.
reintegrar [4] [xẽjnte'gra(x)] *vt* -1. [em cargo etc] to
reinstate. -2. [reconduzir] to readmit.
reiterar [4] [xeite'ra(x)] *vt* to reiterate.
reitor, ra [xej'to(x), ra] *m, f* vice chancellor *UK*,
president *US*.
reitoria [xejto'ria] *f* -1. [cargo] vice-chancellor-
ship *UK*, presidency *US*. -2. [gabinete] vice
chancellor's office *UK*, president's office *US*.
reivindicação [xejvĩndʒika'sãw] *(pl* -ões) *f* claim.
reivindicar [12] [xejvĩndʒi'ka(x)] *vt* to claim.
rejeição [xeʒej'sãw] *(pl* -ões) *f* rejection.
rejeitar [4] [xeʒej'ta(x)] *vt* -1. [recusar] to reject.
-2. [vomitar] to vomit. -3. [desprezar] to ignore.
rejubilar-se [4] [xeʒubi'laxsi] *vp* to rejoice.
rejuvenescer [25] [xeʒuvene'se(x)] ⟨⟩ *vt* to

rejuvenate. ⟨⟩ *vi* to be rejuvenating.
➤ **rejuvenescer-se** *vp* to be rejuvenated.
rejuvenescimento [xeʒuvenesi'mẽntu] *m* rejuvenation.
relação [xela'sãw] *(pl* -ões) *f* -1. [ligação] relationship; **em ~ a** in relation to; ~ **entre/com**
relationship between/with. -2. [listagem] list.
➤ **relações** *fpl* [relacionamento] relationship *(sg)*;
ele não é pessoa de minhas relações he's not sb I
have anything to do with; **cortar relações com
alguém** to break off with sb; **ter relações com alguém** [sexual] to sleep with sb; **relações públicas**
public relations; **relações sexuais** sex, sexual
intercourse.
relacionado, da [xelasjo'nadu, da] *adj* -1. [lista-
do] listed. -2. [ligado] related. -3. [pessoa]: **bem
~** well connected.
relacionamento [xelasjona'mẽntu] *m* -1. [liga-
ção] relationship. -2. [trato]: **é uma garota de
fácil ~** she's a girl who's easy to get on with.
relacionar [4] [xelasjo'na(x)] *vt* -1. [listar] to list.
-2. [confrontar]: ~ **algo com algo** to compare sthg
with sthg. -3. [pessoa] to bring into contact with.
➤ **relacionar-se** *vp* -1. [ligar-se] to be related.
-2. [pessoa]: **~-se com alguém** to mix with sb.
relações-públicas [xela‚sõjʃ'publikaʃ] *mf inv*
[pessoa] PR officer.
relâmpago [xe'lãmpagu] ⟨⟩ *m* METEOR flash of
lightning; **num ~** [rapidamente] in a flash. ⟨⟩ *adj*
[rápido] lightning *(antes de subst)*.
relampejar [4] [xelãnpe'ʒa(x)] *vi*: **relampejou esta
noite** there was lightening last night.
relance [xe'lãnsi] *m*: **ver de ~** to glance at.
relapso, sa [xe'lapsu, sa] ⟨⟩ *adj* negligent. ⟨⟩
m, f negligent person.
relatar [4] [xela'ta(x)] *vt* to relate.
relativamente [xelatʃiva'mẽntʃi] *adv* relatively.
relatividade [xelatʃivi'dadʒi] *f* relativity.
relativo, va [xela'tʃivu, va] *adj* relative; ~ **a algo**
relative to sthg.
relato [xe'latu] *m* account.
relator, ra [xela'to(x), ra] *m, f* report writer.
relatório [xela'tɔrju] *m* report; ~ **anual** annual
report.
relax [xi'lɛkiʃ] *m* relaxation.
relaxado, da [xela'ʃadu, da] *adj* -1. [desleixado]
careless. -2. [descansado] relaxed.
relaxamento [xelaʃa'mẽntu] *m* -1. [desleixo]
carelessness. -2. [repouso] relaxation.
relaxante [xela'ʃãntʃi] *adj* relaxing.
relaxar [4] [xela'ʃa(x)] ⟨⟩ *vt* to relax. ⟨⟩ *vi* -1.
[desleixar-se]: ~ **em algo** to become careless with
sthg. -2. [descansar] to relax. -3. [condescender]: ~
com algo/alguém to relent towards sthg/sb.
➤ **relaxar-se** *vp* -1. [desleixar-se]: **~-se (com algo)** to be careless (with sthg). -2. [distender-se] to
be relaxed.
relegar [14] [xele'ga(x)] *vt* to relegate.
relembrar [4] [xelẽn'bra(x)] *vt* to recall.
relento [xe'lẽntu] *m* dew; **ao ~** outdoors.
reler [42] [xe'le(x)] *vt* to reread.

reles ['xɛliʃ] *adj inv* **-1.** [desprezível] despicable. **-2.** [mero] mere.

relevância [xele'vãnsja] *f* **-1.** [saliência] prominence. **-2.** [importância] relevance; **ser de** ~ to be of importance, to be important.

relevante [xele'vãntʃil] *adj* **-1.** [saliente] prominent. **-2.** [importante] important.

relevar [4] [xele'va(x)] *vt* **-1.** [salientar] to emphasize. **-2.** [aliviar] to alleviate. **-3.** [perdoar] to forgive.

relevo [xe'levul] *m* **-1.** [em superfície] outstanding feature. **-2.** *ARTE* relief. **-3.** *fig* [destaque] importance; **pôr em** ~ to emphasize.

relicário [xeli'karjul] *m* reliquary.

religião [xeli'ʒjãwl] *(pl* **-ões)** *f* religion.

religiosidade [xeliʒjozi'dadʒil] *f* piety; **pagar as contas com** ~ to pay one's debts religiously.

religioso, osa [xeli'ʒozu, ɔzal] <> *adj* religious. <> *m, f* [padre, freira] monk (*f* nun).
  ➡ **religioso** *m* [casamento] church wedding.

relinchar [4] [xelĩn'ʃa(x)] *vi* to neigh.

relincho [xe'lĩnʃul] *m* neigh.

relíquia [xe'likja] *f* relic; ~ **de família** family heirloom.

relógio [xe'lɔʒjul] *m* **-1.** [instrumento] clock; ~ **de pé** grandfather clock; ~ **de ponto** time clock; ~ **de pulso** wrist watch; ~ **de sol** sundial; **correr contra o** ~ to race against the clock. **-2.** [registro] meter.

relojoaria [xeloʒwa'rial] *f* **-1.** *ARTE* watchmaking. **-2.** [loja] watchmaker's.

relojoeiro, ra [xelo'ʒwejru, ral] *m, f* watchmaker.

relutância [xelu'tãnsja] *f* reluctance.

relutante [xelu'tãntʃil] *adj* reluctant.

relutar [4] [xelu'ta(x)] *vi:* ~ **(em fazer algo)** to be reluctant (to do sthg); ~ **(contra algo)** to be reluctant (to accept sthg).

reluzente [xelu'zẽntʃil] *adj* shining.

reluzir [72] [xelu'zi(x)] *vi* [brilhar] to shine.

relva ['xɛwval] *f* grass.

remador, ra [xema'do(x), ral] *m, f* rower.

remanescente [xemane'sẽntʃil] <> *adj* remaining; **isto é** ~ **de práticas antigas** this is what remains of ancient customs. <> *m* remainder.

remanescer [25] [xemane'se(x)] *vi* to remain.

remanso [xe'mãnsul] *m* backwater.

remar [4] [xe'ma(x)] <> *vt* to row. <> *vi* to row; ~ **contra a maré** *fig* to swim against the tide.

remarcação [xemaxka'sãwl] *(pl* **-ões)** *f* adjustment.

remarcar [12] [xemax'ka(x)] *vt* to adjust.

rematado, da [xema'tadu, dal] *adj* [concluído] completed.

rematar [4] [xema'ta(x)] *vt* **-1.** [concluir] to conclude. **-2.** [fazer o acabamento] to finish.

remate [xe'matʃil] *m* **-1.** [conclusão] end. **-2.** [acabamento] finishing touch. **-3.** [de piada] punchline.

remediado, da [xeme'dʒadu, dal] *adj* comfortably off.

remediar [17] [xeme'dʒja(x)] *vt* **-1.** [corrigir, solucionar] to put right. **-2.** [atenuar] to alleviate. **-3.** [evitar] to avoid.

remediável [xeme'dʒjavewl] *(pl* **-eis)** *adj* rectifiable.

remédio [xe'mɛdʒjul] *m* **-1.** [medicamento] remedy. **-2.** [solução] solution.

remela [xe'mɛla] *f* sleep.

remelento, ta [xeme'lẽntu, tal] *adj* bleary-eyed.

remelexo [xeme'leʃul] *m* swaying.

rememorar [4] [xememo'ra(x)] *vt* to remember.

remendar [4] [xemẽn'da(x)] *vt* **-1.** [roupa] to mend. **-2.** [erros] to rectify.

remendo [xe'mẽndul] *m* **-1.** [de pano] patch. **-2.** [de metal, couro] repair. **-3.** [emenda] correction.

remessa [xe'mɛsal] *f* **-1.** [ato] dispatch. **-2.** [de dinheiro] remittance; [de mercadorias] shipment.

remetente [xeme'tẽntʃil] *mf* [de carta] sender.

remeter [5] [xeme'te(x)] *vt* **-1.** [carta, encomenda] to send. **-2.** [dinheiro] to remit.
  ➡ **remeter-se** *vp* [referir-se] to refer to.

remexer [5] [xeme'ʃe(x)] <> *vt* **-1.** [mexer] to move. **-2.** [misturar] to mix. **-3.** [sacudir - braços] to shake; [- papéis, folhas] to shuffle. **-4.** [revolver] to stir up. **-5.** *fam* [rebolar] to roll. <> *vi* [mexer]: ~ **em algo** to rummage through sthg.
  ➡ **remexer-se** *vp* **-1.** [mover-se] to stir. **-2.** [rebolar-se] to roll.

remição [xemi'sãwl] *f* **-1.** [libertação] release. **-2.** [expiação] redemption.

reminiscência [xemini'sẽnsja] *f* reminiscence.

remir [80] [xe'mi(x)] *vt* **-1.** [ger] to redeem. **-2.** [livrar]: ~ **alguém (de algo)** to free sb (from sthg). **-3.** [indenizar] to indemnify.
  ➡ **remir-se** *vp* [redimir-se] to redeem o.s.

remissão [xemi'sãwl] *(pl* **-ões)** *f* **-1.** [ger] remission. **-2.** [em texto] cross-reference.

remo ['xemul] *m* **-1.** [instrumento] oar. **-2.** [esporte] rowing.

remoção [xemo'sãwl] *(pl* **-ões)** *f* removal.

remoçar [13] [xemo'sa(x)] <> *vt* to rejuvenate. <> *vi* to be rejuvenated.

remoer [28] [xe'mwe(x)] *vt* **-1.** [moer novamente] to regrind. **-2.** [remastigar] to chew. **-3.** [refletir muito sobre] to chew over. **-4.** [afligir] to chew at.
  ➡ **remoer-se** *vp* [amofinar-se] to be consumed.

remontar [4] [xemõn'ta(x)] <> *vt* **-1.** [armar de novo] to reassemble. **-2.** *TEATRO* to restage. **-3.** [mobiliar] to refurnish. <> *vi* **-1.** [em cavalo] to remount. **-2.** [no tempo]: ~ **a** to date back to; ~ **ao passado** to return to the past.

remorso [xe'mɔxsul] *m* remorse.

remoto, ta [xe'mɔtu, tal] *adj* remote.

removedor [xemove'do(x)] *m* remover.

remover [5] [xemo've(x)] *vt* **-1.** [ger] to remove. **-2.** [transferir] to transfer. **-3.** [superar] to overcome.

remuneração [xemunera'sãwl] *(pl* **-ões)** *f* remuneration.

remunerador, ra [xemunera'do(x), ral] *adj* [recompensador] remunerative.

remunerar [4] [xemune'ra(x)] *vt* to remunerate.
rena ['xena] *f* reindeer.
renal [xe'naw] (*pl* -ais) *adj* renal.
Renascença [xena'sẽnsal] *f*: **a ~** the Renaissance.
renascentista [xenasẽn'tʃiʃta] *adj* Renaissance (*antes de subst*).
renascer [25] [xena'se(x)] *vi* -**1.** [nascer de novo] to spring up again. -**2.** *fig* [recuperar-se, resurgir] to be reborn.
renascimento [xenasi'mẽntul] *m* rebirth.
⇒ **Renascimento** *m*: **o Renascimento** the Renaissance.
renda ['xẽnda] *f* -**1.** [rendimento] income; **viver de ~** to have a private income; **~ bruta** gross income; **~ fixa** fixed yield; **~ líquida** net income. -**2.** [lucro] profit. -**3.** [tecido] lace.
rendado, da [xẽn'dadu, da] *adj* -**1.** [feito de renda] lace (*antes de subst*). -**2.** [como renda] lacy.
⇒ **rendado** *m* lacework.
rendeiro, ra [xẽn'dejru, ra] *m, f* -**1.** [fabricante de renda] lacemaker. -**2.** [de terra] tenant farmer.
render [5] [xẽn'de(x)] ⟨⟩ *vt* -**1.** [dominar] to overpower. -**2.** [substituir] to relieve. -**3.** [lucrar] to yield. -**4.** [causar] to bring about. -**5.** [prestar] to render. ⟨⟩ *vi* -**1.** [dar lucro] to be profitable. -**2.** [trabalho] to be productive. -**3.** [comida]: **a comida rendeu para toda a semana** there was enough food for the whole week; **vamos fazer sopa porque rende mais** let's make soup because it goes further. -**4.** [durar] to last.
⇒ **render-se** *vp* [entregar-se]: **~-se (a algo/alguém)** to surrender (to sb/sthg).
rendição [xẽndʒi'sãw] *f* -**1.** [capitulação] surrender. -**2.** [substituição] changing.
rendido, da [xẽn'dʒidu, da] *adj fig*: **~ a algo** overcome by sthg.
rendimento [xẽndʒi'mẽntu] *m* -**1.** [renda] rental. -**2.** [lucro] profit. -**3.** [desempenho] performance. -**4.** [juro] interest.
rendoso, osa [xẽn'dozu, ɔza] *adj* -**1.** [lucrativo] profitable. -**2.** [proveitoso] productive.
renegado, da [xene'gadu, da] ⟨⟩ *adj* renegade. ⟨⟩ *m, f* renegade.
renegar [14] [xene'ga(x)] *vt* -**1.** [ger] to renounce. -**2.** [negar] to deny. -**3.** [desprezar] to reject.
renhido, da [xe'ɲidu, da] *adj* hard-fought.
renitente [xeni'tẽntʃi] *adj* persistent.
renomado, da [xeno'madu, da] *adj* renowned.
renome [xe'nɔmi] *m*: **de ~** renowned.
renovação [xenova'sãw] (*pl* -ões) *f* -**1.** [ger] renewal. -**2.** [de ensino, empresa] revamping. -**3.** ARQUIT renovation.
renovador, ra [xeno'vado(x), ra] ⟨⟩ *adj* reformist. ⟨⟩ *m, f* reformist.
renovar [4] [xeno'va(x)] *vt* -**1.** [ger] to renew. -**2.** [ensino, empresa] to revamp. -**3.** ARQUIT to renovate.
rentabilidade [xẽntabili'dadʒi] *f* -**1.** [lucro] profitability. -**2.** [proveito] productiveness.
rentável [xẽn'tavɛw] (*pl* -eis) *adj* profitable.

rente ['xẽntʃi] ⟨⟩ *adj* -**1.** [muito curto] close-cropped. -**2.** [junto]: **~ a** right next to. ⟨⟩ *adv* -**1.** [muito curto] very short. -**2.** [junto]: **ele caiu ~ ao chão** he fell flat on the floor; **ele foi esmagado ~ ao muro** he was crushed right up against the wall.
renúncia [xe'nũnsja] *f* renouncement.
renunciar [16] [xenũn'sja(x)] *vi*: **~ a algo** to renounce sthg.
reorganização [xeoxganiza'sãw] *f* reorganization.
reorganizar [4] [xeoxgani'za(x)] *vt* to reorganize.
reparação [xepara'sãw] (*pl* -ões) *f* -**1.** [conserto] repair. -**2.** [indenização] compensation. -**3.** [retratação] reparation.
reparar [4] [xepa'ra(x)] ⟨⟩ *vt* -**1.** [consertar] to repair. -**2.** [indenizar] to compensate. -**3.** [retratar-se de] to admit. -**4.** [notar] to notice. ⟨⟩ *vi* [notar]: **~ em algo/alguém** to notice sthg/sb; **não repare na bagunça** pay no attention to the mess.
reparo [xe'paru] *m* -**1.** [conserto] repair. -**2.** [crítica] criticism.
repartição [xepaxtʃi'sãw] (*pl* -ões) *f* -**1.** [partilha] distribution. -**2.** [órgão governamental] department; **~ pública** government department.
repartir [6] [xepax'tʃi(x)] *vt* -**1.** [dividir- em partes] to divide up; **~ o cabelo** to part one's hair; [- entre vários] to distribute. -**2.** [compartilhar] to share.
repassar [4] [xepa'sa(x)] *vt* -**1.** [passar de novo] to cross again. -**2.** [revisar] to revise. -**3.** [verbas] to transfer.
repasse [xe'pasi] *m* [de verba] transfer.
repatriação [xepatrja'sãw] (*pl* -ões) *f* repatriation.
repatriar [16] [xepa'trja(x)] *vt* to repatriate.
⇒ **repatriar-se** *vp* to return home.
repelente [xepe'lẽntʃi] ⟨⟩ *adj* [repugnante] repellent. ⟨⟩ *m* [inseticida] repellent.
repelir [57] [xepe'li(x)] *vt* -**1.** [fazer regressar] to drive away. -**2.** [expulsar] to repel. -**3.** [rechaçar, impedir de entrar] to refuse admission to. -**4.** [recusar] to refuse. -**5.** [repudiar] to reject. -**6.** [desmentir] to refute.
repensar [4] [xepẽn'sa(x)] ⟨⟩ *vt* to reconsider. ⟨⟩ *vi*: **~ em algo** to reconsider sthg.
repente [xe'pẽntʃi] *m*: **num ~ tudo escureceu** all of a sudden everything went dark; **um ~ de carinho** a sudden show of affection.
⇒ **de repente** *loc adv* -**1.** [repentinamente] suddenly. -**2.** *fam* [talvez] maybe.
repentinamente [xepẽntʃina'mẽntʃil] *adv* suddenly.
repentino, na [xepẽn'tʃinu, na] *adj* sudden.
repercussão [xepexku'sãw] (*pl* -ões) *f* -**1.** *fig* [de som] reverberation. -**2.** [efeito] repercussion; **o CD teve boa ~ no exterior** the CD was very successful abroad.
repercutir [6] [xepexku'tʃi(x)] ⟨⟩ *vt* [som] to re-echo. ⟨⟩ *vi* -**1.** [som] to reverberate. -**2.** *fig* [afetar]: **~ em** to have repercussions on.

repertório [xepex'tɔrjuł] *m* **-1.** [conjunto] collection. **-2.** *MÚS* repertoire.

repetente [xepe'tẽntʃi] *EDUC* <> *adj* repeating. <> *mf* student who repeats a year.

repetição [xepetʃi'sãw] (*pl* -ões) *f* repetition.

repetido, da [xepe'tʃidu, da] *adj* repeated; **repetidas vezes** repeatedly.

repetir [57] [xepe'tʃi(x)] <> *vt* **-1.** [ger] to repeat. **-2.** [roupa] to wear again. **-3.** [refeição] to have a second helping of, to have seconds. **-4.** [tocar de novo]: ~ **uma música** to play an encore. <> *vi* to repeat.
→ **repetir-se** *vp* **-1.** [fenômeno] to be repeated. **-2.** [pessoa] to repeat o.s.

repetitivo, va [xepetʃi'tʃivu, va] *adj* repetitive.

repicar [12] [xepi'ka(x)] *vt & vi* to ring.

repique [xe'piki] *m* **-1.** [de sino] peal. **-2.** *fig* [alarme] alarm bell; ~ **falso** false alarm.

replay [xi'plej] *m* replay.

repleto, ta [xe'plɛtu, ta] *adj* [cheio]: ~ **(de)** full (of).

réplica ['xɛplika] *f* **-1.** [cópia] replica. **-2.** [resposta] reply.

replicar [12] [xepli'ka(x)] <> *vt* **-1.** [responder] to reply. **-2.** [contestar] to answer. <> *vi* **-1.** [responder] to reply. **-2.** [contestar] to respond.

repolho [xe'poʎu] *m* cabbage.

repor [45] [xe'po(x)] *vt* **-1.** [recolocar] to replace. **-2.** [devolver] to repay.
→ **repor-se** *vp* to recover.

reportagem [xepox'taʒẽ] (*pl* -ns) *f* **-1.** [ato] report. **-2.** [matéria]: ~ **(sobre)** report (on). **-3.** [repórteres] reporters (*pl*), the press.

reportar [4] [xepox'ta(x)] *vt* **-1.** [atribuir] to attribute. **-2.** [retroceder] to take back. **-3.** [relatar] to report.
→ **reportar-se** *vp* [referir-se] to refer.

repórter [xe'pɔxte(x)] (*pl* -es) *mf* reporter.

repórter-fotográfico, ca [xe'pɔxte(x)foto'grafiku, ka] (*pl* -s) *m* press photographer.

reposição [xepozi'sãw] (*pl* -ões) *f* [restituição] return; ~ **salarial** wage adjustment.

repositório [xepozi'tɔrju] *m* repository.

repousante [xepo'zãntʃi] *adj* restful.

repousar [4] [xepo'za(x)] <> *vt* to rest. <> *vi* **-1.** [descansar] to rest. **-2.** [basear-se]: ~ **em/sobre algo** to be based on sthg. **-3.** [não produzir] to rest, to lie fallow.

repouso [xe'pozu] *m* [descanso] rest; **em** ~ at rest.

repreender [5] [xeprjẽn'de(x)] *vt* to reprimand.

repreensão [xeprjẽ'sãw] (*pl* -ões) *f* reprimand.

repreensível [xeprjẽ'sivew] (*pl* -eis) *adj* reprehensible.

represa [xe'preza] *f* dam.

represália [xepre'zalja] *f* reprisal; **em** ~ in reprisal.

representação [xeprezẽnta'sãw] (*pl* -ões) *f* **-1.** [reprodução] representation. **-2.** [queixa]: ~ **contra algo/alguém** complaint against sthg/sb. **-3.** [delegação] representatives (*pl*). **-4.** *TEATRO*

performance. **-5.** *COM*: **ter a** ~ **de algo** to display sthg. **-6.** *fig* [fingimento] pretence *UK*, pretense *US*.

representante [xeprezẽn'tãntʃi] <> *adj* representative. <> *mf* representative.

representar [4] [xeprezẽn'ta(x)] <> *vt* **-1.** [ger] to represent. **-2.** [*TEATRO* - encenar] to perform; [- interpretar] to play. <> *vi* *TEATRO* [interpretar] to perform.

representatividade [xeprezẽntatʃivi'dadʒil] *f* representation.

representativo, va [xeprezẽnta'tʃivu, va] *adj* representative; ~ **de algo** representative of sthg.

repressão [xepre'sãw] (*pl* -ões) *f* repression.

repressivo, va [xepre'sivu, va] *adj* repressive.

repressor, ra [xepre'so(x), ra] *adj* repressive.

reprimido, da [xepri'midu, da] *adj* repressed.

reprimir [6] [xepri'mi(x)] *vt* **-1.** [conter - paixão] to contain; [- pensamento] to suppress. **-2.** [dissimular] to suppress. **-3.** *PSIC* to repress. **-4.** [proibir] to prohibit.
→ **reprimir-se** *vp* [conter-se] to control o.s.

reprisar [4] [xepri'za(x)] *vt* to repeat.

reprise [xe'prizi] *f* repeat.

réprobo, ba ['xɛprobu, ba] <> *adj* reprobate. <> *m, f* reprobate.

reprodução [xeprodu'sãw] (*pl* -ões) *f* reproduction.

reprodutivo, va [xeprodu'tʃivu, va] *adj* reproductive.

reprodutor, ra [xeprodu'to(x), ra] *adj* reproductive.
→ **reprodutor** *m* breeding animal.

reproduzir [72] [xeprodu'zi(x)] *vt* **-1.** [copiar, repetir] to copy. **-2.** [procriar] to breed. **-3.** [reeditar] to republish.
→ **reproduzir-se** *vp* **-1.** [procriar-se] to breed. **-2.** [repetir-se] to be repeated.

reprovação [xeprova'sãw] (*pl* -ões) *f* **-1.** [censura] disapproval. **-2.** [em exame, seleção] failure.

reprovado, da [xepro'vadu, da] <> *adj* failed. <> *m, f* failure.

reprovar [4] [xepro'va(x)] <> *vt* **-1.** [censurar] to disapprove of. **-2.** [rejeitar] to reject. **-3.** [em exame, seleção] to fail. <> *vi* [em exame, seleção] to fail.

réptil ['xɛptʃiw] (*pl* -eis) *m* reptile.

república [xɛ'publika] *f* **-1.** *POL* republic. **-2.** *EDUC* students' residence.

República Centro-Africana [xe,publikasẽntrwafri'kãna] *n* Central African Republic.

República da África do Sul [xepublikada,afrikadu'suw] *n* Republic of South Africa.

República Dominicana [xe,publikadomini'kãna] *n* Dominican Republic.

republicano, na [xepubli'kãnu, na] <> *adj* republican. <> *m, f* republican.

República Tcheca [xe,publika'tʃɛka] *n* Czech Republic.

repudiar [16] [xepu'dʒjar] *vt* to repudiate.

repúdio [xe'pudʒju] *m* repudiation.

repugnância [xepug'nãsja] *f* -**1.** [ger] repugnance. -**2.** [oposição] opposition.

repugnante [xepug'nãntʃi] *adj* repugnant.

repugnar [4] [xepug'na(x)] ⋄ *vt* to disgust. ⋄ *vi*: ~ **(a)** to disgust, to be repugnant (to).

repulsa [xe'puwsa] *f* -**1.** [ato] repulsion. -**2.** [sentimento] repugnance. -**3.** [oposição] rejection.

repulsão [xepuw'sãw] (*pl* -ões) *f* -**1.** [repulsa] repulsion. -**2.** *FÍSICA* rejection.

repulsivo, va [xepuw'sivu, va] *adj* repulsive.

reputação [xeputa'sãw] (*pl* -ões) *f* reputation.

reputado, da [xepu'tadu, da] *adj* renowned.

reputar [4] [xepu'ta(x)] *vt* to consider, to regard as.
➤ **reputar-se** *vp* to consider o.s.

repuxado, da [xepu'ʃadu, da] *adj* -**1.** [esticado] tight; **cabelo** ~ pulled-back hair. -**2.** [amendoado] slanting.

repuxar [4] [xepu'ʃa(x)] ⋄ *vt* [esticar - roupa, pele] to stretch; [- cabelo] to pull back tight. ⋄ *vi* [retesar] to tense.

repuxo [xe'puʃu] *m* fountain.

requebrado [xeke'bradu] *m* swaying.

requebrar [4] [xeke'bra(x)] *vt* to wiggle.
➤ **requebrar-se** *vp* to wiggle one's hips.

requeijão [xekej'ʒãw] (*pl* -ões) *m* soft cheese.

requentado, da [xekẽn'tadu, da] *adj* reheated.

requentar [4] [xekẽn'ta(x)] *vt* to reheat.

requerente [xeke'rẽntʃi] *mf JUR* petitioner.

requerer [38] [xeke're(x)] ⋄ *vt* -**1.** [pedir] to request. -**2.** [exigir] to demand. -**3.** [merecer] to deserve. -**4.** *JUR* to petition for. ⋄ *vi JUR* to make a petition.

requerimento [xekeri'mẽntu] *m* -**1.** [ato de requerer] application. -**2.** [petição] petition.

réquiem ['xɛkjẽ] (*pl* -ns) *m* requiem.

requintado, da [xekĩn'tadu, da] *adj* refined.

requintar [4] [xekĩn'ta(x)] ⋄ *vt* to refine. ⋄ *vi*: ~ **em** to be refined in.
➤ **requintar-se** *vp* to be refined.

requinte [xe'kĩntʃi] *m* -**1.** [refinamento] refinement. -**2.** [excesso] excess.

requisição [xekizi'sãw] (*pl* -ões) *f* requisition.

requisitado, da [xekizi'tadu, da] *adj* -**1.** [pedido] requested. -**2.** [muito procurado] in demand.

requisitar [4] [xekizi'ta(x)] *vt* to demand.

requisito [xeki'zitu] *m* requirement.

rês [xeʃ] (*pl* reses) *m* head of cattle.

rescindir [6] [xesĩn'dʒi(x)] *vt* [contrato] to rescind.

rescrever [5] [xeʃkre've(x)] *vt* to rewrite.

resenha [xe'zaɲa] *f* -**1.** [de livro] review. -**2.** [relatório] report. -**3.** [resumo] summary.

resenhar [xeze'ɲa(x)] *vt* [sumariar] to write a summary of.

reserva [xe'zɛxva] ⋄ *f* -**1.** [ger] reserve; ~ **internacionais** foreign reserves; ~ **natural** nature reserve; ~ **de mercado** protected market. -**2.** [em hotel, avião *etc*] reservation; **fazer** ~ **de algo** to reserve sthg. -**3.** [restrição]: **ter** ~ **a** *ou* **para com** to have reservations about. -**4.** [discrição] discretion. ⋄ *mf ESP* reserve.

➤ **reservas** *fpl* [energia] reserves.

reservado, da [xezex'vadu, da] *adj* -**1.** [ger] reserved. -**2.** [íntimo] private.
➤ **reservado** *m* [privada] private room.

reservar [4] [xezex'va(x)] *vt* -**1.** [fazer reserva] to reserve. -**2.** [poupar] to save. -**3.** [destinar] to allow; **a vida lhe reserva muitas alegrias** life has much joy in store for him.
➤ **reservar-se** *vp* [preservar-se] to save o.s.

reservatório [xezexva'tɔrjul] *m* -**1.** [depósito] tank. -**2.** [de água] reservoir.

reservista [xezex'viʃta] *mf* reservist.

resfriado, da [xeʃfri'adu, da] *adj* -**1.** [pessoa] cold; **estar** ~ to have a cold; **ficar** ~ to catch cold. -**2.** [carne] chilled.
➤ **resfriado** *m* cold; **pegar um** ~ to catch a cold.

resfriar [16] [xeʃ'frja(x)] *vt* [esfriar] to cool.
➤ **resfriar-se** *vp MED* to catch a cold.

resgatar [4] [xeʒga'ta(x)] *vt* -**1.** [ger] to rescue. -**2.** [restituir] to recover. -**3.** [pagar] to pay off. -**4.** [recuperar] to recoup. -**5.** [expiar] to redeem.

resgate [xeʒ'gatʃi] *m* -**1.** [dinheiro] ransom. -**2.** [libertação] release. -**3.** [salvamento] rescue. -**4.** *FIN* [retirada] withdrawal; ~ **automático** automatic withdrawal. -**5.** *COM* redemption.

resguardar [4] [xeʒgwax'da(x)] *vt* -**1.** [proteger]: ~ **(de)** to protect (from). -**2.** [vigiar] to protect.
➤ **resguardar-se** *vp* [proteger-se]: ~-**se de** to protect o.s. from.

resguardo [xeʒ'gwaxdu] *m* -**1.** [proteção] protection. -**2.** [cuidado] care. -**3.** [repouso] rest; **estar/ficar de** ~ to take it easy.

residência [xezi'dẽnsja] *f* residence; **fixar** ~ **em** to take up residence in.

residencial [xezidẽn'sjaw] (*pl* -ais) *adj* residential.

residente [xezi'dẽntʃi] ⋄ *adj* resident. ⋄ *mf* -**1.** [morador] resident. -**2.** [médico] senior registrar *UK*, resident *US*.

residir [6] [xezi'dʒi(x)] *vi* to reside.

resíduo [xe'zidwu] *m* -**1.** [resto] residue. -**2.** [bancário] surplus.

resignação [xezigna'sãw] *f*: ~ **(a/com)** resignation to.

resignadamente [xezignada'mẽntʃi] *adv* resignedly, with resignation.

resignado, da [xezig'nadu, da] *adj* resigned.

resignar-se [4] [xezig'naxsi] *vp* to resign o.s.; ~ **com algo** to resign o.s. to sthg; ~ **a fazer algo** to resign o.s. to doing sthg.

resiliente [xezi'ljẽntʃi] *adj* resilient.

resina [xe'zina] *f* resin.

resistência [xeziʃ'tẽnsja] *f* -**1.** [ger] resistance; **o carro não teve** ~ **para subir a ladeira** the car did not have the power to go up the slope. -**2.** [moral] stamina. -**3.** *fig* [oposição]: ~ **a** resistance to.

resistente [xeziʃ'tẽntʃi] *adj* -**1.** [forte] strong; ~ **ao calor** heat-resistant. -**2.** [durável] durable. -**3.** [que se opõe a]: ~ **a** resistant to.

resistir [6] [xeziʃ'tʃi(x)] *vi*: ~ a algo to resist sthg.
resma ['xeʒmal *f* ream.
resmungão, ona [xeʒmũŋ'gãw, ɔnal (*mpl* -ões, *fpl* -nas) <> *adj* [rabugento] cantankerous. <> *m,f* grouch.
resmungar [14] [xeʒmũŋ'ga(x)] *vt* & *vi* to grumble.
resmungo [xeʒ'mũŋgul *m* grumble.
resolução [xezolu'sãw] (*pl* -ões) *f* -1. [decisão] decision; **tomar uma** ~ to take a decision. -2. [solução] solution. -3. [firmeza] resolve. -4. [de imagem] resolution; **de alta** ~ high-resolution, hi-res.
resoluto, ta [xezo'lutu, ta] *adj* resolute; ~ a fazer algo resolved to do sthg.
resolver [5] [xezow've(x)] <> *vt* -1. [solucionar] to solve. -2. [decidir]: ~ fazer algo to decide to do sthg. <> *vi* -1. [adiantar]: a violência não resolve violence doesn't solve anything. -2. [decidir] to decide.
➡ **resolver-se** *vp* [decidir] to make up one's mind; ~-se a fazer algo to decide to do sthg; ~ -se sobre *ou* quanto a algo to make a decision about sthg.
resolvido, da [xezow'vidu, da] *adj* -1. [pessoa] determined; ~ a fazer algo determined to do sthg. -2. [assunto, questão] resolved.
respaldar [4] [xeʃpaw'da(x)] *vt* [apoiar] to back.
respaldo [xeʃ'pawdul *m* -1. [de cadeira] back. -2. *fig* [apoio] backing.
respectivamente [xeʃpektʃiva'mẽntʃi] *adv* respectively.
respectivo, va [xeʃpek'tʃivu, va] *adj* respective; ~ a in respect of.
respeitador, ra [xeʃpejtado(x), ra] *adj* respectful.
respeitar [4] [xeʃpej'ta(x)] *vt* to respect.
respeitável [xeʃpej'tavɛw] (*pl* -eis) *adj* -1. [digno de respeito] respectable. -2. [considerável] considerable.
respeito [xeʃ'pejtu] *m* -1. [deferência]: ~ a *ou* por respect for; **falta de** ~ lack of respect; **dar-se ao** ~ to command respect; **em** ~ a out of respect for; **faltar ao** ~ com alguém to be rude to sb; **impor** ~ a to command the respect of. -2. [relação] respect; **dizer** ~ a to concern; **a** ~ **de** [sobre] about; **com** ~ a [no tocante a] as regards.
respeitoso, osa [xeʃpej'tozu, ɔzal *adj* respectful.
respingar [14] [xeʃpĩŋ'ga(x)] *vi* to splash.
respingo [xeʃ'pĩŋgul *m* splash.
respiração [xeʃpira'sãw] *f* breathing; ~ artificial artificial respiration.
respirador [xeʃpira'do(x)] *m* respirator.
respirar [4] [xeʃpi'ra(x)] <> *vt* [ar] to breathe. <> *vi* -1. [absorver o ar] to breathe. -2. *fig* [descansar] to have time to breathe; **não deixar alguém** ~ to not give sb breathing space. -3. *fig* [sentir alívio] to breathe freely again.
respiratório, ria [xeʃpira'tɔrju, rja] *adj* respiratory.
respiro [xeʃ'pirul *m* -1. [respiração] breath. -2. *fig* [descanso] rest. -3. [abertura] vent.

resplandecente [xeʃplãnde'sẽntʃi] *adj* -1. [jóia] resplendent. -2. [dia] splendid.
resplandecer [25] [xeʃplãnde'se(x)] *vi* -1. [brilhar] to shine. -2. [sobressair] to outshine.
resplendor [xeʃplẽn'do(x)] *m* brilliance.
respondão, dona [xeʃpõn'dãw, dona] (*mpl* -ões, *fpl* -s) *m, f* cheeky person.
responder [5] [xeʃpõn'de(x)] <> *vt* [dar resposta] to reply. <> *vi* -1. [dar resposta]: ~ (a algo/alguém) to reply to sthg/sb. -2. [replicar] to answer. -3. [ser respondão] to answer back. -4. [reagir]: ~ a algo to respond to sthg. -5. [responsabilizar-se]: ~ por algo/alguém to answer for sthg/sb. -6. [submeter-se a]: ~ a algo to undergo sthg.
responsabilidade [xeʃpõnsabili'dadʒi] *f* -1. [obrigação] responsibility. -2. *JUR* liability.
responsabilizar [4] [xeʃpõnsabili'za(x)] *vt*: ~ alguém (por algo) to hold sthg/sb responsible for sthg.
➡ **responsabilizar-se** *vp*: ~-se (por algo/alguém) to hold o.s. responsible (for sthg/sb).
responsável [xeʃpõn'savɛw] (*pl* -eis) <> *adj*: ~ (por) responsible (for). <> *mf* -1. [encarregado] person in charge. -2. [culpado] person responsible.
resposta [xeʃ'pɔʃta] *f* -1. [de pergunta] answer; **em** ~ a algo in response to sthg. -2. *fig* [reação] response.
resquício [xeʃ'kisju] *m* -1. [vestígio] fragment. -2. [fragmento] fragment.
ressabiado, da [xesa'bjadu, da] *adj* -1. [desconfiado] suspicious. -2. [ressentido] resentful.
ressabiar [xesa'bja(x)] ➡ **ressabiar-se** *vp* -1. [ficar assustado] to be startled. -2. [magoar-se] to be offended.
ressaca [xe'sakal *f* -1. [do mar] rough sea; **estar de** ~ to be rough. -2. *fig* [de bebida] hangover; **estar/ficar de** ~ to have/to get a hangover.
ressaibo [xe'sajbu] *m* -1. [mau gosto] unpleasant taste. -2. *fig* [indício] sign. -3. [ressentimento] resentment.
ressaltar [4] [xesaw'ta(x)] *vt* to emphasize.
ressalva [xe'sawva] *f* -1. [emenda] correction. -2. [restrição] proviso; **fazer uma** ~ a algo to make an exception to sthg.
ressarcimento [xesaxsi'mẽntul *m* [compensação] reparation.
ressarcir [79] [xesax'si(x)] *vt* [compensar]: ~ algo (de) to compensate for sthg (with); ~ alguém (de) to compensate sb (with).
➡ **ressarcir-se** *vp* [compensar-se]: ~-se de to be compensated for.
ressecado, da [xese'kadu, da] *adj* dried up.
ressecar [12] [xese'ka(x)] *vt* & *vi* to dry up.
ressentido, da [xesẽn'tʃidu, da] *adj* resentful.
ressentimento [xesẽntʃi'mẽntul *m* resentment.
ressentir-se [56] [xesẽn'tʃixsi] *vp* -1. [magoar-se]: ~ (de algo) to resent (sthg). -2. [sofrer consequência]: ~ de algo to feel the effects of sthg.
ressequido, da [xese'kidu, da] *adj* dried up.

ressoar [20] [xe'swa(x)] *vi* to resound.

ressonância [xeso'nãnsja] *f* -**1**. [ger] resonance. -**2**. MED: ~ **magnética** magnetic resonance. -**3**. *fig* [repercussão]: **ter ~ em algo** to be a success in sthg.

ressonante [xeso'nãntʃi] *adj* resonant.

ressurgimento [xesuxʒi'mẽntu] *m* resurgence.

ressurgir [52] [xesux'zi(x)] *vi* -**1**. [reaparecer] to reappear. -**2**. [revitalizar-se] to revive. -**3**. [ressuscitar] to be resurrected.

ressurreição [xesuxej'sãw] (*pl* -ões) *f* resurrection.

ressuscitar [4] [xesusi'ta(x)] <> *vt* -**1**. [pessoa, animal] to resuscitate. -**2**. [costume, moda] to revive. <> *vi* -**1**. [pessoa, animal] to be resuscitated. -**2**. [costume, moda] to be revived.

restabelecer [25] [xeʃtabele'se(x)] *vt* to restore.
◆ **restabelecer-se** *vp* to recover.

restabelecimento [xeʃtabelesi'mẽntu] *m* -**1**. [de ordem, tradição] restoration. -**2**. [de doente] recovery.

restante [xeʃ'tãntʃi] <> *adj* remaining. <> *m* [resto] remainder.

restar [4] [xeʃ'ta(x)] *vi* -**1**. [sobrar] to be left over. -**2**. [sobreviver] to survive. -**3**. [subsistir] to remain; **não me resta dúvida de que ...** I no longer have any doubt that ... -**4**. [faltar]: **faltam duas páginas para terminar** there are two pages left to finish.

restauração [xeʃtawra'sãw] (*pl* -ões) *f* restoration.

restaurador, ra [xeʃtawra'do(x), ra] *m, f* restorer.

restaurante [xeʃtaw'rãntʃi] *m* restaurant.

restaurar [4] [xeʃtaw'ra(x)] *vt* -**1**. [ger] to restore. -**2**. [recuperar] to recover.

réstia ['xɛʃtʃja] *m* [de luz] ray.

restinga [xeʃ'tʃĩga] *f* sandbank.

restituição [xeʃtʃitwi'sãw] (*pl* -ões) *f* -**1**. [devolução] return; ~ **do imposto de renda** refunding of income tax. -**2**. [pagamento] repayment.

restituir [74] [xeʃtʃi'twi(x)] *vt* -**1**. [devolver] to return. -**2**. [pagar] to repay. -**3**. [restabelecer] to restore.

resto ['xɛʃtu] *m* -**1**. [ger] remainder. -**2**. [restante] rest; **de ~** [além disso] besides.
◆ **restos** *mpl* [de comida] leftovers.
◆ **restos mortais** *mpl* (mortal) remains.

restrição [xeʃtri'sãw] (*pl* -ões) *f* restriction.

restringir [52] [xeʃtrĩ'ʒi(x)] *vt* to restrict.
◆ **restringir-se** *vp* to restrict o.s.

restrito, ta [xeʃ'tritu, ta] *adj* restricted.

resultado [xezuw'tadu] *m* -**1**. [ger] result. -**2**. [proveito]: **dar ~** to be effective; **o filme deu bom ~ publicitário** the film was good publicity.

resultante [xezuw'tãntʃi] <> *adj* resulting; ~ **de algo** resulting from sthg. <> *f* -**1**. [conseqüência] outcome. -**2**. FÍSICA result.

resultar [46] [xezuw'ta(x)] *vi* -**1**. [originar-se]: ~ **de algo** to result from sthg. -**2**. [redundar] to turn out to be; ~ **em algo** to lead to sthg.

resumido, da [xezu'midu, da] *adj* concise.

resumir [xezu'mi(x)] *vt* to summarize.

◆ **resumir-se** *vp*: ~**-se em** *ou* **a algo** to consist of sthg.

resumo [xe'zumu] *m* summary; **em ~** in short.

resvalar [4] [xeʒva'la(x)] *vi* -**1**. [deslizar]: ~ **(de/por algo)** to slip (from/through sthg). -**2**. *fig* [incidir]: ~ **em algo** to slide into sthg.

reta ['xɛta] *f* ▷ **reto**.

retaguarda [ˌxeta'gwaxda] *f* -**1**. [posição] rear. -**2**. MIL rearguard.

retalhar [4] [xeta'ʎa(x)] *vt* -**1**. [cortar em pedaços] to cut up. -**2**. [golpear] to slash. -**3**. [dividir] to divide.

retalho [xe'taʎu] *m* remnant; **colcha de ~s** patchwork quilt.

retaliação [xetalja'sãw] (*pl* -ões) *f* retaliation.

retaliar [16] [xeta'lja(x)] <> *vt* to repay. <> *vi* to retaliate.

retangular [xetãŋgu'la(x)] *adj* rectangular.

retângulo [xe'tãŋgulu] *m* rectangle.

retardado, da [xetax'dadu, da] <> *adj* -**1**. [atrasado]: **fui ~ pelo trânsito** I was delayed by traffic. -**2**. PSIC retarded. <> *m, f* PSIC retarded person; ~ **mental** mentally retarded person.

retardar [4] [xetax'da(x)] *vt* -**1**. [atrasar] to delay. -**2**. [adiar] to postpone.
◆ **retardar-se** *vp* [atrasar-se] to be delayed.

retardatário, ria [xetaxda'tarju, rja] <> *adj* tardy. <> *m, f* latecomer.

retardo [xe'taxdu] *m* -**1**. [atraso] delay. -**2**. PSIC retardedness.

retenção [xetẽ'sãw] *f* -**1**. [detenção] detention; **a ~ no trânsito é grande** there is a major traffic hold-up. -**2**. MED [de líquidos] retention.

reter [1] [xe'te(x)] *vt* -**1**. [ger] to retain. -**2**. [segurar, prender - rédeas, corda] to hold; [- ladrão, suspeito] to detain. -**3**. [guardar] to keep. -**4**. [reprimir, deter] to hold back.
◆ **reter-se** *vp* [reprimir-se] to restrain o.s.

retesado, da [xete'zadu, da] *adj* taut.

retesar [4] [xete'za(x)] *vt* to tense.
◆ **retesar-se** *vp* to tense.

reticência [xetʃi'sẽnsja] *f* reticence.
◆ **reticências** *fpl* [sinal] ellipsis (*sing*), suspension points.

reticente [xetʃi'sẽntʃi] *adj* reticent.

retidão [xetʃi'dãw] *f* [lisura] rectitude.

retificar [12] [xetʃifi'ka(x)] *vt* -**1**. [corrigir] to rectify. -**2**. [purificar] to purify. -**3**. AUTO to repair.

retina [xe'tʃina] *f* ANAT retina.

retinir [6] [xetʃi'ni(x)] *vi* -**1**. [tinir] to clink. -**2**. [ressoar] to resound.

retinto, ta [xe'tʃĩtu, ta] *adj* [muito escuro] inky.

retirado, da [xetʃi'radu, da] *adj* [pessoa] retiring; [vida] retired; [lugar, casa] isolated.
◆ **retirada** *f* -**1**. [ger] withdrawal; **bater em retirada** [fugir] to beat a retreat. -**2**. [migração] migration.

retirante [xetʃi'rãntʃi] *mf* migrant.

retirar [4] [xetʃi'ra(x)] *vt* -**1**. [ger] to remove. -**2**. [retratar-se de] to take back. -**3**. [ganhar] to make. -**4**. [livrar, salvar] to get out.

➡ **retirar-se** *vp* **-1.** [ger] to leave. **-2.** [refugiar-se] to withdraw.

retiro [xe'tʃiru] *m* retreat.

reto, ta ['xɛtu, ta] *adj* **-1.** [ger] straight; **ângulo** ~ right angle. **-2.** *fig* [justo] straightforward. **-3.** *fig* [honesto] honest.

➡ **reto** *m* ANAT rectum.

➡ **reta** *f* **-1.** MAT straight line. **-2.** [de estrada, pista] straight; **reta de chegada, reta final** home straight.

retocar [12] [xeto'ka(x)] *vt* **-1.** [pintura] to touch up. **-2.** [texto] to tidy up.

retomada [xeto'mada] *f* [recuperação] recovery.

retomar [4] [xeto'ma(x)] *vt* **-1.** [continuar] to resume. **-2.** [reaver] to take back.

retoque [xe'tɔki] *m* finishing touch; **dar um** ~ to add a finishing touch.

retorcer [25] [xetox'se(x)] *vt* **-1.** [torcer de novo] to re-twist. **-2.** [contorcer-se] to twist.

➡ **retorcer-se** *vp* [contorcer-se] to writhe.

retorcido, da [xetox'sidu, da] *adj* **-1.** [muito torto] twisted. **-2.** [empolado] involved.

retórico, ca [xe'tɔriku, ka] *adj* **-1.** [sem conteúdo] rhetorical. **-2.** *fig* [afetado] affected.

➡ **retórico** *m* rhetorician.

➡ **retórica** *f* **-1.** [discurso] rhetoric. **-2.** *pej* [afetação] affectation.

retornar [4] [xetox'na(x)] *vi* [voltar] to return; ~ **de algo** to return from sthg.

retorno [xe'toxnu] *m* **-1.** [ger] return. **-2.** [resposta] response; **dar um** ~ **(sobre algo)** to give one's response (to sthg). **-3.** [em estrada] turning place; **fazer o** ~ to turn back.

retorquir [78] [xetox'ki(x)] <> *vt*: ~ **que** to retort that. <> *vi* to answer back.

retrabalhar [xetraba'ʎa(x)] *vt* [aprimorar] to re-condition.

retração [xetra'sãw] *f* **-1.** [de gengiva, de imagem] receding. **-2.** [em compras] contraction.

retraído, da [xetra'idu, da] *adj fig* [reservado, tímido] reserved.

retraimento [xetraj'mẽntu] *m* [reserva, timidez] reserve.

retrair [68] [xetra'i(x)] *vt* **-1.** [ger] to withdraw. **-2.** [tornar reservado] to make reserved.

➡ **retrair-se** *vp* **-1.** [afastar-se] to withdraw. **-2.** [tornar-se reservado] to become withdrawn.

retransmitir [6] [xetrãnʒmi'tʃi(x)] *vt* to show again.

retrasado, da [xetra'zadu, da] *adj* [ano, semana] before last.

retratar [4] [xetra'ta(x)] *vt* **-1.** [fazer retrato] to depict. **-2.** [descrever] to portray. **-3.** [desdizer] to retract. **-4.** [expressar] to express.

➡ **retratar-se** *vp* **-1.** [representar-se] to portray o.s. **-2.** [desdizer-se] ~**-se de algo** to retract sthg. **-3.** [confessar erro] to admit one's mistake.

retrátil [xe'tratʃiw] (*pl* **-eis**) *adj* retractable.

retratista [xetra'tʃiʃta] *mf* portrait painter.

retrato [xe'tratu] *m* **-1.** [ger] portrait; ~ **falado** Identikit® picture; **ser o** ~ **de alguém** [parecer-se]

to be the (spitting) image of sb. **-2.** *fig* [exemplo] picture.

retribuição [xetribwi'sãw] (*pl* **-ões**) *f* **-1.** [pagamento] remuneration. **-2.** [recompensa] reward. **-3.** [agradecimento] reciprocation.

retribuir [74] [xetri'bwi(x)] *vt* **-1.** [pagar] to pay. **-2.** [agradecer] to return. **-3.** [corresponder] to reciprocate.

retroagir [52] [xetrwa'ʒi(x)] *vi*: ~ **(a algo)** to be retroactive (on sthg).

retroativo, va [xetrwa'tʃivu, va] *adj* retroactive.

retroceder [5] [xetrose'de(x)] *vi* **-1.** [recuar] to step back. **-2.** [desistir] ~ **(em algo)** to withdraw (from sthg). **-3.** [decair] to decline.

retrocesso [xetro'sɛsu] *m* **-1.** [retorno] return. **-2.** [declínio] step backwards. **-3.** [recaída] recurrence. **-4.** [tecla] backspace. **-5.** [na economia] slowdown.

retrógrado, da [xe'trɔgradu, da] *adj* **-1.** [idéia, movimento] retrograde, reactionary. **-2.** [pessoa] reactionary.

retroprojetor [ˌxɛtroproʒe'to(x)] *m* overhead projector.

retrós [xe'trɔʃ] *m* bobbin.

retrospectiva [xetroʃpek'tʃiva] *f* retrospective.

retrospectivamente [xetroʃpektʃiva'mẽntʃi] *adv* retrospectively.

retrospecto [xetroʃ'pɛktu] *m* [retrospetiva] retrospect; **em** ~ in retrospect.

retrovisor [xetrovi'zo(x)] (*pl* **-es**) <> *adj* rear-view. <> *m* rear-view mirror.

réu [xew], **ré** [xɛ] *m, f* accused.

reumático, ca [xewma'tʃiku, ka] <> *adj* rheumatic. <> *m, f* rheumatism sufferer.

reumatismo [xewma'tʃiʒmu] *m* rheumatism.

reumatologia [xewmatolo'ʒia] *f* rheumatology.

reumatologista [xewmatolo'ʒiʃta] *mf* rheumatologist.

reunião [xew'njãw] (*pl* **-ões**) *f* **-1.** [encontro] meeting; ~ **de cúpula** summit; ~ **de diretoria** board meeting. **-2.** [festa] party. **-3.** [coletânea] collection.

reunir [6] [xew'ni(x)] *vt* **-1.** [juntar] to gather. **-2.** [congregar] to join together. **-3.** [aliar] to combine. **-4.** [unir] to unite.

➡ **reunir-se** *vp* **-1.** [juntar-se] to gather. **-2.** [aliar-se] to be combined. **-3.** [realizar reunião] to meet. **-4.** [incorporar-se] to join together.

reutilizar [4] [xewtʃili'za(x)] *vt* to reuse.

revalorizar [4] [xevalori'za(x)] *vt* to revalue.

revanche [xe'vãnʃi] *f* **-1.** [desforra] revenge. **-2.** ESP return match.

revanchismo [xevãn'ʃiʒmu] *m* retaliation.

reveillon [xeve'jõn] *m* New Year's Eve.

revelação [xevela'sãw] (*pl* **-ões**) *f* **-1.** [ger] revelation. **-2.** FOT developing.

revelador, ra [xevela'do(x), ra] *adj* revealing.

revelar [4] [xeve'la(x)] *vt* **-1.** [ger] to reveal. **-2.** [mostrar, demonstrar] to show. **-3.** FOT to develop.

➡ **revelar-se** *vp* [dar-se a conhecer] to turn out to be.

revelia [xeve'lia] f default.
➡ **à revelia** loc adv **-1.** JUR in absentia. **-2.** [despercebidamente] without anybody knowing.
➡ **à revelia de** loc adv without the knowledge/consent of.

revenda [xe'vẽnda] f resale.

revendedor, ra [xevẽnde'do(x), ra] (mpl **-es**, fpl **-s**) ⬥ adj resale (antes de subst). ⬥ m, f [de automóveis] dealer.

revender [5] [xevẽn'de(x)] vt to resell.

rever [40] [xe've(x)] vt **-1.** [tornar a ver] to see again. **-2.** [examinar] to check. **-3.** [revisar] to revise.

reverberação [xevexbera'sãw] (pl **-ões**) f **-1.** [de som] reverberation. **-2.** [de luz, calor] reflection.

reverberar [4] [xevexbe'ra(x)] vt [refletir] to reflect.

reverência [xeve'rẽnsja] f **-1.** [respeito] reverence. **-2.** [saudação]: **fazer uma** ~ to bow.

reverenciar [16] [xeverẽn'sja(x)] vt **-1.** [respeitar] to respect. **-2.** [saudar] to salute.

reverendo [xeve'rẽndu] m priest.

reverente [xeve'rẽntʃi] adj reverent.

reversão [xevex'sãw] (pl **-ões**) f reversion.

reversível [xevex'sivew] (pl **-eis**) adj reversible.

reverso, sa [xe'vexsu, sa] ⬥ adj reverse. ⬥ m [lado contrário] reverse.

reverter [5] [xevex'te(x)] vi **-1.** [retroceder]: ~ **a** to return to. **-2.** [redundar]: ~ **em favor de alguém** to revert in s.o.'s favour; ~ **em benefício de** to benefit.

revertério [xevex'tɛrju] m fam turnabout.

revés [xe'vɛʃ] (pl **-eses**) m **-1.** [reverso] reverse; **ao** ~ [às avessas] inside out. **-2.** fig [infortúnio] setback.
➡ **de revés** loc adv [olhar, sorrir] askance.

revestimento [xeveʃtʃi'mẽntul] m covering.

revestir [54] [xeveʃ'tʃi(x)] vt **-1.** [ger] to cover. **-2.** [munir]: ~ **alguém de algo** to invest sb with sthg. **-3.** [vestir] to don, to put on.
➡ **revestir-se** vp [munir-se] to summon up.

revezamento [xeveza'mẽntul m **-1.** [ato]: **para cuidar do bebê, o casal fez um** ~ the couple took it in turns to look after the baby. **-2.** ESP relay.

revezar [4] [xeve'za(x)] ⬥ vt to swap. ⬥ vi: ~ **(com)** to take turns (with).
➡ **revezar-se** vp to alternate.

revidar [4] [xevi'da(x)] ⬥ vt **-1.** [responder] to return. **-2.** [contestar] to answer. ⬥ vi [responder] to answer back.

revide [xe'vidʒi] m response.

revigorar [4] [xevigo'ra(x)] vt to reinvigorate.
➡ **revigorar-se** vp to regain one's strength.

revirado, da [xevi'radu, da] adj **-1.** [casa] untidy. **-2.** [revolto] choppy.

revirar [4] [xevi'ra(x)] vt **-1.** [tornar a virar] to turn over. **-2.** [mudar] to change. **-3.** [os olhos] to roll. **-4.** [remexer em] to turn out.
➡ **revirar-se** vp [virar-se] to toss and turn.

reviravolta [xe,vira'vɔwtal f **-1.** [mudança] turnabout. **-2.** [pirueta] pirouette.

revisão [xevi'zãw] (pl **-ões**) f **-1.** [de texto] revision; ~ **de provas** proofreading. **-2.** [de máquina - ger]

overhaul; [- carro, motor de carro] service. **-3.** [os revisores] review board. **-4.** JUR review.

revisar [4] [xevi'za(x)] vt **-1.** [texto] to revise. **-2.** [máquina - ger] to overhaul; [- motor de carro] to service. **-3.** [recapitular] to review.

revisor, ra [xevi'zo(x), ra] (mpl **-es**, fpl **-s**) ⬥ adj examining. ⬥ m, f [de provas] proofreader.

revista [xe'viʃta] f **-1.** [publicação] magazine; ~ **feminina** women's magazine; ~ **em quadrinhos** comic. **-2.** [acadêmica] journal. **-3.** MIL [inspeção] review. **-4.** [busca] search. **-5.** TEATRO revue.

revistar [4] [xeviʃ'ta(x)] vt to search.

revisto, ta [xe'viʃtu, ta] ⬥ pp ⊳ **rever**. ⬥ adj checked.

revitalizar [4] [xevitali'za(x)] vt to revitalize.

reviver [5] [xevi've(x)] ⬥ vi **-1.** [doente] to pick up. **-2.** [revigorar-se] to come back to life. ⬥ vt [relembrar] to relive.

revocar [12] [xevo'ka(x)] vt **-1.** [lembrar] to recall. **-2.** [restituir]: ~ **alguém a algo** to bring sb back to sthg. **-3.** [tirar]: ~ **alguém de algo** to remove sb from sthg.

revogação [xevoga'sãw] (pl **-ões**) f repeal.

revogar [14] [xevo'ga(x)] vt to repeal.

revolta [xe'vɔwta] f **-1.** [ger] revolt. **-2.** [rebeldia]: ~ **(contra)** rebellion (against). **-3.** [indignação]: ~ **(diante de** ou **com)** indignation (at).

revolto, ta [xe'vowtu, ta] adj **-1.** [revirado] rough. **-2.** [conturbado] troubled. **-3.** [desarrumado] untidy.

revoltoso, osa [xevow'tozu, ɔza] adj rebellious.
➡ **revoltoso** m rebel.

revolução [xevolu'sãw] (pl **-ões**) f revolution.

revolucionar [4] [xevolusjo'na(x)] vt **-1.** [transformar] to revolutionize. **-2.** [sublevar] to stir up. **-3.** [agitar] to change completely.

revolucionário, ria [xevolusjo'narju, rja] ⬥ adj revolutionary. ⬥ m, f revolutionary.

revolver [5] [xevow've(x)] vt **-1.** [remexer] to rummage through. **-2.** [examinar, investigar] to search. **-3.** [revirar - olhos] to roll; [- corpo, terra] to turn over. **-4.** [agitar] to blow about. **-5.** [relembrar] to recall.
➡ **revolver-se** vp **-1.** [mexer-se] to roll over. **-2.** [agitar-se] to blow about.

revólver [xe'vɔwve(x)] (pl **-es**) m revolver.

reza [ˈxɛza] f prayer.

rezar [4] [xe'za(x)] ⬥ vt **-1.** [orar] to pray. **-2.** [missa] to say mass. **-3.** [afirmar, preceituar] to state. ⬥ vi [orar] to pray.

RG (abrev de **Registro Geral**) m Brazilian identity card, ≃ ID card.

RH (abrev de **Recursos Humanos**) m HR.

riacho [ˈxjaʃul m stream.

Riad [ˈxjadʒil n Riyadh.

ribalta [xi'bawtal f **-1.** [luzes] footlights (pl). **-2.** fig [palco] boards (pl).

ribanceira [xibãn'sejra] f **-1.** [margem elevada] steep river bank. **-2.** [despenhadeiro] ravine. **-3.** [rampa] steep slope.

ribeira [xi'bejral f **-1.** [margem de rio] bank. **-2.** [riacho] stream.

ribeirão [xibej'rãw] (*pl*-ões) *m* stream.

ribeirinho, nha [xibej'riɲu, ɲa] ◇ *adj* river-side. ◇ *m, f* riverside dweller.

ribombar [4] [xibõn'ba(x)] *vi* **-1.** [trovão] to rumble. **-2.** [canhão, granada] to boom.

ricaço, ça [xi'kasu, sa] *m, f* very rich person.

ricamente [xika'mẽntʃil] *adv* richly.

rícino ['xisinu] *m* castor-oil plant; **óleo de** ~ castor oil.

rico, ca ['xiku, ka] ◇ *adj* **-1.** [ger] rich. **-2.** [opulento] opulent. **-3.** [abundante]: ~ **em algo** rich in sthg. **-4.** [esplêndido] splendid. **-5.** [valiosa] precious. ◇ *m, f* [pessoa] rich person.

ricochetear [15] [xikoʃe'tʃja(x)] *vi* to ricochet.

ricota [xi'kɔta] *f* ricotta.

ridicularizar [4] [xidʒikulari'za(x)] *vt* to ridicule.

ridículo, la [xi'dʒikulu, la] *adj* ridiculous.
→ **ridículo** *m* ridicule.

rifa ['xifa] *f* raffle.

rifar [4] [xi'fa(x)] *vt* to raffle.

rifle ['xifli] *m* rifle.

Riga ['xiga] *n* Riga.

rigidez [xiʒi'deʒ] *f* **-1.** [dureza - de metais, parede] rigidity; [- de músculo, corpo] stiffness. **-2.** *fig* [severidade] harshness. **-3.** *fig* [inflexibilidade] strictness.

rígido, da ['xiʒidu, da] *adj* **-1.** [hirto] stiff. **-2.** [resistente] strong. **-3.** [severo - pessoa, rosto] severe; [- disciplina] strict.

rigor [xi'go(x)] (*pl*-es) *m* **-1.** [rigidez] rigour *UK*, rigor *US*. **-2.** [severidade] severity. **-3.** [exatidão] rigour *UK*, rigor *US*. **-4.** [meticulosidade] thoroughness; **com** ~ strictly. **-5.** [preceito] good manners (*pl*). **-6.** [auge] harshness.
→ **a rigor** *loc adv* strictly speaking.

rigorosamente [xigorɔza'mẽntʃil] *adv* rigorously; **chega no trabalho** ~ **às 8 horas** he arrives at work at 8 o'clock sharp.

rigoroso, osa [xigo'rozu, ɔza] *adj* **-1.** [ger] strict. **-2.** [castigo] severe. **-3.** [exato] precise. **-4.** [meticuloso] meticulous. **-5.** *fig* [penoso] severe.

rijo, ja ['xiʒu, ʒa] *adj* **-1.** [rígido] firm. **-2.** [severo] severe.

rim ['xĩ] (*pl*-ns) *m* ANAT kidney.
→ **rins** *mpl fam* [região lombar] lower back (*sg*).

rima ['xima] *f* rhyme.

rimar [4] [xi'ma(x)] ◇ *vt* to set to rhyme. ◇ *vi* to rhyme.

rímel® ['ximɛw] (*pl*-eis) *m* mascara.

rinçagem [xĩ'saʒẽl (*pl*-ns) *f* rinse.

rinçar [xĩ'sa(x)] *vt* to rinse.

ringue ['xĩŋgil *m* ring.

rinha ['xiɲa] *f fam* [briga de galos] cockfight.

rinoceronte [xinose'rõntʃil *m* rhinoceros.

rinque ['xĩŋki] *m* rink.

rins [xĩnʃ] *pl* ▷ **rim**.

rio ['xiw] *m* river; **gastar** ~**s de dinheiro** to spend lots of money.

Rio Branco [ˌxiw'brãŋku] *n* Rio Branco.

Rio de Janeiro [ˌxiwdʒiʒa'nejru] *n* Rio de Janeiro.

RIO DE JANEIRO

Capital of the republic until the foundation of Brasilia in 1960; Rio de Janeiro is one of the most beautiful and traditional icons of Brazil, thanks to its famous beaches, such as Copacabana and Ipanema, as well as the beauty of its natural landmarks, such as the Sugar Loaf Mountain and the Corcovado. In spite of its loss of political power following the move of the capital city, Rio de Janeiro still exerts a powerful influence on the culture of Brazil.

Rio da Prata [ˌxiwda'prata] *n* River Plate.

Rio Grande do Norte [ˌxiwgrãndʒidu'nɔxtʃi] *n* Rio Grande do Norte.

Rio Grande do Sul [ˌxiwgrãndʒidu'suw] *n* Rio Grande do Sul.

rio-platense [ˌxiwpla'tẽnsi] ◇ *adj* River Plate (*antes de subst*). ◇ *mf* person from the River Plate region.

ripa ['xipa] *f* [de madeira] slat; **meter a** ~ **em alguém** *fig* [falar mal] to speak ill of sb.

riqueza [xi'keza] *f* **-1.** [ger] richness. **-2.** [fortuna, bens] wealth. **-3.** [beleza] beauty; **essa igreja é uma** ~! this church is beautiful!

rir [69] ['xi(x)] *vi* to laugh; ~ **de algo/alguém** to laugh at sthg/sb; ~ **para alguém** to smile at sb; **morrer de** ~ **(de algo/alguém)** to laugh one's head off (at sthg/sb), to laugh oneself silly (at sthg/sb).

risada [xi'zada] *f* **-1.** [riso] laughter. **-2.** [gargalhada] guffaw.

risca ['xiʃka] *f* **-1.** [listra] stripe. **-2.** [no cabelo] parting. **-3.** [traço] line.
→ **à risca** *loc adv* to the letter.

riscar [12] [xiʃ'ka(x)] *vt* **-1.** [fazer riscas em - porta, parede] to scratch; [- papel] to draw lines on. **-2.** [esboçar] to sketch. **-3.** [marcar] to draw. **-4.** [apagar] to cross out. **-5.** [acender] to scratch. **-6.** [eliminar]: ~ **alguém/algo de algo** to eliminate sb/sthg from sthg. **-7.** [atritar] to scrape.

risco ['xiʃku] *m* **-1.** [traço] scratch. **-2.** [esboço] sketch. **-3.** [perigo] risk; **correr** ~ **de** to run the risk of; **pôr algo/alguém em** ~ to put sthg/sb at risk.

risco-país [ˌxiʃkupa'jiʃ] *m* ECON country risk.

risível [xi'zivew] (*pl*-eis) *adj* laughable.

riso ['xizu] *m* laugh; ~ **amarelo** forced laugh.

risonho, nha [xi'zoɲu, ɲa] *adj* **-1.** [que sorri] smiling. **-2.** [alegre] cheerful.

risoto [xi'zotu] *m* risotto.

rispidez [xiʃpi'deʒ] *f* harshness.

ríspido, da ['xiʃpidu, da] *adj* harsh.

rissole [xi'sɔli] *m* rissole.

riste ['xiʃtʃi] *m*: **dedo em** ~ pointing finger; **orelhas em** ~ pointed ears.

rítmico, ca ['xitʃmiku, ka] *adj* rhythmic.

ritmo ['xitʃimu] *m* rhythm.

rito ['xitu] *m* rite.

ritual [xi'twaw] (*pl*-ais [xi'twajʃl) ◇ *adj* ritual. ◇ *m* **-1.** [ger] ritual. **-2.** [livro] service book.

rival [xi'vaw] (*pl*-ais) ◇ *adj* rival. ◇ *mf* rival.

rivalidade [xivali'dadʒi] f rivalry.

rivalizar [4] [xivali'za(x)] vi: ~ **com algo/alguém** to compete with sthg/sb; ~ **por algo/alguém** to compete for sthg/sb; ~ **em algo** to compete in sthg.

rixa ['xiʃal f quarrel.

RJ (abrev de **Estado do Rio de Janeiro**) n State of Rio de Janeiro.

RN (abrev de **Estado do Rio Grande do Norte**) n State of Rio Grande do Norte.

RO (abrev de **Estado de Rondônia**) n State of Rondônia.

robalo [ro'balu] m sea bass.

robô [ro'bol m robot.

robótica [xo'bɔtʃikal f robotics (sg).

robustecer [25] [xobuʃte'se(x)] ⟨⟩ vt to strengthen. ⟨⟩ vi to become stronger.
➡ **robustecer-se** vp to become stronger.

robustez [xobuʃ'teʒ] f robustness.

robusto, ta [xo'buʃtu, tal adj robust.

roça ['xɔsal f-1. [plantação] plantation. -2. [campo] country. -3. [mato] clearing.

roçado [xo'sadul m-1. [terreno] cleared land. -2. [clareira] clearing. -3. [plantação] plantation.

rocambole [xokãn'bɔlil m roll.

roçar [13] [xo'sa(x)] ⟨⟩ vt-1. [cortar] to clear. -2. [tocar de leve] to brush. -3. [atritar] to scrape. ⟨⟩ vi [tocar de leve]: ~ **em** to brush against.

roceiro, ra [xo'sejru, ral m, f-1. [lavrador] country worker. -2. [caipira] yokel.

rocha ['xɔʃal f-1. [pedra] rock. -2. [rochedo] crag.

rochedo [xo'ʃedul m crag.

rock ['xɔkil m MÚS rock.

roda ['xɔdal f-1. [ger] wheel. -2. [círculo] circle; **alta** ~ high society; ~ **de samba** circle of samba dancers and musicians; **brincar de** ~ to play in a circle. -3. [de saia] hoop.

roda d'água [xɔdadagwal f waterwheel.

rodado, da [xo'dadu, dal adj-1. [que tem roda] full. -2. [percorrido] on the clock.
➡ **rodada** f-1. [giro] turn; **dar uma rodada** to turn round. -2. [de bebida] round. -3. ESP round.

rodagem [xo'daʒẽ] (pl-ns) f-1. [ato de rodar] driving. -2. [raio de roda] wheel ▷ **estrada**.

roda-gigante [xɔdaʒi'gãntʃil (pl rodas-gigantes) f big wheel, Ferris wheel.

rodamoinho [xɔda'mwiɲul m-1. [de água] whirlpool. -2. [de cabelo] swirl.

rodapé [xɔda'pɛl m-1. [de parede] skirting board. -2. [de página] foot; **nota de** ~ footnote. -3. [artigo] article.

rodar [4] [xo'da(x)] ⟨⟩ vt-1. [fazer girar] to turn. -2. [percorrer] to travel. -3. [imprimir] to print. -4. [filmar] to film. -5. AUTO to do. -6. COMPUT to run. ⟨⟩ vi-1. [girar] to turn. -2. [percorrer]: ~ **por** [a pé] to wander around; [de carro] to drive around. -3. [ser impresso] to be printed. -4. fam [ser reprovado]: ~ **(em algo)** to fail (in sthg). -5. fam [sair]: ~ **(de algo)** to leave (sthg). -6. [decorrer] to move on.

roda-viva [ˌxɔda'vival (pl rodas-vivas) f commotion.

rodear [15] [xo'dʒja(x)] vt-1. [contornar] to go round. -2. [cercar] to surround.
➡ **rodear-se** vp [cercar-se] to surround o.s.

rodeio [xo'dejul m-1. [circunlóquio] circumlocution. -2. [evasiva] evasiveness; **fazer** ~s to beat about the bush; **sem** ~s bluntly. -3. [de gado] rodeo.

rodela [xo'dɛlal f [pedaço] slice.

rodízio [xo'dʒizjul m-1. [revezamento] turn; **fazer** ~ to take turns. -2. [em restaurante] type of service in a restaurant where you are served at your table as much meat or, sometimes, pizza as you can eat, and normally accompanied by a free buffet of salad, etc.

rodo ['xodul m-1. [para puxar água] brush. -2. [agrícola] rake.
➡ **a rodo** loc adv a lot.

rodoanel [rodo'anewl (pl -éis) m ring road UK, beltway US.

rododendro [xodo'dẽndrul m rhododendron.

rodopiar [16] [xodo'pja(x)] vi to spin around.

rodopio [xodo'piwl m spin.

rodovia [xodo'vial f motorway UK, highway US.

rodoviário, ria [xodo'vjarju, rjal adj road.
➡ **rodoviária** f [estação de ônibus] bus station.

roedor, ra [xwe'do(x), ral adj gnawing.
➡ **roedor** m rodent.

roer [28] ['xwe(x)] vt-1. [com dentes] to gnaw; ~ **as unhas** to bite one's nails; **duro de** ~ fam fig a hard nut to crack. -2. [destruir] to eat away. -3. [corroer] to erode. -4. fig [atormentar] to eat away at, to gnaw at.
➡ **roer-se** vp fig [atormentar-se]: ~-**se de algo** to be eaten up with sthg.

rogado, da [xo'gadu, dal adj: **fazer-se de** ~ to play hard to get.

rogar [14] [xo'ga(x)] ⟨⟩ vt to ask; ~ **pragas (contra algo/alguém)** to curse (sthg/sb). ⟨⟩ vi to pray; ~ **a alguém que faça algo** to beg sb to do sthg.

rogo ['xogul m-1. [súplica] request; **a** ~ **de** [a pedido] at the request of. -2. [oração] prayer.

rojão [xo'ʒãwl (pl -ões) m-1. [foguete] rocket. -2. fig [ritmo intenso] hectic pace; **aguentar o** ~ fig [resistir] to stand the pace.

rol [xɔwl (pl róis) m list.

rolagem [xo'laʒẽl (pl -ns) f [de dívida] postponement.

rolamento [xola'mẽntul m MEC ball bearing.

rolar [4] [xo'la(x)] ⟨⟩ vt-1. [fazer girar] to roll. -2. fig [dívida] to run up. ⟨⟩ vi-1. [cair, deslizar] to roll; ~ **de/por/em algo** to roll off/down/on sthg. -2. [na cama] to toss and turn. -3. fam [estender-se] to roll on. -4. fam [ser servido] to be served. -5. fam [acontecer] to go on.

roldana [xow'dãnal f pulley.

roleta [xo'letal f-1. [jogo] roulette. -2. [borboleta] turnstile.

roleta-russa [xoˌleta'xusal (pl roletas-russas) f Russian roulette.

rolha ['xoʎɐ] *f* -**1.** [peça] cork. -**2.** *fam fig* [censura] gag.

roliço, ça [xo'lisu, sa] *adj* -**1.** [redondo] round. -**2.** [gordo] chubby.

rolo ['xolu] *m* -**1.** [ger] roller; ~ **de pastel** rolling pin; ~ **compressor** steam roller. -**2.** [cilindro] roll. -**3.** [almofada] bolster. -**4.** *fam* [bafafá, confusão] brawl; **dar** ~ to cause trouble.

ROM (*abrev de* **Read Only Memory**) *f* ROM.

romã [xo'mã] *f* pomegranate.

Roma ['xoma] *n* Rome.

romance [xo'mãsi] *m* -**1.** *LITER* novel; ~ **policial** detective story. -**2.** *fig* [amoroso] romance. -**3.** *fig* [saga] saga. -**4.** *fig* [exageração]: **fazer um** ~ **de algo** to make a song and dance about sthg.

romanceado, da [xomãn'sjadu, da] *adj* -**1.** *LITER* novelized. -**2.** [fantasiado] romanticized.

romancear [15] [xomãn'sja(x)] *vt* -**1.** *LITER* to novelize. -**2.** [fantasiar] to romanticize.

romancista [xomãn'sifta] *mf* novelist.

românico, ca [xo'mãniku, ka] *adj* -**1.** *LING* Romance. -**2.** *ARQUIT & ARTE* Romanesque.

romano, na [xo'mãnu, na] <> *adj* Roman. <> *m, f* Roman.

romântico, ca [xo'mãntʃiku, ka] <> *adj* -**1.** *ARQUIT & LITER* Romantic. -**2.** [poético, sentimental] romantic. <> *m, f* -**1.** *ARQUIT & LITER* Romantic. -**2.** [pessoa] romantic.

romantismo [xomãn'tʃiʒmu] *m* -**1.** *ARQUIT & LITER* Romanticism. -**2.** [sentimentalismo] romance.

romantizar [4] [xomãntʃi'za(x)] *vt* [fantasiar] to romanticize.

romaria [xoma'ria] *f* -**1.** [peregrinação] pilgrimage. -**2.** [festa] popular festival. -**3.** *fig* [muita gente] flock.

rombo ['xõnbu] *m* -**1.** [furo] hole. -**2.** *fig* [desfalque] embezzlement. -**3.** *fig* [prejuízo] deficit.

rombudo, da [xõn'budu, da] *adj* [faca, agulha] blunt.

romeiro, ra [xo'mejru, ra] *m, f* pilgrim.

Romênia [xo'menja] *n* Rumania.

romeno, na [xo'menu, na] <> *adj* Rumanian. <> *m, f* Rumanian.
  ◆ **romeno** *m* [língua] Rumanian.

romeu-e-julieta [xo,mewiʒu'ljeta] *m* *CULIN* guava preserve on cheese.

rompante [xõn'pãntʃi] *m* outburst.

romper [5] [xõn'pe(x)] <> *vt* to break. <> *vi* -**1.** [quebrar] to burst. -**2.** [rasgar] to tear. -**3.** [despontar] to break. -**4.** [relações]: ~ **(com alguém)** to break up (with sb); ~ **com algo** [tradição] to break from sthg. -**5.** [começar]: ~ **em algo** to break into sthg.
  ◆ **romper-se** *vp* -**1.** [despedaçar-se] to break. -**2.** [interromper-se] to be broken off.

rompimento [xõnpi'mẽntu] *m* -**1.** [de cano, barragem] bursting. -**2.** [de contrato, relações] breaking.

roncar [12] [xõn'ka(x)] *vi* to snore.

ronco ['xõŋku] *m* -**1.** [no sono] snore. -**2.** *MED* rale. -**3.** [ruído] rumble. -**4.** [grunhido] grunt.

ronda ['xõnda] *f* beat; **fazer a** ~ to be on patrol.

rondar [4] [xõn'da(x)] <> *vt* -**1.** [andar vigiando] to patrol. -**2.** [espreitar] to prowl about. -**3.** [andar à volta de] to go round. -**4.** [cifra] to reach. <> *vi:* ~ **(por)** [andar vigiando] to be on patrol (throughout); [espreitar] to prowl (about).

Rondônia [xõn'donja] *n* Rondonia.

ronqueira [xõŋ'kejra] *f* wheeze.

ronrom [xõn'xõ] *m* purr.

ronronar [4] [xõnxo'na(x)] *vi* to purr.

roque ['xɔki] *m* -**1.** *MÚS* rock (and roll). -**2.** [dança] rock and roll.

roqueiro, ra [xo'kejru, ra] *m, f* -**1.** [músico] rock musician. -**2.** [cantor] rock singer.

Roraima [xo'rajma] *n* Roraima.

rosa ['xɔza] <> *adj inv* [cor] pink. <> *f* *BOT* rose. <> *m* [cor] pink.

rosado, da [xo'zadu, da] *adj* pink.

rosa-dos-ventos [,xɔzaduʃ'vẽntuʃ] *f inv* wind rose.

rosário [xo'zarju] *m* -**1.** [colar] string of beads. -**2.** [orações] rosary.

rosa-shocking [xɔza'ʃkĩŋ] *adj inv* shocking pink.

rosbife [xoʒ'bifi] *m* roast beef.

rosca ['xoʃka] *f* -**1.** [de parafuso, porca] thread. -**2.** [pão] twist. -**3.** [biscoito] biscuit.

roseira [xo'zejra] *f* rose bush.

róseo, sea ['xɔzju, zja] *adj* rosy.

roseta [xo'zeta] *f* -**1.** [ger] rosette. -**2.** [de espora] rowel.

rosnar [4] [xoʒ'na(x)] <> *vi* [cão] to growl. <> *m* [de cão] growl.

rosto ['xoʃtul *m* face.

rota ['xɔta] *f* route.

ROTA (*abrev de* **Rondas Ostensivas Tobias de Aguiar**) *f* shock police force of São Paulo.

rotação [xota'sãw] (*pl* -ões) *f* rotation.

rotativa [xota'tʃiva] *f* ⊳ **rotativo**.

rotatividade [xotatʃivi'dadʒi] *f* -**1.** [movimento] turning. -**2.** [rodízio] rotation ⊳ **hotel**.

rotativo, va [xota'tʃivu, va] *adj* -**1.** [giratório] rotary. -**2.** [alternativo] rotating.
  ◆ **rotativa** *f* *TIP* rotary press.

roteador, ra [rotea'do(x),ra] *m* *COMPUT* router.

roteirista [xotej'riʃta] *mf* script writer.

roteiro [xo'tejru] *m* -**1.** [ger] script. -**2.** [de viagem] guide book. -**3.** [de trabalho] schedule.

rotina [xo'tʃina] *f* routine.

rotineiro, ra [xotʃi'nejru, ra] *adj* routine.

roto, ta ['xotu, ta] *adj* -**1.** [rasgado] torn. -**2.** [maltrapilho] ragged.

rótula ['xɔtula] *f* *ANAT* kneecap.

rotular [4] [xotu'la(x)] <> *adj* *ANAT* patellar. <> *vt* -**1.** [etiquetar] to label. -**2.** *fig* [qualificar]: ~ **alguém/algo (de algo)** to label sb/sthg (as sthg).

rótulo ['xɔtulul *m* label.

rotundo, da [xo'tũndu, da] *adj* -**1.** [redondo] round. -**2.** [gordo] rotund.
  ◆ **rotunda** *f* *ARQUIT* rotunda.

roubada [xo'bada] *f* *FUT* [de bola] tackle.

roubalheira [xoba'ʎejra] *f* [outright] robbery.

roubar [4] [xo'ba(x)] <> vt -**1.** [ger] to steal. -**2.** [furtar] to rob. <> vi -**1.** [furtar] to steal. -**2.** [enganar] to cheat.

roubo ['xobu] m -**1.** [ato] theft. -**2.** [produto roubado] stolen goods (pl). -**3.** fig [preço extorsivo]: **ser um ~** to be exorbitant.

rouco, ca ['xoku, ka] adj hoarse.

round ['xawndʒil m ESP round.

roupa ['xopa] f clothes (pl); **~ de baixo** underwear; **~ de cama/mesa** bed/table linen; **~ suja se lava em casa** fig don't wash your dirty linen in public.

roupagem [xo'paʒẽl f clothing.

roupão [xo'pãw] (pl -ões) m dressing gown; **~ de banho** bathrobe.

rouparia [xopa'ria] f -**1.** [roupas] clothes (pl). -**2.** [local] linen room.

rouquidão [xoki'dãw] f hoarseness.

rouxinol [xoʃi'nɔw] (pl -óis) m nightingale.

roxo, xa ['xoʃu, ʃa] adj -**1.** [cor] violet; **~ de inveja** fig green with envy; **estar ~ de saudades** fig to have the blues. -**2.** MED purple. -**3.** [apaixonado]: **ser ~ por** to be passionate about.
    roxo m [cor] violet.

royalty ['xɔjawtʃi] (pl royalties) m royalty.

RP (abrev de Relações Públicas) f PR.

RPM (abrev de Rotações por Minuto) f RPM.

RR (abrev de Estado de Roraima) n State of Roraima.

RS (abrev de Estado do Rio Grande do Sul) n State of Rio Grande do Sul.

RSVP (abrev de répondez s'il vous plaît) RSVP.

rua ['xua] f -**1.** [ger] street; **~ de mão única** one way street; **~ principal** main street; **~ sem saída** dead end. -**2.** loc: **ir para a ~** [sair] to go out; **pôr alguém na ~** [expulsar] to kick sb out; [demitir] to fire sb; **viver na ~** fig to go out a lot.

rubéola [xu'bεwla] f German measles, rubella.

rubi [xu'bi] m ruby.

rubor [xu'bo(x)] (pl -es) m -**1.** [na face] flush. -**2.** [vergonha] blush.

ruborizar [4] [xubori'za(x)] vt [envergonhar] to embarrass.
    ruborizar-se vp to blush.

rubrica [xu'brika] f -**1.** [assinatura] initials (pl). -**2.** [indicação de assunto etc] rubric.

rubricar [12] [xubri'ka(x)] vt to initial.

rubro, bra ['xubru, bra] adj -**1.** [ger] bright red. -**2.** [faces] ruddy.

ruço, ça ['xusu, sa] adj -**1.** [desbotado, surrado] faded. -**2.** fam [difícil] tricky.

rúcula ['xukula] f rocket (salad).

rude ['xudʒi] adj -**1.** [descortês] rude. -**2.** [primitivo] crude.

rudeza [xu'deza] f -**1.** [descortesia] rudeness. -**2.** [primitivismo] crudeness.

rudimentar [xudʒimẽn'ta(x)] adj rudimentary.

rudimentos [xudʒi'mẽntuʃ] mpl rudiments.

rueiro, ra ['xwejru, ra] adj: **ser ~** to be a gadabout.

ruela ['xwεla] f alleyway.

rufar [4] [xu'fa(x)] <> vt [tambor] to beat. <> vi to drum.

rufião, fiona [xu'fjãw, fjona] (mpl -ões, fpl -s) m, f [gigolô] gigolo.

ruga ['xuga] f -**1.** [na pele] wrinkle; **cheio de ~s** covered in wrinkles. -**2.** [na roupa] crease.

rúgbi ['xugbi] m rugby.

ruge ['xuʒi] m rouge.

rugido [xu'ʒidul m roar.

rugir [52] [xu'ʒi(x)] vi to roar.

ruído ['xwidul m noise.

ruidoso, osa [xwi'dozu, ɔza] adj noisy.

ruim ['xuĩ] (pl -ns) adj -**1.** [nocivo] vile. -**2.** [malvado] wicked. -**3.** [imprestável, ineficiente] useless. -**4.** [podre] rotten. -**5.** [defeituoso] faulty. -**6.** [ordinário] poor. -**7.** [desagradável] bad; **achar ~** [zangar-se] to get upset.

ruína [ˌxwinal f -**1.** [ger] ruin; **levar alguém à ~** to ruin sb; **estar em ~s** to be in ruins. -**2.** [causa de destruição, queda] ruination. -**3.** [decadência] downfall.
    ruínas fpl [escombros] ruins.

ruindade [xwĩn'dadʒi] f -**1.** [qualidade] wickedness. -**2.** [ação] sin.

ruins [xu'ĩʃ] pl ⊳ **ruim.**

ruir [74] ['xwi(x)] vi to collapse.

ruivo, va ['xuivu, va] <> adj -**1.** [pessoa] redheaded. -**2.** [cabelo, barba] red. <> m, f redhead.

rulê [xu'le] adj ⊳ **gola.**

rum ['xũ] m rum.

rumar [4] [xu'ma(x)] <> vt: **~ algo para** to steer sthg towards. <> vi: **~ para** to head for.

rumba ['xũnba] f rumba.

ruminante [xumi'nãntʃi] <> adj ruminant. <> m ruminant.

ruminar [4] [xumi'na(x)] <> vt to think over. <> vi to ruminate.

rumo ['xumul m -**1.** [direção] course; **ir ~ a** to head for. -**2.** fig [destino] fate; **sem ~** lit adrift; fig aimless.

rumor [xu'mo(x)] (pl -es) m -**1.** [ruído] noise. -**2.** [boato] rumour.

rumorejante [xumore'ʒãntʃil adj whispering.

ruptura [xup'tural f -**1.** [ger] rupture. -**2.** [de fiação] break. -**3.** [de relações, negociações] break-up. -**4.** [de contrato] breach.

rural [xu'raw] (pl -ais) adj rural.

ruralista [xura'liʃtal <> adj rural. <> mf landowner who protects the interests of rural life, and especially those of landowners themselves.

rusga ['xuʒga] f brawl.

rush ['xãʃil m heavy traffic; **a hora do ~** rush hour.

Rússia ['xusja] n Russia.

russo, sa ['xusu, sa] <> adj Russian. <> m, f Russian.
    russo m [língua] Russian.

rústico, ca ['xuʃtʃiku, ka] adj rustic.

S

s, S [ˈɛsil] m [letra] s, S.

sã [sã] f ▷ **são**.

S.A. (abrev de **Sociedade Anônima**) f limited company, ≃ Ltd.

Saara [saˈaral] n: **o (deserto do)** ~ the Sahara (Desert).

saariano, na [saaˈrjãnu, na] ◇ adj Saharan. ◇ m, f Saharan.

sáb. (abrev de **sábado**) m Sat.

sábado [ˈsabadul] m Saturday; **aos** ~**s** on Saturdays; **cair num** ~ to fall on a Saturday; **esse** ~ **agora** [próximo] next Saturday; **(no)** ~ (on) Saturday; **(no)** ~ **que vem/no próximo** ~ (on) the coming, next Saturday; ~ **de manhã** Saturday morning; ~ **de** ou **á tarde/noite** Saturday afternoon/evening; ~ **passado** ou **retrasado** last Saturday, Saturday just gone; ~ **sim,** ~ **não** every other Saturday; **todos os** ~**s** every Saturday; ~ **de aleluia** Easter Saturday.

sabão [saˈbãw] (pl-ões) m - **1.** [produto] soap; ~ **de coco** coconut soap; ~ **em pó** soap powder. - **2.** [repreensão]: **passar um** ~ **em alguém** to tell sb off.

sabatina [sabaˈtʃina] f revision test.

sabedoria [sabedoˈria] f wisdom; ~ **popular** popular wisdom.

saber [35] [saˈbe(x)] ◇ m knowledge. ◇ vt to know. ◇ vt to know; ~ **de cor** to know (off) by heart; ~ **(como) fazer algo** to know how to do sthg; **que eu saiba** as far as I know; **sei lá!** fam who knows!; **você que sabe** fam it's up to you. ◇ vi - **1.** [ter erudição] to know. - **2.** [estar a par de]: ~ **(de algo)** to know (sthg). - **3.** [ter notícia]: ~ **de alguém** to hear from sb.
➥ **a saber** loc adv namely.

sabiá [saˈbja] m song thrush.

sabichão, chona [sabiˈʃãw, ʃona] (mpl -chões, fpl -s) adj irôn know-all.

sabido, da [saˈbidu, da] adj - **1.** [astuto] wise. - **2.** [conhecedor] knowledgeable. - **3.** [conhecido]: **como é** ~ as is generally known; **é** ~ **que ...** it is known that ...

sábio, bia [ˈsabju, bja] ◇ adj wise. ◇ m, f wise person.

sabões [saˈbõjʃl] pl ▷ **sabão**.

sabonete [saboˈnetʃil] m toilet soap.

saboneteira [saboneˈtejral] f soap dish.

sabor [saˈbo(x)] (pl -es) m taste; **ao** ~ **de** at the mercy of.

saborear [15] [saboˈrja(x)] vt to savour.

saboroso, osa [saboˈrozu, ɔzal] adj tasty.

sabotador, ra [sabotaˈdo(x), ral] m, f saboteur.

sabotagem [saboˈtaʒěl] (pl -ns) f sabotage.

sabotar [4] [saboˈta(x)] vt to sabotage.

sabugo [saˈbugol] m ANAT nail root.

SAC (abrev de **Serviço de Atendimento ao Consumidor**) m Brazilian consumer telephone service.

saca [ˈsakal] f [saco largo] sack.

sacação [sakaˈsãwl] (pl -ões) f fam - **1.** [achado] find. - **2.** [invenção] clever idea.

sacada [saˈkadal] f ARQUIT balcony.

sacado, da [saˈkadu, dal] m, f COM drawee.

sacador, ra [sakaˈdo(x), ral] m, f COM drawer.

sacal [saˈkawl] (pl -ais) adj boring; **ser** ~ to be boring.

sacana [saˈkanal] adj mfam - **1.** [sujo]: **ser** ~ to be a bastard. - **2.** [esperto] sharp. - **3.** [libidinoso] randy. - **4.** [brincalhão] raffish.

sacanagem [sakaˈnaʒěl] (pl -ns) f mfam - **1.** [sujeira] dirty trick. - **2.** [libidinagem] screwing. - **3.** [brincadeira] joke.

sacanear [15] mfam [sakaˈnja(x)] vt - **1.** [amolar] to pester. - **2.** [fazer sujeira com] to screw.

sacar [12] [saˈka(x)] ◇ vt - **1.** [arma, carteira] to pull out; ~ **algo de algo** to draw sthg from sthg. - **2.** [em banco] to draw. - **3.** fam [compreender] to twig. ◇ vi - **1.** [de arma]: ~ **de algo** to whip out sthg. - **2.** [em banco]: ~ **(contra/sobre)** to draw (against/from). - **3.** ESP to serve. - **4.** fam [compreender] to twig. - **5.** fam [mentir] to fib. - **6.** fam [falar sem saber] to talk through one's hat.

sacarina [sakaˈrinal] f saccharin.

saca-rolha [ˌsakaˈxoʎal] (pl saca-rolhas) m corkscrew.

sacerdócio [sasexˈdɔsjul] m priesthood.

sacerdote, tisa [sasexˈdɔtʃi, tʃizal] m, f [pagão] priest (f priestess).
➥ **sacerdote** m RELIG priest.

sachê [saˈʃel] m sachet.

saci-pererê [ˌsaˌsiperˈerel] m figure of Brazilian folklore who typically ambushes travellers.

saciar [16] [saˈsja(x)] vt to satisfy.

saciedade [sasjeˈdadʒil] f [satisfação plena] satisfaction.

saco [ˈsakul] m - **1.** [recipiente] bag. - **2.** [utensílio]: ~ **de água quente** hot-water bottle; ~ **de café** coffee filter; ~ **de dormir** sleeping bag. - **3.** [enseada] cove. - **4.** vulg [testículos] balls. - **5.** fam [amolação]: **encher o** ~ **(de alguém)** to get one's goat; **estar de** ~ **cheio (de alguém/algo)** to have a bellyful (of sb/sthg); **que** ~! what a bore!; **ser/estar um** ~ to be boring. - **6.** fam [paciência]: **haja** ~! keep your knickers on!, don't get your knickers in a twist!; **ter** ~ **(com alguém)** to be cool (with sb). - **7.** fam [disposição]: **estar com/sem**

~ **de fazer algo** to give/not to give a hoot about doing sthg.

sacola [sa'kɔla] f saddlebag.

sacolão [sako'lãw] m greengrocer's.

sacoleiro, ra [sako'lejru, ra] m,f pedlar *UK*, peddler *US*.

sacolejar [4] [sakole'ʒa(x)] vt -1. [sacudir] to shake. -2. [rebolar] to sway.

sacolejo [sako'leʒu] m fam jerk.

sacramentar [4] [sakramẽn'ta(x)] vt -1. *RELIG* to bless. -2. [ultimar] to close.

sacramento [sakra'mẽntu] m *RELIG* sacrament.

sacrificar [12] [sakrifi'ka(x)] vt -1. [ger] to sacrifice. -2. [prejudicar] to damage. -3. [matar] to put down.

➡ **sacrificar-se** vp -1. [ger] to sacrifice o.s. -2. [sujeitar-se] to give in to.

sacrifício [sakri'fisju] m sacrifice.

sacrilégio [sakri'lɛʒju] m sacrilege.

sacrílego, ga [sa'krilegu, ga] adj sacrilegious.

sacristão [sakriʃ'tãw] (pl -ões) m sacristan.

sacristia [sakriʃ'tʃia] f sacristy.

sacro, cra ['sakru, kra] adj -1. [sagrado] sacred. -2. *ANAT* sacral.

➡ **sacro** m *ANAT* sacrum.

sacrossanto, ta [sakro'sãntu, ta] adj sacrosanct.

sacudida [saku'dʒida] f shake.

sacudido, da [saku'dʒidu, da] adj [sacolejado] shaken.

sacudir [41] [saku'dʒi(x)] vt to shake.

➡ **sacudir-se** vp -1. [tremer] to shake. -2. [saracotear] to waggle.

sádico, ca ['sadʒiku, ka] <> adj sadistic. <> m, f sadist.

sadio, dia [sa'dʒiu, dʒia] adj healthy.

sadismo [sa'dʒiʒmu] m sadism.

sadomasoquismo [sadomazo'kiʒmu] m sadomasochism.

sadomasoquista [sadomazo'kiʃta] <> adj sadomasochistic. <> mf sadomasochist.

safadeza [safa'deza] f -1. [ger] mischief. -2. [devassidão] debauchery.

safado, da [sa'fadu, da] adj -1. [ger] mischievous. -2. [devasso] debauched. -3. [com raiva]: ~ **(da vida)** fed up to the back teeth.

safanão [safa'nãw] (pl -ões) m fam -1. [tranco, puxão] tug. -2. [cascudo] box (on the ears).

safári [sa'fari] m safari.

safena [sa'fena] f *ANAT* saphena; **ponte de** ~ coronary bypass.

safira [sa'fira] f sapphire.

safra ['safra] f -1. *AGR* harvest. -2. fig [de cantores etc] crop.

saga ['saga] f saga.

sagacidade [sagasi'dadʒi] f shrewdness.

sagaz [sa'gajʒ] adj shrewd.

sagitariano, na [saʒita'rjãnu, na] <> adj Sagittarian. <> m, f Sagittarian.

Sagitário [saʒi'tarju] <> m [zodíaco] Sagittarius; **ser** ~ to be a Sagittarian. <> mf [pessoa] Sagittarian.

sagrado, da [sa'gradu, da] adj sacred.

saguão [sa'gwãw] (pl -ões) m -1. [entrada] lobby. -2. [pátio] courtyard.

saia ['saja] f -1. [roupa] skirt; ~ **escocesa** kilt. -2. [de mesa] (floor-length) tablecloth. -3. fam fig [mulher] skirt; ~ **justa** tight spot.

saia-calça [ˌsaja'kawsa] (pl saias-calça) f culottes (pl).

saibro ['sajbru] m gravel.

saída [sa'ida] f -1. [ger] way out; **de** ~ straight away; ~ **de emergência** emergency exit. -2. [ato] leaving; **dar uma** ~ to pop out. -3. *COM*: **ter muita** ~ to sell well. -4. [dito]: **ter boas** ~**s** to be witty. -5. [*COMPUT*- de programa] exit; [- de dados] output.

saída-de-praia [saˌidadʒi'praja] (pl saídas-de-praia) f beach wrap.

saideira [saj'dejra] f one for the road.

saiote [sa'jɔtʃi] m petticoat.

sair [68] [sa'i(x)] vi -1. [gen] to come out; ~ **do armário** fig to come out (as being homosexual). -2. [ir para fora - de ônibus, trem, avião] to get off; [- de carro] to get out of. -3. [ir para a rua] to go out. -4. [ir embora, deixar] to leave; ~ **de fininho** to sneak off. -5. [fugir] to get out. -6. [escapar]: ~ **de** to get out of. -7. [aparecer] to appear. -8. [desaparecer]: ~ **de moda** to go out of fashion. -9. [parecer-se]: ~ **a alguém** to take after sb. -10. [resultar] to turn out; ~ **ganhando/perdendo** to end up winning/losing. -11. [custar]: ~ **(a ou por)** to come to; ~ **caro** to be expensive. -12. *COMPUT* to exit.

➡ **sair-se** vp -1. [obter resultado]: ~**-se bem/mal** to come out well/badly. -2. [dizer]: ~**-se com** to come out with.

sal ['saw] (pl sais) m salt; **sem** ~ [manteiga etc] unsalted; [precisando de mais sal] bland; ~ **de banho** bath salts (pl); ~ **de cozinha** kitchen salt; ~ **grosso** rock salt.

sala ['sala] f -1. [aposento] room; ~ **de embarque** departure lounge; ~ **de espera** waiting room; ~ **de estar** living room; ~ **de operações** operating theatre; ~ **de parto** delivery room. -2. [de espetáculos] concert hall. -3. *EDUC*: ~ **(de aula)** classroom; [alunos] class. -4. fig: **fazer** ~ **a alguém** [entreter] to entertain sb.

salada [sa'lada] f -1. *CULIN* salad; ~ **de frutas** fruit salad. -2. fig [confusão]: **fazer uma** ~ **de algo** to make a muddle of sthg.

saladeira [sala'dejra] f salad bowl.

sala-e-quarto [ˌsalaj'kwaxtu] (pl sala-e-quartos) m studio (flat).

salafrário, ria [sala'frarju, rja] m, f fam scoundrel.

salamaleque [salama'lɛki] m exaggerated greeting.

salame [sa'lãmi] m salami.

salaminho [sala'miɲu] m small salami.

salão [sa'lãw] (pl -ões) m -1. [aposento] lounge. -2. [estabelecimento]: ~ **de beleza** beauty salon; ~ **de chá** tea room. -3. [exposição] exhibition hall.

➡ **de salão** loc adj -1. [piada] tasteful. -2. [jogo]

indoor. **-3.** [dança] dance hall *(antes de subst)*.

salarial [sala'rjaw] *(pl* **-ais)** *adj* pay *(antes de subst)*.

salário [sa'larju] *m* wage; ~ **de fome** miserly wage; **décimo terceiro** ~ *Christmas bonus equal to one month's wages*; ~ **mínimo** minimum wage; ~ **líquido** net salary.

salário-base [sa,larju'bazi] *(pl* **salários-base)** *m* basic wage.

salário-família [sa,larjufa'milja] *(pl* **salários-família)** *m extra pro rata pay for employees with dependants*.

saldão [saw'dãw] *(pl* **-ões)** *m* [saldo] sale.

saldar [4] [saw'da(x)] *vt* to settle.

saldo [ˈsawdu] *m* **-1.** [ger] balance; ~ **credor/devedor** credit/debit balance; ~ **negativo/positivo** debit/credit balance; ~ **a receber/pagar** balance due/to pay. **-2.** *fig* [resultado] outcome.

saleiro [sa'lejru] *m* **-1.** [recipiente] salt cellar. **-2.** [moedor] salt mill.

saleta [sa'leta] *f* small living room.

salgadinho [sawga'dʒiɲu] *m* canapé.

salgado, da [saw'gadu, da] *adj* **-1.** [comida - com sal] salted; [- com excesso de sal] salty. **-2.** [anedota] salty. **-3.** [preço] steep.

salgar [14] [saw'ga(x)] *vt* to salt.

salgueiro [saw'gejru] *m* willow.

saliência [sa'ljẽnsja] *f* **-1.** [proeminência] projection. **-2.** *fig* [espevitamento] eagerness.

salientar [4] [saljẽn'ta(x)] *vt* **-1.** [ressaltar] to highlight. **-2.** [enfatizar] to stress.

➡ **salientar-se** *vp* [distinguir-se] to distinguish o.s.

saliente [sa'ljẽntʃi] *adj* **-1.** [ressaltado] salient. **-2.** *fig* [espevitado] eager.

salino, na [sa'linu, na] *adj* saline.

➡ **salina** *f* **-1.** [terreno] salt bed. **-2.** [empresa] salt works.

salitre [sa'litri] *m* saltpetre.

saliva [sa'liva] *f* saliva; **gastar** ~ to waste one's breath.

salivar [4] [sa'liva(x)] *vi* to salivate.

salmão [saw'mãw] *(pl* **-ões)** ◇ *m* [peixe] salmon. ◇ *m inv* [cor] salmon. ◇ *adj inv* [cor] salmon-pink.

salmo [ˈsawmu] *m* psalm.

salmões [saw'mõjʃ] *pl* ▷ **salmão**.

salmonela [sawmo'nɛla] *f* salmonella.

salmoura [saw'mora] *f* brine.

salobro, bra [sa'lobru, bra] *adj* brackish.

salões [sa'lõjʃ] *pl* ▷ **salão**.

salpicão [sawpi'kãw] *(pl* **-ões)** *m* **-1.** [paio] smoked sausage. **-2.** [prato]: ~ **(de galinha)** *cold shredded chicken and vegetable dish*.

salpicar [12] [sawpi'ka(x)] *vt* **-1.:** ~ **algo em algo,** ~ **algo de algo** [temperar] to season sthg with sthg; [sarapintar, sujar] to splash; ~ **alguém de algo** [sujar] to splash sb with sthg. **-2.** [entremear]: ~ **algo com** *ou* **de algo** to pepper sthg with sthg.

salsa [ˈsawsa] *f* **-1.** [erva] parsley. **-2.** *MÚS* salsa.

salsicha [saw'siʃa] *f* sausage.

salsichão [sawsi'ʃãw] *(pl* **-chões)** *m* large sausage.

saltado, da [saw'tadu, da] *adj* prominent.

saltar [4] [saw'ta(x)] ◇ *vt* **-1.** [ger] to jump. **-2.** *fam* [fazer vir] to send for. ◇ *vi* **-1.** [pular]: ~ **(de/sobre)** to jump (from/on). **-2.** [de ônibus, trem, cavalo]: ~ **(de)** to jump (from). **-3.** [brotar]: ~ **de** to pour from. **- 4.** [rolha] to pop.

salteado, da [saw'tʃjadu, da] *adj* [alternado] alternate; **saber de cor e** ~ to know off by heart.

salteador, ra [sawtʃja'do(x), ra] *m, f* mugger.

saltimbanco [sawtʃĩ'bãŋku] *m* travelling acrobat.

saltitante [sawtʃi'tãntʃi] *adj* [ave, criança] hopping; ~ **de alegria** jumping for joy.

saltitar [4] [sawtʃi'ta(x)] *vi* **-1.** [pular] to hop. **-2.** *fig* [divagar]: ~ **de ... para ...** to jump from ... to ...

salto [ˈsawtu] *m* **-1.** [pulo] jump; **dar um** ~ to leap; **dar** ~s **de alegria** to leap for joy. **-2.** *ESP*: ~ **em altura** high jump; ~ **em distância** long jump; ~ **de vara** pole vault. **-3.** [de sapato] heel; ~ **alto/baixo** high/low heel.

salto-mortal [ˌsawtumox'taw] *(pl* **saltos-mortais)** *m* somersault.

salubre [sa'lubri] *adj* salubrious.

salutar [salu'ta(x)] *(pl* **-es)** *adj* **-1.** [saudável] healthy. **-2.** *fig* [moralizador] salutary.

salva [ˈsawva] *f* **-1.** *MIL*: ~ **(de tiros)** salvo (of gunshots). **-2.** *fig*: **uma** ~ **de palmas** a round of applause. **-3.** [bandeja] tray.

salvação [sawva'sãw] *f* salvation; **não ter** ~ to be without hope; **ser a** ~ **da pátria** *fam fig* to be one's salvation.

salvador, ra [sawva'do(x), ra] *m, f* [pessoa] saviour.

Salvador [sawva'do(x)] *n* Salvador.

salvadorenho, nha [sawvado'reɲu, ɲa] ◇ *adj* Salvadorean. ◇ *m, f* Salvadorean.

salvados [saw'vaduʃ] *mpl* salvage *(sg)*.

salvaguarda [sawva'gwaxda] *f* safeguard.

salvaguardar [4] [ˌsawvagwax'da(x)] *vt* to safeguard.

salvamento [sawva'mẽntu] *m* rescue; **equipe de** ~ rescue team!

salvar [4] [saw'va(x)] *vt* to save.

➡ **salvar-se** *vp* [escapar] to escape.

salva-vidas [ˌsalva'vidaʃ] ◇ *adj inv* lifeguard; **lancha** ~ life boat. ◇ *m* **-1.** *inv* [bóia] lifebelt. **-2.** [pessoa] lifeguard. **-3.** [jaqueta] life jacket.

salve [ˈsawvi] *interj* cheers!

sálvia [ˈsawvja] *f* *BOT* sage.

salvo, va [ˈsawvu, va] ◇ *adj* safe; **estar a** ~ to be safe. ◇ *prep* except.

salvo-conduto [ˌsawvukõn'dutu] *(pl* **salvo-condutos, salvos-condutos)** *m* safe conduct.

samambaia [samãn'baja] *f* fern.

samaritano [samari'tãnu] *m*: **bom** ~ *RELIG* good Samaritan; *fig & pej* do-gooder.

samba [ˈsãnba] *m* samba.

SAMBA

Through its catchy rhythm and vitality, samba has become synonymous with Brazilian music. Afro-Brazilian in origin, it developed mainly in Bahia, Rio de Janeiro and São Paulo. It is characterized by a syncopated beat and is generally performed on percussion instruments, guitars and *cavaquinho* (small four-stringed guitar). There are many kinds of samba. One of the more traditional forms is the 'samba-de-roda' from Bahia; another very popular form is the 'sambas-enredo' of the carnival in Rio de Janeiro, which express the theme of each samba school's parade; finally, there is a fairly characteristic form of samba, known as the 'samba de breque', with a generally satirical content.

samba-canção [ˌsãnbakãn'sãw] (*pl* **sambas-canções**) <> *m* MÚS *type of samba.* <> *adj inv*: **cueca** ~ shorts *(pl)*.

samba-de-roda ['sãnbadʒi'xɔdal (*pl* **sambas-de-roda**) *m samba in which the dancers form a circle and each dances in turn.*

samba-enredo [ˌsãnbẽn'xedul (*pl* **sambas-enredo**) *m samba describing the theme chosen by a samba school for the carnival.*

sambar [4] [sãn'ba(x)] *vi* to samba.

sambista [sãn'biʃtal *mf* **-1.** [dançarino] samba dancer. **-2.** [compositor] composer of sambas.

sambódromo [sãn'bɔdromul *m track along which samba schools parade.*

samovar [samo'va(x)] *m* samovar.

Sana ['sanal *n* San'a.

sanar [4] [sa'na(x)] *vt* **-1.** [curar] to cure. **-2.** [remediar] to remedy.

sanatório [sana'tɔrjul *m* sanatorium.

sanável [sa'navewl (*pl* **-eis**) *adj* **-1.** [curável] curable. **-2.** [remediável] remediable.

sanção [sãn'sãwl (*pl* **-ões**) *f* **-1.** [ger] sanction. **-2.** [punição]: ~ **(contra)** sanction (against).

sancionar [4] [sãnsjo'na(x)] *vt* [aprovar] to sanction.

sanções [sãn'sõjʃl *pl* ⊳ **sanção**.

sandália [sãn'daljal *f* sandal.

sândalo ['sãndalul *m* sandalwood.

sanduíche [sãn'dwiʃil *m* sandwich; ~ **americano** double-decker sandwich; ~ **misto** cheese and ham sandwich.

saneamento [sanja'mẽntul *m* **-1.** [limpeza] sanitization. **-2.** *fig* [correção] purge.

sanear [15] [sa'nja(x)] *vt* **-1.** [tornar salubre] to sanitize. **-2.** *fig* [corrigir] to purge.

sanfona [sãn'fonal *f* **-1.** MÚS concertina. **-2.** [em suéter] ribbing.

sanfonado, da [sãnfo'nadu, dal *adj* **-1.** [porta] folding *(antes de subst)*. **-2.** [suéter] ribbed.

sangramento [sãngra'mẽntul *m* **-1.** [de ferida] bleeding. **-2.** [de açude, represa] overflow.

sangrar [4] [sãŋ'gra(x)] <> *vi* [verter sangue] to bleed. <> *vt* **-1.** [ger] to bleed. **-2.** [açude, represa] to drain.

sangrento, ta [sãŋ'grẽntu, tal *adj* **-1.** [ger]

bloody. **-2.** CULIN [carne] rare.

sangria [sãŋ'grial *f* **-1.** [bebida] sangria. **-2.** MED blood-letting. **-3.** *fig* [extorsão] extortion.

sangue ['sãŋgil *m* **-1.** [ger] blood; **de** ~ [exame, transfusão] blood; **começou a sair muito** ~ **do corte** the cut started to bleed a lot; **tirar** ~ to take blood. **-2.** *fig* [raça]: **puro** ~ thoroughbred.

➡ **a sangue frio** *loc adv* in cold blood.

sangue-frio [ˌsãŋgi'friwl *m* sangfroid.

sanguessuga [ˌsãŋgi'sugal *f* leech.

sanguinário, ria [sãŋgi'narju, rjal *adj* bloodthirsty.

sanguíneo, nea [sãŋ'g(w)inju, njal *adj* **-1.** [relativo ao sangue] blood *(antes de subst)*. **-2.** [pessoa] ruddy.

sanha ['sãɲal *f*: ~ **(contra)** anger (against).

sanidade [sani'dadʒil *f* [mental] sanity.

sanitário, ria [sani'tarju, rjal *adj* **-1.** [ger] sanitary. **-2.** [banheiro] bath *(antes de subst)*.

San José [ˌsãnxo'sel *n* San José.

San Marino [ˌsãnma'rinul *n* San Marino.

San Salvador [ˌsãnsawva'do(x)l *n* San Salvador.

Santa Catarina [ˌsãntakata'rinal *n* Santa Catarina.

santidade [sãntʃi'dadʒil *f* sanctity.

➡ **Santidade** *f* [Vossa Santidade] Holiness.

santificar [12] [sãntʃifi'ka(x)] *vt* to sanctify.

Santiago de Cuba [ˌsãnˌtʃjagudʒi'kubal *n* Santiago de Cuba.

Santiago do Chile [sãnˌtʃagudu'ʃilil *n* Santiago de Chile.

santinho [sãn'tʃiɲul *m* **-1.** [figura] religious figurine. **-2.** *fam* [pessoa] goody-goody.

santo, ta ['sãntu, tal <> *adj* **-1.** [sagrado] holy; **todo o** ~ **dia** *fam fig* the whole blessed day long. **-2.** *(antes de subst)* [caridoso] kind. **-3.** [eficaz]: **um** ~ **remédio** an effective medicine. <> *m, f* **-1.** [ger] saint. **-2.** *loc*: ~ **de casa não faz milagre** a prophet is not without honour save in his own country; **ter** ~ **forte** *fam* to have the gods smiling on you.

SANTOS-DUMONT

Aviator and inventor from Minas Gerais; Alberto Santos-Dumont (1873-1832) invented the airship in 1901, with which he flew round the Eiffel Tower. In 1906, he built the 14-Bis, the first plane officially to fly over 25m above ground. Santos-Dumont also invented the wristwatch and is considered by Brazilians to be the inventor of the airplane.

Santo Domingo [ˌsãntudo'mĩŋgul *n* Santo Domingo.

santuário [sãn'twarjul *m* sanctuary.

são, sã ['sãw, 'sãl *adj* **-1.** [ger] healthy. **-2.** PSIC sane. **-3.** [curado] well. **-4.** [ileso]: ~ **e salvo** safe and sound. **-5.** [sensato] sensible.

São [sãwl *m* Saint.

SÃO FRANCISCO

'Old Chico' is the nickname given to the largest river in Brazilian territory; its source is in Minas Gerais and it crosses the states of Bahia, Pernambuco, Alagoas and Sergipe, covering a total of 3,160 km. It is fundamental to the economy of the region, providing significant opportunities for hydroelectric output, fluvial access to certain areas, allowing agricultural activity on its banks and irrigation to distant areas.

São Luís [ˌsãwlu'iʒ] n São Luís.
São Paulo [ˌsãw'pawlu] n São Paulo.
São Tomé [ˌsãwto'mɛ] n São Tomé.
São Tomé e Príncipe [sãwtoˌmɛj'prĩsipil] n São Tomé and Príncipe.
sapata [sa'pata] f - **1.** [suporte] prop. - **2.** [de freio] shoe.
sapatão [sapa'tãw] m mfam pej dyke.
sapataria [sapata'ria] f - **1.** [ofício] shoe trade. - **2.** [loja] shoe shop.
sapateado [sapa'tʃjadu] m tap dance.
sapateador, ra [sapatʃja'do(x), ra] m, f tap dancer.
sapatear [15] [sapa'tʃja(x)] vi - **1.** [dançar] to tap-dance. - **2.** [bater com os pés] to stamp.
sapateiro, ra [sapa'tejru, ra] m, f - **1.** [fabricante] shoemaker. - **2.** [quem conserta] cobbler.
    ➡ **sapateiro** m [loja] shoe shop.
    ➡ **sapateira** f [móvel] shoe cupboard.
sapatilha [sapa'tʃiʎa] f - **1.** [de balé] ballet shoe. - **2.** [sapato baixo] slipper.
sapato [sa'patu] m shoe.
sapê, sapé [sa'pe] m thatch; **telhado de ~** thatched roof.
sapeca [sa'pɛka] adj - **1.** [levado] mischievous. - **2.** [assanhado] irritable.
sapecar [15] [sape'ka(x)] vt [tapa, soco etc]: **~ algo em alguém** to hit sb with sthg.
sapiência [sa'pjẽsja] f - **1.** [erudição] knowledge. - **2.** [bom julgamento] wisdom.
sapiente [sa'pjẽtʃil] adj [erudito] knowledgeable.
sapinho [sa'piɲu] m MED thrush.
sapo ['sapu] m toad; **engolir ~** fig to take the flak.
saque ['sakil m - **1.** FIN withdrawal; **~ a descoberto** overdraft. - **2.** ESP serve. - **3.** [de cidade, loja] ransacking. - **4.** fam [mentira] fib.
saquê [sa'ke] m sake.
saquear [15] [sa'kja(x)] vt to ransack.
saracotear [15] [sarako'tʃja(x)] vt to sway.
saraivada [saraj'vada] f hail storm; **uma ~ de** fig a shower of.
saraivar [4] [saraj'va(x)] vi to hail.
sarampo [sa'rãpu] m measles.
sarapintado, da [sarapĩ'tadu, da] adj dotted.
sarar [4] [sa'ra(x)] ⬦ vt [pessoa, doença, ferida] to heal. ⬦ vi - **1.** [pessoa] to get better. - **2.** [ferida] to heal.
sarau [sa'raw] m soirée.
sarcasmo [sax'kaʒmul m sarcasm.
sarcástico, ca [sax'kaʃtʃiku, ka] adj sarcastic.
sarcófago [sax'kɔfagul m sarcophagus.

sarda ['saxdal f freckle.
Sardenha [sax'deɲa] n Sardinia.
sardento, ta [sax'dẽtu, ta] adj freckly.
sardinha [sax'dʒiɲa] f sardine.
sardônico, ca [sax'doniku, ka] adj sardonic.
sargento [sax'ʒẽtul mf sergeant.
sári ['saril m sari.
sarjeta [sax'ʒeta] f gutter.
sarna ['saxnal f scabies; **procurar ~ para se coçar** to look for trouble.
sarnento, ta [sax'nẽtu, ta] adj [com sarna] mangy.
sarrafo [sa'xaful m batten; **baixar o ~ em alguém** fam to batter sb.
sarro ['saxul m - **1.** [borra] residue. - **2.** [de nicotina] tartar. - **3.** [na língua] fur. - **4.** fam [pessoa, coisa]: **ser um ~** to be fun. - **5.** mfam [bolinagem]: **tirar um ~ (de alguém)** to grope (sb).
Satã [sa'tã], **Satanás** [sata'naʃl m Satan.
satânico, ca [sa'tãniku, ka] adj - **1.** [culto] satanic. - **2.** fig [diabólico] devilish.
satélite [sa'tɛlitʃil] ⬦ m satellite. ⬦ adj [cidade, país] satellite (antes de subst).
sátira ['satʃiral f satire.
satírico, ca [sa'tʃiriku, ka] adj satirical.
satirizar [4] [satʃiri'za(x)] vt to satirize.
satisfação [satʃiʃfa'sãw] (pl -ões) f - **1.** [alegria, prazer] pleasure; **dar ~ a alguém** to give sb pleasure; **ter ~ em fazer algo** to be pleased to do sthg. - **2.** [de desejos, necessidades] satisfaction. - **3.** [explicação] explanation; **dar uma ~ a alguém** to give sb an explanation; **não dar satisfações a ninguém** to owe an explanation to nobody; **tomar satisfações de alguém** to get an explanation from sb.
satisfatório, ria [satʃiʃfa'tɔrju, rja] adj satisfactory.
satisfazer [31] [satʃiʃfa'ze(x)] ⬦ vt to satisfy. ⬦ vi - **1.** [ser satisfatório] to be satisfactory. - **2.** [contentar, convir]: **~ a** to satisfy.
    ➡ **satisfazer-se** vp: **~-se (com)** to be satisfied (with).
satisfeito, ta [satʃiʃ'fejtu, ta] ⬦ pp ⊳ satisfazer. ⬦ adj - **1.** [ger] satisfied. - **2.** [alegre] pleased.
saturação [satura'sãw] f saturation.
saturado, da [satu'radu, da] adj - **1.**: **~ de algo** saturated with sthg. - **2.** fig [enfastiado]: **~ (de algo/alguém)** fed up (with sthg/sb).
saturar [4] [satu'ra(x)] vt - **1.**: **~ algo (de algo)** to saturate sthg (with sthg). - **2.** fig [enfastiar]: **~ alguém de algo** to wear sb out with sthg. - **3.** [saciar] to fill.
Saturno [sa'tuxnul m Saturn.
saudação [sawda'sãw] (pl -ões) f - **1.** [cumprimento] greeting. - **2.** [homenagem] homage.
saudade [saw'dadʒil f - **1.** [de pessoa, país, família] pining. - **2.** [do passado, de época] nostalgia; **estar morrendo de ~(s) de alguém** to be pining for sb; **matar as ~s de alguém** to catch up with sb; **estava louco para as ~s da minha cama** I was dying to sleep in my own bed again; **sentir ~(s) de alguém/algo** to pine for sb/sthg.

saudar [19] [saw'da(x)] *vt* to greet.
saudável [saw'davɛw] (*pl* -eis) *adj* healthy.
saúde [sa'udʒi] ⬦ *f* health; **estado de** ~ state of health; **estar bem/mal de** ~ to be in good/bad health; **não ter** ~ **para fazer algo** *fam fig* to not be fit to do sthg; **brindar à** ~ **de alguém** to drink to sb's health; ~ **pública** public health; [órgão] health service. ⬦ *interj* [para brindar] cheers!; [depois de um espirro] bless you!
saudita [saw'dʒita] (*pl* **sauditas**) ⬦ *adj* Saudi. ⬦ *mf* Saudi.
saudosismo [sawdo'ziʒmul] *m* nostalgia.
saudoso, osa [saw'dozu, ɔza] *adj* -1. [que causa saudades] dearly missed. -2. [que sente saudades]: **estar** ~ **de alguém/algo** to miss sb/sthg. -3. [que denota saudades] grieving.
šauna [l'sawnal] *f* -1. [ger] sauna; **fazer** ~ to have a sauna. -2. *fig*: **estar uma** ~ [estar muito quente] to be like a sauna.
saveiro [sa'vejru] *m* fishing boat.
saxão, xã [sak'sãw, sã] ⬦ *adj* Saxon. ⬦ *mf* Saxon.
saxofone [sakso'foni] *m* saxophone.
saxofonista [saksofo'niʃta] *mf* saxophonist.
sazonado, da [sazo'nadu, da] *adj* ripe.
sazonal [sazo'naw] (*pl* -ais) *adj* seasonal.
sazonalidade [sazonali'dadʒi] *f* seasonal variation.
SBT (*abrev de* **Sistema Brasileiro de Televisão**) *m* the second most popular Brazilian television station.
SC (*abrev de* **Estado de Santa Catarina**) *n State of Santa Catarina.*
scanner [iʃka'ne(x)] (*pl* -s) *m COMPUT* scanner.
script [iʃkriptʃi] (*pl* -s) *m* script.
se [si] ⬦ *pron* -1. [reflexo: pessoa] himself (*f* herself); [você, vocês] yourself, yourselves *pl*; [impessoal] oneself; **lavar-**~ to wash (oneself); **eles** ~ **perderam** they got lost; **vocês se perderam** you got lost. -2. [reflexo: coisa, animal] itself; **o vidro partiu-**~ the glass broke. -3. [recíproco] each other; **escrevem-**~ **regularmente** they write to each other regularly. -4. [com sujeito indeterminado]: **'aluga-**~ **quarto'** 'room to let'; **'vende-**~' 'for sale'; **come-**~ **bem aqui** the food here is very good. ⬦ *conj* -1. [indica condição] if; ~ **tiver tempo, escrevo** I'll write if I have time; ~ **fizer sol, iremos à praia** if it's sunny, we'll go to the beach. -2. [indica causa] if; ~ **você está com fome, coma alguma coisa** if you're hungry, have something to eat; ~ **..., então ...** if ..., then ...; ~ **diminui a oferta, então aumenta o preço** if demand diminishes, the cost goes up. -3. [indica comparação] if; ~ **um é feio, o outro ainda é pior** if you think he's ugly, you should see the other one. -4. [em interrogativas]: **que tal** ~ **fôssemos ao cinema?** how about going to the movies?; **e** ~ **ela não vier?** and what if she doesn't come? -5. [exprime desejo] if; ~ **pelo menos tivesse dinheiro!** if only I had the money! -6. [em interrogativa indireta] if, whether; **avisem-me** ~ **quiserem ir** let me

know if you'd like to go; **perguntei-lhe** ~ **gostou** I asked him if he liked it. -7. [em locuções]: ~ **bem que** even though, although.
sé [l'sɛ] *f* cathedral.
➡ **Santa Sé** *f*: **a Santa Sé** the Holy See.
SE (*abrev de* **Estado de Sergipe**) *n State of Sergipe.*
seara [l'sjara] *f* -1. [terra] sown field. -2. [de cereais] corn field.
sebáceo, cea [se'basju, sja] *adj* sebaceous.
sebento, ta [se'bẽtu, ta] *adj* [sujo] filthy.
sebo [l'sebu] *m* -1. [substância] sebum. -2. [livraria] second-hand bookshop.
seborréia [sebo'xɛja] *f* seborrhoea *UK*, seborrhea *US*.
seboso, osa [se'bozu, ɔza] *adj* -1. [ger] greasy. -2. *fam fig* [pessoa] conceited.
SEBRAE (*abrev de* **Serviço de Apoio às Micro e Pequenas Empresas**) *m Brazilian support body for small and very small businesses.*
seca [l'seka] *f* ⬦ seco.
secador [seka'do(x)] (*pl* -es) *m* dryer; ~ **(de cabelo)** hairdryer; ~ **de pratos** drainer; ~ **de roupa** [varal] clothes line.
secadora [seka'dora] *f* tumble-dryer.
secagem [se'kaʒẽ] *f* drying.
seção [se'sãw] (*pl* -ões) *f* section.
secar [12] [se'ka(x)] ⬦ *vt* & *vi* to dry.
seccionar [4] [seksjo'na(x)] *vt* -1. [cortar] to cut into sections. -2. [dividir] to divide.
secessão [sese'sãw] *f* secession.
seco, ca [l'seku, ka] *adj* -1. [ger] dry. -2. [magro] thin. -3. *fam* [ávido]: **estar** ~ **por algo/para fazer algo** to be dying for sthg/to do sthg.
➡ **seca** *f* drought.

seções [se'sõjʃ] *pl* ⬦ seção.
secreção [sekre'sãw] (*pl* -ões) *f* secretion.
secretaria [sekreta'ria] *f* secretariat.
secretária [sekre'tarja] *f* ⬦ **secretário**.
secretariado [sekreta'rjadu] *m* [cargo, curso] secretarial course.
secretariar [16] [sekreta'rja(x)] ⬦ *vt* to take minutes of. ⬦ *vi* to work as a secretary.
secretário, ria [sekre'tarju, rja] *m, f* [ger] secretary; ~ **de Estado** Secretary of State.
➡ **secretária** *f* -1. [mesa] desk. -2. [aparelho]: ~ **eletrônica** answering machine.
secretário-geral, secretária-geral [sekre,tarjuʒe'raw, sekre,tarjaʒe'raw] (*mpl* **secretários-gerais**, *fpl* **secretárias-gerais**) *m, f* secretary general.

secreto, ta [se'krɛtu, ta] *adj* secret.
sectário, ria [sɛk'tarju, rja] ◇ *adj* sectarian. ◇ *m, f* [seguidor] sectarian.
sectarismo [sekta'riʒmu] *m* sectarianism.
secular [seku'la(x)] (*pl* -es) *adj* -1. [ger] secular. -2. [antigo] age-old.
secularizar [4] [sekulari'za(x)] *vt* to secularize.
século ['sɛkulu] *m* century; **do** ~ [descoberta, romance] of the century.

➤ **séculos** *mpl fig* [longo tempo] ages; **há** ~**s** for ages; **há** ~**s que não viajava** it's ages since I travelled, I haven't travelled for ages; ~**s atrás** ages ago.
secundar [4] [sekũn'da(x)] *vt* -1. [auxiliar] to help. -2. [reforçar] to reinforce.
secundário, ria [sekũn'darju, rja] *adj* secondary.
secura [se'kura] *f* -1. [ger] dryness. -2. *fam* [desejo]: ~ **por algo** longing for sthg.
seda ['seda] *f* -1. [material] silk; **de** ~ silk; ~ **crua/pura** raw/pure silk. -2. *fig* [pessoa]: **estar uma** ~ to be very friendly.
sedã [se'dã] *m* sedan.
sedar [4] [se'da(x)] *vt* to sedate.
sedativo, va [seda'tʃivu, va] *adj* MED sedative; *fig* [música, balanço, silêncio] soothing.

➤ **sedativo** *m* MED sedative.
sede¹ ['sedʒi] *f* -1. [secura] thirst; **estar com** ~ to be thirsty; **matar a** ~ to quench one's thirst. -2. *fig* [desejo]: ~ **de algo** thirst for sthg.
sede² ['sɛdʒi] *f* -1. [estabelecimento] headquarters. -2. [de governo] seat. -3. [centro, local] venue.
sedentário, ria [sedẽn'tarju, rja] *adj* sedentary.
sedento, ta [se'dẽntu, ta] *adj* -1. [de água] thirsty. -2. *fig* [ávido]: ~ **de algo** thirsty for sthg.
SEDEX (*abrev de* **Serviço de Encomenda Expressa**) *m Brazilian express mail delivery service*.
sediar [15] [se'dʒja(x)] *vt* to base.
sedição [sedʒi'sãw] (*pl* -ões) *f* sedition.
sedicioso, osa [sedʒi'sjozu, ɔza] *adj* seditious.
sedimentação [sedʒimẽnta'sãw] (*pl* -ões) *f* sedimentation.
sedimentar [4] [sedʒimẽn'ta(x)] *vi* to sediment.
sedimento [sedʒi'mẽntu] *m* sediment.
sedoso, osa [se'dozu, ɔza] *adj* silky.
sedução [sedu'sãw] (*pl* -ões) *f* -1. [ato] seduction. -2. [atração]: ~ **por algo/alguém** attraction towards sthg/sb.
sedutor, ra [sedu'to(x), ra] (*mpl* -es, *fpl* -s) ◇ *adj* seductive. ◇ *m, f* [sexualmente] seducer.
seduzir [72] [sedu'zi(x)] *vt* -1. [ger] to seduce. -2. [induzir] to encourage.
seg. (*abrev de* **segunda-feira**) *f* Mon.
segmentação [segmẽnta'sãw] (*pl* -ões) *f* segmentation.
segmentar [4] [segmẽn'ta(x)] *vt* to segment.
segmento [seg'mẽntu] *m* segment.
segredar [4] [segre'da(x)] *vt* &*vi* to whisper.
segredo [se'gredu] *m* -1. [ger] secret; **guardar** ~ to keep secret; ~ **de Estado** state secret. -2. [discrição] secrecy; **em** ~ in secret. -3. [dispositivo] secret lock.

segregação [segrega'sãw] *f* segregation.
segregar [14] [segre'ga(x)] *vt* -1. [ger] to segregate. -2. [expelir] to secrete.
seguidamente [se,gida'mẽntʃi] *adv* -1. [com frequência] often. -2. [continuamente] continuously.
seguido, da [se'gidu, da] *adj* -1. [consecutivo] consecutive; **cinco dias** ~**s** five days running; **horas seguidas** hours on end. -2. [adotado] widely adopted. -3. [que se segue]: ~ **a** following. -4. [acompanhado]: ~ **de/por** followed by.

➤ **em seguida** *loc adv* -1. [consecutivamente] shortly after. -2. [imediatamente] straight away, at once.
seguidor, ra [segi'do(x), ra] *m, f* follower.
seguimento [segi'mẽntu] *m* continuation; **dar** ~ **a algo** to continue with sthg.
seguinte [se'gĩntʃi] ◇ *adj* -1. [subseqüente] following, next; ~ **a** following. -2. (*antes de subst)* [citando, explicando] following. ◇ *mf*: **o/a** ~ [numa fila, ordem] the next; [citando, explicando] as follows; **o negócio é o** ~ *fam* the matter is as follows; **pelo** ~ for the following reason.
seguir [55] [se'gi(x)] ◇ *vt* -1. [ger] to follow. -2. [perseguir] to chase. -3. [continuar] to continue. ◇ *vi* -1. [ger] to follow. -2. [continuar] to carry on, to keep going. -3. [direção] to continue; ~ **reto** to go straight ahead.

➤ **seguir-se** *vp* -1. [suceder]: ~**-se (a algo)** to follow on (from sthg); **seguiram-se dias de euforia** there followed days of euphoria. -2. [em citações] to follow.
segunda [se'gũnda] *f* ▷ **segundo**.
segunda-feira [se,gũnda'fejra] (*pl* **segundas-feiras**) *f* Monday; *veja também* **sábado**.
segundanista [segũndã'niʃta] *mf* second year (*university*) *student*.
segundo, da [se'gũndu, da] ◇ *num adj* second; ~ **grau** EDUC secondary education; ~ **tempo** FUT second half. ◇ *num m, f* second. ◇ *adj* -1. [outro] second; **segundas intenções** ulterior motives; **de segunda mão** second-hand. -2. [inferior]: **de** ~ **time** second-rate.

➤ **segundo** ◇ *m* [medida de tempo] second; **(só) um** ~! *fig* just a second!, (just) one second! ◇ *prep* according to. ◇ *conj* [conforme] according to.

➤ **segunda** *f* -1. AUTO second (gear). -2. [segunda-feira] Monday.

➤ **de segunda** ◇ *loc adj* second class. ◇ *loc adv* [viajar] second class.
segurado, da [segu'radu, da] ◇ *adj* insured. ◇ *m, f* person insured.
segurador, ra [segura'do(x), ra] *m, f* [agente] insurance broker.

➤ **seguradora** *f* [companhia] insurance company.
seguramente [se,gura'mẽntʃi] *adv* -1. [com certeza] certainly. -2. [muito provavelmente] surely.
segurança [segu'rãnsa] ◇ *f* -1. [proteção, estabilidade] security; **de** ~ security; **cinto de** ~ safety

belt; ~ **nacional** national security. **-2.** [ausência de perigo] safety. **-3.** [certeza, confiança] assurance. <> *mf* [pessoa] security guard.

segurar [4] [segu'ra(x)] <> *vt* **-1.** [pegar] to hold. **-2.** [firmar] to fix. **-3.** [sustentar] to hold up. **-4.** [pôr no seguro]: ~ **algo/alguém (contra)** to insure sthg/sb (against). <> *vi* [apoiar-se]: ~ **(em)** to hold on (to).

◆ **segurar-se** *vp* **-1.** [apoiar-se]: ~-**se em** to hold on to. **-2.** [fazer seguro] to steady o.s. **-3.** [controlar-se] to control o.s.

seguro, ra [se'guru, ra] *adj* **-1.** [ger] safe. **-2.** [certo] sure; **estar** ~ **de algo** to be sure of sthg. **-3.** [confiante, firme] secure; ~ **de si** self-assured. **-4.** [infalível] foolproof.

◆ **seguro** <> *m* [contrato] insurance policy; **fazer** ~ to take out an insurance policy; ~ **de automóvel** car insurance; ~ **contra incêndio** fire insurance; ~ **de vida** life insurance. <> *adv* steadily.

seguro-desemprego [se,gurudesẽn'pregu] (*pl* **seguros-desemprego**) *m* unemployment benefit *UK*, unemployment compensation *US*.

seguro-saúde [se,gurusa'udʒi] (*pl* **seguros-saúde**) *m* health insurance.

seio ['seju] *m* **-1.** ANAT breast. **-2.** *fig* [meio] heart.

seis ['sejʃ] *num* **-1.** [ger] six; **o (número)** ~ the (number) six; **duzentos e** ~ two hundred and six; **trinta e** ~ thirty-six; **Rua das Acácias, (número)** ~ number six, Rua das Acácias; **pacotes de** ~ packets of six; ~ **de cada vez** six at a time; **somos** ~ we are six, there are six of us; **vieram os** ~ the six of them came; **tirar** ~ [nos estudos] to get (a) six. **-2.** [hora]: **às** ~ **(horas)** at six o'clock; **são** ~ **horas** it is six o'clock; **são** ~ **e meia** it is half past six. **-3.** [data] sixth; **hoje é dia** ~ today is the sixth; **(no) dia** ~ **de janeiro** (on the) sixth of January. **-4.** [idade]: **ele tem** ~ **anos (de idade)** he is six years old. **-5.** [temperatura]: ~ **graus abaixo de zero** six degrees below freezing. **-6.** *ESP* [jogador]: **o número** ~ number six. **-7.** *ESP* [resultado]: **empatar de** ~ **a** ~ to draw six all; ~ **a zero** six nil. **-8.** [em naipes]: ~ **de espadas** six of spades.

seiscentos, tas [sejʃ'sẽntuʃ, taʃ] *num* six hundred; *veja também* **seis**.

seita ['sejta] *f* sect.

seiva ['sejva] *f* sap.

seixo ['sejʃu] *m* pebble.

seja ['seʒa] *conj* whether it be; **ou** ~ that is.

sela ['sɛla] *f* saddle.

selagem [se'laʒẽ] *f* [de carta] postage.

selar [4] [se'la(x)] *vt* **-1.** [ger] to seal. **-2.** [cavalo] to saddle. **-3.** [carta] to stamp.

seleção [sele'sãw] (*pl* **-ões**) *f* **-1.** [escolha] selection. **-2.** [equipe] team; **a** ~ **brasileira** the Brazilian team.

selecionado, da [selesjo'nadu, da] *adj* [escolhido] chosen.

◆ **selecionado** *m* [equipe] team.

selecionar [4] [selesjo'na(x)] *vt* to select.

seleta [se'lɛta] *f* ▷ **seleto**.

seletivo, va [sele'tʃivu, va] *adj* selective.

seleto, ta [se'lɛtu, ta] *adj* select.

◆ **seleta** *f* selection.

selim [se'lĩ] (*pl* **-ns**) *m* saddle.

selo ['selu] *m* **-1.** [carimbo, sinete] seal. **-2.** [postal] stamp. **-3.** *fig* [cunho] seal of approval.

selva ['sɛwva] *f* jungle.

selvagem [sew'vaʒẽ] (*pl* **-ns**) *adj* **-1.** [ger] wild. **-2.** [bárbaro] savage. **-3.** [ermo] desolate. **-4.** *fig* [grosseiro] rude.

selvageria [sewvaʒe'ria] *f* savagery.

sem [sẽ] *prep* without; ~ **algo/fazer algo** without sthg/doing sthg; ~ **ajuda** without help; ~ **dúvida** without doubt; **passar** ~ **algo** to go without sthg.

◆ **sem que** *loc conj* without.

semáforo [se'maforu] *m* **-1.** AUTO traffic lights (*pl*). **-2.** FERRO signal.

semana [se'mãna] *f* week; **há uma** ~ a week ago; **uma** ~ **atrás** a week ago; **a** ~ **passada** last week; **a** ~ **retrasada** the week before last; **por** ~ [número de vezes] per week; [ser pago] weekly.

◆ **Semana Santa** *f* Holy Week.

semanal [sema'naw] (*pl* **-ais**) *adj* weekly.

semanalmente [semanaw'mẽntʃi] *adv* weekly.

semanário [sema'narju] *m* weekly.

semântico, ca [se'mãntʃiku, ka] *adj* semantic.

◆ **semântica** *f* semantics (*pl*).

semblante [sẽn'blãntʃi] *m* [rosto] countenance.

sem-cerimônia [sẽnseri'monja] (*pl* **-s**) *f* **-1.** [informalidade] informality. **-2.** [grosseria] rudeness.

semeadura [semja'dura] *f* [semeação] sowing; **começaram a** ~ **do trigo** they began sowing the wheat.

semear [15] [se'mja(x)] *vt* **-1.** [ger] to sow. **-2.** *fig* [espalhar] to spread.

semelhança [seme'ʎãnsa] *f* resemblance; **ter** ~ **com** to resemble.

semelhante [seme'ʎãntʃi] <> *adj* **-1.** [parecido]: ~ **(a)** similar (to). **-2.** [tal] such. <> *m* (*ger pl*) [próximo] fellow man.

semelhar [4] [seme'ʎa(x)] *vt* to resemble.

sêmen ['semẽ] *m* semen.

semente [se'mẽntʃi] *f* seed.

semestral [semeʃ'traw] (*pl* **-ais**) *adj* half-yearly.

semestralmente [semeʃtraw'mẽntʃi] *adv* every semester, every six months.

semestre [se'mɛʃtri] *m* semester; **todo** ~ every six months; **todo o** ~ the whole semester.

sem-fim [,sẽn'fĩ] *m*: **um** ~ **de** an endless amount of.

semi-aberto, ta [semja'bɛxtu, ta] (*mpl* **-s**, *fpl* **-s**) *adj* **-1.** [ger] half-opened. **-2.** [porta] ajar.

semi-analfabeto, ta [semjanawfa'bɛtu, ta] (*mpl* **-s**, *fpl* **-s**) *adj* semi-literate.

semibreve [semi'brɛvi] *f* MÚS semibreve.

semicerrar [semi'sexa(x)] *vt* to half-close.

semicírculo [semi'sixkulu] *m* semicircle.

semicolcheia [semikow'ʃeja] *f* MÚS semiquaver.

semiconsciente [semikõn'sjẽntʃi] *adj* semi-conscious.

semifinal [semifi'nawl] (*pl* -ais) *f* semi-final.
semifinalista [semifina'liʃta] <> *adj* semi-final (*antes de subst*). <> *mf* semi-finalist.
semi-internato [semiĩntex'natu] (*pl* semi-internatos) *m* day school.
seminal [semi'naw] (*pl* -ais) *adj* seminal.
seminário [semi'narju] *m* -1. *RELIG* seminary. -2. *EDUC* seminar.
seminarista [semina'riʃta] *mf* seminarist.
seminu, nua [semi'nu, nua] *adj* half-naked.
semiótica [se'mjɔtʃika] *f* semiotics.
semiprecioso, osa [semipre'sjozu, ɔza] *adj* semi-precious.
semita [se'mita] <> *adj* Semitic. <> *mf* Semite.
semítico, ca [se'mitʃiku, ka] *adj* Semitic.
semitom [semi'tõ] (*pl* -ns) *m* MÚS semitone.
sem-número [sẽn'numeru] *m*: um ~ de a countless number of.
semolina [semo'lina] *f* semolina.
sem-par [sẽn'pa(x)] *adj inv* peerless.
sempre ['sẽnpri] *adv* always; **como** ~ as always; **de** ~ usual; **para** ~ for ever; **quase** ~ nearly always.
 sempre que *loc conj* whenever.
sem-terra [sẽn'tɛxa] *mf inv* landless farm worker.
sem-teto [sẽn'tɛtu] *mf inv* homeless person.
sem-vergonha [sẽnvex'goɲa] <> *adj inv* shameless. <> *mf inv* shameless person.
SENAC (*abrev de* Serviço Nacional de Aprendizagem Comercial) *m* Brazilian training body for people working in the general business sector.
senado [se'nadu] *m* senate.
senador, ra [sena'do(x), ra] *m, f* senator.
SENAI (*abrev de* Serviço Nacional de Aprendizagem Industrial) *m* Brazilian training body for people working in industry.
senão [se'nãw] (*pl* -ões) <> *prep* [exceto] apart from. <> *conj* [caso contrário] or else. <> *m* hiccup.
senda ['sẽnda] *f* path.
Senegal [sene'gaw] *n*: (o) ~ Senegal.
senhor, ra [se'ɲo(x), ɔra] (*mpl* -es, *fpl* -s) *adj* grand; **uma senhora indigestão** a bad case of indigestion.
 senhor *m* -1. [tratamento - antes de nome, cargo]: ~ X Mr X; o Senhor Ministro (the) Minister; [- você]: o ~ you; [mais formal] sir; [- em cartas]: Prezado Senhor Dear Sir. -2. [homem] man. -3. [cavalheiro] gentleman. -4. [homem idoso]: ~ (de idade) elderly man. -5. [dono] master; ser ~ de seu nariz to be one's own master. -6. [patrão] boss. -7. *RELIG*: o Senhor the Lord.
 senhora *f* -1. [tratamento - antes de nome, cargo]: senhora X Mrs X; [- você]: a senhora you; [mais formal] madam; senhoras e ~ es! ladies and gentlemen!; [- em cartas]: Prezada Senhora Dear Madam. -2. [mulher] woman. -3. [dama] lady. -4. [mulher idosa]: senhora (de idade) elderly woman. -5. [esposa] wife. -6. *RELIG*: Nossa Senhora Our Lady; (Minha) Nossa (Senhora)! *fam* Heavens (above)!, (My/Dear) Lord!

senhoria [seɲo'ria] *f* ⊳ senhorio.
senhoril [seɲo'riw] (*pl* -is) *adj* distinguished.
senhorio, ria [seɲo'riu, ria] *m, f* [proprietário] landlord (*f* landlady).
 Senhoria *f* [em carta]: Vossa Senhoria Your Honour.
senhorita [seɲo'rita] *f* -1. [tratamento - antes de nome]: ~ X Miss X; [- você]: a ~ you. -2. [moça] young lady.
senil [se'niw] (*pl* -is) *adj* senile.
senilidade [senili'dadʒi] *f* senility.
sênior ['sẽnjo(x)] (*pl* -s) <> *adj* senior. <> *m* [desportista] senior.
senões [se'nõjʃ] *mpl* ⊳ senão.
sensação [sẽsa'sãw] (*pl* -ões) *f* -1. [ger] feeling; **ter a** ~ **de que** to have the feeling that. -2. [surpresa, agitação]: **causar** ~ to cause a sensation.
sensacional [sẽsasjo'naw] (*pl* -ais) *adj* sensational.
sensacionalismo [sẽsasjona'liʒmu] *m* sensationalism.
sensacionalista [sẽsasjona'liʃta] *adj* sensationalist.
sensatez [sẽsa'teʒ] *f* common sense.
sensato, ta [sẽn'satu, ta] *adj* sensible.
sensibilidade [sẽnsibili'dadʒi] *f* sensitivity.
sensibilizar [4] [sẽnsibili'za(x)] *vt* -1. [comover] to move. -2. [impressionar] to sensitize.
 sensibilizar-se *vp* [comover-se] to be touched.
sensitivo, va [sẽnsi'tʃivu, va] *adj* sensitive.
sensível [sẽn'sivɛw] (*pl* -eis) *adj* -1. [ger] sensitive. -2. [evidente, considerável] marked.
sensivelmente [sẽnsivew'mẽntʃi] *adv* markedly.
senso ['sẽnsu] *m* [juízo] sense; ~ **de humor** sense of humour; **bom** ~, good sense; ~ **comum** common sense; ~ **de responsabilidade** sense of responsibility.
sensor [sẽn'so(x)] *m* sensor.
sensorial [sẽnso'rjaw] (*pl* -ais) *adj* sensory.
sensual [sẽn'swaw] (*pl* -ais) *adj* sensual.
sensualidade [sẽnswali'dadʒi] *f* sensuality.
sentado, da [sẽn'tadu, da] *adj* -1. [pessoa] sitting. -2. [jantar] sit-down.
sentar [4] [sẽn'ta(x)] *vt & vi* to sit.
 sentar-se *vp* to sit down.
sentença [sẽn'tẽnsa] *f* JUR sentence; ~ **de morte** death sentence.
sentenciar [sẽntẽn'sia(x)] <> *vt* [condenar] to sentence. <> *vi* [decidir] to decide.
sentencioso, sa [sẽntẽ'sjosu, sa] *adj* sententious.
sentido, da [sẽn'tʃidu, da] *adj* -1. [ressentido] offended. -2. [triste] hurt. -3. [lamentoso] sorrowful.
 sentido *m* -1. [ger] sense; **sexto** ~ sixth sense. -2. [significado] meaning; **sem** ~ meaningless; **duplo** ~ double meaning; ~ **figurado** figurative sense; **fazer** ~ to make sense; **ter/ não ter** ~ to make/not make sense. -3. [direção] direction; ~ **horário/anti-horário** clockwise/

anticlockwise. **- 4.** [aspecto] way. **- 5.** [atenção]: **estar com o ~ em algo/alguém** to have one's attention on sthg/sb. **- 6.** [propósito] aim; **no ~ de** towards.

◆ **sentidos** *mpl* [consciência] senses; **perder/recobrar os ~s** to lose/regain consciousness.

sentimental [sēntʃimēn'tawl] (*pl* **-ais**) <> *adj* **-1.** [ger] sentimental. **- 2.** [amoroso] love (*antes de subst*). <> *mf* sentimental person.

sentimentalismo [sēntʃimēnta'liʒmul] *m* sentimentality.

sentimentalóide [sēntʃimēnta'lɔidʒil] *adj* oversentimental.

sentimento [sēntʃi'mēntul] *m* **-1.** [ger] feeling. **- 2.** [emoçāo]: **com ~** with feeling. **- 3.** [senso] sense.

◆ **sentimentos** *mpl* **-1.** [pêsames] condolences. **- 2.** [índole]: **uma pessoa de bons ~s** a well-meaning person.

sentinela [sēntʃi'nɛlal] *f* guard.

sentir [56] [sēn'tʃi(x)] <> *vt* **-1.** [ger] to feel. **-2.** [pelos sentidos] to sense. **-3.** [sofrer com] to be upset by. **- 4.** [melindrar-se com] to resent. **- 5.** [lamentar] to regret. <> *vi* **-1.** [sofrer] to suffer. **-2.** [lamentar] to regret; **sinto muito** I am very sorry. **- 3.** [perceber]: **sem ~** without realizing.

◆ **sentir-se** *vp* to feel.

senzala [sēn'zala] *f* slave quarters (*pl*).

separaçāo [separa'sãw] (*pl* **-ões**) *f* separation; **~ de bens** (*contract of*) *separation of property* (*prior to marriage*).

separado, da [sepa'radu, da] *adj* **-1.** [apartado] separate. **-2.** [do cônjuge] separated.

separar [4] [sepa'ra(x)] *vt* **-1.** [ger] to separate. **-2.** [isolar] to isolate. **-3.** [reservar] to set aside.

◆ **separar-se** *vp* **-1.** [ger] to separate. **-2.** [cônjuges]: **~-se (de alguém)** to separate (from s.o.). **- 3.** [estrada, rio]: **~-se em** to divide into.

separata [sepa'rata] *f* offprint.

separatismo [separa'tʃiʒmul] *m* separatism.

separatista [separa'tʃiʃtal] <> *adj* separatist. <> *mf* separatist.

septicemia [septʃise'mial] *f* septicaemia *UK*, septicemia *US*.

séptico, ca ['sɛptʃiku, ka] *adj* septic.

septuagésimo, ma [septwa'ʒɛzimu, ma] *num* seventieth.

sepulcro [se'puwkrul] *m* tomb.

sepultamento [sepuwta'mēntul] *m* burial.

sepultar [4] [sepuw'ta(x)] *vt* to bury.

sepultura [sepuw'tural] *f* tomb, grave.

seqüela [se'kwɛlal] *f* **-1.** [seqüência] sequel. **-2.** [conseqüência] consequence. **-3.** *MED* sequela.

seqüência [se'kwēsjal] *f* sequence.

seqüenciador [sekwēsia'do(x)] *m* sequencer.

sequer [se'kɛ(x)] *adv* at least; **nem ~** not even; **nāo sabia ~ o nome de seus pais** he didn't even know his parents' name.

seqüestrador, ra [sekweʃtra'do(x), ra] (*mpl* **-res**, *fpl* **-s**) *m, f* **-1.** [de pessoa] kidnapper. **-2.** [de aviāo] hijacker.

seqüestrar [sekweʃ'tra(x)] *vt* **-1.** [pessoa] to kidnap. **-2.** [aviāo] to hijack. **-3.** *JUR* [bens] to sequestrate.

seqüestro [se'kwɛʃtrul] *m* **-1.** [de pessoa] kidnapping. **-2.** [de aviāo] hijacking. **-3.** *JUR* [de bens] sequestration.

seqüestro-relâmpago [se,kweʃtruxe'lānpagul] (*pl* **-gos**) *m kidnapping in which a person is held for a few hours while the kidnappers, having extracted passwords, use his bank cards to withdraw cash.*

sequioso, osa [se'kjozu, ɔza] *adj* thirsty.

séquito ['sɛkitul] *m* retinue.

ser [3] ['se(x)] (*pl* **-res**) <> *m* [criatura] being; **~ humano** human being. <> *vi* **-1.** [para descrever] to be; **é longo demais** it's too long; **sāo bonitos** they're pretty; **sou médico** I'm a doctor. **-2.** [para designar lugar, origem] to be; **ele é do Brasil** he's from Brazil; **é em Sāo Paulo** it's in Sāo Paulo; **sou brasileira** I'm Brazilian. **-3.** [custar] to be; **quanto é? - sāo 100 reais** how much is it? - (it's) 100 reals. **- 4.** [com data, dia, hora] to be; **hoje é sexta** it's Friday today; **que horas sāo?** what time is it?; **sāo seis horas** it's six o'clock. **-5.** [exprime possessāo] to be; **é do Ricardo** it's Ricardo's; **este carro é seu?** is this your car? **- 6.** [em locuções]: **a nāo ~ que** unless; **que foi?** what's wrong?; **ou seja** in other words; **será que ele vem?** will he be coming? <> *v aux* [forma a voz passiva] to be; **ele foi visto na saída do cinema** he was seen on his way out of the cinema. <> *v impess* **-1.** [exprime tempo] to be; **é de dia/noite** it's daytime/night-time; **é tarde/cedo** it's late/early. **-2.** [com adjetivo] to be; **é difícil dizer** it's difficult to say; **é fácil de ver** it's easy to see; **eles sāo Fluminense** they're Fluminense fans.

◆ **ser de** *v + prep* [matéria] to be made of; [ser adepto de] to be a fan of.

◆ **ser para** *v + prep* to be for; **isto nāo é para comer** this isn't for eating.

serāo [se'rãw] (*pl* **-ões**) *m* [trabalho noturno] night duty; **fazer ~** to work late.

sereia [se'rejal] *f* mermaid.

serelepe [sere'lɛpil] *adj* lively.

serenar [4] [sere'na(x)] <> *vt* **-1.** [acalmar] to calm down. **-2.** [suavizar] to relieve. <> *vi* [acalmar] to calm down.

serenata [sere'natal] *f* serenade.

serenidade [sereni'dadʒil] *f* serenity.

sereno, na [se'renu, nal] *adj* **-1.** [tranqüilo] serene. **-2.** [límpido] clear.

◆ **sereno** *m* night air; **apanhar ~** to get a chill; **no ~** in the open air.

seresta [se'rɛʃtal] *f* serenade.

Sergipe [sex'ʒipil] *n* Sergipe.

seriado, da [se'rjadu, dal] *adj* serialized.

◆ **seriado** *m* *TV* series.

serial [se'rjawl] (*pl* **-ais**) *adj* *COMPUT* serial.

série ['sɛrjil] *f* **-1.** [ger] series; **uma ~ de** a series of; **número de ~** serial number. **-2.** *EDUC* year.

em série *loc adv*: **fabricar em** ~ to mass-produce.

fora de série *loc adj* [excepcional] exceptional.

seriedade [serje'dadʒi] *f* -**1**. [ger] seriousness. -**2**. [circunspecção] sobriety. -**3**. [honestidade] integrity.

seringa [se'rĩga] *f* syringe.

seringal [serĩ'gaw] (*pl* -**ais**) *m* rubber-tree plantation.

seringueiro, ra [serĩ'gejru, ra] *m, f* rubber tapper.

seringueira *f* rubber tree.

sério, ria ['sɛrju, rja] <> *adj* -**1**. [ger] serious. -**2**. [sóbrio] sober. -**3**. [sem rir] straight-faced. <> *adv* really; **falando** ~ seriously.

a sério *loc adv* seriously; **levar a** ~ [dedicar-se] to take seriously; [magoar-se com] to take seriously.

sermão [sex'mãw] (*pl* -**ões**) *m* sermon; **levar um** ~ **de alguém** to be given a sermon by sb; **passar um** ~ **em alguém** to give sb a sermon.

serpente [sex'pẽtʃi] *f* -**1**. *ZOOL* serpent, snake. -**2**. *fig* [pessoa] snake (in the grass).

serpentear [15] [sexpẽn'tʃja(x)] *vi* -**1**. [rio, caminho] to meander. -**2**. [cobra] to snake.

serpentina [serpẽn'tʃina] *f* -**1**. [de papel] streamer. -**2**. [conduto] coil.

SERPRO (*abrev de* Serviço Federal de Processamento de Dados) *m Brazilian federal data-processing agency.*

serra ['sɛxa] *f* -**1**. [ferramenta] saw; ~ **circular** circular saw. -**2**. [lâmina] serrated blade. -**3**. [montanhas] mountain range, sierra.

serrado, da [se'xadu, da] *adj* -**1**. [madeira] sawn. -**2**. [folha] serrated.

serragem [se'xaʒẽ] *f* [resíduo] sawdust.

Serra Leoa [ˌsexale'oa] *n* Sierra Leone.

serralheiro, ra [sexa'ʎejru, ra] *m, f* blacksmith.

serralheria [sexaʎe'ria] *f* -**1**. [ofício] smithery. -**2**. [oficina] smithy.

serrano, na [se'xãnu, na] <> *adj* mountain *(antes de subst).* <> *m, f* mountain dweller.

serrar [4] [se'xa(x)] *vt* to saw.

serraria [sexa'ria] *f* sawmill.

serrote [se'xɔtʃi] *m* saw.

sertanejo, ja [sextane'ʒu, ʒa] <> *adj* of the *sertão.* <> *m, f* person who lives in the *sertão.*

sertão [sex'tãw] *m* -**1**. [o interior do país] bush. -**2**. [região agreste] wilderness.

servente [sex'vẽtʃi] *mf* -**1**. [faxineiro] caretaker *UK*, janitor *US*. -**2**. [operário] labourer; ~ **de pedreiro** bricklayer's labourer.

Sérvia ['sɛxvja] *n* Serbia.

serviçal [sexvi'saw] (*pl* -**ais**) <> *adj* [prestativo] obliging. <> *mf* [criado] servant.

serviço [sex'visu] *m* -**1**. [ger] service; ~ **de bordo** ship's roster; ~ **militar** military service; ~ **de informações** information service; **Serviço Nacional de Saúde** National Health Service; **Serviço Público** Civil Service; ~**s públicos** public

services. -**2**. [trabalho, local de trabalho] work; **prestar** ~**s** [trabalhar] to render services; [fazer favores] to help out; **prestação de** ~**s** services rendered; ~ **social** social services (*pl*). -**3**. [iguarias] catering. -**4**. *loc*: **dar o** ~ *fam* to spill the beans; **fazer um** ~ *gír crime* to carry out a contract; **não brincar em** ~ [ser eficiente] to be a stickler; [não desperdiçar oportunidade] to not miss an opportunity.

de serviço *loc adj* [entrada, elevador] tradesmen's (*antes de subst*).

servidão [sexvi'dãw] *f* -**1**. [escravidão] servitude. -**2**. *JUR* [de passagem] right of way.

servido, da [sex'vidu, da] *adj* -**1**. [que se serve] served. -**2**. [provido]: **bem** ~ **de** well-supplied with.

servidor, ra [sex'vido(x), ra] <> *m, f* [funcionário] official; ~ **público** civil servant.

servidor *m COMPUT* server.

servil [sex'viw] (*pl* -**is**) *adj* [subserviente]: ~ **(a)** servile (to).

servir [54] [sex'vi(x)] <> *vt* -**1**. [jantar, bebida] to serve; **pedi para o garçom nos** ~ **duas cervejas** I asked the waiter to bring us a couple of beers; ~ **algo a alguém**, ~ **alguém de algo** to serve sthg to sb, to serve sb with sthg. -**2**. [ajudar] to help. <> *vi* -**1**. [ger] to serve. -**2**. [prestar serviço]: ~ **a** to serve. -**3**. [prestar, ser útil] to be of use. -**4**. [ser adequado] to be good; **qualquer trem serve** any train will do; **não** ~ **para algo** to be no good for. -**5**. [caber] to fit. -**6**. [fazer as vezes de]: ~ **de algo** to act as. -**7**. [ser apto] to be fit.

servir-se *vp* -**1**. [de comida, bebida]: ~**-se (de)** to help o.s. (to). -**2**. [usar]: ~**-se de** to use.

servo, va ['sɛxvu, va] *m, f* -**1**. [escravo] slave. -**2**. [criado] servant.

SESC (*abrev de* Serviço Social do Comércio) *m Brazilian body providing social, sport and cultural facilities to people working in the general business sector.*

sessão [se'sãw] (*pl* -**ões**) *f* -**1**. [ger] session. -**2**. *CINE* performance; **primeira** ~ first performance; ~ **da tarde** matinée.

sessenta [se'sẽta] *num* sixty; **os anos** ~ the sixties; *veja também* **seis**.

sessões [se'sõjʃ] *pl* > **sessão**.

sesta ['sɛʃta] *f* siesta, afternoon nap.

set. (*abrev de* setembro) Sept.

set ['sɛtʃi] *m ESP* set.

seta ['sɛta] *f* arrow.

sete ['sɛtʃi] *num* seven; **pintar o** ~ *fig* to get up to mischief; *veja também* **seis**.

setecentos, tas [sɛtʃi'sẽtuʃ, taʃ] *num* seven hundred; *veja também* **seis**.

sete-e-meio [sɛtʃi'meju] (*pl* sete-e-meios) *m* [jogo] *kind of card game.*

setembro [se'tẽbru] *m* September; **em** ~, **no mês de** ~ in September/in the month of September; **em** ~ **do ano que vem/do ano passado** in September next year/last year; **em meados de** ~ in mid-September; **dia primeiro/dois/**

seis de ~ first/second/sixth of September; **no dia três de** ~ on the third of September; **no início/fim de** ~ at the beginning/end of September; **todo ano em** ~ every year in September.

setenta [se'tẽnta] *num* seventy; **os anos** ~ the seventies; *veja também* **seis.**

setentrional [setẽntrjo'naw] (*pl* **-ais**) *adj* northern.

sétimo, ma ['sɛtʃimu, ma] *num* seventh; **a sétima parte** the seventh part.
➨ **sétima** *f* MÚS seventh.

setor [se'to(x)] (*pl* **-es**) *m* **-1.** [ger] sector. **-2.** [de repartição, estabelecimento] section.

setorial [seto'riaw] (*pl* **-ais**) [raijʃ] *adj* sector.

setorizar [setori'za(x)] *vt* to divide into sectors.

setuagésimo, ma [setwa'ʒɛsimu, ma] *num* seventieth.

seu, sua ['sew, 'sua] <> *adj* **-1.** [dele] his; [dela] her; [de você, vocês] your; [deles, delas] their; **ela trouxe o** ~ **carro** she brought her car; **onde estacionou a sua moto?** where did you park your motorcycle? **-2.** [de coisa, animal: singular] its; **o cachorro foi para o seu canil** the dog went into its kennel **-3.** [de coisa, animal: plural] their. <> *pron:* **o** ~**/a sua** [dele] his; [dela] hers; [deles, delas] theirs; [de coisa, animal: singular] its; [de coisa, animal: plural] theirs; **um amigo** ~ a friend of his/hers; **os** ~**s** [a família de cada um] his/her etc. family. <> *m, f* **-1.** *pej:* **como vai,** ~ **Pedro?** how are you, mister Pedro?; ~ **estúpido!** you fool!; ~**s irresponsáveis!** you irresponsible lot! **-2.** [com malícia]: ~ **malandro!** you cheeky one!, cheeky thing!; **sua danadinha!** you rotter!, rotten thing!

Seul [se'uw] *n* Seoul.

seus [sewʃ] ⊳ **seu.**

severidade [severi'dadʒi] *f* **-1.** [ger] severity. **-2.** [com filho] strictness.

severo, ra [se'vɛru, ra] *adj* **-1.** [castigo] severe. **-2.** [pessoa] strict.

sex. (*abrev de* **sexta-feira**) *f* Fri.

sexagenário, ria [seksaʒe'narjo, rja] <> *adj:* **ser** ~ to be a sexagenarian, to be in one's sixties. <> *m, f* sexagenarian.

sexagésimo, ma [seksa'ʒɛzimu, ma] *num* sixtieth.

sexo ['sɛksu] *m* sex.

sexólogo, ga [sek'sɔlogu, ga] *m, f* sexologist.

sexta ['seʃta] *f* ⊳ **sexto.**

sexta-feira [ˌseʃta'fejra] (*pl* **sextas-feiras**) *f* Friday; *veja também* **sábado.**
➨ **Sexta-feira Santa** *f* Good Friday.

sexto, ta ['seʃtu, ta] *num* sixth; **a sexta parte** the sixth part.
➨ **sexta** *f* [sexta-feira] Friday.

sêxtuplos ['seʃtupluʃ] *mpl* sextuplets.

sexual [sek'swaw] (*pl* **-ais**) *adj* **-1.** [ger] sexual. **-2.** [educação, vida] sex (*antes de subst*).

sexualidade [sekswali'dadʒi] *f* sexuality.

sexualmente [seksuaw'mẽntʃi] *adv* sexually.

sexy ['sɛksi] *adj* sexy.

Seychelles [sej'ʃɛliʃ] *npl:* **as (ilhas)** ~ the Seychelles.

SFH (*abrev de* **Sistema Financeiro de Habitação**) *m Brazilian housing credit advisory service.*

shareware [ʃari'wari] (*pl* **-s**) *m* COMPUT shareware.

shopping ['ʃɔpĩŋ] *m* shopping centre *UK*, shopping mall *US*.

short ['ʃɔxtʃi] *m* shorts (*pl*).

show ['ʃow] *m* **-1.** [espetáculo] show; **ser/estar um** ~ *fig* to be spectacular. **-2.** *fig* [atuação brilhante]: **dar um** ~ **(de algo)** to give a brilliant performance (of sthg). **-3.** *fig* [escândalo]: **dar um** ~ to create a scene.

showroom [ʃow'xũ] *m* showroom.

Sibéria [si'bɛrja] *n:* **(a)** ~ Siberia.

siberiano, na [sibe'rjãnu, na] <> *adj* Siberian. <> *m, f* Siberian.

sibilante [sibi'lãntʃi] *adj* sibilant.

sibilar [sibi'la(x)] *vi* [silvar] to whistle; [zumbir] to buzz.

sicário [si'karju] *m* paid assassin.

Sicília [si'silja] *n* Sicily.

sicrano, na [si'krãnu, na] *m, f:* **fulano e** ~ so-and-so.

sideral [side'raw] (*pl* **-ais**) *adj* sidereal.

siderurgia [si'derux'ʒia] *f* iron and steel industry.

siderúrgico, ca [side'ruxʒiku, ka] *adj* iron and steel (*antes de sust*).
➨ **siderúrgica** *f* [usina] steelworks (*sg*).

sidra ['sidra] *f* cider.

sifão [si'fãw] (*pl* **-ões**) *m* **-1.** [tubo] siphon. **-2.** [de aparelho sanitário] U-bend. **-3.** [garrafa] soda siphon.

sífilis ['sifiliʃ] *f inv* syphilis.

sifilítico, ca [sifi'litʃiku, ka] <> *adj* syphilitic. <> *m, f* syphilitic.

sifões [si'fõjʃ] *pl* ⊳ **sifão.**

sigilo [si'ʒilu] *m* secrecy; ~ **bancário** bank confidentiality.

sigiloso, osa [siʒi'lozu, ɔza] *adj* secret.

sigla ['sigla] *f* **-1.** [abreviatura] acronym. **-2.** [sinal] initial.

signatário, ria [signa'tarju, rja] *m, f* signatory.

significação [signifika'sãw] *f* **-1.** [significado] meaning. **-2.** [importância] significance.

significado [signifi'kadu, da] *m* **-1.** [sentido] meaning. **-2.** LING signified.

significante [signifi'kãntʃi] *adj* **-1.** [significativo] significant. **-2.** LING signifying.

significar [12] [signifi'ka(x)] <> *vt* **-1.** [ger] to mean. **-2.** [indicar] to signify. <> *vi* [ter importância] to mean.

significativo, va [signifika'tʃivu, va] *adj* significant.

signo ['signu] *m* sign; ~ **do zodíaco** sign of the zodiac, star sign.

sílaba ['silaba] *f* syllable.

silenciador [silẽnsja'do(x)] *m* [de arma] silencer.

silenciar [16] [silẽn'sja(x)] <> *vt* **-1.** [calar] to silence. **-2.** [omitir] to conceal. <> *vi* **-1.** [calar-se] to be quiet. **-2.** [omitir-se]: ~ **sobre** to keep quiet about.

silêncio [si'lẽnʒu] *m* silence; **ficar em** ~ to remain silent.

silencioso, osa [silẽ'sjozu, ɔza] *adj* silent.

silhueta [si'ʎweta] *f* **-1.** [ger] silhouette. **-2.** [corpo] outline.

silício [si'lisju] *m* silicon.

silicone [sili'koni] *m* silicone.

silo ['silu] *m* silo.

silvar [4] [siw'va(x)] *vi* **-1.** [ger] to hiss. **-2.** [vento] to whistle.

silvestre [siw'vɛʃtri] *adj* wild.

silvícola [siw'vikola] *mf* forest dweller.

silvo ['siwvu] *m* **-1.** [ger] h̃iss. **-2.** [ventania] whistle.

sim ['sĩ] ⟨⟩ *adv* yes; **acho** *ou* **creio que** ~ I think *ou* believe so; **dizer que** ~ to say yes; **pelo** ~, **pelo não** just in case; **quero,** ~ 'yes, I'd like to; **vou,** ~ yes, I'm going. ⟨⟩ *m*: **dar o** ~ to consent.

simbiose [sĩ'bjɔzi] *f* symbiosis.

simbiótico, ca [sĩbi'ɔtiku, ca] *adj* symbiotic.

simbólico, ca [sĩ'bɔliku, ka] *adj* symbolic.

simbolismo [sĩbo'liʒmu] *m* **-1.** [representação] symbolism. **-2.** *ARTE & LITER* Symbolism.

simbolizar [4] [sĩboli'za(x)] *vt* to symbolize.

símbolo ['sĩbolu] *m* **-1.** [ger] symbol. **-2.** [insígnia] emblem.

simbologia [sĩbolo'ʒia] *f* symbology.

simetria [sime'tria] *f* symmetry.

simétrico, ca [si'mɛtriku, ka] *adj* symmetrical.

similar [simi'la(x)] (*pl* **-es**) *adj*: ~ **(a)** similar (to).

similaridade [similari'dadʒi] *f* similarity.

símile ['simili] *m* **-1.** [de objeto] copy. **-2.** [de palavra] analogy, simile.

similitude [simili'tudʒi] *f* similitude.

simpatia [sĩpa'tʃia] *f* **-1.** [qualidade] warmth. **-2.** [atração - por outrem, lugar] liking; **sentir** ~ **por alguém** to like sb. **-3.** [pessoa]: **ser uma** ~ to be friendly. **-4.** [solidariedade] sympathy. **-5.** [espirit] charm.

simpático, ca [sĩ'patʃiku, ka] *adj* **-1.** [pessoa - atraente] pleasant; [- amável] nice. **-2.** [agradável] pleasant. **-3.** [favorável]: ~ **a algo/alguém** favourable towards sthg/sb. **-4.** *ANAT* sympathetic.

simpatizante [sĩpatʃi'zãntʃi] *adj*: ~ **com** sympathetic towards.

simpatizar [4] [sĩpatʃi'za(x)] *vi*: ~ **com alguém/ algo** to like sb/sthg; ~ **com uma causa** to sympathize with a cause.

simples ['sĩpliʃ] ⟨⟩ *adj* **-1.** [ger] simple. **-2.** *(antes de subst)* [mero] mere; [único] single. ⟨⟩ *adv* simply.

simplesmente [sĩpliʃ'mẽntʃi] *adv* simply.

simplicidade [sĩplisi'dadʒi] *f* simplicity.

simplificação [sĩplifika'sãw] *f* simplification.

simplificar [12] [sĩplifi'ka(x)] *vt* to simplify.

simplista [sĩ'pliʃta] *adj* simplistic.

simplório, ria [sĩ'plɔrju, rja] *adj* simple.

simpósio [sĩ'pɔzju] *m* symposium.

simulação [simula'sãw] (*pl* **-ões**) *f* **-1.** [de combate, salvamento] simulation. **-2.** [de sentimento, desmaio] pretence. **-3.** [de animal, voz] imitation.

simulacro [simu'lakru] *m* **-1.** [ger] pretence. **-2.** [de exame] mock. **-3.** [de bosque] imitation.

simulador [simula'do(x)] *m* simulator.

simular [4] [simu'la(x)] *vt* **-1.** [combate, salvamento] to simulate. **-2.** [sentimento, desmaio] to feign. **-3.** [animal, vozes] to imitate.

simultaneamente [simuwtãnja'mẽntʃi] *adv* simultaneously.

simultâneo, nea [simuw'tãnju, nja] *adj*: ~ **(a** *ou* **com)** simultaneous (with).

sina ['sina] *f* fate.

sinagoga [sina'gɔga] *f* synagogue.

Sinai [si'naj] *n*: **o** ~ Sinai.

sinal [si'naw] (*pl* **-ais**) *m* **-1.** [ger] sign; **fazer um** ~ **(para alguém)** to signal (to sb); **dar** ~ **de vida** to give sign of life; **em** ~ **de** as a sign of. **-2.** [símbolo] signal; ~ **de pontuação** punctuation mark; ~ **de mais/menos** plus/minus sign. **-3.** [aviso]: **dar o** ~ *ESP* [para partida] to give the off; ~ **de alarme** alarm bell. **-4.** *TELEC* tone; ~ **de chamada** ringing tone; ~ **de discar** dialling tone; **dar** ~ **(de discar)** to give the (dialling) tone; **dar** ~ **de ocupado** to give the engaged tone. **-5.** *AUTO*: ~ **(luminoso de tráfego)** traffic lights (*pl*); ~ **verde** green light; **avançar o** ~ to jump the lights. **-6.** [pinta] mole; [de nascença] birthmark. **-7.** *COM* deposit; **de** ~ as a deposit.

➤ **por sinal** *loc adv* **-1.** [a propósito] by the way. **-2.** [aliás] besides.

sinal-da-cruz [si,nawda'kruʒ] (*pl* **sinais-da-cruz**) *m* sign of the cross.

sinaleiro [sina'lejru] *m* *NÁUT* signalman.

sinalização [sinaliza'sãw] *f* **-1.** [sinais de tráfego - *AUTO*] traffic signs (*pl*); [- *FERRO*] signals (*pl*). **-2.** [indicação em estrada *etc*] road sign.

sinalizar [4] [sinali'za(x)] ⟨⟩ *vt* [avenida, estrada] to signpost. ⟨⟩ *vi* [pessoa] to signal.

sinceramente [sĩsera'mẽntʃi] *adv* sincerely.

sinceridade [sĩseri'dadʒi] *f* sincerity; **com toda** ~ in all sincerity.

sincero, ra [sĩ'sɛru, ra] *adj* sincere.

sincopado, da [sĩko'padu, da] *adj* *MÚS* syncopated.

síncope ['sĩkopi] *f* *MED* syncope.

sincronia [sĩkro'nia] *f* synchrony.

sincronizar [4] [sĩkroni'za(x)] *vt* **-1.** [combinar] to synchronize. **-2.** *CINE* to sync.

sindical [sĩdʒi'kaw] (*pl* **-ais**) *adj* trade union *(antes de subst).*

sindicalismo [sĩdʒika'liʒmu] *m* trade unionism.

sindicalista [sĩdʒika'liʃta] ⟨⟩ *adj* trade union *(antes de subst).* ⟨⟩ *mf* trade unionist.

sindicalizado, da [sĩdʒikali'zadu, da] *adj* unionized.

sindicalizar-se [4] [sĩdʒikali'zaxsi] *vp* to join a trade union.

sindicância [sĩndʒi'kãnsja] f[inquérito]: ~ **(de/sobre)** enquiry (into).

sindicato [sĩndʒi'katu] m **-1.** [de profissionais] trade union. **-2.** [financeiro] syndicate.

síndico, ca ['sĩndʒiku, ka] m,f **-1.** [de prédio] residents' representative. **-2.** [de falência] receiver. **-3.** [de inquérito] leader.

síndrome ['sĩndromi] f syndrome; ~ **de abstinência** withdrawal symptoms (pl).

sinecura [sine'kura] f sinecure.

sineta [si'neta] f small bell.

sinfonia [sĩnfo'nia] f symphony.

sinfônico, ca [sĩn'foniku, ka] adj symphonic.
➤ **sinfônica** f[orquestra] symphonic orchestra.

singeleza [sĩnʒe'leza] f simplicity.

singelo, la [sĩn'ʒɛlu, la] adj simple.

singular [sĩngu'la(x)] (pl **-es**) ◇ adj **-1.** [ger] singular. **-2.** [peculiar] strange. ◇ m GRAM singular.

singularidade [sĩngulari'dadʒi] f **-1.** [raridade] singularity. **-2.** [peculiaridade] oddness.

singularizar [4] [sĩngulari'za(x)] vt **-1.** [distinguir] to single out. **-2.** [detalhar] to list.
➤ **singularizar-se** vp [distinguir-se] to distinguish o.s.

sinistro, tra [si'niʃtru, tra] adj sinister.
➤ **sinistro** m **-1.** [acidente] disaster. **-2.** [dano] damage.

sino ['sinu] m bell.

sinônimo, ma [si'nonimu, ma] adj synonymous.
➤ **sinônimo** m synonym.

sinopse [si'nɔpsi] f synopsis.

sintagma [sĩn'tagma] m syntagma.

sintático, ca [sĩn'tatʃiku, ka] adj syntactic.

sintaxe [sĩn'tasi] f syntax.

síntese ['sĩntezi] f **-1.** [ger] synthesis. **-2.** [resumo] summary; **em** ~ in short.

sintético, ca [sĩn'tɛtʃiku, ka] adj **-1.** [artificial] synthetic. **-2.** [conciso] concise.

sintetizador [sĩntetʃiza'do(x)] m synthesizer.

sintetizar [4] [sĩntetʃi'za(x)] vt **-1.** [resumir] to summarize. **-2.** QUÍM to synthesize.

sintoma [sĩn'toma] m **-1.** MED symptom. **-2.** fig [indício] sign.

sintomático, ca [sĩnto'matʃiku, ka] adj symptomatic.

sintonia [sĩnto'nia] f **-1.** ELETRON tuning. **-2.** fig [entrosamento] harmony.

sintonizador [sĩntoniza'do(x)] m tuner.

sintonizar [4] [sĩntoni'za(x)] ◇ vt ELETRON to tune. ◇ vi **-1.** ELETRON: ~ **com** to tune into. **-2.** fig [entrosar-se]: ~ **(com)** to harmonise (with).
➤ **sintonizar-se** vp [harmonizar-se]: ~ **com** to be in tune with.

sinuca [si'nuka] f **-1.** ESP snooker. **-2.** [situação difícil]: **estar numa** ~ **(de bico)** to be snookered.

sinuosidade [sinwozi'dadʒi] f [tortuosidade]: **a** ~ **da estrada** the twistiness of the road.

sinuoso, osa [si'nwozu, ɔza] adj **-1.** [linha] wavy. **-2.** [estrada, rio] meandering. **-3.** [recorte] wavy.

sinusite [sinu'zitʃi] f sinusitis.

sionismo [sjo'niʒmu] m Zionism.

sionista [sjo'niʃta] ◇ adj Zionist. ◇ mf Zionist.

sirene [si'reni] f siren.

siri [si'ri] m crab; **casquinha de** ~ CULIN stuffed crab shells.

Síria ['sirja] n Syria.

sirigaita [siri'gajta] f fam shrew.

sírio, ria ['sirju, rja] ◇ adj Syrian. ◇ m, f Syrian.

sísmico, ca ['siʒmiku, ka] adj seismic.

sismógrafo [siʒ'mɔgraful] m seismograph.

siso ['sizu] m **-1.** [juízo] wisdom. **-2.** [dente]: **(dente de)** ~ wisdom tooth.

sistema [siʃ'tema] m **-1.** [ger] system; ~ **nervoso** nervous system; ~ **solar** solar system; ~ **fiscal** tax system; ~ **operacional** COMPUT operating system. **-2.** [maneira] method.

sistemática [siʃte'matʃikal] f **-1.** [sistematização] systematization. **-2.** [ciência] systematics (sg).

sistemático, ca [siʃte'matʃiku, ka] adj systematic.

sistematização [siʃte'matʃiza'sãw] (pl **-ões**) f systematization.

sistematizar [4] [siʃtematʃi'za(x)] vt to systematize.

sisudo, da [si'zudu, da] adj wise.

site ['sajtʃi] (pl **-s**) m COMPUT site.

sitiante [si'tʃiãntʃi] mf settler.

sitiar [16] [si'tʃja(x)] vt **-1.** [cercar] to besiege. **-2.** [assediar] to harrass.

sítio ['sitʃju] m **-1.** [propriedade] farm. **-2.** MIL siege; **estado de** ~ state of siege; **em estado de** ~ under siege.

situação [sitwa'sãw] (pl **-ões**) f **-1.** [ger] situation. **-2.** [localização] position.

situacionista [sitwasjo'niʃta] ◇ adj ruling party. ◇ mf member of the ruling party.

situado, da [si'twadu, da] adj situated; **estar ou ficar** ~ to be situated.

situar [4] [si'twa(x)] vt to place.
➤ **situar-se** vp **-1.** [localizar-se - casa, filme] to be located; [- pessoa] to place o.s.; **tenho que me** ~ **para saber que rua seguir** I have to get my bearings in order to know which street to take. **-2.** [classificar-se] to be placed. **-3.** [em assunto, questão] to take a position.

skate [iʃ'kejtʃi] m **-1.** [esporte] skateboarding. **-2.** [prancha] skateboard.

slide [iʒ'lajdʒi] m slide, transparency.

slogan [iʒ'logãn] m slogan.

smart card [iʒimaxtʃi'kaxdʒil] (pl **smart cards**) m COMPUT smart card.

smoking [iʒ'mokĩŋ] m dinner jacket.

SNI (abrev de **Serviço Nacional de Informações**) m Brazilian information service concerned particularly with state security, ≃ MI5 UK, ≃ CIA US.

só ['sɔ] ◇ adj **-1.** [sozinho] alone; **a** ~ **s** alone. **-2.** [solitário] lonely. **-3.** [único] single. ◇ adv [somente] only; **é** ~**?** is that all?; **é** ~**!** that's all!

SO (abrev de **Sudoeste**) m SW.

soalho ['swaʎu] *m* = assoalho.

soar [20] ['swa(x)l] ⟷ *vi* -**1**. [ger] to sound; ~ **a algo (a alguém)** to sound like sthg (to s.o.). -**2**. [ser pronunciado] to be voiced. -**3**. [hora] to strike. ⟷ *vt* [suj: horas] to strike.

sob ['sobi] *prep* under; ~ **esse aspecto** from that perspective.

soberania [sobera'nia] *f* -**1**. [de nação] sovereignty. -**2**. *fig* [superioridade] supremacy.

soberano, na [sobe'rãnu, na] ⟷ *adj* -**1**. [independente] sovereign. -**2**. [poderoso] powerful. -**3**. [supremo] supreme. -**4**. [altivo] haughty. ⟷ *m, f* [monarca] sovereign.

soberba [so'bexba] *f* [altivez] arrogance.

soberbo, ba [so'bexbu, ba] *adj* -**1**. [arrogante] arrogant. -**2**. [magnífico] magnificent.

sobra ['sobra] *f* leftover; **dar de** ~ to be more than enough; **ter algo de** ~ to have sthg spare.
   ⇢ **sobras** *fpl* leftovers.

sobraçar [13] [sobra'sa(x)] *vt* to carry under one's arm.

sobrado [so'bradu] *m* floor.

sobranceiro, ra [sobrãn'sejru, ra] *adj* -**1**. [que está acima]: ~ **a** above. -**2**. [arrogante] supercilious.

sobrancelha [sobrãn'seʎa] *f* eyebrow.

sobrar [4] [so'bra(x)] *vi* -**1**. [ger]: ~ to be left over; **me sobra tempo para ir ao cinema** I have some free time to go to the cinema; **o médico examinou duas crianças, sobrou uma** the doctor examined two children, there was one still left; **isso dá e sobra** that is more than enough. -**2**. [ficar de fora] to be left out.

sobre ['sobri] *prep* -**1**. [ger] on. -**2**. [por cima de] over. -**3**. [a respeito de] about.

sobreaviso [sobrja'vizu] *m*: **estar/ficar de** ~ to be on the alert.

sobrecapa [sobre'kapa] *f* dust jacket.

sobrecarga [sobre'kaxga] *f* overload.

sobrecarregar [4] [sobrekaxe'ga(x)] *vt* -**1**. [com carga] to overload. -**2**. [pessoa] to overburden.

sobre-humano, na [sobrju'mãnu, na] (*mpl* -**s**, *fpl* -**s**) *adj* superhuman.

sobreloja [sobre'lɔʒa] *f* mezzanine.

sobremaneira [sobrema'nejra] *adv* excessively.

sobremesa [sobre'meza] *f* dessert; **de** ~ for dessert.

sobrenatural [sobrenatu'raw] (*pl* -**ais**) *adj* supernatural.

sobrenome [sobri'nɔmi] *m* surname.

sobrepor [45] [sobre'po(x)] *vt* -**1**. [pôr em cima]: ~ **algo a algo** to put sthg on top of sthg. -**2**. *fig* [antepor]: ~ **algo a algo** to put sthg before sthg.
   ⇢ **sobrepor-se** *vp* -**1**. [pôr-se em cima] to be put on top. -**2**. *fig* [antepor-se] to come before. -**3**. *fig* [a críticas] to overcome.

sobreposição [sobrepozi'sãw] (*pl* -**ões**) *f* [de objetos] superimposition.

sobreposto, ta [sobre'poʃtu, ta] ⟷ *pp* ⊳ **sobrepor**. ⟷ *adj* [posto em cima]: ~ **a** placed on top of.

sobrepujar [4] [sobrepu'ʒa(x)] *vt* -**1**. [ger] to overcome. -**2**. [ser superior a]: ~ **algo/alguém (em algo)** to outdo sthg/s.o. (in sthg).

sobrescrito [sobreʃ'kritul] *m* address.

sobressair [68] [sobresa'i(x)] *vi* to stand out.
   ⇢ **sobressair-se** *vp* to stand out.

sobressalente [sobresa'lẽntʃil] ⟷ *adj* spare. ⟷ *m* spare.

sobressaltado, da [sobresaw'tadu, da] *adj* -**1**. [assustado] startled; **acordar** ~ to wake up with a start. -**2**. [apreensivo] worried.

sobressaltar [4] [sobresaw'ta(x)] *vt* -**1**. [assustar] to startle. -**2**. [inquietar] to worry.
   ⇢ **sobressaltar-se** *vp* -**1**. [assustar-se] to be startled. -**2**. [inquietar-se] to worry.

sobressalto [sobre'sawtu] *m* -**1**. [ger] start. -**2**. [inquietação] concern.

sobretaxa [sobre'taʃa] *f* surcharge.

sobretudo [sobre'tudu] ⟷ *m* overcoat. ⟷ *adv* especially.

sobrevida [sobre'vida] *f*: **após o transplante, teve uma** ~ **de dez anos** after the transplant, he survived for another ten years.

sobrevir [67] [sobre'vi(x)] *vi*: ~ **(a algo)** to survive (sthg).

sobrevivência [sobrevi'vẽnsja] *f*: ~ **(a)** survival (from).

sobrevivente [sobrevi'vẽntʃil] ⟷ *adj* surviving. ⟷ *mf* survivor.

sobreviver [5] [sobrevi've(x)] *vi*: ~ **(a algo/alguém)** to survive (sthg/s.o.).

sobrevoar [20] [sobre'vwa(x)] *vt* to fly over.

sobrevôo [sobre'vowl] *m* overflying.

sobriedade [sobrje'dadʒil] *f* -**1**. [moderação] moderation. -**2**. [ausência de embriaguez] sobriety.

sobrinho, nha [so'briɲu, ɲal] *m, f* nephew (*f* niece).

sóbrio, bria ['sɔbrju, brja] *adj* -**1**. [ger] sober. -**2**. [moderado]: ~ **(em)** moderate (in).

socado, da [so'kadu, da] *adj* -**1**. [esmagado] crushed. -**2**. [metido] stuck. -**3**. [pessoa] squat.

socador [soka'do(x)] *m* pestle; ~ **de alho** garlic crusher.

soçaite [so'sajtʃil] *m fam* high society.

socar [12] [so'ka(x)] *vt* -**1**. [dar socos em] to punch. -**2**. [esmagar] to crush. -**3**. [calcar] to grind. -**4**. [amassar] to knead. -**5**. [meter] to chuck.

sociabilidade [sosjabili'dadʒil] *f* sociability.

sociabilizar [4] [sosjabili'za(x)] *vt* to socialize.

social [so'sjawl] (*pl* -**ais**) *adj* -**1**. [ger] social. -**2**. [relativo a sócios] members' (*antes de subst*). -**3**. [via de acesso] front (*antes de subst*). -**4**. [banheiro] guest (*antes de subst*). -**5**. [camisa] dress. -**6**. *COM*: **razão** ~ trade name.
   ⇢ **sociais** *fpl* [em hipódromo *etc* - área] members' enclosure; [- cadeiras] members' seats.

socialdemocracia [so,sjawdemokra'sial] *f* social democracy.

socialdemocrata [so,sjawdemo'kratal] ⟷ *adj* social democratic. ⟷ *mf* social democrat.

socialismo [sosja'liʒmul] *m* socialism.

socialista [sosja'liʃta] <> *adj* socialist. <> *mf* socialist.

socialite [sosja'lajtʃi] *mf* socialite.

socializar [4] [sosjali'za(x)] *vt* to socialize.

sociável [so'sjavew] (*pl* -eis) *adj* sociable.

sociedade [sosje'dadʒi] *f* -**1.** [ger] society; ~ **de consumo** consumer society; **a alta** ~ high society; **uma mulher da** ~ a woman of the world; **Sociedade Protetora dos Animais** *society for the protection of animals,* ≃ RSPCA *UK.* -**2.** [COM-empresa] company; [- entre sócios] partnership; ~ **anônima** limited company; ~ **(de responsabilidade) limitada** limited (liability) company. -**3.** [parceria] patnership; **em** ~ **com** in partnership with.

sócio, cia ['sɔsju, sja] *m, f* -**1.** [ger] partner. -**2.** [membro] member.

sociocultural ['sɔsjokuwtu'raw] (*pl* -ais) *adj* sociocultural.

sócio-econômico, ca [sosjoeko'nomiku, ka] (*mpl* -s, *fpl* -s) *adj* socio-economic.

sociolingüística [ˌsɔsjolĩŋ'gwiʃtʃika] *f* sociolinguistics *(sg).*

sociologia [sosjolo'ʒia] *f* sociology.

sociológico, ca [sosjo'lɔʒiku, ka] *adj* sociological.

sociólogo, ga [so'sjɔlogu, ga] *m, f* sociologist.

sóciopolítico, ca [sosjopo'litʃiku, ka] (*mpl* -s, *fpl* -s) *adj* socio-political.

soco ['soku] *m* punch; **dar um** ~ **em algo/alguém** to punch sthg/sb.

soco-inglês [sokwĩ'gleʃ] (*pl* socos-ingleses) *m* knuckleduster.

socorrer [5] [soko'xe(x)] *vt* to rescue.

socorro [so'koxu] *m* rescue; **equipe de** ~ rescue team; **pedir** ~ to ask for help; **socorro!** help!; **primeiros** ~**s** first aid *(sg).*

soda ['sɔda] *f* -**1.** [bebida] soda. -**2.** [substância]: ~ **cáustica** caustic soda.

sódio ['sɔdʒiu] *m* sodium.

sodomia [sodo'mia] *f* sodomy.

sodomizar [sodomi'za(x)] *vt* to sodomize.

sofá [so'fa] *m* sofa.

sofá-cama [soˌfa'kãma] (*pl* sofás-camas) *m* sofa bed.

Sófia ['sɔfja] *n* Sofia.

sofisma [so'fiʒma] *m* -**1.** [em filosofia] sophism. -**2.** [falsidade] false statement.

sofista [so'fiʃta] <> *adj* sophist. <> *mf* sophist.

sofisticação [sofiʃtʃika'sãw] (*pl* -ões) *f* -**1.** [requinte] sophistication. -**2.** [aprimoramento] refinement.

sofisticado, da [sofiʃtʃi'kadu, da] *adj* -**1.** [requintado] sophisticated. -**2.** [aprimorado] fancy. -**3.** [afetado] refined.

sofisticar [12] [sofiʃtʃi'ka(x)] *vt* to refine.

sofredor, ra [sofre'do(x), ra] <> *adj* suffering. <> *m, f* [pessoa] sufferer.

sôfrego, ga ['sofregu, ga] *adj* -**1.** [ávido] eager. -**2.** [ao comer, beber] greedy. -**3.** [impaciente] impatient; **o pai aguardava** ~ **notícias sobre o**

filho the father waited impatiently for news of his son.

sofreguidão [sofregi'dãw] *f* -**1.** [avidez] eagerness. -**2.** [ao comer, beber] greed. -**3.** [impaciência] impatience.

sofrer [5] [so'fre(x)] <> *vt* -**1.** [ger] to suffer. -**2.** [suportar] to bear. -**3.** [receber] to undergo. <> *vi* [padecer] to suffer; ~ **de** MED to suffer from.

sofrido, da [so'fridu, da] *adj* long-suffering.

sofrimento [sofri'mẽtu] *m* suffering.

sofrível [so'frivew] (*pl* -eis) *adj* bearable.

soft ['softʃi], **software** [sof'twe(x)] *m* COMPUT software.

sogro, gra [sogru, gra] *m, f* father-in-law (*f* mother-in-law).

sóis [sɔjʃ] *pl* ⊳ sol.

soja ['sɔʒa] *f* soya.

sol ['sɔw] (*pl* sóis) *m* -**1.** [ger] sun; **fazer** ~ to be sunny; ~ **a pino** mid-day sun; **tomar (banho de)** ~ to sunbathe; **ao** ~ in the sun; **tapar o** ~ **com a peneira** to hide the truth. -**2.** MÚS [nota] soh, sol.

sola ['sɔla] *f* -**1.** [de sapato] sole. -**2.** ANAT: ~ **do pé** sole of the foot. -**3.** *loc:* **entrar de** ~ FUT to make an illegal tackle; [com garra] to enter aggressively.

solado, da [so'ladu, da] *adj* flat.
→ **solado** *m* [de calçado] sole.

solão [so'lãw] *m* [sol quente] very hot sun.

solapar [4] [sola'pa(x)] *vt* -**1.** [minar] to undermine. -**2.** [abalar] to shake. -**3.** *fig* [arruinar] destroy.

solar [4] [so'la(x)] (*pl* -es) <> *adj* solar. <> *m* [moradia] manor house. <> *vt* [sapato] to sole. <> *vi* -**1.** [bolo] to fail to rise. -**2.** MÚS to perform a solo.

solavanco [sola'vãŋku] *m* jolt.

solda ['sowda] *f* -**1.** [substância] solder. -**2.** [soldadura] weld.

soldado [sow'dadu] *mf* -**1.** MIL soldier; ~ **de chumbo** tin soldier; ~ **raso** private (soldier). -**2.** [defensor] defender.

soldador, ra [sowda'do(x), ra] *m, f* welder.

soldadura [sowda'dura] *f* -**1.** [ato] welding. -**2.** [junta] weld.

soldagem [sow'daʒẽ] *f* welding.

soldar [4] [sow'da(x)] *vt* to weld.

soldo ['sowdu] *m* MIL pay.

soleira [so'lejra] *f* -**1.** [de porta] threshold. -**2.** [de ponte] foundation.

solene [so'leni] *adj* solemn.

solenemente [soleni'mẽtʃi] *adv* solemnly.

solenidade [soleni'dadʒi] *f* -**1.** [qualidade] solemnity. -**2.** [cerimônia] ceremony.

soletrar [4] [sole'tra(x)] *vt* -**1.** [letras] to spell. -**2.** [ler devagar] to read out slowly.

solicitação [solisita'sãw] (*pl* -ões) *f* [pedido] request.
→ **solicitações** *fpl* [apelo] appeal *(sg).*

solicitar [4] [solisi'ta(x)] *vt* -**1.** [pedir] to request; ~ **algo a alguém** to ask sb for sthg. -**2.** [requerer] to apply for. -**3.** [atenção, amizade] to seek.

solícito, ta [so'lisitu, ta] *adj* helpful.

solicitude [solisi'tudʒi] *f* -**1.** [zelo] care. -**2.** [boa-vontade] concern. -**3.** [empenho] commitment.

solidão [soli'dãw] *f* -**1.** [isolamento] solitude. -**2.** [ermo] desolation. -**3.** [sentimento] loneliness.

solidariedade [solidarje'dadʒi] *f* solidarity.

solidário, ria [soli'darju, rja] *adj* -**1.** [na dor] united; **mostrar-se** ~ to show one's solidarity; **ser** ~ **com** to stand by. -**2.** [simpático]: **ser** ~ **a** to be sympathetic to.

solidarizar-se [4] [solidari'zaxsi] *vp*: ~-**se com** to sympathise with.

solidez [soli'deʒ] *f* -**1.** [ger] strength. -**2.** [física] solidity. -**3.** [estabilidade] stability.

solidificar [12] [solidʒifi'ka(x)] *vt* -**1.** [fisicamente] to solidify. -**2.** *fig* [laços, amizade] to strengthen.
    ➤ **solidificar-se** *vp* -**1.** [fisicamente] to set. -**2.** *fig* [laços, amizade] to become strong.

sólido, da ['sɔlidu, da] *adj* -**1.** [ger] solid. -**2.** [moralmente] strong. -**3.** *fig* [firme - ger] strong; [- conhecimento] firm; [- argumento] sound.
    ➤ **sólido** *m* MAT solid.

solilóquio [soli'lɔkju] *m* soliloquy.

solista [so'liʃta] *m* MÚS soloist.

solitário, ria [soli'tarju, rja] <> *adj* solitary. <> *m, f* [eremita] solitary person.
    ➤ **solitário** *m* [diamante] solitaire.
    ➤ **solitária** *f* -**1.** [cela] solitary (confinement) cell. -**2.** [verme] tapeworm.

solo ['sɔlu] *m* -**1.** [chão] ground. -**2.** MÚS solo.

solstício [sowʃ'tʃisju] *m* ASTRON solstice; ~ **de inverno/verão** winter/summer solstice.

soltar [4] [sow'ta(x)] *vt* -**1.** [libertar] to release; ~ **os cachorros** *fig* to lash out. -**2.** [desatar] to untie. -**3.** [afrouxar] to loosen. -**4.** [largar] to let go. -**5.** [deixar cair (das mãos)] to drop. -**6.** [emitir] to let out. -**7.** [pronunciar] to utter; ~ **um palavrão** to swear; ~ **o verbo** *fig* to blow one's top. -**8.** [lançar] to let off; ~ **pipa** to fly a kite.
    ➤ **soltar-se** *vp* [desprender-se]: ~-**se (de algo)** to free o.s. (from sthg).

solteira [sow'tejra] *f* ⊳ **solteiro**.

solteirão, rona [sowtej'rãw, rona] (*mpl* -**ões**, *fpl* -**s**) *m, f* bachelor (*f* spinster).

solteiro, ra [sow'tejru, ra] *adj* unmarried, single.

solteirona [sowtej'rona] *f* ⊳ **solteirão**.

solto, ta ['sowtu, ta] <> *pp* ⊳ **soltar**. <> *adj* [ger] loose; **ter a língua solta** *fam fig* to have a loose tongue.
    ➤ **à solta** *loc adv* on the loose.

soltura [sow'tura] *f* -**1.** [libertação] release. -**2.** [desregramento] looseness.

solução [solu'sãw] (*pl* -**ões**) *f* solution; ~ **de continuidade** interruption; **sem** ~ **de continuidade** without interruption.

soluçar [13] [solu'sa(x)] *vi* -**1.** [chorar] to sob. -**2.** MED to hiccup.

solucionar [13] [solusjo'na(x)] *vt* to resolve.

soluço [su'lusu] *m* -**1.** [choro] sob; **aos** ~**s** sobbing. -**2.** MED hiccup.

solúvel [so'luvɛw] (*pl* -**eis**) *adj* soluble.

solvência [sow'vẽnsja] *f* -**1.** FIN [de dívida] solvency. -**2.** [dissolução] solubility.

solvente [sow'vẽntʃi] <> *adj* -**1.** [substância] soluble. -**2.** FIN [devedor] solvent. <> *m* [substância] solvent.

solver [5] [sow've(x)] *vt* -**1.** FIN [dívida] to pay. -**2.** [dissolver] to dissolve.

som ['sõ] (*pl* -**ns**) *m* -**1.** [ger] sound; **fazer um** ~ *fam* to make music; **ao** ~ **de** to the sound of. -**2.** [aparelho] hi-fi.

soma ['soma] *f* -**1.** [ger] sum. -**2.** *fig* [conjunto] combination.

Somália [so'malja] *n* Somalia.

somar [4] [so'ma(x)] <> *vt* -**1.** [adicionar] to add; ~ **algo a algo** to add sthg to sthg. -**2.** [totalizar] to add up to. <> *vi* to add (up).
    ➤ **somar-se** *vp* to gather together.

somatório [soma'tɔrju] *m* -**1.** [soma] sum total. -**2.** *fig* [total] total. -**3.** *fig* [conjunto] series.

sombra ['sõbra] *f* -**1.** [projeção] shadow; **fazer** ~ **a alguém** *fig* to put sb in the shade; **ser a** ~ **de alguém** *fig* to shadow sb. -**2.** [área] shade; **à** ~ **de** in the shade of; *fig* [sob a proteção de] under the protection of; **querer** ~ **e água fresca** *fig* to want an easy life. -**3.** *fig* [sinal] shadow; **sem** ~ **de dúvida** without a shadow of a doubt. -**4.** *fig* [anonimato] in the shade.

sombreado, da [sõ'brjadu, da] *adj* shaded.
    ➤ **sombreado** *m* ARTE shading.

sombrear [15] [sõ'brja(x)] <> *vt* [com sombra] to shade; **a nuvem sombreou a praia** the cloud cast a shadow over the beach. <> *vi* ARTE to shade (in).

sombreiro [sõ'brejru] *m* hat.

sombrinha [sõ'brina] *f* umbrella.

sombrio, bria [sõ'briw, bria] *adj* -**1.** [escuro] dark. -**2.** [triste] gloomy. -**3.** [carrancudo] grim.

somente [sɔ'mẽntʃi] *adv* only.

sonambulismo [sonãbu'liʒmu] *m* sleepwalking.

sonâmbulo, la [so'nãnbulu, la] <> *adj* sleepwalking. <> *m, f* sleepwalker.

sonata [so'nata] *f* sonata.

sonda ['sõda] *f* -**1.** MED probe. -**2.** MED [de alimentação] drip. -**3.** NÁUT depth finder. -**4.** TEC [para mineiração] bore. -**5.** TEC [petrolífera] drill. -**6.** METEOR weather balloon.
    ➤ **sonda espacial** *f* space probe.

sondagem [sõn'daʒẽ] (*pl* -**ns**) *f* -**1.** [com sonda - biliar] exploration; [- marítima, meteorológica] sounding; [- petrolífera] drilling. -**2.** [de opinião] survey.

sondar [4] [sõn'da(x)] *vt* -**1.** [ger] to probe. -**2.** NÁUT to sound. -**3.** TEC [terreno] to bore. -**4.** TEC [petróleo] to drill. -**5.** METEOR [atmosfera] to take soundings of. -**6.** [opinião] to survey. -**7.** *fig* [investigar] to fathom.

soneca [so'nɛka] *f* nap; **tirar uma** ~ to take a nap.

sonegação [sonega'sãw] *f* -**1.** [ocultação] withholding; ~ **de impostos** *ou* fiscal tax evasion. -**2.** [roubo] theft.

sonegador, ra [sonega'do(x), ra] <> *adj* [de impostos] fraudulent. <> *m, f* [de impostos] tax dodger.

sonegar [14] [sone'ga(x)] *vt* -**1.** [dinheiro, bens] to conceal. -**2.** [impostos] to dodge. -**3.** [roubar] to steal. -**4.** [informações] to withhold.

soneto [so'netu] *m* sonnet.

sonhador, ra [soɲa'do(x), ra] (*mpl* -es, *fpl* -s) <> *adj* dreaming. <> *m, f* dreamer.

sonhar [4] [so'ɲa(x)] <> *vt* [ter sonho com] to dream. <> *vi* -**1.** [ter sonho] to dream; ~ **com algo/alguém** to dream about sthg/sb; **nem sonhando!** in your dreams!; ~ **acordado** to daydream. -**2.** [desejar]: ~ **com algo** to dream of sthg; ~ **em fazer algo** to dream of doing sthg.

sonho ['soɲu] *m* -**1.** [ger] dream. -**2.** CULIN doughnut.

sono ['sonu] *m* -**1.** [período] sleep; ~ **leve/pesado** light sleep/heavy sleep; **pegar no** ~ to fall asleep. -**2.** [vontade de dormir]: **estar caindo** *ou* **morrendo de** ~ to be dead on one's feet; **estar com** *ou* **sentir** ~ to be *ou* feel sleepy; **estar sem** ~ not to be sleepy.

sonolência [sono'lẽsja] *f* drowsiness.

sonolento, ta [sono'lẽtu, ta] *adj* sleepy.

sonoridade [sonori'dadʒi] *f* -**1.** [timbre, altura] sound quality. -**2.** [ressonância] resonance.

sonorizar [sonori'za(x)] *vt* -**1.** [filme] to make the soundtrack for. -**2.** [sala] to set up the sound for.

sonoro, ra [so'noru, ra] *adj* -**1.** [de som] resonant. -**2.** GRAM voiced.

sonoterapia [sonotera'pia] *f* sleep therapy.

sons [sõʃ] *pl* ▷ **som**.

sonso, sa ['sõsu, sa] *adj* sly.

sopa ['sopa] *f* -**1.** CULIN soup; ~ **de lentilhas** lentil soup. -**2.** *fam* [facilidade] easy life; **ser** ~ to be a piece of cake. -**3.** *loc*: **dar** ~ [descuidar-se] to be careless; [estar disponível] to be going spare; [abundar] to be in abundance.

sopapo [so'papu] *m* slap; **dar um** ~ **em alguém** to slap sb.

sopé [so'pɛ] *m* foot.

sopeira [so'pejra] *f* (soup) tureen.

soporífero, ra [sopo'riferu, ra], *adj* -**1.** [que faz dormir] soporific. -**2.** *fig* [chato] boring.
   ▶ **soporífero** *m* [substância] soporific.

soporífico [sopo'rifikul] = **soporífero**

soprano [so'prãnul] <> *adj* soprano *(antes de subst)*. <> *mf* soprano.

soprar [4] [so'pra(x)] <> *vt* -**1.** [com sopro] to blow. -**2.** *fig* [segredar] to whisper. <> *vi* [vento] to blow.

sopro ['sopru] *m* -**1.** [ar] puff. -**2.** [som - de vento] sigh; [- de fole] puff; [- de saxofone] soft sound; **instrumento de** ~ wind instrument. -**3.** [aragem] breeze. -**4.** *fig* [ânimo] breath. -**5.** MED murmur; ~ **cardíaco** heart murmur.

soquete [so'kɛtʃi] *f* [meia] ankle sock.

sordidez [soxdʒi'deʒ] *f* -**1.** [imundície] squalor. -**2.** [torpeza] sordidness.

sórdido, da ['sɔrdʒidu, da] *adj* -**1.** [imundo] squalid. -**2.** [torpe] sordid.

soro ['soru] *m* -**1.** MED serum. -**2.** [de leite] whey.

soropositivo, va [soropozi'tʃivu, va] <> *adj* seropositive. <> *m, f* seropositive person.

sóror ['sɔro(x)] *f* RELIG sister.

sorrateiramente [soxatejra'mẽtʃi] *adv* stealthily.

sorrateiro, ra [soxa'tejru, ra] *adj* stealthy.

sorridente [soxi'dẽtʃil] *adj* smiling.

sorrir [69] [so'xi(x)] *vi* to smile; ~ **(para)** to smile (at); [destino, fortuna *etc*] to smile on.

sorriso [so'xizul] *m* smile; **dar um** ~ **(para alguém)** to smile (at sb); ~ **amarelo** wry smile.

sorte ['sɔxtʃi] *f* -**1.** [ventura] luck; **boa** ~! good luck!; **dar** ~ [ter sorte] to be lucky; **dar** ~ **(para alguém)** to bring (sb) luck; **estar com** *ou* **ter** ~ to be lucky; **má** ~ bad luck; **que** ~! what luck!; **de** ~ [sortudo] lucky; **tirar a** ~ to draw lots; **tirar a** ~ **grande** [na loteria] to hit the jackpot; [enriquecer] to become rich; [ser afortunado] to do the right thing. -**2.** [acaso] chance; **tentar a** ~ to try one's luck; **por** ~ by chance. -**3.** [sina] fate. -**4.** [situação] lot. -**5.** [maneira]: **desta** ~ in this way; **de** ~ **que** in such a way that. -**6.** [espécie] sort; **toda** ~ **de iguarias** all sorts of delicacies.

sorteado, da [sox'tʃjadu, da] *adj* winning.

sortear [15] [sox'tʃja(x)] *vt* -**1.** [pessoa, bilhete] to draw lots for. -**2.** [rifar] to raffle.

sorteio [sox'teju] *m* -**1.** [de pessoa, bilhete] draw. -**2.** [rifa] raffle.

sortido, da [sox'tʃidu, da] *adj* -**1.** [abastecido] stocked. -**2.** [variado] assorted.

sortilégio [soxtʃi'lɛʒu] *m* -**1.** [bruxaria] sorcery. -**2.** [encantamento] enchantment.

sortimento [soxtʃi'mẽtul] *m* [provisão] stock.

sortir [60] [sox'tʃi(x)] *vt* -**1.** [abastecer]: ~ **algo com** *ou* **de** to supply sthg with. -**2.** [variar] to vary.
   ▶ **sortir-se** *vp* [abastecer-se]: ~-**se com** *ou* **de** to supply o.s. with.

sortudo, da [sox'tudu, da] <> *adj* lucky. <> *m, f* lucky person.

sorumbático, ca [sorũn'batʃiku, ka] *adj* gloomy.

sorvedouro [soxve'dorul] *m* -**1.** [redemoinho] whirlpool; ~ **de dinheiro** *fig* a drain on resources. -**2.** [abismo] chasm.

sorver [5] [sox've(x)] *vt* -**1.** [ger] to inhale. -**2.** [beber] to sip. -**3.** [absorver] to absorb.

sorvete [sox'vetʃil] *m* -**1.** [com leite] ice cream. -**2.** [sem leite] sorbet.

sorveteiro, ra [soxve'tejru, ra] *m, f* ice-cream man.

sorveteria [soxvete'ria] *f* ice-cream parlour.

sósia ['sɔzja] *mf* double.

soslaio [soʒ'laju] ▶ **de soslaio** *loc adv* sideways.

sossegado, da [sose'gadu, da] *adj* quiet.

sossegar [14] [sose'ga(x)] *vt & vi* to calm down.

sossego [so'segul] *m* peace (and quiet).

sotaina [so'tãjna] *f* cassock.

sótão ['sɔtãwl] (*pl* -**ãos**) *m* attic.

sotaque [so'takil] *m* accent.

sotavento [sɔta'vẽtul] *m* NÁUT lee; **a** ~ leeward.

soterrar [4] [sote'xa(x)] *vt* to bury.

soturno, na [so'tuxnu, na] *adj* **-1.** [triste] sad. **-2.** [amedrontador] frightening.

soutien [su'tʃjã] *m* = **sutiã**.

sova ['sɔva] *f* **-1.** [amassamento - uva, cacau] crushing; [- de massa] keading. **-2.** [surra] beating; **dar uma ~ em alguém** to beat sb up; **levar uma ~ (de alguém)** to take a beating (from sb).

sovaco [so'vaku] *m* armpit.

sovado, da [so'vadu, da] *adj* **-1.** [trabalhado] kneaded. **-2.** [espancado] beaten. **-3.** [usado, fatigado] worn out.

sovar [4] [so'va(x)] *vt* **-1.** [amassar - uva, cacau] to crush; [- massa] to knead. **-2.** [surrar] to beat up. **-3.** *fig* [roupa, couro] to tan.

sovina [so'vina] <> *adj* miserly. <> *mf* miser.

sovinice [sovi'nisil *f* meanness; **ser pura ~** to be utterly mean.

sozinho, nha [so'ziɲu, ɲal *adj* **-1.** [desacompanhado] alone. **-2.** [solitário] all alone. **-3.** [único] by itself. **-4.** [por si só] by myself/yourself/himself etc.

SP (*abrev de* **Estado de São Paulo**) *n* State of São Paulo.

spam ['ijpãm] (*pl* **-s**) *m* COMPUT spam.

SPC (*abrev de* **Serviço de Proteção ao Crédito**) *m* Brazilian service providing information on credit credit rating.

spot [iʃ'pɔtʃi] *m* spotlight.

spray [iʃ'prej] *m* spray.

SQL (*abrev de* **Structured Query Language**) *f* SQL.

Sr. (*abrev de* **senhor**) *m* ≃ Mr.

Sra. (*abrev de* **senhora**) *f* ≃ Mrs.

SRF (*abrev de* **Secretaria da Receita Federal**) *f* department of the Brazilian ministry of finance responsible for taxes and customs and excise.

Sri Lanka [ˌsri'lãŋka] *n* Sri Lanka.

Srs. (*abrev de* **senhores**) *mpl* Messrs, Mr and Mrs.

srta (*abrev de* **senhorita**) *f* ≃ Miss.

staff [iʃ'tafil *m* staff.

standard [iʃ'tãndaxdʒil *adj inv* standard.

status [iʃ'tatus] *m* status; **~ quo** status quo.

STF (*abrev de* **Supremo Tribunal Federal**) *m* Brazilian supreme federal tribunal responsible for the enforcement of the constitution and also heading the judiciary.

STJ (*abrev de* **Superior Tribunal de Justiça**) *m* Brazilian higher court of justice.

strip-tease [iʃˌtripi'tʃizil *m* striptease; **fazer um ~** to do a striptease.

sua ['sua] <> **seu**.

suado, da ['swadu, da] *adj* **-1.** [da suor] sweaty. **-2.** *fam fig* [difícil de obter] hard-earned.

suador, ra [swa'do(x), ra] *m* **-1.** [sudorífero] sudorific. **-2.** [dificuldade, esforço] sweat, hard job.

suar [4] ['swa(x)] <> *vt* **-1.** [transpirar] to sweat. **-2.** [roupa] to make sweaty. <> *vi* **-1.** [transpirar] to sweat; **~ em bicas** to sweat buckets; **~ frio** to come out in a cold sweat. **-2.** [verter umidade] to sweat. **-3.** *fam fig* [esforçar-se]: **~ por algo/para fazer algo** to sweat blood for sthg/to do sthg;

ela suou por esse emprego she had to work hard for that job.

suas ['suaʃ] <> **seu**.

suástica ['swaʃtʃika] *f* swastika.

suave ['swavil *adj* **-1.** [ger] mild. **-2.** [vinho, pele, cabelos] smooth. **-3.** [brisa, ritmo] gentle. **-4.** [cor] delicate. **-5.** [música, tecido] soft. **-6.** [terno - pessoa] charming; [- carícia] gentle; [- voz] soft. **-7.** [leve - trabalho] light; [- vida] easy; **em ~s prestações** in easy instalments.

suavidade [swavi'dadʒil *f* **-1.** [ger] mildness. **-2.** [de pele, cabelos] smoothness. **-3.** [de brisa, música, ritmo] gentleness. **-4.** [de tecido, cor, brisa, música] softness. **-5.** [ternura] charm.

suavizar [4] [swavi'za(x)] *vt* **-1.** [abrandar] to tone down. **-2.** [amenizar] to ease. **-3.** [amaciar - pele, cabelo] to smooth; [- tecido] to soften.

→ **suavizar-se** *vp* [amenizar-se] to ease.

subalimentado, da [subalimẽn'tadu, da] *adj* undernourished.

subalterno, na [subaw'tɛxnu, na] <> *adj* subordinate. <> *m, f* subordinate.

subchefe [sub'ʃɛfil *mf* assistant director.

subconsciente [subkõn'sjẽntʃil <> *adj* subconscious. <> *m* subconscious.

subcutâneo, nea [subku'tãnju, nja] *adj* subcutaneous.

subdesenvolvido, da [subdʒizĩnvow'vidu, da] <> *adj* **-1.** [não-desenvolvido] underdeveloped. **-2.** *pej* [atrasado] moronic. <> *m, f pej* [pessoa] moron.

subdesenvolvimento [subdizĩnvowvi'mẽntul *m* underdevelopment.

subdividir [6] [subdʒivi'dʒi(x)] *vt*: **~ algo (em)** to subdivide sthg (into).

→ **subdividir-se** *vp*: **~-se (em)** to be subdivided (into).

subemprego [subẽn'pregul *m* **-1.** [trabalho] underpaid job. **-2.** [condição] underpaid work.

subentender [5] [subẽntẽn'de(x)] *vt* to infer.

→ **subentender-se** *vp* to be inferred; **subentende-se que ...** it can be inferred that ...

subentendido, da [subẽntẽn'dʒidu, da] *adj* inferred.

→ **subentendido** *m* innuendo.

subestimar [4] [subeʃtʃi'ma(x)] *vt* to underestimate.

subida [su'bida] *f* **-1.** [ato] climb. **-2.** [ladeira] slope. **-3.** [de preços] rise.

subir [61] [su'bi(x)] <> *vt* **-1.** [galgar] to climb (up). **-2.** [ir para cima, percorrer] to go up. **-3.** [escalar] to climb, to scale. **-4.** [aumentar] to raise. **-5.** [ascender] to climb. **-6.** [voz] to raise. <> *vi* **-1.** [ger] to go up; **~ a ou até** to go up to; **~ em** [árvore] to climb (up); [telhado, cadeira] to climb onto; **~ por** to go up; **~ à cabeça** *fig* to go to one's head. **-2.** [ascender - balão, neblina, fumaça] to rise; [- elevador, teleférico] to go up; [- em ônibus] to get on. **-3.** [socialmente] to go up in the world; **~ a/de** to rise from; **~ na vida** to get on in life. **-4.** [aumentar] to rise.

súbito, ta ['subitu, ta] *adj* sudden.
➤ **súbito** *adv* suddenly; **de** ~ suddenly.
subjacente [subʒa'sẽntʃil *adj* underlying.
subjazer [subʒa'ze(x)] *vi*: **as tramas políticas que subjaziam** the underlying political plots.
subjetividade [subʒetʃivi'dadʒil *f* subjectivity.
subjetivo, va [subʒe'tʃivu, va] *adj* subjective.
subjugar [14] [subʒu'ga(x)] *vt* **-1.** [derrotar] to overpower. **-2.** [dominar] to dominate. **-3.** [impor-se a] to supplant. **-4.** [moralmente] to subdue.
subjuntivo [subʒũn'tʃivul *m* subjunctive.
sublevação [subleva'sãw] (*pl* **-ões**) *f* uprising.
sublevar [4] [suble'va(x)] *vt*: ~ **alguém (contra algo)** to stir up sb (against sthg).
➤ **sublevar-se** *vp*: ~**-se (contra algo)** to rebel (against sthg).
sublimação [sublima'sãw] (*pl* **-ões**) *f* **-1.** [engrandecimento] exaltation. **-2.** [de desejos] sublimation.
sublimar [4] [subli'ma(x)] *vt* **-1.** [engrandecer] to exalt. **-2.** [desejos] to sublimate.
sublime [su'blimil *adj* sublime.
sublinhar [4] [subli'ɲa(x)] *vt* **-1.** [palavras] to underline. **-2.** [enfatizar] to emphasize.
sublocar [12] [sublo'ka(x)] *vt* to sublet.
sublocatário, ria [subloka'tarju, rja] *m, f* subtenant.
submarino, na [subma'rinu, na] *adj* underwater.
➤ **submarino** *m* submarine.
submergir [78] [submex'ʒi(x)] *vt* & *vi* to submerge.
submersão [submex'sãw] (*pl* **-ões**) *f* submersion.
submeter [5] [subme'te(x)] *vt* **-1.** [dominar] to subdue. **-2.** [para apreciação]: ~ **algo a** to submit sthg to. **-3.** [sujeitar]: ~ **alguém/algo a algo** to subject sb/sthg to sthg.
➤ **submeter-se** *vp* **-1.** [render-se] to surrender. **-2.** [sujeitar-se]: ~ **a algo** to undergo sthg; ~ **a alguém** to submit to sb.
submissão [submi'sãw] *f* **-1.** [sujeição, obediência] submission. **-2.** [apatia] lack of determination.
submisso, sa [sub'misu, sa] *adj* submissive.
submundo [sub'mũdul *m* underworld.
subnutrição [subnutri'sãw] *f* malnutrition.
subnutrido, da [subnu'tridu, da] *adj* malnourished.
subordinado, da [suboxdʒi'nadu, da] <> *adj* subordinate. <> *m,f* [subalterno] subordinate.
subordinar [4] [suboxdʒi'na(x)] *vt* **-1.** [ger] to subordinate. **-2.** [sujeitar] to subject.
➤ **subordinar-se** *vp* [sujeitar-se]: ~**-se a algo/ alguém** to subject o.s. to sthg/sb.
subornar [4] [subox'na(x)] *vt* to bribe.
suborno [su'boxnu] *m* bribe.
subproduto [subpro'dutul *m* by-product.
sub-reptício, cia [subxep'tʃisju, sja] *adj* surreptitious.
subscrever [5] [subʃkre've(x)] <> *vt* **-1.** [assinar] to sign. **-2.** [aprovar] to subscribe to. **-3.** [arrecadar] to collect. <> *vi* **-1.** [aceder]: ~ **a** to endorse *UK*, to indorse *US*. **-2.** [contribuir]: ~ **(com algo)**

para algo to contribute (sthg) to sthg.
➤ **subscrever-se** *vp* [assinar] to sign; **subscrevemo-nos** *fml* & *COM* we remain; **atenciosamente, subscrevemo-nos** *fml* & *COM* we remain, yours sincerely.
subscrição [subʃkri'sãw] (*pl* **-ões**) *f* **-1.** [ato de assinatura] signing. **-2.** [contribuição] contribution.
subscrito, ta [subʃ'kritu, ta] <> *pp* ▷ **subscrever**. <> *adj* undersigned. <> *m, f* undersigned.
subsecretário, ria [subsekre'tarju, rja] *m, f* undersecretary.
subseqüente [subse'kwẽntʃil *adj* subsequent; ~ **(a)** subsequent (to).
subserviência [subsexvjẽnsja] *f* subservience.
subserviente [subsex'vjẽntʃil *adj* subservient, servile; ~ **(a)** subservient (towards).
subsidiar [15] [subzi'dʒja(x)] *vt* to subsidize.
subsidiário, ria [subzi'dʒjarju, rja] *adj* subsidiary.
➤ **subsidiária** *f* [empresa] subsidiary.
subsídio [sub'zidʒju] *m* **-1.** [contribuição] contribution. **-2.** [estatal] subsidy.
➤ **subsídios** *mpl* [dados, contribuições] information *(sg)*.
subsistência [subziʃ'tẽnsja] *f* [sustento, sobrevivência] subsistence; **de** ~ subsistence *(antes de subst)*.
subsistir [6] [subziʃ'tʃi(x)] *vi* **-1.** [existir] to exist. **-2.** [persistir] to remain. **-3.** [sobreviver] to survive.
subsolo [sub'sɔlu] *m* **-1.** [da terra] subsoil. **-2.** [de prédio] basement.
substância [subʃ'tãnsja] *f* substance; **em** ~ in essence.
substancial [subʃtãn'sjaw] (*pl* **-ais**) <> *adj* substantial. <> *m* [essência] essence.
substantivo, va [subʃtãn'tʃivu, va] *adj* **-1.** [essencial] essential. **-2.** *GRAM* substantive.
➤ **substantivo** *m GRAM* noun.
substituição [subʃtʃitwi'sãw] (*pl* **-ões**) *f* substitution, replacement.
substituir [74] [subʃtʃi'twi(x)] *vt* to substitute, to replace.
substituto, ta [subʃtʃi'tutu, ta] <> *adj* substitute *(antes de subst)*, replacement *(antes de subst)*. <> *m, f* substitute, replacement.
subterfúgio [subtex'fuʒju] *m* subterfuge.
subterrâneo, nea [subte'xãnju, nja] *adj* underground.
➤ **subterrâneos** *mpl* underground movements.
subtítulo [sub'tʃitulu] *m* subtitle.
subtotal [subto'taw] (*pl* **-ais**) *m* subtotal.
subtração [subtra'sãw] (*pl* **-ões**) *f* **-1.** [furto] theft. **-2.** [dedução] deduction. **-3.** *MAT* subtraction.
subtrair [68] [subtra'i(x)] <> *vt* **-1.** [furtar] to steal. **-2.** [deduzir] to deduct. **-3.** *MAT* to subtract. <> *vi MAT* to subtract.
➤ **subtrair-se** *vp* [esquivar-se]: ~**-se a algo** to dodge sthg.
subumano, na [subju'mãnu, na] *adj* subhuman.
suburbano, na [subux'bãnu, na] <> *adj* **-1.** [do subúrbio] suburban. **-2.** *pej* [atrasado] backward.

◇ *m*, *f* **-1**. [morador] suburbanite. **-2**. *pej* [atrasado] moron.

subúrbio [su'buxbju] *m* suburb.

subvenção [subvẽn'sãw] (*pl* -ões) *f* subsidy.

subvencionar [4] [subvẽnsjo'na(x)] *vt* to subsidize.

subversão [subvex'sãw] *f* subversion.

subversivo, va [subvex'sivu, va] ◇ *adj* subversive. ◇ *m*, *f* [pessoa] subversive.

subverter [5] [subvex'te(x)] *vt* **-1**. [desordenar] to subvert. **-2**. [agitar] to incite. **-3**. [arruinar] to upset.

sucata [su'kata] *f* scrap metal.

sucção [suk'sãw] *f* suction.

sucedâneo, nea [suse'dãnju, nja] ◇ *adj* substitute. ◇ *m*, *f* substitute.

suceder [5] [suse'de(x)] *vi* **-1**. [acontecer] to happen. **-2**. [seguir-se a]: ~ **a algo/alguém** to follow (on from) sthg/sb.

    ◆ **suceder-se** *vp* **-1**. [seguir-se]: **sucedem-se os governantes, mas nada muda** rulers come and go but nothing changes. **-2**. [repetir-se]: **os dias se sucediam e ele não regressava** day followed day and still he didn't return.

sucedido, da [suse'dʒidu. da] *m*: **vou lhe contar o** ~ I'll tell you what happened.

sucessão [suse'sãw] (*pl* -ões) *f* succession.

sucessivo, va [suse'sivu, va] *adj* successive; **crimes** ~**s** a succession of crimes.

sucesso [su'sɛsu] *m* **-1**. [êxito] success; **fazer** *ou* **ter** ~ to be successful; **com/sem** ~ successfully/unsuccessfully; **de** ~ successful. **-2**. [música, filme] hit; **ser um** ~ to be a hit.

sucessor, ra [suse'so(x), ra] *m*, *f* successor.

sucinto, ta [su'sĩntu, ta] *adj* succinct.

suco ['suku] *m* juice.

suculento, ta [suku'lẽntu, ta] *adj* succulent.

sucumbir [6] [sukũn'bi(x)] *vi* **-1**. [vergar]: ~ **a algo** to yield to sthg. **-2**. [ceder]: ~ **a algo** to succumb to sthg. **-3**. [morrer]: ~ **(a algo)** to succumb (to sthg).

sucursal [sukux'saw] (*pl* -ais) *f* **-1**. [de empresa, loja] branch. **-2**. [de jornal, emissora] subsidiary.

SUDAM (**Superintendência do Desenvolvimento da Amazônia**) *f body overseeing the use of resources for the development of the Amazon region.*

sudanês, esa [suda'neʃ, eza] ◇ *adj* Sudanese. ◇ *m*, *f* Sudanese.

Sudão [su'dãw] *n* Sudan.

SUDENE (*abrev de* **Superintendência do Desenvolvimento do Nordeste**) *f body responsible for overseeing economic and financial incentives in northeastern Brazil.*

sudeste [su'dɛʃtʃi] ◇ *adj* south-east. ◇ *m* south-east.

súdito, ta ['sudʒitu, ta] *m*, *f* subject.

sudoeste [su'dwɛʃtʃi] ◇ *adj* south-west. ◇ *m* south-west.

Suécia ['swɛsja] *n* Sweden.

sueco, ca ['swɛku, ka] ◇ *adj* Swedish. ◇ *m*, *f* Swede.

◆ **sueco** *m* [língua] Swedish.

suéter ['swɛte(x)] (*pl* -es) *m ou f* sweater.

suficiência [sufi'sjẽnsja] *f* sufficiency.

suficiente [sufi'sjẽntʃi] ◇ *adj* sufficient. ◇ *m*: **tenho o** ~ **até amanhã** I have enough until tomorrow.

sufixo [su'fiksu] *m* suffix.

suflê [su'fle] *m* soufflé.

sufocação [sufoka'sãw] (*pl* -ões) *f* **-1**. [ger] suffocation. **-2**. *fig* [opressão] oppression.

sufocante [sufo'kãntʃi] *adj* **-1**. [ger] suffocating. **-2**. *fig* [opressivo] oppressive.

sufocar [12] [sufo'ka(x)] ◇ *vt* **-1**. [asfixiar] to suffocate. **-2**. *fig* [oprimir] to oppress. **-3**. *fig* [debelar] to crush. ◇ *vi* [asfixiar-se] to be stifled.

◆ **sufocar-se** *vp* [asfixiar-se] to be suffocated.

sufoco [su'foku] *m* **-1**. [aflição] dread; **que** ~! how dreadful!; **ser um** ~ to be dreadful. **-2**. [dificuldade] hassle; **deixar alguém no** ~ to leave sb in the lurch; **passar (por) um** ~ to have a hard time.

sufrágio [su'fraʒju] *m* **-1**. [voto] vote; ~ **universal** universal suffrage. **-2**. [apoio] support.

sugar [14] [su'ga(x)] *vt* **-1**. [por sucção] to suck. **-2**. *fig* [extorquir] to extort; ~ **o sangue de alguém** to get every last drop of blood out of sb.

sugerir [57] [suʒe'ri(x)] *vt* to suggest; ~ **algo a alguém** to suggest sthg to sb.

sugestão [suʒeʃ'tãw] (*pl* -ões) *f* **-1**. [ger] suggestion; **dar uma** ~ to make a suggestion. **-2**. [evocação, insinuação] hint.

sugestionar [4] [suʒeʃtʃjo'na(x)] *vt*: ~ **algo a alguém** to inspire sb with sthg.

◆ **sugestionar-se** *vp*: ~ **se con algo** to experience sthg.

sugestionável [suʒeʃtʃjo'navew] (*pl* -eis) *adj* impressionable.

sugestivo, va [suʒeʃ'tʃivu, va] *adj* **-1**. [evocativo] evocative. **-2**. [insinuante] suggestive.

Suíça ['swisa] *n* Switzerland.

suíças ['swisaʃ] *fpl* sideburns.

suicida [swi'sida] ◇ *adj* suicidal. ◇ *mf* [pessoa] suicidal person.

suicidar-se [7] [swisi'daxsi] *vp* to commit suicide.

suicídio [swi'sidʒju] *m* suicide; **ser** ~ *fig* [ser arriscado] to be suicide.

suíço, ça ['swisu, sa] ◇ *adj* Swiss. ◇ *m*, *f* Swiss.

sui generis [swi'ʒeneriʃ] *adj inv* unique, sui generis.

suingar [swĩ'ga(x)] *vi* to dance the swing.

suingue ['swĩgi] *m* swing.

suíno, na ['swinu, na] *adj* pig *(antes de subst)*.

◆ **suíno** *m* [porco] pig.

suíte ['switʃi] *f* suite.

sujar [4] [su'ʒa(x)] ◇ *vt* **-1**. [tornar sujo] to dirty. **-2**. *fig* [macular] to disgrace. ◇ *vi fam* [dar errado] to go wrong.

◆ **sujar-se** *vp* **-1**. [tornar-se sujo] to get dirty. **-2**. *fig* [macular-se] to disgrace o.s.

sujeição [suʒej'sãw] *f* **-1**. [subordinação] subordination. **-2**. [submissão] submission.

sujeira [su'ʒejra] *f* -**1.** [coisa suja] dirt. -**2.** [estado] dirtiness; **a sala estava uma ~ quando cheguei** the room was a dirty mess when I arrived. -**3.** *fam* [bandalheira] dirty trick; **fazer uma ~ com alguém** to play a dirty trick on sb.

sujeitar [4] [suʒej'ta(x)] *vt* -**1.** [submeter]: **~ algo/ alguém a algo** to subject sthg/sb to sthg. -**2.** [apresentar]: **~ algo a algo** to submit sthg to sthg.
➡ **sujeitar-se** *vp* [submeter-se]: **~-se a algo** to subject o.s. to sthg.

sujeito, ta [su'ʒejtu, ta] <> *adj*: **~ a** subject to. <> *m, f* person.
➡ **sujeito** *m GRAM* subject.

sujo, ja ['suʒu, ʒa] <> *adj* -**1.** [imundo] dirty; **estar/ficar ~ com alguém** *fig* to be/fall out of favour with sb, to be in sb's bad books. -**2.** *fig* [mau-caráter] dishonest. <> *m, f fig* [pessoa] dishonest person.

sul ['suw] <> *adj* southern. <> *m* [região] south; **ao ~ de** to the south of.

sulcar [12] [suw'ka(x)] *vt* -**1.** [abrir sulcos em] to plough *UK*, to plow *US*. -**2.** [rosto] to line. -**3.** [singrar] to cut through.

sulco [suw'ku] *m* furrow.

sulfato [suw'fatu] *m* sulphate.

sulfúrico, ca [suw'furiku, ka] *adj* sulphuric.

sulista [su'liʃta] <> *adj* southern. <> *mf* southerner.

sultão, tana [suw'tãw, tãna] (*pl* -**ões**) *m, f* sultan (*f* sultana).

suma ['suma] ➡ **em suma** *loc adv* in short.

sumamente [suma'mẽntʃi] *adv* [extremamente] extremely.

sumário, ria [su'marju, rja] *adj* -**1.** [breve] brief. -**2.** [julgamento] summary. -**3.** [traje] skimpy.
➡ **sumário** *m* -**1.** [resumo] summary. -**2.** [no início de livro] table of contents. -**3.** *JUR*: **~ de culpa** indictment.

sumiço [su'misu] *m* disappearance; **dar (um) ~ em** to do away with.

sumidade [sumi'dadʒi] *f*: **~ (em algo)** authority (in sthg).

sumido, da [su'midu, da] *adj* -**1.** [desaparecido] vanished; **andar ~** to have disappeared. -**2.** [voz] low. -**3.** [apagado] faint.

sumir [61] [su'mi(x)] *vi* to disappear; **~ com algo** to disappear with sthg.

sumo, ma ['sumu, ma] *adj* extreme; **~ sacerdote** high priest.
➡ **sumo** *m* [suco] juice.

sundae ['sãdej] *m* sundae.

sunga ['sũga] *f* [de banho] (swimming) trunks.

suntuoso, osa [sũn'twozu, ɔza] *adj* sumptuous.

suor ['swɔ(x)] (*pl* -**es**) *m* -**1.** [transpiração] sweat. -**2.** *fig* [trabalho]: **fiz esta casa com o meu próprio ~** I built this house by the sweat of my brow.

super ['supe(x)] *fam* <> *adj* [ótimo] super. <> *interj* super!

superabundante [,superabũn'dãntʃi] *adj* excessive.

superação [supera'sãw] (*pl* -**ões**) *f* overcoming; é fundamental para a **~ do estresse** it's essential for overcoming stress.

superado, da [supe'radu, da] *adj* -**1.** [ultrapassado] outmoded, old-fashioned. -**2.** [resolvido] overcome.

superalimentar [4] [4] [superalimẽn'ta(x)] *vt* -**1.** [animais, pacientes] to overfeed. -**2.** [indústria, sistema] to supercharge.

superaquecer [25] [,superake'se(x)] *vt* & *vi* to overheat.

superaquecimento [,superakesi'mẽntu] *m* overheating.

superar [4] [supe'ra(x)] *vt* -**1.** [sobrepujar]: **~ alguém (em algo)** to outdo sb (in sthg); **~ o inimigo** to defeat an enemy; **superou a todos em velocidade** he surpassed everyone in terms of speed. -**2.** [recorde] to beat. -**3.** [expectativa, objetivos *etc*] to exceed. -**4.** [ultrapassar] to surpass. -**5.** [resolver] to overcome.
➡ **superar-se** *vp* -**1.** [melhorar]: **~-se (em algo)** to excel o.s. (in sthg). -**2.** [exceder-se] to excel o.s.

superávit [supe'ravitʃil] *m COM* surplus.

supercílio [super'silju] *m* eyebrow.

superdotado, da [,supexdo'tadu, da] <> *adj* -**1.** [em inteligência] (exceptionally) gifted. -**2.** *fam* [sexualmente] well endowed. <> *m, f* [em inteligência] (exceptionally) gifted person.

superestimar [4] [,supereʃtʃi'ma(x)] *vt* to overestimate.

superestrutura [,supereʃtru'tura] *f* superstructure.

superficial [supexfi'sjaw] (*pl* -**ais**) *adj* superficial.

superficialidade [supexfisjali'dadʒi] *f* superficiality.

superfície [supex'fisji] *f* -**1.** [parte externa] surface. -**2.** [extensão] area.

supérfluo, lua [su'pɛxflu, lua] *adj* superfluous.
➡ **supérfluo** *m* [gasto]: **vamos cortar o ~** we're going to cut out what is superfluous.

super-homem [,super'ɔmẽ] (*pl* -**ns**) *m* superman.

superintendência [,superĩntẽn'dẽnsja] *f* [órgão] management.

superintendente [,superĩntẽn'dẽntʃi] *mf* manager.

superior [supe'rjo(x)] (*pl* -**es**) <> *adj RELIG* superior. <> *m, f* [em hierarquia] superior.
➡ **superior** *adj* -**1.** [de cima] upper. -**2.** [mais alto] higher. -**3.** [maior] greater. -**4.** [melhor] better; **~ a** better than. -**5.** [excelente] first class. -**6.** *EDUC* higher; **escola ~** senior school; **curso ~** degree course.

superioridade [superjori'dadʒi] *f* superiority.

superlativo, va [supexla'tʃivul *adj* superlative.
➡ **superlativo** *m GRAM* superlative.

superlotado, da [,supexlo'tadu, da] *adj*: **~ (de)** overcrowded (with).

superlotar [,supexlo'ta(x)] *vt* to pack.

supermercado [,supexmex'kadu] *m* supermarket.

◇ *m, f* **-1.** [morador] suburbanite. **-2.** *pej* [atrasado] moron.

subúrbio [su'buxbju] *m* suburb.

subvenção [subvẽ'sãw] (*pl* **-ões**) *f* subsidy.

subvencionar [4] [subvẽsjo'na(x)] *vt* to subsidize.

subversão [subvex'sãw] *f* subversion.

subversivo, va [subvex'sivu, va] ◇ *adj* subversive. ◇ *m, f* [pessoa] subversive.

subverter [5] [subvex'te(x)] *vt* **-1.** [desordenar] to subvert. **-2.** [agitar] to incite. **-3.** [arruinar] to upset.

sucata [su'kata] *f* scrap metal.

sucção [suk'sãw] *f* suction.

sucedâneo, nea [suse'dânju, nja] ◇ *adj* substitute. ◇ *m, f* substitute.

suceder [5] [suse'de(x)] *vi* **-1.** [acontecer] to happen. **-2.** [seguir-se a]: ~ **a algo/alguém** to follow (on from) sthg/sb.

  suceder-se *vp* **-1.** [seguir-se]: **sucedem-se os governantes, mas nada muda** rulers come and go but nothing changes. **-2.** [repetir-se]: **os dias se sucediam e ele não regressava** day followed day and still he didn't return.

sucedido, da [suse'dʒidu, da] *m*: **vou lhe contar o** ~ I'll tell you what happened.

sucessão [suse'sãw] (*pl* **-ões**) *f* succession.

sucessivo, va [suse'sivu, va] *adj* successive; **crimes** ~**s** a succession of crimes.

sucesso [su'sɛsu] *m* **-1.** [êxito] success; **fazer** *ou* **ter** ~ to be successful; **com/sem** ~ successfully/ unsuccessfully; **de** ~ successful. **-2.** [música, filme] hit; **ser um** ~ to be a hit.

sucessor, ra [suse'so(x), ra] *m, f* successor.

sucinto, ta [su'sĩntu, ta] *adj* succinct.

suco ['suku] *m* juice.

suculento, ta [suku'lẽntu, ta] *adj* succulent.

sucumbir [6] [sukũn'bi(x)] *vi* **-1.** [vergar]: ~ **a algo** to yield to sthg. **-2.** [ceder]: ~ **a algo** to succumb to sthg. **-3.** [morrer]: ~ **(a algo)** to succumb (to sthg).

sucursal [sukux'saw] (*pl* **-ais**) *f* **-1.** [de empresa, loja] branch. **-2.** [de jornal, emissora] subsidiary.

SUDAM (**Superintendência do Desenvolvimento da Amazônia**) *f body overseeing the use of resources for the development of the Amazon region.*

sudanês, esa [suda'neʃ, eza] ◇ *adj* Sudanese. ◇ *m, f* Sudanese.

Sudão [su'dãw] *n* Sudan.

SUDENE (*abrev de* **Superintendência do Desenvolvimento do Nordeste**) *f body responsible for overseeing economic and financial incentives in northeastern Brazil.*

sudeste [su'dɛʃtʃi] ◇ *adj* south-east. ◇ *m* south-east.

súdito, ta ['sudʒitu, ta] *m, f* subject.

sudoeste [su'dwɛʃtʃi] ◇ *adj* south-west. ◇ *m* south-west.

Suécia ['swɛsja] *n* Sweden.

sueco, ca ['swɛku, ka] ◇ *adj* Swedish. ◇ *m, f* Swede.

◆ **sueco** *m* [língua] Swedish.

suéter ['swɛte(x)] (*pl* **-es**) *m ou f* sweater.

suficiência [sufi'sjẽnsja] *f* sufficiency.

suficiente [sufi'sjẽntʃi] ◇ *adj* sufficient. ◇ *m*: **tenho o** ~ **até amanhã** I have enough until tomorrow.

sufixo [su'fiksu] *m* suffix.

suflê [su'fle] *m* soufflé.

sufocação [sufoka'sãw] (*pl* **-ões**) *f* **-1.** [ger] suffocation. **-2.** *fig* [opressão] oppression.

sufocante [sufo'kãntʃi] *adj* **-1.** [ger] suffocating. **-2.** *fig* [opressivo] oppressive.

sufocar [12] [sufo'ka(x)] ◇ *vt* **-1.** [asfixiar] to suffocate. **-2.** *fig* [oprimir] to oppress. **-3.** *fig* [debelar] to crush. ◇ *vi* [asfixiar-se] to be stifled.

◆ **sufocar-se** *vp* [asfixiar-se] to be suffocated.

sufoco [su'foku] *m* **-1.** [aflição] dread; **que** ~! how dreadful!; **ser um** ~ to be dreadful. **-2.** [dificuldade] hassle; **deixar alguém no** ~ to leave sb in the lurch; **passar (por) um** ~ to have a hard time.

sufrágio [su'fraʒju] *m* **-1.** [voto] vote; ~ **universal** universal suffrage. **-2.** [apoio] support.

sugar [14] [su'ga(x)] *vt* **-1.** [por sucção] to suck. **-2.** *fig* [extorquir] to extort; ~ **o sangue de alguém** to get every last drop of blood out of sb.

sugerir [57] [suʒe'ri(x)] *vt* to suggest; ~ **algo a alguém** to suggest sthg to sb.

sugestão [suʒeʃ'tãw] (*pl* **-ões**) *f* **-1.** [ger] suggestion; **dar uma** ~ to make a suggestion. **-2.** [evocação, insinuação] hint.

sugestionar [4] [suʒeʃtʃjo'na(x)] *vt*: ~ **algo a alguém** to inspire sb with sthg.

◆ **sugestionar-se** *vp*: ~ **se con algo** to experience sthg.

sugestionável [suʒeʃtʃjo'navew] (*pl* **-eis**) *adj* impressionable.

sugestivo, va [suʒeʃ'tʃivu, va] *adj* **-1.** [evocativo] evocative. **-2.** [insinuante] suggestive.

Suíça ['swisa] *n* Switzerland.

suíças ['swisaʃ] *fpl* sideburns.

suicida [swi'sida] ◇ *adj* suicidal. ◇ *mf* [pessoa] suicidal person.

suicidar-se [7] [swisi'daxsi] *vp* to commit suicide.

suicídio [swi'sidʒju] *m* suicide; **ser** ~ *fig* [ser arriscado] to be suicide.

suíço, ça ['swisu, sa] ◇ *adj* Swiss. ◇ *m, f* Swiss.

sui generis [swi'ʒeneris] *adj inv* unique, sui generis.

suingar [swĩŋ'ga(x)] *vi* to dance the swing.

suingue ['swĩŋgi] *m* swing.

suíno, na ['swinu, na] *adj* pig (*antes de subst*).

◆ **suíno** *m* [porco] pig.

suíte ['switʃi] *f* suite.

sujar [4] [su'ʒa(x)] ◇ *vt* **-1.** [tornar sujo] to dirty. **-2.** *fig* [macular] to disgrace. ◇ *vi fam* [dar errado] to go wrong.

◆ **sujar-se** *vp* **-1.** [tornar-se sujo] to get dirty. **-2.** *fig* [macular-se] to disgrace o.s.

sujeição [suʒej'sãw] *f* **-1.** [subordinação] subordination. **-2.** [submissão] submission.

sujeira [su'ʒejra] f -1. [coisa suja] dirt. -2. [estado] dirtiness; **a sala estava uma ~ quando cheguei** the room was a dirty mess when I arrived. -3. fam [bandalheira] dirty trick; **fazer uma ~ com alguém** to play a dirty trick on sb.

sujeitar [4] [suʒej'ta(x)] vt -1. [submeter]: **~ algo/ alguém a algo** to subject sthg/sb to sthg. -2. [apresentar]: **~ algo a algo** to submit sthg to sthg.
➡ **sujeitar-se** vp [submeter-se]: **~-se a algo** to subject o.s. to sthg.

sujeito, ta [su'ʒejtu, ta] <> adj: **~ a** subject to. <> m, f person.
➡ **sujeito** m GRAM subject.

sujo, ja ['suʒu, ʒa] <> adj -1. [imundo] dirty; **estar/ficar ~ com alguém** fig to be/fall out of favour with sb, to be in sb's bad books. -2. fig [mau-caráter] dishonest. <> m, f fig [pessoa] dishonest person.

sul ['suw] <> adj southern. <> m [região] south; **ao ~ de** to the south of.

sulcar [12] [suw'ka(x)] vt -1. [abrir sulcos em] to plough UK, to plow US. -2. [rosto] to line. -3. [singrar] to cut through.

sulco [suw'ku] m furrow.

sulfato [suw'fatu] m sulphate.

sulfúrico, ca [suw'furiku, ka] adj sulphuric.

sulista [su'liʃta] <> adj southern. <> mf southerner.

sultão, tana [suw'tãw, tãna] (pl -ões) m, f sultan (f sultana).

suma ['suma] ➡ **em suma** loc adv in short.

sumamente [suma'mẽntʃi] adv [extremamente] extremely.

sumário, ria [su'marju, rja] adj -1. [breve] brief. -2. [julgamento] summary. -3. [traje] skimpy.
➡ **sumário** m -1. [resumo] summary. -2. [no início de livro] table of contents. -3. JUR: **~ de culpa** indictment.

sumiço [su'misu] m disappearance; **dar (um) ~ em** to do away with.

sumidade [sumi'dadʒi] f: **~ (em algo)** authority (in sthg).

sumido, da [su'midu, da] adj -1. [desaparecido] vanished; **andar ~** to have disappeared. -2. [voz] low. -3. [apagado] faint.

sumir [61] [su'mi(x)] vi to disappear; **~ com algo** to disappear with sthg.

sumo, ma ['sumu, ma] adj extreme; **~ sacerdote** high priest.
➡ **sumo** m [suco] juice.

sundae ['sãndej] m sundae.

sunga ['sũnga] f [de banho] (swimming) trunks.

suntuoso, osa [sũn'twozu, ɔza] adj sumptuous.

suor ['swɔ(x)] (pl -es) m -1. [transpiração] sweat. -2. fig [trabalho]: **fiz esta casa com o meu próprio ~** I built this house by the sweat of my brow.

super ['supe(x)] fam <> adj [ótimo] super. <> interj super!

superabundante [ˌsuperabũn'dãntʃi] adj excessive.

superação [supera'sãw] (pl -ões) f overcoming; é

fundamental para a ~ do estresse it's essential for overcoming stress.

superado, da [supe'radu, da] adj -1. [ultrapassado] outmoded, old-fashioned. -2. [resolvido] overcome.

superalimentar [4] [4] [superalimẽn'ta(x)] vt -1. [animais, pacientes] to overfeed. -2. [indústria, sistema] to supercharge.

superaquecer [25] [ˌsuperake'se(x)] vt & vi to overheat.

superaquecimento [ˌsuperakesi'mẽntu] m overheating.

superar [4] [supe'ra(x)] vt -1. [sobrepujar]: **~ alguém (em algo)** to outdo sb (in sthg); **~ o inimigo** to defeat an enemy; **superou a todos em velocidade** he surpassed everyone in terms of speed. -2. [recorde] to beat. -3. [expectativa, objetivos etc] to exceed. -4. [ultrapassar] to surpass. -5. [resolver] to overcome.
➡ **superar-se** vp -1. [melhorar]: **~-se (em algo)** to excel o.s. (in sthg). -2. [exceder-se] to excel o.s.

superávit [supe'ravitʃi] m COM surplus.

supercílio [supex'silju] m eyebrow.

superdotado, da [ˌsupexdo'tadu, da] <> adj -1. [em inteligência] (exceptionally) gifted. -2. fam [sexualmente] well endowed. <> m, f [em inteligência] (exceptionally) gifted person.

superestimar [4] [ˌsupereʃtʃi'ma(x)] vt to overestimate.

superestrutura [ˌsupereʃtru'tura] f superstructure.

superficial [supexfi'sjaw] (pl -ais) adj superficial.

superficialidade [supexfisjali'dadʒi] f superficiality.

superfície [supex'fisji] f -1. [parte externa] surface. -2. [extensão] area.

supérfluo, lua [su'pɛxflu, lua] adj superfluous.
➡ **supérfluo** m [gasto]: **vamos cortar o ~** we're going to cut out what is superfluous.

super-homem [ˌsuper'ɔmẽ] (pl -ns) m superman.

superintendência [ˌsuperĩntẽn'dẽnsja] f [órgão] management.

superintendente [ˌsuperĩntẽn'dẽntʃi] mf manager.

superior [supe'rjo(x)] (pl -es) <> adj RELIG superior. <> m, f [em hierarquia] superior.
➡ **superior** adj -1. [de cima] upper. -2. [mais alto] higher. -3. [maior] greater. -4. [melhor] better; **~ a** better than. -5. [excelente] first class. -6. EDUC higher; **escola ~** senior school; **curso ~** degree course.

superioridade [superjori'dadʒi] f superiority.

superlativo, va [supexla'tʃivu] adj superlative.
➡ **superlativo** m GRAM superlative.

superlotado, da [ˌsupexlo'tadu, da] adj: **~ (de)** overcrowded (with).

superlotar [ˌsupexlo'ta(x)] vt to pack.

supermercado [ˌsupexmex'kadu] m supermarket.

superpotência [ˌsupexpoˈtẽnsja] f superpower.
superpovoado, da [ˌsupexpoˈvwadu, da] adj overpopulated.
superprodução [ˌsupexproduˈsãw] (pl -ões) f -1. ECON overproduction. -2. CINE mega-production.
superproteger [26] [ˌsupexproteˈʒe(x)] vt to over-protect.
supersensível [ˌsupexsẽnˈsivew] (pl -eis) adj hypersensitive.
supersônico, ca [ˌsupexˈsoniku, ka] adj supersonic.
superstição [supexʃtʃiˈsãw] (pl -ões) f superstition.
supersticioso, osa [superʃtʃiˈsjozu, ɔza] <> adj superstitious. <> m, f superstitious person.
supervisão [ˌsupexviˈzãw] (pl -ões) f -1. [ato] supervision. -2. [instância] supervisory authority.
supervisionar [4] [ˌsupexvizjoˈna(x)] vt to supervise.
supervisor, ra [ˌsupexviˈzo(x), ra] m, f supervisor.
supetão [supeˈtãw] ◆ **de supetão** loc adv all of a sudden.
suplantar [4] [suplãnˈta(x)] vt [sobrepujar]: ~ algo/alguém (em algo) to supplant sthg/sb (in sthg).
suplementar [4] [suplemẽnˈta(x)] <> adj extra. <> vt -1. [fornecer] to provide. -2. [servir de suplemento a] to supplement.
suplemento [supleˈmẽntul] m -1. [suprimento] supply. -2. [complemento] supplement; ~ policial police reinforcement. -3. JORN supplement.
suplente [suˈplẽntʃil] mf substitute.
súplica [ˈsuplika] f plea.
suplicar [12] [supliˈka(x)] <> vt to beg for; ~ algo a/de alguém to beg sb for sthg. <> vi to plead.
suplício [suˈplisjul] m torture.
supor [45] [suˈpo(x)] vt -1. [ger] to suppose; **suponho que sim** I suppose so; **suponhamos que** let's suppose (that), supposing. -2. [pressupor] to presuppose.
◆ **supor-se** vp to be assumed.
suportar [4] [supoxˈta(x)] vt -1. [sustentar] to support. -2. [resistir a] to withstand. -3. [tolerar] to bear.
suportável [supoxˈtavew] (pl -eis) adj bearable.
suporte [suˈpɔxtʃil] m support.
suposição [supoziˈsãw] (pl -ões) f [conjetura] assumption.
supositório [supoziˈtɔrjul] m suppository.
supostamente [supoʃtaˈmẽntʃil] adv supposedly.
suposto, osta [suˈpoʃtu, oʃta] <> pp ▷ supor. <> adj supposed.
◆ **suposto** m [pressuposto] assumption.
supracitado, da [suprasiˈtadu, da] <> adj aforementioned. <> m, f: o ~ the abovementioned.
supra-sumo [ˌsupraˈsumul] m: o ~ de algo [máximo] the culmination of sthg; [irôn] the height of sthg.
supremacia [supremaˈsia] f supremacy.

supremo, ma [suˈpremu, ma] adj -1. [amor, perdão, tribunal] supreme. -2. [qualidade] superior.
◆ **Supremo** m: **o Supremo** the Supreme Court.
supressão [supreˈsãw] (pl -ões) f -1. [corte] cutback. -2. [eliminação] deletion. -3. [abolição] abolition. -4. [omissão] suppression.
suprimento [supriˈmẽntul] m supply.
suprimir [6] [supriˈmi(x)] vt -1. [cortar] to cut back. -2. [eliminar] to delete. -3. [abolir] to abolish. -4. [omitir] to suppress.
suprir [6] [suˈpri(x)] <> vt -1. [prover]: ~ **alguém de** ou **com algo** to supply sb with sthg. -2. [substituir]: ~ algo **por algo** to substitute sthg with sthg. -3. [fazer as vezes de] to replace. -4. [preencher] to meet; ~ **a falta de algo** to make up for the lack of sthg; ~ **a falta de alguém** to make up for sb's absence. -5. [perfazer] to make up. <> vi -1. [fazer as vezes de]: ~ **por** to stand in for. -2. [preencher]: ~ **a** to meet; ~ **a falta** to make up for the lack.
supurar [4] [supuˈra(x)] vi to suppurate, to fester.
surdez [sux'deʒ] f deafness.
surdina [sux'dʒina] f MÚS mute.
◆ **em surdina** loc adv on the quiet.
surdo, da [ˈsuxdu, da] <> adj -1. MED deaf. -2. [som] muffled. -3. [consoante] voiceless. <> m, f [pessoa] deaf person.
◆ **surdo** m MÚS [de bateria] kind of drum.
surdo-mudo, surda-muda [ˈsuxdu'mudu, ˈsuxda'mudal] (mpl **surdos-mudos**, fpl **surdas-mudas**) <> adj [pessoa] deaf and dumb. <> m, f [pessoa] deaf mute.
surfar [4] [sux'fa(x)] vi to surf.
surfe [ˈsuxfil] m surfing.
surfista [sux'fiʃta] mf surfer.
surgimento [suxʒiˈmẽntul] m emergence.
surgir [52] [sux'ʒi(x)] vi -1. [aparecer] to appear. -2. [sobrevir] to arise; ~ **de** to come from.
Suriname [suri'nãmil] n Surinam.
surpreendente [surprjẽn'dẽntʃil] adj surprising.
surpreender [5] [surprjẽn'de(x)] <> vt -1. [ger] to surprise. -2. [apanhar em flagrante]: ~ **alguém (fazendo algo)** to catch sb (doing sthg). -3. [vislumbrar]: ~ **algo em algo** to glimpse sthg in sthg. <> vi [causar espanto] to be surprising.
◆ **surpreender-se** vp [espantar-se]: ~-se **de/com algo** to be amazed by/at sthg.
surpreso, sa [sux'prezu, za] <> pp ▷ surpreender. <> adj surprised.
◆ **surpresa** f -1. [espanto] amazement. -2. [imprevisto] surprise; **fazer uma surpresa para alguém** to give sb a surprise; **que surpresa!** [em encontro casual] what a surprise!; **ser uma surpresa** to be a surprise; **de surpresa** by surprise. -3. [presente] surprise.
surra [ˈsuxal] f thrashing; **dar uma** ~ **em alguém** to give sb a thrashing; **levar uma** ~ **(de alguém)** to get a thrashing (from sb).
surrado, da [su'xadu, da] adj -1. [espancado] beaten. -2. [muito usado] worn out.

surrar [4] [suˈxa(x)] *vt* -**1.** [espancar] to beat up. -**2.** *ESP* to thrash. -**3.** [usar muito] to wear out.

surrealismo [suxeaˈliʒmul *m* surrealism.

surrealista [suxeaˈliʃtal ◇ *adj* -**1.** *ARTE* surrealist. -**2.** *fig* [fora do normal] surreal. ◇ *mf* *ARTE* surrealist.

surrupiar [16] [suxuˈpja(x)] *vt* to steal.

sursis [suxˈsil *m* (*inv*) *JUR* suspended sentence.

surtar [surˈta(x)] *vi fam* to go berserk.

surtir [6] [suxˈtʃi(x)] ◇ *vt* [produzir] to bring about; ~ **efeito** to be effective. ◇ *vi* [funcionar] to work out.

surto [ˈsuxtul *m* -**1.** [irrupção] outburst. -**2.** [de doença] outbreak. -**3.** [de progresso, industrialização] surge.

suscetibilidade [susetʃibiliˈdadʒil *f* -**1.** [melindre] touchiness. -**2.** [propensão] susceptibility.

suscetível [suseˈtʃivɛw] (*pl* -**eis**) *adj* -**1.** [melindroso] sensitive. -**2.** [propenso]: ~ **a** susceptible to; ~ **de** liable to.

suscitar [4] [susiˈta(x)] *vt* -**1.** [provocar] to provoke. -**2.** [fazer surgir] to arouse. -**3.** [despertar] to awaken.

suspeição [suʃpejˈsãw] (*pl* -**ões**) *f* suspicion.

suspeita [suʃˈpejtal *f* ⊳ **suspeito**.

suspeitar [4] [suʃpejˈta(x)] ◇ *vt* [crer, supor]: ~ **que** to suspect (that). ◇ *vi* [desconfiar]: ~ **de alguém** to suspect sb; ~ **de que** to suspect that.

suspeito, ta [suʃˈpejtu, tal ◇ *adj* -**1.** [que desperta suspeita] suspicious. -**2.** [de ser tendencioso]: **sou ~ para falar, mas ...** I'm biased in saying this but ... ◇ *m, f* [pessoa]: ~ (**de algo**) suspect (of sthg).

➤ **suspeita** *f* suspicion; **estar com suspeita de algo** to be suspected of having sthg.

suspender [6] [suʃpẽnˈde(x)] *vt* -**1.** [ger] to suspend. -**2.** [levantar] to lift up. -**3.** [adiar] to postpone. -**4.** [encomenda] to cancel.

suspensão [suʃpẽnˈsãw] (*pl* -**ões**) *f* -**1.** [ger] suspension. -**2.** [adiamento] postponement. -**3.** [de encomenda] cancellation. -**4.** [de sanções] lifting.

suspense [suʃˈpẽnsil *m* suspense; **estamos assistindo um (filme de)** ~ we are watching a thriller; **fazer** ~ to create suspense.

suspenso, sa [suʃˈpẽnsu, sal ◇ *pp* ⊳ **suspender**. ◇ *adj* -**1.** [ger] suspended. -**2.** [levantado] held up. -**3.** [adiado] postponed. -**4.** [encomenda] cancelled. -**5.** [sanções] lifted.

suspensórios [suʃpẽnˈsɔrjuʃl *mpl* braces *UK*, suspenders *US*.

suspirar [4] [suʃpiˈra(x)] *vi* to sigh; ~ **de alívio** to sigh with relief; ~ **por algo** to long for sthg.

suspiro [suʃˈpirul *m* -**1.** [aspiração] sigh; **dar um** ~ to give a sigh. -**2.** *CULIN* meringue.

sussurrar [4] [susuˈxa(x)] ◇ *vt & vi* to whisper.

sussurro [suˈsuxul *m* whisper.

sustância [suʃˈtãnsjal *f* -**1.** [vigor] strength. -**2.** [de comida] sustenance.

sustar [4] [suʃˈta(x)] *vt & vi* [deter-se] to stop.

sustentáculo [suʃtẽnˈtakulul *m* -**1.** [base] support. -**2.** *fig* [base] mainstay.

sustentar [4] [suʃtẽnˈta(x)] *vt* -**1.** [ger] to support. -**2.** [afirmar]: ~ **que** to maintain (that). -**3.** [defender] to uphold.

➤ **sustentar-se** *vp* -**1.** [ger] to support o.s.; ~ -**se no ar** to hover. -**2.** [alimentar-se] to sustain o.s.

sustento [suʃˈtẽntul *m* -**1.** [alimento] sustenance. -**2.** [manutenção] support.

suster [1] [suʃˈte(x)] *vt* -**1.** [sustentar] to hold up. -**2.** [conter] to keep in check.

➤ **suster-se** *vp* -**1.** [sustentar-se] to be supported. -**2.** [conter-se] to contain o.s. -**3.** [de pé] to hold o.s. up.

susto [ˈsuʃtul *m* fright; **dar um** ~ **em alguém** to give sb a fright; **levar** *ou* **tomar um** ~ to get a fright; **que** ~! what a fright!

sutiã [suˈtʃjãl *m* bra.

sutil [suˈtʃiwl (*pl* -**is**) *adj* subtle.

sutileza [sutʃiˈlezal *f* subtlety.

sutilmente [sutʃiwˈmẽntʃil *adv* subtly.

Suva [ˈsuval *n* Suva.

suvenir [suveˈni(x)l *m* souvenir.

t, T *m* [letra] t, T.

tá [ˈtal *fam* = **está**.

tabacaria [tabakaˈrial *f* tobacconist's.

tabaco [taˈbakul *m* tobacco.

tabagismo [tabaˈʒiʒmul *m* -**1.** [uso do tabaco] nicotine addiction. -**2.** [intoxicação] nicotine poisoning.

tabefe [taˈbɛfil *m fam* slap; **dar um** ~ **em alguém** to slap sb; **levar um** ~ **de alguém** to be slapped by sb.

tabela [taˈbɛlal *f* -**1.** [quadro] table. -**2.** [lista] list; ~ **de preços** price list. -**3.: por** ~ [indiretamente] indirectly. -**4.** *loc*: **estar caindo pelas** ~**s** [estar fatigado, adoentado] to feel out of sorts; [estar em más condições] to be in a bad way.

tabelado, da [tabeˈladu, dal *adj* -**1.** [produtos] price-controlled. -**2.** [preços] controlled. -**3.** [dados] listed.

tabelamento [tabelaˈmẽntul *m* [controle de preços]: ~ **de preços** price control.

tabelar [4] [tabeˈla(x)] *vt* -**1.** [fixar o preço de] to set the price of. -**2.** [dados] to list.

tabelião, liã [tabeˈljãw, ljãl (*mpl* -**ães**, *fpl* -**s**) *m, f* notary public.

taberna [ta'bɛxna] *f* public house *UK*, tavern *US*.

tabique [ta'biki] *m* [parede divisória] dividing wall.

tablado [ta'bladu] *m* -**1.** [palco] stage. -**2.** [palanque] stand. -**3.** [estrado] dais.

tablete [ta'blɛtʃi] *m* -**1.** [de chocolate] bar. -**2.** [de manteiga] pat. -**3.** [medicamento] tablet.

tablóide [ta'blɔjdʒi] *m* tabloid.

tabu [ta'bu] <> *adj* taboo. <> *m* taboo.

tábua ['tabwa] *f* -**1.** [de madeira] board; ~ **corrida** *ARQUIT* wooden floor; ~ **de passar roupa** ironing board; ~ **de salvação** *fig* last resort. -**2.** [de mesa] leaf. -**3.** *MAT* table.

tabuada [ta'bwada] *f* -**1.** [tabela] multiplication table, times table. -**2.** [livro] book of tables.

tabulador [tabula'do(x)] *m* tab key.

tabular [4] [tabu'la(x)] *vt* to tabulate.

tabuleiro [tabu'lejru] *m* -**1.** [bandeja] tray. -**2.** *CULIN* baking tray. -**3.** [de jogo] board.

tabuleta [tabu'leta] *f* notice board.

taça ['tasa] *f* -**1.** [copo] glass. -**2.** [troféu] cup.

tacada [ta'kada] *f* -**1.** *ESP* strike. -**2.** *fig*: **de uma ~ só** [de uma só vez] in one go.

tacanho, nha [ta'kãɲu, ɲa] *adj* -**1.** [baixo] short. -**2.** [mesquinho] mean. -**3.** *fig* [sem visão] obtuse.

tacar [12] [ta'ka(x)] *vt* -**1.** *ESP* to strike. -**2.** [atirar] to hurl; ~ **um soco em alguém** to throw a punch at sb.

tacha ['taʃa] *f* -**1.** [prego] tack. -**2.** [em roupa, cadeira] stud.

tachar [4] [ta'ʃa(x)] *vt*: ~ **alguém/algo de algo** to brand sb/sth as sthg.

tacheado, da [ta'ʃjadu, da] *adj* studded.

tachinha [ta'ʃiɲa] *f* drawing pin *UK*, thumbtack *US*.

tacho ['taʃu] *m* [recipiente] pan, dish.

tácito, ta ['tasitu, ta] *adj* [implícito] tacit.

taciturno, na [tasi'tuxnu, na] *adj* [introverso, sério] taciturn.

taco ['taku] *m* -**1.** [*ESP* - bilhar] cue; [- golfe] club; [- hóquei] stick; [- pólo] mallet. -**2.** [de assoalho] block.

tadinho, nha [ta'dʒiɲu, ɲa] *interj fam* ⊳ **coitado**.

tafetá [tafe'ta] *m* taffeta.

tagarela [taga'rɛla] <> *adj* prattling, chattering. <> *mf* chatterbox.

tagarelar [4] [tagare'la(x)] *vi* to prattle, to chatter.

tagarelice [tagare'lisi] *f* prattle, chatter.

tailandês, esa [tajlãn'deʃ, eza] <> *adj* Thai. <> *m, f* Thai.
 ⇒ **tailandês** *m* [língua] Thai.

Tailândia [taj'lãndʒja] *n* Thailand.

tailleur [taj'ɛ(x)] *m* (woman's) suit.

tainha [ta'iɲa] *f* mullet.

taipa ['tajpa] *f*: **casa de ~** mud hut; **parede de ~** mud wall.

Taipei [taj'pej] *n* Taipei.

tais [tajʃ] *pl* ⊳ **tal**.

Taiti [taj'tʃi] *n* Tahiti.

Taiwan [taj'wã] *n* Taiwan.

taiwanês, esa [tajwãneʃ, eza] <> *adj* Taiwanese. <> *m, f* Taiwanese.

tal ['taw] (*pl* **tais**) <> *adj* -**1.** [ger] such; **eu nunca diria ~ coisa** I would never say such a thing; **não me misturo com tais pessoas** I don't mix with such people; **isso nunca teve ~ repercussão** this never had such an effect; **a dor foi ~, que desmaiei** the pain was such that I fainted. -**2.** [este, aquele]: **não existe ~ hotel** there is no such hotel; **a ~ respeito** on that subject; **o ~ vizinho** that neighbour. -**3.** [valor indeterminado]: **na avenida ~** in such and such street. -**4.** [introduz um exemplo ou uma enumeração]: ~ **como** such as. -**5.** [introduz uma comparação]: ~ **qual** just like; ~ **pai, ~ filho** like father, like son. <> *pron indef* [isto, aquilo]: **por ~** for that reason; **fulano de ~** Joe Bloggs. <> *mf*: **ele se acha o ~** he thinks he's it.
 ➡ **que tal** *loc* [pedindo opinião]: **que ~?** what do you think?; **que ~ (tomarmos) um drinque?** what about (us having) a drink?
 ➡ **e tal** *loc*: **ele é simpático e ~, mas ineficiente** he's nice and all that, but inefficient; **ela tem trinta e ~ anos** she's thirty something.
 ➡ **um tal de** *loc*: **um ~ de João** John what's-his-name; **foi um ~ de gente reclamar** there were loads of people complaining.
 ➡ **a tal ponto que** *loc conj* such a point that.
 ➡ **de tal maneira que** *loc conj* in such a way that.

tala ['tala] *f MED* splint.

talão [ta'lãw] (*pl* -**ões**) *m* -**1.** [bloco] book; ~ **de cheques** cheque book *UK*, check book *US*. -**2.** [canhoto] stub.

talco ['tawku] *m* -**1.** [material] talc. -**2.** [produto de higiene] talcum powder.

talento [ta'lẽntu] *m* -**1.** [aptidão] ability; **uma pessoa de ~** a very able person. -**2.** [pessoa talentosa] talented person.

talentoso, osa [talẽn'tozu, ɔza] *adj* talented.

talhado, da [ta'ʎadu, da] *adj* -**1.** [leite] curdled. -**2.** [madeira] carved. -**3.** [apropriado] appropriate. -**4.** [cortado]: **um terno bem ~** a well-cut suit.

talhar [4] [ta'ʎa(x)] <> *vt* [madeira] to carve. <> *vi* [leite] to curdle.

talharim [taʎa'rĩ] (*pl* -**ns**) *m* tagliatelle.

talhe ['taʎi] *m* [de roupa] cut.

talher [ta'ʎe(x)] (*pl* -**es**) *m* place setting; ~ **es** cutlery (*sg*).

talho ['taʎu] *m* [corte] cut.

talismã [taliʒ'mã] *m* talisman.

talo ['talu] *m BOT* stalk, stem.

talude [ta'ludʒi] *m* slope.

taludo, da [ta'ludu, da] *adj* -**1.** [corpulento - adulto] stout; [- criança] plump. -**2.** [de talo resistente] strong-stalked, thick-stemmed.

talvez [taw'veʒ] *adv* maybe, perhaps; ~ **ele esteja certo** maybe he is right.

tamanco [ta'mãŋku] *m* clog.

tamanduá [tamãn'dwa] *m* anteater.

tamanho, nha [ta'mãɲu, ɲa] *adj* -**1.** [tão grande]: **seu erro foi ~ que ele pediu desculpas** his mistake was so great he apologized. **-2.** [tão notável]: **ele é um ~ escritor** he is such a great author.

➤ **tamanho** *m* size; **de que ~ é?** what size is it?; **em ~ natural** life-size, life-sized; **um prédio que não tem ~** *ou* **do ~ de um bonde** *fam* an enormous building.

tamanho-família [ta͵mãɲufaˈmilja] *adj inv* **-1.** [garrafa, caixa] family-size. **-2.** *fig* [casa, carro] family *(antes de subst)*.

tâmara [ˈtãmara] *f* date.

tamarindo [tamaˈrĩdu] *m* tamarind.

também [tãˈbẽ] *adv* **-1.** [igualmente] too; **ele ~ é inteligente** he's intelligent, too, he too is intelligent; **quero um café – eu ~** I want a coffee – so do I *ou* me too; **sou do Rio, e ele ~** é I'm from Rio, and so is he; **ela não viajou, e eu ~ não** she didn't go, and neither did I; **ele não fala inglês, e eu ~ não** he doesn't speak English, and neither do I. **-2.** [além disso] too. ⬦ *interj* [não é de surpreender] hardly surprising!

tambor [tãˈbo(x)] *(pl -es) m* drum.

tamborete [tãboˈretʃi] *m* [banco] stool.

tamborilar [4] [tãboriˈla(x)] *vi* [tocar] to drum.

tamborim [tãboˈrĩ] *(pl -ns) m* tambourine.

Tâmisa [ˈtãmiza] *n*: **o (rio) ~** the (river) Thames.

tampa [ˈtãpa] *f* **-1.** [de caixa, privada, panela] lid. **-2.** [de garrafa] cap.

tampado, da [tãˈpadu, da] *adj*: **a panela está tampada** the saucepan is covered.

tampão [tãˈpãw] *(pl -ões) m* **-1.** [de pia, banheira] plug. **-2.** *MED* compress. **-3.** [vaginal] tampon. **-4.** [de poço, esgoto] bung.

tampar [4] [tãˈpa(x)] *vt* **-1.** [com tampa - ger] to put a lid on; [- em garrafa] to put a top on. **-2.** [tapar] to cover.

tampinha [tãˈpiɲa] ⬦ *f* [tampa pequena] bottle top. ⬦ *mf fam* [pessoa baixa] dumpy person.

tampo [ˈtãpu] *m* **-1.** [de privada] seat, lid. **-2.** [de mesa] top.

tampouco [͵tãˈpoku] *adv*: **não foi à reunião e ~ justificou sua ausência** he didn't turn up at the meeting, nor did he justify his absence.

Tananarive [tananaˈrivi] *n* Antananarivo.

tanga [ˈtãga] *f* **-1.** [roupa indígena] loincloth. **-2.** [biquíni] G-string.

Tanganica [tãgaˈnika] *n*: **o (lago) ~** Lake Tanganyika.

tangente [tãˈʒẽtʃi] *f* tangent; **escapar pela ~** *fig* to narrowly escape.

tanger [26] [tãˈʒe(x)] ⬦ *vt* [instrumento] to play; [sinos] to ring. ⬦ *vi* **-1.** [sinos] to ring. **-2.** [dizer respeito]: **no que tange a** with regard to, as regards.

tangerina [tãʒeˈrina] *f* tangerine.

tangível [tãˈʒivew] *(pl -eis) adj fig* **-1.** [alcançável] attainable. **-2.** [real] tangible.

tango [ˈtãgu] *m* tango.

tanque [ˈtãki] *m* **-1.** *MIL* tank. **-2.** [de lavar roupa] washtub. **-3.** [reservatório] reservoir.

tantã [tãˈtã] *adj fam* [maluco] crazy.

tanto, ta [ˈtãtu, ta] ⬦ *adj* **-1.** [tão grande] so much; **~ tempo** so much time. **-2.** [tão numeroso] so many; **ela tem trinta e ~s anos** he's thirty something; **~ ... quanto** as many ... as; **tanta gente** so many people. ⬦ *pron* so much; **pode ficar com o lápis, já tenho ~s** you can keep the pencil, I already have so many.

➤ **tanto** ⬦ *m*: **um ~ de** some. ⬦ *adv* so much; **ela trabalha ~** she works so much; **~ quanto** as much as; **~ ... como** both ... and; **nem ~** assim not that much; **~ melhor** all the better; **se ~** if that.

➤ **tantas** *fpl*: **às tantas** the early hours of the morning.

➤ **e tanto** *loc adj*: **é um professor e ~** he's an amazing teacher.

➤ **tanto que** *loc conj* so much so that.

➤ **tanto faz** *loc adv* it's all the same.

➤ **um tanto (ou quanto)** *loc adv*: **uma pessoa um ~ (ou quanto) difícil** a somewhat difficult person.

Tanzânia [tãˈzãnja] *n* Tanzania.

tão [tãw] *adv* so; **~ ... quanto** as... as; **~ logo** as soon as.

tão-só [tãwˈsɔ] *adv* only.

tão-somente [tãwsɔˈmẽtʃi] *adv* only.

tapa [ˈtapa] *m* [tabefe] slap; **dar um ~ em alguém** to slap sb; **levar um ~ de alguém** to be slapped by sb; **no ~** by force.

tapado, da [taˈpadu, da] *adj* **-1.** [ger] covered. **-2.** *fam* [pessoa] thick.

tapar [4] [taˈpa(x)] *vt* **-1.** [ger] to cover. **-2.** [garrafa] to put the lid back on.

tapeação [tapjaˈsãw] *(pl -ões) f* **-1.** [engano] hoax. **-2.** [reparo, limpeza malfeitos] quick going-over.

tapear [15] [taˈpja(x)] *vt* [enganar] to fool.

tapeçaria [tapesaˈria] *f* **-1.** [tapete - de chão] rug; [- de parede] tapestry, wall hanging. **-2.** [loja] carpet shop. **-3.** [arte - de chão] rug-making; [- de parede] tapestry.

tapeceiro, ra [tapeˈsejru, ra] *m, f* **-1.** [vendedor] *seller of carpets and soft furnishings.* **-2.** [fabricante] *manufacturer of carpets and soft furnishings.*

tapete [taˈpetʃi] *m* **-1.** [solto] rug; **~ de banheiro** bathmat. **-2.** [fixo] carpet.

tapioca [taˈpjɔka] *f* tapioca.

tapume [taˈpumi] *m* **-1.** [cerca de sebe] hedge. **-2.** [anteparo de madeira] fence. **-3.** [parede divisória] partition.

taquara [taˈkwara] *f BOT* bamboo; **voz de ~ rachada** gravelly voice.

taquicardia [takikaxˈdʒia] *f* palpitations *(pl)*, tachycardia.

taquigrafar [4] [takigraˈfa(x)] ⬦ *vt* to take shorthand. ⬦ *vi* to write in shorthand.

taquigrafia [takigraˈfia] *f* shorthand *UK*, stenography *US*.

taquígrafo, fa [taˈkigrafu, fa] *m, f* shorthand typist *UK*, stenographer *US*.

tara [ˈtara] *f PSIC* mania.

tarado, da [ta'radu, da] <> *adj* **-1.** [desequilibrado] unbalanced. **-2.** [sexualmente] depraved. **-3.** *fam fig* [fascinado]: **ser ~ por** to be mad about. <> *m, f* [desequilibrado] maniac; **~ (sexual)** (sexual) pervert.

tarar [4] [ta'ra(x)] *vi fam*: **~ por alguém/algo** to fall madly in love with sb/sthg.

tardar [4] [tax'da(x)] <> *vt* [retardar] to put off. <> *vi* [demorar-se, vir tarde] to delay; **~ a fazer algo** to take a long time to do sthg; **o mais ~** at the latest; **sem mais ~** without further delay.

tarde ['taxdʒi] <> *f* afternoon; **às cinco da ~** at five in the afternoon; **boa ~!** good afternoon!; **de** *ou* **à ~** in the afternoon; **hoje à ~** this afternoon; **ontem à ~** yesterday afternoon. <> *adv* late; **~ demais** too late; **mais ~** later; **antes ~ do que nunca** better late than never; **~ da noite** late at night.

tardinha [tax'dʒiɲa] *f* late afternoon; **à** *ou* **de ~** late in the afternoon.

tardio, dia [tax'dʒiu, dʒia] *adj* late.

tarefa [ta'refa] *f* **-1.** [trabalho em geral] task. **-2.** [empreitada] job.

tarifa [ta'rifa] *f* **-1.** [preço - de gás, água] tariff; **~ alfandegária** customs duty; [- de transporte] fare. **-2.** [tabela de preços] price list.

tarifar [4] [tari'fa(x)] *vt* to price.

tarifaço [tari'fasu] *m general price rise in publicly-owned utilities.*

tarimba [ta'rĩba] *f fig* [experiência] experience; **ter ~ (em/como algo)** to be an old hand at/as sthg.

tarimbado, da [tarĩ'badu, da] *adj*: **~ (em)** highly-experienced (in).

tarô [ta'ro] *m* tarot.

tarrafa [ta'xafa] *f* fishing net.

tarraxa [ta'xaʃa] *f* [rosca] screw.

tartaruga [taxta'ruga] *f* **-1.** [grande] turtle. **-2.** [pequena] tortoise; **pente de ~** tortoiseshell comb.

tascar [12] [taʃ'ka(x)] *vt fam*: **~ algo em alguém** to plant sthg on sb.

tasco ['taʃku] *m fam* bit.

Tasmânia [taʒ'mãnja] *n* Tasmania.

tataraneto, ta [tatara'nɛtu] *m* great-great-great-grandson (*f* -granddaughter).

tataravô, vó [tatara'vo, vɔ] *m, f* great-great grandfather (*f* -grandmother).

tatear [15] [ta'tʃja(x)] <> *vt* to feel. <> *vi* to feel one's way.

táteis ['tatejʃ] *pl* ⊳ **tátil**.

tatibitate [tatʃibi'tatʃi] *adj* [que troca consoantes - devido à idade] stumbling; [- por defeito] stammering.

tático, ca ['tatʃiku, ka] *adj* tactical.

➡ **tática** *f* **-1.** MIL tactic. **-2.** [ciência] tactics *(sg).* **-3.** *fam* [plano de ação] strategy.

tátil ['tatʃiw] (*pl* -eis) *adj* tactile.

tato ['tatu] *m* **-1.** [ger] touch. **-2.** *fig* [cautela]: **ter ~** to be tactful.

tatu [ta'tu] *m* armadillo.

tatuador, ra [tatwa'do(x), ra] *m, f* tattooist.

tatuagem [ta'twaʒẽ] (*pl* -ns) *f* **-1.** [desenho] tattoo. **-2.** [técnica] tattooing.

tatuar [4] [ta'twa(x)] *vt* to tattoo.

taurino, na [tawri'nu, na] <> *adj* ASTRO Taurus. <> *m, f* ASTRO Taurus.

tautologia [tawtolo'ʒia] *f* tautology.

taxa ['taʃa] *f* **-1.** [ger] rate; **~ de natalidade/crescimento** birth/growth rate; **~ de câmbio** exchange rate; **~ de conversão** COM conversion rate; **~ de juros** interest rate; **~ de retorno** COM rate of return; **~ bancária** bank rate; **~ fixa** COM flat rate; **~ de inscrição** registration fee; **~ de matrícula** enrolment fee. **-2.** [imposto] tax; **~ de embarque** airport tax; **~ de exportação** COM export duty; **~ rodoviária** road tax.

taxação [taʃa'sãw] *f* **-1.** [de impostos] taxation. **-2.** [de preços] fixing.

taxar [4] [ta'ʃa(x)] *vt* **-1.** [onerar com imposto] to tax. **-2.** [fixar o preço de] to fix.

taxativo, va [taʃa'tʃivu, va] *adj* [categórico] categorical; **ser ~ (em algo)** to be categorical (about sthg).

táxi ['taksi] *m* taxi UK, cab US; **~ aéreo** air taxi.

taxiar [tak'sja(x)] *vi* to taxi.

taxímetro [tak'simetru] *m* taxi meter.

taxinomia [taksino'mia] *f* taxonomy.

taxista [tak'siʃta] *mf* taxi driver UK, cab driver US.

tchã ['tʃã] *m fam* [charme] charm.

tchau ['tʃaw] *interj fam* bye, ciao.

tcheco, ca ['tʃɛku, ka] <> *adj* Czech. <> *m, f* Czech.

➡ **tcheco** *m* [língua] Czech.

tchecoslovaco, ca [tʃɛkoʒlo'vaku, ka] <> *adj* Czechoslovakian. <> *m, f* Czechoslovak.

Tchecoslováquia [tʃɛkoʒlo'vakja] *n* Czechoslovakia.

te ['tʃi] *pron pess* **-1.** [você] you. **-2.** [a, para, em você]: **~ mandei duas cartas** I sent you two letters.

tear [te'a(x)] (*pl* -es) *m* loom.

teatral [tʃja'traw] (*pl* -ais) *adj* **-1.** [ger] theatre (*antes de subst*) UK, theater (*antes de subst*) US. **-2.** *fig* [pessoa, comportamento] theatrical.

teatro ['tʃjatru] *m* **-1.** [ger] theatre UK, theater US; **~ de arena** theatre in the round; **~ de bolso** small theatre; **peça de ~** stage play; **~ de marionetes** puppet theatre; **~ rebolado** burlesque; **~ de variedades** variety show. **-2.** [LITER - gênero] playwriting; [- obras de um autor] plays *(pl).* **-3.** [curso] drama. **-4.** MIL: **~ de operações** theatre of war UK. **-5.** *fig* [palco] scene. **-6.** *fig*: **fazer ~** [exagerar] to dramatize.

teatrólogo, ga [tʃja'trɔlogu, ga] *m, f* dramatist.

teatro-revista [ˌtʃjatruxe' viʃta] (*pl* teatros-revista) *m* theatre review UK, theater review US.

tecelagem [tese'laʒẽ] (*pl* -ns) *f* weaving.

tecelão, lã [tese'lãw, lã] (*mpl* -ões, *fpl* -s) *m, f* weaver.

tecer [25] [te'se(x)] vt **-1.** [ger] to weave. **-2.** fig [fazer]: ~ **elogios a alguém/algo** to praise sb/sthg; ~ **intrigas sobre/contra alguém** to create conspiracies about/against sb.

tecido [te'sidu] m **-1.** [têxtil] material. **-2.** BIOL & ANAT tissue.

tecla ['tɛkla] f **-1.** [ger] key; ~ **de função** function key; ~ **de saída** exit key; ~ **de tabulação** tab key. **-2.** [de máquina de calcular, de gravador] button. **-3.** loc: **bater na mesma** ~ fig to harp on about sthg.

tecladista [tekla'dʒiʃta] mf MÚS keyboard player.

teclado [te'kladu] m keyboard.

teclar [4] ['tekla(x)] <> vt to key (in) <> vi COMPUT: ~ **(com alguém)** to chat (with sb); **você quer** ~? do you want to chat?

técnica ['tɛknika] f ▷ **técnico**.

tecnicamente [tɛknika'mẽntʃil adv technically.

técnico, ca ['tɛkniku, kal <> adj technical. <> m, f **-1.** [profissional] technician. **-2.** [especialista] expert. **-3.** ESP coach.

➡ **técnica** f **-1.** [procedimentos, métodos] technique. **-2.** [conhecimento prático] skill.

tecnicolor [tekni'kɔlo(x)] adj: **em** ~ (in) technicolour UK, (in) technicolor US.

tecnocrata [tekno'krata] mf technocrat.

tecnologia [tɛknolo'ʒia] f technology; ~ **de ponta** latest technology.

tecnológico, ca [tɛkno'lɔʒiku, kal adj technological.

teco ['tɛku] m [batida de uma bola em outra] hit; **dar um** ~ **em** [em bola] to hit; fig [em pessoa] to be angry with.

teco-teco [,tɛku'tɛku] (pl teco-tecos) m light aircraft.

tectônico, ca [katek'toniku, kal adj tectonic.

➡ **tectônica** f GEOL tectonics (sg).

tédio ['tɛdʒiu] m tedium.

tedioso, osa [te'dʒjozu, ɔzal adj tedious.

Teerã [tee'rãl n Teheran.

Tegucigalpa [tegusi'kawpa] n Tegucigalpa.

teia ['tejal f **-1.** [ger] web; ~ **de aranha** spider's web, cobweb. **-2.** fig [organização]: ~ **de espionagem** espionage network.

teima ['tejma] f obstinacy.

teimar [4] [tej'ma(x)] <> vt: ~ **que** to insist that. <> vi [insistir] to persist; ~ **em fazer algo** to persist in doing sthg.

teimosia [tejmo'zia] f stubborness; ~ **em fazer algo** obstinacy in doing sthg.

teimoso, osa [tej'mozu, ɔzal adj **-1.** [adulto] obstinate. **-2.** [criança] stubborn.

teipe ['tejpil m magnetic tape.

Tejo ['tɛʒul n: **o (rio)** ~ the (river) Tagus.

tel. [tell (abrev de **telefone**) m tel.

tela ['tɛlal f **-1.** [ger] canvas. **-2.** [de arame] wire netting. **-3.** CINE, COMPUT & TV screen.

telão [te'lãwl (pl -ões) m big screen.

tele ['tɛlel pref tele.

telecomandar [4] [tɛlekomãn'da(x)] vt to operate by remote control.

telecomando [tɛleko'mãndul m remote control.

telecomunicação [tɛlekomunika'sawl (pl -ões) f telecommunication.

➡ **telecomunicações** fpl telecommunications.

teleconferência [telekõnferẽnsjal f teleconference.

telecurso [tɛle'kuxsul m television course.

teleférico [tele'fɛrikul m **-1.** [de esqui] ski lift. **-2.** [bondinho] cable car.

telefonar [4] [telefo'na(x)] vi to (tele)phone, to call; ~ **para alguém** to (tele)phone sb, to call sb.

telefone [tele'fonil m **-1.** [aparelho, linha] (tele)phone; **estar/falar ao** ~ to be on the phone; ~ **celular** mobile phone UK, cellphone US; ~ **sem fio** cordless phone; ~ **público** public (tele)phone. **-2.** [número] (tele)phone number.

telefonema [telefo'nemal m (tele)phone call; **dar um** ~ **para alguém/algum lugar** to make a call to sb/somewhere.

telefonia [telefo'nial f [sistema] telephone system.

telefônico, ca [tele'foniku, kal adj telephone (antes de subst); **chamada telefônica** (tele)phone call.

telefonista [telefo'niʃtal mf telephonist.

telefoto [tele'fɔtul f telephoto.

telegrafar [4] [telegra'fa(x)] <> vt to telegraph. <> vi to telegraph; ~ **a alguém** to telegraph sb.

telegrafia [telegra'fial f telegraphy.

telegráfico, ca [tele'grafiku, kal adj telegraphic.

telegrafista [telegra'fiʃtal mf telegraphist.

telégrafo [te'lɛgraful m **-1.** [aparelho] telegraph. **-2.** [local] telegraph office.

telegrama [tele'grãmal m telegram; **passar um** ~ to send a telegram; ~ **fonado** telemessage.

teleguiado, da [tɛle'gjadu, dal adj **-1.** [guiado a distância] remote-controlled; **míssil** ~ guided missile. **-2.** fig [influenciado] (easily) led.

teleguiar [16] [tɛle'gja(x)] vt to operate by remote control.

telejornal [,tɛleʒox'nawl (pl -ais) m TV television news (sg).

telejornalismo [tɛleʒoxna'liʒmul m television journalism.

telenovela [,tɛleno'vɛlal f TV soap opera.

TELENOVELA

Telenovelas are very popular; episodes of these dramatized stories are broadcast daily on prime-time television. Although the main plot usually revolves around a love interest, the telenovelas, shown nationwide, often address important social issues. Having reached high technical standards, Brazilian telenovelas are currently exported to around 120 countries.

---

teleobjetiva [,tɛljobʒe'tʃival f telephoto lens.

telepatia [telepa'tʃial f telepathy; **por** ~ by telepathy.

telepático, ca [tele'patʃiku, kal adj telepathic.

teleprocessamento [tɛleprosesa'mẽntul m teleprocessing.

telescópico, ca [teleʃ'kɔpiku, ka] adj telescopic.

telescópio [teleʃ'kɔpju] m telescope.

telespectador, ra [tɛlɛʃpekta'do(x), ra] <> adj viewing. <> m, f viewer.

teletexto [tɛle'teʃtu] m teletext.

teletipo [tɛle'tʃipu] m teletype.

televisão [televi'zãw] (pl -ões) f -1. [ger] television; ~ a cabo cable television; ~ a cores colour television. -2. [empresa] television company.

televisionar [4] [televizjo'na(x)] vt to televise.

televisivo, va [televi'zivu, va] adj television (antes de subst).

televisor [televi'zo(x)] (pl -es) m television.

telex [tɛ'lɛkiʃ] (pl -es) m telex; passar um ~ to send a telex.

telha ['teʎa] f -1. [de casa etc] tile. -2. fam fig [mente]: dar na ~ de alguém fazer algo to get it into sb's head to do sthg; ter uma ~ de menos to have a screw loose.

telhado [te'ʎadu] m roof.

telha-vã [ˌteʎa'vã] (pl telhas-vãs) f unlined roof.

telnet [tel'netji] (pl -s) f COMPUT telnet.

telões [tɛ'lõjʃ] pl = telão.

tema ['tema] m -1. [assunto - de redação, romance] theme; [- de palestra] subject. -2. MÚS theme. -3. [dever de casa] homework.

temático, ca [te'matʃiku, ka] adj thematic.
  ◆ **temática** f thematics (sg).

temer [5] [te'me(x)] <> vt to fear; ~ que to fear that; ~ fazer algo to be afraid to do sthg, to be afraid of doing sthg. <> vi to be afraid; ~ por alguém/algo to fear for sb/sthg.

temerário, ria [teme'rarju, rja] adj -1. [audacioso, destemido] fearless. -2. [perigoso, arriscado] reckless.

temeridade [temeri'dadʒi] f: ser uma ~ [ser arriscado, perigoso] to be a foolhardy act; [ser atemorizador] to be terrifying.

temeroso, osa [teme'rozu, ɔza] adj -1. [medroso, receoso] afraid. -2. [amedrontador] dreadful.

temido, da [te'midu, da] adj [assustador] frightening.

temível [te'mivεw] (pl -eis) adj fearsome.

temor [te'mo(x)] (pl -es) m fear.

tempão [tẽn'pãw] m fam: um ~ ages.

têmpera ['tẽnpera] f -1. [ger] tempera. -2. [de metais] tempering.

temperado, da [tẽnpe'radu, da] adj -1. [ferro, aço] hardened. -2. [clima] temperate. -3. [CULIN - condimentado] seasoned; [- marinado] marinated.

temperamental [tẽnperamẽn'taw] (pl -ais) <> adj temperamental. <> mf temperamental person.

temperamento [tẽnpera'mẽntul] m temperament.

temperança [tẽnpe'rãnsa] f temperance.

temperar [4] [tẽnpe'ra(x)] vt -1. [metal] to temper. -2. [CULIN - condimentar] to season; [- marinar] to marinate.

temperatura [tẽnpera'tura] f temperature; ~

ambiente room temperature.

tempero [tẽn'peru] m -1. [condimento] seasoning. -2. [vinha d'alho] marinade. -3. [sabor] flavour UK, flavor US.

tempestade [tẽnpeʃ'tadʒi] f storm; ~ de areia sandstorm; fazer uma ~ em copo d'água to make a mountain out of a molehill.

tempestuoso, osa [tẽnpeʃ'twozu, ɔza] adj [dia, tempo] stormy.

templo ['tẽnplu] m -1. [pagão] temple. -2. [cristão] church.

tempo ['tẽnpu] m -1. [ger] time; o ~ todo the whole time; quanto ~? how long?; há quanto ~ você mora aqui? how long have you been living here?; não a vejo há muito ~ it's a long time since I saw her; há muito ~ a long time ago; não dá ~ there isn't (enough) time; ~ integral full-time; dar ~ ao ~ to give things time; ganhar/perder ~ to gain/lose time; em seu devido ~ in due course; em ~ hábil in reasonable time; a ~ on time; a ~ e a hora at the appropriate time; nos bons ~s in the good times; nesse meio ~ in the meanwhile; ao mesmo ~ at the same time; de ~s em ~s from time to time; esse vestido é do ~ do Onça that dress went out with the ark. -2. METEOR weather; previsão do ~ weather forecast. -3. GRAM tense. -4. ESP: primeiro/segundo ~ first/second half. -5. [MÚS - divisão de compasso] time; [- velocidade de execução] timing.

tempo-quente [ˌtẽnpu'kẽntʃil] m [briga, discussão] heated words (pl).

têmpora ['tẽnpora] f ANAT temple.

temporada [tẽnpo'rada] f -1. [ger] season; baixa/alta ~ high/low season. -2. [espaço de tempo] time.

temporal [tẽnpo'raw] (pl -ais) <> adj -1. [temporário] temporary. -2. [não-espiritual] temporal. <> m storm.

temporão, rã [tẽnpo'rãw, rã] adj [filho] premature.

temporário, ria [tẽnpo'rarju, rja] adj temporary.

tenacidade [tenasi'dadʒil] f tenacity.

tenaz [te'najʒ] <> adj [pessoa] tenacious. <> f [ferramenta] tongs (pl).

tencionar [4] [tẽnsjo'na(x)] vt: ~ algo/fazer algo to be planning sthg/to do sthg.

tenda ['tẽnda] f tent; ~ de oxigênio oxygen tent.

tendão [tẽn'dãw] (pl -ões) m tendon.

tendência [tẽn'dẽnsja] f -1. [propensão] tendency; ~ a ou para algo tendency to ou towards sthg; ~ a fazer algo tendency to do sthg. -2. [vocação] inclination; ~ a ou para algo inclination towards sthg; ~ a fazer algo inclination to do sthg. -3. [da moda, música] trend.

tendencioso, osa [tẽndẽn'sjozu, ɔza] adj tendentious.

tendente [tẽn'dẽntʃil] adj: ser ~ a fazer algo to tend to do sthg.

tender [5] [tẽn'de(x)] vt -1. [ter tendência]: ~ a ou para algo to be inclined to ou towards sthg; ~

a fazer algo to tend to do sthg. **-2.** [ter vocação]: ~ a ou **para algo** to be inclined towards sthg; ~ a **fazer algo** to intend to do sthg. **-3.** [encaminhar- -se]: ~ a ou **para algo** to move towards sthg; ~ a **fazer algo** to be closer to doing sthg.

tênder ['tẽnde(x)] *m* NÁUT tender.

tendinite [tẽdʒi'nitʃi] *f* MED tendinitis.

tenebroso, sa [tene'brozu, za] *adj* **-1.** [ger] dark. **-2.** *fig* [terrível, horrível] horrendous.

tenente [te'nẽntʃi] *mf* lieutenant.

tenho ['teɲu] ▷ **ter**.

tênis ['teniʃ] *m* **-1.** *inv* ESP tennis; ~ **de mesa** table tennis. **-2.** [calçado] trainer *UK*, sneaker *US*.

tenista [te'niʃta] *mf* tennis player.

tenor [te'no(x)] ◇ *m* tenor. ◇ *adj inv* [instrumento] tenor *(antes de subst)*.

tenro, ra ['tẽnxu, xa] *adj* **-1.** [ger] tender. **-2.** [recente, novo] new.

tensão [tẽ'sãw] *(pl* -ões) *f* **-1.** [ger] tension; ~ **pré-menstrual** pre-menstrual tension, PMT. **-2.** [pressão] pressure. **-3.** [voltagem] voltage.

tenso, sa ['tẽnsu, sa] *adj* **-1.** [ger] taut. **-2.** [pessoa, ambiente] tense.

tentação [tẽnta'sãw] *(pl* -ões) *f* temptation; ~ **de fazer algo** temptation to do sthg.

tentáculo [tẽn'takulu] *m* tentacle.

tentado, da [tẽn'tadu, da] *adj* **-1.** [atraído, seduzido] tempted; **estar** ~ **a fazer algo** to be tempted to do sthg. **-2.** [experimentado] attempted.

tentador, ra [tẽnta'do(x), ra] *(mpl* -es, *fpl* -s) *adj* tempting.

tentar [4] [tẽn'ta(x)] *vt* **-1.** [experimentar] to try. **-2.** [usar de meios para] to attempt; ~ **fazer algo** to try to do sthg. **-3.** [atrair] to tempt.

tentativa [tẽnta'tʃiva] *f* attempt; ~ **de fazer algo** attempt at doing sthg; ~ **de roubo** attempted robbery.

tênue ['tẽnwi] *adj* **-1.** [fraco - luz, voz, desejo] faint; [- sentimento] slight; [- argumento] tenuous. **-2.** [fino] flimsy. **-3.** [leve] slight.

teologia [tʃolo'ʒia] *f* theology.

teológico, ca [tʃolo'lɔʒiku, ka] *adj* theological.

teólogo, ga ['tʃjologu, ga] *m, f* theologian.

teor ['tʃjo(x)] *m* **-1.** [conteúdo, significado] tenor. **-2.** [proporção de uma substância] content; **baixo** ~ **de nicotina** low nicotine content; ~ **alcoólico** alcohol content.

teorema [teo'rema] *m* theorem.

teoria [teo'ria] *f* theory.

teoricamente [ˌtʃjorika'mẽntʃi] *adv* theoretically.

teórico, ca [te'ɔriku, ka] ◇ *adj* theoretical. ◇ *m, f* theorist.

teorizar [4] [teori'za(x)] ◇ *vt* to theorize. ◇ *vi* **-1.** [expor teorias] to expound theories. **-2.** [discorrer teoricamente] to theorize; ~ **sobre algo** to theorize about sthg.

tépido, da ['tɛpidu, da] *adj* tepid, lukewarm.

ter [1] ['te(x)] ◇ *vt* **-1.** [ger] to have; ~ **razão** to be right. **-2.** [obter]: ~ **sucesso em algo** to be successful in sthg. **-3.** [sentir] to be; ~ **fome/ pressa/calor** to be hungry/hurried/hot; **o que é**

que você tem? what's wrong with you? **-4.** [contar]: '**quantos anos você tem?**' - '**tenho 30 anos**' [idade] 'how old are you?' - 'I'm 30'; **ele tem 2 metros de altura** [medida] he is 2 metres tall. **-5.** [proceder com]: ~ **cuidado** to be careful; **tenha calma!** calm down! **-6.** [considerar]: ~ **alguém por** ou **como algo** to consider sb as sthg. ◇ *v impess* [haver]: **tem algo/alguém** there is sthg/sb; **não tem problema** (it's) no problem; **não tem de quê** you're welcome; **tem três meses que não chove** it hasn't rained for three months; **tem três meses que cheguei** it's three months since I arrived. ◇ *v aux*: ~ **que** ou **de fazer algo** to have to do sthg; ~ **como fazer algo** to be able to do sthg; ~ **a ver com** to have sthg to do with; **não tenho nada a ver com isso** I have nothing to do with it; **não** ~ **onde cair morto** to have nowhere to turn.

ter. *(abrev de* terça-feira) *f* Tue.

terabyte [texa'baijtʃi] *(pl* **terabytes**) *m* terabyte.

terapeuta [tera'pewta] *mf* therapist.

terapêutico, ca [tera'pewtʃiku, ka] *adj* therapeutic.
➤ **terapêutica** *f* **-1.** [parte da medicina] therapeutics *(pl)*. **-2.** [tratamento] therapy.

terapia [tera'pia] *f* **-1.** [ger] therapy. **-2.**: ~ **de casal** marriage guidance.

terça ['texsa], **terça-feira** [texsa'fejra] *(pl* **terças- feiras** [texsaʃ'fejraʃ]) *f* Tuesday; ~ **gorda** Shrove Tuesday, Pancake Day; *veja também* **sexta-feira**.

terceirização [texsejriʒa'sãw] *f* outsourcing.

terceirizar [4] [texsejri'za(x)] *vt* to outsource.

terceiro, ra [tex'sejru, ra] ◇ *num* third; **o Terceiro Mundo** the Third World; *veja também* **sexto**. ◇ *m, f* **-1.** [ger] third party. **-2.** [aquele ou aquilo em terceiro lugar] third.
➤ **terceira** *f* AUTO third (gear).
➤ **terceiros** *mpl* [outras pessoas] others.

terciário, ria [tex'sjarju, rja] *adj* tertiary.

terço, ça ['texsu, sa] *num*: **a terça parte** the third part.
➤ **terço** *m* [rosário] rosary.

terçol [tex'sɔw] *(pl* -óis) *m* stye.

Tergal® [tex'gaw] *m* Terylene®.

tergiversar [4] [texʒivex'sa(x)] *vi* [usar de subterfúgios ou evasivas] to avoid the issue.

termas ['tɛxmaʃ] *fpl* spa *(sg)*.

termelétrica [texme'lɛtrika] *f* thermoelectric plant.

térmico, ca [tɛx'miku, ka] *adj* thermal.

terminação [texmina'sãw] *(pl* -ões) *f* **-1.** [ger] end. **-2.** [ato] termination. **-3.** GRAM ending.

terminal [texmi'naw] *(pl* -ais) ◇ *adj* terminal; **em estado** ~ terminally ill. ◇ *m* **-1.** [ger] terminal. **-2.** [fim da linha] terminus; ~ **marítimo** sea terminal.

terminante [texmi'nãntʃi] *adj* **-1.** [categórico] categorical. **-2.** [decisivo, inapelável] final. **-3.** [concludente] concluding.

terminantemente [texminãntʃi'mẽntʃi] *adv* categorically.

terminar [4] [texmi'na(x)] ⟨⟩ *vt* to finish. ⟨⟩ *aux:* ~ **de fazer algo** [finalmente] to finish doing sthg; [há pouco tempo] to have just done sthg. ⟨⟩ *vi* to finish; ~ **em algo** [em local, forma] to end in sthg.

término ['texminu] *m* end.

terminologia [texminolo'ʒia] *f* terminology.

terminológico, ca [texmino'lɔʒiku, ka] *adj* terminological.

termo ['texmu] *m* **-1.** [ger] term. **-2.** [fim] end; **pôr** ~ **a algo** to put an end to sthg; **a longo** ~ in the long term; **meio** ~ compromise.

➡ **termos** *mpl* terms; **em** ~ **s de** in terms of; **em** ~ **s gerais** in general terms; **em** ~ **s** on terms; **estar em bons/maus** ~ **s** to be on good/bad terms.

termodinâmica [texmodʒi'nãmika] *f* thermodynamics *(sg)*.

termômetro [ter'mɔmetru] *m* [instrumento] thermometer.

termonuclear [texmonukle'a(x)] ⟨⟩ *adj* thermonuclear. ⟨⟩ *f* [usina termonuclear] nuclear power station.

termostato [texmoʃ'tatu] *m* thermostat.

terninho [tex'niɲu] *m* trouser suit *UK*, pantsuit *US*.

terno, na ['texnu, na] *adj* tender.

➡ **terno** *m* [traje] suit.

ternura [tex'nura] *f* tenderness.

terra ['texa] *f* **-1.** [ger] earth; ~ **vegetal** compost; **chão de** ~ **batida** earth floor. **-2.** [por oposição ao mar] [terreno] land; ~ **firme** terra firma. **-3.** [região, país]: **já me habituei a viver nesta** ~ I've got used to living in this area; ~ **de ninguém** no-man's-land; **a** ~ **prometida** the promised land; **a Terra Santa** the Holy Land. **-4.** [pátria] homeland; ~ **natal** birthplace.

terraço [te'xasul] *m* **-1.** [varanda] terrace. **-2.** [cobertura plana de um edifício] roof terrace.

terracota [texa'kɔta] *f* [argila] terracotta.

Terra do Fogo [,texadu'fogu] *n* Tierra del Fuego.

Terra Nova [,texa'nɔva] *n* Newfoundland.

terraplenagem [texaple'naʒẽ] *f* site levelling *UK*, site leveling *US*.

terraplenar [texaple'na(x)] *vt* to level.

terreiro [te'xejru] *m* **-1.** [espaço de terra] yard. **-2.** [espirit] *place where Afro-Brazilian rites are performed.*

terremoto [texe'mɔtu] *m* earthquake.

terreno, na [te'xenu, na] *adj* [material, mundano] material.

➡ **terreno** *m* **-1.** [extensão de terra] land. **-2.** [para construção, plantação] site; ~ **baldio** wasteland. **-3.** GEOL terrain. **-4.** *loc*: **ganhar/perder** ~ to lose/gain ground; **sondar o** ~ to check the lie of the land.

térreo, ea ['tɛxju, ja] *adj* [andar, casa] ground level *(antes de subst)*.

➡ **térreo** *m* [andar térreo] ground floor *UK*, first floor *US*.

terrestre [te'xɛʃtri] *adj* **-1.** [relativo ou pertencente à Terra - globo, crosta] earth's, of the earth; [- seres,

fenômenos] earthly. **-2.** [por oposição a aquático] land *(antes de subst)*.

terrificante [texifi'kãntʃi], **terrífico, ca** [te'xifiku, ka] *adj* terrifying.

terrina [te'xina] *f* tureen.

territorial [texito'rjaw] *adj* territorial.

território [texi'tɔrju] *m* **-1.** [ger] territory. **-2.** [parte de uma federação] district.

terrível [te'xivɛw] *(pl* **-eis)** *adj* **-1.** [ger] terrible. **-2.** [muito forte, enorme] dreadful.

terror [te'xo(x)] *(pl* **-es)** *m* [medo] terror; **ser um** ~ [ser amedrontador] to be terrifying; [ser horrível] to be awful.

terrorismo [texo'riʒmu] *m* terrorism.

terrorista [texo'riʃta] ⟨⟩ *adj* terrorist *(antes de subst)*. ⟨⟩ *mf* [pessoa] terrorist.

tesão [te'sãw] *(pl* **-ões)** *m* **-1.** *mfam* [desejo sexual] hots *(pl)*; **estar com** ~ to have the hots, to be horny; **sentir** ~ **por alguém** to have the hots for sb; **ser um** ~ [pessoa] to be sexy; [coisa] to be fantastic. **-2.** [ereção] stiffy, hard-on; **estar com** ~ to have a hard-on.

tese ['tɛzi] *f* thesis.

➡ **em tese** *loc adv* in theory.

teso, sa ['tezu, za] *adj* **-1.** [esticado] taut. **-2.** [ereto] stiff. **-3.** *fam* [sem dinheiro] skint.

tesões [te'zõjʃ] *pl* ⊳ **tesão**.

tesoura [te'zoral] *f* scissors *(pl)*.

tesourar [4] [tezo'ra(x)] *vt* **-1.** [cortar] to cut with scissors. **-2.** *fam* [falar mal de] to slag off.

tesouraria [tezora'ria] *f* **-1.** [departamento] finance department. **-2.** [cargo] finance director.

tesoureiro, ra [tezo'rejru, ra] *m, f* **-1.** [de banco] treasurer. **-2.** [de empresa] financial director.

tesouro [te'zorul] *m* **-1.** [ger] treasure. **-2.** [lugar onde são guardadas as riquezas] treasury.

➡ **Tesouro** *m*: **oTesouro Nacional** the Treasury.

testa ['tɛʃta] *f* forehead; **à** ~ **de** at the head of.

testa-de-ferro [,tɛʃtadʒi'fɛxul] *(pl* **testas-de-ferro)** *mf* figurehead.

testamentário, ria [teʃtamẽntarju, rja] *adj* of a will.

testamento [teʃta'mẽntul] *m* will.

➡ **NovoTestamento** *m* New Testament.

➡ **VelhoTestamento** *m* Old Testament.

testar [4] [teʃ'ta(x)] *vt* **-1.** [submeter a teste] to test. **-2.** [deixar em testamento] to bequeath.

teste ['tɛʃtʃi] *m* test.

testemunha [teʃte'muɲa] *f* witness; ~ **ocular** eye witness; ~ **de acusação** witness for the prosecution.

testemunha-de-Jeová [teʃte'muɲadʒieo'va] *mf* Jehovah's Witness.

testemunhar [4] [teʃte'muɲa(x)] ⟨⟩ *vt* **-1.** [ger] to witness. **-2.** JUR [depor sobre] to testify to. **-3.** [comprovar] to prove. **-4.** [manifestar] to display. ⟨⟩ *vi* JUR to testify; ~ **sobre/a favor de/contra algo** to give evidence about/for/against sthg; ~ **sobre/a favor de/contra alguém** to act as witness regarding/for/against sb.

testemunho [teʃte'muɲul] *m* testimony; **dar** ~

(sobre algo) to give evidence (about sthg).
testículo [teʃ'tʃikulu] *m* testicle.
testudo, da [teʃ'tudu, da] *adj* with a wide forehead.
teta ['teta] *f* [ANAT- de mulher] breast; [- de animal] teat; [- de vaca] udder.
tétano ['tɛtanu] *m* tetanus.
tête-à-tête [,tɛtʃja'tɛtʃil] *m* tête-à-tête.
tetéia [te'teja] *f fam* [pessoa] dish.
teto ['tɛtu] *m* **-1.** [ger] ceiling. **-2.** [de peça da casa] roof; ~ **solar** AUTO sunroof. **-3.** [habitação]: **sem** ~ homeless person.
tetracampeão, peã [tetrakãn'pjãw, pjã] *m, f* four times champion.
tetraplégico, ca [tetra'plɛʒiku, ka] <> *adj* quadriplegic. <> *m, f* quadriplegic.
tétrico, ca ['tɛtriku, ka] *adj* **-1.** [medonho, horrível] grim. **-2.** [triste, fúnebre] gloomy.
teu, tua ['tew, 'tua] <> *adj poss* your. <> *pron poss* yours.
tevê [te've] *f* = **televisão.**
têxtil ['teʃtʃiw] (*pl* **-teis**) *adj* textile.
texto ['teʃtu] *m* text.
textual [teʃ'twaw] *adj* **-1.** [relativo ao texto] textual. **-2.** *fig* [exato]: **foram estas minhas palavras textuais** those were my precise words.
textualmente [teʃtwaw'mẽtʃil] *adv* [exatamente, literalmente] verbatim.
textura [teʃ'tura] *f* texture.
texugo [te'ʃugul] *m* ZOOL badger.
tez ['teʃ] *f* [cútis] complexion.
ti ['tʃil] *pron pess* you; **trouxe este presente para** ~ **I** brought this present for you.
tia ['tʃia] *f* aunt.
tia-avó [,tʃia'vɔl] (*pl* **tias-avós**) *f* great-aunt.
tiara ['tʃjaral] *f* tiara.
tibetano, na [tʃibe'tanu, na] <> *adj* Tibetan. <> *m, f* Tibetan.
　　➡ **tibetano** *m* [língua] Tibetan.
Tibete [tʃi'bɛtʃil] *n* Tibet.
tíbia ['tʃibja] *f* ANAT tibia.
tíbio, bia ['tʃibju, bja] *adj* lukewarm.
tição [tʃi'sãw] (*pl* **-ões**) *m* **-1.** [lenha] ember. **-2.** [negro] *fig* & *pej* nigger.
ticar [4] [tʃi'ka(x)] *vt* to tick.
tico ['tʃikul] *m*: **um** ~ **(de)** a bit (of).
tico-tico [,tʃiku'tʃikul] (*pl* **-s**) *m* ZOOL ruffous-collared sparrow.
tido, da ['tʃidu, da] *adj* [considerado]: ~ **como** considered.
　　➡ **tido** *pp* ⊳ **ter.**
tietagem [tʃje'taʒẽl] (*pl* **-ns**) *f fam*: **fazer** ~ **para** to show admiration towards.
tiete ['tʃjɛtʃil] *mf fam* fan.
tifo ['tʃiful] *m* typhus.
tigela [tʃi'ʒelal] *f* [vasilha] bowl.
tigre ['tʃigril] *m* ZOOL tiger.
tigresa [tʃi'grezal] *f* ZOOL tigress.
tijolo [tʃi'ʒolul] *m* brick; **de** ~ **aparente** brick-faced; ~ **refratário** firebrick.
til ['tʃiwl] *m* tilde.

tilintar [4] [tʃilĩn'ta(x)] <> *vt* [sino, chocalho] to jingle. <> *vi* [sino, moeda] to jingle. <> *m* jingle.
timaço [tʃi'masul] *m fam* [grande time] great team.
timão [tʃi'mãw] (*pl* **-ões**) *m* NÁUT helm, tiller.
timbrado, da [tʃĩn'bradu, da] *adj*: **papel** ~ headed paper.
timbre ['tʃĩnbril] *m* **-1.** [em papel de correspondência] heading. **-2.** [de voz] tone. **-3.** MÚS [tom] timbre. **-4.** [de vogal] sound.
time ['tʃimil] *m* **-1.** [ger] team. **-2.** *fig*: **de segundo** ~ second-rate. **-3.** *fam loc*: **tirar o** ~ **de campo** to pull out.
timer ['tajme(x)] *m* timer.
timidez [tʃimi'deʃl] *f* timidity.
tímido, da ['tʃimidu, da] *adj* **-1.** [avanço, governo] timid. **-2.** [pessoa, temperamento] timid, shy.
timões [tʃi'mõjʃl] *pl* ⊳ **timão.**
timoneiro, ra [tʃimo'nejru, ra] *m, f* NÁUT helmsman.
tímpano ['tʃĩnpanul] *m* **-1.** ANAT eardrum. **-2.** [em campainha] bell.
tina ['tʃina] *f* **-1.** [para lavar roupa] trough. **-2.** [para banho] bathtub. **-3.** [para uso industrial] vat.
tíner ['tʃine(x)] *m* thinner.
tingido, da [tʃĩn'ʒidu, da] *adj* [tinto] dyed.
tingimento [tʃĩnʒi'mẽtul] *m* dyeing.
tingir [52] [tʃĩn'ʒi(x)] *vt* **-1.** [ger] to dye. **-2.** [parede, corpo] to paint.
tinha ['tʃina] ⊳ **ter.**
tinhoso, osa [tʃi'nozu, ɔzal] *adj* **-1.** [teimoso] obstinate. **-2.** [persistente] stubborn.
tinido [tʃi'nidul] *m* ring.
tinir [6] [tʃi'ni(x)] *vi* **-1.** [ger] to ring. **-2.** *loc*: **estar tinindo** [estar em ótimo estado de limpeza] to be sparkling; [estar bem preparado] to be well-primed; [estar em ótimas condições] to be in excellent order; ~ **de fome/raiva** to be extremely hungry/furious.
tinjo ['tʃĩʒul] <> **tingir.**
tino ['tʃinul] *m* **-1.** [juízo] common sense; **perder o** ~ to lose one's common sense. **-2.** [prudência] care. **-3.**: **ter** ~ **para algo** [ter queda para] to have a gift for sthg.
tinta ['tʃĩtal] *f* **-1.** [para imprimir, escrever] ink. **-2.** [para tingir] dye. **-3.** [para pintar] paint; ~ **a óleo** oil paint; ~ **plástica** emulsion.
tinteiro [tʃĩn'tejrul] *m* inkwell.
tintim [tʃĩn'tʃĩl] *m*: **tintim!** cheers!
　　➡ **tintim por tintim** *loc adv* word for word.
tinto ['tʃĩntul] *adj* **-1.** [cabelos] dyed. **-2.**: **vinho** ~ red wine.
tintura [tʃĩn'tural] *f* **-1.** [tinta] dye. **-2.** [ato] dyeing.
tinturaria [tʃĩntura'rial] *f* **-1.** [ramo] dyeing. **-2.** [lavandaria] dry-cleaner's. **-3.** [onde se faz tingimento] dyer's.
tintureiro, ra [tʃĩntu'rejru, ral] *m, f* [profissional - que lava a seco] dry-cleaner; [- que tinge] dyer.
tio ['tʃiwl] *m* uncle; **os meus** ~**s** [casal] my aunt and uncle.
tio-avô ['tʃiwa'vol] (*pl* **tios-avôs**) *m* great-uncle.

tipão [tʃi'pãw] *m* stunner.
tipicamente [tʃipika'mẽntʃil *adv* typically.
típico, ca ['tʃipiku, ka] *adj* typical.
tipificar [12] [tʃipifi'ka(x)] *vt* to typify.
tipo, pa ['tʃipu, pal *m* -**1.** [espécie] type; ~ **sangüíneo** blood group. -**2.** [pessoa] sort. -**3.** *fam* [sujei-
to] guy (*f* girl). -**4.** [*TIP* - peça] type; [- letra] font.
tipografia [tʃipogra'fial *f* -**1.** [arte] typography.
-**2.** [estabelecimento] printer's.
tipográfico, ca [tʃipo'grafiku, ka] *adj* typogra-
phical; **erro** ~ typo.
tipógrafo, fa [tʃi'pɔgrafu, fal *m*, *f* [profissional - que
imprime] printer; [- que compõe] typesetter.
tipóia [tʃi'pɔjal *f* [tira de pano] sling.
tique ['tʃikil *m* tick; ~ **nervoso** nervous tic.
tique-taque [ˌtʃiki'takil (*pl* **tique-taques**) *m*
tick-tock.
tíquete [tʃi'ketʃil *m* ticket, voucher.
tíquete-restaurante ['tʃiketʃixeʃtaw'rãntʃil (*pl*
tíquetes-restaurante) *m* [vale-refeição] luncheon
voucher.
tiquinho [tʃi'kiɲul *m*: **um** ~ (**de**) a shred (of).
tira ['tʃiral ◇ *f* [ger] strip. ◇ *m gír* [agente de po-
lícia] cop.
tiracolo [tʃira'kɔlul *m*: **a** ~ across the shoulder;
com os filhos a ~ with the children in tow.
tirada [tʃi'radal *f* [dito] tirade.
tiragem [tʃi'raʒẽl (*pl* -**ns**) *f* -**1.** [operação de imprimir]
print run. -**2.** [número de exemplares] circulation.
tira-gosto ['tʃira'goʃtul (*pl* **tira-gostos**) *m*
savoury *UK*, savory *US*.
tira-manchas [ˌtʃira'mãnʃaʃl *m inv* stain remover.
Tirana [tʃi'rãnal *n* Tirana.
tirania [tʃira'nial *f* tyranny.
tirânico, ca [tʃi'rãniku, ka] *adj* tyrannical.
tiranizar [4] [tʃirani'za(x)] *vt* to tyrannize.
tirano, na [tʃi'rãnu, nal ◇ *adj* [cruel, injusto]
tyrannical. ◇ *m*, *f* tyrant.
tirante [tʃi'rãntʃil ◇ *adj*: ~ **dois ou três problemas, o resto deu certo** except for a couple of
problems, the rest worked out well; **uma cor** ~
a verde a greenish colour *UK*, a greenish color
US. ◇ *m* -**1.** [correia] harness. -**2.** [viga] tie beam.
-**3.** *MEC* connecting rod.
tirar [4] [tʃi'ra(x)] *vt* -**1.** [ger] to take. -**2.** [retirar] to
take away. -**3.** [de cima] [despir, descalçar] to take
off. -**4.** [de dentro] [sacar] to take out, to withdraw.
-**5.** [trazer abaixo] to take down. -**6.** [extrair] to
extract. -**7.** [eliminar] to remove. -**8.** [obter] to get;
~ **proveito de** to make use of. -**9.** [mesa] to clear.
-**10.** [para dançar] to ask. -**11.** *MÚS* to take down. -**12.**
TIP [imprimir] to print. -**13.**: ~ **algo/alguém de algo**
[afastar, fazer sair] to take sthg/sb away from sthg;
-**14.** [loc]: **sem** ~ **nem pôr** exactly like; **ele é o pai
sem** ~ **nem pôr** he's the spitting image of his
father.
tiririca [tʃiri'rikal *adj fam*: **estar/ficar** ~ to be
hopping mad.
tiritar [4] [tʃiri'ta(x)] *vi* to shiver; ~ **de frio** to
shiver with cold.

tiro ['tʃirul *m* -**1.** [ger] shot; **dar um** ~ (**em**) to fire
a shot (at); **trocar** ~ **s** to exchange fire; ~ **ao alvo**
target practice; **o** ~ **saiu pela culatra** *fig* it
backfired. -**2.** [loc]: **ser** ~ **e queda** to be surefire.
tiro-de-guerra [tʃirudʒi'gɛxal (*pl* **tiros-de-guer-
ra**) *m* army reserve training centre.
tiroteio [tʃiro'tejul *m* -**1.** [tiros amiudados]
shooting. -**2.** [troca de tiros] shootout.
tis [tʃiʃl *pl* ▷ **til.**
tísico, ca ['tʃiziku, ka] ◇ *adj* consumptive. ◇
m, *f* consumptive.
titânio [tʃi'tãnjul *m* titanium.
títere ['tʃiteril *m* [marionete] puppet.
titia [tʃi'tʃial *f fam* aunty; **ficar para** ~ to become
an old maid.
Titicaca [tʃitʃi'kakal *n*: **o (lago)** ~ Lake Titicaca.
titio [tʃi'tʃiwl *m fam* uncle.
tititi [tʃitʃi'tʃil *m* -**1.** *gír* [falatório] tittle-tattle. -**2.**
[badalação] hubbub. -**3.** [discussão, briga] brawl.
titubeante [tʃitu'bjãntʃil *adj* -**1.** [cambaleante]
lurching. -**2.** [hesitante] hesitant.
titubear [15] [tʃitu'bja(x)] *vi* -**1.** [hesitar] to hesitate; ~ **em algo/em fazer algo** to hesitate in
sthg/at doing sthg. -**2.** [cambalear] to lurch.
titular [tʃitu'la(x)] ◇ *adj* [efetivo - juiz] incumbent;
[- professor] tenured; [- oficial] official. ◇ *mf* -**1.**
[ocupante efetivo de função ou cargo] incumbent. -**2.**
POL [de ministério]: **o** ~ **do Ministério da Saúde** the
Health Minister. -**3.** [possuidor] holder.
título ['tʃitulul *m* -**1.** [ger] title. -**2.** [documento]
(title) deed; ~ **ao portador** *COM* bearer bond *ou*
certificate; ~ **de crédito** *COM* bond; ~ **de propriedade** *JUR* title deed. -**3.** [motivo]: **a** ~ **de** by way of;
a ~ **de curiosidade** out of curiosity; **a** ~ **de quê?**
what for?
tive ['tʃivil *v* ▷ **ter.**
tlintlim [tlĩn'tlĩnl *m* tinkle.
TM (*abrev de* **Trademark**) *f* TM.
TO (*abrev de* **Estado de Tocantins**) *n State of
Tocantins.*
toa ['toal *f NÁUT* towline.
◆ **à toa** *loc adv* -**1.** [ger] for no reason; **não é à**
~ **que** it's not by chance that. -**2.** [inutilmente] in
vain. -**3.** [desocupado] at a loose end. -**4.** [sem
rumo] aimlessly.
toada ['twadal *f MÚS* tune, melody.
toalete [twa'lɛtʃil ◇ *m* [banheiro] toilet. ◇ *f* -**1.**
[ato]: **fazer a** ~ to get washed and dressed. -**2.**
[traje] outfit.
toalha [tʃwaʎal *f* towel; ~ **de banho/rosto/praia**
bath/hand/beach towel; ~ **de mesa** tablecloth.
toalheiro [twa'ʎejrul *m* [utensílio] towel rail.
tobogã [tobo'gãl *m* -**1.** [trenó] toboggan. -**2.** [pis-
ta] slide.
toca ['tɔkal *f* -**1.** [covil] den. -**2.** *fig* [refúgio] bolt-
hole.
toca-discos [ˌtɔka'dʒiʃkuʃl *m inv* record player.
tocado, da [to'kadu, dal *adj* -**1.** *fam* [meio embria-
gado] tipsy. -**2.** [expulso] turfed out.
toca-fitas [ˌtɔka'fitaʃl *m inv* cassette player.

tocaia [to'kaja] f ambush.

tocante [to'kãntʃi] adj inv [comovente] touching.
◆ **no tocante a** loc prep when it comes to.

Tocantins [tokãn'tʃĩn] npl Tocantins.

tocar [12] [to'ka(x)] ◇ vt - **1.** [ger] to touch. - **2.** MÚS to play. - **3.** [campainha, sino] to ring. - **4.** [buzina] to hoot. - **5.** [conduzir] to drive. - **6.** [fazer progredir]: ~ **algo (para frente)** to move (sthg) forward. - **7.** [expulsar]: ~ **alguém/algo de algum lugar** to throw sb/sthg out of somewhere. ◇ vi - **1.** [ger] to ring. - **2.** [apalpar, encostar]: ~ **(em) algo/alguém** to touch sthg/sb.
◆ **tocar a** vi [dizer respeito a]: **no** ou **pelo que me toca** as far as I am concerned.
◆ **tocar em** vi - **1.** [referir-se a] to touch (up)on. - **2.** [fazer escala em] to stop off in. - **3.** [caber a]: **toca a você fazer isso** it's up to you to do it.
◆ **tocar para** vi [telefonar] to ring.
◆ **tocar-se** vp - **1.** [pôr-se em contato] to touch. - **2.** [perceber] to notice. - **3.** [ofender-se] to be provoked.

tocha ['tɔʃa] f [facho] torch.

toco ['toku] m - **1.** [de árvore] stump. - **2.** [de cigarro, charuto] butt(-end), stub.

todavia [toda'via] conj however.

todo, da ['todu, da] ◇ adj indef [inteiro] all; **a Europa toda** the whole of Europe; **a equipe toda** the entire team; **o dia ~**, ~ **o dia** the whole day (long). ◇ adv [completamente] completely. ◇ pron indef [qualquer, cada] every; ~ **dia**, ~ **s os dias** every day; **em** ou **por toda parte** everywhere; ~ **mundo** everyone; **em** ~ **caso** in any case; **de** ~ **jeito** all the same.
◆ **todo** m whole; **ao** ~ in all; **de** ~ entirely.
◆ **todos** pron pl [todas as pessoas] everyone (sg).
◆ **a toda (velocidade)** loc adv at top speed.

todo-poderoso, osa [,todupode'rozu, ɔza] adj all-powerful.
◆ **Todo-Poderoso** m: **o Todo Poderoso** the Almighty.

toga ['tɔga] f - **1.** HIST toga. - **2.** [jur] gown.

toicinho [toj'siɲu] m = toucinho.

toldo ['towdu] m awning.

tolerância [tole'rãnsja] f tolerance.

tolerante [tole'rãntʃi] adj tolerant.

tolerar [4] [tole'ra(x)] vt - **1.** [ger] to tolerate. - **2.** [suportar] to bear.

tolerável [tole'ravew] (pl -eis) adj - **1.** [aceitável] tolerable. - **2.** [suportável] bearable.

tolher [5] [to'ʎe(x)] vt - **1.** [dificultar] to impede. - **2.** [impedir]: ~ **alguém de algo/de fazer algo** to prevent sb from sthg/from doing sthg.

tolice [to'lisi] f - **1.** [ato] stupid thing. - **2.** [qualidade] idiocy. - **3.** [dito] rubbish.

tolo, la ['tolu, la] ◇ adj - **1.** [ger] stupid. - **2.** [pessoa - idiota] idiotic; [- ingênuo] foolish. ◇ m, f [pessoa] idiot.

tom ['tõ] (pl -ns) m - **1.** [ger] tone. - **2.** [altura de um som] pitch; ~ **agudo/grave** high/low pitch. - **3.** [matiz] shade. - **4.** [MÚS - intervalo entre duas notas] tone; [- escala] key; ~ **maior/menor** major/minor

key. - **5.** loc: **ser de bom** ~ to be polite.

tomada [to'mada] f - **1.** [ato] taking; ~ **de decisão** decision making; ~ **de preços** tender; ~ **de posse** [de presidente] investiture; ~ **de posto oficial** taking office. - **2.** [ELETR - plugue] plug; [- na parede] socket. - **3.** [ocupação] taking. - **4.** CINE take.

tomar [4] [to'ma(x)] vt - **1.** [ger] to take; ~ **alguém em/por algo** to take sb in/by sthg; ~ **emprestado** to borrow; **toma!** there you are!; ~ **um susto** to get a fright. - **2.** [ocupar] to take. - **3.** [beber] to have. - **4.** [ocupar aspecto] to take up. - **5.** [satisfação]: ~ **satisfação de alguém** to get an explanation from sb. - **6.** [considerar]: ~ **algo como algo** to take sthg as sthg; ~ **alguém por algo** to take sb for sthg.
◆ **tomar-se** vp: ~**-se de algo (por)** [ser invadido por] to be full of sthg (for ou towards); ~**-se (de) horror a** to be filled with horror at.

tomara [to'mara] interj let's hope so!; ~ **que chova!** let's hope it rains!

tomara-que-caia [to,maraki'kaja] ◇ adj inv strapless. ◇ m inv strapless dress.

tomate [to'matʃi] m tomato.

tomateiro [toma'tejru] m tomato plant.

tombadilho [tõnba'dʒiʎu] m (poop) deck.

tombar [4] [tõn'ba(x)] ◇ vt - **1.** [derrubar] to knock down. - **2.** [para preservar] to list (for the preservation of buildings). ◇ vi: ~ **(em/de/para)** [cair] to fall on/off/towards; [cair rolando] to tumble on/off/towards.

tombo ['tõnbu] m [queda] fall; **levar um** ~ to take a tumble.

tomilho [to'miʎu] m thyme.

tomo ['tomu] m - **1.** [parte] tome. - **2.** [volume] volume.

tomografia [tomogra'fia] f MED tomography; ~ **computadorizada** computerized axial tomography, CAT scanning.

tona ['tona] f: **à** ~ to the surface; **vir/trazer à** ~ fig [vir à baila] to come/bring up.

tonal [to'naw] (pl -ais) adj MÚS tonal.

tonalidade [tonali'dadʒi] f - **1.** [ger] shade. - **2.** [mus] tonality.

tonel [to'new] (pl -éis) m [recipiente] cask.

tonelada [tone'lada] f - **1.** [medida] ton. - **2.** fig [grande quantidade de]: **uma** ~ **de** tons of.

tonelagem [tone'laʒẽ] f tonnage.

toner ['tone(x)] m TEC toner.

tônico, ca ['toniku, ka] adj tonic.
◆ **tônico** m [cosmético] tonic; ~ **para o cabelo** hair tonic.
◆ **tonica** f - **1.** [água tônica] tonic water. - **2.** MÚS tonic. - **3.** fig [idéia, assunto principal] keynote.

tonificante [tonifi'kãntʃi] adj invigorating.

tonificar [12] [tonifi'ka(x)] vt to tone.

tons [tõʃ] pl ⊳ **tom**.

tontas ['tõntaʃ] fpl: **às** ~ [atarantadamente] in a fluster.

tontear [15] [tõn'tʃja(x)] ◇ vt - **1.** [suj: bebida, perfume] to make giddy. - **2.** [suj: pessoa, notícia, revelação] to stun. - **3.** [suj: barulho, confusão] to drive mad. <> *vi* **-1.** [bebida, perfume] to be intoxicating. **-2.** [notícia, revelação] to be shocking. **-3.** [barulho, confusão] to be maddening. **-4.** [pessoa - ficar tonto] to become dizzy; [- perturbar-se] to be stunned; [- ficar atordoado] to be maddened.

tonteira [tõn'tejra] *f* [vertigem] giddiness, dizziness; **ter** ~ to suffer a dizzy spell.

tonto, ta ['tõntu, ta] *adj* **-1.** [zonzo] dizzy. **-2.** [perturbado, atordoado] giddy. **-3.** [tolo] giddy.

tontura [tõn'tura] *f* = **tonteira**.

tônus ['tonuʃ] *m inv*: ~ **muscular** muscle tone.

top ['tɔpi] *m* **-1.** [bustiê] bodice. **-2.** [o melhor]: ~ **de linha** top-of-the-range.

topada [to'pada] *f* trip; **dar uma** ~ **em algo** to trip over sthg.

topar [4] [to'pa(x)] <> *vt* [aceitar, concordar com]: ~ **algo/fazer algo** to agree to sthg/to do sthg; **você topa ir à praia?** do you feel like going to the beach? <> *vi* [aceitar, concordar] to agree.
→ **topar com** *vi* [encontrar] to come across.
→ **topar em** *vi* [tropeçar em] to trip over.
→ **topar-se** *vp* [deparar-se]: ~ **com algo/alguém** to come across sthg/sb.

topázio [to'pazju] *m* topaz.

topete [to'pɛtʃi] *m* [cabelo levantado] quiff; **ter o** ~ **de fazer algo** to have the nerve to do sthg.

topetudo, da [topetu'du, da] *adj* **-1.** [que usa topete] with a quiff *(depois de subst)*. **-2.** [destemido] daring.

tópico, ca ['tɔpiku, ka] *adj* [questão, assunto] topical.
→ **tópico** *m* [tema, assunto] topic.

topless [tɔpi'lɛʃ] <> *adj inv* topless. <> *m inv* topless bikini.

topo ['topu] *m* top.

topografia [topogra'fia] *f* topography.

topográfico, ca [topo'grafiku, ka] *adj* topographical.

topônimo [to'ponimu] *m* toponym, place name.

toque ['tɔki] <> *v* ⊳ **tocar**. <> *m* **-1.** [ger] touch. **-2.** [de campainha] ring. **-3.** [de corneta] blast. **-4.** *MED* palpation. **-5.** [pequeno teor ou quantidade]: **um** ~ **de** a touch of. **-6.** [retoque] finishing touch. **-7.** *fam* : **dar um** ~ **em alguém** to have a word with sb. **-8.** *MIL* : ~ **de recolher** curfew. **-9.** *loc*: **a** ~ **de caixa** hurriedly.

Tóquio ['tɔkju] *n* Tokyo.

tora ['tɔra] *f* **-1.** [de madeira] log. **-2.** [pedaço] piece; **tirar uma** ~ [cochilar] to take a nap.

tórax ['tɔrakiʃ] *m inv* thorax.

torção [tox'sãw] *f* **-1.** [ato de torcer] twist(ing). **-2.** *MED* sprain.

torcedor, ra [toxse'do(x), ra] (*mpl* **-es**, *fpl* **-s**) *m, f* *ESP* supporter; **sou** ~ **do Flamengo** I am a Flamengo supporter.

torcedura [toxse'dura] *f* *MED* sprain.

torcer [25] [tox'se(x)] <> *vt* **-1.** [ger] to twist. **-2.** [espremer] to wring. **-3.** *MED* to sprain. <> *vi* **-1.** [ger] to twist **-2.** [num jogo] to do one's bit as a supporter.

→ **torcer por** *vi* *ESP* [ser aficionado de] to be a supporter of.
→ **torcer para, torcer por** *vi* [desejar o êxito de] to back.

torcicolo [toxsi'kɔlu] *m* *MED* stiff neck, wryneck; **estar com** ~ to have a stiff neck.

torcida [tox'sida] *f* [*ESP* - ato] support; [- torcedores] supporters *(pl)*.

tormenta [tox'mẽnta] *f* **-1.** *METEOR* storm. **-2.** *fig* [transtorno] upheaval.

tormento [tox'mẽntu] *m* torment.

tormentoso, sa [toxmẽn'tozu, za] *adj* stormy.

tornado [tox'nadu] *m* tornado.

tornar [4] [tox'na(x)] <> *vt* [fazer ser] to make; ~ **algo em algo** to turn sthg into sthg. <> *vi*: ~ **a fazer algo** to do sthg again; **ela tornou a insistir** she again insisted.
→ **tornar-se** *vp* [vir a ser] to become.

torneado, da [tox'njadu, da] *adj* [arredondado] turned; **bem** ~ *fig* [corpo, pernas] well-turned, shapely.

tornear [15] [tox'nja(x)] *vt* to turn.

torneio [tox'neju] *m* [competição] tournament.

torneira [tox'nejra] *f* tap *UK*, faucet *US*.

torniquete [toxni'ketʃi] *m* *MED* tourniquet.

torno ['toxnu] *m* *TEC* lathe.
→ **en torno de** *loc prep* around.

tornozeleira [toxnoze'lejra] *f* ankle strap.

tornozelo [toxnu'zelu] *m* ankle.

toró [to'rɔ] *m* *METEOR* downpour; **caiu um** ~ there was a heavy downpour.

torpe ['toxpi] *adj* **-1.** [vil] foul. **-2.** [desonesto] shameful. **-3.** [obsceno] disgraceful.

torpedear [15] [toxpe'dʒja(x)] *vt* to torpedo.

torpedo [tox'pedu] *m* torpedo.

torpeza [tox'peza] *f* **-1.** [vileza] foulness. **-2.** [desonestidade] shamefulness. **-3.** [obscenidade] disgrace.

torpor [tox'po(x)] *m* **-1.** [entorpecimento] torpor. **-2.** [indiferença] inertia. **-3.** *MED* unresponsiveness.

torquês [tox'keʃ] *f* (pair of) pliers.

torrada [to'xada] *f* toast.

torradeira [toxa'dejra] *f* toaster.

torrão [to'xãw] (*pl* **-ões**) *m* **-1.** [de terra endurecida] clod. **-2.** [de açúcar] lump. **-3.** : ~ **natal** birthplace.

torrar [4] [to'xa(x)] <> *vt* **-1.** [tostar] to toast. **-2.** [ressecar] to parch. **-3.** *fig* [mercadorias] to dump. **-4.** *fig* [dinheiro] to burn. **-5.** *fam fig* [irritar] to annoy; ~ **a paciência de alguém** to try sb's patience. <> *vi* to be irritating.

torre ['toxi] *f* **-1.** [construção] tower; ~ **de controle** *AERON* control tower; ~ **de vigia** watchtower. **-2.** *ELETR* pylon. **-3.** *RÁDIO & TV* mast. **-4.** [xadrez] castle, rook.

torrefação [toxefa'sãw] (*pl* **-oes**) *f* **-1.** [de café, cacau] roast(ing). **-2.** [estabelecimento] roasting house.

torrencial [toxẽn'sjaw] *adj* torrential.

torrente [to'xẽntʃi] *f* torrent.

torresmo [toˈxeʒmu] *m CULIN* crackling, pork scratchings *(pl)*.

tórrido, da [ˈtɔxidu, da] *adj* torrid.

torrone [toˈxɔnil *m* nougat.

torso [ˈtoxsu] *m* torso.

torta [ˈtɔxta] *f* [empadão, doce] pie; ~ **de limão/maçã** lemon/apple pie/tart.

torto, ta [ˈtoxtu, ta] *adj* **-1.** [ger] crooked. **-2.** *loc:* **a** ~ **e a direito** left, right and centre; **cometer erros a** ~ **e a direito** to make mistakes left, right and centre.

tortuoso, osa [tox'twozu, ɔza] *adj* **-1.** [sinuoso] winding. **-2.** *(fig)* [que não segue uma linha reta] convoluted.

tortura [tox'tura] *f* [ger] torture; [lance difícil]: **ser uma** ~ to be torture.

torturador, ra [toxtura'do(x), ra] *m, f* torturer.

torturante [toxtu'rãntʃi] *adj* **-1.** [dor] excruciating. **-2.** [espera] agonizing. **-3.** [viagem] harrowing.

torturar [4] [toxtu'ra(x)] *vt* [ger] to torment; [incomodar fisicamente] to kill.

torvelinho [toxve'liɲu] *m* [confusão] turmoil.

tosa [ˈtɔza] *f* **-1.** [de pêlo] trimming. **-2.** [de lã] shearing.

tosar [4] [to'za(x)] *vt* **-1.** [pêlo] to clip. **-2.** [cabelo] to crop.

tosco, ca [ˈtoʃku, ka] *adj* crude.

tosquiar [16] [toʃ'kja(x)] *vt* [ovelha] to shear.

tosse [ˈtɔsi] *f* cough; ~ **de cachorro** *ou* **comprida** whooping cough; ~ **seca** dry cough.

tossir [59] [to'si(x)] *vi* **-1.** [ger] to cough. **-2.** [expelir] to cough up.

tostado, da [toʃ'tadu, da] *adj* **-1.** [levemente queimado] browned. **-2.** [moreno] tanned.

tostão [toʃ'tãw] *(pl* **-ões)** *m* [dinheiro] cash; **estava sem um** ~ I didn't have a penny; **fiquei sem um** ~ I was left penniless.

tostar [4] [toʃ'ta(x)] *vt* **-1.** [ger] to brown. **-2.** [pele] to tan.

total [to'taw] *(pl* **-ais)** ◇ *adj* total. ◇ *m* total; **no** ~ in total.

totalidade [totali'dadʒi] *f* entirety; **a** ~ **da população** the entire population; **a** ~ **dos alunos** all the students; **em sua** ~ in its/their entirety.

totalitário, ria [totali'tarju, rja] *adj* totalitarian.

totalitarismo [totalita'riʒmu] *m* totalitarianism.

totalizar [4] [totali'za(x)] *vt* **-1.** [calcular o total de] to total up. **-2.** [atingir o total de] to total.

totalmente [totaw'mẽntʃi] *adv* entirely, totally.

touca [ˈtoka] *f* [de lã, malha] bonnet; ~ **de banho/natação** bathing/swimming cap.

toucador [toka'do(x)] *(mpl* **-es)** *m* [cômoda] dressing table.

toucinho [to'siɲu] *m* uncured bacon; ~ **defumado** smoked bacon.

toupeira [to'pejra] *f* **-1.** *ZOOL* mole. **-2.** *fig* [ignorante] dimwit.

tourada [to'rada] *f* bullfight.

tourear [15] [to'rja(x)] ◇ *vt* to fight *(bulls)*. ◇ *vi* to be a bullfighter.

toureiro, ra [to'rejru, ra] *m, f* bullfighter.

touro [ˈtoru] *m* **-1.** *ZOOL* bull. **-2.** *fig:* **ser um** ~ [ser robusto] to be strong as an ox.

➡ **Touro** *m ASTRO* Taurus.

toxemia [tokse'mia] *f* toxaemia *UK*, toxemia *US*.

tóxico, ca [ˈtɔksiku, ka] *adj* toxic.

➡ **tóxico** *m* **-1.** [veneno] poison. **-2.** [droga] drug.

toxicômano, na [toksi'komanu, na] *m, f* drug addict.

toxina [tok'sina] *f* toxin.

TPM *(abrev de* **Tensão Pré-Menstrual)** *f* PMT.

trabalhadeira [trabaʎa'dejra] *f* ▷ **trabalhador**.

trabalhado, da [traba'ʎadu, da] *adj* worked.

trabalhador, ra [trabaʎa'do(x), ra] *(mpl* **-es**, *fpl* **-s)** ◇ *adj* [laborioso] hard-working; **classe trabalhadora** *POL* working class. ◇ *m, f* worker; **(~) autônomo** freelance (worker); ~ **braçal** manual worker.

trabalhão [traba'ʎãw] *m* = **trabalheira**.

trabalhar [4] [traba'ʎa(x)] ◇ *vt* **-1.** [ger] to work. **-2.** [aprimorar] to work on. **-3.** [elaborar] to develop. ◇ *vi* to work; ~ **em algo** [em projeto] to work at sthg; *TEATRO* to perform in sthg; ~ **com algo** [num ramo] to work in sthg; [comerciar com] to deal in; ~ **como algo** [exercer a profissão de] to work as sthg.

trabalheira [traba'ʎejra] *f* hard work; **ser** *ou* **dar uma** ~ to be a lot of work.

trabalhista [traba'ʎiʃta] ◇ *adj* **-1.** [ger] labour *UK*, labor *US*; **Partido Trabalhista** Labour Party. **-2.** [que é especialista em direito do trabalho] employment *(antes de subst)*. ◇ *mf* [POL - partidário] Labour Party supporter; [- membro] Labour Party member.

trabalho [tra'baʎu] *m* **-1.** [ger] work; ~ **braçal** manual work; ~ **de campo** fieldwork; ~ **doméstico** domestic work; ~**s forçados** forced labour *UK*, forced labor *US*; ~ **de parto** labour *UK*, labor *US*; ~ **artesanal** craftwork. **-2.** [tarefa] job. **-3.** *ECON* labour *UK*, labor *US*. **-4.** *EDUC* homework. **-5.** [espirit] spell; **fazer um** ~ to cast a spell. **-6.**: **dar** ~ **(a alguém)** [exigir esforço] to be a lot of work (for sb); [causar transtorno] to be a bother (to sb).

trabalhoso, osa [traba'ʎozu, ɔza] *adj* arduous.

traça [ˈtrasal *f* **-1.** [de roupa] moth. **-2.** [de livro] bookworm.

traçado [tra'sadu] *m* **-1.** [conjunto de traços] sketch. **-2.** [planta] plan.

tração [tra'sãw] *f* traction; ~ **nas quatro rodas** four-wheel drive.

traçar [13] [tra'sa(x)] *vt* **-1.** [fazer com traços] to sketch. **-2.** [planejar] to draw up. **-3.** [demarcar] to mark out. **-4.** *fam* [devorar] to devour.

traço [tra'sul *m* **-1.** [linha] line. **-2.** [sinal de pontuação] (en) dash. **-3.** [modo de desenhar] style. **-4.** [característica] trait.

➡ **traços** *mpl* **-1.** [feições] features. **-2.** *fig* [vestígio] traces. **-3.** *fig* [laivos] traces. **-4.** [pequena quantidade de substância] traces.

tradição [tradʒi'sãw] *(pl* **-ões)** *f* tradition.

tradicional [tradʒisjo'naw] (*pl* **-ais**) *adj* traditional.

tradicionalista [tradʒisjona'liʃta] <> *adj* traditionalist. <> *mf* traditionalist.

tradicionalmente [tradʒisjonaw'mẽntʃi] *adv* traditionally.

tradução [tradu'sãw] (*pl* **-ões**) *f* **-1.** [ger] translation. **-2.** *COMPUT:* ~ **eletrônica** machine translation, automatic translation.

tradutor, ra [tradu'to(x), ra] (*mpl* **-es**, *fpl* **-s**) <> *adj* translating. <> *m, f* translator; ~ **juramentado** accredited translator.

traduzir [72] [tradu'zi(x)] <> *vt* **-1.** [texto, código] to translate; ~ **algo do português para o inglês** to translate sthg from Portuguese into English. **-2.** [sentimento, pensamento] to express. <> *vi* **-1.** [saber traduzir] to translate. **-2.** [ser tradutor] to work as a translator.

  ◆ **traduzir-se** *vp* [manifestar-se]**: sua tristeza se traduz em agressão** her grief is expressed through aggression.

traduzível [tradu'zivew] (*pl* **-eis**) *adj* translatable.

trafegar [14] [trafe'ga(x)] *vi* [transitar] to be driven.

trafegável [trafe'gavew] (*pl* **-eis**) *adj* passable.

tráfego ['trafegu] *m* traffic; ~ **engarrafado** traffic jam; ~ **aéreo** air traffic.

traficante [trafi'kãntʃi] *mf* trafficker; ~ **de drogas** drug trafficker *ou* dealer.

traficar [12] [trafi'ka(x)] <> *vt* to traffic in. <> *vi* to traffic; ~ **com** to deal in.

tráfico ['trafiku] *m* traffic; ~ **de drogas** drug trafficking; ~ **de influência** backscratching.

tragada [tra'gada] *f* [em cigarro] drag.

tragar [14] [tra'ga(x)] <> *vt* **-1.** [engolir] to swallow. **-2.** [inalar] to inhale. **-3.** *fam* [tolerar] to tolerate. <> *vi* [inalar] to inhale.

tragédia [tra'ʒɛdʒja] *f* tragedy.

trágico, ca [tra'ʒiku, ka] <> *adj* **-1.** [ger] tragic. **-2.** *fig* [dado a fazer drama] over-dramatic. <> *m, f* [ator] tragic actor (*f* actress).

tragicomédia [traʒiko'mɛdʒa] *f* tragicomedy.

tragicômico, ca [traʒi'komiku, ka] *adj* tragicomic.

trago ['tragu] <> *v* ▷ **trazer**. <> *m* **-1.** [gole] mouthful; **de um só** ~ in one gulp. **-2.** [dose pequena] drop. **-3.** [em cigarro] puff; **dar um** ~ **(em)** to take a puff (of).

traguei [tra'gej] *v* ▷ **tragar**.

traição [traj'sãw] (*pl* **-ões**) *f* **-1.** [deslealdade] disloyalty. **-2.** [infidelidade] infidelity. **-3.** *POL* treason.

traiçoeiro, ra [traj'swejru, ra] *adj* **-1.** [pessoa] disloyal. **-2.** [ação] treacherous. **-3.** [mar, passagem] treacherous.

traidor, ra [traj'do(x), ra] (*mpl* **-es**, *fpl* **-s**) <> *adj* **-1.** [infiel] unfaithful. **-2.** [comprometedor] betraying. <> *m, f* [pessoa] traitor.

trailer ['trejle(x)] *m* **-1.** [ger] trailer. **-2.** [tipo casa] caravan *UK*, trailer *US*.

traineira [traj'nejra] *f NÁUT* trawler.

training ['trejnĩŋ] *m* tracksuit.

trair [68] [tra'i(x)] *vt* **-1.** [atraiçoar] to betray. **-2.** [ser infiel a] to be unfaithful to. **-3.** [não cumprir - promessa] to break; [- dever] to fail in. **-4.** [revelar] to betray.

  ◆ **trair-se** *vp:* ~**-se por algo/fazendo algo** [denunciar-se] to give o.s. away by sthg/doing sthg.

trajar [4] [tra'ʒa(x)] *vt* to wear.

  ◆ **trajar-se** *vp:* ~**-se de** to be dressed in.

traje ['traʒi] *m* dress; ~ **de banho** swimsuit; ~ **de passeio** smart dress; ~ **a rigor** evening dress; ~ **s menores** underwear *(sg)*.

trajeto [tra'ʒɛtu] *m* distance, journey.

trajetória [traʒe'tɔrja] *f* **-1.** [trajeto] path. **-2.** *fig* [caminho] course.

tralha ['traʎa] *f* [traste] junk.

trama ['trãma] *f* **-1.** [ger] plot. **-2.** [de tecido] weft.

tramar [4] [tra'ma(x)] <> *vt* **-1.** [tecer] to weave. **-2.** [maquinar] to plot. <> *vi* [conspirar]**:** ~ **contra** to plot against.

trambique [trãn'biki] *m fam* [negócio fraudulento] con; **dar um** ~ **em** [burlar] to con.

trambiqueiro, ra [trãnbi'kejru, ra] <> *adj* slippery. <> *m, f* con artist.

trambolhão [tranbo'ʎãw] (*pl* **-ões**) *m* tumble; **levar um** ~ to be knocked down; **desceu as escadas aos trambolhões** he stumbled down the stairs; **abrir caminho aos trambolhões** to push one's way through.

trambolho [tran'boʎul] *m* [objeto grande e incômodo] encumbrance.

tramitar [4] [trami'ta(x)] *vi* to be dealt with.

trâmites ['trãmitʃiʃ] *mpl fig* [vias] procedures.

tramóia [tra'mɔja] *f* **-1.** [trama] scheme. **-2.** [trapaça] swindle.

trampolim [trãnpo'lĩ] (*pl* **-ns**) *m* **-1.** *ESP* diving board. **-2.** *fig* [meio] springboard.

tranca ['trãnka] *f* **-1.** [de porta] bolt; **passar a** ~ **em** to bolt. **-2.** [de carro] lock; **passar a** ~ **em** to lock.

trança ['trãnsa] *f* **-1.** [ger] plaited bread. **-2.** [trançado] braid.

trançado, da [trãn'sadu, da] *adj* **-1.** [cabelo] plaited. **-2.** [cinto, galão, fita] braided. **-3.** [cesto] woven.

trancado, da [trãnka'du, da] *adj* [fechado] firmly shut.

trancafiar [16] [trãnka'fja(x)] *vt* to lock up.

trancar [12] [trãn'ka(x)] *vt* **-1.** [chavear] to lock. **-2.** [prender] to lock up. **-3.** *EDUC & UNIV* [matrícula] to suspend. **-4.** *FUT* to shove (to one side).

  ◆ **trancar-se** *vp* **-1.** [fechar-se] to shut o.s. away. **-2.** [não se manifestar] to clam up.

trançar [13] [trãn'sa(x)] <> *vt* **-1.** [cabelo] to plait. **-2.** [palha, fita] to weave. <> *vi fam* [zanzar] to mope.

tranco ['trãnku] *m* **-1.** [andadura de cavalo] trot. **-2.** [esbarrão] shove. **-3.** [solavanco] jolt. **-4.** *fam* [advertência] jolt.

  ◆ **aos trancos** *loc adv* [aos solavancos] jolting.

  ◆ **aos trancos e barrancos** *loc adv* [com dificuldade] with great difficulty.

tranqüilamente [trãŋkwila'mẽntʃi] *adv* **-1.** [com

calma] calmly. **-2.** [sossegadamente] peacefully. **-3.** [com facilidade, seguramente] easily.

tranqüilidade [trãŋkwili'dadʒil *f* tranquillity; **preciso de ~ para fazer isso** I need peace and quiet to do this.

tranqüilizador, ra [trãŋkwiliza'do(x), ral *adj* **-1.** [música] soothing. **-2.** [pessoa, notícia] reassuring.

tranqüilizante [trãŋkwili'zãntʃil <> *adj* soothing. <> *m* MED tranquillizer.

tranqüilizar [trãŋkwili'za(x)] *vt* **-1.** [acalmar] to calm (down). **-2.** [despreocupar] to reassure.
➡ **tranqüilizar-se** *vp* to calm down.

tranqüilo, la [trãŋ'kwilu, lal *adj* **-1.** [mulher, criança] calm. **-2.** [lugar, sono] peaceful. **-3.** [consciência] clear. **-4.** [sem dificuldades] easy. **-5.** [certo] certain.

transa ['trãnzal *f fam* **-1.** [combinação] arrangement. **-2.** [relação] relationship. **-3.** [relação sexual] sex. **-4.** [assunto] matter. **-5.** [negócios] business.

transação [trãnza'sãwl (*pl* -ões) *f* **-1.** [combinação, acordo] agreement. **-2.** [negociação] deal. **-3.** COM business.

transamazônico, ca [trãnzama'zoniku, kal *adj* trans-Amazonian.

transar [4] [trãn'za(x)] <> *vt* **-1.** *fam* [combinar] to arrange. **-2.** [arranjar] to obtain. **-3.** [drogas - tomar] to take; [- negociar] to deal in. <> *vi* **-1.** [ter relação sexual] to have sex; **~ com** to have sex with. **-2.** [relacionar-se]: **~ com** to hang out with. **-3.** [negociar, trabalhar]: **~ com** to deal in.

transatlântico, ca [trãnza'tlãntʃiku, kal *adj* transatlantic.
➡ **transatlântico** *m* liner.

transbordamento [trãnʒboxda'mẽntul *m* overflow.

transbordar [4] [trãnʒbox'da(x)] *vi*: **~ (de)** to overflow (from); **~ de felicidade** to be overjoyed.

transbordo [trãnʒ'bɔxdul *m* NÁUT transfer.

transcendência [trãnsẽn'dẽnsjal *f* transcendence.

transcendental [trãnsẽndẽn'tawl (*pl* -ais) *adj* transcendental.

transcender [5] [trãnsẽn'de(x)] *vt*: **~ (a) algo** to transcend sthg.

transcodificar [5] [trãnʒkodʒifi'ka(x)] *vt* [videoteipe] to transcode.

transcorrer [trãnʃko'xe(x)] *vi* **-1.** [decorrer] to go by. **-2.** [decorrer em certo estado ou condição] to pass off.

transcrever [5] [trãnʃkre've(x)] *vt* **-1.** [ger] to transcribe. **-2.** [copiar] to copy.

transcrição [trãnʃkri'sãwl (*pl* -ões) *f* **-1.** [ato] transcription. **-2.** [texto transcrito] transcript; **~ fonética** phonetic transcription.

transcrito, ta [trãnʃ'kritu, tal <> *pp* ▷ transcrever.
➡ **transcrito** *m* transcript.

transcurso [trãnʃ'kuxsul *m* course.

transe ['trãnzil *m* **-1.** [espírito] anguish. **-2.** [situação difícil] ordeal. **-3.** [hipnótico] trance.

transeunte [trãn'zeũntʃil *mf* passer-by.

transferência [trãnʃfe'rẽnsjal *f* **-1.** [ger] transfer. **-2.** PSIC transference. **-3.** [adiamento] postponement.

transferir [57] [trãnʃfe'ri(x)] *vt* **-1.** [deslocar]: **~ algo/alguém para algum lugar** to transfer sthg/sb somewhere. **-2.** [transmitir]: **~ algo para alguém** to transfer sthg to sb; PSIC to transfer sthg onto sb. **-3.** [adiar] to postpone.
➡ **transferir-se** *vp* [mudar-se] to move.

transfigurar [4] [trãnʃfigu'ra(x)] *vt* [pessoa, rosto] to transfigure.
➡ **transfigurar-se** *vp* [pessoa, rosto] to be transfigured.

transformação [trãnʃfoxma'sãwl (*pl* -ões) *f* transformation.

transformador, ra [trãnʃfoxma'do(x), ral (*mpl* -es, *fpl* -s) *m* ELETR transformer.

transformar [4] [trãnʃfox'ma(x)] *vt* **-1.** [dar nova forma, modificar] to transform. **-2.** [converter]: **~ algo/alguémem** to turn sthg/sb into.
➡ **transformar-se** *vp* **-1.** [mudar, transfigurar-se] to be transformed. **-2.** [converter-se]: **~-se em** to turn into, to become. **-3.** [disfarçar-se]: **~-se em** to disguise o.s. as.

transformista [trãnʃfox'miʃtal *m* [travesti] transvestite.

transfusão [trãnʃfu'zãwl (*pl* -ões) *f* transfusion; **~ de sangue** blood transfusion.

transgredir [57] *[trãnʒgre'dʒi(x)] *vt* [infringir] to transgress.

transgressão [trãnʒgre'sãwl (*pl* -ões) *f* transgression.

transgressor, ra [trãʒgre'so(x), ral <> *adj* offending. <> *m*, *f* offender; **~ da lei** offender.

transição [trãnzi'sãwl (*pl* -ões) *f* [passagem de um estado a outro] transition; **fase de ~** transition stage.

transigente [trãnzi'ʒẽntʃil *adj* compliant.

transigir [52] [trãnzi'ʒi(x)] *vi* **-1.** [ceder] to compromise; **~ com alguém** to meet sb halfway. **-2.** [condescender] to condescend; **~ com algo** to yield to sthg.

transitar [4] [trãnzi'ta(x)] *vi*: **~ (por)** [pessoa, carro] to travel (through); [documentos] to work one's way (through).

transitável [trãnzi'tavewl (*pl* -eis) *adj* passable.

transitivo, va [trãnzi'tʃivu, val *adj* GRAM transitive.

trânsito ['trãnzitul *m* **-1.** [ger] passage; **passageiro em ~** transit passenger. **-2.** [tráfego] traffic; **~ impedido** no entry. **-3.** [boa aceitação] acceptance; **ter bom ~ em** to be well-accepted in.

transitório, ria [trãnzi'tɔrju, rjal *adj* transitory.

transladar [4] [trãnʒla'da(x)] *vt* = trasladar.

translado [trãnʒ'ladul *m* = traslado.

translúcido, da [trãnʒ'lusidu, dal *adj* **-1.** [que deixa passar a luz] translucent. **-2.** *fig* [claro] clear.

transmissão [trãnʒmi'sãwl (*pl* -ões) *f* **-1.** [ger]

transmission. -2. [de ordem, notícia, recado] sending; ~ **de pensamento** mind-reading. **-3.** [de bens, cargo] transfer. **-4.** [*RÁDIO & TV* - programa] broadcast; [- ato de transmitir] broadcasting; ~ **ao vivo** live broadcast.

transmissível [trãnʒmi'sivew] (*pl* -eis) *adj* [doença] transmittable.

transmissor, ra [trãnʒmi'so(x), ra] *adj* transmitting.

→ **transmissor** *m* -1. [ger] transmitter. -2. [de doença] carrier.

transmitir [6] [trãnʒmi'tʃi(x)] *vt* -1. [ger] to transmit. -2. [comunicar] to send. -3. [transferir] to transfer. -4. *RÁDIO & TV* to broadcast.

transparecer [25] [trãnʃpare'se(x)] *vi* -1. [aparecer]: ~ **através/por trás de** to be visible through/behind. -2. *fig* [revelar-se]: ~ **(em)** to show through (in).

transparência [trãnʃpa'rênsja] *f* -1. [ger] transparency. -2. [usada em projetor] slide.

transparente [trãnʃpa'rêntʃi] *adj* -1. [ger] transparent. -2. [roupa] see-through. -3. *fig* [claro, evidente - sentimentos, intenções] clear; **o livro é de um moralismo** ~ the book is clearly moralistic; [- pessoa] transparent.

transpassar [4] [trãnʃpa'sa(x)] *vt* -1. [atravessar] to cross. -2. [penetrar, furar] to pierce. -3. [peça de vestuário] to overlap.

transpiração [trãnʃpira'sãw] *f* -1. [ato] perspiration. -2. [suor] perspiration.

transpirar [4] [trãnʃpi'ra(x)] <> *vt* -1. [suar] to perspire. -2. [exprimir] to exude. <> *vi* -1. [suar] to perspire. -2. [revelar-se] to transpire. -3. [divulgar-se] to become known.

transplantar [4] [trãnʃplãn'ta(x)] *vt*: ~ **algo (de/ para)** to transplant sthg (from/to).

transplante [trãnʃ'plãntʃi] *m* transplant.

transpor [45] [trãnʃ'po(x)] *vt* -1. [ger] to transpose. -2. [atravessar] to cross. -3. *fig* [obstáculos] to overcome. -4. [mudar de lugar] to change the position of.

transportadora [trãnʃpoxta'dora] *f* haulage company.

transportar [trãnʃpox'ta(x)] *vt* -1. [levar] to transport. -2. *fig* [remontar mentalmente]: ~ **alguém a algum lugar/tempo** to take sb back to some place/time.

transporte [trãnʃ'poxtʃi] *m* -1. [ato] transport. -2. [condução] haulage; ~ **coletivo** public transport. -3. [soma] amount carried forward.

transposto, osta [trãnʃ'postu, ɔʃta] *pp* ▷ transpor.

transtornado, da [trãnʃtox'nadu, da] *adj* upset.

transtornar [4] [trãnʃtox'na(x)] *vt* -1. [abalar] to upset. -2. [alterar] to disrupt.

→ **transtornar-se** *vp* to get upset.

transtorno [trãnʃ'toxnu] *m* -1. [perturbação] confusion. -2. [desordem, alteração] disruption. -3. [contrariedade, contratempo] upset.

transversal [trãnʒvex'saw] (*pl* -ais) <> *adj* -1. [corte, linha] transverse. -2. [rua]: **esta rua é ~ à**

avenida principal this street crosses the main avenue. <> *f* [rua transversal] cross street.

transverso, sa [trãnʒ'vɛxsu, sa] *adj* transverse.

transviado, da [trãnʒ'vjadu, da] *adj* wayward.

transviar [16] [trãnʒ'vja(x)] *vt* to lead astray.

→ **transviar-se** *vp* -1. [perder-se] to go astray. -2. [corromper-se] to become corrupted.

trapaça [tra'pasa] *f* cheating; **fazer ~s no jogo** to cheat during the game.

trapacear [15] [trapa'sja(x)] *vt & vi* to cheat.

trapaceiro, ra [trapa'sejru, ra] <> *adj* cheating. <> *m, f* cheat.

trapalhada [trapa'ʎada] *f* [confusão] confusion.

trapalhão, ona [trapa'ʎãw, ʎona] (*mpl* -ões, *fpl* -s) *adj* clumsy.

trapeiro, ra [tra'pejru, ra] *m, f* -1. [quem cata trapos] rag-and-bone-man. -2. [quem cata papéis] scavenger.

trapézio [tra'pɛzju] *m* -1. [aparelho] trapeze. -2. *GEOM* trapezium. -3. [*ANAT*- no pescoço] trapezius; [- do carpo] trapezium.

trapezista [trape'ziʃta] *mf* trapeze artist.

trapezoidal [trapezoj'daw] (*pl* -ais) *adj* trapezoidal.

trapo [ˈtrapu] *m* -1. [pedaço de pano] rag. -2. *fig*: **estar um ~** [estar mal física ou moralmente] to be down and out; [estar muito cansado] to be washed out.

→ **trapos** *mpl* [roupa surrada] rags.

traquéia [tra'kɛja] *f* trachea, windpipe.

traquejo [tra'keʒu] *m* experience.

traqueotomia [trakjoto'mia] *f* tracheotomy.

traquinas [tra'kinaʃ] *adj inv* mischievous.

trarei [tra'rej] *v* ▷ trazer.

traria [tra'ria] *v* ▷ trazer.

trás [ˈtrajʃ] *adv & prep* behind; **de ~ para frente** back to front; **andar para ~** to walk backwards; **ficar para ~** to fall behind; **de ~** back; **por ~ de** behind; **dar para ~** to back out.

traseira [tra'zejra] *f* -1. [parte posterior] rear. -2. *fam* [nádegas] bottom.

traseiro, ra [tra'zejru, ra] *adj* rear.

→ **traseiro** *m fam* [nádegas] bottom.

trasladar [4] [trazla'da(x)] *vt* -1. *JUR* to transfer. -2. [transferir]: ~ **algo (de ...) para** to transfer sthg (from ...) to.

traslado [traz'ladu] *m* -1. *JUR* transcript. -2. [transferência] transfer.

traspassar [trazpa'sə(x)] *vt* = transpassar.

traste [ˈtraʃtʃi] *m* -1. [objeto de pouco valor] bauble. -2. [pessoa - inútil] no-hoper; [- de mau caráter] rogue; **estar um ~** [estar mal fisicamente] to be a wreck.

tratado, da [tra'tadu, da] *m* -1. [acordo] treaty; ~ **de paz** peace treaty. -2. [obra] treatise.

tratador, ra [trata'do(x), ra] *m, f*: ~ **de cavalos** groom.

tratamento [trata'mẽntu] *m* -1. [ger] treatment; **forma de** ~ form of address; ~ **médico** medical treatment; ~ **de choque** shock treatment. -2. [de problema, tema] handling.

tratante [tra'tãntʃil *mf* rogue.
tratar [4] [tra'ta(x)] *vt* -**1.** [ger] to treat. -**2.** [combinar] to deal with. -**3.** *MED:* ~ **(de) alguém/algo** to treat sb/sthg. -**4.** [negociar] to organize. -**5.** [abordar] to deal with. - **6.** [forma de tratamento]: ~ **alguém de** *ou* **por algo** to address sb as *ou* by sthg.
 ➡ **tratar com** *vi* [lidar com] to deal with.
 ➡ **tratar de** *vi* -**1.** [cuidar de - pessoa, planta] to care for; [- caso, negócio] to look after. -**2.** [organizar] to organize. -**3.** [discorrer, versar sobre] to deal with. -**4.** [empenhar-se]: ~ **de fazer algo** to try to do sthg.
 ➡ **tratar-se** *vp* -**1.** [cuidar-se] to look after o.s. -**2.** *MED:* ~**-se com alguém** to be under sb's care. -**3.** *loc:* **trata-se de ...** it's a matter of ...; **trata-se de uma moça de origem muito humilde** she happens to be a girl from a very humble background; **de que se trata?** what's it about?
tratável [tra'tavew] (*pl* -**eis**) *adj* -**1.** [pessoa] approachable. -**2.** [doença] treatable.
trato ['tratul *m* -**1.** [tratamento] treatment. -**2.** [convivência, contato] dealings *(pl).* -**3.** [acordo, combinação] agreement. -**4.** [modo]: **mulher de fino ~** a refined woman.
trator [tra'to(x)] (*pl* -**es**) *m* tractor.
trauma ['trawmal *m* -**1.** *MED* injury. -**2.** *PSIC* trauma.
traumático, ca [traw'matʃiku, kal *adj* traumatic.
traumatismo [trawma'tʃiʒmul *m* *MED* injury.
traumatizante [trawmatʃi'zãntʃil *adj* traumatizing.
traumatizar [4] [trawmatʃi'za(x)] *vt* -**1.** *MED* to injure. -**2.** *PSIC* to traumatize. -**3.** *fig* [afetar] to affect.
trava ['traval *f* [peça] stop.
travada [tra'vadal *f* [freada] braking; **dar uma ~ em algo** [frear] to put on the breaks; *fig* [interromper] to put the brakes on sthg.
travado, da [tra'vadu, dal *adj* -**1.** [preso] locked. -**2.** [freado] stopped.
travar [4] [tra'va(x)] <> *vt* -**1.** [fazer parar] to stop. -**2.** [frear] to brake. -**3.** [iniciar, desencadear - conversa, amizade] to strike up; [- luta] to start. -**4.** [movimento] to hinder. -**5.** [segurar] to take hold of. <> *vi* to stop.
trave ['travil *f* -**1.** *CONSTR* beam. -**2.** *ESP* crossbar.
através [tra'vɛʃ] *m:* **olhar de ~ (para)** to look sideways (at).
travessa [tra'vɛsal *f* -**1.** [rua] alleyway. -**2.** [prato] serving dish. -**3.** [prendedor de cabelo] slide.
travessão [trave'sãw] (*pl* -**ões**) *m* *GRAM* (em) dash.
travesseiro [trave'sejrul *m* pillow.
travessia [trave'sial *f* -**1.** [ato] crossing. -**2.** [viagem] journey.
travesso, ssa [tra'vesu, sal *adj* [criança] naughty.
travessura [trave'sural *f* -**1.** [de criança] mischief; **fazer ~s** to get up to mischief. -**2.** [brincadeira] prank.
travesti [trave'ʃtʃil *m* -**1.** [homossexual] transvestite. -**2.** [artista] drag artist.

trazer [30] [tra'ze(x)] *vt* -**1.** [ger] to bring; ~ **de volta** to bring back. -**2.** [ter] to have. -**3.** [usar, trajar] to wear. -**4.** *loc:* ~ **algo à baila** to air sthg.
TRE (*abrev de* **Tribunal Regional Eleitoral**) *m* *Regional Electoral Court*.
trecho ['treʃul *m* -**1.** [parte do espaço de um lugar] stretch. -**2.** *LITER & MÚS* passage.
treco ['trɛkul *m* *fam* [coisa] thing; **ter um ~** [sentir-se mal] to have a nasty turn; [zangar-se] to have a fit.
trégua ['trɛgwal *f* -**1.** *MIL* truce. -**2.** *fig* [descanso] rest.
treinado, da [trej'nadu, dal *adj* -**1.** [animal] trained. -**2.** [atleta] fit. -**3.** [acostumado] practised *UK*, practiced *US*.
treinador, ra [trejna'do(x), ral (*mpl* -**es**, *fpl* -**s**) *m, f* trainer.
treinamento [trejna'mẽntul *m* training.
treinar [4] [trej'na(x)] <> *vt* -**1.** [ger] to train. -**2.** [praticar] to practise *UK*, to practice *US*. <> *vi* [praticar] to train.
treino ['trejnul *m* -**1.** [ger] training. -**2.** [destreza] skill.
trejeito [tre'ʒejtul *m* -**1.** [gesto] gesture. -**2.** [gesto cômico] funny face.
trela ['trɛlal *f:* **dar ~ a** *ou* **para alguém** [conversar com] to keep chatting to sb; [dar confiança a] to encourage sb.
treliça [tre'lisal *f* [para porta, planta] trellis.
trem ['trẽl (*pl* -**ns**) *m* -**1.** *FERRO* train; **ir de ~** to go by train; **pegar um ~** to take a train; ~ **de carga** goods train; ~ **expresso** express train. -**2.** *AERON:* ~ **de aterrissagem** landing gear, undercarriage. -**3.** *loc:* ~ **da alegria** [nepotismo] jobs for the boys.
trema ['tremal *m* diaeresis *UK*, dieresis *US*.
trem-bala [ˌtrẽ'balal (*pl* **trens-bala**) *m* high-speed train.
tremedeira [treme'dejral *f* [tremor] trembling.
tremelicante [tremeli'kãntʃil *adj* -**1.** [pessoa] shivering. -**2.** [bandeira] fluttering.
tremelicar [12] [tremeli'ka(x)] *vi* to tremble; ~ **de frio** to shiver with cold.
tremelique [treme'likil *m* trembling.
tremendo, da [tre'mẽndu, dal *adj* -**1.** [imenso] enormous. -**2.** [terrível] terrible. -**3.** [fantástico] amazing.
tremer [5] [tre'me(x)] *vi* to shake; ~ **de frio/medo** to shake with cold/fear.
tremor [tre'mo(x)] (*pl* -**es**) *m* tremor; ~ **de terra** earthquake.
tremular [4] [tremu'la(x)] *vi* -**1.** [bandeira] to flutter. -**2.** [luz] to flicker.
trêmulo, la ['tremulu, lal *adj* -**1.** [pessoa, mão] trembling. -**2.** [passo, voz] faltering.
trena ['trenal *f* [fita métrica] tape measure.
trenó [tre'nɔl *m* sledge *UK*, sled *US*.
trepada [tre'padal *f* *mfam* leg-over; **dar uma ~** to get laid.
trepadeira [trepa'dejral *f* creeper.
trepar [4] [tre'pa(x)] *vi* -**1.** [subir]: ~ **(em algo)** to

climb (up sthg). **-2.** *mfam* [ter relações sexuais]: ~ **(com alguém)** to get laid.

trepidação [trepida'sãw] *f* shaking.

trepidante [trepi'dãntʃi] *adj* **-1.** [que trepida] shaking. **-2.** *fig* [agitado] restless.

trepidar [4] [trepi'da(x)] *vi* to shake.

três ['trejʃ] <> *num* three. <> *m* three; *veja também* **seis**.

➤ **a três por dois** *loc adv* often.

tresloucado, da [treʒlo'kadu, da] *adj* crazy.

Três-Marias [ˌtrejʃma'riaʃ] *fpl* **-1.** ASTRON Orion's Belt. **-2.** BOT bougainvillea.

três-quartos [trejʃ'kwaxtuʃ] <> *adj inv* [manga, saia] three-quarter length. <> *m* [apartamento] three-room flat *UK* ou apartment *US*.

trevas ['trɛvaʃ] *fpl* [escuridão] darkness *(sg)*.

trevo ['trevu] *m* **-1.** BOT clover. **-2.** [de vias] intersection.

treze ['trezi] <> *num* thirteen. <> *m* [algarismo] thirteen; *veja também* **seis**.

trezentos, tas [tre'zẽntuʃ, taʃ] <> *num* three hundred. <> *m* [algarismo] three hundred; *veja também* **seis**.

triagem ['trjaʒẽ] *f* **-1.** [seleção] selection; **fazer uma** ~ to make a selection. **-2.** [separação] sorting; **fazer uma** ~ to sort out.

triangular [trjãŋgu'la(x)] *adj* triangular.

triângulo ['trjãŋgulu] *m* triangle.

triathlon ['trjatlu] *m* triathlon.

tribal [tri'baw] *adj* tribal.

tribo ['tribu] *m* tribe.

tribulação [tribula'sãw] (*pl* -ões) *f* tribulation.

tribuna [tri'buna] *f* **-1.** [de orador] rostrum. **-2.** [em espetáculos públicos] platform; ~ **da imprensa** press gallery; ~ **de honra** rostrum.

tribunal [tribu'naw] (*pl* -ais) *m* **-1.** [instituição] court; **Tribunal de Contas** Court of Accounts; **Tribunal do Júri** trial by jury; **Tribunal de Justiça** Court of Justice; **Tribunal do Trabalho** Industrial Tribunal. **-2.** [os magistrados] bench.

tributação [tributa'sãw] *f* taxation.

tributar [4] [tribu'ta(x)] *vt* **-1.** [ger] to tax. **-2.** [pagar como tributo] to pay tax on. **-3.** *fig* [render, prestar] to pay.

tributário, ria [tribu'tarju, rja] *adj* **-1.** [relativo a tributo] tax *(antes de subst)*. **-2.** [rio] tributary *(antes de subst)*.

➤ **tributário** *m* [afluente] tributary.

tributável [tribu'tavew] (*pl* -eis) *adj* taxable.

tributo [tri'butu] *m* **-1.** [imposto] tax. **-2.** *fig* [ônus] duty.

tricampeão, peã [trikãn'pjãw, pjã] *m*, *f* three-times champion.

triciclo [tri'siklu] *m* **-1.** [de criança] tricycle. **-2.** [usado para a entrega de mercadorias] (delivery) tricycle.

tricô [tri'ko] *m* knitting; **fazer** ~ to knit; **de** ~ knitted.

tricolor [triko'lo(x)] *adj* **-1.** [desenho, bandeira] three-coloured *UK*, three-colored *US*. **-2.** FUT tricolour *UK*, tricolor *US*.

tricotar [4] [triko'ta(x)] *vt* & *vi* to knit.

tridimensional [tridʒimẽnsjo'naw] (*pl* -ais) *adj* three-dimensional.

trienal [trje'naw] <> *adj* triennial. <> *f* [exposição] triennial.

triênio ['trjenju] *m* three-year period.

trigal [tri'gaw] *m* wheat field.

trigêmeo, mea [tri'ʒemju, mja] <> *adj* [criança] triplet *(antes de subst)*. <> *m*, *f* triplet.

trigésimo, ma [tri'ʒɛzimu, ma] <> *num* thirtieth. <> *m* thirtieth; *veja também* **sexto**.

trigo ['trigu] *m* wheat.

trigonometria [trigonome'tria] *f* trigonometry.

trilha ['triʎa] *f* **-1.** [caminho] path. **-2.** [rasto] trail. **-3.** *fig* [exemplo]: **seguir a** ~ **de alguém** to follow in sb's footsteps. **-4.** COMPUT track. **-5.** CINE: ~ **sonora** soundtrack.

trilhado, da [tri'ʎadu, da] *adj* [percorrido] well-trodden.

trilhão [tri'ʎãw] (*pl* -ões) *num* trillion.

trilhar [4] [tri'ʎa(x)] *vt* [percorrer] to tread.

trilho [tri'ʎu] *m* **-1.** FERRO rail. **-2.** [caminho] track.

trilíngue [tri'liŋgwe] *adj* trilingual.

trilogia [trilo'ʒia] *f* trilogy.

trimestral [trimeʃ'traw] (*pl* -ais) *adj* quarterly.

trimestralidade [trimeʃtrawi'dadʒi] *f* quarterly payment.

trimestralmente [trimeʃtraw'mẽntʃi] *adv* quarterly.

trimestre [tri'mɛʃtri] *m* quarter.

trinca ['trĩŋka] *f* **-1.** [de cartas] set of three. **-2.** *fam* [de pessoas] threesome.

trincar [12] [trĩŋ'ka(x)] <> *vt* **-1.** [cortar com os dentes] to crunch. **-2.** [cerrar] to grit. **-3.** [rachar] to crack. <> *vi* [rachar] to crack.

trinchar [4] [trĩn'ʃa(x)] *vt* [carne] to carve.

trincheira [trĩn'ʃejra] *f* MIL trench.

trinco ['trĩŋku] *m* **-1.** [ferrolho] latch. **-2.** [lingüeta] catch; **passar o** ~ **na porta** to put the door on the latch.

trindade [trĩn'dadʒi] *f*: **a Santíssima Trindade** the Holy Trinity.

➤ **trindades** *fpl* angelus *(sg)*.

Trinidad e Tobago [triniˌdadʒito'bagu] *n* Trinidad and Tobago.

trinta ['trĩnta] <> *num* thirty. <> *m* thirty; *veja também* **sessenta**.

trio ['triw] *m* trio; ~ **elétrico** music float.

tripa [tri'pa] *f* **-1.** [intestino] intestine. **-2.** CULIN tripe *(inv)*. **-3.** *loc*: **fazer das** ~s **coração** to work one's guts out.

tripartir [6] [tripax'tʃi(x)] *vt* to divide into three parts.

tripé [tri'pɛ] *m* [suporte] tripod.

tríplex ['tripleks] <> *adj inv* three-storey *UK*, three-story *US*. <> *m inv* three-storey flat *UK*, three-storey apartment *US*.

triplicar [12] [tripli'ka(x)] <> *vt* **-1.** MAT to treble. **-2.** [aumentar muito] to triple. <> *vi* **-1.** [tornar-se triplo] to treble. **-2.** [aumentar muito] to triple.

tríplice ['triplisi] *adj* triple.

triplo, pla ['triplu, pla] *adj* triple.

➤ **triplo** *m*: 27 é o ~ de 9 27 is three times 9; **este sofá é o ~ daquele** this sofa is three times the size of that one.

Trípoli ['tripoli] *n* Tripoli.

tripulação [tripula'sãw] (*pl* -ões) *f* crew.

tripulado, da [tripula'du, da] *adj* -1. [nave] manned. -2. [barco] crewed.

tripulante [tripu'lãntʃi] *mf* crew member.

tripular [4] [tripu'la(x)] *vt* -1. [prover de tripulação] to man. -2. [governar] to crew.

trisavô, vó [triza'vo, vɔ] *m, f* great-great-grandfather (*f* great-great-grandmother); **os ~s** great-great-grandparents.

triste ['triʃtʃi] *adj* -1. [ger] sad. -2. [entristecedor] depressing. -3. [sombrio, lúgubre] sombre. -4. *fam* [pessoa] sad.

tristeza [triʃ'teza] *f* -1. [de pessoa] sadness. -2. [de lugar] gloominess. -3.: **ser uma ~** [ser terrível] to be appalling.

tristonho, nha [triʃ'toɲu, ɲal *adj* [pessoa, rosto, ar] melancholy.

triturar [4] [tritu'ra(x)] *vt* -1. [reduzir a fragmentos] to grind. -2. *fig* [afligir] to crush.

triunfal [trjũn'faw] (*pl* -ais) *adj* triumphal.

triunfante [trjũn'fãntʃi] *adj* triumphant.

triunfar [4] [trjũn'fa(x)] *vi* [vencer] to triumph.

triunfo ['trjũnfu] *m* triumph.

trivial [tri'vjaw] (*pl* -ais) <> *adj* -1. [comida] ordinary. -2. [assunto, preocupações] trivial. <> *m* [comida cotidiana] everyday food.

trivialidade [trivjali'dadʒi] *f* triviality.

triz ['triʃ] *m*: **por um ~** by a whisker; **escapar por um ~** to escape by the skin of one's teeth.

troca ['trɔka] *f* exchange; **em ~ de** in exchange for.

troça ['trɔsa] *f* [zombaria] ridicule; **fazer ~ de alguém** to make fun of sb.

trocadilho [troka'dʒiʎu] *m* pun.

trocado, da [tro'kadu, da] *adj* -1. [errado] wrong. -2. [dinheiro] in coins.

➤ **trocado** *m* small change.

trocador, ra [troka'do(x), ra] *m, f* [em ônibus] conductor.

trocar [12] [tro'ka(x)] <> *vt* -1. [ger] to change; ~ **alguém/algo de lugar** to change the place of sb/sthg; ~ **dinheiro** to change money. -2. [permutar] to swap. -3. [confundir] to mix up. -4. [cheque] to cash. -5. [reciprocar] to exchange. -6. [permutar]: ~ **algo/alguém por algo, ~ algo/alguém por alguém** to change sthg/sb for sthg, to change sthg/sb for sb; ~ **o dia pela noite** to live at night. -7. [dar preferência]: ~ **algo por algo** to exchange sthg for sthg. -8. *loc*: ~ **as pernas** *fig* to trip over one's (own) feet. <> *vi*: ~ **de algo** to change sthg; ~ **de bem/mal** to make up/fall out.

➤ **trocar-se** *vp* [mudar de roupa] to get changed.

troçar [tro'sa(x)] *vt* to ridicule.

troca-troca [ˌtrɔka'trɔka] *m* swap.

troco ['troku] *m* -1. [dinheiro] change. -2. *fig*

[revide] retort, rejoinder; **dar o ~ a alguém** to get one's own back; **a ~ de que ela fez isso?** [por quê, para quê] what on earth did she do that for?; **a ~ de algo/de fazer algo** [por causa de] by way of sthg/of doing sthg; [por meio de] by means of sthg/of doing sthg; **em ~ de** [em recompensa] in exchange for.

troço ['trɔsul *m* -1. *fam* [coisa] thing; **ter um ~** [sentir-se mal] to feel a pang; [ficar chocado, danado] to get a shock; **ser ~ em algum lugar/em algo** [ser influente] to have influence somewhere/in sthg; **ser um ~** [ser muito bonito, bom] to be amazing.

troféu [tro'fɛw] *m* trophy.

tromba ['trõba] *f* -1. [de elefante] trunk. -2. *fam* [cara amarrada] long face; **estar de ~** to sulk.

trombada [trõ'bada] *f* crash; **dar uma ~** to crash.

tromba-d'água [ˌtrõba'dagwa] (*pl* **trombas-d'água**) *f* [chuva] downpour; **caiu uma ~** there was a huge downpour.

trombadinha [trõba'dʒiɲa] *mf gír* [pivete] very young thief.

trombeta [trõ'beta] *f* MÚS [instrumento] trumpet.

trombone [trõ'boni] *m* -1. MÚS trombone. -2.: **botar a boca no ~** *fam fig* to tell the whole world.

trombose [trõ'bɔzi] *f* thrombosis.

trombudo, da [trõ'budu, da] *adj fig* [emburrado] sulky.

trompa ['trõpa] *f* -1. MÚS horn. -2. ANAT: ~ **de Falópio** Fallopian tube; **ligar as ~s** to have one's tubes tied, to undergo tubal ligation.

troncho, cha ['trõʃu, ʃa] *adj* -1. [torto] crooked. -2. [desajeitado] clumsy. -3. [mutilado]: ~ **de uma perna** one-legged.

tronco ['trõku] *m* -1. [BOT - caule] trunk; [- ramo] branch. -2. ANAT trunk. -3. TELEC trunkline. -4. [de família, raça] lineage.

troncudo, da [trõ'kudu, da] *adj* stocky.

trono ['tronu] *m* -1. [cadeira] throne. -2. *fig* [poder] driving seat. -3. *fam* [latrina] throne.

tropa ['trɔpa] *f* -1. MIL army. -2. [conjunto de pessoas] troop. -3. [polícia]: ~ **de choque** riot squad.

tropeção [trope'sãw] (*pl* -ões) *m* trip; **dar um ~ em algo** to trip over sthg.

tropeçar [13] [trope'sa(x)] *vi* to trip; ~ **em algo** [dar topada em] to trip over sthg; *fig* [esbarrar em] to stumble on sthg.

tropeço [tro'pesul *m fig* [obstáculo] setback.

tropeções [trope'sõjʃ] *pl* ▷ **tropeção**.

trôpego, ga ['tropegu, ga] *adj* unsteady; **estar ~ de sono** to be asleep on one's feet.

tropel [tro'pɛw] *m* -1. [multidão desordenada] mob. -2. [de animais] herd. -3. [ruído] clattering. -4. [grande confusão] hubbub.

tropical [tropi'kaw] (*pl* -ais) *adj* tropical.

tropicalismo [tropika'liʒmu] *m Brazilian musical movement*.

trópico ['trɔpiku] *m* tropic; **Trópico de Câncer/Ca-
pricórnio** Tropic of Cancer/Capricorn.
troquei [tro'kej] *v* ▷ **trocar**.
trotar [4] [tro'ta(x)] *vi* to trot.
trote ['trɔtʃi] *m* **-1.** [de cavalo] trot. **-2.** [por telefone]
hoax; **passar um ~ em alguém** to play a hoax on
sb. **-3.** [em calouro] trick; **dar um ~ em alguém** to
play a trick on sb.
trottoir [tro'twa(x)] *m*: **fazer ~** to walk the
streets.
trouxa ['troʃa] ⬦ *adj fam* [bobo] foolish. ⬦ *mf
fam* [bobo] fool. ⬦ *f* bundle.
trouxe ['trosi] *v* ▷ **trazer**.
trova ['trɔva] *f* **-1.** [cantiga] folksong. **-2.** [poesia]
ballad.
trovador [trova'do(x)] *m* troubadour.
trovão [tro'vãw] (*pl* **-ões**) *m* thunder.
trovejar [4] [trove'ʒa(x)] *vi* METEOR to thunder.
trovoada [tro'vwada] *f* thunderstorm.
trucidar [trusi'da(x)] *vt* to slaughter, to massacre.
truculência [truku'lẽnsja] *f* horror.
truculento, ta [truku'lẽntu, ta] *adj* gruesome.
trufa ['trufa] *f* truffle.
truísmo [tru'iʒmu] *m* truism.
truncar [trũŋ'ka(x)] *vt* **-1.** [texto] to shorten. **-2.**
[discurso] to cut off.
trunfo ['trũnfu] *m* trump card.
trupe ['trupi] *f* **-1.** [de artistas] troop. **-2.** *pej* [gru-
po] buch.
truque ['truki] *m* trick.
truste ['truʃtʃi] *m* **-1.** [organização financeira] trust.
-2. [grupo de empresas] corporation.
truta ['truta] *f* trout.
TSE [te 'ɛsi ɛ] (*abrev de* **Tribunal Superior Eleitoral**)
m Brazilian higher electoral tribunal.
TST [te 'ɛsi te] (*abrev de* **Tribunal Superior do
Trabalho**) *m Brazilian higher employment tribunal.*
tu ['tu] *pron pess* you.
tua ['tua] *f* ▷ **teu**.
tuba ['tuba] *f* MÚS tuba.
tubarão [tuba'rãw] (*pl* **-ões**) *m* shark.
tubário, ria [tu'barju, rja] *adj* [MED - gravidez]
ectopic; [- infecção] tubal.
tuberculose [tubexku'lɔzi] *f* tuberculosis, TB.
tuberculoso, osa [tubexku'lozu, ɔza] ⬦ *adj*
tubercular. ⬦ *m, f* person with TB.
tubinho [tu'biɲu] *m* **-1.** [tubo pequeno] small
tube. **-2.** [vestido] tube dress.
tubo ['tubu] *m* **-1.** [ger] tube; **~ de ensaio** test

tube. **-2.** [canal] pipe. **-3.** ANAT: **~ digestivo**
digestive tract.
 ▸ tubos *mpl*: **gastar/custar os ~s** to spend/
cost a bomb.
tubulação [tubula'sãw] *f* **-1.** [conjunto de tubos]
pipework. **-2.** [colocação de tubos] plumbing.
tubular [tubu'la(x)] *adj* tubular.
TUCA (*abrev de* **Teatro da Universidade Católica**)
*m theatre of the Catholic university in São
Paulo.*
tucano [tu'kãnu] *m* **-1.** ZOOL toucan. **-2.** POL
member of Brazilian Social Democratic Party.
tudo ['tudu] *pron indef* **-1.** [todas as coisas, a totalida-
de] everything; **~ (o) que** *ou* **quanto** everything
that; **é ~** that's all; **~ isso** all that; **~ quanto é
tipo de gente** all kinds of people. **-2.** [a coisa fun-
damental]: **ser ~** to be everything.
 ▸ acima de tudo *loc adv* above all.
 ▸ antes de tudo *loc adv* first of all.
 ▸ apesar de tudo *loc prep* despite everything.
 ▸ depois de tudo *loc adv* after all.
tufão [tu'fãw] (*pl* **-ões**) *m* typhoon.
tufo ['tufu] *m* **-1.** [de planta] shoot. **-2.** [de cabelo]
lock. **-3.** [de terra, pedra] mound.
tulipa [tu'lipa] *f* **-1.** BOT tulip. **-2.** [chope servido em
copo alto] *tall glass of draught beer.*
tumba ['tũnba] *f* [sepultura] tomb.
tumefação [tumefa'sãw] *f* swelling.
tumor [tu'mo(x)] (*pl* **-es**) *m* tumour *UK*, tumor *US*;
~ cerebral brain tumour; **~ maligno/benigno**
malignant/benign tumour.
túmulo ['tumulu] *m* **-1.** [monumento] tomb. **-2.**
[cova] grave. **-3.** *fig*: **ser um ~** [ser lúgubre] to be
like a tomb; [ser discreto] to be very discreet.
tumulto [tu'muwtu] *m* **-1.** [grande movimento]
commotion. **-2.** [confusão, balbúrdia] hubbub. **-3.**
[motim] riot.
tumultuado, da [tumuw'twadu, da] *adj* **-1.** [vida]
turbulent. **-2.** [rua] noisy.
tumultuar [4] [tumuw'twa(x)] ⬦ *vt* [desordenar,
agitar] to disrupt. ⬦ *vi* **-1.** [fazer barulho] to make
a noise. **-2.** [amotinar-se] to rise up.
túnel ['tunɛw] (*pl* **-eis**) *m* tunnel.
túnica ['tunika] *f* [vestimenta] tunic.
Túnis ['tuniʃ] *n* Tunis.
Tunísia [tu'nizja] *f* Tunisia.
tunisino, na [tuni'zinu, na] ⬦ *adj* Tunisian. ⬦
m, f Tunisian.
tupi [tu'pi] ⬦ *adj* Tupi. ⬦ *mf* Tupi Indian. ⬦
m [língua] Tupi.

tupi-guarani [tu͵pigwara'nil (*pl* -**is**) ⬦ *adj* Tupi. ⬦ *mf* [indígena] Tupi (Indian). ⬦ *m* Tupi.

tupiniquim [tupini'kĩl ⬦ *adj* - **1**. [relativo aos tupiniquins] Brazilian Indian. - **2**. *pej* [brasileiro] Brazilian. ⬦ *mf* Brazilian Indian.

turba ['tuxbal *f* - **1**. [multidão em desordem] mob. - **2**. [multidão] mass.

turbante [tux'bãntʃil *m* turban.

turbar [4] [tux'ba(x)] *vt* [perturbar] to trouble.

➥ **turbar-se** *vp* [tornar-se sombrio] to darken.

turbilhão [tuxbi'ʎãw] (*pl* -**ões**) *m* - **1**. [de água] whirlpool. - **2**. [de ar] whirlwind. - **3**. *fig* [agitação] whirl.

turbina [tux'binal *f* turbine.

turbinado, da [tuxbina'du, dal *adj fam* [motor, processador] turbocharged.

turbulência [tuxbu'lẽnsial *f* - **1**. METEOR turbulence. - **2**. [desordem, inquietação] unrest.

turbulento, ta [tuxbu'lẽntu, tal *adj* - **1**. METEOR stormy. - **2**. [tumultuoso] turbulent. - **3**. [que cria desordem] disorderly.

turco, ca ['tuxku, kal ⬦ *adj* Turkish. ⬦ *m, f* Turk.

➥ **turco** *m* [língua] Turkish.

turfa ['tuxfal *f* peat.

turfe ['tuxfil *m ESP* horse-racing.

túrgido, da ['tuxʒidu, dal *adj* swollen, turgid.

turíbulo [tu'ribulul *m* incense-burner.

turismo [tu'riʒmul *m* tourism; **fazer** ~ to go sightseeing.

turista [tu'riʃtal *mf* - **1**. [quem faz turismo] tourist. - **2**. [aluno] persistent absentee.

turístico, ca [tu'riʃtʃiku, kal *adj* tourist *(antes de subst)*.

turma ['tuxmal *f* - **1**. [grupo] group. - **2**. [grupo de trabalhadores] shift. - **3**. EDUC class. - **4**. *fam* [grupo de amigos] gang.

turmalina [tuxma'linal *f* tourmaline.

turnê [tux'nel *f* tour.

turno ['tuxnul *m* - **1**. [turma] group. - **2**. [horário - de trabalho] shift; [- de escola] class; ~ **da noite** night shift; ~ **da manhã** morning shift. - **3**. *ESP* round. - **4**. [de eleição] round. - **5**. [vez] turn; **por** ~ **s** in turns; **por seu** ~ in turn.

turquesa [tux'kezal ⬦ *adj inv* turquoise. ⬦ *m* [cor] turquoise. ⬦ *f* [pedra] turquoise.

Turquia [tux'kial *n* Turkey.

turra ['tuxal *f*: **viver às** ~ **s** to argue all the time.

turrão, ona [tu'xãw, ɔnal *adj fam* [teimoso, pertinaz] stubborn.

turvar [4] [tux'va(x)] ⬦ *vt* - **1**. [água, rio] to stir up. - **2**. [vista] to cloud. ⬦ *vi* - **1**. [água, rio] to grow rough. - **2**. [vista] to become cloudy. - **3**. [vinho] to become cloudy.

turvo, va ['tuxvu, val *adj* cloudy.

tusso ['tusul *v* ▷ tossir.

tutano [tu'tãnul *m ANAT* marrow.

tutela [tu'tɛlal *f* - **1**. JUR guardianship; **estar sob** ~ to be in care. - **2**. [proteção] protection. - **3**. [supervisão] supervision.

tutelar [4] [tute'la(x)] ⬦ *adj* protective. ⬦ *vt* - **1**.

JUR to act as guardian to. - **2**. [proteger] to protect.

tutor, ra [tu'to(x), ral (*mpl* -**es**, *fpl* -**s**) *m, f* guardian.

tutu [tu'tul *m* - **1**. CULIN Brazilian dish consisting of beans, bacon and cassava flour. - **2**. *fam* [dinheiro] cash.

TV [te' vel (*abrev de* **televisão**) *f* TV.

tweed ['twidʒil *m* tweed.

u, U *m* [letra] u, U.

uai ['wajl *interj* - **1**. [espanto, surpresa, terror] oh! - **2**. [reforço, confirmação] yeah!

úbere ['uberil ⬦ *adj* [solo] fertile. ⬦ *m* [mama] udder.

Ubes (*abrev de* **União Brasileira dos Estudantes Secundaristas**) *f* Brazilian union of secondary students.

ubiqüidade [ubikwi'dadʒil *f* ubiquity.

ubíquo, qua [u'bikwu, kwal *adj* ubiquitous.

Ucrânia [u'krãnja] *n* Ukraine.

ué ['wɛl *interj* - **1**. [exprimindo surpresa] what? - **2**. [exprimindo ironia] hey!

UE (*abrev de* **União Européia**) *f* EU.

UEM (*abrev de* **União Econômica e Monetária**) *f* EMU.

UERJ (*abrev de* **Universidade Estadual do Rio de Janeiro**) *f* state university of Rio de Janeiro.

UF (*abrev de* **Unidade Federativa**) *f* state.

ufa ['ufal *interj* phew!

ufanar-se [4] [ufa'naxsil *vp*: ~ **de** to take inordinate pride in.

ufanismo [ufa'niʒmul *m* - **1**. [por feitos pessoais] vainglory. - **2**. [pela pátria] national pride.

UFBA (*abrev de* **Universidade Federal da Bahia**) *f* federal university of Bahia.

UFMG (*abrev de* **Universidade Federal de Minas Gerais**) *f* federal university of Minas Gerais.

UFRGS (*abrev de* **Universidade Federal do Rio Grande do Sul**) *f* federal university of Rio Grande do Sul.

UFRJ (*abrev de* **Universidade Federal do Rio de Janeiro**) *f* federal university of Rio de Janeiro.

Uganda [u'gãndal *n* Uganda.

UHF (*abrev de* **Ultra High Frequency**) *f* UHF.

ui ['ujl *interj* - **1**. [exprimindo dor] ouch! - **2**. [exprimindo surpresa] hey!

uísque ['wiʃkil *m* whisky.

uivada [uj'vadal *f* howl.

uivante [uj'vãntʃi] adj howling.
uivar [4] [uj'va(x)] vi [ger] to howl; ~ **(de)** to howl (with).
uivo ['ujvu] m howl.
UK (abrev de **United Kingdom**) m UK.
Ulan Bator [u͜lãnba'to(x)] n Ulan Bator.
úlcera ['uwsera] f ulcer; ~ **de estômago** gastric ulcer.
ulcerar [4] [uwse'ra(x)] <> vt to ulcerate. <> vi to develop an ulcer.
ulterior [uwte'rjo(x)] adj [que ocorre depois] subsequent.
ulteriormente [uwterjox'mẽntʃi] adv subsequently.
última ['uwtʃima] f ⊳ **último**.
ultimamente [͜uwtʃima'mẽntʃi] adv lately.
ultimar [4] [uwtʃi'ma(x)] vt to conclude.
últimas ['uwtʃimaʃ] fpl ⊳ **último**.
ultimato [uwtʃi'matu], **ultimátum** [uwtʃi'matũ] m ultimatum.
último, ma ['uwtʃimu, ma] <> adj - **1.** [ger] last; **por** ~ [em último lugar] last; [finalmente] lastly. - **2.** [mais recente] latest. - **3.** [o pior] worst. - **4.** [gravíssimo] final. - **5.** [máximo] ultimate. <> m, f [em fila, competição] last.
  ➡ **última** f - **1.** [novidade] latest. - **2.** [asneira] latest blunder.
  ➡ **últimas** fpl: **dizer as últimas a alguém** to vilify sb; **estar nas últimas** [estar moribundo] to be on one's last legs; [estar na miséria] to be down and out.
ultrajante [uwtra'ʒãntʃi] adj outrageous.
ultrajar [4] [uwtra'ʒa(x)] vt to outrage.
ultraje [uw'traʒi] m outrage.
ultraleve [͜uwtra'lɛvi] <> adj ultralight. <> m microlight.
ultramar [͜uwtra'ma(x)] m overseas.
ultramarino, na [͜uwtrama'rinu, na] adj overseas (antes de subst).
ultramoderno, na [͜uwtramo'dɛxnu, na] adj state-of-the-art.
ultrapassado, da [͜uwtrapa'sadu, da] adj out-of-date.
ultrapassagem [͜uwtrapa'saʒẽ] (pl -ns) f overtaking UK, passing US.
ultrapassar [4] [͜uwtrapa'sa(x)] <> vt - **1.** [passar à frente de] to overtake UK, to pass US. - **2.** [transpor] to cross. - **3.** [em qualidade]: ~ **alguém (em algo)** to surpass sb (in sthg). - **4.** [exceder] to exceed. <> vi [passar à frente] to overtake UK, to pass US.
ultra-romântico, ca [͜uwtraxo'mãntʃiku, ka] (pl -s) adj highly romantic.
ultra-secreto, ta [͜uwtrase'krɛtu, ta] (pl -s) adj top secret.
ultra-sensível [͜uwtrasẽn'sivew] (pl -eis) adj hypersensitive.
ultra-som [͜uwtra'sõ] (pl -s) m ultrasound.
ultra-sônico, ca [͜uwtra'soniku, ka] (pl -s) adj - **1.** [onda sonora] ultrasonic. - **2.** MED ultrasound (antes de subst).

ultra-sonografia [͜uwtrasonogra'fia] (pl -s) f ultrasound scanning.
ultravioleta [͜uwtravjo'leta] adj ultraviolet.
ululante [ulu'lãntʃi] adj - **1.** [multidão] screaming. - **2.** fig [gritante] blatant; **o óbvio** ~ the glaring truth.
ulular [4] [ulu'la(x)] <> vt [protestos, insultos] to scream. <> vi - **1.** [vento] to howl. - **2.** [multidão] to scream.
um, uma [ũ, 'uma] (mpl **uns**, fpl **umas**) <> artigo indefinido a, an (antes de vogal ou h mudo); ~ **homem** a man; ʰ**uma casa** a house; **uma mulher** a woman; **uma hora** an hour; **uma maçã** an apple. <> adj - **1.** [exprime quantidade, data indefinida] one, some pl; **comprei uns livros** I bought some books; ~ **dia voltarei** I'll be back one day; **estou saindo umas semanas de férias** I'm going on holidays for a few weeks. - **2.** [para indicar quantidades] one; **trinta e** ~ **dias** thirty-one days; ~ **litro/metro/quilo** one litre/metre/kilo. - **3.** [aproximadamente] about, around; **esperei uns dez minutos** I waited for about ten minutes; **estavam lá umas cinqüenta pessoas** there were about fifty people there. - **4.** [para enfatizar]: **está** ~ **frio/calor** it's so cold/hot; **estou com uma sede** I'm so thirsty; **foi** ~ **daqueles dias!** it's been one of those days! <> pron [indefinido] one, some pl; **me dê** ~ give me one; **pede mais uma** ask for another one; ~ **deles** one of them; ~ **a** ~, ~ **por** ~ one by one; **uns e outros** some/other people. <> num one ⊳ veja também **seis**.
umbanda [ũn'bãnda] f [espirit] Afro-Brazilian cult.
umbigo [ũn'bigu] m navel.
umbilical [ũnbili'kaw] (pl -**ais**) adj ⊳ **cordão**.
umbral [ũn'braw] (pl -**ais**) m - **1.** [de porta] doorway. - **2.** [limiar] threshold.
umedecer [25] [umide'se(x)] vt to dampen.
  ➡ **umedecer-se** vp to mist over.
umedecido, da [umide'sidu, da] adj damp.
umidade [umi'dadʒi] f - **1.** [de clima, ar] humidity. - **2.** [de parede, terra] damp.
úmido, da ['umidu, da] adj damp.
UN (abrev de **United Nations**) f UN.
UnB (abrev de **Universidade de Brasília**) f university of Brasília.
unânime [u'nãnimi] adj unanimous.
unanimidade [unãnimi'dadʒi] f unanimity.
unção [ũn'sãw] f RELIG unction.
undécimo, ma [ũn'dɛsimu, ma] num eleventh.
UNE (abrev de **União Nacional dos Estudantes**) f Brazilian national union of students, ≃ NUS UK.
UNESCO (abrev de **United Nations Educational, Scientific and Cultural Organization**) f UNESCO.
ungir [78] [ũn'ʒi(x)] vt RELIG to anoint.
ungüento [ũn'gwẽntu] m ointment.
unha ['uɲa] f nail; **fazer as** ~**s** [com manicure] to do one's nails; ~ **encravada** ingrowing nail; **ser** ~ **e carne (com alguém)** to be hand in glove (with sb).

unhada [u'ɲada] *f* scratch.

unha-de-fome [‚uɲadʒi'fɔmi] (*pl* **unhas-de-fo-me**) <> *adj* miserly. <> *mf* miser.

unhar [4] [u'ɲa(x)] *vt* to scratch.

união [u'ɲjãw] (*pl* **-ões**) *f* **-1.** [ger] union. **-2.** [junção] joining.

➥ **União** *f* **-1.** [o governo federal]: **a União** the Union. **-2.** [confederação]: **a União Européia** the European Union.

unicamente [‚unika'mẽntʃi] *adv* **-1.** [exclusivamente] exclusively. **-2.** [somente] only.

Unicamp (*abrev de* **Universidade Estadual de Campinas**) *f university of Campinas*.

UNICEF (*abrev de* **United Nations International Children's Emergency Fund**) *m* UNICEF.

único, ca ['uniku, ka] *adj* **-1.** [ger] unique. **-2.** [só] single; **ser filho** ~ to be an only child; **ser o** ~ **que ...** to be the only one to ...

unicórnio [uni'kɔxnju] *m* unicorn.

unidade [uni'dadʒi] *f* **-1.** [ger] unit; ~ **central de processamento** central processing unit; ~ **de CD-ROM** CD-ROM drive; ~ **de disco** disc drive. **-2.** [uniformidade, união, coesão] unity.

unidimensional [unidʒimẽnsjo'naw] (*pl* **-ais**) *adj* one-dimensional.

unido, da [u'nidu, da] *adj* **-1.** [ligado] joined. **-2.** *fig* [pessoas] united.

UNIFESP (*abrev de* **Universidade Federal de São Paulo**) *f federal university of São Paulo*.

unificação [unifika'sãw] *f* unification.

unificar [12] [unifi'ka(x)] *vt* **-1.** [unir] to unite. **-2.** [uniformizar] to unify.

uniforme [uni'fɔxmi] <> *adj* **-1.** [que só tem uma forma, semelhante] uniform. **-2.** [que não varia] regular. <> *m* [roupa] uniform; **de** ~ in uniform.

uniformidade [unifoxmi'dadʒi] *f* uniformity.

uniformizado, da [unifoxmi'zadu, da] *adj* **-1.** [de uniforme] uniformed. **-2.** [uniforme] uniform.

uniformizar [4] [unifoxmi'za(x)] *vt* **-1.** [unificar] to standardize. **-2.** [pessoa] to put into uniform.

➥ **uniformizar-se** *vp* [vestir uniforme] to wear one's uniform.

unilateral [unilate'raw] (*pl* **-ais**) *adj* unilateral.

unir [6] [u'ni(x)] *vt* **-1.** [ger] to unite. **-2.** [juntar] [comunicar cidades] to join (together). **-3.** [combinar] to combine; ~ **o útil ao agradável** to mix business with pleasure.

➥ **unir-se** *vp* **-1.** [juntar-se] to unite; ~**-se a algo/ alguém** to join sthg/sb. **-2.** [afetivamente] to be united. **-3.** [conciliar-se] to be reconciled. **-4.** [casar]: ~**-se em matrimônio** to unite in marriage, to join in matrimony.

unissex [uni'sɛkiʃ] *adj inv* unisex.

uníssono, na [u'nisonu, na] *adj* unison; **em** ~ in unison.

unitário, ria [uni'tarju, rja] *adj* **-1.** [preço] unit (*antes de subst*). **-2.** *POL* unitary.

universal [univex'saw] (*pl* **-ais**) *adj* universal.

universalidade [univexsali'dadʒi] *f* universality.

universalizar [4] [univexsali'za(x)] *vt* to universalize.

universidade [univexsi'dadʒi] *f* **-1.** [ger] university. **-2.** [pessoal] faculty.

universitário, ria [univexsi'tarju, rja] <> *adj* university (*antes de subst*). <> *m, f* **-1.** [professor] faculty member, university lecturer. **-2.** [aluno] university student.

universo [uni'vɛxsu] *m* **-1.** *ASTRON* universe. **-2.** *fig* [mundo] world.

uno, una ['unu, 'una] *adj* single.

uns [ũnʃ] ▷ **um**.

untar [4] [ũn'ta(x)] *vt*: ~ **algo (com)** [fôrma] to grease sthg (with); [corpo] to oil sthg (with).

upa ['upa] *interj* [numa caída] oops!; [para pessoa se levantar] upsy-daisy!; [para incentivar animal] gee up!

update ['apdejtʃi] *m* COMPUT update.

upgrade ['apgrejdʒi] *m* COMPUT: **fazer um** ~ to upgrade.

upload ['aplodʒi] *m* COMPUT: **fazer um** ~ to upload.

Urais [u'rajʃ] *npl*: **os** ~ the Urals.

urânio [u'rãnju] *m* uranium.

Urano [u'rãnu] *n* Uranus.

urbanismo [uxba'niʒmu] *m* town planning.

urbanista [uxba'niʃta] *mf* town planner.

urbanístico, ca [uxba'niʃtʃiku, ka] *adj* town planning (*antes de subst*).

urbanização [uxbaniza'sãw] *f* urbanization.

urbanizado, da [uxbani'zadu, da] *adj* [área] built-up.

urbanizar [4] [uxbani'za(x)] *vt* **-1.** [área] to urbanize. **-2.** [pessoa] to refine.

urbano, na [ux'bãnu, na] *adj* **-1.** [da cidade] urban. **-2.** [pessoa - com hábitos citadinos] urban; [- cortês] urbane.

urbe ['uxbi] *f* city.

urdidura [uxdʒi'dura] *f* **-1.** [conjunto de fios] warp. **-2.** [enredo] plot.

urdir [6] [ux'dʒi(x)] *vt fig* [tramar] to plot.

urdu [ux'du] *m* [língua] Urdu.

uretra [u'rɛtra] *f* urethra.

urgência [ux'ʒẽnsja] *f* urgency; **com** ~ urgently.

urgente [ux'ʒẽntʃi] *adj* urgent.

urgentemente [uxgẽntʃi'mẽntʃi] *adv* urgently.

urgir [52] [ux'ʒi(x)] <> *vt* **-1.** [pressionar]: ~ **alguém (a/para) que** to urge sb to. **-2.** [exigir] to demand. <> *vi* **-1.** [tempo, circunstâncias] to press on. **-2.** [ser urgente] to be pressing; ~ **fazer algo** to have to do sthg; **urge resolver a situação** the situation must be resolved; **uma situação que urge ser contornada** a situation that urgently needs to be turned around.

úrico, ca ['uriku, ka] *adj* [ácido] uric.

urina [u'rina] *f* urine.

urinar [4] [uri'na(x)] <> *vt* **-1.** [sangue] to pass. **-2.** [cama] to wet. <> *vi* [expelir urina] to urinate; ~ **em** to wet.

➥ **urinar-se** *vp* [com urina] to wet o.s.

urinário, ria [uri'narju, rja] *adj* urinary.

urinol [uri'nɔw] (*pl* **-óis**) *m* chamber pot.

URL (*abrev de* **Universal Resources Locator**) *f* URL.

urna ['uxna] *f* [caixa] urn; ~ **eleitoral** ballot box; ~ **eletrônica** computerized vote.

urnas *fpl fig* [pleito eleitoral] polls.
urologia [urolo'ʒial *f* urology.
urologista [urolo'ʒiʃta] *mf* urologist.
urrar [4] [u'xa(x)] ◇ *vt* [gritar] to scream. ◇ *vi* -**1.** [animal] to roar. -**2.** [gritar]: ~ **de dor** to scream with pain.
urro ['uxu] *m* -**1.** [de animal] roar. -**2.** [grito] scream.
ursa ['uxsa] *f* ▷ **urso**.
ursada [ux'sada] *f fam*: **fazer uma** ~ **com alguém** to be disloyal to sb.
urso, sa ['uxsu, sa] *m, f* bear.
➡ **Ursa** *f*: **Ursa Maior/Menor** Ursa Major/Minor.
urso-branco [ˌuxsu'brãŋku] *m* polar bear.
urso-polar [ˌuxsu'pola(x)] (*pl* ursos-polares) *m* polar bear.
urticária [uxtʃi'karja] *f* (nettle) rash, urticaria.
urtiga [ux'tʃiga] *f* nettle.
urubu [uru'bu] *m* black vulture.
urubuzar [urubu'za(x)] *vt fam* [com o olhar] to watch like a hawk.
urucubaca [uruku'baka] *f* bad luck; **estar com** ~ to be unlucky.
Uruguai [uru'gwaj] *n*: (o) ~ Uruguay.
uruguaio, ia [uru'gwaju, ja] ◇ *adj* Uruguayan. ◇ *m, f* Uruguayan.
urze ['uxzil *f* heather.
usado, da [u'zadu, da] *adj* -**1.** [utilizado] used; **muito/pouco** ~ much/little used. -**2.** [comum] usual. -**3.** [na moda] fashionable. -**4.** [gasto] worn out.
usar [4] [u'za(x)] ◇ *vt* -**1.** [ger] to use. -**2.** [gastar] to wear out. -**3.** [vestir, ter] to wear. -**4.** [costumar]: ~ **fazer algo** to be in the habit of doing sthg. ◇ *vi* [servir-se de]: ~ **de algo** to use sthg; **modo de** ~ [em medicamento] directions for use.
Usenet (*abrev de* **Users Network**) [uze'ntʃil *f* Usenet.
username [uzex'nejmil (*pl* usernames) *m* COMPUT username.
usina [u'zina] *f* -**1.** [industrial] factory; ~ **de aço** steelworks (*pl*). -**2.** [agrícola]: ~ **de açúcar** sugar mill. -**3.** [de energia elétrica]: ~ **hidrelétrica** hydroelectric power station; ~ **termonuclear** nuclear power station.
usineiro, ra [uzi'nejru, ra] ◇ *adj* plant (*antes de subst*). ◇ *m, f* sugar mill owner.
uso ['uzul *m* -**1.** [ger] use; **objetos de** ~ **pessoal** personal belongings; **de** ~ **fácil** easy to use; **fazer** ~ **de** to make use of; **para** ~ **externo/interno** FARM for external/internal use. -**2.** [vestir] wearing. -**3.** [costume] common practice. -**4.** [desgaste] wear. -**5.** LING usage.
USP (*abrev de* **Universidade de São Paulo**) *f* university of São Paulo.
usual [u'zwaw] (*pl* -ais) *adj* usual.
usualmente [uzaw'mẽtʃil *adv* usually.
usuário, ria [u'zwarju, rja] *m, f* user.
usucapião [uzuka'pjãw] *m* JUR prescription.
usufruir [74] [uzufru'i(x)] ◇ *vt* -**1.** [desfrutar] to

enjoy. -**2.** JUR to hold in usufruct. ◇ *vi*: ~ **de** [desfrutar] to enjoy.
usufruto [uzu'frutul *m* JUR usufruct.
usura [u'zural *f* -**1.** [avareza] avarice. -**2.** [cobrança alta] usury. -**3.** [desgaste] wear.
usurário, ria [uzu'rarju, rja] ◇ *adj* [avaro] avaricious. ◇ *m, f* [agiota] usurer.
usurpação [uzuxpa'sãw] (*pl* -ões) *f* usurpation.
usurpar [4] [uzux'pa(x)] *vt* to usurp.
úteis ['utejʃ] *pl* ▷ **útil**.
utensílio [utẽ'silju] *m* -**1.** [instrumento] tool. -**2.** [de cozinha, doméstico] utensil.
uterino, na [ute'rinu, na] *adj* uterine.
útero ['uterul *m* uterus, womb.
UTI (*abrev de* **Unidade de Terapia Intensiva**) *f* ICU.
útil ['utʃiw] (*pl* -eis) *adj* -**1.** [ger] useful. -**2.** [reservado ao trabalho]: **dia** ~ working day.
utilidade [utʃili'dadʒil *f* -**1.** [ger] usefulness; **de muita/pouca** ~ of great/little use. -**2.** [utensílio]: ~s **domésticas** domestic appliances.
utilitário, ria [utʃili'tarju, rja] *adj* -**1.** [objetivo, peça etc] practical. -**2.** AUTO & COMPUT utility.
➡ **utilitário** *m* COMPUT utility.
utilização [utʃiliza'sãw] (*pl* -ões) *f* use.
utilizar [4] [utʃili'za(x)] *vt* to use.
➡ **utilizar-se** *vp*: ~-**se de** to make use of.
utilizável [utʃili'zavew] (*pl* -eis) *adj* -**1.** [máquina, instrumento] utilizable. -**2.** [sugestão] practical.
utopia [uto'pial *f* Utopia.
utópico, ca [u'tɔpiku, ka] *adj* Utopian.
UV (*abrev de* **Ultravioleta**) *m* UV.
uva ['uval *f* -**1.** [fruta] grape. -**2.** *fam* [pessoa, coisa]: **que** ~ **de ...!** what a delightful ...!; **uma** ~ a delight; **uma** ~ **de criança** a delightful child.
úvula ['uvula] *f* uvula.

v, V *m* [letra] v, V.
vã [vã] *f* ▷ **vão**.
vaca ['vaka] *f* -**1.** ZOOL cow; **carne de** ~ beef; **couro de** ~ cowhide; ~ **leiteira** dairy cow; **a** ~ **foi para o brejo** it went out the window. -**2.** *fam pej* [pessoa] lump. -**3.** *loc*: **no tempo das** ~s **gordas** in times of plenty; **no tempo das** ~s **magras** during lean times.
vaca-fria [ˌvaka'frial *f*: **voltar à** ~ to get back to the point in question.
vacância [va'kãnsja] *f* vacancy.
vacante [va'kãntʃil *adj* vacant.

vaca-preta [ˌvakaˈpreta] (*pl* **vacas-pretas**) *f* *Coca-Cola®* float.

vacilação [vasilaˈsãw] (*pl* -ões) *f* -**1.** [hesitação] hesitation. -**2.** [oscilação] swaying.

vacilada [vasiˈlada] *f* slip-up; **dar uma** ~ to slip up.

vacilante [vasiˈlãntʃi] *adj* -**1.** [hesitante] hesitant. -**2.** [pouco firme] wobbly.. -**3.** [luz] flickering.

vacilar [4] [vasiˈla(x)] *vi* -**1.** [hesitar] to hesitate; ~ **em algo/em fazer algo** to hesitate in sthg/in doing sthg. -**2.** [oscilar] to sway. -**3.** [cambalear] to totter. -**4.** [luz] to flicker.

vacilo [vaˈsilu] *m fam* -**1.** [hesitação] havering, shilly-shallying. -**2.** [erro, falha] howler, blunder.

vacina [vaˈsina] *f* vaccine.

vacinação [vasinaˈsãw] (*pl* -ões) *f* vaccination.

vacinar [4] [vasiˈna(x)] *vt* -**1.** *MED*: ~ **alguém (contra)** to vaccinate sb (against). -**2.** *fig* [imunizar]: ~ **alguém contra** to protect sb from.

➡ **vacinar-se** *vp* -**1.** *MED*: ~-**se (contra)** to be vaccinated (against). -**2.** *fig* [imunizar-se]: ~-**se contra** to become immune to.

vacum [vaˈkũ] *adj*: **gado** ~ cattle.

vácuo [ˈvakwu] *m* -**1.** *FÍSICA* vacuum; **embalado a** ~ vacuum-packed. -**2.** *METEOR* low. -**3.** [espaço] space. -**4.** *fig* [vazio] void.

vadiagem [vaˈdʒiaʒẽ], **vadiação** [vadʒiaˈsãw] *f* vagrancy.

vadiar [16] [vaˈdʒia(x)] *vi* -**1.** [viver na ociosidade] to lounge about. -**2.** [suj: aluno, professional] to skive. -**3.** [perambular] to roam.

vadio, dia [vaˈdʒiu, ʒia] *adj* -**1.** [ocioso] idle. -**2.** [aluno, professional] skiving. -**3.** [vagabundo] vagrant.

vaga [ˈvaga] *f* ➡ **vago.**

vagabundagem [vagabũnˈdaʒẽ] *f* -**1.** [vagabundismo] roaming. -**2.** [vadiagem] loafing.

vagabundear [15] [vagabũnˈdʒia(x)] *vi* -**1.** [vadiar] to drift. -**2.** [vaguear] to roam.

vagabundo, da [vagaˈbũndu, da] ⬦ *adj* -**1.** [errante] vagabond. -**2.** [vadio] idle. -**3.** [safado] shameless. -**4.** [mulher] easy. -**5.** [produto] shoddy. ⬦ *m, f* -**1.** [pessoa errante] tramp. -**2.** [vadio] idler. -**3.** [safado] rogue.

vagalhão [vagaˈʎãw] (*pl* -ões) *m* breaker.

vaga-lume [ˌvagaˈlumi] (*pl* **vaga-lumes**) *m* -**1.** *ZOOL* glow-worm. -**2.** [cine] usher.

vagão [vaˈgãw] (*pl* -ões) *m* -**1.** [de passageiros] carriage. -**2.** [de carga] wagon.

vagão-leito [vaˌgãwˈlejtu] (*pl* **vagões-leito**) *m* sleeping car.

vagão-restaurante [vaˌgãwxeʃtawˈrãntʃi] (*pl* **vagões-restaurante**) *m* buffet car.

vagar [14] [vaˈga(x)] ⬦ *vi* -**1.** [ficar desocupado] to be vacant. -**2.** [vaguear] to drift. ⬦ *m* [lentidão] slowness; **com mais** ~ at greater leisure.

vagareza [vagaˈreza] *f* slowness.

vagaroso, osa [vagaˈrozu, ɔza] *adj* slow.

vagem [ˈvaʒẽ] (*pl* -ns) *f* green bean.

vagina [vaˈʒina] *f* vagina.

vaginal [vaʒiˈnaw] (*pl* -ais) *adj* vaginal.

vago, ga [ˈvagu, ga] *adj* -**1.** [impreciso] vague. -**2.** [desocupado] vacant; **horas vagas** spare time. -**3.** [desabitado] empty.

➡ **vaga** *f* -**1.** [em hotel] vacancy. -**2.** [em empresa *etc*] vacancy; **abriu uma vaga para gerente** an opening has appeared for manager. -**3.** [para carro] space. -**4.** [onda] wave.

vagões [vaˈgõjʃ] *pl* ➡ **vagão.**

vaguear [15] [vaˈgja(x)] *vi* -**1.** [perambular] to drift. -**2.** [passear] to ramble.

vaia [ˈvaja] *f* boo.

vaiar [4] [vaˈja(x)] *vt & vi* to boo.

vaidade [vajˈdadʒi] *f* -**1.** [orgulho] vanity. -**2.** [futilidade] futility.

vaidoso, osa [vajˈdozu, ɔza] *adj* vain; **ser** ~ **de alguém/algo** to be proud of sb/sthg.

vai-não-vai [vajnãwˈvaj] *m inv* shilly-shallying.

vaivém [vajˈvẽ] (*pl* -ns) *m* -**1.** [de pessoas] to and fro. -**2.** [de pêndulo] swinging. -**3.** [de barco] rocking.

vala [ˈvala] *f* -**1.** [escavação] ditch. -**2.** [sepultura]: ~ **comum** common grave.

vale [ˈvali] *m* -**1.** *GEOGR* valley. -**2.** [documento] receipt. -**3.** [postal] ~ **postal** postal order.

valentão, ona [valẽnˈtãw, ona] (*mpl* -ões, *fpl* -s) ⬦ *adj* burly. ⬦ *m, f* burly person.

valente [vaˈlẽntʃi] *adj* brave.

valentia [valẽnˈtʃia] *f* -**1.** [coragem] courage. -**2.** [ação] feat.

valentona [valẽnˈtona] *f* ➡ **valentão.**

valer [43] [vaˈle(x)] ⬦ *vt* -**1.** [ger] to be worth; ~ **a pena** to be worthwhile. -**2.** [acarretar]: ~ **algo a alguém** to bring sb sthg. ⬦ *vi* -**1.** [ger] to be worth; **mais vale ... (do que)** it is better to ... (than to); **valeu!** *fam* cheers! -**2.** [equivaler]: ~ **por** to be worth the same as; **ou coisa que o valha** or something similar. -**3.** [ser válido] to be valid; [em jogos] to be fair; **assim não vale!** that's unfair!; **fazer** ~ **os direitos** to assert one's rights; **ser para** ~ to be the real thing. -**4.** [vigorar] to be in force.

➡ **para valer** *loc adv* [muito]: **me diverti para** ~ I had a really good time.

➡ **valer-se** *vp* [servir-se]: ~-**se de** to make use of.

vale-refeição [ˌvalixefejˈsãw] (*pl* **vales-refeição**) *m* [tíquete-refeição] meal ticket.

valeta [vaˈleta] *f* gutter.

valete [vaˈlɛtʃi] *m* [carta] jack.

vale-transporte [ˌvalitrãʃˈpɔxtʃi] (*pl* **vales-transporte**) *m* travel voucher.

vale-tudo [ˌvaliˈtudu] *m inv* free-for-all.

valia [vaˈlia] *f* value; **de grande** ~ [de grande valor] very valuable; [de grande utilidade] very useful.

validação [validaˈsãw] *f* validation.

validade [valiˈdadʒi] *f* validity; **prazo de** ~ [em comida] expiry date.

validar [4] [valiˈda(x)] *vt* to validate.

válido, da [ˈvalidu, da] *adj* valid.

valioso, osa [vaˈljozu, ɔza] *adj* valuable.

valise [vaˈlizi] *f* case.

valor [va'lo(x)] (*pl* -**es**) *m* value; **de (grande)** ~ of (great) value; **objetos de** ~ valuables; **sem** ~ worthless; **ter** ~ to be valuable; ~ **de mercado** market value; ~ **nominal** *ECON* face value; **no** ~ **de** to the value of; **dar** ~ **a algo/alguém** to value sthg/sb.
  valores *mpl* -**1.** [princípios] values. -**2.** *BOLSA* securities.
valorização [valoriza'sãw] *f* appreciation.
valorizar [4] [valori'za(x)] *vt* -**1.** [imóvel, moeda] to push up the value of. -**2.** [pessoa, trabalho] to appreciate.
  valorizar-se *vp* to appreciate.
valoroso, osa [valo'rozu, ɔza] *adj* courageous.
valsa ['vawsa] *f* waltz.
valsar [4] [vaw'sa(x)] *vi* to waltz.
válvula ['vawvula] *f* valve; ~ **de escape** *fig* safety valve; ~ **de segurança** safety valve.
vampe ['vãnpi] *f* vamp.
vampiro [vãm'piru] *m* -**1.** [personagem] vampire. -**2.** *ZOOL* vampire bat.
vandalismo [vãnda'liʒmu] *m* vandalism.
vândalo, la ['vãndalu, la] *m, f* vandal.
vangloriar-se [16] [vãŋglo'rjaxsi] *vp*: ~-**se (de)** to boast (about).
vanguarda [vãŋ'gwaxda] *f* -**1.** *MIL* front line. -**2.** [cultural] avant-garde; **de** ~ avant-garde *(antes de subst)*.
vantagem [vãn'taʒẽ] (*pl* -**ns**) *f* -**1.** [ger] advantage; **levar** ~ **(em)** to get the upper hand (in); **tirar** ~ **de** to take advantage from. -**2.** [superioridade]: ~ **(sobre)** advantage (over); **contar** ~ to brag; **levar** ~ **(sobre)** to have an advantage (over).
vantajoso, osa [vãnta'ʒozu, ɔza] *adj* -**1.** [benéfico] advantageous. -**2.** [lucrativo] profitable.
vão, vã ['vãw, 'vã] *adj* -**1.** [frívolo] empty. -**2.** [inútil] vain; **em** ~ in vain. -**3.** [irreal] futile.
  vão *m* -**1.** [espaço] space. -**2.** [de porta *etc*] opening.
vapor [va'po(x)] (*pl* -**es**) *m* -**1.** [de água] steam; **a** ~ [máquina, ferro] steam *(antes de subst)*; **cozinhar no** ~ to steam. -**2.** *FÍSICA* vapour *UK*, vapor *US*.
  a todo o vapor *loc adv* at full speed.
vaporização [vaporiza'sãw] *f* -**1.** [nebulização] spray. -**2.** *FÍSICA* vaporization.
vaporizador [vaporiza'do(x)] (*pl* -**es**) *m* -**1.** [de perfume *etc*] spray. -**2.** *MED* vaporizer.
vaporizar [4] [vapori'za(x)] *vt* -**1.** [nebulizar] to spray. -**2.** *FÍSICA* to vaporize.
vaporoso, osa [vapo'rozu, ɔza] *adj* -**1.** [tecido, cortina] see-through, diaphanous. -**2.** [com vapor] steamy.
vapt-vupt [ˌvaptʃi'vuptʃi] <> *interj* zap! <> *m* [lençol] fitted sheet.
vaqueiro [va'kejru] *m* cowherd *UK*, cowboy *US*.
vaquinha [va'kiɲa] *f*: **fazer uma** ~ to have a whip-round.
vara ['vara] *f* -**1.** [pau] stick; ~ **de condão** magic wand. -**2.** [para salto] pole. -**3.** *TEC* rod. -**4.** [de trombone] slide. -**5.** *JUR* jurisdiction. -**6.** [de porcos] herd.

varal [va'raw] (*pl* -**ais**) *m* [de roupas] clothes line.
varanda [va'rãnda] *f* -**1.** [sacada] verandah. -**2.** [balcão] balcony.
varão [va'rãw] (*pl* -**ões**) <> *adj* male. <> *m* male.
varapau [vara'paw] *mf fam* [pessoa] beanpole.
varar [4] [va'ra(x)] <> *vt* -**1.** [furar] to pierce. -**2.** [passar por] to cross. <> *vi*: ~ **por** [passar por] to pass through; [atravessar] to go through.
varejeira [vare'ʒejra] *f* [mosca] bluebottle.
varejista [vare'ʒiʃta] <> *adj* retail *(antes de subst)*. <> *mf* [vendedor] retailer.
varejo [va'reʒu] *m* *COM* retail trade; **preço no** ~ retail price; **a loja vende a** ~ the shop sells retail.
variação [varja'sãw] (*pl* -**ões**) *f* [alteração] change, variation; ~ **cambial** *ECON* exchange-rate fluctuation.
variado, da [va'rjadu, da] *adj* -**1.** [diverso] varied. -**2.** [sortido] assorted.
variante [va'rjãntʃi] <> *adj* different. <> *f* -**1.** [variação] change. -**2.** [versão] variant.
variar [16] [va'rja(x)] <> *vt* [diversificar] to vary. <> *vi* -**1.** [ger] to vary; ~ **em algo** to vary in sthg. -**2.** [diversificar] to make changes; ~ **de** to change; **para** ~ [para diversificar] for a change; *irôn* and just for a change. -**3.** *fam* [delirar] to unhinge.
variável [va'rjavew] (*pl* -**eis**) <> *adj* changeable, variable. <> *f* *MAT* variable.
varicela [vari'sɛla] *f* chickenpox.
variedade [varje'dadʒi] *f* -**1.** [diversidade] variety. -**2.** [tipo] type.
  variedades *fpl* variety *(sg)*; **espetáculo/teatro de** ~**s** variety show *ou* theatre *UK ou* theater *US*.
varinha [va'riɲa] *f* stick; ~ **de condão** magic wand.
vário, ria ['varju, rja] *adj* [variado] diverse.
  vários <> *adj pl* several. <> *pron pl* several.
varíola [va'riwla] *f* smallpox.
varizes [va'riziʃ] *fpl* varicose veins.
varões [va'rõjʃ] *pl* ▷ **varão**.
varonil [varo'niw] (*pl* -**is**) *adj* virile.
varredor, ra [vaxe'do(x), ra] (*mpl* -**es**, *fpl* -**s**) *m, f* sweeper; ~ **de rua** road sweeper.
varredura [vaxe'dura] *f* -**1.** [ato] sweep. -**2.** *COMPUT* scan.
varrer [5] [va'xe(x)] *vt* -**1.** [com vassoura] to sweep. -**2.** [arrastar] to sweep away. -**3.** *fig* [devastar] to raze. -**4.** *fig* [livrar]: ~ **algo de** to sweep sthg from.
varrido, da [va'xidu, da] *adj*: **doido** ~ raving lunatic.
Varsóvia [vax'sɔvja] *n* Warsaw.
várzea ['vaxzja] *f* [vale] low, flat valley.
vascular [vaʃku'la(x)] (*pl* -**es**) *adj* vascular.
vasculhar [4] [vaʃku'ʎa(x)] *vt* -**1.** [pesquisar] to research. -**2.** [revirar] to rummage through.
vasectomia [vazekto'mia] *f* vasectomy.
vaselina® [vaze'lina] <> *f* [substância] vaseline. <> *mf fam pej* [pessoa]: **ser um** ~ to be smooth talker.

vasilha [va'ziʎa] f vessel.

vasilhame [vazi'ʎãmil] m -1. [para alimentos] storage jars (pl). -2. [garrafa vazia] empties (pl).

vaso ['vazu] m -1. [para plantas] pot; ~ de flores flower vase. -2. [privada] toilet; ~ sanitário toilet bowl. -3. ANAT vessel; ~ sanguíneo blood vessel.

vassalo, la [va'salu, la] m, f vassal.

vassoura [va'sora] f broom.

vastidão [vaʃtʃi'dãw] f vastness.

vasto, ta ['vaʃtu, ta] adj -1. [extenso] vast. -2. fig [considerável] wide.

vatapá [vata'pa] m CULIN a very spicy Bahian dish made with fish, coconut milk, prawns, peanuts and cashew nuts, vatapá.

vaticano, na [vatʃi'kãnu, na] adj Vatican (antes de subst).
➡ **Vaticano** m: o Vaticano the Vatican.

vaticinar [4] [vatʃisi'na(x)] vt to foretell.

vaticínio [vatʃi'sinju] m prophecy.

vau [vaw] m -1. [de rio] ford. -2. NÁUT beam.

vazado, da [va'zadu, da] adj -1. [letra] outlined. -2. [círculo] hollow. -3. [moeda] embossed. -4. [olhos] sunken.

vazamento [vaza'mẽntu] m leakage.

vazante [va'zãntʃi] <> adj ebbing. <> f [maré] ebb tide.

vazão [va'zaw] (pl -ões) f -1. [vazamento] leak. -2. [escoamento] flow. -3. COM [venda] sale. -4. loc: dar ~ a [liberar] to give vent to; [atender a] to deal with; [solucionar] to sort out; COM to clear.

vazar [4] [va'za(x)] <> vi -1. [ger] to leak. -2. [maré] to go out. -3. fig [informação] to leak out. <> vt -1. [esvaziar] to empty. -2. [olhos] to gouge out. -3. [derramar]: ~ algo (em) to spill sthg (on). -4. fig [moldar] to model.

vazio, zia [va'ziu, zia] adj -1. [ger] empty. -2. [com pouca gente] deserted.
➡ **vazio** m -1. [vácuo] vacuum. -2. [lacuna] blank space. -3. fig [sentimento] void.

vazões [va'zõjʃ] pl ⊳ vazão.

veado ['vjadu] m -1. [animal] deer; carne de ~ venison. -2. vulg pej [homossexual] poof(ter) UK, fag(got) US.

vedado, da [ve'dadu, da] adj -1. [proibido, impedido] barred; ~ a prohibited to. -2. [hermeticamente fechado] sealed.

vedar [4] [ve'da(x)] vt -1. [proibir, impedir] to prohibit, to bar. -2. [sangue]: vedou o sangramento com um lenço he stopped the flow of blood with a handkerchief. -3. [hermeticamente] to seal.

vedete [ve'dɛtʃi] f -1. [de teatro] star. -2. fam fig [destaque] star.

veemência [veje'mẽnsja] f vehemence; com ~ vehemently.

veemente [veje'mẽntʃi] adj vehement.

vegetação [veʒeta'sãw] (pl -ões) f vegetation.

vegetal [veʒe'taw] (pl -ais) <> adj plant (antes de subst). <> m plant.

vegetar [4] [veʒe'ta(x)] vi -1. [planta] to grow. -2. fig [pessoa] to vegetate.

vegetarianismo [veʒetarjã'niʒmu] m vegetarianism.

vegetariano, na [veʒeta'rjãnu, na] <> adj vegetarian. <> m, f vegetarian.

vegetativo, va [veʒeta'tʃivu, va] adj fig vegetative.

veia ['veja] f -1. [ger] vein. -2. fig [tendência] streak.

veiculação [vejkula'sãw] (pl -ões) f -1. [de mercadorias, visitantes] transport UK, transportation US. -2. [de doença] transmission. -3. [de idéias, mensagens, doutrinas] spreading.

veicular [4] [vejku'la(x)] vt -1. [publicar, divulgar] to spread. -2. [anúncios] to distribute.

veículo [ve'ikulu] m -1. [de locomoção] vehicle. -2. [de informação] means (sg).

veio ['veju] m -1. [de rocha] vein. -2. [de madeira] grain. -3. [em mina] seam.

vela ['vɛla] f -1. [de cera] candle; segurar ~ fam fig to play gooseberry. -2. NÁUT sail; à ~ sailing; fazer-se à ou de vela to set sail; ~ mestra mainsail. -3. [embarcação] yacht.

velame [velã'mi] m NÁUT sails (pl).

velar [4] [ve'la(x)] <> adj LING velar. <> f LING velar. <> vt -1. [cobrir]: ~ algo (com algo) to cover sthg (with sthg). -2. [ocultar] to hide. -3. [dissimular] to disguise. -4. [doente, sono] to watch over. -5. [defunto] to keep vigil for, to hold a wake for. <> vi -1. [cuidar]: ~ por algo/alguém to watch over sthg/sb. -2. FOT [filme] to be damaged by exposure to light.
➡ **velar-se** vp -1. [cobrir-se] to keep o.s. covered. -2. [ocultar-se] to hide.

veleidade [velej'dadʒi] f -1. [capricho] whim. -2. [inconstância] fickleness.

veleiro [ve'lejru] m NÁUT sailing boat.

velejar [4] [vele'ʒa(x)] vi to sail.

velhaco, ca [ve'ʎaku, ka] <> adj dishonest. <> m, f crook.

velha-guarda [ˌveʎa'gwaxda] f old guard.

velharia [veʎa'ria] f -1. pej [grupo de idosos] old people (pl). -2. [velhos objetos, trastes]: ~ (s) old stuff (sg).

velhice [ve'ʎisi] f old age.

velho, lha ['vɛʎu, ʎa] <> adj old; nos ~s tempos in the old days. <> m, f -1. [pessoa] old person. -2. fam [pai] old man; os ~s [pai e mãe] one's folks. -3. fam [amigo]: meu ~ old chap.

velhote, ta [ve'ʎotʃi, ta] <> adj old. <> m, f old person.

velocidade [velosi'dadʒi] f [ger] speed; aumentar/diminuir a ~ to increase/reduce one's speed; ~ de processamento COMPUT processing speed; ~ máxima maximum speed; a toda ~ at full speed; em alta ~ at high speed.

velocímetro [velo'simetru] m speedometer.

velocípede [velo'sipedʒi] m velocipede.

velocíssimo, ma [velɔ'sisimu, ma] adj superl ⊳ veloz.

velocista [velo'siʃta] mf sprinter.

velódromo [ve'lɔdrumu] m cycle track.

velório [ve'lɔrju] m wake.

veloz [ve'lɔʃ] (pl -es) adj -1. [ger] fast. -2. [movimento] quick.

velozmente [veloʒ'mẽntʃi] adv quickly.

veludo [ve'ludu] m [tecido] velvet; ~ **cotelê** corduroy.

venal [ve'naw] (pl -ais) adj -1. [subornável] corrupt. -2.: **valor** ~ selling price.

vencedor, ra [vẽnse'do(x), ra] (pl -es, fpl -s) <> adj winning. <> m, f winner.

vencer [25] [vẽ'se(x)] <> vt -1. [ger] to win. -2. [superar, dominar, resistir a] to overcome. -3. [derrotar] to defeat. -4. [exceder]: ~ **algo/alguém (em algo)** to outdo sthg/sb (in sthg). -5. [conter] to contain. -6. [percorrer] to cross. <> vi -1. [ganhar] to win. -2. [expirar- prazo, garantia, contrato, validade] to expire; [- pagamento, conta, promissória] to become due.

vencido, da [vẽ'sidu, da] adj -1. [derrotado] beaten; **dar-se por** ~ to give up. -2. [expirado] expired.

vencimento [vẽnsi'mẽntu] m -1. [expiração] expiry. -2. [data] due date.
  ➡ **vencimentos** mpl [salário] earnings.

venda ['vẽnda] f -1. [vendagem] sale; à ~ on ou for sale; **pôr algo à** ~ to put sthg up for sale; **preço de** ~ selling price; ~ **a crédito** credit sale; ~ **a prazo** ou **prestação** sale in instalments. -2. [mercearia] general store. -3. [nos olhos] blindfold.
  ➡ **vendas** fpl [vendagem] sales.

vendagem [vẽn'daʒẽ] f [venda] sale.

vendar [4] [vẽn'da(x)] vt: ~ **(os olhos de) alguém** to blindfold sb.

vendaval [vẽnda'vaw] (pl -ais) m -1. [ventania] gale. -2. fig [turbilhão] whirlwind.

vendável [vẽn'davew] (pl -eis) adj saleable.

vendedor, ra [vẽnde'do(x), ra] (mpl -es, fpl -s) m, f -1. [dono] seller. -2. [em loja] sales assistant; ~ **ambulante** street vendor. -3. [de seguros] salesperson.

vender [5] [vẽn'de(x)] <> vt -1. [pôr à venda] to sell; ~ **no varejo** to sell retail; ~ **no/por atacado** to sell wholesale; **estar vendendo saúde** fig to be bursting with health. -2. [entregar em troca] to sell off; ~ **algo a/para alguém (por)** to sell sb sthg (for); ~ **algo a prazo** ou **prestação** to sell sthg on credit/in instalments; ~ **fiado** to give credit. <> vi to sell.
  ➡ **vender-se** vp -1. [estar à venda]: **vendem-se picolés** ice lollies for sale. -2. [deixar-se subornar]: **ele se vendeu por 30 mil dólares** he accepted a bribe of 30 thousand dollars.

vendeta [vẽn'deta] f vendetta.

vendido, da [vẽn'dʒidu, da] pej <> adj bribed. <> m, f grafter.

vendinha [vẽn'dʒiɲa] f corner shop.

veneno [ve'nenu] m -1. [peçonha] poison; **o cigarro é um** ~ **para a saúde** smoking is a health hazard. -2. [de cobra, inseto] venom. -3. fig [malícia] venom.

venenoso, osa [vene'nozu, ɔza] adj -1. [ger]

poisonous. -2. fig [malicioso] venomous.

veneração [venera'sãw] f: ~ **(por)** veneration (for).

venerar [4] [vene'ra(x)] vt -1. [adorar] to revere. -2. RELIG to worship.

venéreo, rea [ve'nɛrju, rja] adj venereal.

veneta [ve'neta] f: **me deu na** ~ **que ...** [idéia] I took it into my head that ...; [impulso] I had a sudden impulse to ...; **fazer algo de** ~ to do sthg on impulse.

Veneza [ve'neza] n Venice.

veneziana [vene'zjana] f -1. [porta] louvred door UK, louvered door US. -2. [janela] louvred window UK, louvered window US.

veneziano, na [vene'zjãnu, na] <> adj Venetian. <> m, f Venetian.

Venezuela [vene'zwɛla] n Venezuela.

venezuelano, na [venezwe'lanu, na] <> adj Venezuelan. <> m, f Venezuelan.

vênia ['venja] f -1. [permissão] permission. -2. JUR [desculpa] pardon.

venial [ve'njaw] (pl -ais) adj -1. [desculpável] forgiveable. -2. RELIG [pecado] venial.

venta ['vẽta] f [narina] nostril.
  ➡ **ventas** fpl [nariz] nose (sg).

ventania [vẽta'nia] f gale.

ventar [4] [vẽn'ta(x)] vi: **venta muito aqui** it is very windy here; **estar ventando** to be windy.

ventarola [vẽnta'rɔla] f fan.

ventilação [vẽntʃila'sãw] f -1. [de ambiente] ventilation. -2. AUTO [de motor] cooling.

ventilador [vẽntʃila'do(x)] (pl -es) m [elétrico] fan.

ventilar [4] [vẽntʃi'la(x)] vt [arejar] to air.

vento ['vẽntu] m -1. [ar] air. -2. [brisa] wind. -3. loc: **ir de** ~ **em popa** to go very well.

ventoinha [vẽn'twiɲa] f -1. [catavento] windmill. -2. [grimpa] weather vane. -3. AUTO fan.

ventoso, osa [vẽn'tozu, ɔza] adj windy.
  ➡ **ventosa** f -1. MED ventouse. -2. ZOOL sucker.

ventre ['vẽntri] m -1. ANAT belly. -2. euf [útero] womb.

ventríloquo, qua [vẽn'trilokwu, kwa] m, f ventriloquist.

ventura [vẽn'tura] f -1. [destino] fate; **por** ~ by chance. -2. [sorte] good fortune; **boa** ~ good luck.

venturoso, osa [vẽntu'rozu, ɔza] adj [feliz] happy.

Vênus ['venuʃ] n Venus.

ver [40] ['ve(x)] <> vt -1. [ger] to see; **já volto, viu?** I'll be back soon, OK? -2. [assistir] to watch. -3. [resolver] to see to. -4. [tomar cuidado em] to watch. -5. [em remissiva]: **veja ...** look ... <> vi -1. [enxergar] to see; **ela é bonita que só vendo** you wouldn't believe how pretty she is; ~ **em** fig [em situação, pessoa] to see in. -2. [pensar]: **deixa eu** ~ ... let me see ... -3. [ger]: **ter a** ou **que** ~ **com** to have to do with; [ter envolvimento com] to be involved with; **são pessoas muito diferentes, não têm nada a** ~ **uma com a outra** they are two very different people, they are not at all alike; **este trabalho tem muito a** ~ **com você** that work is right up your street. <> *m*: **a meu** ~ in my opinion.

◆ **ver-se** *vp* -**1.** [ger] to see o.s. -**2.** [avistar-se] to see one another. -**3.** [ter contato]: **há anos que não nos víamos** it's years since we saw each other, we hadn't seen each other for years. -**4.** [em dificuldade, lugar] to find o.s. -**5.** [entender-se]: **bem se vê que ...** it's obvious that ...; ~-**se com alguém** to pay sb back.

◆ **pelo visto** *loc adv* by the look of it.

◆ **vai ver que** *loc adv* [talvez] perhaps.

veracidade [verasi'dadʒil] *f* truthfulness.

veranear [vera'nja(x)] *vi* to spend the summer.

veraneio [vera'neju] *m* summer holidays *(pl)* *UK*, summer vacation *US*; **cidade de** ~ holiday resort.

veranista [vera'niʃta] *mf* summer holidaymaker *UK*, summer vacationer *US*.

verão [ve'rãw] *(pl -ões) m* summer.

veraz [ve'rajʒ] *adj* truthful.

verba ['vɛxba] *f* funding.

verbal [vex'baw] *(pl -ais) adj* verbal.

verbalizar [4] [vexbali'za(x)] *vt & vi* to verbalize.

verbalmente [vexbaw'mẽntʃi] *adv* verbally.

verbete [vex'betʃi] *m* [em dicionário] entry.

verbo ['vɛxbu] *m* -**1.** *GRAM* verb; **deitar o** ~ *fam* to make a speech; **soltar o** ~ *fam* to shoot one's mouth off. -**2.** *RELIG*: **o Verbo** the Word.

verborragia [vexboxa'ʒia] *f* waffle.

verborrágico, ca [vexbo'xaʒiku, ka] *adj* verbose.

verdade [vex'dadʒi] *f* truth; **a** ~ **nua e crua** the naked truth; **não é** ~? *fam* isn't that right?; **na** ~ in fact; **para falar a** ~ to tell the truth; ~? *fam* really?

◆ **verdades** *fpl* home truths; **dizer umas** ~s **a alguém** *fam* to tell sb a few home truths.

◆ **de verdade** <> *loc adv* -**1.** [realmente]: **tudo o que relato aconteceu de** ~ everything I'm describing really happened. -**2.** [a sério] seriously. <> *loc adj* [autêntico]: **é um vencedor de** ~ he's a true winner.

verdadeiramente [vexdadejra'mẽntʃi] *adv* truly.

verdadeiro, ra [vexda'dejru, ra] *adj* -**1.** [ger] true. -**2.** [autêntico] real.

verde ['vexdʒi] <> *adj* -**1.** [cor] green; ~ **de fome** weak with hunger; ~ **de raiva** livid. -**2.** [fruta] unripe, green. <> *m* -**1.** [cor] green. -**2.** [natureza] country. -**3.** *loc*: **jogar (um)** ~ **(para colher maduro)** to get at the truth.

verde-abacate [ˌvexdʒiabaˈkatʃi] *adj (inv)* avocado-green.

verde-claro, ra ['vexdʒi'klaru, ra] *(pl -s)* <> *adj* light green. <> *m* light green.

verde-escuro, ra ['vexdʒiiʃ'kuru, ra] *(pl -s)* <> *adj* dark green. <> *m* dark green.

verdejante [vexde'ʒãntʃi] *adj* verdant.

verdejar [4] [vexde'ʒa(x)] *vi* to become green.

verde-oliva ['vexʒjo'liva] <> *adj inv* olive green. <> *m* olive green.

verdor [vex'do(x)] *m* -**1.** [cor verde] greenness. -**2.** [as plantas verdes] greenery. -**3.** *fig* [exuberância]: **o**

~ **da mocidade** the vigour of youth. -**4.** *fig* [inexperiência] inexperience.

verdugo [vex'dugu] *m* -**1.** [carrasco] executioner. -**2.** *fig* [pessoa cruel] beast.

verdura [vex'dura] *f* [hortaliça] greens *(pl)*.

verdureiro, ra [vexdu'rejru, ra] *m, f* greengrocer.

vereador, ra [verja'do(x), ra] *m, f* councillor *UK*, councilor *US*.

vereda [ve'reda] *f* path.

veredicto [vere'dʒiktul] *m* verdict.

verga ['vexga] *f* -**1.** [vara] stick. -**2.** [metálica] rod.

vergão [vex'gãw] *(pl -ões) m* [marca] weal.

vergar [14] [vex'ga(x)] <> *vt* [dobrar] to bend. <> *vi* -**1.** [dobrar] to bend. -**2.** [com peso] to sag.

vergões [vex'gõjʃ] *pl* ⊳ **vergão**.

vergonha [vex'goɲa] *f* -**1.** [acanhamento] shyness; **me dá** ~ **falar em público** I feel shy about speaking in public; **perder a** ~ to overcome one's shyness; **que** ~! how embarrassing!; **sentir** ~ to feel embarrassed; **ter** ~ **de fazer algo** to feel shy about doing sthg. -**2.** [brio, pudor] shame; **que falta de** ~! how disgraceful!; **ter** ~ **na cara** to be shameless; **tomar** ~ to swallow one's pride. -**3.** [desonra] shame. -**4.** [vexame] outrage; **passar por uma** ~ to be outraged.

vergonhoso, osa [vexgo'ɲozu, ɔza] *adj* -**1.** [indigno] disgraceful. -**2.** [indecoroso] indecent. -**3.** [que dá vergonha] shameful.

verídico, ca [ve'ridʒiku, ka] *adj* true.

verificação [verifika'sãw] *(pl -ões) f* -**1.** [averiguação] checking. -**2.** [comprovação] verification.

verificar [12] [verifi'ka(x)] *vt* -**1.** [averiguar] to check. -**2.** [comprovar] to confirm.

◆ **verificar-se** *vp*: **verifica-se um aumento na inflação** an increase in inflation has been confirmed.

verme ['vɛxmi] *m* worm.

vermelhidão [vexmeʎi'dãw] *f* redness.

vermelho, lha [vex'meʎu, ʎa] *adj* -**1.** [ger] red; **ficar** ~ **de raiva/vergonha** to flush with anger/embarrassment. -**2.** [ao chorar]: **olhos** ~s red eyes.

◆ **vermelho** *m* -**1.** [cor] red. -**2.** [déficit]: **estar no** ~ to be in the red.

vermicida [vexmi'sida], **vermífugo** [vex'mifugu] *m* vermicide.

vermute [vex'mutʃi] *m* vermouth.

vernáculo, la [vex'nakulu, la] *adj* vernacular.

◆ **vernáculo** *m* vernacular.

vernissage [vexni'saʒi] *f* opening.

verniz [vex'niʃ] *(pl -es) m* -**1.** [solução] varnish. -**2.** [couro] patent leather; **de** ~ [bolsa, sapatos] patent leather *(antes de subst)*. -**3.** *fig* [polidez] veneer.

verões [ve'rõjʃ] *pl* ⊳ **verão**.

verossímil [vero'simiw] *(pl -eis) adj* -**1.** [crível] credible. -**2.** [provável] likely.

verossimilhança [verosimi'ʎãnsa] *f* -**1.** [credibilidade] credibility. -**2.** [probabilidade] likelihood.

verruga [ve'xuga] *f* wart.

versado, da [vex'sadu, da] *adj*: ~ **em** versed in.

versão [vex'sãw] (*pl* -**ões**) *f* -**1**. [interpretação] version. -**2**. [tradução]: ~ **(para)** translation (into).

versar [4] [vex'sa(x)] *vi*: ~ **sobre** to be about.

versátil [vex'satʃiw] (*pl* -**eis**) *adj* versatile.

versatilidade [vexsatʃili'dadʒi] *f* versatility.

versejar [4] [vexse'ʒa(x)] <> *vt* to versify. <> *vi* to write in verse.

versículo [vex'sikulu] *m* -**1**. [de artigo] paragraph. -**2**. *RELIG* verse.

verso ['vɛxsu] *m* -**1**. [gênero] verse; ~**s brancos** blank verse *(sg)*. -**2**. [linha de poema] line. -**3**. [poema] poem. -**4**. [de página] verso; **vide** ~ see over(leaf).

versões [vex'sõjʃ] *pl* ▷ **versão**.

versus ['vɛxsuʃ] *prep* versus.

vértebra ['vɛxtebra] *f* vertebra.

vertebrado, da [vexte'bradu, da] *adj* vertebrate.
  ➡ **vertebrado** *m* vertebrate.

vertebral [vexte'braw] (*pl* -**ais**) *adj* vertebral.

vertente [vex'tẽntʃi] *f* -**1**. [declive] slope. -**2**. *fig* [aspecto] angle.

verter [5] [vex'te(x)] <> *vt* -**1**. [despejar - líquido] to pour; [- recipiente] to tip. -**2**. [derramar] to spill. -**3**. [lágrimas, sangue] to shed. -**4**. [traduzir]: ~ **(para)** to translate (into). <> *vi* [brotar]: ~ **de** [água] to spring from; [rio] to rise from.

vertical [vextʃi'kaw] (*pl* -**ais**) <> *adj* vertical. <> *f* vertical.

vértice ['vɛxtʃisil] *m* -**1**. *GEOM* vertex. -**2**. [de montanha *etc*] summit.

vertigem [vex'tʃiʒẽl] (*pl* -**ns**) *f* -**1**. *MED* vertigo. -**2**. [tonteira] giddiness, dizziness; **dar** ~ to make dizzy; **ter** ~ to feel giddy, to feel dizzy.

vertiginoso, osa [vextʃiʒi'nozu, ɔza] *adj* vertiginous.

verve ['vɛxvi] *f* verve.

vesgo, ga ['veʒgu, ga] *adj* cross-eyed.

vesícula [ve'zikula] *f*: ~ **(biliar)** gall bladder.

vespa ['veʃpa] *f* wasp.

véspera ['vɛʃpera] *f*: **na** ~ **de** the day before; ~ **de Natal** Christmas Eve.
  ➡ **vésperas** *fpl* [um tempo antes]: **nas** ~**s de** on the eve of; **estar nas** ~**s de** to be about to.

vesperal [veʃpe'raw] (*pl* -**ais**) <> *adj* evening *(antes de subst)*. <> *f* matinee.

vespertino, na [veʃpex'tʃinu, na] *adj* evening *(antes de subst)*.
  ➡ **vespertino** *m* evening paper.

veste ['veʃtʃi] *f* -**1**. [vestido] dress. -**2**. [eclesiástica] vestment.

vestiário [veʃ'tʃarju] *m* -**1**. [onde se troca roupa] changing room. -**2**. [onde se deixa casacos *etc*] cloakroom.

vestibulando, da [veʃtʃibu'lãndu, da] *m, f* university candidate.

vestibular [veʃtʃibu'la(x)] *m* university entrance exam.

vestíbulo [veʃ'tʃibulu] *m* -**1**. [de casa] hall. -**2**. [de teatro] foyer.

vestido, da [veʃ'tʃidu, da] *adj* -**1**. [com roupa]: ~ **(com/de)** dressed in. -**2**. [fantasiado]: ~ **de** dressed as.
  ➡ **vestido** *m* dress; ~ **de noiva** wedding dress.

vestígio [veʃ'tʃiʒju] *m* -**1**. [pegada] trail. -**2**. *fig* [indício] trace.

vestimenta [veʃtʃi'mẽnta] *f* -**1**. [roupa] garment. -**2**. *RELIG* vestment.

vestir [54] [veʃ'tʃi(x)] <> *vt* -**1**. [pôr sobre alguém] to put on. -**2**. [usar] to wear. -**3**. [costurar para] to make clothes for. -**4**. [dar vestuário para] to clothe. -**5**. [fantasiar]: ~ **alguém de** to dress sb as. -**6**. [fronha] to cover. <> *vi* [ter caimento]: ~ **bem/mal** to dress well/badly.
  ➡ **vestir-se** *vp* -**1**. [usar]: **ela só se veste de branco** she only wears white. -**2**. [aprontar-se] to get dressed. -**3**. [comprar roupa]: ~-**se em** to buy clothes in. -**4**. [fantasiar-se]: **vestiu-se de pirata** he was dressed (up) as a pirate.

vestuário [veʃ'twarju] *m* -**1**. [roupas] clothing. -**2**. *TEATRO* costumes *(pl)*.

vetar [4] [ve'ta(x)] *vt* -**1**. [lei, proposta, candidato] to veto. -**2**. [acesso] to forbid.

veterano, na [vete'rãnu, na] <> *adj* veteran *(antes de subst)*. <> *m, f* veteran.

veterinário, ria [veteri'narju, rja] <> *adj* veterinary. <> *m, f* vet, veterinary surgeon.

veto ['vɛtu] *m* veto.

véu ['vɛu] *m* -**1**. [pano] veil. -**2**. *ANAT*: ~ **do paladar** soft palate.

vexame [ve'ʃãmi] *m* -**1**. [vergonha] shame; **dar um** ~ to make a fool of o.s.; **passar um** ~ to be disgraced. -**2**. [humilhação] humiliation. -**3**. [ultraje] outrage.

vexaminoso, sia [veʃami'nozu, za] *adj* -**1**. [vergonhoso] disgraceful. -**2**. [humilhante] humiliating. -**3**. [ultrajante] outrageous.

vexar [4] [ve'ʃa(x)] *vt* -**1**. [envergonhar] to embarrass. -**2**. [humilhar] to humiliate. -**3**. [ultrajar] to outrage.
  ➡ **vexar-se** *vp* [envergonhar-se] to be ashamed.

vexatório [veʃa'torju] *adj* = vexaminoso.

vez ['veʃ] (*pl* -**es**) *f* -**1**. [frequência, quantidade] time; **uma** ~ once; **duas** ~ **es** twice; **três** ~ **es** three times; **algumas** ~ **es** a few times; **às** ~ **es** sometimes; **cada** ~ **mais** more and more; **cada** ~ **mais alto** higher and higher; **cada** ~ **menos** less and less; **de** ~ **em quando** from time to

time; **mais ~ es** more often; **mais uma ~**, **outra ~** (once) again; **raras ~ es** seldom; **uma ~ ou outra** once in a while; **uma ~ na vida e outra na morte** once in a blue moon; **várias ~ es** several times. **-2.** [ocasião] time; **você já sentiu isso alguma ~?** have you ever felt that?; **cada ~ que, toda ~ que** every time; **desta ~** this time; **de uma ~ por todas** once and for all; **de uma ~ só** once only; **de ~** once and for all; **era uma ~ ...** once upon a time ...; **na maioria das ~ es** on most occasions, most times. **-3.** [turno] turn; **ter ~ to** have a chance. **-4.** [multiplicação] times; **2 ~ es 4** 2 times 4.
⇒ vezes *fpl* [função]: **fazer as ~ es de** to stand in for.
⇒ em vez de *loc prep* instead of.
⇒ uma vez que *loc conj* **-1.** [já que] since. **-2.** [se] if.
VHF (*abrev de* Very High Frequency) *f* VHF.
VHS (*abrev de* Video Home System) *m* VHS.
via ['via] ◇ *f* **-1.** [caminho, estrada] road; **~ de acesso** access road; **~ férrea** railway; **~ pública** thoroughfare. **-2.** [transporte]: **por ~ aérea** by air; [postal] by airmail; **por ~ terrestre** by land, overland. **-3.** [meio] route; **por ~ de** through (means of); **por ~ oficial** through official means. **-4.** [processo]: **em ~ (s) de** on the way to. **-5.** [de documento] copy; **primeira/segunda ~** original/duplicate (copy). **-6.** [de drenagem *etc*] channel. **-7.** ANAT tract; **por ~ oral** by mouth. **-8.** *loc*: **chegar às ~s de fato** to come to blows. ◇ *prep* via.
⇒ Via Láctea *f* Milky Way.
⇒ por via das dúvidas *loc adv* just in case.
⇒ via de regra *loc adv*: **(por) ~ de regra** as a general rule.
viabilidade [vjabili'dadʒi] *f* feasibility, viability.
viabilizar [vjabili'za(x)] *vt* to make possible.
viação [vja'sãw] (*pl* -ões) *f* **-1.** [conjunto de estradas] highways, roads (*pl*). **-2.** [companhia] bus company.
viaduto [vja'dutu] *m* viaduct.
viagem ['vjaʒẽ] (*pl* -ns) *f* **-1.** [ger] journey; **boa ~!** have a good journey!; **~ de ida e volta** return trip; **~ inaugural** NÁUT maiden voyage; **~ de negócios** business trip. **-2.** *fig* [sob efeito de droga] trip.
⇒ viagens *fpl* travels.
viajado, da [vja'ʒadu, da] *adj* [pessoa] well-travelled UK, well-traveled US.
viajante [vja'ʒãntʃi] ◇ *adj* travelling UK, traveling US. ◇ *mf* traveller UK, traveler US.
viajar [4] [vja'ʒa(x)] *vi*: **~ (por)** to travel (across/through).
viário, ria ['vjarju, rja] *adj* road (*antes de subst*).
viatura [vja'tura] *f* vehicle.
viável ['vjavɛw] (*pl* -eis) *adj* viable, feasible.
víbora ['vibora] *f* **-1.** ZOOL viper. **-2.** *fig* [pessoa] snake in the grass.
vibração [vibra'sãw] (*pl* -ões) *f* **-1.** [tremor] vibration. **-2.** *fig* [entusiasmo] thrill.

vibrador, ra [vibra'do(x),ra] *adj* [vibratório] vibrating.
⇒ vibrador *m* [estimulador] vibrator.
vibrante [vi'brãntʃi] *adj fig* [entusiasmado] vibrant.
vibrar [4] [vi'bra(x)] ◇ *vt* **-1.** [fazer tremer] to shake. **-2.** [dedilhar] to vibrate. ◇ *vi* **-1.** [tremer] to shake. **-2.** *fig* [entusiasmar-se] to be thrilled.
vibrião [vi'brjãw] (*pl* -ões) *m* vibrio.
vice ['visi] *mf* deputy.
vice- [visi] *prefixo* vice-.
vice-campeão, peã [ˌvisikãn'pjãw, pjã] (*mpl* -ões, *fpl* -s) *m, f* runner-up.
vicejante [vise'ʒãntʃi] *adj* **-1.** [horta, pomar] lush. **-2.** [estilo, poesia] flowery.
vicejar [4] [vise'ʒa(x)] ◇ *vi* [vegetar] to flourish. ◇ *vt* [dar viço a] to cause to flourish.
vice-presidente, ta [ˌvisiprezi'dẽntʃi, ta] (*mpl* -s, *fpl* -s) *m, f* **-1.** POL vice-president. **-2.** [de comitê, empresa] deputy chairman.
vice-rei [ˌvisi'xej] (*pl* vice-reis) *m* viceroy.
vice-reitor, ra [ˌvisixej'to(x), ra] (*mpl* -es, *fpl* -s) *m, f* deputy head.
vice-versa [ˌvisi'vɛxsa] *adv* vice versa.
viciado, da [vi'sjadu, da] *adj* **-1.** [em droga *etc*]: **~ (em)** addicted (to); **ser ~ em drogas** to be hooked on drugs. **-2.** [adulterado] vitiated.
viciante [vi'sjãntʃi] *adj* addictive.
viciar [16] [vi'sja(x)] ◇ *vt* **-1.** [dar vício a] to addict. **-2.** [adulterar] to vitiate. ◇ *vi* [criar vício] to be addictive.
⇒ viciar-se *vp* [tornar-se viciado]: **~-se (em)** to become addicted (to).
vicinal [visi'naw] (*pl* -ais) *adj*: **estrada ~** local route.
vício ['visju] *m* **-1.** [devassidão] vice. **-2.** [em droga, bebida] addiction. **-3.** [mau hábito] bad habit; **~ de linguagem** barbarism.
vicioso, osa [vi'sjozu, ɔza] *adj* **-1.** [sistema, hábito] corrupt. **-2.** [círculo] vicious.
vicissitude [visisi'tudʒi] *f* vicissitude; **as ~s da vida** the ups and downs of life.
viço ['visu] *m* **-1.** [de planta] vigour UK, vigor US. **-2.** [de pele] freshness.
viçoso, osa [vi'sozu, ɔza] *adj* **-1.** [planta] luxuriant. **-2.** [pele] glowing.
Victoria [vik'tɔrja] *n*: **o lago ~** Lake Victoria.
vida ['vida] *f* **-1.** [ger] life; **a outra ~** the life beyond; **dar a ~ por** *fig* to give anything for; **em ~** [doar *etc*] alive; **estar entre a ~ e a morte** to be at death's door; **estilo de ~** lifestyle; **feliz da ~** delighted; **para toda a ~** forever; **padrão de ~** standard of living; **que ~!** what a life!; **tratar da ~** to get on with one's life; **~ de cão** dog's life; **~ conjugal** married life; **~ doméstica** home life; **~ sentimental** love life; **~ útil** [de máquina *etc*] useful life. **-2.** [subsistência]: **custo de ~** cost of living; **estar bem de ~** to be well off; **ganhar a ~** to earn one's living; **meio de ~** means of living; **cheio de ~** full of life; **dar ~ a algo** to liven sthg up; **sem ~** lifeless. **-3.** [direção]: **seguir (reto) toda a ~** to continue straight on as far as you can go. **-4.**

[prostituição]: **cair na** ~ to go on the game; **mulher da** ~ prostitute.

vidão [vi'dãw] *m fam* life of Riley.

vide ['vidʒi] *vt* see; ~ **verso** see over(leaf).

videira [vi'dejra] *f* grapevine.

vidente [vi'dãntʃi] *mf* seer.

vídeo ['vidʒju] *m* **-1.** [ger] video. **-2.** [tela] screen.

videocâmara [vidʒju'kãmara] *f* video camera.

videocassete [‚vidʒjuka'sɛtʃi] *m* **-1.** [aparelho] video cassette recorder, VCR. **-2.** [fita] videotape.

videoclipe [‚vidʒju'klipi] *m* music video.

videoclube [‚vidʒju'klubi] *m* video club.

videoconferência ['vidʒjukõnʃe'rẽnsja] *f TELEC* video-conference.

vídeo game ['vidʒju'gejmi] *m* video game.

videolocadora [‚vidʒjuloka'dora] *f* video rental.

videoteca [‚vidʒju'tɛka] *f* video library.

videoteipe [‚vidʒju'tejpi] *m* **-1.** [fita] videotape. **-2.** [processo] videotaping.

videotexto [‚vidʒju'teʃtu] *m* teletext, video-tex(t).

vidraça [vi'drasa] *f* window pane.

vidraçaria [vidrasa'ria] *f* **-1.** [loja] glazier's. **-2.** [fábrica] glass factory. **-3.** [vidraças] glazing.

vidraceiro [vidra'sejru] *m* glazier.

vidrado, da [vi'dradu, da] *adj* **-1.** [ger] glazed. **-2.** *fam* [encantado]: ~ **em** crazy about.

vidrar [4] [vi'dra(x)] <> *vt* [cerâmica *etc*] to glaze. <> *vi fam* [encantar-se]: ~ **(em)** to fall in love (with).

vidreiro, ra [vi'drejru, ra] *m, f* glass-maker.

vidro ['vidru] *m* **-1.** [material] glass; ~ **aramado** reinforced glass; ~ **fosco** frosted glass; ~ **fumê** smoked glass. **-2.** [frasco] bottle.

viela ['vjɛla] *f* alley(way).

Viena ['vjena] *n* Vienna.

viés [vjɛʃ] *m COST* bias.

➠ **de viés** *loc adv* sideways.

Vietnã [vjɛt'nã] *n*: **(o)** ~ Vietnam.

vietnamita [vjɛtna'mita] <> *adj* Vietnamese. <> *mf* Vietnamese.

➠ **vietnamita** *m* [língua] Vietnamese.

viga ['viga] *f* **-1.** [de madeira] beam. **-2.** [de concreto, ferro] girder.

vigamento [viga'mẽntu] *m* rafters *(pl)*.

vigarice [viga'risi] *f* swindle.

vigário [vi'garju] *m* vicar.

vigarista [viga'riʃta] *mf* swindler.

vigência [vi'ʒẽnsja] *f* validity; **estar em** ~ to be in force.

vigente [vi'ʒẽntʃi] *adj* **-1.** [lei, contrato, norma] in force. **-2.** [situação política, costume] current.

viger [26] [vi'ʒe(x)] *vi* to be in force.

vigésimo, ma [vi'ʒɛzimu, ma] *num* twentieth; *veja também* **sexto**.

vigia [vi'ʒia] <> *f* **-1.** [vigilância] surveillance. **-2.** *NÁUT* porthole. <> *mf* [pessoa] nightwatchman.

vigiar [16] [vi'ʒja(x)] <> *vt* **-1.** [banco, presos] to guard. **-2.** [mala, criança] to keep an eye on. **-3.** [espreitar] to watch. <> *vi* to be on the lookout.

vigilância [viʒi'lãnsja] *f* surveillance.

vigilante [viʒi'lãntʃi] <> *adj* alert. <> *mf* guard.

vigília [vi'ʒilja] *f* **-1.** [privação de sono]: **fez-se uma** ~ **para evitar ataques** a watch was kept in order to avoid attack. **-2.** [prática religiosa] vigil.

vigor [vi'go(x)] *m* **-1.** [energia - de corpo, espírito] vigour; [- para o trabalho] energy. **-2.** [veemência] vigour. **-3.** [vigência]: **em** ~ in force; **entrar em** ~ to come into force.

vigorar [4] [vigo'ra(x)] *vi* to be in force.

vigoroso, osa [vigo'rozu, ɔza] *adj* vigorous.

vil ['viw] *(pl* **vis)** *adj* vile.

vila ['vila] *f* **-1.** [povoação] town. **-2.** [conjunto residencial] residential block. **-3.** [casa] villa.

vilã [vi'lã] *f* ▷ **vilão**.

vilania [vila'nia] *f* villainy.

vilão, lã [vi'lãw, lã] *(mpl* **-ãos, -ães,** *fpl* **-s)** *m, f* villain.

vilarejo [vila'reʒu] *m* hamlet.

vileza [vi'leza] *f* **-1.** [ato] vileness. **-2.** [qualidade] meanness.

vilipendiar [vilipẽn'dʒja(x)] *vt* to belittle.

vime ['vimi] *m* osier, withy; **de** ~ wicker.

vinagre [vi'nagri] *m* vinegar.

vinagreira [vina'grejra] *f* vinegar cruet.

vinagrete [vina'gretʃi] *m* vinaigrette.

vincar [12] [vĩn'ka(x)] *vt* **-1.** [roupa, papel] to crease. **-2.** [rosto] to wrinkle. **-3.** [terra] to furrow.

vinco ['vĩŋku] *m* **-1.** [em roupa, papel] crease. **-2.** [no rosto] wrinkle. **-3.** [sulco] furrow.

vinculação [vĩŋkula'sãw] *f* link, linking; **ele não quer a** ~ **do seu nome aos escândalos** he doesn't want his name to be linked to the scandals.

vincular [4] [vĩŋku'la(x)] *vt* **-1.** [ligar] to tie. **-2.** [por obrigação] to bind.

vínculo ['vĩŋkulu] *m* **-1.** [pessoal, familiar] bond. **-2.** [profissional, entre países] tie; ~ **empregatício** work contract.

vinda ['vĩnda] *f* ▷ **vindo**.

vindicar [12] [vĩndʒi'ka(x)] *vt* **-1.** [vingar] to avenge. **-2.** [defender] to vindicate. **-3.** [reivindicar] to claim.

vindima [vĩn'dʒima] *f* grape harvest.

vindo, da ['vĩndu, da] <> *pp* ▷ **vir.** <> *adj*: ~ **(de)** originating (in).

➠ **vinda** *f* **-1.** [ger] arrival (in). **-2.** [regresso] return.

vindouro, ra [vĩn'doru, ra] *adj* **-1.** [ano, década] coming. **-2.** [geração] future.

vingador, ra [vĩŋga'do(x), ra] <> *adj* avenging. <> *m, f* avenger.

vingança [vĩŋ'gãnsa] *f* revenge.

vingar [4] [vĩŋ'ga(x)] <> *vt* [tirar desforra de] to avenge. <> *vi* **-1.** [medrar] to thrive. **-2.** [dar certo] to be successful.

➠ **vingar-se** *vp* [tirar desforra]: ~**-se (de)** to take revenge (on/for).

vingativo, va [vĩŋga'tʃivu, va] *adj* vindictive.

vinha ['viɲa] *f* **-1.** [vinhedo] vineyard. **-2.** [planta] vine.

vinhedo [vi'ɲedu] *m* vineyard.

vinheta [vi'ɲeta] f vignette.

vinho ['viɲu] ◇ adj inv [cor] burgundy. ◇ m -1. [cor] burgundy. -2. [bebida] wine; ~ **branco** white wine; ~ **espumante** sparkling wine; ~ **de mesa** table wine; ~ **do Porto** port; ~ **rosado** rosé (wine); ~ **tinto** red wine.

vinícola [vi'nikula] adj wine-producing.

vinicultor, ra [ˌvinikuw'to(x), ra] (mpl -es, fpl -s) m, f wine producer.

vinicultura [vinikuw'tura] f winemaking.

vinil [vi'niw] m vinyl.

vinte ['vĩtʃi] num twenty; veja também seis.

vintém [vĩ'tẽl] (pl -ns) m -1. [moeda antiga] old Brazilian coin. -2. [dinheiro] **estar sem um** ~ to be penniless.

vintena [vĩ'tena] f: **uma** ~ **de** a score of.

viola ['vjɔla] f viola.

violação [vjola'sãw] (pl -ões) f -1. [de lei, pacto, direitos] violation. -2. [invasão] ~ **de domicílio** housebreaking. -3. [de pessoa] violation, rape. -4. [de correspondência] interference. -5. [de local sagrado] violation, desecration.

violão [vjo'lãw] (pl -ões) m guitar.

violar [4] [vjo'la(x)] vt -1. [lei, pacto, direitos] to violate. -2. [domicílio] to break in. -3. [pessoa] to violate, to rape. -4. [correspondência] to interfere with. -5. [local sagrado] to violate. -6. [segredo] to breach.

violeiro, ra [vjo'lejru, ra] m, f guitarist.

violência [vjo'lẽsja] f -1. [ato] violence. -2. [agressividade] vehemence. -3. [força - de vendaval] force; [- de paixões] violence.

violentar [4] [vjolẽn'ta(x)] vt -1. [mulher] to violate, to rape. -2. [deturpar] to distort.

violento, ta [vjo'lẽntu, ta] adj violent.

violeta [vjo'leta] ◇ f [flor] violet. ◇ adj inv [cor] violet.

violinista [vjoli'niʃta] mf violinist.

violino [vjo'linu] m violin.

violoncelista [vjolõnse'liʃta] mf cellist.

violoncelo [vjolõn'sɛlu] m cello.

violonista [vjolo'niʃta] mf guitarist.

VIP (abrev de Very Important Person) [vipi] ◇ adj [pessoa, local] VIP. ◇ mf VIP.

vir [67] ['vi(x)] vi -1. [apresentar-se] to come; **veio me ver** he came to see me; **venho visitá-lo amanhã** I'll come and see you tomorrow. -2. [chegar] to arrive; **ele veio atrasado/adiantado** he arrived late/early; **ela veio no ônibus das onze** she came on the eleven o'clock bus. -3. [a seguir no tempo] to come; **a semana/o ano que vem** next week/year, the coming week/year. -4. [estar] to be; **vem escrito em português** it's written in Portuguese; **vinha embalado** it came in a package. -5. [regressar] to come back; **eles vêm de férias amanhã** they're coming back from holidays tomorrow; **hoje, venho mais tarde** today, I'll be coming later than usual. -6. [surgir] to come; **o carro veio não sei de onde** the car came out of nowhere; **veio-me uma idéia** I've got an idea. -7. [provir] ~ **de** to come from; **venho agora mesmo**

de lá I've just come from there. -8. [em locuções]: ~ **a ser** to become; **que vem a ser isto?** what's the meaning of this?; ~ **abaixo** [edifício, construção] to collapse; ~ **ao mundo** [nascer] to come into the world, to be born; ~ **a saber (de algo)** to find out (about sthg); ~ **sobre** [arremeter contra] to lunge at; ~ **a tempo de algo** to arrive in time for sthg; ~ **a tempo de fazer algo** to arrive in time to do sthg.

viração [vira'sãw] (pl -ões) f breeze.

vira-casaca [ˌviraka'zaka] (pl **vira-casacas**) mf turncoat.

virado, da [vi'radu, da] adj [voltado]: ~ **para** facing.

➡ **virado** m CULIN: ~ **de feijão** sautéed beans with fried egg and sausage.

➡ **virada** f -1. [viradela] turning. -2. [guinada] swerve. -3. ESP sudden turnaround. -4. [esforço]: **dar uma virada** to make a last effort.

vira-lata [ˌvira'lata] (pl **vira-latas**) m -1. [cachorro] mongrel. -2. [pessoa] down-and-out.

virar [4] [vi'ra(x)] ◇ vt -1. [volver] ~ **algo (para)** to turn sthg (towards); ~ **as costas** to turn one's back. -2. [mostrar pelo verso] to turn over. -3. [entornar] to tip. -4. [emborcar] to capsize. -5. [contornar] to turn. -6. [apontar] ~ **algo contra alguém** to turn sthg on sb. -7. [meter]: ~ **a mão em alguém** to attack sb. -8. [fazer mudar de opinião] to change. -9. [transformar-se] to turn into. ◇ vi -1. [volver] to turn; ~ **para** to turn towards; ~ **de bruços** to turn on to one's tummy; ~ **de costas** to turn on to one's back; ~ **do avesso** to turn inside out. -2. [emborcar] to capsize. -3. [contornar]: ~ **(em)** to turn (into); ~ **à direita/esquerda** to turn (to the) right/left. -4. [mudar] to change. -5. [mudar de direção] to change direction. -6. [rebelar-se, voltar-se]: ~ **contra** to turn against.

➡ **virar-se** vp -1. [volver-se] to turn around. -2. [rebelar-se] to rebel; ~**-se contra** to turn against. -3. [defender-se] to stand up for o.s. -4. [empenhar-se] to struggle.

viravolta [ˌvira'vɔwta] f -1. [volta inteira] spin. -2. [sobre si mesmo] somersault. -3. fig [mudança] turnabout.

virgem ['vixʒẽ] (pl -ns) ◇ adj -1. [ger] virgin. -2. [fita, filme] blank. -3. [mel] pure. -4. [isento]: ~ **de algo** lacking sthg. ◇ f [pessoa] virgin.

➡ **Virgem** f -1. RELIG Virgin. -2. ARTE madonna. -3. [zodíaco] Virgo; **ser Virgem** to be a Virgo.

virginal [vixʒi'naw] (pl -ais) adj virginal.

virgindade [vixʒĩn'dadʒi] f virginity.

virginiano, na [vixʒi'njãnu, na] ◇ adj Virgo (antes de subst.). ◇ m, f Virgo.

vírgula ['vixgula] f -1. [entre palavras] comma. -2. [entre números] [decimal] point. -3. [mecha] curl. -4. [objetando-se]: **uma** ~! fam my foot!

viril [vi'riw] (pl -is) adj virile.

virilha [vi'riʎa] f groin.

virilidade [virili'dadʒi] f virility.

virose [vi'rɔzi] f viral infection.

virótico, ca [vi'rɔtʃiku, ka] adj viral.

virtual [vix'twaw] (*pl* -ais) *adj* -1. [possível] potential. -2. *COMPUT* virtual; **realidade** ~ virtual reality.

virtualmente [vixtwaw'mēntʃi] *adv* virtually.

virtude [vix'tudʒi] *f*-1. [qualidade] virtue. -2. [capacidade] knack. -3. [razão]: **em** ~ **de** due to.

virtuose [vix'twɔzi] *mf* virtuoso.

virtuosidade [vixtwozi'dadʒi] *f* virtuosity.

virtuosismo [vixtwo'ziʒmu] *m* virtuosity.

virtuoso, osa [vix'twozu, ɔza] <> *adj* [íntegro] virtuous. <> *m, f* [gênio] virtuoso.

virulência [viru'lēnsja] *f* virulence.

virulento, ta [viru'lēntu, ta] *adj* virulent.

vírus ['viruʃ] *m inv* vírus.

vis [viʃ] *pl* ▷ **vil**.

visado, da [vi'zadu, da] *adj* -1. [cheque] valid. -2. [pessoa] watched.

visão [vi'zãw] (*pl* -ões) *f*-1. [sentido] vision, sight. -2. [o que se vê] sight; ~ **de conjunto** overall impression. -3. [alucinação] vision; **ter visões** to have visions. -4. [percepção, ponto de vista]: ~ **(de/sobre)** view (on/about). -5. [revelação] vision.

visar [4] [vi'za(x)] <> *vt*-1. [cheque, passaporte] to stamp. -2. [objetivar] to look for; ~ **(a) fazer algo** to aim to do sthg. <> *vi* [objetivar]: ~ **a algo/a fazer algo** to aim for sthg/to aim to do sthg.

vis-à-vis [viza'viʃ] *adv* vis-à-vis.

víscera ['viseral *f* viscus.

➡ **vísceras** *fpl* viscera, bowels.

visceral [vise'raw] (*pl* -ais) *adj* -1. [ger] visceral. -2. [arraigado] deep-rooted.

visconde, dessa [viʃ'kõndʒi, desa] *m, f* viscount.

viscoso, osa [viʃ'kozu, ɔza] *adj* viscous.

viseira [vi'zejra] *f* visor.

visibilidade [vizibili'dadʒi] *f* visibility.

visionário, ria [vizjo'narju, rja] <> *adj* visionary. <> *m, f* visionary.

visita [vi'zita] *f*-1. [ato] visit; **fazer uma** ~ **a alguém** to pay sb a visit; ~ **de médico** *fig* flying visit. -2. [visitante] visitor; **ter** ~**s** to have visitors; ~ **de cerimônia** official visit. -3. [vistoria] inspection.

visitação [vizita'sãw] (*pl* -ões) *f* [visita] visit; **aberto à** ~ **pública** open to the public.

➡ **Visitação** *f RELIG* Visitation.

visitante [vizi'tãntʃi] *mf* visitor.

visitar [4] [vizi'ta(x)] *vt* -1. [fazer visita a] to visit. -2. [vistoriar] to inspect.

➡ **visitar-se** *vp* [fazer visitas mútuas] to visit one another.

visível [vi'zivεw] (*pl* -eis) *adj* visible.

visivelmente [vizivew'mēntʃi] *adv* visibly.

vislumbrar [viʒlūm'bra(x)] *vt* to glimpse.

vislumbre [viʒ'lūnbril *m* glimpse.

visões [vi'zõjʃ] *pl* ▷ **visão**.

visom [vi'zõ] (*pl* -s) *m* mink; **casaco de** ~ mink coat.

visor [vi'zo(x)] (*pl* -es) *m* viewfinder.

vista ['viʃta] *f* ▷ **visto**.

vista-d'olhos [ˌviʃta'dɔʎuʃ] (*pl* vistas-d'olhos) *f* glance; **passar uma** ~ **(em)** to glance (at).

visto, ta ['viʃtu, ta] <> *pp* ▷ **ver**. <> *adj* -1. [olhado]: ~ **(de)** seen (from). -2. [considerado] thought of. -3. [estudado] looked at.

➡ **visto** *m* -1. [em documento] stamp. -2. [em passaporte] visa.

➡ **vista** *f* -1. [ger] view; **com vista para o mar** with sea view. -2. [sentido] sight. -3. [olhos, olhar] eyesight; **a perder de vista** as far as the eye can see; [pagamento] long-term; **à primeira vista** at first sight; **à vista** [visível] visible; [pagamento] in cash; **pôr à vista** to put on display; **até a vista!** see you later!; **conhecer de vista** to know by sight; **perder de vista** to lose sight of; **vista cansada** tired eyes. -4. [propósito]: **com vista a** with a view to; **ter em vista** to have in mind. -5: *loc*: **dar na vista** to be obvious; **fazer vista grossa (a)** to turn a blind eye (to); **saltar à vista** to be glaringly obvious, to stand out a mile.

➡ **em vista de** *loc prep* in view of.

➡ **pelo visto** *loc adv* by the look of it.

➡ **visto que** *loc conj* seeing.

vistoria [viʃto'rial *f* inspection.

vistoriar [viʃto'rja(x)] *vt* to inspect.

vistoso, osa [viʃ'tozu, ɔza] *adj* eye-catching.

visual [vi'zwaw] (*pl* -ais) <> *adj* visual. <> *m fam* -1. [aspecto] appearance, look. -2. [vista] view.

visualizar [4] [vizwali'za(x)] *vt* to visualize.

visualmente [vizuaw'mēntʃi] *adv* visually; ~ **incapacitado** visually impaired.

vital [vi'taw] (*pl* -ais) *adj* vital.

vitalício, cia [vita'lisju, sja] *adj* lifelong (*antes de subst*).

vitalidade [vitali'dadʒi] *f* vitality.

vitalizar [4] [vitali'za(x)] *vt* to vitalize.

vitamina [vita'mina] *f* vitamin.

vitaminado, da [vitami'nadu, da] *adj* with added vitamins.

vitamínico, ca [vita'miniku, ka] *adj* vitamin (*antes de subst*).

vitela [vi'tεla] *f*-1. *ZOOL* calf. -2. [carne] veal.

vítima ['vitʃima] *f* [pessoa] victim; **fazer-se de** ~ to play the victim; **ser** ~ **de** to be the victim of.

vitimar [4] [vitʃi'ma(x)] *vt* -1. [matar] to claim the life of. -2. [sacrificar] to sacrifice. -3. [danificar] to destroy.

vitória [vi'tɔrja] *f* victory.

Vitória [vi'tɔrja] *n* Vitória.

vitória-régia [viˌtɔrja'xεʒja] (*pl* vitórias-régias) *f* giant water lily.

vitorioso, osa [vito'rjozu, ɔza] *adj* victorious.

vitral [vi'traw] (*pl* -ais) *m* stained-glass window.

vítreo, trea ['vitrju, trja] *adj* -1. [de vidro] glass (*antes de subst*). -2. [aspecto] glassy.

vitrificar [12] [vitrifi'ka(x)] <> *vt*-1. [converter em vidro] to vitrify. -2. [fazer tomar aparência de vidro] to make as smooth as glass. <> *vi* -1. [converter-se em vidro] to turn into glass. -2. [tomar aparência de vidro] to become as smooth as glass.

vitrine [vi'trinil, **vitrina** [vi'trinal *f*-1. [de loja] shop window. -2. [armário] display case.

vitrinista [vitri'niʃta] *mf* window dresser.

vitrola [vi'trɔla] *mf fig fam* gossip.
➤ **vitrola** *f* gramophone.
viuvez [vju've3] *f* widowhood.
viúvo, va ['vjuvu, va] ⬦ *adj* widowed. ⬦ *m, f* widower (*f* widow).
viva ['viva] ⬦ *m* cheer. ⬦ *interj* hooray!; ~ **a rainha!** long live the Queen!
vivacidade [vivasi'dadʒi] *f* vivacity.
vivalma [vi'vawma] *f*: **não tinha** ~ there wasn't a living soul about.
vivamente [viva'mẽntʃi] *adv* **-1.** [descrever, sentir] vividly. **-2.** [debater, discursar, protestar] vigorously.
vivaz [vi'vaʒ] *adj* lively.
viveiro [vi'vejru] *m* **-1.** [de plantas] nursery. **-2.** [de pássarɔs] aviary. **-3.** [de peixes] fish farm.
vivência [vi'vẽsja] *f* **-1.** [existência] existence. **-2.** [experiência] experience; **ter** ~ **em algo** to have experience in sthg.
vivenciar [18] [vivẽ'sja(x)] *vt* to live through.
vivenda [vi'vẽda] *f* (detached) house.
vivente [vi'vẽntʃi] ⬦ *adj* living. ⬦ *mf* living being.
viver [5] [vi've(x)] ⬦ *vt* **-1.** [vida] to live. **-2.** [fase, situação] to experience. ⬦ *vi* **-1.** [ger] to live; ~ **bem** [economicamente] to live comfortably; [em harmonia] to live happily. **-2.** [estar vivo] to be alive. **-3.** [perdurar] to last. **-4.** [sustentar-se]: ~ **de** to live off; ~ **à custa de** to live off. **-5.** [conviver]: ~ **com** to mingle with; [maritalmente] to live with. **-6.** [dedicar-se completamente]: ~ **para** to live for. **-7.** [residir]: ~ **(em)** to live (in). **-8.** [freqüentar muito]: ~ **(em)** to live (in). **-9.** [estar sempre] to always be; ~ **doente/gripado** to always be ill/ have a cold; ~ **trabalhando** to do nothing but work. ⬦ *m* life.
víveres ['viveriʃ] *mpl* provisions.
vivido, da [vi'vidu, da] *adj* [pessoa] experienced.
vívido, da [vi'vidu, da] *adj* **-1.** [ger] vivid. **-2.** [expressivo] vivacious.
vivificar [12] [vivifi'ka(x)] *vt* to revive.
vivo, va ['vivu, va] *adj* **-1.** [ger] bright. **-2.** [existente] living; **estar** ~ to be alive. **-3.** [animado, buliçoso] lively. **-4.** [ardente] fervent.
➤ **vivos** *mpl*: **os** ~**s** the living.
➤ **ao vivo** *loc adv* live.
vizinhança [vizi'ɲãsa] *f* neighbourhood *UK*, neighborhood *US*.
vizinho, nha [vi'ziɲu, ɲal ⬦ *adj* neighbouring *UK*, neighboring *US*. ⬦ *m, f* neighbour *UK*, neighbor *US*.
voador, ra [vwa'do(x), ra] *adj* flying.
voar [20] ['vwa(x)] *vi* **-1.** [ger] to fly; ~ **em algo** to fly in sthg; **fazer algo voando** *fig* to do sthg quickly. **-2.** [explodir]: ~ **pelos ares** to explode; **fazer** ~ **pelos ares** to blow up. **-3.** *loc*: **estar/ficar voando** *fam* [ficar sem entender] to be thrown; ~ **alto** *fig* to aim high; ~ **para cima de alguém** [assediar] to mob sb; [atacar] to fly at sb.
vocabulário [vokabu'larju] *m* vocabulary.
vocábulo [vo'kabulu] *m* word.
vocação [voka'sãw] (*pl* **-ões**) *f* vocation.

vocacional [vokasjo'naw] (*pl* **-ais**) *adj* vocational.
vocal [vo'kaw] (*pl* **-ais**) *adj* vocal.
vocálico, ca [vo'kaliku, ka] *adj* vocal.
vocalista [voka'liʃta] *mf* vocalist.
você [vo'se] (*pl* **vocês**) *pron pess* **-1.** [tratamento] you; ~ **é médico?** are you a doctor?; ~ **está muito elegante** you're looking very elegant; **vocês precisam estudar** you need to study; ~ **mesmo** *ou* **próprio** you yourself. **-2.** (*depois de prep*): **isto pertence a** ~**?** is this yours?; **quero ir com vocês** I want to go with you; **penso muito em** ~ I think about you a lot; **esta carta é para** ~ this letter is for you. **-3.** [em anúncios]: **'o novo Fiat Regatta** ~ **vai adorar'** 'the new Fiat Regatta - you'll love it'; **'o melhor para** ~**'** 'the best thing for you'. **-4.** [alguém qualquer um] one; **na Universidade,** ~ **tem que estudar muito** at university, one has to study a lot.
vocês [vo'seʃ] ⬥ **você**.
vociferar [4] [vosife'ra(x)] ⬦ *vt* [bradar] to shout. ⬦ *vi* [reclamar]: ~ **(contra)** to complain (about).
vodca ['vɔdʒka] *f* vodka.
voga ['vɔga] ⬦ *f* **-1.** [ger] fashion; **estar em** ~ to be in vogue. **-2.** *NÁUT* [cadência] rowing. ⬦ *m* [remador] oarsman.
vogal [vo'gaw] (*pl* **-ais**) *f* *LING* vowel.
vogar [14] [vo'ga(x)] *vi* **-1.** [navegar] to sail. **-2.** [circular] to circulate. **-3.** [estar em moda] to be in vogue. **-4.** [vigorar] to be in force.
voile ['vwaw] (*pl* **voiles**) *m* voile; **cortina de** ~ net curtain.
volante [vo'lãntʃi] *m* **-1.** *AUTO* steering wheel; **estar no** ~ to be at the wheel. **-2.** [motorista, piloto] driver. **-3.** [para apostas] betting slip. **-4.** [de máquina] flywheel.
volátil [vo'latʃiw] (*pl* **-eis**) *adj* volatile.
volatilidade [volatʃili'dadʒi] *f* *ECON* volatility.
vôlei ['volej], **voleibol** [volei'bow] *m* volleyball.
voleio [vo'leju] *m* volley.
volt ['vɔwtʃi] *m* volt.
volta ['vɔwta] *f* **-1.** [giro] turn; **dar a** ~ **(a algo)** to go around (sthg); **dar uma** ~ [sobre si mesmo] to turn round. **-2.** [retorno] return; **de** ~ back; **estar de** ~ to be back; **na** ~ [voltando] on the way back; [ao chegar] on arrival. **-3.** [passeio]: **dar uma** ~ [a pé] to go for a walk; [de carro] to go for a drive. **-4.** *ESP* lap. **-5.** *MIL*: **dar meia** ~ to about-turn *UK*, to about-face *US*. **-6.** *AUTO*: **fazer a** ~ to make a U-turn, to turn back. **-7.** [mudança]: **dar** ~**s** [vida *etc*] to go round in circles. **-8.** [de espiral] twist. **-9.** [contorno] edge. **-10.** [curva] curve. **-11.** *fig* [troco] comeback. **-12.** *loc*: **dar a** ~ **por cima** *fig* to get over (it).
➤ **às voltas com** *loc prep*: **estar/andar às** ~**s com** to be struggling with.
➤ **em volta de** *loc prep* around.
➤ **por volta de** *loc prep* around.
➤ **volta e meia** *loc adv* every now and again.
voltado, da [vow'tadu, da] *adj* **-1.** [de frente para] facing. **-2.** [concentrado]: **estar** ~ **para** to be focussed on.

voltagem [vow'taʒẽ] *f* voltage.

voltar [4] [vow'ta(x)] <> *vt* - **1.** [dirigir]: ~ **algo para** to turn sthg towards. - **2.** [mudar a posição de] to turn. - **3.** [mostrar pelo verso] to turn over. <> *vi* - **1.** [ger] to return; ~ **a si** to come to; ~ **atrás** *fig* to back out. - **2.** [mudar de direção]: ~ **a** *ou* **para** to turn towards. - **3.** [repetir-se] to come back. - **4.** [tratar novamente]: ~ **a algo** to return to sthg. - **5.** [recomeçar]: ~ **a fazer algo** to do sthg again.

voltar-se *vp* - **1.** [virar-se] to turn round. - **2.** [recorrer]: ~**-se para** to turn to. - **3.** [rebelar-se]: ~**-se contra** to turn against.

voltear [15] [vow'tʃja(x)] <> *vt* - **1.** [contornar] to go round. - **2.** [fazer girar] to turn. <> *vi* - **1.** [girar] to revolve. - **2.** [esvoaçar] to flutter.

volteio [vow'teju] *m* - **1.** [rodopio] spin. - **2.** [volta] bend. - **3.** [de equilibrista] movement.

voltímetro [vowt'ʃi'metru] *m ELETR* voltmeter.

volubilidade [volubili'dadʒi] *f* fickleness.

volume [vo'lumi] *m* - **1.** [ger] volume; **aumentar/diminuir o** ~ to turn the volume up/down. - **2.** [pacote] package.

volumoso, osa [volu'mozu, ɔza] *adj* bulky.

voluntário, ria [volũn'tarju, rja] <> *adj* voluntary. <> *m, f* volunteer.

voluntarioso, osa [volũnta'rjozu, ɔza] *adj* headstrong.

volúpia [vo'lupja] *f* - **1.** [sexual] pleasure. - **2.** [ambição] desire.

voluptuoso, osa [volup'twozu, ɔza] *adj* voluptuous.

volúvel [vo'luvew] (*pl* -eis) *adj* changeable.

volver [5] [vow've(x)] <> *vt* to turn. <> *vi*: ~ **a** to return to.

vomitar [4] [vomi'ta(x)] <> *vt* - **1.** [expelir] to vomit, to throw up. - **2.** [sujar com vômito] to vomit on, to be sick on. - **3.** *fig* [proferir] to spew out. <> *vi* [expelir vômito] to vomit, to be sick.

vômito ['vomitu] *m* - **1.** [ato] vomiting, throwing up. - **2.** [substância] vomit, sick.

vontade [võn'tadʒi] *f* - **1.** [determinação] will; **força de** ~ will power; **por** ~ **própria** of one's own accord; ~ **de ferro** iron will. - **2.** [desejo] wish; **dar** ~ **a alguém de fazer algo** to make sb feel like doing sthg; **me deu vontade de sair** I felt like going out; **o filme me deu vontade de viajar** the film made me feel like travelling; **fazer a** ~ **de alguém** to do what sb wants; **ter** ~ **de fazer algo** to feel like doing sthg; **contra a** ~ unwillingly; **sem** ~ reluctantly. - **3.** [necessidade] need. - **4.** [empenho, interesse]: **boa/má** ~ good/ill will; **de boa/má** ~ gladly/grudgingly.

vontades *fpl* [caprichos]: **cheio de** ~**s** wilful; **fazer todas as** ~**s de alguém** to pander to sb.

à vontade *loc adv* - **1.** [sem cerimônia]: **ficar à** ~ to feel at ease; **fique à** ~ make yourself at home. - **2.** [em quantidade] loads. - **3.** [quanto se quiser] as much as one wants.

com vontade *loc adv* [comer *etc*] heartily.

vôo ['vow] *m* flight; **levantar** ~ to take off; ~ **cego** flying blind; ~ **livre** *ESP* hang-gliding.

voragem [vo'raʒẽ] (*pl* -s) *f* - **1.** [abismo] chasm. - **2.** [de águas] maelstrom. - **3.** *fig* [de paixão, ambição] confusion.

voraz [vo'raʃ] (*pl* -es) *adj* - **1.** [pessoa, apetite] voracious. - **2.** *fig* [fogo *etc*] devastating.

vos [vuʃ] *pron pl* [complemento direto] you; [complemento indireto] (to) you; *fml* [reflexo] yourselves; *fml* [recíproco] each other, one another.

vós ['vɔʃ] *pron pess* [sujeito, complemento direto] you; [complemento indireto] (to) you; ~ **mesmos** *ou* **próprios** you, yourselves.

vosso, vossa ['vɔsu, 'vɔsa] <> *adj* your. <> *pron*: **o** ~**/a vossa** yours; **um amigo** ~ a friend of yours; **os** ~**s** [a vossa família] your family.

votação [vota'sãw] (*pl* -ões) *f* [ato] voting; [voto] vote; **decidir algo por** ~ to decide sthg by ballot.

votado, da [vo'tadu, da] *adj*: **o mais** ~ [chapa, senador etc] the one with the highest vote.

votante [vo'tãntʃi] *mf* voter.

votar [4] [vo'ta(x)] <> *vt* - **1.** [eleger] to vote. - **2.** [submeter a votação] to take a vote on. - **3.** [aprovar] to pass. <> *vi* - **1.** [dar voto] to vote; ~ **em/contra/por** to vote on/against/for; ~ **em branco** to abstain. - **2.** [ter direito a voto] to have a vote.

voto ['vɔtu] *m* - **1.** [votação] voting; ~ **nulo/em branco** invalid/blank vote; ~ **secreto** secret ballot. - **2.** [promessa] vow; ~ **de castidade/pobreza** vow of chastity/poverty. - **3.** [desejo] wish; **fazer** ~**s por** to wish for; **fazer** ~**s que** to hope that; ~**s de felicidade** best wishes.

vovó [vo'vɔ] *f* granny.

vovô [vo'vo] *m* grandpa.

voyeur [voj'ɛ(x)] (*pl* -s) *mf* voyeur.

voyeurismo [voje'riʒmu] *m* voyeurism.

voz ['vɔʃ] (*pl* -es) *f* - **1.** [ger] voice; **de viva** ~ orally, viva (voce); ~ **arrastada** drawling voice; **a meia** ~ softly; **em** ~ **alta/baixa** in a loud/low voice; **levantar a** ~ **para alguém** to raise one's voice at sb; ~ **de cana rachada** rasping voice. - **2.** [poder decisório, autoridade]: **ter** ~ **(ativa) em** to have a say in; **dar** ~ **de prisão** to announce an arrest. - **3.** *fig* [conselho]: **a** ~ **da experiência** the voice of experience. - **4.** *MIL*: ~ **de comando** command. - **5.** *GRAM*: ~ **ativa/passiva** active/passive voice.

vozeirão [vozej'rãw] (*pl* -ões) *m* thundering voice.

vozerio [voze'riw] *m* uproar.

vulcânico, ca [vuw'kãniku, ka] *adj* volcanic.

vulcão [vuw'kãw] (*pl* -ões) *m* volcano.

vulgar [vuw'ga(x)] (*pl* -es) *adj* - **1.** [comum] common. - **2.** [baixo, grosseiro] vulgar. - **3.** [medíocre] mediocre.

vulgaridade [vuwgari'dadʒi] *f* vulgarity.

vulgarizar [4] [vuwgari'za(x)] *vt* [popularizar] to popularize.

vulgarizar-se *vp* - **1.** [popularizar-se] to become commonplace. - **2.** [tornar-se reles] to coarsen.

vulgarmente [vuwgax'mẽntʃi] *adv* commonly.

vulgo ['vuwgul] <> *m* common people. <> *adv* otherwise known as.
vulnerabilidade [vuwnerabili'dadʒil] *f* vulnerability.
vulnerável [vuwne'ravɛwl] (*pl* **-eis**) *adj* vulnerable.
vulto ['vuwtul] *m* **-1.** [figura, sombra] figure. **-2.** [semblante] face. **-3.** *fig* [importância] stature; **de** ~ important. **-4.: tomar** ~ [desenvolver-se] to take shape.
vultoso, osa [vuw'tozu, ɔza] *adj* **-1.** [volumoso] bulky. **-2.** [obra, negócio] weighty. **-3.** [quantia] considerable.
vulva ['vuwva] *f* vulva.

w, W *m* [letra] w, W.
walkie-talkie [ˌwɔki'tɔki] (*pl* **walkie-talkies**) *m* walkie-talkie.
walkman® ['wɔkm l] *m* Walkman.
WAN (*abrev de* **Wide Area Network**) *f* WAN.
Washington ['wɔʃintõl] *n* Washington.
watt ['wɔtʃil] *m* watt.
WC (*abrev de* **water closet**) *m* WC.
Web [web] (**world wide web**) *f* COMPUT web.
webcam ['uɛbikãl] (*pl* **webcams**) *f* COMPUT webcam.
webmail ['uɛbimejo] (*pl* **webmails**) *m* COMPUT webmail.
webmaster ['uɛbimaʃtɛ(x)l] (*pl* **webmasters**) *mf* COMPUT webmaster.
webpage ['uɛbipejʒi] (*pl* **webpages**) *f* COMPUT webpage.
western ['wɛʃtexnl] *m* western.
windsurfe [wĩdʒi'suxfi] *m* windsurfing.
windsurfista [wĩdʒisux'fiʃta] *mf* windsurfer.
workshop [woxki'ʃɔpil] *m* workshop.
WWW (*abrev de* **World Wide Web**) *f* WWW.

x, X *m* [letra] x, X.
xá [ʃal] *m* shah.
xadrez [ʃa'dreʃl] <> *m* **-1.** [jogo] chess. **-2.** [desenho] check. **-3.** [tecido] checked cloth; **de** ~ checked. **-4.** *fam* [prisão] clink. <> *adj inv* checked.
xale ['ʃalil] *m* shawl.
xampu [ʃãn'pul] *m* shampoo.
xará [ʃa'ral] *mf* namesake.
xaropada [ʃaro'padal] *f fam* drag.
xarope [ʃa'rɔpil] *m* syrup.
xaveco [ʃa'vɛkul] *m fig* [objeto sem valor] piece of junk.
xaxim [ʃa'ʃĩl] *m* fibrous-stemmed plant.
xeique ['ʃejkil] *m* sheikh.
xelim [ʃe'lĩl] (*pl* **-s**) *m* shilling.
xenofobia [ʃenofo'bial] *f* xenophobia.
xepa ['ʃepal] *f fam* [de feira] scraps (*pl*).
xeque ['ʃɛkil] *m* **-1.** [xadrez] check. **-2.** [xeique] sheikh. **-3.** *loc*: **pôr em** ~ to threaten.
xeque-mate [ˌʃɛki'matʃil] (*pl* **xeque-mates**) *m* checkmate.
xereta [ʃe'retal] *adj fam* [bisbilhoteiro] busybody.
xeretar [4] [ʃere'ta(x)l] <> *vt* to snoop into. <> *vi*: ~ (**em/sobre**) to snoop (into/on).
xerez [ʃe'reʃl] *m* sherry.
xerife [ʃe'rifil] *m* sheriff.
xerocar [12] [ʃero'ka(x)l], *vt* to photocopy.
xerocópia [ʃero'kɔpjal] *f* photocopy.
xerocopiar [16] [ʃeroko'pja(x)l] *vt* = **xerocar**.
xérox® [ʃe'rɔksl] *m* **-1.** [cópia] photocopy. **-2.** [máquina] photocopier.
xexelento, ta [ʃeʃe'lẽntu, tal] *adj fam* gross.
xexéu [ʃe'ʃɛwl] *m fam* pong.
xi [ʃil] *interj* **-1.** [exprimindo espanto] oh no! **-2.** [exprimindo inquietação] oh no!
xícara ['ʃikaral] *f* cup; ~ **de chá** cup of tea.
xiita [ʃi'ital] <> *adj* [muçulmano] Shiite. <> *mf* **-1.** [muçulmano] Shiite. **-2.** *fig* [radical] extremist.
xifópago, ga [ʃi'fɔpagu, gal] *adj* conjoined.
xilofone [ʃilo'fonil] *m* xylophone.
xilografia [ʃilogra'fial] *f* **-1.** [técnica] wood engraving. **-2.** [gravura] woodcut.
xilogravura [ʃilogra'vural] *f* wood engraving.

xingação [ʃĩŋga'sãw] (pl -ões) f swearing.
xingamento [ʃĩŋga'mẽntu] m swearing.
xingar [14] [ʃĩ'ga(x)] ◇ vt to swear at; ~ alguém de algo to call sb sthg. ◇ vi to swear.
xinxim [ʃĩn'ʃĩ] (pl -ns) m: ~ de galinha chicken casserole.
xixi [ʃi'ʃi] m fam pee; fazer ~ to pee.
xodó [ʃo'dɔ] m -1. [pessoa querida] sweetheart. -2. [estima]: ter ~ por alguém/algo to be passionate about sb/sthg. -3. [flerte, namoro]: estar de ~ com alguém to be soft on sb.
xota [ʃɔta] f vulg [vulva] pussy.
xoxota [ʃo'ʃɔta] f vulg [vulva] pussy.
xucro, cra [ʃukru, kra] adj -1. [animal] untamed. -2. [grosseiro] coarse. -3. [ignorante] thick.

Z

z, Z m [letra] z, Z.
zabumba [za'bũnba] m [bombo] (big) bass drum.
zaga [zaga] f FUT fullback.
zagueiro [za'gejru] m FUT fullback.
zaino [zãjnu] adj [cavalo] dark brown.
Zaire [zajri] n Zaire.
Zâmbia [zãnbja] m Zambia.
zanga [zãŋga] f -1. [irritação] annoyance. -2. [briga] anger.
zangado, da [zãŋ'gadu, da] adj -1. [aborrecido] angry; estar ~ com alguém [sem falar] to be angry with sb. -2. [irritado] annoyed. -3. [malhumorado] cross.
zangão [zãŋ'gãw] (pl -ões) m ZOOL drone.
zangar [14] [zãŋ'ga(x)] ◇ vt [irritar] to annoy. ◇ vi -1. [irritar-se] to get angry. -2. [ralhar] to scold; ~ com alguém to tell sb off.
➡ **zangar-se** vp -1. [aborrecer-se] to get angry. -2. [irritar-se] to get annoyed.
zangões [zãŋ'gõjʃ] pl ▷ zangão.
zanzar [4] [zan'za(x)] vi to wander about.
zarcão [zar'kãw] m [tinta] red lead.
zarolho, lha [za'roʎu, ʎa] adj one-eyed.
zarpar [4] [zax'pa(x)] vi -1. [embarcação] to weigh anchor. -2. [partir] to set off. -3. [fugir] to run away.
zebra [zebra] f -1. ZOOL zebra. -2. [faixa para pedestres] zebra crossing. -3. fam pej [pessoa] dunce. -4. loc: dar ~ to turn out badly.
zebu [ze'bu] m ZOOL zebu.
zelador, ra [zela'do(x), ra] (pl -es, fpl -s) m, f [de prédio] caretaker UK, janitor US.

zelar [4] [ze'la(x)] vi: ~ por to care for.
zelo ['zelu] m -1. [cuidado] care. -2. [empenho] zeal.
zeloso, osa [ze'lozu, za] adj -1. [cuidadoso]: ~ (de/por) caring (for), careful (of). -2. [diligente]: ~ em zealous in.
zé-mané [,zɛma'nɛ] (pl -s) m fam [otário, bobalhão] idiot, airhead.
zen [zẽ] adj inv zen.
zen-budismo [zẽn bu'dʒiʒmu] m Zen Buddhism.
zé-ninguém [,zɛnĩŋ'gẽ] (pl zés-ninguém) m: um ~ a nobody.
zênite ['zenitʃi] m zenith.
zepelim [ze'pelĩ] (pl -ns) m [balão] zeppelin.
zé-povinho [,zɛpo'viɲu] (pl -s) m -1. [homem comum] Joe Public, Joe Bloggs. -2. [povo] common people.
zerar [4] [ze'ra(x)] vt -1. [reduzir a zero] to reduce to zero. -2. [liquidar] to wipe out.
zerinho, nha [ze'riɲu, ɲa] adj fam spanking new.
zero ['zɛru] num -1. [ger] zero; ~ erros no mistakes; abaixo/acima de ~ below/above zero. -2. ESP nil; [em tênis] love. -3. loc: começar do ~ to start from scratch; ser um ~ à esquerda to be a nothing.
➡ **a zero** loc adv: estar com a moral a ~ to be at rock bottom; ficar a ~ to end up broke; veja também seis.
zero-quilômetro [,zɛruki'lometru] ◇ adj inv brand new. ◇ m inv brand new car.
ziguezague [,zigi'zagi] m zigzag.
ziguezagueante [zigiza'gjãntʃi] adj zigzagging.
ziguezaguear [zigiza'gja(x)] vi to zigzag.
Zimbábue [zĩn'babwe] n Zimbabwe.
zinco ['zĩŋku] m zinc; folha de ~ corrugated iron.
zipar [4] [zi'pa(x)] vt COMPUT to zip.
zíper ['zipe(x)] (pl -es) m [fecho ecler] zip UK, zipper US.
ziquizira [ziki'zira] f fam bug.
zircônio [zix'konju] m zirconium.
zoada ['zwada] f = zoeira.
zoar ['zwa(x)] ◇ vt [caçoar] to make fun of. ◇ vi -1. [fazer grande ruído] to make a din. -2. [zumbir] to buzz. -3. [fazer troça] to make fun. -4. [promover confusão] to cause trouble.
zodiacal [zodʒja'kaw] adj of the zodiac (depois de subst).
zodíaco [zo'dʒiaku] m zodiac.
zoeira ['zwejra] f din.
zombador, ra [zõnba'do(x), ra] adj mocking.
zombar [4] [zõm'ba(x)] vi -1. [debochar]: ~ de alguém/algo to make fun of sb/sthg. -2. [desdenhar]: ~ de algo to sneer at sthg.
zombaria [zonba'ria] f [deboche] ridicule.
zombeteiro, ra [zõnbe'tejru, ra] ◇ adj [zombador] joking. ◇ m,f joker.
zona ['zona] f -1. [ger] zone; ~ eleitoral electoral district; ~ franca free trade area. -2. fam [bagunça, confusão] mess; fazer ~ to make a mess.
zoneamento [zonja'mẽntu] m [divisão em zonas] zoning.

zonear [15] [zo'nja(x)] <> vt **-1.** *fam* [bagunçar] to mess up. **-2.** [dividir em zonas] to zone. <> *vi fam* [bagunçar] to mess up.

zonzeira [zõn'zejra] *f* dizziness, giddiness; **dar ~ em alguém** to make sb giddy; **sentir ~** to feel giddy.

zonzo, za ['zõnzu, za] *adj* **-1.** [tonto] dizzy. **-2.** [atordoado, confuso] giddy.

zôo ['zow] *m* zoo.

zoologia [zwolo'ʒia] *f* zoology.

zoológico, ca [zo'lɔʒiku, ka] *adj* zoological.
➤ **zoológico** *m* zoo.

zoólogo, ga ['zwɔlogu, ga] *m, f* zoologist.

zoom [zũ] *m* zoom.

zorra ['zoxa] *f fam* mess.

zum [zũ] *m* zoom.

zumbido [zũn'bidu] *m* **-1.** [de inseto] buzz. **-2.** [de motor, vozes *etc*] hum. **-3.** [no ouvido] ringing.

zumbir [6] [zũm'bi(x)] *vi* **-1.** [inseto] to buzz. **-2.** [motor, vozes] to hum. **-3.** [bala, vento] to whistle. **-4.** [ouvido] to ring.

zunido [zu'nidu] *m* **-1.** [de inseto] buzz. **-2.** [de motor] hum. **-3.** [de vento] whistle.

zunir [6] [zu'ni(x)] *vi* **-1.** [inseto] to buzz. **-2.** [motor] to hum. **-3.** [vento *etc*] to whistle.

zunzum [zũn'zũ] (*pl* **-ns**) *m* **-1.** [ruído] humming. **-2.** [boato] rumour.

zureta [zu'reta] *mf* halfwit.

zurrar [4] [zu'xa(x)] *vi* to bray.

zurro ['zuxu] *m* bray.

Vivendo
no Reino Unido e nos Estados Unidos

ÍNDICE

Reino Unido

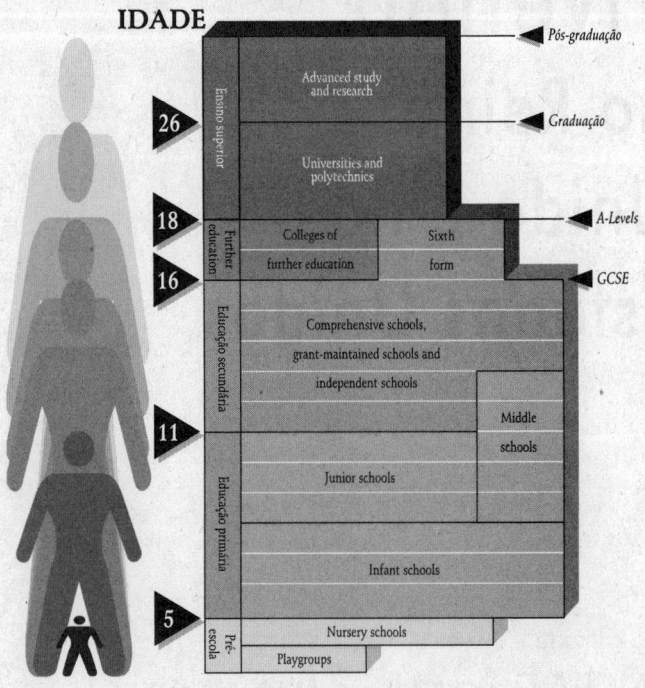

IDADE

- Pós-graduação
- Graduação
- A-Levels
- GCSE

Ensino superior — Advanced study and research / Universities and polytechnics

26

Further education — Colleges of further education / Sixth form

18

16

Educação secundária — Comprehensive schools, grant-maintained schools and independent schools

Middle schools

11

Educação primária — Junior schools / Infant schools

5

Pré-escola — Nursery schools / Playgroups

No Reino Unido, a educação é obrigatória dos 5 aos 16 anos de idade. O sistema educacional é, em grande parte, descentralizado, ou seja, de responsabilidade regional, e estrutura-se da seguinte maneira:

Educação pré-escolar (até 5 anos) Não é obrigatória, embora as crianças possam, a partir de dois anos de idade, matricular-se em escolas maternais (*nursery schools*). Muitas crianças em idade pré-escolar freqüentam grupos de atividades lúdico-educativas (*playgroups*), organizados pelos próprios pais.

Educação primária (dos 5 aos 11 anos) A educação primária subdivide-se em escolas para crianças dos 5 aos 7 anos (*infant schools*) e para aquelas dos 7 aos 11 anos (*junior schools*). Certas regiões optam por oferecer escolas para alunos dos 8 aos 14 anos (*middle schools*), que, depois, ingressam diretamente no nivel secundário (*upper secondary schools*). Alguns institutos particulares de educação primária são chamados *prep* (*preparatory*) *schools*.

Educação secundária (dos 11 aos 16/18 anos) É ministrada tanto em escolas públicas quanto nas escolas privadas.

‣ As **comprehensive schools**, financiadas pelo Estado, oferecem educação genérica e gratuita para todos. Elas são freqüentadas pela maioria dos estudantes britânicos.

‣ As **independent schools** são instituições privadas, financiadas mediante semestralidade paga pelos pais. Elas também são chamadas *private schools* ou *public schools*, e

congregam apenas 16% das crianças em idade escolar. Dentre essas escolas, algumas são famosas, como *Eton* ou *Harrow*.

▸ As **grant-maintained schools** são escolas de administração autônoma, não sujeitas a autoridade regional, mas subvencionadas diretamente pelo Estado.

Currículo Durante os primeiros cinco anos da educação secundária, a maioria dos alunos segue um currículo comum, o chamado *national curriculum*, definido pelo governo central. Aos 16 anos, o aluno presta um exame chamado *General Certificate of Secondary Education (GCSE)*. Cerca de 50% dos estudantes concluem nesse ponto seus estudos, independentemente de seu desempenho no exame.

▸ **A-Levels** Aqueles que desejarem ingressar na universidade devem prosseguir os estudos por mais dois anos, ao longo dos quais se preparam para prestar um exame chamado *GCE Advanced Level*. Em geral, desse exame constam três disciplinas. Os *A-Levels* são prestados na Inglaterra, no País de Gales e na Irlanda do Norte. Na Escócia, que possui sistema educacional próprio, os alunos concluem seus estudos prestando os chamados *Highers*, que são exames de várias disciplinas.

Educação secundária não-obrigatória (*Further Education*, dos 16 aos 18 anos)

Futher Education designa os estudos que se seguem ao ensino obrigatório. Os alunos que prosseguem seus estudos visando à obtenção de *A-Levels* costumam cursar na mesma escola os dois anos adicionais, também chamados *sixth form*. Mas podem ainda cursá-los nos *sixth-form colleges*. Cursos de orientação profissional são ministrados por instituições tais como os *colleges of further education*, que incluem escolas de arte, escolas agrícolas etc.

Ensino superior (dos 18 aos 26 anos)

O ensino superior é ministrado pelas universidades. O acesso à universidade depende de uma quantidade mínima de *A-Levels* obtidos com boas notas, e a disputa por vagas é acirrada. Bolsas de estudo são oferecidas pelas autoridades regionais, mas, em geral, precisam ser complementadas, seja pelo auxílio financeiro dos pais ou por empréstimos bancários para estudantes, a juros menores. Normalmente, os

> ### Oxbridge
>
> *Oxbridge* é uma expressão utilizada para designar conjuntamente as famosas universidades de Oxford e Cambridge. Fundadas no século XIII, elas se distinguem tanto das universidades fundadas no Reino Unido na década de 60 - as *redbrick universities*, que visavam à expansão do número de vagas universitárias -, quanto das ex-escolas politécnicas, transformadas em universidades apenas na década de 1990. Ainda hoje, embora 50% dos alunos de Oxford e Cambridge provenham da escola pública, persiste a crença de que seus estudantes gozam de situação econômica privilegiada. Isso de deve à grande quantidade de graduados em *Oxbridge* que exercem cargos importantes em áreas como economia, política e direito.

cursos universitários estendem-se por três anos, conduzindo ao *undergraduate degree*. A partir daí, aqueles que desejarem prosseguir com seus estudos o fazem na qualidade de *post-graduates*, podendo concluí-los com o *higher degree* ou com um *doctorate*.

Educação de adultos A educação de adultos é proporcionada por centros de educação pós-escolar e por departamentos especiais de algumas universidades. Os adultos podem, ainda, realizar seus estudos na *Open University*, instituição de ensino a distância, fundada em 1969, que oferece cursos universitários de graduação e pós-graduação por correspondência. Para tanto, não existem pré-requisitos, e os estudos baseiam-se em livros e programas de rádio e televisão.

A sigla UK, *United Kingdom* (Reino Unido), é uma forma abreviada de Reino Unido da Grã-Bretanha e Irlanda do Norte. A Grã-Bretanha compõe-se de Inglaterra, País de Gales e Escócia. As chamadas Ilhas Britânicas, por sua vez, são formadas pela Grã-Bretanha, Irlanda e pelas ilhas adjacentes, como as do Canal da Mancha e a Ilha de Man. Os quatro países que integram o Reino Unido têm um governo comum, embora o parlamento escocês e a assembléia galesa cuidem dos assuntos internos da Escócia e do País de Gales, respectivamente. Cada uma dessas nações tem identidade cultural própria. No País de Gales, fala-se também o galês, língua de origem celta (há um canal de televisão que transmite em galês - ver **meios de comunicação** - e a maioria dos sinais de trânsito se vale dessa língua), mas o inglês é o idioma mais utilizado. A Escócia goza de maior autonomia do que o País de Gales, tendo também seu próprio sistema legal e educacional. O gaélico, língua celta da Escócia, tem uso menos generalizado do que o galês, mas é idioma corrente nas Terras Altas (*Highlands*) e nas ilhas escocesas. A Irlanda subdivide-se politicamente em Irlanda do Norte, de maioria protestante, e República da Irlanda (ou *Eire*, em gaélico irlandês), de maioria católica. A República da Irlanda é independente desde 1921.

País	Área (km²)	População
■ Inglaterra	130.400	46.161.000
■ País de Gales	20.800	2.798.000
■ Escócia	78.800	4.957.000
■ Irlanda do Norte	5.452	1.583.000

Geografia Cerca de mil quilômetros separam a costa sul da Inglaterra do extremo norte da Escócia; de leste a oeste do Reino Unido, a distância máxima atinge cerca de quinhentos quilômetros. Na Grã-Bretanha, nunca se está a mais de 120 km do mar. O interior da Inglaterra compõe-se de planícies, à exceção do norte e do sudoeste, ao passo que grande parte da Escócia e do País de Gales apresenta terreno montanhoso. A paisagem da Irlanda do Norte é formada de montanhas baixas e campos ondulados por colinas. Bem no centro, encontra-se Lough Neagh, o maior lago de água doce do Reino Unido, com cerca de 390 km². Nas áreas urbanas entre Londres e Manchester concentra-se 90% da população britânica.

Administração local O Reino Unido divide-se em condados (ou regiões, na Escócia), que, por sua vez, subdividem-se em distritos.

❑ A Inglaterra e o País de Gales têm seis condados metropolitanos (Grande Manchester, Merseyside, South Yorkshire, Tyne and Wear, West Midlands e West Yorkshire), os quais se subdividem em 36 distritos metropolitanos; há, ainda, 39 condados não-metropolitanos, que se subdividem em outros 296 distritos não-metropolitanos.

❑ A Grande Londres é uma área à parte, composta de 32 municípios (*boroughs*) e da *Corporation of the City of London*, o centro financeiro londrino.

❑ A Escócia possui 29 autoridades locais (*unitary authorities*) e três conselhos de ilhas (Órcadas, Shetland e Hébridas).

❑ A Irlanda do Norte subdivide-se em 26 conselhos distritais (*district councils*).

A maioria dos condados, regiões, distritos e municípios possui conselhos próprios. Em geral, seus representantes são eleitos a cada quatro anos. As autoridades metropolitanas, municipais e as dos condados respondem pelos serviços mais importantes: segurança, educação e transporte. As autoridades distritais ocupam-se de questões como habitação e coleta de lixo. Os serviços públicos são subvencionados por impostos municipais que taxam a propriedade de imóveis para habitação (*council tax*) e comércio (*non-domestic rates*).

Ir ao restaurante, ao cinema ou a um *pub* são as atividades preferidas da maioria dos britânicos, no que se refere ao lazer. O teatro e as danceterias são também populares, assim como assistir à televisão, praticar jardinagem ou dedicar-se a trabalhos manuais. Em anos mais recentes, a ginástica aeróbica e os exercícios físicos têm atraído uma maior quantidade de adeptos.

Festas populares A Grã-Bretanha tem poucas festas nacionais, que são também chamadas *bank holidays*, porque, nessas ocasiões, os bancos permanecem fechados, assim como as escolas e boa parte do comércio.

▸ **A Semana Santa e o Natal** são as únicas festas religiosas nacionais. No domingo de Páscoa, é comum presentear amigos e familiares com ovos de chocolate. Como ocorre em outros países europeus, a segunda-feira que sucede à Páscoa também é feriado no Reino Unido, à exceção da Escócia. O Natal é a festa popular mais importante. Costuma-se enviar cartões a parentes e amigos e decorar a árvore de Natal com bolas, fitas e luzes coloridas. A troca de presentes, depositados ao pé da árvore, acontece na

Feriados	
1º de janeiro	Dia de Ano-Novo
2 de janeiro	Feriado de Ano-Novo (somente na Escócia)
17 de março	Dia de São Patrício (somente na Irlanda do Norte)
Março ou abril	Sexta-feira Santa e Páscoa
	Segunda-feira de Páscoa (exceto na Escócia)
Primeira segunda-feira de maio	Dia do trabalho
Última segunda-feira de maio	Feriado de primavera (*Spring Bank Holiday*, exceto na Escócia)
12 de julho	Batalha de Boyne (somente na Irlanda do Norte)
Primeira segunda-feira de agosto	Feriado de verão (*Summer Bank Holiday*, somente na Escócia)
Última segunda-feira de agosto	Feriado de verão (*Summer Bank Holiday*, exceto na Escócia)
25 de dezembro	Dia de Natal
26 de dezembro	*Boxing Day*

manhã de 25 de dezembro, seguindo-se o almoço de Natal, que tradicionalmente consiste em peru recheado ao forno, batatas assadas e legumes. O dia 26, chamado *Boxing Day*, é feriado, e é costume passá-lo em casa, descansando, ou em visita a parentes ou amigos.

▸ **A véspera de Ano-Novo** (*Silvester* ou *Hogmanay*, na Escócia) caracteriza-se pelas festas que atravessam a noite. À meia-noite, é costume cantar uma canção chamada *Auld Lang Syne* ("Os velhos tempos").

Pubs Os *pubs* (forma abreviada de *public house*), os famosos bares da Grã-Bretanha, são parte importante da vida social do país. Em geral, dividem-se em uma área com mesas e cadeiras (*lounge bar*) e outra, em que se bebe em pé (*public bar*). Costuma-se pedir a bebida no balcão e pagar por ela de imediato. Nos *pubs*, não é hábito dar gorjetas. Em muitos deles, pode-se jogar dardos ou bilhar; karaokê e música ao vivo estão também entre as atrações oferecidas.

Off-licenses Bebidas alcoólicas em lata ou garrafa, como cerveja e vinho, podem ser compradas em lojas chamadas *off-licenses*. A maioria delas abre de segunda a sábado, das 10 horas da manhã às 10 horas da noite, ou mesmo aos domingos, em algumas regiões.

Restaurantes Na Grã-Bretanha, é grande a oferta de restaurantes e cafés dotados de excelente cozinha, tanto nacional quanto internacional. As lanchonetes de *fast food* são populares, mas o tradicional *fish and chips*, peixe frito com batatas fritas, continua sendo a opção preferida da maioria. A comida indiana também é muito popular, e são numerosos os restaurantes hindus existentes na Grã-Bretanha. De modo geral, os *pubs* também servem almoço barato e de boa qualidade. Nos restaurantes, o vinho pode custar o triplo do que se paga por ele nas lojas de bebidas, e a conta pode incluir um acréscimo de 10%, cobrado pelo serviço. Quando esse acréscimo não é cobrado, é costume deixar gorjeta correspondente a 10% ou 15% da conta.

Nas horas vagas, ver televisão é a atividade preferida dos britânicos. Em geral, rádio e televisão desfrutam de sólida reputação de imparcialidade política na Grã-Bretanha.

Canais de televisão São cinco os canais nacionais de televisão:

▶ A **BBC** (*British Broadcasting Corporation*) transmite em dois canais para toda a Grã-Bretanha, BBC1 e BBC2, ambos financiados por um imposto anual, pago por todos os proprietários de aparelhos de televisão. A BBC1 oferece uma programação de alta qualidade, dirigida a um amplo público, que inclui filmes, notícias, esportes e programas humorísticos. A BBC2 atinge um público mais restrito, com programação voltada para a educação e a cultura, incluindo-se aí os programas relacionados à *Open University* (ver **educação**).

▶ A **ITV** (*Independent Television* ou canal 3) transmite programas de 15 emissoras regionais independentes, financiadas por publicidade. Em linhas gerais, sua programação se assemelha à da BBC1. Os dois canais travam feroz batalha por audiência.

▶ O **Channel 4**, um canal comercial independente e de alcance nacional (à exceção do País de Gales), apresenta programas especializados para públicos específicos, buscando cobrir temas não explorados pela ITV. Em lugar do *Channel 4*, o País de Gales recebe o *S4C Welsh Fourth Channel*, que transmite seus programas em galês.

▶ O **Channel 5** é um canal comercial com um apelo jovem e descontraído, transmitindo programas culturais e informativos de caráter mais popular do que os de seus concorrentes.

TV por satélite e a cabo A *British Sky Broadcasting* (*BSkyB*) domina as transmissões por satélite, oferecendo programas esportivos, filmes, notícias, serviços de telecompras e concursos televisivos. Ela compete com diversos canais a cabo e companhias cuja programação apresenta atrações similares, além de filmes pelo sistema *pay-per-view*, televisão interativa e acesso à internet. Em 1998, foi introduzida na Grã-Bretanha a televisão digital, que oferece qualidade superior de imagem e de som.

Rádio A BBC tem cinco emissoras nacionais de rádio (ver quadro), além de estações na Escócia, País de Gales e Irlanda do Norte.

A Grã-Bretanha possui duas emissoras independentes: a *Classic FM* e a *Virgin Radio 1215 AM*. A Inglaterra conta ainda com 39 emissoras regionais da BBC, além de mais de uma centena de estações regionais independentes.

Jornais Cerca de 56% dos adultos lêem jornal na Grã-Bretanha. Além dos jornais diários nacionais e das edições dominicais (ver quadro), algumas cidades publicam periódicos vespertinos, e há diversos jornais regionais, como o *Yorkshire Post* (de Leeds), o *Herald* (de Glasgow), *The Scotsman* (de Edimburgo), o *South Wales Echo* (de Cardiff) e *The Belfast Telegraph*.

Radio nacional: BBC

■ *Rádio 1* (1053/1089 kHz MW; 97.6-99.8 MHz FM) Música pop, rock, notícias e informação sobre o trânsito.

■ *Rádio 2* (88-90.2 MHz FM) Música popular, entretenimento, comédias, programas culturais e notícias.

■ *Rádio 3* (1215 kHz MW; 90.2-92.4 MHz FM) Música clássica, radioteatro e documentários.

■ *Rádio 4* (198 kHz LW; 92.4-94.6 MHz FM) Notícias, documentários, atualidades, radioteatro, entretenimento e críquete.

■ *Rádio 5* Live (693/909 kHz OM) Notícias e esportes 24 horas por dia.

Existem também centenas de jornais semanais e numerosas publicações distribuídas

gratuitamente. Os jornais podem ser entregues em domicílio ou podem ser adquiridos nos diversos postos de vendas, em pequenas lojas de bairro, nos supermercados e nos quiosques.

Os jornais britânicos podem ser classificados pelo formato grande ou pequeno. Em geral, os jornais de qualidade têm formato grande (*broadsheet*), embora alguns, como *The Guardian* e *The Times*, tragam suplementos com formato pequeno ou tablóide. Os jornais populares, sempre em formato tablóide, preferem trocar a seriedade das análises por notícias sobre a vida pessoal de personalidades públicas, crimes mórbidos, boatos sobre os famosos e cobertura obsessiva da vida da família real britânica.

▶ Em geral, não há espaço para questões políticas nos tablóides, cujas tiragens são bem maiores do que as da grande imprensa. Pode-se afirmar, contudo, que a maioria dos jornais britânicos situa-se à direita do espectro político.

▶ Os **jornais dominicais** são mais grossos do que os diários e, com freqüência, trazem dois ou mais suplementos, além de uma revista em cores.

Principais jornais britânicos

Jornais populares (diários)
The Sun (1964) D 3.502.923 P
Daily Mail (1896) D 2.489.264 P
Daily Mirror (1903) E 2.164.576 P
Daily Express (1900)D 991.560 P
Daily Star (1978) D 706.554 P
Daily Record (1895) C/E 584.290 P

Jornais populares (dominicais)
News of the World (1843) D 4.086.621 P
The Mail on Sunday (1982)D 2.342.860 P
The Sunday Mirror (1963) D 1.845.860 P
The People (1881) D 1.389.778 P
The Sunday Express (1918) D 834,999 G
Sunday Sport (1988) D 301.000 P

Grande imprensa (diários)
Daily Telegraph (1855) D 1.013.653 G
The Times (1785) D 711,295 G
Financial Times (1888) C 475.475 G
The Guardian (1821) E 411.386 G
The Independent (1985) C/E 224,655 G

Grande imprensa (dominicais)
The Sunday Times (1822) D 1.405.430 G
Sunday Telegraph (1961) D 784.069 G
The Observer (1791) E 449.806 G
The Independent on Sunday (1990)
  C/E 231.869 G

Os números indicam circulação. Entre parênteses: ano de fundação. Orientação política:
E = esquerda, D = direita, C = centro. Fomato: G = grande; P = pequeno (tablóide)

Revistas Os pontos de venda de jornais oferecem também uma ampla gama de revistas, que vão desde os semanários de análise político-econômica, como *The Economist*, até revistas de conteúdo satírico, como *Viz*. Milhares de publicações atendem a todo tipo de interesse. As revistas de maior vendagem são os guias da programação da televisão e publicações como *Reader's Digest*, *Computer Shopper*, *What Car* e *National Geographic*. Revistas femininas como *Woman's Own*, *Bella*, *Best* e *Prima* também vendem milhões de exemplares.

O uso da internet vem se ampliando cada vez mais no Reino Unido. Os domicílios conectados à rede já ultrapassam os 10 milhões, número superior à média européia, ainda que inferior àquele verificado na Escandinávia. Os britânicos passam, em média, mais tempo na rede do que a maioria dos europeus - mais de sete horas semanais. O Reino Unido encontra-se também entre os primeiros países da Europa no tocante às compras pela internet, embora muitos usuários ainda temam usar o cartão de crédito na rede.

Cerca de 74% dos internautas britânicos têm acesso à internet a partir de suas casas. O acesso desde o local de trabalho se dá também em proporções consideráveis, sendo menor o número daqueles que se valem de bibliotecas, centros educacionais ou cafés para o acesso à rede. Os principais provedores de acesso no Reino Unido são Freeserve, AOL, BT Internet, NTL, LineOne e VirginNet. A maioria das conexões se faz ainda por linha discada, mas os serviços de banda larga vêm se difundindo cada vez mais no mercado.

Embora o número de internautas do sexo masculino seja ainda superior ao de mulheres na rede, essa desproporção vem diminuindo progressivamente. No Reino Unido, o usuário típico da internet é do sexo masculino, jovem ou de meia-idade e de alto poder aquisitivo.

Uma grande porcentagem das empresas britânicas está conectada à rede (86%). Muitas fazem uso constante da internet em seus negócios, para envio e recebimento de mensagens de correio eletrônico, nas atividades relacionadas a marketing e publicidade, e nos setores de compras, vendas, administração e formação de pessoal.

Na indústria manufatureira, a semana de trabalho oscila entre 38 e 40 horas, ao passo que, nos escritórios, a carga horária semanal é de 35 a 38 horas. Funcionários de hospitais, restaurantes e hotéis chegam a trabalhar cem horas por semana, embora a média esteja em torno de cinqüenta ou sessenta horas.

▶ Muitas empresas utilizam o sistema de **horário móvel**, sobretudo em escritórios. Seus empregados devem estar presentes em certos horários de maior demanda, o chamado *core time*: das 9 às 11.30 e das 13.30 às 16 horas, por exemplo. As pausas e os horários de entrada, saída e de almoço são flexíveis, podendo-se, assim, chegar mais tarde ao trabalho, desde que a diferença seja compensada ao final do expediente.

Férias A maioria dos britânicos dispõe de férias anuais remuneradas por um período de quatro a seis semanas. Em geral, as férias anuais são gozadas dentro do período correspondente, mas algumas empresas permitem que seus funcionários acumulem férias para o ano seguinte. Além das férias, há também os diversos feriados ao longo do ano (ver **lazer**).

Salários Os trabalhadores britânicos recebem o salário mensal depositado diretamente em suas contas bancárias. O pagamento é acompanhado de um contracheque (*wage slip*), detalhando o salário bruto e eventuais deduções, como o imposto retido, o desconto relativo à previdência social, aos fundos de pensão das empresas e à contribuição sindical. Trabalhadores manuais e temporários costumam receber por semana e em dinheiro. Em geral, o pagamento é realizado às sextas-feiras, também acompanhado de um demonstrativo, contendo os valores da remuneração e dos descontos.

Ausência por doença Em caso de ausência no trabalho por um período inferior a sete dias, basta ao trabalhador preencher um formulário (*self-certification form*) ao retornar, explicando o motivo da ausência. Períodos de tempo maiores, porém, demandam apresentação de atestado médico.

Imposto de renda O imposto é recolhido pelas autoridades fiscais (o *Inland Revenue*) e cobrado sobre o total dos ganhos anuais. O ano fiscal britânico começa em 6 de abril, estendendo-se até 5 de abril do ano seguinte. A maioria das pessoas não faz declaração de renda, uma vez que o imposto é recolhido na fonte pelas empresas, sistema que, no Reino Unido, chama-se *Pay-As-You-Earn* (*PAYE*). Os trabalhadores autônomos pagam seus impostos ao final do ano fiscal. O montante a pagar é definido com base nas informações contidas na declaração de renda, que devem ser devidamente documentadas.

Previdência social A assistência social pública é parcialmente financiada pelas contribuições à previdência social: a chamada *National Insurance* ou *NI*. Essas contribuições dão direito a aposentadoria, seguro-desemprego e outros benefícios. Elas são obrigatórias para a maioria dos residentes na Grã-Bretanha e, em geral, as empresas as deduzem diretamente dos salários.

Seguro-desemprego Para ter direito ao seguro-desemprego, o trabalhador precisa ter contribuído para a previdência social por determinado período de tempo. O benefício é pago a cada duas semanas, mediante cheque postal. Os requerentes devem renovar sua solicitação a cada duas semanas, comprovando sua situação. Aqueles que não são beneficiados pelo seguro-desemprego podem solicitar outros benefícios sociais destinados a pessoas de baixa renda, como o chamado *Income Support*. Centrais de trabalho (*job centres*) congregam ofertas de emprego, assessoram o desempregado em sua busca por uma nova colocação e orientam-no na solicitação dos benefícios.

O Reino Unido é visitado por mais de 25 milhões de pessoas por ano, que procuram seu patrimônio histórico-cultural, seus castelos, as cidades antigas e ruínas históricas, os museus e as galerias de arte, bem como sua beleza natural. A maior parte desses turistas - cerca de 12 milhões ao ano - dirige-se para Londres, atraída pelo caráter cosmopolita da cidade e por seus famosos monumentos. Londres oferece também muitas atrações culturais, como museus, teatros e espetáculos musicais. Muita gente aproveita a estada na capital inglesa para visitar as tradicionais cidades universitárias de Oxford e Cambridge. O interior da Inglaterra oferece muitos outros atrativos: cidades medievais, como York, as termas romanas e a elegância georgiana de Bath; Stratford-upon-Avon - a cidade-natal de William Shakespeare; Stonehenge e seu famoso monumento de pedras pré-históricas; ou a beleza natural de Lake District, a 160 km ao norte de Manchester, que serviu de cenário e inspiração a numerosos pintores e escritores.

Muitos turistas visitam também a Escócia, para desfrutar de sua beleza natural, da fauna e flora locais e, sobretudo, da sensação de amplidão e tranqüilidade propiciada pelas vastas paisagens. Numerosas atividades podem ser praticadas ao ar livre, como golfe, montanhismo, esqui, pesca e esportes aquáticos. Também o País de Gales atrai os que buscam atividade física e a prática de esportes, tais como o *tracking*, o montanhismo e o ciclismo pelas montanhas dos parques naturais de Snowdonia ou Breacon Beacons.

Uma importante categoria de visitantes compõem os estudantes de inglês. Todos os anos, milhares de jovens e adultos dirigem-se a diferentes pontos do Reino Unido com o intuito de fazer cursos de inglês e praticar o idioma. As cidades mais procuradas por esses estudantes de língua são Londres, Oxford, Cambridge, Bristol, Bath, Brighton e Edimburgo.

Boa parte dos visitantes chega ao Reino Unido de avião, embora o Eurostar tenha, nos últimos anos, popularizado o acesso por trem, a partir da França. Muitos ainda preferem cruzar o Canal da Mancha de balsa, sobretudo aqueles que viajam de carro, com suas famílias ou num grupo de pessoas.

Além dos hotéis, os turistas costumam hospedar-se também nos *bed & breakfast* - quartos em casas particulares, com café da manhã. Os *bed & breakfast* oferecem um ambiente mais íntimo e aconchegante do que os hotéis, além de maior economia. Essas acomodações estão sujeitas a inspeção por parte das autoridades responsáveis pelo turismo e por associações como a *AA* (*Automobile Association*, o automóvel-clube britânico). Elas são avaliadas pelo seu conforto, limpeza e qualidade dos serviços e recebem uma classificação, expressa em número de estrelas ou diamantes. Além disso, estão presentes em toda parte, até mesmo em áreas remotas do país.

Outra opção, bastante popular entre as famílias ou grupos que viajam para o campo, é o aluguel de *cottages*. Os *cottages* são, em geral, casas no campo - por vezes moinhos ou silos. Com freqüência, são construções antigas que foram reformadas para esse fim. Pode-se também optar pelo aluguel de uma casa flutuante, quando se deseja viajar pelos muitos rios e canais da Inglaterra.

Estados Unidos

Os Estados Unidos da América ocupam uma área de 9.809.155 km², sendo o quarto país do mundo em extensão territorial. Com 286.488.000 de habitantes, são também o terceiro país mais populoso do mundo, depois de China e Índia. Sua superfície cobre toda a faixa intermediária do continente norte-americano, estendendo-se por cerca de 4 mil quilômetros do Atlântico ao Pacífico, e por quase 2 mil quilômetros de norte a sul, desde a fronteira canadense até o Golfo do México. Fazem parte dos Estados Unidos o Alasca, situado a noroeste do Canadá, e o Havaí, no Pacífico central. Sob administração americana encontram-se, ainda, várias ilhas do Pacífico e do Caribe, incluindo-se aí Porto Rico, Guam, as Ilhas Virgens e a Samoa norte-americana.

As 10 maiores áreas metropolitanas dos EUA		
Cidade	População	Estado
Nova York	20.124.000	Nova York
Los Angeles	15.781.000	Califórnia
Chicago	8.810.000	Illinois
Washington DC-Baltimore	6.726.000	DC/Maryland
São Francisco	6.278.000	Califórnia
Filadélfia	5.893.000	Pensilvânia
Boston	5.455.000	Massachusetts
Detroit	5.187.000	Michigan
Dallas	4.037.000	Texas
Houston	3.731.000	Texas

[Fonte: World Almanac]

Regiões Os EUA dividem-se em quatro regiões geográficas:

❏ Nordeste - Nova Inglaterra (formada pelos estados de Connecticut, New Hampshire, Maine, Massachusetts, Rhode Island e Vermont), Nova Jersey, Nova York, Pensilvânia, Maryland, Delaware e Washington DC.

❏ Centro-oeste (*Midwest*) - Illinois, Indiana, Iowa, Kansas, Michigan, Minnesota, Missouri, Nebraska, Dakota do Norte, Ohio, Dakota do Sul e Wisconsin.

❏ Sul - Alabama, Arkansas, Flórida, Georgia, Kentucky, Louisiana, Mississippi, Carolina do Norte, Oklahoma, Carolina do Sul, Tennessee, Texas, Virgínia e Virgínia Ocidental.

❏ Oeste - Alasca, Arizona, Califórnia, Colorado, Havaí, Idaho, Montana, Nevada, Novo México, Oregon, Utah, Washington e Wyoming.

Governos federal e estadual Os EUA são uma república federativa, formada por cinqüenta estados e o Distrito de Colúmbia, território situado no estado de Maryland, que abriga a capital do país, Washington DC. O poder se divide entre os governos federal, estadual e municipal.

❏ O governo federal constitui-se do presidente da República, do Congresso (formado pela Câmara de Representantes e pelo Senado) e da Corte Suprema. Sob seu controle estão áreas como defesa, relações exteriores, emissão de moeda e regulamentação do comércio.

❏ O poder estadual compõe-se do governador e de um congresso bicameral (*State Congress*). Estão sob sua responsabilidade a cobrança de impostos, a saúde pública, a educação e a legislação civil e penal.

❏ Os estados se dividem em condados, que, por sua vez, subdividem-se em municípios, cada um deles com administração própria. A maioria das cidades é governada por um prefeito e uma Câmara municipal (*city council*). As autoridades locais encarregam-se da administração de escolas, hospitais, serviços de emergência, da limpeza pública, do sistema viário e das leis que regulam a atividade comercial.

Estados Unidos

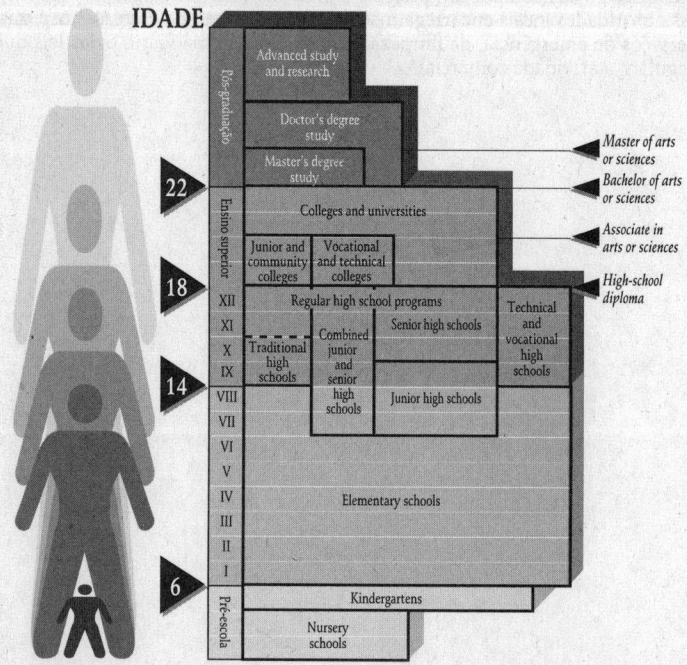

IDADE

O governo central dos EUA exerce pouco controle direto sobre a educação. O sistema educacional varia de uma região para outra. A maioria das instituições de ensino compõe-se de escolas estaduais, mas cerca de 25% dessas escolas e 45% das faculdades estão nas mãos de grupos privados ou religiosos. O ensino é, em geral, obrigatório, e se estende dos 5 ou 6 anos até por volta dos 16 ou 18 anos de idade.

Educação pré-escolar (até 5 anos) Cerca de 35% das crianças de 3 e 4 anos freqüentam escolas maternais (*nursery schools*), e quase todas entre 4 e 5 vão ao jardim da infância.

Escola primária (dos 6 aos 13 anos) e escola secundária (até 18 anos) Nos dois casos, o número de anos de estudo varia de um estado para outro. Os modelos mais comuns são os seguintes:

- ❑ seis anos de escola primária, seguidos por três anos de *junior high school* (ensino fundamental) e três anos de *senior high school* (ensino médio).
- ❑ oito anos de escola primária (ensino fundamental), seguidos por quatro anos de escola secundária (ensino médio).
- ❑ quatro ou cinco anos de escola primária, seguidos por três ou quatro anos de *middle school* (ensino fundamental), e quatro anos de escola secundária ou *high school* (ensino médio).

OS ANOS ESCOLARES

	Escola Secundária		Faculdade
	Idade	Série	Idade
■ estudante de primeiro ano *(freshman)*	14-15	9ª	18
■ estudante de segundo ano *(sophomore)*	15-16	10ª	19
■ estudante de terceiro ano *(junior)*	16-17	11ª	20
■ estudante de último ano *(senior)*	17-18	12ª	21

Currículo Não há um currículo nacional nos EUA. A maioria dos estudantes das escolas secundárias (*high schools*) deve cursar algumas disciplinas obrigatórias, podendo, nas últimas séries, cursar matérias optativas.

Exames Os estudantes fazem provas ao final de cada curso semestral, mas, ao contrário do que ocorre em outros países, inexiste um exame nacional ao término do ensino secundário. As avaliações são contínuas, ao longo dos anos escolares, e o desempenho dos alunos é determinado pela média dessas avaliações, chamada *Grades Point Average* (GPA). Aqueles que desejarem ingressar na universidade fazem exames nacionais, tais como o *American College Test* (ACT) e o *Scholastic Aptitude Test* (SAT).

Escolas privadas Cerca de 12% dos estudantes estadunidenses freqüentam escolas privadas. Seus cursos organizam-se de forma idêntica ao das escolas públicas, mas o currículo tem por alvo prioritário assegurar o ingresso dos alunos nas melhores universidades e faculdades, como as que integram as chamadas *Ivy League* e *Seven Sisters* (ver quadro).

Ensino superior (dos 18 aos 26 anos)
Mais de 50% dos graduados na escola secundária dão prosseguimento aos estudos em nível superior, onde podem obter os seguintes graus: *undergraduate*, *graduate* e *postgraduate*. Cursos superiores são oferecidos por *state colleges*, *community* ou *junior colleges* (que oferecem cursos de dois anos), *undergraduate colleges* (com cursos universitários de quatro anos de duração), escolas técnicas e as prestigiosas universidades e *graduate schools*. Os cursos são pagos pelos estudantes (ou por seus pais), mas cerca de 50% dos alunos conseguem ajuda econômica.

Instituições mais respeitadas de ensino superior	
Universidades	**Faculdades**
Ivy League	*Seven Sisters*
Brown	Barnard
Columbia	Bryn Mawr
Cornell	Mount Holyoke
Dartmouth	Radcliffe
Harvard	Smith
Univ. of Pennsylvania	Vassar
Princeton	Wellesley
Yale	

Educação de adultos Nos EUA, milhões de adultos freqüentam universidades e outras instituições de ensino superior, seja em cursos de tempo integral ou de um único período. Cerca de 40% dos estudantes universitários têm mais de 25 anos.

Os Estados Unidos têm a mais alta porcentagem *per capita* de televisores do mundo. Na prática, todos os lares americanos possuem pelo menos um aparelho de TV, e 70% deles possuem dois ou mais. Uma típica família americana vê sete horas de televisão por dia, e a média por pessoa é de trinta horas semanais.

Canais de televisão Existem quatro redes comerciais nacionais nos EUA:

- ❏ American Broadcasting Company (ABC)
- ❏ Columbia Broadcasting Service (CBS)
- ❏ National Broadcasting Company (NBC)
- ❏ Fox TV

Essas quatro redes respondem por 70% da audiência nos horários de maior demanda. Existem cerca de 1.300 canais comerciais, bem como por volta de quatrocentos canais estatais não-comerciais e canais educativos. A maioria dos canais comerciais é afiliada a uma rede nacional, porém existem mais de quatrocentos canais comerciais independentes, oferecendo uma programação especializada, composta, por exemplo, de filmes antigos.

Programação das redes A programação das tevês baseia-se quase exclusivamente no entretenimento, como competições televisivas, programas de entrevistas, comédias de costumes e filmes. De modo geral, apenas o noticiário local e os grandes eventos esportivos são transmitidos ao vivo.

Os índices de audiência e a publicidade O motor das grandes redes de televisão é sobretudo a publicidade, permitida à razão de 15 minutos por hora. Os índices de audiência são, portanto, o fator mais importante na televisão norte-americana. Índice baixo significa receita publicitária menor, o que pode fazer com que mesmo programas de relativa popularidade sejam tirados do ar, se assim exigirem as estatísticas.

TV a cabo e por satélite Cerca de 60% dos lares americanos possuem TV a cabo. Nas grandes cidades, há uma média de 35 canais disponíveis, além das redes nacionais e do *Public Broadcasting System* (PBS), a rede pública de televisão (ver abaixo). Ao contrário do que ocorre com as redes, a televisão a cabo não está sujeita às leis federais, razão pela qual pode, eventualmente, veicular material considerado impróprio. Em geral, cada canal especializa-se em determinado tema, como esportes, filmes, religião, notícias (como é o caso da CNN), compras, música (como a MTV), saúde, pornografia ou programas em língua estrangeira. Muitos hotéis, bares e clubes oferecem TV a cabo em seus estabelecimentos, um atrativo sobretudo quando da transmissão ao vivo de eventos esportivos.

Rede pública de televisão (*Public Broadcasting System*, PBS) O PBS compõe-se de uma rede de canais não-comerciais, financiada por fundos federais, pelo patrocínio de empresas e por doações de particulares. Suas transmissões oferecem programas de conteúdo educativo e cultural.

Rádio Há mais de 10 mil estações de rádio nos EUA, sendo que as principais cidades chegam a ter de cinqüenta a cem estações. Muitas delas são afiliadas a redes nacionais como a ABC, a NBC e a CBS, mas há também cerca de 100 redes regionais. Programas de conteúdo diferenciado podem ser encontrados na *National Public Radio* (NPR), especializada em notícias e em temas da atualidade, e na *American Public Radio* (APR), cuja especialidade são os programas de entretenimento. Assim como o PBS, a NPR e a APR sobrevivem com a ajuda de subsídios governamentais e do patrocínio privado.

Jornais Existem por volta de 1.700 jornais diários e 850 jornais dominicais nos EUA, perfazendo uma tiragem total superior a 68 milhões de exemplares. Jornais semanais e quinzenais somam cerca de 7.500 títulos. Os principais grupos étnicos têm também seus próprios jornais, e todas as regiões distribuem jornais gratuitos, contendo notícias das comunidades locais.

> **Identificação das estações de rádio**
>
> As estações de rádio são identificadas por um prefixo de quatro letras, KLMN ou WBNS, por exemplo. As estações a leste do Mississippi e das Montanhas Rochosas têm por primeira letra o "W", e aquelas situadas a oeste, o "K". Em geral, a indicação AM ou FM sucede ao prefixo, como em WBNS FM.

▸ **Imprensa nacional?** A maioria dos jornais americanos possui caráter regional. *Christian Science Monitor*, *USA Today* e *Wall Street Journal* são os únicos com circulação nacional, embora alguns jornais de prestígio, como o *New York Times*, o *Washington Post* e o *Los Angeles Times* publiquem edições nacionais. O *USA Today* destaca-se entre os jornais populares, com uma vendagem superior a 5 milhões de exemplares por dia. O *Wall Street Journal*, a mais importante publicação sobre negócios, é impresso em diversas cidades e tem quatro edições regionais, sendo o jornal de maior circulação nos EUA. Outras publicações regionais de qualidade, sobretudo em formato grande, são o *Boston Globe*, o *Chicago Tribune*, o *Denver Post*, o *Miami Herald* e o *San Francisco Herald*.

> **A compra do jornal**
>
> Um terço dos norte-americanos recebe seu jornal na porta de casa. Jornais são vendidos também em quiosques e máquinas. Nas máquinas, introduz-se o valor correspondente e retira-se o exemplar pelo qual se pagou.

▸ Os leitores podem optar entre jornais de formato grande ou pequeno. Assim como no Reino Unido, os jornais de conteúdo mais diferenciado são aqueles de formato grande, ao passo que os tablóides se concentram em temas como sexo, escândalos e esportes. A maioria das cidades publica seus próprios tablóides. Exemplos disso são o *Herald* (Boston), o *Sun Times* (Chicago) e o *Daily News* (Nova York). Os semanários mais escandalosos são o *National Enquirer*, o *Globe* e o *Star*.

▸ A maioria dos diários publica uma edição dominical, normalmente com diversas seções. Os jornais dominicais podem ser adquiridos no sábado à tarde (à exceção da seção de notícias), chegando a custar o triplo dos diários, embora, de modo geral, os jornais sejam baratos.

As revistas semanais de notícias, como *Newsweek*, *Time* e *US News and World Report*, são bastante populares e oferecem boa cobertura jornalística. Contudo, as revistas mais populares são as que tratam de moda, delinqüência, guerras e pessoas famosas.

Internet Nos EUA, muitas pessoas se conectam diariamente à internet, de suas casas, do trabalho ou da escola, enviando e recebendo milhões de mensagens de correio eletrônico - o serviço mais utilizado. Há centenas de provedores de acesso, dentre os quais destacam-se a *America Online* (AOL) e a MSN, que proporcionam aos usuários notícias de política, economia, finanças ou esportes, além de informações sobre os espetáculos em cartaz. Boa parte dos internautas conecta-se à rede por linha discada, mas é cada vez maior o número de usuários que se valem de modalidades mais rápidas de conexão, como ADSL e cabo. Bastante populares são os programas de troca de mensagens em tempo real, como o ICQ e o Instant Messenger, que permitem a comunicação rápida, por intermédio de texto ou de voz, além de possibilitar a transferência de arquivos em geral.

A semana de trabalho nos EUA tem de quarenta a 45 horas, embora os trabalhadores industriais cheguem a trabalhar 53 horas semanais. O horário típico de expediente vai das 8 às 17 horas, com uma hora para almoço.

▸ O sistema de horário móvel é menos utilizado nos EUA do que na Grã-Bretanha.

Férias Nos EUA, é comum ter apenas uma ou duas semanas de férias remuneradas ao ano, e muitos trabalhadores não têm direito a férias remuneradas durante o primeiro ano de trabalho. Cada ano de permanência num mesmo posto resulta num acréscimo do tempo de férias.

Imposto de renda Existem dois tipos de impostos: o federal e o estadual. Os impostos são recolhidos pelo *Internal Revenue Service* (IRS). O sistema baseia-se em cálculo individual (*self-assessment*), de responsabilidade exclusiva dos contribuintes. Às empresas, cabe deduzir o imposto do salário de seus empregados. Esse sistema de retenção do imposto na fonte chama-se *withholding*. Todos aqueles que recebem salário sujeito a retenção devem preencher uma declaração de renda relativa ao ano fiscal anterior (de janeiro a dezembro) e apresentá-la antes de 15 de abril. O imposto de renda recolhido pelos estados é, em geral, menor do que o imposto federal e varia de um estado a outro. Alguns estados não recolhem impostos.

> **Green Card**
>
> Todos os estrangeiros que desejem permanecer nos EUA necessitam de um visto. Em linhas gerais, existem dois tipos de visto: os concedidos para imigrantes (residência permanente) e os concedidos para não-imigrantes (residência temporária). Os imigrantes recebem um documento chamado *Alien Registration Receipt Card*, mais conhecido como *Green Card*, embora sua cor atual seja rosa. O trâmite para obtenção do *Green Card* é demorado e complicado. Para consegui-lo, o solicitante deve ser parente próximo de um cidadão americano ou funcionário de uma empresa sediada nos EUA. Do contrário, terá de comprovar que possui recursos suficientes para investir significativa importância em dinheiro na economia do país.

Previdência social A previdência norte-americana cobre a aposentadoria, compulsória ou por doença, pensões por invalidez e viuvez, e o programa de assistência chamado *Medicare*. Todos os cidadãos estadunidenses, bem como residentes estrangeiros, recebem uma carteira da chamada *social security*, contendo um número de identificação composto de nove dígitos. O pré-requisito para o direito à assistência consiste num número mínimo de anos de trabalho, que, em geral, é de cerca de dez anos.

As contribuições à previdência social são feitas por empregados e empresas, cada qual destinando ao sistema certa porcentagem do salário bruto. A contribuição dos trabalhadores é descontada diretamente pela empresa. Trabalhadores autônomos contribuem anualmente.

Desemprego Um fundo administrado conjuntamente pelo governo federal e pelos governos estaduais garante uma renda semanal por tempo limitado (em geral, 26 semanas) aos desempregados, que, para recebê-la, precisam se inscrever no órgão competente. O montante do auxílio depende da renda anterior do trabalhador, mas procura-se proporcionar-lhe uma renda equivalente à metade de seu salário semanal prévio.

O tempo livre de que desfrutam os norte-americanos é relativamente pequeno (ver **trabalho**).

Festas nacionais Além das festas nacionais, muitos estados têm suas próprias datas comemorativas.

▸ **Natal e Ano-Novo** No Natal, costuma-se enviar cartões a parentes e amigos e decorar a árvore de Natal com bolas, fitas e luzes coloridas. A troca de presentes, depositados ao pé da árvore, acontece na manhã de 25 de dezembro, seguindo-se o almoço de Natal, que tradicionalmente consiste em peru recheado ao forno, batatas assadas e legumes. A véspera de Ano-Novo (*Silvester*) caracteriza-se pelas festas que atravessam a noite.

▸ **Semana Santa** Nos EUA, as crianças associam a data ao coelho da Páscoa, que entrega cestas de doces e ovos de chocolate (*Easter baskets*) na manhã do domingo de Páscoa.

Feriados nacionais	
1º de janeiro	Dia de Ano-Novo
Terceira segunda-feira de janeiro	Dia de Martin Luther King
Terceira segunda-feira de fevereiro	Dia dos presidentes (comemoram-se os aniversários de nascimento de Lincoln e Washington
Última segunda-feira de maio	*Memorial Day* (comemoração dos mortos na guerra)
4 de julho	Dia da independência
Primeira segunda-feira de setembro	Dia do trabalho
Segunda segunda-feira de outubro	Dia da hispanidade (Cristóvão Colombo)
11 de novembro	Dia do armistício
Quarta quinta-feira de novembro	Dia de ação de graças
25 de dezembro	Dia de Natal

▸ **O dia de ação de graças** comemora, em sua origem, a colheita na colônia de Plymouth no ano de 1621, após um inverno de grandes privações. Hoje em dia, toda a família se reúne para compartilhar um almoço tradicional, que consiste, entre outros pratos, em peru recheado, purê de batatas e tortas de abóbora e maçã.

Bares O melhor lugar para uma conversa tranquila são os bares onde se servem coquetéis (*cocktail lounge*). A bebida é servida nas mesas e a conta pode ser paga a cada rodada ou ao final. Nos EUA, a prática mais comum é cada um pagar o que consumiu, e costuma-se deixar gorjeta, algo entre 15% a 20% do valor total da conta.

Restaurantes Os norte-americanos comem fora com bastante frequência: cerca de 40% do orçamento de uma família típica americana são gastos em restaurantes. Os pratos são servidos em porções generosas e é bem ampla a oferta de comidas de diversos países. Em geral, a conta não inclui o serviço, sendo hábito deixar gorjeta equivalente a 15% ou 20% do valor total.

Esportes Os esportes individuais de maior popularidade são a natação, o ciclismo, o esqui, a pesca, a corrida para manter a forma, o *tracking* e a ginástica aeróbica. Os esportes coletivos que atraem maior público são o beisebol (o esporte nacional), o futebol americano e o basquetebol.

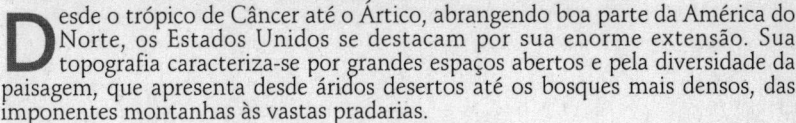

Desde o trópico de Câncer até o Ártico, abrangendo boa parte da América do Norte, os Estados Unidos se destacam por sua enorme extensão. Sua topografia caracteriza-se por grandes espaços abertos e pela diversidade da paisagem, que apresenta desde áridos desertos até os bosques mais densos, das imponentes montanhas às vastas pradarias.

Esse país gigantesco divide-se em cinqüenta estados, e viajar por eles significa apreciar as diferenças geográficas e culturais que os distinguem, cada um com seu sabor individual, mas todos contribuindo para o amálgama vital e dinâmico que deu forma ao país ao longo de sua história.

O turismo concentra-se sobretudo nos estados da Flórida, Califórnia e Havaí, nos centros de esqui em meio às montanhas e nas metrópoles. Mas são também bastante visitados os parques nacionais, como Yosemite e Yellowstone, os Grandes Lagos, e a impressionante paisagem dos cânions no Colorado e em Monument Valley. Entre as cidades norte-americanas destacam-se Nova York, com seus imponentes arranha-céus e suas muitas atrações culturais, além da energia e do dinamismo de sua gente; Nova Orleans, onde se pode desfrutar da típica cultura sulista e ouvir o jazz em sua terra-natal; e Las Vegas, um oásis no meio do deserto, com seus palácios de neon dedicados ao jogo e ao divertimento.

Viajar pelos Estados Unidos é fácil, ainda que as distâncias sejam grandes. A maneira mais simples de percorrer o país é por avião, sobretudo quando se deseja atravessar grandes extensões. Ônibus e trens são uma boa opção para aqueles que pretendem percorrer sem pressa uma área menor, como o noroeste do país, entre Boston e Washington. Mas o melhor meio de transporte para viajar pelo território americano é o carro, porque permite explorar as cidades pequenas e conhecer os locais de menor afluência turística. Além disso, o aluguel de veículos é simples, com preços bastante acessíveis, e o custo da gasolina é barato.

Não é difícil encontrar hospedagem, disponível em todos os níveis, desde pequenos motéis ao longo das estradas e nas cercanias das cidades até as grandes cadeias de hotéis. Outra opção de hospedagem são os *bed & breakfast*, ou *b&b*, normalmente situados em casas antigas transformadas em hospedarias. Muitos desses *b&b* são famosos pelos esplêndidos cafés-da-manhã que servem a seus hóspedes.

Living in
Brazil

CONTENTS

Brazil is a country the size of a continent, with an area of 8,514,205 km². Situated in South America, it is the largest country in the southern hemisphere. With the Atlantic Ocean on its east coast, Brazil shares borders with Argentina, Paraguay, Bolivia, Peru and Colombia in the west, Uruguay in the south and Venezuela, Guyana, Suriname and French Guyana in the north. The official language is Portuguese and its 170 million inhabitants make it the fifth most populous country in the world, after China, India, the USA and Indonesia.

Brazil is world famous for its natural beauty and talented football players; it is also becoming a valuable contributor to the world's scientific knowledge, supplying important research into agriculture, space, engineering, geosciences and physics. In addition, it has one of the most powerful economies in the world due to the size and strength of its industries, agriculture and cattle ranching.

The population of Brazil is characterized by its great ethnic and cultural diversity. It has developed from three basic ethnic groups: the indigenous, the White and the African (Black). The intensive intermarriage between these groups resulted in a large mixed-race population, and was added to in turn by various immigrant peoples, thus further broadening and diversifying the ethnic composition of the Brazilian population. Since independence from Portugal in 1822 there has been a huge influx of immigrants, coming mainly from Italy, Spain, Germany, Poland, Ukraine and Japan.

Indians In 1500, the indigenous population, speaking around one thousand different languages, exceeded 3 million. By the 1950s, this figure had been reduced to less than 100,000; this has since risen so that by 2001 there were 358,000 Indians, accounting for 0.21% of the Brazilian population. They live in 561 government-acknowledged reservations, which cover 1 million km^2, that is 12.26% of the entire country. These are spread throughout the country except for the states of Piauí and Rio Grande do Norte. Most of the indigenous people live in so-called Constitutional Amazonia (*Amazônia Legal*), comprising the states of Amazonas, Acre, Amapá, Pará, Rondônia, Roraima, Tocantins, Mato Grosso and part of Maranhão. Some tribes, such as the Ticuna, the Guarani and the Ianomâmi, are still quite large; others however, such as the Juma, the Xeta, the Caripuna and the Avá-canoeiro, are greatly reduced in number.

Black population In 1800, 47% of the Brazilian population was black, 30% mixed-race and 23% white. By 1880 this had changed: 20% were black, 38% white and 42% mixed-race. The ethnic composition of the Brazilian people was profoundly affected by a number of factors, including the end of the slave trade (slavery in Brazil was only abolished in 1888), the high mortality rate among the Black population, intense European immigration during the growth of the coffee industry, and the intense intermarrying between Whites and Blacks. The data from 2000 show that Blacks and mixed-race people make up 45.3% of the population in a proportion of 6.2% Black and 39.1 % mixed-race.

Immigration In 1808 the king of Portugal, Dom João VI, passed a decree permitting non-Portuguese to own land in Brazil. The first to take advantage of this were the Swiss, who founded the city of Nova Friburgo in the state of Rio de Janeiro in 1818. Throughout the 19th century, waves of immigrants entered the country. The Germans headed towards the states of Santa Catarina and Espírito Santo; the Italians went to São Paulo. The Japanese arrived in 1908, along with significant contingents of Swiss, Spaniards, Poles and Syrian-Lebanese. Over half these immigrants settled in the

> **Black Awareness Day**
> During the time Brazil was a colony, there were many conflicts between black slaves and whites. Rebellious slaves gathered in quilombos, fortified settlements. The most noteworthy quilombo was Palmares, situated in lands belonging to the states of Pernambuco and Alagoas. It contained up to eleven settlements, spread over an area of around 350 km^2. In the seventeenth century, Macaco, the most important centre of Palmares, comprised 1,500 dwellings and approximately 8,000 inhabitants. The chief of this quilombo, Zumbi, was killed in 1695 and became a symbol of the Black struggle against racial oppression; the date of his death – 20th November – is now Black Awareness Day.

state of São Paulo, to work in the coffee plantations, replacing slave labour. In other areas of Brazil, immigration was characterized by the settling of the colonists in

small properties, as opposed to the vast fazendas of São Paulo. Nowadays, immigrants, for the most part Koreans and Bolivians, seek out the big cities, where they work illegally. There is also a significant number of highly qualified workers who are settling in Brazil in order to work for multinational firms.

Total population growth and proportion by sex				
	1980	**1990**	**1996**	**2000**
Total Population	119,002,706	146,825,475	157,070,163	169,799,170
% Men	49.68	49.36	49.30	49.22
% Women	50.31	50.63	50.69	50.78

Source: IBGE (Instituto Brasileiro de Geografia e Estatística)

The majority of the Brazilian population is Roman Catholic. There are indicators, however, that show a decline in the number of practising Catholics, with a significant drift towards other Christian Protestant or free churches. Between 1970 and 1990, the number of Protestants increased by 10%; other free-church Christians, by 9%; and the number of Catholics by a mere 2%. One of the striking characteristics of Brazilian society is its religious syncretism. A large number of people not only profess the Christian faith, but also believe in spiritualism and the worship of Afro-Brazilian deities.

Religions in Brazil	
Religion/Doctrine	**Number of adherents (% of total population)**
■ Roman Catholicism	73.60
■ Evangelical	15.41
■ Spiritualist (*espírita*)	1.38
■ Spiritualist (*espiritualista*)	0.02
■ Umbanda	0.25
■ Candomblé	0.08
■ Judaism	0.06
■ Buddhism	0.14
■ Other oriental religions	0.11
■ Islam	0.01
■ Hindu	--
■ Esoteric traditions	0.04
■ Indigenous traditions	0.01
■ Other religions	1.17
■ No religion	7.26
■ Indeterminate	0.23

Source: IBGE, Demographic Census 2000

The Regions of Brazil Brazil is divided into five regions, according to the physical, population and economic features of the states that make up the country:

▶ *Região Norte (Northern Region)*: Rondônia, Acre, Amazonas, Roraima, Pará, Amapá and Tocantins

▶ *Região Nordeste (North-Eastern Region)*: Maranhão, Piauí, Ceará, Rio Grande do Norte, Paraíba, Pernambuco, Alagoas, Sergipe and Bahia

▶ *Região Centro-Oeste (Central-Western Region)*: Mato Grosso do Sul, Mato Grosso, Goiás, and Distrito Federal

▶ *Região Sudeste (South-Eastern Region)*: Minas Gerais, Espírito Santo, Rio de Janeiro and São Paulo

▶ *Região Sul (Southern Region)*: Paraná, Santa Catarina and Rio Grande do Sul

Norte The Northern Region has an area of 3,852,968 km² and a population of 12,893,561 (2000). The climate is equatorial, hot and humid, providing the ideal conditions for the survival of the Amazon forest, which covers nearly the whole region. The rubber boom, begun in the mid-nineteenth century, drew waves of people from the North-Eastern Region who settled along the region's rivers, which, until then, had remained practically undiscovered. In the 1970s, with the opening up of roadways and new projects in agriculture, livestock production and mineral exploitation, the population was enticed into the south of Pará, the north of Tocantins, the west of Amazonia, Rondônia and Acre. The economy of the region is based on plant produce such as latex, the Assai palm, various woods and cashew nuts, and on the extraction of minerals – most of the iron ore exported from Brazil comes from Carajás, in the state of Pará.

Nordeste The North-Eastern Region covers 1,553,918 km² and has a population of 47,693,253 (2000). This region is subdivided into four distinct areas, according to their geo-economic features: the *zona da mata*, *agreste*, the *sertão* and the *meio-norte*. The *zona da mata* corresponds to the coastal strip that stretches from the state of Rio Grande do Norte to the south of Bahia; most of the region's population is concentrated in this area, where the main urban centres of the *Nordeste* are to be found. The soil is fertile, due to the large rainfall, and it is here that the great sugarcane plantations are located, as well as the oil fields, the production of cocoa and the region's main industrial centres. The *agreste* is a narrow strip of land situated between the *zona da mata* and the *sertão*, stretching from Rio Grande do Norte to the north-east of Bahia. Although it is an area of lower rainfall, it is nevertheless very fertile. The *sertão*, on the other hand, is characterized by its semi-arid climate, with scarce and irregular rainfall; the harshness of this climate adversely affects the economic activities in the area, especially agriculture. The *sertão* covers a large part of the *Nordeste* region, forming a significant part of Piauí and almost the whole of Ceará. In spite of a greater vitality of the *Nordeste* economy over the past few years, the region still struggles with poverty and high infant mortality rates.

Centro-Oeste The Central-Western Region covers an area of 1,606,445 km² and has a population of 11,616,745 (2000). It includes most of the Central Plateau (*Planalto Central*), with extensive areas of wooded grassland and a tropical climate with a clearly-defined dry season. The vast plain of Pantanal is situated in Mato Grosso do Sul and provides natural pasture land, which is flooded by the river Paraguay and its tributaries during the rainy season. Part of the region is covered in equatorial forest, and shares features with the Amazon Rainforest. The main economy is agriculture, and the area produces vast quantities of soya, sorghum, cotton, sunflower, rice and corn. Beef farming is also an important endeavour here, with the country's largest herd, 57 million head of cattle, based mainly in the Mato Grosso do Sul. There are large mineral resources too, particularly manganese. The region is developing a growing tourist trade, encouraging interest in picturesque historic towns like Goiás and Pirenópolis, as well as the capital of Brazil, modern Brasilia.

Sudeste The South-Eastern Region is the most populous of the five Brazilian regions, with 72,297,351 inhabitants (2000). Its 924,574 km² are home to the largest cities of the country: São Paulo, Rio de Janeiro and Belo Horizonte. Interest in the area was first stimulated by the gold rush in Minas Gerais during the 18th century. The end of the mining boom saw the development of livestock production and agriculture, especially the cultivation of coffee, which spread from the *Baixada Fluminense* (the alluvial plain in the state of Rio de Janeiro), through the valley of Paraíba (which runs between the states of São Paulo and Rio de Janeiro), expanding then throughout the south of Minas Gerais, Espírito Santo and finally into the interior of São Paulo. Brazilian industrialization started at the turn of the 19th century in the Sudeste region, mainly in São Paulo, where the largest concentration of industries in the country is to be found. The *Sudeste* is considered the economic heart of Brazil, with its diverse industrial production, productive agriculture intensive, modern cattle farming and numerous mineral deposits. These deposits are concentrated in the Serra do Espinhaço (MG), where there is iron and manganese, and in the basin of Campos (RJ), where there is oil. The region has always attracted immigrants, especially from the *Nordeste*, although the influx has slowed recently.

Sul The Southern Region covers 576,300 km² and has a population of 25,089,783 (2000). The climate is colder than the rest of the country, with occasional frosts and snow in some parts of Rio Grande do Norte and Santa Catarina. The region was first settled by Portuguese missionaries, who remained only at certain isolated points along the coast and in the interior. European immigrants started to establish small farms in the region in the 19th century, and agriculture and livestock production formed the basis of its economy until the development of a car industry in Curitiba and Porto Alegre in the 1990s. However, agriculture and beef production remain important for the local economy, and Sul has some of the country's highest indices in health and education.

The Brazilian states and their capital cities

State	Abbr.	Capital City
ACRE	AC	Rio Branco
ALAGOAS	AL	Maceió
AMAPÁ	AP	Macapá
AMAZONAS	AM	Manaus
BAHIA	BA	Salvador
CEARÁ	CE	Fortaleza
DISTRITO FEDERAL	DF	Brasília
ESPÍRITO SANTO	ES	Vitória
GOIÁS	GO	Goiânia
MARANHÃO	MA	São Luís
MATO GROSSO	MT	Cuiabá
MATO GROSSO DO SUL	MS	Campo Grande
MINAS GERAIS	MG	Belo Horizonte
PARÁ	PA	Belém
PARAÍBA	PB	João Pessoa
PARANÁ	PR	Curitiba
PERNAMBUCO	PE	Recife
PIAUÍ	PI	Teresina
RIO DE JANEIRO	RJ	Rio de Janeiro
RIO GRANDE DO NORTE	RN	Natal
RIO GRANDE DO SUL	RS	Porto Alegre
RONDÔNIA	RO	Porto Velho
RORAIMA	RR	Boa Vista
SANTA CATARINA	SC	Florianópolis
SÃO PAULO	SP	São Paulo
SERGIPE	SE	Aracaju
TOCANTINS	TO	Palmas

Main cities of Brazil by population

São Paulo	10,405,867
Rio de Janeiro	5, 851,914
Salvador	2,440,828
Belo Horizonte	2,232,747
Fortaleza	2,138,234
Brasília	2,043,169
Curitiba	1,586,848
Recife	1,421,993
Manaus	1,403,796
Porto Alegre	1,360,033

Source: Almanaque Abril, data from 2000

Environment Between 15% and 20% of the earth's biological diversity is found in Brazil. It is estimated that, from a world total of 250,000 plant species, 55,000 can be found in Brazil, as can the world's greatest variety of primates, amphibians and vertebrates. This natural wealth could be exploited by the pharmaceutical or cosmetic industries, which represents a huge economic potential. However, these resources also attract plant and animal trafficking. Every year, 38 million animals are captured illegally in the country and 10% of international animal trafficking targets the fauna of Brazil.

In an effort to protect Brazilian fauna and flora the government has established so-called 'conservation units'. According to official figures, 5.05% of national territory is environmentally protected by these federal conservation units, which include national parks and biological reservations, as well as ecological stations and reserves.

Brazil's varied natural landscapes – the forests, bush, *caatinga*, the *Pantanal* (swamps) of Mato Grosso, fields, mangroves, sandbanks, coconut and pine plantations – are essential for the survival of its abundant flora. Some of the following areas form part of the greatest concentration of biodiversity in the world and deserve special mention:

Amazon Rainforest The largest tropical rainforest in the world, it has an area of 4.9 million km^2 and covers 54.4% of the country. Large projects such as the building of roads and hydroelectric plants have already resulted in the destruction of around 13.9% of its original area. Government organizations and the Brazilian scientific community have developed plans for the conservation and sustainable exploitation of species, in an attempt to broaden knowledge of the forest's biodiversity and how to protect it.

Atlantic woods Another important forested region, the Atlantic woods are now reduced to 7% of the area they occupied at the time the Portuguese arrived in Brazil. This is due to the fact that this area has been settled and populated the longest, and holds the greatest concentration of inhabitants in the country – from the coastline of the *Nordeste* to the interior of Rio Grande do Sul, stretching westwards through the states of São Paulo and Paraná. Once rich in rare woods such as Brazilian copal, peroba and tauari, the depletion of the region's riches began with the deforestation of Brazilwood, which is nowadays all but extinct. However, the Atlantic woods are still home to significant numbers of animal and plant species.

Pantanal The Pantanal, or swamp, is the largest floodplain in the world and has a wealth of relatively heterogeneous fauna and flora, with 650 species of birds, 80 species of mammals, 260 species of fish and 50 species of reptiles. Its rivers are thought to be the richest in fish in the world. In 2001, the Pantanal was declared a site of natural heritage for humanity by Unesco.

Cerrado This wooded grassland is a form of savannah, with abundant grasses and small, twisted, thick-barked trees. Around 20% of Brazilian territory is covered by this form of vegetation, which covers the whole of the country's central plateau (*Planalto Central*); it can also be found, less strikingly, in Amazônia, Minas Gerais, parts of São Paulo, Bahia, Maranhão and Piauí. An estimated 10,000 plant species, over 800 species of birds and 161 species of mammals are thought to live in the *cerrado*. Nowadays, extensive beef production, monocultures and road-building present the main threats to this environment.

Caatinga The *caatinga* has been reduced to half its original size and covers a mere 10% of the national territory. It is characteristic of the Brazilian *Nordeste*, and its vegetation is particularly adapted to a dry climate and poor, stony soil. The long periods of drought and the irregular rainfall in-between make life extremely hard for the *sertanejos*, as the inhabitants of the *sertão* (or *caatinga*) are known.

Apart from this wealth of vegetation, Brazil also has one of the world's largest river networks, due to its size, flatness and high rainfall in most regions. The more important water systems are the Amazon basin, with 3,904,393 km^2 in national territory (from a total of 7,050,000 km^2). The Amazon river is 6,868 km long and has around 7,000 tributaries; it is the largest river in the world in terms of water flow, and second only to the Nile in length. Other important water systems are formed by the basins of the rivers Paraná, Paraguai, Uruguai, São Francisco, Parnaíba and Tocantins-Araguaia. The São Francisco river is the longest river entirely within Brazilian territory.

Political administration The Federal Republic of Brazil comprises 26 states, 1 federal district and 5,561 municipalities; it has a presidential government. The political organization in Brazil is based on three independent bodies: the executive, the legislative and the judicial.

Executive body Within the federal framework, the executive body's leader is the President of the Republic, who has a four-year mandate, with a right to stand for re-election. Within the states, governors centralize executive power and, in the municipalities, this power is held by mayors (*prefeitos*). The President must be Brazilian-born and over 35 years of age to be eligible for election; he or she is elected through direct voting. If no candidate gets an absolute majority in the first round, a second round is held. The Vice-President is elected at the same time as the President.

Legislative body Responsible for making the laws that govern the country, the legislative body is formed at federal level by the National Congress, made up of the Chamber of Deputies and the Senate. At state level, it consists of Legislative Assemblies, led by state deputies. In the municipalities, it consists of Municipal Chambers, or town halls, led by councillors. The Chamber of Deputies is made up of 513 representatives elected by direct vote and proportional representation, for four-year mandates. Three Senators per state are elected to the Senate, with eight-year mandates. The Senate alternates the representation by one- and two-thirds every four years.

Judicial body At federal level, judicial power is exercised by the Supreme Federal Tribunal (the highest court in the country), the High Court of Justice, Regional Federal Tribunals, the Labour High Court, the Electoral High Court, the Military High Court and the Union Accounts Court. At regional level, there are Regional Labour Courts, Regional Electoral Courts and Military Courts.

Armed forces The Brazilian Armed Forces are made up of the Navy, the Army and the Air Force. Military service is compulsory for all male citizens. Young men are called up during the year of their eighteenth birthday. Nowadays, the three forces allow the voluntary enrolment of women in auxiliary roles.

The Brazilian economy In the past, the Brazilian economy was characterized by monoculture for exportation (Brazilwood, sugarcane, cotton, coffee, cocoa, rubber). Beef production and ore extraction have also been of great economic significance, being directly responsible for the development of Brazil's interior and for building up a transport network between its various regions. The cultivation of coffee was developed after independence and brought about the first stages of industrialization in the country during the nineteenth century. The crisis that followed the Wall Street Crash of 1929 saw the price of coffee plummet, yet it promoted industrialization by forcing the Brazilian government to take measures that were to accelerate the country's development. Since then, industry has continued to expand to such an extent that it overtook agriculture in terms of economic importance in the mid-1950s. Today, Brazil's GDP places the country amongst the top ten economies in the world, with the largest industrial park amongst so-called emergent countries.

GDP:	US$ 529.3 billion (1999)
GDP per sector:	Services 55.1%
	Industry 37.1%
	Agriculture 7.8%

Source: Banco Central do Brasil

Inflation Inflation has been a constant subject for debate in Brazilian economy, especially since the 1940s. Between 1915 and 1940, the rates of inflation varied greatly, though rarely reaching two figures, something that subsequently became a regular occurrence. In the 1960s, for the first time in history, the inflation index came very close to 100% per year. After the military coup in 1964 measures to fight inflation were implemented, especially wage control, which caused inflation indices to drop. In 1973, Brazilian inflation was 13.7% per year. However, international crises led to an increase in this rate, until it reached 76% per year in 1979. In the 1980s, rates of inflation increased dramatically, reaching three figures – in 1981, Brazilian inflation was 100% per year. In an attempt to contain the instability of the monetary system, there followed a number of governmental plans – the 'Cruzado' plan, the 'Collor 1' plan and the 'Collor 2' plan – but these were only partially successful. Finally, the 'Real' plan, implemented in July 1994, managed to contain inflation and provided the country with relative economic stability.

Income distribution In 2000, UN data relating to 174 nations placed Brazil amongst the countries of greatest income concentration in the world. The average income of the wealthiest 20% is 25.5 times greater than the average income of the poorest 20%. The first group receives 63.8% of national income, whereas the second receives a mere 2.5% of the total. This strong concentration of the country's wealth means that around 15% of Brazilians live in conditions of extreme poverty, a condition that affects mainly the Black and rural populations. Regional differences also have to be taken into consideration when looking at poverty in the country: the *Nordeste* region, with 30% of the national population, is home to 62% of the poorest people in Brazil. In spite of the social programmes that have been implemented, poverty in Brazil in 2002 has similar indices to those of the 1970s. One of the main factors in this unequal distribution of the country's wealth is the difficulty in gaining access to adequate education. In spite of the progress made in education in recent times, only a small proportion of the population can attend good schools and universities, thereby getting better jobs and higher income.

Work and employment Most labour relations in Brazil are ruled by the CLT ('Consolidation of Labour Laws'), created during the government of Getúlio Vargas (1930-1945). Since 1940, there has also been a minimum national wage, whose value is set by the federal government. The working day must not exceed 8 hours, or 44 hours a week. Data from 1999 shows an economically active population of 79.3 million people, and an unemployment figure of 9.6%. The Brazilian workplace has seen a dramatic fall in formal employment between 1989 and 1999: in 1999, there were around 38.9 million casual workers.

Women's social position There have been significant changes in the profile of the Brazilian woman and the family model. The census in 2000 and other studies have shown an increase in the number of women as principal earners in the family: in 1991, the proportion was 8.5%; by 2000, the number had increased to 13%. There has also been a dramatic fall in the birth rate and this coincides with the greater presence of women in the workplace. In spite of the continued difference in wages between men and women, women are increasingly active in the Brazilian workplace.

The Brazilian education system is divided into basic education and higher education. The former includes infant, primary and intermediate education. Higher education includes undergraduate and post-graduate studies, other university courses and further studies. These 'further studies', implemented in 1999, lead to earlier qualification than an undergraduate degree, but do not give access to post-graduate studies. Ongoing education for young people and adults, including professional and special training, are also supplied. Education is provided by both the public sector (municipal, state or federal) and by private schools and universities.

Infant education (*up to age 6*) This includes day-care nurseries for children from birth up to 3, and pre-school for children aged 4 to 6. Since 1996, infant education is no longer seen as a social service, being now considered part of basic education and, in the case of public schools, the responsibility of the municipalities. Nevertheless, infant education is not compulsory, and it remains a weak spot in the Brazilian education system: it provides for the needs of only a third of all children aged 6 or under. The Southern region has the highest proportion of pre-school attendance (99%), while the South-Eastern region has the most children in nurseries (78%). According to the schools' census of 2001, 6 million children aged 6 and under have access to infant education.

Basic education (*from age 7 to 14*) Basic education lasts eight academic years, or *series* – 1st to 4th *series* for children aged between 7 and 10, and 5th to 8th *series* for children between 11 and 14. According to the constitution of 1988, it is the duty of the state to provide free and compulsory basic education. There is a core curriculum common to the whole of Brazil, which is determined by the Federal Education Council of Brazil and takes regional differences into account, in order to make allowances for local characteristics. Many children fail to pass their final school exams, and many are forced to stay away from school. These problems have been addressed with some success by the educational policies of recent years. Data from 2000 shows that 94.9% of children aged between 7 and 14 attend school.

Intermediate education (*from age 15 to 17*) This takes place over three academic years, and most of those who attend go to public-sector schools. Figures from Unesco show that only 33.4% of the relevant age group attend school at this level in Brazil, though there has been some increase over the last decade.

Higher education (*from age 18 to 24*) There are 1,097 institutions for higher education in Brazil, provided by both private organisations and municipal, state and federal universities. In contrast to the other tiers of education, the public sector accounts for the majority of places – 65%. University candidates are selected primarily through an entrance exam, the *vestibular*, which is taken at the end of intermediate education.

Public Universities of Brazil

The Faculties of Law in São Paulo (1827) and Recife (1854), the Mining School of Ouro Preto (1854) and the Polytechnic of Rio de Janeiro (1870) developed from institutions that have existed in the country since 1808, and were the first universities in Brazil. Nowadays, with the exception of Tocantins, all Brazilian states have a public federal university. The more prominent of these are:

- Federal University of Bahia (UFBA)
- University of Brasília (UnB)
- Federal University of Minas Gerais (UFMG)
- Federal University of Rio de Janeiro (UFRJ)
- Federal University of Rio Grande do Sul (UFRGS)

The state of São Paulo also has three state public universities, which are among the most respected higher-education institutions in the country:

- São Paulo University (USP)
- Campinas State University (UNICAMP)
- São Paulo State University (UNESP)

Young people and adult education There are also courses and exams available for both young people and adults who did not finish their basic or intermediate education during their school years. The Brazilian education system thus enables these people to attend adult classes and resume their studies, so affording them greater professional possibilities.

Professional education Courses leading to professional qualifications are provided mainly by SENAC ('National Service for Commercial Training') and SENAI ('National Service for Industrial Training'), as well as by companies who are willing to take on trainees. These courses are geared towards employment. In 1999, there were 33,000 professional training courses in the whole country.

Special education Special education is intended for young people and adults with special needs; it is officially part of government policy, but its practical implementation is, as yet, in its early stages.

Illiteracy The 1999 data indicate 22.8 million illiterates in Brazil, that is, 13.8% of the population aged 15 or over. The country also has a rate of 30.5% functional illiterates, namely people aged 15 or over who have had less than four years of schooling, and who therefore read and write well below standard.

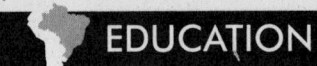

Schooling in Brazil				
Illiteracy rates	**1996**	**1997**	**1998**	**1999**
People aged 10 & over	13.7	13.9	12.9	12.3
People between 10 & 14	8.3	8.7	6.9	5.5
Years at school (people aged 10 or over) (% in 1999)	**Total**	**Men**	**Women**	
No education or less than 1 year	13.4	13.6	13.2	
1 to 3 years	18.3	19.4	17.2	
4 to 7 years	34.2	34.5	34.0	
8 to 10 years	14.8	14.7	14.9	
11 and over	19.0	17.5	20.4	

Source: IBGE

School curriculum The national curriculum includes: Portuguese, social studies (history and geography), mathematics, physics, biology and physical education. From the age of 11 (fifth *serie*), it is obligatory to learn at least one foreign language. In 1997, the Ministry of Education established educational guidelines ('National Curriculum Parameters', or PCNs), in an effort to redefine teaching in Brazil. They aim to encourage the critical and creative spirit of the pupil, stimulate ethical awareness and develop concern for health, the environment and multiculturalism, as well as to provide sex education.

Education versus work In Brazil, many young people are forced to leave school in order to work and help support the family. In the 1990s, however, there was a drop in the number of pupils forced to study part-time, or leave school altogether. Amongst 15 to 17 year-olds, the percentage of students who do not need to work as well rose from 38.9% in 1992 to 55.7% in 1999. Amongst young people aged between 20 and 24, the percentage of those who study full-time rose from 6.9% in 1992 to 10.9% in 1999.

Television In Brazil, the most popular means of communication, and the most far-reaching, is television; most advertising funds are channelled into this medium. The first televised broadcast took place in 1950, made by São Paulo's *TV Tupi*. In 1956, Brazilians watched their first football match on television and in 1972, colour television arrived. In 1996, subscription television was introduced, and now includes cable and satellite transmissions. Studies made in 2001 show that 97% of the population over the age of 10 watch television at least once a week. The biggest broadcasting station, *Rede Globo*, reaches most Brazilian municipalities (99.77%), and is famous for the quality of its soaps, which are exported to several countries worldwide. Other national commercial networks are *Rede Bandeirantes*, *Rede Record*, SBT (*Sistema Brasileiro de Televisão*) and *Rede TV!* Apart from these open-signal commercial stations, the country also has a public network of educational stations such as *TV Cultura* (in São Paulo) and *TVE* (in Rio de Janeiro).

Radio Much has changed since Brazil's first radio transmission, on September 7th 1922, when the speech of the then President of the Republic was broadcast over the airwaves while the country celebrated its first 100 years of Independence. Since then, radio has become the second most wide-reaching medium in the country after television, and it has evolved with the market, being also transmitted on the Brazilian internet. According to the Ministry of Communication, there are currently around 2,965 radio stations in the country.

Main Brazilian newspapers

The *Correio Braziliense* was the first Portuguese language newspaper to be distributed in Brazil; it was first published in London by Hipólito José da Costa between June 1808 and December 1822. The newspaper went against the interests of the Portuguese Crown. Free from censorship, it openly criticized Portuguese policies in Brazil and greatly influenced political journalism around Independence. Hipólito José da Costa was also the first famous Brazilian to defend the abolition of slavery.

Among the main present-day Brazilian newspapers are the following:

‣ *Folha de São Paulo* (SP)
‣ *O Estado de São Paulo* (SP)
‣ *O Globo* (RJ)
‣ *Jornal do Brasil* (RJ)
‣ *O Estado de Minas* (MG)
‣ *Correio Braziliense* (DF)
‣ *Zero Hora* (RS)

The press The history of the press in Brazil dates only from the nineteenth century, as Portugal would not allow it to exist in its colony. When the Portuguese Court moved to Brazil in 1808, it brought a printing plant with it; in the same year, the Royal Press was created. Editorial censorship was brought along too, and only came to an end in 1821. With the end of censorship, important newspapers emerged in opposition to the Portuguese Crown. During the reign of Dom Pedro II (1831-1889), there came a period of freedom and prosperity for the press; abolitionist and republican newspapers were printed, as were more humorous publications. Since the beginning of the 20th century the Brazilian press has gone from strength to strength; in 2000, there were around 500 daily newspapers being printed, with an average circulation in excess of 7 million, while weekly news and information magazines represent 32% of market: *Veja*, *Época* and *IstoÉ* being the three most widely-distributed. There are also specialized publications dedicated to a wide variety of subjects, which account for 22% of the market.

Telephone In 1877, just one year after Alexander Graham Bell's invention, some telephones were made in Rio de Janeiro by the Western and Brazilian Telegraph Company; one was installed in the residence of Emperor Dom Pedro II. Two years later the first grant to establish a telephone network was conceded, in Rio de Janeiro and Niterói (RJ). Phone networks in Brazil were managed by private foreign concession until 1970, and the service was unreliable; however, in 1972 the Ministry of Communication created *Telebrás* to manage the planning of public telecommunications services. By the 1990s, *Telebrás* had installed 10 million phone outlets in the country. Since 1995 the telecommunications network has been gradually privatized and in 1998 the *Telebrás* system, by then divided into 12 regional holdings for fixed and mobile telephony, was taken over by private enterprise. According to 2001 figures, Brazil now has 43.77 million land lines, around 26 million mobile phones and 1.3 million public telephones.

Internet Until 1994, the internet in Brazil was restricted to universities. However, once it became available to the general public, in 1996, and once the telephone lines had been improved, the internet grew rapidly. The country is already in the leading position in Latin America, both in terms of providers and of users, and is ninth in the world ranking of internet users. In 2001, 11.9 million people owned a home computer with access to the net, although these people belong mainly to the more affluent classes of the population – classes A (34%) and B (50%). The installation of broadband services, especially from 2000 onwards, has allowed faster navigation and file transfer. It is estimated that by the end of 2002, the number of users of this kind of service will have reached 634,000. At present, a huge effort is being made to take the internet into public-sector schools, in order to avoid so-called digital exclusion, namely the marginalizing of the poorer social layers in relation to access to information and technology. Brazil is also the third Latin American country to have access to Internet 2, a project that allows communication amongst the international scientific community via a high-tech network.

The Internet in South America		
	Country	No. of hosts
1st	**Brazil (.br)**	**1,644,575**
2nd	Argentina (.ar)	465,359
3rd	Chile (.cl)	122,727
4th	Uruguay (.uy)	70,892
5th	Columbia (.co)	57,419
6th	Venezuela (.ve)	22,614
7th	Peru (.pe)	13,504
8th	Ecuador (.ec)	3,383
9th	Paraguay (.py)	2,704
10th	Bolivia (.bo)	1,522

Source: Network Wizards, January 2002

The calendar of Brazilian feast days is intimately linked to Christianity and, more especially, to Roman Catholicism. The celebrations of Easter, Christmas and the feast days in June (*festas juninas*) are popular. There are also secular celebrations such as Carnival, the greatest of all feasts in Brazil, and other civic feast days. The religious syncretism that characterizes the country becomes quite apparent during many religious feast days, when both Catholic saints and their Afro-Brazilian counterparts are honoured at the same time.

Carnival This is without doubt the most famous of all Brazilian celebrations. It was probably introduced into the country in the 17th century under the name of *entrudo*. This was a form of merrymaking where people pelted each other with water, dust, chalk and anything else that was to hand. However, the rel-

> **Groups and troupes: the birth of the samba schools**
>
> Groups (or *blocos*) were the most democratic way of celebrating Carnival. They were neither planned nor choreographed, and brought together friends, family and neighbours. Troupes (or *ranchos*) formed a much more organized parade, with a greater number of women and more instruments such as *cavaquinhos*, guitars, clarinets and flutes that played music especially composed for the occasion. The troupes also contained an element that was to become a feature of the samba schools: the standard-bearer. These groups and troupes were later to give rise to the samba schools. In 1899, the first *marcha-rancho* – a musical genre typical of carnival celebrations – to be recorded in the history of Brazilian carnivals was composed: Ô *abre alas*, by Chiquinha Gonzaga.

ative violence of this activity soon encountered strong opposition. Little by little, the missiles were replaced by more harmless ones, such as paper streamers and confetti. In 1840, in Rio de Janeiro, the first documented fancy-dress ball took place, inspired by similar events in European cities. In 1846, *Zé Pereira* emerged, a group of jesters that took to the streets, banging on *bumbos* and drums. Since then, Carnival has become a tradition in Rio de Janeiro. Its popularity helped it to spread throughout the various regions of the country. It officially takes place during the four days preceding Ash Wednesday (Saturday until Shrove Tuesday).

> **National Bank Holidays**
>
> ■ January 1st - *New Year's Day*
> ■ Moveable Date - *Good Friday*
> ■ April 21st - *Tiradentes**
> ■ May 1st - *Labour Day*
> ■ September 7th - *Independence Day*
> ■ October 12th - *Nossa Senhora Aparecida***
> ■ November 15th - *Proclamation of the Republic*
> ■ December 25th - *Christmas Day*
> * national hero, freedom fighter
> ** Patron saint of Brazil

Festas Juninas The *festas juninas* are also celebrated throughout the country, in commemoration of Saints Anthony, John and Peter. Originally these feast days were called *joaninas*, having reached Brazil through the Jesuits in the hope of luring the natives they intended to convert. The feast days occurred during the same period that the indigenous people celebrated their fertility rituals, namely the harvest season. The *festas juninas* became quite popular and the tradition spread. During these days, it is customary to have bonfires, fireworks, dancing and bunting, as well as traditional food and drink.

Feast of the Divine This feast is of Portuguese origin and was introduced into

Brazil during the 16th century; it celebrates the descent of the divine Holy Spirit to the apostles of Jesus Christ. It takes place on Whit Sunday, 50 days after Easter. The way it is celebrated varies very much from region to region, but all festivities have as a high point the crowning of the Emperor of the Divine. In the city of Pirenópolis (GO), where it is celebrated with great pomp, jousts are held as well, representing the battles between Christians and Moors. Some commemorations are accompanied by music and dances typical of the day, along with a glut of food for all.

Optional Bank Holidays

- Moveable Date - *Carnival*
- Moveable Date - *Ash Wednesday*
- Moveable Date - *Corpus Christi*
- November 2nd - *All Souls' Day*
- December 24th - *Christmas Eve*
- December 31st - *New Year's Eve*

Círio de Nazaré Our Lady of Nazareth is the patron saint of the city of Belém (Bethlehem), in Pará. Her feast day is one of the most important in the region and brings together thousands of locals and people from other regions as well. The procession of the Círio (candle) wends through the streets of Belém to the sound of prayers and chants, starting from the city's baroque cathedral and ending up at the basilica of Nazaré (Nazareth).

Christian Celebrations

The Epiphany: January 6th
Ash Wednesday
Palm Sunday
Holy Saturday
Easter Sunday
Ascension Day
Pentecost
Corpus Christi
St John: June 24th
St Peter: June 29th
Nossa Senhora Aparecida: October 12th; patron saint of Brazil
All Souls' Day: November 2nd
Christmas Day: December 25th

Bom Jesus dos Navegantes This celebration takes place on the São Francisco river in Alagoas and Salvador (BA). In Salvador, the statue of *Bom Jesus dos Navegantes* is taken by boat across the Baía de Todos os Santos accompanied by thousands of other highly-decorated sailing vessels, to the beach of Boa Viagem. A similar celebration takes place in Aracaju (SE). In Porto Alegre (RS), the celebration is held in honour of *Nossa Senhora dos Navegantes.*

Afro-Brazilian Celebrations

January 1st: *Day of Oxalá*
January 20th: *Day of Oxóssi (St Sebastian)*
February 2nd: *Day of Iemanjá*
April 23rd: *Ogum (St George)*
September 27th: *Ibeji (SS Cosmas and Damian)*

Manual de comunicação em inglês

Cartas

Início e término

A fórmula de despedida, utilizada ao término de uma carta, depende da saudação empregada em seu início.

Quando se sabe o nome do destinatário:
Dear Sir
Dear Madam

Quando não se sabe se o destinatário é homem ou mulher:
Dear Sir or Madam
ou
Dear Sir/Madam

Quando o destinatário é uma empresa ou organização:
Dear Sirs (UK)
Gentlemen (US)

Assim se conclui uma carta, quando não se sabe o nome do destinatário:
Yours faithfully (UK)

No inglês americano, a ordem das palavras é a inversa:
Faithfully yours (US)

Quando se sabe o nome do destinatário:
Dear Mr Robertson
Dear Mrs Dent
Dear Miss Carrington
Dear Ms Paton
Se o destinatário é uma mulher, a abreviatura *Ms* é cada vez mais utilizada, porque não especifica se ela é casada (*Mrs*) ou solteira (*Miss*).

Dear Dr Howells

Nos Estados Unidos, a abreviatura é normalmente seguida de um ponto: Mr., Mrs., Ms., Dr.

Yours sincerely (UK)
Sincerely yours (US)
Sincerely (US)

Mais amigável:
Yours very sincerely (UK)

Menos formal:
With best wishes
With kind regards
K indest regards

Essas frases podem encerrar a carta ou preceder qualquer uma das fórmulas de despedida acima.

Quando o destinatário é um amigo ou parente:
Dear Bob
Dear Jane
Dear Martin and Kathryn
Dear All
Dear Mum and Dad
Dear Uncle John/Auntie Annie
My dear Chris
Dearest/My dearest Ruth

With love
Love
Love from
Love and best wishes

Mais afetuoso:
With all my/our love
Much love

Mais informal:
Lots of love

Mais formal:
Yours
All the best (UK)
Best wishes
Regards

Ao se escrever para o editor de um jornal:
Sir

Quando não se sabe o nome do destinatário:
Yours faithfully (UK)
Faithfully yours (US)

Para um membro do parlamento britânico:
Dear Mr/Mrs Brown

Quando se sabe o nome do destinatário:
Yours sincerely (UK)
Sincerely yours (US)
Sincerely (US)

Para um membro da Câmara ou do Senado americano:
Sir/Madam
Dear Congressman/
Congresswoman Fox
Dear Senator Mitcham

Menos comum:
Yours respectfully (UK)
Respectfully yours (US)
Respectfully (US)

Carta impressa formal

Os parágrafos não têm margem e são separados por um espaço.

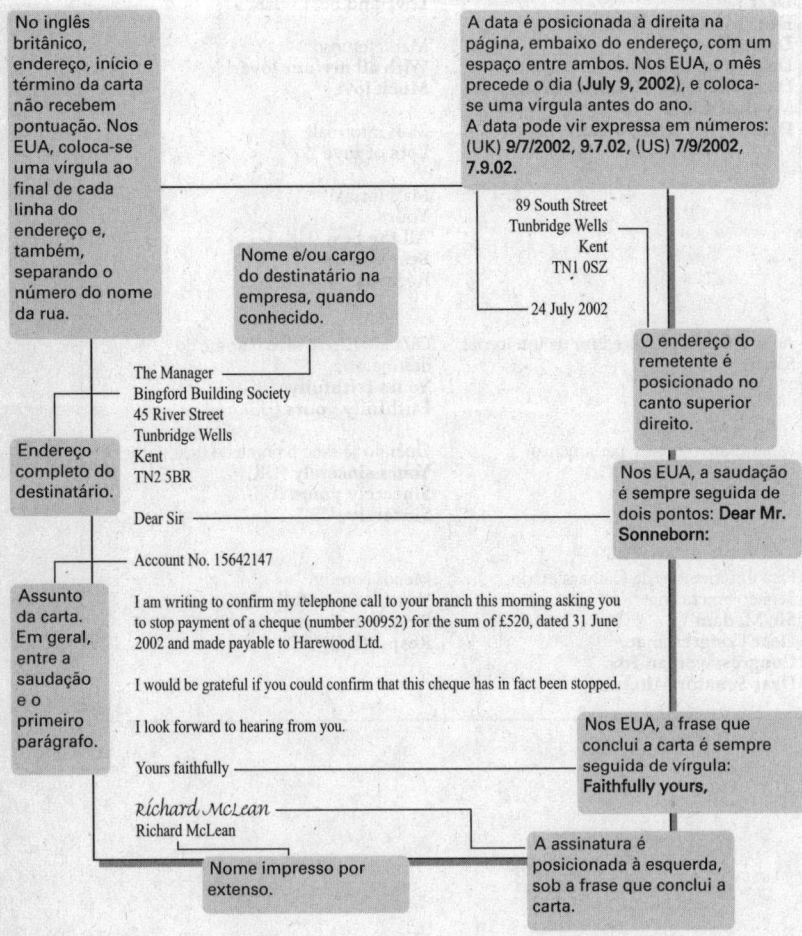

No inglês britânico, endereço, início e término da carta não recebem pontuação. Nos EUA, coloca-se uma vírgula ao final de cada linha do endereço e, também, separando o número do nome da rua.

A data é posicionada à direita na página, embaixo do endereço, com um espaço entre ambos. Nos EUA, o mês precede o dia (**July 9, 2002**), e coloca-se uma vírgula antes do ano.
A data pode vir expressa em números: (UK) **9/7/2002**, **9.7.02**, (US) **7/9/2002**, **7.9.02**.

Nome e/ou cargo do destinatário na empresa, quando conhecido.

89 South Street
Tunbridge Wells
Kent
TN1 0SZ

24 July 2002

O endereço do remetente é posicionado no canto superior direito.

The Manager
Bingford Building Society
45 River Street
Tunbridge Wells
Kent
TN2 5BR

Endereço completo do destinatário.

Dear Sir

Nos EUA, a saudação é sempre seguida de dois pontos: **Dear Mr. Sonneborn:**

Account No. 15642147

Assunto da carta. Em geral, entre a saudação e o primeiro parágrafo.

I am writing to confirm my telephone call to your branch this morning asking you to stop payment of a cheque (number 300952) for the sum of £520, dated 31 June 2002 and made payable to Harewood Ltd.

I would be grateful if you could confirm that this cheque has in fact been stopped.

I look forward to hearing from you.

Nos EUA, a frase que conclui a carta é sempre seguida de vírgula: **Faithfully yours,**

Yours faithfully

Richard McLean
Richard McLean

Nome impresso por extenso.

A assinatura é posicionada à esquerda, sob a frase que conclui a carta.

Carta para um amigo

Deixa-se uma margem no início de cada parágrafo.

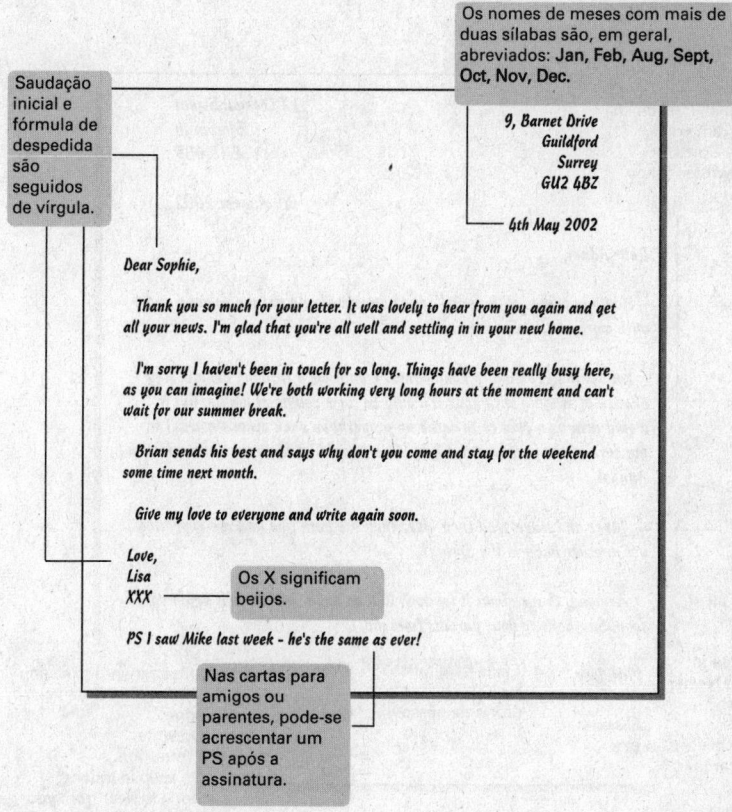

Os nomes de meses com mais de duas sílabas são, em geral, abreviados: Jan, Feb, Aug, Sept, Oct, Nov, Dec.

Saudação inicial e fórmula de despedida são seguidos de vírgula.

9, Barnet Drive
Guildford
Surrey
GU2 4BZ

4th May 2002

Dear Sophie,

Thank you so much for your letter. It was lovely to hear from you again and get all your news. I'm glad that you're all well and settling in in your new home.

I'm sorry I haven't been in touch for so long. Things have been really busy here, as you can imagine! We're both working very long hours at the moment and can't wait for our summer break.

Brian sends his best and says why don't you come and stay for the weekend some time next month.

Give my love to everyone and write again soon.

Love,
Lisa
XXX

Os X significam beijos.

PS I saw Mike last week - he's the same as ever!

Nas cartas para amigos ou parentes, pode-se acrescentar um PS após a assinatura.

Outro exemplo de carta para um amigo

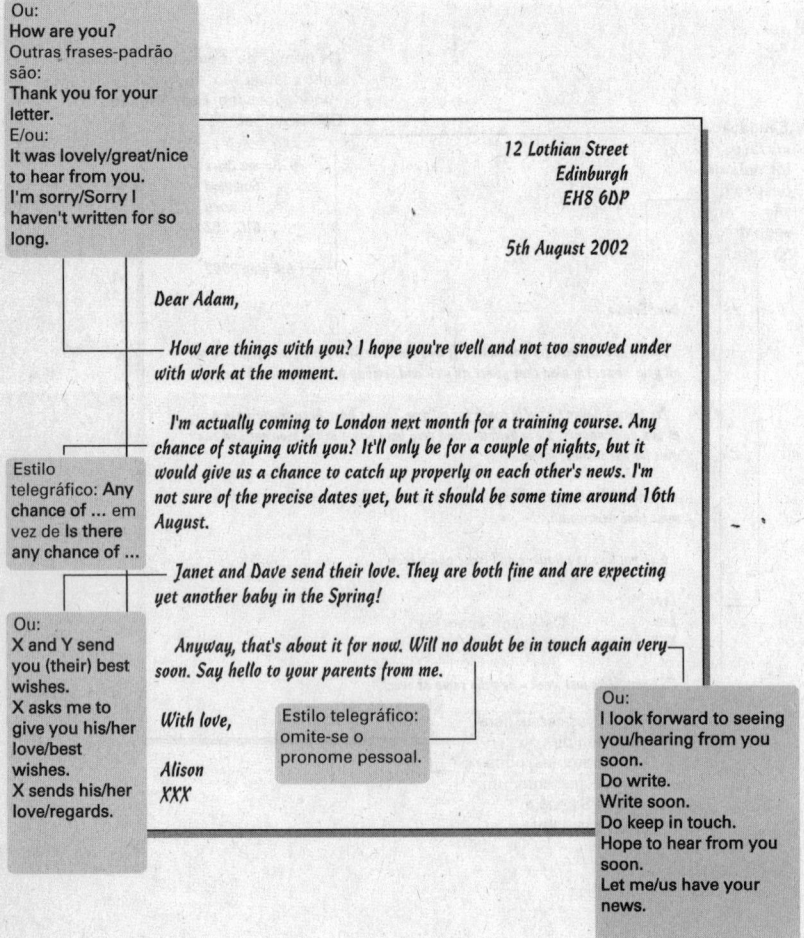

Ou:
How are you?
Outras frases-padrão são:
Thank you for your letter.
E/ou:
It was lovely/great/nice to hear from you.
I'm sorry/Sorry I haven't written for so long.

12 Lothian Street
Edinburgh
EH8 6DP

5th August 2002

Dear Adam,

How are things with you? I hope you're well and not too snowed under with work at the moment.

I'm actually coming to London next month for a training course. Any chance of staying with you? It'll only be for a couple of nights, but it would give us a chance to catch up properly on each other's news. I'm not sure of the precise dates yet, but it should be some time around 16th August.

Estilo telegráfico: **Any chance of ...** em vez de **Is there any chance of ...**

Janet and Dave send their love. They are both fine and are expecting yet another baby in the Spring!

Anyway, that's about it for now. Will no doubt be in touch again very soon. Say hello to your parents from me.

Ou:
X and Y send you (their) best wishes.
X asks me to give you his/her love/best wishes.
X sends his/her love/regards.

With love,

Alison
XXX

Estilo telegráfico: omite-se o pronome pessoal.

Ou:
I look forward to seeing you/hearing from you soon.
Do write.
Write soon.
Do keep in touch.
Hope to hear from you soon.
Let me/us have your news.

Convite de casamento

Modelo de convite

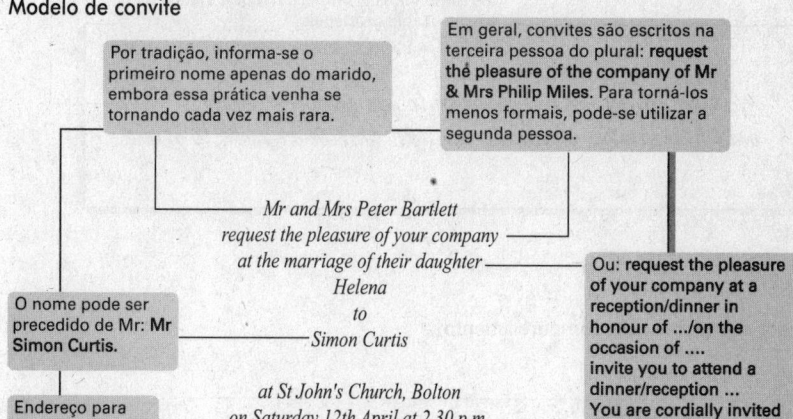

Por tradição, informa-se o primeiro nome apenas do marido, embora essa prática venha se tornando cada vez mais rara.

Em geral, convites são escritos na terceira pessoa do plural: **request thé pleasure of the company of Mr & Mrs Philip Miles**. Para torná-los menos formais, pode-se utilizar a segunda pessoa.

Ou: **request the pleasure of your company at a reception/dinner in honour of .../on the occasion of ....**
invite you to attend a dinner/reception ...
You are cordially invited to attend...

O nome pode ser precedido de Mr: **Mr Simon Curtis.**

Endereço para resposta.

Mr and Mrs Peter Bartlett
request the pleasure of your company
at the marriage of their daughter
Helena
to
Simon Curtis

at St John's Church, Bolton
on Saturday 12th April at 2.30 p.m.
and afterwards at the reception
at the Crown Hotel

RSVP
11 York Road
Bolton BL2 3XR

Pode-se especificar uma data:
Please RSVP by 12th March.
Ou: **Your RSVP would be appreciated by 12th March.**

Para aceitar o convite

Não é necessário datar ou assinar a resposta. Se o convite estiver na terceira pessoa do plural, a resposta também deve empregar a terceira pessoa: **Mr & Mrs Mark Payne thank Mr & Mrs Peter Bartlett for their kind invitation to the marriage of their daughter Helena on 12th April, and to the reception afterwards. They have great pleasure in accepting.**

A resposta deve ser escrita à mão.

We thank you for your kind invitation to the marriage of your daughter Helena on 12th April, and to the reception afterwards. We have great pleasure in accepting.

Ou: **It is with great/much pleasure that we/they accept.**

Para declinar do convite

Ou, na terceira pessoa do plural: **Mr and Mrs Crosbie thank Mr and Mrs Bartlett for their kind invitation to their daughter's wedding, and to the reception afterwards, but regret that they will be unable to attend.**

We thank you for the kind invitation to your daughter's wedding, and to the reception afterwards, but regret that we are unable to attend.

Para agradecer pelo comparecimento

45 Talbot Road
Leeds
LS11 9KY

1st February 2002

Dear Chris and Natalie,

Ou: **bought us ...**

Thank you so much for the beautiful coffee set you sent us as a wedding present. You must come and visit next week so that you can be the first to enjoy them.

Ou: **We were both delighted you could come...; It was really nice to see you at the wedding.**

I was so glad that you could come to the wedding. It was nice to have all our friends and family there, even Uncle George! Give my thanks to Tom for the catering: he did us proud.

Ou: **Say thank you to ...**

We had a wonderful honeymoon in the Maldives and are now trying to settle down to work again. Let us known when is good for you to come to dinner.

Many thanks once again!

With much love,

Sheila & Sam

XXX

Reservas

Cada vez mais, reservas de passagens ou hotel são feitas pela internet e por e-mail. Toda reserva feita por telefone precisa ser confirmada por escrito.

Para fazer uma reserva

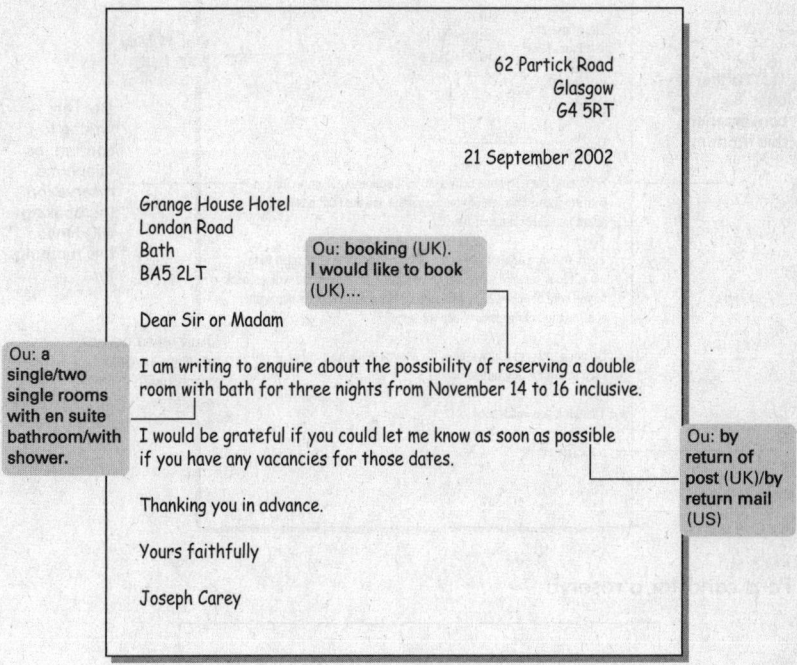

62 Partick Road
Glasgow
G4 5RT

21 September 2002

Grange House Hotel
London Road
Bath
BA5 2LT

Ou: booking (UK).
I would like to book
(UK)...

Dear Sir or Madam

Ou: a
single/two
single rooms
with en suite
bathroom/with
shower.

I am writing to enquire about the possibility of reserving a double room with bath for three nights from November 14 to 16 inclusive.

I would be grateful if you could let me know as soon as possible if you have any vacancies for those dates.

Ou: by
return of
post (UK)/by
return mail
(US)

Thanking you in advance.

Yours faithfully

Joseph Carey

Para confirmar a reserva

> 622 Monroe Street
> Philadelphia
> PA 19145
> USA
>
> Tel: 215.617.1439
>
> May 11, 2002

Nos EUA, a saudação é seguida de dois pontos, e a fórmula de despedida, de vírgula.

Ou: 11 May 2002 (UK)

The Manager
The Pines Hotel
Denver
CO 80348
USA

Ou: Further to our conversation this morning, ...

Dear Sir:

Ou: I am writing to confirm the telephone reservation (ou booking UK) I made this morning for...

Following our telephone conversation this morning, I am writing to confirm the reservation of your restaurant and bar facilities for the afternoon and evening of June 22.

There will be a total of 300 guests requiring a four-course meal with wine. I look forward to receiving copies of your menus and will get back to you with our choices as soon as possible. I would appreciate written confirmation of the price which we agreed.

Do not hesitate to contact me at the above telephone number, if you need to discuss any further details.

Ou: Please do not hesitate to get in touch (with me/us) ...

Thanking you in advance.

Sincerely yours,

Joel Stein

Para cancelar a reserva

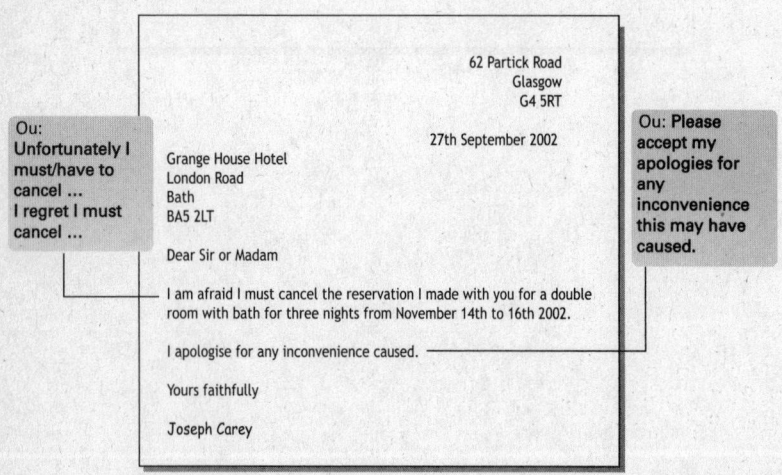

> 62 Partick Road
> Glasgow
> G4 5RT
>
> 27th September 2002

Ou: Unfortunately I must/have to cancel ... I regret I must cancel ...

Grange House Hotel
London Road
Bath
BA5 2LT

Ou: Please accept my apologies for any inconvenience this may have caused.

Dear Sir or Madam

I am afraid I must cancel the reservation I made with you for a double room with bath for three nights from November 14th to 16th 2002.

I apologise for any inconvenience caused.

Yours faithfully

Joseph Carey

Para solicitar informação

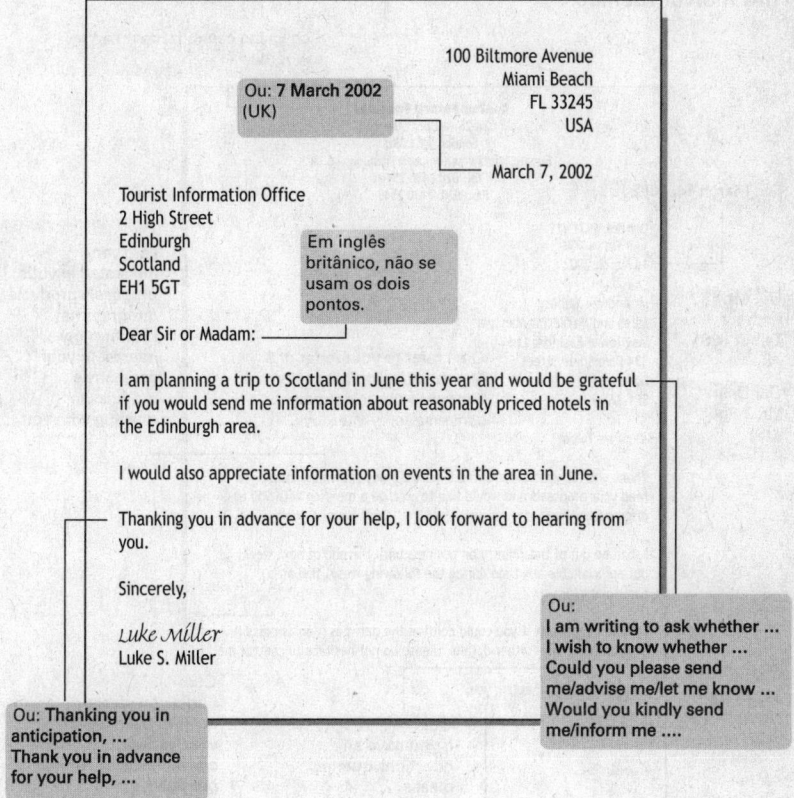

100 Biltmore Avenue
Miami Beach
FL 33245
USA

Ou: **7 March 2002**
(UK)

March 7, 2002

Tourist Information Office
2 High Street
Edinburgh
Scotland
EH1 5GT

Em inglês britânico, não se usam os dois pontos.

Dear Sir or Madam:

I am planning a trip to Scotland in June this year and would be grateful if you would send me information about reasonably priced hotels in the Edinburgh area.

I would also appreciate information on events in the area in June.

Thanking you in advance for your help, I look forward to hearing from you.

Sincerely,

Luke Miller
Luke S. Miller

Ou:
I am writing to ask whether ...
I wish to know whether ...
Could you please send me/advise me/let me know ...
Would you kindly send me/inform me ....

Ou: **Thanking you in anticipation, ...**
Thank you in advance for your help, ...

Correspondência comercial

Para marcar reunião

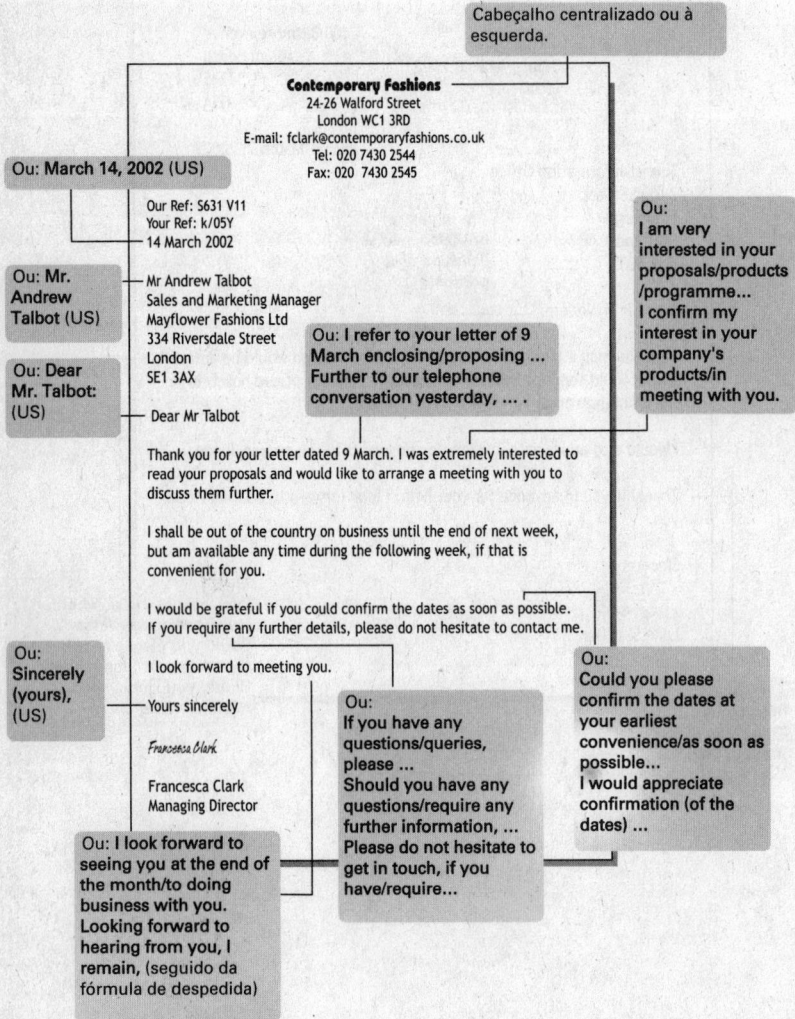

Cabeçalho centralizado ou à esquerda.

Contemporary Fashions
24-26 Walford Street
London WC1 3RD
E-mail: fclark@contemporaryfashions.co.uk
Tel: 020 7430 2544
Fax: 020 7430 2545

Ou: **March 14, 2002** (US)

Our Ref: S631 V11
Your Ref: k/05Y
14 March 2002

Ou: **Mr. Andrew Talbot** (US)

Mr Andrew Talbot
Sales and Marketing Manager
Mayflower Fashions Ltd
334 Riversdale Street
London
SE1 3AX

Ou: **Dear Mr. Talbot:** (US)

Dear Mr Talbot

Ou: **I refer to your letter of 9 March enclosing/proposing ... Further to our telephone conversation yesterday, ...**

Ou: **I am very interested in your proposals/products /programme... I confirm my interest in your company's products/in meeting with you.**

Thank you for your letter dated 9 March. I was extremely interested to read your proposals and would like to arrange a meeting with you to discuss them further.

I shall be out of the country on business until the end of next week, but am available any time during the following week, if that is convenient for you.

I would be grateful if you could confirm the dates as soon as possible. If you require any further details, please do not hesitate to contact me.

I look forward to meeting you.

Ou: **Sincerely (yours),** (US)

Yours sincerely

Francesca Clark

Francesca Clark
Managing Director

Ou: **If you have any questions/queries, please ... Should you have any questions/require any further information, ... Please do not hesitate to get in touch, if you have/require...**

Ou: **Could you please confirm the dates at your earliest convenience/as soon as possible... I would appreciate confirmation (of the dates) ...**

Ou: **I look forward to seeing you at the end of the month/to doing business with you. Looking forward to hearing from you, I remain,** (seguido da fórmula de despedida)

Para responder a um pedido de informação

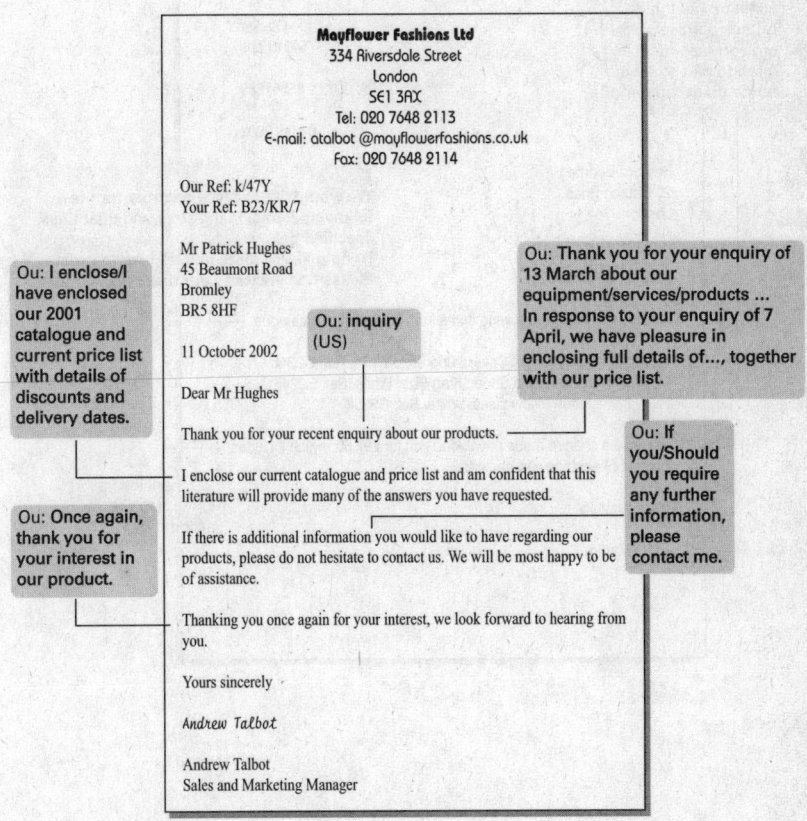

Mayflower Fashions Ltd
334 Riversdale Street
London
SE1 3AX
Tel: 020 7648 2113
E-mail: atalbot @mayflowerfashions.co.uk
Fax: 020 7648 2114

Our Ref: k/47Y
Your Ref: B23/KR/7

Mr Patrick Hughes
45 Beaumont Road
Bromley
BR5 8HF

11 October 2002

Dear Mr Hughes

Thank you for your recent enquiry about our products.

I enclose our current catalogue and price list and am confident that this literature will provide many of the answers you have requested.

If there is additional information you would like to have regarding our products, please do not hesitate to contact us. We will be most happy to be of assistance.

Thanking you once again for your interest, we look forward to hearing from you.

Yours sincerely

Andrew Talbot

Andrew Talbot
Sales and Marketing Manager

Ou: I enclose/I have enclosed our 2001 catalogue and current price list with details of discounts and delivery dates.

Ou: inquiry (US)

Ou: Thank you for your enquiry of 13 March about our equipment/services/products ... In response to your enquiry of 7 April, we have pleasure in enclosing full details of..., together with our price list.

Ou: If you/Should you require any further information, please contact me.

Ou: Once again, thank you for your interest in our product.

Para fazer um pedido de compra

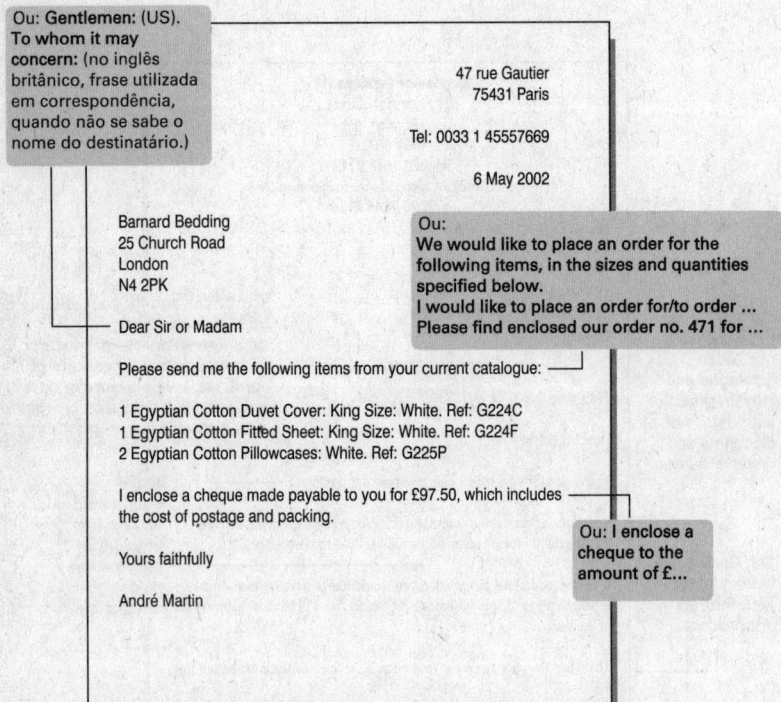

Ou: **Gentlemen:** (US). **To whom it may concern:** (no inglês britânico, frase utilizada em correspondência, quando não se sabe o nome do destinatário.)

47 rue Gautier
75431 Paris

Tel: 0033 1 45557669

6 May 2002

Barnard Bedding
25 Church Road
London
N4 2PK

Dear Sir or Madam

Please send me the following items from your current catalogue:

1 Egyptian Cotton Duvet Cover: King Size: White. Ref: G224C
1 Egyptian Cotton Fitted Sheet: King Size: White. Ref: G224F
2 Egyptian Cotton Pillowcases: White. Ref: G225P

I enclose a cheque made payable to you for £97.50, which includes the cost of postage and packing.

Yours faithfully

André Martin

Ou:
We would like to place an order for the following items, in the sizes and quantities specified below.
I would like to place an order for/to order ...
Please find enclosed our order no. 471 for ...

Ou: **I enclose a cheque to the amount of £...**

Emprego

Nos países de língua inglesa, cartas escritas com o intuito de candidatar-se a um emprego devem ser datilografadas ou impressas, a não ser quando em resposta a um anúnico solicitando que sejam escritas à mão.

Para candidatar-se a um estágio

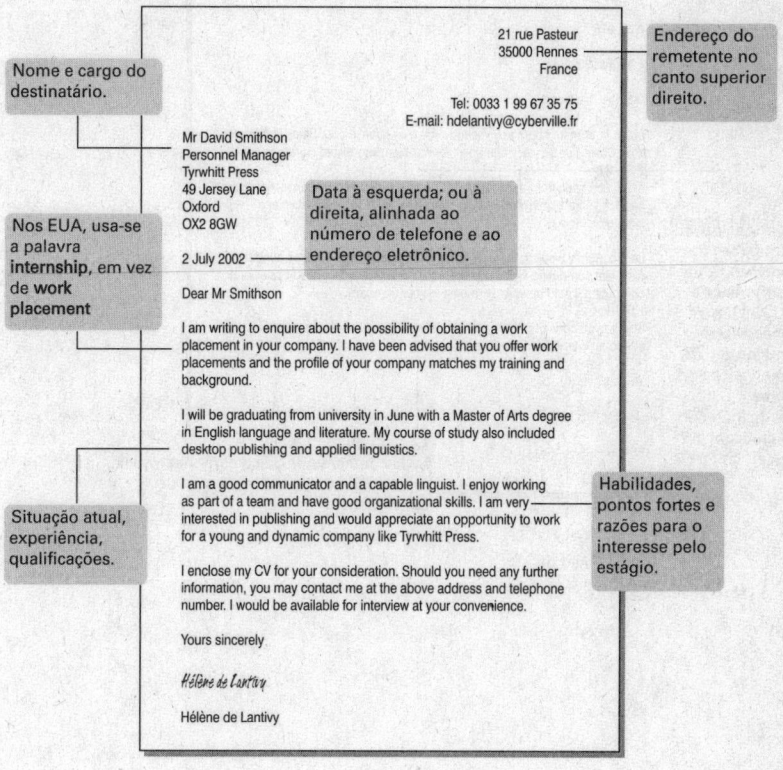

Nome e cargo do destinatário.

Nos EUA, usa-se a palavra internship, em vez de work placement

Situação atual, experiência, qualificações.

21 rue Pasteur
35000 Rennes
France

Tel: 0033 1 99 67 35 75
E-mail: hdelantivy@cyberville.fr

Endereço do remetente no canto superior direito.

Mr David Smithson
Personnel Manager
Tyrwhitt Press
49 Jersey Lane
Oxford
OX2 8GW

2 July 2002

Data à esquerda; ou à direita, alinhada ao número de telefone e ao endereço eletrônico.

Dear Mr Smithson

I am writing to enquire about the possibility of obtaining a work placement in your company. I have been advised that you offer work placements and the profile of your company matches my training and background.

I will be graduating from university in June with a Master of Arts degree in English language and literature. My course of study also included desktop publishing and applied linguistics.

I am a good communicator and a capable linguist. I enjoy working as part of a team and have good organizational skills. I am very interested in publishing and would appreciate an opportunity to work for a young and dynamic company like Tyrwhitt Press.

Habilidades, pontos fortes e razões para o interesse pelo estágio.

I enclose my CV for your consideration. Should you need any further information, you may contact me at the above address and telephone number. I would be available for interview at your convenience.

Yours sincerely

Hélène de Lantivy

Hélène de Lantivy

Para saber sobre vagas

Ou: I would like to/I wish to inquire about the possibility of becoming a … at your factory/ facility/in your company.

Se já se conhece alguém na empresa, deve-se mencioná-lo.

Ou: As you will note from the enclosed CV (UK)/résumé (US), I have specialized /majored (US) in physics and have participated in significant research.

Ou: at your convenience.
I will contact your office early next week to arrange an appointment at your convenience.

Indica envio de anexo.

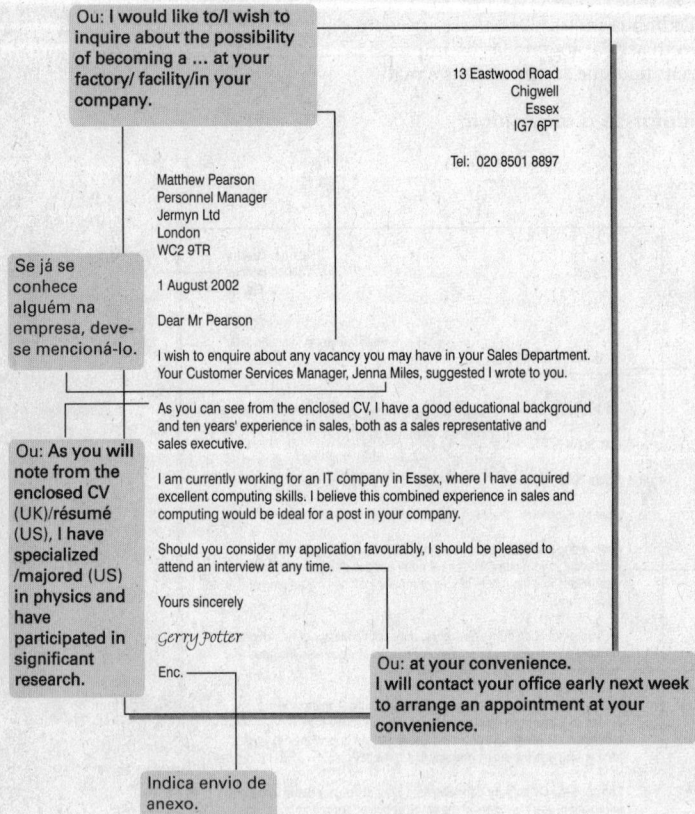

13 Eastwood Road
Chigwell
Essex
IG7 6PT

Tel: 020 8501 8897

Matthew Pearson
Personnel Manager
Jermyn Ltd
London
WC2 9TR

1 August 2002

Dear Mr Pearson

I wish to enquire about any vacancy you may have in your Sales Department. Your Customer Services Manager, Jenna Miles, suggested I wrote to you.

As you can see from the enclosed CV, I have a good educational background and ten years' experience in sales, both as a sales representative and sales executive.

I am currently working for an IT company in Essex, where I have acquired excellent computing skills. I believe this combined experience in sales and computing would be ideal for a post in your company.

Should you consider my application favourably, I should be pleased to attend an interview at any time.

Yours sincerely

Gerry Potter

Enc.

Para responder a um anúncio de jornal

Ou: I would like to apply for the above post as recently advertised in the July issue of.../which was advertised in today's "Daily Post".
I am writing to apply for the above post/for the post of ... (as) advertised in ....
I am writing in response to your advertisement in ... for ...
I would like to be considered for the above post which your company advertised in ...

12 Beaconsfield Street
London
W1 9JB

Tel: 020 7580 7095

Mr Nathan Richards
Chief Analyst
Pritchard Investments
Albert Street
London EC1 2KM

31 May 2002

Assunto da carta: função ou cargo.

Ou: and (I) enclose my (current) CV (UK)/résumé (US) for your consideration.

Dear Mr Richards

Financial Analyst

I would like to apply for the above post as advertised in "The Financial Times" of 25 May, and I enclose my CV for your attention.

As you can see from my CV, I am an experienced financial analyst and consultant, having worked extensively in this sector in both London and Frankfurt. I am currently looking for a position that will allow me to develop my skills and experience in a dynamic environment such as Pritchard Investments.

I believe that my financial and academic background would be of benefit to your company. Should you consider me suitable for the post, I can provide the names of three referees.

Ou:
Thank you for considering my application. If you would like to schedule an interview, please call me at .... I will be available at your convenience.
I would appreciate the chance to meet you (UK)/meet with you (US). You may reach me at the above telephone number or e-mail address.

I thank you for your consideration and remain at your disposal for any further information. I look forward to meeting you in the near future.

Your sincerely

Michael Griffin

Michael Griffin

Enc.

Ou: I look forward to talking with you/to discussing matters with you (at a future interview).

Frases úteis:

I know how to/I can operate a cash register/computer/power equipment.
I am computer literate/a good communicator/a good organizer.
I am a capable linguist/can speak fluent English and German.
I have good computer/IT/language/editing/communication/organisational skills.
I can learn new tasks and enjoy/can accept a challenge.
I enjoy working/can work with a variety of people.
I work well in team, and can also work under pressure.
I perform well under stress/am good with difficult customers.
I can handle multiple tasks simultaneously.

Curriculum Vitae

Recém-formado, com alguma experiência (UK)

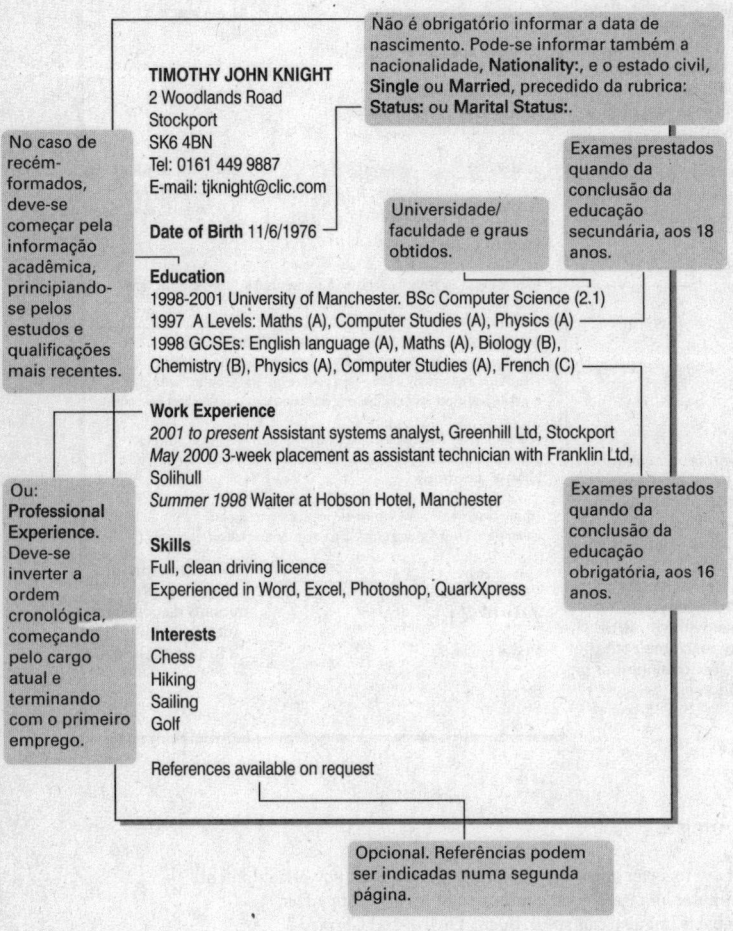

No caso de recém-formados, deve-se começar pela informação acadêmica, principiando-se pelos estudos e qualificações mais recentes.

TIMOTHY JOHN KNIGHT
2 Woodlands Road
Stockport
SK6 4BN
Tel: 0161 449 9887
E-mail: tjknight@clic.com

Date of Birth 11/6/1976

Não é obrigatório informar a data de nascimento. Pode-se informar também a nacionalidade, **Nationality:**, e o estado civil, **Single** ou **Married**, precedido da rubrica: **Status:** ou **Marital Status:**.

Education
1998-2001 University of Manchester. BSc Computer Science (2.1)
1997 A Levels: Maths (A), Computer Studies (A), Physics (A)
1998 GCSEs: English language (A), Maths (A), Biology (B), Chemistry (B), Physics (A), Computer Studies (A), French (C)

Universidade/faculdade e graus obtidos.

Exames prestados quando da conclusão da educação secundária, aos 18 anos.

Work Experience
2001 to present Assistant systems analyst, Greenhill Ltd, Stockport
May 2000 3-week placement as assistant technician with Franklin Ltd, Solihull
Summer 1998 Waiter at Hobson Hotel, Manchester

Ou: **Professional Experience.** Deve-se inverter a ordem cronológica, começando pelo cargo atual e terminando com o primeiro emprego.

Skills
Full, clean driving licence
Experienced in Word, Excel, Photoshop, QuarkXpress

Exames prestados quando da conclusão da educação obrigatória, aos 16 anos.

Interests
Chess
Hiking
Sailing
Golf

References available on request

Opcional. Referências podem ser indicadas numa segunda página.

Cargo de gerência (UK)

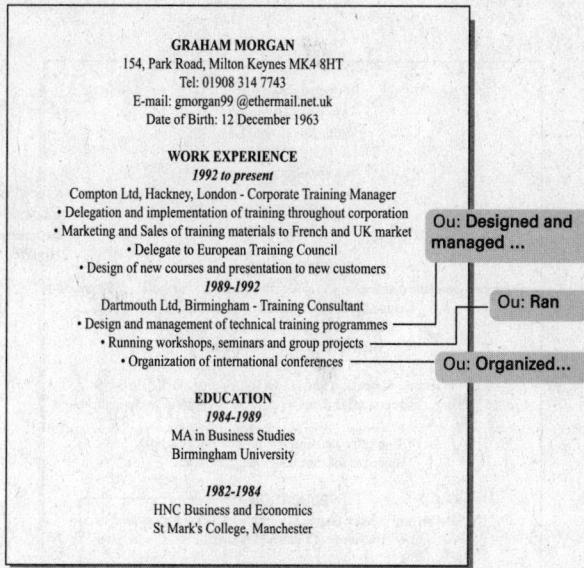

GRAHAM MORGAN
154, Park Road, Milton Keynes MK4 8HT
Tel: 01908 314 7743
E-mail: gmorgan99 @ethermail.net.uk
Date of Birth: 12 December 1963

WORK EXPERIENCE
1992 to present
Compton Ltd, Hackney, London - Corporate Training Manager
• Delegation and implementation of training throughout corporation
• Marketing and Sales of training materials to French and UK market
• Delegate to European Training Council
• Design of new courses and presentation to new customers
1989-1992
Dartmouth Ltd, Birmingham - Training Consultant
• Design and management of technical training programmes
• Running workshops, seminars and group projects
• Organization of international conferences

EDUCATION
1984-1989
MA in Business Studies
Birmingham University

1982-1984
HNC Business and Economics
St Mark's College, Manchester

> Ou: Designed and managed ...

> Ou: Ran

> Ou: Organized...

Recém-formado, com alguma experiência (US)

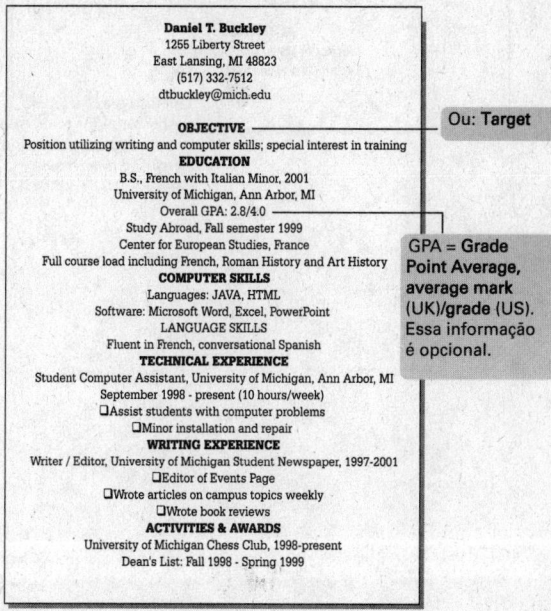

Daniel T. Buckley
1255 Liberty Street
East Lansing, MI 48823
(517) 332-7512
dtbuckley@mich.edu

OBJECTIVE
Position utilizing writing and computer skills; special interest in training
EDUCATION
B.S., French with Italian Minor, 2001
University of Michigan, Ann Arbor, MI
Overall GPA: 2.8/4.0
Study Abroad, Fall semester 1999
Center for European Studies, France
Full course load including French, Roman History and Art History
COMPUTER SKILLS
Languages: JAVA, HTML
Software: Microsoft Word, Excel, PowerPoint
LANGUAGE SKILLS
Fluent in French, conversational Spanish
TECHNICAL EXPERIENCE
Student Computer Assistant, University of Michigan, Ann Arbor, MI
September 1998 - present (10 hours/week)
❏ Assist students with computer problems
❏ Minor installation and repair
WRITING EXPERIENCE
Writer / Editor, University of Michigan Student Newspaper, 1997-2001
❏ Editor of Events Page
❏ Wrote articles on campus topics weekly
❏ Wrote book reviews
ACTIVITIES & AWARDS
University of Michigan Chess Club, 1998-present
Dean's List: Fall 1998 - Spring 1999

> Ou: Target

> GPA = Grade Point Average, average mark (UK)/grade (US). Essa informação é opcional.

Cargo de gerência (US)

TESSA PARKS
437 West 94th Street,
Chicago, IL 60637
(733) 702-1336
tessaparks@chicol.com

OBJECTIVE
Product Designer/Manager

Ou: Work Experience Employment History.

EXPERIENCE
Computer Consultant and Systems Designer, Oakwood Inc., Chicago, IL, 1994-present
Troubleshoot hardware and software problems
Design and test new operating systems
Head up large team of consultants

Assistant Systems Consultant, Jones Davis Inc., Springfield, IL, 1990-1994
Created Web pages and customized computer systems for clients in the Springfield area

Intern, Roseberry Inc., Chicago, IL, June - August 1990
Worked as software design engineer intern.

EDUCATION
Bachelor of Science Degree in Computer Science, May 1990
University of Chicago, Chicago, IL

COMPUTER SKILLS
Languagues and Software : B, CC, Java, HTML, Excel, Word
Operating Systems : Unix, Windows, Mac OS

ACTIVITIES
Society of Manufacturing Engineers
Aircraft Owners and Pilots Association

Quando a experiência profissional for mais relevante, não é necessário detalhar a formação acadêmica.

E-mail

Como o e-mail é uma forma bastante rápida de comunicação, o estilo das mensagens é, em geral, informal e telegráfico, contendo muitas abreviações e acrônimos.

As convenções que regem a comunicação pela internet - a chamada netiqueta - recomendam que não se escrevam mensagens em letras maiúsculas, pois isso é entendido como sinal de raiva.

Em geral, não se empregam as formas tradicionais de saudação (**Dear ...**). Quando se conhece bem o destinatário da mensagem, pode-se iniciá-la com uma saudação informal, **Hello** ou **Hi**, seguida do primeiro nome da pessoa em questão.

Na empresa

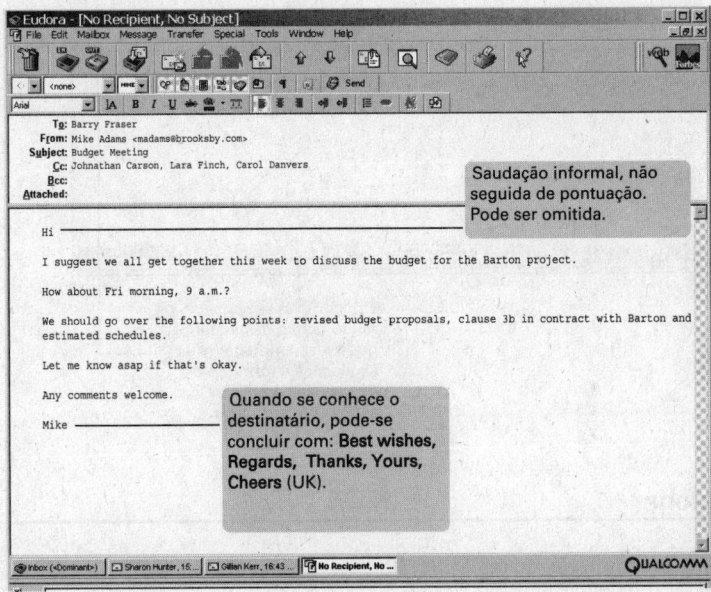

Entre empresas

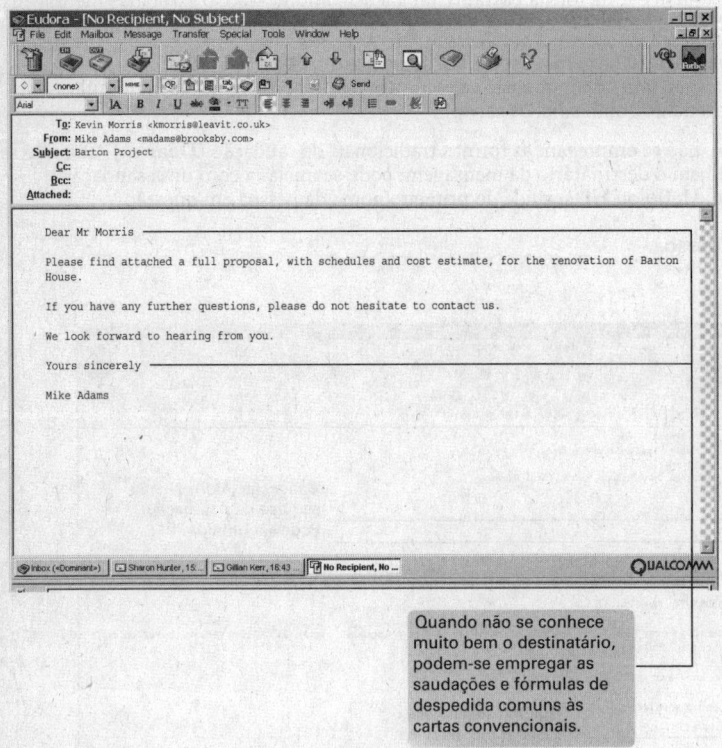

```
To: Kevin Morris <kmorris@leavit.co.uk>
From: Mike Adams <madams@brooksby.com>
Subject: Barton Project
Cc:
Bcc:
Attached:

Dear Mr Morris

Please find attached a full proposal, with schedules and cost estimate, for the renovation of Barton
House.

If you have any further questions, please do not hesitate to contact us.

We look forward to hearing from you.

Yours sincerely

Mike Adams
```

> Quando não se conhece muito bem o destinatário, podem-se empregar as saudações e fórmulas de despedida comuns às cartas convencionais.

Ao telefone

Pronúncia dos números de telefone:

20995 = Two oh double nine five (UK)
Two zero double nine five (US)

Frases típicas

Para pedir informação à telefonista:

- Can I have directory enquiries (UK)/directory assistance (US) please?
- I'm trying to get through to a London number.
- What is the (country) code for Canada?
- How do I get an outside line?

Para chamar alguém:
Hello,
- could I speak to …?
- can I speak to …?
- I'd like to speak to …
- (could I have) extension 593 please?

Para atender a uma chamada:
- Robert McQueen speaking, can I help you?
- Hello, this is …
- Yes, speaking *(confirmando que se é a pessoa chamada)*
- Hold on/hold please, I'll (just) get him/her.
- I'm sorry, he's/she's not here. Can I take a message?
- I'm afraid he's away on business/out of the office/off sick/on holiday/on vacation (US)

Para deixar um recado
Na secretária eletrônica:
- I'm returning your call…
- I'll be in London next week, perhaps we can…
- I'd like to talk to you about…
- Could you call me back, so we can discuss…?

Com outra pessoa:
- Could you ask him/her to call me on …?
- Could you tell him/her I won't be able to…?
- I'll call back later.
- I need to speak to … urgently
- Please ask him/her to confirm… . Thank you.

Para entender melhor:
- Could you spell that please?
- Could you speak a bit more slowly please?
- I'm sorry I didn't catch that. Could you repeat that please?
- Let me check, 11 a.m. Wednesday 10th … Yes, that's fine.

Para concluir a chamada:
- Thank you, I look forward to seeing you on Wednesday. Goodbye.
- Thank you for your help.

Mensagem de secretária eletrônica:
- We are unable to take your call at the moment/I am not here at the moment. Please leave a message after the tone.

Portuguese Communication Guide

Letters

In Portuguese, informal letters to friends or relatives do not follow a very rigid pattern. But commercial letters and letters that require more formality are written according to given formats and rules, depending on their purpose. There are also specific ways for heading correspondence and addressing envelopes to given posts and authorities, as well as specific modes of address for a specific authority.

Beginnings and endings of formal letters

When you know the name of the person you are writing to:	Endings:
Prezado sr. Antonio	Atenciosamente
Prezada sra. Carmem	Muito atenciosamente
	Cordialmente
When you do not know whether it is a man or woman that you are writing to:	Cordiais saudações
	Respeitosamente
Prezado sr(a).	This is the abbreviation for **senhor(a)**. In Portuguese, pronouns agree with gender (masculine or feminine) and number (singular and plural).
When you are writing to a company or organization:	
Prezados senhores	

Letters to authorities

In the case of authorities, letters should be headed and addressed according to the following conventions:

Presidents, governors, mayors, senators, deputies, councillors, ministers, ambassadors, judges, high-ranking military (general, admiral, marshal), university rectors:	*Pronouns of address:*
Exmo. Sr.	V. Exa. (Vossa Excelência), *with*
Exmo. Sr. Governador	*verbs and pronouns inflected in the*
Exmo. Sr. Deputado	*third person*
Exmo. Sr. Marechal	
Exmo. Sr. Ministro	
Other authorities:	V.Sa. (Vossa Senhoria), senhor, senhora, *with verbs and pronouns*
Ilmo. Sr.	*inflected in the third person*
Ilma. Sra.	

Informal letters

To friends and relatives, letters may start as follows:	And end as follows:
Querido Pedro	Um abraço
Meu querido Pedro	Um grande abraço
Querida Laura	Seu sobrinho/sua sobrinha
Minha querida Laura	
Queridos Pedro e Laura	*More affectionately:*
Meus queridos	Um beijo
Minha cara	Um grande beijo
Querido irmão/querida irmã	Muitos beijos
Querida mamãe/querido papai	Abraços e beijos
Queridos pais	Com muito carinho
Querido tio/querida tia	Com saudades
Queridos tios	Seu/sua
Caro/cara	
	More formally:
Or simply:	Com votos de
Pedro	Sinceramente
Laura	

Letters to friends

Below are two examples of letters to friends:

The date is usually preceded by the name of the place where the letter is being written, and can be placed either on the left or on the right. The date can also be abbreviated to 5/7/02 or 5.7.02.

Both here and at the end, the comma is required.

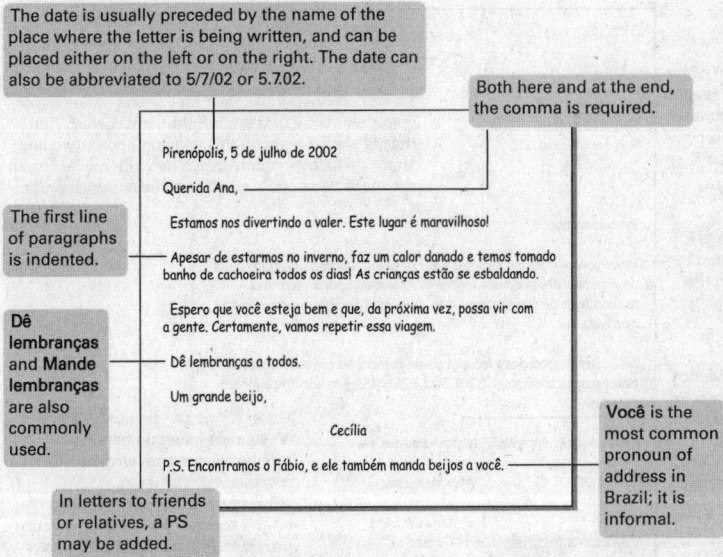

The first line of paragraphs is indented.

Dê lembranças and Mande lembranças are also commonly used.

Pirenópolis, 5 de julho de 2002

Querida Ana,

Estamos nos divertindo a valer. Este lugar é maravilhoso!

Apesar de estarmos no inverno, faz um calor danado e temos tomado banho de cachoeira todos os dias! As crianças estão se esbaldando.

Espero que você esteja bem e que, da próxima vez, possa vir com a gente. Certamente, vamos repetir essa viagem.

Dê lembranças a todos.

Um grande beijo,

Cecília

P.S. Encontramos o Fábio, e ele também manda beijos a você.

Você is the most common pronoun of address in Brazil; it is informal.

In letters to friends or relatives, a PS may be added.

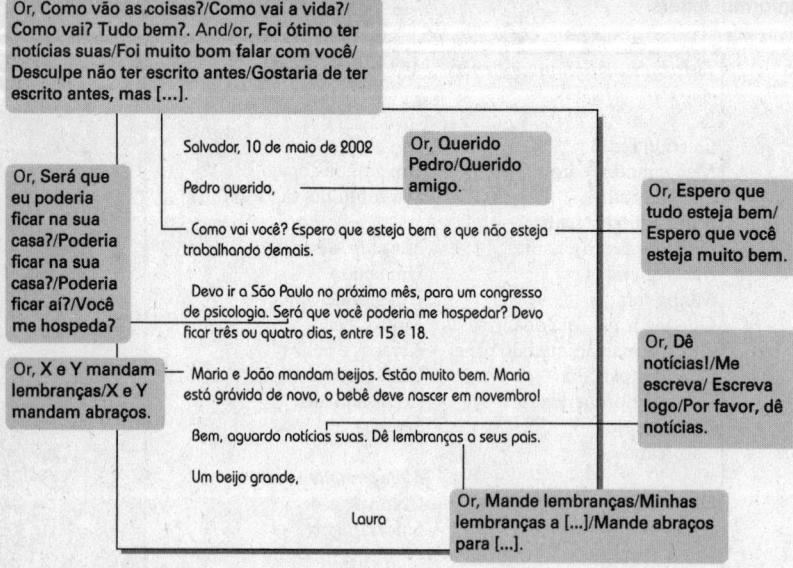

Or, Como vão as coisas?/Como vai a vida?/Como vai? Tudo bem?. And/or, Foi ótimo ter notícias suas/Foi muito bom falar com você/Desculpe não ter escrito antes/Gostaria de ter escrito antes, mas [...].

Or, Será que eu poderia ficar na sua casa?/Poderia ficar na sua casa?/Poderia ficar aí?/Você me hospeda?

Or, X e Y mandam lembranças/X e Y mandam abraços.

Salvador, 10 de maio de 2002

Pedro querido,

Or, Querido Pedro/Querido amigo.

Como vai você? Espero que esteja bem e que não esteja trabalhando demais.

Devo ir a São Paulo no próximo mês, para um congresso de psicologia. Será que você poderia me hospedar? Devo ficar três ou quatro dias, entre 15 e 18.

Maria e João mandam beijos. Estão muito bem. Maria está grávida de novo, o bebê deve nascer em novembro!

Bem, aguardo notícias suas. Dê lembranças a seus pais.

Um beijo grande,

Laura

Or, Espero que tudo esteja bem/Espero que você esteja muito bem.

Or, Dê notícias!/Me escreva/ Escreva logo/Por favor, dê notícias.

Or, Mande lembranças/Minhas lembranças a [...]/Mande abraços para [...].

Commercial letters: format and language

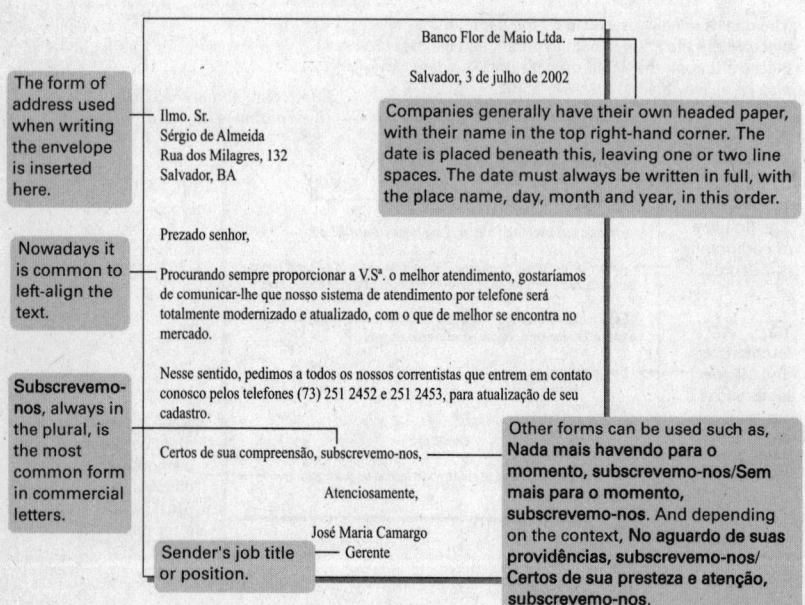

Banco Flor de Maio Ltda.

Salvador, 3 de julho de 2002

The form of address used when writing the envelope is inserted here.

Ilmo. Sr.
Sérgio de Almeida
Rua dos Milagres, 132
Salvador, BA

Companies generally have their own headed paper, with their name in the top right-hand corner. The date is placed beneath this, leaving one or two line spaces. The date must always be written in full, with the place name, day, month and year, in this order.

Nowadays it is common to left-align the text.

Prezado senhor,

Procurando sempre proporcionar a V.Sª. o melhor atendimento, gostaríamos de comunicar-lhe que nosso sistema de atendimento por telefone será totalmente modernizado e atualizado, com o que de melhor se encontra no mercado.

Nesse sentido, pedimos a todos os nossos correntistas que entrem em contato conosco pelos telefones (73) 251 2452 e 251 2453, para atualização de seu cadastro.

Subscrevemo-nos, always in the plural, is the most common form in commercial letters.

Certos de sua compreensão, subscrevemo-nos,

Atenciosamente,

José Maria Camargo
Gerente

Sender's job title or position.

Other forms can be used such as, Nada mais havendo para o momento, subscrevemo-nos/Sem mais para o momento, subscrevemo-nos. And depending on the context, No aguardo de suas providências, subscrevemo-nos/ Certos de sua presteza e atenção, subscrevemo-nos.

Requerimentos

A *requerimento* is a letter of petition to an authority. This also follows more rigid rules in terms of the structure and layout of the text.

This is the more commonly used form of address to people in this position; it is followed by the name of the institution. It could be, for instance, **Ilmo. Sr. Secretário da Saúde da Prefeitura do Município de São Paulo**, or **Ilmo. Sr. Diretor da Eletropaulo.**

> Exmo. Sr. Reitor da Universidade Padre Manoel da Nóbrega
>
> Mônica Batista, estudante do 3º ano da Faculdade de Economia desta Universidade, encontrando-se em sérias dificuldades financeiras, vem respeitosamente requerer a V. Exa. uma bolsa de estudo para que possa terminar seu curso.
>
> Nestes termos,
> pede deferimento.
>
> Belo Horizonte, 5 de janeiro de 2002.
>
> _____
> (Assinatura)

Wedding invitation

Sample invitation

Or a more formal, somewhat pompous expression, **enlace matrimonial.**

If there is no reception after the ceremony, the wording could be, **Após a cerimónia, os noivos despedem-se na igreja/recebem os cumprimentos na sala proquial.**

Nowadays, the telephone number could also be added.

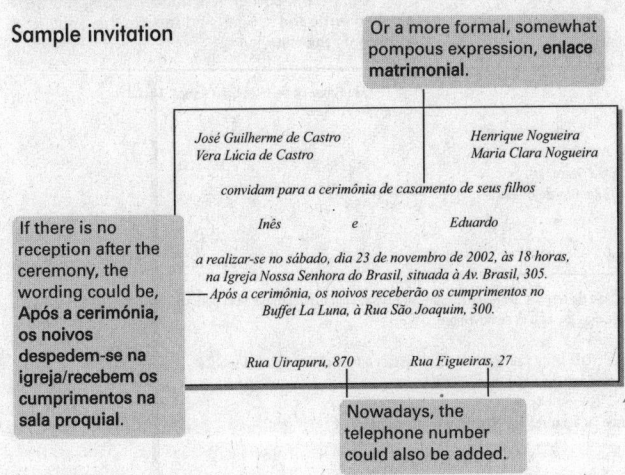

José Guilherme de Castro
Vera Lúcia de Castro

Henrique Nogueira
Maria Clara Nogueira

convidam para a cerimónia de casamento de seus filhos

Inês   e   Eduardo

a realizar-se no sábado, dia 23 de novembro de 2002, às 18 horas, na Igreja Nossa Senhora do Brasil, situada à Av. Brasil, 305.
Após a cerimónia, os noivos receberão os cumprimentos no Buffet La Luna, à Rua São Joaquim, 300.

Rua Uirapuru, 870   Rua Figueiras, 27

To thank someone for coming

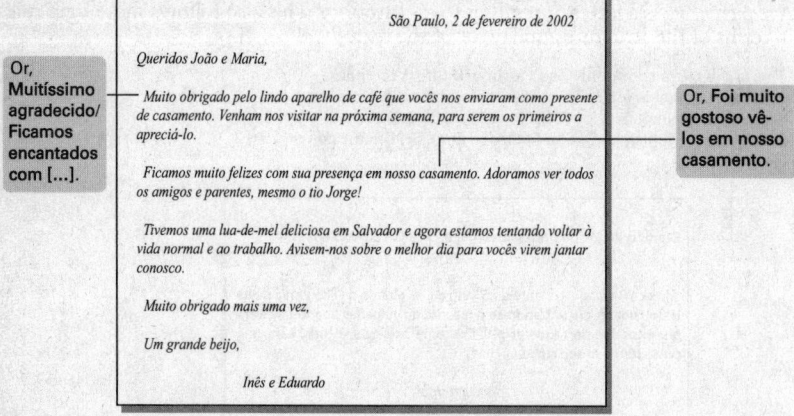

Or,
Muitíssimo agradecido/ Ficamos encantados com [...].

São Paulo, 2 de fevereiro de 2002

Queridos João e Maria,

Muito obrigado pelo lindo aparelho de café que vocês nos enviaram como presente de casamento. Venham nos visitar na próxima semana, para serem os primeiros a apreciá-lo.

Ficamos muito felizes com sua presença em nosso casamento. Adoramos ver todos os amigos e parentes, mesmo o tio Jorge!

Tivemos uma lua-de-mel deliciosa em Salvador e agora estamos tentando voltar à vida normal e ao trabalho. Avisem-nos sobre o melhor dia para vocês virem jantar conosco.

Muito obrigado mais uma vez,

Um grande beijo,

Inês e Eduardo

Or, **Foi muito gostoso vê-los em nosso casamento.**

Reservations

Travel and hotel reservations are increasingly being made by email or via the internet. However, reservations made by phone need to be confirmed in writing.

Making a reservation

Companies usually have their own headed notepaper, with their name or logo in the top right-hand corner. It is not common practice to write the sender's address in this spot; only the date.

São Paulo, 21 de setembro de 2002

Hotel Pitanga
Av. Ponta Negra, 450
Natal - Rio Grande do Norte

Or, **com cama de casal/um apartamento de solteiro/dois apartamentos de solteiro/uma suíte para casal/uma suíte para solteiro.**

Prezados senhores,

Gostaria de reservar um apartamento para casal, com banheiro, para um período de três dias, de 14 a 16 de novembro.

Agradeceria se os senhores me respondessem o mais rápido possível sobre a disponibilidade de vagas nessas datas.

Desde já, agradeço sua atenção e subscrevo-me,

Atenciosamente,

Paula Moraes

Confirming a reservation

São Paulo, 3 de julho de 2002

Ilmo. Sr.
Mário Loureiro
Gerente
Hotel Pinheiro

Prezado senhor,

De acordo com nossa conversa ao telefone esta manhã, escrevo para confirmar a reserva de seu restaurante para o dia 24 julho. Serão 300 pessoas, para três refeições. Assim que recebermos cópias de seu cardápio, entraremos em contato novamente para informá-lo de nossas escolhas. Gostaria que o senhor confirmasse por escrito o orçamento combinado.

Em caso de necessidade, queira entrar em contato comigo pelo telefone 7905643.

Desde já agradeço sua atenção,

Atenciosamente,

Miriam Muniz

> Or, **Não deixe de entrar em contato comigo pelo telefone [...] caso necessário.**

> Or, **Certa(o) de sua atenção e pronto atendimento, subscrevo-me [...].**

Cancelling a reservation

São Paulo, 29 de setembro de 2002

Hotel Pitanga
Av. Ponta Negra, 450
Natal - Rio Grande do Norte

Prezados senhores,

Infelizmente, gostaria de cancelar a reserva que havia feito de um apartamento de casal, para os dias 14 a 16 de novembro.

Queiram me desculpar pelo aborrecimento.

Sinceramente,

Paula Moraes

> Or, **Lamento informar que devo cancelar/ Lamentavel- mente/sou obrigada(o) a cancelar[...]**

> Or, **Por favor, aceitem minhas sinceras desculpas.**

Requesting information

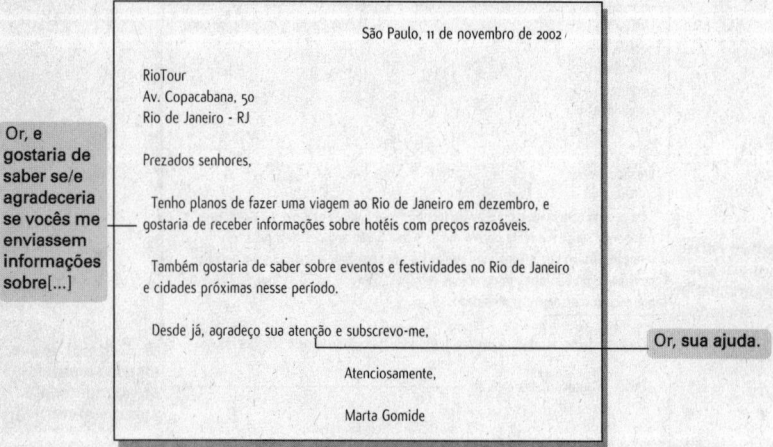

Or, e gostaria de saber se/e agradeceria se vocês me enviassem informações sobre[...]

São Paulo, 11 de novembro de 2002

RioTour
Av. Copacabana, 50
Rio de Janeiro - RJ

Prezados senhores,

Tenho planos de fazer uma viagem ao Rio de Janeiro em dezembro, e gostaria de receber informações sobre hotéis com preços razoáveis.

Também gostaria de saber sobre eventos e festividades no Rio de Janeiro e cidades próximas nesse período.

Desde já, agradeço sua atenção e subscrevo-me,

Or, sua ajuda.

Atenciosamente,

Marta Gomide

Business correspondence

Arranging a meeting

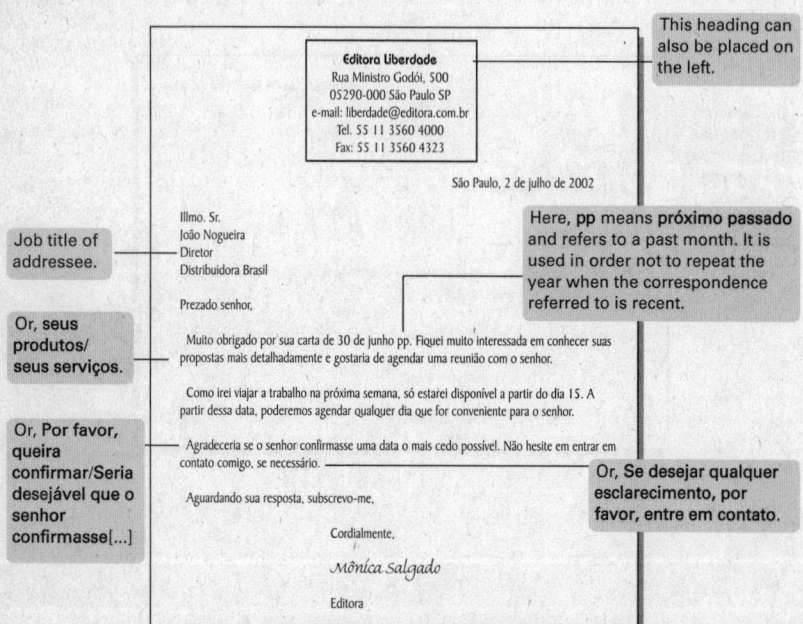

This heading can also be placed on the left.

Editora Liberdade
Rua Ministro Godói, 500
05290-000 São Paulo SP
e-mail: liberdade@editora.com.br
Tel. 55 11 3560 4000
Fax: 55 11 3560 4323

São Paulo, 2 de julho de 2002

Illmo. Sr.
João Nogueira
Diretor
Distribuidora Brasil

Job title of addressee.

Prezado senhor,

Muito obrigado por sua carta de 30 de junho pp. Fiquei muito interessada em conhecer suas propostas mais detalhadamente e gostaria de agendar uma reunião com o senhor.

Here, pp means **próximo passado** and refers to a past month. It is used in order not to repeat the year when the correspondence referred to is recent.

Or, **seus produtos/ seus serviços.**

Como irei viajar a trabalho na próxima semana, só estarei disponível a partir do dia 15. A partir dessa data, poderemos agendar qualquer dia que for conveniente para o senhor.

Or, **Por favor, queira confirmar/Seria desejável que o senhor confirmasse[...]**

Agradeceria se o senhor confirmasse uma data o mais cedo possível. Não hesite em entrar em contato comigo, se necessário.

Or, **Se desejar qualquer esclarecimento, por favor, entre em contato.**

Aguardando sua resposta, subscrevo-me,

Cordialmente,

Mônica Salgado

Editora

Placing an order

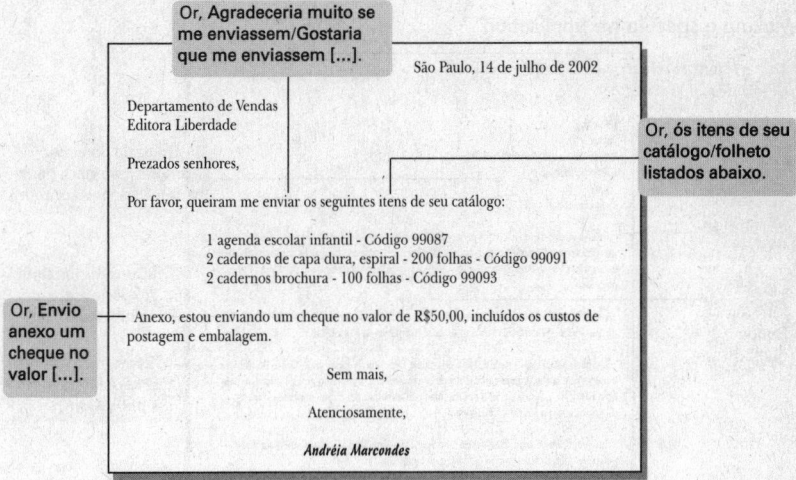

Or, **Agradeceria muito se me enviassem/Gostaria que me enviassem [...]**.

São Paulo, 14 de julho de 2002

Departamento de Vendas
Editora Liberdade

Prezados senhores,

Por favor, queiram me enviar os seguintes itens de seu catálogo:

Or, **ós itens de seu catálogo/folheto listados abaixo.**

1 agenda escolar infantil - Código 99087
2 cadernos de capa dura, espiral - 200 folhas - Código 99091
2 cadernos brochura - 100 folhas - Código 99093

Or, **Envio anexo um cheque no valor [...]**.

Anexo, estou enviando um cheque no valor de R$50,00, incluídos os custos de postagem e embalagem.

Sem mais,

Atenciosamente,

Andréia Marcondes

Replying to a request for information

Milflores Moda Ltda.
Rua Fiandeiras, 300
03090-000 São Paulo SP
tel. 6790 4321
fax: 6790 4322
e-mail: moreira@milflores.com.br

São Paulo, 12 de julho de 2002

Ilmo. Sr.
Patrício Moraes

Or, **por ter entrado em contato conosco em junho pp./19 de junho pp.**

Prezado senhor,

Or, **nossos serviços/nossos equipamentos.**

Gostaríamos de agradecer por ter entrado em contato conosco e solicitado informações sobre nossos produtos.

Em anexo, enviamos nosso catálogo e lista de preços, na certeza de que eles atenderão a suas necessidades.

Or, **Por favor, entre em contato conosco sempre que desejar.**

Para mais detalhes e informações referentes a nossos produtos, não deixe de entrar em contato conosco. Teremos enorme prazer em atendê-lo.

Or, **Será um prazer atendê-lo/ Teremos grande satisfação em atendê-lo.**

Agradecemos seu interesse, e ficamos à sua disposição para qualquer esclarecimento,

Muito atenciosamente,

José Batista
Gerente de Marketing e Vendas

Or, **Mais uma vez, agradecemos seu interesse.**

Employment

Making a speculative application

Department in which the addressee works, or job title, if known.

Or, de Vendas/de Marketing/ de Arte.

Less formally, Soube que[...]

Or, Gostaria de saber sobre/Escrevo para pedir-lhe informações sobre[...]

Current position, experience and education.

Personal qualities and reasons for the application.

Or, Contando com sua compreensão e atenção[...]

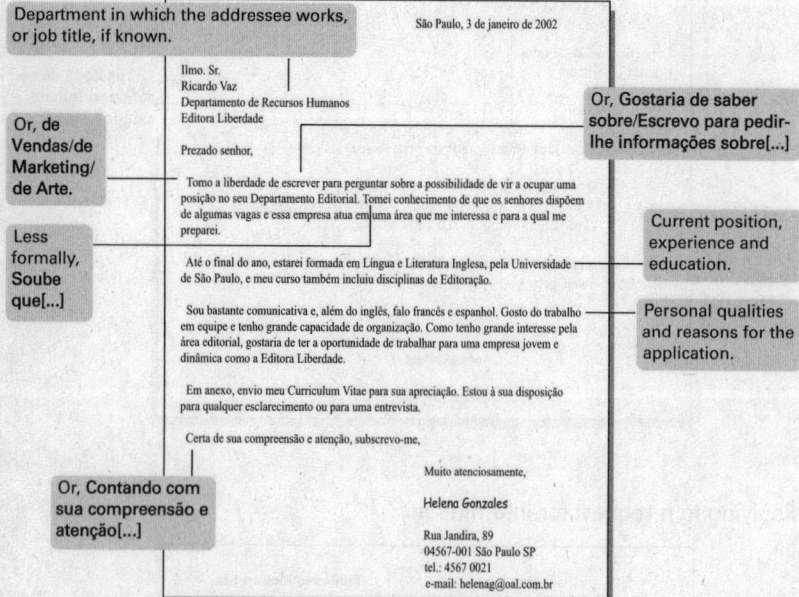

São Paulo, 3 de janeiro de 2002

Ilmo. Sr.
Ricardo Vaz
Departamento de Recursos Humanos
Editora Liberdade

Prezado senhor,

Tomo a liberdade de escrever para perguntar sobre a possibilidade de vir a ocupar uma posição no seu Departamento Editorial. Tomei conhecimento de que os senhores dispõem de algumas vagas e essa empresa atua em uma área que me interessa e para a qual me preparei.

Até o final do ano, estarei formada em Língua e Literatura Inglesa, pela Universidade de São Paulo, e meu curso também incluiu disciplinas de Editoração.

Sou bastante comunicativa e, além do inglês, falo francês e espanhol. Gosto do trabalho em equipe e tenho grande capacidade de organização. Como tenho grande interesse pela área editorial, gostaria de ter a oportunidade de trabalhar para uma empresa jovem e dinâmica como a Editora Liberdade.

Em anexo, envio meu Curriculum Vitae para sua apreciação. Estou à sua disposição para qualquer esclarecimento ou para uma entrevista.

Certa de sua compreensão e atenção, subscrevo-me,

Muito atenciosamente,

Helena Gonzales

Rua Jandira, 89
04567-001 São Paulo SP
tel.: 4567 0021
e-mail: helenag@oal.com.br

Enquiring about vacancies

Or, para solicitar informações sobre[...]

Or, Sou muito qualificado e tenho mais de dez/cinco anos/muitos anos de[...]

Or, à sua inteira disposição.

Or, O sr. (name), (job title) nessa empresa, sugeriu-me que lhe escrevesse sobre/para[...]

Or, para uma entrevista, quando melhor lhe convier.

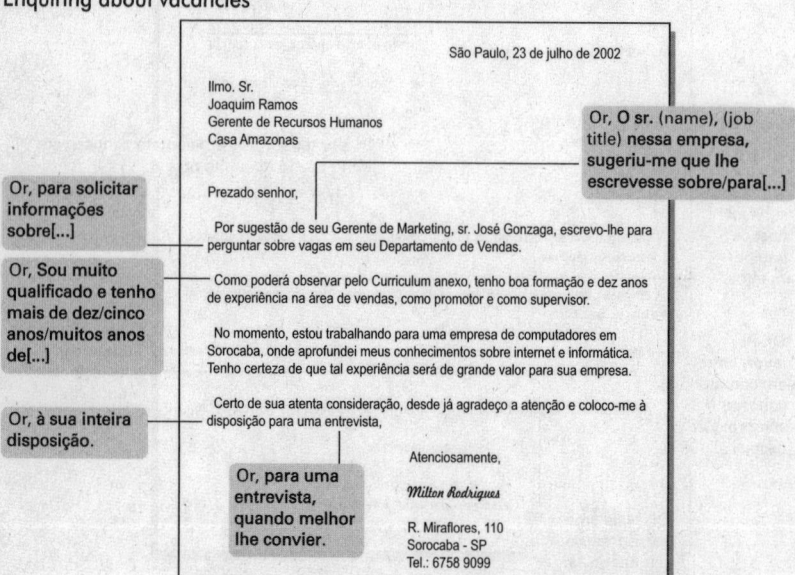

São Paulo, 23 de julho de 2002

Ilmo. Sr.
Joaquim Ramos
Gerente de Recursos Humanos
Casa Amazonas

Prezado senhor,

Por sugestão de seu Gerente de Marketing, sr. José Gonzaga, escrevo-lhe para perguntar sobre vagas em seu Departamento de Vendas.

Como poderá observar pelo Curriculum anexo, tenho boa formação e dez anos de experiência na área de vendas, como promotor e como supervisor.

No momento, estou trabalhando para uma empresa de computadores em Sorocaba, onde aprofundei meus conhecimentos sobre internet e informática. Tenho certeza de que tal experiência será de grande valor para sua empresa.

Certo de sua atenta consideração, desde já agradeço a atenção e coloco-me à disposição para uma entrevista,

Atenciosamente,

Milton Rodrigues

R. Miraflores, 110
Sorocaba - SP
Tel.: 6758 9099

Replying to a job advertisement

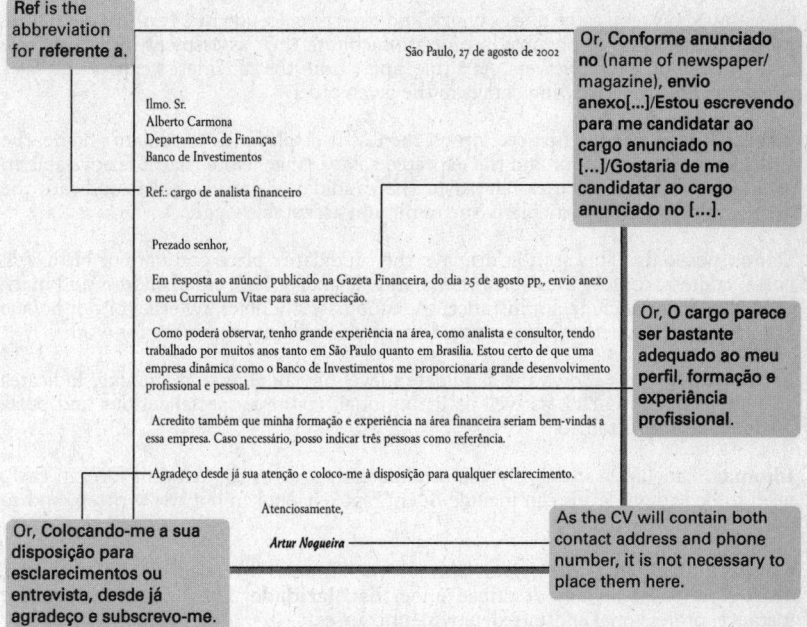

Ref is the abbreviation for **referente a**.

Or, **Conforme anunciado no** (name of newspaper/magazine), **envio anexo[...]/Estou escrevendo para me candidatar ao cargo anunciado no [...]/Gostaria de me candidatar ao cargo anunciado no [...].**

São Paulo, 27 de agosto de 2002

Ilmo. Sr.
Alberto Carmona
Departamento de Finanças
Banco de Investimentos

Ref.: cargo de analista financeiro

Prezado senhor,

Em resposta ao anúncio publicado na Gazeta Financeira, do dia 25 de agosto pp., envio anexo o meu Curriculum Vitae para sua apreciação.

Como poderá observar, tenho grande experiência na área, como analista e consultor, tendo trabalhado por muitos anos tanto em São Paulo quanto em Brasília. Estou certo de que uma empresa dinâmica como o Banco de Investimentos me proporcionaria grande desenvolvimento profissional e pessoal.

Acredito também que minha formação e experiência na área financeira seriam bem-vindas a essa empresa. Caso necessário, posso indicar três pessoas como referência.

Agradeço desde já sua atenção e coloco-me à disposição para qualquer esclarecimento.

Atenciosamente,

Artur Nogueira

Or, **O cargo parece ser bastante adequado ao meu perfil, formação e experiência profissional.**

Or, **Colocando-me a sua disposição para esclarecimentos ou entrevista, desde já agradeço e subscrevo-me.**

As the CV will contain both contact address and phone number, it is not necessary to place them here.

Useful phrases:

Tenho experiência em/no/na/com [...].
Sou bastante comunicativo(a)/muito organizado(a).
Sou fluente/Tenho fluência em inglês/espanhol/alemão/francês.
Tenho bons conhecimentos de informática/editoração/telecomunicações.
Estou apto a aprender novas tarefas/aceitar novos desafios.
Gosto de trabalhar em equipe/com pessoas diferentes.
Sou competente em [...].
Tenho competência para lidar com várias tarefas simultaneamente.
Meus pontos fortes são [...].
Tenho grande capacidade de organização/planejamento.

Currículum Vitae or Currículo

CVs nowadays tend to be quite concise and objective documents. Personal details are presented as clearly as possible in order to facilitate their assessment by prospective employers and/or interviewers. As a rule, apart from the candidate's experience, CVs should include the following details in the given order.

Cabeçalho: This is the first section on the CV. It displays the candidate's name, the title of the job applied for and the expected salary range. Note that it is advisable to insert up to three job titles related to the candidate's profile, and to indicate the desired salary, noting particularly the minimum acceptable wage.

Dados pessoais: This section displays the candidate's place and date of birth, full postal address, contact numbers (phone, mobile and/or fax), email address and marital status. It can include, for instance, the candidate's hobbies, whether or not he/she is a smoker, and whether he/she would accept to travel or even move for work.

Escolaridade: This shows the candidate's level of schooling and training, indicates any university attended, as well as listing qualifications, specializations and postgraduate degrees attained.

Idiomas: Languages spoken by the candidate, as well as the relevant level in each, need to be shown; levels can include fluent, spoken, spoken but not written, and so on.

Cursos: A list can also be given of any other courses attended by the candidate, apart from those already described under **Escolaridade**. These could include, for instance, professional and/or redeployment courses.

Experiência profissional: This section lists the posts held previously by the candidate, from the latest to the earliest, mentioning one or two past jobs or responsibilities of interest or relevance to the post applied for.

Habilidades/qualificações: This section describes the areas in which the candidate has the most aptitude and ability, and indicates the time spent acquiring each.

Capacitação profissional: A brief description is given here of the length of time the candidate has been working, the field he/she is currently working in, knowledge acquired, previously held posts, as well as training programmes and courses attended that are of relevance to his/her career.

Sample CV

It is important to date the CV or to indicate an update, such as **atualização: 15/07/02**, to show when the CV was either written or updated.

BERENICE BUENO

15/07/2002

Analista de cobrança
Analista de orçamentos

Mínimo aceitável: R$ 1.500,00/mês
Salário pretendido: R$ 2.000,00/mês

Dados pessoais

Data de nascimento: 21 de janeiro de 1970
Experiência profissional: 10 anos
Atualmente empregado
Hobbies: teatro, cinema e leitura
Não fumante

This is not obligatory, but nowadays this piece of information can be important for the prospective employer.

Endereço: R. José Vicente, 700
06543-000 São Paulo-SP
Tel. (11) 899-7766
e-mail: berebueno@oal.com.br

Aceita: transferência de cidade, de estado; viajar a trabalho
Informática: Word, Excel, Power Point, Access

Here you can indicate the level of knowledge of or proficiency in (**bom/ótimo/médio**) such programs.

Escolaridade

Pós-graduação incompleta – Contabilidade e Finanças – Unifesp - 2001/2003 – São Paulo
Superior completo – Ciências Contábeis – Universidade São Judas – 1991/1995 – São Paulo

Idiomas

Inglês: fluente
Espanhol: fluente

Cursos

Análise de risco – Universidade do Paraná – 1998 – 1 semana
Contabilidade Avançada – Senac – 1993 – 1 mês
Inglês - Cultura Inglesa – 1990 – 2 anos

You can list as many details as you want, provided they are relevant.

Experiência profissional

	Empresa	Cargo ocupado	Período
Emprego atual	Banco DBC	Consultor financeiro	De 1999 até hoje
Anterior	Cia. VVV	Analista financeiro	De 1995 a 1999
Outros:	Banco Finans	Analista financeiro	De 1990 a 1995

Habilidades/Qualificações

Área fiscal (ótimo) – última atualização: 1999 – Experiência: 9 anos
Área contábil (ótimo) – última atualização: 2001 – Experiência: 10 anos

Capacitação profissional

Profissional com 10 anos de experiência no mercado, sempre atuando na área financeira e contábil em empresas de médio e grande porte. Bons conhecimentos na área fiscal: ativo imobilizado, tesouraria, logística e expedição. Atuação na área contábil de contas patrimoniais, classificação e reclassificação contábil, participação em processos de diligências, fusões e aquisições.

Email

As emailing is a rapid and concise means of communication, the style of the messages themselves tends to be informal and telegraphic. According to internet conventions (netiquette), messages should never be written in capital letters, as this is interpreted as a sign of anger. Formal methods of address, such as, **Prezado(a) senhor(a)** are not normally used. If you are sending an email to someone you know well, the message can begin with a simple **Ola** or **Oi**, followed by the recipient's first name.

Within a company

Informal opener, followed by a comma. **Bom dia/ Boa tarde** can also be used.

Or, when you know the person, **um abraço/até mais**.

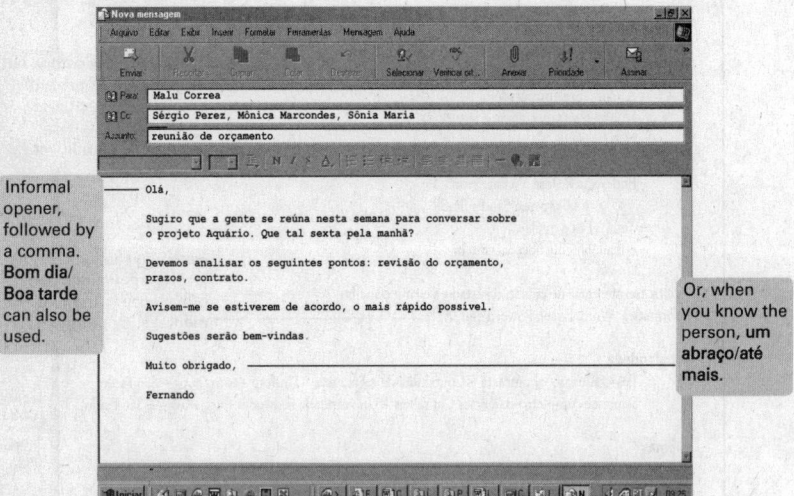

Business to business

When you don't know the person, it is best to choose **Prezado senhor(a)**.

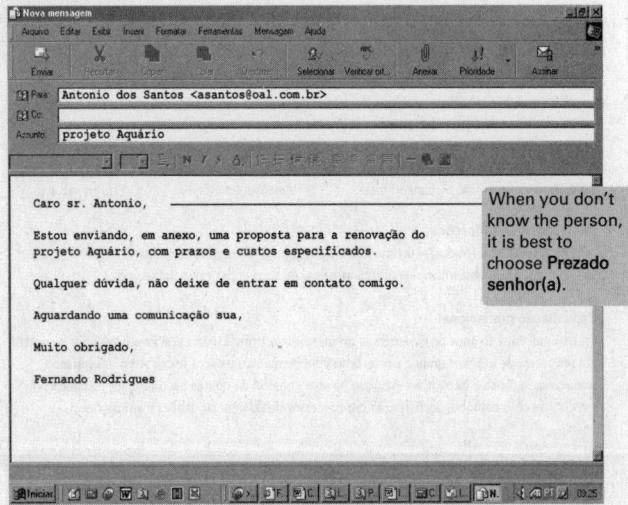

Between friends

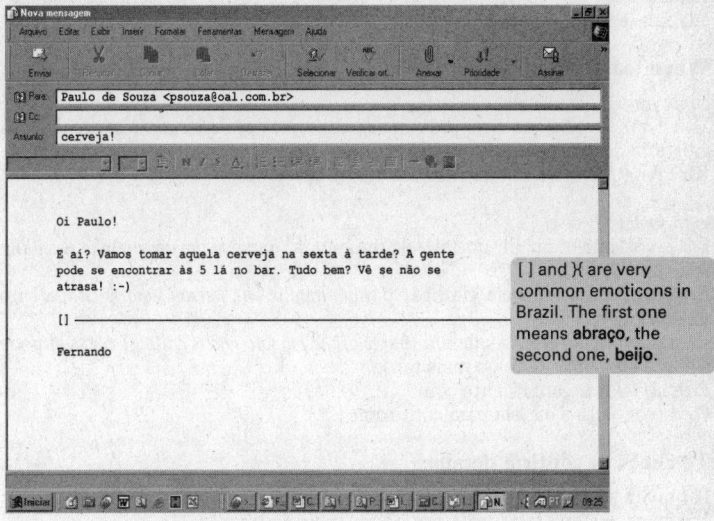

[ ] and }{ are very common emoticons in Brazil. The first one means **abraço**, the second one, **beijo**.

Telephone calls

This is how to say a telephone number in Brazil:

3719 4465

três-sete-um-nove, quatro-quatro-meia-cinco

In Brazil, when giving a telephone number, you normally say **meia** (from **meia dúzia**, or 'half a dozen') instead of **seis**.

Useful phrases

Asking the operator for information:

Por favor, telefonista, quero falar com [...].
Por favor, telefonista, estou tentando falar com [...].
Por favor, qual é o código do DDD/o código para [...] (*long-distance calls*).
Por favor, qual é o código do DDI/o código para [...] (*international calls*).

When asking to speak to someone:

Alô!

Poderia falar com [...]?
Gostaria de falar com [...].
Ana Maria, por favor.
Ramal 257, por favor.

When answering a call:

Alô! Aqui é [...] (*confirming who you are*)
Alô, quem fala? Alô, com quem deseja falar? (*to find out who the person wants to speak to*)
Marco Aurélio, pois não?/o que deseja?
Um minuto, por favor./Um instante, por favor.

Desculpe, ele/ela não está. Deseja/Quer deixar um recado?
Ele/ela saiu da sala um instante/não se encontra no escritório/não se encontra em sua sala/está viajando.

When leaving a message:

on an answering machine:
Vou estar em São Paulo na próxima semana, nós poderíamos/a gente poderia [...]
Gostaria de/Queria falar com você sobre [...]
Por favor, me ligue. Precisamos conversar sobre [...]

with somebody else:
Por favor, poderia pedir que ele/ela ligue para (*name of the person who is calling*) no telefone (*number*)[...]?
Por favor, peça para ele/ela ligar para (*name of the person who is calling*) no telefone (*number*)[...].
Por favor, diga a ele/ela que o/a (*name of the person who is calling*) não vai poder [...]
Volto a ligar/ligo de novo mais tarde.
Preciso falar urgentemente com [...].
Por favor, peça a ele/ela para confirmar [...].

To check or confirm details:

Por favor, poderia soletrar?
Por favor, poderia falar mais/um pouco mais devagar?
Desculpe, não entendi. Poderia repetir, por favor?
Confirmando: 11 horas, quarta-feira, dia 10... Certo? Ótimo.

To end a telephone conversation:

Men say **obrigado**; women say **obrigada**.

Obrigado(a). Vejo você na quarta. Até lá.
Obrigado(a) pela ajuda.

Or, **Até quarta, então. Tchau.**

Message left on an answering machine:

Não posso/podemos atendê-lo agora. Por favor, deixe seu recado após/logo após o sinal.

ENGLISH-PORTUGUESE
INGLÊS - PORTUGUÊS

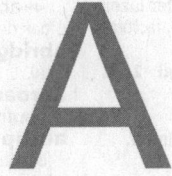

a¹ (*pl* as OR a's), **A** (*pl* As OR A's) [eɪ] *n* [letter] a, A *m*; **to get from A to B** ir de um lugar para outro; **from A to Z** de A a Z, de cabo a rabo.

➤ **A** *n* -**1.** MUS [note] lá *m* -**2.** SCH [mark] A *m*.

a² [stressed eɪ, unstressed ə] (*before vowel or silent 'h' an*) [stressed æn, unstressed ən] *indef art* -**1.** [non-specific] um *m*, uma *f*; ~ **boy** um garoto; ~ **table** uma mesa; **an orange** uma laranja -**2.** [referring to occupation]: **she's** ~ **teacher/actress** ela é professora/atriz -**3.** [one] um, uma; ~ **hundred/thousand pounds** cem/mil libras -**4.** [to express prices, ratios etc] por; **£10** ~ **day/person** £10 por dia/pessoa; **twice** ~ **week/month** duas vezes por semana/mês; **50 km an hour** 50 km por hora -**5.** [to express prices, ratios etc]: **20 cents** ~ **kilo** 20 centavos o quilo -**6.** [preceding person's name]: ~ **Mr Smith phoned** um certo senhor Smith ligou; **do you know** ~ **Miss Costa?** você conhece alguma senhora Costa?

a. acre.

A-1 *adj inf* de primeira.

A4 *n UK* A4.

AA <> *adj* (*abbr of* **anti-aircraft**) antiaéreo(rea). <> *n* -**1.** (*abbr of* **Automobile Association**) associação britânica que presta serviço de emergência a seus filiados em situações de problemas e acidentes automobilísticos, ≃ Touring *m* Club do Brasil. -**2.** (*abbr of* **Associate in Arts**) (*titular de*) diploma em ciências humanas nos Estados Unidos. -**3.** (*abbr of* **Alcoholics Anonymous**) AA *mpl*.

AAA *n* -**1.** (*abbr of* **Amateur Athletic Association**) federação britânica de atletas amadores. -**2.** (*abbr of* **American Automobile Association**) associação automobilística americana.

AAU *n* (*abbr of* **Amateur Athletic Union**) confederação norte-americana de atletas amadores.

AAUP (*abbr of* **American Association of University Professors**) *n* associação norte-americana de professores universitários, ≃ ANDES *f*.

AB <> *n* (*abbr of* **Bachelor of Arts**) (*titular de*) graduação em ciências humanas nos Estados Unidos. <> *abbr of* **Alberta**.

aback [ə'bæk] *adv*: **to be taken** ~ **(by sthg)** ficar surpreso(sa) (com algo), ser surpreendido(da) (por algo).

abacus ['æbəkəs] (*pl* **-cuses** OR **-ci** [-saɪ]) *n* ábaco *m*.

abandon [ə'bændən] <> *vt* -**1.** [leave, desert] abandonar -**2.** [give up] desistir de. <> *n (U)*: **with** ~ sem inibição, desenfreado(da).

abandoned [ə'bændənd] *adj* [deserted] abandonado(da).

abashed [ə'bæʃt] *adj* envergonhado(da).

abate [ə'beɪt] *vi fml* [storm, noise, wind] abrandar; [pain, fear, anxiety] diminuir.

abattoir ['æbətwɑː^r] *n* matadouro *m*.

abbess ['æbes] *n* abadessa *f*.

abbey ['æbɪ] *n* abadia *f*.

abbot ['æbət] *n* abade *m*.

abbreviate [ə'briːvɪeɪt] *vt* abreviar.

abbreviation [ə,briːvɪ'eɪʃn] *n* [short form] abreviatura *f*.

ABC *n* -**1.** [alphabet] abc *m*. -**2.** *fig* [basics]: **the** ~ **of** o abc de. -**3.** (*abbr of* **American Broadcasting Company**) rede de televisão norte-americana, ABC *f*.

abdicate ['æbdɪkeɪt] <> *vi* abdicar. <> *vt* [responsibility] abrir mão de.

abdication [,æbdɪ'keɪʃn] *n* [of throne] abdicação *f*.

abdomen ['æbdəmen] *n* abdome *m*.

abdominal [æb'dɒmɪnl] *adj* abdominal.

abduct [əb'dʌkt] *vt* raptar.

abduction [əb'dʌkʃn] *n* rapto *m*.

aberration [,æbə'reɪʃn] *n* aberração *f*; **a mental** ~ um desatino.

abet [ə'bet] (*pt* & *pp* **-ted**, *cont* **-ting**) *vt* ▷ **aid**.

abeyance [ə'beɪəns] *n fml*: **in** ~ em estado jacente.

abhor [əb'hɔː^r] (*pt* & *pp* **-red**, *cont* **-ring**) *vt* abominar.

abhorrent [əb'hɒrənt] *adj* abominável.

abide [ə'baɪd] *vt* suportar.

➤ **abide by** *vt fus* sujeitar-se a.

abiding [ə'baɪdɪŋ] *adj* duradouro(ra).

ability [ə'bɪlətɪ] (*pl* -ies) *n* -1. *(U)* [capacity, level of capability] capacidade *f*; **to do sthg to the best of one's** ~ fazer algo da melhor maneira possível -2. [skill, talent] habilidade *f*.

abject ['æbdʒekt] *adj* -1. [miserable, depressing] abjeto(ta) -2. [humble] servil.

ablaze [ə'bleɪz] *adj* -1. [on fire] em chamas -2. *fig* [bright]: **to be** ~ **with** estar iluminado(da) com.

able ['eɪbl] *adj* -1. [capable] capaz; **to be** ~ **to do sthg** ser capaz de fazer algo; [in a position to] poder fazer algo; [manage to] conseguir fazer algo -2. [accomplished, talented] competente.

able-bodied [-,bɒdɪd] *adj* -1. robusto(ta) -2. MIL (fisicamente) apto(ta).

ablutions [ə'blu:ʃnz] *npl fml* abluções *fpl*.

ably ['eɪblɪ] *adv* competentemente, habilmente.

abnormal [æb'nɔ:ml] *adj* anormal.

abnormality [,æbnɔ:'mælətɪ] (*pl* -ies) *n* anormalidade *f*.

abnormally [æb'nɔ:məlɪ] *adv* -1. [behave, develop, grow] irregularmente, de modo anormal -2. [cold, wide, loud]: **it's** ~ **cold for this time of the year** não é normal este frio nesta época do ano.

aboard [ə'bɔ:d] <> *adv* [on ship, plane] a bordo. <> *prep* [ship, plane] a bordo de; [bus, train] em.

abode [ə'bəud] *n fml*: **of no fixed** ~ sem domicílio fixo.

abolish [ə'bɒlɪʃ] *vt* abolir.

abolition [,æbə'lɪʃn] *n* abolição *f*.

A-bomb (*abbr of* atom bomb) *n* bomba *f* atômica.

abominable [ə'bɒmɪnəbl] *adj* abominável.

abominable snowman *n*: **the** ~ o abominável homem das neves.

abominably [ə'bɒmɪnəblɪ] *adv* abominavelmente.

aborigine [,æbə'rɪdʒənɪ] *n* aborígine *mf*.

abort [ə'bɔ:t] *vt & vi* abortar.

abortion [ə'bɔ:ʃn] *n* [of pregnancy] aborto *m*; **to have an** ~ abortar.

abortive [ə'bɔ:tɪv] *adj* fracassado(da).

abound [ə'baund] *vi* -1. [be plentiful] existir em abundância, abundar -2. [be full]: **to** ~ **with** OR **in sthg** ser rico(ca) em algo, ser cheio(cheia) de algo.

about [ə'baut] <> *adv* -1. [approximately] cerca de; ~ **fifty/a hundred/a thousand** quase OR cerca de cinqüenta/cem/mil; **to be just** ~ **ready** estar quase pronto(ta); **at** ~ **five o'clock** por volta das cinco horas -2. [referring to place] por perto; **to walk** ~ andar por perto; **to jump** ~ saltitar -3. [on the point of]: **to be** ~ **to do sthg** estar prestes a fazer algo. <> *prep* -1. [relating to, concerning] sobre; **a film** ~ **Paris** um filme sobre Paris; **what is it** ~? de que se trata?; **to talk** ~ **sthg** falar sobre algo -2. [referring to place] por; **to wander** ~ **the streets** vagar pelas ruas.

about-turn *esp UK*, **about-face** *esp US n* -1. MIL meia-volta *f* -2. *fig* [change of attitude] guinada *f* de 180 graus.

above [ə'bʌv] <> *adv* -1. [on top, higher up] de cima -2. [in text] acima; **the items mentioned** ~ os itens acima mencionados -3. [more, over] acima de; **children aged five and** ~ crianças de cinco anos ou mais. <> *prep* acima de.

→ **above all** *adv* acima de tudo.

aboveboard [ə,bʌv'bɔ:d] *adj* -1. legítimo(ma) -2. limpo(pa).

abracadabra [,æbrəkə'dæbrə] *excl* abracadabra!

abrasion [ə'breɪʒn] *n fml* [graze] esfolamento *m*.

abrasive [ə'breɪsɪv] <> *adj* -1. [cleaner, cloth] abrasivo(va) -2. *fig* [person, manner] mordaz. <> *n* abrasivo *m*.

abreast [ə'brest] *adv* lado a lado.

→ **abreast of** *prep*: **to keep** ~ **of sthg** estar a par de algo.

abridged [ə'brɪdʒd] *adj* resumido(da), compacto(ta).

abroad [ə'brɔ:d] *adv* [overseas]: **to live** ~ viver/morar no exterior; **to go** ~ ir para o exterior.

abrupt [ə'brʌpt] *adj* -1. [sudden] repentino(na) -2. [brusque, rude] brusco(ca).

abruptly [ə'brʌptlɪ] *adv* -1. [suddenly] repentinamente -2. [brusquely, rudely] bruscamente.

ABS (*abbr of* anti-lock breaking system) *n* ABS *m*.

abscess ['æbsɪs] *n* abcesso *m*.

abscond [əb'skɒnd] *vi* esconder-se; **to** ~ **with sthg** sumir com algo.

abseil ['æbseɪl] *vi* praticar rappel; **to** ~ **down a rock** praticar rappel numa rocha.

absence ['æbsəns] *n* -1. [of person] ausência *f*; **in sb's** ~ na ausência de alguém -2. [lack] falta *f*; **in the** ~ **of sthg** na falta de algo.

absent ['æbsənt] *adj* -1. [not present]: ~ **(from)** ausente (de); **to be** ~ **without leave** MIL estar ausente sem autorização -2. [absent-minded] desatento(ta).

absentee [,æbsən'ti:] *n* ausente *mf*.

absenteeism [,æbsən'ti:ɪzm] *n* absenteísmo *m*.

absent-minded [-'maɪndɪd] *adj* distraído(da).

absent-mindedness *n* distração *f*.

absent-mindedly [-'maɪndɪdlɪ] *adv* distraidamente.

absinth(e) ['æbsɪnθ] *n* absinto *m*.

absolute ['æbsəlu:t] *adj* -1. [complete, utter] absoluto(ta) -2. [totalitarian] arbitrário(ria).

absolutely ['æbsəlu:tlɪ] <> *adv* [completely, utterly] absolutamente. <> *excl* [expressing agreement] sem dúvida.

absolute majority *n* maioria *f* absoluta.

absolution [,æbsə'lu:ʃn] *n* RELIG absolvição *f*.

absolve [əb'zɒlv] *vt* [free, clear]: **to** ~ **sb (of sthg)** absolver alguém (de algo).

absorb [əb'sɔ:b] *vt* -1. [soak up] absorver -2. *fig* [learn] assimilar -3. [interest] absorver; **to be** ~**ed in sthg** estar absorvido(da) em algo -4. [take over] incorporar.

absorbent [əb'sɔ:bənt] *adj* absorvente.

absorbing [əb'sɔ:bɪŋ] *adj* cativante.

absorption [əb'sɔ:pʃn] *n* -1. [soaking up] absorção *f* -2. [interest] concentração *f* -3. [taking over] incorporação *f*.

abstain [əb'steɪn] *vi* -1. [refrain]: **to** ~ **from sthg** abster-se de algo -2. [in vote] abster-se.

abstemious [æb'sti:mjəs] *adj fml* abstêmio(mia).

abstention [əb'stenʃn] *n* [in vote] abstenção *f*.

abstinence ['æbstɪnəns] *n*: ~ **(from sthg)** abstinência *f* (de algo).

abstract [adj & n 'æbstrækt, vb æb'strækt] <> adj abstrato(ta). <> n [summary] resumo m. <> vt [summarize] resumir.

abstraction [æb'strækʃn] n **-1.** (U) [distractedness] distração f. **-2.** [abstract idea] abstração f.

abstruse [æb'stru:s] adj confuso(sa).

absurd [əb'sɜ:d] adj absurdo(da).

absurdity [əb'sɜ:dətɪ] (pl -ies) n absurdo m.

absurdly [əb'sɜ:dlɪ] adv incrivelmente.

ABTA (abbr of Association of British Travel Agents) n associação britânica de agentes de viagens, ≃ ABAV f.

Abu Dhabi [ˌæbu:'dɑ:bɪ] n Abu Dabi.

abundance [ə'bʌndəns] n abundância f.

abundant [ə'bʌndənt] adj abundante.

abundantly [ə'bʌndəntlɪ] adv **-1.** [manifestly] suficientemente; **it is ~ clear that ...** está suficientemente claro que ...; **he made it ~ clear that ...** ele deixou mais do que claro que ... **-2.** [in large amounts] em abundância.

abuse [n ə'bju:s, vb ə'bju:z] <> n **-1.** [offensive remarks] insultos mpl **-2.** [maltreatment, misuse] abuso m. <> vt **-1.** [insult] insultar **-2.** [maltreat] maltratar **-3.** [misuse] abusar de.

abusive [ə'bju:sɪv] adj abusivo(va).

abut [ə'bʌt] (pt & pp **-ted**, cont **-ting**) vi: **to ~ on to** ser limítrofe a.

abysmal [ə'bɪzml] adj abismal.

abysmally [ə'bɪzməlɪ] adv terrivelmente.

abyss [ə'bɪs] n **-1.** abismo m **-2.** fig [gap] abismo m.

Abyssinia [ˌæbɪ'sɪnɪə] n Abissínia; **in/to ~** na/à Abissínia.

Abyssinian adj & n abissínio(nia).

a/c (abbr of account (current)) c.c. f.

AC (abbr of alternating current) n CA f.

acacia [ə'keɪʃə] n acácia f.

academic [ˌækə'demɪk] <> adj **-1.** [of college, university] acadêmico(ca) **-2.** [studious] intelectual **-3.** [hypothetical] conjetural. <> n [teacher, researcher] acadêmico m, -ca f.

academic year n ano m letivo.

academy [ə'kædəmɪ] (pl -ies) n **-1.** [school, college] academia f, escola f **-2.** [institution, society] academia f.

ACAS (abbr of Advisory Conciliation and Arbitration Service) n organização britânica para conciliação entre sindicatos e empregadores.

accede [æk'si:d] vi **-1.** fml [agree]: **to ~ to sthg** aceder a algo **-2.** [monarch]: **to ~ to the throne** subir ao trono.

accelerate [ək'seləreɪt] <> vt apressar. <> vi **-1.** [car, driver] acelerar **-2.** [inflation, growth] disparar.

acceleration [ək,selə'reɪʃn] n **-1.** [of car] aceleração f **-2.** [of inflation, growth] disparada f.

accelerator [ək'seləreɪtəʳ] n acelerador m.

accent ['æksent] n **-1.** [when speaking] sotaque m **-2.** [in writing] acento m **-3.** fig [emphasis] ênfase f.

accentuate [æk'sentjʊeɪt] vt [emphasize, stress] acentuar.

accept [ək'sept] vt **-1.** [agree to take, receive] aceitar **-2.** [agree to follow] assentir **-3.** [recognize as satisfactory] aprovar **-4.** [get used to] reconhecer **-5.** [admit, recognize as one's own] assumir **-6.** [person - as

part of group] acolher; [- for job, as member of club] aceitar **-7.** [agree, believe]: **to ~ that** aceitar que **-8.** [process] aceitar.

acceptable [ək'septəbl] adj **-1.** [permissible] aceitável **-2.** [passable] admissível.

acceptably [ək'septəblɪ] adv apropriadamente.

acceptance [ək'septəns] n **-1.** [gen] aceitação f **-2.** [recognizing as satisfactory] aprovação f.

accepted [ək'septɪd] adj [recognized as correct, true] aceito(ta).

access ['ækses] <> n **-1.** [entry, way in] acesso m; **to gain ~ to** [place, building] obter acesso a **-2.** [opportunity to use, see]: **to have ~ to sthg** ter acesso a algo. <> vt COMPUT acessar.

accessibility [ək,sesə'bɪlətɪ] n **-1.** [of place] acessibilidade f **-2.** [availability] acesso m.

accessible [ək'sesəbl] adj **-1.** [reachable, understandable] acessível **-2.** [available] disponível.

accession [æk'seʃn] n [of monarch] ascensão f.

accessory [ək'sesərɪ] (pl -ies) n **-1.** [extra part, device] acessório m **-2.** JUR cúmplice mf.

  ➤ **accessories** npl [to outfit] acessórios mpl.

access road n **-1.** [gen] rua f de acesso **-2.** UK [to motorway] via f de acesso.

access time n COMPUT tempo m de acesso.

accident ['æksɪdənt] n **-1.** acidente m; **to have an ~** sofrer um acidente **-2.** (U) [chance]: **by ~** por acaso; **it was an ~** foi sem querer.

accidental [ˌæksɪ'dentl] adj acidental.

accidentally [ˌæksɪ'dentəlɪ] adv **-1.** [drop, break] sem querer **-2.** [meet, find, discover] acidentalmente.

accident-prone adj propenso(sa) a acidentes.

acclaim [ə'kleɪm] <> n (U) aclamação f. <> vt aclamar.

acclamation [ˌæklə'meɪʃn] n aclamação f.

acclimatize, -ise [ə'klaɪmətaɪz], **acclimate** US ['ækləmeɪt] vi: **to ~ (to sthg)** aclimatar-se (a algo).

accolade ['ækəleɪd] n honra f.

accommodate [ə'kɒmədeɪt] vt **-1.** [provide room for] acomodar **-2.** [oblige] comprazer a.

accommodating [ə'kɒmədeɪtɪŋ] adj complacente.

accommodation UK [əˌkɒmə'deɪʃn] n, **accommodations** US [əˌkɒmə'deɪʃnz] npl **-1.** [lodging] alojamento m, acomodação f **-2.** [work space] instalações fpl.

accompaniment [ə'kʌmpənɪmənt] n MUS acompanhamento m. ·

accompanist [ə'kʌmpənɪst] n MUS pessoa que canta ou toca junto com alguém.

accompany [ə'kʌmpənɪ] (pt & pp -ied) vt **-1.** acompanhar **-2.** MUS [with instrument]: **to ~ sb (on sthg)** acompanhar alguém (em algo).

accomplice [ə'kʌmplɪs] n cúmplice m.

accomplish [ə'kʌmplɪʃ] vt [achieve, manage] conseguir; [carry out, effect] realizar; [reach, attain] alcançar.

accomplished [ə'kʌmplɪʃt] adj [skilled] excelente, competente.

accomplishment [ə'kʌmplɪʃmənt] n **-1.** [achievement, finishing] realização f, conclusão f **-2.** [feat, deed] feito m.

  ➤ **accomplishments** npl [skills] habilidades fpl.

accord [əˈkɔːd] n -1. [settlement] acordo m -2. [agreement, harmony]: **to be in ~ (with sb/sthg)** estar de acordo com alguém algo; **with one ~** unanimamente; **to do sthg of one's own ~** fazer algo por iniciativa própria.

accordance [əˈkɔːdəns] n: **in ~ with sthg** de acordo com algo.

according to prep -1. [as stated or shown by] segundo; **to go ~ to plan** sair conforme o planejado -2. [with regard to, depending on] conforme.

accordingly [əˈkɔːdɪŋlɪ] adv -1. [appropriately] de modo apropriado -2. [consequently] conseqüentemente.

accordion [əˈkɔːdjən] n acordeão m, sanfona f.

accordionist [əˈkɔːdjənɪst] n acordeonista mf, sanfoneiro m, -ra f.

accost [əˈkɒst] vt abordar.

account [əˈkaunt] n -1. [with bank, company] conta f -2. [with shop]: **I have an ~ at the butcher's** tenho conta no açougue -3. [report]: **to give an ~ of sthg** fazer um relato de algo -4. phr: **to call sb to ~** fazer alguém se explicar; **to give a good ~ of o.s.** causar boa impressão; **to take ~ of sthg, to take sthg into ~** levar algo em consideração; **to be of no ~** não ter importância; **on no ~** de modo algum.

◆ **accounts** npl [of business] contabilidade f.
◆ **by all accounts** adv de acordo com a opinião geral.
◆ **on account of** prep devido a; **on my ~** por minha causa.
◆ **account for** vt fus -1. [explain] justificar; **a theory that ~s for all the facts** uma teoria que justifique os fatos -2. [represent] representar.

accountability [ə,kauntəˈbɪlətɪ] n responsabilidade f.

accountable [əˈkauntəbl] adj [responsible]: **to be held ~ for sthg** ser responsabilizado(da) por algo; **~ to sb** [answerable] obrigado(da) a prestar contas a alguém.

accountancy [əˈkauntənsɪ] n [profession, business] contabilidade f.

accountant [əˈkauntənt] n contador m, -ra f.

accounting [əˈkauntɪŋ] n [skill, practice of accountancy] contabilidade f.

accounts department n setor m de contabilidade.

accoutrements UK [əˈkuːtrəmənts], **accouterments** US [əˈkuːtərmənts] npl hum [baggage] parafernália f.

accredited [əˈkredɪtɪd] adj [authorized, recognized] acreditado(da).

accrue [əˈkruː] vt & vi FIN render.

accumulate [əˈkjuːmjuleɪt] ◇ vt acumular. ◇ vi acumular-se.

accumulation [ə,kjuːmjuˈleɪʃn] n -1. (U) [accumulating] acumulação f -2. [group of things] monte m.

accuracy [ˈækjʊrəsɪ] n -1. [truth, correctness] exatidão f -2. [precision - of weapon, marksman] precisão f; [- of typing, figures, estimate] exatidão f.

accurate [ˈækjʊrət] adj -1. [true, correct] exato(ta) -2. [precise - shot, marksman] preciso(sa); [- typist, figures, estimate] exato(ta).

accurately [ˈækjʊrətlɪ] adv -1. [truthfully, correctly] com exatidão -2. [precisely - aim] com precisão; [- type, estimate] com exatidão.

accusation [,ækjuːˈzeɪʃn] n -1. [charge, criticism] acusação f -2. JUR [formal charge] incriminação f.

accuse [əˈkjuːz] vt -1. [charge, criticize]: **to ~ sb of sthg/of doing sthg** acusar alguém de algo/de fazer algo -2. JUR: **to ~ sb of sthg/of doing sthg** incriminar alguém por algo/por fazer algo.

accused [əˈkjuːzd] n JUR: **the ~** [defendant] o réu(a ré).

accusing [əˈkjuːzɪŋ] adj acusador(ra).

accusingly [əˈkjuːzɪŋlɪ] adv acusatoriamente.

accustomed [əˈkʌstəmd] adj: **to be ~ to sthg/to doing sthg** estar acostumado(da) a algo/a fazer algo.

ace [eɪs] ◇ n -1. [playing card] ás m -2. TENNIS ace m -3. phr: **to be within an ~ of victory** estar a um passo da vitória. ◇ adj [top-class]: **he's an ~ tennis player** ele é um tenista de primeira.

acerbic [əˈsɜːbɪk] adj acerbo(ba).

acetate [ˈæsɪteɪt] n acetato m.

acetic acid [əˈsiːtɪk-] n (U) ácido m acético.

acetone [ˈæsɪtəun] n (U) acetona f.

acetylene [əˈsetɪliːn] n (U) acetileno m.

ache [eɪk] ◇ n [dull pain] dor f. ◇ vi -1. [be painful] doer -2. fig [want]: **to be aching for sthg/to do sthg** estar morrendo de vontade de algo/de fazer algo.

achieve [əˈtʃiːv] vt [success] conseguir ; [goal, ambition] realizar ; [victory, fame] conquistar.

achievement [əˈtʃiːvmənt] n -1. [feat, deed] conquista f -2. [process of achieving] realização f.

Achilles' heel [əˈkɪliːz-] n calcanhar m de Aquiles.

Achilles' tendon n tendão m de Aquiles.

acid [ˈæsɪd] ◇ adj -1. ácido(da) -2. fig [remark, tone] áspero(ra). ◇ n -1. ácido m -2. inf [LSD] ácido m.

acidic [əˈsɪdɪk] adj CHEM acidífero(ra).

acidity [əˈsɪdətɪ] n -1. CHEM acidez f -2. fig [of remark, tone] aspereza f.

acid rain n chuva f ácida.

acid test n fig [test of worth] prova f dos nove.

acknowledge [əkˈnɒlɪdʒ] vt -1. [accept, recognize] reconhecer; **to ~ sb as sthg** reconhecer alguém como algo -2. [letter]: **to ~ (receipt of) sthg** acusar (o recebimento de algo) -3. [greet] cumprimentar.

acknowledg(e)ment [əkˈnɒlɪdʒmənt] n -1. [acceptance, recognition] reconhecimento m -2. [of letter] aviso m de recebimento -3. [thanks, gratitude] retribuição f.

◆ **acknowledg(e)ments** npl [in book] agradecimentos mpl.

ACLU (abbr of **American Civil Liberties Union**) n associação norte-americana para a defesa das liberdades civis.

acme [ˈækmɪ] n apogeu m.

acne [ˈæknɪ] n acne f.

acorn [ˈeɪkɔːn] n bolota f, glande m.

acoustic [əˈkuːstɪk] adj acústico(ca).

◆ **acoustics** npl [of room, auditorium] acústica f.

acoustic guitar n violão m acústico.

acquaint [ə'kweɪntl] *vt*: **to ~ sb with sthg** [information] informar alguém sobre algo; **to be ~ed with sthg** [method, technique] estar por dentro de algo; **to be ~ed with sb** *fml* conhecer alguém.

acquaintance [ə'kweɪntəns] *n* -**1.** [personal associate] conhecido *m*, -da *f* -**2.** *(U) fml*: **to make sb's ~** conhecer alguém.

acquiesce [ˌækwɪ'es] *vi*: **to ~ (to** OR **in sthg)** aquiescer-se (a algo).

acquiescence [ˌækwɪ'esns] *n* aquiescência *f*.

acquire [ə'kwaɪə^r] *vt* -**1.** [obtain] [property, company, object] adquirir -**2.** [information, document] obter -**3.** [skill, knowledge, habit] adquirir.

acquired taste [ə'kwaɪəd-] *n* gosto *m* adquirido.

acquisition [ˌækwɪ'zɪʃn] *n* -**1.** [of property, company, object] aquisição *f* -**2.** *(U)* [of information, document] obtenção *f* -**3.** *(U)* [of skill, knowlege, habit] aquisição *f*.

acquisitive [ə'kwɪzɪtɪv] *adj* ambicioso(sa), consumista.

acquit [ə'kwɪt] *(pt & pp* -**ted**, *cont* -**ting)** *vt* -**1.** JUR: **to ~ sb of sthg** absolver alguém de algo -**2.** [conduct]: **to ~ o.s. well/badly** desempenhar-se bem/mal.

acquittal [ə'kwɪtl] *n* JUR absolvição *f*.

acre ['eɪkə^r] *n* [unit of measurement] acre *m (4046,9 m²)*.

acreage *n* [size in acres] área *f* medida em acres.

acrid ['ækrɪd] *adj* -**1.** [smoke, smell, taste] acre -**2.** *fig* [remark] mordaz.

acrimonious [ˌækrɪ'məʊnjəs] *adj* acrimonioso(sa).

acrobat ['ækrəbæt] *n* [circus performer] acrobata *mf*.

acrobatic [ˌækrə'bætɪk] *adj* -**1.** [somersault, display] acrobático(ca) -**2.** [person] astuto(ta).

   → **acrobatics** *npl* acrobacias *fpl*.

acronym ['ækrənɪm] *n* acrônimo *m*.

across [ə'krɒs] ◇ *adv* -**1.** [from one side to the other]: **they came ~ in a small boat** eles atravessaram num barco pequeno -**2.** [in the direction of]: **she looked ~ at me** ela olhou em minha direção; **he went ~ to speak to her** ele foi em sua direção para lhe falar -**3.** [in measurements] de um lado a outro -**4.** [in crosswords] cruzado(da) -**5.** *phr*: **to get sthg ~ (to sb)** fazer-se entender (por alguém). ◇ *prep* -**1.** [from one side to the other] de um lado a outro; **he drew a line ~ the page** ele traçou uma linha de um lado a outro da página; **there is a bridge ~ the river** há uma ponte sobre o rio; **she walked/ran ~ the road** ela atravessou a estrada caminhando/correndo; **he looked ~ the street** ele olhou pela rua -**2.** [on the other side of] no outro lado de.

   → **across from** *prep* na frente de.

acrylic [ə'krɪlɪk] ◇ *adj* [fibre, jumper, paint] acrílico(-ca). ◇ *n (U)* [fibre] acrílico *m*.

act [ækt] ◇ *n* -**1.** [action, deed] ato *m*; **to catch sb in the ~** pegar alguém em flagrante -**2.** JUR lei *f* -**3.** [of play, opera] ato *m*; [in cabaret etc] número *m* -**4.** *fig* [pretence] fingimento *m*; **to put on an ~** agir com fingimento -**5.** *phr*: **to get in on the ~** aproveitar-se de algo iniciado por outrem; **to get one's ~ together** organizar-se. ◇ *vi* -**1.** [gen] agir; **to ~ as if/like** agir como se/como -**2.** [in play, film] representar, atuar -**3.** *fig* [pretend] fingir -**4.** [fulfil function]: **to ~ as sthg** atuar como algo; **to ~ for** OR

on behalf of sb representar alguém. ◇ *vt* [role] desempenhar; **to ~ the fool/innocent** fazer-se de bobo/inocente.

   → **act out** *vt sep* -**1.** [feeling] expressar -**2.** [event] representar.

   → **act up** *vi inf* -**1.** [machine] emperrar -**2.** [person] comportar-se mal.

ACT *(abbr of* **American College Test)** *n exame realizado ao final do ensino médio em escolas norte-americanas.*

acting ['æktɪŋ] ◇ *adj* [interim] interino(na). ◇ *n (U)* [in play, film] atuação *f*; **to enjoy ~** gostar de atuar.

action ['ækʃn] *n* -**1.** *(U)* [fact of doing sthg] ação *f*; **to take ~** agir; **to put sthg into ~** pôr algo em ação; **in ~** [person, machine] em atividade; **out of ~** [person] fora de combate; [machine] desativado(da) -**2.** [deed] atividade *f* -**3.** *(U)* [in battle, war] ação *f*; **to be killed in ~** ser morto(ta) em ação -**4.** JUR ação *f* judicial; **to bring an ~ against sb** entrar com uma ação judicial contra alguém -**5.** [in play, book, film] história *f* -**6.** [effect] efeito *m*.

action group *n* [lobby] grupo *m* de ação.

action replay *n* replay *m*.

activate ['æktɪveɪt] *vt* [set off] ativar.

active ['æktɪv] *adj* -**1.** [lively, energetic] ativo(va) -**2.** [involved, hardworking] dinâmico(ca) -**3.** [positive] incessante -**4.** [volcano] ativo(va).

actively ['æktɪvlɪ] *adv* -**1.** [promote] ativamente -**2.** [seek, encourage] incessantemente.

active service *n (U)* MIL serviço *m* ativo; **to be killed on ~** ser morto(ta) em serviço.

activist ['æktɪvɪst] *n* [political campaigner] ativista *mf*.

activity [æk'tɪvətɪ] *(pl* -**ies)** *n (U)* atividade *f*.

   → **activities** *npl* [actions, doings] ações *fpl*.

act of God *n* força *f* maior.

actor ['æktə^r] *n* ator *m*.

actress ['æktrɪs] *n* atriz *f*.

actual ['æktʃʊəl] *adj* real; **in ~ fact** na verdade.

actuality [ˌæktʃʊ'ælətɪ] *n*: **in ~** de fato.

actually ['æktʃʊəlɪ] *adv* -**1.** [really, in truth] na verdade, realmente -**2.** [by the way] a propósito -**3.** [contradicting sb] pensando bem, de fato; **that's not true, ~** pensando bem, aquilo não é verdade.

actuary ['æktʃʊərɪ] *(pl* -**ies)** *n* [statistician] estatístico *m*, -ca *f*.

actuate ['æktʃʊeɪt] *vt* [activate] acionar.

acuity [ə'kju:ətɪ] *n fml* acuidade *f*.

acumen ['ækjʊmen] *n (U)*: **business ~** tino para os negócios.

acupuncture ['ækjʊpʌŋktʃə^r] *n (U)* acupuntura *f*.

acute [ə'kju:t] *adj* -**1.** [severe, extreme] agudo(da) -**2.** [perceptive, intelligent] engenhoso(sa) -**3.** [keen, sensitive] aguçado(da) -**4.** LING: **e ~** e agudo -**5.** MATH agudo(da).

acute accent *n* acento *m* agudo.

acutely [ə'kju:tlɪ] *adv* [extremely] acentuadamente.

ad *(abbr of* **advertisement)** *n fam* -**1.** [in newspaper] anúncio *m* -**2.** [on TV] propaganda *f*.

AD *(abbr of* **Anno Domini)** d.C.

adage ['ædɪdʒ] *n* adágio *m*.

adamant ['ædəmənt] *adj* [determined]: **to be ~**

(about sthg/that) estar inflexível (em relação a algo).

Adam's apple ['ædəmz-] n pomo-de-adão m.

adapt [ə'dæptl] ⟨⟩ vt adaptar. ⟨⟩ vi: **to ~ to sthg** adaptar-se a algo.

adaptability [ə,dæptə'bɪlətɪl] n adaptabilidade f.

adaptable [ə'dæptəbll] adj [person] maleável.

adaptation [,ædæp'teɪʃn] n [of book, play] adaptação f.

adapter, adaptor [ə'dæptə'] n ELEC adaptador m.

ADAS (abbr of **Agricultural Development and Advisory Service**) n organização britânica de pesquisa e consultoria para as indústrias do setor agrícola.

ADC (abbr of **analogue to digital converter**) n ADC m, conversor m analógico-digital.

add [æd] vt -1.: **to ~ sthg to sthg** adicionar algo a algo -2. [total] somar; **6 ~ 3 equals 9** US 6 mais 3 é igual a 9 -3. [say as an afterthought] acrescentar.
◆ **add in** vt sep [include] incluir.
◆ **add on** vt sep: **to ~ sthg on (to sthg)** [to building] anexar algo (a algo); [to bill, total] incluir algo (em algo).
◆ **add to** vt fus [increase] aumentar.
◆ **add up** ⟨⟩ vt sep [total up] adicionar. ⟨⟩ vi -1. [make sense] fazer sentido -2. [accumulate] acumular.
◆ **add up to** vt fus [represent] representar.

addendum [ə'dendəm] (pl -da) n [additional section] adendo m.

adder ['ædə'] n [snake] víbora f.

addict ['ædɪkt] n -1. [to drug, harmful substance] viciado m, -da f, dependente mf -2. [exercise, TV etc.] fanático m, -ca f.

addicted [ə'dɪktɪd] adj -1. [to drug, harmful substance]: **~ (to sthg)** viciado(da) (em algo), dependente de algo -2. fig [to exercise, TV] fanático(ca) (por algo).

addiction [ə'dɪkʃn] n (U) -1. [to drug, harmful substance] vício m, dependência f; **~ to sthg** vício em algo, dependência de algo -2. fig [to exercise, food, TV] fanatismo m; **~ to sthg** fanatismo por algo.

addictive [ə'dɪktɪv] adj -1. [drug, harmful substance] que vicia -2. fig [exercise, food, TV] que vicia.

Addis Ababa ['ædɪs 'æbəbə] n Adis-Abeba; **in/to ~** em/para Adis-Abeba.

addition [ə'dɪʃn] n -1. (U) MATH adição f -2. [extra thing] acréscimo m -3. (U) [act of adding] adicionamento m; **in ~** além disso; **in ~ to** além de.

additional [ə'dɪʃənl] adj [extra] adicional.

additive ['ædɪtɪv] n aditivo m.

addled ['ædldl] adj -1. [rotten] podre -2. inf [confused] confuso(sa).

add-on COMPUT ⟨⟩ adj adicional. ⟨⟩ n add-on m, software ou hardware acrescentado a um computador para melhorar seu desempenho.

address [ə'dres] ⟨⟩ n -1. [location] endereço m -2. [speech] discurso m. ⟨⟩ vt -1. [letter, parcel] endereçar -2. [give a speech to] discursar -3. [speak to, accost]: **to ~ sb as** dirigir-se a alguém como -4. [deal with] tratar; **to ~ o.s. to sthg** interessar-se por algo.

address book n agenda f de endereços.

addressee [,ædre'si:] n [of letter, parcel] destinatário m, -ria f.

Aden ['eɪdn] n Áden; **in/to ~** em/à Áden.

adenoids ['ædɪnɔɪdz] npl adenóides fpl.

adept ['ædept] adj: **to be ~ at sthg/at doing sthg** ser perito(ta) em algo/em fazer algo.

adequacy ['ædɪkwəsɪl] n (U) -1. [sufficiency] suficiência f -2. [competence] adequação f.

adequate ['ædɪkwət] adj -1. [sufficient] suficiente -2. [competent] adequado(da).

adequately ['ædɪkwətlɪl] adv -1. [sufficiently] suficientemente -2. [competently] adequadamente.

adhere [əd'hɪə'] vi -1. [to surface, principle]: **to ~ (to sthg)** aderir (a algo) -2. [to regulation, decision]: **to ~ to sthg** respeitar algo.

adherence [əd'hɪərəns] n : **~ (to sthg)** [surface] aderência f (a algo); [principle] adesão f (a algo); [regulation, decision] respeito m (a algo).

adhesive [əd'hi:sɪv] ⟨⟩ adj [sticky] adesivo(va). ⟨⟩ n [glue] cola f.

adhesive tape n fita f adesiva.

ad hoc [,æd'hɒk] adj ad hoc.

ad infinitum [,ædɪnfɪ'naɪtəm] adv ad infinitum.

adjacent [ə'dʒeɪsənt] adj adjacente; **~ to sthg** adjacente a algo.

adjective ['ædʒɪktɪv] n adjetivo m.

adjoin [ə'dʒɔɪn] vt unir.

adjoining [ə'dʒɔɪnɪŋ] ⟨⟩ adj [next-door] vizinho(nha). ⟨⟩ prep ao lado de.

adjourn [ə'dʒɜ:n] ⟨⟩ vt [postpone] adiar. ⟨⟩ vi -1. [come to a temporary close] ser/estar suspenso(sa) -2. hum [go]: **to ~ (to)** ir para.

adjournment [ə'dʒɜ:nmənt] n adiamento m, suspensão f.

Adjt (abbr of **adjutant**) assistente administrativo de oficial do exército.

adjudge [ə'dʒʌdʒ] vt -1. [declare] decretar -2. JUR sentenciar.

adjudicate [ə'dʒu:dɪkeɪt] ⟨⟩ vt [contest, claim] adjudicar. ⟨⟩ vi [serve as judge, arbiter in contest] julgar; **to ~ on** or **upon sthg** deliberar sobre algo.

adjudication [ə,dʒu:dɪ'keɪʃn] n adjudicação f.

adjunct ['ædʒʌŋkt] n [something added] acessório m.

adjust [ə'dʒʌst] ⟨⟩ vt [alter, correct] ajustar. ⟨⟩ vi: **to ~ (to sthg)** adaptar-se (a algo).

adjustable [ə'dʒʌstəbl] adj [machine, chair] regulável.

adjustable spanner n chave f inglesa.

adjusted [ə'dʒʌstɪd] adj [emotionally stable]: **to be well ~** estar equilibrado(da).

adjustment [ə'dʒʌstmənt] n -1. [to heat, speed, machine] ajuste m; **to make an ~ to sthg** fazer um ajuste em algo -2. (U) [change of attitude] mudança f; **~ to sthg** adaptação a algo.

adjutant ['ædʒʊtənt] n ajudante mf.

ad lib [,æd'lɪb] (pt & pp **ad-libbed**, cont **ad-libbing**) ⟨⟩ adj [improvised] espontâneo(nea). ⟨⟩ adv [freely] de improviso. ⟨⟩ n [improvised joke, remark] improviso m.
◆ **ad-lib** vi [improvise] improvisar.

adman ['ædmæn] (pl **admen** ['ædmen]) n anunciante m.

admin ['ædmɪn] n UK inf administração f.

administer [əd'mɪnɪstə'] vt -1. [company, business]

administrar - **2.** [justice, punishment] aplicar - **3.** [drug, medication] ministrar.

administration [əd͵mɪnɪ'streɪʃn] n - **1.** (U) [of company, business] administração f - **2.** (U) [of justice, punishment] aplicação f.

➤ **Administration** n US [government]: **the Administration** o Governo.

administrative [əd'mɪnɪstrətɪv] adj [job, work, staff] administrativo(va).

administrator [əd'mɪnɪstreɪtə͵ʳ] n administrador m, -ra f.

admirable ['ædmərəbl] adj admirável.

admirably ['ædmərəblɪ] adv admiravelmente.

admiral ['ædmərəl] n almirante mf.

Admiralty ['ædmərəltɪ] n UK: **the** ~ o Ministério da Marinha.

admiration [͵ædmə'reɪʃn] n admiração f.

admire [əd'maɪə͵ʳ] vt - **1.** [respect, like] admirar; **to** ~ **sb for sthg** admirar alguém por algo - **2.** [look at with pleasure] apreciar.

admirer [əd'maɪərə͵ʳ] n - **1.** [suitor] pretendente mf - **2.** [enthusiast, fan] fã mf.

admiring [əd'maɪərɪŋ] adj [look] de admiração.

admiringly [əd'maɪərɪŋlɪ] adv [gaze] com admiração.

admissible [əd'mɪsəbl] adj JUR [evidence] aceitável.

admission [əd'mɪʃn] n - **1.** [permission to enter] admissão f - **2.** [cost of entrance] entrada f - **3.** [confession] confissão f; **by his/her own** ~ conforme ele/ela mesmo(ma) admitiu.

admit [əd'mɪt] (pt & pp **-ted**, cont **-ting**) ⟨⟩ vt - **1.** [acknowledge, confess] confessar, admitir; **to** ~ **that** admitir que; **to** ~ **doing sthg** admitir/confessar ter feito algo; **to** ~ **defeat** fig dar-se por vencido(da) - **2.** [allow to enter] admitir; **to be admitted to hospital** UK OR **to the hospital** US dar entrada no hospital - **3.** [allow to join] admitir; **to** ~ **sb to sthg** admitir alguém em algo. ⟨⟩ vi: **to** ~ **to sthg/to doing sthg** admitir algo/fazer algo.

admittance [əd'mɪtəns] n [right to enter, entrance]: **to gain** ~ **to sthg** ser admitido(da) em algo; 'no ~' 'entrada proibida'.

admittedly [əd'mɪtɪdlɪ] adv reconhecidamente.

admixture n fml mistura f.

admonish [əd'mɒnɪʃ] vt fml [tell off] repreender.

ad nauseam [͵æd'nɔːzɪæm] adv exaustivamente.

ado [ə'duː] n: **without further** OR **more** ~ sem mais delongas OR preâmbulos.

adolescence [͵ædə'lesns] n adolescência f.

adolescent [͵ædə'lesnt] ⟨⟩ adj - **1.** [teenage] adolescente - **2.** pej [immature] imaturo(ra). ⟨⟩ n [teenager] adolescente mf.

adopt [ə'dɒpt] ⟨⟩ vt [recommendation, suggestion] aceitar. ⟨⟩ vi [give a home to a child] adotar.

adoption [ə'dɒpʃn] n (U) adoção f.

adoptive [ə'dɒptɪv] adj adotivo(va).

adorable [ə'dɔːrəbl] adj adorável.

adoration [͵ædə'reɪʃn] n adoração f.

adore [ə'dɔː͵ʳ] vt adorar.

adoring [ə'dɔːrɪŋ] adj - **1.** [look] de admiração - **2.** [smile, person] encantador(ra).

adorn [ə'dɔːn] vt [decorate] adornar.

adornment [ə'dɔːnmənt] n [decoration] adorno m.

ADP (abbr of **automatic data processing**) n PAD m, processamento m automático de dados.

adrenalin [ə'drenəlɪn] n (U) adrenalina f.

Adriatic [͵eɪdrɪ'ætɪk] n: **the** ~ **(Sea)** o (Mar) Adriático.

adrift [ə'drɪft] ⟨⟩ adj [boat, ship] à deriva. ⟨⟩ adv: **to go** ~ fig [go wrong] ir por água abaixo.

adroit [ə'drɔɪt] adj hábil.

ADT (abbr of **Atlantic Daylight Time**) n horário de verão na costa leste dos Estados Unidos.

adulation [͵ædjʊ'leɪʃn] n (U) adulação f.

adult ['ædʌlt] ⟨⟩ adj - **1.** [mature, responsible] adulto(ta) - **2.** [for adults] para adultos, para maiores. ⟨⟩ n [person, animal] adulto m, -ta f.

adult education n (U) educação f para adultos.

adulterate [ə'dʌltəreɪt] vt adulterar.

adulteration [ə͵dʌltə'reɪʃn] n (U) adulteração f.

adulterer [ə'dʌltərə͵ʳ] n adúltero m, -ra f.

adultery [ə'dʌltərɪ] n (U) adultério m.

adulthood ['ædʌlthʊd] n maioridade f.

advance [əd'vɑːns] ⟨⟩ n - **1.** [gen] avanço m - **2.** [money] adiantamento m. ⟨⟩ comp - **1.** [early] antecipado(da) - **2.** [prior]: ~ **warning** aviso prévio. ⟨⟩ vt - **1.** [improve] progredir - **2.** [bring forward in time] adiantar - **3.** [money]: **to** ~ **sb sthg** adiantar algo a alguém. ⟨⟩ vi - **1.** [go forward] avançar; **to** ~ **on sb** avançar em alguém - **2.** [improve] progredir.

➤ **advances** npl: **to make** ~**s to sb** [sexual] assediar alguém; [business] propor um bom negócio para alguém.

➤ **in advance** adv com antecedência; **to book in** ~ reservar antecipadamente; **to know in** ~ saber de antemão; **half an hour in** ~ meia hora antes.

➤ **in advance of** prep - **1.** [superior to] superior a - **2.** [prior to] antes de.

advanced [əd'vɑːnst] adj avançado(da); ~ **in years** euph [elderly] em idade avançada.

advancement [əd'vɑːnsmənt] n - **1.** (U) [promotion in job] promoção f - **2.** [improvement] avanço m.

advantage [əd'vɑːntɪdʒ] n - **1.** vantagem f; **to be to one's** ~ ser conveniente para alguém; **to have** OR **hold the** ~ **(over sb)** ter OR levar vantagem (sobre alguém) - **2.** phr: **to take** ~ **of sthg/sb** aproveitar-se de algo/alguém.

advantageous [͵ædvən'teɪdʒəs] adj vantajoso(sa).

advent ['ædvənt] n [of invention, person, period] advento m.

➤ **Advent** n RELIG Advento m.

Advent calendar n calendário com figuras decorativas em cada dia das quatro semanas antecedentes ao Natal, marcando o período do Advento.

adventure [əd'ventʃə͵ʳ] n aventura f; **to have no sense of** ~ não ter espírito de aventura.

adventure holiday n férias fpl de aventura.

adventure playground n área de lazer para crianças que oferece materiais diversos para montar e brincar.

adventurer [əd'ventʃərə͵ʳ] n - **1.** [adventurous person] aventureiro m, -ra f - **2.** [unscrupulous person] inescrupuloso m, -sa f.

adventurous [əd'ventʃərəs] *adj* **-1.** [person] intrépido(da) - **2.** [life, project] aventureiro(ra) - **3.** [menu, programme etc.] atraente, interessante.

adverb ['ædvɜːb] *n* advérbio *m*.

adverbial <> *adj* adverbial. <> *n* adjunto *m* adverbial.

adversary ['ædvəsərɪ] (*pl* -ies) *n* adversário *m*, -ria *f*.

adverse ['ædvɜːs] *adj* adverso(sa).

adversely ['ædvɜːslɪ] *adv* negativamente.

adversity [əd'vɜːsətɪ] *n (U)* adversidade *f*.

advert ['ædvɜːt] *n UK* = advertisement.

advertise ['ædvətaɪz] <> *vt* [job, car, product] anunciar. <> *vi* [in newspaper, on TV, in shop window]: **they're advertising for sales representatives** estão anunciando vaga para representantes comerciais.

advertisement [əd'vɜːtɪsmənt] *n* - **1.** [in newspaper, on TV, in shop window] anúncio *m* - **2.** *fig* [recommendation] propaganda *f*.

advertiser ['ædvətaɪzə[r]] *n* anunciante *mf*.

advertising ['ædvətaɪzɪŋ] *n (U)* - **1.** [advertisements] propaganda *f* - **2.** [industry] publicidade *f*.

advertising agency *n* agência *f* de publicidade.

advertising campaign *n* campanha *f* publicitária.

advice [əd'vaɪs] *n (U)* conselho *m*; **to give sb** ~ dar conselhos a alguém; **to take sb's** ~ aceitar conselhos de alguém; **a piece of** ~ um conselho.

advice note *n* aviso *m* de envio.

advisability [əd,vaɪzə'bɪlətɪ] *n (U)* conveniência *f*.

advisable [əd'vaɪzəbl] *adj* aconselhável.

advise [əd'vaɪz] <> *vt* - **1.** [give advice to]: **to** ~ **sb to do sthg/not to do sthg** aconselhar alguém a fazer algo/a não fazer algo - **2.** [professionally]: **to** ~ **sb on sthg** assessorar alguém em algo - **3.** *fml* [inform] avisar; **to** ~ **sb of sthg** avisar alguém sobre algo. <> *vi* - **1.** [give advice]: **to** ~ **against sthg/against doing sthg** desaconselhar algo/a fazer algo - **2.** [act as adviser]: **to** ~ **on sthg** assessorar em algo.

advisedly [əd'vaɪzɪdlɪ] *adv* deliberadamente.

adviser *UK*, **advisor** *US* [əd'vaɪzə[r]] *n* assessor *m*, -ra *f*.

advisory [əd'vaɪzərɪ] *adj* [group, organization] de assessoria; **in an** ~ **capacity** *OR* **role** com função *OR* no papel de assessor(ra).

advocacy ['ædvəkəsɪ] *n (U)* [support] defesa *f*.

advocate [*n* 'ædvəkət, *vb* 'ædvəkeɪt] <> *n* - **1.** *Scot JUR* advogado *m*, -da *f* - **2.** [supporter] defensor *m*, -ra *f*. <> *vt fml* [recommend] defender.

AEC (*abbr of* Atomic Energy Commission) *n* organismo norte-americano de energia nuclear, ≃ CNEN *f*.

Aegean [iː'dʒiːən] *n*: **the** ~**(Sea)** o (Mar) Egeu; **in the** ~ no Egeu.

aegis ['iːdʒɪs] *n*: **under the** ~ **of** sob a égide de.

aeon *UK*, **eon** *US* ['iːən] *n* - **1.** *GEOL* éon *m* - **2.** *fig* [very long time] século *m*.

aerial ['eərɪəl] <> *adj* [of, from, in the air] aéreo(rea). <> *n UK* [antenna] antena *f*.

aerobatics [,eərəʊ'bætɪks] *n (U)* acrobacias *fpl* aéreas.

aerobics [eə'rəʊbɪks] *n (U)* aeróbica *f*, ginástica *f* aeróbica.

aerodrome ['eərədrəʊm] *n esp UK* aeródromo *m*.

aerodynamic [,eərəʊdaɪ'næmɪk] *adj* aerodinâmico(ca).

aerodynamics <> *n (U) SCIENCE* aerodinâmica *f*. <> *npl* [aerodynamic qualities] aerodinâmicas *f*.

aerogramme ['eərəgræm] *n* aerograma *m*.

aeronautics [,eərə'nɔːtɪks] *n (U)* aeronáutica *f*.

aeroplane *UK* ['eərəpleɪn], **airplane** ['eəpleɪn] *US n* avião *m*.

aerosol ['eərəsɒl] *n* aerossol *m*.

aerospace ['eərəʊspeɪs] *n*: **the** ~ **industry** a indústria aeroespacial.

aesthete, esthete *US* ['iːsθiːt] *n* esteta *mf*.

aesthetic, esthetic *US* [iːs'θetɪk] *adj* estético(ca).

aesthetically, esthetically *US* [iːs'θetɪklɪ] *adv* esteticamente.

aesthetics, esthetics *US* [iːs'θetɪks] *n (U)* estética *f*.

afar [ə'fɑː[r]] *adv*: **from** ~ à distância.

AFC (*abbr of* Association Football Club) *n* futebol clube britânico, FC *f*.

AFDC (*abbr of* Aid to Families with Dependent Children) *n* associação norte-americana para auxílio a famílias com crianças portadoras de necessidades especiais, ≃ APAE *f*.

affable ['æfəbl] *adj* [pleasant] afável.

affair [ə'feə[r]] *n* - **1.** [event] acontecimento *m* - **2.** [concern] assunto *m* - **3.** [extramarital relationship] caso *m*.

affairs *npl* - **1.** [business, personal interests] negócios *mpl* - **2.** [matters] questões *fpl*.

affect [ə'fekt] *vt* - **1.** [influence, act upon] afetar - **2.** [imitate, put on] imitar - **3.** [feign] fingir.

affectation [,æfek'teɪʃn] *n* - **1.** [mannerism] afetação *f* - **2.** [pretence] fingimento *m*.

affected [ə'fektɪd] *adj* [mannered] afetado(da).

affection [ə'fekʃn] *n* afeição *f*.

affectionate [ə'fekʃnət] *adj* afetuoso(osa).

affectionately [ə'fekʃnətlɪ] *adv* afetuosamente.

affidavit [,æfɪ'deɪvɪt] *n* juramento *m*.

affiliate [*n* ə'fɪlɪət, *vb* ə'fɪlɪeɪt] <> *n* filiado *m*, -da *f*. <> *vt*: **to be** ~**d to** *OR* **with sthg** ser filiado(da) a algo.

affiliation [ə,fɪlɪ'eɪʃn] *n* afiliação *f*.

affinity [ə'fɪnətɪ] (*pl* -ies) *n* - **1.** *(U)* [attraction] atração *f*; **to have an** ~ **with sb/sthg** sentir atração por alguém/algo - **2.** [connection, similarity] afinidade *f*; **to have an** ~ **with sb/sthg** ter afinidade com alguém/algo.

affirm [ə'fɜːm] *vt* afirmar.

affirmation [,æfə'meɪʃn] *n* afirmação *f*.

affirmative [ə'fɜːmətɪv] <> *adj* afirmativo(va). <> *n* afirmativa *f*; **to reply in the** ~ responder que sim/positivamente.

affix [ə'fɪks] *vt* [stamp] afixar.

afflict [ə'flɪkt] *vt* afligir; **to be** ~**ed with sthg** sofrer de algo.

affliction [ə'flɪkʃn] *n* - **1.** [distress] aflição *f* - **2.** [physical] doença *f*.

affluence ['æfluəns] *n (U)* riqueza *f*.

affluent ['æfluəntl *adj* rico(ca).

affluent society *n* sociedade *f* afluente.

afford [ə'fɔːdl *vt* -**1.** [have enough money for]: **to be able to** ~ **sthg** poder pagar por algo -**2.** [time, energy]: **to be able to** ~ **the time (to do sthg)** ter tempo (para fazer algo) -**3.** [allow]: **we can't** ~ **to let this happen** não podemos nos dar ao luxo de deixar que isto aconteça -**4.** *fml* [provide, give] oferecer.

affordable [ə'fɔːdəbl] *adj* acessível.

afforestation [æˌfɒrɪ'steɪʃn] *n (U)* florestamento *m*.

affray [ə'freɪ] *n UK fml* [disturbance] desordem *f*.

affront [ə'frʌnt] ⟨⟩ *n* afronta *f*. ⟨⟩ *vt* ofender.

Afghan ['æfgæn], **Afghani** [æf'gænl ⟨⟩ *adj* afegão(gã) ⟨⟩ *n* afegão *m*, -gã *f*, afegane *mf*.

Afghan hound *n* Afghan hound *mf*.

Afghani *adj* & *n* = Afghan.

Afghanistan [æf'gænɪstæn] *n* Afeganistão; **in** ~ no Afeganistão.

afield [ə'fiːld] *adv*: **far** ~ longe.

AFL-CIO (*abbr of* **American Federation of Labor and Congress of Industrial Organizations**) *n* federação norte-americana de sindicatos da indústria.

afloat [ə'fləʊt] *adj* -**1.** [above water] flutuante -**2.** *fig* [out of debt] em dia.

afoot [ə'fʊt] *adj* [present, happening] em ação.

aforementioned [əˌfɔː'menʃənd], **aforesaid** [ə'fɔːsed] *adj fml* acima mencionado(da).

afraid [ə'freɪd] *adj* -**1.** [frightened] assustado(da); **to be** ~ **(of sb/sth)** ter medo (de alguém/algo); **to be** ~ **of doing** *OR* **to do sthg** ter medo de fazer algo -**2.** [reluctant, apprehensive] apreensivo(va); **to be** ~ **(that)** ter medo (que); **to be** ~ **of sthg** ter medo de algo; **he was** ~ **of losing his job** tinha medo de perder seu emprego -**3.** [in apologies]: **to be** ~ **(that)** ter receio (que); **I'm** ~ **so/not** receio que sim/não.

afresh [ə'freʃ] *adv* novamente.

Africa ['æfrɪkə] *n* África; **in** ~ na África.

African ['æfrɪkən] ⟨⟩ *adj* africano(na). ⟨⟩ *n* africano *m*, -na *f*.

African American ⟨⟩ *adj* afro-americano(na). ⟨⟩ *n* afro-americano *m*, -na *f*.

African violet *n* violeta *f* africana.

Afrikaans [ˌæfrɪ'kɑːns] *n* africâner *m*.

Afrikaner [ˌæfrɪ'kɑːnəʳ] *n* africâner *mf*.

aft [ɑːft] *adv* à popa *OR* ré.

after ['ɑːftəʳ] ⟨⟩ *prep* -**1.** [following - in time] após; [- in order] após; ~ **you!** atrás de você! -**2.** [as a result of] depois -**3.** [in spite of] apesar de -**4.** *inf* [in search of, looking for] atrás de -**5.** [with the name of] em homenagem a -**6.** [directed at sb moving away] atrás de -**7.** *ART* à moda de -**8.** *US* [telling the time]: **it's twenty** ~ **three** são três e vinte. ⟨⟩ *adv* em seguida, depois. ⟨⟩ *conj* depois que/de; ~ **she left university ...** depois que deixou/de deixar a universidade, ela ...

➡ **afters** *npl UK* sobremesa *f*.

➡ **after all** *adv* -**1.** [in spite of everything] apesar de tudo -**2.** [it should be remembered] afinal.

afterbirth ['ɑːftəbɜːθ] *n* placenta *f*.

aftercare ['ɑːftəkeəʳ] *n (U)* ajuda oficial para quem acabou de sair do hospital ou da prisão.

after-effects *npl* efeitos *mpl* secundários, conseqüências *fpl*.

afterlife ['ɑːftəlaɪf] (*pl* -**lives** [-laɪvzl) *n* vida *f* após a morte.

aftermath ['ɑːftəmæθ] *n* conseqüências *fpl*.

afternoon [ˌɑːftə'nuːn] *n* tarde *f*; **good** ~ boa tarde.

➡ **afternoons** *adv esp US* à tarde.

after-sales service *n* serviço *m* pós-venda.

aftershave ['ɑːftəʃeɪv] *n* loção *f* após-barba.

aftershock ['ɑːftəʃɒk] *n* pequenos tremores *mpl* (após terremoto).

aftersun (lotion) *n* creme *m* hidratante após-sol.

aftertaste ['ɑːftəteɪst] *n* [of food, drink] ressaibo *m*, mau sabor *m*.

afterthought ['ɑːftəθɔːt] *n* pensamento *m* a posteriori.

afterwards, afterward *US* ['ɑːftəwəd(z)] *adv* posteriormente, depois.

again [ə'gen] *adv* -**1.** [one more time] outra vez; ~ **and** ~ repetidas vezes; **all over** ~ tudo de novo; **time and** ~ mil vezes -**2.** [once more as before] de novo -**3.** [asking for information to be repeated]: **what was that** ~? o que foi mesmo que você disse? -**4.** *phr*: **half as much** ~ cinqüenta por cento a mais; **(twice) as much** ~ (duas) vezes mais; **come** ~? *inf* o que?; **then** *OR* **there** ~ por outro lado.

against [ə'genst] ⟨⟩ *prep* -**1.** [gen] contra -**2.** [in contrast to]: **as** ~ em comparação com, em vez de. ⟨⟩ *adv* contra.

age [eɪdʒ] (*cont* **ageing** *OR* **aging**) ⟨⟩ *n* -**1.** [of person, animal, thing] idade *f*; **what** ~ **are you?** quantos anos você tem?; **to be of** ~ *US* ser maior de idade; **to come of** ~ atingir à maioridade; **to be under** ~ ser menor de idade; **act your** ~! pare de agir como criança! -**2.** *(U)* [state or process of ageing - of person] idade *f*; [- of object, cheese, wine] tempo *m*; **wine improves with** ~ o vinho melhora com o tempo -**3.** [stage - of person's life] idade *f*, hora *f*; [- of history] era *f*. ⟨⟩ *vt* envelhecer. ⟨⟩ *vi* envelhecer.

➡ **ages** *npl* [a long time]: ~**s ago** séculos atrás; **for** ~**s** há séculos.

aged [*adj sense* 1 eɪdʒd, *adj sense* 2 *& npl* 'eɪdʒɪd] ⟨⟩ *adj* -**1.** [of the stated age] da idade de; **a person** ~ **30** uma pessoa de 30 anos; **to be** ~ **20** ter 20 anos (de idade) -**2.** [very old] envelhecido(da), antigo(ga). ⟨⟩ *npl*: **the** ~ [the elderly] os idosos.

age group *n* grupo *m* etário.

ageing ['eɪdʒɪŋ] ⟨⟩ *adj* -**1.** [getting old - person] idoso(sa); **the** ~ **population** a população de idosos; [- thing] velho(lha), ultrapassado(da) -**2.** [thing] velho(lha), ultrapassado(da). ⟨⟩ *n (U)* [process of getting old] envelhecimento *m*.

ageless ['eɪdʒlɪs] *adj* [person, thing] imutável, eterno(na).

agency ['eɪdʒənsɪ] (*pl* -**ies**) *n* -**1.** [gen] agência *f* -**2.** [government organisation] órgão *m*.

agenda [ə'dʒendə] (*pl* -**s**) *n* pauta *f*, agenda *f*.

agent ['eɪdʒənt] *n* -**1.** [person] agente *mf* -**2.** [substance] reagente *m*.

age-old *adj* [very old] antigo(ga).

aggravate ['ægrəveɪt] *vt* **-1.** [make worse] agravar - **2.** [annoy] irritar.

aggravating ['ægrəveɪtɪŋ] *adj* [person, behaviour, problem] agravante, irritante.

aggravation [,ægrə'veɪʃn] *n (U)* [irritation] agravo *m*, irritação *f*.

aggregate ['ægrɪgət] <> *adj* total. <> *n* **-1.** [total] total *m* **-2.** [material] agregado *m*.

aggression [ə'greʃn] *n (U)* agressão *f*.

aggressive [ə'gresɪv] *adj* **-1.** [belligerent] agressivo(-va) - **2.** [forceful - campaign] agressivo(va); [- person] audaz, empreendedor(ra).

aggressively [ə'gresɪvlɪ] *adv* [belligerently] agressivamente.

aggressor [ə'gresəʳ] *n* agressor *m*, -ra *f*.

aggrieved [ə'gri:vd] *adj* [upset, hurt] magoado(da).

aggro ['ægrəʊ] *n UK inf* arruaça *f*.

aghast [ə'gɑ:st] *adj* [horrified] espantado(da); ~ **at** sthg espantado(da) (com algo).

agile [*UK* 'ædʒaɪl, *US* 'ædʒəl] *adj* [body, person, mind] ágil.

agility [ə'dʒɪlətɪ] *n (U)* agilidade *f*.

aging *adj* & *n* = ageing.

agitate ['ædʒɪteɪt] <> *vt* **-1.** [disturb, worry] perturbar - **2.** [shake] agitar. <> *vi* [campaign actively]: **to** ~ **for/against sthg** fazer campanha pró/contra algo.

agitated ['ædʒɪteɪtɪd] *adj* [disturbed, anxious] agitado(da).

agitation [,ædʒɪ'teɪʃn] *n* [anxiety] agitação *f*.

agitator ['ædʒɪteɪtəʳ] *n* [political activist] agitador *m*, -ra *f*.

AGM (*abbr of* **annual general meeting**) *n UK* assembléia *f* geral anual (*de clube, empresa etc*).

agnostic [æg'nɒstɪk] <> *adj* agnóstico(ca). <> *n* agnóstico *m*, -ca *f*.

ago [ə'gəʊ] *adv* atrás; **three days** ~ três dias atrás; **years/long** ~ anos/tempos atrás.

agog [ə'gɒg] *adj* ansioso(osa), impaciente; **to be all** ~ (**with**) estar ansioso(sa) (com).

agonize, -ise ['ægənaɪz] *vi* agonizar; **to** ~ (**over** *OR* **about** sth) atormentar-se (com algo).

agonized ['ægənaɪzd] *adj* [faces, screams] agoniado(da).

agonizing ['ægənaɪzɪŋ] *adj* **-1.** [decision, wait] angustiante - **2.** [pain] agonizante.

agonizingly ['ægənaɪzɪŋlɪ] *adv* [difficult, painful] angustiosamente, dolorosamente.

agony ['ægənɪ] (*pl* **-ies**) *n* **-1.** [physical pain] dores *fpl*, agonia *f*; **to be in** ~ estar morrendo de dor - **2.** [mental pain] angústia *f*; **to be in** ~ estar angustiado(da).

agony aunt *n UK inf* conselheira *f* sentimental.

agony column *n UK inf* consultório *m* sentimental.

agoraphobia [,ægərə'fəʊbjəl] *n* agorafobia *f*.

agree [ə'gri:] <> *vi* **-1.** [concur] concordar; **to** ~ **with sb/sthg** concordar com alguém/algo; **to** ~ **on sthg** chegar a um acordo sobre algo; **to** ~ **about sthg** concordar sobre algo - **2.** [consent] concordar; **to** ~ **to sthg** concordar com algo - **3.** [statements] conferir - **4.** [food]: **to** ~ **with sb** combinar com alguém - **5.** *GRAMM* : **to** ~ (**with**) concordar (com). <> *vt* **-1.** [price, terms] concordar - **2.** [concur]: **to** ~ **that** concordar que - **3.** [arrange]: **to** ~ **to do sthg** combinar para fazer algo - **4.** [concede]: **to** ~ (**that**) concordar (que).

agreeable [ə'gri:əbl] *adj* **-1.** [weather, experience] agradável - **2.** [willing]: **to be** ~ **to sthg** ser favorável a algo.

agreeably [ə'gri:əblɪ] *adv* [pleasantly] agradavelmente.

agreed [ə'gri:d] <> *adj*: **to be** ~ **on sthg** estar de acordo sobre algo. <> *adv* **-1.** [decided] de acordo - **2.** [admittedly]: ~ (**that**) sem dúvida (que).

agreement [ə'gri:mənt] *n* **-1.** [accord] acordo *m*; **to be in** ~ **with sb/sthg** estar de acordo com alguém/algo - **2.** [settlement, contract] acordo *m*; **to reach an** ~ chegar a um acordo - **3.** [consent] aceitação *f* - **4.** *GRAMM* concordância *f*.

agricultural [,ægrɪ'kʌltʃərəl] *adj* agrícola.

agriculture ['ægrɪkʌltʃəʳ] *n* [farming] agricultura *f*.

aground [ə'graʊnd] *adv*: **to run** ~ encalhar.

ah [ɑ:] *excl* ah!

aha [ɑ:'hɑ:] *excl* ah! ah!

ahead [ə'hed] *adv* **-1.** [in front] à frente; **right** *OR* **straight** ~ direto em frente - **2.** [forwards] em frente; **to go on** ~ ir na frente; **to be sent on** ~ ser mandado(da) antes *OR* primeiro - **3.** [in competition, game] à frente - **4.** [indicating success]: **to get** ~ ir adiante, prosperar - **5.** [in time] à frente.
  ➡ **ahead of** *prep* **-1.** [gen] à frente de - **2.** [in time] antes de; ~ **of schedule** adiantado(da).

ahoy [ə'hɔɪ] *excl NAUT* à vista!; **land/ship** ~! terra/barco à vista!

AI *n* **-1.** (*abbr of* **Amnesty International**) AI *f*. - **2.** (*abbr of* **artificial intelligence**) IA *f*. - **3.** (*abbr of* **artificial insemination**) IA *f*.

aid [eɪd] <> *n* **-1.** [help] socorro *m*, assistência *f*; **to go to the** ~ **of sb** socorrer alguém; **in** ~ **of sb/sthg** em benefício de alguém/algo; **with the** ~ **of sb/sthg** com a ajuda de alguém/algo - **2.** [device - for teaching, learning] ferramenta *f*; [- for walking, hearing etc] aparelho *m*. <> *vt* **-1.** [help] socorrer - **2.** *JUR* : **to** ~ **and abet** ser cúmplice de.

aide [eɪd] *n POL* assistente *mf*.

aide-de-camp [eɪddə'kɑ:] (*pl* **aides-de-camp**) *n* ajudante-de-ordens *mf*.

AIDS, Aids (*abbr of* **acquired immune deficiency syndrome**) <> *n* AIDS *f*. <> *comp*: ~ **specialist** médico *mf* especialista em AIDS; ~ **patient** aidético *m*, -ca *f*.

aid worker *n* pessoa *f* que presta assistência em áreas atingidas por catástrofes ou guerras.

AIH (*abbr of* **artificial insemination by husband**) *n* inseminação artificial com sêmen do marido.

ail [eɪl] *vi* [be ill] estar doente.

ailing ['eɪlɪŋ] *adj* **-1.** [ill] doente - **2.** *fig* [economy] debilitado(da).

ailment ['eɪlmənt] *n* [illness] doença *f*.

AIM (*abbr of* **alternative investment market**) *n* mercado financeiro britânico de investimentos alternativos.

aim [eɪm] <> *n* **-1.** [objective] objetivo *m* - **2.** [in firing gun, arrow] mira *f*; **to take** ~ **at sthg** apontar para algo. <> *vt* **-1.** [gun, camera]: **to** ~ **sthg at sb/sthg** mirar algo em alguém/algo - **2.** [plan, programme]:

to be ~ed at doing sthg ser OR estar voltado(da) para algo **-3.** [remark, criticism]**: to be ~ed at sb** ser OR estar direcionado(da) para alguém. ◇ *vi* **-1.** [point weapon] mirar; **to ~ at sthg** mirar em algo **-2.** [intend]**: to ~ at** OR **for sthg** visar a algo; **to ~ to do sthg** pretender fazer algo.

aimless ['eɪmlɪs] *adj* [person, life, work] sem objetivo.

aimlessly ['eɪmlɪslɪ] *adv* [wander, look] a esmo, sem rumo.

ain't [eɪnt] *inf*= am not, are not, is not, have not, has not.

air [eəʳ] ◇ *n* **-1.** [for breathing] ar *m* **-2.** [sky]**: to be seen from the ~** ser visto(ta) do alto OR de cima; **to throw sthg into the ~** mandar algo pelos ares; **by ~** [travel] de avião; **to be (up) in the ~** *fig* ser avoado(da) **-3.** [distinctive quality] ar *m* **-4.** *literary* [tune] melodia *f* **-5.** RADIO & TV**: to be on the ~** estar no ar **-6.** *phr***: to clear the ~** *fig* esclarecer as coisas. ◇ *comp* aéreo(rea). ◇ *vt* **-1.** [washing, room, bed] arejar **-2.** [feelings, opinions] manifestar **-3.** [broadcast] anunciar. ◇ *vi* [washing] arejar.

➡ **airs** *npl*: **~s and graces** ares *mpl*; **to give o.s. ~s, to put on ~s** fazer pose.

airbag ['eəbæg] *n* AUT airbag *m*.

airbase ['eəbeɪs] *n* base *f* aérea.

airbed ['eəbed] *n* UK [inflatable mattress] colchão *m* inflável.

airborne ['eəbɔ:n] *adj* **-1.** [troops, regiment] transportado(da) por via aérea **-2.** [plane] em vôo.

airbrake ['eəbreɪk] *n* freio *m* de ar comprimido.

airbrush ['eəbrʌʃ] ◇ *n* ART aerógrafo *m*. ◇ *vt* **-1.** ART pintar com aerógrafo **-2.** PHOT retocar com aerógrafo **-3.** *fig*: **an ~ed version** uma versão melhorada.

airbus ['eəbʌs] *n* airbus *m*.

air-conditioned [-kən'dɪʃnd] *adj* climatizado(da).

air-conditioning [-kən'dɪʃnɪŋ] *n* ar *m* condicionado.

aircraft ['eəkrɑ:ft] (*pl inv*) *n* aeronave *f*, avião *m*.

aircraft carrier *n* porta-aviões *m inv.*

air cushion *n* **-1.** [inflatable cushion] almofada *f* inflável **-2.** [of hovercraft etc] colchão *m* de ar.

airfield ['eəfi:ld] *n* aeródromo *m*.

air force ◇ *n* força *f* aérea. ◇ *comp* da força aérea.

air freight *n* frete *m* aérea.

air freshener [-'freʃnəʳ] *n* purificador *m* de ar.

airgun ['eəgʌn] *n* pistola *f* de ar comprimido.

air hostess *n* UK aeromoça *f.*

airily ['eərɪlɪ] *adv* [light-heartedly, casually] despreocupadamente, alegremente.

airing ['eərɪŋ] *n*: **to give sthg an ~** [clothes] dar uma arejada em algo; [room] ventilar algo; *fig* [opinion] refrescar algo.

airing cupboard *n* UK armário *m* para secar roupa.

air lane *n* rota *f* aérea.

airless ['eəlɪs] *adj* abafado(da).

air letter *n* aerograma *m*.

airlift ['eəlɪft] ◇ *n* transporte *m* aéreo. ◇ *vt* transportar por via aérea.

airline ['eəlaɪn] *n* companhia *f* aérea.

airliner ['eəlaɪnəʳ] *n* avião *m* de passageiros.

airlock ['eəlɒk] *n* **-1.** [in tube, pipe] retentor *m* de ar **-2.** [airtight chamber] câmara *f* de compressão.

airmail ['eəmeɪl] *n* correio *m* aéreo; **by ~** por via aérea.

airman ['eəmən] (*pl* **-men** [-mən]) *n* [aviator] aviador *m.*

air mattress *n* colchão *m* de ar.

air miles *npl* milhas *fpl* aéreas.

airplane ['eəpleɪn] *n* US **=** aeroplane.

airplay ['eəpleɪ] *n* [on radio] divulgação *m*.

air pocket *n* bolsa *f* de ar.

airport ['eəpɔ:t] ◇ *n* aeroporto *m*. ◇ *comp* de aeroporto.

air raid *n* ataque *m* aéreo.

air-raid shelter *n* abrigo *m* antiaéreo.

air rifle *n* espingarda *f* de ar comprimido.

airship ['eəʃɪp] *n* dirigível *m*.

airsick ['eəsɪk] *adj*: **to be ~** estar enjoado(da).

airspace ['eəspeɪs] *n* espaço *m* aéreo.

airspeed ['eəspi:d] *n* velocidade *f* no ar.

air steward *n* comissário *m* de bordo.

air stewardess *n* aeromoça *f.*

air strike *n* MIL ataque *m* aéreo.

airstrip ['eəstrɪp] *n* campo *m* de pouso.

air terminal *n* terminal *m* aéreo.

airtight ['eətaɪt] *adj* hermético(ca).

airtime ['eətaɪm] *n* [on radio] tempo *m* de transmissão.

air-to-air *adj* [missile] do ar para o ar.

air-traffic control *n* controle *m* de tráfego aéreo.

air-traffic controller *n* controlador *m* de tráfego aéreo.

air travel *n* viagem *f* aérea; **~ is cheaper now** viajar de avião é mais barato agora.

airwaves ['eəweɪvz] *npl* ondas *fpl* de rádio.

airy ['eərɪ] (*compar* **-ier**, *superl* **-iest**) *adj* **-1.** [room] arejado(da) **-2.** [notions, promises] leviano(na) **-3.** [nonchalant] indiferente.

aisle [aɪl] *n* **-1.** [in church] nave *f* lateral **-2.** [in plane, theatre, shop] corredor *m*.

ajar [ə'dʒɑ:ʳ] *adj* [door] entreaberto(ta).

AK *abbr of* Alaska.

aka (*abbr of* also known as) também conhecido(da) como.

akin [ə'kɪn] *adj* semelhante.

AL *abbr of* Alabama.

Alabama [ˌæləˈbæmə] *n* Alabama.

alabaster [ˌæləˈbɑ:stəʳ] *n* alabastro *m*.

à la carte *adj* & *adv* à la carte.

alacrity [ə'lækrətɪ] *n fml* [eagerness] prontidão *f.*

alarm [ə'lɑ:m] ◇ *n* **-1.** [fear] susto *m* **-2.** [device] alarme *m*; **to raise** OR **sound the ~** dar OR soar o alarme. ◇ *vt* [scare] alarmar.

alarm clock *n* despertador *m*.

alarming [ə'lɑ:mɪŋ] *adj* alarmante.

alarmingly [ə'lɑ:mɪŋlɪ] *adv* [worryingly] de forma alarmante.

alarmist [ə'lɑ:mɪst] *adj* [person, ideas] alarmista.

alas [ə'læs] *excl literary* ai!

Alaska [ə'læskə] *n* Alasca.

Albania [æl'beɪnjə] n Albânia; **in** ~ na Albânia.
Albanian [æl'beɪnjən] ◇ adj albanês(nesa). ◇ n
-1. [person] albanês m, -sa f -2. [language] albanês m.
albatross ['ælbətrɒs] (pl inv OR -es) n albatroz m.
albeit [ɔ:l'bi:ɪt] conj fml embora.
Alberta [æl'bɜ:tə] n Alberta.
Albert Hall n: **the** ~ o Albert Hall.
alderman ['ɔ:ldəmən] (pl -men [-mən]) n vereador
m.
ale [eɪl] n cerveja f.
alert [ə'lɜ:t] ◇ adj -1. [vigilant, aware] alerta; **to be**
~ **to sthg** estar alerta para algo -2. [perceptive]
atento(ta). ◇ n [warning] alerta f; **on the** ~
[watchful] em estado de alerta; **on** ~ MIL em estado
de alerta; **to give the** ~ dar o sinal de alerta.
◇ vt -1. [warn] alertar, avisar -2. [make aware]: **to**
~ **sb to sthg** alertar alguém sobre algo.
Aleutian Islands [ə'lu:ʃjən-] npl: **the** ~ as Ilhas
Aleutas.
A level (abbr of **Advanced level**) n SCH exame feito
ao final do ensino médio na Grã-Bretanha

Alexander technique n: **the** ~ a técnica de
Alexander.
Alexandria [,ælɪg'zɑ:ndrɪə] n Alexandria; **in** ~ em
Alexandria.
alfalfa [æl'fælfə] n alfalfa f.
alfresco [æl'freskəʊ] adj, adv [meal, eat] ao ar livre.
algae ['ældʒi:] npl algas fpl.
Algarve [æl'gɑ:v] n: **the** ~ o Algarve; **in the** ~ no
Algarve.
algebra ['ældʒɪbrə] n álgebra f.
Algeria [æl'dʒɪərɪə] n Argélia; **in** ~ na Argélia.
Algerian [æl'dʒɪərɪən] ◇ adj argelino(na). ◇ n
argelino m, -na f.
Algiers [æl'dʒɪəz] n Argel; **in** ~ em Argel.
algorithm ['ælgərɪðm] n algoritmo m.
alias ['eɪlɪəs] (pl -es) ◇ adv vulgo. ◇ n nome m
falso.
alibi ['ælɪbaɪ] n álibi m.
alien ['eɪljən] ◇ adj -1. [foreign] estrangeiro(ra) -2.
[from outer space] alienígena -3. [unfamiliar] estra-
nho(nha). ◇ n -1. [from outer space] alienígena mf
-2. JUR [foreigner] estrangeiro m, -ra f.
alienate ['eɪljəneɪt] vt [estrange] alienar.
alienation [,eɪljə'neɪʃn] n -1. [estrangement] afastamento m -2. [feeling of not belonging] alienação f.
alight [ə'laɪt] (pt & pp -ed OR alit) ◇ adj [on fire] em
chamas. ◇ vi fml -1. [land] pousar -2. [from train,
bus] descer; **to** ~ **from sthg** descer de algo.
align [ə'laɪn] vt -1. [line up] alinhar -2. [ally]: **to** ~ **o.s.**
with sb aliar-se a alguém.

alignment [ə'laɪnmənt] n -1. [of car wheels, brakes,
books] alinhamento m -2. [with an ally] aliança f.
alike [ə'laɪk] ◇ adj [two people, things] semelhante,
parecido(da). ◇ adv [in a similar way] de forma
semelhante; **they look** ~ eles são parecidos.
alimentary canal [,ælɪ'mentərɪ-] n tubo m digestivo.
alimony ['ælɪmənɪ] n pensão f (alimentícia).
A-line adj evasê.
alive [ə'laɪv] adj -1. [living] vivo(va); **to come** ~
ganhar vida -2. [aware]: **to be** ~ **to sthg** estar
consciente de algo -3. [full]: **to be** ~ **with sthg**
estar cheio(cheia) de algo, fervilhar de algo.
alkali ['ælkəlaɪ] (pl -s OR -es) n álcali m.
alkaline ['ælkəlaɪn] adj alcalino(na).
all [ɔ:l] ◇ adj -1. [with singular noun] todo(da); ~ **the**
money o dinheiro todo; ~ **the time** sempre; **we**
were out ~ **day** estivemos fora o dia inteiro. -2.
[with plural noun] todos(das); ~ **the houses** todas as
casas; ~ **trains stop at Trenton** todos os trens
param em Trenton. ◇ adv -1. [completely]
completamente; ~ **alone** completamente só. -2.
[in scores]: **it's two** ~ dois a dois (empate). -3. [in
phrases]: ~ **but empty** quase vazio(zia); ~ **over**
[finished] terminado(da). ◇ pron -1. [everything]
tudo; [people, things] todos mpl, -das fpl; **is that** ~?
[in store] mais alguma coisa?; **the best of** ~ o
melhor de todos. -2. [everybody] todos, todo o
mundo; ~ **of us went** fomos todos. -3. [in
phrases]: **can I help you at** ~ posso ajudar em
alguma coisa?; **in** ~ [in total] ao todo; **in** ~ **it was a**
great success resumindo, foi um grande êxito.
Allah ['ælə] n Alá m.
all-around adj US = **all-round**.
allay [ə'leɪ] vt fml -1. [calm] abrandar -2. [solve, settle]
dirimir.
all clear n -1. [signal] sinal de fim de estado de
alerta -2. fig [go-ahead] permissão f para prosseguir.
allegation [,ælɪ'geɪʃn] n alegação f; **to make** ~**s**
(about sb/sthg) fazer alegações (sobre alguém/
algo).
allege [ə'ledʒ] vt [claim] alegar; **to** ~ **that** alegar
que.
alleged [ə'ledʒd] adj suposto(ta).
allegedly [ə'ledʒɪdlɪ] adv supostamente.
allegiance [ə'li:dʒəns] n: ~ **(to sb/sthg)** lealdade
(a alguém/algo).
allegorical [,ælɪ'gɒrɪkl] adj alegórico(ca).
allegory ['ælɪgɒrɪ] (pl -ies) n alegoria f.
alleluia [,ælɪ'lu:jə] excl aleluia!
allergic [ə'lɜ:dʒɪk] adj alérgico(ca); ~ **to sthg** lit &
fig alérgico(ca) a algo.
allergy ['ælədʒɪ] (pl -ies) n alergia f; **to have an** ~
to sthg ter alergia a algo.
alleviate [ə'li:vɪeɪt] vt [ease] aliviar.
alley(way) ['ælɪ(weɪ)] n [narrow path] beco m.
alliance [ə'laɪəns] n -1. [agreement] acordo m -2. [un-
ion] aliança f.
allied ['ælaɪd] adj -1. [powers, troops] aliado(da) -2.
[related] relacionado(da).
alligator ['ælɪgeɪtə'] (pl inv OR -s) n aligátor m.
all-important adj [crucial] crucial.

all-in *adj UK* [price] tudo incluído.
➤ **all in** ⬦ *adj inf* [tired] exausto(ta). ⬦ *adv UK* [inclusive] com extras incluído.

all-in-one *n* [garment - underwear or for cycling] macaquinho *m*; [- top and trousers] macacão *m*.

all-in wrestling *n* luta *f* livre.

alliteration [ə,lɪtə'reɪʃn] *n* aliteração *f*.

all-night *adj* [party, vigil, session] que dura toda a noite; [chemist's, shop] 24 horas.

allocate ['æləkeɪt] *vt*: **to ~ sthg to sb/sthg** [money, resources, items] alocar algo para alguém/algo; [task] atribuir algo para alguém/algo.

allocation [,ælə'keɪʃn] *n* -**1.** [sharing out - of money, resources, items] alocação *f*; [- of task, responsibility] atribuição *f*- **2.** [share - of money, resources] alocação *f*; [- of tickets, seats, places] atribuição *f*.

allot [ə'lɒt] (*pt & pp* -**ted**, *cont* -**ting**) *vt* [allocate - task] distribuir; [- money, resources] repartir; [- time] dedicar.

allotment [ə'lɒtmənt] *n* -**1.** *UK* [garden] lote *m* -**2.** [sharing out - of tasks, resources] distribuição *f*; [- of money] partilha *f*; [- of time] dedicação *f*-**3.** [share - of money, resources] cota *f*; [- of time] alocação *f*.

all-out *adj* [effort] supremo(ma) ; [war] total ; [attack] resoluto(ta).

allow [ə'lau] *vt* -**1.** [permit] permitir; **to ~ sb to do sthg** permitir *OR* deixar alguém fazer algo; **~ me** permita-me, deixe-me -**2.** [allocate] destinar -**3.** [admit]: **to ~ (that)** admitir que.
➤ **allow for** *vt fus* levar em conta *OR* consideração.

allowable [ə'lauəbl] *adj* [acceptable] aceitável, permitido(da).

allowance [ə'lauəns] *n* -**1.** [grant] subsídio *m*, auxílio *m* -**2.** *Am* [pocket money] mesada *f*-**3.** *FIN* [tax exemption] isenção *f*-**4.** [excuse]: **to make ~s for sb/sthg** fazer concessões para alguém *OR* algo.

alloy ['ælɔɪ] *n* [metal] liga *f*.

all-powerful *adj* onipotente, todo-poderoso(sa).

all right ⬦ *adv* -**1.** [gen] bem -**2.** [indicating agreement] sim, o.k. -**3.** [do you understand?]: **all right?** certo? -**4.** [now then] certo, o.k. ⬦ *adj* -**1.** [healthy, unharmed]: **to be ~** estar bem -**2.** *inf* [acceptable, satisfactory]: **how was the film? - ~, I suppose** como foi o filme? - legal, imagino; **sorry I'm late - that's ~** desculpe, estou atrasada - não tem importância -**3.** [permitted]: **is it ~ if ...?** tudo bem se ...?, posso ...?

all-round *UK*, **all-around** *US adj* -**1.** [athlete, worker] versátil -**2.** [improvement] global.

all-rounder [-'raundə'] *n* -**1.** [versatile person] pessoa *f* versátil -**2.** *SPORT*: **he is an ~ at football** no futebol, ele se destaca em várias posições.

all-terrain vehicle *n* (veículo) *m* fora-de-estrada *m*.

all-time *adj* [record, best]: **it was an ~ record** foi um recorde insuperável; **one of the ~ greatest songs** uma das mais canções de todos os tempos.

allude [ə'luːd] *vi*: **to ~ to sthg** aludir a algo.

allure [ə'ljʊə'] *n* [attraction] fascinação *f*, encanto *m*.

alluring [ə'ljʊərɪŋ] *adj* [attractive] fascinante, encantador(ra).

allusion [ə'luːʒn] *n* [reference] alusão *f*.

ally [*n* 'ælaɪ, *vb* ə'laɪ] (*pl* -**ies**, *pt & pp* -**ied**) ⬦ *n* -**1.** *MIL & POL* aliado *m*, -da *f*-**2.** [associate, helper] associado *m*, -da *f*. ⬦ *vt*: **to ~ o.s. with sb** aliar-se a alguém.

almanac ['ɔːlmənæk] *n* [book] almanaque *m*.

almighty [ɔːl'maɪtɪ] *adj inf* [enormous] enorme.
➤ **Almighty** ⬦ *adj* onipotente. ⬦ *n*: **the Almighty** o Todo-Poderoso.

almond ['ɑːmənd] *n* -**1.** [nut] amêndoa *f*-**2.** [tree] amendoeira *f*.

almond paste *n* pasta *f* de amêndoas.

almost ['ɔːlməʊst] *adv* quase, praticamente.

alms [ɑːmz] *npl dated* esmola *f*.

aloft [ə'lɒft] *adv* -**1.** [in the air] no ar, nas alturas -**2.** *NAUT* no topo do mastro.

alone [ə'ləʊn] ⬦ *adj* [without others] só, sozinho (nha); **to be ~ with sb** estar a sós com alguém. ⬦ *adv* -**1.** [without others] só; **to go it ~** fazer algo por conta própria -**2.** [only] somente, só; **he knows the answer** só *OR* somente ele sabe a resposta -**3.** [untouched, unchanged]: **to leave sthg ~** deixar algo em paz, parar de mexer em algo; **leave me ~!** deixe-me em paz!
➤ **let alone** *conj* sem falar em.

along [ə'lɒŋ] ⬦ *adv*: **they went ~ to the demonstration** eles foram *OR* se dirigiram para a demonstração; **she insisted on coming ~** ela insistiu em vir junto *OR* também; **I took her ~ to the concert** levei-a comigo ao concerto. ⬦ *prep* -**1.** [from one end to the other] ao longo de -**2.** [beside] ao lado de, junto de -**3.** [in] em.
➤ **all along** *adv* o tempo todo.
➤ **along with** *prep* junto com.

alongside [ə,lɒŋ'saɪd] ⬦ *prep* [next to] junto a; [beside] ao lado de. ⬦ *adv* lado a lado.

aloof [ə'luːf] ⬦ *adj* [reserved] reservado(da). ⬦ *adv* [distant]: **to remain ~ (from sthg)** ficar indiferente (a algo).

aloud [ə'laʊd] *adv* alto, em voz alta.

alpaca [æl'pækə] *n* -**1.** [animal] alpaca *f*-**2.** [material] lã *f* de alpaca.

alphabet ['ælfəbet] *n* alfabeto *m*.

alphabetical [,ælfə'betɪkl] *adj* alfabético(ca); **in ~ order** em ordem alfabética.

alphabetically [,ælfə'betɪklɪ] *adv* alfabeticamente, em ordem alfabética.

alphabetize, -ise ['ælfəbətaɪz] *vt* alfabetizar.

alphanumeric key *n COMPUT* tecla *f* alfanumérica.

alpine ['ælpaɪn] *adj* alpino(na).

Alps [ælps] *npl*: **the ~** os Alpes; **in the ~** nos Alpes.

already [ɔːl'redɪ] *adv* já.

alright [,ɔːl'raɪt] *adv & adj* = **all right**.

Alsace [æl'sæs] *n* Alsácia; **in ~** na Alsácia.

Alsatian [æl'seɪʃn] ⬦ *adj* alsaciano(na). ⬦ *n* -**1.** [person] alsaciano *m*, -na *f* -**2.** [dog] pastor *m* alemão.

also ['ɔːlsəʊ] *adv* [as well] também.

also-ran *n* -**1.** [gen] perdedor *m*, -ra *f*-**2.** [horseracing] *cavalo que não chega entre os três primeiros.*

Alta *abbr of* **Alberta**.

altar ['ɔːltə'] *n* altar *m*.

alter ['ɔːltəʳ] ◇ vt [change, modify] alterar. ◇ vi alterar-se.

alteration [ˌɔːltəˈreɪʃn] n **-1.** [act of changing] alteração f, modificação f **-2.** [change] alteração f, mudança f; **to make an ~ or ~s to sthg** fazer uma alteração or alterações em algo.

altercation [ˌɔːltəˈkeɪʃn] n fml altercação f.

alter ego (pl -s) n alter ego m.

alternate [adj UK ɔːlˈtɜːnət, US ˈɔːltərnət, vb ˈɔːltərneɪt] ◇ adjalternado(da). ◇ vtalternar. ◇ vi: **to ~ (with)** alternar(com); **to ~ between sthg and sthg** alternar entre uma coisa e outra.

alternately [ɔːlˈtɜːnətlɪ] adv [by turns] alternadamente.

alternating current ['ɔːltəneɪtɪŋ-] n ELEC corrente f alternada.

alternation [ˌɔːltəˈneɪʃn] n alternação f, alternância f.

alternative [ɔːlˈtɜːnətɪv] ◇ adj alternativo(va). ◇ n alternativa f; **an ~ to sb/sthg** uma alternativa a alguém/algo; **to have no ~ (but to do sthg)** não ter alternativa (a não ser fazer algo).

alternatively [ɔːlˈtɜːnətɪvlɪ] adv por outro lado, de outro modo.

alternative medicine n medicina f alternativa.

alternator ['ɔːltəneɪtəʳ] n ELEC alternador m.

although [ɔːlˈðəʊ] conj embora, apesar de.

altitude ['æltɪtjuːd] n altitude f.

alto ['æltəʊ] (pl -s) ◇ n contralto m. ◇ comp [flute, saxophone] alto.

altogether [ˌɔːltəˈgeðəʳ] adv **-1.** [completely] completamente, totalmente **-2.** [in general] de modo geral, no geral **-3.** [in total] ao todo, no total.

altruism ['æltrʊɪzm] n altruismo m.

altruistic [ˌæltrʊˈɪstɪk] adj altruista.

aluminium UK [ˌæljʊˈmɪniəm], **aluminum** US [əˈluːmɪnəm] ◇ n alumínio m. ◇ comp de alumínio; **~ foil** papel-alumínio m.

alumnus [əˈlʌmnəs] (pl -ni [-naɪ]) n ex-aluno m, -na f.

always ['ɔːlweɪz] adv sempre.

am [æm] vb ▷ **be**.

a.m. (ante meridiem): **at three ~** às três da manhã.

AM (abbr of amplitude modulation) n **-1.** AM f. **-2.** (abbr of Master of Arts) (titular de) diploma de mestre em ciências humanas nos Estados Unidos.

AMA (abbr of American Medical Association) n associação norte-americana de médicos, ≈ AMB f.

amalgam [əˈmælgəm] n **-1.** fml [combination] amálgama m or f. **-2.** TECH [of metals] amálgama m or f.

amalgamate [əˈmælgəmeɪt] ◇ vt [unite] amalgamar, misturar. ◇ vi [unite] unir-se.

amalgamation [əˌmælgəˈmeɪʃn] n [process] amalgamação f.

amass [əˈmæs] vt [fortune, power, information] acumular.

amateur ['æmətəʳ] ◇ adj amador(ra). ◇ n amador m, -ra f.

amateurish [ˌæməˈtɜːrɪʃ] adj pej [unprofessional]

malfeito(ta), mal-acabado(da).

amaze [əˈmeɪz] vt [astonish] surpreender, assombrar.

amazed [əˈmeɪzd] adj surpreso(sa), assombrado(da).

amazement [əˈmeɪzmənt] n surpresa f, assombro m.

amazing [əˈmeɪzɪŋ] adj [incredible] incrível, surpreendente.

amazingly [əˈmeɪzɪŋlɪ] adv [very] surpreendentemente.

Amazon ['æməzn] n **-1.** [river]: **the ~** o Amazonas **-2.** [region]: **in the ~** na Amazônia; **the ~ (Basin)** a bacia amazônica; **the ~ rainforest** a floresta amazônica **-3.** [woman] amazona f.

Amazonian [ˌæməˈzəʊnjən] adj amazônico(ca).

ambassador [æmˈbæsədəʳ] n embaixador m, -ra f.

amber ['æmbəʳ] ◇ adj **-1.** [amber-coloured] ambárico(ca), ambariano(na) **-2.** UK [traffic light] amarelo(la). ◇ n **-1.** [substance] âmbar m **-2.** UK [colour of traffic light] amarelo m. ◇ comp [made of amber] de âmbar.

ambiance ['æmbɪəns] n = ambience.

ambidextrous [ˌæmbɪˈdekstrəs] adj ambidestro(tra).

ambience ['æmbɪəns] n [atmosphere] ambiente m, atmosfera f.

ambiguity [ˌæmbɪˈgjuːətɪ] (pl -ies) n ambigüidade f.

ambiguous [æmˈbɪgjʊəs] adj ambíguo(gua).

ambiguously [æmˈbɪgjʊəslɪ] adv de modo ambíguo.

ambition [æmˈbɪʃn] n ambição f.

ambitious [æmˈbɪʃəs] adj ambicioso(sa).

ambivalence [æmˈbɪvələns] n **-1.** [uncertainty] incerteza f **-2.** [ambiguity] ambivalência f.

ambivalent [æmˈbɪvələnt] adj **-1.** [uncertain] incerto(ta) **-2.** [ambiguous] ambivalente.

amble ['æmbl] vi [walk] passear.

ambulance ['æmbjʊləns] ◇ n ambulância f. ◇ comp [service, driver] de ambulância.

ambush ['æmbʊʃ] ◇ n emboscada f. ◇ vt [attack] emboscar.

ameba n US = amoeba.

ameliorate [əˈmiːljəreɪt] vt & vi fml melhorar.

amen [ˌɑːˈmen] excl [at end of prayer] amém!

amenable [əˈmiːnəbl] adj: **~ (to sthg)** receptivo(va) (a algo).

amend [əˈmend] vt [change] emendar, corrigir.

➡ **amends** npl: **to make ~s (for sthg)** compensar (por algo).

amendment [əˈmendmənt] n **-1.** [change] correção f **-2.** [act of changing] emenda f.

amenities [əˈmiːnətɪz] npl comodidades fpl, conforto m.

America [əˈmerɪkə] n América, Estados Unidos (da América); **in ~** na América, nos Estados Unidos (da América).

➡ **Americas** npl: **the ~s** as Américas, a América.

American [əˈmerɪkn] ◇ adj americano(na), estadunidense. ◇ n americano m, -na f, estadunidense mf.

American football *n UK* futebol *m* americano.

American Indian *n* ameríndio *m*.

Americanism [ə'merɪkənɪzm] *n* [word, phrase] americanismo *m*.

americanize, -ise [ə'merɪkənaɪz] *vt* americanizar.

amethyst ['æmɪθɪst] *n* ametista *f*.

Amex *n* (*abbr of* American Stock Exchange) *segunda maior bolsa de valores dos Estados Unidos.*

amiable ['eɪmjəbl] *adj* [pleasant, likable] amável.

amiably ['eɪmjəblɪ] *adv* amavelmente.

amicable ['æmɪkəbl] *adj* [friendly] amigável.

amicably ['æmɪkəblɪ] *adv* amigavelmente.

amid(st) [ə'mɪd(st)] *prep fml* [among] entre, no meio de.

amino acid [ə'mi:nəʊ-] *n* aminoácido *m*.

amiss [ə'mɪs] <> *adj* [wrong] errado(da). <> *adv* [wrongly]: **to take sthg ~** levar algo a mal.

Amman *n* Amã; **in ~** em Amã.

ammo ['æməʊ] *n inf* MIL munição *f*.

ammonia [ə'məʊnjə] *n* [liquid] amônia *f*; [gas] amoníaco *m*.

ammunition [,æmjʊ'nɪʃn] *n* **-1.** [bombs, bullets] munição *f* **-2.** *fig* [information, argument] argumento *m*.

ammunition dump *n* paiol *m*, depósito *m* de munição.

amnesia [æm'ni:zjə] *n* amnésia *f*.

amnesty ['æmnəstɪ] (*pl* -ies) *n* anistia *f*.

Amnesty International *n* Anistia *f* Internacional.

amniocentesis *n* amniocentese *f*.

amoeba *UK* (*pl* -bas OR -bae [-bi:]), **ameba** *US* (*pl* -bas OR -bae [-bi:]) [ə'mi:bə] *n* ameba *f*.

amok [ə'mɒk] *adv*: **to run ~** *correr cega e furiosamente com o intuito de matar.*

among(st) [ə'mʌŋ(st)] *prep* **-1.** [surrounded by, in middle of] no meio de, entre **-2.** [within, between, included in] entre.

amoral [,eɪ'mɒrəl] *adj* [person, behaviour] amoral.

amorous ['æmərəs] *adj* amoroso(sa).

amorphous [ə'mɔ:fəs] *adj* amorfo(fa).

amortize [ə'mɔ:taɪz] *vt* FIN amortizar.

amount [ə'maʊnt] *n* **-1.** [quantity] quantidade *f*, volume *m* **-2.** [sum of money] quantia *f*.

◆ amount to *vt fus* **-1.** [total] totalizar, atingir a quantia de **-2.** [be equivalent to] equivaler.

amp *n* **-1.** (*abbr of* ampere) A. **-2.** *fam* (*abbr of* amplifier) amplificador *m*.

amperage ['æmpərɪdʒ] *n* ELEC amperagem *f*.

ampere ['æmpeə'] *n* ampère *m*.

ampersand ['æmpəsænd] *n* ampersand *m* (*nome do sinal gráfico '&'*)

amphetamine [æm'fetəmi:n] *n* anfetamina *f*.

amphibian [æm'fɪbɪən] *n* anfíbio *m*.

amphibious [æm'fɪbɪəs] *adj* [animal, vehicle] anfíbio(bia).

amphitheatre *UK*, **amphitheater** *US* ['æmfɪ,θɪətə'] *n* anfiteatro *m*.

ample ['æmpl] *adj* **-1.** [enough] suficiente **-2.** [large] amplo(pla).

amplification [,æmplɪfɪ'keɪʃn] *n* **-1.** [of sound] amplificação *f* **-2.** [of idea, statement] ampliação *f*.

amplifier ['æmplɪfaɪə'] *n* [for radio, stereo] amplificador *m*.

amplify ['æmplɪfaɪ] (*pt* & *pp* -ied) <> *vt* **-1.** [sound] amplificar **-2.** [idea, statement] ampliar. <> *vi* [expand]: **to ~ (on sthg)** complementar (algo).

amply ['æmplɪ] *adv* **-1.** [sufficiently] amplamente **-2.** [considerably] consideravelmente.

ampoule *UK*, **ampule** *US* ['æmpu:l] *n* ampola *f*.

amputate ['æmpjʊteɪt] <> *vt* [limb] amputar. <> *vi* [perform amputation] amputar.

amputation [,æmpjʊ'teɪʃn] *n* amputação *f*.

Amsterdam [,æmstə'dæm] *n* Amsterdã; **in ~** em Amsterdã.

Amtrak ['æmtræk] *n empresa pública de trens mais importante dos Estados Unidos no transporte de passageiros.*

amuck [ə'mʌk] *adv* = amok.

amulet ['æmjʊlɪt] *n* amuleto *m*.

amuse [ə'mju:z] *vt* **-1.** [cause to laugh, smile] divertir **-2.** [entertain] entreter; **to ~ o.s. (by doing sthg)** entreter-se (fazendo algo).

amused [ə'mju:zd] *adj* **-1.** [entertained, delighted] divertido(da), entretido(da); **to be ~ at** OR **by sthg** estar entretido(da) com algo **-2.** [entertained]: **to keep o.s. ~** entreter-se.

amusement [ə'mju:zmənt] *n* **-1.** [enjoyment] divertimento *m* **-2.** [diversion, game] diversão *f*, entretenimento *m*.

amusement arcade *n* fliperama *m*.

amusement park *n* parque *m* de diversões.

amusing [ə'mju:zɪŋ] *adj* [funny] divertido(da).

an [stressed æn, unstressed ən] *indef art* ▷ **a**[2].

anabolic steroid [,ænə'bɒlɪk-] *n* esteróide *m* anabólico OR anabolizante.

anachronism [ə'nækrənɪzm] *n* anacronismo *m*.

anachronistic [ə,nækrə'nɪstɪk] *adj* anacrônico(ca).

anaemia *UK*, **anemia** *US* [ə'ni:mjə] *n* anemia *f*.

anaemic *UK*, **anemic** *US* [ə'ni:mɪk] *adj* [suffering from anaemia] anêmico(ca).

anaesthesia *UK*, **anesthesia** *US* [,ænɪs'θi:zjə] *n* anestesia *f*.

anaesthetic *UK*, **anesthetic** *US* [,ænɪs'θetɪk] *n* anestésico *m*; **under ~** anestesiado(da).

anaesthetist *UK*, **anesthetist** *US* [æ'ni:sθətɪst] *n* anestesista *mf*.

anaesthetize *UK*, **-ise** *UK*, **anesthetize** *US* [æ'ni:sθətaɪz] *vt* anestesiar.

anagram ['ænəgræm] *n* anagrama *m*.

anal ['eɪnl] *adj* anal.

analgesic [,ænæl'dʒi:sɪk] <> *adj* analgésico(ca). <> *n* analgésico *m*.

analog *adj* & *n US* = analogue.

analogous [ə'næləgəs] *adj fml* [comparable]: **~ (to sthg)** análogo OR semelhante (a algo).

analogue, analog *US* ['ænəlɒg] <> *adj* [watch, clock] analógico(ca). <> *n fml* [similar object, device] análogo *m*.

analogy [ə'nælədʒɪ] (*pl* -ies) *n* [similarity] analogia *f*; **to draw an ~ with/between** fazer uma analogia com/entre; **by ~** por analogia.

analyse *UK*, **analyze** *US* ['ænəlaɪz] *vt* [examine] analisar.

analysis [ə'næləsɪs] (*pl* **analyses** [ə'næləsiːz]) *n* **-1.** análise *f* **-2.** *phr:* **in the final** *OR* **last** ~ afinal de contas.

analyst ['ænəlɪst] *n* **-1.** [political, computer, statistics] analista *mf* **-2.** [psychoanalyst] psicanalista *mf.*

analytic(al) [,ænə'lɪtɪk(l)] *adj* [person, study, approach] analítico(ca).

analyze *vt US* = **analyse.**

anarchic [æ'nɑːkɪk] *adj* [lacking control] anárquico(ca).

anarchist ['ænəkɪst] *n* POL anarquista *mf.*

anarchy ['ænəkɪ] *n* [lawlessness, disorder] anarquia *f.*

anathema [ə'næθəmə] *n* [object of dislike, disapproval] anátema *m.*

anatomical [,ænə'tɒmɪkl] *adj* anatômico(ca).

anatomy [ə'nætəmɪ] (*pl* **-ies**) *n* anatomia *f.*

ANC (*abbr of* **African National Congress**) *n* Congresso *m* Nacional Africano.

ancestor ['ænsestə'] *n* **-1.** [person] ancestral *mf,* antepassado *m,* -da *f* **-2.** *fig* [of machine, vehicle] antecessor *m,* -ra *f.*

ancestral home [æn'sestrəl-] *n* casa *f* dos antepassados.

ancestry ['ænsestrɪ] (*pl* **-ies**) *n* linhagem *f.*

anchor ['æŋkə'] <> *n* **-1.** NAUT âncora *f;* **to drop/weigh** ~ lançar/içar âncora **-2.** TV [presenter] âncora *mf.* <> *vt* **-1.** [secure] assegurar **-2.** TV [present] apresentar. <> *vi* NAUT ancorar.

anchorage ['æŋkərɪdʒ] *n* **-1.** NAUT ancoradouro *m* **-2.** [means of securing] ancoragem *f.*

anchorman ['æŋkəmæn] (*pl* **-men** [-men]) *n* TV âncora *m.*

anchorwoman ['æŋkə,wʊmən] (*pl* **women** [-,wɪmɪn]) *n* TV âncora *f.*

anchovy ['æntʃəvɪ] (*pl inv OR* **-ies**) *n* anchova *f.*

ancient ['eɪnʃənt] *adj* **-1.** [dating from distant past] antigo(ga) **-2.** *hum* [very old] pré-histórico(ca).

ancillary [æn'sɪlərɪ] *adj* [staff, workers, device] auxiliar.

and [strong form ænd, weak form ənd, ən] *conj* **-1.** [as well as, in addition to] e **-2.** [in numbers] e **-3.** (*with infinitive*) [in order to]: **come** ~ **see!** venha ver!; **try** ~ **come!** tente vir!; **to wait** ~ **see** esperar para ver.
➡ **and all that** *adv* e (todas) essas coisas.
➡ **and so on, and so forth** *adv* e assim por diante.

Andes ['ændiːz] *n:* **the** ~ os Andes; **in** ~ nos Andes.

Andorra [æn'dɔːrə] *n* Andorra; **in** ~ em Andorra.

androgynous [æn'drɒdʒɪnəs] *adj* andrógino(na).

android ['ændrɔɪd] *n* andróide *mf.*

anecdote ['ænɪkdəʊt] *n* anedota *f.*

anemia *n US* = **anaemia.**

anemic *adj US* = **anaemic.**

anemone [ə'nemənɪ] *n* anêmona *f.*

anesthetic *etc n US* = **anaesthetic** etc.

anew [ə'njuː] *adv* novamente.

angel ['eɪndʒəl] *n* **-1.** RELIG anjo *m* **-2.** *fig inf* [delightful person] anjo *m.*

Angeleno [,ændʒə'liːnəʊ] *n habitante de ou nascido em Los Angeles.*

angelic [æn'dʒelɪk] *adj* angélico(ca).

anger ['æŋgə'] <> *n* raiva *f.* <> *vt* irritar, zangar.

angina [æn'dʒaɪnə] *n* angina *f.*

angle ['æŋgl] <> *n* **-1.** MATH ângulo *m* **-2.** [corner] canto *m,* ângulo *m* **-3.** [point of view] ângulo *m* **-4.** [slope] ladeira *f;* **at an** ~ [aslant] em ângulo. <> *vt* [slant] apresentar tendenciosamente. <> *vi* **-1.** [fish] pescar **-2.** [manoeuvre]: **to** ~ **for sthg** tramar para obter algo.

Anglepoise (lamp)® ['æŋglpɔɪz-] *n* luminária *f* de mesa (*flexível*).

angler ['æŋglə'] *n* pescador *m,* -ra *f* (de linha e anzol).

Anglican ['æŋglɪkən] <> *adj* anglicano(na). <> *n* anglicano *m,* -na *f.*

anglicism ['æŋglɪsɪzm] *n* anglicismo *m.*

angling ['æŋglɪŋ] *n* [fishing] pesca *f* (com linha e anzol).

Anglo- *prefix* anglo-.

Anglo-Saxon [,æŋgləʊ'sæksn] <> *adj* anglo-saxão(ônica). <> *n* **-1.** [person] anglo-saxão *m,* -ônica *f* **-2.** [language] anglo-saxão *m.*

Angola [æŋ'gəʊlə] *n* Angola; **in** ~ em Angola.

Angolan [æŋ'gəʊlən] <> *adj* angolano(na). <> *n* angolano *m,* -na *f.*

angora [æŋ'gɔːrə] *n* **-1.** [goat] angorá *f;* [rabbit] angorá *mf* **-2.** [material] angorá *m.*

angrily ['æŋgrəlɪ] *adv* com irritação *OR* raiva.

angry ['æŋgrɪ] (*compar* **-ier,** *superl* **-iest**) *adj* zangado(da), furioso(sa); **to be** ~ **(with sb)** estar zangado(da) (com alguém); **to get** ~ **(with sb)** zangar-se (com alguém).

angst [æŋst] *n* ânsia *f.*

anguish ['æŋgwɪʃ] *n* angústia *f.*

anguished ['æŋgwɪʃt] *adj* angustiado(da).

angular ['æŋgjʊlə'] *adj* [face, jaw, body] angular.

animal ['ænɪml] <> *adj* animal. <> *n* **-1.** [living creature] animal *m* **-2.** *inf pej* [brutal person] animal *m.*

animate ['ænɪmət] *adj* animado(da).

animated ['ænɪmeɪtɪd] *adj* animado(da).

animated cartoon *n* desenho *m* animado.

animation [,ænɪ'meɪʃn] *n* animação *f.*

animosity [,ænɪ'mɒsətɪ] (*pl* **-ies**) *n* animosidade *f.*

aniseed ['ænɪsiːd] *n* semente *f* de anis.

ankle ['æŋkl] <> *n* tornozelo *m.* <> *comp:* ~ **deep** até o tornozelo.

annals ['ænlz] *npl fml* anais *mpl.*

annex ['æneks] *vt* anexar.

annexation [,ænek'seɪʃn] *n* anexação *f.*

annexe ['æneks] *n* [building] anexo *m.*

annihilate [ə'naɪəleɪt] *vt* [destroy] aniquilar.

annihilation [ə,naɪə'leɪʃn] *n* [destruction] aniquilação *f.*

anniversary [,ænɪ'vɜːsərɪ] (*pl* **-ies**) *n* aniversário *m* (*de casamento, de independência, etc.*).

annotate ['ænəteɪt] *vt fml* comentar.

annotated *adj:* ~ **edition** edição *f* comentada.

announce [ə'naʊns] *vt* anunciar.

announcement [ə'naʊnsmənt] *n* [public statement] anúncio *m.*

announcer [ə'naʊnsə'] *n:* **television/radio** ~ locutor de televisão/rádio.

annoy [ə'nɔɪ] *vt* [irritate] irritar, amolar.

annoyance [ə'nɔɪəns] *n* irritação *f,* aborrecimento *m.*

annoyed [ə'nɔɪd] *adj* irritado(da); **to be** ~ **at sthg**

estar irritado(da) com algo; **to be ~ with sb** estar irritado(da) com alguém; **to get ~** irritar-se.
annoying [ə'nɔɪŋ] *adj* irritante.
annual ['ænjʊəl] <> *adj* anual. <> *n* -**1.** [plant] planta *f* sazonal - **2.** [book] anuário *m*, publicação *f* anual.
annual general meeting *n* reunião *f* geral anual.
annually ['ænjʊəlɪ] *adv* anualmente.
annuity [ə'njuːɪtɪ] (*pl* -**ies**) *n* FIN anuidade *m*.
annul [ə'nʌl] (*pt* & *pp* -**led**, *cont* -**ling**) *vt* anular, invalidar.
annulment [ə'nʌlmənt] *n* anulação *f*.
annum ['ænəm] *n*: **per ~** por ano.
Annunciation [ə,nʌnsɪ'eɪʃn] *n*: **the ~** a Anunciação.
anode ['ænəʊd] *n* TECH ânodo *m*.
anoint [ə'nɔɪnt] *vt* RELIG ungir.
anomalous [ə'nɒmələs] *adj fml* anômalo(la).
anomaly [ə'nɒməlɪ] (*pl* -**ies**) *n* [different thing, person] anomalia *f*.
anon. (*abbr of* anonymous) anônimo(ma).
anonymity [,ænə'nɪmətɪ] *n* anonimato *m*, anonímia *f*.
anonymous [ə'nɒnɪməs] *adj* anônimo(ma).
anonymously [ə'nɒnɪməslɪ] *adv* anonimamente.
anorak ['ænəræk] *n esp* UK anoraque *m*.
anorexia (nervosa) [,ænə'reksɪə(nɜː'vəʊsə)] *n* anorexia *f* nervosa.
anorexic [,ænə'reksɪk] <> *adj* anoréxico(ca). <> *n* anoréxico *m*, -ca *f*.
another [ə'nʌðə'] <> *adj* -**1.** [additional] outro(tra); **in ~ few minutes ...** dentro de alguns minutos ... - **2.** [different] outro(tra). <> *pron* -**1.** [an additional one] outro *m*, -tra *f*; **one after ~** um(a) depois do(da) outro(tra) - **2.** [a different one] outro *m*, -tra *f*; **to argue with one ~** discutir um com o outro/ uma com a outra; **to love one ~** amar-se.
ANSI (*abbr of* American National Standards Institute) *n* instituto norte-americano de padronização, ≃ ABNT *f*.
answer ['ɑːnsə'] <> *n* [reply] resposta *f*; **in ~ to sthg** em resposta a algo. <> *vt* -**1.** responder - **2.** [respond to]: **to ~ the door/phone** atender a porta/o telefone. <> *vi* [reply] responder.
   ◆ **answer back** <> *vt sep* retrucar. <> *vi* retrucar.
   ◆ **answer for** *vt fus* responder por.
answerable ['ɑːnsərəbl] *adj* [accountable] responsável; **~ to sb** adequado(da) a alguém; **~ for sthg** responsável por algo.
answering machine, answerphone ['ɑːnsərɪŋ-] *n* secretária *f* eletrônica.
ant [ænt] *n* formiga *f*.
antacid [,ænt'æsɪd] *n* antiácido *m*.
antagonism [æn'tægənɪzm] *n* antagonismo *m*.
antagonist [æn'tægənɪst] *n* antagonista *mf*.
antagonistic [æn,tægə'nɪstɪk] *adj* antagônico(ca).
antagonize, -ise [æn'tægənaɪz] *vt* hostilizar.
Antarctic [æn'tɑːktɪk] <> *n*: **the ~** o Antártico; **in the ~** no Antártico. <> *adj* antártico(ca).
Antarctica [æn'tɑːktɪkə] *n* Antártica *f*.

Antarctic Circle *n*: **the ~** o Círculo Polar Antártico.
Antarctic Ocean *n*: **the ~** o Oceano Antártico.
ante ['æntɪ] *n inf fig inf*: **to up** OR **raise the ~** jogar alto.
anteater ['ænt,iːtə'] *n* tamanduá *m*.
antecedent [,æntɪ'siːdənt] *n fml* [earlier event] antecedente *m*.
antediluvian [,æntɪdɪ'luːvjən] *adj hum* [outdated] antidiluviano(na).
antelope ['æntɪləʊp] (*pl inv* OR -**s**) *n* antílope *m*.
antenatal [,æntɪ'neɪtl] *adj* pré-natal.
antenatal clinic *n* clínica *f* pré-natal.
antenna [æn'tenə] (*pl sense 1* -**nae** [-niː], *pl sense 2* -**s**) *n* -**1.** [of insect, lobster] antena *f* - **2.** US [aerial] antena *f*.
anteroom ['æntɪrʊm] *n* -**1.** [antechamber] ante-sala *f* - **2.** [waiting room] sala *f* de espera.
anthem ['ænθəm] *n* [song, hymn] hino *m*.
anthill ['ænthɪl] *n* formigueiro *m*.
anthology [æn'θɒlədʒɪ] (*pl* -**ies**) *n* antologia *f*.
anthrax ['ænθræks] *n* antraz *m*.
anthropologist [,ænθrə'pɒlədʒɪst] *n* antropólogo *m*, -ga *f*.
anthropology [,ænθrə'pɒlədʒɪ] *n* antropologia *f*.
anti- ['æntɪ] *prefix* anti.
anti-aircraft [,æntɪ'eəkrɑːft] *adj* antiaéreo(a).
antiapartheid *adj* antiapartheid.
antiballistic missile [,æntɪbə'lɪstɪk-] *n* míssil *m* antibalístico.
antibiotic [,æntɪbaɪ'ɒtɪk] *n* [medicine] antibiótico *m*.
antibody ['æntɪ,bɒdɪ] (*pl* -**ies**) *n* BIOL anticorpo *m*.
anticipate [æn'tɪsɪpeɪt] *vt* -**1.** [expect, experience prematurely] prever - **2.** [preempt] antecipar-se a.
anticipation [æn,tɪsɪ'peɪʃn] *n* -**1.** [advance action] antecipação *f*; **thanking you in ~** antecipadamente grato(ta) - **2.** [expectation] expectativa *f*; **in ~ of** na expectativa de - **3.** [foresight] pressentimento *m*.
anticlimax [,æntɪ'klaɪmæks] *n* [disappointment] anticlímax *m*.
anticlockwise UK [,æntɪ'klɒkwaɪz] <> *adj* [direction] em sentido anti-horário. <> *adv* em sentido anti-horário.
antics ['æntɪks] *npl* -**1.** [of children, animals] palhaçadas *fpl* - **2.** *pej* [of politician etc] trapaças *fpl*.
anticyclone [,æntɪ'saɪkləʊn] *n* METEOR anticiclone *m*.
antidepressant [,æntɪdɪ'presnt] <> *adj* antidepressivo(va). <> *n* [drug] antidepressivo *m*.
antidote ['æntɪdəʊt] *n* -**1.** [drug, medicine] antídoto *m*; **~ to sthg** antídoto contra algo - **2.** *fig* [relief] antídoto.
antifreeze ['æntɪfriːz] *n* anticongelante *m*.
Antigua [æn'tiːgə] *n* Antígua; **in ~** em Antígua.
antihero ['æntɪ,hɪərəʊl] (*pl* -**es**) *n* [in literature] anti-herói *m*.
antihistamine [,æntɪ'hɪstəmɪn] <> *adj* anti-histamínico(ca). <> *n* anti-histamínico *m*.
antinuclear *adj* antinuclear.
antipathy [æn'tɪpəθɪ] *n* antipatia *f*; **~ to** OR **towards sb/sthg** antipatia por alguém/algo.
antipersonnel ['æntɪ,pɜːsə'nell] *adj* MIL contra pessoas.

antiperspirant [ˌæntɪˈpɜːspərənt] n desodorante m.

Antipodes [ænˈtɪpədiːz] npl: **the ~** as Antípodas (Austrália e Nova Zelândia).

antiquarian [ˌæntɪˈkweərɪən] ⬦ adj [bookshop, bookseller] de antiguidades. ⬦ n [antique collector] antiquário m.

antiquated [ˈæntɪkweɪtɪd] adj antiquado(da).

antique [ænˈtiːk] ⬦ adj [furniture, object] antigo(ga). ⬦ n [pece of furniture, object] antiguidade f.

antique dealer n antiquário m.

antique shop n loja f de antiguidades.

antiquity [ænˈtɪkwətɪ] (pl -ies) n antiguidade f.

anti-Semitic [-sɪˈmɪtɪk] adj anti-semita.

anti-Semitism [ˌæntɪˈsemɪtɪzm] n anti-semitismo m.

antiseptic [ˌæntɪˈseptɪk] ⬦ adj anti-séptico(ca). ⬦ n anti-séptico m.

antisocial [ˌæntɪˈsəʊʃl] adj anti-social.

antistatic [ˌæntɪˈstætɪk] adj antiestático(ca).

anti-tank adj MIL antitanque.

antithesis [ænˈtɪθɪsɪs] (pl -theses [-θɪsiːz]) n fml [direct opposite] antítese f.

antlers [ˈæntləz] npl cornos mpl.

antonym [ˈæntənɪm] n antônimo m.

Antrim n [county] Antrim; **in ~** em Antrim.

Antwerp [ˈæntwɜːp] n Antuérpia; **in ~** em Antuérpia.

anus [ˈeɪnəs] n ânus m.

anvil [ˈænvɪl] n bigorna f.

anxiety [æŋˈzaɪətɪ] (pl -ies) n -1. [worry] ansiedade f -2. [cause of worry] angústia f -3. [keenness] anseio m.

anxious [ˈæŋkʃəs] adj -1. [worried] preocupado(da); **to be ~ about sb/sthg** estar preocupado(da) com alguém/algo -2. [keen]: **to be ~ to do sthg** estar ansioso(sa) por fazer algo; **to be ~ that** estar ansioso(sa) para que.

anxiously [ˈæŋkʃəslɪ] adv -1. [nervously] nervosamente -2. [eagerly] ansiosamente.

any [ˈenɪ] ⬦ adj -1. (with negative) nenhum(ma); **I haven't got ~ money** não tenho dinheiro nenhum; **he never does ~ work** ele nunca faz trabalho algum -2. [some] (with sg n) algum(ma); (with pl n) alguns(mas); **can I be of ~ help?** posso ajudar (em algo)?; **have you got ~ money?** você tem algum dinheiro? -3. [no matter which] qualquer; **~ box will do** qualquer caixa serve. ⬦ pron -1. (with negative) nenhum(ma); **I didn't buy ~ of them** não comprei nenhum deles -2. [some] algum(ma); **do you have ~?** você tem (algum)?; **if ~** se é que algum -3. [no matter which one or ones] qualquer um (uma); **take ~ you like** pegue qualquer um que você queira. ⬦ adv -1. (with negative): **I don't want it ~ more** não quero mais isto; **I can't stand it ~ longer** não agüento mais isto -2. [some, a little] um pouco; **is that ~ better/different?** está um pouco melhor/diferente?

anybody [ˈenɪˌbɒdɪ] pron = **anyone**.

anyhow [ˈenɪhaʊ] adv -1. [in spite of that] assim mesmo -2. [carelessly] de qualquer jeito -3. [returning to topic in conversation] seja como for.

anyone [ˈenɪwʌn] pron -1. (in negative statements) alguém -2. (in questions) alguém -3. [someone]

alguém -4. [any person] qualquer pessoa.

anyplace adv US = **anywhere**.

anything [ˈenɪθɪŋ] pron -1. (in negative statements) nada -2. (in questions) algo -3. [something] algo, qualquer coisa -4. [any object, event] qualquer coisa.

➤ **anything but** adv: **he wasn't friendly when I saw him, ~ but** ele não foi amigável quando o vi, muito pelo contrário; **she was ~ but complimentary about my painting** ela não foi nada elogiosa sobre meus quadros.

anyway [ˈenɪweɪ] adv [in any case] de qualquer forma.

anywhere [ˈenɪweəʳ], **anyplace** US [ˈenɪpleɪs] adv -1. (in negative statements) nenhum lugar -2. (in questions) em/a algum lugar -3. [any place] (em) qualquer lugar -4. [unspecified amount, number] aproximadamente; **to last ~ from three weeks to two months** durar algo entre três semanas e dois meses.

Anzac (abbr of Australia–New Zealand Army Corps) n corporação de soldados australianos ou neozelandeses.

AOB, a.o.b. (abbr of any other business) questão que não foi incluída na pauta principal de uma reunião.

Apache [əˈpætʃɪ] n [native American] apache m.

apart [əˈpɑːt] adv -1. [separated in space] à parte, separadamente, distante; **we're living ~** estamos vivendo separados; **the houses were only a few yards ~ from each other** as casas ficavam a apenas algumas jardas de distância uma da outra; **I had to keep them ~** eu tinha que mantê-los à distância -2. [to pieces] em pedaços -3. [aside, excepted] à parte.

➤ **apart from** ⬦ prep [except for] exceto, a não ser (por). ⬦ conj [in addition to] além de.

apartheid [əˈpɑːtheɪt] n apartheid m.

apartment [əˈpɑːtmənt] n apartamento m.

apartment building n prédio m de apartamentos.

apathetic [ˌæpəˈθetɪk] adj apático(ca).

apathy [ˈæpəθɪ] n apatia f.

APB (abbr of all points bulletin) n US mensagem de rádio da polícia sobre pessoa que está sendo procurada.

ape [eɪp] ⬦ n [animal] macaco m, -ca f. ⬦ vt pej [imitate] imitar.

Apennines [ˈæpɪnaɪnz] npl: **the ~** os Apeninos.

aperitif [əperəˈtiːf] n aperitivo m.

aperture [ˈæpəˌtjʊəʳ] n abertura f.

apex [ˈeɪpeks] (pl -es OR apices) n [top] ápice m.

Apex (abbr of advance purchase excursion) n UK passagem comprada com antecedência e que oferece descontos.

aphid [ˈeɪfɪd] n pulgão m.

aphorism [ˈæfərɪzm] n aforismo m.

aphrodisiac [ˌæfrəˈdɪzɪæk] ⬦ adj afrodisíaco(ca). ⬦ n afrodisíaco m.

apices [ˈeɪpɪsiːz] pl ➤ **apex**.

apiece [əˈpiːs] adv [each] cada.

aplomb [əˈplɒm] n [composure] compostura f.

apocalypse [əˈpɒkəlɪps] n apocalípse m.

apocalyptic [əˌpɒkəˈlɪptɪk] *adj* apocalíptico(ca).
apogee [ˈæpədʒiː] *n fig* & *fml* [peak] apogeu *m*.
apolitical [ˌeɪpəˈlɪtɪkəl] *adj* [non-political] apolítico (ca).
apologetic [əˌpɒləˈdʒetɪk] *adj* arrependido(da); **to be ~ about sthg** estar arrependido(da) em relação a algo, desculpar-se por algo.
apologetically [əˌpɒləˈdʒetɪklɪ] *adv* em tom de desculpas.
apologize, -ise [əˈpɒlədʒaɪz] *vi* [say sorry]: **to ~ to sb for sthg** pedir desculpas a alguém por algo.
apology [əˈpɒlədʒɪ] (*pl* -ies) *n* [spoken, written] desculpa *f*.
apoplectic [ˌæpəˈplektɪk] *adj* -1. MED apoplético(ca) -2. *inf* [very angry] furioso(sa).
apoplexy [ˈæpəpleksɪ] *n* MED apoplexia *f*.
apostle [əˈpɒsl] *n* RELIG apóstolo *m*.
apostrophe [əˈpɒstrəfɪ] *n* GRAMM apóstrofe *f*.
appal (UK *pt* & *pp* -led, *cont*-ling), **appall** US [əˈpɔːl] *vt* [shock deeply] horrorizar.
Appalachian [ˌæpəˈleɪtʃən] *n*: the **~s** os Apalaches; the **~ Mountains** os Montes Apalache.
appall *vt* US = appal.
appalled [əˈpɔːld] *adj* horrorizado(da).
appalling [əˈpɔːlɪŋ] *adj* -1. [shocking] espantoso(sa) -2. *inf* [very bad] terrível.
appallingly [əˈpɔːlɪŋlɪ] *adv* -1. [shockingly] espantosamente -2. *inf* [very badly] terrivelmente.
apparatus [ˌæpəˈreɪtəs] (*pl inv* OR -es) *n* -1. [equipment] aparelho *m* -2. [system, organization] organização *f*.
apparel [əˈpærəl] *n* US traje *m*.
apparent [əˈpærənt] *adj* aparente; **for no ~ reason** sem nenhuma razão aparente.
apparently [əˈpærəntlɪ] *adv* aparentemente.
apparition [ˌæpəˈrɪʃn] *n fml* [ghost] aparição *f*.
appeal [əˈpiːl] <> *vi* -1. [request] apelar; **to ~ to sb for sthg** apelar a alguém por algo -2. [to sb's honour, common sense]: **to ~ to sthg** apelar para algo -3. [contest a decision or verdict] recorrer; **to ~ against sthg** recorrer contra algo -4. [attract, interest]: **to ~ to (sb)** agradar a alguém. <> *n* -1. [request] apelo *m* -2. [contesting a decision or verdict] apelação *m* -3. [charm, interest] encanto *m*.
appealing [əˈpiːlɪŋ] *adj* [attractive] encantador(ra).
appear [əˈpɪəʳ] <> *vi* -1. [become visible, of person] aparecimento *m*; [- of object] chegada *f*; [- of rash etc. on skin] surgimento *m*; **to make an ~** aparecer; **to put in an ~** marcar presença -3. [outward aspect] aparência *f*; **to keep up ~s** manter as aparências; **by** OR **to all ~s** a julgar pelas aparências -4. [bodily features] aspecto *m* -5. [in play, film, on TV] participação *f*.
appease [əˈpiːz] *vt* -1. [placate] apaziguar -2. [satisfy] saciar.
appeasement [əˈpiːzmənt] *n* -1. [placating, pol] apaziguamento *m*, conciliação *f* -2. [satisfaction] satisfação *f*.

append [əˈpend] *vt fml* [add]: **to ~ sthg (to sthg)** anexar algo a algo.
appendage [əˈpendɪdʒ] *n* anexo *m*.
appendices [əˈpendɪsiːz] *pl* ▷ **appendix**.
appendicitis [əˌpendɪˈsaɪtɪs] *n* apendicite *f*.
appendix [əˈpendɪks] (*pl* -dixes OR -dices) *n* apêndice *m*; **to have one's ~ out** OR **removed** sofrer a remoção do apêndice.
appertain *vi fml*: **to ~ to sthg** ser pertinente a algo.
appetite [ˈæpɪtaɪt] *n* -1. [for food] apetite *m*; **~ for sthg** desejo por algo -2. *fig* [enthusiasm]: **~ for sthg** gosto por algo.
appetizer, -iser [ˈæpɪtaɪzəʳ] *n* [food] entrada *f*; [drink] aperitivo *m*.
appetizing, -ising [ˈæpɪtaɪzɪŋ] *adj* [food] apetitoso(sa).
applaud [əˈplɔːd] <> *vt* -1. [clap for] aplaudir -2. *fig* [approve] aplaudir. <> *vi* [clap] aplaudir.
applause [əˈplɔːz] *n* aplauso *m*.
apple [ˈæpl] *n* maçã *f*; **to be the ~ of sb's eye** ser a menina dos olhos de alguém.
apple pie *n* torta *f* de maçã.
apple tree *n* macieira *f*.
appliance [əˈplaɪəns] *n* [device] utensílio *m*.
applicable [əˈplɪkəbl] *adj* apropriado(da); **~ to sb/sthg** apropriado(da) a alguém/algo.
applicant [ˈæplɪkənt] *n* candidato *m*, -ta *f*; **~ for sthg** [job] candidato(ta) a algo; [state benefit] pretendente a algo *m*.
application [ˌæplɪˈkeɪʃn] *n* -1. [gen] aplicação *f* -2. [for job, college, club] inscrição *f*; **~ for sthg** inscrição para algo -3. COMPUT aplicativo *m*.
application form *n* ficha *f* de inscrição.
applicator [ˈæplɪkeɪtəʳ] *n* aplicador *m*.
applied [əˈplaɪd] *adj* [science] aplicado(da).
appliqué [əˈpliːkeɪ] *n* SEWING aplique *m*.
apply [əˈplaɪ] (*pt* & *pp* -ied) <> *vt* -1. [rule, skill] aplicar; **to ~ o.s. (to sthg)** dedicar-se a algo; **to ~ one's mind to sthg** concentrar-se em algo -2. [paint, ointment] aplicar -3. [brakes] usar. <> *vi* -1. [for work, grant] candidatar-se; **to ~ for sthg** candidatar-se a algo; **to ~ to sb for sthg** recorrer a alguém para algo -2. [be relevant] aplicar-se; **to ~ to sb/sthg** aplicar-se a alguém/algo.
appoint [əˈpɔɪnt] *vt* -1. [to job, position] nomear; **to ~ sb to/as sthg** nomear alguém para/como algo -2. *fml* [time, place] marcar.
appointment [əˈpɔɪntmənt] *n* -1. (U) [to job, position] nomeação *f*; **'by ~ to Her Majesty the Queen'** 'por indicação de Sua Majestade, a Rainha' -2. [job, position] posição *f* -3. [with doctor, hairdresser, in business] hora *f* marcada; **to have an ~** ter uma hora marcada; **to make an ~** marcar uma hora; **by ~** com hora marcada; **the doctor only sees patients by ~** o médico só atende (pacientes) com hora marcada.
apportion [əˈpɔːʃn] *vt* [money, blame] dividir.
apposite [ˈæpəzɪt] *adj fml* apropriado(da).
appraisal [əˈpreɪzl] *n* [report, opinion] apreciação *f*.
appraise [əˈpreɪz] *vt fml* [evaluate] apreciar.
appreciable [əˈpriːʃəbl] *adj* [noticeable] apreciável.

appreciably [ə'priːʃəblɪ] *adv* [noticeably] visivelmente.

appreciate [ə'priːʃɪeɪt] ◇ *vt* -**1.** [value] valorizar -**2.** [recognize, understand] reconhecer -**3.** [be grateful for] reconhecer. ◇ *vi FIN* [increase in value] valorizar.

appreciation [ə,priːʃɪ'eɪʃn] *n* -**1.** *(U)* [liking] apreciação *m* -**2.** *(U)* [recognition, understanding] reconhecimento *f* -**3.** *(U)* [gratitude] gratidão *m* -**4.** *FIN* [increase in value] valorização *f* -**5.** [assessment] avaliação *f*.

appreciative [ə'priːʃjətɪv] *adj* apreciativo(va).

apprehend [,æprɪ'hend] *vt fml* [arrest] deter.

apprehension [,æprɪ'henʃn] *n* [anxiety] apreensão *f*.

apprehensive [,æprɪ'hensɪv] *adj* [anxious]: ~ **(about sthg)** apreensivo(va) com algo.

apprehensively [,æprɪ'hensɪvlɪ] *adv* apreensivamente.

apprentice [ə'prentɪs] ◇ *n* [trainee] aprendiz *mf*, estagiário(ria). ◇ *vt*: **to be ~d to sb** tornar-se aprendiz de alguém.

apprenticeship [ə'prentɪʃɪp] *n* estágio *m*.

appro. (*abbr of* **approval**) *n fam*: **on** ~ sujeito(ta) à aprovação.

approach [ə'prəʊtʃ] ◇ *n* -**1.** [arrival] chegada *f* -**2.** [way in, access] acesso *m* -**3.** [method] abordagem *m* -**4.** [proposal]: **to make an** ~ **to sb** fazer uma proposta a alguém. ◇ *vt* -**1.** [come near to] aproximar-se de -**2.** [speak to]: **to** ~ **sb about sthg** abordar alguém sobre algo; *COMM* sondar alguém sobre algo -**3.** [deal with] abordar -**4.** [approximate, reach] alcançar. ◇ *vi* aproximar-se.

approachable [ə'prəʊtʃəbl] *adj* acessível.

approaching [ə'prəʊtʃɪŋ] *adj* [in time] próximo(ma) ; [in space] que se aproxima.

approbation [,æprə'beɪʃn] *n fml* [approval] sanção *f*.

appropriate [*adj* ə'prəʊprɪət, *vb* ə'prəʊprɪeɪt] ◇ *adj* [suitable] apropriado(da). ◇ *vt* -**1.** [steal] apropriar-se de -**2.** [allocate] destinar.

appropriately [ə'prəʊprɪətlɪ] *adv* adequadamente.

appropriation [ə,prəʊprɪ'eɪʃn] *n* -**1.** [stealing] apropriação *f* -**2.** [allocation] alocação *f*.

approval [ə'pruːvl] *n* -**1.** [liking, admiration] aprovação *f* -**2.** [official agreement] sanção *f* -**3.** *COMM*: **on** ~ sob condição.

approve [ə'pruːv] ◇ *vi*: **to** ~ **(of sb/sthg)** ser a favor de alguém/algo. ◇ *vt* [ratify] aprovar.

approved [ə'pruːvd] *adj* aprovado(da).

approving [ə'pruːvɪŋ] *adj* [favourable] favorável.

approx. (*abbr of* **approximately**) aprox.

approximate [*adj* ə'prɒksɪmət, *vb* ə'prɒksɪmeɪt] ◇ *adj* aproximado(da). ◇ *vi*: **to** ~ **to sthg** aproximar-se de algo.

approximately [ə'prɒksɪmətlɪ] *adv* aproximadamente.

approximation [ə,prɒksɪ'meɪʃn] *n* -**1.** [estimate] aproximação *f* -**2.** [similar thing]: ~ **(to sthg)** semelhança com algo.

Apr. (*abbr of* **April**) abr.

APR *n* -**1.** (*abbr of* **annualized percentage rate**) taxa *f* de juros anual. -**2.** (*abbr of* **annual purchase rate**) taxa *f* de aquisição anual.

après-ski [,æpreɪ'skiː] *n* après-ski *m*, *entretenimento noturno e atividades sociais que ocorrem nos lugares em que se costuma ir esquiar*.

apricot ['eɪprɪkɒt] ◇ *n* -**1.** [fruit] damasco *m* -**2.** [colour] laranja claro *m*. ◇ *comp* de damasco.

apricot tree *n* damasqueiro *m*.

April ['eɪprəl] *n* abril *m*; *see also* **September**.

April Fools' Day *n* primeiro *m* de abril.

APRIL FOOLS' DAY

Assim como no Brasil, também na Grã-Bretanha e nos Estados Unidos é costume pregar peças em amigos e conhecidos no 1º de abril. Nessa data, até mesmo os jornais mais sérios e as estações de rádio e TV brincam com seus leitores, ouvintes e espectadores, divulgando notícias falsas.

---

apron ['eɪprən] *n* -**1.** [clothing] avental *m*; **to be tied to sb's** ~ **strings** *inf* estar preso(sa) à saia de alguém -**2.** *AERON* pátio *m* de manobras.

apropos ['æprəpəʊ] *fml* ◇ *adj* [pertinent] concernente. ◇ *prep*: ~ **(of)** a propósito de.

apt [æpt] *adj* -**1.** [pertinent] adequado(da) -**2.** [likely]: **to be** ~ **to do sthg** costumar fazer algo.

Apt. (*abbr of* **apartment**) apto.

aptitude ['æptɪtjuːd] *n* [skill] aptidão *f*; **to have an** ~ **for sthg** ter aptidão para algo.

aptitude test *n* teste *m* de aptidão.

aptly ['æptlɪ] *adv* [suitably] apropriadamente.

aqualung ['ækwəlʌŋ] *n* aqualung *m*.

aquamarine [,ækwəmə'riːn] *n* [colour] azul-turquesa *m*.

aquaplane ['ækwəpleɪn] *vi UK AUT* aquaplanar.

aquarium [ə'kweərɪəm] (*pl* -**riums** OR -**ria** [-rɪə]) *n* aquário *m*.

Aquarius [ə'kweərɪəs] *n* -**1.** [sign] Aquário *m* -**2.** [person] aquariano *m*, -na *f*.

aquatic [ə'kwætɪk] *adj* aquático(ca).

aqueduct ['ækwɪdʌkt] *n* aqueduto *m*.

AR *abbr of* **Arkansas**.

ARA (*abbr of* **Associate of the Royal Academy**) *n* membro associado da Royal Academy, *academia real britânica de artes*.

Arab ['ærəb] ◇ *adj* árabe. ◇ *n* [person, horse] árabe *mf*.

Arabia [ə'reɪbjə] *n* Arábia; **in** ~ na Arábia.

Arabian [ə'reɪbjən] ◇ *adj* árabe. ◇ *n* [person] árabe *mf*.

Arabian desert *n*: **the** ~ o deserto da Arábia.

Arabian Peninsula *n*: **the** ~ a Península Arábica.

Arabian Sea *n*: **the** ~ o Mar das Arábias.

Arabic ['ærəbɪk] ◇ *adj* arábico(ca). ◇ *n* [language] arábico *m*.

Arabic numeral *n* algarismo *m* arábico.

arable ['ærəbl] *adj* cultivável.

Arab League *n*: **the** ~ a Liga Árabe.

arbiter ['ɑːbɪtə[r]] *n fml* [judge] árbitro *m*.

arbitrary ['ɑːbɪtrərɪ] *adj* [random] arbitrário(ria).

arbitrate ['ɑːbɪtreɪt] *vi* arbitrar.

arbitration [ˌɑːbɪ'treɪʃn] n arbitragem f; **to go to ~** ir à arbitragem.

arc [ɑːk] n [curve] arco m.

ARC (abbr of **AIDS-related complex**) n ARC m, complexo m relacionado à AIDS.

arcade [ɑː'keɪd] n arcada f.

arch [ɑːtʃ] <> adj [knowing] travesso(sa). <> n arco m. <> vt [back, eyebrow] arquear. <> vi arquear-se.

arch- [ɑːtʃ] prefix [chief] arqui.

archaeological [ˌɑːkɪə'lɒdʒɪkl] adj arqueológico(-ca).

archaeologist [ˌɑːkɪ'ɒlədʒɪst] n arqueólogo m, -ga f.

archaeology [ˌɑːkɪ'ɒlədʒɪ] n arqueologia f.

archaic [ɑː'keɪɪk] adj **-1.** [ancient] arcaico(ca) **-2.** [old-fashioned] antiquado(da).

archangel ['ɑːkˌeɪndʒəl] n arcanjo m.

archbishop [ˌɑːtʃ'bɪʃəp] n arcebispo m.

archduchess [ˌɑːtʃ'dʌtʃɪs] n arquiduquesa f.

archduke [ˌɑːtʃ'djuːk] n arquiduque m.

arched [ɑːtʃt] adj **-1.** ARCHIT em arco **-2.** [curved] arqueado(da).

archenemy [ˌɑːtʃ'enɪmɪ] (pl **-ies**) n arqui-inimigo m, -ga f.

archeology etc [ˌɑːkɪ'ɒlədʒɪ] n = **archaeology etc.**

archer ['ɑːtʃəʳ] n arqueiro m.

archery ['ɑːtʃərɪ] n arco-e-flecha m.

archetypal [ˌɑːkɪ'taɪpl] adj [typical] arquetípico(ca).

archetype ['ɑːkɪtaɪp] n arquétipo m.

archipelago [ˌɑːkɪ'pelɪgəʊ] (pl **-es** OR **-s**) n arquipélago m.

architect ['ɑːkɪtekt] n **-1.** [of buildings] arquiteto m, -ta f **-2.** fig [of plan, event] idealizador m, -ra f.

architectural [ˌɑːkɪ'tektʃərəl] adj arquitetônico(-ca).

architecture ['ɑːkɪtektʃəʳ] n arquitetura f.

archive file ['ɑːkaɪv-] n COMPUT arquivo m armazenado.

archives ['ɑːkaɪvz] npl [of documents] arquivo m.

archivist ['ɑːkɪvɪst] n arquivista mf.

archway ['ɑːtʃweɪ] n passagem f em arco.

Arctic ['ɑːktɪk] <> adj **-1.** GEOGR ártico(ca) **-2.** inf [very cold] gélido(da). <> n: **the ~** o Ártico; **in the ~** no Ártico.

Arctic Circle n: **the ~** o Círculo Polar Ártico.

Arctic Ocean n: **the ~** o Oceano Ártico.

ardent ['ɑːdənt] adj [passionate] ardente.

ardour UK, **ardor** US ['ɑːdəʳ] n [zeal] ardor m.

arduous ['ɑːdjʊəs] adj [difficult] árduo(a).

are [stressed ɑːʳ, unstressed əʳ] (cf **a, an**) vb ⊳**be.**

area ['eərɪə] n **-1.** [gen] área f; **in the ~** na área **-2.** fig [approximate size, number]: **in the ~ of** ao redor de.

area code n US código m de área.

arena [ə'riːnə] n **-1.** SPORT estádio m **-2.** fig [area of activity] área f.

aren't [ɑːnt] = **are not.**

Argentina [ˌɑːdʒən'tiːnə] n Argentina; **in ~** na Argentina.

Argentine ['ɑːdʒəntaɪn], **Argentinian** <> adj argentino(na). <> n [person] argentino m, -na f.

arguable ['ɑːgjʊəbl] adj [questionable] questionável.

arguably ['ɑːgjʊəblɪ] adv indubitavelmente.

argue ['ɑːgjuː] <> vi **-1.** [quarrel] discutir; **to ~ (with sb about sthg)** discutir (com alguém sobre algo) **-2.** [reason] argumentar; **to ~ for/against sthg** argumentar a favor/contra algo. <> vt [case, point] afirmar; **to ~ that** afirmar que.

argument ['ɑːgjʊmənt] n **-1.** [quarrel] discussão f; **to have an ~ (with sb)** ter uma discussão (com alguém) **-2.** [reason] argumento m **-3.** [reasoning] argumentação f.

argumentative [ˌɑːgjʊ'mentətɪv] adj questionador(ra).

aria ['ɑːrɪə] n ária f.

arid ['ærɪd] adj **-1.** [land] árido(da) **-2.** fig [subject, writing] árido(da).

Aries ['eəriːz] n **-1.** [sign] Áries f **-2.** [person] ariano(-na).

arise [ə'raɪz] (pt **arose**, pp **arisen** [ə'rɪzn]) vi [appear] surgir; **to ~ from sthg** surgir de algo; **if the need ~s** se houver necessidade.

aristocracy [ˌærɪ'stɒkrəsɪ] (pl **-ies**) n aristocracia f.

aristocrat [UK 'ærɪstəkræt, US ə'rɪstəkrætl] n aristocrata mf.

aristocratic [UK ˌærɪstə'krætɪk, US əˌrɪstə'krætɪk] adj aristocrático(ca).

arithmetic [ə'rɪθmətɪk] <> adj aritmético(ca). <> n aritmética f.

Arizona [ˌærɪ'zəʊnə] n Arizona; **in ~** no Arizona.

ark [ɑːk] n [ship] arca f.

Arkansas ['ɑːkənsɔː] n Arkansas; **in ~** no Arkansas.

arm [ɑːm] <> n **-1.** [of person] braço m; **~ in ~** de braços dados; **to keep sb at ~'s length** fig manter alguém à distância; **to welcome sb/sthg with open ~s** fig receber alguém/algo de braços abertos; **to twist sb's ~** fig forçar alguém a fazer algo; **to cost an ~ and a leg** fig custar os olhos da cara **-2.** [of garment] manga f **-3.** [of chair] braço m **-4.** [of organization] ramo m. <> vt [with weapons] armar.
   ➦ **arms** npl [weapons] armas fpl; **to take up ~s** pegar em armas; **to be up in ~s (about sthg)** estar furioso(sa) em relação a algo.

armada [ɑː'mɑːdə] n [fleet of boats, ships] armada f.

armadillo [ˌɑːmə'dɪləʊ] (pl **-s**) n tatu m.

Armageddon [ˌɑːmə'gednl n armagedom m.

armaments ['ɑːməmənts] npl [weapons] armamento m.

armband ['ɑːmbænd] n braçadeira f.

armchair ['ɑːmtʃeəʳ] n poltrona f.

armed [ɑːmd] adj **-1.** [with weapon] armado(da) **-2.** fig [with information]: **~ with sthg** munido(da) de algo.

armed forces npl forças fpl armadas.

armed robbery n roubo m a mão armada.

Armenia [ɑː'miːnjə] n Armênia; **in ~** na Armênia.

Armenian [ɑː'miːnjən] <> adj armênio(a). <> n **-1.** [person] armênio m, -a f **-2.** [language] armênio m.

armhole ['ɑːmhəʊl] n cava f.

armistice ['ɑːmɪstɪs] n armistício m.

armour UK, **armor** US ['ɑːməʳ] n **-1.** [for person] armadura f **-2.** [for military vehicle] blindagem f.

armoured *UK*, **armored** *US* ['ɑːməd] *adj MIL* blindado(da).

armoured car [ɑːməd-] *n MIL* carro *m* blindado.

armour-plated [-'pleɪtɪd] *adj MIL* blindado(da).

armoury *UK* (*pl* -ies), **armory** *US* (*pl* -ies) ['ɑːmərɪ] *n* arsenal *m*.

armpit ['ɑːmpɪt] *n* axila *f*.

armrest ['ɑːmrest] *n* braço *m*.

arms control ['ɑːmz-] *n* controle *m* armamentista.

army ['ɑːmɪ] (*pl* -ies) *n* -**1**. *MIL* exército *m* -**2**. *fig* [large group] exército *m*.

A road *n UK* rodovia principal.

aroma [ə'rəʊmə] *n* [smell] aroma *m*.

aromatherapy [ərəʊmə'θerəpɪ] *n* aromaterapia *f*.

aromatic [,ærə'mætɪk] *adj* aromático(ca).

arose [ə'rəʊz] *pt* ▷ **arise**.

around [ə'raʊnd] ◇ *adv* -**1**. [about, around] por aí -**2**. [on all sides] ao redor -**3**. [in circular movement] ao redor -**4**. *phr*: **to have been** ~ *inf* ter experiência. ◇ *prep* -**1**. [encircling] ao redor de -**2**. [through, throughout] por todo(da) -**3**. [near] perto -**4**. [approximately] cerca de.

arousal [ə'raʊzl] *n (U)* [of feelings, emotions] despertar *m*.

arouse [ə'raʊz] *vt* -**1**. [excite - feeling] provocar; [- person] estimular -**2**. [wake] despertar.

arrange [ə'reɪndʒ] *vt* -**1**. [flowers, books, furniture] arrumar -**2**. [event, meeting, party] organizar; **to** ~ **to do sthg** combinar para fazer algo; **to** ~ **sthg for sb** arranjar algo para alguém; **to** ~ **for sb to do sthg** combinar com alguém para que faça algo -**3**. *MUS* fazer um arranjo.

arranged marriage [ə'reɪndʒd-] *n* casamento *m* arranjado.

arrangement [ə'reɪndʒmənt] *n* -**1**. [agreement] acordo *m*; **to come to an** ~ chegar a um acordo -**2**. [of objects] arranjo *m*; **flower** ~ arranjo de flores -**3**. *MUS* arranjo *m*.
➡ **arrangements** *npl* providências *fpl*; **to make** ~**s** tomar providências.

array [ə'reɪ] ◇ *n* -**1**. [of objects, people, ornaments] série *f* -**2**. *COMPUT* array *m*. ◇ *vt* [ornaments] enfeitar.

arrears [ə'rɪəz] *npl* [money owed] dívida *f*; **in** ~ [retrospectively] retroativamente; [late] em atraso.

arrest [ə'rest] ◇ *n* [by police] prisão *f*; **under** ~ preso(sa). ◇ *vt* -**1**. [subj: police] prender -**2**. *fml* [sb's attention] prender -**3**. *fml* [stop] deter.

arresting [ə'restɪŋ] *adj* [striking] impressionante.

arrival [ə'raɪvl] *n* [gen] chegada *f*; **late** ~ [of train, bus, mail] chegada atrasada; **new** ~ [person] recém-chegado(da); [baby] recém-nascido(da).

arrive [ə'raɪv] *vi* -**1**. [gen] chegar; **to** ~ **at a conclusion/decision** chegar a uma conclusão/decisão -**2**. [baby] nascer.

arrogance ['ærəgəns] *n* arrogância *f*.

arrogant ['ærəgənt] *adj* arrogante.

arrogantly ['ærəgəntlɪ] *adv* presunçosamente.

arrow ['ærəʊ] *n* -**1**. [weapon] flecha *f* -**2**. [symbol] seta *f*.

arrowroot *n* araruta *f*.

arse [*UK* ɑːs], **ass** [*US* æs] *n vulg* [bottom] bunda *f*.

arsenal ['ɑːsənl] *n* [of weapons] arsenal *m*.

arsenic ['ɑːsnɪk] *n* arsênico *m*.

arson ['ɑːsn] *n* incêndio *m* premeditado.

arsonist ['ɑːsənɪst] *n* incendiário *m*, -ria *f*.

art [ɑːt] ◇ *n (U)* arte *f*. ◇ *comp* de artes.
➡ **arts** ◇ *npl* -**1**. *SCH* & *UNIV* [humanities] artes *fpl* -**2**. [fine arts]: **the** ~**s** as belas artes. ◇ *comp SCH* & *UNIV* de belas artes.
➡ **arts and crafts** *n* [school subject] artes *fpl*.

art deco [-'dekəʊ] *n* arte *f* deco.

artefact ['ɑːtɪfækt] *n* = **artifact**.

arterial [ɑː'tɪərɪəl] *adj* -**1**. [blood] arterial -**2**. [road] principal.

arteriosclerosis [ɑː,tɪərɪəʊsklɪ'rəʊsɪs] *n* arterioesclerose *f*.

artery ['ɑːtərɪ] (*pl* -ies) *n* artéria *f*.

artful ['ɑːtfʊl] *adj* [cunning] astuto(ta).

art gallery *n* -**1**. [public] museu *m* de arte -**2**. [for selling paintings] galeria *f* de arte.

arthritic [ɑː'θrɪtɪk] *adj* artrítico(ca).

arthritis [ɑː'θraɪtɪs] *n* artrite *f*.

artic [ɑː'tɪk] *n UK inf* = **articulated lorry**.

artichoke ['ɑːtɪtʃəʊk] *n* alcachofra *f*.

article ['ɑːtɪkl] *n* artigo *m*.

articled clerk ['ɑːtɪkld-] *n UK* estagiário *m* de advocacia.

articles of association ['ɑːtɪklz-] *npl* estatutos *mpl*.

articulate [*adj* ɑː'tɪkjʊlət, *vb* ɑː'tɪkjʊleɪt] ◇ *adj* [eloquent - person] articulado(da); [- speech] claro(ra). ◇ *vt* [give clear expression to] articular.

articulated lorry [ɑː'tɪkjʊleɪtɪd-] *n UK* caminhão *m* articulado.

articulation [ɑː,tɪkjʊ'leɪʃn] *n* -**1**. [enunciation] articulação *f* -**2**. [expression in words] expressão *f*.

artifact ['ɑːtɪfækt] *n* artefato *m*.

artifice ['ɑːtɪfɪs] *n* artifício *m*.

artificial [,ɑːtɪ'fɪʃl] *adj* artificial.

artificial insemination *n* inseminação *f* artificial.

artificial intelligence *n* inteligência *f* artificial.

artificially [,ɑːtɪ'fɪʃəlɪ] *adv* artificialmente.

artificial respiration *n* respiração *f* artificial.

artillery [ɑː'tɪlərɪ] *n* [guns] artilharia *f*.

artisan [,ɑːtɪ'zæn] *n* artesão *m*, -sã *f*.

artist ['ɑːtɪst] *n* artista *mf*.

artiste [ɑː'tiːst] *n* artista *mf*.

artistic [ɑː'tɪstɪk] *adj* artístico(ca).

artistically [ɑː'tɪstɪklɪ] *adv* artisticamente.

artistry ['ɑːtɪstrɪ] *n* [creative skill] talento *m* artístico.

artless ['ɑːtlɪs] *adj* [naive, simple] ingênuo(nua), simples.

art nouveau [,ɑːnuː'vəʊ] *n* art nouveau *m*.

as [stressed æz, unstressed əz] ◇ *conj* -**1**. [referring to time] enquanto; **she rang (just)** ~ **I was leaving** ela ligou (bem) na hora em que eu estava saindo; ~ **time goes by** com o passar do tempo -**2**. [referring to manner, way] como; **do** ~ **I say** faça como eu digo; ~ **it is** como está; ~ **it turns/turned out** no final; ~ **things stand** pelo jeito -**3**. [introducing a statement] como; ~ **you see, ...** como você pode ver; ~ **you know, ...** como você sabe -**4**. [because]

como. ⬦ *prep* **-1.** [referring to function, characteristic]: **he lived in Africa ~ a boy** ele viveu na África quando garoto; **he made his name ~ an actor** ele fez seu nome como ator; **she works ~ a nurse** ela trabalha como enfermeira **-2.** [referring to attitude, reaction] como; **she treats it ~ a game** ela trata isto como um jogo. ⬦ *adv (in comparisons)*: **~ ... ~** tão ... quanto; **~ red ~ a tomato** tão vermelho quanto um tomate; **he's ~ tall ~ I am** ele é tão alto quanto eu; **~ much/many ~** tanto ... quanto; **~ much wine/chocolate ~ you want** tanto vinho/chocolate quanto você queira.
➡ **as it were** *adv* por assim dizer.
➡ **as for, as to** *prep* quanto a.
➡ **as from, as of** *prep* a partir de.
➡ **as if, as though** *conj* como se.
➡ **as to** *prep* sobre.

AS ⬦ *n* (*abbr of* **Associate in Science**) (*titular de*) *graduação em ciências em universidade norte-americana*. ⬦ *abbr of* **American Samoa**.

ASA (*abbr of* **American Standards Association**) *n* **-1.** *associação norte-americana de padronização*, ≃ ABNT *f*. **-2.** (*abbr of* **Advertising Standards Authority**) *órgão britânico que regula a propaganda*, ≃ CONAR *m*. **-3.** (*abbr of* **Amateur Swimming Association**) *associação britânica de nadadores amadores*.

asap (*abbr of* **as soon as possible**) o mais rápido possível.

asbestos [æs'bestəs] *n* asbesto *m*.

asbestosis [ˌæsbes'təʊsɪs] *n* asbestose *f*.

ascend [ə'send] ⬦ *vt fml* [hill, staircase, ladder] subir; **to ~ the throne** ascender ao trono. ⬦ *vi* [climb] subir, elevar-se.

ascendancy [ə'sendənsɪ] *n* [dominance] domínio *m*.

ascendant [ə'sendənt] *n*: **to be in the ~** [rising in power] estar em ascensão.

ascendency [ə'sendənsɪ] *n* = **ascendancy**.

ascending [ə'sendɪŋ] *adj* [increasing] ascendente; **in ~ order** em ordem ascendente.

ascension [ə'senʃn] *n* [to throne] ascensão *f*.
➡ **Ascension** *n* RELIG Ascensão *f*.

Ascension Island *n* Ilha *f* da Ascensão.

ascent [ə'sent] *n* **-1.** [climb] escalada *f* **-2.** [upward slope] subida *f* **-3.** *(U) fig* [progress] escalada *f*.

ascertain [ˌæsə'teɪn] *vt* averiguar.

ascetic [ə'setɪk] ⬦ *adj* ascético(ca). ⬦ *n* asceta *mf*.

ASCII (*abbr of* **American Standard Code for Information Interchange**) *n* ASCII *m*.

ascorbic acid [ə'skɔ:bɪk-] *n* ácido *m* ascórbico.

ascribe [ə'skraɪb] *vt* [attribute]: **to ~ sthg to sthg/sb** atribuir algo a algo/alguém.

aseptic [ˌeɪ'septɪk] *adj* [germ-free] asséptico(ca).

asexual [ˌeɪ'sekʃʊəl] *adj* BIOL assexuado(da).

ash [æʃ] *n* **-1.** [from cigarette, fire] cinza *f* **-2.** [tree] freixo *m*.
➡ **ashes** *npl* [from cremation] cinzas *fpl*.

ASH (*abbr of* **Action on Smoking and Health**) *n grupo britânico de combate ao tabagismo*.

ashamed [ə'ʃeɪmd] *adj* [embarrassed] envergonhado(da); **to be ~ of sb/sthg** estar envergonhado(-da) por alguém/algo; **to be ~ to do sthg** estar com vergonha de fazer algo.

ashcan [ˈæʃkæn] *n US* lixeira *f*.

ashen-faced [ˈæʃnˌfeɪst] *adj* pálido(da).

ashore [ə'ʃɔ:ʳ] *adv* [go, swim] em direção à costa.

ashtray [ˈæʃtreɪ] *n* cinzeiro *m*.

Ash Wednesday *n* Quarta-feira *f* de Cinzas.

Asia [ˈeɪʒə] *n* Ásia; **in ~** na Ásia.

Asia Minor *n* Ásia Menor.

Asian [ˈeɪʒn] ⬦ *adj* asiático(ca). ⬦ *n* [person] asiático *m*, -ca *f*.

Asiatic [UK ˌeɪʒɪ'ætɪk, US ˌeɪʒɪ'ætɪk] *adj* asiático(ca).

aside [ə'saɪd] ⬦ *adv* **-1.** [to one side] para o lado; **to take sb ~** chamar alguém à parte; **to brush** OR **sweep sthg ~** ignorar algo **-2.** [apart] à parte; **~ from** com exceção de. ⬦ *n* **-1.** [in play] aparte *m* **-2.** [remark] observação *f*.

ask [ɑ:sk] ⬦ *vt* **-1.** [question] perguntar; **to ~ sb sthg** perguntar algo a alguém; **if you ~ me ...** se você quer saber ... **-2.** [enquire] perguntar; **to ~ a question** fazer uma pergunta **-3.** [request] pedir; **to ~ sb for sthg** pedir algo a alguém; **to ~ sb to do sthg** pedir a alguém para fazer algo **-4.** [invite] convidar **-5.** [set a price of]: **how much are they asking?** quanto estão pedindo? ⬦ *vi* **-1.** [enquire] perguntar **-2.** [request] pedir.
➡ **ask after** *vt fus*: **to ~ sb** perguntar por alguém.
➡ **ask for** *vt fus* **-1.** [person] pedir por, chamar por **-2.** [thing] pedir por.

askance [ə'skæns] *adv* [disapprovingly]: **to look ~ at sb/sthg** olhar alguém/algo com desconfiança, olhar de soslaio para alguém/algo.

askew [ə'skju:] *adj* [not straight] torto(ta).

asking price [ˈɑ:skɪŋ-] *n* [for house, car, item in sale] preço *m* estipulado.

asleep [ə'sli:p] *adj* [sleeping] adormecido(da); **to fall ~** pegar no sono; **to be fast** OR **sound ~** estar em sono profundo.

ASM (*abbr of* **air-to-surface missile**) *n* ASM *m*, míssil *m* ar-superfície.

asparagus [ə'spærəgəs] *n* aspargo *m*.

ASPCA (*abbr of* **American Society for the Prevention of Cruelty to Animals**) *n sociedade norte-americana protetora dos animais*, ≃ SUIPA *f*.

aspect [ˈæspekt] *n* **-1.** aspecto *m* **-2.** ARCHIT posição *f*.

aspen [ˈæspən] *n* álamo *m*.

aspersions [ə'spɜ:ʃnz] *npl*: **to cast ~ (on sb)** levantar calúnias (sobre alguém); **to cast ~ (on sthg)** levantar suspeitas (sobre algo).

asphalt [ˈæsfælt] *n* asfalto *m*.

asphyxiate [əs'fɪksɪeɪt] *vt* asfixiar.

aspic [ˈæspɪk] *n* geléia *f* (*de carne ou peixe*).

aspidistra *n* aspidistra *f*.

aspirate [ˈæspərət] ⬦ *adj* LING aspirado(da). ⬦ *vt* MED, LING aspirar.

aspiration [ˌæspə'reɪʃn] *n* aspiração *f*.

aspire [ə'spaɪəʳ] *vi*: **to ~ to sthg/to do sthg** aspirar algo, aspirar fazer algo.

aspirin [ˈæsprɪn] *n* aspirina *f*.

aspiring [ə'spaɪərɪŋ] *adj* aspirante.

ass [æs] *n* **-1.** [donkey] jumento *m* **-2.** *UK inf* [idiot] burro *m*, -ra *f* **-3.** *US vulg* = **arse**.

assail [ə'seɪl] *vt* **-1.** [attack physically] atacar **-2.** *fig* [beset] acometer.

assailant [ə'seɪlənt] n [attacker] agressor m, -ra f.

assassin [ə'sæsɪn] n assassino m, -na f.

assassinate [ə'sæsɪneɪt] vt assassinar; **to be ~ed** ser assassinado(da).

assassination [ə,sæsɪ'neɪʃn] n assassinato m.

assault [ə'sɔ:lt] <> n - **1.** MIL ataque m; **~ on sthg** ataque a algo - **2.** [physical attack] agressão f; **~ on sb** agressão a alguém; **~ and battery** JUR agressão f seguida de lesões. <> vt [attack - physically] agredir; [- sexually] violentar, estuprar.

assault course n pista f de combate.

assemble [ə'sembl] <> vt - **1.** [gather] reunir - **2.** [fit together] montar. <> vi [gather] reunir.

assembler language n = **assembly language**.

assembly [ə'semblɪ] (pl -ies) n - **1.** [meeting] reunião f - **2.** [law-making body] assembléia f, parlamento m - **3.** (U) [gathering together] assembléia f - **4.** (U) [fitting together] montagem f.

assembly language n COMPUT linguagem f assembly, linguagem f assembler.

assembly line n linha f de montagem.

assent [ə'sent] <> n [agreement] acordo m, aprovação f. <> vi concordar; **to ~ to sthg** aceitar algo.

assert [ə'sɜ:t] vt - **1.** [fact, belief] afirmar - **2.** [authority] impor; **to ~ o.s.** firmar-se.

assertion [ə'sɜ:ʃn] n [claim] afirmação f.

assertive [ə'sɜ:tɪv] adj positivo(va).

assess [ə'ses] vt - **1.** [judge] avaliar - **2.** [estimate] estimar.

assessment [ə'sesmənt] n - **1.** [judgment] avaliação f - **2.** [estimate] estimativa f.

assessor [ə'sesə'] n FIN analista mf.

asset ['æset] n ativo m.
  ➡ **assets** npl COMM ativos mpl; **~s and liabilities** ativo m e passivo.

asset-stripping [-,strɪpɪŋ] n compra de uma empresa em baixa e venda lucrativa de seu capital, seguida de seu fechamento.

assiduous [ə'sɪdjʊəs] adj [diligent] assíduo(dua).

assiduously [ə'sɪdjʊəslɪ] adv [diligently] com assiduidade.

assign [ə'saɪn] vt - **1.** [allot, allocate]: **to ~ sthg (to sb/sthg)** designar algo (a alguém/algo) - **2.** [appoint]: **to ~ sb (to sthg/to do sthg)** designar alguém (para algo/fazer algo).

assignation [,æsɪg'neɪʃn] n fml [secret meeting] encontro m amoroso.

assignment [ə'saɪnmənt] n - **1.** [task] tarefa f - **2.** (U) [act of appointing] designação f - **3.** [law] partilha f, transferência f de bens.

assimilate [ə'sɪmɪleɪt] vt - **1.** [ideas, facts] assimilar - **2.** [people]: **to ~ sb (into sthg)** absorver alguém (em algo) - **3.** [nutrients, food] absorver.

assimilation [ə,sɪmɪ'leɪʃn] n - **1.** [of ideas, facts] assimilação f - **2.** [of people, food] absorção f.

assist [ə'sɪst] vt [help] auxiliar; **to ~ sb with sthg/in doing sthg** auxiliar alguém em algo/a fazer algo.

assistance [ə'sɪstəns] n [help] auxílio m, ajuda f; **to be of ~ (to sb)** ser de alguma ajuda (para alguém).

assistant [ə'sɪstənt] <> n - **1.** [helper] assistente mf - **2.** [in shop] balconista mf, atendente mf. <> comp assistente mf; **~ manager** gerente adjunto.

assistant referee n árbitro m assistente, -tra assistente f.

associate [adj & n ə'səʊʃɪət, vb ə'səʊʃɪeɪt] <> adj [member] associado(da). <> n [business partner] sócio m, -cia f. <> vt [connect] associar-se; **to ~ o.s. with sb/sthg** associar-se a alguém/algo; **to ~ sthg with sb/sthg** associar algo a alguém/algo; **to be ~d with sb/sthg** ser associado a alguém/algo. <> vi: **to ~ with sb** relacionar-se com alguém.

association [ə,səʊsɪ'eɪʃn] n - **1.** [organization] associação f - **2.** (U) [relationship, of ideas] associação f; **in ~ with sb/sthg** em associação com alguém/algo.

assonance ['æsənəns] n assonância f.

assorted [ə'sɔ:tɪd] adj [of various types] sortido(da), variado(da).

assortment [ə'sɔ:tmənt] n [mixture] diversidade f.

Asst (abbr of **assistant**) assistente mf.

assuage [ə'sweɪdʒ] vt fml [relieve] minorar.

assume [ə'sju:m] vt - **1.** [suppose] supor - **2.** [take on] assumir.

assumed name [ə'sju:md-] n nome m falso.

assuming [ə'sju:mɪŋ] conj: **~ that** supondo que.

assumption [ə'sʌmpʃn] n - **1.** [supposition] suposição f - **2.** [of power] tomada f.
  ➡ **Assumption** n RELIG: **the Assumption** a Ascensão f.

assurance [ə'ʃʊərəns] n - **1.** [promise] promessa f - **2.** (U) [confidence] segurança f - **3.** (U) FIN [insurance] seguro m.

assure [ə'ʃʊə'] vt [reassure] assegurar; **to ~ sb of sthg** assegurar alguém de algo; **to be ~d of sthg** [be certain] estar seguro(ra de algo).

assured [ə'ʃʊəd] adj [confident] autoconfiante.

AST (abbr of **Atlantic Standard Time**) n horário de inverno na costa leste dos Estados Unidos.

asterisk ['æstərɪsk] n asterisco m.

astern [ə'stɜ:n] adv NAUT à popa.

asteroid ['æstərɔɪd] n asteróide m.

asthma ['æsmə] n asma f.

asthmatic [æs'mætɪk] <> adj asmático(ca). <> n asmático m, -ca f.

astigmatism [ə'stɪgmətɪzm] n astigmatismo m.

astonish [ə'stɒnɪʃ] vt [amaze] surpreender.

astonished adj surpreso(sa).

astonishing [ə'stɒnɪʃɪŋ] adj extraordinário(ria), surpreendente.

astonishment [ə'stɒnɪʃmənt] n espanto m, surpresa f.

astound [ə'staʊnd] vt [amaze] pasmar.

astounded adj pasmado(da).

astounding [ə'staʊndɪŋ] adj espantoso(sa).

astrakhan [,æstrə'kæn] n astracã m.

astray [ə'streɪ] adv: **to go ~** [become lost] extraviar-se; **to lead sb ~** fig [into bad ways] levar alguém para o mal caminho.

astride [ə'straɪd] prep: **sitting ~ a horse** montado(da) em um cavalo; **sitting ~ a chair** sentado(da) numa cadeira com uma perna de cada lado.

astringent [ə'strɪndʒənt] <> adj - **1.** [cosmetic lotion] adstringente - **2.** [criticism] severo(ra). <> n [cosmetic] adstringente m.

astrologer [ə'strɒlədʒə'] n astrólogo m, -ga f.

astrological [,æstrə'lɒdʒɪkl] adj astrológico(ca).

astrologist [ə'strɒlədʒɪst] *n* = **astrologer**.
astrology [ə'strɒlədʒɪ] *n* astrologia *f.*
astronaut ['æstrənɔːt] *n* astronauta *mf.*
astronomer [ə'strɒnəməʳ] *n* astrônomo *m*, -ma *f.*
astronomical [ˌæstrə'nɒmɪkl] *adj* - 1. ASTRON astronômico(ca) - 2. *inf fig* [very large] astronômico(ca).
astronomy [ə'strɒnəmɪ] *n* astronomia *f.*
astrophysics [ˌæstrəʊ'fɪzɪks] *n* astrofísica *f.*
astute [ə'stjuːt] *adj* [shrewd] perspicaz.
asunder [ə'sʌndəʳ] *adv literary* [apart]: **to tear** ~ dilacerar.
ASV (*abbr of* **American Standard Version**) *n tradução da Bíblia adotada nos Estados Unidos.*
asylum [ə'saɪləm] *n* - 1. *dated* [mental hospital] hospício *m* - 2. *(U)* [protection] asilo *m.*
asymmetrical [ˌeɪsɪ'metrɪkl] *adj* assimétrico(ca).
at [stressed æt, unstressed ət] *prep* - 1. [indicating place, position] em; ~ **work** no trabalho; ~ **my father's** na casa do meu pai; ~ **home** em casa; ~ **the top of the house** em cima de casa; ~ **the bottom of the hill** ao pé da colina - 2. [indicating direction] para, em direção a; **to smile** ~ **sb** sorrir para alguém; **to stare** ~ **sb/sthg** olhar para alguém/algo; **to shoot** ~ **sb/sthg** atirar em (direção a) alguém/algo - 3. [indicating a particular time] em; ~ **midnight/noon** à meia-noite, ao meio-dia; ~ **eleven o'clock** às onze horas; ~ **Christmas** no Natal; ~ **night** à noite - 4. [indicating age, speed, rate] a, em; ~ **your age** na sua idade; ~ **high speed** em alta velocidade; ~ **52 (years of age)** aos 52 anos (de idade); ~ **100 mph** a 100 milhas por hora - 5. [indicating price] a; ~ **£50** a OR por 50 libras - 6. [indicating particular state, condition] a, em; ~ **liberty** em liberdade; ~ **my invitation** a meu convite; ~ **peace/war** em paz/guerra; ~ **lunch/dinner** no almoço/jantar - 7. [indicating tentativeness, noncompletion] em; **to snatch** ~ **sthg** tentar pegar algo; **to nibble** ~ **sthg** beliscar/mordiscar algo - 8. (*after adjectives*) com; **amused/appalled/puzzled** ~ **sthg** entretido(da)/apavorado(da)/embaraçado(da) com algo; **to be bad/good** ~ **sthg** ser ruim/bom(boa) em algo.
➥ **at all** *adv* - 1. *(with negative)*: **not** ~ **all** [when thanked] não há de que; [when answering a question] de forma alguma; **she's not** ~ **all happy** ela não está nem um pouco feliz - 2. [in the slightest]: **anything** ~ **all will do** qualquer coisa está bem; **do you know her** ~ **all?** você a conhece de algum lugar?
ATC (*abbr of* **Air Training Corps**) *n unidade de formação e treinamento das forças aéreas britânicas.*
ate [UK et, US eɪt] *pt* ⊳ **eat.**
atheism ['eɪθɪɪzm] *n* ateísmo *m.*
atheist ['eɪθɪɪst] *n* ateu *m*, -téia *f.*
Athenian [ə'θiːnjən] <> *adj* ateniense *mf.* <> *n* ateniense *mf.*
Athens ['æθɪnz] *n* Atenas *f*; **in** ~ em Atenas.
athlete ['æθliːt] *n* atleta *mf.*
athlete's foot *n* MED pé-de-atleta *f.*
athletic [æθ'letɪk] *adj* atlético(ca).
➥ **athletics** *npl* atletismo *m.*
Atlantic [ət'læntɪk] <> *adj* atlântico(ca). <> *n*: **the** ~ **(Ocean)** o (Oceano) Atlântico.

Atlantis [ət'læntɪs] *n* Atlântida.
atlas ['ætləs] *n* atlas *m inv.*
Atlas ['ætləs] *n*: **the** ~ **Mountains** os Montes Atlas.
atm. (*abbr of* **atmosphere**) atm.
ATM (*abbr of* **automated teller machine**) *n* caixa *m* automático.
atmosphere ['ætməˌsfɪəʳ] *n* atmosfera *f.*
atmospheric [ˌætməs'ferɪk] *adj* - 1. [relating to the atmosphere] atmosférico(ca) - 2. [attractive, mysterious] envolvente.
ATOL (*abbr of* **Air Travel Organisers' Licence**) *n organização britânica mantida pela CAA que defende os interesses das pessoas que utilizam a aviação comercial no Reino Unido.*
atoll ['ætɒl] *n* atol *m.*
atom ['ætəm] *n* - 1. TECH átomo *m* - 2. *fig* [tiny amount] ponta *f* pingo *m.*
atom bomb *n* bomba *f* atômica.
atomic [ə'tɒmɪk] *adj* atômico(ca).
atomic bomb *n* = **atom bomb.**
atomic energy *n* energia *f* atômica.
atomic number *n* PHYS número *m* atômico.
atomizer, -iser ['ætəmaɪzəʳ] *n* vaporizador *m.*
atone [ə'təʊn] *vi*: **to** ~ **for sthg** redimir-se por algo.
atonement [ə'təʊnmənt] *n* remissão *f*; ~ **for sthg** punição por algo.
A to Z *n* A a Z *m.*
ATP (*abbr of* **automatic train protection**) *n* - 1. *sistema britânico para frear automaticamente um trem.* - 2. (*abbr of* **Association of Tennis Professionals**) ATP *f.*
atrocious [ə'trəʊʃəs] *adj* - 1. [cruel] desumano(na), atroz - 2. [very bad] atroz.
atrocity [ə'trɒsətɪ] (*pl* **-ies**) *n* [terrible act] atrocidade *f.*
attach [ə'tætʃ] *vt* - 1. [fasten] prender; **to** ~ **sthg to sthg** prender algo em algo - 2. [to document] anexar; **to** ~ **sthg to sthg** anexar algo a algo - 3. [importance, blame] atribuir; **to** ~ **sthg to sthg** atribuir algo a algo - 4. COMPUT atachar, anexar.
attaché [ə'tæʃeɪ] *n* adido *m.*
attaché case [ə'tæʃeɪ-] *n* pasta *f.*
attached [ə'tætʃt] *adj* - 1. [included] anexado(da) - 2. [fastened]: ~ **to sthg** preso(sa) a OR em algo - 3. [assigned]: ~ **to sthg** designado(da) para algo - 4. [fond]: ~ **to sb/sthg** apegado(da) a alguém/algo.
attachment [ə'tætʃmənt] *n* - 1. [device] dispositivo *m* - 2. [fondness]: ~ **(to sb/sthg)** apego (a alguém/algo) - 3. COMPUT anexo *m.*
attack [ə'tæk] <> *n* - 1. [gen] ataque *f*; ~ **on sthg** ataque contra OR a alguém/algo - 2. [physical, verbal] agressão *f*; ~ **on sb** agressão a alguém <> *vt* - 1. [gen] atacar - 2. [physically, verbally] agredir. <> *vi* atacar.
attacker [ə'tækəʳ] *n* - 1. [assailant] agressor *m*, -ra *f* - 2. SPORT atacante *mf.*
attain [ə'teɪn] *vt* [reach] atingir.
attainment [ə'teɪnmənt] *n* - 1. *(U)* [act of achieving] conquista *f* - 2. [skill] capacitação *f*, qualificação *f.*
attempt [ə'tempt] <> *n* [try] tentativa *m*; ~ **at sthg** tentativa de fazer algo; ~ **on sb's life** atentado

contra a vida de alguém. ◇ *vt* [try] tentar; **to ~ to do sthg** tentar fazer algo.

attend [əˈtend] ◇ *vt* **-1.** [meeting, party] comparecer **-2.** [school, church] freqüentar. ◇ *vi* **-1.** [be present] comparecer **-2.** [pay attention]**: to ~ (to sthg)** prestar atenção (a algo).
➡ **attend to** *vt fus* **-1.** [deal with] cuidar de **-2.** [look after] atender a.

attendance [əˈtendəns] *n* **-1.** [number of people present] audiência *f* **-2.** *(U)* [presence] presença *f*.

attendant [əˈtendənt] ◇ *adj* [accompanying] relacionado(da). ◇ *n* [at museum, petrol station] atendente *mf*.

attention [əˈtenʃn] ◇ *n* **-1.** [gen] atenção *f*; **to attract sb's ~** atrair a atenção de alguém; **to bring sthg to sb's ~**, **to draw sb's ~ to sthg** chamar a tenção de alguém para algo; **to pay ~ to sb/sthg** prestar atenção a alguém/algo; **to pay no ~ to sb/sthg** não prestar atenção a alguém/algo **-2.** [care] atenção *f*, cuidados *mpl* **-3.** *COMM*: **for the ~ of** aos cuidados de **-4.** *MIL*: **to stand to ~** ficar em posição de sentido. ◇ *excl MIL* sentido!

attentive [əˈtentɪv] *adj* **-1.** [paying attention] atento(ta) **-2.** [politely helpful] atencioso(sa).

attentively [əˈtentɪvlɪ] *adv* **-1.** [with attention] atentamente **-2.** [helpfully] cuidadosamente.

attenuate [əˈtenjʊeɪt] *fml* ◇ *vt* atenuar. ◇ *vi* atenuar.

attest [əˈtest] ◇ *vt* [affirm] atestar. ◇ *vi*: **to ~ to sthg** [prove] dar testemunho de algo.

attic [ˈætɪk] *n* sótão *m*.

attire [əˈtaɪər] *n fml* [clothing] traje *m*.

attitude [ˈætɪtjuːd] *n* **-1.** [way of thinking/acting] atitude *f*; **~ to(wards) sb/sthg** atitude frente a alguém/algo **-2.** [posture] postura *f*.

attn (*abbr of* for the attention of) a/c.

attorney [əˈtɜːnɪ] *n US* [lawyer] advogado *m*, -da *f*.

attorney general (*pl* attorneys general) *n* procurador *m*, -ra *f* público, -ca *f*.

attract [əˈtrækt] *vt* atrair; **to be ~ed to sb/sthg** ser atraído(da) por alguém/algo.

attraction [əˈtrækʃn] *n* **-1.** *(U)* [liking] atração *f*; **~ to sb** atração por alguém **-2.** *(U)* [appeal, charm] graça *f* **-3.** [attractive feature, event] atração *f*.

attractive [əˈtræktɪv] *adj* atraente.

attractively [əˈtræktɪvlɪ] *adv* de modo atraente.

attributable [əˈtrɪbjʊtəbl] *adj*: **~ to sb/sthg** atribuível a alguém/algo.

attribute [*vb* əˈtrɪbjuːt, *n* ˈætrɪbjuːt] ◇ *vt*: **to ~ sthg to sb/sthg** atribuir algo a alguém/algo. ◇ *n* [quality] atributo *m*.

attribution *n* atribuição *f*; **~ to sb/sthg** atribuição a alguém/algo.

attrition [əˈtrɪʃn] *n* desgaste *m*; **war of ~** guerra de desgaste.

attuned [əˈtjuːnd] *adj* **-1.** [accustomed] acostumado(da); **~ to sthg** familiarizado(da) a algo **-2.** [tuned in] sintonizado(da); **~ to sthg** ligado(da) em algo.

ATV *n* (*abbr of* all-terrain vehicle) off-road *m*.

atypical [ˌeɪˈtɪpɪkl] *adj* atípico(ca).

atypically [ˌeɪˈtɪpɪklɪ] *adv* atipicamente.

aubergine [ˈəʊbəʒiːn] *n UK* beringela *f*.

auburn [ˈɔːbən] *adj* [hair] castanho avermelhado(da).

auction [ˈɔːkʃn] ◇ *n* [sale] leilão *m*; **at** *OR* **by ~** em leilão; **to put sthg up for ~** pôr algo em leilão. ◇ *vt* leiloar.
➡ **auction off** *vt sep* leiloar.

auctioneer [ˌɔːkʃəˈnɪər] *n* leiloeiro *m*, -ra *f*.

audacious [ɔːˈdeɪʃəs] *adj* [daring, impudent] audacioso(sa).

audacity [ɔːˈdæsətɪ] *n* audácia *f*.

audible [ˈɔːdəbl] *adj* audível.

audience [ˈɔːdjəns] *n* **-1.** [of play, film, TV programme] platéia *f* **-2.** [formal meeting] audiência *f*.

audio [ˈɔːdɪəʊ] *adj* áudio, auditivo(va).

audio frequency *n* freqüência *f* auditiva.

audiotyping *n* transcrição *f* de fitas de áudio.

audiotypist [ˈɔːdɪəʊˌtaɪpɪst] *n* transcritor *m*, -ra *f* de fitas (de áudio).

audio-visual [ˈɔːdɪəʊ-] *adj* audiovisual.

audit [ˈɔːdɪt] ◇ *n* [of accounts] auditoria *f*. ◇ *vt* [accounts] auditorar.

audition [ɔːˈdɪʃn] ◇ *n* audição *f*. ◇ *vi*: **she is ~ing for a part in a film** ela está fazendo um teste para um papel num filme.

auditor [ˈɔːdɪtər] *n* [of accounts] auditor *m*, -ra *f*.

auditorium [ˌɔːdɪˈtɔːrɪəm] (*pl* -riums *OR* -ria [-rɪə]) *n* auditório *m*.

au fait [ˌəʊˈfeɪ] *adj*: **~ with sthg** estar a par de algo.

Aug. (*abbr of* August) ago.

augment [ɔːgˈment] *vt* [increase] aumentar.

augur [ˈɔːgər] *vi*: **to ~ well/badly** ser um bom/ mau sinal.

august [ɔːˈgʌst] *adj literary* [dignified] augusto(ta).

August [ˈɔːgəst] *n* agosto *m*; *see also* **September**.

Auld Lang Syne [ˌɔːldlæŋˈsaɪn] *n* canção escocesa tradicionalmente cantada no ano-novo.

aunt [ɑːnt] *n* tia *f*.

auntie, aunty [ˈɑːntɪ] (*pl* -ies) *n inf* titia *f*.

au pair [ˌəʊˈpeər] *n* au pair *mf*.

aura [ˈɔːrə] *n* aura *f*.

aural [ˈɔːrəl] *adj* auditivo(va), auricular.

aurally [ˈɔːrəlɪ] *adv* auditivamente.

auspices [ˈɔːspɪsɪz] *npl*: **under the ~ of** sob o patrocínio de.

auspicious [ɔːˈspɪʃəs] *adj* [promising] promissor(ra).

Aussie [ˈɒzɪ] *inf* ◇ *adj* australiano(na). ◇ *n* australiano *m*, -na *f*.

austere [ɒˈstɪər] *adj* **-1.** [person, life] duro(ra), austero(ra) **-2.** [room, building] austero(ra).

austerity [ɒˈsterətɪ] *n* austeridade *f*.

austerity measures *npl* medidas *fpl* austeras.

Australasia [ˌɒstrəˈleɪʒə] *n* Australásia.

Australia [ɒˈstreɪljə] *n* Austrália; **in ~** na Austrália.

Australian [ɒˈstreɪljən] ◇ *adj* australiano(na). ◇ *n* australiano *m*, -na *f*.

Austria [ˈɒstrɪə] *n* Áustria; **in ~** na Áustria.

Austrian [ˈɒstrɪən] ◇ *adj* austríaco(ca). ◇ *n* austríaco *m*, -ca *f*.

authentic [ɔːˈθentɪk] *adj* **-1.** [genuine] autêntico(ca) **-2.** [accurate] fidedigno(na).

authenticate [ɔːˈθentɪkeɪt] *vt* autenticar.

authentication [ɔːˌθentɪˈkeɪʃn] *n* autenticação *f*.

authenticity [ˌɔːθenˈtɪsətɪ] *n* autenticidade *f*.

author [ˈɔːθəʳ] *n* autor *m*, -ra *f*.

authoritarian [ɔːˌθɒrɪˈteərɪən] *adj* autoritário(ria).

authoritative [ɔːˈθɒrɪtətɪv] *adj* **-1.** [person, voice] autoritário(ria) - **2.** [report] oficial.

authority [ɔːˈθɒrətɪ] (*pl* **-ies**) *n* **-1.** [gen] autoridade *f*; ~ **on sthg** autoridade em algo - **2.** (*U*) [power] autoridade *f*; **in** ~ com autoridade - **3.** (*U*) [permission] autorização *f* - **4.** *phr*: **to have it on good** ~ receber de fonte segura.
  ➡ **authorities** *npl* [people in power]: **the authorities** as autoridades.

authorize, -ise [ˈɔːθəraɪz] *vt* autorizar; **to** ~ **sb to do sthg** autorizar alguém a fazer algo.

Authorized Version [ˈɔːθəraɪzd-] *n*: **the** ~ a Versão Autorizada (*da Bíblia*).

authorship [ˈɔːθəʃɪp] *n* autoria *f*.

autistic [ɔːˈtɪstɪk] *adj* autista.

auto [ˈɔːtəʊ] (*pl* **-s**) *n US* [car] auto *m*.

autobiographical [ˈɔːtəˌbaɪəˈɡræfɪkl] *adj* autobiográfico(ca).

autobiography [ˌɔːtəbaɪˈɒɡrəfɪ] (*pl* **-ies**) *n* autobiografia *f*.

autocrat [ˈɔːtəkræt] *n* autocrata *mf*.

autocratic [ˌɔːtəˈkrætɪk] *adj* autocrático(ca).

autocross [ˈɔːtəʊkrɒs] *n UK* autocross *m*.

Autocue® [ˈɔːtəʊkjuː] *n UK* teleprompter *m*.

autofocus *n* autofoco *m*.

autograph [ˈɔːtəɡrɑːf] <> *n* autógrafo *m*. <> *vt* autografar.

Automat® *n* [restaurant] *tipo de restaurante americano comum nos anos 50 e 60, onde a comida era vendida em máquinas com a inserção de moedas.*

automata [ɔːˈtɒmətə] *pl* ⊳ **automaton**.

automate [ˈɔːtəmeɪt] *vt* automatizar.

automatic [ˌɔːtəˈmætɪk] <> *adj* **-1.** [gen] automático(ca) - **2.** [fine, right of appeal] imediato(ta). <> *n* **-1.** [car] carro *n* automático - **2.** [gun] pistola *f* automática - **3.** [washing machine] máquina *f* de lavar automática.

automatically [ˌɔːtəˈmætɪklɪ] *adv* automaticamente.

automatic pilot *n AERON* & *NAUT* piloto *m* automático; **on** ~ *fig* no automático.

automation [ˌɔːtəˈmeɪʃn] *n* [of process] automação *f*, automatização *f*.

automaton [ɔːˈtɒmətən] (*pl* **-tons** OR **-ta**) *n* **-1.** [robot] autômata *mf*, robô *m* - **2.** *pej* [person] robô *m*.

automobile [ˈɔːtəməbiːl] *n US* [car] automóvel *m*.

automotive [ˌɔːtəˈməʊtɪv] *adj* [relating to automobiles] automotivo(va).

autonomous [ɔːˈtɒnəməs] *adj* autônomo(ma).

autonomy [ɔːˈtɒnəmɪ] *n* autonomia *f*.

autopilot [ˈɔːtəʊpaɪlɒt] *n* = **automatic pilot**.

autopsy [ˈɔːtɒpsɪ] (*pl* **-ies**) *n* autópsia *f*.

autumn [ˈɔːtəm] <> *n* outono *m*; **in** ~ no outono. <> *comp* de outono, outonal.

autumnal [ɔːˈtʌmnəl] *adj* outonal, de outono.

auxiliary [ɔːɡˈzɪljərɪ] (*pl* **-ies**) <> *adj* auxiliar. <> *n* [person] auxiliar *mf*.

AV <> *n* (*abbr of* **Authorized Version**) versão *f* autorizada. <> (*abbr of* **audio-visual**) audiovisual.

avail [əˈveɪl] <> *n*: **to no** ~ em vão. <> *vt*: **to** ~ **o.s. of sthg** aproveitar-se de algo.

availability [əˌveɪləˈbɪlətɪ] *n* disponibilidade *f*.

available [əˈveɪləbl] *adj* disponível.

avalanche [ˈævəlɑːnʃ] *n* avalanche *f*.

avant-garde [ˌævɒnˈɡɑːd] <> *n* vanguarda *f*. <> *adj* de vanguarda.

avarice [ˈævərɪs] *n* avareza *f*.

avaricious [ˌævəˈrɪʃəs] *adj* avarento(ta).

avdp. (*abbr of* **avoirdupoids**) *sistema inglês de pesos baseado na libra.*

Ave. (*abbr of* **avenue**) Av.

avenge [əˈvendʒ] *vt* vingar.

avenue [ˈævənjuː] *n* [wide road] avenida *f*.

average [ˈævərɪdʒ] <> *adj* **-1.** [mean] média(dio) - **2.** [typical] comum - **3.** *pej* [mediocre] mediano(na). <> *n* [mean] média *f*; **on** ~ em média. <> *vt* [speed, distance, quantity]: **they** ~ **300 cars a day** eles atingem uma média de 300 carros por dia.
  ➡ **average out** <> *vt sep* calcular a média. <> *vi*: **to** ~ **out at** chegar à média de.

averse [əˈvɜːs] *adj*: **to be** ~ **to sthg/to doing sthg** ser contrário(ria) a algo/fazer algo.

aversion [əˈvɜːʃn] *n* **-1.** [dislike] aversão *f*; ~ **to sthg** aversão a algo - **2.** [object of dislike] aversão *f*.

avert [əˈvɜːt] *vt* [avoid] evitar.

aviary [ˈeɪvjərɪ] (*pl* **-ies**) *n* aviário *m*.

aviation [ˌeɪvɪˈeɪʃn] *n* aviação *f*.

aviator [ˈeɪvɪeɪtəʳ] *n dated* aviador *m*, -ra *f*.

avid [ˈævɪd] *adj* [keen] ávido(da); ~ **for sthg** ávido (da) de/por algo.

avocado [ˌævəˈkɑːdəʊ] (*pl* **-s** OR **-es**) *n*: ~ **(pear)** abacate *m*.

avoid [əˈvɔɪd] *vt* evitar; **to** ~ **doing sthg** evitar fazer algo.

avoidable [əˈvɔɪdəbl] *adj* evitável.

avoidance [əˈvɔɪdəns] *n* ⊳ **tax avoidance**.

avowed [əˈvaʊd] *adj* declarado(da).

AWACS (*abbr of* **airborne warning and control system**) *n sistema aéreo de monitoramento terrestre por radar*; ~ **planes** aviões *mpl* AWACS.

await [əˈweɪt] *vt* **-1.** [wait for] esperar - **2.** [be ready for] estar pronto(ta) para.

awake [əˈweɪk] (*pt* **awoke** OR **awaked**, *pp* **awoken**) <> *adj* [not sleeping] acordado(da); **to be wide** ~ estar totalmente desperto(ta). <> *vt* **-1.** [wake up] acordar - **2.** *fig* [provoke] despertar. <> *vi* [wake up] acordar.

awakening [əˈweɪknɪŋ] *n* **-1.** [from sleep] despertar *m* - **2.** *fig* [of feeling] despertar *m*.

award [əˈwɔːd] <> *n* **-1.** [prize] prêmio *m* - **2.** [compensation] recompensa *f*. <> *vt* [give] premiar; **to** ~ **sb sthg, to** ~ **sthg to sb** conceder algo a alguém.

aware [əˈweəʳ] *adj* **-1.** [conscious]: ~ **of sthg** consciente de algo; ~ **that** ciente de que - **2.** [informed, sensitive] consciente; ~ **of sthg** informado(da) sobre algo.

awareness [əˈweənɪs] *n* consciência *f*.

awash [əˈwɒʃ] *adj*: ~ **(with sthg)** cheio(a) (de algo).

away [əˈweɪ] <> *adv* **-1.** [indicating movement] embora; ~ **from** longe de; **to look/turn** ~

virar-se **- 2.** [at a distance - in space]**: she lives 3 miles**
~ **ela mora a três milhas daqui; we live 4 miles** ~
from the city centre moramos a 4 milhas do centro
da cidade; [- in time]**: the exams were only two
days** ~ faltavam apenas dois dias para os
exames **- 3.** [separate from]**: to be kept** ~ **from
sthg** ser mantido(da) afastado(da) de algo; **to
give sthg** ~ dar algo; **to take sthg** ~ levar algo
- 4. [absent]**: to be** ~ estar fora **- 5.** [in a safe place]**:
to put sthg** ~ guardar algo **- 6.** [indicating disappearance, cessation]**: the stain has faded** ~ a
mancha desapareceu; **the wood had rotted** ~ a
madeira tinha apodrecido **- 7.** [continuously]**: to
sing/work** ~ cantar/trabalhar sem parar. ◇
adj SPORT: ~ **team** time *m* visitante; ~ **game** jogo
fora de casa.

awe [ɔː] *n* temor *m*; **to be in** ~ **of sb** estar
intimidado(da) por alguém.

awesome ['ɔːsəm] *adj* [impressive] terrível.

awestruck ['ɔːstrʌk] *adj* aterrorizado(da).

awful ['ɔːfʊl] *adj* **-1.** [terrible] horrível **- 2.** *inf* [very
great]**: to have an** ~ **lot of work to do** ter um
bocado de coisas para fazer.

awfully ['ɔːflɪ] *adv inf* [very] pra caramba; **to be** ~
difficult ser difícil pra caramba.

awhile [ə'waɪl] *adv literary* durante um tempo.

awkward ['ɔːkwəd] *adj* **-1.** [clumsy] desajeitado(da)
- 2. [embarassing] embaraçoso(sa) **- 3.** [embarrassed]**: to
feel** ~ sentir-se embaraçado(da) **- 4.** [difficult to deal
with] complicado(da) **- 5.** [inconvenient] inadequado(-
da).

awkwardly ['ɔːkwədlɪ] *adv* **-1.** [clumsily] desajeitadamente **- 2.** [in an embarrassed way] embaraçosa-
mente **- 3.** [inconveniently] inconvenientemente.

awkwardness ['ɔːkwədnɪs] *n* **-1.** [clumsiness - of
movement, position] falta *f* de jeito; [- of person]
indelicadeza *f* **- 2.** [unease] dificuldade *f* **- 3.** [inconve-
nience] embaraço *m*.

awl [ɔːl] *n* furador *m*.

awning ['ɔːnɪŋ] *n* **-1.** [of tent] cobertura *f* **- 2.** [of shop]
toldo *m*.

awoke [ə'wəʊk] *pt* ▷ **awake**.

awoken [ə'wəʊkn] *pp* ▷ **awake**.

AWOL (*abbr of* **absent without leave**)**: to go** ~ MIL
sair sem permissão; **the cat has gone** ~ *hum* o
gato sumiu.

awry [ə'raɪ] ◇ *adj* [twisted] desajeitado(da). ◇
adv: **to go** ~ [wrong] dar errado.

axe UK, **ax** US [æks] ◇ *n* machado *m*; **to have an**
~ **to grind** ter um interesse pessoal. ◇ *vt* [pro-
ject, jobs] cortar.

axes ['æksiːz] *pl* ▷ **axis**.

axiom ['æksɪəm] *n* axioma *m*.

axis ['æksɪs] (*pl* **axes**) *n* eixo *m*.

axle ['æksl] *n* [shaft] eixo *m*.

ayatollah [ˌaɪə'tɒlə] *n* aiatolá *m*.

aye [aɪ] ◇ *adv* [yes] sim. ◇ *n* [affirmative vote] sim
m.

AYH (*abbr of* **American Youth Hostels**) *n* Albergues
mpl da Juventude (*nos Estados Unidos*).

A-Z *n* guia que contém mapas de ruas das
cidades britânicas.

AZ *abbr of* **Arizona**.

azalea [ə'zeɪljə] *n* azaléia *f*.

Azerbaijan [ˌæzəbaɪ'dʒɑːn] *n* Azerbaijão; **in** ~ no
Azerbaijão.

Azerbaijani [ˌæzəbaɪ'dʒɑːnɪ] ◇ *adj* azerbaijano(-
na). ◇ *n* azerbaijano *m*, -na *f*.

Azeri [ə'zerɪ] ◇ *adj* azeri. ◇ *n* azeri *mf*.

Azores [ə'zɔːz] *npl*: **the** ~ os Açores; **in the** ~ nos
Açores.

AZT (*abbr of* **azidothymidine**) *n* AZT® *m*.

Aztec ['æztek] ◇ *adj* asteca. ◇ *n* asteca *mf*.

azure ['æʒəʳ] *adj* [bright blue] azul-celeste.

B

b (*pl* **b's** OR **bs**)**, B** (*pl* **B's** OR **Bs**) [biː] *n* [letter] b, B *m*.
◆ **B** *n* **- 1.** MUS si *m* **- 2.** SCH [mark] B *m*.

b. (*abbr of* **born**) n.

BA *n* **-1.** (*abbr of* **Bachelor of Arts**) *titular de
graduação em ciências humanas.* **- 2.** (*abbr of* **British Academy**) *organismo público britânico para
fomento de pesquisa em ciências humanas.*

BAA (*abbr of* **British Airports Authority**) *n organismo independente que controla os aeroportos
britânicos,* ≃ INFRAERO *f.*

babble ['bæbl] ◇ *n* [noise] balbucio *m*. ◇ *vi* [per-
son] balbuciar.

babe [beɪb] *n* **-1.** *literary* [baby] nenê *mf* **- 2.** *inf* [term of
affection] garota *f* **- 3.** *inf* [beautiful woman] boneca *f.*

baboon [bə'buːn] *n* [animal] babuíno *m.*

baby ['beɪbɪ] (*pl* **-ies**) *n* **-1.** [child] bebê *mf*, nenê *mf* **- 2.**
pej [feeble person]**: don't be such a** ~ ! não seja tão
criança! **- 3.** *esp US inf* [term of affection] pequeno(-
na).

baby boomer [-ˌbuːməʳ] *n* US *pessoa nascida
num período de explosão demográfica nos
Estados Unidos, especialmente entre 1946 e
1954.*

baby buggy UK, **baby carriage** UK *n* [foldable
pushchair] carrinho *m* de bebê

baby food *n* comida *f* de nenê.

babyish ['beɪbɪʃ] *adj pej* infantil.

baby-sit *vi* tomar conta de crianças, trabalhar
como babá.

baby-sitter [-ˌsɪtəʳ] *n* babá *f*, baby-sitter *f.*

bachelor ['bætʃələʳ] *n* [unmarried man] solteirão *m*;
confirmed ~ solteirão convicto.

Bachelor of Arts *n* [person]; [degree] *bacharelado em Artes, Ciências Humanas ou Sociais.*

Bachelor of Science *n* [person] Bacharel *m* em
Ciências ; [degree] bacharelado *m* em ciências.

bachelor's degree *n* grau *m* de bacharel.

back [bæk] ◇ *adj* (*in compounds*) **-1.** [rear] traseiro (ra); ~ **legs** patas traseiras **- 2.** [at the back] de trás, dos fundos; ~ **seat** assento de trás; ~ **garden** jardim dos fundos **- 3.** [overdue] atrasado(da). <> *adv* **-1.** [backwards] para trás **- 2.** [indicating return to former position or state] de volta; **is he** ~ **yet?** ele já está de volta?, ele já voltou?; **to go** ~ **to sleep** voltar a dormir; **to go** ~ **and forth** ficar indo e vindo **- 3.** [earlier]: ~ **in January** em janeiro passado **- 4.** [in reply, in return] de volta; **to phone** ~ ligar de volta; **to pay** ~ reembolsar; **to write** ~ responder **- 5.** [in fashion again]: **to be** ~ **(in fashion)** estar de volta (à moda). <> *n* **-1.** [of person, animal] costas *fpl*; **to break the** ~ **of sthg** *fig* conseguir terminar algo; **to do sthg behind sb's** ~ fazer algo pelas costas de alguém; **to know somewhere like the** ~ **of one's hand** conhecer um lugar como a palma da mão; **to put sb's** ~ **up** encher o saco de alguém; **to stab sb in the** ~ apunhalar pelas costas; **to turn one's** ~ **on sb/sthg** virar as costas para alguém/algo **- 2.** [reverse side - of page, envelope] verso *m*; [- of head] parte *f* de trás, parte *f* anterior **- 3.** [furthest point away from front - of room] fundos *mpl*; [- of cupboard, fridge]: **in the** ~ **of the fridge** na parte de trás geladeira; [- of car] traseira *f*; [- of chair] encosto *m*; **at the** ~ **of, in the** ~ **of** *US* atrás de; **in the** ~ **of beyond** *UK* no fim do mundo **- 4.** *SPORT* [player] zagueiro(ra). <> *vt* **-1.** [reverse] recuar **- 2.** [support] apoiar **- 3.** [bet on] apostar **- 4.** [provide lining for] forrar. <> *vi* [reverse] retornar; ~ **into sthg** [walking] voltar-se para algo; [in vehicle] entrar de ré em algo.

◆ **back to back** *adv* [with backs touching]: **to stand** ~ **to** ~ ficar costas com costas.

◆ **back to front** *adv* [the wrong way round] de trás para frente, ao contrário.

◆ **back away** *vi* afastar-se.

◆ **back down** *vi* voltar atrás.

◆ **back off** *vi* afastar-se.

◆ **back onto** *vt fus UK* dar (com os fundos) para.

◆ **back out** *vi* [of promise, arrangement] dar para trás.

◆ **back up** <> *vt sep* **-1.** [support] apoiar **- 2.** [reverse] dar marcha à ré **- 3.** *COMPUT* fazer cópia de segurança de. <> *vi* **-1.** [reverse] dar marcha à ré **- 2.** *COMPUT* fazer cópia de segurança.

backache ['bækeik] *n* dor *f* nas costas.

backbencher [‚bæk'bentʃəʳ] *n UK POL* membro do *Parlamento Britânico*, *sem cargo oficial no governo ou na oposição*.

backbenches [‚bæk'bentʃiz] *npl UK POL*: **the** ~ *as cadeiras reservadas aos membros do Parlamento Britânico, sem cargo oficial no governo ou na oposição*.

backbiting ['bækbaitiŋ] *n* (U) falar *m* pelas costas.

backbone ['bækbəʊn] *n* **-1.** [spine] coluna *f* vertebral **- 2.** (U) *fig* [courage, force] tutano *m* **- 3.** *fig* [main support]: **the** ~ **of** a espinha dorsal de.

backbreaking ['bæk‚breikiŋ] *adj* [exhausting] estafante.

back burner *n*: **to put sthg on the** ~ *fig* deixar algo em segundo plano.

backchat *UK* ['bæktʃæt], **backtalk** *US* ['bæktɔːk] *n* (U) *inf* contestações *fpl*.

backcloth ['bækklɒθ] *n UK* = backdrop.

backcomb ['bækkəʊm] *vt UK* pentear o cabelo em direção ao couro cabeludo para fazê-lo parecer mais volumoso.

back copy *n* = back number.

backdate [‚bæk'deit] *vt* antedatar.

back door *n* porta *f* dos fundos; **to get in through** *or* **by the** ~ *fig* conseguir algo por baixo do pano.

backdrop ['bækdrɒp] *n* **-1.** *THEATRE* pano *m* de fundo **- 2.** *fig* [background] pano *m* de fundo.

backer ['bækəʳ] *n FIN* avalista *mf*.

backfire [‚bæk'faiəʳ] *vi* **-1.** [motor vehicle] engasgar **- 2.** [go wrong] dar errado; **his plans** ~**d (on him)** seus planos não deram o resultado esperado.

backgammon ['bæk‚gæmən] *n* (U) gamão *m*.

background ['bækgraʊnd] <> *n* **-1.** [in picture, view] fundo *m*; **in the** ~ *lit* ao fundo; *fig* [unnoticeable] em segundo plano **- 2.** [of event, situation] cenário *m* **- 3.** [upbringing] background *m*. <> *comp* **-1.** [music, noise] de fundo **- 2.** [reading, information] preliminar.

backhand ['bækhænd] *n* backhand *m*.

backhanded ['bækhændid] *adj fig* [equivocal] falso(-sa).

backhander ['bækhændəʳ] *n UK inf* [bribe] suborno *m*.

backing ['bækiŋ] *n* **-1.** (U) [support] suporte *m* **- 2.** [lining] forro *m* **- 3.** *MUS* acompanhamento *m*.

backing group *n MUS* grupo *m* de acompanhamento.

back issue *n* = back number.

backlash ['bæklæʃ] *n* [adverse reaction] revolta *f*.

backless ['bæklis] *adj* frente-única.

backlog ['bæklɒg] *n* acúmulo *m*.

back number *n* número *m* atrasado.

backpack ['bækpæk] *n* mochila *f*.

backpacker ['bækpækəʳ] *n* mochileiro *m*, -ra *f*.

backpacking ['bækpækiŋ] *n*: **to go** ~ viajar com a mochila nas costas.

back passage *n euphemism* reto *m*.

back pay *n* (U) salário *m* atrasado.

backpedal [‚bæk'pedl] (*UK pt* & *pp* **-led**, *cont* **-ling**, *US pt* & *pp* **-ed**, *cont* **-ing**) *vi fig* [change one's mind]: **to** ~ **(on sthg)** dar pra trás (em algo).

back seat *n* [in car] banco *m* de trás; **to take a** ~ *fig* desempenhar um papel secundário.

back-seat driver *n* carona que fica dizendo ao motorista como dirigir.

backside [‚bæk'said] *n inf* traseiro *m*.

backslapping *n* (U) *inf* [congratulations] saudações *mpl*.

backslash ['bækslæʃ] *n COMPUT* barra *f* invertida.

backslide [‚bæk'slaid] (*pt* & *pp* **-slid** [-'slid]) *vi* ter uma recaída.

backspace ['bækspeis] <> *n* [key] tecla *f* de retorno. <> *vi* [in typing] clicar o retorno, retornar.

backstage [‚bæk'steidʒ] *adv* nos bastidores.

back street *n UK* ruela *f*.

back-street abortion *n UK* aborto *m* clandestino.

backstroke ['bækstrəʊk] *n* [in swimming] nado *m* (de) costas.

backtalk *n US* = backchat.

backtrack ['bæktræk] *vi* = backpedal.

backup ['bækʌp] ◇ *adj* -**1.** [reserve] de reserva -**2.** *COMPUT* de segurança. ◇ *n* -**1.** [support] suporte *m* -**2.** *COMPUT* backup *m*, cópia *f* de segurança.

backward ['bækwəd] ◇ *adj* -**1.** [directed towards the rear] para trás -**2.** *pej* [late in development - person] retardado(da); [- society, ideas] atrasado(da). ◇ *adv US* = **backwards**.

backward-looking [-,lʊkɪŋ] *adj pej* retrógrado(-da).

backwards ['bækwədz], **backward** *US* ['bækwəd] *adv* -**1.** [towards the rear] de trás para a frente; ~ **and forwards** de um lado para outro -**2.** [back to front] de trás para a frente, ao contrário.

backwash ['bækwɒʃ] *n* [of event, situation] repercussão *f*.

backwater ['bæk,wɔ:tə^r] *n fig* & *pej* [place behind the times] lugar *m* atrasado; **cultural** ~ atraso *m* cultural.

backwoods ['bækwʊdz] *npl* [remote place] confins *mpl*.

backyard [,bæk'jɑ:d] *n* -**1.** *UK* [yard] pátio *m*, quintal *m* -**2.** *US* [garden] jardim *m*.

bacon ['beɪkən] *n (U)* bacon *m*.

bacteria [bæk'tɪərɪə] *npl* bactérias *fpl*.

bacteriology [bæk,tɪərɪ'ɒlədʒɪ] *n (U)* bacteriologia *f*.

bad [bæd] (*compar* **worse**, *superl* **worst**) ◇ *adj* -**1.** [gen] ruim; **not** ~ nada mal; **too** ~ uma pena; **to be** ~ **at sthg** ser ruim em algo -**2.** [unfavourable] mau (má); **to go from** ~ **to worse** ir de mal a pior -**3.** [severe] grave, severo(ra) -**4.** [inadequate] ruim -**5.** [guilty]: **to feel** ~ **about sthg** sentir-se mal por algum motivo -**6.** [food, milk, meat] mal; **to go** ~ ir mal. ◇ *adv US* = **badly**.

bad blood *n (U)* [anger] ódio *m*.

bad cheque *UK*, **bad check** *US n* cheque *m* sem fundo.

bad debt *n* dívida *f* perdida.

baddy (*pl* -**ies**) *n inf* vilão *m*, vilã *f*.

bade [bæd] *pt* ▷ **bid**.

bad feeling *n (U)* [resentment] rancor *m*, ressentimento *m*.

badge [bædʒ] *n* -**1.** [metal, plastic] crachá *m* -**2.** [sewn on] distintivo *m* -**3.** [on car] selo *m*.

badger ['bædʒə^r] ◇ *n* [animal] texugo *m*. ◇ *vt* [pester]: **to** ~ **sb (to do sthg)** convencer alguém (a fazer algo).

badly ['bædlɪ] (*compar* **worse**, *superl* **worst**) *adv* -**1.** [poorly] mal; **to think** ~ **of sb** pensar mal de alguém -**2.** [severely] gravemente -**3.** [improperly] indevidamente -**4.** [cruelly] mal -**5.** [very much]: **to be** ~ **in need of sthg** precisar muito de algo.

badly-off *adj* -**1.** [poor] carente -**2.** [lacking]: **to be** ~ **for sthg** estar carente de algo.

bad-mannered [-'mænəd] *adj* mal-educado(da).

badminton ['bædmɪntən] *n (U)* badminton *m*.

bad-mouth *vt esp US inf* falar mal de.

badness ['bædnɪs] *n (U)* maldade *f*.

bad-tempered [-'tempəd] *adj* -**1.** [by nature] genioso(sa) -**2.** [in a bad mood] mal-humorado(da).

baffle ['bæfl] *vt* [puzzle] desnortear.

baffling ['bæflɪŋ] *adj* [puzzling] desnorteante.

BAFTA (*abbr of* **British Academy of Film and Television Arts**) *n organização britânica que promove e premia os melhores em filmes, televisão e outras mídias interativas.*

bag [bæg] (*pt* & *pp* -**ged**, *cont* -**ging**) ◇ *n* -**1.** [container] saco *m*; ~ **of bones** saco de ossos; **in the** ~ *inf* no papo; **to pack one's** ~**s** *fig* [leave] fazer as malas -**2.** [handbag] bolsa *f*; [when travelling] mala *f* -**3.** [bagful] sacola *f*. ◇ *vt* -**1.** [put into bags] ensacar -**2.** *UK inf* [get] pegar -**3.** *UK inf* [reserve] marcar.
➡ **bags** *npl* -**1.** [under eyes] bolsas *fpl* -**2.** [lots]: ~ **s of sthg** *inf* um montão de algo.

bagel ['beɪgl] *n* pão *m* enrolado.

baggage ['bægɪdʒ] *n (U)* bagagem *f*.

baggage car *n US* vagão *m* de bagagens.

baggage reclaim *n* esteira *f* de bagagem.

baggage room *n US* guarda-volumes *m inv*.

baggy ['bægɪ] (*compar* -**ier**, *superl* -**iest**) *adj* largo(ga).

Baghdad [bæg'dæd] *n* Bagdá; **in** ~ em Bagdá.

bag lady *n inf* mulher *f* de rua.

bagpipes ['bægpaɪps] *npl* gaita *f* de foles.

bagsnatcher ['bægsnætʃə^r] *n* batedor *m* de carteira.

baguette [bə'get] *n* [loaf] baguete *f*.

bah [bɑ:] *excl* bah!

Bahamas [bə'hɑːməz] *npl*: **the** ~ as Bahamas; **in the** ~ nas Bahamas.

Bahrain, Bahrein [bɑː'reɪn] *n* Barein; **in** ~ em Barein.

Bahraini, Bahreini [bɑː'reɪnɪ] ◇ *adj* & *n* baraini. ◇ *n* baraini *mf*.

bail [beɪl] *n (U)* *JUR* fiança *f*; **on** ~ sob fiança.
➡ **bail out** ◇ *vt sep* -**1.** *JUR* [pay bail for] afiançar -**2.** [rescue] resgatar -**3.** [boat] tirar água. ◇ *vi* [from plane] saltar de pára-quedas.

bailiff ['beɪlɪf] *n* -**1.** [in court] oficial *mf* de justiça -**2.** [in charge of repossession] administrador *m*, -ra *f* de propriedades.

bait [beɪt] ◇ *n (U)* [food] isca *f*; **to rise to** *OR* **take the** ~ *fig* morder a isca. ◇ *vt* -**1.** [hook] pôr isca em -**2.** [mousetrap] armar -**3.** [tease, torment - person] atormentar; [- bear, badger] provocar.

baize [beɪz] *n (U)* feltro *m*.

bake [beɪk] ◇ *vt* -**1.** [cook] assar -**2.** [dry, harden] queimar. ◇ *vi* [food] assar.

baked beans [beɪkt-] *npl* feijão cozido em molho de tomate.

baked potato [beɪkt-] *n batata grande assada com casca e servida com recheio.*

Bakelite® ['beɪkəlaɪt] *n* baquelita *f*.

baker ['beɪkə^r] *n* padeiro *m*; ~'**s (shop)** padaria *f*.

bakery ['beɪkərɪ] (*pl* -**ies**) *n* padaria *f*.

baking ['beɪkɪŋ] ◇ *adj inf* [hot] escaldante. ◇ *n* [process] cozimento *m*.

baking powder *n (U)* fermento *m* em pó.

baking tin *n* fôrma *f*.

baking tray *n* assadeira *f*.

balaclava (helmet) [bælə'klɑːvə-] *n UK* balaclava *f*.

balance ['bæləns] ◇ *n* -**1.** [equilibrium] equilíbrio *m*; **to keep/lose one's** ~ manter/perder o equilíbrio; **off** ~ desequilibrado(da) -**2.** *fig* [counterweight] contra-peso *m* -**3.** *fig* [weight, force]: ~ **of evidence**

peso *m* da evidência - **4.** [scales] balança *f*; **to be** OR **hang in the** ~ estar na balança - **5.** [remainder] restante *m* - **6.** [of bank account] saldo *m*. ◇ *vt* - **1.** [keep in balance] balancear - **2.** [compare]: **to** ~ **sthg against sthg** contrabalançar algo em relação a algo - **3.** [in accounting]: **to** ~ **the books/a budget** fazer o balanço dos livros/do orçamento. ◇ *vi* - **1.** [maintain equilibrium] equilibrar-se - **2.** [in accounting] fechar, bater.

➡ **on balance** *adv* de um modo geral.

balanced ['bælənst] *adj* equilibrado(da).

balanced diet ['bælənst-] *n* dieta *f* equilibrada.

balance of payments *n* balança *f* de pagamentos.

balance of power *n* equilíbrio *m* de forças.

balance of trade *n* balança *f* comercial.

balance sheet *n* balancete *m*.

balancing act ['bælənsıŋ-] *n* fig [careful manoeuvre] malabarismo *m*.

balcony ['bælkənɪ] (*pl* -ies) *n* - **1.** [on building] sacada *f* - **2.** [in theatre] balcão *m*, galeria *f*.

bald [bɔːld] *adj* - **1.** [head, man, tyre] careca - **2.** *fig* [unadorned] curto(ta) e grosso(sa).

bald eagle *n* águia *f* americana (*símbolo dos Estados Unidos que aparece em todos os emblemas oficiais*).

balding ['bɔːldɪŋ] *adj* careca, calvo(va).

baldness ['bɔːldnɪs] *n* (U) calvície *f*.

bale [beɪl] *n* fardo *m*.

➡ **bale out** UK *vt sep* = **bail out**.

Balearic Islands [,bælɪ'ærɪk-], **Balearics** [,bælɪ'ærɪks] *npl*: **the** ~ as Ilhas Baleares; **in the** ~ nas Ilhas Baleares.

baleful ['beɪlfʊl] *adj* fulminante.

Bali ['bɑːlɪ] *n* Bali; **in** ~ em Bali.

balk [bɔːk] *vi* [recoil]: **to** ~ **(at sthg)** [person] recusar-se (a fazer algo).

Balkan ['bɔːlkən] *adj* balcânico(ca).

Balkans ['bɔːlkənz], **Balkan States** *npl*: **the** ~ os Balcãs; **in the** ~ nos Balcãs.

ball [bɔːl] *n* - **1.** [in game] bola *f*; **to start/keep the** ~ **rolling** *fig* pôr/manter a bola em jogo; **to be on the** ~ *fig* estar ligado(da) em tudo; **to play** ~ **with sb** *fig* colaborar (com alguém) - **2.** [sphere] novelo *m* - **3.** [dance] baile *m*; **to have a** ~ *fig* divertir-se.

➡ **balls** *vulg* ◇ *n* [nonsense] merda *f*. ◇ *npl* [testicles] saco *m*; *fig* [courage]: **to have** ~ ter colhões. ◇ *excl* caralho!

ballad ['bæləd] *n* balada *f*.

ball-and-socket joint *n* junta *f* articulada (*bola-e-soquete*).

ballast ['bæləst] *n* (U) lastro *m*.

ball bearing *n* rolamento *m*.

ball boy *n* gandula *m*.

ballcock ['bɔːlkɒk] *n* bóia *f*.

ballerina [,bælə'riːnə] *n* bailarina *f*.

ballet ['bæleɪ] *n* (U) balé *m*.

ballet dancer *n* bailarino(na).

ball game *n* - **1.** US [baseball match] jogo *m* de beisebol - **2.** *fig* [situation]: **it's a whole new** ~ *inf* é outra história.

ball girl *n* gandula *f*.

ballistic missile *n* míssil *m* balístico.

ballistics [bə'lɪstɪks] *n* (U) balística *f*.

balloon [bə'luːn] ◇ *n* balão *m*. ◇ *vi* [swell] inflar.

ballooning [bə'luːnɪŋ] *n* (U) balonismo *m*.

ballot ['bælət] ◇ *n* - **1.** [voting paper] voto *m* - **2.** [voting process] votação *f*. ◇ *vt* [canvass] caçar votos. ◇ *vi* [vote]: **to** ~ **for sthg** votar para algo.

ballot box *n* - **1.** [container] urna *f* - **2.** [voting process] urnas *fpl*.

ballot paper *n* cédula *f* de votação.

ball park *n* US estádio *m* de beisebal.

ball-park figure *n* *inf* [estimate] valor *m* estimado.

ballpoint (pen) ['bɔːlpɔɪnt-] *n* caneta *f* esferográfica.

ballroom ['bɔːlrʊm] *n* salão *m* de baile.

ballroom dancing *n* (U) dança *f* de salão.

balls-up UK, **ball-up** US *n* *v inf* cagada *f*.

balm [bɑːm] *n* bálsamo *m*.

balmy ['bɑːmɪ] (*compar* -ier, *superl* -iest) *adj* suave.

baloney [bə'ləʊnɪ] *n* - **1.** *inf* [rubbish] asneira *f* - **2.** US [sausage] mortadela *f*.

balsa ['bɒlsə] *n* = **balsawood**.

balsam ['bɔːlsəm] *n* (U) [substance] bálsamo *m*.

balsawood ['bɒlsəwʊd] *n* balsa *f*.

Baltic ['bɔːltɪk] ◇ *adj* [port, coast] báltico(ca). ◇ *n*: **the** ~ **(Sea)** o (mar) Báltico.

Baltic Republic *n*: **the** ~**s** as Repúblicas Bálticas.

Baltic State *n*: **the** ~**s** os Estados Bálticos.

balustrade [,bæləs'treɪd] *n* balaustrada *f*.

bamboo [bæm'buː] *n* bambu *m*.

bamboozle [bæm'buːzl] *vt inf* lograr.

ban [bæn] (*pt* & *pp* -ned, *cont* -ning) ◇ *n* proibição *f*; **on sthg** proibição de algo. ◇ *vt* banir; **to** ~ **sb from doing sthg** proibir alguém de fazer algo.

banal [bə'nɑːl] *adj* *pej* banal.

banana [bə'nɑːnə] *n* banana *f*.

banana republic *n* república *f* das bananas.

banana split *n* banana *f* split.

band [bænd] *n* - **1.** [musical group] banda *f* - **2.** [gang] bando *m* - **3.** [long strip] correia *f* - **4.** [broad stripe, range] faixa *f*.

➡ **band together** *vi* unir-se.

bandage ['bændɪdʒ] ◇ *n* faixa *f*. ◇ *vt* enfaixar.

Band-Aid® *n* band-aid *m*.

bandan(n)a [bæn'dænə] *n* bandana *f*.

b and b, B and B (*abbr of* **bed and breakfast**) *n* tipo de acomodação típica da Grã-Bretanha em que residências privadas oferecem serviço de quarto e café da manhã.

bandit ['bændɪt] *n* bandido *m*.

bandmaster ['bænd,mɑːstəʳ] *n* maestro *m*, -trina *f*.

band saw *n* serra *f* de fita.

bandsman ['bændzmən] (*pl* -men [-mən]) *n* músico *m*.

bandstand ['bændstænd] *n* palanque *m*.

bandwagon ['bændwægən] *n*: **to jump on the** ~ pegar carona na idéia.

bandy ['bændɪ] (*compar* -ier, *superl* -iest, *pt* & *pp* -ied) *adj* [bandy-legged] cambaio(a).

➡ **bandy about, bandy around** *vt sep* ficar repetindo.

bandy-legged [-ˌlegd] *adj* = bandy.

bane [beɪn] *n*: **the ~ of sb's life** a cruz da vida de alguém.

bang [bæŋ] ◇ *adv* - 1. [right]: **~ in the middle** bem no meio; **~ on** certeiro(ra) - 2. *phr*: **~ goes/go ...** *inf* lá se vai/vão ... ◇ *n* - 1. [blow] golpe *m* - 2. [loud noise] estrondo *m*; **to go with a ~** *inf fig* ser um estouro. ◇ *vt* - 1. [hit] bater - 2. [move noisily] bater. ◇ *vi* - 1. [knock]: **to ~ on sthg** dar pancadas - 2. [make a loud noise] bater - 3. [crash]: **to ~ into sb/ sthg** bater em alguém/algo. ◇ *excl* bum.

◆ **bangs** *npl US* franjas *fpl*.

◆ **bang down** *vt sep*: **to ~ sthg down on** bater algo com força em.

banger ['bæŋəʳ] *n UK* - 1. *inf* [sausage] salsicha *f* - 2. *inf* [old car] carroça *f* - 3. [firework] rojão *m*.

Bangkok [bæŋ'kɒk] *n* Bangkok; **in ~** em Bangkok.

Bangladesh [ˌbæŋglə'deʃ] *n* Bangladesh; **in ~** em Bangladesh.

Bangladeshi [ˌbæŋglə'deʃɪ] ◇ *adj* bangladeshiano(na). ◇ *n* bangladeshiano *m*, -na *f*.

bangle ['bæŋgl] *n* pulseira *f*.

banish ['bænɪʃ] *vt* - 1. [gen, fig] banir - 2. *literary* [dismiss] afugentar.

banister ['bænɪstəʳ] *n*, **banisters** ['bænɪstəz] *npl* corrimão *m*.

banjo ['bændʒəʊ] (*pl* -s *OR* -es) *n* banjo *m*.

bank [bæŋk] ◇ *n* - 1. [gen & *FIN*] banco *m*; **blood/ data ~** banco *m* de sangue/dados - 2. [alongside river, lake] margem *m* - 3. [slope] monte *m* - 4. [of clouds, fog] massa *f*. ◇ *vt FIN* depositar. ◇ *vi* - 1. *FIN*: **to ~ with sb** ser correntista de - 2. [plane] inclinar lateralmente.

◆ **bank on** *vt fus* contar com.

bank account *n* conta *f* corrente.

bank balance *n* saldo *m* bancário.

bankbook ['bæŋkbʊk] *n* extrato *m* bancário.

bank card *n* cartão *m* de garantia de cheque.

bank charges *npl* tarifas *fpl* bancárias.

bank draft *n* ordem *f* bancária.

banker ['bæŋkəʳ] *n FIN* banqueiro *m*, -ra *f*.

banker's order *n UK* débito *m* em conta.

bank holiday *n UK* feriado *m* bancário.

banking ['bæŋkɪŋ] *n (U)* serviços *mpl* bancários.

bank loan *n* empréstimo *m* bancário.

bank manager *n* gerente *mf* de banco.

bank note *n* cédula *f*.

bank rate *n* taxa *f* referencial de juros.

bankrupt ['bæŋkrʌpt] ◇ *adj* [financially] falido(da); **to go ~** ir à falência; **to be morally ~** *fig* estar desmoralizado(da). ◇ *n* falido *m*, -da *f*. ◇ *vt* falir.

bankruptcy ['bæŋkrəptsɪ] (*pl* -ies) *n* falência *f*; **moral ~** *fig* desmoralização *f*.

bank statement *n* extrato *m* bancário.

banner ['bænəʳ] *n* [made of cloth] faixa *f*.

bannister ['bænɪstəʳ] *n*, **bannisters** ['bænɪstəz] *npl* = banister.

banns [bænz] *npl*: **to publish the ~** proclamar os votos.

banquet ['bæŋkwɪt] *n* banquete *m*.

bantam ['bæntəm] *n* garnisé *m*.

bantamweight ['bæntəmweɪt] *n* peso-galo *m*.

banter ['bæntəʳ] ◇ *n (U)* brincadeiras *fpl*. ◇ *vi* brincar.

bap [bæp] *n UK* bisnaguinha *f*.

baptism ['bæptɪzm] *n* batismo *m*; **~ of fire** *fig* batismo de fogo.

Baptist ['bæptɪst] *n* batista *mf*.

baptize, -ise [*UK* bæp'taɪz, *US* 'bæptaɪz] *vt* batizar.

bar [bɑːʳ] (*pt* & *pp* -red, *cont*-ring) ◇ *n* - 1. [of wood, metal, chocolate, soap etc] barra *f*; **to be behind ~s** estar atrás das grades - 2. *fig* [obstacle] barreira *f* - 3. [drinking place] bar *m* - 4. [counter] balcão *m* - 5. *MUS* compasso *m*. ◇ *vt* - 1. [bolt] trancar - 2. [block off] bloquear; **to ~ sb's way** bloquear a passagem de alguém - 3. [ban] barrar; **to ~ sb (from somewhere/from doing sthg)** impedir alguém (de entrar em algum lugar/fazer algo). ◇ *prep* [except] excepto; **~ none** sem exceção.

◆ **Bar** *n* - 1. *UK*: **the Bar** [barristers] o Magistrado; [profession] a Magistratura - 2. *US*: **the Bar** [lawyers] advogados(das); [profession] a Advocacia.

Barbados [bɑː'beɪdɒs] *n* Barbados; **in ~** em Barbados.

barbarian [bɑː'beərɪən] *n* - 1. *HIST* bárbaro *m* - 2. *pej* & *fig* [uncultured person] bárbaro *m*, -ra *f*.

barbaric [bɑː'bærɪk] *adj pej* bárbaro(ra).

barbarous ['bɑːbərəs] *adj pej* bárbaro(ra).

barbecue ['bɑːbɪkjuː] ◇ *n* - 1. [grill] churrasqueira *f* - 2. [party] churrasco *m*. ◇ *vt* assar *(na churrasqueira)*.

barbed [bɑːbd] *adj* - 1. [pointed, spiked] farpado(da) - 2. [unkind] espinhento(ta).

barbed wire [bɑːbd-] *n UK (U)* arame *m* farpado.

barber ['bɑːbəʳ] *n* barbeiro *m*; **~'s (shop)** barbearia *f*.

barbiturate [bɑː'bɪtjʊrət] *n* barbitúrico *m*.

Barcelona [ˌbɑːsə'ləʊnə] *n* Barcelona; **in ~** em Barcelona.

bar chart, bar graph *US n* gráfico *m* de barras.

bar code *n* código *m* de barras.

bare [beəʳ] ◇ *adj* - 1. [without covering] descoberto(ta) - 2. [basic] mínimo(ma); **the ~ essentials** o mínimo necessário - 3. [empty] vazio(a) ◇ *vt* [reveal - chest, limbs] exibir, mostrar; **to ~ one's teeth** mostrar os dentes **to ~ one's head** tirar o chapéu.

bareback ['beəbæk] ◇ *adj* em pêlo. ◇ *adv* em pêlo.

barefaced ['beəfeɪst] *adj* deslavado(da).

barefoot(ed) [ˌbeə'fʊt(ɪd)] ◇ *adj* descalço(ça). ◇ *adv* descalço.

bareheaded [ˌbeə'hedɪd] ◇ *adj* sem chapéu. ◇ *adv* sem chapéu.

barelegged [ˌbeə'legd] ◇ *adj* de pernas de fora. ◇ *adv* de pernas de fora.

barely ['beəlɪ] *adv* [scarcely] mal.

bargain ['bɑːgɪn] ◇ *n* - 1. [agreement] barganha *f*; **into the ~** ainda por cima - 2. [good buy] pechincha *f*. ◇ *vi* barganhar; **to ~ with sb for sthg** pechinchar com alguém por algo.

◆ **bargain for, bargain on** *vt fus* esperar.

bargaining ['bɑːgɪnɪŋ] *n (U)* barganha *f*.

bargaining power *n (U)* poder *m* de barganha.

barge [bɑːdʒ] ◇ *n* barca *f*. ◇ *vi inf* **to ~ into sb/**

sthg esbarrar em alguém/algo; **to ~ past sb/ sthg** passar empurrando alguém/algo.

➡ **barge in** *vi*: **to ~ in (on sb/sthg)** interromper (alguém/algo).

barge pole *n inf*: **I wouldn't touch it with a ~** não quero nem de graça.

bar graph *n US* = **bar chart**.

baritone ['bærɪtəʊn] *n* barítono *m*.

barium meal ['beərɪəm-] *n UK* (líquido de) contraste *m*.

bark [bɑːk] ◇ *n* **-1.** [of dog] latido *m*; **his ~ is worse than his bite** *inf* cão que late não morde **-2.** [on tree] casca *f.* ◇ *vt* [order] gritar. ◇ *vi* [dog] latir; **to ~ at sb/sthg** xingar alguém/algo.

barking ['bɑːkɪŋ] ◇ *n* (U) latidos *mpl.* ◇ *adj & adv*: **to be ~ (mad)** *UK inf* ser/estar completamente louco(ca); **to go ~ mad** *UK inf* pirar de vez.

barley ['bɑːlɪ] *n* (U) cevada *f.*

barley sugar *n UK bala feita com caramelo e cevada.*

barley water *n UK* (U) *bebida à base de cevada e suco de fruta.*

barmaid ['bɑːmeɪd] *n* garçonete *f.*

barman ['bɑːmən] (*pl* **-men** [-mən]) *n* barman *m.*

barmy ['bɑːmɪ] (*compar* **-ier,** *superl* **-iest**) *adj UK inf* doido(da).

barn [bɑːn] *n* celeiro *m.*

barnacle ['bɑːnəkl] *n* cirrípede *m.*

barn dance *n* **-1.** [occasion] ≃ baile *m* caipira **-2.** *UK* [type of dance] ≃ dança *f* caipira.

barn owl *n* coruja *f* branca.

barnstorm *US vi* **-1.** [politician] viajar em campanha (pelo país) **-2.** [performer] sair em turnê.

barnstorming *UK adj* vigoroso(sa).

barometer [bə'rɒmɪtə^r] *n* **-1.** [instrument] barômetro *m* **-2.** *fig* [way of measuring] ≃ termômetro *m.*

baron ['bærən] *n* barão *m*; **oil/press ~** *fig* magnata da imprensa/do petróleo.

baroness ['bærənɪs] *n* baronesa *f.*

baronet ['bærənɪt] *n* baronete *m.*

baroque [bə'rɒk] *adj* barroco(ca).

barrack ['bærək] *vt UK* interromper com gritos.

➡ **barracks** *npl* quartel *m.*

barracking ['bærəkɪŋ] *n* (U) *UK* gritaria *f.*

barracuda [ˌbærə'kuːdə] *n* barracuda *f.*

barrage ['bærɑːʒ] *n* **-1.** [of firing] bombardeio *m* **-2.** [of questions] bombardeio *m* **-3.** *UK* [dam] barragem *f.*

barred [bɑːd] *adj* [window, door] trancado(da).

barrel ['bærəl] *n* **-1.** [container] barril *m* **-2.** [of gun] cano *m.*

barrel organ *n* realejo *m.*

barren ['bærən] *adj* **-1.** [unable to have children] estéril **-2.** [unable to produce crops] improdutivo(va) **-3.** [dull] enfadonho(nha).

barrette [bə'ret] *n US* [for hair] fivela *f* passador *m.*

barricade [ˌbærɪ'keɪd] ◇ *n* barricada *f.* ◇ *vt* bloquear, obstruir com barricadas; **to ~ o.s. in** entrincheirar-se em.

barrier ['bærɪə^r] *n* **-1.** [fence, wall] barreira *f* **-2.** *fig* [obstacle] obstáculo *m.*

barrier cream *n UK* loção *f* protetora.

barring ['bɑːrɪŋ] *prep*: **~ accidents** a menos que

haja imprevistos; **~ further complications** se não houver complicações.

barrister ['bærɪstə^r] *n UK* advogado *m*, -da *f.*

barroom ['bɑːrʊm] *n US* sala *f* de bar.

barrow ['bærəʊ] *n* [market stall] carrinho *m* de frutas/verduras.

bar stool *n* tamborete *m* de bar.

bartender ['bɑːtendə^r] *n US* garçom *m*, -nete *f.*

barter ['bɑːtə^r] ◇ *n* barganha *f*, troca *f.* ◇ *vt* trocar; **to ~ sthg for sthg** trocar algo por algo. ◇ *vi* barganhar.

base [beɪs] ◇ *n* base *f.* ◇ *vt* **-1.** [use as starting point]: **to ~ sthg (up)on sthg** basear algo em algo **-2.** [locate] estabelecer; **to be ~d in** viver/trabalhar em; **a New York-based company** uma empresa sediada em Nova York. ◇ *adj pej* [dishonourable] desprezível.

baseball ['beɪsbɔːl] *n* (U) beisebol *m.*

baseball cap *n* boné *m* de beisebol.

base camp *n* acampamento *m* de base.

baseless ['beɪslɪs] *adj* infundado(da).

baseline ['beɪslaɪn] *n SPORT* linha *f* de base.

basement ['beɪsmənt] *n* porão *m.*

base metal *n dated* metal *m* não-precioso.

base rate *n* taxa *f* de base.

bases ['beɪsiːz] *pl* ▷ **basis**.

bash [bæʃ] *inf* ◇ *n* **-1.** [painful blow] pancada *f* **-2.** [attempt]: **to have a ~ (at sthg)** tentar fazer (algo) **-3.** [party] farra *f.* ◇ *vt* **-1.** [hit] bater **-2.** [criticize] xingar.

bashful ['bæʃfʊl] *adj* tímido(da).

basic ['beɪsɪk] *adj* [fundamental] básico(ca).

➡ **basics** *npl* **-1.** [rudiments] princípios *mpl* básicos **-2.** [essential foodstuffs] ≃ cesta *f* básica.

BASIC (*abbr of* Beginners' All-purpose Symbolic Instruction Code) *n* BASIC *m.*

basically ['beɪsɪklɪ] *adv* [essentially] basicamente, no fundo.

basic rate *n UK* taxa *f* básica.

basic wage *n* salário *m* base.

basil ['bæzl] *n* (U) manjericão *m.*

basin ['beɪsn] *n* **-1.** *UK* [bowl, container] tigela *f*; [for washing] pia *f* **-2.** *GEOGR* bacia *f.*

basis ['beɪsɪs] (*pl* **-ses**) *n* **-1.** [gen] base *f*; **on the ~ that** com base no fato de que, considerando que **-2.** [arrangement]: **on a weekly/monthly ~** numa base semanal/mensal; **on the ~ of** com base em.

bask [bɑːsk] *vi* **-1.** [sunbathe]: **to ~ in the sun** tomar banho de sol **-2.** *fig* [take pleasure]: **to ~ in sb's praise/approval** gozar do elogio/da aprovação de alguém.

basket ['bɑːskɪt] *n* [container - for rubbish] cesto *m*; [- for shopping] cesta *f.*

basketball ['bɑːskɪtbɔːl] ◇ *n* (U) basquete *m.* ◇ *comp* de basquete.

basket case *n inf* **-1.** [person] bagaço *m* **-2.** [failure] ruína *f.*

basketwork ['bɑːskɪtwɜːk] *n* **-1.** (U) [craft, activity] trabalho *m* em vime **-2.** (U) [articles] artigos *mpl* de vime.

basking shark ['bɑːskɪŋ-] *n* tubarão-frade *m.*

Basle [bɑːl] *n* Basiléia; **in ~** na Basiléia.

Basque [bɑːsk] ⟨⟩ *adj* basco(ca). ⟨⟩ *n* - **1.** [person] basco *m*, -ca *f* - **2.** [language] basco *m*.

bass¹ [beɪs] ⟨⟩ *adj* [part, singer] baixo(xa). ⟨⟩ *n* - **1.** [singer] baixo *m*, -xa *f* - **2.** [double bass] duplo baixo *m* - **3.** = bass guitar.

bass² [bæs] (*pl inv OR* -es) *n* [fish] perca *f*.

bass clef [beɪs-] *n MUS* clave *f* de fá.

bass drum [beɪs-] *n MUS* tambor *m* baixo.

basset (hound) ['bæsɪt-] *n* cão *m* bassê.

bass guitar [beɪs-] *n MUS* baixo *m*.

bassoon [bə'suːn] *n MUS* fagote *m*.

bassoonist *n MUS* fagotista *mf*.

bastard ['bɑːstəd] *n* - **1.** [illegitimate child] bastardo *m*, -da *f* - **2.** *v inf pej* [person] canalha *mf*, filho *m* da mãe.

baste [beɪst] *vt CULIN* regar.

bastion ['bæstɪən] *n fig* bastião *m*.

bat [bæt] (*pt & pp* -ted, *cont* -ting) ⟨⟩ *n* - **1.** [animal] morcego *m* - **2.** [SPORT - for cricket] pá *f*; [- for baseball] bastão *m*; [- for table tennis] raquete *f* - **3.** *phr*: to do sthg off one's own ~ fazer algo sem auxílio. ⟨⟩ *vt & vi* rebater.

batch [bætʃ] *n* - **1.** [of papers, letters] pilha *f* - **2.** [of work] porção *f* - **3.** [of products] lote *m* - **4.** [of people] grupo *m* - **5.** [of bread, cakes etc] fornada *f*.

batch file *n COMPUT* arquivo *m* em lote.

batch processing *n* (*U*) COMPUT processamento *m* em lote.

bated ['beɪtɪd] *adj*: with ~ breath [expectantly] segurando a respiração.

bath [bɑːθ] ⟨⟩ *n* - **1.** [bathtub] banheira *f* - **2.** [act of washing] banho *m*; to have OR take a bath tomar (um) banho. ⟨⟩ *vt* dar banho em.
➡ **baths** *npl UK* [public] banhos *mpl* públicos.

bath chair *n* cadeira *f* de banho.

bath cube *n* cubos *mpl* de sais de banho.

bathe [beɪð] ⟨⟩ *vt* - **1.** [wound] lavar - **2.** [in light, sweat] banhar; to be ~d in sthg estar coberto(ta) de algo. ⟨⟩ *vi* - **1.** [swim] nadar - **2.** *US* [take a bath] tomar (um) banho.

bather ['beɪðə'] *n* [swimmer] banhista *m*.

bathing ['beɪðɪŋ] *n* (*U*) banho *m*; safe for ~ próprio(pria) para banho; to go ~ dar um mergulho.

bathing cap *n* touca *f* de banho.

bathing costume, bathing suit *n* maiô *m*.

bathing trunks *npl* calção *m* de banho.

bath mat *n* tapete *m* de banheiro.

bath oil *n* óleo *m* de banho.

bathrobe ['bɑːθrəʊb] *n* - **1.** [made of towelling] roupão *m* de banho - **2.** [dressing gown] *US* chambre *m*.

bathroom ['bɑːθrʊm] *n UK* banheiro *m*.

bath salts *npl* sais *mpl* de banho.

bath towel *n* toalha *f* de banho.

bathtub ['bɑːθtʌb] *n* banheira *f*.

batik [bə'tiːk] *n* batique *m*.

baton ['bætən] *n* - **1.** [of conductor] batuta *f* - **2.** [in relay race] bastão *m* - **3.** *UK* [of policeman] cassetete *m*.

baton charge *n UK* [by police] investida *f* policial.

batsman ['bætsmən] (*pl* -men [-mən]) *n CRICKET* batedor *m*.

battalion [bə'tæljən] *n* batalhão *m*.

batten ['bætn] *n* [piece of wood] tábua *f*.
➡ **batten down** *vt fus fig*: to ~ down the

hatches preparar-se para momentos difíceis/ enfrentar uma crise.

batter ['bætə'] ⟨⟩ *n* - **1.** CULIN massa *f* (mole) - **2.** SPORT batedor *m*, -ra *f*. ⟨⟩ *vt* [child, woman] surrar. ⟨⟩ *vi* [beat] bater.
➡ **batter down** *vt sep* botar abaixo.

battered ['bætəd] *adj* - **1.** [child, woman] maltratado(-da) - **2.** [old, worn-out - car] arruinado(da); [- hat] surrado(da) - **3.** CULIN misturado(da).

battering ['bætərɪŋ] *n*: to take a ~ sofrer uma derrota.

battering ram *n* aríete *m*.

battery ['bætərɪ] (*pl* -ies) *n* - **1.** [gen] bateria *f* - **2.** [ELEC - of car] bateria *f*; [- of radio, torch etc] pilha *f* - **3.** [group - of people] grupo *m*; [- of things] série *f*, conjunto *m*.

battery charger *n* carregador *m* de bateria.

battery hen *n* frango *m* de granja.

battle ['bætl] ⟨⟩ *n* batalha *f*; ~ for/against/with sthg batalha por/contra/com algo; ~ of wits disputa de intelectos; to be half the ~ ser a metade do caminho; to be fighting a losing ~ estar lutando em vão. ⟨⟩ *vi* [fight] lutar; to ~ for/ against/with sthg lutar por/contra/com algo.

battledress ['bætldres] *n UK* uniforme *m* de combate.

battlefield ['bætlfiːld], **battleground** ['bætl-graʊnd] *n MIL & fig* campo *m* de batalha.

battlements ['bætlmənts] *npl* [of castle] ameias *fpl*.

battleship ['bætlʃɪp] *n* couraçado *m*.

bauble ['bɔːbl] *n* bugiganga *f*.

baud [bɔːd] *n COMPUT* baud *m*.

baud rate *n COMPUT* baud rate *m*, taxa *f* de bauds.

baulk [bɔːk] *vi* = balk.

Bavaria [bə'veərɪə] *n* Baviera; in ~ na Baviera.

Bavarian [bə'veərɪən] ⟨⟩ *adj* bávaro(ra). ⟨⟩ *n* bávaro *m*, -ra *f*.

bawdy ['bɔːdɪ] (*compar* -ier, *superl* -iest) *adj* obsceno(na).

bawl [bɔːl] ⟨⟩ *vt* [shout] gritar. ⟨⟩ *vi* - **1.** [shout] gritar - **2.** [weep] berrar.

bay [beɪ] ⟨⟩ *n* - **1.** GEOGR baía *f* - **2.** [for loading] zona *m* de carga e descarga - **3.** [for parking] vaga *f* - **4.** [horse] baio *m* - **5.** *phr*: to keep sb/sthg at ~ manter alguém/algo à distância. ⟨⟩ *vi* [dog, wolf] latir.

bay leaf *n* folha *f* de louro.

Bay of Biscay *n*: the ~ o Golfo de Biscaia.

bayonet ['beɪənɪt] *n* baioneta *f*.

bay tree *n* loureiro *m*.

bay window *n* bay window *f* janela *f* saliente.

bazaar [bə'zɑː'] *n* - **1.** [market] bazar *m* - **2.** *UK* [charity sale] bazar *m* beneficente.

bazooka [bə'zuːkə] *n* bazuca *f*.

B & B *n abbr of* bed and breakfast

BBC (*abbr of* British Broadcasting Corporation) *n* companhia estatal britânica de rádio e televisão, BBC *f*.

BC - **1.** (*abbr of* before Christ) a.C. - **2.** *abbr of* British Columbia.

BCG (*abbr of* Bacillus Calmette-Guérin) *n* BCG *f*.

BD (*abbr of* Bachelor of Divinity) *n* (*titular de*) graduação em teologia cristã protestante.

BDS (*abbr of* Bachelor of Dental Science) *n* (*titular de*) graduação em odontologia.

be [bi:] (*pt* was OR were, *pp* been) ◇ *aux vb* **-1.** (*in combination with ppr: to form cont tense*) estar; **what is he doing?** o que ele está fazendo?; **it's snowing** está nevando **-2.** (*in combination with pp: to form passive*) ser; **to ~ loved** ser amado(da) **-3.** (*in question tags*) ser, estar; **the meal was delicious, wasn't it?** a comida estava deliciosa, não estava? **-4.** (*followed by to + infin*) dever; **I'm to ~ promoted** devo ser promovido(da); **you're not to tell anyone** você não deve contar a ninguém. ◇ *copulative vb* **-1.** (*with adj, n*) ser, estar; **to ~ a doctor/lawyer/plumber** ser médico/advogado/bombeiro; **she's intelligent/attractive** ela é inteligente/atraente; **~ quiet!** fique quieto!; **1 and 1 are 2** 1 e 1 são 2 **-2.** [referring to health] estar; **how are you?** como vai você? **-3.** [referring to age] ter; **how old are you?** quantos anos você tem? **-4.** [cost] custar; **how much was it?** quanto custou?; **that will ~ £10, please** são £10, por favor. ◇ *vi* **-1.** [exist] existir, haver, ser; **~ that as it may** seja como for **-2.** [referring to place] estar; **Toulouse is in France** Toulouse fica na França; **he will ~ here tomorrow** ele estará aqui amanhã **-3.** [referring to movement] estar; **I've been to the cinema/to France/to the butcher's** fui ao cinema/para a França/ao açougue. ◇ *v impers* **-1.** [referring to time, dates] ser; **it's two o'clock** são duas horas **-2.** [referring to distance] ser; **it's 3 km to the next town** são 3 quilômetros até a próxima cidade **-3.** [referring to the weather] estar; **it's hot/cold/windy** está quente OR frio OR ventando **-4.** [for emphasis] ser; **it's me** sou eu; **it's the milkman** é o leiteiro.

beach [bi:tʃ] ◇ *n* praia *f*. ◇ *vt* [boat, whale] encalhar.

beach ball *n* bola *f* de praia.

beach buggy *n* buggy *m*.

beachcomber ['bi:tʃ,kəʊməʳ] *n* pessoa *que ganha a vida catando e vendendo artigos deixados na praia*.

beachhead ['bi:tʃhed] *n* MIL cabeça-de-ponte *f*.

beachwear ['bi:tʃweəʳ] *n* (U) roupa *f* de praia.

beacon ['bi:kən] *n* **-1.** [warning fire] fogaréu *m* **-2.** [lighthouse] farol *m* **-3.** [radio beacon] radiofarol *m*.

bead [bi:d] *n* **-1.** [of wood, glass] conta *f* **-2.** [of sweat] gota *f*.

beaded *adj* [decorated with beads] enfeitado(da) com contas.

beading ['bi:dɪŋ] *n* [wood] moldura *f*.

beady ['bi:dɪ] (*compar* -ier, *superl* -iest) *adj* [eyes] pequeno(na) e brilhante; **to keep a ~ eye on sb/sthg** *fig* ficar de olho em alguém/algo.

beagle ['bi:gl] *n* bigle *m*.

beak [bi:k] *n* [of bird] bico *m*.

beaker ['bi:kəʳ] *n* copo *m* (*de plástico*).

be-all *n*: **the ~ and end-all** a razão de ser.

beam [bi:m] ◇ *n* **-1.** [of wood, concrete] viga *f* **-2.** [of light] raio *m*, feixe *m* **-3.** US AUT: **high/low ~ s** luz alta/baixa. ◇ *vt* [signal, news] transmitir. ◇ *vi* **-1.** [smile] irradiar-se **-2.** [shine] irradiar.

beaming ['bi:mɪŋ] *adj* radiante.

bean [bi:n] *n* CULIN feijão *m*, grão *m*; **to be full of ~ s** *inf* estar cheio (cheia) de vida; **to spill the ~ s** *inf* dar com a língua nos dentes.

beanbag ['bi:nbæg] *n* [seat] *almofada grande e*

redonda, feita de flocos de espuma que se adapta ao corpo de quem senta.

beanshoot ['bi:nʃu:t], **beansprout** ['bi:nspraʊt] *n* broto *m* de feijão.

bear [beəʳ] (*pt* bore, *pp* borne) ◇ *n* **-1.** [animal] urso *m*, -sa *f* **-2.** ST EX baixista *mf*. ◇ *vt* **-1.** [carry] carregar **-2.** [sustain] suportar **-3.** [accept] aceitar **-4.** [show] exibir **-5.** [produce, interest] produzir **-6.** [give birth to] parir **-7.** [feeling] guardar. ◇ *vi* **-1.** [turn] virar **-2.** [have effect]: **to bring pressure/influence to ~ on sb** exercer pressão/influência sobre alguém.

➥ **bear down** *vi*: **to ~ down on sb/sthg** abater-se sobre algo/alguém.

➥ **bear out** *vt sep* confirmar.

➥ **bear up** *vi* resistir.

➥ **bear with** *vt fus* tolerar.

bearable ['beərəbl] *adj* [tolerable] suportável.

beard [bɪəd] *n* [of man] barba *f*.

bearded *adj* [man, face] com barba.

bearer ['beərəʳ] *n* **-1.** [of stretcher, coffin] carregador *m*, -ra *f* **-2.** [of news, document] portador *m*, -ra *f* **-3.** [of name, title] detentor *m*, -ra *f*.

bear hug *n* *inf* abraço *m* forte.

bearing ['beərɪŋ] *n* **-1.** [connection] relação *f*; **~ on sthg** relação com algo **-2.** [deportment] conduta *f* **-3.** TECH mancal *m* **-4.** [on compass] direção *f*; **to get/lose one's ~ s** *fig* achar/perder o rumo.

bear market *n* ST EX mercado *m* em baixa.

bearskin ['beəskɪn] *n* **-1.** [fur] pele *f* de urso **-2.** [hat] barretina *f* (de pele).

beast [bi:st] *n* **-1.** [animal] besta *m* **-2.** *inf pej* [person] besta *f*.

beastly ['bi:stlɪ] (*compar* -ier, *superl* -iest) *adj dated* abominável.

beat [bi:t] (*pt* beat, *pp* beaten) ◇ *n* **-1.** [gen] batida *f* **-2.** [of heart, pulse] batimento *m* **-3.** MUS [rhythm] ritmo *m* **-4.** [of policeman] ronda *f*. ◇ *adj inf* [exhausted] nocauteado(da). ◇ *vt* **-1.** [hit] bater em **-2.** [defeat] derrotar; **it ~ s me** *inf* isto acaba comigo **-3.** [arrive ahead of] chegar antes; **she ~ me to it** ela me venceu **-4.** [be better than] superar **-5.** [eggs, wings] bater **-6.** MUS [time] marcar **-7.** *phr*: **~ it!** *inf* [go away] caia fora! ◇ *vi* **-1.** [rain] cair **-2.** [heart, pulse] bater.

➥ **beat down** ◇ *vi* **-1.** [sun] bater **-2.** [rain] cair uma pancada. ◇ *vt sep* [force to lower price] fazer baixar.

➥ **beat off** *vt sep* [resist] repelir.

➥ **beat up** *vt sep inf* [person] espancar.

beaten *adj* **-1.** [metal] forjado(da) **-2.** [path] batido(-da).

beater ['bi:təʳ] *n* **-1.** [for eggs, cream etc] batedeira *f* **-2.** [for carpet] batedor *m* **-3.** [of woman, child] agressor *m*, -ra *f*.

beat generation *n* geração *f* beat.

beating ['bi:tɪŋ] *n* [defeat, punishment] surra *f*; **to take a ~** levar uma surra; **to take some ~** *inf* ser difícil de superar.

beating up (*pl* beatings up) *n* *inf* [thrashing] espancamento *m*.

beatnik ['bi:tnɪk] *n* beatnik *m*.

beat-up *adj inf* [shabby] caindo aos pedaços.

beautician [bju:'tɪʃn] *n* esteticista *mf*.

beautiful ['bju:tɪfʊl] *adj* **-1.** [gen] bonito(ta) **-2.** [well executed] belo(la).

beautifully ['bju:təflɪ] *adv* **-1.** [attractively] belamente **-2.** *inf* [very well] esplendidamente.

beauty ['bju:tɪ] (*pl* **-ies**) ⟨⟩ *n* **-1.** (*U*) [attractiveness] beleza *f* **-2.** [beautiful woman] beldade *f* **-3.** *inf* [very good thing] maravilha *f.* ⟨⟩ *comp* [product] de beleza.

beauty contest *n* concurso *m* de beleza.

beauty parlour *n* salão *m* de beleza.

beauty queen *n* miss *f.*

beauty salon *n* = beauty parlour.

beauty spot *n* **-1.** [place] recanto *m* **-2.** [on skin] sinal *m.*

beaver ['bi:vəʳ] *n* castor *m.*
➤ **beaver away** *vi*: to ~ away (at sthg) dar duro (em algo).

becalmed [bɪ'kɑ:md] *adj* [ship] parado(da) por falta de vento.

became [bɪ'keɪm] *pt* ▷ **become**.

because [bɪ'kɒz] *conj* porque.
➤ **because of** *prep* por causa de.

béchamel sauce [ˌbeɪʃə'mel-] *n* molho *m* bechamel or branco.

beck [bek] *n*: to be at sb's ~ and call estar sempre à disposição de alguém.

beckon ['bekən] ⟨⟩ *vt* **-1.** [make a signal to] acenar **-2.** *fig* [call] chamar. ⟨⟩ *vi* [signal]: to ~ to sb acenar para alguém.

become [bɪ'kʌm] (*pt* **became**, *pp* **become**) *vt* **-1.** [grow] ficar; **what has ~ of ...?** o que foi feito de ...? **-2.** [acquire post of] tornar-se **-3.** [suit, be appropriate to] combinar com, ficar bem em; **sarcasm doesn't ~ you** o sarcasmo não combina com você.

becoming [bɪ'kʌmɪŋ] *adj* **-1.** [attractive] elegante **-2.** [appropriate] adequado(da).

bed [bed] (*pt* & *pp* **-ded**, *cont* **-ding**) *n* **-1.** [to sleep on] cama *f*; **to go to ~** ir para a cama; **to make the ~** arrumar a cama; **to make one's (own) ~** *fig* fazer a própria cama; **to go to ~ with sb** *euphemism* ir para a cama com alguém **-2.** [flowerbed] canteiro *m*; **a ~ of roses** *fig* [easy, pleasant] um mar de rosas **-3.** [bottom - of sea] fundo *m*; [- of river] leito *m.*
➤ **bed down** *vt* & *vi* acolher.

BEd (*abbr of* **Bachelor of Education**) *n* (*titular de*) *graduação que habilita para o magistério.*

bed and breakfast *n* **-1.** [service] hospedagem *f* com café da manhã **-2.** [hotel] bed and breakfast *m*, *acomodação típica da Grã-Bretanha (geralmente em casa de família) acompanhada de café da manhã.*

bed-bath *n* banho *m* na cama.

bedbug ['bedbʌg] *n* percevejo *m.*

bedclothes ['bedkləʊðz] *npl* roupa *f* de cama.

bedcover ['bedˌkʌvəʳ] *n* colcha *f.*

bedding ['bedɪŋ] *n* = bedclothes.

bedding plant *n* planta *f* de canteiro.

bedeck [bɪ'dek] *vt*: to ~ sthg with sthg decorar algo com algo.

bedevil [bɪ'devl] (*UK pt* & *pp* **-led**, *cont* **-ling**, *US pt* & *pp* **-ed**, *cont* **-ing**) *vt*: to be bedevilled with sthg estar atormentado(da) com algo.

bedfellow ['bedˌfeləʊ] *n fig* [colleague] aliado *m*, -da *f.*

bedlam ['bedləm] *n* [chaos] tumulto *m.*

bed linen *n* roupa *f* de cama.

Bedouin, Beduin ['bedʊɪn] ⟨⟩ *adj* beduíno(na). ⟨⟩ *n* beduíno *m*, -na *f.*

bedpan ['bedpæn] *n* comadre *f.*

bedraggled [bɪ'drægld] *adj* enlameado(da).

bedridden ['bedˌrɪdn] *adj* acamado(da).

bedrock ['bedrɒk] *n* (*U*) **-1.** GEOL leito *m* de rocha firme **-2.** *fig* [solid foundation] alicerce *m.*

bedroom ['bedrʊm] *n* quarto *m.*

bedside ['bedsaɪd] ⟨⟩ *n* beira *f* da cama. ⟨⟩ *comp* [lamp, table] de cabeceira.

bedside manner *n* [of doctor] jeito *m* para lidar com doentes.

bedside table *n* mesa *f* de cabeceira, criado-mudo *m.*

bed-sit(ter) *n UK* conjugado *m.*

bedsore ['bedsɔ:ʳ] *n* assadura *f.*

bedspread ['bedspred] *n* colcha *f.*

bedtime ['bedtaɪm] *n* hora *f* de dormir.

Beduin *adj* & *n* = Bedouin.

bed-wetting [-ˌwetɪŋ] *n* incontinência *f* urinária.

bee [bi:] *n* abelha *f*; **to have a ~ in one's bonnet about sthg** *fig* estar obcecado(da) por algo.

Beeb [bi:b] *n UK inf*: **the ~** a BBC.

beech [bi:tʃ] *n* faia *f.*

beef [bi:f] ⟨⟩ *n* (*U*) [meat] carne *f* de vaca. ⟨⟩ *vi inf* [complain]: to ~ about sthg reclamar de algo.
➤ **beef up** *vt sep inf* [strengthen] reforçar.

beefburger ['bi:fˌbɜ:gəʳ] *n* hambúrguer *m* bovino.

Beefeater ['bi:fˌi:təʳ] *n guarda da Torre de Londres.*

beefsteak ['bi:fˌsteɪk] *n* bife *m.*

beehive ['bi:haɪv] *n* **-1.** [for bees] colméia *f* **-2.** [hairstyle] ≃ pixaim *m.*

beekeeper ['bi:ˌki:pəʳ] *n* apicultor *m*, -ra *f.*

beeline ['bi:laɪn] *n*: to make a ~ for sb/sthg *inf* ir direto a alguém/algo.

been [bi:n] *pp* ▷ **be**.

beep [bi:p] *inf* ⟨⟩ *n* bipe *m.* ⟨⟩ *vi* bipar.

beeper ['bi:pəʳ] *n* [device] bipe *m.*

beer [bɪəʳ] *n* cerveja *f.*

beer garden *n terraço de um bar em que geralmente se admite a presença de crianças.*

beer mat *n* bolacha *f.*

beeswax ['bi:zwæks] *n* (*U*) cera *f* de abelha.

beet [bi:t] *n* **-1.** [sugar beet] acelga *f* **-2.** *US* [beetroot] beterraba *f.*

beetle ['bi:tl] *n* besouro *m.*

beetroot ['bi:tru:t] *n* beterraba *f.*

befall [bɪ'fɔ:l] (*pt* **-fell** [-'fel], *pp* **-fallen** [-'fɔ:lən]) *literary* ⟨⟩ *vt* suceder. ⟨⟩ *vi* acontecer.

befit [bɪ'fɪt] (*pt* & *pp* **-ted**, *cont* **-ting**) *vt fml* convir a.

before [bɪ'fɔ:ʳ] ⟨⟩ *adv* [previously] antes. ⟨⟩ *prep* **-1.** [preceding in time] antes de **-2.** [in front of]: **the road stretched out ~ them** a estrada se abria diante or à frente deles; **~ my very eyes** diante de meus próprios olhos; **standing ~ the door** parado(da) em frente à porta **-3.** [confronting] perante **-4.** [in the presence of] diante de, perante a. ⟨⟩

conj: ~ **leaving the country** antes de deixar o país; ~ **he entered the house** antes de entrar na casa.

beforehand [bɪˈfɔːhænd] *adv* [in advance] de antemão.

befriend [bɪˈfrend] *vt* **-1.** [make friends with] fazer amizade com **-2.** [support] favorecer.

befuddled [bɪˈfʌdld] *adj* [confused] atordoado(da).

beg [beg] (*pt* & *pp* **-ged,** *cont* **-ging**) ◇ *vt* **-1.** [money, food] mendigar, pedir **-2.** [favour, forgiveness, mercy] pedir; **I ~ your pardon** desculpe-me; **to ~ sb for sthg** pedir algo a alguém ; **to ~ sb to do sthg** pedir a alguém para fazer algo. ◇ *vi* **-1.** [for money, food] mendigar, pedir; **to ~ for sthg** mendigar *OR* pedir algo **-2.** [for favour, forgiveness, mercy] pedir; **to ~ for sthg** pedir algo.

began [bɪˈgæn] *pt* ⊳ **begin.**

beggar [ˈbegəʳ] *n* mendigo *m*, -ga *f*.

begin [bɪˈgɪn] (*pt* **began,** *pp* **begun,** *cont* **-ning**) ◇ *vt* **-1.** [start] começar; **to ~ doing** *OR* **to do sthg** começar a fazer algo **-2.** [initiate] começar. ◇ *vi* [start] começar; **to ~ with, ...** para começar, ...

beginner [bɪˈgɪnəʳ] *n* [learner] principiante *mf*, aprendiz *mf*.

beginning [bɪˈgɪnɪŋ] *n* **-1.** [start] começo *m*; **in the ~** no começo **-2.** [origin] início *m*, origem *f*.

begonia [bɪˈgəʊnjə] *n* begônia *f*.

begrudge [bɪˈgrʌdʒ] *vt* **-1.** [envy]: **to ~ sb sthg** invejar algo de alguém **-2.** [give, do unwillingly]: **to ~ doing sthg** fazer algo de má vontade.

beguile [bɪˈgaɪl] *vt* [charm] encantar.

beguiling [bɪˈgaɪlɪŋ] *adj* [charming] encantador(ra).

begun [bɪˈgʌn] *pp* ⊳ **begin.**

behalf [bɪˈhɑːf] *n*: **on ~ of sb** *UK*, **in ~ of sb** *US* em nome de alguém.

behave [bɪˈheɪv] ◇ *v refl*: **to ~ o.s.** comportar-se bem. ◇ *vi* **-1.** [in a particular way] comportar-se **-2.** [in an acceptable way] comportar-se bem.

behaviour *UK*, **behavior** *US* [bɪˈheɪvjəʳ] *n* comportamento *m*.

behaviourism *UK*, **behaviorism** *US* [bɪˈd heɪvjərɪzm] *n* behaviorismo *m*.

behead [bɪˈhed] *vt* degolar.

beheld [bɪˈheld] *pt* & *pp* ⊳ **behold.**

behind [bɪˈhaɪnd] ◇ *prep* **-1.** [at the back of] atrás de **-2.** [causing, responsible for] por trás de **-3.** [supporting]: **to be ~ sb** apoiar alguém, estar com alguém **-4.** [indicating deficiency, delay] atrás de; **to run ~ schedule** estar atrasado(da). ◇ *adv* **-1.** [at, in the back] atrás **-2.** [late] para trás; **~ with sthg** com atraso em algo. ◇ *n inf* [buttocks] traseiro *m*.

behold [bɪˈhəʊld] (*pt* & *pp* **beheld**) *vt literary* contemplar.

beige [beɪʒ] ◇ *adj* bege. ◇ *n* bege *m*; **in ~** em bege.

Beijing [ˌbeɪˈdʒɪŋ] *n* Beijing; **in ~** em Beijing.

being [ˈbiːɪŋ] *n* **-1.** [creature] ser *m* **-2.** (*U*) [state of existing]: **in ~** em vigor; **to come into ~** nascer; **for the time ~** por enquanto.

Beirut [ˌbeɪˈruːt] *n* Beirute; **in ~** em Beirute.

belated [bɪˈleɪtɪd] *adj* tardio(dia).

belatedly [bɪˈleɪtɪdlɪ] *adv* tardiamente.

belch [beltʃ] ◇ *n* arroto *m*. ◇ *vt* [smoke, fire] expelir. ◇ *vi* [person] arrotar.

beleaguered [bɪˈliːgəd] *adj* **-1.** [*MIL* - city] sitiado (da); [- troops] cercado(da) **-2.** *fig* [harassed] assediado(da).

belfry [ˈbelfrɪ] (*pl* **-ies**) *n* campanário *m*.

Belgian [ˈbeldʒən] ◇ *adj* belga. ◇ *n* belga *mf*.

Belgium [ˈbeldʒəm] *n* Bélgica; **in ~** na Bélgica.

Belgrade [ˌbelˈgreɪd] *n* Belgrado; **in ~** em Belgrado.

belie [bɪˈlaɪ] (*cont* **belying**) *vt* **-1.** [disprove] desmentir **-2.** [give false idea of] esconder, disfarçar.

belief [bɪˈliːf] *n* **-1.** (*U*) crença *f*; **~ in sthg** crença em algo; **beyond ~** inacreditável **-2.** [opinion] opinião *f*; **in the ~ that** na certeza de que.

believable [bɪˈliːvəbl] *adj* **-1.** [creditable] crível **-2.** [possible] possível.

believe [bɪˈliːv] ◇ *vt* **-1.** [think] achar; **I ~ so** acho que sim **-2.** [person, statement] acreditar em; **~ it or not** acredite ou não. ◇ *vi* **-1.** [be religious] crer em **-2.** [know to exist]: **to ~ in sb/sthg** acreditar em alguém/algo.

believer [bɪˈliːvəʳ] *n* **-1.** *RELIG* crente *mf* **-2.** [supporter]: **~ in sthg** partidário(ria) de algo.

Belisha beacon [bɪˈliːʃə-] *n UK* sinal laranja intermitente identificando local de travessia de pedestres.

belittle [bɪˈlɪtl] *vt* [disparage] depreciar.

Belize [beˈliːz] *n* Belize; **in ~** em Belize.

bell [bel] *n* **-1.** [of church] sino *m* **-2.** [on door, bicycle] campainha *f*; **to ring a ~** *fig* trazer à lembrança.

bell-bottoms *npl* calça *f* boca-de-sino.

bellhop [ˈbelhop] *n US* mensageiro *m*, -ra *f* (de hotel).

belligerence [bɪˈlɪdʒərəns] *n* [aggression] agressividade *f*.

belligerent [bɪˈlɪdʒərənt] *adj* **-1.** [at war] beligerante **-2.** [aggressive] agressivo(va).

bellow [ˈbeləʊ] ◇ *vt* [order] gritar. ◇ *vi* **-1.** [person] gritar **-2.** [bull] mugir.

bellows [ˈbeləʊz] *npl* fole *m*.

bell push *n UK* campainha *f*.

bell-ringer *n* sineiro *m*, -ra *f*.

belly [ˈbelɪ] (*pl* **-ies**) *n* barriga *f*.

bellyache [ˈbelɪeɪk] ◇ *n* [stomachache] dor *f* de estômago. ◇ *vi inf* [complain] reclamar.

belly button *n inf* [navel] umbigo *m*.

belly dancer *n* dançarina *f* do ventre.

belly dancing *n* dança *f* do ventre.

belong [bɪˈlɒŋ] *vi* **-1.** [be property]: **to ~ to sb** pertencer a alguém **-2.** [be a member]: **to ~ to sthg** fazer parte *OR* ser membro de algo **-3.** [be situated in right place] encaixar-se.

belongings [bɪˈlɒŋɪŋz] *npl* pertences *mpl*.

Belorussia [ˌbeləʊˈrʌʃə] *n* Bielo-Rússia; **in ~** na Bielo-Rússia.

beloved [bɪˈlʌvd] ◇ *adj* amado(da), querido(da). ◇ *n* amado *m*, -da *f*.

below [bɪˈləʊ] ◇ *adv* **-1.** [in a lower position] de baixo **-2.** [in text or with numbers, quantities] abaixo **-3.** *NAUT*: **to go ~** descer. ◇ *prep* abaixo de.

belt [belt] ◇ *n* **-1.** [for clothing] cinto *m*; **to be below the ~** *fig* ser cruel, ser um golpe baixo; **to have sthg under one's ~** [as experience] ter algo como experiência; [qualification] ter algo no currículo; **to tighten one's** ~ apertar o cinto **-2.** TECH correia f **-3.** [of land, sea] faixa f, cinturão m. ⟨⟩ vt **-1.** inf[hit with a belt] dar uma surra de cinto em **-2.** inf [punch, beat] meter o couro em. ⟨⟩ vi UK inf [move at speed]: **to** ~ **along/down sthg** ir à toda por.

➤ **belt out** vt sep inf cantar a plenos pulmões.
➤ **belt up** vi UK inf[be quiet] botar zíper na boca, calar o bico.

beltway ['belt,weɪ] n US anel m viário, rodoanel m.
bemused [bɪ'mju:zd] adj bestificado(da).
bench [bentʃ] n **-1.** [seat] banco m **-2.** [in laboratory, workshop] bancada f **-3.** UK JUR magistratura f.
benchmark n **-1.** [standard] referência f **-2.** COMPUT padrão m de desempenho **-3.** ECON benchmark m, indicador m.
bend [bend] (pt & pp bent) ⟨⟩ n **-1.** curva f **-2.** phr: **round the** ~ inf pirado(da), maluco(ca); **to drive sb round the** ~ inf deixar alguém maluco(ca). ⟨⟩ vt dobrar. ⟨⟩ vi **-1.** [arm, leg] dobrar-se ; [tree, person] inclinar-se **-2.** [river, road] fazer uma curva.
➤ **bends** npl MED : **the** ~ **s** o mal da descompressão.
➤ **bend down** vi curvar-se.
➤ **bend over** vi inclinar-se; **to** ~ **over backwards for sb** fig fazer todo o possível por alguém.
bendy ['bendɪ] (compar -ier, superl -iest) adj UK flexível.
beneath [bɪ'ni:θ] ⟨⟩ adv[below] debaixo. ⟨⟩ prep **-1.** [under] debaixo de, sob **-2.** [unworthy of]: **he felt the job was** ~ **him** ele sentia que o emprego estava aquém dele; **to be** ~ **sthg** não ser digno(na) de algo.
benediction [,benɪ'dɪkʃn] n RELIG bênção f.
benefactor ['benɪfæktəʳ] n benfeitor m.
benefactress ['benɪfæktrɪs] n benfeitora f.
beneficial [,benɪ'fɪʃl] adj benéfico(ca); ~ **to sb/ sthg** benéfico(ca) para alguém/algo.
beneficiary [,benɪ'fɪʃərɪ] (pl -ies) n JUR beneficiário m, -ria f.
benefit ['benɪfɪt] ⟨⟩ n **-1.** [advantage] benefício m; **to be to sb's** ~, **to be of** ~ **to sb** ser benéfico(ca) para alguém; **for the** ~ **of** em benefício OR prol de **-2.** [good point] vantagem f **-3.** ADMIN [allowance of money] auxílio m. ⟨⟩ comp [concert, match, performance] beneficente. ⟨⟩ vt beneficiar. ⟨⟩ vi: **to** ~ **from sthg** beneficiar-se de algo.
Benelux ['benɪlʌks] n Benelux; **the** ~ **countries** os países Benelux.
benevolent [bɪ'nevələnt] adj [kind, generous] benevolente.
BEng [,bi:'eŋ] (abbr of Bachelor of Engineering) n (titular de) graduação em engenharia.
Bengal [,beŋ'gɔ:l] n Bengala; **in** ~ em Bengala; **the Bay of** ~ a Baía de Bengala.
benign [bɪ'naɪn] adj **-1.** [gen] benévolo(la) **-2.** [influence, conditions] agradável, propício(cia) **-3.** MED benigno(na).
Benin [be'nɪn] n Benim; **in** ~ em Benim.
bent [bent] ⟨⟩ pt & pp ▷ **bend**. ⟨⟩ adj **-1.** [wire, bar] torto(ta) **-2.** [person, body] curvado(da) **-3.** UK inf [dishonest] corrupto(ta) **-4.** [determined]: **to be** ~ **on sthg/on doing sthg** ter inclinação para algo/

fazer algo. ⟨⟩ n [natural aptitude] inclinação f; **to have a** ~ **for sthg** ter uma inclinação para algo.
bequeath [bɪ'kwi:ð] vt **-1.** [money, property] deixar; **to** ~ **sb sthg, to** ~ **sthg to sb** deixar algo para alguém **-2.** fig [idea, system] passar; **to** ~ **sb sthg, to** ~ **sthg to sb** passar algo para alguém.
bequest [bɪ'kwest] n [in will] herança f.
berate [bɪ'reɪt] vt [rebuke] repreender.
Berber ['bɜːbəʳ] ⟨⟩ adj berbere. ⟨⟩ n **-1.** [person] berbere mf **-2.** [language] berbere m.
bereaved [bɪ'ri:vd] (pl inv) ⟨⟩ adj enlutado(da). ⟨⟩ npl: **the** ~ os enlutados.
bereavement [bɪ'ri:vmənt] n luto m.
bereft [bɪ'reft] adj literary desolado(da); ~ **of sthg** privado(da) de algo.
beret ['bereɪ] n boina f.
Bering Sea ['berɪŋ-] n: **the** ~ o Mar de Bering.
Bering Strait ['berɪŋ-] n: **the** ~ o Estreito de Bering.
berk [bɜːk] n UK inf palhaço m, -ça f.
Berlin [bɜː'lɪn] n Berlim; **in** ~ em Berlim; **in East/ West** ~ na Berlim Oriental/Ocidental; **the** ~ **Wall** o Muro de Berlim.
Berliner [bɜː'lɪnəʳ] n berlinense mf.
berm [bɜːm] n US berma f.
Bermuda [bə'mju:də] n (Ilhas) Bermudas fpl.
Bermuda shorts npl bermuda f.
Bern [bɜːn] n Berna; **in** ~ em Berna.
berry ['berɪ] (pl -ies) n baga f.
berserk [bə'zɜːk] adj: **to go** ~ ficar furioso(sa).
berth [bɜːθ] ⟨⟩ n **-1.** [in harbour] ancoradouro m **-2.** [in ship, train] beliche m **-3.** phr: **to give sb a wide** ~ fig manter distância de alguém. ⟨⟩ vt NAUT ancorar, atracar. ⟨⟩ vi [ship] ancorar, atracar.
beseech [bɪ'si:tʃ] (pt & pp besought OR beseeched) vt literary [implore] suplicar; **to** ~ **sb to do sthg** suplicar a alguém para que faça algo.
beset [bɪ'set] (pt & pp beset, cont -ting) ⟨⟩ adj: ~ **with** OR **by sthg** cercado (cercada) de algo. ⟨⟩ vt envolver.
beside [bɪ'saɪd] prep **-1.** [next to] ao lado de **-2.** [compared with] comparado(da) com **-3.** phr: **to be** ~ **o.s. with sthg** estar louco(ca) de algo.
besides [bɪ'saɪdz] ⟨⟩ adv além disso. ⟨⟩ prep [in addition to] além de.
besiege [bɪ'si:dʒ] vt **-1.** [town, fortress] sitiar **-2.** fig: **to be** ~ **d by people** ser/estar assediado(da) de pessoas; **to be** ~ **d with calls/complaints** ser bombardeado(da) com ligações/reclamações.
besotted [bɪ'sɒtɪd] adj: ~ **(with sb)** obcecado(da) (por alguém).
besought [bɪ'sɔːt] pt & pp ▷ **beseech**.
bespectacled [bɪ'spektəkld] adj com óculos.
bespoke [bɪ'spəuk] adj UK dated **-1.** [clothes] feito (feita) sob medida **-2.** [tailor] que costura sob medida.
best [best] ⟨⟩ adj [in quality] melhor. ⟨⟩ adv **-1.** [better than all the others] melhor; **whoever does** ~ **in the exam** quem se sair melhor no exame **-2.** [more than all the others] mais; **which one did you like** ~? de qual deles você gostou mais? ⟨⟩ n **-1.** [highest standard possible] melhor m; **to do one's** ~ fazer o melhor possível; **he is the** ~ **of friends**

ele é o melhor amigo do mundo **-2.** [utmost] máximo *m*; **she tried her best** ~ ela fez o tudo o que podia **-3.** [most outstanding person, thing etc] melhor *mf-***4.** *phr*: **to make the** ~ **of sthg** tirar o máximo de proveito de algo; **to be for the** ~ ser melhor; **all the** ~**!** um abraço!; **the** ~ **of both worlds** o melhor de ambas as partes.
➡ **at best** *adv* na melhor das hipóteses.

bestial ['bestjəl] *adj* [disgusting] bestial.

best man *n* padrinho *m* de casamento.

bestow [bɪ'stəʊ] *vt fml*: **to** ~ **sthg on sb** outorgar *OR* conceder algo a alguém.

best-seller *n* **-1.** [article sold] mais vendido *m*, -da *f***-2.** [book] best-seller *m*.

best-selling *adj* mais vendido(da).

bet [bet] (*pt* & *pp* bet *OR* **-ted**, *cont* **-ting**) ◇ *n* **-1.** [wager] aposta *f*; **a** ~ **on sthg** uma aposta em algo; **to hedge one's** ~**s** resguardar-se **-2.** *fig* [prediction] aposta *f*; **it's a safe** ~ **that ...** é certo que ...; **your best** ~ **is to ...** o melhor a se fazer é ... ◇ *vt* apostar. ◇ *vi* apostar; **to** ~ **on sthg** apostar em algo; **you** ~**!** *inf* pode apostar!, com certeza!

beta-blocker ['bi:tə,blɒkəʳ] *n* bloqueador-beta *m*.

Bethlehem ['beθlɪhem] *n* Belém; **in** ~ em Belém.

betray [bɪ'treɪ] *vt* **-1.** [person, principles] trair **-2.** [secret, emotion] revelar.

betrayal [bɪ'treɪəl] *n* **-1.** [of person, principles] traição *f* **-2.** [of secret, emotion] revelação *f*.

betrothed [bɪ'trəʊðd] *adj dated* [engaged to be married] prometido(da); ~ **to sb** prometido(da) para alguém.

better ['betəʳ] ◇ *adj* melhor; **to get** ~ melhorar; **to get** ~ **and** ~ ficar cada vez melhor. ◇ *adv* **-1.** [gen] melhor **-2.** [when giving advice, stating intention]: **you'd** ~ **phone her** é melhor você ligar para ela; **I'd** ~ **go now** é melhor eu ir embora. ◇ *n* [best one] melhor *mf*; **to get the** ~ **of sb** apoderar-se *OR* tomar conta de alguém; **her emotions got the** ~ **of her** suas emoções tomaram conta dela. ◇ *vt* [improve] melhorar; **to** ~ **o.s.** melhorar de vida, aprimorar-se.

better half *n inf* cara-metade *mf*.

better off *adj* **-1.** [financially] melhor de vida **-2.** [in a better situation] melhor; **you're** ~ **taking a taxi** será melhor você pegar um táxi.

betting ['betɪŋ] *n* **-1.** [bets] apostar *m* **-2.** [odds] chance *f*.

betting shop *n UK* casa *f* de apostas.

between [bɪ'twi:n] ◇ *prep* entre. ◇ *adv*: **(in)** ~ entre.

bevelled *UK*, **beveled** *US* ['bevld] *adj* chanfrado(da).

beverage ['bevərɪdʒ] *n fml* [drink] bebida *f*.

bevy ['bevɪ] (*pl* **-ies**) *n* [group] bando *m*.

beware [bɪ'weəʳ] *vi* tomar cuidado, ter cautela; **to** ~ **of sthg** tomar cuidado com algo.

bewildered [bɪ'wɪldəd] *adj* [confused] confuso(sa), desnorteado(da).

bewildering [bɪ'wɪldərɪŋ] *adj* [confusing] desnorteante, desconcertante.

bewitched [bɪ'wɪtʃt] *adj* encantado(da).

bewitching [bɪ'wɪtʃɪŋ] *adj* encantador(ra).

beyond [bɪ'jɒnd] ◇ *prep* **-1.** além de; **it is** ~ **my**

responsibility vai além de minha responsabilidade **-2.** [outside the range of] fora de; **it is** ~ **my control** está fora de meu controle; **the town has changed** ~ **all recognition** a cidade ficou irreconhecível. ◇ *adv* **-1.** [in space] mais além, mais adiante **-2.** [in time] mais além, mais um pouco.

b.f. (*abbr of* brought forward) cont.

BFPO (*abbr of* British Forces Post Office) *n código utilizado em cartas escritas para membros das forças britânicas.*

b.h.p. (*abbr of* brake horsepower) b.h.p.

bi- [baɪ] *prefix* bi.

biannual [baɪ'ænjʊəl] *adj* semestral.

bias ['baɪəs] *n* **-1.** [prejudice] preconceito *m* **-2.** [tendency] propensão *f*, tendência *f*.

biased ['baɪəst] *adj* **-1.** [prejudiced] preconceituoso(sa); **to be** ~ **against sthg/sb** ser preconceituoso(sa) em relação a algo/alguém **-2.** [tendentious] tendencioso(sa); **to be** ~ **towards sthg** ser tendencioso(sa) em relação a algo; **to be** ~ **towards sb** pender para o lado de alguém.

bib [bɪb] *n* [for baby] babador *m*.

Bible ['baɪbl] *n*: **the** ~ a Bíblia.
➡ **bible** *n* [copy of the Bible] bíblia *f*.

biblical ['bɪblɪkl] *adj* bíblico(ca).

bibliography [,bɪblɪ'ɒɡrəfɪ] (*pl* **-ies**) *n* [list of books] bibliografia *f*.

bicarbonate of soda [baɪ'kɑ:bənət-] *n* bicarbonato *m* de sódio.

bicentenary *UK* [,baɪsen'ti:nərɪ] (*pl* **-ies**), **bicentennial** *US* [,baɪsen'tenjəll] *n* bicentenário *m*.

biceps ['baɪseps] (*pl inv*) *n* bíceps *m*.

bicker ['bɪkəʳ] *vi* [quarrel] brigar.

bickering ['bɪkərɪŋ] *n* (U) [quarrelling] briga *f*.

bicycle ['baɪsɪkl] ◇ *n* bicicleta *f*. ◇ *vi* andar de bicicleta.

bicycle path *n* ciclovia *f*.

bicycle pump *n* bomba *f* de ar *(para bicicleta)*.

bid [bɪd] (*pt* & *pp vt sense* 1 & *vi* bid, *cont* bidding, *pt vt senses* 2 & 3 bid *OR* bade, *pp vt senses* 2 & 3 bid *OR* bidden [*bɪdn*], *cont* bidding) ◇ *n* **-1.** [attempt] tentativa *f*, intento *m*; **a** ~ **for power** uma busca pelo poder **-2.** [at auction] licitação *f* **-3.** *COMM* proposta *f*. ◇ *vt* **-1.** [at auction] licitar **-2.** *literary* [request]: **to** ~ **sb do sthg** convidar alguém a fazer algo **-3.** *fml* [say]: **to** ~ **sb good morning/farewell** dizer bom dia/adeus a alguém. ◇ *vi* **-1.** [at auction]: **to** ~ **(for sthg)** abrir licitação (para algo) **-2.** [attempt]: **to** ~ **for sthg** tentar algo.

bidder ['bɪdəʳ] *n* [at auction] licitante *mf*.

bidding ['bɪdɪŋ] *n* [at auction] licitação *f*.

bide [baɪd] *vt*: **to** ~ **one's time** esperar a vez.

bidet ['bi:deɪ] *n* bidê *m*.

biennial [baɪ'enɪəl] ◇ *adj* [every two years] bienal. ◇ *n* **-1.** [plant] planta *f* bienal **-2.** [festival] bienal *f*.

bier [bɪəʳ] *n* caixão *m*.

bifocals [,baɪ'fəʊklz] *npl* lentes *fpl* bifocais.

big [bɪɡ] (*compar* **-ger**, *superl* **-gest**) *adj* **-1.** [gen] grande **-2.** [older] mais velho(lha) **-3.** [successful] importante **-4.** *phr*: **in a** ~ **way** em grande estilo.

bigamist *n* bígamo *m*, -ma *f*.

bigamy ['bɪgəmɪ] *n (U)* bigamia *f.*
Big Apple *n*: the ~ a Big Apple, Nova York.
Big Bang *n*: the ~ **theory** a teoria do big-bang.
Big Ben *n* Big Ben *m.*
big business *n (U)* [large companies] grandes negócios *mpl.*
big cat *n* animal grande da família dos felinos.
big deal *inf* ◇ *n* grande coisa *f*; **it's no** ~ não é nada de mais; **what's the** ~? e daí? ◇ *excl* grande coisa!
Big Dipper [-'dɪpə'] *n* **-1.** *UK* [rollercoaster] montanha-russa *f* **-2.** *US ASTRON*: **the** ~ a Ursa Maior.
big end *n AUT* cabeça *f* de biela.
big fish *n inf* [important person] peixe *m* grande.
big game *n (U)* animais *mpl* de grande porte.
big hand *n* **-1.** [on clock] ponteiro *m* dos minutos **-2.** *inf* [applause] salva *f* de palmas.
bighead ['bɪghed] *n inf* metido *m* a besta.
big-headed *adj inf* metido(da).
big-hearted [-'hɑːtɪd] *adj* gentil, generoso(sa).
big money *n (U) inf* bolada *f*; **to make** ~ ganhar um dinheirão *ou* uma bolada.
big mouth *n inf* **-1.** [tendency to gossip] língua *f* solta **-2.** [person] linguarudo *m*, -da *f.*
big name *n inf* grande figura *f.*
bigot ['bɪgət] *n* fanático *m*, -ca *f.*
bigoted ['bɪgətɪd] *adj* fanático(ca).
bigotry ['bɪgətrɪ] *n (U)* fanatismo *m.*
big shot *n inf* figurão *m*, costa-larga *m.*
big time *n inf*: **the** ~ o auge.
big toe *n* dedão *m* do pé.
big top *n* (lona do) circo *m.*
big wheel *n* **-1.** *UK* [at fairground] roda-gigante *f* **-2.** *inf* [big shot] peixe *m* grande.
bigwig ['bɪgwɪg] *n inf pej* figurão *m*, -rona *f.*
bike [baɪk] *n inf* **-1.** [cycle] bike *f*, bicicleta *f* **-2.** [motorcycle] moto *f.*
bikeway ['baɪkweɪ] *n US* ciclovia *f.*
bikini [bɪ'kiːnɪ] *n* biquíni *m.*
bilateral [ˌbaɪ'lætərəl] *adj* [talks] bilateral.
bilberry ['bɪlbərɪ] *(pl* -ies*) n* uva-do-monte *f*, mirtilo *m.*
bile [baɪl] *n* **-1.** [fluid] bílis *f* **-2.** [anger] irritação *f.*
bilingual [baɪ'lɪŋgwəl] *adj* bilíngüe.
bilious ['bɪljəs] *adj* **-1.** [sickening] bilioso(sa) **-2.** [nauseous] nauseado(da).
bill [bɪl] ◇ *n* **-1.** [statement of cost] conta *f*; ~ **for sthg** conta de algo **-2.** [in parliament] projeto *m* de lei **-3.** [of show, concert] programa *m* **-4.** *US* [bank note] nota *f* **-5.** [poster]: **'post** *OR* **stick no** ~ **s'** 'proibido colar cartazes' **-6.** [beak] bico *m* **-7.** *phr*: **to be given a clean** ~ **of health** *MED* obter um atestado de boa saúde. ◇ *vt* [send a bill to]: **to** ~ **sb (for sthg)** cobrar (algo) de alguém.
billboard ['bɪlbɔːd] *n* quadro *m* de anúncios.
billet ['bɪlɪt] ◇ *n* boleto *m*, alojamento *m.* ◇ *vt* aboletar, alojar.
billfold ['bɪlfəʊld] *n US* carteira *f.*
billiards ['bɪljədz] *n (U)* bilhar *m.*
billion ['bɪljən] *num* **-1.** [thousand million] bilhão *m* **-2.** *UK dated* [million million] trilhão *m.*
billionaire [ˌbɪljə'neə'] *n* bilionário *m*, -ria *f.*

bill of exchange *n* letra *f* de câmbio.
bill of lading [-'leɪdɪŋ] *n* conhecimento *m* de embarque marítimo.
Bill of Rights *n*: **the** ~ *as dez primeiras emendas da Constituição norte-americana.*

BILL OF RIGHTS

É o nome que se dá às dez primeiras emendas da Constituição norte-americana, as quais garantem direitos fundamentais, tais como a liberdade de expressão, de credo e de reunião.

bill of sale *n* contrato *m* de venda.
billow ['bɪləʊ] ◇ *n* [of smoke] nuvem *f.* ◇ *vi* **-1.** [smoke, steam] formar nuvens **-2.** [skirt, sail] ondular.
billposter *n* **-1.** pessoa *f* que cola cartazes **-2.** [unauthorised] pichador *m*, -ra *f.*
billycan ['bɪlɪkæn] *n* caldeirão *m.*
billy goat ['bɪlɪ-] *n* bode *m.*
BIM *(abbr of* **British Institute of Management***) n* instituto britânico de administração.
bimbo ['bɪmbəʊ] *(pl* -s *OR* -es*) n inf pej* ≃ burra *f* gostosa.
bimonthly [ˌbaɪ'mʌnθlɪ] ◇ *adj* **-1.** [every two months] bimestral **-2.** [twice a month] bimensal. ◇ *adv* **-1.** [every two months] bimestralmente **-2.** [twice a month] bimensalmente.
bin [bɪn] *(pt & pp* -ned, *cont* -ning*)* ◇ *n* **-1.** *UK* [for rubbish] lixeira *f* **-2.** [for storage] lata *f.* ◇ *vt inf* [discard] descartar.
binary ['baɪnərɪ] *adj* [system, code] binário(ria).
bind [baɪnd] *(pt & pp* bound*)* ◇ *vt* **-1.** [tie up] amarrar **-2.** [unite] ligar **-3.** [bandage] atar **-4.** [book] encadernar **-5.** [constrain] comprometer. ◇ *n inf* **-1.** *UK* [nuisance] saco *m* **-2.** [difficult situation] aperto *m.*
➡ **bind over** *vt sep JUR* obrigar legalmente.
binder ['baɪndə'] *n* **-1.** [machine] encadernadora *f* **-2.** [person] encadernador *m*, -ra *f* **-3.** [cover] encadernação *f.*
binding ['baɪndɪŋ] ◇ *adj* comprometedor(ra), obrigatório(ria). ◇ *n* **-1.** [of book - process] encadernação *f*; [- cover] capa *f* **-2.** [on dress, tablecloth] laço *m.*
binge [bɪndʒ] *inf* ◇ *n*: **to go on a** ~ ir à farra. ◇ *vi*: **to** ~ **on sthg** empanturrar-se de algo.
bingo ['bɪŋgəʊ] *n* bingo *m.*
bin-liner *n UK* saco *m* de lixo.
binoculars [bɪ'nɒkjʊləz] *npl* binóculo *m.*
biochemistry [ˌbaɪəʊ'kemɪstrɪ] *n (U)* bioquímica *f.*
biodegradable [ˌbaɪəʊdɪ'greɪdəbll] *adj* biodegradável.
biodiversity [ˌbaɪəʊdaɪ'vɜːsətɪ] *n (U)* biodiversidade *f.*
bioethics [ˌbaɪəʊ'eθɪks] *n (U)* bioética *f.*
biographer [baɪ'ɒgrəfə'] *n* biógrafo *m*, -fa *f.*
biographic(al) [ˌbaɪə'græfɪk(l)] *adj* biográfico(ca).
biography [baɪ'ɒgrəfɪ] *(pl* -ies*) n* biografia *f.*
biofuel ['baɪəfjʊəl] *n* biocombustível *m.*
biological [ˌbaɪə'lɒdʒɪkl] *adj* biológico(ca); ~ **washing powder** sabão em pó com enzimas.
biological clock *n* relógio *m* biológico.

biological warfare n guerra f biológica.

biological weapon n arma f biológica.

biologist [baɪˈɒlədʒɪst] n biólogo m, -ga f.

biology [baɪˈɒlədʒɪ] n (U) biologia f.

biopic [ˈbaɪəʊpɪk] n inf filme m biográfico.

biopsy [ˈbaɪɒpsɪ] (pl -ies) n biópsia f.

biosphere [ˈbaɪəʊˌsfɪəˡ] n biosfera f.

biotech company [ˈbaɪəʊtek-] n empresa f de biotecnologia.

biotechnology [ˌbaɪəʊtekˈnɒlədʒɪ] n (U) biotecnologia f.

bioterrorism [ˌbaɪəʊˈterərɪzm] n bioterrorismo m.

bipartite [ˌbaɪˈpɑːtaɪt] adj [treaty] bipartido(da).

biplane [ˈbaɪpleɪn] n biplano m.

birch [bɜːtʃ] n -1. [tree] bétula f -2. [for punishment]: the ~ a vara.

bird [bɜːd] n -1. [creature] pássaro m, ave f; to kill two ~s with one stone ≃ matar dois coelhos com uma cajadada só -2. inf [woman] perua f.

birdcage [ˈbɜːdkeɪdʒ] n gaiola f.

birdie [ˈbɜːdɪ] n -1. [bird] passarinho m -2. [in golf] birdie m.

bird of paradise n ave-do-paraíso f.

bird of prey n ave f de rapina.

birdseed [ˈbɜːdsiːd] n (U) alpiste m.

bird's-eye view n vista f panorâmica.

birdwatcher n obeservador m, -ra f de pássaros.

biro® n caneta f esferográfica.

birth [bɜːθ] n nascimento m; to give ~ (to) dar à luz (a); fig [of idea, system, country] dar origem(a).

birth certificate n certidão f de nascimento.

birth control n (U) controle m de natalidade.

birthday [ˈbɜːθdeɪ] ⟨> n aniversário m. ⟨> comp de aniversário.

birthmark [ˈbɜːθmɑːk] n sinal m de nascença.

birthplace [ˈbɜːθpleɪs] n local m de nascimento.

birthrate [ˈbɜːθreɪt] n taxa f de natalidade.

birthright [ˈbɜːθraɪt] n direito m inato.

Biscay [ˈbɪskɪ] n: the Bay of ~ a Baía de Biscaia.

biscuit [ˈbɪskɪt] n -1. UK [crisp] biscoito m, bolacha f -2. US [bread-like cake] bolacha f.

bisect [baɪˈsekt] vt -1. GEOM cortar ao meio -2. [cut in two] dividir em duas partes.

bisexual [ˌbaɪˈsekʃʊəl] ⟨> adj bissexual. ⟨> n bissexual mf.

bishop [ˈbɪʃəp] n bispo m.

bison [ˈbaɪsn] (pl inv OR -s) n búfalo f.

bistro [ˈbɪstrəʊ] (pl -s) n bistrô m.

bit [bɪt] ⟨> pt ▷ bite. ⟨> n -1. [small piece] pedaço m; ~s and pieces UK inf bugigangas; to ~s aos pedaços -2. [unspecified amount]: a ~ of um pouco de; quite a ~ of um bocado de -3. [short time]: for a ~ por um instante/momento -4. [of drill] broca f -5. [of bridle] freio m -6. COMPUT bit m -7. phr: to do one's ~ UK fazer a sua parte; every ~ as ... as exatamente tão ... quanto; it's a ~ much [overwhelming] é um pouco demais; not a ~ nem um pouco.

➡ **a bit** adv um pouco.

➡ **bit by bit** adv pouco a pouco.

bitch [bɪtʃ] ⟨> n -1. [female dog] cadela f -2. vinf pej [unpleasant woman] vaca f. ⟨> vi inf -1. [complain] emputecer-se -2. [talk unpleasantly]: to ~ about sb falar mal de alguém.

bitchy [ˈbɪtʃɪ] (compar -ier, superl -iest) adj inf malicioso(sa).

bite [baɪt] (pt bit, pp bitten) ⟨> n -1. [act of biting] mordida f, dentada f -2. inf [food]: a ~ (to eat) algo (para beliscar) -3. [wound] picada f -4. UK [sharp flavour] sabor m picante. ⟨> vt -1. [subj: person, animal] morder; to ~ one's nails roer as unhas -2. [subj: insect, snake] picar. ⟨> vi -1. [animal, person] morder; to ~ into sthg morder algo; to ~ off sthg abocanhar algo; to ~ off more than one can chew ≃ dar um passo maior que a perna; to ~ the hand that feeds one ≃ cuspir no prato em que comeu -2. [insect, snake] picar -3. [tyres, clutch] furar -4. fig [sanction, law] morder.

biting [ˈbaɪtɪŋ] adj -1. [very cold] cortante -2. [caustic] mordaz.

bitmap n COMPUT bitmap m.

bit part n ponta f.

bitten [ˈbɪtn] pp ▷ bite.

bitter [ˈbɪtəˡ] ⟨> adj -1. [gen] amargo(ga); to the ~ end até o fim -2. [acrimonious] pungente -3. [resentful] amargurado(da) -4. [icy] gelado(da). ⟨> n UK [beer] cerveja f amarga.

bitter lemon n batida f de limão.

bitterly [ˈbɪtəlɪ] adv -1. [cold] amargamente -2. [intensely] duramente.

bitterness [ˈbɪtənɪs] n (U) -1. [gen] amargor m -2. [of wind, weather] rigor m.

bittersweet [ˈbɪtəswiːt] adj agridoce.

bitty [ˈbɪtɪ] (compar-ier, superl-iest) adj UK inf sem pé nem cabeça.

bitumen [ˈbɪtjʊmɪn] n (U) betume m.

bivouac [ˈbɪvʊæk] (pt & pp -ked, cont -king) ⟨> n acampamento m sem barracas. ⟨> vi dormir ao relento (acampando).

biweekly [ˌbaɪˈwiːklɪ] ⟨> adj -1. [every two weeks] quinzenal -2. [twice a week]: ~ magazine revista publicada duas vezes por semana. ⟨> adv -1. [every two weeks] quinzenalmente -2. [twice a week] duas vezes por semana.

bizarre [bɪˈzɑːˡ] adj bizarro(rra), estranho(nha).

BL n -1. (abbr of Bachelor of Law(s)) (titular de) graduação em direito. -2. (abbr of Bill of Lading) conhecimento de embarque marítimo.

blab [blæb] (pt & pp -bed, cont -bing) vi inf fazer fofoca.

black [blæk] ⟨> adj -1. [in colour] preto(ta); to be beaten ~ and blue ficar roxo(xa) de pancada; ~ and white [films, photos] preto-e-branco -2. [person, skin] negro(gra) -3. [without milk] puro(ra), preto(ta) -4. [grim] sombrio(a); ~ humour humor negro -5. [angry] furioso(sa). ⟨> n -1. (U) [colour] preto m; in ~ and white [in writing] o preto no branco, por escrito; in the ~ [solvent] sem dívidas -2. [person] negro m, -gra f. ⟨> vt UK [boycott] boicotar.

➡ **black out** ⟨> vt sep -1. [put out lights] ficar no escuro -2. [suppress] tirar do ar. ⟨> vi [faint] desmaiar.

blackball [ˈblækbɔːl] vt votar contra (para excluir alguém de um clube).

black belt *n* faixa-preta *mf*.
blackberry ['blækbərɪ] (*pl* -ies) *n* amora *f*.
blackbird ['blækbɜːd] *n* melro *m*.
blackboard ['blækbɔːd] *n* quadro-negro *m*, lousa *f*.
black box *n* [flight recorder] caixa-preta *f*.
black comedy *n* tragicomédia *f*, comédia *f* de humor negro.
blackcurrant [ˌblæk'kʌrənt] *n* groselha-preta *f*.
black economy *n* economia *f* informal.
blacken ['blækn] ⇔ *vt* -1. pretejar -2. *fig* [reputation, name] denegrir. ⇔ *vi* [sky] escurecer.
black eye *n* olho *m* roxo.
Black Forest *n*: the ~ a Floresta Negra.
blackhead ['blækhed] *n* cravo *m*.
black hole *n* ASTRON buraco *m* negro.
black ice *n* (U) camada fina e transparente de gelo sobre as ruas que dificulta a passagem de carros.
blackjack ['blækdʒæk] *n* -1. (U) [card game] blackjack *m* -2. Am [weapon] cassetete *m*.
blackleg ['blækleg] *n* pej fura-greve *mf*.
blacklist ['blæklɪst] ⇔ *n* lista *f* negra. ⇔ *vt* incluir na lista negra.
black magic *n* (U) magia *f* negra.
blackmail ['blækmeɪl] ⇔ *n* lit & fig chantagem *f*. ⇔ *vt* chantagear.
blackmailer ['blækmeɪlə'] *n* chantagista *mf*.
Black Maria [-mə'raɪə] *n* inf camburão *m*.
black mark *n* mancha *f* negra.
black market *n* mercado *m* negro.
blackout ['blækaʊt] *n* -1. [in wartime] blecaute *m* -2. [power cut] blecaute *m*, apagão *m* -3. [suppression of news] censura *f* -4. [fainting fit] desmaio *m*.
Black Power *n* movimento que marcou a luta dos negros norte-americanos pelo direito à igualdade e liberdade.
black pudding *n* UK morcela *f* preta.
Black Sea *n*: the ~ o Mar Negro.
black sheep *n* fig ovelha *f* negra.
blacksmith ['blæksmɪθ] *n* ferreiro *m*.
black spot *n* ponto *m* cego.
black-tie *adj* black-tie, de gala.
bladder ['blædə'] *n* ANAT bexiga *f*.
blade [bleɪd] *n* -1. [of knife, saw] lâmina *f* -2. [of propeller] pá *f* -3. [of grass] folha *f*.
blame [bleɪm] ⇔ *n* (U) [responsibility] culpa *f*; **to take the ~ for sthg** assumir a culpa por algo. ⇔ *vt* culpar; **to ~ sthg on sb/sthg, to ~ sb/sthg for sthg** culpar alguém/algo de alguma coisa; **to be to ~ for sthg** ser culpado(da) por algo.
blameless ['bleɪmlɪs] *adj* [innocent] inocente, irrepreensível.
blanch [blɑːntʃ] ⇔ *vt* CULIN escaldar. ⇔ *vi* [go white] empalidecer.
blancmange [blə'mɒndʒ] *n* manjar-branco *m*.
bland [blænd] *adj* -1. [person] agradável, meigo(ga) -2. [food] insosso(sa) -3. [music, style] suave.
blank [blæŋk] ⇔ *adj* -1. em branco -2. *fig* [look] vazio(a). ⇔ *n* -1. [empty space] espaço *m* em branco -2. MIL [cartridge] cartucho *m* -3. *phr*: **to draw a ~** tirar leite de pedra.
blank cheque *n* -1. cheque *m* em branco

-2. *fig* [free hand] carta *f* branca.
blanket ['blæŋkɪt] ⇔ *adj* [comprehensive] na íntegra, completo(ta). ⇔ *n* -1. [bed cover] cobertor *m*, colcha *f* -2. [layer] camada *f*. ⇔ *vt* [cover] cobrir.
blanket bath *n* UK MED banho *m* na cama.
blankly ['blæŋklɪ] *adv* [stare] inexpressivamente.
blank verse *n* (U) verso *m* branco.
blare [bleə'] *vi* soar.
⇒ **blare out** *vi* soar.
blasé [UK 'blɑːzeɪ, US ˌblɑː'zeɪ] *adj* [unconcerned] indiferente.
blasphemous ['blæsfəməs] *adj* blasfemo(ma).
blasphemy ['blæsfəmɪ] (*pl* -ies) *n* blasfêmia *f*.
blast [blɑːst] ⇔ *n* -1. [of bomb] explosão *f* -2. [of air] corrente *f* -3. US inf [celebration] farra *f*. ⇔ *vt* [hole, tunnel] dinamitar. ⇔ *excl* UK inf diabos!
⇒ **(at) full blast** *adv* -1. [maximum volume] a todo volume -2. [maximum effort, speed] a todo vapor.
⇒ **blast off** *vi* SPACE decolar.
blasted ['blɑːstɪd] *adj* inf [for emphasis] maldito(ta).
blast furnace *n* alto-forno *m*.
blast-off *n* (U) SPACE decolagem *f*.
blatant ['bleɪtənt] *adj* [shameless] descarado(da).
blatantly ['bleɪtntlɪ] *adv* descaradamente.
blaze [bleɪz] ⇔ *n* -1. [fire] incêndio *m* -2. *fig* [of colour, light] explosão *f*; **a ~ of publicity** uma grande onda de publicidade. ⇔ *vi* -1. [fire] arder -2. *fig* [with colour, emotion] resplandecer.
blazer ['bleɪzə'] *n* [jacket] blazer *m*.
blazing ['bleɪzɪŋ] *adj* -1. [sun, heat] abrasador(ra); **it was ~ hot** fazia um calor infernal -2. [row] acalorado(da).
bleach [bliːtʃ] ⇔ *n* [chemical] alvejante *m*. ⇔ *vt* -1. [hair] clarear -2. [clothes] alvejar. ⇔ *vi* desbotar.
bleached [bliːtʃt] *adj* -1. [hair] descolorido(da), clareado(da) -2. [jeans] desbotado(da).
bleachers ['bliːtʃəz] *npl* US SPORT arquibancadas *fpl*.
bleak [bliːk] *adj* -1. [future] sombrio(a) -2. [place] escuro(ra) -3. [weather] gélido(da) -4. [face, person] triste.
bleary ['blɪərɪ] (*compar* -ier, *superl* -iest) *adj* [eyes] turvo(va).
bleary-eyed [ˌblɪərɪ'aɪd] *adj* com os olhos turvos.
bleat [bliːt] ⇔ *n* [of sheep, goat] balido *m*. ⇔ *vi* -1. [sheep, goat] balir -2. *fig* [person - speak] tagarelar; [- complain] balbuciar.
bleed [bliːd] (*pt* & *pp* bled) ⇔ *vt* [drain] esvaziar. ⇔ *vi* sangrar.
bleep [bliːp] ⇔ *n* apito *m*. ⇔ *vt* & *vi* apitar.
bleeper ['bliːpə'] *n* bipe *m*.
blemish ['blemɪʃ] ⇔ *n* -1. [flaw] mancha *f* -2. [pimple, scar] cicatriz *f* -3. *fig* [on name, reputation] mancha *f*. ⇔ *vt* [reputation] manchar.
blend [blend] ⇔ *n* mistura *f*. ⇔ *vt* [mix] misturar; **to ~ sthg with sthg** misturar algo com algo. ⇔ *vi* [colours, sounds] misturar-se; **to ~ with sthg** misturar com algo.
⇒ **blend in** *vi* -1. [person] confundir-se -2. [colours, sounds] confundir-se.
⇒ **blend into** *vt fus* confundir-se com.
blender ['blendə'] *n* [food mixer] liquidificador *m*.
bless [bles] (*pt* & *pp* -ed OR blest) *vt* RELIG & *fig*

abençoar; **to be ~ed with sthg** ser abençoado(-da) com algo; **~ you!** [after sneezing] saúde!; [thank you] obrigado(da)!

blessed ['blesɪd] *adj* **-1.** *RELIG & fig* abençoado(da) **-2.** *inf* [for emphasis] bendito(ta).

blessing ['blesɪŋ] *n* benção *f*; **to count one's ~s** dar graças a Deus pelo que se tem; **a ~ in disguise** um mal que vem para bem; **to be a mixed ~** ter seus prós e contras.

blest [blest] *pt & pp* ▷ **bless.**

blew [blu:] *pt* ▷ **blow.**

blight [blaɪt] ◇ *n* **-1.** [plant disease] ferrugem *f* **-2.** *fig* [curse] desgraça *f* **-3.** *(U) fig* [decay] declínio *m.* ◇ *vt* arruinar.

blimey ['blaɪmɪ] *excl UK inf* minha nossa!, caramba!

blind [blaɪnd] ◇ *adj* **-1.** [gen] cego(ga) **-2.** *fig* [unaware]: **~ to sthg** cego(ga) para algo **-3.** *UK inf* [for emphasis]: **it doesn't make a ~ bit of difference to me** isso não faz a menor diferença para mim. ◇ *adv*: **~ drunk** completamente bêbado. ◇ *n* [for window] persiana *f.* ◇ *npl*: **the ~** os cegos. ◇ *vt* **-1.** cegar **-2.** *fig* [make unobservant] ofuscar; **to ~ sb to sthg** impedir alguém de ver algo.

blind alley *n* **-1.** [street] beco *m* **-2.** *fig* [dead end] beco *m* sem saída.

blind corner *n* curva *f* sem visibilidade.

blind date *n* encontro *m* às cegas.

blinders ['blaɪndəz] *npl US* antolhos *mpl.*

blindfold ['blaɪndfəʊld] ◇ *adv* de olhos vendados. ◇ *n* venda *f.* ◇ *vt* vendar.

blinding ['blaɪndɪŋ] *adj* **-1.** [light] ofuscante **-2.** [severe]: **~ headache** dor de cabeça de matar.

blindingly ['blaɪndɪŋlɪ] *adv* [clearly]: **~ obvious** totalmente óbvio(via).

blindly ['blaɪndlɪ] *adv* **-1.** [without seeing] às cegas **-2.** *fig* [without knowing] sem saber.

blindness ['blaɪndnɪs] *n (U)* cegueira *f*; **~ to sthg** falta *f* de visão para algo.

blind spot *n* [when driving] ponto *m* cego.

blink [blɪŋk] ◇ *n* **-1.** piscar *m*; **in the ~ of an eye** num piscar de olhos **-2.** *inf* [machine]: **on the ~** enguiçado(da). ◇ *vt* **-1.** [eyes] piscar **-2.** *Am AUT*: **to ~ one's lights** dar farol alto *OR* luz alta. ◇ *vi* **-1.** [person] piscar **-2.** [light] cintilar.

blinkered ['blɪŋkəd] *adj fig* [view, attitude] bitolado(-da).

blinkers ['blɪŋkəz] *npl UK* [for horse] antolhos *mpl.*

blinking ['blɪŋkɪŋ] *adj UK inf* [for emphasis]: **that ~ phone!** que droga de telefone!

blip [blɪp] *n* **-1.** [sound] bipe *m* **-2.** [on radar] luz *f* intermitente **-3.** *fig* [temporary problem] problema *m* temporário.

bliss [blɪs] *n* êxtase *m*, bem-aventurança *f.*

blissful ['blɪsfʊl] *adj* abençoado(da); **~ ignorance** santa ignorância.

blissfully ['blɪsfʊlɪ] *adv* **-1.** [contentedly] maravilhosamente **-2.** [unknowingly]: **~ unaware** *OR* **ignorant** totalmente sem saber.

blister ['blɪstə'] ◇ *n* [on skin] bolha *f.* ◇ *vi* formar bolhas.

blistering ['blɪstərɪŋ] *adj* **-1.** [very hot] abrasador(ra) **-2.** [scathing] mordaz.

blister pack *n* blíster *m.*

blithe [blaɪð] *adj* **-1.** [unworried] despreocupado(da) **-2.** *dated* [cheerful] alegre.

blithely ['blaɪðlɪ] *adv* **-1.** [without a care] despreocupadamente **-2.** [casually] tranqüilamente.

BLitt (*abbr of* **Bachelor of Letters (Baccalaureus Litterarum)**) *n (titular de) graduação em letras.*

blitz [blɪts] *n* **-1.** *MIL* bombardeio *m* aéreo **-2.** *UK fig* [attack]: **to have a ~ on sthg** dar uma geral em algo.

blizzard ['blɪzəd] *n* nevasca *f.*

BLM (*abbr of* **Bureau of Land Management**) *n instituto norte-americano de gestão territorial,* ≃ INCRA *m.*

bloated ['bləʊtɪd] *adj* **-1.** [swollen] inchado(da) **-2.** [having eaten too much] empanturrado(da).

blob [blɒb] *n* **-1.** [drop] pingo *m* **-2.** [shapeless thing] borrão *m*, mancha *f.*

bloc [blɒk] *n POL* bloco *m.*

block [blɒk] ◇ *n* **-1.** [gen] bloco *m* **-2.** [of buildings] quadra *f*, quarteirão *m* **-3.** [obstruction] bloqueio *m* **-4.** *TECH*: **~ and tackle** talha *f* patente. ◇ *vt* **-1.** bloquear **-2.** [hinder] barrar.

◆ **block off** *vt sep* bloquear.

◆ **block out** *vt sep* bloquear.

◆ **block up** ◇ *vt sep* [obstruct] entupir. ◇ *vi* entupir.

blockade [blɒ'keɪd] ◇ *n* bloqueio *m.* ◇ *vt* bloquear.

blockage ['blɒkɪdʒ] *n* [obstruction] obstrução *f.*

block booking *n* reserva *f* conjunta.

blockbuster ['blɒkbʌstə'] *n inf* [book, film] estouro *m.*

block capitals *npl* maiúsculas *fpl.*

blockhead ['blɒkhed] *n inf* cabeça-dura *mf.*

block letters *npl* maiúsculas *fpl.*

block release *n UK na Inglaterra, liberação de estagiários de fábricas do trabalho para que possam estudar numa faculdade durante várias semanas.*

block vote *n UK* voto *m* em bloco.

bloke [bləʊk] *n UK inf* cara *m.*

blond [blɒnd] *adj* [hair, man] loiro(ra), claro(ra).

blonde [blɒnd] ◇ *adj* [hair, woman] loiro(ra), claro(ra). ◇ *n* [woman] loira *f.*

blood [blʌd] *n* sangue *m*; **new** *OR* **fresh ~** sangue novo; **in cold ~** a sangue frio; **it's in his ~** está em seu sangue; **to make one's ~ boil** deixar alguém danado(da) da vida; **to make sb's ~ run cold** gelar a alma de alguém.

blood bank *n* banco *m* de sangue.

bloodbath ['blʌdbɑːθ] *n* banho *m* de sangue.

blood brother *n* irmão *m* de sangue.

blood cell *n* glóbulo *m* sangüíneo.

blood count *n* contagem *f* de glóbulos sangüíneos.

blood-curdling *adj* de gelar o sangue.

blood donor *n* doador *m*, -ra *f* de sangue.

blood group *n* grupo *m* sangüíneo.

bloodhound ['blʌdhaʊnd] *n* cão *m* de Santo Humberto.

bloodless ['blʌdlɪs] *adj* **-1.** [face, lips] pálido(da) **-2.** [coup, victory] sem derramamento de sangue.

bloodletting ['blʌd,letɪŋ] *n* [killing] matança *f.*

blood money *n* [money paid to killer] *dinheiro pago a um assassino.*

blood orange *n* laranja *f* sangüínea.

blood poisoning *n* septicemia *f.*

blood pressure *n* pressão *f* sangüínea OR arterial.

blood relation, blood relative *n* parente *mf* consangüíneo, -nea.

bloodshed ['blʌdʃed] *n* derramamento *m* de sangue.

bloodshot ['blʌdʃɒt] *adj* [eyes] injetado(da).

blood sports *npl esportes que envolvem a matança de animais.*

bloodstained ['blʌdsteɪnd] *adj* manchado(da) de sangue.

bloodstream ['blʌdstri:m] *n* corrente *f* sangüínea.

blood test *n* exame *m* de sangue.

bloodthirsty ['blʌd,θɜ:stɪ] *adj* sanguinário(ria).

blood transfusion *n* transfusão *f* de sangue.

blood type *n* tipo *m* sangüíneo.

blood vessel *n* vaso *m* sangüíneo.

bloody ['blʌdɪ] (*compar* -ier, *superl* -iest) ◇ *adj* -1. [war, conflict] sangrento(ta) -2. [face, hands] ensangüentado(da) -3. *UK v inf* [for emphasis]: **that ~ ...** essa droga de ...; **you ~ idiot!** seu imbecil! ◇ *adv UK v inf:* **~ good** bom pra caramba; **~ difficult** difícil para burro.

bloody-minded [-'maɪndɪd] *adj UK inf* do contra.

bloom [blu:m] ◇ *n* [flower] flor *f.* ◇ *vi* [plant, tree] florir.

blooming ['blu:mɪŋ] ◇ *adj* -1. *UK inf* [for emphasis]: **~ heck!** esse inferno miserável! -2. [healthy, attractive] radiante. ◇ *adv UK inf* pra caramba.

blossom ['blɒsəm] ◇ *n* [of tree] flor *f*; **in ~** em flor. ◇ *vi* -1. [tree] florescer -2. *fig* [person] desabrochar.

blot [blɒt] (*pt & pp* -ted, *cont* -ting) ◇ *n* -1. [of ink etc] borrão *m* -2. *fig* [- on character, reputation] mancha *f*; [- on landscape] estrago *m.* ◇ *vt* -1. [dry] secar -2. [stain with ink] borrar.

➡ **blot out** *vt sep* -1. [obscure] ocultar -2. [erase] apagar.

blotch *n* mancha *f.*

blotchy ['blɒtʃɪ] (*compar* -ier, *superl* -iest) *adj* manchado(da).

blotting paper ['blɒtɪŋ-] *n* papel *m* mata-borrão.

blouse [blaʊz] *n* blusa *f.*

blouson ['blu:zɒn] *n UK* blusão *m.*

blow [bləʊ] (*pt* blew, *pp* blown) ◇ *vi* -1. [wind] ventar -2. [through mouth] soprar -3. [fuse] estourar -4. [whistle] assoviar. ◇ *vt* -1. [subj: wind] soprar -2. [whistle, horn, trumpet] soar -3. *inf* [money] torrar -4. [clear]: **to ~ one's nose** assoar o nariz -5. *phr:* **to ~ bubbles** fazer bolas OR bolhas. ◇ *n* -1. [hit] golpe *m*; **to come to ~s** começar a brigar; **to strike a ~ for sthg** *fig* lutar por algo -2. [shock] choque *m*; **to soften the ~** amortecer o golpe.

➡ **blow away** *vi* [in wind] voar longe, sair voando.

➡ **blow out** ◇ *vt sep* apagar. ◇ *vi* -1. [candle] apagar -2. [tyre] estourar.

➡ **blow over** *vi* -1. [storm] cessar -2. [argument] esquecer-se.

➡ **blow up** ◇ *vt sep* -1. [inflate] encher -2. [with bomb] explodir -3. [enlarge] ampliar. ◇ *vi* [explode] explodir.

blow-by-blow *adj* detalhado(da).

blow-dry ◇ *n* secagem *f.* ◇ *vt* secar.

blowfly ['bləʊflaɪ] (*pl* -flies) *n* mosca-varejeira *f.*

blowgun *n US* = blowpipe.

blowlamp *UK* ['bləʊlæmp], **blowtorch** ['bləʊtɔ:tʃ] *n* maçarico *m.*

blown [bləʊn] *pp* ▻ blow.

blowout ['bləʊaʊt] *n* -1. [of tyre] furo *m* -2. *inf* [big meal] comilança *f.*

blowpipe *UK* ['bləʊpaɪp], **blowgun** *US* ['bləʊɡʌn] *n* zarabatana *f.*

blowtorch *n* = blowlamp.

blowzy ['blaʊzɪ] (*compar* -ier, *superl* -iest) *adj Br:* **a ~ woman** uma mulher desalinhada.

BLS (*abbr of* Bureau of Labor Statistics) *n instituto norte-americano de economia e estatística do trabalho.*

BLT (*abbr of* bacon, lettuce and tomato) *n fam sanduíche de bacon, alface e tomate.*

blubber ['blʌbə^r] ◇ *n* [of whale] gordura *f.* ◇ *vi pej* [weep] choramingar.

bludgeon ['blʌdʒən] *vt* espancar; **to ~ sb into doing sthg** *fig* ameaçar alguém para que faça algo.

blue [blu:] ◇ *adj* -1. [in colour] azul -2. *inf* [sad] triste -3. [pornographic - film, movie] pornográfico(-ca); [- joke] obsceno(na). ◇ *n* azul *m*; **dressed in ~** vestido(da) de azul; **out of the ~** inesperadamente.

➡ **blues** *npl* **the ~s** *MUS* o blues; *inf* [sad feeling] a melancolia.

blue baby *n MED* bebê *m* cianótico.

bluebell ['blu:bel] *n* campainha *f* (azul).

blueberry ['blu:bərɪ] (*pl* -ies) *n* mirtilo *m.*

bluebird ['blu:bɜ:d] *n* azulão *m* norte-americano.

blue-black *adj* azul-ferrete.

blue-blooded [-'blʌdɪd] *adj* de sangue azul.

bluebottle ['blu:,bɒtl] *n* mosca-varejeira *f.*

blue channel *n: the ~ acesso direto utilizado pelos membros da Comunidade Européia ao passar pelo controle de passaportes.*

blue cheese *n* queijo *m* azul.

blue chip *n ST EX* blue chip *f*, ação *f* de primeira ordem.

➡ **blue-chip** *comp ST EX* de primeira ordem.

blue-collar *adj* operário(ria).

blue-eyed boy [-aɪd-] *n inf* queridinho *m.*

blue jeans *npl US* jeans *m*, calça *f* jeans.

blue moon *n inf:* **once in a ~** uma vez a cada século.

blueprint ['blu:prɪnt] *n* -1. *CONSTR* planta *f* -2. *fig* [plan, programme] projeto *m.*

bluestocking ['blu:,stɒkɪŋ] *n pej* sabichona *f.*

blue tit *n UK* chapim-azul *m.*

blue whale *n* baleia *f* azul.

bluff [blʌf] ◇ *adj* [person, manner] expansivo(va). ◇ *n* -1. [deception] blefe *m*; **to call sb's ~** pagar para ver (o que alguém está ameaçando fazer)

-2. [cliff] penhasco m. ⬦ vt: **to ~ one's way into/ out of sthg** trapacear para entrar em/sair de algo. ⬦ vi blefar.

blunder ['blʌndə'] ⬦ n gafe f. ⬦ vi **-1.** [make mistake] cometer um grande equívoco **-2.** [move clumsily] cambalear ; [stumble] tropeçar.

blundering ['blʌndərɪŋ] adj [stupid] desajeitado(-da).

blunt [blʌnt] ⬦ adj **-1.** [gen] obtuso(sa) **-2.** [pencil] sem ponta **-3.** [knife] cego(ga) **-4.** [forthright] direto(ta). ⬦ vt **-1.** [knife] cegar **-2.** fig [enthusiam, interest etc] murchar **-3.** [impact] amortecer.

bluntly ['blʌntlɪ] adv [say, reply] com franqueza, sem rodeios.

bluntness ['blʌntnɪs] n [forthrightness] franqueza f.

blur [blɜ:'] (pt & pp -red, cont -ring) ⬦ n borrão m, névoa f. ⬦ vt **-1.** [outline, photograph] desfocar **-2.** [distinction, memory, vision] embaçar **-3.** [confuse] obscurecer.

blurb [blɜ:b] n inf [on book] sinopse f.

blurred [blɜ:d] adj **-1.** [outline, photograph] desfocado(da) **-2.** [distinction, memory, vision] obscuro(ra).

blurt [blɜ:t] ➡ **blurt out** vt sep falar sem pensar.

blush [blʌʃ] ⬦ n rubor m. ⬦ vi corar.

blusher ['blʌʃə'] n ruge m.

bluster ['blʌstə'] ⬦ n **-1.** [angry talk] discussão f **-2.** [boasting] bazófia f. ⬦ vi **-1.** [speak angrily] vociferar **-2.** [boast] fanfarronar.

blustery ['blʌstərɪ] adj ventoso(sa).

BM n **-1.** (abbr of Bachelor of Medicine) (titular de) graduação em medicina. **-2.** (abbr of British Museum) Museu m Britânico.

BMA (abbr of British Medical Association) n associação britânica de medicina, ≃ AMB f.

BMJ (abbr of British Medical Journal) n publicação da associação britânica de medicina.

BMus (abbr of Bachelor of Music) n (titular de) graduação em música.

BNP (abbr of British National Party) n partido britânico de extrema direita.

BO (abbr of body odour) n cê-cê m.

boa constrictor ['bəʊəkən'strɪktə'] n jibóia f.

boar [bɔ:'] n **-1.** [male pig] barrão m **-2.** [wild pig] javali m.

board [bɔ:d] ⬦ n **-1.** [plank] tábua f **-2.** [for notices] quadro m (de avisos) **-3.** [for games] tabuleiro m **-4.** [blackboard] quadro-negro m **-5.** ADMIN direção f; **~ of directors** conselho m de diretores; **examining ~** banca f examinadora; **~ of enquiry** comissão f de inquérito **-6.** UK [at hotel, guesthouse] pensão f; **~ and lodging** casa e comida; **full ~** pensão completa; **half ~** meia pensão **-7.** phr: **above ~** honesto(ta); **to go by the ~** ir por água abaixo; **to sweep the ~** ganhar todas. ⬦ vt [get onto] embarcar em.
➡ **across the board** ⬦ adj generalizado(da). ⬦ adv de forma generalizada.
➡ **on board** ⬦ adj a bordo. ⬦ adv a bordo; **to take sthg on ~** aceitar algo.
➡ **board up** vt sep fechar com tábuas.

boarder ['bɔ:də'] n **-1.** [lodger] pensionista mf **-2.** [at school] interno m, -na f.

board game n jogo m de tabuleiro.

boarding card ['bɔ:dɪŋ-] n cartão m de embarque.

boarding house n hospedaria f.

boarding school ['bɔ:dɪŋ-] n colégio m interno.

board meeting n reunião f de conselho.

Board of Trade n UK: **the ~** ≃ Câmara f do Comércio, na Inglaterra, comissão governamental responsável pela supervisão do comércio e pelo estímulo às exportações.

boardroom ['bɔ:drʊm] n sala f da diretoria.

boardwalk ['bɔ:dwɔ:k] n US passeio m de tábuas.

boast [bəʊst] ⬦ n alarde m. ⬦ vt [special feature] ostentar. ⬦ vi [show off] vangloriar-se; **to ~ about sthg** gabar-se de algo.

boastful ['bəʊstfʊl] adj presunçoso(sa).

boasting n presunção f, ostentação f.

boat [bəʊt] n [ship] barco m; [for rowing] bote m; [for sailing] veleiro m; **by ~** de barco; **in the same ~** fig no mesmo barco; **to rock the ~** fig complicar as coisas.

boater ['bəʊtə'] n [hat] chapéu m de palha.

boating ['bəʊtɪŋ] n passeio m de barco.

boat people npl refugiados que escapam de seu país de barco.

boatswain ['bəʊsn] n NAUT contramestre m.

boat train n trem que leva as pessoas para embarcar num navio ou que recolhe as que desembarcaram.

bob [bɒb] (pt & pp -bed, cont -bing) ⬦ n **-1.** [hairstyle] corte m chanel **-2.** UK inf dated [shilling] xelim m **-3.** = **bobsleigh.** ⬦ vi [boat, ship] balouçar-se.

bobbin ['bɒbɪn] n [spool] bobina f.

bobble ['bɒbl] n [fluffy ball] pompom m.

bobby ['bɒbɪ] (pl -ies) n UK inf [policeman] tira m.

bobby pin n US grampo m (de cabelo).

bobby socks, bobby sox npl US meias fpl soquete.

bobsleigh ['bɒbsleɪ] n trenó m de esporte.

bode [bəʊd] vi literary: **to ~ ill/well (for sb/ sthg)** ser de mau/bom agouro (para alguém/ algo).

bodice ['bɒdɪs] n [of dress] corpete f.

bodily ['bɒdɪlɪ] ⬦ adj [needs] físico(ca). ⬦ adv [carry, lift] em peso.

body ['bɒdɪ] (pl -ies) n **-1.** [gen] corpo m; **to keep ~ and soul together** ganhar o suficiente só para pagar as contas **-2.** [corpse] cadáver m; **over my dead ~!** só por cima do meu cadáver! **-3.** [organization] entidade f **-4.** [of car] carroceria f **-5.** [of plane] fuselagem f **-6.** (U) [of wine] corpo m **-7.** [garment] body m.

body bag n saco m mortuário.

body building n fisiculturismo m.

bodyguard ['bɒdɪgɑ:d] n guarda-costas mf inv.

body odour UK, **body odor** US n odor m corporal.

body search n revista f corporal.

body shop n **-1.** [garage] oficina f mecânica **-2.** Am inf [gym] academia f (de ginástica).

body stocking n macaquinho m colante (para ginástica, dança).

bodywork ['bɒdɪwɜ:k] n [of car] carroçeria f.

boffin ['bɒfɪn] n UK inf cientista mf.

bog [bɒg] n -1. [marsh] lodaçal m -2. UK v inf [toilet] privada f.

bogey ['bəʊgɪ] n -1. [spectre]: **the ~ of recession** o fantasma da recessão -2. inf [in nose] meleca f.

bogeyman n ≃ bicho-papão m.

bogged down [ˌbɒgd-] adj atolado(da).

boggle ['bɒgl] vi: **the mind ~s!** não dá para acreditar!

boggy ['bɒgɪ] (compar -ier, superl -iest) adj lamacento(ta), pantanoso(sa).

bogie n RAIL truque m.

Bogotá [ˌbɒgə'tɑ:] n Bogotá; **in ~** em Bogotá.

bog-standard adj inf comum.

bogus ['bəʊgəs] adj falso(sa).

Bohemia [bəʊ'hi:mjə] n Boêmia; **in ~** na Boêmia.

bohemian [bəʊ'hi:mɪən] <> adj boêmio(mia). <> n boêmio m, -mia f.

➡ **Bohemian** <> adj boêmio(mia). <> n boêmio m, -mia f.

boil [bɔɪl] <> n -1. MED [on skin] furúnculo m -2. [boiling point]: **to bring sthg to the ~** deixar algo ferver; **to come to the ~** começar a ferver. <> vt -1. [water, kettle] ferver -2. [food] cozinhar. <> vi [water, kettle] ferver.

➡ **boil away** vi [evaporate] evaporar.

➡ **boil down to** vt fus fig reduzir-se a.

➡ **boil over** vi -1. [liquid] derramar -2. fig [feelings] descontrolar-se.

boiled [bɔɪld] adj cozido(da); **~ sweet** UK caramelo m; **~ egg** ovo m cozido.

boiler ['bɔɪləʳ] n boiler m.

boiler suit n UK macacão m.

boiling ['bɔɪlɪŋ] adj -1. [liquid] fervente -2. inf [hot person] morto(ta) de calor; [- weather] abrasador(ra) -3. [angry]: **~ with rage** fervendo de raiva.

boiling point n ponto m de ebulição.

boisterous ['bɔɪstərəs] adj [child, behaviour] irriquieto(ta).

bold [bəʊld] adj -1. [confident] audacioso(sa) -2. [brave] corajoso(sa) -3. ART [lines, design] arrojado(da) -4. [colour] nítido(da) -5. TYPO: **in ~ type** OR **print** em negrito.

boldly ['bəʊldlɪ] adv corajosamente.

Bolivia [bə'lɪvɪə] n Bolívia; **in ~** na Bolívia.

Bolivian [bə'lɪvɪən] <> adj boliviano(na). <> n boliviano m, -na f.

bollard ['bɒlɑ:d] n [on road] poste m de sinalização.

bollocks ['bɒləks] UK vulg <> npl saco m. <> excl saco!

Bolshevik ['bɒlʃɪvɪk] <> adj bolchevique. <> n bolchevique mf.

bolster ['bəʊlstəʳ] <> n [pillow] travesseiro m longo. <> vt [encourage] alentar.

➡ **bolster up** vt fus [support] sustentar.

bolt [bəʊlt] <> n -1. [on door, window] ferrolho m, trinco m -2. [type of screw] parafuso m. <> adv : **to sit ~ upright** sentar direito. <> vt -1. [fasten together] aparafusar -2. [close] trancar -3. [food] devorar. <> vi [run] disparar.

bomb [bɒm] <> n [explosive device] bomba f. <> vt bombardear.

bombard [bɒm'bɑ:d] vt MIL & fig bombardear, **to ~ sb with sthg** bombardear alguém com algo.

bombardment [bɒm'bɑ:dmənt] n bombardeio m.

bombastic [bɒm'bæstɪk] adj bombástico(ca).

bomb disposal squad n esquadrão m anti-bombas.

bomber ['bɒmәʳ] n -1. [plane] bombardeiro m -2. [person] pessoa que pratica atentados a bomba.

bomber jacket n jaqueta curta ajustada ao peito e aos quadris.

bombing ['bɒmɪŋ] n bombardeio m.

bombproof adj [shelter] à prova de bombas.

bombshell ['bɒmʃel] n fig [unpleasant surprise] bomba f; **to come as a ~** cair como uma bomba.

bombsite n área f bombardeada.

bona fide ['bəʊnə'faɪd] adj [genuine] legítimo(ma).

bonanza [bə'nænzə] n fonte, muitas vezes repentina ou inesperada, de sorte ou riqueza.

bond [bɒnd] <> n -1. [emotional link] laço m -2. [binding promise] compromisso m -3. FIN título m -3. [glue]: **to ~ sthg to sthg** colar algo a algo -2. fig [people] unir. <> vi -1. [stick together]: **to ~ (together)** colar -2. fig [people] unir-se.

bondage n literary [servitude] servidão f.

bonded warehouse ['bɒndɪd-] n depósito m da alfândega.

bone [bəʊn] <> n -1. [of body, material] osso m; **~ of contention** pomo m da discórdia; **to feel sthg in one's ~s** sentir algo na pele; **to know sthg in one's ~s** saber algo intuitivamente; **to make no ~s about sthg** não fazer cerimônia sobre algo -2. [of fish] espinha f. <> vt [fish, meat] desossar.

bone china n porcelana fina e branca feita com cinzas de ossos.

bone-dry adj completamente seco(ca).

bone-idle adj inf encostado(da).

boneless ['bəʊnlɪs] adj sem osso.

bone marrow n tutano m.

bonfire ['bɒnˌfaɪəʳ] n fogueira f ao ar livre.

bonfire night n UK noite de 5 de novembro, quando os ingleses lançam fogos de artifício e queimam a figura de Guy Fawkes numa fogueira ao ar livre.

bongo ['bɒŋgəʊ] (pl -s OR -es) n: **~ (drum)** bongô m.

bonk [bɒŋk] inf <> vt [have sex with] transar com. <> vi [have sex] transar.

Bonn [bɒn] n Bonn; **in ~** em Bonn.

bonnet ['bɒnɪt] n -1. UK [of car] capô m -2. [hat] touca f.

bonus ['bəʊnəs] (pl -es) n -1. [extra money] bônus m inv -2. fig [added treat] vantagem f adicional.

bonus issue n UK FIN emissão f de títulos de bonificação.

bony ['bəʊnɪ] (compar -ier, superl -iest) adj -1. [person, hand, face] ossudo(da) -2. [meat] com osso; [fish] cheio (cheia) de espinhas.

boo [bu:] (pl -s) <> excl bu! <> n vaia f. <> vt & vi vaiar.

boob [bu:b] n inf [mistake] gafe f.

➡ **boobs** npl UK inf [breasts] tetas fpl.

boob tube n -1. UK [garment] tomara-que-caia m inv -2. US inf [TV] telinha f.

booby prize ['bu:bɪ-] n prêmio m de consolação.

booby trap ['bu:bɪ-] n -1. [bomb] bomba f camuflada -2. [prank] armadilha f.

➨ **booby-trap** *vt* [car, building] colocar explosivos em.

boogie ['bu:gɪ] *inf* ◇ *n* [dance]: **let's have a ~** vamos sacudir. ◇ *vi* [dance] sacudir.

book [bʊk] ◇ *n* -**1.** [for reading] livro *m*; **to do sthg by the ~** fazer algo como manda o figurino; **to throw the ~ at sb** fazer todas as acusações possíveis a alguém -**2.** [pack - of stamps] bloco *m*; [- of matches] caixa *f*; [- of cheques, tickets] talão *m*. ◇ *vt* -**1.** [reserve] reservar; **to be fully ~ed** estar totalmente cheio (cheia) *OR* esgotado(da) -**2.** *inf* [subj: police] autuar -**3.** *UK FTBL* dar cartão amarelo *OR* vermelho a. ◇ *vi* reservar, fazer uma reserva.

➨ **books** *npl COMM* registros *mpl*; **to do the ~s** escriturar, fazer a contabilidade; **to be in sb's good/bad ~s** ser bem/mal visto por alguém.

➨ **book in** ◇ *vt sep* registrar-se. ◇ *vi* [at hotel] registrar-se.

➨ **book up** *vt sep*: **to be ~ed up** [fully booked] estar completamente cheio (cheia); **the hotel is ~ed up** o hotel está lotado.

bookable ['bʊkəbl] *adj* -**1.** [seats, tickets] a ser reservado(da) -**2.** *FTBL*: **a ~ offence** uma falta digna de cartão.

book bag *n US* = **booksack**.

bookbinding ['bʊk,baɪndɪŋ] *n* encadernação *f*.

bookcase ['bʊkkeɪs] *n* estante *f* (para livros).

book club *n* clube *m* do livro.

bookends *npl* prateleiras *fpl*.

bookie ['bʊkɪ] *n inf* bookmaker *m*.

booking ['bʊkɪŋ] *n* -**1.** *esp UK* [reservation] reserva *f* -**2.** *esp UK FTBL* cartão *m* amarelo *OR* vermelho.

booking clerk *n esp UK* vendedor *m*, -ra *f* de ingressos.

booking office *n esp UK* bilheteria *f*.

bookish ['bʊkɪʃ] *adj* [person] aficionado(da) pelos livros.

bookkeeper ['bʊk,ki:pəʳ] *n COMM* contador *m*, -ra *f*.

bookkeeping ['bʊk,ki:pɪŋ] *n COMM* contabilidade *f*.

booklet ['bʊklɪt] *n* [pamphlet] folheto *m*.

bookmaker ['bʊk,meɪkəʳ] *n* bookmaker *m*.

bookmark ['bʊkmɑ:k] *n* marcador *m* de páginas.

booksack *n US* mochila *f*.

bookseller ['bʊk,seləʳ] *n* vendedor *m*, -ra *f* de livros.

bookshelf ['bʊkʃelf] (*pl* -**shelves** [-ʃelvz]) *n* prateleira *f OR* estante *f* (para livros).

bookshop *UK* ['bʊkʃɒp], **bookstore** *US* ['bʊkstɔ:ʳ] *n* livraria *f*.

bookstall ['bʊkstɔ:l] *n UK* banca *f* de jornal.

bookstore *n US* = **bookshop**.

book token *n esp UK* vale-livro *m*.

bookworm ['bʊkwɜ:m] *n fig* [person] rato *m* de biblioteca.

boom [bu:m] ◇ *n* -**1.** [loud noise] estrondo *m* -**2.** [increase] boom *m*, crescimento *m* -**3.** *NAUT* retranca *f* -**4.** [for TV camera, microphone] bum *m*. ◇ *vi* -**1.** [make noise] ribombar -**2.** *ECON* [grow] crescer rapidamente.

boomerang ['bu:məræŋ] *n* bumerangue *m*.

boon [bu:n] *n* [help, advantage] ajuda *f*.

boor [bʊəʳ] *n* pessoa *f* rude.

boorish ['bʊərɪʃ] *adj* rude.

boost [bu:st] ◇ *n* -**1.** [increase] incremento *m*; **to give a ~ to sthg** dar um empurrão em algo -**2.** [improvement] impulso *m*. ◇ *vt* -**1.** [increase] incrementar -**2.** [improve] levantar -**3.** *US inf* [steal] afanar.

booster ['bu:stəʳ] *n MED* [vaccine] reforço *m*.

booster seat *n* cadeirinha *f* para automóvel, bebê-conforto *m*.

boot [bu:t] ◇ *n* -**1.** [footwear] bota *f* -**2.** *UK* [of car] porta-bagagem *m*. ◇ *vt* -**1.** *inf* [kick] dar um pé na bunda de -**2.** *COMPUT* inicializar, dar boot em.

➨ **to boot** *adv* também.

➨ **boot out** *vt sep inf* mandar às favas.

➨ **boot up** *vi COMPUT* inicializar, dar boot.

booth [bu:ð] *n* -**1.** [at fair] barraca *f* -**2.** [telephone booth] cabine *f* (telefônica) -**3.** [voting booth] cabine *f* eleitoral.

bootleg ['bu:tleg] *adj* [alcohol] de contrabando; [recording] pirata.

bootlegger ['bu:t,legəʳ] *n inf* contrabandista *mf*.

booty ['bu:tɪ] *n literary* butim *m*.

booze [bu:z] *inf* ◇ *n* [alcohol] trago *m*. ◇ *vi* [drink alcohol] tomar umas e outras.

boozer ['bu:zəʳ] *n inf* -**1.** [person] bebum *mf* -**2.** *UK* [pub] bar *m*.

bop [bɒp] (*pt & pp* -**ped**, *cont* -**ping**) *inf* ◇ *n* -**1.** [hit] batida *f* -**2.** [disco, dance] festa *f* dançante. ◇ *vt* [hit] bater. ◇ *vi* [dance] dançar.

border ['bɔ:dəʳ] ◇ *n* -**1.** [between countries] fronteira *f* -**2.** [edge] borda *f* -**3.** [hem] orla *f* -**4.** [outer boundary] limite *m* -**5.** [bank, shore] margem *f* -**6.** [for flowers] bordadura *f*. ◇ *vt* -**1.** [country] limitar-se com -**2.** [surround] cercar.

➨ **border on** *vt fus* [verge on] beirar em.

border collie *n* border collie *m*.

borderline ['bɔ:dəlaɪn] ◇ *adj*: **~ case** caso-limite *m*. ◇ *n fig* [division] limite *m*.

bore [bɔ:ʳ] ◇ *pt* ▷ **bear**. ◇ *n* -**1.** *pej* [tedious person] chato *m*, -ta *f*; [tedious situation, event] chatice *f* -**2.** [of gun] calibre *m*. ◇ *vt* -**1.** [not interest] entediar; **to ~ sb stiff** *OR* **to tears** *OR* **to death** *inf* matar alguém de tédio -**2.** [drill] furar.

bored [bɔ:d] *adj* entediado(da); **to be ~ with sthg** estar entediado(da) com algo.

boredom ['bɔ:dəm] *n* tédio *m*.

boring ['bɔ:rɪŋ] *adj* chato(ta).

born [bɔ:n] *adj* -**1.** [given life] nascido(da); **to be ~** nascer; **~ and bred (in)** nascido e criado (em), nascida e criada (em) -**2.** [for emphasis] nato(ta).

born-again *adj* -**1.** [Christian] convertido(da) -**2.** *fig* [earnestly enthusiastic] fanático(ca).

borne [bɔ:n] *pp* ▷ **bear**.

Borneo ['bɔ:nɪəʊ] *n* Bornéu *f*; **in ~** em Bornéu.

borough ['bʌrə] *n* município *m*, distrito *m*.

borrow ['bɒrəʊ] *vt* [property, money] tomar emprestado(da); **to ~ sthg from sb** pegar algo emprestado de alguém.

borrower ['bɒrəʊəʳ] *n* [of money] tomador *m*, -ra *f* de empréstimo.

borrowing ['bɒrəʊɪŋ] *n* [of money] empréstimo *m*.

borstal ['bɔ:stl] n UK instituto m correcional para jovens.

Bosnia ['bɒznɪə] n Bósnia; **in** ~ na Bósnia.

Bosnia-Herzegovina [-ˌhɜ:tsəgə'vi:nə] n Bósnia-Herzegovina.

Bosnian ['bɒznɪən] <> adj bósnio(nia). <> n bósnio m, -nia f.

bosom ['bʊzəm] n **-1.** [of woman] peito m **-2.** fig [centre] seio m; ~ **friend** amigo m, -ga f do peito.

Bosporus ['bɒspərəs], **Bosphorus** ['bɒsfərəs] n: **the** ~ o Bósforo.

boss [bɒs] <> n **-1.** [of company, department, organization] chefe mf; **to be one's own** ~ trabalhar por conta própria **-2.** fig [of gang] chefão m; **you're the** ~**!** você é quem manda! <> vt pej [give orders to] mandar.

➡ **boss about, boss around** vt sep mandar em.

bossy ['bɒsɪ] (compar -ier, superl -iest) adj mandão(ona).

bosun ['bəʊsn] n = boatswain.

botanic(al) [bə'tænɪk(l)] adj botânico(ca).

botanical garden n jardim m botânico.

botanist ['bɒtənɪst] n botânico m, -ca f.

botany ['bɒtənɪ] n botânica f.

botch [bɒtʃ] ➡ **botch up** vt sep inf fazer nas coxas.

both [bəʊθ] <> adj ambos(bas), os dois, as duas; **we** ~ **left** nós dois (duas) saímos, ambos saímos; ~ **my brother and myself will be there** tanto meu irmão quanto eu estaremos lá, nós dois estaremos lá. <> adv não apenas ... como; **she is** ~ **witty and intelligent** ela não só é espirituosa, como também inteligente. <> pron ambos mpl, -bas fpl; ~ **of us** nós dois (duas).

bother ['bɒðə] <> vt **-1.** [worry] preocupar; **I can't be** ~**ed to do that** não me disponho a fazer isso **-2.** [irritate, annoy] incomodar. <> vi [trouble o.s.] incomodar-se; **to** ~ **about sthg** incomodar-se com algo; **to** ~ **doing** OR **to do sthg** incomodar-se em fazer algo. <> n **-1.** (U) [inconvenience] aborrecimento m **-2.** [nuisance] incômodo m **-3.** [difficulty] dificuldade f **-4.** [obstacle] estorvo m. <> excl (que) droga!

bothered ['bɒðəd] adj **-1.** [worried] preocupado(da) **-2.** [annoyed] chateado(da).

Botswana [bɒ'tswɑ:nə] n Botsuana; **in** ~ em Botsuana.

bottle ['bɒtl] <> n **-1.** [gen] garrafa f **-2.** [of medicine] frasco m **-3.** [of perfume] vidro m **-4.** [for baby] mamadeira f **-5.** (U) UK inf [courage]: **he didn't have the** ~ **to do it** ele não teve coragem de fazer isso. <> vt **-1.** [wine] engarrafar **-2.** [fruit] enfrascar.

➡ **bottle out** vi UK inf dar para trás.

➡ **bottle up** vt sep [feelings] reprimir.

bottle bank n container no qual se recolhem garrafas de vidro vazias para reciclagem.

bottled ['bɒtld] adj engarrafado(da).

bottle-feed vt [baby] dar mamadeira para.

bottleneck ['bɒtlnek] n **-1.** [in traffic] engarrafamento m **-2.** [in production] gargalo m.

bottle-opener n abridor m (de garrafa).

bottle party n festa informal em que cada convidado leva bebida.

bottom ['bɒtəm] <> adj **-1.** [lowest] de baixo **-2.** [least successful] último(ma). <> n **-1.** [lowest part - of glass, bag, lake] fundo m; [- of page] fim m, final m; [- of mountain, hill] sopé m; **at the** ~ **embaixo; at the** ~ **of** no fundo de **-2.** [far end] fim m, final m **-3.** [least successful level] nível m mais baixo **-4.** [buttocks] traseiro m **-5.** fig [root, cause]: **at the** ~ **of** por trás de; **to get to the** ~ **of sthg** ir até o fundo de algo.

➡ **bottom out** vi [prices, recession] estabilizar-se.

bottomless ['bɒtəmlɪs] adj **-1.** [very deep] sem fundo **-2.** [endless] infinito(ta).

bottom line n fig: **the** ~ **is that ...** a questão toda é que ...

botulism n (U) botulismo m.

bough [baʊ] n [of tree] galho m.

bought [bɔ:t] pt & pp ➡ buy.

boulder ['bəʊldə] n pedregulho m.

boulevard ['bu:ləvɑ:d] n alameda f.

bounce [baʊns] <> vi **-1.** [ball] quicar **-2.** [light, sound] refletir **-3.** [person - with energy, enthusiasm]: **she was bouncing with energy/enthusiasm** ela estava pulando de alegria/entusiasmo; **she bounced into the room, singing** ela entrou na sala radiante, cantando; [- jump up and down]: **to** ~ **on sthg** saltar sobre algo **-4.** inf [cheque] ser devolvido(da). <> vt [ball] bater. <> n **-1.** [of ball] pulo m **-2.** fig [vigour] vigor m, vivacidade f.

➡ **bounce back** vi [after illness, setback] recuperar-se.

bouncer ['baʊnsə] n inf [at club etc] leão-de-chácara m.

bouncy ['baʊnsɪ] (compar -ier, superl -iest) adj **-1.** [lively] vivaz **-2.** [bed, trampoline] com bom molejo **-3.** [ball] saltitante.

bound [baʊnd] <> pt & pp ➡ bind. <> adj **-1.** [certain]: **to be** ~ **to do sthg** fazer algo na certa **-2.** [forced, morally obliged]: ~ **by sthg/to do sthg** obrigado(da) por algo/fazer algo; **I'm** ~ **to say/admit** devo dizer/admitir **-3.** [en route]: **to be** ~ **for** estar a caminho de. <> n [leap] salto m. <> vt [border]: **to be** ~**ed by** ser limitado(da) por. <> vi [leap] correr aos pulos.

➡ **bound up with** prep [connected] estreitamente ligado a.

➡ **bounds** npl [limits] limites mpl; **out of** ~**s** interditado(da).

boundary ['baʊndərɪ] (pl -ies) n **-1.** [of area of land] fronteira f **-2.** fig [of science, knowledge] fronteiras fpl.

boundless ['baʊndlɪs] adj ilimitado(da).

bountiful ['baʊntɪfʊl] adj literary [ample] abundante.

bounty ['baʊntɪ] n (U) literary [generosity] generosidade f.

bouquet [bəʊ'keɪ] n **-1.** [bunch] buquê m **-2.** [smell] buquê m.

bouquet garni ['bu:keɪgɑ:'ni:] n bouquet garni m (ervas para tempero).

bourbon ['bɜ:bən] n bourbon m (uísque norte-americano).

bourgeois ['bɔ:ʒwɑ:] adj pej burguês(esa).

bourgeoisie [ˌbɔ:ʒwɑ:'zi:] n pej: **the** ~ a burguesia.

bout [baʊt] *n* -**1.** [attack] ataque *m* -**2.** [session] período *m* -**3.** [boxing match] assalto *m*.

boutique [buːˈtiːk] *n* butique *f*.

bow¹ [baʊ] ⬦ *n* -**1.** [act of bowing] reverência *f*-**2.** [of ship] proa *f*. ⬦ *vt* [lower] inclinar. ⬦ *vi* -**1.** [make a bow] inclinar-se -**2.** [defer]: **to ~ to** sthg submeter-se a algo.

➡ **bow down** *vi* [give in]: **to ~ down (to sb)** render-se(a alguém).

➡ **bow out** *vi* afastar-se.

bow² [bəʊ] *n* -**1.** [gen & *MUS*] arco *m* -**2.** [knot] laço *m*.

bowels [ˈbaʊəlz] *npl* -**1.** [intestines] intestinos *mpl* -**2.** *fig* [deepest part] entranhas *fpl*.

bowl [bəʊl] ⬦ *n* -**1.** [container - gen] tigela *f*; [- for sugar] açucareiro *m*; [- for fruit] fruteira *f*-**2.** [bowl-shaped part - of toilet, sink] bacia *f*; [- of pipe] fornilho *m* -**3.** [bowlful] prato *m*. ⬦ *vt & vi* [in cricket] atirar.

➡ **bowls** *n (U)* jogo *m* de bocha.

➡ **bowl over** *vt sep* -**1.** [knock over] derrubar -**2.** *fig* [surprise, impress] surpreender.

bow-legged [ˌbəʊˈlegɪd] *adj* cambota.

bowler [ˈbəʊlə'] *n* -**1.** [in cricket, bowls] lançador *m* -**2.** [headgear]: **~ (hat)** chapéu-coco *m*.

bowling [ˈbəʊlɪŋ] *n*: **(tenpin) ~** jogo *m* de boliche.

bowling alley *n* -**1.** [building] boliche *m* -**2.** [alley] pista *f* de boliche.

bowling green *n* cancha *m* de bocha.

bow tie [bəʊ-] *n* gravata-borboleta *f*.

bow window [bəʊ-] *n* janela *f* em arco.

box [bɒks] ⬦ *n* -**1.** [gen] caixa *f* -**2.** [in theatre] camarote *m* -**3.** [in car races] box *m* -**4.** *UK inf* [television]: **the ~** a TV -**5.** [shrub, tree] buxo *m*. ⬦ *vt* -**1.** [punch] esmurrar -**2.** [put in boxes] colocar em caixas. ⬦ *vi* [fight] lutar.

➡ **box in** *vt sep* -**1.** [hem in]: **to get ~ed in** ficar espremido(da) -**2.** [build a box around] encaixotar, encaixar.

boxed [bɒkst] *adj* empacotado(da).

boxer [ˈbɒksə'] *n* -**1.** [fighter] boxeador *m*, -ra *f*-**2.** [dog] boxer *mf*.

boxer shorts *npl* cuecas *fpl* samba-canção.

boxing [ˈbɒksɪŋ] *n (U)* boxe *m*.

Boxing Day *n* dia seguinte ao Natal em que é feriado nacional no Reino Unido. Tradicionalmente, era o dia em que os empregados recebiam os presentes dos patrões, geralmente uma caixinha em dinheiro.

boxing glove *n* luva *f* de boxe.

boxing ring *n* ringue *m* de boxe.

box junction *n UK* cruzamento de ruas demarcado com faixas amarelas sobre o qual um veículo não pode avançar a menos que seu caminho esteja livre.

box number *n* caixa *f* postal.

box office *n* bilheteria *f*.

boxroom [ˈbɒksrʊm] *n UK* quarto *m* de despejo.

boy [bɔɪ] ⬦ *n* -**1.** [young male] menino *m* -**2.** [adult male] rapaz *m* -**3.** [son] filho *m* -**4.** [male friend]: **the ~s** os caras. ⬦ *excl*: **(oh) ~!** *inf* nossa!

boycott [ˈbɔɪkɒt] ⬦ *n* boicote *m*. ⬦ *vt* boicotar.

boyfriend [ˈbɔɪfrend] *n* namorado *m*.

boyish [ˈbɔɪʃ] *adj* juvenil.

boy scout *n* escoteiro *m*.

Bp (*abbr of* **Bishop**) bispo *m*.

Br (*abbr of* **Brother**) *RELIG* Ir.

bra [brɑː] *n* sutiã *f*.

brace [breɪs] (*pl sense 3 inv*) ⬦ *n* -**1.** *MED* aparelho *m* -**2.** [pair] par *m*. ⬦ *vt lit & fig* **to ~ o.s. (for** sthg**):** preparar-se (para algo).

➡ **braces** *npl UK* [for trousers] suspensórios *mpl*.

bracelet [ˈbreɪslɪt] *n* bracelete *m*.

bracing [ˈbreɪsɪŋ] *adj* revigorante.

bracken [ˈbrækn] *n (U)* samambaia *f*.

bracket [ˈbrækɪt] ⬦ *n* -**1.** [support] suporte *m*, mão-francesa *f*-**2.** [parenthesis] parêntese *m*; **in ~s** entre parênteses -**3.** [group] faixa *f*. ⬦ *vt*-**1.** [enclose in brackets] colocar entre parênteses -**2.** [group]: **to ~** sb/sth **(together) with** sb/sthg equiparar alguém/algo a alguém/algo.

brackish [ˈbrækɪʃ] *adj* salobre.

brag [bræg] (*pt & pp* -**ged**, *cont* -**ging**) *vi* [boast] gabar-se.

braid [breɪd] ⬦ *n* -**1.** [on uniform] galão *m* -**2.** *US* [hairstyle] trança *f*. ⬦ *vt US* trançar.

braille [breɪl] *n (U)* braile *m*.

brain [breɪn] *n* -**1.** [organ] cérebro *m* -**2.** [mind] cabeça *f*; **to have sthg on the ~** estar com algo na cabeça -**3.** *inf* [clever person] gênio *m*.

➡ **brains** *npl* [intelligence] sabedoria *f*; **to pick sb's ~s** recorrer à sabedoria de alguém; **to rack** *UK* OR **cudgel** *US* one's **~s** *fig* queimar OR gastar os neurônios.

brainchild [ˈbreɪntʃaɪld] *n* invenção *f*.

brain death *n (U)* morte *f* cerebral.

brain drain *n* evasão *f* de cérebros.

brainless [ˈbreɪnlɪs] *adj* idiota, tolo(la).

brainstorm [ˈbreɪnstɔːm] *n* -**1.** *UK* [moment of aberration] bobeira *f*-**2.** *US* [brilliant idea] idéia *f* luminosa.

brainstorming [ˈbreɪnˌstɔːmɪŋ] *n (U)* brainstorming *m*.

brainteaser [ˈbreɪnˌtiːzə'] *n* quebra-cabeça *m*.

brainwash [ˈbreɪnwɒʃ] *vt* fazer lavagem cerebral em.

brainwave [ˈbreɪnweɪv] *n* idéia *f* luminosa.

brainy [ˈbreɪnɪ] (*compar* -**ier**, *superl* -**iest**) *adj inf* sabichão(chona).

braise [breɪz] *vt* refogar.

brake [breɪk] ⬦ *n* -**1.** [on vehicle] freio *m* -**2.** *fig* [restraint] freio *m*. ⬦ *vi* frear.

brake fluid *n (U)* líquido *m* de freio.

brake light *n* luz *f* de freio.

brake lining *n* lona *f* de freio.

brake pedal *n* pedal *m* do freio.

brake shoe *n* sapata *f* de freio.

bramble [ˈbræmbl] *n* [bush] amoreira *f* silvestre; [fruit] amora *f* silvestre.

bran [bræn] *n (U)* farelo *m*.

branch [brɑːntʃ] ⬦ *n* -**1.** [of tree] galho *m* -**2.** [of river] braço *m* -**3.** [of railway] ramal *m* -**4.** [of company, bank, organization] sucursal *f* -**5.** [of subject] ramo *m*. ⬦ *vi* [road] bifurcar-se.

➡ **branch off** *vi* [road, track] ramificar-se.

➡ **branch out** *vi* [person, company] expandir-se em nova direção.

branch line *n* [railway] ramal *m* secundário.

brand [brænd] ⬦ *n* -**1.** *COMM* marca *f* -**2.** *fig* [type] tipo *m* - **3.** [mark on cattle] marca *f* de ferro em brasa. <> *vt* - **1.** [cattle] marcar com ferro em brasa - **2.** *fig* [classify]: **to ~ sb (as) sthg** rotular alguém de algo.

brandish ['brændıʃ] *vt* brandir.

brand leader *n* marca *f* dominante.

brand name *n* marca *f* registrada.

brand-new *adj* novo(va) em folha.

brandy ['brændı] (*pl* -ies) *n* conhaque *m*.

brash [bræʃ] *adj pej* atrevido(da).

Brasilia [brə'zıljə] *n* Brasília; **in ~** em Brasília.

brass [brɑːs] *n* - **1.** (*U*) [type of metal] latão *m* - **2.** MUS: **the ~** os metais.
➤ **brasses** *npl* [ornaments] objetos *mpl* decorativos em latão.

brass band *n* fanfarra *f*.

brasserie ['bræsərı] *n restaurante simples e barato que serve comida em estilo francês.*

brassiere [*UK* 'bræsıə^r, *US* brə'zır] *n* sutiã *m*.

brass knuckles *npl Am* soco-inglês *m*.

brass rubbing *n* [picture] gravura *f* em latão.

brass tacks *npl inf:* **to get down to ~** ir direto ao assunto.

brat [bræt] *n inf pej* capeta *m*.

bravado [brə'vɑːdəʊ] *n* (*U*) bravata *f*.

brave [breıv] <> *adj* corajoso(sa). <> *n* [warrior] guerreiro *m* índio, bravo *m*. <> *vt* enfrentar.

bravely ['breıvlı] *adv* bravamente.

bravery ['breıvərı] *n* (*U*) bravura *f*.

bravo [‚brɑː'vəʊ] *excl* bravo!

brawl [brɔːl] *n* briga *f*.

brawn [brɔːn] *n* (*U*) [muscle] músculo *m*

brawny ['brɔːnı] (*compar* -ier, *superl* -iest) *adj* musculoso(sa).

bray [breı] *vi* [donkey] zurrar.

brazen ['breızn] *adj* descarado(da).
➤ **brazen out** *vt sep:* **to ~ it out** encarar.

brazier ['breızjə^r] *n* braseiro *m*.

Brazil [brə'zıl] *n* Brasil; **in ~** no Brasil.

Brazilian [brə'zıljən] <> *adj* brasileiro(ra). <> *n* brasileiro *m*, -ra *f*.

brazil nut *n* castanha-do-pará *f*.

breach [briːtʃ] <> *n* - **1.** [act of disobedience] quebra *f*; **a ~ of an agreement** o rompimento de um acordo; **a ~ of the law** uma transgressão da lei; **to be in ~ of sthg** estar transgredindo algo; **~ of contract** quebra de contrato - **2.** [opening, gap] brecha *f*; **to step into the ~** *fig* ficar no lugar de alguém temporariamente - **3.** *fig* [in friendship, marriage] rompimento *m*. <> *vt* - **1.** [disobey] romper - **2.** [make hole in] abrir uma brecha em.

breach of the peace *n* atentado *m* à ordem pública.

bread [bred] *n* - **1.** [food] pão *m*; **~ and butter** [food] pão com manteiga, *fig* [main income] sustento *m* - **2.** *inf* [money] ganha-pão *m*.

bread bin *UK*, **bread box** *US n* caixa *f* para pão.

breadboard ['bredbɔːd] *n* tábua *f* de pão.

breadcrumbs ['bredkrʌmz] *npl* farinha *f* de rosca.

breaded ['bredıd] *adj* empanado(da).

breadline ['bredlaın] *n:* **to be on the ~** estar no limite da pobreza.

breadth [bretθ] *n* - **1.** [in measurements] largura *f* - **2.** *fig* [scope] alcance.

breadwinner ['bred‚wınə^r] *n* arrimo *m* (de família).

break [breık] (*pt* broke, *pp* broken) <> *n* - **1.** [interruption] interrupção *f*; **a ~ in transmission** uma queda na transmissão - **2.** [gap] brecha *f* - **3.** [fracture] fratura *f* - **4.** [change] rompimento *m*; **~ with sthg** rompimento *m* com algo - **5.** [pause] pausa *f*; **tea/coffee/lunch ~** pausa para o chá/café/almoço; [rest] descanso *m*; **a weekend ~** um feriado curto; **give me a ~!** me dá um tempo/uma trégua!; **to have a ~ from sthg** dar uma parada em algo; **without a ~** sem parar - **6.** SCOL recreio *m* - **7.** *inf* [luck, chance] chance *f*; **lucky ~** golpe de sorte - **8.** *literary* [of day]: **at ~ of day** ao alvorecer, ao raiar do dia - **9.** COMPUT [key] tecla *f* break. <> *vt* - **1.** [gen] quebrar - **2.** [fracture] fraturar - **3.** [cause to malfunction] danificar - **4.** [burst through] romper; **to ~ sb's hold** esquivar-se de alguém - **5.** [interrupt] interromper - **6.** [destroy, cause to fail] arruinar - **7.** [undermine, cause to fail] furar - **8.** [announce]: **to ~ the news (of sthg to sb)** dar a notícia (de algo a alguém) - **9.** TENNIS: **to ~ sb's serve** quebrar o serviço de alguém. <> *vi* - **1.** [gen] quebrar - **2.** [split] partir-se - **3.** [burst through] romper - **4.** [pause] parar - **5.** [day] raiar - **6.** [weather] mudar - **7.** [escape]: **to ~ loose** *OR* **free** escapar - **8.** [voice - with emotion] perturbar-se; [- at puberty] mudar - **9.** [become known] ser divulgado(da) - **10.** *phr:* **to ~ even** ficar em ponto de equilíbrio.
➤ **break away** *vi* - **1.** [escape] escapar - **2.** [end relationship]: **to ~ away (from sb)** romper (com alguém).
➤ **break down** <> *vt sep* - **1.** [destroy, demolish] derrubar - **2.** [analyse] analisar - **3.** [bring to an end] acabar com. <> *vi* - **1.** [stop working] estragar - **2.** [end unsuccessfully] concluir sem sucesso - **3.** [collapse, disintegrate] terminar - **4.** [MED: collapse] sofrer um colapso; **to ~ down in tears** romper em lágrimas - **5.** [decompose] decompor-se.
➤ **break in** <> *vi* - **1.** [enter by force] arrombar - **2.** [interrupt] interromper; **to ~ in on sb/sthg** interromper alguém/algo. <> *vt sep* - **1.** [horse] domar - **2.** [person] acostumar - **3.** [shoes] amaciar.
➤ **break into** *vt fus* - **1.** [enter by force] arrombar - **2.** [begin suddenly] romper em - **3.** [become involved in] entrar em.
➤ **break off** <> *vt sep* - **1.** [detach] quebrar - **2.** [put an end to] acabar. <> *vi* - **1.** [become detached] quebrar-se - **2.** [stop talking] deter-se - **3.** [stop working] parar-se.
➤ **break out** *vi* - **1.** [begin suddenly] rebentar - **2.** [become covered]: **to ~ out in spots/a rash** aparecer com manchas/uma erupção; **to ~ out in a cold sweat** começar a suar frio - **3.** [escape]: **to ~ out (of)** fugir (de).
➤ **break through** <> *vt fus* [force a way through] abrir caminho por. <> *vi* [force a way through] romper.
➤ **break up** <> *vt sep* - **1.** [separate into smaller pieces - ice] partir; [- soil] repartir; [- car] desmontar - **2.** [bring to an end] acabar. <> *vi* - **1.** [separate into smaller pieces] partir-se - **2.** [come to an end] acabar-se; **to ~ up with sb** acabar com alguém - **3.**

[disperse] dispersar-se **-4.** [for school holiday] terminar.
➜ **break with** *vt fus* romper com.
breakable ['breɪkəbl] *adj* quebradiço(ça).
breakage ['breɪkɪdʒ] *n* quebra *f.*
breakaway ['breɪkəweɪ] *adj* dissidente.
break dancing *n (U)* break *m.*
breakdown ['breɪkdaʊn] *n* **-1.** [failure, ending] quebra *f* **-2.** [analysis] detalhamento *m* **-3.** MED **nervous ~** colapso *m* nervoso.
breaker ['breɪkə^r] *n* [wave] rebentação *f.*
breakeven *n (U)* ponto *m* de equilíbrio.
breakfast ['brekfəst] <> *n* café *m* da manhã. <> *vi:* **to ~ (on sthg)** tomar (algo no) café da manhã.
breakfast cereal *n* cereal *m* matinal.
breakfast television *n* UK programa *m* de tv matutino.
break-in *n* arrombamento *m.*
breaking ['breɪkɪŋ] *n (U):* **~ and entering** JUR invasão *m* de domicílio.
breaking point *n* limite *m.*
breakneck ['breɪknek] *adj:* **at ~ speed** em altíssima velocidade.
breakthrough ['breɪkθru:] *n* avanço *m.*
breakup ['breɪkʌp] *n* **-1.** [of system, group] dissociação *f* **-2.** [of relationship] rompimento *m.*
breakup value *n* COMM valor *m* de liquidação.
bream [bri:m] *(pl inv OR* **-s)** *n* brema *f*; **sea ~** pargo *m.*
breast [brest] *n* **-1.** [gen] peito *m* **-2.** [of woman] seio *m* **-3.** *fig:* **to make a clean ~ of it** desabafar.
breast-feed <> *vt & vi* amamentar.
breast pocket *n* bolso *m* superior.
breaststroke ['breststrəʊk] *n (U)* nado *m* de peito.
breath [breθ] *n* **-1.** *(U)* [air taken into lungs] respiração *f;* **out of ~** sem fôlego; **to get one's ~ back** retomar o fôlego; **to hold one's ~** [stop breathing] prender o fôlego; *fig* [wait anxiously] ficar apreensivo(va); **to save one's ~** poupar seu fôlego; **to say sthg under one's ~** dizer algo ao pé do ouvido; **to take one's ~ away** ser surpreendente; **to waste one's ~** gastar sua saliva; **to go out for a ~ of (fresh) air** sair para tomar ar (fresco) **-2.** [air breathed out] hálito *m*; **bad ~** mau hálito.
breathalyse UK, **-yze** US ['breθəlaɪz] *vt* aplicar o teste do bafômetro em.
Breathalyser® UK, **-yzer**® US ['breθəlaɪzə^r] *n* bafômetro *m.*
breathe [bri:ð] <> *vi* respirar; **to ~ more easily** *fig* respirar aliviado(da). <> *vt* **-1.** [inhale] inalar **-2.** [whisper] murmurar.
➜ **breathe in** <> *vi* [inhale] respirar. <> *vt sep* [inhale] inalar.
➜ **breathe out** *vi* [exhale] exalar.
breather ['bri:ðə^r] *n inf* respirada *f*, descanso *m.*
breathing ['bri:ðɪŋ] *n (U)* respiração *f.*
breathing space *n fig* pausa *f.*
breathless ['breθlɪs] *adj* **-1.** [physically] ofegante **-2.** [with excitement] radiante.
breathtaking ['breθ,teɪkɪŋ] *adj* **-1.** [beautiful] surpreendente **-2.** [extreme] incrível.
breath test *n* teste *m* de bafômetro.
breed [bri:d] *(pt & pp* bred [bred]) <> *n* **-1.** [of

animal] raça *f* **-2.** *fig* [sort, style] tipo *m.* <> *vt* **-1.** [cultivate] criar **-2.** *fig* [provoke] gerar. <> *vi* [produce young] procriar.
breeder ['bri:də^r] *n* [of animals] criador *m.*
breeder reactor *n* reator *m* regenerador.
breeding ['bri:dɪŋ] *n (U)* **-1.** [raising animals, plants] criação *f* **-2.** [manners] boa educação *f*; **a person of good ~** uma pessoa de berço.
breeding-ground *n fig* [of ideas, activity] fonte *f.*
breeze [bri:z] <> *n* [light wind] brisa *f.* <> *vi:* **to ~ in/out** entrar/sair calmamente.
breezeblock ['bri:zblɒk] *n* UK tijolo *m* leve.
breezy ['bri:zɪ] *(compar* **-ier,** *superl* **-iest)** *adj* **-1.** [windy] ventoso(sa) **-2.** [cheerful] alegre.
Breton ['bretn] <> *adj* bretão(tã). <> *n* **-1.** [person] bretão *m*, -tã *f* **-2.** [language] bretão *m.*
brevity ['brevɪtɪ] *n* **-1.** [shortness] brevidade *f* **-2.** [conciseness] concisão *f.*
brew [bru:] <> *vt* [beer] fermentar; [tea] preparar. <> *vi* **-1.** [infuse] preparar-se **-2.** *fig* [develop - crisis, trouble] armar-se; [- storm] formar-se.
brewer ['bru:ə^r] *n* fabricante *mf* de cerveja.
brewery ['brʊərɪ] *(pl* **-ies)** *n* cervejaria *f.*
briar ['braɪə^r] *n* BOT urze *f* branca.
bribe [braɪb] <> *n* suborno *m.* <> *vt* subornar; **to ~ sb to do sthg** subornar alguém para fazer algo.
bribery ['braɪbərɪ] *n (U)* suborno *m.*
bric-a-brac ['brɪkəbræk] *n (U)* bugiganga *f.*
brick [brɪk] *n* [for building] tijolo *m.*
➜ **brick up** *vt sep* fechar com tijolos.
bricklayer ['brɪk,leɪə^r] *n* pedreiro *m.*
brickwork ['brɪkwɜːk] *n (U)* alvenaria *f.*
bridal ['braɪdl] *adj* de noiva.
bride [braɪd] *n* noiva *f.*
bridegroom ['braɪdgrʊm] *n* noivo *m.*
bridesmaid ['braɪdzmeɪd] *n* dama *f* de honra.
bridge [brɪdʒ] <> *n* **-1.** [gen] ponte *f*; **I'll cross that ~ when I come to it** *fig* só vou me preocupar quando chegar a hora **-2.** [on ship] ponte *f* de comando **-3.** [of nose] cavalete *m* **-4.** [card game] bridge *m* **-5.** [for teeth] ponte *f.* <> *vt* [gap] transpor.
bridging loan ['brɪdʒɪŋ-] *n* UK empréstimo *m* bancário *(a curto prazo).*
bridle ['braɪdl] <> *n* [of horse] cabresto *m.* <> *vt* [put a bridle on] colocar cabresto em. <> *vi:* **to ~ (at sthg)** indignar-se (diante de algo).
bridle path *n* trilha *f.*
brief [bri:f] <> *adj* **-1.** [short, concise] breve; **in ~** em suma **-2.** [revealing, skimpy] reduzido(da). <> *n* **-1.** JUR [statement] declaração *f* **-2.** UK [instructions] instrução *f.* <> *vt* informar; **to ~ sb on sthg** [bring up to date] pôr alguém a par de algo; [instruct] treinar alguém sobre/em algo.
➜ **briefs** *npl* [underwear] cuecas *fpl.*
briefcase ['bri:fkeɪs] *n* pasta *f* executiva.
briefing ['bri:fɪŋ] *n* instruções *fpl.*
briefly ['bri:flɪ] *adv* **-1.** [for a short time] brevemente **-2.** [concisely] rapidamente.
Brig. *(abbr of* **brigadier)** brig..
brigade ['brɪgeɪd] *n* brigada *f.*
brigadier [,brɪgə'dɪə^r] *n* brigadeiro *m.*
bright [braɪt] *adj* **-1.** [full of light] claro(ra) **-2.** [colour] vivo(va) **-3.** [lively, cheerful] alegre **-4.** [intelligent]

inteligente **- 5.** [hopeful, promising] radioso(sa).
➤ **brights** *npl US inf AUT* luz f alta.
➤ **bright and early** *adv* de manhã cedo.
brighten [ˈbraɪtn] *vi* **-1.** [become lighter] iluminar-se **- 2.** [become more cheerful] alegrar-se.
➤ **brighten up** ◇ *vt sep* alegrar. ◇ *vi* **-1.** [become more cheerful] alegrar-se **- 2.** [weather] melhorar.
brightly [ˈbraɪtlɪ] *adv* **-1.** [shine] fortemente **- 2.** [cheerfully] alegremente **- 3.** [coloured] em cores vivas.
brightness [ˈbraɪtnɪs] *n (U)* brilho *m*.
brilliance [ˈbrɪljəns] *n* **-1.** [cleverness] inteligência *f* **- 2.** [of light, colour] brilho *m*.
brilliant [ˈbrɪljənt] *adj* **-1.** [clever, successful] brilhante **- 2.** [colour] vivo(va) **- 3.** [light] brilhante **- 4.** *inf* [wonderful, enjoyable] genial.
brilliantly [ˈbrɪljəntlɪ] *adv* **-1.** [cleverly] inteligentemente, de forma brilhante **- 2.** [coloured] em cores vivas **- 3.** [shine] fortemente.
Brillo pad [ˈbrɪləʊ-] *n* esfregão *m (de aço com sabão).*
brim [brɪm] (*pt* & *pp* **-med**, *cont* **-ming**) ◇ *n* **-1.** [edge] borda *f* **- 2.** [of hat] aba *f*. ◇ *vi*: **to ~ with enthusiasm** transbordar de entusiasmo.
➤ **brim over** *vi*: **to ~ over (with sthg)** transbordar (de algo).
brine [braɪn] *n (U)* salmoura *f*.
bring [brɪŋ] (*pt* & *pp* **brought**) *vt* **-1.** [gen] trazer; **to ~ sthg to an end** acabar com algo **- 2.** *JUR*: **to ~ charges against sb** acusar alguém; **to be brought to trial** ser levado(da) a julgamento **- 3.** *phr*: **I couldn't ~ myself to do it** não tive coragem de fazê-lo.
➤ **bring about** *vt sep* produzir.
➤ **bring along** *vt sep* trazer.
➤ **bring around** *vt sep* [make conscious]: **to bring sb around** fazer alguém recuperar os sentidos.
➤ **bring back** *vt sep* **-1.** [hand over] devolver **- 2.** [carry, transport] trazer de volta **- 3.** [recall] relembrar **- 4.** [reinstate] trazer de volta.
➤ **bring down** *vt sep* **-1.** [cause to fall] derrubar **- 2.** [reduce] baixar.
➤ **bring forward** *vt sep* **-1.** [in time] adiantar **- 2.** [in bookkeeping] transportar.
➤ **bring in** *vt sep* **-1.** [introduce] apresentar **- 2.** [earn] render **- 3.** *JUR* [verdict] apresentar.
➤ **bring off** *vt sep* conseguir.
➤ **bring on** *vt sep* [cause] causar; **to ~ sthg on o.s.** causar algo a si próprio(pria).
➤ **bring out** *vt sep* **-1.** [produce and sell] lançar **- 2.** [reveal] ressaltar.
➤ **bring round, bring to** *vt sep* = **bring around**.
➤ **bring up** *vt sep* **-1.** [educate] educar **- 2.** [mention] mencionar **- 3.** [vomit] vomitar.
brink [brɪŋk] *n*: **on the ~ of** à beira de.
brisk [brɪsk] *adj* **-1.** [walk, swim] rápido(da) **- 2.** [business, trading] ativo(va) **- 3.** [manner, tone] enérgico(ca) **- 4.** [wind, weather] forte.
brisket [ˈbrɪskɪt] *n* carne *f* de peito.
briskly [ˈbrɪsklɪ] *adv* **-1.** [walk] rapidamente **- 2.** [speak, act] desembaraçadamente.

bristle [ˈbrɪsl] ◇ *n* **-1.** [hair] pêlo *m* **- 2.** [on brush] cerda *f*. ◇ *vi* **-1.** [stand up] ficar em pé **- 2.** [react angrily]: **to ~ (at sthg)** eriçar-se (diante de algo).
➤ **bristle with** *vt fus* estar apinhado(da) de.
bristly [ˈbrɪslɪ] (*compar* **-ier**, *superl* **-iest**) *adj* [hairy] cabeludo(da).
Brit (*abbr of* **Briton**) *n fam* britânico *m*, -ca *f*.
Britain [ˈbrɪtn] *n* Grã-Bretanha; **in ~** na Grã-Bretanha.
British [ˈbrɪtɪʃ] ◇ *adj* britânico(ca). ◇ *npl*: **the ~** os britânicos.
British Columbia *n* Colúmbia Britânica.
British Council *n*: **the ~** o British Council, o Conselho Britânico.
British Isles *npl*: **the ~** as Ilhas Britânicas.
British Summer Time *n (U)* horário *m* britânico de verão.
British Telecom *n* principal empresa britânica de telecomunicações.
Briton [ˈbrɪtn] *n* britânico *m*, -ca *f*.
Britpop [ˈbrɪtpɒp] *n (U)* tipo de música pop tocada por bandas britânicas, muito popular em meados dos anos 90.
Brittany [ˈbrɪtənɪ] *n* Bretanha; **in ~** na Bretanha.
brittle [ˈbrɪtl] *adj* [easily broken] quebradiço(ça).
Bro = **Br.**
broach [brəʊtʃ] *vt* [subject] abordar.
broad [brɔːd] ◇ *adj* **-1.** [physically wide] largo(ga) **- 2.** [wide-ranging, extensive] amplo(pla) **- 3.** [general, unspecific] geral **- 4.** [hint] explícito(ta) **- 5.** [accent] forte. ◇ *n US inf* [woman] sujeita *f*.
➤ **in broad daylight** *adv* em plena luz do dia.
B road *n UK* estrada *f* secundária.
broad bean *n* fava *f*.
broadcast [ˈbrɔːdkɑːst] (*pt* & *pp* **broadcast**) ◇ *n* transmissão *f*. ◇ *vt* transmitir.
broadcaster [ˈbrɔːdkɑːstəʳ] *n* locutor *m*, -ra *f*.
broadcasting [ˈbrɔːdkɑːstɪŋ] *n (U)* transmissão *f*.
broaden [ˈbrɔːdn] ◇ *vt* **-1.** [make physically wider] alargar **- 2.** [make more general, wide-ranging] ampliar. ◇ *vi* [become physically wider] alargar-se.
➤ **broaden out** *vi* ampliar-se.
broadly [ˈbrɔːdlɪ] *adv* **-1.** [generally] em geral; **~ speaking** em termos gerais **- 2.** [smile] abertamente.
broadly-based [-ˈbeɪst] *adj* de bases amplas.
broadminded [ˌbrɔːdˈmaɪndɪd] *adj* tolerante.
broadsheet [ˈbrɔːdʃiːt] *n* jornal *m (de tamanho grande).*

BROADSHEET/BROADSIDE

Broadsheet, na Grã-Bretanha, e *broadside*, nos Estados Unidos, são os termos empregados para designar os jornais de maior reputação e prestígio. Trata-se dos jornais impressos em formato grande, que apresentam as notícias com seriedade e oferecem seções importantes sobre cultura, esportes e finanças. De modo geral, esses jornais gozam de maior respeito do que os tablóides, que tendem a usar uma linguagem mais simples e direta, e são publicados em formato pequeno.

brocade [brəˈkeɪd] *n (U)* brocado *m*.
broccoli [ˈbrɒkəlɪ] *n* brócolis *mpl*.

brochure ['brəʊʃəʳ] n folheto m.

brogue n -1. [accent] sotaque m -2. [shoe] chanca f.

broil [brɔɪl] vt US grelhar.

broiler ['brɔɪləʳ] n -1. [chicken for broiling] galeto m -2. Am [pan] grelha f.

broke [brəʊk] <> pt ▷ break. <> adj inf [penniless] falido(da); **to go** ~ ir à falência; **to go for** ~ arriscar tudo.

broken ['brəʊkn] <> pp ▷ break. <> adj -1. [damaged, in pieces] quebrado(da) -2. [fractured] fraturado(da) -3. [not working] estragado(da) -4. [interrupted] interrompido(da) -5. [unfulfilled] rompido(da) -6. [marriage, home] desfeito(ta) -7. [hesitant, inaccurate] incorreto(ta).

broken-down adj -1. [not working] avariado(da) -2. [dilapidated] arruinado(da).

broker ['brəʊkəʳ] n corretor m, -ra f.

brokerage ['brəʊkərɪdʒ] n (U) -1. [business] corretora f -2. [fee] corretagem f.

brolly ['brɒlɪ] (pl -ies) n UK inf guarda-chuva m.

bromine n bromo m.

bronchitis [brɒŋ'kaɪtɪs] n (U) bronquite f.

bronze [brɒnz] <> n -1. (U) [metal] bronze m -2. [sculpture] escultura f em bronze -3. = **bronze medal**. <> comp [made of bronze] em bronze. <> adj [bronze-coloured] bronzeado(da).

bronzed adj bronzeado(da).

bronze medal n medalha f de bronze.

brooch [brəʊtʃ] n broche m.

brood [bru:d] <> n -1. [of animals] ninhada f -2. inf [of children] penca f. <> vi: **to** ~ **(over** OR **about** sthg)** matutar (sobre algo).

broody ['bru:dɪ] (compar-ier, superl-iest) adj -1. [sad] pensativo(va) -2. [bird] choco(ca).

brook [brʊk] <> n riacho m. <> vt fml tolerar.

broom [bru:m] n -1. [brush] vassoura f -2. [shrub] giesta f.

broomstick ['bru:mstɪk] n cabo m de vassoura.

Bros, bros (abbr of **brothers**) irmãos.

broth [brɒθ] n (U) caldo m.

brothel ['brɒθl] n bordel m.

brother ['brʌðəʳ] <> n -1. [gen & RELIG] irmão m -2. fig [associate, comrade] irmão m. <> excl US inf puxa vida!

brotherhood ['brʌðəhʊd] n -1. (U) [companionship] fraternidade f -2. [organization] irmandade f.

brother-in-law (pl **brothers-in-law**) n cunhado m.

brotherly ['brʌðəlɪ] adj fraternal.

brought [brɔːt] pt & pp ▷ bring.

brow [braʊ] n -1. [forehead] testa f -2. [eyebrow] sobrancelha f; **to knit one's** ~s franzir a testa -3. [of hill] topo m.

browbeat ['braʊbi:t] (pt browbeat, pp -en) vt intimidar.

browbeaten ['braʊbi:tn] adj intimidado(da).

brown [braʊn] <> adj -1. [colour - hair, eyes] castanho(nha); [- object] marrom; ~ **bread** pão m integral -2. [tanned] bronzeado(da). <> n [colour] marrom m; **in** ~ em marrom. <> vt [food] tostar.

Brownie (Guide) n escoteira junior de sete a dez anos.

brownie point n fig: **to earn** ~s fazer média.

brown paper n (U) papel m pardo.

brown rice n (U) arroz m integral.

brown sugar n (U) açúcar m mascavo.

browse [braʊz] <> vt COMPUT: **to** ~ **the Web** navegar na Web. <> vi -1. [in shop] dar uma olhada -2. [read]: **to** ~ **through sthg** dar uma olhada em algo -3. [graze] pastar.

browser ['braʊzəʳ] n COMPUT navegador m.

bruise [bru:z] <> n equimose f. <> vt -1. [leave a bruise on] machucar -2. fig [hurt, offend] ferir. <> vi machucar-se.

bruised [bru:zd] adj -1. [having bruise] machucado(da) -2. fig [hurt, offended] ferido(da).

Brummie, Brummy ['brʌmɪ] UK inf <> adj de Birmingham. <> n habitante mf de Birmimgham.

brunch [brʌntʃ] n brunch m, combinação de café da manhã e almoço servido ao meio-dia.

Brunei ['bru:naɪ] n Brunei; **in** ~ em Brunei.

brunette [bru:'net] n morena f.

brunt [brʌnt] n: **to bear** OR **take the** ~ **of sthg** suportar OR sofrer a força de algo.

brush [brʌʃ] <> n -1. [for hair] escova f -2. [of artist, for shaving, paint] pincel m -3. [encounter] atrito m. <> vt -1. [clean with brush] escovar -2. [move with hand] sacudir -3. [touch lightly] roçar.
➡ **brush aside** vt sep desprezar.
➡ **brush off** vt sep [dismiss] desprezar.
➡ **brush up** <> vt sep [revise] recapitular. <> vi: **to** ~ **up on sthg** treinar OR praticar algo.

brushed [brʌʃt] adj [fabric]: ~ **cotton** fio m de algodão penteado.

brush-off n inf: **to give sb the** ~ dar um chega pra lá em alguém, botar alguém de escanteio.

brush-up n (U) inf: **to have a wash and** ~ dar uma geral.

brushwood ['brʌʃwʊd] n (U) graveto m.

brushwork ['brʌʃwɜ:k] n (U) pincelada f.

brusque [bru:sk] adj brusco(ca).

Brussels ['brʌslz] n Bruxelas; **in** ~ em Bruxelas.

brussels sprout n couve-de-bruxelas f.

brutal ['bru:tl] adj brutal.

brutality [bru:'tælətɪ] (pl -ies) n -1. (U) [cruelty] brutalidade f -2. [cruel act] brutalidade f.

brutalize, -ise ['bru:təlaɪz] vt -1. [make brutal] brutalizar -2. [treat brutally] maltratar.

brute [bru:t] <> adj bruto(ta). <> n -1. [large animal] besta f -2. [bully] animal mf.

BS (abbr of **Bachelor of Science**) n (titular de) graduação em ciências nos Estados Unidos.

BSA (abbr of **Boy Scouts of America**) n associação de escoteiros norte-americanos, ≃ UEB f.

BSc (abbr of **Bachelor of Science**) n (titular de) graduação em ciências.

BSE (abbr of **bovine spongiform encephalopathy**) n EEB f.

BSI (abbr of **British Standards Institution**) n instituto britânico de normatização, ≃ ABNT f.

B-side n lado-B m.

BST (abbr of **British Summer Time**) horário de verão britânico.

BT (abbr of **British Telecom**) n empresa de telefonia britânica.

Btu (*abbr of* British thermal unit) *n unidade de calor britânica*, btu *m*.

bubble ['bʌbll] <> *n* bolha *f*. <> *vi* borbulhar.

bubble bath *n* **-1.** [liquid] espuma *f* de banho **-2.** [bath] banho *m* de espuma.

bubble gum *n* (*U*) chiclete *m* de bola.

bubblejet printer ['bʌbldʒet-] *n* impressora *f* a jato de tinta.

bubbly ['bʌbll] (*compar* -ier, *superl* -iest) <> *adj* [person] efervescente. <> *n inf* champanhe *m*.

Bucharest [ˌbuːkəˈrest] *n* Bucareste; **in** ~ em Bucareste.

buck [bʌk] (*pl sense 1 inv OR* -s) <> *n* **-1.** [male animal] macho *m* **-2.** *US inf* [dollar] pila *mf*; **to make a fast** ~ fazer grana fácil *OR* rápido **-3.** *inf* [responsibility]: **the** ~ **stops here** a responsabilidade pára aqui; **to pass the** ~ passar *OR* transferir a responsabilidade. <> *vt* **-1.** [subj: horse] derrubar **-2.** *inf* [oppose] ir contra. <> *vi* [horse] corcovear.

➡ **buck up** *inf* <> *vt sep* **-1.** [make more positive] avivar **-2.** [cheer up] animar. <> *vi* **-1.** [hurry up] apressar-se **-2.** [cheer up, become more positive] animar-se.

bucket ['bʌkɪt] *n* **-1.** [container] balde *m* **-2.** [bucketful] balde *m*.

➡ **buckets** *npl inf fig* [large quantity]: ~s **of sthg** baldes de algo.

Buckingham Palace ['bʌkɪŋəm-] *n* Palácio *m* de Buckingham.

buckle ['bʌkl] <> *n* fivela *f*. <> *vt* **-1.** [fasten] afivelar **-2.** [bend] arquear. <> *vi* [bend] arquear-se, vergar-se.

➡ **buckle down** *vi* [work harder]: **to** ~ **down (to sthg)** empenhar-se (em algo).

buckshot ['bʌkʃɒt] *n* (*U*) chumbo *m* (de espingarda).

buckskin ['bʌkskɪn] *n* (*U*) pele *f* de cervo.

buckteeth [bʌk'tiːθ] *npl* dentes *mpl* salientes.

buckthorn *n* escambroeiro *m*, espinheiro *m*.

buckwheat ['bʌkwiːt] *n* (*U*) fagopiro *m*, trigomouro *m*.

bud [bʌd] (*pt & pp* -ded, *cont* -ding) <> *n* botão *m*; **to nip sthg in the** ~ *fig* cortar algo pela raiz. <> *vi* florescer.

Budapest [ˌbjuːdə'pest] *n* Budapeste; **in** ~ em Budapeste.

Buddha ['budə] *n* Buda *m*.

Buddhism ['budɪzm] *n* (*U*) budismo *m*.

Buddhist ['budɪst] <> *adj* budista. <> *n* budista *mf*.

budding ['bʌdɪŋ] *adj* [aspiring] principiante.

buddy ['bʌdɪ] (*pl* -ies) *n US inf* [friend] camarada *mf*.

budge [bʌdʒ] <> *vt* **-1.** [move] mexer **-2.** [change mind of] dissuadir. <> *vi* **-1.** [move - object] mover-se; [- person] mudar-se **-2.** [change mind] mudar de opinião.

budgerigar ['bʌdʒərɪgaːʳ] *n* periquito *m* (australiano).

budget ['bʌdʒɪt] <> *adj* [cheap] econômico(ca). <> *n* orçamento *m*; **the Budget** *UK POL* o Orçamento. <> *vt* estimar. <> *vi* calcular.

➡ **budget for** *vt fus* planejar os gastos com.

budget account *n* **-1.** [with shop] conta *f* (crediário) **-2.** [at bank] conta *f* orçamentária.

budgetary ['bʌdʒɪtrɪ] *adj* orçamentário(ria).

budgie ['bʌdʒɪ] *n inf* periquito *m* (australiano).

Buenos Aires [ˌbwenəs'aɪrɪz] *n* Buenos Aires; **in** ~ em Buenos Aires.

buff [bʌf] <> *adj* [brown] pardo(da). <> *n inf* [expert] expert *mf*.

buffalo ['bʌfələʊ] (*pl inv OR* -es *OR* -s) *n* búfalo *m*.

buffer ['bʌfəʳ] *n* **-1.** [for trains] pára-choque *m* **-2.** [protection] proteção *f* **-3.** *COMPUT* buffer *m*.

buffer state *n* estado-tampão *m*.

buffet¹ [*UK* 'bufeɪ, *US* bə'feɪ] *n* **-1.** [meal] bufê *m* **-2.** [cafeteria] cantina *f*.

buffet² ['bʌfɪt] *vt* [physically] bater.

buffet car ['bufeɪ-] *n* vagão-restaurante *m*.

buffoon [bə'fuːn] *n* palhaço *m*.

bug [bʌg] (*pt & pp* -ged, *cont* -ging) <> *n* **-1.** *US* [small insect] inseto *m* **-2.** *inf* [germ] vírus *m* **-3.** *inf* [listening device] grampo *m* **-4.** *COMPUT* [fault in program] bug *m* **-5.** [enthusiasm]: **the travel** ~ a febre de viajar. <> *vt inf* **-1.** [spy on] grampear **-2.** *Am* [annoy] chatear.

bugbear ['bʌgbeəʳ] *n* bicho-papão *m*.

bugger ['bʌgəʳ] *UK v inf* <> *n* **-1.** [unpleasant person, task] porre *mf* **-2.** [particular type of person] infeliz *mf*. <> *excl* merda! <> *vt*: ~ **it!** dane-se!

➡ **bugger off** *vi*: ~ **off!** vá à merda!

buggy ['bʌgɪ] (*pl* -ies) *n* [pushchair, stroller] carrinho *m* de bebê.

bugle ['bjuːgl] *n* trombeta *f*.

build [bɪld] (*pt & pp* built) <> *vt* construir. <> *n* corpo *m*, constituição *f* física.

➡ **build into** *vt sep* embutir em.

➡ **build on** <> *vt fus* [further] ampliar. <> *vt sep* [base on] alicerçar.

➡ **build up** <> *vt sep* [strengthen] fortalecer. <> *vi* [increase] intensificar.

➡ **build upon** *vt fus & vt sep* = build on.

builder ['bɪldəʳ] *n* construtor.

building ['bɪldɪŋ] *n* **-1.** [structure] edifício *m*, prédio *m* **-2.** (*U*) [profession] construção *f*.

building and loan association *n US* associação *f* de financiamento imobiliário, ≃ sistema *m* financeiro de habitação.

building block *n* **-1.** [toy] bloco *m* para montar **-2.** *fig* [element] alicerce *f*.

building contractor *n* construtor *m*, -ra *f*.

building site *n* canteiro *m* de obras.

building society *n UK* sociedade *f* de financiamento imobiliário.

BUILDING SOCIETY

As *building societies* funcionam como bancos, embora não possuam um sistema de compensação. Elas se dedicam a conceder financiamentos imobiliários e, no passado, desempenharam papel muito importante na Grã-Bretanha. Hoje, muitas delas converteram-se em bancos.

---

build-up *n* [increase] intensificação *f*.

built [bɪlt] <> *pt & pp* ⊳ **build**. <> *adj* [person]: **heavily** ~ de forte constituição; ~ **for sthg** de constituição apropriada para algo.

built-in adj -1. CONSTR embutido(da) -2. [inherent] embutido(da).

built-up adj: ~ **area** área f urbanizada.

bulb [bʌlb] n -1. [for lamp] lâmpada f -2. [of plant] bulbo m.

bulbous ['bʌlbəs] adj bulboso(sa).

Bulgaria [bʌl'geərɪə] n Bulgária; **in** ~ na Bulgária.

Bulgarian [bʌl'geərɪən] <> adj búlgaro(ra). <> n -1. [person] búlgaro m, -ra f -2. [language] búlgaro m.

bulge [bʌldʒ] <> n -1. [lump] protuberância f -2. [sudden increase] aumento m. <> vi: **to** ~ **(with sthg)** estar estourando(de algo).

bulging ['bʌldʒɪŋ] adj -1. abarrotado(da) -2. musculoso(sa).

bulimia (nervosa) [bjʊ'lɪmɪə-] n (U) bulimia f nervosa.

bulk [bʌlk] <> n -1. [mass] volume m -2. [of person] massa f -3. COMM: **in** ~ a granel -4. [majority, most of]: **the** ~ **of** a maior parte de. <> adj a granel.

bulk buying [-'baɪɪŋ] n (U) compra f a granel.

bulkhead ['bʌlkhed] n biombo m.

bulky ['bʌlkɪ] (compar -ier, superl -iest) adj volumoso(osa).

bull [bʊl] n -1. [male cow] touro m -2. [male animal] macho m -3. ST EX especulador m, -ra f -4. (U) v inf US [nonsense] tolice f.

bulldog ['bʊldɒg] n buldogue m.

bulldog clip n prendedor m de papel, clipe m buldogue.

bulldoze ['bʊldəʊz] vt -1. [with bulldozer] aplainar -2. fig [force]: **to** ~ **one's way** forçar sua passagem; **to** ~ **sb into sthg/into doing sthg** obrigar alguém a algo/a fazer algo.

bulldozer ['bʊldəʊzə'] n escavadeira f.

bullet ['bʊlɪt] n -1. [for gun] bala f -2. [in text] marcador m.

bulletin ['bʊlətɪn] n -1. [brief report] boletim m -2. [regular publication] boletim m.

bulletin board n -1. US quadro m de avisos -2. COMPUT sistema m BBS.

bullet-proof adj à prova de bala.

bullfight ['bʊlfaɪt] n tourada f.

bullfighter ['bʊl,faɪtə'] n toureiro m.

bullfighting ['bʊl,faɪtɪŋ] n touradas fpl.

bullion ['bʊljən] n (U) barras fpl de ouro ou prata.

bullish ['bʊlɪʃ] adj -1. ST EX: ~ **market** mercado em alta -2. [optimistic] otimista.

bull market n mercado m em alta.

bullock ['bʊlək] n boi m.

bullring ['bʊlrɪŋ] n arena f de touros.

bullrush ['bʊlrʌʃ] n = bulrush.

bull's-eye n -1. [target] mosca f -2. [shot] mosca f.

bullshit ['bʊlʃɪt] (pt & pp -ted, cont -ting) vulg <> n papo m furado. <> vi falar abobrinhas.

bull terrier n bull terrier mf.

bully ['bʊlɪ] (pl -ies, pt & pp -ied) <> n brigão m, -gona f. <> vt amedrontar; **to** ~ **sb into doing sthg** amedrontar alguém para que faça algo.

bullying ['bʊlɪŋ] n (U) maus-tratos mpl.

bulrush ['bʊlrʌʃ] n papiro m.

bum [bʌm] (pt & pp -med, cont -ming) n -1. esp UK v inf [bottom] traseiro m -2. US inf pej [tramp] vagabundo m -3. US inf pej [idler] desocupado m, -da f.

bum around esp US vi inf -1. [waste time] vadiar -2. [travel aimlessly] perambular.

bum bag n inf pochete f.

bumblebee ['bʌmblbi:] n abelhão m.

bumbling ['bʌmblɪŋ] adj inf inútil; ~ **incompetence** incompetência extraordinária.

bumf [bʌmf] n UK inf papelada f.

bump [bʌmp] <> n -1. [road] elevação f -2. [head] galo m -3. [leg] inchaço m -4. [knock, blow] batida f -5. [noise] pancada f. <> vt [knock, damage] bater. <> vi -1. [move unevenly] solavancar -2. [knock, hit]: **to** ~ **into sthg** topar em algo.

bump into vt fus [meet by chance]: **to** ~ **into sb** topar com alguém.

bump off vt sep inf apagar.

bump up vt sep inf aumentar.

bumper ['bʌmpə'] <> adj super-. <> n -1. [on car] pára-choque m -2. US RAIL pára-choque m.

bumper-to-bumper adj: ~ **traffic** trânsito congestionado e lento.

bumph [bʌmf] n = bumf.

bumptious ['bʌmpʃəs] adj pej presunçoso(sa).

bumpy ['bʌmpɪ] (compar -ier, superl -iest) adj -1. [surface] esburacado(da) -2. [ride, journey] turbulento(ta).

bun [bʌn] n -1. [cake] bolo m doce (pequeno e com passas) -2. [bread roll] pãozinho m -3. [hairstyle] coque m.

bunch [bʌntʃ] <> n [group - of people] grupo m; [- of flowers] ramalhete m; [- of fruit] cacho m; [- of keys] molho m. <> vt agrupar. <> vi unir.

bunches npl [hairstyle] maria-chiquinha f.

bundle ['bʌndl] <> n -1. [clothes] trouxa -2. [paper] maço -3. [wood] feixe. <> vt socar.

bundle off vt sep mandar, enviar.

bundle up vt sep -1. [put into bundles] entrouxar -2. [dress warmly] agasalhar(-se).

bundled software ['bʌndld-] n COMPUT software m incluído.

bung [bʌŋ] <> n tampo m. <> vt UK inf -1. [give] passar -2. [put] deixar -3. [toss] jogar.

bungalow ['bʌŋgələʊ] n [single-storey house] casa f térrea.

bunged up [bʌŋd-] adj -1. [nose] congestionado -(da) -2. [sink, drains] entupido(da).

bungee jump n bungee jump m.

bungee-jumping ['bʌndʒɪ-] n bungee jumping m.

bungle ['bʌŋgl] vt fracassar.

bunion ['bʌnjən] n joanete m.

bunk [bʌŋk] n -1. [bed] beliche m -2. inf [nonsense] besteira f -3. phr: **to do a** ~ inf dar no pé.

bunk bed n beliche m.

bunker ['bʌŋkə'] n -1. MIL [shelter] abrigo m -2. [for coal] carvoeira f -3. [in golf] bunker m.

bunkhouse n alojamento m.

bunny ['bʌnɪ] (pl -ies) n: ~ **(rabbit)** coelhinho m.

bunny hill n US SKIING morro baixo e sem obstáculos utilizado como pista para a prática de esqui na neve.

Bunsen burner ['bʌnsn-] n bico m de Bunsen.

bunting ['bʌntɪŋ] n [flags] bandeirolas fpl.

buoy [UK bɔɪ, US 'bu:ɪ] n [float] bóia f.

buoy up *vt sep* [encourage] animar.

buoyancy ['bɔɪənsɪ] *n (U)* **-1.** [ability to float] capacidade *f* de flutuar **-2.** [optimism] otimismo *m*.

buoyant ['bɔɪənt] *adj* **-1.** [able to float] capaz de flutuar, flutuante **-2.** [optimistic] otimista.

BUPA (*abbr of* British United Provident Association) *n plano de saúde privado existente na Grã-Bretanha.*

burden ['bɜːdn] ◇ *n* **-1.** [physical load] carga *f* **-2.** *fig* [heavy responsibility] fardo *m*; **to be a ~ on sb** ser um peso para alguém; **to relieve the ~ on sb** aliviar a carga sobre alguém. ◇ *vt* : **to ~ sb with sthg** sobrecarregar alguém com algo.

bureau ['bjʊərəʊ] (*pl* -x) *n* **-1.** *US* [government department] departamento *m* **-2.** [office, branch] agência *f*, escritório *m* **-3.** *UK* [desk] escrivaninha *f* **-4.** *US* [chest of drawers] cômoda *f*.

bureaucracy [bjʊəˈrɒkrəsɪ] (*pl* -ies) *n* **-1.** [system] burocracia *f* **-2.** *(U) pej* [rules] burocracia *f*.

bureaucrat ['bjʊərəkræt] *n pej* burocrata *mf*.

bureaucratic [ˌbjʊərəˈkrætɪk] *adj pej* burocrático(ca).

bureau de change [ˌbjʊərəʊdəˈʃɒndʒ] (*pl* bureaux de change [ˌbjʊərəʊdəˈʃɒndʒ]) *n* casa *f* de câmbio.

bureaux ['bjʊərəʊz] *pl* ▷ **bureau**.

burger ['bɜːgəˈ] *n* [hamburger] hambúrguer *m*.

burglar ['bɜːgləˈ] *n* ladrão *m*, -dra *f*.

burglar alarm *n* alarme *m* anti-roubo.

burglarize *vt US* = burgle.

burglary ['bɜːglərɪ] (*pl* -ies) *n* **-1.** [event] roubo *m* (*de casa*), arrombamento *m* (*de casa*) **-2.** [activity] roubo *m* (*de casa*), arrombamento *m* (*de casa*).

burgle ['bɜːgl], **burglarize** ['bɜːgləraɪz] *US vt* roubar (*casa*), arrombar (*casa*).

Burgundy *n* Borgonha.

burial ['berɪəl] *n* enterro *m*.

burial ground *n* cemitério *m*.

burk [bɜːk] *n UK inf* idiota *mf*.

Burkina Faso [bɜːˌkiːnəˈfæsəʊ] *n* Burquina Faso; **in ~** em Burquina Faso.

burly ['bɜːlɪ] (*compar* -ier, *superl* -iest) *adj* robusto(ta).

Burma ['bɜːmə] *n* Birmânia.

Burmese [ˌbɜːˈmiːz] ◇ *adj* birmanês(esa). ◇ *n* **-1.** [person] birmanês *m*, -esa *f* **-2.** [language] birmanês *m*.

burn [bɜːn] (*pt & pp* burnt *OR* -ed) ◇ *vt* **-1.** [gen] queimar; **to ~ o.s.** queimar-se **-2.** [destroy by fire] incendiar ◇ *vi* **-1.** [gen] queimar **-2.** [be on fire] incendiar-se **-3.** *fig* [feel strong emotion]: **to ~ with sthg** arder de algo. ◇ *n* **-1.** [wound, injury] queimadura *f* **-2.** [mark] queimadura *f*.
◆ **burn down** ◇ *vt sep* [destroy by fire] incendiar. ◇ *vi* **-1.** [be destroyed by fire] incendiar-se **-2.** [burn less brightly] extinguir-se.
◆ **burn out** ◇ *vt sep* [exhaust]: **to ~ o.s. out** esgotar-se. ◇ *vi* [die down] extinguir-se.
◆ **burn up** ◇ *vt sep* [use up] queimar. ◇ *vi* [be destroyed by fire, heat] carbonizar.

burner ['bɜːnəˈ] *n* [on cooker] queimador *m*.

burning ['bɜːnɪŋ] *adj* **-1.** [on fire] em chamas **-2.** [very hot] escaldante; **to be ~ hot** estar ardendo

OR derretendo de calor **-3.** [very red] em brasa **-4.** [intense] ardente.

burnish ['bɜːnɪʃ] *vt* lustrar.

burnout *n* **-1.** *TECH* combustão *f* **-2.** *fig* [of person] exaustão *f*.

Burns Night *n festa celebrada na Escócia em 25 de janeiro para comemorar o aniversário do poeta Robert Burns.*

burnt [bɜːnt] *pt & pp* ▷ **burn**.

burnt-out *adj* **-1.** [by fire] carbonizado(da) **-2.** *fig* [exhausted] esgotado(da).

burp [bɜːp] *inf* ◇ *n* arroto *m*. ◇ *vi* arrotar.

burrow ['bʌrəʊ] ◇ *n* toca *f*. ◇ *vi* **-1.** [dig] entocar-se **-2.** *fig* [in order to search] remexer.

bursar ['bɜːsəˈ] *n* tesoureiro *m*, -ra *f*.

bursary ['bɜːsərɪ] (*pl* -ies) *n UK* [scholarship, grant] bolsa *f* (*de estudos*).

burst [bɜːst] (*pt & pp* burst) ◇ *vi* **-1.** [break open] estourar **-2.** [explode] explodir **-3.** [door, lid]: **to ~ open** abrir-se de repente **-4.** [go suddenly] irromper. ◇ *vt* [break open] estourar. ◇ *n* [bout] estouro *m*.
◆ **burst into** *vt fus* **-1.** [gen] irromper em **-2.** [flower, leaf, blossom] desabrochar.
◆ **burst out** *vt fus* **-1.** [say suddenly] exclamar **-2.** [begin suddenly]: **to ~ out laughing/crying** começar a gargalhar/chorar.

bursting ['bɜːstɪŋ] *adj* **-1.** [full] repleto(ta) **-2.** [with emotion]: **~ with sthg** repleto(ta) de algo **-3.** [eager]: **to be ~ to do sthg** estar morrendo de vontade de fazer algo.

Burundi [bʊˈrʊndɪ] *n* Burundi; **in ~** em Burundi.

bury ['berɪ] (*pt & pp* -ied) *vt* **-1.** [gen] enterrar **-2.** [hide - face, hands] esconder **-3.** *fig* [immerse]: **to ~ o.s. in sthg** enterrar-se em algo.

bus [bʌs] *n* ônibus *m*; **by ~** de ônibus.

bus conductor *n* cobrador *m*, -ra *f* de ônibus.

bus driver *n* motorista *mf* de ônibus.

bush [bʊʃ] *n* **-1.** [plant] arbusto *m* **-2.** [open country]: **the ~** a selva **-3.** *phr*: **to beat about the ~** fazer rodeios.

bushel ['bʊʃl] *n* alqueire *m*.

bushy ['bʊʃɪ] (*compar* -ier, *superl* -iest) *adj* espesso(sa).

business ['bɪznɪs] ◇ *n* **-1.** *(U)* [commerce] negócios *mpl*; **on ~** a negócios; **to mean ~** *inf* falar sério; **to go out of ~** ir a falência **-2.** [company] negócio *m* **-3.** *(U)* [concern, duty] assunto *m*; **to have no ~ doing** *OR* **to do sthg** não ter o direito de fazer algo; **mind your own ~!** *inf* meta-se com sua vida! **-4.** [affair, matter] negócio *m*, assunto *m*. ◇ *comp* comercial *mf*.

business address *n* endereço *m* comercial.

business card *n* cartão *m* de visita.

business class *n (U)* classe *f* executiva.

businesslike ['bɪznɪslaɪk] *adj* profissional.

businessman ['bɪznɪsmæn] (*pl* -men [-men]) *n* [occupation] empresário *m*, homem *m* de negócios.

business school *n* escola *f* de comércio.

business trip *n* viagem *f* de negócios.

businesswoman ['bɪznɪsˌwʊmən] (*pl* -women [-ˌwɪmɪn]) *n* [occupation] empresária *f*, mulher *f* de negócios.

busker ['bʌskəˈ] *n UK* artista *mf* de rua.

bus lane n faixa f exclusiva para ônibus.

bus shelter n abrigo m de ônibus.

bus station n estação f rodoviária.

bus stop n parada f OR ponto m de ônibus.

bust [bʌst] (pt & pp bust OR -ed) <> adj inf -1. [broken] quebrado(da) -2. [bankrupt]: **to go ~** quebrar. <> n -1. [gen] busto m -2. police sl [raid] batida f. <> vt inf -1. [break] quebrar -2. [arrest] prender -3. police sl [raid] revistar. <> vi inf quebrar.

bustle ['bʌsl] <> n [activity] movimento m. <> vi apressar-se.

bustling ['bʌslɪŋ] adj movimentado(da).

bust-up n inf -1. [quarrel, fight] quebra-pau m -2. [breakup] rompimento m.

busy ['bɪzɪ] (compar -ier, superl -iest) <> adj -1. [gen & TELEC] ocupado(da); **to be ~ doing sthg** estar ocupado(da) fazendo algo -2. [hectic - time] agitado(da); [- place] movimentado(da) <> vt: **to ~ o.s. (doing sthg)** ocupar-se fazendo algo.

busybody ['bɪzɪˌbɒdɪ] (pl -ies) n pej intrometido m, -da f.

busy lizzie n maria-sem-vergonha f.

busy signal n US TELEC sinal m de ocupado.

but [bʌt] <> conj mas <> prep senão, a não ser; **you've been nothing ~ trouble** você só tem me dado trabalho; **the last ~ one** o penúltimo (a penúltima).
◆ **but for** prep se não fosse.

butane ['bjuːteɪn] n (U) butano m.

butch [bʊtʃ] adj UK inf [woman] sapatão.

butcher ['bʊtʃəʳ] <> n -1. [shopkeeper] açougueiro m, -ra f; **~'s (shop)** açougue m -2. fig [indiscriminate killer] carniceiro m, -ra f. <> vt -1. [kill for meat] abater -2. fig [kill indiscriminately] exterminar, fazer uma carnificina com.

butchery ['bʊtʃərɪ] n (U) fig [indiscriminate killing] carnificina f.

butler ['bʌtləʳ] n mordomo m.

butt [bʌt] <> n -1. [of cigarette, cigar] bagana f -2. [of rifle] coronha f -3. [for water] tina m -4. [target] alvo m -5. esp US inf [bottom] traseiro m. <> vt [hit with head] dar cabeçada em.
◆ **butt in** vi [interrupt] atrapalhar, interromper; **to ~ in on sb/sthg** atrapalhar OR interromper alguém/algo.

butter ['bʌtəʳ] <> n (U) manteiga f; **~ wouldn't melt in her mouth** inf parece uma mosca morta. <> vt passar manteiga.
◆ **butter up** vt sep inf bajular.

butter bean n feijão-manteiga m, feijão-de-lima m.

buttercup ['bʌtəkʌp] n botão-de-ouro m.

butter dish n manteigueira f.

buttered ['bʌtəd] adj com manteiga.

butterfingers ['bʌtəˌfɪŋgəz] (pl inv) n inf estabanado m, -da f.

butterfly ['bʌtəflaɪ] (pl -ies) n -1. [insect] borboleta f; **to have butterflies in one's stomach** inf estar com frio na barriga -2. (U) [swimming style] nado m borboleta.

buttermilk ['bʌtəmɪlk] n (U) soro m (do leite).

butterscotch ['bʌtəskɒtʃ] n (U) doce m de manteiga.

buttocks ['bʌtəks] npl nádegas fpl.

button ['bʌtn] <> n -1. [on clothes] botão m -2. [on machine] botão m -3. US [badge] button m. <> vt = button up.
◆ **button up** vt sep [fasten] abotoar.

button-down <> adj abotoado(da). <> n.

buttonhole ['bʌtnhəʊl] <> n -1. [hole] casa f (de botão) -2. UK [flower] flor f (de lapela). <> vt inf pegar para conversar.

button mushroom n cogumelo m de Paris.

buttress ['bʌtrɪs] <> n contraforte m. <> vt [wall] reforçar.

buxom ['bʌksəm] adj de corpo e seios grandes.

buy [baɪ] (pt & pp bought) <> vt -1. lit & fig comprar; **to ~ sthg from sb** comprar algo de alguém <> n compra f, aquisição f.
◆ **buy in** vt sep UK provisionar.
◆ **buy into** vt fus investir em.
◆ **buy off** vt sep subornar.
◆ **buy out** vt sep -1. [in business] comprar a parte de -2. [from army] pagar para sair; **he bought himself out** ele comprou sua saída do exército.
◆ **buy up** vt sep comprar a totalidade de.

buyer ['baɪəʳ] n -1. [purchaser] comprador m, -ra f -2. [profession] gerente mf de compras.

buyout ['baɪaʊt] n compra f majoritária de ações.

buzz [bʌz] <> n [noise - of insect, machinery] zumbido m; [- of conversation] murmúrio m; **to give sb a ~** inf [on phone] dar uma ligada para alguém. <> vi -1. zunir; lit & fig **to ~ (with sthg)** zunir (de algo) <> vt [on intercom] ligar, chamar.
◆ **buzz off** vi UK inf: **~ off!** dê o fora!

buzzard ['bʌzəd] n -1. UK [hawk] gavião m -2. US [vulture] abutre m.

buzzer ['bʌzəʳ] n campainha f.

buzzing ['bʌzɪŋ] n zumbido m.

buzzword ['bʌzwɜːd] n inf palavra f da moda.

by [baɪ] <> prep -1. [expressing cause, agent] por; **he's worried ~ her absence** está preocupado com a sua ausência; **he was hit ~ a car** ele foi atropelado por um carro; **a book ~ Stephen King** um livro de Stephen King; **funded ~ the government** financiado pelo governo. -2. [expressing method, means]: **~ car/bus/plane** de carro/ônibus/avião; **~ phone/mail** pelo telefone/correio; **to pay ~ credit card/check** pagar com cartão de crédito/cheque; **to win ~ cheating** ganhar trapaceando. -3. [near to, beside] junto a; **~ the sea** à beira-mar, junto ao mar. -4. [past] por; **a car went ~ the house** um carro passou pela casa. -5. [via] por; **exit ~ the door on the left** saia pela porta do lado esquerdo. -6. [with time]: **be there ~ nine** esteja lá às nove horas; **~ day** de dia; **it should be ready ~ now** já deve estar pronto. -7. [expressing quantity] a; **sold ~ the dozen** vende-se à dúzia; **prices fell ~ 20%** os preços baixaram 20%; **we charge ~ the hour** cobramos por hora. -8. [expressing meaning] com; **what do you mean ~ that?** que quer dizer com isso? -9. [in division, multiplication] por; **about six feet ~ fifteen** aproximadamente dois metros por cinco. -10. [according to] segundo; **~ law** segundo a lei; **it's fine ~ me** por mim tudo bem. -11. [expressing gradual process] a; **one ~ one** um a um; **day ~ day** dia a dia. **-12.** [in phrases]: **~ mistake** por engano; **~ oneself** sozinho; **~ profession** por profissão. <> *adv* [past]: **to go/drive ~** passar.

bye (-bye) [baɪ(baɪ)] *excl inf* tchau!

bye-election *n* = by-election.

byelaw [ˈbaɪlɔː] *n* = bylaw.

by-election *n* eleição suplementar realizada para substituir um político que renunciou ao cargo parlamentar ou morreu.

Byelorussia [bɪˌeləʊˈrʌʃə] *n* = Belorussia.

bygone [ˈbaɪgɒn] *adj* decorrido(da).
 ➡ **bygones** *npl*: **to let ~s be ~s** deixar o que passou para trás.

bylaw [ˈbaɪlɔː] *n* estatuto *m*.

by-line *n* linha no início de um artigo de jornal ou revista dando o nome do autor.

BYOB (*abbr of* **bring your own bottle**) traga sua própria bebida.

bypass [ˈbaɪpɑːs] <> *n* **-1.** [road] rodoanel *m* **-2.** *MED*: **~ (operation)** (cirurgia de) ponte *f* de safena. <> *vt* **-1.** [place] passar ao redor de **-2.** [issue, person] passar por cima de.

by-product *n* **-1.** [product] subproduto *m* **-2.** *fig* [consequence] subproduto *m*.

bystander [ˈbaɪˌstændə'] *n* espectador *m*, -ra *f*.

byte [baɪt] *n* COMPUT byte *m*.

byword [ˈbaɪwɜːd] *n* [symbol]: **to be a ~ for sthg** ser um exemplo de algo.

c¹ (*pl* **c's** OR **cs**), **C** (*pl* **C's** OR **Cs**) [siː] *n* [letter] c, C *m*.
 ➡ **C** *n* **-1.** MUS dó *m* **-2.** SCH [mark] C *m*, regular *m* **-3.** (*abbr of* **celsius, centigrade**) C.

c² **-1.** (*abbr of* **century**) séc. **-2.** (*abbr of* **cent(s)**) cent.

c., ca. (*abbr of* **circa**) c.

C/A -1. (*abbr of* **capital account**) conta de empréstimos e investimentos. **- 2.** (*abbr of* **credit account**) conta *f* de crédito. **- 3.** (*abbr of* **current account**) c/c *f*.

CA <> *n* (*abbr of* **chartered accountant**) contador com certificado de qualificação profissional na Escócia e no Canadá. <> **-1.** (*abbr of* **Central America**) América *f* Central. **- 2.** *abbr of* **California.**

CAA *n* **-1.** (*abbr of* **Civil Aviation Authority**) organismo regulador da aviação civil na Grã-Bretanha. **- 2.** (*abbr of* **Civil Aeronautics Authority**) autoridade de aviação civil nos Estados Unidos.

cab [kæb] *n* **-1.** [taxi] táxi *m* **-2.** [of lorry] cabine *f*.

CAB (*abbr of* **Citizens' Advice Bureau**) *n* centro

britânico de informação e assistência ao cidadão.

cabaret [ˈkæbəreɪ] *n* cabaré *m*.

cabbage [ˈkæbɪdʒ] *n* [vegetable] repolho *m*.

cabbie, cabby [ˈkæbɪ] *n inf* taxista *mf*.

caber [ˈkeɪbə'] *n*: **tossing the ~** esporte praticado na Escócia no qual o vencedor é aquele que arremessar um tronco de pinheiro à maior distância.

cabin [ˈkæbɪn] *n* **-1.** [on ship] camarote *m* **-2.** [in aircraft] cabine *f* **-3.** [house] cabana *f*.

cabin class *n* classe *f* cabina.

cabin crew *n* tripulação *f*.

cabin cruiser *n* iate *m*.

cabinet [ˈkæbɪnɪt] *n* **-1.** [cupboard] armário *m* **-2.** POL gabinete *m*.

cabinet-maker *n* marceneiro *m*, -ra *f*.

cabinet minister *n* ministro *m*, -tra *f* de gabinete.

cable [ˈkeɪbl] <> *n* **-1.** [rope] cabo *m* **-2.** [telegram] telegrama *m* **-3.** ELEC cabo *m* **-4.** TV = **cable television.** <> *vt* [telegraph] telegrafar.

cable car *n* teleférico *m*.

cablegram *n* cabograma *m*.

cable railway *n* ferrovia *f* funicular.

cable television, cable TV *n* (U) televisão *f* a cabo.

caboodle [kəˈbuːdl] *n inf*: **the whole (kit and) ~** a tralha toda.

cabriolet [ˈkæbrɪəʊleɪ] *n* [car] conversível *m*.

cache [kæʃ] <> *n* **-1.** [store] esconderijo *m* **-2.** COMPUT cache *f*. <> *vt* COMPUT armazenar em cache.

cachet [ˈkæʃeɪ] *n fml* prestígio *m*.

cackle [ˈkækl] <> *n* **-1.** [of hen] cacarejo *m* **-2.** [of person] gargalhada *f*. <> *vi* **-1.** [hen] cacarejar **-2.** [person] gargalhar.

cacophony [kæˈkɒfənɪ] *n* balbúrdia *f*.

cactus [ˈkæktəs] (*pl* **-tuses** OR **-ti** [-taɪ]) *n* cacto *m*.

CAD (*abbr of* **computer-aided design**) *n* CAD *m*.

caddie [ˈkædɪ] <> *n* carregador *m*, -ra *f* de tacos. <> *vi*: **to ~ for sb** carregar os tacos de golfe para alguém.

caddy [ˈkædɪ] (*pl* **-ies**) *n* porta-chá *m*.

cadence [ˈkeɪdəns] *n* [of voice] cadência *f*.

cadet [kəˈdet] *n* [in police] cadete *m*.

cadge [kædʒ] UK inf <> *vt*: **to ~ sthg (off** OR **from sb)** filar algo (de alguém). <> *vi*: **to ~ off** OR **from sb** pedir esmolas a OR para alguém.

Cadiz [kəˈdɪz] *n* Cádiz.

Caesar [ˈsiːzə'] *n* César *m*.

caesarean (section) UK, **cesarean (section)** US [sɪˈzeərɪən-] *n* cesariana *f*; **she had a ~** ela fez uma cesariana.

CAF (*abbr of* **cost and freight**) custo *m* e frete.

cafe, café [ˈkæfeɪ] *n* café *m*.

cafeteria [ˌkæfɪˈtɪərɪə] *n* cantina *f*.

caffeine [ˈkæfiːn] *n* (U) cafeína *f*.

cage [keɪdʒ] *n* **-1.** [for animals] jaula *f* **-2.** [for birds] gaiola *f*.

caged [keɪdʒd] *adj* **-1.** [animals] enjaulado(da) **-2.** [birds] engaiolado(da).

cagey [ˈkeɪdʒɪ] (*compar* **-ier**, *superl* **-iest**) *adj inf* cauteloso(sa), cuidadoso(sa).

cagoule [kə'gu:l] *n UK* capa *f* de chuva.

cahoots [kə'hu:ts] *n inf*: **to be in ~ with/against sb** estar de armação com/contra alguém.

CAI (*abbr of* **computer-aided instruction**) *n* CAI *f*, instrução *f* assistida por computador.

cairn [keən] *n* [heap of stones] marco *m* de pedras.

Cairo ['kaɪərəʊ] *n* Cairo.

cajole [kə'dʒəʊl] *vt*: **to ~ sb out of sthg** persuadir alguém a desistir de algo; **to ~ sb into doing sthg** persuadir alguém a fazer algo.

cake [keɪk] *n* - **1.** [type of sweet food] bolo *m*; **to sell like hot ~s** vender como água; **you can't have your ~ and eat it** não dá para assobiar e chupar cana ao mesmo tempo; **a piece of ~** *inf* uma moleza *OR* barbada - **2.** [of fish, potato] bolinho *m* (*achatado*) - **3.** [of soap] sabonete *m*.

caked [keɪkt] *adj*: **~ with sthg** empastado(da) de algo, coberto(ta) de algo.

cake pan *n US* fôrma *f* (*de bolo*).

cake tin *n UK* [for baking] fôrma *f* (*de bolo*); [for storing] pote *m*.

cal (*abbr of* **calorie**) *n* cal.

CAL (*abbr of* **computer-assisted learning**) *n* CAL *f*, aprendizagem *f* assistida por computador.

calamine lotion [kæləmaɪn-] *n* (*U*) loção *f* de calamina.

calamitous [kə'læmɪtəs] *adj fml* calamitoso(sa).

calamity [kə'læmɪtɪ] (*pl* -**ies**) *n fml* calamidade *f*.

calcium ['kælsɪəm] *n* (*U*) cálcio *m*.

calculate ['kælkjʊleɪt] *vt* - **1.** [work out - figures, result etc] calcular; [- consequences, risk etc] medir - **2.** [plan, intend]: **to be ~d to do sthg** ter o intuito de fazer algo.

calculate on *vi*: **to ~ on sthg** contar com algo; **to ~ on sb doing sthg** contar com que alguém faça algo.

calculated ['kælkjʊleɪtɪd] *adj* [planned, intentional - risk] calculado(da); [- crime, deception] premeditado(da); [- insult] intencional.

calculating ['kælkjʊleɪtɪŋ] *adj pej* calculista.

calculation [,kælkjʊ'leɪʃn] *n MATH* cálculo *m*.

calculator ['kælkjʊleɪtə^r] *n* calculadora *f*.

calculus [,kælkjʊləs] *n* (*U*) *MATH* cálculo *m*.

calendar ['kælɪndə^r] *n* calendário *m*.

calendar month *n* mês *m* civil.

calendar year *n* ano *m* civil.

calf [kɑ:f] (*pl* **calves**) *n* - **1.** [young animal - cow] bezerro *m*, -ra *f*; [- elephant, whale] filhote *m* - **2.** (*U*) [leather] couro *m* de bezerro - **3.** [of leg] panturrilha *f*, barriga *f* da perna.

calf-length *adj* três-quartos.

calfskin *n* couro *m* de bezerro.

caliber *n US* = **calibre** *m*.

calibrate ['kælɪbreɪt] *vt* - **1.** [mark out] graduar - **2.** [adjust] calibrar.

calibre, caliber *US* ['kælɪbə^r] *n* - **1.** [quality] nível *m* - **2.** [size] calibre *m*.

calico ['kælɪkəʊ] *n* (*U*) morim *m*.

California [,kælɪ'fɔːnjə] *n* Califórnia.

Californian [,kælɪ'fɔːnjən] <> *adj* californiano (na). <> *n* californiano *m*, -na *f*.

calipers *npl US* = **callipers**.

call [kɔːl] <> *n* - **1.** [cry - of person] grito *m*; [- of animal,

bird] canto *m* - **2.** [visit] visita *f*; **to pay a ~ on sb** fazer uma visita a alguém - **3.** [for flight] chamada *f*; **final ~** última chamada - **4.** [demand] pedido *m*; **~ for sthg** solicitação por algo; **there's no ~ for that** não há razão para isso - **5.** [summons] chamado *m* - **6.** [standby]: **on ~** de plantão - **7.** [telephone call] telefonema *m*, ligação *f*; **long-distance ~** chamada de longa distância; **to give sb a ~** telefonar para alguém, dar uma ligada para alguém - **8.** [lure, fascination] encanto *m*. <> *vt* - **1.** [gen] chamar; **disgraceful, I'd ~ it!** uma vergonha, eu diria!; **would you ~ what he does art?** você chamaria o que ele faz de arte?; **he ~ed me a liar** ele me chamou de mentiroso; **let's ~ it £10 a** gente faz por £10 - **2.** [telephone] ligar para. <> *vi* - **1.** [shout] chamar - **2.** [animal, bird] cantar - **3.** [by telephone] ligar - **4.** [visit] visitar.

call back <> *vt sep* - **1.** [on telephone] ligar de volta - **2.** [ask to return] chamar de volta. <> *vi* - **1.** [on phone] ligar de volta - **2.** [visit again] voltar outra vez.

call by *vi inf* dar uma passada.

call for *vt fus* - **1.** [collect] ir buscar - **2.** [demand] exigir.

call in <> *vt sep* - **1.** [send for] chamar - **2.** *COMM* [goods] fazer um recall de; *FIN* [loan] resgatar. <> *vi*: **could you ~ in at the butcher's on your way home?** você pode passar no açougue ao voltar para casa?

call off *vt sep* - **1.** [cancel] cancelar - **2.** [order not to attack] mandar voltar.

call on *vt fus* - **1.** [visit] visitar - **2.** [ask]: **to ~ on sb to do sthg** convocar alguém para fazer algo.

call out <> *vt sep* - **1.** [gen] convocar - **2.** [cry out] gritar. <> *vi* [cry out] gritar.

call round *vi* dar uma passada.

call up *vt sep* - **1.** *MIL* convocar - **2.** [on telephone] dar uma ligada - **3.** *COMPUT* chamar, buscar.

call box *n UK* cabine *f* telefônica, ≈ orelhão *m*.

caller ['kɔːlə^r] *n* - **1.** [visitor] visita *f* - **2.** [on telephone]: **I'm sorry ~, the number is engaged** sinto muito, senhor(ra), a linha está ocupada.

caller (ID) display *n* [on telephone] identificador *m* de chamadas.

call girl *n* garota *f* de programa.

calligraphy [kə'lɪgrəfɪ] *n* (*U*) caligrafia *f*.

call-in *n US RADIO & TV* programa *com participação por telefone de ouvintes ou telespectadores*.

calling ['kɔːlɪŋ] *n* - **1.** [profession, trade] profissão *f* - **2.** [vocation] vocação *f*.

calling card *n US* cartão *m* de visita.

callipers *UK*, **calipers** *US* ['kælɪpəz] *npl* - **1.** *MATH* compasso *m* de calibre - **2.** *MED* aparelho *m* ortopédico.

callous ['kæləs] *adj* insensível.

callously ['kæləslɪ] *adv* insensivelmente.

callousness ['kæləsnɪs] *n* (*U*) insensibilidade *f*.

call-up *n UK* convocação *f*.

callus ['kæləs] (*pl* -**es**) *n* calo *m*.

calm [kɑːm] <> *adj* [person, voice, weather] calmo(ma), tranqüilo(la). <> *n* (*U*) [peaceful state] tranqüilidade *f*, calmaria *f*. <> *vt* acalmar, tranqüilizar.

calm down ⬦ *vt sep* acalmar, tranqüilizar. ⬦ *vi* acalmar-se, tranqüilizar-se.

calmly ['kɑ:mlɪ] *adv* calmamente, tranqüilamente.

calmness ['kɑ:mnɪs] *n (U)* tranqüilidade *f*.

Calor gas® ['kælə'-] *n UK (U)* ≃ butano *m*.

calorie ['kælərɪ] *n* [in food] caloria *f*.

calorific [‚kælə'rɪfɪk] *adj* [fattening] calórico(ca).

calumny *adj fml* calúnia *f*.

calve [kɑ:v] *vi* [cow] dar cria.

calves [kɑ:vz] *pl* ⊳ **calf**.

cam [kæm] *n* came *f*.

CAM (*abbr of* **computer-aided manufacturing**) *n* CAM *f*, produção *f* assistida por computador.

camaraderie [‚kæmə'rɑ:dərɪ] *n (U)* camaradagem *f*.

camber ['kæmbə'] *n* inclinação *f*.

Cambodia [kæm'bəʊdjə] *n* Camboja; **in** ~ no Camboja.

Cambodian [kæm'bəʊdjən] ⬦ *adj* cambojano(-na). ⬦ *n* cambojano *m*, -na *f*.

camcorder ['kæm‚kɔ:də'] *n* filmadora *f*.

came [keɪm] *pt* ⊳ **come**.

camel ['kæml] ⬦ *adj*: ~-**coloured** da cor de camelo; **a** ~ **coat** um casaco de pele de camelo. ⬦ *n* [animal] camelo *m*.

camellia [kə'mi:ljə] *n* camélia *f*.

cameo ['kæmɪəʊ] (*pl* **-s**) *n* **-1.** [piece of jewellery] camafeu *m* **-2.** [in writing] descrição *f* breve e inteligente **-3.** [in acting] ponta *f*.

camera ['kæmərə] *n* câmera *f*.

in camera *adv fml* em câmara.

cameraman ['kæmərəmæn] (*pl* **-men** [-men]) *n* cameraman *m*, câmera *m*.

Cameroon [‚kæmə'ru:n] *n* Camarões; **in** ~ nos Camarões.

Cameroonian [‚kæmə'ru:nɪən] ⬦ *adj* camaronês(esa). ⬦ *n* camaronês *m*, -esa *f*.

camisole ['kæmɪsəʊl] *n* camisola *f*.

camomile ['kæməmaɪl] ⬦ *n* [plant, herb] camomila *f*. ⬦ *comp*: ~ **tea** chá de camomila.

camouflage ['kæməflɑ:ʒ] ⬦ *n* comuflagem *f* ⬦ *vt* camuflar.

camp [kæmp] ⬦ *n* **-1.** [gen] acampamento *m*; **holiday** ~ acampamento de férias; **training** ~ campo *m* de treinamento; **concentration/refugee** ~ campo de concentração/refugiados **-2.** *fig* [faction] facção *f*. ⬦ *vi* acampar.

camp out *vi* acampar.

campaign [kæm'peɪn] ⬦ *n* campanha *f*. ⬦ *vi*: **to** ~ **(for/against sthg)** fazer campanha (a favor de/contra algo).

campaigner [kæm'peɪnə'] *n* [activist] ativista *mf*; **old** ~ veterano *m*, -na *f*.

camp bed *n* cama *f* de armar.

camper ['kæmpə'] *n* **-1.** [person] campista *mf* **-2.** [vehicle]: ~ **(van)** trailer *m*.

campground ['kæmpgraʊnd] *n US* camping *m*.

camphor ['kæmfə'] *n* cânfora *f*.

camping ['kæmpɪŋ] *n (U)* acampamento *m*; **to go** ~ ir acampar.

camping site, campsite ['kæmpsaɪt] *n* camping *m*.

campus ['kæmpəs] (*pl* **-es**) *n* campus *m*.

camshaft ['kæmʃɑ:ft] *n* eixo *m* de came.

can¹ [kæn] ⬦ *n* [container] lata *f*. ⬦ *vt* enlatar.

can² [*weak form* kən, *strong form* kæn] (*pt* **was, were,** *pt & conditional* **could**) *aux vb* **-1.** [be able to] poder; ~ **you help me?** pode me ajudar?; **I** ~ **see the mountains** posso ver as montanhas **-2.** [know how to] saber; ~ **you drive?** você sabe dirigir?; **I** ~ **speak Portuguese** eu sei falar português **-3.** [be allowed to] poder; **you can't smoke here** você não pode fumar aqui **-4.** [in polite requests] poder; ~ **you tell me the time?** pode me dizer as horas?; ~ **I speak to the manager?** posso falar com o gerente? **-5.** [expressing occasional occurrence] poder; **it** ~ **get cold at night** às vezes a temperatura diminui bastante à noite **-6.** [expressing possibility] poder; **they could be lost** eles podem estar perdidos.

Canada ['kænədə] *n* Canadá; **in** ~ no Canadá.

Canadian [kə'neɪdjən] ⬦ *adj* canadense. ⬦ *n* canadense *mf*.

canal [kə'næl] *n* [waterway] canal *m*.

Canaries *npl*: **the** ~ as Canárias.

canary [kə'neərɪ] (*pl* **-ies**) *n* canário *m*.

Canary Islands, Canaries [kə'neərɪz] *npl*: **the** ~ as Ilhas Canárias; **in the** ~ nas Ilhas Canárias.

Canberra *n* Canberra; **em** ~ em Camberra.

cancel ['kænsl] (*UK* *pt* & *pp* **-led,** *cont*-**ling,** *US* *pt* & *pp* **-ed,** *cont*-**ing**) *vt* [call off, invalidate] cancelar.

cancel out *vt sep* anular.

cancellation [‚kænsə'leɪʃn] *n* cancelamento *m*.

cancer ['kænsə'] ⬦ *n* [disease] câncer *m*. ⬦ *comp*: ~ **cell** célula cancerosa; ~ **research** pesquisa sobre câncer; ~ **specialist** especialista em câncer.

Cancer *n* **-1.** [sign] Câncer *m* **-2.** [person] canceriano *m*, -na *f*; **I'm** ~ sou de Câncer.

cancerous ['kænsərəs] *adj* canceroso(sa).

candelabra [‚kændɪ'lɑ:brə] *n* candelabro *m*.

candid ['kændɪd] *adj* [frank] sincero(ra), franco(ca).

candidacy ['kændɪdəsɪ] *n (U)* candidatura *f*.

candidate ['kændɪdət] *n* **-1.** [for job]: ~ **for sthg** candidato(ta) a algo **-2.** [taking exam] candidato *m*, -ta *f*.

candidature ['kændɪdətʃə'] *n* candidatura *f*.

candidly ['kændɪdlɪ] *adv* sinceramente, francamente.

candidness ['kændɪdnɪs] *n* = **candour**.

candied ['kændɪd] *adj* cristalizado(da).

candle ['kændl] *n* vela *f*; **to burn the** ~ **at both ends** *inf* dar duro dia e noite.

candlelight ['kændllaɪt] *n (U)* luz *f* de vela.

candlelit ['kændllɪt] *adj* à luz de velas.

candlestick ['kændlstɪk] *n* castiçal *m*.

candour *UK*, **candor** *US* ['kændə'] *n (U)* sinceridade *f*, franqueza *f*.

candy ['kændɪ] (*pl* **-ies**) *n esp US (U)* [confectionery] doce *m*, guloseima *f*.

candy bar *n US* barra *f* de doce.

candy box *n US* caixa *f* de doces.

candyfloss *UK* ['kændɪflɒs], **cotton candy** *US n (U)* algodão-doce *m*.

candy store *n US* confeitaria *f*.

cane [keɪn] ◇ n -1. (U) [for making furniture] palhinha f -2. [walking stick] bengala f -3. [for punishment]: **the ~** ≃ a palmatória -4. [for supporting plant] vara f. ◇ comp de palhinha. ◇ vt bater com vara em.

cane sugar n (U) cana-de-açúcar f.

canine [ˈkeɪnaɪn] ◇ adj canino(na). ◇ n: **~ (tooth)** (dente m) canino m.

canister [ˈkænɪstəʳ] n lata f de metal; **a ~ of tear gas** uma bomba de gás lacrimogênio; **a smoke ~** uma bomba de fumaça.

cannabis [ˈkænəbɪs] n (U) maconha f.

canned [kænd] adj -1. [tinned - food] enlatado(da); [- drink] em lata, de latinha -2. **inf** fig [music] gravado(da).

cannelloni [ˌkænɪˈləʊnɪ] n (U) canelone m.

cannery (pl -ies) n fábrica f de enlatados.

cannibal [ˈkænɪbl] n canibal mf.

cannibalize, -ise [ˈkænɪbəlaɪz] vt [vehicle, machine] desmanchar.

cannon [ˈkænən] (pl inv OR -s) n -1. [on ground] canhão m -2. [on aircraft] canhão m.
➤ **cannon into** vt fus UK esbarrar.

cannonball [ˈkænənbɔːl] n bala f de canhão.

cannot [ˈkænɒt] vb fml ▷ **can²**.

canny [ˈkænɪ] (compar -ier, superl -iest) adj [shrewd] astuto(ta).

canoe [kəˈnuː] ◇ n canoa f. ◇ vi andar de canoa.

canoeing [kəˈnuːɪŋ] n (U): **to go ~** praticar canoagem.

canon [ˈkænən] n -1. [clergyman] cônego m -2. [general principle] cânone m.
➤ **Canon** n [of Mass]: **the Canon** o cânon.

canonize, -ise [ˈkænənaɪz] vt canonizar.

canoodle [kəˈnuːdl] vi UK inf amassar-se.

can opener n abridor m de lata.

canopy [ˈkænəpɪ] (pl -ies) n -1. [over bed, seat] dossel m -2. [of trees, branches] cobertura f.

cant [kænt] n pej [insincere talk] papo-furado m.

can't [kɑːnt] = **cannot**.

Cantab (abbr of **Cantabrigiensis**) da Universidade de Cambridge.

Cantabrian Mountains [kænˈteɪbrɪən-] npl: **the ~** as Montanhas Cantábricas.

cantaloup UK, **cantaloupe** US [ˈkæntəluːp] n cantalupo m.

cantankerous [kænˈtæŋkərəs] adj rabugento(ta).

canteen [kænˈtiːn] n -1. [restaurant] cantina f -2. [box of cutlery] faqueiro m.

canter [ˈkæntəʳ] ◇ n meio m galope. ◇ vi andar a meio galope.

cantilever [ˈkæntɪliːvəʳ] n viga f em balanço, cantiléver.

Canton [kænˈtɒn] n Cantão.

Cantonese [ˌkæntəˈniːz] ◇ adj cantonês(esa). ◇ n [language] cantonês m. ◇ npl: **the ~** os cantoneses.

canvas [ˈkænvəs] n -1. (U) [cloth] lona f; **under ~** [in a tent] em uma barraca -2. ART tela f.

canvass [ˈkænvəs] ◇ vt -1. POL pedir -2. [investigate] sondar. ◇ vi POL [campaign] pedir votos.

canvasser [ˈkænvəsəʳ] n -1. POL [campaigner] cabo mf eleitoral -2. [investigator] pesquisador m, -ra f.

canvassing [ˈkænvəsɪŋ] n -1. POL [campaigning] angariação f de votos -2. [investigation] pesquisa f.

canyon [ˈkænjən] n desfiladeiro m.

cap [kæp] (pt & pp -ped, cont -ping) ◇ n -1. [hat] boné m -2. [swimming, shower] touca f; **to go ~ in hand to sb** fig dirigir-se a alguém com o chapéu na mão -3. [lid, top] tampa f -4. UK [contraceptive device] diafragma m. ◇ vt -1. [cover top of] cobrir -2. [improve on]: **to ~ it all** para arrematar.

CAP (abbr of **Common Agricultural Policy**) n política que permite que todos os países da União Européia organizem e controlem sua produção agrícola conjuntamente.

capability [ˌkeɪpəˈbɪlətɪ] (pl -ies) n -1. [ability] capacidade f -2. MIL poderio m.

capable [ˈkeɪpəbl] adj -1. [able, having capacity]: **to be ~ of sthg/of doing sthg** ser capaz de algo/de fazer algo -2. [competent, skilful] competente, hábil.

capably [ˈkeɪpəblɪ] adv habilmente.

capacious [kəˈpeɪʃəs] adj fml espaçoso(sa).

capacitor [kəˈpæsɪtəʳ] n capacitor m.

capacity [kəˈpæsɪtɪ] (pl -ies) ◇ n -1. (U) [limit, ability] capacidade f; **to be filled to ~** estar com a lotação esgotada; **~ for sthg** capacidade para algo; **~ for doing** OR **to do sthg** capacidade para fazer algo -2. [position] qualidade f; **in my ~ as** ... na qualidade de ...; **in a ... ~** na condição de ... ◇ comp máximo(ma).

cape [keɪp] n -1. GEOGR cabo m -2. [cloak] capa f.

Cape Canaveral [-kəˈnævərəl] n Cabo m Canaveral.

Cape of Good Hope n: **the ~** o Cabo da Boa Esperança.

caper [ˈkeɪpəʳ] ◇ n -1. [for flavouring food] alcaparra f -2. inf [escapade] mutreta f. ◇ vi fazer travessuras, pular.

Cape Town n Cidade f do Cabo.

Cape Verde [-vɜːd] n: **the ~ Islands** as Ilhas de Cabo Verde; **in ~** em Cabo Verde.

capillary [kəˈpɪlərɪ] (pl -ies) n capilar m.

capita ▷ **per capita**.

capital [ˈkæpɪtl] ◇ adj -1. [letter] maiúsculo(la) -2. [punishable by death] capital. ◇ n -1. [of country]: **~ (city)** capital f -2. fig [centre] capital f -3. TYPO **~ (letter)** (letra) maiúscula; **in ~s** em letras maiúsculas -4. [money] capital m; **to make ~ (out) of sthg** fig aproveitar-se de algo.

capital allowance n margem f fiscal para investimentos.

capital assets npl ativos mpl fixos.

capital expenditure n (U) dispêndio m com ativos fixos.

capital gains tax n imposto m sobre lucros de capital.

capital goods npl bens mpl de capital.

capital-intensive adj de capital intensivo.

capitalism [ˈkæpɪtəlɪzm] n (U) capitalismo m.

capitalist [ˈkæpɪtəlɪst] ◇ adj capitalista. ◇ n capitalista mf.

capitalize, -ise [ˈkæpɪtəlaɪz] vi: **to ~ on sthg** [make most of] tirar proveito de algo, capitalizar algo.

capital punishment n (U) pena f de morte.
capital stock n estoque m de capital.
capital transfer tax n imposto m sobre transferência de capital.
Capitol ['kæpɪtl] n: the ~ o Capitólio.
Capitol Hill ['kæpɪtl-] n congresso norte-americano.
capitulate [kə'pɪtjuleɪt] vi: to ~ (to sthg) render-se (a algo), ceder (frente a algo).
capitulation [kə,pɪtju'leɪʃn] n (U) capitulação f.
cappuccino [,kæpu'tʃiːnəu] (pl -s) n cappuccino m.
capricious [kə'prɪʃəs] adj inconstante.
Capricorn ['kæprɪkɔːn] n -1. [sign] Capricórnio m -2. [person]: I'm ~ sou de Capricórnio.
caps (abbr of capital letters) npl maiúsc.
capsicum ['kæpsɪkəm] n pimentão m.
capsize [kæp'saɪz] ⬦ vt emborcar. ⬦ vi emborcar-se.
capsule ['kæpsjuːl] n cápsula f.
Capt. (abbr of captain) cap.
captain ['kæptɪn] ⬦ n -1. [gen] capitão m -2. [of airliner] comandante mf. ⬦ vt [ship] comandar.
caption ['kæpʃn] n legenda f.
captivate ['kæptɪveɪt] vt cativar.
captivating ['kæptɪveɪtɪŋ] adj cativante.
captive ['kæptɪv] ⬦ adj -1. [imprisoned] de cativeiro -2. fig [unable to leave] cativo(va); ~ audience audiência cativa. ⬦ n prisioneiro m, -ra f.
captivity [kæp'tɪvətɪ] n: in ~ em cativeiro.
captor ['kæptər] n capturador m, -ra f.
capture ['kæptʃər] ⬦ vt -1. [gen] capturar -2. [gain, take control of] conquistar. ⬦ n (U) captura f.
car [kɑːr] ⬦ n -1. [motor car] carro m -2. [on train] vagão m. ⬦ comp de automóvel.
Caracas [kə'rækəs] n Caracas; **em** ~ em Caracas.
carafe [kə'ræf] n garrafa f de mesa.
car alarm n alarme m de carro.
caramel ['kærəmel] n -1. (U) [burnt sugar] caramelo m -2. [sweet] caramelo m.
carat ['kærət] n UK quilate m.
caravan ['kærəvæn] ⬦ n -1. UK [vehicle - towed by car] trailer m; [- towed by horse] carruagem m -2. [travelling group] caravana f. ⬦ comp de trailer; ~ holiday férias de trailer.
caravanning ['kærəvænɪŋ] n UK viagem f de trailer.
caravan site n UK área f para trailers.
caraway seed ['kærəweɪ-] n semente f de alcaravia.
carbohydrate [,kɑːbəu'haɪdreɪt] n (U) [chemical substance] carboidrato m.
⬥ **carbohydrates** npl [food] carboidratos mpl.
carbon ['kɑːbən] n -1. (U) [element] carbono m -2. = carbon copy -3. = carbon paper.
carbonated ['kɑːbəneɪtɪd] adj com gás.
carbon copy n -1. [document] cópia f em papel carbono -2. fig [exact copy] cópia f perfeita.
carbon dating [-'deɪtɪŋ] n (U) datação f por carbono 14.
carbon dioxide [-daɪ'ɒksaɪd] n (U) dióxido m de carbono.
carbon fibre n (U) fibra f de carbono.

carbon monoxide [-mɒ'nɒksaɪd] n monóxido m de carbono.
carbon paper n papel-carbono m.
car-boot sale n UK feira em que objetos usados são vendidos no porta-malas de um carro.
carburettor UK, **carburetor** US [,kɑːbə'retər] n carburador m.
carcass ['kɑːkəs] n [of animal] carcaça f.
carcinogenic [,kɑːsɪnə'dʒenɪk] adj cancerígeno(-na).
card [kɑːd] n -1. [playing card] carta f; **to play one's** ~s **right** fig agir de forma inteligente; **to put** OR **lay one's** ~s **on the table** fig pôr as cartas na mesa -2. [for information, greetings] cartão m -4. [postcard] postal m, cartão m postal -5. (U) [cardboard] papelão m.
⬥ **cards** npl [game] cartas fpl.
⬥ **on the cards** UK, **in the cards** US adv inf: to be on the ~ estar na cara.
cardamom ['kɑːdəməm] n cardamomo m.
cardboard ['kɑːdbɔːd] ⬦ n (U) papelão m. ⬦ comp [made of cardboard] de papelão m.
cardboard box n caixa f de papelão.
card-carrying [-'kærɪŋ] adj ativo(va).
card catalog n US fichário m.
cardiac ['kɑːdɪæk] adj cardíaco(ca), do coração.
cardiac arrest n ataque m cardíaco.
cardigan ['kɑːdɪgən] n cardigã m.
cardinal ['kɑːdɪnl] ⬦ adj primordial. ⬦ n RELIG cardeal m.
cardinal number, cardinal numeral n número m cardinal.
card index n UK fichário m.
cardiograph ['kɑːdɪəgrɑːf] n cardiógrafo m.
cardiology [,kɑːdɪ'ɒlədʒɪ] n (U) cardiologia f.
cardiovascular [,kɑːdɪəu'væskjulər] adj cardiovascular.
cardphone ['kɑːdfəun] n telefone m (público) de cartão.
cardsharp ['kɑːd,ʃɑːp] n trapaceiro m, -ra f.
card table n mesa f de jogo.
card vote n UK voto m representativo da classe.
care [keər] ⬦ n -1. (U) [protection, looking after] cuidado m; **to be taken into** ~ ser entregue aos cuidados de uma instituição social; **to take** ~ **of sb** [look after] cuidar de alguém; **to take** ~ **of sthg** [deal with] cuidar de algo; **take** ~! inf [when saying goodbye] cuide-se! -2. (U) [caution, carefulness] cuidado m; **to take** ~ **to do sthg** ter o cuidado de fazer algo; **take** ~! [be careful] tenha cuidado! -3. [cause of worry] preocupação f. ⬦ vi -1. [be concerned] preocupar-se; **to** ~ **about sb/sthg** preocupar-se com alguém/algo -2. [mind] importar-se; **I couldn't** ~ **less** inf não dou a mínima.
⬥ **care of** prep aos cuidados de.
⬥ **care for** vt fus [like] gostar de.
CARE (abbr of Cooperative for American Relief Everywhere) n organização humanitária norte-americana.
career [kə'rɪər] ⬦ n carreira f. ⬦ comp [professional] de carreira f. ⬦ vi desgovernar-se; **to** ~ **into sthg** ir desgovernado(da) em direção a algo.
careerist [kə'rɪərɪst] n pej carreirista mf.

careers [kə'rɪəz] *comp* de orientação vocacional.

careers adviser *n* orientador *m*, -ra *f* vocacional.

career woman *n* mulher *f* de carreira.

carefree ['keəfri:] *adj* despreocupado(da).

careful ['keəfʊl] *adj* -1. [cautious] cuidadoso(sa); ~ with sthg cuidadoso(sa) com algo; to be ~ to do sthg ter o cuidado de fazer algo -2. [thorough] cuidadoso(sa).

carefully ['keəflɪ] *adv* -1. [cautiously] cuidadosamente, com cuidado -2. [thoroughly] cuidadosamente.

careless ['keəlɪs] *adj* -1. [inattentive] desatento(ta), descuidado(da) -2. [unconcerned] despreocupado(da).

carelessly ['keəlɪslɪ] *adv* -1. [inattentively] sem atenção, descuidadamente -2. [unconcernedly] despreocupadamente.

carelessness ['keəlɪsnɪs] *n* (U) -1. [inattention] desatenção *f* -2. [lack of concern] descuido *m*.

carer ['keərə] *n* pessoa que cuida de um familiar incapacitado ou doente.

caress [kə'res] <> *n* carícia *f*. <> *vt* acariciar.

caretaker ['keə,teɪkə] *n* UK zelador *m*, -ra *f*.

caretaker government *n* governo *m* de transição.

car ferry *n* balsa *f*.

cargo ['kɑ:gəʊ] (*pl*-es OR-s) <> *n* carregamento *m*. <> *comp* de carga.

car hire *n* UK (U) aluguel *m* de carros.

Carib ['kærɪb] *n* Caribe *m*.

Caribbean [UK kærɪ'bɪən, US kə'rɪbɪən] <> *adj* caribenho(nha). <> *n* -1. [sea]: the ~ (Sea) o (Mar do) Caribe -2. [region]: the ~ o Caribe; in the ~ no Caribe.

caribou ['kærɪbu:] (*pl inv* OR-s) *n* caribu *m*.

caricature ['kærɪkə,tjʊə] <> *n* [cartoon, travesty] caricatura *f*. <> *vt* fazer caricatura de.

caries ['keəri:z] *n* (U) cárie *f*.

caring ['keərɪŋ] *adj* afetuoso(sa).

caring professions *npl*: the ~ as profissões humanitárias.

carnage ['kɑ:nɪdʒ] *n* (U) carnificina *f*.

carnal ['kɑ:nl] *adj literary* carnal.

carnation [kɑ:'neɪʃn] *n* craveiro *m*.

carnival ['kɑ:nɪvl] *n* -1. [festive occasion] carnaval *m* -2. [fair] parque *m* de diversões.

carnivore ['kɑ:nɪvɔ:] *n* carnívoro *m*, -ra *f*.

carnivorous [kɑ:'nɪvərəs] *adj* carnívoro(ra).

carol ['kærəl] *n*: (Christmas) ~ cântico *m* de Natal.

carouse [kə'raʊz] *vi* farrear.

carousel [,kærə'sel] *n* -1. *esp US* [at fair] carrossel *m* -2. [at airport] esteira *f*.

carp [kɑ:p] (*pl inv* OR -s) <> *n* carpa *f*. <> *vi* queixar-se; to ~ about sthg queixar-se de algo.

car park *n* UK estacionamento *m*.

Carpathians [kɑ:'peɪθɪənz] *npl*: the ~ os Cárpatos.

carpenter ['kɑ:pəntə] *n* carpinteiro *m*, -ra *f*.

carpentry ['kɑ:pəntrɪ] *n* (U) carpintaria *f*.

carpet ['kɑ:pɪt] <> *n* -1. [floor covering] carpete *m*; to sweep sthg under the ~ *fig* varrer algo para baixo do tapete -2. *fig* [of flowers, snow] tapete *m*.

<> *vt* -1. [fit with floor covering] acarpetar -2. *fig* [with flowers, snow] cobrir.

carpet slipper *n* pantufas *fpl*.

carpet sweeper [-'swi:pə] *n* limpador *m* de carpete, feiticeira *f*.

car phone *n* telefone *m* para automóvel.

car pool *n* UK [fleet of cars] frota *f*.

carport ['kɑ:,pɔ:t] *n* garagem *f*.

car radio *n* rádio *m* de carro.

car rental *n* Am aluguel *m* de carro.

carriage ['kærɪdʒ] *n* -1. [horsedrawn vehicle] carruagem *f* -2. UK [railway coach] vagão -3. (U) [transport of goods] carregamento *m*; ~ paid OR free UK frete pago; ~ forward UK frete ao portador -4. [on typewriter] carro *m* -5. (U) *literary* [deportment] postura *f*.

carriage clock *n* relógio *m* com alça.

carriageway ['kærɪdʒweɪ] *n* UK pista *f* simples.

carrier ['kærɪə] *n* -1. COMM transportador *m*, -ra *f* -2. [of disease] portador *m*, -ra *f* -3. MIL: (aircraft) ~ porta-aviões *m inv* -4. [on bicycle] cestinha *f* -5. = carrier bag.

carrier bag *n* sacola *f*.

carrier pigeon *n* pombo-correio *m*.

carrion ['kærɪən] *n* (U) carniça *f*.

carrot ['kærət] *n* -1. [vegetable] cenoura *f* -2. *inf fig* [incentive] incentivo *m*.

carry ['kærɪ] (*pt* & *pp* -ied) <> *vt* -1. [transport - subj: person, animal] carregar; [- subj: water, wind, vehicle] levar -2. [be equipped with] dispor de; all planes ~ lifejackets todos os aviões dispõem de coletes salva-vidas -3. [weapon] portar -4. [disease] transmitir -5. [involve as a consequence] implicar; the job carries considerable responsibility o emprego implica em responsabilidades consideráveis -6. [motion, proposal] aprovar -7. [be pregnant with] carregar -8. MATH sobrar. <> *vi* [sound] projetar-se.

◆ **carry away** *vt sep*: to get carried away entrar no embalo.

◆ **carry forward** *vt sep* transportar.

◆ **carry off** *vt sep* -1. [make a success of] tornar um sucesso -2. [win] sair-se bem.

◆ **carry on** <> *vt fus* [continue] continuar; to ~ on doing sthg continuar a fazer algo. <> *vi* -1. [continue] continuar; to ~ on with sthg continuar algo -2. *inf* [make a fuss] criar caso -3. *inf* [have an affair]: to ~ on with sb estar de caso com alguém.

◆ **carry out** *vt fus* -1. [task, plan, experiment] levar a cabo -2. [promise, order, threat] cumprir.

◆ **carry through** *vt sep* [accomplish] completar.

carryall ['kærɔ:l] *n* US bolsa *f* de viagem.

carrycot ['kærɪkɒt] *n esp UK* moisés *m inv*.

carry-on *n* UK *inf* bagunça *f*.

carryout *n* US & *Scot* -1. [food] comida *f* para viagem OR para levar -2. [drink] bebida *f* para viagem OR para levar.

carsick ['kɑ:,sɪk] *adj* enjoado(da) (*em carro*).

cart [kɑ:t] <> *n* -1. [vehicle] carroça *f* -2. (*abbr of* cartridge) COMPUT cartucho *m* -3. US [for shopping]: (shopping OR grocery) ~ carrinho *m* (de compras). <> *vt inf* carregar.

carte blanche ['kɑ:tblɑ̃ʃ] *n* (U) carta *f* branca.

cartel [kɑ:'tel] *n* cartel *m*.

cartilage ['kɑ:tɪlɪdʒ] *n* (U) cartilagem *f*.

carton ['kɑ:tn] *n* -**1.** [brick-shaped] caixa *f* -**2.** [plastic] frasco *m*.

cartoon [kɑ:'tu:n] *n* -**1.** [satirical drawing] cartum *m* -**2.** [comic strip] tira *f*, tirinha *f* -**3.** [film] desenho *m* animado.

cartoonist [kɑ:'tu:nɪst] *n* cartunista *mf*.

cartridge ['kɑ:trɪdʒ] *n* -**1.** [for gun] cartucho *m* -**2.** [for pen] recarga *f* -**3.** [for camera] rolo *m* de filme -**4.** [for record player] cápsula *f*.

cartridge paper *n* (U) papel-manilha *m*.

cartwheel ['kɑ:twi:l] *n* [movement] pirueta *f*.

car valeting *n* lavagem *f* completa.

carve [kɑ:v] <> *vt* -**1.** [shape, sculpt] esculpir -**2.** [slice] fatiar -**3.** [cut into surface] gravar. <> *vi* [slice joint] fatiar a carne.

➡ **carve out** *vt sep* [create, obtain] criar.

➡ **carve up** *vt sep* [divide] dividir.

carving ['kɑ:vɪŋ] *n* [art, work, object] entalhe *m*.

carving knife *n* faca *f* de trinchar.

car wash *n* -**1.** [process] lavagem *f* de carro -**2.** [place] lava-rápido *m*.

cascade [kæ'skeɪd] <> *n* -**1.** [waterfall] cascata *f* -**2.** [of blossom, information] chuva *f*. <> *vi* [flow downwards] cair em cascatas.

case [keɪs] *n* -**1.** [gen] caso *m*; **a ~ in point** um exemplo típico; **to be the ~** ser o caso; **in that ~** nesse caso; **he may still come, in which ~ we can all leave together** pode ser que ele ainda venha, e neste caso todos podemos partir juntos; **as** OR **whatever the ~ may be** seja qual for o caso; **in ~ of** em caso de -**2.** [argument] razões *fpl*; **~ for/ against sthg** razões a favor de/contra algo -**3.** JUR [trial, inquiry] causa *f* -**4.** [container, holder] estojo *m* -**5.** UK [suitcase] mala *f*.

➡ **in any case** *adv* seja como for.

➡ **in case** <> *conj* caso. <> *adv* : (just) **in ~** só por precaução.

case-hardened *adj* [person] calejado(da).

case history *n* prontuário *m*.

casement window *n* janela *f* de batente.

case study *n* estudo *m* de caso.

cash [kæʃ] <> *n* (U) -**1.** [notes and coins] dinheiro *m*; **to pay (in) ~** pagar em dinheiro -**2.** *inf* [money] dinheiro *m* -**3.** [payment]: **~ in advance** pagamento *m* adiantado/antecipado; **~ on delivery** pagamento contra entrega. <> *vt* descontar.

➡ **cash in** *vi*: **to ~ in on sthg** *inf* tirar proveito de algo.

cash and carry *n* sistema *f* pague e leve.

cashbook ['kæʃbʊk] *n* livro-caixa *m*.

cash box *n* cofre *m*.

cash card *n* cartão *m* de saque.

cash crop *n* plantação *f* para venda direta.

cash desk *n* UK caixa *m*.

cash discount *n* desconto *m* no pagamento à vista.

cash dispenser [-dɪ'spensə^r] *n* = **cashpoint**

cashew (nut) ['kæʃu:-] *n* castanha *f* de caju.

cash flow *n* fluxo *m* de caixa.

cashier [kæ'ʃɪə^r] *n* caixa *mf*.

cash machine *n* = **cash point**.

cashmere [kæʃ'mɪə^r] <> *n* (U) caxemira *f*. <> *comp* de caxemira.

cashpoint ['kæʃpɔɪnt] *n* caixa *m* automático.

cash price *n* preço *m* à vista.

cash register *n* caixa *f* registradora.

cash sale *n* venda *f* à vista.

casing ['keɪsɪŋ] *n* [protective cover] invólucro *m*.

casino [kə'si:nəʊ] (*pl* -**s**) *n* cassino *m*.

cask [kɑ:sk] *n* barril *m*.

casket ['kɑ:skɪt] *n* -**1.** [for jewels] porta-jóias *m inv* -**2.** US [coffin] caixão *m*.

Caspian Sea ['kæspɪən-] *n*: **the ~** o mar Cáspio.

casserole ['kæsərəʊl] *n* -**1.** [stew] ensopado *m* (no forno) -**2.** [pot] prato *f* de ir ao forno.

cassette [kæ'set] *n* cassete *f*.

cassette deck *n* deck *m*.

cassette player *n* toca-fitas *m inv*.

cassette recorder *n* gravador *m*.

cassock ['kæsək] *n* batina *f*.

cast [kɑ:st] (*pt* & *pp* **cast**) <> *n* -**1.** [of play, film] elenco *m* -**2.** MED gesso *m*. <> *vt* -**1.** [turn, direct] dar uma espiada em; **to ~ doubt on sthg** pôr algo em dúvida; **to ~ a spell (on sb)** lançar um feitiço (sobre alguém) -**2.** [light, shadow] lançar -**3.** [throw] arremessar -**4.** [choose for play, film] dar o papel a; **she ~ him in the role of Hamlet** ela deu-lhe o papel de Hamlet -**5.** POL: **to ~ one's vote** votar -**6.** [metal] moldar -**7.** [lose, shed] trocar. <> *vi* [in fishing] lançar.

➡ **cast about, cast around** *vi*: **to ~ about for sthg** procurar algo.

➡ **cast aside** *vt sep* rejeitar.

➡ **cast down** *vt sep* *fml* [make sad] deixar deprimido(da).

➡ **cast off** <> *vt* -**1.** *fml* [old practices, habits, burden] livrar-se de -**2.** [in knitting] arrematar. <> *vi* -**1.** NAUT soltar as amarras -**2.** [in knitting] arrematar os pontos.

➡ **cast on** <> *vt* [in knitting] montar. <> *vi* [in knitting] montar os pontos.

castanets [,kæstə'nets] *npl* castanholas *fpl*.

castaway ['kɑ:stəweɪ] *n* náufrago *m*, -ga *f*.

caste [kɑ:st] *n* [class] casta *f*.

caster ['kɑ:stə^r] *n* [wheel] rodízio *m*.

caster sugar *n* (U) UK açúcar *m* refinado.

castigate ['kæstɪgeɪt] *vt fml* [punish] castigar; [criticize severely] criticar severamente.

casting ['kɑ:stɪŋ] *n* [object] peça *f* fundida.

casting vote ['kɑ:stɪŋ-] *n* voto *m* de minerva.

cast iron *n* (U) ferro *m* fundido.

➡ **cast-iron** *adj* -**1.** [made of cast iron] de ferro fundido -**2.** *fig* [indisputable] incontestável.

castle ['kɑ:sl] *n* -**1.** [building] castelo *m* -**2.** [in chess] torre *f*.

castoff *n*: **to wears sb's ~s** usar as roupas velhas de alguém.

castor ['kɑ:stə^r] *n* = **caster**.

castor oil *n* (U) óleo *m* de rícino.

castor sugar *n* = **caster sugar**.

castrate [kæ'streɪt] *vt* castrar.

castration [kæ'streɪʃn] *n* (U) castração *f*.

casual ['kæʒʊəl] *adj* -**1.** [relaxed, uninterested] despreocupado(da) -**2.** *pej* [offhand] deselegante, informal

- 3. [chance] ocasional **- 4.** [clothes] informal **- 5.** [irregular] temporário(ria).

casually ['kæʒʊəlɪ] *adv* **- 1.** [in a relaxed manner, without interest] casualmente **- 2.** [dress] informalmente.

casualty ['kæʒjʊəltɪ] (*pl* **-ies**) *n* **- 1.** [dead or injured person] vítima *mf*; MIL baixa *f* **- 2.** MED = **casualty department** **- 3.** *fig* [of change, policy, system] vítima *f*.

casualty department *n* pronto-socorro *m*.

cat [kæt] *n* **- 1.** [domestic animal] gato *m*, -ta *f*; **to let the ~ out of the bag** abrir o bico; **to be like a ~ on hot bricks** UK OR **on a hot tin roof** US não estar à vontade; **to put the ~ among the pigeons** UK criar confusão; **to rain ~s and dogs** chover canivetes; **to think one is the ~'s whiskers** UK achar-se muito especial; **there's no room to swing a ~** não há espaço nem para respirar; **to play ~ and mouse** brincar de gato e rato **- 2.** [wild animal] felino *m*, -na *f* **- 3.** (*abbr of* **catalytic converter**) AUT catalisador *m*.

CAT (*abbr of* **computer-assisted testing**) *n* **- 1.** CAT *f*, verificação *f* assistida por computador. **- 2.** (*abbr of* **computer-assisted translation**) tradução *f* assistida por computador. **- 3.** (*abbr of* **computerized axial tomography**) tomografia *f* axial computadorizada.

cataclysmic [ˌkætə'klɪzmɪk] *adj* cataclísmico(ca).

catacombs ['kætəkuːmz] *npl* catacumbas *fpl*.

Catalan ['kætəˌlæn] <> *adj* catalão(lã). <> *n* **- 1.** [person] catalão *m*, -lã *f* **- 2.** [language] catalão *m*.

catalogue UK, **catolog** US ['kætəlɒg] <> *n* **- 1.** [of items for sale] catálogo *m* **- 2.** [in library, museum] catálogo *m* **- 3.** *fig* [list] lista *f*. <> *vt* catalogar.

Catalonia [ˌkætə'ləʊnɪə] *n* Catalunha; **in ~** na Catalunha.

Catalonian [ˌkætə'ləʊnɪən] <> *adj* catalão(lã). <> *n* [person] catalão *m*, -lã *f*.

catalyst ['kætəlɪst] *n* **- 1.** CHEM catalisador *m* **- 2.** *fig* [cause] motivo *m*.

catalytic converter *n* conversor *m* catalítico.

catamaran [ˌkætəmə'ræn] *n* catamarã *f*.

catapult UK ['kætəpʊlt] <> *n* **- 1.** [hand-held] atiradeira *f*, estilingue *m* **- 2.** HIST [machine] catapulta *f*. <> *vt* **- 1.** [hurl] catapultar **- 2.** *fig* [promote] projetar.

cataract ['kætərækt] *n* catarata *f*.

catarrh [kə'tɑːʳ] *n* (U) catarro *m*.

catastrophe [kə'tæstrəfɪ] *n* catástrofe *f*.

catastrophic [ˌkætə'strɒfɪk] *adj* catastrófico(ca).

catatonic *adj* catatônico(ca).

cat burglar *n* UK *gatuno que entra e sai pela janela ou telhado*.

catcall ['kætkɔːl] *n* vaia *f*.

catch [kætʃ] (*pt* & *pp* **caught**) <> *vt* **- 1.** [gen] pegar **- 2.** [ball etc] apanhar **- 3.** [discover, surprise] flagrar; **to ~ sb doing sthg** flagrar alguém fazendo algo; **to ~ sb unawares** pegar alguém desprevenido(da) **- 4.** [hear clearly] compreender **- 5.** [interest, imagination, attention] despertar **- 6.** [sight]: **to ~ sight of sb/sthg, to ~ a glimpse of sb/sthg** conseguir avistar alguém/algo **- 7.** [on hook, in door, in trap] prender **- 8.** [strike] atingir. <> *vi* **- 1.** [become hooked, get stuck] ficar preso(sa) em **- 2.** [start to burn] pegar. <> *n* **- 1.** [of ball etc] pegada *f* **- 2.** [thing or amount caught] pesca *f* **- 3.** [fastener] trinco *m* **- 4.** [snag] armadilha *f*.

➤ **catch at** *vt fus* tentar agarrar.

➤ **catch on** *vi* **- 1.** [become popular] pegar **- 2.** *inf* [understand] entender; **to ~ on to sthg** dar-se conta de algo.

➤ **catch out** *vt sep* [trick] apanhar em erro.

➤ **catch up** <> *vt sep* **- 1.** [come level with] alcançar **- 2.** [involve]: **to get caught up in sthg** ser envolvido(da) em algo. <> *vi* alcançar; **to ~ up on sthg** por algo em dia.

➤ **catch up with** *vt fus* **- 1.** [get to same point as] alcançar **- 2.** [catch, find] pegar.

catch-22 *n* (U): **it's a ~ situation** é um beco sem saída.

catch-all *adj* que engloba tudo.

catching ['kætʃɪŋ] *adj* [infectious] contagioso(sa).

catchment area ['kætʃmənt-] *n* região atendida por uma escola ou um hospital.

catchphrase ['kætʃfreɪz] *n* [of entertainer] bordão *m*.

catchword ['kætʃwɜːd] *n* [slogan] slogan *m*.

catchy ['kætʃɪ] (*compar* **-ier**, *superl* **-iest**) *adj* que pega com facilidade.

catechism ['kætəkɪzml] *n* catecismo *m*.

categorical [ˌkætɪ'gɒrɪkl] *adj* categórico(ca).

categorically [ˌkætɪ'gɒrɪklɪ] *adv* categoricamente.

categorize, -ise ['kætəgəraɪz] *vt* [classify]: **to ~ sb (as sthg)** classificar alguém (como algo).

category ['kætəgərɪ] (*pl* **-ies**) *n* categoria *f*.

cater ['keɪtəʳ] *vi* [provide food] fornecer comida.

➤ **cater for** *vt fus* UK **- 1.** [provide for] satisfazer; **the magazine ~ s for independent working women** a revista se destina a mulheres autônomas **- 2.** [anticipate] contar com.

➤ **cater to** *vt fus* servir de instrumento a.

caterer ['keɪtərəʳ] *n* [serviço *m* de] bufê *m*.

catering ['keɪtərɪŋ] *n* bufê *m*; **a ~ college** uma escola de culinária.

caterpillar ['kætəpɪləʳ] *n* [insect] lagarta *f*.

catfish (*pl inv* OR **-es**) *n* peixe-gato *m*.

cat flap *n* UK portinhola *f* para gatos.

catgut *n* (U) categute *m*.

catharsis [kə'θɑːsɪs] (*pl* **catharses** [kə'θɑːsiːz]) *n* *fml* [relief of tension] catarse *f*.

cathedral [kə'θiːdrəl] *n* catedral *f*.

catheter ['kæθɪtəʳ] *n* catéter *m*.

cathode ray tube ['kæθəʊd-] *n* tubo *m* de raios catódicos.

Catholic ['kæθlɪk] <> *adj* católico(ca). <> *n* católico *m*, -ca *f*.

➤ **catholic** *adj* [broad] eclético(ca).

Catholicism [kə'θɒlɪsɪzm] *n* (U) catolicismo *m*.

catkin ['kætkɪn] *n* amento *m*.

cat litter *n* granulado *m* higiênico (para gatos).

Catseyes® ['kætsaɪz] *npl* UK olhos-de-gato *mpl*.

catsuit ['kætsuːt] *n* UK colante *m* feminino (de corpo inteiro).

catsup ['kætsəp] *n* US ketchup *m*.

cattle ['kætl] *npl* gado *m*.

cattle grid *n* UK mata-burro *m*.

catty ['kætɪ] (*compar* **-ier**, *superl* **-iest**) *adj inf pej* [spiteful] rancoroso(sa).

catwalk ['kætwɔːk] *n* passarela *f*.

Caucasian [kɔː'keɪʒən] <> *adj* caucásio(sia). <> *n* **- 1.** GEOGR caucásio *m*, -sia *f* **- 2.** [white person] pessoa *f* de raça branca.

Caucasus ['kɔːkəsəs] *n*: the ~ o Cáucaso.
caucus ['kɔːkəs] *n POL* **-1.** *US* [meeting] cáucus *m* **-2.** [interest group] ala *f.*
caught [kɔːt] *pt* & *pp* ▷ catch.
cauldron *n* caldeirão *m.*
cauliflower ['kɒlɪˌflaʊəʳ] *n* couve-flor *f.*
causal ['kɔːzl] *adj* causal.
cause [kɔːz] ◇ *n* **-1.** [gen] causa *f* **-2.** [grounds] razão *f*; **to have** ~ **for sthg** ter razão para algo; **to have** ~ **to do sthg** ter razão para fazer algo ◇ *vt* causar; **to** ~ **sb to do sthg** fazer com que alguém faça algo; **to** ~ **sthg to be done** fazer com que algo seja feito.
causeway ['kɔːzweɪ] *n* caminho *m* elevado *(sobre a água).*
caustic ['kɔːstɪk] *adj* **-1.** *CHEM* cáustico(ca) **-2.** *fig* [comment] mordaz.
caustic soda *n* soda *f* cáustica.
cauterize, -ise ['kɔːtəraɪz] *vt* cauterizar.
caution ['kɔːʃn] ◇ *n* **-1.** (U) [care] cuidado *m*; **to do sthg with** ~ fazer algo com cautela **-2.** [warning] aviso *m* **-3.** *UK JUR* injunção *f.* ◇ *vt* **-1.** [warn]: **to** ~ **sb against doing sthg** prevenir alguém para não fazer algo **-2.** *UK JUR* advertir; **to** ~ **sb for sthg** advertir alguém por algo.
cautionary ['kɔːʃənərɪ] *adj* preventivo(va).
cautious ['kɔːʃəs] *adj* cauteloso(sa).
cautiously ['kɔːʃəslɪ] *adv* com cautela.
cautiousness ['kɔːʃəsnɪs] *n* (U) cautela *f.*
cavalier [ˌkævəˈlɪəʳ] *adj* [offhand] arrogante.
cavalry ['kævlrɪ] *n* (U) **-1.** [on horseback] cavalaria *f* **-2.** [in armoured vehicles] cavalaria *f.*
cave [keɪv] *n* gruta *f*, caverna *f.*
 ➡ **cave in** *vi* **-1.** [physically collapse] desabar **-2.** [yield, stop arguing]: **to** ~ **in (to sthg)** ceder (a algo).
caveman ['keɪvmæn] *(pl* **-men** [-menl) *n* troglodita *mf.*
cavern ['kævən] *n* caverna *f.*
cavernous ['kævənəs] *adj* imenso(sa).
caviar(e) ['kævɪɑːʳ] *n* (U) caviar *m.*
caving ['keɪvɪŋ] *n* (U) *UK* espeleologia *f*; **to go** ~ ir explorar cavernas.
cavity ['kævətɪ] *(pl* **-ies)** *n* **-1.** [in object, structure, body] cavidade *f*; **buccal** ~ cavidade bucal; **nasal** ~ fossas *fpl* nasais **-2.** [in tooth] cárie *f.*
cavort [kəˈvɔːt] *vi* saracotear.
cayenne (pepper) [keɪˈen-] *n* (U) pimenta-de--caiena *f.*
CB *n* **-1.** (*abbr of* Citizens' Band) CB, faixa *f* do cidadão. **- 2.** (*abbr of* Companion of (the Order of) the Bath) *(titular de) distinção britânica de honra.*
CBC (*abbr of* Canadian Broadcasting Corporation) *n rede canadense de rádio e televisão.*
CBE (*abbr of* Companion of (the Order of) the British Empire) *n (beneficiário de) distinção britânica de honra.*
CBI (*abbr of* Confederation of British Industry) *n confederação britânica de empresários,* ≃ CNI *f.*
CBS (*abbr of* Columbia Broadcasting System) *n rede norte-americana de rádio e televisão,* CBS *f.*
cc ◇ *n* (*abbr of* cubic centimetre) *cm.* ◇ (*abbr of* carbon copy) cópia *f* carbono.

CC (*abbr of* County Council) *n* **-1.** *autoridade de estados administrativos britânicos.* **- 2.** (*abbr of* City Council) *corpo administrativo de cidade britânica.*
CCTV (*abbr of* closed-circuit television) *n* CFT *m.*
CD ◇ *n* (*abbr of* compact disc) CD *m.* ◇ (*abbr of* Corps Diplomatique) corpo *m* diplomático.
CD-I (*abbr of* compact disc (interactive)) *n* CD-I *m.*
CD player *n* tocador *m* de CD.
Cdr. (*abbr of* commander) *n* com.
CD-R (*abbr of* compact disc (rewritable)) *n* CD-R *m.*
CD-R drive *n* unidade *f* de CD-R.
CD rewriter ['siːdiːˈriːˌraɪtə] = **CD-RW drive.**
CD-ROM (*abbr of* compact disc read-only memory) *n* CD-ROM *m.*
CD-RW (*abbr of* compact disc rewritable) *n* CD-RW *m.*
CD-RW drive *n* gravador *m* de CD.
CDT (*abbr of* Central Daylight Time) ◇ *n horário de verão na região central dos Estados Unidos.* ◇ (*abbr of* craft, design and technology) *disciplina de artes, desenho e tecnologia ensinada em escolas britânicas.*
CD tower *n* torre *f* para CDs.
CDV (*abbr of* compact disc video) *n* CDV *m.*
CE (*abbr of* Church of England) igreja anglicana.
cease [siːs] *fml* ◇ *vt* cessar; **to** ~ **doing** *OR* **to do sthg** parar de fazer algo; ~ **fire!** cessar fogo! ◇ *vi* parar.
ceasefire *n* cessar-fogo *m.*
ceaseless ['siːslɪs] *adj fml* incessante.
ceaselessly ['siːslɪslɪ] *adv fml* incessantemente.
cedar *n* cedro *m.*
cede [siːd] *vt* [yield] ceder; **to** ~ **sthg to sb** ceder algo a alguém.
cedilla *n* cedilha *f.*
CEEB (*abbr of* College Entry Examination Board) *n organismo responsável pelo acesso ao ensino superior nos Estados Unidos.*
Ceefax® ['siːfæks] *n UK serviço de teletexto da BBC.*
ceilidh ['keɪlɪ] *n festa realizada na Escócia e na Irlanda na qual as pessoas cantam e dançam músicas regionais e contam histórias.*
ceiling ['siːlɪŋ] *n* **-1.** [of room] teto *m* **-2.** *fig* [limit] teto *m* máximo.
celebrate ['selɪbreɪt] ◇ *vt* celebrar. ◇ *vi* comemorar.
celebrated ['selɪbreɪtɪd] *adj* célebre, famoso(sa).
celebration [ˌselɪˈbreɪʃn] *n* **-1.** (U) [activity, feeling] celebração *f* **-2.** [event] comemoração *f.*
celebrity [sɪˈlebrətɪ] *(pl* **-ies)** *n* [star] celebridade *f.*
celeriac [sɪˈlerɪæk] *n* aipo-rábano *m.*
celery ['selərɪ] *n* (U) aipo *m.*
celestial [sɪˈlestjəl] *adj* celestial.
celibacy ['selɪbəsɪ] *n* (U) celibato *m.*
celibate ['selɪbət] *adj* celibatário(ria).
cell [sel] *n* **-1.** *BIOL* & *COMPUT* célula *f* **-2.** [small room] cela *f* **-3.** [secret group] unidade *f.*
cellar ['selə] *n* **-1.** [basement] porão *m* **-2.** [stock of wine] adega *f.*
cellist ['tʃelɪst] *n* violoncelista *mf.*
cello ['tʃeləʊ] *(pl* **-s)** *n* [instrument] violoncelo *m.*

Cellophane® ['seləfeɪn] *n (U)* celofane *m.*

cellphone ['selfəʊn], **cellular phone** ['seljʊləʳ-] *n* (telefone *m*) celular *m.*

cellulite ['seljʊlaɪt] *n* celulite *f.*

celluloid *n (U)* [plastic] celulóide *m.*

cellulose ['seljʊləʊs] *n (U)* celulose *f.*

Celsius ['selsɪəs] *adj* Célsius.

Celt [kelt] *n* celta *mf.*

Celtic ['keltɪk] <> *adj* celta. <> *n* [language] celta *m.*

cement [sɪ'ment] <> *n (U)* **- 1.** [for concrete] cimento *m*, argamassa *f* **- 2.** [glue] cola *f.* <> *vt* **- 1.** [cover with cement] cimentar **- 2.** [glue] colar **- 3.** *fig* [reinforce] fortalecer.

cement mixer *n* betoneira *f.*

cemetery ['semɪtrɪ] *(pl* **-ies)** *n* cemitério *m.*

cenotaph ['senəta:f] *n* cenotáfio *m.*

censor ['sensəʳ] <> *n* [of films, books, letters] censor *m*, -ra *f.* <> *vt* [film, book, letter] censurar.

censorship ['sensəʃɪp] *n (U)* censura *f.*

censure ['senʃəʳ] <> *n (U)* repreensão *f.* <> *vt* repreender.

census ['sensəs] *(pl* **censuses)** *n* [population survey] censo *m.*

cent [sent] *n* centavo *m.*

centenary UK [sen'ti:nərɪ] *(pl* **-ies)**, **centennial** US [sen'tenjəl] *n* centenário *m.*

center *n, adj & vt* US = **centre.**

centigrade ['sentɪɡreɪd] *adj* centígrado(da).

centigram(me) ['sentɪɡræm] *n* centigrama *m.*

centilitre UK, **centiliter** US ['sentɪ li:təʳ] *n* centilitro *m.*

centimetre UK, **centimeter** US ['sentɪ mi:təʳ] *n* centímetro *m.*

centipede ['sentɪpi:d] *n* centopéia *f.*

central ['sentrəl] *adj* central; ~ **to sthg** [crucial] essencial para algo.

Central African <> *adj* centro-africano(na). <> *n* centro-africano *m*, -na *f.*

Central African Republic *n*: **the** ~ a República Centro-Africana; **in the** ~ na República Centro-Africana.

Central America *n* América Central.

Central American <> *adj* centro-americano(na). <> *n* centro-americano *m*, -na *f.*

Central Asia *n* Ásia Central.

Central Europe *n* Europa Central.

central government *n (U)* governo *m* central.

central heating *n (U)* aquecimento *m* central.

centralization [sentrəlaɪ'zeɪʃn] *n (U)* centralização *f.*

centralize, -ise ['sentrəlaɪz] *vt* centralizar.

centralized ['sentrəlaɪzd] *adj* centralizado(da).

central locking [-'lɒkɪŋ] *n* travamento *f* central (das portas).

centrally ['sentrəlɪ] *adv* no centro.

centrally heated *adj* com aquecimento central.

central nervous system *n* sistema *f* nervoso central.

central processing unit *n* COMPUT unidade *f* central de processamento.

central reservation *n* UK canteiro *m* central.

centre UK, **center** US ['sentəʳ] <> *n* **- 1.** [gen] centro *m*; **health/leisure** ~ centro de saúde/lazer; ~ **of attention** centro das atenções; ~ **of gravity** centro de gravidade; **the** ~ POL o centro **- 2.** SPORT [player] pivô. <> *adj* **- 1.** [middle] central, do meio **- 2.** POL de centro. <> *vt* [place centrally] centralizar.

➤ **centre around, centre on** *vt fus* centrar em.

centre back *n* SPORT centromédio *m.*

centrefold *n* página *f* central.

centre forward *n* SPORT centroavante *m.*

centre half *n* = **centre back.**

centrepiece UK, **centerpiece** US ['sentəpi:s] *n* **- 1.** [decoration] centro *m* de mesa **- 2.** [principal element] peça-chave *f.*

centre spread *n* = **centrefold.**

centrifugal force [sentrɪ'fju:gl-] *n* força *f* centrífuga.

century ['sentʃʊrɪ] *(pl* **-ies)** *n* **- 1.** [one hundred years] século *m* **- 2.** CRICKET: **to score a** ~ marcar cem pontos.

CEO *(abbr of* **chief executive officer)** *n* executivo *m*, -va *f* -chefe.

ceramic [sɪ'ræmɪk] *adj* de cerâmica, cerâmico(ca).

➤ **ceramics** *n* [craft, objects] cerâmica *f.*

cereal ['sɪərɪəl] *n* [crop, breakfast food] cereal *m.*

cerebral ['serɪbrəl] *adj* cerebral.

cerebral palsy *n (U)* MED paralisia *f* cerebral.

ceremonial [serɪ'məʊnjəl] <> *adj* cerimonial, de cerimônia. <> *n* **- 1.** [event] cerimônia *f* OR *m* **- 2.** [pomp, formality] cerimonial *m.*

ceremonious [serɪ'məʊnjəs] *adj* cerimonioso(sa).

ceremony ['serɪmənɪ] *(pl* **-ies)** *n* **- 1.** [event] cerimônia *f;* **degree** ~ cerimônia *f* de colação de grau **- 2.** *(U)* [pomp, formality] formalidade *f;* **without** ~ sem cerimônia; **to stand on** ~ fazer cerimônia.

cert. [sɜ:t] *n* UK *inf* [certainty] barbada *f.*

cert. *(abbr of* **certificate)** certificado *m.*

certain ['sɜ:tn] *adj* **- 1.** [gen] certo(ta); **she is** ~ **to be late** ela certamente vai se atrasar; **to be** ~ **of sthg/of doing sthg** ter a certeza de algo/fazer algo; **to make** ~ **of sthg/of doing sthg** assegurar-se de algo/fazer algo; **for** ~ com certeza; **to a** ~ **extent** até certo ponto **- 2.** [named person]: **a** ~ ... um certo ... (uma certa ...).

certainly ['sɜ:tnlɪ] *adv* com certeza; **do you agree? - I** ~ **do** com certeza (que sim); ~ **not!** de modo algum.

certainty ['sɜ:tntɪ] *(pl* **-ies)** *n (U)* certeza *f.*

CertEd *(abbr of* **Certificate in Education)** *n diploma universitário em educação.*

certifiable [sɜ:tɪ'faɪəbl] *adj* [insane] demente.

certificate [sə'tɪfɪkət] *n* **- 1.** [gen] certificado *m* **- 2.** [of birth, marriage] certidão *f;* **death** ~ atestado *m* de óbito.

certification [sɜ:tɪfɪ'keɪʃn] *n* certificação *f.*

certified ['sɜ:tɪfaɪd] *adj* **- 1.** [professional person] habilitado(da) **- 2.** [document] autenticado(da).

certified mail *n* US postagem *f* registrada.

certified public accountant *n* US perito-contador *m*, -ra *f.*

certify ['sɜ:tɪfaɪ] *(pt & pp* **-ied)** *vt* **- 1.** [declare true]: **to** ~ **that** certificar OR atestar que **- 2.** [give certificate of qualification to]: **to be certified as** receber certificado de -**3.** [declare insane]: **to be certified** ser declarado(da) incapacitado(da).

cervical [sə'vaɪkl] *adj* cervical; ~ **cancer** câncer *m* de colo de útero.

cervical smear *n* exame *f* de lâmina.

cervix ['sɜːvɪks] (*pl* -**ices** [-ɪsiːz]) *n* colo *m* do útero.

cesarean (section) *n US* = **caesarean (section)**.

cessation [se'seɪʃn] *n fml* [stopping] suspensão *f.*

cesspit ['sespɪt], **cesspool** ['sespuːl] *n* fossa *f.*

CET (*abbr of* **Central European Time**) *n* horário da Europa Central.

cf. (*abbr of* **confer**) cf., cfr.

CFC (*abbr of* **chlorofluorocarbon**) *n* CFC *m.*

cg (*abbr of* **centigram**) cg.

CGT (*abbr of* **capital gains tax**) *n imposto sobre ganhos de capital.*

ch (*abbr of* **central heating**) aquecimento *m* central.

ch. (*abbr of* **chapter**) cap.

CH (*abbr of* **Companion of Honour**) *n (beneficiário de) distinção de honra britânica.*

Chad [tʃæd] *n* Chade.

chafe [tʃeɪf] <> *vt* [rub] roçar. <> *vi* -**1.** [be sore] esfolar -**2.** *fig* [be annoyed]: **to** ~ **at** sthg irritar--se com algo.

chaff [tʃɑːf] *n* [husks] palhiço *m.*

chaffinch ['tʃæfɪntʃ] *n* tentilhão *m.*

chain [tʃeɪn] <> *n* -**1.** [metal] corrente *f*; ~ **of office** *condecoração usada por oficiais em cerimônias* -**2.** [of islands] série *f*; ~ **of events** rede *f* de acontecimentos -**3.** [of mountains] cadeia *f* -**4.** [of shops, hotels] cadeia *f*, rede *f.* <> *vt* -**1.** [prisoner, bicycle] acorrentar -**2.** [hands] algemar -**3.** [dog] amarrar.

chain letter *n* carta *f* de corrente.

chain reaction *n* reação *f* em cadeia.

chainsaw *n* serra *f* articulada.

chain-smoke *vi* fumar um cigarro atrás do outro.

chain-smoker *n* fumante *mf* inveterado, -da.

chain store *n* filial *f.*

chair [tʃeəʳ] <> *n* -**1.** [for sitting in] cadeira *f* -**2.** [university post] cátedra *f* -**3.** [of meeting, organization - position] presidência *f*; **to take the** ~ presidir; [-person] presidente *mf.* <> *vt* [meeting, discussion] presidir.

chairlift *n* teleférico *m.*

chairman ['tʃeəmən] (*pl* -**men** [-mən]) *n* presidente *m.*

chairmanship ['tʃeəmənʃɪp] *n* presidência *f.*

chairperson ['tʃeə,pɜːsn] (*pl* -**s**) *n* presidente *mf.*

chairwoman ['tʃeə,wʊmən] (*pl* -**women** [,wɪmɪn]) *n* presidenta *f.*

chaise longue [ʃeɪz'lɒŋ] (*pl* **chaises longues** [ʃeɪz'lɒŋ]) *n* espreguiçadeira *f.*

chalet ['ʃæleɪ] *n* chalé *f.*

chalice ['tʃælɪs] *n* cálice *m.*

chalk [tʃɔːk] *n* -**1.** *(U)* [mineral] greda *f* -**2.** [for drawing] giz *m.*

➡ **by a long chalk** *adv* de longe.

➡ **not by a long chalk** *adv* nem de longe.

➡ **chalk up** *vt sep* [attain] obter.

chalkboard ['tʃɔːkbɔːd] *n UK* quadro-negro *m.*

challenge ['tʃælɪndʒ] <> *n* desafio *m.* <> *vt* -**1.** [to fight, competition]: **to** ~ **sb (to** sthg**)** desafiar alguém (para algo); **to** ~ **sb to do** sthg desafiar alguém a fazer algo -**2.** [question] questionar.

challenger ['tʃælɪndʒəʳ] *n* competidor *m*, -ra *f.*

challenging ['tʃælɪndʒɪŋ] *adj* -**1.** [difficult] desafiador(ra) -**2.** [aggressive] provocador(ra).

chamber ['tʃeɪmbəʳ] *n* -**1.** [room] gabinete *m*; **the council** ~ o gabinete do conselho -**2.** [body] câmara *f* -**3.** [of gun] tambor *m.*

➡ **chambers** *npl* [of barrister] sala *f* de audiências.

chambermaid ['tʃeɪmbəmeɪd] *n* camareira *f.*

chamber music *n (U)* música *f* de câmara.

chamber of commerce *n* câmara *f* de comércio.

chamber orchestra *n* orquestra *f* de câmara.

chameleon [kə'miːljən] *n* [animal] camaleão *m*, -oa *f.*

chamois¹ ['ʃæmɪ] (*pl inv*) *n* [animal] cabra *f* montês.

chamois² ['ʃæmɪ] *n*: ~ **(leather)** camurça *f.*

champ [tʃæmp] <> *n inf* [champion] campeão *m*, -ã *f.* <> *vi* [horse] mascar.

champagne [,ʃæm'peɪn] *n (U)* champanha *m.*

champion ['tʃæmpjən] *n* -**1.** [of competition] campeão *f*, -ã -**2.** [of cause] defensor *m*, -ra *f.*

championship ['tʃæmpjənʃɪp] *n* campeonato *m.*

chance [tʃɑːns] <> *n* -**1.** *(U)* [luck] acaso *m*, sorte *f*; **by** ~ por acaso; **by any** ~ por acaso -**2.** [likelihood, opportunity] chance *f*; **not to stand a** ~ **(of doing** sthg**)** não ter a menor chance (de fazer algo); **on the off-**~ **(that)** na esperança de que -**3.** [risk] risco *m*; **to take a** ~ **(on** sthg/**on doing** sthg**)** arriscar-se (em algo/a fazer algo). <> *adj* acidental. <> *vt* -**1.** [risk] arriscar -**2.** [happen]: **to** ~ **to do** sthg acontecer algo por acaso.

chancellor ['tʃɑːnsələʳ] *n* -**1.** [chief minister] chanceler *m* -**2.** *UNIV* reitor *m*, -ra *f.*

Chancellor of the Exchequer *n UK* ≃ Ministro *m*, -tra *f* da Fazenda.

chancy ['tʃɑːnsɪ] (*compar* -**ier**, *superl* -**iest**) *adj inf* [risky] arriscado(da).

chandelier [,ʃændə'lɪəʳ] *n* lustre *m.*

change [tʃeɪndʒ] <> *n* -**1.** [alteration, difference] mudança *f*, alteração *f*; ~ **in** sb/sthg mudança em alguém/algo -**2.** [contrast, for variety] diferença *f*; **to make a** ~ fazer diferença; **Peter arriving on time? That makes a** ~ **!** Peter chegando na hora? Que mudança!; **for a** ~ para variar -**3.** [switch, replacement] mudança *f*; ~ **of clothes** muda *f* de roupa -**4.** *(U)* [money returned after payment, smaller units of money] troco *m* -**5.** *(U)* [coins] trocado *m.* <> *vt* -**1.** [gen] mudar; **to** ~ sthg **into** sthg transformar algo em algo; **to** ~ **one's mind** mudar de idéia; **to get** ~**d** mudar de roupa; **to** ~ **hands** *COMM* mudar de dono -**2.** [replace, exchange] trocar. <> *vi* -**1.** [gen] mudar; **to** ~ **into** sthg transformar-se em algo -**2.** [put on different clothes] trocar-se; **to** ~ **into** sthg trocar algo -**3.** [move to different train, bus] fazer conexão.

➡ **change over** *vi* [convert] trocar para; **to** ~ **over to** sthg trocar para algo.

➡ **change round** *vt sep* trocar.

changeable ['tʃeɪndʒəbl] *adj* -**1.** [mood] inconstante -**2.** [weather] instável.

changed [tʃeɪndʒd] *adj* [person] mudado(da); **to be a ~ person** ser uma outra pessoa.

change machine *n* máquina *f* de troco.

change of life *n*: **the ~ a** menopausa.

changeover ['tʃeɪndʒ,əʊvə'] *n*: **~ (to sthg)** mudança *f* (para algo).

change purse *n US* porta-níqueis *m inv*, niqueleira *f*.

changing ['tʃeɪndʒɪŋ] *adj* variável, instável.

changing room *n* vestiário *m*.

channel ['tʃænl] (*UK pt* & *pp* -**led**, *cont* -**ling**, *US pt* & *pp* -**ed**, *cont* -**ing**) <> *n* canal *m*. <> *vt* canalizar.
➡ **Channel** *n*: **the (English) Channel** o Canal da Mancha.
➡ **channels** *npl*: **to go through the proper ~ s** seguir os trâmites legais.

channel-hopping *n TV* troca *f* rápida de canal, zapping *m*.

Channel Islands *npl*: **the ~ as** Ilhas Normandas.

Channel Tunnel *n*: **the ~ o** Túnel do Canal da Mancha.

chant [tʃɑːnt] <> *n* -**1.** RELIG [song] canto *m* -**2.** [repeated words] coro *m*. <> *vt* -**1.** RELIG cantar, entoar -**2.** [words] entoar. <> *vi* -**1.** RELIG [sing] cantar -**2.** [repeat words] entoar.

chaos ['keɪɒs] *n* caos *m*.

chaotic [keɪˈɒtɪk] *adj* caótico(ca).

chap [tʃæp] *n UK inf* [man] cara *m*, chapa *m*.

chapat(t)i [tʃəˈpætɪ] *n* pão indiano feito de farinha, água e sal, de formato arrendondado.

chapel ['tʃæpl] *n* capela *f*.

chaperon(e) ['ʃæpərəʊn] <> *n* acompanhante *mf*. <> *vt* acompanhar.

chaplain ['tʃæplɪn] *n* capelão *m*.

chapped [tʃæpt] *adj* rachado(da).

chapter ['tʃæptə'] *n* -**1.** capítulo *m* -**2.** *phr*: **to give sb ~ and verse on sthg** falar tudo a alguém sobre algo.

char [tʃɑː'] (*pt* & *pp* -**red**, *cont* -**ring**) <> *vt* [burn] carbonizar, torrar. <> *vi* [work as cleaner] trabalhar como diarista.

character ['kærəktə'] *n* -**1.** [nature - of place] jeito *m*; [- of person] caráter *m*; **out of ~** atípico; **in ~** típico -**2.** (*U*) [unusual quality, style] estilo *m* -**3.** [in film, book, play] personagem *mf* -**4.** *inf* [unusual person] tipo *m* -**5.** [letter, symbol] caractere *m*.

character code *n COMPUT* código *m* de caracteres.

characteristic [,kærəktəˈrɪstɪk] <> *adj* [typical] característico(ca). <> *n* [attribute] característica *f*.

characteristically [,kærəktəˈrɪstɪklɪ] *adv* [typically] caracteristicamente.

characterization [,kærəktəraɪˈzeɪʃn] *n* caracterização *f*.

characterize, -ise ['kærəktəraɪz] *vt* -**1.** [typify] caracterizar -**2.** [portray]: **to ~ sthg as** caracterizar algo como.

charade [ʃəˈrɑːd] *n* charada *f*.
➡ **charades** *n* (*U*) mímica *f*.

charcoal ['tʃɑːkəʊl] *n* carvão *m* (vegetal).

charge [tʃɑːdʒ] <> *n* -**1.** [cost] preço *m*; **admission**

~ entrada *f*; **telephone ~ s** tarifas *fpl* telefônicas; **delivery ~ taxa** *f* de entrega; **free of ~ grátis** -**2.** [command, control] responsabilidade *f*; **to have ~ of sthg** estar no comando de algo; **to take ~ (of sthg)** tomar conta (de algo); **in ~ encarregado(da)**; **in ~ of** no comando de -**3.** JUR acusação *f* -**4.** ELEC & MIL carga *f*. <> *vt* -**1.** [sum of money] cobrar; **to ~ sthg to sb/sthg** debitar algo de alguém/algo -**2.** [suspect, criminal] acusar; **to ~ sb with sthg** acusar alguém de algo -**3.** [attack] investir contra -**4.** ELEC carregar. <> *vi* -**1.** [ask for payment]: **to ~ (for sthg)** cobrar (por algo) -**2.** [rush] correr -**3.** [attack] investir.

chargeable ['tʃɑːdʒəbl] *adj* -**1.** [costs]: **~ (to sb/sthg)** debitável (de alguém/algo) -**2.** [offence] imputável.

charge account *n* conta *f* aberta.

charge card *n* cartão *m* de crédito de um estabelecimento comercial.

charged [tʃɑːdʒd] *adj* [tense] carregado(da).

chargé d'affaires [,ʃɑːzeɪdæˈfeə] (*pl* chargés d'affaires [,ʃɑːzeɪdæˈfeə]) *n* encarregado *m*, -da *f* de negócios.

charge hand *n UK* capataz *m*.

charge nurse *n UK* enfermeiro *m*, -ra *f* -chefe.

charger ['tʃɑːdʒə'] *n* -**1.** [for batteries] carregador *m* -**2.** *literary* [soldier's horse] cavalo *m* de batalha.

charge sheet *n UK* boletim *m* de ocorrência.

chariot ['tʃærɪət] *n* biga *f*.

charisma [kəˈrɪzmə] *n* carisma *m*.

charismatic [,kærɪzˈmætɪk] *adj* [charming] carismático(ca).

charitable ['tʃærətəbl] *adj* -**1.** [person, remark] generoso(sa) -**2.** [organization] de caridade, beneficente.

charity ['tʃærətɪ] (*pl* -**ies**) *n* -**1.** (*U*) [gifts, money] caridade *f* -**2.** [organization] instituição *f* de caridade -**3.** [kindness] simpatia *f*.

charity shop *n* loja *f* beneficente.

charlatan ['ʃɑːlətən] *n* charlatão *m*, -tona *f*.

charm [tʃɑːm] <> *n* -**1.** (*U*) [appeal, attractiveness] charme *m*, encanto *m* -**2.** [spell] feitiço *m* -**3.** [on bracelet] amuleto *m*. <> *vt* encantar.

charm bracelet *n* pulseira *f* com berloques.

charmer ['tʃɑːmə'] *n* [charming person] sedutor *m*, -ra *f*.

charming ['tʃɑːmɪŋ] *adj* encantador(ra).

charmingly ['tʃɑːmɪŋlɪ] *adv* encantadoramente.

charred [tʃɑːd] *adj* carbonizado(da).

chart [tʃɑːt] <> *n* -**1.** [diagram] gráfico *m* -**2.** [map] mapa *m*, carta *f*; **a star/sea ~ uma** carta celeste/marítima. <> *vt* -**1.** [plot, map] cartografar -**2.** *fig* [record] registrar.
➡ **charts** *npl*: **the ~ s as** paradas de sucesso.

charter ['tʃɑːtə'] <> *n* [document] carta *f*. <> *vt* [plane, boat] fretar.

chartered accountant ['tʃɑːtəd-] *n UK* contador *m* diplomado, contadora *f* diplomada.

charter flight *n* vôo *m* fretado.

charter plane *n* avião *m* fretado.

chary ['tʃeərɪ] (*compar* -**ier**, *superl* -**iest**) *adj*: **to be ~ of doing sthg** ser cuidadoso(sa) ao fazer algo.

chase [tʃeɪs] <> *n* -**1.** [pursuit] perseguição *f*; **to give ~ dar** perseguição -**2.** [hunt] caça *f*. <> *vt*

-1. [pursue] perseguir **-2.** [drive away] enxotar **-3.** [money, jobs] correr atrás de. ◇ *vi*: **to ~ after sb/sthg** correr atrás de alguém/algo.

➡ **chase up** *vt sep UK* [person, information] correr *OR* sair atrás de.

chaser ['tʃeɪsəʳ] *n* [drink] *bebida suave tomada após uma bebida alcoólica mais forte ou mais fraca.*

chasm ['kæzml *n* abismo *m.*

chassis ['ʃæsɪ] (*pl inv*) *n* [of vehicle] chassi *m.*

chaste [tʃeɪst] *adj* casto(ta).

chasten ['tʃeɪsnl *vt* disciplinar.

chastise [tʃæ'staɪz] *vt fml* [scold] repreender.

chastity ['tʃæstətɪl *n* castidade *f.*

chat [tʃætl (*pt & pp* **-ted**, *cont* **-ting**) ◇ *n* bate-papo *m*, conversa *f*; **to have a ~** bater papo. ◇ *vi* bater papo, conversar.

➡ **chat up** *vt sep UK inf* bater papo.

chatiquette ['tʃætɪketl *n COMPUT* etiqueta *f* no bate-papo, chatiqueta *f.*

chat room *n COMPUT* sala *f* de bate-papo.

chat show *n UK* programa *m* de entrevistas.

chatter ['tʃætəʳ] ◇ *n* **-1.** [of person] tagarelice *f* **-2.** [of animal, bird] chilro *m.* ◇ *vi* **-1.** [person] tagarelar **-2.** [animal, bird] chilrar **-3.** [teeth] bater.

chatterbox ['tʃætəbɒksl *n inf* tagarela *mf.*

chattering classes *npl UK*: **the ~** os pseudo-formadores de opinião.

chatty ['tʃætɪl (*compar* **-ier**, *superl* **-iest**) *adj* **-1.** [person] tagarela **-2.** [letter] informal.

chauffeur ['ʃəʊfəʳ] ◇ *n* chofer *m.* ◇ *vt* trabalhar como chofer.

chauvinist ['ʃəʊvɪnɪst] *n* chauvinista *mf.*

chauvinistic ['ʃəʊvɪnɪstɪk] *adj* chauvinista.

cheap [tʃiːp] ◇ *adj* **-1.** [gen] barato(ta) **-2.** [despicable, vulgar] de mau gosto. ◇ *adv* barato. ◇ *n*: **on the ~** por uma ninharia.

cheapen ['tʃiːpnl *vt* [degrade] rebaixar; **to ~ o.s.** rebaixar-se.

cheaply ['tʃiːplɪl *adv* [at a low price] barato.

cheapness ['tʃiːpnɪsl *n* **-1.** [low cost] baixo preço *m* **-2.** [vulgarity] mau gosto *m.*

cheapskate ['tʃiːpskeɪtl *n inf pej* pão-duro *m.*

cheat [tʃiːtl ◇ *n* trapaceiro *m*, -ra *f.* ◇ *vt* trapacear; **to ~ sb out of sthg** passar alguém para trás em algo; **to feel ~ed** sentir-se passado(da) para trás. ◇ *vi* [be dishonest] trapacear.

➡ **cheat on** *vt fus inf* [be unfaithful to] trair.

cheating ['tʃiːtɪŋl *n* **-1.** [at cards] blefe *m* **-2.** [in exam] cola *f.*

check [tʃekl ◇ *n* **-1.** [gen]: **~ (on sthg)** checagem *f* (de algo) **-2.** [restraint]: **~ (on sthg)** controle *m* (sobre algo); **in ~** sob controle **-3.** *US* [bill] conta *f* **-4.** [pattern] xadrez *m* **-5.** [in chess] xeque *m.* ◇ *vt* **-1.** [test, verify] verificar, conferir **-2.** [restrain, stop] conter. ◇ *vi* verificar; **to ~ for sthg** verificar se há algo, procurar por algo; **to ~ on sthg** examinar algo.

➡ **check in** ◇ *vt sep* [luggage, coat] despachar. ◇ *vi* **-1.** [at hotel] registrar-se **-2.** [at airport] fazer check-in.

➡ **check off** *vt sep* [names on a list] marcar.

➡ **check out** ◇ *vt sep* **-1.** [luggage, coat] dar

baixa em **-2.** [investigate] averiguar. ◇ *vi* [from hotel] fechar a conta e sair.

➡ **check up** *vi* informar-se; **to ~ up on sb/sthg** informar-se sobre alguém/algo.

checkbook *n US* = chequebook.

checked [tʃektl *adj* [patterned] quadriculado(da).

checkered *adj US* = chequered.

checkers ['tʃekəzl *n US* (jogo *m* de) damas *fpl.*

check guarantee card *n US* cartão *m* de garantia de cheque.

check-in *n* check-in *m.*

checking account ['tʃekɪŋ-] *n US* conta *f* corrente.

checklist ['tʃeklɪstl *n* lista *f* de verificação.

checkmate ['tʃekmeɪtl *n* [in chess] xeque-mate *m.*

checkout ['tʃekaʊtl *n* **-1.** [in supermarket] caixa *m* **-2.** [in hotel] saída *f*, checkout *m.*

checkpoint ['tʃekpɔɪntl *n* [place] posto *m* de controle.

check-up *n* check-up *m.*

Cheddar (cheese) ['tʃedəʳ-] *n* queijo *m* Cheddar.

cheek [tʃiːk] ◇ *n* **-1.** [of face] bochecha *f* **-2.** [buttock] nádega *f* **-3.** *inf* [impudence] audácia *f.* ◇ *vt inf* atrever-se a.

cheekbone ['tʃiːkbəʊnl *n* osso *m* malar, maçã *f* do rosto.

cheekily ['tʃiːkɪlɪl *adv* descaradamente.

cheekiness ['tʃiːkɪnɪsl *n* descaramento *m.*

cheeky ['tʃiːkɪl (*compar* **-ier**, *superl* **-iest**) *adj* descarado(da).

cheep *vi* piar.

cheer [tʃɪəʳ] ◇ *n* [shout] vivas *fpl.* ◇ *vt* **-1.** [shout approval, encouragement at] ovacionar **-2.** [gladden] animar. ◇ *vi* aclamar, aplaudir.

➡ **cheers** *excl* **-1.** [said before drinking] saúde! **-2.** *UK inf* [goodbye] tchau! **-3.** *UK inf* [thank you] valeu!

➡ **cheer on** *vt sep* torcer por.

➡ **cheer up** ◇ *vt sep* animar. ◇ *vi* animar-se.

cheerful ['tʃɪəfʊll *adj* alegre.

cheerfully ['tʃɪəfʊlɪl *adv* **-1.** [happily] alegremente **-2.** [willingly] de boa vontade.

cheerfulness ['tʃɪəfʊlnɪsl *n* [happiness] alegria *f.*

cheering ['tʃɪərɪŋl ◇ *adj* [gladdening] animado(da). ◇ *n* animação *f.*

cheerio [,tʃɪərɪ'əʊl *excl UK inf* tchau!

cheerleader ['tʃɪə,liːdəʳ] *n* animador *m*, -ra *f* de torcida.

cheerless ['tʃɪəlɪsl *adj* triste.

cheery ['tʃɪərɪl (*compar* **-ier**, *superl* **-iest**) *adj* cordial.

cheese [tʃiːzl *n* queijo *m.*

cheeseboard ['tʃiːzbɔːdl *n* **-1.** [board] tábua *f* de queijos **-2.** [on menu] variedade *f* de queijos.

cheeseburger ['tʃiːz,bɜːgəʳ] *n* xisburguer *m.*

cheesecake ['tʃiːzkeɪkl *n CULIN* torta *f* de queijo.

cheesed off *adj inf* chateado(da).

cheesy ['tʃiːzɪl (*compar* **-ier**, *superl* **-iest**) *adj* **-1.** [tasting of cheese] de queijo **-2.** [grin] de chulé **-3.** *inf* [cheap, unpleasant] cafona.

cheetah ['tʃiːtəl *n* guepardo *m.*

chef [ʃefl *n* cozinheiro *m*, -ra *f*-chefe.

chemical ['kemɪkll ◇ *adj* químico(ca). ◇ *n* substância *f* química.

chemically ['kemɪklɪl *adv* quimicamente.

chemical weapons *npl* armas *fpl* químicas.

chemist ['kemɪst] *n* -**1.** *UK* [pharmacist] farmacêutico *m*, -ca *f*; ~'s (shop) farmácia *f*- **2.** [scientist] químico *m*, -ca *f*.

chemistry ['kemɪstrɪ] *n* química *f*.

chemotherapy [ˌkiːməʊˈθerəpɪ] *n* quimioterapia *f*.

cheque *UK*, **check** *US* [tʃek] *n* cheque *m*; **to pay by** ~ pagar com cheque.

cheque account *n* [at bank, building society] conta *f* corrente.

chequebook *UK*, **checkbook** *US* ['tʃekbʊk] *n* talão *m* de cheques.

cheque (guarantee) card *n UK* cartão *m* de garantia de cheque.

chequered *UK* ['tʃekəd], **checkered** *US* ['tʃekerd] *adj* -**1.** [patterned] xadrez - **2.** *fig* [varied] cheio (cheia) de altos e baixos.

cherish ['tʃerɪʃ] *vt* [treasure - hope, memory] acalentar; [- privilege, right] apreciar; [- person, thing] acariciar.

cherished ['tʃerɪʃt] *adj* [dear] precioso(sa).

cherry ['tʃerɪ] (*pl* -ies) *n* -**1.** [fruit] cereja *f* - **2.**: ~ (tree) cerejeira *f*.

cherry-pick *vt adquirir as empresas mais lucrativas durante a privatização de um setor da economia.*

cherub ['tʃerəb] (*pl* -s *OR* -im [-ɪm]) *n* -**1.** [angel] querubim *m* - **2.** [child] anjinho *m*, -nha *f*.

chervil ['tʃɜːvɪl] *n* (U) [herb] cerefólio *m*.

chess [tʃes] *n* xadrez *m*.

chessboard ['tʃesbɔːd] *n* tabuleiro *m* de xadrez.

chessman ['tʃesmæn] (*pl* -men [-men]), **chess piece** *n* peça *f* do jogo de xadrez.

chest [tʃest] *n* -**1.** *ANAT* peito *m*; **to get sthg off one's** ~ *inf* desabafar - **2.** [box, trunk] caixa *f* - **3.** [coffer] baú *m*.

chestnut ['tʃesnʌt] <> *adj* [colour] castanho(nha). <> *n* -**1.** [nut] castanha *f* - **2.**: ~ (tree) castanheiro *m*.

chest of drawers (*pl* chests of drawers) *n* [piece of furniture] cômoda *f*.

chesty ['tʃestɪ] (*compar* -ier, *superl* -iest) *adj* [cough] com catarro.

chevron ['ʃevrən] *n* -**1.** [on road] placa *f* de sinalização - **2.** [on uniform] divisa *f*.

chew [tʃuː] <> *n* [biting] mastigação *f*. <> *vt* -**1.** [food] mastigar - **2.** [nails, carpet] roer.

➤ **chew over** *vt sep fig* [think over] ponderar, refletir sobre.

➤ **chew up** *vt sep* [food, slippers] roer.

chewing gum ['tʃuːɪŋ-] *n* chiclete *m*.

chewy ['tʃuːɪ] (*compar* -ier, *superl* -iest) *adj* [food] duro(ra).

chic [ʃiːk] <> *adj* chique. <> *n* elegância *f*.

chicanery [ʃɪˈkeɪnərɪ] *n* [trickery] tramóia *f*; [deception] ilusão *f*.

chick [tʃɪk] *n* -**1.** [baby bird] filhote *m* (de pássaro) - **2.** *inf* [woman] garota *f*.

chicken ['tʃɪkɪn] <> *adj inf* [cowardly] galinha. <> *n* -**1.** [bird] galinha *f*; **it's a** ~ **and egg situation** é a história do ovo e da galinha - **2.** (U) [food] frango *m* - **3.** *inf* [coward] galinha *m*.

➤ **chicken out** *vi inf*: **to** ~ **out (of sthg/of doing sthg)** acovardar-se (de algo/de fazer algo).

chicken feed *n fig* [small sum of money] ninharia *f*.

chickenpox ['tʃɪkɪnpɒks] *n* catapora *f*.

chicken wire *n* tela *f* de arame (*para galinheiros*).

chickpea ['tʃɪkpiː] *n* grão-de-bico *m*.

chicory ['tʃɪkərɪ] *n* [vegetable] chicória *f*.

chide [tʃaɪd] (*pt* chided *OR* chid [tʃɪd], *pp* chid *OR* chidden ['tʃɪdn]) *vt literary* repreender.

chief [tʃiːf] <> *adj* -**1.** [most important] principal - **2.** [head] chefe; ~ **accountant** contador *m*, -ra *f* chefe. <> *n* -**1.** [of organization] chefe *mf*- **2.** [of tribe] chefe *m*, cacique *m*.

chief constable *n UK* chefe *mf* de polícia.

chief executive *n* [head of company] presidente *mf* executivo, -va.

➤ **Chief Executive** *n US* [US president]: **the Chief Executive** o (a) Chefe de Governo.

chief justice *n Am* ≃ presidente *mf* do Supremo Tribunal.

chiefly ['tʃiːflɪ] *adv* [mainly] principalmente.

chief of staff *n* chefe *mf* do estado-maior.

chieftain ['tʃiːftən] *n* líder *m*, chefe *m*.

chiffon ['ʃɪfɒn] *n* chiffon *m*.

chihuahua [tʃɪˈwaːwə] *n* chihuahua *m*.

chilblain ['tʃɪlbleɪn] *n* frieira *f*.

child [tʃaɪld] (*pl* children) *n* -**1.** [boy, girl] criança *f* - **2.** [son, daughter] filho *m*, -lha *f*.

childbearing ['tʃaɪldˌbeərɪŋ] *n* (U) parto *m*.

child benefit *n UK* benefício pago pelo governo britânico a todas as famílias de acordo com o número de filhos.

childbirth ['tʃaɪldbɜːθ] *n* (U) parto *m*.

childcare ['tʃaɪldkeəʳ] *n* assistência *f* à infância; **they share the** ~ eles dividem as responsabilidades relativas às crianças.

childhood ['tʃaɪldhʊd] *n* infância *f*.

childish ['tʃaɪldɪʃ] *adj pej* infantil.

childishly ['tʃaɪldɪʃlɪ] *adv pej* de modo infantil.

childless ['tʃaɪldlɪs] *adj* sem filhos.

childlike ['tʃaɪldlaɪk] *adj* ingênuo(nua).

childminder ['tʃaɪldˌmaɪndəʳ] *n UK* babá *mf*.

child prodigy *n* criança *f* prodígio.

childproof ['tʃaɪldpruːf] *adj* seguro(ra) para crianças, à prova de crianças.

children ['tʃɪldrən] *pl* ⊏> **child**.

Chile ['tʃɪlɪ] *n* Chile; **in** ~ no Chile.

Chilean ['tʃɪlɪən] <> *adj* chileno(na). <> *n* chileno *m*, -na *f*.

chili ['tʃɪlɪ] *n* = **chilli**.

chill [tʃɪl] <> *adj* glacial. <> *n* -**1.** [illness] resfriado *m* - **2.** [in temperature]: **a** ~ **in the air** uma friagem - **3.** [feeling of fear] calafrio *m*. <> *vt* -**1.** [drink, food] gelar - **2.** [person] arrepiar-se de. <> *vi* [drink, food] esfriar.

chilli ['tʃɪlɪ] (*pl* -ies) *n* [vegetable] pimenta-malagueta *f*.

chilling ['tʃɪlɪŋ] *adj* -**1.** [very cold] gelado(da) - **2.** [frightening] arrepiante.

chilli powder *n* pimenta *f* em pó.

chilly ['tʃɪlɪ] (*compar* -ier, *superl* -iest) *adj* frio(fria).

chime [tʃaɪm] <> *n* [of bell, clock] batida *f*. <> *vt* [time] bater. <> *vi* [bell, clock] tocar.

◆ **chime in** *vi* concordar.

chimney ['tʃɪmnɪl] *n* chaminé *f*.

chimneypot ['tʃɪmnɪpɒt] *n* cano *m* de chaminé.

chimneysweep ['tʃɪmnɪswiːp] *n* limpador *m*, -ra *f* de chaminé.

chimp [tʃɪmp] *inf*, **chimpanzee** [ˌtʃɪmpənˈziː] *n* chimpanzé *mf*.

chin [tʃɪn] *n* queixo *m*.

china ['tʃaɪnə] ◇ *n* (U) - **1.** [substance] porcelana *f* - **2.** [crockery] louças *fpl* de porcelana. ◇ *comp* de porcelana.

China ['tʃaɪnə] *n* China; **in** ~ na China; **the People's Republic of** ~ a República Popular da China.

china clay *n* (U) caulim *m*.

China Sea *n*: **the** ~ o Mar da China.

Chinatown ['tʃaɪnətaʊn] *n* bairro *m* chinês.

chinchilla [tʃɪnˈtʃɪlə] *n* chinchila *f*.

Chinese [ˌtʃaɪˈniːz] ◇ *adj* chinês(esa). ◇ *n* [language] chinês *m*. ◇ *npl*: **the** ~ os chineses.

Chinese cabbage *n* repolho *m* chinês.

Chinese lantern *n* [light] lanterna *f* chinesa.

Chinese leaf *n* UK = **Chinese cabbage**.

chink [tʃɪŋk] ◇ *n* - **1.** [narrow opening] fresta *f* - **2.** [sound] tinido *m*. ◇ *vi* tilintar.

chinos ['tʃiːnəʊz] *npl* calça de algodão grosso.

chintz [tʃɪnts] ◇ *n* (U) tecido *m* de algodão estampado, chita *f*. ◇ *comp* de algodão estampado, de chita.

chinwag ['tʃɪnwæg] *n* inf: **to have a** ~ bater um papo.

chip [tʃɪp] (*pt* & *pp* -ped, *cont* -ping) ◇ *n* - **1.** UK [hot, fried potato strip] batata *f* frita em palito - **2.** US [snack] batata *f* frita de pacote - **3.** [fragment] lasca *f* - **4.** [flaw] defeito *m* - **5.** COMPUT chip *m* - **6.** [token] ficha *f*; **when the** ~ **s are down** quando chega a hora da verdade - **7.** SPORT tacada *f* - **8.** *phr*: **to have a** ~ **on one's shoulder** ficar ressentido(da). ◇ *vt* [damage] lascar.

◆ **chip in** *inf* ◇ *vt fus* [contribute] contribuir com. ◇ *vi* - **1.** [contribute] fazer uma vaquinha - **2.** [interrupt] interromper.

◆ **chip off** *vt sep* lascar.

chipboard ['tʃɪpbɔːd] *n* (U) compensado *m*.

chipmunk ['tʃɪpmʌŋk] *n* tâmia *m*.

chipped ['tʃɪpt] *adj* [flawed] lascado(da).

chippings ['tʃɪpɪŋz] *npl* cavacos *mpl*; **'loose** ~ **'** 'cascalho solto'.

chip shop *n* UK loja onde se compram peixe com batatas fritas.

chiropodist [kɪˈrɒpədɪst] *n* quiropodista *mf*.

chiropody [kɪˈrɒpədɪ] *n* (U) quiropodia *f*.

chiropractor *n* quiroprático *m*, -ca *f*.

chirp [tʃɜːp] *vi* chilrar, piar.

chirpy ['tʃɜːpɪ] (*compar* -ier, *superl* -iest) *adj esp* UK *inf* [cheerful] animado(da).

chisel ['tʃɪzl] (UK *pt* & *pp* -led, *cont* -ling, US *pt* & *pp* -ed, *cont* -ing) ◇ *n* - **1.** [for wood] formão *m* - **2.** [for stone] cinzel *m*. ◇ *vt* - **1.** [wood] esculpir com formão - **2.** [stone] cinzelar.

chit [tʃɪt] *n* [note] vale *m*.

chit-chat *n* (U) *inf* bate-papo *m*.

chivalrous ['ʃɪvlrəs] *adj* cavalheiresco(ca).

chivalry ['ʃɪvlrɪ] *n* - **1.** *literary* [of knights] cavalaria *f* - **2.** [courtesy] cavalheirismo *m*.

chives [tʃaɪvz] *npl* cebolinha *f*.

chivvy (*pt* & *pp* -ied), **chivvy** (*pt* & *pp* -ied) ['tʃɪvɪ] *vt* inf: **to** ~ **sb along** dar uma apressada em alguém.

chloride ['klɔːraɪd] *n* cloreto *m*.

chlorinated ['klɔːrɪneɪtɪd] *adj* clorado(da).

chlorine ['klɔːriːn] *n* (U) cloro *m*.

chlorofluorocarbon ['klɔːrəʊˌflʊərəʊ'kɑːbən] *n* clorofluorcarbono *m*.

chloroform ['klɒrəfɔːm] *n* (U) clorofórmio *m*.

chlorophyll *n* clorofila *f*.

choc-ice ['tʃɒkaɪs] *n* UK bola de sorvete com cobertura de chocolate.

chock [tʃɒk] *n* calço *m* (para roda de veículo).

chock-a-block, chock-full *adj* inf: ~ **(with)** [people] apinhado(da) (de); [things] entupido(da) (de).

chocolate ['tʃɒkələt] ◇ *n* (U) chocolate *m*; **plain/ milk** ~ chocolate amargo/ao leite; **a box of** ~ **s** uma caixa de bombons. ◇ *comp* [biscuit, cake, mousse] de chocolate.

choice [tʃɒɪs] ◇ *n* - **1.** [gen] escolha *f*, opção *f*; **to have no** ~ **but to do sthg** não ter outra escolha a não fazer algo; **it was my first** ~ foi a minha primeira opção; **to do sthg by** ~ fazer algo por vontade própria - **2.** [variety, selection] variedade *f*. ◇ *adj* selecionado(da).

choir ['kwaɪə'] *n* [singers] coro *m*.

choirboy ['kwaɪəbɔɪ] *n* menino *m* de coro.

choke [tʃəʊk] ◇ *n* AUT afogador *m*. ◇ *vt* - **1.** [subj: person] estrangular - **2.** [subj: smoke, fumes] asfixiar, sufocar - **3.** [block] entupir, obstruir. ◇ *vi* [on food, water] engasgar.

◆ **choke back** *vt fus* segurar, controlar.

choker *n* gargantilha *f*.

cholera ['kɒlərə] *n* (U) cólera *f*.

cholesterol [kəˈlestərɒl] *n* (U) colesterol *m*.

choose [tʃuːz] (*pt* chose, *pp* chosen) ◇ *vt* - **1.** [select] escolher; **there's little** OR **not much to** ~ **between them** não há muito o que escolher entre eles (elas) - **2.** [opt]: **to** ~ **to do sthg** optar por fazer algo. ◇ *vi* [select]: **to** ~ **(from sthg)** escolher (entre algo).

choos(e)y ['tʃuːzɪ] (*compar* -ier, *superl* -iest) *adj* exigente.

chop [tʃɒp] (*pt* & *pp* -ped, *cont* -ping) ◇ *n* - **1.** [meat] costeleta *f* - **2.** [blow] pancada *f*; **to be for the** ~ [person] estar para ser demitido(da); [project] estar para ser cancelado(da). ◇ *vt* - **1.** [wood] retalhar - **2.** [vegetables, apple] picar - **3.** inf [funding, budget] cortar - **4.** *phr*: **to** ~ **and change** ser inconstante.

◆ **chop down** *vt sep* derrubar.

◆ **chop up** *vt sep* - **1.** [vegetables, fruit] picar - **2.** [wood, meat] cortar.

chopper ['tʃɒpə'] *n* - **1.** [axe] machadinha *f* - **2.** inf [helicopter] helicóptero *m*.

chopping board ['tʃɒpɪŋ-] *n* tábua *f* de cozinha.

choppy ['tʃɒpɪ] (*compar* -ier, *superl* -iest) *adj* [sea] agitado(da).

chopsticks ['tʃɒpstɪks] *npl* hashi *mpl*.

choral ['kɔːrəl] *adj* de coral.

chord [kɔːd] n MUS acorde m; **to strike a ~ (with sb)** tocar fundo (em alguém).

chore [tʃɔː˞] n afazeres mpl; **household ~s** afazeres domésticos.

choreographer [ˌkɒrɪˈɒɡrəfə˞] n coreógrafo m, -fa f.

choreography [ˌkɒrɪˈɒɡrəfɪ] n (U) coreografia f.

chortle [ˈtʃɔːtl] vi dar gargalhadas.

chorus [ˈkɔːrəs] n -1. [gen] coro m -2. [part of song] refrão m.

chose [tʃəʊz] pt ⊳ choose.

chosen [ˈtʃəʊzn] pp ⊳ choose.

choux pastry [ʃuː-] n (U) doce feito com ovos e em cujo interior se acrescenta creme.

chow [tʃaʊl] n [dog] chow-chow m inv.

chowder [ˈtʃaʊdə˞] n (U) sopa f (de frutos do mar); **clam ~** sopa de mariscos.

Christ [kraɪst] <> n Cristo m. <> excl Jesus Cristo!, Minha Nossa!

christen [ˈkrɪsn] vt batizar.

christening [ˈkrɪsnɪŋ] <> n batizado m. <> comp de batismo.

Christian [ˈkrɪstʃən] <> adj cristão(tã). <> n cristão m, -tã f.

Christian Democrat n POL democrata mf cristão, -tã.

Christianity [ˌkrɪstɪˈænətɪ] n (U) cristianismo m.

Christian name n nome m de batismo.

Christmas [ˈkrɪsməs] <> n Natal m; **Happy** OR **Merry ~!** Feliz Natal! <> comp de Natal.

Christmas cake n UK bolo escuro e decorado que contém muitas frutas secas e que é coberto com marzipã e glacê e servido no Natal.

Christmas card n cartão m de Natal.

Christmas carol n cântico m de Natal.

Christmas cracker n UK cilindro de papel que produz um estalido ao ser aberto e que contém dentro um presente de Natal.

Christmas Day n dia m de Natal.

Christmas Eve n noite f de Natal.

Christmas Island n Ilha de Natal.

Christmas pudding n UK pudim rico e escuro feito com frutas secas, condimentos e gordura animal, servido no Natal.

Christmas stocking n meias fpl de Natal (penduradas na lareira).

Christmas tree n árvore f de Natal.

chrome [krəʊm], **chromium** [ˈkrəʊmɪəm] <> n (U) cromo m. <> comp de cromo, cromado(da).

chrome-plated adj cromado(da).

chromosome [ˈkrəʊməsəʊm] n cromossomo m.

chronic [ˈkrɒnɪk] adj -1. [long-lasting] crônico(ca) -2. [habitual] inveterado(da).

chronically [ˈkrɒnɪklɪ] adv [ill] cronicamente.

chronicle [ˈkrɒnɪkl] <> n crônica f. <> vt narrar.

chronological [ˌkrɒnəˈlɒdʒɪkl] adj cronológico(-ca).

chronologically [ˌkrɒnəˈlɒdʒɪklɪ] adv cronologicamente.

chronology [krəˈnɒlədʒɪ] n [sequence] cronologia f.

chrysalis [ˈkrɪsəlɪs] (pl -lises [-lɪsiːzl]) n [insect] crisálida f.

chrysanthemum [krɪˈsænθəməm] (pl -s) n crisântemo m.

chub (pl inv OR -s) n espécie de carpa.

chubbiness n (U) fofice f.

chubby [ˈtʃʌbɪ] (compar -ier, superl -iest) adj rechonchudo(da).

chuck [tʃʌk] vt inf -1. [throw] jogar, atirar -2. inf: **to ~ sb** dar o fora em alguém; **to ~ sthg** largar algo.

   ➤ **chuck away, chuck out** vt sep inf jogar fora; **to ~ sthg out** botar algo fora; **to ~ sb out** botar alguém para fora.

chuckle [ˈtʃʌkl] <> n risadinha f. <> vi rir discretamente.

chuffed [tʃʌft] adj UK inf: **~ (with sthg/to do sthg)** muito contente (com algo/por fazer algo).

chug [tʃʌg] (pt & pp -ged, cont -ging) vi ratear.

chum [tʃʌm] n inf camarada mf, companheiro m, -ra f.

chummy [ˈtʃʌmɪ] (compar -ier, superl -iest) adj inf: **to be ~ (with sb)** ser legal (com alguém).

chump [tʃʌmp] n inf [fool] tonto m, -ta f.

chunk [tʃʌŋk] n -1. [piece] pedaço m -2. inf [large amount] grande parte f.

chunky [ˈtʃʌŋkɪ] (compar -ier, superl -iest) adj -1. [person] parrudo(da) -2. [jewellery, furniture] maciço(-ça) -3. [cardigan] grosso(sa).

church [tʃɜːtʃ] n -1. [building] igreja f; **to go to ~** freqüentar a igreja -2. [organization]: **the Church** a Igreja.

churchgoer [ˈtʃɜːtʃˌɡəʊə˞] n fiel m, devoto m, -ta f.

churchman [ˈtʃɜːtʃmən] (pl -men [-mən]) n clérigo m, eclesiástico m.

Church of England n: **the ~** a Igreja Anglicana.

CHURCH OF ENGLAND

A Igreja Anglicana originou-se da disputa entre o rei Henrique VIII, que desejava divorciar-se, e a Igreja Católica, que lhe negou o divórcio, em meados do século XVI. Autoproclamando-se chefe da Igreja Anglicana, Henrique VIII separou-a da Igreja Católica. O chefe laico da Igreja Anglicana é o monarca, e seu chefe espiritual, o arcebispo de Canterbury.

Church of Scotland n: **the ~** a Igreja Presbiteriana da Escócia.

churchyard [ˈtʃɜːtʃjɑːd] n cemitério ao redor de uma igreja.

churlish [ˈtʃɜːlɪʃ] adj indelicado(da).

churn [tʃɜːn] <> n -1. [for making butter] batedeira f de manteiga -2. [for transporting milk] latão m. <> vt [stir up] agitar. <> vi revolver-se.

   ➤ **churn out** vt sep inf produzir em larga escala.

   ➤ **churn up** vt sep -1. [mud] agitar -2. [water] revolver.

chute [ʃuːt] n -1. [waterfall] queda f d'água, cachoeira f -2. [for escape] rampa f -3. [for rubbish] calha f -4. [in a pool] tobogã m.

chutney [ˈtʃʌtnɪ] n (U) molho feito à base de frutas, sementes picantes e açúcar que se come com carne ou queijo.

CI *abbr of* **Channel Islands**.

CIA (*abbr of* **Central Intelligence Agency**) *n* CIA *f*.

cicada [sɪ'kɑːdə] *n* cigarra *f*.

CID (*abbr of* **Criminal Investigation Department**) *n* departamento de investigação criminal da polícia britânica.

cider ['saɪdə'] *n* sidra *f*. •

c.i.f. (*abbr of* **cost, insurance and freight**) c.i.f., custo, seguro e frete.

cigar [sɪ'gɑː'] *n* charuto *m*.

cigarette [ˌsɪgə'ret] *n* cigarro *m*.

cigarette butt, cigarette end *UK n* bagana *f*.

cigarette holder *n* piteira *f*.

cigarette lighter *n* isqueiro *m*.

cigarette paper *n* mortalha *f*.

C-in-C (*abbr of* **commander in chief**) *n* comandante-em-chefe *m*.

cinch [sɪntʃ] *n inf*: **it's a** ~ é sopa *or* canja.

cinder ['sɪndə'] *n* cinza *f*.

cinderblock ['sɪndəblɒk] *n US* bloco *m* de cimento e cinzas.

Cinderella [ˌsɪndə'relə] *n* Cinderela *f* gata-borralheira *f*.

cine camera *n* filmadora *f*.

cine film *n* filme *m*, película *f*.

cinema ['sɪnəmə] *n* [place, art] cinema *m*.

cinematic [ˌsɪnɪ'mætɪk] *adj* cinematográfico(ca).

cinnamon ['sɪnəmən] *n (U)* canela *f*.

cipher ['saɪfə'] *n* -**1**. [secret writing system] cifra *f* - **2**. *fig* [person] nulidade *f*.

circa ['sɜːkə] *prep* cerca de, aproximadamente.

circle ['sɜːkl] ◇ *n* -**1**. [gen] círculo *m*; **to come full** ~ voltar ao ponto de partida; **to go round in** ~s andar em círculos - **2**. [seats in theatre, cinema] galeria *f*. ◇ *vt* -**1**. [draw a circle round] marcar com círculo - **2**. [move round] circundar. ◇ *vi* mover-se em círculos.

circuit ['sɜːkɪt] *n* -**1**. [gen] circuito *m* - **2**. [lap, movement round] volta *f*.

circuit board *n* placa *f* de circuito.

circuit breaker *n* disjuntor *m*.

circuitous [sə'kjuːɪtəs] *adj* tortuoso(sa).

circular ['sɜːkjʊlə'] ◇ *adj* -**1**. [shape, object] redondo(da) - **2**. [argument] circular. ◇ *n* circular *f*.

circulate ['sɜːkjʊleɪt] ◇ *vi* circular. ◇ *vt* circular.

circulation [ˌsɜːkjʊ'leɪʃn] *n* circulação *f*; **in** ~ em circulação.

circumcise ['sɜːkəmsaɪz] *vt* circuncidar.

circumcision [ˌsɜːkəm'sɪʒn] *n* circuncisão *f*.

circumference [sə'kʌmfərəns] *n* circunferência *f*.

circumflex ['sɜːkəmfleks] *n*: ~ **(accent)** (acento) *m* circunflexo *m*.

circumnavigate [ˌsɜːkəm'nævɪgeɪt] *vt* circunavegar.

circumscribe ['sɜːkəmskraɪb] *vt fml* [restrict] circunscrever.

circumspect ['sɜːkəmspekt] *adj* circunspecto(ta).

circumstances *npl* circunstâncias *fpl*; **under** *or* **in no** ~ sob *or* em nenhuma circunstância; **under** *or* **in the** ~ nas *or* nestas circunstâncias.

circumstantial [ˌsɜːkəm'stænʃl] *adj fml*: ~ evidence evidência *f* circunstancial.

circumvent [ˌsɜːkəm'vent] *vt fml* burlar.

circus ['sɜːkəs] *n* -**1**. [for entertainment] circo *m* - **2**. [in place names] no Reino Unido, praça circular à qual convergem várias ruas.

cirrhosis [sɪ'rəʊsɪs] *n (U)* cirrose *f*.

CIS (*abbr of* **Commonwealth of Independent States**) *n* CEI *f*.

cissy ['sɪsɪ] (*pl* -**ies**) *n UK inf* maricas *m inv*.

cistern ['sɪstən] *n* -**1**. *UK* [in roof] cisterna *f* - **2**. [on lavatory] caixa *f* de descarga.

citation [saɪ'teɪʃn] *n* -**1**. [quotation] citação *f* - **2**. [official praise]: ~ **(for sthg)** menção *f* honrosa (por algo).

cite [saɪt] *vt* citar.

citizen ['sɪtɪzn] *n* [of country, of town] cidadão *m*, -dã *f*.

Citizens' Advice Bureau *n* Centro *m* de Apoio ao Cidadão.

Citizens' Band *n (U)* banda *f* do cidadão.

citizenship ['sɪtɪznʃɪp] *n (U)* cidadania *f*.

citric acid ['sɪtrɪk-] *n (U)* ácido *m* cítrico.

citrus fruit ['sɪtrəs-] *n* fruta *f* cítrica.

city ['sɪtɪ] (*pl* -**ies**) *n* cidade *f*.
➤ **City** *n UK*: **the City** o bairro financeiro de Londres.

THE CITY

A *City*, o bairro financeiro de Londres, compõe uma unidade administrativa autônoma da capital inglesa, dotada inclusive de sua própria polícia. É o bairro mais antigo da cidade, conhecido também como *Square Mile*, pelo fato de sua área total ter uma milha quadrada (ou 2,6 km²). Por extensão, *the City* é hoje termo empregado para designar o mundo financeiro britânico.

---

city centre *n* centro *m* da cidade.

city hall *n US* prefeitura *f*.

city technology college *n UK* centro de formação técnica profissional custeada por indústrias.

civic ['sɪvɪk] *adj* cívico(ca).

civic centre *n UK* centro *m* cívico.

civil ['sɪvl] *adj* -**1**. [involving ordinary citizens] civil - **2**. [polite] educado(da).

civil defence *n (U)* defesa *f* civil.

civil disobedience *n (U)* desobediência *f* civil.

civil engineer *n* engenheiro *m*, -ra *f* civil.

civil engineering *n (U)* engenharia *f* civil.

civilian [sɪ'vɪljən] ◇ *n* civil *mf*. ◇ *comp* civil.

civility [sɪ'vɪlətɪ] *n (U)* civilidade *f*.

civilization [ˌsɪvɪlar'zeɪʃn] *n (U)* civilização *f*.

civilize, -ise ['sɪvɪlaɪz] *vt* civilizar.

civilized ['sɪvɪlaɪzd] *adj* civilizado(da).

civil law *n (U)* [relating to private case] direito *m* civil.

civil liberties *npl* liberdades *fpl* civis.

Civil List *n UK* verba anual designada pelo Parlamento inglês à Família Real.

civil rights *npl* direitos *mpl* civis.

civil servant *n* funcionário *m* público, funcionária *f* pública.

civil service *n* serviço *m* público.

civil war *n* guerra *f* civil.

CJD (*abbr of* Creutzfeldt-Jakob disease) *n forma humana da doença da vaca louca*, doença *f* de Creutzfeldt-Jakob.

cl (*abbr of* centilitre) *n* cl.

clad [klæd] *adj literary* [dressed]: ~ **in sthg** vestido(da) de algo.

cladding ['klædɪŋ] *n (U) UK* revestimento *m*.

claim [kleɪm] ⟨⟩ *n* **- 1.** [assertion] alegação *f* **- 2.** [demand] reivindicação *f* **- 3.** [rightful]: **to have a** ~ **on sb** ter direitos sobre alguém; **to have a** ~ **on sb's attention** reivindicar a atenção de alguém; **to lay** ~ **to sthg** reivindicar algo **- 4.** [financial] reclamação *f*. ⟨⟩ *vt* **- 1.** [assert, maintain] alegar; **to** ~ **(that)** alegar que **- 2.** [apply for, assert one's rights to] reivindicar **- 3.** [take] levar. ⟨⟩ *vi*: **to** ~ **on one's insurance** acionar o seguro; **to** ~ **for sthg** reclamar algo.

claimant ['kleɪmənt] *n* **- 1.** [to the throne] pretendente *mf* **- 2.** [of benefit, in law case] requerente *mf*.

claim form *n* formulário *m* de reclamação.

clairvoyant [kleə'vɔɪənt] ⟨⟩ *adj* clarividente. ⟨⟩ *n* vidente *mf*.

clam [klæm] (*pt & pp* -med, *cont* -ming) *n* marisco *m*.

◆ **clam up** *vi inf* fechar a boca.

clamber ['klæmbə^r] *vi* subir com dificuldade.

clammy ['klæmɪ] (*compar* -ier, *superl* -iest) *adj inf* melado(da).

clamor *n & vi US* = clamour.

clamorous ['klæmərəs] *adj* clamoroso(sa).

clamour *UK*, **clamor** *US* ['klæmə^r] ⟨⟩ *n (U)* **- 1.** [noise] clamor *m* **- 2.** [demand]: ~ **for sthg** queixa *f* por algo. ⟨⟩ *vi*: **to** ~ **for sthg** queixar-se por algo.

clamp [klæmp] ⟨⟩ *n* **- 1.** [fastener] presilha *f*, braçadeira *f* **- 2.** MED & TECH grampo *m*. ⟨⟩ *vt* **- 1.** [with fastener] apertar **- 2.** [parked car] pôr travas em.

◆ **clamp down** *vi*: **to** ~ **down (on sthg)** impor restrições (a algo).

clampdown ['klæmpdaʊn] *n*: ~ **(on sthg)** restrição *f* (sobre algo).

clan [klæn] *n* clã *m*.

clandestine [klæn'destɪn] *adj* clandestino(na).

clang [klæŋ] ⟨⟩ *n* som *m* metálico, tinido *m*. ⟨⟩ *vi* tinir.

clanger ['klæŋə^r] *n UK inf* mancada *f*; **to drop a** ~ dar uma mancada.

clank [klæŋk] ⟨⟩ *n* ruído *m* metálico grave. ⟨⟩ *vi* retinir.

clap [klæp] (*pt & pp* -ped, *cont* -ping) ⟨⟩ *n* **- 1.** [of hands] palmas *fpl* **- 2.** [of thunder] estrondo *m*. ⟨⟩ *vt* **-1.**: **to** ~ **one's hands** bater palmas **- 2.** *inf*: **to** ~ **eyes on sb/sthg** botar os olhos em alguém/algo. ⟨⟩ *vi* aplaudir.

clapboard ['klæpbɔːd] *n US* tábua para revestimento externo da casa ou do edifício.

clapped-out [klæpt-] *adj UK inf* [machine] caindo aos pedaços.

clapperboard ['klæpəbɔːd] *n* indicador *m* de cenas.

clapping ['klæpɪŋ] *n (U)* aplauso *m*.

claptrap ['klæptræp] *n (U) inf* conversa *f* mole.

claret ['klærət] *n* **- 1.** [wine] clarete *m* **- 2.** [colour] cor-de-vinho *f*.

clarification [ˌklærɪfɪ'keɪʃn] *n* [explanation] esclarecimento *m*.

clarify ['klærɪfaɪ] .(*pt & pp* -ied) *vt* [explain, expand on] esclarecer.

clarinet [ˌklærə'net] *n* clarinete *m*.

clarity ['klærətɪ] *n (U)* clareza *f*.

clash [klæʃ] ⟨⟩ *n* **- 1.** [of interests, personality] choque *m*; ~ **with sb** choque com alguém **- 2.** [disagreement] divergência *f*; ~ **with sb** divergência com alguém **- 3.** [noise] estrépito *m*. ⟨⟩ *vi* **-1.** [be incompatible - ideas, beliefs] chocar-se; [- colours] destoar; **to** ~ **with sthg** destoar de algo **- 2.** [fight] chocar-se; **to** ~ **with sb** chocar-se com alguém **- 3.** [disagree] divergir; **to** ~ **with sb** divergir de alguém **- 4.** [coincide] coincidir; **to** ~ **with sthg** coincidir com algo **- 5.** [make noise] soar.

clasp [klɑːsp] ⟨⟩ *n* [fastener] fecho *m*. ⟨⟩ *vt* [hold tight] apertar.

class [klɑːs] ⟨⟩ *n* **- 1.** [gen] classe *f* **- 2.** [lesson] aula *f* **- 3.** [category] espécie *f*; **to be in a** ~ **of one's own** ser excelente. ⟨⟩ *comp* [relating to social groups] de classes. ⟨⟩ *vt* classificar; **to** ~ **sb as sthg** classificar alguém como algo.

class-conscious *adj pej* esnobe.

classic ['klæsɪk] ⟨⟩ *adj* clássico(ca). ⟨⟩ *n* clássico *m*.

◆ **classics** *npl*: **the** ~ os clássicos.

classical ['klæsɪkl] *adj* clássico(ca).

classical music *n (U)* música *f* clássica.

classicism *n (U)* classicismo *m*.

classicist *n (U)* classicista *mf*.

classification [ˌklæsɪfɪ'keɪʃn] *n* classificação *f*.

classified ['klæsɪfaɪd] *adj* [secret] confidencial.

classified ad *n* [anúncio *m*] classificado *m*.

classify ['klæsɪfaɪ] (*pt & pp* -ied) *vt* classificar.

classless ['klɑːslɪs] *adj* sem classes.

classmate ['klɑːsmeɪt] *n* colega *mf* de classe.

classroom ['klɑːsrʊm] *n* sala *f* de aula.

classy ['klɑːsɪ] (*compar* -ier, *superl* -iest) *adj inf* bacana, chique.

clatter ['klætə^r] ⟨⟩ *n* **- 1.** [of pans, dishes] tinido *m* **- 2.** [of hooves] repique *m*. ⟨⟩ *vi* **-1.** [pans, dishes] retinir **- 2.** [hooves] repicar **- 3.** [person]: **to** ~ **in/out/down** entrar/sair/descer fazendo barulho.

clause [klɔːz] *n* **- 1.** [in legal document] cláusula *f* **- 2.** GRAMM oração *f*.

claustrophobia [ˌklɔːstrə'fəʊbjə] *n (U)* claustrofobia *f*.

claustrophobic [ˌklɔːstrə'fəʊbɪk] *adj* claustrofóbico(ca).

claw [klɔː] ⟨⟩ *n* **- 1.** [of wild animal, bird] garra *f* **- 2.** [of cat, dog] unha *f* **- 3.** [of sea creature] pinça *f* **- 4.** [of insect] ferrão *f*. ⟨⟩ *vt* arranhar; **to** ~ **one's way to** galgar seu caminho para. ⟨⟩ *vi*: **to** ~ **at sthg** agarrar-se a algo.

◆ **claw back** *vt sep UK* recuperar.

clay [kleɪ] *n* argila *f*, barro *m*.

clay pigeon shooting *n (U)* tiro *m* ao prato.

clean [kliːn] ⟨⟩ *adj* **-1.** [gen] limpo(pa); **to come** ~ **about sthg** *inf* confessar algo **-2.** [blank] em branco **-3.** [inoffensive] inofensivo(va) **-4.** [cut, break] preciso(sa). <> *adv* [completely] completamente. <> *vt* [make clean] limpar; **to ~ one's teeth** *UK* escovar os dentes. <> *vi* fazer faxina. <> *n* faxina *f*; **to give sthg a ~** dar uma limpada em algo.

● **clean out** *vt sep* **-1.** [clear out] fazer uma limpeza (em) **-2.** *inf fig* [leave penniless] deixar sem um centavo **-3.** *inf* [take everything from] depenar.

● **clean up** <> *vt sep* [clear up] arrumar. <> *vi inf* [win] limpar.

cleaner ['kli:nə^r] *n* **-1.** [person] faxineiro *m*, -ra *f* **-2.** [substance] produto *m* de limpeza **-3.** [shop]: **~'s** lavanderia *f*.

cleaning ['kli:nɪŋ] *n (U)* limpeza *f*, faxina *f*.

cleaning lady *n* faxineira *f*.

cleanliness ['klenlɪnɪs] *n (U)* limpeza *f*, asseio *m*.

clean-living *adj* de vida limpa.

cleanly ['kli:nlɪ] *adv* com precisão.

cleanness ['kli:nnɪs] *n (U)* limpeza *f*, asseio *m*.

cleanse [klenz] *vt* **-1.** [make clean] limpar **-2.** [make pure] purificar; **to ~ sb/sthg of sthg** livrar alguém/algo de algo.

cleanser ['klenzə^r] *n* **-1.** [for skin] creme *m* de limpeza **-2.** [detergent] detergente *m*.

clean-shaven [-'ʃeɪvn] *adj* de barba feita.

cleanup ['kli:nʌp] *n* limpeza *f*.

clear [klɪə^r] <> *adj* **-1.** [gen] claro(ra); **to make sthg ~ (to sb)** tornar algo claro (para alguém); **to make it ~ that** deixar claro que; **to make o.s. ~** fazer-se entender; **to be ~ about sthg** [understand] entender algo com clareza; [explain clearly] fazer-se entender sobre algo; **~ head mente *f* lúcida -2.** [obvious, unmistakable] óbvio(via) **-3.** [transparent] transparente **-4.** [water] límpido(da) **-5.** [unobstructed, free] livre **-6.** [conscience] tranqüilo(la) **-7.** [profit] líquido(da). <> *adv* [out of the way]: **to step ~** ficar fora do caminho; **stand ~!** afaste-se!; **to stay** *OR* **steer ~ of sb/sthg** afastar-se de alguém/algo. <> *n*: **in the ~** [out of danger] fora de perigo; [free from suspicion] acima de qualquer suspeita. <> *vt* **-1.** [remove obstacles from - way, path] desimpedir; [- pipe] limpar; [- table] tirar **-2.**: **to ~ one's throat** limpar a garganta **-3.** [take out of the way] retirar **-4.** [jump] transpor **-5.** [pay] saldar **-6.** [authorize] autorizar **-7.** [prove not guilty] livrar de culpa; **to be ~ed of sthg** ser declarado(da) inocente de algo **-8.** [accept for payment] liberar **-9.** [customs] desembaraçar. <> *vi* **-1.** [disperse, diminish - fog, smoke] dissipar-se; [- headache] passar **-2.** [brighten up] clarear.

● **clear away** *vt sep* arrumar.

● **clear off** *vi UK inf* dar o fora.

● **clear out** <> *vt sep* [tidy up] arrumar. <> *vi inf* [leave] dar o fora.

● **clear up** <> *vt sep* **-1.** [tidy] arrumar **-2.** [solve, settle] resolver. <> *vi* **-1.** [weather] clarear **-2.** [illness] desaparecer **-3.** [tidy up] arrumar.

clearance ['klɪərəns] *n (U)* **-1.** [removal] retirada *f*; **the ~ of mines** a remoção de minas terrestres; **land ~** a limpeza da terra **-2.** [of contents of house] desocupação *f* **-3.** [permission] autorização *f*; **customs ~** desembaraço *m* alfandegário **-5.** [free space] vão *m* livre; **the bridge has a 12m ~** a ponte tem um vão livre de 12m.

clearance sale *n* liquidação *f*.

clear-cut *adj* bem definido(da).

clear-headed [-'hedɪd] *adj* esperto(ta).

clearing ['klɪərɪŋ] *n* [in forest] clareira *f*.

clearing bank *n UK* banco *m* compensador.

clearing house *n* **-1.** [organization] central *f* de informações **-2.** [bank] carteira *f* de compensação.

clearing up *n (U)* limpeza *f*, arrumação *f*.

clearly ['klɪəlɪ] *adv* **-1.** [distinctly, lucidly] claramente **-2.** [obviously] evidentemente.

clearout ['klɪəraʊt] *n esp UK inf* faxina *f* geral.

clear-sighted [-'saɪtɪd] *adj* [person] perspicaz.

clearway ['klɪəweɪ] *n UK AUT* via *f* expressa.

cleavage ['kli:vɪdʒ] *n* **-1.** [between breasts] decote *m* **-2.** [division] rachadura *f*.

cleave *literary* <> *vt* [split] rachar. <> *vi* [be very attached to]: **to ~ to sb/sthg** ser fiel a alguém/algo.

cleaver ['kli:və^r] *n* cutelo *m* de açougueiro.

clef [klef] *n* clave *f*.

cleft [kleft] *n* fenda *f*, rachadura *f*.

cleft palate *n* fenda *f* palatina.

clematis ['klemətɪs] *n* clematite *f*.

clemency ['klemənsɪ] *n (U) fml* [mercy] clemência *f*.

clementine ['kleməntaɪn] *n* clementina *f*.

clench [klentʃ] *vt* cerrar; **to have sthg ~ed between one's teeth** ter algo preso entre os dentes.

clergy ['klɜ:dʒɪ] *npl*: **the ~** o clero.

clergyman ['klɜ:dʒɪmən] (*pl* -men [-mən]) *n* clérigo *m*.

cleric ['klerɪk] *n* clérigo *m*.

clerical ['klerɪkl] *adj* **-1.** [in office] de escritório **-2.** [in church] clerical.

clerk [*UK* klɑ:k, *US* klɜ:rk] *n* **-1.** [in office] auxiliar *mf* de escritório **-2.** [in court] escriturário *m*, -ria *f*, escrevente *mf* **-3.** *US* [shop assistant] balconista *mf*.

clever ['klevə^r] *adj* **-1.** [intelligent] inteligente **-2.** [ingenious] engenhoso(sa); **that's ~!** que engenhoso! **-3.** [skilful] hábil.

cleverly ['klevəlɪ] *adv* **-1.** [intelligently] inteligentemente **-2.** [ingeniously] engenhosamente **-3.** [skilfully] habilmente.

cleverness ['klevənɪs] *n* **-1.** [intelligence] esperteza *f*, inteligência *f* **-2.** [ingenuity] engenhosidade *f* **-3.** [skill] habilidade *f*.

cliché ['kli:ʃeɪ] *n* clichê *m*.

click [klɪk] <> *n* **-1.** [gen] clique *m* **-2.** [of tongue] estalo *m*. <> *vt* estalar. <> *vi* **-1.** [gen] estalar; **the door ~ed shut** a porta se fechou com um clique **-2.** *inf* [fall into place] cair a ficha **-3.** *COMPUT* clicar.

client ['klaɪənt] *n* cliente *mf*.

clientele [ˌkli:ən'tel] *n (U)* clientela *f*, freguesia *f*.

cliff [klɪf] *n* penhasco *m*.

cliffhanger ['klɪfˌhæŋə^r] *n inf* suspense *m*.

climactic [klaɪ'mæktɪk] *adj* culminante.

climate ['klaɪmɪt] *n* clima *m*.

climatic [klaɪ'mætɪk] *adj* climático(ca).

climate change *n* mudança *f* climática.

climax ['klaɪmæks] *n* clímax *m*.

climb [klaɪm] ◇ *n* [ascent] escalada *f.* ◇ *vt* [go up - tree, ladder] subir em; [- hill, mountain] escalar; [- fence] transpor. ◇ *vi* -**1.** [person]: **to ~ up/down/over sthg** subir em/decer de/transpor algo; **to ~ into/out of sthg** subir em/descer de algo -**2.** [plant] trepar -**3.** [road, plane, prices] subir.
➡ **climb down** *vi* [back down] admitir o erro.
climb-down *n* retratação *f.*
climber [ˈklaɪməʳ] *n* -**1.** [person] alpinista *mf* -**2.** [plant] trepadeira *f.*
climbing [ˈklaɪmɪŋ] ◇ *adj* [plant] trepadeira. ◇ *n (U)* alpinismo *m.*
climbing frame *n UK* estrutura feita de metal, madeira ou corda na qual as crianças sobem para brincar.
climes [klaɪmz] *npl literary* clima *m.*
clinch [klɪntʃ] *vt* [settle] fechar.
cling [klɪŋ] (*pt* & *pp* **clung**) *vi* -**1.** [person]: **to ~ to sb/sthg** [physically] agarrar-se a alguém/algo; *fig* [emotionally: to person] apegar-se a alguém/algo; [to beliefs, ideas, principles] aferrar-se a alguém/algo -**2.** [clothes]: **to ~ (to sb)** ajustar-se bem (a alguém) -**3.** [smell] impregnar.
clingfilm [ˈklɪŋfɪlm] *n (U) UK* filme *m* de PVC transparente.
clinging [ˈklɪŋɪŋ] *adj* -**1.** [person, child] apegado(da) -**2.** [clothes] colado(da).
clinic [ˈklɪnɪk] *n* [building] clínica *f.*
clinical [ˈklɪnɪkl] *adj* -**1.** *MED* clínico(ca) -**2.** *pej* [coldly rational] analítico(ca) -**3.** [functional] impessoal.
clinically [ˈklɪnɪklɪ] *adv* -**1.** *MED* clinicamente -**2.** *pej* [coldly] analiticamente.
clink [klɪŋk] ◇ *n* tilintar *m.* ◇ *vi* tilintar.
clip [klɪp] (*pt* & *pp*-**ped**, *cont*-**ping**) ◇ *n* -**1.** [fastener - for paper] clipe *m*; [- for hair] grampo *m*; [- for earring] fecho *m* -**2.** *TV* & *CINEMA* videoclipe *m* -**3.** *inf* [smack]: **to give sb a ~ around the ear** dar um tapa na orelha de alguém. ◇ *vt* -**1.** [fasten] prender -**2.** [cut - lawn, hedge, nails] cortar; [- newspaper cutting] recortar -**3.** *inf* [hit - person] dar um tapa em; [- car] bater em.
➡ **clip on** *vi* [fasten] segurar, prender.
clipboard [ˈklɪpbɔːd] *n* prancheta *f* com prendedor.
clip-on *adj* de prender; **~ earrings** brincos *mpl* de pressão; **~ badge** button *m*; **~ bow tie** gravata-borboleta *f.*
clipped [klɪpt] *adj* [speech] entrecortado(da).
clippers [ˈklɪpəz] *npl* -**1.** [for hair] máquina *f* de cortar cabelo -**2.** [for nails] cortador *m* de unhas -**3.** [for plants, hedges] tesoura *f* de podar.
clipping [ˈklɪpɪŋ] *n* [newspaper cutting] recorte *m.*
➡ **clippings** *npl* [small pieces] fragmentos *mpl*; **grass/nail ~s** restos *mpl* de grama/unha cortada.
clique [kliːk] *n pej* panelinha *f.*
clitoris [ˈklɪtərɪs] *n* clítoris *m inv.*
cloak [kləʊk] ◇ *n* -**1.** [garment] capa *f* -**2.** *fig* [cover for secret] disfarce *m.* ◇ *vt* [hide, disguise] ocultar; **to be ~ed in** estar envolto(ta) em.
cloak-and-dagger *adj* misterioso(sa).
cloakroom [ˈkləʊkrʊm] *n* -**1.** [for clothes] guarda-volumes *m inv* -**2.** *UK* [toilet - in public place] banheiro *m*; [- in house] lavabo *m.*

clobber [ˈklɒbəʳ] *inf* ◇ *n* -**1.** *(U)* [things] tralhas *fpl* -**2.** *(U)* [clothes] trapos *mpl.* ◇ *vt inf* -**1.** [hit] bater -**2.** [defeat] massacrar -**3.** [affect very badly] afetar.
clock [klɒk] ◇ *n* -**1.** [timepiece] relógio *m*; **round the ~** dia e noite; **to put the ~ back** *lit* atrasar o relógio; *fig* fazer de conta que nada mudou; **to put the ~ forward** adiantar o relógio -**2.** [in vehicle - mileometer] hodômetro *m*; [- speedometer] velocímetro *m.* ◇ *vt* [reach time or speed] marcar.
➡ **clock in, clock on** *vi UK* [at work] bater o ponto *OR* cartão-de-ponto na entrada.
➡ **clock off, clock out** *vi UK* [at work] bater o ponto *OR* cartão-de-ponto na saída.
➡ **clock up** *vt fus* [amass] acumular.
clock radio *n* rádio-relógio *m.*
clockwise [ˈklɒkwaɪz] ◇ *adj* em sentido horário. ◇ *adv* em sentido horário.
clockwork [ˈklɒkwɜːk] ◇ *n (U)*: **to go like ~** funcionar como um relógio. ◇ *comp* de corda.
clod [klɒd] *n* [of earth] torrão *m.*
clog [klɒg] (*pt* & *pp* -**ged**, *cont* -**ging**) *vt* entupir, bloquear.
➡ **clogs** *npl* tamancos *mpl.*
➡ **clog up** ◇ *vt sep* -**1.** [drains] entupir -**2.** [nose] congestionar. ◇ *vi* [drains] entupir; [roads] bloquear; [pores] fechar.
clogged [klɒgd] *adj* [drains] entupido(da); [roads] bloqueado(da); [pores] fechado(da).
cloister [ˈklɔɪstəʳ] *n ARCHIT* claustro *m.*
cloistered *adj literary* [secluded] enclausurado(da), recluso(sa).
clone [kləʊn] ◇ *n* clone *m.* ◇ *vt BIOL* clonar.
close¹ [kləʊs] ◇ *adj* -**1.** [near] próximo(ma), perto; **~ to sb/sthg** perto de alguém/algo; **~ to tears** à beira das lágrimas; **it was a ~ shave** foi por um fio *OR* triz; **~ up, ~ to** de perto; **~ by, ~ at hand** bem perto -**2.** [in relationship] íntimo(ma); **~ to sb** apegado(da) a alguém -**3.** [in degree of connection - resemblance, family] próximo(ma); [- link, connection] estreito(ta) -**4.** [careful]: **a ~ watch** um olhar atento; **to pay ~ attention** prestar muita atenção; **~ questioning** uma pergunta detalhada; **a ~r look** um olhar mais de perto; **a ~r examination** um exame minucioso -**5.** [oppressive] carregado(da) -**6.** [almost equal] com uma pequena margem de diferença. ◇ *adv* perto. ◇ *n* [street] rua *f* sem saída.
➡ **close on, close to** *prep* [almost] cerca de.
close² [kləʊz] ◇ *vt* -**1.** [shut, shut down] fechar -**2.** [bring to an end] encerrar, concluir. ◇ *vi* -**1.** [shut] fechar -**2.** [heal] cicatrizar -**3.** [end] terminar. ◇ *n* [end] fim *m*, final *m.*
➡ **close down** ◇ *vt sep* [shut] fechar. ◇ *vi* -**1.** [shut down] fechar -**2.** [end] terminar.
➡ **close in** *vi* -**1.** [night, fog] fechar -**2.** [person] cercar; **to ~ in on sb/sthg** cercar alguém/algo.
➡ **close off** *vt sep* interditar.
close-cropped [ˌkləʊs-] *adj* rente.
closed [kləʊzd] *adj* fechado(da).
closed circuit television *n* televisão *f* em circuito fechado.
closedown [ˈkləʊzdaʊn] *n* -**1.** *UK* [of TV, radio station] encerramento *m* da programação -**2.** [of factory, mine] fechamento *m.*

closed shop n estabelecimento em que todos os trabalhadores devem pertencer a um determinado sindicato.

close-fitting [ˌkləʊs-] adj justo(ta).

close-knit [ˌkləʊs-] adj muito unido(da).

closely ['kləʊslɪ] adv **-1.** [in degree of connection] intimamente; **to resemble sb/sthg** ~ parecer muito com alguém/algo **-2.** [carefully] atentamente.

closeness ['kləʊsnɪs] n (U) **-1.** [of shops, facilities] proximidade f **-2.** [of relationship] intimidade f.

closeout ['kləʊzaʊt] n US liquidação f.

close quarters [ˌkləʊs-] npl: **at** ~ [very close] muito próximo(ma); MIL em contato direto (com o inimigo).

close season ['kləʊs-] n UK temporada f de caça proibida.

closet ['klɒzɪt] <> adj inf inconfesso(sa). <> n **-1.** Am closet m, armário m **-2.** fig: **to come out of the** ~ sair do armário. <> vt: **to be** ~**ed with sb** ficar trancado(da) com alguém.

close-up ['kləʊs-] n primeiro plano m.

closing ['kləʊzɪŋ] adj [final] final, de encerramento.

closing price n preço m OR cotação f de fechamento.

closing time n horário m de fechamento.

closure ['kləʊʒəʳ] n **-1.** [of business, company] fechamento m **-2.** [of road, railway line: temporarily] interdição f.

clot [klɒt] (pt & pp -ted, cont -ting) <> n **-1.** [of blood] coágulo m **-2.** UK inf [fool] idiota mf. <> vi [blood] coagular.

cloth [klɒθ] n **-1.** (U) [fabric] tecido m **-2.** [for cleaning] pano m **-3.** [tablecloth] toalha f.

clothe [kləʊð] vt fml [dress] vestir; ~**d in** vestido(da) de.

clothes [kləʊðz] npl roupa f; **to put one's** ~ **on** vestir-se; **to take one's** ~ **off** tirar a roupa.

clothes basket n cesto m de roupa.

clothes brush n escova f de roupa.

clothes horse n **-1.** [for drying clothes] estendedor m de roupa **-2.** pej [person] pessoa que só se preocupa em andar na moda, pouco inteligente e sem habilidades.

clothesline ['kləʊðzlaɪn] n varal m.

clothes peg UK, **clothespin** US ['kləʊðzpɪn] n prendedor m de roupa.

clothing ['kləʊðɪŋ] n (U) roupa f; ~ **allowance** auxílio-vestuário m.

clotted cream [ˌklɒtɪd-] n (U) UK creme feito de nata muito espesso, típico da Cornualha.

cloud [klaʊd] <> n [gen] nuvem f; **to be under a** ~ ter má fama. <> vt **-1.** [mist up] embaçar **-2.** [make less pleasant] estragar **-3.** [make less clear]: **to** ~ **the issue** obscurecer a questão.

⬥ **cloud over** vi **-1.** [sky] encobrir-se **-2.** [face] entristecer-se.

cloudburst ['klaʊdbɜːst] n temporal m repentino.

cloudless ['klaʊdlɪs] adj limpo(pa), sem nuvens.

cloudy ['klaʊdɪ] (compar -ier, superl -iest) adj **-1.** [sky] nublado(da) **-2.** [liquid] turvo(va).

clout [klaʊt] inf <> n **-1.** [blow] bofetão m **-2.** (U)

[influence] influência f. <> vt [hit] dar um bofetão em.

clove [kləʊv] n: **a** ~ **of garlic** um dente de alho.

⬥ **cloves** npl [spice] cravo-da-índia m.

clover ['kləʊvəʳ] n (U) trevo m.

clown [klaʊn] <> n **-1.** [performer] palhaço m **-2.** [fool] palhaço m, -ça f. <> vi fazer palhaçadas.

cloying ['klɔɪŋ] adj enjoativo(va).

club [klʌb] (pt & pp -bed, cont -bing) <> n **-1.** [association] clube m **-2.** [nightclub] boate f, casa f noturna **-3.** [weapon] bastão m **-4.** SPORT [equipment]: **(golf)** ~ taco m (de golfe). <> comp do clube. <> vt [hit] espancar.

⬥ **clubs** npl [playing cards] paus mpl.

⬥ **club together** vi UK fazer vaquinha.

club car n US RAIL vagão-restaurante m.

clubhouse ['klʌbhaʊs] n clube m.

cluck [klʌk] vi [hen, person] cacarejar.

clue [kluː] n **-1.** [in crime] pista f, vestígio m; **I haven't (got) a** ~ não tenho (a menor) idéia **-2.** [hint] dica f **-3.** [key to problem]: **the** ~ **(to sthg)** a chave (para algo) **-4.** [in crossword] pista f.

clued-up [kluːd-] adj UK inf antenado(da).

clueless ['kluːlɪs] adj UK inf tapado(da); **she's completely** ~ ela é completamente tapada; **to be** ~ **about sth** não ter a menor idéia sobre algo.

clump [klʌmp] <> n [group - of trees] arvoredo m; [- of bushes] moita m; [- of flowers] ramalhete m. <> vi [move heavily] mover-se pesadamente.

clumsily ['klʌmzɪlɪ] adv **-1.** [move, express o.s.] desajeitadamente **-2.** [designed, executed] grosseiramente.

clumsy ['klʌmzɪ] (compar -ier, superl -iest) adj **-1.** [gen] desajeitado(da) **-2.** [unwieldy] tosco(ca).

clung [klʌŋ] pt & pp ⊳ **cling.**

cluster ['klʌstəʳ] <> n [group - of people, houses, trees] grupo m; [- of grapes] cacho m; [- of flowers] ramalhete m. <> vi **-1.** [people] agrupar-se, reunir-se **-2.** [things] amontoar-se.

clutch [klʌtʃ] <> n AUT embreagem f. <> vt [with hands - object] agarrar; [- part of body] apertar. <> vi: **to** ~ **at sb/sthg** agarrar-se a alguém/algo.

⬥ **clutches** npl: **in the** ~**es of** nas garras de.

clutch bag n bolsa f feminina.

clutter ['klʌtəʳ] <> n bagunça f. <> vt bagunçar.

cm (abbr of centimetre) n cm.

CNAA (abbr of Council for National Academic Awards) n organismo britânico que outorga diplomas de cursos superiores de instituições que não possuem status de universidade.

CND (abbr of Campaign for Nuclear Disarmament) n organização britânica que realiza campanhas contra o armamento nuclear.

c/o (abbr of care of) a/c.

co- [kəʊ] prefix co.

Co. **-1.** (abbr of Company) Cia. **-2.** (abbr of County) área administrativa britânica, usada, em alguns casos, na representação de endereços.

CO <> n **-1.** (abbr of commanding officer) com. **-2.** (abbr of Commonwealth Office) ministério para as relações com o Commonwealth britânico. **-3.** (abbr of conscientious objector) aquele que não é voluntário para entrar nas forças armadas por *razões morais.* <> *abbr of* **Colorado**.

coach [kəʊtʃ] <> n -**1.** UK [bus] ônibus m inv -**2.** RAIL vagão m -**3.** [horsedrawn] carruagem f -**4.** SPORT treinador m, -ra f -**5.** [tutor] professor m, -ra f particular. <> vt -**1.** SPORT treinar -**2.** [tutor] preparar; **to ~ sb in sthg** preparar alguém em algo.

coaching [ˈkəʊtʃɪŋ] n (U) -**1.** SPORT treinamento m -**2.** [tutoring] preparação f.

coach station n UK (estação f) rodoviária f.

coach trip n UK passeio m de ônibus.

coagulate [kəʊˈægjʊleɪt] vi coagular.

coal [kəʊl] n (U) carvão m.

coalesce [ˌkəʊəˈles] vi fml fundir-se.

coalface [ˈkəʊlfeɪs] n veio m de carvão.

coalfield [ˈkəʊlfiːld] n jazida f de carvão.

coal gas n (U) gás m de carvão.

coalition [ˌkəʊəˈlɪʃn] n POL coalizão f.

coal mine n mina f de carvão.

coal miner n minerador m, -ra f de carvão.

coal mining n (U) mineração f de carvão.

coarse [kɔːs] adj -**1.** [rough] áspero(ra) -**2.** [vulgar] grosseiro(ra).

coarsen [ˈkɔːsn] <> vt -**1.** [make vulgar] deixar grosso(sa) -**2.** [make rough] deixar áspero(ra). <> vi -**1.** [become vulgar] vulgarizar-se -**2.** [become rough] tornar-se áspero(ra).

coast [kəʊst] <> n costa f. <> vi -**1.** [car] ir em ponto morto -**2.** fig [through life, exam] passar; **to ~ through life** deixar a vida passar; **to be ~ing happily along** estar curtindo o momento.

coastal [ˈkəʊstl] adj costeiro(ra); **a ~ town** uma cidade litorânea.

coaster [ˈkəʊstəʳ] n -**1.** [small mat] descanso m para copos -**2.** UK [ship] navio m costeiro.

coastguard [ˈkəʊstgɑːd] n -**1.** [person] guarda mf costeiro, -ra -**2.** [organization]: **the ~** a guarda costeira.

coastline [ˈkəʊstlaɪn] n litoral m.

coat [kəʊt] <> n -**1.** [garment] casaco m -**2.** [of animal] pêlo m -**3.** [of paint, varnish] demão f. <> vt: **to ~ sthg (with sthg)** revestir algo (com algo).

coat hanger n cabide m.

coating [ˈkəʊtɪŋ] n [covering - of chocolate, icing] cobertura f; [- of dust] camada f.

coat of arms (pl **coats of arms**) n brasão m.

coat stand n cabide m.

coat-tails npl -**1.** abas fpl (de casaca); **on sb's ~** fig na esteira de alguém.

co-author <> n co-autor m, -ra f. <> vt: **to ~** ser co-autor(ra) de.

coax [kəʊks] vt: **to ~ sb (to do** OR **into doing sthg)** persuadir alguém (a fazer algo); **to ~ sthg out of sb** conseguir algo de alguém com jeitinho.

coaxial cable [kəʊˈæksɪəl-] n COMPUT cabo m coaxial.

cobalt [ˈkəʊbɔːlt] n cobalto m.

cobble ➠ **cobble together** vt sep deixar alinhavado(da).

cobbled [ˈkɒbld] adj de pedras arredondadas.

cobbler [ˈkɒbləʳ] n sapateiro m, -ra f.

cobbles [ˈkɒblz], **cobblestones** [ˈkɒblstəʊnz] npl pedras arredondadas (para pavimentação).

COBOL (abbr of **Common Business Oriented Language**) n (U) COMPUT COBOL.

cobra [ˈkəʊbrə] n naja f.

cobweb [ˈkɒbweb] n teia f de aranha.

Coca-Cola® [ˌkəʊkəˈkəʊlə] n Coca-Cola® f.

cocaine [kəʊˈkeɪn] n (U) cocaína f.

cock [kɒk] <> n -**1.** UK [male chicken] galo m -**2.** [male bird] pássaro m macho -**3.** vulg [penis] pinto m. <> vt -**1.** [gun] engatilhar -**2.** [head] virar.

➠ **cock up** vt sep UK vulg: **the project was going fine, but they ~ed it up** o projeto estava indo bem, mas eles acabaram fodendo tudo.

cock-a-hoop adj inf [delighted] exultante.

cock-and-bull story n inf história f para boi dormir.

cockatoo [ˌkɒkəˈtuː] n (pl -s) n cacatua f.

cockerel [ˈkɒkrəl] n frango m.

cocker spaniel [ˌkɒkə-] n cocker spaniel mf.

cockeyed [ˈkɒkaɪd] adj inf -**1.** [not straight] torto(ta) -**2.** [unlikely to succeed] absurdo(da).

cockfight [ˈkɒkfaɪt] n rinha f.

cockle [ˈkɒkl] n [shellfish] berbigão m.

Cockney [ˈkɒknɪ] (pl **Cockneys**) <> n -**1.** [person] pessoa vinda da área leste de Londres, em geral da classe trabalhadora -**2.** [accent] cockney m. <> comp de cockney.

cockpit [ˈkɒkpɪt] n -**1.** [in plane] cabine f de comando -**2.** [in F1 car] cockpit m.

cockroach [ˈkɒkrəʊtʃ] n barata f.

cocksure [ˌkɒkˈʃʊəʳ] adj convencido(da).

cocktail [ˈkɒkteɪl] n [drink] coquetel m.

cocktail party n coquetel m.

cocktail shaker [-ˌʃeɪkəʳ] n coqueteleira f.

cocktail stick n garfo m para coquetéis.

cock-up n vinf cagada f.

cocky [ˈkɒkɪ] (compar -ier, superl -iest) adj inf petulante.

cocoa [ˈkəʊkəʊ] n (U) -**1.** [powder] cacau m -**2.** [drink] chocolate m.

coconut [ˈkəʊkənʌt] n coco m.

cocoon [kəˈkuːn] <> n casulo m. <> vt [protect from reality] preservar.

cod [kɒd] (pl inv OR -s) n bacalhau m.

COD -1. (abbr of **cash on delivery**) entrega contra pagamento. -**2.** (abbr of **collect on delivery**) entrega contra pagamento.

code [kəʊd] <> n código m. <> vt -**1.** [encode] codificar -**2.** [give identifier to] identificar como.

coded [ˈkəʊdɪd] adj [written in code] em código.

codeine [ˈkəʊdiːn] n (U) codeína f.

code name n pseudônimo m.

code of practice n código m de conduta.

cod-liver oil n (U) óleo m de fígado de bacalhau.

codswallop [ˈkɒdzˌwɒləp] n (U) UK inf asneira f.

coed [ˌkəʊˈed] <> adj (abbr of **co-educational**) relativo à escola mista. <> n -**1.** (abbr of **co-educational student**) aluno de escola mista nos Estados Unidos. -**2.** (abbr of **co-educational school**) escola mista na Grã-Bretanha.

coeducational [ˌkəʊedjuːˈkeɪʃənl] adj [school] misto(ta).

coefficient [ˌkəʊɪˈfɪʃnt] n coeficiente m.

coerce [kəʊˈɜːs] vt: **to ~ sb (into doing sthg)**

coagir alguém(a fazer algo).

coercion [kəʊˈɜːʃn] n (U) coerção f.

coexist [ˌkəʊɪɡˈzɪst] vi coexistir.

coexistence [ˌkəʊɪɡˈzɪstəns] n (U) coexistência f.

C. of E. (abbr of **Church of England**) n igreja anglicana.

coffee [ˈkɒfi] n [drink] café m.

coffee bar n UK lanchonete f.

coffee beans npl grãos mpl de café.

coffee break n intervalo m para o café, coffee break m.

coffee cup n xícara f de café.

coffee-maker n cafeteira f.

coffee mill n moedor m de café.

coffee morning n UK evento social, realizado durante o café da manhã, cuja finalidade é arrecadar dinheiro para organizações beneficentes.

coffee pot n bule m para café.

coffee shop n - 1. UK [café] café m - 2. US [restaurant] cafeteria f - 3. [shop selling coffee] cafeteria f.

coffee table n mesinha f de centro.

coffee-table book n livro m de gravuras.

coffers [ˈkɒfəz] npl fundos mpl, quantia f disponível.

coffin [ˈkɒfɪn] n caixão m.

cog [kɒg] n [tooth on wheel] dente m de engrenagem; [wheel] roda f dentada; a ~ in the machine fig uma peça secundária.

cogent [ˈkəʊdʒənt] adj irrefutável.

cogitate [ˈkɒdʒɪteɪt] vi fml cogitar.

cognac [ˈkɒnjæk] n conhaque m.

cognitive [ˈkɒgnɪtɪv] adj cognitivo(va).

cogwheel [ˈkɒgwiːl] n roda f dentada.

cohabit [ˌkəʊˈhæbɪt] vi: to ~ (with sb) coabitar (com alguém).

coherent [kəʊˈhɪərənt] adj coerente.

coherently [kəʊˈhɪərəntlɪ] adv coerentemente.

cohesion [kəʊˈhiːʒn] n (U) [unity] coesão f.

cohesive [kəʊˈhiːsɪv] adj [united] coeso(sa).

cohort [ˈkəʊhɔːt] n - 1. pej [companion] bando m - 2. [in statistics] grupo m.

COI (abbr of **Central Office of Information**) n serviço de informação do governo britânico.

coil [kɔɪl] <> n - 1. [of rope, wire] rolo m - 2. [of smoke] espiral f - 3. ELEC bobina f - 4. UK [contraceptive device] DIU m. <> vt enrolar. <> vi enrolar-se, enroscar-se.

◆ **coil up** vt sep enrolar-se.

coiled [kɔɪld] adj enrolado(da).

coin [kɔɪn] <> n moeda f. <> vt [invent] criar; to ~ a phrase como se pode dizer.

coinage [ˈkɔɪnɪdʒ] n - 1. (U) [currency] moeda f - 2. (U) [system] sistema m monetário - 3. [invented word, phrase] invenção f.

coincide [ˌkəʊɪnˈsaɪd] vi - 1. [occur simultaneously]: to ~ (with sthg) coincidir (com algo) - 2. [be in agreement] coincidir.

coincidence [kəʊˈɪnsɪdəns] n [chance event] coincidência f.

coincidental [kəʊˌɪnsɪˈdentl] adj coincidente.

coincidentally [kəʊˌɪnsɪˈdentəlɪ] adv coincidentemente.

coin-operated [-ˈɒpəˌreɪtɪd] adj que funciona com moedas.

coitus [ˈkəʊɪtəs] n (U) fml coito m.

coke [kəʊk] n - 1. [fuel] coque m - 2. inf [cocaine] coca f.

Coke® [kəʊk] n Coca® f.

Col. (abbr of **colonel**) cel.

cola [ˈkəʊlə] n refrigerante m de cola.

COLA (abbr of **cost-of-living adjustment**) n na Grã-Bretanha, atualização salarial feita de acordo com o custo de vida.

colander [ˈkʌləndəʳ] n coador m.

cold [kəʊld] <> adj frio (fria); to feel ~ [person] sentir frio; to be ~ [person] estar com frio; it's ~ today está frio hoje; to get ~ [person] ficar com frio; [food] esfriar. <> n - 1. [illness] resfriado m; to catch (a) ~ pegar um resfriado - 2. (U) [low temperature]: the ~ o frio.

cold-blooded [-ˈblʌdɪd] adj - 1. BIOL de sangue frio - 2. [unfeeling] frio (fria) - 3. [ruthless - killer, murderer] de sangue frio; [- killing, murder] a sangue frio.

cold cream n (U) creme m para a pele.

cold cuts npl US frios mpl.

cold feet npl: to have OR get ~ inf amarelar.

cold-hearted [-ˈhɑːtɪd] adj insensível.

coldly [ˈkəʊldlɪ] adv friamente.

coldness [ˈkəʊldnɪs] n (U) - 1. [low temperature] friagem f - 2. [attitude, response] frieza f.

cold shoulder n: to give sb the ~ inf dar um gelo em alguém.

cold sore n herpes m inv bucal.

cold storage n (U) [of food] refrigeração f.

cold sweat n suor m frio; to be in a ~ about sthg suar frio por causa de algo.

cold war n: the ~ a guerra fria.

coleslaw [ˈkəʊlslɔː] n (U) salada f de repolho.

colic [ˈkɒlɪk] n (U) cólica f.

collaborate [kəˈlæbəreɪt] vi - 1. [work together] colaborar; to ~ with sb colaborar com alguém - 2. pej [with enemy] conspirar; to ~ with sb conspirar com alguém.

collaboration [kəˌlæbəˈreɪʃn] n - 1. (U) [teamwork] colaboração f; ~ with sb colaboração com alguém - 2. pej [with enemy] conspiração f; ~ with sb conspiração com alguém.

collaborative [kəˈlæbərətɪv] adj conjunto(ta).

collaborator [kəˈlæbəreɪtəʳ] n - 1. [colleague] colaborador m, -ra f - 2. pej [traitor] traidor m, -ra f.

collage [ˈkɒlɑːʒ] n colagem f.

collagen [ˈkɒlədʒən] n (U) colágeno m.

collapse [kəˈlæps] <> n (U) - 1. [gen] colapso m - 2. [of building, roof] desmoronamento m. <> vi - 1. [gen] desmoronar - 2. [fail] fracassar - 3. [person] ter um colapso; his lung ~d o pulmão dele entrou em falência; to ~ with a heart attack ter um ataque do coração; I ~d into bed desfaleci na cama - 4. [folding table, chair] desmontar-se.

collapsible [kəˈlæpsəbl] adj desmontável.

collar [ˈkɒləʳ] <> n - 1. [on garment - shirt] colarinho m; [- dress, jacket] gola f - 2. [for dog] coleira f - 3. TECH anel m. <> vt inf [detain] segurar.

collarbone [ˈkɒləbəʊn] n clavícula f.

collate [kəˈleɪt] vt - 1. [compare] confrontar - 2. [put in order] ordenar.

collateral [kɒ'lætərəl] n (U) garantia f de empréstimo, caução f.

collation [kə'leɪʃn] n (U) - **1.** [comparison] confrontação f - **2.** [ordering] ordenação f.

colleague ['kɒliːg] n colega mf.

collect [kə'lekt] ◇ vt - **1.** [gather together - wood, bottles, belongings] juntar; [- material for book] colher, coletar: **to ~ o.s.** OR **one's thoughts** recompor-se - **2.** [as a hobby] colecionar - **3.** [fetch, pick up] buscar - **4.** [money, taxes] cobrar; **~ on delivery** US cobrar na entrega. ◇ vi - **1.** [crowd, people] reunir-se - **2.** [dust, dirt] juntar - **3.** [for charity, gift] arrecadar. ◇ adv US TELEC: **to call (sb) ~** ligar (para alguém) a cobrar.
  ◆ **collect up** vt sep juntar.

collectable [kə'lektəbl] ◇ adj [desirable to collectors] de coleção. ◇ n [desirable object] colecionável m.

collected [kə'lektɪd] adj - **1.** [person] controlado(da) - **2.** [works, poems] completo(ta).

collecting [kə'lektɪŋ] n (U) [hobby] coleção f; **stamp ~** colecionar selos.

collection [kə'lekʃn] n - **1.** [of objects] coleção f - **2.** [anthology] antologia f - **3.** (U) [act of collecting] coleta f - **4.** [of money] arrecadação f, vaquinha f; **they made a ~ to buy flowers for her** fizeram uma vaquinha para comprar flores para ela.

collective [kə'lektɪv] ◇ adj coletivo(va). ◇ n cooperativa f.

collective bargaining n (U) negociações fpl (entre empregadores e sindicatos).

collectively [kə'lektɪvlɪ] adv coletivamente.

collective ownership n (U) propriedade f conjunta.

collector [kə'lektə'] n - **1.** [as a hobby] colecionador m, -ra f - **2.** [of taxes] coletor m, -ra f - **3.** [of debts, rent] cobrador m, -ra f.

collector's item n peça f de coleção.

college ['kɒlɪdʒ] n - **1.** [for further education] escola f; **a ~ of technology** um instituto de tecnologia; **art ~** escola de artes; **community ~** US escola politécnica - **2.** UK [of university] instituição dentro de certas universidades britânicas que possui corpo docente, instalações e estudantes próprios - **3.** [organized body] colégio m; **electoral ~** colégio eleitoral.

college of education n faculdade f de educação.

collide [kə'laɪd] vi: **to ~ (with sb/sthg)** colidir (com alguém/algo).

collie ['kɒlɪ] n collie m.

colliery ['kɒljərɪ] (pl -ies) n UK mina f de carvão (incluindo suas instalações).

collision [kə'lɪʒn] n - **1.** [crash]: **~ (with sb/sthg)** colisão f (com alguém/algo); **~ between** colisão de - **2.** fig [conflict] conflito m; **head-on ~** colisão f frontal.

collision course n: **to be on a ~** estar em rota de colisão.

colloquial [kə'ləʊkwɪəl] adj coloquial.

colloquialism [ka'ləʊkwɪəlɪzm] n coloquialismo m.

collude [kə'luːd] vi: **to ~ with sb** entrar em conluio com alguém.

collusion [kə'luːʒn] n: **in ~ with** em conluio com.

cologne [kə'ləʊn] n (U) água-de-colônia f.

Colombia [kə'lɒmbɪə] n Colômbia; **in ~** na Colômbia.

Colombian [kə'lɒmbɪən] ◇ adj colombiano(na). ◇ n colombiano m, -na f.

colon ['kəʊlən] n - **1.** ANAT cólon m - **2.** [punctuation mark] dois-pontos mpl.

colonel ['kɜːnl] n coronel m.

colonial [kə'ləʊnjəl] adj [rule, power] colonial.

colonialism [kə'ləʊnjəlɪzm] n (U) colonialismo m.

colonist ['kɒlənɪst] n colonizador m, -ra f.

colonize, -ise ['kɒlənaɪz] vt colonizar.

colonnade [ˌkɒlə'neɪd] n colunata f.

colony ['kɒlənɪ] (pl -ies) n - **1.** [gen] colônia f - **2.** [of artists] retiro m.

color etc US = colour etc.

colorado beetle n doríforo m.

colossal [kə'lɒsl] adj colossal.

colostomy [kə'lɒstəmɪ] (pl -ies) n colostomia f.

colour UK, **color** US ['kʌlə'] ◇ n cor f; **red/blue in ~** na cor vermelha/azul; **the photos are in ~** as fotos são coloridas. ◇ adj colorido(da); **~ television/diagram** televisão/diagrama em cores. ◇ vt - **1.** [food, liquid] tingir; [with pen, crayon] pintar, colorir - **2.** [dye] tingir - **3.** fig [affect] influenciar. ◇ vi [blush] corar.
  ◆ **colours** npl - **1.** [of school, team] cores fpl - **2.** [flag] bandeira f.
  ◆ **colour in** vt sep colorir.

colour bar n discriminação f racial.

colour blind adj - **1.** daltônico(ca) - **2.** fig [racially unprejudiced] que não faz discriminação racial.

colour-coded adj identificado(da) OR codificado(da) por cores.

coloured UK, **colored** US ['kʌləd] adj - **1.** [having colour] colorido(da) - **2.** [having stated colour]: **a cream-~ ed jacket** uma jaqueta cor de creme; **a brightly ~ ed shirt** uma camisa de cores vivas.

colourfast UK, **colorfast** US ['kʌləfɑːst] adj de cores firmes.

colourful UK, **colorful** US ['kʌləfʊl] adj - **1.** [brightly coloured] colorido(da) - **2.** [story] vivo(va) - **3.** [person] animado(da).

colouring UK, **coloring** US ['kʌlərɪŋ] n - **1.** [dye] corante m - **2.** (U) [complexion, hair] tonalidade f - **3.** [colours] cor m.

colourless UK, **colorless** US ['kʌləlɪs] adj - **1.** [not coloured] incolor - **2.** fig [uninteresting] sem graça.

colour scheme n distribuição f de cores.

colour supplement n UK suplemento m em cores.

colt [kəʊlt] n [young horse] potro m.

column ['kɒləm] n - **1.** [gen] coluna f - **2.** [of people, vehicles] fila f.

columnist ['kɒləmnɪst] n colunista mf.

coma ['kəʊmə] n coma m.

comatose ['kəʊmətəʊs] adj [in a coma] em coma.

comb [kəʊm] ◇ n [for hair] pente m. ◇ vt - **1.** [hair] pentear - **2.** fig [search] vasculhar.

combat ['kɒmbæt] ◇ n combate m. ◇ vt [fight] combater.

combative ['kɒmbətɪv] adj combativo(va).

combination [ˌkɒmbɪˈneɪʃn] n combinação f.
combination lock n fechadura f com segredo.
combine [vb kəmˈbaɪn, n ˈkɒmbaɪn] ⇔ vt [join together] agrupar; **to ~ sthg with sthg** [two substances] combinar algo com algo; [two qualities] reunir; [two activities] conjugar. ⇔ vi [businesses, political parties]: **to ~ (with sb/sthg)** aliar-se (a alguém/algo). ⇔ n -1. [group] associação f -2. = combine harvester.
combined adj: **~ (with sb/sthg)** conjunto(ta) (com alguém/algo).
combine harvester [-ˈhɑːvɪstəʳ] n colheitadeira f.
combustible [kəmˈbʌstəbl] adj [substance] combustível.
combustion [kəmˈbʌstʃn] n (U) combustão f.
come [kʌm] (pt came, pp come) vi -1. [move] vir; [arrive] chegar; **the news came as a shock** a notícia foi um choque; **coming!** estou indo; **the time has ~** chegou a hora; **he doesn't know whether he's coming or going** fig ele não sabe o que fazer -2. [reach]: **to ~ up/down to** chegar a -3. [happen] chegar a; **how did you ~ to fail your exam?** como que você foi rodar no exame?; **~ what may** haja o que houver -4. [become]: **to ~ true** tornar-se realidade; **to ~ undone/unstuck** se desfazer/soltar -5. [begin gradually]: **to ~ to do sthg** passar a fazer algo -6. [be placed in order] classificar-se; **P ~s before Q** o P vem antes do Q; **she came second in the exam** ela se classificou em segundo lugar no exame -7. v inf [sexually] gozar -8. phr: **~ to think of it** pensando bem.
to come adv vindouro(ra); **in (the) days/years to ~** nos dias/anos vindouros.
come about vi [happen] acontecer.
come across ⇔ vt fus [find] encontrar. ⇔ vi [speaker, message] apresentar-se; **to ~ across as** parecer.
come along vi -1. [arrive by chance] aparecer -2. [improve] desenvolver-se; **the project is coming along nicely** o projeto está se desenvolvendo bem -3. phr: **~ along!** [expressing encouragement] anda!; [hurry up] anda logo!
come apart vi -1. [fall to pieces] desfazer-se -2. [come off] cair.
come at vt fus [attack] avançar para.
come back vi -1. [in talk, writing]: **to ~ back to sthg** voltar a algo -2. [memory]: **to ~ back (to sb)** lembrar(-se) de -3. [become fashionable again] voltar.
come by vt fus -1. [get, obtain] conseguir -2. US [visit, drop in on] dar uma chegada.
come down vi -1. [unemployment, prices] baixar -2. [aeroplane, parachutist] descer -3. [rain] cair.
come down to vt fus resumir-se a.
come down with vt fus [cold, flu] apanhar.
come forward vi [witnesses, volunteers] apresentar-se.
come from vt fus vir de.
come in vi -1. [enter] entrar -2. [arrive, be received] chegar -3. [be involved] entrar.
come in for vt fus [criticism] receber.
come into vt fus -1. [inherit] receber -2. [begin to be]: **to ~ into being** surgir; **to ~ into sight** aparecer.

come of vt fus [result from] dar em; **no good will ~ of it** isso não vai acabar bem.
come off vi -1. [button, label, lid] abrir -2. [attempt, joke] dar certo -3. [finish]: **to ~ off well/badly** sair-se bem/mal -4. [stain] sair -5. phr: **~ off it!** inf deixa disso!
come on vi -1. [start] começar -2. [light, heating] ligar-se -3. [progress, improve] ir; **how's the work coming on?** como está indo o trabalho? -4. phr: **~ on!** [expressing encouragement] vamos lá!; [hurry up] vamos; [expressing disbelief] que é isso.
come out vi -1. [truth, fact] revelar-se -2. [product, book, film] ser lançado -3. [finish] acabar; **to ~ out well/badly** sair-se bem/mal -4. [go on strike] entrar em greve -5. [declare publicly]: **to ~ out for/against sthg** manifestar-se a favor/contra algo -6. [photograph] sair -7. [sun, moon, stars] aparecer.
come out in vt fus: **to ~ out in spots** ficar com manchas.
come out with vt fus [remark] sair com.
come over vt fus [subj: sensation, emotion] tomar conta de.
come round vi -1. [change opinion]: **to ~ round (to sthg)** concordar (com algo) -2. [regain consciousness] voltar a si -3. [Christmas, birthday, summer] chegar.
come through ⇔ vt fus [survive] sobreviver a. ⇔ vi -1. [news, reports, results] chegar -2. [survive] sobreviver.
come to ⇔ vt fus -1. [reach]: **to ~ to an end** chegar ao fim; **to ~ to power** chegar ao poder; **to ~ to a decision** chegar a uma decisão -2. [amount to] chegar a. ⇔ vi [regain consciousness] voltar a si.
come under vt fus -1. [be governed by] ser de competência de -2. [heading] aparecer em -3. [suffer]: **to ~ under attack (from)** sofrer ataque (de).
come up vi -1. [gen] surgir -2. [be imminent] estar próximo.
come up against vt fus [opposition, difficulties] enfrentar.
come upon vt fus [find] encontrar.
come up to vt fus -1. [in space] chegar até; [in time] estar chegando -2. [equal] comparar-se.
come up with vt fus [answer, idea, solution] aparecer com.
comeback [ˈkʌmbæk] n [return] reaparecimento m; **to make a ~** reaparecer.
comedian [kəˈmiːdjən] n [comic] comediante m.
comedienne [kəˌmiːdɪˈen] n [comic] comediante f.
comedown [ˈkʌmdaʊn] n inf [anticlimax] retrocesso m.
comedy [ˈkɒmədɪ] (pl -ies) n comédia f.
comely [ˈkʌmlɪ] adj literary atraente.
come-on n inf: **to give sb the ~** estar a fim de alguém.
comet [ˈkɒmɪt] n cometa m.
come-uppance [ˌkʌmˈʌpəns] n inf: **to get one's ~** levar o troco.
comfort [ˈkʌmfət] ⇔ n -1. (U) [ease] conforto m;

too close for ~ desconfortável devido à proximidade **- 2.** [luxury] luxo *m* **- 3.** [solace] consolo *m*. ◇ *vt* consolar.

comfortable ['kʌmftəbl] *adj* **- 1.** [chair, room] confortável **- 2.** [at ease] à vontade **- 3.** [financially secure] bem de vida **- 4.** [after operation, accident] bem **- 5.** [ample] amplo(pla).

comfortably ['kʌmftəbl] *adv* **- 1.** [sit, sleep] confortavelmente **- 2.** [without financial difficulty] bem; **I can manage** ~ **on £50 a week** posso me virar bem com 50 libras por semana; ~ **off** em boa situação **- 3.** [win] com facilidade.

comforter ['kʌmfətəˀ] *n* **- 1.** [person] consolador *m*, -ra *f* **- 2.** *US* [quilt] edredon *m*.

comforting ['kʌmfətɪŋ] *adj* [thought, words] consolador(ra), confortante.

comfort station *n US euph* banheiro *m* público.

comfy ['kʌmfɪ] (*compar* **-ier**, *superl* **-iest**) *adj inf* **- 1.** [chair, room] confortável **- 2.** [person] à vontade.

comic ['kɒmɪk] ◇ *adj* [amusing] engraçado(da). ◇ *n* **- 1.** [comedian] comediante *m* **- 2.** [magazine] história *f* em quadrinhos, gibi *m*.
◆ **comics** *npl US* [in newspaper] tira *f* em quadrinhos.

comical ['kɒmɪkl] *adj* [amusing] engraçado(da).

comic strip *n* tira *f* em quadrinhos.

coming ['kʌmɪŋ] ◇ *adj* [future] próximo(ma). ◇ *n*: ~ **s and goings** idas *fpl* e vindas.

comma ['kɒmə] *n* vírgula *f*.

command [kə'mɑːnd] ◇ *n* **- 1.** [order] comando *m* **- 2.** (*U*) [control] comando *m*; **in** ~ **of sthg** no comando de algo **- 3.** [mastery] domínio *m*; **at one's** ~ à disposição; **she has four languages at her** ~ ela domina quatro idiomas **- 4.** *COMPUT* comando *m*. ◇ *vt* **- 1.** [order] mandar; **to** ~ **sb to do sthg** mandar alguém fazer algo **- 2.** *MIL* [control] comandar **- 3.** [deserve] merecer.

commandant [ˌkɒmən'dænt] *n* comandante *mf*.

commandeer [ˌkɒmən'dɪəˀ] *vt* confiscar.

commander [kə'mɑːndəˀ] *n* **- 1.** [in army] comandante *mf* **- 2.** [in navy] capitão *m*, -tã *f*.

commander in chief (*pl* **commanders in chief**) *n* comandante-chefe *m*.

commanding [kə'mɑːndɪŋ] *adj* **- 1.** [lead, position] de comando **- 2.** [voice, manner] autoritário(ria) **- 3.** [view] dominante.

commanding officer *n* comandante *mf*.

commandment [kə'mɑːndmənt] *n* RELIG mandamento *m*.

command module *n* módulo *m* de comando.

commando [kə'mɑːndəʊ] (*pl* **-s** OR **-es**) *n* **- 1.** [unit] unidade *f* de assalto **- 2.** [soldier] soldado *m* da unidade de assalto.

command performance *n* no *Reino Unido, espetáculo feito por ordem superior.*

commemorate [kə'meməreɪt] *vt* homenagear.

commemoration [kəˌmemə'reɪʃn] *n*: **in** ~ **of** em homenagem a.

commemorative [kə'memərətɪv] *adj* comemorativo(va).

commence [kə'mens] *fml* ◇ *vt* principiar; **to** ~ **doing sthg** principiar algo. ◇ *vi* principiar.

commencement [kə'mensmənt] *n fml* [beginning] princípio *m*.

commend [kə'mend] *vt* **- 1.** [praise]: **to** ~ **sb (on** OR **for sthg)** elogiar alguém (por algo) **- 2.** [recommend]: **to** ~ **sthg (to sb)** recomendar algo (a alguém); **we** ~ **our souls to God** encomendamos nossas almas a Deus.

commendable [kə'mendəbl] *adj* louvável.

commendation [ˌkɒmen'deɪʃn] *n* [special award] condecoração *f*.

commensurate [kə'menʃərət] *adj fml*: ~ **with** sthg proporcional a algo.

comment ['kɒment] ◇ *n* comentário *m*; **no** ~ sem comentários. ◇ *vt*: **to** ~ **that** comentar que. ◇ *vi* comentar; **to** ~ **on** sthg comentar algo.

commentary ['kɒməntrɪ] (*pl* **-ies**) *n* **- 1.** RADIO & TV comentário *m* **- 2.** [written explanation, comment] crítica *f*.

commentate ['kɒmənteɪt] *vi* RADIO & TV: **to** ~ **(on** sthg) narrar (algo).

commentator ['kɒmənteɪtəˀ] *n* **- 1.** [RADIO & TV - making comments] comentarista *mf*; [- describing] narrador *m*, -ra *f* **- 2.** [expert] analista *mf*; **political** ~ analista político.

commerce ['kɒmɜːs] *n* (*U*) comércio *m*.

commercial [kə'mɜːʃl] ◇ *adj* comercial. ◇ *n* [advertisement] comercial *m*.

commercial bank *n* banco *m* comercial.

commercial break *n* [intervalo *m*] comercial *m*.

commercialism [kə'mɜːʃəlɪzm] *n* (*U*) *pej* mercantilismo *m*.

commercialize, -ise [kə'mɜːʃəlaɪz] *vt* comercializar.

commercialized [kə'mɜːʃəlaɪzd] *adj pej* comercializado(da).

commercially [kə'mɜːʃəlɪ] *adv* comercialmente.

commercial vehicle *n UK* veículo *m* comercial.

commie ['kɒmɪ] *inf pej* ◇ *adj* comuna. ◇ *n* comuna *mf*.

commiserate [kə'mɪzəreɪt] *vi*: **to** ~ **(with** sb) compadecer-se (de alguém).

commiseration [kəˌmɪzə'reɪʃn] *n* compadecimento *m*, comiseração *f*.

commission [kə'mɪʃn] ◇ *n* **- 1.** [gen] comissão *f* **- 2.** [piece of work] encomenda *f*. ◇ *vt* [work] encomendar; **to** ~ **sb (to do sthg)** encarregar alguém (de fazer algo).

commissionaire [kəˌmɪʃə'neəˀ] *n UK* porteiro *m*, -ra *f*.

commissioner [kə'mɪʃnəˀ] *n* **- 1.** [high-ranking public official] comissário *m*, -ria *f* **- 2.** [member of commission] membro *m* de uma comissão, delegado *m*, -da *f*.

commit [kə'mɪt] (*pt* & *pp* **-ted**, *cont* **-ting**) *vt* **- 1.** [carry out] cometer **- 2.** [promise] comprometer; **to** ~ **o.s. (to sthg/to doing sthg)** comprometer-se (a algo/a fazer algo) **- 3.** [person to institution] confinar **- 4.**: **to** ~ **sthg to memory** confiar algo à memória.

commitment [kə'mɪtmənt] *n* **- 1.** (*U*) [dedication] dedicação *f* **- 2.** [responsibility] compromisso *m*.

committed [kə'mɪtɪd] *adj* [writer, artist, Christian] comprometido(da); ~ **to** sb/sthg comprometido(da) com alguém/algo.

committee [kə'mɪtɪ] *n* comitê *m*.

commode [kə'məʊd] *n* comadre *f*.
commodity [kə'mɒdətɪl] *(pl* -ies) *n* **- 1.** [gen] mercadoria *f* **- 2.** *ECON* commodity *f*.
commodity exchange *n* bolsa *f* de mercadorias.
common ['kɒmən] <> *adj* **- 1.** [gen] comum; ~ **to** comum a **- 2.** *UK pej* [vulgar] vulgar. <> *n* [land] área *f* pública.
➤ **in common** *adv* em comum.
common denominator *n* **- 1.** *MATH* denominador *m* comum **- 2.** [characteristic in common] característica *f* em comum.
commoner ['kɒmənəʳ] *n* plebeu *m*, -béia *f*.
common good *n*: for the ~ pelo bem comum.
common ground *n (U)* ponto *m* pacífico.
common knowledge *n (U)* conhecimento *m* geral.
common land *n (U)* área *f* pública.
common law *n* direito *m* consuetudinário, lei *f* comum.
➤ **common-law** *adj* concubinário(ria).
commonly ['kɒmənlɪ] *adv* [generally] geralmente.
commonplace ['kɒmənpleɪs] <> *adj* [everyday] trivial. <> *n* [frequent phenomenon] lugar-comum *m*.
common room *n* [in school, college] sala *f* de recreação.
Commons ['kɒmənz] *npl UK*: the ~ a Câmara dos Comuns.
common sense *n (U)* senso *m* comum.
Commonwealth ['kɒmənwelθ] *n* [former British colonies]: the ~ a Comunidade Britânica.
Commonwealth of Independent States *n*: the ~ a Comunidade dos Estados Independentes.
commotion [kə'məʊʃn] *n* comoção *f*.
communal ['kɒmjʊnl] *adj* comum.
commune [*n* 'kɒ'mju:n, *vb* kə'mju:n] <> *n* [group of people] comuna *f*. <> *vi*: to ~ with comungar com.
communicate [kə'mju:nɪkeɪt] <> *vt* comunicar. <> *vi* comunicar-se, relacionar-se; to ~ with comunicar-se com.
communicating [kə'mju:nɪkeɪtɪŋ] *adj* [doors, rooms] com comunicação.
communication [kə,mju:nɪ'keɪʃn] *n (U)* comunicação *f*.
➤ **communications** *npl* comunicações *fpl*.
communications satellite *n* satélite *m* de comunicações.
communications technology *n* tecnologia *f* de comunicação.
communicative [kə'mju:nɪkətɪv] *adj* [talkative] comunicativo(va).
communicator [kə'mju:nɪkeɪtəʳ] *n*: a good/bad ~ um bom/mau comunicador, uma boa/má comunicadora.
communion [kə'mju:njən] *n (U)* [communication] comunhão *f*.
➤ **Communion** *n (U) RELIG* comunhão *f*.
communiqué [kə'mju:nɪkeɪ] *n* comunicado *m*.
communism *n (U)* comunismo *m*.
communist <> *adj* comunista. <> *n* comunista *mf*.

community [kə'mju:nətɪl] *(pl* -ies) *n* [group] comunidade *f*; the ~ a comunidade.
community centre *n* centro *m* comunitário.
community home *n UK* ≃ Febem *f*.
community policing *n (U)* policiamento *m* comunitário.
community service *n (U)* **- 1.** [imposed on offender] prestação *m* de serviços à comunidade **- 2.** *UK* [voluntary] trabalho *m* voluntário.
community spirit *n (U)* espírito *m* comunitário.
commutable [kə'mju:təbl] *adj JUR* [sentence] comutável.
commutation ticket [,kɒmju:'teɪʃn-] *n US* passagem *f* integrada.
commute [kə'mju:t] <> *vt JUR* comutar. <> *vi* [to work] *viajar regularmente entre a casa e o trabalho, especialmente de trem.*
commuter [kə'mju:təʳ] *n pessoa que viaja regularmente entre a casa e o trabalho, especialmente de trem.*
commy ['kɒmɪ] *(pl* -ies) *adj* & *n* = **commie**.
Comoro Islands *npl*: the ~ as Ilhas de Comoro.
compact [*adj* & *vb* kəm'pækt, *n* 'kɒmpækt] <> *adj* [small and neat] compacto(ta). <> *n* **- 1.** [for face powder] estojo *m* **- 2.** *US AUT*: ~ **(car)** carro *m* de médio porte. <> *vt* compactar.
compact disc *n* disco *m* compacto, CD *m*.
compact disc player *n* CD-player *m*, toca-CD *m*.
companion [kəm'pænjən] *n* **- 1.** [gen] companheiro *m*, -ra *f* **- 2.** [book] compêndio *m*.
companionable [kəm'pænjənəbl] *adj* amigável.
companionship [kəm'pænjənʃɪp] *n (U)* camaradagem *f*.
company ['kʌmpənɪ] *(pl* -ies) *n* **- 1.** [gen] companhia *f*; to keep sb ~ fazer companhia a alguém; to part ~ **(with sb)** romper relações (com alguém) **- 2.** [business] companhia *f*, empresa *f*.
company car *n* carro *m* da empresa.
company director *n* diretor *m*, -ra *f* de empresa *OR* companhia.
company secretary *n* secretário *m*, -ria *f* geral da empresa *OR* companhia.
comparable ['kɒmprəbl] *adj* comparável; ~ **to** *OR* **with** comparável a *OR* com.
comparative [kəm'pærətɪv] *adj* **- 1.** [relative] relativo(va) **- 2.** [study, literature] comparado(da) **- 3.** *GRAM* comparativo(va).
comparatively [kəm'pærətɪvlɪ] *adv* [relatively] relativamente.
compare [kəm'peəʳ] <> *vt* comparar; to ~ **sb/ sthg with** *OR* **to** comparar alguém/algo com *OR* a; ~**d with** *OR* **to** comparado com *OR* a. <> *vi*: to ~ **(with sb/sthg)** comparar-se (com alguém/algo); to ~ **favourably/unfavourably with sthg** ser melhor/pior que algo.
comparison [kəm'pærɪsn] *n* comparação *f*; in ~ **(with** *OR* **to)** em comparação(com *OR* a).
compartment [kəm'pɑ:tmənt] *n* compartimento *m*.
compartmentalize, -ise [,kɒmpɑ:t'mentəlaɪz] *vt* compartimentar.
compass ['kʌmpəs] *n* **- 1.** [for finding direction] bússola

f - **2.** *fml* [scope] alcance *f*; **within the** ~ **of sb/sthg** ao alcance de alguém/algo.

➡ **compasses** *npl* compasso *m*; **a pair of** ~**es** um compasso.

compassion [kəm'pæʃn] *n (U)* compaixão *f*.

compassionate [kəm'pæʃənət] *adj* compassível.

compassionate leave *n* tempo que o empregador permite que o funcionário se ausente do trabalho por razões pessoais.

compatibility [kəm,pætə'bɪlətɪ] *n (U)* ~ **(with)** compatibilidade *f* (com).

compatible [kəm'pætəbl] *adj* ~ **(with)** compatível (com).

compatriot [kəm'pætrɪət] *n* compatriota *mf*.

compel [kəm'pel] (*pt & pp* **-led**, *cont* **-ling**) *vt* - **1.** [force] compelir; **to** ~ **sb to do sthg** compelir alguém a fazer algo - **2.** [demand] impelir.

compelling [kəm'pelɪŋ] *adj* - **1.** [argument, reason] convincente - **2.** [book, film, performance] envolvente.

compendium [kəm'pendɪəm] (*pl* **-diums** OR **-dia** [-dɪəl]) *n* [book] compêndio *m*.

compensate ['kɒmpenseɪt] ◇ *vt*: **to** ~ **sb for sthg** [financially] compensar alguém por algo. ◇ *vi*: **to** ~ **for sthg** compensar algo.

compensation [,kɒmpen'seɪʃn] *n*: ~ **(for sthg)** compensação *f* (por algo).

compere ['kɒmpeə'] *UK* ◇ *n* apresentador *m*, -ra *f*. ◇ *vt* apresentar.

compete [kəm'piːt] *vi* - **1.** [vie]: **to** ~ **(for sthg)** competir (por algo); **to** ~ **with** OR **against sb (for sthg)** competir com OR contra alguém (por algo) - **2.** COMM: **to** ~ **(with sb/sthg)** concorrer (com alguém/algo); **to** ~ **for sthg** disputar algo - **3.** [take part]: **to** ~ **(in sthg)** participar (de algo).

competence ['kɒmpɪtəns] *n (U)* [proficiency] competência *f*.

competent ['kɒmpɪtənt] *adj* competente.

competently ['kɒmpɪtəntlɪ] *adv* competentemente.

competing [kəm'piːtɪŋ] *adj* [conflicting] conflitante.

competition [,kɒmpɪ'tɪʃn] *n* - **1.** [gen] competição *f* - **2.** *(U)* COMM concorrência *f*.

competitive [kəm'petətɪv] *adj* competitivo(va).

competitively [kəm'petətɪvlɪ] *adv* competitivamente.

competitor [kəm'petɪtə'] *n* - **1.** [in business] concorrente *mf* - **2.** [in race, contest] competidor *m*, -ra *f*.

compilation [,kɒmpɪ'leɪʃn] *n* compilação *f*.

compile [kəm'paɪl] *vt* compilar.

complacency [kəm'pleɪsnsɪ] *n (U)* complacência *f*.

complacent [kəm'pleɪsnt] *adj* complacente.

complacently [kəm'pleɪsntlɪ] *adv* com complacência.

complain [kəm'pleɪn] *vi* [moan] queixar-se; **to** ~ **about sthg** queixar-se de algo.

complaining [kəm'pleɪnɪŋ] *adj* que reclama.

complaint [kəm'pleɪnt] *n* queixa *f*.

complement [*n* 'kɒmplɪmənt, *vb* 'kɒmplɪ,ment] ◇ *n* - **1.** [gen & GRAM] complemento *m* - **2.** [accompaniment] acompanhamento *m* - **3.** [number]: **a full** ~ **of** a totalidade de. ◇ *vt* - **1.** [gen] complementar - **2.** [accompany] acompanhar.

complementary [,kɒmplɪ'mentərɪ] *adj* complementar.

complete [kəm'pliːt] ◇ *adj* - **1.** [total, thorough] completo(ta); ~ **with** completo(ta) com - **2.** [finished, ended] concluído(da). ◇ *vt* - **1.** [collection, set, form] completar - **2.** [work, painting, book] concluir.

completely [kəm'pliːtlɪ] *adv* [totally] completamente.

completion [kəm'pliːʃn] *n (U)* [of work] conclusão *f*.

complex ['kɒmpleks] ◇ *adj* complexo(xa). ◇ *n* complexo *m*.

complexion [kəm'plekʃn] *n* - **1.** [of face] aparência *f* - **2.** [aspect] caráter *m*.

complexity [kəm'pleksətɪ] (*pl* **-ies**) *n* complexidade *f*.

compliance [kəm'plaɪəns] *n (U)* [obedience] cumprimento *m*; ~ **with sthg** de acordo com algo.

compliant [kəm'plaɪənt] *adj* obediente.

complicate ['kɒmplɪkeɪt] *vt* complicar.

complicated ['kɒmplɪkeɪtɪd] *adj* complicado(da).

complication [,kɒmplɪ'keɪʃn] *n* complicação *f*.

complicity [kəm'plɪsətɪ] *n (U)*: ~ **(in sthg)** cumplicidade *f* (em algo).

compliment [*n* 'kɒmplɪmənt, *vb* 'kɒmplɪment] ◇ *n* cumprimento *m*, elogio *m*. ◇ *vt*: **to** ~ **sb (on sthg)** cumprimentar alguém (por algo).

➡ **compliments** *npl fml* cumprimentos *mpl*.

complimentary [,kɒmplɪ'mentərɪ] *adj* - **1.** [admiring] lisonjeiro(ra) - **2.** [free] gratuito(ta).

complimentary ticket *n* bilhete *m* gratuito.

compliments slip *n* bilhete *m* de saudação.

comply [kəm'plaɪ] (*pt & pp* **-ied**) *vi*: **to** ~ **with sthg** cumprir algo.

component [kəm'pəʊnənt] *n* componente *m*.

compose [kəm'pəʊz] *vt* - **1.** [constitute] compor; **to be** ~**d of sthg** ser composto(ta) por algo - **2.** [write, create] escrever - **3.** [make calm]: **to** ~ **o.s.** recompor-se.

composed [kəm'pəʊzd] *adj* [calm] tranqüilo(la).

composer [kəm'pəʊzə'] *n* compositor *m*, -ra *f*.

composite ['kɒmpəzɪt] ◇ *adj* composto(ta). ◇ *n* composto *m*.

composition [,kɒmpə'zɪʃn] *n* composição *f*.

compost [*UK* 'kɒmpɒst, *US* 'kɒmpəʊst] *n (U)* adubo *m*.

composure [kəm'pəʊʒə'] *n (U)* compostura *f*.

compound [*adj & n* 'kɒmpaʊnd, *vb* kəm'paʊnd] ◇ *adj* composto(ta). ◇ *n* - **1.** [gen] composto *m* - **2.** [enclosed area] complexo *m*. ◇ *vt* - **1.** [exacerbate] agravar - **2.** [mixture, substance]: **to be** ~**ed of sthg** ser composto(ta) por algo.

compound fracture *n* MED fratura *f* exposta.

compound interest *n (U)* juros *mpl* compostos.

comprehend [,kɒmprɪ'hend] *vt* [understand] compreender.

comprehension [,kɒmprɪ'henʃn] *n* - **1.** *(U)* [understanding] compreensão *f* - **2.** SCH [exercise] interpretação *f*.

comprehensive [,kɒmprɪ'hensɪv] ◇ *adj* - **1.** [wide-ranging] abrangente - **2.** [insurance] total. ◇ *n UK* [school] = **comprehensive school**.

comprehensively [ˌkɒmprɪˈhensɪvlɪ] *adv* completamente.

comprehensive school *n* escola estadual de ensino médio que abrange todas as habilidades.

compress [kəmˈpres] ⇔ *n* MED compressa *f.* ⇔ *vt* -**1.** [squeeze, press] comprimir -**2.** [condense] sintetizar.

compression [kəmˈpreʃn] *n (U)* -**1.** [of air] compressão *f* -**2.** [of text] redução *f.*

comprise [kəmˈpraɪz] *vt* -**1.** [consist of]: **to be ~ d of** ser constituído(da) de -**2.** [constitute] constituir.

compromise [ˈkɒmprəmaɪz] ⇔ *n* [concession, agreement] meio-termo *m.* ⇔ *vt* [undermine integrity of] comprometer; **to ~ o.s.** comprometer-se. ⇔ *vi* [make concessions] fazer concessões.

compromising [ˈkɒmprəmaɪzɪŋ] *adj* [embarrassing] comprometedor(ra).

compulsion [kəmˈpʌlʃn] *n* -**1.** [strong desire] compulsão *f* -**2.** *(U)* [force] coação *f.*

compulsive [kəmˈpʌlsɪv] *adj* -**1.** [behaviour, gambler, liar] compulsivo(va) -**2.** [compelling] envolvente.

compulsory [kəmˈpʌlsəri] *adj* compulsório(ria).

compulsory purchase *n* UK desapropriação *f.*

compunction [kəmˈpʌŋkʃn] *n (U)* compunção *f.*

computation [ˌkɒmpjuːˈteɪʃn] *n* cômputo *m.*

compute [kəmˈpjuːt] *vt* computar.

computational linguistics *n (U)* lingüística *f* computacional.

computer [kəmˈpjuːtəʳ] ⇔ *n* computador *m.* ⇔ *comp* de computador.

computer dating [-ˈdeɪtɪŋ] *n* agência *f* de namoro por computador.

computer game *n* jogo *m* de computador.

computer graphics *npl* infografia *f.*

computerization [kəmˌpjuːtəraɪˈzeɪʃn] *n (U)* informatização *f.*

computerize, -ise [kəmˈpjuːtəraɪz] *vt* informatizar.

computerized [kəmˈpjuːtəraɪzd] *adj* informatizado(da).

computer-literate *adj* com conhecimentos de informática.

computer science *n* ciência *f* da computação.

computing [kəmˈpjuːtɪŋ] *n (U)* computação *f,* informática *f.*

comrade [ˈkɒmreɪd] *n* companheiro *m,* -ra *f.*

comradeship [ˈkɒmreɪdʃɪp] *n (U)* companheirismo *m,* camaradagem *f.*

con (*pt* & *pp* -**ned,** *cont* -**ning**) *fam* *n* (*abbr* of **convict**) *fam* presidiário *m,* -a *f.*

concave [ˌkɒnˈkeɪv] *adj* côncavo(va).

conceal [kənˈsiːl] *vt* [hide - object, substance] esconder; [- information, feelings] ocultar; **to ~ sthg from sb** esconder algo de alguém.

concede [kənˈsiːd] ⇔ *vt* [admit] conceder. ⇔ *vi* aceitar.

conceit [kənˈsiːt] *n (U)* [arrogance] presunção *f.*

conceited [kənˈsiːtɪd] *adj* presunçoso(sa).

conceivable [kənˈsiːvəbl] *adj* concebível.

conceivably [kənˈsiːvəblɪ] *adv* possivelmente.

conceive [kənˈsiːv] ⇔ *vt* conceber. ⇔ *vi* -**1.** MED conceber -**2.** [imagine]: **to ~ of sthg** conceber algo.

concentrate [ˈkɒnsəntreɪt] ⇔ *vt* concentrar. ⇔ *vi* concentrar-se; **to ~ on sthg** concentrar-se em algo.

concentrated [ˈkɒnsəntreɪtɪd] *adj* concentrado(-da).

concentration [ˌkɒnsənˈtreɪʃn] *n* concentração *f.*

concentration camp *n* campo *m* de concentração.

concentric [kənˈsentrɪk] *adj* concêntrico(ca).

concept [ˈkɒnsept] *n* conceito *m.*

conception [kənˈsepʃn] *n* concepção *f.*

conceptual art *n* arte *f* conceitual.

conceptualize, -ise [kənˈseptʃʊəlaɪz] *vt* conceituar.

concern [kənˈsɜːn] ⇔ *n* -**1.** [worry, anxiety] preocupação *f* -**2.** [matter of interest] assunto *m;* **it's no ~ of mine!** não é da minha conta! -**3.** COMM [company] negócio *m.* ⇔ *vt* -**1.** [worry]: **to be ~ ed (about sb/ sthg)** estar preocupado(da) (com alguém/ algo) -**2.** [involve] dizer respeito(a); **to be ~ ed with sthg** [subj: person] estar envolvido(da) com algo; **to ~ o.s. with sthg** preocupar-se com algo; **as far as ... is ~ ed** no que diz respeito a ... -**3.** [subj: book, report, film] tratar de.

concerning [kənˈsɜːnɪŋ] *prep* acerca de, sobre.

concert [ˈkɒnsət] *n* concerto *m.*
↪ in concert *adv* -**1.** MUS em concerto -**2.** *fml* [acting as one] conjuntamente.

concerted [kənˈsɜːtɪd] *adj* [effort] conjunto(ta).

concertgoer [ˈkɒnsətˌgəʊəʳ] *n* freqüentador *m,* -ra *f* de concertos.

concert hall *n* casa *f* de concertos.

concertina [ˌkɒnsəˈtiːnə] (*pt* & *pp* -**ed,** *cont* -**ing**) ⇔ *n* concertina *f.* ⇔ *vi* engavetar-se.

concerto [kənˈtʃeətəʊ] (*pl* -**s**) *n* concerto *m.*

concession [kənˈseʃn] *n* -**1.** [allowance, point won] concessão *f* -**2.** COMM [franchise] franquia *f* -**3.** [special price] desconto *m.*

concessionaire *n* concessionário *m,* -ria *f.*

concessionary [kənˈseʃnərɪ] *adj* [fare, price] com desconto.

conciliation [kənˌsɪlɪˈeɪʃn] *n (U)* conciliação *f.*

conciliatory [kənˈsɪlɪətrɪ] *adj* conciliatório(ria).

concise [kənˈsaɪs] *adj* conciso(sa).

concisely [kənˈsaɪslɪ] *adv* concisamente.

conclave [ˈkɒnkleɪv] *n* conclave *m.*

conclude [kənˈkluːd] ⇔ *vt* -**1.** [bring to an end] concluir -**2.** [deduce]: **to ~ (that)** concluir (que) -**3.** [agree on] firmar. ⇔ *vi* [finish] concluir.

conclusion [kənˈkluːʒn] *n* [ending, decision] conclusão *f;* **to jump to the wrong ~** chegar à conclusão errada; **a foregone ~** uma conclusão previsível.

conclusive [kənˈkluːsɪv] *adj* conclusivo(va).

concoct [kənˈkɒkt] *vt* -**1.** [story, excuse, alibi] forjar -**2.** [mixture, drink] preparar.

concoction [kənˈkɒkʃn] *n* [mixture, drink] mistura *f.*

concord [ˈkɒŋkɔːd] *n (U)* [peaceful agreement] acordo *m.*

concourse [ˈkɒŋkɔːs] *n* [hall] hall *m.*

concrete [ˈkɒŋkriːt] ⇔ *adj* concreto(ta). ⇔ *n (U)* [building material] concreto *m.* ⇔ *comp* [made of concrete] de concreto. ⇔ *vt* [path, garden] concretar.

confined

concrete mixer *n* betoneira *f.*

concur [kən'kɜː^r] (*pt* & *pp* -red, *cont* -ring) *vi* [agree]: to ~ (with sthg) concordar (com algo).

concurrent *adj* simultâneo(nea).

concurrently [kən'kʌrəntlɪ] *adv* simultaneamente, concomitantemente.

concussed [kən'kʌst] *adj* que sofreu concussão.

concussion [kən'kʌʃn] *n (U)* concussão *f.*

condemn [kən'dem] *vt* -1. condenar; to ~ sb for sthg condenar alguém por algo -2. [force]: to ~ sb to sthg/to do sthg condenar alguém a algo/a fazer algo -3. *JUR* [sentence]: to ~ sb to sthg condenar alguém a algo.

condemnation [ˌkɒndem'neɪʃn] *n (U)* condenação *f.*

condemned [kən'demd] *adj* condenado(da).

condensation [ˌkɒnden'seɪʃn] *n (U)* condensação *f.*

condense [kən'dens] ◇ *vt* condensar. ◇ *vi* [gas, liquid] condensar-se.

condensed milk [kən'denst-] *n (U)* leite *m* condensado.

condescend [ˌkɒndɪ'send] *vi* -1. [behave patronizingly]: to ~ to sb condescender-se a alguém -2. [lower o.s.]: to ~ to do sthg condescender em fazer algo.

condescending [ˌkɒndɪ'sendɪŋ] *adj* condescendente.

condiments ['kɒndɪmənts] *npl fml* condimentos *mpl.*

condition [kən'dɪʃn] ◇ *n* -1. [of person] forma *f*; out of ~ fora de forma -2. [of car] estado *m*; in good/bad ~ em bom/mau estado -3. *MED* [disease, complaint] problema *m* -4. [provision] condição *f*; on one ~ sob *OR* com uma condição; on ~ that desde que; to agree to do sthg on one ~ concordar em fazer algo sob *OR* com uma condição. ◇ *vt* -1. condicionar -2. [hair] hidratar.

➡ **conditions** *npl* [circumstances] condições *fpl.*

conditional [kən'dɪʃənl] ◇ *adj* condicional; ~ (up)on sthg condicionado(da) a algo. ◇ *n GRAM* condicional *m.*

conditionally [kən'dɪʃnəlɪ] *adv* condicionalmente.

conditioner [kən'dɪʃnə^r] *n* -1. [for hair] condicionador *m* -2. [for clothes] amaciante *m.*

conditioning [kən'dɪʃnɪŋ] *n (U) PSYCH* condicionamento *m.*

condolences [kən'dəʊlənsɪz] *npl* condolências *fpl*, pêsames *mpl.*

condom ['kɒndəm] *n* camisinha *f*, preservativo *m.*

condominium [ˌkɒndə'mɪnɪəm] *n US* [apartment, building] condomínio *m.*

condone [kən'dəʊn] *vt* tolerar.

condor ['kɒndɔː^r] *n* condor *m.*

conducive [kən'djuːsɪv] *adj*: ~ to sthg/to doing sthg conducente a algo/a fazer algo.

conduct [*n* 'kɒndʌkt, *vb* kən'dʌkt] ◇ *n (U)* conduta *f.* ◇ *vt* -1. [research, survey & *PHYS*] conduzir -2. [behave]: to ~ o.s. well/badly comportar-se bem/mal -3. *MUS* reger. ◇ *vi MUS* reger.

conducted tour [kən'dʌktɪd-] *n* excursão *f* guiada.

conductor [kən'dʌktə^r] *n* -1. [on bus] cobrador *m* -2. [on train] *US* condutor *m* -3. *PHYS* condutor *m* -4. *MUS* maestro *m*, -trina *f.*

conductress [kən'dʌktrɪs] *n* [on bus] cobradora *f.*

conduit ['kɒndɪt] *n* conduto *m.*

cone [kəʊn] *n* -1. [gen] cone *m* -2. [for ice cream] casquinha *f* -3. [from tree] pinha *f.*

➡ **cone off** *vt sep UK* bloquear com cones (*uma estrada*).

confectioner [kən'fekʃnə^r] *n* confeiteiro *m*, -ra *f*; ~'s (shop) confeitaria *f.*

confectionery [kən'fekʃnərɪ] *n (U)* confeito *m.*

confederacy *n* confederação *f.*

confederate *n* cúmplice *mf.*

confederation [kən,fedə'reɪʃn] *n* [group] confederação *f.*

Confederation of British Industry *n*: the ~ a Confederação das Indústrias Britânicas.

confer [kən'fɜː^r] (*pt* & *pp* -red, *cont* -ring) ◇ *vt fml*: to ~ sthg (on sb) conferir algo (a alguém). ◇ *vi*: to ~ (with sb on *OR* about sthg) confabular (com alguém sobre *OR* a respeito de algo).

conference ['kɒnfərəns] *n* conferência *f*; in ~ em reunião.

conference call *n* teleconferência *f.*

conference centre *n* centro *m* de conferências.

conference hall *n* salão *m* de conferências.

conferencing ['kɒnfərənsɪŋ] *n (U)* (sistema *m* de) teleconferência *f.*

confess [kən'fes] ◇ *vt* confessar; to ~ (that) confessar que. ◇ *vi* [gen] confessar; to ~ to sthg confessar *OR* admitir algo.

confession [kən'feʃn] *n* confissão *f.*

confessional [kən'feʃənl] *n* confessionário *m.*

confetti [kən'fetɪ] *n (U)* confete *m.*

confidant [ˌkɒnfɪ'dænt] *n* confidente *m.*

confidante [ˌkɒnfɪ'dænt] *n* confidente *f.*

confide [kən'faɪd] ◇ *vt* confiar ◇ *vi*: to ~ in sb confiar em alguém.

confidence ['kɒnfɪdəns] *n* -1. (U) [assurance] autoconfiança *f* -2. (U) [trust] confiança *f*; to have ~ in sb ter confiança em alguém -3. [secrecy]: in ~ em segredo -4. [secret] confidência *f.*

confidence trick *n* conto-do-vigário *m.*

confident ['kɒnfɪdənt] *adj* -1. [assured] autoconfiante -2. [sure] confiante; ~ of sthg confiante em algo.

confidential [ˌkɒnfɪ'denʃl] *adj* confidencial.

confidentiality ['kɒnfɪˌdenʃɪ'ælətɪ] *n (U)* sigilo *m*; a breach of ~ uma quebra de sigilo.

confidentially [ˌkɒnfɪ'denʃəlɪ] *adv* -1. [in confidence] confidencialmente -2. [in private] em particular.

confidently ['kɒnfɪdəntlɪ] *adv* -1. [with assurance] com autoconfiança -2. [with certainty] com confiança.

configuration [kən,fɪgə'reɪʃn] *n* configuração *f.*

confine [kən'faɪn] *vt* confinar; to be ~d to estar confinado(da) a; to ~ o.s. to sthg/to doing sthg confinar-se a algo/a fazer algo.

➡ **confines** *npl* confins *mpl.*

confined [kən'faɪnd] *adj* [space, area] confinado(da).

confinement [kən'faɪnmənt] *n* -**1.** (U) [imprisonment] confinamento *m* -**2.** *dated* & MED (trabalho *m* de) parto *m*.

confirm [kən'fɜ:m] *vt* -**1.** [gen] confirmar -**2.** RELIG crismar.

confirmation [ˌkɒnfə'meɪʃn] *n* -**1.** [gen] confirmação *f* -**2.** RELIG crisma *f*.

confirmed [kən'fɜ:md] *adj* [habitual] convicto(ta).

confiscate ['kɒnfɪskeɪt] *vt* confiscar.

confiscation [ˌkɒnfɪ'skeɪʃn] *n* (U) confisco *m*.

conflagration [ˌkɒnflə'greɪʃn] *n* fml conflagração *f*.

conflate *vt* fml fundir.

conflict [*n* 'kɒnflɪkt, *vb* kən'flɪkt] <> *n* [fighting, clash] conflito *m*; ~ **of interest** conflito de interesses. <> *vi* [clash] entrar em conflito; **to** ~ **with sb/sthg** entrar em conflito com alguém/algo.

conflicting [kən'flɪktɪŋ] *adj* [contradictory] conflitante.

confluence *n* [of rivers] confluência *f*.

conform [kən'fɔ:m] *vi* -**1.** [behave as expected] conformar-se -**2.** [be in accordance]: **to** ~ **(to** OR **with sthg)** conformar-se (com algo).

conformist [kən'fɔ:mɪst] *pej* <> *adj* conformista. <> *n* conformista *mf*.

conformity [kən'fɔ:mətɪ] *n* (U) conformidade *f*; ~ **to** OR **with sthg** conformidade com algo.

confound [kən'faʊnd] *vt* [confuse, defeat] confundir.

confounded [kən'faʊndɪd] *adj* inf [for emphasis] maldito(ta).

confront [kən'frʌnt] *vt* -**1.** [person] defrontar-se com -**2.** [task, problem] enfrentar -**3.** [present]: **to** ~ **sb (with sthg)** confrontar alguém (com algo).

confrontation [ˌkɒnfrʌn'teɪʃn] *n* confrontação *f*.

confrontational *adj* de confrontamento.

confuse [kən'fju:z] *vt* -**1.** [bewilder] confundir -**2.** [mix up]: **to** ~ **sb/sthg (with)** confundir alguém/ algo (com) -**3.** [complicate, make less clear] complicar.

confused [kən'fju:zd] *adj* confuso(sa).

confusing [kən'fju:zɪŋ] *adj* confuso(sa).

confusion [kən'fju:ʒn] *n* confusão *f*.

conga ['kɒŋgə] *n*: **the** ~ a conga.

congeal [kən'dʒi:l] *vi* -**1.** [blood] coagular -**2.** [food] congelar.

congenial [kən'dʒi:njəl] *adj* agradável.

congenital [kən'dʒenɪtl] *adj* MED congênito(ta).

conger eel ['kɒŋgər-] *n* enguia *f* marinha.

congested [kən'dʒestɪd] *adj* congestionado(da).

congestion [kən'dʒestʃn] *n* (U) -**1.** [overcrowding] congestionamento *m* -**2.** MED congestão *f*.

conglomerate [kən'glɒmərət] *n* COMM conglomerado *m*.

conglomeration [kənˌglɒmə'reɪʃn] *n* fml conglomeração *f*.

Congo ['kɒŋgəʊ] *n* -**1.** [country]: **the** ~ o Congo; **in the** ~ no Congo -**2.** [river]: **the** ~ o Congo.

Congolese [ˌkɒŋgə'li:z] <> *adj* congolês(esa). <> *n* congolês *m*, -esa *f*.

congratulate [kən'grætʃʊleɪt] *vt*: **to** ~ **sb (on)** felicitar alguém (por); **to** ~ **o.s. (on)** congratular-se (por).

congratulations [kənˌgrætʃʊ'leɪʃənz] <> *npl* felicitações *fpl*. <> *excl* parabéns!

congratulatory [kən'grætʃʊlətrɪ] *adj* de felicitações.

congregate ['kɒŋgrɪgeɪt] *vi* congregar-se.

congregation [ˌkɒŋgrɪ'geɪʃn] *n* RELIG congregação *f*.

congress ['kɒŋgres] *n* [meeting] congresso *m*.
➡ **Congress** *n* US POL Congresso *m*.

congressional [kən'greʃənl] *adj* US POL parlamentar.

congressman ['kɒŋgresmən] (*pl* -men [-mən]) *n* US POL congressista *m*.

congresswoman ['kɒŋgresˌwʊmən] (*pl* -women [-ˌwɪmɪn]) *n* US POL congressista *f*.

conical ['kɒnɪkl] *adj* cônico(ca).

conifer ['kɒnɪfər] *n* conífera *f*.

coniferous [kə'nɪfərəs] *adj* conífero(ra).

conjecture [kən'dʒektʃər] <> *n* conjectura *f*. <> *vt*: **to** ~ **(that)** prever (que). <> *vi* conjecturar.

conjugal ['kɒndʒʊgl] *adj* fml conjugal.

conjugate ['kɒndʒʊgeɪt] *vt* conjugar.

conjugation [ˌkɒndʒʊ'geɪʃn] *n* conjugação *f*.

conjunction [kən'dʒʌŋkʃn] *n* -**1.** GRAM conjunção *f* -**2.** [combination] combinação *f*; **in** ~ **with** em conjunto com.

conjunctivitis [kənˌdʒʌŋktɪ'vaɪtɪs] *n* (U) conjuntivite *f*.

conjure ['kʌndʒər] <> *vt* [by magic] fazer aparecer. <> *vi* [by magic] fazer truques.
➡ **conjure up** *vt sep* [evoke] evocar.

conjurer ['kʌndʒərər] *n* [magician] mágico *m*, -ca *f*.

conjuring trick ['kʌndʒərɪŋ-] *n* [magic trick] truque *m* de mágica.

conjuror ['kʌndʒərər] *n* = conjurer.

conk [kɒŋk] *n* inf [nose] narigão *m*.
➡ **conk out** *vi* inf -**1.** [person] estar em frangalhos -**2.** [car, machine] escangalhar-se.

conker ['kɒŋkər] *n* UK castanha-da-índia *f*.

con man (*pl* -men) *n* vigarista *m*.

connect [kə'nekt] <> *vt* -**1.** [gen] ligar, conectar; **to** ~ **sthg (to sthg)** ligar algo (a algo); **I'm just** ~**ing you** [on telephone] estou completando sua ligação -**2.** [associate]: **to** ~ **sb/sthg to** OR **with** relacionar alguém/algo a OR com -**3.** ELEC [to power supply]: **to** ~ **sthg to** conectar algo a. <> *vi* [train, plane, bus]: **to** ~ **(with)** conectar com.

connected [kə'nektɪd] *adj* [related, associated] relacionado(da); ~ **with** conectado(da) com.

Connecticut [kə'netɪkət] *n* Connecticut.

connecting [kə'nektɪŋ] *adj* [flight, train] de conexão.

connecting rod *n* AUT biela *f*.

connection [kə'nekʃn] *n* -**1.** [relationship] conexão *f*, relação *f*; ~ **between/with sthg** relação entre /com algo; **in** ~ **with** em relação a -**2.** [plane, train, bus & *ELEC*] conexão *f* - **3.** [on telephone] ligação *f* - **4.** [influential contact] contato *m*.

connective tissue [kə'nektɪv-] *n* tecido *m* conjuntivo.

connexion [kə'nekʃn] *n UK* = connection.

connive [kə'naɪv] *vi* - **1.** [plot] conspirar; **to ~ with sb** tramar com alguém - **2.** [allow to happen]: **to ~ at sthg** ser conivente em algo.

conniving [kə'naɪvɪŋ] *adj pej* traidor(ra).

connoisseur [ˌkɒnə'sɜːʳ] *n* conhecedor *m*, -ra *f*, especialista *mf*.

connotation [ˌkɒnə'teɪʃn] *n* conotação *f*.

conquer ['kɒŋkəʳ] *vt* - **1.** [take by force] conquistar - **2.** *fig* [overcome] dominar.

conqueror ['kɒŋkərəʳ] *n* conquistador *m*, -ra *f*.

conquest ['kɒŋkwest] *n* conquista *f*.

cons *npl* - **1.** *Br fam* (*abbr of* **conveniences**): **all mod ~** com todas as comodidades. - **2.** ⊳ **pro**.

Cons. (*abbr of* **Conservative**) *partido político britânico de centro-direita*.

conscience ['kɒnʃəns] *n* consciência *f*; **to have a guilty ~** ter a consciência pesada; **in all ~** em sã consciência.

conscientious [ˌkɒnʃɪ'enʃəs] *adj* consciencioso(-sa).

conscientiously [ˌkɒnʃɪ'enʃəslɪ] *adv* conscienciosamente.

conscientiousness *n* (*U*) consciência *f*, escrúpulo *m*.

conscientious objector *n pessoa que, por razões morais ou religiosas, recusa-se a servir nas forças armadas.*

conscious ['kɒnʃəs] *adj* consciente; **~ of sthg** consciente de algo; **fashion-~** conhecedor(ra) da moda.

consciously ['kɒnʃəslɪ] *adv* [intentionally] deliberadamente.

consciousness ['kɒnʃəsnɪs] *n* (*U*) consciência *f*; **to lose/regain ~** perder/recobrar os sentidos.

conscript [*n* 'kɒnskrɪpt, *vb* kən'skrɪpt] *MIL* ⇔ *n* recruta *mf*. ⇔ *vt* recrutar.

conscription [kən'skrɪpʃn] *n* (*U*) serviço *m* militar obrigatório.

consecrate ['kɒnsɪkreɪt] *vt* - **1.** *RELIG* [make holy] consagrar - **2.** *fig* [dedicate] dedicar.

consecration [ˌkɒnsɪ'kreɪʃn] *n RELIG* consagração *f*.

consecutive [kən'sekjʊtɪv] *adj* consecutivo(va).

consecutively [kən'sekjʊtɪvlɪ] *adv* consecutivamente.

consensus [kən'sensəs] *n* consenso *m*.

consent [kən'sent] ⇔ *n* (*U*) consentimento *m*. ⇔ *vi*: **to ~ (to sthg)** consentir (em algo).

consenting [kən'sentɪŋ] *adj*: **~ adults** *adultos que aceitam ter relações sexuais.*

consequence ['kɒnsɪkwəns] *n* - **1.** [result] conseqüência *f*; **to face the ~s** encarar as conseqüências; **in ~** em conseqüência - **2.** [importance] importância *f*; **to be of little ~** não ter importância.

consequent ['kɒnsɪkwənt] *adj* conseqüente.

consequently ['kɒnsɪkwəntlɪ] *adv* conseqüentemente.

conservation [ˌkɒnsə'veɪʃn] *n* conservação *f*.

conservation area *n* área *f* de preservação permanente.

conservationist [ˌkɒnsə'veɪʃənɪst] *n* conservacionista *mf*.

conservatism [kən'sɜːvətɪzm] *n* (*U*) conservadorismo *m*.

➧ **Conservatism** *n* (*U*) *UK POL* Conservadorismo *m*.

conservative [kən'sɜːvətɪv] ⇔ *adj* - **1.** [traditional] conservador(ra) - **2.** [cautious] cauteloso(sa). ⇔ *n* conservador *m*, -ra *f*.

➧ **Conservative** *POL UK* ⇔ *adj* conservador(ra). ⇔ *n* conservador *m*, -ra *f*.

Conservative Party *n UK*: **the ~** o Partido Conservador.

conservatory [kən'sɜːvətrɪ] (*pl* -**ies**) *n* estufa *f*.

conserve [*n* 'kɒnsɜːv, *vb* kən'sɜːv] ⇔ *n* conserva *f*. ⇔ *vt* conservar.

consider [kən'sɪdəʳ] *vt* - **1.** [gen] considerar; **all things ~ed** considerando tudo - **2.** [believe] achar.

considerable [kən'sɪdrəbl] *adj* considerável.

considerably [kən'sɪdrəblɪ] *adv* consideravelmente.

considerate [kən'sɪdərət] *adj* [thoughtful] atencioso(sa); **that's very ~ of you** é muita consideração de sua parte.

consideration [kənˌsɪdə'reɪʃn] *n* - **1.** (*U*) [gen] consideração *f*; **to take sthg into ~** levar algo em consideração; **to show no ~ for others** não mostrar consideração pelos outros - **2.** [factor] fator *m* - **3.** [discussion]: **under ~** em consideração; **your proposal is under ~** sua proposta está sendo considerada.

considered [kən'sɪdəd] *adj*: **~ opinion** opinião *f* sincera.

considering [kən'sɪdərɪŋ] ⇔ *prep* considerando, em vista de. ⇔ *conj* considerando que. ⇔ *adv* apesar de tudo, pensando bem.

consign [kən'saɪn] *vt* [relegate]: **to ~ sb/sthg to sthg** consignar alguém/algo a algo.

consignee [ˌkɒnsaɪ'niː] *n* consignatário *m*, -ria *f*.

consignment [kən'saɪnmənt] *n* [load] remessa *f*, despacho *m*.

consignment note *n* nota *f* de expedição.

consist [kən'sɪst] ➧ **consist in** *vt fus*: **to ~ in sthg/in doing sthg** consistir em algo/em fazer algo.

➧ **consist of** *vt fus* consistir em.

consistency [kən'sɪstənsɪ] (*pl* -**ies**) *n* - **1.** (*U*) [coherence] consistência *f*, coerência *f* - **2.** [texture] consistência *f*.

consistent [kən'sɪstənt] *adj* - **1.** [gen] constante - **2.** [growth, improvement] consistente - **3.** [argument, facts, position]: **~ (with)** coerente (com).

consistently [kən'sɪstəntlɪ] *adv* - **1.** [gen] constantemente - **2.** [argue, reason] coerentemente.

consolation [ˌkɒnsə'leɪʃn] *n* consolação *f*.

consolation prize *n* [in competition] prêmio *m* de consolação.

console [*n* 'kɒnsəʊl, *vt* kən'səʊl] ⇔ *n* [control panel] console *m*. ⇔ *vt* consolar; **to ~ o.s. with sthg** contentar-se com algo.

consolidate [kən'sɒlɪdeɪt] ⇔ *vt* - **1.** [strengthen]

consolidar - **2.** *COMM* [merge] fundir-se. ◇ *vi COMM* fundir-se.

consolidation [kənˌsɒlɪ'deɪʃn] *n (U)* - **1.** [strengthening] consolidação *f* - **2.** *COMM* [merging] fusão *f.*

consommé [*UK* kən'sɒmeɪ, *US* ˌkɒnsə'meɪ] *n (U)* consomê *m.*

consonant ['kɒnsənənt] *n* consoante *f.*

consort [*vb* kən'sɔːt, *n* 'kɒnsɔːt] ◇ *n* - **1.** [spouse] consorte *mf* - **2.** *MUS* grupo *m.* ◇ *vi fml:* to ~ with sb ter ligações com alguém.

consortium [kən'sɔːtjəm] (*pl* -tiums *OR* -tia [-tjəl] *n* consórcio *m.*

conspicuous [kən'spɪkjʊəs] *adj* conspícuo(cua).

conspicuously [kən'spɪkjʊəslɪ] *adv* conspicuamente.

conspiracy [kən'spɪrəsɪ] (*pl* -ies) *n* conspiração *f.*

conspirator [kən'spɪrətəʳ] *n* conspirador *m*, -ra *f.*

conspiratorial [kənˌspɪrə'tɔːrɪəl] *adj* conspiratório(ria).

conspire [kən'spaɪəʳ] ◇ *vt:* to ~ to do sthg conspirar para fazer algo. ◇ *vi* - **1.** [plan secretly]: to ~ against/with sb conspirar contra/com alguém - **2.** [combine] cooperar.

constable ['kʌnstəbl] *n UK* [policeman] guarda *m.*

constabulary [kən'stæbjʊlərɪ] (*pl* -ies) *n UK* força *f* policial.

constancy ['kɒnstənsɪ] *n (U)* - **1.** [continuity] constância *f* - **2.** *literary* [faithfulness] fidelidade *f.*

constant ['kɒnstənt] *adj* - **1.** [gen] constante - **2.** *literary* [faithful] fiel.

constantly ['kɒnstəntlɪ] *adv* constantemente.

constellation [ˌkɒnstə'leɪʃn] *n ASTRON* constelação *f.*

consternation [ˌkɒnstə'neɪʃn] *n (U)* consternação *f.*

constipated ['kɒnstɪpeɪtɪd] *adj* constipado(da).

constipation [ˌkɒnstɪ'peɪʃn] *n (U)* constipação *f*, prisão *f* de ventre.

constituency [kən'stɪtjʊənsɪ] (*pl* -ies) *n* - **1.** [area] distrito *m* eleitoral - **2.** [group] eleitorado *m.*

constituency party *n UK* partido *m* local.

constituent [kən'stɪtjʊənt] ◇ *adj* constituinte. ◇ *n* - **1.** [voter] eleitor *m*, -ra *f* - **2.** [element] constituinte *m.*

constitute ['kɒnstɪtjuːt] *vt* constituir.

constitution [ˌkɒnstɪ'tjuːʃn] *n* - **1.** [health] constituição *f* (física) - **2.** [composition] constituição *f.*
➡ **Constitution** *n:* the (United States) Constitution a Constituição (dos Estados Unidos).

CONSTITUTION

Ao contrário da Constituição norte-americana, expressa num texto escrito e definitivo, a Constituição britânica não é um documento propriamente dito, mas resulta do conjunto das leis ao longo da história, tendo por base o princípio da jurisprudência.

constitutional [ˌkɒnstɪ'tjuːʃənl] *adj* constitucional.

constrain [kən'streɪn] *vt* - **1.** [person] coagir; to ~ sb to do sthg forçar alguém a fazer algo - **2.** [process, development] impedir, restringir.

constrained [kən'streɪnd] *adj* [inhibited] constrangido(da), contido(da).

constraint [kən'streɪnt] *n* - **1.** [restriction] restrição *f*; ~ on sthg restrição a algo - **2.** *(U)* [control] força *f* - **3.** [coercion] coação *f.*

constrict [kən'strɪkt] *vt* - **1.** [part of body] apertar - **2.** [person] restringir.

constricting [kən'strɪktɪŋ] *adj* - **1.** [clothes] apertado(da) - **2.** [circumstances, lifestyle] limitado(da).

construct [*vb* kən'strʌkt, *n* 'kɒnstrʌkt] ◇ *vt* - **1.** [edifice, object] construir - **2.** [sentence, argument] formar. ◇ *n fml* [concept] constructo *m.*

construction [kən'strʌkʃn] ◇ *n* - **1.** [gen] construção *f* - **2.** *(U)* [building industry] construção *f* (civil). ◇ *comp* de construção.

construction industry *n* setor *m* da construção civil.

constructive [kən'strʌktɪv] *adj* construtivo(va).

constructively [kən'strʌktɪvlɪ] *adv* construtivamente.

construe [kən'struː] *vt fml* [interpret]: to ~ sthg as interpretar algo como.

consul ['kɒnsəl] *n* [envoy] cônsul *m*, consulesa *f.*

consular ['kɒnsjʊləʳ] *adj* consular.

consulate ['kɒnsjʊlət] *n* [building] consulado *m.*

consult [kən'sʌlt] ◇ *vt* consultar. ◇ *vi:* to ~ with sb consultar-se com alguém.

consultancy [kən'sʌltənsɪ] (*pl* -ies) *n* [company] empresa *f* de consultoria.

consultancy fee *n* taxa *f* de consultoria.

consultant [kən'sʌltənt] *n* - **1.** [expert] consultor *m*, -ra *f* - **2.** *UK* [medical specialist] especialista *mf.*

consultation [ˌkɒnsəl'teɪʃn] *n* - **1.** [gen] consulta *f* - **2.** [of book, map] consultação *f.*

consulting room [kən'sʌltɪŋ-] *n* consultório *m.*

consume [kən'sjuːm] *vt* consumir.

consumer [kən'sjuːməʳ] ◇ *n* consumidor *m*, -ra *f.* ◇ *comp* do consumidor.

consumer credit *n (U)* crédito *m* ao consumidor.

consumer durables *npl* bens *mpl* duráveis.

consumer goods *npl* bens *mpl* de consumo.

consumerism [kən'sjuːmərɪzml] *n (U) pej* [theory] consumismo *m.*

consumer society *n (U)* sociedade *f* de consumo.

consumer spending *n (U)* gastos *mpl* com bens de consumo.

consuming *adj* profundo(da); a ~ passion uma paixão ardente.

consummate [*adj* kən'sʌmət, *vb* 'kɒnsəmeɪt] ◇ *adj* - **1.** [perfect] consumado(da) - **2.** [highly skilled] perfeito(ta). ◇ *vt* consumar.

consummation [ˌkɒnsə'meɪʃn] *n (U)* consumação *f.*

consumption [kən'sʌmpʃn] *n (U)* - **1.** [use] consumo *m* - **2.** *dated* [tuberculosis] tuberculose *f.*

cont. (*abbr of* continued): ~ on page 10 continua na página 10.

contact ['kɒntækt] ◇ *n* - **1.** *(U)* [physical, eye, communication] contato *m*; to lose ~ with sb perder contato com alguém; to make ~ with sb fazer contato com alguém; in ~ em contato; in ~ with

sb em contato com alguém **- 2.** [person] contato *m*.
◇ *vt* contatar, entrar em contato com.

contact lens *n* lente *f* de contato.

contact number *n* telefone *m* para contato.

contagion *n* contágio *m*.

contagious [kən'teɪdʒəs] *adj* **- 1.** MED contagioso(sa)
- 2. *fig* [laughter, good humour] contagiante.

contain [kən'teɪn] *vt* conter; **to ~ o.s.** conter-se.

contained [kən'teɪnd] *adj* [unemotional] contido(da).

container [kən'teɪnəʳ] *n* **- 1.** [box, bottle etc] recipiente *m* **- 2.** COMM [for transporting goods] contêiner *m*.

containerize, -ise [kən'teɪnəraɪz] *vt* COMM **-1.**
[transport] transportar em contêiner **- 2.** [pack]
acondicionar em contêiner.

container ship *n* navio *m* de carga.

containment [kən'teɪnmənt] *n* contenção *f*.

contaminate [kən'tæmɪneɪt] *vt* contaminar. .

contaminated [kən'tæmɪneɪtɪd] *adj* contamina-
do(da).

contamination [kən,tæmɪ'neɪʃn] *n (U)* contaminação *f*.

cont'd (*abbr of* **continued**) cont.

contemplate ['kɒntempleɪt] ◇ *vt* **- 1.** [scheme,
idea, proposal] considerar; **to ~ doing sthg** pensar
em fazer algo **- 2.** *literary* [sunset, flower] contemplar. ◇ *vi* [meditate] contemplar.

contemplation [,kɒntem'pleɪʃn] *n (U)* contemplação *f*.

contemplative [kən'templətɪv] *adj* contemplati-
vo(va).

contemporary [kən'tempərərɪ] (*pl* -ies) ◇ *adj*
contemporâneo(nea). ◇ *n* contemporâneo *m*,
-nea *f*.

contempt [kən'tempt] *n (U)* **- 1.** [gen] desprezo *m*; **~
for sb/sthg** desprezo por alguém/algo; **to hold sb
in ~** menosprezar alguém **- 2.** JUR : **~ (of court)**
desacato *m* (à autoridade do tribunal).

contemptible [kən'temptəbl] *adj* vil.

contemptuous [kən'temptʃʊəs] *adj* desdenhoso(-
sa); **to be ~ of sthg** fazer pouco caso de algo.

contend [kən'tend] ◇ *vt* **- 1.** [deal]: **to ~ with sthg**
lidar com algo; **to have enough to ~ with** ter
muitos problemas para resolver **- 2.** [compete]: **to
~ for sthg** disputar algo; **to ~ against sb** disputar
com alguém. ◇ *vt fml* [claim]: **to ~ that** sustentar
que.

contender [kən'tendəʳ] *n* **- 1.** [in fight, race] oponente
mf **- 2.** [for political office] candidato *m*, -ta *f*.

content [*n* 'kɒntent, *adj* & *vb* kən'tent] ◇ *adj*
contente; **~ with sthg** contente com algo; **to be
~ to do sthg** estar a fim de fazer algo. ◇ *n* **- 1.**
[amount contained] teor *m* **- 2.** [subject matter] conteúdo *m*. ◇ *vt*: **to ~ o.s. with sthg/with doing sthg**
contentar-se com algo/em fazer algo.

◆ **contents** *npl* **- 1.** [of container, document] conteúdo *m* **- 2.** [at front of book] sumário *m*.

contented [kən'tentɪd] *adj* satisfeito(ta).

contentedly [kən'tentɪdlɪ] *adv* com satisfação.

contention [kən'tenʃn] *n* **- 1.** [argument, assertion]
argumentação *f* **- 2.** *(U)* [disagreement] discussão *f*
- 3. *(U)* [competition]: **to be in ~** estar em discussão;
the bone of ~ o pomo da discórdia.

contentious [kən'tenʃəs] *adj fml* contencioso(sa).

contentment [kən'tentmənt] *n (U)* contentamento
m.

contest [*n* 'kɒntest, *vb* kən'test] ◇ *n* **- 1.** [competi-
tion] concurso *m* **- 2.** [for power, control] disputa *f*.
◇ *vt* **- 1.** [compete for] concorrer **- 2.** [dispute]
questionar.

contestant [kən'testənt] *n* concorrente *mf*.

context ['kɒntekst] *n* contexto *m*; **out of ~** fora de
contexto.

continent ['kɒntɪnənt] *n* GEOGR continente *m*.

◆ **Continent** *n* UK: **the Continent** o *Continente
Europeu (excluindo-se a Grã-Bretanha)*.

continental [,kɒntɪ'nentl] ◇ *adj* **- 1.** GEOGR continental **- 2.** UK [European] europeu(péia) (do continente). ◇ *n* UK *inf* europeu *m*, -péia *f* (do
continente).

continental breakfast *n* café *m* da manhã
continental.

contingency [kən'tɪndʒənsɪ] (*pl* -ies) *n* contingência *f*.

contingency plan *n* plano *m* de contingência.

contingent [kən'tɪndʒənt] ◇ *adj fml*: **~ (up)on**
sthg dependente de algo. ◇ *n* contingente *m*.

continual [kən'tɪnjʊəl] *adj* contínuo(nua).

continually [kən'tɪnjʊəlɪ] *adv* continuamente.

continuation [kən,tɪnjʊ'eɪʃn] *n* **- 1.** *(U)* [act of ex-
tending] prolongamento *m* **- 2.** [sequel] continuação
f.

continue [kən'tɪnju:] ◇ *vt* **- 1.** [carry on] continuar,
prosseguir; **to ~ doing** OR **to do sthg** continuar a
fazer algo **- 2.** [begin again] recomeçar **- 3.** [resume
speaking] prosseguir. ◇ *vi* **- 1.** [carry on] continuar;
to ~ with sthg continuar com algo **- 2.** [begin again]
recomeçar **- 3.** [resume speaking, travelling] prosseguir.

continuity [,kɒntɪ'nju:ətɪ] *n (U)* [gen] continuidade
f; **~ announcer** anunciante *m* (*que oferece um
programa*); **~ boy/girl** continuísta *mf*.

continuous [kən'tɪnjʊəs] *adj* [uninterrupted] contí-
nuo(nua).

continuous assessment *n (U)* avaliação *f*
contínua.

continuously [kən'tɪnjʊəslɪ] *adv* [without interrup-
tion] continuamente.

contort [kən'tɔ:t] *vt* contorcer.

contortion [kən'tɔ:ʃn] *n* contorção *f*.

contour ['kɒn,tʊəʳ] ◇ *n* **- 1.** [outline] contorno *m*
- 2. [on map] relevo *m*. ◇ *comp* de relevo.

contraband ['kɒntrəbænd] ◇ *adj* contrabandea-
do(da). ◇ *n (U)* contrabando *m*.

contraception [,kɒntrə'sepʃn] *n (U)* contracepção
f.

contraceptive [,kɒntrə'septɪv] ◇ *adj* anticoncepcional. ◇ *n* anticoncepcional *m*.

contraceptive pill *n* pílula *f* anticoncepcional.

contract [*n* 'kɒntrækt, *vb* kən'trækt] ◇ *n* contrato
m. ◇ *vt* **- 1.** [through legal agreement] contratar; **to
~ to do sthg** contratar para fazer algo **- 2.** COMM:
to ~ sb (to do sthg) contratar alguém (para fazer
algo) **- 3.** *fml* [illness, disease] contrair **- 4.** [word]
abreviar. ◇ *vi* [metal, plastic] contrair-se.

◆ **contract in** *vi esp* UK comprometer-se *(por
contrato)*.

contract out ◇ *vt sep* terceirizar. ◇ *vi esp UK*: **to ~ out (of sthg)** desmanchar (algo).

contraction [kən'trækʃn] *n* contração *f.*

contractor [kən'træktə'] *n* contratante *mf.*

contractual [kən'træktʃʊəl] *adj* contratual.

contradict [ˌkɒntrə'dɪkt] *vt* -**1.** [challenge] contradizer -**2.** [conflict with]: **to ~ each other** contradizer-se.

contradiction [ˌkɒntrə'dɪkʃn] *n* contradição *f;* ~ **in terms** contradição em termos.

contradictory [ˌkɒntrə'dɪktərɪ] *adj* contraditório(-ria).

contraflow ['kɒntrəfləʊl] *n* contrafluxo *m.*

contralto [kən'træltəʊ] (*pl* -s) *n* contralto *m.*

contraption [kən'træpʃn] *n* geringonça *f.*

contrary ['kɒntrərɪ, *adj sense 2* kən'treərɪ] ◇ *adj* [opposing] contrário(ria); ~ **to sthg** contrário(ria) a algo. ◇ *n* contrário *m*; **on the ~** pelo contrário; **to the ~** em contrário.

contrary to *prep* contrário a.

contrast [*n* 'kɒntrɑːst, *vb* kən'trɑːst] ◇ *n* -**1.** [difference]: ~ **(between/with)** contraste *m* (entre/com); **by** *OR* **in** ~ em comparação, por outro lado; **in** ~ **with** *OR* **to sthg** em comparação com algo -**2.** [something different]: ~ **(to sb/sthg)** oposto *m*, -ta *f* (a alguém/algo). ◇ *vt*: **to ~ sthg with sthg** contrastar algo com algo. ◇ *vi*: **to ~ (with sthg)** contrastar *OR* dar contraste (com algo).

contrasting [kən'trɑːstɪŋ] *adj* contrastante.

contravene [ˌkɒntrə'viːn] *vt* violar.

contravention [kɒntrə'venʃn] *n* violação *f.*

contribute [kən'trɪbjuːt] ◇ *vt* -**1.** [give] contribuir com -**2.** [to magazine, newspaper] colaborar com. ◇ *vi* -**1.** [give money]: **to ~ (to sthg)** contribuir (para algo) -**2.** [be part of cause]: **to ~ to sthg** contribuir para algo -**3.** [write material]: **to ~ to sthg** colaborar com algo.

contributing [kən'trɪbjuːtɪŋ] *adj* [factor] contribuinte.

contribution [ˌkɒntrɪ'bjuːʃn] *n* -**1.** [gen]: ~ **(to sthg)** contribuição *f* (para algo) -**2.** [written article] colaboração *f.*

contributor [kən'trɪbjʊtə'] *n* -**1.** [of money] contribuinte *mf*-**2.** [to magazine, newspaper] colaborador *m*, -ra *f.*

contributory [kən'trɪbjʊtərɪ] *adj* [factor] contribuinte.

contrite ['kɒntraɪt] *adj literary* contrito(ta).

contrivance [kən'traɪvns] *n* -**1.** [contraption] dispositivo *m* -**2.** [ploy] manobra *f*, artimanha *f.*

contrive [kən'traɪv] *fml vt* -**1.** [manoeuvre to put in place] manipular -**2.** [manage]: **to ~ to do sthg** dar um jeito de fazer algo -**3.** [invent, construct] improvisar.

contrived [kən'traɪvd] *adj pej* arranjado(da).

control [kən'trəʊl] ◇ *n* -**1.** [gen] controle *m*; **to gain ~ (of sthg)** obter o controle (de algo); **to take ~ (of sthg)** tomar o controle (de algo); **beyond** *OR* **outside one's ~** fora do controle de alguém; **in ~ of** no controle de, no comando de; **out of ~** fora de controle; **under ~** sob controle; **to lose ~** [of emotions] perder o controle -**2.** *COMPUT* comando *m.* ◇ *vt*

controlar. ◇ *comp* de controle.

controls *npl* [of machine, vehicle] controles *mpl.*

control code *n COMPUT* código *m* de controle.

control group *n* [in experiment, survey] grupo *m* de controle.

control key *n COMPUT* tecla *f* control.

controlled [kən'trəʊld] *adj* controlado(da).

controller [kən'trəʊlə'] *n* [person responsible] controller *mf*, diretor *m*, -ra *f*; **financial ~** contador *m*, -ra *f.*

controlling *adj* [factor] de controle.

controlling interest *n* controle *m* acionário.

control panel *n* painel *m* de controle.

control room *n* sala *f* de controle.

control tower *n* torre *f* de controle.

controversial [ˌkɒntrə'vɜːʃl] *adj* controverso(sa), polêmico(ca).

controversy ['kɒntrəvɜːsɪ, *UK* kən'trɒvəsɪ] (*pl* -ies) *n* controvérsia *f*, polêmica *f.*

conundrum [kə'nʌndrəm] (*pl* -s) *n* *fml* [problem] enigma *m.*

conurbation [ˌkɒnɜː'beɪʃn] *n* conurbação *f.*

convalesce [ˌkɒnvə'les] *vi* convalescer.

convalescence [ˌkɒnvə'lesns] *n (U)* convalescença *f.*

convalescent [ˌkɒnvə'lesnt] ◇ *adj* convalescente. ◇ *n* convalescente *mf.*

convection [kən'vekʃn] *n (U)* convecção *f.*

convector *n*: ~ **heater** aquecedor *m* de convecção.

convene [kən'viːn] ◇ *vt* [meeting, conference] convocar. ◇ *vi* [court, parliament] reunir-se.

convenience [kən'viːnjəns] *n* -**1.** *(U)* [gen] conveniência *f*; **at your earliest ~** assim que possível -**2.** [facility] comodidade *f.*

convenience food *n* alimentos *mpl* pré-prontos.

convenience store *n US* loja *f* de conveniências.

convenient [kən'viːnjənt] *adj* -**1.** [suitable] conveniente -**2.** [handy] cômodo(da); ~ **for sthg** conveniente para algo.

conveniently [kən'viːnjəntlɪ] *adv* convenientemente.

convent ['kɒnvənt] *n* [building] convento *m.*

convention [kən'venʃn] *n* convenção *f.*

conventional [kən'venʃənl] *adj* convencional; ~ **person** *pej* pessoa *f* sem graça; ~ **weapons** armas *fpl* não-nucleares.

conventionally [kən'venʃnəlɪ] *adv* de maneira convencional.

convent school *n* colégio *m* de freiras.

converge [kən'vɜːdʒ] *vi* convergir; **to ~ on sb/sthg** [to move towards] dirigir-se para alguém/algo.

convergence [kən'vɜːdʒəns] *n* [in EU] convergência *f*; ~ **criteria** critérios *mpl* de convergência.

conversant [kən'vɜːsənt] *adj fml*: ~ **with sthg** familiarizado(da) com algo.

conversation [ˌkɒnvə'seɪʃn] *n* conversação *f*, conversa *f*; **to make ~** puxar conversa.

conversational [ˌkɒnvə'seɪʃənl] *adj* [chatty] conversador(ra).

conversationalist [ˌkɒnvəˈseɪʃnəlɪst] n conversador m, -ra f.

converse [n & adj ˈkɒnvɜːs, vb kənˈvɜːs] ⬦ adj fml [opposing] inverso(sa). ⬦ n [opposite]: **the** ~ o inverso. ⬦ vi fml [talk] conversar; **to** ~ **with sb** conversar com alguém.

conversely [kənˈvɜːslɪ] adv fml inversamente.

conversion [kənˈvɜːʃn] n -**1.** [gen] conversão f -**2.** [converted building, room] reforma f.

conversion table n tabela f de conversão.

convert [vb kənˈvɜːt, n ˈkɒnvɜːt] ⬦ vt: **to** ~ **sthg (in)to sthg** converter algo em algo; **to** ~ **sb (to sthg)** converter alguém (para algo); **I didn't like jazz much but she** ~ **ed me to it** eu não gostava muito de jazz, mas ela me converteu. ⬦ vi -**1.** [change]: **she's** ~ **ed to Catholicism** ela se converteu ao catolicismo; **the seating** ~ **s to a double bed** o sofá se transforma numa cama de casal -**2.** SPORT converter. ⬦ n convertido m, -da f.

converted [kənˈvɜːtɪd] adj -**1.** [building, room, ship] transformado(da), adaptado(da) -**2.** RELIG [person] convertido(da).

convertible [kənˈvɜːtəbl] ⬦ adj -**1.** [car, currency] conversível -**2.** [bed, sofa] dobrável. ⬦ n [car] conversível m.

convex [kɒnˈveks] adj convexo(xa).

convey [kənˈveɪ] vt -**1.** fml [people, cargo] conduzir -**2.** [feelings, ideas, thoughts] expressar; **to** ~ **sthg to sb** transmitir algo a alguém.

conveyancing [kənˈveɪənsɪŋ] n (U) transferência f de posse.

conveyer belt [kənˈveɪəʳ-], **conveyor belt** n esteira f transportadora.

convict [n ˈkɒnvɪkt, vb kənˈvɪkt] ⬦ n condenado m, -da f. ⬦ vt JUR: **to** ~ **sb of sthg** condenar alguém por algo.

convicted [kənˈvɪktɪd] adj JUR condenado(da).

conviction [kənˈvɪkʃn] n -**1.** [gen] convicção f -**2.** JUR condenação f.

convince [kənˈvɪns] vt [persuade] convencer; **to** ~ **sb of sthg** convencer alguém de algo; **to** ~ **sb to do sthg** convencer alguém a fazer algo.

convinced [kənˈvɪnst] adj: ~ **(of sthg)** convencido(da) (de algo).

convincing [kənˈvɪnsɪŋ] adj convincente.

convivial [kənˈvɪvɪəl] adj alegre, festivo(va).

convoluted [ˈkɒnvəluːtɪd] adj [tortuous] enrolado(da).

convoy [ˈkɒnvɔɪ] n [group] comboio m; **in** ~ em comboio.

convulse [kənˈvʌls] vt: **to be** ~**d with** [laughter, pain] dobrar-se de.

convulsion [kənˈvʌlʃn] n MED convulsão f.

convulsive [kənˈvʌlsɪv] adj convulsivo(va).

coo [kuː] vi -**1.** [bird] arrulhar -**2.** [person] sussurrar.

cook [kʊk] ⬦ n cozinheiro m, -ra f. ⬦ vt -**1.** [food, meal] cozinhar; **I'll** ~ **dinner** vou preparar o jantar -**2.** inf [books, accounts] falsificar. ⬦ vi cozinhar.

➣ **cook up** vt sep [plan, scheme, excuse] inventar.

cookbook [ˈkʊkˌbʊk] n = **cookery book**.

cooked [kʊkt] adj [food] cozido(da).

cooker [ˈkʊkəʳ] n esp UK [stove] fogão m.

cookery [ˈkʊkərɪ] n (U) culinária f.

cookery book n livro m de receitas.

cookie [ˈkʊkɪ] n -**1.** esp US [biscuit] biscoito m -**2.** COMPUT cookie m.

cooking [ˈkʊkɪŋ] ⬦ n (U) -**1.** [activity] culinária f; **do you like** ~? você gosta de cozinhar? -**2.** [food] cozinha f; **her** ~ **is awful!** ela cozinha mal pra caramba! ⬦ comp -**1.** [oil, utensils, salt] de cozinha -**2.** [sherry, chocolate] para cozinhar.

cooking apple n maçã f para cozinhar.

cookout [ˈkʊkaʊt] n US refeição f ao ar livre.

cool [kuːl] ⬦ adj -**1.** [not warm] frio (fria) -**2.** [calm] tranqüilo(la) -**3.** [unfriendly] frio (fria) -**4.** inf [excellent] legal -**5.** inf [trendy] bacana. ⬦ vt esfriar. ⬦ vi -**1.** [food, liquid, room] esfriar -**2.** [enthusiasm, ardour] arrefecer. ⬦ n inf [calm]: **to keep / lose one's** ~ manter/perder a calma.

➣ **cool down** ⬦ vt sep -**1.** [make less warm] esfriar -**2.** [make less angry] acalmar-se. ⬦ vi -**1.** [become less warm] esfriar -**2.** [become less angry] acalmar-se.

➣ **cool off** vi -**1.** [become less warm] esfriar -**2.** [become less angry] acalmar-se.

coolant [ˈkuːlənt] n líquido m refrigerante.

cool bag n bolsa f térmica.

cool box UK, **cooler** US n caixa f de gelo.

cool-headed [-ˈhedɪd] adj calmo(ma), de sangue-frio.

cooling-off period [ˈkuːlɪŋ-] n período m de calmaria.

cooling tower [ˈkuːlɪŋ-] n torre f de resfriamento.

coolly [ˈkuːlɪ] adv -**1.** [calmly] calmamente -**2.** [coldly] friamente.

coolness [ˈkuːlnɪs] n (U) -**1.** [in temperature] friagem f -**2.** [unfriendliness] frieza f.

coop [kuːp] n gaiola f; **chicken** ~ galinheiro m.

➣ **coop up** vt sep inf trancafiar.

co-op [abbr of cooperative] n fam coop.

cooperate [kəʊˈɒpəreɪt] vi cooperar; **to** ~ **with sb / sthg** cooperar com alguém/algo.

cooperation [kəʊˌɒpəˈreɪʃn] n (U) cooperação f.

cooperative [kəʊˈɒpərətɪv] ⬦ adj cooperativo(va). ⬦ n [enterprise] cooperativa f.

co-opt vt: **to** ~ **sb (into/onto sthg)** cooptar alguém (em algo).

coordinate [n kəʊˈɔːdɪnət, vt kəʊˈɔːdɪneɪt] ⬦ n [on map, graph] coordenada f. ⬦ vt coordenar.

➣ **coordinates** npl [clothes] conjuntos mpl.

coordination [kəʊˌɔːdɪˈneɪʃn] n (U) coordenação f.

coot n [bird] galeirão m.

co-ownership n (U) co-propriedade f.

cop [kɒp] (pt & pp -ped, cont -ping) n inf [policeman] tira m.

➣ **cop out** vi inf: **to** ~ **out (of sthg)** cair fora (de algo).

cope [kəʊp] vi suportar; **to** ~ **with sthg** lidar com algo.

Copenhagen [ˌkəʊpənˈheɪgən] n Copenhague.

copier [ˈkɒpɪəʳ] n [photocopier] copiadora f.

copilot [ˈkəʊˌpaɪlət] n co-piloto m, -ta f.

copious [ˈkəʊpjəs] adj copioso(sa).

cop-out n inf desculpa f furada.

copper [ˈkɒpəʳ] n **-1.** (U) [metal] cobre m **-2.** UK inf [policeman] tira m.

coppice [ˈkɒpɪs], **copse** [kɒps] n capão m.

copulate [ˈkɒpjʊleɪt] vi fml: **to ~(with)** copular (com).

copulation [ˌkɒpjʊˈleɪʃn] n (U) cópula f.

copy [ˈkɒpɪ] (pt & pp **-ied**) <> n cópia f. <> vt copiar. <> vi [cheat] colar.
➡ **copy down** vt sep anotar.
➡ **copy out** vt sep copiar.

copycat [ˈkɒpɪkæt] <> n inf maria-vai-com-as-outras mf inv. <> comp [crime, killing] idêntico(ca) a outro mais famoso.

copy protect vt COMPUT proteger contra cópias.

copyright [ˈkɒpɪraɪt] n (U) direitos mpl autorais, copyright m.

copy typist n UK digitador m, -ra f.

copywriter [ˈkɒpɪˌraɪtəʳ] n redator m, -ra f de material publicitário.

coral [ˈkɒrəl] <> n(U) coral m. <> comp de coral; **a ~ pink** uma rosa coral.

coral reef n recife m de corais.

Coral Sea n: **the ~** o Mar de Coral.

cord [kɔːd] <> n **-1.** [string] cordão m **-2.** [wire] fio m **-3.** [fabric] veludo m cotelê. <> comp de veludo cotelê.
➡ **cords** npl inf calça f de veludo cotelê.

cordial [ˈkɔːdjəl] <> adj cordial. <> n cordial m.

cordially [ˈkɔːdɪəlɪ] adv cordialmente.

cordless adj sem-fio.

cordon [ˈkɔːdn] n [barrier] cordão m de isolamento.
➡ **cordon off** vt sep isolar (com cordão).

cordon bleu [-ˈblɜː] adj: **a ~ cook** cozinheiro m, -ra f de alto nível.

corduroy [ˈkɔːdərɔɪ] <> n veludo m cotelê. <> comp de veludo cotelê.

core [kɔːʳ] <> n **-1.** [gen] centro m **-2.** [of apple, pear] caroço m **-3.** [of argument, policy] âmago m **-4.** phr: **to be English/royalist to the ~** ser inglês(esa)/monarquista até morrer; **to be shaken to the ~** ficar muito comovido(da). <> vt [fruit] descaroçar.

CORE (abbr of Congress on Racial Equality) n organização norte-americana contra o racismo.

corer [ˈkɔːrəʳ] n [for fruit] descaroçador m.

co-respondent n JUR co-responsável mf (em caso de divórcio por adultério).

Corfu [kɔːˈfuː] n Corfu; **in ~** em Corfu.

corgi [ˈkɔːgɪ] (pl **-s**) n pequeno cão do País de Gales de nariz alongado e pernas curtas.

coriander [ˌkɒrɪˈændəʳ] n (U) **-1.** [herb] coriandro m **-2.** [spice] coentro m.

cork [kɔːk] n **-1.** (U) [material] cortiça f **-2.** [stopper] rolha f.

corkage [ˈkɔːkɪdʒ] n (U) taxa cobrada num restaurante pela abertura das garrafas trazidas pelos clientes.

corked [kɔːkt] adj com gosto de rolha.

corkscrew [ˈkɔːkskruː] n saca-rolhas m.

cormorant [ˈkɔːmərənt] n cormorão m.

corn [kɔːn] n **-1.** (U) UK [wheat, barley, oats] cereais mpl **-2.** (U) esp Am [maize] milho m **-3.** [callus] calo m.

corn bread n broa f de milho.

cornea [ˈkɔːnɪə] (pl **-s**) n córnea f.

corned beef [kɔːnd-] n (U) carne f bovina enlatada.

corner [ˈkɔːnəʳ] <> n **-1.** [gen] canto m; **to cut ~s** fig pular etapas **-2.** [in street, road] esquina f **-3.** FTBL escanteio m. <> vt **-1.** [trap] encurralar **-2.** [monopolize] monopolizar.

corner flag n FTBL bandeirinha f de escanteio.

corner kick n FTBL cobrança f de escanteio.

corner shop n pequeno armazém de esquina que vende comida e artigos de limpeza.

cornerstone [ˈkɔːnəstəʊn] n fig [basis] fundamento m.

cornet [ˈkɔːnɪt] n **-1.** [instrument] corneta f **-2.** UK [ice-cream cone] casquinha f.

cornfield [ˈkɔːnfiːld] n **-1.** UK [of wheat] campo m de trigo **-2.** esp US [of maize] milharal m.

cornflakes [ˈkɔːnfleɪks] npl flocos mpl de cereais.

cornflour UK [ˈkɔːnflaʊəʳ], **cornstarch** US [ˈkɔːnstɑːtʃ] n (U) amido m de milho.

cornice [ˈkɔːnɪs] n cornija f.

Cornish [ˈkɔːnɪʃ] <> adj da Cornualha.

corn oil n óleo m de milho.

corn on the cob n milho m cozido.

cornstarch n US = cornflour.

cornucopia [ˌkɔːnjʊˈkəʊpjə] n literary cornucópia f.

Cornwall [ˈkɔːnwɔːl] n Cornualha f; **in ~** na Cornualha.

corny [ˈkɔːnɪ] (compar **-ier**, superl **-iest**) adj inf batido(da).

corollary [kəˈrɒlərɪ] (pl **-ies**) n corolário m.

coronary [ˈkɒrənrɪ] (pl **-ies**), **coronary thrombosis** [-θrɒmˈbəʊsɪs] (pl **coronary thromboses** [-θrɒmˈbəʊsiːz]) n trombose f coronária.

coronation [ˌkɒrəˈneɪʃn] n coroação f.

coroner [ˈkɒrənəʳ] n oficial responsável por investigar as mortes das pessoas que morreram de forma violenta, brusca ou incomum.

Corp. (abbr of corporation) Corp.

corpora [ˈkɔːpərə] pl ▷ corpus.

corporal [ˈkɔːpərəl] n cabo m.

corporal punishment n (U) castigo m corporal.

corporate [ˈkɔːpərət] adj **-1.** [business] corporativo(-va) **-2.** [collective] coletivo(va).

corporate hospitality n diversão proporcionada por uma empresa a seus clientes, como refeições especiais ou drinks em locais agradáveis.

corporate identity, corporate image n imagem f da empresa.

corporation [ˌkɔːpəˈreɪʃn] n **-1.** [council] associação f **-2.** [large company] corporação f.

corporation tax n UK imposto m sobre renda de corporações.

corps [kɔːʳ] (pl inv) n **-1.** MIL unidade f **-2.** [group] corpo m.

corpse [kɔːps] n cadáver m.

corpulent [ˈkɔːpjʊlənt] adj fml corpulento(ta).

corpus [ˈkɔːpəs] (pl **-pora** OR **-puses**) n [collection of writings] corpus m.

corpuscle [ˈkɔːpʌsl] n corpúsculo m.

corral [kɒˈrɑːl] *n esp US* curral *m*.
correct [kəˈrekt] ◇ *adj* -1. [right, accurate] certo(ta) -2. [appropriate, suitable] adequado(da). ◇ *vt* corrigir.
correction [kəˈrekʃn] *n* -1. *(U)* [act of correcting] correção *f*-2. [change] emenda *f*.
correctly [kəˈrektlɪ] *adv* -1. [accurately] corretamente -2. [appropriately, suitably] adequadamente.
correlate [ˈkɒrəleɪt] ◇ *vt* correlacionar. ◇ *vi*: to ~ (with sthg) corresponder (a algo).
correlation [ˌkɒrəˈleɪʃn] *n*: ~ (between) correlação (entre).
correspond [ˌkɒrɪˈspɒnd] *vi* -1. [be equivalent]: to ~ (with *or* to sthg) corresponder (com *or* a algo) -2. [tally]: to ~ (with *or* to sthg) ajustar-se (a algo) -3. [write letters]: to ~ (with sb) corresponder-se (com alguém).
correspondence [ˌkɒrɪˈspɒndəns] *n* -1. [letters] correspondência *f*-2. [letter-writing]: ~ with/between sb correspondência com/entre alguém -3. [relationship, similarity]: ~ with sthg relação com algo.
correspondence course *n* curso *m* por correspondência.
correspondent [ˌkɒrɪˈspɒndənt] *n* [reporter] correspondente *mf*.
corresponding [ˌkɒrɪˈspɒndɪŋ] *adj* [relevant] correspondente.
corridor [ˈkɒrɪdɔː⁻] *n* [in building] corredor *m*.
corroborate [kəˈrɒbəreɪt] *vt* corroborar.
corroboration [kəˌrɒbəˈreɪʃn] *n (U)* corroboração *f*.
corrode [kəˈrəʊd] ◇ *vt* corroer. ◇ *vi* corroer-se.
corrosion [kəˈrəʊʒn] *n (U)* [of metal] corrosão *f*.
corrosive [kəˈrəʊsɪv] *adj* [poison, substance] corrosivo(sa).
corrugated [ˈkɒrəgeɪtɪd] *adj* ondulado(da).
corrugated iron *n (U)* ferro *m* corrugado.
corrupt [kəˈrʌpt] ◇ *adj* -1. [dishonest] corrupto(ta) -2. [depraved] depravado(da) -3. *COMPUT* [damaged] corrompido(da). ◇ *vt* corromper.
corruption [kəˈrʌpʃn] *n (U)*-1. [gen] corrupção *f*-2. [depravity] depravação *f*.
corsage [kɔːˈsɑːʒ] *n* [flowers] *pequeno buquê utilizado pelas mulheres à altura dos ombros*.
corset [ˈkɔːsɪt] *n* [undergarment] espartilho *m*.
Corsica [ˈkɔːsɪkə] *n* Córsega; in ~ na Córsega.
Corsican [ˈkɔːsɪkən] ◇ *adj* córsico(ca). ◇ *n* -1. [person] córsico *m*, -ca *f*, -2. [language] córsico *m*.
cortege, cortège [kɔːˈteɪʒ] *n* séquito *m*.
cortisone [ˈkɔːtɪzəʊn] *n (U)* cortisona *f*.
cos¹ [kɒz] *conj UK inf* = because.
cos² [kɒs] *n* = cos lettuce.
cosh [kɒʃ] ◇ *n* cacete *m*. ◇ *vt* dar cacetadas.
cosignatory [ˌkəʊˈsɪgnətrɪ] *(pl* -ies) *n* co-signatário(ria).
cosine [ˈkəʊsaɪn] *n* co-seno *m*.
cos lettuce [kɒs-] *n UK* alface *f* romana.
cosmetic [kɒzˈmetɪk] ◇ *adj fig* [superficial] superficial. ◇ *n* cosmético *m*.
cosmetic surgery *n (U)* cirurgia *f* estética.
cosmic [ˈkɒzmɪk] *adj* cósmico(ca).

cosmonaut [ˈkɒzmənɔːt] *n* cosmonauta *mf*.
cosmopolitan [ˌkɒzməˈpɒlɪtn] *adj* cosmopolita.
cosmos [ˈkɒzmɒs] *n*: the ~ o cosmos.
Cossack [ˈkɒsæk] *n* cossaco *m*.
cosset [ˈkɒsɪt] *vt* acarinhar.
cost [kɒst] *(pt & pp senses 1 & 3* cost, *pt & pp sense 2-* ed) ◇ *n* -1. custo *m*; at all ~s a qualquer custo -2. ◇ *vt* -1. [in financial transactions - sum of money] custar; [- person] custar a -2. *COMM* [estimate price of] orçar; to ~ a product orçar um produto; the work was ~ed at £65 o trabalho foi orçado em £65. ◆ **costs** *npl JUR* custas *fpl*.
cost accountant *n* contador *m*, -ra *f* de custos.
co-star [ˈkəʊ-] ◇ *n* coadjuvante *mf*. ◇ *vt* atuar como coadjuvante. ◇ *vi*: to ~ (with) contracenar (com).
Costa Rica [ˌkɒstəˈriːkə] *n* Costa Rica; in ~ na Costa Rica.
Costa Rican [ˌkɒstəˈriːkən] ◇ *adj* costarriquenho(nha). ◇ *n* costarriquenho *m*, -nha *f*.
cost-benefit analysis *n (U)* análise *f* de custo-benefício.
cost-effective *adj* rentável, lucrativo(va).
cost-effectiveness *n (U)* rentabilidade *f*.
costing [ˈkɒstɪŋ] *n* estimativa *f* de custos.
costly [ˈkɒstlɪ] *(compar* -ier, *superl* -iest) *adj* -1. [expensive] oneroso(sa) -2. *fig* [involving loss, damage] dispendioso(sa).
cost of living *n*: the ~ o custo de vida.
cost-of-living index *n* ≃ índice *m* de preços ao consumidor.
cost price *n* preço *m* de custo.
costume [ˈkɒstjuːm] *n* -1. *THEATRE* roupa *f*; lion ~ fantasia de leão; in ~ and make-up vestido(da) e maquiado(da) -2. *(U)* [dress] traje *m*; swimming ~ maiô *m*.
costume jewellery *n (U)* bijuteria *f*.
cosy *UK*, **cozy** *US* [ˈkəʊzɪ] *(compar* -ier, *superl* -iest, *pl* -ies) ◇ *adj* -1. [clothes] confortável -2. [person] aconchegado(da); to feel ~ sentir-se aconchegado(da) -3. [chat, atmosphere] aconchegante. ◇ *n* [for teapot] abafador *m*.
cot [kɒt] *n* -1. *UK* [for child] berço *m* -2. *US* [folding bed] cama *f* de campanha.
cot death *n* morte *f* no berço.
cottage [ˈkɒtɪdʒ] *n* cabana *f*, chalé *m*; a country ~ uma casa de campo.
cottage cheese *n (U)* requeijão *m*.
cottage hospital *n UK* hospital *m* pequeno no campo.
cottage industry *n* indústria *f* caseira.
cottage pie *n UK* bolo de carne picada coberto com purê de batata.
cotton [ˈkɒtn] ◇ *n (U)* -1. [fabric, plants] algodão *m* -2. [thread] linha *f*. ◇ *comp* de algodão. ◆ **cotton on** *vi inf*: to ~ on (to sthg) sacar (algo).
cotton bud *UK*, **cotton swab** *US* *n* cotonete *m*.
cotton candy *n US* = candyfloss.
cotton swab *n US* = cotton bud.
cotton wool *n (U)* chumaço *m* de algodão.
couch [kaʊtʃ] ◇ *n* -1. [gen] sofá *m* -2. [psychiatrist's]

divã *m.* ◇ *vt fig* : **to ~ sthg in** [express] formular algo em.

couchette [ku:'ʃet] *n UK* cama *f (em trem ou navio).*

couch potato *n inf* folgado *m,* -da *f.*

cougar ['ku:gəʳ] *(pl inv OR* -**s)** *n* puma *m.*

cough [kɒf] ◇ *n* -**1.** [noise] tossida *f* -**2.** [illness] tosse *f.* ◇ *vi* tossir. ◇ *vt* expelir tossindo.
➤ **cough up** *vt sep* -**1.** [bring up] expelir tossindo -**2.** *v inf* [pay up] desembolsar.

coughing ['kɒfɪŋ] *n* tosse *f.*

cough mixture *n UK* xarope *m* para a tosse.

cough sweet *n UK* pastilha *f* para tosse.

cough syrup *n* = cough mixture.

could [kʊd] *pt* ▷ **can².**

couldn't ['kʊdnt] = could not.

could've ['kʊdəv] = could have.

council ['kaʊnsl] ◇ *n* -**1.** [local authority] câmara *f* municipal -**2.** [group, organization] conselho *m* -**3.** [meeting] assembléia *f.* ◇ *comp* [of local authority] de conselho.

council estate *n UK conjunto de casas de propriedade do município destinado à locação.*

council flat *n UK apartamento de propriedade do município para ser alugado a baixo custo.*

council house *n UK casa de propriedade do município para ser alugada a baixo custo.*

councillor ['kaʊnsələʳ] *n* vereador *m,* -ra *f.*

Council of Europe *n* Conselho *m* da Europa.

council of war *n* conselho *m* de guerra.

council tax *n UK* ≃ imposto *m* territorial urbano.

counsel ['kaʊnsl] *(UK pt & pp* -**led,** *cont* -**ling,** *US pt & pp* -**ed,** *cont* -**ing)** ◇ *n* -**1.** *(U) fml* [advice] parecer *m* -**2.** [lawyer] conselheiro *m,* -ra *f,* advogado *m,* -da *f.* ◇ *vt* aconselhar; **to ~ sb to do sthg** *fml* aconselhar alguém a fazer algo.

counselling *UK,* **counseling** *US* ['kaʊnsəlɪŋ] *n (U)* aconselhamento *m,* orientação *f.*

counsellor *UK,* **counselor** *US* ['kaʊnsələʳ] *n* -**1.** [adviser, helper] conselheiro *m,* -ra *f,* orientador(ra) ra -**2.** *US* [lawyer] advogado *m,* -da *f.*

count [kaʊnt] ◇ *n* -**1.** [total] conta *f;* **to keep ~ of** sthg registrar algo; **to lose ~ of** sthg perder a conta de algo -**2.** [point] ponto *m* -**3.** *JUR* [charge] enquadramento *m* -**4.** [aristocrat] conde *m.* ◇ *vt* -**1.** [add up] contar -**2.** [consider, include]: **to ~ sb/ sthg as sthg** considerar alguém/algo como algo. ◇ *vi* contar; **to ~ for** contar (para); **to ~ (up) to** contar até; **to ~ as sthg** contar como algo.
➤ **count against** *vt fus* pesar contra.
➤ **count in** *vt sep inf* incluir.
➤ **count on** *vt fus* [rely on, expect] contar com.
➤ **count out** *vt sep* -**1.** [money] contar um a um -**2.** *inf* [leave out] excluir.
➤ **count up** *vt fus* contar.
➤ **count upon** *vt fus* = count on.

countdown ['kaʊntdaʊn] *n* contagem *f* regressiva.

countenance ['kaʊntənəns] ◇ *n literary* [face] semblante *m.* ◇ *vt* [approve of] aprovar.

counter ['kaʊntəʳ] ◇ *n* -**1.** [in shop, kitchen] balcão *m* -**2.** [in board game] ficha *f* -**3.** [in post office, bank]

guichê *m.* ◇ *vt* : **to ~ sthg with sthg** [respond to] responder algo com algo; **to ~ sthg by doing** sthg responder algo fazendo algo. ◇ *vi* : **to ~ with sthg/by doing sthg** responder com/fazendo algo.
➤ **counter to** *adv* ao contrário de; **to run ~ to** sthg ir contra algo/ser contrário a algo.

counteract [ˌkaʊntə'rækt] *vt* neutralizar.

counter-attack ◇ *n* contra-ataque *m.* ◇ *vt &* *vi* contra-atacar.

counterbalance [ˌkaʊntə'bæləns] *vt fig* [correct, balance] contrapeso *m.*

counterclaim ['kaʊntəkleɪm] *n* reivindicação *f.*

counterclockwise *US* [ˌkaʊntə'klɒkwaɪz] ◇ *adj* anti-horário(ria). ◇ *adv* em sentido anti-horário.

counter-espionage *n (U)* contra-espionagem *f.*

counterfeit ['kaʊntəfɪt] ◇ *adj* falsificado(da). ◇ *vt* falsificar.

counterfoil ['kaʊntəfɔɪl] *n* canhoto *m.*

counter-intelligence *n (U)* contra-espionagem *f.*

countermand [ˌkaʊntə'mɑːnd] *vt* revogar.

counter-measure *n* contramedida *f.*

counter-offensive *n* contra-ofensiva *f.*

counterpane ['kaʊntəpeɪn] *n* colcha *f.*

counterpart ['kaʊntəpɑːt] *n* contraparte *f.*

counterpoint ['kaʊntəpɔɪnt] *n (U) MUS* contraponto *m.*

counter-productive *adj* contraproducente.

counter-revolution *n* contra-revolução *f.*

countersank ['kaʊntəsæŋk] *pt* ▷ **countersink.**

countersign ['kaʊntəsaɪn] *vt* [document] -**1.** referendar -**2.** [cheque] endossar.

countersink ['kaʊntəsɪŋk] *(pt* -**sank,** *pp* -**sunk** [-sʌŋk]) *vt* escarear.

countess ['kaʊntɪs] *n* condessa *f.*

countless ['kaʊntlɪs] *adj* inúmero(ra).

countrified ['kʌntrɪfaɪd] *adj pej* rústico(ca).

country ['kʌntrɪ] *(pl* -**ies)** ◇ *n* -**1.** [nation] país *m;* **to go to the ~** *UK POL* fazer uma eleição -**2.** [countryside]: **the ~** o campo -**3.** [area of land, region] região *f.* ◇ *comp* do campo.

country and western ◇ *n (U)* música *f* country. ◇ *comp* country *inv.*

country club *n* clube *m* de campo, country club *m.*

country dancing *n (U)* dança *f* tradicional.

country house *n* casa *f* de campo.

countryman ['kʌntrɪmən] *(pl* -**men** [-mən]) *n* [from same country] compatriota *m.*

country music *n & comp* = country and western.

country park *n UK* parque *m* regional.

countryside ['kʌntrɪsaɪd] *n (U)* campo *m.*

countrywoman ['kʌntrɪˌwʊmən] *(pl* -**women** [-ˌwɪmɪn]) *n* [from same country] compatriota *f.*

county ['kaʊntɪ] *(pl* -**ies)** *n* condado *m.*

county council *n UK* conselho *m* regional.

county court *n UK* tribunal *m* regional.

county town *UK,* **county seat** *US n capital de um condado.*

coup [ku:] *n* -**1.** [rebellion]: **~ (d'état)** golpe de

estado -2. [masterstroke] golpe *m* de mestre.

coupé [ˈkuːpeɪ] *n AUT* cupê *m*.

couple [ˈkʌpl] ⟨⟩ *n* **-1.** [in relationship] casal *m* **-2.** [small number]: **a** ~ alguns, algumas; **a** ~ **of** dois, duas. ⟨⟩ *vt***-1.** [join]: **to** ~ **sthg (to sthg)** unir algo (a algo) **-2.** *fig* [associate]: **to** ~ **sthg with sthg** associar algo a algo; ~**d with** aliado(da) a.

couplet [ˈkʌplɪt] *n* dístico *m*.

coupling [ˈkʌplɪŋ] *n RAIL* engate *m*.

coupon [ˈkuːpɒn] *n* **-1.** [voucher] vale *m* **-2.** [form] cupom *m*.

courage [ˈkʌrɪdʒ] *n (U)* coragem *f*; **to take** ~ **(from sthg)** tirar coragem (de algo); **to have the** ~ **of one's convictions** ter coragem de manter suas opiniões.

courageous [kəˈreɪdʒəs] *adj* corajoso(sa).

courageously [kəˈreɪdʒəslɪ] *adv* corajosamente.

courgette [kɔːˈʒet] *n UK* abobrinha *f*.

courier [ˈkʊrɪəˈ] *n* **-1.** [on holiday tour] *representante de uma agência de viagens que cuida das pessoas que estão a passeio* **-2.** [delivering letters, packages] mensageiro *m*, -ra *f*, courier *m*.

course [kɔːs] ⟨⟩ *n* **-1.** [gen] curso *m* **-2.** *MED* [of treatment] tratamento *m* **-3.** [path, route] rota *f*; **to run** OR **take its** ~ seguir OR tomar o curso natural; **to be on** ~ **for** [ship, plane] estar rumando para; *fig* [on target] em curso; **off** ~ fora de curso **-4.** [plan]: ~ **(of action)** curso (de ação) **-5.** [of time]: **in due** ~ no tempo devido; **in the** ~ **of** no decorrer de **-6.** [in meal] prato *m* **-7.** *SPORT* campo *m*. ⟨⟩ *vi literary* [flow] correr.

➡ of course *adv* **-1.** [inevitably, not surprisingly] evidentemente **-2.** [certainly] claro que sim; **of** ~ **you can!** claro que pode!; **'do you want the job?'** - **'of** ~ **I do!'** 'você quer o trabalho?' - 'claro que quero!'; **of** ~ **not** claro que não.

coursebook [ˈkɔːsbʊk] *n* livro *m* de curso.

coursework [ˈkɔːswɜːk] *n (U)* trabalho *m* de curso.

court [kɔːt] ⟨⟩ *n* **-1.** JUR tribunal *m*; **to appear in** ~ comparecer perante um tribunal; **to settle out of** ~ resolver fora dos tribunais; **to go to** ~ processar; **to take sb to** ~ levar alguém a julgamento; **the** ~ o tribunal **-2.** *SPORT* quadra *f*; **on** ~ na quadra **-3.** [courtyard] pátio *m* **-4.** [of king, queen etc] corte *f*. ⟨⟩ *vt* [seek] procurar. ⟨⟩ *vi dated* [go out together] cortejar.

court circular *n UK* ≃ diário *m* da corte.

courteous [ˈkɜːtjəs] *adj* cortês.

courtesan [ˌkɔːtɪˈzæn] *n* cortesã *f*.

courtesy [ˈkɜːtɪsɪ] *n (U)* [polite behaviour] cortesia *f*.

➡ (by) courtesy of *prep* [thanks to] por cortesia de.

courtesy car *n* carro *m* de cortesia.

courtesy coach *n* ônibus *m* de cortesia.

courthouse [ˈkɔːthaʊs] *n US* palácio *m* da justiça.

courtier [ˈkɔːtjəˈ] *n* cortesão *m*.

court-martial (*pl* court-martials OR courts-martial, *UK pt & pp* -led, *cont* -ling, *US pt & pp* -ed, *cont* -ing) ⟨⟩ *n* corte *m* marcial. ⟨⟩ *vt* submeter a uma corte marcial.

court of appeal *UK*, **court of appeals** *US n* tribunal *m* de apelação.

court of inquiry *n* **-1.** [investigation] tribunal *m*

de investigação **-2.** [investigating group] comissão *f* de inquérito.

court of law *n* tribunal *m*.

courtroom [ˈkɔːtrʊm] *n* sala *f* de tribunal.

courtship [ˈkɔːtʃɪp] *n (U)* **-1.** [of people] galanteio *m* **-2.** [of animals] requesta *f*.

court shoe *n* escarpim *m*.

courtyard [ˈkɔːtjɑːd] *n* pátio *m*.

cousin [ˈkʌzn] *n* primo *m*, -ma *f*.

couture [kuːˈtʊəˈ] *n*: **haute** ~ alta-costura *f*.

cove [kəʊv] *n* [bay] enseada *f*.

coven [ˈkʌvən] *n* grupo *m* de bruxas.

covenant [ˈkʌvənənt] *n* **-1.** [promise of money] convênio *m* **-2.** [pact] pacto *m*.

Covent Garden [ˌkɒvənt-] *n área comercial e artística coberta no centro de Londres, que também inclui o Royal Opera House.*

Coventry [ˈkɒvəntrɪ] *n*: **to send sb to** ~ pôr alguém no ostracismo.

cover [ˈkʌvəˈ] ⟨⟩ *n* **-1.** [covering] capa *f* **-2.** [lid] tampa *f* **-3.** [blanket] coberta *f* **-4.** [protection, shelter] abrigo *m*; **to take** ~ [from weather] abrigar-se; [from gunfire] proteger-se; **under** ~ [from weather] abrigado(da); **under** ~ **of darkness** sob o manto da escuridão; **to break** ~ sair do esconderijo **-5.** [disguise, front or insurance] cobertura *f*. ⟨⟩ *vt* cobrir; **to** ~ **sthg with sthg** cobrir algo com algo; **to** ~ **sb against sthg** [give insurance] cobrir alguém contra algo.

➡ cover up *vt sep* **-1.** [person, animal] cobrir **-2.** *fig* [story, scandal] encobrir.

coverage [ˈkʌvərɪdʒ] *n (U)* [of news] cobertura *f*.

coveralls [ˈkʌvərɔːlz] *npl US* macacão *m*.

cover charge *n* couvert *m*.

cover girl *n* garota *f* da capa.

covering [ˈkʌvərɪŋ] *n* cobertura *f*.

covering letter *UK*, **cover letter** *US n carta ou nota contendo explicações ou informações adicionais que acompanha uma encomenda ou outra carta.*

cover note *n UK* nota *f* de cobertura.

cover price *n* [of book, magazine] preço *m* de capa.

covert [ˈkʌvət] *adj* secreto(ta), oculto(ta).

cover-up *n* encobrimento *m*.

cover version *n* regravação *f* de música.

covet [ˈkʌvɪt] *vt fml* ambicionar.

cow [kaʊ] ⟨⟩ *n* **-1.** [female type of cattle] vaca *f* **-2.** [female elephant, whale, seal] fêmea *f* **-3.** *UK inf pej* [woman] vaca *f*. ⟨⟩ *vt* intimidar.

coward [ˈkaʊəd] *n* covarde *mf*.

cowardice [ˈkaʊədɪs] *n (U)* covardia *f*.

cowardly [ˈkaʊədlɪ] *adj* covarde.

cowboy [ˈkaʊbɔɪ] ⟨⟩ *n* **-1.** [cattlehand] vaqueiro **-2.** *UK inf* [dishonest workman] patife *m*. ⟨⟩ *comp* [western] caubói *m*.

cower [ˈkaʊəˈ] *vi* encolher-se de medo.

cowhide [ˈkaʊhaɪd] *n (U)* couro *m* de vaca.

cowl neck *n* capuz *m*.

co-worker *n* colega *mf* de trabalho.

cowpat [ˈkaʊpæt] *n* estrume *m* de vaca.

cowshed [ˈkaʊʃed] *n* estábulo *m*.

cox [kɒks], **coxswain** [ˈkɒksən] *n* timoneiro *m*, -ra *f*.

coy [kɔɪ] *adj* recatado(da).

coyly ['kɔɪlɪ] *adv* recatadamente.

coyote [kɔɪ'əʊtɪ] *n* coiote *m*.

cozy *adj* & *n US* = cosy.

CP (*abbr of* Communist Party) *n* partido *m* comunista.

CPA (*abbr of* certified public accountant) *n* contador público certificado nos Estados Unidos.

Cpl. (*abbr of* corporal) corporal.

cps (*abbr of* characters per second) cps.

CPS (*abbr of* Crown Prosecution Service) *n* organismo britânico que decide quais casos policiais devem ser levados ao tribunal.

CPU (*abbr of* central processing unit) *n* COMPUT CPU *f*.

Cr - **1.** *abbr of* Councillor. - **2.** *abbr of* credit.

crab [kræb] *n* - **1.** [sea creature] caranguejo *m* - **2.** [food] siri *m*.

crab apple *n* - **1.** [fruit] maçã *f* silvestre - **2.** [tree] macieira *f* silvestre.

crabby (*compar* -ier, *superl* -iest) *adj* mal-humorado(da).

crack [kræk] <> *n* - **1.** [fault - in cup, glass, mirror] trinca *f*; [- in wall, ceiling] rachadura *f*; [- in skin] arranhão *m* - **2.** [small opening, gap] fresta *f*; **at the ~ of dawn** no raiar do dia - **3.** [sharp noise] estalo *m* - **4.** [joke] piada *f* - **5.** *inf* [attempt]: **to have a ~ at sthg** tentar (fazer) algo - **6.** [cocaine] crack *m*. <> *adj* de primeira. <> *vt* - **1.** [damage - gen] arranhar; [- cup, glass] trincar; [- wall, ceiling] rachar - **2.** [open - egg] quebrar; [- bottle] abrir; [- safe] arrombar - **3.** [cause to make sharp noise] estalar - **4.** [bang, hit] bater - **5.** [solve - problem] resolver; [- code] decifrar - **6.** *inf* [make]: **to ~ a joke** soltar uma piada. <> *vi* - **1.** [split, be damaged - gen] arranhar; [- cup, glass] trincar; [- wall, ceiling,] rachar - **2.** [make sharp noise] estalar - **3.** [give way, collapse] ruir - **4.** *UK inf* [act quickly]: **to get ~ing** pôr mãos à obra.

◆ **crack down** *vi*: **to ~ down (on sb/sthg)** fazer linha dura (contra alguém/algo).

◆ **crack up** *vi* ter um colapso nervoso.

crackdown ['krækdaʊn] *n*: **~ (on sthg)** endurecimento *m* (em relação a algo).

cracked ['krækt] *adj* - **1.** [damaged - cup, glass, skin] arranhado(da); [- wall, ceiling] rachado(da) - **2.** *inf* [mad] doido(da).

cracker ['krækə^r] *n* - **1.** [biscuit] biscoito *m* - **2.** *UK* [for Christmas] tubo colorido que faz barulho ao abrir e contém um presente surpresa.

crackers ['krækəz] *adj UK inf* [mad] doido(da).

cracking ['krækɪŋ] *adj inf*: **to walk at a ~ pace** andar a passos largos.

crackle ['krækl] <> *n* - **1.** [of fire, cooking] crepitação *f* - **2.** [of phone, radio] interferência *f*. <> *vi* - **1.** [fire, cooking] crepitar - **2.** [phone, radio] estar com interferência.

crackling ['kræklɪŋ] *n (U)* - **1.** [noise - on phone] tilintar *m*; [- on radio] interferência *f* - **2.** [pork skin] torresmo *m*.

crackpot ['krækpɒt] *inf* <> *adj* maluco(ca). <> *n* excêntrico *m*, -ca *f*.

cradle ['kreɪdl] <> *n* - **1.** [baby's bed, birthplace] berço *m* - **2.** [hoist] pedestal *m*. <> *vt* - **1.** [person] embalar - **2.** [object] segurar cuidadosamente.

craft [krɑːft] (*pl sense 2 inv*) *n* - **1.** [trade, skill] arte *f* - **2.** [boat] barco *m*.

craftsman ['krɑːftsmən] (*pl* -men [-mən]) *n* artesão *m*.

craftsmanship ['krɑːftsmənʃɪp] *n* destreza *f*, habilidade *f*.

craftsmen *pl* ▷ craftsman.

crafty ['krɑːftɪ] (*compar* -ier, *superl* -iest) *adj* astuto(ta).

crag [kræg] *n* penhasco *m*.

craggy ['krægɪ] (*compar* -ier, *superl* -iest) *adj* - **1.** [rock] escarpado(da) - **2.** [face] de traços fortes.

Crakow ['krækaʊ] *n* Cracóvia *f*; **in ~** em Cracóvia.

cram [kræm] (*pt* & *pp* -med, *cont* -ming) <> *vt* abarrotar; **to ~ sthg with sthg** abarrotar algo com algo; **to be crammed (with sthg)** estar abarrotado(da) (de algo). <> *vi* [study hard] rachar de estudar.

cramp [kræmp] <> *n* - **1.** [in leg, arm] cãibra *f* - **2.** [in stomach] cólica *f*. <> *vt* [restrict, hinder] limitar.

cramped [kræmpt] *adj* [confined] apertado(da).

crampon ['kræmpən] *n* ganho *m* de ferro.

cranberry ['krænbərɪ] (*pl* -ies) *n* uva-do-monte *f*.

crane [kreɪn] <> *n* - **1.** [machine] guindaste *m* - **2.** [bird] grou *m*. <> *vt* espichar. <> *vi* espichar-se.

crane fly *n* mosquito-berne *m*.

cranium ['kreɪnjəm] (*pl* -niums *OR* -nia [-njəl]) *n* crânio *m*.

crank [kræŋk] <> *n* - **1.** TECH manivela *f* - **2.** *inf* [eccentric] extravagante *mf*. <> *vt* - **1.** [gen] dar manivela em - **2.** *AUT* dar partida em.

crankshaft ['kræŋkʃɑːft] *n* virabrequim *m*.

cranky ['kræŋkɪ] (*compar* -ier, *superl* -iest) *adj inf* - **1.** [odd] esquisito(ta) - **2.** [bad-tempered] irritadiço(ça).

cranny ['krænɪ] (*pl* -ies) *n* ▷ nook.

crap [kræp] *n (U) vulg* - **1.** [excrement] bosta *f* - **2.** *fig* [rubbish] asneira *f*.

crappy ['kræpɪ] (*compar* -ier, *superl* -iest) *adj vulg* de péssima qualidade.

crash [kræʃ] <> *n* - **1.** [accident] acidente *m* - **2.** [loud noise] estrépito *m* - **3.** *FIN* crash *m*. <> *vt* [cause to collide] bater com. <> *vi* - **1.** [collide] colidir; **to ~ into sthg** colidir em algo - **2.** [make loud noise - drums] soar; [- cymbals] retinir; [- waves] quebrar; [- china] espatifar - **3.** *FIN* [collapse] entrar em colapso - **4.** *COMPUT* dar pane.

crash barrier *n* cerca *f* de proteção.

crash course *n* curso *m* intensivo.

crash diet *n* dieta *f* rigorosa.

crash-dive *vi* submersão *f* súbita.

crash helmet *n* elmo *m*.

crash-land <> *vt* aterrisar forçosamente. <> *vi* aterrisar forçosamente.

crash-landing *n* aterrissagem *f* forçada.

crass [kræs] *adj* crasso(sa).

crate [kreɪt] *n* - **1.** [for carrying things] caixote *m* - **2.** [crateful] engradado *m*.

crater ['kreɪtə^r] *n* cratera *f*.

cravat [krə'væt] *n* cachecol *m*.

crave [kreɪv] <> *vt* ansiar. <> *vi*: **to ~ for sthg** ansiar por algo.

craving ['kreɪvɪŋ] *n*: **~ (for sthg/to do sthg)** desejo incontrolável (por algo/fazer algo).

crawl [krɔːl] ⟨⟩ *vi* -**1.** [on hands and knees] engatinhar -**2.** [move slowly - insect] rastejar; [- vehicle, traffic] arrastar-se -**3.** *inf*: **to be** ~**ing with sthg** estar infestado(da) de algo -**4.** *inf* [grovel]: **to** ~ **(to sb)** rastejar (aos pés de alguém). ⟨⟩ *n* -**1.** [slow pace]: **at a** ~ vagarosamente -**2.** *(U)* [swimming stroke]: **the** ~ o crawl.

crawler lane [ˈkrɔːləʳ-] *n UK* faixa *f* para veículos lentos.

crayfish [ˈkreɪfɪʃ] *(pl inv OR* **-es)** *n* -**1.** [fish] lagostim *m* -**2.** [food] camarão-d'água-doce *m*.

crayon [ˈkreɪɒn] *n* lápis *m* de cera.

craze [kreɪz] *n* [fashion] moda *f*.

crazed [kreɪzd] *adj* enlouquecido(da); ~ **with** louco(ca) de.

crazy [ˈkreɪzɪ] *(compar* -**ier**, *superl* -**iest)** *adj inf* [mad, enthusiastic] louco(ca); **to be** ~ **about sthg/sb** ser/estar louco(ca) por algo/alguém.

crazy paving *n UK* pavimento *m* irregular.

CRC *(abbr of* **camera-ready copy)** *PRINT n* versão pronta para impressão.

CRE *(abbr of* **Commission for Racial Equality)** *n* commissão para combater a desigualdade racial.

creak [kriːk] ⟨⟩ *n* rangido *m*. ⟨⟩ *vi* ranger.

creaky [ˈkriːkɪ] *(compar* -**ier**, *superl* -**iest)** *adj* que range.

cream [kriːm] ⟨⟩ *adj* [in colour] creme. ⟨⟩ *n* -**1.** creme *m* -**2.** [elite] **the** ~ a nata. ⟨⟩ *vt* [puree] fazer purê com.

➠ **cream off** *vt sep* tirar o melhor de.

cream cake *n UK* bolo *m* de creme.

cream cheese *n (U)* queijo *m* cremoso.

cream cracker *n UK* bolacha *f* cream cracker.

cream of tartar *n (U)* cremor *m* de tártaro.

cream tea *n UK* chá acompanhado de bolinhos com presunto, geléia e creme, comum na Inglaterra.

creamy [ˈkriːmɪ] *(compar* -**ier**, *superl* -**iest)** *adj* -**1.** [texture, taste] cremoso(sa) -**2.** [colour] creme.

crease [kriːs] ⟨⟩ *n* [in fabric - deliberate] friso *m*; [- accidental] dobra *f.* ⟨⟩ *vt* [deliberately] amassar; [accidentally] amarrotar. ⟨⟩ *vi* -**1.** [fabric] amassar -**2.** [face, forehead] franzir-se.

creased [kriːst] *adj* -**1.** [fabric] amarrotado(da) -**2.** [face] franzido(da).

crease-resistant *adj*: ~ **fabric** tecido *m* que não amassa.

create [kriːˈeɪt] *vt* -**1.** [gen] criar -**2.** [noise, fuss, impression] causar.

creation [kriːˈeɪʃn] *n* criação *f.*

creative [kriːˈeɪtɪv] *adj* criativo(va); ~ **writing** produção *f* literária.

creativity [ˌkriːeɪˈtɪvətɪ] *n (U)* criatividade *f.*

creator [kriːˈeɪtəʳ] *n* [person] criador *m*, -ra *f.*

creature [ˈkriːtʃəʳ] *n* -**1.** [animal] criatura *f* -**2.** *literary* [person] ser *m.*

crèche [kreʃ] *n UK* creche *f.*

credence [ˈkriːdns] *n (U)* credibilidade *f*; **to give** *OR* **lend** ~ **to sthg** conferir credibilidade a algo.

credentials [krɪˈdenʃlz] *npl* -**1.** [papers] credenciais *fpl* -**2.** *fig* [qualifications] credenciais *fpl* -**3.** [references] referências *fpl.*

credibility [ˌkredəˈbɪlətɪ] *n (U)* credibilidade *f.*

credible [ˈkredəbl] *adj* crível.

credit [ˈkredɪt] ⟨⟩ *n* -**1.** *(U)* [financial aid] crédito *m*; **in** ~ com saldo positivo; **on** ~ a prazo -**2.** *(U)* [praise] honras *fpl*; **to his/her** ~ [successfully completed] a seu favor; [in his/her favour] para o seu próprio bem; **to do sb** ~ dizer muito em favor de alguém; **to give sb** ~ **for sthg** crer que alguém seja capaz de algo -**3.** *SCH & UNIV* crédito *m* -**4.** *FIN* [money credited] saldo *m* positivo. ⟨⟩ *vt* -**1.** *FIN* creditar -**2.** *inf* [believe] acreditar -**3.** [attribute]: **to** ~ **sb with sthg** atribuir a alguém o mérito por algo.

➠ **credits** *npl CINEMA* créditos *mpl.*

creditable [ˈkredɪtəbl] *adj fml* louvável.

credit account *n UK* conta *f* de crédito.

credit broker *n* intermediário *m* financeiro, intermediária *f* financeira.

credit card *n* cartão *m* de crédito.

credit control *n (U)* controle *m* de crédito.

credit facilities *npl* facilidades *fpl* de crédito.

credit limit *UK*, **credit line** *US n* limite *m* de crédito.

credit note *n* -**1.** *COMM* nota *f* promissória -**2.** *FIN* letra *f* de câmbio.

creditor [ˈkredɪtəʳ] *n* credor *m*, -ra *f.*

credit rating *n* índice *f* de crédito.

credit squeeze *n* contenção *f* de crédito.

credit transfer *n* transferência *f* bancária.

creditworthy [ˈkredɪtˌwɜːðɪ] *adj* merecedor(ra) de crédito.

credulity [krɪˈdjuːlətɪ] *n (U) fml* credulidade *f.*

credulous [ˈkredjʊləs] *adj* crédulo(la).

creed [kriːd] *n* -**1.** [political] doutrina *f* -**2.** *RELIG* credo *m.*

creek [kriːk] *n* -**1.** [inlet] enseada *f* -**2.** *US* [stream] riacho *m.*

creep [kriːp] *(pt & pp* **crept)** ⟨⟩ *vi* -**1.** [move slowly] arrastar-se -**2.** [move stealthily] andar furtivamente -**3.** [grovel]: **to** ~ **(to sb)** rastejar-se (diante de alguém). ⟨⟩ *n inf* [person] pegajoso *m*, -sa *f.*

➠ **creeps** *npl*: **to give sb the** ~**s** *inf* dar arrepios *mpl* em alguém.

➠ **creep in** *vi* [mistakes, doubts] surgir.

➠ **creep up on** *vt* ~ -**1.** [subj: person, animal] aproximar-se furtivamente -**2.** [subj: feeling, state] aproximar-se.

creeper [ˈkriːpəʳ] *n* [plant] trepadeira *f.*

creeping *adj* [gradual] gradual.

creepy [ˈkriːpɪ] *(compar* -**ier**, *superl* -**iest)** *adj inf* horripilante.

creepy-crawly [-ˈkrɔːlɪ] *(pl* **creepy-crawlies)** *n inf* bicho *m* rastejante.

cremate [krɪˈmeɪt] *vt* cremar.

cremation [krɪˈmeɪʃn] *n (U)* cremação *f.*

crematorium *UK* [ˌkreməˈtɔːrɪəm] *(pl* -**riums** *OR* -**ria** [-rɪə]), **crematory** *US* [ˈkremətrɪ] *(pl* -**ies)** *n* crematório *m.*

creosote [ˈkrɪəsəʊt] ⟨⟩ *n (U)* creosoto *m.* ⟨⟩ *vt* aplicar creosoto em.

crepe [kreɪp] *n* crepe *m.*

crepe bandage *n UK* atadura *f.*

crepe paper *n (U)* papel *m* crepom.

crepe-soled shoes [-səʊld-] *npl UK* calçado *m* com sola emborrachada.

crept [krept] *pt & pp* ▷ **creep**.

Cres. *abbr of* Crescent.

crescendo [krɪˈʃendəʊ] (*pl* **-s**) *n* crescendo *m*.

crescent [ˈkresnt] ◇ *adj* [shaped] crescente. ◇ *n* **-1.** [shape] crescente *mf* **-2.** [street] rua *f* em forma de arco.

cress [kres] *n (U)* agrião *m*.

crest [krest] *n* **-1.** [on bird's head, of wave] crista *f* **-2.** [of hill] cume *m* **-3.** [on coat of arms] brasão *m*.

crestfallen [ˈkrest,fɔːln] *adj* desanimado(da).

Crete [kriːt] *n* Creta; **in** ~ em Creta.

cretin [ˈkretɪn] *n inf offensive* [idiot] cretino *m*, -na *f*.

crevasse [krɪˈvæs] *n* fissura *f*, fenda *f*.

crevice [ˈkrevɪs] *n* fenda *f*, rachadura *f*.

crew [kruː] *n* **-1.** [of ship, plane, ambulance] tripulação *f* **-2.** CINEMA & TV equipe *f* **-3.** *inf* [gang] bando *m*.

crew cut *n* corte *m* de cabelo à escovinha.

crewman [ˈkruːmæn] (*pl* **-men** [-men]) *n* **-1.** [of aircraft] tripulante *mf* **-2.** [of film set] membro *m* da equipe.

crew neck *n* [on sweater] gola *f* redonda.

crew-neck(ed) [-nek(t)] *adj* de gola redonda.

crib [krɪb] (*pt & pp* **-bed**, *cont* **-bing**) ◇ *n* berço *m*. ◇ *vt inf* [copy]: **to** ~ **sthg off** OR **from sb** copiar algo de alguém.

cribbage [ˈkrɪbɪdʒ] *n (U)* jogo de cartas em que a pontuação é marcada com madeira num tabuleiro.

crick [krɪk] ◇ *n* [in neck] torcicolo *m*. ◇ *vt* dar mau jeito em.

cricket [ˈkrɪkɪt] ◇ *n* **-1.** (U) [game] críquete *m* **-2.** [insect] grilo *m*. ◇ *comp* de críquete.

cricketer [ˈkrɪkɪtəʳ] *n* jogador *m*, -ra *f* de críquete.

crikey [ˈkraɪkɪ] *excl UK inf dated* caramba!

crime [kraɪm] ◇ *n* crime *m*. ◇ *comp*: ~ **prevention** prevenção *f* contra o crime; ~ **novel** novela *f* policial.

Crimea *n*: **the** ~ a Criméia; **in the** ~ na Criméia.

crime wave *n* onda *f* de criminalidade.

criminal [ˈkrɪmɪnl] ◇ *adj* **-1.** [JUR - act] criminal; [- lawyer] criminalista; [offence] penal **-2.** *inf* [shameful] vergonhoso(sa). ◇ *n* criminoso *m*, -sa *f*.

criminalize, -ise [ˈkrɪmɪnəlaɪz] *vt* criminalizar.

criminal law *n (U)* direito *m* penal.

criminology [ˌkrɪmɪˈnɒlədʒɪ] *n (U)* criminologia *f*.

crimped *adj* ondulado(da).

crimson [ˈkrɪmzn] ◇ *adj* **-1.** [in colour] carmesim **-2.** [with embarrassment] vermelho(lha). ◇ *n* carmesim *mf*.

cringe [krɪndʒ] *vi* **-1.** [out of fear] encolher-se **-2.** *inf* [with embarrassment]: **to** ~ **(at sthg)** encolher-se de vergonha (por algo).

crinkle [ˈkrɪŋkl] ◇ *n* ruga *f*. ◇ *vt* enrugar. ◇ *vi* enrugar-se.

cripple [ˈkrɪpl] ◇ *n offensive* aleijado *m*, -da *f*. ◇ *vt* **-1.** MED [disable] aleijar **-2.** [put out of action] inutilizar **-3.** *fig* [bring to a halt] paralisar.

crippling [ˈkrɪplɪŋ] *adj* **-1.** MED [disease] devastador(ra) **-2.** [taxes, prices, debts] excessivo(va).

crisis [ˈkraɪsɪs] (*pl* **crises** [ˈkraɪsiːz]) *n* crise *f*.

crisp [krɪsp] *adj* **-1.** [pastry, bacon] crocante; [fruit, vegetables] fresco(ca); [banknote] liso(sa); [snow] quebradiço(ça) **-2.** [weather] revigorante **-3.** [manner, toner] seco(ca).

◆ **crisps** *npl UK* batatas *fpl* fritas *(em pacote)*.

crispbread [ˈkrɪspbred] *n (U)* biscoito de centeio ou trigo, que substitui o pão para quem está de dieta.

crispy [ˈkrɪspɪ] (*compar* **-ier**, *superl* **-iest**) *adj* [pastry, bacon] crocante; [fruit, vegetables] fresco(ca).

criss-cross ◇ *adj* [pattern] xadrez. ◇ *vt* [subj: roads] entrecruzar. ◇ *vi* [lines, pattern] entrecruzar-se.

criterion [kraɪˈtɪərɪən] (*pl* **-ria** [-rɪə], **-rions**) *n* critério *m*.

critic [ˈkrɪtɪk] *n* crítico *m*, -ca *f*.

critical [ˈkrɪtɪkl] *adj* **-1.** [serious] crítico(ca), grave **-2.** [crucial] fundamental **-3.** [analytical, disparaging] crítico(ca); **to be** ~ **of sb/sthg** criticar alguém/ algo.

critically [ˈkrɪtɪklɪ] *adv* **-1.** [seriously] criticamente, gravemente **-2.** [crucially] fundamentalmente **-3.** [analytically, disparagingly] criticamente.

criticism [ˈkrɪtɪsɪzm] *n* crítica *f*.

criticize, -ise [ˈkrɪtɪsaɪz] ◇ *vt* [judge unfavourably] criticar. ◇ *vi* [make unfavourable comments] criticar.

critique [krɪˈtiːk] *n* crítica *f*.

croak [krəʊk] ◇ *n* **-1.** [of frog] coaxo *m* **-2.** [of bird] grasnido *m* **-3.** [hoarse voice] rouquidão *f*. ◇ *vt* grunhir. ◇ *vi* **-1.** [animal] coaxar **-2.** [bird] granir **-3.** [person] ter rouquidão.

Croat [ˈkrəʊæt], **Croatian** [krəʊˈeɪʃn] ◇ *adj* croata. ◇ *n* **-1.** [person] croata *mf* **-2.** [language] croata *m*.

Croatia [krəʊˈeɪʃə] *n* Croácia; **in** ~ na Croácia.

crochet [ˈkrəʊʃeɪ] ◇ *n (U)* crochê *m*. ◇ *vt* fazer de crochê.

crockery [ˈkrɒkərɪ] *n (U)* louça *f (de barro)*.

crocodile [ˈkrɒkədaɪl] (*pl inv* OR **-s**) *n* [animal] crocodilo *m*.

crocus [ˈkrəʊkəs] (*pl* **-cuses**) *n* açafrão *m*.

croft [krɒft] *n UK* sítio *m*.

croissant [ˈkrwæsæ] *n* croissant *m*.

crony [ˈkrəʊnɪ] (*pl* **-ies**) *n inf* [friend] camarada *mf*.

crook [krʊk] *n* **-1.** [criminal] vigarista *mf* **-2.** *inf* [dishonest person] trapaceiro *m*, -ra *f* **-3.** [angle] curvatura *f* **-4.** [shepherd's staff] cajado *m*. ◇ *vt* entortar, dobrar.

crooked [ˈkrʊkɪd] *adj* **-1.** [not straight - back] arqueado(da); [- teeth, smile] torto(ta); [- path] sinuoso(sa) **-2.** *inf* [dishonest] desonesto(ta).

croon [kruːn] ◇ *vt* [sing softly] cantarolar. ◇ *vi* [sing softly] cantarolar.

crop [krɒp] (*pt & pp* **-ped**, *cont* **-ping**) ◇ *n* **-1.** [kind of plant] cultura *f* **-2.** [harvested produce] colheita *f* **-3.** *inf fig* [group]: **a** ~ **of books** uma coleção de livros; **a** ~ **of graduates** um grupo de formandos **-4.** [whip] chicote *m* **-5.** [of bird] papo *m* **-6.** [haircut] cabelo *m* curto. ◇ *vt* **-1.** [cut short] tosar **-2.** [eat] mascar.

◆ **crop up** *vi* surgir.

cropper [ˈkrɒpəʳ] *n inf*: **to come a** ~ [fall] levar um tombo; [fail] entrar pelo cano.

crop spraying [-ˌspreɪɪŋ] n (U) pulverização f.
croquet [ˈkrəʊkeɪ] n (U) croqué m.
croquette [krɒˈket] n croquete m.
cross [krɒs] ◇ adj zangado(da). ◇ n -1. [gen] cruz f -2. [mixture] cruzamento m; **a Labrador ~** um cruzamento de labrador; **a ~ between two things** uma mistura de duas coisas. ◇ vt -1. [gen] cruzar -2. [move across - street, room] atravessar; [- subj: expression] trespassar; **a look of distaste ~ed her face** um olhar de desagrado trespassou-lhe o rosto -3. RELIG : **to ~ o.s.** fazer o sinal da cruz -4. UK [cheque] cruzar -5. [thwart] frustrar, impedir. ◇ vi -1. [intersect] cruzar-se -2. [traverse] fazer uma travessia.
➡ **cross off, cross out** vt sep riscar.
crossbar [ˈkrɒsbɑːˁ] n -1. [of goal] trave f -2. [of bicycle] barra f transversal.
crossbow [ˈkrɒsbəʊ] n besta f.
crossbreed [ˈkrɒsbriːd] n cruza f.
cross-Channel adj [ferry, route] do Canal da Mancha; **~ travel** viagem pelo Canal da Mancha.
cross-check ◇ n verificação f cruzada. ◇ vt verificar de forma cruzada.
cross-country ◇ adj & adv através do campo. ◇ n [race, running] esporte praticado através dos campos.
cross-cultural adj intercultural.
cross-dress vi -1. [man] vestir-se de mulher -2. [woman] vestir-se de homem.
crossed line [krɒst-] n linha f cruzada.
cross-examination n -1. JUR interrogatório m (para confirmar veracidade) -2. fig [close questioning] interrogatório m.
cross-examine vt -1. JUR interrogar (para confirmar veracidade) -2. fig [question closely] interrogar.
cross-eyed [ˈkrɒsaɪd] adj vesgo(ga).
cross-fertilize vt [plant] fecundar por cruzamento.
crossfire [ˈkrɒsˌfaɪəˁ] n (U) fogo m cruzado.
crosshead [ˈkrɒsˌhed] adj [screw] com cabeça Philips®; **~ screwdriver** chave f de fenda Philips®.
crossing [ˈkrɒsɪŋ] n -1. [place to cross] faixa f de segurança -2. [sea journey] travessia f.
cross-legged [ˈkrɒslegd] adv de pernas cruzadas.
crossly [ˈkrɒslɪ] adv com irritação.
cross-ply (pl -ies) adj [tyre] de carcaça diagonal.
cross-purposes npl mal-entendido m; **to be at ~** não se entender.
cross-question vt interrogar novamente.
cross-refer ◇ vt remeter. ◇ vi fazer uma referência.
cross-reference n referência f cruzada.
crossroads [ˈkrɒsrəʊdz] (pl inv) n cruzamento m, encruzilhada f; **to be at a ~** fig estar numa encruzilhada.
cross-section n -1. [drawing] corte m transversal -2. [of population] amostra f representativa.
crosswalk [ˈkrɒswɔːk] n US faixa f de segurança.
crossways [ˈkrɒsweɪz] adv = **crosswise**.
crosswind [ˈkrɒswɪnd] n vento m contrário.

crosswise [ˈkrɒswaɪz] adv em diagonal, transversalmente.
crossword (puzzle) [ˈkrɒswɜːd-] n palavras fpl cruzadas.
crotch [krɒtʃ] n -1. [of person] entreperna f -2. [of garment] gancho m.
crotchet [ˈkrɒtʃɪt] n semínima f.
crotchety [ˈkrɒtʃɪtɪ] adj UK inf rabugento(ta).
crouch [kraʊtʃ] vi -1. [person] agachar-se -2. [animal] armar o bote.
croup [kruːp] n -1. [illness] crupe m -2. [of horse] garupa f.
croupier [ˈkruːpɪəˁ] n crupiê mf.
crouton [ˈkruːtɒn] n pão torrado cortado em cubos que acompanha a sopa.
crow [krəʊ] ◇ n corvo m; **as the ~ flies** em linha reta. ◇ vi -1. [cock] cantar -2. inf [gloat] gabar-se.
crowbar [ˈkrəʊbɑːˁ] n pé-de-cabra m.
crowd [kraʊd] ◇ n -1. [mass of people] multidão f -2. [social group] turma f. ◇ vi aglomerar-se. ◇ vt -1. [fill] lotar -2. [force into small space] empurrar; **to ~ everyone in** colocar todo mundo para dentro.
crowded [ˈkraʊdɪd] adj cheio (cheia), lotado(da); **~ with** cheio (cheia) de, repleto(ta) de.
crown [kraʊn] ◇ n -1. [gen] coroa f -2. [top - of hat] copa f; [- of head] topo m; [- of hill] cume m. ◇ vt -1. [monarch] coroar -2. [tooth] pôr uma coroa em -3. [cover top of] cobrir.
➡ **Crown** ◇ n: **the Crown** [monarchy] a Coroa. ◇ comp da Coroa.
crown court n tribunal m (com júri).
crowning [ˈkraʊnɪŋ] adj supremo(ma).
Crown Jewels npl: **the ~** as jóias da Coroa.
crown prince n príncipe m herdeiro.
crow's feet npl pés-de-galinha mpl.
crow's nest n cesto m de gávea.
crucial [ˈkruːʃl] adj [vital] crucial.
crucially [ˈkruːʃlɪ] adv [vitally] crucialmente; **~ important** de vital importância.
crucible [ˈkruːsɪbl] n [container] cadinho m.
crucifix [ˈkruːsɪfɪks] n crucifixo m.
Crucifixion [ˌkruːsɪˈfɪkʃn] n: **the ~** a Crucificação.
crucify [ˈkruːsɪfaɪ] (pt & pp -ied) vt lit & fig crucificar.
crude [kruːd] ◇ adj -1. [commodity] cru (crua) -2. [joke, person] grosseiro(ra) -3. [sketch] tosco(ca) -4. [method, shelter] primitivo(va). ◇ n = **crude oil**.
crudely [ˈkruːdlɪ] adj -1. [vulgarly] de maneira grosseira -2. [clumsily] toscamente.
crude oil n (U) petróleo m bruto.
cruel [kruəl] (compar -ler, superl -lest) adj -1. [sadistic] cruel -2. [painful, harsh - disappointment] doloroso(sa); [- winter] rigoroso(sa).
cruelly [ˈkruəlɪ] adv -1. [sadistically] cruelmente -2. [painfully, harshly] dolorosamente.
cruelty [ˈkruəltɪ] n (U) crueldade f.
cruet [ˈkruːɪt] n galheta f.
cruise [kruːz] ◇ n cruzeiro m. ◇ vi -1. [sail] fazer um cruzeiro -2. [drive] ir à velocidade de cruzeiro -3. [fly] voar.
cruise missile n míssil m de cruzeiro.
cruiser [ˈkruːzəˁ] n -1. [warship] cruzador m -2. [cabin cruiser] iate m.

crumb [krʌm] *n* **-1.** [of food] migalha *f*- **2.** [of information] fragmento *m*.

crumble ['krʌmbl] <> *n* doce de frutas coberto com uma mistura de farinha, manteiga e açúcar e cozido no forno. <> *vt* esmigalhar. <> *vi* **-1.** [disintegrate - bread, cheese] esmigalhar-se; [- building, cliff] desmoronar - **2.** *fig* [collapse] desmoronar.

crumbly ['krʌmblɪ] (*compar* **-ier,** *superl* **-iest**) *adj* farelento(ta).

crummy ['krʌmɪ] (*compar* **-ier,** *superl* **-iest**) *adj inf* [bad] fajuto(ta).

crumpet ['krʌmpɪt] *n* **-1.** [food] fatias de bolo tostadas que se come com manteiga - **2.** (U) *inf offensive* [women] gostosona *f*.

crumple ['krʌmpl] <> *vt* amassar. <> *vi* **-1.** [crease, dent] amassar - **2.** [collapse] desmoronar.
* **crumple up** *vt sep* amassar.

crunch [krʌntʃ] <> *n* [sound] mastigação *f* barulhenta; **if/when it comes to the ~** *inf* se/quando chegar a hora da verdade. <> *vt* **-1.** [with teeth] mastigar ruidosamente - **2.** [underfoot] esmagar com o pé ao caminhar. <> *vi* [snow, gravel] estalar.

crunchy ['krʌntʃɪ] (*compar* **-ier,** *superl* **-iest**) *adj* **-1.** [food] crocante - **2.** [snow, gravel] que estala.

crusade [kru:'seɪd] <> *n* **-1.** [war] cruzada *f*- **2.** *fig* [campaign] campanha *f*. <> *vi*: **to ~ for/against** sthg fazer campanha em favor de/contra algo.

crusader [kru:'seɪdə'] *n* **-1.** *HIST* cavaleiro *m* das cruzadas - **2.** *fig* [campaigner] defensor *m*, -ra *f*.

crush [krʌʃ] <> *n* **-1.** [crowd] aglomeração *f*- **2.** *inf* [infatuation]: **to have a ~ on sb** estar obcecado(da) por alguém - **3.** *UK* [drink] batida *f*. <> *vt* **-1.** [squash, press, smash] esmagar - **2.** *fig* [destroy] acabar com.

crush barrier *n UK* barreira *f*.

crushing ['krʌʃɪŋ] *adj* esmagador(ra).

crust [krʌst] *n* **-1.** [on bread] casca *f*- **2.** [on pie] crosta *f* torrada - **3.** [hard covering] crosta *f*.

crustacean [krʌ'steɪʃn] *n* crustáceo *m*.

crusty ['krʌstɪ] (*compar* **-ier,** *superl* **-iest**) *adj* **-1.** [food] crocante - **2.** [person] ríspido(da).

crutch [krʌtʃ] *n* **-1.** [stick] muleta *f*- **2.** *fig* [support] apoio *m* - **3.** [crotch] gancho *m*.

crux [krʌks] *n* ponto *m* crucial.

cry [kraɪ] (*pl* **cries,** *pt* & *pp* **cried**) <> *n* **-1.** [weep] choro *m* - **2.** [shout] grito *m*; **to be a far ~ from** não se parecer em nada com - **3.** [of bird] canto *m*. <> *vt* **-1.** [weep] chorar - **2.** [shout] gritar. <> *vi* **-1.** [weep] chorar - **2.** [shout] gritar.
* **cry off** *vi* desistir de.
* **cry out** <> *vt* gritar. <> *vi* [call out] gritar.
* **cry out for** *vt fus* [be in need of]: **to be ~ ing out for** sthg precisar de algo.

crybaby ['kraɪ,beɪbɪ] (*pl* **-ies**) *n inf pej* chorão *m*, -rona *f*.

crying ['kraɪɪŋ] <> *adj inf*: **it's a ~ shame** é uma vergonha enorme; **a ~ need for** sthg uma necessidade evidente de algo. <> *n* (U) choro *m*.

crypt [krɪpt] *n* cripta *f*.

cryptic ['krɪptɪk] *adj* [mysterious] enigmático(ca).

crypto- *prefix*: **a ~-communist** um comunista enrustido.

crystal ['krɪstl] <> *n* cristal *m*. <> *comp* [glass] de cristal.

crystal ball *n* bola *f* de cristal.

crystal clear *adj* **-1.** [water, voice] cristalino(na) - **2.** [motive, meaning] claro(ra).

crystallize, -ise ['krɪstəlaɪz] <> *vi* **-1.** [substance] cristalizar - **2.** [idea, plan] clarear. <> *vt* **-1.** [idea, plan] clarear - **2.** [fruit] cristalizar.

CSA (*abbr of* **Child Support Agency**) *n* agência britânica responsável pela coleta de doações para auxílio a crianças carentes.

CSC (*abbr of* **Civil Service Commission**) *n* organização britânica responsável pela contratação de funcionários públicos.

CSE (*abbr of* **Certificate of Secondary Education**) *n* antigo certificado de conclusão de ensino médio na Grã-Bretanha.

CS gas *n* gás *m* lacrimogêneo.

CST (*abbr of* **Central Standard Time**) *n* horário oficial no centro dos Estados Unidos e do Canadá.

ct (*abbr of* **carat**) ql.

CT *abbr of* **Connecticut**.

CTC (*abbr of* **city technology college**) *n* escola de ensino médio que tem parceria com empresas e com o governo para ensino de tecnologia na Grã-Bretanha.

cu. (*abbr of* **cubic**) cúbico(ca).

cub [kʌb] *n* **-1.** [young animal] filhote *m* - **2.** [boy scout] lobinho *m*.

Cuba ['kju:bə] *n* Cuba; **in ~** em Cuba.

Cuban ['kju:bən] <> *adj* cubano(na). <> *n* cubano *m*, -na *f*.

cubbyhole ['kʌbɪhəʊl] *n* cubículo *m*.

cube [kju:b] <> *n* cubo *m*. <> *vt MATH* elevar ao cubo.

cube root *n* raiz *f* cúbica.

cubic ['kju:bɪk] *adj* cúbico(ca).

cubicle ['kju:bɪkl] *n* **-1.** [shower] boxe *m* - **2.** [in shop] provador *m*.

cubism ['kju:bɪzm] *n* (U) cubismo *m*.

cubist ['kju:bɪst] *n* cubista *mf*.

cub reporter *n* jornalista *mf* novato, -ta.

Cub Scout *n* lobinho *m*.

cuckoo ['kuku:] *n* cuco *m*.

cuckoo clock *n* (relógio *m* de) cuco *m*.

cucumber ['kju:kʌmbə'] *n* pepino *m*.

cud [kʌd] *n*: **to chew the ~** *lit* & *fig* ruminar.

cuddle ['kʌdl] <> *n* abraço *m*. <> *vt* abraçar. <> *vi* abraçar-se.
* **cuddle up** *vi*: **to ~ up (to sb)** aconchegar-se (em alguém).

cuddly ['kʌdlɪ] (*compar* **-ier,** *superl* **-iest**) *adj* [person] mimoso(sa).

cuddly toy ['kʌdlɪ-] *n* bicho *m* de pelúcia.

cudgel ['kʌdʒəl] (*UK pt* & *pp* **-led,** *cont* **-ling,** *US pt* & *pp* **-ed,** *cont* **-ing**) <> *n* cacete *m*; **to take up the ~s for sb/sthg** sair em defesa de alguém/algo. <> *vt* dar cacetadas.

cue [kju:] *n* **-1.** *RADIO , THEATRE* & *TV* deixa *f*; **on ~** no momento certo; **to take one's ~ from sb** seguir o exemplo de alguém - **2.** *fig* [stimulus, signal] sinal *f* - **3.** [in snooker, pool] taco *m*.

cuff [kʌf] <> *n* **-1.** [of sleeve] punho *m* - **2.** *US* [of trouser] barra *f* **- 3.** [blow] tapa *m.* ◇ *vt* [hit] bater.

cufflink *n* abotoadura *f.*

cu. in. *abbr of* cubic inch(es).

cuisine [kwɪˈziːn] *n (U)* arte *f* culinária.

cul-de-sac [ˈkʌldəsæk] *n* beco *m* sem saída.

culinary [ˈkʌlɪnərɪ] *adj* culinária.

cull [kʌl] ◇ *n* [kill] extermínio *m.* ◇ *vt* **- 1.** [kill] exterminar **- 2.** *fml* [gather] reunir.

culminate [ˈkʌlmɪneɪt] *vi*: **to** ~ **in** sthg culminar em algo.

culmination [ˌkʌlmɪˈneɪʃn] *n* culminação *f.*

culottes [kjuːˈlɒts] *npl* saia-calça *f.*

culpable [ˈkʌlpəbll] *adj fml* culpável; ~ **homicide** homicídio *m* culposo.

culprit [ˈkʌlprɪt] *n* culpado *m,* -da *f.*

cult [kʌlt] ◇ *n* **- 1.** *RELIG* culto *m* **- 2.** [book, film] objeto *m* de culto. ◇ *comp* [book, film] de culto.

cultivate [ˈkʌltɪveɪt] *vt* **- 1.** [gen] cultivar **- 2.** [get to know] fazer amizade com.

cultivated [ˈkʌltɪveɪtɪd] *adj* **- 1.** [land] cultivado(da) **- 2.** [person, accent] culto(ta).

cultivation [ˌkʌltɪˈveɪʃn] *n (U)* [farming] cultivo *m.*

cultural [ˈkʌltʃərəl] *adj* cultural.

culture [ˈkʌltʃəˈ] *n* cultura *f.*

cultured [ˈkʌltʃəd] *adj* [educated] culto(ta).

cultured pearl *n* pérola *f* cultivada.

culture shock *n* choque *m* cultural.

culture vulture *n* *inf* amante *mf* da cultura.

culvert [ˈkʌlvət] *n* bueiro *m.*

cumbersome [ˈkʌmbəsəm] *adj* **- 1.** [object] de difícil manejo **- 2.** [system] ineficiente.

Cumbria *n* Cúmbria.

cumin [ˈkʌmɪn] *n (U)* cominho *m.*

cumulative [ˈkjuːmjʊlətɪv] *adj* cumulativo(va).

cunning [ˈkʌnɪŋ] ◇ *adj* **- 1.** [person] astuto(ta) **- 2.** [method, idea] engenhoso(sa). ◇ *n (U)* astúcia *f.*

cup [kʌp] (*pt & pp* **-ped,** *cont* **-ping**) ◇ *n* **- 1.** [gen] xícara *f;* **it's not my** ~ **of tea** *inf* não faz o meu gênero **- 2.** [as prize, of bra] taça *f* **- 3.** [competition] copa *f.* ◇ *vt* dispor (as mãos) em forma de concha.

cupboard [ˈkʌbəd] *n* armário *m.*

cupcake [ˈkʌpkeɪk] *n* bolinho *m* coberto com glacê.

Cup Final *n*: **the** ~ o jogo final da copa.

cup holder *n SPORT* atual campeão *m,* -ã *f* da copa.

cupid [ˈkjuːpɪd] *n* [figure] cupido *m.*

cupola [ˈkjuːpələ] (*pl* **-s**) *n ARCHIT* cúpula *f.*

cup tie *n UK* jogo *m* eliminatório.

curable [ˈkjʊərəbll] *adj* curável.

curate [ˈkjʊərət] ◇ *n RELIG* coadjutor *m,* -ra *f.* ◇ *vt* [exhibition] organizar.

curator [ˌkjʊəˈreɪtəˈ] *n* [of museum] curador *m,* -ra *f.*

curb [kɜːb] ◇ *n* **- 1.** [control]: ~ **(on** sthg) controle *m* (sobre algo) **- 2.** *US* [of road] meio-fio *m.* ◇ *vt* controlar.

curd cheese [kɜːd-] *n (U) UK* requeijão *m.*

curdle [ˈkɜːdll] *vi* **- 1.** [milk] coalhar **- 2.** [blood] coagular.

cure [kjʊəˈ] ◇ *n* **- 1.** *MED*: ~ **(for** sthg) cura *f* (de algo) **- 2.** [solution]: ~ **(for** sthg) solução *f* (para algo). ◇ *vt* **- 1.** *MED* curar *f* **- 2.** [solve] remediar **- 3.**

[rid]: **to** ~ **sb of** sthg *fig* livrar alguém de algo **- 4.** [preserve] curtir.

cure-all *n* panacéia *f.*

curfew [ˈkɜːfjuː] *n* toque *m* de recolher.

curio [ˈkjʊərɪəʊl] (*pl* **-s**) *n* raridade *f,* curiosidade *f.*

curiosity [ˌkjʊərɪˈɒsətɪ] *n* **- 1.** *(U)* [inquisitiveness] curiosidade *f* **- 2.** [rarity] raridade *f.*

curious [ˈkjʊərɪəs] *adj* curioso(sa); ~ **about** sb/sthg curioso(sa) sobre alguém/algo.

curiously [ˈkjʊərɪəslɪ] *adv* curiosamente.

curl [kɜːl] ◇ *n* **- 1.** [of hair] cacho *m* **- 2.** [of smoke] onda *f.* ◇ *vt* **- 1.** [hair] encrespar, encaracolar **- 2.** [tail, ribbon] enrolar. ◇ *vi* **- 1.** [hair] encrespar, encaracolar **- 2.** [paper, leaf, road, smoke, snake] enrolar; **to** ~ **into a ball** enrolar-se numa bola.
  ◆ **curl up** *vi* [person, animal] enrolar-se.

curler [ˈkɜːləˈ] *n* rolo *m.*

curling [ˈkɜːlɪŋ] *n SPORT* jogo escocês que consiste em deslizar pedras sobre o gelo.

curling tongs *npl* ferros *mpl* de frisar.

curly [ˈkɜːlɪ] (*compar* **-ier,** *superl* **-iest**) *adj* [hair] encaracolado(da).

currant [ˈkʌrənt] *n* [dried grape] uva *f* passa.

currency [ˈkʌrənsɪ] (*pl* **-ies**) *n* **- 1.** [money] moeda *f* corrente; **foreign** ~ moeda *f* estrangeira **- 2.** *fml* [acceptability]: **to gain** ~ ganhar aceitação.

current [ˈkʌrənt] ◇ *adj* atual; **in** ~ **use** de uso corrente. ◇ *n* corrente *f.*

current account *n UK* conta *f* corrente.

current affairs *npl* atualidades *fpl.*

current assets *npl* ativo *m* corrente.

current liabilities *npl* passivo *m* circulante.

currently [ˈkʌrəntlɪ] *adv* atualmente.

curricular *adj* curricular.

curriculum [kəˈrɪkjələm] (*pl* **-lums** OR **-la** [-lə]) *n* [course of study] currículo *m.*

curriculum vitae [-ˈviːtaɪ] (*pl* **curricula vitae**) *n* currículo *m,* curriculum *m* (vitae).

curried [ˈkʌrɪd] *adj* com molho de caril.

curry [ˈkʌrɪ] (*pl* **-ies**) *n* caril *m.*

curry powder *n (U)* caril *m* em pó.

curse [kɜːs] ◇ *n* **- 1.** [evil charm]: ~ **(on** sb/sthg) maldição *f* OR praga *f* (sobre alguém/algo) **- 2.** [swearword] palavrão *m* **- 3.** [source of problems] desgraça *f.* ◇ *vt* **- 1.** [wish misfortune on] maldizer **- 2.** [complain about] xingar. ◇ *vi* [swear] praguejar.

cursor [ˈkɜːsəˈ] *n COMPUT* cursor *m.*

cursory [ˈkɜːsərɪ] *adj* apressado(da); **a** ~ **glance** um olhada por cima.

curt [kɜːt] *adj* brusco(ca).

curtail [kɜːˈteɪl] *vt* **- 1.** [cut short] encurtar **- 2.** [restrict, reduce] reduzir.

curtailment [kɜːˈteɪlmənt] *n (U) fml* [reduction] redução *f.*

curtain [ˈkɜːtn] *n* cortina *f.*
  ◆ **curtain off** *vt sep* separar com uma cortina.

curtain call *n* chamada à frente do palco para receber aplausos.

curtain raiser *n* *fig* [warm-up] preâmbulo *m,* prelúdio *m.*

curts(e)y [ˈkɜːtsɪ] (*pt & pp* **curtsied**) ◇ *n* reverência *f (feita por mulher).* ◇ *vi* fazer reverência.

curvaceous [kɜ:'veɪʃəs] *adj inf* bom (boa) de curvas.

curvature ['kɜ:vətjəᶜ] *n (U)* curvatura *f.*

curve [kɜ:v] ◇ *n* curva *f.* ◇ *vi* fazer uma curva.

curved [kɜ:vd] *adj* curvo(va).

curvy ['kɜ:vɪ] (*compar* -ier, *superl* -iest) *adj*: a ~ blond uma loira cheia de curvas.

cushion ['kʊʃn] ◇ *n* -1. [for sitting on] almofada *f* -2. [protective layer] colchão *m.* ◇ *vt* amortecer; **to be ~ed against sthg** estar protegido(da) de algo.

cushy ['kʊʃɪ] (*compar* -ier, *superl* -iest) *adj inf* mole.

custard ['kʌstəd] *n* [sauce] creme *m (para doces).*

custard pie *n* torta *f* de creme.

custard powder *n (U)* pó desidratado que se mistura ao leite e ao açúcar para fazer creme.

custodial *adj* [sentence] custódio(dia).

custodian [kʌ'stəʊdjən] *n* [of building, museum] guarda *m.*

custody ['kʌstədɪ] *n (U)* -1. [of child] custódia *f* -2. [of suspect]: **in ~** sob custódia.

custom ['kʌstəm] *n* -1. [tradition, habit] costume *m*, hábito *m* -2. *(U)* COMM [trade] preferência *f*; **thank you for your ~** agradecemos a preferência.

➡ **customs** *n (U)* [place, organization] alfândega *f*; **to go through ~** passar pela alfândega.

customary ['kʌstəmrɪ] *adj* costumeiro(ra), habitual.

custom-built *adj* personalizado(da).

customer ['kʌstəməᶜ] *n* -1. [client] cliente *mf* -2. *inf* [person] tipo *m*; **an awkward ~** um tipo complicado.

customer services *npl* serviço *m* de atendimento ao consumidor.

customize, -ise ['kʌstəmaɪz] *vt* -1. [gen] personalizar -2. COMPUT customizar.

custom-made *adj* feito(ta) sob medida.

Customs and Excise *n (U)* UK *departamento do governo britânico responsável por coletar impostos sobre a compra e venda de bens e serviços ou sobre bens importados.*

customs duty *n (U)* imposto *m* alfandegário.

customs officer *n* fiscal *mf* de alfândega.

cut [kʌt] (*pt & pp* cut, *cont* -ting) ◇ *n* -1. [gen] corte *m*; ~ **(in sthg)** corte (em algo) -2. *inf* [share] parte *f* -3. *phr*: **a ~ above (the rest)** melhor que os outros. ◇ *vt* -1. [gen] cortar -2. [tooth] romper -3. *inf* [miss] matar -4. *phr*: **to ~ sb dead** fazer que não se vê alguém; ~ **and dried** definitivo(va). ◇ *vi* -1. cortar -2. *phr*: **to ~ both ways** ser uma faca de dois gumes.

➡ **cut across** *vt fus* -1. [as short cut] cortar caminho por -2. [transcend] transcender, estar acima de.

➡ **cut back** ◇ *vt sep* -1. [tree, bush] podar -2. [expenditure, budget] reduzir, diminuir. ◇ *vi*: **to ~ back (on sthg)** reduzir (algo).

➡ **cut down** ◇ *vt sep* -1. [chop down] cortar, derrubar -2. [reduce] reduzir, diminuir. ◇ *vi*: **to ~ down on sthg** reduzir algo.

➡ **cut in** *vi* -1. [interrupt]: **to ~ in (on sb)** interromper (alguém) -2. [in car] cortar (a frente de), fechar.

➡ **cut off** *vt sep* -1. [sever] cortar fora -2. [sever supply of] cortar; **I got ~ off** [on telephone] cortaram

meu telefone -3. [isolate]: **to be ~ off (from sb/sthg)** ficar isolado(da) (de alguém/algo).

➡ **cut out** ◇ *vt sep* -1. [gen] cortar; **to ~ out the light** cortar a entrada de luz; ~ **it out!** pare com isso! -2.: **to be ~ out for sthg** *fig* ser feito(ta) para algo. ◇ *vi* [stall] morrer.

➡ **cut up** *vt sep* [chop up] picar.

cut and paste COMPUT ◇ *vt* recortar e colar. ◇ *vi* recortar e colar.

cutback ['kʌtbæk] *n*: ~ **(in sthg)** corte *m* (em algo).

cute [kju:t] *adj esp US* [appealing] bonitinho(nha).

cut glass ◇ *n (U)* vidro *m* lapidado. ◇ *comp* de vidro lapidado.

cuticle ['kju:tɪkl] *n* cutícula *f.*

cutlery ['kʌtləri] *n (U)* talheres *mpl.*

cutlet ['kʌtlɪt] *n* costeleta *f.*

cut-off (point) *n* [limit] (ponto *m*) limite *m.*

cut-out *n* -1. [on machine] disjuntor *m* -2. [shape] figura *f* para recortar.

cut-price, cut-rate *US adj* com desconto.

cutter ['kʌtəᶜ] *n* [tool] cortador *m.*

cut-throat *adj* [ruthless] acirrado(da).

cutting ['kʌtɪŋ] ◇ *adj* [sarcastic] mordaz. ◇ *n* -1. [of plant] chantão *m* -2. [from newspaper] recorte *m* -3. *UK* [for road, railway] corte *m.*

cutting edge *n* centro *m.*

cutting room *n* CINEMA sala *f* de edição.

cuttlefish ['kʌtlfɪʃ] (*pl inv*) *n* siba *m.*

cut up *adj UK inf* [upset] chateado(da).

CV (*abbr of* **curriculum vitae**) *n* UK CV *m.*

c.w.o. (*abbr of* **cash with order**) *pagamento no ato da ordem de compra.*

cwt. *abbr of* **hundredweight**.

cyanide ['saɪənaɪd] *n (U)* cianeto *m*, cianureto *m.*

cybercafé *n* COMPUT cibercafé *m.*

cybernetics [ˌsaɪbə'netɪks] *n (U)* cibernética *f.*

cyberspace ['saɪbəspeɪs] *n* COMPUT ciberespaço *m.*

cyclamen ['sɪkləmən] (*pl inv*) *n* ciclâmen *m.*

cycle ['saɪkl] ◇ *n* -1. [process] ciclo *m* -2. [bicycle] bicicleta *f.* ◇ *comp*: ~ **path** ciclovia *f*; ~ **track** pista *f* para ciclismo; ~ **race** corrida *f* de bicicletas. ◇ *vi* andar de bicicleta.

cyclic(al) ['saɪklɪk(l)] *adj* cíclico(ca).

cycling ['saɪklɪŋ] *n (U)* ciclismo *m*; **to go ~** andar de bicicleta.

cycling helmet *n* capacete *m* de ciclismo.

cyclist ['saɪklɪst] *n* ciclista *mf.*

cyclone ['saɪkləʊn] *n* ciclone *m.*

cygnet ['sɪgnɪt] *n* filhote *m* de cisne.

cylinder ['sɪlɪndəᶜ] *n* -1. [gen] cilindro *m* -2. [container] tambor *m.*

cylinder block *n* bloco *m* de cilindros.

cylinder head *n* cabeça *f* de cilindro, culatra *f.*

cylindrical [sɪ'lɪndrɪkl] *adj* cilíndrico(ca).

cymbals ['sɪmblz] *npl* címbalos *mpl.*

cynic ['sɪnɪk] *n* cético *m*, -ca *f.*

cynical ['sɪnɪkl] *adj* cético(ca).

cynically ['sɪnɪklɪ] *adv* ceticamente.

cynicism ['sɪnɪsɪzm] *n (U)* ceticismo *m.*

cypher ['saɪfəᶜ] *n* = **cipher**.

cypress ['saɪprəs] *n* cipreste *m.*

Cypriot ['sɪprɪət] ◇ *adj* cipriota. ◇ *n* cipriota

mf; **Greek** ~ cipriota grego(ga); **Turkish** ~ cipriota turco(ca).
Cyprus ['saɪprəs] *n* Chipre; **in** ~ em Chipre.
cyst [sɪst] *n* cisto *m*.
cystic fibrosis [ˌsɪstɪkfaɪ'brəʊsɪs] *n* (U) fibrose *f* cística.
cystitis [sɪs'taɪtɪs] *n* (U) cistite *f*.
cytology [saɪ'tɒlədʒɪ] *n* (U) citologia *f*.
czar [zɑː'] *n* czar *m*.
Czech [tʃek] ◇ *adj* tcheco(ca). ◇ *n* -**1.** [person] tcheco *m*, -ca *f*-**2.** [language] tcheco *m*.
Czechoslovak *adj* & *n* = **Czechoslovakian**.
Czechoslovakia [ˌtʃekəslə'vækɪə] *n* Tchecoslováquia; **in** ~ na Tchecoslováquia.
Czechoslovakian [ˌtʃekəslə'vækɪən] ◇ *adj* tchecoslovaco(ca). ◇ *n* tchecoslovaco *m*, -ca *f*.
Czech Republic *n*: **the** ~ a República Tcheca.

D

d (*pl* **d's** OR **ds**), **D** (*pl* **D's** OR **Ds**) [diː] *n* [letter] d, D *m*.
◆ **D** ◇ *n* -**1.** MUS ré *m* -**2.** SCH [mark] D *m*. ◇ US *abbr of* **Democrat(ic)**.
d. (*abbr of* **died**) *m*.
DA (*abbr of* **district attorney**) *n* promotor nos *Estados Unidos*.
D/A (*abbr of* **digital to analogue**) *adj* D/A.
dab [dæb] (*pt* & *pp* -**bed**, *cont* -**bing**) ◇ *n* [small amount - of powder, ointment] pitada *f*; [- of paint] pincelada *f*. ◇ *vt* -**1.** [skin, wound] aplicar de leve -**2.** [eyes] tocar de leve -**3.** [cream, ointment]: to ~ sthg on(to) sthg aplicar algo em algo.
dabble ['dæbl] ◇ *vt* agitar (*com as mãos ou os pés*). ◇ *vi*: **to** ~ **(in sthg)** atuar como amador (em algo).
dab hand *n* UK *inf*: **to be a** ~ **(at sthg)** ser um craque (em algo).
Dacca ['dækə] *n* Dacca.
dachshund ['dækshʊnd] *n* dachshund *m*.
dad [dæd] *n* *inf* pai *m*.
daddy ['dædɪ] (*pl* -**ies**) *n* *inf* papai *m*.
daddy longlegs [-'lɒŋlegz] (*pl inv*) *n* pernilongo *m*.
daffodil ['dæfədɪl] *n* narciso *m*.
daft [dɑːft] *adj* UK *inf* bobo(ba).
dagger ['dægə'] *n* adaga *f*.
dahlia ['deɪljə] *n* dália *f*.
daily ['deɪlɪ] (*pl* -**ies**) ◇ *adj* diário(ria). ◇ *adv* diariamente; **twice** ~ duas vezes por dia. ◇ *n* -**1.** [newspaper] diário *m* -**2.** *esp* UK [cleaning woman] diarista *f*.

daintily ['deɪntɪlɪ] *adv* delicadamente, suavemente; **to eat** ~ comer com delicadeza.
dainty ['deɪntɪ] (*compar* -**ier**, *superl* -**iest**) *adj* delicado(da).
dairy ['deərɪ] (*pl* -**ies**) *n* leiteria *f*.
dairy cattle *npl* gado *m* leiteiro.
dairy farm *n* fazenda *f* de gado leiteiro.
dairy products *npl* lacticínios *mpl*.
dais ['deɪs] *n* estrado *m*.
daisy ['deɪzɪ] (*pl* -**ies**) *n* margarida *f*.
daisy wheel *n* margarida *f* (de impressão).
daisy-wheel printer *n* impressora *f* de margarida.
Dakar ['dækɑː] *n* Dacar.
dale [deɪl] *n* *literary* vale *m*.
dalmatian [dæl'meɪʃn] *n* [dog] dálmata *m*.
dam [dæm] (*pt* & *pp* -**med**, *cont* -**ming**) ◇ *n* [across river] represa *f*, barragem *f*. ◇ *vt* [river] represar.
◆ **dam up** *vt sep* -**1.** [river] represar -**2.** [feelings] conter.
damage ['dæmɪdʒ] ◇ *n*: ~ **(to sthg)** [gen] dano *m* (a algo); [to health, skin] mal *m* (a algo). ◇ *vt* -**1.** [object] danificar -**2.** [person] machucar -**3.** *fig* [chances, reputation] prejudicar.
◆ **damages** *npl* JUR danos *mpl*.
damaging ['dæmɪdʒɪŋ] *adj* *fig* prejudicial, danoso(sa); ~ **to sthg** prejudicial a algo.
Damascus [də'mæskəs] *n* Damasco.
Dame [deɪm] *n* UK *título honorífico concedido a uma mulher pelos serviços prestados à sociedade*.
damn [dæm] ◇ *adj* *inf* maldito(ta). ◇ *adv* *inf* muito. ◇ *n* *inf*: **not to give** OR **care a** ~ **(about sthg)** não estar nem aí (para algo). ◇ *vt* -**1.** RELIG [condemn] condenar -**2.** *inf* [curse] amaldiçoar; ~ **you!** maldito seja! ◇ *excl* *inf* droga!
damnable ['dæmnəbl] *adj* *dated* [appalling] execrável.
damnation [dæm'neɪʃn] *n* (U) RELIG danação *f*.
damned [dæmd] *inf* ◇ *adj* maldito(ta); **I'm** ~ **if I'll do it** bem capaz que eu vou fazer isso; **well I'll be** OR **I'm** ~! ora veja só! ◇ *adv* muito.
damning ['dæmɪŋ] *adj* condenatório(ria), incriminatório(ria).
damp [dæmp] ◇ *adj* úmido(da). ◇ *n* (U) umidade *f*. ◇ *vt* [make wet] umedecer.
◆ **damp down** *vt sep* [restrain] controlar.
damp course *n* UK impermeabilização *f*.
dampen ['dæmpən] *vt* -**1.** [make wet] umedecer -**2.** *fig* [emotion] esfriar.
damper ['dæmpə'] *n* [for fire] abafador *m*; **to put a** ~ **on sthg** *inf* jogar um balde de água fria em algo.
dampness ['dæmpnɪs] *n* umidade *f*.
damp-proof course *n* = **damp course**.
damson ['dæmzn] *n* abrunheiro *m*.
dance [dɑːns] ◇ *n* -**1.** [gen] dança *f*; **shall we have a** ~? vamos dançar? -**2.** [social event] baile *m*. ◇ *vt* dançar. ◇ *vi* dançar.
dance floor *n* pista *f* de dança.
dance hall *n* salão *m* de baile.
dancer ['dɑːnsə'] *n* dançarino *m*, -na *f*.
dancing ['dɑːnsɪŋ] *n* (U) dança *f*; **to go** ~ ir dançar.

D & C (*abbr of* dilation and curettage) *n* D&C.

dandelion ['dændɪlaɪən] *n* dente-de-leão *m*.

dandruff ['dændrʌf] *n (U)* caspa *f*.

dandy ['dændɪ] (*pl* -ies) *n* almofadinha *m*.

Dane [deɪn] *n* dinamarquês *m*, -esa *f*.

danger ['deɪndʒər] *n* perigo *m*; in ~ em perigo; out of ~ fora de perigo; ~ to sb/sthg perigo para alguém/algo; to be in ~ of doing sthg perigar fazer algo.

danger list *n UK*: to be on the ~ estar em estado grave.

danger money *n (U) UK* adicional *m* por periculosidade.

dangerous ['deɪndʒərəs] *adj* perigoso(sa).

dangerous driving *n (U) JUR* direção *f* perigosa.

dangerously ['deɪndʒərəslɪ] *adv* -1. [riskily] perigosamente - 2. *MED*: ~ ill em estado grave.

danger zone *n* zona *f* de perigo.

dangle ['dæŋɡl] *vt, vi* balançar.

Danish ['deɪnɪʃ] <> *adj* dinamarquês(quesa). <> *n* -1. [language] dinamarquês *m* - 2. *US* = Danish pastry. <> *npl*: the ~ os dinamarqueses.

Danish blue *n* tipo de queijo azul.

Danish pastry, Danish *US n* torta recheada com maçãs, glacê e marzipã.

dank [dæŋk] *adj* úmido e frio, úmida e fria.

Danube ['dænju:b] *n*: the ~ o Danúbio.

dapper ['dæpər] *adj* garboso(sa).

dappled ['dæpld] *adj* -1. [animal] pintado(da), malhado(da) - 2. [shade] pintado(da).

Dardanelles *npl*: the ~ o estreito de Dardanelos.

dare [deər] <> *vt* -1. [be brave enough]: to ~ to do sthg ousar fazer algo - 2. [challenge]: to ~ sb to do sthg desafiar alguém a fazer algo - 3. *phr*: I ~ say ouso dizer (que). <> *vi* atrever-se; how ~ you! como se atreve! <> *n* desafio *m*.

daredevil ['deə,devl] *n* intrépido *m*, -da *f*.

daren't [deənt] = dare not.

Dar es-Salaam [,dɑːresə'lɑːm] *n* Dar es-Salaam.

daring ['deərɪŋ] <> *adj* ousado(da). <> *n (U)* ousadia *f*.

dark [dɑːk] <> *adj* -1. [gen] escuro(ra) - 2. [gloomy] obscuro(ra) - 3. [sinister] sombrio(bria). <> *n* -1. *(U)* [darkness]: the ~ a escuridão, o escuro; to be in the ~ about sthg estar às escuras sobre algo - 2. [night]: before/after ~ antes/depois de escurecer.

Dark Ages *npl*: the ~ a Idade Média.

darken ['dɑːkn] <> *vt* escurecer. <> *vi* -1. escurecer - 2. *fig* [face] anuviar-se.

dark glasses *npl* óculos *m inv* escuros.

dark horse *n fig* [person] pessoa *f* enigmática.

darkness ['dɑːknɪs] *n (U)* escuridão *f*, trevas *fpl*.

darkroom ['dɑːkrʊm] *n* câmara *f* escura.

darling ['dɑːlɪŋ] <> *adj* -1. [dear] querido(da) - 2. *inf* [cute] adorável. <> *n* -1. [loved person] querido *m*, -da *f*; she's a little ~ é uma graça de criança - 2. [favourite] preferido *m*, -da *f*.

darn [dɑːn] <> *adj inf* maldito(ta). <> *adv inf* pra caramba. <> *n* remendo *m*. <> *vt* [repair] remendar, cerzir. <> *excl inf* [damn] que droga!

darning ['dɑːnɪŋ] *n (U)* [work] remendagem *f*,

cerzidura *f*; I hate ~ odeio cerzir.

darning needle *n* agulha *f* de cerzir.

dart [dɑːt] <> *n* -1. [arrow] dardo *m* - 2. *SEWING* pence *f*. <> *vt* lançar. <> *vi* [move quickly] lançar-se.
darts *n (U)* [game] dardos *mpl*.

dartboard ['dɑːtbɔːd] *n* alvo *m* para dardos.

dash [dæʃ] <> *n* -1. [of liquid] pingo *m* - 2. [in punctuation] travessão *m* - 3. *AUT* painel *m* (de instrumentos) - 4. [rush]: to make a ~ for sthg sair em disparada por algo. <> *vt* -1. *literary* [hurl] arremessar - 2. [hopes] frustar. <> *vi* correr; I must ~! preciso correr!
dash off <> *vt sep* [write quickly] rabiscar. <> *vi* [rush off] chispar.

dashboard ['dæʃbɔːd] *n* painel *m* de instrumentos.

dashing ['dæʃɪŋ] *adj* [handsome, energetic] atraente.

dastardly ['dæstədlɪ] *adj dated* cruel.

DAT [dæt] (*abbr of* digital audio tape) *n* DAT *m*.

data ['deɪtə] *n* dados *mpl*.

databank ['deɪtəbæŋk] *n* banco *m* de dados.

database ['deɪtəbeɪs] *n* base *f* de dados.

data capture *n (U)* captura *f* de dados.

data management *n COMPUT* gerenciamento *m* de dados.

data processing *n (U)* processamento *m* de dados.

data protection *n COMPUT* proteção *f* de dados.

data recovery *n COMPUT* recuperação *f* de dados.

data transmission *n (U)* transmissão *f* de dados.

date [deɪt] <> *n* -1. [in time] data *f*; what's today's ~? que dia é hoje?; at a later ~ um outro dia; to bring sb/sthg up to ~ atualizar alguém/algo; to keep sb/sthg up to ~ manter alguém/algo atualizado(da); to be out of ~ [dictionary, database] estar desatualizado(da); [passport] estar vencido(da); to ~ até agora - 2. [appointment] encontro *m* - 3. [person] par *m* - 4. [fruit] tâmara *f*, datil *m*. <> *vt* -1. [put a date on] datar - 2. [go out with] sair com. <> *vi* [go out of fashion] cair de moda.
date back to, date from *vt fus* datar de.

datebook *n US* agenda *f*.

dated ['deɪtɪd] *adj* antiquado(da).

date of birth *n* data *f* de nascimento.

date rape *n* estupro realizado por um homem após ter se relacionado socialmente com uma mulher.

date stamp *n* -1. [device] carimbo *m* datador - 2. [mark] data *f* carimbada.

daub [dɔːb] *vt*: to ~ sthg with sthg manchar algo.

daughter ['dɔːtər] *n* filha *f*.

daughter-in-law (*pl* daughters-in-law) *n* nora *f*.

daunt [dɔːnt] *vt* desalentar.

daunting ['dɔːntɪŋ] *adj* desalentador(ra).

dawdle ['dɔːdl] *vi* fazer cera.

dawn [dɔːn] <> *n* -1. [of day] amanhecer *m*, alvorada *f*; at ~ ao amanhecer; from ~ to dusk do amanhecer ao pôr-do-sol - 2. *fig* [of era, period] aurora *f*. <> *vi* -1. [day] amanhecer - 2. *fig* [era, period] despertar.
dawn (up)on *vt fus* dar-se conta de; it finally

~ed on me that ... finalmente me dei conta de que ...

dawn chorus n canto m dos pássaros ao amanhecer.

day [deɪ] n -**1.** [gen] dia m; the ~ before a véspera; the ~ after o dia seguinte; the ~ before Christmas a véspera de Natal; the ~ before yesterday anteontem; the ~ after tomorrow depois de amanhã; any ~ now qualquer dia destes; let's call it a ~ por hoje chega; to make sb's ~ ganhar o dia, guardar algo para dias mais difíceis; it's early ~s yet: to save sthg for a rainy ~ é cedo para saber; his ~s are numbered seus dias estão contados; ~ and night dia e noite -**2.** [age, era] tempo m; in this ~ and age hoje em dia; one ~, some ~, one of these ~s um dia (desses).
◆ **days** adv [work] durante o dia.

dayboy ['deɪbɔɪ] n UK SCH aluno m de semi-internato.

daybreak ['deɪbreɪk] n romper m do dia; at ~ ao romper do dia.

day care n assistência diurna proporcionada a idosos e/ou portadores de deficiência.

day centre n UK centro assistencial que proporciona cuidados e recreação durante o dia a idosos e/ou portadores de deficiência.

daydream ['deɪdriːm] ◇ n devaneio m. ◇ vi devanear, sonhar acordado(da).

daygirl ['deɪɡɜːl] n UK SCH aluna f de semi-internato.

Day-Glo® ['deɪɡləʊ] adj fluorescente.

daylight ['deɪlaɪt] n -**1.** (U) [light] luz f do dia -**2.** [dawn] amanhecer m -**3.** phr inf: to scare the (living) ~s out of sb quase matar alguém de susto.

daylight robbery n (U) inf: 50 pounds? that's ~! 50 libras? isso é um roubo!

daylight saving time n esp US horário m de verão.

day nursery n creche f.

day off (pl days off) n dia m de folga.

day pupil n UK aluno m, -na f de semi-internato.

day release n UK sistema na Inglaterra que permite que os trabalhadores se ausentem um dia por semana do serviço para estudar.

day return n UK passagem f de ida e volta (no mesmo dia).

day room n sala f de estar (em hospital, asilo).

day school n escola f diurna (particular).

day shift n turno m do dia.

daytime ['deɪtaɪm] ◇ n dia m; in the ~ durante o dia. ◇ comp de dia; ~ flight vôo m diurno.

day-to-day adj diário(ria).

daytrader ['deɪtreɪdər] n ST EX day-trader mf.

day trip n viagem f de um dia.

day-tripper n UK pessoa que sai em viagem de um dia.

daze [deɪz] ◇ n: in a ~ atordoado(da). ◇ vt atordoar.

dazed [deɪzd] adj [lit & fig] atordoado(da).

dazzle ['dæzl] vt -**1.** [blind] ofuscar -**2.** [impress] deslumbrar.

dazzling ['dæzlɪŋ] adj -**1.** [blinding] ofuscante -**2.** [impressive] deslumbrante.

DBE (abbr of Dame Commander of the Order of the British Empire) n (beneficiária de) distinção de honra britânica.

DBS n -**1.** (abbr of direct broadcasting by satellite) transmissão f direta via satélite. -**2.** (abbr of direct-broadcast satellite) satélite f de transmissão direta.

DC ◇ n (abbr of direct current) CC f. ◇ abbr of District of Columbia.

DD (abbr of Doctor of Divinity) n (titular de) doutorado em teologia.

D-day ['diːdeɪ] n dia m D.

DDT (abbr of dichlorodiphenyltrichloroethane) n DDT m.

DE abbr of Delaware.

DEA (abbr of Drug Enforcement Administration) n departamento da polícia norte-americana encarregado do controle de questões relacionadas a drogas, ≃ DENARC m.

deacon ['diːkn] n -**1.** [minister] diácono m -**2.** [lay assistant] acólito m.

deaconess [ˌdiːkə'nes] n diaconisa f.

deactivate [ˌdiː'æktɪveɪt] vt desativar.

dead [ded] ◇ adj -**1.** [not alive] morto(ta); to shoot sb ~ matar alguém com um tiro; he wouldn't be seen ~ doing that inf nunca seria visto fazendo aquilo -**2.** [numb] dormente, adormecido(da) -**3.** [ELEC - battery] descarregado(da); [- radio, TV] quebrado(da); [- telephone line] mudo(da) -**4.** [complete]: ~ silence silêncio m mortal; ~ stop parada f repentina -**5.** [not lively] morto(ta). ◇ adv -**1.** [directly, precisely] diretamente; ~ on time bem na hora -**2.** inf [completely, very] totalmente; to be ~ set on doing sthg estar totalmente determinado(da) a fazer algo; to be ~ against sthg/doing sthg ser totalmente contra algo/fazer algo -**3.** [suddenly]: to stop ~ parar repentinamente. ◇ n: at ~ of night na calada da noite. ◇ npl: the ~ os mortos.

deadbeat ['dedbiːt] n US inf malandro m, -dra f.

dead-beat adj inf morto(ta).

dead centre n ponto m morto.

dead duck n inf fracasso m.

deaden ['dedn] vt -**1.** [noise] amortecer -**2.** [feeling] abrandar.

dead end n -**1.** [street] rua f sem saída -**2.** fig [course of action] impasse m.

dead-end job n emprego m sem perspectivas.

deadhead ['dedhed] vt podar.

dead heat n empate m.

dead letter n fig [rule, law] letra f morta.

deadline ['dedlaɪn] n prazo m final.

deadlock ['dedlɒk] n impasse m.

deadlocked ['dedlɒkt] adj paralisado(da).

dead loss n inf -**1.** [person] traste m -**2.** [thing] porcaria f.

deadly ['dedlɪ] (compar -ier, superl -iest) ◇ adj -**1.** [lethal] letal -**2.** [mortal] mortal -**3.** [fatally precise] fatal. ◇ adv [extremely] terrivelmente.

deadly nightshade [-'naɪtʃeɪd] n (U) beladona f.

deadpan ['dedpæn] ◇ adj supostamente sério(ria). ◇ adv afetadamente sério(ria).

Dead Sea n: the ~ o Mar Morto.

dead wood UK, **deadwood** US ['dedwʊd] n (U) fig estorvo m.

deaf [def] <> adj -1. [unable to hear] surdo(da) -2. fig [unwilling to hear]: **to be ~ to sthg** ser surdo(da) a algo. <> npl: **the ~ os surdos**.

deaf-aid n UK aparelho m de surdez.

deafen ['defn] vt ensurdecer.

deafening ['defnɪŋ] adj ensurdecedor(ra).

deaf mute <> adj surdo-mudo(da). <> n surdo-mudo m, -da f.

deafness ['defnɪs] n (U) surdez f.

deal [diːl] (pt & pp dealt) <> n -1. [business agreement] transação f, acordo m; **to do** OR **strike a ~ with sb** fazer um acordo com alguém -2. inf [treatment] tratamento m; **big ~!** iron grande coisa! -3. [quantity]: **a good** OR **great ~** muito; **a good** OR **great ~ of work** muito trabalho. <> vt -1. [strike]: **to ~ sb/sthg a blow** dar um golpe em alguém/algo; **to ~ a blow to sthg** fig ser um golpe em/para algo -2. [cards] repartir. <> vi -1. [in cards] repartir -2. [trade] negociar.

◆ **deal in** vt fus COMM negociar.

◆ **deal out** vt sep repartir.

◆ **deal with** vt fus -1. [handle, cope with, be faced with] lidar com -2. [be concerned with] tratar de.

dealer ['diːləʳ] n -1. [trader] negociante m -2. [in cards] carteador m, -ra f.

dealership ['diːləʃɪp] n revendendor m, -ra f.

dealings npl [relations]: **~s with sb** relações mpl com alguém.

dealt [delt] pt & pp ▷ deal.

dean [diːn] n -1. [of church, cathedral] deão m -2. [of university] decano m, -na f.

dear [dɪəʳ] <> adj -1. [loved] querido(da); **to be ~ to sb** ser precioso(sa) para alguém -2. [in letter]: **Dear Sir/Madam** Prezado Senhor/Prezada Senhora -3. esp UK [expensive] caro(ra). <> n: **my ~** meu querido, minha querida. <> excl: **oh ~!** oh céus!

dearly ['dɪəlɪ] adv -1.: **to love sb ~** amar muito alguém -2. [very much] muito; **I would ~ love to know ...** eu adoraria saber ... -3. [pay, cost] caro.

dearth [dɜːθ] n carência f.

death [deθ] n morte f; **to frighten/worry sb to ~** quase matar alguém de susto/preocupação; **to be bored to ~ with sthg** inf morrer de tédio com algo; **to be sick to ~ of sthg/of doing sthg** inf estar de saco cheio de algo/de fazer algo; **to be put to ~** ser morto(ta); **to be at ~'s door** estar à beira da morte.

deathbed ['deθbed] n leito m de morte.

death certificate n certidão f de óbito.

death duty UK, **death tax** US n imposto m de transmissão causa mortis.

death knell n fig: **to sound the ~ for sb/sthg** soar o alarme para alguém/algo.

deathly ['deθlɪ] (compar -ier, superl -iest) <> adj [silence, hush] mortal. <> adv [pale, cold] mortalmente.

death penalty n pena f de morte.

death rate n taxa f de mortalidade.

death row n US corredor m da morte.

death sentence n sentença f de morte.

death squad n esquadrão m da morte.

death tax n US = death duty.

death toll n número m de mortos.

death trap n inf: **this car is a ~** este carro é um perigo.

Death Valley n Vale m da Morte.

deathwatch beetle ['deθwɒtʃ-] n caruncho f.

death wish n desejo m de morrer.

deb [deb] n UK inf debutante mf.

debacle n fracasso m.

debar [diːˈbɑːʳ] (pt & pp -red, cont -ring) vt: **to ~ sb (from somewhere/from doing sthg)** privar alguém (do acesso a algum lugar/de fazer algo).

debase [dɪˈbeɪs] vt [person, sport] degradar; **to ~ o.s.** degradar-se.

debasement [dɪˈbeɪsmənt] n [of person, sport] degradação f.

debatable [dɪˈbeɪtəbl] adj contestável, controverso(sa).

debate [dɪˈbeɪt] <> n (U) debate m; **open to ~** aberto(ta) ao debate. <> vt [issue] debater; **to ~ whether to do sthg** discutir sobre o que fazer. <> vi debater.

debating society [dɪˈbeɪtɪŋ-] n grupo m de discussão.

debauched [dɪˈbɔːtʃt] adj devasso(sa), depravado(da).

debauchery [dɪˈbɔːtʃərɪ] n (U) depravação f.

debenture [dɪˈbentʃəʳ] n debênture f.

debilitate [dɪˈbɪlɪteɪt] vt enfraquecer.

debilitating [dɪˈbɪlɪteɪtɪŋ] adj enfraquecedor(ra).

debility [dɪˈbɪlətɪ] n (U) fraqueza f.

debit ['debɪt] <> n débito m. <> vt [account, sum of money] debitar.

debit card n cartão m de débito.

debonair [ˌdebəˈneəʳ] adj garboso(sa).

debrief [ˌdiːˈbriːf] vt interrogar (ao se terminar uma missão).

debriefing [ˌdiːˈbriːfɪŋ] n interrogatório m (após o término de uma missão).

debris ['deɪbriː] n -1. escombros mpl -2. GEOL fragmento m de rocha.

debt [det] n -1. dívida f; **to be in ~** estar endividado(da) -2. [feeling of gratitude] dívida f; **to be in sb's ~** estar em débito com alguém.

debt collector n cobrador m, -ra f de dívidas.

debtor ['detəʳ] n devedor m, -ra f.

debug [ˌdiːˈbʌg] (pt & pp -ged, cont -ging) vt -1. [room] tirar microfones escondidos de -2. COMPUT [program] depurar.

debunk [ˌdiːˈbʌŋk] vt derrubar.

debut ['deɪbjuː] n debute m.

debutante ['debjʊtɑːnt] n debutante mf.

dec. (abbr of deceased) m.

Dec. (abbr of December) dez.

decade ['dekeɪd] n década f.

decadence ['dekədəns] n decadência f.

decadent ['dekədənt] adj decadente.

decaf n inf café m descafeinado.

decaffeinated [dɪˈkæfɪneɪtɪd] adj descafeinado(da).

decal ['diːkæl] n US adesivo m, decalque m.

decamp [dɪˈkæmp] vi inf safar-se.

decant [dɪ'kænt] *vt* decantar.

decanter [dɪ'kæntəʳ] *n* [container] licoreira *f.*

decapitate [dɪ'kæpɪteɪt] *vt* decapitar.

decathlete [dɪ'kæθliːt] *n* decatleta *mf.*

decathlon [dɪ'kæθlɒn] *n* decatlo *m.*

decay [dɪ'keɪ] <> *n* **-1.** [of tooth] cárie *f* **-2.** [of body, plant] decomposição *f* **-3.** *fig* [of building, society]: **to fall into** ~ [building] cair em ruínas; [system] entrar em decadência; [society] entrar em declínio; **urban** ~ decadência *f* urbana. <> *vi* **-1.** [tooth] criar cáries **-2.** [body, plant] decompor-se **-3.** *fig* [building, society] entrar em declínio.

deceased [dɪ'siːst] (*pl inv*) *fml* <> *adj* falecido(da). <> *n*: **the** ~ o falecido, a falecida. <> *npl*: **the** ~ os mortos.

deceit [dɪ'siːt] *n* engano *m.*

deceitful [dɪ'siːtfʊl] *adj* enganoso(sa).

deceive [dɪ'siːv] *vt* enganar; **to** ~ **o.s.** enganar-se.

decelerate [ˌdiː'seləreɪt] *vi* desacelerar.

December [dɪ'sembəʳ] *n* dezembro; *see also* **September.**

decency ['diːsnsɪ] *n* **-1.** [respectability] decência *f* **-2.** [consideration]: **to have the** ~ **to do sthg** ter a decência de fazer algo.

decent ['diːsnt] *adj* decente.

decently ['diːsntlɪ] *adv* decentemente.

decentralization [diːˌsentrəlaɪ'zeɪʃn] *n* descentralização *f.*

decentralize, -ise [ˌdiː'sentrəlaɪz] *vt* descentralizar.

deception [dɪ'sepʃn] *n* **-1.** [lie, pretence] engano *m* **-2.** [act of lying, pretending] embuste *m.*

deceptive [dɪ'septɪv] *adj* enganoso(sa).

deceptively [dɪ'septɪvlɪ] *adv* enganosamente.

decibel ['desɪbell] *n* decibel *m.*

decide [dɪ'saɪd] <> *vt* **-1.** [resolve, determine] decidir; **to** ~ **to do sthg** decidir fazer algo; **to** ~ **that** decidir que **-2.** [settle] decidir, resolver. <> *vi* [make up one's mind] decidir-se.

➤ **decide (up)on** *vt fus* decidir-se por.

decided [dɪ'saɪdɪd] *adj* **-1.** [distinct] evidente **-2.** [resolute] decidido(da).

decidedly [dɪ'saɪdɪdlɪ] *adv* decididamente.

deciding [dɪ'saɪdɪŋ] *adj*: ~ **vote** voto *m* de Minerva.

deciduous [dɪ'sɪdjʊəs] *adj* decíduo(dua).

decimal ['desɪmll] <> *adj* decimal. <> *n* (número *m*) decimal *m.*

decimal currency *n* moeda *f* de sistema decimal.

decimalize, -ise ['desɪməlaɪz] *vt* converter em decimal.

decimal place *n* casa *f* decimal.

decimal point *n* vírgula *f* decimal.

decimate ['desɪmeɪt] *vt* dizimar.

decipher [dɪ'saɪfəʳ] *vt* decifrar.

decision [dɪ'sɪʒn] *n* **-1.** [gen] decisão *f*; **to make a** ~ tomar uma decisão **-2.** [decisiveness] determinação *f.*

decision-maker *n* tomador *m*, -ra *f* de decisões.

decision-making *n* tomada *f* de decisão.

decisive [dɪ'saɪsɪv] *adj* **-1.** [person] decidido(da)

-2. [factor, event] decisivo(va).

decisively [dɪ'saɪsɪvlɪ] *adv* **-1.** [confidently] decididamente **-2.** [conclusively] claramente.

decisiveness [dɪ'saɪsɪvnɪs] *n* [of person] determinação *f.*

deck [dek] <> *n* **-1.** [of ship] convés *m* **-2.** [of bus] piso *m* **-3.** [of cards] baralho *m* **-4.** *US* [of house] *área com piso e sem telhado junto a uma casa.* <> *vt* [decorate]: **to** ~ **sthg with** decorar algo com.

➤ **deck out** *vt sep* enfeitar.

deckchair ['dektʃeəʳ] *n* espreguiçadeira *f.*

deckhand ['dekhænd] *n* taifeiro *m.*

declaration [ˌdeklə'reɪʃn] *n* declaração *f.*

Declaration of Independence *n*: **the** ~ *a declaração da independência norte-americana em 1776.*

declare [dɪ'kleəʳ] *vt* declarar.

declared [dɪ'kleəd] *adj* [intention] declarado(da).

declassify [ˌdiː'klæsɪfaɪ] (*pt* & *pp* **-ied**) *vt* revelar, tornar público(ca).

decline [dɪ'klaɪn] <> *n* declínio *m*; **to be in** ~ estar em declínio; **on the** ~ em declínio. <> *vt* [refuse] recusar, declinar; **to** ~ **to do sthg** recusar-se a fazer algo. <> *vi* **-1.** [deteriorate] decair **-2.** [refuse] recusar-se.

declutch [dɪ'klʌtʃ] *vi* AUT soltar a embreagem.

decode [ˌdiː'kəʊd] *vt* decodificar.

decoder [ˌdiː'kəʊdəʳ] *n* decodificador *m.*

decommission [ˌdiːkə'mɪʃn] *vt* desmontar.

decompose [ˌdiːkəm'pəʊz] *vi* [decay] decompor.

decomposition [ˌdiːkɒmpə'zɪʃn] *n* [decay] decomposição *f.*

decompression chamber [ˌdiːkəm'preʃn-] *n* câmara *f* de descompressão.

decompression sickness [ˌdiːkəm'preʃn-] *n* mal *m* da descompressão.

decongestant [ˌdiːkən'dʒestənt] *n* descongestionante *m.*

decontaminate [ˌdiːkən'tæmɪneɪt] *vt* descontaminar.

décor ['deɪkɔːʳ] *n* decoração *f.*

decorate ['dekəreɪt] *vt* **-1.** [gen] decorar; **to** ~ **sthg with** decorar algo com **-2.** [with medal] condecorar.

decoration [ˌdekə'reɪʃn] *n* **-1.** [ornament] enfeite *m* **-2.** [activity, appearance] decoração *f* **-3.** [medal] condecoração *f.*

decorative ['dekərətɪv] *adj* decorativo(va).

decorator ['dekəreɪtəʳ] *n* decorador *m*, -ra *f.*

decorous ['dekərəs] *adj fml* decoroso(sa).

decorum [dɪ'kɔːrəm] *n* (*U*) decoro *m.*

decoy [*n* 'diːkɔɪ, *vb* dɪ'kɔɪ] <> *n* chamariz *m*, isca *f.* <> *vt* atrair.

decrease [*n* 'diːkriːs, *vb* dɪ'kriːs] <> *n* diminuição *f*; ~ **in sthg** diminuição de algo. <> *vt* diminuir. <> *vi* diminuir.

decreasing [diː'kriːsɪŋ] *adj* decrescente.

decree [dɪ'kriː] <> *n* **-1.** [order, decision] decreto *m* **-2.** *US* [judgment] sentença *f.* <> *vt* decretar; **to** ~ **that** decretar que.

decree absolute (*pl* **decrees absolute**) *n* UK JUR sentença *f* definitiva de divórcio.

decree nisi [-'naɪsaɪ] (*pl* **decrees nisi**) *n* UK JUR sentença *f* provisória de divórcio.

decrepit [dɪˈkrepɪt] *adj* decrépito(ta).

decry [dɪˈkraɪ] (*pt* & *pp* -ied) *vt fml* depreciar, censurar.

dedicate [ˈdedɪkeɪt] *vt* -1. [book, song, poem]: **to ~ sthg to sb** dedicar algo a alguém - 2. [life, career] dedicar; **to ~ o.s. to sthg** dedicar-se a algo.

dedicated [ˈdedɪkeɪtɪd] *adj* [gen & COMPUT] dedicado(da).

dedication [ˌdedɪˈkeɪʃn] *n* dedicação *f*.

deduce [dɪˈdjuːs] *vt* deduzir; **to ~ sthg from sthg** deduzir algo de algo.

deduct [dɪˈdʌkt] *vt* deduzir; **to ~ sthg from sthg** descontar OR deduzir algo de algo.

deduction [dɪˈdʌkʃn] *n* -1. [conclusion] dedução *f* - 2. [sum deducted] desconto *m*.

deed [diːd] *n* -1. [action] ação *f*, feito *m* - 2. JUR escritura *f*.

deed poll (*pl* deed polls OR deeds poll) *n* UK: **to change one's name by ~** trocar oficialmente de nome.

deem [diːm] *vt fml* julgar; **the building was ~ed to be unsafe** o edifício foi considerado inseguro; **to ~ it wise to do sthg** julgar sensato fazer algo.

deep [diːp] <> *adj* -1. [gen] profundo(da); **to be thrown in at the ~ end** *fig* ser posto(ta) numa situação nova sem preparação - 2. [in measurements] de profundidade - 3. [colour] intenso(sa) - 4. [sound, voice] grave. <> *adv* fundo; **to go ~ into the forest** embrenhar-se floresta adentro; **to be ~ in thought** estar imerso(sa) em pensamentos; **to know ~ down** *fig* saber bem no fundo.

deepen [ˈdiːpn] <> *vt* [hole, channel] aprofundar. <> *vi* -1. [river, sea] aprofundar-se - 2. [crisis, recession, feeling] agravar-se - 3. [darkness] tornar-se mais profundo(da).

deepening [ˈdiːpnɪŋ] *adj* [crisis, recession] cada vez mais grave.

deep-fat fryer *n* fritadeira *f* por imersão.

deep freeze *n* freezer *m*.
  ➻ **deep-freeze** *vt* congelar.

deep-fry *vt* fritar *(com muito óleo)*.

deeply [ˈdiːplɪ] *adv* -1. [dig, sigh] fundo - 2. [profoundly, sincerely] profundamente.

deep-rooted *adj* arraigado(da).

deep-sea *adj* submarino(na).

deep-seated *adj* [belief, fear] profundamente arraigado(da).

deep-set *adj* [eyes] encovado(da).

deer [dɪəʳ] (*pl inv*) *n* veado *m*, cervo *m*.

deerstalker [ˈdɪəˌstɔːkəʳ] *n* [hat] boné *m* com abas.

de-escalate [ˌdiːˈeskəleɪt] <> *vt* suavizar. <> *vi* suavizar.

deface [dɪˈfeɪs] *vt* danificar.

defamation [ˌdefəˈmeɪʃn] *n fml* difamação *f*.

defamatory [dɪˈfæmətrɪ] *adj fml* difamatório(ria).

default [dɪˈfɔːlt] <> *n* -1. JUR falta *f*; **to declare s.o. in ~** declarar alguém inadimplente; **by ~** à revelia - 2. COMPUT default *m*, padrão *m*. <> *adj* COMPUT default, OR padrão <> *vi* FIN, JUR: **to ~ on sthg** estar/ficar inadimplente com algo.

defaulter [dɪˈfɔːltəʳ] *n* [on payment] inadimplente *mf*.

default value *n* COMPUT valor-padrão *m*, valor *m* default.

defeat [dɪˈfiːt] <> *n* [gen] derrota *f*; **to admit ~** admitir a derrota. <> *vt* -1. [team, opponent] derrotar - 2. [motion, proposal] rechaçar - 3. [plans] frustrar.

defeatism [dɪˈfiːtɪzml] *n* derrotismo *m*.

defeatist [dɪˈfiːtɪst] <> *adj* derrotista. <> *n* derrotista *mf*.

defecate [ˈdefəkeɪt] *vi fml* defecar.

defect [*n* ˈdiːfekt, *vb* dɪˈfekt] <> *n* [fault] defeito *m*. <> *vi* POL: **to ~ to the other side** ≃ passar para o outro lado, virar a casaca.

defection [dɪˈfekʃn] *n* deserção *f*.

defective [dɪˈfektɪv] *adj* defeituoso(sa).

defector [dɪˈfektəʳ] *n* desertor *m*, -ra *f*.

defence UK, **defense** US [dɪˈfens] *n* -1. [gen & SPORT] defesa *f*; **~ against sb/sthg** defesa contra alguém/algo - 2. [protective device, system] proteção *f*; **~ against sb/sthg** proteção *f* contra alguém/algo - 3. [JUR - lawyers]: **the ~** a defesa; [- denial of charge] defesa *f*; **in sb's ~** em defesa de alguém.
  ➻ **defences** *npl* [of country] defesas *fpl*.

defenceless UK, **defenseless** US [dɪˈfenslɪs] *adj* indefeso(sa).

defend [dɪˈfend] <> *vt* defender; **to ~ sb/sthg against sb/sthg** defender alguém/algo de alguém/algo; **to ~ o.s.** defender-se. <> *vi* SPORT defender-se.

defendant [dɪˈfendənt] *n* réu *m*, ré *f*.

defender [dɪˈfendəʳ] *n* -1. [gen] defensor *m*, -ra *f* - 2. [SPORT - player] zagueiro *m*, -ra *f*; [- of title] defensor *m*, -ra *f*.

defense *n* US = defence.

defenseless *adj* US = defenceless.

defensive [dɪˈfensɪv] <> *adj* -1. [weapons, tactics] defensivo(va) - 2. [person] receoso(sa). <> *n*: **on the ~** na defensiva.

defer [dɪˈfɜːʳ] (*pt* & *pp* -red, *cont* -ring) <> *vt* adiar, protelar. <> *vi*: **to ~ to sb** deferir a alguém.

deference [ˈdefərəns] *n* deferência *f*.

deferential [ˌdefəˈrenʃl] *adj* deferente.

defiance [dɪˈfaɪəns] *n* desafio *m*; **in ~ of sb/sthg** a despeito de alguém/algo.

defiant [dɪˈfaɪənt] *adj* desafiador(ra).

defiantly [dɪˈfaɪəntlɪ] *adv* desafiadoramente.

deficiency [dɪˈfɪʃnsɪ] (*pl* -ies) *n* -1. [lack] deficiência *f* - 2. [inadequacy] deficiência *f*, imperfeição *f*.

deficient [dɪˈfɪʃnt] *adj* -1. [lacking]: **~ in sthg** deficiente em algo - 2. [inadequate] deficiente.

deficit [ˈdefɪsɪt] *n* déficit *m*.

defile [dɪˈfaɪl] *vt* -1. [grave, church] profanar - 2. [mind, purity] corromper.

define [dɪˈfaɪn] *vt* definir.

definite [ˈdefɪnɪt] *adj* -1. [date, plan] definido(da) - 2. [improvement, difference] claro(ra) - 3. [person] seguro(ra).

definitely [ˈdefɪnɪtlɪ] *adv* sem dúvida.

definition [ˌdefɪˈnɪʃn] *n* -1. [of word, expression, concept] definição *f*; **by ~** por definição - 2. [of problem, function] explicação *f* - 3. [clarity] nitidez *f*.

definitive [dɪˈfɪnɪtɪv] *adj* definitivo(va).

deflate [dɪˈfleɪt] <> *vt* -1. [balloon, tyre] esvaziar - 2.

fig [person] diminuir **- 3.** *ECON* deflacionar. ⬦ *vi* [balloon, tyre] esvaziar-se.

deflation [dɪˈfleɪʃn] *n ECON* deflação *f*.

deflationary [dɪˈfleɪʃnərɪ] *adj ECON* deflacionário(-ria).

deflect [dɪˈflekt] *vt* desviar.

deflection [dɪˈflekʃn] *n* desvio *m*.

defog [ˌdiːˈfɒg] *vt US AUT* desembaçar.

defogger [ˌdiːˈfɒgəʳ] *n US AUT* desembaçador *m*.

deforest [ˌdiːˈfɒrɪst] *vt* desflorestar.

deforestation [diːˌfɒrɪˈsteɪʃn] *n* desflorestamento *m*.

deform [diːˈfɔːm] *vt* deformar.

deformed [dɪˈfɔːmd] *adj* deformado(da).

deformity [dɪˈfɔːmətɪ] (*pl* -ies) *n* **- 1.** [state of being deformed] deformidade *f* **- 2.** [deformed part] máformação *f* (congênita).

DEFRA (*abbr of* **Department for the Environment, Food and Rural Affairs**) *n divisão do governo britânico que trata de questões agrárias e do meio ambiente*.

defraud [dɪˈfrɔːd] *vt* fraudar.

defray [dɪˈfreɪ] *vt* custear.

defrost [ˌdiːˈfrɒst] ⬦ *vt* **- 1.** [fridge] degelar **- 2.** [frozen food] descongelar **- 3.** *US* [AUT - de-ice] descongelar. ⬦ *vi* **- 1.** [fridge] degelar **- 2.** [frozen food] descongelar.

deft [deft] *adj* **- 1.** [movement, fingers] ágil **- 2.** [handling of situation] hábil.

deftly [ˈdeftlɪ] *adv* **- 1.** [move] agilmente **- 2.** [deal with situation] habilmente.

defunct [dɪˈfʌŋkt] *adj* extinto(ta).

defuse [ˌdiːˈfjuːz] *vt UK* **- 1.** [bomb] desativar **- 2.** *fig* [situation] acalmar.

defy [dɪˈfaɪ] (*pt* & *pp* -ied) *vt* **- 1.** [disobey] desafiar **- 2.** [challenge]: **to ~ sb to do sthg** desafiar alguém a fazer algo **- 3.** *fig* [elude - description] impossibilitar; [- efforts] tornar inútil.

degenerate [*adj* & *n* dɪˈdʒenərət, *vb* dɪˈdʒenəreɪt] ⬦ *adj* degenerado(da). ⬦ *n* degenerado *m*, -da *f*. ⬦ *vi* degenerar; **to ~ into** degenerar para.

degradation [ˌdegrəˈdeɪʃn] *n* degradação *f*.

degrade [dɪˈgreɪd] *vt* [debase] degradar.

degrading [dɪˈgreɪdɪŋ] *adj* [debasing] degradante.

degree [dɪˈgriː] *n* **- 1.** [unit of measurement, amount] grau *m*; **by ~ s** gradualmente **- 2.** [qualification] título *m* universitário; **to have/take a ~ (in sthg)** ter/obter graduação (em algo).

dehumanize, -ise [diːˈhjuːmənaɪz] *vt* desumanizar.

dehydrated [ˌdiːhaɪˈdreɪtɪd] *adj* desidratado(da).

dehydration [ˌdiːhaɪˈdreɪʃn] *n* desidratação *f*.

de-ice [diːˈaɪs] *vt* descongelar.

de-icer [diːˈaɪsəʳ] *n* substância *f* descongelante.

deign [deɪn] *vi*: **to ~ to do sthg** dignar-se a fazer algo.

deity [ˈdiːɪtɪ] (*pl* -ies) *n* divindade *f*, deidade *f*.

déjà vu [ˌdeʒɑːˈvjuː] *n* déjà vu *m*.

dejected [dɪˈdʒektɪd] *adj* abatido(da), desanimado(da).

dejection [dɪˈdʒekʃn] *n* abatimento *m*, desânimo *m*.

Del. *abbr of* **Delaware**.

Delaware [ˈdeləweəʳ] *n* Delaware; **in ~** em Delaware.

delay [dɪˈleɪ] ⬦ *n* atraso *m*; **without ~** sem demora. ⬦ *vt* **- 1.** [cause to be late] atrasar **- 2.** [postpone] adiar; **to ~ doing sthg** adiar (fazer) algo. ⬦ *vi* demorar-se; **to ~ in doing sthg** demorar-se para fazer algo.

delayed [dɪˈleɪd] *adj* atrasado(da).

delayed-action [dɪˈleɪd-l] *adj* de ação retardada; **~ shutter** *PHOT* obturador *m* automático.

delectable [dɪˈlektəbl] *adj* **- 1.** [food] delicioso(sa) **- 2.** [person] fabuloso(sa).

delegate [*n* ˈdelɪgət, *vb* ˈdelɪgeɪt] ⬦ *n* delegado *m*, -da *f*. ⬦ *vt* **- 1.** [appoint to do job] delegar; **to ~ sb to do sthg** delegar alguém para fazer algo **- 2.** [hand over responsibility for] delegar; **to ~ sthg to sb** delegar algo a alguém. ⬦ *vi* delegar responsabilidades.

delegation [ˌdelɪˈgeɪʃn] *n* delegação *f*.

delete [dɪˈliːt] *vt* **- 1.** [remove] apagar **- 2.** *COMPUT* deletar.

deletion [dɪˈliːʃn] *n* exclusão *f*.

Delhi [ˈdelɪ] *n* Delhi.

deli [ˈdelɪ] (*abbr of* **delicatessen**) *n fam loja onde se vendem bebidas, frios, conservas e pães*.

deliberate [*adj* dɪˈlɪbərət, *vb* dɪˈlɪbəreɪt] ⬦ *adj* **- 1.** [intentional] deliberado(da) **- 2.** [slow] pausado(da). ⬦ *vi fml* deliberar.

deliberately [dɪˈlɪbərətlɪ] *adv* **- 1.** [on purpose] deliberadamente **- 2.** [slowly] pausadamente.

deliberation [dɪˌlɪbəˈreɪʃn] *n* **- 1.** [careful consideration] deliberação *f* **- 2.** [slowness] morosidade *f*.
➤ **deliberations** *npl* deliberações *fpl*.

delicacy [ˈdelɪkəsɪ] (*pl* -ies) *n* **- 1.** *(U)* [gracefulness, tact] delicadeza *f* **- 2.** [food] iguaria *f*.

delicate [ˈdelɪkət] *adj* **- 1.** [gen] delicado(da) **- 2.** [flavour, colour] suave **- 3.** [instrument] delicado(da), sensível.

delicately [ˈdelɪkətlɪ] *adv* **- 1.** [made, drawn] com delicadeza **- 2.** [flavoured, coloured] suavemente **- 3.** [hint, suggest] delicadamente.

delicatessen [ˌdelɪkəˈtesn] *n* delicatessen *f*.

delicious [dɪˈlɪʃəs] *adj* **- 1.** [tasty] delicioso(sa) **- 2.** *fig* [delightful] encantador(ra).

delight [dɪˈlaɪt] ⬦ *n* **- 1.** [great pleasure] prazer *m*, deleite *m*; **to take ~ in doing sthg** ter prazer em fazer algo **- 2.** [wonderful thing, person] encanto *m*. ⬦ *vt* encantar. ⬦ *vi*: **to ~ in sthg/in doing sthg** encantar-se em algo/em fazer algo.

delighted [dɪˈlaɪtɪd] *adj* muito contente; **~ by** *or* **with sthg** encantado(da) com algo; **to be ~ to do sthg** estar muito feliz por fazer algo; **to be ~ that** ficar contente que.

delightful [dɪˈlaɪtfʊl] *adj* encantador(ra).

delightfully [dɪˈlaɪtfʊlɪ] *adv* encantadoramente.

delimit [diːˈlɪmɪt] *vt fml* delimitar.

delineate [dɪˈlɪnɪeɪt] *vt fml* delinear.

delinquency [dɪˈlɪŋkwənsɪ] *n* delinqüência *f*.

delinquent [dɪˈlɪŋkwənt] ⬦ *adj* delinqüente. ⬦ *n* delinqüente *mf*.

delirious [dɪˈlɪrɪəs] *adj* delirante; **to be ~** estar delirando.

delirium [dɪˈlɪrɪəm] *n* delírio *m*.

deliver [dɪ'lɪvəʳ] ◇ *vt* - **1.** [distribute]: **to ~ sthg (to sb)** entregar algo (a alguém) - **2.** [give - speech, lecture] proferir; [- message] entregar; [- warning, ultimatum] dar - **3.** [blow] desferir - **4.** [baby] trazer ao mundo - **5.** *fml* [liberate]: **to ~ sb (from sthg)** libertar alguém (de algo) - **6.** *US POL* [votes] captar. ◇ *vi* - **1.** *COMM* repartir - **2.** [fulfil promise] cumprir (o prometido).

deliverance [dɪ'lɪvərəns] *n fml* libertação *f.*

delivery [dɪ'lɪvərɪ] (*pl* -**ies**) *n* - **1.** [of goods, letters] entrega *f* - **2.** [goods delivered] remessa *f* - **3.** [way of speaking] elocução *f* - **4.** [birth] parto *m.*

delivery note *n* guia *f* de remessa.

delivery van *UK,* **delivery truck** *US n* camionete *f* de entrega.

delphinium [del'fɪnɪəm] (*pl* -**s**) *n* espora *f* de jardim.

delta ['deltə] (*pl* -**s**) *n GEOGR* delta *m.*

delude [dɪ'luːd] *vt* enganar; **to ~ o.s.** enganar-se.

deluge ['deljuːdʒ] ◇ *n* - **1.** [flood] dilúvio *m* - **2.** *fig* [huge number] mar *m.* ◇ *vt*: **to be ~d with sthg** ser inundado(da) por algo.

delusion [dɪ'luːʒn] *n* ilusão *f;* **~s of grandeur** delírios *mpl* de grandeza.

de luxe [də'lʌks] *adj* de luxo.

delve [delv] *vi* - **1.** [into mystery] pesquisar; **to ~ into sthg** investigar algo - **2.** [in bag, cupboard] remexer; **to ~ into** *OR* **inside sthg** revolver dentro de algo.

Dem. - **1.** (*abbr of* **Democrat**) Democrata *mf.* - **2.** (*abbr of* **Democratic**) Democrático(ca).

demagogue *UK,* **demagog** *US* ['deməgɒg] *n* demagogo *m,* -ga *f.*

demand [dɪ'mɑːnd] ◇ *n* - **1.** [gen] exigência *f;* **wage ~** reivindicação *f* salarial; **on ~** [gen] a pedido; *COMM* sob demanda - **2.** [need & *COMM*]: **~ for sthg** demanda *f* por algo; **in ~** solicitado(da). ◇ *vt* - **1.** [gen] exigir; **to ~ to do sthg** exigir fazer algo - **2.** [enquire forcefully] inquirir.

demanding [dɪ'mɑːndɪŋ] *adj* - **1.** [exhausting] que exige muito esforço - **2.** [not easily satisfied] exigente.

demarcation [ˌdiːmɑː'keɪʃn] *n* demarcação *f.*

demarcation dispute *n disputa entre sindicatos sobre as funções a serem realizadas por seus membros.*

dematerialize, -ise [diːmə'tɪərəlaɪz] *vi* desmaterializar-se.

demean [dɪ'miːn] *vt* rebaixar; **to ~ o.s.** rebaixar-se, humilhar-se.

demeaning [dɪ'miːnɪŋ] *adj* humilhante.

demeanour *UK,* **demeanor** *US* [dɪ'miːnəʳ] *n fml* comportamento *m.*

demented [dɪ'mentɪd] *adj* demente.

dementia [dɪ'menʃə] *n* demência *f.*

demerara sugar [ˌdeməˈreərə-] *n UK* açúcar *m* mascavo.

demigod ['demɪgɒd] *n* semideus *m.*

demijohn ['demɪdʒɒn] *n* garrafão *m.*

demilitarized zone, demilitarised zone [ˌdiːˈmɪlɪtəraɪzd-] *n* zona *f* desmilitarizada.

demise [dɪ'maɪz] *n fml* - **1.** [death] falecimento *m* - **2.** *fig* [end] fim *m.*

demist [ˌdiː'mɪst] *vt UK AUT* desembaçar *m.*

demister [ˌdiː'mɪstəʳ] *n UK AUT* desembaçador *m.*

demo ['deməʊ] (*pl* -**s**) (*abbr of* **demonstration**) *n* - **1.** *fam* [protest] manifestação *f.* - **2.** [tape, video] demo *f.*

demobilize, -ise [ˌdiː'məʊbɪlaɪz] *vt fml* desmobilizar.

democracy [dɪ'mɒkrəsɪ] (*pl* -**ies**) *n* democracia *f.*

democrat ['deməkræt] *n* democrata *mf.*
➡ **Democrat** *n US* democrata *mf.*

democratic [deməˈkrætɪk] *adj* democrático(ca).
➡ **Democratic** *adj US* democrata.

democratically [ˌdeməˈkrætɪklɪ] *adv* democraticamente.

Democratic Party *n US*: **the ~** o Partido Democrata (dos Estados Unidos).

democratize, -ise [dɪ'mɒkrətaɪz] *vt* democratizar.

demographic [ˌdeməˈgræfɪk] *adj* demográfico(ca).

demolish [dɪ'mɒlɪʃ] *vt* - **1.** [knock down] demolir - **2.** [prove wrong] destruir, acabar com - **3.** *inf* [eat] acabar com.

demolition [ˌdeməˈlɪʃn] *n* - **1.** [knocking down] demolição *f* - **2.** [proving wrong] destruição *f.*

demon ['diːmən] ◇ *n* [evil spirit] demônio *m.* ◇ *comp inf* [skilled] fantástico(ca).

demonstrable [dɪ'mɒnstrəbl] *adj* demonstrável.

demonstrably [dɪ'mɒnstrəblɪ] *adv* decididamente.

demonstrate ['demənstreɪt] ◇ *vt* - **1.** [gen] demonstrar - **2.** [appliance, machine] mostrar o funcionamento de. ◇ *vi* manifestar-se; **to ~ for/against sthg** manifestar-se a favor de/contra algo.

demonstration [demən'streɪʃn] *n* - **1.** [gen] demonstração *f* - **2.** [protest gathering, march] manifestação *f.*

demonstrative [dɪ'mɒnstrətɪv] *adj* efusivo(va).

demonstrator ['demənstreɪtəʳ] *n* - **1.** [of machine, product] demonstrador *m,* -ra *f* - **2.** [protester] manifestante *mf.*

demoralize, -ise [dɪ'mɒrəlaɪz] *vt* desmoralizar.

demoralized [dɪ'mɒrəlaɪzd] *adj* desmoralizado(da).

demote [ˌdiː'məʊt] *vt* rebaixar (na carreira profissional).

demotion [ˌdiː'məʊʃn] *n* rebaixamento *m* (na carreira profissional).

demotivate [ˌdiː'məʊtɪveɪt] *vt* desmotivar.

demure [dɪ'mjʊəʳ] *adj* recatado(da).

demystify [ˌdiː'mɪstɪfaɪ] (*pt* & *pp* -**ied**) *vt* desmistificar.

den [den] *n* [lair] toca *f.*

denationalization ['diːˌnæʃnəlarˈzeɪʃn] *n* desnacionalização *f.*

denationalize, -ise [ˌdiː'næʃnəlaɪz] *vt* desnacionalizar.

denial [dɪ'naɪəl] *n* - **1.** [refutation] contestação *f* - **2.** (U) [refusal] negação *f.*

denier ['denɪəʳ] *n* [of stockings, tights] denier *m, medida da espessura do fio de náilon ou de seda usado na fabricação de roupas.*

denigrate ['denɪgreɪt] *vt fml* difamar, denegrir.

denim ['denɪm] *n* brim *m.*
➡ **denims** *npl* jeans *m inv.*

denim jacket n jaqueta f jeans.

denizen ['denɪzn] n *literary or hum* habitante mf.

Denmark ['denmɑ:k] n Dinamarca; **in ~ na** Dinamarca.

denomination [dɪˌnɒmɪ'neɪʃn] n -**1.** RELIG denominação f, seita f -**2.** FIN valor m.

denominator [dɪ'nɒmɪneɪtəʳ] n denominador m.

denote [dɪ'nəʊt] vt fml denotar.

denouement [deɪ'nu:mɒn] n desfecho m.

denounce [dɪ'naʊns] vt denunciar.

dense [dens] adj -**1.** [thick - trees, undergrowth] denso(sa); [- mist, fog] espesso(sa) -**2.** inf [stupid] estúpido(da).

densely ['denslɪ] adv [thickly] densamente.

density ['densətɪ] (pl -ies) n densidade f.

dent [dent] <> n amassado m. <> vt [surface] amassar.

dental ['dentl] adj dentário(ria); **a ~ problem** um problema nos dentes.

dental floss n (U) fio m dental.

dental plate n dentadura f postiça, chapa f.

dental surgeon n cirurgião-dentista m, cirurgiã-dentista f.

dental surgery n cirurgia f dentária.

dental treatment n (U) tratamento m dentário.

dented ['dentɪd] adj amassado(da).

dentist ['dentɪst] n dentista mf; **to go to the ~'s** ir ao dentista.

dentistry ['dentɪstrɪ] n (U) odontologia f.

dentures ['dentʃəz] npl dentadura f.

denude vt fml: **to ~ sthg (of sthg)** despojar algo (de algo).

denunciation [dɪˌnʌnsɪ'eɪʃn] n denúncia f.

deny [dɪ'naɪ] (pt & pp -ied) vt negar; **to ~ sb sthg** negar algo a alguém.

deodorant [di:'əʊdərənt] n desodorante m.

depart [dɪ'pɑ:t] vi fml -**1.** [leave] partir; **to ~ from** partir de -**2.** [differ]: **to ~ from sthg** afastar-se de algo.

department [dɪ'pɑ:tmənt] n -**1.** [gen] departamento m -**2.** [of government] ministério m.

departmental [ˌdi:pɑ:t'mentl] adj de departamento.

department store n loja f de departamentos.

departure [dɪ'pɑ:tʃəʳ] n -**1.** [leaving] partida f -**2.** [variation]: **~ (from sthg)** abandono m (de algo) -**3.** [orientation] início m.

departure lounge n sala f de embarque.

depend [dɪ'pend] vi -**1.** [rely - financially]: **to ~ on sb/ sthg** depender de alguém/algo; [- emotionally]: **to ~ on sb** confiar em alguém -**2.** [be determined]: **it ~s** depende; **it ~s on** depende de; **~ing on** dependendo de.

dependable [dɪ'pendəbl] adj confiável.

dependant [dɪ'pendənt] n dependente mf.

dependence [dɪ'pendəns] n -**1.** [reliance]: **~ (on sb/sthg)** dependência f (de alguém/algo) -**2.** [addiction]: **~ (on sthg)** dependência (de algo).

dependent [dɪ'pendənt] adj -**1.** [reliant]: **to be ~ (on sb/sthg)** ser dependente (de alguém/algo) -**2.** [addicted] dependente -**3.** [determined by]: **to be ~ on sb/sthg** depender de alguém/algo.

depict [dɪ'pɪkt] vt -**1.** [show in picture] retratar -**2.**

[describe]: **to ~ sb/sthg as sthg** retratar alguém/ algo como algo.

depilatory [dɪ'pɪlətrɪ] adj depilatório(ria).

deplete [dɪ'pli:t] vt reduzir.

depletion [dɪ'pli:ʃn] n (U) redução f.

deplorable [dɪ'plɔ:rəbl] adj deplorável.

deplore [dɪ'plɔ:ʳ] vt deplorar.

deploy [dɪ'plɔɪ] vt dispor.

deployment [dɪ'plɔɪmənt] n (U) disposição f.

depopulated [ˌdi:'pɒpjʊleɪtd] adj despovoado(-da).

depopulation [di:ˌpɒpjʊ'leɪʃn] n (U) despovoamento m.

deport [dɪ'pɔ:t] vt deportar.

deportation [ˌdi:pɔ:'teɪʃn] n deportação f.

deportation order n ordem f de deportação.

depose [dɪ'pəʊz] vt [king, ruler] depor.

deposit [dɪ'pɒzɪt] <> n -**1.** GEOL [of gold, oil] jazida f -**2.** [of sediment, silt] depósito m -**3.** [fin] depósito m; **to make a ~** fazer um depósito -**4.** [down payment - on house, car] entrada f; [- on hotel room] depósito m -**5.** [returnable payment - on hired goods] caução f; [- on bottle, container] depósito m. <> vt -**1.** [gen] depositar -**2.** [bag, case, shopping] colocar.

deposit account n UK conta f remunerada.

depositor [də'pɒzɪtəʳ] n depositante mf.

depot ['depəʊ] n -**1.** [storage facility - for goods] armazém m; [- for vehicles] garagem f -**2.** US [bus or train terminus] terminal m.

depraved [dɪ'preɪvd] adj depravado(da).

depravity [dɪ'prævətɪ] n (U) depravação f.

deprecate ['deprɪkeɪt] vt fml censurar.

deprecating ['deprɪkeɪtɪŋ] adj desaprovador(ra).

depreciate [dɪ'pri:ʃɪeɪt] vi depreciar.

depreciation [dɪˌpri:ʃɪ'eɪʃn] n (U) depreciação f.

depress [dɪ'pres] vt -**1.** [sadden, discourage] deprimir -**2.** ECON depreciar -**3.** [slow down, reduce] reduzir.

depressant [dɪ'presənt] n MED sedativo m.

depressed [dɪ'prest] adj -**1.** [person] deprimido(da) -**2.** ECON em depressão -**3.** [area]: **~ point** ponto inferior.

depressing [dɪ'presɪŋ] adj deprimente.

depression [dɪ'preʃn] n depressão f.

➡ **Depression** n: **the (Great) Depression** a Grande Depressão.

depressive [dɪ'presɪv] adj depressivo(va).

deprivation [ˌdeprɪ'veɪʃn] n [privation] privação f.

deprive [dɪ'praɪv] vt: **to ~ sb of sthg** privar alguém de algo.

deprived [dɪ'praɪvd] adj necessitado(da).

Dept. (abbr of **department**) Dep.

depth [depθ] n -**1.** profundidade f; **to be out of one's ~** [lit & fig] não dar pé para alguém; **in ~** em profundidade -**2.** [severity] gravidade f; **the ~ of sthg** a gravidade de algo.

➡ **depths** npl: **the ~s** [of sea, memory] as profundezas; [of winter] o auge; **to be in the ~s of despair** estar no auge do desespero.

depth charge n carga f de profundidade.

deputation [ˌdepjʊ'teɪʃn] n delegação f.

deputize, -ise ['depjʊtaɪz] vi: **to ~ (for sb)** substituir oficialmente (alguém).

deputy ['depjʊtɪ] (pl -ies) <> adj adjunto(ta); **~**

head subdiretor *m*, -ra *f*; ~ **chairman** vice-presidente *m*. ⬦ *n* -**1**. [second-in-command] suplente *mf* -**2**. *US* [deputy sheriff] ajudante *mf* do delegado.

derail [dɪ'reɪl] *vt* [train] descarrilhar.

derailment [dɪ'reɪlmənt] *n* descarrilhamento *m*.

deranged [dɪ'reɪndʒd] *adj* perturbado(da), transtornado(da).

derby [*UK* 'dɑːbɪ, *US* 'dɜːbɪl (*pl* -**ies**) *n* -**1**. [sports event] jogo *m* local -**2**. *US* [hat] chapéu-coco *m*.

deregulate [ˌdiː'regjʊleɪt] *vt* desregulamentar.

deregulation [ˌdiːregjʊ'leɪʃn] *n(U)* desregulamentação *f*.

derelict ['derəlɪkt] *adj* abandonado(da).

deride [dɪ'raɪd] *vt* escarnecer de, zombar de.

derision [dɪ'rɪʒn] *n (U)* escárnio *m*, zombaria *f*.

derisive [dɪ'raɪsɪv] *adj* zombeteiro(ra).

derisory [də'raɪzərɪ] *adj* -**1**. [ridiculous] irrisório(ria) -**2**. [scornful] zombeteiro(ra).

derivation [ˌderɪ'veɪʃn] *n* [of word] origem *f*.

derivative [dɪ'rɪvətɪv] ⬦ *adj pej* pouco original. ⬦ *n* derivado *m*.

derive [dɪ'raɪv] ⬦ *vt* -**1**. [pleasure]: **to ~ sthg from sthg** encontrar algo em algo -**2**. [word, expression]: **to be ~d from sthg** derivar de algo. ⬦ *vi* [word, expression]: **to ~ from sthg** derivar-se de algo.

dermatitis [ˌdɜːmə'taɪtɪs] *n (U)* dermatite *f*.

dermatologist [ˌdɜːmə'tɒlədʒɪst] *n* dermatologista *mf*.

dermatology [ˌdɜːmə'tɒlədʒɪl *n (U)* dermatologia *f*.

derogatory [dɪ'rɒgətrɪ] *adj* depreciativo(va).

derrick ['derɪk] *n* -**1**. [crane] guindaste *m* -**2**. [over oil well] torre *f* de perfuração.

derv [dɜːv] *n UK* gasóleo *m*.

desalination [diːˌsælɪ'neɪʃn] *n (U)* dessalinização *f*.

descant ['deskænt] *n* [tune] contraponto *m*.

descend [dɪ'send] ⬦ *vi* -**1**. *fml* [go down] descer -**2**. [fall]: **to ~ (on sb/sthg)** recair (sobre alguém/algo) -**3**. [invade]: **to ~ on** invadir -**4**. [stoop, lower o.s.]: **to ~ to sthg/to doing sthg** rebaixar-se a algo/a fazer algo. ⬦ *vt fml* [go down] descer.

descendant [dɪ'sendənt] *n* [family member] descendente *mf*.

descended [dɪ'sendɪd] *adj*: **to be ~ from sb** ser descendente *OR* descender de alguém.

descending [dɪ'sendɪŋ] *adj*: **in ~ order** em ordem decrescente.

descent [dɪ'sent] *n* -**1**. [downwards movement] descida *f* -**2**. *(U)* [origin] ascendência *f*.

describe [dɪ'skraɪb] *vt* [recount] descrever.

description [dɪ'skrɪpʃn] *n* -**1**. [account] descrição *f* -**2**. [type] tipo *m*.

descriptive [dɪ'skrɪptɪv] *adj* descritivo(va).

desecrate ['desɪkreɪt] *vt* profanar.

desecration [ˌdesɪ'kreɪʃn] *n (U)* profanação *f*.

desegregate [diː'segrɪgeɪt] *vt* dessegregar.

deselect [ˌdiːsɪ'lekt] *vt UK POL* [rejeitar (uma candidatura).

desert [*n* 'dezət, *vb & npl* dɪ'zɜːt] ⬦ *n* -**1**. *GEOGR* deserto *m* -**2**. *fig* [boring place] deserto *m*; **a cultural ~** um deserto cultural. ⬦ *vt* abandonar. ⬦ *vi MIL* desertar.

➡ **deserts** *npl*: **to get one's just ~s** receber aquilo que se merece.

deserted [dɪ'zɜːtɪd] *adj* [place] deserto(ta), abandonado(da).

deserter [dɪ'zɜːtə^r] *n* desertor *m*, -ra *f*.

desertion [dɪ'zɜːʃn] *n* -**1**. *(U) MIL* deserção *f* -**2**. [of person] abandono *m*.

desert island ['dezət-] *n* ilha *f* deserta.

deserve [dɪ'zɜːv] *vt* merecer; **to ~ sthg** merecer algo; **we ~ to win** merecemos vencer.

deserved [dɪ'zɜːvd] *adj* merecido(da).

deservedly [dɪ'zɜːvɪdlɪ] *adv* merecidamente.

deserving [dɪ'zɜːvɪŋ] *adj* merecedor(ra); **~ of sthg** *fml* merecedor(ra) de algo.

desiccated ['desɪkeɪtɪd] *adj* desidratado(da).

design [dɪ'zaɪn] ⬦ *n* -**1**. [plan, drawing] projeto *m* -**2**. *(U)* [art] design *m* -**3**. [pattern, motif] padrão *m* -**4**. [structure, shape] modelo *m* -**5**. *fml* [intention] intenção *f*; **by ~** por intenção; **to have ~s on sb/sthg** ter más intenções com relação a alguém/algo. ⬦ *vt* -**1**. [building, car] projetar -**2**. [clothes, costumes] desenhar -**3**. [plan, system, test] projetar, criar; **to be ~ed for sthg/to do sthg** ser projetado(da) para algo/para fazer algo.

designate [*adj* 'dezɪgnət, *vb* 'dezɪgneɪt] ⬦ *adj* designado(da). ⬦ *vt* [appoint] designar; **to ~ sb as sthg/to do sthg** designar alguém como algo/para fazer algo.

designation [ˌdezɪg'neɪʃn] *n fml* [name] designação *f*.

designer [dɪ'zaɪnə^r] ⬦ *adj* [jeans, glasses, stubble] de marca. ⬦ *n* -**1**. [of building, machine] projetista *mf* -**2**. [of theatre set] cenógrafo *m*, -fa *f* -**3**. [of clothes] estilista *mf*.

desirable [dɪ'zaɪərəbl] *adj* -**1**. *fml* [appropriate] apropriado(da) -**2**. [attractive] agradável -**3**. [sexually attractive] desejável.

desire [dɪ'zaɪə^r] ⬦ *n* -**1**. [wish] desejo *m*, vontade *f*; **~ for sthg/to do sthg** desejo por algo/de fazer algo, vontade de algo/de fazer algo -**2**. *(U)* [sexual longing] desejo *m*. ⬦ *vt* desejar; **it leaves a lot to be ~d** isso deixa muito a desejar.

desirous [dɪ'zaɪərəs] *adj fml*: **~ of sthg/of doing sthg** desejoso(sa) de algo/de fazer algo.

desist [dɪ'zɪst] *vi fml*: **to ~ (from doing sthg)** desistir (de fazer algo).

desk [desk] *n* -**1**. [piece of furniture - in office, study] escrivaninha *f*; [- in school] carteira *f* -**2**. [service point] balcão *m*.

desk clerk *n US* recepcionista *mf (de hotel)*.

desk diary *n* agenda *f (de mesa)*.

desk lamp *n* luminária *f (de mesa)*.

desktop ['desk.tɒp] *adj* [computer]: **a ~ computer** um computador de mesa *OR* desktop.

desktop publishing *n (U)* editoração *f* eletrônica.

desolate ['desələt] *adj* desolado(da).

desolation [ˌdesə'leɪʃn] *n* -**1**. [gen] desolação *f* -**2**. [despair] aflição *f*.

despair [dɪ'speə^r] ⬦ *n (U)* desespero *m*; **in ~** desesperado(da). ⬦ *vi* desesperar-se; **to ~ of**

sb/sthg perder a esperança com alguém/algo; **to ~ of doing sthg** perder a esperança de fazer algo.

despairing [dɪ'speərɪŋ] *adj* desesperador(ra).

despairingly [dɪ'speərɪŋlɪ] *adv* desesperadamente.

despatch [dɪ'spætʃ] *n* & *vt* = **dispatch**.

desperate ['despratl] *adj* -**1.** [gen] desesperado(da); **to feel ~** sentir-se desesperado(da) -**2.** [situation, problem] desesperador(ra) -**3.** [criminal] implacável -**4.** [in great need]: **to be ~ for sthg** estar louco(ca) por algo.

desperately ['desprətlɪ] *adv* -**1.** [gen] desesperadamente -**2.** [busy, sorry, in love] muito.

desperation [ˌdespə'reɪʃn] *n (U)* desespero *m*; **in ~** em desespero.

despicable [dɪ'spɪkəbl] *adj* desprezível.

despise [dɪ'spaɪz] *vt* desprezar.

despite [dɪ'spaɪt] *prep* apesar de.

despondent [dɪ'spɒndənt] *adj* desanimado(da).

despot ['despɒt] *n* déspota *mf*.

despotic [de'spɒtɪk] *adj* despótico(ca).

dessert [dɪ'zɜːt] *n* sobremesa *f*.

dessertspoon [dɪ'zɜːtspuːn] *n* -**1.** [spoon] colher *f* de sobremesa -**2.** [spoonful] colherada *f* de sobremesa.

dessert wine *n* vinho *m* doce *(servido com a sobremesa)*.

destabilize, -ise [ˌdiː'steɪbɪlaɪz] *vt* desestabilizar.

destination [ˌdestɪ'neɪʃn] *n* destino *m*.

destined ['destɪnd] *adj* -**1.** [intended]: **~ for sthg/to do sthg** predestinado(da) a algo/a fazer algo -**2.** [bound]: **to be ~ for** estar indo para.

destiny ['destɪnɪ] *(pl* -**ies)** *n* destino *m*.

destitute ['destɪtjuːt] *adj* [extremely poor] necessitado(da), miserável.

destroy [dɪ'strɔɪ] *vt* -**1.** [gen] destruir -**2.** [animal] acabar com.

destroyer [dɪ'strɔɪəʳ] *n* -**1.** [ship] contratorpedeiro *m* -**2.** [person, thing] destruidor *m*, -ra *f*.

destruction [dɪ'strʌkʃn] *n (U)* destruição *f*.

destructive [dɪ'strʌktɪv] *adj* [harmful] destrutivo(va).

destructively [dɪ'strʌktɪvlɪ] *adv* destrutivamente.

desultory ['desəltrɪ] *adj fml* sem propósito, desinteressado(da).

Det. *(abbr of* **Detective)** detetive *mf*.

detach [dɪ'tætʃ] *vt* -**1.** [remove] tirar; **to ~ sthg from sthg** tirar algo de algo ; [tear off] destacar -**2.** [dissociate]: **to ~ o.s. from sthg** afastar-se de algo.

detachable [dɪ'tætʃəbl] *adj* removível.

detached [dɪ'tætʃt] *adj* [unemotional] imparcial.

detached house *n* casa *f* separada.

detachment [dɪ'tætʃmənt] *n* -**1.** *(U)* [aloofness] desinteresse *m*, desapego *m* -**2.** *MIL* destacamento *m*.

detail ['diːteɪl] ◇ *n* -**1.** [small point] detalhe *m* -**2.** *(U)* [collection of facts, points] detalhe *m*, particularidade *f*; **to go into ~** entrar em detalhes; **in ~** detalhadamente -**3.** *MIL* destacamento *m*. ◇ *vt* [list] detalhar.

➡ **details** *npl* -**1.** [information] dados *mpl* -**2.** [personal information] dados *mpl* (pessoais).

detailed ['diːteɪld] *adj* detalhado(da).

detain [dɪ'teɪn] *vt* -**1.** [in hospital, police station] deter -**2.** [delay] retardar.

detainee [ˌdiːteɪ'niː] *n* detento *m*, -ta *f*.

detect [dɪ'tekt] *vt* -**1.** [subj: person] perceber -**2.** [subj: device] detectar.

detection [dɪ'tekʃn] *n* -**1.** *(U)* [discovery] detecção *f* -**2.** [investigation] investigação *f*.

detective [dɪ'tektɪv] *n* detetive *mf*.

detective novel *n* romance *m* policial.

detector [dɪ'tektəʳ] *n* detector *m*.

détente [deɪ'tɒnt] *n POL* détente *f*.

detention [dɪ'tenʃn] *n* -**1.** *(U)* [of suspect, criminal] detenção *f*; **in ~** em detenção -**2.** [at school] castigo *m (depois da aula)*; **to be in ~** ficar de castigo.

detention centre *n UK* centro *m* de detenção.

deter [dɪ'tɜːʳ] *(pt* & *pp* -**red,** *cont* -**ring)** *vt* dissuadir; **to ~ sb from doing sthg** dissuadir alguém de fazer algo.

detergent [dɪ'tɜːdʒənt] *n* detergente *m*.

deteriorate [dɪ'tɪərɪəreɪt] *vi* piorar.

deterioration [dɪˌtɪərɪə'reɪʃn] *n* -**1.** *(U)* [in health, economic situation] agravamento *f* -**2.** *(U)* [in weather] piora *f*.

determination [dɪˌtɜːmɪ'neɪʃn] *n* -**1.** *(U)* [resolve] determinação *f* -**2.** [establishing, fixing] definição *f*.

determine [dɪ'tɜːmɪn] *vt* -**1.** [gen] determinar -**2.** *fml* [resolve]: **to ~ to do sthg** determinar-se a fazer algo -**3.** [fix, settle] definir.

determined [dɪ'tɜːmɪnd] *adj* [person, effort] determinado(da); **~ to do sthg** determinado(da) a fazer algo.

deterrent [dɪ'terənt] ◇ *adj* dissuasivo(va). ◇ *n* dissuasão *f*.

detest [dɪ'test] *vt* detestar.

detestable [dɪ'testəbl] *adj* detestável.

dethrone [dɪ'θrəʊn] *vt* destronar.

detonate ['detəneɪt] ◇ *vt* detonar. ◇ *vi* detonar.

detonator ['detəneɪtəʳ] *n* detonador *m*.

detour ['diːˌtʊəʳ] *n* desvio *m*.

detox ['diːtɒks] *n inf* desintoxicação *f*.

detoxification *n* desintoxicação *f*.

detract [dɪ'trækt] *vi*: **to ~ from** [quality, achievement] depreciar; [enjoyment] perturbar.

detractor [dɪ'træktəʳ] *n* detrator *m*, -ra *f*.

detrain *vi* desembarcar *(de trem)*.

detriment ['detrɪmənt] *n*: **to the ~ of sb/sthg** em detrimento de alguém/algo.

detrimental [ˌdetrɪ'mentl] *adj* prejudicial.

detritus [dɪ'traɪtəs] *n (U)* detrito *m*.

deuce [djuːs] *n TENNIS* empate *m*.

Deutschmark ['dɔɪtʃˌmaːk] *n* marco *m* alemão.

devaluation [ˌdiːvæljʊ'eɪʃn] *n FIN* desvalorização *f*.

devalue [ˌdiː'væljuː] *vt* desvalorizar.

devastate ['devəsteɪt] *vt* -**1.** [place] devastar -**2.** *fig* [person] arrasar.

devastated ['devəsteɪtɪd] *adj* -**1.** [place] devastado(da) -**2.** *fig* [person] arrasado(da).

devastating ['devəsteɪtɪŋ] *adj* -**1.** [disastrous] devastador(ra) -**2.** [very effective, attractive] avassalador(ra).

devastation [ˌdevə'steɪʃn] n (U) [destruction] devastação f.

develop [dɪ'veləp] <> vt -1. [gen] desenvolver -2. [land, area, resources] explorar -3. [illness] contrair -4. PHOT revelar. <> vi -1. [gen] desenvolver -2. [problem, illness] aparecer.

developer [dɪ'veləpəʳ] n -1. [of land] empreendedor m imobiliário, empreendedora f imobiliária -2. [person]: **an early/a late** ~ criança f com desenvolvimento precoce/tardio -3. PHOT [chemical] revelador m.

developing country [dɪ'veləpɪŋ-] n país m em desenvolvimento.

development [dɪ'veləpmənt] n -1. (U) [expansion, growth, conception - gen] desenvolvimento m; [- of business, company] crescimento m -2. (U) [of land, area] exploração f -3. [developed land] loteamento m -4. [further incident] acontecimento m -5. (U) [of illness, fault, habit] desenvolvimento m -6. PHOT revelação f.

development area n UK zona f de desenvolvimento urbano.

deviant ['di:vjənt] <> adj anormal, pervertido(da). <> n pervertido m, -da f.

deviate ['di:vɪeɪt] vi: **to** ~ **(from sthg)** desviar-se (de algo).

deviation [ˌdi:vɪ'eɪʃn] n desvio m; **sexual** ~ perversão f sexual.

device [dɪ'vaɪs] n -1. [apparatus] dispositivo m, aparelho m -2. [plan, method] artifício m; **to leave sb to their own** ~s deixar alguém à própria sorte -3. [bomb]: **(incendiary)** ~ bomba f incendiária.

devil ['devl] n -1. [evil spirit] demônio m -2. inf [person] diabo m, -ba f; **poor** ~! pobre diabo! -3. [for emphasis]: **who/where/why the** ~ ...? que/onde/por que diabos ...?
➡ **Devil** n [Satan]: **the Devil** o Diabo.

devilish ['devlɪʃ] adj [fiendish] diabólico(ca).

devil-may-care adj inconseqüente, imprudente.

devil's advocate n advogado m do diabo.

devious ['di:vjəs] adj -1. [gen] desonesto(ta) -2. [route] sinuoso(sa).

deviousness n (U) [dishonesty] desonestidade f.

devise [dɪ'vaɪz] vt conceber.

devoid [dɪ'vɔɪd] adj fml: ~ **of sthg** desprovido(da) de algo.

devolution [ˌdi:və'lu:ʃn] n (U) POL descentralização f.

devolve [dɪ'vɒlv] vi fml: **to** ~ **(up)on sb** ser incumbência de alguém.

devote [dɪ'vəʊt] vt: **to** ~ **sthg to sthg** dedicar algo a algo; **to** ~ **o.s. to sthg** dedicar-se a algo.

devoted [dɪ'vəʊtɪd] adj [person] dedicado(da); ~ **to sb/sthg** dedicado(da) a alguém/algo.

devotee [ˌdevə'ti:] n -1. [disciple] devoto m, -ta f -2. [fan] fã mf -3. [enthusiast] entusiasta mf.

devotion [dɪ'vəʊʃn] n -1. (U) [commitment]: ~ **to sb/sthg** dedicação f a alguém/algo -2. RELIG devoção f.

devour [dɪ'vaʊəʳ] vt -1. [eat, read avidly] devorar -2. fig [subj: fire] consumir.

devout [dɪ'vaʊt] adj RELIG devoto(ta).

dew [dju:] n (U) orvalho m.

dexterity [dek'sterətɪ] n (U) agilidade f, destreza f.

dexterous ['dekstrəs] adj ágil.

dextrose ['dekstrəʊs] n (U) dextrose f.

dextrous ['dekstrəs] adj = **dexterous**.

diabetes [ˌdaɪə'bi:ti:z] n (U) diabete f.

diabetic [ˌdaɪə'betɪk] <> adj -1. [person] diabético(ca) -2. [jam, chocolate] para diabéticos. <> n diabético m, -ca f.

diabolic(al) [ˌdaɪə'bɒlɪk(l)] adj -1. [evil] diabólico(-ca) -2. inf [very bad] horroroso(sa).

diaeresis UK, **dieresis** US (pl -eses) [daɪ'erɪsɪs] n diérese f.

diagnose ['daɪəgnəʊz] vt diagnosticar.

diagnosis [ˌdaɪəg'nəʊsɪs] (pl -oses [-əʊsi:z]) n diagnóstico m.

diagnostic [ˌdaɪəg'nɒstɪk] adj MED diagnóstico(ca).

diagonal [daɪ'ægənl] <> adj [line] diagonal. <> n diagonal f.

diagonally [daɪ'ægənəlɪ] adv diagonalmente.

diagram ['daɪəgræm] n diagrama m.

diagrammatic [ˌdaɪəgrə'mætɪk] adj diagramático(ca).

dial ['daɪəl] (UK pt & pp -led, cont -ling, US pt & pp -ed, cont -ing) <> n -1. [of watch, clock, meter] mostrador m -2. [of radio] dial m -3. [of telephone] teclado m. <> vt [number] discar.

dialect ['daɪəlekt] n dialeto m.

dialling code UK, **dialing code** US ['daɪəlɪŋ-] n código m de discagem.

dialling tone UK ['daɪəlɪŋ-], **dial tone** US n linha f (no telefone).

dialogue UK, **dialog** US ['daɪəlɒg] n diálogo m.

dial tone n US = **dialling tone**.

dialysis [daɪ'ælɪsɪs] n (U) diálise f.

diamanté adj de vidrilhos.

diameter [daɪ'æmɪtəʳ] n diâmetro m.

diametrically [ˌdaɪə'metrɪklɪ] adv: ~ **opposed** diametralmente oposto(ta).

diamond ['daɪəmənd] n -1. [gem] diamante m -2. [shape] losango m.
➡ **diamonds** npl [cards] ouros mpl.

diamond wedding n bodas fpl de diamante.

diaper ['daɪpəʳ] n US fralda f.

diaphanous [daɪ'æfənəs] adj transparente.

diaphragm ['daɪəfræm] n diafragma m.

diarrh(o)ea [ˌdaɪə'rɪə] n (U) diarréia f.

diary ['daɪərɪ] (pl -ies) n -1. [appointment book] agenda f -2. [personal record] diário m.

diatribe ['daɪətraɪb] n crítica f violenta.

dice [daɪs] (pl inv) <> n [for games] dado m; **no** ~ US inf de jeito nenhum. <> vt cortar em cubinhos.

dicey ['daɪsɪ] (compar -ier, superl -iest) adj UK inf incerto(ta).

dichotomy [daɪ'kɒtəmɪ] (pl -ies) n fml dicotomia f.

Dictaphone® ['dɪktəfəʊn] n dictafone® m.

dictate [vb dɪk'teɪt, n 'dɪkteɪt] <> vt -1. [letter] ditar; **to** ~ **sthg to sb** ditar algo para alguém -2. [conditions, terms] ditar, impor. <> vi: **to** ~ **to sb** [read aloud] ditar para alguém; [give orders] impor a alguém. <> n ditado m.

dictation [dɪk'teɪʃn] n ditado m.

dictator [dɪk'teɪtə'] n POL ditador m, -ra f.
dictatorship [dɪk'teɪtəʃɪp] n ditadura f.
diction ['dɪkʃn] n (U) [pronunciation] dicção f.
dictionary ['dɪkʃənrɪ] (pl -ies) n dicionário m.
did [dɪd] pt ▷ do.
didactic [dɪ'dæktɪk] adj didático(ca).
diddle ['dɪdl] vt UK inf passar a perna em.
didn't ['dɪdnt] = did not.
die [daɪ] (pt & pp died, cont dying, pl sense 2 only dice)
◇ vi -1. [person, animal, plant] morrer; **to be dying** estar morrendo; **to be dying for sthg/to do sthg** inf estar morrendo de vontade de algo/de fazer algo -2. fig [love, anger, memory] morrer. ◇ n -1. [for shaping metal] molde m -2. [dice] dado m.
➡ **die away** vi [sound, wind] desvanecer-se.
➡ **die down** vi -1. [fire] arrefecer -2. [sound, wind] abrandar.
➡ **die out** vi -1. [family, custom] desaparecer -2. [species] ser extinto(ta).
diehard ['daɪhɑːd] n teimoso(sa).
dieresis n US = diaeresis.
diesel ['diːzl] n -1. (U) [fuel, oil] diesel m -2. [vehicle] veículo m a diesel.
diesel engine n motor m a diesel.
diesel fuel, diesel oil n óleo m diesel.
diet ['daɪət] ◇ n -1. [gen] dieta f -2. [in order to lose weight] dieta f, regime m; **to be/go on a** ~ estar de/entrar em dieta. ◇ comp [low-calorie] de baixa caloria; **a** ~ **Coke®** uma Coca® light. ◇ vi [in order to lose weight] fazer regime.
dietary ['daɪətrɪ] adj alimentar.
dietary fibre n (U) fibra f alimentar.
dieter ['daɪətə'] n pessoa f de regime.
dietician [ˌdaɪə'tɪʃn] n nutricionista mf.
differ ['dɪfə'] vi -1. [be different] diferir; **to** ~ **from sb/ sthg** diferir/distinguir-se de alguém/algo -2. [disagree]: **to** ~ **with sb (about sthg)** discordar de alguém (sobre algo); **to agree to** ~ parar de discutir.
difference ['dɪfrəns] n diferença f; **it doesn't make any** ~ não faz a menor diferença; **to make all the** ~ fazer toda a diferença.
different ['dɪfrənt] adj diferente; ~ **from** diferente de.
differential [ˌdɪfə'renʃl] ◇ adj diferencial. ◇ n diferencial m.
differentiate [ˌdɪfə'renʃɪeɪt] ◇ vt: **to** ~ **sthg from sthg** diferenciar algo de algo. ◇ vi: **to** ~ **(between)** diferenciar (entre).
differently ['dɪfrəntlɪ] adv diferentemente.
difficult ['dɪfɪkəlt] adj difícil.
difficulty ['dɪfɪkəltɪ] (pl -ies) n dificuldade f; **to have** ~ **in doing sthg** ter dificuldade em fazer algo; **with** ~ com dificuldade.
diffidence ['dɪfɪdəns] n (U) acanhamento m.
diffident ['dɪfɪdənt] adj acanhado(da).
diffuse [adj dɪ'fjuːs, vb dɪ'fjuːz] ◇ adj difuso(sa). ◇ vt -1. [light] difundir -2. [information] divulgar. ◇ vi difundir-se.
diffusion [dɪ'fjuːʒn] n (U) -1. [of light] difusão f -2. [of information] divulgação f.
dig [dɪg] (pt & pp dug, cont digging) ◇ n -1. fig [unkind remark] zombaria f -2. ARCHAEOL escavação f.

◇ vt -1. [in ground] cavar -2. [press, jab]: **to** ~ **sthg into sb/sthg** fincar algo em alguém/algo; **to** ~ **sb in the ribs** cutucar alguém. ◇ vi -1. [in ground] enterrar-se -2. [press, jab]: **to** ~ **into sthg** cravar-se em algo; **my strap's** ~ **ging into me** a alça do vestido está me apertando.
➡ **dig out** vt sep -1. [car, accident victims] resgatar -2. inf [letter, document] desencavar.
➡ **dig up** vt sep -1. [from ground] desenterrar -2. inf [information] desencavar.
digest [n 'daɪdʒest, vb dɪ'dʒest] ◇ n [book] resenha f. ◇ vt [food, information] digerir.
digestible [dɪ'dʒestəbl] adj digerível.
digestion [dɪ'dʒestʃn] n digestão f.
digestive [dɪ'dʒestɪv] adj digestivo(va).
digestive biscuit [dɪ'dʒestɪv-] n UK biscoito liso levemente adocicado muito comum na Grã-Bretanha.
digestive system n sistema m digestivo.
digger n [machine] escavadeira f.
digit ['dɪdʒɪt] n -1. [figure] dígito m -2. [finger, toe] dedo m.
digital ['dɪdʒɪtl] adj [watch, readout] digital.
digital camera n câmera f digital.
digital recording n gravação f digital.
digital television, digital TV n televisão f digital.
digital watch n relógio m digital.
digitize, -ise ['dɪdʒɪtaɪz] vt digitalizar.
dignified ['dɪgnɪfaɪd] adj digno(na).
dignify ['dɪgnɪfaɪ] (pt & pp -ied) vt honrar.
dignitary ['dɪgnɪtrɪ] (pl -ies) n dignitário m, -ria f.
dignity ['dɪgnətɪ] n dignidade f.
digress [daɪ'gres] vi fugir do assunto, divagar; **to** ~ **(from sthg)** desviar-se (de algo).
digression [daɪ'greʃn] n digressão f.
digs [dɪgz] npl UK inf quarto m alugado.
dike [daɪk] n -1. [wall, bank] dique m -2. inf pej [lesbian] sapatão m.
diktat n [pol] imposição f.
dilapidated [dɪ'læpɪdeɪtɪd] adj em ruínas.
dilate [daɪ'leɪt] ◇ vt dilatar. ◇ vi dilatar-se.
dilated [daɪ'leɪtɪd] adj dilatado(da).
dilemma [dɪ'lemə] n dilema m.
dilettante [ˌdɪlɪ'tæntɪ] (pl -tes OR -ti [-tɪ]) n pej amador m, -ra f.
diligence ['dɪlɪdʒəns] n (U) [hard work] diligência f.
diligent ['dɪlɪdʒənt] adj diligente, aplicado(da).
dill [dɪl] n (U) aneto m.
dillydally ['dɪlɪdælɪ] (pt & pp -ied) vi inf dated embromar-se.
dilute [daɪ'luːt] ◇ adj diluído(da). ◇ vt: **to** ~ **sthg (with sthg)** diluir algo (com algo).
dilution [daɪ'luːʃn] n: ~ **(with sthg)** diluição f (com algo).
dim [dɪm] (compar -mer, superl -mest, pt & pp -med, cont -ming) ◇ adj -1. [dark] sombrio(bria) -2. [indistinct - shape] indistinto(ta); [- sight, sound] fraco(ca); [- memory] vago(ga) -3. [weak] fraco(ca) -4. [gloomy]: **to take a** ~ **view of sthg** não levar fé em algo -5. inf [stupid] idiota. ◇ vt [light] diminuir. ◇ vi [beauty, hope, memory] extinguir-se.
dime [daɪm] n US moeda de 10 centavos de dólar;

cars are a ~ a **dozen in the world today** [common] hoje tem carros a dar com pau no mundo.

dimension [dɪ'menʃn] n dimensão f.

➤ **dimensions** pl [of room, object] dimensões fpl.

-dimensional [dɪ'menʃənl] suffix dimensional.

diminish [dɪ'mɪnɪʃ] ⟨⟩ vt [make less important] diminuir. ⟨⟩ vi diminuir.

diminished [dɪ'mɪnɪʃt] adj -**1.** [profits, budget] reduzido(da) -**2.** [reputation] em baixa -**3.** [person] menosprezado(da).

diminished responsibility n (U) JUR responsabilidade f diminuída.

diminishing returns [dɪ'mɪnɪʃɪŋ] npl rendimentos mpl decrescentes.

diminutive [dɪ'mɪnjʊtɪv] ⟨⟩ adj fml [tiny] diminuto(ta). ⟨⟩ n GRAMM diminutivo m.

dimly ['dɪmlɪ] adv -**1.** [shine] fracamente -**2.** [see, remember] vagamente.

dimmer ['dɪmə'] n [switch] dimmer m.

➤ **dimmers** npl US -**1.** [dipped headlights] faróis mpl baixos -**2.** [parking lights] pisca-alerta m.

dimmer switch n = dimmer.

dimple ['dɪmpl] n covinha f (no rosto).

dimwit ['dɪmwɪt] n inf estúpido m, -da f, anta mf.

dim-witted [-'wɪtɪd] adj inf estúpido(da).

din [dɪn] n inf zoeira f.

dine [daɪn] vi fml jantar.

➤ **dine out** vi jantar fora.

diner ['daɪnə'] n -**1.** [person] cliente mf (de restaurante) -**2.** US [restaurant] lanchonete f (em beira de estrada).

dingdong [ˌdɪŋ'dɒŋ] ⟨⟩ adj inf [battle, argument] tumultuado(da). ⟨⟩ n [of bell] badalada f.

dinghy ['dɪŋɡɪ] (pl -ies) n [for sailing] barco m a vela (pequeno); [for rowing] bote m a remo.

dingo ['dɪŋɡəʊ] (pl -es) n dingo m.

dingy ['dɪndʒɪ] (compar -ier, superl -iest) adj [dirty, drab] sujo(ja).

dining car ['daɪnɪŋ-] n vagão-restaurante m.

dining room ['daɪnɪŋ-] n sala f de jantar.

dining table ['daɪnɪŋ-] n mesa f de jantar.

dinner ['dɪnə'] n -**1.** [meal - in evening] jantar m; [- at midday] almoço m -**2.** [formal event] jantar m.

dinner dance n jantar m dançante.

dinner jacket n UK smoking m.

dinner party n jantar m (para poucas pessoas).

dinner service n aparelho m de jantar.

dinner table n: the ~ a mesa de jantar.

dinnertime ['dɪnətaɪm] n hora f do jantar.

dinosaur ['daɪnəsɔː'] n [reptile] dinossauro m.

dint [dɪnt] n fml: **by** ~ **of** por meio de.

diocese ['daɪəsɪs] n diocese f.

diode ['daɪəʊd] n diodo m.

dip [dɪp] (pt & pp -ped, cont -ping) ⟨⟩ n -**1.** [in road, ground] depressão f -**2.** [sauce] molho m cremoso -**3.** [swim]: **to go for a** ~ dar um mergulho. ⟨⟩ vt -**1.** [into liquid]: **to** ~ **sthg in (to) sthg** mergulhar algo em algo -**2.** UK [headlights] baixar. ⟨⟩ vi -**1.** [sun, wing] baixar -**2.** [road, ground] descer -**3.** [temperature, price] cair.

Dip. UK abbr of diploma.

Dip. Ed. (abbr of Diploma in Education) (titular de)

diploma em educação na Grã-Bretanha.

diphtheria [dɪf'θɪərɪə] n (U) difteria f.

diphthong ['dɪfθɒŋ] n LING ditongo m.

diploma [dɪ'pləʊmə] (pl -s) n diploma m.

diplomacy [dɪ'pləʊməsɪ] n diplomacia f.

diplomat ['dɪpləmæt] n diplomata mf.

diplomatic [ˌdɪplə'mætɪk] adj diplomático(ca).

diplomatic bag n mala f diplomática.

diplomatic corps n corpo m diplomático.

diplomatic immunity n imunidade f diplomática.

diplomatic relations npl relações fpl diplomáticas.

dipsomaniac [ˌdɪpsə'meɪnɪæk] n dipsomaníaco m, -ca f.

dipstick ['dɪpstɪk] n AUT vareta f do nível do óleo.

dipswitch ['dɪpswɪtʃ] n UK AUT chave f de luz alta e baixa.

dire ['daɪə'] adj [serious] terrível.

direct [dɪ'rekt] ⟨⟩ adj -**1.** [gen] direto(ta) -**2.** [insurance] sem intermediários. ⟨⟩ vt -**1.** [aim]: **to** ~ **sthg at sb** dirigir algo a alguém -**2.** [person to place] guiar -**3.** [group, project, film, play] dirigir -**4.** [order]: **to** ~ **sb to do sthg** mandar alguém fazer algo. ⟨⟩ adv direto.

direct action n ação f direta.

direct current n corrente f contínua.

direct debit n UK débito m automático (em conta corrente).

direct dialling [-'daɪəlɪŋ] n discagem f direta.

direct hit n: **to score a** ~ **on the target** acertar em cheio no alvo.

direction [dɪ'rekʃn] n -**1.** [spatial] direção f -**2.** fig [orientation] rumo m -**3.** [of group, project, play, film] direção f; **under the** ~ **of** sob a direção de.

➤ **directions** npl -**1.** [instructions to place] indicações fpl -**2.** [instructions for use] instruções fpl.

directive [dɪ'rektɪv] n diretriz f.

directly [dɪ'rektlɪ] adv -**1.** [in straight line] diretamente, direto -**2.** [frankly, openly] diretamente -**3.** [exactly] logo, bem -**4.** [very soon] imediatamente.

direct mail n mala-direta f.

director [dɪ'rektə'] n diretor m, -ra f.

directorate [dɪ'rektərət] n [board of directors] diretoria f.

director-general (pl **directors-general** OR **director-generals**) n diretor-geral m, diretora-geral f.

Director of Public Prosecutions n UK ≃ Procurador m, -ra f da República.

directorship [dɪ'rektəʃɪp] n -**1.** [position] cargo m de diretor, -ra f -**2.** [period] diretorado m.

directory [dɪ'rektərɪ] (pl -ies) n -**1.** [book, list] lista f -**2.** COMPUT diretório m.

directory enquiries n UK (serviço m de) auxílio m à lista.

direct rule n governo m central.

direct selling n vendas f diretas.

direct speech n discurso m direto.

direct taxation n imposto m direto.

dire straits npl: **in** ~ em apuros.

dirge [dɜːdʒ] n música m fúnebre.

dirt [dɜːt] n -**1.** [mud, dust] sujeira f -**2.** [earth] terra f.

dirt cheap *inf* <> *adj* bem barato(ta). <> *adv* bem barato; **this was** ~ isso foi uma ninharia.

dirt track *n* estrada *f* de terra.

dirty ['dɜːtɪ] (*compar* -**ier**, *superl* -**iest**, *pt* & *pp* -**ied**) <> *adj* -**1.** [not clean] sujo(ja) - **2.** [unfair] baixo(xa); ~ **trick** golpe *m* baixo - **3.** [smutty] obsceno(na); ~ **joke** piada *f* suja. <> *vt* sujar.

disability [ˌdɪsə'bɪlətɪ] (*pl* -**ies**) *n* deficiência *f.*

disable [dɪs'eɪbl] *vt* [injure] incapacitar.

disabled [dɪs'eɪbld] <> *adj* [person] incapacitado(-da). <> *npl*: **the** ~ os deficientes.

disablement [dɪs'eɪblmənt] *n* [of person] incapacidade *f,* deficiência *f.*

disabuse [ˌdɪsə'bjuːz] *vt fml*: **to** ~ **sb (of sthg)** desiludir alguém (sobre algo).

disadvantage [ˌdɪsəd'vɑːntɪdʒ] *n* desvantagem *f;* **to be at a** ~ estar em desvantagem; **to be to one's** ~ pesar contra alguém.

disadvantaged [ˌdɪsəd'vɑːntɪdʒd] *adj* desfavorecido(da).

disadvantageous [ˌdɪsædvɑːn'teɪdʒəs] *adj* desvantajoso(sa).

disaffected [ˌdɪsə'fektɪd] *adj* insatisfeito(ta).

disaffection [ˌdɪsə'fekʃn] *n* (U) insatisfação *f.*

disagree [ˌdɪsə'griː] *vi* -**1.** [have different opinions] discordar, não estar de acordo; **to** ~ **with sb** discordar de alguém; **to** ~ **with sthg** discordar de algo - **2.** [differ] divergir - **3.** [subj: food, drink]: **to** ~ **with sb** fazer mal a alguém.

disagreeable [ˌdɪsə'griːəbl] *adj* desagradável.

disagreement [ˌdɪsə'griːmənt] *n* -**1.** [of opinions, records] divergência *f* - **2.** [argument] discussão *f.*

disallow [ˌdɪsə'laʊ] *vt* -**1.** *fml* [appeal, claim] rejeitar - **2.** [goal] anular.

disappear [ˌdɪsə'pɪə'] *vi* desaparecer.

disappearance [ˌdɪsə'pɪərəns] *n* -**1.** [of person, object] desaparecimento *m* - **2.** [of species, civilization] extinção *f.*

disappoint [ˌdɪsə'pɔɪnt] *vt* [fail to satisfy] desapontar, decepcionar.

disappointed [ˌdɪsə'pɔɪntɪd] *adj* desapontado(da), decepcionado(da); ~ **in** OR **with sthg** decepcionado(da) com algo.

disappointing [ˌdɪsə'pɔɪntɪŋ] *adj* desapontador(-ra), decepcionante.

disappointment [ˌdɪsə'pɔɪntmənt] *n* -**1.** (U) [feeling] desapontamento *m* - **2.** [letdown] decepção *f.*

disapproval [ˌdɪsə'pruːvl] *n* (U) desaprovação *f.*

disapprove [ˌdɪsə'pruːv] *vi*: **to** ~ **(of sb/sthg)** desaprovar (algo/alguém).

disapproving [ˌdɪsə'pruːvɪŋ] *adj* desaprovador(-ra).

disarm [dɪs'ɑːm] *vt* & *vi* desarmar.

disarmament [dɪs'ɑːməmənt] *n* (U) desarmamento *m.*

disarming [dɪs'ɑːmɪŋ] *adj* [smile, person] que desarma, irresistível.

disarray [ˌdɪsə'reɪ] *n* (U): **in** ~ *fml* [clothes, hair] em desalinho; [room] em desordem; POL em desacordo.

disassociate [ˌdɪsə'səʊʃɪeɪt] *vt*: **to** ~ **o.s. from sb/sthg** desligar-se de alguém/algo.

disaster [dɪ'zɑːstə'] *n* -**1.** [gen] desastre *m*; **natural** ~ desastre *m* natural - **2.** (U) [misfortune] azar *m*; **to court** ~ procurar encrenca.

disaster area *n* [after natural disaster] área *f* de calamidade pública.

disastrous [dɪ'zɑːstrəs] *adj* [catastrophic] desastroso(sa).

disastrously [dɪ'zɑːstrəslɪ] *adv* [catastrophically] desastrosamente.

disband [dɪs'bænd] <> *vt* dispersar. <> *vi* dispersar-se.

disbelief [ˌdɪsbɪ'liːf] *n* (U): **in** OR **with** ~ com descrença.

disbelieve [ˌdɪsbɪ'liːv] *vt* [person, words] não acreditar em.

disc UK, **disk** US [dɪsk] *n* disco *m.*

discard [dɪ'skɑːd] *vt* desfazer-se de, pôr fora.

discarded [dɪ'skɑːdɪd] *adj* posto(ta) fora.

disc brake *n* freio *m* a disco.

discern [dɪ'sɜːn] *vt* -**1.** [see] discernir - **2.** [detect] perceber.

discernible [dɪ'sɜːnəbl] *adj* -**1.** [visible] discernível - **2.** [detectable] perceptível.

discerning [dɪ'sɜːnɪŋ] *adj* perspicaz.

discharge [*n* 'dɪstʃɑːdʒ, *vb* dɪs'tʃɑːdʒ] <> *n* -**1.** [of patient] alta *f*; [of prisoner, defendant] libertação *f*; [from armed forces] dispensa *f* - **2.** *fml* [fulfilment] cumprimento *m* - **3.** [toxic emission] descarga *f* - **4.** MED [from nose, wound] secreção *f* - **5.** [payment] quitação *f.* <> *vt* -**1.** [allow to leave - patient] dar alta para; [- prisoner, defendant] libertar; [- from armed forces] dispensar - **2.** *fml* [fulfil] cumprir - **3.** [emit] emitir - **4.** [pay] quitar.

discharged bankrupt [dɪs'tʃɑːdʒd-] *n* pessoa falida que cumpriu as disposições legais e pode retornar aos negócios.

disciple [dɪ'saɪpl] *n* -**1.** RELIG apóstolo *m* - **2.** *fig* [follower] discípulo *m,* -la *f.*

disciplinarian [ˌdɪsɪplɪ'neərɪən] *n* disciplinador *m,* -ra *f.*

disciplinary ['dɪsɪplɪnərɪ] *adj* disciplinar; **to take** ~ **action against sb** tomar ações disciplinares contra alguém.

discipline ['dɪsɪplɪn] <> *n* disciplina *f.* <> *vt* -**1.** [train] disciplinar - **2.** [punish] punir.

disciplined ['dɪsɪplɪnd] *adj* [controlled] disciplinado(da).

disc jockey *n* disc-jóquei *mf.*

disclaim [dɪs'kleɪm] *vt fml* negar.

disclaimer [dɪs'kleɪmə'] *n* negação *f.*

disclose [dɪs'kləʊz] *vt* divulgar.

disclosure [dɪs'kləʊʒə'] *n* -**1.** (U) [act of disclosing] divulgação *f* - **2.** [revealed fact] revelação *f.*

disco ['dɪskəʊ] (*pl* -**s**) (*abbr of* **discotheque**) *n* casa *f* noturna.

discoloration [dɪsˌkʌlə'reɪʃn] *n* [fading, staining] descoloração *f.*

discolour UK, **discolor** US [dɪs'kʌlə'] *vt* & *vi* descolorir.

discoloured UK, **discolored** US [dɪs'kʌləd] *adj* descolorido(da).

discomfort [dɪs'kʌmfət] *n* -**1.** [gen] desconforto *m* - **2.** (U) [physical pain] mal-estar *m.*

disconcert [ˌdɪskən'sɜːt] *vt* desconcertar.

disconcerting [ˌdɪskən'sɜ:tɪŋ] *adj* desconcertante.

disconnect [ˌdɪskə'nekt] *vt* -**1.** [detach] desconectar -**2.** [from gas, electricity - appliance] desconectar, desligar; [- house, building] cortar -**3.** [on phone] cortar.

disconnected [ˌdɪskə'nektɪd] *adj* -**1.** [remarks, thoughts, events] desconexo(xa) -**2.** [telephone, wire] desconectado(da).

disconsolate [dɪs'kɒnsələt] *adj* inconsolável.

discontent [ˌdɪskən'tent] *n (U)*: ~ **(with sthg)** descontentamento *m* (com algo).

discontented [ˌdɪskən'tentɪd] *adj*: ~ **(with sthg)** descontente (com algo).

discontentment [ˌdɪskən'tentmənt] *n (U)*: ~ **(with sthg)** descontentamento *m* (com algo).

discontinue [ˌdɪskən'tɪnju:] *vt* suspender.

discontinued line [ˌdɪskən'tɪnju:d-] *n COMM* (produto *m*) fora *f* de linha.

discord ['dɪskɔ:d] *n* -**1.** *(U) fml* [conflict] discórdia *f* -**2.** *MUS* dissonância *f*.

discordant [dɪ'skɔ:dənt] *adj* -**1.** [conflicting] discordante -**2.** *MUS* dissonante.

discotheque ['dɪskəʊtek] *n* discoteca *f*.

discount [*n* 'dɪskaʊnt, *vb UK* dɪs'kaʊnt, *US* 'dɪskaʊnt] <> *n* [price reduction] desconto *m*. <> *vt* -**1.** [disregard] desconsiderar -**2.** *COMM* [offer at lower price] dar desconto em; [price] abater.

discount house *n* -**1.** *FIN* casa *f* de câmbio -**2.** *COMM* [store] loja *f* que vende com descontos.

discount rate *n* taxa *f* de desconto.

discount store *n COMM* loja *f* que vende com descontos.

discourage [dɪ'skʌrɪdʒ] *vt* -**1.** [dishearten] desencorajar -**2.** [dissuade] dissuadir; to ~ **sb from doing sthg** desestimular alguém de fazer algo.

discouraging [dɪ'skʌrɪdʒɪŋ] *adj* desencorajador(ra).

discourse ['dɪskɔ:s] *n*: ~ **(on sthg)** discurso *m* (sobre algo).

discourteous [dɪs'kɜ:tjəs] *adj fml* descortês.

discourtesy [dɪs'kɜ:tɪsɪ] *n (U)* descortesia *f*.

discover [dɪ'skʌvər] *vt* -**1.** [gen] descobrir -**2.** [realize] perceber, dar-se conta de.

discoverer [dɪ'skʌvərər] *n* descobridor *m*, -ra *f*.

discovery [dɪ'skʌvərɪ] *(pl* -**ies)** *n* -**1.** [gen] descoberta *f*; the ~ **of America** o descobrimento da América -**2.** [realization] compreensão *f*.

discredit [dɪs'kredɪt] <> *n (U)* [shame] descrédito *m*. <> *vt* -**1.** [person] desonrar -**2.** [idea, belief, theory] desacreditar.

discredited [dɪskredɪtɪd] *adj* desacreditado(da).

discreet [dɪ'skri:t] *adj* discreto(ta).

discreetly [dɪ'skri:tlɪ] *adv* discretamente.

discrepancy [dɪ'skrepənsɪ] *(pl* -**ies)** *n*: ~ **(in/between)** discrepância *f* (em/entre).

discrete [dɪs'kri:t] *adj fml* distinto(ta).

discretion [dɪ'skreʃn] *n* -**1.** [tact] discrição *f* -**2.** [judgment] ponderação *f*; at the ~ **of** a critério de.

discretionary [dɪ'skreʃənərɪ] *adj* discricionário(ria).

discriminate [dɪ'skrɪmɪneɪt] *vi* -**1.** [distinguish] discriminar; to ~ **between** fazer distinção entre -**2.** [treat unfairly]: to ~ **against sb** discriminar alguém.

discriminating [dɪ'skrɪmɪneɪtɪŋ] *adj* [discerning] criterioso(sa).

discrimination [dɪˌskrɪmɪ'neɪʃn] *n (U)* -**1.** [prejudice] discriminação *f* -**2.** [good judgment] discernimento *m*.

discus ['dɪskəs] *(pl* -**es)** *n* [sport] disco *m*.

discuss [dɪ'skʌs] *vt* discutir; to ~ **sthg with sb** discutir algo com alguém.

discussion [dɪ'skʌʃn] *n* -**1.** *(U)* [act of discussing] discussão *f*; under ~ em discussão -**2.** [talk] debate *f*.

disdain [dɪs'deɪn] *fml* <> *n (U)* desdém *m*; ~ **for sb/sthg** desprezo *m* por alguém/algo. <> *vt* desdenhar. <> *vi*: to ~ **to do sthg** não se dar ao trabalho de fazer algo.

disdainful [dɪs'deɪnfʊl] *adj* desdenhoso(sa).

disease [dɪ'zi:z] *n* doença *f*.

diseased [dɪ'zi:zd] *adj* doente.

disembark [ˌdɪsɪm'bɑ:k] *vi* desembarcar.

disembarkation [ˌdɪsembɑ:'keɪʃn] *n (U)* desembarque *m*.

disembodied [ˌdɪsɪm'bɒdɪd] *adj* -**1.** [spirit] desencarnado(da) -**2.** [voice] desincorporado(da).

disembowel [ˌdɪsɪm'baʊəl] *(UK pt & pp* -**led,** *cont* -**ling,** *US pt & pp* -**ed,** *cont* -**ing)** *vt* estripar.

disenchanted [ˌdɪsɪn'tʃɑ:ntɪd] *adj*: ~ **(with sthg)** desencantado(da) (com algo).

disenchantment [ˌdɪsɪn'tʃɑ:ntmənt] *n (U)* desencantamento *m*.

disenfranchise [ˌdɪsɪn'fræntʃaɪz] *vt* = disfranchise.

disengage [ˌdɪsɪn'geɪdʒ] *vt* -**1.** [release]: to ~ **sthg (from sthg)** desprender algo (de algo); to ~ **o.s. (from sthg)** soltar-se (de algo) -**2.** *TECH* [gears, mechanism] desengatar.

disengagement *n* desligamento *m*.

disentangle [ˌdɪsɪn'tæŋgl] *vt*: to ~ **sthg from sthg** desemaranhar algo de algo; to ~ **o.s. from sthg** desenredar-se de algo.

disfavour *UK*, **disfavor** *US* [dɪs'feɪvər] *n*: to look on sthg with ~ olhar para algo com desaprovação; to fall into ~ with sb cair em desgraça com alguém.

disfigure [dɪs'fɪgər] *vt* desfigurar.

disfranchise [ˌdɪs'fræntʃaɪz] *vt* caçar o direito de voto de.

disgorge [dɪs'gɔ:dʒ] *vt* despejar.

disgrace [dɪs'greɪs] <> *n* -**1.** *(U)* [shame] desgraça *f*; in ~ com vergonha -**2.** [cause for shame - thing] desgraça *f*; [- person] vergonha *f*. <> *vt* envergonhar; to ~ **o.s.** envergonhar-se.

disgraceful [dɪs'greɪsfʊl] *adj* vergonhoso(sa).

disgruntled [dɪs'grʌntld] *adj* decepcionado(da).

disguise [dɪs'gaɪz] <> *n* disfarce *m*; in ~ disfarçado(da). <> *vt* disfarçar; to ~ **o.s. as sb/sthg** disfarçar-se de alguém/algo.

disgust [dɪs'gʌst] <> *n* nojo *m*; ~ **at sthg** nojo de algo; in ~ com nojo. <> *vt* enojar.

disgusting [dɪs'gʌstɪŋ] *adj* [very unpleasant] nojento(ta).

dish [dɪʃ] *n* [container, food] prato *m*.
 dishes *npl* louça *f*; to do *or* wash the ~ **es** lavar a louça.

- **dish out** vt sep inf distribuir.
- **dish up** vt sep inf pôr na mesa.

dish aerial UK, **dish antenna** US n antena f parabólica.

disharmony [ˌdɪsˈhɑːmənɪ] n (U) desarmonia f.

dishcloth [ˈdɪʃklɒθ] n pano m de prato.

disheartened [dɪsˈhɑːtnd] adj desanimado(da).

disheartening [dɪsˈhɑːtnɪŋ] adj desanimador(ra).

dishevelled UK, **disheveled** US [dɪˈʃevəld] adj desalinhado(da).

dishonest [dɪsˈɒnɪst] adj desonesto(ta).

dishonesty [dɪsˈɒnɪstɪ] n (U) desonestidade f.

dishonor n & vt US = dishonour.

dishonorable adj US = dishonourable.

dishonour UK, **dishonor** US [dɪsˈɒnəʳ] fml <> n desonra f. <> vt desonrar.

dishonourable UK, **dishonorable** US [dɪsˈɒnərəbll] adj desonroso(sa).

dish soap n US detergente m (para lavar louça).

dish towel n US pano m de prato.

dishwasher [ˈdɪʃˌwɒʃəʳ] n [machine] lava-louças fpl inv.

dishy [ˈdɪʃɪ] (compar-ier, superl-iest) adj UK inf [attractive] gato m, -ta f.

disillusioned [ˌdɪsɪˈluːʒnd] adj desiludido(da); ~ with sb/sthg desiludido(da) com alguém/algo.

disillusionment [ˌdɪsɪˈluːʒnmənt] n (U): ~ (with sb/sthg) desilusão f (com alguém/algo).

disincentive [ˌdɪsɪnˈsentɪv] n desestímulo m.

disinclined [ˌdɪsɪnˈklaɪnd] adj: to be ~ to do sthg estar pouco disposto(ta) a fazer algo.

disinfect [ˌdɪsɪnˈfekt] vt desinfetar.

disinfectant [ˌdɪsɪnˈfektənt] n desinfetante m.

disinformation [ˌdɪsɪnfəˈmeɪʃn] n (U) desinformação f.

disingenuous [ˌdɪsɪnˈdʒenjʊəsl] adj dissimulado(da).

disinherit [ˌdɪsɪnˈherɪt] vt deserdar.

disintegrate [dɪsˈɪntɪɡreɪt] vi -1. [object] desintegrar-se -2. fig [project, marriage] desmoronar.

disintegration [dɪsˌɪntɪˈɡreɪʃn] n (U) -1. [of object] desintegração f -2. fig [of project, marriage] desmoronamento m.

disinterested [ˌdɪsˈɪntrəstɪd] adj -1. [objective] neutro(tra) -2. [uninterested]: ~ (in sb/sthg) desinteressado(da) (em alguém/algo).

disinvestment [ˌdɪsɪnˈvestmənt] n (U) desinvestimento m.

disjointed [dɪsˈdʒɔɪntɪd] adj desconjuntado(da).

disk [dɪsk] n COMPUT: floppy ~ disquete m; hard ~ disco m rígido.

disk drive UK, **diskette drive** US n COMPUT drive m, unidade f de disco.

diskette [dɪskˈet] n COMPUT disquete m.

diskette drive n US = disk drive.

disk operating system [-ˈɒpəreɪtɪŋ-] n COMPUT sistema m operacional de disco.

dislike [dɪsˈlaɪk] <> n -1. (U) [feeling] aversão f; ~ of sb/sthg aversão a alguém/algo; to take a ~ to sb não simpatizar com alguém; to take a ~ to sthg ter aversão a algo -2. [thing not liked] desgosto m. <> vt não gostar de.

dislocate [ˈdɪsləkeɪt] vt -1. MED deslocar -2. [disrupt] desorganizar.

dislodge [dɪsˈlɒdʒ] vt [remove - person]: to ~ sb (from) desalojar alguém (de); [- thing]: to ~ sthg (from) remover algo (de).

disloyal [ˌdɪsˈlɔɪəl] adj: ~ (to sb) desleal (a alguém).

dismal [ˈdɪzml] adj -1. [gloomy, depressing] sombrio(bria), deprimente -2. [unsuccessful] frustrante.

dismantle [dɪsˈmæntl] vt [machine, structure] desmantelar.

dismay [dɪsˈmeɪ] <> n (U) consternação f; to sb's ~ para desespero de alguém. <> vt consternar.

dismember [dɪsˈmembəʳ] vt desmembrar.

dismiss [dɪsˈmɪs] vt -1. [from job]: to ~ sb (from sthg) despedir alguém (de algo) -2. [refuse to take seriously] descartar -3. [allow to leave] dispensar -4. [JUR - case] encerrar; [- jury] dispensar.

dismissal [dɪsˈmɪsl] n -1. [from job] demissão f -2. [refusal to take seriously] descartamento m -3. [JUR - of case] encerramento m; [- of jury] dispensa f.

dismissive [dɪsˈmɪsɪv] adj [attitude, tone] de menosprezo; to be ~ of sb/sthg menosprezar algo/alguém.

dismount [ˌdɪsˈmaʊnt] vi: to ~ (from sthg) descer (de algo).

disobedience [ˌdɪsəˈbiːdjəns] n desobediência f.

disobedient [ˌdɪsəˈbiːdjənt] adj desobediente.

disobey [ˌdɪsəˈbeɪ] <> vt [person, rule] desobedecer a. <> vi desobedecer.

disorder [dɪsˈɔːdəʳ] n -1. [disarray]: in ~ em desordem -2. [rioting] tumulto m -3. MED distúrbio m.

disordered [dɪsˈɔːdəd] adj -1. [in disarray] desordenado(da) -2. MED: mentally ~ mentalmente perturbado(da).

disorderly [dɪsˈɔːdəlɪ] adj -1. [untidy] desordenado(da) -2. [unruly] indisciplinado(da).

disorderly conduct n JUR perturbação f da ordem.

disorganized, -ised [dɪsˈɔːɡənaɪzd] adj desorganizado(da).

disorientated UK [dɪsˈɔːrɪənteɪtɪd], **disoriented** US [dɪsˈɔːrɪəntɪd] adj desorientado(da).

disown [dɪsˈəʊn] vt renegar.

disparage [dɪˈspærɪdʒ] vt depreciar.

disparaging [dɪˈspærɪdʒɪŋ] adj depreciativo(va).

disparate [ˈdɪspərət] adj fml diverso(sa).

disparity [dɪˈspærətɪ] (pl -ies) n: ~ (between/in) disparidade f (entre/em).

dispassionate [dɪˈspæʃnət] adj imparcial.

dispatch [dɪˈspætʃ] <> n [message] envio m. <> vt [send] enviar, despachar.

dispatch box n UK POL -1. [box] caixa na qual se transporta documentos oficiais -2. [in House of Commons]: the ~ local onde os parlamentares mais importantes fazem seus discursos.

dispatch rider n emissário m, -ria f.

dispel [dɪˈspel] (pt & pp -led, cont -ling) vt [feeling] dissipar.

dispensable [dɪˈspensəbl] adj dispensável.

dispensary [dɪˈspensərɪ] (pl -ies) n dispensário m.

dispensation [ˌdɪspenˈseɪʃn] n [permission] dispensa f.

dispense [dɪ'spens] *vt* **-1.** [justice] administrar **-2.** [advice] oferecer **-3.** [drugs, medicine] preparar.
➡ **dispense with** *vt fus* dispensar.

dispenser [dɪ'spensə^r] *n* [machine, container] máquina *f* automática; **cash** ~ caixa *m* automático; **soap** ~ saboneteira *f* líquido *(em banheiro público)*.

dispensing chemist *UK*, **dispensing pharmacist** *US* [dɪ'spensɪŋ-] *n* farmacêutico *m*, -ca *f*.

dispersal [dɪ'spɜːsll] *n* dispersão *f*.

disperse [dɪ'spɜːs] <> *vt* **-1.** [crowd] dispersar **-2.** [knowledge, news] disseminar **-3.** [substance, gas, oil slick] dispersar. <> *vi* [crowd] dispersar-se.

dispirited [dɪ'spɪrɪtɪd] *adj* desalentado(da).

dispiriting [dɪ'spɪrɪtɪŋ] *adj* desalentador(ra).

displace [dɪs'pleɪs] *vt* **-1.** [supplant] substituir **-2.** *CHEM & PHYS* deslocar.

displaced person [dɪs'pleɪst-] *n* exilado *m*, -da *f*.

displacement [dɪs'pleɪsmənt] *n* deslocamento *m*.

display [dɪ'spleɪ] <> *n* **-1.** [of goods, merchandise, or-naments] exposição *f*; **on** ~ em exposição; **window** ~ vitrine *f* **-2.** [of feeling, courage, skill] demonstração *f* **-3.** [performance] exibição *f* **-4.** *COMPUT* exibição *f*. <> *vt* **-1.** [gen] expor **-2.** [feeling, courage, skill] demonstrar.

display advertising *n* propaganda *f* artística.

displease [dɪs'pliːz] *vt* descontentar.

displeasure [dɪs'pleʒə^r] *n (U)* descontentamento *m*.

disposable [dɪ'spəʊzəbl] *adj* **-1.** [to be thrown away after use] descartável; ~ **nappy** *UK*, ~ **diaper** *US* fralda *f* descartável **-2.** [available] disponível.

disposal [dɪ'spəʊzl] *n (U)* **-1.** [getting rid of] descarte *f* **-2.** [availability]: **at sb's** ~ à disposição de alguém.

dispose ➡ **dispose of** *vt fus* [get rid of - rubbish, nuclear waste] descartar-se de; [- problem] livrar-se de.

disposed [dɪ'spəʊzd] *adj* **-1.** [willing]: **to be** ~ **to do sth** estar disposto(ta) a fazer algo **-2.** [positive]: **to be well-** ~ **to** *OR* **towards sb** estar bem-intencionado(da) com/em relação a alguém.

disposition [ˌdɪspə'zɪʃn] *n* **-1.** [temperament] temperamento *m* **-2.** [willingness, tendency]: ~ **to do sth** disposição *f* para fazer algo.

dispossess [ˌdɪspə'zes] *vt fml*: **to** ~ **sb of sth** despojar alguém de algo.

disproportion [ˌdɪsprə'pɔːʃn] *n* desproporção *f*.

disproportionate [ˌdɪsprə'pɔːʃnət] *adj* despro-porcional; ~ **to sth** desproporcional a algo.

disprove [ˌdɪs'pruːv] *vt* [theory, idea]: **to** ~ **sth** mostrar que algo está errado.

dispute [dɪ'spjuːt] <> *n* **-1.** [quarrel] disputa *f* **-2.** *(U)* [disagreement] discussão *f*; **in** ~ em discussão. <> *vt* **-1.** [question, challenge] discutir **-2.** [fight for] disputar.

disqualification [dɪsˌkwɒlɪfɪ'keɪʃn] *n*: ~ **(from sth)** desqualificação *f* (de algo); ~ **from a sporting event** desqualificação de um evento esportivo; ~ **from standing for election** inelegibilidade *f* para uma eleição; ~ **from driving** *UK* proibição *f* para dirigir.

disqualify [ˌdɪs'kwɒlɪfaɪ] *(pt & pp* **-ied)** *vt* **-1.** [subj: authority, illness, criminal record]: **to** ~ **sb (from doing sth)** desqualificar alguém (para fazer algo) **-2.**

SPORT desqualificar **-3.** *UK* [from driving] ser proibido de.

disquiet [dɪs'kwaɪət] *n (U)* inquietação *f*.

disregard [ˌdɪsrɪ'gɑːd] <> *n*: ~ **(for sthg)** des-consideração *f OR* indiferença *f* (por algo). <> *vt* desconsiderar.

disrepair [ˌdɪsrɪ'peə^r] *n (U)* mau estado *m* de conservação; **to fall into** ~ estar caindo aos pedaços.

disreputable [dɪs'repjʊtəbll] *adj* desacreditado(-da).

disrepute [ˌdɪsrɪ'pjuːt] *n*: **to bring sthg into** ~ desacreditar algo; **to fall into** ~ cair em descré-dito.

disrespectful [ˌdɪsrɪ'spektfʊl] *adj* desrespeitoso(-sa).

disrupt [dɪs'rʌpt] *vt* transtornar.

disruption [dɪs'rʌpʃn] *n* transtorno *m*.

disruptive [dɪs'rʌptɪv] *adj* perturbador(ra).

dissatisfaction [ˈdɪsˌsætɪs'fækʃn] *n (U)* insatisfa-ção *f*.

dissatisfied [ˌdɪs'sætɪsfaɪd] *adj* insatisfeito(ta); ~ **with sthg** insatisfeito(ta) com algo.

dissect [dɪ'sekt] *vt* dissecar.

dissection [dɪ'sekʃn] *n* dissecação *f*.

disseminate [dɪ'semɪneɪt] *vt* [information] dissemi-nar.

dissemination [dɪˌsemɪ'neɪʃn] *n (U)* [of information] disseminação *f*.

dissension [dɪ'senʃn] *n* divergência *f*.

dissent [dɪ'sent] <> *n (U)* [disagreement] divergência *f*. <> *vi*: **to** ~ **(from sthg)** divergir (de algo).

dissenter [dɪ'sentə^r] *n* [protester] dissidente *mf*.

dissenting [dɪ'sentɪŋ] *adj* [not in agreement] dissi-dente.

dissertation [ˌdɪsə'teɪʃn] *n* dissertação *f*.

disservice [ˌdɪs'sɜːvɪs] *n*: **to do sb a** ~ fazer um desserviço a alguém.

dissident ['dɪsɪdənt] *n* dissidente *mf*.

dissimilar [ˌdɪ'sɪmɪlə^r] *adj* diferente; ~ **to** diferente de.

dissipate ['dɪsɪpeɪt] <> *vt* **-1.** [heat] dissipar **-2.** [ef-forts, money] dispersar. <> *vi* [heat, crowd] dissi-par-se.

dissipated ['dɪsɪpeɪtɪd] *adj* [person, life] desregrado(-da).

dissociate [dɪ'səʊʃɪeɪt] *vt* dissociar; **to** ~ **o.s. from sthg** dissociar-se de algo.

dissolute ['dɪsəluːt] *adj* dissoluto(ta).

dissolution [ˌdɪsə'luːʃn] *n (U)* [of organization, relation-ship] dissolução *f*.

dissolve [dɪ'zɒlv] <> *vt* dissolver. <> *vi* **-1.** [sub-stance] dissolver-se **-2.** *fig* [disappear] desaparecer.
➡ **dissolve in(to)** *vt fus* [tears, laughter] dissol-ver-se em.

dissuade [dɪ'sweɪd] *vt*: **to** ~ **sb (from doing sthg)** dissuadir alguém (de fazer algo).

distance ['dɪstəns] *n* **-1.** [between two places] distância *f* **-2.** [distant point]: **at a** ~ à distância; **from a** ~ de longe; **in the** ~ ao longe. <> *vt*: **to** ~ **o.s. from sb/sthg** distanciar-se de alguém/algo.

distant ['dɪstənt] *adj* distante; ~ **from** distante de.

distaste [dɪsˈteɪst] *n (U)* repugnância *f*; ~ **for sthg** repugnância a algo.

distasteful [dɪsˈteɪstfʊl] *adj* [unpleasant] desagradável, repugnante.

distemper [dɪˈstempəʳ] *n (U)* **-1.** [paint] pintura *f* à têmpera **-2.** [disease] cinomose *f*.

distended [dɪˈstendɪd] *adj* dilatado(da).

distil *UK* (*pt* & *pp* **-led**, *cont* **-ling**), **distill** *US* [dɪˈstɪl] *vt* destilar.

distiller [dɪˈstɪləʳ] *n* destilador *m*.

distillery [dɪˈstɪlərɪ] (*pl* **-ies**) *n* destilaria *f*.

distinct [dɪˈstɪŋkt] *adj* **-1.** [different] distinto(ta); ~ **from** distinto(ta de); **as** ~ **from** em oposição a **-2.** [clear] nítido(da).

distinction [dɪˈstɪŋkʃn] *n* **-1.** [difference, excellence] distinção *f*; **to draw** *OR* **make a** ~ **between** fazer uma distinção entre **-2.** [in exam result] destaque *m*.

distinctive [dɪˈstɪŋktɪv] *adj* [flavour, voice] característico(ca).

distinctly [dɪˈstɪŋktlɪ] *adv* **-1.** [clearly] claramente **-2.** [considerably] excessivamente.

distinguish [dɪˈstɪŋgwɪʃ] <> *vt* **-1.** [tell apart]: **to** ~ **sthg from sthg** distinguir algo de algo **-2.** [discern, perceive, make different] distinguir; **to** ~ **o.s.** [perform well] distinguir-se. <> *vi*: **to** ~ **between** distinguir-se entre.

distinguished [dɪˈstɪŋgwɪʃt] *adj* ilustre.

distinguishing [dɪˈstɪŋgwɪʃɪŋ] *adj* [feature, mark] peculiar.

distort [dɪˈstɔːt] *vt* distorcer.

distorted [dɪˈstɔːtɪd] *adj* distorcido(da).

distortion [dɪˈstɔːʃn] *n* distorção *f*.

distract [dɪˈstrækt] *vt* [person, attention]: **to** ~ **sb (from sthg)** distrair alguém(de algo).

distracted [dɪˈstræktɪd] *adj* [preoccupied] atordoado(da).

distraction [dɪˈstrækʃn] *n* **-1.** [gen] distração *f* **-2.** (U): **to drive sb to** ~ levar alguém à loucura.

distraught [dɪˈstrɔːt] *adj* transtornado(da).

distress [dɪˈstres] <> *n* **-1.** [suffering - mental] aflição *f*; [- physical] agonia *f*, dor *f*; **to be in** ~ estar em agonia **-2.** [danger]: **in** ~ em perigo. <> *vt* [upset] afligir.

distressed [dɪˈstrest] *adj* [anxious, upset] angustiado(da).

distressing [dɪˈstresɪŋ] *adj* [news, account, image] angustiante.

distress signal *n* pedido *m* de socorro.

distribute [dɪˈstrɪbjuːt] *vt* distribuir.

distribution [ˌdɪstrɪˈbjuːʃn] *n* distribuição *f*.

distributor [dɪˈstrɪbjʊtəʳ] *n* **-1.** *COMM* distribuidor *m*, -ra *f* **-2.** *AUT* distribuidor *m*.

district [ˈdɪstrɪkt] *n* **-1.** [of country] distrito *m* **-2.** [of town] bairro *m*.

district attorney *n US JUR* promotor *m* público, promotora *f* pública.

district council *n UK ADMIN* conselho *m* de bairro.

district nurse *n UK* enfermeira *encarregada de atender a domicílio os pacientes de uma área.*

District of Columbia *n* Distrito *m* de Colúmbia.

distrust [dɪsˈtrʌst] <> *n* desconfiança *f*. <> *vt* desconfiar.

distrustful [dɪsˈtrʌstfʊl] *adj* desconfiado(da).

disturb [dɪˈstɜːb] *vt* **-1.** [interrupt] incomodar **-2.** [upset, worry] preocupar **-3.** [cause to change] mexer em.

disturbance [dɪˈstɜːbəns] *n* **-1.** [fight] distúrbio *m* **-2.** [interruption, disruption]: ~ **of the peace** *JUR* perturbação *f* da ordem **-3.** [distress, upset] perturbação *f*.

disturbed [dɪˈstɜːbd] *adj* perturbado(da).

disturbing [dɪˈstɜːbɪŋ] *adj* [news, image] perturbador(ra).

disunity *n (U)* desunião *f*.

disuse [ˌdɪsˈjuːs] *n*: **to fall into** ~ cair em desuso.

disused [ˌdɪsˈjuːzd] *adj* [factory, railway line] abandonado(da).

ditch [dɪtʃ] <> *n* fosso *m*. <> *vt inf* **-1.** [boyfriend, girlfriend] livrar-se de **-2.** [plan] descartar **-3.** [old car, clothes] desfazer-se de.

dither [ˈdɪðəʳ] *vi* [be indecisive] hesitar.

ditto [ˈdɪtəʊ] *adv* idem.

diuretic [ˌdaɪjʊˈretɪk] *n* diurético *m*.

diva [ˈdiːvə] (*pl* **-s**) *n* diva *f*.

divan [dɪˈvæn] *n* divã *m*.

divan bed *n* divã *m*.

dive [daɪv] (*UK pt* & *pp* **-d**, *US pt* & *pp* **-d** *OR* **dove**) <> *vi* **-1.** [gen] mergulhar; **to** ~ **(into sthg)** mergulhar (em algo) **-2.** [as sport] mergulhar, saltar **-3.** [into pocket, bag]: **to** ~ **into sthg** enfiar a mão em algo. <> *n* **-1.** [gen] mergulho *m* **-2.** [sudden movement] movimento *m* brusco **-3.** *inf pej* [bar, restaurant] espelunca *f*.

dive-bomb *vt* bombardear com caça de mergulho.

diver [ˈdaɪvəʳ] *n* mergulhador *m*, -ra *f*.

diverge [daɪˈvɜːdʒ] *vi* **-1.** [opinions, interests] divergir; **to** ~ **from sthg** divergir de algo **-2.** [roads, paths] separar-se.

divergence [daɪˈvɜːdʒəns] *n* [of opinions, interests] divergência *f*.

divergent [daɪˈvɜːdʒənt] *adj* [opinions, interests] divergente.

diverse [daɪˈvɜːs] *adj* diferente.

diversification [daɪˌvɜːsɪfɪˈkeɪʃn] *n (U)* [in industry] diversificação *f*.

diversify [daɪˈvɜːsɪfaɪ] (*pt* & *pp* **-ied**) <> *vt* [products] diversificar. <> *vi* [in industry] diversificar-se.

diversion [daɪˈvɜːʃn] *n* **-1.** (U) [gen] desvio *m* **-2.** [distraction] diversão *f*.

diversionary [daɪˈvɜːʃnrɪ] *adj* [tactics] diversivo(va).

diversity [daɪˈvɜːsətɪ] *n (U)* diversidade *f*.

divert [daɪˈvɜːt] *vt* **-1.** [gen] desviar **-2.** [distract] distrair.

divest [daɪˈvest] *vt fml*: **to** ~ **sb of sthg** [take away] privar alguém de algo; **to** ~ **o.s. of sthg** [get rid of] livrar-se de algo.

divide [dɪˈvaɪd] <> *vt* **-1.** dividir; **to** ~ **sthg between** *OR* **among** dividir algo entre **-2.** [split up]: **to** ~ **sthg into** dividir algo em **-3.** *MATH*: **to** ~ **sthg by** dividir algo por. <> *vi* [split into two] dividir-se. <> *n* [difference] divisão *f*.
  ➡ **divide up** *vt sep* dividir.

divided [dɪˈvaɪdɪd] *adj* [disunited] dividido(da).

dividend [ˈdɪvɪdend] *n* [profit] dividendo *m*; **to pay ~s** trazer benefícios.

dividers [dɪˈvaɪdəz] *npl* compasso *m*.

dividing line [dɪˈvaɪdɪŋ-] *n* linha *f* divisória.

divine [dɪˈvaɪn] <> *adj* divino(na). <> *vt* **-1.** [gen] adivinhar **- 2.** [water] descobrir.

diving [ˈdaɪvɪŋ] *n* [from board] salto *m (de trampolim)*; [underwater] mergulho *m*.

diving board *n* trampolim *m*.

diving suit *n* escafandro *m*.

divinity [dɪˈvɪnətɪ] *(pl -ies) n* **-1.** *(U)* [godliness] divindade *f* **- 2.** *(U)* [study] teologia *f* **- 3.** [god, goddess] deidade *f*.

divisible [dɪˈvɪzəbl] *adj* MATH divisível; **~ by** divisível por.

division [dɪˈvɪʒn] *n* **-1.** [gen] divisão *f* **- 2.** *(U)* [sharing out, distribution] repartição *f* **- 3.** [disagreement] discórdia *f*.

division sign *n* sinal *m* de divisão.

divisive [dɪˈvaɪsɪv] *adj* que causa divisão.

divorce [dɪˈvɔːs] <> *n* JUR divórcio *m*. <> *vt* **-1.** JUR [husband, wife] divorciar-se de **- 2.** [separate]: **to ~ sthg from sthg** separar algo de algo.

divorced [dɪˈvɔːst] *adj* **-1.** JUR divorciado(da) **- 2.** *fig* [separated]: **to be ~ from sthg** estar distante de algo.

divorcee [dɪvɔːˈsiː] *n* divorciado *m*, -da *f*.

divulge [daɪˈvʌldʒ] *vt* [information, secret] divulgar.

DIY *(abbr of* **do-it-yourself)** *n UK conceito utilizado para atividades do tipo faça-você-mesmo, como montar objetos ou fazer reparos em casa.*

dizziness [ˈdɪzɪnɪs] *n (U)* vertigem *f*, tontura *f*.

dizzy [ˈdɪzɪ] *(compar -ier, superl -iest) adj* **-1.** [giddy] tonto(ta) **- 2.** *fig* [height, speed] vertiginoso(sa).

DJ *n* **-1.** *(abbr of* **disc jockey)** DJ *mf*. **- 2.** *(abbr of* **dinner jacket)** smoking *m*.

Djakarta [dʒəˈkɑːtə] *n* Jacarta; **in ~** em Jacarta.

Djibouti [dʒɪˈbuːtɪ] *n* Djibouti; **in ~** no Djibouti.

dl *(abbr of* **decilitre)** dl.

DLit(t) [ˌdiːˈlɪt] *(abbr of* **Doctor of Letters)** *n (titular de)* doutorado em letras.

dm *(abbr of* **decimetre)** dm.

DM *(abbr of* **Deutschmark)** marco *m* alemão.

DMA *(abbr of* **direct memory access)** *n* DMA *m*.

DMus [ˌdiːˈmjuːz] *(abbr of* **Doctor of Music)** *n (titular de)* doutorado em música.

DMZ *(abbr of* **demilitarized zone)** *n US* zona *f* desmilitarizada.

DNA *(abbr of* **deoxyribonucleic acid)** *n* DNA *m*.

D-notice *n UK pedido oficial à imprensa para que uma determinada informação não se torne pública por razões de segurança nacional.*

DNS *(abbr of* **Domain Name System)** *n* COMPUT DNS *m*.

do¹ [duː] *(pt* **did**, *pp* **done)** *aux vb* **-1.** [in negatives]: **don't ~ that!** não faça isso!; **she didn't see it** ela não o viu. **- 2.** [in questions]: **~ you like it?** você gosta?; **how ~ you do it?** como é que se faz? **- 3.** [referring to previous verb]: **~ you smoke? - yes, I ~ /no, I don't** você fuma? sim/não; **I eat more than you ~** eu como mais do que você; **no, I didn't do it!** não fiz, não!; **so ~ I** eu também. **- 4.** [in question tags]: **so, you like Scotland, ~ you?** então você gosta da Escócia, não gosta?; **the train leaves at**

five o'clock, doesn't it? o trem sai às cinco, não é (verdade)? **- 5.** [for emphasis]: **I ~ like this bedroom** eu realmente gosto deste quarto; **~ come in!** faça o favor de entrar!

<> *vt* **-1.** [perform] fazer; **to ~ one's homework** fazer o dever de casa; **what is she doing?** o que ela está fazendo?; **what can I ~ for you?** em que posso ajudá-lo? **- 2.** [clean, brush, etc]: **to ~ one's hair** pentear-se; **to ~ one's make-up** maquiar-se; **to ~ one's teeth** escovar os dentes. **- 3.** [cause] fazer; **to ~ damage** fazer estragos; **to ~ sb good** fazer bem a alguém. **- 4.** [have as job]: **what do you ~?** o que você faz? **- 5.** [provide, offer] fazer; **we ~ pizzas for under $5** vendemos pizzas por menos de 5 dólares. **- 6.** [subj: vehicle] ir a; **the car was ~ing 50mph** o carro ia a 80 km/h. **- 7.** *inf* [visit] visitar; **we're doing Scotland next week** para a semana vamos visitar a Escócia.

<> *vi* **-1.** [behave, act] fazer; **~ as I say** faça como eu lhe digo. **- 2.** [progress]: **he did badly/well on his test** ele foi mal/bem no exame; **how did you ~?** como é que foi? **- 3.** [be sufficient] chegar; **will $10 ~?** 10 dólares chega? **- 4.** [in phrases]: **how ~ you ~?** [greeting] (muito) prazer (em conhecê-lo); **how are you ~ing?** como é que vão as coisas?; **what does that have to ~ with it?** o que é que isso tem a ver?

<> *n* [party] festa *f*; **~s and don'ts** o que fazer e não fazer.

<> **do up** *vt sep* [coat, shirt] abotoar; [shoes, laces] apertar, atar; [zip] fechar; [decorate] renovar.

<> **do with** *vt fus* [need]: **I could ~ with a drink** eu bem que beberia alguma coisa.

<> **do without** *vt fus* passar sem.

do² *(abbr of* **ditto)** ditto *m*.

DOA *(abbr of* **dead on arrival)** *adj diz-se do corpo que chega sem vida ao hospital.*

doable [ˈduːəbl] *adj inf* exequível.

d.o.b. *(abbr of* **date of birth)** data *f* de nascimento.

Doberman [ˈdəʊbəmən] *(pl -s) n*: **~ (pinscher)** dobermann *m* pinscher.

docile [*UK* ˈdəʊsaɪl, *US* ˈdɒsəl] *adj* dócil.

dock [dɒk] <> *n* **-1.** [in harbour] doca *f* **- 2.** [in court] banco *m* dos réus. <> *vt* [wages] descontar. <> *vi* **-1.** [ship] atracar **- 2.** [passengers] chegar.

docker [ˈdɒkəʳ] *n* estivador *m*, -ra *f*.

docket [ˈdɒkɪt] *n* **-1.** *UK documento que descreve o conteúdo de algo sendo entregue ou transportado* **- 2.** *US* JUR lista *f* das sentenças.

docklands [ˈdɒkləndz] *npl UK* região *f* das docas.

dock worker *n* = docker.

dockyard [ˈdɒkjɑːd] *n* estaleiro *m*.

doctor [ˈdɒktəʳ] <> *n* **-1.** [of medicine] médico *m*, -ca *f*; **to go to the ~'s** ir ao médico **- 2.** [holder of PhD] doutor *m*, -ra *f*. <> *vt* **-1.** [change, tamper with] adulterar **- 2.** *UK* [neuter] castrar.

doctorate [ˈdɒktərət], **doctor's degree** *n* doutorado *m*.

Doctor of Medicine *n* doutor *m*, -ra *f* em medicina.

doctrinaire [ˌdɒktrɪˈneəʳ] *adj* doutrinário(ria).

doctrine [ˈdɒktrɪn] *n* doutrina *f*.

docudrama [ˌdɒkjʊˈdrɑːmə] *(pl -s) n* TV dramatização *f*.

document [n 'dɒkjʊmənt, vb dɒkjʊ'ment] <> n documento m. <> vt [record, detail] documentar.

documentary [ˌdɒkjʊ'mentərɪ] (pl -ies) <> adj [evidence] documental. <> n documentário m.

documentation [ˌdɒkjʊmen'teɪʃn] n (U) [evidence] documentação f.

DOD (abbr of **Department of Defense**) n departamento m de defesa (norte-americano).

doddering ['dɒdərɪŋ], **doddery** ['dɒdərɪ] adj inf senil.

doddle ['dɒdl] n UK inf barbada f.

Dodecanese [ˌdəʊdɪkə'niːz] npl: **the ∼** o Dodecaneso.

dodge [dɒdʒ] <> n inf mutreta f; **a tax ∼** uma mutreta para não pagar impostos. <> vt [avoid] fugir de. <> vi esquivar-se.

Dodgems® ['dɒdʒəmz] npl UK carros m de batida (em parques de diversão).

dodgy ['dɒdʒɪ] adj UK inf -1. [dishonest] desonesto(ta) -2. [risky, unreliable] arriscado(da) -3. [weak, unhealthy] fraco(ca).

doe [dəʊ] n -1. [female deer] corça f -2. [female rabbit] coelha f.

doer ['duːəᵣ] n inf: **he's a ∼!** ele põe a mão na massa!

does [weak form dəz, strong form dʌz] vb ⊳ **do**.

doesn't ['dʌznt] = **does not**.

dog [dɒg] (pt & pp -ged, cont -ging) <> n -1. [animal] cão m, cachorro m; **it's a ∼'s life** é uma vida de cão; **to go to the ∼s** inf entrar pelo cano; **let sleeping ∼s lie** não mexa em casa de marimbondo -2. UK [sport]: **the ∼s** corrida f de cachorros -3. US [hot dog] cachorro-quente m. <> vt -1. [follow closely] seguir -2. [subj: problems, bad luck] atormentar.

dog biscuit n biscoito m canino.

dog collar n -1. [of dog] coleira f de cachorro -2. [of clergyman] gola f de padre.

dog-eared [-ɪəd] adj [book, page] com orelhas.

dog-eat-dog adj muito competitivo(va).

dog-end n inf [of cigarette] guimba f, bagana f.

dogfight ['dɒgfaɪt] n -1. [between dogs] briga f de cachorro -2. [between aircraft] combate m aéreo.

dogfish (pl inv) n cação m.

dog food n ração f para cachorro.

dogged ['dɒgɪd] adj [resistance, perseverance] persistente.

doggone ['dɒgɒn], **doggoned** ['dɒgɒnd] adj US inf maldito(ta).

doggy ['dɒgɪ] (pl -ies) n inf cachorrinho m.

doggy bag n ≃ quentinha f, pequena sacola que os restaurantes oferecem para o cliente levar a comida que sobrou.

dogma ['dɒgmə] n dogma m.

dogmatic [dɒg'mætɪk] adj dogmático(ca).

do-gooder [-'gʊdəᵣ] n pej pessoa bem-intencionada, mas que acaba atrapalhando.

dog paddle n nado m cachorrinho.

dogsbody ['dɒgzˌbɒdɪ] (pl -ies) n UK inf faz-tudo mf, burro m de carga.

dog tag n US placa de identificação usada no pescoço de um soldado.

doing ['duːɪŋ] n: **is this your ∼?** foi vòcê que fez isso?

doings npl [activities] atividades fpl.

do-it-yourself n (U) sistema m faça-você-mesmo.

doldrums ['dɒldrəmz] npl: **to be in the ∼** fig estar estagnado(da).

dole [dəʊl] n UK [unemployment benefit] ≃ seguro-desemprego m; **to be on the ∼** estar recebendo seguro-desemprego.

dole out vt sep [food, money] repartir.

doleful ['dəʊlfʊl] adj lúgubre.

doll [dɒl] n [toy] boneca f.

dollar ['dɒləᵣ] n dólar m.

dolled up [dɒld-] adj inf enfeitado(da), produzido(da).

dollhouse n US = **doll's house**.

dollop ['dɒləp] n inf monte m.

doll's house UK, **dollhouse** US ['dɒlhaʊs] n casa f de bonecas.

dolly ['dɒlɪ] (pl -ies) n -1. [doll] bonequinha f -2. TECH [for TV or film camera] plataforma f móvel.

Dolomites ['dɒləmaɪts] npl: **the ∼** os Dolomíticos.

dolphin ['dɒlfɪn] n golfinho m.

domain [də'meɪn] n [sphere of interest, land] domínio m.

domain name n COMPUT nome m de domínio.

dome [dəʊm] n ARCHIT domo m.

domestic [də'mestɪk] <> adj -1. [gen - flight] doméstico(ca); [- production] nacional -2. [person] caseiro(ra). <> n doméstico m, -ca f.

domestic appliance n eletrodoméstico m.

domesticated [də'mestɪkeɪtɪd] adj -1. [animal] domesticado(da) -2. hum [person] caseiro(ra).

domesticity [ˌdəʊme'stɪsətɪ] n (U) [home life] vida f caseira.

domicile ['dɒmɪsaɪl] n fml domicílio m.

dominance ['dɒmɪnəns] n (U) -1. [control, power] dominância f -2. [importance] predominância f.

dominant ['dɒmɪnənt] adj -1. [colour] predominante -2. [personality, group] influente.

dominate ['dɒmɪneɪt] vt dominar.

dominating ['dɒmɪneɪtɪŋ] adj [person] dominador(ra).

domination [ˌdɒmɪ'neɪʃn] n (U) domínio m.

domineering [ˌdɒmɪ'nɪərɪŋ] adj [person, personality] dominador(ra).

Dominica [də'mɪnɪkə] n Domínica; **in ∼** na Domínica.

Dominican Republic [də'mɪnɪkən-] n: **the ∼** a República Dominicana; **in the ∼** na República Dominicana.

dominion [də'mɪnjən] n -1. (U) [power] dominação f -2. [land] domínio m.

domino ['dɒmɪnəʊ] (pl -es) n peça f de dominó.

dominoes npl [game] dominó m.

domino effect n efeito m dominó.

don [dɒn] (pt & pp -ned, cont -ning) <> n UK UNIV professor m, -ra f universitário, -ria f. <> vt fml [clothing] vestir.

donate [də'neɪt] vt [give] doar.

donation [də'neɪʃn] n doação f.

done [dʌn] <> pp ⊳ **do**. <> adj -1. [finished] pronto(ta) -2. [cooked] assado(da) -3. [socially acceptable] socialmente aceito(ta); **it's not ∼ to insult**

your host não é de bom tom insultar seu anfitrião; **it's the ~ thing to thank your host when leaving** é de bom tom agradecer seu anfitrião ao partir. <> *excl* [to conclude deal] combinado!

donkey ['dɒŋkɪ] (*pl* **donkeys**) *n* burro *m*, -ra *f.*

donkey jacket *n UK jaqueta feita de material resistente.*

donkey work *n UK inf* maçada *f*; **to do the ~** fazer a pior parte.

donor ['dəʊnə^r] *n* doador *m*, -ra *f.*

donor card *n* carteira *f* de doador.

don't [dəʊnt] = **do not**.

doodle ['du:dl] <> *n* rabisco *m.* <> *vi* rabiscar.

doom [du:m] *n* destino *m.*

doomed [du:md] *adj* [plan, mission] condenado(da); **to be ~ to sthg/to do sthg** estar destinado(da) a algo/a fazer algo; **to be ~ to failure** estar fadado(da) ao fracasso.

door [dɔ:^r] *n* porta *f*; **the next ~ neighbour** o vizinho do lado; **the house next ~** a casa ao lado; **she showed him the ~** ela pediu para que ele saísse; **out of ~s** ao ar livre; **it's three miles ~ to ~** são três milhas de um ponto a outro; **as one ~ closes another one opens** quando se fecha uma porta, se abre uma janela; **to open the ~ to sthg** *fig* abrir as portas para algo.

doorbell ['dɔ:bel] *n* campainha *f.*

doorhandle ['dɔ:hændl] *n* maçaneta *f.*

doorknob ['dɔ:nɒb] *n* maçaneta *f.*

doorknocker ['dɔ:ˌnɒkə^r] *n* aldrava *f.*

doorman ['dɔ:mən] (*pl* -**men** [-mən]) *n* porteiro *m.*

doormat ['dɔ:mæt] *n* -**1.** [mat] capacho *m* -**2.** *fig* [person] capacho *m.*

doorstep ['dɔ:step] *n* [step] degrau *m*; **there's a cinema right on the ~** há um cinema bem próximo de casa.

doorstop ['dɔ:stɒp] *n* encosto *m* para porta.

door-to-door *adj* [salesman, selling] de porta em porta.

doorway ['dɔ:weɪ] *n* vão *m* da porta.

dope [dəʊp] <> *n* -**1.** *drugs sl* [cannabis] maconha *f* -**2.** [for athlete, horse] estimulante *m* -**3.** *inf* [fool] babaca *mf.* <> *vt* [drug] dopar.

dope test *n SPORT* exame *m* antidoping.

dopey ['dəʊpɪ] (*compar* -**ier**, *superl* -**iest**) *adj inf* -**1.** [groggy] grogue -**2.** [stupid] tonto(ta).

dormant ['dɔ:mənt] *adj* inativo(va).

dormer (window) ['dɔ:mə^r-] *n* água-furtada *f.*

dormice ['dɔ:maɪs] *pl* ▷ **dormouse**.

dormitory ['dɔ:mətrɪ] (*pl* -**ies**) *n* -**1.** [room] dormitório *m* -**2.** *US* [in university] casa *f* de estudante.

Dormobile® ['dɔ:məˌbi:l] *n* motocasa *f.*

dormouse ['dɔ:maʊs] (*pl* -**mice**) *n* rato-silvestre *m*, rata-silvestre *f.*

DOS [dɒs] (*abbr of* **disk operating system**) *n* DOS *m.*

dosage ['dəʊsɪdʒ] *n* -**1.** [amount] dosagem *f* -**2.** [on label] posologia *f.*

dose [dəʊs] <> *n* -**1.** [of medicine, drug] dose *f* -**2.** [of illness] ataque *f.* <> *vt* [person]: **to ~ sb (with sthg)** medicar alguém (com algo).

doss [dɒs] ▶ **doss down** *vi UK inf* ajeitar-se para dormir *(num lugar qualquer).*

dosser ['dɒsə^r] *n UK inf* pessoa que não tem onde

morar e dorme na rua ou em pensões baratas.

dosshouse ['dɒshaʊs, *pl* -haʊzɪz] *n UK inf* pensão *f* barata *(para os sem-teto).*

dossier ['dɒsɪeɪ] *n* dossiê *m.*

dot [dɒt] (*pt & pp* -**ted**, *cont* -**ting**) <> *n* -**1.** [on material] mancha *f* -**2.** [in punctuation] ponto *m*; **since the year ~** desde que o mundo é mundo. <> *vt* [scatter - over surface] salpicar; [- over town, area, country] espalhar.

▶ **on the dot** *adv* em ponto.

DOT (*abbr of* **Department of Transportation**) *n departamento de transportes do governo norte-americano.*

dotage ['dəʊtɪdʒ] *n*: **to be in one's ~** estar fraco(ca) da cabeça.

dotcom ['dɒtkɒm] *adj* ponto-com.

dote ▶ **dote on** *vt fus* adorar; **to ~ on sb/sthg** babar por alguém/algo.

doting ['dəʊtɪŋ] *adj* babão(ona).

dot-matrix printer *n* impressora *f* matricial.

dotted line ['dɒtɪd-] *n* linha *f* pontilhada; **to sign on the ~** *fig* assinar na linha pontilhada.

dotty ['dɒtɪ] (*compar* -**ier**, *superl* -**iest**) *adj inf* [mad] doido(da).

double ['dʌbl] <> *adj* duplo(pla). <> *adv* -**1.** [twice] dobro -**2.** [two of the same] em dobro -**3.** [in two] em dois; **to bend ~** dobrar ao meio. <> *n* -**1.** [twice the amount] dobro *m* -**2.** [of alcohol] duplo *m*, -**pla** *f* -**3.** [look-alike] cópia *f* -**4.** *CINEMA* dublê *mf.* <> *vt* [increase twofold] dobrar. <> *vi* -**1.** [increase twofold] duplicar -**2.** [serve two purposes]: **to ~ as** fazer as vezes de.

▶ **doubles** *npl TENNIS* dupla *f.*

▶ **double up** <> *vt sep*: **to be ~d up with laughter** rachar de tanto rir; **to be ~d up in pain** dobrar-se de dor. <> *vi* [bend over] curvar-se, dobrar-se.

double act *n* dupla *f* cômica.

double agent *n* agente *mf* duplo.

double-barrelled *UK*, **double-barreled** *US* [-'bærəld] *adj* -**1.** [shotgun] de dois canos -**2.** [plan, question] de duplo sentido -**3.** [name]: **a ~ surname** um sobrenome composto.

double bass [-beɪs] *n* contrabaixo *m.*

double bed *n* cama *f* de casal.

double-breasted [-'brestɪd] *adj* [jacket] trespassado(da).

double-check <> *vt* verificar duas vezes. <> *vi* verificar duas vezes.

double chin *n* papada *f.*

double-click *COMPUT* <> *n* duplo clique *m.* <> *vt* dar um duplo clique em. <> *vi* dar um duplo clique.

double cream *n UK* creme *m* muito espesso.

double-cross *vt* passar para trás.

double-dealer *n* hipócrita *mf.*

double-decker [-'dekə^r] *n* [bus] ônibus *m inv* de dois andares.

double-density *adj COMPUT* [disk] de dupla densidade.

double-dutch *n UK hum*: **to talk ~** falar grego.

double-edged *adj* -**1.** [blade] de dois gumes -**2.** *fig* [remark, compliment] ambíguo(gua).

double entendre [ˌduːblɑːˈtɑːndr] *n* duplo sentido *m*.

double fault *n* TENNIS falta *f* dupla.

double figures *npl* números *mpl* de dois algarismos.

double-glazing [-ˈgleɪzɪŋ] *n* vidros *mpl* duplos.

double-jointed [-ˈdʒɔɪntɪd] *adj* [person, joint] de articulações flexíveis.

double-park *vi* AUT estacionar em fila dupla.

double-quick *inf* ⇔ *adj* acelerado(da). ⇔ *adv* de forma acelerada.

double room *n* quarto *m* de casal.

double-sided *adj* COMPUT [disk] de dupla face.

double standards *npl* critérios *mpl* tendenciosos; **to have** ~ não medir as coisas segundo os mesmos critérios.

double take *n*: **to do a** ~ dar uma segunda olhada.

double-talk *n* linguagem *f* confusa, algaravia *f*.

double time *n* pagamento *m* em dobro.

double vision *n* visão *f* dupla.

double whammy [-ˈwæmɪ] *n* golpe *m* duplo.

doubly [ˈdʌblɪ] *adv* duplamente.

doubt [daʊt] ⇔ *n* dúvida *f*; **there is no** ~ **that** não há dúvida de que; **to cast** ~ **on sthg** lançar dúvida sobre algo; **no** ~ sem dúvida; **without (a)** ~ sem dúvida; **beyond (all)** ~ sem dúvida alguma; **in** ~ em dúvida. ⇔ *vt* -**1.** [distrust] desconfiar de -**2.** [consider unlikely] duvidar; **to** ~ **whether** OR **if** duvidar se.

doubtful [ˈdaʊtfʊl] *adj* -**1.** [unlikely] improvável -**2.** [uncertain] incerto(ta); **to be** ~ **about** OR **of sthg** estar em dúvida sobre algo -**3.** [dubious] duvidoso(sa).

doubtless [ˈdaʊtlɪs] *adv* sem dúvida.

dough [dəʊ] *n* (*U*) -**1.** [for baking] massa *f* -**2.** *inf* [money] grana *f*.

doughnut [ˈdəʊnʌt] *n* -**1.** [without hole] sonho *m* -**2.** [with hole] rosca *f*.

dour [dʊəʳ] *adj* austero(ra).

douse [daʊs] *vt* -**1.** [put out] jogar água em -**2.** [drench] encharcar.

dove¹ [dʌv] *n* [bird] pomba *f*.

dove² [dəʊv] *pt US* ⊳ **dive**.

dovecot(e) [ˈdʌvkɒt] *n* pombal *m*.

dovetail [ˈdʌvteɪl] ⇔ *vt* combinar com. ⇔ *vi* combinar.

dovetail joint *n* ensambladura *f* em cauda de andorinha.

dowager [ˈdaʊədʒəʳ] *n literary* [old lady] senhora *f* digna.

dowdy [ˈdaʊdɪ] (*compar* -**ier**, *superl* -**iest**) *adj* deselegante.

Dow-Jones average [ˌdaʊˈdʒəʊnz-] *n*: **the** ~ o índice Dow Jones.

down [daʊn] ⇔ *adv* -**1.** [downwards] para baixo; **to fall** ~ cair; ~ **here/there** aqui/ali em baixo -**2.** [along]: **I'm going** ~ **to the shops** estou indo fazer compras; **we walked** ~ **to the park** fomos até o parque -**3.** [southwards]: **we flew** ~ **from Recife to Rio** viajamos para o sul, do Recife até o Rio -**4.** [reduced, lower] baixo; **prices are coming** ~ os preços estão baixando; ~ **to the last detail** até o último detalhe -**5.** [as deposit]: **to pay £5** ~ pagar £5 de entrada -**6.** [in written form]: **get sthg** ~ **in writing** conseguir algo por escrito; **write it** ~ tome nota. ⇔ *prep* -**1.** [downwards] para baixo; **they ran** ~ **the hill** eles correram morro abaixo -**2.** [along]: **we walked** ~ **the street** caminhamos pela rua. ⇔ *adj* -**1.** *inf* [depressed] desanimado(da) -**2.** [behind] por trás -**3.** [lower in amount] mais baixo(xa) -**4.** [not in operation] fora de operação. ⇔ *n* -**1.** (*U*) [feathers, hair] penugem *f* -**2.** *US* SPORT tempo *m*. ⇔ *vt* -**1.** [knock over] abater -**2.** [swallow] engolir.

◆ **Downs** *npl UK*: **the Downs** *chapada ao sul da Inglaterra*.

◆ **down with** *excl*: ~ **with the king!** abaixo o rei!

down-and-out ⇔ *adj* sem futuro. ⇔ *n* mendigo *m*, -ga *f*.

down-at-heel *adj esp UK* desleixado(da).

downbeat [ˈdaʊnbiːt] *adj inf* [gloomy] sombrio(bria).

downcast [ˈdaʊnkɑːst] *adj fml* -**1.** [person] abatido(da) -**2.** [eyes] cabisbaixo(xa).

downer [ˈdaʊnəʳ] *n inf* -**1.** [drug] calmante *m* -**2.** [depressing event or situation] droga *f*; **to be on a** ~ estar de baixo-astral.

downfall [ˈdaʊnfɔːl] *n* -**1.** (*U*) [ruin] queda *f* -**2.** [cause of ruin] ruína *f*.

downgrade [ˈdaʊngreɪd] *vt* rebaixar.

downhearted [ˌdaʊnˈhɑːtɪd] *adj* desacorçoado(da).

downhill [ˌdaʊnˈhɪl] ⇔ *adj* -**1.** [path] íngreme -**2.** *fig* [easy] canja; **it's** ~ **all the way now** daqui pra frente, é canja -**3.** [skier]: **he's a** ~ **skier** ele esquia morro abaixo. ⇔ *adv* -**1.** [downwards] para baixo -**2.** *fig* [from bad to worse] de mau a pior. ⇔ *n* SKIING descida *f*.

Downing Street [ˈdaʊnɪŋ-] *n* rua no centro de Londres onde fica a residência oficial do primeiro-ministro inglês, governo *m* britânico.

DOWNING STREET

Situada no centro de Londres, e fechada ao público, a *Downing Street* abriga, no número 10, a residência oficial do primeiro-ministro britânico, e, no número 11, a do ministro das finanças. Por isso, a expressão é utilizada com freqüência para designar o governo britânico como um todo.

---

download [ˌdaʊnˈləʊd] *vt* COMPUT baixar, fazer download.

downmarket ⇔ *adj* barato(ta), de baixa qualidade. ⇔ *adv*: **to go** ~ produzir mais barato com qualidade inferior.

down payment *n* entrada *f*.

downplay [ˈdaʊnpleɪ] *vt* minimizar.

downpour [ˈdaʊnpɔːʳ] *n* aguaceiro *m*.

downright [ˈdaʊnraɪt] ⇔ *adj* [lie, fool] inequívoco(ca). ⇔ *adv* completamente.

downside [ˈdaʊnsaɪd] *n* [disadvantage] desvantagem *f*.

downsize ⇔ *vt* [workforce] reduzir o número

de. ◇ *vi* [subj: company] reduzir o número de empregados.

Down's syndrome *n (U)* síndrome *f* de Down.

downstairs [,daʊn'steəz] ◇ *adj* do andar de baixo. ◇ *adv*: **to come** ~ vir para *or* andar de baixo; **to go** ~ ir para *or* andar de baixo; **to live** ~ morar no andar de baixo.

downstream [,daʊn'stri:m] *adv* a jusante, rio abaixo.

downtime ['daʊntaɪm] *n* tempo *m* ocioso.

down-to-earth *adj* realista.

downtown [,daʊn'taʊn] *esp US* ◇ *adj* do centro; ~ **New York** Nova York central. ◇ *adv*: **to go** ~ ir ao centro; **to live** ~ viver no centro.

downtrodden ['daʊn,trɒdn] *adj* oprimido(da).

downturn ['daʊntɜ:n] *n* decréscimo *m*; ~ **in sthg** queda em algo.

down under *adv* na *or* para Austrália/Nova Zelândia.

downward ['daʊnwəd] ◇ *adj* **-1.** [towards ground] para baixo **-2.** [decreasing] descendente. ◇ *adv* *US* = **downwards**.

downwards ['daʊnwədz] *adv* **-1.** [look, move] para baixo; **the overall trend is** ~ a tendência geral é de baixa **-2.** [in hierarchy] para baixo.

downwind [,daʊn'wɪnd] *adv* a favor do vento.

dowry ['daʊərɪ] (*pl* **-ies**) *n* dote *m*.

doz. (*abbr of* **dozen**) dz.

doze [dəʊz] ◇ *n* soneca *f*; **to have a** ~ tirar uma soneca. ◇ *vi* dormitar.

◆ **doze off** *vi* cochilar.

dozen ['dʌzn] ◇ *num adj* dúzia *f*. ◇ *n* [twelve] dúzia *f*; **50p a** ~ 50p a dúzia.

◆ **dozens** *npl inf*: ~ **s of** um montão de.

dozy ['dəʊzɪ] (*compar* **-ier**, *superl* **-iest**) *adj* **-1.** [sleepy] sonolento(ta) **-2.** *UK inf* [stupid] retardado(da).

DP (*abbr of* **data processing**) *n* PD *m*.

DPhil [,di:'fɪl] (*abbr of* **Doctor of Philosophy**) *n* (*titular de*) doutorado em ciências humanas.

DPP (*abbr of* **Director of Public Prosecutions**) *n* fiscal geral do estado na Grã-Bretanha.

DPT (*abbr of* **diphtheria, pertussis, tetanus**) *n* (vacina *f*) tríplice *f*.

Dr (*abbr of* **Doctor**) Dr. (Dra.).

Dr. (*abbr of* **Drive**) *usado em nomes de rua na Grã-Bretanha*.

drab [dræb] (*compar* **-ber**, *superl* **-best**) *adj* **-1.** [buildings] sombrio(bria) **-2.** [colour, garment] apagado(da) **-3.** [life] monótono(na).

draconian [drə'kəʊnjən] *adj fml* draconiano(na).

draft [drɑ:ft] ◇ *n* **-1.** [early version] rascunho *m* **-2.** [money order] ordem *f* de pagamento **-3.** *US MIL*: **the** ~ o destacamento **-4.** *US* = **draught**. ◇ *vt* **-1.** [write] rascunhar, fazer um rascunho de **-2.** *US MIL* recrutar **-3.** [transfer] deslocar.

draft dodger [-'dɒdʒər] *n US* o que tenta fugir do serviço militar.

draftee [,drɑ:f'ti:] *n US* recruta *m*.

draftsman *n US* = **draughtsman**.

draftsmanship *n US* = **draughtsmanship**.

drafty *adj US* = **draughty**.

drag [dræg] (*pt* & *pp* **-ged**, *cont* **-ging**) ◇ *vt* **-1.** [gen] arrastar **-2.** [search] dragar. ◇ *vi* **-1.** [trail] arrastar

-2. [pass slowly] arrastar-se. ◇ *n* **-1.** *inf* [bore] chatice *f*; **what a** ~! que pé no saco! **-2.** *inf* [on cigarette] tragada *f* **-3.** [air resistance] resistência *f* aerodinâmica **-4.** (*U*) [cross-dressing]: **in** ~ vestido como mulher.

◆ **drag down** *vt sep fig* [debase]: **to** ~ **sb down** levar alguém para o buraco.

◆ **drag in(to)** *vt sep* [involve] meter em; **don't** ~ **me into this!** não me meta nisso!

◆ **drag on** *vi* arrastar-se.

◆ **drag out** *vt sep* **-1.** [protract] prolongar-se em demasia **-2.** [extract]: **to** ~ **sthg out of sb** arrancar algo de alguém.

dragnet ['drægnet] *n* **-1.** [net] rede *f* de arrasto **-2.** *fig* [to catch criminal] batida *f*.

dragon ['drægən] *n* **-1.** [beast] dragão *m* **-2.** *inf* [woman] bruxa *f*.

dragonfly ['drægnflaɪ] (*pl* **-ies**) *n* libélula *f*.

dragoon [drə'gu:n] ◇ *n* dragão *m*. ◇ *vt*: **to** ~ **sb into doing sthg** forçar alguém a fazer algo.

drag racing *n (U)* corrida *f* de carros envenenados.

dragster ['drægstər] *n* carro *m* envenenado.

drain [dreɪn] ◇ *n* **-1.** [pipe] cano *m* de esgoto; **to go down the** ~ ir para o brejo; [grating in street] bueiro *m* **-2.** [depletion]: ~ **on sthg** sorvedouro de algo; **it's a** ~ **on my energy** esgota todas as minhas forças. ◇ *vt* **-1.** [remove water from] drenar **-2.** [deplete] esgotar, exaurir **-3.** [drink, glass] beber até o fim. ◇ *vi* **-1.** [dry] escoar **-2.** [disappear] desaparecer.

drainage ['dreɪnɪdʒ] *n* **-1.** [pipes, ditches] esgoto *m* **-2.** [draining] drenagem *f*.

draining board *UK* ['dreɪnɪŋ-], **drainboard** *US* ['dreɪnbɔ:rd] *n* escorredor *m* de louça.

drainpipe ['dreɪnpaɪp] *n* cano *m* de esgoto.

drake [dreɪk] *n* pato *m* (macho).

dram [dræm] *n* [of whisky] trago *m*.

drama ['drɑ:mə] ◇ *n* **-1.** [play, excitement] drama *f* **-2.** (*U*) [art] teatro *m*. ◇ *comp* de teatro.

dramatic [drə'mætɪk] *adj* **-1.** [concerned with theatre] teatral **-2.** [exciting] dramático(ca) **-3.** [sudden, noticeable] drástico(ca).

dramatically [drə'mætɪklɪ] *adv* **-1.** [noticeably] drasticamente **-2.** [theatrically] teatralmente.

dramatist ['dræmətɪst] *n* dramaturgo *m*, -ga *f*.

dramatization [,dræmətaɪ'zeɪʃn] *n* [for theatre, film, television] dramatização *f*.

dramatize, -ise ['dræmətaɪz] *vt* **-1.** [rewrite as play] dramatizar **-2.** *pej* [make exciting] tornar dramático(ca).

drank [dræŋk] *pt* ▷ **drink**.

drape [dreɪp] *vt* colocar suavemente; **to be** ~ **d with** *or* **in sthg** estar/ser coberto(ta) com algo.

◆ **drapes** *npl US* cortinas *fpl*.

draper ['dreɪpər] *n*: ~ **'s (shop)** loja *f* de cortinas e tecidos.

drastic ['dræstɪk] *adj* drástico(ca).

drastically ['dræstɪklɪ] *adv* drasticamente.

draught *UK*, **draft** *US* [drɑ:ft] *n* **-1.** [air current] corrente *f* **-2.** *literary* [gulp] golfada *f* **-3.** [from barrel]: **on** ~ [beer] de barril.

◆ **draughts** *n UK* damas *fpl*.

draught beer n UK chope m.

draughtboard ['drɑ:ftbɔ:d] n UK tabuleiro m de damas.

draughtsman UK, **draftsman** US ['drɑ:ftsmən] (pl -men [-mən]) n [of technical drawings] desenhista m industrial.

draughtsmanship UK, **draftsmanship** US ['drɑ:ftsmənʃip] n -1. [of artist] habilidade f para o desenho -2. [of work] desenho m industrial.

draughtswoman UK, **draftswoman** US (pl -women [-wimin]) n [of technical drawings] desenhista f industrial.

draughty UK (compar -ier, superl -iest), **drafty** US (compar -ier, superl -iest) ['drɑ:fti] adj pouco protegido(da) do frio.

draw [drɔ:] (pt drew, pp drawn) <> vt -1. [sketch] desenhar -2. [pull] puxar; to ~ the curtains [open] abrir as cortinas; [close] fechar as cortinas -3. [breath] inalar -4. [pull out] sacar -5. [arrive at, form] chegar a -6. [formulate] estabelecer -7. [attract] atrair; to be OR feel drawn to ser/sentir-se atraído(da) por; to ~ sb's attention to sthg chamar a atenção de alguém para algo. <> vi -1. [sketch] esboçar -2. [move]: to ~ near aproximar-se; to ~ away afastar-se; to ~ to an end OR a close tender para um final -3. SPORT empatar; to ~ with sb empatar com alguém. <> n -1. SPORT [result] empate m -2. [lottery] sorteio m -3. [attraction] atração f.
 ➡ **draw in** vi [days] declinar.
 ➡ **draw into** vt sep: to ~ sb into sthg envolver alguém em algo.
 ➡ **draw on** vt fus -1. = draw upon -2. [smoke] tragar.
 ➡ **draw out** vt sep -1. [encourage] desinibir -2. [prolong] prolongar -3. [withdraw] sacar.
 ➡ **draw up** <> vt sep [draft] redigir, preparar. <> vi [stop] parar.
 ➡ **draw upon** vt fus recorrer a.

drawback ['drɔ:bæk] n inconveniente m.

drawbridge ['drɔ:brɪdʒ] n ponte f levadiça.

drawer [drɔ:ʳ] n [in desk, chest] gaveta f.

drawing ['drɔ:ɪŋ] n -1. [picture] desenho m, croqui m -2. (U) [skill, act] ato m de desenhar.

drawing board n prancheta f de desenho; **back to the ~!** inf de volta ao ponto de partida!

drawing pin n UK percevejo m.

drawing room n [living room] sala-de-estar f.

drawl [drɔ:l] <> n fala f arrastada. <> vt arrastar. <> vi falar de forma arrastada.

drawn [drɔ:n] <> pp ▷ draw. <> adj -1. [curtain, blind] fechado(da) -2. [face, person] abatido(da).

drawn-out adj esticado(da).

drawstring ['drɔ:strɪŋ] n cordão m.

dread [dred] <> n (U) medo m, pavor m. <> vt temer; to ~ doing sthg ter medo de fazer algo; I ~ to think tenho medo de pensar.

dreaded ['dredɪd] adj [feared] temido(da).

dreadful ['dredful] adj -1. [terrible] terrível -2. [unpleasant] desagradável -3. [ill] horrível -4. [embarrassed] envergonhado(da) -5. [poor] fraco(ca) -6. [for emphasis] horroroso(sa).

dreadfully ['dredfulɪ] adv -1. [badly] terrivelmente -2. [extremely] extremamente.

dreadlocks ['dredlɒksl npl cabelo m rastafári.

dream [dri:m] (pt & pp -ed OR dreamt) <> n -1. [during sleep] sonho m; **bad** ~ pesadelo m -2. [aspiration] sonho m; **to be beyond one's wildest** ~**s** ser muito melhor do que o esperado. <> adj almejado(da). <> vt [during sleep]: **to** ~ **(that)** sonhar que; I never ~ ed this would happen jamais imaginei que isso pudesse acontecer. <> vi -1. [during sleep] sonhar; **to** ~ **of** OR **about sthg** sonhar com algo; I wouldn't ~ of it fig nem pensar, de maneira nenhuma -2. [aspire]: **to** ~ **of sthg/of doing sthg** sonhar com algo/em fazer algo.
 ➡ **dream up** vt sep bolar.

dreamer ['dri:məʳ] n [unrealistic person] sonhador m, -ra f.

dreamily ['dri:mɪlɪ] adv como nos sonhos.

dreamlike ['dri:mlaɪk] adj de sonho.

dreamt [dremt] pt & pp ▷ dream.

dream world n mundo m de sonhos.

dreamy ['dri:mɪ] (compar -ier, superl -iest) adj -1. [look, smile] distraído(da), sonhador(ra) -2. [music, feeling] sentimental.

dreary ['drɪərɪ] (compar -ier, superl -iest) adj -1. [gloomy, depressing] sombrio(a) -2. [dull, boring] chato(ta).

dredge [dredʒ] vt [lake, harbour, river] dragar.
 ➡ **dredge up** vt sep -1. [with dredger] dragar -2. fig [from past] trazer à tona.

dredger ['dredʒəʳ] n [ship, machine] draga f.

dregs [dregz] npl -1. [of liquid] borra f -2. fig [of society] ralé f.

drench [drentʃ] vt encharcar; **to be** ~**ed in** OR **with sthg** estar encharcado(da) de algo.

Dresden ['drezdən] n Dresden; **in** ~ em Dresden.

dress [dres] <> n -1. [frock] vestido m -2. [type of clothing] roupa f. <> vt -1. [clothe] vestir; **to be** ~**ed** estar vestido(da); **to be** ~**ed in** estar vestido(da) de; **to get** ~**ed** vestir-se -2. [bandage] fazer curativo em -3. CULIN temperar. <> vi vestir-se.
 ➡ **dress up** <> vt sep -1. [in costume] disfarçar-se -2. [in best clothes] vestir-se elegantemente -3. [in formal clothes] vestir-se a rigor -4. fig [embellish] enfeitar. <> vi -1. [in costume] fantasiar-se -2. [in best clothes] vestir-se elegantemente -3. [in formal clothes] vestir-se a rigor.

dressage ['dresɑ:ʒ] n (U) adestramento m.

dress circle n THEATRE balcão m nobre.

dresser ['dresəʳ] n -1. [for dishes] aparador m -2. US [chest of drawers] cômoda f -3. [person]: **to be a smart** ~ vestir-se bem -4. THEATRE camareiro m, -ra f.

dressing ['dresɪŋ] n -1. [bandage] curativo m -2. [for salad] tempero m, molho m -3. US [for turkey etc] molho m.

dressing gown n -1. [man's] roupão m -2. [woman's] robe f.

dressing room n -1. SPORT vestiário m -2. THEATRE camarim m.

dressing table n penteadeira f.

dressmaker ['dres,meɪkəʳ] n costureiro m, -ra f.

dressmaking ['dres,meɪkɪŋ] n (U) costura f.

dress rehearsal n THEATRE ensaio m geral.

dress shirt n camisa f social.

dressy ['dresɪ] (*compar* -**ier**, *superl* -**iest**) *adj* [smart] chique.

drew [dru:] *pt* ▷ **draw**.

dribble ['drɪbl] ◇ *n* -**1**. *(U)* [of saliva] filete *m* -**2**. [of other liquid] gota *f.* ◇ *vt* -**1**. *SPORT* [ball] driblar -**2**. [liquid] pingar. ◇ *vi* -**1**. [drool] babar -**2**. [trickle] derramar.

dribs [drɪbz] *npl*: **in ~ and drabs** aos poucos.

dried [draɪd] ◇ *pt & pp* ▷ **dry**. ◇ *adj* -**1**. [powdered] em pó -**2**. [fruit, herbs, flowers] seco(ca).

dried fruit *n (U)* fruta *f* seca.

dried-up *adj* seco(ca).

drier ['draɪə^r] *n* = **dryer**.

drift [drɪft] ◇ *n* -**1**. [movement, trend] tendência *f* -**2**. [of current] fluxo *m* -**3**. [geol] pressão *f* -**4**. [of people] curso *m* -**5**. [of snow, leaves, sand] monte *m* -**6**. [meaning] sentido *m*; **to get the general ~** pegar a idéia geral. ◇ *vi* -**1**. [boat] estar à deriva -**2**. [snow, sand, leaves] acumular-se -**3**. [person]: **they're ~ing towards bankruptcy** eles estão indo a caminho da falência; **to ~ into marriage** acabar se casando; **to ~ apart** acabar se afastando.

◆ **drift off** *vi* [fall asleep] cair de sono.

drifter ['drɪftə^r] *n* [person] nômade *mf*.

driftwood ['drɪftwʊd] *n (U)* madeira *f* flutuante.

drill [drɪl] ◇ *n* -**1**. [tool] furadeira *f* -**2**. [industrial] perfuradora *f* -**3**. [dentist's] broca *f* -**4**. [exercise, training] treinamento *m*. ◇ *vt* -**1**. [metal, wood, hole] perfurar *f* -**2**. [instruct] instruir; **to ~ sthg into sb** ensinar algo a alguém *(repetindo a lição regularmente)*. ◇ *vi* furar; **to ~ into sthg** penetrar em algo; **to ~ for sthg** procurar algo *(perfurando com broca)*.

drilling platform ['drɪlɪŋ-] *n* plataforma *f* de perfuração.

drily ['draɪlɪ] *adv* = **dryly**.

drink [drɪŋk] (*pt* **drank**, *pp* **drunk**) ◇ *n* -**1**. [non-alcoholic beverage] bebida *f* -**2**. [alcoholic beverage] bebida *f* alcoólica; **to have a ~** tomar um drinque -**3**. *(U)* [alcohol] bebida *f.* ◇ *vt* beber. ◇ *vi* beber; **to ~ to sb/sb's success** brindar a alguém/ao sucesso de alguém.

drinkable ['drɪŋkəbl] *adj* -**1**. [safe to drink] potável -**2**. [tasty] saboroso(sa).

drink-driving *UK*, **drunk-driving** *US n (U)* ato *m* de dirigir bêbado, -da *f*.

drinker ['drɪŋkə^r] *n* -**1**. [of alcohol] beberrão *m*, -rona *f* -**2**. [of tea, coffee]: **he's a great tea/coffee ~** ele gosta muito de tomar chá/café.

drinking ['drɪŋkɪŋ] ◇ *adj*: **I'm not a ~ man** não sou um homem que bebe; **~ laws** leis de consumo de bebida alcoólica. ◇ *n*: **to go ~** ir beber; **heavy ~** embriagamento.

drinking companion *n* companheiro *m*, -ra *f* de bebida.

drinking fountain *n* bebedouro *m*.

drinking-up time *n UK inf tempo concedido nos bares para acabar os drinks antes de fechar*.

drinking water ['drɪŋkɪŋ-] *n (U)* água *f* potável.

drip [drɪp] (*pt & pp* -**ped**, *cont* -**ping**) ◇ *n* -**1**. [drop] gota *f* -**2**. *MED* aparelho *m* de soro -**3**. *inf* [wimp] sonso *m*, -sa *f.* ◇ *vt* pingar. ◇ *vi* -**1**. [gen] pingar -**2**. [nose] escorrer -**3**. [person]: **to be ~ping with** [sweat, blood] estar encharcado(da) de; [diamonds, furs] *fig* estar coberto(ta) de.

drip-dry *adj* que não amarrota ao secar.

drip-feed ◇ *n* alimentação *f* por conta-gotas. ◇ *vt* alimentar por conta-gotas.

dripping ['drɪpɪŋ] ◇ *adj* -**1**. [person, clothes, hair]: **~ (wet)** encharcado(da) -**2**. [tap] que pinga. ◇ *n CULIN* [from meat] banha *f (de carne)*.

drive [draɪv] (*pt* **drove**, *pp* **driven**) ◇ *n* -**1**. [journey] passeio *m*, volta *f* de carro -**2**. [urge] ímpulso *m* -**3**. [campaign] campanha *f* -**4**. *(U)* [energy] ímpeto *m* -**5**. [road to house] caminho *m* -**6**. *SPORT* [stroke] tacada *f* -**7**. *US AUT* [in automatic car] transmissão *f* automática. ◇ *vt* -**1**. [vehicle] dirigir; [passenger] levar *(de carro)* -**2**. *TECH* [operate] operar -**3**. [chase] seguir -**4**. [motivate] motivar -**5**. [force]: **to ~ sb to sthg/to do sthg** levar alguém a algo/a fazer algo; **to ~ sb mad** *OR* **crazy** [make insane] deixar alguém louco(ca) *OR* maluco(ca); [irritate] deixar alguém furioso(sa) -**6**. [hammer] bater -**7**. *SPORT* [hit] rebater. ◇ *vi AUT* -**1**. [driver] dirigir -**2**. [travel by car] viajar.

◆ **drive at** *vt fus* querer dizer, insinuar.

◆ **drive out** *vt sep* fazer sair.

drive-in *esp US* ◇ *adj* drive-in. ◇ *n* -**1**. [restaurant] drive-in *m* -**2**. [cinema] autocine *m*.

drivel ['drɪvl] *n inf* bobagem *f*.

driven ['drɪvn] *pp* ▷ **drive**.

driver ['draɪvə^r] *n* -**1**. [of vehicle] motorista *mf* -**2**. *COMPUT* driver *m*.

driver's license *n US* = **driving licence**.

drive shaft *n* eixo *m* de transmissão.

driveway ['draɪvweɪ] *n* acesso *m*.

driving ['draɪvɪŋ] ◇ *adj* [rain, wind] forte; **~ rain** chuva *f* torrencial. ◇ *n (U)* direção *f*.

driving force *n* força *f* motriz.

driving instructor *n* instrutor *m*, -ra *f* de direção.

driving lesson *n* aula *f* de direção.

driving licence *UK*, **driver's license** *US n* carteira *f* de motorista.

driving mirror *n* (espelho *m*) retrovisor *m*.

driving school *n* auto-escola *f*.

driving test *n* exame *m* de direção.

drizzle ['drɪzl] ◇ *n* garoa *f*, chuvisco *m*. ◇ *v impers* garoar, chuviscar.

drizzly ['drɪzlɪ] (*compar* -**ier**, *superl* -**iest**) *adj* chuvoso(sa); **~ rain** garoa *f* fina.

droll [drəʊl] *adj* engraçado(da).

dromedary ['drɒmədrɪ] (*pl* -**ies**) *n* dromedário *m*.

drone [drəʊn] ◇ *n* -**1**. [sound] zunido *m* -**2**. [bee] zangão *m*. ◇ *vi* zunir.

◆ **drone on** *vi* falar de forma monótona; **to ~ on about sthg** falar de forma monótona sobre algo.

drool [dru:l] *vi* -**1**. [dribble] babar -**2**. *fig* [admire]: **to ~ over sb/sthg** babar por alguém/algo.

droop [dru:p] *vi* -**1**. [hang down - shoulders] encurvar-se; [- head] inclinar-se; [- eyelids] fechar-se; [- flowers] murchar-se -**2**. *fig* [weaken, flag] desanimar-se.

drop [drɒp] (*pt & pp* -**ped**, *cont* -**ping**) ◇ *n* -**1**. [of liquid - water, blood, rain] gota *f*; [- tea, coffee, milk] gole *m*; [- alcohol] dose *f* - **2.** [sweet] bala *f* - **3.** [decrease] queda *f*; ~ **in sthg** queda de algo - **4.** [vertical distance] descida *f*. ◇ *vt* - **1.** [let fall - gen] deixar cair; [- bombs] lançar; [- stitch]: **she ~ped a stitch** escapou um ponto - **2.** [decrease, lower] reduzir - **3.** [voice] baixar - **4.** [leave, abandon] deixar - **5.** [leave out] excluir - **6.** [hint, remark] lançar - **7.** TENNIS [lose] perder - **8.** [write]: **to ~ sb a line** OR **note** escrever a alguém umas linhas OR um bilhete. ◇ *vi* - **1.** [fall] cair; **to ~ to one's knees** ajoelhar-se; **~ dead!** vai tomar banho! - **2.** [fall] baixar - **3.** [wind, attendance] diminuir.

◆ **drops** *npl* MED gotas *fpl*.

◆ **drop by** *vi inf* dar um pulo *(como visita)*.

◆ **drop in** *vi inf* passar na casa de; **to ~ in on sb** passar na casa de alguém.

◆ **drop off** ◇ *vt sep* deixar. ◇ *vi* - **1.** [fall asleep] cair no sono - **2.** [grow less] diminuir.

◆ **drop out** *vi* [withdraw] retirar-se; **to ~ out of** OR **from sthg** desligar-se de algo.

drop-in centre *n centro mantido pelos serviços sociais, pela igreja, etc., que as pessoas podem freqüentar se desejarem.*

droplet ['drɒplɪt] *n* gotícula *f*.

dropout ['drɒpaʊt] *n* - **1.** [from society] marginalizado *m*, -da *f* - **2.** [from university] pessoa *f* que largou os estudos.

dropper ['drɒpəʳ] *n* conta-gotas *m inv*.

droppings ['drɒpɪŋz] *npl* excremento *m (de animais)*.

drop shot *n* TENNIS deixada *f*.

dross [drɒs] *n* - **1.** TECH [waste material] refugo *m* - **2.** *fig* [rubbish] porcaria *f*.

drought [draʊt] *n* seca *f*.

drove [drəʊv] ◇ *pt* ▷ **drive**. ◇ *n* [of people] multidão *f*.

drown [draʊn] ◇ *vt* - **1.** [kill] afogar - **2.** [sound]: **to ~ sb/sthg (out)** abafar alguém/algo. ◇ *vi* afogar-se.

drowsy ['draʊzɪ] *(compar* -**ier,** *superl* -**iest)** *adj* [person] sonolento(ta).

drudge [drʌdʒ] *n* escravo *m*, -va *f* do trabalho.

drudgery ['drʌdʒərɪ] *n (U)* trabalho *m* pesado.

drug [drʌg] *(pt & pp* -**ged,** *cont* -**ging)** ◇ *n* - **1.** [medication] remédio *m* - **2.** [illegal substance] droga *f*. ◇ *vt* - **1.** [person, animal] drogar - **2.** [food, drink] adicionar droga a.

drug abuse *n (U)* abuso *m* de drogas.

drug addict *n* drogado *m*, -da *f*, viciado *m*, -da *f* em drogas.

drug addiction *n (U)* vício *m* em drogas, toxicomania *f*.

drug dealer *n* traficante *mf* de drogas.

druggist ['drʌgɪst] *n* US farmacêutico *m*, -ca *f*.

drugstore ['drʌgstɔːʳ] *n* US farmácia *f*, drogaria *f*.

druid ['druːɪd] *n* druida *m*.

drum [drʌm] *(pt & pp* -**med,** *cont* -**ming)** ◇ *n* - **1.** [instrument] tambor *m* - **2.** [container, cylinder] barril *m*. ◇ *vt* [fingers] tamborilar. ◇ *vi* - **1.** [on drums] tocar - **2.** [rain, fingers] tamborilar - **3.** [hooves] bater.

◆ **drums** *npl* [set of drums] bateria *f*.

◆ **drum into** *vt sep*: **to ~ sthg into sb** incutir algo em alguém.

◆ **drum up** *vt sep* angariar.

drumbeat ['drʌmbiːt] *n* rufo *m (de tambores)*.

drum brake *n* freio *m* de tambor.

drummer ['drʌməʳ] *n* baterista *mf*.

drumming ['drʌmɪŋ] *n* - **1.** [of drums] rufar *m* - **2.** [of rain, fingers] tamborilo *m* - **3.** [of hooves] batida *f*.

drum roll *n* rufar *m* de tambor.

drumstick ['drʌmstɪk] *n* - **1.** [for drum] baqueta *f* - **2.** [food] coxa *f*.

drunk [drʌŋk] ◇ *pp* ▷ **drink**. ◇ *adj* - **1.** [on alcohol] bêbado(da); **to get ~** embebedar-se; **to be charged with being ~ and disorderly** JUR ser acusado(da) de estar embriagado(do) - **2.** *fig* [excited, carried away]: **to be ~ with** OR **on sthg** estar encantado(da) com algo. ◇ *n* bêbado *m*, -da *f*.

drunkard ['drʌŋkəd] *n* beberrão *m*, -rona *f*.

drunk-driving *n* US = **drink-driving**.

drunken ['drʌŋkn] *adj* - **1.** [person] bêbado(da) - **2.** [state, event] = **de bêbado**.

drunken driving *n* = **drink-driving**.

drunkenness ['drʌŋkənnɪs] *n (U)* embriaguez *f*.

dry [draɪ] *(compar* -**ier,** *superl* -**iest,** *pt & pp* dried) ◇ *adj* - **1.** [gen] seco(ca) - **2.** [climate] árido(da) - **3.** [sense of humour] sarcástico(ca) - **4.** [tedious] monótono(na).

◇ *vt & vi* secar.

◆ **dry out** ◇ *vt sep* secar completamente. ◇ *vi* [get dry - gen] secar; [- person] secar-se.

◆ **dry up** ◇ *vt sep* [dishes] secar. ◇ *vi* - **1.** [gen] secar - **2.** [supplies, inspiration] esgotar-se - **3.** [actor, speaker] calar-se.

dry-clean *vt* lavar a seco.

dry cleaner *n*: **~'s** tinturaria *f*.

dry cleaning *n* [work, service] lavagem *f* a seco.

dry dock *n* dique *m* seco.

dryer ['draɪəʳ] *n* [for clothes] secadora *f*.

dry ginger *n (U)* ginger ale *m*.

dry goods *npl* artigos *mpl* de armarinho.

dry ice *n (U)* gelo-seco *m*.

dry land *n* terra *f* firme.

dryly ['draɪlɪ] *adv* [wryly] secamente.

dryness ['draɪnɪs] *n (U)* - **1.** [lack of water] aridez *f* - **2.** [wryness] secura *f* - **3.** [tedium] monotonia *f*.

dry rot *n (U)* apodrecimento *m* da madeira *(de casa)*.

dry run *n* [practice] ensaio *m*.

dry ski slope *n* rampa *f* de esqui artificial.

dry-stone wall *n* parede *f* de pedra.

DSc *(abbr of* **Doctor of Science)** *n (titular de)* doutorado em ciências.

DST *(abbr of* **daylight saving time)** *horário de verão nos Estados Unidos.*

DTI *(abbr of* **Department of Trade and Industry)** *ministério britânico da indústria e do comércio,* ≃ MDIC *m*.

DTLR *(abbr of* **Department for Transport, Local Government and the Regions)** *n departamento dos transportes do governo britânico e dos governos locais.*

DTP *(abbr of* **desktop publishing)** *n* DTP *f*.

DTs [ˌdiːˈtiːz] *(abbr of* **delirium tremens)** *npl fam*: **to have the ~** estar em crise de abstinência.

dual ['djuːəl] *adj* duplo(pla).

dual carriageway *n* UK pista *f* dupla.

dual control *n* controle *m* duplo.

dual nationality *n* dupla nacionalidade *f.*

dual-purpose *adj* que tem dupla finalidade.

Dubai [,duː'baɪ] *n* Dubai.

dubbed [dʌbd] *adj* **-1.** CINEMA dublado(da) **-2.** [nicknamed] apelidado(da).

dubious ['djuːbjəs] *adj* **-1.** [suspect, questionable] duvidoso(sa) **-2.** [uncertain, undecided]: **to be ~ about doing sthg** estar indeciso(sa) sobre fazer algo.

Dublin ['dʌblɪn] *n* Dublin; **in ~** em Dublin.

Dublin Bay prawn *n* camarão *m* à Dublin Bay.

Dubliner ['dʌblɪnər] *n* dublinense *mf.*

duchess ['dʌtʃɪs] *n* duquesa *f.*

duchy ['dʌtʃɪ] *(pl* **-ies)** *n* ducado *m.*

duck [dʌk] <> *n* **-1.** [bird] pato *m*, -ta *f*; **to take to sthg like a ~ to water** tirar algo de letra; **like water off a ~'s back** sem nenhum efeito **-2.** *(U)* [food] pato *m.* <> *vt* **-1.** [lower] curvar **-2.** [try to avoid] esquivar-se de; **to ~ the issue** evitar a questão **-3.** [submerge] mergulhar. <> *vi* **-1.** [lower head] curvar-se **-2.** [move down quickly] abaixar-se.
◆ duck out *vi*: **to ~ out (of sthg/of doing sthg)** safar-se (de algo/de fazer algo).

duckling ['dʌklɪŋ] *n* **-1.** [animal] patinho *m*, -nha *f* **-2.** [food] pato *m* novo.

duct [dʌkt] *n* **-1.** [pipe - heating] tubo *m*; [- water] canal *m* **-2.** ANAT ducto *m.*

dud [dʌd] <> *adj* **-1.** [banknote, coin, cheque] falso(sa) **-2.** [machine, idea] imprestável **-3.** [bomb, shell, bullet] que falhou. <> *n* negação *f*; **to be a ~ at sthg** [person] ser uma negação em algo; **to be a ~** [banknote, cheque] não ter fundos; [bomb, shell, bullet] não prestar.

dude [djuːd] *n* US *inf* [man] cara *m.*

dude ranch *n* US rancho *m* para turistas.

due [djuː] <> *adj* **-1.** [expected] previsto(ta); **she's ~ back shortly** espera-se que ela volte logo; **when is the next train ~?** quando chega o próximo trem? **-2.** [proper] devido(da); **in ~ course** no tempo devido **-3.** [owed, owing]: **the rent is ~** o aluguel venceu; **she's ~ a pay rise** ela deve ganhar um aumento de salário; **how much are you ~?** quanto te devem? <> *n* [deserts] direito *m*; **to give him his ~, ...** para lhe fazer justiça, ... <> *adv* exatamente; **~ north** bem ao norte.
◆ dues *npl* direitos *mpl.*
◆ due to *prep* devido a.

due date *n* [data *f* de] vencimento *m.*

duel ['djuːəl] *n* duelo *m.*

duet [djuː'et] *n* dueto *m.*

duff [dʌf] *adj* UK *inf* inútil.
◆ duff up *vt sep* UK *inf* dar uma surra em.

duffel bag ['dʌfl-] *n* mochila *f.*

duffel coat ['dʌfl-] *n* casaco *m* grosso *(com capuz).*

duffle bag ['dʌfl-] *n* = **duffel bag.**

duffle coat ['dʌfl-] *n* = **duffel coat.**

dug [dʌg] *pt & pp* ▷ **dig.**

dugout ['dʌgaʊt] *n* **-1.** [canoe] canoa *f* **-2.** SPORT fosso *m.*

duke [djuːk] *n* duque *m.*

dull [dʌl] <> *adj* **-1.** [boring] entediante **-2.** [colour,

light] opaco(ca) **-3.** [day, weather] nublado(da) **-4.** [thud, boom] surdo(da) **-5.** [ache, pain] incômodo(da). <> *vt* **-1.** [deaden - pain] aliviar; [- senses, memory] enfraquecer; [- pleasure] diminuir **-2.** [make less bright] embaciar.

duly ['djuːlɪ] *adv* **-1.** [properly] devidamente **-2.** [as expected] como era de se esperar.

dumb [dʌm] *adj* **-1.** [unable to speak] mudo(da) **-2.** *esp* US *inf* [stupid] estúpido(da).

dumbbell ['dʌmbell] *n* [weight] haltere *m.*

dumbfound [dʌm'faʊnd] *vt* pasmar; **to be ~ed** ficar pasmado(da).

dumbstruck ['dʌmstrʌk] *adj* chocado(da), pasmado(da).

dumbwaiter [,dʌm'weɪtəʳ] *n* [lift] elevador *m* de comida.

dumdum (bullet) ['dʌmdʌm-] *n* bala *f* dundum.

dummy ['dʌmɪ] *(pl* **-ies)** <> *adj* [fake] falso(sa). <> *n* **-1.** [model of human figure - tailor's] manequim *m*; [- ventriloquist's] boneco *m* **-2.** [copy, fake object] imitação *f* **-3.** UK [for baby] chupeta *f* **-4.** SPORT drible *m.* <> *vt* SPORT driblar.

dummy run *n* prova *f*, ensaio *m.*

dump [dʌmp] <> *n* **-1.** [for rubbish] lixeira *f* **-2.** [for ammunition] depósito *m* **-3.** *inf pej* [ugly place] espelunca *f.* <> *vt* **-1.** [put down] deixar cair **-2.** [dispose of] descarregar **-3.** COMM liquidar **-4.** COMPUT mover de um dispositivo para outro **-5.** *inf* [jilt] romper com.
◆ dumps *npl*: **to be (down) in the ~s** estar na fossa.

dumper (truck) ['dʌmpəʳ-] *UK,* **dump truck** *US n* caminhão *m* basculante.

dumping ['dʌmpɪŋ] *n (U)* descarregamento *m*; **'no ~'** 'proibido jogar lixo'.

dumping ground *n* depósito *m.*

dumpling ['dʌmplɪŋ] *n* CULIN bolinho *m* de massa de pão.

dumpster *n* US caçamba *f* de lixo.

dump truck *n* US = **dumper (truck).**

dumpy ['dʌmpɪ] *(compar* **-ier,** *superl* **-iest)** *adj inf* atarracado(da).

dunce [dʌns] *n* burro *m*, -ra *f*, ignorante *mf.*

dune [djuːn] *n* duna *f.*

dung [dʌŋ] *n (U)* esterco *m.*

dungarees [,dʌŋgə'riːz] *npl* UK macacão *m.*

dungeon ['dʌndʒən] *n* masmorra *f.*

dunk [dʌŋk] *vt inf* molhar.

Dunkirk [dʌn'kɜːk] *n* Dunquerque.

duo ['djuːəʊ] *n* **-1.** MUS dueto *m* **-2.** [couple] casal *m.*

duodenal ulcer ['djuːəʊ'diːnl-] *n* úlcera *f* duodenal.

dupe [djuːp] <> *n* [person] otário *m*, -ria *f.* <> *vt* [trick]: **to ~ sb (into doing sthg)** iludir alguém (a fazer algo).

duplex ['djuːpleks] *n* US dúplex *m inv.*

duplicate [*adj & n* 'djuːplɪkət, *vb* 'djuːplɪkeɪt] <> *adj* [document] duplicado(da); **~ key** cópia *f* de chave. <> *n* [of document] cópia *f*; **in ~** em duplicata. <> *vt* **-1.** [document] copiar **-2.** [double, repeat] repetir.

duplication [,djuːplɪ'keɪʃn] *n (U)* **-1.** [copying] duplicação *f* **-2.** [doubling, repetition] repetição *f.*

duplicity [dju:'plɪsətɪ] *n (U) fml* [deceit] duplicidade *f.*

durability [ˌdjʊərə'bɪlətɪ] *n (U)* durabilidade *f.*

durable ['djʊərəbl] *adj* durável, duradouro(ra).

duration [djʊ'reɪʃn] *n (U)* duração *f*; **for the ~ of** durante.

duress [djʊ'res] *n (U)* : **under ~** sob coerção.

Durex® ['djʊəreks] *n* [condom] preservativo *m*, camisinha *f.*

during ['djʊərɪŋ] *prep* durante.

dusk [dʌsk] *n (U)* crepúsculo *m*, anoitecer *m.*

dusky ['dʌskɪ] (*compar* **-ier**, *superl* **-iest**) *adj literary* [skin] moreno(na).

dust [dʌst] <> *n (U)* **-1.** [gen] pó *m*; **to gather ~** [get dusty] pegar pó; *fig* [be ignored] ser privado(da); **to let the ~ settle** deixar a poeira baixar; **to have bitten the ~** ser derrubado(da) por terra **-2.** [earth, sand] poeira *f*, pó *m.* <> *vt* **-1.** [clean] tirar o pó de **-2.** [cover]: **to ~ sthg with sthg** polvilhar algo com algo.
  ◆ **dust off** *vt sep* **-1.** [clean] sacudir a poeira de **-2.** *fig* [re-use] reaproveitar.

dustbin ['dʌstbɪn] *n UK* lata *f* de lixo.

dustbowl ['dʌstbəʊl] *n* zona *f* de desertificação.

dustcart ['dʌstkɑ:t] *n UK* caminhão *m* de lixo.

dust cover *n* **-1.** [for book] = **dust jacket -2.** [for furniture] = **dust sheet.**

duster ['dʌstə^r] *n* **-1.** [cloth] espanador *m* de pó **-2.** *US* [overall] guarda-pó *m.*

dust jacket, dust cover *n* [on book] sobrecapa *f.*

dustman ['dʌstmən] (*pl* **-men** [-mən]) *n UK* lixeiro *m.*

dust mite *n* ácaro *m (da poeira doméstica).*

dustpan ['dʌstpæn] *n* pá *f* de lixo.

dust sheet, dust cover *n UK* capa *f (para os móveis).*

dust storm *n* tempestade *f* de poeira.

dust-up *n inf* briga *f*, rinha *f.*

dusty ['dʌstɪ] (*compar* **-ier**, *superl* **-iest**) *adj* [covered in dust] empoeirado(da).

Dutch [dʌtʃ] <> *adj* holandês(esa). <> *n* [language] holandês *m.* <> *npl*: **the ~** os holandeses. <> *adv*: **let's go ~** cada um paga a sua parte.

Dutch auction *n UK* leilão *no qual vai se baixando o preço de venda até que haja um comprador.*

Dutch barn *n UK* celeiro *m* holandês.

Dutch cap *n UK* diafragma *m.*

Dutch courage *n* coragem *f (produzida pela embriaguez).*

Dutch elm disease *n (U)* doença *f* do olmo holandês.

Dutchman ['dʌtʃmən] (*pl* **-men** [-mən]) *n* holandês *m.*

Dutchwoman ['dʌtʃˌwʊmən] (*pl* **-women** [-ˌwɪmɪn]) *n* holandesa *f.*

dutiable ['dju:tjəbl] *adj* tributável.

dutiful ['dju:tɪfʊl] *adj* zeloso(sa).

duty ['dju:tɪ] (*pl* **-ies**) *n* **-1.** *(U)* [moral, legal responsibility] dever *m*; **to do one's ~** cumprir com o dever **-2.** *(U)* [work] obrigação *f*; **to be on/off ~** estar de plantão/folga **-3.** [tax] imposto *m.*
  ◆ **duties** *npl* [tasks, part of job] funções *fpl.*

duty bound *adj* [obliged] obrigado(da); **to be ~ to do sthg** ser obrigado(da) a fazer algo.

duty-free <> *n* **-1.** [goods] artigo *m* isento de impostos **-2.** [shop] loja *f* duty-free. <> *adj* [whisky, cigarettes] isento(ta) de impostos.

duty-free shop *n* loja *f* duty-free.

duty officer *n* oficial *mf* em serviço.

duvet ['du:veɪ] *n UK* edredom *m*, acolchoado *m.*

duvet cover *n UK* capa *f* do edredom.

DVD (*abbr of* Digital Versatile Disk) *n* DVD *m.*

DVD player *n* (reprodutor *m* de) DVD *m.*

DVD ROM (*abbr of* Digital Versatile Disk read only memory) *n* DVD-ROM *m.*

DVLA (*abbr of* Driver and Vehicle Licensing Agency) *n órgão britânico responsável pelo registro de automóveis e emissão de carteiras de motorista,* ≃ DENATRAN *m.*

DVM (*abbr of* Doctor of Veterinary Medicine) *n (titular de) doutorado em medicina veterinária.*

dwarf [dwɔ:f] (*pl* **-s** OR **dwarves** [dwɔ:vz]) <> *adj* [plant, animal] anão (anã). <> *n* anão *m*, anã *f.* <> *vt* [tower over] sobrepujar.

dwell [dwel] (*pt & pp* **dwelt** OR **-ed**) *vi literary* [live] morar.
  ◆ **dwell on** *vt fus* [past, problem] ficar dando voltas com.

-dweller ['dwelə^r] *suffix* [inhabitant] habitante *mf*; **city-~** habitante *mf* da cidade.

dwelling ['dwelɪŋ] *n literary* morada *f.*

dwelt [dwelt] *pt & pp* ⊳ **dwell.**

dwindle ['dwɪndl] *vi* [decrease, grow smaller] ir diminuindo.

dwindling ['dwɪndlɪŋ] *adj* [decreasing, growing smaller] decrescente.

DWP (*abbr of* Department for Work and Pensions) *n departamento britânico para administração de trabalhadores e pensionistas.*

dye [daɪ] <> *n* [colouring] tintura *f.* <> *vt* [change colour of] tingir.

dyed [daɪd] *adj* tingido(da).

dying ['daɪɪŋ] <> *cont* ⊳ **die.** <> *adj* **-1.** [about to die - person] agonizante; [- species] em vias de extinção **-2.** *fig* [declining] que está desaparecendo. <> *npl*: **the ~** os moribundos.

dyke [daɪk] *n* = **dike.**

dynamic [daɪ'næmɪk] *adj* [energetic] dinâmico(ca).
  ◆ **dynamics** *npl* [forces of change] dinâmica *f.*

dynamism ['daɪnəmɪzml] *n (U)* [energy] dinamismo *m.*

dynamite ['daɪnəmaɪt] <> *n (U)* **-1.** [explosive] dinamite *f* **-2.** *inf fig* [person, story, news]: **to be ~** ser uma bomba **-3.** *inf fig* [excellent] excelente. <> *vt* [blow up] dinamitar.

dynamo ['daɪnəməʊ] (*pl* **-s**) *n TECH* dínamo *m.*

dynasty [*UK* 'dɪnəstɪ, *US* 'daɪnəstɪ] (*pl* **-ies**) *n* [ruling family] dinastia *f.*

dysentery ['dɪsntrɪ] *n (U)* disenteria *f.*

dyslexia [dɪs'leksɪə] *n (U)* dislexia *f.*

dyslexic [dɪs'leksɪk] *adj* disléxico(ca).

dyspepsia [dɪs'pepsɪə] *n (U) MED* dispepsia *f.*

dystrophy ['dɪstrəfɪ] *n* ⊳ **muscular dystrophy.**

e (*pl* e's *OR* es), **E** (*pl* E's *OR* Es) [i:] *n* [letter] e, E *m*.
➡ **E** *n* -**1**. *MUS* mi *m* -**2**. (*abbr of* east) l -**3**. (*abbr of* ecstasy) ecstasy *m*.

E111 *n* formulário que garante seguro saúde a cidadãos britânicos em estadas temporárias em outros países da União Européia.

ea. (*abbr of* each) cada.

each [i:tʃ] ⬦ *adj* [every] cada. ⬦ *pron* [every one] cada um (uma); **two of** ~ dois de cada; ~ **other** um ao outro; **we know** ~ **other** nós nos conhecemos.

eager ['i:gəʳ] *adj* [keen, enthusiastic] animado(da); **to be** ~ **for sthg/to do sthg** estar ansioso(sa) por algo/para fazer algo.

eagerly ['i:gəlɪ] *adv* [talk, plan] animadamente.

eagle ['i:gl] *n* [bird] águia *f*.

eagle-eyed [-'aɪd] *adj* [person] com olhos de lince.

eaglet ['i:glɪt] *n* águia *f* nova.

E and OE (*abbr of* errors and omissions excepted) ≃ SEO, salvo erro ou omissão.

ear [ɪəʳ] *n* -**1**. [of person, animal] orelha *f*; **by** ~ *MUS* de ouvido; **to go in one** ~ **and out the other** *inf* entrar por um ouvido e sair pelo outro; **to have** *OR* **keep one's** ~ **to the ground** *inf* estar/manter-se atento(ta) aos últimos acontecimentos; **to have an** ~ **for sthg** ter ouvido para algo; **to play it by** ~ *fig* nadar de acordo com a maré -**2**. [of corn] espiga *f*.

earache ['ɪəreɪk] *n* dor *f* de ouvido.

eardrum ['ɪədrʌm] *n* tímpano *m*.

earl [ɜ:l] *n* conde *m*.

earlier ['ɜ:lɪəʳ] ⬦ *adj* -**1**. [previous] anterior -**2**. [according to clock]: **let's take the** ~ **train** vamos pegar o trem que tem antes. ⬦ *adv* antes; ~ **on** antes; ~ **that day** mais cedo naquele dia; **they arrived** ~ **than expected** eles chegaram antes do esperado.

earliest ['ɜ:lɪəst] ⬦ *adj* -**1**. [first] primeiro(ra); **at your** ~ **convenience** assim que puder -**2**. [according to clock] primeiro(ra). ⬦ *adv*: **at the** ~ no mínimo.

earlobe ['ɪələʊb] *n* lóbulo *m* da orelha.

early ['ɜ:lɪ] (*compar* -ier, *superl* -iest) ⬦ *adj* -**1**. [gen] adiantado(da); **the** ~ **train** o primeiro trem; **to make an** ~ **start** começar na primeira hora -**2**. [of the beginning of a period of time - old] antigo(ga);

[- period]: **this chair is** ~ **Victorian** esta cadeira é do início da era Vitoriana; [- in career, life] os primeiros anos de; [- in time] no começo de; ~- **morning** da madrugada; **the** ~ **chapters** os primeiros capítulos. ⬦ *adv* -**1**. [before expected time] antes da hora -**2**. [in the morning, in a period of time] cedo; **to get up** ~ madrugar; **as** ~ **as 1950** já em 1950; ~ **on** cedo.

early closing *n* meio-feriado *m* (*para as lojas*).

early retirement *n* aposentadoria *f* antecipada.

early warning system *n* *MIL* sistema *m* de alerta imediato.

earmark ['ɪəmɑ:k] *vt*: **to be** ~ **ed for sthg** ser destinado(da) para algo.

earn [ɜ:n] *vt* -**1**. [as salary] ganhar -**2**. *COMM* gerar -**3**. *fig* [respect, praise] merecer.

earned income [ɜ:nd-] *n* rendimento *m* do trabalho.

earner ['ɜ:nəʳ] *n* -**1**. [person] assalariado *m*, -da *f* -**2**. [product] fonte *f* de recursos -**3**. *UK inf* [business]: **a nice little** ~ um negócio da China.

earnest ['ɜ:nɪst] *adj* [serious, sincere] sério(ria), sincero(ra).
➡ **in earnest** ⬦ *adj* convicto(ta). ⬦ *adv* para valer.

earnestly ['ɜ:nɪstlɪ] *adv* -**1**. [talk] seriamente -**2**. [wish] de todo o coração.

earnings ['ɜ:nɪŋz] *npl* [of person, business] rendimentos *mpl*.

earnings-related *adj* [pension, payment, benefit] proporcional aos rendimentos.

ear, nose and throat specialist *n* otorrinolaringologista *mf*.

earphones ['ɪəfəʊnz] *npl* [headset] fones *mpl* de ouvido.

earpiece *n* audiofone *m*.

earplugs ['ɪəplʌgz] *npl* protetores *mpl* de ouvido.

earring ['ɪərɪŋ] *n* brinco *m*.

earshot ['ɪəʃɒt] *n*: **within/out of** ~ dentro/fora do alcance do ouvido.

ear-splitting *adj* ensurdecedor(ra).

earth [ɜ:θ] ⬦ *n* -**1**. [gen] terra *f*; **how/what on** ~ ...? como/o que é que ...?; **where/why on** ~ ...? onde/por que diabos ...?; **to cost the** ~ *UK* custar uma fortuna -**2**. (*U*) [soil] solo *m* -**3**. *UK* [in electric plug, appliance] terra *m*. ⬦ *vt UK*: **to be** ~ **ed** estar aterrado(da).

earthenware ['ɜ:θnweəʳ] ⬦ *adj* de barro, de louça. ⬦ *n* (*U*) cerâmica *f*.

earthling ['ɜ:θlɪŋ] *n* habitante *mf* da terra.

earthly ['ɜ:θlɪ] *adj* -**1**. [of material world] terreno(na) -**2**. *inf* [possible] concreto(ta).

earthquake ['ɜ:θkweɪk] *n* terremoto *m*.

earth-shattering *adj UK inf* surpreendente.

earth tremor *n* tremor *m* de terra.

earthward(s) ['ɜ:θwəd(z)] *adv* em direção à terra.

earthworm ['ɜ:θwɜ:m] *n* minhoca *f*.

earthy ['ɜ:θɪ] (*compar* -ier, *superl* -iest) *adj* -**1**. [humour, person] direto(ta) -**2**. [taste, smell] de terra.

earwax ['ɪəwæks] *n* (*U*) cera *f* de ouvido.

earwig ['ɪəwɪg] *n* lacraia *f*.

ease [i:z] ⟷ n (U)-**1.** [lack of difficulty] facilidade f; **to do sthg with** ~ fazer algo com facilidade -**2.** [comfort] comodidade f; **at** ~ à vontade; **ill at** ~ pouco(ca) à vontade. ⟷ vt -**1.** [make less severe - pain, restrictions] aliviar; [- problems] atenuar -**2.** [move carefully] ajeitar; **to** ~ **sthg open** abrir algo com cuidado. ⟷ vi [become less severe] aliviar; **to show signs of easing** mostrar sinais de alívio.
➡ **ease off** vi diminuir.
➡ **ease up** vi -**1.** [rain] acalmar -**2.** [relax] relaxar; **to** ~ **up on sb** inf ser menos duro(ra) com alguém.

easel ['i:zl] n cavalete m.

easily ['i:zɪlɪ] adv -**1.** [without difficulty] facilmente -**2.** [undoubtedly] sem sombra de dúvida -**3.** [in a relaxed manner] tranqüilamente.

easiness ['i:zɪnɪs] n [lack of difficulty] facilidade f.

east [i:st] ⟷ adj -**1.** [in the east, facing the east] oriental -**2.** [from the east] leste. ⟷ adv a leste; ~ **of** ao leste de. ⟷ n -**1.** [direction] leste m -**2.** [region]: **the** ~ o leste.
➡ **East** n: **the East** [of country] o leste; [Asia, Eastern bloc] o Oriente.

eastbound ['i:stbaʊnd] adj em direção ao leste.

East End n: **the** ~ o leste de Londres.

Easter ['i:stə'] n Páscoa f.

Easter egg n ovo m de Páscoa.

Easter Island n Ilha da Páscoa.

easterly ['i:stəlɪ] adj -**1.** [towards the east, in the east] a leste -**2.** [from the east] do leste.

eastern ['i:stən] adj [part of country, continent] oriental, do leste.
➡ **Eastern** adj oriental.

Eastern bloc [-'blɒk] n: **the** ~ o bloco Oriental.

Easter Sunday n Domingo m de Páscoa.

East German ⟷ adj da Alemanha Oriental. ⟷ n [person] alemão m, -mã f oriental.

East Germany n: **(the former)** ~ (a antiga) Alemanha Oriental; **in** ~ na Alemanha Oriental.

eastward ['i:stwəd] ⟷ adj ao leste. ⟷ adv = eastwards.

eastwards ['i:stwədz] adv em direção ao leste.

easy ['i:zɪ] (compar -ier, superl -iest) ⟷ adj -**1.** [not difficult] fácil -**2.** [comfortable] cômodo(da) -**3.** [relaxed] sossegado(da). ⟷ adv: **to go** ~ **on sb/sthg** inf [treat more kindly] ir com calma com alguém/algo; **to take it** OR **things** ~ inf levar isso OR as coisas com calma.

easy-care adj UK [clothes] que não precisa ser passado(da).

easy chair n [armchair] poltrona f.

easygoing [,i:zɪ'gəʊɪŋ] adj [person, manner] descontraído(da).

eat [i:t] (pt ate, pp eaten) ⟷ vt & vi comer.
➡ **eat away** vt sep, **eat into** vt fus -**1.** [corrode away] corroer -**2.** [deplete] destruir.
➡ **eat out** vi [at restaurant] comer fora.
➡ **eat up** vt sep -**1.** [food] comer tudo -**2.** fig [money, time] consumir um monte de.

eatable ['i:təbl] adj [palatable] comestível.

eaten ['i:tn] pp ▷ **eat**.

eater ['i:tə'] n comedor m, -ra f.

eatery ['i:tərɪ] (pl -ies) n restaurante m.

eating apple ['i:tɪŋ-] n maçã f (para a sobremesa).

eau de cologne [,əʊdəkə'ləʊn] n água-de-colônia f, colônia f.

eaves ['i:vz] npl [of house] beirado m.

eavesdrop ['i:vzdrɒp] (pt & pp -ped, cont -ping) vi [listen, spy] bisbilhotar; **to** ~ **on sb** bisbilhotar alguém.

ebb [eb] ⟷ n (U) [of tide, sea] vazante f; **the** ~ **and flow of sthg** fig os altos e baixos de algo; **to be at a low** ~ fig estar cabisbaixo(xa). ⟷ vi -**1.** [tide, sea] baixar -**2.** literary [strength, pain, feeling]: **to** ~ **(away)** desaparecer.

ebb tide n maré f baixa.

ebony ['ebənɪ] ⟷ adj literary [colour] da cor do ébano. ⟷ n (U) [wood] ébano m.

ebullient [ɪ'bʊljənt] adj [lively] entusiasmado(da).

e-business n -**1.** [company] empresa f de e-business -**2.** [electronic commerce] e-business m.

EC (abbr of European Community) n CE f.

e-cash n COMPUT dinheiro m eletrônico.

ECB (abbr of European Central Bank) n BCE m.

eccentric [ɪk'sentrɪk] ⟷ adj [odd] excêntrico(ca). ⟷ n [person] excêntrico m, -ca f.

eccentricity [,eksen'trɪsətɪ] (pl -ies) n excentricidade f.

ecclesiastic(al) [ɪ,kli:zɪ'æstɪ(l)] adj [of Christian church] eclesiástico(ca).

ECG n -**1.** (abbr of electrocardiogram) ECG m. -**2.** (abbr of electrocardiograph) eletrocardiógrafo m.

ECH (abbr of electric central heating) n aquecimento m central elétrico.

echelon ['eʃəlɒn] n fml [level in organization] escalão m.

echo ['ekəʊ] (pl -es, pt & pp -ed, cont -ing) ⟷ n eco m. ⟷ vt [repeat - words] repetir; [- opinion] repercurtir. ⟷ vi ecoar.

éclair [eɪ'kleə'] n [cake] bomba f.

eclectic [ɪ'klektɪk] adj eclético(ca).

eclipse [ɪ'klɪps] ⟷ n -**1.** [of sun, moon] eclipse m; **total/partial** ~ eclipse total/parcial -**2.** fig [decline] declínio m. ⟷ vt fig [overshadow] eclipsar.

ECM (abbr of European Common Market) n US MCE m.

eco-friendly ['i:kəʊ'frendlɪ] adj ecológico(ca).

ecological [,i:kə'lɒdʒɪkl] adj ecológico(ca).

ecologically [,i:kə'lɒdʒɪklɪ] adv [from ecological point of view] ecologicamente.

ecologist [ɪ'kɒlədʒɪst] n ecologista mf.

ecology [ɪ'kɒlədʒɪ] n (U) ecologia f.

e-commerce n comércio m eletrônico.

economic [,i:kə'nɒmɪk] adj econômico(ca).

economical [,i:kə'nɒmɪkl] adj econômico(ca).

Economic and Monetary Union n União f Monetária e Econômica.

economics [,i:kə'nɒmɪks] ⟷ n (U) [study] economia f. ⟷ npl [of plan, business, trade] aspectos mpl econômicos.

economist [ɪ'kɒnəmɪst] n [expert] economista mf.

economize, -ise [ɪ'kɒnəmaɪz] vi [save money, resources] economizar; **to** ~ **on sthg** economizar em algo.

economy [ɪ'kɒnəmɪ] (*pl* **-ies**) *n* economia *f*; **economies of scale** economias de escala.

economy class *n* classe *f* econômica.

economy-size(d) *adj* [pack, jar] de tamanho econômico.

ecosystem ['i:kəʊˌsɪstəm] *n* ecossistema *m*.

ecotax ['i:kəʊtæks] *n* ecotaxa *f*.

ecotourism [ˌi:kəʊ'tʊərɪzm] *n* ecoturismo *m*.

ecstasy ['ekstəsɪ] (*pl* **-ies**) *n* **-1.** (*U*) [great happiness] êxtase *m* **-2.** [feeling of happiness]: **to go into ecstasies about sthg** entrar em êxtase por algo **-3.** [drug] ecstasy *m*.

ecstatic [ek'stætɪk] *adj* extasiado(da).

ecstatically [ek'stætɪklɪ] *adv* em êxtase.

ECT (*abbr of* **electroconvulsive therapy**) *n* terapia *f* de eletrochoque.

ectoplasm ['ektəplæzm] *n* (*U*) [of cell] ectoplasma *m*.

ECU, Ecu ['ekju:] (*abbr of* **European Currency Unit**) *n* Unidade *f* Monetária Européia.

Ecuador ['ekwədɔ:ʳ] *n* Equador; **in** ~ no Equador.

Ecuadoran [ˌekwə'dɔ:rən], **Ecuadorian** [ˌekwə'dɔ:rɪən] <> *adj* equatoriano(na). <> *n* equatoriano *m*, -na *f*.

ecumenical [i:kjʊ'menɪkl] *adj* RELIG ecumênico(ca).

eczema ['eksɪmə] *n* (*U*) eczema *m*.

ed. -1. (*abbr of* **edited**) ed. **-2.** (*abbr of* **edition**) Ed. **-3.** (*abbr of* **editor**) ed.

eddy ['edɪ] (*pl* **-ies**, *pt* & *pp* **-ied**) <> *n* redemoinho *m*. <> *vi* redemoinhar.

Eden ['i:dn] *n*: **(the Garden of)** ~ (o Jardim do) Éden.

edge [edʒ] <> *n* **-1.** [outer limit] borda *f*; **to be on the** ~ **of sthg** estar à beira de algo **-2.** [of blade] fio *m* **-3.** [advantage]: **to have an** ~ **over sb/sth, to have the** ~ **on sb/sthg** levar ligeira vantagem sobre alguém/algo **-4.** (*U*) *fig* [in voice] rispidez *f*. <> *vi* [move slowly] avançar lentamente.

on edge *adj* **-1.** [person] nervoso(sa) **-2.** [nerves] à flor da pele.

edged [edʒd] *adj*: ~ **with sthg** orlado(da) por algo.

edgeways ['edʒweɪz], **edgewise** ['edʒwaɪz] *adv* [sideways] de lado.

edging ['edʒɪŋ] *n* borda *f*.

edgy ['edʒɪ] (*compar* **-ier**, *superl* **-iest**) *adj* impaciente.

edible ['edɪbl] *adj* [safe to eat] comestível.

edict ['i:dɪkt] *n* [decree] edital *m*.

edifice ['edɪfɪs] *n fml* [building] edifício *m*.

edify ['edɪfaɪ] (*pt* & *pp* **-ied**) *vt fml* edificar.

edifying ['edɪfaɪɪŋ] *adj fml* edificante.

Edinburgh ['edɪnbrə] *n* Edimburgo.

Edinburgh Festival *n*: **the** ~ o Festival de Edimburgo.

edit ['edɪt] *vt* **-1.** [gen] editar **-2.** [correct] revisar; **to need** ~ **ing** precisar de revisão.

edit out *vt sep* [word, sentence, passage] cortar.

edition [ɪ'dɪʃn] *n* edição *f*.

editor ['edɪtəʳ] *n* **-1.** [gen] editor *m*, -ra *f* **-2.** [copy editor] revisor *m*, -ra *f* **-3.** COMPUT editor *m* (de texto).

editorial [ˌedɪ'tɔ:rɪəl] <> *adj* editorial. <> *n* editorial *m*.

EDP (*abbr of* **electronic data processing**) *n* PED *m*.

EDT (*abbr of* **Eastern Daylight Time**) *n* horário de verão na zona leste dos Estados Unidos.

educate ['edʒʊkeɪt] *vt* **-1.** SCH & UNIV educar **-2.** [inform] informar.

educated ['edʒʊkeɪtɪd] *adj* [cultured] educado(da), culto(ta).

education [ˌedʒʊ'keɪʃn] *n* (*U*) **-1.** [activity, sector] educação *f*, ensino *m* **-2.** [process or result of teaching] educação *f*.

educational [ˌedʒʊ'keɪʃənl] *adj* **-1.** [establishment, policy] educacional **-2.** [toy, experience] educativo(-va).

educationalist [ˌedʒʊ'keɪʃnəlɪst] *n* especialista *mf* em educação.

educator ['edʒʊkeɪtəʳ] *n* US fml [teacher] educador *m*, -ra *f*.

Edwardian [ed'wɔ:dɪən] *adj* eduardiano(na), da época do rei Eduardo VII.

EEC (*abbr of* **European Economic Community**) *n* CEE *f*.

EEG *n* **-1.** (*abbr of* **electroencephalogram**) EEG *m*. **-2.** (*abbr of* **electroencephalograph**) eletrencefalógrafo *m*.

eel [i:l] *n* enguia *f*.

EEOC (*abbr of* **Equal Employment Opportunity Commission**) *n* comissão norte-americana para a prevenção da discriminação no trabalho.

eerie ['ɪərɪ] *adj* lúgubre, sinistro(tra).

EET (*abbr of* **Eastern European Time**) *n* horário da Europa Oriental.

efface [ɪ'feɪs] *vt* apagar.

effect [ɪ'fekt] <> *n* **-1.** [gen] efeito *m*; **to have an** ~ **on sb/sthg** ter um efeito sobre alguém/algo; **to take** ~ [law, rule] entrar em vigor; [drug] fazer efeito; **to put sthg into** ~ pôr algo em prática; **for** ~ para impressionar **-2.** [meaning]: **to the** ~ **that** no sentido de que; **to that** ~ neste sentido. <> *vt* **-1.** [recovery, change] causar **-2.** [reconcilition, comeback, repairs] fazer.

effects *npl* **-1.**: **(special)** ~ **s** efeitos (especiais) **-2.** [property] bens *mpl*.

in effect *adv* na prática; **the law is in** ~ a lei está em vigor.

effective [ɪ'fektɪv] *adj* **-1.** [successful] eficaz **-2.** [actual, real] efetivo(va) **-3.** [in operation] em vigor.

effectively [ɪ'fektɪvlɪ] *adv* **-1.** [well, successfully] eficazmente **-2.** [in fact] efetivamente.

effectiveness [ɪ'fektɪvnɪs] *n* (*U*) [success, efficiency] eficácia *f*.

effeminate [ɪ'femɪnət] *adj pej* efeminado(da).

effervesce [ˌefə'ves] *vi* efervescer.

effervescent [ˌefə'vesnt] *adj* [liquid] efervescente.

effete [ɪ'fi:t] *adj pej* [weak, effeminate] efeminado(da).

efficacious [efɪ'keɪʃəs] *adj fml* eficaz.

efficacy ['efɪkəsɪ] *n* (*U*) [effectiveness] eficácia *f*.

efficiency [ɪ'fɪʃənsɪ] *n* (*U*) eficiência *f*.

efficient [ɪ'fɪʃənt] *adj* eficiente.

efficiently [ɪ'fɪʃəntlɪ] *adv* [competently] eficientemente.

effigy ['efɪdʒɪ] (*pl* **-ies**) *n* efígie *f*.

effluent ['efluənt] *n* efluente *m*.

effort ['efət] *n* **-1.** (*U*) [physical or mental exertion] esforço *m*; **to be worth the** ~ valer o esforço; **to make the** ~ **to do sthg** esforçar-se para fazer algo; **with** ~ com esforço **-2.** [attempt] esforço *m*, tentativa *f*; **to make an/no ~ to do sthg** empenhar-se/não se empenhar em fazer algo.

effortless ['efətlıs] *adj* fácil, com desenvoltura.

effortlessly ['efətlıslı] *adv* facilmente, sem esforço.

effrontery [ı'frʌntərı] *n (U)* atrevimento *m*.

effusive [ı'fju:sıv] *adj* efusivo(va).

effusively [ı'fju:sıvlı] *adv* efusivamente.

EFL (*abbr of* **English as a Foreign Language**) *n* inglês *para estrangeiros*.

EFTA ['eftə] (*abbr of* **European Free Trade Association**) *n associação para o livre comércio europeu*.

EFTS (*abbr of* **electronic funds transfer system**) *n sistema que processa transferência eletrônica de fundos de uma conta para a outra*.

e.g. (*abbr of* **exempli gratia**) *adv* e.g.

egalitarian [ı,gælı'teərıən] *adj* igualitário(ria).

egg [eg] *n* **-1.** [gen] ovo *m* **-2.** [of woman] óvulo *m*.
  ◆ **egg on** *vt sep* instigar.

eggcup ['egkʌp] *n* oveiro *m*.

eggplant ['egplɑ:nt] *n US* berinjela *f*.

eggshell ['egʃel] *n* casca *f* de ovo.

egg timer *n* ampulheta *f (para marcar tempo de cozimento de um ovo)*.

egg whisk *n* batedor *m* de ovos.

egg white *n* clara *f* de ovo.

egg yolk [-jəʊk] *n* gema *f* de ovo.

EGM (*abbr of* **extraordinary general meeting**) *n assembléia geral extraordinária*, AGE *f*.

ego ['i:gəʊ] (*pl* **-s**) *n* [opinion of self] ego *m*.

egocentric [,i:gəʊ'sentrık] *adj fml & pej* [selfish] egocêntrico(ca).

egoism ['i:gəʊızm] *n (U)* [self-interest] egoísmo *m*.

egoist ['i:gəʊıst] *n* [self-centred person] egoísta *mf*.

egoistic [,i:gəʊ'ıstık] *adj* [self-centred] egoísta.

egotism ['i:gətızm] *n (U)* egotismo *m*, egoísmo *m*.

egotist ['i:gətıst] *n* egotista *mf*, egoísta *mf*.

egotistic(al) [,i:gə'tıstık(l)] *adj* egotista, egoísta.

ego trip *n inf* massagem *f* no ego.

Egypt ['i:dʒıpt] *n* Egito *m*; **in ~** no Egito.

Egyptian [ı'dʒıpʃn] ◇ *adj* egípcio(cia). ◇ *n* [person] egípcio *m*, -cia *f*.

eh [eı] *excl UK inf* **-1.** [inviting reply, agreement] ahã! **-2.** [what did you say?] hmm? **-3.** [expressing astonishment] ah!

eiderdown ['aıdədaʊn] *n UK* [bed cover] edredom *m*.

eight [eıt] *num* oito; *see also* **six**.

eighteen [,eı'ti:n] *num* dezoito; *see also* **six**.

eighteenth [,eı'ti:nθ] *num* décimo oitavo, décima oitava; *see also* **sixth**.

eighth [eıtθ] *num* oitavo(va); *see also* **sixth**.

eightieth ['eıtııθ] *num* octagésimo(ma); *see also* **sixth**.

eighty ['eıtı] (*pl* **-ies**) *num* oitenta; *see also* **sixty**.

Eire ['eərə] *n* (República da) Irlanda.

either ['aıðə', 'i:ðə'] ◇ *adj* **-1.** [one or the other] qualquer; **~ side could win** qualquer um dos lados poderia ganhar; **she couldn't find ~ jumper** ela não conseguia achar nenhuma das blusas; **~ way** de qualquer jeito; **I don't mind ~ way** por mim tanto faz **-2.** [each] cada; **on ~ side** de cada

lado. ◇ *pron*: **~ (of them) will do** qualquer um (deles) serve; **I don't like ~ (of them)** não gosto de nenhum (dos dois). ◇ *adv (after negative)* também não; **they don't smoke ~** eles também não fumam. ◇ *conj*: **~ ... or ...** [in positive sentence] ou ...ou ...; [in negative sentence] nem ...nem ...; **~ he leaves or I do** ou ele sai ou saio eu; **you are not being ~ clever or funny** você não está sendo nem inteligente nem engraçado.

ejaculate [ı'dʒækjʊleıt] ◇ *vt* [exclaim] exclamar. ◇ *vi* [have orgasm] ejacular.

eject [ı'dʒekt] *vt* **-1.** [object] ejetar **-2.** [person]: **to ~ sb (from)** expulsar alguém (de).

ejector seat *UK* [ı'dʒektə'-], **ejection seat** *US* [ı'dʒekʃn-] *n* assento *m* ejetor.

eke [i:k] ◆ **eke out** ◇ *vt sep* [save - money] esticar; [- food, supply] racionar. ◇ *vt fus*: **to ~ out a living** ganhar a vida com dificuldade.

EKG (*abbr of* **electrocardiogram**) *n US* ECG *m*.

el (*abbr of* **elevated railroad**) *n US fam* elevado *m* férreo.

elaborate [*adj* ı'læbrət, *vb* ı'læbəreıt] ◇ *adj* [complicated, detailed] elaborado(da). ◇ *vi*: **to ~ (on sthg)** detalhar (algo).

elaborately [ı'læbərətlı] *adv* [in detail] detalhadamente.

elapse [ı'læps] *vi* [time] transcorrer.

elastic [ı'læstık] ◇ *adj* **-1.** [material, skin] elástico(ca) **-2.** *fig* [plan, timetable] elástico(ca). ◇ *n (U)* [material] elástico *m*.

elasticated [ı'læstıkeıtıd] *adj* [waistband] elástico(ca).

elastic band *n UK* elástico *m*.

elasticity [,elæ'stısətı] *n (U)* [stretchiness] elasticidade *f*.

elated [ı'leıtıd] *adj* exultante.

elation [ı'leıʃn] *n (U)* exultação *f*.

elbow ['elbəʊ] ◇ *n* cotovelo *m*. ◇ *vt*: **to ~ sb aside** empurrar alguém com os cotovelos.

elbow grease *n (U) inf* duro *m* danado.

elbowroom ['elbəʊrʊm] *n inf* [physical space] espaço *m (para trabalhar)*.

elder ['eldə'] ◇ *adj* [older] mais velho(lha), primogênito(ta). ◇ *n* **-1.** [older person] velho *m*, -lha *f* **-2.** [of tribe] ancião *m*, -ã *f* **-3.** [of church] presbítero *m* **-4.** *BOT*: **~ (tree)** sabugueiro *m*.

elderberry ['eldə,berı] (*pl* **-ies**) *n* **-1.** [fruit] fruto *m* do sabugueiro **-2.** [tree] sabugueiro *m*.

elderly ['eldəlı] ◇ *adj* [old - person] idoso(sa); [- thing] velho(lha), antigo(ga). ◇ *npl*: **the ~** os idosos.

elder statesman *n* estadista *mf* experiente.

eldest ['eldıst] *adj* [oldest] mais velho(lha).

El Dorado *n* El Dorado.

elect [ı'lekt] ◇ *adj* eleito(ta). ◇ *vt* **-1.** [by voting] eleger; **to ~ sb (as)** eleger alguém (como) algo **-2.** *fml* [choose]: **to ~ to do sthg** escolher fazer algo.

elected [ı'lektıd] *adj* [president, chairperson] eleito(ta).

election [ı'lekʃn] *n* eleição *f*; **to have OR hold an ~** ter OR fazer uma eleição; **local ~s** eleições locais.

ELECTION

Nos EUA, as eleições presidenciais realizam-se a cada quatro anos. Por lei, o presidente não pode permanecer no cargo por mais de dois mandatos consecutivos. As eleições gerais britânicas realizam-se a cada cinco anos, mas o primeiro-ministro pode convocar eleições a qualquer momento. Tanto nos Estados Unidos como na Grã-Bretanha, o voto não é obrigatório.

election campaign n campanha f eleitoral.
electioneering [ɪˌlekʃəˈnɪərɪŋ] n (U) pej propaganda f eleitoral, eleitoralismo m.
elective [ɪˈlektɪv] n SCH & UNIV disciplina f opcional.
elector [ɪˈlektəʳ] n [voter] eleitor m, -ra f.
electoral [ɪˈlektərəl] adj eleitoral.
electoral college n POL colégio m eleitoral.
electoral register, electoral roll n: the ~ o registro dos eleitores.
electorate [ɪˈlektərət] n: the ~ o eleitorado.
electric [ɪˈlektrɪk] adj -1. [using or producing electricity] elétrico(ca) -2. fig [exciting] eletrizante.
➡ **electrics** npl UK inf [in car, machine] partes fpl elétricas.
electrical [ɪˈlektrɪkl] adj elétrico(ca).
electrical engineer n engenheiro m, -ra f eletricista.
electrical engineering n (U) engenharia f elétrica.
electrically [ɪˈlektrɪklɪ] adv [by electricity] eletricamente.
electrical shock n US = electric shock.
electric blanket n cobertor m elétrico.
electric chair n: the ~ a cadeira elétrica.
electric cooker n fogão m elétrico.
electric current n corrente f elétrica.
electric drill n furadeira f elétrica.
electric fence n cerca f elétrica.
electric fire n estufa f elétrica.
electric guitar n guitarra f elétrica.
electrician [ˌɪlekˈtrɪʃn] n eletricista mf.
electricity [ˌɪlekˈtrɪsətɪ] n -1. ELEC eletricidade f -2. fig [excitement] excitação f.
electric light n (U) luz f elétrica.
electric shock UK, **electrical shock** US n choque m elétrico.
electric storm n tempestade f elétrica.
electrify [ɪˈlektrɪfaɪ] (pt & pp -ied) vt -1. [convert to electric power] eletrificar -2. fig [excite] deixar eletrizado(da).
electrifying [ɪˈlektrɪfaɪŋ] adj fig [exciting] eletrizante.
electro- [ɪˈlektrəʊ] prefix eletro-.
electrocardiogram n MED eletrocardiograma m.
electrocardiograph [ɪˌlektrəʊˈkɑːdɪəgrɑːf] n MED eletrocardiógrafo m.
electrocardiography n MED eletrocardiografia f.
electrocute [ɪˈlektrəkjuːt] vt eletrocutar; to ~ o.s eletrocutar-se.
electrode [ɪˈlektrəʊd] n eletrodo m.

electroencephalogram n MED eletrencefalograma m.
electroencephalograph [ɪˌlektrəʊenˈsefələgrɑːf] n MED eletrencefalógrafo m.
electroencephalography n MED eletrencefalografia f.
electrolysis [ˌɪlekˈtrɒləsɪs] n (U) eletrólise f.
electromagnet n eletroímã m.
electromagnetic [ɪˌlektrəʊmægˈnetɪk] adj eletromagnético(ca).
electron [ɪˈlektrɒn] n elétron m.
electronic [ˌɪlekˈtrɒnɪk] adj eletrônico(ca).
➡ **electronics** ⬦ n (U) [technology] eletrônica f. ⬦ npl [equipment] componentes mpl eletrônicos.
electronic banking n serviço m bancário via internet.
electronic data processing n (U) processamento m eletrônico de dados.
electronic mail n (U) correio m eletrônico.
electronic organizer n agenda f eletrônica.
electron microscope n microscópio m eletrônico.
electroplated [ɪˈlektrəʊˌpleɪtɪd] adj galvanizado(da).
elegance [ˈelɪgəns] n (U) elegância f.
elegant [ˈelɪgənt] adj -1. [stylish, beautiful] elegante -2. [clever, neat] brilhante.
elegantly [ˈelɪgəntlɪ] adv -1. [stylishly, beautifully] elegantemente -2. [cleverly, neatly] brilhantemente.
elegy [ˈelɪdʒɪ] (pl -ies) n elegia f.
element [ˈelɪmənt] n -1. SCIENCE elemento m -2. [small amount, proportion] parcela f -3. [in heater, kettle] resistência f -4. pej [in society, group] elemento m -5. phr: to be in one's ~ estar em seu meio.
➡ **elements** npl -1. [basics] conhecimentos mpl básicos -2. [weather]: the ~s os fenômenos atmosféricos.
elementary [ˌelɪˈmentərɪ] adj elementar.
elementary school n US escola f primária.
elephant [ˈelɪfənt] (pl inv OR -s) n elefante m
elevate [ˈelɪveɪt] vt -1. [give importance to, promote]: to ~ sb/sthg to sthg, to ~ sb/sthg into sthg elevar alguém/algo a algo -2. [raise physically] levantar.
elevated [ˈelɪveɪtɪd] adj fml -1. [person, situation] digno(na) -2. [idea, sentiment] elevado(da) -3. [platform, position] alto(ta).
elevated railway n ferrovia f elevada.
elevation [ˌelɪˈveɪʃn] n fml -1. (U) [promotion, raising of person] promoção f; [- of standards] elevação f -2. [of hill, land] altitude f.
elevator [ˈelɪveɪtəʳ] n US elevador m.
eleven [ɪˈlevn] num onze; see also six.
elevenses [ɪˈlevnzɪz] n (U) UK lanche m rápido (às 11 da manhã).
eleventh [ɪˈlevnθ] num décimo primeiro, décima primeira; see also sixth.
eleventh hour n fig: the ~ a última hora.
elf [elf] (pl elves) n elfo m.
elicit [ɪˈlɪsɪt] vt fml -1. [response, reaction]: to ~ sthg (from sb) obter algo (de alguém) -2. [information]: to ~ sthg (from sb) extrair algo (de alguém).

eligibility [ˌelɪdʒə'bɪlətɪ] *n (U)* **-1.** [suitability] eligibilidade *f* **-2.** *dated* [of bachelor] aptidão *f (para o casamento).*

eligible ['elɪdʒəbl] *adj* **-1.** [suitable, qualified] elegível; **to be ~ for sthg/to do sthg** estar habilitado(da) a algo/a fazer algo **-2.** *dated* [marriageable]: **to be ~** ser um bom partido.

eliminate [ɪ'lɪmɪneɪt] *vt* **-1.** [remove]: **to ~ sb/sthg (from)** eliminar alguém/algo (de) **-2.** [in sport, competition]: **to be ~d from sthg** ser eliminado(da) de algo.

elimination [ɪˌlɪmɪ'neɪʃn] *n (U)* eliminação *f.*

elite [ɪ'liːt] *<>* *adj* de elite. *<>* *n* elite *f.*

elitism [ɪ'liːtɪzm] *n (U) pej* elitismo *m.*

elitist [ɪ'liːtɪst] *pej* *<>* *adj* elitista. *<>* *n* elitista *mf.*

elixir [ɪ'lɪksəʳ] *n literary* **-1.** [magic drink] elixir *m* **-2.** *fig* [magic cure] poção *f* mágica.

Elizabethan [ɪˌlɪzə'biːθn] *<>* *adj* elizabetano(na). *<>* *n* elizabetano *m,* -na *f.*

elk [elk] *(pl inv OR* **-s)** *n* alce *m.*

ellipse [ɪ'lɪps] *n* elípse *f.*

elliptical [ɪ'lɪptɪkl] *adj* **-1.** [in shape] elíptico(ca) **-2.** *fml* [phrase, remark] obscuro(ra).

elm [elm] *n:* **~ (tree)** olmo *m.*

elocution [ˌelə'kjuːʃn] *n (U)* elocução *f.*

elongated ['iːlɒŋgeɪtɪd] *adj* alongado(da).

elope [ɪ'ləʊp] *vi:* **to ~ (with sb)** fugir para casar (com alguém).

elopement [ɪ'ləʊpmənt] *n* fuga *f (com o namorado).*

eloquence ['eləkwəns] *n (U)* eloqüência *f.*

eloquent ['eləkwənt] *adj* eloqüente.

eloquently ['eləkwəntlɪ] *adv* eloqüentemente.

El Salvador [ˌel'sælvədɔːʳ] *n* El Salvador; **in ~** em El Salvador.

else [els] *adv:* **anything ~** mais alguma coisa; **he doesn't need anything ~** ele não precisa de nada mais; **everyone ~** todos os outros, todas as outras; **nothing ~** nada mais; **someone ~** alguma outra pessoa; **something ~** outra coisa; **somewhere ~** outro lugar; **who/what/where~?** quem/que/onde mais?

➡ **or else** *conj* **-1.** [or if not] ou então, senão **-2.** [as threat] senão.

elsewhere [els'weəʳ] *adv* em outro lugar.

ELT *(abbr of* **English Language Teaching)** *n.* ensino *m* de língua inglese

elucidate [ɪ'luːsɪdeɪt] *fml* *<>* *vt* elucidar. *<>* *vi* elucidar.

elude [ɪ'luːd] *vt* escapar de; **his name ~s me completely** o nome dele me escapa totalmente.

elusive [ɪ'luːsɪv] *adj* esquivo(va), evasivo(va).

elves [elvz] *pl* ⊳ **elf.**

'em [əm] *cont inf* = them.

emaciated [ɪ'meɪʃɪeɪtɪd] *adj* emagrecido (da).

e-mail *n COMPUT* e-mail *m,* correio *m* eletrônico.

e-mail address *n* endereço *m* (de correio) eletrônico, e-mail *m.*

e-mail phone *n* telefone *m* com correio eletrônico.

emanate ['eməneɪt] *fml* *<>* *vt* emanar. *<>* *vi:* to **~ from** emanar de.

emancipate [ɪ'mænsɪpeɪt] *vt:* **to ~ sb (from sthg)** emancipar alguém (de algo).

emancipation [ɪˌmænsɪ'peɪʃn] *n (U):* **~ (from sthg)** emancipação *f* (de algo).

emasculate [ɪ'mæskjʊleɪt] *vt fml* [weaken] enfraquecer.

emasculation [ɪˌmæskjʊ'leɪʃn] *n (U) fml* [weakening] enfraquecimento *m.*

embalm [ɪm'bɑːm] *vt* [body] embalsamar.

embankment [ɪm'bæŋkmənt] *n* **-1.** [along road, railway] barreira *f* **-2.** [along river] margem *f.*

embargo [em'bɑːgəʊ] *(pl* **-es,** *pt & pp* **-ed,** *cont* **-ing)** *<>* *n* **-1.** [gen]: **~ (on sthg)** embargo *m* (de algo) **-2.** *fig* [ban]: **~ (on sthg)** proibição *f* (de algo). *<>* *vt* **-1.** *COMM & POL* embargar **-2.** *fig* [ban] proibir.

embark [ɪm'bɑːk] *vi* **-1.** [board ship]: **to ~ (on)** embarcar(em) **-2.** [start]: **to ~ (up)on sthg** dar início (a algo).

embarkation [ˌembɑː'keɪʃn] *n* embarque *m.*

embarkation card *n UK* cartão *m* de embarque.

embarrass [ɪm'bærəs] *vt* [shame] envergonhar.

embarrassed [ɪm'bærəst] *adj* [self-conscious] envergonhado(da).

embarrassing [ɪm'bærəsɪŋ] *adj* [shameful] embaraçoso(sa).

embarrassment [ɪm'bærəsmənt] *n* vergonha *f.*

embassy ['embəsɪ] *(pl* **-ies)** *n* embaixada *f.*

embattled [ɪm'bætld] *adj* [troubled] em dificuldade.

embedded [ɪm'bedɪd] *adj* **-1.** [buried]: **~ in sthg** enterrado(da) em algo **-2.** *COMPUT:* **~ in sthg** embutido(da) em algo **-3.** *fig* [ingrained] enraizado(da).

embellish [ɪm'belɪʃ] *vt* **-1.** [room, garment]: **to ~ sthg with sthg** embelezar algo com algo **-2.** *fig* [story, account] enfeitar.

embers ['embəz] *npl* brasa *f.*

embezzle [ɪm'bezl] *vt* [money] desviar.

embezzlement [ɪm'bezlmənt] *n (U)* desvio *m (de dinheiro).*

embezzler [ɪm'bezləʳ] *n* defraudador *m,* -ra *f.*

embittered [ɪm'bɪtəd] *adj* amargurado(da).

emblazoned [ɪm'bleɪzndl] *adj:* **~ (on sthg)** gravado(da) (em algo); **~ (with sthg)** ornado(da) (com algo).

emblem ['embləm] *n* [symbolic design] emblema *m.*

embodiment [ɪm'bɒdɪmənt] *n* [epitome] personificação *f.*

embody [ɪm'bɒdɪ] *(pt & pp* **-ied)** *vt* **-1.** [epitomize] personificar **-2.** [include]: **to be embodied in sthg** estar incorporado(da) em algo.

embolism ['embəlɪzm] *n* embolia *f.*

embossed [ɪm'bɒst] *adj* **-1.** [material] em relevo **-2.** [design, lettering]: **~ (on sthg)** em relevo (sobre algo).

embrace [ɪm'breɪs] *<>* *n* abraço *m.* *<>* *vt* **-1.** [person] abraçar **-2.** *fml* [religion, way of life] converter-se a **-3.** *fml* [aspects, elements] conter. *<>* *vi* abraçar-se.

embrocation [ˌembrə'keɪʃn] *n (U) fml* [liquid] embrocação *f.*

embroider [ɪm'brɔɪdəʳ] *<>* *vt* **-1.** *SEWING* bordar **-2.** *pej* [embellish] enfeitar. *<>* *vi SEWING* bordar.

embroidered [ɪm'brɔɪdəd] *adj SEWING* bordado(da).

embroidery [ɪm'brɔɪdərɪ] n (U) bordado m.

embroil [ɪm'brɔɪl] vt: **to get/be** ~**ed (in sthg)** envolver-se/ser envolvido(da) (em algo).

embryo ['embrɪəʊ] (pl -s) n -1. BIOL embrião m -2. fig [beginnings]: **in** ~ em estado embrionário.

embryonic [,embrɪ'ɒnɪk] adj fig [emergent] embrionário(ria).

emcee (abbr of master of ceremonies) n US mestre mf de cerimônias.

emend [ɪ'mend] vt corrigir.

emerald ['emərəld] <> adj [colour] esmeralda. <> n [stone] esmeralda f.

emerge [ɪ'mɜːdʒ] <> vi -1. [come out] aparecer; **to** ~ **from sthg** surgir de algo -2. [from experience, situation]: **to** ~ **from** surgir de -3. [become known - facts, truth] vir à tona; [- writer, movement] surgir. <> vt: **it** ~**s that** vem à tona que.

emergence [ɪ'mɜːdʒəns] n (U) surgimento m, aparecimento m.

emergency [ɪ'mɜːdʒənsɪ] (pl -ies) <> adj de emergência. <> n emergência f.

emergency brake n US [of car] freio m de mão.

emergency exit n saída f de emergência.

emergency landing n pouso m de emergência.

emergency number n número m de emergência.

emergency room n US [in hospital] sala f de emergência.

emergency services npl serviços mpl de emergência.

emergency stop n parada f de emergência.

emergent [ɪ'mɜːdʒənt] adj emergente.

emery board ['emərɪ-] n lixa f (de unhas).

emetic [ɪ'metɪk] <> adj que provoca vômitos. <> n vomitório m.

emigrant ['emɪgrənt] n emigrante mf.

emigrate ['emɪgreɪt] vi emigrar; **to** ~ **to/from** emigrar para/de.

emigration [,emɪ'greɪʃn] n (U) emigração f.

émigré ['emɪgreɪ] n fml exilado m político, exilada f política.

eminence ['emɪnəns] n (U) [prominence] eminência f.

eminent ['emɪnənt] adj [distinguished] eminente.

eminently ['emɪnəntlɪ] adv fml [extremely] eminentemente.

emir [e'mɪə'] n emir m.

emissary ['emɪsərɪ] (pl -ies) n fml emissário m, -ria f.

emission [ɪ'mɪʃn] n fml emissão f.

emit [ɪ'mɪt] (pt & pp -ted, cont -ting) vt fml emitir.

emollient [ɪ'mɒlɪənt] n fml emoliente m.

emolument [ɪ'mɒljʊmənt] n fml [payment fee] honorários mpl; [salary] remuneração f.

emoticon [ɪ'məʊtɪkɒn] n COMPUT emoticon m.

emotion [ɪ'məʊʃn] n emoção f.

emotional [ɪ'məʊʃənl] adj -1. [easily moved] emotivo(va) -2. [charged with emotion] emocionado(da) -3. [appealing to the emotions] comovente.

emotionally [ɪ'məʊʃnəlɪ] adv emocionalmente.

emotionless [ɪ'məʊʃnlɪs] adj sem emoção.

emotive [ɪ'məʊtɪv] adj emotivo(va), emocionante.

empathy ['empəθɪ] n (U) : ~ **(with sb)** empatia f (com alguém).

emperor ['empərə'] n imperador m.

emphasis ['emfəsɪs] (pl -ases [-əsiːz]) n: ~ **(on sthg)** ênfase f (em algo); **to lay** OR **place** ~ **on sthg** dar ênfase a algo.

emphasize, -ise ['emfəsaɪz] vt enfatizar.

emphatic [ɪm'fætɪk] adj [forceful] enfático(ca).

emphatically [ɪm'fætɪklɪ] adv -1. [with emphasis] enfaticamente -2. [definitely] terminantemente.

emphysema [,emfɪ'siːmə] n (U) enfisema m.

empire ['empaɪə'] n império m.

empire building n desenvolvimento m de impérios econômicos.

empirical [ɪm'pɪrɪkl] adj empírico(ca).

empiricism [ɪm'pɪrɪsɪzm] n (U) empirismo m.

employ [ɪm'plɔɪ] vt -1. [give work to] empregar; **to be** ~**ed as sthg** estar empregado(da) como algo -2. fml [use] empregar; **to** ~ **sthg as sthg/to do sthg** empregar algo como algo/para fazer algo.

employable [ɪm'plɔɪəbl] adj empregável.

employee [ɪm'plɔɪiː] n empregado m, -da f.

employer [ɪm'plɔɪə'] n empregador m, -ra f.

employment [ɪm'plɔɪmənt] n -1. [being in work] emprego m; **to be in** ~ estar empregado(da) -2. [work] trabalho m.

employment agency n agência f de empregos.

employment office n agência m de empregos.

emporium [em'pɔːrɪəml] n empório m.

empower [ɪm'paʊə'] vt fml: **to be** ~**ed to do sthg** receber autoridade para fazer algo.

empress ['emprɪs] n imperatriz f.

emptiness ['emptɪnɪs] n (U) vazio m.

empty ['emptɪ] (compar -ier, superl -iest, pt & pp -ied, pl -ies) <> adj vazio(zia). <> vt esvaziar; **to** ~ **sthg into/out of sthg** despejar algo em/de dentro de algo. <> vi [become empty] esvaziar. <> n inf casco m.

empty-handed [-'hændɪd] adv de mãos vazias.

empty-headed [-'hedɪd] adj pej de cabeça vazia.

EMS (abbr of European Monetary System) n SMT m.

emu ['iːmjuː] (pl inv OR -s) n emu f.

EMU (abbr of Economic and Monetary Union) n UME f.

emulate ['emjʊleɪt] vt -1. [gen] imitar -2. COMPUT emular.

emulsion [ɪ'mʌlʃn] <> n -1.: ~ **(paint)** tinta f plástica -2. PHOT emulsão f. <> vt UK [paint] pintar (com tinta plástica).

enable [ɪ'neɪbl] vt: **to** ~ **sb to do sthg** permitir que alguém faça algo.

enact [ɪ'nækt] vt -1. JUR promulgar -2. [act] representar.

enactment [ɪ'næktmənt] n -1. JUR promulgação f -2. [of scene, play] representação f.

enamel [ɪ'næml] n (U) esmalte m.

enamelled UK, **enameled** US [ɪ'næmld] adj esmaltado(da).

enamel paint n (U) tinta f esmalte.

enamoured UK, **enamored** US [ɪ'næməd] adj: ~ **of sb/sthg** encantado(da) por alguém/algo.

en bloc [ɑː'blɒk] adv fml em bloco.

enc. - 1. (*abbr of* enclosure) anexo *m.* **- 2.** (*abbr of* enclosed) anexo(xa).

encamp *vi* acampar, acampar-se.

encampment [ɪnˈkæmpmənt] *n* [of soldiers, gipsies] acampamento *m.*

encapsulate [ɪnˈkæpsjʊleɪt] *vt fig* [philosophy, idea]: **to ~ sthg (in)** resumir algo (em).

encase [ɪnˈkeɪs] *vt*: **~d in sthg** envolvido(da) em algo.

encash [ɪnˈkæʃ] *vt UK* [cheque] descontar.

enchanted [ɪnˈtʃɑːntɪd] *adj* **- 1.** [delighted]: **~ (by** OR **with sthg)** encantado(da) (por OR com algo) **- 2.** [under a spell] encantado(da).

enchanting [ɪnˈtʃɑːntɪŋ] *adj* encantador(ra).

encircle [ɪnˈsɜːkl] *vt* cercar.

enclave [ˈenkleɪv] *n* [of country] enclave *m.*

enclose [ɪnˈkləʊz] *vt* **- 1.** [surround, contain] cercar; **~d by** OR **with sthg** cercado(da) por OR com algo **- 2.** [put in envelope] anexar; **please find ~d ...** segue anexo(xa) ...

enclosure [ɪnˈkləʊʒəʳ] *n* **- 1.** [place] cercado *m* **- 2.** [in letter] anexo *m.*

encompass [ɪnˈkʌmpəs] *vt fml* **- 1.** [include] abranger **- 2.** [surround] cercar.

encore [ˈɒŋkɔːʳ] ⋄ *n* [by singer, performer] bis *m.* ⋄ *excl* bis!

encounter [ɪnˈkaʊntəʳ] ⋄ *n* encontro *m.* ⋄ *vt fml* **- 1.** [person] encontrar, encontrar-se com **- 2.** [problem, difficulty etc.] deparar-se com.

encourage [ɪnˈkʌrɪdʒ] *vt* **- 1.** [give confidence to]: **to ~ sb (to do sthg)** incentivar alguém (a fazer algo) **- 2.** [foster] incentivar, estimular.

encouragement [ɪnˈkʌrɪdʒmənt] *n (U)* incentivo *m,* estímulo *m.*

encouraging [ɪnˈkʌrɪdʒɪŋ] *adj* incentivador(ra).

encroach [ɪnˈkrəʊtʃ] *vi*: **to ~ (up)on sthg** apossar-se de algo; [rights] abusar de algo; [privacy] invadir algo.

encrusted [ɪnˈkrʌstɪd] *adj*: **~ with sthg** incrustado(da) de algo.

encrypt [ɪnˈkrɪpt] *vt* COMPUT criptografar.

encumber [ɪnˈkʌmbəʳ] *vt fml*: **to be ~ed with sthg** estar carregado(da) de algo; [debts] estar sobrecarregado(da) de algo.

encyclop(a)edia [ɪnˌsaɪkləˈpiːdjə] *n* enciclopédia *f.*

encyclop(a)edic [ɪnˌsaɪkləˈpiːdɪk] *adj* enciclopédico(ca).

end [end] ⋄ *n* **- 1.** [last part, finish] fim *m,* final *m;* **to be at an ~** estar no fim; **to come to an ~** acabar, chegar ao fim; **to put an ~ to sthg** pôr fim a algo; **at the ~ of the day** *fig* no final das contas; **in the ~** [finally] finalmente **- 2.** [tip, edge] extremidade *f* **- 3.** [point, final section] ponta *f;* **from ~ to ~** de ponta a ponta **- 4.** [side, one of two ends, of phone line] lado *m;* **which ~ does it open?** de que lado abre?; **to make ~s meet** conseguir que o dinheiro chegue **- 5.** *fml* [purpose] fim *m,* objetivo *m;* **an ~ in itself** um fim em si mesmo **- 6.** *literary* [death] fim *m.* ⋄ *vt* acabar, terminar; **to ~ sthg with** acabar OR terminar algo com. ⋄ *vi* [finish] acabar, terminar; **to ~ in** acabar em; **to ~ with** acabar OR terminar com.

◆ on end *adv* **- 1.** [upright] em pé **- 2.** [continuously] a fio.

◆ no end *adv inf*: **it cheered me up no ~** me alegrou o tempo inteirinho.

◆ no end of *prep inf* um mar de.

◆ end up *vi* acabar, terminar; **to ~ up doing sthg** acabar fazendo algo.

endanger [ɪnˈdeɪndʒəʳ] *vt* pôr em perigo.

endangered species [ɪnˈdeɪndʒəd-] *n* espécie *f* em perigo de extinção.

endear [ɪnˈdɪəʳ] *vt*: **to ~ sb to sb** fazer com que alguém conquiste alguém; **to ~ o.s. to sb** conquistar a afeição de alguém.

endearing [ɪnˈdɪərɪŋ] *adj* simpático(ca).

endearment [ɪnˈdɪəməntl] *n fml* palavra *f* carinhosa.

endeavour UK, **endeavor** US [ɪnˈdevəʳ] *fml* ⋄ *n* tentativa *f,* esforço *m.* ⋄ *vt*: **to ~ to do sthg** tentar fazer algo.

endemic [enˈdemɪk] *adj* endêmico(ca).

ending [ˈendɪŋ] *n* **- 1.** [gen] final *m* **- 2.** GRAM terminação *f.*

endive [ˈendaɪv] *n* **- 1.** [salad vegetable] endívia *f* **- 2.** [chicory] chicória *f.*

endless [ˈendlɪs] *adj* **- 1.** [unending] interminável **- 2.** [inexhaustible] inesgotável **- 3.** [vast] sem fim.

endlessly [ˈendlɪslɪ] *adv* **- 1.** [in time] interminavelmente **- 2.** [in amount, degree] infinitamente.

endorse [ɪnˈdɔːs] *vt* **- 1.** [approve] endossar **- 2.** UK [driving licence]: **to have one's licence ~d** receber pontos na carteira.

endorsement [ɪnˈdɔːsmənt] *n* **- 1.** (*U*) [gen] endosso *m* **- 2.** UK [on driving licence] pontos *mpl.*

endow [ɪnˈdaʊ] *vt* **- 1.** [equip]: **to be ~ed with sthg** ser dotado(da) de algo **- 2.** [donate money to] dotar.

endowment [ɪnˈdaʊmənt] *n* dote *m.*

endowment insurance *n* seguro *m* dotal.

endowment mortgage *n UK* hipoteca *f* dotal.

end product *n* produto *m* final.

end result *n* resultado *m* final.

endurable [ɪnˈdjʊərəbl] *adj* suportável.

endurance [ɪnˈdjʊərəns] *n (U)* resistência *f.*

endurance test *n* teste *m* de resistência.

endure [ɪnˈdjʊəʳ] ⋄ *vt* resistir, suportar. ⋄ *vi fml* perdurar.

enduring [ɪnˈdjʊərɪŋ] *adj fml* perdurável.

end user *n* usuário *m,* -ria *f* final.

endways UK [ˈendweɪz], **endwise** US [ˈendwaɪz] *adv* **- 1.** [lengthways] de frente **- 2.** [end to end] ponta a ponta.

enema [ˈenɪmə] *n* MED enema *m.*

enemy [ˈenɪmɪ] (*pl* -ies) ⋄ *n* **- 1.** [person] inimigo *m,* -ga *f* **- 2.** MIL: **the ~** o inimigo. ⋄ *comp* inimigo(ga).

energetic [ˌenəˈdʒetɪk] *adj* **- 1.** [lively] ativo(va) **- 2.** [physically taxing] vigoroso(sa) **- 3.** [enthusiastic] ativo(va).

energy [ˈenədʒɪ] (*pl* -ies) *n (U)* energia *f.*

energy-saving *adj* [device] que poupa energia.

enervating [ˈenəveɪtɪŋ] *adj fml* desgastante.

enfold [ɪnˈfəʊld] *vt literary* **- 1.** [engulf] envolver **- 2.** [embrace]: **to ~ sb (in sthg)** envolver alguém (em algo).

enforce [ɪnˈfɔːs] vt -1. [law] fazer cumprir, aplicar -2. [standards, discipline] impor.

enforceable [ɪnˈfɔːsəbl] adj aplicável.

enforced [ɪnˈfɔːst] adj -1. [obligatory] compulsório(-ria) -2. [unavoidable] inevitável.

enforcement [ɪnˈfɔːsmənt] n (U) aplicação f.

enfranchise [ɪnˈfræntʃaɪz] vt -1. [give vote to] conferir o direito de voto a -2. [set free] emancipar.

engage [ɪnˈɡeɪdʒ] <> vt -1. [attract] atrair; **to ~ sb in conversation** travar conversa com alguém -2. TECH engrenar -3. fml [employ] contratar; **to be ~d in OR on sthg** dedicar-se a algo; [busy with] estar ocupado(da) em algo. <> vi [be involved]: **to ~ in** envolver-se em.

engaged [ɪnˈɡeɪdʒd] adj -1. [couple] noivo(va); **~ to sb** noivo(va) de alguém; **to get ~** noivar -2. [busy, occupied] ocupado(da); **~ in sthg** envolvido(da) em algo -3. [phone, toilet] ocupado(da).

engaged tone n UK sinal m de ocupado.

engagement [ɪnˈɡeɪdʒmənt] n -1. [of couple] noivado m -2. [appointment] compromisso m.

engagement ring n anel m de noivado.

engaging [ɪnˈɡeɪdʒɪŋ] adj atraente.

engender [ɪnˈdʒendər] vt fml gerar.

engine [ˈendʒɪn] n -1. [of car, plane, ship] motor m -2. RAIL locomotiva f.

engine driver n UK maquinista mf.

engineer [ˌendʒɪˈnɪər] <> n -1. [of roads, machines, bridges] engenheiro m, -ra f -2. [on ship] técnico m, -ca f -3. US [engine driver] maquinista mf. <> vt -1. [construct] construir -2. [contrive] tramar.

engineering [ˌendʒɪˈnɪərɪŋ] n engenharia f.

England [ˈɪŋɡlənd] n Inglaterra; **in ~** na Inglaterra.

English [ˈɪŋɡlɪʃ] <> adj inglês(esa). <> n [language] inglês m. <> npl: **the ~** os ingleses.

English breakfast n café m da manhã inglês.

English Channel n: **the ~** o Canal da Mancha.

Englishman [ˈɪŋɡlɪʃmən] (pl -men [-mən]) n inglês m.

English muffin n US pãozinho redondo e chato que se costuma torrar antes de comer.

Englishwoman [ˈɪŋɡlɪʃˌwʊmən] (pl -women [-ˌwɪmɪn]) n inglesa f.

engrave [ɪnˈɡreɪv] vt -1. [metal, glass] gravar -2. [design]: **to ~ sthg (on sthg)** gravar algo (em algo) -3. fig [on memory] gravar.

engraver [ɪnˈɡreɪvər] n gravador m, -ra f.

engraving [ɪnˈɡreɪvɪŋ] n -1. [design] gravura f -2. (U) [skill] gravação f.

engrossed [ɪnˈɡrəʊst] adj: **to be ~ (in sthg)** estar absorto(ta) (em algo).

engrossing [ɪnˈɡrəʊsɪŋ] adj absorvente.

engulf [ɪnˈɡʌlf] vt -1. [cover, surround - subj:fire] devorar; [- subj:water] tragar -2. fig [overwhelm] tomar conta de.

enhance [ɪnˈhɑːns] vt -1. [increase] aumentar -2. [improve] melhorar -3. [heighten: beauty, graphics] realçar.

enhancement [ɪnˈhɑːnsmənt] n -1. (U) [increase] aumento m -2. [improvement] melhoria f -3. COMPUT realçamento m.

enigma [ɪˈnɪɡmə] n enigma m.

enigmatic [ˌenɪɡˈmætɪk] adj enigmático(ca).

enjoy [ɪnˈdʒɔɪ] <> vt -1. [like] gostar de; **to ~ doing sthg** gostar de fazer algo; **to ~ o.s.** divertir-se -2. fml [possess] desfrutar de. <> vi US: **~!** [enjoy yourself] divirta-se!; [before meal] bom apetite!

enjoyable [ɪnˈdʒɔɪəbl] adj agradável.

enjoyment [ɪnˈdʒɔɪmənt] n -1. (U) prazer m -2. (U) fml [possession] gozo m, desfrute m.

enlarge [ɪnˈlɑːdʒ] vt ampliar.

→ **enlarge (up)on** vt fus desenvolver.

enlargement [ɪnˈlɑːdʒmənt] n -1. (U) [gen] ampliação f -2. MED dilatação f.

enlighten [ɪnˈlaɪtn] vt fml esclarecer.

enlightened [ɪnˈlaɪtnd] adj esclarecido(da).

enlightening [ɪnˈlaɪtnɪŋ] adj esclarecedor(ra).

enlightenment [ɪnˈlaɪtnmənt] n (U) esclarecimento m.

→ **Enlightenment** n: **the Enlightenment** o Iluminismo.

enlist [ɪnˈlɪst] <> vt -1. MIL [recruit] recrutar -2. [support, help] angariar. <> vi MIL: **to ~ (in)** alistar-se(em).

enlisted man [ɪnˈlɪstɪd-] n US recruta m.

enliven [ɪnˈlaɪvn] vt animar.

en masse [ˌɒnˈmæs] adv em massa.

enmeshed [ɪnˈmeʃt] adj: **to be ~ in sthg** estar enredado(da) em algo.

enmity [ˈenmətɪ] (pl -ies) n (U) inimizade f.

ennoble [ɪˈnəʊbl] vt -1. [elevate to nobility] nobilitar -2. [dignify] enobrecer.

enormity [ɪˈnɔːmətɪ] n (U) enormidade f.

enormous [ɪˈnɔːməs] adj enorme.

enormously [ɪˈnɔːməslɪ] adv enormemente.

enough [ɪˈnʌf] <> adj suficiente. <> pron suficiente; **to have had ~ (of sthg)** [expressing annoyance] estar farto(ta) (de algo); **more than ~** mais que suficiente; **~ is ~** já chega; **that's ~ (of that)!** chega! <> adv -1. [sufficiently] suficientemente, bastante; **to suffer ~** sofrer o bastante; **he hasn't tried hard ~** ele ainda não tentou o suficiente; **to be good ~ to do sthg** fml ter a bondade de fazer algo -2. [rather] bastante; **strangely ~** curiosamente.

enquire [ɪnˈkwaɪər] vt & vi = inquire.

enquiry [ɪnˈkwaɪərɪ] (pl -ies) n = inquiry.

enraged [ɪnˈreɪdʒd] adj enfurecido(da).

enrich [ɪnˈrɪtʃ] vt enriquecer.

enrol UK (pt & pp -led, cont -ling), **enroll** US [ɪnˈrəʊl] <> vt matricular. <> vi: **to ~ (on OR in sthg)** matricular-se (em algo).

enrolment UK, **enrollment** US [ɪnˈrəʊlmənt] n -1. (U) [act of registering] inscrição f -2. [entry in register] matrícula f.

en route [ˌɒnˈruːt] *adv*: ~ **(from)** vindo de: ~ **(to)** a caminho de.

ensconced [ɪnˈskɒnst] *adj fml* [in chair] acomodado(-da).

enshrine [ɪnˈʃraɪn] *vt*: **to be** ~**d in sthg** estar amparado(da) em algo, ser garantido(da) por algo.

ensign [ˈensaɪn] *n* **-1.** [flag] bandeira *f*-**2.** *US* [sailor] guarda-marinha *mf*.

enslave [ɪnˈsleɪv] *vt* escravizar.

ensue [ɪnˈsjuː] *vi fml* resultar.

ensuing [ɪnˈsjuːɪŋ] *adj fml* subseqüente.

ensure [ɪnˈʃʊəʳ] *vt* assegurar; **to** ~ **(that)** assegurar que.

ENT (*abbr of* **ear, nose and throat**) *n* otorrino *mf*.

entail [ɪnˈteɪl] *vt* [involve] implicar.

entangled [ɪnˈtæŋgld] *adj* **-1.** [ensnared]: **to be** ~ **in sthg** estar emaranhado(da) em algo **-2.** [involved]: **to be** ~ **in sthg** estar envolvido(da) em algo; **to be** ~ **with sb** estar envolvido(da) com alguém.

entanglement [ɪnˈtæŋglmənt] *n* [involvement] envolvimento *m*.

enter [ˈentəʳ] <> *vt* **-1.** [come or go into] entrar em **-2.** [join - competition, race, the church] entrar em; [- school, politics, parliament] ingressar em; [- armed forces] alistar-se em; [- university] matricular-se em **-3.** [register]: **to** ~ **sb/sthg for sthg** inscrever alguém/algo em algo **-4.** [write down] registrar **-5.** *COMPUT* inserir; ~ **your name, please** insira seu nome. <> *vi* **-1.** [come or go in] entrar **-2.** [register]: **to** ~ **(for sthg)** inscrever-se (para algo).

➡ **enter into** *vt fus* **-1.** [begin] iniciar **-2.** [become involved in] comprometer-se em **-3.** [affect]: **money shouldn't** ~ **into it** o dinheiro não deveria contar aqui.

enteritis [ˌentəˈraɪtɪs] *n* (*U*) enterite *f*.

enter key *n COMPUT* tecla *f* enter.

enterprise [ˈentəpraɪz] *n* **-1.** [company, business] empresa *f*-**2.** [venture] aventura *f*-**3.** (*U*) [initiative] empreendimento *m*.

enterprise culture *n* cultura *f* empresarial.

enterprise zone *n UK* zona do Reino Unido na qual se fomenta a atividade cultural e empresarial.

enterprising [ˈentəpraɪzɪŋ] *adj* empreendedor(-ra).

entertain [ˌentəˈteɪn] <> *vt*-**1.** [amuse] entreter -**2.** [have as guest] receber -**3.** *fml* [consider] considerar -**4.** *fml* [harbour] nutrir. <> *vi* -**1.** [amuse] divertir -**2.** [have guests] receber.

entertainer [ˌentəˈteɪnəʳ] *n* animador *m*, -ra *f*.

entertaining [ˌentəˈteɪnɪŋ] <> *adj* divertido(da). <> *n* (*U*) [receiving guests]: **she does a lot of** ~ ela sempre recebe muitos convidados.

entertainment [ˌentəˈteɪnmənt] <> *n* **-1.** (*U*) [amusement] divertimento *m*, entretenimento *m* **-2.** [show] espetáculo *m*. <> *comp* do espetáculo.

entertainment allowance *n* verba *f* de representação.

enthral (*pt* & *pp* **-led**, *cont* **-ling**), **enthrall** *US* [ɪnˈθrɔːl] *vt* fascinar.

enthralling [ɪnˈθrɔːlɪŋ] *adj* fascinante.

enthrone [ɪnˈθrəʊn] *vt fml* entronizar.

enthuse [ɪnˈθjuːz] *vi*: **to** ~ **(about sthg)** entusiasmar-se (com algo).

enthusiasm [ɪnˈθjuːzɪæzml] *n* **-1.** (*U*) [passion, eagerness] entusiasmo *m*; ~ **for sthg** entusiasmo por algo **-2.** [interest, hobby] paixão *f*, interesse *m*.

enthusiast [ɪnˈθjuːzɪæst] *n* [fan] entusiasta *mf*.

enthusiastic [ɪnˌθjuːzɪˈæstɪk] *adj* entusiástico(ca).

enthusiastically [ɪnˌθjuːzɪˈæstɪklɪ] *adv* entusiasticamente.

entice [ɪnˈtaɪs] *vt* atrair; **to** ~ **sb away from sthg** desviar alguém de algo; **to** ~ **sb into sthg** instigar alguém a algo.

enticing [ɪnˈtaɪsɪŋ] *adj* tentador(ra).

entire [ɪnˈtaɪəʳ] *adj* inteiro(ra).

entirely [ɪnˈtaɪəlɪ] *adv* inteiramente; **that's** ~ **different** isso é completamente diferente.

entirety [ɪnˈtaɪrətɪ] *n* (*U*) *fml*: **in its** ~ em sua totalidade.

entitle [ɪnˈtaɪtl] *vt* [allow]: **to** ~ **sb to sthg** dar a alguém o direito a algo; **to** ~ **sb to do sthg** autorizar alguém a fazer algo.

entitled [ɪnˈtaɪtld] *adj* **-1.** [having a right to]: **to be** ~ **to sthg/to do sthg** ter direito a algo/a fazer algo **-2.** [called] intitulado(da).

entitlement [ɪnˈtaɪtlmənt] *n* direito *m*.

entity [ˈentətɪ] (*pl* **-ies**) *n* entidade *f*.

entomology [ˌentəˈmɒlədʒɪ] *n* (*U*) entomologia *f*.

entourage [ˌɒntuˈrɑːʒ] *n* [of politician, popstar] séquito *m*.

entrails [ˈentreɪlz] *npl* entranhas *fpl*.

entrance [*n* ˈentrəns, *vb* ɪnˈtrɑːns] <> *n* **-1.** [arrival] entrada *f*-**2.** [way in]: ~ **(to sthg)** entrada (para *OR* de algo) **-3.** (*U*) [entry]: **to gain** ~ **to sthg** *fml* [to building] obter acesso a algo; [to society, university] ingressar em algo. <> *vt* [delight] encantar.

entrance examination *n* [for school, profession] exame *m* de admissão; [for university] ≃ vestibular *m*.

entrance fee *n* **-1.** [gen] (preço *m* do) ingresso *m* **-2.** [to club] taxa *f* de admissão.

entrancing [ɪnˈtrɑːnsɪŋ] *adj* encantador(ra).

entrant [ˈentrənt] *n* **-1.** [gen] participante *mf*-**2.** [to profession] novato *m*, -ta *f*-**3.** [to university] calouro *m*, -ra *f*.

entreat [ɪnˈtriːt] *vt*: **to** ~ **sb (to do sthg)** suplicar a alguém (para que faça algo).

entreaty [ɪnˈtriːtɪ] (*pl* **-ies**) *n* súplica *f*.

entrenched *adj* [firm] arraigado(da).

entrepreneur [ˌɒntrəprəˈnɜːʳ] *n* empresário *m*, -ria *f*.

entrepreneurial [ˌɒntrəprəˈnɜːrɪəl] *adj* empresarial.

entrust [ɪnˈtrʌst] *vt*: **to** ~ **sthg to sb, to** ~ **sb with sthg** confiar algo a alguém.

entry [ˈentrɪ] (*pl* **-ies**) *n* **-1.** [gen] entrada *f*; ~ **(into)** entrada (em) **-2.** (*U*) [admission]: ~ **(to)** acesso *m* (a); **to gain** ~ **to** conseguir acesso a; **'no** ~' [to room, building] 'proibida a entrada'; *AUT* 'não entre' **-3.** [in competition] inscrição *f*-**4.** [in diary] anotação *f*-**5.** [in ledger] lançamento *m* **-6.** *fig* [joining] ingresso *m*.

entry fee *n* ingresso *m*.

entry form *n* ficha *f* de inscrição.

entry phone *n* porteiro *m* eletrônico.

entryway ['entrɪˌweɪ] *n US* passagem *f* de entrada.
entwine [ɪn'twaɪn] <> *vt* entrelaçar. <> *vi* entrelaçar-se.
E number *n* na Europa, *número que representa a substância química adicionada a um alimento.*
enumerate [ɪ'nju:məreɪt] *vt* enumerar.
enunciate [ɪ'nʌnsɪeɪt] <> *vt* **-1.** [pronounce clearly] pronunciar **-2.** [express clearly] expor, enunciar. <> *vi* [speak clearly] enunciar.
envelop [ɪn'veləp] *vt*: to ~ sb/sthg in sthg envolver alguém/algo em algo.
envelope ['envələʊp] *n* [for letter] envelope *m*.
enviable ['envɪəbl] *adj* invejável.
envious ['envɪəs] *adj* invejoso(sa); ~ (of sb/ sthg) invejoso(sa) (de alguém/algo).
enviously ['envɪəslɪ] *adv* com inveja.
environment [ɪn'vaɪərənmənt] *n* **-1.** [gen] ambiente *m* **-2.** [natural world]: the ~ o meio ambiente; **Department of the Environment** *UK* ≃ Ministério *m* do Meio Ambiente.
environmental [ɪnˌvaɪərən'mentl] *adj* ambiental.
environmentalist [ɪnˌvaɪərən'mentəlɪst] *n* ambientalista *mf.*
environmentally [ɪnˌvaɪərən'mentəlɪ] *adv* ecologicamente; ~ **friendly** que não prejudica o meio ambiente, ecológico(ca).
Environmental Protection Agency *n US*: **the** ~ a Secretaria Especial do Meio Ambiente.
environs [ɪn'vaɪərənz] *npl* [of town, place] arredores *mpl.*
envisage [ɪn'vɪzɪdʒ], **envision** *US* [ɪn'vɪʒn] *vt* prever.
envoy ['envɔɪ] *n* enviado *m*, -da *f.*
envy ['envɪ] (*pt & pp* -ied) <> *n (U)* inveja *f*; to be the ~ of ser objeto de inveja de; to be green with ~ estar morrendo de inveja. <> *vt* invejar; to ~ sb sthg invejar algo a alguém.
enzyme ['enzaɪm] *n* enzima *f.*
EOC (*abbr of* Equal Opportunities Commission) *n organismo do governo britânico que trata da discriminação sexual.*
eon *n US* = aeon.
EPA (*abbr of* Environmental Protection Agency) *n agência norte-americana de proteção ambiental,* ≃ APA *f.*
epaulet(te) ['epəˈlet] *n* dragona *f.*
ephemeral [ɪ'femərəl] *adj* efêmero(ra).
epic ['epɪk] <> *adj* épico(ca). <> *n* [book, film] épico *m.*
epicentre *UK*, **epicenter** *US* ['epɪsentə'] *n* epicentro *m.*
epidemic [ˌepɪ'demɪk] *n* [of disease] epidemia *f.*
epidural [ˌepɪ'djʊərəl] *n* [injection] epidural *f.*
epigram ['epɪgræm] *n* epigrama *f.*
epilepsy ['epɪlepsɪ] *n (U)* epilepsia *f.*
epileptic [ˌepɪ'leptɪk] <> *adj* [fit, person] epilético(ca). <> *n* epilético *m*, -ca *f.*
epilogue *UK*, **epilog** *US* ['epɪlɒg] *n* [to play, book] epílogo *m.*
Epiphany [ɪ'pɪfənɪ] *n*: **(the)** ~ **(a)** Epifania.
episcopal [ɪ'pɪskəpl] *adj* [of bishop] episcopal.
episode ['epɪsəʊd] *n* episódio *m.*

episodic [ˌepɪ'sɒdɪk] *adj* episódico(ca).
epistle [ɪ'pɪsl] *n literary* [letter] epístola *f.*
epitaph ['epɪtɑːf] *n* epitáfio *m.*
epithet ['epɪθet] *n* epíteto *m.*
epitome [ɪ'pɪtəmɪ] *n*: **the** ~ **of sb/sthg** [person] o exemplo vivo de alguém/algo, a personificação de alguém/algo; **this hotel is the** ~ **of luxury** este hotel é o número um em termos de luxo.
epitomize, -ise [ɪ'pɪtəmaɪz] *vt* personificar, representar o paradigma de.
epoch ['iːpɒk] *n* época *f.*
epoch-making *adj* que marcou época.
eponymous [ɪ'pɒnɪməs] *adj* epônimo(ma).
EPOS (*abbr of* electronic point of sale) *n* ponto *m* eletrônico de venda, EPOS *m.*
equable ['ekwəbl] *adj* [calm, reasonable] calmo(ma).
equal ['iːkwəl] (*UK pt & pp*-led, *cont*-ling, *US pt & pp*-ed, *cont*-ing) <> *adj* **-1.** igual; ~ **to sthg** [sum] igual a algo; **on** ~ **terms** em igualdade de condições **-2.** [capable]: to be ~ to sthg estar à altura de algo. <> *n* [person] igual *mf*; **he's her** ~ **in everything** ele é igual a ela em tudo. <> *vt* **-1.** *MATH* ser igual a **-2.** [in standard] igualar-se a.
equality [iː'kwɒlətɪ] *n (U)* igualdade *f.*
equalize, -ise ['iːkwəlaɪz] <> *vt* igualar. <> *vi SPORT* empatar.
equalizer ['iːkwəlaɪzə'] *n SPORT* gol *m* de empate.
equally ['iːkwəlɪ] *adv* **-1.** [to the same extent] igualmente **-2.** [in equal amounts] por igual **-3.** [by the same token] da mesma forma.
equal opportunities *npl* oportunidades *fpl* iguais.
Equal Opportunities Commission *n*: **the** ~ *organismo do governo britânico que trata da discriminação sexual.*
equal(s) sign *n* sinal *m* de igual.
equanimity [ˌekwə'nɪmətɪ] *n (U)* equanimidade *f.*
equate [ɪ'kweɪt] *vt*: to ~ sthg with sthg equiparar algo com algo.
equation [ɪ'kweɪʒn] *n MATH* equação *f.*
equator [ɪ'kweɪtə'] *n*: **the** ~ o equador.
equatorial [ˌekwə'tɔːrɪəl] *adj* equatorial.
Equatorial Guinea *n* Guiné Equatorial.
equestrian [ɪ'kwestrɪən] *adj* eqüestre.
equidistant [ˌiːkwɪ'dɪstənt] *adj*: ~ **(from)** eqüidistante (de).
equilateral triangle [ˌiːkwɪ'lætərəl-] *n* triângulo *m* equilátero.
equilibrium [ˌiːkwɪ'lɪbrɪəm] *n* equilíbrio *m.*
equine ['ekwaɪn] *adj* eqüino(na).
equinox ['iːkwɪnɒks] *n* equinócio *m.*
equip [ɪ'kwɪp] (*pt & pp* -ped, *cont* -ping) *vt* **-1.** [provide with equipment] equipar; **to** ~ **sb/sthg with sthg** equipar alguém/algo com algo **-2.** [prepare mentally]: **to** ~ **sb for sthg** preparar alguém psicologicamente para algo.
equipment [ɪ'kwɪpmənt] *n (U)* equipamento *m.*
equitable ['ekwɪtəbl] *adj* eqüitativo(va).
equity ['ekwətɪ] *n FIN* [market value] patrimônio *m* líquido.
→ **equities** *npl ST EX* ações *fpl* ordinárias.
equivalent [ɪ'kwɪvələnt] <> *adj* equivalente; **to be**

~ **to sthg** ser equivalente a algo. <> *n* equivalente *m*.

equivocal [ɪˈkwɪvəkl] *adj* **-1.** [statement, remark] ambíguo(gua) **-2.** [behaviour, event] duvidoso(sa).

equivocate [ɪˈkwɪvəkeɪt] *vi* usar expressões ambíguas.

er [ɜːʳ] *excl* **-1.** [in hesitation] ãhn! **-2.** [to attract attention] ei!

ER -1. (*abbr of* **Elizabeth Regina**) *emblema da rainha Elizabete* **-2.** *n US* (*abbr of* **emergency room**) *MED* pronto-socorro *m*.

era [ˈɪərə] (*pl* **-s**) *n* era *f*.

ERA (*abbr of* **Equal Rights Amendment**) *n lei norte-americana de igualdade de direitos para as mulheres*.

eradicate [ɪˈrædɪkeɪt] *vt* erradicar.

eradication [ɪˌrædɪˈkeɪʃn] *n* (*U*) erradicação *f*.

erase [ɪˈreɪz] *vt* **-1.** [rub out] apagar **-2.** *fig* [drive away, eliminate] eliminar, extinguir.

eraser [ɪˈreɪzəʳ] *n US* borracha *f*.

erect [ɪˈrekt] <> *adj* ereto(ta). <> *vt* **-1.** [building, statue] erigir **-2.** [tent, roadblock] montar.

erection [ɪˈrekʃn] *n* **-1.** (*U*) [of building, statue] construção *f* **-2.** [erect penis] ereção *f*; **to get/have an** ~ conseguir/ter uma ereção.

ergonomic [ˌɜːɡəˈnɒmɪk] *adj* ergonômico(ca).

ergonomics [ˌɜːɡəˈnɒmɪks] *n* (*U*) ergonomia *f*.

ERISA (*abbr of* **Employee Retirement Income Security Act**) *n lei norte-americana que trata de questões de aposentadoria*.

Eritrea [ˌerɪˈtreɪə] *n* Eritréia; **in** ~ na Eritréia.

Eritrean [ˌerɪˈtreɪən] <> *adj* eritreu(tréia). <> *n* eritreu *m*, -tréia *f*.

ERM (*abbr of* **Exchange Rate Mechanism**) *n* MTC *m*.

ermine [ˈɜːmɪn] *n* (*U*) [fur] arminho *m*.

erode [ɪˈrəʊd] <> *vt* **-1.** *GEOL* causar erosão em **-2.** *fig* [destroy] destruir. <> *vi* **-1.** *GEOL* sofrer erosão **-2.** *fig* [be destroyed] ser destruído(da).

erogenous zone [ɪˈrɒdʒɪnəs-] *n* zona *f* erógena.

erosion [ɪˈrəʊʒn] *n* **-1.** *GEOL* erosão *f* **-2.** *fig* [destruction] destruição *f*.

erotic [ɪˈrɒtɪk] *adj* erótico(ca).

eroticism [ɪˈrɒtɪsɪzm] *n* (*U*) erotismo *m*.

err [ɜːʳ] *vi* errar; **to** ~ **on the side of caution** pecar por excesso de cautela; **to** ~ **is human** errar é humano.

errand [ˈerənd] *n* **-1.** [task] tarefa *f*; **to go on** *OR* **run an** ~ **(for sb)** encarregar-se de alguma tarefa (para alguém) **-2.** [message] recado *m*.

errand boy *n* menino *m* de recados.

erratic [ɪˈrætɪk] *adj* irregular.

erroneous [ɪˈrəʊnjəs] *adj fml* errôneo(nea).

error [ˈerəʳ] *n* **-1.** [mistake] erro *m*; ~ **of judgment** erro de julgamento; **in** ~ por engano **-2.** *FIN*: ~ **s and omissions excepted** salvo erro ou omissão.

error message *n* *COMPUT* mensagem *f* de erro.

erstwhile [ˈɜːstwaɪl] *adj literary* anterior, antigo(ga).

erudite [ˈeruːdaɪt] *adj* erudito(ta).

erupt [ɪˈrʌpt] *vi* **-1.** [volcano] entrar em erupção **-2.** *fig* [violence, war] explodir.

eruption [ɪˈrʌpʃn] *n* **-1.** [of volcano] erupção *f* **-2.** [of violence, war] explosão *f*.

ESA (*abbr of* **European Space Agency**) *n agência espacial européia*.

escalate [ˈeskəleɪt] *vi* **-1.** [conflict, violence] intensificar-se **-2.** [costs, prices] aumentar.

escalation [ˌeskəˈleɪʃn] *n* **-1.** [of conflict, violence] intensificação *f* **-2.** [of costs, prices] aumento *m*.

escalator [ˈeskəleɪtəʳ] *n* escada *f* rolante.

escalator clause *n* cláusula *f* de indexação.

escapade [ˌeskəˈpeɪd] *n* escapada *f*.

escape [ɪˈskeɪp] <> *n* **-1.** [gen] fuga *f*; ~ **(from sb/sthg)** fuga (de alguém/algo); **one's** ~ **(from)** fugir (de); **we had a narrow** ~ escapamos por um triz **-2.** [leakage] escapamento *m* **-3.** *COMPUT* tecla *f* Esc. <> *vt* **-1.** [gen] fugir de **-2.** [death, injury] escapar a; **to** ~ **notice** passar desapercebido(da) **-3.** [subj: fact, name] escapar. <> *vi* **-1.** [from person, place, situation]: **to** ~ **(from sb/sthg)** fugir (de alguém/algo) **-2.** [from danger] escapar **-3.** [leak] vazar.

escape clause *n* cláusula *f* de exceção, *cláusula que permite revogação de um contrato*.

escape key *n* *COMPUT* tecla *f* Esc.

escape route *n* **-1.** [from prison] rota *f* de fuga **-2.** [from fire] saída *f* de emergência.

escapism [ɪˈskeɪpɪzm] *n* (*U*) escapismo *m*.

escapist [ɪˈskeɪpɪst] *adj* escapista.

escapologist [ˌeskəˈpɒlədʒɪst] *n* ilusionista *mf*.

escarpment [ɪˈskɑːpmənt] *n* escarpa *f*.

eschew [ɪsˈtʃuː] *vt fml* evitar.

escort [n ˈeskɔːt, vb ɪˈskɔːt] <> *n* **-1.** [guard] escolta *f*; **under** ~ sob escolta **-2.** [companion] acompanhante *mf*. <> *vt* [accompany] acompanhar.

escort agency *n* agência *f* de acompanhantes.

Eskimo [ˈeskɪməʊ] (*pl* **-s**) <> *adj* esquimó. <> *n* **-1.** [person] esquimó *mf* **-2.** [language] esquimó *m*.

ESL (*abbr of* **English as a Second Language**) *n inglês para imigrantes que vivem permanentemente no Reino Unido e obtiveram cidadania britânica*.

esophagus *n US* = oesophagus.

esoteric [ˌesəˈterɪk] *adj* esotérico(ca).

esp. (*abbr of* **especially**) espec.

ESP *n* **-1.** (*abbr of* **extrasensory perception**) percepção *f* extrasensorial. **-2.** (*abbr of* **English for Special Purposes**) *inglês para fins específicos*.

espadrille [ˌespəˈdrɪl] *n* alpargata *f*.

especial *adj* especial.

especially [ɪˈspeʃəlɪ] *adv* **-1.** [in particular, specifically] especialmente **-2.** [more than usually] excepcionalmente.

Esperanto [ˌespəˈræntəʊ] *n* esperanto *m*.

espionage [ˈespɪəˌnɑːʒ] *n* (*U*) espionagem *f*.

esplanade [ˌespləˈneɪd] *n* esplanada *f*.

espouse [ɪˈspaʊz] *vt fml* abraçar.

espresso [eˈspresəʊ] (*pl* **-s**) *n* café *m* expresso.

Esq. (*abbr of* **esquire**) *n título formal utilizado após um nome masculino, especialmente se ele não tiver nenhum outro título*.

Esquire [ɪˈskwaɪəʳ] *n*: **James Smith,** ~ Sr. James Smith.

essay [ˈeseɪ] *n* **-1.** *SCH & UNIV* trabalho *m* **-2.** *LITERATURE* ensaio *m*.

essayist [ˈeseɪɪst] *n* ensaísta *mf*.

essence [ˈesns] *n* essência *f*; **in** ~ em essência.

essential [ɪˈsenʃl] *adj* essencial; ~ **(to** OR **for sthg)** essencial (para algo).
➥ **essentials** *npl* - **1.** [basic commodities] o essencial - **2.** [most important elements] fundamentos *mpl*, elementos *mpl* essenciais.
essentially [ɪˈsenʃəlɪ] *adv* [basically] essencialmente, basicamente.
essential oil *n* óleo *m* essencial.
est. - **1.** (*abbr of* **established**) estabelecido(da). - **2.** (*abbr of* **estimated**) estimado(da).
EST (*abbr of* **Eastern Standard Time**) *n* horário oficial na zona oriental dos Estados Unidos.
establish [ɪˈstæblɪʃ] *vt* - **1.** [create, found] criar, estabelecer - **2.** [initiate]: **to ~ contact with sb** estabelecer contato com alguém - **3.** [ascertain] provar - **4.** [cause to be accepted] firmar; **to ~ o.s. (as)** estabelecer-se (como).
established [ɪˈstæblɪʃt] *adj* - **1.** [accepted] aceito(ta) - **2.** [founded] fundado(da).
establishment [ɪˈstæblɪʃmənt] *n* - **1.** (*U*) [creation, foundation] fundação *f*, criação *f* - **2.** [shop, business] estabelecimento *m*.
➥ **Establishment** *n* [status quo]: **the Establishment** a classe governante.
estate [ɪˈsteɪt] *n* - **1.** [land, property] propriedade *f* - **2.**: **housing ~** loteamento *m* - **3.**: **industrial ~** zona *f* industrial - **4.** JUR [inheritance] herança *f*.
estate agency *n* UK agência *f* imobiliária.
estate agent *n* UK corretor *m*, -ra *f* de imóveis; **~ 's** agência *f* imobiliária.
estate car *n* UK van *f*, perua *f*.
estd., est'd. (*abbr of* **established**) estabelecido(-da).
esteem [ɪˈstiːm] ⟨⟩ *n* estima *f*; **to hold sb/sthg in high ~** ter alguém/algo em alta estima. ⟨⟩ *vt* [respect] estimar.
esthetic etc US = **aesthetic etc.**
estimate [*n* ˈestɪmət, *vb* ˈestɪmeɪt] ⟨⟩ *n* - **1.** [calculation, reckoning] cálculo *m*, estimativa *f* - **2.** COMM orçamento *m*. ⟨⟩ *vt* calcular, estimar. ⟨⟩ *vi* COMM: **to ~ for sthg** fazer um orçamento de algo.
estimated [ˈestɪmeɪtɪd] *adj* estimado(da); **an ~ 5,000 people died** estima-se que 5.000 pessoas morreram.
estimation [ˌestɪˈmeɪʃn] *n* - **1.** [opinion] opinião *f* - **2.** [calculation] cálculo *m*, estimativa *f*.
Estonia [eˈstəʊnɪə] *n* Estônia; **in ~** na Estônia.
Estonian [eˈstəʊnɪən] ⟨⟩ *adj* estoniano(na). ⟨⟩ *n* - **1.** [person] estoniano *m*, -na *f* - **2.** [language] estoniano *m*.
estranged [ɪˈstreɪndʒd] *adj* separado(da); **his ~ son** o filho com o qual ele não fala.
estrogen *n* US = **oestrogen**.
estuary [ˈestjʊərɪ] (*pl* -**ies**) *n* estuário *m*.
ETA (*abbr of* **estimated time of arrival**) *n* hora *f* prevista de chegada.
e-tailer [ˈiːteɪləʳ] *n* varejista *mf* eletrônico(ca), e-tailer *mf*.
et al. [ˌetˈæl] (*abbr of* **et alii**) et al.
etc. (*abbr of* **etcetera**) etc.
etcetera [ɪtˈsetərə] *adv* et cetera.
etch [etʃ] *vt* - **1.** [engrave] gravar com água-forte - **2.** *fig* [imprint]: **to be ~ed on sb's memory** estar

gravado(da) na memória de alguém.
etching [ˈetʃɪŋ] *n* gravura *f* de água-forte.
ETD (*abbr of* **estimated time of departure**) *n* hora *f* prevista de partida.
eternal [ɪˈtɜːnl] *adj* - **1.** [gen] eterno(na) - **2.** [truth, value] absoluto(ta).
eternally [ɪˈtɜːnəlɪ] *adv* [forever] eternamente.
eternity [ɪˈtɜːnətɪ] *n* (*U*) eternidade *f*.
eternity ring *n* UK aliança que simboliza o amor eterno.
ether [ˈiːθəʳ] *n* (*U*) [solvent, anaesthetic] éter *m*.
ethereal [ɪˈθɪərɪəl] *adj literary* [unearthly] etéreo(rea).
ethic [ˈeθɪk] *n* ética *f*.
➥ **ethics** ⟨⟩ *n* (*U*) [study] ética *f*. ⟨⟩ *npl* [morals] moral *f*.
ethical [ˈeθɪkl] *adj* [morally right] ético(ca).
Ethiopia [ˌiːθɪˈəʊpɪə] *n* Etiópia; **in ~** na Etiópia.
Ethiopian [ˌiːθɪˈəʊpɪən] ⟨⟩ *adj* etíope. ⟨⟩ *n* etíope *mf*.
ethnic [ˈeθnɪk] *adj* - **1.** [traditions, groups, conflict] étnico(ca) - **2.** [clothes, food] folclórico(ca).
ethnic cleansing [-ˈklensɪŋ] *n* limpeza *f* étnica.
ethnic minority *n* minoria *f* étnica.
ethnology [eθˈnɒlədʒɪ] *n* (*U*) etnologia *f*.
ethos [ˈiːθɒs] *n* sistema *m* de valores.
etiquette [ˈetɪket] *n* etiqueta *f*.
ETV (*abbr of* **Educational Television**) *n* rede norte-americana de televisão especializada em programas culturais e educacionais.
etymology [ˌetɪˈmɒlədʒɪ] (*pl* -**ies**) *n* etimologia *f*.
EU (*abbr of* **European Union**) *n* UE *f*.
eucalyptus [ˌjuːkəˈlɪptəs] (*pl* -**tuses**) *n* eucalipto *m*.
eulogize, -ise [ˈjuːlədʒaɪz] *vt fml* elogiar, louvar.
eulogy [ˈjuːlədʒɪ] (*pl* -**ies**) *n fml* elogio *m*.
eunuch [ˈjuːnək] *n* eunuco *m*.
euphemism [ˈjuːfəmɪzml] *n* eufemismo *m*.
euphemistic [ˌjuːfəˈmɪstɪk] *adj* eufemístico(ca).
euphoria [juːˈfɔːrɪə] *n* euforia *f*.
euphoric [juːˈfɒrɪk] *adj* eufórico(ca).
Eurasia [jʊəˈreɪʒə] *n* Eurásia; **in ~** na Eurásia.
Eurasian [jʊəˈreɪʒən] ⟨⟩ *adj* - **1.** [of Europe and Asia] eurásico(ca) - **2.** [of mixed European and Asian descent] eurasiático(ca). ⟨⟩ *n* eurasiático *m*, -ca *f*.
eureka [jʊəˈriːkə] *excl* heureca!
Euro- [ˈjʊərəʊ] *prefix* euro-.
Eurocheque [ˈjʊərəʊˌtʃek] *n* eurocheque *m*.
Eurocrat [ˈjʊərəˌkræt] *n* eurocrata *mf*.
Eurocurrency [ˈjuːrəʊˌkʌrənsɪl] (*pl* -**ies**) *n* moeda *f* européia.
Eurodollar [ˈjʊərəʊˌdɒləʳ] *n* eurodólar *m*.
Euro-elections *npl* eleições *fpl* do Parlamento Europeu.
Euro MP *n* membro *m* do Parlamento Europeu.
Europe [ˈjʊərəp] *n* Europa; **in ~** na Europa.
European [ˌjʊərəˈpiːən] ⟨⟩ *adj* europeu(péia). ⟨⟩ *n* europeu *m*, -péia *f*.
European Central Bank *n*: **the ~** o Banco Central Europeu.
European Community *n*: **the ~** a Comunidade Européia.
European Court of Human Rights *n*: **the ~** o Tribunal Europeu de Direitos Humanos.

European Court of Justice *n*: the ~ o Tribunal Europeu de Justiça.

European Currency Unit *n* Unidade *f* Monetária Européia.

Europeanism [ˌjʊərəˈpiːənɪzml] *n* europeísmo *m*.

Europeanize, -ise [ˌjʊərəˈpiːənaɪz] *vt* europeizar.

European Monetary System *n*: the ~ o Sistema Monetário Europeu.

European Parliament *n*: the ~ o Parlamento Europeu.

European Union *n*: the ~ a União Européia.

Eurosceptic [ˈʊərəʊˌskeptɪk] <> *adj* eurocético(-ca). <> *n* eurocético *m*, -ca *f*.

Eurostar [ˈʊərəʊstɑːʳ] *n* Eurostar *m, trem de alta velocidade que vai da Inglaterra à França passando sob o Canal da Mancha.*

euthanasia [ˌjuːθəˈneɪzjə] *n* eutanásia *f*.

evacuate [ɪˈvækjʊeɪt] *vt* evacuar.

evacuation [ɪˌvækjʊˈeɪʃn] *n* evacuação *f*.

evacuee [ɪˌvækjuːˈiː] *n* evacuado *m*, -da *f* (*devido a uma guerra*).

evade [ɪˈveɪd] *vt* **-1.** [pursuers, capture] fugir a **-2.** [issue, question] fugir de **-3.** [subj: love, success] escapar de.

evaluate [ɪˈvæljʊeɪt] *vt* avaliar.

evaluation [ɪˌvæljʊˈeɪʃn] *n* avaliação *f*.

evangelical [ˌiːvænˈdʒelɪkl] *adj* evangélico(ca).

evangelism [ɪˈvændʒəlɪzm] *n* (U) evangelismo *m*.

evangelist [ɪˈvændʒəlɪst] *n* evangelista *mf*.

evangelize, -ise [ɪˈvændʒəlaɪz] *vt* evangelizar.

evaporate [ɪˈvæpəreɪt] *vi* **-1.** [liquid] evaporar **-2.** *fig* [feeling] evaporar-se, dissipar-se.

evaporated milk [ɪˈvæpəreɪtɪd-] *n* tipo de leite condensado por evaporação que não contém açucar.

evaporation [ɪˌvæpəˈreɪʃn] *n* **-1.** [of liquid] evaporação *f* - **2.** *fig* [of feeling] dissipação *f*.

evasion [ɪˈveɪʒn] *n* **-1.** (U) [of responsibility, payment etc] evasão *f* - **2.** [lie] evasiva *f*.

evasive [ɪˈveɪsɪv] *adj* **-1.** [to avoid question, subject] evasivo(va) **-2.** [to avoid being hit]: **to take ~ action** tomar uma ação defensiva.

evasiveness [ɪˈveɪsɪvnəs] *n* (U) atitude *f* evasiva.

eve [iːv] *n* [day before] véspera *f*.

even [ˈiːvn] <> *adj* **-1.** [regular] regular **-2.** [calm] equilibrado(da) **-3.** [flat, level] plano(na) **-4.** [equal] igual; **to get ~ with sb** ficar quite com alguém **-5. :** ~ **number** número par. <> *adv* **-1.** [for emphasis] mesmo; ~ **I** mesmo eu; ~ **now** mesmo agora; ~ **then** [at that time] mesmo então; [in spite of that] mesmo assim **-2.** [in comparisons] ainda **-3.** [indeed] até.

◆ **even as** *conj* [while] enquanto.

◆ **even if** *conj* mesmo se.

◆ **even so** *adv* [in spite of that] mesmo assim.

◆ **even though** *conj* ainda que.

◆ **even out** <> *vt sep* nivelar. <> *vi* nivelar-se.

even-handed [-ˈhændɪd] *adj* justo(ta).

evening [ˈiːvnɪŋ] *n* **-1.** [end of day - from 5 pm until 8 pm] tardinha *f*; **good ~** boa tarde; **in the ~** à tarde; [- from 8 pm onwards] noite *f*; **good ~** boa noite; **in the ~** à noite, ao anoitecer **-2.** [event, entertainment] noite *f*.

◆ **evenings** *adv US* à noite.

evening class *n* aula *f* noturna.

evening dress *n* **-1.** (U) [formal clothes] traje *m* a rigor **-2.** [woman's garment] vestido *m* de gala.

evening star *n*: the ~ a estrela vespertina.

evenly [ˈiːvnlɪ] *adv* **-1.** [regularly] regularmente **-2.** [equally] igualmente **-3.** [calmly] tranqüilamente.

evenness [ˈiːvnnɪs] *n* **-1.** [regularity] regularidade *f* - **2.** [equality] igualdade *f*.

evensong [ˈiːvnsɒŋ] *n* culto *m* da tarde.

event [ɪˈvent] *n* **-1.** [happening] acontecimento *m*; **social ~** evento *m* social **-2.** *SPORT* evento *m* **-3.** [case] caso *m*; **in the ~ of** em caso de; **in the ~ that the train is cancelled** na eventualidade de o trem ser cancelado.

◆ **in any event** *adv* [all the same] em todo o caso.

◆ **in the event** *adv UK* na realidade.

even-tempered [-ˈtempəd] *adj* equilibrado(da).

eventful [ɪˈventfʊl] *adj* movimentado(da), agitado(da).

eventide home [ˈiːvntaɪd-] *n UK euphemism* lar *m* de idosos.

eventing [ɪˈventɪŋ] *n UK* [horseriding]: **(three-day) ~** concurso *m* hípico (de três dias).

eventual [ɪˈventʃʊəl] *adj* final.

eventuality [ɪˌventʃʊˈælətɪ] (*pl* -ies) *n* eventualidade *f*.

eventually [ɪˈventʃʊəlɪ] *adv* finalmente, no fim.

ever [ˈevəʳ] *adv* **-1.** [already, at some time] já, alguma vez; **have you ~ been to Scotland?** você já/alguma vez foi para a Escócia?; **the worst film I've ~ seen** o pior filme que eu já vi; **if ~** se por acaso **-2.** [with negative - gen] nunca; **no one ~ calls these days** ninguém nunca telefona por esses dias; **hardly ~** quase nunca; [- emphatic] jamais; **don't ~ speak to me like that!** jamais fale comigo desse jeito **-3.** [all the time] sempre; **as ~** como sempre; **for ~** para sempre **-4.** [for emphasis]: **why ~ did you do that?** por que cargas d'água você fez isso?; **how ~ did he get back?** como será que ele voltou?; ~ **so kind** tão gentil; ~ **such a mess** tamanha bagunça.

◆ **ever since** <> *adv* desde então. <> *conj* desde que. <> *prep* desde.

Everest [ˈevərɪst] *n*: Mount ~ o Monte Everest.

Everglades [ˈevəˌgleɪdz] *npl*: the ~ *região pantanosa da Flórida.*

evergreen [ˈevəgriːn] <> *adj* sempre-verde. <> *n* sempre-verde *m*.

everlasting [ˌevəˈlɑːstɪŋ] *adj* [lasting forever] eterno(na).

every [ˈevrɪ] *adj* **-1.** [each] cada **-2.** [to express frequency]: ~ **three hours** a cada três horas; ~ **day** cada dia **-3.** [all] todo (da); ~ **day** todos os dias.

◆ **every now and then, every so often** *adv* de vez em quando.

◆ **every other** *adj* [every alternate]: ~ **other day** dia sim, dia não; ~ **other week** cada duas semanas.

◆ **every which way** *adv US* para todos os lados.

everybody [ˈevrɪˌbɒdɪ] *pron* = everyone.

everyday [ˈevrɪdeɪ] *adj* diário(ria).

everyone ['evrɪwʌn] *pron* todo mundo, todos *mpl* -das *fpl*.

everyplace *adv US* = **everywhere**.

everything ['evrɪθɪŋ] *pron* tudo.

everywhere ['evrɪweə'], **everyplace** *US* ['evrɪ,-pleɪs] *adv* por todo o lado; [with verbs of motion] para todo o lado; ~ **you go it's the same** onde quer que se vá é o mesmo.

evict [ɪ'vɪkt] *vt*: **to ~ sb (from)** despejar alguém (de).

eviction [ɪ'vɪkʃn] *n* despejo *m*.

eviction notice *n* aviso *m* de despejo.

evidence ['evɪdəns] *n* - **1.** [proof] evidência *f* - **2.** *JUR* prova *f*; **to give** ~ prestar depoimento.

➡ **in evidence** *adj* [noticeable] em evidência.

evident ['evɪdənt] *adj* evidente.

evidently ['evɪdəntlɪ] *adv* evidentemente.

evil ['iːvl] ⬦ *adj* [morally bad] mau(má). ⬦ *n* - **1.** *(U)* [wicked behaviour] maldade *f* - **2.** [wicked thing] mal *m*.

evildoer *n* malfeitor *m*, -ra *f*.

evil-minded [-'maɪndɪd] *adj* malvado(da).

evince [ɪ'vɪns] *vt fml* evidenciar.

evocation [,evəʊ'keɪʃn] *n* evocação *f*.

evocative [ɪ'vɒkətɪv] *adj* evocativo(va).

evoke [ɪ'vəʊk] *vt* - **1.** [call up, summon] chamar - **2.** [elicit, provoke] evocar.

evolution [,iːvə'luːʃn] *n* evolução *f*.

evolve [ɪ'vɒlv] ⬦ *vt* [develop] desenvolver. ⬦ *vi* - **1.** *BIOL*: **to ~ (into/from)** evoluir (para/de) - **2.** [develop] desenvolver-se.

ewe [juː] *n* ovelha *f*.

ex- [eks] *prefix* ex-.

exacerbate [ɪg'zæsəbeɪt] *vt* exacerbar.

exact [ɪg'zækt] ⬦ *adj* [precise] exato(ta); **to be ~** para ser exato(ta). ⬦ *vt*: **to ~ sthg (from sb)** exigir algo (de alguém).

exacting [ɪg'zæktɪŋ] *adj* [demanding, rigorous] exigente.

exactitude [ɪg'zæktɪtjuːd] *n (U) fml* exatidão *f*.

exactly [ɪg'zæktlɪ] ⬦ *adv* [precisely] exatamente; **not ~** [not really] não exatamente. ⬦ *excl* exatamente!

exaggerate [ɪg'zædʒəreɪt] ⬦ *vt* exagerar. ⬦ *vi* exagerar.

exaggerated [ɪg'zædʒəreɪtɪd] *adj* exagerado(da).

exaggeration [ɪg,zædʒə'reɪʃn] *n* exagero *m*.

exalted [ɪg'zɔːltɪd] *adj* [important] sublime.

exam [ɪg'zæm] *(abbr of* **examination***) n* - **1.** *SCH* prova *f*; **to take** *OR* **sit an ~** fazer uma prova. - **2.** *MED US* exame *m*.

examination [ɪg,zæmɪ'neɪʃn] *n* - **1.** [gen] exame *m* - **2.** [inspection] investigação *f* - **3.** [consideration] análise *f* - **4.** *JUR* [of witness, suspect] interrogatório *m*.

examination board *n* banca *f* examinadora.

examination paper *n UK* [test] prova *f*, exame *m*.

examine [ɪg'zæmɪn] *vt* - **1.** [gen] examinar - **2.** [consider] estudar - **3.** *JUR* interrogar.

examiner [ɪg'zæmɪnə'] *n* examinador *m*, -ra *f*; **internal/external ~** examinador externo/interno, examinadora externa/interna.

example [ɪg'zɑːmpl] *n* exemplo *m*; **for ~** por exemplo; **to follow sb's ~** seguir o exemplo de

alguém; **to make an ~ of sb** fazer exemplo de alguém.

exasperate [ɪg'zæspəreɪt] *vt* exasperar.

exasperating [ɪg'zæspəreɪtɪŋ] *adj* exasperador(-ra), irritante.

exasperation [ɪg,zæspə'reɪʃn] *n (U)* exasperação *f*.

excavate ['ekskəveɪt] *vt* escavar.

excavation [,ekskə'veɪʃn] *n* escavação *f*.

excavator ['ekskə,veɪtə'] *n UK* [machine] escavadeira *f*.

exceed [ɪk'siːd] *vt* - **1.** [be bigger than] exceder - **2.** [go beyond, go over - limit] ultrapassar; [- expectations] superar.

exceedingly [ɪk'siːdɪŋlɪ] *adv* extremamente.

excel [ɪk'sel] *(pt & pp* **-led**, *cont* **-ling***)* ⬦ *vi*: **to ~ (in** *OR* **at sthg)** sobressair-se (em algo). ⬦ *vt*: **to ~ o.s.** *UK* superar-se.

excellence ['eksələns] *n (U)* excelência *f*.

Excellency ['eksələnsɪ] *(pl* **-ies***) n*: **Your/His ~** Sua Excelência.

excellent ['eksələnt] ⬦ *adj* excelente. ⬦ *excl* excelente!

except [ɪk'sept] ⬦ *prep* exceto. ⬦ *conj* exceto. ⬦ *vt*: **to ~ sb (from sthg)** excluir alguém (de algo).

➡ **except for** ⬦ *prep* com exceção de. ⬦ *conj* exceto.

excepted [ɪk'septɪd] *prep*: **Jenny ~, everyone agreed** com a exceção de Jenny, todos concordaram.

excepting [ɪk'septɪŋ] *prep & conj* = **except**.

exception [ɪk'sepʃn] *n* - **1.** [exclusion] exceção *f*; **~ to sthg** exceção a algo; **with the ~ of** com a exceção de; **without ~** sem exceção - **2.** [offence]: **to take ~ to sthg** ofender-se com algo.

exceptional [ɪk'sepʃənl] *adj* [unusually clever, talented] excepcional.

exceptionally [ɪk'sepʃnəlɪ] *adv* [unusually] excepcionalmente.

excerpt ['eksɜːpt] *n*: **~ (from sthg)** excerto *m* de algo.

excess [ɪk'ses, *before nouns* 'ekses] ⬦ *adj* excessivo(va). ⬦ *n* excesso *m*; **to ~** em excesso; **debts in ~ of £200,000** débitos de mais de £200.000. ⬦ *vt* *RAIL* sobretaxar.

excess baggage *n* excesso *m* de bagagem.

excess fare *n UK* sobretaxa *f*.

excessive [ɪk'sesɪv] *adj* excessivo(va).

excess luggage *n* = **excess baggage**.

exchange [ɪks'tʃeɪndʒ] ⬦ *n* - **1.** *(U)* [act of swapping] troca *f*, intercâmbio *m*; **in ~** em troca; **in ~ for** em troca de - **2.** [swap] troca *f* - **3.** *FIN*: **stock ~** bolsa *f* (de valores) - **4.** *FIN*: **(foreign) ~** câmbio *m*, divisas *fpl* - **5.** *TELEC*: **(telephone) ~** central *f* telefônica - **6.** [educational visit] intercâmbio *m* - **7.** *fml* [conversation] diálogo *m*. ⬦ *vt* [swap] trocar; **to ~ sthg for sthg** trocar algo por algo; **to ~ sthg with sb** trocar algo com alguém.

exchange rate *n FIN* taxa *f* de câmbio.

Exchequer [ɪks'tʃekə'] *n UK*: **the ~** o Ministério da Fazenda britânico.

excise ['eksaɪz] ⬦ *n (U)* imposto *m*; **Customs and Excise** ≃ a Receita Federal. ⬦ *vt fml* extrair.

excise duties *npl* impostos *mpl* indiretos *OR* de consumo.

excitable [ɪk'saɪtəbl] *adj* excitável.

excite [ɪk'saɪt] *vt* **-1.** [person] entusiasmar **-2.** [nerves, heart] agitar **-3.** [interest, suspicion] despertar.

excited [ɪk'saɪtɪd] *adj* **-1.** [enthused] entusiasmado(da) **-2.** [agitated] agitado(da).

excitement [ɪk'saɪtmənt] *n* **-1.** *(U)* [state - enthusiasm] entusiasmo *m*; [- agitation] agitação *f* **-2.** [exciting thing] emoção *f*.

exciting [ɪk'saɪtɪŋ] *adj* emocionante.

excl. *(abbr of* **excluding)** exc.

exclaim [ɪk'skleɪm] ⟨⟩ *vt & vi* exclamar.

exclamation [ˌeksklə'meɪʃn] *n* exclamação *f*.

exclamation mark *UK*, **exclamation point** *US n* ponto *m* de exclamação.

exclude [ɪk'sklu:d] *vt* excluir; **to ~ sb/sthg (from sthg)** excluir alguém/algo (de algo).

excluding [ɪk'sklu:dɪŋ] *prep* excluindo.

exclusion [ɪk'sklu:ʒn] *n (U)* exclusão *f*; **~ (from)** exclusão (de); **to the ~ of** a ponto de excluir.

exclusion clause *n COMM* cláusula *f* de exclusão.

exclusive [ɪk'sklu:sɪv] ⟨⟩ *adj* exclusivo(va). ⟨⟩ *n PRESS* artigo *m* exclusivo.

➡ **exclusive of** *prep*: **~ of sales tax** imposto sobre vendas não-incluído.

exclusively [ɪk'sklu:sɪvlɪ] *adv* exclusivamente.

excommunicate [ˌekskə'mju:nɪkeɪt] *vt* excomungar.

excommunication ['ekskəˌmju:nɪ'keɪʃn] *n* excomungação *f*.

excrement ['ekskrɪmənt] *n fml* excremento *m*.

excrete [ɪk'skri:t] *vt* excretar.

excruciating [ɪk'skru:ʃɪeɪtɪŋ] *adj* **-1.** [pain] insuportável **-2.** [emotion, performance] terrível.

excursion [ɪk'skɜ:ʃn] *n* [trip] excursão *f*.

excusable [ɪk'skju:zəbl] *adj* desculpável.

excuse [*n* ɪk'skju:s, *vb* ɪk'skju:z] ⟨⟩ *n* **-1.** [reason, explanation] desculpa *f* **-2.** [justification]: **~ (for sthg)** desculpa (para algo). ⟨⟩ *vt* **-1.** desculpar; **to ~ sb for sthg/for doing sthg** desculpar alguém por algo/por fazer algo **-2.** [let off, free] dispensar; **to ~ sb from sthg** dispensar alguém de algo **-3.** [allow to leave] dar licença **-4.** *phr*: **~ me** [to attract attention] com licença; [forgive me] desculpe; *US* [sorry] perdão.

ex-directory *adj UK* que não consta na lista telefônica.

exec [ɪg'zek] *(abbr of* **executive)** executivo(va).

execrable ['eksɪkrəbl] *adj fml* execrável.

execute ['eksɪkju:t] *vt* executar.

execution [ˌeksɪ'kju:ʃn] *n* execução *f*.

executioner [ˌeksɪ'kju:ʃnə'] *n* carrasco *m*, -ca *f*.

executive [ɪg'zekjʊtɪv] ⟨⟩ *adj* executivo(va). ⟨⟩ *n* **-1.** *COMM* executivo *m*, -va *f* **-2.** [of government] executivo *m* **-3.** [of political party] executiva *f*.

executive director *n* diretor *m* executivo, diretora *f* executiva.

executive toy *n brinquedo usado por executivos para ajudar na concentração*.

executor [ɪg'zekjʊtə'] *n* [of will] testamenteiro *m*, -ra *f*.

exemplary [ɪg'zemplərɪ] *adj* [perfect] exemplar.

exemplify [ɪg'zemplɪfaɪ] *(pt & pp* **-ied)** *vt* **-1.** [typify] ilustrar **-2.** [give example of] exemplificar.

exempt [ɪg'zempt] ⟨⟩ *adj*: **to be ~ (from sthg)** [tax] estar isento(ta) (de algo); [duty, rules] estar livre (de algo); [military service] estar dispensado(da) (de algo). ⟨⟩ *vt*: **to ~ sb/sthg (from sthg)** [tax] isentar alguém/algo (de algo); [duty, rules, military service] dispensar alguém/algo (de algo).

exemption [ɪg'zempʃn] *n* **-1.** [from tax] isenção *f* **-2.** [from military service] dispensa *f*.

exercise ['eksəsaɪz] ⟨⟩ *n* exercício *m*; **to take ~** fazer exercício; **an ~ in sthg** um exercício de algo. ⟨⟩ *vt* **-1.** exercitar; **to ~ sb's mind** exercitar a mente de alguém **-2.** *fml* [use, practise] exercer. ⟨⟩ *vi* exercitar-se.

exercise bike *n* bicicleta *f* ergométrica.

exercise book *n* **-1.** [for notes] caderno *m (de anotações)* **-2.** [published book] livro *m* de exercícios.

exert [ɪg'zɜ:t] *vt* exercer; **to ~ o.s.** esforçar-se.

exertion [ɪg'zɜ:ʃn] *n* **-1.** [physical effort] esforço *m* **-2.** *fig* [committed effort] empenho *m* **-3.** *(U)* [of power, influence] exercício *m*.

ex gratia [eks'greɪʃə] *adj UK*: **~ payment** gratificação *f*.

exhale [eks'heɪl] ⟨⟩ *vt* exalar. ⟨⟩ *vi* exalar.

exhaust [ɪg'zɔ:st] ⟨⟩ *n* **-1.** [fumes] descarga *f*, escapamento *m* **-2.** [tube]: **~ (pipe)** (cano *m* de) descarga *f*. ⟨⟩ *vt* **-1.** [person, patience, subject] esgotar **-2.** [supply, money] usar.

exhausted [ɪg'zɔ:stɪd] *adj* exausto(ta).

exhausting [ɪg'zɔ:stɪŋ] *adj* exaustivo(va).

exhaustion [ɪg'zɔ:stʃn] *n (U)* exaustão *f*.

exhaustive [ɪg'zɔ:stɪv] *adj* exaustivo(va).

exhibit [ɪg'zɪbɪt] ⟨⟩ *n* **-1.** *ART* objeto *m* exposto **-2.** *JUR* [piece of evidence] prova *f*, evidência *f*. ⟨⟩ *vt* **-1.** *fml* [demonstrate] demonstrar **-2.** *ART* expor. ⟨⟩ *vi ART* expor.

exhibition [ˌeksɪ'bɪʃn] *n* **-1.** *ART* exposição *f* **-2.** [demonstration] demonstração *f* **-3.** *phr*: **to make an ~ of o.s.** *UK* fazer um escândalo.

exhibitionist [ˌeksɪ'bɪʃnɪst] *n* exibicionista *mf*.

exhibitor [ɪg'zɪbɪtə'] *n* expositor *m*, -ra *f*.

exhilarating [ɪg'zɪləreɪtɪŋ] *adj* estimulante.

exhort [ɪg'zɔ:t] *vt fml*: **to ~ sb to do sthg** exortar alguém a fazer algo.

exhume [eks'hju:m] *vt fml* exumar.

exile ['eksaɪl] ⟨⟩ *n* **-1.** [condition] exílio *m*; **in ~** no exílio **-2.** [person] exilado *m*, -da *f*. ⟨⟩ *vt*: **to ~ sb (from/to)** exilar alguém (de/para).

exiled ['eksaɪld] *adj* exilado(da).

exist [ɪg'zɪst] *vi* existir.

existence [ɪg'zɪstəns] *n (U)* existência *f*; **to come into ~** entrar em vigor; **to be in ~** existir.

existentialism [ˌegzɪ'stenʃəlɪzm] *n (U)* existencialismo *m*.

existentialist [ˌegzɪ'stenʃəlɪst] ⟨⟩ *adj* existencialista. ⟨⟩ *n* existencialista *mf*.

existing [ɪg'zɪstɪŋ] *adj* existente, atual.

exit ['eksɪt] ⟨⟩ *n* saída *f*. ⟨⟩ *vi* sair.

exit poll *n UK POL* pesquisa *f* de boca-de-urna.

exit visa *n* visto *m* de saída.

exodus ['eksədəs] n êxodo m.

ex officio [eksə'fɪʃɪəʊ] fml <> adj ex officio. <> adv em ex officio.

exonerate [ɪg'zɒnəreɪt] vt : to ~ sb (from sthg) exonerar alguém (de algo).

exorbitant [ɪg'zɔ:bɪtənt] adj exorbitante.

exorcism n exorcismo m.

exorcist ['eksɔ:sɪst] n exorcista mf.

exorcize, -ise ['eksɔ:saɪz] vt exorcizar.

exotic [ɪg'zɒtɪk] adj exótico(ca).

expand [ɪk'spænd] <> vt -1. [gen] expandir -2. [department, area] ampliar -3. [influence] aumentar <> vi -1. [gen] expandir-se -2. [influence] aumentar -3. PHYS dilatar.
 ◆ **expand (up)on** vt fus entrar em detalhes.

expanse [ɪk'spæns] n vastidão f.

expansion [ɪk'spænʃn] n -1. (U) [gen] expansão f -2. [of department, area] ampliação f -3. [of influence] aumento m -4. PHYS dilatação f.

expansion card n COMPUT cartão m de expansão.

expansionism n (U) expansionismo m.

expansionist [ɪk'spænʃənɪst] adj expansionista.

expansion slot n COMPUT slot m de expansão.

expansive [ɪk'spænsɪv] adj [relaxed, talkative] expansivo(va).

expatriate [eks'pætrɪət] <> adj expatriado(da). <> n expatriado m, -da f.

expect [ɪk'spekt] <> vt -1. [gen] esperar; to ~ to do sthg esperar fazer algo; to ~ sb to do sthg esperar que alguém faça algo; to ~ sthg from sb esperar algo de alguém -2. [suppose]: to ~ (that) supor que; I ~ so suponho que sim; what do you ~? e o que você queria? <> vi [be pregnant]: to be ~ing estar esperando bebê.

expectancy n ⊳ life expectancy.

expectant [ɪk'spektənt] adj [crowd, person] ansioso(-sa).

expectantly [ɪk'spektəntlɪ] adv ansiosamente.

expectant mother n gestante f.

expectation [,ekspek'teɪʃn] n -1. [hope] expectativa f -2. [belief] convicção f; against OR contrary to all ~(s) ao contrário de todas as expectativas.

expectorant [ɪk'spektərənt] n expectorante m.

expedient [ɪk'spi:djənt] fml <> adj pertinente, conveniente. <> n expediente m.

expedite ['ekspɪdaɪt] vt fml expedir.

expedition [,ekspɪ'dɪʃn] n -1. [organized journey] expedição f -2. [short trip, outing] passeio m.

expeditionary force [,ekspɪ'dɪʃnərɪ-] n força f expedicionária.

expel [ɪk'spel] (pt & pp -led, cont -ling) vt -1. [from school, country]: to ~ sb (from) expulsar alguém (de) -2. [from container]: to ~ sthg (from) expelir algo (de).

expend [ɪk'spend] vt : to ~ sthg (on sthg) gastar algo (com/em algo).

expendable [ɪk'spendəbl] adj -1. [person] dispensável -2. [resources] consumível.

expenditure [ɪk'spendɪtʃəʳ] n -1. [of money] gastos mpl -2. [of energy, resource] gasto m.

expense [ɪk'spens] n -1. [amount spent] despesa f, gasto m -2. (U) [cost] custo m; to go to great ~ (to do sthg) ter uma grande despesa (para fazer algo); at the ~ of em detrimento de, à custa de; at his/her own ~ [financial] do seu próprio bolso; at sb's ~ fig [in order to mock] às custas de alguém.
 ◆ **expenses** npl COMM despesas fpl; on ~s nas despesas.

expense account n relatório m de despesas.

expensive [ɪk'spensɪv] adj [financially] caro(ra).

experience [ɪk'spɪərɪəns] <> n experiência f. <> vt experimentar.

experienced [ɪk'spɪərɪənst] adj [well-practised] experiente; ~ at OR in sthg experiente em algo.

experiment [ɪk'sperɪmənt] <> n -1. SCIENCE experimento m; to carry out an ~ conduzir um experimento -2. [exploratory attempt] tentativa f. <> vi SCIENCE fazer experiências; to ~ with sthg fazer experiências com algo; to ~ on sb/sthg fazer experiências em alguém/algo.

experimental [ɪk,sperɪ'mentl] adj SCIENCE experimental.

expert ['ekspɜ:t] <> adj especializado(da), perito(ta); ~ at sthg/at doing sthg perito(ta) em algo/em fazer algo. <> n especialista mf, perito m, -ta f.

expertise [,ekspɜ:'ti:z] n (U) excelência f, perícia f.

expert system n COMPUT sistema m especialista.

expiate vt fml expiar.

expire [ɪk'spaɪəʳ] vi [run out] vencer.

expiry [ɪk'spaɪərɪ] n (U) vencimento m.

expiry date n data f de vencimento.

explain [ɪk'spleɪn] <> vt -1. [describe, clarify] explicar; to ~ sthg to sb explicar algo a alguém -2. [account for] justificar. <> vi explicar-se; to ~ to sb (about sthg) justificar-se (para alguém) sobre algo.
 ◆ **explain away** vt sep justificar.

explanation [,eksplə'neɪʃn] n -1. (U) [act of explaining] explicação f -2. [account]: ~ (for sthg) justificativa f (por algo) -3. [description, clarification] explanação f.

explanatory [ɪk'splænətrɪ] adj explicativo(va).

expletive [ɪk'spli:tɪv] n fml imprecação f.

explicit [ɪk'splɪsɪt] adj [clearly expressed] explícito(ta).

explode [ɪk'spləʊd] <> vt -1. [set off] explodir -2. fig [disprove] derrubar. <> vi -1. [blow up] explodir -2. fig [with feeling] explodir.

exploit [n 'eksplɔɪt, vb ɪk'splɔɪt] <> n façanha f. <> vt explorar.

exploitation [,eksplɔɪ'teɪʃn] n (U) [of workers, resources] exploração f.

exploration [,eksplə'reɪʃn] n [of space, countries] exploração f.

exploratory [ɪk'splɒrətrɪ] adj exploratório(ria).

explore [ɪk'splɔ:ʳ] <> vt explorar. <> vi explorar.

explorer [ɪk'splɔ:rəʳ] n explorador m, -ra f.

explosion [ɪk'spləʊʒn] n explosão f.

explosive [ɪk'spləʊsɪv] <> adj -1. [gen] explosivo(-va) -2. [controversial] controverso(sa). <> n explosivo m.

explosive device n dispositivo m explosivo.

exponent [ɪk'spəʊnənt] n -1. [gen] expoente mf -2. [supporter] defensor m, -ra f.

exponential [,ekspə'nenʃl] adj fml [growth] exponencial.

export [*n* & *comp* 'ekspɔːt, *vb* ɪk'spɔːt] <> *n (U)* exportação *f.* <> *comp* de exportação. <> *vt* exportar.

➡ **exports** *npl* [goods] exportações *fpl.*

exportable [ɪk'spɔːtəbl] *adj* exportável.

exportation [ˌekspɔː'teɪʃn] *n (U)* exportação *f.*

exporter [ek'spɔːtə^r] *n* exportador *m*, -ra *f.*

export licence *n UK COMM* licença *f* de exportação.

expose [ɪk'spəʊz] *vt* -**1.** [gen] expor; **to be ~d to sthg** estar exposto(ta) a algo; **to ~ o.s.** mostrar-se -**2.** [unmask] desmascarar.

exposé [eks'pəʊzeɪ] *n* exposição *f (de fatos reveladores).*

exposed [ɪk'spəʊzd] *adj* [unsheltered] desprotegido(-da).

exposition [ˌekspə'zɪʃn] *n fml* exposição *f.*

exposure [ɪk'spəʊʒə^r] *n* -**1.** [gen] exposição *f* -**2.** *MED* [hypothermia]: **to die from ~** morrer de frio -**3.** [unmasking - of person] desmascaramento *m*; [- of corruption] descoberta *f* -**4.** [*PHOT* - time] exposição *f*; [- photograph] pose *f.*

exposure meter *n* fotômetro *m.*

expound [ɪk'spaʊnd] *fml* <> *vt* expor. <> *vi*: **to ~ on sthg** explanar sobre algo.

express [ɪk'spres] <> *adj* -**1.** *UK* [urgent letter, parcel] expresso(sa) -**2.** [transport] expresso(sa) -**3.** *fml* [specific] explícito(ta). <> *adv* por correio expresso. <> *n*: ~ **(train)** (trem *m*) expresso *m.* <> *vt* -**1.** [show, state] expressar, exprimir; **to ~ o.s.** expressar-se -**2.** *MATH* representar.

expression [ɪk'spreʃn] *n* expressão *f.*

expressionism [ɪk'spreʃənɪzm] *n (U)* expressionismo *m.*

expressionist [ɪk'spreʃənɪst] <> *adj* expressionista. <> *n* expressionista *mf.*

expressionless [ɪk'spreʃənlɪs] *adj* sem expressão, inexpressivo(va).

expressive [ɪk'spresɪv] *adj* [full of feeling] expressivo(va).

expressively [ɪk'spresɪvlɪ] *adv* expressivamente.

expressly [ɪk'spreslɪ] *adv* [specifically] expressamente.

expressway [ɪk'spresweɪ] *n* via *f* expressa.

expropriate [eks'prəʊprɪeɪt] *vt fml* expropriar.

expropriation [eksˌprəʊprɪ'eɪʃn] *n fml* expropriação *f.*

expulsion [ɪk'spʌlʃn] *n* expulsão *f*; ~ **(from)** expulsão (de).

exquisite [ɪk'skwɪzɪt] *adj* -**1.** [beautiful] fino(na) -**2.** [very pleasing] delicado(da).

exquisitely [ɪk'skwɪzɪtlɪ] *adv* [beautifully] finamente.

ex-serviceman *n UK* ex-combatente *m.*

ex-servicewoman *n UK* ex-combatente *f.*

ext., extn. *(abbr of* extension) extens.

extant [ek'stænt] *adj* existente.

extemporize, -ise [ɪk'stempəraɪz] *vi fml* improvisar.

extend [ɪk'stend] <> *vt* -**1.** [make bigger] ampliar -**2.** [make longer - in space] estender; [- in time] prolongar -**3.** [postpone] prorrogar -**4.** [make more wide-ranging] estender -**5.** *fml* [stretch out] esticar -**6.** [offer - welcome, help] estender; [- credit] conceder. <> *vi*

-**1.** [stretch, reach] extender-se -**2.** [rule, law]: **to ~ to sb/sthg** extender-se a alguém/algo -**3.** [protrude] extender-se.

extendable [ɪk'stendəbl] *adj* -**1.** [in time] prorrogável -**2.** [in space] expansível.

extended-play [ɪk'stendɪd-] *adj* de grande duração.

extension [ɪk'stenʃn] *n* -**1.** [gen] aumento *m* -**2.** [longer time limit] prorrogação *f* -**3.** [development, growth] expansão *f* -**4.** *TELEC & ELEC* extensão *f* -**5.** *COMPUT*: **filename** ~ extensão do arquivo.

extension cable, extension lead *n ELEC* extensão *f.*

extensive [ɪk'stensɪv] *adj* -**1.** [in amount] amplo(pla) -**2.** [in area, range] extenso(sa).

extensively [ɪk'stensɪvlɪ] *adv* -**1.** [in amount] amplamente -**2.** [in range] extensivamente.

extent [ɪk'stent] *n* -**1.** [gen] extensão *f* -**2.** [degree]: **to what ~ ...?** até que ponto ...?; **to the ~ that** [in that, in so far as] na medida em que; [to the point where] até o ponto em que; **to a certain ~** até um certo ponto; **to a large** *OR* **great ~** em grande parte; **to some ~** até certo ponto.

extenuating circumstances [ɪk'stenjʊeɪtɪŋ-] *npl* circunstâncias *fpl* atenuantes.

exterior [ɪk'stɪərɪə^r] <> *adj* externo(na). <> *n* exterior *m.*

exterminate [ɪk'stɜːmɪneɪt] *vt* exterminar.

extermination [ɪkˌstɜːmɪ'neɪʃn] *n (U)* exterminação *f.*

external [ɪk'stɜːnl] *adj* -**1.** [outside] externo(na) -**2.** [foreign] exterior(ra).

➡ **externals** *npl* aparências *fpl.*

externally [ɪk'stɜːnəlɪ] *adv* externamente.

extinct [ɪk'stɪŋkt] *adj* extinto(ta).

extinction [ɪk'stɪŋkʃn] *n (U)* [of species] extinção *f.*

extinguish [ɪk'stɪŋgwɪʃ] *vt* -**1.** *fml* [put out] apagar -**2.** *fig* [eliminate] extinguir.

extinguisher [ɪk'stɪŋgwɪʃə^r] *n*: **(fire)** ~ extintor *m* (de incêndio).

extol (*pt* & *pp* -**led**, *cont* -**ling**), **extoll** *US* [ɪk'stəʊl] *vt* enaltecer.

extort [ɪk'stɔːt] *vt*: **to ~ sthg from sb** extorquir algo de alguém.

extortion [ɪk'stɔːʃn] *n* extorção *f.*

extortionate [ɪk'stɔːʃnət] *adj* extorsivo(va).

extra ['ekstrə] <> *adj* [additional] extra; ~ **charge** sobrecarga *f.* <> *n* -**1.** [addition] acessório *m* -**2.** *CINEMA & THEATRE* extra *mf.* <> *adv* extra.

➡ **extras** *npl* [in price] extras *mpl.*

extra- ['ekstrə] *prefix* extra.

extract [*n* 'ekstrækt, *vb* ɪk'strækt] <> *n* -**1.** [excerpt] trecho *m* -**2.** *CHEM & CULIN* extrato *m.* <> *vt* -**1.** [take out]: **to ~ sthg (from sthg)** extrair algo (de algo) -**2.** [obtain, elicit]: **to ~ sthg (from sb)** arrancar algo (de alguém).

extraction [ɪk'strækʃn] *n* -**1.** [origin, descent] origem *f* -**2.** [removal] extração *f.*

extractor (fan) [ɪk'stræktə^r-] *n UK* exaustor *m.*

extracurricular [ˌekstrəkə'rɪkjʊlə^r] *adj* extracurricular.

extradite ['ekstrədaɪt] *vt*: **to ~ sb (from/to)** extraditar alguém (de/para).

extradition [ˌekstrəˈdɪʃn] ◇ n extradição f. ◇ comp de extradição.

extramarital [ˌekstrəˈmærɪtl] adj extraconjugal.

extramural [ˌekstrəˈmjʊərəl] adj UNIV de extensão universitária.

extraneous [ɪkˈstreɪnjəs] adj -1. [irrelevant] irrelevante -2. [outside] externo(na).

extraordinary [ɪkˈstrɔːdnrɪ] adj -1. [special] extraordinário(ria) -2. [strange] exquisito(ta).

extraordinary general meeting n assembléia f geral extraordinária.

extrapolate [ɪkˈstræpəleɪt] ◇ vt -1. MATH: to ~ sthg from sthg extrapolar algo a partir de algo -2. [deduce]: to ~ sthg from sthg inferir algo de algo. ◇ vi -1. MATH: to ~ from sthg extrapolar a partir de algo -2. [deduce]: to ~ from sthg inferir de algo.

extrasensory perception [ˌekstrəˈsensərɪ-] n (U) percepção f extrasensorial.

extraterrestrial [ˌekstrətəˈrestrɪəl] adj extraterrestre.

extra time n UK SPORT prorrogação f.

extravagance [ɪkˈstrævəgəns] n -1. [luxury] extravagância f -2. (U) [excessive spending] gasto m excessivo.

extravagant [ɪkˈstrævəgənt] adj -1. [excessive] extravagante -2. [elaborate] caprichado(da).

extravaganza [ɪkˌstrævəˈgænzə] n espetáculo público de pompa.

extreme [ɪkˈstriːm] ◇ adj extremo(ma). ◇ n [furthest limit] extremo m; in the ~ ao extremo; to ~s aos extremos.

extremely [ɪkˈstriːmlɪ] adv [very] extremamente.

extreme sports npl esportes mpl radicais.

extremism [ɪkˈstriːmɪzml] n (U) extremismo m.

extremist [ɪkˈstriːmɪst] ◇ adj extremista. ◇ n extremista mf.

extremity [ɪkˈstremətɪ] (pl -ies) n -1. (U) fml [extreme adversity] suma gravidade f -2. (U) [extremeness] extremismo m -3. fml [end] extremidade f.
◆ **extremities** npl [of body] extremidades fpl.

extricate [ˈekstrɪkeɪt] vt: to ~ sthg (from) soltar algo (de); to ~ o.s. (from) livrar-se (de).

extrovert [ˈekstrəvɜːt] ◇ adj extrovertido(da). ◇ n extrovertido m, -da f.

extruded [ɪkˈstruːdɪd] adj TECH prensado(da).

exuberance [ɪgˈzjuːbərəns] n (U) exuberância f.

exuberant [ɪgˈzjuːbərənt] adj exuberante.

exude [ɪgˈzjuːd] ◇ vt -1. [ooze, give off] exsudar -2. fig [be full of] exalar. ◇ vi exsudar.

exult [ɪgˈzʌlt] vi: to ~ (at OR in sthg) alegrar-se (com algo).

exultant [ɪgˈzʌltənt] adj exultante.

eye [aɪ] (cont eyeing OR eying) ◇ n -1. , [gen & ANAT] olho m; before my (very) ~s bem debaixo dos meus olhos; in my ~s a meu ver; to cast OR run one's ~ over sthg passar os olhos em algo; to catch sb's ~ chamar a atenção de alguém; to clap OR lay OR set ~s on sb pôr os olhos em alguém; to cry one's ~s out inf chorar muito; to feast one's ~s on sthg alimentar os olhos com algo; to have an ~ for sthg ter bons olhos para algo; to have one's ~ on sb/sthg ter os olhos sobre alguém/algo; to keep one's ~s open (for), to keep an ~ out (for) ficar de olhos abertos (em); to keep an ~ on sb/sthg dar uma olhada em alguém/algo; there is more to this than meets the ~ a coisa é mais complicada do que parece; to open sb's ~s (to sthg) abrir os olhos de alguém (em relação a algo); not to see ~ to ~ with sb não ver as coisas com os mesmos olhos de alguém; to close OR shut one's ~s to sthg fechar os olhos para algo; to turn a blind ~ (to sthg) fazer vista grossa (para algo); to be up to one's ~s in sthg UK inf estar até aqui de algo -2. [of needle] buraco m. ◇ vt olhar.
◆ **eye up** vt sep UK encarar, comer com os olhos.

eyeball [ˈaɪbɔːl] ◇ n globo m ocular. ◇ vt US inf encarar.

eyebath [ˈaɪbɑːθ] n copinho m para lavar os olhos.

eyebrow [ˈaɪbraʊ] n sobrancelha f; to raise one's ~s (at sthg) fig ficar surpreendido(da) (com algo).

eyebrow pencil n lápis m inv de sobrancelha.

eye-catching adj chamativo(va).

eye contact n (U): to make/avoid ~ (with sb) fazer/evitar contato direto (com alguém).

eyedrops [ˈaɪdrɒps] npl colírio m.

eyeglasses [ˈaɪglɑːsɪz] npl US óculos m inv.

eyelash [ˈaɪlæʃ] n cílio m.

eyelet [ˈaɪlɪt] n ilhó m.

eye-level adj à altura dos olhos.

eyelid [ˈaɪlɪd] n pálpebra f; not to bat an ~ inf não dar a mínima.

eyeliner [ˈaɪˌlaɪnər] n delineador m (para os olhos).

eye-opener n inf revelação f.

eyepatch [ˈaɪpætʃ] n tapa-olho m.

eye shadow n sombra f (para os olhos).

eyesight [ˈaɪsaɪt] n visão f.

eyesore [ˈaɪsɔːr] n horror m, monstruosidade f.

eyestrain [ˈaɪstreɪn] n vista f cansada.

eyetooth [ˈaɪtuːθ] (pl -teeth) n: to give one's eyeteeth for sthg/to do sthg dar tudo por algo/para fazer algo.

eyewash [ˈaɪwɒʃ] n (U) inf [nonsense] disparates mpl.

eyewitness [ˌaɪˈwɪtnɪs] n testemunha mf ocular.

eyrie [ˈɪərɪ] n ninho m de águia.

e-zine [ˈiːziːn] n revista f eletrônica.

F

f (pl f's OR fs), **F** (pl F's OR Fs) [ef] n [letter] f, F m.
◆ **F** n -1. MUS fá m -2. (abbr of Fahrenheit) F.

FA (abbr of Football Association) n confederação de

futebol da Inglaterra e do País de Gales, ≃ CBF f.

FAA (*abbr of* **Federal Aviation Administration**) *n* órgão federal norte-americano de aviação civil.

fable ['feɪbl] *n* [traditional story] fábula f.

fabled ['feɪbld] *adj* lendário(ria).

fabric ['fæbrɪk] *n* **-1.** [cloth] tecido *m* **-2.** *fig* [of building, society] estrutura f.

fabricate ['fæbrɪkeɪt] *vt* **-1.** [invent] inventar **-2.** [manufacture] fabricar.

fabrication [ˌfæbrɪ'keɪʃn] *n* **-1.** [lie, lying] invenção f **-2.** (*U*) [manufacture] fabricação f.

fabulous ['fæbjʊləs] *adj* fabuloso(sa).

fabulously ['fæbjʊləslɪ] *adv* fabulosamente.

facade [fə'sɑ:d] *n* fachada f.

face [feɪs] ◇ *n* **-1.** [of person] rosto *m*, cara f; ~ to ~ cara a cara; **to fall flat on one's** ~ cair de cara no chão; **to look sb in the** ~ olhar alguém na cara; **to say sthg to sb's** ~ dizer algo na cara de alguém; **to show one's** ~ mostrar a cara; **it was staring me in the** ~ saltava aos meus olhos **-2.** [expression] expressão f; **to make** OR **pull a** ~ fazer careta **-3.** [of building] fachada f **-4.** [of coin] lado *m* **-5.** [of clock, watch] mostrador *m* **-6.** [appearance, nature] cara f **-7.** [surface] face f; **on the** ~ of it à primeira vista **-8.** [respect]: **to lose** ~ perder a reputação; **to save** ~ livrar a cara **-9.** *phr:* **to fly in the** ~ of sthg ir de encontro a algo. ◇ *vt* **-1.** [gen] encarar **-2.** [look on to, point towards] dar para **-3.** [confront] enfrentar.

➡ **face down** *adv* [person] de bruços; [object] para baixo.

➡ **face up** *adv* [person] de costas; [object] para cima.

➡ **in the face of** *prep* [confronted with] diante de.

➡ **face up to** *vt fus* enfrentar.

facecloth ['feɪsklɒθ] *n UK* toalhinha f de rosto.

face cream *n* (*U*) creme *m* para o rosto.

faceless ['feɪslɪs] *adj* sem rosto, anônimo(ma).

facelift *n* **-1.** [on face] lifting *m* **-2.** *fig:* **to give sthg a** ~ dar uma cara nova para algo.

face pack *n* máscara f facial.

face powder *n* (*U*) pó-de-arroz *m*.

face-saving [-'seɪvɪŋ] *adj* para salvar as aparências.

facet ['fæsɪt] *n* faceta f.

facetious [fə'si:ʃəs] *adj* brincalhão(lhona).

facetiously *adv* de forma brincalhona.

face-to-face *adj* cara a cara.

face value *n* [of coin, stamp] valor *m* nominal; **to take sthg at** ~ *fig* levar algo ao pé da letra.

facial ['feɪʃl] ◇ *adj* facial. ◇ *n* limpeza f de pele.

facile [*UK* 'fæsaɪl, *US* 'fæsl] *adj pej* [trivial] trivial.

facilitate [fə'sɪlɪteɪt] *vt fml* facilitar.

facility [fə'sɪlətɪ] (*pl* -ies) *n* **-1.** [ability]: **to have a** ~ **for sthg** ter facilidade para algo **-2.** [feature] recurso *m*.

➡ **facilities** *npl* **-1.** [amenities] instalações *fpl* **-2.** [services] serviços *mpl*.

facing ['feɪsɪŋ] *adj* [opposite] oposto(ta).

facsimile [fæk'sɪmɪlɪ] *n* fac-símile *m*; **a** ~ **edition** uma edição fac-similar.

facsimile machine *n fml* aparelho *m* de fax.

fact [fækt] *n* fato *m*; **the** ~ **is, ...** o fato é que ...; **the** ~ **remains that ...** a verdade que fica é que ...; **to know sthg for a** ~ ter certeza de algo.

➡ **in fact** ◇ *conj* na verdade. ◇ *adv* na verdade.

fact-finding [-'faɪndɪŋ] *adj* de investigação.

faction ['fækʃn] *n* facção f.

factional ['fækʃənl] *adj* [dispute] faccional.

fact of life *n* fato *m* consumado.

➡ **facts of life** *npl euphemism:* **to tell sb (about) the** ~ **s of life** contar a alguém como nascem as crianças.

factor ['fæktə'] *n* fator *m*.

factory ['fæktərɪ] (*pl* -ies) *n* fábrica f.

factory farming *n* (*U*) criação f intensiva.

factory ship *n* navio-fábrica *m*.

factotum [fæk'təʊtəm] (*pl* -s) *n* factótum *m*.

fact sheet *n UK* informativo *m*.

factual ['fæktʃʊəl] *adj* real, concreto(ta).

faculty ['fæklʊ] (*pl* -ies) *n* **-1.** [gen] faculdade f **-2.** *US* [in college]: **the** ~ o corpo docente.

fad [fæd] *n* mania f, capricho *m*.

faddy ['fædɪ] (*compar* -ier, *superl* -iest) *adj inf pej* chato(ta).

fade [feɪd] ◇ *vt* [remove colour] desbotar. ◇ *vi* **-1.** [colour] desbotar **-2.** [sound] diminuir **-3.** [hope, memory, feeling] esvaecer **-4.** [smile, flower] murchar.

➡ **fade away, fade out** *vi* esvaecer.

faded ['feɪdɪd] *adj* desbotado(da).

faeces *UK*, **feces** *US* ['fi:si:z] *npl* fezes *fpl*.

Faeroe, Faroe ['feərəʊ] *n:* **the** ~ **Islands, the** ~ **s** as Ilhas Feroé; **in the** ~ **Islands** nas Ilhas Feroé.

faff [fæf] ➡ **faff about, faff around** *vi UK inf* enrolar.

fag [fæg] *n* **-1.** *UK inf* [cigarette] cigarro *m* **-2.** *UK inf* [chore] tarefa f chata **-3.** *US inf pej* [homosexual] bicha f.

fag end *n UK inf* bagana f.

fagged out [fægd-] *adj UK inf* acabado(da), moído(da).

faggot, fagot *US* ['fægət] *n* **-1.** *UK CULIN* almôndega f **-2.** *US inf pej* [homosexual] bicha f.

Fahrenheit ['færənhaɪt] *adj* Fahrenheit *inv.*

fail [feɪl] ◇ *vt* **-1.** [not succeed in]: **to** ~ **to do sthg** não conseguir fazer algo **-2.** [SCH & UNIV- exam, test] não passar em; [- candidate] rodar **-3.** [neglect]: **to** ~ **to do sthg** deixar de fazer algo **-4.** [let down] falhar. ◇ *vi* **-1.** [not succeed] não conseguir **-2.** *SCH & UNIV* rodar **-3.** [stop functioning] falhar **-4.** [weaken] enfraquecer.

failed [feɪld] *adj* [singer, writer etc] fracassado(da).

failing ['feɪlɪŋ] ◇ *n* [weakness] fraqueza f. ◇ *prep* na falta de; **or,** ~ **that, ...** ou, caso contrário, ...

fail-safe *adj* [device, system] protegido(da) contra falhas.

failure ['feɪljə'] *n* **-1.** fracasso *m* **-2.** [to attend, appear, act]: **I was surprised by her** ~ **to attend the meeting** fiquei surpreso pelo fato de ela não ter comparecido à reunião **-3.** [breakdown, malfunction] falha f **-4.** *MED:* **heart** ~ falência f do coração.

faint [feɪntl] <> adj -1. [slight] vago(ga) -2. [half-hearted] desmaiado(da) -3. [dizzy] fraco(ca). <> vi desmaiar.

faint-hearted [-'hɑːtɪd] adj covarde.

faintly ['feɪntlɪ] adv -1. [gen] tenuemente -2. [slightly] levemente.

faintness ['feɪntnɪs] n (U)-1. [dizziness] fraqueza f-2. [dimness - of image] imprecisão f; [- of sound, hope, memory] debilidade f.

fair [feəʳ] <> adj -1. [just] justo(ta); it's not ~ ! não é justo!; to be ~, ... para ser franco(ca), ... -2. [quite large] considerável -3. [quite good] bom (boa) -4. [hair, person] loiro(ra) -5. [skin, complexion] claro(ra) -6. [weather] claro(ra), bom (boa). <> n -1. UK [funfair] parque m de diversões -2. [trade fair] feira f. <> adv [fairly] limpo.
◆ **fair enough** excl UK inf tudo bem.

fair copy n cópia f passada a limpo.

fair game n (U) alvo m fácil; ~ for sb/sthg alvo fácil para alguém/algo.

fairground ['feəgraʊnd] n parque m de exposições.

fair-haired [-'heədl] adj [person] loiro(ra).

fairly ['feəlɪ] adv -1. [rather] bastante -2. [justly] justamente.

fair-minded [-'maɪndɪd] adj justo(ta).

fairness ['feənɪs] n (U) [justness] imparcialidade f, justiça f; in ~ to sb para ser justo(ta) com alguém.

fair play n (U) jogo m limpo.

fairway ['feəweɪ] n [on golf course] parte lisa do campo de golfe entre os buracos.

fairy ['feərɪ] (pl -ies) n [imaginary creature] fada f.

fairy lights npl UK lâmpadas fpl decorativas.

fairy tale n conto m de fadas.

fait accompli [ˌfeɪtə'kɒmplɪ] (pl faits accomplis [ˌfeɪtə'kɒmplɪ]) n fato m consumado.

faith [feɪθ] n -1. (U) [trust] fé f; ~ in sb/sthg fé em alguém/algo; in good/bad ~ de boa/má fé -2. [religion] crença f, fé f.

faithful ['feɪθfʊl] <> adj fiel. <> npl RELIG: the ~ os fiéis.

faithfully ['feɪθfʊlɪ] adv [loyally] fielmente; Yours ~ UK [in letter] atenciosamente, cordialmente.

faithfulness ['feɪθfʊlnɪs] n (U) fidelidade f.

faith healer n curandeiro m, -ra f.

faithless ['feɪθlɪs] adj [disloyal] infiel.

fake [feɪk] <> adj falso(sa). <> n -1. [object, painting] falsificação f-2. [person] falsário m, -ria f. <> vt -1. [falsify] falsificar -2. [simulate] fingir. <> vi [pretend] fingir.

falcon ['fɔːlkən] n falcão m.

Falkland Islands ['fɔːklənd-], **Falklands** ['fɔːkləndz] npl: the ~ as (Ilhas) Malvinas; in the ~ nas (Ilhas) Malvinas.

fall [fɔːl] (pt fell, pp fallen) <> vi -1. [gen] cair; to ~ flat [joke] não surtir efeito -2. [become] ficar; to ~ in love apaixonar-se; to ~ open cair aberto(ta) -3. [be classified]: to ~ into/under pertencer a -4. [disintegrate]: to ~ to bits OR pieces cair aos pedaços -5. [city, country]: to ~ (to sb) cair (nas mãos de alguém) -6. [occur]: to ~ on cair em -7. UK POL [constituency]: to ~ to sb passar ao controle de

alguém -8. [light, shadow] bater. <> n -1. [accident] tombo m, caída f-2. [of snow] nevasca f-3. [from power] queda f-4. [decrease] queda f; ~ in sthg queda de algo -5. US [autumn] outono m.
◆ **falls** npl [waterfall] cataratas fpl.
◆ **fall about** vi UK inf: to ~ about (laughing) cair na risada.
◆ **fall apart** vi -1. [book, chair] cair aos pedaços -2. fig [country, person] desmoronar.
◆ **fall away** vi -1. [plaster, paint] descolar -2. [land, slope] descer.
◆ **fall back** vi -1. [retreat, recede] retroceder -2. [lag behind] recuar.
◆ **fall back on** vt fus [resort to] recorrer a.
◆ **fall behind** vi -1. [in race] ficar para trás -2. [with rent, with work] atrasar-se.
◆ **fall down** vi -1. [person, picture, building] desabar -2. [fail] falhar.
◆ **fall for** vt fus -1. inf [fall in love with] ficar caído(da) por -2. [be deceived by] deixar-se enganar por.
◆ **fall in** vi -1. [roof, ceiling] desabar -2. MIL entrar em forma.
◆ **fall in with** vt fus [go along with] concordar com.
◆ **fall off** vi -1. [drop off] desprender-se -2. [diminish] diminuir.
◆ **fall on** vt fus -1. [subj: eyes, gaze] dirigir-se para -2. [attack] atacar, lançar-se sobre.
◆ **fall out** vi -1. [drop out] cair -2. [quarrel]: to ~ out (with sb) brigar (com alguém) -3. MIL sair de forma.
◆ **fall over** <> vt fus tropeçar em; to be ~ing over o.s. to do sthg inf desdobrar-se para fazer algo. <> vi [lose balance] cair.
◆ **fall through** vi [plan, deal] fracassar.
◆ **fall to** vt fus [devolve upon] recair; it ~s to me to make a speech toca para mim fazer o discurso.

fallacious [fə'leɪʃəs] adj fml falacioso(sa).

fallacy ['fæləsɪ] (pl -ies) n [misconception] falácia f.

fallen ['fɔːln] pp ▷ fall.

fall guy n US inf [scapegoat] bode m expiatório.

fallible ['fæləbl] adj falível.

falling ['fɔːlɪŋ] adj [decreasing] em declínio.

fallopian tube [fə'ləʊpɪən-] n trompa f de Falópio.

fallout ['fɔːlaʊt] n (U) [radiation] chuva f radioativa.

fallout shelter n abrigo m antinuclear.

fallow ['fæləʊ] adj [land] alqueivado(da); to lie ~ ficar sem cultivo.

false [fɔːls] adj -1. [gen] falso(sa) -2. [artificial] postiço(ça).

false alarm n alarme m falso.

falsehood ['fɔːlshʊd] n fml -1. [lie] mentira f-2. (U) [lack of truth] falsidade f.

falsely ['fɔːlslɪ] adv -1. [wrongly] erroneamente -2. [insincerely] falsamente.

false start n tentativa f frustrada.

false teeth npl dentadura f postiça.

falsetto [fɔːl'setəʊ] (pl -s) <> n MUS falsete m. <> adv [sing] em falsete.

falsify ['fɔːlsɪfaɪ] (pt & pp -ied) vt [facts, accounts] falsificar.

falter ['fɔːltə'] *vi* -**1.** [gen] vacilar -**2.** [hesitate, lose confidence] hesitar.

faltering ['fɔːltərɪŋ] *adj* [steps, voice] vacilante.

fame [feɪm] *n (U)* fama *f.*

familiar [fə'mɪljə'] *adj* -**1.** [known] familiar; ~ **to sb** familiar para alguém -**2.** [conversant]: ~ **with sthg** familiarizado(da) com algo; **to be on** ~ **terms with sb** ter relações amigáveis com alguém -**3.** *pej* [overly informal - person] que se dá muitas liberdades; [- tone, manner] amigável em excesso.

familiarity [fə,mɪlɪ'ærətɪ] *n* -**1.** [with book, rules, subject]: ~ **with sthg** conhecimento *m* de algo -**2.** [of place, face] familiaridade *f* -**3.** *pej* [excessive informality] liberdades *fpl.*

familiarize, -ise [fə'mɪljəraɪz] *vt*: **to** ~ **o.s. with sthg** familiarizar-se com algo; **to** ~ **sb with sthg** familiarizar alguém com algo.

family ['fæmlɪ] (*pl* -**ies**) <> *n* família *f.* <> *comp* -**1.** [belonging to family] familiar; ~ **car** carro da família -**2.** [suitable for all ages] para toda a família.

family business *n* negócio *m* familiar.

family credit *n (U) UK* auxílio-família *m.*

family doctor *n* médico *m,* -ca *f* de família.

family life *n (U)* vida *f* familiar.

family planning *n (U)* planejamento *m* familiar.

family tree *n* árvore *f* genealógica.

famine ['fæmɪn] *n* fome *f* extrema e coletiva.

famished ['fæmɪʃt] *adj inf* [very hungry] faminto(ta), morto(ta) de fome.

famous ['feɪməs] *adj* famoso(sa); ~ **for** famoso(sa) por algo.

famously ['feɪməslɪ] *adv dated*: **to get on** *OR* **along** ~ **with sb** ficar íntimo(ma) de alguém.

fan [fæn] (*pt & pp* -**ned**, *cont* -**ning**) <> *n* -**1.** [of paper, silk] leque *m* -**2.** [electric or mechanical] ventilador *m* -**3.** [enthusiast] fã *mf,* admirador *m,* -ra *f.* <> *vt* -**1.** [cool] abanar; **to** ~ **o.s.** abanar-se -**2.** [stimulate] atiçar.

➡ **fan out** *vi* [army, search party] espalhar-se.

fanatic [fə'nætɪk] *n* fanático *m,* -ca *f.*

fanatical [fə'nætɪkl] *adj* fanático(ca).

fanaticism [fə'nætɪsɪzm] *n (U)* fanatismo *m.*

fan belt *n* correia *f* do ventilador.

fanciful ['fænsɪfʊl] *adj* -**1.** [odd] estapafúrdio(dia) -**2.** [elaborate] extravagante.

fan club *n* fã-clube *m.*

fancy ['fænsɪ] (*compar* -**ier**, *superl* -**iest**, *pl* -**ies**, *pt & pp* -**ied**) <> *adj* -**1.** [elaborate] caprichado(da) -**2.** [expensive] extravagante. <> *n* -**1.** [liking] gosto *m*; **to take a** ~ **to sb/sthg** ter simpatia por alguém/ algo; **to take sb's** ~ cair nas graças de alguém -**2.** [whim] capricho *m* -**3.** [fantasy] fantasia *f.* <> *vt* -**1.** *inf* [want] querer; **I** ~ **going to the cinema** me agrada a idéia de ir ao cinema -**2.** [like] agradar-se de; **to** ~ **o.s.** estar cheio (cheia) de si -**3.** [imagine] imaginar; ~ **meeting you here!** imagina só, te encontrar por aqui!; **to** ~ **o.s. as sthg** imaginar-se como alguém; ~ **that!** imagina só!, quem diria!

fancy dress *n (U)* fantasia *f.*

fancy-dress party *n* festa *f* à fantasia.

fancy goods *npl* artigos *mpl* de luxo.

fanfare ['fænfeə'] *n MUS* fanfarra *f.*

fang [fæŋ] *n* -**1.** [of snake] presa *f* -**2.** [of carnivore] colmilho *m.*

fan heater *n* aquecedor *m* de ventoinha.

fanlight ['fænlaɪt] *n UK* clarabóia *f.*

fan mail *n (U)* cartas *fpl* de fãs.

fanny ['fænɪ] *n US inf* [backside] bunda *f.*

fanny pack *n US* pochete *f.*

fantasize, -ise ['fæntəsaɪz] *vi* fantasiar; **to** ~ **about sthg/about doing sthg** fantasiar sobre algo/sobre fazer algo.

fantastic [fæn'tæstɪk] *adj* -**1.** *inf* [gen] fantástico(ca) -**2.** [bizarre, strange] exótico(ca).

fantastically [fæn'tæstɪklɪ] *adv* -**1.** [extremely] extremamente -**2.** [bizarrely, strangely] exoticamente.

fantasy ['fæntəsɪ] (*pl* -**ies**) <> *n* fantasia *f.* <> *comp* de sonhos, imaginário(ria).

fanzine ['fænziːn] *n* fanzine *m.*

fao (*abbr of* **for the attention of**) a/c.

FAO (*abbr of* **Food and Agriculture Organization**) *n* FAO *f.*

FAQ (*abbr of* **frequently asked questions**) *n* perguntas *fpl* mais freqüentes, FAQ *f.*

far [fɑː'] (*compar* **farther** *OR* **further**, *superl* **farthest** *OR* **furthest**) <> *adv* -**1.** [in distance] longe; **how** ~ **is it?** a que distância fica?; **how** ~ **have you come?** até onde você veio?; **is it** ~ **?** é longe?; ~ **away** *OR* **off** muito longe; ~ **and wide** por todo o lugar; **as** ~ **as** até; **we walked as** ~ **as the river** caminhamos até o rio -**2.** [in time]: ~ **away** *OR* **off** muito longe; **as** ~ **back as 1900** já em 1900; **so** ~ até agora -**3.** [in degree or extent] muito; **how** ~ **have you got with your novel?** até onde você já foi no romance?; **he's not** ~ **wrong** *OR* **out** *OR* **off** ele não está tão errado; **as** ~ **as I know** até onde eu sei; **as** ~ **as I'm concerned** no que me diz respeito; **as** ~ **as possible** até onde é possível; ~ **and away, by** ~ de longe; ~ **from it** pelo contrário; **so** ~ até este ponto; **so** ~ **so good** até agora tudo bem; **to go so** ~ **as to do sthg** chegar ao ponto de fazer algo; **to go too** ~ ir longe demais. <> *adj* -**1.** [distant, extreme] extremo(ma) -**2.** [remote] distante, remoto(ta).

faraway ['fɑːrəweɪ] *adj* -**1.** [distant] distante -**2.** [dreamy] ausente.

farce [fɑːs] *n* farsa *f.*

farcical ['fɑːsɪkl] *adj* ridículo(la).

fare [feə'] <> *n* -**1.** [payment, rate] tarifa *f* -**2.** [price of ticket] preço *m* -**3.** [person] passageiro *m,* -ra *f* -**4.** *fml* [food] comida *f.* <> *vi* [manage]: **to** ~ **well/badly** passar bem/mal.

Far East *n*: **the** ~ o Extremo Oriente.

fare stage *n UK parada na qual aumenta o preço da passagem.*

farewell [feə'wel] <> *n* despedida *f,* adeus *m.* <> *excl literary* adeus!

farfetched [,fɑː'fetʃt] *adj* forçado(da).

far-flung *adj* -**1.** [remote] longínquo(qua) -**2.** [extensive] vasto(ta).

farm [fɑːm] <> *n* fazenda *f.* <> *vt* cultivar. <> *vi* cultivar a terra.

➡ **farm out** *vt sep* mandar fazer.

farmer ['fɑːmə'] *n* fazendeiro *m,* -ra *f.*

farmhand ['fɑːmhænd] *n* peão *m,* -oa *f.*

farmhouse ['fɑ:mhaʊs, *pl* -haʊzɪz] *n* granja *f*, quinta *f*.

farming ['fɑ:mɪŋ] *n (U)* **-1.** [activity] agricultura *f* **-2.** [of animals] criação *f* **-3.** [of crops] cultivo *m*.

farmland ['fɑ:mlænd] *n (U)* terra *f* cultivada.

farmstead ['fɑ:msted] *n US* granja *f*.

farmyard ['fɑ:mjɑ:d] *n* terreiro *m (de fazenda)*.

Faroe *n* = Faeroe.

far-off *adj* distante.

far-reaching [-'ri:tʃɪŋ] *adj* **-1.** [implications] de longo alcance **-2.** [changes] abrangente.

farrier ['færɪə'] *n* ferrador *m*, -ra *f*.

far-sighted *adj* **-1.** [person] prudente; [plan] perspicaz **-2.** *US* [longsighted] hipermetrope.

fart [fɑ:t] vulg <> *n* **-1.** [wind] peido *m* **-2.** [person] pé-no-saco *m*. <> *vi* peidar.

farther ['fɑ:ðə'] *compar* ⊳ far.

farthest ['fɑ:ðəst] *superl* ⊳ far.

fascia ['feɪʃə] *n* **-1.** [on shop] fachada *m* **-2.** AUT painel *m* **-3.** [for mobile phone] frente *f*.

fascinate ['fæsɪneɪt] *vt* fascinar.

fascinating ['fæsɪneɪtɪŋ] *adj* fascinante.

fascination [,fæsɪ'neɪʃn] *n (U)* fascinação *f*.

fascism ['fæʃɪzm] *n (U)* fascismo *m*.

fascist ['fæʃɪst] <> *adj* fascista. <> *n* fascista *mf*.

fashion ['fæʃn] <> *n* **-1.** [current style] moda *f*; ~ **model** modelo *mf* (de passarela); **in/out of** ~ [vogue] na/fora de moda **-2.** [manner] maneira *f*; **after a** ~ até certo ponto. <> *vt fml* [shape] moldar.

fashionable ['fæʃnəbl] *adj* [in vogue] da moda.

fashion-conscious *adj* atento(ta) às tendências da moda.

fashion designer *n* estilista *mf*.

fashion show *n* desfile *m* de modas.

fast [fɑ:st] <> *adj* **-1.** [rapid] rápido(da); **she's in the** ~ **track** ela está indo pelo caminho mais rápido; **to pull a** ~ **one on sb** *inf* passar a perna em alguém **-2.** [clock, watch] adiantado(da) **-3.** [dye] permanente. <> *adv* **-1.** [rapidly] depressa; **how** ~ **does this car go?** a que velocidade este carro chega?; **I need help** ~ preciso de ajuda rápido **-2.** [firmly] firmemente; **to hold** ~ **to sthg** [grip firmly] segurar firme algo; *fig* [stick to] manter-se firme em algo; **to be** ~ **asleep** dormir profundamente. <> *n* jejum *m*. <> *vi* jejuar.

fast breeder reactor *n* reator *m* super-regenerador.

fasten ['fɑ:sn] <> *vt* **-1.** [close - jacket, bag] fechar; [- seat belt] apertar **-2.** [attach]: **to** ~ **sthg to sthg** fixar algo em algo **-3.** [grasp] prender. <> *vi*: **to** ~ **on to sb/sthg** agarrar-se a alguém/algo.

fastener ['fɑ:snə'] *n* **-1.** [dress, bag] fecho *m* **-2.** [necklace] presilha *f* **-3.** [door] fechadura *f*.

fastening ['fɑ:snɪŋ] *n* **-1.** [gen] fechadura *f* **-2.** [on window] trinco *m*.

fast food *n (U)* fast-food *m*.

fast-forward <> *n* avanço *m* rápido. <> *vt* avançar rapidamente. <> *vi* avançar rapidamente.

fastidious [fə'stɪdɪəs] *adj* [fussy] meticuloso(sa).

fast lane *n* **-1.** [on motorway] pista *f* de alta velocidade **-2.** *fig* [exciting lifestyle]: **life in the** ~ vida *f* excitante.

fat [fæt] (*compar* **-ter**, *superl* **-test**) <> *adj* **-1.** [person, animal, face, legs, meat] gordo(da); **to get** ~ engordar **-2.** [volume, file, wallet] pesado(da) **-3.** [FIN - profit, fee] avultado(da); [- cheque, bank account] gordo(da) **-4.** *iro* [small]: **that was a** ~ **lot of good** OR **use** não foi nada bom o que você fez!; ~ **chance!** nem pensar! <> *n* **-1.** *(U)* ANAT gordura *f* **-2.** *(U)* [in food - raw] banha *f*; [- cooked] sebo *m*; [- in cooking, diet] gordura *f*.

fatal ['feɪtl] *adj* **-1.** [ruinous] fatal **-2.** [mortal] mortal.

fatalism ['feɪtəlɪzm] *n (U)* fatalismo *m*.

fatalistic [,feɪtə'lɪstɪk] *adj* fatalista.

fatality [fə'tælətɪ] (*pl* **-ies**) *n* [accident victim] fatalidade *f*; [fatalism] fatalismo *m*.

fatally ['feɪtəlɪ] *adv* **-1.** [ruinously] fatalmente **-2.** [mortally] mortalmente.

fate [feɪt] *n* **-1.** *(U)* [destiny] destino *m*; **to tempt** ~ brincar com a sorte **-2.** [of person, thing] sina *f*.

fated ['feɪtɪd] *adj* **-1.** [destined] predestinado(da); **to be** ~ **to do sthg** estar fadado(da) a fazer algo **-2.** [doomed] condenado(da).

fateful ['feɪtfʊl] *adj* [decisive] fatídico(ca).

fathead *n inf* estúpido *m*, -da *f*.

father ['fɑ:ðə'] <> *n lit, fig* pai *m*. <> *vt* ser o pai de.

➡ **Father** *n* **-1.** [priest] padre *m* **-2.** [God]: **our Father** nosso Pai.

Father Christmas *n UK* Papai *m* Noel.

fatherhood ['fɑ:ðəhʊd] *n (U)* paternidade *f*.

father-in-law (*pl* **father-in-laws** OR **fathers-in-law**) *n* sogro *m*.

fatherly ['fɑ:ðəlɪ] *adj* paternal.

Father's Day *n* Dia *f* dos Pais.

fathom ['fæðəm] <> *n* braça *f*. <> *vt*: **to** ~ **sthg (out)** desvendar algo; **to** ~ **sb (out)** compreender alguém.

fatigue [fə'ti:g] <> *n (U)* fadiga *f*. <> *vt* [weary] fatigar.

➡ **fatigues** *npl* farda *f* de serviço.

fatless *adj* sem gordura.

fatness ['fætnɪs] *n (U)* [of person] gordura *f*.

fatten ['fætn] *vt* engordar.

➡ **fatten up** *vt sep* engordar.

fattening ['fætnɪŋ] *adj* que engorda; **to be very** ~ engordar muito.

fatty ['fætɪ] (*compar* **-ier**, *superl* **-iest**, *pl* **-ies**) <> *adj* **-1.** [food] gorduroso(sa) **-2.** BIOL [tissue] adiposo(sa). <> *n inf pej* gorducho *m*, -cha *f*.

fatuous ['fætjʊəs] *adj* fátuo(tua).

fatuously *adv* tolamente.

fatwa ['fætwə] *n* mandado *m* religioso islâmico.

faucet ['fɔ:sɪt] *n US* torneira *f*.

fault [fɔ:lt] <> *n* **-1.** [responsibility] culpa *f* **-2.** [defect] defeito *m* **-3.** [mistake, imperfection] falha *f*; **to find** ~ **with sb/sthg** criticar algo/alguém; **to be at** ~ equivocar-se; **through no** ~ **of my own I missed the train** perdi o trem, mas não foi culpa minha **-4.** GEOL falha *f* **-5.** [in tennis] falta *f*. <> *vt*: **to** ~ **sb (on sthg)** criticar alguém (em algo).

faultless ['fɔ:ltlɪs] *adj* impecável.

faulty ['fɔ:ltɪ] (*compar* **-ier**, *superl* **-iest**) *adj* **-1.** [machine, system] defeituoso(sa) **-2.** [reasoning, logic] falho(lha).

fauna ['fɔːnə] *n* fauna *f*.

faux pas [ˌfəʊ'pɑː] (*pl inv*) *n* gafe *f*.

favour *UK*, **favor** *US* ['feɪvə'] ⬦ *n* **-1.** (*U*) [approval] aprovação *f*; **in sb's ~** em favor de alguém; **to be in ~ (with sb)** contar com o apoio (de alguém); **to be out of ~ (with sb)** não contar com o apoio (de alguém); **to curry ~ with sb** puxar o saco de alguém **-2.** [kind act] favor *m*; **to do sb a ~** fazer um favor a alguém **-3.** (*U*) [favouritism] favoritismo *m* **-4.** [advantage]: **to rule in sb's ~** decidir a favor de alguém. ⬦ *vt* **-1.** [gen] favorecer **-2.** *iro* [honour]: **to ~ sb with sthg** honrar alguém com algo.
  ➡ **in favour** *adv* [in agreement] a favor.
  ➡ **in favour of** *prep* **-1.** [in preference to] em favor de **-2.** [in agreement with]: **to be in ~ of sthg/ of doing sthg** estar a favor de algo/de fazer algo.

favourable *UK*, **favorable** *US* ['feɪvrəbl] *adj* favorável.

favourably *UK*, **favorably** *US* ['feɪvrəblɪ] *adv* [well] favoralmente.

favoured *UK*, **favored** *US* ['feɪvəd] *adj* [with special advantages] favorecido(da).

favourite *UK*, **favorite** *US* ['feɪvrɪt] ⬦ *adj* [preferred] favorito(ta). ⬦ *n* favorito(ta).

favouritism *UK*, **favoritism** *US* ['feɪvrɪtɪzm] *n* (*U*) favoritismo *m*.

fawn [fɔːn] ⬦ *adj* castanho(nha) claro(ra). ⬦ *n* [animal] cervato *m*. ⬦ *vi*: **to ~ on sb** bajular alguém.

fax [fæks] ⬦ *n* fax *m*. ⬦ *vt* **-1.** [send fax to] enviar um fax para **-2.** [send by fax] enviar por fax.

fax machine *n* (máquina *f* de) fax *m*.

fax number *n* número *m* de fax.

faze [feɪz] *vt inf* grilar.

FBI (*abbr of* Federal Bureau of Investigation) *n* FBI *m*.

FC (*abbr of* Football Club) *n* FC.

FCC (*abbr of* Federal Communications Commission) *n* comissão federal norte-americana de comunicação audiovisual.

FCO (*abbr of* Foreign and Commonwealth Office) *n* ministério britânico de relações exteriores e com o Commonwealth, ≃ MRE *m*.

FDA *n* (*abbr of* Food and Drug Administration) órgão norte-americano que controla os medicamentos e produtos alimentícios.

FE (*abbr of* Further Education) *n* estudos de educação continuada após o término do ensino superior na Grã-Bretanha.

fear [fɪə'] ⬦ *n* **-1.** [gen] medo *m* **-2.** [risk] risco *m*, perigo *m*; **for ~ of** por medo de. ⬦ *vt* **-1.** [be afraid of] ter medo de, temer **-2.** [anticipate] temer, recear; **to ~ (that)** recear que. ⬦ *vi* [be afraid]: **to ~ for sb/sthg** temer por alguém/algo.

fearful ['fɪəfʊl] *adj* **-1.** *fml* [frightened] temeroso(sa); **~ of sthg/of doing sthg** temeroso(sa) de algo/de fazer algo **-2.** [frightening] terrível, pavoroso(sa).

fearless ['fɪəlɪs] *adj* sem medo, destemido(da).

fearlessly ['fɪəlɪslɪ] *adv* destemidamente, sem medo.

fearsome ['fɪəsəm] *adj* terrível.

feasibility [ˌfiːzə'bɪlətɪ] *n* (*U*) [of plan] viabilidade *f*.

feasibility study *n* estudo *m* de viabilidade.

feasible ['fiːzəbl] *adj* [plan] viável.

feast [fiːst] ⬦ *n* [meal] banquete *m*. ⬦ *vi*: **to ~ on** *OR* **off sthg** banquetear-se com algo.

feat [fiːt] *n* façanha *f*.

feather ['feðə'] *n* pena *f*; **a ~ in one's cap** motivo de muito orgulho.

feather bed *n* cama *f* de penas.

feather-brained *adj* disparatado(da); **a ~ person** um cabeça-de-vento.

featherweight ['feðəweɪt] *n* [boxer] peso-pena *m*.

feature ['fiːtʃə'] ⬦ *n* **-1.** [characteristic - of house] característica *f*; [- of machine] recurso *m*; [- of style, landscape] aspecto *m*; [- of face, personality] traço *m* **-2.** [article] reportagem *f* especial **-3.** RADIO & TV [programme] especial *m* **-4.** CINEMA longa-metragem *m*. ⬦ *vt* [subj: film, exhibition] ter como atração principal; **a film featuring Juliette Binoche** um filme estrelando Juliette Binoche. ⬦ *vi*: **to ~ (in sthg)** [appear, figure] figurar (em algo).

feature film *n* longa-metragem *m*.

featureless ['fiːtʃəlɪs] *adj* sem traços característicos.

Feb. [feb] (*abbr of* February) fev.

February ['februərɪ] *n* fevereiro *m*; *see also* September.

feces *npl US* = faeces.

feckless ['feklɪs] *adj* displicente.

fed [fed] *pt* & *pp* ⊳ feed.

Fed [fed] ⬦ *n* **-1.** *fam* (*abbr of* Federal agent/official) oficial ou agente oficial norte-americano, especialmente do FBI. **- 2.** *fam* (*abbr of* Federal Reserve Board) órgão de controle do banco central norte-americano. ⬦ **-1.** (*abbr of* federal) fed. **- 2.** (*abbr of* federation) Fed.

federal ['fedrəl] *adj* federal.

Federal Bureau of Investigation *n* polícia federal americana, FBI *m*.

federalism ['fedrəlɪzm] *n* (*U*) federalismo *m*.

federation [ˌfedə'reɪʃn] *n* **-1.** [country] federação *f* **-2.** [association] liga *f*.

fed up *adj* farto(ta), cheio(a); **to be ~ with sb/ sthg** estar cheio de alguém/algo.

fee [fiː] *n* [payment - school] (taxa *f* de) matrícula *f*; [- doctor] preço *m* da consulta; [- lawyer] honorários *mpl*; [- monthly membership] mensalidade *f*; [- annual membership] anuidade *f*; [- entrance] taxa *f* de admissão.

feeble ['fiːbl] *adj* **-1.** [weak] fraco(ca) **-2.** [lacking conviction] débil.

feeble-minded *adj* [stupid] imbecil, de idéias curtas.

feebleness ['fiːblnɪs] *n* (*U*) **-1.** [weakness] fraqueza *f* **-2.** [lack of conviction] debilidade *f*.

feebly ['fiːblɪ] *adv* **-1.** [weakly] fracamente **-2.** [without conviction] sem convicção.

feed [fiːd] (*pt* & *pp* fed) ⬦ *vt* **-1.** [give food to] alimentar **-2.** *fig* [fuel] alimentar **-3.** [put, insert]: **to ~ sthg into sthg** inserir algo em algo. ⬦ *vi* **-1.** [take food] alimentar-se; **to ~ on** *OR* **off sthg** alimentar-se de algo **-2.** *fig* [be fuelled]: **to ~ on** *OR* **off sthg** crescer com algo. ⬦ *n* **-1.** [meal] comida *f* **-2.** (*U*) [animal food] ração *f*.

feedback ['fiːdbæk] *n* (*U*) **-1.** [reaction] reação *f* **-2.** ELEC feedback *m*.

feedbag ['fi:dbæg] n US embornal m.
feeder road n via f de alimentação.
feeding bottle ['fi:dɪŋ-] n UK mamadeira f.
feel [fi:l] (pt & pp felt) ⋄ vt -1. [touch] tocar -2. [believe, think] achar, acreditar; **to ~ (that)** achar que -3. [experience, be aware of] sentir; **to ~ o.s. doing sthg** sentir-se fazendo algo -4. phr: **I'm not ~ing myself today** não estou me sentindo bem hoje. ⋄ vi -1. [have sensation, emotion] sentir--se; **to ~ like sthg/like doing sthg** [be in mood for] ter vontade de algo/de fazer algo -2. [seem] parecer -3. [by touch]: **to ~ for sthg** procurar algo com as mãos. ⋄ n -1. [sensation, touch] sensação f -2. [atmosphere] clima m -3. phr: **to get/have a ~ for sthg** acostumar-se a algo.
feeler ['fi:lə'] n -1. [of insect, snail] antena f -2. [of octopus] tentáculo m.
feeling ['fi:lɪŋ] n -1. [emotion] sensação f; **bad ~** mau pressentimento -2. [physical - of nausea, vertigo etc] sensação f; [- sensation] sensibilidade f -3. [awareness, impression] impressão f -4. [understanding] disposição f; **to have a ~ for sthg** levar jeito para algo.
 ➡ **feelings** npl sentimentos mpl; **to hurt sb's ~s** magoar alguém, magoar os sentimentos de alguém; **no hard ~s!** sem ressentimentos!
fee-paying [-'peɪɪŋ] adj UK pago(ga).
feet [fi:t] pl ⊳ foot.
feign [feɪn] vt fml fingir.
feint [feɪnt] ⋄ n finta f. ⋄ vi fintar.
feisty ['faɪstɪ] (compar -ier, superl -iest) adj esp US inf determinado(da).
felicitous [fɪ'lɪsɪtəs] adj fml [fortunate] oportuno(na).
feline ['fi:laɪn] ⋄ adj felino(na). ⋄ n fml felino m, -na f.
fell [fel] ⋄ pt ⊳ fall. ⋄ vt -1. [tree] cortar -2. [person] derrubar.
 ➡ **fells** npl GEOGR charneca f.
fellow ['feləʊ] ⋄ adj companheiro m, -ra f. ⋄ n -1. dated [man] cara mf -2. [comrade, peer] camarada mf -3. [of society or college] membro m honorário.
fellowship ['feləʊʃɪp] n -1. (U) [comradeship] companheirismo m -2. [organization] sociedade f -3. [in university - grant] bolsa f de pesquisa; [- post] pesquisador m, -ra f.
felony ['felənɪ] (pl -ies) n JUR delito m grave.
felt [felt] ⋄ pt & pp ⊳ feel. ⋄ n (U) [textile] feltro m.
felt-tip pen n pincel m atômico.
female ['fi:meɪl] ⋄ adj -1. [gen] feminino(na) -2. [plant] fêmeo(mea). ⋄ n -1. [female animal] fêmea f -2. inf pej [woman] fêmea f.
feminine ['femɪnɪn] ⋄ adj feminino(na). ⋄ n GRAMM feminino m.
femininity [femɪ'nɪnətɪ] n (U) feminilidade f.
feminism ['femɪnɪzml] n (U) feminismo m.
feminist ['femɪnɪst] n feminista.
fence [fens] ⋄ n [barrier] cerca f; **to sit on the ~** fig ficar em cima do muro. ⋄ vt cercar.
 ➡ **fence in** vt sep -1. [garden] cercar -2. fig [person] prender; **she feels completely ~d in** ela se sente totalmente presa.
 ➡ **fence off** vt sep isolar.

fencing ['fensɪŋ] n (U) -1. SPORT esgrima f -2. [fences] cerca f -3. [material] material m para fazer cerca.
fend [fend] vi: **to ~ for o.s.** saber se virar.
 ➡ **fend off** vt sep rechaçar.
fender ['fendə'] n -1. [round fireplace] guarda-fogo m -2. [on boat] proteção f -3. US [on car] pára-lama f.
fennel ['fenl] n (U) erva-doce f.
fens [fenz] npl UK pântano m.
feral ['fɪərəl] adj selvagem.
ferment [n 'fɜ:ment, vb fə'ment] ⋄ n (U) [unrest] grande agitação f, polvorosa f; **in ~** em polvorosa. ⋄ vi [change chemically] fermentar.
fermentation [fɜ:mən'teɪʃn] n (U) fermentação f.
fermented [fə'mentɪd] adj fermentado(da).
fern [fɜ:n] n samambaia f.
ferocious [fə'rəʊʃəs] adj feroz.
ferociously [fə'rəʊʃəslɪ] adv ferozmente.
ferocity [fə'rɒsətɪ] n (U) ferocidade f.
ferret ['ferɪt] n [animal] furão m.
 ➡ **ferret about, ferret around** vi inf vasculhar.
 ➡ **ferret out** vt sep inf desenterrar.
ferris wheel ['ferɪs-] n esp US roda-gigante f.
ferry ['ferɪ] (pl -ies, pt & pp -ied) ⋄ n balsa f. ⋄ vt transportar.
ferryboat ['ferɪbəʊt] n = ferry.
ferryman ['ferɪmən] (pl -men [-mən]) n balseiro m.
fertile ['fɜ:taɪl] adj fértil.
fertility [fɜ:'tɪlətɪ] n (U) fertilidade f.
fertility drug n remédio f para infertilidade.
fertilization [fɜ:tɪlaɪ'zeɪʃn] n (U) -1. [enrichment] fertilização f -2. [insemination] fecundação f.
fertilize, -ise ['fɜ:tɪlaɪz] vt -1. [enrich] fertilizar -2. [inseminate] fecundar.
fertilizer ['fɜ:tɪlaɪzə'] n fertilizante m.
fervent ['fɜ:vənt] adj -1. [admirer, believer] fervoroso(-sa) -2. [belief, desire, hope] ardente.
fervour UK, **fervor** US ['fɜ:və'] n (U) fervor m.
fester ['festə'] vi -1. [wound] inflamar, inflamar-se -2. fig [situation, problem, feeling] inflamar.
festival ['festəvl] n -1. [series of organized events] festival m -2. [holiday] feriado m, dia m festivo.
festive ['festɪv] adj festivo(va).
festive season n: the **~** a época do Natal.
festivities [fes'tɪvətɪz] npl festividades fpl.
festoon [fe'stu:n] vt enfeitar; **to be ~ed with sthg** estar enfeitado(da) com algo.
fetal ['fi:tl] adj = foetal.
fetch [fetʃ] vt -1. [go and get] ir buscar -2. [sell for] alcançar.
fetching ['fetʃɪŋ] adj atraente.
fete, fête [feɪt] ⋄ n festa f beneficente. ⋄ vt festejar (em honra de alguém).
fetid ['fetɪd] adj fétido(da).
fetish ['fetɪʃ] n -1. [sexual obsession] fetiche m -2. [mania] mania f -3. [object] amuleto m.
fetishism ['fetɪʃɪzml] n (U) fetichismo m.
fetlock ['fetlɒk] n machinho m.
fetter ['fetə'] vt restringir.
 ➡ **fetters** npl fig [constraints] restrição f.
fettle ['fetl] n (U): **in fine ~** [person] em forma.
fetus ['fi:təs] n = foetus.

feud [fju:d] <> *n* contenda *f.* <> *vi* brigar.

feudal ['fju:dl] *adj* feudal.

fever ['fi:vəʳ] *n* **-1.** MED febre *f* **-2.** *fig* [frenzy] frenesi *m.*

fevered ['fi:vəd] *adj* **-1.** [hot] febril **-2.** [wild, excited] exaltado(da).

feverish ['fi:vərıʃ] *adj* **-1.** MED febril **-2.** [frenzied] frenético(ca).

fever pitch *n* (*U*) ponto *m* máximo.

few [fju:] <> *adj* [not many] pouco(ca); **a ~ alguns(mas); a ~ more** mais alguns(mas); **quite a ~, a good ~** bastante; **and far between** pouquíssimos(mas). <> *pron* poucos *mpl*, -cas *fpl*; **a ~** poucos(cas); **quite a ~, a good ~** bastante.

fewer ['fju:əʳ] <> *adj* menos; **no ~ than** não menos do que. <> *pron* menos.

fewest ['fju:əst] *adj* o menos possível.

FHA (*abbr of* **Federal Housing Administration**) *n* órgão norte-americano que controla a habitação social.

fiancé [fı'ɒnseı] *n* noivo *m.*

fiancée [fı'ɒnseı] *n* noiva *f.*

fiasco [fı'æskəʊ] (*UK pl* **-s**, *US pl* **-s** OR **-es**) *n* fiasco *m.*

fib [fıb] (*pt & pp* **-bed**, *cont* **-bing**) *inf* <> *n* lorota *f.* <> *vi* contar lorotas.

fibber ['fıbəʳ] *n inf* mentiroso(sa).

fibre UK, **fiber** US ['faıbəʳ] *n* **-1.** (*U*) [material, substance] fibra *f* **-2.** [thread] filamento *m* **-3.** (*U*) [strength] força *f.*

fibreboard UK, **fiberboard** US ['faıbəbɔ:d] *n* (*U*) madeira *f* compensada.

fibreglass UK, **fiberglass** US ['faıbəgla:s] <> *n* (*U*) fibra *f* de vidro. <> *comp* de fibra de vidro.

fibre optics *n* (*U*) fibra *f* óptica.

fibrositis [ˌfaıbrə'saıtıs] *n* (*U*) fibrosite *f.*

FICA (*abbr of* **Federal Insurance Contributions Act**) *n* lei norte-americana que regulamenta o pagamento obrigatório de contribuição social mensal por parte dos trabalhadores.

fickle ['fıkl] *adj* inconstante, volúvel.

fiction ['fıkʃn] *n* **-1.** (*U*) [literature] ficção *f* **-2.** [fabrication, lie] invenção *f.*

fictional ['fıkʃənl] *adj* **-1.** [literary] ficcional **-2.** [invented] imaginário(ria).

fictionalize, -ise ['fıkʃənəlaız] *vt* romancear.

fictitious [fık'tıʃəs] *adj* [false] fictício(cia).

fiddle ['fıdl] <> *n* **-1.** [violin] rabeca *f*; **(as) fit as a ~** em excelente forma; **to play second ~ (to sb)** estar em segundo plano (para alguém) **-2.** UK inf [fraud] embuste *m.* <> *vt* UK inf falsificar. <> *vi* **-1.** [fidget]: **to ~ (about** OR **around)** enrolar; **to ~ (about** OR **around) with sthg** mexer em algo **-2.** [waste time]: **to ~ about** OR **around** perder tempo.

fiddler ['fıdləʳ] *n* [violinist] violinista *mf.*

fiddly ['fıdlı] (*compar* **-ier**, *superl* **-iest**) *adj* UK inf trabalhoso(sa).

fidelity [fı'delətı] *n* (*U*) **-1.** [loyalty] fidelidade *f* **-2.** [accuracy] veracidade *f.*

fidget ['fıdʒıt] *vi* estar irrequieto(ta), mover-se sem parar.

fidgety ['fıdʒıtı] *adj inf* inquieto(ta).

fiduciary [fı'du:ʃjərı] (*pl* **-ies**) <> *adj* fiduciário

(ria). <> *n* fiduciário *m*, -ria *f.*

field [fi:ld] <> *n* **-1.** [gen] campo *m* **-2.** [of knowledge] área *f* **-3.** [real environment]: **in the ~** no campo de batalha **-4. : ~ of vision** campo visual. <> *vt* [avoid answering] responder. <> *vi* SPORT interceptar.

field day *n* [for study, sport] dia *m* de atividades externas; **to have a ~** *fig* fazer a festa.

fielder ['fi:ldəʳ] *n* **-1.** [in baseball] jardineiro *m* **-2.** [in cricket] interceptador *m.*

field event *n* esporte *m* de campo.

field glasses *npl* binóculos *mpl.*

field marshal *n* marechal-de-campo *m.*

field mouse *n* ratazana *f.*

field trip *n* viagem *f* de estudos.

fieldwork ['fi:ldwɜ:k] *n* (*U*) pesquisa *f* de campo.

fieldworker ['fi:ldwɜ:kəʳ] *n* pesquisador *m*, -ra *f* de campo.

fiend [fi:nd] *n* **-1.** [cruel person] demônio *m* **-2.** *inf* [fanatic] fanático *m*, -ca *f.*

fiendish ['fi:ndıʃ] *adj* **-1.** [evil] diabólico(ca) **-2.** *inf* [very difficult] cabeludo(da).

fierce [fıəs] *adj* **-1.** [aggressive, ferocious] feroz **-2.** [wild, uncontrolled] violento(ta) **-3.** [intense - competition, battle] árduo(a); [- heat] intenso(sa); [- criticism] ferrenho(nha).

fiercely ['fıəslı] *adv* **-1.** [aggressively, ferociously] ferozmente **-2.** [wildly] violentamente **-3.** [intensely] arduamente.

fiery ['faıərı] (*compar* **-ier**, *superl* **-iest**) *adj* **-1.** [burning] ardente **-2.** [spicy] picante **-3.** [volatile] explosivo(-va) **-4.** [bright red] cor-de-fogo.

FIFA (*abbr of* **Fédération Internationale de Football Association**) *n* FIFA *f.*

fifteen [fıf'ti:n] *num* quinze; *see also* **six.**

fifteenth [fıf'ti:nθ] *num* décimo quinto, décima quinta; *see also* **sixth.**

fifth [fıfθ] *num* quinto, quinta; *see also* **sixth.**

Fifth Amendment *n*: **the ~** a Quinta Emenda, emenda constitucional americana que estabelece direitos civis aos criminosos.

fifth column *n* quinta-coluna *f.*

fiftieth ['fıftıəθ] *num* qüinquagésimo, qüinquagésima; *see also* **sixth.**

fifty ['fıftı] (*pl* **-ies**) *num* cinqüenta; *see also* **sixty.**

fifty-fifty <> *adj*: **to have a ~ chance** ter cinqüenta por cento de chance. <> *adv* : **to split sthg ~** dividir algo meio a meio.

fig [fıg] *n* figo *m.*

fight [faıt] (*pt & pp* **fought**) <> *n* **-1.** [physical] briga *f*, luta *f*; **to have a ~ (with sb)** ter uma briga (com alguém); **to put up a ~** desencadear uma luta **-2.** *fig* [battle, struggle] luta *f*, batalha *f* **-3.** [argument] discussão *f*; **to have a ~ (with sb)** ter uma discussão (com alguém). <> *vt* **-1.** [gen] lutar (com), combater; [physically] brigar com **-2.** [combat, struggle against] lutar contra. <> *vi* **-1.** [physically, in war] lutar **-2.** *fig* [battle, struggle]: **to ~ for/against sthg** lutar por/contra algo **-3.** [argue] discutir sobre; **to ~ about** OR **over sthg** discutir sobre algo.

➡ **fight back** <> *vt fus* segurar. <> *vi* revidar.

➡ **fight off** *vt sep* **-1.** [deter physically] rechaçar **-2.** *fig* [overcome] superar.

➡ **fight out** *vt sep*: **to ~ it out** resolver a questão.

fighter ['faɪtə^r] *n* **-1.** [plane] caça *m* **-2.** [soldier] guerreiro *m*, -ra *f* **-3.** [combative person] lutador *m*, -ra *f*.

fighting ['faɪtɪŋ] *n (U)* [in war, punch-up] luta *f*.

fighting chance *n*: **to have a ~** ter uma boa chance.

figment ['fɪgmənt] *n*: **a ~ of sb's imagination** um produto da imaginação de alguém.

figurative ['fɪgərətɪv] *adj* [language, art] figurado(da).

figuratively ['fɪgərətɪvlɪ] *adv* metaforicamente.

figure [*UK* 'fɪgə^r, *US* 'fɪgjər] *n* **-1.** [statistic] índice *m*; **to put a ~ on sth** declarar o valor total de algo **-2.** [symbol of number] número *m*; **in single/double ~s** em valores até dez/acima de dez **-3.** [human shape, outline] silhueta *f* **-4.** [diagram, representative personality] figura *f* **-5.** [famous person] personalidade *f* **-6.** [aesthetic shape of body] forma *f* **-7.** ⋄ *vt esp US* [suppose] supor. ⋄ *vi* **-1.** [feature] figurar **-2.** *US* [make sense]: **that ~ s!** faz sentido!

➡ **figure out** *vt sep* compreender.

figure eight *n US* = figure of eight.

figurehead ['fɪgəhed] *n* **-1.** [on ship] carranca *f* de proa **-2.** [leader without real power] testa-de-ferro *m*.

figure of eight *UK*, **figure eight** *US n* forma *f* de oito.

figure of speech *n* figura *f* de linguagem.

figure-skating *n (U)* patinação *f* artística.

figurine [*UK* 'fɪgəri:n, *US* ˌfɪgjə'ri:n] *n* estatueta *f (de metal ou cerâmica)*.

Fiji ['fi:dʒi:] *n* Fiji; **in ~** em Fiji.

Fijian [ˌfi:'dʒi:ən] ⋄ *adj* fijiano(na). ⋄ *n* fijiano *m*, -na *f*.

filament ['fɪləmənt] *n* [in light bulb] filamento *m*.

filch [fɪltʃ] *vt inf* surrupiar.

file [faɪl] ⋄ *n* **-1.** [folder] pasta *f* **-2.** [report] relatório *m*; **on ~, on the ~ s** em arquivo, arquivado(da) **-3.** *COMPUT* arquivo *m* **-4.** [tool] lixa *f* **-5.** [line]: **in single ~** em fila indiana. ⋄ *vt* **-1.** [put in folder] pôr na pasta **-2.** *JUR* dar entrada em **-3.** [shape, smooth] lixar. ⋄ *vi* **-1.** [walk in single file] andar em fila única **-2.** *JUR*: **to ~ for divorce** dar entrada no divórcio.

file clerk *n US* = filing clerk.

filename ['faɪlˌneɪm] *n COMPUT* nome *m* de arquivo.

filet *n US* = fillet.

filibuster ['fɪlɪbʌstə^r] *vi esp US POL* fazer discursos obstrucionistas.

filigree ['fɪlɪgri:] ⋄ *adj* filigranado(da). ⋄ *n (U)* filigrana *f*.

filing cabinet ['faɪlɪŋ-] *n* fichário *m*.

filing clerk *UK* ['faɪlɪŋ-], **file clerk** *US n* arquivista *mf*.

Filipino [ˌfɪlɪ'pi:nəʊ] (*pl* -s) ⋄ *adj* filipino(na). ⋄ *n* filipino *m*, -na *f*.

fill [fɪl] ⋄ *vt* **-1.** [make full - container] encher; [- room, street] ocupar; **to ~ sthg (with sthg)** encher algo com algo **-2.** [fulfill] preencher **-3.** [tooth] obturar. ⋄ *vi* encher-se. ⋄ *n*: **to have had one's ~ of sthg** estar até o pescoço de algo; **to eat one's ~** fartar-se.

➡ **fill in** ⋄ *vt sep* **-1.** [form] preencher **-2.** [hole] tapar **-3.** [inform]: **to ~ sb in (on sthg)** informar alguém (sobre algo). ⋄ *vt fus*: **to be ~ing in time** fazer tempo. ⋄ *vi* [substitute]: **to ~ in (for sb)** substituir alguém.

➡ **fill out** ⋄ *vt sep* [complete] completar. ⋄ *vi* [get fatter] engordar.

➡ **fill up** ⋄ *vt sep* encher. ⋄ *vi* lotar.

filled [fɪld] *adj* **-1.** [with sandwich filling] recheado(da) **-2.** [with emotion]: **~ (with sthg)** cheio(a) (de algo).

filler ['fɪlə^r] *n (U)* [for cracks] enchimento *m*.

filler cap *n UK* tampa *f* do tanque de combustível.

fillet *UK*, **filet** *US* ['fɪlɪt] *n* **-1.** [piece of meat] filé *m* **-2.** *(U)* [type of meat] lombo *m*.

fillet steak *n* filé *m*.

fill-in *n inf* [stopgap] tapa-buraco *m*.

filling ['fɪlɪŋ] ⋄ *adj* [satisfying] que satisfaz. ⋄ *n* **-1.** [in tooth] obturação *f* **-2.** [in cake, sandwich] recheio *m*.

filling station *n* posto *m* de gasolina.

fillip ['fɪlɪp] *n* estímulo *m*.

filly ['fɪlɪ] (*pl* -ies) *n* potranca *f*.

film [fɪlm] ⋄ *n* **-1.** [cinema, TV, photographic] filme *m* **-2.** *(U)* [footage] cobertura *f* **-3.** [layer] película *f*. ⋄ *vt* filmar. ⋄ *vi* filmar.

filming ['fɪlmɪŋ] *n (U)* filmagem *f*.

film-maker *n* cineasta *mf*.

film star *n* astro *m* de cinema, estrela *f* de cinema.

filmstrip ['fɪlmˌstrɪp] *n* diafilme *m*.

film studio *n* estúdio *m* de cinema.

Filofax® ['faɪləʊfæks] *n* agenda *f (de folhas descartáveis)*.

filter ['fɪltə^r] ⋄ *n* filtro *m*. ⋄ *vt* **-1.** [water, petrol] filtrar **-2.** [coffee] coar. ⋄ *vi* [people] infiltrar-se.

➡ **filter out** *vt sep* [remove by filtering] filtrar.

➡ **filter through** *vi* infiltrar-se.

filter coffee *n* café *m* coado.

filter lane *n UK* faixa *f* de conversão *(à direita ou esquerda)*.

filter paper *n* filtro *m* de papel *(para café)*.

filter-tipped [-'tɪpt] *adj* com filtro.

filth [fɪlθ] *n (U)* **-1.** [dirt] sujeira *f* **-2.** [obscenity] obscenidade *f*.

filthy ['fɪlθɪ] (*compar* -ier, *superl* -iest) *adj* **-1.** [very dirty] imundo(da) **-2.** [obscene] obsceno(na).

filtration plant [fɪl'treɪʃn-] *n* unidade *f* de filtragem.

fin [fɪn] *n* **-1.** [on fish] barbatana *f* **-2.** *US* [for swimmer] nadadeira *f*.

final ['faɪnl] ⋄ *adj* **-1.** [last in order] último(ma) **-2.** [at end, definitive] final. ⋄ *n* final *f*.

➡ **finals** *npl UNIV* exames *mpl* finais; **to sit one's ~ s** prestar os exames finais.

final demand *n* último aviso *m*.

finale [fɪ'nɑ:lɪ] *n* final *m*.

finalist ['faɪnəlɪst] *n* finalista *mf*.

finalize, -ise ['faɪnəlaɪz] *vt* finalizar.

finally ['faɪnəlɪ] *adv* **-1.** [at last] finalmente **-2.** [lastly] finalmente, por fim.

finance [*n* 'faɪnæns, *vb* faɪ'næns] ⋄ *n (U)* **-1.** [money] financiamento *m* **-2.** [money management] finanças *fpl*. ⋄ *vt* financiar.

➡ **finances** *npl* finanças *fpl*.

financial [fɪˈnænʃl] *adj* financeiro(ra).

financial adviser *n* assessor *m* financeiro, assessora *f* financeira.

financially [fɪˈnænʃəlɪ] *adv* financeiramente.

financial services *npl* serviços *mpl* financeiros.

financial year *UK*, **fiscal year** *US* *n* ano *m* fiscal.

financier [fɪˈnænsɪəʳ] *n UK* financista *mf*.

finch [fɪntʃ] *n* tentilhão *m*.

find [faɪnd] (*pt* & *pp* **found**) <> *vt* **-1.** [gen] encontrar, achar; **to ~ one's way** achar o caminho **-2.** [realize, discover]: **to ~ (that)** descobrir que **-3.** *JUR*: **to be found guilty/not guilty of sthg** ser declarado(da) culpado(da)/inocente de algo. <> *n* descoberta *f.*
  find out <> *vi* descobrir. <> *vt fus* **-1.** [information] informar-se **-2.** [truth] desmascarar. <> *vt sep* [person] descobrir.

findings [ˈfaɪndɪŋz] *npl* constatações *fpl.*

fine [faɪn] <> *adj* **-1.** [good, high-quality] excelente **-2.** [perfectly satisfactory] ótimo(ma) **-3.** [healthy] bem **-4.** [not rainy] bom(boa) **-5.** [thin, smooth] fino(na) **-6.** [minute, exact] sutil. <> *adv* [quite well] bem. <> *n* multa *f.* <> *vt* multar.

fine arts *npl* belas-artes *fpl.*

finely [ˈfaɪnlɪ] *adv* **-1.** [thinly, smoothly]: **to cut ~** cortar fino(na) **-2.** [tuned, balanced] com precisão.

fineness [ˈfaɪnnɪs] *n (U)* **-1.** [high quality] excelência *f* **-2.** [thinness, smoothness] finura *f* **-3.** [precision] minúcia *f.*

finery [ˈfaɪnərɪ] *n (U)* refinamento *m.*

finesse [fɪˈnes] *n (U)* finura *f*, delicadeza *f.*

fine-tooth comb [ˈfaɪntuːθ-] *n*: **to go over sthg with a ~** passar o pente fino em algo.

fine-tune [ˈfaɪntjuːn] *vt* ajustar.

finger [ˈfɪŋgəʳ] <> *n* dedo *m*; **to keep one's ~s crossed** manter os dedos cruzados; **she didn't lay a ~ on him** ela não encostou um dedo nele; **he didn't lift a ~ to help** ele não levantou um dedo para ajudar; **to point a** *OR* **the ~ at sb** apontar um *OR* o dedo para alguém; **to put one's ~ on sthg** colocar o dedo na ferida de algo, identificar algo corretamente; **to slip through one's ~s** escorrer pelos dedos; **to twist sb round one's little ~** fazer alguém de gato e sapato. <> *vt* [feel] tocar com os dedos.

fingermark [ˈfɪŋgəmɑːk] *n* marca *f* de dedo.

fingernail [ˈfɪŋgəneɪl] *n* unha *f (dos dedos da mão).*

fingerprint [ˈfɪŋgəprɪnt] *n* impressão *f* digital; **to take sb's ~s** tirar as impressões digitais de alguém.

fingertip [ˈfɪŋgətɪp] *n* ponta *f* do dedo; **at one's ~s** ao alcance da mão.

finicky [ˈfɪnɪkɪ] *adj pej* [- person] meticuloso(sa); [- task] minucioso(sa).

finish [ˈfɪnɪʃ] <> *n* **-1.** [end] final *m* **-2.** [texture] acabamento *m.* <> *vt* **-1.** [conclude, complete] terminar; **to ~ doing sthg** terminar de fazer algo **-2.** [consume] acabar **-3.** [leave] terminar, acabar. <> *vi* **-1.** [gen] terminar **-2.** [complete task] terminar, acabar.
  finish off *vt sep* [conclude, complete, consume] terminar.
  finish up *vi* acabar, terminar.

  finish with *vt fus* [break off with] terminar com.

finished [ˈfɪnɪʃt] *adj* **-1.** [ready, completed] terminado(da), pronto(ta) **-2.** [no longer interested]: **to be ~ with sthg** não estar mais interessado(da) em algo **-3.** [over, no longer in existence] liquidado(da) **-4.** *inf* [done for] acabado(da).

finishing line [ˈfɪnɪʃɪŋ-] *n* linha *f* de chegada.

finishing school [ˈfɪnɪʃɪŋ-] *n* ≃ colégio privado no qual se preparam as alunas da alta classe para entrar na sociedade.

finite [ˈfaɪnaɪt] *adj* **-1.** [limited] finito(ta) **-2.** *GRAMM* conjugado(da).

Finland [ˈfɪnlənd] *n* Finlândia; **in ~** na Finlândia.

Finn [fɪn] *n* [inhabitant of Finland] finlandês *m*, -esa *f.*

Finnish [ˈfɪnɪʃ] <> *adj* [of or relating to Finland] finlandês(esa). <> *n* [language] finlandês *m.*

fiord [fjɔːd] *n* = **fjord**.

fir [fɜːʳ] *n* abeto *m.*

fire [faɪəʳ] <> *n* **-1.** *(U)* [flames, burning] fogo *m*; **on ~** em chamas; **to catch ~** pegar fogo; **to set ~ to sthg** pôr fogo em algo **-2.** [for warmth, cooking] fogueira *f* **-3.** [blaze, conflagration] incêndio *m* **-4.** *UK* [heater, apparatus] aquecedor *m*, estufa *f* **-5.** *(U)* [shooting] fogo *m*; **to open ~ (on sb)** abrir fogo (contra alguém). <> *vt* **-1.** [shoot] disparar **-2.** [rap out] lançar **-3.** *esp US* [dismiss] demitir, despedir. <> *vi*: **to ~ (on** *OR* **at)** atirar em.

fire alarm *n* alarme *m* contra incêndio.

firearm [ˈfaɪərɑːm] *n* arma *f* de fogo.

fireball [ˈfaɪəbɔːl] *n* bola *f* de fogo.

firebomb [ˈfaɪəbɒm] <> *n* bomba *f* incendiária. <> *vt* lançar bombas incendiárias em.

firebreak [ˈfaɪəbreɪk] *n* aceiro *m.*

fire brigade *UK*, **fire department** *US* *n* corpo *m* de bombeiros.

fire chief *n US* = **fire master**.

firecracker [ˈfaɪəˌkrækəʳ] *n* rojão *m.*

fire-damaged *adj* deteriorado(da) por incêndio.

fire department *n US* = **fire brigade**.

fire door *n* porta *f* corta-fogo.

fire drill *n* simulação *f* de incêndio.

fire-eater *n* [performer] engolidor *m*, -ra *f* de fogo.

fire engine *n* carro *m* de bombeiros.

fire escape *n* escada *f* de incêndio.

fire extinguisher *n* extintor *m* de incêndio.

fire fighter *n* bombeiro *m*, -ra *f.*

fireguard [ˈfaɪəgɑːd] *n* guarda-fogo *m.*

fire hazard *n* risco *m* de incêndio.

fire hydrant [-ˈhaɪdrənt], **fireplug** *US* [ˈfaɪəplʌg] *n* hidrante *m.*

firelight [ˈfaɪəlaɪt] *n (U)* luz *f* de fogo.

firelighter [ˈfaɪəlaɪtəʳ] *n* acendedor *m* de fogo.

fireman [ˈfaɪəmən] (*pl* -men [-mən]) *n* bombeiro *m.*

fire master *UK*, **fire chief** *US* *n* chefe *mf* do corpo de bombeiros.

fireplace [ˈfaɪəpleɪs] *n* lareira *f.*

fireplug *n US* = **fire hydrant**.

firepower [ˈfaɪəˌpaʊəʳ] *n (U)* potência *f* de fogo.

fireproof [ˈfaɪəpruːf] *adj* à prova de fogo.

fire-raiser [-ˌreɪzəʳ] *n UK* incendiário *m*, -ria *f.*

fire regulations *npl* medidas *fpl* contra incêndio.
fire service *n UK* corpo *m* de bombeiros.
fireside ['faɪəsaɪd] *n*: **by the** ~ ao calor da lareira.
fire station *n* posto *m* de bombeiros.
firewood ['faɪəwʊd] *n (U)* lenha *f.*
firework ['faɪəwɜːk] *n* fogo *m* de artifício.
➡ **fireworks** *npl fig* [outburst of anger] fogos *mpl*
de artifício.
firework display *n* espetáculo *m* pirotécnico.
firing ['faɪərɪŋ] *n (U)* MIL tiroteio *m.*
firing squad *n* pelotão *m* de fuzilamento.
firm [fɜːm] <> *adj* **-1.** [gen] firme; **to stand** ~
manter-se firme **-2.** [definite] claro(ra) **-3.** [invest-
ment, rate] estável. <> *n* empresa *f.*
➡ **firm up** <> *vt sep* [make clearer, finalize] firmar.
<> *vi* firmar.
firmly ['fɜːmlɪ] *adv* firmemente.
firmness ['fɜːmnɪs] *n (U)* firmeza *f.*
first [fɜːst] <> *adj* primeiro(ra); **for the** ~ **time**
pela primeira vez; ~ **thing (in the morning)** à
primeira hora (da manhã); ~ **things** ~ primeiro
o mais importante; **I don't know the** ~ **thing about**
it não tenho a mais remota idéia sobre isso. <>
adv **-1.** [before anyone, anything else] primeiro; ~ **of**
all antes de mais nada, em primeiro lugar **-2.** [for
the first time] pela primeira vez **-3.** [firstly, in list of
points] primeiramente. <> *n* **-1.** [person] primeiro
m, -ra *f* **-2.** [unprecedented event] acontecimento *m*
sem precedentes **-3.** *UK* UNIV diploma *m* universitário **-4.** AUT: ~ **(gear)** primeira *f* (marcha).
➡ **at first** *adv* no princípio.
➡ **at first hand** *adv* em primeira mão.
first aid *n (U)* primeiros socorros *mpl.*
first-aider [-'eɪdər] *n* socorrista *mf.* •
first-aid kit *n* kit *m* de primeiros socorros.
first-class *adj* **-1.** [excellent] de primeira **-2.** *UK*
UNIV com louvor **-3.** [letter, ticket] de primeira
classe.
first-class mail *n (U)* correio *m de primeira*
classe.
first course *n* entrada *f.*
first cousin *n* primo-irmão *m*, prima-irmã *f.*
first-day cover *n* envelope com carimbo comemorativo de lançamento de um selo.
first-degree *adj* **-1.** MED: ~ **burn** queimadura *f*
de primeiro grau **-2.** *US* JUR: ~ **murder** homicídio
m em primeiro grau.
first floor *n* **-1.** *UK* [above ground level] primeiro
andar *m* **-2.** *US* [at ground level] andar *m* térreo.
firsthand [ˌfɜːst'hænd] <> *adj* de primeira mão.
<> *adv* em primeira mão.
first lady *n* POL primeira-dama *f.*
first language *n* língua *f* materna.
first lieutenant *n* primeiro-tenente *m.*
firstly ['fɜːstlɪ] *adv* primeiramente.
first mate *n* primeiro piloto *m*, imediato *m.*
first name *n* nome *m* de batismo, nome *m.*
➡ **first-name** *adj*: **to be on first-name terms**
(with sb) relacionar-se intimamente (com alguém).
first night *n* noite *f* de estréia.
first offender *n* delinqüente *mf* primário, -ria.

first officer *n* = **first mate**.
first-past-the-post system *n UK* sistema *m*
de eleição por voto majoritário.
first-rate *adj* de primeira.
first refusal *n* primeira opção *f* de compra.
First World War *n*: **the** ~ a Primeira Guerra
Mundial.
firtree ['fɜːtriː] *n* = **fir**.
fiscal ['fɪskl] *adj* fiscal.
fiscal year *n US* = **financial year**.
fish [fɪʃ] *(pl inv)* <> *n* peixe *m.* <> *vt* pescar em.
<> *vi* **-1.** [try to catch fish] pescar; **to** ~ **for sthg**
pescar algo **-2.** [try to obtain]: **to** ~ **for sthg** buscar
algo.
➡ **fish out** *vt sep inf* [bring out] sacar.
fish and chips *npl UK* peixe *m* frito com batatas
fritas.
fish and chip shop *n UK* barraca *f* de peixe
frito com batatas fritas.
fishbowl ['fɪʃbəʊl] *n* aquário *m.*
fishcake ['fɪʃkeɪk] *n* bolinho *m* de peixe.
fisherman ['fɪʃəmən] *(pl* -men [-mən]) *n* pescador
m.
fishery ['fɪʃərɪ] *(pl* -ies) *n* pescaria *f.*
fish-eye lens *n* lente *f* objetiva *(na câmera).*
fish farm *n* viveiro *m* de peixes.
fish fingers *UK*, **fish sticks** *US npl* porções *fpl*
de peixe empanado.
fishhook ['fɪʃhʊk] *n* anzol *m.*
fishing ['fɪʃɪŋ] *n (U)* pesca *f*; **to go** ~ ir pescar.
fishing boat *n* barco *m* de pesca.
fishing line *n* linha *f* de pesca.
fishing rod *n* vara *f* de pescar.
fishmonger ['fɪʃˌmʌŋɡər] *n esp UK* peixeiro *m*; ~'**s**
(shop) peixaria *f.*
fishnet ['fɪʃnet] *n* **-1.** [for fishing] rede *f* de pesca **-2.**
(U) [material]: ~ **stockings/tights** malhas *fpl/*
meias *fpl* de malha.
fish pond *n* lagoa *f* de peixe.
fish shop *n* peixaria *f.*
fish slice *n UK* escumadeira *f.*
fish sticks *npl US* = **fish fingers**.
fish tank *n* aquário *m (usado como viveiro).*
fishwife ['fɪʃwaɪf] *(pl* -wives [-waɪvz]) *n pej*: **to be-**
have like a ~ comportar-se como uma lavadeira.
fishy ['fɪʃɪ] *(compar* -ier, *superl* -iest) *adj* **-1.** [like fish] de
peixe **-2.** *fig* [suspicious] duvidoso(sa).
fission ['fɪʃn] *n (U)* fissão *f.*
fissure ['fɪʃər] *n* fissura *f.*
fist [fɪst] *n* punho *m.*
fit [fɪt] *(pt & pp* -ted, *cont* -ting) <> *adj* **-1.** [suitable]
adequado(da); **to be** ~ **for sthg** estar apto(ta)
para algo; **to be** ~ **to do sthg** estar apto(ta) a fazer
algo; **to see** OR **think** ~ **(to do sthg)** julgar OR achar
conveniente (fazer algo); **do as you think** ~ faça
como você achar melhor **-2.** [healthy] em forma;
to keep ~ manter-se em forma. <> *n* **-1.** [of
clothes, shoes etc.] tamanho *m*; **it's a good** ~ fica
bem; **it's a tight** ~ fica justo **-2.** [epileptic seizure]
ataque *m*; **to have a** ~ MED ter um ataque; *fig* [be
angry] ter um ataque (de fúria) **-3.** [bout - of crying,
depression] crise *f*; [- of rage, sneezing, giggles] acesso
m; **in** ~**s and starts** aos trancos e barrancos. <>

vt -**1.** [be correct size for] servir - **2.** [place]: **to ~ sthg into sthg** encaixar algo em algo - **3.** [provide]: **to ~ sthg with sthg** equipar algo com algo; **to have sthg ~ted** instalar algo - **4.** [be suitable for] adequar-se. ◇ *vi* -**1.** [be correct size] servir - **2.** [go] encaixar - **3.** [into container] caber.

◆ **fit in** ◇ *vt sep* [accommodate] arranjar tempo para. ◇ *vi* adaptar-se; **to ~ in with sb/sthg** adaptar-se com alguém/algo; **that ~s in with what she told me** isso vem ao encontro do que ela me contou.

◆ **fit out** *vt sep* equipar.

◆ **fit together** *vt sep* -**1.** [assemble] unir-se - **2.** [make sense] fazer sentido.

fitful [ˈfɪtfʊl] *adj* intermitente.

fitment [ˈfɪtmənt] *n* móvel *m (da casa)*.

fitness [ˈfɪtnɪs] *n (U)* -**1.** [health] bom estado *m* físico - **2.** [suitability] aptidão *f*; **~ for sthg** aptidão para algo.

fitted [ˈfɪtəd] *adj* -**1.** [suited]: **~ for** OR **to sthg** adequado(da) para algo; **to be ~ to do sthg** ser adequado(da) para fazer algo - **2.** [tailored] na medida - **3.** UK [built-in] embutido(da).

fitted carpet [ˈfɪtəd-] *n* carpete *m*.

fitted kitchen [ˈfɪtəd-] *n* UK cozinha *f* de módulos.

fitted sheet *n* lençol *m* com elástico.

fitter [ˈfɪtər] *n* [mechanic] mecânico *m*, -ca *f*.

fitting [ˈfɪtɪŋ] ◇ *adj fml* apropriado(da). ◇ *n* -**1.** [part] acessório *m* - **2.** [for clothing] prova *f*.

◆ **fittings** *npl* acessórios *mpl*.

fitting room *n* provador *m*.

five [faɪv] *num* cinco; *see also* **six**.

five-day week *n* semana *f* de cinco dias.

fiver [ˈfaɪvər] *n* inf -**1.** UK [amount] *cinco libras*; [note] *cédula de cinco libras* - **2.** US [amount] *cinco dólares*; [note] *cédula de cinco dólares*.

five-star *adj* [of highest standard]: **~ hotel** hotel cinco estrelas; **~ treatment** tratamento de primeira.

fix [fɪks] ◇ *vt* -**1.** [attach, concentrate] fixar; **to ~ sthg to sthg** fixar algo em algo - **2.** [set, arrange] arranjar - **3.** [repair] consertar - **4.** inf [rig] manipular - **5.** esp US [food, drink] preparar. ◇ *n* -**1.** inf [difficult situation]: **to be in a ~** estar em apuro - **2.** drugs sl dose *f* de entorpecente.

◆ **fix up** *vt sep* -**1.** [provide]: **to ~ sb up with sthg** arranjar algo para alguém - **2.** [arrange] organizar, preparar.

fixation [fɪkˈseɪʃn] *n* fixação *f*; **~ on** OR **about sb/ sthg**, **~** fixação em OR por alguém/algo.

fixed [fɪkst] *adj* fixado(da).

fixed assets *npl* ativo *m* fixo.

fixture [ˈfɪkstʃər] *n* -**1.** [in building] instalação *f* - **2.** fig [permanent feature] figura *f* constante - **3.** [sports event] encontro *m*.

fizz [fɪz] ◇ *vi* -**1.** [drink] espumar - **2.** [firework] crepitar. ◇ *n* -**1.** [sound] chiado *m* - **2.** (U) [of drinks] efervescência *f*.

fizzle [ˈfɪzl] ◆ **fizzle out** *vi* -**1.** [firework] falhar - **2.** fig [interest] sumir.

fizzy [ˈfɪzɪ] (compar -ier, superl -iest) *adj* gasoso(sa).

fjord [fjɔːd] *n* fiorde *m*.

FL *abbr of* **Florida**.

flab [flæb] *n (U)* flacidez *f (do corpo)*.

flabbergasted [ˈflæbəɡɑːstɪd] *adj* estarrecido(da), pasmado(da).

flabby [ˈflæbɪ] (compar -ier, superl -iest) *adj* flácido(da), gordo(da).

flaccid [ˈflæsɪd] *adj* flácido(da).

flag [flæɡ] (pt & pp -ged, cont -ging) ◇ *n* [banner] bandeira *f*. ◇ *vi* -**1.** [person] desanimar - **2.** [spirts] decair - **3.** [conversation] acabar.

◆ **flag down** *vt sep* fazer sinal para.

Flag Day *n* 14 de junho, dia da bandeira nos Estados Unidos.

flag of convenience *n* bandeira *f* de conveniência.

flagon [ˈflæɡən] *n* -**1.** [bottle] garrafão *m* - **2.** [jug] jarro *m*.

flagpole [ˈflæɡpəʊl] *n* mastro *m* de bandeira.

flagrant [ˈfleɪɡrənt] *adj* flagrante.

flagship [ˈflæɡʃɪp] *n* -**1.** [ship] nau *f* capitânia - **2.** [main asset] carro-chefe *m*.

flagstone [ˈflæɡstəʊn] *n* laje *f*.

flail [fleɪl] ◇ *vt* agitar. ◇ *vi* agitar-se.

flair [fleər] *n* -**1.** [talent] dom *m*; **to have a ~ for sthg** ter um dom para algo - **2.** (U) [stylishness] habilidade *f*.

flak [flæk] *n (U)* -**1.** [gunfire] fogo *m* antiaéreo - **2.** inf [criticism] críticas *fpl*.

flake [fleɪk] ◇ *n* [small piece - of snow] floco *m*; [- of paint, plaster] lasca *f*; [- of skin] pedaço *m*. ◇ *vi* descascar.

◆ **flake out** *vi* inf desfalecer.

flaky [ˈfleɪkɪ] (compar -ier, superl -iest) *adj* -**1.** [flaking - skin] com escamas; [- paintwork] lascado(da); [- texture] folhado(da) - **2.** US inf [person, idea] extravagante.

flaky pastry *n (U)* massa *f* folhada, mil-folhas *m* inv.

flambé [ˈflɑːmbeɪ] (pt & pp -ed, cont -ing) ◇ *adj* flambado(da). ◇ *vt* flambar.

flamboyant [flæmˈbɔɪənt] *adj* -**1.** [person, behaviour] extravagante - **2.** [clothes, design] chamativo(va).

flame [fleɪm] *n* chama *f*; **in ~s** em chamas; **to burst into ~s** irromper em chamas. ◇ *vi* -**1.** [be on fire] estar queimando - **2.** [redden] inflamar-se.

flameproof [ˈfleɪmpruːf] *adj* à prova de fogo.

flame-retardant [-rɪˈtɑːdənt] *adj* resistente ao fogo.

flame-thrower [-ˈθrəʊər] *n* lança-chamas *m inv.*

flaming [ˈfleɪmɪŋ] *adj* -**1.** [fire-coloured] em cor de fogo - **2.** UK [very angry] acalorado(da) - **3.** UK inf [for emphasis] maldito(ta).

flamingo [fləˈmɪŋɡəʊ] (pl -s OR -es) *n* flamingo *m.* .

flammable [ˈflæməbl] *adj* inflamável.

flan [flæn] *n* torta *f*.

Flanders [ˈflɑːndəz] *n* Flanders; **in ~** em Flanders.

flange [flændʒ] *n* rebordo *m*.

flank [flæŋk] ◇ *n* -**1.** [of animal] lado *m* - **2.** [of army] flanco *m*. ◇ *vt*: **to be ~ed by sb/sthg** ser ladeado(da) por alguém/algo.

flannel [ˈflænl] *n* -**1.** (U) [fabric] flanela *f* - **2.** UK [face-cloth] luva *f* de banho.

➡ **flannels** *npl* calças *fpl* de flanela.

flannelette [ˌflænə'let] *n (U)* baetilha *f.*

flap [flæp] (*pt* & *pp* -**ped**, *cont* -**ping**) ◇ *n* -**1.** [piece] dobra *f* -**2.** *inf* [state of panic]: **to get in a ~** ficar estérico(ca). ◇ *vt* -**1.** [wings] bater -**2.** [arms] agitar, mexer. ◇ *vi* -**1.** [wave - skirt, jacket] ondear, agitar-se; [- wings, bird] bater -**2.** *inf* [panic] estar estérico(ca).

flapjack ['flæpdʒæk] *n* -**1.** *UK* [biscuit] biscoito *m* de aveia -**2.** *US* [pancake] panqueca *f.*

flare [fleə'] ◇ *n* [distress signal] sinal *m* luminoso. ◇ *vi* -**1.**: **to ~ (up)** [fire] chamejar; [person] enfurecer-se; [war, revolution, disease] deflagrar-se -**2.** [trousers, skirt] alargar-se -**3.** [nostrils] abrir-se.

➡ **flares** *npl UK* [trousers] calças *fpl* boca-de-sino.

flared [fleəd] *adj* [trousers, skirt] boca-de-sino.

flash [flæʃ] ◇ *adj* -**1.** *PHOT* com flash -**2.** *inf* [expensive-looking] ostentoso(sa). ◇ *n* -**1.** [of light, colour] brilho *m* -**2.** *PHOT* flash *m* -**3.** [sudden moment] instante *m*; **in a ~** num instante; **quick as a ~** rápido(da) como um raio. ◇ *vt* -**1.** [light, torch] brilhar (*numa direção específica*) -**2.** [look, smile]: **she flashed a smile at him** ela sorriu rapidamente para ele -**3.** [show on screen] projetar -**4.** [show briefly] mostrar rapidamente. ◇ *vi* -**1.** [gen] reluzir -**2.** [move fast] irromper; **it ~ed through his mind that ...** imediatamente lhe ocorreu que ...; **to ~ past** passar feito um raio.

flashback ['flæʃbæk] *n* flashback *m.*

flashbulb ['flæʃbʌlb] *n* [lâmpada *f* de] flash *m.*

flash card *n* cartão no qual se aparecem uma *palavra ou um desejo e que se utiliza como material didático.*

flashcube ['flæʃkjuːb] *n* flash *m* de cubo.

flasher ['flæʃə'] *n UK* -**1.** [light] pisca-pisca *m* -**2.** *inf* [man] exibicionista *m.*

flash flood *n* enchente *f.*

flashgun ['flæʃgʌn] *n* disparador *m* de flash.

flashlight ['flæʃlaɪt] *n* [torch] lanterna *f* (elétrica).

flashpoint *n* -**1.** [moment] ponto *m* de fulgor -**2.** [place] zona *f* de conflito.

flashy ['flæʃɪ] (*compar* -**ier**, *superl* -**iest**) *adj inf* ostentoso(sa).

flask [flɑːsk] *n* -**1.** [to keep drinks hot] garrafa *f* térmica -**2.** [used in chemistry] frasco *m* -**3.** [hip flask] cantil *m.*

flat [flæt] (*compar* -**ter**, *superl* -**test**) ◇ *adj* -**1.** [level] plano(na); **~ feet** pés *mpl* chatos -**2.** [shoes] sem salto -**3.** [punctured] vazio(zia) -**4.** [categorical] categórico(ca) -**5.** [business, trade] estagnado(da) -**6.** [monotonous - voice] monótono(na); [- performance, writing] uniforme -**7.** [*MUS* - lower than correct note] abaixo do tom; [- lower than stated note] abemolado(da) -**8.** *COMM* [fare, fee] único(ca) -**9.** [no longer fizzy - beer] choco(ca); [- lemonade] que passou do ponto -**10.** [battery] descarregado(da). ◇ *adv* -**1.** [level] horizontalmente -**2.** [absolutely]: **~ broke** completamente quebrado(da) -**3.** [categorically] terminantemente -**4.** [exactly] precisamente -**5.** *MUS* abaixo do tom. ◇ *n* -**1.** *UK* [apartment] flat *m* -**2.** *MUS* bemol *m.*

➡ **flat out** *adv* a todo vapor.

flat cap *n UK* gorro *m.*

flat-chested [-'tʃestɪd] *adj* de seios pequenos.

flatfish ['flætfɪʃ] (*pl inv*) *n* linguado *m.*

flat-footed [-'fʊtɪd] *adj* [with flat feet] de pés chatos.

flatlet *n UK* flat *m.*

flatly ['flætlɪ] *adv* -**1.** [absolutely] categoricamente -**2.** [dully] de forma monótona.

flatmate ['flætmeɪt] *n UK* colega *mf* que divide o apartamento com outro.

flat-packed *adj* [furniture] para montar.

flat racing *n (U)* corrida *f* de cavalos sem obstáculos.

flat rate *n* preço *m* único.

flatscreen television, flatscreen TV ['flæt,-skriːn] *n* tv *f* de tela plana.

flatten ['flætn] *vt* -**1.** [make flat - steel, bumps] aplanar; [- wrinkles] esticar; [- paper] alisar; **to ~ o.s. against** sthg prensar-se contra algo -**2.** [building] demolir -**3.** *inf* [opponent] esmagar.

➡ **flatten out** ◇ *vi* aplanar-se, nivelar-se. ◇ *vt sep* [wrinkles] esticar ; [lumps, bumps] aplanar.

flatter ['flætə'] *vt* -**1.** [compliment] adular, bajular; **I'm ~ed** sinto-me lisonjeado(da); **to ~ o.s. (that)** congratular-se de que -**2.** [suit] cair bem.

flatterer ['flætərə'] *n* bajulador *m*, -ra *f.*

flattering ['flætərɪŋ] *adj* [remark, offer] lisonjeiro(ra); [dress, colour, neckline] que cai bem.

flattery ['flætərɪ] *n (U)* bajulação *f.*

flatulence ['flætjʊləns] *n (U)* flatulência *f.*

flatware ['flætweə'] *n US* talheres *mpl.*

flaunt [flɔːnt] *vt* ostentar.

flautist *UK* ['flaʊtɪst], **flutist** *US* ['fluːtɪst] *n* flautista *mf.*

flavour *UK*, **flavor** *US* ['fleɪvə'] ◇ *n* -**1.** [taste] sabor *m* -**2.** *fig* [atmosphere] ar *m*, toque *m.* ◇ *vt* [food, drink] condimentar.

flavouring *UK*, **flavoring** *US* ['fleɪvərɪŋ] *n (U)* condimento *m.*

flaw [flɔː] *n* [fault] imperfeição *f*; **~ in sthg** imperfeição em algo.

flawed [flɔːd] *adj* imperfeito(ta), defeituoso(sa).

flawless ['flɔːlɪs] *adj* impecável.

flax [flæks] *n* linho *m.*

flay [fleɪ] *vt* [skin] pelar.

flea [fliː] *n* pulga *f*; **to send sb away with a ~ in his/her ear** mandar alguém embora com forte reprovação.

flea market *n* mercado *m* das pulgas.

fleck [flek] ◇ *n* mancha *f.* ◇ *vt* : **~ed with sthg** manchado(da) com algo.

fled [fled] *pt* & *pp* ⊳ **flee.**

fledg(e)ling ['fledʒlɪŋ] ◇ *adj* [new, young] novato(ta). ◇ *n* ave *f* recém-emplumada.

flee [fliː] (*pt* & *pp* **fled**) ◇ *vt* [country, enemy] fugir de. ◇ *vi* fugir.

fleece [fliːs] ◇ *n* -**1.** [material, of sheep] velo *m* -**2.** [garment] sobretudo *m* de lã. ◇ *vt inf* [cheat] trapacear.

fleet [fliːt] *n* frota *f.*

fleeting ['fliːtɪŋ] *adj* fugaz.

Fleet Street *n* Fleet Street *f.*

Fleming [ˈflemɪŋ] *n* flamengo *m*, -ga *f*.

Flemish [ˈflemɪʃ] <> *adj* flamengo(ga). <> *n* [language] flamengo *m*. <> *npl*: **the** ~ os flamengos.

flesh [fleʃ] *n* -**1.** [of body] carne *f*; **to be only** ~ **and blood** ser de carne e osso; **to be sb's own** ~ **and blood** ser sangue do sangue de alguém; **in the** ~ em carne e osso -**2.** [of fruit, vegetable] polpa *f*.
◆ **flesh out** *vt sep* detalhar.

flesh wound *n* ferimento *m* superficial.

fleshy [ˈfleʃɪ] (*compar* -**ier**, *superl* -**iest**) *adj* [fat] carnudo(da).

flew [fluː] *pt* ▷ **fly.**

flex [fleks] <> *n ELEC* fio *m*, cabo *m*. <> *vt* [bend] flexionar.

flexibility [ˌfleksəˈbɪlətɪ] *n* (U) flexibilidade *f*.

flexible [ˈfleksəbl] *adj* flexível.

flexitime [ˈfleksɪtaɪm] *n* (U) horário *m* flexível.

flick [flɪk] <> *n* -**1.** [of whip, towel] pancada leve -**2.** [with finger] peteleco *m*. <> *vt* -**1.** [whip, towel] dar uma pancada leve em -**2.** [with finger] dar um peteleco em -**3.** [switch - turn on] ligar; [- turn off] desligar.
◆ **flicks** *npl inf*: **the** ~ **s** o cinema.
◆ **flick through** *vt fus* folhear.

flicker [ˈflɪkəʳ] <> *n* -**1.** [of light, candle] oscilação *f* -**2.** *fig* [of hope, interest] centelha *f*. <> *vi* -**1.** [candle, light] tremeluzir -**2.** [shadow, eyelids] tremer.

flick knife *n UK* canivete *f* de mola.

flier [ˈflaɪəʳ] *n* -**1.** [pilot] aviador *m* -**2.** [advertising leaflet] folheto *m* publicitário.

flight [flaɪt] *n* -**1.** [gen] vôo *m*; ~ **of fancy** OR **of the imagination** *fig* vôo da imaginação -**2.** [of steps, stairs] lance *m* -**3.** [escape] fuga *f*.

flight attendant *n* comissário *m*, -ria *f* de bordo.

flight crew *n* tripulação *f* de vôo.

flight deck *n* -**1.** [of aircraft carrier] pista *f* de aterrissagem -**2.** [of aircraft] cabine *f* de comando.

flight path *n* trajetória *f* de vôo.

flight recorder *n* caixa-preta *f*.

flighty [ˈflaɪtɪ] (*compar* -**ier**, *superl* -**iest**) *adj* volúvel.

flimsy [ˈflɪmzɪ] (*compar* -**ier**, *superl* -**iest**) *adj* -**1.** [fabric, structure] frágil -**2.** [excuse, argument] furado(da).

flinch [flɪntʃ] *vi* encolher-se; **to** ~ **from sthg/from doing sthg** vacilar diante de algo/em fazer algo; **without** ~ **ing** sem pestanejar.

fling [flɪŋ] (*pt* & *pp* **flung**) <> *n* [affair] caso *m*. <> *vt* [throw] atirar; **to** ~ **o.s. into an armchair/onto the ground** atirar-se numa poltrona/no chão.

flint [flɪnt] *n* -**1.** (U) [rock] sílex *m* -**2.** [in lighter] pedra *f*.

flip [flɪp] (*pt* & *pp* -**ped**, *cont* -**ping**) <> *vt* -**1.** [move with a flick] mover rapidamente, sacudir; **to** ~ **a coin** tirar cara ou coroa; **to** ~ **sthg open** abrir algo de supetão; **to** ~ **sthg over** virar algo bruscamente; **to** ~ **through sthg** folhear algo -**2.** [switch]: **to** ~ **on** ligar; **to** ~ **off** desligar -**3.** [throw] atirar, jogar. <> *vi inf* [become angry] perder o controle. <> *n* -**1.** [of coin] arremesso *m* rápido -**2.** [somersault] piparote *m* -**3.** *phr*: **at the** ~ **of a switch** ao toque de um interruptor.

flipchart *n* quadro *m* de folhas móveis.

flip-flop *n UK* [shoe] sandália *f* de dedo.

flippant [ˈflɪpənt] *adj* leviano(na).

flippantly [ˈflɪpəntlɪ] *adv* levianamente.

flipper [ˈflɪpəʳ] *n* -**1.** [of animal] barbatana *f* -**2.** [for swimmer, diver] pé-de-pato *m*.

flipping [ˈflɪpɪŋ] *UK inf* <> *adj* maldito(ta). <> *adv* absolutamente.

flip side *n* [of record] lado *m* B.

flirt [flɜːt] <> *n* [person] paquerador *m*, -ra *f*. <> *vi* -**1.** [with person] flertar; **to** ~ **with sb** flertar com alguém -**2.** [with idea] interessar-se por; **to** ~ **with sthg** interessar-se por algo.

flirtation [flɜːˈteɪʃn] *n* -**1.** (U) [flirting] flerte *m* -**2.** [love affair] caso *m* -**3.** [brief interest]: ~ **with sthg** interesse *m* em algo.

flirtatious [flɜːˈteɪʃəs] *adj* galanteador(ra).

flit [flɪt] (*pt* & *pp* -**ted**, *cont* -**ting**) *vi* [move quickly - bird] esvoaçar; [- expression, idea] passar rapidamente.

float [fləʊt] <> *n* -**1.** [on fishing line, net] bóia *f* -**2.** [in procession] carro *m* alegórico -**3.** [money] caixa *m*. <> *vt* -**1.** [on water] fazer boiar -**2.** [idea, project] lançar. <> *vi* -**1.** [on water] boiar -**2.** [through air] flutuar.

floating [ˈfləʊtɪŋ] *adj* flutuante.

floating voter *n UK* eleitor *m* indeciso, eleitora *f* indecisa.

flock [flɒk] <> *n* -**1.** [of birds, people] bando *m* -**2.** [of sheep] rebanho *m*. <> *vi*: **to** ~ **to** ir em massa para.

floe [fləʊ] *n* banquisa *f*.

flog [flɒg] (*pt* & *pp* -**ged**, *cont* -**ging**) *vt* -**1.** [whip] chicotear -**2.** *UK inf* [sell] pôr no prego.

flood [flʌd] <> *n* -**1.** [of water] enchente *f* -**2.** *fig* [great amount] dilúvio *m*. <> *vt* -**1.** [with water] inundar -**2.** *fig* [overwhelm]: **to** ~ **sthg (with)** inundar algo (com); **to** ~ **the market** inundar o mercado -**3.** [with light] encher -**4.** AUT [engine] afogar. <> *vi* -**1.** [river] transbordar -**2.** [street, land] inundar-se -**3.** *fig* [arrive in great amounts] chegar aos montes; **to** ~ **back** retornar.
◆ **floods** *npl* -**1.** [from river, rain] enchentes *fpl* -**2.** *fig* [of tears] torrente *f*.

floodgates [ˈflʌdgeɪts] *npl*: **to open the** ~ *fig* abrir caminho.

flooding [ˈflʌdɪŋ] *n* (U) [from river, rain] enchente *f*, inundação *f*.

floodlight [ˈflʌdlaɪt] *n* holofote *m*.

floodlit [ˈflʌdlɪt] *adj* iluminado(da) por holofotes.

flood tide *n* preamar *f*, maré *f* alta.

floor [flɔːʳ] <> *n* -**1.** [of room] piso *m*, chão *m* -**2.** [bottom] fundo *m* -**3.** [storey] andar *m*; **first** *US* OR **ground** *UK* ~ andar térreo -**4.** [at meeting, debate]: **from the** ~ da platéia; **to have/give the** ~ ter/dar a palavra -**5.** [for dancing] pista *f* -**6.** [of stock exchange] sala *f* de pregões; **to go through the** ~ [share prices] atingir a cotação mais baixa. <> *vt* -**1.** [knock down] nocautear -**2.** [baffle] confundir.

floorboard [ˈflɔːbɔːd] *n* tábua *f* de assoalho.

floor cloth *n UK* pano *m* de chão.

flooring [ˈflɔːrɪŋ] *n (U)* pavimentação *f.*

floor lamp *n US* abajur *m* de pé.

floor show *n* espetáculo *m* noturno *(em bar, restaurante, cabaré).*

floorwalker [ˈflɔːˌwɔːkəʳ] *n esp US* supervisor *m*, -ra *f* de seção *(em lojas).*

floozy [ˈfluːzɪ] *(pl* -ies) *n dated & pej* mulher *f* promíscua.

flop [flɒp] *(pt &* pp -ped, *cont* -ping) *inf* ◇ *n* [failure] fracasso *m.* ◇ *vi* -1. [fail] fracassar -2. [fall] esparramar-se; **the book** ~ed open at page 20 o livro caiu aberto na página 20.

floppy [ˈflɒpɪ] *(compar* -ier, *superl* -iest) *adj* desengonçado(da).

floppy (disk) *n* disquete *m.*

flora [ˈflɔːrə] *n* flora *f;* ~ and fauna flora e fauna.

floral [ˈflɔːrəl] *adj* -1. [made of flowers] floral -2. [patterned with flowers] florido(da), de flores.

Florence [ˈflɒrəns] *n* Florença; **in** ~ em Florença.

floret [ˈflɒrɪt] *n* florzinha *f.*

florid [ˈflɒrɪd] *adj* -1. [face, complexion] corado(da) -2. [style] florido(da).

Florida [ˈflɒrɪdə] *n* Flórida; **in** ~ na Flórida.

florist [ˈflɒrɪst] *n* florista *mf;* ~'s (shop) floricultura *f.*

floss [flɒs] ◇ *n (U)* -1. [dental floss] fio-dental -2. [for embroidery] seda *f* crua. ◇ *vt* limpar com fio-dental. ◇ *vi* limpar os dentes com fio-dental.

flotation [fləˈteɪʃn] *n ST EX* levantamento *m* de capital.

flotilla [fləˈtɪlə] *n* flotilha *f.*

flotsam [ˈflɒtsəm] *n (U):* ~ and jetsam [debris] entulho *m;* [people] gente *f* desocupada.

flounce [flaʊns] ◇ *n* [in cloth] babado *m.* ◇ *vi* [move] mover-se com ar de indignação; **he** ~d out of the room ele saiu indignado.

flounder [ˈflaʊndəʳ] *(pl inv OR* -s) ◇ *n* [fish] linguado *m.* ◇ *vi* -1. [in water, mud] debater-se -2. [in conversation, speech] atrapalhar-se.

flour [ˈflaʊəʳ] *n (U)* farinha *f.*

flourish [ˈflʌrɪʃ] ◇ *vi* -1. [grow healthily - plants, garden] florescer; [- child] crescer -2. [be successful] prosperar. ◇ *vt* movimentar. ◇ *n* -1. [movement]: **to do sthg with a** ~ fazer algo de maneira a ser notado(da) -2. [of trumpets] fanfarra *f.*

flourishing [ˈflʌrɪʃɪŋ] *adj* -1. [growing healthily] viçoso(sa) -2. [successful] próspero(ra).

flout [flaʊt] *vt* desrespeitar.

flow [fləʊ] ◇ *n* fluxo *m.* ◇ *vi* -1. [liquid, electricity, air] correr *f* -2. [traffic, words, ideas] fluir -3. [tide] baixar -4. [hair, dress] ondear -5. [result]: **to** ~ from sthg brotar de algo.

flow chart, flow diagram *n* fluxograma *m.*

flower [ˈflaʊəʳ] ◇ *n BOT* flor *f;* **in** ~ em flor. ◇ *comp* de flores. ◇ *vi* florescer.

flowerbed [ˈflaʊəbed] *n* canteiro *m* de flores.

flowered *adj* florido(da).

flowering [ˈflaʊərɪŋ] ◇ *adj BOT* florido(da). ◇ *n fig* [of artistic movement, talents] florescência *f.*

flowerpot [ˈflaʊəpɒt] *n* vaso *m* de flores.

flowery [ˈflaʊərɪ] *(compar* -ier, *superl* -iest) *adj* -1. [patterned] florido(da) -2. *pej* [elaborate] floreado(da)

-3. [sweet-smelling] com odor de flores.

flowing [ˈfləʊɪŋ] *adj* -1. *fig* [writing, style] fluente -2. *fig* [hair, robes] esvoaçante.

flown [fləʊn] *pp* ▷ **fly**.

fl. oz. *abbr of* fluid ounce.

flu [fluː] *n (U)* gripe *m;* **to have** ~ estar com gripe.

fluctuate [ˈflʌktʃʊeɪt] *vi* oscilar, flutuar.

fluctuation [ˌflʌktʃʊˈeɪʃn] *n* [act of fluctuating] oscilação *f,* flutuação *f.*

flue [fluː] *n* fumeiro *m.*

fluency [ˈfluːənsɪ] *n (U)* [in a foreign language] fluência *f.*

fluent [ˈfluːənt] *adj* fluente; **he speaks** ~ Spanish ele fala espanhol fluentemente; **to be** ~ **in sthg** ser fluente em algo.

fluently [ˈfluːəntlɪ] *adv* fluentemente.

fluff [flʌf] ◇ *n (U)* -1. [down] felpa *f* -2. [dust] penugem *f.* ◇ *vt* -1. [puff up]: **to** ~ sthg (up) afofar -2. *inf* [do badly] fazer mal, não acertar.

fluffy [ˈflʌfɪ] *(compar* -ier, *superl* -iest) *adj* [downy] macio(cia).

fluid [ˈfluːɪd] ◇ *n* fluido *m.* ◇ *adj* -1. [flowing] fluido(da) -2. [unfixed] mutável.

fluid ounce *n* onça *f* fluida *(0,028 litro).*

fluke [fluːk] *n inf* [chance] obra *f* do acaso.

flummox [ˈflʌməks] *vt esp UK inf* bestificar.

flung [flʌŋ] *pt & pp* ▷ **fling**.

flunk [flʌŋk] *esp US inf* ◇ *vt* [SCH & UNIV - exam, test] não passar em; [- student] reprovar. ◇ *vi* levar pau, ser reprovado(da).

fluorescent [flʊəˈresnt] *adj* [colour] fluorescente.

fluorescent light *n* luz *f* fluorescente.

fluoridate *vt* adicionar flúor a.

fluoride [ˈflʊəraɪd] *n* fluoreto *m.*

fluorine [ˈflʊəriːn] *n (U)* flúor *m.*

flurry [ˈflʌrɪ] *(pl* -ies) *n* -1. [shower] lufada *f* -2. [sudden burst] erupção *f.*

flush [flʌʃ] ◇ *adj* -1. [level]: ~ with sthg nivelado(da) com -2. *inf* [not short of money]: **to be** ~ with money estar sentado(da) no dinheiro. ◇ *n* -1. [in toilet] descarga *f* -2. [blush] rubor *m* -3. [sudden feeling] acesso *m;* **in the first** ~ **of sthg** *literary* no primeiro afluxo de algo. ◇ *vt* -1. [with water]: **to** ~ **the toilet** dar a descarga na privada; **to** ~ **sthg down the toilet** deixar algo cair na privada -2. *fig* [force out of hiding]: **to** ~ **sb out** fazer alguém sair. ◇ *vi* -1. [toilet] dar a descarga -2. [blush] ruborizar.

flushed [flʌʃt] *adj* -1. [red-faced] ruborizado(da) -2. [excited]: ~ with sthg empolgado(da) com algo.

fluster [ˈflʌstəʳ] ◇ *n* atrapalhação *f.* ◇ *vt* atrapalhar.

flustered [ˈflʌstəd] *adj* atrapalhado(da).

flute [fluːt] *n MUS* flauta *f.*

fluted [ˈfluːtɪd] *adj ARCHIT* acanalado(da).

flutist *n US* = flautist.

flutter [ˈflʌtəʳ] ◇ *n* -1. [of wings] bater *m* -2. [of eyelashes] pestanejo *m* -3. [of heart] pulso *m* -4. *inf* [sudden feeling] agito *m* -5. *inf* [bet] aposta *f.* ◇ *vt* -1. [wings] bater, agitar -2. [eyelashes] pestanejar. ◇ *vi* -1. [bird, insect, wings] agitar -2. [flag] tremular -3. [dress] esvoaçar -4. [heart, pulse] pulsar.

flux [flʌks] n -**1.** (U) [change] fluxo m; **to be in a state of** ~ mudar continuamente -**2.** TECH fundente m.

fly [flaɪ] (pl **flies**, pt **flew**, pp **flown**) ◇ n -**1.** [insect] mosca f; **a** ~ **in the ointment** fig ≃ um pequeno problema -**2.** [of trousers] braguilha f. ◇ vt -**1.** [cause to fly] fazer voar -**2.** [transport by air] transportar em avião -**3.** [flag] tremular. ◇ vi -**1.** [bird, insect, plane] voar -**2.** [pilot] pilotar -**3.** [travel by plane] ir de avião -**4.** [move fast] voar; **time flies** o tempo voa -**5.** [attack]: **to** ~ **at sb** voar para cima de alguém -**6.** [flag] tremular.
◆ **fly away** vi ir-se embora.
◆ **fly in** ◇ vt sep trazer em avião. ◇ vi chegar.
◆ **fly into** vt fus: **to** ~ **into a rage/temper** enfurecer-se.
◆ **fly out** ◇ vt sep levar de avião. ◇ vi sair de avião.

flyby n US = flypast.

fly-fishing n (U) pesca f com iscas artificiais.

fly half n UK no rúgbi, jogador rápido cujo objetivo é passar a bola para uma linha de jogadores.

flying ['flaɪŋ] ◇ adj -**1.** [able to fly] voador(ra) -**2.** [running] veloz. ◇ n [in plane]: **I hate** ~ odeio viajar de avião.

flying colours npl: **to pass (sthg) with** ~ passar (em algo) com louvor.

flying doctor n médico que utiliza o avião para visitar seus pacientes em áreas mais isoladas.

flying officer n UK tenente-aviador m.

flying saucer n disco m voador.

flying squad n UK radiopatrulha f.

flying start n: **to get off to a** ~ começar muito bem.

flying visit n visita f rápida.

flyleaf ['flaɪliːf] (pl **-leaves**) n guarda f.

flyover ['flaɪˌəʊvəʳ] n UK viaduto m.

flypast UK ['flaɪˌpɑːst], **flyby** US ['flaɪˌbaɪ] n apresentação f aérea.

flysheet ['flaɪʃiːt] n [on tent] teto m duplo.

fly spray n inseticida f.

flyweight ['flaɪweɪt] n peso-mosca m.

flywheel ['flaɪwiːl] n TECH volante m.

FM -**1.** (abbr of **frequency modulation**) FM f. -**2.** (abbr of **field marshal**) mestre-de-campo m.

FMCS (abbr of **Federal Mediation and Conciliation Services**) n serviço federal norte-americano que oferece serviços de conciliação entre empregadores e sindicatos em disputas industriais.

FO (abbr of **Foreign Office**) n ≃ MRE m.

foal [fəʊl] n potro m.

foam [fəʊm] ◇ n -**1.** [bubbles] espuma f -**2.** [material]: ~ **rubber** espuma de borracha. ◇ vi espumar.

foamy ['fəʊmɪ] (compar -**ier**, superl -**iest**) adj [with bubbles] espumoso(sa), espumante.

fob [fɒb] (pt & pp **-bed**, cont **-bing**) ◆ **fob off** vt sep: **to** ~ **sthg off on sb** empurrar algo para alguém; **to** ~ **sb off with sthg** enrolar alguém com algo.

FOB, f.o.b. (abbr of **free on board**) FOB m.

fob watch n relógio m de corrente.

focal ['fəʊkl] adj focal.

focal point ['fəʊkl-] n -**1.** [of view, room] ponto m central -**2.** fig [of report, study] foco m.

focus ['fəʊkəs] (pl **-cuses** OR **-ci** [-saɪ]) ◇ n [gen] foco m; **out of/in** ~ fora de/em foco; ~ **of attention** foco de atenção. ◇ vt -**1.** [lens, camera] focar; **to** ~ **sthg on sb/sthg** [lens, camera, eyes] focar algo em alguém/algo -**2.** [mentally]: **to** ~ **one's attention on sb/sthg** concentrar a atenção em alguém/algo. ◇ vi -**1.**: **to** ~ **on sb/sthg** enfocar alguém/algo -**2.** [mentally]: **to** ~ **on sthg** concentrar-se em algo.

focussed adj [mentally] concentrado(da).

fodder ['fɒdəʳ] n [feed] forragem f.

foe [fəʊ] n literary inimigo m, -ga f, antagonista mf.

FOE n (abbr of **Friends of the Earth**) ≃ NAT f.

foetal ['fiːtl] adj fetal.

foetus ['fiːtəs] n feto m.

fog [fɒg] n [mist] nevoeiro m, neblina f.

fogbound ['fɒgbaʊnd] adj fechado(da) por causa de nevoeiro.

fogey ['fəʊgɪ] n = fogy.

foggiest ['fɒgɪəst] n inf: **I haven't the** ~ não tenho a menor idéia.

foggy ['fɒgɪ] (compar -**ier**, superl -**iest**) adj [misty] nevoento(ta).

foghorn ['fɒghɔːn] n buzina f de nevoeiro.

fog lamp n farol m de neblina.

fogey ['fəʊgɪ] (pl **-ies**) n inf: **old** ~ raposa mf velha.

foible ['fɔɪbl] n ponto m fraco.

foil [fɔɪl] ◇ n -**1.** (U) [metal sheet] papel m alumínio -**2.** [contrast]: **to act as a** ~ **to** OR **for sb/sthg** complementar alguém/algo, ser um complemento de alguém/algo. ◇ vt frustrar.

foist [fɔɪst] vt: **to** ~ **sthg on sb** impingir algo a alguém.

fold [fəʊld] ◇ vt -**1.** [gen] dobrar; **to** ~ **one's arms** cruzar os braços -**2.** [wrap] abraçar. ◇ vi -**1.** [bed, chair] dobrar -**2.** inf [newspaper, play] fracassar -**3.** inf [business] falir. ◇ n -**1.** [in material, paper] dobra f -**2.** [for animals] curral m -**3.** fig [group of people]: **the** ~ o grupo.
◆ **fold up** ◇ vt sep dobrar. ◇ vi -**1.** dobrar -**2.** inf [newspaper, play] fracassar -**3.** inf [business] falir.

foldaway ['fəʊldəweɪ] adj dobrável.

folder ['fəʊldəʳ] n -**1.** [gen & COMPUT] pasta f -**2.** [binder] fichário f -**3.** [brochure] folheto f.

folding ['fəʊldɪŋ] adj [chair, table] dobrável.

foliage ['fəʊlɪdʒ] n (U) folhagem f.

folk [fəʊk] ◇ adj popular. ◇ n [music] música f folk. ◇ npl [people] gente f.
◆ **folks** npl inf -**1.** [relatives] parentes mpl -**2.** [everyone] pessoal m.

folklore ['fəʊklɔːʳ] n (U) folclore m.

folk music n (U) música m folk.

folk singer n cantor m, -ra f folk.

folk song n canção f folk.

folksy ['fəʊksɪ] (compar -**ier**, superl -**iest**) adj US inf amigável.

follicle ['fɒlɪkl] n folículo m.

follow ['fɒləʊ] ◇ vt -**1.** [gen] seguir; ~ **that taxi!** siga aquele táxi!; **(to be)** ~**ed by sthg** ser/vir acompanhado(da) por algo, ser seguido(da) de algo - **2.** [pursue] perseguir - **3.** [go along with, understand] acompanhar. ⬦ *vi* - **1.** [come after] seguir-se; **as** ~**s** conforme segue, da seguinte forma - **2.** [happen as logical result] vir em seguida - **3.** [be logical] proceder; **it** ~**s that** isso quer dizer que - **4.** [understand] acompanhar.

➥ **follow up** *vt sep* - **1.** [pursue] acompanhar - **2.** [supplement]: **to** ~ **sthg up with** responder a algo com.

follower ['fɒləʊəʳ] *n* [disciple, believer] seguidor *m*, -ra *f*.

following ['fɒləʊɪŋ] ⬦ *adj* seguinte. ⬦ *n* [group of supporters, fans] séquito *m*. ⬦ *prep* [after] depois de.

follow-up ⬦ *adj* complementar. ⬦ *n* [to visit, treatment, programme] continuação *f*.

folly ['fɒlɪ] *n (U)* [foolishness] loucura *f*.

foment [fəʊ'ment] *vt fml* fomentar.

fond [fɒnd] *adj* - **1.** [affectionate] carinhoso(sa); **to be** ~ **of sb** gostar muito de alguém; **to be** ~ **of sthg/ of doing sthg** gostar muito de algo/de fazer algo - **2.** *fml* [hope, wish] ingênuo(nua).

fondle ['fɒndl] *vt* acariciar.

fondly ['fɒndlɪ] *adv* - **1.** [affectionately] carinhosamente - **2.** [naively] ingenuamente.

fondness ['fɒndnɪs] *n (U)* afeição *f*, carinho *m*; ~ **for sb/sthg** gosto por alguém/algo.

fondue ['fɒndjuː] *n CULIN* fondue *m*.

font [fɒnt] *n* - **1.** [in church] pia *f* batismal - **2.** *COMPUT & TYPO* fonte *f*.

food [fuːd] *n* comida *f*; ~ **for thought** assunto para reflexão.

food chain *n* cadeia *f* alimentar.

food mill *n* processador *m* de alimentos.

food mixer *n* batedeira *f*.

food poisoning [-'pɔɪznɪŋ] *n (U)* intoxicação *f* alimentar.

food processor [-ˌprəʊsesəʳ] *n* multiprocessador *m*.

food stamp *n US* vale-alimentação *m (fornecido pelo governo)*.

foodstuffs ['fuːdstʌfs] *npl* gêneros *mpl* alimentícios.

fool [fuːl] ⬦ *n* - **1.** [idiot] idiota *mf*; **to make a** ~ **of sb** fazer alguém de bobo; **to make a** ~ **of o.s.** fazer papel de bobo; **to act** *OR* **play the** ~ bancar o bobo - **2.** *UK* [dessert] musse *f*. ⬦ *vt* enganar; **to** ~ **sb into doing sthg** enrolar alguém para que faça algo. ⬦ *vi* brincar.

➥ **fool about, fool around** *vi* - **1.** [behave foolishly]: **to** ~ **about (with sthg)** fazer-se de bobo (em relação a algo) - **2.** [be unfaithful]: **to** ~ **about (with sb)** pular a cerca (com alguém) - **3.** *US* [tamper]: **to** ~ **around with sthg** brincar com algo.

foolhardy ['fuːlˌhɑːdɪ] *adj* temerário(ria).

foolish ['fuːlɪʃ] *adj* - **1.** [unwise, silly] bobo(ba), idiota - **2.** [laughable, undignified] tolo(la).

foolishly ['fuːlɪʃlɪ] *adv* - **1.** [unwisely, in a silly manner] de maneira idiota - **2.** [laughably, in an undignified manner] estupidamente.

foolishness ['fuːlɪʃnɪs] *n (U)* idiotice *f*.

foolproof ['fuːlpruːf] *adj* infalível.

foolscap ['fuːlzkæp] *n (U)* papel *m* ofício.

foot [fʊt] (*pl senses 1 and 2* feet, *pl sense 3 inv OR* feet) ⬦ *n* - **1.** [of animal] pata *f* - **2.** [of person] pé *m*; **on** ~ a pé; **to be on one's feet, to get to one's feet** ficar de pé; **to be back on one's feet** estar logo de pé; **to have/get cold feet** não ter coragem suficiente; **to have itchy feet** ter formiga nos pés; **to put one's** ~ **down** bater pé; **to put one's** ~ **in it** meter os pés pelas mãos; **to put one's feet up** descansar; **to be rushed off one's feet** ser massacrado(da); **to set** ~ **in** pôr os pés em; **to stand on one's own two feet** ser dono de seu próprio nariz - **3.** [bottom] pé *m* - **4.** [of hill] sopé *m* - **5.** [unit of measurement] pé *m* *(30,48 cm)*. ⬦ *vt inf*: **to** ~ **the bill (for sthg)** pagar a conta (por algo).

footage ['fʊtɪdʒ] *n (U)* metragem *f*.

foot-and-mouth disease *n (U)* febre *f* aftosa.

football ['fʊtbɔːl] *n* - **1.** *UK* [game] futebol *m* - **2.** *US* [American football] futebol *m* americano - **3.** [ball] bola *f* de futebol.

football club *n UK* time *m* de futebol.

footballer ['fʊtbɔːləʳ] *n UK* jogador *m*, -ra *f* de futebol, futebolista *mf*.

football field *n US* campo *m* de futebol americano.

football game *n US* partida *f* de futebol americano.

football ground *n UK* campo *m* de futebol.

football match *n UK* partida *f* de futebol.

football player *n* jogador *m*, -ra *f* de futebol.

football pools *npl UK* ≃ loteria *f* esportiva.

football supporter *n* torcedor *m*, -ra *f*.

footbrake ['fʊtbreɪk] *n* freio *m* de pé.

footbridge ['fʊtbrɪdʒ] *n* passarela *f*.

footer ['fʊtəʳ] *n COMPUT* rodapé *m*.

foot fault *n TENNIS* falta *f* de saque *(pé dentro da linha)*.

foothills ['fʊthɪlz] *npl* contraforte *m*.

foothold ['fʊthəʊld] *n* apoio *m* para os pés; **to get a** ~ [on mountain, rockface] ter um ponto de apoio; [in organization, company] base *f* de operações.

footing ['fʊtɪŋ] *n* - **1.** [foothold] lugar *m* onde pôr o pé; **to lose one's** ~ escorregar, perder a base - **2.** [basis] base *f*; **on an equal** ~ **(with sb/sthg)** em pé de igualdade (com alguém/algo).

footlights ['fʊtlaɪts] *npl* ribalta *f*.

footling ['fʊtlɪŋ] *adj dated & pej* néscio(cia).

footman ['fʊtmən] (*pl* -men [-mən]) *n* lacaio *m*.

footmark ['fʊtmɑːk] *n* pegada *f*.

footmen ['fʊtmən] *pl* ➭ **footman**.

footnote ['fʊtnəʊt] *n* nota *f* de rodapé.

footpath ['fʊtpɑːθ, *pl* -pɑːðz] *n* trilha *f*.

footprint ['fʊtprɪnt] *n* pegada *f*.

footsie *n*: **to play** ~ tocar o pé de alguém com o próprio pé demonstrando interesse afetivo ou sexual.

Footsie *n UK FIN inf* = FTSE

footsore ['fʊtsɔːʳ] *adj* com os pés doloridos.

footstep ['fʊtstep] *n* - **1.** [sound] passo *m* - **2.** [footprint] pegada *f*; **to follow in sb's** ~**s** seguir os passos de alguém.

footwear ['fʊtweəʳ] *n (U)* calçado *m*.

footwork ['fʊtwɜːk] *n SPORT* jogo *m* de pernas.

for [fɔːr] *prep* **-1.** [expressing intention, purpose, reason] para; **this book is** ~ **you** este livro é para você; **what did you do that** ~**?** para que você fez isso?; **what's it** ~**?** para que é?; **to go** ~ **a walk** ir dar um passeio; '~ **sale'** 'vende-se'; **a town famous** ~ **its wine** uma cidade famosa pelo vinho; ~ **this reason** por esta razão **- 2.** [during] durante; **I'm going away** ~ **a while** vou estar fora durante *or* por algum tempo; **I've lived here** ~ **ten years** vivo aqui há dez anos; **we talked** ~ **hours** falamos horas e horas **-3.** [by, before] para; **it'll be ready** ~ **tomorrow** estará pronto (para) amanhã; **be there** ~ **8 p.m.** esteja lá antes das oito da noite **- 4.** [on the occasion of] por; **I got socks** ~ **Christmas** ganhei meias de Natal; ~ **the first time** pela primeira vez; **what's** ~ **dinner?** o que há para jantar?; ~ **the moment** no momento **- 5.** [on behalf of] por; **to do sthg** ~ **sb** fazer algo para alguém; **to work** ~ **sb** trabalhar para alguém **- 6.** [with time and space] para; **there's no room** ~ **it** não há espaço para isso; **to have time** ~ **sthg** ter tempo para algo **-7.** [expressing distance]: **roadwork** ~ **20 miles** obras na estrada ao longo de 32 quilômetros; **we drove** ~ **miles** dirigimos quilômetros e mais quilômetros **- 8.** [expressing destination] para; **a ticket** ~ **Boston** um bilhete para Boston; **this train is** ~ **Newark only** este trem só vai até Newark **- 9.** [expressing price] por; **I bought it** ~ **five dollars** comprei-o por cinco dólares **-10.** [expressing meaning]: **what's the Portuguese** ~ **boy?** como é que se diz boy em português? **-11.** [with regard to] para; **it's warm** ~ **November** para novembro está quente; **it's easy** ~ **you** para você é fácil; **respect** ~ **human rights** respeito pelos direitos humanos; **I feel sorry** ~ **them** sinto pena deles; **it's too far** ~ **us to walk** é longe demais para irmos a pé; **it's time** ~ **dinner** está na hora do jantar.

FOR (*abbr of* free on rail) FOR.

forage ['fɒrɪdʒ] *vi* [search] procurar; **to** ~ **for sthg** sair à procura de algo.

foray ['fɒreɪ] *n* **-1.** [raid] incursão *f* **- 2.** *fig* [excursion] incursão *f*; ~ **into sthg** incursão em algo.

forbad [fəˈbæd], **forbade** [fəˈbeɪd] *pt* ▷ **forbid**.

forbearing [fɔːˈbeərɪŋ] *adj* indulgente.

forbid [fəˈbɪd] (*pt* **-bade** *or* **-bad**, *pp* **forbid** *or* **-bid-den**, *cont* **-bidding**) *vt* [not allow] proibir; **to** ~ **sb to do sthg** proibir alguém de fazer algo; **God** *or* **Heaven** ~! Deus me livre!

forbidden [fəˈbɪdn] ◇ *pp* ▷ **forbid**. ◇ *adj* proibido(da).

forbidding [fəˈbɪdɪŋ] *adj* **-1.** [severe] repulsivo(va) **- 2.** [threatening] ameaçador(ra).

force [fɔːs] ◇ *n* **-1.** [gen] força *f*; ~ **of habit** força do hábito; **by** ~ à força **- 2.** [power, influence] poder *m*; **a** ~ **to be reckoned with** um poder a ser reconhecido **-3.** [group] equipe *f*; **sales** ~ a equipe de vendas; **security** ~ **s** as equipes de segurança; **task** ~ orça-tarefa *f*; **in** ~ em grande número **- 4.** [effect]: **to be in/come into** ~ estar/entrar em vigor. ◇ *vt* **-1.** [compel] forçar; **to** ~ **sb to do sthg** obrigar alguém a fazer algo; **to** ~ **sthg on sb** impor algo a alguém; **to** ~ **o.s.** forçar-se **- 2.** [break open] forçar **- 3.** [push] empurrar; **to** ~ **sthg open** forçar algo; **to** ~ **one's way through/into**

abrir caminho (por entre) **- 4.** [hurry] apressar **- 5.** [smile, answer] arrancar.

➥ **forces** *npl*: **the** ~ **s** as Forças Armadas; **to join** ~ **s (with sb)** unir forças (com alguém).

➥ **by force of** *prep* mediante, por meio de.

➥ **force back** *vt sep* **-1.** [push back] fazer recuar **- 2.** [suppress] reprimir.

➥ **force down** *vt sep* **-1.** [swallow] forçar-se a comer **- 2.** [force to land] forçar a aterrissar.

forced [fɔːst] *adj* forçado(da).

forced landing *n* aterrissagem *f* forçada.

force-feed *vt* alimentar à força.

forceful ['fɔːsfʊl] *adj* **-1.** [strong, powerful] forte **- 2.** [words, ideas] contundente **- 3.** [support, recommendation] enérgico(ca).

forcefully ['fɔːsfʊlɪ] *adv* vigorosamente, energicamente.

forcemeat ['fɔːsmiːt] *n esp UK* recheio *m* de carne.

forceps ['fɔːseps] *npl* fórceps *m*.

forcible ['fɔːsəbl] *adj* **-1.** [using physical force] feito(ta) à força **- 2.** [powerful] eficaz **- 3.** [recommendation, argument] enérgico(ca).

forcibly ['fɔːsəblɪ] *adv* **-1.** [using physical force] à força **- 2.** [powerfully] eficazmente **- 3.** [eagerly] energicamente.

ford [fɔːd] ◇ *n* vau *m*. ◇ *vt* vadear.

fore [fɔːr] ◇ *adj NAUT* dianteiro(ra). ◇ *n*: **to come to the** ~ *fig* tornar-se influente.

forearm ['fɔːrɑːm] *n* antebraço *m*.

forebears ['fɔːbeəz] *npl fml* antepassados *mpl*.

foreboding [fɔːˈbəʊdɪŋ] *n* mau pressentimento *m*.

forecast ['fɔːkɑːst] (*pt & pp* **forecast** *or* **-ed**) ◇ *n* [prediction] previsão *f*. ◇ *vt* [predict] prever.

forecaster ['fɔːkɑːstər] *n* **-1.** *ECON* analista *mf* **- 2.** *METEOR* meteorologista *mf*.

foreclose [fɔːˈkləʊz] ◇ *vt* executar. ◇ *vi*: **to** ~ **on sb** privar alguém do direito de resgatar uma hipoteca.

foreclosure [fɔːˈkləʊʒər] *n* execução *f* de uma hipoteca.

forecourt ['fɔːkɔːt] *n* área *f* para estacionamento.

forefathers ['fɔːˌfɑːðəz] *npl* antepassados *mpl*.

forefinger ['fɔːˌfɪŋgər] *n* indicador *m*.

forefront ['fɔːfrʌnt] *n*: **in** *or* **at the** ~ **of sthg** em primeiro plano de algo.

forego [fɔːˈgəʊ] *vt* = **forgo**.

foregoing [fɔːˈgəʊɪŋ] ◇ *adj* anterior, precedente. ◇ *n fml*: **the** ~ o supracitado.

foregone conclusion ['fɔːgɒn-] *n*: **it's a** ~ é um resultado inevitável.

foreground ['fɔːgraʊnd] *n* primeiro plano *m*; **in the** ~ em primeiro plano.

forehand ['fɔːhænd] *n* [tennis stroke] golpe *m* com a frente da mão.

forehead ['fɔːhed] *n* testa *f*.

foreign ['fɒrən] *adj* **-1.** [from abroad] estrangeiro(ra) **- 2.** [external] exterior **- 3.** [alien] estranho(nha).

foreign affairs *npl* relações *fpl* exteriores.

foreign aid *n* (U) ajuda *f* internacional.

foreign body *n* corpo *m* estranho.

foreign competition *n* (U) competição *f* internacional.

foreign currency *n* moeda *m* estrangeira.
foreigner ['fɒrənə'] *n* [from abroad] estrangeiro *m*, -ra *f.*
foreign exchange *n (U)* câmbio *m;* ~ **markets** mercados de câmbio; ~ **rates** taxas de câmbio.
foreign investment *n (U)* investimento *m* estrangeiro.
Foreign Legion *n:* **the** ~ a Legião Estrangeira.
foreign minister *n* ministro *m* de relações exteriores.
Foreign Office *n UK:* **the** ~ ≃ o Ministério das Relações Exteriores.
Foreign Secretary *n UK* ≃ Ministro *m* das Relações Exteriores.
foreleg ['fɔːleg] *n* perna *f* dianteira.
foreman ['fɔːmən] *(pl* **-men** *n* **-1.** [of workers] capataz *m* **-2.** [of jury] primeiro jurado *m.*
foremost ['fɔːməʊst] <> *adj* principal. <> *adv:* **first and** ~ antes de mais nada.
forename ['fɔːneɪm] *n* prenome *m.*
forensic [fə'rensɪk] *adj* forense.
forensic medicine *n (U)* medicina *f* legal.
forensic science *n (U)* ciência *f* forense.
forerunner ['fɔːˌrʌnə'] *n* [precursor] precursor *m*, -ra *f.*
foresee [fɔː'siː] *(pt* **-saw** [-'sɔː], *pp* **-seen)** *vt* prever.
foreseeable [fɔː'siːəbl] *adj* previsível; **for/in the** ~ **future** num futuro próximo.
foreseen [fɔː'siːn] *pp* ⊳ foresee.
foreshadow [fɔːˈʃædəʊ] *vt* prenunciar.
foreshortened [fɔːˈʃɔːtnd] *adj* condensado(da).
foresight ['fɔːsaɪt] *n (U)* previdência *f.*
foreskin ['fɔːskɪn] *n* prepúcio *m.*
forest ['fɒrɪst] *n* floresta *f.*
forestall [fɔː'stɔːl] *vt* prevenir.
forestry ['fɒrɪstrɪ] *n (U)* silvicultura *f.*
Forestry Commission *n UK:* **the** ~ *departamento do governo britânico responsável pela proteção e pelo desenvolvimento das florestas e matas do país.*
foretaste ['fɔːteɪst] *n* [sample] amostra *f.*
foretell [fɔː'tel] *(pt & pp* **-told)** *vt* predizer, prenunciar.
forethought ['fɔːθɔːt] *n (U)* premeditação *f.*
foretold [fɔː'təʊld] *pt & pp* ⊳ foretell.
forever [fə'revə'] *adv* **-1.** [eternally] para sempre **-2.** *inf* [incessantly] sem parar, sempre **-3.** *inf* [a long time] para sempre.
forewarn [fɔː'wɔːn] *vt* prevenir.
foreword ['fɔːwɜːd] *n* apresentação *f.*
forfeit ['fɔːfɪt] <> *n* **-1.** [penalty] prenda *f* **-2.** [fine] multa *f.* <> *vt* [lose] perder.
forgave [fə'geɪv] *pt* ⊳ forgive.
forge [fɔːdʒ] <> *n* [place] forja *f.* <> *vt* **-1.** [industry] forjar *f* **-2.** *fig* [create] forjar **-3.** [make illegal copy of] falsificar.
➡ **forge ahead** *vi* avançar continuamente.
forger ['fɔːdʒə'] *n* falsificador *m*, -ra *f.*
forgery ['fɔːdʒərɪ] *(pl* **-ies)** *n* falsificação *f.*
forget [fə'get] *(pt* **- got,** *pp* **-gotten,** *cont* **-getting)** <> *vt* **-1.** [gen] esquecer; **to** ~ **to do sthg** esquecer-se de fazer algo; **to** ~ **o.s.** esquecer-se de si mesmo **-2.** [leave behind] esquecer-se de. <>

vi esquecer-se; **to** ~ **about sthg** esquecer-se de algo.
forgetful [fə'getfʊl] *adj* esquecido(da).
forgetfulness [fə'getfʊlnɪs] *n (U)* esquecimento *m.*
forget-me-not *n* não-te-esqueças-de-mim *f,* miosótis *f.*
forgive [fə'gɪv] *(pt* **-gave,** *pp* **-given)** *vt* perdoar; **to** ~ **sb for sthg/for doing sthg** perdoar alguém por algo/por fazer algo.
forgiveness [fə'gɪvnɪs] *n (U)* perdão *m.*
forgiving [fə'gɪvɪŋ] *adj* que perdoa, clemente.
forgo [fɔː'gəʊ] *(pt* **-went,** *pp* **-gone** [-'gɒn]) *vt* renunciar a, abrir mão de.
forgot [fə'gɒt] *pt* ⊳ forget.
forgotten [fə'gɒtn] *pp* ⊳ forget.
fork [fɔːk] <> *n* **-1.** [for food] garfo *m* **-2.** [for gardening] forquilha *f* **-3.** [in road, river] bifurcação *f.* <> *vi* bifurcar-se.
➡ **fork out** *inf* <> *vt fus* desembolsar; **to** ~ **out money on** *or* **for sthg** desembolsar dinheiro em ou para algo. <> *vi:* **to** ~ **out (for sthg)** desembolsar uma grana (para algo).
forklift truck ['fɔːklɪft-] *n* empilhadeira *f.*
forlorn [fə'lɔːn] *adj* **-1.** [face, expression, cry] desesperado(da) **-2.** [desolate - person] desolado(da); [- place] abandonado(da) **-3.** [hope, attempt] desesperança do(da).
form [fɔːm] <> *n* **-1.** [shape] forma *f;* **in the** ~ **of** na forma de; **to take the** ~ **of** tomar a forma de **-2.** [type] tipo *m* **-3.** *(U)* [fitness] aparência *f;* **on** ~ *UK,* **in** ~ *US* em forma; **off** ~ fora de forma **-4.** [questionnaire] formulário *m* **-5.** [figure] imagem *f* **-6.** *UK SCH* [class] série *f* **-7.** *(U)* [usual behaviour]: **true to** ~ como era de se esperar. <> *vt* **-1.** [gen] formar **-2.** [constitute] constituir. <> *vi* formar-se.
formal ['fɔːml] *adj* **-1.** [gen] formal **-2.** [official] oficial.
formality [fɔː'mælətɪ] *(pl* **-ies)** *n* formalidade *f.*
formalize, -ise ['fɔːməlaɪz] *vt* formalizar.
formally ['fɔːməlɪ] *adv* **-1.** formalmente **-2.** [officially] oficialmente.
format ['fɔːmæt] *(pt & pp* **-ted,** *cont* **-ting)** <> *n* **-1.** [of book, magazine] formato *m* **-2.** [of meeting] estilo *m* **-3.** *COMPUT* formato. <> *vt COMPUT* formatar.
formation [fɔː'meɪʃn] *n* **-1.** [gen] formação *f* **-2.** *(U)* [establishment] estrutura *f.*
formative ['fɔːmətɪv] *adj* formativo(va).
former ['fɔːmə'] <> *adj* **-1.** [earlier, previous] ex-; ~ **husband** ex-marido *m* **-2.** [time] passado(da) **-3.** [first] anterior. <> *n:* **the** ~ o primeiro.
formerly ['fɔːməlɪ] *adv* antigamente.
form feed *n* alimentação *f* de formulário.
Formica® [fɔː'maɪkə] *n (U)* fórmica® *f.*
formidable ['fɔːmɪdəbl] *adj* **-1.** [frightening] pavoroso(sa) **-2.** [impressive] impressionante.
formless ['fɔːmlɪs] *adj* [shapeless] disforme, sem forma.
Formosa [fɔː'məʊsə] *n* Formosa *f;* **in** ~ em Formosa.
formula ['fɔːmjʊlə] *(pl* **-as** *OR* **-ae** [-iː]) *n* fórmula *f.*
formulate ['fɔːmjʊleɪt] *vt* formular.
formulation [ˌfɔːmjʊ'leɪʃn] *n* formulação *f.*

fornicate ['fɔːnɪkeɪt] *vi fml* fornicar.

forsake [fə'seɪk] (*pt* **-sook**, *pp* **-saken**) *vt literary* abandonar.

forsaken [fə'seɪkn] *adj* abandonado(da).

forsook [fə'sʊk] *pt* ⊳ **forsake**.

forsythia [fɔː'saɪθjəl] *n (U)* forsítia *f*.

fort [fɔːt] *n* forte *m*; **to hold the ~ (for sb)** tomar conta de algo (para alguém).

forte ['fɔːtɪ] *n* forte *m*.

forth [fɔːθ] *adv literary* **-1.** [outwards, onwards] adiante **-2.** [into future]: **from that day ~** daquele dia em diante.

forthcoming [fɔːθ'kʌmɪŋ] *adj* **-1.** [imminent] próximo(ma) **-2.** [available] disponível **-3.** [helpful] prestimoso(sa).

forthright ['fɔːθraɪt] *adj* franco(ca).

forthwith [ˌfɔːθ'wɪθ] *adv fml* incontinenti.

fortieth ['fɔːtɪɪθ] *num* quadragésimo(ma); *see also* sixth.

fortification [ˌfɔːtɪfɪ'keɪʃn] *n MIL* **-1.** [act of fortifying] fortificação *f* **-2.** [structure] forte *m*.

fortified wine ['fɔːtɪfaɪd-] *n* vinho *m* licoroso.

fortify ['fɔːtɪfaɪ] (*pt & pp* **-ied**) *vt* **-1.** [place] fortificar **-2.** *fig* [person, resolve] fortalecer.

fortitude ['fɔːtɪtjuːd] *n (U)* fortaleza *f*.

fortnight ['fɔːtnaɪt] *n* quinzena *f*.

fortnightly ['fɔːtˌnaɪtlɪ] ⟨⟩ *adj* quinzenal. ⟨⟩ *adv* quinzenalmente.

fortress ['fɔːtrɪs] *n* fortaleza *f*.

fortuitous [fɔː'tjuːɪtəs] *adj fml* [accidental] fortuito(ta).

fortunate ['fɔːtʃnət] *adj* feliz; **it's ~ that ...** por sorte ...

fortunately ['fɔːtʃnətlɪ] *adv* felizmente.

fortune ['fɔːtʃuːn] *n* **-1.** [large amount of money] fortuna *f* **-2.** [luck] sorte *f* **-3.** [future]: **to tell sb's ~** ler a sorte de alguém.

   ➡ **fortunes** *npl* vicissitudes *fpl*.

fortune-teller [-ˌteləʳ] *n* **-1.** adivinho *m*, -nha *f* **-2.** [using cards] cartomante *mf*.

forty ['fɔːtɪ] *num* quarenta; *see also* sixty.

forum ['fɔːrəm] (*pl* **-s**) *n* **-1.** *HISTORY* praça *f* pública **-2.** [meeting place] fórum *m*.

forward ['fɔːwəd] ⟨⟩ *adj* **-1.** [position] dianteiro(ra) **-2.** [movement] para frente **-3.** [advanced] avançado(da) **-4.** [impudent] impudente. ⟨⟩ *adv* **-1.** [in space] para a frente **-2.** [to earlier time]: **to bring sthg ~** trazer algo à baila **-3.** [to later time]: **to put a clock ~** adiantar um relógio. ⟨⟩ *n SPORT* atacante *mf*. ⟨⟩ *vt* **-1.** [send on - letter] remeter; [- parcels, goods] expedir; [- information] enviar; **please ~** favor enviar para novo endereço **-2.** [further] desenvolver.

forwarding address ['fɔːwədɪŋ-] *n* endereço *m* para envio.

forward-looking [-'lʊkɪŋ] *adj* de visão.

forwardness ['fɔːwədnɪs] *n (U)* [boldness] audácia *f*.

forwards ['fɔːwədz] *adv* = forward.

forward slash *n TYPO* barra *f* inclinada (*para frente*).

forwent [fɔː'went] *pt* ⊳ **forgo**.

fossil ['fɒsl] *n GEOL* fóssil *m*.

fossil fuel *n* combustível *m* fóssil.

fossilized, -ised ['fɒsɪlaɪzd] *adj GEOL* fossilizado(-da).

foster ['fɒstəʳ] ⟨⟩ *adj* de criação; **~ brother** irmão de criação. ⟨⟩ *vt* **-1.** [child] criar, cuidar de **-2.** [idea, hope] fomentar.

foster child *n* filho *m*, -lha *f* de criação.

foster parent *n* pais *mpl* de criação.

fought [fɔːt] *pt & pp* ⊳ **fight**.

foul [faʊl] ⟨⟩ *adj* **-1.** [dirty - linen] enlameado(da); [- water] imundo(da); [- air] poluído(da) **-2.** [food] estragado(da), podre; [taste] nojento(ta); [smell, breath] fétido(da) **-3.** [very unpleasant] péssimo(ma), horrível **-4.** [obscene] obsceno(na) **-5.** *phr*: **to fall ~ of sb** entrar em choque com alguém. ⟨⟩ *n SPORT* falta *f*. ⟨⟩ *vt* **-1.** [make dirty] sujar **-2.** *SPORT* cometer falta em **-3.** [entangle] enredar.

   ➡ **foul up** *vt sep inf* estragar.

foul-mouthed [-'maʊðd] *adj* desbocado(da).

foul play *n* **-1.** *SPORT* jogo *m* sujo **-2.** [criminal act] crime *m*.

found [faʊnd] ⟨⟩ *pt & pp* ⊳ **find**. ⟨⟩ *vt* **-1.** [provide funds for] fundar **-2.** [start building] assentar os alicerces de **-3.** [base]: **to ~ sthg on** basear algo em.

foundation [faʊn'deɪʃn] *n* **-1.** *(U)* [gen] fundação *f* **-2.** [basis] base *f* **-3.** *(U)* [cosmetic]: **~ (cream)** base *f*.

   ➡ **foundations** *npl CONSTR* alicerces *mpl*.

founder ['faʊndəʳ] ⟨⟩ *n* [person] fundador *m*, -ra *f*. ⟨⟩ *vi* **-1.** [sink] afundar **-2.** *fig* [fail] fracassar.

founder member *n* sócio-fundador *m*, sócia-fundadora *f*.

founding father *n* [founder] fundador *m*.

foundry ['faʊndrɪ] (*pl* **-ies**) *n* fundição *f*.

fount [faʊnt] *n* [origin] fonte *f*.

fountain ['faʊntɪn] *n* **-1.** [man-made] chafariz *m* **-2.** *fig* [source] fonte *f*.

fountain pen *n* caneta-tinteiro *f*.

four [fɔːʳ] *num* quatro; *see also* six; **on all ~s** de quatro.

four-leaved clover [-liːvd-] *n* trevo *m* de quatro folhas.

four-letter word *n* palavrão *m*.

four-poster (bed) *n* cama *f* com dossel.

foursome ['fɔːsəm] *n* quarteto *m*.

four-star *adj* (de) quatro estrelas.

fourteen [ˌfɔː'tiːn] *num* quatorze; *see also* six.

fourteenth [ˌfɔː'tiːnθ] *num* décimo quarto, décima quarta; *see also* sixth.

fourth [fɔːθ] *num* quarto(ta); *see also* sixth.

Fourth of July *n*: **the ~ o** 4 de julho (*dia da Independência norte-americana*).

FOURTH OF JULY ▮

O 4 de julho, o dia da independência, é uma das mais importantes festas nacionais nos Estados Unidos. Como parte das comemorações, muitas cidades organizam paradas nas ruas e, à noite, queimas de fogos de artifício, em que predominam as cores azul, vermelho e branco. Os edifícios são decorados com enfeites nessas mesmas cores e com bandeiras americanas. Muita gente sai da cidade para fazer piquenique com a família e, conforme a tradição, comer cachorros-quentes e melancia.

four-way stop *n US* cruzamento *m* (*de quatro vias*).

four-wheel drive *n* -**1.** [vehicle] veículo *m* com tração nas quatro rodas -**2.** [system] tração *f* nas quatro rodas.

fowl [faʊl] (*pl inv OR* -s) *n* -**1.** *CULIN* ave *f* -**2.** [bird] ave *f* (doméstica).

fox [fɒks] <> *n* [animal] raposa *f.* <> *vt* -**1.** [outwit] lograr -**2.** [baffle] deixar atordoado(da).

foxcub *n* filhote *m* de raposa.

foxglove ['fɒksglʌv] *n* dedaleira *f.*

foxhole ['fɒkshəʊl] *n* -**1.** [for soldier] trincheira *f* -**2.** [for animal] toca *f* de raposa.

foxhound ['fɒkshaʊnd] *n* cão *m* de caça à raposa.

foxhunt ['fɒkshʌnt] *n* caça *f* à raposa.

foxhunting ['fɒks,hʌntɪŋ] *n* (*U*) caça *f* à raposa.

fox terrier *n* fox terrier *m.*

foxy ['fɒksɪ] *adj* [sexy] sexy.

foyer ['fɔɪeɪ] *n* -**1.** [of hotel, theatre] saguão *m* -**2.** *US* [of house] vestíbulo *m.*

FP *n* -**1.** (*abbr of* former pupil) ex-aluno *m*, -na *f.* -**2.** *US* (*abbr of* fireplug) hidrante *m.*

FPA (*abbr of* Family Planning Association) *n* associação britânica que oferece serviço de planejamento familiar.

fr. (*abbr of* franc) franco *m.*

Fr. (*abbr of* father) Pe.

fracas ['fræka:, *US* 'freɪkəs] (*UK pl inv*, *US pl* fracases) *n* rixa *f.*

fraction ['frækʃn] *n* -**1.** [gen] fração *f* -**2.** [a little bit]: it's a ~ **too big** é um pouquinho maior.

fractionally ['frækʃnəlɪ] *adv* levemente.

fractious ['frækʃəs] *adj* irritadiço(ça).

fracture ['fræktʃəʳ] *MED* <> *n* fratura *f.* <> *vt* fraturar.

fragile ['frædʒaɪl] *adj* frágil.

fragility [frə'dʒɪlətɪ] *n* fragilidade *f.*

fragment [*n* 'frægmənt, *vb* 'frægment] <> *n* fragmento *m.* <> *vi* fragmentar-se.

fragmentary ['frægməntrɪ] *adj* fragmentário(ria).

fragmented [fræg'mentɪd] *adj* fragmentado(da).

fragrance ['freɪgrəns] *n* fragrância *f.*

fragrant ['freɪgrənt] *adj* perfumado(da).

frail [freɪl] *adj* frágil.

frailty ['freɪltɪ] (*pl* -ies) *n* -**1.** (*U*) [gen] fragilidade *f* -**2.** [imperfection] fraqueza *f.*

frame [freɪm] <> *n* -**1.** [of picture] moldura *f* -**2.** [of glasses] armação *f* -**3.** [structure - of door] marco *m*; [- of boat] estrutura *f*; [- of window, bicycle] quadro *m*; [- of bed, chair] armação *f* -**4.** [physique] constituição *f.* <> *vt* -**1.** [put in a frame] emoldurar -**2.** *fig* [surround] cercar -**3.** [formulate, express] expressar -**4.** *inf* [falsely incriminate] incriminar falsamente.

frame of mind *n* estado *m* de espírito.

framework ['freɪmwɜ:k] *n* -**1.** [physical structure] estrutura *f* -**2.** [basis] base *f.*

France [frɑ:ns] *n* França; **in** ~ na França.

franchise ['fræntʃaɪz] *n* -**1.** *POL* [right to vote] direito *m* de voto -**2.** *COMM* [right to sell goods] franquia *f.*

franchisee [,fræntʃaɪ'zi:] *n* franqueado *m*, -da *f.*

franchisor *n* franqueador *m*, -ra *f.*

frank [fræŋk] <> *adj* franco(ca). <> *vt* franquear.

Frankfurt ['fræŋkfət] *n*: ~ (**am Main**) Frankfurt (am Main); **in** ~ em Frankfurt.

frankfurter ['fræŋkfɜ:təʳ] *n* salsicha *f* defumada.

frankincense ['fræŋkɪnsens] *n* (*U*) olíbano *m.*

franking machine ['fræŋkɪŋ-] *n* máquina *f* de selagem.

frankly ['fræŋklɪ] *adv* francamente.

frankness ['fræŋknɪs] *n* (*U*) franqueza *f.*

frantic ['fræntɪk] *adj* frenético(ca); **she was** ~ ela estava fora de si.

frantically ['fræntɪklɪ] *adv* -**1.** [in an upset manner] furiosamente -**2.** [busily] ativamente.

fraternal [frə'tɜ:nl] *adj* -**1.** [brotherly] fraterno(na) -**2.** [friendly] fraternal.

fraternity [frə'tɜ:nətɪ] (*pl* -ies) *n* -**1.** [community] comunidade *f* -**2.** *US* [of students] fraternidade *f* -**3.** (*U*) [friendship] fraternidade *f.*

FRATERNITY

Os clubes de estudantes, masculinos (*fraternities*) e femininos (*sororities*), são elementos de destaque na vida universitária norte-americana. Muitos estudantes associam-se a eles desde o primeiro ano da faculdade, permanecendo membros desses clubes mesmo após o término dos estudos. Cada clube possui seu próprio nome, composto de letras do alfabeto grego, e tem sua sede no edifício em que reside a maioria de seus membros. Os clubes realizam trabalhos para instituições de assistência social, mas são famosos também por suas bebedeiras e cerimônias secretas. Algumas universidades proibiram essas cerimônias de iniciação, porque elas promoviam trotes cruéis e perigosos.

fraternize, -ise ['frætənaɪz] *vi* [be on friendly terms] confraternizar; **to** ~ **with sb** confraternizar-se com alguém.

fraud [frɔ:d] *n* -**1.** (*U*) [crime] fraude *f* -**2.** [deceitful act] trapaça *f* -**3.** *pej* [impostor] impostor *m*, -ra *f.*

fraudulent ['frɔ:djʊlənt] *adj* fraudulento(ta).

fraught [frɔ:t] *adj* -**1.** [full]: ~ **with sthg** repleto(ta) de algo -**2.** *UK* [frantic] preocupado(da); **a** ~ **weekend** um fim de semana enlouquecido.

fray [freɪ] <> *vi* -**1.** [clothing, fabric, rope] esfiapar-se -**2.** *fig* [nerves, temper] desgastar-se. <> *n literary* rixa *f.*

frayed [freɪd] *adj* -**1.** [clothing, fabric, rope] esfiapado(da) -**2.** *fig* [nerves, temper] desgastado(da).

frazzled ['fræzld] *adj inf* [harassed] estafado(da).

FRB (*abbr of* Federal Reserve Board) *n* fundo de reserva federal norte-americano.

FRCP (*abbr of* Fellow of the Royal College of Physicians) *membro do Royal College of Physicians, associação britânica de médicos.*

FRCS (*abbr of* Fellow of the Royal College of Surgeons) *membro do Royal College of Surgeons, associação britânica de cirurgiões.*

freak [fri:k] <> *adj* imprevisto(ta). <> *n* -**1.** [strange creature - in appearance] aberração *f*; [- in behaviour] excêntrico *m*, -ca *f* -**2.** [unusual event] anomalia *f* -**3.** *inf* [fanatic] fanático *m*, -ca *f.*
　➡ **freak out** *inf* <> *vi* -**1.** [get angry] baratinar-se -**2.** [panic] apavorar-se. <> *vt sep* baratinar.

freakish ['fri:kɪʃ] *adj* [strange] esquisito(ta).

freckle ['frekl] *n* sarda *f.*

free [fri:] (*compar* **freer**, *superl* **freest**, *pt* & *pp* **freed**) <> *adj* -**1.** [gen] livre; **to be** ~ **to do sthg** ser livre para fazer algo; **feel** ~! sinta-se à vontade!; **to set sb/sthg** ~ libertar alguém/algo; **to give sb a** ~ **hand** dar a alguém carta branca -**2.** [not paid for] grátis; ~ **of charge** sem despesas -**3.** [unattached] solto(ta) -**4.** [not affected by]: ~ **of additives** sem aditivos; ~ **from worry** sem preocupação -**5.** [generous]: **to be** ~ **with sthg** [money] ser generoso(sa) com algo; [advice, affection] ser generoso(sa) em algo. <> *adv* -**1.** [without payment] gratuitamente; **for** ~ de graça -**2.** [without restraint] livremente. <> *vt* -**1.** [release] pôr em liberdade, libertar -**2.** [make available] liberar -**3.** [remove] livrar; **to** ~ **sb of** OR **from sthg** livrar alguém de algo.

-free [fri:] *suffix*: **a salt-**~ **diet** uma dieta sem sal.

freebie ['fri:bi] *n inf* brinde *m*.

freedom ['fri:dəm] *n* liberdade *f*; ~ **from sthg** ausência *f* de algo; **the right to** ~ **from hunger** o direito de não se passar fome.

freedom fighter *n* lutador *m*, -ra *f* pela liberdade.

free enterprise *n* (U) livre iniciativa *f*.

free-fall *n* (U) queda *f* livre.

Freefone® ['fri:fəun] *n* UK (U) discagem *f* gratuita.

free-for-all *n* -**1.** [brawl] tumulto *m* generalizado -**2.** [argument] discussão *f* generalizada.

free gift *n* oferta *f*.

freehand ['fri:hænd] <> *adj* à mão livre. <> *adv* à mão livre.

freehold ['fri:həʊld] <> *adv*: **to buy** ~ comprar como propriedade alodial. <> *n* propriedade *f* alodial.

freeholder ['fri:həʊldəʳ] *n* possuidor *m*, -ra *f* de propriedade alodial.

free house *n* bar não-controlado por uma única cervejaria.

free kick *n* tiro *m* livre; **to take a** ~ bater OR cobrar um tiro livre.

freelance ['fri:lɑ:ns] <> *adj* frila, autônomo(ma). <> *adv* como frila. <> *n* frila *mf*, autônomo *m*, -ma *f*. <> *vi* trabalhar como frila OR autônomo(-ma).

freeloader ['fri:ləʊdəʳ] *n inf* bicão *m*.

freely ['fri:lɪ] *adv* -**1.** [without constraint] livremente; ~ **available** fácil de obter -**2.** [generously] generosamente.

freeman ['fri:mən] (*pl* **-men** [-mən]) *n* [citizen] cidadão *m* honorário.

free-market economy *n* economia *f* de livre mercado.

Freemason ['fri:ˌmeɪsn] *n* maçom *m*.

Freemasonry ['fri:ˌmeɪsnrɪ] *n* maçonaria *f*.

freemen ['fri:mən] *pl* ▷ **freeman**.

freephone ['fri:fəʊn] *n* = **freefone**.

freepost ['fri:pəʊst] *n* porte *m* pago.

free-range *adj* UK caipira; ~ **eggs** ovos caipira.

free sample *n* amostra *f* grátis.

freesia ['fri:zjə] *n* frésia *f*.

free speech *n* (U) liberdade *f* de expressão.

freestanding [ˌfri:'stændɪŋ] *adj* independente.

freestyle ['fri:staɪl] *n* [in swimming] estilo *m* livre.

freethinker [ˌfri:'θɪŋkəʳ] *n* livre-pensador *m*, -ra *f*.

free time *n* tempo *m* livre.

free trade *n* (U) livre comércio *m*.

freeway ['fri:weɪ] *n* US auto-estrada *f*.

freewheel [ˌfri:'wi:l] *vi* -**1.** [cyclist] andar sem pedalar -**2.** [motorist] ir em ponto morto.

freewheeling [ˌfri:'wi:lɪŋ] *adj inf* [style, attitude] liberal.

free will *n* (U) vontade *f* própria; **to do sthg of one's own** ~ fazer algo por vontade própria.

free world *n*: **the** ~ o mundo livre.

freeze [fri:z] (*pt* **froze**, *pp* **frozen**) <> *vt* -**1.** [gen] congelar -**2.** [engine, lock] emperrar -**3.** [pipes] entupir. <> *vi* -**1.** [turn to ice] congelar-se -**2.** METEOR esfriar muito -**3.** [stop moving] parar -**4.** *inf* [be cold] congelar. <> *n* -**1.** [cold weather] frio *m* intenso -**2.** [of wages, prices] congelamento *m*.

➤ **freeze over** *vi* congelar (*na superfície*).

➤ **freeze up** *vi* -**1.** [river, lake] congelar -**2.** [lock, engine] emperrar.

freeze-dried [-'draɪd] *adj* congelado(da) a vácuo.

freeze frame *n* -**1.** [photograph] pose *f* -**2.** [on video] imagem *f* congelada.

freezer ['fri:zəʳ] *n* -**1.** [machine] freezer *m*, frízer *m* -**2.** [part of fridge] congelador *m*.

freezing ['fri:zɪŋ] <> *adj* gelado(da); **it's** ~ **in here** está um gelo aqui; **I'm** ~ estou congelando. <> *n* congelamento *m*; **5 degrees below** ~ *inf* 5 graus abaixo de zero.

freezing point *n* ponto *m* de congelamento.

freight [freɪt] *n* (U) [goods] carga *f*.

freight train *n* trem *m* de carga.

French [frentʃ] <> *adj* francês(esa). <> *n* francês *m*, -esa *f*. <> *npl*: **the** ~ os franceses.

French bean *n* vagem *f*.

French bread *n* (U) pão *m* francês, bisnaga *f*.

French Canadian <> *adj* franco-canadense. <> *n* [person] franco-canadense *mf*.

French chalk *n* (U) giz *m* de alfaiate.

French doors *npl* = **French windows**.

French dressing *n* -**1.** [in UK] molho *m* vinagrete -**2.** [in US] molho *m* rosé.

French fries *npl esp* US batatas *fpl* fritas.

Frenchman ['frentʃmən] (*pl* **-men** [-mən]) *n* francês *m*.

French polish *n* (U) verniz *m* (*para móveis*).

French Riviera *n*: **the** ~ a Riviera Francesa.

French stick *n* UK baguete *f*.

French toast *n* (U) rabanada *f*.

French windows *npl* janela *f* de batente.

Frenchwoman ['frentʃˌwʊmən] (*pl* **-women** [ˌwɪmɪn]) *n* francesa *f*.

frenetic [frə'netɪk] *adj* frenético(ca).

frenzied ['frenzɪd] *adj* agitado(da), incontrolável.

frenzy ['frenzɪ] (*pl* **-ies**) *n* frenesi *m*.

frequency ['fri:kwənsɪ] (*pl* **-ies**) *n* freqüência *f*.

frequency modulation *n* (U) freqüência *f* modulada.

frequent [*adj* 'fri:kwənt, *vb* frɪ'kwent] <> *adj* freqüente. <> *vt* freqüentar.

frequently ['fri:kwəntlɪ] *adv* freqüentemente.

fresco ['freskəʊ] (*pl* **-es** OR **-s**) *n* afresco *m*.

fresh [freʃ] <> *adj* -**1.** [gen] fresco(ca); ~ **from**

recém-saído(da) de **-2.** [water] doce **-3.** [another] novo(va); **to make a ~ start** começar tudo de novo **-4.** [not tired] bem-disposto(ta) **-5.** [complexion] revigorado(da) **-6.** [refreshing] refrescante **-7.** [original] original **-8.** *inf dated* [cheeky] atrevido(da); **to get ~ with sb** ser atrevido(da) com alguém **-9.** [bright] vivo(va). <> *adv* [recently] recém-; **~ cut flowers** flores recém-cortadas; **to be ~ out of sthg** *inf* acabar de ficar sem algo.

freshen ['freʃn] <> *vt* [refresh] renovar. <> *vi* [wind] tornar-se mais frio (fria).
➡ **freshen up** <> *vt sep* **-1.** [person] refrescar **-2.** [room, house] tornar mais atrativo(va). <> *vi* [person] refrescar-se *(com água).*

fresher ['freʃəʳ] *n UK inf* calouro *m*, -ra *f.*

freshly ['freʃlɪ] *adv* [recently] recentemente, recém-.

freshman ['freʃmən] (*pl* -men [-mən]) *n* calouro *m.*

freshness ['freʃnɪs] *n* **-1.** [gen] frescor *m* **-2.** [originality] originalidade *f.*

freshwater ['freʃ,wɔːtəʳ] *adj* de água doce.

fret [fret] (*pt* & *pp* **-ted**, *cont* **-ting**) *vi* [worry] preocupar-se.

fretful ['fretful] *adj* irritadiço(ça); **a ~ night** uma noite agitada.

fretsaw ['fretsɔː] *n* serra *f* tico-tico.

Freudian *adj* freudiano(na); **~ slip** ato *m* falho.

FRG (*abbr of* **Federal Republic of Germany**) *n* RFA *f.*

Fri. (*abbr of* **Friday**) sex.

friar ['fraɪəʳ] *n* frei *m.*

friction ['frɪkʃn] *n (U)* **-1.** [rubbing] fricção *f* **-2.** [conflict] atrito *m.*

Friday ['fraɪdɪ] *n* sexta-feira *f*; *see also* **Saturday.**

fridge [frɪdʒ] *n esp UK* refrigerador *m.*

fridge-freezer *n UK* refrigerador *m* com freezer.

fried [fraɪd] <> *pt* & *pp* ⊳ **fry.** <> *adj* frito(ta); **~ egg** ovo frito.

friend [frend] *n* amigo *m*, -ga *f*; **to be ~s (with sb)** ser amigo(ga) (de alguém); **to make ~s (with sb)** fazer amizade (com alguém).

friendless ['frendlɪs] *adj* sem amigos.

friendly ['frendlɪ] (*compar* -ier, *superl* -iest, *pl* -ies) <> *adj* **-1.** [kind, pleasant] amável; **to be ~ with sb** ser amigável com alguém **-2.** [not enemy] amigo(-ga) **-3.** [not serious] amistoso(sa). <> *n esp UK SPORT* amistoso *m.*

friendly society *n UK* organização com a qual as pessoas contribuem regularmente e que lhes dá dinheiro quando se aposentam ou ficam doentes.

friendship ['frendʃɪp] *n* **-1.** [between people] amizade *f* **-2.** [between countries] boas relações *fpl.*

fries [fraɪz] *npl* = **French fries.**

Friesian (cow) ['friːzjən-] *n* vaca *f* holandesa.

frieze [friːz] *n* friso *m.*

frigate ['frɪgət] *n* fragata *f.*

fright [fraɪt] *n* **-1.** *(U)* [fear] medo *m*; **to take ~** ter medo **-2.** [shock] susto *m*; **to give sb a ~** dar um susto em alguém.

frighten ['fraɪtn] *vt* assustar; **to ~ sb into doing sthg** forçar alguém a fazer algo por medo.
➡ **frighten away** *vt sep* espantar.
➡ **frighten off** *vt sep* espantar.

frightened ['fraɪtnd] *adj* amedrontado(da); **to be ~ of sthg/of doing sthg** ter medo de algo/de fazer algo.

frightening ['fraɪtnɪŋ] *adj* assustador(ra).

frightful ['fraɪtful] *adj dated* horrendo(da).

frigid ['frɪdʒɪd] *adj* [sexually cold] frígido(da).

frill [frɪl] *n* **-1.** [decoration] babado *m* **-2.** *inf* [extra] frescura *f.*

frilly ['frɪlɪ] (*compar* -ier, *superl* -iest) *adj* com babados.

fringe [frɪndʒ] <> *n* **-1.** [gen] franja *f* **-2.** *fig* [edge] orla *f*, margem *f* **-3.** *fig* [extreme] facção *f.* <> *vt* [border] cercar.

fringe benefit *n* benefício *m* adicional.

fringe group *n* facção *f.*

fringe theatre *n UK* teatro *m* de vanguarda.

Frisbee® ['frɪzbɪ] *n* jogo *m* de Frisbee®.

Frisian Islands ['frɪʒən-] *npl*: **the ~** as Ilhas Frísias.

frisk [frɪsk] <> *vt* [search] revistar. <> *vi* [play] brincar.

frisky ['frɪskɪ] (*compar* -ier, *superl* -iest) *adj inf* brincalhão(lhona).

fritter ['frɪtəʳ] *n CULIN* bolinho *m* frito.
➡ **fritter away** *vt sep* desperdiçar; **to ~ money/time away on sthg** desperdiçar dinheiro/tempo com algo.

frivolity [frɪ'vɒlətɪ] (*pl* -ies) *n* frivolidade *f.*

frivolous ['frɪvələs] *adj* frívolo(la).

frizzy ['frɪzɪ] (*compar* -ier, *superl* -iest) *adj* crespo(pa).

fro [frəʊ] *adv* ⊳ **to.**

frock [frɒk] *n dated* vestido *m.*

frog [frɒg] *n* [animal] rã *f*; **to have a ~ in one's throat** estar com a garganta irritada.

frogman ['frɒgmən] (*pl* -men [-mən]) *n* homem-rã *m.*

frogmarch ['frɒgmɑːtʃ] *vt* levar à força.

frogspawn ['frɒgspɔːn] *n (U)* ova *f* de rã.

frolic ['frɒlɪk] (*pt* & *pp* **-ked**, *cont* **-king**) <> *n* brincadeira *f.* <> *vi* brincar.

from [frɒm] *prep* **-1.** [expressing origin, source] de; **I'm ~ California** sou da Califórnia; **the train ~ Chicago** o trem de Chicago; **I bought it ~ a supermarket** comprei-o num supermercado **-2.** [expressing removal, deduction] de; **away ~ home** longe de casa; **to take sthg (away) ~ sb** tirar algo de alguém; **10% will be deducted ~ the total** será deduzido 10% do total **-3.** [expressing distance] de; **five miles ~ here** a oito quilômetros daqui; **it's not far ~ here** não é longe daqui **-4.** [expressing position] de; **~ here you can see the valley** daqui se vê o vale **-5.** [expressing what sthg is made with] de; **it's made ~ stone** é feito de pedra **-6.** [expressing starting time] desde; **~ the moment you arrived** desde que chegou; **~ now on** de agora em diante; **~ next year** a partir do próximo ano; **open ~ nine to five** aberto das nove às cinco **-7.** [expressing change] de; **the price has gone up ~ $1 to $2** o preço subiu de um dólar para dois; **to translate ~ German into English** traduzir do alemão para o inglês **-8.** [expressing range] de; **it could take ~ two to six months** pode levar de dois a seis meses **-9.** [as a result of] de; **I'm tired ~ walking**

estou cansado de andar **-10.** [expressing protec-
tion] de; **sheltered** ~ **the wind** protegido do
vento **-11.** [in comparisons]: **different** ~ diferente
de.
frond [frɒnd] *n* fronde *m*.
front [frʌnt] ⬦ *n* **-1.** [gen] frente *f*; **at the** ~ **of** à
frente de **-2.** MIL front *m*, frente *f* **-3.** [promenade]:
(sea) ~ orla *f* marítima **-4.** [outward appearance]
fachada *f* **-5.** [of book] capa *f.* ⬦ *adj* [at front] da
frente; ~ **page** primeira página; ~ **cover** capa.
⬦ *vt* **-1.** [stand before] ser de frente para **-2.** [TV
programme] estar à frente de. ⬦ *vi*: **to** ~ **onto**
sthg dar de frente para algo.
▸ **in front** *adv* **-1.** [further forward] na frente **-2.**
[winning]: **to be in** ~ estar na frente.
▸ **in front of** *prep* **-1.** [close to front of] em
frente de **-2.** [in the presence of] na frente de.
frontage [ˈfrʌntɪdʒ] *n* fachada *f* principal.
frontal [ˈfrʌntl] *adj* frontal.
frontbench [ˈfrʌntˈbentʃ] *n cadeiras dianteiras
no parlamento britânico nas quais se sentam
os líderes do governo e da oposição.*
front desk *n* recepção *f.*
front door *n* porta *f* da frente.
frontier [ˈfrʌn.tɪəʳ, US frʌnˈtɪərl *n* **-1.** [border] fronteira *f* **-2.** *fig* [furthest limit] fronteira *f.*
frontispiece [ˈfrʌntɪspiːsl *n* frontispício *m.*
front line *n*: **the** ~ a linha de frente.
front man *n* **-1.** [of group] representante *mf* **-2.** [of
programme] apresentador *m*, -ra *f.*
front-page *adj* de primeira página.
front room *n* sala *f* de estar.
front-runner *n* favorito *m*, -ta *f.*
front-wheel drive *n* **-1.** [vehicle] veículo *m* com
tração dianteira **-2.** [system] tração *f* dianteira.
frost [frɒst] ⬦ *n* **-1.** (*U*) [layer of ice] geada *f* **-2.**
[weather] frio *m* intenso. ⬦ *vi*: **to** ~ **over** OR **up**
cobrir-se de geada.
frostbite [ˈfrɒstbaɪt] *n* (*U*) enregelamento *m.*
frostbitten [ˈfrɒstˌbɪtn] *adj* enregelado(da).
frosted [ˈfrɒstɪd] *adj* **-1.** [opaque] fosco(ca) **-2.** US CU-
LIN coberto(ta) com glacê.
frosting [ˈfrɒstɪŋ] *n* (*U*) US CULIN cobertura *f* (*de
glacê).*
frosty [ˈfrɒstɪ] (*compar* **-ier**, *superl* **-iest**) *adj* **-1.** [very
cold] gelado(da) **-2.** [covered with frost] coberto(ta)
de geada **-3.** *fig* [unfriendly] glacial.
froth [frɒθ] ⬦ *n* (*U*) espuma *f.* ⬦ *vi* espumar.
frothy [ˈfrɒθɪ] (*compar* **-ier**, *superl* **-iest**) *adj* [covered in
froth] espumante.
frown [fraʊn] ⬦ *n* cenho *m.* ⬦ *vi* franzir as
sobrancelhas.
▸ **frown (up)on** *vt fus* não ver com bons
olhos.
froze [frəʊz] *pt* ⊳ **freeze**.
frozen [ˈfrəʊzn] ⬦ *pp* ⊳ **freeze**. ⬦ *adj* **-1.** [gen]
congelado(da) **-2.** [feeling very cold] gelado(da) **-3.** *fig*
[rigid]: ~ **with fear** gelado(da) de medo **-4.** [prices,
salaries, assets] congelado(da).
FRS *n* **-1.** (*abbr of* **Fellow of the Royal Society**)
*membro da Royal Society, organização britânica
para pesquisa científica.* **- 2.** (*abbr of* **Federal Reserve System**) ≃ BACEN *m.*

frugal [ˈfruːgl] *adj* **-1.** [small] frugal **-2.** [careful]
regrado(da).
fruit [fruːt] (*pl inv* OR **fruits**) ⬦ *n* **-1.** [food] fruta *f*
-2. *fig* [result] fruto *m*; **to bear** ~ dar resultados.
⬦ *comp* de frutas; **a** ~ **tree** uma árvore frutífera.
⬦ *vi* frutificar.
fruitcake [ˈfruːtkeɪk] *n* **-1.** bolo *m* com passas **-2.**
inf [mad person] maluco *m*, -ca *f.*
fruiterer [ˈfruːtərəʳ] *n UK* fruteiro *m*, -ra *f*; ~ **'s
(shop)** fruteira *f.*
fruitful [ˈfruːtfʊl] *adj* [successful] produtivo(va), pro-
veitoso(sa).
fruition [fruːˈɪʃn] *n* (*U*): **to come to** ~ realizar-se.
fruit juice *n* suco *m* de fruta.
fruitless [ˈfruːtlɪs] *adj* [wasted] infrutífero(ra), vão
(vã).
fruit machine *n UK* caça-níqueis *m inv.*
fruit salad *n* salada *f* de frutas.
frumpy [ˈfrʌmpɪ] (*compar* **-ier**, *superl* **-iest**) *adj inf*
antiquado(da).
frustrate [frʌˈstreɪt] *vt* frustrar.
frustrated [frʌˈstreɪtɪd] *adj* frustrado(da).
frustrating [frʌˈstreɪtɪŋ] *adj* frustrante.
frustration [frʌˈstreɪʃn] *n* frustração *f.*
fry [fraɪ] (*pt* & *pp* **fried**) ⬦ *vt* [food] fritar. ⬦ *vi*
[food] fritar.
frying pan [ˈfraɪŋ-] *n* frigideira *f*; **to jump out of
the** ~ **into the fire** saltar da frigideira e cair no
fogo, ir de mal a pior.
ft. *abbr of* **foot, feet.**
FT (*abbr of* **Financial Times**) *n jornal diário britânico
de economia.*
FTC (*abbr of* **Federal Trade Commission**) *n órgão
norte-americano responsável por se fazer cumprir a legislação sobre monopólios.*
FTSE (*abbr of* **Financial Times Stock Exchange**) *n*
FTSE *m*; **the** ~ **index** o índice FTSE; **the** ~ **100**
*as ações das 100 maiores empresas britânicas
ponderadas com base em seu valor de mercado.*
fuchsia [ˈfjuːʃə] *n* fúcsia *f.*
fuck [fʌk] *vulg* ⬦ *vt* [have sex with] trepar OR foder
com. ⬦ *vi* trepar, foder. ⬦ *excl* merda!
▸ **fuck off** *vulg* ⬦ *vi* foder-se. ⬦ *excl* vá se
foder!
fucking [ˈfʌkɪŋ] *adj vulg* [for emphasis] de merda; **a** ~
idiot um idiota de merda.
fuddled [ˈfʌdld] *adj* [confused] confuso(sa).
fuddy-duddy [ˈfʌdɪˌdʌdɪ] (*pl* **fuddy-duddies**) *n inf*
careta *mf.*
fudge [fʌdʒ] ⬦ *n* (*U*) [sweet] fondant *m*, doce de
açúcar, leite e manteiga. ⬦ *vt* **-1.** *inf* [falsify, tamper with] falsificar **-2.** [avoid, confuse] escapar-se de.
fuel [fjʊəl] (*UK* *pt* & *pp* **-led**, *cont* **-ling**, *US* *pt* & *pp* **-ed**,
cont **-ing**) ⬦ *n* combustível *m*; **to add** ~ **to the
fire** *fig* botar lenha na fogueira. ⬦ *vt* **-1.** [supply
with fuel] abastecer **-2.** [increase] aumentar.
fuel cell *n* célula *f* a combustível.
fuel pump *n* bomba *f* de combustível.
fuel tank *n* tanque *m* de combustível.
fugitive [ˈfjuːdʒətɪv] *n* fugitivo *m*, -va *f.*
fugue [fjuːg] *n* MUS fuga *f.*
fulcrum [ˈfʊlkrəm] (*pl* **-crums** OR **-cra** [-krə]) *n*
fulcro *m.*

fulfil (*pt* & *pp* **-led**, *cont* **-ling**), **fulfill** US [fʊl'fɪl] *vt*
-1. [carryout] cumprir; **to ~ one's role** desempenhar
seu papel **-2.** [satisfy] satisfazer; **to ~ o.s.** realizar-
se.

fulfilling [fʊl'fɪlɪŋ] *adj* gratificante.

fulfilment, fulfillment US [fʊl'fɪlmənt] *n (U)* **-1.**
[satisfaction] satisfação *f* **-2.** [carrying through - of ambition, dream] realização *f*; [- of role] desempenho *m*;
[- of need, promise] cumprimento *m*.

full [fʊl] <> *adj* **-1.** [gen] cheio (cheia); **~ of** cheio
(cheia) de **-2.** [with food] satisfeito(ta) **-3.** [complete -
employment, use] integral; [- explanation, name, day, re-
covery] completo(ta), efetivo(va); [- member, profes-
sor] titular **-4.** [maximum] máximo(ma) **-5.** [sound]
forte **-6.** [flavour] rico(ca) **-7.** [plump - mouth] cheio
(cheia); [- figure] voluptuoso(sa) **-8.** [ample, wide]
largo(ga). <> *adv* **-1.** [directly] em cheio **-2.** [very]:
to know ~ well that ... saber muito bem que ...
-3. [at maximum] no máximo. <> *n*: **in ~** [payment]
na totalidade; [write] por extenso; **to the ~** ao
máximo.

fullback [ˈfʊlbæk] *n* zagueiro *m*, -ra *f*.

full-blooded [-ˈblʌdɪd] *adj* **-1.** [pure-blooded] de
raça pura **-2.** [wholehearted] vigoroso(sa).

full-blown [-ˈbləʊn] *adj* bem-caracterizado(da); **a
~ disease** uma doença bem-desenvolvida.

full board *n (U)* diária *f* completa.

full-bodied [-ˈbɒdɪd] *adj* [wine] encorpado(da).

full dress *n (U)* traje *m* a rigor.

full-face *adj* [portrait, photo] de frente.

full-fashioned *adj* US = **fully-fashioned**.

full-fledged *adj* US = **fully-fledged**.

full-frontal *adj* [photo, appearance] em nu frontal.

full-grown [-ˈgrəʊn] *adj* adulto(ta).

full house *n* [at show, event] casa *f* cheia.

full-length <> *adj* **-1.** [portrait, mirror] de corpo
inteiro **-2.** [dress, curtains] comprido(da) **-3.** [novel,
film] extenso(sa); **a ~ film** um longa-metragem.
<> *adv* ao comprido, completamente.

full moon *n* lua *f* cheia.

fullness [ˈfʊlnɪs] *n* **-1.** [of details, information] riqueza
f **-2.** [of face, figure, lips] largura *f* **-3.** [of skirt, sleeves]
comprimento *m* **-4.** *phr*: **in the ~ of time** no
momento oportuno.

full-page *adj* de página inteira.

full-scale *adj* **-1.** [model, drawing, copy] em tamanho natural **-2.** [inquiry] completo(ta) **-3.** [war] total
-4. [attack] maciço(ça).

full-size(d) *adj* **-1.** [life-size] de tamanho natural
-2. [adult] adulto(ta) **-3.** US AUT: **~ car** carro *m* de
passeio.

full stop <> *n* ponto *m* final. <> *adv* UK ponto
final.

full time *n* UK SPORT final *m* de jogo.
full-time <> *adj* de tempo integral. <> *adv*
em tempo integral.

full up *adj* **-1.** [after meal] cheio(cheia) **-2.** [bus, train]
lotado(da).

fully [ˈfʊlɪ] *adv* **-1.** [completely] completamente,
totalmente; **to be ~ booked** estar com as reservas
esgotadas **-2.** [in detail] em detalhes.

fully-fashioned UK, **full-fashioned** US [-
ˈfæʃnd] *adj* justo(ta); **~ tights** meia-calça *f* justa.

fully-fledged UK, **full-fledged** US [-ˈfledʒd] *adj*
fig [doctor, lawyer] experiente.

fulness [ˈfʊlnɪs] *n* = **fullness**.

fulsome [ˈfʊlsəm] *adj* exagerado(da).

fumble [ˈfʌmbl] *vi* tatear; **to ~ for sthg** procurar
desajeitadamente por algo; **he ~d in his pockets
for his keys** ele vasculhou os bolsos desajeitadamente à procura das chaves.

fume [fjuːm] *vi* [with anger] fumegar.
fumes *npl* [gas - from car, fire] fumaça *f*; [- of
paint] vapor *m*.

fumigate [ˈfjuːmɪgeɪt] *vt* desinfetar.

fun [fʌn] <> *n (U)* **-1.** [pleasure, amusement] diversão
f; **we really had ~ at the party** nós realmente nos
divertimos na festa; **what ~!** que divertido!; **for
~, for the ~ of it** por prazer, por brincadeira
-2. [playfulness] alegria *f* **-3.** [ridicule]: **to make ~ of
sb** caçoar de alguém; **to poke ~ at sb** zombar de
alguém. <> *adj* divertido(da).

function [ˈfʌŋkʃn] <> *n* **-1.** [gen] função *f* **-2.** [for-
mal social event] cerimônia *f*. <> *vi* funcionar; **to ~
as sthg** funcionar como algo.

functional [ˈfʌŋkʃnəl] *adj* **-1.** [furniture, design]
funcional **-2.** [machine, system] operacional.

functionary [ˈfʌŋkʃnərɪ] (*pl* **-ies**) *n* funcionário *m*
público, funcionária *f* pública.

function key *n* COMPUT tecla *f* de função.

fund [fʌnd] <> *n* **-1.** [amount of money] fundo *m* **-2.**
fig [reserve] reserva *f*. <> *vt* financiar.
funds *npl* recursos *mpl*.

fundamental [ˌfʌndəˈmentl] *adj* **-1.** [basic] básico(-
ca), fundamental **-2.** [vital] fundamental; **~ to
sthg** fundamental para algo.
fundamentals *npl* fundamentos *mpl*.

fundamentalism [ˌfʌndəˈmentəlɪzm] *n (U)* fundamentalismo *m*.

fundamentally [ˌfʌndəˈmentəlɪ] *adv* **-1.** [basically]
basicamente, fundamentalmente **-2.** [radically]
radicalmente.

funding [ˈfʌndɪŋ] *n (U)* recursos *mpl*.

fund-raising [-ˌreɪzɪŋ] <> *n (U)* angariação *f* de
fundos. <> *comp* de angariação de fundos.

funeral [ˈfjuːnərəl] *n* funeral *m*.

funeral director *n* agente *mf* funerário, -ria.

funeral parlour *n* casa *f* funerária.

funeral service *n* cerimônia *f* de enterro.

funereal [fjuːˈnɪərɪəl] *adj* fúnebre.

funfair [ˈfʌnfeəʳ] *n* parque *m* de diversões.

fungus [ˈfʌŋɡəs] (*pl* **-gi** [-ɡaɪ], **-es**) *n* BOT fungo *m*.

funk [fʌŋk] *n (U)* **-1.** MUS funk *m* **-2.** *dated* [fear] pavor
m.

funky [ˈfʌŋkɪ] (*compar* **-ier**, *superl* **-iest**) *adj* MUS
ritmado(da), vibrante.

funnel [ˈfʌnl] (UK *pt* & *pp* **-led**, *cont* **-ling**, US *pt* & *pp*
-ed, *cont* **-ing**) <> *n* **-1.** [tube] funil *m* **-2.** [on ship]
chaminé *f*. <> *vt* **-1.** [liquid] passar por funil **-2.**
[crowd, money] encaminhar. <> *vi* [crowd, people]
encaminhar-se.

funnily [ˈfʌnɪlɪ] *adv* [strangely] estranhamente; **~
enough** curiosamente.

funny [ˈfʌnɪ] (*compar* **-ier**, *superl* **-iest**) *adj* **-1.** [amus-
ing] engraçado(da) **-2.** [odd] esquisito(ta) **-3.** [ill]: **to
feel ~** não se sentir bem.

funnies *npl US* quadrinhos *mpl.*

funny bone *n* osso *m* do cotovelo.

funny farm *n esp US inf hum* pinel *f*, manicômio *m*.

fun run *n maratona que tem por objetivo angariar recursos para instituições de caridade.*

fur [fɜːʳ] *n* -1. [on animal] pêlo *m* -2. [garment] pele *f*.

fur coat *n* casaco *m* de pele.

furious ['fjʊərɪəs] *adj* -1. [very angry] furioso(sa) -2. [violent] violento(ta).

furiously ['fjʊərɪəslɪ] *adv* -1. [angrily] furiosamente -2. [fight, work, drive] violentamente.

furled [fɜːld] *adj* dobrado(da).

furlong ['fɜːlɒŋ] *n medida correspondente a um oitavo de milha.*

furnace ['fɜːnɪs] *n* [fire] fornalha *f*.

furnish ['fɜːnɪʃ] *vt* -1. [fit out] mobiliar -2. *fml* [provide] fornecer; **to ~ sb with sthg** fornecer algo a alguém.

furnished ['fɜːnɪʃt] *adj* [fitted out] mobiliado(da).

furnishings ['fɜːnɪʃɪŋz] *npl* mobiliário *m*.

furniture ['fɜːnɪtʃəʳ] *n (U)* móvel *m*.

furniture polish *n* lustrador *m* de móveis.

furore *UK* [fjʊˈrɔːrɪ], **furor** *US* ['fjʊrɔːr] *n* furor *m*.

furrier ['fʌrɪəʳ] *n* peleiro *m*, -ra *f*.

furrow ['fʌrəʊ] *n* -1. [in field] sulco *m* -2. [on forehead] ruga *f*.

furrowed ['fʌrəʊd] *adj* -1. [field, land] lavrado(da) -2. [brow] enrugado(da).

furry ['fɜːrɪ] (*compar* -ier, *superl* -iest) *adj* -1. [animal] peludo(da) -2. [material, toy] de pelúcia.

further ['fɜːðəʳ] <> *compar* ⊳ **far.** <> *adv* -1. [gen] mais adiante; **how much ~ is it?** a que distância fica?; **~ on/back** mais adiante/atrás -2. [complicate, develop, enquire] mais; **to take sth ~** levar algo adiante; **to go ~** ir adiante; **this mustn't go any ~** isso tem que ficar entre nós -3. [in addition] além disso. <> *adj* adicional, novo(va); **until ~ notice** até novas ordens. <> *vt* [career, cause, aims] impulsionar.

further to *prep fml* com referência a.

further education *n UK educação para adultos após deixar a escola excluindo-se a universidade.*

furthermore [ˌfɜːðəˈmɔːʳ] *adv* além do mais, além disso.

furthermost ['fɜːðəməʊst] *adj* mais longe.

furthest ['fɜːðɪst] <> *superl* ⊳ **far.** <> *adj* -1. [in distance] mais afastado(da) -2. [greatest] maior. <> *adv* -1. [in distance] mais longe -2. [to greatest degree, extent] maior.

furtive ['fɜːtɪv] *adj* furtivo(va).

furtively ['fɜːtɪvlɪ] *adv* furtivamente.

fury ['fjʊərɪ] *n* fúria *f*; **in a ~** num acesso de fúria.

fuse *esp UK*, **fuze** *US* [fjuːz] <> *n* -1. *ELEC* fusível *m* -2. [of bomb, firework] detonador *m*. <> *vt* -1. [gen] fundir -2. *ELEC* queimar. <> *vi* -1. [gen] fundir-se -2. *ELEC* queimar.

fusebox *n* caixa *f* de fusíveis.

fused [fjuːzd] *adj ELEC* [fitted with a fuse] com fusível.

fuselage ['fjuːzəlɑːʒ] *n* fuselagem *f*.

fuse wire *n* fio *m* de chumbo (*para fusível*).

fusillade [ˌfjuːzəˈleɪd] *n* fuzilaria *f*.

fusion ['fjuːʒn] *n* fusão *f*.

fuss [fʌs] <> *n* [bother, agitation] alvoroço *m*; **to make a ~** fazer um estardalhaço; **to kick up** *OR* **to make a ~ about sthg** causar *OR* fazer confusão por algo; **to make a ~ of sb** *UK* tratar alguém com atenção. <> *vi* [become agitated] alvoroçar-se.

fuss over *vt fus* alvoroçar-se com.

fusspot ['fʌspɒt] *n inf* exagerado *m*, -da *f*.

fussy ['fʌsɪ] (*compar* -ier, *superl* -iest) *adj* -1. [fastidious] exigente -2. [over-ornate] exagerado(da).

fusty ['fʌstɪ] (*compar* -ier, *superl* -iest) *adj* -1. [room, clothes] com cheiro de mofo -2. [person, idea, attitude] antiquado(da).

futile ['fjuːtaɪl] *adj* fútil.

futility [fjuːˈtɪlətɪ] *n (U)* futilidade *f*.

futon ['fuːtɒn] *n* colchão japonês.

future ['fjuːtʃəʳ] <> *n* -1. [time ahead] futuro *m*; **in (the) ~** no futuro -2. *GRAMM*: **~ (tense)** futuro *m*. <> *adj* futuro(ra).

futures *npl COMM* mercado *m* de futuros.

futuristic [ˌfjuːtʃəˈrɪstɪk] *adj* [design] futurístico(ca).

fuze *n, vt & vi US* = **fuse.**

fuzz [fʌz] *n* -1. [hair] penugem *f* -2. *inf* [police]: **the ~** os tiras.

fuzzy ['fʌzɪ] (*compar* -ier, *superl* -iest) *adj* -1. [hair] encrespado(da) -2. [image, ideas] difuso(sa).

fwd. (*abbr of* **forward**) encaminhar.

fwy (*abbr of* **freeway**) *US* auto-estrada *f*.

FY (*abbr of* **fiscal year**) *n* -1. *US* ano *m* fiscal. -2. (*abbr of* **financial year**) *UK* ano *m* fiscal.

FYI (*abbr of* **for your information**) para sua informação.

G

g¹ (*pl* **g's** *OR* **gs**), **G** (*pl* **G's** *OR* **Gs**) [dʒiː] *n* [letter] g, G *m.*

G <> *n MUS* sol *m.* <> -1. (*abbr of* **good**) B *m* -2. [film certificate] *US* (*abbr of* **general (audience)**) censura *f* livre.

g² -1. (*abbr of* **gram**) g -2. (*abbr of* **gravity**) G.

GA *abbr of* **Georgia.**

gab [gæb] *n* ⊳ **gift.**

gabardine [ˌgæbəˈdiːn] *n* -1. *(U)* [material] gabardine *f* -2. [raincoat] gabardina *f*.

gabble ['gæbl] <> *vt* tagarelar. <> *vi* tagarelar. <> *n* tagarelice *f*.

gable ['geɪbl] *n* oitão *m.*

Gabon [gæˈbɒn] *n* Gabão; **in ~** no Gabão.

Gabonese [ˌgæbəˈniːz] <> *adj* gabonense. <> *npl*: **the ~** os gabonenses.

gad ◆ **gad about** (pt & pp -**ded**, cont -**ding**) vi inf badalar.

gadget ['gædʒɪt] n aparelho m.

gadgetry ['gædʒɪtrɪ] n (U) aparelhagem f.

Gaelic ['geɪlɪk] ◇ adj gaélico(ca). ◇ n gaélico m, -ca f.

gaffe [gæf] n gafe f.

gaffer ['gæfəʳ] n UK inf [boss] chefe mf.

gag [gæg] (pt & pp -**ged**, cont -**ging**) ◇ n -**1.** [for mouth] mordaça f -**2.** inf [joke] piada f. ◇ vt [put gag on] amordaçar. ◇ vi amordaçar.

gage n & vt US = gauge.

gaiety ['geɪətɪ] n (U) alegria f.

gaily ['geɪlɪ] adv -**1.** [cheerfully] alegremente -**2.** [without thinking] despreocupadamente.

gain [geɪn] ◇ n -**1.** [profit] ganho m -**2.** (U) [making a profit] lucro m -**3.** [increase] aumento m. ◇ vt -**1.** [gen] ganhar -**2.** [subj: watch, clock] adiantar-se; **my watch has** ~**ed ten minutes** meu relógio adiantou-se em dez minutos. ◇ vi -**1.** [increase]: **to** ~ **in sthg** crescer em algo -**2.** [profit] lucrar; **to** ~ **from/by sthg** lucrar com algo -**3.** [watch, clock] adiantar-se.
◆ **gain on** vt fus aproximar-se de.

gainful ['geɪnful] adj fml [activity, employment] lucrativo(va), vantajoso(sa).

gainfully ['geɪnfulɪ] adv fml vantajosamente.

gainsay [ˌgeɪn'seɪ] (pt & pp -**said**) vt fml contradizer.

gait [geɪt] n maneira f de andar.

gaiters ['geɪtəz] npl polainas fpl.

gal. abbr of **gallon**.

gala ['gɑːlə] ◇ n -**1.** [celebration] festival m -**2.** UK SPORT festival m. ◇ comp [performance, occasion] de gala.

Galapagos Islands [gə'læpəgəs-] npl: **the** ~ as Ilhas Galápagos; **in the** ~ nas Ilhas Galápagos.

galaxy ['gæləksɪ] (pl -**ies**) n [group of planets and stars] galáxia f.

gale [geɪl] n [wind] ventania f.

Galicia [gə'lɪʃɪə] n -**1.** [in Central Europe] Galícia; **in** ~ na Galícia -**2.** [in Spain] Galiza; **in** ~ na Galiza.

gall [gɔːl] ◇ n (U) [nerve]: **to have the** ~ **to do sthg** ter a audácia de fazer algo. ◇ vt incomodar.

gall. abbr of **gallon**.

gallant [sense 1 'gælənt, sense 2 gə'lænt] adj -**1.** [courageous] valente -**2.** [polite to women] galante.

gallantry ['gæləntrɪ] n (U) -**1.** [courage] valentia f -**2.** [politeness to women] galanteio m.

gall bladder n vesícula f biliar.

galleon ['gælɪən] n galeão m.

gallery ['gælərɪ] (pl -**ies**) n galeria f.

galley ['gælɪ] (pl **galleys**) n -**1.** [ship] galé f -**2.** [kitchen] cozinha f (de navio ou avião) -**3.** TYPO: ~ (**proof**) prova f de granel.

Gallic ['gælɪk] adj gaulês(lesa).

galling ['gɔːlɪŋ] adj -**1.** [annoying] irritante -**2.** [humiliating] vergonhoso(sa).

gallivant [ˌgælɪ'vænt] vi inf perambular.

gallon ['gælən] n galão m.

gallop ['gæləp] ◇ n -**1.** [pace of horse] galope m -**2.** [horse ride] galopada f. ◇ vi galopar.

galloping ['gæləpɪŋ] adj fig [soaring] galopante.

gallows ['gæləʊz] (pl inv) n forca f.

gallstone ['gɔːlstəʊn] n cálculo m biliar.

Gallup poll® ['gæləp-] n UK ≃ pesquisa f do ibope.

galore [gə'lɔːʳ] adv em abundância.

galoshes [gə'lɒʃɪz] npl galocha f.

galvanize, -ise ['gælvənaɪz] vt -**1.** TECH galvanizar -**2.** [impel]: **to** ~ **sb into action** estimular alguém a uma ação.

Gambia ['gæmbɪə] n: **(the)** ~ a Gâmbia; **in (the)** ~ na Gâmbia.

Gambian ['gæmbɪən] ◇ adj gambiano(na). ◇ n gambiano m, -na f.

gambit ['gæmbɪt] n -**1.** [remark, ploy] lábia f -**2.** [in chess] tática f, estratégia f.

gamble ['gæmbl] ◇ n [calculated risk] aposta f; **to take a** ~ assumir o risco. ◇ vi -**1.** [bet] apostar; **to** ~ **on sthg** apostar em algo -**2.** [take risk]: **to** ~ **on sthg** arriscar em algo.

gambler ['gæmbləʳ] n jogador m, -ra f.

gambling ['gæmblɪŋ] n (U) jogo m (de azar).

gambol ['gæmbl] (UK pt & pp -**led**, cont -**ling**, US pt & pp -**ed**, cont -**ing**) vi cabriolar, saltar.

game [geɪm] ◇ n -**1.** [sport, amusement] jogo m; **a children's** ~ uma brincadeira de criança -**2.** [contest, match] jogo m, partida f -**3.** [division of match - in tennis] game m; [- in bridge] jogada f -**4.** [playing equipment] brinquedo m -**5.** [scheme, trick] truque m; **stop playing** ~**s with me!** pare de brincar comigo! -**6.** (U) [hunted animals] caça f -**7.** phr: **to beat sb at their own** ~ derrotar alguém usando suas próprias armas; **the** ~**'s up** acabou a brincadeira; **to give the** ~ **away** entregar o jogo. ◇ adj -**1.** [brave] corajoso(sa) -**2.** [willing] disposto(-ta); ~ **for sthg/to do sthg** pronto(ta) para algo/ para fazer algo.
◆ **games** ◇ n SCH [physical education] jogos mpl. ◇ npl [sporting contest] jogos mpl.

gamekeeper ['geɪmˌkiːpəʳ] n guarda-caça mf.

gamely ['geɪmlɪ] adv [bravely] corajosamente.

game reserve n reserva f de caça.

gamesmanship ['geɪmzmənʃɪp] n (U) artimanha f (no jogo).

gamma rays ['gæmə-] npl raios mpl gama.

gammon ['gæmən] n (U) presunto m.

gammy ['gæmɪ] (compar -**ier**, superl -**iest**) adj UK inf manco(ca).

gamut ['gæmət] n gama f; **to run the** ~ **of sthg** recorrer a toda a gama de algo.

gander ['gændəʳ] n [male goose] ganso m.

gang [gæŋ] n -**1.** [of criminals] quadrilha f, gangue f -**2.** [of young people] turma f.
◆ **gang up** vi inf mancomunar-se; **to** ~ **up on sb** mancomunar-se contra alguém.

Ganges ['gændʒiːz] n: **the (River)** ~ o Rio Ganges.

gangland ['gæŋlænd] n (U) submundo m (do crime).

gangling ['gæŋglɪŋ], **gangly** ['gæŋglɪ] (compar -**ier**, superl -**iest**) adj desajeitado(da).

gangplank ['gæŋplæŋk] n prancha f (de desembarque), passadiço m.

gangrene ['gæŋgriːn] n (U) gangrena f.

gangrenous ['gæŋgrɪnəs] adj gangrenado(da).

gangster ['gæŋstəʳ] n gângster mf.

gangway ['gæŋweɪ] *n* -1. *UK* [aisle] corredor *m* -2. [gangplank] passadiço *m*.

gannet ['gænɪt] (*pl inv OR* -s) *n* [bird] ganso-patola *m*.

gantry ['gæntrɪ] (*pl* -ies) *n* [for crane] cavalete *m*.

GAO (*abbr of* General Accounting Office) *n* departamento *m* de finanças públicas (*norte-americano*).

gaol [dʒeɪl] *n* & *vt UK* = **jail**.

gap [gæp] *n* -1. [empty space] espaço *m*, brecha *f*; **her death left a ~ in our lives** sua morte deixou um vazio em nossas vidas; **fill in the ~s** preencher as lacunas -2. [in time] intervalo *m* -3. *fig* [in knowledge, report] falha *f* -4. *fig* [between theory and practice etc.] disparidade *f*.

gape [geɪp] *vi* -1. [person]: **to ~ (at sb/ sthg)** ficar boquiaberto(ta) (diante de alguém/algo) -2. [hole, shirt] abrir.

gaping ['geɪpɪŋ] *adj* -1. [person] boquiaberto(ta) -2. [hole, shirt, wound] todo aberto, toda aberta.

garage [*UK* 'gærɑ:ʒ, *US* gə'rɑ:ʒ] *n* -1. [for keeping car] garagem *f* -2. *UK* [for fuel] posto *m* de gasolina -3. [for car repair] oficina *f* (*mecânica*) -4. [for selling cars] revendedora *f*.

garage sale *n US* venda *f* de garagem.

garb [gɑ:b] *n* (*U*) *fml* traje *m*.

garbage ['gɑ:bɪdʒ] *n esp US* (*U*) -1. [refuse] lixo *m* -2. *inf* [nonsense] besteira *f*.

garbage can *n US* lata *f* de lixo.

garbage collector *n US* lixeiro *m*, -ra *f*.

garbage truck *n US* caminhão *m* de lixo.

garbled ['gɑ:bld] *adj* [message, account] adulterado(-da).

Garda (Síochána) *n Irish*: **the ~** a polícia irlandesa.

garden ['gɑ:dn] <> *n* jardim *m*. <> *comp* de jardim. <> *vi* jardinar.

   • **gardens** *npl* jardim *m*.

garden centre *n* loja *f* de jardinagem.

garden city *n UK* cidade-jardim *f*.

gardener ['gɑ:dnəʳ] *n* jardineiro *m*, -ra *f*.

gardenia [gɑ:'di:njə] *n* gardênia *f*.

gardening ['gɑ:dnɪŋ] <> *n* (*U*) jardinagem *f*. <> *comp* de jardinagem; **~ expert** perito *m*, -ta *f* em jardinagem.

garden party *n* festa *f* ao ar livre.

gargantuan [gɑ:'gæntjʊən] *adj* gigantesco(ca).

gargle ['gɑ:gl] *vi* gargarejar.

gargoyle ['gɑ:gɔɪl] *n* gárgula *f*.

garish ['geərɪʃ] *adj* espalhafatoso(sa).

garland ['gɑ:lənd] *n* guirlanda *f* (*de flores*).

garlic ['gɑ:lɪk] *n* alho *m*.

garlic bread *n* pão *m* de alho.

garlicky ['gɑ:lɪkɪ] *adj inf* -1. [in smell] com cheiro de alho -2. [in taste] com gosto de alho.

garment ['gɑ:mənt] *n* peça *f* de roupa.

garner ['gɑ:nəʳ] *vt fml* colher.

garnet ['gɑ:nɪt] *n* [red stone] granada *f*.

garnish ['gɑ:nɪʃ] *CULIN* <> *n* decoração *f*. <> *vt* decorar.

garret ['gærət] *n* sótão *m*.

garrison ['gærɪsn] <> *n* [soldiers] guarnição *f*. <> *vt* guarnecer.

garrulous ['gærələs] *adj* tagarela.

garter ['gɑ:təʳ] *n* -1. [band round leg] liga *f* -2. *US* [suspender] suspensório *m*.

gas [gæs] (*pl* gases *OR* gasses, *pt* & *pp* -sed, *cont* -sing) <> *n* -1. *CHEM* gás *m* -2. [domestic fuel] gás *m* (*de cozinha*) -3. *US* [fuel for vehicle] gasolina *f*; **to step on the ~** *inf* pisar no acelerador. <> *vt* [poison] envenenar (com gás).

gas chamber *n* câmara *f* de gás.

gas cooker *n UK* fogão *m* a gás.

gas cylinder *n* botijão *m* de gás.

gaseous *adj TECH* gasoso(sa).

gas fire *n UK* aquecedor *m* a gás.

gas fitter *n* encanador *m*, -ra *f* de gás.

gas gauge *n US* medidor *m* de gás.

gash [gæʃ] <> *n* corte *m* (*na pele*), ferida *f*. <> *vt* cortar (*a pele*), ferir.

gasket ['gæskɪt] *n* gaxeta *f*.

gasman ['gæsmæn] (*pl* -men [-men]) *n* vendedor *m*, -ra *f* de gás.

gas mask *n* máscara *f* antigás.

gasmen *pl* >> **gasman**.

gas meter *n* medidor *m* de gás.

gasoline ['gæsəli:n] *n US* (*U*) gasolina *f*.

gasometer [gæ'sɒmɪtəʳ] *n* gasômetro *m*.

gas oven *n* -1. [for cooking] forno *m* a gás -2. [gas chamber] câmara *f* de gás.

gasp [gɑ:sp] <> *n* arfada *f*. <> *vi* ofegar.

gas pedal *n US* acelerador *m*.

gasping ['gɑ:spɪŋ] *adj UK inf* [in great need]: **to be ~ for sthg** estar louco(ca) por algo.

gas pump attendant *n US* frentista *mf*.

gas station *n US* posto *m* de gasolina.

gas stove *n* = **gas cooker**.

gassy ['gæsɪ] (*compar* -ier, *superl* -iest) *adj pej* [water, beer] com muito gás.

gas tank *n US* tanque *m* de gasolina.

gas tap *n* torneira *f* de gás.

gastric ['gæstrɪk] *adj* gástrico(ca).

gastric ulcer *n* úlcera *f* gástrica.

gastritis [gæs'traɪtɪs] *n* (*U*) gastrite *f*.

gastroenteritis ['gæstrəʊˌentə'raɪtɪs] *n* (*U*) gastroenterite *f*.

gastronomic [ˌgæstrə'nɒmɪk] *adj* gastronômico(-ca).

gastronomy [gæs'trɒnəmɪ] *n* (*U*) gastronomia *f*.

gasworks ['gæswɜ:ks] (*pl inv*) *n* fábrica *f* de gás.

gate [geɪt] *n* portão *m*.

-GATE

Desde o escândalo de Watergate, em 1972, que resultou na primeira renúncia de um presidente dos Estados Unidos - Richard Nixon -, o sufixo *-gate* vem sendo acrescentado a outras palavras, para designar escândalos políticos nos Estados Unidos e na Grã-Bretanha. Assim, a palavra *Irangate* foi cunhada para referir-se á venda ilegal de armas dos Estados Unidos para o Irã, na década de 1980; e, ao final da década de 1990, a palavra *Monicagate* foi inventada para designar o escândalo sexual envolvendo o presidente Bill Clinton e a ex-estagiária da Casa Branca, Monica Lewinski.

---

gâteau ['gætəʊ] (*pl* -x [-z]) *n UK* bolo *m* recheado.

gatecrash ['geɪtkræʃ] *inf* ◇ *vt* entrar como penetra em. ◇ *vi* entrar como penetra.

gatecrasher ['geɪt,kræʃə'] *n inf* penetra *mf*.

gatehouse ['geɪthaʊs, *pl* -haʊzɪz] *n* portaria *f*.

gatekeeper ['geɪt,ki:pə'] *n* porteiro *m*, -ra *f*.

gatepost ['geɪtpəʊst] *n* mourão *m*.

gateway ['geɪtweɪ] *n* -**1**. [entrance] portão *m* -**2**. *fig* [means of access]: ~ to entrada *f* para; ~ airport aeroporto *m* de entrada.

gather ['gæðə'] ◇ *vt* -**1**. [collect - gen] colher; [- courage, strength] reunir: **to ~ together** reunir -**2**. [speed, momentum] ganhar -**3**. [understand]: **to ~ (that)** compreender que -**4**. [into folds] franzir. ◇ *vi* [come together] reunir.

➡ **gather up** *vt sep* [objects] juntar.

gathering ['gæðərɪŋ] *n* [meeting] assembléia *f*.

GATT [gæt] (*abbr of* **General Agreement on Tariffs and Trade**) *n acordo geral de tarifas e comércio*, GATT *m*.

gauche [gəʊʃ] *adj* desajeitado(da).

gaudy ['gɔ:dɪ] (*compar* -**ier**, *superl* -**iest**) *adj* chamativo(va).

gauge, gage *US* [geɪdʒ] ◇ *n* -**1**. [measuring instrument - for rain] pluviômetro *m*; [- for tyre pressure] calibrador *m*; [- for fuel] medidor *m* de combustível -**2**. [calibre] calibre *m* -**3**. [of rail] bitola *f*. ◇ *vt* -**1**. [estimate, measure] estimar, calcular -**2**. [predict] prever.

Gaul [gɔ:l] *n* -**1**. [country] Gália -**2**. [person] gaulês *m*, -lesa *f*.

gaunt [gɔ:nt] *adj* -**1**. [person, face] esquelético(ca) -**2**. [landscape, building] desolado(da).

gauntlet ['gɔ:ntlɪt] *n* [medieval glove] manopla *f*; [for motorcyclist] luva *f* (*de material resistente e punho largo*); **to run the ~ of sthg** expor-se a algo; **to throw down the ~ (to sb)** lançar um desafio (a alguém).

gauze [gɔ:z] *n* (*U*) [fabric] gaze *f*.

gave [geɪv] *pt* ▷ **give**.

gawky ['gɔ:kɪ] (*compar* -**ier**, *superl* -**iest**) *adj* desengonçado(da).

gawp [gɔ:p] *vi* embasbacar-se; **to ~ at sb/sthg** embasbacar-se diante de alguém/algo.

gay [geɪ] ◇ *adj* -**1**. [homosexual] gay -**2**. [cheerful, brightly coloured] alegre. ◇ *n* [homosexual] gay *mf*.

Gaza Strip ['gɑ:zə-] *n*: **the ~** a Faixa de Gaza.

gaze [geɪz] ◇ *n* olhar *m* fixo. ◇ *vi*: **to ~ (at sb/sthg)** olhar fixamente (para alguém/algo).

gazebo [gə'zi:bəʊ] (*pl* -**s**) *n* mirante *m*.

gazelle [gə'zel] (*pl inv OR* -**s**) *n* gazela *f*.

gazette [gə'zet] *n* [newspaper] gazeta *f*.

gazetteer [,gæzɪ'tɪə'] *n* dicionário *m* geográfico.

gazump [gə'zʌmp] *vt UK inf* concordar em vender uma casa a alguém e depois vendê-la a outro por um preço mais alto; **to be ~ed** ser passado(da) pra trás na compra de um imóvel.

GB (*abbr of* **Great Britain**) *n* GB.

GBH (*abbr of* **grievous bodily harm**) *n UK* lesão *f* corporal grave.

GC (*abbr of* **George Cross**) *n* (*titular da*) *maior condecoração de bravura concedida a civis na Grã-Bretanha.*

GCE (*abbr of* **General Certificate of Education**) *n*

antigo exame final do ensino médio na Grã-Bretanha.

GCH (*abbr of* **gas central heating**) *n UK* aquecimento *m* central a gás.

GCHQ (*abbr of* **Government Communications Headquarters**) *n centro de informações dos serviços secretos britânicos.*

GCSE (*abbr of* **General Certificate of Secondary Education**) *n exame final do ensino médio na Grã-Bretanha, em substituição ao nível O do GCE.*

Gdns (*abbr of* **Gardens**) Jd.

GDP (*abbr of* **gross domestic product**) *n* PIB *m*.

GDR (*abbr of* **German Democratic Republic**) *n* RDA *f*.

gear [gɪə'] ◇ *n* -**1**. TECH [mechanism] engrenagem *f* -**2**. [on car, bicycle] marcha *f*; **in ~** engatado(da), engrenado(da); **out of ~** desengatado(da), fora de funcionamento -**3**. (*U*) [equipment, clothes] apetrechos *mpl*. ◇ *vt*: **to ~ sthg to sb/sthg** encaminhar algo a alguém/algo.

➡ **gear up** *vi*: **to ~ up for sthg/to do sthg** preparar-se para algo/para fazer algo.

gearbox ['gɪəbɒks] *n* caixa *f* de câmbio.

gearing *n* [assembly of gears] engrenagem *f*.

gear lever, gear stick *UK*, **gear shift** *US n* alavanca *f* de mudança.

gear wheel *n* roda *f* de engrenagem.

gee [dʒi:] *excl* -**1**. [to horse]: ~ **up!** eia! -**2**. *US inf* [expressing surprise, excitement]: ~ **(whizz)!** puxa!, nossa!

geese [gi:s] *pl* ▷ **goose**.

Geiger counter ['gaɪgə'-] *n* contador *m* Geiger.

geisha (girl) ['geɪʃə-] *n* gueixa *f*.

gel [dʒel] (*pt & pp* -**led**, *cont* -**ling**) ◇ *n* [for hair] gel *m*. ◇ *vi* -**1**. *fig* [idea, plan] tomar forma -**2**. [liquid] engrossar.

gelatin ['dʒelətɪn], **gelatine** [,dʒelə'ti:n] *n* gelatina *f*.

gelding ['geldɪŋ] *n* cavalo *m* castrado.

gelignite ['dʒelɪgnaɪt] *n* (*U*) gelignite *f*.

gem [dʒem] *n* -**1**. [jewel] gema *f*, pedra *f* preciosa -**2**. *fig* [person, thing] jóia *f*.

Gemini ['dʒemɪnaɪ] *n* -**1**. [sign] Gêmeos -**2**. [person] geminiano *m*, -na *f*; **I'm ~** sou de Gêmeos.

gemstone ['dʒemstəʊn] *n* pedra *f* preciosa.

gen [dʒen] (*pt & pp* -**ned**, *cont* -**ning**) *n UK inf* informações *fpl*.

➡ **gen up** *vi UK inf*: **to ~ up (on sthg)** informar-se (sobre algo).

gen. -**1**. (*abbr of* **general**) ger. -**2**. (*abbr of* **generally**) em geral.

Gen. (*abbr of* **General**) Gen.

gender ['dʒendə'] *n* -**1**. [sex] sexo *m* -**2**. GRAMM gênero *m*.

gene [dʒi:n] *n* gene *m*.

genealogist [,dʒi:nɪ'ælədʒɪst] *n* genealogista *mf*.

genealogy [,dʒi:nɪ'ælədʒɪ] (*pl* -**ies**) *n* genealogia *f*.

genera ['dʒenərə] *pl* ▷ **genus**.

general ['dʒenərəl] ◇ *adj* geral. ◇ *n MIL* general *mf*.

➡ **in general** *adv* -**1**. [as a whole] em geral -**2**. [usually] geralmente.

general anaesthetic *n* anestesia *f* geral.

general delivery n (U) US posta-restante f.
general election n eleições fpl gerais.
generality [ˌdʒenəˈrælətɪ] (pl -ies) n -1. [generalization] generalidade f-2. [majority] maioria f.
generalization [ˌdʒenərəlaɪˈzeɪʃn] n generalização f.
generalize, -ise [ˈdʒenərəlaɪz] vi generalizar; to ~ about sthg generalizar sobre algo.
general knowledge n (U) cultura m geral.
generally [ˈdʒenərəlɪ] adv -1. [usually] geralmente -2. [by most people] comumente -3. [in a general way] em geral.
general manager n gerente mf geral.
general practice n clínica f geral.
general practitioner n clínico m, -ca f geral.
general public n: the ~ o público em geral.
general-purpose adj de uso geral.
general strike n greve f geral.
generate [ˈdʒenəreɪt] vt-1. [energy, power, heat] gerar -2. [interest, excitement] provocar ; [jobs, employment] gerar.
generation [ˌdʒenəˈreɪʃn] n geração f; first/second ~ primeira/segunda geração.
generation gap n conflito m de gerações.
generator [ˈdʒenəreɪtəˈ] n gerador m.
generic [dʒɪˈnerɪk] adj [of whole group] genérico(ca).
generosity [ˌdʒenəˈrɒsətɪ] n (U) generosidade f.
generous [ˈdʒenərəs] adj generoso(sa).
generously [ˈdʒenərəslɪ] adv generosamente.
genesis [ˈdʒenəsɪs] (pl -eses [-əsiːz]) n [origin] gênese f.
genetic [dʒɪˈnetɪk] adj genético(ca).
➡ **genetics** n (U) genética f.
genetically modified [dʒɪˈnetɪkəlɪˈmɒdɪfaɪd] adj geneticamente modificado(da).
genetic engineering n (U) engenharia f genética.
genetic fingerprinting [-ˈfɪŋɡəprɪntɪŋ] n impressão f genética.
Geneva [dʒɪˈniːvə] n Genebra; in ~ em Genebra.
Geneva convention n: the ~ a convenção de Genebra.
genial [ˈdʒiːnjəl] adj cordial, simpático(ca).
genie [ˈdʒiːnɪ] (pl genies OR genii [ˈdʒiːnɪaɪ]) n gênio m.
genitals [ˈdʒenɪtlz] npl genitais mpl.
genius [ˈdʒiːnjəs] (pl -es) n -1. [person] gênio m -2. [special ability]: a stroke of ~ um golpe de mestre; ~ for sthg/for doing sthg dom para algo/para fazer algo.
Genoa [dʒəˈnəʊə] n Gênova; in ~ em Gênova.
genocide [ˈdʒenəsaɪd] n (U) genocídio m.
genre [ˈʒrəl] n [in art, literature, film] gênero m.
gent [dʒentl] n UK dated inf cavalheiro m.
➡ **gents** n UK [toilets] banheiro m masculino.
genteel [dʒenˈtiːl] adj -1. [refined] fino(na), refinado(da) -2. [affected] afetado(da).
gentile [ˈdʒentaɪl] <> adj gói, não-judeu(dia). <> n gói mf.
gentle [ˈdʒentl] adj -1. [gen] suave -2. [kind] gentil -3. [discreet] leve.
gentleman [ˈdʒentlmən] (pl -men [-mən]) n -1. [well-bred man] cavalheiro m, gentleman m; ~'s

agreement acordo m de cavalheiros -2. [man] senhor m.
gentlemanly [ˈdʒentlmənlɪ] adj cavalheiresco(ca).
gentleness [ˈdʒentlnɪs] n -1. [gen] suavidade f-2. [kindness] delicadeza f.
gently [ˈdʒentlɪ] adv -1. [gen] suavemente -2. [kindly] delicadamente, gentilmente -3. [slowly] lentamente.
gentry [ˈdʒentrɪ] n alta burguesia f.
genuflect [ˈdʒenjuːflekt] vi fml genuflectir.
genuine [ˈdʒenjuɪn] adj -1. [antique, work of art] genuíno(na) -2. [person, feeling, mistake] autêntico(ca).
genuinely [ˈdʒenjuɪnlɪ] adv -1. [surprised, disappointed] genuinamente -2. [spoken, believed] sinceramente.
genus [ˈdʒiːnəs] (pl genera [ˈdʒenərəl] n gênero m.
geographer [dʒɪˈɒɡrəfəˈ] n geógrafo m, -fa f.
geographical [ˌdʒɪəˈɡræfɪkl] adj geográfico(ca).
geography [dʒɪˈɒɡrəfɪ] n geografia f.
geological [ˌdʒɪəˈlɒdʒɪkl] adj geológico(ca).
geologist [dʒɪˈɒlədʒɪst] n geólogo m, -ga f.
geology [dʒɪˈɒlədʒɪ] n geologia f.
geometric(al) [ˌdʒɪəˈmetrɪk(l)] adj geométrico(ca).
geometry [dʒɪˈɒmətrɪ] n (U) geometria f.
geophysics [ˌdʒɪːəʊˈfɪzɪks] n (U) geofísica f.
Geordie [ˈdʒɔːdɪ] <> adj de ou relativo a Tyneside. <> n [person] natural ou habitante de Tyneside.
George Cross [ˈdʒɔːdʒ-] n UK medalha de honra ao mérito.
Georgia [ˈdʒɔːdʒə] n [in US, CIS] Geórgia f.
Georgian [ˈdʒɔːdʒən] <> adj -1. UK [of Georgian period] georgiano(na) -2. GEOGR: [US, CIS] georgiano(na). <> n [in US, CIS] georgiano m, -na f.
geranium [dʒɪˈreɪnjəm] (pl -s) n gerânio m.
gerbil [ˈdʒɜːbɪl] n gerbo m.
geriatric [ˌdʒerɪˈætrɪk] adj -1. [of old people] geriátrico(ca) -2. pej [very old, inefficient] ultrapassado(da).
germ [dʒɜːml] n -1. BIO germe m -2. MED bactéria f-3. fig [of idea, plan] embrião m.
German [ˈdʒɜːmən] <> adj alemão(mã). <> n -1. [person] alemão m, -mã f-2. [language] alemão m.
Germanic [dʒɜːˈmænɪk] adj germânico(ca).
German measles n (U) rubéola f.
German shepherd (dog) n pastor m alemão.
Germany [ˈdʒɜːmənɪ] (pl -ies) n Alemanha; in ~ na Alemanha.
germicide [ˈdʒɜːmɪsaɪd] n germicida f, bactericida f.
germinate [ˈdʒɜːmɪneɪt] <> vt germinar. <> vi germinar.
germination [ˌdʒɜːmɪˈneɪʃn] n (U) germinação f.
germ warfare n (U) guerra f bacteriológica.
gerrymandering [ˈdʒerɪmændərɪŋ] n (U) divisão de uma zona eleitoral de forma a beneficiar um partido em prejuízo de outro.
gerund [ˈdʒerənd] n GRAM gerúndio m.
gestation [dʒeˈsteɪʃn] n gestação f.
gestation period n período m de gestação.
gesticulate [dʒesˈtɪkjʊleɪt] vi gesticular.

gesticulation [dʒe,stıkjʊ'leıʃn] n gesticulação f.

gesture ['dʒestʃəʳ] <> n gesto m. <> vi: **to ~ to** OR **towards sb** fazer gestos a alguém

get [getl] (pt & pp **got**, US pp **gotten**) vt **-1.** [obtain] obter; [buy] comprar; **she got a job** ela arranjou emprego **-2.** [receive] receber; **I got a book for Christmas** ganhei um livro no Natal **-3.** [means of transportation] apanhar; **let's ~ a taxi** vamos apanhar um táxi **-4.** [find] ir buscar; **could you ~ me the manager?** [in store] podia chamar o gerente?; [on phone] pode me passar o gerente? **-5.** [illness] apanhar; **I got the flu over Christmas** peguei uma gripe no Natal **-6.** [cause to become]: **to ~ sthg done** mandar fazer algo; **to ~ sthg ready** preparar algo; **can I ~ my car repaired here?** posso mandar consertar o meu carro aqui? **-7.** [ask, tell]: **to ~ sb to do sthg** arranjar alguém para fazer algo **-8.** [move]: **to ~ sthg out of sthg** tirar algo de algo; **I can't ~ it through the door** não consigo passar com isso na porta **-9.** [understand] compreender; **to ~ a joke** contar uma piada **-10.** [time, chance] ter; **we didn't ~ the chance to see everything** não tivemos oportunidade de ver tudo **-11.** [idea, feeling] ter; **I ~ a lot of enjoyment from it** me divirto à beça com isso **-12.** [phone] atender **-13.** [in phrases]: **you ~ a lot of rain here in winter** chove muito aqui no inverno ▷ **have**. <> vi **-1.** [become] ficar; **it's getting late** está ficando tarde; **to ~ ready** preparar-se; **to ~ lost** perder-se; **~ lost!** não enche o saco!, desapareça! **-2.** [into particular state, position] meter-se; **how do you ~ to El Paso from here?** como se vai daqui para El Paso?; **to ~ into the car** entrar no carro **-3.** [arrive] chegar; **when does the train ~ here?** quando é que o trem chega aqui? **-4.** [in phrases]: **to ~ to do sthg** ter a oportunidade de fazer algo. <> aux vb ser; **to ~ delayed** atrasar-se; **to ~ killed** ser morto.

➤ **get along (with sb)** vi dar-se bem (com alguém).

➤ **get back** vi [return] voltar.

➤ **get in** vi [arrive] chegar; (enter) entrar.

➤ **get off** vi [leave] sair.

➤ **get on** vi [enter train, bus] entrar.

➤ **get out** vi [of car, bus, train] sair.

➤ **get through** vi [on phone] completar a ligação.

➤ **get up** vi levantar-se.

getaway ['getəweı] n fuga f; **to make one's ~** escapar.

getaway car n carro m de fuga.

get-together n inf encontro m informal (entre amigos).

getup ['getʌp] n inf traje m.

get-up-and-go n (U) inf iniciativa f.

get-well card n cartão m de melhoras.

geyser ['gi:zəʳ] n [hot spring] gêiser m.

Ghana ['gɑ:nə] n Gana; **in ~** em Gana.

Ghan(a)ian [gɑ:'neıən] <> adj ganense. <> n ganense mf.

ghastly ['gɑ:stlı] (compar -ier, superl -iest) adj **-1.** inf [very bad, unpleasant] horrível **-2.** [horrifying, macabre] macabro(bra), horroroso(sa) **-3.** [ill] abatido(da).

gherkin ['gɜ:kın] n pepino m em conserva.

ghetto ['getəʊ] (pl -s OR -es) n gueto m.

ghetto blaster [-'blɑ:stəʳ] n inf minisystem portátil de grande potência.

ghost [gəʊst] <> n [spirit] fantasma m; **he doesn't have a ~ of a chance** ele não tem a menor chance. <> vt = **ghostwrite**.

ghostly ['gəʊstlı] (compar -ier, superl -iest) adj fantasmagórico(ca).

ghost town n cidade-fantasma f.

ghostwrite ['gəʊstraıt] (pt -wrote, pp -written) vt escrever anonimamente para outra pessoa.

ghostwriter ['gəʊst,raıtəʳ] n ghost-writer mf.

ghostwritten ['gəʊst,rıtn] pp ▷ **ghostwrite**.

ghostwrote ['gəʊstrəʊt] pt ▷ **ghostwrite**.

ghoul [gu:l] n **-1.** [spirit] espírito m do mal **-2.** pej [ghoulish person] demônio m.

ghoulish ['gu:lıʃ] adj [morbid] macabro(bra).

GHQ (abbr of general headquarters) n QG m.

GI (abbr of government issue) n soldado raso norte-americano.

giant ['dʒaıənt] <> adj gigantesco(ca). <> n **-1.** [gen] gigante m **-2.** [business, organization] gigante mf.

giant-size(d) adj de tamanho família.

gibber ['dʒıbəʳ] vi tagarelar.

gibberish ['dʒıbərıʃ] n (U) asneira f.

gibbon ['gıbən] n gibão m.

gibe [dʒaıb] <> n zombaria f. <> vi: **to ~ at sb/sthg** zombar de alguém/algo.

giblets ['dʒıblıts] npl miúdos mpl (de ave).

Gibraltar [dʒı'brɔ:ltəʳ] n Gibraltar; **in ~** em Gibraltar; **the Rock of ~** o Rochedo de Gibraltar.

giddy ['gıdı] (compar -ier, superl -iest) adj [dizzy] tonto(ta).

gift [gıft] n **-1.** [present] presente m **-2.** [talent] dom m; **to have a ~ for sthg/for doing sthg** ter o dom para algo/para fazer algo; **to have the ~ of the gab** ter o dom da fala; pej ter lábia.

GIFT (abbr of gamete in fallopian transfer) n técnica de inseminação artificial.

gift certificate n US = **gift token**.

gifted ['gıftıd] adj **-1.** [gen] talentoso(sa), de talento **-2.** [child] superdotado(da).

gift token, gift voucher UK, **gift certificate** US n vale-presente m.

gift wrap n papel m de presente.

gift-wrapped [-ræpt] adj enrolado(da) para presente.

gig [gıg] n inf [concert] show m.

gigabyte ['gaıgəbaıt] n COMPUT gigabyte m.

gigantic [dʒaı'gæntık] adj gigantesco(ca).

giggle ['gıgl] <> n **-1.** [laugh] risadinha f, risada f **-2.** UK inf [fun] diversão f; **to do sthg for a ~** divertir-se fazendo algo tolo; **to have the ~s** ter um ataque de riso. <> vi [laugh] dar risadinhas bobas.

giggly ['gıglı] (compar -ier, superl -iest) adj com riso bobo.

GIGO ['gaıgəʊ] (abbr of garbage in, garbage out) COMPUT GIGO m, entra lixo, sai lixo.

gigolo ['ʒıgələʊ] (pl -s) n pej gigolô m.

gigot ['ʒi:gəʊ] n perna f de carneiro.

gilded ['gıldıd] adj = **gilt**.

gill [dʒɪl] *n* [unit of measurement] *0,142 litros.*
gills [gɪlz] *npl* [of fish] guelras *fpl.*
gilt [gɪlt] ⟨⟩ *adj* [covered in gold] dourado(da). ⟨⟩ *n* (U) [gold layer] dourado *m.*
● **gilts** *npl* FIN títulos *mpl* de máxima garantia.
gilt-edged *adj* FIN de máxima garantia.
gimme ['gɪmɪ] *inf* = give me.
gimmick ['gɪmɪk] *n pej* artimanha *f.*
gin [dʒɪn] *n* [drink] gim *m*; ~ **and tonic** gim-tônica *m.*
ginger ['dʒɪndʒə'] ⟨⟩ *adj* UK [colour - of hair] ruivo(va); [- of cat] avermelhado(da). ⟨⟩ *n* (U) -1. [root] gengibre *m* - 2. [powder] gengibre *m* em pó.
ginger ale *n* [mixer] jinjibirra *f.*
ginger beer *n* [slightly alcoholic] cerveja *f* de gengibre.
gingerbread ['dʒɪndʒəbredl] *n* (U) -1. [cake] pão *m* de gengibre - 2. [biscuit] biscoito *m* de gengibre.
ginger group *n* UK grupo *m* de pressão.
ginger-haired [-'heədl] *adj* ruivo(va).
gingerly ['dʒɪndʒəlɪ] *adv* cuidadosamente.
gingham ['gɪŋəm] *n* (U) [cloth] guingão *m.*
gingivitis [,dʒɪndʒɪ'vaɪtɪs] *n* (U) MED gengivite *f.*
ginseng ['dʒɪnseŋ] *n* (U) ginseng *m.*
gipsy ['dʒɪpsɪ] (*pl*-ies) ⟨⟩ *adj* cigano(na). ⟨⟩ *n* [nomad] cigano *m*, -na *f.*
giraffe [dʒɪ'rɑːf] (*pl inv* OR -s) *n* girafa *f.*
gird [gɜːd] (*pt* & *pp* -ed OR girt) *vt* ▷ loin.
girder ['gɜːdə'] *n* viga *f.*
girdle ['gɜːdl] *n* [corset] espartilho *m.*
girl [gɜːl] *n* -1. [young female child] menina *f*, garota *f* - 2. [young woman] moça *f* - 3. [daughter] menina *f* - 4. [female friend]: **the** ~ **s** as amigas, as meninas.
girl Friday *n* auxiliar *f* de escritório.
girlfriend ['gɜːlfrend] *n* -1. [female lover] namorada *f* - 2. [female friend] amiga *f.*
girl guide UK, **girl scout** US *n* [individual] escoteira *f*, bandeirante *f.*
girlie magazine ['gɜːlɪ-] *n inf* revista *f* erótica.
girlish ['gɜːlɪʃ] *adj* de menininha.
girl scout *n* US = girl guide.
giro ['dʒaɪrəʊ] (*pl* -s) *n* UK -1. (U) [system] transferência *f* de crédito - 2.: *inf* ~ (**cheque**) seguro-desemprego *m.*
girt *pt* & *pp* ▷ gird.
girth [gɜːθ] *n* -1. [circumference] circunferência *f* - 2. [of horse] cincha *f.*
gist [dʒɪst] *n* essência *f*; **to get the** ~ (**of sthg**) pegar a essência (de algo).
give [gɪv] (*pt* gave, *pp* given) ⟨⟩ *vt* -1. [gen] dar; **to** ~ **sb sthg** dar algo para OR a alguém - 2. [hand over, pass] entregar; **to** ~ **sb sthg**, **to** ~ **sthg to sb** entregar algo para OR a alguém - 3. [pay]: **to** ~ **sthg (for sthg)** dar OR pagar algo (por algo) - 4. *phr:* **to be given to believe** OR **understand that** *fml* ser levado(da) a acreditar OR entender que; **I'd** ~ **anything** OR **my right arm to do that** eu daria tudo OR qualquer coisa para fazer isso. ⟨⟩ *vi* [collapse, break] ceder. ⟨⟩ *n* (U) [elasticity] elasticidade *f.*
● **give or take** *prep* mais ou menos.
● **give away** *vt sep* -1. [get rid of] desfazer-se de - 2. [reveal] revelar.
● **give back** *vt sep* [return] devolver.

● **give in** *vi* -1. [admit defeat] render-se, dar-se por vencido(da) - 2. [agree unwillingly]: **to** ~ **in to sthg** ceder frente a algo.
● **give off** *vt fus* [produce] exalar.
● **give out** ⟨⟩ *vt sep* [distribute] distribuir. ⟨⟩ *vi* -1. [be exhausted] esgotar-se - 2. [fail] falhar, não funcionar.
● **give over** ⟨⟩ *vt sep* [dedicate]: **to be given over to sthg** ser destinado(da) a algo. ⟨⟩ *vi* UK *inf* [stop]: ~ **over!** (já) chega!
● **give up** *vt sep* -1. [stop, abandon] abandonar; **to** ~ **up smoking** parar de fumar; **to** ~ **up chocolate** deixar de comer chocolate - 2. [surrender]: **to** ~ **o.s. up (to sb)** render-se (a alguém). ⟨⟩ *vi* [admit defeat] render-se.
● **give up on** *vt fus* [abandon] abandonar *(por muito difícil).*
give-and-take *n* (U) [compromise] toma-lá-dá-cá *m.*
giveaway ['gɪvə,weɪ] ⟨⟩ *adj* -1. [telltale] revelador(ra) - 2. [very cheap] dado(da). ⟨⟩ *n* [telltale sign] sinal *m* óbvio.
given ['gɪvn] ⟨⟩ *pp* ▷ give. ⟨⟩ *adj* -1. [set, fixed] dado(da); **at any** ~ **time** num determinado momento - 2. [prone]: **to be** ~ **to sthg/to doing sthg** ser dado(da) a algo/a fazer algo. ⟨⟩ *prep* [taking into account] dado(da); ~ **the circumstances** dadas as circunstâncias; ~ **that** dado que.
given name *n* US prenome *m.*
giver ['gɪvə'] *n* doador *m*, -ra *f.*
glacé cherry ['glæseɪ-] *n* cereja *f* glaçada.
glacial ['gleɪsjəl] *adj* glacial.
glacier ['glæsjə'] *n* geleira *f.*
glad [glæd] (*compar* -der, *superl* -dest) *adj* -1. [happy, pleased] feliz; **to be** ~ **about sthg** estar feliz por algo; **to be** ~ **that** estar feliz que - 2. [willing]: **to be** ~ **to do sthg** ter vontade de fazer algo, desejar fazer algo - 3. [grateful]: **to be** ~ **of sthg** ficar agradecido(da) por algo.
gladden ['glædn] *vt literary* contentar.
glade [gleɪd] *n literary* clareira *f.*
gladiator ['glædɪeɪtə'] *n* gladiador *m.*
gladioli [,glædɪ'əʊlaɪ] *npl* gladíolos *mpl.*
gladly ['glædlɪ] *adv* -1. [happily, eagerly] com prazer, alegremente - 2. [willingly] com satisfação.
glamor *n* US = glamour.
glamorize, -ise ['glæməraɪz] *vt* fantasiar.
glamorous ['glæmərəs] *adj* [gen] glamouroso(sa); [job] atraente.
glamour UK, **glamor** US ['glæmə'] *n* (U) [gen] glamour *m*; [of job] encanto *m.*
glance [glɑːns] ⟨⟩ *n* [quick look] olhadela *f*; **to cast** OR **take a** ~ **at sthg** dar uma olhada rápida em algo; **at a** ~ de relance; **at first** ~ à primeira vista. ⟨⟩ *vi* [look quickly]: **to** ~ **at sb/sthg** olhar alguém/algo de relance; **to** ~ **at** OR **through sthg** passar os olhos em algo.
● **glance off** *vt fus* -1. [light] desviar - 2. [ball] rebater - 3. [bullet] ricochetear.
glancing ['glɑːnsɪŋ] *adj* [oblique] oblíquo(qua).
gland [glænd] *n* glândula *f.*
glandular fever ['glændjʊlə'-] *n* (U) mononucleose *f* infecciosa.
glare [gleə'] ⟨⟩ *n* -1. [scowl] olhar *m* penetrante,

encarada *f* - **2.** *(U)* [blaze, dazzle] brilho *m* - **3.** [of publicity] foco *m*. ◇ *vi* - **1.** [scowl]: **to ~ at sb/sthg** fulminar alguém/algo com o olhar, lançar um olhar fulminante sobre alguém/algo - **2.** [blaze, dazzle] ofuscar.

glaring ['gleərɪŋ] *adj* - **1.** [very obvious] evidente - **2.** [blazing, dazzling] ofuscante.

glasnost ['glæznɒst] *n (U)* glasnost *f*.

glass [glɑːs] ◇ *n* - **1.** *(U)* [material] vidro *m* - **2.** [for drinking] copo *m* - **3.** *(U)* [glassware] objetos *mpl* de cristal. ◇ *comp* de vidro.
➡ **glasses** *npl* [spectacles] óculos *m inv*; [binoculars] binóculos *mpl*.

glassblowing ['glɑːsˌbləʊɪŋ] *n (U)* modelagem *f* de vidro a quente.

glass fibre *n (U) UK* fibra *f* de vidro.

glasshouse ['glɑːshaʊs, *pl* -haʊzɪz] *n UK* - **1.** [greenhouse] estufa *f* - **2.** *fig inf* [military prison] prisão *f* militar.

glassware ['glɑːsweə'] *n (U)* objetos *mpl* de cristal.

glassy ['glɑːsɪ] (*compar* -ier, *superl* -iest) *adj* - **1.** [smooth, shiny] cristalino(na) - **2.** [blank, lifeless] vidrado(da).

Glaswegian [glæz'wiːdʒən] ◇ *adj* de ou relativo a Glasgow. ◇ *n* - **1.** [person] *natural ou habitante de Glasgow* - **2.** [dialect] *dialeto falado em Glasgow*.

glaucoma [glɔːˈkəʊmə] *n (U)* glaucoma *m*.

glaze [gleɪz] ◇ *n* - **1.** [on pottery] verniz *m*, esmalte *m* - **2.** CULIN glacê *m*. ◇ *vt* - **1.** [pottery] envernizar - **2.** CULIN cristalizar.
➡ **glaze over** *vi* apagar-se.

glazed [gleɪzd] *adj* - **1.** [dull, bored] vidrado(da) - **2.** [pottery] vitrificado(da) - **3.** CULIN cristalizado(da) - **4.** [with glass] envidraçado(da).

glazier ['gleɪzjə'] *n* vidraceiro *m*, -ra *f*.

gleam [gliːm] ◇ *n* - **1.** [glow] lampejo *m* - **2.** [fleeting expression] olhar *m*. ◇ *vi* - **1.** [surface, object] reluzir - **2.** [light] brilhar - **3.** [face, eyes] olhar.

gleaming ['gliːmɪŋ] *adj* - **1.** [surface, object] reluzente - **2.** [light] brilhante - **3.** [face, eyes] reluzente.

glean [gliːn] *vt* [gather] coletar.

glee [gliː] *n (U)* [joy, delight] alegria *f*; [gloating] regozijo *m*.

gleeful ['gliːfʊl] *adj* [joyful] alegre; [gloating] de regozijo.

glen [glen] *n Scot & Irish* vale *m*.

glib [glɪb] (*compar* -ber, *superl* -best) *adj pej* - **1.** [answer, excuse] de momento - **2.** [person] de muita lábia.

glibly ['glɪblɪ] *adv pej* [talk, reply] com muita lábia.

glide [glaɪd] *vi* - **1.** [move smoothly] deslizar - **2.** [fly] planar.

glider ['glaɪdə'] *n* [plane] planador *m*.

gliding ['glaɪdɪŋ] *n (U)* [sport] vôo *m* sem motor; **to go ~** voar de planador.

glimmer ['glɪmə'] ◇ *n* - **1.** [faint light] luz *f* fraca - **2.** *fig* [trace, sign] sinal *m* mínimo; **a ~ of hope** um fio de esperança. ◇ *vi* tremeluzir.

glimpse [glɪmps] ◇ *n* - **1.** [sight, look] vislumbre *m*; **to catch a ~ of sb/sthg** ver alguém/algo de relance - **2.** [perception, idea, insight] noção *f*. ◇ *vt*

- **1.** [catch sight of] ver de relance - **2.** [perceive] vislumbrar.

glint [glɪnt] ◇ *n* brilho *m*. ◇ *vi* - **1.** [metal, sunlight] brilhar - **2.** [eyes - greed, anger] faiscar; [- amusement] brilhar.

glisten ['glɪsn] *vi* brilhar.

glitch [glɪtʃ] *n inf* [in plan] falha *f* técnica, pane *f*.

glitter ['glɪtə'] ◇ *n* [gen] brilho *m*. ◇ *vi* - **1.** [object, light] brilhar - **2.** [eyes - with excitement] cintilar; [- with fury] faiscar.

glittering ['glɪtərɪŋ] *adj* - **1.** [object, light] reluzente, brilhante - **2.** [eyes] brilhante - **3.** [glamorous] deslumbrante.

glitzy ['glɪtsɪ] (*compar* -ier, *superl* -iest) *adj inf* [glamorous] deslumbrante.

gloat [gləʊt] *vi*: **to ~ (over sthg)** tripudiar (de algo).

global ['gləʊbl] *adj* [worldwide] mundial.

globalization [ˌgləʊbəlaɪˈzeɪʃn] *n* globalização *f*.

globally ['gləʊbəlɪ] *adv* - **1.** [worldwide] mundialmente - **2.** [generally] em geral.

global warming [-ˈwɔːmɪŋ] *n (U)* aquecimento *m* global.

globe [gləʊb] *n* - **1.** [Earth]: **the ~** o globo - **2.** [spherical shape] globo *m*.

globetrotter ['gləʊbˌtrɒtə'] *n inf* globe-trotter *mf*.

globule ['glɒbjuːl] *n* gota *f*.

gloom [gluːm] *n* - **1.** [darkness] escuro *m*, escuridão *f* - **2.** [unhappiness] desânimo *m*.

gloomy ['gluːmɪ] (*compar* -ier, *superl* -iest) *adj* - **1.** [place, landscape] sombrio(bria) - **2.** [weather] sombrio(bria), escuro(ra) - **3.** [atmosphere] deprimente; [mood] pessimista - **4.** [outlook, news] desanimador(ra).

glorification [ˌglɔːrɪfɪˈkeɪʃn] *n (U)* [act of glorifying] glorificação *f*.

glorified ['glɔːrɪfaɪd] *adj pej* [jumped-up] incrementado(da).

glorify ['glɔːrɪfaɪ] (*pt & pp* -ied) *vt* [overpraise, overesteem] glorificar.

glorious ['glɔːrɪəs] *adj* - **1.** [illustrious] glorioso(sa) - **2.** [wonderful] magnífico(ca).

glory ['glɔːrɪ] (*pl* -ies) *n* - **1.** [gen] glória *f* - **2.** *(U)* [splendour] esplendor *m*.
➡ **glories** *npl* glórias *fpl*.
➡ **glory in** *vt fus* [relish] desfrutar de.

gloss [glɒs] *n* - **1.** *(U)* [shine - of wood, furniture] lustre *m*; [- of hair] brilho *m* - **2.**: **~ (paint)** esmalte *m*.
➡ **gloss over** *vt fus* falar por alto sobre.

glossary ['glɒsərɪ] (*pl* -ies) *n* glossário *m*.

glossy ['glɒsɪ] (*compar* -ier, *superl* -iest) *adj* - **1.** [gen] lustroso(sa) - **2.** *fig* [spectacle, display] de luxo.

glossy magazine *n* revista *f* impressa em papel de luxo.

glove [glʌv] *n* luva *f*.

glove compartment *n* porta-luvas *m inv*.

glove puppet *n UK* fantoche *m*.

glow [gləʊ] ◇ *n* - **1.** [light] fulgor *m*, brilho *m* - **2.** [flush] rubor *m* - **3.** *fig* [feeling] arrebatamento *m*. ◇ *vi* - **1.** [fire] arder - **2.** [sky, light, brass] brilhar - **3.** [with colour] resplandecer - **4.** [person]: **to ~ (with sthg)** resplanceder (de algo).

glower ['glaʊə'] *vi*: **to ~ (at sb/sthg)** olhar

ameaçadoramente (para alguém/algo).

glowing ['gləʊɪŋ] adj [very favourable] inflamado(da).

glow-worm n vaga-lume m.

glucose ['glu:kəʊs] n (U) glicose f.

glue [glu:] (cont **glueing** OR **gluing**) ⬦ n (U) cola f. ⬦ vt [stick with glue] colar; **to ~ sthg to sthg** colar algo em algo; **to be ~d to sthg** fig [absorbed by] ficar grudado(da) em algo.

glue-sniffing [-ˌsnɪfɪŋ] n (U) inalação f de cola.

glum [glʌm] (compar **-mer**, superl **-mest**) adj [unhappy] melancólico(ca).

glut [glʌt] n excesso m.

gluten ['glu:tən] n (U) glúten m.

glutinous ['glu:tɪnəs] adj **-1.** [mud] pegajoso(sa) **-2.** [milk pudding, stew] glutinoso(sa) **-3.** [rice] empapado(da).

glutton ['glʌtn] n [greedy person] glutão m, -tona f; **to be a ~ for punishment** gostar de sofrer.

gluttony ['glʌtənɪ] n (U) gula f.

glycerin ['glɪsərɪn], **glycerine** ['glɪsəri:n] n (U) glicerina f.

gm (abbr of **gram**) g.

GMAT (abbr of **Graduate Management Admissions Test**) n exame de admissão no segundo ciclo do ensino superior nos Estados Unidos.

GM foods npl alimentos mpl geneticamente modificados.

GMO (abbr of **genetically modified organism**) ⬦ adj OGM. ⬦ n OGM m.

GMT (abbr of **Greenwich Mean Time**) n horário oficial de Greenwich, GMT m.

gnarled [nɑ:ld] adj **-1.** [tree] nodoso(sa) **-2.** [hands] áspero(ra).

gnash [næʃ] vt : **to ~ one's teeth** ranger os dentes.

gnat [næt] n mosquito m.

gnaw [nɔ:] ⬦ vt [chew] roer. ⬦ vi [worry] atormentar-se; **to ~ (away) at sb** atormentar alguém.

gnome [nəʊm] n gnomo m.

GNP (abbr of **gross national product**) n PNB m.

gnu [nu:] (pl inv OR **-s**) n gnu m.

GNVQ (abbr of **General National Vocational Qualification**) n EDUC curso de formação profissional com duração de dois anos para maiores de 16 anos na Inglaterra e no País de Gales.

go [gəʊ] (pt **went**, pp **gone**, pl **goes**) vi **-1.** [move, travel] ir; **to ~ home** ir para casa; **to ~ to Brazil** ir ao Brasil; **to ~ by bus** ir de ônibus; **to ~ for a walk** fazer um passeio; **to ~ and do sthg** ir fazer algo; **to ~ in** entrar; **to ~ out** sair **-2.** [leave] ir-se; **it's time for us to ~** é hora de irmos embora; **when does the bus ~?** quando é que ônibus sai?; **~ away!** vá embora! **-3.** [attend] ir; **to ~ to school** ir para a escola; **which school do you ~ to?** para que escola você vai? **-4.** [become] ficar; **she went pale** empalideceu; **the milk has gone sour** o leite azedou **-5.** [expressing future tense]: **to be going to do sthg** ir fazer algo **-6.** [function] funcionar; **the car won't ~** o carro não pega **-7.** [stop working] ir-se; **the fuse has gone** o fusível queimou **-8.** [time] passar **-9.** [progress] correr; **to ~ well** correr bem **-10.** [bell, alarm] tocar **-11.** [match] condizer; **to ~ with** condizer com; **red wine doesn't ~ with fish** vinho tinto não combina com peixe **-12.** [be sold] ser vendido; **'everything must ~'** 'liquidação total' **-13.** [fit] caber **-14.** [lead] ir; **where does this path ~?** aonde vai dar este caminho? **-15.** [belong] ir, ser **-16.** [in phrases]: **to let ~ of sthg** [drop] largar algo; **there are two days to ~** faltam dois dias; **to ~ US** [to take away] para levar. ⬦ n **-1.** [turn] vez f; **it's your ~** é a sua vez **-2.** [attempt] tentativa f; **to have a ~ at sthg** experimentar algo; **'50 cents a ~'** [for game] '50 centavos cada vez'.

➤ **go ahead** vi [take place] realizar-se; **~ ahead!** vá em frente!

➤ **go around** vi [revolve] rodar; **there isn't enough cake to ~ around** não tem bolo (suficiente) para todo mundo.

➤ **go back** vi voltar.

➤ **go down** vi [decrease] diminuir; [sun] pôr-se; [tire] esvaziar-se.

➤ **go in** vi entrar.

➤ **go off** vi [alarm, bell] tocar, soar; [go bad] azedar; [light, heating] apagar-se.

➤ **go on** vi [happen] passar-se; [light, heating] acender-se; **to ~ on doing sthg** continuar a fazer algo.

➤ **go out** vi [leave house] sair; [light, fire, cigarette] apagar-se; [have relationship]: **to ~ out with sb** sair com alguém; **to ~ out to eat** ir comer fora.

➤ **go over** vt fus [check] rever.

➤ **go through** vt fus [experience] passar por; [spend] gastar; [search] revistar.

➤ **go up** vi [increase] subir.

➤ **go without** vt fus passar sem.

goad [gəʊd] vt [provoke] provocar; **to ~ sb into doing sthg** incitar alguém a fazer algo.

go-ahead ⬦ adj [dynamic] dinâmico(ca), empreendedor(ra). ⬦ n [permission] permissão f; **give sb the ~ (for sthg)** dar a luz verde a alguém (para algo).

goal [gəʊl] n **-1.** SPORT gol m; **to score a ~** fazer um gol, marcar um gol **-2.** [aim] meta f, objetivo m.

goalie ['gəʊlɪ] n inf goleiro m, -ra f.

goalkeeper ['gəʊlˌki:pə[r]] n goleiro m, -ra f.

goalless ['gəʊllɪs] adj: **~ draw** empate sem gols.

goalmouth ['gəʊlmaʊθ, pl -maʊðz] n boca f do gol.

goalpost ['gəʊlpəʊst] n trave f.

goat [gəʊt] n [animal] cabra f, bode m; **to act the ~** UK comportar-se de forma tola; **to get (on) sb's ~** encher o saco de alguém.

goatee (beard) n cavanhaque m.

goat's cheese n queijo m de cabra.

gob [gɒb] (pt & pp **-bed**, cont **-bing**) v inf ⬦ n **-1.** UK [mouth] matraca f, bico m **-2.** UK [spit] escarro m. ⬦ vi [spit] escarrar.

gobble ['gɒbl] vt devorar.

➤ **gobble down, gobble up** vt sep engolir rapidamente.

gobbledygook ['gɒbldɪgu:k] n **-1.** [incomprehensible language] linguagem f incompreensível, palavreado m sem sentido **-2.** inf [nonsense] asneiras fpl.

go-between n intermediário m, -ria f.

Gobi ['gəʊbɪ] n: **the ~ Desert** o Deserto de Gobi.

goblet ['gɒblɪt] n cálice m.

goblin ['gɒblɪn] *n* duende *m*.

gobsmacked ['gɒbsmækt] *adj UK v inf* embasbacado(da).

go-cart *n* = go-kart.

god [gɒd] *n* deus *m*.
 ➨ **God** ◇ *n* Deus *m*; **God knows** só Deus sabe; **for God's sake!** pelo amor de Deus!; **thank God** graças a Deus; **God willing** se Deus quiser. ◇ *excl*: **(my) God!** (meu) Deus!
 ➨ **gods** *npl UK inf*: **the ~s** THEATRE as galerias.

godchild ['gɒdtʃaɪld] (*pl* -**children** [-ˌtʃɪldrən]) *n* afilhado *m*, -da *f*.

goddam(n) ['gɒdæm] *esp US v inf* ◇ *adj* maldito(ta); **where's the ~ key?** cadê a porcaria da chave?; **what a ~ waste of time!** que perda de tempo imbecil! ◇ *excl* maldito!, maldita!

goddaughter ['gɒdˌdɔːtəʳ] *n* afilhada *f*.

goddess ['gɒdɪs] *n* deusa *f*.

godfather ['gɒdˌfɑːðəʳ] *n* padrinho *m*.

godforsaken ['gɒdfəˌseɪkn] *adj* abandonado(da) por Deus, que Deus esqueceu.

godmother ['gɒdˌmʌðəʳ] *n* madrinha *f*.

godparents ['gɒdˌpeərənts] *npl* padrinhos *mpl*.

godsend ['gɒdsend] *n* dádiva *f* de Deus.

godson ['gɒdsʌn] *n* afilhado *m*.

goes [gəʊz] *vb* ▷ go.

gofer ['gəʊfəʳ] *n US inf* serviçal *m*.

go-getter [-ˈgetəʳ] *n* pessoa *f* dinâmica.

goggle ['gɒgl] *vi*: **to ~ (at sb/sthg)** arregalar os olhos (para alguém ou algo).

goggles ['gɒglz] *npl* óculos *m* de proteção.

go-go dancer *n* dançarina *sexy (de bar, boite)*.

going ['gəʊɪŋ] ◇ *adj* -**1.** [rate, salary] em vigor, atual -**2.** *UK* [available, in existence] disponível; **she's the biggest fool ~** ela é a maior trouxa do momento. ◇ *n* -**1.** [progress] avanço *m*, marcha *f*; **that's good ~** isso é que é andar rápido; **it was slow ~** estava indo devagar; **to be heavy ~** ser pesado(da); **to be easy ~** ser fácil (de lidar) -**2.** [in riding, horse-racing] condições *fpl* (do chão de corrida).

going concern *n* empresa *f* lucrativa e próspera.

goings-on *npl inf* coisas *fpl* estranhas.

go-kart [-kɑːt] *n UK* kart *m*.

Golan Heights ['gəʊˌlæn-] *npl*: **the ~** os Altos de Golan.

gold [gəʊld] ◇ *adj* [gold-coloured] dourado(da). ◇ *n* -**1.** *(U)* [metal] ouro *m*; **to be as good as ~** ser bem comportado(da), ser de ouro -**2.** *(U)* [gold jewellery, ornaments, coins] riquezas *fpl* -**3.** [medal] dobrão *m*. ◇ *comp* [made of gold] de ouro.

golden ['gəʊldən] *adj* -**1.** [made of gold] de ouro -**2.** [gold-coloured] dourado(da).

golden age *n* idade *f* de ouro.

golden eagle *n* águia-real *f*.

golden handshake *n* bolada *f*.

golden opportunity *n* oportunidade *f* de ouro.

golden retriever *n* golden retriever *m*.

golden rule *n* regra *f* de ouro.

golden wedding *n* bodas *fpl* de ouro.

goldfish ['gəʊldfɪʃ] (*pl inv*) *n* peixe-dourado *m*.

goldfish bowl *n* aquário *m* para peixes-dourados.

gold leaf *n (U)* ouro *m* em folha.

gold medal *n* medalha *f* de ouro.

goldmine ['gəʊldmaɪn] *n lit, fig* mina *f* de ouro.

gold-plated [-ˈpleɪtɪd] *adj* banhado(da) a ouro.

gold standard *adj* padrão-ouro *m*.

goldsmith ['gəʊldsmɪθ] *n* ourives *mf*.

golf [gɒlf] *n (U)* golfe *m*.

golf ball *n* -**1.** [for golf] bola *f* de golfe -**2.** [for typewriter] esfera *f*.

golf club *n* -**1.** [association, place] clube *m* de golfe -**2.** [stick] taco *m* de golfe.

golf course *n* campo *m* de golfe.

golfer ['gɒlfəʳ] *n* jogador *m*, -ra *f* de golfe.

golly ['gɒlɪ] *excl inf dated* Deus do céu!

gondola ['gɒndələ] *n* [boat] gôndola *f*.

gondolier [ˌgɒndəˈlɪəʳ] *n* gondoleiro *m*, -ra *f*.

gone [gɒn] ◇ *pp* ▷ **go**. ◇ *adj* [no longer here] que já se foi. ◇ *prep* [past]: **it's just ~ mid-day** já passa do meio-dia; **she's ~ fifty** ela já passou dos cinquenta.

gong [gɒŋ] *n* gongo *f*.

gonna ['gɒnə] *cont inf* = going to.

gonorrh(o)ea [ˌgɒnəˈrɪə] *n (U)* gonorréia *f*.

goo [guː] *n (U) inf* meleca *f*.

good [gʊd] (*compar* better, *superl* best) ◇ *adj* -**1.** [gen] bom, boa; **it feels ~ to be in the fresh air** faz bem estar ao ar livre; **it's ~ that ...** é bom que ...; **to be ~ at sthg** ser bom em algo, ser boa em algo; **to be ~ with** [children, animals] ter jeito com; [one's hands] ter habilidade com -**2.** [kind] gentil; **to be ~ to sb** ser bom para alguém, ser boa para alguém; **to be ~ enough to do sthg** fazer o favor de fazer algo; **a ~ number of people** um bom número de pessoas -**3.** [morally correct] correto(ta) -**4.** [well-behaved] bem-comportado(da); **be ~!** comporte-se bem! -**5.** [beneficial]: **it's ~ for you** faz bem para você -**6.** [attractive] bonito(ta) -**7.** *phr*: **it's a ~ job** OR **thing (that) ...** ainda bem que ...; **~ for you!** que bom para você!; **to give as ~ as one gets** pagar na mesma moeda; **to make sthg ~** reparar algo. ◇ *n* -**1.** *(U)* [benefit, welfare] bem *m*; **for the ~ of** para o bem de; **for your own ~** para o seu próprio bem; **it will do him ~** fará bem a ele -**2.** [use]: **it's no ~** não adianta; **what's the ~ of ...?** qual é a vantagem de ...?; **will this be any ~?** isto serve? -**3.** [morality, virtue] bem *m*; **to be up to no ~** estar com más intenções. ◇ *excl* que bom!
 ➨ **goods** *npl* [merchandise] mercadorias *fpl*; **to come up with** OR **deliver the ~s** *UK inf* fazer o esperado.
 ➨ **as good as** *adv* quase; **it's as ~ as new** está praticamente novo.
 ➨ **for good** *adv* [forever] para sempre.
 ➨ **good afternoon** *excl* boa tarde!
 ➨ **good day** *excl dated* OR *Austr* tenha um bom dia!
 ➨ **good evening** *excl* boa noite!
 ➨ **good morning** *excl* bom dia!
 ➨ **good night** *excl* boa noite!

good behaviour *n* bom comportamento *m*.

goodbye [ˌgʊdˈbaɪ] ◇ *excl* até logo! ◇ *n* adeus *m*.

good deed *n* boa ação *f.*

good-for-nothing ◇ *adj* imprestável. ◇ *n* imprestável *mf.*

good fortune *n* boa sorte *f.*

Good Friday *n* Sexta-Feira *f* Santa.

good-humoured [-'hju:məd] *adj* bem-humorado(da).

good-looking [-'lʊkɪŋ] *adj* [person] bonito(ta).

good manners *npl* boas maneiras *fpl.*

good-natured [-'neɪtʃəd] *adj* **-1.** [person] de bom coração **-2.** [rivalry, argument] amigável.

goodness ['gʊdnɪs] ◇ *n* **-1.** [kindness] bondade *f* **-2.** [nutritive quality] valor *m* nutritivo. ◇ *excl*: **(my) ~!** minha nossa!; **for ~ sake!** pelo amor de Deus!; **thank ~** graças a Deus!; **~ gracious!** Santo Deus!

goods train [gʊdz-] *n UK* trem *m* de carga.

good-tempered [-'tempəd] *adj* calmo(ma).

good turn *n*: **to do sb a ~** fazer um favor a alguém.

goodwill [gʊd'wɪl] *n* **-1.** [kind feelings] boa vontade *f* **-2.** *COMM* fundo *m* de comércio.

goody ['gʊdɪ] (*pl* **-ies**) ◇ *n inf* [good person] mocinho *m*, -nha *f.* ◇ *excl* que ótimo!
➡ goodies *npl inf* **-1.** [delicious food] guloseimas *fpl* **-2.** [desirable objects] coisas *fpl* atraentes.

gooey ['gu:ɪ] (*compar* **gooier**, *superl* **gooiest**) *adj inf* [sticky] grudento(ta).

goof [gu:f] *US inf* ◇ *n* **-1.** [mistake] mancada *f* **-2.** [person] palerma *mf.* ◇ *vi* dar uma mancada.
➡ goof off *vi US inf* vadear.

goofy ['gu:fɪ] (*compar* **-ier**, *superl* **-iest**) *adj* **-1.** *inf* [person] pateta **-2.** *inf* [behaviour, clothes] simplório(ria).

goose [gu:s] (*pl* **geese** [gi:s]) *n* [bird] ganso *m*, -sa *f.*

gooseberry ['gʊzbərɪ] (*pl* **-ies**) *n* **-1.** [fruit] groselha *f* **-2.** *UK inf* [unwanted person]: **to play ~** segurar a vela.

gooseflesh ['gu:sfleʃ], **goose pimples** *UK n*, **goosebumps** *US* ['gu:sbʌmps] *npl* arrepio *m.*

goosestep ['gu:sˌstep] (*pt* & *pp* **-ped**, *cont* **-ping**) ◇ *n* passo *m* de ganso. ◇ *vi* andar a passo de ganso.

GOP (*abbr of* **Grand Old Party**) *n US partido republicano norte-americano.*

gopher ['gəʊfəʳ] *n pequeno roedor semelhante a uma ratazana encontrado nos Estados Unidos.*

gore [gɔ:ʳ] ◇ *n* (*U*) *literary* [blood] sangue *m* (*derramado*). ◇ *vt* [subj: bull] ferir com os chifres.

gorge [gɔ:dʒ] ◇ *n* garganta *f*, desfiladeiro *m.* ◇ *vt*: **to ~ o.s. on** *OR* **with sthg** empanturrar-se com algo.

gorgeous ['gɔ:dʒəs] *adj* **-1.** [place, present, weather] magnífico(ca), maravilhoso(sa) **-2.** *inf* [person] deslumbrante.

gorilla [gə'rɪlə] *n* gorila *m.*

gormless ['gɔ:mlɪs] *adj UK inf* burro(ra).

gorse [gɔ:s] *n* (*U*) tojo *m.*

gory ['gɔ:rɪ] (*compar* **-ier**, *superl* **-iest**) *adj* sangrento(ta).

gosh [gɒʃ] *excl inf* por Deus!

go-slow *n UK* operação *f* tartaruga.

gospel ['gɒspl] ◇ *n* **-1.** [doctrine] evangelho *m* **-2.**: **~ (truth)** verdade absoluta. ◇ *comp* gospel *inv*; **~ music/singer** música/cantor(ra) gospel.
➡ Gospel *n* [in Bible] Evangelho *m.*

gossamer ['gɒsəməʳ] *n* **-1.** [spider's thread] teia *f* de aranha **-2.** [material] *tecido muito fino.*

gossip ['gɒsɪp] ◇ *n* **-1.** [conversation] conversa *f*, bate-papo *m*; **to have a ~** bater papo **-2.** [person] fofoca *f.* ◇ *vi* fofocar.

gossip column *n* coluna *f* social.

got [gɒt] *pt* & *pp* ▷ **get**.

Gothic ['gɒθɪk] *adj* gótico(ca).

gotta ['gɒtə] *cont inf* = **got to**.

gotten ['gɒtn] *pp US* ▷ **get**.

gouge [gaʊdʒ] **➡ gouge out** *vt sep* **-1.** [hole] abrir **-2.** [eyes] arrancar.

goulash ['gu:læʃ] *n* (*U*) gulash *m* (*prato típico húngaro*).

gourd [gʊəd] *n* cabaço *m.*

gourmet ['gʊəmeɪ] ◇ *n* gourmet *m.* ◇ *comp* gastrônomo *m*, -ma *f.*

gout [gaʊt] *n* (*U*) gota *f.*

govern ['gʌvən] ◇ *vt* **-1.** *POL* governar **-2.** [determine] controlar. ◇ *vi POL* governar.

governable *adj POL* governável.

governess ['gʌvənɪs] *n* governanta *f.*

governing ['gʌvənɪŋ] *adj POL* governante.

governing body *n* conselho *m* administrativo.

government ['gʌvnmənt] ◇ *n* **-1.** [group of people] governo *m* **-2.** (*U*) [process] governo *m*; **the art of ~** a arte de governar. ◇ *comp* do governo.

governmental [ˌgʌvn'mentl] *adj* governamental.

government stock *n* títulos *mpl* do governo.

governor ['gʌvənəʳ] *n* **-1.** *POL* governador *m*, -ra *f* **-2.** [of school] diretor *m*, -ra *f* **-3.** [of prison] diretor *m*, -ra *f.*

governor-general (*pl* **governor-generals** *OR* **governors-general**) *n* governador geral *m.*

govt (*abbr of* **government**) *gov.*

gown [gaʊn] *n* **-1.** [dress] vestido *m* **-2.** *UNIV* & *JUR* beca *f* **-3.** *MED* avental *m.*

GP (*abbr of* **general practitioner**) *n* clínico *m* geral.

GPO *n* **-1.** (*abbr of* **General Post Office**) *antigo serviço britânico de correios.* **-2.** (*abbr of* **Government Printing Office**) *departamento de imprensa do governo (norte-americano).*

gr. -1. *abbr of* **gross**. **-2.** (*abbr of* **gram**) g.

grab [græb] (*pt* & *pp* **-bed**, *cont* **-bing**) ◇ *vt* **-1.** [with hands - person, arm] agarrar; [- money] pegar **-2.** *fig* [opportunity, sandwich] pegar; **to ~ the chance to do sthg** aproveitar a oportunidade de fazer algo **-3.** *inf* [appeal to] arrebatar; **how does this ~ you?** o que você me diz disso? ◇ *vi*: **to ~ at sthg** [with hands] tentar agarrar. ◇ *n*: **to make a ~ at** *OR* **for sthg** tentar apoderar-se de algo.

grace [greɪs] ◇ *n* **-1.** (*U*) [elegance] graça *f*, elegância *f* **-2.** [graciousness]: **to have the ~ to do sthg** ter finura para fazer algo; **to do sthg with good ~** fazer algo de bom grado **-3.** (*U*) [extra time] prazo *m* **-4.** [prayer] graças *fpl.* ◇ *vt* **-1.** *fml* [honour] agraciar **-2.** [adorn] enfeitar.

➤ Grace n [title] Eminência f.
graceful [ˈgreɪsfʊl] adj -1. [beautiful] elegante -2. [gracious] amável.
graceless [ˈgreɪslɪs] adj -1. [lacking charm] sem graça -2. [ill-mannered] deselegante.
gracious [ˈgreɪʃəs] <> adj -1. [polite] afável -2. [elegant] elegante. <> excl: **(good)** ~! Santo Deus!, Nossa (Senhora)!
graciously [ˈgreɪʃəslɪ] adv [politely] afavelmente.
gradation [grəˈdeɪʃn] n [of colour, light] gradação f.
grade [greɪd] <> n -1. [level] nível m -2. [quality] qualidade f; **high-~** de alta qualidade; **low-~** de baixa qualidade; **to make the ~** obter sucesso -3. US [in school] série f -4. [mark] classificação f -5. US [gradient] declive m. <> vt -1. [classify] classificar -2. [mark, assess] avaliar.
grade crossing n US passagem f de nível.
grade school n US escola f primária.
grade school teacher n US professor m, -ra f de nível primário.
gradient [ˈgreɪdjənt] n -1. [of road] declive m -2. MATH gradiente m.
gradual [ˈgrædʒʊəl] adj gradual.
gradually [ˈgrædʒʊəlɪ] adv gradualmente.
graduate [n ˈgrædʒʊət, vb ˈgrædʒʊeɪt] <> n -1. [person with a degree] graduado m, -da f, licenciado m, -da f -2. US: **to be a high-school ~** ter completado o segundo grau. <> comp US [postgraduate] pós-graduado(da). <> vi -1. [with a degree]: **to ~** graduar-se -2. US [from high school]: **to ~** formar-se -3. [progress]: **to ~ from sthg (to sthg)** passar OR evoluir de algo (para algo).
graduated [ˈgrædʒʊeɪtɪd] adj [gen] graduado(da); [pension, tax] retroativo(va).
graduate school n US escola f de pós-graduação.
graduation [ˌgrædʒʊˈeɪʃn] n -1. [completion of course] formatura f -2. [ceremony - at university] colação f de grau; US [at high school] formatura f.
graffiti [grəˈfiːtɪ] n (U) pichação f.
graft [grɑːft] <> n -1. [gen] enxerto m -2. UK inf [hard work] labuta f -3. US inf [corruption] suborno m. <> vt -1. enxertar; **to ~ sthg onto sthg** enxertar algo em algo -2. [idea, system] combinar; **to ~ sthg onto sthg** combinar algo com algo.
grain [greɪn] n -1. [of corn, rice, salt] grão m -2. (U) [crops] cereais mpl -3. fig [small amount] parcela f mínima; **there wasn't a ~ of truth in what he said** não havia uma palavra de verdade no que ele disse -4. (U) [of wood] veio m; **it goes against the ~ for me** fig vai contra a minha natureza.
gram [græm] n grama f.
grammar [ˈgræmər] n gramática f.
grammar school n -1. [in UK] ginásio m -2. [in US] escola f primária.
grammatical [grəˈmætɪkl] adj gramatical.
gramme [græm] n UK = gram.
gramophone [ˈgræməfəʊn] dated <> n gramofone m. <> comp de gramofone.
gran [græn] n UK inf vovó f.
Granada [grəˈnɑːdə] n Granada; **in ~** em Granada.
granary [ˈgrænərɪ] (pl -ies) n celeiro m.

granary bread n pão m de trigo.
grand [grænd] (pl inv) <> adj -1. [impressive, imposing] magnífico(ca) -2. [ambitious, large-scale] ambicioso(-sa) -3. [socially important] ilustre -4. inf dated [excellent] excelente. <> n inf [thousand pounds] mil libras fpl; [thousand dollars] mil dólares mpl.
grandad n inf vovô m.
Grand Canyon n: the ~ o Grand Canyon.
grandchild [ˈgræntʃaɪld] (pl -children [-ˌtʃɪldrən]) n neto m, -ta f.
granddad [ˈgrændæd] n inf = grandad.
granddaughter [ˈgrænˌdɔːtər] n neta f.
grand duchess n [noblewoman] grã-duquesa f.
grand duke n [nobleman] grão-duque m.
grandeur [ˈgrændʒər] n grandeza f.
grandfather [ˈgrændˌfɑːðər] n avô m.
grandfather clock n relógio m de pêndulo.
grandiose [ˈgrændɪəʊz] adj pej espalhafatoso(sa).
grand jury n US júri m principal.
grandma [ˈgrænmɑː] n inf vovó f, vó f.
grand master n grão-mestre m.
grandmother [ˈgrænˌmʌðər] n avó f.
Grand National n: the ~ a Grand National, corrida de cavalos realizada anualmente em Liverpool, na Inglaterra.
grandpa [ˈgrænpɑː] n inf vovô m, vô m.
grandparents [ˈgrænˌpeərənts] npl avós mpl.
grand piano n piano m de cauda.
grand prix [ˌgrɒnˈpriː] (pl grands prix) n grande prêmio m.
grand slam n SPORT grand slam m.
grandson [ˈgrænsʌn] n neto m.
grandstand [ˈgrændstænd] n tribuna f de honra.
grand total n total m geral.
granite [ˈgrænɪt] n (U) granito m.
granny [ˈgrænɪ] (pl -ies) n inf vovó f, vó f.
granny flat n UK local dentro ou próximo à casa de uma pessoa, feito para que um parente de idade possa viver nele.
granola [grəˈnəʊlə] n US granola f.
grant [grɑːnt] <> n [money - for renovations] subsídio m; [- for study] bolsa f. <> vt fml -1. [agree to] conceder -2. [accept as true] admitir; **I ~ (that) ...** eu admito que ... -3. phr: **to take sb/sthg for ~** não dar o devido valor a alguém/algo; **to take it for ~ed that ...** tomar como certo que ...
granulated sugar [ˈgrænjʊleɪtɪd-] n (U) açúcar m -cristal.
granule [ˈgrænjuːl] n grânulo m.
grape [greɪp] n uva f.
grapefruit [ˈgreɪpfruːt] (pl inv OR -s) n pomelo m.
grape picking [-ˈpɪkɪŋ] n (U) colheita f de uvas.
grapevine [ˈgreɪpvaɪn] n -1. [plant] parreira f -2. fig [information channel]: **I heard on the ~ that ...** um passarinho me contou que ...
graph [grɑːf] n gráfico m.
graphic [ˈgræfɪk] adj -1. [vivid] vívido(da) -2. ART pitoresco(ca).
➤ graphics npl [pictures] artes fpl gráficas; **computer ~s** gráfico m de computador.
graphic artist n artista mf gráfico, -ca.
graphic design n (U) projeto m gráfico.

graphic designer n projetista mf gráfico, -ca.

graphic equalizer n equalizador m gráfico.

graphics card n COMPUT placa f gráfica.

graphite ['græfaɪt] n (U) grafita f.

graphology [græ'fɒlədʒɪ] n (U) grafologia f.

graph paper n (U) papel m quadriculado.

grapple ['græpl] ➡ **grapple with** vt fus -1. [physically] atracar-se com -2. fig [mentally] estar às voltas com.

grappling iron ['græplɪŋ-] n arpéu m.

grasp [grɑːsp] <> n -1. [grip] agarramento m -2. [power to achieve]: **in** OR **within one's** ~ ao alcance de alguém -3. [understanding] compreensão f; **to have a good** ~ **of sthg** ter um bom domínio de algo. <> vt -1. [with hands] segurar -2. [understand] compreender -3. fig [seize] agarrar.

grasping ['grɑːspɪŋ] adj pej [greedy - person] ganancioso(sa); [- attitude] avaro(ra).

grass [grɑːs] <> n -1. [common green plant] grama f -2. (U) drugs sl [marijuana] maconha f. <> vi UK crime sl: **to** ~ **(on sb)** dedurar alguém.

grasshopper ['grɑːsˌhɒpəʳ] n gafanhoto m.

grassland ['grɑːslænd] n pastagem f.

grass roots <> npl [ordinary people] plebe f. <> comp popular.

grass snake n cobra f d'água.

grassy ['grɑːsɪ] (compar -ier, superl -iest) adj coberto(ta) de grama.

grate [greɪt] <> n [fireplace] grade f. <> vt CULIN ralar. <> vi [irritate] irritar; **to** ~ **on sb's nerves** deixar alguém com os nervos à flor da pele.

grateful ['greɪtfʊl] adj agradecido(da); **to be** ~ **to sb (for sthg)** ser grato(ta) a alguém (por algo).

gratefully ['greɪtfʊlɪ] adv agradecidamente.

grater ['greɪtəʳ] n ralador m.

gratification [ˌgrætɪfɪ'keɪʃn] n -1. [pleasure] gratificação f -2. [satisfaction] satisfação f.

gratify ['grætɪfaɪ] (pt & pp -ied) vt -1. [please]: **to be gratified** sentir-se gratificado(da) -2. [satisfy] satisfazer.

gratifying ['grætɪfaɪɪŋ] adj [pleasing] gratificante.

grating ['greɪtɪŋ] <> adj áspero(ra). <> n [grille] grade f.

gratitude ['grætɪtjuːd] n (U) gratidão f; ~ **to sb (for sthg)** gratidão por alguém (por algo).

gratuitous [grə'tjuːɪtəs] adj fml [unjustified] gratuito(ta).

gratuity [grə'tjuːɪtɪ] (pl -ies) n fml [tip] gratificação f.

grave [greɪv] <> adj grave. <> n túmulo m; **to turn in one's** ~ revirar-se no túmulo; **to dig one's own** ~ cavar a própria sepultura.

grave accent [grɑːv-] n acento m grave.

gravedigger ['greɪvˌdɪgəʳ] n coveiro m, -ra f.

gravel ['grævl] <> n (U) cascalho m. <> comp de cascalho.

gravelled UK, **graveled** US ['grævld] adj de cascalho.

gravestone ['greɪvstəʊn] n lápide f.

graveyard ['greɪvjɑːd] n cemitério m.

gravitate ['grævɪteɪt] vi: **to** ~ **towards sb/sthg** fig [be attracted to] ser atraído(da) por alguém/algo.

gravity ['grævətɪ] n -1. [force] gravidade f -2. fml [seriousness, worrying nature] seriedade f, gravidade

f -3. [solemnity] gravidade f.

gravy ['greɪvɪ] n -1. [meat juice] molho m de carne; [sauce] caldo m de carne -2. US v inf [easy money] grana f fácil.

gravy boat n molheira f.

gravy train n inf: **the** ~ a mina de ouro.

gray adj & n US = grey.

grayscale n US = greyscale.

graze [greɪz] <> n [wound] machucado m, ferimento m. <> vt -1. [feed on] pastar -2. [cause to feed] pastorear -3. [break surface of] esfolar -4. [touch lightly] tocar de leve. <> vi [animals] pastar.

grease [griːs] <> n -1. [animal fat] gordura f -2. [lubricant] graxa f -3. [dirt] sebo m. <> vt -1. [gen] engraxar -2. [baking tray] untar.

grease gun n bomba f engraxadeira.

greasepaint ['griːspeɪnt] n (U) maquilagem f para o teatro.

greaseproof paper [ˌgriːspruːf-] n (U) UK papel m parafinado.

greasy ['griːzɪ] (compar -ier, superl -iest) adj -1. [food] gorduroso(sa); [tools] engordurado(da); [hair, hands, skin] seboso(sa) -2. [clothes] sujo(ja) -3. [road] escorregadio(dia).

greasy spoon n hum [cafe] boteco m.

great [greɪt] <> adj -1. [gen] grande -2. inf [really good, really nice] ótimo(ma). <> n grande mf. <> excl ótimo!

Great Barrier Reef n: **the** ~ a Grande Barreira.

Great Bear n: **the** ~ (a) Ursa Maior.

Great Britain n Grã-Bretanha; **in** ~ na Grã-Bretanha.

greatcoat ['greɪtkəʊt] n sobretudo m pesado.

Great Dane n pastor m dinamarquês.

Great Depression n: **the** ~ a Grande Depressão.

great-grandchild n bisneto m, -ta f.

great-grandfather n bisavô m.

great-grandmother n bisavó f.

Great Lakes npl: **the** ~ os Grandes Lagos.

greatly ['greɪtlɪ] adv imensamente; ~ **exaggerated** muito exagerado(da); ~ **different** extremamente diferente.

greatness ['greɪtnɪs] n grandeza f.

Great Wall of China n: **the** ~ a Grande Muralha da China.

Great War n: **the** ~ a Grande Guerra.

Greece [griːs] n Grécia f; **in** ~ na Grécia.

greed [griːd] n -1. [for food] gula f -2. fig [for money, power]: ~ **(for sthg)** ganância (por algo).

greedily ['griːdɪlɪ] adv gulosamente.

greedy ['griːdɪ] (compar -ier, superl -iest) adj -1. [for food] guloso(sa) -2. fig [for money, power]: ~ **for sthg** ganancioso(sa) por algo.

Greek [griːk] <> adj grego(ga); **the** ~ **Islands** as Ilhas Gregas. <> n -1. [person] grego m, -ga f -2. [language] grego m.

green [griːn] <> adj -1. [gen] verde -2. inf [with nausea, fear] pálido(da) -3. inf [inexperienced] novato(ta) -4. inf [jealous]: ~ **(with envy)** morto(ta) de ciúme. <> n -1. [colour] verde; **in** ~ de verde -2. [in village] praça f -3. GOLF green m.

Green n *POL* Verde; **the Greens** os Verdes.
greens *npl* [vegetables] verduras *fpl*.
greenback ['gri:nbæk] n *US inf* [banknote] nota *f* de dólar.
green bean n vagem *f*.
green belt n *UK* área *f* verde.
Green Beret n *US inf*: **the ~s** os Green Berets, *membros das Forças Especiais norte-americanas*.
green card n - **1.** *UK* [for insuring vehicle] *seguro que protege veículos e motoristas no exterior* - **2.** *US* [resident's permit] green card *m*, visto *m* permanente *(nos Estados Unidos)*.

GREEN CARD

Assim se denomina o documento que permite a um estrangeiro viver e trabalhar nos Estados Unidos. A despeito do nome, hoje o *green card* já não é verde. O processo para sua obtenção é longo e complexo. O interessado deve possuir um parente próximo que seja cidadão estadunidense ou estar empregado numa companhia do país. Do contrário, precisará comprovar que tem condições de fazer investimentos financeiros nos Estados Unidos.

greenery ['gri:nəri] n (U) folhagem *f*.
green fingers *npl UK*: **to have ~** ter dom/mão boa para jardinagem.
greenfly ['gri:nflaɪ] (*pl inv OR* -**ies**) n pulgão *m*.
greengage ['gri:ngeɪdʒ] n rainha-cláudia *f*.
greengrocer ['gri:n,grəʊsəʳ] n verdureiro(ra); **~'s** **(shop)** quitanda *f*.
greenhorn ['gri:nhɔ:n] n *US* - **1.** [immigrant, new arrival] recém-chegado *m*, -da *f* - **2.** [novice] novato *m*, -ta *f*.
greenhouse ['gri:nhaʊs, *pl* -haʊzɪz] n estufa *f*.
greenhouse effect n: **the ~** o efeito estufa.
greenhouse gas n gás *m* de efeito estufa.
greenish ['gri:nɪʃ] *adj* esverdeado(da).
Greenland ['gri:nlənd] n Groenlândia; **in ~** na Groenlândia.
Greenlander ['gri:nləndəʳ] n groenlandês *m*, -esa *f*.
green light n: **the ~** o sinal verde.
green paper n *POL* projeto de lei.
Green Party n: **the ~** o Partido Verde.
green salad n salada *f* verde.
green thumb n *US*: **to have a ~** ter dom/mão boa para jardinagem.
greet [gri:t] *vt* - **1.** [say hello to] cumprimentar - **2.** [speech, announcement, remark] saudar - **3.** [subj: sight, smell] receber.
greeting ['gri:tɪŋ] n [salutation] cumprimento *m*, saudação *f*.
greetings *npl* [on card] votos *mpl*.
greetings card *UK* ['gri:tɪŋz-], **greeting card** *US* n cartão *m* de comemoração.
gregarious [grɪ'geərɪəs] *adj* gregário(ria).
gremlin ['gremlɪn] n *inf* duende *m* que supostamente provoca o mau funcionamento de motores ou outros equipamentos, gremlin *m*.
Grenada [grə'neɪdə] n Granada; **in ~** em Granada.

grenade [grə'neɪd] n: **(hand) ~** granada *f* (de mão).
Grenadian [grə'neɪdjən] <> *adj* granadino(na). <> n granadino *m*, -na *f*.
grenadier [,grenə'dɪəʳ] n granadeiro *m*.
grew [gru:] *pt* ⊳ **grow**.
grey *UK*, **gray** *US* [greɪ] <> *adj* - **1.** [colour, weather] cinzento(ta) - **2.** [hair, beard] grisalho(lha); **to go ~** ficar grisalho(lha) - **3.** [complexion - with fatigue, nausea] desolado(da); [- skin] envelhecido(da) - **4.** *fig* [life, situation] preto(ta). <> n cinza *m*; **in ~** de cinza.
grey area n área *f* cinzenta.
grey-haired [-'heəd] *adj* grisalho(lha).
greyhound ['greɪhaʊnd] n galgo *m*.
greying *UK*, **graying** *US* ['greɪɪŋ] *adj* acinzentado(da).
grey matter n - **1.** *MED* massa *f* cinzenta - **2.** *inf* [brain power] inteligência *f*.
greyscale *UK*, **grayscale** *US* ['greɪskeɪl] n *COMPUT* escala *f* de tons.
grey squirrel n esquilo *m* cinzento.
grid [grɪd] n - **1.** [grating] gradeamento *m* - **2.** [system of squares] grade *f* - **3.** *ELEC* rede *f*.
griddle ['grɪdl] n chapa *f* de ferro *(para assar)*.
gridiron ['grɪd,aɪən] n - **1.** [in cooking] grelha *f* - **2.** *US* [game] futebol *m* americano; [field] campo *m* de futebol americano.
gridlock ['grɪdlɒk] n empasse *m*.
grid reference n coordenadas *fpl*.
grief [gri:f] n - **1.** [sorrow] pesar *m*, tristeza *f* - **2.** *inf* [trouble] chateação *f* - **3.** *phr*: **to come to ~** fracassar; **good ~!** credo!
grief-stricken *adj* agoniado(da).
grievance ['gri:vns] n [complaint] queixa *f*, agravo *m*.
grieve [gri:v] <> *vt fml*: **it ~s me to say that** me dói dizer que. <> *vi*: **to ~ (for sb/sthg)** estar de luto por alguém/algo.
grieving ['gri:vɪŋ] n (U) luto *m*.
grievous ['gri:vəs] *adj fml* [serious, harmful] doloroso(sa).
grievous bodily harm n (U) lesão *f* corporal.
grievously ['gri:vəslɪ] *adv fml* gravemente.
grill [grɪl] <> n - **1.** [for cooking] grelha *f* - **2.** [food] grelhado *m*. <> *vt* - **1.** [cook on grill] grelhar - **2.** *inf* [interrogate] interrogar.
grille [grɪl] n grade *f*.
grim [grɪm] (*compar* -**mer**, *superl* -**mest**) *adj* - **1.** [stern] severo(ra), rígido(da) - **2.** [gloomy] deprimente.
grimace [grɪ'meɪs] <> n careta *f*. <> *vi* fazer caretas.
grime [graɪm] n (U) sujeira *f*.
grimly ['grɪmlɪ] *adv* - **1.** [unhappily] severamente - **2.** [with determination] rigidamente.
grimy ['graɪmɪ] (*compar* -**ier**, *superl* -**iest**) *adj* imundo(da).
grin [grɪn] (*pt & pp* -**ned**, *cont* -**ning**) <> n sorriso *m* aberto. <> *vi*: **to ~ (at sb/sthg)** abrir um sorriso (para alguém/algo); **to ~ and bear it** aceitar (algo) e aguentar firme.
grind [graɪnd] (*pt & pp* **ground**) <> *vt* - **1.** [coffee, pepper, grain] moer; **freshly ground coffee** café

moído na hora **- 2.** [ash, dirt]**: to ~ sthg into sthg**
esmagar algo em algo **- 3.** [rub together] ranger.
◇ *vi* [scrape] arranhar. ◇ *n* **-1.** [hard, boring work]
rotina *f* **- 2.** *US inf***: to go ~** ficar grisalho(lha).

➤ **grind down** *vt sep* [oppress] oprimir.

➤ **grind up** *vt sep* **-1.** [bottles] triturar **- 2.** [knife]
afiar **- 3.** *US* [meat] picar **- 4.** [gemstone] lapidar.

grinder [ˈɡraɪndə^r] *n* [machine] moedor *m*.

grinding [ˈɡraɪndɪŋ] *adj* [oppressive] opressivo(va).

grinning *adj* sorridente.

grip [ɡrɪp] (*pt & pp* -**ped**, *cont* -**ping**) ◇ *n* **-1.** [phy-
sical hold]**: to have a ~ on sb/sthg** ter o controle
sobre algúem/algo; **to keep a ~ on the handrail**
segurar-se no corrimão; **to get a good ~** dar um
bom aperto; **to release one's ~ on sb/sthg** deixar
de controlar algúem/algo **- 2.** [control, domination]
domínio *m*; **~ on sb/sthg** controle sobre algúem/
algo; **in the ~ of sthg** nas garras de algo; **to get to
~ s with sthg** encarar algo; **to get a ~ on o.s.**
controlar-se; **to lose one's ~** *fig* perder a eficiência
- 3. *(U)* [adhesion] aderência *f* **- 4.** [handle] punho *m*
- 5. *dated* [bag] valise *f*. ◇ *vt* **-1.** [grasp] agarrar **- 2.**
[subj: tyres] ter aderência a **- 3.** [imagination, atten-
tion] controlar.

gripe [ɡraɪp] *inf* ◇ *n* [complaint] queixa *f*; **the ~ s**
cólicas *fpl*. ◇ *vi***: to ~ (about sthg)** resmungar
(por causa de algo).

gripping [ˈɡrɪpɪŋ] *adj* [story, film] emocionante.

grisly [ˈɡrɪzlɪ] (*compar* -**ier**, *superl* -**iest**) *adj* [horrible,
macabre] horrendo(da), medonho(nha).

grist [ɡrɪst] *n (U)***: it's all ~ to sb's** *OR* **the mill** tudo
vale *OR* serve.

gristle [ˈɡrɪsl] *n (U)* cartilagem *f*.

gristly [ˈɡrɪslɪ] (*compar* -**ier**, *superl* -**iest**) *adj* cartila-
ginoso(sa).

grit [ɡrɪt] (*pt & pp* -**ted**, *cont* -**ting**) ◇ *n* **-1.** [stones]
areia *f* **- 2.** *inf* [courage] coragem *f*. ◇ *vt* [road,
steps] pôr areia em.

➤ **grits** *npl* *US* canjica *f*.

gritter [ˈɡrɪtə^r] *n* veículo que espalha areia nas
estradas congeladas.

gritty [ˈɡrɪtɪ] (*compar* -**ier**, *superl* -**iest**) *adj* **-1.** [stony]
arenoso(sa) **- 2.** *inf* [brave] corajoso(sa).

grizzled [ˈɡrɪzld] *adj* acinzentado(da).

grizzly [ˈɡrɪzlɪ] (*pl* -**ies**) *n*: **~ (bear)** urso-cinzento
m.

groan [ɡrəʊn] ◇ *n* gemido *m*. ◇ *vi* **-1.** [moan]
gemer **- 2.** [creak] ranger **- 3.** [complain] resmungar.

grocer [ˈɡrəʊsə^r] *n* dono *m*, -na *f* de mercearia; **~ 's
(shop)** mercearia *f*.

groceries [ˈɡrəʊsərɪz] *npl* [foods] comestíveis *mpl*.

grocery [ˈɡrəʊsərɪ] (*pl* -**ies**) *n* [shop] mercearia *f*.

groggy [ˈɡrɒɡɪ] (*compar* -**ier**, *superl* -**iest**) *adj* grogue.

groin [ɡrɔɪn] *n ANAT* virilha *f*.

groom [ɡruːm] ◇ *n* **-1.** [of horses] cavalariço *m* **- 2.**
[bridegroom] noivo *m*. ◇ *vt* **-1.** [horse, dog] tratar **- 2.**
[candidate]**: to ~ sb (for sthg)** preparar algúem
(para algo).

groomed *adj*: **well/badly ~** bem/mal tratado(-
da).

groove [ɡruːv] *n* **-1.** [in metal, wood] entalhe *m* **- 2.** [in
record] ranhura *f*.

grope [ɡrəʊp] ◇ *vt* **-1.** [sexually] acariciar **- 2.** [try to

find]**: to ~ one's way** tatear o caminho. ◇ *vi***: to
~ (about) for sthg** [object] tatear por algo; *fig* [so-
lution, remedy] tentar algo às cegas.

gross [ɡrəʊs] (*pl inv OR* -**es**) ◇ *adj* **-1.** [total] bruto(ta)
- 2. *fml* [serious, inexcusable] grave **- 3.** *inf* [coarse, vul-
gar] indecente **- 4.** *inf* [obese] balofo(fa) **- 5.** *inf* [dis-
gusting] nojento(ta). ◇ *n* grosa *f*. ◇ *vt* [subj:
person] receber em bruto; [subj: store, film] arrecadar em bruto.

gross domestic product *n* produto *m* interno
bruto.

grossly [ˈɡrəʊslɪ] *adv* [for emphasis] extremamente.

gross national product *n* produto *m* nacional
bruto.

gross profit *n* lucro *m* bruto.

grotesque [ɡrəʊˈtesk] *adj* [strange, unnatural] grotes-
co(ca).

grotto [ˈɡrɒtəʊ] (*pl* -**es** *OR* -**s**) *n* gruta *f*.

grotty [ˈɡrɒtɪ] (*compar* -**ier**, *superl* -**iest**) *adj UK inf*
asqueroso(sa).

grouchy [ˈɡraʊtʃɪ] (*compar* -**ier**, *superl* -**iest**) *adj inf*
mal-humorado(da).

ground [ɡraʊnd] ◇ *pt & pp* ➤ grind. ◇ *n* **-1.**
[surface of earth] terra *f*, chão *m*; **above/below ~**
em cima/embaixo da terra; **on the ~** no chão; **to
be thin on the ~** ser pouco numeroso(sa); **to get
sthg off the ~** *fig* iniciar algo com sucesso **- 2.** *(U)*
[area of land] terreno *m* **- 3.** [area used for a particular
purpose] campo *m* **- 4.** [subject area] área *f*; **to break
fresh** *OR* **new ~** dar o primeiro passo **- 5.** [advan-
tage]**: to gain/lose ~** ganhar/perder terreno **- 6.**
*phr***: to cut the ~ from under sb's feet** puxar o
tapete de alguém; **to go to ~** esconder-se; **to run
sb/sthg to ~** encontrar alguém/algo; **to run o.s.
into the ~** trabalhar até a exaustão; **to stand
one's ~** defender seu ponto de vista. ◇ *vt* **-1.**
[base]**: to be ~ed on** *OR* **in sthg** ter algo como
base; **to be well-~ed in sthg** estar bem baseado
em algo **- 2.** [aircraft, pilot] ficar retido(da) **- 3.** *esp US*
inf [child] ficar de castigo **- 4.** *US ELEC***: to be ~ ed** ter
um fio-terra.

➤ **grounds** *npl* **-1.** [reason] razão *f*, motivo *m*;
~ s for sthg/for doing sthg motivo para algo/
para fazer algo; **on the ~ s of** com o pretexto de;
on the ~ s that com o motivo de que **- 2.** [land round
building] jardins *mpl* **- 3.** [area for specific purpose] área
f **- 4.** [of coffee] borra *f*.

ground control *n* controle *m* de terra.

ground cover *n (U)* vegetação *f* rasteira.

ground crew *n* equipe *f* de terra.

ground floor *n* (andar *m*) térreo *m*.

ground-in *adj* impregnado(da).

grounding [ˈɡraʊndɪŋ] *n*: **~ (in sthg)** conhecimentos *mpl* básicos (sobre algo).

groundless [ˈɡraʊndlɪs] *adj* infundado(da).

ground level *n*: **at ~** ao nível do solo.

groundnut [ˈɡraʊndnʌt] *n* amendoim *m*.

ground plan *n* [of building] planta *f* baixa.

ground rent *n* aluguel *m* residencial.

ground rules *npl* regras *fpl* básicas.

groundsheet [ˈɡraʊndʃiːt] *n* lona *f*.

groundsman [ˈɡraʊndzmən] (*pl* -**men** [-mən]) *n UK*
zelador *m* de campo esportivo.

ground staff n -1. [at sports ground] equipe f de campo -2. UK [at airport] pessoal m de terra.

groundswell ['graʊndswell] n [of feeling] acirramento m.

groundwork ['graʊndwɜːk] n (U) base f, fundamento m.

group [gruːp] ◇ n -1. [gen] grupo m -2. MUS banda f. ◇ vt agrupar; [classify] classificar. ◇ vi: to ~ (together) agrupar-se.

group captain n UK ≃ coronel m (de aviação).

groupie ['gruːpɪ] n inf tiete mf.

group practice n prática médica empreendida por um grupo de médicos associados que trabalham juntos como colegas ou como especialistas de áreas diferentes.

group therapy n (U) terapia f de grupo.

grouse [graʊs] (pl sense 1 inv OR -s, pl sense 2 -s) ◇ n -1. [bird] galo-silvestre m -2. inf [complaint] queixa f. ◇ vi inf queixar-se.

grove [grəʊv] n -1. [of trees] arvoredo m -2. [of fruit trees] pomar m.

grovel ['grɒvl] (UK pt & pp -led, cont -ling, US pt & pp -ed, cont -ing) vi -1. pej [humble o.s.] humilhar-se; to ~ to sb humilhar-se diante de alguém -2. [crawl on floor] rastejar.

grow [grəʊ] (pt grew, pp grown) ◇ vt -1. [plants] cultivar -2. [hair, beard] deixar crescer. ◇ vi -1. [plant, hair, person] crescer; [company, city, economy, plan] desenvolver-se -2. [seeds] germinar -3. [increase] aumentar -4. [become] tornar-se; to ~ tired of sthg cansar-se de algo -5. [do eventually]: to ~ to do sthg passar a fazer algo.

　◆ **grow apart** vi [become less friendly] distanciar-se.

　◆ **grow into** vt fus [clothes, shoes] crescer o suficiente para poder vestir.

　◆ **grow on** vt fus inf [please more and more]: this book is growing on me gosto cada vez mais deste livro.

　◆ **grow out** vi [perm, dye] desbotar.

　◆ **grow out of** vt fus -1. [clothes, shoes]: he's grown out of all his clothes as roupas dele ficaram pequenas -2. [habit] perder.

　◆ **grow up** vi crescer.

grower ['grəʊə^r] n [person] produtor m, -ra f, agricultor m, -ra f.

growl [graʊl] ◇ n -1. [of dog] rosnar m -2. [of lion] rugido m -3. [of engine] rangido m -4. [of person] resmungo m. ◇ vi -1. [dog] rosnar -2. [lion] rugir -3. [engine] ranger -4. [person] resmungar.

grown [grəʊn] ◇ pp ▷ grow. ◇ adj crescido(-da).

grown-up ◇ adj -1. [fully grown, full-sized] crescido(da) -2. [mature, sensible] maduro(ra). ◇ n adulto m, -ta f.

growth [grəʊθ] n -1. (U) [development, increase] crescimento m -2. MED [lump] tumor m, abscesso m.

growth rate n taxa f de crescimento.

grub [grʌb] n -1. [insect] larva f -2. (U) inf [food] rango m.

grubby ['grʌbɪ] (compar -ier, superl -iest) adj encardido(da).

grudge [grʌdʒ] ◇ n ressentimento m; to bear sb a ~, to bear a ~ against sb guardar rancor contra alguém. ◇ vt ressentir, lamentar; to ~ sb sthg invejar alguém por algo; to ~ doing sthg fazer algo com má vontade.

grudging ['grʌdʒɪŋ] adj relutante.

grudgingly ['grʌdʒɪŋlɪ] adv com relutância.

gruelling UK, **grueling** US ['grʊəlɪŋ] adj árduo(-dua).

gruesome ['gruːsəm] adj horrível.

gruff [grʌf] adj -1. [hoarse] rouco(ca) -2. [rough, unfriendly] brusco(ca).

grumble ['grʌmbl] ◇ n -1. [complaint] resmungo m -2. [rumble - thunder, stomach] ronco m; [- train] rebôo m. ◇ vi -1. [complain] resmungar; to ~ about sthg resmungar por algo -2. [rumble - thunder, stomach] roncar; [- train] reboar.

grumbling ['grʌmblɪŋ] n -1. [complaining] resmungo m -2. [rumbling] ronco m.

grumpy ['grʌmpɪ] (compar -ier, superl -iest) adj -1. inf [person] resmungão(ona) -2. inf [face] rabugento(ta).

grunt [grʌnt] ◇ n -1. [of pig] grunhido m -2. [of person] resmungo m. ◇ vi -1. [pig] grunhir -2. [person] resmungar.

G-string n -1. MUS corda f G -2. [clothing] tanga f tapa-sexo.

Guadeloupe [ˌgwɑːdə'luːp] n Guadalupe; in ~ em Guadalupe.

Guam n Guam; in ~ em Guam.

guarantee [ˌgærən'tiː] ◇ n garantia f; under ~ sob garantia. ◇ vt -1. COMM dar garantia para -2. [promise] garantir.

guarantor [ˌgærən'tɔː^r] n fiador m, -ra f.

guard [gɑːd] ◇ n -1. [person] guarda mf -2. [group of guards] guarda f -3. [supervision] proteção f; to be on ~ estar em guarda; to stand ~ estar de guarda; to be on (one's) ~ (against sthg) estar alerta (em relação a algo); to catch sb off ~ pegar alguém desprevenido(da) -4. UK RAIL chefe mf de trem -5. [protective device] dispositivo m de segurança -6. [in boxing] proteção f. ◇ vt -1. [protect] proteger -2. [prevent from escaping] vigiar.

　◆ **guard against** vt fus prevenir-se contra.

guard dog n cão m de guarda.

guarded ['gɑːdɪd] adj [careful] cauteloso(sa).

guardian ['gɑːdjən] n -1. JUR [of child] guardião m, -diã f -2. [protector] curador m, -ra f.

guardian angel n anjo m da guarda.

guardianship ['gɑːdjənʃɪp] n (U) tutela f.

guard rail n US [on road] proteção f lateral.

guardsman ['gɑːdzmən] (pl -men [-mən]) n sentinela mf.

guard's van n UK vagão m de freio.

Guatemala [ˌgwɑːtə'mɑːlə] n Guatemala; in ~ na Guatemala.

Guatemalan [ˌgwɑːtə'mɑːlən] ◇ adj guatemalteco(ca). ◇ n guatemalteco m, -ca f.

guava ['gwɑːvə] n -1. [fruit] goiaba f -2. [tree] goiabeira f.

guerilla [gə'rɪlə] n = guerrilla.

Guernsey ['gɜːnzɪ] n -1. [place] Guernsey; in ~ em Guernsey -2. [sweater] pulôver m de lã (originalmente usado por pescadores) -3. [cow] Guernsey.

guerrilla [gə'rɪlə] n guerrilheiro m, -ra f; **urban ~** guerrilheiro urbano, guerrilheira urbana.

guerrilla warfare n (U) guerrilha f.

guess [ges] ◇ n -**1.** [at facts, figures] suposição f; **to take a ~** adivinhar -**2.** [hypothesis] hipótese f; **it's anybody's ~** não há como saber. ◇ vt [assess correctly] adivinhar; **~ what!** adivinha! ◇ vi -**1.** [attempt to answer] chutar; **to ~ at sthg** tentar adivinhar algo; **to keep sb ~ing** não contar a alguém -**2.** [think, suppose]: **I ~ (so)** eu acho (que sim).

guesstimate ['gestɪmət] n inf estimativa f aproximada.

guesswork ['gesw3:k] n (U) adivinhação f.

guest [gest] n -**1.** [visitor - at home] visita mf; [- at club, restaurant, concert] convidado m, -da f -**2.** [at hotel] hóspede mf -**3.** [in show] convidado m, -da f especial -**4.** phr: **be my ~!** seja meu convidado!

guesthouse ['gesthaʊs, pl -haʊzɪz] n pensão f.

guest of honour n convidado m, -da f de honra.

guestroom ['gestrʊm] n quarto m de hóspedes.

guest star n ator m convidado, atriz f convidada.

guffaw [gʌ'fɔ:] ◇ n gargalhada f. ◇ vi gargalhar, dar gargalhadas.

Guiana [gaɪ'ænə] n Guiana; **in ~** na Guiana.

guidance ['gaɪdəns] n -**1.** [help] orientação f -**2.** [leadership] liderança f; **under the ~ of** sob a orientação de.

guide [gaɪd] ◇ n -**1.** [person, book for tourist] guia mf -**2.** [manual] manual m -**3.** [indication] estimativa f (aproximada) -**4.** = **girl guide.** ◇ vt -**1.** [show by leading] guiar; **the waiter ~d them to a table** o garçom os conduziu até a mesa -**2.** [plane, missile] orientar -**3.** [influence]: **to be ~d by sb/sthg** ser orientado(da) por alguém/algo.

Guide Association n: **the ~** as Escoteiras.

guide book n guia m.

guided missile ['gaɪdɪd-] n míssil m guiado.

guide dog n cão-guia m.

guided tour n -**1.** [of city] excursão f guiada -**2.** [of cathedral, museum etc] visita f guiada.

guidelines ['gaɪdlaɪnz] npl princípios mpl, diretrizes fpl.

guiding ['gaɪdɪŋ] adj norteador(ra).

guild [gɪld] n -**1.** HIST guilda f -**2.** [association] associação f.

guildhall ['gɪldhɔ:l] n guilda f.

guile [gaɪl] n (U) literary astúcia f.

guileless ['gaɪllɪs] adj literary cândido(da).

guillotine ['gɪlə,ti:n] ◇ n -**1.** [gen] guilhotina f -**2.** UK POL estipulação de um tempo determinado para discutir um projeto de lei. ◇ vt guilhotinar.

guilt [gɪlt] n culpa f.

guiltily ['gɪltɪlɪ] adv com a consciência pesada.

guilty ['gɪltɪ] (compar -ier, superl -iest) adj -**1.** [remorseful] culpado(da); **to have a ~ conscience** ter a consciência pesada -**2.** [causing remorse] condenável, que causa remorso -**3.** JUR culpado(da); **to be found ~/not ~** ser declarado culpado(da)/inocente -**4.** fig [culpable] culpável; **to be ~ of sthg** ser culpado(da) de algo.

guinea ['gɪnɪ] n guinéu m.

Guinea ['gɪnɪ] n Guiné; **in ~** em Guiné.

Guinea-Bissau [-bɪ'saʊ] n Guiné-Bissau; **in ~** em Guiné-Bissau.

guinea fowl n galinha f d'angola.

guinea pig ['gɪnɪ-] n -**1.** [animal] porquinho-da-índia m -**2.** [subject of experiment] cobaia mf.

guise [gaɪz] n fml aparência f, aspecto m.

guitar [gɪ'tɑ:ʳ] n violão m, guitarra f.

guitarist [gɪ'tɑ:rɪst] n violonista mf, guitarrista mf.

gulch [gʌltʃ] n US ravina f.

gulf [gʌlf] n -**1.** [sea] golfo m -**2.** [deep hole]: **~ (between)** abismo (entre) -**3.** fig [separation] abismo m.

◆ **Gulf** n: **the Gulf** o Golfo Pérsico; **the Gulf of Aden** o Golfo de Áden; **the Gulf of Mexico** o Golfo do México.

Gulf States npl: **the ~** [around Persian Gulf] os países do Golfo Pérsico; [in US] os estados norte-americanos que têm costa para o Golfo do México (Flórida, Alabama, Mississippi, Louisiana e Texas).

Gulf Stream n: **the ~** a corrente do Golfo.

gull [gʌl] n [bird] gaivota f.

gullet ['gʌlɪt] n esôfago m.

gullible ['gʌləbl] adj ingênuo(nua).

gully ['gʌlɪ] (pl -ies) n -**1.** [valley] barranco m -**2.** [ditch] vala f.

gulp [gʌlp] ◇ n gole m. ◇ vt engolir. ◇ vi engolir em seco.

◆ **gulp down** vt sep engolir.

gum [gʌm] (pt & pp -med, cont -ming) ◇ n -**1.** (U) [chewing gum] chiclete m -**2.** [adhesive] goma f -**3.** ANAT gengiva f. ◇ vt -**1.** [cover with adhesive] passar goma em -**2.** [stick] colar.

gumboil ['gʌmbɔɪl] n abscesso m nas gengivas.

gumboots ['gʌmbu:ts] npl UK galocha f.

gummed adj adesivo(va).

gumption ['gʌmpʃn] n (U) inf [resourcefulness] senso m prático.

gumshoe ['gʌmʃu:] n US crime sl detetive mf.

gun [gʌn] (pt & pp -ned, cont -ning) n -**1.** [gen] arma f -**2.** [specific type - revolver] revólver m; [- pistol] pistola f; [- shotgun] espingarda m; [- rifle] rifle m; [- cannon] canhão m; **to stick to one's ~s** não dar o braço a torcer -**3.** SPORT [starting pistol] revólver m; **to jump the ~** fig precipitar-se -**4.** [tool] pistola f.

◆ **gun down** vt sep balear.

gunboat ['gʌnbəʊt] n canhoeira f.

gundog ['gʌndɒg] n cão m de caça.

gunfire ['gʌnfaɪəʳ] n (U) tiroteio m.

gunge [gʌndʒ] n (U) UK inf substância f nojenta e pegajosa.

gung-ho [gʌŋ'həʊ] adj UK inf impulsivo(va).

gunk [gʌŋk] n inf meleca f.

gunman ['gʌnmən] (pl -men [-mən]) n pistoleiro m.

gunner ['gʌnəʳ] n MIL artilheiro m, -ra f.

gunpoint ['gʌnpɔɪnt] n: **at ~** na mira.

gunpowder ['gʌn,paʊdəʳ] n (U) pólvora f.

gunrunning ['gʌn,rʌnɪŋ] n (U) contrabando m de armas.

gunshot ['gʌnʃɒt] n [firing of gun] tiro m.

gunsmith ['gʌnsmɪθ] n armeiro m, -ra f.

gurgle ['gɜ:gl] ◇ n -**1.** [of water] gorgolejo m -**2.** [of baby] gugu *m*. <> *vi* -**1**. [water] gorgolejar -**2**. [baby] fazer gugu.

guru ['guru:] *n* -**1**. [spiritual leader] guru *m* -**2**. [adviser] conselheiro *m*, -ra *f*.

gush [gʌʃ] <> *n* jorro *m*. <> *vt* jorrar. <> *vi* -**1**. [flow out] verter -**2**. *pej* [enthuse] entusiasmar-se.

gushing ['gʌʃɪŋ] *adj pej* [over-enthusiastic] efusivo(va).

gusset ['gʌsɪt] *n* -**1**. *SEWING* nesga *f* -**2**. [in tights] entreperna *m*.

gust [gʌst] <> *n* rajada *f*. <> *vi* dar uma rajada.

gusto ['gʌstəʊ] *n (U)*: **with** ~ com garra.

gusty ['gʌstɪ] (*compar* -**ier**, *superl* -**iest**) *adj* tempestuoso(sa).

gut [gʌt] (*pt* & *pp* -**ted**, *cont* -**ting**) <> *n* -**1**. *MED* intestino *m* -**2**. *inf* [stomach] bucho *m*. <> *vt* -**1**. [remove organs from] destripar -**2**. [destroy] destruir.
→ **guts** *npl inf* -**1**. [intestines] tripas *fpl*; **to hate sb's** ~ **s** ter alguém atravessado(da) na garganta -**2**. [courage] coragem *f*; **to have** ~ **s** ter estômago.

gut feeling *n* pressentimento *m*.

gut reaction *n* reação *f* instintiva.

gutter ['gʌtə^r] *n* -**1**. [ditch] sarjeta *f* -**2**. [on roof] calha *f*.

guttering ['gʌtərɪŋ] *n (U)* calhas *fpl*.

gutter press *n pej* imprensa-marrom *f*.

guttural ['gʌtərəl] *adj* gutural.

guv [gʌv] *n UK inf* chefe *m*.

guy [gaɪ] *n* -**1**. *inf* [man] cara *mf* -**2**. *esp US* [person] galera *f inv* -**3**. *UK* [dummy] *boneco que se queima na Grã-Bretanha na Noite da Conspiração da Pólvora.*

Guyana [gaɪˈænə] *n* Guiana *f*; **in** ~ na Guiana.

Guy Fawkes Night *n* Noite *f* da Conspiração da Pólvora.

---

guy rope *n* amarra *f*.

guzzle ['gʌzl] <> *vt pej* - [food] devorar com gula; [- drink] beber com gula. <> *vi* engolir com gula.

gym [dʒɪm] *n inf* -**1**. [gymnasium - in school] ginásio *m*; [- in hotel, health club] sala *f* de ginástica -**2**. *(U)* [exercises] ginástica *f*, ginásio *m*.

gymkhana [dʒɪmˈkɑːnə] *n* gincana *f*.

gymnasium [dʒɪmˈneɪzjəm] (*pl* -**siums** OR -**sia** [-zjə]) *n* ginásio *m*.

gymnast ['dʒɪmnæst] *n* ginasta *mf*.

gymnastics [dʒɪmˈnæstɪks] *n (U)* ginástica *f*.

gym shoes *npl* sapatilha *f* de ginástica.

gymslip ['dʒɪmˌslɪp] *n UK* bata *f* escolar.

gynaecological *UK*, **gynecological** *US* [ˌgaɪnəkəˈlɒdʒɪkl] *adj* ginecológico(ca).

gynaecologist *UK*, **gynecologist** *US* [ˌgaɪnəˈkɒlədʒɪst] *n* ginecologista *mf*.

gynaecology *UK*, **gynecology** *US* [ˌgaɪnəˈkɒlədʒɪl] *n (U)* ginecologia *f*.

gypsy ['dʒɪpsɪl] (*pl* -**ies**) *adj* & *n* = **gipsy**.

gyrate [dʒaɪˈreɪt] *vi* girar.

gyration [dʒaɪˈreɪʃn] *n* giro *m*, rotação *f*.

gyroscope ['dʒaɪrəskəʊp] *n* giroscópio *m*.

h (*pl* **h's** OR **hs**), **H** (*pl* **H's** OR **Hs**) [eɪtʃ] *n* [letter] h, H *m*.

ha [hɑː] *excl* ah!

habeas corpus [ˌheɪbjəsˈkɔːpəs] *n (U)* habeas corpus *m*.

haberdashery ['hæbədæʃərɪ] (*pl* -**ies**) *n* -**1**. *(U)* [goods] materiais *mpl* de costura, artigos *mpl* de armarinho -**2**. [shop] armarinho *m*.

habit ['hæbɪt] *n* -**1**. [customary practice] hábito *m*, costume *m*; **to be in the** ~ **of doing sthg** ter o hábito de fazer algo, ter o costume de fazer algo; **to make a** ~ **of sthg** tornar algo um hábito; **to make a** ~ **of doing sthg** ter por hábito fazer algo -**2**. [drug addiction] vício *m* -**3**. [garment] hábito *m*.

habitable ['hæbɪtəbl] *adj* habitável.

habitat ['hæbɪtæt] *n* hábitat *m*.

habitation [hæbɪˈteɪʃn] *n* -**1**. *(U)* [occupation] habitação *f* -**2**. *fml* [house] moradia *f*.

habit-forming [-ˌfɔːmɪŋ] *adj* que vicia; **marijuana is** ~ a maconha vicia.

habitual [həˈbɪtʃʊəl] *adj* -**1**. [customary] habitual, costumeiro(ra) -**2**. [offender, smoker, drinker] inveterado(da).

habitually [həˈbɪtʃʊəli] *adv* habitualmente.

hack [hæk] <> *n* -**1**. *pej* [writer] escritorzinho *m*, -razinha *f* -**2**. *US inf* [taxi] táxi *m*. <> *vt* -**1**. [cut] cortar -**2**. *inf* [cope with] enfrentar. <> *vi* [cut] talhar.
→ **hack into** *vt fus COMPUT* invadir ilegalmente.
→ **hack through** *vt fus* [cut] abrir caminho; **to** ~ **(one's way) through sthg** abrir caminho através de algo.

hacker ['hækə^r] *n COMPUT*: **(computer)** ~ hacker *mf* (de computador).

hackie *n US inf* taxista *mf*.

hacking ['hækɪŋ] *n COMPUT* invasão *m* ilegal de sistemas de computação.

hacking cough *n* tosse *f* seca.

hackles ['hæklz] *npl* [on animal] pêlos *mpl* eriçados do dorso; **to make sb's** ~ **rise** enfurecer alguém.

hackney cab, hackney carriage ['hæknɪ-] *n fml* [taxi] carro *m* de praça.

hackneyed ['hæknɪd] *adj pej* batido(da), banal.

hacksaw ['hæksɔː] *n* serra *f* para metais.

had [*weak form* həd, *strong form* hæd] *pt* & *pp* ▷ have.

haddock ['hædək] (*pl inv*) *n* hadoque *m*.

hadn't ['hædntl] = **had not**.

haematology [ˌhiːmə'tɒlədʒɪ] *n* = **hematology**.

haemoglobin [ˌhiːmə'gləʊbɪn] *n* = **hemoglobin**.

haemophilia [ˌhiːmə'fɪlɪə] *n* = **hemophilia**.

haemophiliac [ˌhiːmə'fɪlɪæk] *n* = **hemophiliac**.

haemorrhage ['hemərɪdʒ] *n* & *vi* = **hemorrhage**.

haemorrhoids ['hemərɔɪdz] *npl* = **hemorrhoids**.

hag [hæg] *n pej* bruxa *f*, megera *f*.

haggard ['hægəd] *adj* abatido(da).

haggis ['hægɪs] *n* lingüiça escocesa, normalmente com o formato de uma bola, feita de carne de carneiro picada e embutida na pele do estômago do carneiro.

haggle ['hægl] *vi* pechinchar, regatear; **to ~ over** *OR* **about sthg** pechinchar acerca de algo; **to ~ with sb** pechinchar com alguém.

haggling ['hæglɪŋ] *n (U)* regateio *m*.

Hague [heɪg] *n*: **The ~** Haia.

hail [heɪl] ◇ *n* **-1.** *(U)* [frozen rain] granizo *m* **-2.** *fig* [torrent - of bullets] rajada *f*; [- of criticism] chuva *f*; [- of abuse] onda *f*. ◇ *vt* **-1.** [call] chamar **- 2.** [acclaim]: **to ~ sb/sthg as sthg** aclamar alguém/algo como algo. ◇ *v impers METEOR* chover granizo.

hailstone ['heɪlstəʊn] *n* granizo *m*.

hailstorm *n* chuva *f* de granizo.

hair [heə^r] ◇ *n* **-1.** *(U)* [on human head] cabelo *m*; **to do one's ~** pentear-se; **to let one's ~ down** relaxar e curtir; **to make sb's ~ stand on end** deixar alguém de cabelos em pé; **to split ~s** debater minúcias **- 2.** [on animal, insect, plant] pêlo *m* **-3.** [on human skin] pêlo *m*. ◇ *comp* **-1.** [oil, lotion] capilar **- 2.** [conditioner] de cabelos.

hairbrush ['heəbrʌʃ] *n* escova *f* de cabelo.

haircut ['heəkʌt] *n* corte *m* de cabelo.

hairdo ['heəduː] (*pl* -s) *n inf* penteado *m*.

hairdresser ['heəˌdresə^r] *n* cabeleireiro *m*, -ra *f*; **~'s (salon)** (salão *m* de) cabeleireiro *m*.

hairdressing ['heəˌdresɪŋ] *n (U)* profissão *f* do cabeleireiro. ◇ *comp* de cabeleireiro.

hairdryer ['heəˌdraɪə^r] *n* secador *m* de cabelos.

hair gel *n (U)* gel *m* fixador.

hairgrip ['heəgrɪp] *n UK* grampo *m* de cabelo.

hairline ['heəlaɪn] *n* [of the hair] contorno *m* do cabelo.

hairline fracture *n* fratura *f* muito fina.

hairnet ['heənet] *n* rede *f* de cabelo.

hairpiece ['heəpiːs] *n* cabelo *m* postiço.

hairpin ['heəpɪn] *n* grampo *m* de cabelo.

hairpin bend *n* curva *f* fechada.

hair-raising [-ˌreɪzɪŋ] *adj* assustador(ra); **a ~ story** uma história de deixar os cabelos em pé.

hair remover [-rɪˌmuːvə^r] *n* (creme *m*) depilatório *m*.

. **hair-restorer** *n* loção *f* capilar.

hair's breadth *n*: **by a ~** por um triz.

hair slide *n UK* passador *m*, presilha *f*.

hair-splitting *n (U) pej* sutilezas *fpl*.

hairspray ['heəspreɪ] *n* laquê *m*.

hairstyle ['heəstaɪl] *n* penteado *m*.

hairstylist ['heəˌstaɪlɪst] *n* cabeleireiro *m*, -ra *f*.

hairy ['heərɪ] (*compar* -ier, *superl* -iest) *adj* **-1.** [covered in hair - person] cabeludo(da); [- animal, legs] peludo(-da) **- 2.** *inf* [dangerous] arriscado(da).

Haiti ['heɪtɪ] *n* Haiti; **in ~** no Haiti.

Haitian ['heɪʃn] ◇ *adj* haitiano(na). ◇ *n* haitiano *m*, -na *f*.

hake [heɪk] (*pl inv OR* -s) *n* merluza *f*.

halal [hə'lɑːl] ◇ *adj* que foi abatido conforme a lei islâmica. ◇ *n (U)* carne de animal abatido conforme a lei islâmica.

halcyon *adj literary*: **~ days** dias *mpl* venturosos.

hale [heɪl] *adj*: **~ and hearty** firme e forte.

half [*UK* hɑːf, *US* hæf] (*pl senses 1, 2 and 3* **halves**, *pl senses 4, 5 and 6* **halves** *OR* **halfs**) ◇ *adj* meio (meia); **~ my salary** metade *f* do meu salário. ◇ *adv* **-1.** [partly, almost] meio, quase; **I ~ expected him to say yes** eu meio que esperava que ele dissesse sim; **not ~!** *UK inf* e como! **- 2.** [by half]: **to increase sthg by ~** acrescentar a metade ao valor de algo **- 3.** [in equal measure] meio; **~-and-~** meio a meio **- 4.** [in telling the time]: **~ past ten** *UK*, **~ after ten** *US* dez e meia; **it's ~ past ten/one** são dez e meia/é uma e meia. ◇ *n* **-1.** [one of two equal parts] metade *f*; **by ~** pela metade; **in ~** ao meio; **to be too clever by ~** *pej* ser muito astuto(ta); **he doesn't do things by halves** ele não faz as coisas pela metade; **to go halves (with sb)** rachar as despesas (com alguém) **- 2.** [fraction] meio *m* **-3.** *SPORT* [of sports match] tempo *m* **- 4.** *SPORT* [halfback] meio-campo *mf* **- 5.** [of beer] meia cerveja *f* **- 6.** [child's ticket] meia entrada *f*. ◇ *pron* [one of two equal parts] metade de; **~ of** metade de.

halfback ['hɑːfbæk] *n* meio-campo *mf*.

half-baked [-'beɪkt] *adj inf* mal-elaborado(da).

half board *n (U) UK* meia pensão *f*.

half-breed ◇ *adj* mestiço(ça). ◇ *n* mestiço *m*, -ça *f*.

half-brother *n* meio-irmão *m*.

half-caste [-kɑːst] ◇ *adj* mestiço(ça). ◇ *n* mestiço *m*, -ça *f*.

half cock *n*: **to go off (at) ~** ir com muita sede ao pote.

half-day *n* meio turno *m*.

half-fare *n* meia passagem *f*.

half-hearted [-'hɑːtɪd] *adj* desanimado(da).

half-heartedly [-'hɑːtɪdlɪ] *adv* sem entusiasmo.

half hour *n* meia hora *f*.

➡ **half-hour** *adj* = **half-hourly**.

half-hourly *adj* a cada meia hora.

half-length *adj* de meio corpo.

half-light *n (U)* meia-luz *f*.

half-mast *n UK*: **at ~** [flag] a meio pau.

half measures *npl* meios-termos *mpl*.

half moon *n* meia-lua *f*.

half note *n US MUS* mínima *f*.

halfpenny ['heɪpnɪ] (*pl* -pennies *OR* -pence) *n* meio pêni *m*.

half-price *adj* a metade do preço.

➡ **half price** *adv* pela metade do preço.

half-sister *n* meia-irmã *f*.

half step *n US MUS* semitom *m*.

half term *n UK* recesso *m* escolar.

half time n (U) meio-tempo m.
half tone n US MUS meio-tom m, semitom m.
half-truth n meia verdade f.
halfway [hɑːˈfweɪ] <> adj no meio do caminho. <> adv - **1.** [in space] a meio caminho - **2.** [in time] no meio - **3.** phr: **to meet sb ~** fig [compromise] chegar a um acordo com alguém.
half-wit n idiota mf.
half-yearly adj semestral.
  ◆ **half yearly** adv semestralmente.
halibut [ˈhælɪbət] (pl inv OR -s) n halibute m.
halitosis [ˌhælɪˈtəʊsɪs] n (U) halitose f.
hall [hɔːl] n - **1.** [in house] entrada f, hall m - **2.** [meeting room] salão m - **3.** [public building] sala f; **town ~** prédio m da prefeitura - **4.** UK [UNIV & hall of residence] alojamento m, casa f do estudante; **to live in ~** morar em casa do estudante - **5.** [country house] mansão m.
halleluja [ˌhælɪˈluːjə] excl aleluia!
hallmark [ˈhɔːlmɑːk] n - **1.** [typical feature] marca f distintiva - **2.** [on metal] selo m de autenticidade.
hallo [həˈləʊ] excl = hello.
hall of residence (pl halls of residence) n UK UNIV casa f do estudante.
hallowed [ˈhæləʊd] adj [respected] sagrado(da), santo(ta).
Hallowe'en, Halloween, [ˌhæləʊˈiːn] n Dia m das Bruxas.

hallucinate [həˈluːsɪneɪt] vi alucinar.
hallucination [ˌhəluːsɪˈneɪʃn] n alucinação f.
hallucinogenic [həˌluːsɪnəˈdʒenɪk] adj alucinógeno(na).
hallway [ˈhɔːlweɪ] n - **1.** [at entrance of house] saguão m, hall m - **2.** [corridor] corredor m.
halo [ˈheɪləʊ] (pl -es OR -s) n - **1.** [of saint, angel] auréola f - **2.** fig [circle of light] halo m.
halogen [ˈhælədʒen] <> n (U) halogênio m. <> comp halógeno m, -na f.
halt [hɔːlt] <> n [stop]: **to come to a ~** [vehicle, horse] fazer uma parada; [development, activity] interromper-se; **to call a ~ to sthg** pôr fim a algo; **to grind to a ~** [stop moving] parar lentamente; [stop working] estagnar-se. <> vt [stop - person] deter; [- development, activity] interromper. <> vi [stop - person, train] parar; [- development, activity] interromper-se.
halter [ˈhɔːltər] n [for horse] cabresto m.
halterneck [ˈhɔːltənek] adj: **~ dress** vestido m de frente-única.
halting [ˈhɔːltɪŋ] adj vacilante.
halve [UK hɑːv, US hæv] vt - **1.** [reduce by half] reduzir à metade - **2.** [divide] partir ao meio.
halves [UK hɑːvz, US hævz] pl ⊳ **half**.
ham [hæm] (pt & pp -med, cont -ming) <> n - **1.** [meat] presunto m - **2.** pej [actor] canastrão m - **3.** [radio fanatic]: **(radio) ~** radioamador m, -ra f. <> comp de presunto. <> vt: **to ~ it up** THEATRE exagerar na atuação.
Hamburg [ˈhæmbɜːg] n Hamburgo.
hamburger [ˈhæmbɜːgər] n - **1.** [burger] hambúrguer m - **2.** US [mince] carne f moída.
ham-fisted [-ˈfɪstɪd] adj desajeitado(da).
hamlet [ˈhæmlɪt] n aldeia f.
hammer [ˈhæmər] <> n [tool] martelo m. <> vt - **1.** [with tool] martelar - **2.** [with fist] bater em - **3.** inf fig [fact, order]: **to ~ sthg into sb** meter algo na cabeça de alguém - **4.** inf fig [defeat] dar uma surra em. <> vi - **1.** [with tool] martelar - **2.** [with fist]: **to ~ (on sthg)** bater com insistência (em algo) - **3.** phr: **to ~ away at sthg** fig [task] trabalhar com afinco em algo.
  ◆ **hammer into** vt sep: **to ~ sthg into sb** fig meter algo na cabeça de alguém.
  ◆ **hammer out** <> vt fus [draw up] alcançar com muito esforço. <> vt sep [with tool] malhar.
hammock [ˈhæmək] n rede f de dormir.
hamper [ˈhæmpər] <> n - **1.** [for picnic] cesta f - **2.** US [for laundry] cesto m de roupa. <> vt [impede] dificultar.
hamster [ˈhæmstər] n hamster m.
hamstring [ˈhæmstrɪŋ] (pt & pp -strung [-strʌŋ]) <> n ANAT tendão m do jarrete. <> vt fig [thwart] impedir, dificultar.
hand [hænd] <> n - **1.** [part of body] mão f; **to hold ~s** dar as mãos; **by ~** à mão; **~ in ~** [people] de mãos dadas; **with his bare ~s** com suas próprias mãos; **at the ~s of** nas mãos de; **~s up!** mãos ao alto!; **to change ~s** trocar de mãos; **to force sb's ~** forçar alguém a agir; **to get OR lay one's ~s on sb** colocar OR pôr as mãos em alguém; **to get OR lay one's ~s on sthg** colocar OR pôr as mãos em algo; **to give sb a free ~** dar carta branca a alguém; **to go ~ in ~** [things] andar de mãos dadas; **to have one's ~s full** estar muito atarefado(da); **to try one's ~ at sthg** tentar fazer algo; **to wait on sb ~ and foot** dar tudo de bandeja para alguém; **to wash one's ~s of sthg** lavar as mãos sobre algo - **2.** [help] mão f; **to give OR lend sb a ~ (with sthg)** dar uma mão para alguém (em algo) - **3.** [control, management] mão f; **in the ~s of** nas mãos de; **to take sb in ~** controlar alguém - **4.** [influence] dedo m; **to have a ~ in sthg/in doing sthg** interferir em algo/ao se fazer algo - **5.** [worker - on farm] peão m, -ona f; [- on ship] tripulante mf - **6.** [of clock, watch] ponteiro m - **7.** [handwriting] caligrafia f - **8.** [of cards] mão f; **I overplayed my ~** fig superestimei minha situação - **9.** inf [applause] palmas fpl. <> vt: **to ~ sthg to sb, to ~ sb sthg** entregar algo a alguém.
  ◆ **(close) at hand** adv próximo.
  ◆ **in hand** adv - **1.** [time, money]: **to have sthg in ~** ter algo sobrando - **2.** [problem, situation]: **to have sb/sthg in ~** ter alguém/algo sob controle.
  ◆ **on hand** adv em prontidão.
  ◆ **on the one hand** adv por um lado.
  ◆ **on the other hand** adv por outro lado.
  ◆ **out of hand** <> adj [situation]: **to get out of ~** sair de controle. <> adv [completely] completamente.
  ◆ **to hand** adv à mão.

→ **hand down** vt sep [to next generation] legar.
→ **hand in** vt sep entregar.
→ **hand on** vt sep passar adiante.
→ **hand out** vt sep distribuir.
→ **hand over** ◇ vt sep -1. [baton, money] entregar -2. [responsibility, power] transferir, ceder -3. TELEC passar a ligação. ◇ vi [government minister, chairman] transferir; **to ~ over to sb** transferir para alguém.

handbag ['hændbæg] n bolsa f.
handball ['hændbɔ:l] n (U) [game] handebol m.
handbill ['hændbɪl] n panfleto m.
handbook ['hændbʊk] n manual m.
handbrake ['hændbreɪk] n freio m de mão.
handclap ['hændklæp] n: **slow ~** aplauso lento e ritmado em forma de protesto.
handcrafted ['hænd,krɑ:ftɪd] adj artesanal.
handcuff ['hændkʌf] vt algemar.
handcuffs ['hændkʌfs] npl algemas fpl.
handful ['hændfʊl] n -1. lit & fig punhado m -2. inf [difficult person, animal]: **to be a ~** ser um demônio.
handgun ['hændgʌn] n arma f de mão.
handheld PC ['hændheld-] n computador m de bolso, handheld m.
handicap ['hændɪkæp] (pt & pp -ped, cont -ping) ◇ n -1. [physical or mental disability] deficiência f-2. fig [disadvantage] obstáculo m -3. SPORT handicap m. ◇ vt [hinder] estorvar, atrapalhar.
handicapped ['hændɪkæpt] ◇ adj [physically or mentally disabled] deficiente. ◇ npl: **the ~** os deficientes.
handicraft ['hændɪkrɑ:ft] n [skill] artesanato m.
handiwork ['hændɪwɜ:k] n (U) [work produced by o.s.] trabalho m manual.
handkerchief ['hæŋkətʃɪf] (pl -chiefs OR -chieves [-tʃi:vz]) n lenço m.
handle ['hændl] ◇ n -1. [for opening and closing - of window] trinco m; [- of door] maçaneta f-2. [for holding] cabo m -3. [for carrying] alça f; **to fly off the ~** perder a cabeça. ◇ vt -1. [with hands] manusear -2. [control, operate - car] guiar; [- ship] comandar; [- gun] manejar; [- words] articular -3. [manage, process] manejar -4. [cope with] tratar de. ◇ vi -1. governar -2. [ship] comandar -3. [car] guiar.
handlebars ['hændlbɑ:z] npl guidom m.
handler ['hændlə'] n -1. [of animal] treinador m, -ra f -2. [of luggage]: **(baggage) ~** carregador m, -ra f (de bagagem) -3. [of stolen goods] receptor m, -ra f.
handling charges ['hændlɪŋ-] npl [at bank] taxas fpl de manutenção.
hand lotion n creme m para as mãos.
hand luggage n UK bagagem f de mão.
handmade [,hænd'meɪd] adj feito(ta) à mão.
hand-me-downs npl inf roupas fpl usadas.
handout ['hændaʊt] n -1. [gift] donativo m -2. [leaflet] folheto m informativo -3. [for lecture, discussion] polígrafo m.
handover ['hændəʊvə'] n transferência f.
handpicked [,hænd'pɪkt] adj [people] escolhido(da) a dedo.
handrail ['hændreɪl] n corrimão m.
handset ['hændset] n TELEC fone m (do telefone).
handshake ['hændʃeɪk] n aperto m de mão.

hands-off adj sem interferência.
handsome ['hænsəm] adj -1. [man] bonito(ta) -2. literary [woman] bela, bonita -3. [reward, profit] considerável.
handsomely ['hænsəmlɪ] adv [generously] generosamente.
hands-on adj [training, experience] prático(ca).
handstand ['hændstænd] n: **to do a ~** plantar bananeira.
hand-to-mouth adj precário(ria).
→ **hand to mouth** adv precariamente.
hand towel n toalha f de mão.
handwriting ['hænd,raɪtɪŋ] n letra f, caligrafia f.
handwritten ['hænd,rɪtn] adj escrito(ta) à mão.
handy ['hændɪ] (compar -ier, superl -iest) adj inf -1. [useful] prático(ca); **to come in ~** vir a calhar -2. [skilful] hábil -3. [near] à mão; **to keep sthg ~** manter algo à mão.
handyman ['hændɪmæn] (pl -men [-men]) n faz-tudo mf.
hang [hæŋ] (pt & pp sense 1 hung, pt & pp sense 2 hung OR hanged) ◇ vt -1. [suspend] pendurar -2. [execute] enforcar. ◇ vi -1. [be suspended] estar suspenso(sa) -2. [be executed] ser enforcado(da). ◇ n: **to get the ~ of sthg** inf pegar o jeito de algo.
→ **hang about, hang around** vi -1. [loiter] demorar-se -2. [wait] rondar.
→ **hang down** vi pender.
→ **hang on** ◇ vt fus [depend on] depender de. ◇ vi -1. [keep hold]: **to ~ on (to sb/sthg)** segurar-se (em alguém/algo) -2. inf [continue waiting] aguardar -3. [persevere] resistir, agüentar.
→ **hang onto** vt fus -1. [keep hold of] segurar-se a -2. [keep] manter.
→ **hang out** ◇ vt sep [washing] estender. ◇ vi inf [spend time] passar um tempo, frequentar.
→ **hang round** vi = hang about.
→ **hang together** vi [alibi, argument] ser consistente.
→ **hang up** ◇ vt sep [suspend] pendurar. ◇ vi [on telephone] desligar.
→ **hang up on** vt fus TELEC desligar; **he hung up on me** ele desligou o telefone na minha cara.
hangar ['hæŋə'] n hangar m.
hangdog ['hæŋdɒg] adj envergonhado(da).
hanger ['hæŋə'] n [coat hanger] cabide m.
hanger-on (pl hangers-on) n bajulador m, -ra f, aproveitador m, -ra f.
hang glider n [apparatus] asa-delta f.
hang gliding n (U) vôo m livre (com asa delta).
hanging ['hæŋɪŋ] n -1. (U) [form of punishment] forca f -2. [execution] enforcamento m -3. [drapery] tapeçaria f (para parede).
hangman ['hæŋmən] (pl -men [-mən]) n carrasco m, -ca f.
hangover ['hæŋ,əʊvə'] n -1. [from drinking] ressaca f; **to have a ~** estar de ressaca -2. [from past]: **~ (from sthg)** vestígio m (de algo).
hang-up n inf PSYCH complexo m.
hank n -1. [of wool] novelo m -2. [of rope, wire] meada m.
hanker ['hæŋkə'] → **hanker after, hanker for** vt fus ansiar por, desejar ardentemente.

hankering ['hæŋkərɪŋ] n: ~ **after** OR **for** anseio m por.

hankie, hanky ['hæŋkɪ] (pl -ies) (abbr of **handkerchief**) n inf lencinho m.

hanky-panky n inf [sexual behaviour] sem-vergonhice f.

Hanoi [hæ'nɔɪ] n Hanói.

Hansard ['hænsɑːd] n atas oficiais dos debates realizados no parlamento britânico, ≃ Diário Oficial.

haphazard [ˌhæp'hæzəd] adj caótico(ca), desordenado(da).

haphazardly [ˌhæp'hæzədlɪ] adv desordenadamente, de qualquer maneira.

hapless ['hæplɪs] adj literary desafortunado(da).

happen ['hæpən] vi -1. [occur] acontecer; **to** ~ **to sb** acontecer com alguém -2. [chance]: **I** ~ **ed to see him yesterday** por acaso eu o vi ontem; **do you** ~ **to have a pen on you?** você não teria por acaso uma caneta?; **as it** ~ **s** por acaso.

happening ['hæpənɪŋ] n [occurrence] acontecimento m.

happily ['hæpɪlɪ] adv -1. [contentedly]: **to be** ~ **doing sthg** fazer algo alegremente -2. [fortunately] felizmente -3. [willingly] com satisfação.

happiness ['hæpɪnɪs] n (U) felicidade f.

happy ['hæpɪ] (compar -ier, superl -iest) adj -1. [contented] feliz, contente -2. [causing contentment] feliz; **Happy Christmas/New Year/Birthday!** Feliz Natal/Ano Novo/Aniversário!; **to be** ~ **with** OR **about sthg** estar feliz com algo; **to be** ~ **to do sthg** estar muito disposto(ta) a fazer algo; **I'd be** ~ **to do it** eu faria isso com muito gosto.

happy event n nascimento m; **when's the** ~ **event** quando nasce a criança?

happy-go-lucky adj despreocupado(da).

happy hour n inf happy hour f.

happy medium n meio-termo m.

harangue [hə'ræŋ] <> n arenga f, ladainha f. <> vt arengar.

Harare [hə'rɑːrɪ] n Harare.

harass ['hærəs] vt [pester - with questions, problems] atormentar; [- sexually] molestar.

harassed ['hærəst] adj [stressed] tenso(sa).

harassment ['hærəsmənt] n -1. [persecution] perseguição f -2. [sexual] assédio m.

harbinger ['hɑːbɪndʒə^r] n literary precursor m, -ra f.

harbour UK, **harbor** US ['hɑːbə^r] <> n porto m. <> vt -1. [feeling] abrigar -2. [person] dar refúgio a.

harbour master n capitão m, -tã f do porto.

hard [hɑːd] <> adj -1. [very firm, not soft] duro(ra) -2. [difficult] difícil -3. [strenuous, stressful] duro(ra), pesado(da) -4. [forceful] forte -5. [harsh, unkind] ríspido(da); **to be** ~ **on sb/sthg** ser duro com alguém/algo -6. [winter, frost] rigoroso(sa) -7. [water] duro(ra) -8. [fact, news] concreto(ta) -9. UK POL [extreme]: ~ **left/right** extrema esquerda/direita. <> adv -1. [strenuously] muito, duro -2. [forcefully] com força -3. [rain, snow] intensamente -4. phr: **to be** ~ **pushed** OR **put** OR **pressed to do sthg** ver-se em apuros para fazer algo; **to feel** ~ **done by** sentir-se injustiçado(da) por.

hard-and-fast adj rígido(da).

hardback ['hɑːdbæk] <> adj de capa dura. <> n [book] edição f de capa dura.

hard-bitten adj duro(ra), inflexível.

hardboard ['hɑːdbɔːd] n (U) madeira f compensada.

hard-boiled adj -1. [egg] cozido(da) -2. [person] impassível.

hard cash n (U) dinheiro m vivo.

hard cider n US sidra f.

hard copy n COMPUT cópia f impressa.

hard-core adj [pornography] explícito(ta).
➡ **hard core** n [of group] núcleo m.

hard court n quadra f rápida.

hard currency n moeda f forte.

hard disk n disco m rígido.

hard drugs npl drogas fpl pesadas.

harden ['hɑːdn] <> vt -1. [steel, arteries] endurecer -2. fig [person] endurecer -3. [attitude, ideas, opinion] fortalecer. <> vi -1. [glue, concrete, arteries] endurecer, endurecer-se -2. fig [person] endurecer-se -3. [attitude, ideas, opinion] fortalecer-se.

hardened ['hɑːdnd] adj -1. [steel, arteries] endurecido(da) -2. [criminal] habitual -3. [accustomed]: ~ **to sthg** acostumado(da) a algo.

hardening ['hɑːdnɪŋ] n -1. [of steel, arteries] endurecimento m -2. [of attitude, ideas, opinion] fortalecimento m.

hard hat n [for protection] capacete m.

hard-headed [-'hedɪd] adj realista.

hard-hearted [-'hɑːtɪd] adj insensível; **a** ~ **person** uma pessoa sem coração.

hard-hitting [-'hɪtɪŋ] adj chocante.

hard labour n (U) trabalhos mpl forçados.

hard line n: **to take a** ~ **on sthg** manter a linha dura em relação a algo.
➡ **hard-line** adj linha-dura.
➡ **hard lines** npl UK: **hard lines!** que azar!

hard-liner n linha-dura mf.

hardly ['hɑːdlɪ] adv -1. [scarcely, not really] dificilmente; ~ **ever/anything** quase nunca/nada; **I can** ~ **move/wait** mal posso me mover/esperar -2. [only just] apenas.

hardness ['hɑːdnɪs] n -1. [firmness, also of water] dureza f -2. [difficulty] dificuldade f -3. [of heart, person] insensibilidade f.

hard-nosed [-'nəʊzd] adj obstinado(da), contundente.

hard return n COMPUT retorno m de hardware.

hard sell n venda f agressiva.

hardship ['hɑːdʃɪp] n -1. (U) [difficult conditions] privações fpl -2. [difficult circumstance] dificuldade f.

hard shoulder n UK AUT acostamento m.

hard up adj inf desprovido(da); ~ **for sthg** desprovido(da) de algo.

hardware ['hɑːdweə^r] n -1. [tools, equipment] ferragens fpl -2. COMPUT hardware m.

hardware shop n ferragem f.

hardwearing [ˌhɑːd'weərɪŋ] adj UK resistente.

hardwood ['hɑːdwʊd] n (U) madeira f de lei.

hardworking [ˌhɑːd'wɜːkɪŋ] adj trabalhador(ra).

hardy ['hɑːdɪ] (compar -ier, superl -iest) adj -1. [person, animal] forte, robusto(ta) -2. [plant] resistente.

hare [heə^r] ◇ *n* lebre *f.* ◇ *vi UK inf*: **to ~ off** correr a toda.

harebell *n* campainha *f.*

harebrained ['heə,breɪnd] *adj inf* tolo(la).

harelip [,heə'lɪp] *n* lábio *m* leporino.

harem [*UK* haː'riːm, *US* 'hærəm] *n* harém *m.*

haricot (bean) ['hærɪkəʊ-] *n* feijão *m.*

hark [haːk] ◆ **hark back** *vi*: **to ~ back to sthg** voltar a algo.

harlequin ['haːləkwɪn] ◇ *n* arlequim *m.* ◇ *comp* arlequinal, de arlequim.

Harley Street ['haːlɪ-] *n* rua no centro de Londres famosa pelos seus médicos especialistas.

harm [haːm] ◇ *n* [physical] mal *m*; [psychological] dano *m*; **to do ~ to sb/sthg, to do sb/sthg ~** fazer mal a alguém/algo; **to mean no ~** não ter má intenção; **there's no ~ in it** não há mal nenhum nisso; **to be out of ~'s way** estar a salvo; **to come to no ~** [person] chegar são e salvo, chegar sã e salva; [thing] ficar a salvo. ◇ *vt* [physically] ferir; [psychologically] danificar, prejudicar.

harmful ['haːmfʊl] *adj* [physically] nocivo(va) ; [psychologically] prejudicial.

harmless ['haːmlɪs] *adj* inofensivo(va).

harmlessly ['haːmlɪslɪ] *adv* [without causing damage] sem causar dano.

harmonic [haː'mɒnɪk] *adj* harmônico(ca).

harmonica [haː'mɒnɪkə] *n* gaita-de-boca *f.*

harmonious [haː'məʊnjəs] *adj* harmonioso(sa).

harmonium [haː'məʊnjəm] (*pl* -s) *n* harmônio *m.*

harmonize, -ise ['haːmənaɪz] ◇ *vt* harmonizar. ◇ *vi* harmonizar; **to ~ with sthg** harmonizar-se com algo.

harmony ['haːmənɪ] (*pl* -ies) *n* harmonia *f*; **in ~ with sthg** em harmonia com algo.

harness ['haːnɪs] ◇ *n* -**1.** [for horse] arreio *m* -**2.** [for person, child] andador *m.* ◇ *vt* -**1.** [horse] arrear, pôr arreios em -**2.** [energy, solar power] aproveitar.

harp [haːp] *n MUS* harpa *f.* ◆ **harp on** *vi*: **to ~ on (about sthg)** bater sempre na mesma tecla (sobre algo).

harpist ['haːpɪst] *n* harpista *mf.*

harpoon [haː'puːn] ◇ *n* arpão *m.* ◇ *vt* arpoar.

harpsichord ['haːpsɪkɔːd] *n* clavicórdio *m.*

harrowing ['hærəʊɪŋ] *adj* angustiante.

harry ['hærɪ] (*pt* & *pp* -ied) *vt* -**1.** [badger] importunar; **to ~ sb for sthg** importunar alguém para obter algo -**2.** *MIL* [attack] saltear.

harsh [haːʃ] *adj* -**1.** [cruel, severe] severo(ra), duro(ra) -**2.** [conditions, weather] duro(ra) -**3.** [cry, voice] áspero(ra) -**4.** [colour, contrast, light] forte -**5.** [landscape] desolado(da) -**6.** [taste] azedo(da).

harshly ['haːʃlɪ] *adv* -**1.** [treat, punish, judge] severamente, duramente -**2.** [cry, shout] asperamente -**3.** [shine] ofuscantemente.

harshness ['haːʃnɪs] *n* (*U*) -**1.** [of person, treatment] severidade *f*, dureza *f* -**2.** [of climate] rigor *m* -**3.** [of cry, voice] aspereza *f* -**4.** [of colour, contrast, light] forte constraste *m* -**5.** [of landscape] desolação *f.*

harvest ['haːvɪst] ◇ *n* colheita *f.* ◇ *vt* [crops] colher.

harvest festival *n* festividade religiosa que celebra o início da colheita.

has [weak form həz, strong form hæz] *vb* ⊳ **have**.

has-been *n inf pej*: **that man is a ~** aquele homem já era.

hash [hæʃ] *n* -**1.** (*U*) [meat] picadinho *m* -**2.** *inf* [mess]: **to make a ~ of sthg** fazer uma confusão em algo -**3.** *drugs sl* [hashish] haxixe *m.* ◆ **hash up** *vt sep UK inf* [make a mess of] fazer uma confusão em.

hash browns *npl US* prato feito com batatas esmagadas e fritas.

hashish ['hæʃiːʃ] *n* (*U*) haxixe *m.*

hasn't ['hæznt] = **has not**.

hassle ['hæsl] *inf* ◇ *n* [annoyance] amolação *f.* ◇ *vt* amolar, aborrecer.

haste [heɪst] *n* (*U*) -**1.** [rush] pressa *f*; **to do sthg in ~** fazer algo às pressas -**2.** [speed] rapidez *f*; **to make ~** *dated* apressar-se.

hasten ['heɪsn] ◇ *vt* acelerar. ◇ *vi* apressar-se; **I ~ to add that ...** apresso-me a acrescentar que ...

hastily ['heɪstɪlɪ] *adv* -**1.** [rashly] apressadamente -**2.** [quickly] rapidamente, às pressas.

hasty ['heɪstɪ] (*compar* -ier, *superl* -iest) *adj* -**1.** [rash] precipitado(da) -**2.** [quick] breve.

hat [hæt] *n* chapéu *m*; **keep it under your ~** mantenha isso entre nós; **to be talking through one's ~** só dizer besteira; **that's old ~** isso é mais velho que andar para frente.

hatbox ['hæt,bɒks] *n* chapeleira *f.*

hatch [hætʃ] ◇ *vt* -**1.** [chick] incubar -**2.** [egg] chocar -**3.** *fig* [scheme, plot] conceber, idealizar. ◇ *vi* -**1.** [chick] sair do ovo -**2.** [egg] chocar. ◇ *n* [for serving food] portinhola *f*, janela *f* de comunicação.

hatchback ['hætʃ,bæk] *n* carro *m* com porta traseira.

hatchet ['hætʃɪt] *n* machadinha *f*; **to bury the ~** fazer as pazes.

hatchet job *n inf* crítica *f* destrutiva.

hatchway ['hætʃ,weɪ] *n* escotilha *f.*

hate [heɪt] ◇ *n* -**1.** [emotion] ódio *m* -**2.** [person, thing hated] aversão *f.* ◇ *vt* [dislike] detestar, odiar; **to ~ doing sthg** odiar fazer algo.

hateful ['heɪtfʊl] *adj* detestável.

hatred ['heɪtrɪd] *n* (*U*) ódio *m.*

hat trick *n SPORT* série de três pontos marcados pelo mesmo jogador na mesma partida.

haughty ['hɔːtɪ] (*compar* -ier, *superl* -iest) *adj* arrogante.

haul [hɔːl] ◇ *n* -**1.** [of drugs, stolen goods] carregamento *m* -**2.** [distance]: **long ~** longo trajeto *m.* ◇ *vt* -**1.** [pull] arrastar, puxar -**2.** [by lorry] transportar.

haulage ['hɔːlɪdʒ] *n* -**1.** [gen] transporte *m* -**2.** [cost] gasto *m* com transporte.

haulage contractor *n* transportadora *f.*

haulier *UK* ['hɔːlɪə^r], **hauler** *US* ['hɔːlər] *n* -**1.** [business] transportadora *f* -**2.** [person] transportador *m*, -ra *f.*

haunch [hɔːntʃ] *n* -**1.** [of person] quadril *m* -**2.** [of animal] lombo *m.*

haunt [hɔːnt] ◇ *n* [place] lugar *m* preferido. ◇ *vt* -**1.** [subj: ghost] assombrar -**2.** [subj: memory, fear, problem] perseguir.

haunted [ˈhɔːntɪd] *adj* **-1.** [house, castle] assombrado(da) **-2.** [look] espantado(da).

haunting [ˈhɔːntɪŋ] *adj* inesquecível, obcecante.

Havana [həˈvænə] *n* Havana; **in ~** em Havana.

have [hæv] (*pt & pp* had) *aux vb* **-1.** [to form perfect tenses]: **I ~ finished** acabei; **~ you been there? - no, I ~ n't** você já esteve lá? - não; **they hadn't seen it** não o tinham visto; **we had already left** nós já tínhamos saído **-2.** [must]: **to ~ (got) to do sthg** ter de fazer algo; **do you ~ to pay?** é preciso pagar? ◇ *vt* **-1.** [possess]: **to ~ (got)** ter; **do you ~ OR ~ you got a double room?** você tem um quarto de casal?; **she's got brown hair** ela tem o cabelo castanho **-2.** [experience] ter; **to ~ a cold** estar resfriado; **to ~ a great time** divertir-se a valer **-3.** [replacing other verbs] ter; **to ~ breakfast** tomar o café da manhã; **to ~ dinner** jantar; **to ~ lunch** almoçar; **to ~ a bath** tomar banho; **to ~ a drink** tomar qualquer coisa, tomar um drinque; **to ~ a shower** tomar um banho; **to ~ a swim** nadar **-4.** [feel] ter; **I ~ no doubt about it** não tenho dúvida alguma *OR* nenhuma sobre isso **-5.** [cause to be]: **to ~ sthg done** mandar fazer algo; **to ~ one's hair cut** cortar o cabelo **-6.** [be treated in a certain way]: **I've had my wallet stolen** roubaram a minha carteira.

haven [ˈheɪvn] *n* [refuge] abrigo *m*.

haven't [ˈhævnt] = have not.

haversack [ˈhævəsæk] *n dated* mochila *f*.

havoc [ˈhævək] *n* (*U*) destruição *f*, estragos *mpl*; **to play ~ with sthg** causar estragos em algo.

Hawaii [həˈwaiiː] *n* Havaí; **in ~** no Havaí.

Hawaiian [həˈwaiːən] ◇ *adj* havaiano(na). ◇ *n* havaiano *m*, -na *f*.

hawk [hɔːk] ◇ *n* **-1.** [bird] falcão *m*; **to watch sb like a ~** observar alguém com olhos de lince **-2.** *POL* não-pacifista *mf*. ◇ *vt* [in the street] vender de forma ambulante; [door to door] vender *(de porta em porta)*.

hawker [ˈhɔːkəʳ] *n* **-1.** [street vendor] camelô *mf* **-2.** [door-to-door] vendedor *m*, -ra *f* ambulante.

hawthorn [ˈhɔːθɔːn] *n* pilriteiro *m*.

hay [heɪ] *n* (*U*) feno *m*; **to make ~ while the sun shines** aproveitar uma oportunidade.

hay fever *n* (*U*) febre *f* do feno.

haymaking *n* (*U*) preparo *m* do feno.

haystack [ˈheɪˌstæk] *n* feixe *m* de feno.

haywire [ˈheɪˌwaɪəʳ] *adj inf*: **to go ~** ficar louco (ca).

hazard [ˈhæzəd] ◇ *n* [danger] perigo *m*. ◇ *vt* **-1.** [life, reputation] arriscar, pôr em perigo **-2.** [guess, suggestion] atrever-se a fazer.

hazardous [ˈhæzədəs] *adj* perigoso(sa), arriscado(da).

hazard warning lights *npl UK* pisca-alerta *m*.

haze [heɪz] *n* **-1.** [mist] neblina *f* **-2.** [state of confusion] confusão *f* mental.

hazel [ˈheɪzl] ◇ *adj* castanho-claro. ◇ *n* [tree] aveleira *f*.

hazelnut [ˈheɪzlˌnʌt] *n* avelã *f*.

hazy [ˈheɪzɪ] (*compar* -ier, *superl* -iest) *adj* **-1.** [misty] nebuloso(sa) **-2.** [vague, confused - ideas, memory] vago(ga); [- person, facts] confuso(sa).

H-bomb *n* bomba *f* H.

h & c (*abbr of* hot and cold (water)) (água) q e f.

HCA (*abbr of* health care assistant) *n* auxiliar *mf* de enfermagem.

he [hiː] ◇ *pers pron* ele; **he's tall** ele é alto.

HE -1. (*abbr of* high explosive) altamente explosivo(va). **- 2.** (*abbr of* His (or Her) Excellency) S.Exª.

head [hed] ◇ *n* **-1.** [gen] cabeça *f*; **a** *OR* **per ~ por** pessoa, por cabeça; **off the top of one's ~** de improviso; **to bite** *OR* **snap sb's ~ off** xingar/ insultar alguém sem motivos; **to laugh/sing/ shout one's ~ off** rir/cantar/gritar a plenos pulmões; **to be banging one's ~ against a brick wall** dar murro em ponta de faca; **I can't make ~ nor tail of it** isto não tem pé nem cabeça; **on your own ~ be it** que seja por sua própria conta e risco, você que arque com as conseqüências; **to have a ~ for heights** não ter medo de altura; **to be off one's ~** *UK*, **to be out of one's ~** *US* estar fora de seu juízo; **we put our ~s together** tratamos de resolver juntos; **to go to one's ~** subir à cabeça; **to keep one's ~** manter a cabeça no lugar; **to lose one's ~** perder a cabeça; **to be soft in the ~** ter o miolo mole **-2.** [of table, bed, river] cabeceira *f* **-3.** [of page] cabeçalho *m* **-4.** [of stairs] topo *m* **-5.** [of queue, procession] frente *f* **-6.** [of flower] corola *f* **-7.** [head teacher] diretor *m*, -ra *f* **-8.** *ELEC* cabeçote *m* **-9.** *phr*: **to come to a ~** chegar a um ponto crítico. ◇ *vt* **-1.** [be at front of, top of] encabeçar **-2.** [be in charge of] comandar **-3.** *FTBL* cabecear. ◇ *vi* dirigir-se, ir; **we gave up and ~ed home** nós desistimos e fomos para casa; **the ship was ~ing due north** o navio rumava para o norte.

→ **heads** *npl* [on coin] cara *f*; **~s or tails?** cara ou coroa?

→ **head for** *vt fus* **-1.** [place] dirigir-se para **-2.** *fig* [trouble, disaster] encaminhar-se para.

→ **head off** ◇ *vt sep* **-1.** [intercept] deter **-2.** [forestall] antecipar-se a. ◇ *vi* [leave] esquivar-se.

headache [ˈhedeɪk] *n dor f* de cabeça; **to have a ~** ter uma dor de cabeça.

headband [ˈhedbænd] *n* faixa *f (para a cabeça)*.

headboard [ˈhedˌbɔːd] *n* cabeceira *f*.

head boy *n UK* [at school] representante *m* discente.

head cold *n* resfriado *m*.

head count *n* contagem *f (das pessoas presentes)*.

headdress [ˈhedˌdres] *n* touca *f*.

header [ˈhedəʳ] *n* **-1.** *FTBL* cabeçada *f* **-2.** [at top of page] cabeçalho *m*.

headfirst [ˌhedˈfɜːst] *adv* de cabeça.

headgear [ˈhedˌgɪəʳ] *n* proteção *f* para a cabeça.

head girl *n UK* [in school] representante *f* discente.

headhunt [ˈhedhʌnt] *vt* [recruit] contratar *(novos talentos)*.

headhunter [ˈhedˌhʌntəʳ] *n* [recruiter] caça-talentos *mf inv*.

heading [ˈhedɪŋ] *n* título *m*, cabeçalho *m*.

headlamp [ˈhedlæmp] *n UK* farol *m (de carro)*.

headland [ˈhedlənd] *n* promontório *m*.

headlight [ˈhedlaɪt] *n* farol *m (de carro)*.

headline [ˈhedlaɪn] *n* **-1.** [in newspaper] manchete *f* **-2.** [of news broadcast] notícia *f* principal.

headlong ['hedlɒŋ] <> *adv* **-1.** [at great speed] apressadamente **-2.** [impetuously] precipitadamente **-3.** [dive, fall] abruptamente. <> *adj* [impetuous] precipitado(da).

headmaster [ˌhed'mɑːstəʳ] *n* diretor *m (de colégio).*

headmistress [ˌhed'mɪstrɪs] *n* diretora *f (de colégio).*

head office *n* sede *f.*

head-on <> *adj* frontal, de frente. <> *adv* de frente.

headphones ['hedfəʊnz] *npl* fones *mpl* de ouvido.

headquarters [ˌhed'kwɔːtəz] *npl* **-1.** FIN sede *f,* matriz *f* -**2.** MIL quartel-general *m.*

headrest ['hedrest] *n* apoio *m* para a cabeça.

headroom ['hedrʊm] *n (U)* **-1.** [in car] espaço *m (entre a cabeça e o teto)* -**2.** [below bridge] altura *f* livre.

headscarf ['hedskɑːf] *(pl* **-scarves** [-skɑːvz] OR -scarfs) *n* lenço *m (para a cabeça).*

headset ['hedset] *n* fones *mpl* de ouvido com microfone.

headship ['hedʃɪp] *n* direção *f (de colégio).*

head start *n* vantagem *f* inicial; ~ **on** OR **over sb** vantagem sobre alguém.

headstone ['hedstəʊn] *n* lápide *f.*

headstrong ['hedstrɒŋ] *adj* cabeça-dura, obstinado(da).

head teacher *n* diretor *m,* -ra *f* de colégio.

head waiter *n* mâître *m.*

headway ['hedweɪ] *n*: **to make** ~ fazer progressos.

headwind ['hedwɪnd] *n* vento *m* contrário.

headword *n* [in dictionary, reference book] entrada *f,* verbete *m.*

heady ['hedɪ] *(compar* -**ier,** *superl* -**iest)** *adj* **-1.** [exciting] emocionante **-2.** [causing giddiness] inebriante, estonteante.

heal [hiːl] <> *vt* **-1.** [mend, cure - person] curar; [- wound] cicatrizar **-2.** *fig* [breach, division] cicatrizar. <> *vi* [be mended, cured] cicatrizar.

➡ **heal up** *vi* [be mended, cured] cicatrizar.

healing ['hiːlɪŋ] <> *adj* curativo(va). <> *n (U)* cura *f.*

health [helθ] *n (U)* -**1.** [condition of body] saúde *f;* **to be in good/poor** ~ estar bem/mal de saúde; **to drink (to) sb's** ~ brindar à saúde de alguém -**2.** *fig* [of country, organization] bom estado *m.*

health centre *n* centro *m* de saúde.

health-conscious *adj* preocupado(da) com a saúde.

health farm *n* spa *m.*

health food *n* alimentos *mpl* naturais.

health food shop *n* loja *f* de alimentos naturais.

health hazard *n* risco *m* à saúde.

health service *n* serviço *m* de saúde.

health visitor *n* UK enfermeiro *m* comunitário, enfermeira *f* comunitária.

healthy ['helθɪ] *(compar* -**ier,** *superl* -**iest)** *adj* -**1.** [gen] saudável -**2.** *fig* [thriving] saneado(da) -**3.** [substantial] substancial.

heap [hiːp] <> *n* monte *m,* pilha *f;* **in a** ~

amontoado(da). <> *vt* -**1.** [pile up] amontoar; **to** ~ **sthg on (to) sthg** amontoar algo sobre algo -**2.** *fig* [lavish]: **to** ~ **sthg on sb** cobrir alguém de algo.

➡ **heaps** *npl inf*: ~ **s of** montes OR pilhas de.

hear [hɪəʳ] *(pt* & *pp* **heard** [hɜːd]) <> *vt* -**1.** [perceive] ouvir -**2.** [learn of] escutar; **to** ~ **(that)** ouvir dizer que -**3.** JUR [listen to] ver. <> *vi* -**1.** [perceive sound] ouvir -**2.** [know]: **to** ~ **about sthg** ouvir falar sobre algo -**3.** [receive news] ter notícias de; **to** ~ **from sb** ter notícias de alguém -**4.** *phr*: **I've never heard of him/it!** nunca ouvi falar dele/disto!; **I won't** ~ **of it!** não quero saber nada sobre isto!

➡ **hear out** *vt sep* escutar *(sem interromper).*

hearing ['hɪərɪŋ] *n* -**1.** [sense] audição *f;* **hard of** ~ com problemas de audição; **in/within sb's** ~ ao alcance dos ouvidos de alguém -**2.** JUR [trial] audiência *f,* julgamento *m;* **to give sb a fair** ~ *fig* dar a alguém a oportunidade de falar.

hearing aid *n* aparelho *m* auditivo.

hearsay ['hɪəseɪ] *n (U)* rumor *m,* boato *m.*

hearse [hɜːs] *n* carro *m* funerário.

heart [hɑːt] *n* -**1.** [gen] coração *m;* **to have a** ~ **of gold** ter um coração de ouro; **his** ~ **isn't in it** ele não colocou o coração nisto; **it's a subject close to my** ~ é um assunto que me encanta; **from the** ~ de coração; **from the bottom of my** ~ do fundo do meu coração; **in one's** ~ **of** ~ **s** no fundo do coração; **to do sthg to one's** ~ **'s content** fazer algo até que se tenha vontade; **my** ~ **leapt/sank** meu coração pulou/entristeceu-se; **to break sb's** ~ partir o coração de alguém; **to set one's** ~ **on sthg/on doing sthg** colocar o coração em algo/ ao fazer algo; **to take sthg to** ~ levar algo a sério -**2.** *(U)* [courage]: **to have the** ~ **to do sthg** ter coragem de fazer algo; **to lose** ~ perder o ímpeto -**3.** [of problem] centro *m* -**4.** [of cabbage, celery, lettuce] miolo *m.*

➡ **hearts** *npl* [playing cards] copas *fpl;* **the six of** ~ **s** o seis de copas.

➡ **at heart** *adv* de coração.

➡ **by heart** *adv* de cor.

heartache ['hɑːteɪk] *n* sofrimento *m,* angústia *f.*

heart attack *n* ataque *m* cardíaco.

heartbeat ['hɑːtbiːt] *n* pulsação *f.*

heartbreaking ['hɑːtˌbreɪkɪŋ] *adj* de partir o coração.

heartbroken ['hɑːtˌbrəʊkn] *adj* de coração partido.

heartburn ['hɑːtbɜːn] *n (U)* azia *f.*

heart disease *n (U)* doença *f* cardíaca.

heartening ['hɑːtnɪŋ] *adj* animador(ra).

heart failure *n (U)* parada *f* cardíaca.

heartfelt ['hɑːtfelt] *adj* sincero(ra), de todo coração.

hearth [hɑːθ] *n* -**1.** [of fireplace] base *f* -**2.** [fireplace] lareira *f.*

heartland ['hɑːtlænd] *n* área *f* central.

heartless ['hɑːtlɪs] *adj* desumano(na); ~ **person** pessoa sem coração.

heartrending ['hɑːtˌrendɪŋ] *adj* consternador(ra).

heart-searching *n (U)* exame *m* de consciência.

heartthrob ['hɑːtθrɒb] *n* galã *m.*

heart-to-heart <> *adj* franco(ca). <> *n* conversa *f* franca.

heart transplant n transplante m de coração.
heartwarming ['hɑ:t,wɔ:mɪŋ] adj enternecedor(-ra), gratificante.
hearty ['hɑ:tɪ] (compar -ier, superl -iest) adj -1. [loud, energetic] caloroso(sa) -2. [substantial - meal] farto(ta); [- appetite] bom (boa) -3. [strongly felt] profundo(da).
heat [hi:t] ⇔ n -1. (U) [gen] calor m -2. (U) [specific temperature] temperatura f -3. (U) [fire, source of heat] fogo m -4. (U) fig: in the ~ of the moment no calor do momento -5. [eliminating round] rodada f -6. ZOOL: on ~ UK, in ~ no cio. ⇔ vt esquentar.
◆ **heat up** ⇔ vt sep [make warm] esquentar. ⇔ vi [become warm] ficar quente, esquentar.
heated ['hi:tɪd] adj -1. [room, swimming pool] aquecido(da) -2. [argument, discussion, person] esquentado(da).
heater ['hi:təʳ] n aquecedor m.
heath [hi:θ] n [open place] charneca f.
heathen ['hi:ðn] ⇔ adj pagão(gã). ⇔ n pagão m, -gã f.
heather ['heðəʳ] n (U) urze f.
heating ['hi:tɪŋ] n (U) calefação f.
heat rash n brotoeja f (pelo calor).
heat-resistant adj refratário(ria), resistente ao calor.
heat-seeking [-,si:kɪŋ] adj detector(ra) de calor.
heatstroke ['hi:tstrəʊk] n (U) insolação f.
heat wave n onda f de calor.
heave [hi:v] ⇔ vt -1. [pull] puxar, arrastar; [push] empurrar -2. inf [throw] atirar, arremessar -3. [give out]: to ~ a sigh dar um suspiro. ⇔ vi -1. [pull] puxar -2. [rise and fall - boat, shoulders] sacudir-se; [- waves] ondular; [- chest] arfar -3. [retch] embrulhar. ⇔ n -1. [pull] puxão m -2. [push] empurrão m.
heaven ['hevn] n -1. [Paradise] paraíso m; ~ (alone) knows! sabe Deus! -2. (U) [something delightful] paraíso m.
◆ **heavens** ⇔ npl: the ~s literary os céus. ⇔ excl: (good) ~s! céus!
heavenly ['hevnlɪ] adj -1. inf dated [delightful] divino(na) -2. literary [of the skies] celestial.
heavily ['hevɪlɪ] adv -1. [for emphasis - to rain, smoke, drink, tax] excessivamente; [- laden, booked, dependent] totalmente; [- in debt] seriamente; [- populated] densamente -2. [solidly] solidamente -3. [noisily, ponderously] pesadamente -4. [deeply] profundamente.
heaviness ['hevɪnɪs] n -1. [of object] peso m -2. [of sleep] profundidade f -3. [of movement] dureza f, intensidade f -4. [of mixture] densidade f -5. [of feeling] abatimento f.
heavy ['hevɪ] (compar -ier, superl -iest) adj -1. [gen] pesado(da); how ~ is it? quanto pesa? -2. [intense, deep] intenso(sa); to be a ~ sleeper ter o sono muito profundo -3. [in quantity] em grande número -4. [person - fat] gordo(da); [- solidly built] sólido(da) -5. [laden]: ~ with fruit literary carregado(da) de fruta -6. [ponderous - movement] brusco(ca); [- fall] feio (feia) -7. [oppressive] carregado(da) -8. [sad]: with a ~ heart com o coração partido -9. [excessive]: to be a ~ smoker/drinker fumar/ beber em excesso; this car's ~ on petrol este carro consome muita gasolina -10. [grave, serious]

grande -11. [busy] cheio (cheia).
heavy cream n US nata f para enfeitar.
heavy-duty adj para grandes cargas/esforços; [máterial] resistente.
heavy goods vehicle n UK veículo m de carga pesada.
heavy-handed [-'hændɪd] adj [clumsy - tactics, policy, person] desastrado(da); [- compliment, treatment] grosseiro(ra).
heavy industry n indústria f pesada.
heavy metal n (U) MUS heavy-metal m.
heavyweight ['hevɪweɪt] ⇔ adj SPORT peso pesado. ⇔ n peso m pesado.
Hebrew ['hi:bru:] ⇔ adj hebraico(ca). ⇔ n -1. [person] hebraico m, -ca f -2. [language] hebraico m.
Hebrides ['hebrɪdɪ:z] npl: the ~ as Hébridas; in the ~ nas Hébridas.
heck [hek] excl: what/where/why the ~ ...? o que/ onde/por que diabos ...?; a ~ of a lot of uma montanha de; a ~ of a nice guy um cara e tanto.
heckle ['hekl] ⇔ vt ficar interrompendo. ⇔ vi ficar interrompendo.
heckler ['hekləʳ] n pessoa que fica interrompendo (um orador, um comediante, um político etc).
hectare ['hekteəʳ] n hectare m.
hectic ['hektɪk] adj muito agitado(da).
hector ['hektəʳ] ⇔ vt intimidar com bravatas. ⇔ vi bravatear.
he'd [hi:d] = he had, he would.
hedge [hedʒ] ⇔ n [shrub] cerca f viva. ⇔ vi [prevaricate] dar evasivas.
hedgehog ['hedʒhɒg] n porco-espinho m.
hedgerow ['hedʒrəʊ] n linha f de cerca viva.
hedonism ['hi:dənɪzm] n (U) hedonismo m.
hedonist ['hi:dənɪst] n hedonista mf.
heed [hi:d] ⇔ n: to pay ~ to sb prestar atenção em alguém; to take ~ of sthg levar algo em consideração. ⇔ vt fml ter em conta.
heedless ['hi:dlɪs] adj: to be ~ of sthg não fazer caso de algo.
heel [hi:l] n -1. [of foot] calcanhar m; to dig one's ~s in fincar o pé; to follow hard on the ~s (of sb/sthg) ficar na cola (de alguém/algo); to take to one's ~s dar no pé; to turn on one's ~ dar meia volta -2. [of shoe] salto m.
hefty ['heftɪ] (compar -ier, superl -iest) adj inf -1. [person] robusto(ta) -2. [salary, fee, fine] vultoso(sa), alto(ta).
heifer ['hefəʳ] n vitela f, novilha f.
height [haɪt] n -1. [gen] altura f; in ~ de altura; what ~ is it/are you? que altura tem isto/você tem?; to gain/lose ~ ganhar/perder altura -2. [zenith] apogeu m; the ~ of [fight, fame, tourist season] o auge de; [stupidity, ignorance, bad manners] o cúmulo de.
◆ **heights** npl -1. [limits] limites mpl -2. [high places] alto m; are you afraid of ~? você tem medo de altura?; the Golan Heights o Planalto do Golã.
heighten ['haɪtn] ⇔ vt intensificar. ⇔ vi intensificar-se.
heinous ['heɪnəs] adj fml hediondo(da).

heir [eəʳ] *n* herdeiro *m*.

heir apparent (*pl* **heirs apparent**) *n* sucessor *m* direto.

heiress ['eərɪs] *n* herdeira *f*.

heirloom ['eəlu:m] *n* herança *f* de família.

heist [haɪst] *n inf* roubo *m*.

held [held] *pt & pp* ▷ **hold**.

helices ['helɪsi:z] *pl* ▷ **helix**.

helicopter ['helɪkɒptəʳ] *n* hepicóptero *m*.

heliport ['helɪpɔ:t] *n* heliporto *m*.

helium ['hi:lɪəm] *n* (*U*) hélio *m*.

helix ['hi:lɪks] (*pl* **-es** OR **helices**) *n* [spiral] hélice *f*.

hell [hell] ◇ *n* **-1.** inferno *m*. **-2.** *inf* [for emphasis]: **what/where/why the ~ ...?** o que/onde/por que diabos ...?; **it was one ~ of a mess** estava uma bagunça total; **he's a ~ of a nice guy** ele é um cara simpático e tanto; **like ~** como o diabo; **like ~ you will!** com os diabos que você vai!; **let's get the ~ out (of here!)** vamos cair fora daqui! **-3.** *phr*: **to ~ with ...!** *v inf* pro inferno com ...!; **all ~ broke loose** *inf* o mundo veio abaixo; **to do sthg for the ~ of it** *inf* fazer algo por gosto; **to give sb ~** *inf* [verbally] fazer alguém passar poucas e boas; **go to ~!** *v inf* vá para o inferno!; **to play ~ with sthg** *inf* infernizar algo. ◇ *excl inf* diabos!, droga!

he'll [hi:l] = **he will**.

hell-bent *adj*: **to be ~ on doing sthg** estar totalmente decidido(da) a fazer algo.

hellish ['helɪʃ] *adj inf* infernal.

hello [hə'ləʊ] *excl* [greeting] olá!, oi!; [answering telephone, attracting attention] alô!

helm [helm] *n* **-1.** [of ship] leme *m*, timão *m* **-2.** *fig* [of company, organization] direção *f*; **at the ~** na direção.

helmet ['helmɪt] *n* capacete *m*.

helmsman ['helmzmən] (*pl* **-men** [-mən]) *n* NAUT timoneiro *m*, -ra *f*.

help [help] ◇ *n* **-1.** (*U*) [assistance] ajuda *f*; **to be of ~** ajudar; **with the ~ of sb/sthg** com a ajuda de alguém/algo **-2.** (*U*) [in an emergency] socorro *m* **-3.** [useful person or object]: **to be a ~** ser útil. ◇ *vt* **-1.** [gen] ajudar; **to ~ sb (to) do sthg** ajudar alguém a fazer algo; **can I ~ you?** [in shop, at reception] pois não? **-2.** [avoid] evitar; **I can't ~ feeling sad** não posso evitar ficar triste; **I couldn't ~ laughing** eu não conseguia parar de rir **-3.** *phr*: **to ~ o.s. (to sthg)** servir-se (de algo). ◇ *vi* [gen] ajudar; **to ~ with sthg** ajudar em algo. ◇ *excl* socorro!

➡ **help out** ◇ *vt sep* dar uma mão para. ◇ *vi* dar uma mão.

helper ['helpəʳ] *n* ajudante *mf*.

helpful ['helpfʊl] *adj* **-1.** [willing to help] prestativo(va) **-2.** [useful] proveitoso(sa).

helping ['helpɪŋ] *n* porção *f* (*de comida*); **would you like a second ~?** quer repetir?

helping hand *n*: **if you need a ~, just call** se precisar de uma mãozinha, é só chamar.

helpless ['helplɪs] *adj* indefeso(sa).

helplessly ['helplɪslɪ] *adv* **-1.** [uncontrollably] sem parar **-2.** [in a helpless manner] sem se poder fazer nada.

helpline ['helplaɪn] *n* (linha *f* de) suporte *m*.

Helsinki ['helsɪŋkɪ] *n* Helsinque; **in ~** em Helsinque.

helter-skelter [,heltə'skeltəʳ] UK ◇ *n* tobogã *m* gigante. ◇ *adv* desordenadamente.

hem [hem] (*pt & pp* **-med**, *cont* **-ming**) ◇ *n* bainha *f*. ◇ *vt* abainhar, fazer a bainha de.

➡ **hem in** *vt sep* cercar.

he-man *n inf hum* macho *m*.

hematology [,hi:mə'tɒlədʒɪ] *n* (*U*) hematologia *f*.

hemisphere ['hemɪ,sfɪəʳ] *n* [of Earth] hemisfério *m*.

hemline ['hemlaɪn] *n* (altura *f* da) bainha *f*.

hemoglobin [,hi:mə'gləʊbɪn] *n* (*U*) hemoglobina *f*.

hemophilia [,hi:mə'fɪlɪə] *n* (*U*) hemofilia *f*.

hemophiliac [,hi:mə'fɪlɪæk] *n* hemofílico *m*, -ca *f*.

hemorrhage ['hemərɪdʒ] ◇ *n* hemorragia *f*. ◇ *vi* ter uma hemorragia.

hemorrhoids ['hemərɔɪdz] *npl* hemorróidas *fpl*.

hemp [hemp] *n* (*U*) [plant or fibre] cânhamo *m*.

hen [hen] *n* **-1.** [female chicken] galinha *f* **-2.** [female bird] fêmea *f*.

hence [hens] *adv fml* **-1.** [therefore] por isso, assim **-2.** [from now]: **ten years ~** daqui a dez anos.

henceforth [,hens'fɔ:θ] *adv fml* doravante.

henchman ['hentʃmən] (*pl* **-men** [-mən]) *n pej* capanga *m*, jagunço *m*.

henna ['henə] ◇ *n* (*U*) hena *f*. ◇ *vt* passar OR aplicar hena em.

hen party *n* UK *inf* despedida *f* de solteira.

henpecked ['henpekt] *adj pej* submisso(sa), dominado(da).

hepatitis [,hepə'taɪtɪs] *n* (*U*) hepatite *f*.

her [hɜːʳ] ◇ *pers pron* **-1.** (*direct*) a; **I know ~** eu a conheço **-2.** (*indirect*) lhe; **send it to ~** mande isso para ela; **tell ~** diga-lhe **-3.** (*after prep*) ela; **Lucy brought it with ~** a Lucy trouxe-o consigo OR com ela. ◇ *poss adj* o seu (a sua), dela; **~ books** os livros dela, os seus livros.

herald ['herəld] ◇ *n* [messenger] mensageiro *m*, -ra *f*. ◇ *vt fml* **-1.** [signify, usher in] anunciar **-2.** [proclaim] conclamar.

heraldry ['herəldrɪ] *n* (*U*) heráldica *f*.

herb [UK hɜːb, US ɜːb] *n* erva *f*.

herbaceous [hɜː'beɪʃəs] *adj* herbáceo(cea).

herbal [UK 'hɜːbl, US ɜːbl] *adj* à base de ervas.

herbalist ['hɜːblɪst] *n* herbanário *m*, -ria *f*.

herbicide *n* herbicida *f*.

herbivore ['hɜːbɪvɔːʳ] *n* herbívoro *m*, -ra *f*.

herb tea *n* (*U*) infusão *f* de ervas.

herd [hɜːd] ◇ *n* **-1.** [gen] rebanho *m*; [of elephants] manada *f* **-2.** [of people] multidão *f*. ◇ *vt* **-1.** [drive] pastorear **-2.** *fig* [push] conduzir (*em grupo*).

herdsman ['hɜːdzmən] (*pl* **-men** [-mən]) *n* **-1.** [of sheep, goats] pastor *m* **-2.** [of cattle] boiadeiro *m*, vaqueiro *m*.

here [hɪəʳ] *adv* **-1.** [in, at this place] aqui; **~ he is/they are** aqui está ele/estão eles; **~ it is** aqui está; **~ you are!** toma!; **Christmas is nearly ~** o Natal está próximo; **~ and there** aqui e acolá **-2.** [from this place]: **from ~** daqui; **he left ~ a while ago** ele saiu daqui há pouco **-3.** [to this place]: **come ~!** vem aqui!; **~ they come** lá vêm eles **-4.** [in toasts]: **~'s to** um brinde a.

hereabouts UK [ˈhɪərəˌbaʊts], **hereabout** US [ˌhɪərəˈbaʊt] adv por aqui.

hereafter [ˌhɪərˈɑːftəʳ] ◇ adv fml de agora em diante, a partir de agora. ◇ n: **the** ~ o além.

hereby [ˌhɪəˈbaɪ] adv **-1.** fml [in documents] por meio deste (desta) **-2.** fml [when speaking]: **I** ~ **declare this theatre open** neste momento, declaro este teatro aberto.

hereditary [hɪˈredɪtrɪ] adj hereditário(ria).

heredity [hɪˈredətɪ] n (U) hereditariedade f.

heresy [ˈherəsɪ] (pl -ies) n heresia f.

heretic [ˈherətɪk] n **-1.** RELIG herege mf **-2.** fig [unorthodox thinker] rebelde mf.

herewith [ˌhɪəˈwɪð] adv fml [with letter]: **please find** ~ ... segue anexo ...

heritage [ˈherɪtɪdʒ] n (U) herança f.

heritage centre n museu m (em local histórico).

hermaphrodite [hɜːˈmæfrədaɪt] ZOOL ◇ adj hermafrodita. ◇ n hermafrodita mf.

hermetic [hɜːˈmetɪk] adj [airtight] hermético(ca).

hermetically [hɜːˈmetɪklɪ] adv: ~ **sealed** hermeticamente fechado(da).

hermit [ˈhɜːmɪt] n eremita mf.

hernia [ˈhɜːnjə] n hérnia f.

hero [ˈhɪərəʊl] (pl -es) n **-1.** [gen] herói m **-2.** [idol] ídolo m.

heroic [hɪˈrəʊɪk] adj heróico(ca).
➡ **heroics** npl pej patetices fpl.

heroin [ˈherəʊɪn] n [drug] (U) heroína f.

heroine [ˈherəʊɪn] n heroína f.

heroism [ˈherəʊɪzml] n (U) heroísmo m.

hero worship n (U) idolatria f, veneração f.

heron [ˈherən] (pl inv OR -s) n garça f real.

herpes [ˈhɜːpiːz] n (U) herpes m inv.

herring [ˈherɪŋ] (pl inv OR -s) n arenque m.

herringbone [ˈherɪŋbəʊn] adj [pattern] em espinha de peixe.

hers [hɜːz] poss pron o seu (a sua), (o/a) dela; **a friend of** ~ um amigo dela OR seu; **those shoes are** ~ estes sapatos são dela OR seus; **these are mine - where are** ~? estes são os meus - onde estão os dela?

herself [hɜːˈself] pron **-1.** (reflexive) se; **she hurt** ~ ela se machucou **-2.** (after prep) si própria OR mesma; **she did it** ~ foi ela mesma que o fez.

he's [hiːz] = **he is, he has.**

hesitant [ˈhezɪtənt] adj hesitante.

hesitate [ˈhezɪteɪt] vi [pause] hesitar; **to** ~ **to do sthg** hesitar em fazer algo.

hesitation [ˌhezɪˈteɪʃn] n hesitação f; **without** ~ sem hesitação; **to have no** ~ **in doing sthg** não ter dúvidas ao fazer algo.

hessian [ˈhesɪən] n UK aniagem f, juta f.

heterogeneous [ˌhetərəˈdʒiːnjəs] adj fml heterogêneo(nea).

heterosexual [ˌhetərəʊˈsekʃʊəl] ◇ adj heterossexual. ◇ n heterossexual mf.

het up [het-] adj inf nervoso(sa), como uma pilha de nervos.

hew [hjuː] (pt -ed, pp -ed OR hewn) vt literary [stone, wood] talhar.

HEW (abbr of (Department of) Health, Education and Welfare) n ministério norte-americano de educação, saúde e bem-estar social.

hex [heks] n **-1.** [curse] praga f, urucubaca f **-2.** COMPUT: ~ **(code)** (código m) hexadecimal m.

hexagon [ˈheksəgən] n hexágono m.

hexagonal [hekˈsægənl] adj hexagonal.

hey [heɪ] excl ei!

heyday [ˈheɪdeɪ] n auge m, apogeu m.

hey presto [-ˈprestəʊ] excl tadá!

HF (abbr of high frequency) HF.

HGV (abbr of heavy goods vehicle) n veículos pesados, como ônibus e caminhão; **an** ~ **licence** ≃ uma carteira categoria C.

hi [haɪ] excl inf [hello] oi!, olá!

HI abbr of Hawaii.

hiatus [haɪˈeɪtəs] (pl -es) n fml [pause] pausa f.

hibernate [ˈhaɪbəneɪt] vi hibernar.

hibernation [ˌhaɪbəˈneɪʃn] n (U) hibernação f; **to be in** ~ estar hibernando.

hiccough, hiccup [ˈhɪkʌp] (pt & pp -ped, cont -ping) ◇ n **-1.** [sound] soluço m; **to have** ~s estar com soluços **-2.** fig [difficulty] contratempo m. ◇ vi soluçar.

hick [hɪk] n esp US inf pej caipira mf.

hid [hɪd] pt ▷ hide.

hidden [ˈhɪdn] ◇ pp ▷ hide. ◇ adj **-1.** [from view] escondido(da) **-2.** [not apparent - disadvantages, dangers] escondido(da); [- problems] não aparente; [- cost] embutido(do) **-3.** [deliberately concealed - weapons] secreto; [- feelings] oculto.

hidden agenda n pej segunda intenção f.

hide [haɪd] (pt hid, pp hidden) ◇ n **-1.** [animal skin] pele f **-2.** [for watching birds, animals] esconderijo m. ◇ vt **-1.** [conceal] esconder; **to** ~ **sthg (from sb)** esconder algo (de alguém) **-2.** [cover] cobrir. ◇ vi [conceal o.s.] esconder-se.

hide-and-seek n (U) esconde-esconde m; **to play** ~ brincar de esconde-esconde.

hideaway [ˈhaɪdəweɪ] n inf refúgio m.

hidebound [ˈhaɪdbaʊnd] adj pej **-1.** [institution] antiquado(da) **-2.** [person] careta.

hideous [ˈhɪdɪəs] adj horrível.

hideout [ˈhaɪdaʊt] n esconderijo m.

hiding [ˈhaɪdɪŋ] n **-1.** (U) [concealment]: **to be in** ~ estar escondido(da) **-2.** inf [beating]: **to give sb a (good)** ~ dar uma (boa) surra em alguém; **to get a (good)** ~ **from sb** levar uma (boa) surra de alguém.

hiding place n esconderijo m.

hierarchical [ˌhaɪəˈrɑːkɪkl] adj hierárquico(ca).

hierarchy [ˈhaɪərɑːkɪ] (pl -ies) n hierarquia f.

hieroglyphics [ˌhaɪərəˈglɪfɪks] npl hieróglifos mpl.

hi-fi [ˈhaɪfaɪ] n sistema f hi-fi.

higgledy-piggledy [ˌhɪgldɪˈpɪgldɪ] inf ◇ adj desordenado(da). ◇ adv desordenadamente, de qualquer maneira.

high [haɪ] ◇ adj **-1.** [gen] alto(ta); **to have a** ~ **opinion of sb/sthg** ter alguém/algo em alta conta; **how** ~ **is it?** qual é a altura? **-2.** [greater than normal - speed] alto(ta); [- wind] forte; [- prices, unemployment] elevado(da); **temperatures in the** ~ **twenties** temperaturas bem acima dos 20 graus **-3.** [important, influential] importante **-4.** [honourable] nobre **-5.** [high-pitched] agudo(da) **-6. drugs sl** [on drugs] baratinado(da) **-7. inf** [drunk] alto(ta). <> adv **-1.** [above ground level] a grande altura **-2.** [in degrees] em alto grau; **to search ~ and low** procurar em tudo quanto é lugar. <> n [highest point] pico m; **to reach a new ~** atingir um novo pico; **to be on a ~** estar animadíssimo(ma).

highball ['hɔːbɔːl] n **US** uísque m com soda e gelo.

highbrow ['haɪbraʊ] adj erudito(ta).

high chair n cadeira f de bebê.

high-class adj [superior - person] de alta classe; [- hotel, restaurant] de alta categoria; [- performance] de alto nível.

high command n alto comando m.

high commission n alta comissão f.

high commissioner n alto comissário m, alta comissária f.

High Court n **UK** **JUR** Corte f Suprema.

high-density adj **COMPUT** de alta densidade.

higher ['haɪə'] adj [exam, qualification] superior(ra).

➡ **Higher** n: **Higher (Grade)** **SCH** na Escócia, exame realizado ao final da escola secundária.

higher education n (U) ensino m superior.

high explosive n explosivo m de alta potência.

high-fidelity adj de alta-fidelidade.

high finance n altas finanças fpl.

high-flier n pessoa f ambiciosa.

high-flying adj [ambitious] ambicioso(sa).

high ground n: **to have OR hold the ~** ter OR levar vantagem; **to take the moral ~** acreditar possuir valores morais superiores.

high-handed [-'hændɪd] adj despótico(ca).

high-heeled [-'hiːld] adj de salto alto.

high horse n inf: **to get on one's ~** estar por cima.

high jump n **SPORT** salto m em altura; **to be for the ~ UK** inf merecer uma punição.

Highland Games ['haɪlənd-] npl Jogos mpl das Terras Altas.

Highlands ['haɪləndz] npl: **the ~** [of Scotland] as Terras Altas.

high-level adj **-1.** [talks, discussions] de alto nível **-2.** [diplomats, officials] do alto escalão.

high life n (U): **the ~** a vida da alta sociedade.

highlight ['haɪlaɪt] <> n [of event, occasion] ponto m alto, destaque m. <> vt **-1.** [with pen] realçar **-2.** [emphasize] enfatizar.

➡ **highlights** npl [in hair] realces mpl.

highlighter (pen) ['haɪlaɪtə'-] n caneta f marca-texto.

highly ['haɪlɪ] adv **-1.** [very, extremely] altamente **-2.** [very well, at high level] muito bem **-3.** [favourably] favoravelmente; **I ~ recommend** it realmente recomendo isso.

highly-strung adj irritadiço(ça).

high mass n missa f solene.

high-minded [-'maɪndɪd] adj nobre.

Highness ['haɪnɪs] n: **His/Her/Your (Royal) ~** Sua Alteza (Real); **Their (Royal) ~es** Suas Altezas (Reais).

high-octane adj de alto índice de octana.

high-pitched [-'pɪtʃt] adj [shrill] agudo(da).

high point n [of occasion] ponto m alto.

high-powered [-'paʊəd] adj **-1.** [powerful] de alta potência **-2.** [dynamic] dinâmico(ca).

high-pressure adj **-1.** [air, gas] de alta pressão **-2.** [persuasive] persuasivo(va).

high priest n **RELIG** sumo sacerdote m.

high-ranking [-'ræŋkɪŋ] adj de destaque.

high-resolution adj **COMPUT** de alta resolução.

high-rise adj de muitos andares; **a ~ building** um espigão.

high-risk adj de alto risco.

high school n **-1. UK** [for 11- to 18-year-olds] ≃ escola f secundária **-2. US** [for 15- to 18-year-olds] ≃ segundo grau m.

high seas npl: **the ~** o alto-mar.

high season n (U) alta estação f.

high-speed adj **-1.** [train] de alta velocidade **-2. PHOT** [film] para alta velocidade.

high-spirited adj [person] alegre, vivaz.

high spot n ponto m de relevo.

high street n **UK** avenida f principal.

hightail ['haɪteɪl] vt esp **US**: **they ~ed it back home** eles se mandaram rapidinho para casa.

high tea n (U) **UK** chá f ao fim da tarde (servido no lugar do jantar).

high-tech <> adj [method, industry] de alta tecnologia. <> n (abbr of **high technology**) alta tecnologia f.

high technology n (U) alta tecnologia f.

high-tension adj de alta tensão.

high tide n (U) [of sea] maré f alta.

high treason n (U) alta traição f.

high water n (U) preamar f.

highway ['haɪweɪ] n **-1. US** [main road between cities] auto-estrada f **-2. UK** [any main road] rodovia f.

Highway Code n **UK**: **the ~** ≃ o Código Nacional de Trânsito.

high wire n cabo m de aço.

hijack ['haɪdʒæk] <> n [of aircraft, car] seqüestro m. <> vt [aircraft, car] seqüestrar.

hijacker ['haɪdʒækə'] n seqüestrador m, -ra f.

hike [haɪk] <> n [long walk] caminhada f. <> vi [go for a long walk] caminhar.

hiker ['haɪkə'] n caminhante mf, andarilho m.

hiking ['haɪkɪŋ] n (U) excursões fpl a pé; **to go ~** fazer excursões.

hilarious [hɪ'leərɪəs] adj hilariante, engraçado(da).

hilarity [hɪ'lærətɪ] n (U) **fml** hilaridade f; **to cause much ~** causar muitos risos.

hill [hɪl] n **-1.** [mound] colina f **-2.** [slope] ladeira f.

hillbilly ['hɪl,bɪlɪ] (pl **-ies**) n **US** inf pej jeca m.

hillock ['hɪlək] n pequena colina f, outeiro m.

hillside ['hɪlsaɪd] n encosta f.

hill start n partida f do carro em uma lomba.

hilltop ['hɪltɒp] <> adj no topo do morro. <> n topo m do morro.

hilly ['hɪlɪ] (compar **-ier**, superl **-iest**) adj montanhoso(sa).

hilt [hɪlt] n punho m; **to the ~** ao extremo; **to support/defend sb to the ~** apoiar/defender alguém com unhas e dentes.

him [hɪm] pers pron **-1.** (direct) o; **I know ~** eu o conheço **- 2.** *(indirect)* lhe; **tell** ~ diga-lhe **- 3.** *(after prep)* ele; **send it to** ~ mande isso para ele; **Tony brought it with** ~ Tony trouxe-o consigno *OR* com ele.

Himalayan [ˌhɪməˈleɪən] *adj* do Himalaia, himalaico(ca).

Himalayas [ˌhɪməˈleɪəz] *npl*: **the** ~ as montanhas do Himalaia; **in the** ~ nas montanhas do Himalaia.

himself [hɪmˈself] *pron* **-1.** *(reflexive)* se; **he hurt** ~ machucou-se **- 2.** *(after prep)* si próprio *OR* mesmo; **he did it** ~ foi ele mesmo que o fez.

hind [haɪnd] *(pl inv OR* **-s)** <> *adj* traseiro(ra). <> *n* [deer] corça *f*.

hinder [ˈhɪndə'] *vt* retardar, atrapalhar.

Hindi [ˈhɪndɪ] *n (U)* [language] hindi *m*.

hindmost [ˈhaɪndməʊst] *adj* último(ma).

hindquarters [ˈhaɪndkwɔːtəz] *npl* traseiro *m*.

hindrance [ˈhɪndrəns] *n* **-1.** [obstacle] obstáculo *m* **- 2.** *(U)* [delay] atrasos *mpl*.

hindsight [ˈhaɪndsaɪt] *n (U)*: **with the benefit of** ~ olhando em retrospecto.

Hindu [ˈhɪnduː] *(pl* **-s)** <> *adj* hindu. <> *n* hindu *m*.

Hinduism [ˈhɪnduːɪzm] *n (U)* hinduísmo *m*.

hinge [hɪndʒ] *(cont* **hingeing)** *n* [on door, window, lid] dobradiça *f*.

→ **hinge (up)on** *vt fus* [depend on] depender de.

hint [hɪnt] <> *n* **-1.** [indirect suggestion] alusão *f*; **to drop a** ~ dar uma indireta; **to take the** ~ pegar uma indireta **- 2.** [useful suggestion, tip] dica *f* **- 3.** [small amount, trace] sinal *m*. <> *vi*: **to** ~ **at sthg** fazer alusão a algo. <> *vt*: **to** ~ **that** insinuar que.

hinterland [ˈhɪntəlænd] *n* [area around coast, river] hinterlândia *f*, interior *m*.

hip [hɪp] <> *adj inf* [fashionable] moderno(na). <> *n* [part of body] quadril *m*.

hip bath *n* banheira *f* de assento.

hip bone *n* osso *m* ilíaco.

hip flask *n* garrafa *f* de bolso.

hip-hop *n (U)* [music] hip-hop *m*.

hippie [ˈhɪpɪ] *n* hippie *m*.

hippo [ˈhɪpəʊ] *(pl* **-s)** *n* hipopótamo *m*.

hippopotamus [ˌhɪpəˈpɒtəməs] *(pl* **-muses** *OR* **-mi** [-maɪl] *)n* hipopótamo *m*.

hippy [ˈhɪpɪ] *(pl* **-ies)** *n* = **hippie**.

hire [ˈhaɪə'] <> *n (U)* [of car, equipment] aluguel *m*; **for** ~ aluga-se; **bicycles for** ~ alugam-se bicicletas; **taxi for** ~ táxi livre. <> *vt* **-1.** [rent] alugar **- 2.** [employ] contratar.

→ **hire out** *vt sep* alugar.

hire car *n UK*: **to have a** ~ alugar um carro.

hired help *n* [domestic staff] assessoria *f* doméstica.

hire purchase *n (U) UK* compra *f* a prazo; **to buy sthg on** ~ comprar algo a prazo.

his [hɪz] <> *poss pron* o seu (a sua), (o/a) dele; ~ **books** os livros dele, os seus livros <> *poss adj* o seu (a sua), dele; **a friend of** ~ um amigo dele *OR* seu; **these shoes are** ~ estes sapatos são dele *OR* seus; **these are mine - where are** ~**?** estes são os meus - onde estão os dele?

Hispanic [hɪˈspænɪk] <> *adj* hispânico(ca). <> *n esp US* hispânico *m*, -ca *f*.

hiss [hɪs] <> *n* **-1.** [of animal, person] silvo *m* **- 2.** [of audience] vaia *f* **- 3.** [of steam, gas] assobio *m*. <> *vt* [actor, speaker] vaiar. <> *vi* **- 1.** [animal, person] silvar; **she** ~**ed angrily at him** ela o vaiou irritada **- 2.** [steam, gas] assobiar.

histogram [ˈhɪstəgræm] *n* histograma *m*.

historian [hɪˈstɔːrɪən] *n* historiador *m*, -ra *f*.

historic [hɪˈstɒrɪk] *adj* [significant] histórico(ca).

historical [hɪˈstɒrɪkəl] *adj* histórico(ca).

history [ˈhɪstərɪ] *(pl* **-ies)** *n* **-1.** [gen] história *f*; **to go down in** ~ entrar para a história; **to make** ~ fazer história **- 2.** [past record] histórico *m*.

histrionics [ˌhɪstrɪˈɒnɪks] *npl pej* melodrama *m*.

hit [hɪt] *(pt & pp* **hit,** *cont* **-ting)** <> *n* **-1.** [blow] golpe *m*, pancada *f* **- 2.** [successful strike] tiro *m* certeiro **- 3.** [success] sucesso *m* **- 4.** *COMPUT* [of website] visita *f*. <> *comp* de sucesso. <> *vt* **-1.** [strike a blow at] bater em **- 2.** [crash into] bater contra **- 3.** [score] ferir **- 4.** [reach] alcançar; **the thought suddenly** ~ **me that** ... de repente me dei conta de que ... **- 5.** [affect badly] atingir **- 6.** *phr*: **to** ~ **it off (with sb)** dar-se bem (com alguém).

→ **hit back** *vi*: **to** ~ **back (at sb/sthg)** *fig* revidar aos ataques (de alguém/algo).

→ **hit on** *vt fus* **-1.** = **hit upon - 2.** *US inf* [chat up] dar uma cantada em.

→ **hit out** *vi*: **to** ~ **out at sb/sthg** [physically] tentar bater em alguém/algo; [in speech, writing] rebater veementemente.

→ **hit upon** *vt fus* [think of] achar, descobrir.

hit-and-miss *adj* = **hit-or-miss**.

hit-and-run <> *adj* **-1.** [driver] que não presta socorro **- 2.** [accident] em que não se presta socorro. <> *n* [accident] acidente no qual não se presta socorro.

hitch [hɪtʃ] <> *n* [problem, snag] dificuldade *f*. <> *vt* **-1.** [solicit]: **to** ~ **a lift** pegar carona **- 2.** [fasten]: **to** ~ **sthg on(to) sthg** amarrar algo em algo. <> *vi* [hitchhike] viajar de carona.

→ **hitch up** *vt sep* [pull up] levantar.

hitchhike [ˈhɪtʃhaɪk] *vi* viajar de carona.

hitchhiker [ˈhɪtʃhaɪkə'] *n* caroneiro *m*, -ra *f*.

hi-tech [ˌhaɪˈtek] *adj* = **high-tech**.

hither [ˈhɪðə'] *adv literary* aqui; ~ **and thither** em muitas direções, aqui e acolá.

hitherto [ˌhɪðəˈtuː] *adv fml* até agora.

hit list *n* lista *f* negra.

hit man *n* matador *m* de aluguel.

hit-or-miss *adj* aleatório(ria).

hit parade *n dated* parada *f* de sucessos.

HIV *(abbr of* **human immunodeficiency virus)** *n (U)* HIV *m*; **to be** ~ **-positive** ser soropositivo(va).

hive [haɪv] *n* [for bees] colméia *f*; **a** ~ **of activity** *fig* um centro de atividades.

→ **hive off** *vt sep* [separate] transferir.

HK *(abbr of* **Hong Kong)** HK.

hl *(abbr of* **hectolitre)** hl.

HM *(abbr of* **His (or Her) Majesty)** S.M.

HMG *(abbr of* **His (or Her) Majesty's Government)** *expressão utilizada nos documentos oficiais da Grã-Bretanha*, governo *m* de sua majestade.

HMI (*abbr of* **His (or Her) Majesty's Inspector**) *n inspetor de escolas na Grã-Bretanha.*

HMO (*abbr of* **health maintenance organization**) *n* órgão norte-americano de saúde pública.

HMS (*abbr of* **His (or Her) Majesty's Ship**) *prefixo utilizado nos navios da marinha real britânica,* navio *m* de sua majestade.

HMSO (*abbr of* **His (or Her) Majesty's Stationery Office**) *n* serviço oficial de imprensa da Grã-Bretanha.

HNC (*abbr of* **Higher National Certificate**) *n certificado de qualificação em disciplinas técnicas na Grã-Bretanha.*

HND (*abbr of* **Higher National Diploma**) *n diploma de qualificação em disciplinas técnicas na Grã-Bretanha.*

hoard [hɔ:d] <> *n* [store] provisão *f.* <> *vt* [collect, save] estocar.

hoarding ['hɔ:dɪŋ] *n UK* [for advertisements, posters] outdoor *m.*

hoarfrost ['hɔ:frɒst] *n (U)* geada *f.*

hoarse [hɔ:s] *adj* rouco(ca).

hoax [həʊks] *n* trote *m.*

hoaxer ['həʊksə[r]] *n* trotador *m,* -ra *f;* **bomb ~** *pessoa que passa um trote de bomba.*

hob [hɒb] *n UK* [on cooker] mesa *f.*

hobble ['hɒbl] *vi* [limp] coxear.

hobby ['hɒbɪ] (*pl* -**ies**) *n* [leisure activity] hobby *m.*

hobby horse *n* -**1.** [toy] cavalinho-de-pau *m* -**2.** [favourite topic] assunto *m* favorito.

hobnob ['hɒbnɒb] (*pt* & *pp* -**bed**, *cont* -**bing**) *vi* [socialize]: **to ~ with sb** enturmar-se com alguém.

hobo ['həʊbəʊ] (*pl* -**es** *OR* -**s**) *n US* [tramp] vagabundo *m,* -da *f.*

Ho Chi Minh City ['həʊˌtʃiːˈmɪn-] *n* Ho Chi Minh.

hock [hɒk] *n (U)* [wine] vinho *m* branco do Reno.

hockey ['hɒkɪ] *n* -**1.** [on grass] hóquei *m* -**2.** *US* [ice hockey] hóquei *m* no gelo.

hockey stick *n* bastão *m* de hóquei.

hocus-pocus [ˌhəʊkəsˈpəʊkəs] *n (U)* [trickery] tapeação *f.*

hod [hɒd] *n* [for bricks] cocho *m (de pedreiro).*

hodgepodge *n US* = hotchpotch.

hoe [həʊ] <> *n* enxada *f.* <> *vt* capinar.

hog [hɒg] (*pt* & *pp* -**ged**, *cont* -**ging**) <> *n* -**1.** *US lit* & *fig* porco *m,* -ca *f* -**2.** *phr:* **to go the whole ~** ir até o fim. <> *vt inf* [monopolize] monopolizar.

Hogmanay ['hɒgməneɪ] *n denominação escocesa para a Noite de Ano Novo.*

hoi-polloi *npl pej:* **the ~** a gentalha, a ralé.

hoist [hɔɪst] <> *n* guindaste *f.* <> *vt* -**1.** [load, person] levantar - **2.** [sail, flag] içar.

hokum ['həʊkəm] *n US inf* palhaçada *f.*

hold [həʊld] (*pt* & *pp* **held**) <> *n* -**1.** [grasp, grip]: **to have a firm ~ on sthg** segurar algo firme; **to keep ~ of sthg** segurar algo; **to take** *OR* **lay ~ of sthg** começar a ter efeito de algo; **to get ~ of sthg** [obtain] arranjar algo; **to get ~ of sb** [find] encontrar - **2.** [of ship, aircraft] porão *m* -**3.** [control, influence] influência *f;* **to take ~** [fire] tomar conta. <> *vt* -**1.** [in hand, arms] segurar - **2.** [maintain in position] manter; **to ~ sb prisoner** manter alguém como

prisioneiro(ra); **to ~ sb hostage** tomar alguém como refém - **3.** [have, possess] ter, possuir - **4.** [conduct, stage] conduzir - **5.** *fml* [consider] julgar; **to ~ (that)** sustentar que; **to ~ sb responsible for sthg** responsabilizar alguém por algo; **to ~ sthg dear** ter afeição por algo - **6.** [on telephone]: **please ~ the line** aguarde na linha, por favor - **7.** [keep, sustain] manter - **8.** *MIL* ocupar - **9.** [support, have space for] suportar - **10.** [contain] guardar - **11.** *phr:* **~ it!,** **~ everything!** espera aí!; **to ~ one's own** virar-se. <> *vi* -**1.** [remain unchanged] manter-se; **to ~ still** *OR* **steady** segurar firme - **2.** [on phone] esperar.

◆ **hold against** *vt sep:* **to ~ sthg against sb** *fig* ter algo que pese contra alguém.

◆ **hold back** <> *vi* [hesitate] hesitar; **to ~ back from doing sthg** hesitar em fazer algo. <> *vt sep* -**1.** [gen] reter - **2.** [prevent progress of]: **to ~ sb back (from doing sthg)** impedir alguém (de fazer algo) .

◆ **hold down** *vt sep* [job] manter.

◆ **hold off** <> *vt sep* [fend off] manter à distância. <> *vi* [rain] parar.

◆ **hold on** *vi* -**1.** [gen] esperar - **2.** [grip]: **to ~ on (to sthg)** segurar-se firme (em algo).

◆ **hold onto** *vt fus* [retain] reter.

◆ **hold out** <> *vt sep* [hand, arms] estender. <> *vi* -**1.** [last] durar - **2.** [resist]: **to ~ out (against sb/sthg)** resistir (a alguém/algo).

◆ **hold out for** *vt fus* insistir em.

◆ **hold up** *vt sep* -**1.** [raise] levantar - **2.** [delay] atrasar - **3.** *inf* [rob] assaltar.

◆ **hold with** *vt fus* [approve of] aprovar.

holdall ['həʊldɔ:l] *n UK* mochila *f.*

holder ['həʊldə[r]] *n* -**1.** [gen] suporte *m,* recipiente *m;* **cigarette ~** boquilha *f;* **candle ~** castiçal *m* -**2.** [owner - gen] titular *mf;* [- of ticket] portador *m,* -ra *f;* [- position, title] detentor *m,* -ra *f.*

holding ['həʊldɪŋ] <> *adj* [action, operation] controlador(ra). <> *n* -**1.** [investment] participação *f* acionária - **2.** [farm] propriedade *f.*

holding company *n* empresa *f* controladora, holding *f.*

hold-up *n* -**1.** [robbery] assalto *m* à mão armada - **2.** [delay] empecilho *m,* atraso *m.*

hole [həʊl] *n* -**1.** [gen] buraco *m;* **~ in one** um buraco numa só tacada; **to pick ~ s in sthg** [criticize] achar defeito em algo; [in sock, shoe] furo *m* -**2.** *inf* [horrible place] buraco *m* -**3.** *inf* [predicament] apuro *m.*

◆ **hole up** *vi* [hide, take shelter] hibernar.

holiday ['hɒlɪdeɪ] *n* -**1.** [vacation] férias *fpl;* **to be/go on ~** estar de/sair de férias - **2.** [public holiday] feriado *m.*

holiday camp *n UK* colônia *f* de férias.

holidaymaker ['hɒlɪdeɪˌmeɪkə[r]] *n UK* excursionista *mf.*

holiday pay *n UK* férias *fpl* remuneradas.

holiday resort *n UK* cidade *f* turística.

holiday season *n US* temporada *f* de férias.

holiness ['həʊlɪnɪs] *n (U)* [holy quality] santidade *f.*

◆ **Holiness** *n* [in titles]: **His/Your Holiness** Sua Santidade.

holistic [həʊˈlɪstɪk] *adj* holístico(ca).

Holland ['hɒlənd] *n* Holanda *f;* **in ~** na Holanda.

hollandaise sauce [ˌhɒlən'deɪz-] *n (U)* molho *m* holandês.

holler ['hɒlə'] *inf* ⬦ *vt* gritar. ⬦ *vi esp US* gritar.

hollow ['hɒləʊ] ⬦ *adj* **-1.** [gen] oco (oca), vazio(-zia) **-2.** [gaunt - eyes] fundo(da); [- cheeks] magro(gra) **-3.** [empty of meaning or value - laugh, optimism] falso(sa); [- promise, victory] vão (vã). ⬦ *n* **-1.** [gen] buraco *m* **-2.** [in ground, pillow] buraco *m*, cavidade *f*.
➡ **hollow out** *vt sep* **-1.** [make hollow] tornar oco (oca) **-2.** [make by hollowing] escavar.

holly ['hɒlɪ] *n (U)* azevinho *m*.

hollyhock *n* malva-rosa *f*.

Hollywood ['hɒlɪwʊd] ⬦ *n* [film industry] Hollywood. ⬦ *comp* de Hollywood.

holocaust ['hɒləkɔːst] *n* [destruction] holocausto *m*.
➡ **Holocaust** *n*: **the Holocaust** o Holocausto.

hologram ['hɒləgræm] *n* holograma *m*.

hols [hɒlz] *npl UK inf* folgas *fpl*.

holster ['həʊlstə'] *n* coldre *m*.

holy ['həʊlɪ] (*compar* -**ier**, *superl* -**iest**) *adj* **-1.** [sacred] sagrado(da), santo(ta); ~ **water** água *f* benta **-2.** [pure and good] puro(ra).

Holy Communion *n (U)* Sagrada Comunhão *f*.

Holy Father *n*: **the** ~ o Papa.

Holy Ghost *n*: **the** ~ o Espírito Santo.

Holy Grail [-'greɪl] *n*: **the** ~ o Santo Graal.

Holy Land *n*: **the** ~ a Terra Santa.

holy orders *npl* votos *mpl* sagrados; **to take** ~ ordenar-se sacerdote.

Holy Spirit *n*: **the** ~ o Espírito Santo.

homage ['hɒmɪdʒ] *n fml* **-1.** [respect] homenagem *f*; **to pay** ~ **to sb/sthg** prestar homenagem a alguém/algo **-2.** [tribute] tributo *m*.

home [həʊm] ⬦ *adj* **-1.** [not foreign] nacional **-2.** *SPORT* interno(na). ⬦ *adv* **-1.** [to or at one's house] para casa **-2.** [from abroad] para casa (do exterior) **-3.** *phr*: **to bring sthg** ~ **(to sb)** fazer alguém enxergar algo; **to drive** *OR* **hammer sthg** ~ **(to sb)** deixar algo bem claro (para alguém). ⬦ *n* **-1.** [one's house, place of residence] casa *f*; **to make one's** ~ fazer a casa; **it's a** ~ **from** ~ *UK*, **it's a** ~ **away from** ~ *US* é um lugar onde a gente se sente em casa **-2.** [place of origin] terra *f* natal **-3.** [family unit, institution] lar *m*; **to leave** ~ sair de casa.
➡ **at home** *adv* **-1.** [gen] em casa; **at** ~ **with sthg** à vontade com algo; **to make o.s. at** ~ sentir-se à vontade *OR* em casa **-2.** [in one's own country] no meu país **-3.** *SPORT*: **to play at** ~ jogar em casa.
➡ **home in** *vi*: **to** ~ **in on sthg** dirigir-se diretamente a algo.

home address *n* endereço *m* residencial.

home banking *n (U)* home banking *m*.

home brew *n (U)* [beer] cerveja *f* caseira.

homecoming ['həʊmˌkʌmɪŋ] *n* **-1.** [return] volta *f* ao lar **-2.** *US SCH & UNIV* regresso *m* dos ex-alunos às suas faculdades.

home computer *n* computador *m* pessoal.

home cooking *n* comida *f* caseira.

Home Counties *npl UK*: **the** ~ os condados ao redor de Londres.

home delivery *n* entrega *m* a domicílio.

home economics *n (U)* economia *f* doméstica.

home fries *npl US* batatas *fpl* fritas.

home ground *n* **-1.** [gen]: **to be on** ~ estar em seu território **-2.** *SPORT* campo *m* do time da casa.

home-grown *adj* plantado(da) em casa.

home help *n UK* empregada *que auxilia pessoas idosas ou doentes*.

home improvements *npl* reformas *fpl* na casa.

homeland ['həʊmlænd] *n* **-1.** [country of birth] terra *f* natal **-2.** [in South Africa] gueto *m*.

homeless ['həʊmlɪs] ⬦ *adj* sem-teto. ⬦ *npl*: **the** ~ os sem-teto, os desabrigados.

homelessness ['həʊmlɪsnəs] *n (U)*: **the problem of** ~ o problema dos sem-teto.

home loan *n* financiamento *m* para habitação.

homely ['həʊmlɪ] *adj* **-1.** [simple, unpretentious] simples **-2.** [ugly] feio (feia).

home-made *adj* caseiro(ra); ~ **bread** pão *m* feito em casa.

home movie *n* filmagem *f* caseira.

Home Office *n UK*: **the** ~ ≃ o Ministério do Interior.

homeopathic [ˌhəʊmɪəʊ'pæθɪk] *adj* homeopático(ca).

homeopathy [ˌhəʊmɪ'ɒpəθɪ] *n (U)* homeopatia *f*.

homeowner ['həʊmˌəʊnə'] *n* proprietário *m*, -ria *f* da casa.

home page *n COMPUT* homepage *f*, página *f* inicial.

home rule *n (U)* autonomia *f* interna.

home run *n US inf* tacada *que permite ao jogador de beisebol completar o circuito das bases*.

Home Secretary *n UK* ≃ Ministro *m*, -tra *f* do Interior.

homesick ['həʊmsɪk] *adj* com saudade de casa; **to feel** ~ estar com saudades de casa.

homesickness ['həʊmˌsɪknɪs] *n (U)* saudade *f* de casa.

homespun ['həʊmspʌn] *adj fig* [unsophisticated] tosco(ca).

homestead ['həʊmsted] *n US* fazenda *f*.

home straight *n*: **the** ~ [of race] a reta de chegada; [of task] última etapa *f*.

hometown ['həʊmtaʊn] *n* cidade *f* natal.

home truth *n* verdades *fpl* desagradáveis; **to tell sb a few** ~**s** dizer algumas verdades para alguém.

homeward ['həʊmwəd] ⬦ *adj* de regresso. ⬦ *adv* = homewards.

homewards ['həʊmwədz] *adv* para casa.

homework ['həʊmwɜːk] *n* **-1.** *SCH* dever *m* de casa, tema *m* **-2.** *inf fig* [preparation] dever *m* de casa.

homey, homy ['həʊmɪ] *US adj US* familiar.

homicidal ['hɒmɪsaɪdl] *adj* homicida.

homicide ['hɒmɪsaɪd] *n fml (U)* homicídio *m*.

homily ['hɒmɪlɪ] (*pl* -**ies**) *n* [lecture] homilia *f*.

homing ['həʊmɪŋ] *adj* **-1.** [instinct] que se refere ao instinto do lar; ~ **instinct** instinto *m* doméstico **-2.** [device] autodirecional.

homing pigeon *n* pombo-correio *m*.

homoeopathy *etc n* = homeopathy *etc*.

homogeneous [ˌhɒmə'dʒiːnjəs] *adj* homogêneo(-nea).

homogenize, -ise [hə'mɒdʒənaɪz] *vt UK* homogeneizar.

homophobic ['həʊməʊ'fəʊbɪk] *adj* homofóbico(-ca).

homosexual [ˌhɒmə'sekʃʊəl] ◇ *adj* homossexual. ◇ *n* homossexual *mf*.

homosexuality [ˌhɒmə,sekʃʊ'ælətɪ] *n (U)* homossexualidade *f*.

homy *adj US* = **homey**.

Hon. -1. (*abbr of* **Honourable**) honorável **-2.** (*abbr of* **Honorary**) hon.

Honduran [hɒn'djʊərən] ◇ *adj* hondurenho(-nha). ◇ *n* hondurenho *m*, -nha *f*.

Honduras [hɒn'djʊərəs] *n* Honduras; **in** ~ em Honduras.

hone [həʊn] *vt* **-1.** [knife, sword] afiar **-2.** [intellect, wit] aprimorar.

honest ['ɒnɪst] ◇ *adj* **-1.** [trustworthy] honesto(ta) **-2.** [frank, truthful] sincero(ra); **to be** ~, ... para ser franco(ca), ... **-3.** [legal] legal. ◇ *adv inf*: **I didn't steal your pencil,** ~! eu não roubei o seu lápis, juro!

honestly ['ɒnɪstlɪ] ◇ *adv* **-1.** [in a trustworthy manner] honestamente **-2.** [frankly, truthfully] sinceramente. ◇ *excl* [expressing impatience, disapproval] ora, francamente!

honesty ['ɒnɪstɪ] *n* **-1.** *(U)* [trustworthiness] honestidade *f* **-2.** [frankness, truthfulness] sinceridade *f*.

honey ['hʌnɪ] *n* **-1.** *(U)* [food] mel *m* **-2.** *esp US* [dear] querido *m*, -da *f*.

honeybee ['hʌnɪbiː] *n* abelha *f* operária.

honeycomb ['hʌnɪkəʊm] *n* **-1.** [in wax] favo *m (de mel)* **-2.:** ~ **pattern** formato *m* de favo de mel.

honeymoon ['hʌnɪmuːn] ◇ *n lit & fig* lua-de-mel *f*. ◇ *vi* sair em lua-de-mel.

honeysuckle ['hʌnɪ,sʌkl] *n* madressilva *f*.

Hong Kong [ˌhɒŋ'kɒŋ] *n* Hong Kong; **in** ~ em Hong Kong.

honk [hɒŋk] ◇ *n* **-1.** [of horn] buzinada *f* **-2.** [of goose] grasnada *f*. ◇ *vi* **-1.** [motorist] buzinar **-2.** [goose] grasnar. ◇ *vt*: **to** ~ **a horn** tocar a buzina.

honky ['hɒŋkɪ] (*pl* **-ies**) *n US vinf offensive* branquelo *m*, -la *f*.

Honolulu [ˌhɒnə'luːluː] *n* Honolulu; **in** ~ em Honolulu.

honor etc *n & vt US* = **honour etc**.

honorary [*UK* 'ɒnərərɪ, *US* ɒnə'reərɪ] *adj* honorário(-ria).

honor roll *n US* [sch] [univ] relação *f* dos melhores alunos.

honour *UK*, **honor** *US* ['ɒnər] ◇ *n* honra *f*; **in** ~ **of sb/sthg** em honra de alguém/algo. ◇ *vt* honrar.

 ◆ **Honour** *n* [in titles]: **Your** ~ Vossa Senhoria, Vossa Excelência.

 ◆ **honours** *npl* **-1.** [gen] honras *fpl* **-2.** *UNIV tipo de grau universitário concedido por universidades britânicas* **-3.** *phr*: **to do the** ~**s** fazer as honras da casa.

honourable *UK*, **honorable** *US* ['ɒnrəbl] *adj* honrado(da).

 ◆ **Honourable** *adj* [in titles]: **the Honourable** ... o Honorável ...

honourably *UK*, **honorably** *US* ['ɒnərəblɪ] *adv* honrosamente.

honour bound *adj*: **to be** ~ **to do sthg** ver-se moralmente obrigado(da) a fazer algo.

honours degree *n UK* [univ] = **honours 2**.

honours list *n UK na Inglaterra, relação de pessoas importantes que recebem condecorações como sinal de respeito.*

Hons. (*abbr of* **honours degree**) *n tipo de grau universitário concedido por universidades britânicas.*

Hon. Sec. (*abbr of* **honorary secretary**) *n* secretário *m* honorário, secretária *f* honorária.

hooch [huːtʃ] *n inf* bebida *f* alcoólica ilegal.

hood [hʊd] *n* **-1.** [on cloak, jacket] capuz *f* **-2.** *US* [of car] capota *f* **-3.** [of pram] toldo *m* **-4.** [of cooker] aba *f* **-5.** *US* [car bonnet] capô *m*.

hooded ['hʊdɪd] *adj* **-1.** [wearing a hood] encapuzado(da) **-2.** [eyes] mascarado(da).

hoodlum ['huːdləm] *n* [youth] *US inf* arruaceiro *m*, -ra *f*; [gangster] gângster *mf*.

hoodwink ['hʊdwɪŋk] *vt* lograr.

hooey ['huːɪ] *n US inf* bobagem *f*.

hoof [huːf, hʊf] (*pl* **-s** *OR* **hooves**) *n* pata *f*, casco *m*.

hook [hʊk] ◇ *n* **-1.** [for coat, picture, curtain] gancho *m* **-2.** [for catching fish] anzol *m* **-3.** [fastener] fecho *m*; ~ **and eye** colchete *m*. ◇ *vt* **-1.** [fasten with hook] enganchar **-2.** [fish] fisgar **-3.** [arm, leg] dar um gancho em.

 ◆ **off the hook** *adv* **-1.** [phone] fora do gancho **-2.** [out of trouble] sem problemas; **to get sb off the** ~ livrar alguém de um problema.

 ◆ **hook up** *vt sep*: **to** ~ **sthg up to sthg** *COMPUT & TELEC* conectar algo em algo.

hooked [hʊkt] *adj* **-1.** [shaped like a hook] curvado(da) **-2.** *inf* [addicted]: **to be** ~ **(on sthg)** ser viciado(da) (em algo).

hooker ['hʊkər] *n US inf* prostituta *f*.

hook(e)y ['hʊkɪ] *n (U) US inf*: **to play** ~ matar aula.

hooligan ['huːlɪgən] *n* arruaceiro *m*, -ra *f*, hooligan *m*.

hooliganism ['huːlɪgənɪzm] *n (U)* arruaça *f*.

hoop [huːp] *n* argola *f*.

hoop-la ['huːplɑː] *n (U)* [game] jogo *m* de argolas.

hooray [hʊ'reɪ] *excl* = **hurray**.

hoot [huːt] ◇ *n* **-1.** [of owl] pio *m* **-2.** [of horn] buzinada *f* **-3.** [of laughter] grito *m* **-4.** *UK inf* [amusing thing, person]: **she's a real** ~ ela é o máximo. ◇ *vi* **-1.** [owl] piar **-2.** [horn] buzinar **-3.** *inf* [person] gritar. ◇ *vt* [horn] buzinar.

hooter ['huːtər] *n* **-1.** [horn - of car] buzina *f*; [- of factory] sirene *f* **-2.** *UK inf* [nose] narigão *m*.

Hoover® ['huːvər] *n UK* aspirador *m*.

 ◆ **hoover** ◇ *vt* passar o aspirador em. ◇ *vi* passar o aspirador.

hooves [huːvz] *pl* ⊳ **hoof**.

hop [hɒp] (*pt & pp* **-ped**, *cont* **-ping**) ◇ *n* **-1.** [of person] pulo *m* num pé só **-2.** [of small animal, bird] pulinho *m* **-3.** *inf* [trip] viagem *f* rápida. ◇ *vt inf*

-1. US [bus, train] pegar **-2.** phr: ~ it! dê o fora. ◇ vi **-1.** [jump on one leg] pular com um pé só **-2.** [small animal, bird] dar pulinhos **-3.** inf [move nimbly] pular; **she ~ped on a plane to New York** ela foi dar um pulo em Nova York.

hops npl [for making beer] lúpulos mpl.

hope [həʊp] ◇ n esperança f; **in the ~ of** na esperança de; **I don't hold out much ~** não tenho muita esperança; **to pin one's ~s on sb/sthg** depositar a esperança em alguém/algo; **to raise sb's ~s** dar esperança a alguém. ◇ vt: **to ~ (that)** esperar que; **to ~ to do sthg** esperar fazer algo. ◇ vi esperar; **to ~ for sthg** esperar (por) algo; **I ~ so/not** espero que sim/não; **to ~ for the best** esperar que tudo dê certo.

hope chest n US baú m do enxoval.

hopeful [ˈhəʊpfʊl] ◇ adj **-1.** [full of hope] esperançoso(sa), otimista; **to be ~ of sthg/of doing sthg** ter esperanças de algo/de fazer algo **-2.** [encouraging] promissor(ra). ◇ n aspirante mf (a um cargo).

hopefully [ˈhəʊpfəlɪ] adv **-1.** [in a hopeful way] esperançosamente **-2.** [with luck] com sorte.

hopeless [ˈhəʊplɪs] adj **-1.** [despairing] desesperado(da) **-2.** [impossible] impossível **-3.** inf [useless] inútil.

hopelessly [ˈhəʊplɪslɪ] adv **-1.** [despairingly] desesperançosamente **-2.** [completely] totalmente.

hopper [ˈhɒpəʳ] n [bin] tremonha f.

hopping [ˈhɒpɪŋ] adv: **to be ~ mad** estar soltando fogo pelas ventas.

hopscotch [ˈhɒpskɒtʃ] n (U) amarelinha f.

horde [hɔːd] n horda f.

hordes npl: **~s of** uma multidão de.

horizon [həˈraɪzn] n [of sky] horizonte m; **on the ~** no horizonte.

horizons npl: **to broaden one's ~s** ampliar os horizontes.

horizontal [ˌhɒrɪˈzɒntl] ◇ adj horizontal. ◇ n: **the ~** a horizontal.

hormone [ˈhɔːməʊn] n hormônio m.

hormone replacement therapy n terapia f de reposição hormonal.

horn [hɔːn] n **-1.** [of animal] chifre m **-2.** MUS [instrument] trompa f **-3.** [of car] buzina f **-4.** [of ship] apito m.

hornet [ˈhɔːnɪt] n vespão m.

horn-rimmed [-ˈrɪmd] adj feito(ta) com aros de chifre.

horny [ˈhɔːnɪ] (compar -ier, superl -iest) adj **-1.** [scale, body, armour] feito(ta) de chifre **-2.** [hand] calejado(da) **-3.** vinf [sexually excited] com tesão.

horoscope [ˈhɒrəskəʊp] n horóscopo m.

horrendous [hɒˈrendəs] adj horrendo(da).

horrible [ˈhɒrəbl] adj horrível.

horribly [ˈhɒrəblɪ] adv **-1.** [horrifically] horrivelmente **-2.** inf [very] terrivelmente, muito.

horrid [ˈhɒrɪd] adj **-1.** esp UK [person] antipático(ca) **-2.** [idea, place] horroroso(sa).

horrific [hɒˈrɪfɪk] adj horroroso(sa), horrível.

horrify [ˈhɒrɪfaɪ] (pt & pp -ied) vt horrorizar.

horrifying [ˈhɒrɪfaɪɪŋ] adj horripilante.

horror [ˈhɒrəʳ] n **-1.** [gen] horror m; **to my/his ~** para o meu/seu espanto **-2.** [strong dislike]: **to**

have a ~ of sthg ter horror a algo.

horror film n filme m de terror.

horror-struck adj horrorizado(da).

hors d'oeuvre [ɔːˈdɜːvr] (pl -s) n hors d'oeuvre m, entrada f.

horse [hɔːs] n [animal] cavalo m.

horseback [ˈhɔːsbæk] ◇ adj: **~ riding** US equitação f. ◇ n: **on ~** a cavalo.

horsebox UK [ˈhɔːsbɒks], **horsecar** US [ˈhɔːskɑːʳ] n reboque m para transportar cavalos.

horse chestnut n **-1.** [tree]: **~ (tree)** castanheiro-da-índia m **-2.** [nut] castanha-da-índia f.

horse-drawn adj puxado(da) a cavalo.

horsefly [ˈhɔːsflaɪ] (pl -flies) n mutuca f.

horsehair [ˈhɔːsheəʳ] n (U) pêlo m de cavalo.

horseman [ˈhɔːsmən] (pl -men [-mən]) n **-1.** [non-professional] cavaleiro m **-2.** [professional] ginete m.

horse opera n US hum filme m de faroeste.

horseplay [ˈhɔːspleɪ] n (U) grosseria f.

horsepower [ˈhɔːsˌpaʊəʳ] n (U) cavalo-vapor m.

horse racing n (U) corrida f de cavalos.

horseradish [ˈhɔːsˌrædɪʃ] n (U) [plant] raiz-forte f.

horse riding n (U) equitação f; **to go ~** andar a cavalo, montar.

horseshoe [ˈhɔːsʃuː] n ferradura f.

horse show n concurso m hípico, rodeio m.

horse-trading n (U) fig & pej negociação f.

horse trials npl concurso m hípico, rodeio m.

horsewhip [ˈhɔːswɪp] (pt & pp -ped, cont -ping) vt chicotear.

horsewoman [ˈhɔːsˌwʊmən] (pl -women [-ˌwɪmɪn]) n amazona f.

horticultural [ˌhɔːtɪˈkʌltʃərəl] adj hortícola.

horticulture [ˈhɔːtɪkʌltʃəʳ] n (U) horticultura f.

hose [həʊz] ◇ n [hosepipe] mangueira f. ◇ vt regar com mangueira.

hose down vt sep lavar com mangueira.

hosepipe [ˈhəʊzpaɪp] n mangueira f.

hosiery [ˈhəʊzɪərɪ] n (U) artigos mpl de malha, lingeries fpl.

hospice [ˈhɒspɪs] n [for the terminally ill] hospício m.

hospitable [hɒˈspɪtəbl] adj hospitaleiro(ra).

hospital [ˈhɒspɪtl] n hospital m.

hospitality [ˌhɒspɪˈtælətɪ] n (U) hospitalidade f.

hospitality suite n copa f livre (em conferência, hotel).

hospitalize, -ise [ˈhɒspɪtəlaɪz] vt hospitalizar.

host [həʊst] ◇ n **-1.** [at private party] anfitrião m, -ã f **-2.** [place, organization] sede f; **~ city/country** cidade-/país-sede **-3.** [compere] apresentador m, -ra f **-4.** literary [large number]: **a ~ of sthg** um monte de algo. ◇ vt apresentar.

Host n RELIG: **the ~** a hóstia.

hostage [ˈhɒstɪdʒ] n refém mf; **to be taken/held ~** ser levado(a)/mantido(a) como refém.

hostel [ˈhɒstl] n albergue m, alojamento m; **(youth) ~** albergue (da juventude).

hostelry [ˈhɒstəlrɪ] (pl -ries) n hum [pub] estalagem f.

hostess [ˈhəʊstes] n **-1.** [at party] anfitriã f **-2.** [escort] acompanhante f.

hostile [*UK* 'hɒstaɪl, *US* 'hɒstl] *adj* -**1.** [gen] hostil; ~ to sb/sthg hostil com alguém/algo -**2.** [unfavourable] adverso(sa), desfavorável.

hostility [hɒ'stɪlətɪ] *n (U)* [antagonism, unfriendliness] hostilidade *f*.
➤ **hostilities** *npl* hostilidades *fpl*.

hot [hɒt] (*compar* -**ter**, *superl* -**test**, *pt* & *pp* -**ted**, *cont* -**ting**) *adj* -**1.** [gen] quente; I'm ~ estou com calor -**2.** [spicy] picante -**3.** *inf* [expert] bom (boa); to be ~ on *or* at sthg ser bom (boa) em algo -**4.** [recent] recente, quente -**5.** [temper] veemente.
➤ **hot up** *vi inf* -**1.** [situation, campaign] esquentar -**2.** [party] animar-se -**3.** [pace]: **the pace is ~ting up** as coisas estão indo rápido demais.

hot-air balloon *n* balão *m* de ar quente.

hotbed ['hɒtbed] *n fig* [centre] foco *m*.

hotchpotch *UK* ['hɒtʃpɒtʃ], **hodgepodge** *US* ['hɒdʒpɒdʒ] *n inf* mixórdia *f*.

hot-cross bun *n* pão doce feito com passas e enfeitado com uma cruz que se come na Semana Santa.

hot dog *n* cachorro-quente *m*.

hotel [həʊ'tel] <> *n* hotel *m*. <> *comp* de hotel; ~ **industry** setor *m* hoteleiro.

hotelier [həʊ'telɪəʳ] *n* hoteleiro *m*, -ra *f*.

hot flush *UK*, **hot flash** *US* *n* calorão *m* (*da menopausa*).

hotfoot *adv literary* apressadamente.

hotheaded [ˌhɒt'hedɪd] *adj* temerário(ria).

hothouse ['hɒthaʊs, *pl* -haʊzɪz] <> *n* [greenhouse] estufa *f*. <> *comp* de estufa.

hot line *n* -**1.** [between government heads] linha *f* direta -**2.** [24-hour phone line] linha *f* de emergência.

hotly ['hɒtlɪ] *adv* -**1.** [argue, debate] calorosamente -**2.** [deny] veementemente -**3.** [pursue]: **to be ~ pursued** ser seguido(da) de perto.

hotplate ['hɒtpleɪt] *n* chapa *f* elétrica.

hotpot ['hɒtpɒt] *n UK* ensopado de cordeiro típico de Lancashire.

hot potato *n inf fig* [controversial topic] batata *f* quente.

hot rod *n AUT* carro *m* envenenado.

hot seat *n inf*: **to always be in the ~** ser sempre quem tem de descascar o abacaxi.

hot spot *n* -**1.** [exciting place] lugar *m* da moda -**2.** [politically unsettled area] área *f* de tensão.

hot-tempered *adj* esquentado(da).

hot water *n (U) inf fig*: **to be in/get into ~** estar/ficar em maus lençóis.

hot-water bottle *n* bolsa *f* de água quente.

hot-wire *vt inf*: **to ~ a car** dar partida num carro fazendo ligação direta.

hound [haʊnd] <> *n* [dog] cão *m* de caça. <> *vt* -**1.** [persecute] perseguir -**2.** [drive out]: **to ~ sb out (of somewhere)** conseguir tirar alguém (de algum lugar).

hour ['aʊəʳ] *n* -**1.** [gen] hora *f*; **half an ~** meia hora; **per** *or* **an ~** por hora; **on the ~** nas horas cheias, nas horas fechadas; **in the small ~s** em altas horas da madrugada -**2.** *literary* [specific moment] momento *m*.
➤ **hours** *npl* -**1.** [of business] expediente *m*; **bank** ~ **expediente bancário** -**2.** [routine] horário *m*; **to work long ~** trabalhar por horas a fio.

hourly ['aʊəlɪ] <> *adj* -**1.** [happening every hour] de hora em hora, a cada hora -**2.** [per hour] por hora. <> *adv* -**1.** [every hour] a cada hora -**2.** [per hour] por hora -**3.** *fig* [constantly] continuamente.

house [*n* & *adj* haʊs, *pl* 'haʊzɪz, *vb* haʊz] <> *adj* -**1.** *COMM* caseiro(ra) -**2.** [wine] da casa. <> *n* -**1.** [gen] casa *f*; **it's on the ~** é oferta da casa; **to put** *or* **set one's ~ in order** pôr *or* colocar as coisas em ordem; **to bring the ~ down** *inf* fazer a casa vir abaixo, ser muito aplaudido(da) -**2.** [people in house] família *f* -**3.** *POL* câmara *f* -**4.** [in debates]: **this ~ believes that ...** os participantes do debate acreditam que ... -**5.** [in school] dormitório *m*. <> *vt* [accommodate - people, family] alojar; [- department, library, office] abrigar.

house arrest *n (U)*: **under ~** sob prisão domiciliar.

houseboat ['haʊsbəʊt] *n* casa *f* flutuante.

housebound ['haʊsbaʊnd] *adj* confinado(da) em casa.

housebreaking ['haʊsˌbreɪkɪŋ] *n (U)* arrombamento *m* da casa.

housebroken ['haʊsˌbrəʊkn] *adj US* [pet] domesticado(da).

housecoat ['haʊskəʊt] *n* chambre *m*.

household ['haʊshəʊld] <> *adj* -**1.** [domestic] doméstico(ca) -**2.** [familiar] familiar. <> *n* família *f*, lar *m*.

householder ['haʊsˌhəʊldəʳ] *n* -**1.** [owner] dono *m*, -na *f* da casa -**2.** [head of family] chefe *mf* da casa.

househunting ['haʊsˌhʌntɪŋ] *n (U)* procura *f* de casa; **to go ~** procurar casa para morar/alugar.

househusband *n* dono *m* de casa.

housekeeper ['haʊsˌkiːpəʳ] *n* governanta *f*.

housekeeping ['haʊsˌkiːpɪŋ] *n* -**1.** [work] tarefas *fpl* domésticas -**2.** [budget]: **~ (money)** dinheiro *m* para os gastos da casa.

houseman ['haʊsmən] (*pl* -**men** [-mən]) *n UK* interno *m*, -na *f*.

house martin *n* andorinha-de-casa *f*.

housemen *pl* ⊳ **houseman**.

house music *n* house music *f*.

House of Commons *n UK*: **the ~** a Câmara dos Comuns.

HOUSE OF COMMONS

House of Commons e *House of Lords* são as duas casas que compõem o Parlamento britânico. A *House of Commons*, com seus 650 membros, é a que desfruta de maior poder. Seus *Members of Parliament* (MPs) são eleitos pelo povo para um mandato de cinco anos. O governo é formado pelos MPs pertencentes ao partido que obteve maioria nas eleições.

House of Lords *n UK*: **the ~** a Câmara dos Lordes.

HOUSE OF LORDS ▬▬▬▬

A *House of Lords* conta com mais de mil membros. Seus componentes não são eleitos: em sua maioria, eles ou herdaram seus títulos de nobreza ou desfrutam do título em caráter vitalício, mas não hereditário. A *House of Lords* tem menos poder do que a *House of Commons*, mas possui a prerrogativa de modificar leis aprovadas por essa última. É a mais alta corte de apelações do Reino Unido, excetuando-se a Escócia, que desfruta de sistema jurídico próprio.

House of Representatives *n US*: the ~ a Câmara dos Representantes.

HOUSE OF REPRESENTATIVES ▬▬▬▬

Juntamente com o Senado, a *House of Representatives* constitui o corpo legislativo dos Estados Unidos. Seus deputados são eleitos em sistema de votação proporcional, de acordo com a população de cada estado.

house-owner *n* proprietário *m*, -ria *f (da casa)*.

houseplant ['haʊsplɑːnt] *n* planta *f* de interior.

house-proud *adj* fanático(ca) pela aparência da casa.

Houses of Parliament *npl UK*: the ~ o Parlamento britânico.

house-to-house *adj* de casa em casa.

house-train *vt UK* ensinar o local onde fazer as necessidades a *(gato, cachorro)*.

housewarming (party) ['haʊsˌwɔːmɪŋ-] *n* festa *f* de inauguração de uma casa.

housewife ['haʊswaɪf] *(pl* -wives [-waɪvz]) *n* dona *f* de casa.

housework ['haʊswɜːk] *n (U)* afazeres *mpl* domésticos.

housing ['haʊzɪŋ] <> *n* -1. *(U)* [accommodation] alojamento *m* -2. *(U)* [topic, study] habitação *f* -3. TECH cárter *m*. <> *comp* habitacional.

housing association *n UK* organização que possui casas e ajuda seus membros a alugá-las ou comprá-las por um preço mais barato.

housing benefit *n UK* auxílio-moradia *m*.

housing development *n* conjunto *m* habitacional.

housing estate *UK*, **housing project** *US n* conjunto *m* habitacional.

hovel ['hɒvl] *n* [house] choupana *f*.

hover ['hɒvəʳ] *vi* -1. [fly] pairar, flutuar no ar -2. [linger] permanecer.

hovercraft ['hɒvəkrɑːft] *(pl inv OR* -s) *n* aerodeslizador *m*.

hoverport ['hɒvəpɔːt] *n* porto *m* para aerodeslizador.

how [haʊ] *adv* -1. [referring to way or manner] como; ~ do you get there? como se chega lá?; ~ does it work? como funciona?; tell me ~ to do it me diga como fazer isso. -2. [referring to health, quality] como; ~ are you? como vai?; ~ are you doing? como vai você?; ~ are things? como vão as coisas?; ~ is your room? como é o seu quarto? -3. [referring to degree, amount] quanto; ~ far? a que distância?; ~ long? quanto tempo?; ~ many?

quantos?; ~ much? quanto?; ~ much is it? quanto custa?; ~ old are you? quantos anos você tem? -4. [in phrases]: ~ about a drink? que tal uma bebida?; ~ lovely! que lindo!

howdy ['haʊdɪ] *excl US inf* olá!

however [haʊˈevəʳ] <> *conj* [in whatever way] como quer que; ~ you want como quiser. <> *adv* -1. [nevertheless] contudo, no entanto -2. [no matter how]: ~ difficult it is por mais difícil que seja; ~ many/much não importa quantos/quanto -3. [how] de que modo, como.

howl [haʊl] <> *n* -1. [of pain, anger] grito *m* -2. [of laughter] gargalhada *f*. <> *vi* -1. [animal, wind] uivar -2. [person - in pain] gritar; [- with laughter] gargalhar.

howler ['haʊləʳ] *n inf* asneira *f*.

howling ['haʊlɪŋ] *adj inf* [success] imenso(sa).

hp *(abbr of* horsepower) *n* hp *m*.

HP *n* -1. *UK (abbr of* hire purchase) a prazo; to buy sthg on ~ comprar algo a prazo -2. = hp.

HQ *(abbr of* headquarters) *n* QG.

hr *(abbr of* hour) h.

HRH *(abbr of* His/Her Royal Highness) Sua A. Real.

hrs *(abbr of* hours) h.

HRT *(abbr of* hormone replacement therapy) *n* TRH *f*.

HS *(abbr of* high school) *US escola de ensino médio*.

HST *(abbr of* Hawaiian Standard Time) *horário oficial do Havaí*.

ht *(abbr of* height) altura *f*.

HT *(abbr of* high tension) ELEC alta-tensão *f*.

hub [hʌb] *n* -1. [of wheel] cubo *m* -2. [of activity] centro *m*.

hub airport *n US* aeroporto *m* principal.

hubbub ['hʌbʌb] *n* algazarra *f*.

hubcap ['hʌbkæp] *n* calota *f*.

huddle ['hʌdl] <> *vi* -1. [crouch, curl up] amontoar-se -2. [crowd together] apertar-se uns contra os outros. <> *n* [of people] amontoado *m*.

hue [hjuː] *n* [colour] matiz *f*.

huff [hʌf] <> *n*: in a ~ com raiva. <> *vi*: to ~ and puff estar ofegante, bufar.

huffy ['hʌfɪ] *(compar* -ier, *superl* -iest) *adj inf* -1. [offended] ressentido(da) -2. [touchy] sensível.

hug [hʌg] *(pt & pp* -ged, *cont* -ging) <> *n* abraço *m*; to give sb a ~ dar um abraço em alguém. <> *vt* -1. [embrace] abraçar -2. [stay close to] manter-se perto de.

huge [hjuːdʒ] *adj* enorme.

huh [hʌ] *excl* -1. [after questions] hein! -2. [expressing surprise] como!, hein! -3. [expressing scorn] hum!

hulk [hʌlk] *n* -1. [of ship] carcaça *f* -2. [person] brutamontes *mpl*.

hulking ['hʌlkɪŋ] *adj* gigantesco(ca).

hull [hʌl] *n* [of ship] casco *m*.

hullabaloo [ˌhʌləbə'luː] *n inf* bagunça *f*.

hullo [hə'ləʊ] *excl* = hello.

hum [hʌm] *(pt & pp* -med, *cont* -ming) <> *vi* -1. [buzz] zumbir -2. [sing] cantarolar -3. [be busy] estar em atividade -4. *phr*: to ~ and haw gaguejar, titubear. <> *vt* [tune] zunir. <> *n (U)* -1. [of bee, machine] zumbido *m* -2. [of car] barulho *m* -3. [of conversation] murmúrio *m*.

human ['hjuːmən] <> *adj* humano(na). <> *n*: ~ (being) (ser *m*) humano *m*.

humane [hju:'meɪn] *adj* [compassionate] humano(na), humanitário(ria).

humanely [hju:'meɪnlɪ] *adv* humanamente.

human error *n* (U) erro *m* humano.

humanist ['hju:mənɪst] *n* PHILOSOPHY humanista *mf*.

humanitarian [hju:ˌmænɪ'teərɪən] <> *adj* humanitário(ria). <> *n* pessoa *f* que luta pela justiça social.

humanity [hju:'mænətɪ] *n* humanidade *f*.
➡ **humanities** *npl*: **the humanities** as humanidades.

humanly ['hju:mənlɪ] *adv*: ~ **possible** humanamente possível.

human nature *n* (U) natureza *f* humana.

human race *n*: **the** ~ **a** raça humana.

human resources *npl* recursos *mpl* humanos.

human rights *npl* direitos *mpl* humanos.

humble ['hʌmbl] <> *adj* humilde. <> *vt* humilhar; **to** ~ **o.s.** humilhar-se.

humbly ['hʌmblɪ] *adv* humildemente.

humbug ['hʌmbʌg] *n* -1. (U) dated [hypocrisy] hipocrisia *f* -2. UK [sweet] caramelo *m* de menta.

humdrum ['hʌmdrʌm] *adj* monótono(na).

humid ['hju:mɪd] *adj* úmido(da).

humidity [hju:'mɪdətɪ] *n* (U) umidade *f*.

humiliate [hju:'mɪlɪeɪt] *vt* humilhar.

humiliating [hju:'mɪlɪeɪtɪŋ] *adj* humilhante.

humiliation [hju:ˌmɪlɪ'eɪʃn] *n* (U) humilhação *f*.

humility [hju:'mɪlətɪ] *n* (U) humildade *f*.

hummingbird ['hʌmɪŋbɜ:d] *n* beija-flor *m*.

humor *n* & *vt* US = humour.

humorist ['hju:mərɪst] *n* humorista *mf*.

humorous ['hju:mərəs] *adj* humorístico(ca).

humour UK, **humor** US ['hju:mə^r] <> *n* (U) [gen] humor *m*; **in bad/good** ~ dated de mau/bom humor. <> *vt* fazer a vontade de.

hump [hʌmp] <> *n* -1. [hill] elevação *f* -2. [on back of animal, person] corcova *f*. <> *vt* inf [carry] carregar.

humpbacked bridge ['hʌmpbækt-] *n* ponte *f* encurvada.

humus ['hju:məs] *n* (U) humo *m*.

hunch [hʌntʃ] <> *n* inf pressentimento *m*. <> *vt* curvar. <> *vi* curvar-se.

hunchback ['hʌntʃbæk] *n* corcunda *mf*.

hunched [hʌntʃt] *adj* encurvado(da).

hundred ['hʌndrəd] *num* cem; **a** OR **one hundred** cem; see also **six**.
➡ **hundreds** *npl* centenas *fpl*.

hundredth ['hʌndrətθ] *num* centésimo(ma); see also **sixth**.

hundredweight ['hʌndrədweɪt] *n* -1. [in UK] quintal *m* métrico (50,8 kg) -2. [in US] quintal *m* métrico (45,3 kg).

hung [hʌŋ] <> *pt* & *pp* ▷ hang. <> *adj* POL sem maioria.

Hungarian [hʌŋ'geərɪən] <> *adj* húngaro(ra). <> *n* -1. [person] húngaro *m*, -ra *f* -2. [language] húngaro *m*.

Hungary ['hʌŋgərɪ] *n* Hungria; **in** ~ na Hungria.

hunger ['hʌŋgə^r] *n* -1. [desire for food, starvation] fome *f* -2. literary [strong desire] sede *f*.
➡ **hunger after, hunger for** *vt fus literary* ter fome de.

hunger strike *n* greve *f* de fome.

hung over *adj* inf: **to be** ~ estar com ressaca.

hungry ['hʌŋgrɪ] (compar -ier, superl -iest) *adj* -1. [for food] faminto(ta); **to go** ~ ficar com fome -2. literary [eager]: **to be** ~ **for sthg** ter sede de algo.

hung up *adj* inf: **to be** ~ (on sb/sthg), **to be** ~ (about sb/sthg) ficar complexado(da) (por causa de alguém/algo).

hunk [hʌŋk] *n* -1. [large piece] naco *m* -2. inf [attractive man] pedaço *m* de mau caminho.

hunky-dory [ˌhʌŋkɪ'dɔ:rɪ] *adj* inf satisfatório(ria) para todos.

hunt [hʌnt] <> *n* -1. [SPORT- activity] caça *f*; [- hunters] grupo *m* de caçadores -2. [search] busca *f*. <> *vi* -1. [for food, sport] caçar -2. [search]: **to** ~ (for sthg) procurar (algo). <> *vt* -1. [animals, birds] caçar -2. [person] procurar.
➡ **hunt down** *vt sep* encurralar.

hunter ['hʌntə^r] *n* caçador *m*, -ra *f*.

hunting ['hʌntɪŋ] *n* -1. SPORT caça *f* -2. UK [fox-hunting] caça *f* à raposa -3. [pursuit] busca *f*. <> comp de caça.

huntsman ['hʌntsmən] (pl -men [-mən]) *n* caçador *m*.

hurdle ['hɜ:dl] <> *n* -1. [in race] barreira *f* -2. [obstacle] obstáculo *m*. <> *vt* [jump over] saltar.
➡ **hurdles** *npl* SPORT corrida *f* de obstáculos.

hurl [hɜ:l] *vt* -1. [throw] arremessar -2. [shout] proferir.

hurrah [hʊ'rɑ:] *excl dated* viva!, hurra!

hurray [hʊ'reɪ] *excl* viva!

hurricane ['hʌrɪkən] *n* furacão *m*.

hurried ['hʌrɪd] *adj* [hasty] apressado(da), precipitado(da).

hurriedly ['hʌrɪdlɪ] *adv* apressadamente, precipitadamente.

hurry ['hʌrɪ] (pt & pp -ied) <> *vt* apressar. <> *vi* apressar-se; **to** ~ **to do sthg** apressar-se para fazer algo. <> *n* [rush] pressa *f*; **to be in a** ~ estar com pressa; **to do sthg in a** ~ fazer algo com pressa; **to be in no** ~ **to do sthg** [unwilling] não estar com pressa nenhuma de fazer algo.
➡ **hurry off** *vi* sair correndo.
➡ **hurry up** <> *vi* apressar-se; **hurry!** vamos de uma vez! <> *vt sep* apressar, acelerar.

hurt [hɜ:t] (pt & pp **hurt**) <> *vt* -1. [cause physical pain to] machucar -2. [injure] ferir -3. [upset] magoar -4. [be detrimental to] prejudicar. <> *vi* -1. [be painful] doer; **my feet** ~ os meus pés doem; **ouch, you're** ~**ing** ai, você está me machucando -2. [be detrimental] prejudicar. <> *adj* -1. [injured] machucado(da) -2. [upset] magoado(da). <> *n* (U) [emotional pain] dor *f*.

hurtful ['hɜ:tfʊl] *adj* ofensivo(va).

hurtle ['hɜ:tl] *vi* precipitar-se; **to** ~ **over** precipitar-se por; **to** ~ **past** passar como um raio.

husband ['hʌzbənd] *n* marido *m*.

husbandry ['hʌzbəndrɪ] *n* (U) fml criação *f*.

hush [hʌʃ] <> *n* [quietness] silêncio *m*. <> *vt* [silence] silenciar. <> *excl* silêncio!
➡ **hush up** *vt sep* -1. [affair] silenciar a respeito de -2. [noisy person] ficar quieto(ta).

hush money *n* (U) inf suborno *m* (para comprar o silêncio de alguém).

husk [hʌsk] *n* [of seed, grain] casca *f.*
husky ['hʌskɪ] (*compar* -**ier**, *superl* -**iest**) ◇ *adj* [hoarse] rouco(ca). ◇ *n* [dog] husky *m.*
hustings ['hʌstɪŋz] *npl UK* campanha *f* eleitoral.
hustle ['hʌsl] ◇ *vt* -**1.** [hurry] empurrar -**2.** *US* [persuade, trick]: **to ~ sb into doing sthg** pressionar alguém a fazer algo *OR* para que faça algo. ◇ *n (U)* [business]: **~ and bustle** grande atividade *f.*
hut [hʌt] *n* -**1.** [rough house] cabana *f* -**2.** [shed] barraca *f.*
hutch [hʌtʃ] *n* arapuca *f.*
hyacinth ['haɪəsɪnθ] *n* jacinto *m.*
hybrid ['haɪbrɪd] ◇ *adj* híbrido(da). ◇ *n* híbrido *m.*
hydrangea [haɪ'dreɪndʒə] *n* hortênsia *f.*
hydrant ['haɪdrənt] *n* hidrante *m.*
hydraulic [haɪ'drɔːlɪk] *adj* hidráulico(ca).
 ➡ **hydraulics** *n (U)* hidráulica *f.*
hydro *n UK* [spa] estância *f* hidromineral.
hydrocarbon [ˌhaɪdrə'kɑːbən] *n* hidrocarboneto *m.*
hydrochloric acid [ˌhaɪdrə'klɔːrɪk-] *n (U)* ácido *m* clorídrico.
hydroelectric [ˌhaɪdrəʊɪ'lektrɪk] *adj* hidrelétrico(-ca).
hydroelectricity [ˌhaɪdrəʊɪlek'trɪsətɪ] *n (U)* hidreletricidade *f.*
hydrofoil ['haɪdrəfɔɪl] *n* embarcação *f* com hidrofólio.
hydrogen ['haɪdrədʒən] *n (U)* hidrogênio *m.*
hydrogen bomb *n* bomba *f* de hidrogênio.
hydrophobia [ˌhaɪdrə'fəʊbjə] *n (U) fml* [rabies] hidrofobia *f.*
hydroplane ['haɪdrəpleɪn] *n* [speedboat] hidroplano *m.*
hyena [haɪ'iːnə] *n* hiena *f.*
hygiene ['haɪdʒiːn] *n (U)* higiene *f.*
hygienic [haɪ'dʒiːnɪk] *adj* higiênico(ca).
hygienist [haɪ'dʒiːnɪst] *n* [at dentist's] higienista *mf* bucal.
hymn [hɪm] *n* hino *m.*
hymn book *n* hinário *m.*
hype [haɪp] *inf* ◇ *n (U)* propaganda *f* exagerada. ◇ *vt* fazer propaganda exagerada de.
hyped up [haɪpd-] *adj inf* como uma pilha de nervos.
hyper ['haɪpə'] *adj inf* enérgico(ca), ativo(va).
hyperactive [ˌhaɪpər'æktɪv] *adj* hiperativo(va).
hyperbole [haɪ'pɜːbəlɪ] *n (U)* hipérbole *f.*
hyperinflation *n (U)* hiperinflação *f.*
hyperlink ['haɪpə‚lɪŋk] *n COMPUT* hyperlink *m.*
hypermarket ['haɪpə‚mɑːkɪt] *n* hipermercado *m.*
hypersensitive [ˌhaɪpə'sensɪtɪv] *adj* -**1.** [easily offended]: **~ (to/about sthg)** hipersensível (a algo) -**2.** *MED* hipersensível.
hypertension [ˌhaɪpə'tenʃn] *n MED (U)* hipertensão *f.*
hypertext ['haɪpətekst] *n COMPUT* hipertexto *m.*
hyperventilate [ˌhaɪpə'ventɪleɪt] *vi* hiperventilar.
hyphen ['haɪfn] *n* hífen *m.*
hyphenate ['haɪfəneɪt] *vt* hifenizar.

hypnosis [hɪp'nəʊsɪs] *n (U)* hipnose *f*; **under ~** hipnotizado(da).
hypnotic [hɪp'nɒtɪk] *adj* hipnótico(ca).
hypnotism ['hɪpnətɪzml] *n (U)* hipnotismo *m.*
hypnotist ['hɪpnətɪst] *n* hipnotizador *m*, -ra *f.*
hypnotize, -ise ['hɪpnətaɪz] *vt* hipnotizar.
hypoallergenic ['haɪpəʊ‚ælə'dʒenɪk] *adj* hipoalergênico(ca).
hypochondriac [ˌhaɪpə'kɒndrɪæk] *n* hipocondríaco *m*, -ca *f.*
hypocrisy [hɪ'pɒkrəsɪ] *n (U)* hipocrisia *f.*
hypocrite ['hɪpəkrɪt] *n* hipócrita *mf.*
hypocritical [ˌhɪpə'krɪtɪkl] *adj* hipócrita.
hypodermic needle [ˌhaɪpə'dɜːmɪk-] *n* agulha *f* hipodérmica.
hypodermic syringe [ˌhaɪpə'dɜːmɪk-] *n* seringa *f* hipodérmica.
hypothermia [ˌhaɪpəʊ'θɜːmɪə] *n (U)* hipotermia *f.*
hypothesis [haɪ'pɒθɪsɪs] (*pl* -**theses** [-θɪsiːz]) *n* hipótese *f.*
hypothesize, -ise [haɪ'pɒθɪsaɪz] ◇ *vt* fazer hipóteses sobre. ◇ *vi* fazer hipóteses.
hypothetical [ˌhaɪpə'θetɪkl] *adj* hipotético(ca).
hysterectomy [ˌhɪstə'rektəmɪ] (*pl* -**ies**) *n* histerectomia *f.*
hysteria [hɪs'tɪərɪə] *n* histeria *f.*
hysterical [hɪs'terɪkl] *adj* -**1.** [gen] histérico(ca) -**2.** *inf* [very funny] hilariante.
hysterics [hɪs'terɪks] *npl* -**1.** [panic, excitement] crise *f* histérica, histeria *f* -**2.** *inf* [fits of laughter] ataque *m* de riso; **to be in ~** arrebentar-se de tanto rir.
Hz (*abbr of* hertz) Hz.

i (*pl* **i's** *OR* **is**), **I** (*pl* **I's** *OR* **Is**) [aɪ] *n* [letter] i, I *m.*
I[1] [aɪ] (*abbr of* **Island, Isle**) ilha *f.*
I[2] [aɪ] *pers pron* eu; **she and ~ were at college together** eu e ela fomos ao colégio juntos(tas); **it is ~** *fml* sou eu; **~ can't do it** eu não posso fazer isso.
IA *abbr of* **Iowa.**
IAEA (*abbr of* **International Atomic Energy Agency**) *n* AIEA *f.*
IATA (*abbr of* **International Air Transport Association**) *n* associação internacional de transporte aéreo, IATA *f.*
IBA (*abbr of* **Independent Broadcasting Authority**) *n* órgão britânico de regulamentação das redes privadas de rádio e televisão.
Iberian [aɪ'bɪːrɪən] ◇ *adj* ibérico(ca). ◇ *n* ibérico *m*, -ca *f.*

Iberian peninsula *n*: the ~ a Península Ibérica.

ibid (*abbr of* **ibidem**) ib.

i/c (*abbr of* **in charge**) resp.; **to be** ~ **sthg** ser responsável por.

ICA (*abbr of* **Institute of Contemporary Arts**) *n* *instituto de arte contemporânea de Londres*.

ICBM (*abbr of* **intercontinental ballistic missile**) *n* míssil *m* balístico intercontinental.

ICC *n* **-1.** (*abbr of* **International Chamber of Commerce**) ICC *f*, Câmara *f* de Comércio Internacional **-2.** (*abbr of* **Interstate Commerce Commission**) *órgão federal norte-americano que regula o comércio entre os estados*.

ice [aɪs] ⬦ *n* **-1.** (*U*)[gen] gelo *m*; **to break the** ~ *fig* quebrar o gelo; **to put sthg on** ~ *fig* colocar algo de lado **-2.** *UK* [ice cream] sorvete *m*. ⬦ *vt UK* [cover with icing] cobrir com glacê.

➡ **ice over, ice up** *vi* congelar.

ice age *n* era *f* glacial.

iceberg ['aɪsbɜːg] *n* iceberg *m*.

iceberg lettuce *n* alface *f* americana.

icebox ['aɪsbɒks] *n* **-1.** *UK* [in refrigerator] congelador *m* **-2.** *US* [refrigerator] geladeira *f*, refrigerador *m*.

icebreaker ['aɪsˌbreɪkəʳ] *n* [ship] navio *m* quebra-gelo.

ice bucket *n* balde *m* de gelo.

ice cap *n* calota *f* glacial.

ice-cold *adj* gelado(da).

ice cream *n* sorvete *m*.

ice cream bar *n US* picolé *m* com casquinha de chocolate.

ice cube *n* cubo *m* de gelo.

iced [aɪst] *adj* **-1.** [cooled with ice] com gelo **-2.** [covered in icing] coberto(ta) com glacê.

ice floe *n* banquisa *f*.

ice hockey *n* (*U*) hóquei *m* sobre o gelo.

Iceland ['aɪslənd] *n* Islândia; **in** ~ na Islândia.

Icelander ['aɪsləndəʳ] *n* islandês *m*, -esa *f*.

Icelandic [aɪs'lændɪk] ⬦ *adj* islandês(esa). ⬦ *n* [language] islandês *m*.

ice lolly *n UK* picolé *m*.

ice pick *n* picador *m* de gelo.

ice rink *n* rinque *m* (de patinação).

ice skate *n* patim *m* para o gelo.

➡ **ice-skate** *vi* patinar sobre o gelo.

ice-skater *n* patinador *m*, -ra *f* sobre o gelo.

ice-skating *n* (*U*) patinação *f* sobre o gelo; **to go** ~ praticar patinação.

icicle ['aɪsɪkl] *n* pingente *m* de gelo.

icily ['aɪsɪlɪ] *adv* [in unfriendly way] friamente.

icing ['aɪsɪŋ] *n* (*U*) glacê *m*; **the third goal was the** ~ **on the cake** *fig* o terceiro gol foi para coroar a vitória.

icing sugar *n UK* açúcar *m* de confeiteiro.

ICJ (*abbr of* **International Court of Justice**) *n* TIJ *m*.

icon ['aɪkɒn] *n* ícone *m*.

iconoclast [aɪ'kɒnəklæst] *n* iconoclasta *mf*.

ICR (*abbr of* **Institute for Cancer Research**) *n* instituto norte-americano para pesquisa do câncer, ≃ INCA *m*.

ICU (*abbr of* **intensive-care unit**) *n* UTI *f*.

icy ['aɪsɪ] (*compar* **-ier**, *superl* **-iest**) *adj* **-1.** [very cold]

gelado(da) **-2.** [covered in ice] coberto(ta) de gelo **-3.** *fig* [unfriendly] frio (fria).

id [ɪd] *n* id *m*.

I'd [aɪd] = I would, I had.

ID ⬦ *n* (*abbr of* **identification**) identificação *f*; ~ **card** (carteira *f* de) *f* identidade, ≃ RG *m*. ⬦ *abbr of* **Idaho**.

Idaho ['aɪdəˌhəʊ] *n* Idaho.

ID card *n* = **identity card**.

IDD (*abbr of* **international direct dialling**) *n* DDI *m*.

idea [aɪ'dɪə] *n* **-1.** [gen] idéia *f*; **to get the** ~ *inf* pegar a idéia; **wherever did you get the** ~ **that I don't like him?** de onde você tirou a idéia de que eu não gosto dele?; **to have an** ~ **of sthg** ter idéia de algo; **to have no** ~ não ter idéia; **the** ~ **is to ...** a idéia é ... **-2.** [suspicion] impressão *f*.

ideal [aɪ'dɪəl] ⬦ *adj* [perfect] ideal; **to be** ~ **for sthg** ser ideal para algo. ⬦ *n* [principle] ideal *m*.

idealism [aɪ'dɪəlɪzm] *n* [high principles] idealismo *m*.

idealist [aɪ'dɪəlɪst] *n* idealista *mf*.

idealize, -ise [aɪ'dɪəlaɪz] *vt* idealizar.

ideally [aɪ'dɪəlɪ] *adv* **-1.** [perfectly] perfeitamente **-2.** [preferably] idealmente.

identical [aɪ'dentɪkl] *adj* idêntico(ca).

identical twins *npl* gêmeos *mpl* idênticos.

identifiable [aɪ'dentɪfaɪəbl] *adj* identificável.

identification [aɪˌdentɪfɪ'keɪʃn] *n* identificação *f*; ~ **with sb/sthg** identificação com alguém/algo.

identify [aɪ'dentɪfaɪ] (*pt* & *pp* **-ied**) ⬦ *vt* **-1.** [gen] identificar **-2.** [connect]: **to** ~ **sb with sthg** relacionar alguém a algo. ⬦ *vi* [empathize]: **to** ~ **with sb/sthg** identificar-se com alguém/algo.

Identikit picture® [aɪ'dentɪkɪt-] *n* retrato *m* falado.

identity [aɪ'dentətɪ] (*pl* **-ies**) *n* identidade *f*.

identity card *n* (carteira *f* de) identidade *f*.

identity parade *n* identificação *f* (*de um criminoso*).

ideological [ˌaɪdɪə'lɒdʒɪkl] *adj* ideológico(ca).

ideology [ˌaɪdɪ'ɒlədʒɪ] (*pl* **-ies**) *n* ideologia *f*.

idiom ['ɪdɪəm] *n* **-1.** [phrase] expressão *f* idiomática **-2.** *fml* [style, language] linguagem *f*.

idiomatic [ˌɪdɪə'mætɪk] *adj* [natural-sounding] idiomático(ca).

idiosyncrasy [ˌɪdɪə'sɪŋkrəsɪ] (*pl* **-ies**) *n* idiossincrasia *f*.

idiot ['ɪdɪət] *n* [fool] idiota *mf*.

idiotic [ˌɪdɪ'ɒtɪk] *adj* idiota.

idle ['aɪdl] ⬦ *adj* **-1.** [person - inactive] ocioso(sa); [- lazy] preguiçoso(sa) **-2.** [not in use] parado(da) **-3.** [empty] vão (vã) **-4.** [casual] casual **-5.** [futile] inútil. ⬦ *vi* [engine] estar em ponto morto.

➡ **idle away** *vt sep* desperdiçar.

idleness ['aɪdlnɪs] *n* (*U*) [laziness] preguiça *f*.

idler ['aɪdləʳ] *n* preguiçoso(sa), desocupado(da).

idly ['aɪdlɪ] *adv* **-1.** [lazily] preguiçosamente **-2.** [casually] casualmente.

idol ['aɪdl] *n* ídolo *m*.

idolize, -ise ['aɪdəlaɪz] *vt* idolatrar.

idyl(l) ['ɪdɪl] *n* idílio *m*.

idyllic [ɪ'dɪlɪk] *adj* idílico(ca).

i.e. (*abbr of* **id est**) i.e.

IEE (*abbr of* **Institution of Electrical Engineers**) *n* *instituto britânico de engenheiros eletricistas.*

if [ɪf] ⬦ *conj* **-1.** [gen] se; ~ **I were you** se eu fosse você **-2.** [though] ainda que; **a good,** ~ **rather expensive, restaurant** um bom restaurante, ainda que caro **-3.** [that] que. ⬦ *n:* ~ **s and buts** poréns *mpl.*
➡ **if not** *conj* se não.
➡ **if only** ⬦ *conj* **-1.** [providing a reason] ao menos, nem que seja; **let's stop at the next services,** ~ **to stretch our legs** vamos parar no próximo posto, ao menos *or* nem que seja para esticar as pernas **-2.** [expressing regret] se ao menos. ⬦ *excl* quem dera!

iffy [ˈɪfɪ] (*compar* **-ier,** *superl* **-iest**) *adj inf* inseguro(ra).

igloo [ˈɪɡluː] (*pl* **-s**) *n* iglu *m.*

ignite [ɪɡˈnaɪt] ⬦ *vt* acender. ⬦ *vi* acender, acender-se.

ignition [ɪɡˈnɪʃn] *n* ignição *f.*

ignition key *n* chave *f* de ignição.

ignoble [ɪɡˈnəʊbl] *adj fml* ignóbil.

ignominious [ˌɪɡnəˈmɪnɪəs] *adj fml* ignominioso(sa).

ignominy [ˈɪɡnəmɪnɪ] *n (U) fml* ignomínia *f.*

ignoramus [ˌɪɡnəˈreɪməs] (*pl* **-es**) *n* ignorante *mf.*

ignorance [ˈɪɡnərəns] *n (U)* ignorância *f.*

ignorant [ˈɪɡnərənt] *adj* **-1.** [uneducated] ignorante; [lacking information] desinformado(da) **-2.** *fml* [unaware]: **to be** ~ **of sthg** ignorar algo **-3.** *inf* [rude] ignorante.

ignore [ɪɡˈnɔːʳ] *vt* [take no notice of] ignorar.

iguana [ɪˈɡwɑːnə] (*pl inv OR* **-s**) *n* iguana *f.*

ikon [ˈaɪkɒn] *n* = **icon**.

IL *abbr of* **Illinois**.

ILEA (*abbr of* **Inner London Education Authority**) *n* *antigo órgão responsável pela educação em Londres.*

ileum [ˈɪlɪəm] (*pl* **ilea** [ˈɪlɪə]) *n* íleo *m.*

ilk [ɪlk] *n fml:* **of that** ~ [of that sort] do mesmo tipo.

ill [ɪl] ⬦ *adj* **-1.** [sick, unwell] doente; **to feel** ~ sentir-se doente; **to be taken** ~, **to fall** ~ ficar doente **-2.** [bad, unfavourable] mau (má). ⬦ *adv* mal; **to speak/think** ~ **of sb** falar/pensar mal de alguém; **we can** ~ **afford such luxuries** mal conseguimos pagar esses luxos.
➡ **ills** *npl* males *mpl.*

ill. (*abbr of* **illustration**) il.

I'll [aɪl = I will, I shall.

ill-advised [-ədˈvaɪzd] *adj* **-1.** [not sensible] imprudente, insensato(ta); **to be** ~ **to do sthg** ser imprudente fazer algo **-2.** [unwise] pouco aconselhável.

ill at ease *adj:* **he always felt shy and** ~ **at parties** ele sempre se sentia intimidado e pouco àvontade nas festas.

ill-bred *adj* malcriado(da).

ill-considered *adj* imponderado(da).

ill-disposed *adj:* **to be** ~ **towards sb** estar de má vontade com alguém.

illegal [ɪˈliːɡl] *adj* ilegal; ~ **immigrant/alien** imigrante/estrangeiro ilegal.

illegally [ɪˈliːɡəlɪ] *adv* ilegalmente.

illegible [ɪˈledʒəbl] *adj* ilegível.

illegitimate [ˌɪlɪˈdʒɪtɪmət] *adj* ilegítimo(ma).

ill-equipped [-ɪˈkwɪpt] *adj* despreparado(da).

ill-fated [-ˈfeɪtɪd] *adj* malfadado(da).

ill feeling *n (U)* ressentimento *f*, rancor *m.*

ill-founded [-ˈfaʊndɪd] *adj* infundado(da).

ill-gotten gains [-ˈɡɒtən-] *npl fml* ganhos *mpl* ilícitos.

ill health *n (U)* má saúde *f.*

illicit [ɪˈlɪsɪt] *adj* ilícito(ta).

illicitly [ɪˈlɪsɪtlɪ] *adv* ilicitamente.

ill-informed *adj* mal informado(da).

Illinois *n* Illinois; **in** ~ em Illinois.

illiteracy [ɪˈlɪtərəsɪ] *n (U)* analfabetismo *m.*

illiterate [ɪˈlɪtərət] ⬦ *adj* analfabeto(ta). ⬦ *n* analfabeto *m*, -ta *f.*

ill-mannered *adj* mal-educado(da).

illness [ˈɪlnɪs] *n* doença *f.*

illogical [ɪˈlɒdʒɪkl] *adj* ilógico(ca).

ill-suited *adj* inadequado(da); **an** ~ **couple** um casal desajustado; **to be** ~ **to sthg** ser inadequado(da) para algo.

ill-tempered *adj* mal-humorado(da), genioso(sa).

ill-timed [-ˈtaɪmd] *adj* inoportuno(na).

ill-treat *vt* maltratar.

ill-treatment *n (U)* maus tratos *mpl.*

illuminate [ɪˈluːmɪneɪt] *vt* **-1.** [light up] iluminar **-2.** [explain] ilustrar, esclarecer.

illuminated [ɪˈluːmɪneɪtɪd] *adj* [sign, notice] iluminado(da).

illuminating [ɪˈluːmɪneɪtɪŋ] *adj* [enlightening] esclarecedor(ra).

illumination [ɪˌluːmɪˈneɪʃn] *n (U)* [lighting] iluminação *f.*
➡ **illuminations** *npl UK* luzes *fpl* decorativas.

illusion [ɪˈluːʒn] *n* **-1.** [gen] ilusão *f*; **to have no** ~ **s about sb/sthg** não ter ilusões com alguém/algo; **to be under the** ~ **that** estar com a ilusão de que **-2.** [magic trick] truque *m* de ilusionismo.

illusionist [ɪˈluːʒənɪst] *n fml* ilusionista *mf.*

illusory [ɪˈluːsərɪ] *adj fml* ilusório(ria).

illustrate [ˈɪləstreɪt] *vt* ilustrar.

illustration [ˌɪləˈstreɪʃn] *n* ilustração *f.*

illustrator [ˈɪləstreɪtəʳ] *n* ilustrador *m*, -ra *f.*

illustrious [ɪˈlʌstrɪəs] *adj fml* ilustre.

ill will *n (U)* animosidade *f.*

ill wind [-wɪnd] *n:* **it's an** ~ **(that blows nobody any good)** *proverb* há males que vêm para o bem.

ILO (*abbr of* **International Labour Organization**) *n* OIT *f.*

I'm [aɪm] = **I am**.

image [ˈɪmɪdʒ] *n* [gen] imagem *f*; **to be the** ~ **of sb** ser a cara de alguém.

imagery [ˈɪmɪdʒrɪ] *n* imagens *fpl.*

imaginable [ɪˈmædʒɪnəbl] *adj* imaginável.

imaginary [ɪˈmædʒɪnrɪ] *adj* imaginário(ria).

imagination [ɪˌmædʒɪˈneɪʃn] *n* imaginação *f.*

imaginative [ɪˈmædʒɪnətɪv] *adj* imaginativo(va).

imagine [ɪˈmædʒɪn] *vt* imaginar; **to** ~ **doing sthg** imaginar fazer algo; ~ **(that)!** imagine!

imaginings [ɪˈmædʒɪnɪŋz] *npl literary* fantasias *fpl.*

imbalance [ˌɪmˈbæləns] *n* desequilíbrio *m.*

imbecile ['ɪmbɪsi:l] *n* imbecil *mf*.

imbue [ɪm'bju:] *vt fml*: **to be ~d with sthg** estar imbuído(da) de algo.

IMF (*abbr of* **International Monetary Fund**) *n* FMI *m*.

imitate ['ɪmɪteɪt] *vt* imitar.

imitation [ˌɪmɪ'teɪʃn] <> *n* imitação *f*. <> *adj* de imitação.

imitator ['ɪmɪteɪtə'] *n* imitador *m*, -ra *f*.

immaculate [ɪ'mækjʊlət] *adj* **-1.** [clean and tidy] imaculado(da) **-2.** [impeccable] impecável.

immaculately [ɪ'mækjʊlətlɪ] *adv* **-1.** [cleanly, tidily] de maneira imaculada **-2.** [impeccably] impecavelmente.

immaterial [ˌɪmə'tɪərɪəl] *adj* [irrelevant, unimportant] irrelevante.

immature [ˌɪmə'tjʊə'] *adj* **-1.** [childish] imaturo(ra) **-2.** *BOT & ZOOL* jovem.

immaturity [ˌɪmə'tjʊərətɪ] *n* **-1.** [childishness] imaturidade *f* **-2.** *BOT & ZOOL* juventude *f*.

immeasurable [ɪ'meʒrəbl] *adj* incomensurável.

immediacy [ɪ'mi:djəsɪ] *n (U)* imediatidade *f*, urgência *f*.

immediate [ɪ'mi:djət] *adj* **-1.** [gen] imediato(ta) **-2.** [closest in relationship] próximo(ma).

immediately [ɪ'mi:djətlɪ] <> *adv* **-1.** [gen] imediatamente **-2.** [directly, closely] diretamente. <> *conj* [as soon as] assim que.

immemorial [ˌɪmɪ'mɔːrɪəl] *adj*: **from time ~** desde tempos imemoráveis.

immense [ɪ'mens] *adj* imenso(sa).

immensely [ɪ'menslɪ] *adv* imensamente.

immensity [ɪ'mensətɪ] *n (U)* imensidão *f*.

immerse [ɪ'mɜːs] *vt* **-1.** [plunge into liquid]: **to ~ sthg in sthg** mergulhar algo em algo **-2.** *fig* [involve]: **to ~ o.s. in sthg** envolver-se em algo.

immersion heater [ɪ'mɜː.ʃn-] *n* ebulidor *m*.

immigrant ['ɪmɪgrənt] <> *n* imigrante *mf*. <> *comp* de imigrantes.

immigration [ˌɪmɪ'greɪʃn] <> *n (U)* imigração *f*. <> *comp* de imigração; **~ restrictions** restrições *fpl* para imigração.

imminence ['ɪmɪnəns] *n (U)* iminência *f*.

imminent ['ɪmɪnənt] *adj* iminente.

immobile [ɪ'məʊbaɪl] *adj* imóvel.

immobilization [ɪˌməʊbɪlaɪ'zeɪʃn] *n (U)* imobilização *f*.

immobilize, -ise [ɪ'məʊbɪlaɪz] *vt* imobilizar.

immobilizer *n AUT* corta-corrente *m*.

immodest [ɪ'mɒdɪst] *adj* **-1.** [vain] vaidoso(sa) **-2.** [indecent] indecente.

immoral [ɪ'mɒrəl] *adj* imoral.

immorality [ˌɪmə'rælətɪ] *n (U)* imoralidade *f*.

immortal [ɪ'mɔːtl] <> *adj* imortal. <> *n* **-1.** [god] deus *m* **-2.** [hero] imortal *mf*.

immortality [ˌɪmɔː'tælətɪ] *n* imortalidade *f*.

immortalize, -ise [ɪ'mɔːtəlaɪz] *vt* imortalizar.

immovable [ɪ'muːvəbl] *adj* **-1.** [fixed] fixo(xa) **-2.** [obstinate] inflexível.

immune [ɪ'mjuːn] *adj* **-1.** *MED* imune; **to be ~ to sthg** ser imune a algo **-2.** *fig* [impervious]: **to be ~ to sthg** não ser suscetível a algo **-3.** [exempt] isento(ta), livre; **to be ~ from sthg** estar protegido(da) de algo.

immune system *n* sistema *m* imunológico.

immunity [ɪ'mjuːnətɪ] *n* **-1.** *(U) MED*: **~ (to sthg)** imunidade *f* (a algo) **-2.** *(U) fig* [imperviousness]: **~ to sthg** falta *f* de suscetibilidade a algo **-3.** [exemption] isenção *f*; **~ from sthg** proteção *f* contra algo.

immunization [ˌɪmjuːnaɪ'zeɪʃn] *n MED* imunização *f*.

immunize, -ise [ɪ'mjuːnaɪz] *vt*: **to ~ sb (against sthg)** *MED* imunizar alguém (contra algo).

immunodeficiency [ˌɪmjuːnəʊdɪ'fɪʃənsɪ] *n (U)* imunodeficiência *f*.

immunology [ˌɪmjuːn'ɒlədʒɪ] *n (U)* imunologia *f*.

immutable [ɪ'mjuːtəbl] *adj fml* imutável.

imp [ɪmp] *n* **-1.** [creature] diabinho *m* **-2.** [naughty child] diabinho *m*, -nha *f*.

impact [*n* 'ɪmpækt, *vb* ɪm'pækt] <> *n* impacto *m*; **on ~** ao impacto; **to make an ~ on sb/sthg** causar impacto em alguém/algo. <> *vt* **-1.** [collide with] colidir com **-2.** [influence] influenciar.

impair [ɪm'peə'] *vt* prejudicar, debilitar.

impaired [ɪm'peəd] *adj* prejudicado(da), debilitado(da).

impale [ɪm'peɪl] *vt* perfurar; **to ~ sb/sthg on sthg** empalar alguém/algo em algo.

impart [ɪm'pɑːt] *vt fml* **-1.** [information]: **to ~ sthg (to sb)** transmitir algo (a alguém) **-2.** [feeling, quality] conferir; **to ~ flavour to the dish** conferir sabor ao prato.

impartial [ɪm'pɑːʃl] *adj* imparcial.

impartiality [ɪmˌpɑːʃɪ'ælətɪ] *n (U)* imparcialidade *f*.

impassable [ɪm'pɑːsəbl] *adj* intransitável.

impasse [æm'pɑːs] *n* impasse *m*; **to reach an ~** chegar a um impasse.

impassioned [ɪm'pæʃnd] *adj* veemente.

impassive [ɪm'pæsɪv] *adj* impassível.

impatience [ɪm'peɪʃns] *n* impaciência *f*.

impatient [ɪm'peɪʃnt] *adj* impaciente; **to be ~ to do sthg** estar impaciente para fazer algo; **to be ~ for sthg** esperar algo com impaciência.

impatiently [ɪm'peɪʃntlɪ] *adv* impacientemente.

impeach [ɪm'piːtʃ] *vt JUR* impugnar.

impeachment [ɪm'piːtʃmənt] *n (U) JUR* impeachment *m*.

impeccable [ɪm'pekəbl] *adj* impecável.

impeccably [ɪm'pekəblɪ] *adv* impecavelmente.

impecunious [ˌɪmpɪ'kjuːnjəs] *adj fml* indigente.

impede [ɪm'piːd] *vt* impedir.

impediment [ɪm'pedɪmənt] *n* impedimento *m*; **a speech ~** um defeito de fala.

impel [ɪm'pel] (*pt & pp* -led, *cont* -ling) *vt*: **to ~ sb to do sthg** impelir alguém a fazer algo.

impending [ɪm'pendɪŋ] *adj* iminente.

impenetrable [ɪm'penɪtrəbl] *adj* **-1.** [impossible to penetrate] impenetrável **-2.** [impossible to understand] incompreensível.

imperative [ɪm'perətɪv] <> *adj* [essential] indispensável. <> *n* imperativo *m*.

imperceptible [ˌɪmpə'septəbl] *adj* imperceptível.

imperfect [ɪm'pɜːfɪkt] <> *adj* [not perfect] imperfeito(ta). <> *n GRAM*: **~ (tense)** (pretérito *m*) imperfeito *m*.

imperfection [ˌɪmpəˈfekʃn] *n* imperfeição *f.*

imperial [ɪmˈpɪərɪəl] *adj* -1. [of an empire or emperor] imperial -2. [system of measurement]: ~ **system** *sistema británico de medidas.*

imperialism [ɪmˈpɪərɪəlɪzml] *n (U)* imperialismo *m.*

imperialist [ɪmˈpɪərɪəlɪst] <> *adj* imperialista. <> *n* imperialista *mf.*

imperil [ɪmˈperɪl] (*UK pt* & *pp* -**led**, *cont* -**ling**, *US pt* & *pp* -**ed**, *cont* -**ing**) *vt fml* pôr em perigo.

imperious [ɪmˈpɪərɪəs] *adj* imperioso(sa).

impersonal [ɪmˈpɜːsnl] *adj* impessoal.

impersonate [ɪmˈpɜːsəneɪt] *vt* -1. [mimic, imitate] imitar -2. [pretend to be] fazer-se passar por.

impersonation [ɪmˌpɜːsəˈneɪʃn] *n* [by mimic] imitação *f*; to do ~s (of sb) fazer imitações (de alguém).

impersonator [ɪmˈpɜːsəneɪtəʳ] *n* -1. [mimic] imitador *m*, -ra *f* -2. [impostor] impostor *m*, -ra *f.*

impertinence [ɪmˈpɜːtɪnəns] *n (U)* impertinência *f.*

impertinent [ɪmˈpɜːtɪnənt] *adj* [rude] impertinente.

imperturbable [ˌɪmpəˈtɜːbəbl] *adj* imperturbável.

impervious [ɪmˈpɜːvjəs] *adj* [not influenced]: ~ **to** sthg imune a algo.

impetuous [ɪmˈpetʃʊəs] *adj* impetuoso(sa).

impetus [ˈɪmpɪtəs] *n* -1. [momentum] ímpeto *m* -2. [stimulus] estímulo *m.*

impinge [ɪmˈpɪndʒ] *vi*: **to** ~ **on sb/sthg** afetar alguém/algo.

impish [ˈɪmpɪʃ] *adj* travesso(sa).

implacable [ɪmˈplækəbl] *adj* implacável.

implant [*n* ˈɪmplɑːnt, *vb* ɪmˈplɑːntl] <> *n* implante *m.* <> *vt*: **to** ~ **sthg in(to) sb** implantar algo em alguém.

implausible [ɪmˈplɔːzəbl] *adj* implausível.

implement [*n* ˈɪmplɪmənt, *vt* ˈɪmplɪment] <> *n* [tool] ferramenta *f.* <> *vt* implementar.

implementation [ˌɪmplɪmenˈteɪʃn] *n (U)* implementação *f.*

implicate [ˈɪmplɪkeɪt] *vt*: **to** ~ **sb in sthg** implicar alguém em algo.

implication [ˌɪmplɪˈkeɪʃn] *n* -1. *(U)* [involvement] implicação *f*, envolvimento *m* -2. [inference] implicação *f*; by ~ por conseqüência.

implicit [ɪmˈplɪsɪt] *adj* -1. [inferred] implícito(ta) -2. [inherent]: ~ **in sthg** inerente a algo -3. [complete] absoluto(ta).

implicitly [ɪmˈplɪsɪtlɪ] *adv* -1. [by inference] implicitamente -2. [completely] absolutamente.

implied [ɪmˈplaɪd] *adj* subentendido(da).

implode [ɪmˈpləʊd] *vi* implodir.

implore [ɪmˈplɔːʳ] *vt*: **to** ~ **sb (to do sthg)** implorar a alguém (para que faça algo).

imply [ɪmˈplaɪ] (*pt* & *pp* -**ied**) *vt* -1. [suggest] pressupor -2. [involve] implicar.

impolite [ˌɪmpəˈlaɪt] *adj* descortês, indelicado(da).

imponderable [ɪmˈpɒndrəbl] *adj* imponderável.
 ◆ **imponderables** *npl* imponderáveis *mpl.*

import [*n* ˈɪmpɔːt, *vt* ɪmˈpɔːtl] <> *n* -1. COMM importação *f* -2. *fml* [meaning] significado *m*, sentido *m* -3. *(U) fml* [importance] importância *f.* <>

comp de importação. <> *vt* importar.

importance [ɪmˈpɔːtns] *n (U)* importância *f.*

important [ɪmˈpɔːtnt] *adj* importante; **to be** ~ **to sb** ser importante para alguém.

importantly [ɪmˈpɔːtntlɪ] *adv*: **more** ~ o que é mais importante.

importation [ˌɪmpɔːˈteɪʃn] *n (U)* importação *f.*

imported [ɪmˈpɔːtɪd] *adj* importado(da).

importer [ɪmˈpɔːtəʳ] *n* importador *m*, -ra *f.*

impose [ɪmˈpəʊz] <> *vt* [force]: **to** ~ **sthg (on sb/ sthg)** impor algo (a alguém/algo). <> *vi* [cause trouble]: **to** ~ **(on sb)** causar problemas (para alguém).

imposing [ɪmˈpəʊzɪŋ] *adj* imponente.

imposition [ˌɪmpəˈzɪʃn] *n* imposição *f.*

impossibility [ɪmˌpɒsəˈbɪlətɪ] (*pl* -**ies**) *n* impossibilidade *f.*

impossible [ɪmˈpɒsəbl] <> *adj* impossível. <> *n*: **to do the** ~ fazer o impossível.

impostor, imposter *US* [ɪmˈpɒstəʳ] *n* impostor *m*, -ra *f.*

impotence [ˈɪmpətəns] *n* impotência *f.*

impotent [ˈɪmpətənt] *adj* impotente.

impound [ɪmˈpaʊnd] *vt* JUR apreender.

impoverished [ɪmˈpɒvərɪʃt] *adj lit* & *fig* empobrecido(da).

impracticable [ɪmˈpræktɪkəbl] *adj* impraticável.

impractical [ɪmˈpræktɪkl] *adj* pouco prático(ca).

imprecation [ˌɪmprɪˈkeɪʃn] *n fml* imprecação *f.*

imprecise [ɪmprɪˈsaɪs] *adj* impreciso(sa).

impregnable [ɪmˈpregnəbl] *adj* -1. [impenetrable] invulnerável -2. *fig* [in very strong position] imbatível.

impregnate [ˈɪmpregneɪt] *vt* -1. [introduce substance into]: **to** ~ **sthg with sthg** impregnar algo de algo -2. *fml* [fertilize] fecundar.

impresario [ˌɪmprɪˈsɑːrɪəʊl] (*pl* -**s**) *n* empresário *m*, -ria *f* teatral.

impress [ɪmˈpres] <> *vt* -1. [influence, affect] impressionar -2. [make clear]: **to** ~ **sthg on sb** convencer alguém da importância de algo. <> *vi* impressionar.

impression [ɪmˈpreʃn] *n* -1. [gen] impressão *f*; **to make an** ~ impressionar; **to be under the** ~ **(that)** ter a impressão de que -2. [impersonation] imitação *f.*

impressionable [ɪmˈpreʃnəbl] *adj* impressionável.

Impressionism *n (U)* ART Impressionismo *m.*

impressionist [ɪmˈpreʃənɪst] *n* [entertainer] imitador *m*, -ra *f.*
 ◆ **Impressionist** ART <> *adj* impressionista. <> *n* impressionista *mf.*

impressive [ɪmˈpresɪv] *adj* impressionante.

imprint [ˈɪmprɪnt] <> *n* -1. [mark] marca *f*, impressão *f* -2. [publisher's name] ≃ selo *m* da editora. <> *vt* [mark] imprimir, marcar.

imprinted [ɪmˈprɪntɪd] *adj* -1. [marked] marcado(da) -2. *fig* [on mind, memory]: ~ **on sthg** impresso(sa) em algo, marcado(da) em algo.

imprison [ɪmˈprɪzn] *vt* [put in prison] aprisionar.

imprisonment [ɪmˈprɪznmənt] *n (U)* aprisionamento *m.*

improbable [ɪmˈprɒbəbl] *adj* **-1.** [unlikely] improvável **-2.** [strange] estranho(nha).

impromptu [ɪmˈprɒmptju:] *adj* de improviso, improvisado(da).

improper [ɪmˈprɒpəʳ] *adj* **-1.** [unsuitable] inadequado(da) **-2.** [dishonest] desonesto(ta) **-3.** [rude, shocking] impróprio(pria).

impropriety [ˌɪmprəˈpraɪətɪ] *n* indecoro *m*.

improve [ɪmˈpru:v] <> *vi* [get better] melhorar; **to ~ (up)on sthg** melhorar algo. <> *vt* **-1.** [gen] melhorar **-2.** [cultivate] desenvolver.

improved [ɪmˈpru:vd] *adj* [better] melhorado(da).

improvement [ɪmˈpru:vmənt] *n* melhoria *f*; **~ in/on sthg** melhoria em algo.

improvisation [ˌɪmprəvaɪˈzeɪʃn] *n* improvisação *f*.

improvise [ˈɪmprəvaɪz] *vt & vi* improvisar.

imprudent [ɪmˈpru:dnt] *adj* imprudente.

impudence *n* impudência *f*.

impudent [ˈɪmpjʊdnt] *adj* impudente.

impugn [ɪmˈpju:n] *vt fml* impugnar.

impulse [ˈɪmpʌls] *n* impulso *m*; **on ~** sem pensar.

impulse buying [-ˈbaɪɪŋ] *n (U)* compra *f* impulsiva.

impulsive [ɪmˈpʌlsɪv] *adj* impulsivo(va).

impunity [ɪmˈpju:nətɪ] *n* impunidade *f*; **with ~** impunemente.

impure [ɪmˈpjʊəʳ] *adj* impuro(ra).

impurity [ɪmˈpjʊərətɪ] *(pl -ies) n* impureza *f*.

IMRO [ˈɪmrəʊ] *(abbr of* **Investment Management Regulatory Organization)** *n órgão britânico regulador de empresas que lidam com fundos de investimento e pensões.*

in [ɪn] *prep* **-1.** [indicating place, position] em; **it comes ~ a box** vem numa caixa; **~ the hospital** no hospital; **~ Scotland** na Escócia; **~ Boston** em Boston; **~ the middle** no meio; **~ the sun/rain** no sol/na chuva; **~ here/there** aqui/ali (dentro); **~ front** à frente. **-2.** [appearing in] em; **who's ~ the play?** quem está na peça? **-3.** [indicating arrangement] em; **they come ~ packs of three** vêm em embalagens de três; **~ a row** em fila; **cut it ~ half** corte-o ao meio. **-4.** [during]: **~ April** em abril; **~ the afternoon** à *or* de tarde; **~ the morning** de manhã; **ten o'clock ~ the morning** dez (horas) da manhã; **~ 1994** em 1994; **~ summer/winter** no verão/inverno. **-5.** [within] em; [after] dentro de, daqui a; **it'll be ready ~ an hour** estará pronto daqui a *or* dentro de uma hora; **she did everything ~ ten minutes** ela fez tudo em dez minutos; **they're arriving ~ two weeks** chegam dentro de *or* daqui a duas semanas. **-6.** [indicating means]: **~ writing** por escrito; **they were talking ~ English** estavam falando (em) inglês; **write ~ ink** escreva a tinta. **-7.** [wearing] de; **dressed ~ red** vestido de vermelho; **the man ~ the blue suit** o homem com o terno azul. **-8.** [indicating state] em; **to be ~ a hurry** estar com pressa; **to be ~ pain** ter dores; **to cry out ~ pain** gritar de dor *or* com dores; **~ ruins** em ruínas; **~ good health** com boa saúde. **-9.** [with regard to] de; **a rise ~ prices** uma subida dos preços; **to be 50 meters ~ length** ter 50 metros de comprimento. **-10.** [with numbers]: **one ~ ten** um em cada dez. **-11.** [indicating age]: **she's ~ her twenties** ela está na casa dos vinte. **-12.** [with colours]: **it comes ~ green or blue** vem em verde ou azul. **-13.** [with superlatives] de; **the best ~ the world** o melhor do mundo. <> *adv* **-1.** [inside] dentro; **you can go ~ now** pode entrar agora. **-2.** [at home, work]: **she's not ~** (ela) não está; **to stay ~** ficar em casa. **-3.** [train, bus, plane]: **the train's not ~ yet** o trem ainda não chegou. **-4.** [tide]: **the tide is ~** a maré está cheia. <> *adj inf* [fashionable] na moda, in *(inv)*.

in. *abbr of* **inch**.

IN *abbr of* **Indiana**.

inability [ˌɪnəˈbɪlətɪ] *n* incapacidade *f*; **~ to do sthg** incapacidade para fazer algo.

inaccessible [ˌɪnækˈsesəbl] *adj* inacessível.

inaccuracy [ɪnˈækjʊrəsɪ] *(pl -ies) n* imprecisão *f*.

inaccurate [ɪnˈækjʊrət] *adj* impreciso(sa).

inaction [ɪnˈækʃn] *n* inação *f*.

inactive [ɪnˈæktɪv] *adj* inativo(va).

inactivity [ˌɪnækˈtɪvətɪ] *n (U)* inatividade *f*.

inadequacy [ɪnˈædɪkwəsɪ] *(pl -ies) n* **-1.** *(U)* [state of being inadequate] insuficiência *f* **-2.** [weakness - of system] imperfeição *f*; [- of person] incapacidade *f*.

inadequate [ɪnˈædɪkwət] *adj* **-1.** [insufficient] insuficiente **-2.** [person] incapaz.

inadmissible [ˌɪnədˈmɪsəbl] *adj* inadmissível.

inadvertent [ˌɪnədˈvɜːtnt] *adj* acidental.

inadvertently [ˌɪnədˈvɜːtəntlɪ] *adv* acidentalmente.

inadvisable [ˌɪnədˈvaɪzəbl] *adj* desaconselhável.

inalienable [ɪnˈeɪljənəbl] *adj fml* inalienável.

inane [ɪˈneɪn] *adj* vazio(zia), fútil.

inanely [ɪˈneɪnlɪ] *adv* futilmente.

inanimate [ɪnˈænɪmət] *adj* inanimado(da).

inanity [ɪˈnænətɪ] *n (U)* futilidade *f*.

inapplicable [ˌɪnəˈplɪkəbl] *adj* inaplicável.

inappropriate [ˌɪnəˈprəʊprɪət] *adj* inapropriado(da).

inarticulate [ˌɪnɑːˈtɪkjʊlət] *adj* **-1.** [person] incapaz de se expressar (bem) **-2.** [words, sounds] inarticulado(da).

inasmuch [ˌɪnəzˈmʌtʃ] **➧ inasmuch as** *conj fml* [because] visto que; [to the extent that] na medida em que.

inattention [ˌɪnəˈtenʃn] *n (U)* desatenção *f*; **~ to sthg** desatenção a algo.

inattentive [ˌɪnəˈtentɪv] *adj* desatento(ta); **~ to sthg** desatento(ta) a algo.

inaudible [ɪˈnɔːdɪbl] *adj* inaudível.

inaugural [ɪˈnɔːgjʊrəl] *adj* [opening] inaugural.

inaugurate [ɪˈnɔːgjʊreɪt] *vt* **-1.** [leader, president] empossar **-2.** [building, system] inaugurar.

inauguration [ɪˌnɔːgjʊˈreɪʃn] *n* **-1.** [of leader, president] posse *f* **-2.** [of building, system] inauguração *f*.

inauspicious [ˌɪnɔːˈspɪʃəs] *adj* de mau agouro, pouco propício(cia).

in-between *adj* intermediário(ria).

inboard *adj* interno(na).

inborn [ˌɪnˈbɔːn] *adj* inato(ta).

inbound [ˈɪnbaʊnd] *adj US*: **an ~ ship** um navio que se aproxima; **the ~ flight from Miami** o vôo que chega de Miami.

inbred [ˌɪn'bred] *adj* **-1.** [family, group] endogâmico(-ca), consangüíneo(nea) **-2.** [characteristic, quality] inato(ta).

inbreeding ['ɪnˌbriːdɪŋ] *n (U)* endogamia *f*.

inbuilt [ˌɪn'bɪlt] *adj* **-1.** [device] embutido(da), incorporado(da) **-2.** [quality, defect] inerente.

inc. (*abbr of* **inclusive**) inclusive.

Inc. [ɪŋk] (*abbr of* **incorporated**) ≃ S.A.

Inca ['ɪŋkə] ⟨⟩ *adj* inca. ⟨⟩ *n* inca *mf*.

incalculable [ɪn'kælkjʊləbl] *adj* [very great] incalculável.

incandescent [ˌɪnkæn'desnt] *adj lit* incandescente ; *fig* [with rage] vermelho(lha).

incantation [ˌɪnkæn'teɪʃn] *n* **-1.** [magic words] palavras *fpl* mágicas **-2.** [spell] feitiço *m*.

incapable [ɪn'keɪpəbl] *adj* **-1.** [unable]: **to be ~ of sthg/of doing sthg** ser incapaz de algo/de fazer algo **-2.** [incompetent] incompetente.

incapacitate [ˌɪnkə'pæsɪteɪt] *vt* incapacitar.

incapacitated [ˌɪnkə'pæsɪteɪtɪd] *adj* incapacitado(-da).

incapacity [ˌɪnkə'pæsətɪ] *n (U)* incapacidade *f*; **~ for sthg** incapacidade para algo.

incarcerate [ɪn'kɑːsəreɪt] *vt fml* encarcerar.

incarceration [ɪnˌkɑːsə'reɪʃn] *n (U) fml* encarceramento *m*.

incarnate [ɪn'kɑːneɪt] *adj* encarnado(da); **he is generosity ~** ele é a generosidade em pessoa.

incarnation [ˌɪnkɑː'neɪʃn] *n* encarnação *f*.

incendiary device [ɪn'sendjərɪ-] *n* artefato *m* incendiário.

incense [*n* 'ɪnsens, *vt* ɪn'sens] ⟨⟩ *n (U)* [perfume] incenso *m*. ⟨⟩ *vt* [anger] enfurecer, enraivecer.

incentive [ɪn'sentɪv] *n* incentivo *m*.

incentive scheme *n* plano *m* de incentivos.

inception [ɪn'sepʃn] *n fml* começo *m*, origem *f*.

incessant [ɪn'sesnt] *adj* incessante.

incessantly [ɪn'sesntlɪ] *adv* incessantemente.

incest ['ɪnsest] *n* incesto *m*.

incestuous [ɪn'sestjʊəs] *adj* **-1.** [sexual] incestuoso(-sa) **-2.** *fig* [too close] fechado em si mesmo, fechada em si mesma.

inch [ɪntʃ] ⟨⟩ *n* polegada *f*. ⟨⟩ *vi* avançar gradualmente.

incidence ['ɪnsɪdəns] *n* incidência *f*.

incident ['ɪnsɪdənt] *n* [occurrence, event] incidente *m*.

incidental [ˌɪnsɪ'dentl] *adj* [minor] acessório(ria), secundário(ria).

incidentally [ˌɪnsɪ'dentəlɪ] *adv* **-1.** [by chance] por acaso **-2.** [by the way] a propósito.

incidental music *n* música *f* de fundo.

incinerate [ɪn'sɪnəreɪt] *vt* incinerar.

incinerator [ɪn'sɪnəreɪtər] *n* incinerador *m*.

incipient [ɪn'sɪpɪənt] *adj fml* incipiente.

incision [ɪn'sɪʒn] *n fml* incisão *f*.

incisive [ɪn'saɪsɪv] *adj* incisivo(va).

incisor [ɪn'saɪzər] *n* incisivo *m*.

incite [ɪn'saɪt] *vt* incitar; **to ~ sb to do sthg** incitar alguém a fazer algo.

incitement [ɪn'saɪtmənt] *n (U)* incitamento *m*; **~ to sthg/to do sthg** incitamento a algo/a fazer algo.

incl. -1. (*abbr of* **including**) incluindo **-2.** (*abbr of* **inclusive**) inclusive.

inclement [ɪn'klemənt] *adj fml* [weather] inclemente.

inclination [ˌɪnklɪ'neɪʃn] *n* **-1.** *(U)* [liking, preference] vontade *f* **-2.** [tendency]: **~ to do sthg** tendência *f* OR inclinação *f* para fazer algo.

incline [*n* 'ɪnklaɪn, *vb* ɪn'klaɪn] ⟨⟩ *n* [slope] ladeira *f*. ⟨⟩ *vt* [lean, bend] inclinar. ⟨⟩ *vi* [tend]: **to ~ to sthg** tender para algo.

inclined [ɪn'klaɪnd] *adj* **-1.** [tending] inclinado(da), propenso(sa); **to be ~ to sthg** estar propenso(sa) a algo; **to be ~ to do sthg** estar inclinado(da) a fazer algo **-2.** [wanting, willing]: **to be ~ to do sthg** estar disposto(ta) a fazer algo **-3.** [sloping] inclinado(da).

include [ɪn'kluːd] *vt* **-1.** [contain] abranger **-2.** [add, count] incluir.

included [ɪn'kluːdɪd] *adj* incluído(da).

including [ɪn'kluːdɪŋ] *prep* inclusive; **six died, ~ a child** seis morreram, incluindo uma criança.

inclusion [ɪn'kluːʒn] *n* inclusão *f*.

inclusive [ɪn'kluːsɪv] *adj* inclusive; **1 to 9, ~** de um a nove, inclusive; **£150 ~** £150, tudo incluído; **~ of** incluindo.

incognito [ˌɪnkɒg'niːtəʊ] *adv* incógnito(ta).

incoherent [ˌɪnkəʊ'hɪərənt] *adj* incoerente.

income ['ɪŋkʌm] *n* **-1.** [earnings] renda *f* **-2.** [profit] lucro *m*.

incomes policy *n UK* política *f* de rendimentos.

income support *n UK* auxílio dado pelo governo a pessoas desempregadas ou de renda muito baixa.

income tax *n* imposto *m* de renda.

incoming ['ɪnˌkʌmɪŋ] *adj* **-1.** [tide] ascendente **-2.** [plane, passengers] de chegada **-3.** [mail, report, phone call] recebido(da) **-4.** [government, official] novo(va).

incommunicado [ˌɪnkəmjuːnɪ'kɑːdəʊ] *adv* incomunicável.

incomparable [ɪn'kɒmpərəbl] *adj* incomparável.

incompatible [ˌɪnkəm'pætɪbl] *adj* incompatível; **~ with sb/sthg** incompatível com alguém/algo.

incompetence [ɪn'kɒmpɪtəns] *n (U)* incompetência *f*.

incompetent [ɪn'kɒmpɪtənt] *adj* incompetente.

incomplete [ˌɪnkəm'pliːt] *adj* incompleto(ta).

incomprehensible [ɪnˌkɒmprɪ'hensəbl] *adj* incompreensível.

inconceivable [ˌɪnkən'siːvəbl] *adj* inconcebível.

inconclusive [ˌɪnkən'kluːsɪv] *adj* **-1.** [meeting, outcome, debate] sem conclusões claras **-2.** [evidence, argument] pouco convincente.

incongruous [ɪn'kɒŋgrʊəs] *adj* incongruente.

inconsequential [ˌɪnkɒnsɪ'kwenʃl] *adj* [insignificant] insignificante.

inconsiderable [ˌɪnkən'sɪdərəbl] *adj*: **not ~** nada desprezível.

inconsiderate [ˌɪnkən'sɪdərət] *adj* **-1.** [attitude, treatment] impensado(da), irrefletido(da) **-2.** [person] sem consideração.

inconsistency [ˌɪnkən'sɪstənsɪ] (*pl* **-ies**) *n* **-1.** *(U)*

[state of being inconsistent] inconsistência *f* **-2.** [contradictory point] contradição *f*.
inconsistent [ˌɪnkən'sɪstənt] *adj* **-1.** [not agreeing, contradictory] inconsistente; ~ **with sthg** contraditório(ria) com algo **-2.** [erratic] irregular.
inconsolable [ˌɪnkən'səʊləbl] *adj* inconsolável.
inconspicuous [ˌɪnkən'spɪkjʊəs] *adj* discreto(ta).
incontinence [ɪn'kɒntɪnəns] *n (U)* incontinência *f*.
incontinent [ɪn'kɒntɪnənt] *adj* incontinente.
incontrovertible [ˌɪnkɒntrə'vɜːtəbl] *adj* incontestável.
inconvenience [ˌɪnkən'viːnjəns] <> *n* **-1.** *(U)* [difficulty, discomfort] incômodo *m* **-2.** [inconvenient thing] inconveniência *f*. <> *vt* incomodar.
inconvenient [ˌɪnkən'viːnjənt] *adj* inconveniente.
incorporate [ɪn'kɔːpəreɪt] *vt* **-1.** [include] incorporar; **to** ~ **sb/sthg in (to) sthg** incluir alguém/algo em algo **-2.** [blend] combinar.
incorporated company *n* COMM sociedade *f* anônima.
incorporation [ɪnˌkɔːpə'reɪʃn] *n* **-1.** [integration] integração *f* **-2.** COMM [of company] incorporação *f*.
incorrect [ˌɪnkə'rekt] *adj* incorreto(ta).
incorrigible [ɪn'kɒrɪdʒəbl] *adj* incorrigível.
incorruptible [ˌɪnkə'rʌptəbl] *adj* [person] incorruptível.
increase [*n* 'ɪnkriːs, *vb* ɪn'kriːs] <> *n*: ~ **(in sthg)** aumento *m* (de algo); **to be on the** ~ estar aumentando, estar em crescimento. <> *vt & vi* aumentar.
increased [ɪn'kriːst] *adj* intensificado(da), em crescimento.
increasing [ɪn'kriːsɪŋ] *adj* crescente.
increasingly [ɪn'kriːsɪŋlɪ] *adv* cada vez mais.
incredible [ɪn'kredəbl] *adj inf* incrível.
incredulous [ɪn'kredjʊləs] *adj* incrédulo(la).
increment ['ɪnkrɪmənt] *n* incremento *m*.
incriminate [ɪn'krɪmɪneɪt] *vt* incriminar; **to** ~ **o.s.** incriminar-se.
incriminating [ɪn'krɪmɪneɪtɪŋ] *adj* incriminatório(ria).
incrusted *adj* = encrusted.
incubate ['ɪnkjʊbeɪt] *vt & vi* **-1.** [gen] incubar **-2.** [egg] chocar.
incubation [ˌɪnkjʊ'beɪʃn] *n* incubação *f*.
incubator ['ɪnkjʊbeɪtə'] *n* [for baby] incubadora *f*.
inculcate ['ɪnkʌlkeɪt] *vt fml*: **to** ~ **sthg in (to) sb** inculcar algo em alguém.
incumbent [ɪn'kʌmbənt] *fml* <> *adj*: **to be** ~ **(up)on sb to do sthg** incumbir alguém de fazer algo. <> *n* [postholder] titular *mf*.
incur [ɪn'kɜː'] (*pt & pp* -**red**, *cont* -**ring**) *vt* **-1.** [wrath, criticism] incorrer em **-2.** [expenses] contrair.
incurable [ɪn'kjʊərəbl] *adj lit & fig* incurável.
incursion [UK ɪn'kɜːʃn, US ɪn'kɜːʒn] *n* MIL incursão *f*; *fig* [unwelcome] invasão *f*.
indebted [ɪn'detɪd] *adj* **-1.** [grateful]: **to be** ~ **to sb** estar em dívida com alguém **-2.** [owing money]: **to be** ~ **to sb** estar devendo a alguém.
indecency [ɪn'diːsnsɪ] *n (U)* indecência *f*.
indecent [ɪn'diːsnt] *adj* **-1.** [obscene] indecente **-2.** [unreasonable] inadequado(da).

indecent assault *n* atentado *m* contra o pudor.
indecent exposure *n (U)* ato *m* obsceno.
indecipherable [ˌɪndɪ'saɪfərəbl] *adj* indecifrável.
indecision [ˌɪndɪ'sɪʒn] *n (U)* indecisão *f*.
indecisive [ˌɪndɪ'saɪsɪv] *adj* indeciso(sa).
indeed [ɪn'diːd] *adv* **-1.** [certainly] realmente, certamente **-2.** [in fact] na verdade **-3.** [for emphasis] realmente; **very big** ~ estupidamente grande; **very few** ~ pouquíssimos(mas) **-4.** [to express surprise, disbelief] mesmo; ~? é mesmo?
indefatigable [ˌɪndɪ'fætɪgəbl] *adj* incansável.
indefensible [ˌɪndɪ'fensəbl] *adj* [behaviour, argument] indefensável.
indefinable [ˌɪndɪ'faɪnəbl] *adj* indefinível.
indefinite [ɪn'defɪnɪt] *adj* **-1.** [indeterminate] indefinido(da) **-2.** [imprecise] impreciso(sa).
indefinitely [ɪn'defɪnətlɪ] *adv* [for indeterminate period] indefinidamente.
indelible [ɪn'deləbl] *adj* **-1.** [gen] indelével **-2.** [memory] que não se pode apagar.
indelicate [ɪn'delɪkət] *adj* indelicado(da).
indemnify [ɪn'demnɪfaɪ] (*pt & pp* -**ied**) *vt* **-1.** [insure]: **to** ~ **sb for** OR **against sthg** segurar alguém contra algo **-2.** [compensate]: **to** ~ **sb for sthg** indenizar alguém por algo.
indemnity [ɪn'demnətɪ] *n* **-1.** *(U)* [insurance] garantia *f* **-2.** [compensation] indenização *f*.
indent [ɪn'dent] *vt* **-1.** [text] recuar **-2.** [edge, surface] recortar.
indentation [ˌɪnden'teɪʃn] *n* **-1.** [in text] recuo *m* de parágrafo novo **-2.** [in edge, coastline, surface] reentrância *f*.
indenture [ɪn'dentʃə'] *n* contrato *m* de aprendizagem.
independence [ˌɪndɪ'pendəns] *n* independência *f*.
Independence Day *n festa nos Estados Unidos em comemoração à sua independência, no dia 4 de julho em 1776.*
independent [ˌɪndɪ'pendənt] *adj* independente; ~ **of sb/sthg** independente de alguém/algo.
independently [ˌɪndɪ'pendəntlɪ] *adv* **-1.** [govern, rule] independentemente; ~ **of sb/sthg** independentemente de alguém/algo **-2.** [live, think, act] de forma independente.
independent school *n UK* escola *f* privada.
in-depth *adj* em profundidade, exaustivo(va).
indescribable [ˌɪndɪ'skraɪbəbl] *adj* indescritível.
indestructible [ˌɪndɪ'strʌktəbl] *adj* indestrutível.
indeterminate [ˌɪndɪ'tɜːmɪnət] *adj* [indefinite] indeterminado(da).
index ['ɪndeks] (*pl senses 1 and 2* -**es**, *pl sense 3* -**es** OR **indices**) <> *n* **-1.** [of book] índice *m* remissivo **-2.** [in library] catálogo *m* **-3.** ECON [value system] índice *m*. <> *vt* **-1.** [book] acrescentar índice remissivo a **-2.** [econ] indexar.
index card *n* ficha *f* de indexação.
index finger *n* [dedo *m*] indicador *m*.
index-linked [-lɪŋkt] *adj* indexado(da).
India ['ɪndjə] *n* Índia *f*; **in** ~ na Índia.
India ink *n US* = Indian ink.
Indian ['ɪndjən] <> *adj* **-1.** [from India] indiano(na) **-2.** [from the Americas] índio(dia). <> *n* **-1.** [from India]

indiano *m*, **-na** *f* **-2.** [from the Americas] índio *m*, -dia *f*.

Indiana [ˌɪndɪˈænəl *n* Indiana; **in ~** em Indiana.

Indian ink *UK*, **India ink** *US n* (tinta *f*) nanquim *m*.

Indian Ocean *n*: **the ~** o Oceano Índico.

Indian summer *n* [warm weather] veranico *m*.

india rubber *n* borracha *f*.

indicate [ˈɪndɪkeɪt] <> *vt* **-1.** [gen] indicar **-2.** [suggest] sugerir. <> *vi* [when driving]: **to ~ left/right** sinalizar à esquerda/direita.

indication [ˌɪndɪˈkeɪʃn] *n* **-1.** [suggestion] indicação *f* **-2.** [sign] indício *m*.

indicative [ɪnˈdɪkətɪv] <> *adj*: **~ of sthg** indicativo(va) de algo. <> *n GRAM* indicativo *m*.

indicator [ˈɪndɪkeɪtəʳ] *n* **-1.** [sign] indicador *m* **-2.** [on car] pisca-pisca *m*.

indices [ˈɪndɪsiːz] *pl* ⊳ **index**.

indict [ɪnˈdaɪt] *vt* indiciar; **to ~ sb for sthg** indiciar alguém por algo.

indictable [ɪnˈdaɪtəbl] *adj* passível de ser indiciado(da).

indictment [ɪnˈdaɪtmənt] *n* **-1.** *JUR* indiciamento *m* **-2.** [criticism] crítica *f* dura.

indie [ˈɪndɪ] *adj inf* independente.

indifference [ɪnˈdɪfrəns] *n (U)* indiferença *f*.

indifferent [ɪnˈdɪfrənt] *adj* **-1.** [uninterested] indiferente; **~ to sthg** indiferente a algo **-2.** [mediocre] medíocre.

indigenous [ɪnˈdɪdʒɪnəs] *adj* nativo(va), indígena.

indigestible [ˌɪndɪˈdʒestəbl] *adj* **-1.** [food] indigesto(ta) **-2.** [facts] incompreensível.

indigestion [ˌɪndɪˈdʒestʃn] *n (U)* indigestão *f*.

indignant [ɪnˈdɪgnənt] *adj* indignado(da); **to be ~ at sthg** estar indignado(da) com algo.

indignantly [ɪnˈdɪgnəntlɪ] *adv* com indignação.

indignation [ˌɪndɪgˈneɪʃn] *n (U)* indignação *f*.

indignity [ɪnˈdɪgnətɪ] (*pl* **-ies**) *n* **-1.** *(U)* [feeling of humiliation] afronta *f* **-2.** [humiliating situation] indignidade *f*.

indigo [ˈɪndɪgəʊ] <> *adj* [in colour] da cor de anil. <> *n* [colour] anil *m*.

indirect [ˌɪndɪˈrekt] *adj* indireto(ta).

indirect costs *npl* gastos *mpl* indiretos.

indirect lighting *n* luz *f OR* iluminação *f* indireta.

indirectly [ˌɪndɪˈrektlɪ] *adv* indiretamente.

indirect speech *n GRAM* discurso *m* indireto.

indirect taxation *n* impostos *mpl* indiretos.

indiscreet [ˌɪndɪˈskriːt] *adj* indiscreto(ta); [tactless] indelicado(da).

indiscretion [ˌɪndɪˈskreʃn] *n* indiscrição *f*.

indiscriminate [ˌɪndɪˈskrɪmɪnət] *adj* indiscriminado(da).

indiscriminately [ˌɪndɪˈskrɪmɪnətlɪ] *adv* indiscriminadamente.

indispensable [ˌɪndɪˈspensəbl] *adj* indispensável.

indisposed [ˌɪndɪˈspəʊzd] *adj fml* [unwell] indisposto(ta).

indisputable [ˌɪndɪˈspjuːtəbl] *adj* inquestionável.

indistinct [ˌɪndɪˈstɪŋkt] *adj* **-1.** [words] indistinto(ta) **-2.** [memory] confuso(sa) **-3.** [picture, marking] borrado(da).

indistinguishable [ˌɪndɪˈstɪŋgwɪʃəbl] *adj* indistinguível; **~ from sb/sthg** indistinguível de alguém/algo.

individual [ˌɪndɪˈvɪdʒʊəl] <> *adj* **-1.** [gen] individual **-2.** [private] particular **-3.** [distinctive] pessoal. <> *n* indivíduo *m*.

individualist [ˌɪndɪˈvɪdʒʊəlɪst] *n* individualista *mf*.

individualistic [ˈɪndɪˌvɪdʒʊəˈlɪstɪk] *adj* individualista.

individuality [ˈɪndɪˌvɪdʒʊˈælətɪl] *n (U)* individualidade *f*.

individually [ˌɪndɪˈvɪdʒʊəlɪ] *adv* [separately] individualmente.

indivisible [ˌɪndɪˈvɪzəbl] *adj* indivisível.

Indochina [ˌɪndəʊˈtʃaɪnə] *n* Indochina; **in ~** na Indochina.

indoctrinate [ɪnˈdɒktrɪneɪt] *vt* doutrinar.

indoctrination [ɪnˌdɒktrɪˈneɪʃn] *n (U)* doutrinação *f*.

indolent [ˈɪndələnt] *adj fml* indolente.

indomitable [ɪnˈdɒmɪtəbl] *adj* indomável.

Indonesia [ˌɪndəˈniːzjəl *n* Indonésia; **in ~** na Indonésia.

Indonesian [ˌɪndəˈniːzjən] <> *adj* indonésio(sia). <> *n* **-1.** [person] indonésio *m*, -sia *f* **-2.** [language] indonésio *m*.

indoor [ˈɪndɔːʳ] *adj* **-1.** [plant] de interior **-2.** [shoes] para dentro de casa **-3.** [sports] em local coberto; **~ swimming pool** piscina *f* coberta.

indoors [ˌɪnˈdɔːz] *adv* dentro de casa; **to go ~** entrar, ir para dentro.

indubitably [ɪnˈdjuːbɪtəblɪ] *adv* indubitavelmente, sem dúvida.

induce [ɪnˈdjuːs] *vt*: **to ~ sb to do sthg** induzir alguém a fazer algo.

inducement [ɪnˈdjuːsmənt] *n* [incentive] estímulo *m*, incentivo *m*.

induction [ɪnˈdʌkʃn] *n* **-1.** [into official position]: **~ into sthg** posse *m* em algo **-2.** *(U) MED, ELEC* indução *f* **-3.** [introduction to job] apresentação *f*.

induction course *n* curso *m* de integração *OR* de iniciação.

indulge [ɪnˈdʌldʒ] <> *vt* **-1.** [whim, passion] satisfazer **-2.** [child, person] fazer a vontade de; **to ~ o.s.** permitir-se um luxo. <> *vi*: **to ~ in sthg** permitir-se algo.

indulgence [ɪnˈdʌldʒəns] *n* **-1.** *(U)* [tolerance, kindness] indulgência *f* **-2.** [special treat] vício *m*, prazer *m*.

indulgent [ɪnˈdʌldʒənt] *adj* [liberal, kind] indulgente.

Indus *n*: **the (River) ~** o (Rio) Indus.

industrial [ɪnˈdʌstrɪəl] *adj* **-1.** [of industry] industrial **-2.** [industrialized] industrializado(da).

industrial action *n*: **to take ~** declarar-se em greve.

industrial estate *UK*, **industrial park** *US n* parque *m* industrial.

industrial injury *n* acidente *m* de trabalho.

industrialist [ɪnˈdʌstrɪəlɪst] *n* industrialista *mf*.

industrialization [ɪnˌdʌstrɪəlaɪˈzeɪʃn] *n* industrialização *f*.

industrialize, -ise [ɪnˈdʌstrɪəlaɪz] <> *vt* industrializar. <> *vi* industrializar-se.

industrial park n US = industrial estate.
industrial relations npl relações fpl de trabalho.
industrial revolution n revolução f industrial.
industrial tribunal n justiça f do trabalho.
industrious [ɪn'dʌstrɪəs] adj trabalhador(ra), diligente.
industry ['ɪndəstrɪ] (pl -ies) n -1. [gen] indústria f; the coal ~ o setor carvoeiro -2. (U) [hard work] laboriosidade f.
inebriated [ɪ'ni:brɪeɪtɪd] adj fml inebriado(da).
inedible [ɪn'edɪbl] adj -1. [unpleasant to eat] não-comestível -2. [poisonous] venenoso(sa).
ineffective [ˌɪnɪ'fektɪv] adj ineficaz, inútil.
ineffectual [ˌɪnɪ'fektʃʊəl] adj ineficaz, inútil.
inefficiency [ˌɪnɪ'fɪʃnsɪ] n (U) ineficiência f.
inefficient [ˌɪnɪ'fɪʃnt] adj ineficiente.
inelegant [ɪn'elɪɡənt] adj deselegante.
ineligible [ɪn'elɪdʒəbl] adj inelegível; to be ~ for sthg não estar qualificado(da) para algo.
inept [ɪ'nept] adj -1. [incompetent] inepto(ta); ~ at sthg incapaz de algo -2. [clumsy] malfeito(ta).
ineptitude [ɪ'neptɪtju:d] n (U) [incompetence] inépcia f, incompetência f.
inequality [ˌɪnɪ'kwɒlətɪ] (pl -ies) n desigualdade f.
inequitable [ɪn'ekwɪtəbl] adj fml injusto(ta).
ineradicable adj fml inextirpável.
inert [ɪ'nɜ:t] adj inerte.
inertia [ɪ'nɜ:ʃə] n inércia f.
inertia-reel seat belt n cinto m de segurança retrátil.
inescapable [ˌɪnɪ'skeɪpəbl] adj inevitável.
inessential [ˌɪnɪ'senʃl] adj: ~ (to sthg) dispensável (para algo).
inestimable [ɪn'estɪməbl] adj fml inestimável.
inevitable [ɪn'evɪtəbl] <> adj inevitável. <> n: the ~ o inevitável.
inevitably [ɪn'evɪtəblɪ] adv inevitavelmente.
inexact [ˌɪnɪɡ'zækt] adj inexato(ta).
inexcusable [ˌɪnɪk'skju:zəbl] adj imperdoável.
inexhaustible [ˌɪnɪɡ'zɔ:stəbl] adj inesgotável.
inexorable [ɪn'eksərəbl] adj fml [unpreventable] inexorável.
inexorably [ɪn'eksərəblɪ] adv inexoravelmente.
inexpensive [ˌɪnɪk'spensɪv] adj barato(ta), econômico(ca).
inexperience [ˌɪnɪk'spɪərɪəns] n (U) inexperiência f.
inexperienced [ˌɪnɪk'spɪərɪənst] adj inexperiente.
inexpert [ɪn'eksps:t] adj inábil.
inexplicable [ˌɪnɪk'splɪkəbl] adj inexplicável.
inexplicably [ˌɪnɪk'splɪkəblɪ] adv inexplicavelmente.
inextricably [ˌɪnɪk'strɪkəblɪ] adv inextricavelmente.
infallible [ɪn'fæləbl] adj infalível.
infamous ['ɪnfəməs] adj infame.
infamy n (U) fml infâmia f.
infancy ['ɪnfənsɪ] n (U) primeira infância f; to be in its ~ fig estar engatinhando.
infant ['ɪnfənt] n -1. [baby] bebê m -2. [young child] criança f pequena.

infantile ['ɪnfəntaɪl] adj infantil.
infant mortality n mortalidade f infantil.
infantry ['ɪnfəntrɪ] n (U) infantaria f.
infantryman ['ɪnfəntrɪmən] (pl -men [-mən]) n soldado m de infantaria.
infant school n UK na Grã-Bretanha, escola para crianças entre 5 e 7 anos.
infatuated [ɪn'fætjʊeɪtɪd] adj: ~ (with sb/sthg) obcecado(da) (por alguém/algo).
infatuation [ɪnˌfætjʊ'eɪʃn] n: ~ (with sb/sthg) obsessão f (por alguém/algo).
infect [ɪn'fekt] vt -1. MED infectar; to become ~ed [wound] infeccionar; to ~ sb with sthg infectar alguém com algo -2. fig [spread to] contagiar.
infected [ɪn'fektɪd] adj -1. [food, patient] infectado(-da); ~ with sthg infectado(da) por algo -2. [wound] infeccionado(da).
infection [ɪn'fekʃn] n -1. [disease] infecção f -2. (U) [spreading of germs] contágio m.
infectious [ɪn'fekʃəs] adj -1. [disease] infeccioso(sa) -2. fig [feeling, laugh] contagioso(sa).
infer [ɪn'fɜ:'] (pt & pp -red, cont -ring) vt -1. [deduce]: to ~ (that) inferir que; to ~ sthg (from sthg) deduzir OR inferir algo (de algo) -2. inf [insinuate] insinuar.
inference ['ɪnfərəns] n -1. [conclusion] conclusão f -2. (U) [deduction]: by ~ por dedução.
inferior [ɪn'fɪərɪə'] <> adj [gen] inferior; ~ to sb/sthg inferior a alguém/algo. <> n [in status] inferior mf.
inferiority [ɪnˌfɪərɪ'ɒrətɪ] n (U) inferioridade f.
inferiority complex n complexo m de inferioridade.
infernal adj inf dated infernal.
inferno [ɪn'fɜ:nəʊ] (pl -s) n inferno m, incêndio m incontrolável.
infertile [ɪn'fɜ:taɪl] adj -1. [woman, animal] estéril -2. [soil] infértil.
infertility [ˌɪnfə'tɪlətɪ] n (U) -1. [of woman, animal] esterilidade f -2. [of soil] infertilidade f.
infestation [ˌɪnfe'steɪʃn] n infestação f, praga f.
infested [ɪn'festɪd] adj: ~ with sthg infestado(da) por algo.
infidelity [ˌɪnfɪ'delətɪ] n [of partner] infidelidade f.
infighting ['ɪnˌfaɪtɪŋ] n (U) disputa f interna.
infiltrate ['ɪnfɪltreɪt] <> vt infiltrar. <> vi: to ~ into sthg infiltrar-se em algo.
infinite ['ɪnfɪnət] adj infinito(ta).
infinitely ['ɪnfɪnətlɪ] adv infinitamente.
infinitesimal [ˌɪnfɪnɪ'tesɪml] adj infinitesimal.
infinitive [ɪn'fɪnɪtɪv] n GRAM infinitivo m.
infinity [ɪn'fɪnətɪ] n -1. (U) [gen] infinito m -2. MATH [incalculable number] infinidade f.
infirm [ɪn'fɜ:m] <> adj [unhealthy] enfermo(ma). <> npl: the ~ os enfermos.
infirmary [ɪn'fɜ:mərɪ] (pl -ies) n -1. [hospital] hospital m -2. [room] enfermaria f.
infirmity [ɪn'fɜ:mətɪ] (pl -ies) n enfermidade f.
inflamed [ɪn'fleɪmd] adj MED inflamado(da).
inflammable [ɪn'flæməbl] adj [burning easily] inflamável.
inflammation [ˌɪnflə'meɪʃn] n MED inflamação f.

inflammatory [ɪnˈflæmətrɪ] adj [provocative] incendiante.

inflatable [ɪnˈfleɪtəbl] adj inflável.

inflate [ɪnˈfleɪt] vt -1. [fill with air] inflar -2. ECON [increase] inflacionar.

inflated [ɪnˈfleɪtɪd] adj -1. [filled with air] inflado(da) -2. pej [exaggerated] exagerado(da) -3. ECON [unreasonably high] inflacionado(da).

inflation [ɪnˈfleɪʃn] n (U) ECON inflação f.

inflationary [ɪnˈfleɪʃnrɪ] adj ECON inflacionário(ria).

inflationary spiral n espiral f inflacionária.

inflation-proof adj que não é afetado(da) pela inflação.

inflation rate n ECON taxa f de inflação.

inflection n GRAM flexão f.

inflexible [ɪnˈfleksəbl] adj -1. [gen] inflexível -2. [fixed] imutável.

inflict [ɪnˈflɪkt] vt: to ~ sthg on sb infligir algo a alguém.

in-flight adj de bordo.

inflow [ˈɪnfləʊ] n afluência f.

influence [ˈɪnfluəns] <> n -1. (U) [power]: ~ (on sb/sthg), ~ (over sb/sthg) influência f (sobre alguém/algo); **under the ~ of** [person, group] sob a influência de; [alcohol, drugs] sob o efeito de -2. [influential person, thing]: ~ (on sb/sthg) influência para alguém/algo. <> vt influenciar.

influential [ˌɪnfluˈenʃl] adj influente.

influenza [ˌɪnfluˈenzə] n (U) fml influenza f.

influx [ˈɪnflʌks] n afluxo m.

info [ˈɪnfəʊ] (abbr of information) n (U) inf info f.

inform [ɪnˈfɔːm] vt informar; to ~ sb of/about sthg informar alguém de/sobre algo.

➡ **inform on** vt fus denunciar, delatar.

informal [ɪnˈfɔːml] adj informal.

informally [ɪnˈfɔːməlɪ] adv informalmente.

informant [ɪnˈfɔːmənt] n informante mf.

information [ˌɪnfəˈmeɪʃn] n (U) informações fpl; **to give sb ~** dar informações a alguém; **to get ~** obter informações; **that's a useful piece of ~** esta é uma informação útil; **to have some~ on** OR **about sthg** ter alguma informação sobre algo; **'Information'** 'Informações'; **for your ~** para seu conhecimento.

information desk n (balcão m de) informações fpl.

information office n (balcão m de) informações fpl.

information retrieval n recuperação f de informações.

information technology n tecnologia f da informação.

informative [ɪnˈfɔːmətɪv] adj instrutivo(va).

informed [ɪnˈfɔːmd] adj -1. [having information] informado(da) -2. [based on good information] bem-informado(da); ~ **guess** conjectura f bem-fundamentada.

informer [ɪnˈfɔːməʳ] n [denouncer] informante mf, delator m, -ra f.

infrared [ˌɪnfrəˈred] adj infravermelho(lha).

infrastructure [ˈɪnfrəˌstrʌktʃəʳ] n infra-estrutura f.

infrequent [ɪnˈfriːkwənt] adj infreqüente.

infringe [ɪnˈfrɪndʒ] (cont infringeing) <> vt -1. [right] transgredir, violar -2. [law, agreement] infringir. <> vi -1. [on right]: to ~ on sthg transgredir OR violar algo -2. [on law, agreement]: to ~ on sthg infringir algo.

infringement [ɪnˈfrɪndʒmənt] n -1. [of right] transgressão f, violação f -2. [of law, agreement] infração f.

infuriate [ɪnˈfjʊərɪeɪt] vt enfurecer.

infuriating [ɪnˈfjʊərɪeɪtɪŋ] adj enfurecedor(ra).

infuse [ɪnˈfjuːz] <> vt: to ~ sb with sthg infundir algo em alguém. <> vi estar em infusão.

infusion [ɪnˈfjuːʒn] n infusão f.

ingenious [ɪnˈdʒiːnjəs] adj engenhoso(sa).

ingenuity [ˌɪndʒɪˈnjuːətɪ] n (U) engenhosidade f.

ingenuous [ɪnˈdʒenjʊəs] adj fml ingênuo(nua).

ingest [ɪnˈdʒest] vt fml ingerir.

ingot [ˈɪŋgət] n lingote m.

ingrained [ˌɪnˈgreɪnd] adj -1. [ground in] entranhado(da) -2. [deeply rooted] arraigado(da).

ingratiate [ɪnˈgreɪʃɪeɪt] vt: to ~ o.s. with sb congraçar-se com alguém.

ingratiating [ɪnˈgreɪʃɪeɪtɪŋ] adj insinuante, lisonjeiro(ra).

ingratitude [ɪnˈgrætɪtjuːd] n (U) ingratidão f.

ingredient [ɪnˈgriːdjənt] n ingrediente m.

ingrowing [ˈɪnˌgrəʊɪŋ], **ingrown** [ˈɪnˌgrəʊn] adj encravado(da).

inhabit [ɪnˈhæbɪt] vt habitar.

inhabitant [ɪnˈhæbɪtənt] n habitante mf.

inhalation [ˌɪnhəˈleɪʃn] n (U) inalação f.

inhale [ɪnˈheɪl] <> vt inalar. <> vi [breathe in - smoker] tragar; [- patient] inspirar.

inhaler [ɪnˈheɪləʳ] n MED inalador m.

inherent [ɪnˈhɪərənt, ɪnˈherənt] adj inerente; ~ **in** sthg inerente a algo.

inherently [ɪnˈhɪərəntlɪ, ɪnˈherəntlɪ] adv intrinsecamente.

inherit [ɪnˈherɪt] <> vt: to ~ sthg (from sb) herdar algo (de alguém). <> vi herdar.

inheritance [ɪnˈherɪtəns] n herança f.

inheritor [ɪnˈherɪtəʳ] n [of debt, problem, tradition] herdeiro m, -ra f.

inhibit [ɪnˈhɪbɪt] vt -1. [restrict] impedir -2. PSYCH [repress] inibir.

inhibited [ɪnˈhɪbɪtɪd] adj inibido(da).

inhibition [ˌɪnhɪˈbɪʃn] n inibição f.

inhospitable [ˌɪnhɒˈspɪtəbl] adj -1. [unwelcoming] inospitaleiro(ra) -2. [climate, area] inóspito(ta).

in-house <> adj -1. [journal, report, magazine] de circulação interna -2. [staff, group] interno(na), da casa; ~ **staff** quadro m interno. <> adv internamente.

inhuman [ɪnˈhjuːmən] adj -1. [cruel] desumano(na) -2. [not human] inumano(na).

inhumane [ˌɪnhjuːˈmeɪn] adj desumano(na).

inimitable [ɪˈnɪmɪtəbl] adj inimitável.

iniquitous [ɪˈnɪkwɪtəs] adj fml iníquo(qua).

iniquity [ɪˈnɪkwətɪ] (pl -ies) n -1. (U) fml [wickedness, injustice] iniqüidade f -2. [wicked or unjust act] injustiça f.

initial [ɪˈnɪʃl] (UK pt & pp -led, cont -ling, US pt & pp -ed, cont -ing) <> adj inicial. <> vt rubricar.

➡ **initials** npl iniciais fpl.

initialize, -ise [ɪ'nɪʃəlaɪz] *vt COMPUT* inicializar.
initially [ɪ'nɪʃəlɪ] *adv* inicialmente.
initiate [ɪ'nɪʃɪeɪt] ⬦ *vt* -1. [start] iniciar -2. [teach]:
to ~ sb (into sthg) iniciar alguém (em algo). ⬦
n iniciado *m*, -da *f.*
initiation [ɪˌnɪʃɪ'eɪʃn] *n (U)* -1. [start] início *m* -2. [introduction, teaching] iniciação *f.*
initiative [ɪ'nɪʃətɪv] *n* -1. [gen] iniciativa *f*; **to use one's ~** fazer uso de sua própria iniciativa; **on one's own ~** por iniciativa própria -2. [first move]: **to take the ~** tomar a iniciativa -3. [advantage]: **to have the ~** ter a vantagem.
inject [ɪn'dʒekt] *vt* -1. *MED*: **to ~ sb with sthg, to ~ sthg into sb** injetar algo em alguém -2. *fig* [add]: **to ~ sthg into sthg** injetar algo em algo.
injection [ɪn'dʒekʃn] *n* injeção *f.*
injudicious [ˌɪndʒuː'dɪʃəs] *adj fml* injudicioso(sa).
injunction [ɪn'dʒʌŋkʃn] *n JUR* mandado *m* judicial, interdito *m.*
injure ['ɪndʒəʳ] *vt* -1. [hurt physically] machucar; **to ~ o.s.** machucar-se, ferir-se -2. [reputation, chances] prejudicar -3. [offend] ferir.
injured ['ɪndʒəd] ⬦ *adj* -1. [physically hurt] machucado(da), ferido(da) -2. [reputation, chances] prejudicado(da) -3. [offended] ferido(da). ⬦ *npl*: **the ~ os** feridos.
injurious [ɪn'dʒʊərɪəs] *adj fml*: **~ (to sb/sthg)** pernicioso(sa) (a alguém/algo).
injury ['ɪndʒərɪ] *(pl* -ies) *n* -1. *(U)* [physical harm] lesão *f* -2. [wound] ferimento *m*; **to do o.s. an ~** machucar-se -3. *(U)* [to one's reputation] dano *m* -4. [to one's pride, feelings] golpe *m.*
injury time *n (U)* tempo *m* de descontos *(num jogo).*
injustice [ɪn'dʒʌstɪs] *n* injustiça *f*; **to do sb an ~** fazer uma injustiça a alguém.
ink [ɪŋk] ⬦ *n (U)* tinta *f.* ⬦ *comp* de tinta; **~ pen** caneta-tinteiro *f.*
➡ **ink in** *vt sep* repassar a caneta.
ink-jet printer *n* impressora *f* jato de tinta.
inkling ['ɪŋklɪŋ] *n*: **to have an ~ of sthg** ter uma vaga idéia de algo; **to have an ~ that** ter a vaga idéia de que.
inkpad ['ɪŋkpæd] *n* almofada *f* para carimbos.
inkwell ['ɪŋkwel] *n* tinteiro *m.*
INLA *(abbr of Irish National Liberation Army) n grupo terrorista que luta pela reunificação da Irlanda*, Exército *m* de Libertação Nacional Irlandês.
inlaid [ˌɪn'leɪd] *adj* incrustado(da); **~ with sthg** incrustado(da) de algo.
inland [*adj* 'ɪnlənd, *adv* ɪn'lænd] ⬦ *adj* interior. ⬦ *adv* -1. [drive, head, walk] para o interior -2. [be positioned] no interior.
Inland Revenue *n UK*: **the~** o fisco, ≃ a Receita Federal.
in-laws *npl inf* sogros *mpl.*
inlet ['ɪnlet] *n* -1. [stretch of water] enseada *f* -2. [way in] entrada *f.*
inmate ['ɪnmeɪt] *n* -1. [mental hospital] interno *m*, -na *f* -2. [prison] preso *m*, -sa *f.*
inmost ['ɪnməʊst] *adj literary* [deepest] mais íntimo(-ma).

inn [ɪn] *n* pousada *f.*
innards ['ɪnədz] *npl* entranhas *fpl.*
innate [ˌɪ'neɪt] *adj* inato(ta).
inner ['ɪnəʳ] *adj* -1. [most central] interno(na); **Inner London** o centro de Londres -2. [unexpressed, secret - feelings, doubts] íntimo(ma); [- peace, meaning] interior.
inner city ⬦ *n*: **the ~** o centro urbano decadente. ⬦ *comp* do centro urbano decadente.
innermost ['ɪnəməʊst] *adj* = inmost.
inner tube *n* câmara *f* de ar.
innings ['ɪnɪŋz] *(pl inv) n UK* [in cricket] turno *m*; **to have had a good ~** *fig* ter aproveitado bem a vida.
innocence ['ɪnəsəns] *n (U)* -1. *JUR* [gen] inocência *f* -2. [naivety] ingenuidade *f.*
innocent ['ɪnəsənt] ⬦ *adj* -1. [gen] inocente; **~ of sthg** inocente de algo -2. [harmless] ingênuo(nua). ⬦ *n* [naive person] inocente *mf.*
innocuous [ɪ'nɒkjʊəs] *adj* [harmless] inócuo(cua).
innovation [ˌɪnə'veɪʃn] *n* inovação *f.*
innovative ['ɪnəvətɪv] *adj* inovador(ra).
innovator ['ɪnəveɪtəʳ] *n* inovador *m*, -ra *f.*
innuendo [ˌɪnju:'endəʊ] *(pl* -es *OR* -s) *n* -1. [individual remark] insinuação *f*, indireta *f* -2. *(U)* [style of speaking] insinuações *fpl.*
innumerable [ɪ'nju:mərəbl] *adj* inumerável.
inoculate [ɪ'nɒkjʊleɪt] *vt* inocular; **to ~ sb with sthg** inocular algo em alguém; **to ~ sb against sthg** vacinar alguém contra algo.
inoculation [ɪˌnɒkjʊ'leɪʃn] *n* -1. [injection] inoculação *f* -2. *(U)* [disease prevention] vacinação *f.*
inoffensive [ˌɪnə'fensɪv] *adj* inofensivo(va).
inoperable [ɪn'ɒprəbl] *adj* -1. *MED* que não se pode operar -2. *fml* [unworkable] impraticável.
inoperative [ɪn'ɒprətɪv] *adj* -1. [unworkable] impraticável -2. [not working] que não funciona.
inopportune [ɪn'ɒpətju:n] *adj fml* inoportuno(na).
inordinate [ɪ'nɔ:dɪnət] *adj fml* -1. [gen] excessivo(-va) -2. [pleasure] desmesurado(da).
inordinately [ɪ'nɔ:dɪnətlɪ] *adv fml* [extremely] de forma desmesurada.
inorganic [ˌɪnɔ:'gænɪk] *adj* [substance] inorgânico(-ca).
in-patient *n* paciente *mf* interno, -na.
input ['ɪnpʊt] *(pt & pp input OR* -ted, *cont* -ting) ⬦ *n (U)* -1. [contribution] contribuição *f* -2. *COMPUT, ELEC* entrada *f.* ⬦ *vt COMPUT* entrar.
input/output *n COMPUT* entrada/saída *f.*
inquest ['ɪnkwest] *n JUR* inquérito *m.*
inquire [ɪn'kwaɪəʳ] ⬦ *vt*: **to ~ when/whether/if/how ...** inquirir quando/se/como ... ⬦ *vi* [ask for information] informar-se; **to ~ about sthg** pedir informações sobre algo.
➡ **inquire after** *vt fus* perguntar por.
➡ **inquire into** *vt fus* investigar.
inquiring [ɪn'kwaɪərɪŋ] *adj* inquisitivo(va); **an ~ mind** uma mente curiosa.
inquiry [ɪn'kwaɪərɪ] *(pl* -ies) *n* -1. [question] pergunta *f*; **'Inquiries'** 'Informações' -2. [investigation] investigação *f*, inquérito *m* -3. *(U)* [questioning]: **this spirit of ~** este espírito de questionar.

inquiry desk n (balcão m de) informações fpl.

inquisition [ˌɪnkwɪˈzɪʃn] n pej inquisição f.
→ **Inquisition** n: **the Inquisition** a Inquisição.

inquisitive [ɪnˈkwɪzətɪv] adj curioso(sa).

inroads [ˈɪnrəʊdz] npl: **to make ~ into sthg** abrir caminho em algo.

insane [ɪnˈseɪn] ◇ adj **-1.** MED [mad] insano(na) **-2.** fig [very stupid] louco(ca). ◇ npl: **the ~** os deficientes mentais.

insanitary [ɪnˈsænɪtrɪ] adj insalubre, anti-higiênico(ca).

insanity [ɪnˈsænətɪ] n (U) **-1.** MED [madness] insanidade f **-2.** fig [great stupidity] loucura f.

insatiable [ɪnˈseɪʃəbl] adj insaciável.

inscribe [ɪnˈskraɪb] vt **-1.** [on wall, headstone, plaque] escrever; **to ~ sthg with sthg** escrever algo com algo; **to ~ sthg on sthg** gravar algo em algo **-2.** [in book]: **to ~ sthg in sthg** escrever algo em algo.

inscription [ɪnˈskrɪpʃn] n **-1.** [gen] inscrição f **-2.** [in book] dedicatória f.

inscrutable [ɪnˈskruːtəbl] adj inescrutável, impenetrável.

insect [ˈɪnsekt] n inseto m.

insect bite n picada f de inseto.

insecticide [ɪnˈsektɪsaɪd] n inseticida m.

insect repellent n repelente m para insetos.

insecure [ˌɪnsɪˈkjʊəʳ] adj **-1.** [not confident] inseguro(ra) **-2.** [not safe] pouco seguro(ra).

insecurity [ˌɪnsɪˈkjʊərətɪ] n (U) **-1.** [lack of confidence] insegurança f **-2.** [uncertainty] instabilidade f.

insensible [ɪnˈsensəbl] adj **-1.** [unconscious] inconsciente **-2.** [unaware]: **to be ~ of sthg** não ter consciência de algo **-3.** [unable to feel]: **to be ~ to sthg** ser insensível a algo.

insensitive [ɪnˈsensətɪv] adj **-1.** [unkind, thoughtless] insensível **-2.** [unresponsive]: **~ to sthg** indiferente a algo **-3.** [unable to feel]: **~ to sthg** insensível a algo.

insensitivity [ɪnˌsensəˈtɪvətɪ] n (U) **-1.** [unkindness, thoughtlessness] insensibilidade f **-2.** [lack of sensation]: **~ to sthg** insensibilidade a algo.

inseparable [ɪnˈseprəbl] adj **-1.** [subjects, facts]: **~ (from sthg)** inseparável (de algo) **-2.** [people] inseparável.

insert [vb ɪnˈsɜːt, n ˈɪnsɜːt] ◇ n encarte m. ◇ vt [put in]: **to ~ sthg (in OR into sthg)** inserir algo (em algo).

insertion [ɪnˈsɜːʃn] n (U) inserção f.

in-service training n UK treinamento m no serviço.

inset [ˈɪnset] n [detail] detalhe m.

inshore [adj ˈɪnʃɔːʳ, adv ɪnˈʃɔːʳ] ◇ adj costeiro(ra). ◇ adv **-1.** [towards shore] em direção à costa **-2.** [close to shore] perto da costa.

inside [ɪnˈsaɪd] ◇ adj [interior, near centre] interno(na). ◇ adv **-1.** [in, within - place, object, building] para dentro; **there was sthg ~** havia alguma coisa dentro; [- body, mind] por dentro **-2.** [prison] sl preso(sa). ◇ prep dentro de; **get some food ~ you!** coma alguma coisa!; **~ three weeks** em menos de três semanas. ◇ n **-1.** [interior, inner part]: **the ~** o lado de dentro; **~ out** [clothes] do avesso; **to know sthg ~ out** fig conhecer algo de

cabo a rabo; **to turn sthg ~ out** virar algo do avesso **-2.** AUT: **the ~** [in UK] a faixa da esquerda; [in mainland Europe, US, Brazil etc] a faixa da direita.
→ **insides** npl inf [intestines] tripas fpl.
→ **inside of** prep US [building, object] dentro de.

inside information n (U) informação f confidencial.

inside job n inf roubo cometido com a ajuda de um empregado da empresa ou do local roubado.

inside lane n AUT **-1.** [in UK] faixa f da esquerda **-2.** [in mainland Europe, US, Brazil etc] faixa f da direita.

insider [ˌɪnˈsaɪdəʳ] n pessoa f bem-informada (numa organização).

insider dealing, insider trading n (U) uso indevido de informações privilegiadas na bolsa de valores.

inside story n história f íntima.

insidious [ɪnˈsɪdɪəs] adj insidioso(sa).

insight [ˈɪnsaɪt] n **-1.** (U) [wisdom]: **~ (into sthg)** discernimento m (sobre algo) **-2.** [glimpse]: **~ (into sthg)** insight m (sobre algo); **the book gave me an ~ into the problem** o livro me fez ter algumas idéias sobre o problema.

insignia [ɪnˈsɪgnɪə] (pl inv) n insígnia f.

insignificance [ˌɪnsɪgˈnɪfɪkəns] n insignificância f.

insignificant [ˌɪnsɪgˈnɪfɪkənt] adj insignificante.

insincere [ˌɪnsɪnˈsɪəʳ] adj insincero(ra).

insincerity [ˌɪnsɪnˈserətɪ] n (U) insinceridade f.

insinuate [ɪnˈsɪnjʊeɪt] pej vt **-1.** [imply]: **to ~ (that)** insinuar que **-2.** [install]: **to ~ o.s. into sthg** infiltrar-se em algo.

insinuation [ɪnˌsɪnjʊˈeɪʃn] n pej **-1.** [suggestion] insinuação f **-2.** (U) [act of insinuating] insinuação f.

insipid [ɪnˈsɪpɪd] adj pej **-1.** [dull, boring] insosso(sa) **-2.** [flavourless - drink] insípido(da); [- food] insosso(sa).

insist [ɪnˈsɪst] ◇ vt: **to ~ (that)** insistir que. ◇ vi: **to ~ on sthg** insistir em algo; **to ~ on doing sthg** insistir em fazer algo.

insistence [ɪnˈsɪstəns] n (U) [act of demanding] insistência f; **~ on sthg/on doing sthg** insistência em algo/em fazer algo.

insistent [ɪnˈsɪstənt] adj insistente; **~ on sthg** insistente em algo.

in situ [ˌɪnˈsɪtjuː] adv no local.

insofar [ˌɪnsəʊˈfɑːʳ] → **insofar as** conj na medida em que.

insole [ˈɪnsəʊl] n [in shoe] palmilha f.

insolence [ˈɪnsələns] n (U) insolência f.

insolent [ˈɪnsələnt] adj insolente.

insoluble UK [ɪnˈsɒljʊbl], **insolvable** US [ɪnˈsɒlvəbl] adj insolúvel.

insolvable adj US insolúvel.

insolvency [ɪnˈsɒlvənsɪ] n (U) insolvência f.

insolvent [ɪnˈsɒlvənt] adj insolvente.

insomnia [ɪnˈsɒmnɪə] n (U) insônia f.

insomniac [ɪnˈsɒmnɪæk] n insone mf.

insomuch [ˌɪnsəʊˈmʌtʃ] → **insomuch as** conj fml na medida em que.

inspect [ɪnˈspekt] vt **-1.** [letter, person] examinar **-2.** [factory] inspecionar, vistoriar **-3.** [troops] passar revista em.

inspection [ɪn'spekʃn] n -**1.** [examination] exame m -**2.** [official check] inspeção f, vistoria f.

inspector [ɪn'spektər] n -**1.** [official] fiscal mf -**2.** [of police] inspetor m, -ra f.

inspector of taxes n fiscal mf da Receita.

inspiration [ˌɪnspə'reɪʃn] n -**1.** (U) [source of ideas] inspiração f; ~ **(for sthg)** inspiração (para algo) -**2.** [brilliant idea] idéia f.

inspire [ɪn'spaɪər] vt [stimulate, encourage]: **to** ~ **sb (to do sthg)** inspirar alguém (a fazer algo); **to** ~ **sb with sthg, to** ~ **sthg in sb** inspirar algo a alguém.

inspired [ɪn'spaɪəd] adj inspirado(da).

inspiring [ɪn'spaɪərɪŋ] adj [stimulating, exciting] inspirador(ra).

inst. [ɪnst] (abbr of **instant**) do corrente mês.

instability [ˌɪnstə'bɪlətɪ] n (U) instabilidade f.

install UK, **instal** US [ɪn'stɔːl] vt -**1.** [machinery, equipment] instalar -**2.** [appoint]: **to** ~ **sb (as sthg)** nomear alguém (como algo) -**3.** [settle] instalar-se; **to** ~ **o.s. in front of the fire** acomodar-se em frente ao fogo.

installation [ˌɪnstə'leɪʃn] n instalação f.

installment n US = **instalment**.

installment plan n US compra f a prazo.

instalment UK, **installment** US [ɪn'stɔːlmənt] n -**1.** [payment] prestação f; **in** ~**s** em prestações -**2.** [episode] episódio m.

instance [ɪnstəns] n [example, case] caso m, exemplo m; **for** ~ por exemplo; **in the first** ~ fml em primeira instância.

instant ['ɪnstənt] <> adj instantâneo(nea). <> n [moment] instante m; **the** ~ **(that)** ... no mesmo instante em que ...; **at that** OR **the same** ~ naquele OR no mesmo instante; **this** ~ agora mesmo.

instantaneous [ˌɪnstən'teɪnjəs] adj instantâneo(nea).

instantly ['ɪnstəntlɪ] adv instantaneamente.

instead [ɪn'sted] adv em vez disso.

instead of prep em vez de, em lugar de.

instep ['ɪnstep] n [of foot] peito m do pé.

instigate ['ɪnstɪgeɪt] vt [initiate] instigar.

instigation [ˌɪnstɪ'geɪʃn] n: **at the** ~ **of** por solicitação de.

instigator ['ɪnstɪgeɪtər] n instigador m, -ra f.

instil UK (pt & pp -led, cont -ling), **instill** US (pt & pp -ed, cont -ing) [ɪn'stɪl] vt: **to** ~ **sthg in(to) sb** instilar algo em alguém.

instinct ['ɪnstɪŋkt] n instinto m; **first** ~ primeiro impulso m.

instinctive [ɪn'stɪŋktɪv] adj instintivo(va).

instinctively [ɪn'stɪŋktɪvlɪ] adv instintivamente.

institute ['ɪnstɪtjuːt] <> n [establishment] instituto m. <> vt instituir.

institution [ˌɪnstɪ'tjuːʃn] n instituição f.

institutional [ˌɪnstɪ'tjuːʃənl] adj -**1.** [of organization] institucional -**2.** [of psychiatric hospital, children's home] para uma instituição beneficente.

institutionalize vt institucionalizar.

institutionalized, -ised [ˌɪnstɪ'tjuːʃnə.laɪzd] adj institucionalizado(da).

instruct [ɪn'strʌkt] vt -**1.** [tell, order]: **to** ~ **sb to do sthg** instruir alguém a fazer algo -**2.** [teach]

instruir; **to** ~ **sb in sthg** instruir alguém em algo.

instruction [ɪn'strʌkʃn] n instrução f.

instructions npl [for use] instruções fpl.

instruction manual n manual m de instruções.

instructive [ɪn'strʌktɪv] adj instrutivo(va).

instructor [ɪn'strʌktər] n -**1.** [in driving, skiing] instrutor m -**2.** [in swimming] professor m.

instructress [ɪn'strʌktrɪs] n -**1.** [in driving, skiing] instrutora f -**2.** [in swimming] professora f.

instrument ['ɪnstrəmənt] n -**1.** instrumento m -**2.** literary [means] instrumento m.

instrumental [ˌɪnstrʊ'mentl] <> adj -**1.** [important, helpful]: **to be** ~ **in sthg** desempenhar um papel fundamental em algo -**2.** [music] instrumental. <> n MUS instrumental m.

instrumentalist [ˌɪnstrʊ'mentəlɪst] n MUS instrumentalista mf.

instrument panel n painel m de instrumentos.

insubordinate [ˌɪnsə'bɔːdɪnət] adj fml insubordinado(da).

insubordination ['ɪnsə.bɔːdɪ'neɪʃn] n (U) fml insubordinação f.

insubstantial [ˌɪnsəb'stænʃl] adj -**1.** [fragile] frágil -**2.** [unsatisfying] pouco substancioso(sa).

insufferable [ɪn'sʌfərəbl] adj insuportável.

insufficient [ˌɪnsə'fɪʃnt] adj fml insuficiente; ~ **for sthg/to do sthg** insuficiente para algo/para fazer algo.

insular ['ɪnsjʊlər] adj -**1.** [narrow-minded] limitado(da) -**2.** [isolated] isolado(da).

insulate ['ɪnsjʊleɪt] vt isolar; **to** ~ **sb against** OR **from sthg** isolar alguém de algo.

insulating tape ['ɪnsjʊleɪtɪŋ-] n (U) UK fita f isolante.

insulation [ˌɪnsjʊ'leɪʃn] n (U) [material, substance] isolamento m.

insulin ['ɪnsjʊlɪn] n (U) insulina f.

insult [vt ɪn'sʌlt, n 'ɪnsʌlt] <> n insulto m; **to add** ~ **to injury** para piorar ainda mais as coisas. <> vt insultar, ofender.

insulting [ɪn'sʌltɪŋ] adj ofensivo(va).

insuperable [ɪn'suːprəbl] adj fml insuperável.

insurance [ɪn'ʃʊərəns] <> n -**1.** [against fire, accident, theft] seguro m; ~ **against sthg** seguro contra algo -**2.** fig [safeguard, protection] proteção f; ~ **against sthg** proteção contra algo. <> comp de seguro.

insurance broker n corretor m, -ra f de seguros.

insurance policy n apólice f de seguros.

insurance premium n prêmio m do seguro.

insure [ɪn'ʃʊər] <> vt -**1.** [against fire, accident, theft]: **to** ~ **sb/sthg against sthg** segurar alguém/algo contra algo -**2.** US [make certain] assegurar. <> vi [protect]: **to** ~ **against sthg** prevenir-se contra algo.

insured [ɪn'ʃɔːd] <> adj -**1.** [against fire, accident, theft]: ~ **(against** OR **for sthg)** segurado(da) (contra algo) -**2.** US [certain] assegurado(da). <> n: **the** ~ o segurado, a segurada.

insurer [ɪn'ʃʊərər] n segurador m, -ra f.

insurgent [ɪn'sɜːdʒəntl *n* insurgente *mf*.

insurmountable [ˌɪnsə'maʊntəbll *adj* intransponível.

insurrection [ˌɪnsə'rekʃn] *n* insurreição *f*.

intact [ɪn'tæktl *adj* intacto(ta).

intake ['ɪnteɪk] *n* **-1.** [amount consumed] ingestão *f* **-2.** [people recruited - *SCH, UNIV*] ingresso *m*; [- *MIL*] recrutamento *m* **-3.** [inlet] entrada *f*.

intangible [ɪn'tændʒəbll *adj* intangível.

integral ['ɪntɪgrəl] *adj* [essential] essencial; **to be ~ to sthg** ser parte integrante de algo.

integrate ['ɪntɪgreɪt] <> *vi* integrar; **to ~ with** *OR* **into sthg** integrar-se em algo. <> *vt* integrar; **to ~ sb with** *OR* **into sthg** integrar alguém em algo; **to ~ sthg with** *OR* **into sthg** integrar algo em algo.

integrated ['ɪntɪgreɪtɪd] *adj* [multiracial] integrado(da).

integrated circuit *n* circuito *m* integrado.

integration [ˌɪntɪ'greɪʃn] *n (U)*; **~ (with** *OR* **into sthg)** integração *f* (em algo).

integrity [ɪn'tegrətɪ] *n (U)* **-1.** [honour] integridade *f* **-2.** *fml* [wholeness] integridade *f*.

intellect ['ɪntəlekt] *n* **-1.** [gen] inteligência *f*, intelecto *m* **-2.** [mind] inteligência *f*.

intellectual [ˌɪntə'lektjʊəll <> *adj* intelectual. <> *n* [person] intelectual *mf*.

intellectualize, -ise [ˌɪntə'lektjʊəlaɪz] *vt* intelectualizar.

intelligence [ɪn'telɪdʒəns] *n (U)* **-1.** [ability to think and reason] inteligência *f* **-2.** [information service] serviço *m* de inteligência **-3.** [information] informações *fpl* secretas.

intelligence quotient *n* quociente *m* de inteligência.

intelligence test *n* teste *m* de inteligência.

intelligent [ɪn'telɪdʒənt] *adj* [clever] inteligente.

intelligent card *n* cartão *m* inteligente.

intelligently [ɪn'telɪdʒəntlɪ] *adv* inteligentemente.

intelligentsia [ɪnˌtelɪ'dʒentsɪə] *n*: **the ~** a intelligentsia.

intelligible [ɪn'telɪdʒəbll *adj* inteligível.

intemperate [ɪn'tempərət] *adj fml* **-1.** [excessive] excessivo(va) **-2.** [uncontrolled] descomedido(da) **-3.** [climate] intemperado(da).

intend [ɪn'tend] *vt* [mean] pretender, propor-se a; **to be ~ed for/as sthg** ser destinado(da) para algo; **to be ~ed for sb** ser destinado(da) a alguém; **it wasn't ~ed to be a criticism** não pretendia ser uma crítica; **it was ~ed to be a surprise** era para ser uma surpresa; **to ~ doing sthg/to do sthg** pretender fazer algo.

intended [ɪn'tendɪd] *adj* [planned] planejado(da); **the ~ victim** a vítima almejada.

intense [ɪn'tens] *adj* **-1.** [gen] intenso(sa) **-2.** [person - serious] muito sério(ria); [- emotional] forte.

intensely [ɪn'tenslɪ] *adv* **-1.** [very] enormemente **-2.** [very much] intensamente.

intensify [ɪn'tensɪfaɪ] *(pt & pp -ied)* <> *vt* intensificar. <> *vi* intensificar-se.

intensity [ɪn'tensətɪ] *n* **-1.** [gen] intensidade *f* **-2.** [of person - seriousness] seriedade *f*; [- of emotional nature] força *f*.

intensive [ɪn'tensɪv] *adj* [concentrated] intensivo(va).

intensive care *n (U)* tratamento *m* intensivo.

intensive care unit *n* unidade *f* de tratamento intensivo.

intent [ɪn'tentl <> *adj* **-1.** [absorbed] atento(ta) **-2.** [determined]: **to be ~ (up)on doing sthg** estar determinado(da) a fazer algo. <> *n fml* [intention] intenção *f*; **to all ~s and purposes** para todos os efeitos.

intention [ɪn'tenʃn] *n* intenção *f*.

intentional [ɪn'tenʃənl] *adj* intencional.

intentionally [ɪn'tenʃənəlɪ] *adv* intencionalmente.

intently [ɪn'tentlɪ] *adv* atentamente.

inter [ɪn'tɜː'] *(pt & pp -red, cont -ring)* *vt fml* sepultar.

interact [ˌɪntər'ækt] *vi* **-1.** [people]: **to ~ (with sb)** interagir (com alguém) **-2.** [forces, ideas]: **to ~ (with sthg)** interagir (com algo).

interaction [ˌɪntər'ækʃn] *n* interação *f*.

interactive [ˌɪntər'æktɪv] *adj COMPUT* interativo(va).

intercede [ˌɪntə'siːd] *vi fml*: **to ~ (with/for sb)** interceder (junto a/em favor de alguém).

intercept [ˌɪntə'sept] *vt* [message, missile] interceptar.

interception [ˌɪntə'sepʃn] *n (U)* interceptação *f*.

interchange [*n* 'ɪntətʃeɪndʒ, *vb* ˌɪntə'tʃeɪndʒ] <> *n* **-1.** [exchange] intercâmbio *m* **-2.** [road junction] trevo *m* rodoviário. <> *vt* trocar, intercambiar; **to ~ sthg with sb/sthg** trocar algo com alguém/algo.

interchangeable [ˌɪntə'tʃeɪndʒəbll *adj*: **~ (with sb/sthg)** intercambiável (com alguém/algo).

intercity [ˌɪntə'sɪtɪ] *adj UK* intermunicipal.

intercom ['ɪntəkɒm] *n* interfone *m*.

interconnect [ˌɪntəkə'nekt] *vi* interligar-se; **to ~ with sthg** interligar-se com algo.

interconnecting *adj* [rooms] interligado(da).

intercontinental ['ɪntəˌkɒntɪ'nentl] *adj* intercontinental.

intercontinental ballistic missile *n* míssil *m* balístico intercontinental.

intercourse ['ɪntəkɔːs] *n (U)* [sexual] relação *f* sexual.

interdenominational ['ɪntədɪˌnɒmɪ'neɪʃənl] *adj* de diferentes grupos religiosos.

interdepartmental ['ɪntəˌdiːpɑːt'mentl] *adj* interdepartamental.

interdependent [ˌɪntədɪ'pendənt] *adj* interdependente.

interdict ['ɪntədɪkt] *n* **-1.** *JUR* interdição *m* **-2.** *RELIG* interdito *m*.

interest ['ɪntrəst] <> *n* **-1.** [gen] interesse *m*; **~ in sb/sthg** interesse em alguém/algo **-2.** [hobby] hobby *m*; **in the ~s of** [in order to benefit] em benefício de; [in order to achieve] com a finalidade de; **in the ~s of peace** em nome da paz **-3.** *(U)* [financial charge] juro *m* **-4.** [share in company] participação *f*. <> *vt* [appeal to] interessar; **to ~ sb in sthg/in doing sthg** chamar alguém para algo/para fazer algo; **can I ~ you in a drink?** posso te convidar para um drinque?

interested ['ɪntrəstɪd] *adj* interessado(da); **to be ~ in sb/sthg** estar interessado(da) em alguém/algo; **to be ~ in doing sthg** estar interessado(da) em fazer algo.

interest-free *adj* sem juros.

interesting ['ɪntrəstɪŋ] *adj* interessante.

interest rate *n* taxa *f* de juros.

interface [*n* 'ɪntəfeɪs, *vb* ɪntə'feɪs] ◇ *n* - **1.** COMPUT interface *f* - **2.** [junction, boundary] zona *f* de interação. ◇ *vt* COMPUT conectar por interface.

interfere [ˌɪntə'fɪə'] *vi* - **1.** [meddle] interferir, intrometer-se; **to ~ in sthg** interferir em algo, intrometer-se em algo - **2.** [cause disruption] interferir; **to ~ with sthg** interferir em algo.

interference [ˌɪntə'fɪərəns] *n (U)* - **1.** [meddling]: **~ (with** OR **in sthg)** intrometimento *m* (em algo) - **2.** RADIO & TV interferência *f*.

interfering [ˌɪntə'fɪərɪŋ] *adj pej* intrometido(da).

intergalactic *adj* intergaláctico(ca).

interim ['ɪntərɪm] ◇ *adj* provisório(ria). ◇ *n*: **in the ~** neste ínterim.

interior [ɪn'tɪərɪə'] ◇ *adj* - **1.** [inner] interno(na), interior - **2.** POL do interior. ◇ *n* - **1.** [inside] interior *m* - **2.** [of country]: **the ~** [inland part] o interior.

interior decorator *n* decorador *m*, -ra *f* de interiores.

interior designer *n* decorador *m*, -ra *f* de interiores.

interject [ˌɪntə'dʒekt] *fml* ◇ *vt* - **1.** [add] interpor - **2.** [interrupt] interromper. ◇ *vi* intervir.

interjection [ˌɪntə'dʒekʃn] *n* - **1.** [remark] interrupção *f* - **2.** GRAM interjeição *f*.

interleave [ˌɪntə'li:v] *vt*: **to ~ sthg with sthg** intercalar algo com algo.

interlock [ˌɪntə'lɒk] ◇ *vi* - **1.** TECH encaixar; **to ~ with sthg** encaixar com algo - **2.** [entwine] entrelaçar. ◇ *vt* - **1.** TECH engatar; **to ~ sthg with sthg** engatar algo em algo - **2.** [entwine] entrelaçar.

interloper ['ɪntələʊpə'] *n* intruso *m*, -sa *f*.

interlude ['ɪntəlu:d] *n* - **1.** [gen] intervalo *m* - **2.** MUS interlúdio *m*.

intermarry [ˌɪntə'mærɪ] (*pt* & *pp* -ied) *vi*: **to ~ (with sb)** unir-se (com alguém) pelo casamento (*parentes ou pessoas de raças, religiões, etc. distintas*).

intermediary [ˌɪntə'mi:djərɪ] (*pl* -ies) *n* intermediário *m*, -ria *f*, mediador *m*, -ra *f*.

intermediate [ˌɪntə'mi:djət] *adj* intermediário *m*, -ria *f*.

interminable [ɪn'tɜ:mɪnəbl] *adj* interminável.

intermingle [ˌɪntə'mɪŋgl] *vi*: **to ~ (with people)** misturar-se (com as pessoas).

intermission [ˌɪntə'mɪʃn] *n* intervalo *m*.

intermittent [ˌɪntə'mɪtənt] *adj* intermitente.

intern [*vb* ɪn'tɜ:n, *n* 'ɪntɜ:n] ◇ *n* US [trainee - teacher] estagiário *m*, -ria *f*; [- doctor] interno *m*, -na *f*. ◇ *vt* internar.

internal [ɪn'tɜ:nl] *adj* interno(na); **~ affairs** relações *fpl* interiores.

internal-combustion engine *n* motor *m* de combustão interna.

internally [ɪn'tɜ:nəlɪ] *adv* internamente.

Internal Revenue *n* US: **the ~** a receita pública.

international [ˌɪntə'næʃənl] ◇ *adj* internacional. ◇ *n* UK SPORT - **1.** [match] partida *f* internacional - **2.** [player] atleta *mf* da seleção.

international date line *n*: **the ~** a linha internacional de data.

internationally [ˌɪntə'næʃnəlɪ] *adv* internacionalmente.

International Monetary Fund *n*: **the ~** o Fundo Monetário Internacional.

international relations *npl* relações *fpl* internacionais.

internecine [UK ˌɪntə'ni:saɪn, US ˌɪntər'ni:sn] *adj fml* interno(na); **the ~ quarrels in the party** as disputas internas no partido.

internee [ˌɪntɜ:'ni:] *n* recluso *m*, -sa *f* (*por motivos políticos*).

Internet ['ɪntənet] *n*: **the ~** a Internet.

Internet access *n* acesso *m* à Internet.

Internet café *n* cibercafé *m*.

Internet connection *n* conexão *f* com a Internet.

Internet Service Provider *n* provedor *m* de serviços de Internet.

Internet start-up company *n* empresa *f* eletrônica que surgiu com a Internet.

Internet television, Internet TV *n* televisão *f* via Internet.

internment [ɪn'tɜ:nmənt] *n (U)* reclusão *f* (*por motivos políticos*).

interpersonal [ˌɪntə'pɜ:sənl] *adj* interpessoal.

interplay ['ɪntəpleɪ] *n (U)*: **~ (of/between)** interação *f* (de/entre).

Interpol ['ɪntəpɒl] *n* Interpol *f*.

interpolate [ɪn'tɜ:pəleɪt] *vt fml* - **1.** [add]: **to ~ sthg (into sthg)** interpolar algo (em algo) - **2.** [interrupt] interpolar.

interpose [ˌɪntə'pəʊz] *vt fml* - **1.** [add] interpor - **2.** [interrupt] intervir.

interpret [ɪn'tɜ:prɪt] ◇ *vt* - **1.** [understand] interpretar; **to ~ sthg as** interpretar algo como - **2.** [translate] servir de intérprete em - **3.** *fml* [perform] interpretar. ◇ *vi* [translate] interpretar.

interpretation [ɪnˌtɜ:prɪ'teɪʃn] *n* interpretação *f*.

interpreted language *n* COMPUT linguagem *f* de programação interpretada.

interpreter [ɪn'tɜ:prɪtə'] *n* [person] intérprete *mf*.

interpreting [ɪn'tɜ:prɪtɪŋ] *n* [occupation] interpretação *f*.

interracial [ˌɪntə'reɪʃl] *adj* inter-racial.

interrelate [ˌɪntərɪ'leɪt] ◇ *vt* correlacionar. ◇ *vi*: **to ~ (with sthg)** correlacionar-se (com algo).

interrogate [ɪn'terəgeɪt] *vt* - **1.** [question] interrogar - **2.** COMPUT consultar.

interrogation [ɪnˌterə'geɪʃn] *n* - **1.** *(U)* [questioning] interrogação *f* - **2.** [interview] interrogatório *m*.

interrogation mark *n* US ponto *m* de interrogação.

interrogative [ˌɪntə'rɒgətɪv] GRAM ◇ *adj* interrogativo(va). ◇ *n* - **1.** [form]: **the ~** a forma interrogativa - **2.** [word] pronome *m* interrogativo.

interrogator [ɪn'terəgeɪtə'] *n* interrogador *m*, -ra *f*.

interrupt [ˌɪntə'rʌpt] ◇ *vt* interromper. ◇ *vi* interromper, incomodar.

interruption [ˌɪntə'rʌpʃn] *n* interrupção *f*.

interrupter *n* ELEC interruptor *m*.

intersect [ˌɪntə'sekt] ◇ vi cruzar-se. ◇ vt cruzar.

intersection [ˌɪntə'sekʃn] n [junction] interseção f.

intersperse [ˌɪntə'spɜːs] vt: to be ~ed with sthg ser entremeado(da) por algo.

interstate (highway) n US rodovia f interestadual.

interval ['ɪntəvl] n -1. [period of time]: ~ (between) intervalo m (entre); at ~s em intervalos; at monthly/yearly ~s em intervalos de um mês/um ano -2. UK [at play, concert] intervalo m -3. MUS pausa f.

intervene [ˌɪntə'viːn] ◇ vt intervir. ◇ vi -1. [gen] intervir; to ~ in sthg intervir em algo -2. [time] transcorrer -3. [interrupt] interferir.

intervening [ˌɪntə'viːnɪŋ] adj [period of time] transcorrido(da).

intervention [ˌɪntə'venʃn] n intervenção f.

interventionist [ˌɪntə'venʃənɪst] ◇ adjintervencionista. ◇ n intervencionista mf.

interview ['ɪntəvjuː] ◇ n entrevista f. ◇ vt entrevistar.

interviewee [ˌɪntəvjuː'iː] n entrevistado m, -da f.

interviewer ['ɪntəvjuːə'] n entrevistador m, -ra f.

interweave [ˌɪntə'wiːv] (pt -wove, pp -woven) fig ◇ vt entrelaçar. ◇ vi entrelaçar-se.

intestate [ɪn'testeɪt] adj: to die ~ morrer intestado(da).

intestine [ɪn'testɪn] n intestino m.
➡ **intestines** npl intestinos mpl.

intimacy ['ɪntɪməsɪ] (pl -ies) n (U) [closeness]: ~ (between/with) intimidade f (entre/com).
➡ **intimacies** npl [personal thoughts] intimidades fpl.

intimate [adj & n 'ɪntɪmət, vb 'ɪntɪmeɪt] ◇ adj -1. íntimo(ma) -2. fml [sexually]: to be ~ with sb ter intimidades com alguém -3. [personal] pessoal -4. [thorough] profundo(da) -5. [direct] direto(ta). ◇ n fml [close friend] amigo m íntimo, amiga f íntima. ◇ vt fml [hint, imply] insinuar; to ~ that insinuar que, dar a entender que.

intimately ['ɪntɪmətlɪ] adv intimamente.

intimation [ˌɪntɪ'meɪʃn] n fml [suggestion] insinuação f.

intimidate [ɪn'tɪmɪdeɪt] vt intimidar.

intimidation [ɪnˌtɪmɪ'deɪʃn] n (U) intimidação f.

into ['ɪntʊ] prep -1. [inside - referring to object] em; [- referring to place, vehicle] em direção a; to get ~ a car entrar num carro -2. [against] contra; to bump ~ sb/sthg tropeçar em alguém/algo; to crash ~ sb/sthg chocar-se com alguém/algo -3. [indicating transformation, change] em; to translate ~ Spanish traduzir para o espanhol -4. [concerning, about] sobre -5. MATH [indicating division] por; 6 ~ 2 is 3 6 dividido por 2 é 3 -6. [indicating elapsed time]: ~ the night noite adentro; I was a week ~ my holiday when ... eu estava há uma semana de férias quando ... -7. inf [interested in]: to be ~ sthg gostar de algo.

intolerable [ɪn'tɒlrəbl] adj fml intolerável.

intolerance [ɪn'tɒlərəns] n (U) [lack of respect] intolerância f.

intolerant [ɪn'tɒlərənt] adj intolerante; to be ~ of sb/sthg ser intolerante com alguém/algo.

intonation [ˌɪntə'neɪʃn] n entonação f.

intone vt literary entoar.

intoxicated [ɪn'tɒksɪkeɪtɪd] adj -1. [drunk]: to be ~ estar embriagado(da) -2. fig [excited]: to be ~ by OR with sthg estar inebriado(da) com algo.

intoxicating [ɪn'tɒksɪkeɪtɪŋ] adj -1. [alcoholic] embriagante -2. fig [exciting] inebriante.

intoxication [ɪnˌtɒksɪ'keɪʃn] n (U) fml -1. [drunkenness] embriaguez f -2. [excitement] excitação f.

intractable [ɪn'træktəbl] adj fml -1. [stubborn] intratável -2. [insoluble] insolúvel.

intramural adj intramuros.

Intranet n COMPUT Intranet f.

intransigent [ɪn'trænzɪdʒənt] adj fml intransigente.

intransitive [ɪn'trænzətɪv] adj intransitivo(va).

intrauterine device [ˌɪntrə'juːtəraɪn-] n dispositivo m intra-uterino.

intravenous [ˌɪntrə'viːnəs] adj intravenoso(sa).

in-tray n bandeja f de entrada (para documentos em escritório).

intrepid [ɪn'trepɪd] adj literary intrépido(da).

intricacy ['ɪntrɪkəsɪ] (pl -ies) n -1. (U) [complexity] complexidade f -2. [detail] pormenor m.

intricate ['ɪntrɪkət] adj intricado(da).

intrigue [ɪn'triːg] ◇ n intriga f. ◇ vt intrigar. ◇ vi: to ~ against sb fazer intriga contra alguém.

intriguing [ɪn'triːgɪŋ] adj intrigante.

intrinsic [ɪn'trɪnsɪk] adj intrínseco(ca).

intro ['ɪntrəʊ] (pl -s) (abbr of introduction) n inf introdução f.

introduce [ˌɪntrə'djuːs] vt -1. [present, make aware of] apresentar; to ~ sb to sb/sthg apresentar alguém a alguém/algo -2. [bring in]: to ~ sthg (to OR into) introduzir algo (em).

introduction [ˌɪntrə'dʌkʃn] n -1. [start, initiation] introdução f; ~ to sthg introdução a algo -2. [presentation]: ~ (to sb) apresentação f (a alguém).

introductory [ˌɪntrə'dʌktrɪ] adj introdutório(ria).

introspective [ˌɪntrə'spektɪv] adj introspectivo(va).

introvert ['ɪntrəvɜːt] n introvertido m, -da f.

introverted ['ɪntrəvɜːtɪd] adj introvertido(da).

intrude [ɪn'truːd] vi intrometer-se; to ~ (up)on sb/sthg intrometer-se em alguém/algo.

intruder [ɪn'truːdə'] n intruso m, -sa f.

intrusion [ɪn'truːʒn] n intrometimento m.

intrusive [ɪn'truːsɪv] adj -1. [person] intrometido(da) -2. [presence, interest] inoportuno(na).

intuition [ˌɪntjuː'ɪʃn] n intuição f.

intuitive [ɪn'tjuːɪtɪv] adj intuitivo(va).

Inuit ['ɪnʊɪt] ◇ adj inuit. ◇ n inuit mf.

inundate ['ɪnʌndeɪt] vt inundar; to be ~d with sthg estar cheio (cheia) de algo.

inured [ɪ'njʊəd] adj fml: to be/become ~ to sthg estar habituado(da)/habituar-se a algo.

invade [ɪn'veɪd] vt invadir.

invader [ɪn'veɪdə'] n MIL invasor m, -ra f.

invading adj invasor(ra).

invalid [adj ɪn'vælɪd n & vb 'ɪnvəlɪd] ◇ adj [not

acceptable] inválido(da). <> *n* [ill person] inválido *m*, -da *f*.

invalid out *vt sep*: **to be** ~**ed out (of)** aposentar-se por invalidez (por).

invalidate [ɪnˈvælɪdeɪt] *vt* **-1.** [claim, theory] invalidar, refutar **-2.** [contract, agreement] anular.

invalid chair *n* cadeira *f* de rodas.

invaluable [ɪnˈvæljʊəbl] *adj*: ~ **(to sb/sthg)** inestimável (para alguém/algo).

invariable [ɪnˈveərɪəbl] *adj* invariável.

invariably [ɪnˈveərɪəblɪ] *adv* [always] invariavelmente.

invasion [ɪnˈveɪʒn] *n* invasão *f*.

invective [ɪnˈvektɪv] *n (U) fml* invectiva *f*.

inveigle [ɪnˈveɪgl] *vt*: **to** ~ **sb into sthg** aliciar alguém para algo; **to** ~ **sb into doing sthg** enganar alguém para que faça algo.

invent [ɪnˈvent] *vt* inventar.

invention [ɪnˈvenʃn] *n* invenção *f*.

inventive [ɪnˈventɪv] *adj* inventivo(va).

inventor [ɪnˈventə[r]] *n* inventor *m*, -ra *f*.

inventory [ˈɪnvəntrɪ] (*pl* -**ies**) *n* **-1.** [list] inventário *m* **-2.** *US* [goods] estoque *m*.

inventory control *n* controle *m* de estoque.

inverse [ɪnˈvɜːs] <> *adj* [proportion, relation] inverso(sa). <> *n fml* inverso *m*.

invert [ɪnˈvɜːt] *vt fml* inverter.

invertebrate [ɪnˈvɜːtɪbreɪt] *n* invertebrado *m*.

inverted commas [ɪnˈvɜːtɪd-] *npl UK* aspas *fpl*; **in** ~ entre aspas.

inverted snob [ɪnˈvɜːtɪd-] *n pessoa que finge não gostar de coisas caras ou de boa qualidade.*

invest [ɪnˈvest] <> *vt* **-1.** [gen]: **to** ~ **sthg in sthg/in doing sthg** investir algo em algo/para fazer algo **-2.** *fml* [endow]: **to** ~ **sb with sthg** outorgar algo a alguém, investir alguém de algo. <> *vi* **-1.** [financially] investir; **to** ~ **in sthg** investir em algo **-2.** *fig* [in sthg useful]: **to** ~ **in sthg** investir em algo.

investigate [ɪnˈvestɪgeɪt] *vt & vi* investigar.

investigation [ɪnˌvestɪˈgeɪʃn] *n*: ~ **(into sthg)** investigação *f* (sobre algo).

investigative [ɪnˈvestɪgətɪv] *adj* investigador(ra), de investigação.

investigator [ɪnˈvestɪgeɪtə[r]] *n* investigador *m*, -ra *f*.

investiture [ɪnˈvestɪtʃə[r]] *n* investidura *f*.

investment [ɪnˈvestmənt] *n* investimento *m*.

investment analyst *n* analista *mf* financeiro, -ra.

investment trust *n* fundo *m* de investimento.

investor [ɪnˈvestə[r]] *n* investidor *m*, -ra *f*.

inveterate [ɪnˈvetərət] *adj* inveterado(da).

invidious [ɪnˈvɪdɪəs] *adj* **-1.** [unfair] injusto(ta) **-2.** [unpleasant] desagradável.

invigilate [ɪnˈvɪdʒɪleɪt] *UK* <> *vt* fiscalizar *(um exame)*. <> *vi* fiscalizar um exame.

invigilator [ɪnˈvɪdʒɪleɪtə[r]] *n UK* fiscal *mf*.

invigorating [ɪnˈvɪgəreɪtɪŋ] *adj* **-1.** [gen] revigorante **-2.** [experience] estimulante.

invincible [ɪnˈvɪnsɪbl] *adj* [unbeatable] invencível.

inviolate *adj* inviolado(da).

invisible [ɪnˈvɪzɪbl] *adj* invisível.

invisible assets *npl* ativos *mpl* intangíveis.

invisible earnings *npl* ganhos *mpl* invisíveis.

invisible ink *n (U)* tinta *f* invisível.

invitation [ˌɪnvɪˈteɪʃn] *n* convite *m*; **an** ~ **to sthg/ to do sthg** um convite para algo/para fazer algo.

invite [ɪnˈvaɪt] *vt* **-1.** [request to attend] convidar; **to** ~ **sb to sthg** convidar alguém para algo **-2.** [ask politely]: **to** ~ **sb to do sthg** convidar alguém para fazer algo **-3.** [solicit] solicitar **-4.** [encourage] estimular.

inviting [ɪnˈvaɪtɪŋ] *adj* convidativo(va), tentador(-ra).

in vitro fertilization [ˌɪnˈviːtrəʊ-] *n (U)* fertilização *f* in vitro.

invoice [ˈɪnvɔɪs] <> *n* fatura *f*. <> *vt* **-1.** [send an invoice to] enviar uma fatura para **-2.** [prepare an invoice for] faturar.

invoke [ɪnˈvəʊk] *vt* **-1.** *fml* [quote as justification] invocar **-2.** [cause] evocar, suscitar.

involuntary [ɪnˈvɒləntrɪ] *adj* [unintentional] involuntário(ria).

involve [ɪnˈvɒlv] *vt* **-1.** [entail, require] envolver; **to** ~ **doing sthg** envolver fazer algo **-2.** [concern, affect] atingir, afetar; **to be** ~ **in sthg** estar envolvido(-da) em algo **-3.** [make part of sthg]: **to** ~ **sb in sthg** envolver alguém em algo; **to** ~ **o.s. in sthg** meter-se em algo.

involved [ɪnˈvɒlvd] *adj* **-1.** [complex] complicado(da) **-2.** [participating]: **to be** ~ **in sthg** estar metido(da) em algo **-3.** [in a relationship]: **to be/get** ~ **with sb** envolver-se com alguém **-4.** [entailed]: ~ **(in sthg)** envolvido(da) (em algo).

involvement [ɪnˈvɒlvmənt] *n (U)* [gen] envolvimento *m*; ~ **in sthg** envolvimento em algo.

invulnerable [ɪnˈvʌlnərəbl] *adj*: **to be** ~ **(to sthg)** ser invulnerável (a algo).

inward [ˈɪnwəd] <> *adj* **-1.** [feelings, satisfaction] interno(na), interior **-2.** [flow, movement] para dentro. <> *adv US* = **inwards**.

inward investment *n* investimento *m* externo.

inwardly [ˈɪnwədlɪ] *adv* [pleased, upset] por dentro.

inwards [ˈɪnwədz], **inward** *US adv* para dentro.

I/O (*abbr of* **input-output**) *n* E/S *f*.

IOC (*abbr of* **International Olympic Committee**) *n* COI *m*.

iodine [*UK* ˈaɪədiːn, *US* ˈaɪədaɪn] *n (U)* iodo *m*.

ion [ˈaɪən] *n* íon *m*.

Ionian Sea [aɪˈəʊnjən-] *n*: **the** ~ o Mar Jônio.

iota [aɪˈəʊtə] *n* pouquinho *m*; **not an** ~ nem um pouquinho.

IOU (*abbr of* **I owe you**) *n documento assinado no qual se reconhece uma dívida.*

Iowa [ˈaɪəʊə] *n* Iowa; **in** ~ em Iowa.

IPA (*abbr of* **International Phonetic Alphabet**) *n* AFI *m*.

IQ (*abbr of* **intelligence quotient**) *n* QI *m*.

IRA *n* **-1.** (*abbr of* **Irish Republican Army**) IRA *m* **-2.** (*abbr of* **individual retirement account**) *plano de previdência privada nos Estados Unidos.*

Iran [ɪˈrɑːn] *n* Irã; **in** ~ no Irã.

Iranian [ɪˈreɪnjən] <> *adj* iraniano(na). <> *n* [person] iraniano *m*, -na *f*.

Iraq [ɪˈrɑːk] *n* Iraque; **in** ~ no Iraque.

Iraqi [ɪ'rɑːkɪ] <> adj iraquiano(na). <> n [person] iraquiano, -na f.

irascible [ɪ'ræsəbl] adj irascível.

irate [aɪ'reɪt] adj irado(da).

Ireland ['aɪələnd] n Irlanda; **in** ~ na Irlanda; **the Republic of** ~ a República da Irlanda.

iridescent [,ɪrɪ'desənt] adj literary iridescente.

iris ['aɪərɪs] (pl -es) n MED, BOT íris f inv.

Irish ['aɪrɪʃ] <> adj irlandês(esa). <> n [language] gaélico-irlandês m. <> npl: **the** ~ os irlandeses.

Irish coffee n café m irlandês.

Irishman ['aɪrɪʃmən] (pl -men [-mən]) n irlandês m.

Irish Sea n: **the** ~ o Mar da Irlanda.

Irish setter n séter m irlandês.

Irish stew n ensopado de carne e verduras típico da Irlanda.

Irish wolfhound n wolfhound m irlandês.

Irishwoman ['aɪrɪʃ,wʊmən] (pl -women [-,wɪmɪn]) n irlandesa f.

irk [ɜːk] vt dated aborrecer.

irksome ['ɜːksəm] adj fml aborrecido(da).

IRO n -1. (abbr of International Refugee Organization) organização humanitária para refugiados -2. (abbr of Inland Revenue Office) departamento británico de arrecadação de impostos, ≃ Secretaria f da Fazenda.

iron ['aɪən] <> adj -1. [made of iron] de ferro -2. fig [very strict] duro(ra). <> n -1. (U) [metal] ferro m -2. [for clothes] ferro m (de passar roupa) -3. [golf club] ferro m. <> vt passar (a ferro).
→ **iron out** vt sep fig [overcome] resolver.

Iron Age <> n: **the** ~ a Idade do Ferro. <> comp da Idade do Ferro.

Iron Curtain n: **the** ~ a Cortina de Ferro.

ironic(al) [aɪ'rɒnɪk(l)] adj irônico(ca); **how** ~! que ironia!

ironically [aɪ'rɒnɪklɪ] adv ironicamente.

ironing ['aɪənɪŋ] n (U) -1. [activity]: **to do the** ~ passar roupa -2. [clothes to be ironed] roupa f para passar.

ironing board n tábua f de passar roupa.

iron lung n pulmão m de aço.

ironmonger ['aɪən,mʌŋgəʳ] n UK ferrageiro m, -ra f; ~'s (shop) ferragem f.

ironworks ['aɪənwɜːks] (pl inv) n siderúrgica f.

irony ['aɪrənɪ] (pl -ies) n ironia f; **the** ~ **of it all is that ...** o curioso disso tudo é que ...

irradiate [ɪ'reɪdɪeɪt] vt irradiar.

irrational [ɪ'ræʃənl] adj irracional.

irreconcilable [ɪ,rekən'saɪləbl] adj [completely different] irreconciliável.

irredeemable [,ɪrɪ'diːməbl] adj fml -1. [irreplaceable] irrecuperável -2. [hopeless] irreparável.

irrefutable [,ɪrɪ'fjuːtəbl] adj fml irrefutável.

irregular [ɪ'regjʊləʳ] adj irregular.

irregularity [ɪ,regjʊ'lærətɪ] (pl -ies) n irregularidade f.

irregularly [ɪ'regjʊləlɪ] adv [spasmodically] de forma irregular.

irrelevance [ɪ'reləvəns], **irrelevancy** [ɪ'reləvənsɪ] (pl -ies) n irrelevância f.

irrelevant [ɪ'reləvənt] adj irrelevante.

irreligious [,ɪrɪ'lɪdʒəs] adj descrente.

irremediable [,ɪrɪ'miːdjəbl] adj fml irremediável.

irreparable [ɪ'repərəbl] adj irreparável.

irreplaceable [,ɪrɪ'pleɪsəbl] adj insubstituível.

irrepressible [,ɪrɪ'presəbl] adj irreprimível.

irreproachable [,ɪrɪ'prəʊtʃəbl] adj irrepreensível.

irresistible [,ɪrɪ'zɪstəbl] adj irresistível.

irresolute [ɪ'rezəluːt] adj fml irresoluto(ta).

irrespective → **irrespective of** prep independente de.

irresponsible [,ɪrɪ'spɒnsəbl] adj irresponsável.

irretrievable [,ɪrɪ'triːvəbl] adj -1. [data] irrecuperável -2. [loss, situation] irreparável.

irreverent [ɪ'revərənt] adj irreverente.

irreversible [,ɪrɪ'vɜːsəbl] adj irreversível.

irrevocable [ɪ'revəkəbl] adj irrevogável.

irrigate ['ɪrɪgeɪt] vt [land] irrigar.

irrigation [,ɪrɪ'geɪʃn] <> n (U) [of land] irrigação f. <> comp de irrigação.

irritable ['ɪrɪtəbl] adj [bad-tempered] irritável.

irritant ['ɪrɪtənt] <> adj irritante. <> n -1. [irritating situation, person] motivo m de irritação -2. [substance] agente m irritante.

irritate ['ɪrɪteɪt] vt irritar.

irritated adj irritado(da).

irritating ['ɪrɪteɪtɪŋ] adj irritante.

irritation [ɪrɪ'teɪʃn] n -1. [gen] irritação f -2. [cause of anger] motivo m de irritação.

IRS (abbr of Internal Revenue Service) n departamento norte-americano de arrecadação de impostos, ≃ Secretaria f da Fazenda.

is [ɪz] vb ⊳ be.

ISA (abbr of individual savings account) n sistema británico de aplicações financeiras isentas de impostos.

ISBN (abbr of International Standard Book Number) n ISBN m.

ISDN (abbr of Integrated Services Delivery Network) n COMPUT RDSI f, ISDN f.

Islam ['ɪzlɑːm] n (U) [religion] Islã m.

Islamabad [ɪz'lɑːməbæd] n Islamabad; **in** ~ em Islamabad.

Islamic [ɪz'læmɪk] adj islâmico(ca).

island ['aɪlənd] n -1. [in water] ilha f -2. [in traffic] passagem m para pedestres.

islander ['aɪləndəʳ] n ilhéu m, ilhoa f.

isle [aɪl] n ilha f, ilhota f.

Isle of Man n: **the** ~ a Ilha de Man.

Isle of Wight [-waɪt] n: **the** ~ a Ilha de Wight.

Isles of Scilly npl = Scilly Isles.

isn't ['ɪznt] = is not.

ISO (abbr of International Organization for Standardization) n ISO f.

isobar ['aɪsəbɑːʳ] n METEOR isóbara f.

isolate ['aɪsəleɪt] vt: **to** ~ **sthg/sb (from sthg)** isolar algo/alguém (de algo).

isolated ['aɪsəleɪtɪd] adj isolado(da).

isolation [aɪsə'leɪʃn] n (U) [solitariness] isolamento m; **in** ~ [live] em isolamento; [happen, consider] isoladamente.

isolationism [,aɪsə'leɪʃnɪzml] n isolacionismo m.

isosceles triangle [aɪ'sɒsɪliːz-] n triângulo m isósceles.

isotope [ˈaɪsətəʊp] n isótopo m.

ISP (abbr of Internet Service Provider) n ISP m.

Israel [ˈɪzreɪəl] n Israel; **in** ~ em Israel.

Israeli [ɪzˈreɪlɪ] <> adj israelense. <> n israelense mf.

Israelite [ˈɪzrəlaɪt] <> adj israelita. <> n israelita mf.

issue [ˈɪʃuː] <> n **-1.** [important subject] assunto m, questão f; **at** ~ em questão; **to make an** ~ **of sthg** dar importância demasiada a algo **-2.** [edition] número m, edição f **-3.** [bringing out] emissão f. <> vt **-1.** [statement, decree, warning] expedir **-2.** [stamps, bank notes, shares] emitir, pôr em circulação **-3.** [passport, documents, uniforms] expedir; **to** ~ **sthg to sb, to** ~ **sb with sthg** expedir algo a alguém. <> vi fml [come out, go out]: **to** ~ **from** vir de.

Istanbul [ˌɪstænˈbʊl] n Istambul; **in** ~ em Istambul.

isthmus [ˈɪsməs] n istmo m.

it [ɪt] pron **-1.** [referring to specific thing, subject after prep] ele m, ela f **-2.** [direct object] o m, a f **-3.** [indirect object] lhe; **a free book came with** ~ veio acompanhado de um livro grátis; **give** ~ **to me** me dê isso; **he gave** ~ **a kick** ele deu um chute nele; ~ **'s big** é grande; ~ **'s here** está aqui; **she hit** ~ ela deu uma pancada nele; **she lost** ~ ela o perdeu. **-4.** [referring to situation, fact]: ~ **'s a difficult question** é uma questão difícil; **I can't remember** ~ não me lembro; **tell me about** ~ conte-me. **-5.** [used impersonally]: ~ **'s hot** está calor; ~ **'s six o'clock** são seis horas; ~ **'s Sunday** é domingo. **-6.** [referring to person]: ~ **'s me** sou eu; **who is** ~ **?** quem é?

IT (abbr of information technology) n TI f.

Italian [ɪˈtæljən] <> adj italiano(na). <> n **-1.** [person] italiano m, -na f **-2.** [language] italiano m.

italic [ɪˈtælɪk] adj itálico m.

➡ **italics** npl: **in** ~ em itálico.

Italy [ˈɪtəlɪ] n Itália; **in** ~ na Itália.

ITC (abbr of Independent Television Commission) n órgão britânico que monitora todos os canais de televisão independentes, a cabo e via satélite.

itch [ɪtʃ] <> n coceira f. <> vi **-1.** [be itchy] coçar **-2.** fig [be impatient]: **to be** ~ **ing to do sthg** estar se coçando para fazer algo.

itchy [ˈɪtʃɪ] (compar -ier, superl -iest) adj que coça.

it'd [ˈɪtəd] = it would, it had.

item [ˈaɪtəm] n **-1.** [single thing] item m **-2.** [article in newspaper] artigo m.

itemize, -ise [ˈaɪtəmaɪz] vt detalhar, especificar.

itemized bill [ˈaɪtəmaɪzd-] n conta f discriminada.

itinerant [ɪˈtɪnərənt] adj itinerante.

itinerary [aɪˈtɪnərərɪ] (pl -ies) n itinerário m.

it'll [ɪtl] = it will.

ITN (abbr of Independent Television News) n agência britânica de notícias para os canais independentes de televisão.

its [ɪts] poss adj o seu (a sua), dele (dela).

it's [ɪts] = it is, it has.

itself [ɪtˈself] pron **-1.** (reflexive) se **-2.** (after prep) si mesmo m, -ma f **-3.** (stressed): **the house** ~ **is fine** o casa em sí e boa.

ITV (abbr of Independent Television) n canal privado de televisão na Grã-Bretanha.

IUCD (abbr of intrauterine contraceptive device) n DIU m.

IUD (abbr of intrauterine device) n DIU m.

I've [aɪv] = I have.

IVF (abbr of in vitro fertilization) n FIV f.

ivory [ˈaɪvərɪ] <> adj [ivory-coloured] marfim inv. <> n (U) marfim m. <> comp [made of ivory] de marfim.

Ivory Coast n: **the** ~ a Costa do Marfim; **in the** ~ na Costa do Marfim.

ivory tower n fig ≃ torre f de marfim.

ivy [ˈaɪvɪ] n (U) hera f.

Ivy League n US grupo formado pelas oito universidades mais prestigiadas do leste norte-americano.

j (pl j's OR js) **J** (pl J's OR Js) [dʒeɪ] n [letter] j, J m.

J/A (abbr of joint account) conta f conjunta.

jab [dʒæb] (pt & pp -bed, cont -bing) <> n **-1.** [push] golpe m **-2.** UK inf [injection] injeção f. <> vt: **to** ~ **sthg at sb/sthg** espetar algo em alguém/algo; **to** ~ **sthg into sb/sthg** cravar algo em alguém/algo. <> vi: **to** ~ **at sb/sthg** apunhalar alguém/algo.

jabber [ˈdʒæbəʳ] <> vt algaraviar. <> vi tagarelar.

jack [dʒæk] n **-1.** [device] macaco m **-2.** [playing card] valete m.

➡ **jack in** vt sep UK inf largar.

➡ **jack up** vt sep **-1.** [lift with a jack] macaquear **-2.** [force up] aumentar.

jackal [ˈdʒækəl] n chacal m.

jackdaw [ˈdʒækdɔː] n gralha f.

jacket [ˈdʒækɪt] n **-1.** [garment] casaco m, jaqueta f **-2.** [potato skin] casca f **-3.** [book cover] sobrecapa f **-4.** US [of record] capa f **-5.** [of boiler] camisa f.

jacket potato n batata f assada com pele.

jackhammer [ˈdʒækˌhæməʳ] n US britadeira f.

jack-in-the-box n caixa f de surpresa.

jack knife n [tool] canivete m grande.

➡ **jack-knife** vi [truck, lorry] derrapar a parte dianteira.

jack-of-all-trades (pl jacks-of-all-trades) n pau-para-toda-obra m.

jack plug n pino m.

jackpot [ˈdʒækpɒt] n bolada f.

Jack Russell (terrier) n Jack Russell terrier m.

Jacobean [ˌdʒækəˈbɪən] adj jacobino(na).

Jacobite [ˈdʒækəbaɪt] <> adj jacobita. <> n jacobita mf.

Jacuzzi® [dʒəˈkuːzɪ] n banheira f de hidromassagem.

jade [dʒeɪd] <> adj [jade-coloured] jade inv. <> n -1. [stone] jade f -2. [colour] cor f jade. <> comp [made of jade] de jade.

jaded [ˈdʒeɪdɪd] adj estafado(da).

jagged [ˈdʒægɪd] adj dentado(da).

jaguar [ˈdʒægjʊəˡ] n jaguar m.

jail [dʒeɪl] <> n prisão f, cadeia f. <> vt prender.

jailbird [ˈdʒeɪlbɜːd] n inf preso m, -sa f reincidente.

jailbreak [ˈdʒeɪlbreɪk] n fuga f da prisão.

jailer [ˈdʒeɪləˡ] n carcereiro m, -ra f.

Jakarta [dʒəˈkɑːtə] n Jacarta; **in** ~ em Jacarta.

jam [dʒæm] (pt & pp -med, cont -ming) <> n -1. (U) [preserve] geléia f -2. [of traffic] engarrafamento m -3. inf [difficult situation]: **to get into/be in a** ~ meter-se/estar em apuros. <> vt -1. [place roughly]: **to** ~ **sthg onto sthg** enfiar algo em algo -2. [fix, cause to stick - window]: **to** ~ **the window shut** trancar a janela; [- mechanism] emperrar -3. [fill, pack tightly] apinhar, abarrotar; **to** ~ **sthg into sthg** socar algo em algo -4. TELEC bloquear -5. RADIO interferir. <> vi [stick] emperrar.
 jam on vt [brakes] pisar.

Jamaica [dʒəˈmeɪkə] n Jamaica; **in** ~ na Jamaica.

Jamaican [dʒəˈmeɪkn] <> adj jamaicano(na). <> n jamaicano m, -na f.

jamb [dʒæm] n batente m.

jamboree [ˌdʒæmbəˈriː] n [celebration] farra f.

jamming [ˈdʒæmɪŋ] n RADIO interferência f.

jam-packed [-ˈpækt] adj inf apinhado(da).

jam session n sessão improvisada de jazz ou de rock.

Jan. [dʒæn] (abbr of January) jan.

jangle [ˈdʒæŋgl] <> n [of keys, bells] som m estridente, estrépido m. <> vt fazer soar de forma estridente. <> vi retinir.

janitor [ˈdʒænɪtəˡ] n US & Scot [caretaker] zelador m, -ra f.

January [ˈdʒænjʊərɪ] n janeiro; see also **September**.

Japan [dʒəˈpæn] n Japão; **in** ~ no Japão.

Japanese [ˌdʒæpəˈniːz] (pl inv) <> adj japonês(esa). <> n -1. [person] japonês m, -esa f -2. [language] japonês m. <> npl [people]: **the** ~ os japoneses.

jape [dʒeɪp] n dated pilhéria f.

jar [dʒɑːˡ] (pt & pp -red, cont -ring) <> n pote m. <> vt [shake] sacudir. <> vi -1. [noise, voice]: **to** ~ **(on sb)** dar nos nervos (de alguém) -2. [colours] destoar.

jargon [ˈdʒɑːgən] n (U) jargão m.

jarring [ˈdʒɑːrɪŋ] adj -1. [noise, voice] enervante -2. [colours] destoante.

jasmine [ˈdʒæzmɪn] n jasmim m.

jaundice [ˈdʒɔːndɪs] n (U) icterícia f.

jaundiced [ˈdʒɔːndɪst] adj fig [attitude, view] pessimista.

jaunt [dʒɔːnt] n excursão f.

jaunty [ˈdʒɔːntɪ] (compar -ier, superl -iest) adj -1. [hat, wave] vistoso(sa) -2. [person] animado(da).

Java [ˈdʒɑːvə] n Java; **in** ~ em Java.

javelin [ˈdʒævlɪn] n dardo m.

jaw [dʒɔː] <> n -1. [of person] maxilar m -2. [of animal] mandíbula f. <> vi inf tagarelar.

jawbone [ˈdʒɔːbəʊn] n osso m maxilar.

jay [dʒeɪ] n gaio m.

jaywalk [ˈdʒeɪwɔːk] vi atravessar a rua imprudentemente.

jaywalker [ˈdʒeɪwɔːkəˡ] n pedestre mf imprudente.

jazz [dʒæz] n -1. MUS jazz m -2. US inf [insincere talk] balela f.
 jazz up vt sep inf alegrar, animar.

jazz band n banda f de jazz.

jazz singer n cantor m, -ra f de jazz.

jazzy [ˈdʒæzɪ] (compar -ier, superl -iest) adj -1. [bright] chamativo(va) -2. [music] jazzístico(ca).

JCS (abbr of Joint Chiefs of Staff) n conselho militar do presidente dos Estados Unidos.

jealous [ˈdʒeləs] adj -1. [envious]: **to be** ~ **(of sb/ sthg)** ter inveja (de alguém/algo) -2. [possessive]: **to be** ~ **(of sb/sthg)** estar com ciúmes (de alguém/algo).

jealously [ˈdʒeləslɪ] adv -1. [enviously] invejosamente -2. [possessively] zelosamente.

jealousy [ˈdʒeləsɪ] n (U) -1. [envy] inveja f -2. [resentment] ciúmes mpl.

jeans [dʒiːnz] npl jeans m inv.

Jeep® n jipe m.

jeer [dʒɪəˡ] <> vt -1. [mock] zombar de -2. [boo] vaiar. <> vi -1. [boo] vaiar; **to** ~ **at sb** vaiar alguém -2. [mock] zombar; **to** ~ **at sb** zombar de alguém.
 jeers npl vaias fpl.

jeering [ˈdʒɪərɪŋ] <> adj zombeteiro(ra). <> n zombarias fpl.

Jehovah's Witness [dʒɪˈhəʊvəz-] n Testemunha f de Jeová.

Jello® n (U) US ≃ gelatina f.

jelly [ˈdʒelɪ] (pl -ies) n -1. [dessert] gelatina f -2. [jam] geléia f.

jelly baby n UK caramelo em forma de boneco.

jelly bean n bala f de jujuba.

jellyfish [ˈdʒelɪfɪʃ] (pl inv OR -es) n água-viva f.

jelly roll n US rocambole m.

jemmy UK [ˈdʒemɪ], **jimmy** US [ˈdʒɪmɪ] (pl -ies) n pé-de-cabra m.

jeopardize, -ise [ˈdʒepədaɪz] vt pôr em perigo, arriscar.

jeopardy [ˈdʒepədɪ] n: **in** ~ em perigo.

jerk [dʒɜːk] <> n -1. [movement] guinada f, movimento m brusco -2. inf pej [fool] estúpido m, -da f. <> vt mover abruptamente; **he** ~**ed the door open** ele abriu a porta bruscamente. <> vi dar solavancos.

jerkily [ˈdʒɜːkɪlɪ] adv abruptamente.

jerkin [ˈdʒɜːkɪn] n colete m.

jerky [ˈdʒɜːkɪ] (compar -ier, superl -iest) adj abrupto(-ta).

jerry-built [ˈdʒerɪ-] adj mal construído(da).

jerry can n lata f.

jersey [ˈdʒɜːzɪ] (pl jerseys) n -1. [sweater] suéter m -2. (U) [cloth] jérsei m.

Jersey [ˈdʒɜːzɪ] n Jersey; **in** ~ em Jersey.

Jerusalem [dʒəˈruːsələm] n Jerusalém; **in** ~ em Jerusalém.

Jerusalem artichoke n tupinambor m.

jest [dʒest] n brincadeira f; **in** ~ de brincadeira.

jester [ˈdʒestəˡ] n bufão m.

Jesuit ['dʒezjʊɪt] ◇ *adj* jesuíta. ◇ *n* jesuíta *m*.
Jesus (Christ) ['dʒiːzəs-] ◇ *n* Jesus Cristo. ◇ *interj inf* Jesus Cristo!
jet [dʒet] (*pt* & *pp* -**ted**, *cont* -**ting**) ◇ *n* -**1.** [gen] jato *m* -**2.** [nozzle, outlet] cano *m* de descarga. ◇ *vi* [travel by jet] voar num avião a jato.
jet-black *adj* da cor de azeviche.
jet engine *n* motor *m* a jato.
jetfoil ['dʒetfɔɪl] *n* hidroavião *m*.
jet lag *n* (*U*) jet lag *m*.
jet-propelled [-prə'peld] *adj* de propulsão a jato.
jetsam ['dʒetsəm] *n* ⊏ **flotsam.**
jet set *n*: the ~ o jet set.
jettison ['dʒetɪsən] *vt* -**1.** [cargo, bombs] alijar -**2.** *fig* [discard] descartar.
jetty ['dʒetɪ] (*pl* -**ies**) *n* quebra-mar *m*.
Jew [dʒuː] *n* judeu *m*.
jewel ['dʒuːəl] ◇ *n* -**1.** [gemstone] pedra *f* preciosa -**2.** [piece of jewellery] jóia *f* -**3.** [in watch] rubi *m*. ◇ *comp* de jóias.
jeweller *UK*, **jeweler** *US* ['dʒuːələʳ] *n* joalheiro *m*, -ra *f*; ~'s (shop) joalheria *f*.
jewellery *UK*, **jewelry** *US* ['dʒuːəlrɪ] *n* (*U*) jóias *fpl*.
Jewish ['dʒuːɪʃ] *adj* judeu(dia).
JFK (*abbr of* John Fitzgerald Kennedy International Airport) *n* (aeroporto *m*) JFK *m*.
jib [dʒɪb] (*pt* & *pp* -**bed**, *cont* -**bing**) ◇ *n* -**1.** [NAUT - beam] vau *m*; [- sail] bujarrona *f* -**2.** [of crane] braço *m* de guindaste. ◇ *vi*: to ~ at sthg hesitar em fazer algo.
jibe [dʒaɪb] *n* zombaria *f*.
jiffy ['dʒɪfɪ] *n inf*: in a ~ num instante.
Jiffy bag® *n* envelope *m* acolchoado.
jig [dʒɪg] (*pt* & *pp* -**ged**, *cont* -**ging**) ◇ *n* [dance] jiga *f*. ◇ *vi* -**1.** [dance] dançar jiga -**2.** [jump] saracotear, gingar.
jiggle ['dʒɪgl] *vt* sacudir.
jigsaw (puzzle) ['dʒɪgsɔː-] *n* quebra-cabeça *m*.
jihad [dʒɪ'hɑːd] *n* jihad *f*.
jilt [dʒɪlt] *vt* deixar plantado(da).
jimmy *n US* = **jemmy.**
jingle ['dʒɪŋgl] ◇ *n* -**1.** [sound] tilintar *m* -**2.** [song] jingle *m*. ◇ *vi* tilintar.
jingoism ['dʒɪŋgəʊɪzm] *n* (*U*) jingoísmo *m*.
jinx [dʒɪŋks] *n* pé-frio *m*.
jinxed ['dʒɪŋkst] *adj* de má sorte.
jitters ['dʒɪtəz] *npl inf*: to have the ~ ficar com os nervos à flor da pele.
jittery ['dʒɪtərɪ] *adj inf* nervoso(sa).
jive [dʒaɪv] ◇ *n* -**1.** [dance] swing *m* -**2.** *US inf* [glib talk] burburinho *m*. ◇ *vi* dançar swing.
job [dʒɒb] *n* -**1.** [paid employment] emprego *m* -**2.** [task, piece of work] trabalho *m*; **to do a good** ~ fazer um bom trabalho; **to make a good** ~ **of** sthg fazer algo muito bem -**3.** [difficult time]: **to have a** ~ **doing** sthg ter trabalho para fazer algo -**4.** [function, role] tarefa *f*, função *f* -**5.** *inf* [plastic surgery]: **to have a nose** ~ fazer uma plástica no nariz -**6.** *inf* [crime] trabalho *m* -**7.** *phr*: **that's just the** ~ *UK inf* isso vem bem a calhar.
jobbing ['dʒɒbɪŋ] *adj UK* que trabalha por empreitada.
job centre *n UK* agência *f* de empregos.

job creation scheme *n* projeto *m* de geração de empregos.
job description *n* descrição *f* do cargo.
jobless ['dʒɒblɪs] ◇ *adj* desempregado(da). ◇ *npl*: the ~ os desempregados.
job lot *n* lote *m* (*de mercadorias variadas*).
job satisfaction *n* (*U*) satisfação *f* profissional.
job security *n* (*U*) segurança *f* no trabalho.
Job Seekers Allowance *n UK* seguro-desemprego concedido a pessoas que comprovadamente estão buscando um novo trabalho.
jobsharing ['dʒɒbˌʃeərɪŋ] *n* (*U*) prática de dividir um trabalho de tempo integral entre duas pessoas de forma que cada uma cumpra apenas meio turno, especialmente para permitir que mulheres com filhos possam trabalhar.
Joburg, Jo'burg ['dʒəʊbɜːg] *n inf* Joanesburgo; in ~ em Joanesburgo.
jockey ['dʒɒkɪ] (*pl* -**s**) ◇ *n* jóquei *m*. ◇ *vi*: to ~ **for position** competir por uma melhor posição.
jockstrap ['dʒɒkstræp] *n* sunga *m*.
jocular ['dʒɒkjʊləʳ] *adj* -**1.** [person] divertido(da) -**2.** [remark] engraçado(da).
jodhpurs ['dʒɒdpəz] *npl* culote *m*.
Joe Public [dʒəʊ-] *n UK inf* população *f* em geral.
jog [dʒɒg] (*pt* & *pp* -**ged**, *cont* -**ging**) ◇ *n* [run] corrida *f*, jogging *m*. ◇ *vt* [nudge] cutucar; **to** ~ **the table** sacudir a mesa; **to** ~ **sb's memory** refrescar a memória de alguém. ◇ *vi* [run] fazer cooper.
jogger ['dʒɒgəʳ] *n* [runner] corredor *m*, -ra *f*, praticante *mf* de cooper.
jogging ['dʒɒgɪŋ] *n* [running] cooper *m*.
joggle ['dʒɒgl] *vt* embalar.
Johannesburg [dʒəʊ'hænɪsbɜːg] *n* Joanesburgo; in ~ em Joanesburgo.
john [dʒɒn] *n US inf* [toilet] banheiro *m*.
John Hancock [-'hænkɒk] *n US inf* assinatura *f*, jamegão *m*.
join [dʒɔɪn] ◇ *n* junção *f*. ◇ *vt* -**1.** [connect] juntar -**2.** [get together with] juntar-se a; **do** ~ **us for lunch** venha almoçar com a gente -**3.** [become a member of - political party] filiar-se a; [- club] associar-se a; [- army] alistar-se em -**4.** [take part in] unir-se a; **to** ~ **a queue** *UK*, **to** ~ **a line** *US* entrar numa fila; **to** ~ **forces** juntar forças; ~ **the club!** juntem-se ao clube! ◇ *vi* -**1.** [connect - rivers] unir-se; [- pieces] encaixar-se -**2.** [become a member - of library] inscrever-se; [- of club] associar-se.
➨ **join in** *vt fus* & *vi* participar.
➨ **join up** *vi MIL* alistar-se.
joiner ['dʒɔɪnəʳ] *n* marceneiro *m*, -ra *f*.
joinery ['dʒɔɪnərɪ] *n* (*U*) marcenaria *f*.
joint [dʒɔɪnt] ◇ *adj* conjunto(ta). ◇ *n* -**1.** ANAT articulação *f* -**2.** [where things are joined] encaixe *m* -**3.** *UK* [of meat] corte *m* -**4.** *inf pej* [place] espelunca *f* -**5.** *drugs sl* [cannabis cigarette] baseado *m*.
joint account *n* conta *f* conjunta.
Joint Chiefs of Staff *npl*: the ~ o Alto Comando das Forças Armadas (*nos Estados Unidos*).
jointed ['dʒɔɪntɪd] *adj* articulado(da).

jointly ['dʒɔɪntlɪ] *adv* conjuntamente.
joint ownership *n* (U) co-propriedade *f*.
joint-stock company *n* ≃ sociedade *f* anônima.
joint venture *n* joint-venture *f*.
joist [dʒɔɪst] *n* viga *f* de madeira.
jojoba [hə'həʊbə] *n* (U) jojoba *f*.
joke [dʒəʊk] ◇ *n* -1. [funny story or action] piada *f*, anedota *f*; **to go beyond a** ~ perder a graça; **to play a** ~ **on sb** pregar uma peça em alguém; **it's no** ~ [not easy] não é fácil -2. [referring to situation, person]: **to be a** ~ ser uma piada. ◇ *vi* brincar; **to** ~ **about sthg** brincar em relação a algo; **to** ~ **with sb** brincar com alguém.
joker ['dʒəʊkə'] *n* -1. [person] brincalhão *m*, -lhona *f* -2. [playing card] curinga *m*.
jollity ['dʒɒlətɪ] *n* (U) alegria *f*.
jolly ['dʒɒlɪ] (*compar* -ier, *superl* -iest) ◇ *adj* alegre, divertido(da). ◇ *adv UK inf* muito; ~ **easy!** barbada!; ~ **good!** excelente!
jolt [dʒəʊlt] ◇ *n* -1. [jerk] empurrão *m*, solavanco *m* -2. [shock] sacudida *f*. ◇ *vt* -1. [jerk] sacudir -2. [shock] chocar; **to** ~ **sb into doing sthg** forçar alguém a fazer algo. ◇ *vi* sacolejar.
Joneses ['dʒəʊnzɪz] *npl*: **to keep up with the** ~ não ser menos que os outros.
Jordan ['dʒɔ:dn] *n* Jordânia *f*; **in** ~ na Jordânia; **the (River)** ~ o (Rio) Jordão.
Jordanian [dʒɔ:'demjən] ◇ *adj* jordaniano(na). ◇ *n* jordaniano *m*, -na *f*.
joss stick [dʒɒs-] *n* incenso *m* aromático.
jostle ['dʒɒsl] ◇ *vt* acotovelar. ◇ *vi* acotovelar-se.
jot [dʒɒt] (*pt* & *pp* -ted, *cont* -ting) *n* tiquinho *m*; **there isn't a** ~ **of truth in ...** não há um pingo de verdade em ...; **I don't care a** ~ **what the rest of you think** não ligo a mínima para o que vocês pensam.
◆ **jot down** *vt sep* anotar.
jotter ['dʒɒtə'] *n* bloco *m* de anotações.
jottings ['dʒɒtɪŋz] *npl* recadinhos *mpl*.
journal ['dʒɜ:nl] *n* -1. [magazine] revista *f* especializada -2. [diary] diário *m*.
journalese [,dʒɜ:nə'li:z] *n* (U) *pej* jargão *m* jornalístico, jornalês *m*.
journalism ['dʒɜ:nəlɪzm] *n* (U) jornalismo *m*.
journalist ['dʒɜ:nəlɪst] *n* jornalista *mf*.
journey ['dʒɜ:nɪ] (*pl* -s) *n* jornada *f*.
joust [dʒaʊst] ◇ *n* justa *f*. ◇ *vi* justar.
jovial ['dʒəʊvjəl] *adj* jovial.
jowls [dʒaʊlz] *npl* bochechas *fpl*.
joy [dʒɔɪ] *n* -1. (U) [happiness] alegria *f* -2. [cause of happiness] prazer *m*, deleite *m*.
joyful ['dʒɔɪfʊl] *adj* alegre.
joyfully ['dʒɔɪfʊlɪ] *adv* alegremente.
joyous ['dʒɔɪəs] *adj literary* deleitante, jubiloso(sa).
joyously ['dʒɔɪəslɪ] *adv literary* com deleite.
joypad *n COMPUT* joystick *m*.
joyride ['dʒɔɪraɪd] ◇ *n* volta *f* num carro roubado. ◇ *vi* andar num carro roubado.
joyrider ['dʒɔɪraɪdə'] *n* ladrão *m*, -dra *f* de carro.
joystick ['dʒɔɪstɪk] *n* -1. [in aircraft] manche *m* -2. [for computers, video games] joystick *m*.

JP *n abbr of* Justice of the Peace.
Jr. (*abbr of* Junior) Jr.
jubilant ['dʒu:bɪlənt] *adj* jubilante.
jubilation [,dʒu:bɪ'leɪʃn] *n* (U) júbilo *m*.
jubilee ['dʒu:bɪli:] *n* jubileu *m*.
Judaism ['dʒu:deɪɪzml *n* (U) judaísmo *m*.
judder ['dʒʌdə'] *vi UK* sacudir intensamente.
judge [dʒʌdʒ] ◇ *n* juíz *m*, -za *f*. ◇ *vt* -1. *JUR* julgar -2. [decide result of] sentenciar -3. [estimate] estimar. ◇ *vi* [decide] julgar; **to** ~ **from** *OR* **by** a julgar por, julgando-se por.
judg(e)ment ['dʒʌdʒmənt] *n* -1. *JUR* julgamento *m*; **to pass** ~ **(on sb)** condenar (alguém) -2. [opinion] parecer *m*; **to pass** ~ **(on sb/sthg)** julgar (alguém/algo); **to reserve** ~ adiar um julgamento -3. (U) [ability to form opinion] opinião *f*; **against my better** ~ contra a minha vontade -4. [punishment] sentença *f*.
judg(e)mental [dʒʌdʒ'mentl] *adj pej* crítico(ca).
judicial [dʒu:'dɪʃl] *adj* judicial.
judiciary [dʒu:'dɪʃərɪ] *n*: **the** ~ o judiciário.
judicious [dʒu:'dɪʃəs] *adj* judicioso(sa).
judo ['dʒu:dəʊ] *n* (U) judô *m*.
jug [dʒʌg] *n* [container] jarro *m*.
juggernaut ['dʒʌgənɔ:t] *n* [truck] jamanta *f*.
juggle ['dʒʌgl] ◇ *vt* -1. [throw] fazer malabarismos com -2. [rearrange] reorganizar -3. [commitments] equilibrar -4. [figures, ideas] maquiar. ◇ *vi* [as entertainment] fazer malabarismos.
juggler ['dʒʌglə'] *n* malabarista *mf*.
jugular (vein) ['dʒʌgjʊlə'-] *n* (veia *f*) jugular *f*.
juice [dʒu:s] *n* -1. [from fruit, vegetables] suco *m* -2. [from meat] molho *m*.
◆ **juices** *npl* [in stomach] suco *m* gástrico.
juicy ['dʒu:sɪ] (*compar* -ier, *superl* -iest) *adj* -1. [full of juice] suculento(ta) -2. *inf* [scandalous] escandaloso(sa) -3. *inf* [enjoyable, desirable] desejável.
jujitsu [dʒu:'dʒɪtsu:] *n* (U) jiu-jitsu *m*.
jukebox ['dʒu:kbɒks] *n* juke-box *f*.
Jul. (*abbr of* July) jul.
July [dʒu:'laɪ] *n* julho *m*; *see also* September.
jumble ['dʒʌmbl] ◇ *n* [mixture] mistura *f*. ◇ *vt*: **to** ~ **(up)** confundir.
jumble sale *n UK* venda *f* de objetos usados.
jumbo jet ['dʒʌmbəʊ-] *n* jumbo *m*.
jumbo-sized ['dʒʌmbəʊsaɪzd] *adj* gigantesco(ca).
jump [dʒʌmp] ◇ *n* -1. [leap] salto *m* -2. [fence in horse-jumping] obstáculo *m* -3. [rapid increase] alta *m* -4. *phr*: **to keep one** ~ **ahead of sb** manter um passo à frente de alguém. ◇ *vt* -1. [cross by leaping] pular; **the train** ~ **ed the rails** o trem descarrilhou -2. *inf* [attack] atacar -3. *US* [train, bus] viajar sem passagem em. ◇ *vi* -1. [leap] saltar -2. [make a sudden movement] sobressaltar; **the noise made me** ~ o barulho me fez dar um sobressalto -3. [increase rapidly] ter uma alta.
◆ **jump at** *vt fus fig* agarrar.
◆ **jump in** *vi* [get in quickly]: ~ **in!** entra rápido!
◆ **jump out** *vi* [get out quickly]: ~ **out!** salta fora!
◆ **jump up** *vi* [rise hurriedly] levantar-se rapidamente.
jumped-up ['dʒʌmpt-] *adj UK inf pej* pretencioso(sa).

jumper ['dʒʌmpəʳ] *n* -**1.** *UK* [pullover] suéter *m* -**2.** *US* [dress] avental *m*.

jump jet *n* aeronave *f* de decolagem vertical.

jump leads *npl* cabos *mpl* para ligação da bateria.

jump-start *vt* fazer ligação direta.

jumpsuit ['dʒʌmpsuːt] *n* macacão *m*.

jumpy ['dʒʌmpɪ] (*compar* -ier, *superl* -iest) *adj* nervoso(sa).

Jun. -**1.** (*abbr of* June) jun. -**2.** = **Junr**.

junction ['dʒʌŋkʃn] *n* [meeting point] junção *f*, entroncamento *m*.

junction box *n* caixa *f* de ligação.

juncture ['dʒʌŋktʃəʳ] *n fml*: **at this ~** nesta conjuntura.

June [dʒuːn] *n* junho; *see also* **September**.

jungle ['dʒʌŋgl] *n* selva *f*; **the Amazon ~** a floresta amazônica.

jungle gym *n US* trepa-trepa *f*.

junior ['dʒuːnjəʳ] <> *adj* -**1.** [younger] jovem -**2.** [lower in rank] júnior -**3.** *US* [after name] júnior. <> *n* -**1.** [person of lower rank] júnior *mf* -**2.** [younger person] jovem *mf*; **he's five years her ~** ele é cinco anos mais jovem que ela -**3.** *US SCH & UNIV* aluno *m*, -na *f* do penúltimo ano.

junior college *n US escola universitária para os dois primeiros anos de curso*.

junior doctor *n* médico *m*, -ca *f* residente.

junior high school *n US* escola *f* de ensino intermediário (*para alunos de 13 a 15 anos*).

junior minister *n UK* subsecretário *m*, -ria *f*.

junior school *n UK* escola *f* primária.

juniper ['dʒuːnɪpəʳ] *n* junípero *m*.

junk [dʒʌŋk] <> *n* -**1.** *inf* [unwanted things] traste *m* -**2.** [boat] junco *m*. <> *vt* jogar fora.

junket ['dʒʌŋkɪt] *n* -**1.** (U) [pudding] espécie de pudim feito com leite e coalho -**2.** *inf pej* [trip] viagem *f* às custas do governo.

junk food *n pej comida pronta e pouco saudável*.

junkie ['dʒʌŋkɪ] *n drugs sl* drogado *m*, -da *f*.

junk mail *n pej* junk mail *m*.

junk shop *n* brechó *m*, brique *m*.

Junr (*abbr of Junior*) Jr.

junta [*UK* 'dʒʌntə, *US* 'hʊntə] *n* junta *f*.

Jupiter ['dʒuːpɪtəʳ] *n* [planet] Júpiter.

jurisdiction [,dʒʊərɪs'dɪkʃn] *n* (U) jurisdição *f*.

jurisprudence [,dʒʊərɪs'pruːdəns] *n* (U) jurisprudência *f*.

juror ['dʒʊərəʳ] *n* jurado *m*, -da *f*.

jury ['dʒʊərɪ] (*pl* -ies) *n* júri *m*.

jury box *n* tribunal *f* do júri.

jury service *n* (U) trabalho *m* de jurado (num tribunal).

just [dʒʌst] <> *adj* [fair] justo(ta). <> *adv* -**1.** [recently] agora mesmo; **he's ~ left** ele acabou de sair -**2.** [at this or that moment]: **I was ~ about to go**

out eu estava quase saindo; **I'm ~ going to do it** vou fazer isso agora mesmo; **~ then there was a knock at the door** naquele momento houve uma batida na porta; **she arrived ~ as I was leaving** ela chegou no exato momento em que eu estava saindo; **why do you always arrive ~ as I'm leaving?** por que você sempre chega justamente quando estou saindo? -**3.** [only, simply] apenas, simplesmente; **in ~ a minute** *OR* **moment** *OR* **second** num minuto *OR* instante *OR* segundo; **~ a minute!** espera aí um pouquinho! -**4.** [barely, almost not] mal; **I can only ~ hear you** mal consigo ouvir você; **I only ~ caught the train** quase perdi o trem; **we have ~ enough time** quase não temos tempo -**5.** [for emphasis] simplesmente; **I ~ can't believe it!** simplesmente não consigo acreditar!; **~ look at this mess!** dá só uma olhada na bagunça! -**6.** [exactly, precisely] precisamente; **~ here** exatamente aqui -**7.** [in requests]: **could I ~ borrow your pen?** poderia me emprestar sua caneta, por favor?

➡ **just about** *adv* mais ou menos.

➡ **just as** *adv* [in comparisons]: **~ as well as you** tão bem quanto você; **~ as bad as ever** mal como sempre.

➡ **just now** *adv* -**1.** [a short time ago] agora mesmo -**2.** [at this moment] neste momento.

justice ['dʒʌstɪs] *n* -**1.** [gen] justiça *f* -**2.** [of a cause, claim] razão *f* -**3.** [judge] juíz *m* -**4.** *phr*: **to do ~ to sthg** [to a job] fazer justiça a algo; [to a meal] apreciar devidamente; **to do ~ to sb** fazer justiça a alguém; **to do o.s. ~** desempenhar-se à altura.

Justice of the Peace (*pl* **Justices of the Peace**) *n* Juíz *m*, -za *f* de Paz.

justifiable ['dʒʌstɪfaɪəbl] *adj* justificável.

justifiable homicide *n* homicídio *m* em legítima defesa.

justifiably ['dʒʌstɪfaɪəblɪ] *adv* justificavelmente.

justification [,dʒʌstɪfɪ'keɪʃn] *n* -**1.** [good reason] justificativa *f* -**2.** *COMPUT*: **right-hand ~** alinhamento *m* justificado à direita.

justify ['dʒʌstɪfaɪ] (*pt & pp* -**ied**) *vt* -**1.** [give reasons for] justificar; **to ~ doing sthg** ter razões para fazer algo -**2.** *COMPUT & TYPO* justificar.

justly ['dʒʌstlɪ] *adv* merecidamente, imparcialmente.

justness *n* (U) justiça *f*.

jut [dʒʌt] (*pt & pp* -**ted**, *cont* -**ting**) *vi*: **to ~ (out)** projetar-se.

jute [dʒuːt] *n* (U) juta *f*.

juvenile ['dʒuːvənaɪl] <> *adj* -**1.** *JUR* juvenil -**2.** *pej* [childish] infantil. <> *n JUR* [young person] menor *mf*.

juvenile court *n* juizado *m* de menores.

juvenile delinquent *n* delinquente *mf* juvenil.

juxtapose [,dʒʌkstə'pəʊz] *vt*: **to ~ sthg with sthg** justapor algo com algo.

juxtaposition [,dʒʌkstəpə'zɪʃn] *n* (U) justaposição *f*.

K

k (*pl* **k's** *OR* **ks**), **K** (*pl* **K's** *OR* **Ks**) [keɪl] *n* [letter] k, K *m*.

➡ **K** *n* **-1.** (*abbr of* **kilobyte**) K **-2.** (*abbr of* **Knight**) Cavaleiro *m* **-3.** (*abbr of* **thousand**) mil.

Kabul ['kɑ:bʊl] *n* Cabul; **in** ~ em Cabul.

kaftan ['kæftæn] *n* cafetã *f*.

Kalahari Desert [ˌkælə'hɑ:rɪ-] *n*: **the** ~ o Deserto de Kalahari.

kale [keɪl] *n* (*U*) couve *f* crespa.

kaleidoscope [kə'laɪdəskəʊp] *n* caleidoscópio *m*.

Kampala [kæm'pɑ:lə] *n* Campala; **in** ~ em Campala.

Kampuchea [ˌkæmpʊ'tʃɪə] *n* Camboja; **in** ~ em Camboja.

Kampuchean ◇ *adj* cambojano(na). ◇ *n* cambojano *m*, -na *f*.

kangaroo [ˌkæŋgə'ru:] *n* canguru *m*.

Kansas ['kænzəs] *n* Kansas; **in** ~ no Kansas.

kaolin ['keɪəlɪn] *n* (*U*) caulim *m*.

kaput [kə'pʊt] *adj inf* acabado(da).

karaoke [kɑ:rə'əʊkɪ] *n* karaokê *m*.

karat ['kærət] *n US* quilate *m*.

karate [kə'rɑ:tɪ] *n* (*U*) karatê *m*.

Kashmir [kæʃ'mɪə] *n* Cachemira; **in** ~ na Cachemira.

Katmandu [ˌkætmæn'du:] *n* Katmandu; **in** ~ em Katmandu.

kayak ['kaɪæk] *n* caiaque *m*.

Kazakhstan [ˌkæzæk'stɑ:n] *n* Cazaquistão; **in** ~ no Cazaquistão.

KB (*abbr of* **kilobyte(s)**) *n COMPUT* KB.

KBE (*abbr of* **Knight Commander of the Order of the British Empire**) *n* (*titular de*) *distinção britânica*.

KC (*abbr of* **King's Counsel**) *n título conferido a advogados de prestígio na Grã-Bretanha*.

kcal (*abbr of* **kilocalorie**) Kcal.

kebab [kɪ'bæb] *n churrasquinho picante servido com pão árabe e acompanhado de vegetais picados*, kebab *m*.

kedgeree ['kedʒəri:] *n* (*U*) *UK prato indiano feito com arroz, peixe e ovos*, kedgeree *m*.

keel [ki:l] *n* quilha *f*; **on an even** ~ em perfeito equilíbrio.

➡ **keel over** *vi* **-1.** [ship] emborcar **-2.** [person] desmaiar.

keen [ki:n] *adj* **-1.** [enthusiastic] entusiasta; **to be** ~

on sthg gostar muito de algo, ser aficionado(da) por algo; **to be** ~ **on sb** gostar muito de alguém; **to be** ~ **to do** *OR* **on doing sthg** estar muito a fim de fazer algo; **I'm not madly** ~ **on going** não estou com toda essa vontade de ir **-2.** [intense] intenso(-sa) **-3.** [sharp, well-developed] apurado(da) **-4.** [wind] forte.

keenly ['ki:nlɪ] *adv* **-1.** [intensely] profundamente **-2.** [intently] atentamente.

keenness ['ki:nnɪs] *n* (*U*) **-1.** [enthusiasm] entusiasmo *m* **-2.** [intensity] intensidade *f* **-3.** [sharpness] perspicácia *f*.

keep [ki:p] (*pt* & *pp* **kept**) ◇ *vt* **-1.** [maintain in a particular place or state or position] manter; **to** ~ **sb waiting** fazer alguém esperar **-2.** [retain] ficar com; **please** ~ **the change** pode ficar com o troco; **they're** ~**ing the house in Scotland** eles estão mantendo a casa na Escócia **-3.** [continue]: **to** ~ **doing sthg** continuar fazendo algo; **to** ~ **talking** continuar falando; **to** ~ **going** continuar indo **-4.** [put aside, store] guardar **-5.** [prevent]: **to** ~ **sb/sthg from doing sthg** impedir alguém/algo de fazer algo **-6.** [detain] manter; **to** ~ **sb (from sthg)** privar alguém (de algo); **what kept you here?** o que te segurou aqui? **-7.** [fulfil, observe] cumprir; **to** ~ **a secret** guardar um segredo **-8.** [withhold news or fact of]: **to** ~ **sthg from sb** ocultar algo de alguém; ~ **it to yourself for the moment** não conta isso para ninguém por enquanto **-9.** [diary, record, account] ter **-10.** [own - farm animals] criar; [- shop, car] ter **-11.** *phr*: **they** ~ **themselves to themselves** eles são muito reservados. ◇ *vi* **-1.** [remain, stay] manter-se **-2.** [continue moving] manter-se a **-3.** [last, stay fresh] conservar-se **-4.** *UK* [in health] manter-se. ◇ *n* (*U*) [food, board etc] sustento *m*.

➡ **for keeps** *adv* para valer.

➡ **keep at** *vt fus*: **to** ~ **at it** [work hard] empenhar-se.

➡ **keep back** *vt sep* conter.

➡ **keep down** *vt sep* **-1.** [stop from increasing] limitar **-2.** [food] controlar.

➡ **keep off** ◇ *vt sep* [fend off] manter afastado(da). ◇ *vt fus* [avoid] evitar; '~ **off the grass'** 'não pise na grama'.

➡ **keep on** ◇ *vi* **-1.** [continue] continuar **-2.** [talk incessantly]: **to** ~ **on (about sthg)** falar incessantemente (sobre algo). ◇ *vt* [continue]: **to** ~ **on doing sthg** [without stopping] continuar fazendo algo; [repeatedly] continuar fazendo algo sem parar.

➡ **keep on at** *vt fus UK* importunar.

➡ **keep out** ◇ *vt sep* manter-se fora. ◇ *vi*: '~ **out'** 'entrada proibida'.

➡ **keep to** ◇ *vt fus* **-1.** [observe, respect] respeitar **-2.** [not deviate from] manter-se em **-3.** [stay in] ficar em. ◇ *vt sep* [limit] limitar.

➡ **keep up** ◇ *vt sep* **-1.** [prevent from falling] segurar **-2.** [maintain, continue] manter **-3.** [prevent from going to bed] manter acordado(da). ◇ *vi* **-1.** [maintain pace, level] acompanhar; **to** ~ **up with sb/sthg** acompanhar alguém/algo **-2.** [remain in contact]: **to** ~ **up with sb** manter-se em contato com alguém.

keeper ['ki:pə'] *n* **-1.** [in zoo] zelador *m*, -ra *f*, guarda *mf* **-2.** [curator] curador *m*, -ra *f*.

keep-fit *UK* <> *n (U)* ginástica *f.* <> *comp* de ginástica.

keeping [ˈkiːpɪŋ] *n* **-1.** [care] cuidado *m* **-2.** [conformity, harmony]: **in/out of** ~ **with sthg** [rules, regulations, decision] em acordo/desacordo com algo; [clothes, furniture, style] combinando/não combinando com algo.

keepsake [ˈkiːpseɪk] *n* lembrança *f.*

keg [keg] *n* barrilote *m.*

kelp [kelp] *n (U)* alga *f* marinha.

ken [ken] *n*: **beyond one's** ~ além do alcance de alguém.

kennel [ˈkenl] *n* **-1.** [shelter for dog] canil *m* **-2.** *US* = **kennels**.
➤ **kennels** *npl UK* [for boarding pets] canil *m.*

Kentucky [kenˈtʌkɪ] *n* Kentucky; **in** ~ em Kentucky.

Kenya [ˈkenjə] *n* Quênia; **in** ~ no Quênia.

Kenyan [ˈkenjən] <> *adj* queniano(na). <> *n* queniano *m,* -na *f.*

kept [kept] *pt & pp* ▷ **keep.**

kerb [kɜːb] *n UK* meio-fio *m.*

kerb crawler [-ˌkrɔːləʳ] *n UK* *pessoa que dirige o carro vagarosamente junto ao meio-fio em busca de prostitutas.*

kerbstone [ˈkɜːbstəʊn] *n UK* marco *m* de pedra.

kerfuffle [kəˈfʌfl] *n UK inf* escarcéu *m.*

kernel [ˈkɜːnl] *n* [of nut] amêndoa *f*; **the** ~ **of the issue** o cerne da questão.

kerosene [ˈkerəsiːn] *n (U)* querosene *f.*

kestrel [ˈkestrəl] *n* falcão *m* europeu.

ketch *n* brigue *m.*

ketchup [ˈketʃəp] *n (U)* ketchup *m.*

kettle [ˈketl] *n* chaleira *f.*

kettledrum [ˈketldrʌm] *n* tímpano *m.*

key [kiː] <> *n* **-1.** [for lock] chave *f* **-2.** [of typewriter, computer] tecla *f* **-3.** [explanatory list] legenda *f* **-4.** [solution, answer]: ~ **(to sthg)** chave (para algo) **-5.** [MUS - of piano, organ] tom *m*; [- scale of notes] clave *f.* <> *adj* [main] principal; ~ **position** posição-chave; ~ **issue** questão-chave.
➤ **key in** *vt sep* digitar.

keyboard [ˈkiːbɔːd] <> *n* teclado *m.* <> *vt* digitar.

keyboarder [ˈkiːbɔːdəʳ] *n* digitador *m,* -ra *f.*

keyed up [kiːd-] *adj* excitado(da).

keyhole [ˈkiːhəʊl] *n* buraco *m* da fechadura.

keynote [ˈkiːnəʊt] <> *n* [main point] tônica *f.* <> *comp*: ~ **speech** conferência *f* de abertura.

keypad [ˈkiːpæd] *n COMPUT* teclado *m.*

keypunch [ˈkiːpʌntʃ] *n US* máquina *f* de perfurar cartões.

key ring *n* chaveiro *m.*

keystone [ˈkiːstəʊn] *n* pedra *f* angular.

keystroke [ˈkiːstrəʊk] *n COMPUT* pressionamento *m* de tecla.

keyword *n* palavra-chave *f.*

kg (*abbr of* **kilogram**) Kg.

KGB *n* KGB *f.*

khaki [ˈkɑːkɪ] <> *adj* cáqui *inv.* <> *n* **-1.** [colour] cáqui *m* **-2.** [cloth] tecido *m* cor de cáqui.

kHz (*abbr of* **kilohertz**) *n* kHz.

kibbutz [kɪˈbʊts] *n* (*pl* **kibbutzim** [ˌkɪbʊtˈsiːm], **-es**) *n* kibutz *m.*

kick [kɪk] <> *n* **-1.** [with foot] chute *m* **-2.** *inf* [excitement]: **to do sthg for** ~ **s** fazer algo para se divertir; **to get a** ~ **from sthg** desfrutar de algo **-3.** *inf* [of drink] efeito *m* estimulante. <> *vt* **-1.** [with foot] chutar; **to** ~ **o.s.** *fig* morder-se de raiva **-2.** *inf* [give up] largar. <> *vi* [person, baby, animal] dar pontapés.
➤ **kick about, kick around** *vi UK inf* [lie around] rodear.
➤ **kick in** *vi* fazer efeito.
➤ **kick off** *vi* **-1.** *FTBL* dar o pontapé inicial **-2.** *inf fig* [start] começar.
➤ **kick out** *vt sep inf* expulsar.
➤ **kick up** *vt fus inf* protestar com violência.

kickoff [ˈkɪkɒf] *n* pontapé *m* inicial.

kick-start *vt* dar partida em; **to give sthg a** ~ dar um grande impulso a algo.

kid [kɪd] (*pt & pp* **-ded**, *cont*-**ding**) <> *n* **-1.** *inf* [child, young person] criança *f*; **I've got four** ~ **s** tenho quatro filhos **-2.** [young goat] cabrito *m* **-3.** [leather] pelica *f.* <> *comp inf* [brother, sister]: **my** ~ **brother** meu irmão mais novo; **my** ~ **sister** minha irmã mais nova. <> *vt inf* **-1.** [tease] caçoar **-2.** [delude]: **to** ~ **o.s.** iludir-se. <> *vi inf*: **to be kidding** estar brincando; **no kidding!** [in emphasis] não brinca!; [in disbelief] não acredito!

kiddie, kiddy [ˈkɪdɪ] (*pl* **-ies**) *n inf* guri *m,* -ria *f.*

kid gloves *npl*: **to treat** *OR* **handle sb with** ~ tratar alguém com luvas de pelica.

kidnap [ˈkɪdnæp] (*UK pt & pp* **-ped**, *cont*-**ping**, *US pt & pp* **-ed**, *cont*-**ing**) *vt* seqüestrar.

kidnapper *UK*, **kidnaper** *US* [ˈkɪdnæpəʳ] *n* seqüestrador *m,* -ra *f.*

kidnapping *UK*, **kidnaping** *US* [ˈkɪdnæpɪŋ] *n* seqüestro *m.*

kidney [ˈkɪdnɪ] (*pl* **-s**) *n* rim *m.*

kidney bean *n* feijão *m* roxo.

kidney machine *n* hemodialisador *m.*

Kilimanjaro [ˌkɪlɪmənˈdʒɑːrəʊ] *n* Kilimanjaro.

kill [kɪl] <> *n* **-1.** [of animal] abate *m*; **to move** *OR* **close in for the** ~ dar o bote; *fig* dar o bote **-2.** [dead animal] presa *f.* <> *vt* **-1.** [gen] matar; **my feet are** ~ **ing me** meus pés estão me matando; **to** ~ **o.s.** matar-se **-2.** [murder] assassinar **-3.** *fig* [cause to end, fail] acabar com **-4.** [pass]: **to** ~ **time** matar tempo. <> *vi* assassinar.
➤ **kill off** *vt sep* **-1.** [cause death of] aniquilar **-2.** *fig* [cause to end, fail] destruir.

killer [ˈkɪləʳ] *n* **-1.** [person] assassino *m,* -na *f* **-2.** [animal] matador *m,* -ra *f* **-3.** [disease] doença *f* fatal.

killer whale *n* orca *f,* baleia-assassina *f.*

killing [ˈkɪlɪŋ] <> *adj inf* [very funny] de matar. <> *n* **-1.** [of one person] assassinato *m* **-2.** [of several people] matança *f* **-3.** *inf* [profit]: **to make a** ~ faturar uma grana.

killjoy [ˈkɪldʒɔɪ] *n* estraga-prazer *mf.*

kiln [kɪln] *n* fornalha *f.*

kilo [ˈkiːləʊ] (*pl* **-s**) (*abbr of* **kilogram**) *n* quilo *m.*

kilo- [kɪlə] *prefix* quilo.

kilobyte [ˈkɪləbaɪt] *n* quilobyte *m.*

kilocalorie [ˈkɪləˌkælərɪ] *n* quilocaloria *f.*

kilogram(me) [ˈkɪləgræm] *n* quilograma *m.*

kilohertz [ˈkɪləhɜːtz] (*pl inv*) *n* quilohertz *m.*

kilojoule [ˈkɪlədʒuːl] n quilojoule m.

kilometre UK [ˈkɪləˌmiːtə^r], **kilometer** US [kɪˈlɒmɪtə^r] n quilômetro m.

kilowatt [ˈkɪləwɒt] n quilowatt m.

kilt [kɪlt] n kilt m.

kimono [kɪˈməʊnəʊl (pl -s) n quimono m.

kin [kɪn] n ▷ **kith**.

kind [kaɪnd] ◇ adj gentil, amável; **would you be so ~ as to ...?** será que você me faria a gentileza de ...? ◇ n espécie f, tipo m; **a ~ of** uma espécie de; **~ of** inf de certo modo; **I ~ of thought that ...** eu meio que achei que ...; **of a ~** [sort of] do estilo; **an agreement of a ~** um acordo do estilo; [of same kind] do mesmo tipo; **in ~** [payment] em espécie; **nothing of the ~!** de jeito nenhum!; **it's one of a ~** é um em um milhão; **they're two of a ~** os dois são muito semelhantes.

kindergarten [ˈkɪndəˌgɑːtn] n jardim-de-infância m.

kind-hearted [-ˈhɑːtɪd] adj de bom coração.

kindle [ˈkɪndl] vt **-1.** [fire] pôr fogo em **-2.** fig [idea, feeling] inflamar.

kindling [ˈkɪndlɪŋ] n (U) [to light fire] gravetos mpl.

kindly [ˈkaɪndlɪ] (compar -ier, superl -iest) ◇ adj bondoso(sa), gentil. ◇ adv **-1.** [gen] bondosamente, gentilmente; **to look ~ on sb/sthg** olhar alguém/algo com bons olhos **-2.** [in sarcasm]: **~ leave the room!** faça o favor de sair da sala!; **will you ~ stop calling me that name!** pode fazer o favor de parar de me chamar por esse nome! **-3.** phr: **not to take ~ to sthg** não simpatizar com algo.

kindness [ˈkaɪndnɪs] n **-1.** (U) [gentleness] gentileza f, bondade f **-2.** [helpful act] generosidade f.

kindred [ˈkɪndrɪd] adj [similar] afim; **~ spirit** alma f gêmea.

kinetic [kɪˈnetɪk] adj cinético(ca).

kinfolk(s) [ˈkɪnfəʊk(s)] npl US = **kinsfolk**.

king [kɪŋ] n rei m.

kingdom [ˈkɪŋdəm] n reino m.

kingfisher [ˈkɪŋˌfɪʃə^r] n martim-pescador m.

kingpin [ˈkɪŋpɪn] n **-1.** TECH pino-mestre m **-2.** fig [person] manda-chuva m.

king prawn n camarão m real.

king-size(d) [-saɪz(d)] adj de tamanho grande; **~ bed** cama f king-size.

kink [kɪŋk] n [in rope, hair] dobra f.

kinky [ˈkɪŋkɪ] (compar -ier, superl -iest) adj **-1.** inf [idea, behaviour] excêntrico(ca) **-2.** [sex] pervertido(da).

kinsfolk [ˈkɪnzfəʊk] npl parentes mpl.

kinship [ˈkɪnʃɪp] n **-1.** [relationship] parentesco m **-2.** [closeness] afinidade f.

kiosk [ˈkiːɒsk] n **-1.** [small shop] banca f **-2.** UK [telephone box] cabine f telefônica.

kip [kɪp] (pt & pp -ped, cont -ping) UK inf ◇ n sesta f. ◇ vi sestear.

kipper [ˈkɪpə^r] n arenque m defumado.

Kirk [kɜːk] n. Scot: **the ~** a igreja nacional escocesa.

kirsch [kɪəʃ] n quirche m.

kiss [kɪs] ◇ n beijo m; **to give sb a ~** dar um beijo em alguém. ◇ vt beijar; **to ~ sb goodbye** dar um beijo de despedida em alguém. ◇ vi beijar-se.

kiss curl n UK pequeno anel de cabelo que se penteia para ficar reto na testa, na nuca ou na frente da orelha.

kiss of death n fig: **the ~** o beijo da morte.

kiss of life n [to resuscitate sb]: **to give sb the ~** fazer respiração boca-a-boca em alguém.

kissogram [ˈkɪsəgræm] n beijograma m, forma de homenagear uma pessoa contratando alguém para lhe dar um beijo, ao estilo das telemensagens.

kit [kɪt] (pt & pp -ted, cont -ting) n **-1.** [set] estojo m **-2.** (U) [clothes] equipamento m **-3.** [to be assembled] kit m, modelo m.

◆ **kit out** vt sep UK equipar.

kit bag n mochila f de viagem.

kitchen [ˈkɪtʃɪn] n cozinha f.

kitchenette [ˌkɪtʃɪˈnet] n kitchenette f, copa-cozinha f.

kitchen garden n horta f.

kitchen roll n papel-toalha m.

kitchen sink n pia f de cozinha.

kitchen unit n módulo m de cozinha.

kitchenware [ˈkɪtʃɪnweə^r] n utensílios mpl para cozinha.

kite [kaɪt] n **-1.** [toy] pipa f **-2.** [bird] milhafre m.

Kite-mark n UK marca f de padrão de qualidade.

kith [kɪθ] n: **~ and kin** amigos mpl e parentes.

kitsch [kɪtʃ] n (U) kitsch mf.

kitten [ˈkɪtn] n gatinho m, -nha f.

kitty [ˈkɪtɪ] (pl -ies) n **-1.** [shared fund - for bills, drinks] vaquinha f; [- in card games] bolo m **-2.** [cat] gatinho m, -nha f.

kiwi [ˈkiːwiː] n **-1.** [bird] quivi m **-2.** inf [New Zealander] neozelandês m, -esa f.

kiwi fruit n quivi m.

KKK (abbr of Ku Klux Klan) n Ku Klux Klan f.

klaxon [ˈklæksn] n buzina f elétrica.

Kleenex® [ˈkliːneks] n lenço m de papel.

kleptomaniac [ˌkleptəˈmeɪnɪæk] n cleptomaníaco m, -ca f.

km (abbr of kilometre) km.

km/h (abbr of kilometres per hour) km/h.

knack [næk] n inclinação m, queda f; **to have the ~ (of doing sthg)** levar jeito (para fazer algo); **to have a ~ (for doing sthg)** ter uma queda (para fazer algo).

knacker [ˈnækə^r] UK ◇ n [horse slaughterer] matador m, -ra f de cavalos velhos. ◇ vt inf [tire, break] acabar.

knackered [ˈnækəd] adj UK vinf [tired, broken] acabado(da).

knapsack [ˈnæpsæk] n mochila f.

knave [neɪv] n [playing card] valete m.

knead [niːd] vt [dough, clay] misturar.

knee [niː] n ANAT joelho m; **to be on one's ~s** [kneeling] ajoelhar-se; **to bring sb to their ~s** pôr alguém de joelhos.

kneecap [ˈniːkæp] n rótula f.

knee-deep adj **-1.** [snow, water] até o joelho **-2.** [person] enterrado(da) até o joelho.

knee-high adj à altura dos joelhos.

kneel [niːl] (UK pt & pp knelt, US pt & pp knelt OR -ed) vi ajoelhar-se.

➤ **kneel down** *vi* ajoelhar, ajoelhar-se.
knee-length *adj* até o joelho.
knees-up *n UK inf* festa *f* barulhenta.
knell [nel] *n* -**1.** dobre *m* dos sinos -**2.** *fig*: **to sound the death ~ for sthg** decretar a sentença de morte para algo.
knelt [nelt] *pt & pp* ▷ **kneel**.
knew [nju:] *pt* ▷ **know**.
knickers ['nɪkəz] *npl* -**1.** *UK* [underwear] calcinha *f* -**2.** *US* [knickerbockers] calções *mpl* (presos à altura dos joelhos).
knick-knack ['nɪknæk] *n* penduricalho *m*.
knife [naɪf] (*pl* **knives**) ◇ *n* faca *f*. ◇ *vt* esfaquear.
knifing *n* facada *f*.
knight [naɪt] ◇ *n* -**1.** [gen] cavaleiro *m* -**2.** [in chess] cavalo *m*. ◇ *vt* nomear cavaleiro(ra).
knighthood ['naɪthʊd] *n* título *m* da classe dos cavaleiros.
knit [nɪt] (*pt & pp* knit *OR* -**ted**, *cont* -**ting**) ◇ *adj*: **closely** *OR* **tightly ~** *fig* fortemente unido(da). ◇ *vt* [make with wool] tricotar. ◇ *vi* -**1.** [with wool] fazer tricô, tricotar -**2.** [join] juntar-se.
knitted ['nɪtɪd] *adj* [scarf, hat] de malha.
knitting ['nɪtɪŋ] *n (U)* -**1.** [activity] trabalho *m* de tricô -**2.** [work produced] tricô *m*.
knitting machine *n* máquina *f* de tricô.
knitting needle *n* agulha *f* de tricô.
knitting pattern *n* molde *m* de tricô.
knitwear ['nɪtweəʳ] *n (U)* roupa *f* de tricô.
knives [naɪvz] *pl* ▷ **knife**.
knob [nɒb] *n* -**1.** [on door] maçaneta *f* -**2.** [on drawer] puxador *m* -**3.** [on walking stick, furniture] nó *m* -**4.** [on TV, radio] botão *m*.
knobbly *UK* ['nɒblɪ], **knobby** *US* ['nɒbɪ] (*compar* -**ier**, *superl* -**iest**) *adj* -**1.** [gen] nodoso(sa) -**2.** [knees] ossudo(da).
knock [nɒk] ◇ *n* -**1.** [blow] pancada *f*, batida *f* -**2.** *inf* [piece of bad luck] azar *m*. ◇ *vt* -**1.** [gen] bater contra; **to ~ one's head on sthg** bater com a cabeça em algo; **to ~ a hole in the wall** abrir um buraco na parede; **to ~ a nail into sthg** pregar um prego em algo -**2.** *inf fig* [criticize] criticar. ◇ *vi* -**1.** [on door]: **to ~ at** *OR* **on sthg** bater em algo -**2.** [car engine] bater.
➤ **knock about, knock around** *inf* ◇ *vt sep* [beat up] tratar com violência. ◇ *vi* -**1.** *inf* [wander about] perambular -**2.** *inf* [spend time]: **to ~ about with sb** perder tempo com alguém.
➤ **knock back** *vt sep inf* -**1.** [drink] enxugar -**2.** *inf* [cost] custar a.
➤ **knock down** *vt sep* -**1.** [subj: car, driver] atropelar -**2.** [building] derrubar -**3.** [price] abater.
➤ **knock off** ◇ *vt sep* -**1.** [lower price by] abaixar -**2.** *UK inf* [steal] abafar -**3.** *vinf* [sleep with] dormir com. ◇ *vi inf* [stop working] parar de trabalhar.
➤ **knock out** *vt sep* -**1.** [make unconscious - subj: person, punch] pôr a nocaute; [- subj: drug] derrubar -**2.** [from competition] eliminar.
➤ **knock over** *vt sep* -**1.** [push over] derrubar -**2.** [in car] atropelar.
➤ **knock up** ◇ *vt sep* [produce hurriedly] preparar apressadamente. ◇ *vi TENNIS* bater bola.
knocker ['nɒkəʳ] *n* [on door] aldrava *f*.

knocking ['nɒkɪŋ] *n* -**1.** *(U)* [noise] pancadas *fpl* -**2.** *inf* [defeat] nocaute *m*; [criticism] crítica *f*.
knock-kneed [-'ni:d] *adj* de pernas tortas.
knock-on effect *n UK* efeito *m* dominó.
knockout ['nɒkaʊt] *n* -**1.** [in boxing] nocaute *m* -**2.** *inf* [sensation]: **she's a real ~** ela é de arrasar.
knockout competition *n UK* competição *f* com eliminatórias.
knock-up *n TENNIS* bate-bola *f*.
knot [nɒt] (*pt & pp* -**ted**, *cont* -**ting**) ◇ *n* -**1.** [gen] nó *m*; **to tie/untie a ~** fazer/desfazer um nó -**2.** [of people] grupo *m*. ◇ *vt* [rope, string] dar um nó em.
knotted *adj* -**1.** [tied in or with a knot] atado(da) com nós, emaranhado(da) -**2.** *phr UK*: **get ~!** *inf* te arranca!
knotty ['nɒtɪ] (*compar* -**ier**, *superl* -**iest**) *adj* [difficult] cabeludo(da).
know [nəʊ] (*pt* knew, *pp* known) ◇ *vt* -**1.** [become acquainted with] conhecer; **to get to ~ sb** conhecer alguém -**2.** [fact, information] saber; **to ~ (that)** saber que; **to get to ~ sthg** saber algo -**3.** [language, skill] ter conhecimento de; **to ~ how to do sthg** saber fazer algo -**4.** [recognize] reconhecer -**5.** [distinguish] diferenciar -**6.** [nickname, call]: **to be known as** ser conhecido(da) como. ◇ *vi* saber; **to ~ of sthg** saber de algo; **to ~ about sthg** [be aware of] saber sobre algo; [be expert in] saber de algo; **you ~** [for emphasis, to add information] você sabe; **there is no ~ing ...** é impossível saber ...; **to ~ sthg backwards** conhecer algo de cor e salteado; **not to ~ when one is well off** não saber a sorte que se tem; **to ~ better** não cair nessa. ◇ *n*: **to be in the ~** estar bem-informado(da) sobre.
know-all *n UK* sabichão *m*, -ona *f*.
know-how *n* experiência *f*, know-how *m*.
knowing ['nəʊɪŋ] *adj* [look, smile] de cumplicidade.
knowingly ['nəʊɪŋlɪ] *adv* -**1.** [look, smile] conscientemente -**2.** [act] de propósito.
know-it-all *n* = **know-all**.
knowledge ['nɒlɪdʒ] *n* conhecimento *m*; **it's common ~ that** é do senso comum que; **to my ~** que eu saiba; **to the best of my ~** até onde eu sei.
knowledgeable ['nɒlɪdʒəbl] *adj* entendido(da).
known [nəʊn] ◇ *pp* ▷ **know**. ◇ *adj* conhecido(da).
knuckle ['nʌkl] *n* -**1.** *ANAT* nó *m (do dedo)* -**2.** [of meat] mocotó *m*.
➤ **knuckle down** *vi*: **to ~ down to sthg/to doing sthg** dedicar-se com afinco a algo/a fazer algo.
➤ **knuckle under** *vi* dar-se por vencido(da).
knuckle-duster *n* soqueira *f* de metal.
KO (*abbr of* knockout) *n* K.O. *m*, nocaute *m*.
koala (bear) [kəʊ'ɑ:lə-] *n* coala *m*.
kohl *n* cosmético usado no Oriente para escurecer as áreas acima e abaixo dos olhos.
kook [ku:k] *n US inf* biruta *mf*.
kooky ['ku:kɪ] (*compar* -**ier**, *superl* -**iest**) *adj US inf* biruta.
Koran [kɒ'rɑ:n] *n*: **the ~** o Alcorão.
Korea [kə'rɪə] *n* Coréia *f*; **in ~** na Coréia.

Korean [kəˈrɪən] ◇ *adj* coreano(na). ◇ *n* **-1.** [person] coreano *m*, -na *f* **-2.** [language] coreano *m*.

kosher [ˈkəʊʃəˈ] *adj* **-1.** [meat] kosher **- 2.** *fig inf* [reputable] limpo(pa), puro(ra).

Kosovan [ˈkɒsəvən], **Kosovar** [ˈkɒsəvɑː(r)] ◇ *adj* kosovar. ◇ *n* kosovar *mf*.

Kosovar Albanian ◇ *adj* albano-kosovar. ◇ *n* albano-kosovar *mf*.

Kosovo [ˈkɒsəvəʊ] *n* Kosovo; **in** ~ em Kosovo.

Koweit *n* = Kuwait; **in** ~ no Kuwait.

kowtow [ˌkaʊˈtaʊ] *vi*: **to** ~ **(to sb)** [behave humbly] humilhar-se (diante de alguém).

Krakow [ˈkrækaʊ] *n* = Cracow; **in** ~ em Cracow.

Kremlin [ˈkremlɪn] *n*: **the** ~ o Kremlin.

KS *abbr of* Kansas.

Kt (*abbr of* Knight) cav.

Kuala Lumpur [ˌkwɑːləˈlʊmpəˈ] *n* Cuala Lumpur; **in** ~ no Cuala Lumpur.

kudos [ˈkjuːdɒs] *n (U)* glória *f*.

Ku Klux Klan [kuːklʌksˈklæn] *n*: **the** ~ a Ku Klux Klan.

kumquat [ˈkʌmkwɒt] *n* árvore cítrica da China.

kung fu [ˌkʌŋˈfuː] *n (U)* kung fu *m*.

Kurd [kɜːd] *n* curdo *m*, -da *f*.

Kurdish [ˈkɜːdɪʃ] *adj* curdo(da).

Kurdistan [kɜːdɪˈstɑːn] *n* Curdistão; **in** ~ no Curdistão.

Kuwait [kjuːˈweɪt] *n* **-1.** [country] Kuwait; **in** ~ no Kuwait **- 2.** [city] Kuwait.

Kuwaiti [kjuːˈweɪtɪ] ◇ *adj* kuwaitiano(na). ◇ *n* kuwaitiano *m*, -na *f*.

kW (*abbr of* kilowatt) Kw.

kWh (*abbr of* kilowatt-hour) kWh.

KY *abbr of* Kentucky.

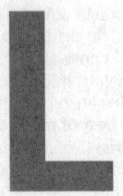

l¹ (*pl* **l's** *OR* **ls**), **L** (*pl* **L's** *OR* **Ls**) [el] *n* [letter] l, L *m*.
➡ **L -1.** (*abbr of* lake) lago *m* **- 2.** (*abbr of* large) G **- 3.** (*abbr of* left) esq. **- 4.** (*abbr of* learner) aprendiz *mf*.
l² (*abbr of* litre) l.

L

Na Grã-Bretanha, a letra L, afixada na traseira de um veículo, indica que seu motorista está aprendendo a dirigir (é um *learner*, ou aprendiz) e, portanto, ainda não possui carteira de motorista.

La *abbr of* Louisiana.

LA ◇ *n abbr of* Los Angeles. ◇ *abbr of* Louisiana.

lab [læb] *n inf* laboratório *m*.

label [ˈleɪbl] (*UK pt* & *pp* **-led**, *cont* **-ling**, *US pt* & *pp* **-ed**, *cont* **-ing**) ◇ *n* **-1.** [identification - on bottle] rótulo *m*; [- on luggage, clothing] etiqueta *f* **- 2.** [of record] selo *m*. ◇ *vt* **-1.** [fix label to - bottle] rotular; [- luggage, clothing] etiquetar **- 2.** [describe] descrever; **to** ~ **sb as sthg** rotular alguém de algo.

labor *etc n US* = labour.

laboratory [*UK* ləˈbɒrətrɪ, *US* ˈlæbrəˌtɔːrɪ] (*pl* **-ies**) ◇ *n* laboratório *m*. ◇ *comp* de laboratório.

Labor Day *n US* Dia *m* do Trabalho.

LABOR DAY

Nos Estados Unidos, o dia do trabalho é comemorado na primeira segunda-feira de setembro. Não há desfiles ou manifestações: a data marca apenas o último feriado prolongado do verão, e muita gente tem o dia livre. Como a maior parte das escolas retoma suas aulas na semana que se segue ao dia do trabalho, a data marca também o fim das férias escolares e o início do ano letivo.

laborious [ləˈbɔːrɪəs] *adj* trabalhoso(sa).

labor union *n US* sindicato *m* (*de trabalhadores*).

labour *UK*, **labor** *US* [ˈleɪbəˈ] ◇ *n* **-1.** [work] trabalho *m*; **manual** ~ trabalho manual; **to withdraw one's** ~ abandonar o trabalho **- 2.** [effort] esforço *m* **- 3.** *(U)* [work force] mão-de-obra *f*; **parts and** ~ peças e mão-de-obra **- 4.** *MED* [giving birth] trabalho *m* de parto; **to go into** ~ entrar em trabalho de parto. ◇ *vt* [insist on] insistir em. ◇ *vi* **-1.** [work] trabalhar **- 2.** [struggle]: **to** ~ **at** *OR* **over sthg** trabalhar em algo; **to** ~ **under a delusion/misapprehension** estar redondamente enganado(da).
➡ **Labour** *UK POL* ◇ *adj* trabalhista. ◇ *n UK* o Partido Trabalhista.

labour camp *n* campo *m* de trabalhos forçados.

labour costs *npl* custos *mpl* com pessoal.

laboured *UK*, **labored** *US* [ˈleɪbəd] *adj* **-1.** [breathing] forçado(da) **- 2.** [style] elaborado(da).

labourer *UK*, **laborer** *US* [ˈleɪbərəˈ] *n* peão *m*.

labour force *n* mão-de-obra *f*.

labour-intensive *adj* que exige muita mão-de-obra.

labour market *n* mercado *m* de trabalho.

labour of love *n* trabalho *m* por amor à arte.

labour pains *npl* dores *fpl* do parto.

Labour Party *n UK*: **the** ~ o Partido Trabalhista.

labour relations *npl* relações *fpl* trabalhistas.

laboursaving *UK*, **laborsaving** *US* [ˈleɪbəˌseɪvɪŋ] *adj*: ~ **device** mecanismo *m* que poupa trabalho.

Labrador [ˈlæbrədɔːˈ] *n* **-1.** [dog] labrador *m* **- 2.** *GEOGR* Labrador.

laburnum *n* laburno *m*.

labyrinth [ˈlæbərɪnθ] *n* labirinto *m*.

lace [leɪs] ◇ *n* **-1.** *(U)* [fabric] renda *f* **- 2.** [shoelace] cadarço *m*. ◇ *comp* de renda. ◇ *vt* **-1.** [shoe, boot] amarrar **- 2.** [drink, food] misturar álcool em.
➡ **lace up** *vt sep* amarrar.

lacemaking [ˈleɪsˌmeɪkɪŋ] *n (U)* fabricação *f* de renda.

laceration [ˌlæsəˈreɪʃn] *n fml* & *MED* laceração *f*.

lace-up ◇ *adj* de cordões. ◇ *n UK* sapato *m* de amarrar.

lack [læk] ◇ *n* falta *f*; **for** *OR* **through ~ of** por falta de; **with no ~ of** sem falta de. ◇ *vt* sentir falta de, carecer de. ◇ *vi*: **you're ~ing in experience** te falta experiência; **to be ~ing** estar faltando.

lackadaisical [,lækə'deɪzɪkl] *adj pej* desinteressado(da), apático(ca).

lackey ['lækɪ] (*pl* -s) *n pej* pau-mandado *m*.

lacklustre *UK*, **lackluster** *US* ['læk,lʌstə'] *adj* sem brilho.

laconic [lə'kɒnɪk] *adj* lacônico(ca).

lacquer ['lækə'] ◇ *n* -1. [for wood, metal] verniz *m* -2. [for hair] fixador *m*. ◇ *vt* -1. [wood, metal] envernizar -2. [hair] aplicar fixador em.

lacrosse [lə'krɒs] *n* (*U*) *jogo canadense semelhante ao hóquei.*

lactic acid ['læktɪk-] *n* ácido *m* láctico.

lacy ['leɪsɪ] (*compar* -ier, *superl* -iest) *adj* rendado(da).

lad [læd] *n inf* -1. [young boy] rapaz *m* -2. [male friend] amigo *m*; **he went out for a drink with the ~ s** ele saiu para beber com a rapazeada -3. *UK* [stable boy] empregado *m* de estábulo.

ladder ['lædə'] ◇ *n* -1. [for climbing] escada *f* de mão -2. *UK* [in tights] defeito *m*. ◇ *vt UK* [tights] puxar fio em. ◇ *vi UK* [tights] puxar fio.

laden ['leɪdn] *adj* carregado(da); **~ with sthg** carregado com algo.

la-di-da [,lɑ:dɪ'dɑ:] *adj inf pej* afetado(da).

ladies *UK* ['leɪdɪz], **ladies room** *US n* senhoras *fpl*, damas *fpl*.

lading ['leɪdɪŋ] *n* ▷ **bill**.

ladle ['leɪdl] ◇ *n* concha *f*. ◇ *vt* servir com concha.

lady ['leɪdɪ] (*pl* -ies) ◇ *n* -1. [woman] senhora *f* -2. [by birth or upbringing] dama *f* -3. *US inf* [used to address woman] senhora *f*. ◇ *comp*: **~ doctor** médica *f*.
  ▬ **Lady** *n* -1. [member of nobility] Lady *f* -2. *RELIG*: **Our Lady** Nossa Senhora.

ladybird *UK* ['leɪdɪbɜːd], **ladybug** *US* ['leɪdɪbʌg] *n* joaninha *f*.

lady-in-waiting [-'weɪtɪŋ] (*pl* ladies-in-waiting) *n* dama *f* de companhia.

lady-killer *n inf* mulherengo *m*, -ga *f*, conquistador *m*, -ra *f*.

ladylike ['leɪdɪlaɪk] *adj* elegante, refinado(da).

Ladyship ['leɪdɪʃɪp] *n*: **her/your ~** Vossa Senhoria.

lag [læg] (*pt & pp* -ged, *cont* -ging) ◇ *n* [in time] atraso *m*, demora *f*. ◇ *vt* revestir com material isolante. ◇ *vi* [move more slowly]: **to ~ (behind)** ficar (para trás).

lager ['lɑːgə'] *n* cerveja *m* tipo Pilsen.

lager lout *n UK* beberrão *m*, -rona *f* jovem.

lagging ['lægɪŋ] *n* (*U*) revestimento *m*.

lagoon [lə'gu:n] *n* lagoa *f*.

Lagos ['leɪgɒs] *n* Lagos; **in ~** em Lagos.

lah-di-dah [,lɑ:dɪ'dɑ:] *adj* = **la-di-da**.

laid [leɪd] *pt & pp* ▷ **lay**.

laid-back *adj inf* descontraído(da).

lain [leɪn] *pp* ▷ **lie**.

lair [leə'] *n* toca *f*.

laissez-faire [,leɪseɪ'feə'] ◇ *adj* do laissez-faire. ◇ *n* (*U*) laissez-faire *m*.

laity ['leɪətɪ] *n RELIG*: **the ~** os laicos.

lake [leɪk] *n GEOGR* lago *m*.

Lake District *n*: **the ~** a Região dos Lagos.

Lake Geneva *n* o Lago de Gênova.

lakeside ['leɪksaɪd] *adj* às margens do lago.

lama (*pl* -s) *n* lama *m*.

lamb [læm] *n* [animal, meat] cordeiro *m*.

lambast [læm'bæst], **lambaste** [læm'beɪst] *vt* criticar severamente.

lamb chop *n* costeleta *f* de cordeiro.

lambing ['læmɪŋ] *n* (*U*) parição *f* (*de ovelhas*).

lambskin ['læmskɪn] *n* pele *f* de cordeiro.

lambswool ['læmzwʊl] ◇ *n* (*U*) lã *f* de cordeiro. ◇ *comp* de lã de cordeiro.

lame [leɪm] *adj* -1. [person, horse] manco(ca) -2. [excuse, argument] pouco convincente.

lamé ['lɑːmeɪ] *n* (*U*) lamê *m*.

lame duck ◇ *adj US fig* [president] em final de mandato. ◇ *n* -1. *fig* [business] fracasso *m* -2. *fig* [person] inútil *mf*.

lamely ['leɪmlɪ] *adv* [unconvincingly] de forma não-convincente.

lament [lə'ment] ◇ *n* lamento *m*. ◇ *vt* lamentar.

lamentable ['læməntəbl] *adj* lamentável.

laminated ['læmɪneɪtɪd] *adj* laminado(da).

lamp [læmp] *n* lâmpada *f*.

lamplight ['læmplaɪt] *n* luz *f* de lâmpada.

lampoon [læm'pu:n] ◇ *n* sátira *f*. ◇ *vt* satirizar.

lamppost ['læmppəʊst] *n* poste *m* de iluminação.

lampshade ['læmpʃeɪd] *n* quebra-luz *m*.

lance [lɑːns] ◇ *n* [spear] lança *f*. ◇ *vt MED* lancetar.

lance corporal *n UK* ≃ cabo *m*.

lancet ['lɑːnsɪt] *n MED* bisturi *m*, lanceta *f*.

land [lænd] ◇ *n* -1. [gen] terra *f* -2. [property, estate] terreno *m* -3. [nation] país *m*. ◇ *vt* -1. [plane] aterrissar -2. [cargo, passengers] desembarcar -3. [fish] recolher -4. *inf* [job, contract] fechar -5. *inf* [put, place]: **to ~ sb in trouble** pôr alguém em apuros; **to ~ sb in jail** fazer com que alguém acabe na cadeia -6. *inf* [encumber]: **to ~ sb with sb/sthg** incomodar alguém com alguém/algo. ◇ *vi* -1. [plane, passenger] aterrissar -2. [fall] cair -3. [from ship] desembarcar.
  ▬ **land up** *vi inf* acabar; **to ~ up in serious debt** acabar com um monte de dívidas; **to ~ up in** *OR* **at** [place] acabar em, ir parar em.

landed gentry ['lændɪd-] *npl* proprietários *mpl* de terra.

landing ['lændɪŋ] *n* -1. [of stairs] patamar *m* -2. [of aeroplane] aterrissagem *f* -3. [of goods from ship] desembarque *m*.

landing card *n* cartão *m* de desembarque.

landing craft *n* navio *m* de desembarque.

landing gear *n* (*U*) trem *m* de aterrissagem.

landing stage *n* cais *m inv* de desembarque.

landing strip *n* pista *f* de aterrissagem.

landlady ['lænd,leɪdɪ] (*pl* -ies) *n* [gen] senhoria *f*; [in guesthouse, pub] proprietária *f*.

landlocked ['lændlɒkt] *adj* cercado(da) de terra.

landlord ['lændlɔ:d] *n* -1. [in lodgings] senhorio *m* -2. [of pub] proprietário *m*.

landmark ['lændmɑ:k] *n* -1. [prominent feature] ponto *m* de referência -2. *fig* [in history] marco *m* divisório.

landmine ['lændmaɪn] *n* mina *f* terrestre.

landowner ['lænd,əʊnəʳ] *n* proprietário *m*, -ria *f* de terras.

landscape ['lændskeɪp] ⟨⟩ *n* paisagem *f*. ⟨⟩ *vt* ajardinar.

landscape gardener *n* paisagista *mf*.

landslide ['lændslaɪd] ⟨⟩ *n* -1. [of earth, rocks] desmoronamento *m* -2. POL vitória *f* esmagadora. ⟨⟩ *comp* POL esmagador(ra).

landslip ['lændslɪp] *n* deslizamento *m* de terra.

lane [leɪn] *n* -1. [road - in country] senda *f*; [- in town, village] ruela *f* -2. [division of road] pista *f*, faixa *f*; 'get/keep in ~' 'entrar/manter-se na pista' -3. [in swimming pool, on racetrack] raia *f* -4. [for shipping, aircraft] pista *f*.

langoustine *n* lagostim *m*.

language ['læŋgwɪdʒ] *n* -1. [spoken, foreign] língua *f* -2. [style, mode of communication] linguagem *f*.

language laboratory *n* laboratório *m* de línguas.

languid ['læŋgwɪd] *adj* lânguido(da).

languish ['læŋgwɪʃ] *vi* -1. [suffer] sofrer -2. [become weak] debilitar-se.

languorous ['læŋgərəs] *adj literary* langoroso(sa).

lank [læŋk] *adj* liso(sa).

lanky ['læŋkɪ] (*compar* -ier, *superl* -iest) *adj* magricela.

lanolin(e) ['lænəlɪn] *n (U)* lanolina *f*.

lantern ['læntən] *n* lanterna *f*.

Laos [laʊs] *n* Laos; **in** ~ em Laos.

Laotian ['laʊʃən] ⟨⟩ *adj* laosiano(na). ⟨⟩ *n* -1. [person] laosiano *m*, -na *f* -2. [language] laosiano *m*.

lap [læp] (*pt* & *pp* -ped, *cont* -ping) ⟨⟩ *n* -1. [knees] colo *m* -2. SPORT volta *f*. ⟨⟩ *vt* -1. [subj: animal] lamber -2. SPORT [runner, car] estar uma volta à frente de. ⟨⟩ *vi* [water, waves] marulhar.

➡ **lap up** *vt sep* -1. [drink] beber com volúpia -2. *fig* [compliments, lies, information] receber com impaciência.

laparoscopy [,læpə'rɒskəpɪ] (*pl* -ies) *n* laparoscopia *f*.

La Paz [læ'pæz] *n* La Paz; **in** ~ em La Paz.

lapdog ['læpdɒg] *n* [dog] cão *m* de estimação.

lapel [lə'pel] *n* lapela *f*.

Lapland ['læplænd] *n* Lapônia; **in** ~ na Lapônia.

Lapp [læp] ⟨⟩ *adj* lapão(ona). ⟨⟩ *n* -1. [person] lapão *m*, -ona *f* -2. [language] lapão *m*.

lapse [læps] ⟨⟩ *n* -1. [failing] lapso *m* -2. [in behaviour] deslize *m* -3. [of time] intervalo *m*. ⟨⟩ *vi* -1. [custom, licence] caducar -2. [passport] expirar -3. [law] prescrever -4. [deteriorate] decair -5. [subj: person]: **to** ~ **into** [coma] entrar em; [silence, dialect] mergulhar em; [bad habits] adquirir.

lapsed [læpst] *adj* descrente.

lap-top (computer) *n* (computador *m*) laptop *m*.

larceny ['lɑ:sənɪ] *n (U)* furto *m*.

larch [lɑ:tʃ] *n* larício *m*.

lard [lɑ:d] *n (U)* toicinho *m*, banha *f* (*de porco*).

larder ['lɑ:dəʳ] *n* despensa *f*.

large [lɑ:dʒ] *adj* grande.

➡ **at large** *adj* [escaped prisoner, animal] em liberdade. ⟨⟩ *adv* [as a whole] em geral.

largely ['lɑ:dʒlɪ] *adv* em grande parte.

larger-than-life ['lɑ:dʒəʳ-l] *adj* exagerado(da).

large-scale *adj* -1. [wide-ranging] de grande escala -2. [map, diagram] em grande escala.

largesse, largess *US* [lɑ:'dʒes] *n (U)* grandeza *f*.

lark [lɑ:k] *n* -1. [bird] cotovia *f* -2. *inf* [joke] brincadeira *f*; **for a** ~ de brincadeira.

➡ **lark about** *vi* fazer palhaçadas.

larva ['lɑ:və] (*pl* -vae [-vi:]) *n* larva *f*.

laryngitis [,lærɪn'dʒaɪtɪs] *n (U)* laringite *f*.

larynx ['lærɪŋks] (*pl* -es) *n* laringe *f*.

lasagna, lasagne [lə'zænjə] *n (U)* lasanha *f*.

lascivious [lə'sɪvɪəs] *adj* lascivo(va).

laser ['leɪzəʳ] *n* laser *m*.

laser beam *n* raio *m* laser.

laser printer *n* impressora *f* a laser.

laser show *n* show *m* com laser.

lash [læʃ] ⟨⟩ *n* -1. [eyelash] cílio *m* -2. [part of whip] chicote *m* -3. [blow with whip] chicotada *f*. ⟨⟩ *vt* -1. [whip] chicotear -2. [subj: wind, rain, waves] fustigar -3. [tie] atar; **to** ~ **sthg to sthg** atar algo em algo.

➡ **lash out** *vi* -1. [physically]: **to** ~ **out (at** OR **against sb)** atacar alguém com extrema violência -2. [verbally]: **to** ~ **out (at** OR **against sb)** atacar alguém verbalmente -3. *UK inf* [spend money]: **to** ~ **out (on sthg)** esbanjar dinheiro (em algo).

lass [læs] *n* [girl] moça *f*.

lasso [læ'su:] (*pl* -s, *pt* & *pp* -ed, *cont* -ing) ⟨⟩ *n* laço *m*. ⟨⟩ *vt* laçar.

last [lɑ:st] ⟨⟩ *adj* -1. [gen] último(ma); ~ **but one** penúltimo(ma); ~ **but two** antepenúltimo(ma) -2. [with dates, time of day] último(ma), passado(da); ~ **week** na semana passada, na última semana; ~ **year** no ano passado -3. [least likely]: **you're the** ~ **person I expected to see** você é a última pessoa que eu esperava ver. ⟨⟩ *adv* -1. [in final place] em último lugar -2. [most recently]: **when did you** ~ **visit them?** quando você os visitou pela última vez?; **at** ~ finalmente; **at** ~! até que enfim! ⟨⟩ *pron* o último, a última; **to leave sthg till** ~ deixar algo para o fim; **the week before** ~ na semana retrasada; **the day before** ~ anteontem. ⟨⟩ *n* [final thing]: **the** ~ **I saw/heard of him** a última coisa que eu soube dele. ⟨⟩ *vi* -1. [gen] durar; **they only had food to** ~ **another week** eles só tinham comida para mais uma semana -2. [survive] sobreviver.

➡ **at (long) last** *adv* por fim.

last-ditch *adj* derradeiro(ra).

lasting ['lɑ:stɪŋ] *adj* duradouro(ra).

lastly ['lɑ:stlɪ] *adv* -1. [to conclude] por fim -2. [at the end] finalmente.

last-minute *adj* de última hora.

last name *n* sobrenome *m*.

last post *n* -1. [postal collection] última coleta *f* -2. MIL toque *m* de recolher.

last rites *npl* últimos sacramentos *mpl*.
last straw *n*: it was the ~ foi a gota d'água.
Last Supper *n*: the ~ a Última Ceia.
last word *n*: to have the ~ ter a palavra final.
Las Vegas *n* Las Vegas; **in** ~ em Las Vegas.
lat. (*abbr of* **latitude**) lat.
latch [lætʃ] *n* trinco *m*; **on the** ~ fechado(da) com o trinco.
◆ **latch onto** *vt fus inf* agarrar-se a.
latchkey ['lætʃki:] (*pl* -s) ◇ *adj* [child] que fica sozinho(nha) em casa. ◇ *n* tranca *f (para porta exterior)*.
late [leɪt] ◇ *adj* -1. [delayed] atrasado(da); **to be ~ for sthg** estar atrasado(da) para algo -2. [later than normal] tarde -3. [near end of]: **in ~ December** no final de dezembro -4. [dead] falecido(da). ◇ *adv* [not on time] tarde; **he arrived 20 minutes ~** ele chegou 20 minutos atrasado; ~ **in December** no final de dezembro; **to work ~** trabalhar até tarde.
◆ **of late** *adv* recentemente.
latecomer ['leɪtˌkʌmə'] *n* retardatário *m*, -ria *f*.
lately ['leɪtlɪ] *adv* ultimamente.
lateness ['leɪtnɪs] *n* -1. [of person, train] atraso *m* -2. [of meeting, event] hora *f* avançada.
late-night *adj* noturno(na), da noite; ~ **opening** aberto(ta) até tarde da noite.
latent ['leɪtənt] *adj* latente.
later ['leɪtə'] ◇ *adj* -1. [last, final] último(ma) -2. [subsequent, following] posterior -3. [train, bus, boat] que sai mais tarde. ◇ *adv* [at a later time]: ~ **(on)** mais tarde.
lateral ['lætərəl] *adj* lateral.
latest ['leɪtɪst] ◇ *adj* [most recent] último(ma). ◇ *n*: **at the** ~ no mais tardar.
latex ['leɪteks] ◇ *n (U)* látex *m inv*. ◇ *comp* de látex.
lath [lɑ:θ] *n* ripa *f*, sarrafo *m*.
lathe [leɪð] *n* torno *m* mecânico.
lather ['lɑ:ðə'] ◇ *n* espuma *f*. ◇ *vt* ensaboar. ◇ *vi* fazer espuma.
Latin ['lætɪn] ◇ *adj* latino(na). ◇ *n* [language] latim *m*.
Latin America *n* América Latina; **in** ~ na América Latina.
Latin American ◇ *adj* latino-americano(na). ◇ *n* [person] latino-americano *m*, -na *f*.
latitude ['lætɪtju:d] *n* -1. GEOGR latitude *f* -2. *fml* [freedom] liberdade *f (de expressão)*.
latrine [lə'tri:n] *n* latrina *f*.
latter ['lætə'] ◇ *adj* -1. [later] último(ma) -2. [second] segundo(da). ◇ *n*: **the** ~ o último, a última; **we prefer the** ~ **house to the former** preferimos esta casa àquela.
latter-day *adj* contemporâneo(nea).
latterly ['lætəlɪ] *adv* recentemente.
lattice ['lætɪs] *n* [fence, frame] treliça *f*.
lattice window *n* janela *f* de treliça.
Latvia ['lætvɪə] *n* Letônia *f*; **in** ~ na Letônia.
Latvian ['lætvɪən] ◇ *adj* letão(ona). ◇ *n* -1. [person] letão *m*, -ona *f* -2. [language] letão *m*.
laudable ['lɔ:dəbl] *adj* louvável.
laugh [lɑ:f] ◇ *n* -1. [sound] riso *m*, risada *f*; **to**

have the last ~ rir por último -2. *inf* [fun, joke] piada *f*; **to do sthg for** ~ **s** OR **a** ~ fazer algo por prazer. ◇ *vi* rir, gargalhar.
◆ **laugh at** *vt fus* [mock] rir-se de, gozar com.
◆ **laugh off** *vt sep* [dismiss] disfarçar com um sorriso.
laughable ['lɑ:fəbl] *adj pej* [absurd] risível.
laughing gas ['lɑ:fɪŋ-] *n (U)* gás *m* hilariante.
laughingstock *n* motivo *m* de riso.
laughter ['lɑ:ftə'] *n (U)* risada *f*, risos *mpl*.
launch [lɔ:ntʃ] ◇ *n* -1. [gen] lançamento *m* -2. [start, initiation] início *m*. ◇ *vt* -1. [gen] lançar -2. [start, initiate] iniciar.
◆ **launch into** *vt fus* -1. [attack, fight] empreender -2. [lecture, explanation] proferir.
launching ['lɔ:ntʃɪŋ] *n* lançamento *m*.
launch(ing) pad ['lɔ:ntʃ(ɪŋ)-] *n* [for rocket, missile, satellite] plataforma *f* de lançamento.
launder ['lɔ:ndə'] *vt* -1. [clothes] lavar e passar -2. *inf* [money] lavar.
laund(e)rette [lɔ:n'dret], **Laundromat**® US ['lɔ:ndrəmæt] *n* lavanderia *f* automatizada.
laundry ['lɔ:ndrɪ] (*pl* -ies) *n* -1. *(U)* [clothes - about to be washed] roupa *f* suja; [- newly washed] roupa *f* lavada -2. [room, business] lavanderia *f*.
laundry basket *n* cesto *m* de roupa suja.
laureate ['lɔ:rɪət] *n* ▷ **poet laureate**.
laurel *n* louro *m*.
◆ **laurels** *npl*: **to rest on one's** ~ **s** deitar na própria fama.
lava ['lɑ:və] *n (U)* lava *f*.
lavatory ['lævətrɪ] (*pl* -ies) *n* -1. [receptacle] privada *f* -2. [room] toalete *f*.
lavatory paper *n UK* papel *m* higiênico.
lavender ['lævəndə'] ◇ *adj* [colour] da cor da alfazema. ◇ *n* -1. [plant] alfazema *f*, lavanda *f* -2. [colour] lavanda *f*.
lavish ['lævɪʃ] ◇ *adj* -1. [generous] generoso(sa); **to be** ~ **with sthg** ser generoso(sa) com algo -2. [sumptuous] suntuoso(sa). ◇ *vt*: **to** ~ **sthg on sb/sthg** encher alguém/algo de algo.
lavishly ['lævɪʃlɪ] *adv* -1. [generously] generosamente -2. [sumptuously] suntuosamente.
law [lɔ:] *n* -1. [gen] lei *f*; **to break the** ~ transgredir a lei; **against the** ~ contra a lei; ~ **and order** lei e ordem; **the** ~ **of the jungle** a lei da selva -2. [system, subject] direito *m* -3. *(U) inf* [police]: **the** ~ a lei -4. *phr*: **to lay down the** ~ *pej* ditar as ordens. ◇ *comp* de direito.
law-abiding [-əˌbaɪdɪŋ] *adj* obediente à lei.
law-breaker *n* infrator *m*, -ra *f* da lei.
law court *n* tribunal *m* de justiça.
lawful ['lɔ:fʊl] *adj fml* lícito(ta).
lawfully ['lɔ:fʊlɪ] *adv fml* licitamente.
lawless ['lɔ:lɪs] *adj* -1. *fml* [illegal] ilegal -2. [without laws] sem lei -3. [person] indisciplinado(da).
Law Lords *npl UK* JUR: **the** ~ ≃ o Supremo Tribunal Federal.
lawmaker ['lɔ:ˌmeɪkə'] *n* legislador *m*, -ra *f*.
lawn [lɔ:n] *n* [grass] gramado *m*.
lawnmower ['lɔ:nˌməʊə'] *n* cortador *m* de grama.
lawn party *n US* recepção *f* ao ar livre.
lawn tennis *n* tênis *m inv* de gramado.

law school n escola f de direito.
lawsuit ['lɔːsuːt] n ação f judicial.
lawyer ['lɔːjəʳ] n advogado m, -da f.
lax [læks] adj negligente.
laxative ['læksətɪv] n laxante m.
laxity ['læksətɪ], **laxness** ['læksnɪs] n (U) negligência f.
lay [leɪ] (pt & pp laid) ⇔ pt ⊳lie. ⇔ vt -1. [in specified position] colocar - 2. [prepare - trap, snare] armar; [- plans] traçar; **to ~ the table** pôr a mesa - 3. [bricks] assentar; [carpet] colocar; [cable] afixar; [pipes, foundations] preparar - 4. [egg] pôr - 5. [blame, emphasis] aplicar. ⇔ adj -1. RELIG leigo(ga) - 2. [untrained, unqualified] desqualificado(da).
➡ **lay aside** vt sep -1. [save] poupar - 2. [put down, abandon] abandonar.
➡ **lay before** vt sep [present] apresentar.
➡ **lay down** vt sep -1. [formulate] formular - 2. [put down] depor.
➡ **lay into** vt fus inf [attack - physically] surrar; [- verbally] dar uma bronca em.
➡ **lay off** ⇔ vt sep [make redundant] dispensar. ⇔ vt fus inf -1. [leave alone] deixar sozinho(nha) - 2. [stop, give up] parar de.
➡ **lay on** vt sep UK [provide, supply] providenciar.
➡ **lay out** vt sep -1. [arrange, spread out] dispor - 2. [plan, design] projetar.
➡ **lay over** vi US pernoitar.
layabout ['leɪəbaʊt] n UK inf vadio m, -dia f.
lay-by (pl -s) n UK acostamento m.
lay days npl prazo estipulado para carga e descarga de um navio.
layer ['leɪəʳ] n -1. [of substance, material] camada f - 2. fig [level] nível m.
layette [leɪˈet] n enxoval m do bebê.
layman ['leɪmən] (pl -men [-mən]) n leigo m; **in ~'s terms** em termos gerais.
lay-off n [redundancy] demissão f.
layout ['leɪaʊt] n [design] leiaute m.
layover ['leɪəʊvəʳ] n US parada f (durante uma viagem).
laze [leɪz] vi: **to ~** (about OR around) vadiar.
lazily ['leɪzɪlɪ] adv [without effort] preguiçosamente.
laziness ['leɪzɪnɪs] n [idleness] preguiça f.
lazy ['leɪzɪ] (compar -ier, superl -iest) adj -1. [person] preguiçoso(sa) - 2. [action] ocioso(sa).
lazybones ['leɪzɪbəʊnz] (pl inv) n inf preguiçoso m, -sa f.
lb abbr of pound.
lbw (abbr of leg before wicket) proteção ilegal do gol com a perna no jogo de cricket.
l.c. (abbr of lower case) caixa-baixa f.
L/C (abbr of letter of credit) carta f de crédito.
LCD (abbr of liquid crystal display) n tela f de cristal líquido, LCD m.
Ld (abbr of Lord) Lorde.
L-driver (abbr of learner driver) n UK ≃ auto-escola f (indicação no veículo).
LDS (abbr of Licentiate in Dental Surgery) n (titular de) graduação em odontologia na Grã-Bretanha.
LEA (abbr of local education authority) n órgão responsável pela educação numa área da Grã-Bretanha.

lead¹ [liːd] (pt & pp led) ⇔ n -1. (U) [winning position] dianteira f; **to be in** OR **have the ~** estar na frente - 2. [amount ahead] vantagem f - 3. (U) [initiative, example] exemplo m; **to take the ~** [do sthg first] tomar a iniciativa - 4. (U) [most important role]: **the ~** o papel principal - 5. [clue] pista f - 6. [for dog] correia f - 7. [wire, cable] fio m. ⇔ adj [most important] principal. ⇔ vt -1. [be in front of] dirigir - 2. [take, guide] conduzir - 3. [head, be in charge of] chefiar, comandar - 4. [organize] organizar; **to ~ the way** assumir a direção - 5. [life, existence] reger - 6. [cause, influence]: **to ~ sb to do sthg** induzir alguém a fazer algo. ⇔ vi -1. [go] levar - 2. [give access to]: **that door ~s to the kitchen** aquela porta dá para a cozinha - 3. [be winning] estar na frente - 4. [result in]: **to ~ to sthg** resultar em algo.
➡ **lead off** ⇔ vt fus [subj: door, room] começar a partir de. ⇔ vi -1. [road, corridor]: **to ~ off (from)** começar (a partir de) - 2. [begin] começar.
➡ **lead up to** vt fus -1. [precede] conduzir a - 2. [in conversation] levar a.
lead² [led] ⇔ n -1. (U) [metal] chumbo m - 2. [in pencil] grafite m. ⇔ comp [made of or with lead] de chumbo.
leaded ['ledɪd] adj -1. [petrol] com chumbo - 2. [window] com almofada de vidro.
leaden ['ledn] adj -1. literary [dark grey] plúmbeo(bea) - 2. literary [heavy] soturno(na) - 3. [very dull] moroso(sa).
leader ['liːdəʳ] n -1. [gen] líder mf - 2. UK [in newspaper] editorial m.
leadership ['liːdəʃɪp] n -1. [people in charge]: **the ~** a liderança - 2. [position of leader] liderança f.
lead-free [led-] adj sem chumbo.
leading ['liːdɪŋ] adj -1. [prominent] destacado(da) - 2. [main, principal]: **to play the ~ part** OR **role in sthg** lit & fig desempenhar o papel principal em algo - 3. SPORT [at front] primeiro(ra).
leading article n UK editorial m.
leading lady n atriz f principal, protagonista f.
leading light n figura f central.
leading man n ator m principal.
leading question n pergunta f com resposta induzida.
lead pencil [led-] n lápis m inv de grafita.
lead poisoning [led-] n saturnismo m.
lead time [liːd-] n COMM prazo m de entrega.
leaf [liːf] (pl leaves) n -1. [gen] folha f - 2. [of table] aba f.
➡ **leaf through** vt fus folhear.
leaflet ['liːflɪt] ⇔ n folder m, folheto m. ⇔ vt distribuir folhetos em.
leafy ['liːfɪ] (compar -ier, superl -iest) adj -1. [with many leaves] frondoso(sa) - 2. [with many trees] arborizado(da).
league [liːg] n liga f; **to be in ~ with sb** [work with] estar confabulado(da) com alguém.
league table n tabela f de classificação da liga.
leak [liːk] ⇔ n -1. [gen] vazamento m; **a ~ in the roof** uma goteira - 2. fig [disclosure] vazamento m (de informações). ⇔ vt [make known] vazar. ⇔ vi -1. [gen] vazar; [boat, shoe]: **to be ~ing** estar com infiltração - 2. [roof] ter goteiras.

➡ **leak out** *vi* [gen] vazar; **to ~ (out) from sthg** vazar de dentro de algo.

leakage ['li:kɪdʒ] *n* vazamento *m*.

leaky ['li:kɪ] (*compar* -**ier**, *superl* -**iest**) *adj* com furos; **a ~ roof** um teto com goteiras.

lean [li:n] (*pt* & *pp* **leant** *OR* -**ed**) ◇ *adj* -**1.** [gen] magro(gra) -**2.** *fig* [harvest, year] improdutivo(va). ◇ *vt* [support, prop]: **to ~ sthg against sthg** apoiar algo contra algo. ◇ *vi* -**1.** [bend, slope] inclinar-se -**2.** [rest]: **to ~ on/against sthg** apoiar-se em/contra algo.

➡ **lean back** *vi* [person] recostar-se.

leaning ['li:nɪŋ] *n*: **~ (towards sthg)** inclinação *f* (para algo).

leant [lent] *pt* & *pp* ▷ **lean**.

lean-to (*pl* -**s**) *n* alpendre *m*.

leap [li:p] (*pt* & *pp* **leapt** *OR* -**ed**) ◇ *n* -**1.** [jump] salto *m*, pulo *m* -**2.** [increase] pulo *m*; **in ~s and bounds** com extrema rapidez. ◇ *vi* -**1.** [jump] saltar, pular -**2.** [increase] disparar; **to ~ to the eye** saltar aos olhos.

➡ **leap at** *vt fus fig* não deixar escapar.

leapfrog ['li:pfrɒg] (*pt* & *pp* -**ged**, *cont* -**ging**) ◇ *n* (*U*) jogo *m* de pular carniça; **to play ~** brincar de pular carniça. ◇ *vi* -**1.** [jump]: **to ~ over sthg** saltar por cima de algo -**2.** *fig* aproveitar-se de.

leapt [lept] *pt* & *pp* ▷ **leap**.

leap year *n* ano *m* bissexto.

learn [lɜ:n] (*pt* & *pp* -**ed** *OR* **learnt**) ◇ *vt* -**1.** [gen] aprender; **to ~ (how) to do sthg** aprender a fazer algo -**2.** [hear] ouvir; **to ~ that** ficar sabendo que. ◇ *vi* -**1.** [acquire knowledge, skill] aprender -**2.** [hear]: **to ~ of** *OR* **about sthg** ficar sabendo de algo.

learned ['lɜ:nɪd] *adj* -**1.** [person] culto(ta), erudito(-ta) -**2.** [journal, paper, book] erudito(ta).

learner ['lɜ:nə'] *n* aprendiz *mf*.

learner (driver) *n* aprendiz *mf* de direção.

learning ['lɜ:nɪŋ] *n* -**1.** [knowledge] erudição *f* -**2.** [study] aprendizagem *f*.

learning curve *n* curva *f* de aprendizagem.

learnt [lɜ:nt] *pt* & *pp* ▷ **learn**.

lease [li:s] ◇ *n* JUR arrendamento *m*, contrato *m* de locação; **to give sb a new ~ of life** UK, **to give a new ~ on life** to *sb* US dar uma nova vida a alguém. ◇ *vt* [premises] arrendar, alugar; **to ~ sthg from/to sb** arrendar algo de/para alguém; [car] fazer um leasing.

leaseback ['li:sbæk] *n* contrato pelo qual o comprador aluga a propriedade comprada ao ex-proprietário.

leasehold ['li:shəʊld] ◇ *adj* arrendado(da). ◇ *adv* em arrendamento.

leaseholder ['li:s,həʊldə'] *n* arrendatário *m*, -ria *f*.

leash [li:ʃ] *n* [for dog] coleira *f*.

least [li:st] ◇ *adj* (*superl of little*) [smallest in amount, degree]: **the ~** o (a) menor; **he earns the ~ money of all** de todos ele é o que ganha menos. ◇ *pron* (*superl of little*) [smallest amount]: **the ~** o mínimo; **it's the ~ we'll have to spend** é o mínimo que teremos de gastar; **that's the ~ of my worries!** essa é a menor das minhas preocupações!; **it's the ~ (that) he can do** é o mínimo que ele podia fazer; **not in the ~** em absoluto, de modo algum;

to say the ~ para não dizer outra coisa. ◇ *adv* [to the smallest amount, degree] menos; **to aim for the ~ possible expenditure** desejar alcançar o menor gasto possível.

➡ **at least** *adv* -**1.** [gen] pelo menos, no mínimo -**2.** [qualifying sthg one has said] pelo menos.

➡ **least of all** *adv* muito menos.

➡ **not least** *adv* *fml* em especial.

leather ['leðə'] ◇ *n* (*U*) couro *m*. ◇ *comp* de couro.

➡ **leathers** *npl* [of motorbike rider] roupas *fpl* de couro.

leatherette [,leðə'ret] *n* (*U*) couro *m* sintético.

leave [li:v] (*pt* & *pp* **left**) ◇ *n* -**1.** [time off] licença *f*; **to be on ~** estar de licença -**2.** *fml* [permission] licença *f*, permissão *f*. ◇ *vt* -**1.** [gen] deixar; **~ me alone!** me deixa em paz!; **it ~s me cold** isso me deixa indiferente; **it ~s a lot to be desired** isso deixa muito a desejar -**2.** [depart from] sair de -**3.** [entrust]: **to ~ it to sb to do sthg** deixar que alguém faça algo; **to ~ sthg/with sb** deixar algo com alguém; **~ it with me!** deixa (isso) comigo!; **to ~ sb sthg**, **to ~ sthg to sb** deixar algo para alguém -**4.** [husband, wife] deixar, largar. ◇ *vi* -**1.** [gen] partir, ir embora -**2.** [end relationship] ir embora.

➡ **leave behind** *vt sep* -**1.** [abandon] abandonar -**2.** [forget] esquecer.

➡ **leave off** ◇ *vt sep* -**1.** [omit] deixar fora, não incluir -**2.** [stop] parar de; **to ~ off doing sthg** parar de fazer algo; **~ off!** *inf* corta essa! ◇ *vi* [stop] deixar; **to carry on from where one left off** continuar de onde se havia parado.

➡ **leave out** *vt sep* [omit] excluir, deixar de fora; **to feel left out** sentir-se ignorado(da).

leave of absence *n* licença *f*.

leaves [li:vz] *pl* ▷ **leaf**.

Lebanese [,lebə'ni:z] (*pl inv*) ◇ *adj* libanês(esa). ◇ *n* [person] libanês *m*, -esa *f*.

Lebanon ['lebənən] *n* Líbano *m*; **in (the) ~** no Líbano.

lecherous ['letʃərəs] *adj* lascivo(va).

lechery ['letʃərɪ] *n* (*U*) lascívia *f*.

lectern ['lektən] *n* atril *m*.

lecture ['lektʃə'] ◇ *n* -**1.** [talk - at university] aula *f*; [- at conference] palestra *f*, conferência *f*; **to give a ~ (on sthg)** dar uma palestra (sobre algo) -**2.** [criticism, reprimand] sermão *m*. ◇ *vt* [scold] dar um sermão em. ◇ *vi* [university]: **to ~ (on/in sthg)** dar uma aula (sobre algo); [at conference] dar uma palestra (sobre algo).

lecture hall *n* [in conference centre] -**1.** sala *f* de conferências -**2.** [in university] sala *f* de aula.

lecturer ['lektʃərə'] *n* -**1.** [teacher] professor *m*, -ra *f* -**2.** [speaker] palestrante *mf*, conferencista *mf*.

lecture theatre *n* anfiteatro *m*.

led [led] *pt* & *pp* ▷ **lead** [^1].

LED (*abbr of* **light-emitting diode**) *n* LED *m*.

ledge [ledʒ] *n* -**1.** [of window] parapeito *m* -**2.** [of mountain] saliência *f*.

ledger ['ledʒə'] *n* livro *m* contábil.

lee [li:] *n* [shelter]: **in the ~ of sthg** ao abrigo de algo.

leech [li:tʃ] *n* -**1.** [creature] sanguessuga *f* -**2.**

fig & pej [person] sanguessuga *f.*

leek [li:k] *n* alho-poró *m.*

leer [lɪəʳ] ◇ *n* olhar *m* malicioso. ◇ *vi*: **to ~ at sb** olhar maliciosamente para alguém.

Leeward Islands [ˈli:wəd-] *npl*: **the ~** as Ilhas de Sotavento.

leeway [ˈli:weɪ] *n* (U) **-1.** [room to manoeuvre] liberdade *f* de ação **-2.** [time lost]: **to make up ~** recuperar o tempo perdido.

left [left] ◇ *pt* & *pp* ▷ **leave.** ◇ *adj* **-1.** [remaining] sobrando; **do you have any money ~?** tem algum dinheiro sobrando?; **to be ~** sobrar; **there's no milk ~** não sobrou leite **-2.** [side, hand, foot] esquerdo(da). ◇ *adv* para a esquerda. ◇ *n* (U) [direction]: **on/to the ~** à esquerda; **keep ~** mantenha-se à esquerda.
➡ **Left** *n* POL: **the Left** a esquerda.

left-hand *adj* esquerdo(da); **~ side** lado *m* esquerdo.

left-hand drive ◇ *adj* com direção do lado esquerdo. ◇ *n* veículo *m* com direção do lado esquerdo.

left-handed [-ˈhændɪd] ◇ *adj* **-1.** [person] canhoto(ta) **-2.** [implement] para canhotos **-3.** US [compliment] com duplo sentido. ◇ *adv* com a (mão) esquerda.

left-hander [-ˈhændəʳ] *n* canhoto *m*, -ta *f.*

Leftist POL ◇ *adj* esquerdista, de esquerda. ◇ *n* esquerdista *mf.*

left luggage (office) *n* UK guarda-bagagem *m.*

leftover [ˈleftəʊvəʳ] *adj* restante.
➡ **leftovers** *npl* sobras *fpl.*

left wing *n* POL esquerda *f.*
➡ **left-wing** *adj* POL esquerdista, de esquerda.

left-winger *n* POL esquerdista *mf.*

lefty [ˈleftɪ] (*pl* -ies) *n* **-1.** UK *inf pej* & POL esquerdista *mf* **-2.** US [left-handed person] canhoto *m*, -ta *f.*

leg [leg] *n* **-1.** [gen] perna *f*; **to be on one's last ~s** estar nas últimas; **you don't have a ~ to stand on** você não tem em que se basear; **to pull sb's ~** pegar no pé de alguém; [of animal, bird, insect] pata *f* **-2.** [CULIN - of chicken] coxa *f*; [- of frog, lamb] perna *f*; [- of pork] pernil *m* **-3.** [of journey, tournament] etapa *f.*

legacy [ˈlegəsɪ] (*pl* -ies) *n* **-1.** [gift of money] legado *m* **-2.** *fig* [consequence] herança *f.*

legal [ˈli:gl] *adj* **-1.** [concerning the law] jurídico(ca) **-2.** [lawful] legal.

legal action *n* ação *f* legal; **to take ~ against sb** iniciar uma ação legal contra alguém.

legal aid *n* (U) auxílio *m* oficial de um advogado.

legality [li:ˈgælətɪ] *n* (U) legalidade *f.*

legalize, -ise [ˈli:gəlaɪz] *vt* legalizar.

legally [ˈli:gəlɪ] *adv* legalmente; **~ binding** com força da lei.

legal tender *n* (U) moeda *f* corrente.

legation [lɪˈgeɪʃn] *n* legação *f.*

legend [ˈledʒənd] *n* **-1.** [myth] lenda *f* **-2.** *fig* [person] lenda *f.*

legendary [ˈledʒəndrɪ] *adj* lendário(ria).

leggings [ˈlegɪŋz] *npl* calças *fpl* stretch.

leggy [ˈlegɪ] (*compar* -ier, *superl* -iest) *adj* **-1.** [person] de pernas compridas e bonitas **-2.** [plant] de longo caule.

legible [ˈledʒəbl] *adj* legível.

legibly [ˈledʒəblɪ] *adv* de forma legível.

legion [ˈli:dʒən] ◇ *adj fml*: **to be ~** ser inumerável. ◇ *n* **-1.** MIL legião *f* **-2.** *fig* [large number] legião *f.*

legionnaire's disease [ˌli:dʒəˈneəz-] *n* (U) doença *f* do legionário, *doença muito rara semelhante à pneumonia.*

legislate [ˈledʒɪsleɪt] *vi* legislar, elaborar leis; **to ~ for/against sthg** elaborar leis a favor de/contra algo.

legislation [ˌledʒɪsˈleɪʃn] *n* (U) legislação *f.*

legislative [ˈledʒɪslətɪv] *adj* legislativo(va).

legislator [ˈledʒɪsleɪtəʳ] *n* legislador *m*, -ra *f.*

legislature [ˈledʒɪsleɪtʃəʳ] *n* legislatura *f.*

legitimacy [lɪˈdʒɪtɪməsɪ] *n* legitimidade *f.*

legitimate [lɪˈdʒɪtɪmət] *adj* legítimo(ma).

legitimately [lɪˈdʒɪtɪmətlɪ] *adv* legitimamente.

legitimize, -ise [lɪˈdʒɪtəmaɪz] *vt* [make legal] legitimar.

legless [ˈleglɪs] *adj* UK *inf* [drunk] bêbado(da) como um gambá.

legroom [ˈlegrʊm] *n* (U) espaço *m* para as pernas.

leg-warmers [-ˌwɔ:məz] *npl* polainas *fpl.*

legwork [ˈlegwɜ:k] *n* (U): **to do the ~** fazer o trabalho de campo.

leisure [UK ˈleʒəʳ, US ˈli:ʒəʳ] *n* (U) lazer *m*; **do it at (your) ~** faça quando puder.

leisure centre *n* centro *m* de lazer.

leisurely [UK ˈleʒəlɪ, US ˈli:ʒərlɪ] ◇ *adj* calmo(ma). ◇ *adv* calmamente.

leisure time *n* (tempo *m* de) lazer *m.*

lemming [ˈlemɪŋ] *n* **-1.** [animal] lemingue *m* **-2.** *fig* [person] marionete *f.*

lemon [ˈlemən] *n* [fruit] limão *m.*

lemonade [ˌleməˈneɪd] *n* **-1.** UK [fizzy] soda *f* limonada **-2.** [made with fresh lemons] limonada *f.*

lemon curd *n* (U) UK *espécie de geléia ou creme feito com suco de limão, açúcar, ovos e manteiga.*

lemon juice *n* suco *m* de limão.

lemon sole *n* solha-limão *m.*

lemon squash *n* UK suco *m* de limão.

lemon squeezer [-ˈskwi:zəʳ] *n* espremedor *m* de limão.

lemon tea *n* chá *m* com limão.

lend [lend] (*pt* & *pp* lent) *vt* **-1.** [money, book] emprestar; **to ~ sb sthg, to ~ sthg to sb** emprestar algo para alguém **-2.** [support, assistance]: **to ~ sthg (to sb)** dar algo (a alguém) **-3.** [credibility, quality]: **to ~ sthg to sthg** conferir algo a algo **-4.** *phr*: **it doesn't ~ itself to that** não se presta para isso.

lender [ˈlendəʳ] *n* [of money] emprestador *m*, -ra *f.*

lending library [ˈlendɪŋ-] *n* biblioteca *f* pública.

lending rate [ˈlendɪŋ-] *n* taxa *f* de empréstimo.

length [leŋθ] *n* **-1.** [gen] comprimento *m*; **what ~ is it?** quanto tem de comprimento?; **it's five metres in ~** são cinco metros de comprimento; **she walked the ~ and breadth of England** ela caminhou por toda a Inglaterra **-2.** [of swimming pool] piscina *f* **-3.** [piece] pedaço *m* **-4.** (U) [duration] duração *f* **-5.** *phr*: **to go to great ~s to do sthg** não medir esforços para fazer algo.

at length adv **-1.** [eventually] no final das contas **-2.** [in detail] detalhadamente.

lengthen ['leŋθən] <> vt **-1.** [skirt] alongar **-2.** [life] prolongar. <> vi alongar-se, ficar mais longo(ga).

lengthways ['leŋθweɪz] adv ao comprido.

lengthy ['leŋθɪ] (compar -ier, superl -iest) adj longo(-ga).

leniency ['liːnjənsɪ] n (U) leniência f, indulgência f.

lenient ['liːnjənt] adj leniente, indulgente.

lens [lenz] n **-1.** [made of glass] lente f **-2.** [contact lens] lente f (de contato).

lent [lent] pt & pp ▷ **lend**.

Lent [lent] n (U) quaresma f.

lentil ['lentɪl] n lentilha f.

Leo ['liːəʊ] n **-1.** [sign] leão m **-2.** [person] leonino(na); I'm ~ sou de Leão.

leopard ['lepəd] n leopardo m.

leopardess ['lepədɪs] n leoparda f.

leotard ['liːətɑːd] n malha f (usada por dançarinos, acrobatas).

leper ['lepəʳ] n [person with leprosy] leproso m, -sa f.

leprechaun ['leprəkɔːn] n leprechaun m, duende m.

leprosy ['leprəsɪ] n (U) lepra f.

lesbian ['lezbɪən] <> adj lésbico(ca). <> n lésbica f.

lesbianism ['lezbɪənɪzm] n (U) lesbianismo m.

lesion ['liːʒn] n MED lesão f.

Lesotho [ləˈsəʊtəʊ] n Lesoto; in ~ no Lesoto.

less [les] (compar of little) <> adj [not as much] menos; ~ ... than menos ... (do) que; ~ and ~ cada vez menos. <> pron [not as much] menos; ~ than menos (do) que; the ~ you work the ~ you earn quanto menos você trabalha, menos você ganha; no ~ than nada menos que. <> adv [to a smaller extent] menos; ~ and ~ cada vez menos. <> prep [minus] menos.

lessee [leˈsiː] n fml arrendatário m, -ria f, locatário m, -ria f.

lessen ['lesn] vt & vi diminuir.

lesser ['lesəʳ] adj menor; to a ~ extent OR degree em menor grau.

lesson ['lesn] n **-1.** [class] aula f; to give/take ~ s (in sthg) dar/receber aulas (de algo) **-2.** [example] lição f; to teach sb a ~ ensinar uma lição a alguém.

lessor [leˈsɔːʳ] n fml arrendador m, -ra f.

lest [lest] conj fml para que não; I did what she asked, ~ she become even angrier fiz o que ela pediu, temendo que ela ficasse ainda mais irritada.

let [let] (pt & pp let, cont -ting) vt **-1.** [allow]: to ~ sb do sthg deixar alguém fazer algo; she ~ her hair grow ela deixou o cabeço crescer; to ~ go of sb/sthg, to ~ sb/sthg go soltar alguém/algo; [release] soltar alguém/algo; to ~ sb know sthg informar alguém de algo, informar algo a alguém **-2.** (in verb forms): ~'s go! vamos!; ~'s see agora vejamos; ~ them wait! eles que esperem! **-3.** [rent out] alugar; **'to ~'** 'aluga-se'.

let alone conj [much less]: he couldn't walk, ~ alone jump ele não conseguia caminhar, que dirá pular.

let down vt sep **-1.** [deflate] esvaziar **-2.** [disappoint] desapontar.

let in vt sep **-1.** [admit] deixar entrar **-2.** [air, water] deixar entrar.

let in for vt sep: to ~ o.s. in for sthg meter-se em algo.

let in on vt sep: he ~ me in on his secret ele me revelou o seu segredo.

let off vt sep **-1.** [excuse, allow not to do]: to ~ sb off sthg eximir alguém de algo **-2.** [criminal, pupil, child] deixar impune **-3.** [bomb, explosive] detonar **-4.** [firework] estourar.

let on vi contar (um segredo); don't ~ on! não conta nada!

let out vt sep **-1.** [gen] deixar sair **-2.** [sound, cry, laugh] emitir **-3.** [garment] alargar.

let up vi **-1.** [heat, rain] cessar **-2.** [person] relaxar.

letdown ['letdaʊn] n inf decepção f.

lethal ['liːθl] adj letal.

lethargic [ləˈθɑːdʒɪk] adj letárgico(ca).

lethargy ['leθədʒɪ] n (U) letargia f.

Letraset® n (U) letraset® f.

let's [lets] = **let us**.

letter ['letəʳ] n **-1.** [written message] carta f **-2.** [of alphabet] letra f.

letters npl fml [literature] letras fpl.

letter bomb n carta-bomba f.

letterbox ['letəbɒks] n UK **-1.** [in door] portinhola f para cartas **-2.** [in street] caixa f de correio.

letterhead ['letəhed] n cabeçalho m em papel timbrado.

lettering ['letərɪŋ] n (U) [characters] letras fpl.

letter of credit n carta f de crédito.

letter opener n abridor m de cartas.

letter-perfect adj US impecável.

letter quality n COMPUT qualidade f carta.

letters patent npl **-1.** JUR carta f patente **-2.** [of inventor] patente f.

lettuce ['letɪs] n alface f.

letup ['letʌp] n pausa f, intervalo m.

leuk(a)emia [luːˈkiːmɪə] n leucemia f.

levee ['levɪ] n US [embankment] barragem f.

level ['levl] (UK pt & pp -led, cont -ling, US pt & pp -ed, cont -ing) <> adj **-1.** [equal in height] nivelado(-da); to be ~ (with sthg) estar nivelado(da) (com algo) **-2.** [equal in standard] em pé de igualdade **-3.** [flat - floor, field] plano(na); [- spoon, cup] raso(sa). <> adv: to draw ~ with sb empatar com alguém, alcançar alguém. <> n **-1.** [gen] nível m; to be on a ~ (with sthg) estar no mesmo nível (de algo) **-2.** US [spirit level] nível m (de bolha) **-3.** [storey] andar m **-4.** phr: to be on the ~ inf ser sincero(ra). <> vt **-1.** [make flat] nivelar, aplainar **-2.** [demolish] derrubar **-3.** [aim]: to ~ a gun at sb/sthg apontar uma arma para alguém/algo; to ~ an accusation at OR against sb lançar uma acusação contra OR sobre alguém.

level off, level out vi estabilizar-se.

level with vt fus inf [be honest with] ser sincero(ra) com.

level crossing n UK passagem f de nível.

level-headed [-ˈhedɪd] adj equilibrado(da), sensato(ta).

level pegging [-'peɡɪŋ] adj UK: **to be ~** estar igualado(da).

lever [UK 'li:vəʳ, US 'levər] n alavanca f.

leverage [UK 'li:vərɪdʒ, US 'levərɪdʒ] n (U) - **1.** fig [influence] influência f - **2.** [force] alavancagem f, força f.

leviathan [lɪ'vaɪəθn] n [large body, organization] leviatã m, gigante m.

levitation [ˌlevɪ'teɪʃn] n (U) levitação f.

levity ['levətɪ] n (U) leviandade f.

levy ['levɪ] (pt & pp -**ied**) <> n [financial contribution, tax]: **~ (on sthg)** taxa f (sobre algo). <> vt [demand, collect] arrecadar.

lewd [lju:d] adj [behaviour] lascivo(va), obsceno(na).

lexical ['leksɪkl] adj lexical.

liability [ˌlaɪə'bɪlətɪ] (pl -**ies**) n - **1.** [hindrance] estorvo m - **2.** JUR (U) [legal responsibility]: **~ (for sthg)** responsabilidade f (por algo).

◆ **liabilities** npl FIN [debts] passivos mpl, obrigações fpl.

liable ['laɪəbl] adj - **1.** [likely]: **she is ~ to do something stupid** é bem provável que ela faça algo estúpido - **2.** [prone]: **to be ~ to sthg** estar propenso(sa) a algo - **3.** JUR: **to be ~ (for sthg)** [legally responsible] ser legalmente responsável(- por algo); **to be ~ to sthg** [punishable] estar sujeito(ta) a algo.

liaise [lɪ'eɪz] vi: **to ~ (with)** fazer contato (com); **to ~ (between)** criar vínculos (entre).

liaison [lɪ'eɪzɒn] n - **1.** (U) [contact, cooperation]: **~ (with/between)** relação f (com/entre) - **2.** [affair, relationship]: **~ (with/between)** ligação f OR caso m (com/entre).

liar ['laɪəʳ] n mentiroso m, -sa f.

Lib - **1.** (abbr of Liberal) liberal - **2.** (abbr of liberation) liberação f.

libel ['laɪbl] (UK pt & pp -**led**, cont -**ling**, US pt & pp -**ed**, cont -**ing**) <> n libelo m. <> vt difamar.

libellous UK, **libelous** US ['laɪbələs] adj difamatório(ria).

liberal ['lɪbərəl] <> adj - **1.** [tolerant] liberal - **2.** [generous] generoso(sa). <> n liberal mf.
◆ **Liberal** POL <> adj liberal. <> n liberal mf.

liberal arts npl esp US ciências fpl humanas.

Liberal Democrat <> adj liberal democrata. <> n liberal democrata mf.

liberalize, -ise ['lɪbərəlaɪz] vt liberalizar.

liberal-minded [-'maɪndɪd] adj liberal.

Liberal Party n: **the ~** o Partido Liberal.

liberate ['lɪbəreɪt] vt libertar.

liberation [ˌlɪbə'reɪʃn] n (U) - **1.** [release] libertação f - **2.** fig [emancipation] libertação f.

liberator ['lɪbəreɪtəʳ] n libertador m, -ra f.

Liberia [laɪ'bɪərɪə] n Libéria f; **in ~** na Libéria.

Liberian [laɪ'bɪərɪən] <> adj liberiano(na). <> n liberiano m, -na f.

libertine ['lɪbəti:n] n libertino m, -na f.

liberty ['lɪbətɪ] (pl -**ies**) n [gen] liberdade f; **at ~** em liberdade; **to be at ~ to do sthg** ter liberdade para fazer algo; **to take liberties (with sb)** tomar liberdades (com alguém).

libido [lɪ'bi:dəʊ] (pl -**s**) n [sexual urge] libido f.

Libra ['li:brə] n - **1.** [sign] libra f - **2.** [person] libriano m, -na f; **I'm ~** sou de Libra.

librarian [laɪ'breərɪən] n bibliotecário m, -ria f.

librarianship [laɪ'breərɪənʃɪp] n (U) biblioteconomia f.

library ['laɪbrərɪ] (pl -**ies**) n biblioteca f.

library book n livro m de biblioteca.

libretto [lɪ'bretəʊ] (pl -**s**) n libreto m.

Libya ['lɪbɪə] n Líbia f; **in ~** na Líbia.

Libyan ['lɪbɪən] <> adj líbio(bia). <> n líbio m, -bia f.

lice [laɪs] pl ⊏> **louse**.

licence ['laɪsəns] <> n - **1.** [permit - gen] licença f; [- for marriage] autorização f; [- for pilot] brevê m - **2.** COMM licença f; **under ~ from** com permissão de. <> vt US = **license**.

license ['laɪsəns] <> vt COMM autorizar. <> n US = **licence**.

licensed ['laɪsənst] adj - **1.** [person]: **to be ~ to do sthg** estar autorizado(da) a fazer algo - **2.** [object - car, dog] com licença; [- gun] registrado(da) - **3.** UK [premises] autorizado(da) a vender álcool.

licensee [ˌlaɪsən'si:] n licenciado m, -da f.

license plate n US placa f (de automóvel).

licensing hours ['laɪsənsɪŋ-] npl UK horário de funcionamento dos bares.

LICENSING HOURS

Tradicionalmente, o horário de funcionamento dos pubs na Grã-Bretanha sempre esteve sujeito a regulamentação bastante estrita, vinculada à legislação sobre a venda de bebidas alcoólicas. Mas, a partir de 1988, as regras se tornaram mais flexíveis. Em vez de abrirem das 11:30 às 14:30h, e das 18 às 23:00h, os pubs passaram a abrir das 11 às 23h, menos aos domingos, quando funcionam das 11 às 15h e das 19 às 22:30h. Na Escócia, os horários são menos rigorosos.

---

licensing laws ['laɪsənsɪŋ-] npl UK leis que controlam a venda de bebidas alcoólicas.

licentious [laɪ'senʃəs] adj fml & pej licencioso(sa).

lichen ['laɪkən] n líquen m.

lick [lɪk] <> n - **1.** [act of licking] lambida f - **2.** inf [small amount]: **a ~ of paint** uma demão de tinta. <> vt - **1.** [with tongue] lamber; **to ~ one's lips** lamber os beiços - **2.** fig [subj: flames, waves] lamber - **3.** inf [defeat] derrotar.

licorice ['lɪkərɪs] n = **liquorice**.

lid [lɪd] n - **1.** [cover] tampa f - **2.** [eyelid] pálpebra f.

lido ['li:dəʊ] (pl -**s**) n - **1.** UK [swimming pool] piscina f pública - **2.** [beach] praia f.

lie [laɪ] (pt sense 1 **lied**, pt senses 2-7 **lay**, pp sense 1 **lied**, pp senses 2-7 **lain**, cont all senses **lying**) <> n mentira f; **to tell ~s** contar mentiras. <> vi - **1.** [tell untruth] mentir; **to ~ to sb** mentir para alguém - **2.** [to be lying down] estar deitado(da) - **3.** [lie down] deitar - **4.** [be situated] encontrar-se - **5.** [corpse] jazer - **6.** : **who knows what ~s ahead?** quem sabe o que nos espera? - **7.** phr: **to ~ low** ficar escondido(da).

◆ **lie about, lie around** vi - **1.** [people] andar sem fazer nada, vadiar - **2.** [things] estar jogado(da).

◆ **lie down** vi deitar-se; **he won't take it lying down** ele não vai ficar agüentando isso.

◆ **lie in** vi UK ficar na cama até tarde.

Liechtenstein ['lɪktən‚staɪn] *n* Liechtenstein; **in ~** em Liechtenstein.

lie detector *n* detector *m* de mentiras.

lie-down *n UK*: **to have a ~** repousar.

lie-in *n UK*: **to have a ~** ficar na cama até tarde.

lieu [lju:‚ lu:] ◆ **in lieu** *adv* em troca; **in ~ of** em vez de.

Lieut. (*abbr of* **lieutenant**) Ten.

lieutenant [*UK* lef'tenənt, *US* lu:'tenəntl] *n* tenente *m*.

lieutenant colonel *n* tenente-coronel *m*.

life [laɪf] (*pl* **lives**) ◇ *n* **-1.** [gen] vida *f*; **to breathe ~ into sthg** dar vida a algo; **to come to ~** criar vida; **that's ~!** é a vida!; **for ~** para toda a vida; **for the ~ of me** *inf* por mais que eu tente; **to lay down one's ~** entregar a vida; **to risk ~ and limb** arriscar a pele; **to scare the ~ out of sb** quase matar alguém do coração; **to take sb's/one's own ~** tirar a vida de alguém/a própria vida **-2.** (*U*) *inf* [life imprisonment] prisão *f* perpétua. ◇ *comp* vitalício(cia).

life-and-death *adj* de vida ou morte.

life annuity *n* renda *f* vitalícia.

life assurance *n* = **life insurance**.

life belt *n* cinto *m* salva-vidas.

lifeblood ['laɪfblʌd] *n* (*U*) *fig* [source of strength] força *f* vital.

lifeboat ['laɪfbəʊt] *n* **-1.** [on ship] bote *m* salva-vidas **-2.** [on shore] lancha *f* de salvamento.

lifeboatman [-man] (*pl* **-men**) *n* salva-vidas *m inv* (*de barco*).

life buoy *n* bóia *f* salva-vidas.

life cycle *n* ciclo *m* vital.

life expectancy *n* espectativa *f* de vida.

lifeguard ['laɪfgɑ:d] *n* salva-vidas *mf inv*.

life imprisonment [-ɪm'prɪznmənt] *n* prisão *f* perpétua.

life insurance *n* (*U*) seguro *m* de vida.

life jacket *n* colete *m* salva-vidas.

lifeless ['laɪflɪs] *adj* **-1.** [dead] sem vida, morto(ta) **-2.** [listless] apagado(da).

lifelike ['laɪflaɪk] *adj* **-1.** [statue, doll] realista **-2.** [portrait] fiel.

lifeline ['laɪflaɪn] *n* **-1.** [rope] corda *f* de segurança **-2.** *fig* [with outside] cordão *m* umbilical.

lifelong ['laɪflɒŋ] *adj* de toda a vida.

life peer *n UK* nobre britânico com título não-hereditário.

life preserver [-prɪ‚zɜ:vəʳ] *n US* **-1.** [belt] cinto *m* salva-vidas **-2.** [jacket] colete *m* salva-vidas.

life raft *n* balsa *f* salva-vidas.

lifesaver ['laɪf‚seɪvəʳ] *n* **-1.** [person] salva-vidas *mf inv* **-2.** *fig* [relief, help] ajuda *f*.

life sentence *n* pena *f* de prisão perpétua.

life-size(d) [-saɪz(d)] *adj* em tamanho natural.

lifespan ['laɪfspæn] *n* **-1.** [of person, animal, plant] vida *f* **-2.** [of product, machine] vida *f* útil.

lifestyle ['laɪfstaɪl] *n* estilo *m* de vida.

life-support system *n* sistema *m* de respiração artificial.

lifetime ['laɪftaɪm] *n* [length of time] vida *f*.

lift [lɪft] ◇ *n* **-1.** [ride] carona *f* **-2.** *UK* [elevator] elevador *m*. ◇ *vt* **-1.** [gen] levantar; **he ~ed the** books off the shelf ele tirou os livros da estante **-2.** [ban, embargo] revogar **-3.** [plagiarize] plagiar **-4.** *inf* [steal] levantar. ◇ *vi* **-1.** [lid, top] levantar **-2.** [mist, fog, clouds] dissipar-se **-3.** [heart, spirits] melhorar.

◆ **lift up** ◇ *vt sep* [bag, baby, books] levantar. ◇ *vi* [lid, top] levantar.

lift-off *n* decolagem *f*.

ligament ['lɪgəmənt] *n* ANAT ligamento *m*.

light [laɪt] (*pt & pp* **lit** *OR* **-ed**) ◇ *adj* **-1.** [gen] leve **-2.** [not dark] claro(ra). ◇ *adv*: **to travel ~** viajar com pouca bagagem. ◇ *n* **-1.** [gen] luz *f* **-2.** [for cigarette, pipe] fogo *m*; **to set ~ to sthg** atear fogo em algo **-3.** [perspective]: **in the ~ of** *UK*, **in ~ of** *US* à luz de; **to see sb/sthg in a different ~** ver alguém/algo de forma diferente **-4.** *literary* [in sb's eyes] brilho *m* **-5.** *phr*: **to come to ~** vir à luz; **to see the ~** [understand] ver claramente; **to throw** *OR* **cast** *OR* **shed ~ on sthg** lançar luz sobre algo; **there's a ~ at the end of the tunnel** há uma luz no fim do túnel; **to make ~ of sthg** não dar a devida importância a algo. ◇ *vt* **-1.** [ignite] acender **-2.** [illuminate] iluminar.

◆ **light out** *vi US inf* dar no pé.

◆ **light up** ◇ *vt sep* **-1.** [illuminate] iluminar **-2.** [start smoking] acender. ◇ *vi* **-1.** [look happy] iluminar-se **-2.** *inf* [start smoking] pôr-se a fumar.

light aircraft (*pl inv*) *n* pequeno aeroplano *m*.

light ale *n* (*U*) *UK tipo de cerveja escura e suave*.

light bulb *n* lâmpada *f*.

light cream *n US* creme *m* light.

lighted ['laɪtɪd] *adj* **-1.** [illuminated] iluminado(da) **-2.** [on fire] aceso(sa).

light-emitting diode [-ɪ'mɪtɪŋ-] *n* diodo *m* emissor de luz.

lighten ['laɪtn] ◇ *vt* **-1.** [make brighter] clarear **-2.** [make less heavy] aliviar. ◇ *vi* **-1.** [brighten] iluminar-se **-2.** [become happier, more relaxed] alegrar-se.

◆ **lighten up** *vi inf* levar na brincadeira.

lighter ['laɪtəʳ] *n* [cigarette lighter] isqueiro *m*.

light-fingered [-'fɪŋgəd] *adj inf* gatuno(na); **to be ~** ter mão leve.

light-headed [-'hedɪd] *adj* tonto(ta).

light-hearted [-'hɑ:tɪd] *adj* **-1.** [cheerful] despreocupado(da) **-2.** [amusing] alegre.

lighthouse ['laɪthaʊs, *pl* -haʊzɪz] *n* farol *m*.

light industry *n* indústria *f* leve.

lighting ['laɪtɪŋ] *n* (*U*) iluminação *f*.

lighting-up time *n* (*U*) hora *f* de acendimento da iluminação pública.

lightly ['laɪtlɪ] *adv* **-1.** [tap, knock] suavemente **-2.** [cook, grill] ligeiramente **-3.** [remark, say] levianamente.

light meter *n* PHOT fotômetro *m*.

lightning ['laɪtnɪŋ] *n* (*U*) raio *m*, relâmpago *m*.

lightning conductor *UK*, **lightning rod** *US* *n* pára-raios *m inv*.

lightning strike *n UK* greve-relâmpago *f*.

light opera *n* opereta *f*.

light pen *n* caneta *f* óptica.

lightship *n* navio-farol *m*.

lights-out *n* (*U*) hora em que se apagam as luzes.

lightweight ['laɪtweɪt] <> adj -**1.** [object] leve -**2.** fig & pej [person] de pouca expressão. <> n -**1.** [boxer] peso m leve -**2.** fig & pej [person] joão-ninguém m.

light year n ano-luz m.

likable ['laɪkəbl] adj simpático(ca), agradável.

like [laɪk] <> prep -**1.** [similar to] como; **to look** ~ **sb/sthg** parecer-se com alguém/algo, parecer alguém/algo; **what did it taste** ~? tinha gosto de quê?; **what did it look** ~? como era?; **what did it sound** ~? como era o barulho?; ~ **this/that** assim -**2.** [typical of]: **that's just** ~ **him** isso é típico dele -**3.** [such as] (tal) como. <> vt -**1.** [enjoy, find pleasant, approve of] gostar; **to** ~ **doing** OR **to do sthg** gostar de fazer algo -**2.** [want, wish] querer; **to** ~ **to do sthg** desejar fazer algo; **to** ~ **sb to do sthg** desejar que alguém faça algo; **I'd** ~ **you to come** gostaria que você viesse. <> adj [similar] igual. <> n: **the** ~ **of sb/sthg** alguém/algo do estilo; **and the** ~ e similares, e coisas do estilo.
◆ **likes** npl [things one likes] gostos mpl.

likeable ['laɪkəbl] adj = **likable**.

likelihood ['laɪklɪhʊd] n (U) probabilidade f; **in all** ~ com toda certeza.

likely ['laɪklɪ] adj -**1.** [probable] provável; **rain is** ~ **later on** é provável que chova mais tarde; **to be** ~ **to do sthg** ser provável que algo aconteça; **he's** ~ **to come** é provável que ele venha; **a** ~ **story!** iro pura invenção! -**2.** [suitable] indicado(da).

like-minded [-'maɪndɪd] adj de mesma opinião.

liken ['laɪkn] vt: **to** ~ **sb/sthg to** comparar alguém/algo a.

likeness ['laɪknɪs] n semelhança f; ~ **to sb/sthg** semelhança com alguém/algo.

likewise ['laɪkwaɪz] adv [similarly] da mesma maneira; **to do** ~ fazer o mesmo.

liking ['laɪkɪŋ] n: ~ **for sb/sthg** afeição f por alguém/algo; **to have a** ~ **for sb/sthg** ter afeição por alguém/algo; **to be to sb's** ~ estar ao gosto de alguém; **he's too confident for my** ~ ele é muito atrevido para o meu gosto.

lilac ['laɪlək] <> adj [colour] lilás. <> n -**1.** [tree] lilás m -**2.** (U) [colour] lilás m.

Lilo® ['laɪləʊ] (pl -s) n UK colchão m inflável.

lilt [lɪlt] n [in voice] melodia f; [in melody] cadência f.

lilting ['lɪltɪŋ] adj [voice] melodioso(sa); [melody] cadenciado(da).

lily ['lɪlɪ] (pl -ies) n lírio m.

lily of the valley (pl lilies of the valley) n lírio-do-vale m.

Lima ['liːmə] n Lima.

limb [lɪm] n -**1.** [of body] membro m -**2.** [of tree] ramo m -**3.** phr: **to be out on a** ~ estar em apuros.

limber ['lɪmbəʳ] ◆ **limber up** vi fazer aquecimento, aquecer.

limbo ['lɪmbəʊ] (pl -s) n -**1.** (U) [uncertain state]: **to be in** ~ estar no limbo -**2.** [dance]: **the** ~ dança caribenha na qual se passa por baixo de uma barra com o corpo inclinado para trás, dança f da cordinha.

lime [laɪm] n -**1.** [fruit] lima f; ~ **(juice)** (suco m de) lima f -**2.** [linden tree] tília f -**3.** (U) [substance] cal f.

lime cordial n refresco m de lima.

lime-green adj de cor verde-limão.

limelight ['laɪmlaɪt] n: **to be in the** ~ estar no/ser o centro das atenções.

limerick ['lɪmərɪk] n poema humorístico de cinco linhas.

limestone ['laɪmstəʊn] n (U) calcário m, pedra f calcária.

limey ['laɪmɪ] (pl -s) n US inf termo pejorativo que designa um inglês.

limit ['lɪmɪt] <> n limite m; **to be off** ~ **s** ser/estar proibido(da); **within** ~ **s** [to a certain extent] até certo ponto; **he's/she's the** ~! inf ele/ela é o cúmulo! <> vt limitar, restringir; **to** ~ **o.s. to sthg** limitar-se a algo.

limitation [ˌlɪmɪ'teɪʃn] n limitação f.

limited ['lɪmɪtɪd] adj [restricted] limitado(da); **to be** ~ **to sthg** estar limitado(da) a algo.

limited company n companhia f limitada.

limited edition n edição f limitada.

limited liability company n = **limited company**.

limitless ['lɪmɪtlɪs] adj ilimitado(da).

limo ['lɪməʊ] n inf limusine f.

limousine ['lɪməziːn] n limusine f.

limp [lɪmp] <> adj -**1.** [hand, handshake] sem firmeza -**2.** [body, lettuce] murcho(cha) -**3.** [excuse] mole. <> n manqueira f. <> vi mancar.

limpet ['lɪmpɪt] n lapa f.

limpid adj literary límpido(da).

limply ['lɪmplɪ] adv -**1.** [lie, hang] sem firmeza -**2.** [reply] de forma vacilante.

linchpin ['lɪntʃpɪn] n fig [important person, thing] peça-chave f.

linctus ['lɪŋktəs] n (U) UK expectorante m.

line [laɪn] <> n -**1.** [gen] linha f; **washing** ~ corda f de varal; **power** ~ cabo m de força; **to draw the** ~ **at doing sthg** fig estabelecer limites para fazer algo -**2.** [row] fileira f, linha f -**3.** [queue] fila f; **to stand** OR **wait in** ~ ficar OR esperar em fila; **to be in** ~ **for promotion** estar a caminho da promoção -**4.** [alignment] alinhamento m; **in** ~ alinhado(da); **in** ~ **with** em linha com; **to step out of** ~ sair da linha -**5.** [RAIL - railway track] linha f (férrea); [- route] linha f -**6.** NAUT: **shipping** ~ companhia f marítima -**7.** [in writing - of text] linha f; **to read between the** ~ **s** ler nas entrelinhas; [- of poetry, song] verso m -**8.** [wrinkle] ruga f -**9.** TELEC [telephone connection] linha f (telefônica) -**10.** inf [short letter]: **to drop sb a** ~ escrever umas linhas para alguém -**11.** [of ideas, reasoning] linha f de raciocínio; **along the same** ~ **s** seguindo a mesma linha; **to be on the right** ~ **s** estar num bom caminho -**12.** inf [field of activity] ramo m -**13.** [lineage, ancestry] linhagem f. <> vt -**1.** [form rows along] alinhar-se ao longo de; **crowds** ~ **d the street** a multidão lotava a rua -**2.** [cover inside surface of] forrar.
◆ **lines** npl -**1.** SCH castigo que consiste em escrever a mesma frase inúmeras vezes -**2.** [actor's words] texto m.
◆ **on the line** adv: **to put sthg on the** ~ pôr algo em jogo.
◆ **out of line** adj inaceitável.
◆ **line up** <> vt sep -**1.** [in rows] alinhar -**2.** inf [organize] arranjar, organizar. <> vi -**1.** [in a row]

alinhar-se **-2.** [in a queue] pôr-se na fila.

lineage ['lɪnɪdʒ] n *fml* linhagem f.

linear ['lɪnɪəʳ] adj linear.

lined [laɪnd] adj **-1.** [paper] pautado(da) **-2.** [face] enrugado(da).

line drawing n desenho m a traço.

line feed n *COMPUT* avanço m de linha.

linen ['lɪnɪn] (U) ⟨⟩ n **-1.** [cloth] linho m **-2.** [sheets] roupa f de cama **-3.** [tablecloths] toalha f (de mesa). ⟨⟩ comp **-1.** [suit, napkins] de linho **-2.** [cupboard, drawer]: ~ **cupboard** armário no qual se guardam as roupas de cama e de mesa.

linen basket n cesto m de roupa suja.

line-out n *RUGBY* formação para recomeço do jogo quando a bola saiu de campo.

line printer n *COMPUT* impressora f de linha.

liner ['laɪnəʳ] n [ship] transatlântico m.

linesman ['laɪnzmən] (pl -men [-mən]) n *SPORT* juiz m de linha.

line-up n **-1.** [of players, competitors] seleção f **-2.** *US* [identification parade] fila f de identificação.

linger ['lɪŋgəʳ] vi **-1.** [dawdle] demorar-se **-2.** [persist] persistir.

lingerie ['lænʒərɪ] n (U) lingerie f.

lingering ['lɪŋgrɪŋ] adj **-1.** [persistent] persistente **-2.** [slow] lento(ta) **-3.** [long] prolongado(da).

lingo ['lɪŋgəʊ] (pl -es) n inf idioma f.

linguist ['lɪŋgwɪst] n **-1.** [someone good at languages] pessoa f com facilidade para os idiomas **-2.** [student or teacher of linguistics] lingüista mf.

linguistic [lɪŋ'gwɪstɪk] adj lingüístico(ca).

➡ **linguistics** n (U) lingüística f.

liniment ['lɪnɪmənt] n (U) linimento m.

lining ['laɪnɪŋ] n **-1.** [of coat, curtains, box] forro m **-2.** [of stomach, nose] paredes fpl internas **-3.** *AUT* [of brakes] revestimento m.

link [lɪŋk] ⟨⟩ n **-1.** [of chain] elo m **-2.** *COMPUT* linque m **-3.** [connection] conexão f; ~ **between sb/sthg** vínculo m OR ligação f entre alguém/algo; ~ **with sb/sthg** vínculo OR ligação com alguém/algo. ⟨⟩ vt **-1.** [relate] ligar, relacionar; **to** ~ **sb/sthg with** OR **to sb/sthg** ligar alguém/algo com OR a alguém/algo, relacionar alguém/algo com OR a alguém/algo **-2.** [connect physically] enlaçar.

➡ **link up** ⟨⟩ vt sep [connect] conectar; **to** ~ **sthg up with sthg** conectar algo a algo. ⟨⟩ vi [connect]: **to** ~ **up (with sb/sthg)** conectar-se (a alguém/algo).

linkage ['lɪŋkɪdʒ] n [connection] conexão f, vínculo m.

linked [lɪŋkt] adj **-1.** [related] relacionado(da) **-2.** [connected physically] enlaçado(da); **arms** ~ **ed** de braços dados.

links [lɪŋks] (pl inv) n *SPORT* campo m de golfe.

link-up n conexão f.

lino ['laɪnəʊ], **linoleum** [lɪ'nəʊljəm] n (U) linóleo m.

linseed oil ['lɪnsiːd-] n (U) óleo m de linhaça.

lint [lɪnt] n **-1.** [dressing] gaze f **-2.** *US* [fluff] fiapo m.

lintel ['lɪntl] n verga f (de porta ou janela).

lion ['laɪən] n leão m.

lion cub n filhote m de leão.

lioness ['laɪənes] n leoa f.

lionize, -ise ['laɪənaɪz] vt tratar como celebridade, endeusar.

lip [lɪp] n **-1.** [of mouth] lábio m; **to keep a stiff upper** ~ manter-se firme; **my** ~ **s are sealed** eu sou um túmulo **-2.** [of container] borda f.

liposuction ['lɪpəʊˌsʌkʃən] n lipoaspiração f.

lip-read vi ler nos lábios.

lip-reading n (U) leitura f dos lábios.

lip salve [-sælv] n *UK* pomada f para lábios.

lip service n: **to pay** ~ **to sthg** concordar com algo da boca para fora.

lipstick ['lɪpstɪk] n batom m.

liquefy ['lɪkwɪfaɪ] (pt & pp -ied) ⟨⟩ vt liquefazer. ⟨⟩ vi liquefazer-se.

liqueur [lɪ'kjʊəʳ] n licor m.

liquid ['lɪkwɪd] ⟨⟩ adj [fluid] líquido(da). ⟨⟩ n [fluid] líquido m.

liquid assets npl ativo m disponível.

liquidate ['lɪkwɪdeɪt] vt liquidar.

liquidation [ˌlɪkwɪ'deɪʃn] n (U) *FIN* falência f; **to go into** ~ abrir falência.

liquidator ['lɪkwɪdeɪtəʳ] n *FIN* liquidante mf.

liquid crystal display n tela f de cristal líquido.

liquidity [lɪ'kwɪdətɪ] n (U) **-1.** [having money] liquidez f **-2.** [being liquid] condição f de ser líquido.

liquidize, -ise ['lɪkwɪdaɪz] vt *UK CULIN* liquidificar.

liquidizer ['lɪkwɪdaɪzəʳ] n *UK* liquidificador m.

liquor ['lɪkəʳ] n *US* [alcohol] álcool m; [spirits] bebida f alcoólica.

liquorice ['lɪkərɪʃ, 'lɪkərɪs] n (U) alcaçuz m.

liquor store n *US* armazém m de bebidas alcoólicas.

lira ['lɪərə] n [Italian] lira f.

Lisbon ['lɪzbən] n Lisboa; **in** ~ em Lisboa.

lisp [lɪsp] ⟨⟩ n ceceio m. ⟨⟩ vi cecear.

lissom(e) ['lɪsəm] adj *literary* grácil, esbelto(ta).

list [lɪst] ⟨⟩ n lista f. ⟨⟩ vt [in writing, speech] listar. ⟨⟩ vi *NAUT* adernar.

listed building [ˌlɪstɪd-] n *UK* prédio m tombado.

listed company [ˌlɪstɪd-] n *UK* sociedade f de capital aberto.

listen ['lɪsn] vi **-1.** [give attention] escutar, ouvir; **to** ~ **to sb/sthg** escutar alguém/algo; **to** ~ **for sthg** estar atento(ta) a algo **-2.** [heed advice] dar atenção a; **to** ~ **to sb/sthg** escutar alguém/algo.

➡ **listen in** vi **-1.** *RADIO* escutar um programa numa estação; **to** ~ **in to sthg** sintonizar em algo **-2.** [eavesdrop] escutar a conversa alheia; **to** ~ **in on sthg** [conversation] prestar atenção em algo; [phone call] interceptar algo.

➡ **listen up** vi *US* inf prestar atenção.

listener ['lɪsnəʳ] n ouvinte mf.

listing ['lɪstɪŋ] n listagem f.

➡ **listings** npl [of events] programação f cultural.

listless ['lɪstlɪs] adj apático(ca).

list price n preço m de catálogo.

lit [lɪt] pt & pp ▷ light.

litany ['lɪtənɪ] (pl -ies) n **-1.** *RELIG* ladainha f, litania f **-2.** [series] ladainha f.

liter n *US* = litre.

literacy ['lɪtərəsɪ] n (U) alfabetização f.

literal ['lɪtərəl] *adj* literal.

literally ['lɪtərəlɪ] *adv* literalmente; **to take sthg ~** levar algo ao pé da letra.

literary ['lɪtərərɪ] *adj* literário(ria); **a ~ man** um literato.

literate ['lɪtərət] *adj* **-1.** [able to read and write] alfabetizado(da); **computer-~** que tem conhecimentos de informática **-2.** [well-read] letrado(da), culto(ta).

literature ['lɪtrətʃəʳ] *n (U)* **-1.** [novels, plays, poetry] literatura *f* **-2.** [books on a particular subject] literatura *f*, bibliografia *f* **-3.** [printed information] informações *fpl*.

lithe [laɪð] *adj* ágil.

lithium ['lɪθɪəm] *n* lítio *m*.

lithograph ['lɪθəgrɑːf] *n* litografia *f*.

lithography *n (U)* litografia *f*.

Lithuania [ˌlɪθjʊ'eɪnɪə] *n* Lituânia; **in ~** na Lituânia.

Lithuanian [ˌlɪθjʊ'eɪnjən] <> *adj* lituano(na). <> *n* **-1.** [person] lituano *m*, -na *f* **-2.** [language] lituano *m*.

litigant ['lɪtɪgənt] *n fml* litigante *mf*.

litigate ['lɪtɪgeɪt] *vi fml* litigar.

litigation [ˌlɪtɪ'geɪʃn] *n (U) fml* litígio *m*.

litmus paper ['lɪtməs-] *n* papel *m* tornassol.

litre *UK*, **liter** *US* ['liːtəʳ] *n* **-1.** [metric unit] litro *m* **-2.** [capacity of engine] cilindrada *f*.

litter ['lɪtəʳ] <> *n* **-1.** *(U)* [waste material] lixo *m* **-2.** [newborn animals] ninhada *f* **-3.** [for litter tray]: **(cat) ~** areia *f* química *(para fezes de gato)*. <> *vt*: **to be ~ed with sthg** estar coberto(ta) de algo.

litter bin *n UK* cesto *m* de lixo.

litter lout *UK*, **litterbug** *n inf* pessoa que suja as vias públicas.

litter tray *n* recipiente com areia química para o gato fazer suas necessidades.

little ['lɪtl] <> *adj* **-1.** [gen] pequeno(na) **-2.** [younger] menor; **my ~ brother** meu irmão mais novo **-3.** [short in time or distance] curto(ta) **-4.** [not much] pouco(ca); **she has a ~ money left** ela tem pouco dinheiro sobrando. <> *pron* [small amount] pouco(ca); **a ~** um pouco; **a ~ (bit)** um pouquinho. <> *adv* **-1.** [to a limited extent] pouco; **he's ~ more than a waiter** ele é pouco mais do que um garçom; **~ by ~** pouco a pouco **-2.** [rarely] raramente; **we go there as ~ as possible** vamos lá o mínimo possível.

little finger *n* dedo *m* mínimo, minguinho *m*.

little-known *adj* pouco conhecido(da).

liturgy ['lɪtədʒɪ] *(pl -ies) n* [form of worship] liturgia *f*.

live [lɪv] <> *vi* **-1.** [gen] viver **-2.** [reside] morar, viver. <> *vt* viver; **to ~ it up** *inf* curtir a vida.
➤ **live down** *vt sep* redimir-se de.
➤ **live for** *vt fus* viver para.
➤ **live in** *vi* **-1.** [student] ser interno(na) **-2.** [servant, nanny] dormir na casa.
➤ **live off** *vt fus* **-1.** [savings] viver de **-2.** [parents, family] viver às custas de.
➤ **live on** <> *vt fus* **-1.** [money] viver **-2.** [food] viver de. <> *vi* [memory, feeling, works] perdurar.
➤ **live out** <> *vt fus* acabar; **she won't ~ out the month** ela não chega até o final do mês. <> *vi* dormir fora.

➤ **live together** *vi* [cohabit] viver juntos(tas).
➤ **live up to** *vt fus* estar à altura de.
➤ **live with** *vt fus* **-1.** [cohabit with] viver com **-2.** *inf* [accept] conviver com.

live [laɪv] <> *adj* **-1.** [living] vivo(va) **-2.** [burning] aceso(sa) **-3.** [unexploded] carregado(da) **-4.** *ELEC* com eletricidade **-5.** *MUS, RADIO & TV* ao vivo. <> *adv* ao vivo.

live-in [lɪv-] *adj* residente.

livelihood ['laɪvlɪhʊd] *n* meio *m* de vida, sustento *m*.

liveliness ['laɪvlɪnɪs] *n* **-1.** [of person] vivacidade *f* **-2.** [of debate] ânimo *m* **-3.** [of mind] sagacidade *f*.

lively ['laɪvlɪ] *(compar -ier, superl -iest) adj* **-1.** [gen] animado(da) **-2.** [mind, curiosity, imagination] sagaz, perspicaz **-3.** [colour] vivo(va).

liven ['laɪvn] ➤ **liven up** <> *vt sep* animar. <> *vi* [person] animar-se.

liver ['lɪvəʳ] *n* fígado *m*.

Liverpudlian [ˌlɪvə'pʌdlɪən] <> *adj* de ou relativo a Liverpool. <> *n* morador ou residente de Liverpool.

liver sausage *UK*, **liverwurst** *US* ['lɪvəwɜːst] *n (U)* salsicha *f* de fígado.

livery ['lɪvərɪ] *(pl -ies) n* **-1.** [uniform] libré *f* **-2.** [of a company] marca *f* distintiva.

lives [laɪvz] *pl* ⊳ **life**.

livestock ['laɪvstɒk] *n (U)* animais *mpl* de uma fazenda.

live wire [laɪv-] *n* **-1.** [wire] cabo *m* com corrente **-2.** *inf* [person] pessoa *f* dinâmica, empreendedor *m*, -ra *f*.

livid ['lɪvɪd] *adj* **-1.** *inf* [angry] furioso(sa) **-2.** [blue-grey] roxo(xa).

living ['lɪvɪŋ] <> *adj* vivo(va); **~ proof** prova *f* viva. <> *n* **-1.** [people]: **the ~** os vivos **-2.** [means of earning money]: **what do you do for a ~?** o que você faz para ganhar a vida?; **to scrape a ~** mal ganhar a vida **-3.** *(U)* [lifestyle] (estilo *m* de) vida *f*; **healthy ~** vida *f* saudável.

living conditions *npl* condições *fpl* de vida.

living expenses *npl* despesas *fpl* básicas.

living room *n* sala *f* de estar.

living standards *npl* padrão *m* de vida.

living wage *n* salário *m* básico.

lizard ['lɪzəd] *n* **-1.** [large] lagarto *m* **-2.** [small] lagartixa *f*.

llama ['lɑːmə] *(pl inv OR -s) n* lhama *m*.

LLB *(abbr of Bachelor of Laws) n (titular de) graduação em direito.*

LLD *(abbr of Doctor of Laws) n (titular de) doutorado em direito.*

LMT *(abbr of Local Mean Time) n* horário *m* local.

lo [ləʊ] *excl*: **~ and behold** olha só!

load [ləʊd] <> *n* **-1.** [gen] carga *f*; **to take a ~ off one's mind** tirar um peso da consciência **-2.** [burden] fardo *m* **-3.** [large amount]: **~s of**, **a ~ of** *inf* um monte de; **a ~ of rubbish** *inf* um monte de bobagem. <> *vt* **-1.** [container, vehicle, person] carregar; **to ~ sb/sthg with sthg** carregar alguém/algo de algo **-2.** [gun]: **to ~ sthg (with sthg)** carregar algo (com algo) **-3.** [in camera, video recorder]: **to ~ a film** colocar filme *(na câmera)*;

to ~ a tape colocar fita *(na filmadora)* - **4.** COMPUT [program] carregar.

➡ **load up** ⬦ *vt sep* carregar. ⬦ *vi* [with furniture, boxes] carregar.

loaded ['ləʊdɪd] *adj* -**1.** [question, statement] com duplo sentido - **2.** [gun, camera] carregado(da) - **3.** *inf* [rich] forrado(da).

loading bay ['ləʊdɪŋ-] *n* zona *f* de carga e descarga.

loaf [ləʊf] *(pl* **loaves)** *n* [of bread] (pedaço *m* de) pão *m*.

➡ **loaf about** *vi* vagabundear.

loafer ['ləʊfə^r] *n* - **1.** [shoe] mocassim *m* - **2.** [lazy person] vadio *m*, -dia *f*.

loam [ləʊm] *n (U)* marga *f*.

loan [ləʊn] ⬦ *n* empréstimo *m*; **on ~** por empréstimo. ⬦ *vt* emprestar; **to ~ sthg to sb**, **to ~ sb sthg** emprestar algo a alguém.

loan account *n* conta *f* de empréstimo.

loan capital *n (U)* capital *f* de empréstimo.

loan shark *n inf pej* agiota *mf*.

loath [ləʊθ] *adj*: **to be ~ to do sthg** estar pouco inclinado(da) a fazer algo.

loathe [ləʊð] *vt* odiar, detestar; **to ~ doing sthg** odiar fazer algo.

loathing ['ləʊðɪŋ] *n (U)* ódio *m*.

loathsome ['ləʊðsəm] *adj* repugnante.

loaves [ləʊvz] *pl* ⊳ **loaf**.

lob [lɒb] *(pt & pp* -**bed**, *cont* -**bing)** ⬦ *n* TENNIS lob *m*. ⬦ *vt* -**1.** [throw] lançar - **2.** [TENNIS - ball] rebater com um lob; [- opponent] dar um lob em.

lobby ['lɒbɪ] *(pl* -**ies**, *pt & pp* -**ied)** ⬦ *n* - **1.** [hall] saguão *m* - **2.** [pressure group] lobby *m*, grupo *m* de pressão. ⬦ *vt* pressionar.

lobbyist ['lɒbɪɪst] *n* lobista *mf*.

lobe [ləʊb] *n* ANAT lóbulo *m*.

lobelia [lə'bi:ljə] *n* lobélia *f*.

lobotomy [lə'bɒtəmɪ] *(pl* -**ies**) *n* lobotomia *f*.

lobster ['lɒbstə^r] *n* lagosta *f*.

lobster pot *n* armadilha *f* para pegar lagostas.

local ['ləʊkl] ⬦ *adj* local. ⬦ *n inf* - **1.** [person]: **the ~ s** os habitantes do lugar - **2.** UK [pub] pub *m* local - **3.** US [bus, train] municipal *m*.

local anaesthetic *n* anestesia *f* local.

local area network *n* COMPUT rede *f* local.

local authority *n* UK autoridade *f* local.

local call *n* chamada *f* local.

local colour *n (U)* cor *f* local.

local derby *n* UK clássico *m* local.

locale [ləʊ'ka:l] *n fml* local *m*.

local government *n (U)* governo *m* local.

locality [ləʊ'kælətɪ] *(pl* -**ies**) *n* localidade *f*.

localized, -ised ['ləʊkəlaɪzd] *adj* localizado(da).

locally ['ləʊkəlɪ] *adv* [in region] localmente ; [in neighbourhood] na região.

local time *n (U)* hora *f* local.

locate [UK ləʊ'keɪt, US 'ləʊkeɪt] ⬦ *vt* localizar. ⬦ *vi* US [settle] localizar-se.

location [ləʊ'keɪʃn] *n* - **1.** [place] localização *f* - **2.** CINEMA: **on ~** em locação.

loc. cit. *(abbr of* **loco citato)** loc. cit.

loch [lɒk] *n* Scot lago *m*.

lock [lɒk] ⬦ *n* - **1.** [of door, window, box] fechadura *f*; **under ~ and key** fechado(da) a sete chaves - **2.** [on canal] eclusa *f* - **3.** AUT [steering lock] ângulo *m* de giro - **4.** [of hair] mecha *f* - **5.** *phr*: **~, stock and barrel** com tudo. ⬦ *vt* - **1.** [fasten securely] fechar com chave - **2.** [keep safely] trancar - **3.** [immobilize] bloquear - **4.** [hold firmly]: **to be ~ ed in an embrace** estar fortemente abraçado(da); **to be ~ ed in combat** estar envolvido(da) em disputa. ⬦ *vi* -**1.** [fasten securely] fechar com chave, chavear - **2.** [become immobilized] trancar.

➡ **locks** *npl literary* [hair] cachos *mpl*.

➡ **lock away** *vt sep* trancar a sete chaves.

➡ **lock in** *vt sep* encerrar.

➡ **lock out** *vt sep* -**1.** [accidentally] trancar do lado de fora - **2.** [deliberately] deixar na rua.

➡ **lock up** *vt sep* - **1.** [person] trancafiar - **2.** [house] trancar - **3.** [valuables] fechar com chave - **4.** [with padlock] fechar com cadeado. ⬦ *vi* trancar-se.

lockable ['lɒkəbl] *adj* com fechadura.

locker ['lɒkə^r] *n* [for clothes, luggage, books] compartimento *m* com chave.

locker room *n* US vestiário *m*.

locket ['lɒkɪt] *n* medalhão *m*.

lockjaw *n (U)* tétano *m*.

lockout ['lɒkaʊt] *n* greve *f* patronal, lockout *m*.

locksmith ['lɒksmɪθ] *n* serralheiro *m*, -ra *f*.

lock-up *n* - **1.** [prison] prisão *f*, cárcere *m* - **2.** UK [garage] garagem *f*.

loco ['ləʊkəʊ] *(pl* -**s**) *inf* ⬦ *adj* US louco(ca). ⬦ *n* UK [locomotive] locomotiva *f*.

locomotive ['ləʊkə,məʊtɪv] *n* locomotiva *f*.

locum ['ləʊkəm] *(pl* -**s**) *n* interino *m*, -na *f*.

locust ['ləʊkəst] *n* gafanhoto *m*.

lodge [lɒdʒ] ⬦ *n* - **1.** [caretaker's room] portaria *f* - **2.** [of manor house] guarita *f* - **3.** [of Freemasons] loja *f* - **4.** [for hunting] região *f* de caça. ⬦ *vt fml* [register] apresentar. ⬦ *vi* - **1.** [stay, live]: **to ~ with sb** hospedar-se na casa de alguém - **2.** [become stuck] alojar-se - **3.** *fig* [in mind] gravar-se na mente.

lodger ['lɒdʒə^r] *n* pensionista *mf (em casa de família)*.

lodging ['lɒdʒɪŋ] *n* ⊳ **board**.

➡ **lodgings** *npl* alojamentos *mpl*.

loft [lɒft] *n* [attic] sótão *m*; **~ (apartment)** *apartamento transformado na cobertura de um armazém ou de uma fábrica, em geral amplo e sem divisórias internas.*

lofty ['lɒftɪ] *(compar* -**ier**, *superl* -**iest)** *adj* -**1.** [noble] elevado(da), nobre - **2.** *pej* [haughty] arrogante - **3.** *literary* [high] elevado(da).

log [lɒg] *(pt & pp* -**ged**, *cont* -**ging)** ⬦ *n* -**1.** [of wood] tronco *m* - **2.** [written record - of ship] diário *m* de bordo; [- of plane] diário *m* de vôo. ⬦ *vt* -**1.** [information - on paper] registrar; [- in computer] registrar em log - **2.** [speed, distance, time] anotar.

➡ **log in** *vi* COMPUT entrar (no sistema), efetuar login.

➡ **log out** *vi* COMPUT sair (do sistema), efetuar logout.

loganberry ['ləʊgənbərɪ] *(pl* -**ies**) *n tipo de framboesa de maior tamanho.*

logarithm ['lɒgərɪðm] *n* logaritmo *m*.

logbook ['lɒgbʊk] n -1. [of ship] diário m de bordo -2. [of plane] diário m de vôo -3. [of car] documentação f.

log cabin n cabana f.

log fire n fogueira f.

loggerheads ['lɒgəhedz] n: at ~ with em desavença com.

logic ['lɒdʒɪk] n lógica f.

logical ['lɒdʒɪkl] adj lógico(ca).

logically ['lɒdʒɪklɪ] adv logicamente.

logistical [lə'dʒɪstɪkl] adj logístico(ca).

logistics [lə'dʒɪstɪks] <> n MIL logística f. <> npl fig [organization] logística f.

logjam ['lɒgdʒæm] n fig problema f crônico.

logo ['ləʊgəʊ] (pl -s) n logotipo m.

logrolling ['lɒgrəʊlɪŋ] n (U) US troca f de favores.

logy adj US inf vagaroso(sa).

loin [lɔɪn] n lombo m.

➤ **loins** npl ANAT quadris mpl; to gird one's ~s fig preparar-se para a batalha.

loincloth ['lɔɪnklɒθ] n tanga f.

loiter ['lɔɪtəʳ] vi -1. [hang about] demorar-se -2. [dawdle] vadiar.

loll [lɒl] vi -1. [sit, lie about] recostar-se, refestelar-se -2. [hang down] estar pendente.

lollipop ['lɒlɪpɒp] n pirulito m.

lollipop lady n UK guarda f escolar.

lollipop man n UK guarda m escolar.

lolly ['lɒlɪ] (pl -ies) n -1. [lollipop] pirulito m -2. UK [ice cream] picolé m -3. (U) UK inf [money] grana f.

London ['lʌndən] n Londres; in ~ em Londres.

Londoner ['lʌndənəʳ] n londrino m, -na f.

lone [ləʊn] adj solitário(ria).

loneliness ['ləʊnlɪnɪs] n (U) solidão f.

lonely ['ləʊnlɪ] (compar -ier, superl -iest) adj -1. [gen] solitário(ria), só -2. [place] isolado(da).

lone parent n UK pai m solteiro, mãe f solteira.

loner ['ləʊnəʳ] n solitário m, -ria f.

lonesome ['ləʊnsəm] adj US inf -1. [person] solitário(ria), só -2. [place] isolado(da).

long [lɒŋ] <> adj -1. [in time] longo(ga); two days ~ de dois dias de duração; how ~ will it take? quanto tempo vai demorar? -2. [in space] comprido(da), longo(ga); 10 metres ~ com 10 metros de comprimento; it's five hundred pages ~ tem quinhentas páginas. <> adv [for a long time] por muito tempo; how ~ have you been waiting? há quanto tempo você está esperando?; as OR so ~ as desde que; before ~ agora; for ~ muito tempo; no ~er não mais; I can't wait any ~er não posso mais esperar; so ~! inf até logo! <> n: the ~ and the short of it is that ... em poucas palavras, o que aconteceu é que ... <> vt: to ~ to do sthg ansiar por fazer algo.

➤ **as long as, so long as** conj [if] desde que; as ~ as you're happy about it desde que você esteja feliz com isso.

➤ **long for** vt fus ansiar por.

long. (abbr of longitude) long.

long-awaited [-ə'weɪtɪd] adj tão esperado(da).

long-distance adj de longa distância.

long-distance call n chamada f de longa distância.

long division n (U) divisão f detalhada.

long-drawn-out adj interminável.

long drink n bebida resultante da mistura de álcool e refresco.

longevity [lɒn'dʒevətɪ] n [of person] longevidade f.

long-haired adj -1. [rabbit, sheep] de pêlo comprido -2. [person] de cabelo comprido.

longhand ['lɒŋhænd] n (U) escrita f à mão.

long-haul adj de grande distância.

longing ['lɒŋɪŋ] <> adj ansioso(sa). <> n desejo m; ~ (for sthg) ânsia f (por algo).

longingly ['lɒŋɪŋlɪ] adv ansiosamente.

Long Island n Long Island.

longitude ['lɒndʒɪtjuːd] n GEOGR (U) longitude f.

long johns npl ceroulas fpl.

long jump n salto m em distância.

long-lasting adj de longa duração, duradouro(-ra).

long-life adj longa-vida.

long-lost adj perdido(da) há muito tempo.

long-playing record [-'pleɪɪŋ-] n LP m.

long-range adj -1. [missile, bomber] de longo alcance -2. [plan, forecast] a longo prazo.

long-running adj -1. [play] de muita duração -2. [dispute] que já dura muito tempo -3. [programme] há muito tempo no ar.

longshoreman ['lɒŋʃɔːmən] (pl -men [-mən]) n US estivador m.

long shot n fig possibilidade f remota.

long-sighted adj -1. MED presbita -2. fig [having foresight] previdente.

long-standing adj de longa data.

long-suffering adj sofrido(da).

long term n: in the ~ a longo prazo.

➤ **long-term** adj a longo prazo.

long vacation n UK UNIV férias fpl de verão.

long wave n (U) onda f longa.

longways ['lɒŋweɪz] adv ao comprido, longitudinalmente.

long-wearing adj US resistente, duradouro(ra).

long weekend n feriadão m.

long-winded adj cansativo(va).

loo [luː] (pl -s) n UK inf toalete m.

loofa(h) ['luːfə] n esponja f vegetal.

look [lʊk] <> n -1. [with eyes] olhada f; to give sb a ~ dar uma olhada em alguém; to have a ~ (for sthg) dar uma olhada (procurando algo); to take OR have a ~ (at sthg) dar uma olhada (em algo) -2. [appearance] aparência f; by the ~ (s) of things pelo jeito. <> vi -1. [with eyes] olhar; to ~ at sb/sthg olhar alguém/algo -2. [search] procurar -3. [have stated appearance] parecer; to ~ like parecer como; it ~s like rain parece que vai chover; to ~ as if parecer como se; you ~ as if you haven't slept parece que você não dormiu. <> vt -1. [look at] olhar -2. [appear]: to ~ one's age aparentar a idade que se tem; to ~ one's best vestir-se elegantemente. <> excl: ~ (here)! olha (só)!

➤ **looks** npl [attractiveness] aparência f, beleza f.

➤ **look after** vt fus [take care of] cuidar de; to ~ after o.s. cuidar-se.

➡ **look at** *vt fus* **- 1.** [examine] examinar **- 2.** [analise] analisar **- 3.** [regard, consider] olhar para.

➡ **look back** *vi* [reminisce] recordar; **she's never ~ed back** ela nunca retrocedeu.

➡ **look down on** *vt fus* [condescend to] desdenhar de, depreciar.

➡ **look for** *vt fus* procurar (por).

➡ **look forward to** *vt fus* aguardar (ansiosamente).

➡ **look into** *vt fus* [examine] analisar, examinar.

➡ **look on** ⬦ *vt fus* = **look upon**. ⬦ *vi* [watch] observar.

➡ **look onto** *vi* [face] ter vista para, dar para.

➡ **look out** *vi* [take care] tomar cuidado; **~ out!** cuidado!

➡ **look out for** *vt fus* [try to spot] estar atento(ta) a.

➡ **look round** ⬦ *vt fus* [visit] visitar. ⬦ *vi* **- 1.** [look at surroundings] percorrer com o olhar ao redor **- 2.** [turn] virar-se.

➡ **look through** *vt fus* [report, document] examinar o conteúdo de.

➡ **look to** *vt fus* **- 1.** [depend on] contar com **- 2.** [think about] pensar em.

➡ **look up** ⬦ *vt sep* **- 1.** [in book] consultar **- 2.** [visit] visitar. ⬦ *vi* [improve] melhorar.

➡ **look upon** *vt fus* [consider]: **I ~ upon him as my father** eu o considerava meu pai.

➡ **look up to** *vt fus* [admire] prezar, respeitar.

look-alike *n* sósia *mf*.

look-in *n UK*: **to get a ~** [chance to participate] ter a possibilidade de participar *OR* fazer parte.

lookout ['lʊkaʊt] *n* **- 1.** [place] posto *m* de observação, guarita *f* **- 2.** [person] vigia *mf* **- 3.** [search]: **to be on the ~ for sthg** estar à espreita de algo.

look-up table *n COMPUT* tabela *f* de consulta.

loom [luːm] ⬦ *n* tear *m*. ⬦ *vi* **- 1.** [rise up] erguer-se **- 2.** *fig* [be imminent] aproximar-se, ser iminente; **to ~ large** crescer em tamanho.

➡ **loom up** *vi* despontar sombriamente.

looming ['luːmɪŋ] *adj* iminente.

loony ['luːnɪ] (*compar* **-ier**, *superl* **-iest**, *pl* **-ies**) *inf* ⬦ *adj* lunático(ca). ⬦ *n* lunático *m*, -ca *f*.

loop [luːp] ⬦ *n* **- 1.** [shape] laço *m* **- 2.** [contraceptive] DIU *m* **- 3.** *COMPUT* loop *m*, laço *m*. ⬦ *vt* [rope, string] enlaçar. ⬦ *vi* [road, river] fazer uma curva acentuada.

loophole ['luːphəʊl] *n* furo *m* (*na lei*).

loo roll *n UK inf* rolo *m* de papel higiênico.

loose [luːs] ⬦ *adj* **- 1.** [not firmly fixed] frouxo(xa) **- 2.** [unattached, unpackaged - sheets of paper] avulso(sa); [- sweets, nails] solto(ta) **- 3.** [not tight-fitting] folgado(da) **- 4.** [free, not restrained] solto(ta) **- 5.** *pej* & *dated* [promiscuous] promíscuo(cua) **- 6.** [inexact] impreciso(sa) **- 7.** [informal] informal **- 8.** *US inf* [relaxed]: **to stay ~** ficar relaxado(da). ⬦ *n* (*U*): **to be on the ~** andar solto(ta).

loose change *n* (*U*) trocado *m*.

loose end *n* ponta *f* solta; **yet another~ we can't explain** outra incógnita que a gente não consegue explicar; **to be at a ~** *UK*, **to be at ~s** *US* estar entediado(da), não ter o que fazer.

loose-fitting *adj* folgado(da).

loose-leaf binder *n* pasta *f* de folhas soltas.

loosely ['luːslɪ] *adv* **- 1.** [not firmly] sem apertar **- 2.** [inexactly] imprecisamente.

loosen ['luːsn] ⬦ *vt* [make less tight] afrouxar. ⬦ *vi* [become less tight] afrouxar.

➡ **loosen up** *vi* **- 1.** [before game, race] aquecer-se **- 2.** *inf* [relax] relaxar.

loot [luːt] ⬦ *n* (*U*) saque *m*. ⬦ *vt* saquear.

looter ['luːtə͡ʳ] *n* saqueador *m*, -ra *f*.

looting ['luːtɪŋ] *n* (*U*) saque *m*.

lop [lɒp] (*pt* & *pp* **-ped**, *cont* **-ping**) *vt* podar.

➡ **lop off** *vt sep* cortar.

lope [ləʊp] *vi* **- 1.** [animal] trotar **- 2.** [person] andar a passos largos e ligeiros.

lop-sided [-'saɪdɪd] *adj* **- 1.** [uneven] assimétrico(ca) **- 2.** *fig* [biased] distorcido(da).

lord [lɔːd] *n UK* [man of noble rank] lorde *m*. ⬦ *vt*: **to ~ it over** humilhar.

➡ **Lord** *n* **- 1.** *RELIG*: **the Lord** [God] o Senhor; **good Lord!** *UK* Deus meu! **- 2.** [in titles] lorde *m* **- 3.** [as form of address]: **my Lord** [bishop] Reverendíssimo *m*; [judge] Meritíssimo *m*, -ma *f*.

➡ **Lords** *npl UK POL*: **the (House of) Lords** a Câmara dos Lordes.

Lord Chancellor *n UK POL* presidente *da* Câmara *dos Lordes e responsável pela Justiça na Inglaterra e no País de Gales*.

lordly ['lɔːdlɪ] (*compar* **-ier**, *superl* **-iest**) *adj* **- 1.** [noble] nobre **- 2.** *pej* [arrogant] arrogante.

Lord Mayor *n UK* prefeito *da cidade de Londres e outras metrópoles*.

Lordship ['lɔːdʃɪp] *n*: **your/his ~** Vossa/Sua Senhoria.

Lord's Prayer *n*: **the ~** o Pai Nosso.

lore [lɔː͡ʳ] *n* (*U*) crença *f* popular.

lorry ['lɒrɪ] (*pl* **-ies**) *n UK* caminhão *m*.

lorry driver *n UK* motorista *mf* de caminhão.

lose [luːz] (*pt* & *pp* **lost**) ⬦ *vt* **- 1.** [gen] perder; **to ~ sight of sb/sthg** perder alguém/algo de vista; **to ~ one's way** [get lost] perder-se; **to ~ weight** emagrecer, perder peso; **you have nothing to ~ inf** você não tem nada a perder **- 2.** [subj: clock, watch]: **my watch ~s 5 minutes a day** meu relógio atrasa 5 minutos por dia **- 3.** [elude, shake off] escapar de. ⬦ *vi* **- 1.** [fail to win] perder **- 2.** [time] atrasar-se.

➡ **lose out** *vi* sair perdendo; **to ~ out on sthg** sair perdendo em algo.

loser ['luːzə͡ʳ] *n* [gen] perdedor *m*, -ra *f*; **to be a good/bad ~** saber/não saber perder, ser um bom/mau perdedor.

losing ['luːzɪŋ] *adj* vencido(da).

loss [lɒs] *n* **- 1.** [gen] perda *f* **- 2.** [failure to win] derrota *f* **- 3.** *COMM* [of money] prejuízo *m*; **to make a ~** ter prejuízo; **to cut one's ~es** cortar a fonte de prejuízos **- 4.** *phr*: **to be at a ~to explain sthg** não saber como explicar algo.

loss adjuster [-ə'dʒʌstə͡ʳ] *n* perito *m*, -ta *f* na determinação de avarias.

loss leader *n COMM* artigo *m* em liquidação, chamariz *m*.

lost [lɒst] ⬦ *pt* & *pp* ⬅ **lose**. ⬦ *adj* **- 1.** [gen] perdido(da); **to get ~** [lose way] perder-se; **get ~! inf** te some! **- 2.** [wasted]: **to be ~ on sb** não surtir efeito em alguém.

lost-and-found office n US setor m de acha-dos e perdidos.

lost cause n causa f perdida.

lost property n (U) achados mpl e perdidos.

lost property office n UK setor m de achados e perdidos.

lot [lɒt] n -1. [large amount]: **a ~ of, ~s of** muito(ta); **a ~ of people** muita gente, muitas pessoas; **~s of problems** muitos problemas; **he talks a ~** ele fala muito -2. inf [group of things]: **I bought two ~s of shares last week** comprei dois lotes de ações na semana passada; **put this ~ in my office** inf coloca tudo isso no meu escritório -3. inf [group of people]: **one ~ of refugees arrived yesterday** um grupo de refugiados chegou ontem; **what a mean ~ you are!** inf são todos uns mesquinhos! -4. [destiny] destino m, sorte f -5. [at auction] lote m -6. [entire amount]: **the ~** tudo -7. US [of land] lote m; [car park] estacionamento m -8. phr: **to draw ~s** tirar à sorte.

→ **a lot** adv muito; **~ better** muito melhor.

loth [ləʊθ] adj = loath.

lotion ['ləʊʃn] n loção f.

lottery ['lɒtərɪ] (pl -ies) n loteria f.

LOTTO® ['lɒtəʊ] n loteria f nacional (britânica), ≃ loto f.

lotus position ['ləʊtəs-] n posição f de lótus.

loud [laʊd] <> adj -1. [person] barulhento(ta) -2. [voice, music, TV] alto(ta) -3. [bang] forte -4. [emphatic]: **to be ~ in sthg** ser enfático(ca) em algo -5. [garish] espalhafatoso(sa). <> adv alto; **~ and clear** alto e claro; **out ~** em voz alta.

loudhailer [ˌlaʊd'heɪləʳ] n UK megafone m.

loudly ['laʊdlɪ] adv -1. [shout] alto -2. [talk] em voz alta -3. [garishly] de forma espalhafatosa.

loudmouth ['laʊdmaʊθ, pl -maʊðz] n inf tagarela mf, gasguita mf.

loudness ['laʊdnɪs] n (U) intensidade f do som.

loudspeaker [ˌlaʊd'spiːkəʳ] n alto-falante m.

lough n Irish lago m.

Louisiana [luːˌiːzɪ'ænə] n Louisiana; **in ~** em Louisiana.

lounge [laʊndʒ] (cont loungeing) <> n -1. [in house] sala f de estar -2. [in airport] sala f de espera -3. UK [bar] = lounge bar. <> vi recostar-se.

→ **lounge about, lounge around** vi vadiar.

lounge bar n UK sala f mais confortável (num bar).

lounge lizard n parasita mf social.

lounge suit n UK traje m social, terno m.

louse [laʊs] (pl sense 1 lice, pl sense 2 -s) n -1. [insect] piolho m -2. inf pej [person] canalha mf.

→ **louse up** vt sep US vinf melar.

lousy ['laʊzɪ] (compar -ier, superl -iest) adj inf -1. [poor-quality] péssimo(ma); **his performance was ~** a apresentação dele foi uma porcaria -2. [ill]: **to feel ~** sentir-se mal.

lout [laʊt] n mal-educado m.

louvre UK, **louver** US ['luːvəʳ] n: **~ door** porta f de veneziana; **~ window** veneziana f.

lovable ['lʌvəbl] adj amável, encantador(ra).

love [lʌv] <> n -1. (U) [affection for person] amor m; **give her my ~** dá um abraço nela por mim; **a ~-hate relationship** uma relação de amor e ódio; **~ from** [at end of letter] um abraço, um beijo; **to be in ~** estar apaixonado(da); **to fall in ~** apaixonar-se; **to make ~** fazer amor -2. [liking for sthg, for activity] paixão f; **to have a ~ of** OR **for sthg** ter paixão por algo -3. [beloved person, thing] amor m -4. inf [term of address] amor m -5. (U) TENNIS: **30 ~** 30 a zero. <> vt -1. [gen] amar -2. [like] adorar; **to ~ to do sthg** OR **doing sthg** adorar fazer algo.

love affair n caso m (de amor).

lovebite ['lʌvbaɪt] n chupão m.

loveless ['lʌvlɪs] adj [marriage] sem amor.

love letter n carta f de amor.

love life n vida f amorosa.

lovely ['lʌvlɪ] (compar -ier, superl -iest) adj -1. [person, child - in looks] encantador(ra); [- in character] amável -2. [view, day, weather] adorável; [dress, surprise, holiday] maravilhoso(sa), adorável.

love-making n (U) relação f sexual.

lover ['lʌvəʳ] n -1. [sexual partner] amante mf -2. [enthusiast] amante mf, apaixonado m, -da f.

lovesick ['lʌvsɪk] adj doente de amor (não-correspondido).

love song n canção f de amor.

love story n história f de amor.

loving ['lʌvɪŋ] adj carinhoso(sa), afetuoso(sa).

lovingly ['lʌvɪŋlɪ] adv carinhosamente, afetuosamente.

low [ləʊ] <> adj -1. [gen] baixo(xa); **we are ~ on milk** estamos com pouco leite -2. [poor - intelligence] pouco(ca); [- opinion] pobre; [- standard, quality, esteem] baixo(xa); [- health] debilitado(da) -3. [not loud or high] baixo(xa) -4. [light] fraco(ca) -5. [neckline] decotado(da) -6. [depressed] deprimido(da) -7. [vulgar] baixo(xa). <> adv -1. [gen] baixo -2. [situated, built] embaixo. <> n -1. [low point] baixa f -2. METEOR área f de baixa pressão.

low-alcohol adj de baixo teor alcoólico.

lowbrow ['ləʊbraʊ] adj de baixo nível intelectual.

low-calorie adj de baixa caloria.

Low Church n corrente evangélica da Igreja Anglicana.

Low Countries npl: **the ~** os Países Baixos.

low-cut adj decotado(da).

low-down adj inf: **~ trick** truque m baixo.

→ **lowdown** n inf: **to give sb the lowdown (on sthg)** dar os detalhes concretos (sobre algo) a alguém.

lower[1] ['ləʊəʳ] <> adj inferior. <> vt -1. [gen] baixar -2. [reduce] reduzir.

lower[2] ['laʊəʳ] vi -1. [be dark] estar escuro(ra) -2. [frown]: **to ~ at sb** fechar a cara para alguém.

Lower Chamber [ˌləʊəʳ-] n POL ≃ Câmara f Baixa.

lower class [ˌləʊəʳ-] n: **the ~(es)** as classes baixas.

Lower House [ˌləʊəʳ-] n POL Câmara f Baixa.

lowest common denominator ['ləʊɪst-] n: **the ~** o menor denominador comum.

low-fat adj com baixo teor de gordura.

low-flying adj de vôo rasante.

low frequency n baixa freqüência f.

low gear n US primeira f (marcha).

low-key *adj* discreto(ta).

Lowlands [ˈləʊləndz] *npl*: **the** ~ [of Scotland] as Terras Baixas *(da Escócia)*.

low-level language *n* COMPUT linguagem *f* de baixo nível.

low-loader *n* veículo *m* com baixa plataforma de carga.

lowly [ˈləʊlɪ] (*compar* -ier, *superl* -iest) *adj* humilde.

low-lying *adj* [land] baixo(xa).

Low Mass *n* missa *f* baixa.

low-necked [-ˈnekt] *adj* decotado(da).

low-paid *adj* mal pago(ga).

low-rise *adj* baixo(xa).

low season *n* baixa estação *f*.

low tide *n* maré *f* baixa.

loyal [ˈlɔɪəl] *adj* leal, fiel.

loyalist [ˈlɔɪəlɪst] *n* leal *mf (ao governo)*.

◆ **Loyalist** *n* POL [in Northern Ireland] *protestante que acredita que a Irlanda do Norte deva continuar fazendo parte do Reino Unido.*

loyalty [ˈlɔɪəltɪ] (*pl* -ies) *n* lealdade *f*, fidelidade *f*.

loyalty card *n* cartão *f* de fidelização.

lozenge [ˈlɒzɪndʒ] *n* -1. [tablet] pastilha *f* -2. [shape] losango *m*.

LP (*abbr of* long-playing record) *n* LP *m*.

L-plate *n UK* ≃ auto-escola *f (indicação no veículo), placa que contém a letra L em vermelho fixada no veículo conduzido por pessoa que está aprendendo a dirigir.*

LPN (*abbr of* licensed practical nurse) *n* técnico em enfermagem nos Estados Unidos.

LPO (*abbr of* London Philharmonic Orchestra) *n* Orquestra *f* Filarmônica de Londres.

LRAM (*abbr of* Licentiate of the Royal Academy of Music) *n* membro da academia britânica de música.

LRB (*abbr of* London Review of Books) *n* jornal britânico de resenhas literárias e humanidades.

LSAT (*abbr of* Law School Admissions Test) *n* exame de acesso às escolas de direito nos Estados Unidos.

LSD *n* (*abbr of* lysergic acid diethylamide) LSD *m*.

LSE (*abbr of* London School of Economics) *n* escola londrina de ciências políticas e econômicas.

LSO (*abbr of* London Symphony Orchestra) *n* Orquestra *f* Sinfônica de Londres.

Lt. (*abbr of* lieutenant) Ten.

LT (*abbr of* low tension) *n* ELEC baixa tensão *f*.

Ltd, ltd (*abbr of* limited) Ltda.

lubricant [ˈluːbrɪkənt] *n* lubrificante *m*.

lubricate [ˈluːbrɪkeɪt] *vt* lubrificar.

lubrication [ˌluːbrɪˈkeɪʃn] *n (U)* lubrificação *f*.

lucid [ˈluːsɪd] *adj* -1. [easily understood] nítido(da) -2. [clear-headed] lúcido(da).

lucidly [ˈluːsɪdlɪ] *adv* claramente, lucidamente.

luck [lʌk] *n (U)* sorte *f*; **good** ~! boa sorte!; **bad** ~ [misfortune] azar *m*; **bad** ~! [said to commiserate] que azar!; **hard** ~! azar!; **to be in** ~ estar com sorte; **to try one's** ~ **at sthg** tentar a sorte em algo; **with (any)** ~ com (um pouco de) sorte.

◆ **luck out** *vi US inf* ter sorte.

luckily [ˈlʌkɪlɪ] *adv* afortunadamente.

luckless [ˈlʌklɪs] *adj* desafortunado(da).

lucky [ˈlʌkɪ] (*compar* -ier, *superl* -iest) *adj* -1. [fortunate - person] sortudo(da), com sorte; [- event] feliz -2. [bringing good luck] da sorte.

lucky charm *n* amuleto *m*.

lucky dip *n UK* saco *m* de surpresas.

lucrative [ˈluːkrətɪv] *adj* lucrativo(va).

ludicrous [ˈluːdɪkrəs] *adj* -1. [appearance, situation] ridículo(la) -2. [decision, suggestion] absurdo(da).

ludo [ˈluːdəʊ] *n (U) UK* ludo *m*.

lug [lʌg] (*pt* & *pp* -ged, *cont* -ging) *vt inf* arrastar, tirar com dificuldade.

luggage [ˈlʌgɪdʒ] *n (U) UK* bagagem *f*.

luggage rack *n UK* porta-bagagem *m*.

luggage van *n UK* RAIL vagão *m* de bagagem.

lugubrious [luˈguːbrɪəs] *adj fml* lúgubre.

lukewarm [ˈluːkwɔːm] *adj* -1. [tepid] morno(na) -2. [unenthusiastic] desanimado(da), indiferente.

lull [lʌl] <> *n* -1. [in activity] pausa *f*; **the** ~ **before the storm** *fig* a bonança antes da tempestade -2. [in fighting] trégua *f*. <> *vt* -1. [make sleepy]: **to** ~ **sb to sleep** ninar alguém para dormir -2. [reassure]: **to** ~ **sb into a false sense of security** passar a alguém uma falsa sensação de segurança.

lullaby [ˈlʌləbaɪ] (*pl* -ies) *n* cantiga *f* de ninar.

lumbago [lʌmˈbeɪgəʊ] *n (U)* lumbago *m*.

lumber [ˈlʌmbəʳ] <> *n* -1. *US* [timber] madeira *f* serrada, tábua *f* -2. *UK* [bric-a-brac] trastes *mpl*. <> *vi* [large person, animal, vehicle] andar a custo.

◆ **lumber with** *vt sep UK inf* [encumber] encarregar.

lumbering [ˈlʌmbərɪŋ] *adj* desengoçado(da).

lumberjack [ˈlʌmbədʒæk] *n* lenhador *m*, -ra *f*.

lumbermill [ˈlʌmbə,mɪl] *n US* serraria *f*.

lumber-room *n UK* quarto *f* para guardar tralhas.

lumberyard [ˈlʌmbəjɑːd] *n* madeireira *f*.

luminous [ˈluːmɪnəs] *adj* luminoso(sa).

lump [lʌmp] <> *n* -1. [piece - of coal] pedaço *m*; [- earth, sugar] torrão *m*; [- in sauce, soup] caroço *m* -2. MED [on body] tumor *m*. <> *vt*: **to** ~ **sthg together** agrupar algo; **you'll just have to** ~ **it** *inf*! você vai ter de engolir isso!

lumpectomy [ˌlʌmˈpektəmɪ] (*pl* -ies) *n* cirurgia para remoção de tumor do seio.

lump sum *n* soma *f* global.

lumpy [ˈlʌmpɪ] (*compar* -ier, *superl* -iest) *adj* encaroçado(da).

lunacy [ˈluːnəsɪ] *n (U)* loucura *f*.

lunar [ˈluːnəʳ] *adj* lunar.

lunatic [ˈluːnətɪk] <> *adj pej* lunático(ca). <> *n* -1. *pej* [fool] idiota *mf* -2. [insane person] lunático *m*, -ca *f*.

lunatic asylum *n* hospício *m*, manicômio *m*.

lunatic fringe *n* minoria *f* extremista.

lunch [lʌntʃ] <> *n* almoço *m*; **to have** ~ almoçar. <> *vi* almoçar.

luncheon [ˈlʌntʃən] *n fml* almoço *m*.

luncheonette *n US* lanchonete *f*.

luncheon meat *n (U)* fiambre *m*.

luncheon voucher *n UK* tíquete-refeição *m*.

lunch hour *n* hora *f* do almoço.

lunchtime [ˈlʌntʃtaɪm] *n* hora *f* do almoço.

lung [lʌŋ] *n* pulmão *m*.

lung cancer *n (U)* câncer *m* de pulmão.
lunge [lʌndʒ] *vi* arremessar-se; **to ~ at sb** investir contra alguém.
lupin *UK* ['lu:pɪn], **lupine** *US* ['lu:paɪn] *n* tremoço *m*.
lurch [lɜ:tʃ] <> *n* [movement] cambaleio *m*, solavanco *m*; **to leave sb in the ~** deixar alguém na mão. <> *vi* [in movement] cambalear, balançar.
lure [ljʊəʳ] <> *n* [attraction] fascínio *m*. <> *vt* [tempt] fascinar.
lurid ['ljʊərɪd] *adj* -**1.** [brightly coloured] sensacional -**2.** [shockingly unpleasant] chocante.
lurk [lɜ:k] *vi* espreitar.
lurking ['lɜ:kɪŋ] *adj* que segue rondando.
Lusaka [lu:'sɑ:kə] *n* Lusaka; **in ~** em Lusaka.
luscious ['lʌʃəs] *adj* -**1.** [fruit] suculento(ta) -**2.** [colour] vistoso(sa).
lush [lʌʃ] <> *adj* -**1.** [healthy, thick] viçoso(sa) -**2.** *inf* [sumptuous] luxuoso(sa). <> *n US inf* [drunkard] bêbado *m*, -da *f*.
lust [lʌst] *n* -**1.** *(U)* [sexual desire] luxúria *f* -**2.** [greed]: **~ for sthg** cobiça *f* por algo.
➡ **lust after, lust for** *vt fus* -**1.** [money, power] cobiçar -**2.** [person] desejar.
luster *n US* = lustre.
lustful ['lʌstfʊl] *adj* luxurioso(sa).
lustre *UK*, **luster** *US* ['lʌstəʳ] *n* [brightness] brilho *m*.
lusty ['lʌstɪ] (*compar*-**ier**, *superl*-**iest**) *adj* vigoroso(sa), forte.
lute [lu:t] *n* alaúde *m*.
luv [lʌv] *n UK inf* amor *m*.
Luxembourg ['lʌksəmˌbɜ:g] *n* Luxemburgo; **in ~** em Luxemburgo.
luxuriant [lʌg'zʊərɪənt] *adj* viçoso(sa), exuberante.
luxuriate [lʌg'zʊərɪeɪt] *vi* deleitar-se; **to ~ in sthg** deleitar-se com algo.
luxurious [lʌg'zʊərɪəs] *adj* -**1.** [expensive] luxuoso(sa) -**2.** [voluptuous] esplêndido(da).
luxury ['lʌkʃərɪ] (*pl*-**ies**) <> *n* luxo *m*. <> *comp* de luxo.
luxury goods *npl* artigos *mpl* de luxo.
LV (*abbr of* **luncheon voucher**) *n* vale-refeição *m*.
LW (*abbr of* **long wave**) *n* onda *f* longa.
lychee [ˌlaɪ'tʃi:] *n* lichia *f*.
Lycra® ['laɪkrə] <> *n (U)* lycra® *f*. <> *comp* de lycra.
lying ['laɪɪŋ] <> *adj* [dishonest] mentiroso(sa), falso(sa). <> *n* [dishonesty] mentiras *fpl*.
lymph gland [lɪmf-] *n* glândula *f* linfática.
lynch [lɪntʃ] *vt* linchar.
lynx [lɪŋks] (*pl inv* OR -**es**) *n* lince *m*.
lyre ['laɪəʳ] *n* lira *f*.
lyric ['lɪrɪk] *adj* lírico(ca).
➡ **lyrics** *npl* letra *f* (*de música*).
lyrical ['lɪrɪkl] *adj* -**1.** [poetic] lírico(ca) -**2.** [enthusiastic] entusiasmado(da).

m¹ (*pl* **m's** OR **ms**), **M** (*pl* **M's** OR **Ms**) [em] *n* [letter] m, M *m*.
➡ **M** -**1.** *UK* (*abbr of* **motorway**) rodovia *f* -**2.** (*abbr of* **medium**) M.
m² -**1.** (*abbr of* **metre**) m -**2.** (*abbr of* **million**) milhão *m*. -**3.** *abbr of* **mile**.
ma [mɑ:] *n inf* mamã *f*.
MA <> *n* (*abbr of* **Master of Arts**) (*titular de*) diploma de mestre em ciências humanas. <> *abbr of* **Massachusetts**.
ma'am [mæm] *n* madame *f*.
mac [mæk] (*abbr of* **mackintosh**) *n UK inf* [coat] capa *f* de chuva.
macabre [mə'kɑ:brə] *adj* macabro(bra).
Macao [mə'kaʊ] *n* Macau; **in ~** em Macau.
macaroni [ˌmækə'rəʊnɪ] *n (U)* macarrão *m*.
macaroni cheese *n (U)* macarrão *m* com molho de queijo.
macaroon [ˌmækə'ru:n] *n* biscoito doce preparado com amêndoas e coco.
mace [meɪs] *n* -**1.** [ornamental rod] maça *f* -**2.** *(U)* [spice] macis *m inv*.
Macedonia [ˌmæsɪ'dəʊnɪə] *n* Macedônia; **in ~** na Macedônia.
Macedonian [ˌmæsɪ'dəʊnɪən] <> *adj* macedônico(ca). <> *n* macedônico *m*, -ca *f*.
machete [mə'ʃetɪ] *n* machete *m*.
Machiavellian [ˌmækɪə'velɪən] *adj* maquiavélico(ca).
machinations [ˌmækɪ'neɪʃnz] *npl* maquinações *fpl*.
machine [mə'ʃi:n] <> *n* máquina *f*. <> *vt* -**1.** SEWING costurar à maquina -**2.** TECH usinar.
machine code *n* COMPUT código *m* de máquina.
machinegun [mə'ʃi:ngʌn] (*pt & pp* -**ned**, *cont* -**ning**) <> *n* metralhadora *f*. <> *vt* metralhar.
machine language *n* COMPUT linguagem *f* de máquina.
machine-readable *adj* COMPUT legível por máquina.
machinery [mə'ʃi:nərɪ] *n (U)* -**1.** [machines] maquinário *m* -**2.** *fig* [system] mecanismo *m*.
machine shop *n* oficina *f* de máquinas.
machine tool *n* máquina *f* operatriz.
machine-washable *adj* lavável à máquina.

machinist [mə'ʃiːnɪst] n operador m, -ra f de máquina.
machismo [mə'tʃɪzməʊ] n (U) machismo m.
macho ['mætʃəʊ] adj inf machista.
mackerel ['mækrəl] (pl inv OR -s) n cavala f.
mackintosh ['mækɪntɒʃ] n UK capa f de chuva.
macramé [mə'krɑːmɪ] n (U) macramé m.
macro ['mækrəʊ] n COMPUT macro f.
macrobiotic [ˌmækrəʊbaɪ'ɒtɪk] adj macrobiótico(-ca).
macrocosm ['mækrəʊkɒzm] n macrocosmo m.
macroeconomics ['mækrəʊˌiːkə'nɒmɪks] n (U) macroeconomia f.
mad [mæd] (compar -der, superl -dest) adj -1. [insane] louco(ca); to go ~ enlouquecer -2. pej [foolish] maluco(ca) -3. [furious] doido(da); to go ~ at sb ficar louco(ca) com alguém -4. [hectic] exasperado(da); like ~ feito louco(ca) -5. [very enthusiastic]: to be ~ about sb/sthg ser louco(ca) por alguém/algo.
Madagascan [ˌmædə'gæskən] <> adj malgaxe. <> n -1. [person] malgaxe mf- 2. [language] malgaxe m.
Madagascar [ˌmædə'gæskər] n Madagascar; in ~ em Madagascar.
madam ['mædəm] n fml [form of address] senhora f.
madcap ['mædkæp] adj doido(da).
madden ['mædn] vt enfurecer, exasperar.
maddening ['mædnɪŋ] adj enlouquecedor(ra).
made [meɪd] pt & pp ⊳ make.
-made [meɪd] suffix: French ~ feito(ta) na França.
Madeira [mə'dɪərə] n -1. (U) [wine] madeira m - 2. GEOGR Ilha f da Madeira; in ~ na Ilha da Madeira.
made-to-measure adj feito(ta) sob medida.
made-up adj -1. [with make-up] maquiado(da) -2. [prepared] já preparado(da) -3. [invented] falso(sa), esfarrapado(da).
madhouse ['mædhaʊs, pl -haʊzɪz] n fig inf hospício m.
madly ['mædlɪ] adv [frantically] alucinadamente; ~ in love loucamente apaixonado(da).
madman ['mædmən] (pl -men [-mən]) n louco m.
madness ['mædnɪs] n (U) loucura f.
Madonna [mə'dɒnə] n -1. RELIG: the ~ a Nossa Senhora -2. ART madona f.
Madrid [mə'drɪd] n Madrid; in ~ em Madrid.
madrigal ['mædrɪgl] n madrigal m.
madwoman ['mædˌwʊmən] (pl -women [-ˌwɪmɪn]) n louca f.
maestro ['maɪstrəʊ] (pl -tros OR -tri [-trɪ]) n maestro m.
MAFF (abbr of Ministry of Agriculture, Fisheries, and Food) n ministério britânico da agricultura, da pesca e dos alimentos, ≃ Ministério m da Agricultura.
Mafia ['mæfɪə] n: the ~ a Máfia.
mag [mæg] (abbr of magazine) n inf revista f.
magazine [ˌmægə'ziːn] n -1. [periodical] revista f- 2. [news programme] programa m de variedades -3. [on a gun] câmara f.
magenta [mə'dʒentə] <> adj magenta. <> n (U) magenta m.
maggot ['mægət] n larva f.

Maghreb ['mʌgreb] n: the ~ o Magrebe.
magic ['mædʒɪk] <> adj -1. [gen] mágico(ca) -2. [referring to conjuring] de mágica. <> n (U) -1. [gen] magia f- 2. [conjuring] mágica f.
magical ['mædʒɪkl] adj [using sorcery] mágico(ca).
magic carpet n tapete m mágico.
magic eye n UK olho m mágico.
magician [mə'dʒɪʃn] n -1. [conjurer] mágico m, -ca f -2. [wizard] mago m, -ga f.
magic wand n varinha f mágica.
magisterial [ˌmædʒɪ'stɪərɪəl] adj -1. fml [authoritative] dominador(ra) -2. JUR magistral.
magistrate ['mædʒɪstreɪt] n magistrado m, -da f.
magistrates' court n UK tribunal m.
Magna Carta [ˌmægnə'kɑːtə] n: the ~ a Carta Magna.
magnanimous [mæg'nænɪməs] adj magnânimo(-ma).
magnate ['mægneɪt] n magnata mf.
magnesium [mæg'niːzɪəm] n (U) magnésio m.
magnet ['mægnɪt] n -1. PHYSICS ímã m -2. fig [attraction] atrativo m.
magnetic [mæg'netɪk] adj -1. PHYSICS magnético(ca) -2. fig [personality] atraente, carismático(ca).
magnetic disk n disco m magnético.
magnetic field n campo m magnético.
magnetic tape n (U) fita f magnética.
magnetism ['mægnɪtɪzm] n (U) magnetismo m.
magnification [ˌmægnɪfɪ'keɪʃn] n (U) -1. [process] ampliação f- 2. [degree of enlargement] aumento m.
magnificence [mæg'nɪfɪsəns] n (U) magnificência f.
magnificent [mæg'nɪfɪsənt] adj -1. [clothes, splendour, building] grandioso(sa) -2. [idea, book, game] magnífico(ca), brilhante.
magnify ['mægnɪfaɪ] (pt & pp -ied) vt -1. [TECH - image] ampliar; [- sound] amplificar -2. fig [exaggerate] exagerar.
magnifying glass ['mægnɪfaɪŋ-] n lupa f, lente f de aumento.
magnitude ['mægnɪtjuːd] n magnitude f.
magnolia [mæg'nəʊljə] n -1. [tree, flower] magnólia f- 2. [colour] creme m.
magnum ['mægnəm] (pl -s) n garrafa de 1,5 litro de capacidade.
magpie ['mægpaɪ] n pega f (ave).
maharaja(h) [ˌmɑːhə'rɑːdʒə] n marajá m.
mahogany [mə'hɒgənɪ] n mogno m.
maid [meɪd] n [servant] empregada f doméstica.
maiden ['meɪdn] <> adj [voyage, speech] de estréia, inaugural. <> n literary [young girl] donzela f; [virgin] virgem f.
maiden aunt n tia f solteirona.
maiden name n nome m de solteira.
maiden speech n POL discurso m inaugural.
mail [meɪl] <> n -1. [letters, parcels] correio m; by ~ pelo correio -2. [system] correios mpl. <> vt -1. [send] mandar pelo correio -2. [put in mail box] postar.
mailbag ['meɪlbæg] n sacola f do carteiro.
mailbox ['meɪlbɒks] n -1. US [for letters] caixa f de correio -2. COMPUT caixa f de entrada.
mailing list ['meɪlɪŋ-] n lista f de endereços.

mailman ['meɪlmən] (pl -men [-mən]) n US carteiro m.

mail order n (U) pedido m por reembolso postal.

mailshot ['meɪlʃɒt] n mala-direta f.

mail train n trem-correio m, trem m postal.

mail truck n US caminhão m dos correios.

mail van n [for delivering mail - by road] carro-correio m; [- by rail] vagão-correio m.

maim [meɪm] vt mutilar.

main [meɪn] <> adj principal. <> n [pipe] tubulação f.
→ **mains** npl: **the** ~**s** [gas, water] as tubulações; [electric] a rede elétrica.
→ **in the main** adv em geral.

main course n prato m principal.

Maine [meɪn] n Maine; **in** ~ em Maine.

mainframe (computer) ['meɪnfreɪm-] n computador m mainframe.

mainland ['meɪnlənd] <> adj continental. <> n: **the** ~ o continente.

main line n RAIL linha-tronco f.
→ **mainline** <> adj [train, station] de linha-tronco. <> vt & vi drugs sl injetar-se na veia.

mainly ['meɪnlɪ] adv principalmente.

main road n rodovia f principal.

mainsail ['meɪnseɪl] n vela-mestra f.

mainstay ['meɪnsteɪ] n meio m de subsistência.

mainstream ['meɪnstriːm] <> adj predominante. <> n: **the** ~ a tendência geral.

maintain [meɪn'teɪn] vt -1. [gen] manter -2. [support, provide for] sustentar, manter -3. [look after] manter em bom estado -4. [assert]: **to** ~ **(that)** sustentar que.

maintenance ['meɪntənəns] n (U) -1. [gen] manutenção f -2. [money] pensão f.

maintenance order n UK JUR obrigação f de pensão alimentícia.

maisonette [ˌmeɪzə'net] n duplex m inv.

maize [meɪz] n (U) milho m.

Maj. (abbr of **Major**) Maj.

majestic [mə'dʒestɪk] adj majestoso(sa).

majestically [mə'dʒestɪklɪ] adv majestosamente.

majesty ['mædʒəstɪ] (pl -ies) n [grandeur] majestade f.
→ **Majesty** n: **His** OR **Her/Your Majesty** Sua/Vossa Majestade.

major ['meɪdʒə'] <> adj -1. [gen] principal -2. MUS maior. <> n [MIL - in army] major m; [- in air force] major-aviador m. <> vi US UNIV: **to** ~ **in sthg** especializar-se em algo.

Majorca [mə'jɔːkə, mə'dʒɔːkəl] n Maiorca; **in** ~ em Maiorca.

Majorcan [mə'jɔːkən, mə'dʒɔːkən] <> adj maiorquino(na). <> n maiorquino m, -na f.

majorette [ˌmeɪdʒə'ret] n baliza f.

major general n general-de-divisão m.

majority [mə'dʒɒrətɪ] (pl -ies) n maioria f; **in a** OR **the** ~ na maioria; **age of** ~ maioridade f.

majority shareholder n acionista mf majoritário, -ria.

major road n estrada f principal.

make [meɪk] (pt & pp made) vt -1. [produce, manufacture] fazer; **to be made of** ser feito de; **to** ~ **lunch/dinner** fazer o almoço/jantar; **made in Japan** fabricado no Japão. -2. [perform, do] fazer; **to** ~ **a mistake** cometer um erro, enganar-se; **to** ~ **a phone call** dar um telefonema. -3. [cause to be] tornar; **to** ~ **sthg better** melhorar algo; **to** ~ **sb happy** fazer alguém feliz; **to** ~ **sthg safer** tornar algo mais seguro. -4. [cause to do, force] fazer; **to** ~ **sb do sthg** obrigar alguém a fazer algo; **it made her laugh** isso a fez rir. -5. [amount to, total] ser; **that** ~**s $5** são 5 dólares. -6. [calculate]: **I** ~ **it seven o'clock** calculo que sejam sete horas; **I** ~ **it $4** segundo os meus cálculos são 4 dólares. -7. [profit, loss] ter. -8. inf [arrive in time for]: **we didn't** ~ **the 10 o'clock train** não conseguimos apanhar o trem das 10. -9. [friend, enemy] fazer. -10. [have qualities for] dar; **this would** ~ **a lovely bedroom** isto dava um lindo quarto. -11. [bed] fazer. -12. [in phrases]: **to** ~ **do** contentar-se; [damage] reparar; **to** ~ **it** [arrive on time] conseguir chegar a tempo; [be able to go] poder ir; [survive a crisis] recuperar-se. <> n [of product] marca f.
→ **make out** vt sep [check, receipt] passar; [form] preencher; [see] distinguir; [hear] perceber, entender.
→ **make up** vt sep [invent] inventar; [comprise] constituir; [difference, extra] cobrir.
→ **make up for** vt fus compensar.

make-believe n (U) faz-de-conta m.

makeover ['meɪkəʊvə'] n -1. [for person] tratamento m -2. [for company] aperfeiçoamento m.

maker ['meɪkə'] n -1. [of film] produtor m, -ra f -2. [of product] fabricante mf.

makeshift ['meɪkʃɪft] adj -1. [temporary] provisório(ria) -2. [improvised] improvisado(da).

make-up n (U) -1. [cosmetics] maquiagem f; ~ **bag** nécessaire m; ~ **remover** removedor m de maquiagem -2. [person's character] caráter m -3. [composition] composição f.

makeweight n contrapeso m.

making ['meɪkɪŋ] n [of cake] fabricação f; [of film] produção f; **in the** ~ em desenvolvimento; **this is history in the** ~ isto passará para a história; **your problems are of your own** ~ teus problemas são todos coisas da tua cabeça; **to be the** ~ **of sb/sthg** ser a causa do êxito de alguém/algo; **you have the** ~**s of a diplomat** você tem tudo para ser um diplomata.

maladjusted [ˌmælə'dʒʌstɪd] adj desajustado(da).

malaise [mæ'leɪz] n (U) fml [unease] mal-estar m.

malaria [mə'leərɪə] n (U) malária f.

Malawi [mə'lɑːwɪ] n Maláui; **in** ~ no Maláui.

Malawian [mə'lɑːwɪən] <> adj malauiano(na). <> n malauiano m, -na f.

Malay [mə'leɪ] <> adj malaio(ia). <> n -1. [person] malaio m, -ia f -2. [language] malaio m.

Malaya [mə'leɪə] n Malásia; **in** ~ na Malásia.

Malayan [mə'leɪən] <> adj malaio(ia). <> n malaio m, -ia f.

Malaysia [mə'leɪzɪə] n Malásia; **in** ~ na Malásia.

Malaysian [mə'leɪzɪən] <> adj malaio(ia). <> n malaio m, -ia f.

malcontent n fml descontente mf.

Maldives ['mɔːldɪvz] npl: **the** ~ as Maldivas; **in the** ~ nas Maldivas.

male [meɪl] ⟨⟩ adj **-1.** [animal] macho; ~ **kangaroo** canguru *m* macho **-2.** [human] masculino(na) **-3.** [concerning men] do homem, masculino(na). ⟨⟩ *n* **-1.** [animal] macho *m* **-2.** [human] homem *m*.

male chauvinist (pig) *n pej* porco *m* chauvinista.

male nurse *n* enfermeiro *m*.

malevolent [mə'levələnt] adj malévolo(la).

malformed [mæl'fɔːmd] adj malformado(da).

malfunction [mæl'fʌŋkʃn] ⟨⟩ *n* mau funcionamento *m*. ⟨⟩ *vi* funcionar mal.

Mali ['mɑːlɪ] *n* Mali; **in** ~ em Mali.

malice ['mælɪs] *n (U)* malícia *f*.

malicious [mə'lɪʃəs] adj malicioso(sa).

malign [mə'laɪn] ⟨⟩ adj maligno(na). ⟨⟩ *vt* difamar, falar mal de.

malignant [mə'lɪgnənt] adj **-1.** [full of hate] malvado(da) **-2.** MED maligno(na).

malinger [mə'lɪŋgə'] *vi pej* fazer-se de doente.

malingerer [mə'lɪŋgərə'] *n pej* doente *mf* fingido, -da.

mall [mɔːl] *n esp US*: **(shopping)** ~ shopping *m* *(center)*.

mallard *n* marreco *m*.

malleable ['mælɪəbll] adj **-1.** [easily influenced] influenciável **-2.** [that can be shaped] maleável.

mallet ['mælɪt] *n* [hammer] marreta *f*.

malnourished [,mæl'nʌrɪʃt] adj subnutrido(da).

malnutrition [,mælnjuː'trɪʃn] *n (U)* subnutrição *f*.

malpractice [,mæl'præktɪs] *n (U)* JUR falta *f* profissional.

malt [mɔːlt] *n* **-1.** *(U)* [grain] malte *m* **-2.** [whisky] uísque *m* de malta.

Malta ['mɔːltə] *n* Malta; **in** ~ em Malta.

Maltese [,mɔːl'tiːz] *(pl inv)* ⟨⟩ adj maltês(esa). ⟨⟩ *n* **-1.** [person] maltês *m*, -esa *f* **-2.** [language] maltês *m*.

maltreat [,mæl'triːt] *vt* maltratar.

maltreatment [,mæl'triːtmənt] *n (U)* maus-tratos *mpl*.

malt whisky *n* uísque *m* de malte.

mammal ['mæml] *n* mamífero *m*.

Mammon *n fig* riqueza *f* maléfica.

mammoth ['mæməθ] ⟨⟩ adj gigantesco(ca), descomunal. ⟨⟩ *n* mamute *m*.

man [mæn] *(pl* men, *pt &* pp -ned, *cont* -ning) ⟨⟩ *n* **-1.** [gen] homem *m*; **the** ~ **in the street** o homem comum; **to talk** ~ **to** ~ conversar de homem para homem; **to be** ~ **enough to do sthg** ser homem suficiente para fazer algo **-2.** [as form of address] cara *m*. ⟨⟩ *vt* **-1.** [ship, plane] tripular **-2.** [machine, switchboard, telephone] manejar.

manacles ['mænəklz] *npl* algemas *fpl*.

manage ['mænɪdʒ] ⟨⟩ *vi* **-1.** [cope] arranjar-se **-2.** [financially] virar-se. ⟨⟩ *vt* **-1.** [be responsible for, control - organization, business] dirigir, gerenciar; [- money] administrar; [- another person] representar; [- time] organizar **-2.** [succeed]: **to** ~ **to do sthg** conseguir fazer algo **-3.** [be available for] poder: **I can only** ~ **an hour tonight** eu só disponho de uma hora esta noite.

manageable ['mænɪdʒəbll] adj **-1.** [hair, inflation] controlável **-2.** [children] dominável **-3.** [task, operation] viável.

management ['mænɪdʒmənt] *n* **-1.** *(U)* [control, running] administração *f*, gestão *f* **-2.** [people in control] gerência *f*, direção *f*.

management consultant *n* assessor *m*, -ra *f* de administração.

manager ['mænɪdʒə'] *n* **-1.** [of organization] gerente *mf*, diretor *m*, -ra *f* **-2.** [of popstar] empresário *m*, -ria *f* **-3.** SPORT treinador *m*, -ra *f*.

manageress [,mænɪdʒə'res] *n UK* gerente *f*.

managerial [,mænɪ'dʒɪərɪəl] adj gerencial.

managing director ['mænɪdʒɪŋ-] *n* diretor-gerente *m*, diretora-gerente *f*.

Managua [mə'nægwə] *n* Manágua; **in** ~ em Manágua.

Mancunian [mæŋ'kjuːnjən] ⟨⟩ adj manchesteriano(na). ⟨⟩ *n* [person] manchesteriano *m*, -na *f*.

mandarin ['mændərɪn] *n* **-1.** [fruit] tangerina *f* **-2.** [civil servant] mandarim *m*, -na *f*.

mandate ['mændeɪt] *n* **-1.** [elected right or authority] mandato *m* **-2.** [task] incumbência *f*, missão *f*.

mandatory ['mændətrɪ] adj obrigatório(ria).

mandolin [mændə'lɪn] *n* bandolim *m*.

mane [meɪn] *n* **-1.** [of horse] crina *f* **-2.** [of lion] juba *f*.

man-eating [-,iːtɪŋ] adj antropófago(ga).

maneuver US = manoeuvre.

manfully ['mænfʊlɪ] adv valentemente.

manganese *n (U)* manganês *m*.

mange [meɪndʒ] *n (U)* sarna *f*.

manger ['meɪndʒə'] *n* manjedoura *f*.

mangetout (pea) [,mɑːʒ'tuː-] *n UK* ervilha-torta *f*.

mangle ['mæŋgl] *vt* **-1.** [body, car] destroçar **-2.** *fig* [text] assassinar.

mango ['mæŋgəʊ] *(pl -es* OR *-s)* *n* manga *f*.

mangrove ['mæŋgrəʊv] *n* mangue *m*.

mangy ['meɪndʒɪ] *(compar -ier, superl -iest)* adj sarnento(ta).

manhandle ['mæn,hændl] *vt* maltratar.

manhole ['mænhəʊl] *n* poço *m* de inspeção, boca-de-lobo *m*.

manhood ['mænhʊd] *n (U)* **-1.** [age] idade *f* adulta **-2.** [virility] virilidade *f*.

man-hour *n* hora-homem *f*.

manhunt ['mænhʌnt] *n* perseguição *f (a um criminoso)*.

mania ['meɪnjə] *n* **-1.** *(U)* PSYCH mania *f* **-2.** [excessive liking]: ~ **(for sthg)** gosto *m* excessivo (por algo).

maniac ['meɪnɪæk] *n* **-1.** [madman] maníaco *m*, -ca *f* **-2.** [fanatic] fanático *m*, -ca *f*.

manic ['mænɪk] adj **-1.** [overexcited] doido(da) **-2.** PSYCH maníaco(ca).

manic-depressive ⟨⟩ adj maníaco-depressivo(va). ⟨⟩ *n* maníaco-depressivo *m*, -va *f*.

manicure ['mænɪ,kjʊə'] ⟨⟩ *n* [individual treatment]: **to give sb a** ~ fazer as unhas de alguém. ⟨⟩ *vt*: **to** ~ **one's nails** fazer as unhas.

manifest ['mænɪfest] *fml* ⟨⟩ adj manifesto(ta). ⟨⟩ *vt* manifestar.

manifestation [,mænɪfes'teɪʃn] *n fml* manifestação *f*.

manifestly ['mænɪfestlɪ] adv *fml* evidentemente, claramente.

manifesto [ˌmænɪˈfestəʊl] (*pl* -s OR -es) *n* manifesto *m*.

manifold [ˈmænɪfəʊld] <> *adj literary* múltiplo(-pla). <> *n* AUT coletor *m*; **exhaust** ~ cano *m* de descarga.

manila *adj* de papel manilha.

Manila [məˈnɪlə] *n* Manila; **in** ~ em Manila.

manilla [məˈnɪlə] *adj* = **manila**.

manipulate [məˈnɪpjʊleɪt] *vt* **- 1.** [control for personal benefit] manipular **- 2.** [operate - machine, controls] operar; [- lever] acionar.

manipulation [məˌnɪpjʊˈleɪʃn] *n* (U) **- 1.** [control for personal benefit] manipulação *f* **- 2.** [operation - of machine, controls] operação *f*; [- of lever] acionamento *m*.

manipulative [məˈnɪpjʊlətɪv] *adj* manipulador(-ra).

Manitoba [ˌmænɪˈtəʊbə] *n* Manitoba; **in** ~ em Manitoba.

mankind [mænˈkaɪnd] *n* (U) humanidade *f*.

manly [ˈmænlɪ] (*compar* -ier, *superl* -iest) *adj* másculo(la), viril.

man-made *adj* **- 1.** [problem, disaster] produzido(-da) pelo homem **- 2.** [fibre, environment] artificial.

manna [ˈmænə] *n* (U) maná *m*.

manned [mænd] *adj* tripulado(da).

mannequin [ˈmænɪkɪn] *n* [dummy] manequim *m*.

manner [ˈmænəʳ] *n* **- 1.** [method] maneira *f*, forma *f*; **in a** ~ **of speaking** por assim dizer **- 2.** [bearing, attitude] jeito *m*, comportamento *m* **- 3.** *literary* [type, sort]: **all** ~ **of** todos os tipos de.
➭ **manners** *npl* maneiras *fpl*; **to be good/bad** ~**s to do sthg** ser de boa/má educação fazer algo.

mannered [ˈmænəd] *adj fml* afetado(da).

mannerism [ˈmænərɪzm] *n* trejeito *m*.

mannish [ˈmænɪʃ] *adj* [woman] masculino(na).

manoeuvrable UK, **maneuverable** US [məˈnuːvrəbl] *adj* manobrável.

manoeuvre UK, **maneuver** US [məˈnuːvəʳ] <> *n* **- 1.** [movement] manobra *f* **- 2.** *fig* [clever move] manobra *f*. <> *vt* [control physically] manobrar, manejar. <> *vi* [move physically] manobrar.
➭ **manoeuvres** *npl* MIL manobras *fpl*.

manor [ˈmænəʳ] *n* [house] solar *m*.

manpower [ˈmænˌpaʊəʳ] *n* (U) mão-de-obra *f*.

manservant [ˈmænsɜːvənt] (*pl* menservants) *n* da-ted criado *m*.

mansion [ˈmænʃn] *n* mansão *f*.

man-size(d) *adj* de tamanho extragrande.

manslaughter [ˈmænˌslɔːtəʳ] *n* (U) homicídio *m* involuntário.

mantelpiece [ˈmæntlpiːs] *n* consolo *m* de lareira.

mantle [ˈmæntl] *n* **- 1.** [layer, covering] camada *f* **- 2.** [of leadership, high office] posição *f* (*de comando*).

man-to-man *adj* de homem para homem.

manual [ˈmænjʊəl] <> *adj* manual. <> *n* [handbook] manual *m*.

manually [ˈmænjʊəlɪ] *adv* manualmente.

manual worker *n* operário *m*, -ria *f*.

manufacture [ˌmænjʊˈfæktʃəʳ] <> *n* (U) manufatura *f*, fabricação *f*. <> *vt* **- 1.** [make] manufaturar, fabricar **- 2.** [invent] inventar.

manufacturer [ˌmænjʊˈfæktʃərəʳ] *n* fabricante *mf*.

manufacturing [ˌmænjʊˈfæktʃərɪŋ] *n* (U) manufatura *f*, fabricação *f*.

manufacturing industries *npl* indústrias *fpl* manufatureiras.

manure [məˈnjʊəʳ] *n* (U) esterco *m*.

manuscript [ˈmænjʊskrɪpt] *n* manuscrito *m*.

Manx [mæŋks] <> *adj* manx. <> *n* [language] manx *m*.

many [ˈmenɪ] (*compar* more, *superl* most) <> *adj* [a lot of, plenty of] muitos(tas); ~ **people** muitas pessoas, muita gente; **how** ~ **...?** quantos(tas) ...?; **too** ~ **...** demais; **there are too** ~ **books for me to read** há livros demais para eu ler; **as** ~ **... as** tantos ... quantos, tantas ... quantas; **bring as** ~ **cups as you can** traga tantas xícaras quantas você puder; **so** ~ **...** tantos(tas) ...; **a good** OR **great** ~ **...** muitíssimos(mas) ..., um grande número de ... <> *pron* [a lot, plenty] muitos(tas); **how** ~**?** quantos(tas)?; **too** ~ muitos(tas); **as** ~ **as** tantos(-tas) quanto; **so** ~ tantos(tas); **a good** OR **great** ~ muitos(tas), um grande número.

Maori [ˈmaʊrɪ] <> *adj* maori. <> *n* maori *mf*.

map [mæp] (*pt* & *pp* -ped, *cont* -ping) <> *n* mapa *m*; **to put sb/sthg on the** ~ colocar alguém/algo no mapa. <> *vt* **- 1.** [chart] fazer o mapa de **- 2.** COMPUT associar.
➭ **map out** *vt sep* planejar, planificar.

maple [ˈmeɪpl] *n* bordo *m*.

maple leaf *n* folha *f* de bordo.

maple syrup *n* (U) xarope *m* de bordo.

Maputo [məˈpuːtəʊ] *n* Maputo; **in** ~ em Maputo.

mar [maːʳ] (*pt* & *pp* -red, *cont* -ring) *vt* prejudicar, frustrar.

Mar. (*abbr of* **March**) mar.

marathon [ˈmærəθn] <> *adj* exaustivo(va). <> *n* maratona *f*.

marathon runner *n* maratonista *mf*.

marauder [məˈrɔːdəʳ] *n* gatuno *m*, -na *f*, saqueador *m*, -ra *f*.

marauding [məˈrɔːdɪŋ] *adj* saqueador(ra).

marble [ˈmaːbl] *n* **- 1.** (U) [stone] mármore *m* **- 2.** [for game] bolita *f* de gude.
➭ **marbles** *n* (U) [game] jogo *m* de gude.

march [maːtʃ] <> *n* **- 1.** [gen] marcha *f* **- 2.** [steady progress] avanço *m*. <> *vi* **- 1.** [gen] marchar **- 2.** [approach] avançar. <> *vt* conduzir, levar à força.

March [maːtʃ] *n* março; *see also* **September**.

marcher [ˈmaːtʃəʳ] *n* [protester] manifestante *mf*.

marching orders [ˈmaːtʃɪŋ-] *npl*: **to give sb his** ~ mandar alguém passear, dar cartão vermelho para alguém.

marchioness [ˌmaːʃəˈnes] *n* [aristocrat] marquesa *f*.

march-past *n* parada *f*.

Mardi Gras [ˌmaːdɪˈgraː] *n* Terça-Feira *f* de Carnaval.

mare [meəʳ] *n* égua *f*.

marg. (*abbr of* **margarine**) *n inf* margarina *f*.

margarine [ˌmaːdʒəˈriːn, ˌmaːgəˈriːnl] *n* (U) margarina *f*.

marge [maːdʒ] *n* (U) *inf* margarina *f*.

margin [ˈmaːdʒɪn] *n* **- 1.** [gen] margem *f* **- 2.** [of desert, forest] limite *m*.

marginal ['mɑːdʒɪnl] adj -**1.** [unimportant] secundário(ria) -**2.** UK POL: ~ **seat** OR **constituency** cadeira f ganha por uma pequena maioria de votos.

marginally ['mɑːdʒɪnəlɪ] adv ligeiramente.

marigold ['mærɪgəʊld] n calêndula f.

marihuana, marijuana [ˌmærɪ'wɑːnə] n (U) maconha f.

marina [mə'riːnə] n marina f.

marinade [ˌmærɪ'neɪd] <> n marinada f. <> vt & vi = **marinate**.

marinate ['mærɪneɪt] <> vt marinar. <> vi ficar em marinada.

marine [mə'riːn] <> adj -**1.** [underwater] marinho(nha) -**2.** [seafaring] marítimo(ma). <> n MIL fuzileiro m naval.

marionette [ˌmærɪə'net] n marionete f.

marital ['mærɪtl] adj conjugal.

marital status n estado m civil.

maritime ['mærɪtaɪm] adj marítimo(ma).

Maritime Provinces, Maritimes npl: the ~ as Províncias Marítimas.

marjoram ['mɑːdʒərəm] n (U) manjerona f.

mark [mɑːk] <> n -**1.** [stain] mancha f; [scratch] marca f -**2.** [in exam] nota f -**3.** [stage, level]: **the half-way** ~ o meio caminho; **beyond the billion** ~ acima de um bilhão -**4.** [sign, indication] sinal f -**5.** [currency] marco m -**6.** CULIN nível m de temperatura -**7.** phr: **to make one's** ~ deixar a marca; **to be quick/slow off the** ~ reagir rapidamente/lentamente; **wide of the** ~ longe da verdade. <> vt -**1.** [gen] marcar -**2.** [exam, essay] corrigir -**3.** [commemorate] comemorar, celebrar -**4.** [stain] manchar.

➡ **mark down** vt sep -**1.** [COMM - prices] rebaixar; [- goods] baixar o preço de -**2.** [downgrade] baixar a nota de.

➡ **mark off** vt sep [cross off] assinalar.

➡ **mark up** vt sep [COMM - prices] aumentar; [- goods] remarcar.

marked [mɑːkt] adj [noticeable] notável.

markedly ['mɑːkɪdlɪ] adv [noticeably] notavelmente.

marker ['mɑːkə'] n -**1.** [sign] indicador m -**2.** SPORT marcador m -**3.** [of exam] avaliador m, -ra f.

marker pen n caneta f marcadora.

market ['mɑːkɪt] <> n [gen] mercado m; **on the** ~ à venda. <> vt comercializar, vender. <> vi US [shop]: **to go** ~**ing** ir às compras.

marketable ['mɑːkɪtəbl] adj vendável, comercializável.

market analysis n (U) análise f de mercado.

market day n dia f da feira.

market forces npl COMM tendências fpl do mercado.

market garden n esp UK horta f.

marketing ['mɑːkɪtɪŋ] n (U) COMM marketing m.

marketplace ['mɑːkɪtpleɪs] n mercado m.

market price n COMM preço m de mercado.

market research n (U) pesquisa f de mercado.

market town n cidade f com feira livre.

market value n COMM valor m de mercado.

marking ['mɑːkɪŋ] n (U) SCH & UNIV correção f.

➡ **markings** npl -**1.** [of flower] manchas fpl -**2.** [of animal] pintas fpl -**3.** [of road] sinais mpl.

marksman ['mɑːksmən] (pl -men [-mən]) n atirador m.

marksmanship ['mɑːksmənʃɪp] n (U) pontaria f.

markup ['mɑːkʌp] n margem m de lucro.

marmalade ['mɑːməleɪd] n (U) geléia f.

maroon [mə'ruːn] adj de cor castanho-avermelhado.

marooned [mə'ruːnd] adj abandonado(da).

marquee [mɑː'kiː] n toldo m.

marquess ['mɑːkwɪs] n = **marquis**.

marquetry n (U) marchetaria f.

marquis ['mɑːkwɪs] n marquês m.

marriage ['mærɪdʒ] n casamento m.

marriage bureau n UK agência f matrimonial.

marriage certificate n certidão m de casamento.

marriage guidance n (U) orientação f para casais.

marriage guidance counsellor n terapeuta mf para casais.

married ['mærɪd] adj -**1.** [having a spouse] casado(da) -**2.** [of marriage] de casado.

marrow ['mærəʊ] n -**1.** UK [vegetable] abóbora f -**2.** (U) [in bones] medula f.

marry ['mærɪ] (pt & pp -ied) <> vt casar; **will you** ~ **me?** quer se casar comigo? <> vi [get married] casar-se.

Mars [mɑːz] n [planet] Marte.

marsh [mɑːʃ] n pântano m.

marshal ['mɑːʃl] (UK pt & pp -led, cont -ling, US pt & pp -ed, cont -ing) <> n -**1.** MIL marechal m -**2.** [assistant] oficial m -**3.** US [law officer] oficial mf de justiça. <> vt -**1.** [people] dirigir, conduzir -**2.** [support, thoughts] ordenar, organizar.

marshalling yard ['mɑːʃlɪŋ-] n pátio m ferroviário.

marshland ['mɑːʃlænd] n (U) pantanal m.

marshmallow [UK ˌmɑːʃ'mæləʊ, US 'mɑːrʃˌmeləʊ] n -**1.** [sweet] marshmallow m -**2.** (U) [substance] de marshmallow.

marshy ['mɑːʃɪ] (compar -ier, superl -iest) adj pantanoso(sa).

marsupial [mɑː'suːpjəl] n marsupial m.

martial ['mɑːʃl] adj marcial.

martial arts [ˌmɑːʃl-] npl artes fpl marciais.

martial law [ˌmɑːʃl-] n (U) lei f marcial.

Martian ['mɑːʃn] <> adj marciano(na). <> n marciano m, -na f.

martin ['mɑːtɪn] n martinete m.

martini [mɑː'tiːnɪ] n [cocktail] martini m.

Martinique [ˌmɑːtɪ'niːk] n Martinica; **in** ~ na Martinica.

martyr ['mɑːtə'] n mártir mf.

martyrdom ['mɑːtədəm] n (U) martírio m.

martyred ['mɑːtəd] adj martirizado(da).

marvel ['mɑːvl] (UK pt & pp -led, cont -ling, US pt & pp -ed, cont -ing) <> n -**1.** [gen] maravilha f -**2.** [surprise, miracle] milagre m. <> vt: **to** ~ **that** admirar-se que. <> vi: **to** ~ (**at sthg**) maravilhar-se (com algo).

marvellous UK, **marvelous** US ['mɑːvələs] adj maravilhoso(sa).

Marxism ['mɑːksɪzm] n (U) marxismo m.

Marxist ['mɑːksɪst] ⬦ *adj* marxista. ⬦ *n* marxista *mf*.

Maryland ['meərɪlænd] *n* Maryland; **in** ~ em Maryland.

marzipan ['mɑːzɪpæn] *n (U)* maçapão *m*.

mascara [mæsˈkɑːrə] *n (U)* rímel *m*.

mascot ['mæskət] *n* mascote *f*.

masculine ['mæskjʊlɪn] *adj* masculino(na).

masculinity [ˌmæskjʊˈlɪnətɪ] *n (U)* masculinidade *f*.

mash [mæʃ] *vt* triturar, amassar.

MASH [mæʃ] (*abbr of* **mobile army surgical hospital**) *n hospital militar de campanha norte-americano*.

mashed potatoes [mæʃt-] *npl* purê *m* de batatas.

mask [mɑːsk] ⬦ *n* **-1.** [covering face] máscara *f* **-2.** *fig* [dissimulation] máscara *f*. ⬦ *vt* **-1.** [cover] mascarar **-2.** [conceal] disfarçar.

masked [mɑːskt] *adj* [face, man] mascarado(da).

masking tape ['mɑːskɪŋ-] *n (U)* fita *f* adesiva.

masochism ['mæsəkɪzm] *n (U)* masoquismo *m*.

masochist ['mæsəkɪst] *n* masoquista *mf*.

masochistic [ˌmæsəˈkɪstɪk] *adj* masoquista.

mason ['meɪsn] *n* **-1.** [stonemason] pedreiro *m*, -ra *f* **-2.** [Freemason] maçom *m*.

masonic [məˈsɒnɪk] *adj* maçônico(ca).

masonry ['meɪsnrɪ] *n (U)* [stones] alvenaria *f*.

masquerade [ˌmæskəˈreɪd] *vi:* **to** ~ **as** fazer-se passar por; **to** ~ **under the name of ...** esconder-se sob o nome de ...

mass [mæs] ⬦ *n* **-1.** GEOGR, PHYSICS massa *f* **-2.** [large amount] grande quantidade *f* **-3.** [main part, majority]: **the** ~ **of** a maioria de. ⬦ *adj* em massa. ⬦ *vt* concentrar. ⬦ *vi* concentrar-se.
➡ **Mass** *n* RELIG missa *f*.
➡ **masses** *npl* **-1.** *inf* [lots, plenty] montes *mpl*; ~**es of sthg** montes de algo **-2.** [ordinary people]: **the** ~ **es** as massas.

Massachusetts [ˌmæsəˈtʃuːsɪts] *n* Massachusetts.

massacre ['mæsəkəʳ] ⬦ *n* massacre *m*. ⬦ *vt* massacrar.

massage [UK 'mæsɑːʒ, US məˈsɑːʒ] ⬦ *n* massagem *f*. ⬦ *vt* massagear.

massage parlour *n* **-1.** [for massage] clínica *f* de massagem **-2.** *euphemism* [brothel] casa *f* de massagens.

masseur [mæˈsɜːr] *n* massagista *m*.

masseuse [mæˈsɜːz] *n* massagista *f*.

massive ['mæsɪv] *adj* [in size, amount] enorme; ~ **majority** maioria em massa.

massively ['mæsɪvlɪ] *adv* enormemente.

mass-market *adj* para mercados de massa.

mass media *n or npl:* **the** ~ os meios de comunicação de massas.

mass-produce *vt* produzir em série.

mass production *n (U)* produção *f* em série.

mast [mɑːst] *n* **-1.** [on boat] mastro *m* **-2.** RADIO & TV antena *f*.

mastectomy (*pl* -ies) *n* mastectomia *f*.

master ['mɑːstəʳ] ⬦ *n* **-1.** [person in charge] senhor *m*; **a** ~ **and his servants** um amo e seus servos **-2.** *fig* [of subject, situation] dono *m* **-3.** UK [teacher]

mestre *m* **-4.** [of ship] capitão *m* **-5.** [original copy] original *m*. ⬦ *adj* **-1.** [in trade] mestre **-2.** [original] original. ⬦ *vt* **-1.** [gain control of] dominar, controlar **-2.** [perfect] dominar.

master bedroom *n* quarto *m* principal.

master disk *n* COMPUT disco-mestre *m*.

masterful ['mɑːstəfʊl] *adj* dominante, autoritário(ria).

master key *n* chave-mestra *f*.

masterly ['mɑːstəlɪ] *adj* magistral.

mastermind ['mɑːstəmaɪnd] ⬦ *n* cabeça *mf*; **he is the** ~ **behind the plan** ele é o cabeça do plano. ⬦ *vt* ser o cabeça de.

Master of Arts (*pl* **Masters of Arts**) *n* **-1.** [degree] mestrado *m* em ciências humanas, *diploma de mestre em ciências humanas* **-2.** [person] mestre *mf* em ciências humanas, *titular de diploma de mestre em ciências humanas*.

master of ceremonies (*pl* **masters of ceremonies**) *n* mestre-de-cerimônias *mf*.

Master of Science (*pl* **Masters of Science**) *n* **-1.** [degree] mestrado *m* em ciências exatas, *diploma de mestre em ciências exatas* **-2.** [person] mestre *mf* em ciências exatas, *titular de diploma de mestre em ciências exatas*.

masterpiece ['mɑːstəpiːs] *n* obra-prima *f*.

master plan *n* plano-mestre *m*.

master's degree *n* mestrado *m*.

masterstroke ['mɑːstəstrəʊk] *n* golpe *m* de mestre.

master switch *n* chave *f* geral.

masterwork ['mɑːstəwɜːk] *n* obra-prima *f*.

mastery ['mɑːstərɪ] *n (U)* domínio *m*.

mastic ['mæstɪk] *n (U)* almécega *f*.

masticate ['mæstɪkeɪt] *fml vt & vi* mastigar.

mastiff ['mæstɪf] *n* mastim *m*.

masturbate ['mæstəbeɪt] *vi* masturbar-se.

masturbation [ˌmæstəˈbeɪʃn] *n (U)* masturbação *f*.

mat [mæt] *n* **-1.** [on floor] tapete *m*; **door** ~ capacho *m* **-2.** [on table]: **beer** ~ porta-copos *m inv*; **table** ~ jogo *m* americano.

match [mætʃ] ⬦ *n* **-1.** [game] partida *f* **-2.** [for lighting] fósforo *m* **-3.** [equal]: **to be no** ~ **for sb** não ser páreo para alguém. ⬦ *vt* **-1.** [be the same as] coincidir com **-2.** [coordinate with] combinar com **-3.** [equal] equiparar-se a. ⬦ *vi* [be the same] combinar.

matchbox ['mætʃbɒks] *n* caixa *f* de fósforos.

matched [mætʃt] *adj:* **to be well** ~ [well suited] combinar bem; [equal in strength] estar igualado(da); **they are well** ~ **(as a couple)** eles formam um belo casal.

matching ['mætʃɪŋ] *adj* que combina bem.

matchless ['mætʃlɪs] *adj literary* incomparável, ímpar.

matchmaker ['mætʃˌmeɪkəʳ] *n* casamenteiro *m*, -ra *f*.

match play *n* GOLF partida de golfe entre duas equipes.

match point *n* TENNIS **-1.** *(U)* [situation] match point *m* **-2.** [score] match point *m*, ponto *m* do jogo.

matchstick ['mætʃstɪk] *n* palito *m*.

mate [meɪt] ◇ n -**1.** inf [friend] amigo m, -ga f, companheiro m, -ra f -**2.** UK inf [form of address] colega mf -**3.** [of animal] parceiro m, -ra f -**4.** NAUT: (first) ~ contramestre m. ◇ vi [animals] acasalar-se; **to ~ with** acasalar-se com.

material [mə'tɪərɪəl] ◇ adj -**1.** material -**2.** [important] substancial. ◇ n material m.
 ➡ **materials** npl materiais mpl.

materialism [mə'tɪərɪəlɪzm] n (U) [desire for possessions] materialismo m.

materialist [mə'tɪərɪəlɪst] n [person greedy for possessions] materialista mf.

materialistic [mə,tɪərɪə'lɪstɪk] adj materialista.

materialize, -ise [mə'tɪərɪəlaɪz] vi -**1.** [happen] concretizar-se -**2.** [appear] materializar-se.

materially [mə'tɪərɪəlɪ] adv -**1.** [physically] materialmente -**2.** [importantly, essentially] essencialmente.

maternal [mə'tɜ:nl] adj maternal.

maternity [mə'tɜ:nətɪ] n (U) maternidade f.

maternity benefit n (U) auxílio-maternidade m.

maternity dress n vestido m de gestante.

maternity hospital n maternidade f (no hospital).

maternity leave n licença-maternidade f.

maternity ward n maternidade f.

math n US = maths.

mathematical [,mæθə'mætɪkl] adj matemático(-ca).

mathematician [,mæθəmə'tɪʃn] n matemático m, -ca f.

mathematics [,mæθə'mætɪks] n (U) [subject] matemática f.

maths UK [mæθs], **math** US [mæθ] (abbr of **mathematics**) inf ◇ n (U) [subject] matemática f. ◇ comp de matemática.

maths coprocessor [-,kəʊ'prəʊsesəʳ] n COMPUT coprocessador m matemático.

matinée ['mætɪneɪ] n matinê f.

matinée jacket n UK casaquinho m de bebê.

mating call ['meɪtɪŋ-] n chamado m do macho (para acasalamento).

mating season ['meɪtɪŋ-] n época f de acasalamento.

matriarch ['meɪtrɪɑ:k] n -**1.** [of a society] matriarca f -**2.** literary [of a family] matriarca f.

matrices ['meɪtrɪsi:z] pl ▷ matrix.

matriculate [mə'trɪkjʊleɪt] vi UNIV matricular-se.

matriculation [mə,trɪkjʊ'leɪʃn] n (U) UNIV matrícula f.

matrimonial [,mætrɪ'məʊnjəl] adj matrimonial.

matrimony ['mætrɪmənɪ] n (U) matrimônio m.

matrix ['meɪtrɪks] (pl matrices OR -es) n -**1.** [gen] matriz f -**2.** TECH molde m para fundição.

matron ['meɪtrən] n -**1.** UK [in hospital] enfermeira-chefe f -**2.** [in school] enfermeira f -**3.** US [in prison] superintendente f -**4.** [middle-aged woman] matrona f.

matronly ['meɪtrənlɪ] adj euph matronal.

matt UK, **matte** US [mæt] adj fosco(ca).

matted ['mætɪd] adj embaraçado(da).

matter ['mætəʳ] ◇ n -**1.** [question, situation] questão f, assunto m; **a ~ of life and death** uma questão

de vida ou morte; **the fact** OR **truth of the ~ is ...** o xis da questão é ...; **that's another** OR **a different ~** isso é outra questão/coisa; **a ~ of opinion** uma questão de opinião; **a ~ of time** uma questão de tempo; **to make ~s worse** piorar as coisas; **and to make ~s worse, ...** e para piorar (ainda mais) as coisas, ...; **as a ~ of course** como algo natural; **as a ~ of principle** por uma questão de princípios; **within a ~ of hours** numa questão de horas -**2.** [trouble, cause of pain] problema m; **what's the ~?** qual é o problema?, o que (é que) houve?; **what's the ~ with it/her?** qual é o problema com isso /ela? -**3.** (U) PHYSICS matéria f -**4.** (U) [material] material/ m; **vegetable ~** matéria vegetal. ◇ vi [be important] importar; **it doesn't ~** não importa; **it doesn't ~ what you decide** não interessa o que você decidir.
 ➡ **as a matter of fact** adv aliás, na verdade.
 ➡ **for that matter** adv quanto a isso.
 ➡ **no matter** adv: **no ~ how hard I try** ... não importa quanto eu tente ...; **no ~ what** aconteça o que acontecer.

Matterhorn ['mætə,hɔ:n] n: **the ~** a Montanha Matterhorn.

matter-of-fact adj sem sentimento, prosaico(-ca).

matting ['mætɪŋ] n (U) esteira f.

mattress ['mætrɪs] n colchão m.

mature [mə'tjʊəʳ] ◇ adj -**1.** [person] maduro(ra) -**2.** [food, drink] envelhecido(da), maturado(da) -**3.** [cheese] curado(da). ◇ vi -**1.** [gen] amadurecer -**2.** [animal, plant] crescer -**3.** [wine, spirit] envelhecer -**4.** [cheese] curar -**5.** [insurance policy] vencer.

mature student n UK UNIV estudante mf adulto, -ta.

maturity [mə'tjʊərətɪ] n maturidade f.

maudlin ['mɔ:dlɪn] adj choroso(sa).

maul [mɔ:l] vt [attack, savage] atacar gravemente.

Mauritania [,mɒrɪ'teɪnɪə] n Mauritânia f; **in ~** na Mauritânia.

Mauritanian [,mɒrɪ'teɪnɪən] ◇ adj mauritano(-na). ◇ n mauritano m, -na f.

Mauritian [mə'rɪʃən] ◇ adj mauriciano(na). ◇ n mauriciano m, -na f.

Mauritius [mə'rɪʃəs] n Maurício; **in ~** em Maurício.

mausoleum [,mɔ:sə'lɪəm] (pl -s) n mausoléu m.

mauve [məʊv] ◇ adj da cor de malva. ◇ n (U) malva f.

maverick ['mævərɪk] ◇ adj inconformista. ◇ n inconformista mf.

mawkish ['mɔ:kɪʃ] adj piegas.

max. [mæks] (abbr of **maximum**) máx.

maxim ['mæksɪm] (pl -s) n máxima f.

maxima ['mæksɪmə] pl ▷ **maximum**.

maximize, -ise ['mæksɪmaɪz] vt maximizar.

maximum ['mæksɪməm] (pl maxima OR -s) ◇ adj [highest, largest] máximo(ma). ◇ n [upper limit] máximo m.

may [meɪ] modal vb -**1.** poder; **you ~ like it** talvez você goste; **he ~ well have said that** ele pode muito bem ter dito aquilo; **it ~ rain** pode ser que chova; **be that as it ~** seja como for; **I would like to add, if I ~ ...** eu gostaria de acrescentar, se possível ... **-2.** *fml* [to express wish, hope]: **long ~ it last!** que dure por muito tempo!; **~ they be very happy!** que eles sejam muito felizes!; ⊳ **might**.

May [meɪ] *n* maio; *see also* **September**.

Maya ['maɪə] *n*: **the ~** os Maias.

maybe ['meɪbi:] *adv* talvez.

Mayday *n* [SOS] mayday, sinal *m* de socorro.

May Day *n* Primeiro *m* de Maio.

mayfly ['meɪflaɪ] (*pl* **-flies**) *n* efemérida *f*.

mayhem ['meɪhem] *n* (*U*) caos *m inv*.

mayn't = may not.

mayonnaise [ˌmeɪə'neɪz] *n* (*U*) maionese *f*.

mayor [meə²] *n* prefeito *m*.

mayoress ['meərɪs] *n* [female mayor] prefeita *f*; [wife of mayor] esposa *f* do prefeito.

maypole ['meɪpəʊl] *n* mastro erigido para o dia 1° de maio ao redor do qual se dança.

may've *cont* = may have.

maze [meɪz] *n* **-1.** [system of paths] labirinto *m* **-2.** *fig* [tangle] confusão *f*.

MB ⟨⟩ *n* (*abbr of* **Bachelor of Medicine**) (*titular de*) bacharelado em medicina. ⟨⟩ **-1.** (*abbr of* **megabyte**) MB **-2.** *abbr of* **Manitoba**.

MBA (*abbr of* **Master of Business Administration**) *n* MBA *m*.

MBBS (*abbr of* **Bachelor of Medicine and Surgery**) *n* (*titular de*) bacharelado em medicina e cirurgia.

MBE (*abbr of* **Member of the Order of the British Empire**) *n* (*beneficiário da*) ordem do Império Britânico.

MC (*abbr of* **master of ceremonies**) *n* mestre-de-cerimônias *m*.

MCAT (*abbr of* **Medical College Admissions Test**) *n* exame de admissão para a faculdade de medicina nos Estados Unidos.

MCC (*abbr of* **Marylebone Cricket Club**) *n* clube londrino de críquete, responsável pelas regras do jogo.

McCarthyism [məˈkɑːrθɪɪzəm] *n* macartismo *m*.

McCoy [məˈkɔɪ] *n* (*U*) *inf*: **the real ~** o produto genuíno.

MCP (*abbr of* **male chauvinist pig**) *n inf* machista *m*.

MD ⟨⟩ *n* **-1.** (*abbr of* **Doctor of Medicine**) (*titular de*) doutorado em medicina **-2.** (*abbr of* **managing director**) diretor-gerente *m*. ⟨⟩ *abbr of* **Maryland**.

MDT (*abbr of* **Mountain Daylight Time**) *n* horário de verão na zona das Montanhas Rochosas nos Estados Unidos.

me [mi:] *pers pron* **-1.** (*direct, indirect*) me; **she knows ~** ela me conhece; **it's ~** sou eu; **send it to ~** mande-o para mim; **tell ~** diga-me; **-2.** (*after prep*) mim; **with ~** comigo; **it's for ~** é para mim.

ME ⟨⟩ *n* (*abbr of* **myalgic encephalomyelitis**) EM *f*. ⟨⟩ *abbr of* **Maine**.

meadow ['medəʊ] *n* campina *f*.

meagre *UK*, **meager** *US* ['mi:gə²] *adj* magro(gra), insuficiente.

meal [mi:l] *n* refeição *f*; **to go out for a ~** sair para jantar; **to make a ~ of sthg** *UK fig* & *pej* fazer algo parecer mais cansativo do que realmente é.

meals on wheels *npl UK* serviço de entrega domiciliar de refeições para idosos e necessitados.

mealtime ['mi:ltaɪm] *n* hora *f* da refeição; **at ~s** na hora das refeições.

mealy-mouthed [ˌmi:lɪˈmaʊðd] *adj pej* evasivo(va), fingido(da).

mean [mi:n] (*pt* & *pp* **meant**) ⟨⟩ *adj* **-1.** [miserly] mesquinho(nha); **to be ~ with sthg** ser avarento com algo **-2.** [unkind] grosseiro(ra); **to be ~ to sb** ser malvado(da) com alguém **-3.** [average] médio(dia) **-4.** *iro* [inferior] inferior; **she's no ~ singer** [excellent] ela é uma cantora de primeira; **it's no ~ task** não é pouca coisa. ⟨⟩ *n* [average] meio-termo *m*; ⊳ **means**. ⟨⟩ *vt* **-1.** [signify, represent] significar **-2.** [have in mind, intend] querer dizer; **to ~ to do sthg** ter a intenção de fazer algo, tencionar fazer algo; **to be meant for sb/sthg** ser feito(ta) para alguém/algo; **they're not meant to be there** eles não deveriam estar lá; **it was meant as a compliment** era para ser um elogio; **to be meant to do sthg** dever fazer algo; **to ~ well** ter boa vontade **-3.** [be serious about] falar sério; **she meant every word she said** tudo o que ela disse era a sério **-4.** [entail] acarretar **-5.** *phr*: **I ~** quer dizer.

meander [mɪˈændə²] *vi* **-1.** [river, road] serpentear **-2.** [in walking] vagar **-3.** [in speaking] divagar.

meaning ['mi:nɪŋ] *n* **-1.** [sense] sentido *m*, significado *m* **-2.** (*U*) [purpose, importance] sentido *m*.

meaningful ['mi:nɪŋfʊl] *adj* **-1.** [expressive] significativo(va) **-2.** [deep, profound] sério(ria).

meaningless ['mi:nɪŋlɪs] *adj* **-1.** [devoid of sense] sem sentido **-2.** [futile] fútil.

meanness ['mi:nnɪs] *n* (*U*) **-1.** [stinginess] avareza *f* **-2.** [unkindness] maldade *f*.

means [mi:nz] (*pl inv*) ⟨⟩ *n* [method, way] meio *m*; **a ~ to an end** um meio para um fim; **by ~ of** por meio de. ⟨⟩ *npl* [money] recursos *mpl*.

➥ **by all means** *adv* claro que sim.

➥ **by no means** *adv* de modo algum.

means test *n esp UK* averiguação oficial quanto à carência de renda para fins de recebimento de pensão do governo.

meant [ment] *pt* & *pp* ⊳ **mean**.

meantime ['mi:nˌtaɪm] *n*: **in the ~** enquanto isso.

meanwhile ['mi:nˌwaɪl] *adv* **-1.** [at the same time] enquanto isso **-2.** [between two events] nesse ínterim.

measles ['mi:zlz] *n*: **to catch ~** pegar sarampo.

measly ['mi:zlɪ] (*compar* **-ier**, *superl* **-iest**) *adj inf* miserável.

measurable ['meʒərəbl] *adj* [significant] considerável.

measurably ['meʒərəblɪ] *adv* consideravelmente.

measure ['meʒə²] ⟨⟩ *n* **-1.** [step, action] medida *f* **-2.** (*U*) [degree, amount] grau *m*; **the film had a ~ of success** o filme até que teve sucesso; **for good ~** para se certificar **-3.** [of alcohol] dose *f* **-4.** [indication] indicação *f* **-5.** [device] régua *f*. ⟨⟩ *vt* [determine size of, gauge] medir. ⟨⟩ *vi* [be of stated size] medir.

➥ **measure up** *vi* [be good enough] estar à altura; **to ~ up to sthg** estar à altura de algo.

measured ['meʒəd] *adj literary* ponderado(da).

measurement ['meʒəmənt] *n* **-1.** [figure, amount]

medida *f*-**2.** *(U)* [act of measuring] medição *f.*
➡ **measurements** *npl* [of sb's body] medidas *fpl.*
measuring jug ['meʒərɪŋ-] *n* jarro *m* de medidas.
measuring tape ['meʒərɪŋ-] *n* fita *f* métrica.
meat [mi:t] *n (U)* carne *f.*
meatball ['mi:tbɔ:l] *n* almôndega *f.*
meat pie *n UK* torta *f* de carne.
meaty ['mi:tɪ] *(compar* -**ier***, superl* -**iest)** *adj fig* [full of ideas] rico(ca), sólido(da).
Mecca ['mekə] *n* - **1.** GEOGR Meca - **2.** *fig* [paradise]: **a ~ for** um paraíso para.
mechanic [mɪ'kænɪk] *n* mecânico *m,* -ca *f.*
➡ **mechanics** ◇ *n (U)* [study] mecânica *f.* ◇ *npl* [way sthg works] mecânica *f.*
mechanical [mɪ'kænɪkl] *adj* mecânico(ca).
mechanical engineering *n (U)* engenharia *f* mecânica.
mechanism ['mekənɪzml] *n* mecanismo *m.*
mechanization *n* mecanização *f.*
mechanize, -ise ['mekənaɪz] ◇ *vt* mecanizar. ◇ *vi* mecanizar-se.
Med *(abbr of* Mediterranean Sea) *n UK inf* Mediterrâneo *m.*
MEd [ˌem'ed] *(abbr of* Master of Education) *n (titular de)* mestrado em educação.
medal ['medl] *n* medalha *f.*
medallion [mɪ'dæljən] *n* medalhão *m.*
medallist *UK,* **medalist** *US* ['medəlɪst] *n* medalhista *mf.*
meddle ['medl] *vi* meter-se; **to ~ in/with sthg** meter-se em/com algo.
meddlesome ['medlsəm] *adj* metido(da), intrometido(da).
media ['mi:djə] ◇ *pl* ⊏> **medium**. ◇ *n or npl:* **the ~** a mídia.
mediaeval [ˌmedɪ'i:vl] *adj* = **medieval**.
media event *n* evento *m* da mídia.
median ['mi:djən] ◇ *adj* MATH mediano(na). ◇ *n US* [of road] canteiro *m* divisor.
mediate ['mi:dɪeɪt] ◇ *vt* [produce by arbitration] negociar. ◇ *vi* [arbitrate]: **to ~ between** ser mediador(ra) entre.
mediation [ˌmi:dɪ'eɪʃn] *n (U)* [arbitration] mediação *f.*
mediator ['mi:dɪeɪtə] *n* mediador *m,* -ra *f.*
medic ['medɪk] *n inf* - **1.** [medical student] estudante *mf* de medicina - **2.** [doctor] médico *m,* -ca *f.*
Medicaid ['medɪkeɪd] *n (U) US* auxílio-saúde *m.*

medical ['medɪkl] ◇ *adj* médico(ca). ◇ *n* [checkup] exame *m* médico, check-up *m.*
medical certificate *n* [result of medical exam] atestado *m* médico.
medical insurance *n (U)* seguro-saúde *m.*
medical student *n* estudante *mf* de medicina.
Medicare ['medɪkeə[r]] *n (U) US* seguro-saúde *m (para idosos).*
medicated ['medɪkeɪtɪd] *adj* medicinal.
medication [ˌmedɪ'keɪʃn] *n* medicação *f.*
medicinal [me'dɪsɪnl] *adj* [drink, herb, tea] medicinal.
medicine ['medsɪn] *n* - **1.** *(U)* [treatment of illness] medicina *f*-**2.** [substance] medicamento *m,* remédio *m.*
medicine man *n* curandeiro *m.*
medieval [ˌmedɪ'i:vl] *adj* medieval.
mediocre [ˌmi:dɪ'əʊkə[r]] *adj* medíocre.
mediocrity [ˌmi:dɪ'ɒkrətɪ] *n (U)* [poor quality] mediocridade *f.*
meditate ['medɪteɪt] *vi* - **1.** [reflect, ponder] refletir; **to ~ (up)on sthg** refletir sobre algo - **2.** [practise meditation] meditar.
meditation [ˌmedɪ'teɪʃn] *n* meditação *f.*
Mediterranean [ˌmedɪtə'reɪnjən] ◇ *n* - **1.** [sea]: **the ~ (Sea)** o (Mar) Mediterrâneo - **2.** [area around sea]: **the ~** o mediterrâneo. ◇ *adj* mediterrâneo(nea).
medium ['mi:djəm] *(pl sense 1* -**dia***, pl sense 2* -**diums)** ◇ *adj* [middle, average] médio(dia). ◇ *n* - **1.** [way of communicating] meio *m* de comunicação - **2.** [spiritualist] médium *mf.*
medium-dry *adj* semi-seco(ca).
medium-size(d) [-saɪzd] *adj* de tamanho médio.
medium wave *n (U)* onda *f* média.
medley ['medlɪ] *(pl* -**s)** *n* - **1.** [mixture] mistura *f*-**2.** [selection of music] coletânea *f.*
meek [mi:k] *adj* dócil, meigo(ga).
meekly ['mi:klɪ] *adv* docilmente.
meet [mi:t] *(pt &* pp **met)** ◇ *n US* [meeting] encontro *m,* competição *f.* ◇ *vt* - **1.** [gen] encontrar; **she met his gaze defiantly** ela encarou o olhar dele de forma desafiadora - **2.** [by arrangement] encontrar-se com, reunir-se com - **3.** [make acquaintance of] conhecer; **I met a really interesting guy** conheci um cara muito interessante - **4.** [wait for - person] ir esperar; [- train, plane, bus, boat] esperar - **5.** [fulfil, satisfy] satisfazer, cumprir - **6.** [deal with] enfrentar - **7.** [pay] pagar em dia - **8.** [experience, come across] deparar-se com - **9.** [hit, touch] ir de encontro a. ◇ *vi* - **1.** [gen] encontrar-se; **their eyes met across the room** os olhos deles se cruzaram na sala - **2.** [committee] reunir-se - **3.** [become acquainted] conhecer-se - **4.** [hit, touch] bater-se.
➡ **meet up** *vi* [by arrangement] encontrar-se; **to ~ up with sb** encontrar-se com alguém.
➡ **meet with** *vt fus* - **1.** [encounter] experimentar - **2.** *US* [by arrangement] encontrar.
meeting ['mi:tɪŋ] *n* - **1.** [gen] reunião *f*-**2.** [coming together] encontro *m.*
meeting place *n* ponto *m* de encontro.
mega- [megə] *prefix* - **1.** [in measurements] mega - **2.** *inf* [very big] mega.

megabit n *COMPUT* megabit m.

megabyte ['megəbaɪt] n *COMPUT* megabyte m.

megahertz ['megəhɜ:ts] n *RADIO* megahertz m.

megalomania [ˌmegələ'meɪnjə] n (U) megalomania f.

megalomaniac [ˌmegələ'meɪnɪæk] n megalomaníaco m, -ca f.

megaphone ['megəfəʊn] n megafone m.

megaton ['megətʌn] n megaton m.

megawatt ['megəwɒt] n megawatt m. .

melamine ['meləmi:n] n (U) melanina f.

melancholy ['melənkəlɪ] <> adj [sad] melancólico(ca). <> n (U) melancolia f.

mellow ['meləʊ] <> adj -1. [gen] suave -2. [smooth, pleasant] melodioso(sa) -3. [gentle, relaxed] alegre, tranqüilo(la). <> vt: **to be ~ed by sthg** sentir-se amadurecido(da) por algo; **to be ~ed by wine** ficar alegre por causa do vinho. <> vi [become more gentle or relaxed] suavizar-se, tranqüilizar-se.

melodic [mɪ'lɒdɪk] adj *MUS* melódico(ca).

melodious [mɪ'ləʊdjəs] adj melodioso(sa).

melodrama ['melədrɑ:mə] n melodrama m.

melodramatic [ˌmelədrə'mætɪk] adj melodramático(ca).

melody ['melədɪ] (pl -ies) n [tune] melodia f.

melon ['melən] n melão m.

melt [melt] <> vt -1. [make liquid] derreter -2. fig [soften] amolecer. <> vi -1. [become liquid] derreter -2. fig [soften] amolecer -3. fig [disappear]: **to ~ into sthg** desaparecer em algo, fundir-se em algo; **to ~ away** dissipar-se; **his savings ~ed away** suas economias se acabaram.

➡ **melt down** vt sep fundir-se.

meltdown ['meltdaʊn] n -1. (U) [act of melting] fusão f -2. [incident] acidente m nuclear.

melting point ['meltɪŋ-] n ponto m de fusão.

melting pot ['meltɪŋ-] n fig [of cultures, races, ideas] cadinho m cultural.

member ['membəʳ] <> adj -membro. <> n membro m.

Member of Congress (pl Members of Congress) n *US* Membro m do Congresso.

Member of Parliament (pl Members of Parliament) n [in UK] Membro m do Parlamento.

membership ['membəʃɪp] n -1. [gen - of party, union] associação f; [- of club] qualidade f de sócio; **I have to renew my ~** tenho que renovar o meu título -2. [number of members] número m de sócios -3. [people themselves]: **the ~** os sócios, os membros.

membership card n carteira f de sócio.

membrane ['membreɪn] n *ANAT* membrana f.

memento [mɪ'mentəʊ] (pl -s) n lembrança f.

memo ['meməʊ] (pl -s) n [at work] memorando m.

memoirs ['memwɑ:z] npl memórias fpl.

memo pad n rascunho m de memorando.

memorabilia [ˌmemərə'bɪlɪə] npl memorabília f.

memorable ['memərəbl] adj memorável.

memorandum [ˌmemə'rændəm] (pl -da, -dums) n fml memorando m.

memorial [mɪ'mɔ:rɪəl] <> adj comemorativo(va). <> n memorial m.

memorize, -ise ['meməraɪz] vt memorizar, decorar.

memory ['memərɪ] (pl -ies) n -1. [gen] memória f; **in ~ of** em memória de; **to lose one's ~** perder a memória; **from ~** de memória; **within living ~** de que se tem memória -2. [sthg remembered] lembrança f.

memory card n *COMPUT* placa f de memória.

men [men] pl ⊳ **man**.

menace ['menəs] <> n -1. [gen] ameaça f -2. inf [nuisance, pest] praga f. <> vt ameaçar.

menacing ['menəsɪŋ] adj ameaçador(ra).

menacingly ['menəsɪŋlɪ] adv de forma ameaçadora.

menagerie [mɪ'nædʒərɪ] n reserva f particular de animais selvagens.

mend [mend] <> n (U) inf: **to be on the ~** estar convalescendo. <> vt [repair] consertar; **to ~ one's ways** corrigir-se.

mending ['mendɪŋ] n -1. [repairing]: **to do the ~** consertar -2. [clothes] roupas fpl a consertar.

menfolk ['menfəʊk] npl homens mpl em geral.

menial ['mi:njəl] adj simplório(ria), baixo(xa).

meningitis [ˌmenɪn'dʒaɪtɪs] n (U) *MED* meningite f.

menopause ['menəpɔ:z] n (U): **the ~** a menopausa.

menservants ['mensɜ:vənts] pl ⊳ **manservant**.

men's room n *US*: **the ~** o banheiro dos homens.

menstrual ['menstrʊəl] adj menstrual.

menstruate ['menstrʊeɪt] vi menstruar.

menstruation [ˌmenstrʊ'eɪʃn] n (U) menstruação f.

menswear ['menzweəʳ] n (U) roupa f masculina.

mental ['mentl] adj mental.

mental age n idade f mental.

mental block n: **to have a ~ about sthg** ter um bloqueio mental sobre algo.

mental hospital n hospital m psiquiátrico.

mentality [men'tælətɪ] n (U) [way of thinking] mentalidade f.

mentally ['mentlɪ] adv mentalmente.

mentally handicapped ['mentəlɪ-] npl: **the ~** os deficientes mentais.

➡ **mentally-handicapped** adj com deficiência mental.

mental note n: **to make a ~ to do sthg** gravar na memória para fazer algo.

menthol ['menθɒl] n (U) mentol m.

mentholated ['menθəleɪtɪd] adj mentolado(da).

mention ['menʃn] <> vt [say, talk about] mencionar; **to ~ sthg to sb** mencionar algo para alguém; **not to ~** sem falar em; **don't ~ it!** não tem de quê! <> n [reference] menção f.

mentor ['mentɔ:ʳ] n fml mentor m, -ra f.

menu ['menju:] n -1. [in restaurant] menu m, cardápio m -2. *COMPUT* menu m.

menu-driven adj *COMPUT* orientado(da) por menu.

meow n & vi *US* = miaow.

MEP (abbr of Member of the European Parliament) n membro do parlamento europeu.

mercantile ['mɜ:kəntaɪl] adj mercantil.

mercenary ['mɜːsɪnrɪ] (*pl* **-ies**) <> *adj* mercenário(ria). <> *n* [soldier] mercenário *m*.

merchandise ['mɜːtʃəndaɪz] *n (U)* COMM mercadoria *f*.

merchant ['mɜːtʃənt] <> *adj* mercantil. <> *n* comerciante *mf*.

merchant bank *n* UK banco *m* mercantil.

merchant navy UK, **merchant marine** US *n* marinha *f* mercante.

merciful ['mɜːsɪfʊl] *adj* -**1**. [person] piedoso(sa) -**2**. [death, release] misericordioso(sa).

mercifully ['mɜːsɪfʊlɪ] *adv* -**1**. [fortunately] graças a Deus -**2**. [with clemency] com clemência.

merciless ['mɜːsɪlɪs] *adj* impiedoso(sa).

mercilessly ['mɜːsɪlɪslɪ] *adv* impiedosamente.

mercurial [mɜːˈkjʊərɪəl] *adj literary* volúvel.

mercury ['mɜːkjʊrɪ] *n (U)* mercúrio *m*.

Mercury ['mɜːkjʊrɪ] *n* [planet] Mercúrio.

mercy ['mɜːsɪ] (*pl* **-ies**) *n* -**1**. *(U)* [kindness, pity] piedade *f*; **at the ~ of** *fig* à mercê de -**2**. [blessing] bênção *f*.

mercy killing *n* eutanásia *f*.

mere [mɪər] *adj* -**1**. [just, no more than] mero(ra); **she's a ~ child!** ela é só uma criança! -**2**. [for emphasis] simples, mero(ra) -**3**. [amount, quantity] apenas.

merely ['mɪəlɪ] *adv* -**1**. [simply, just, only] meramente, simplesmente -**2**. [of amount, quantity] apenas.

meretricious *adj fml* falacioso(sa).

merge [mɜːdʒ] <> *n* COMPUT intercalamento *m*. <> *vt* -**1**. COMM fundir -**2**. COMPUT intercalar. <> *vi* -**1**. COMM fundir-se; **to ~ with sthg** unir-se com algo -**2**. [roads, lines] unir-se -**3**. [blend, melt] misturar; **to ~ into sthg** incorporar-se em algo.

merger ['mɜːdʒər] *n* COMM fusão *f*.

meridian [məˈrɪdɪən] *n* GEOGR meridiano *m*.

meringue [məˈræŋ] *n* merengue *m*.

merino [məˈriːnəʊ] *adj* merino(na).

merit ['merɪt] <> *n (U)* [value] mérito *m*. <> *vt* merecer.

➡ **merits** *npl* [advantages, qualities] méritos *mpl*; **to judge sthg on its ~s** julgar algo por seus méritos.

meritocracy [ˌmerɪˈtɒkrəsɪ] (*pl* **-ies**) *n* [system] meritocracia *f*.

mermaid ['mɜːmeɪd] *n* sereia *f*.

merrily ['merɪlɪ] *adv* -**1**. [gen] divertidamente -**2**. *iro* [blithely] alegremente.

merriment ['merɪmənt] *n (U) literary* [laughter] risadas *fpl*.

merry ['merɪ] (*compar* -**ier**, *superl* -**iest**) *adj* -**1**. *literary* [laugh, joke, person] alegre, divertido(da) -**2**. [fire, party] agradável; **Merry Christmas!** Feliz Natal! -**3**. *inf* [tipsy] alegre.

merry-go-round *n* carrossel *m*.

merrymaking ['merɪˌmeɪkɪŋ] *n (U) literary* pândega *f*, folia *f*.

mesh [meʃ] <> *n (U)* [netting] malha *f*. <> *vi* -**1**. [fit together] combinar -**2**. TECH encaixar.

mesmerize, -ise ['mezməraɪz] *vt*: **to be ~d by sb/sthg** ser hipnotizado(da) por alguém/algo.

mess [mes] *n* -**1**. [gen] bagunça *f*; **to be (in) a ~** estar uma bagunça, estar de pernas para o ar -**2**. [muddle, problem] confusão *f* -**3**. MIL rancho *m*.

➡ **mess about, mess around** *inf* <> *vt sep* embromar. <> *vi* -**1**. [gen] matar tempo -**2**. [tinker]: **to ~ about with sthg** mexer em algo.

➡ **mess up** *vt sep inf* -**1**. [make untidy, dirty - room, papers, objects] bagunçar; [- clothes] sujar -**2**. [spoil] estragar.

➡ **mess with** *vt fus inf* meter-se com.

message ['mesɪdʒ] *n* -**1**. [piece of information] mensagem *f* -**2**. [idea, moral] moral *m* -**3**. *phr*: **to get the ~** *inf* receber o recado.

message switching *n* COMPUT comutação *f* de mensagem.

messenger ['mesɪndʒər] *n* mensageiro *m*, -ra *f*; **by ~** por mensageiro.

Messiah [mɪˈsaɪə] *n*: **the ~** o Messias.

Messrs, Messrs. ['mesəz] (*abbr of* **messieurs**) Srs.

messy ['mesɪ] (*compar* -**ier**, *superl* -**iest**) *adj* -**1**. [dirty, untidy] desarrumado(da) -**2**. [person, activity] confuso(sa) -**3**. [job] sujo(ja) -**4**. *inf* [complicated, confused] complicado(da).

met [met] *pt & pp* ⊳ **meet**.

Met [met] (*abbr of* **Metropolitan Opera**) *n*: **the ~ a** Ópera Metropolitana de Nova Iorque.

metabolism [məˈtæbəlɪzm] *n* metabolismo *m*.

metal ['metl] <> *n* metal *m*. <> *adj* de metal.

metallic [mɪˈtælɪk] *adj* -**1**. [gen] metálico(ca) -**2**. TECH [of metal] metalífero(ra).

metallurgist *n* metalúrgico *m*, -ca *f*.

metallurgy [məˈtælədʒɪ] *n (U)* metalurgia *f*.

metalwork ['metəlwɜːk] *n (U)* [craft] trabalho *m* em metal.

metalworker ['metəlˌwɜːkər] *n* metalurgista *mf*.

metamorphose [ˌmetəˈmɔːfəʊz] *vi*: **to ~ (into sthg)** metamorfosear-se (em algo).

metamorphosis [ˌmetəˈmɔːfəsɪs, ˌmetəməˈfəʊsɪs] (*pl* **-phoses** [-siːz]) *n* metamorfose *f*.

metaphor ['metəfər] *n* metáfora *f*.

metaphorical [ˌmetəˈfɒrɪkl] *adj* metafórico(ca).

metaphysical [ˌmetəˈfɪzɪkl] *adj* PHILOSOPHY metafísico(ca).

metaphysics [ˌmetəˈfɪzɪks] *n (U)* metafísica *f*.

mete [miːt] ➡ **mete out** *vt sep*: **to ~ sthg out to sb** impor algo a alguém.

meteor ['miːtɪər] *n* meteoro *m*.

meteoric [ˌmiːtɪˈɒrɪk] *adj fig* [rapid] meteórico(ca).

meteorite ['miːtjəraɪt] *n* meteorito *m*.

meteorological [ˌmiːtjərəˈlɒdʒɪkl] *adj* meteorológico(ca).

meteorologist [ˌmiːtjəˈrɒlədʒɪst] *n* meteorologista *mf*.

meteorology [ˌmiːtjəˈrɒlədʒɪ] *n (U)* meteorologia *f*.

meter ['miːtər] <> *n* -**1**. [device] medidor *m*; **taxi ~** taxímetro *m*; **electricity ~** relógio *m* de luz; **parking ~** parquímetro *m* -**2**. US = **metre**. <> *vt* [measure] medir.

methadone ['meθədəʊn] *n (U)* metadona *f*.

methane ['miːθeɪn] *n (U)* metano *m*.

method ['meθəd] *n* [way, system] método *m*.

methodical [mɪˈθɒdɪkl] *adj* metódico(ca).

methodically [mɪˈθɒdɪklɪ] *adv* metodicamente.

Methodist ['meθədɪst] <> *adj* metodista. <> *n* metodista *mf*.

methodology [ˌmeθə'dɒlədʒɪ] (pl-ies) n fml metodologia f.

meths [meθs] n UK inf álcool m metilado.

methylated spirits ['meθɪleɪtɪd-] n (U) álcool m metilado.

meticulous [mɪ'tɪkjʊləs] adj meticuloso(sa).

meticulously [mɪ'tɪkjʊləslɪ] adv meticulosamente.

Met Office (abbr of Meteorological Office) n instituto britânico de meteorologia.

metre UK, **meter** US ['mi:tə^r] n -1. [unit of measurement] metro m -2. [in poetry] métrica f.

metric ['metrɪk] adj métrico(ca).

metrication [ˌmetrɪ'keɪʃn] n UK conversão f ao sistema métrico.

metric system n: the ~ o sistema métrico.

metric ton n tonelada f métrica.

metro ['metrəʊ] (pl-s) n metrô m.

metronome ['metrənəʊm] n metrônomo m.

metropolis [mɪ'trɒpəlɪs] (pl-es) n [large city] metrópole f.

metropolitan [ˌmetrə'pɒlɪtn] adj [of a metropolis] metropolitano(na).

Metropolitan Police npl: the ~ a Polícia de Londres.

mettle ['metl] n (U): to be on one's ~ estar preparado(da) para agir da melhor forma possível; to show OR prove one's ~ provar seu próprio valor.

mew [mju:] n & vi = miaow.

mews [mju:z] (pl inv) n UK estrebaria f.

Mexican ['meksɪkn] <> adj mexicano(na). <> n mexicano m, -na f.

Mexico ['meksɪkəʊ] n México; in ~ no México.

Mexico City n Cidade f do México.

mezzanine ['metsəni:n] n mezanino m.

MFA (abbr of Master of Fine Arts) n (titular de) bacharelado em belas artes.

mfr (abbr of manufacturer) fabr. mf.

mg (abbr of milligram) mg.

Mgr -1. (abbr of Monseigneur, Monsignor) Mons. -2. (abbr of manager) gerente mf.

MHR (abbr of Member of the House of Representatives) n membro do congresso norte-americano, ≃ deputado m, -da f federal.

MHz (abbr of megahertz) MHz.

MI abbr of Michigan.

MI5 (abbr of Military Intelligence 5) n órgão do serviço secreto britânico de contra-espionagem.

MI6 (abbr of Military Intelligence 6) n órgão do serviço secreto britânico de espionagem.

MIA (abbr of missing in action) US desaparecido em combate.

miaow UK [mi:'aʊ], **meow** US [mɪ'aʊ] <> n miado m, miau m. <> vi miar.

mice [maɪs] pl ▷ mouse.

Mich. abbr of Michigan.

Michigan ['mɪʃɪgən] n Michigan; in ~ em Michigan.

mickey ['mɪkɪ] n: to take the ~ out of sb UK inf tirar sarro de alguém.

MICR (abbr of magnetic ink character recognition) n MICR f.

micro ['maɪkrəʊ] (pl-s) n micro m.

micro- ['maɪkrəʊ] prefix micro.

microbe ['maɪkrəʊb] n micróbio m.

microbiologist [ˌmaɪkrəʊbaɪ'ɒlədʒɪst] n microbiologista mf.

microbiology [ˌmaɪkrəʊbaɪ'ɒlədʒɪ] n (U) microbiologia f.

microchip ['maɪkrəʊtʃɪp] n microchip m.

microcircuit ['maɪkrəʊˌsɜ:kɪt] n microcircuito m.

microclimate n microclima m.

microcomputer [ˌmaɪkrəʊkəm'pju:tə^r] n microcomputador m.

microcosm ['maɪkrəkɒzm] n microcosmo m.

microfiche ['maɪkrəʊfi:ʃ] (pl inv OR -s) n microficha f.

microfilm ['maɪkrəʊfɪlm] n microfilme m.

microlight ['maɪkrəlaɪt] n ultraleve m.

micron ['maɪkrɒn] n mícron m.

microorganism [ˌmaɪkrəʊ'ɔ:gənɪzm] n microorganismo m.

microphone ['maɪkrəfəʊn] n microfone m.

microprocessor ['maɪkrəʊˌprəʊsesə^r] n microprocessador m.

micro scooter n patinete m.

microscope ['maɪkrəskəʊp] n microscópio m.

microscopic [ˌmaɪkrə'skɒpɪk] adj -1. [very small] microscópico(ca) - 2. [detailed] minucioso(sa).

microsecond n microssegundo m.

microsurgery [ˌmaɪkrə'sɜ:dʒərɪ] n (U) microcirurgia f.

microwave (oven) n forno m de microondas.

mid- [mɪd] prefix: ~ height de meia altura; in ~ morning no meio da manhã; in ~ August em meados de agosto; in ~ winter em pleno inverno; she's in her ~ twenties ela tem uns vinte e poucos anos.

midair [mɪd'eə^r] <> adj no ar. <> n (U): in ~ no ar.

midday ['mɪddeɪ] n (U) meio-dia m.

middle ['mɪdl] <> adj -1. [centre] do meio - 2. [in time]: he was in his ~ forties ele estava nos seus quarenta e poucos anos. <> n -1. [centre] meio m, centro m; in the ~ (of sthg) no meio (de algo); in the ~ of nowhere no meio do nada - 2. [in time] meio m; to be in the ~ of sthg estar no meio de algo; to be in the ~ of doing sthg estar fazendo algo; in the ~ of the night no meio da noite, em plena madrugada; in the ~ of September em meados de setembro - 3. [waist] cintura f.

middle age n (U) meia-idade f.

middle-aged adj de meia-idade.

Middle Ages npl: the ~ a Idade Média.

middle-class adj da classe média.

middle classes npl: the ~ a classe média.

middle distance n: in the ~ em segundo plano.

Middle East n: the ~ o Oriente Médio.

Middle Eastern adj do Oriente Médio.

middle finger n dedo m médio.

middleman ['mɪdlmæn] (pl -men [-men]) n intermediário m.

middle management n (U) administração f intermediária.

middle name n segundo nome m *(num nome composto)*.

middle-of-the-road adj moderado(da).

middle school n UK escola para crianças de 9 a 13 anos.

middleweight ['mɪdlweɪt] n peso m médio.

middling ['mɪdlɪŋ] adj médio(dia), regular.

Mideast n US: the ~ o Oriente Médio.

midfield [ˌmɪd'fiːld] n FTBL meio-campo m.

midge [mɪdʒ] n mosquito-pólvora m.

midget ['mɪdʒɪt] n anão m, -nã f.

MIDI *(abbr of musical instrument digital interface)* n MIDI f.

midi system ['mɪdɪ-] n sistema m MIDI.

Midlands ['mɪdləndz] npl: the ~ a região central da Inglaterra.

midnight ['mɪdnaɪt] <> n (U) meia-noite f. <> comp da meia-noite.

midriff ['mɪdrɪf] n diafragma m.

midst [mɪdst] n [in space, time]: **in the ~ of** *literary* no meio de; **in our ~** entre nós.

midstream [mɪd'striːm] n -1. [of river]: **in ~** no meio da corrente -2. fig [when talking]: **in ~** no meio da conversa.

midsummer ['mɪdˌsʌmər] n (U) pleno verão m.

Midsummer Day n Dia m de São João *(24 de junho)*.

midway [ˌmɪd'weɪ] adv -1. [in space]: ~ **(between)** a meio caminho (entre) -2. [in time]: ~ **(through)** na metade (de).

midweek [adj mɪd'wiːk, adv 'mɪdwiːk] <> adj do meio da semana. <> adv no meio da semana.

Midwest [ˌmɪd'west] n: the ~ o Meio Oeste *(dos Estados Unidos)*.

Midwestern [ˌmɪd'westən] adj do Meio-Oeste *(dos Estados Unidos)*.

midwife ['mɪdwaɪf] *(pl -wives* [-waɪvz]*)* n parteira f.

midwifery ['mɪdˌwɪfərɪ] n (U) trabalho m de parteira.

miffed [mɪft] adj inf amuado(da).

might [maɪt] <> modal vb -1. [expressing possibility]: **I think I ~ go to the pub tonight** acho que é possível eu ir ao bar hoje; **he ~ be armed** ele poderia estar armado -2. [expressing suggestion]: **you ~ have told me** você poderia ter me contado; **it ~ be better to wait** talvez fosse melhor esperar -3. *(past tense of may) fml* [asking permission]: **he asked if he ~ leave the room** ele me pediu permissão para sair da sala -4. [in polite questions, suggestions]: ~ **I ...?** podia ...? -5. [contradicting a point of view]: **you ~ well be right, but ...** é bem possível que você tenha razão, mas ... -6. *phr:* **I ~ have known** OR **guessed** eu deveria ter suspeitado. <> n -1. [power] poder m -2. [physical strength] força f.

mightn't ['maɪtənt] = might not.

might've ['maɪtəv] = might have.

mighty ['maɪtɪ] *(compar -ier, superl -iest)* <> adj -1. [powerful] poderoso(sa) -2. [very large] enorme. <> adv US inf muito.

migraine ['miːɡreɪn, 'maɪɡreɪn] n enxaqueca f.

migrant ['maɪɡrənt] <> adj -1. [bird, animal] migratório(ria) -2. [worker] migrante. <> n -1. [bird,

animal] migratório m, -ria f -2. [person] emigrante mf.

migrate [UK maɪ'ɡreɪt, US 'maɪɡreɪt] vi -1. [bird, animal] migrar -2. [person] emigrar.

migration [maɪ'ɡreɪʃn] n -1. [of birds, animals] migração f -2. [of people] emigração f.

migratory ['maɪɡrətrɪ] adj [bird, animal] migratório(-ria).

mike [maɪk] *(abbr of* microphone*)* n inf mike m.

mild [maɪld] <> adj -1. [food, shampoo, sedative] suave -2. [person, manner] sereno(na) -3. [weather] temperado(da) -4. [surprise, criticism, reproach] moderado(da) -5. [illness] leve. <> n tipo de cerveja suave.

mildew ['mɪldjuː] n -1. (U) [gen] mofo m -2. (U) BOT míldio m.

mildly ['maɪldlɪ] adv -1. [talk, complain, criticize] moderadamente; **to put it ~** para não dizer coisa pior -2. [slightly] bastante.

mild-mannered adj gentil, educado(da).

mildness ['maɪldnɪs] n -1. [of food, shampoo, sedative] suavidade f -2. [of person, manner] serenidade f -3. [of weather] calmaria f -4. [of criticism, reproach] moderação f.

mile [maɪl] n milha f; **we could see for ~s** conseguíamos ver quilômetros à frente; **to be ~s away** fig estar bem longe.
➠ **miles** adv *(in comparisons)* muito; **this is ~ better** sem dúvida alguma isto é realmente melhor.

mileage ['maɪlɪdʒ] n -1. [distance travelled] quilometragem f -2. (U) inf [advantage] vantagem f.

mileage allowance n pagamento m por quilômetros rodados.

mileometer [maɪ'lɒmɪtər] n odômetro m.

milestone ['maɪlstəʊn] n -1. [marker stone] marco m miliário -2. fig [event] marco m.

milieu [UK 'miːljɜː, US miːl'juː] *(pl -s* OR *-x)* n meio m (social).

militant ['mɪlɪtənt] <> adj militante. <> n militante mf.

militarism ['mɪlɪtərɪzm] n (U) militarismo m.

militarist ['mɪlɪtərɪst] n militarista mf.

militarized zone, militarised zone ['mɪlɪtəraɪzd-] n zona f militarizada.

military ['mɪlɪtrɪ] <> adj militar. <> n: the ~ as forças armadas, os militares.

military police npl polícia f militar.

militate ['mɪlɪteɪt] vi fml: **to ~ against sthg** militar contra algo.

militia [mɪ'lɪʃə] n milícia f.

milk [mɪlk] <> n leite m. <> vt -1. [get milk from] ordenhar -2. fig [use for one's own ends] explorar.

milk chocolate <> n (U) chocolate m ao leite. <> comp de chocolate ao leite.

milk float UK, **milk truck** US n veículo usado na entrega domiciliar do leite.

milking ['mɪlkɪŋ] n (U) ordenha f.

milkman ['mɪlkmən] *(pl -men* [-mən]*)* n leiteiro m.

milk round n UK -1. [by milkman] entrega f de leite -2. UNIV [recruitment drive] recrutamento m de pessoal.

milk shake n milk-shake m.

milk tooth n dente-de-leite m.

milk truck n US = milk float.

milky ['mɪlkɪ] (compar -ier, superl -iest) adj - 1. UK [with milk] com leite - 2. [like milk] leitoso(sa) - 3. [pale white] pálido(da).

Milky Way n: the ~ a Via Láctea.

mill [mɪl] ⬦ n - 1. [flour mill] moinho m - 2. [factory] fábrica f - 3. [grinder] moedor m. ⬦ vt [grain] moer.
➡ **mill about, mill around** vi aglomerar-se.

millennium [mɪ'lenɪəm] (pl -nnia [-nɪəl) n [thousand years] milênio m.

miller ['mɪləʳ] n moleiro m, -ra f.

millet ['mɪlɪt] n painço m.

milli- ['mɪlɪl] prefix mili.

millibar ['mɪlɪbɑːʳ] n milibar m.

milligram(me) ['mɪlɪgræm] n miligrama m.

millilitre UK, **milliliter** US ['mɪlɪˌliːtəʳ] n mililitro m.

millimetre UK, **millimeter** US ['mɪlɪˌmiːtəʳ] n milímetro m.

millinery ['mɪlɪnrɪ] n (U) chapelaria f (para senhoras).

million ['mɪljən] n - 1. [1,000,000] milhão m - 2. [enormous number]: a ~, ~s of milhões de.

millionaire [ˌmɪljə'neəʳ] n milionário m, -ria f.

millionairess [ˌmɪljə'neərɪs] n milionária f.

millipede ['mɪlɪpiːd] n embuá m.

millisecond ['mɪlɪˌsekənd] n milissegundo m.

millstone ['mɪlstəʊn] n [for grinding] pedra f de moinho; a ~ round one's neck fig um grande peso sobre os ombros.

millwheel ['mɪlwiːl] n roda f de azenha.

milometer [maɪ'lɒmɪtəʳ] n = mileometer.

mime [maɪm] ⬦ n (U) mímica f. ⬦ vt imitar. ⬦ vi fazer mímica.

mimic ['mɪmɪk] (pt & pp -ked, cont -king) ⬦ n [person] imitador m, -ra f. ⬦ vt [person, voice, gestures] imitar.

mimicry ['mɪmɪkrɪ] n (U) imitação f.

mimosa [mɪ'məʊzə] n mimosa f.

min. [mɪn] - 1. (abbr of minute) min. - 2. (abbr of minimum) mín.

Min. (abbr of ministry) Min.

mince [mɪns] ⬦ n (U) UK carne f picada. ⬦ vt picar; not to ~ one's words não ter papas na língua. ⬦ vi andar com passinhos.

mincemeat ['mɪnsmiːt] n (U) - 1. [fruit] iguaria feita de sebo, frutas cristalizadas e passas - 2. US [minced meat] picadinho m.

mince pie n torta com recheio de frutas secas preparada geralmente no Natal.

mincer ['mɪnsəʳ] n moedor m de carne.

mind [maɪnd] ⬦ n - 1. [gen] mente f; great ~s think alike duas cabeças pensam melhor que uma; to broaden one's ~ ampliar os horizontes de alguém; state of ~ estado de espírito - 2. [thoughts] memória f; to come into/cross sb's ~ passar pela cabeça de alguém; to have sthg on one's ~ estar preocupado(da) com algo; to take sb's ~ off sthg fazer alguém esquecer algo; that was a load OR weight off my ~ isso tirou um peso da minha consciência; to put OR set sb's ~ at rest tranqüilizar alguém - 3. [attention]: to concentrate the ~ concentrar a mente; to keep one's ~ on sthg concentrar-se em algo; to put one's ~ to sthg colocar empenho em algo - 4. [opinion]: to my ~ na minha opinião; to change one's ~ mudar de idéia; to keep an open ~ manter a mente aberta; to make one's ~ up tomar uma decisão; to speak one's ~ dizer o que se pensa; to be in two ~s about sthg estar com dois corações sobre algo - 5. [memory] memória f; to bear sthg in ~ ter algo em mente; to call sthg to ~ trazer algo à memória; to cast one's ~ back pensar no que já aconteceu (no passado); to slip one's ~ fugir da memória - 6. [intention]: to have sthg in ~ ter algo em mente; to have a ~ to do sthg estar pensando em fazer algo. ⬦ vi - 1. [care, worry] importar-se; do you ~ if ...? você se importaria se ...?; I don't ~ eu não me importo; never ~ [don't worry] não faz mal; [it's not important] não tem importância - 2. [be careful]: ~ out! UK cuidado! ⬦ vt - 1. [object to] importar-se em; I don't ~ waiting não me importo em esperar; I wouldn't ~ a ... eu aceitaria um ... - 2. [bother about] preocupar-se com - 3. [pay attention to] prestar atenção com - 4. [take care of] tomar conta de.
➡ **mind you** adv: he didn't give me a Christmas present this year - ~, he never does ele não me deu um presente de Natal neste ano - bom, mas ele nunca dá mesmo.

mind-bending adj inf confuso(sa).

minder ['maɪndəʳ] n - 1. [of child] pessoa f que cuida de crianças - 2. UK [bodyguard] guarda-costas m inv.

mindful ['maɪndfʊl] adj: ~ of sthg ciente de algo.

mindless ['maɪndlɪs] adj - 1. [stupid] absurdo(da), sem sentido - 2. [not requiring thought] tedioso(sa).

mind reader n: I'm not a ~! eu não leio pensamentos!

mindset ['maɪndset] n mentalidade f.

mind's eye n: in one's ~ na imaginação de alguém.

mine[1] [maɪn] ⬦ n - 1. [gen] mina f - 2. [source]: a ~ of information uma fonte de informação. ⬦ vt - 1. [excavate] extrair - 2. [lay mines in] minar.

mine[2] [maɪn] poss pron o meu (a minha); a friend of mine um amigo meu; those shoes are mine esses sapatos são meus; mine are here - where are yours? os meus estão aqui - onde estão os seus?

mine detector n detector m de minas.

minefield ['maɪnfiːld] n - 1. [area containing mines] campo m minado - 2. fig [dangerous topic] campo m minado.

minelayer ['maɪnˌleɪəʳ] n lança-minas m inv.

miner ['maɪnəʳ] n mineiro m, -ra f.

mineral ['mɪnərəl] ⬦ adj GEOL mineral. ⬦ n GEOL mineral m.

mineralogy [ˌmɪnə'rælədʒɪ] n (U) mineralogia f.

mineral water n (U) água f mineral.

minestrone [ˌmɪnɪ'strəʊnɪ] n (U) sopa f minestrone.

minesweeper ['maɪnˌswiːpəʳ] n caça-minas m inv.

mingle ['mɪŋgl] ⬦ vt: to ~ sthg with sthg misturar algo com algo. ⬦ vi - 1. [combine] misturar-se; to ~ with sthg misturar-se com algo - 2. [socially] misturar-se; to ~ with sb misturar-se com alguém.

mini ['mɪnɪ] *n* [skirt, dress] minissaia *f.*

miniature ['mɪnətʃə^r] ◇ *adj* [reduced-scale] em miniatura. ◇ *n* **-1.** [painting] miniatura *f* **-2.** [of alcohol] garrafa *f* em miniatura **-3.** [small scale]: **in ~** em miniatura.

minibus ['mɪnɪbʌs] *(pl* **-es)** *n* microônibus *m inv.*

minicab ['mɪnɪkæb] *n UK* radiotáxi *m.*

minicomputer [,mɪnɪkəm'pju:tə^r] *n* minicomputador *m.*

MiniDisc® ['mɪdɪsk] *n* MiniDisc® *m.*

MiniDisc player® *n* reprodutor *m* de MiniDisc®.

minidish [m'ɪnɪdɪʃ] *n* miniparabólica *f.*

minim ['mɪnɪm] *n MUS* mínima *f.*

minima ['mɪnɪmə] *pl* ▷ **minimum**.

minimal ['mɪnɪml] *adj* mínimo(ma).

minimize, -ise ['mɪnɪmaɪz] *vt* [reduce] minimizar.

minimum ['mɪnɪməm] *(pl* **-mums** OR **-ma)** ◇ *adj* mínimo(ma). ◇ *n* mínimo *m.*

minimum lending rate [-'lendɪŋ-] *n* taxa *f* mínima de empréstimo.

minimum wage *n* salário *m* mínimo.

mining ['maɪnɪŋ] ◇ *adj* mineiro(ra); **~ engineer** engenheiro *m*, -ra *f* de minas. ◇ *n* mineração *f.*

minion ['mɪnjən] *n hum* or *pej* lacaio *m*, -a *f.*

miniseries ['mɪnɪsɪərɪz] *(pl inv)* *n* minissérie *f.*

miniskirt ['mɪnɪskɜ:t] *n* minissaia *f.*

minister ['mɪnɪstə^r] *n* **-1.** POL: **~ (for sthg)** ministro *m*, -tra *f* (de algo) **-2.** RELIG pastor *m*, -ra *f.*
   ➡ **minister to** *vt fus* **-1.** [person] atender **-2.** [needs] atender a.

ministerial [,mɪnɪ'stɪərɪəl] *adj POL* ministerial.

minister of state *n*: **~ (for sthg)** secretário *m*, -ria *f* de estado (para algo).

ministry ['mɪnɪstrɪ] *(pl* **-ies)** *n* **-1.** POL ministério *m*; **Ministry of Defence** Ministério da Defesa **-2.** RELIG [clergy]: **the ~** o sacerdócio.

mink [mɪŋk] *(pl inv)* *n* **-1.** (U) [fur] pele *f* de visom **-2.** [animal] visom *m.*

mink coat *n* casaco *m* de visom.

Minnesota [,mɪnɪ'səʊtə] *n* Minnesota; **in ~** em Minnesota.

minnow ['mɪnəʊ] *n* [fish] peixinho *m (de água doce).*

minor ['maɪnə^r] ◇ *adj* [gen] menor. ◇ *n* [in age] menor *mf* de idade.

Minorca [mɪ'nɔ:kə] *n* Minorca; **in ~** em Minorca.

minority [maɪ'nɒrətɪ] *(pl* **-ies)** ◇ *adj* minoritário(-ria). ◇ *n* [gen] minoria *f*; **to be in a** OR **the ~** estar em minoria, ser minoria.

minority government *n* governo *m* minoritário.

minor road *n* caminho *m* secundário.

minster ['mɪnstə^r] *n* catedral *f.*

minstrel ['mɪnstrəl] *n* menestrel *m.*

mint [mɪnt] ◇ *n* **-1.** (U) [herb] hortelã *f* **-2.** [sweet] bala *f* de hortelã **-3.** [for coins]: **the Mint** a Casa da Moeda; **in ~ condition** novo(va) em folha. ◇ *vt* [coins] cunhar.

mint sauce *n* (U) molho *m* de hortelã.

minuet [,mɪnjʊ'et] *n* minueto *m.*

minus ['maɪnəs] *(pl* **-es)** ◇ *prep* **-1.** MATH [less]: **4 ~ 2 is 2** 4 menos 2 é 2 **-2.** [in temperatures]: **it's ~ 5 degrees** está fazendo 5 graus abaixo de zero. ◇

adj **-1.** MATH [less than zero] negativo(va) **-2.** SCH [in grades] menos. ◇ *n* **-1.** MATH sinal *m* de menos **-2.** [disadvantage] desvantagem *f.*

minuscule ['mɪnəskju:l] *adj* minúsculo(la).

minus sign *n* sinal *m* de menos.

minute¹ ['mɪnɪt] *n* [gen] minuto *m*; **at any ~** a qualquer momento; **at the last ~** no último minuto; **this ~** agora mesmo; **up to the ~** [news, design] de última hora; [technology] de ponta; **wait a ~!** espere um pouco!
   ➡ **minutes** *npl* [of meeting] ata *f.*

minute² [maɪ'nju:t] *adj* [tiny] mínimo(ma).

minutiae [maɪ'nju:ʃɪaɪ] *npl* minúcias *fpl.*

miracle ['mɪrəkl] *n* milagre *m.*

miraculous [mɪ'rækjʊləs] *adj* milagroso(sa).

miraculously [mɪ'rækjʊləslɪ] *adv fig* [surprisingly] milagrosamente.

mirage [mɪ'rɑ:ʒ] *n* miragem *f.*

mire [maɪə^r] *n* (U) lamaçal *m.*

mirror ['mɪrə^r] ◇ *n* espelho *m.* ◇ *vt* **-1.** [copy] espelhar **-2.** *litérary* [reflect] refletir.

mirror image *n* imagem *f* refletida.

mirth [mɜ:θ] *n* (U) *literary* alegria *f.*

misadventure [,mɪsəd'ventʃə^r] *n fml* [unfortunate accident] desventura *f*; **death by ~** JUR morte *f* acidental.

misanthropist [mɪs'ænθrəpɪst] *n* misantropo *m*, -pa *f.*

misapplication *n* má aplicação *f*, abuso *m.*

misapprehension ['mɪs,æprɪ'henʃn] *n* mal-entendido *m.*

misappropriate [,mɪsə'prəʊprɪeɪt] *vt* desviar.

misappropriation ['mɪsə,prəʊprɪ'eɪʃn] *n* desvio *m.*

misbehave [,mɪsbɪ'heɪv] *vi* comportar-se mal.

misbehaviour UK, **misbehavior** US [,mɪsbɪ'heɪvjə^r] *n* (U) mau comportamento *m*, má conduta *f.*

misc *(abbr of* **miscellaneous)** variado(da).

miscalculate [,mɪs'kælkjʊleɪt] *vt* & *vi* calcular mal.

miscalculation [,mɪskælkjʊ'leɪʃn] *n* erro *m* de cálculo.

miscarriage [,mɪs'kærɪdʒ] *n* aborto *m* natural.

miscarriage of justice *n* erro *m* judicial.

miscarry [,mɪs'kærɪ] *(pt* & *pp* **-ied)** *vi* **-1.** [woman] abortar naturalmente **-2.** [plan] fracassar.

miscellaneous [,mɪsə'leɪnjəs] *adj* diverso(sa).

miscellany [UK mɪ'selənɪ, US 'mɪsələɪnɪ] *(pl* **-ies)** *n* miscelânea *f.*

mischance [,mɪs'tʃɑ:ns] *n fml* azar *m*, infortúnio *m*; **by ~** por azar.

mischief ['mɪstʃɪf] *n* (U) **-1.** [playfulness] malícia *f* **-2.** [naughty behaviour] travessuras *fpl* **-3.** [harm] dano *m.*

mischievous ['mɪstʃɪvəs] *adj* **-1.** [playful] cheio (cheia) de malícia **-2.** [naughty] travesso(sa).

misconceived [,mɪskən'si:vd] *adj* [plan, idea] mal concebido(da).

misconception [,mɪskən'sepʃn] *n* conceito *m* falho, idéia *f* equivocada.

misconduct [,mɪs'kɒndʌkt] *n* [bad behaviour] má conduta *f.*

misconstrue [ˌmɪskən'stru:] vt *fml* interpretar erroneamente.

miscount [ˌmɪs'kaʊnt] vt & vi contar mal.

misdeed [ˌmɪs'di:d] n *literary* delito m.

misdemeanour UK, **misdemeanor** US [ˌmɪsdɪ'mi:nɔ'] n JUR contravenção f.

misdirected [ˌmɪsdɪ'rektɪd] adj - **1.** [letter] mal endereçado(da) - **2.** [misused] mal dirigido(da).

miser ['maɪzə'] n avarento m, -ta f.

miserable ['mɪzrəbl] adj - **1.** [unhappy] infeliz, triste - **2.** [depressing - conditions, life] miserável; [- weather, holiday, evening] horrível - **3.** [failure] lamentável.

miserably ['mɪzrəblɪ] adv - **1.** [unhappily] tristemente - **2.** [in depressing fashion] miseravelmente - **3.** [fail] de forma lamentável.

miserly ['maɪzəlɪ] adj mesquinho(nha), miserável.

misery ['mɪzərɪ] (pl -ies) n - **1.** [unhappiness] tristeza f - **2.** [poverty] miséria f - **3.** [gloomy person] desgraça f.

misfire [ˌmɪs'faɪə'] vi - **1.** [gun] não disparar - **2.** [car engine] não dar partida - **3.** [plan] fracassar.

misfit ['mɪsfɪt] n desajustado m, -da f.

misfortune [mɪs'fɔːtʃuːn] n - **1.** (U) [bad luck] azar m - **2.** [piece of bad luck] infortúnio m, desgraça f.

misgivings [mɪs'gɪvɪŋz] npl receio m, desconfiança f.

misguided [ˌmɪs'gaɪdɪd] adj - **1.** [person] desencaminhado(da) - **2.** [attempt, opinion] equivocado(da).

mishandle [ˌmɪs'hændl] vt - **1.** [person, animal] maltratar - **2.** [negotiations, business] administrar mal.

mishap ['mɪshæp] n - **1.** (U) [accident]: **without ~** sem incidentes - **2.** [unfortunate event] incidente m, percalço m.

mishear [ˌmɪs'hɪə'] (pt & pp -heard [-'hɜːd]) vt & vi ouvir mal.

mishmash ['mɪʃmæʃ] n *inf* mixórdia f.

misinform [ˌmɪsɪn'fɔːm] vt informal mal.

misinformation [ˌmɪsɪnfə'meɪʃn] n (U) informação f errada.

misinterpret [ˌmɪsɪn'tɜːprɪt] vt interpretar mal.

misjudge [ˌmɪs'dʒʌdʒ] vt - **1.** [calculate wrongly] calcular mal - **2.** [appraise wrongly] julgar mal.

misjudg(e)ment [ˌmɪs'dʒʌdʒmənt] n julgamento m errado.

mislay [ˌmɪs'leɪ] (pt & pp -laid) vt perder, extraviar.

mislead [ˌmɪs'liːd] (pt & pp -led) vt enganar.

misleading [ˌmɪs'liːdɪŋ] adj enganoso(sa).

misled [ˌmɪs'led] pt & pp ▷ **mislead**.

mismanage [ˌmɪs'mænɪdʒ] vt administrar mal.

mismanagement [ˌmɪs'mænɪdʒmənt] n (U) má administração f.

mismatch [ˌmɪs'mætʃ] vt: **to be ~ed** [colours] combinar mal; [in marriage] estar desencontrado(-da).

misnomer [ˌmɪs'nəʊmə'] n termo m impróprio.

misogynist [mɪ'sɒdʒɪnɪst] n misógino m, -na f.

misplace [ˌmɪs'pleɪs] vt extraviar, perder.

misplaced [ˌmɪs'pleɪst] adj [trust, confidence] inapropriado(da).

misprint ['mɪsprɪnt] n erro m de impressão.

mispronounce [ˌmɪsprə'naʊns] vt pronunciar mal.

misquote [ˌmɪs'kwəʊt] vt citar erroneamente.

misread [ˌmɪs'riːd] (pt & pp -read) vt - **1.** [read wrongly] ler erroneamente - **2.** [misinterpret] interpretar mal.

misrepresent ['mɪsˌreprɪ'zent] vt - **1.** [person] dar uma imagem equivocada de - **2.** [facts] deturpar.

misrepresentation ['mɪsˌreprɪzen'teɪʃn] n - **1.** (U) [wrong interpretation] má interpretação f - **2.** [false account] deturpação f.

misrule [ˌmɪs'ruːl] n [misgovernment] mau governo m.

miss [mɪs] ⬦ vt - **1.** [gen] perder - **2.** [fail to see] não ver, perder - **3.** [fail to hit] errar; **to ~ the target** não acertar o alvo - **4.** [feel absence of - person, home, family] sentir/estar com saudades de; [- things] sentir falta de - **5.** [fail to be present at] faltar a - **6.** [escape] evitar; **I just ~ed being run over** escapei de ser atropelado por pouco. ⬦ vi [fail to hit] não acertar. ⬦ n: **to give sthg a ~** inf deixar algo.
➡ **miss out** ⬦ vt sep omitir. ⬦ vi: **to ~ out (on sthg)** perder (algo).

Miss [mɪs] n senhorita f.

misshapen [ˌmɪs'ʃeɪpn] adj - **1.** [hands, fingers] deformado(da) - **2.** [object] disforme.

missile [UK 'mɪsaɪl, US 'mɪsəl] n - **1.** [weapon] míssil m - **2.** [thrown object] projétil m.

missile launcher [-ˌlɔːntʃə'] n lança-mísseis m inv.

missing ['mɪsɪŋ] adj - **1.** [object] perdido(da) - **2.** [person] desaparecido(da) - **3.** [not present] que falta; **who's ~?** quem está faltando?; **to go ~** desaparecer.

missing link n: **here was the ~ between ...** aqui está o elo que faltava entre ...

missing person n pessoa f desaparecida.

mission ['mɪʃn] n missão f.

missionary ['mɪʃənrɪ] (pl -ies) n missionário m, -ria f.

Mississippi [ˌmɪsɪ'sɪpɪ] n - **1.** [river]: **the ~ (River)** (Rio) Mississippi - **2.** [state] Mississippi; **in ~** em Mississippi.

missive ['mɪsɪv] n missiva f.

Missouri [mɪ'zʊərɪ] n Missouri; **in ~** em Missouri.

misspell [ˌmɪs'spel] (pt & pp -spelt OR -spelled) vt soletrar erroneamente.

misspelling [ˌmɪs'spelɪŋ] n erro m de ortografia.

misspelt [ˌmɪs'spelt] pt & pp ▷ **misspell**.

misspend (pt & pp -spent) vt [money, talent, youth] desperdiçar.

mist [mɪst] n neblina f.
➡ **mist over, mist up** vi embaçar.

mistake [mɪ'steɪk] (pt -took, pp -taken) ⬦ n erro m; **to make a ~** cometer um erro, equivocar-se; **by ~** por engano. ⬦ vt - **1.** [misunderstand] entender mal - **2.** [fail to distinguish]: **to ~ sb/sthg for** confundir alguém/algo com; **there's no mistaking ...** não tem como confundir ...

mistaken [mɪ'steɪkn] ⬦ pp ▷ **mistake**. ⬦ adj - **1.** [person] equivocado(da), enganado(da); **to be ~ about sb/sthg** estar enganado(da) sobre alguém/algo - **2.** [belief, idea] equivocado(da).

mistaken identity n: **a case of ~** um caso de identificação equivocada.

mistakenly [mɪs'teɪknlɪ] adv equivocadamente.

mister ['mɪstə^r] *n inf* amigo *m*.
◆ **Mister** *n* Senhor *m*.

mistime [,mɪs'taɪm] *vt* calcular mal o tempo de.

mistletoe ['mɪsltəʊ] *n (U)* visco *m*.

mistook [mɪ'stʊk] *pt* ➭ **mistake**.

mistranslation [,mɪstræns'leɪʃn] *n* tradução *f* incorreta.

mistreat [,mɪs'triːt] *vt* maltratar.

mistreatment [,mɪs'triːtmənt] *n (U)* maus tratos *mpl*.

mistress ['mɪstrɪs] *n* -**1**. [of house, situation] dona *f* -**2**. [female lover] amante *f* -**3**. [schoolteacher] professora *f*.

mistrial ['mɪstraɪəl] *n* processo *m* nulo.

mistrust [,mɪs'trʌst] ⟨⟩ *n (U)* desconfiança *f*, receio *m*. ⟨⟩ *vt* desconfiar de.

mistrustful [,mɪs'trʌstfʊl] *adj* desconfiado(da); ~ of sb/sthg desconfiado(da) de alguém/algo.

misty ['mɪstɪ] (*compar* -**ier**, *superl* -**iest**) *adj* nebuloso(sa).

misunderstand [,mɪsʌndə'stænd] (*pt* & *pp* -**stood**) *vt* & *vi* entender mal.

misunderstanding [,mɪsʌndə'stændɪŋ] *n* -**1**. *(U)* [lack of understanding] equívoco *m* -**2**. [wrong interpretation] mal-entendido *m* -**3**. [disagreement] desentendimento *m*.

misunderstood [,mɪsʌndə'stʊd] *pt* & *pp* ➭ **misunderstand**.

misuse [*n* ,mɪs'juːs, *vb* ,mɪs'juːz] ⟨⟩ *n* -**1**. *(U)* [wrong use] uso *m* indevido -**2**. [abuse] abuso *m*. ⟨⟩ *vt* -**1**. [use wrongly] usar indevidamente -**2**. [abuse] abusar de.

MIT (*abbr of* Massachusetts Institute of Technology) *n* MIT *m*.

mite [maɪt] *n* -**1**. *ZOOL* ácaro *m* -**2**. *inf* [small amount]: a ~ um pouquinho -**3**. *inf* [small child] criancinha *f*.

miter *n US* = **mitre**.

mitigate ['mɪtɪgeɪt] *vt fml* mitigar.

mitigating ['mɪtɪgeɪtɪŋ] *adj fml*: ~ **circumstances** circunstâncias *fpl* atenuantes.

mitigation [,mɪtɪ'geɪʃn] *n (U) fml* mitigação *f*, atenuante *f*.

mitre *UK*, **miter** *US* ['maɪtə^r] *n* -**1**. [hat] mitra *f* -**2**. [joint] meia-esquadria *f*.

mitt [mɪt] *n* -**1**. = **mitten** -**2**. [in baseball] luva *f*.

mitten ['mɪtn] *n* [with fingers joined] luva *f (com separação somente para o polegar)*; [with fingers cut off] mitene *f*.

mix [mɪks] ⟨⟩ *vt* misturar; **to** ~ **sthg with sthg** misturar algo com algo. ⟨⟩ *vi* misturar-se, combinar-se; **to** ~ **with sb** misturar-se com alguém. ⟨⟩ *n* -**1**. [gen] mistura *f* -**2**. *COMM*: **marketing** ~ mix *m* de marketing, composto *m* mercadológico.
◆ **mix up** *vt sep* -**1**. [confuse] confundir -**2**. [disorder] misturar.

mixed [mɪkst] *adj* -**1**. [of different kinds] misturado(da) -**2**. [of different sexes] misto(ta).

mixed-ability *adj UK* de vários níveis.

mixed blessing *n*: it was a ~ teve um lado bom e um lado ruim.

mixed doubles *n (U)* duplas *fpl* mistas.

mixed economy *n* economia *f* mista.

mixed grill *n* prato grelhado com carnes e vegetais.

mixed marriage *n* casamento *m* misto.

mixed up *adj* -**1**. [confused] confuso(sa) -**2**. [involved]: **to be** ~ **in sthg** estar envolvido(da) em algo.

mixer ['mɪksə^r] *n* -**1**. [machine - for food] *f* batedeira; [- for drinks] misturador *m*; [- for cement] betoneira *f* -**2**. [soft drink] *bebida não-alcoólica usada para se misturar com bebidas alcoólicas.*

mixer tap *n UK* torneira *f (para o fluxo de água fria e quente)*.

mixing bowl ['mɪksɪŋ-] *n* tigela *f*.

mixture ['mɪkstʃə^r] *n* mistura *f*.

mix-up *n inf* engano *m*, confusão *f*.

mk, MK (*abbr of* mark) marco *m*.

mkt (*abbr of* market) mercado *m*.

ml (*abbr of* millilitre) *n* ml.

MLitt [,em'lɪt] (*abbr of* Master of Literature, Master of Letters) *n (titular de)* mestrado em literatura.

MLR (*abbr of* minimum lending rate) *taxa mínima de juros praticada para empréstimos pelo Banco da Inglaterra, referência para os demais bancos.*

mm (*abbr of* millimetre) mm.

MMR (*abbr of* measles, mumps, and rubella) *n* MMR *f*, SCR *f*.

MN ⟨⟩ *n* (*abbr of* Merchant Navy) marinha *f* mercante. ⟨⟩ *abbr of* Minnesota.

mnemonic [nɪ'mɒnɪk] *n* mnemônica *f*.

MO ⟨⟩ *n* (*abbr of* medical officer) *médico encarregado dos serviços de saúde*. ⟨⟩ *abbr of* Missouri.

moan [məʊn] ⟨⟩ *n* -**1**. [of pain, sadness] gemido *m* -**2**. *inf* [complaint] resmungo *m*, queixa *f*. ⟨⟩ *vi* -**1**. [in pain, sadness] gemer -**2**. *inf* [complain] resmungar, queixar-se; **to** ~ **about sb/sthg** resmungar *OR* queixar-se sobre alguém/algo.

moaning ['məʊnɪŋ] *n* -**1**. [pain, sadness] gemidos *mpl* -**2**. *(U)* [complaining] reclamação *f*, queixas *fpl*.

moat [məʊt] *n* fosso *m*.

mob [mɒb] (*pt* & *pp* -**bed**, *cont* -**bing**) ⟨⟩ *n* -**1**. multidão *f* -**2**. *pej*: **the** ~ a ralé, a plebe. ⟨⟩ *vt* cercar, amontoar-se ao redor de.

mobile ['məʊbaɪl] ⟨⟩ *adj* -**1**. [able to move] móvel -**2**. *inf* [having transport] motorizado(da). ⟨⟩ *n* -**1**. [phone] (telefone) celular *m* -**2**. [decoration] móbile *m*.

mobile home *n* trailer *m*.

mobile library *n* biblioteca *f* móvel *OR* ambulante.

mobile phone *n* (telefone) celular *m*.

mobile shop *n* unidade *f* móvel de vendas.

mobility [mə'bɪlətɪ] *n* mobilidade *f*.

mobility allowance *n UK ajuda financeira que recebem os deficientes físicos para poderem se locomover.*

mobilization [,məʊbɪlaɪ'zeɪʃn] *n* mobilização *f*.

mobilize, -ise ['məʊbɪlaɪz] ⟨⟩ *vt* mobilizar. ⟨⟩ *vi* mobilizar-se.

moccasin ['mɒkəsɪn] *n* mocassim *m*.

mock [mɒk] ⟨⟩ *adj* falso(sa); **a** ~ **exam** um simulado. ⟨⟩ *vt* [deride] zombar de. ⟨⟩ *vi* zombar.

mockery ['mɒkərɪ] n -1. (U) [scorn] zombaria f -2. [travesty] paródia f; **to make a ~ of sthg** pôr algo em ridículo.

mocking ['mɒkɪŋ] adj zombeteiro(ra).

mockingbird ['mɒkɪŋbɜːd] n tordo m imitador.

mock-up n modelo m em tamanho natural.

mod [mɒd] n jovem britânico dos anos 60 que vestia roupas alinhadas e gostava da música soul americana.

MoD (abbr of Ministry of Defence) n ministério m da defesa (britânico).

mod cons [ˌmɒd-] (abbr of modern conveniences) npl UK inf: all ~ todas as comodidades modernas.

mode [məʊd] n -1. [gen] modo m -2. [of transport] meio m.

model ['mɒdl] (UK pt & pp -led, cont -ling, US pt & pp -ed, cont -ing) <> adj -1. [miniature] em miniatura -2. [exemplary] modelo. <> n [gen] modelo m. <> vt -1. [shape] moldar -2. [in fashion show] desfilar com -3. [copy]: **to ~ o.s. on sb** ter alguém como modelo, espelhar-se em alguém. <> vi [in fashion show] desfilar.

modem ['məʊdem] COMPUT n modem m.

moderate [adj & n 'mɒdərət, vb 'mɒdəreɪt] <> adj moderado(da). <> n POL moderado m, -da f. <> vt moderar. <> vi moderar-se.

moderately ['mɒdərətlɪ] adv moderadamente.

moderation [ˌmɒdə'reɪʃn] n moderação f; **in ~** com moderação.

moderator ['mɒdəreɪtə'] n -1. [of debate] moderador m, -ra f -2. RELIG presidente duma assembleia protestante.

modern ['mɒdən] adj moderno(na).

modern-day adj dos dias de hoje.

modernism ['mɒdənɪzm] n (U) modernismo m.

modernization [ˌmɒdənaɪ'zeɪʃn] n modernização f.

modernize, -ise ['mɒdənaɪz] <> vt modernizar. <> vi modernizar-se.

modern languages npl línguas fpl modernas.

modest ['mɒdɪst] adj modesto(ta).

modestly ['mɒdɪstlɪ] adv -1. [to small extent] ligeiramente -2. [not proudly] modestamente.

modesty ['mɒdɪstɪ] n (U) modéstia f.

modicum ['mɒdɪkəm] n fml quantia f módica; **a ~ of** um mínimo de.

modification [ˌmɒdɪfɪ'keɪʃn] n -1. [minor alteration] modificação f -2. (U) [alteration] alteração f, modificação f.

modify ['mɒdɪfaɪ] (pt & pp -ied) vt -1. [alter] modificar -2. [tone down] moderar.

modular ['mɒdjʊlə'] adj -1. [furniture] modular -2. [course] em módulos.

modulated ['mɒdjʊleɪtɪd] adj [voice] modulado(da).

modulation [ˌmɒdjʊ'leɪʃn] n TECH modulação f.

module ['mɒdjuːl] n módulo m.

Mogadishu [ˌmɒgə'dɪʃuː] n Mogadíscio; **in ~** em Mogadíscio.

moggy ['mɒgɪ] (pl -ies) n UK inf gato m, -ta f.

mogul ['məʊgl] n [magnate] magnata m.

MOH (abbr of Medical Officer of Health) n secretário municipal de saúde na Grã-Bretanha.

mohair ['məʊheə'] <> n mohair m. <> comp de mohair.

Mohammedan [mə'hæmɪdn] <> adj maometano(na). <> n maometano m, -na f.

Mohican [məʊ'hiːkən] <> adj moicano(na). <> n -1. [indian] moicano m, -na f -2. [haircut] corte de cabelo punk em que a cabeça é raspada nas laterais.

moist [mɔɪst] adj úmido(da); **~ cake** bolo m fofo.

moisten ['mɔɪsn] vt umedecer.

moisture ['mɔɪstʃə'] n (U) umidade f.

moisturize, -ise ['mɔɪstʃəraɪz] vt umectar.

moisturizer ['mɔɪstʃəraɪzə'] n (creme) hidratante m.

molar ['məʊlə'] n molar m.

molasses [mə'læsɪz] n (U) melaço m.

mold etc n & vt US = mould.

Moldavia [mɒl'deɪvɪə] n Moldávia; **in ~** na Moldávia.

mole [məʊl] n -1. [animal] toupeira f -2. [on skin] sinal m -3. [spy] espião m, -ã f.

molecular [mə'lekjʊlə'] adj molecular.

molecule ['mɒlɪkjuːl] n molécula f.

molehill ['məʊlhɪl] n montículo de terra deixado pelas toupeiras ao cavar seus túneis.

molest [mə'lest] vt -1. [attack sexually - child] molestar; [- person] assediar -2. [bother] incomodar.

molester [mə'lestə'] n molestador m, -ra f; **child ~** perversor m, -ra f de menores.

mollify ['mɒlɪfaɪ] (pt & pp -ied) vt fml tranquilizar.

mollusc, mollusk US ['mɒləsk] n molusco m.

mollycoddle ['mɒlɪˌkɒdl] vt inf mimar.

Molotov cocktail ['mɒlətɒf-] n coquetel m Molotov.

molt vt & vi US = moult.

molten ['məʊltn] adj derretido(da), fundido(da).

mom [mɒm] n US inf mãe f.

moment ['məʊmənt] n -1. [gen] momento m; **~ of truth** hora f da verdade; **for one ~** por um momento; **at any ~** a qualquer momento; **at the ~** no momento; **at the last ~** no último momento; **for the ~** por enquanto -2. [importance] importância f.

momentarily ['məʊməntərɪlɪ] adv -1. [for a short time] momentaneamente -2. US [immediately] imediatamente.

momentary ['məʊməntrɪ] adj momentâneo(nea).

momentous [mə'mentəs] adj significativo(va).

momentum [mə'mentəm] n -1. PHYSICS momento m -2. fig [speed, force] força f.

momma ['mɒmə], **mommy** ['mɒmɪ] n US mamãe f, mãezinha f.

Mon. (abbr of Monday) seg.

Monaco ['mɒnəkəʊ] n Mônaco; **in ~** em Mônaco.

monarch ['mɒnək] n monarca mf.

monarchist ['mɒnəkɪst] n monarquista mf.

monarchy ['mɒnəkɪ] (pl -ies) n monarquia f; **the ~** a monarquia.

monastery ['mɒnəstrɪ] (pl -ies) n monastério m.

monastic [mə'næstɪk] adj monástico(ca).

Monday ['mʌndɪ] n segunda-feira f; see also **Saturday**.

monetarism ['mʌnɪtərɪzm] n (U) monetarismo m.

monetarist [ˈmʌnɪtərɪst] n monetarista mf.

monetary [ˈmʌnɪtrɪ] adj monetário(ria).

money [ˈmʌnɪ] n (U) dinheiro m; **to make ~** ganhar dinheiro; **to get one's ~'s worth** fazer o dinheiro OR investimento valer a pena.

moneybox [ˈmʌnɪbɒks] n cofrinho m.

moneyed adj fml abastado(da).

moneylender [ˈmʌnɪˌlendəʳ] n prestamista mf.

moneymaker [ˈmʌnɪˌmeɪkəʳ] n mina f (de ouro).

moneymaking [ˈmʌnɪˌmeɪkɪŋ] adj rentável, lucrativo(va).

money market n mercado m financeiro.

money order n ordem f de pagamento.

money-spinner [-ˌspɪnəʳ] n esp UK inf mina f (de ouro).

money supply n oferta f de moeda.

mongol [ˈmɒŋgəll] *dated & offensive* <> adj mongolóide. <> n mongolóide mf.
➡ **Mongol** adj & n = **Mongolian**.

Mongolia [mɒŋˈgəʊlɪə] n Mongólia; **in ~** na Mongólia.

Mongolian [mɒŋˈgəʊlɪən] <> adj mongol. <> n -1. [person] mongol mf -2. [language] mongol m.

mongoose [ˈmɒŋguːs] (pl -s) n mangusto m.

mongrel [ˈmʌŋgrəl] n [dog] vira-lata m.

monitor [ˈmɒnɪtəʳ] <> n TECH monitor m. <> vt monitorar.

monk [mʌŋk] n monge m.

monkey [ˈmʌŋkɪ] (pl -s) n [animal] macaco m, -ca f.

monkey nut n amendoim m.

monkey wrench n chave f inglesa.

monkfish (pl inv OR -es) n peixe-pescador m.

mono [ˈmɒnəʊ] <> adj monofônico(ca), mono inv. <> n inf -1. [sound] som m mono -2. US [glandular fever] mononucleose f infecciosa.

monochrome [ˈmɒnəkrəʊm] adj [TV, photograph] monocromo(ma).

monocle [ˈmɒnəkl] n monóculo m.

monogamous [mɒˈnɒgəməs] adj monógamo(ma).

monogamy [mɒˈnɒgəmɪ] n (U) monogamia f.

monogrammed [ˈmɒnəgræmd] adj bordado(da) com as iniciais.

monolingual [ˌmɒnəˈlɪŋgwəl] adj monolíngüe.

monolithic [ˌmɒnəˈlɪθɪk] adj monolítico(ca).

monologue, monolog US [ˈmɒnəlɒg] n -1. THEATRE monólogo m -2. inf [long speech] palestra f longa.

mononucleosis [ˈmɒnəʊˌnjuːklɪˈəʊsɪs] n US mononucleose f.

monoplane [ˈmɒnəpleɪn] n monoplano m.

monopolize, -ise [məˈnɒpəlaɪz] vt monopolizar.

monopoly [məˈnɒpəlɪ] (pl -ies) n monopólio m; **~ on** OR **of sthg** monopólio em OR de algo; **the Monopolies and Mergers Commission** UK organização que investiga a possível formação de monopólio pelas empresas.

monorail [ˈmɒnəreɪl] n monotrilho m.

monosodium glutamate [ˌmɒnəˈsəʊdjəmˈgluːtəmeɪt] n (U) glutamato m monossódico.

monosyllabic [ˌmɒnəsɪˈlæbɪk] adj monossilábico(ca).

monosyllable [ˈmɒnəˌsɪləbl] n monossílabo m.

monotone [ˈmɒnətəʊn] n: **he speaks in a ~** ele fala com uma voz monótona.

monotonous [məˈnɒtənəs] adj [voice, job, life] monótono(na).

monotonously [məˈnɒtənəslɪ] adv de forma monótona.

monotony [məˈnɒtənɪ] n (U) monotonia f.

monoxide [mɒˈnɒksaɪd] n monóxido m.

Monrovia [mɒnˈrəʊvɪə] n Monróvia; **in ~** em Monróvia.

Monsignor [ˌmɒnˈsiːɲəʳ] n Monsenhor m.

monsoon [mɒnˈsuːn] n [rainy season] monção f.

monster [ˈmɒnstəʳ] <> adj gigantesco(ca), enorme. <> n monstro m.

monstrosity [mɒnˈstrɒsətɪ] (pl -ies) n monstruosidade f.

monstrous [ˈmɒnstrəs] adj -1. [appalling] espantoso(sa) -2. [hideous] monstruoso(sa) -3. [very large] gigantesco(ca).

montage [ˈmɒntɑːʒ] n montagem f.

Montana [mɒnˈtænə] n Montana; **in ~** em Montana.

Mont Blanc [mɒntl] n Monte m Branco.

Montenegro [ˌmɒntɪˈniːgrəʊ] n Montenegro; **~** em Montenegro.

Montevideo [ˌmɒntɪvɪˈdeɪəʊ] n Montevidéu; **in ~** em Montevidéu.

month [mʌnθ] n mês m.

monthly [ˈmʌnθlɪ] (pl -ies) <> adj mensal. <> adv mensalmente. <> n [publication] revista f mensal.

Montreal [mɒntrɪˈɔːl] n Montreal; **in ~** em Montreal.

monument [ˈmɒnjʊmənt] n monumento m.

monumental [ˌmɒnjʊˈmentl] adj -1. [gen] monumental -2. [extremely bad] descomunal.

moo [muː] (pl -s) <> n mugido m. <> vi mugir.

mooch [muːtʃ] ➡ **mooch about, mooch around** vi inf perambular, vaguear.

mood [muːd] n [state of feelings] humor m; **in a (bad) ~** de mau humor; **in a good ~** de bom humor.

moody [ˈmuːdɪ] (compar -ier, superl -iest) adj pej -1. [changeable] temperamental, de humor variável -2. [bad-tempered] mal-humorado(da).

moon [muːn] n lua f; **to be over the ~** inf dar pulos de alegria.

moonbeam [ˈmuːnbiːm] n raio m de luar.

moonlight [ˈmuːnlaɪt] (pt & pp -ed) <> n (U) luar m, luz f da lua. <> vi inf [have second job] ter um trabalho extra.

moonlighting [ˈmuːnlaɪtɪŋ] n (U) [illegal work] trabalho m extra, bico m.

moonlit [ˈmuːnlɪt] adj enluarado(da).

moonscape [ˈmuːnskeɪp] n paisagem f lunar.

moon shot n viagem para a lua em espaçonave.

moonstone n pedra-da-lua f.

moonstruck [ˈmuːnstrʌk] adj inf lunático(ca).

moony (compar -ier, superl -iest) adj UK inf sonhador(ra).

moor [mɔːʳ] <> n esp UK brejo m vt & vi atracar, ancorar.

Moor [mɔːʳ] n mouro m, -ra f.

moorhen n frango-d'água m.

moorings ['mɔ:rɪŋz] *npl* [of boat, ship - ropes, chains] amarras *fpl*; [- place] ancoradouro *m*.

Moorish ['mɔ:rɪʃ] *adj* mouro(ra), mourisco(ca).

moorland ['mɔ:lənd] *n (U) esp UK* charneca *f*.

moose [mu:s] *(pl inv) n* [North American] alce *m*.

moot [mu:t] *vt* propor.

moot point *n* questão *f* controversa.

mop [mɒp] *(pt & pp* **-ped,** *cont* **-ping)** ⋄ *n* **-1.** [for cleaning] esfregão *m* **- 2.** *inf* [of hair] mecha *f*. ⋄ *vt* **-1.** [floor] esfregar, passar o esfregão em **- 2.** [brow, face] enxugar.

◆ **mop up** *vt sep* **-1.** [clean up] limpar *(com esfregão)* **- 2.** *fig* [clear away] eliminar.

mope [məʊp] *vi pej* lastimar-se.

◆ **mope about, mope around** *vi pej* vaguear desanimado(da).

moped ['məʊped] *n* bicicleta *f* motorizada.

moral ['mɒrəl] ⋄ *adj* moral; ~ **support** apoio *m* moral. ⋄ *n* [lesson] moral *f*.

◆ **morals** *npl* [principles] princípios *mpl*.

morale [mə'rɑ:l] *n (U)* moral *m*.

moralistic [ˌmɒrə'lɪstɪk] *adj pej* moralista.

morality [mə'rælətɪ] *(pl* **-ies)** *n* moralidade *f*.

moralize, -ise ['mɒrəlaɪz] *vi pej:* **to ~ (about** OR **on** **sthg)** moralizar (sobre algo).

morally ['mɒrəlɪ] *adv* moralmente.

Moral Majority *n* grupo de pressão ultracon-servador apoiado pelas igrejas fundamentalis-tas nos EUA.

morass [mə'ræs] *n* [mass] emaranhado *m*, confusão *f*.

moratorium [ˌmɒrə'tɔ:rɪəm] *(pl* **-ria** [-rɪə]) *n fml* moratória *f*; ~ **on sthg** moratória em algo.

morbid ['mɔ:bɪd] *adj* [unhealthy] mórbido(da).

more [mɔ:r] ⋄ *adj* **-1.** [a larger amount of] mais; **there are ~ tourists than usual** há mais turistas que o normal. **- 2.** [additional] mais; **is there any ~ cake?** tem mais bolo?; **I'd like two ~ bottles** queria mais duas garrafas; **there's no ~ wine** já não tem mais vinho. ⋄ *adv* **-1.** [in comparatives] mais; **it's ~ difficult than before** é mais difícil do que antes; **speak ~ clearly** fale de forma mais clara; **we go there ~ often now** agora vamos lá mais freqüentemente. **- 2.** [to a greater degree] mais; **we ought to go to the movies ~** devíamos ir mais vezes ao cinema. **- 3.** [in phrases]: **once ~** mais uma vez; **we'd be ~ than happy to help** teríamos muito prazer em ajudar.

◆ **more and more** *adv, adj &* **pron** cada vez mais.

◆ **more or less** *adv* mais o menos.

moreover [mɔ:'rəʊvər] *adv fml* além disso.

morgue [mɔ:g] *n* [mortuary] necrotério *m*.

MORI ['mɔ:rɪ] *(abbr of* **Market & Opinion Research Institute)** *n instituto britânico de pesquisa de mercado e opinião.*

moribund ['mɒrɪbʌnd] *adj fml* moribundo(da).

Mormon ['mɔ:mən] *n* mórmon *mf*.

morning ['mɔ:nɪŋ] *n* **-1.** [first part of day] manhã *f*; **in the ~** [before lunch] de OR pela manhã; [tomorrow morning] pela manhã **- 2.** [between midnight and noon] manhã *f*.

◆ **mornings** *adv US* de manhã.

morning-after pill *n* pílula *f* do dia seguinte.

morning dress *n esp UK* [formal clothes] *paletó preto com calça listrada*.

morning sickness *n (U)* náusea *f* matinal.

Moroccan [mə'rɒkən] ⋄ *adj* marroquino(na). ⋄ *n* marroquino *m*, -na *f*.

Morocco [mə'rɒkəʊ] *n* Marrocos; **in ~** em Marro-cos.

moron ['mɔ:rɒn] *n inf* [stupid person] idiota *mf*, imbecil *mf*.

moronic [mə'rɒnɪk] *adj* [stupid] idiota, imbecil.

morose [mə'rəʊs] *adj* melancólico(ca).

morphing *n* morphing *m*.

morphine ['mɔ:fi:n] *n (U)* morfina *f*.

morris dancing ['mɒrɪs-] *n (U) dança folclórica inglesa em que os homens representam perso-nagens lendários*.

Morse (code) [mɔ:s-] *n (U)* código *m* Morse.

morsel ['mɔ:sl] *n* pedacinho *m*.

mortal ['mɔ:tl] ⋄ *adj* mortal. ⋄ *n* mortal *mf*.

mortality [mɔ:'tælətɪ] *n (U)* mortalidade *f*.

mortality rate *n* taxa *f* de mortalidade.

mortally ['mɔ:təlɪ] *adv* **-1.** [fatally] mortalmente **- 2.** [deeply] profundamente.

mortar ['mɔ:tər] *n* **-1.** *(U)* [cement mixture] argamassa *f* **- 2.** [gun] morteiro *m* **- 3.** [bowl] almofariz *m*.

mortarboard ['mɔ:təbɔ:d] *n* **-1.** CONSTR padiola *f (para argamassa)* **- 2.** UNIV barrete *m* de forma-tura.

mortgage ['mɔ:gɪdʒ] ⋄ *n* hipoteca *f*. ⋄ *comp* hipotecário(ria). ⋄ *vt* hipotecar.

mortgagee [ˌmɔ:gɪ'dʒi:] *n* credor *m* hipotecário, credora *f* hipotecária.

mortgagor [ˌmɔ:gɪ'dʒɔ:'] *n* devedor *m* hipotecá-rio, devedora *f* hipotecária.

mortician [mɔ:'tɪʃn] *n US* agente *mf* funerário, -ria.

mortified ['mɔ:tɪfaɪd] *adj* mortificado(da).

mortify *vt* mortificar.

mortise lock ['mɔ:tɪs-] *n* fechadura *f* embutida.

mortuary ['mɔ:tʃʊərɪ] *(pl* **-ies)** *n* necrotério *m*.

mosaic [mə'zeɪk] *n* mosaico *m*.

Moscow ['mɒskəʊ] *n* Moscou; **in ~** em Moscou.

Moslem ['mɒzləm] *adj & n* = **Muslim**.

mosque [mɒsk] *n* mesquita *f*.

mosquito [mə'ski:təʊ] *(pl* **-es** OR **-s)** *n* mosquito *m*.

mosquito net *n* mosquiteiro *m*.

moss [mɒs] *n (U)* musgo *m*.

mossy ['mɒsɪ] *(compar* **-ier,** *superl* **-iest)** *adj* coberto(-ta) de musgo.

most [məʊst] ⋄ *adj (superl of* **many & much) -1.** [the majority of] a maioria de; ~ **people** a maioria das pessoas **- 2.** [largest amount of]: **(the) ~** mais; **who's got (the) ~ money?** quem é que tem mais dinheiro?; **what gave me (the) ~ satisfaction was ...** o que me deu a maior satisfação foi ... ⋄ *pron* **-1.** [the majority] a maioria; ~ **of** a maioria de; ~ **of the time** a maior parte do tempo **- 2.** [largest amount]: **(the) ~** o máximo; **at ~** no máximo **- 3.** *phr:* **to make the ~ of sthg** tirar o máximo de algo. ⋄ *adv* **-1.** [to the greatest extent]: **what I like (the) ~** o que eu mais gosto **- 2.** *fml* [very] muito; ~ **certainly** com toda a certeza **- 3.** *US* [almost] quase.

mostly ['məʊstlɪ] *adv* -**1.** [in the main] principalmente -**2.** [usually] normalmente.

MOT ⋄ *n* (*abbr of* **Ministry of Transport** (**test**)) *vistoria anual obrigatória realizada pelo Ministério dos Transportes britânico em carros com mais de 3 anos de fabricação.* ⋄ *vt*: **to have one's car ~ 'd** realizar a vistoria no carro.

motel [məʊ'tell] *n* hotel *m* de beira de estrada.

moth [mɒθ] *n* -**1.** ZOOL mariposa *f*-**2.** [in clothes] traça *f*.

mothball ['mɒθbɔːl] *n* (bola de) naftalina *f*.

moth-eaten *adj* roído(da) pelas traças.

mother ['mʌðə'] ⋄ *n* mãe *f* ⋄ *vt pej* [spoil] mimar.

motherboard ['mʌðə,bɔːd] *n* COMPUT placa-mãe *f*.

motherhood ['mʌðəhʊd] *n* (U) maternidade *f*.

Mothering Sunday ['mʌðərɪŋ-] *n* Dia *m* das Mães.

mother-in-law (*pl* **mothers-in-law** OR **mother-in-laws**) *n* sogra *f*.

motherland ['mʌðəlænd] *n* pátria *f*.

motherless ['mʌðəlɪs] *adj* órfão(fã) de mãe.

motherly ['mʌðəlɪ] *adj* maternal, materno(na).

Mother Nature *n* Mãe *f* Natureza.

mother-of-pearl ⋄ *n* (U) madrepérola *f*. ⋄ *comp* de madrepérola.

Mother's Day *n* Dia *m* das Mães.

mother ship *n* nave-mãe *f*.

mother superior *n* madre *f* superiora.

mother-to-be (*pl* **mothers-to-be**) *n* futura mãe *f*.

mother tongue *n* língua *f* materna.

motif [məʊ'tiːf] *n* motivo *m*.

motion ['məʊʃn] ⋄ *n* -**1.** (U) [process of moving] movimento *m*; **to set sthg in ~** colocar algo em marcha; **to go through the ~s** [act insincerely] fingir, mostrar um falso interesse - **2.** [proposal] proposta *f*. ⋄ *vt*: **to ~ sb to do sthg** fazer sinal para alguém fazer algo. ⋄ *vi*: **to ~ to sb** fazer sinal (*com a mão*) para alguém.

motionless ['məʊʃənlɪs] *adj* imóvel.

motion picture *n* US filme *m*.

motivate ['məʊtɪveɪt] *vt* -**1.** [give cause] motivar - **2.** [give incentive] incentivar; **to ~ sb to do sthg** incentivar alguém a fazer algo.

motivated ['məʊtɪveɪtɪd] *adj* motivado(da).

motivation [,məʊtɪ'veɪʃn] *n* -**1.** [cause] razão *f* - **2.** (U) [sense of purpose] motivação *f*.

motive ['məʊtɪv] *n* motivo *m*, razão *f*.

motley ['mɒtlɪ] *adj pej* heterogêneo(nea).

motocross ['məʊtəkrɒs] *n* (U) motocross *m*.

motor ['məʊtə'] ⋄ *adj* UK [relating to cars - industry, accident] automobilístico(ca); [- mechanic] de automóveis. ⋄ *n* [engine] motor *m*. ⋄ *vi dated* viajar de automóvel.

Motorail® ['məʊtəreɪl] *n* UK serviço ferroviário de transporte de automóveis.

motorbike ['məʊtəbaɪk] *n* moto *f*.

motorboat ['məʊtəbəʊt] *n* barco *m* a motor.

motorcade ['məʊtəkeɪd] *n* caravana *f*.

motorcar ['məʊtəkɑː'] *n* UK fml automóvel *m*.

motorcycle ['məʊtə,saɪkl] *n* motocicleta *f*.

motorcyclist ['məʊtə,saɪklɪst] *n* motociclista *mf*.

motoring ['məʊtərɪŋ] ⋄ *adj* UK automobilístico

(ca); **~ offence** infração *f* de trânsito. ⋄ *n* (U) *dated* automobilismo *m*.

motorist ['məʊtərɪst] *n* motorista *mf*.

motorize, -ise ['məʊtəraɪz] *vt* motorizar.

motor lodge *n* US hotel *m* em beira de estrada.

motor racing *n* (U) corrida *f* automobilística.

motor scooter *n* lambreta *f*.

motor vehicle *n* veículo *m* motorizado.

motorway ['məʊtəweɪ] ⋄ *n* UK auto-estrada *f*. ⋄ *comp* na auto-estrada.

mottled ['mɒtld] *adj* com manchas, pintado(da).

motto ['mɒtəʊ] (*pl* -s OR -es) *n* [maxim] lema *m*.

mould, mold US [məʊld] ⋄ *n* -**1.** (U) BOT mofo *m* - **2.** [shape] fôrma *f*, molde *m*. ⋄ *vt* -**1.** [influence] moldar - **2.** [shape physically] moldar, modelar.

moulding, molding US ['məʊldɪŋ] *n* [decoration] cornija *f*.

mouldy, moldy US (*compar* -ier, *superl* -iest) ['məʊldɪ] *adj* mofado(da).

moult, molt US [məʊlt] ⋄ *vt* trocar. ⋄ *vi* -**1.** [bird] trocar as penas - **2.** [dog] trocar o pêlo.

mound [maʊnd] *n* -**1.** [small hill] morro *m* - **2.** [untidy pile] montanha *f*.

mount [maʊnt] ⋄ *n* -**1.** [support, frame] moldura *f* - **2.** [horse, pony] montaria *f*-**3.** [mountain] monte *m*. ⋄ *vt* -**1.** [climb onto] montar - **2.** *fml* [climb up] subir - **3.** [organize] montar; **to ~ guard over sb/sthg** montar guarda para vigiar alguém/algo - **4.** [photograph] emoldurar - **5.** [trophy] pôr em posição de destaque - **6.** [jewel] engastar. ⋄ *vi* -**1.** [increase] aumentar - **2.** [climb on horse] montar.

◆ **mount up** *vi* [increase] aumentar.

mountain ['maʊntɪn] *n* [gen] montanha *f*; **to make a ~ out of a molehill** fazer uma tempestade num copo d'água.

mountain bike *n* mountain bike *f*.

mountaineer [,maʊntɪ'nɪə'] *n* montanhista *mf*, alpinista *mf*.

mountaineering [,maʊntɪ'nɪərɪŋ] *n* (U) montanhismo *m*, alpinismo *m*.

mountainous ['maʊntɪnəs] *adj* [full of mountains] montanhoso(sa).

mountain range *n* cadeia *f* de montanhas, cordilheira *f*.

mountain rescue *n* (U) resgate *m* nas montanhas.

mounted ['maʊntɪd] *adj* [on horseback] montado(-da).

Mountie ['maʊntɪ] *n inf* membro da polícia montada canadense.

mourn [mɔːn] ⋄ *vt* -**1.** [the loss of] lamentar - **2.** [the death of] lamentar a morte de. ⋄ *vi*: **to ~ for sb** fazer luto por alguém.

mourner ['mɔːnə'] *n* enlutado *m*, -da *f*.

mournful ['mɔːnfʊl] *adj* lamuriento(ta), desolado(da).

mourning ['mɔːnɪŋ] *n* -**1.** [period] luto *m* - **2.** [clothes] traje *m* de luto; **in ~** em luto.

mouse [maʊs] (*pl* **mice**) *n* -**1.** [animal] camundongo *m* - **2.** COMPUT mouse *m*.

mouse mat, mouse pad *n* COMPUT mouse pad *m*.

mousetrap ['maʊstræp] *n* ratoeira *f*.

moussaka [mu:'sɑːkə] *n prato grego à base de beringela e carne moída.*

mousse [mu:s] *n* -**1.** [food] musse *f* -**2.** [for hair] mousse *m.*

moustache *UK* [mə'stɑːʃ], **mustache** *US* ['mʌstæʃ] *n* bigode *m.*

mouth [*n* maʊθ, *vt* maʊð] ⟨⟩ *n* -**1.** *ANAT* boca *f*; **to keep one's** ~ **shut** *inf* ficar de boca fechada -**2.** [entrance - of cave, hole] boca *f*; [- of river] foz *f.* ⟨⟩ *vt* -**1.** [silently]: **to** ~ **a reply** articular uma resposta -**2.** [pompously] dizer pomposamente.

mouthful ['maʊθfʊl] *n* -**1.** [amount - of food] bocado *m*; [- of water] gole *m* -**2.** *inf* [difficult word] palavra *f* difícil de ser pronunciada, palavrão *m.*

mouthorgan ['maʊθ,ɔːgən] *n* harmônica *f*, gaita-de-boca *f.*

mouthpiece ['maʊθpiːs] *n* -**1.** [of object] bocal *m* -**2.** [spokesperson] porta-voz *mf.*

mouth-to-mouth *adj*: ~ **resuscitation** respiração *f* boca-a-boca.

mouth ulcer *n* úlcera *f* bucal.

mouthwash ['maʊθwɒʃ] *n* antiséptico *m* bucal.

mouth-watering [-,wɔːtərɪŋ] *adj* de dar água na boca.

movable ['muːvəbl] *adj* móvel.

move [muːv] ⟨⟩ *n* -**1.** [movement] movimento *m*; **to be always on the** ~ [travelling around] estar sempre viajando; [beginning to move] estar a caminho; **to get a** ~ **on** *inf* apressar-se -**2.** [change] mudança *f* -**3.** [in board game - turn to play] vez *f*; [- action] jogada *f* -**4.** [course of action] medida *f.* ⟨⟩ *vt* -**1.** [shift] mudar, mexer; **to** ~ **the car** tirar o carro -**2.** [change - job, office] mudar de; [- house] mudar-se de -**3.** [affect emotionally] tocar, comover -**4.** [in debate]: **to** ~ **that ...** sugerir que ... -**5.** *fml* [cause]: **to** ~ **sb to do sthg** impelir alguém a fazer algo. ⟨⟩ *vi* -**1.** [shift] mover-se, mexer-se -**2.** [act] agir -**3.** [to new house, job] mudar-se.

→ **move about** *vi* -**1.** [fidget] remexer-se, ir de lá para cá -**2.** [travel] viajar.

→ **move along** ⟨⟩ *vt sep* circular. ⟨⟩ *vi* continuar andando.

→ **move around** *vi* = **move about**.

→ **move away** *vi* -**1.** [go in opposite direction] afastar-se -**2.** [live elsewhere] ir-se embora.

→ **move in** ⟨⟩ *vt sep* [troops] chegar. ⟨⟩ *vi* -**1.** [to new house] instalar-se -**2.** [take control, attack] preparar-se para o ataque.

→ **move off** *vi* [train, bus, car] sair.

→ **move on** ⟨⟩ *vt sep* fazer circular. ⟨⟩ *vi* -**1.** [after stopping] prosseguir -**2.** [in discussion] passar para outro tema.

→ **move out** ⟨⟩ *vt sep* [troops] retirar. ⟨⟩ *vi* [from house] mudar-se.

→ **move over** *vi* chegar mais para lá/cá.

→ **move up** *vi* [on seat] chegar mais para lá/cá.

moveable *adj* = **movable**.

movement ['muːvmənt] *n* -**1.** [gen] movimento *m* -**2.** [transportation] movimentação *f.*

movie ['muːvɪ] *n esp US* filme *m.*

movie camera *n* câmara *f* cinematográfica.

moviegoer ['muːvɪ,gəʊəˈ] *n US* cinéfilo *m*, -la *f.*

movie star *n US* estrela *f* de cinema.

movie theater *n US* cinema *f.*

moving ['muːvɪŋ] *adj* -**1.** [touching] tocante, comovente -**2.** [not fixed] móvel.

moving staircase *n* escada *f* rolante.

mow [məʊ] (*pt* -ed, *pp* -ed *OR* mown) *vt* [cut - grass, lawn] cortar; [- corn, wheat] ceifar.

→ **mow down** *vt sep* dizimar.

mower ['məʊəˈ] *n* [machine] ceifadeira *f.*

mown [məʊn] *pp* ⟩ **mow**.

Mozambican [,məʊzəm'biːkən] ⟨⟩ *adj* moçambicano(na). ⟨⟩ *n* moçambicano *m*, -na *f.*

Mozambique [,məʊzəm'biːk] *n* Moçambique; **in** ~ em Moçambique.

MP *n* -**1.** (*abbr of* Member of Parliament) *membro do Parlamento Britânico* -**2.** (*abbr of* Military Police) *polícia militar*, ≃ PE *f* -**3.** *Can* (*abbr of* Mounted Police) Polícia *f* Montada.

MP3 (*abbr of* MPEG-1 Audio Layer-3) *n COMPUT* MP3 *m.*

MPEG (*abbr of* Moving Pictures Expert Group) *n COMPUT* MPEG *m.*

mpg (*abbr of* miles per gallon) *n* milhas *fpl* por galão.

mph (*abbr of* miles per hour) *n* milhas *fpl* por hora.

MPhil [,em'fɪl] (*abbr of* Master of Philosophy) *n (titular de) mestrado em filosofia.*

MPS (*abbr of* Member of the Pharmaceutical Society) *n membro da sociedade britânica de farmacêuticos.*

Mr ['mɪstəˈ] (*abbr of* Mister) *n* Sr.

MRC (*abbr of* Medical Research Council) *n organização do governo britânico de incentivo à pesquisa médica.*

MRCP (*abbr of* Member of the Royal College of Physicians) *n membro do colégio real de médicos britânicos.*

MRCS (*abbr of* Member of the Royal College of Surgeons) *n membro do colégio real de cirurgiões britânicos.*

MRCVS (*abbr of* Member of the Royal College of Veterinary Surgeons) *n membro do colégio real de veterinários britânicos.*

Mrs ['mɪsɪz] (*abbr of* Missus) *n* Sra.

ms. (*abbr of* manuscript) *n* manuscrito *m.*

Ms [mɪz] *n abreviatura usada diante do nome de mulher quando não se quer especificar seu estado civil, válida para senhora ou senhorita.*

MS ⟨⟩ *n* -**1.** (*abbr of* manuscript) manuscrito *m* -**2.** (*abbr of* Master of Science) *(titular de) mestrado em ciências* -**3.** (*abbr of* multiple sclerosis) esclerose *f* múltipla. ⟨⟩ *abbr of* Mississippi.

MSA (*abbr of* Master of Science in Agriculture) *n (titular de) mestrado em agronomia.*

MSB (*abbr of* most significant bit/byte) *n* MSB *m.*

MSc (*abbr of* Master of Science) *n (titular de) mestrado em ciências.*

MSC (*abbr of* Manpower Services Commission) *n antiga organização do governo britânico que tratava de mão-de-obra.*

MSG (*abbr of* monosodium glutamate) glutamato *m* monossódico.

Msgr (*abbr of* Monsignor) Mons.

MST (*abbr of* Mountain Standard Time) *n horário oficial da região das Montanhas Rochosas nos Estados Unidos.*

MSW (*abbr of* **Master of Social Work**) *n* (*titular de*) mestrado em serviço social.

Mt (*abbr of* **mount**) Mte.

MT ◇ *n* (*abbr of* **machine translation**) tradução *f* automática. ◇ *abbr of* **Montana**.

much [mʌtʃ] (*compar* **more**, *superl* **most**) ◇ *adj* muito(ta); **as** ~ (...) **as** tanto (...) quanto; **how** ~ ...? quanto ...?; **too** ~ ... demais. ◇ *pron* muito; **how** ~ **have you got?** quanto você tem?; **I don't think** ~ **of it** não me parece grande coisa; **as** ~ **as** tanto quanto; **how** ~? quanto?; **too** ~ demais; **this isn't** ~ **of a party** essa festa não está grande coisa; **I'm not** ~ **of a cook** não sou um grande cozinheiro; **so** ~ **for my hard work!** tanto desgaste por meu trabalho!; **I thought as** ~ já imaginava; **it's not up to** ~ *inf* não é nenhuma maravilha, não é aquilo tudo. ◇ *adv* muito; **thank you very** ~ muito obrigado(da); **it's** ~ **too cold** está frio demais; **it's** ~ **the same** é praticamente a mesma coisa; **'what did you think of the film?' - 'not** ~ **'** 'o que você achou do filme?' - 'não gostei muito'; **he's not so** ~ **stupid as lazy** ele é muito mais preguiçoso que bobo; **too** ~ demais; **without so** ~ **as ...** sem nem sequer ...; ~ **as** (exatamente) como; **nothing** ~ nada de mais.

muchness [mʌtʃnɪs] *n*: **to be much of a** ~ vir a ser a mesma coisa.

muck [mʌk] *n* *inf* **-1.** [dirt] sujeira *f* **-2.** [manure] esterco *m*.
◆ **muck about, muck around** *UK inf* ◇ *vt sep* fazer perder tempo. ◇ *vi* fazer cera.
◆ **muck in** *vi* *UK inf* trabalhar juntos(tas).
◆ **muck out** *vt sep* limpar.
◆ **muck up** *vt sep* *UK inf* estragar.

muckraking [mʌkreɪkɪŋ] *n* (*U*) *fig* sensacionalismo *m*.

mucky [mʌkɪ] (*compar* **-ier**, *superl* **-iest**) *adj* *inf* sujo(ja).

mucus [mju:kəs] *n* (*U*) muco *m*.

mud [mʌd] *n* (*U*) lama *f*, barro *m*.

muddle [mʌdl] ◇ *n* **-1.** [disorder] desordem *f*; **to be in a** ~ estar em desordem **-2.** [confusion] confusão *f*; **to be in a** ~ estar confuso(sa). ◇ *vt* **-1.** [put into disorder] desordenar **-2.** [confuse] confundir, misturar.
◆ **muddle along** *vi* prosseguir de forma confusa.
◆ **muddle through** *vi* conseguir de qualquer jeito.
◆ **muddle up** *vt sep* misturar.

muddle-headed [-ˌhedɪd] *adj* **-1.** [person] incapaz de pensar com clareza **-2.** [thinking] confuso(sa).

muddy [mʌdɪ] (*compar* **-ier**, *superl* **-iest**, *pt* & *pp* **-ied**) ◇ *adj* **-1.** [covered with mud - floor, boots] embarrado(da); [- river] lamacento(ta) **-2.** [in colour] turvo(va). ◇ *vt* *fig* [issue, situation] complicar.

mudflap [mʌdflæp] *n* pára-lama *m*.

mudflat [mʌdflæt] *n* estirâncio *m*.

mudguard [mʌdgɑ:d] *n* pára-lama *m*.

mud pack *n* lama *f* medicinal.

mud-slinging *n* (*U*) *fig* difamação *f*.

muesli [mju:zlɪ] *n* *UK* granola *f*.

muff [mʌf] ◇ *n* [for hands] regalo *m*; [for ears]

protetor *m* de orelhas (*contra o frio*). ◇ *vt inf* perder.

muffin [mʌfɪn] *n* **-1.** *UK* [bread roll] pãozinho redondo e chato que se come quente com manteiga **-2.** *US* [cake] bolinho *m* doce com frutas/chocolate.

muffle [mʌfl] *vt* [quieten] abafar.

muffled [mʌfld] *adj* **-1.** [sound] abafado(da) **-2.** [wrapped up warmly]: ~ **(up)** agasalhado(da).

muffler [mʌflər] *n* *US* [for car] silenciador *m*.

mug [mʌg] (*pt* & *pp* **-ged**, *cont* **-ging**) ◇ *n* **-1.** caneca *f* **-2.** *inf* [fool] tolo *m*, -la *f.* ◇ *vt* [attack and rob] assaltar.

mugger [mʌgər] *n* assaltante *mf*.

mugging [mʌgɪŋ] *n* assalto *m*.

muggy [mʌgɪ] (*compar* **-ier**, *superl* **-iest**) *adj* mormacento(ta), quente e úmido(da).

mugshot [mʌgʃɒt] *n* *inf* fotografia tirada pela polícia de frente e de perfil quando se é fichado.

mujaheddin [ˌmu:dʒəheˈdi:n] *npl* mujaheddin *mpl*.

mulatto [mju:ˈlætəʊ] (*pl* **-s** *OR* **-es**) *n* mulato *m*, -ta *f*.

mule [mju:l] *n* **-1.** [animal] mula *f* **-2.** [slipper] tamanco *m*.

mull [mʌl] ◆ **mull over** *vt sep* refletir sobre.

mullah [mʌlə] *n* mulá *m*.

mulled [mʌld] *adj*: ~ **wine** quentão *m*.

mullet [mʌlɪt] (*pl inv OR* **-s**) *n* tainha *f*.

mulligatawny [ˌmʌlɪgəˈtɔ:nɪ] *n* (*U*) sopa indiana feita com caril.

mullioned *adj* de caixilhos.

multi- [mʌltɪ] *prefix* mult(i)-.

multi-access *adj* *COMPUT* de multiacesso.

multicoloured *UK*, **multicolored** *US* [ˌmʌltɪˈkʌləd] *adj* multicor.

multicultural [ˌmʌltɪˈkʌltʃərəl] *adj* multicultural.

multifarious [ˌmʌltɪˈfeərɪəs] *adj* variado(da).

multilateral [ˌmʌltɪˈlætərəl] *adj* multilateral.

multilingual *adj* multilíngüe.

multimedia [ˌmʌltɪˈmi:djə] *adj* multimídia.

multimillionaire [ˈmʌltɪˌmɪljəˈneər] *n* multimilionário *m*, -ria *f*.

multinational [ˌmʌltɪˈnæʃənl] ◇ *adj* multinacional. ◇ *n* multinacional *f*.

multiple [mʌltɪpl] ◇ *adj* múltiplo(pla). ◇ *n* *MATH* múltiplo *m*.

multiple-choice *adj* de múltipla escolha.

multiple injuries *npl* lesões *fpl* múltiplas.

multiple pileup *n* acidentes *mpl* múltiplos (*de veículos*).

multiple sclerosis [-sklɪˈrəʊsɪs] *n* (*U*) esclerose *f* múltipla.

multiplex cinema [mʌltɪpleks-] *n* cinema *m* multi-salas, cinema *m* multiplex.

multiplication [ˌmʌltɪplɪˈkeɪʃn] *n* multiplicação *f*.

multiplication sign *n* sinal *m* de multiplicação.

multiplication table *n* tabuada *f*.

multiplicity [ˌmʌltɪˈplɪsətɪ] *n* multiplicidade *f*.

multiply [mʌltɪplaɪ] (*pt* & *pp* **-ied**) ◇ *vt* multiplicar. ◇ *vi* **-1.** *MATH* multiplicar **-2.** [increase] multiplicar-se.

multi-purpose *adj* multiuso.

multiracial [ˌmʌltɪˈreɪʃl] *adj* multirracial.

multiscreen cinema *n* cinema *m* multi-salas.

multi-storey *UK*, **multistory** *US* <> *adj* com muitos andares. <> *n* edifício-garagem *m*.

multitude [ˈmʌltɪtjuːd] *n* **-1.** [large number] multiplicidade *f* **-2.** [crowd] multidão *f*.

mum [mʌm] *UK inf* <> *n* [mother] mamãe *f*. <> *adj*: **to keep ~** não dar um pio.

mumble [ˈmʌmbl] *vt* & *vi* murmurar.

mumbo jumbo [ˈmʌmbəʊˈdʒʌmbəʊl] *n* (U) *pej* palavreado *m*, enrolação *f*.

mummify [ˈmʌmɪfaɪ] (*pt* & *pp* -ied) *vt* mumificar.

mummy [ˈmʌmɪ] (*pl* -ies) *n* **-1.** *UK inf* [mother] mamãe *f*, mãe *f* **-2.** [preserved body] múmia *f*.

mumps [mʌmps] *n* (U) caxumba *f*.

munch [mʌntʃ] *vt* & *vi* mascar.

mundane [mʌnˈdeɪn] *adj* trivial.

mung bean [mʌŋ-] *n* feijão-fradinho *m*.

municipal [mjuːˈnɪsɪpl] *adj* municipal.

municipality [mjuːˌnɪsɪˈpælətɪ] (*pl* -ies) *n* [city, district] município *m*.

munificent [mjuːˈnɪfɪsənt] *adj fml* munificente.

munitions [mjuːˈnɪʃnz] *npl* munições *fpl*.

mural [ˈmjuːərəl] *n* (pintura *f*) mural *m*.

murder [ˈmɜːdəʳ] <> *n* assassinato *m*; **to get away with ~** fazer o que bem entender sem ser punido(da). <> *vt* assassinar.

murderer [ˈmɜːdərəʳ] *n* assassino *m*.

murderess [ˈmɜːdərɪs] *n* assassina *f*.

murderous [ˈmɜːdərəs] *adj* assassino(na), homicida.

murky [ˈmɜːkɪ] (*compar* -ier, *superl* -iest) *adj* **-1.** [gen] sombrio(bria) **-2.** [water] turvo(va).

murmur [ˈmɜːməʳ] <> *n* **-1.** [low sound] murmúrio *m* **-2.** *MED* [of heart] sopro *m*. <> *vt* & *vi* murmurar.

MusB, MusBac (*abbr of* Bachelor of Music) *n* (*titular de*) *bacharelado em música*.

muscle [ˈmʌsl] *n* **-1.** músculo *m* **-2.** (U) *fig* [power] poder *m*.
➭ **muscle in** *vi* intrometer-se.

muscleman [ˈmʌslmən] (*pl* -men [-mən]) *n* [strong man] homem *m* musculoso.

Muscovite [ˈmʌskəvaɪt] <> *adj* moscovita. <> *n* moscovita *mf*.

muscular [ˈmʌskjʊləʳ] *adj* **-1.** [of muscles] muscular **-2.** [strong] musculoso(sa).

muscular dystrophy [-ˈdɪstrəfɪ] *n* (U) distrofia *f* muscular.

MusD, MusDoc (*abbr of* Doctor of Music) *n* (*titular de*) *doutorado em música*.

muse [mjuːz] <> *n* [source of inspiration] musa *f*. <> *vi* meditar, refletir.

museum [mjuːˈziːəm] *n* museu *m*.

mush [mʌʃ] *n* (U) *inf* **-1.** [gunge] mingau *m* **-2.** [drivel] pieguice *f*.

mushroom [ˈmʌʃrʊm] <> *n* cogumelo *m*. <> *vi* [grow quickly] expandir-se rapidamente.

mushroom cloud *n* cogumelo *m* nuclear.

mushy [ˈmʌʃɪ] (*compar* -ier, *superl* -iest) *adj* **-1.** [very soft] mole **-2.** [over-sentimental] água-com-açúcar, sentimentalóide.

music [ˈmjuːzɪk] *n* **-1.** [gen] música *f* **-2.** [written set of notes] partitura *f*.

musical [ˈmjuːzɪkl] <> *adj* **-1.** [relating to music] [melodious] musical **-2.** [talented in music] com talento para música. <> *n* musical *m*.

musical box *UK*, **music box** *US* *n* caixinha *f* de música.

musical chairs *n* (U) dança *f* da cadeira.

musical instrument *n* instrumento *m* musical.

music box *n US* = musical box.

music centre *n* [machine] aparelho *m* de som.

music hall *n UK* **-1.** [theatre] sala *f* de espetáculo **-2.** (U) [variety entertainment] teatro *m* de variedades.

musician [mjuːˈzɪʃn] *n* músico *m*, -ca *f*.

music stand *n* atril *m* (*para partituras*).

musk [mʌsk] *n* (U) almíscar *m*.

musket [ˈmʌskɪt] *n* mosquete *m*.

muskrat [ˈmʌskræt] *n* rato-almiscarado *m*.

Muslim [ˈmʊzlɪm] <> *adj* muçulmano(na). <> *n* muçulmano *m*, -na *f*.

muslin [ˈmʌzlɪn] *n* (U) musselina *f*.

musquash [ˈmʌskwɒʃ] *n* **-1.** [animal] rato-almiscarado *m* **-2.** (U) [fur] pele *f* de rato-almiscarado.

muss [mʌs] *vt US*: **to ~ sthg (up)** desarrumar algo.

mussel [ˈmʌsl] *n* mexilhão *m*.

must [mʌst] <> *modal vb* **-1.** [have to] dever, ter que; **I ~ go** eu preciso ir **-2.** [intend to] ter que **-3.** [as suggestion] precisar, ter que **-4.** [to express likelihood] dever. <> *n* (U) *inf* [necessity]: **the film is a ~** você tem que ver o filme.

mustache *n US* = moustache.

mustard [ˈmʌstəd] *n* (U) mostarda *f*; **~ and cress** *UK* brotos *mpl* de mostarda e agrião.

mustard gas *n* (U) gás *m* de mostarda.

muster [ˈmʌstəʳ] <> *vt* **-1.** [assemble] reunir **-2.** [summon - strength, energy] juntar; [- support] reunir. <> *vi* reunir-se.
➭ **muster up** *vt fus* **-1.** [courage] armar-se de **-2.** [strength] juntar **-3.** [support] reunir.

mustn't [ˈmʌsnt] = must not.

must've [ˈmʌstəv] = must have.

musty [ˈmʌstɪ] (*compar* -ier, *superl* -iest) *adj* **-1.** [gen] mofado(da) **-2.** [smell] com cheiro de mofo.

mutant [ˈmjuːtənt] <> *adj* mutante. <> *n* mutante *mf*.

mutate [mjuːˈteɪt] *vi* mutar; **to ~ into sthg** mutar-se para algo.

mutation [mjuːˈteɪʃn] *n* mutação *f*.

mute [mjuːt] <> *adj* mudo(da). <> *n* [person who cannot speak] mudo *m*, -da *f*. <> *vt* [muffle] abafar, amortecer.

muted [ˈmjuːtɪd] *adj* **-1.** [soft] suave **-2.** [less strong - reaction] discreto(ta); [- feelings] contido(da).

mutilate [ˈmjuːtɪleɪt] *vt* mutilar.

mutilation [ˌmjuːtɪˈleɪʃn] *n* mutilação *f*.

mutineer [ˌmjuːtɪˈnɪəʳ] *n* amotinado *m*, -da *f*.

mutinous [ˈmjuːtɪnəs] *adj* [disobedient] rebelde.

mutiny [ˈmjuːtɪnɪ] (*pl* -ies, *pt* & *pp* -ied) <> *n* motim *m*. <> *vi* amotinar-se.

mutt [mʌt] *n inf* **-1.** [fool] tolo *m*, -la *f*, bobo *m*, -ba *f* **-2.** *US* [dog] vira-lata *m*.

mutter ['mʌtə'] <> *vt* murmurar. <> *vi* resmungar; **to ~ to sb** sussurrar para alguém; **to ~ to o.s.** ficar resmungando.

muttering ['mʌtərɪŋ] *n* **-1.** [muttered remark] resmungo *m* **-2.** *(U)* [muttering sound] murmúrio *m*.

mutton ['mʌtn] *n (U)* [carne *f* de] carneiro *m*; **~ dressed as lamb** *UK* lobo *m* em pele de cordeiro.

mutual ['mju:tʃʊəl] *adj* **-1.** [reciprocal] mútuo(tua) **-2.** [common] comum.

mutual fund *n US* fundo *m* mútuo.

mutually ['mju:tʃʊəlɪ] *adv* [reciprocally] mutuamente; **~ exclusive** mutuamente excludente.

Muzak® ['mju:zæk] *n (U)* gravação de música suave que toca contiuamente em locais públicos.

muzzle ['mʌzl] <> *n* **-1.** [dog's nose and jaws] focinho *m* **-2.** [wire guard] focinheira *f* **-3.** [of gun] boca *f*. <> *vt* **-1.** [put guard on] colocar focinheira em **-2.** *fig* [silence] amordaçar.

muzzy ['mʌzɪ] (*compar* **-ier**, *superl* **-iest**) *adj* [groggy] atordoado(da), confuso(sa).

MVP (*abbr of* **most valuable player**) *n nos Estados Unidos, título dado ao melhor jogador de um time.*

MW (*abbr of* **medium wave**) onda *f* média.

my [maɪ] *poss adj* meu (minha); **~ books** os meus livros; **~ name is Joe** o meu nome é Joe.

mynah bird *n* mainá *m*.

myopic [maɪ'ɒpɪk] *adj* míope.

myriad ['mɪrɪəd] *literary* <> *adj* incontável. <> *n* miríade *f*.

myrrh [mɜ:'] *n (U)* mirra *f*.

myrtle ['mɜ:tl] *n* mirto *m*.

myself [maɪ'self] *pron* **-1.** *(reflexive)* me; **I hurt ~** machuquei-me **-2.** *(after prep)* mim **-3.** *(stressed)* eu mesmo (eu mesma); **I did it ~** eu mesmo o fiz.

mysterious [mɪ'stɪərɪəs] *adj* misterioso(sa); **to be ~ about sthg** andar cheio (cheia) de mistérios sobre algo.

mysteriously [mɪ'stɪərɪəslɪ] *adv* misteriosamente.

mystery ['mɪstərɪ] (*pl* **-ies**) <> *adj* misterioso(sa). <> *n* mistério *m*.

mystery story *n* história *f* de suspense.

mystery tour *n* viagem *f* surpresa, *passeio turístico de ônibus no qual as pessoas não conhecem o roteiro.*

mystic ['mɪstɪk] <> *adj* místico(ca). <> *n* místico *m*, -ca *f*.

mystical ['mɪstɪkl] *adj* [spiritual] místico(ca).

mysticism ['mɪstɪsɪzm] *n (U)* misticismo *m*.

mystified ['mɪstɪfaɪd] *adj* [puzzled] perplexo(xa), desconcertado(da).

mystifying ['mɪstɪfaɪɪŋ] *adj* [puzzling] desconcertante.

mystique [mɪ'sti:k] *n (U)* mística *f*.

myth [mɪθ] *n* mito *m*.

mythic ['mɪθɪk] *adj* [like a myth] mítico(ca).

mythical ['mɪθɪkl] *adj* **-1.** [imaginary] mítico(ca) **-2.** [untrue] falso(sa).

mythological [ˌmɪθə'lɒdʒɪkl] *adj* [legendary] mitológico(ca).

mythology [mɪ'θɒlədʒɪ] (*pl* **-ies**) *n* **-1.** *(U)* [collection of myths] mitologia *f* **-2.** [set of false beliefs] mito *m*.

myxomatosis [ˌmɪksəmə'təʊsɪs] *n (U)* mixomatose *f*.

n (*pl* **n's** OR **ns**), **N** (*pl* **N's** OR **Ns**) [en] *n* [letter] n, N *m*.
➡ **N** (*abbr of* **north**) N.

n/a, N/A -1. (*abbr of* **not applicable**) não-aplicável **-2.** (*abbr of* **not available**) n/d.

NA (*abbr of* **Narcotics Anonymous**) *n organização norte-americana de ajuda a toxicômanos.*

NAACP (*abbr of* **National Association for the Advancement of Colored People**) *n organização norte-americana de defesa dos direitos de pessoas negras.*

NAAFI ['næfɪ] (*abbr of* **Navy, Army & Air Force Institute**) *n organização governamental encarregada das provisões das forças armadas britânicas.*

nab [næb] (*pt & pp* **-bed**, *cont* **-bing**) *vt inf* **-1.** [arrest] pegar **-2.** [claim quickly] pegar rapidamente.

NACU (*abbr of* **National Association of Colleges and Universities**) *n associação nacional de faculdades e universidades norte-americanas.*

nadir ['neɪˌdɪə'] *n* **-1.** ASTRON nadir *m* **-2.** *fig* [low point] ponto *m* mais baixo.

naff [næf] *adj UK inf* **-1.** [untrendy] brega **-2.** [mediocre] medíocre **-3.** [stupid] idiota.

NAFTA (*abbr of* **North American Free Trade Agreement**) *n* NAFTA *m*.

nag [næg] (*pt & pp* **-ged**, *cont* **-ging**) <> *n inf* **-1.** [person] estorvo *m* **-2.** *UK* [horse] rocim *m*. <> *vt* [pester, find fault with] incomodar; **to ~ sb to do sthg/into doing sthg** incomodar alguém para fazer algo. <> *vi*: **to ~ (at sb)** incomodar (alguém).

nagging ['nægɪŋ] *adj* **-1.** [thought, doubt, pain] perturbador(ra), persistente **-2.** [person] briguento(ta).

nail [neɪl] <> *n* **-1.** [for fastening] prego *m*; **to hit the ~ on the head** acertar na mosca **-2.** [of finger, toe] unha *f*. <> *vt* [fasten]: **to ~ sthg to sthg** pregar algo em algo.
➡ **nail down** *vt sep* **-1.** [fasten] pregar **-2.** *fig* [person]: **to ~ sb down to a date** pressionar alguém a fixar uma data.
➡ **nail up** *vt sep* **-1.** [fasten on wall] fixar **-2.** [close with nails] pregar.

nail-biting *adj* cheio (cheia) de suspense, muito emocionante.

nail brush *n* escova *f* de unhas.

nail clippers *npl* cortador *m* de unhas.

nail file *n* lixa *f* de unha.

nail polish *n (U)* esmalte *m* de unhas.

nail scissors *npl* tesoura *f* para unhas.

nail varnish *n (U)* esmalte *m* de unhas.

nail varnish remover [-rɪ'mu:vəʳ] *n (U)* removedor *m* de esmalte.

Nairobi [naɪ'rəʊbɪ] *n* Nairóbi.

naive, naïve [naɪ'i:v] *adj* ingênuo(nua).

naivety, naïvety [naɪ'i:vtɪ] *n (U)* ingenuidade *f*.

naked ['neɪkɪd] *adj* -1. [nude] nu (nua), pelado(da) -2. [exposed] descoberto(ta); ~ **truth** verdade *f* nua e crua; ~ **flame** chama *f* sem proteção; **with the** ~ **eye** a olho nu -3. [obvious, blatant - emotions] óbvio(via); [- aggression] aberto(ta).

NALGO ['nælgəʊ] (*abbr of* National and Local Government Officers' Association) *n* antigo sindicato de funcionários britânicos.

Nam [næm] (*abbr of* Vietnam) *n US* Vietnam *m*.

name [neɪm] <> *n* nome *m*; **what's your** ~**?** como você se chama?; **by** ~ pelo nome; **is there anyone here by the** ~ **of ...?** há alguém aqui que se chame ...?; **in the** ~ **of** em nome de; **in my/his** ~ em meu/seu nome; **in** ~ **only** só de nome; **to call sb** ~**s** chamar alguém de tudo; **to make a** ~ **for o.s.** conquistar uma boa reputação. <> *vt* -1. [christen] batizar; **to** ~ **sb after sb** *UK*, **to** ~ **sb for sb** *US* dar nome a alguém em homenagem a alguém; **to** ~ **sthg after sthg** *UK*, **to** ~ **sthg for sthg** *US* dar um nome a algo em homenagem a algo -2. [reveal identity of] dizer o nome de -3. [choose] escolher.

name-dropping *n (U)* menção do nome de pessoas famosas que se conheceu, com o intuito de impressionar.

nameless ['neɪmlɪs] *adj* -1. [unknown - person] anônimo(ma); [- disease] desconhecido(da) -2. [indescribable] indescritível.

namely ['neɪmlɪ] *adv* a saber.

nameplate ['neɪmpleɪt] *n* placa *f* de identificação (*em portas*).

namesake ['neɪmseɪk] *n* [with same name] xará *mf*.

Namibia [na:'mɪbɪə] *n* Namíbia; **in** ~ na Namíbia.

Namibian [na:'mɪbɪən] <> *adj* namibiano(na). <> *n* namibiano *m*, -na *f*.

nan(a) [næn(a)] *n UK inf* vó *f*.

nan bread [næn-] *n (U)* pão indiano sem fermento.

nanny ['nænɪ] (*pl* -ies) *n* [childminder] babá *f*.

nanny goat *n* cabra *f*.

nanny state *n* estado *m* protetor.

nap [næp] (*pt* & *pp* -ped, *cont* -ping) <> *n* [sleep] soneca *f*, cochilo *m*; **to take** *OR* **have a** ~ tirar uma soneca *OR* um cochilo. <> *vi* [sleep] cochilar; **to be caught napping** *inf* ser pego de surpresa.

napalm ['neɪpa:m] *n (U)* napalm *m*.

nape [neɪp] *n*: ~ **(of the neck)** nuca *f*.

napkin ['næpkɪn] *n* [serviette] guardanapo *m*.

nappy ['næpɪ] (*pl* -ies) *n UK* fralda *f*.

nappy liner *n* espécie de papel descartável que mantém o bebê seco quando o restante da fralda está molhada.

narcissi [na:'sɪsaɪ] *pl* ▷ **narcissus**.

narcissism ['na:sɪsɪzm] *n (U)* narcisismo *m*.

narcissistic [ˌna:sɪ'sɪstɪk] *adj* narcisista.

narcissus [na:'sɪsəs] (*pl* -cissuses *OR* -cissi) *n* narciso *m*.

narcotic [na:'kɒtɪk] *n* narcótico *m*.

nark [na:k] *UK inf* <> *n* [police informer] informante *mf*, dedo-duro *mf*. <> *vt* irritar.

narky ['na:kɪ] (*compar* -ier, *superl* -iest) *adj UK inf* enjoado(da), mal-humorado(da).

narrate [*UK* nə'reɪt, *US* 'næreɪt] *vt* narrar.

narration [*UK* nə'reɪʃn, *US* næ'reɪʃn] *n* narração *f*.

narrative ['nærətɪv] <> *adj* narrativo(va). <> *n* narrativa *f*.

narrator [*UK* nə'reɪtəʳ, *US* 'næreɪtər] *n* [speaker] narrador *m*, -ra *f*.

narrow ['nærəʊ] <> *adj* -1. [thin, not wide] estreito(ta) -2. [limited, restricted] limitado(da) -3. [marginal, close - victory, majority] apertado(da); [- escape]: **to have a** ~ **escape** escapar por um triz. <> *vt* -1. [eyes] apertar -2. [difference] diminuir, reduzir. <> *vi* -1. [road, river] estreitar-se -2. [eyes] estreitar-se -3. [difference] diminuir, reduzir.

➤ **narrow down** *vt sep* [restrict] diminuir, reduzir.

narrow-gauge *adj RAIL* de bitola estreita.

narrowly ['nærəʊlɪ] *adv* -1. [win, lose, miss] por muito pouco -2. [escape, miss] por um triz.

narrow-minded [-'maɪndɪd] *adj* de visão limitada.

NAS (*abbr of* National Academy of Sciences) *n* organização norte-americana de incentivo à pesquisa científica.

NASA ['næsə] (*abbr of* National Aeronautics and Space Administration) *n* NASA *f*.

nasal ['neɪzl] *adj* nasal.

nascent ['neɪsənt] *adj fml* nascente.

NASDAQ (*abbr of* National Association of Securities Dealers Automated Quotations) *n* NASDAQ *f*.

nastily ['na:stɪlɪ] *adv* [unkindly] com má intenção; **to fall** ~ ter uma queda feia.

nastiness ['na:stɪnɪs] *n (U)* [unkindness] má intenção *f*.

nasturtium [nəs'tɜ:ʃəm] (*pl* -s) *n* capuchinha *f*.

nasty ['na:stɪ] (*compar* -ier, *superl* -iest) *adj* -1. [unkind, unpleasant] mal-intencionado(da) -2. [disgusting, unattractive] horrível, desagradável; **cheap and** ~ barato(ta) e de mau gosto -3. [tricky] complicado(da) -4. [serious - injury, disease] sério(ria); [- fall, accident] feio (feia).

Natal [nə'tæl] *n* Natal; **in** ~ em Natal.

nation ['neɪʃn] *n* [country] nação *f*.

national ['næʃənl] <> *adj* nacional. <> *n* cidadão *m*, -dã *f*.

national anthem *n* hino *m* nacional.

national curriculum *n*: **the** ~ o currículo nacional do ensino na Inglaterra e no País de Gales.

national debt *n* dívida *f* pública.

national dress *n (U)* roupas *fpl* típicas (*de um país*).

National Front *n UK* Frente *f* Nacional, partido político minoritário de extrema direita na Grã-Bretanha.

national grid *n UK* rede *f* elétrica.

National Guard *n US:* the ~ a Guarda Nacional norte-americana.

National Health Service *n (U) UK:* the ~ o Serviço Nacional de Saúde, *órgão britânico gestor da saúde pública.*

National Heritage Minister *n ministro da cultura, do turismo e do desporto britânico.*

National Insurance *n (U) UK* **-1.** [system] ≃ Instituto Nacional de Seguro Social **-2.** [payments] contribuição *f* para a previdência social.

nationalism ['næʃnəlɪzm] *n (U)* nacionalismo *m.*

nationalist ['næʃnəlɪst] ⟨⟩ *adj* [pro-independence] nacionalista. ⟨⟩ *n* [supporter of independence movement] nacionalista *mf.*

nationality [ˌnæʃə'nælətɪ] *(pl* -ies) *n* nacionalidade *f.*

nationalization [ˌnæʃnəlaɪ'zeɪʃn] *n* [of company, industry] nacionalização *f.*

nationalize, -ise ['næʃnəlaɪz] *vt* [company, industry] nacionalizar.

nationalized ['næʃnəlaɪzd] *adj* [company, industry] nacionalizado(da).

National Lottery *n:* the ~ a loteria britânica.

national park *n* parque *m* nacional.

national service *n (U) MIL* serviço *m* militar.

National Trust *n (U) UK:* the ~ *organização britânica que promove a preservação e o acesso público a edifícios de interesse histórico ou arquitetônico e a locais de beleza natural,* ≃ o Patrimônio Nacional.

nation state *n* estado *m* nação.

nationwide ['neɪʃənwaɪd] ⟨⟩ *adj* em âmbito nacional. ⟨⟩ *adv* **-1.** [travel] por todo o país **-2.** [being shown] em todo o país **-3.** [being broadcast] para todo o país.

native ['neɪtɪv] ⟨⟩ *adj* **-1.** [country, area] natal **-2.** nativo(va); ~ **language** língua *f* materna; ~ **to** nativo(va) de. ⟨⟩ *n* **-1.** [person born in area, country] natural *mf* **-2.** *offensive* [original inhabitant] nativo *m,* -va *f.*

Native American ⟨⟩ *adj* indígena norte-americano(na). ⟨⟩ *n* indígena *mf* norte-americano, -na.

NATIVE AMERICAN

Entre os séculos XVII e XIX, as tribos aborígenes que povoavam o território norte-americano viram-se obrigadas a defender suas terras dos colonos europeus, muitas vezes tendo de lutar para mantê-las. Muitos índios morreram em combate ou por contrair doenças trazidas pelos europeus para a América. Outros foram obrigados a viver em reservas, territórios destinados especialmente a eles. Ao longo do século XX, o governo dos EUA procurou conceder mais direitos aos grupos étnicos nativos, demonstrando cada vez maior interesse por sua história e cultura tradicional.

Nativity [nə'tɪvətɪ] *n:* the ~ a Natividade.

nativity play *n* natividade *f.*

NATO ['neɪtəʊ] *(abbr of* North Atlantic Treaty Organization) *n* OTAN *f.*

natter ['nætə'] *UK inf* ⟨⟩ *n:* to have a ~ bater um papo, trovar fiado. ⟨⟩ *vi* papear, bater um papo.

natty ['nætɪl] *(compar* -ier, *superl* -iest) *adj* **-1.** *inf* [person] boa-pinta **-2.** [dresser, appearance] elegante, chique.

natural ['nætʃrəl] ⟨⟩ *adj* **-1.** [gen] natural; **to die of** ~ **causes** morrer de causas naturais **-2.** [inborn, instinctive] nato(ta) **-3.** [biological] biológico(ca) **-4.** : **C** ~ dó bequadro. ⟨⟩ *n* [talented person]: **to be a** ~ ter um talento natural.

natural childbirth *n (U)* parto *m* natural.

natural gas *n (U)* gás *m* natural.

natural history *n (U)* história *f* natural.

naturalist ['nætʃrəlɪst] *n* [biologist] naturalista *mf.*

naturalize, -ise ['nætʃrəlaɪz] *vt* [make citizen] naturalizar; **to be** ~ **d** naturalizar-se.

naturally ['nætʃrəlɪ] *adv* **-1.** [as expected, understandably] naturalmente **-2.** [unaffectedly] com naturalidade **-3.** [instinctively] por natureza; **to come** ~ **to sb** ser inato(ta) em alguém.

naturalness ['nætʃrəlnɪs] *n (U)* naturalidade *f.*

natural resources *npl* recursos *mpl* naturais.

natural science *n* ciências *fpl* naturais.

natural wastage *n* demissão *f* voluntária.

natural yoghurt *n* iogurte *m* natural.

nature ['neɪtʃə'] *n* natureza *f;* **by** ~ por natureza.

nature reserve *n* reserva *f* natural.

nature trail *n* trilha *f* ecológica.

naturist ['neɪtʃərɪst] *n* naturista *mf.*

naughty ['nɔːtɪ] *(compar* -ier, *superl* -iest) *adj* **-1.** [badly behaved] malcriado(da) **-2.** [rude, indecent] obsceno(na), atrevido(da).

nausea ['nɔːsjə] *n (U)* náusea *f.*

nauseam ['nɔːzɪæm] ⟾ **ad nauseam.**

nauseate ['nɔːsɪeɪt] *vt* **-1.** [cause nausea in] nausear, causar náuseas em **-2.** *fig* [disgust]: **it really** ~ **s** me isso (realmente) me dá nojo.

nauseating ['nɔːsɪeɪtɪŋ] *adj* **-1.** [sickening] enjoativo(va) **-2.** *fig* [disgusting] repugnante.

nauseous ['nɔːsjəs] *adj* **-1.** [sick] enjoado(da) **-2.** *fig* [revolting] repugnante.

nautical ['nɔːtɪkl] *adj* náutico(ca).

nautical mile *n* milha *f* náutica.

naval ['neɪvl] *adj* naval.

naval officer *n* oficial *mf* da marinha.

nave [neɪv] *n* nave *f (da igreja).*

navel ['neɪvl] *n* umbigo *m.*

navigable ['nævɪɡəbl] *adj* [deep, wide] navegável.

navigate ['nævɪɡeɪt] ⟨⟩ *vt* **-1.** [steer - plane] pilotar; [- ship] comandar **-2.** [travel safely across] navegar por. ⟨⟩ *vi* **-1.** [ship] comandar **-2.** [car] ser co-piloto(ta) **-3.** [plane] pilotar.

navigation [ˌnævɪ'ɡeɪʃn] *n (U)* [piloting, steering - plane] pilotagem *f;* [- ship] navegação *f.*

navigator ['nævɪɡeɪtə'] *n* **-1.** [on a ship] navegador *m,* -ra *f* **-2.** [on a plane] comandante *mf.*

navvy ['nævɪ] *(pl* -ies) *n UK inf* operário *m (em escavações).*

navy ['neɪvɪ] *(pl* -ies) ⟨⟩ *adj* [in colour] azul-marinho. ⟨⟩ *n* **-1.** [armed force] marinha *f* (de guerra) **-2.** = navy blue.

navy blue ⟨⟩ *adj* azul-marinho. ⟨⟩ *n* azul-marinho *m.*

Nazareth *n* Nazaré; **in** ~ em Nazaré.

Nazi ['nɑːtsɪ] *(pl* -s) ⟨⟩ *adj* nazista. ⟨⟩ *n* nazista *mf.*

NB -1. (*abbr of* **nota bene**) NB **-2.** *abbr of* **New Brunswick**.

NBA *n* **-1.** (*abbr of* **National Basketball Association**) NBA *f* **-2.** (*abbr of* **National Boxing Association**) *federação de boxe norte-americana.*

NBC (*abbr of* **National Broadcasting Company**) *n rede de televisão norte-americana,* NBC *f.*

NBS (*abbr of* **National Bureau of Standards**) *n organização norte-americana de normatiza- ção de unidades de medida.*

NC -1. (*abbr of* **no charge**) grátis **-2.** *abbr of* **North Carolina**.

NCC (*abbr of* **National Curriculum Council**) *n na Grã- Bretanha, órgão responsável pelo currículo escolar,* ≃ Conselho *m* Nacional de Educação.

NCCL (*abbr of* **National Council for Civil Liberties**) *n organização britânica que defende os direitos do cidadão.*

NCO (*abbr of* **non-commissioned officer**) *n* oficial *m* subalterno.

ND *abbr of* **North Dakota**.

NE -1. *abbr of* **Nebraska -2.** *abbr of* **New England - 3.** (*abbr of* **northeast**) NE.

Neanderthal [nɪˈændətɑːl] ⋄ *adj* neandertal. ⋄ *n* (homem *m* de) neandertal *m.*

neap tide [niːp-] *n* maré *f* morta *OR* de quadra- tura.

near [nɪəʳ] ⋄ *adj* **-1.** [in space] perto **-2.** [in time, relationship] próximo(ma); **in the ~ future** em breve; **the nearest thing to sthg** o mais próximo de algo **-3.** [almost happened] quase; **it was a ~ thing** faltou pouco. ⋄ *adv* **-1.** [in space] perto; **come ~er!** chegue mais perto! **-2.** [in time] próximo(ma) **-3.** [almost] quase; **we're nowhere ~ finding a solution** não estamos nem perto de encontrar uma solução. ⋄ *prep* **-1. : ~ (to)** perto de; **phone ~er the time** ligue quando chegar a hora **-2.** [on the point of]: **~ (to)** à beira de **-3.** [similar to]: **~ (to)** próximo(ma) de. ⋄ *vt* aproximar-se de. ⋄ *vi* aproximar-se.

nearby [nɪəˈbaɪ] ⋄ *adj* próximo(ma). ⋄ *adv* perto, nas redondezas.

Near East *n*: **the ~** o Oriente Próximo.

nearly [ˈnɪəlɪ] *adv* [almost] quase; **I ~ cried** quase chorei; **not ~** nem de longe; **not ~ enough** muito pouco; **you don't make ~ enough effort** você não se esforça o suficiente *OR* o bastante; **he doesn't study ~ enough** ele não estuda o suficiente.

near miss *n* [nearly a collision] quase-colisão *f.*

nearness [ˈnɪənɪs] *n* [in distance] proximidade *f.*

nearside [ˈnɪəsaɪd] ⋄ *adj* do lado oposto ao do condutor. ⋄ *n* lado *m* oposto ao do condutor.

nearsighted [ˌnɪəˈsaɪtɪd] *adj US* míope.

neat [niːt] *adj* **-1.** [tidy] arrumado(da) **-2.** [skilful] hábil **- 3.** [undiluted] puro(ra) **-4.** *US inf* [very good] ótimo(- ma), maravilhoso(sa).

neatly [ˈniːtlɪ] *adv* **-1.** [tidily] com capricho **-2.** [skil- fully] habilmente.

neatness [ˈniːtnɪs] *n* **-1.** [of room] arrumação *f* **-2.** [of appearance] asseio *m* **-3.** [of handwriting] clareza *f.*

Nebraska [nɪˈbræskə] *n* Nebrasca; **in ~** em Ne- brasca.

nebulous [ˈnebjʊləs] *adj fml* nebuloso(sa).

NEC (*abbr of* **National Exhibition Centre**) *n centro de convenções em Birmingham, Inglaterra.*

necessarily [*UK* ˈnesəsrəlɪ, ˌnesəˈserəlɪ] *adv* inevita- velmente, necessariamente; **not ~** não necessa- riamente.

necessary [ˈnesəsrɪ] *adj* **-1.** [required] necessário(- ria) **-2.** [inevitable] inevitável.

necessitate [nɪˈsesɪteɪt] *vt fml* necessitar de.

necessity [nɪˈsesətɪ] (*pl* **-ies**) *n* necessidade *f*; **of ~** por necessidade.

neck [nek] ⋄ *n* **-1.** *ANAT* pescoço *m*; **to be up to one's ~ (in sthg)** estar até o pescoço (de algo); **to breathe down sb's ~** ficar na cola de alguém; **to stick one's ~ out** arriscar-se **-2.** [of shirt, dress] gola *f* **-3.** [of bottle] gargalo *m*. ⋄ *vi inf* agarrar-se.
➡ **neck and neck** *adj* **-1.** [horses] cabeça a cabeça **-2.** [competitors] emparelhado(da).

neckerchief [ˈnekətʃɪf] (*pl* **-chiefs** *OR* **-chieves** [-tʃɪvz]) *n* echarpe *f.*

necklace [ˈneklɪs] *n* colar *m.*

neckline [ˈneklaɪn] *n* decote *m.*

necktie [ˈnektaɪ] *n US* gravata *f.*

nectar [ˈnektəʳ] *n* (*U*) [from flowers] néctar *m.*

nectarine [ˈnektərɪn] *n* [fruit] nectarina *f.*

née [neɪ] *adj* em solteira.

need [niːd] ⋄ *n* necessidade *f*; **~ for sthg** necessidade por algo; **~ to do sthg** necessidade de fazer algo; **to be in** *OR* **have ~ of sthg** necessitar de algo; **to have no ~ of sthg** não precisar de algo; **if ~ be** se necessário; **for**; **in ~** em necessidade. ⋄ *vt* precisar de, necessitar de; **to ~ to do sthg** precisar fazer algo. ⋄ *modal vb*: **~ we go?** precisamos ir mesmo?; **it ~ not happen** não tem que ser assim.
➡ **needs** *adv*: **if ~ s must** se preciso for.

needle [ˈniːdl] ⋄ *n* agulha *f*; **it's like looking for a ~ in a haystack** é como procurar uma agulha em um palheiro. ⋄ *vt inf* alfinetar, importunar.

needlecord [ˈniːdlkɔːd] *n* (*U*) veludo *m* cotelê.

needlepoint [ˈniːdlpɔɪnt] *n* (*U*) bordado *m.*

needless [ˈniːdlɪs] *adj* desnecessário(ria); **~ to say** ... desnecessário dizer que ...

needlessly [ˈniːdlɪslɪ] *adv* desnecessariamente.

needlework [ˈniːdlwɜːk] *n* (*U*) **-1.** [work produced] bordado *m* **-2.** [activity] costura *f.*

needn't [ˈniːdnt] = need not.

needy [ˈniːdɪ] (*compar* **-ier**, *superl* **-iest**) ⋄ *adj* necessitado(da), carente. ⋄ *npl*: **the ~** os necessitados.

nefarious [nɪˈfeərɪəs] *adj fml* execrável.

negate [nɪˈgeɪt] *vt fml* [cancel out] anular, invalidar.

negation [nɪˈgeɪʃn] *n fml* [cancelling out] anulação *f*, invalidação *f.*

negative [ˈnegətɪv] ⋄ *adj* negativo(va). ⋄ *n* **-1.** *PHOT* negativo *m* **-2.** *LING* negação *f*; **to answer in the ~** dizer não.

neglect [nɪˈglekt] ⋄ *n* **-1.** [of duty] não-cumpri- mento *m* **-2.** [of work, children] desleixo *m*, descuido *m*; **in a state of ~** num estado de total abandono. ⋄ *vt* **-1.** [not take care of] abandonar **-2.** [not do - duty] não cumprir com; [- work] não fazer; **to ~ to do sthg** deixar de fazer algo.

neglected [nɪ'glektɪd] *adj* [child, garden] abandona-do(da).

neglectful [nɪ'glektfʊl] *adj* negligente; ~ **of sb/ sth** negligente com alguém/algo.

negligee ['neglɪʒeɪ] *n* chambre *m*.

negligence ['neglɪdʒəns] *n (U)* negligência *f*.

negligent ['neglɪdʒənt] *adj* negligente.

negligently ['neglɪdʒəntlɪ] *adv* negligentemente.

negligible ['neglɪdʒəbl] *adj* insignificante.

negotiable [nɪ'gəʊʃjəbl] *adj* [which can be discussed] negociável.

negotiate [nɪ'gəʊʃɪeɪt] <> *vt* **- 1.** [obtain through ne-gotiation] negociar **- 2.** [get over] transpor **- 3.** [get around - obstacle] contornar; [- bend] tomar. <> *vi* negociar; **to ~ with sb for sth** negociar algo com alguém.

negotiation [nɪˌgəʊʃɪ'eɪʃn] *n (U)* [talking, discussion] negociação *f*.

◆ **negotiations** *npl* negociações *fpl*.

negotiator [nɪ'gəʊʃɪeɪtəʳ] *n* negociador *m*, -ra *f*.

neigh [neɪ] *vi* relinchar.

neighbor etc *n US* = neighbour etc.

neighbour *UK*, **neighbor** *US* ['neɪbəʳ] *n* vizinho *m*, -nha *f*.

neighbourhood *UK*, **neighborhood** *US* ['neɪbəhʊd] *n* **- 1.** [of town] vizinhança *f*; **in the ~** na vizinhança; **in the ~ of sth** nas proximidades de algo **- 2.** [approximate area]: **in the ~ of** [approxi-mately] por volta de.

neighbourhood watch *n UK* vigilância *f* comunitária.

neighbouring *UK*, **neighboring** *US* ['neɪbərɪŋ] *adj* vizinho(nha).

neighbourly *UK*, **neighborly** *US* ['neɪbəlɪ] *adj* de boa vizinhança; **to be ~** ser um bom vizinho.

neither ['naɪðəʳ, 'niːðəʳ] <> *adj* nenhum(ma). <> *adv* nem; **~ ... nor ...** nem ... nem ...; **that's ~ here nor there** isso não importa. <> *pron* nenhum(ma) dos dois; **~ of us** nenhum de nós dois. <> *conj*: **~ do I** nem eu.

neo- ['niːəʊ] *prefix* neo-.

neoclassical [ˌniːəʊ'klæsɪkl] *adj* neoclássico(ca).

neolithic [ˌniːəʊ'lɪθɪk] *adj* neolítico(ca).

neologism [niː'ɒlədʒɪzm] *n* neologismo *m*.

neon ['niːɒn] *n (U)* neônio *m*.

neon light *n* lâmpada *f or* luz *f* de néon.

neon sign *n* letreiro *m* de néon.

Nepal [nɪ'pɔːl] *n* Nepal; **in ~** no Nepal.

Nepalese [ˌnepə'liːz] (*pl inv*) <> *adj* nepalês(esa). <> *n* [person] nepalês *m*, -esa *f*.

Nepali [nɪ'pɔːlɪ] *n* [language] nepali *m*, nepalês *m*.

nephew ['nefjuː] *n* sobrinho *m*.

nepotism ['nepətɪzm] *n (U)* nepotismo *m*.

Neptune ['neptjuːn] *n* [planet] Netuno *m*.

nerd *n* pessoa estúpida e ridícula.

nerve [nɜːv] *n* **- 1.** ANAT nervo *m* **- 2.** [courage] coragem *f*; **to lose one's ~** perder a coragem **- 3.** [cheek] petulância *f*; **to have the ~ to do sth** ter a petulância de fazer algo.

◆ **nerves** *npl* nervos *mpl*; **to get on sb's ~s** dar nos nervos de alguém.

nerve centre *n* **- 1.** ANAT centro *m* nervoso **- 2.** *fig* [headquarters] centro *m* nevrálgico.

nerve gas *n (U)* gás *m* asfixiante.

nerve-racking [-ˌrækɪŋ] *adj* angustiante.

nervous ['nɜːvəs] *adj* nervoso(sa); **to be ~ of sth/ of doing sth** ter medo de algo/de fazer algo; **to be ~ about sth** ficar nervoso(sa) por algo.

nervous breakdown *n* crise *f* nervosa.

nervously ['nɜːvəslɪ] *adv* nervosamente.

nervousness ['nɜːvəsnɪs] *n* nervosismo *m*.

nervous system *n* sistema *m* nervoso.

nervous wreck *n* pilha *f* de nervos.

nervy ['nɜːvɪ] (*compar* -ier, *superl* -iest) *adj inf* - **1.** [ner-vous] nervoso(sa) **- 2.** *US* [cheeky] petulante *mf*.

nest [nest] <> *n* **- 1.** [gen] ninho *m* **- 2.** [of ants] formigueiro *m* **- 3.** [of wasps] vespeiro *m* **- 4.** [of tables] conjunto *m*. <> *vi* [make a nest] fazer um ninho, aninhar-se.

nest egg *n* pé-de-meia *m*.

nestle ['nesl] *vi* **- 1.** [make o.s. comfortable] aconche-gar-se **- 2.** [be sheltered] estar abrigado(da).

nestling ['neslɪŋ] *n* [baby bird] filhote *m*.

net [net] (*pt* & *pp* -ted, *cont* -ting) <> *adj* - **1.** [gen] líquido(da) **- 2.** [final] final. <> *n* - **1.** [gen] rede *f* - **2.** [type of fabric] malha *f*. <> *vt* - **1.** [catch] enredar - **2.** *fig* [acquire because of skill] alcançar **- 3.** [bring in as profit] render.

◆ **Net** *n*: **the Net** COMPUT a Rede.

netball ['netbɔːl] *n (U)* *esporte feminino seme-lhante ao basquete*, bola-ao-cesto *m*.

net curtains *npl* cortinas *fpl* de voile.

Netherlands ['neðələndz] *npl*: **the ~** os Países Baixos; **in the ~** nos Países Baixos.

netiquette ['netɪket] *n* COMPUT netiqueta *f*.

net profit *n* lucro *m* líquido.

net revenue *n* receita *f* líquida.

nett *adj* = net.

netting ['netɪŋ] *n (U)* - **1.** [of metal, plastic] tela *f* - **2.** [fabric] voile *m*.

nettle ['netl] <> *n* urtiga *f*. <> *vt* [irritate] irritar.

network ['netwɜːk] <> *n* - **1.** [gen] rede *f* - **2.** [group of people] grupo *m*; **a ~ of contacts** uma rede de contatos. <> *vt* - **1.** RADIO & TV [broadcast] transmitir em rede - **2.** COMPUT ligar em rede. <> *vi* [give mu-tual aid] criar uma rede de contatos.

networking ['netwɜːkɪŋ] *n* COMM estabelecimento *m* de uma rede de contatos.

neuralgia [njʊə'rældʒə] *n (U)* neuralgia *f*.

neurological [ˌnjʊərə'lɒdʒɪkl] *adj* neurológico (ca).

neurologist [ˌnjʊə'rɒlədʒɪst] *n* neurologista *mf*.

neurology [njʊə'rɒlədʒɪ] *n (U)* neurologia *f*.

neurosis [ˌnjʊə'rəʊsɪs] (*pl* -ses [-siːz]) *n* neurose *f*.

neurosurgery [ˌnjʊərəʊ'sɜːdʒərɪ] *n (U)* neurociru-gia *f*.

neurotic [ˌnjʊə'rɒtɪk] <> *adj* [person] neurótico(ca). <> *n* neurótico *m*, -ca *f*.

neuter ['njuːtəʳ] <> *adj* - **1.** GRAM neutro(tra) - **2.** [sexless] castrado(da). <> *vt* castrar.

neutral ['njuːtrəl] <> *adj* - **1.** [non-allied] [pale grey-brown & ELEC] neutro(tra) - **2.** [inexpressive] indiferente - **3.** [colourless] incolor. <> *n* - **1.** *(U)* AUT ponto *m* morto - **2.** [POL - country] país *m* neutro; [- person] pessoa *f* neutra.

neutrality [njuː'trælətɪ] *n (U)* POL neutralidade *f*.

neutralize, -ise ['nju:trəlaɪz] vt [effects] neutrali-zar.

neutron ['nju:trɒn] n nêutron m.

neutron bomb n bomba f de nêutrons.

Nevada [nɪ'vɑ:də] n Nevada; **in** ~ em Nevada.

never ['nevəʳ] adv -**1.** [at no time] nunca; ~ **ever** jamais -**2.** inf [in surprise, disbelief] nunca; **you** ~ **did!** não (me diga)! -**3.** phr: **well I** ~**!** não acredito!

never-ending adj interminável.

never-never n UK inf: **on the** ~ a perder de vista.

never-never land n país m das maravilhas.

nevertheless [ˌnevəðə'les] adv contudo, todavia.

new [nju:] adj novo(va); **as good as** ~ como se fosse novo; **to be** ~ **to sthg** ser novo em algo.
◆ **news** n (U) -**1.** [information] notícia f; **the** ~**s** as notícias; **a piece of** ~**s** uma notícia; **that's** ~**s to me** isto é novidade para mim; **to break the** ~**s to sb** dar a má notícia a alguém -**2.** RADIO & TV noticiário m.

New Age n New Age f, Nova Era f.

new blood n (U) fig sangue m novo.

newborn ['nju:bɔ:n] adj recém-nascido(da).

New Brunswick [-'brʌnzwɪk] n New Brunswick.

New Caledonia [-ˌkælɪ'dəʊnjə] n Nova Caledô-nia; **in** ~ em Nova Caledônia.

New Caledonian [-ˌkælɪ'dəʊnjən] <> adj neoca-ledônio(nia). <> n neocaledônio m, -nia f.

newcomer ['nju:ˌkʌməʳ] n: ~ **(to sthg)** novato m, -ta f (em algo); ~ **(to somewhere)** recém-chegado m, -da f (em algum lugar).

New Delhi n Nova Déhli; **in** ~ em Nova Délhi.

New England n Nova Inglaterra; **in** ~ na Nova Inglaterra.

newfangled [ˌnju:'fæŋgld] adj inf pej modernoso(-sa).

new-found adj recém-descoberto(ta); ~ **friend** amigo m recente.

Newfoundland ['nju:fəndlənd] n Terra f Nova.

New Guinea n Nova Guiné; **in** ~ na Nova Guiné.

New Hampshire [-'hæmpʃəʳ] n New Hampshire; **in** ~ em New Hampshire.

New Hebrides npl: **the** ~ as Novas Hébridas; **in the** ~ nas Novas Hébridas.

New Jersey n Nova Jérsei; **in** ~ em Nova Jérsei.

newly ['nju:lɪ] adv recém-.

newly-weds npl recém-casados mpl, -das fpl.

New Mexico n Novo México; **in** ~ no Novo México.

new moon n lua f nova.

New Orleans [-'ɔ:lɪənz] n Nova Orleans; **in** ~ em Nova Orleans.

New Quebec n Nova Quebec; **in** ~ em Nova Quebec.

news agency n agência f de notícias.

newsagent UK ['nju:zeɪdʒənt], **newsdealer** US ['nju:zdi:lər] n [person] jornaleiro m, -ra f; ~'**s (shop)** banca f de jornais.

news bulletin n boletim m de notícias.

newscast ['nju:zka:st] n noticiário m, jornal m.

newscaster ['nju:zka:stəʳ] n -**1.** [television] apresen-tador m, -ra f de jornal -**2.** [radio] locutor(ra).

news conference n entrevista f coletiva.

newsdealer n US = newsagent.

newsflash ['nju:zflæʃ] n plantão m de notícias.

newsgroup ['nju:zgru:p] n COMPUT grupo m de notícias.

newshound ['nju:zhaʊnd] n repórter mf, caçador m, -ra f de notícias.

newsletter ['nju:zˌletəʳ] n boletim m de notícias.

newsman ['nju:zmæn] (pl -**men** [-men]) n repórter m.

New South Wales n Nova Gales do Sul.

newspaper ['nju:zˌpeɪpəʳ] n jornal m.

newspaperman ['nju:zˌpeɪpəmæn] (pl -**men** [-men]) n [journalist] -**1.** jornalista m -**2.** [seller] jornaleiro m, -ra f.

newsprint ['nju:zprɪnt] n (U) papel m jornal.

newsreader ['nju:zˌri:dəʳ] n -**1.** [TV] apresentador m, -ra f de jornal -**2.** [radio] locutor(ra).

newsreel ['nju:zri:l] n cinejornal m.

newsroom ['nju:zrʊm] n sala f de redação.

news-sheet n folheto m informativo.

news-stand n banca f de revistas.

newsworthy ['nju:zˌwɜ:ðɪ] adj que vale a pena ser noticiado(da), de interesse jornalístico.

newt [nju:t] n tritão m.

new technology n (U) nova tecnologia f.

New Testament n: **the** ~ o Novo Testamento.

new town n UK cidade f planejada.

new wave n -**1.** CINEMA nova onda f -**2.** [in pop music] new wave f.

New World n: **the** ~ o Novo Mundo.

New Year n Ano m Novo; **Happy** ~**!** Feliz Ano Novo!

New Year's Day n dia m de Ano Novo, primeiro m do ano.

New Year's Eve n véspera f de Ano Novo.

New York [-'jɔ:k] n -**1.** [city] Nova Iorque; ~ **(City)** (cidade f de) Nova Iorque -**2.** [state]: ~ **(State)** (Estado m de) Nova Iorque.

New Yorker [-'jɔ:kəʳ] n nova-iorquino m, -na f.

New Zealand [-'zi:lənd] n Nova Zelândia; **in** ~ na Nova Zelândia.

New Zealander [-'zi:ləndəʳ] n neozelandês(esa).

next [nekst] <> adj -**1.** [in time] próximo(ma); ~ **week** semana que vem; **the** ~ **week** na semana que vem; **the day after** ~ depois de amanhã; **the week after** ~ sem ser a próxima semana, na outra -**2.** [in space - turning, page, street] próximo(ma); [- room] ao lado. <> adv -**1.** [afterwards] depois; **when are you** ~ **going to Brazil?** quando você irá novamente ao Brasil? -**2.** [next time] da próxima vez (que); **when we** ~ **meet** da próxima vez que nos encontrarmos -**3.** (with superlatives): ~ **best / biggest** o segundo melhor/maior. <> prep US ao lado de. <> n próximo m, -ma f.
◆ **next to** prep -**1.** [physically near] ao lado de, junto a -**2.** (in comparisons) próximo(ma) de -**3.** [al-most] quase; ~ **to nothing** quase nada.

next-door <> adj: ~ **neighbour** vizinho m, -nha f do lado. <> adv ao lado.

next of kin n parente m mais próximo.

NF <> n (abbr of National Front) pequeno partido político britânico de extrema direita. <> abbr of Newfoundland.

NFL (*abbr of* **National Football League**) *n federação norte-americana de futebol americano*.

NG (*abbr of* **National Guard**) *n força militar existente em cada estado norte-americano*, ≃ Guarda *f* Nacional.

NGO (*abbr of* **non-governmental organization**) *n* ONG *f*.

NH *abbr of* **New Hampshire**.

NHL (*abbr of* **National Hockey League**) *n federação norte-americana de hóquei sobre o gelo*.

NHS (*abbr of* **National Health Service**) *n órgão estatal britânico de saúde pública*.

NI ⟨⟩ *n* (*abbr of* **National Insurance**) *sistema britânico de seguridade social*, ≃ INSS *m*. ⟨⟩ *abbr of* **Northern Ireland**.

Niagara [naɪˈægrə] *n*: ~ **Falls** as cataratas do Niágara.

nib [nɪb] *n* pena *f* (*de caneta*).

nibble [ˈnɪbl] ⟨⟩ *vt* **-1.** [subj: person, caterpillar] beliscar; [subj: rodent, goat, sheep] roer **-2.** [playfully] mordiscar. ⟨⟩ *vi*: **to ~ at sthg** mordiscar algo.

Nicaragua [ˌnɪkəˈrægjʊə] *n* Nicarágua; **in ~** na Nicarágua.

Nicaraguan [ˌnɪkəˈrægjʊən] ⟨⟩ *adj* nicaraguano(-na). ⟨⟩ *n* nicaraguano *m*, -na *f*.

nice [naɪs] *adj* **-1.** [expressing approval - dress, picture] belo(la); [- day, weather] agradável; [- car, food] bom (boa) **-2.** [kind, pleasant] gentil; **it was ~ of you to help** foi muita gentileza de sua parte ajudar.

nice-looking [-ˈlʊkɪŋ] *adj* [attractive] bonito(ta); ~ **person** pessoa *f* atraente.

nicely [ˈnaɪslɪ] *adv* **-1.** [well, attractively, satisfactorily] bem; **that will do ~** será o suficiente **-2.** [politely] educadamente.

nicety [ˈnaɪsətɪ] (*pl* -**ies**) *n* [refinement] delicadeza *f*.

niche [niːʃ] *n* **-1.** [gen] nicho *m* **-2.** [in life] boa colocação *f*.

nick [nɪk] ⟨⟩ *n* **-1.** [cut] talha *f*, corte *m* **-2.** *UK inf* [jail]: **he did four days in the ~ for burglary** ele ficou quatro dias enjaulado por roubo **-3.** *inf* [condition]: **in good/bad ~** *UK* em bom/mau estado **-4.** *phr*: **in the ~ of time** em cima da hora. ⟨⟩ *vt* **-1.** [cut] talhar, cortar **-2.** *UK inf* [steal] passar a mão em **-3.** *UK inf* [arrest] enjaular.

nickel [ˈnɪkl] *n* **-1.** (*U*) [metal] níquel *m* **-2.** *US* [coin] moeda *f* de 5 centavos.

nickname [ˈnɪkneɪm] ⟨⟩ *n* apelido *m*. ⟨⟩ *vt* apelidar.

Nicosia [ˌnɪkəˈsiːə] *n* Nicósia.

nicotine [ˈnɪkətiːn] *n* (*U*) nicotina *f*.

niece [niːs] *n* sobrinha *f*.

nifty [ˈnɪftɪ] (*compar* -**ier**, *superl* -**iest**) *adj inf* chique.

Niger [ˈnaɪdʒəʳ] *n* **-1.** [country] Níger *m*; **in ~** em Níger **-2.** [river]: **the (River) ~** o (Rio) Níger.

Nigeria [naɪˈdʒɪərɪə] *n* Nigéria; **in ~** na Nigéria.

Nigerian [naɪˈdʒɪərɪən] ⟨⟩ *adj* nigeriano(na). ⟨⟩ *n* nigeriano *m*, -na *f*.

Nigerien [naɪˈdʒɪərɪən] ⟨⟩ *adj* nigerino(na). ⟨⟩ *n* nigerino *m*, -na *f*.

niggardly [ˈnɪgədlɪ] *adj* **-1.** [person] mesquinho(-nha) **-2.** [amount] miserável.

niggle [ˈnɪgl] ⟨⟩ *n* [worry] preocupação *f*. ⟨⟩ *vt* **-1.** [worry] preocupar **-2.** [criticize] incomodar. ⟨⟩ *vi*

-1. [worry]: **it ~d at me all day** isso ficou me dando volta o dia inteiro **-2.** [criticize] reclamar.

nigh [naɪ] *adv* **-1.** *literary* [near] próximo(ma) **-2.** : **well ~** [almost] praticamente.

night [naɪt] *n* **-1.** [not day] noite *f*; **at ~** à *OR* de noite; ~ **and day, day and** ~ noite e dia, dia e noite **-2.** *phr*: **to have an early/a late ~** ir dormir cedo/tarde.

➡ **nights** *adv* **-1.** *US* [at night] à *OR* de noite **-2.** *UK* [night shift]: **to work ~s** trabalhar durante a noite.

nightcap [ˈnaɪtkæp] *n* **-1.** [drink] *bebida que se toma antes de se ir dormir* **-2.** [hat] touca *f* de dormir.

nightclothes [ˈnaɪtkləʊðz] *npl* roupa *f* de dormir.

nightclub [ˈnaɪtklʌb] *n* casa *f* noturna, nightclub *m*.

nightdress [ˈnaɪtdres] *n* camisola *f*.

nightfall [ˈnaɪtfɔːl] *n* (*U*) anoitecer *m*.

nightgown [ˈnaɪtgaʊn] *n* camisola *f*.

nightie [ˈnaɪtɪ] *n inf* camisola *f*.

nightingale [ˈnaɪtɪŋgeɪl] *n* rouxinol *m*.

nightlife [ˈnaɪtlaɪf] *n* (*U*) vida *f* noturna.

nightlight [ˈnaɪtlaɪt] *n* luz *f* fraca (*que se deixa acesa à noite*).

nightly [ˈnaɪtlɪ] ⟨⟩ *adj* noturno(na). ⟨⟩ *adv* à noite.

nightmare [ˈnaɪtmeəʳ] *n lit* & *fig* pesadelo *m*.

nightmarish [ˈnaɪtmeərɪʃ] *adj* horripilante.

night owl *n fig* notívago *m*, -ga *f*, coruja *mf*.

night porter *n* porteiro *m*, -ra *f* do turno da noite.

night safe *n caixa externo de banco para depósitos fora do horário de expediente*.

night school *n* (*U*) escola *f* noturna.

night shift *n* [period] turno *m* da noite.

nightshirt [ˈnaɪtʃɜːt] *n* camisolão *m*.

nightspot [ˈnaɪtspɒt] *n* clube *m* noturno.

nightstick [ˈnaɪtstɪk] *n US* cassetete *m*.

night-time *n* (*U*) noite *f*.

night watchman *n* guarda-noturno *m*.

nightwear *n* (*U*) roupa *f* de dormir.

nihilism [ˈnaɪəlɪzm] *n* (*U*) [rejection of authority] niilismo *m*.

nil [nɪl] *n* (*U*) **-1.** [nothing] nada *m* **-2.** *UK SPORT* zero *m*.

Nile [naɪl] *n*: **the ~** o Nilo.

nimble [ˈnɪmbl] *adj* ágil.

nimbly [ˈnɪmblɪ] *adv* agilmente.

nine [naɪn] *num* nove; *see also* **six**.

nineteen [ˌnaɪnˈtiːn] *num* dezenove; *see also* **six**.

nineteenth [naɪnˈtiːnθ] *num* décimo nono, décima nona; *see also* **sixth**.

ninetieth [ˈnaɪntɪəθ] *num* nonagésimo(ma); *see also* **sixth**.

ninety [ˈnaɪntɪ] *num* noventa; *see also* **sixty**.

ninny (*pl* -**ies**) *n inf* bobo(ba).

ninth [naɪnθ] *num* nono(na); *see also* **sixth**.

nip [nɪp] (*pt* & *pp* -**ped**, *cont* -**ping**) ⟨⟩ *n* **-1.** [pinch] beliscão *m* **-2.** [bite] mordiscada *f* **-3.** [of drink] trago *m*. ⟨⟩ *vt* **-1.** [pinch] beliscar **-2.** [bite] mordiscar. ⟨⟩ *vi UK inf* [dash] dar uma saída.

nipper [ˈnɪpəʳ] *n UK inf* criancinha *f*.

nipple ['nɪpl] n -1. [of breast] mamilo m -2. [of baby's bottle] bico m.

nippy ['nɪpɪ] (compar -ier, superl -iest) adj -1. [cold] fresquinho(nha) -2. [quick] rápido(da).

NIREX (abbr of Nuclear Industry Radioactive Waste Executive) n órgão britânico que regula o lixo radiativo da indústria nuclear, ≃ CNEN m.

Nissen hut n refúgio m militar.

nit [nɪt] n -1. [in hair] lêndea f -2. UK inf [idiot] idiota mf.

nit-picking inf <> adj minucioso(sa). <> n (U) detalhismo m.

nitrate ['naɪtreɪt] n nitrato m.

nitric acid ['naɪtrɪk-] n (U) ácido m nítrico.

nitrogen ['naɪtrədʒən] n (U) nitrogênio m.

nitroglycerin(e) [,naɪtrəʊ'glɪsəri:n] n (U) nitroglicerina f.

nitty-gritty [,nɪtɪ'grɪtɪ] n inf: to get down to the ~ ir ao que interessa.

nitwit ['nɪtwɪt] n inf idiota mf.

NJ abbr of New Jersey.

NLF (abbr of National Liberation Front) n FLN f.

NLRB (abbr of National Labor Relations Board) n órgão norte-americano de justiça do trabalho.

NM abbr of New Mexico.

no [nəʊ] (pl -es) <> adv [gen] não; ~, thanks não obrigado(da). <> adj nenhum(ma), algum(ma); I have ~ money left não tehno mais um tostão. <> n não m.

No., no. (abbr of number) no.

Noah's ark ['nəʊəz-] n arca f de Noé.

nobble ['nɒbl] vt UK inf -1. [racehorse] drogar -2. [bribe] subornar -3. [grab, catch] apanhar.

Nobel prize [nəʊ'bel-] n prêmio m Nobel.

nobility [nə'bɪlətɪ] n -1. [aristocracy]: the ~ a nobreza -2. (U) [nobleness] nobreza f.

noble ['nəʊbl] <> adj -1. [aristocratic, distinguished] nobre -2. [brave] grandioso(osa). <> n nobre mf.

nobleman ['nəʊblmən] (pl -men [-mən]) n homem m nobre.

noblewoman ['nəʊbl,wʊmən] (pl -women [-,wɪmɪn]) n mulher f nobre.

nobly ['nəʊblɪ] adv [generously] generosamente.

nobody ['nəʊbədɪ] <> pron ninguém. <> n pej [insignificant person] joão-ninguém m.

no-claim(s) bonus n bonificação f de seguro.

nocturnal [nɒk'tɜ:nl] adj noturno(na).

nod [nɒd] (pt & pp -ded, cont -ding) <> n inclinação f de cabeça. <> vt [in agreement]: to ~ one's head assentir com a cabeça; [as greeting] cumprimentar com a cabeça. <> vi -1. [in agreement] assentir com a cabeça -2. [to indicate sthg] indicar com a cabeça -3. [as greeting]: to ~ to sb cumprimentar alguém com a cabeça.
→ **nod off** vi cabecear.

node [nəʊd] n -1. [gen] nó m -2. COMPUT nó m, nodo m.

nodule ['nɒdju:l] n nódulo m.

no-fly zone n zona f de exclusão aérea.

no-go area n UK zona f proibida.

noise [nɔɪz] n [sound] barulho m.

noiseless ['nɔɪzlɪs] adj silencioso(osa).

noiselessly ['nɔɪzlɪslɪ] adv silenciosamente.

noisily ['nɔɪzɪlɪ] adv ruidosamente, fazendo barulho.

noisy ['nɔɪzɪ] (compar -ier, superl -iest) adj barulhento(ta).

nomad ['nəʊmæd] n nômade mf.

nomadic [nə'mædɪk] adj nômade.

no-man's-land n (U) terra f de ninguém.

nom de plume n pseudônimo m.

nominal ['nɒmɪnl] adj -1. [in name only] apenas no nome; a ~ Catholic um católico só no nome; a ~ leader um líder de fachada -2. [very small] simbólico(ca).

nominally ['nɒmɪnəlɪ] adv [in theory] teoricamente.

nominate ['nɒmɪneɪt] vt -1. [propose]: to ~ sb (for/ as sthg) designar alguém (para algo) -2. [appoint]: to ~ sb (sthg) nomear alguém (algo); to ~ sb (to sthg) nomear alguém (para algo).

nomination [,nɒmɪ'neɪʃn] n -1. [proposal] indicação f -2. (U) [appointment]: ~ (to sthg) nomeação f (para algo).

nominee [,nɒmɪ'ni:] n nomeado m, -da f.

non- [nɒn] prefix [not] não-.

non-addictive adj que não provoca dependência.

non-aggression n (U) não-agressão f.

non-alcoholic adj não alcoólico(ca).

non-aligned adj não-alinhado(da).

non-believer n descrente mf.

nonchalant [UK 'nɒnʃələnt, US ,nɒnʃə'lɑ:ntl adj indiferente.

nonchalantly [UK 'nɒnʃələntlɪ, US ,nɒnʃə'lɑ:ntlɪ] adv com indiferença.

non-combatant n não-combatente mf.

non-commissioned officer n oficial mf subalterno, -na, funcionário m, -ria f não-comissionado, -da f.

non-committal adj evasivo(va).

non-competitive adj não-competitivo(va).

non compos mentis [-,kɒmpəs'mentɪs] adj fora do juízo perfeito, que não está em posse de suas faculdades mentais.

nonconformist [,nɒnkən'fɔ:mɪst] <> adj inconformista. <> n inconformista mf.

nonconformity n (U) inconformismo m.

noncontributory [,nɒnkən'trɪbjʊtərɪ] adj não--contributivo(va).

non-cooperation n (U) não-cooperação f.

nondescript [UK 'nɒndɪskrɪpt, US ,nɒndɪ'skrɪptl adj desinteressante.

non-drinker n abstêmio m, -mia f.

non-drip adj que não pinga.

non-driver n: he's a ~ ele não sabe dirigir.

none [nʌn] pron nehum m, -ma f; there's ~ left não resta nada; ~ of this is your fault nada disso foi culpa sua.

nonentity [nɒ'nentətɪ] (pl -ies) n nulidade f, zero mf à esquerda.

non-essential adj supérfluo(flua).

nonetheless [,nʌnðə'les] adv contudo, não obstante.

non-event n decepção f, fracasso m.

non-executive director n diretor ou diretora não-responsável pela tomada de decisões *em sua instituição ou empresa.*

non-existent *adj* inexistente.

non-fattening *adj* que não engorda.

non-fiction *n (U)* não-ficção *f*.

non-flammable *adj* não-inflamável.

non-infectious *adj* não-infeccioso(sa).

non-inflammable *adj* não-inflamável.

non-interference, non-intervention *n (U)* não-intervenção *f*.

non-iron *adj* que não precisa passar.

non-malignant *adj* não-maligno(na).

non-member *n* não-sócio *m*, não-membro *m*.

non-negotiable *adj* não-negociável.

no-no *n inf*: it's a ~ isso é algo que não se faz.

no-nonsense *adj* prático(ca).

non-operational *adj* inoperante.

non-participation *n (U)* não-participação *f*.

non-payment *n (U)* inadimplência *f*, não-pagamento *m*.

nonplussed, nonplused US [ˌnɒn'plʌst] *adj* perplexo(xa).

non-profit-making UK, **non-profit** US *adj* sem fins lucrativos.

non-proliferation *n (U)* não-proliferação *f*.

non-renewable *adj* - **1.** [contract, agreement] não-prorrogável - **2.** [natural resources, fossil fuels] não-renovável.

non-resident *n* - **1.** [of country] não-residente *mf* - **2.** [of hotel]: **open to** ~ **s** aberto ao público.

non-returnable *adj* [bottle] não-retornável, sem retorno.

nonsense ['nɒnsəns] <> *n (U)* - **1.** [meaningless words] bobagem *f*, asneira *f* - **2.** [foolish idea] besteira *f*; **it is** ~ **to suggest that ...** é um absurdo sugerir que ... - **3.** [foolish behaviour] idiotice *f*; **stop this** ~ **at once** pára com essas criancices agora mesmo; **to make (a)** ~ **of sthg** ridicularizar algo. <> *excl* bobagem!, que nada!

nonsensical [nɒn'sensɪkl] *adj* sem sentido, absurdo(da).

non sequitur [-'sekwɪtəʳ] *n* non sequitur *m*, incoerência *f*.

non-shrink *adj* que não encolhe.

non-skid *adj* antiderrapante.

non-slip *adj* antiderrapante.

non-smoker *n* não-fumante *mf*.

non-starter *n* UK inf [plan]: **to be a** ~ estar condenado(da) ao fracasso.

non-stick *adj* antiaderente.

non-stop <> *adj* - **1.** [gen] contínuo(nua), incessante - **2.** [flight] sem escalas. <> *adv* sem parar, continuamente.

non-taxable *adj* isento(ta) de impostos.

non-toxic *adj* atóxico(ca).

non-transferable *adj* não-transferível.

non-U *adj* UK dated popular, pouco refinado(da).

non-violence *n (U)* não-violência *f*.

non-voter *n* pessoa *f* que não vota.

non-voting *adj* - **1.** [person] que não vota - **2.** FIN [shares] sem direito a voto.

non-white <> *adj* que não é da raça branca. <> *n* pessoa *f* que não é da raça branca.

noodles ['nu:dlz] *npl* talharim *m*.

nook [nʊk] *n* [of room] canto *m*; **every** ~ **and cranny** todos os cantos.

noon [nu:n] <> *n (U)* meio-dia *m*. <> *comp* do meio-dia.

noonday ['nu:ndeɪ] <> *n* meio-dia *m*. <> *comp* do meio-dia.

no one *pron* = **nobody**.

noose [nu:s] *n* [lasso] nó *m* corrediço.

no-place *adv* US = **nowhere**.

nor [nɔːʳ] *conj* - **1.** ▷ **neither** - **2.** [and not] nem; **I don't smoke -** ~ **do I** eu não fumo - nem eu; **I don't know,** ~ **do I care** não sei, nem quero saber.

Nordic ['nɔːdɪk] *adj* nórdico(ca).

norm [nɔːm] *n* norma *f*; **the** ~ o normal.

normal ['nɔːml] *adj* normal.

normality [nɔː'mælɪtɪ], **normalcy** US ['nɔːmlsɪ] *n (U)* normalidade *f*.

normalize, -ise ['nɔːməlaɪz] <> *vt* normalizar. <> *vi* normalizar-se.

normally ['nɔːməlɪ] *adv* normalmente.

Norman <> *adj* normando(da). <> *n* normando(da).

Normandy ['nɔːməndɪ] *n* Normandia; **in** ~ na Normandia.

Norse [nɔːs] *adj* nórdico(ca).

north [nɔːθ] <> *adj* norte; **North London** o norte de Londres. <> *adv* para o norte; ~ **of** ao norte de. <> *n* [direction] norte *m*.

North Africa *n* África do Norte; **in** ~ na África do Norte.

North America *n* América do Norte; **in** ~ na América do Norte.

North American <> *adj* - **1.** da América do Norte - **2.** [of USA] norte-americano(na). <> *n* - **1.** pessoa *f* da América do Norte - **2.** [of USA] norte-americano *m*, -na *f*.

northbound ['nɔːθbaʊnd] *adj* com direção norte.

North Carolina [-ˌkærə'laɪnə] *n* Carolina *f* do Norte; **in** ~ na Carolina do Norte.

North Country *n*: **the** ~ UK a região norte da Inglaterra.

North Dakota [-də'kəʊtə] *n* Dakota do Norte; **in** ~ em Dakota do Norte.

northeast [ˌnɔːθ'iːst] <> *adj* nordeste. <> *n* [direction] nordeste *m*. <> *adv* para o nordeste; ~ **of** ao nordeste de.

northeasterly [ˌnɔːθ'iːstəlɪ] *adj* - **1.** [towards northeast, in northeast] a nordeste - **2.** [from northeast] do nordeste.

northerly ['nɔːðəlɪ] *adj* - **1.** [towards north, in north] ao norte - **2.** [from north] do norte.

northern ['nɔːðən] *adj* do norte.

Northerner ['nɔːðənəʳ] *n* pessoa *que nasceu ou vive no norte.*

Northern Ireland *n* Irlanda do Norte; **in** ~ na Irlanda do Norte.

Northern Lights *npl*: **the** ~ a aurora boreal.

northernmost ['nɔːðənməʊst] *adj* mais setentrional, mais ao norte.

Northern Territory *n* Território *m* do Norte.

North Korea *n* Coréia do Norte; **in** ~ na Coréia do Norte.

North Korean ⬦ *adj* norte-coreano(na). ⬦ *n* norte-coreano *m*, -na *f*.

North Pole *n*: the ~ o Pólo Norte.

North Sea ⬦ *n*: the ~ o Mar do Norte. ⬦ *comp* -**1.** [oil, oilrig] do Mar do Norte -**2.** [fishing] no Mar do Norte.

North Star *n*: the ~ a estrela Polar.

North Vietnam *n* Vietnã do Norte; **in** ~ no Vietnã do Norte.

North Vietnamese ⬦ *adj* norte-vietnamita. ⬦ *n* norte-vietnamita *mf*.

northward ['nɔːθwəd] ⬦ *adj* para o norte. ⬦ *adv* = **northwards**.

northwards ['nɔːθwədz] *adv* para o norte.

northwest [ˌnɔːθ'west] ⬦ *adj* -**1.** [in the northwest, facing the northwest] noroeste -**2.** [from the northwest] do noroeste. ⬦ *n* [direction] noroeste *m*. ⬦ *adv* para noroeste; ~ **of** a noroeste de.

northwesterly [ˌnɔːθ'westəlɪ] *adj* -**1.** [towards northwest, in northwest] a noroeste -**2.** [from northwest] do noroeste.

Northwest Territories *npl Can*: the ~ os Territórios do Noroeste.

North Yemen *n* Iêmen do Norte; **in** ~ no Iêmen do Norte.

Norway ['nɔːweɪ] *n* Noruega; **in** ~ na Noruega.

Norwegian [nɔː'wiːdʒən] ⬦ *adj* norueguês(esa). ⬦ *n* -**1.** [person] norueguês *m*, -esa *f* -**2.** [language] norueguês *m*.

Nos., nos. (*abbr of* numbers) *n*.

nose [nəʊz] *n* -**1.** ANAT nariz *m*; **under one's** ~ debaixo do nariz de alguém; **to cut one's** ~ **off to spite one's face** prejudicar-se ao tentar prejudicar outra pessoa; **to have a** ~ **for sthg** sentir o cheiro de algo; **he gets up my** ~ *inf* ele me deixa muito irritado(da); **to keep one's** ~ **out of sthg** não meter o nariz em algo; **to look down one's** ~ **at sb/sthg** *fig* olhar de cima para alguém/algo; **to pay through the** ~ pagar os olhos da cara; **to poke** OR **stick one's** ~ **into sthg** *inf* meter o nariz em algo; **to turn up one's** ~ **at sthg** torcer o nariz para algo -**2.** [of car] ponta *f*.

➡ **nose about, nose around** *vi* bisbilhotar.

nosebag ['nəʊzbæg] *n* embornal *m*.

nosebleed ['nəʊzbliːd] *n* hemorragia *f* nasal.

nosecone ['nəʊzkəʊn] *n* ogiva *f*.

nosedive ['nəʊzdaɪv] ⬦ *n* [of plane] mergulho *m*. ⬦ *vi* -**1.** [plane] mergulhar -**2.** *fig* [prices, popularity] despencar.

nose ring *n* argola *f* de nariz.

nose stud *n* piercing *m* de nariz.

nosey ['nəʊzɪ] *adj* = **nosy**.

nosh [nɒʃ] *n UK inf* [food] rango *m*.

nosh-up *n UK inf* comilança *f*.

nostalgia [nɒ'stældʒə] *n* (*U*): ~ **(for sthg)** nostalgia *f* (de algo).

nostalgic [nɒ'stældʒɪk] *adj* nostálgico(ca).

nostril ['nɒstrəl] *n* narina *f*.

nosy ['nəʊzɪ] (*compar* -**ier**, *superl* -**iest**) *adj* curioso(sa), abelhudo(da).

not [nɒt] *adv* não; **I hope** ~ espero que não; ~ **a** nem um (uma); ~ **even a** nem mesmo um (uma); ~ **all/every** nem todos(das); ~ **always** nem

sempre; **it's** ~ **every day we get sunshine** não é todo dia que tem sol; **it's** ~ **that I'm jealous, but ...** não que eu seja ciumento, mas ...; ~ **at all** em absoluto, de maneira nenhuma; [to acknowledge thanks] de nada.

notable ['nəʊtəbl] ⬦ *adj* notável; **to be** ~ **for sthg** destacar-se por algo. ⬦ *n fml* celebridade *f*.

notably ['nəʊtəblɪ] *adv* -**1.** [in particular] especialmente -**2.** [noticeably] claramente, obviamente.

notary ['nəʊtərɪ] (*pl* -**ies**) *n*: ~ **(public)** notário *m*, -ria *f*.

notation [nəʊ'teɪʃn] *n* notação *f*.

notch [nɒtʃ] *n* -**1.** [cut] corte *m*, entalhe *m* -**2.** *fig* [on scale] ponto *m*.

➡ **notch up** *vt fus* conseguir.

note [nəʊt] *n* -**1.** [gen] nota *f* -**2.** [written reminder, record] anotação *f*, nota *f*; **to take** ~ **of sthg** prestar atenção em algo; **to compare** ~**s** trocar idéias -**3.** [short letter] bilhete *m* -**4.** [tone] tom *m* -**5.** [importance]: **of** ~ digno(na) de nota. ⬦ *vt* -**1.** [observe] notar, observar -**2.** [mention] apontar, mencionar.

➡ **notes** *npl* [in book] anotações *fpl*.

➡ **note down** *vt sep* anotar.

notebook ['nəʊtbʊk] *n* -**1.** [for writing in] caderno *m* -**2.** COMPUT notebook *m*.

noted ['nəʊtɪd] *adj* conhecido(da), destacado(da); ~ **for sthg** conhecido(da) por algo.

notepad ['nəʊtpæd] *n* bloco *m* de notas.

notepaper ['nəʊtpeɪpə'] *n* (*U*) papel *m* de carta.

noteworthy ['nəʊtˌwɜːðɪ] (*compar* -**ier**, *superl* -**iest**) *adj* digno(na) de menção.

nothing ['nʌθɪŋ] ⬦ *pron* nada; ~ **new/interesting** nada de novo/interessante; **she did** ~ ela não fez nada; **for** ~ [free] de graça; [in vain] para nada.

nothingness ['nʌθɪŋnɪs] *n* (*U*) nada *m*.

notice ['nəʊtɪs] ⬦ *n* -**1.** (*U*) [attention] atenção *f*; **to come to one's** ~ chegar até alguém; **to escape one's** ~ passar desapercebido(da); **to take** ~ **(of sb/sthg)** dar bola (para alguém/algo); **to take no** ~ **(of sb/sthg)** não dar bola (para alguém/algo), fazer pouco caso (de alguém/algo); **he didn't take a blind bit of** ~ ele não fez nem mesmo o mais remoto caso -**2.** (*U*) [warning, announcement] aviso *m*; **at short** ~ em cima da hora; **until further** ~ até segunda ordem -**3.** (*U*) [at work]: **to be given one's** ~ receber aviso prévio; **to hand in one's** ~ apresentar pedido de demissão. ⬦ *vt* perceber, notar; **to** ~ **sb doing sthg** ver que alguém está fazendo algo. ⬦ *vi* perceber.

noticeable ['nəʊtɪsəbl] *adj* notável, digno(na) de nota.

noticeably ['nəʊtɪsəblɪ] *adv* notavelmente.

notice board *n* quadro *m* de avisos.

notification [ˌnəʊtɪfɪ'keɪʃn] *n* (*U*) notificação *f*.

notify ['nəʊtɪfaɪ] (*pt* & *pp* -**ied**) *vt*: **to** ~ **sb (of sthg)** notificar alguém (de algo).

notion ['nəʊʃn] *n* [concept, idea] noção *f*.

➡ **notions** *npl US* [haberdashery] aviamentos *mpl*.

notional ['nəʊʃənl] *adj* [hypothetical] hipotético(ca).

notoriety [ˌnəʊtə'raɪətɪ] *n* (*U*) notoriedade *f*.

notorious [nəʊ'tɔːrɪəs] *adj* notório(ria); ~ **for sthg** notório(ria) por algo.

notoriously [nəʊˈtɔːrɪəslɪ] *adv* notoriamente.

notwithstanding [ˌnɒtwɪθˈstændɪŋ] *fml* ◇ *prep* não obstante. ◇ *adv* no entanto, não obstante.

nougat [ˈnuːgɑː] *n* nugá *m*.

nought [nɔːt] *num* zero *m*; ~ **s and crosses** jogo *m* da velha.

noun [naʊn] *n* substantivo *m*.

nourish [ˈnʌrɪʃ] *vt* -**1.** [feed] nutrir - **2.** [entertain, foster] alimentar.

nourishing [ˈnʌrɪʃɪŋ] *adj* nutritivo(va).

nourishment [ˈnʌrɪʃmənt] *n (U)* alimento *m*.

nouveau riche ◇ *adj* de novo-rico. ◇ *n* novo-rico *m*, nova-rica *f*.

Nov. (*abbr of* **November**) nov.

Nova Scotia [ˌnəʊvəˈskəʊʃə] *n* Nova Escócia; **in** ~ na Nova Escócia.

Nova Scotian [ˌnəʊvəˈskəʊʃn] ◇ *adj* neoescocês(esa). ◇ *n* neoescocês *m*, -esa *f*.

novel [ˈnɒvl] ◇ *adj* original. ◇ *n* romance *m*.

novelist [ˈnɒvəlɪst] *n* romancista *mf*.

novelty [ˈnɒvltɪ] (*pl* -**ies**) *n* - **1.** (*U*) [quality] originalidade *f* - **2.** [unusual object, event] novidade *f* - **3.** [cheap object] bugiganga *f*.

November [nəˈvembə^r] *n* novembro *m*; *see also* **September**.

novice [ˈnɒvɪs] *n* - **1.** [inexperienced person] novato *m*, -ta *f*, principiante *mf* - **2.** RELIG noviço *m*, -ça *f*.

Novocaine® [ˈnəʊvəkeɪn] *n* (*U*) novocaína® *f*.

now [naʊ] ◇ *adv* - **1.** [at this time] agora; **from** ~ **on I'm in charge** de agora em diante eu estou no comando; **any day** ~ qualquer dia destes; **any time** ~ a qualquer momento; ~ **and then** OR **again** de vez em quando; **for** ~ por ora - **2.** [already, before this time] já; **they should be here by** ~ eles já deveriam ser estar aqui; **he's been away for two weeks** ~ já faz duas semanas que ele foi embora - **3.** [at a particular time in the past] então; **we were all singing** ~ estavámos todos cantando naquele momento - **4.** [to introduce statement] agora - **5.** [nowadays] atualmente; ~ **many people use computers to work** atualmente muitas pessoas usam computadores para trabalhar. ◇ *conj:* ~ **(that)** agora que.

NOW [naʊ] (*abbr of* **National Organization for Women**) *n importante organização feminista norte-americana*.

nowadays [ˈnaʊədeɪz] *adv* hoje em dia, atualmente.

nowhere UK [ˈnəʊweə^r], **no-place** US *adv* em nenhum lugar; **to appear out of** OR **from** ~ aparecer do nada; ~ **near** nem de longe; **to be getting** ~ indo a lugar nenhum; **this is getting us** ~ isto não está nos levando a nada.

no-win situation *n* beco *m* sem saída.

noxious [ˈnɒkʃəs] *adj* nocivo(va).

nozzle [ˈnɒzl] *n* bocal *m*, bico *m*.

NP (*abbr of* **notary public**) tabelião *m*, -liã *f*.

NS *abbr of* **Nova Scotia**.

NSC (*abbr of* **National Security Council**) *n conselho federal que coordena a defesa e a política externa norte-americanas*.

NSF ◇ *n* (*abbr of* **National Science Foundation**) *fundação norte-americana de pesquisa científica.* ◇ (*abbr of* **not sufficient funds**) sem fundos.

NSPCC (*abbr of* **National Society for the Prevention of Cruelty to Children**) *n organização britânica de prevenção a maus tratos a crianças.*

NSU (*abbr of* **non-specific urethritis**) *n* uretrite *f* não-específica.

NSW *abbr of* **New South Wales**.

NT *n* - **1.** (*abbr of* **New Testament**) NT *m* - **2.** (*abbr of* **National Trust**) *organização britânica encarregada da preservação de edifícios históricos e locais de interesse público.*

nth [enθ] *adj inf* [umpteenth] enésimo(ma).

nuance [njuːˈɑːns] *n* [of word, meaning] nuança *f*.

nub [nʌb] *n* [crux] essência *f*.

Nubian Desert *n:* **the** ~ o Deserto Núbio.

nubile [UK ˈnjuːbaɪl, US ˈnuːbəl] *adj fml or hum* núbil.

nubuck *n* nubuck *m*, tipo de camurça muito fina usada na fabricação de sapatos.

nuclear [ˈnjuːklɪə^r] *adj* nuclear.

nuclear bomb *n* bomba *f* nuclear.

nuclear disarmament *n* (*U*) desarmamento *m* nuclear.

nuclear energy *n* (*U*) energia *f* nuclear.

nuclear family *n* família *f* nuclear.

nuclear fission *n* (*U*) fissão *f* nuclear.

nuclear-free zone *n* zona *f* livre de energia nuclear.

nuclear fusion *n* (*U*) fusão *f* nuclear.

nuclear physics *n* (*U*) física *f* nuclear.

nuclear power *n* (*U*) energia *f* nuclear.

nuclear reactor *n* reator *m* nuclear.

nuclear war *n* guerra *f* nuclear.

nuclear winter *n* inverno *m* nuclear.

nucleus [ˈnjuːklɪəs] (*pl* -**lei** [-lɪaɪ]) *n* núcleo *m*.

nude [njuːd] ◇ *adj* nu (nua). ◇ *n* [figure, painting] nu *m*; **in the** ~ em pêlos.

nudge [nʌdʒ] ◇ *n* - **1.** [with elbow] cutucada *f* - **2.** *fig* [to encourage] empurrada *f*. ◇ *vt* - **1.** [with elbow] cutucar - **2.** *fig* [to encourage] empurrar; **to** ~ **sb's memory** puxar a memória de alguém.

nudist [ˈnjuːdɪst] ◇ *adj* nudista. ◇ *n* nudista *mf*.

nudity [ˈnjuːdətɪ] *n* (*U*) nudez *f*.

nugget [ˈnʌgɪt] *n* - **1.** [of gold] pepita *f* - **2.** *fig* [valuable piece] pérola *f*.

nuisance [ˈnjuːsns] *n* - **1.** [annoying thing, situation] chatice *f* - **2.** [annoying person] chato *m*, -ta *f* de galocha; **to make a** ~ **of o.s.** amolar.

nuke [njuːk] *inf* ◇ *n* arma *f* nuclear. ◇ *vt* bombardear com armas nucleares.

null [nʌl] *adj:* ~ **and void** nulo e sem valor.

nullify [ˈnʌlɪfaɪ] (*pt* & *pp* -**ied**) *vt* anular.

numb [nʌm] ◇ *adj* [shoulder, hand] adormecido(da); [person] paralisado(da); **to be** ~ **with cold** estar congelado(da) de frio. ◇ *vt* [subj: cold, anaesthetic] paralisar.

number [ˈnʌmbə^r] ◇ *n* - **1.** [gen] número *m*; **a** ~ **of** vários(as); **I've told you any** ~ **of times ...** já te disse um milhão de vezes ... - **2.** [of car] placa *f* - **3.** [song] música *f*. ◇ *vt* - **1.** [amount to] chegar a - **2.** [give a number to] numerar - **3.** [include]: **to be** ~ **ed among** figurar entre.

number-crunching [-ˌkrʌntʃɪŋ] *n (U) inf* cálculo *m* em grande escala.

numberless [ˈnʌmbəlɪs] *adj* inumerável.

number one ◇ *adj* [main] número um, principal. ◇ *n* **-1.** [priority] o mais importante **-2.** *inf* [oneself]: **to look after** ~ cuidar de si mesmo(ma).

numberplate [ˈnʌmbəpleɪt] *n* placa *f* do carro.

Number Ten *n*: ~ **(Downing Street)** *a casa número 10 de Downing Street, residência oficial do primeiro ministro britânico*; *fig* o governo britânico.

numbness [ˈnʌmnɪs] *n* **-1.** dormência *f* **-2.** *fig* [with shock, fear] paralisia *f*.

numbskull [ˈnʌmskʌl] *n* = **numskull**.

numeracy [ˈnjuːmərəsɪ] *n UK* facilidade *f* com números.

numeral [ˈnjuːmərəl] *n* algarismo *m*.

numerate [ˈnjuːmərət] *adj UK* que sabe fazer cálculos elementares.

numerical [njuːˈmerɪkl] *adj* numérico(ca).

numerous [ˈnjuːmərəs] *adj* inúmero(ra).

numskull [ˈnʌmskʌl] *n inf* besta *mf*, imbecil *mf*.

nun [nʌn] *n* freira *f*.

nuptial [ˈnʌpʃl] *adj fml* nupcial.

nurse [nɜːs] ◇ *n* enfermeiro *m*, -ra *f*. ◇ *vt* **-1.** *MED* [care for] cuidar de, atender **-2.** [harbour, foster] nutrir **-3.** [breast-feed] amamentar.

nursemaid [ˈnɜːsmeɪd] *n* babá *f*.

nursery [ˈnɜːsərɪ] *(pl* **-ies)** ◇ *adj* pré-escolar. ◇ *n* **-1.** [for children] creche *f* **-2.** [for plants, trees] viveiro *m* **-3.** [at home] quarto *m* das crianças.

nursery nurse *n UK* ama-seca *f*.

nursery rhyme *n* cantiga *f* infantil.

nursery school *n* pré-escola *f*.

nursery slopes *npl SKIING* pista *f* para principiantes.

nursing [ˈnɜːsɪŋ] *n* **-1.** [profession] enfermagem *f* **-2.** [care] cuidados *mpl*.

nursing auxiliary *n* auxiliar *mf* de enfermagem.

nursing home *n* **-1.** [for old people] clínica *f* de repouso **-2.** [for childbirth] maternidade *f (privada)*.

nurture [ˈnɜːtʃəʳ] *vt* **-1.** [children, plants] criar **-2.** [hope, desire, plan] alimentar.

nut [nʌt] *n* **-1.** [to eat] noz *f* **-2.** *TECH* porca *f*; **the ~s and bolts** *fig* [basics] o básico **-3.** *inf* [mad person] maluco *m*, -ca *f* **-4.** *inf* [enthusiast] aficionado *m*, -da *f* **-5.** *inf* [head] cuca *f*.
➡ **nuts** *inf* ◇ *adj*: **to be ~s** estar louco(ca). ◇ *excl US* maldito seja!

nutcase [ˈnʌtkeɪs] *n inf* pirado *m*, -da *f*.

nutcrackers [ˈnʌtˌkrækəz] *npl* quebra-nozes *m*.

nutmeg [ˈnʌtmeg] *n (U)* noz-moscada *f*.

nutrient [ˈnjuːtrɪənt] *n* nutriente *m*.

nutrition [njuːˈtrɪʃn] *n (U)* nutrição *f*.

nutritional [njuːˈtrɪʃənl] *adj* nutritivo(va).

nutritionist [njuːˈtrɪʃənɪst] *n* nutricionista *mf*.

nutritious [njuːˈtrɪʃəs] *adj* nutritivo(va).

nutshell [ˈnʌtʃel] *n* casca *f* de noz; **in a ~** em poucas palavras.

nutter [ˈnʌtəʳ] *n UK inf* louco *m*, -ca *f*.

nuzzle [ˈnʌzl] ◇ *vt* [with nose] fuçar. ◇ *vi* [nestle]:

---

to ~ (up) against sb/sthg aconchegar-se em alguém/algo.

NV *abbr of* Nevada.

NVQ *(abbr of* National Vocational Qualification) *n na Inglaterra e no País de Gales, certificado de qualificação vocacional obtido pelos estudantes de 15 a 16 anos*, ≃ diploma *m* de segundo grau.

NW *(abbr of* northwest) NO.

NY *abbr of* New York.

Nyasaland *n* Nyasaland; **in ~** em Nyasaland.

NYC *abbr of* New York City.

nylon [ˈnaɪlɒn] ◇ *n (U)* [fabric] náilon *m*. ◇ *comp* de náilon.
➡ **nylons** *npl dated* [stockings] meias *fpl* de náilon.

nymph [nɪmf] *n* ninfa *f*.

nymphomaniac [ˌnɪmfəˈmeɪnɪæk] ◇ *adj* ninfomaníaco(ca). ◇ *n* ninfomaníaco *m*, -ca *f*.

NYRB *(abbr of* New York Review of Books) *n conceituada revista norte-americana com artigos de crítica literária*.

NYSE *(abbr of* New York Stock Exchange) *n* Bolsa *f* de Nova Iorque.

NZ *abbr of* New Zealand.

o *(pl* o's *OR* os), **O** *(pl* O's *OR* Os) [əʊ] *n* **-1.** [letter] o, O *m* **-2.** [zero] zero *m*.

oaf [əʊf] *n* imbecil *mf*.

oak [əʊk] ◇ *n*: ~ **(tree)** carvalho *m*. ◇ *comp* de carvalho.

OAP *(abbr of* old age pensioner) *n UK* idoso que recebe pensão do estado.

oar [ɔːʳ] *n* remo *m*; **to put** *OR* **stick one's** ~ **in** *fig* meter o bedelho em.

oarlock [ˈɔːlɒk] *n US* [rowlock] tolete *m*.

oarsman [ˈɔːzmən] *(pl* **-men** [-mən]) *n* remador *m*.

oarswoman [ˈɔːzˌwʊmən] *(pl* **-women** [-ˌwɪmɪn]) *n* remadora *f*.

OAS *(abbr of* Organization of American States) *n* OEA *f*.

oasis [əʊˈeɪsɪs] *(pl* oases [əʊˈeɪsiːz]) *n* **-1.** [in desert] oásis *m inv* **-2.** *fig* [pleasant place] oásis *m inv*.

oatcake [ˈəʊtkeɪk] *n* biscoito *m* de aveia.

oath [əʊθ] *n* **-1.** [promise] juramento *m*; **on** *OR* **under** ~ sob juramento **-2.** [swearword] blasfêmia *f*.

oatmeal [ˈəʊtmiːl] ◇ *n* [food] farinha *f* de aveia. ◇ *comp* de aveia.

oats [əʊts] *npl* [grain] aveia *f*.

OAU (*abbr of* **Organization of African Unity**) *n* OUA *f*.

obdurate [ˈɒbdjʊrət] *adj fml* contumaz.

OBE (*abbr of* **Order of the British Empire**) *n* (*beneficiário da*) *ordem honorífica do Império Britânico*.

obedience [əˈbiːdjəns] *n (U)*: ~ **(to sb)** obediência *f* (a alguém).

obedient [əˈbiːdjənt] *adj* obediente.

obediently [əˈbiːdjəntli] *adv* obedientemente.

obelisk [ˈɒbəlɪsk] *n* [column] obelisco *m*.

obese [əʊˈbiːs] *adj* obeso(sa).

obesity [əʊˈbiːsəti] *n (U)* obesidade *f*.

obey [əˈbeɪ] <> *vt* obedecer a. <> *vi* obedecer.

obituary [əˈbɪtjʊəri] (*pl* -ies) *n* obituário *m*.

object [*n* ˈɒbdʒɪkt, *vb* ɒbˈdʒekt] <> *n* - **1.** [gen] objeto *m* - **2.** [aim] objetivo *m* - **3.** *GRAM* objeto *m*, complemento *m*. <> *vt*: **to** ~ **(that)** objetar (que). <> *vi* objetar; **to** ~ **to sthg/to doing sthg** opor a algo/a fazer algo.

objection [əbˈdʒekʃn] *n* [argument against] objeção *f*; **to have no** ~ **to sthg/to doing sthg** não ter nenhuma objeção a algo/a fazer algo.

objectionable [əbˈdʒekʃənəbl] *adj* desagradável.

objective [əbˈdʒektɪv] <> *adj* objetivo(va). <> *n* objetivo *m*.

objectively [əbˈdʒektɪvli] *adv* objetivamente.

objectivity [ˌɒbdʒekˈtɪvəti] *n (U)* objetividade *f*.

object lesson [ˈɒbdʒɪkt-] *n*: **an** ~ **in sthg** um exemplo perfeito de algo.

objector [əbˈdʒektər] *n* opositor *m*, -ra *f*.

obligate [ˈɒbligeɪt] *vt fml* obrigar; **to** ~ **sb to do sthg** obrigar alguém a fazer algo.

obligation [ˌɒblɪˈgeɪʃn] *n* obrigação *f*.

obligatory [əˈblɪgətri] *adj* obrigatório(ria).

oblige [əˈblaɪdʒ] <> *vt* - **1.** [force]: **to** ~ **sb to do sthg** obrigar alguém a fazer algo - **2.** *fml* [do a favour to] fazer um favor a. <> *vi* fazer um favor.

obliging [əˈblaɪdʒɪŋ] *adj* prestativo(va).

oblique [əˈbliːk] <> *adj* - **1.** [indirect - look] enviesado(da); [- reference, hint, compliment] indireto(ta) - **2.** [slanting] oblíquo(qua). <> *n TYPO* barra *f*.

obliquely [əˈbliːkli] *adv* [indirectly] indiretamente.

obliterate [əˈblɪtəreɪt] *vt* [destroy] obliterar.

obliteration [əˌblɪtəˈreɪʃn] *n (U)* [destruction] obliteração *f*.

oblivion [əˈblɪvɪən] *n (U)* - **1.** [unconsciousness] inconsciência *f* - **2.** [state of being forgotten] esquecimento *m*.

oblivious [əˈblɪvɪəs] *adj* inconsciente; **to be** ~ **to** *OR* **of sthg** não ter consciência de algo.

oblong [ˈɒblɒŋ] <> *adj* oblongo(ga). <> *n* retângulo *m*.

obnoxious [əbˈnɒkʃəs] *adj* repulsivo(va), repugnante.

o.b.o. (*abbr of* **or best offer**) ou a melhor oferta.

oboe [ˈəʊbəʊ] *n* oboé *m*.

oboist [ˈəʊbəʊɪst] *n* oboísta *mf*.

obscene [əbˈsiːn] *adj* obsceno(na).

obscenity [əbˈsenəti] (*pl* -ies) *n* obscenidade *f*.

obscure [əbˈskjʊər] <> *adj* - **1.** [not well-known] desconhecido(da) - **2.** [difficult to see/understand] obscuro(ra). <> *vt* - **1.** [make difficult to understand] obscurecer - **2.** [hide] esconder.

obscurity [əbˈskjʊərəti] *n (U)* obscuridade *f*.

obsequious [əbˈsiːkwɪəs] *adj fml* & *pej* servil.

observable [əbˈzɜːvəbl] *adj* visível, observável.

observably [əbˈzɜːvəbli] *adv* visivelmente.

observance [əbˈzɜːvns] *n (U)* observância *f*, cumprimento *m*.

observant [əbˈzɜːvnt] *adj* observador(ra).

observation [ˌɒbzəˈveɪʃn] *n* observação *f*.

observation post *n* ponto *m* de observação.

observatory [əbˈzɜːvətri] (*pl* -ies) *n* observatório *m*.

observe [əbˈzɜːv] *vt* observar.

observer [əbˈzɜːvər] *n* - **1.** [gen] observador *m*, -ra *f* - **2.** [political commentator] analista *mf*.

obsess [əbˈses] *vt* obsedar, obcecar; **to be** ~ **ed by** *OR* **with sb/sthg** estar obcecado(da) com *OR* por alguém/algo.

obsession [əbˈseʃn] *n* obsessão *f*.

obsessional [əbˈseʃənl] *adj* obsessivo(va).

obsessive [əbˈsesɪv] *adj* obsessivo(va).

obsolescence [ˌɒbsəˈlesns] *n (U)* obsolescência *f*.

obsolescent [ˌɒbsəˈlesnt] *adj* antiquado(da).

obsolete [ˈɒbsəliːt] *adj* obsoleto(ta).

obstacle [ˈɒbstəkl] *n* obstáculo *m*.

obstacle race *n* corrida *f* de obstáculos.

obstetrician [ˌɒbstəˈtrɪʃn] *n* obstetra *mf*.

obstetrics [ɒbˈstetrɪks] *n (U)* obstetrícia *f*.

obstinacy [ˈɒbstɪnəsi] *n* [stubbornness] obstinação *f*, teimosia *f*.

obstinate [ˈɒbstənət] *adj* - **1.** [stubborn] obstinado(da), teimoso(sa) - **2.** [persistent] persistente.

obstinately [ˈɒbstənətli] *adv* [stubbornly] obstinadamente, teimosamente.

obstreperous [əbˈstrepərəs] *adj fml or hum* escandaloso(sa).

obstruct [əbˈstrʌkt] *vt* - **1.** [road, path, traffic] obstruir, bloquear - **2.** [progress, justice] impedir.

obstruction [əbˈstrʌkʃn] *n* - **1.** [blockage, obstacle] obstrução *f*, obstáculo *m* - **2.** *(U)* [act of impeding] impedimento *m* - **3.** *SPORT* obstrução *f*.

obstructive [əbˈstrʌktɪv] *adj* obstrutivo(va).

obtain [əbˈteɪn] *vt* [get] obter.

obtainable [əbˈteɪnəbl] *adj* disponível.

obtrusive [əbˈtruːsɪv] *adj* - **1.** [person, behaviour] inconveniente - **2.** [smell] penetrante - **3.** [colour] gritante.

obtrusively [əbˈtruːsɪvli] *adv* indiscretamente, inconvenientemente.

obtuse [əbˈtjuːs] *adj* obtuso(sa).

obverse [ˈɒbvɜːs] *n* - **1.** [front side] reverso *m* - **2.** [opposite] contrapartida *f*.

obviate [ˈɒbvɪeɪt] *vt fml* evitar, prevenir.

obvious [ˈɒbvɪəs] <> *adj* - **1.** [evident] óbvio(via) - **2.** [unsubtle] evidente. <> *n*: **to state the** ~ afirmar o óbvio.

obviously [ˈɒbvɪəsli] *adv* - **1.** [of course] evidentemente, obviamente; ~ **not** claro que não - **2.** [clearly] evidentemente; **he's** ~ **lying** é óbvio que ele está mentindo.

obviousness [ˈɒbvɪəsnəs] *n (U)* obviedade *f*.

OCAS (*abbr of* **Organization of Central American**

States) n Organização f dos Estados da América Central.

occasion [ə'keɪʒn] ◇ n -1. [circumstance, time] ocasião f; **on several** ~s em várias ocasiões; **on** ~ *fml* de vez em quando; **special** ~ ocasião especial; **to rise to the** ~ mostrar-se à altura da ocasião -2. *fml* [reason, motive] razão f. ◇ vt *fml* [cause] ocasionar.

occasional [ə'keɪʒənl] adj ocasional.

occasionally [ə'keɪʒnəlɪ] adv de vez em quando, ocasionalmente.

occasional table n mesa f auxiliar.

occluded front n METEOR frente f oclusa.

occult [ɒ'kʌlt] ◇ adj oculto(ta). ◇ n: **the** ~ o oculto.

occupancy ['ɒkjʊpənsɪ] n (U) *fml* ocupação f.

occupant ['ɒkjʊpənt] n ocupante mf.

occupation [ˌɒkjʊ'peɪʃn] n -1. [job] ocupação f, emprego m -2. [pastime] passatempo m -3. (U) MIL ocupação f.

occupational [ˌɒkjʊ'peɪʃənl] adj ocupacional.

occupational disease n MED doença f ocupacional.

occupational hazard n risco m da profissão.

occupational therapist n terapeuta mf ocupacional.

occupational therapy n (U) terapia f ocupacional.

occupied ['ɒkjʊpaɪd] adj ocupado(da).

occupier ['ɒkjʊpaɪə[r]] n ocupante mf.

occupy ['ɒkjʊpaɪ] (pt & pp -ied) vt -1. [gen] ocupar -2. [keep busy]: **to** ~ **o.s.** ocupar-se.

occur [ə'kɜː[r]] (pt & pp -red, cont -ring) vi -1. [happen] ocorrer -2. [exist] existir -3. [be found] ser encontrado(da) -4. [come to mind]: **to** ~ **to sb** ocorrer a alguém.

occurrence [ə'kʌrəns] n -1. [event] acontecimento m -2. (U) [fact or instance of occurring] ocorrência f.

ocean ['əʊʃn] n oceano m.

oceangoing ['əʊʃnˌgəʊɪŋ] adj de grande autonomia.

Oceania [ˌəʊʃɪ'ɑːnɪə] n Oceania; **in** ~ na Oceania.

Oceanian [ˌəʊʃɪ'ɑːnɪən] ◇ adj oceânico(ca). ◇ n oceânico m, -ca f.

ochre UK, **ocher** US ['əʊkə[r]] adj [colour] ocre.

o'clock [ə'klɒk] adv: **five** ~ cinco horas; **it's four** ~ são quatro horas; **it's one** ~ é uma hora.

OCR n -1. (abbr of optical character reader) OCR m -2. (abbr of optical character recognition) OCR f.

Oct. (abbr of October) out.

octagon ['ɒktəgən] n octógono m.

octagonal [ɒk'tægənl] adj octogonal.

octane ['ɒkteɪn] n octano m.

octane number, octane rating n índice m de octana.

octave ['ɒktɪv] n MUS oitava f.

octet [ɒk'tet] n MUS octeto m.

October [ɒk'təʊbə[r]] n outubro m; see also September.

octogenarian [ˌɒktəʊdʒɪ'neərɪən] n octogenário m, -ria f.

octopus ['ɒktəpəs] (pl -puses OR -pi [-paɪ]) n polvo m.

OD ◇ n inf (abbr of overdose) overdose f. ◇ vi -1.

inf (abbr of overdose) tomar uma overdose -2. fig, hum exagerar. ◇ adj (abbr of overdrawn) no negativo, referente a conta bancária.

odd [ɒd] adj -1. [strange] estranho(nha) -2. [not part of pair] sem par -3. [number] ímpar -4. [leftover] avulso(sa) -5. [occasional] ocasional -6. inf [approximately]: **20** ~ **years** 20 e tantos anos.

➦ **odds** npl -1. [probability] probabilidades fpl; **the** ~**s are that ...** as previsões são de que ...; **against the** ~**s** apesar de todas as dificuldades -2. [bits]: ~**s and ends** miudezas fpl -3. phr: **to be at** ~**s with sb/sthg** discordar de algo/alguém.

oddball ['ɒdbɔːl] n inf esquisitão m, -tona f.

oddity ['ɒdɪtɪ] (pl -ies) n -1. [strange person, thing] esquisitice f -2. (U) [strangeness] estranheza f.

odd-job man UK, **odd-jobber** US n faz-tudo mf.

odd jobs npl biscates mpl.

oddly ['ɒdlɪ] adv [strangely] estranhamente; ~ **enough, I didn't care** surpreendentemente, não me importei.

oddments ['ɒdmənts] npl retalhos mpl.

odds-on ['ɒdz-] adj inf: **the** ~ **favourite** o grande favorito.

ode [əʊd] n ode f.

odious ['əʊdjəs] adj odioso(sa).

odometer [əʊ'dɒmɪtə[r]] n [in car] velocímetro m.

odor n US = odour.

odorless adj US = odourless.

odour UK, **odor** US ['əʊdə[r]] n odor m.

odourless UK, **odorless** US ['əʊdəlɪs] adj inodoro(ra).

odyssey ['ɒdɪsɪ] (pl -s) n literary odisséia f.

OECD (abbr of Organization for Economic Cooperation and Development) n organização que reúne um grupo de países desenvolvidos que trabalham pelo desenvolvimento do comércio e crescimento econômico, OECD f.

oesophagus UK, **esophagus** US [ɪ'sɒfəgəs] n esôfago m.

oestrogen UK, **estrogen** US [iː'strədʒən] n (U) estrogênio m.

of [ɒv] prep -1. [belonging to] de; **the colour** ~ **the car** a cor do carro. -2. [expressing amount] de; **a piece** ~ **cake** uma fatia de bolo; **a fall** ~ **20%** uma queda de 20%; **lots** ~ **people** muita gente. -3. [containing, made from] de; **a glass** ~ **beer** um copo de cerveja; **a house** ~ **stone** uma casa de pedra; **it's made** ~ **wood** é de madeira. -4. [regarding, relating to, indicating cause] de; **fear** ~ **spiders** medo de aranhas; **he died** ~ **cancer** ele morreu de câncer. -5. [referring to time] de; **the summer** ~ **1969** o verão de 1969; **the 26th** ~ **August** o 26 de agosto. -6. [with cities, countries] de; **the city** ~ **San Francisco** a cidade de San Francisco. -7. [on the part of] de; **that was very kind** ~ **you** foi muito amável da sua parte. -8. US [in telling the time] menos, para; **it's ten** ~ **four** são dez para as quatro.

off [ɒf] ◇ adv -1. [away]: **to drive/walk** ~ ir-se embora; **to get** ~ [from bus, train, etc] descer; **we're** ~ **to Austria next week** vamos para a Áustria na próxima semana. -2. [expressing removal]: **to take sthg** ~ tirar algo. -3. [so as to stop working]: **to turn sthg** ~ [TV, radio, engine] desligar algo; [tap]

fechar algo. **- 4.** [expressing distance or time away]: **it's a long way** ~ [in distance] é muito longe; [in time] ainda falta muito; **it's two months** ~ é daqui a dois meses. **- 5.** [not at work] de folga; **I'm taking a week** ~ vou tirar uma semana de férias. <> *prep* **-1.** [away from]: **to get** ~ **sthg** descer de algo; ~ **the coast** ao largo da costa; **just** ~ **the main road** perto da estrada principal. **- 2.** [indicating removal]: **take the lid** ~ **the jar** tire a tampa do frasco; **we'll take $20** ~ **the price** descontaremos 20 dólares do preço. **- 3.** [absent from]: **to be** ~ **work** não estar trabalhando. **- 4.** *inf* [from] a; **I bought it** ~ **her** eu comprei isso dela. <> *adj* **-1.** [TV, radio, light] apagado(da), desligado(da); [tap] fechado(da); [engine] desligado(da). **- 2.** [cancelled] cancelado(da).

offal ['ɒfl] *n (U)* vísceras *fpl (do animal abatido)*.

off-balance *adv* **-1.** [not standing firmly] sem equilíbrio **- 2.** [unprepared] desprevenido(da).

offbeat ['ɒfbiːt] *adj inf* original, excêntrico(ca).

off-centre <> *adj* descentralizado(da). <> *adv* fora do centro.

off-chance *n*: he called on the ~ of seeing her ele ligou com a remota esperança de vê-la.

off-colour *adj* **- 1.** [ill] indisposto(ta) **- 2.** [rude, offensive] ofensivo(va).

offcut ['ɒfkʌt] *n* retalho *m*.

off-day *n inf* dia *m* de folga.

off duty *adv*: when do you get ~? quando você fica de folga?
  off-duty *adj* de folga.

offence *UK*, **offense** *US* [ə'fens] *n* **-1.** [crime] infração *f*, delito *m* **- 2.** [displeasure, hurt] insulto *m*, ofensa *f*; **to take** ~ ofender-se.

offend [ə'fend] <> *vt* [upset] ofender. <> *vi* **-1.** [contravene]: **to** ~ **against** transgredir; [decency] pecar contra **- 2.** [commit a crime] cometer (um) crime.

offended [ə'fendɪd] *adj* ofendido(da).

offender [ə'fendə'] *n* **-1.** [criminal] transgressor *m*, -ra *f* **- 2.** [culprit] infrator *m*, -ra *f*.

offending [ə'fendɪŋ] *adj* ofensor(ra).

offense [*sense 2* 'ɒfens] *n US* **-1.** = offence **- 2.** *SPORT* ataque *m*.

offensive [ə'fensɪv] <> *adj* **-1.** [causing offence] ofensivo(va) **- 2.** [aggressive] agressivo(va). <> *n* **-1.** *MIL* ofensiva *f* **- 2.** *fig* [attack]: **to go on** *OR* **take the** ~ partir para a ofensiva.

offensiveness [ə'fensɪvnɪs] *n (U)* caráter *m* ofensivo.

offer ['ɒfə'] <> *n* **-1.** [something offered] oferta *f*; **on** ~ [available] em oferta **- 2.** [bid, proposal] proposta *f*. <> *vt* **-1.** [present, give] oferecer; **to** ~ **sthg to sb, to** ~ **sb sthg** oferecer algo a alguém **- 2.** [propose]: **to** ~ **to do sthg** oferecer-se para fazer algo. <> *vi* oferecer-se.

offering ['ɒfərɪŋ] *n* **-1.** [something offered] oferta *f* **- 2.** *RELIG* [sacrifice] oferenda *f*.

off guard *adv* desprevenido(da).

off-hand <> *adj* [unfriendly] brusco(ca). <> *adv* [at this moment] de imediato.

office ['ɒfɪs] *n* **-1.** [room] escritório *m*, gabinete *m* **- 2.** [building] edifício *m* de escritórios **- 3.** [staff] pessoal *m* **- 4.** [government department] departamento

m **- 5.** [distribution point - for tickets] bilheteria *f*; [- for information] guichê *m*; [- for enquiries] serviço *m* de informações **- 6.** [position of authority] cargo *m*; **in** ~ no poder; **to take** ~ tomar posse.

office automation *n* automatização *f*.

office block *n* prédio *m* de escritórios.

office boy *n* contínuo *m*, bói *m*.

officeholder ['ɒfɪs,həʊldə'] *n* detentor *m*, -ra *f* de cargo público.

office hours *npl* horário *m* de expediente.

office junior *n UK* assistente *mf* de escritório.

Office of Fair Trading *n* ≃ Delegacia *f* de Defesa do Consumidor.

officer ['ɒfɪsə'] *n* **-1.** *MIL* oficial *mf* **- 2.** [in organization] diretor *m*, -ra *f* **- 3.** [in police force] (agente) policial *m*.

office work *n (U)* trabalho *m* de escritório.

office worker *n* funcionário *m*, -ria *f* de escritório.

official [ə'fɪʃl] <> *adj* oficial. <> *n* [public] funcionário *m*, -ria *f*; *SPORT* oficial *mf*.

officialdom [ə'fɪʃəldəm] *n (U)* burocracia *f*.

officially [ə'fɪʃəlɪ] *adv* oficialmente.

official receiver *n* síndico *m*, -ca *f* em falências.

officiate [ə'fɪʃɪeɪt] *vi* oficiar; **to** ~ **at sthg** celebrar algo.

officious [ə'fɪʃəs] *adj pej* intrometido(da).

offing ['ɒfɪŋ] *n*: **in the** ~ num futuro próximo.

off-key *MUS* <> *adj* desafinado(da). <> *adv* de maneira desafinada.

off-licence *n UK* loja *f* de bebidas alcoólicas.

off limits *adj esp US* proibido(da).

off-line *adj COMPUT* off-line, desconectado(da).

offload ['ɒf'ləʊd] *vt inf*: **to** ~ **sthg (onto sb)** livrar-se de algo (passando para alguém).

off-peak <> *adj* de tarifa reduzida. <> *adv* fora do horário de pico.

off-putting [-,pʊtɪŋ] *adj* desconcertante.

off sales *npl UK* venda *f* de bebidas alcoólicas.

off season *n*: **the** ~ a baixa temporada.
  off-season *adj* de baixa temporada.

offset ['ɒfset] (*pt & pp* offset, *cont* -ting) *vt* contrabalançar.

offshoot ['ɒfʃuːt] *n* [spin-off] ramificação *f*; **to be an** ~ **of sthg** ser uma ramificação de algo.

offshore ['ɒfʃɔː'] <> *adj* **-1.** [in or on the sea] em alto mar **- 2.** [near coast] costeiro(ra). <> *adv* **-1.** [out at sea] ao largo **- 2.** [near coast] a pouca distância da costa.

offside [*adj & adv* ,ɒf'saɪd, *n* 'ɒfsaɪd] <> *adj* **-1.** [part of vehicle] do lado do motorista **- 2.** *SPORT* impedido(da). <> *n* [of vehicle] lado *m* do motorista.

offspring ['ɒfsprɪŋ] (*pl inv*) *n* **-1.** *fml or hum* [of people] descendência *f* **- 2.** [of animals] prole *f*.

offstage [,ɒf'steɪdʒ] <> *adj* dos bastidores. <> *adv* nos bastidores.

off-the-cuff <> *adj* improvisado(da). <> *adv* de improviso.

off-the-peg *adj UK* pronto(ta), confeccionado(da).

off-the-record <> *adj* extra-oficial. <> *adv* extra-oficialmente.

off-the-wall *adj* não usual, excêntrico(ca).

off-white *adj* de cor não totalmente branca.

OFSTED (*abbr of* **Office for Standards in Education**) *n órgão britânico que inspeciona a educação.*

OFT (*abbr of* **Office of Fair Trading**) *n órgão britânico que controla as transações comerciais.*

often ['ɒfn, 'ɒftn] *adv* **-1.** [many times] muitas vezes; **how ~?** quantas vezes?; **how ~ do you visit her?** com que freqüência você a visita? **-2.** [in many cases] freqüentemente.

➡ **as often as not** *adv* geralmente.

➡ **every so often** *adv* de vez em quando.

➡ **more often than not** *adv* freqüentemente.

ogle ['əʊgl] *vt pej* comer com os olhos.

ogre ['əʊgə] *n* [in fairy tales] ogro *m*.

oh [əʊ] *excl* **-1.** [to introduce comment] ah!; **~ really?** é mesmo? **-2.** [expressing emotion] ah!; **~ no!** essa não!

OH *abbr of* **Ohio**.

Ohio [əʊ'haɪəʊ] *n* Ohio; **in ~** em Ohio.

ohm [əʊm] *n* ohm *m*.

OHMS (*abbr of* **On His (or Her) Majesty's Service**) *na Grã-Bretanha, expressão que indica o caráter oficial de um documento.*

oil [ɔɪl] ◇ *n* **-1.** [gen] óleo *m* **-2.** (*U*) [petroleum] petróleo *m* **-3.** (*U*) [olive oil] azeite *m*. ◇ *vt* [lubricate] lubrificar.

➡ **oils** *npl* ART tintas *fpl* a óleo.

oilcan ['ɔɪlkæn] *n* almotolia *f*.

oil change *n* troca *f* de óleo.

oilcloth ['ɔɪlklɒθ] *n* (*U*) oleado *m*.

oilfield ['ɔɪlfiːld] *n* campo *m* petrolífero.

oil filter *n* filtro *m* de óleo.

oil-fired [-,faɪəd] *adj* a óleo.

oil industry *n*: **the ~** a indústria petrolífera, o setor petroleiro.

oilman ['ɔɪlmən] (*pl* **-men** [-mən]) *n* **-1.** [worker] trabalhador *m* do setor petroleiro **-2.** [businessman] executivo *m* do setor petroleiro.

oil paint *n* tinta *f* a óleo.

oil painting *n* **-1.** [art] pintura *f* a óleo **-2.** [picture] quadro *m* a óleo.

oilrig ['ɔɪlrɪg] *n* plataforma *f* petrolífera.

oilskins ['ɔɪlskɪnz] *npl* capa *f* de oleado.

oil slick *n* mancha *f* de óleo.

oil tanker *n* **-1.** [ship] petroleiro *m* **-2.** [lorry] caminhão *m* -tanque.

oil well *n* poço *m* de petróleo.

oily ['ɔɪlɪ] (*compar* **-ier**, *superl* **-iest**) *adj* **-1.** [covered in oil] gorduroso(sa) **-2.** *pej* [smarmy] bajulador(ra).

ointment ['ɔɪntmənt] *n* pomada *f*.

oiro (*abbr of* **offers in the region of**) ofertas em torno de.

OK (*pl* **OKs**, *pt* & *pp* **OKed**, *cont* **OKing**), **okay** [,əʊ'keɪ] *inf* ◇ *adj*: **are you ~?** você está bem?; **to be ~ with** *or* **by sb** estar tudo bem com alguém. ◇ *adv* [well] bem. ◇ *n*: **to give (sb) the ~** dar sinal verde (a alguém). ◇ *excl* **-1.** [asking for, expressing agreement] está bem!, tá (bem/bom)! **-2.** [fair enough] certo! **-3.** [to introduce new topic] bom! ◇ *vt* aprovar.

Oklahoma [,əʊklə'həʊmə] *n* Oklahoma; **in ~** em Oklahoma.

okra ['əʊkrə] *n* (*U*) quiabo *m*.

old [əʊld] ◇ *adj* **-1.** [aged, ancient, longstanding]

velho(lha) **-2.** [referring to age]: **how ~ are you?** quantos anos você tem? **-3.** [former, ancient, out-of-date] antigo(ga); **in the ~ days** antigamente **-4.** *inf* [for emphasis]: **any ~ clothes will do** qualquer roupa serve; **any ~ how** de qualquer jeito. ◇ *npl*: **the ~** os idosos.

old age *n* (*U*) velhice *f*.

old age pension *n* UK pensão *f* por idade.

old age pensioner *n* UK aposentado *m*, -da *f* por idade.

Old Bailey [-'beɪlɪ] *n*: **the ~** o prédio do Tribunal Criminal (de Londres).

olden ['əʊldn] *adj*: **in the ~ days** antigamente.

old-fashioned [-'fæʃnd] *adj* **-1.** [outmoded] antiquado(da) **-2.** [traditional] tradicional.

old flame *n* paixão *f* antiga.

old hat *adj inf pej*: **to be ~** estar fora de moda.

old maid *n pej* [spinster] solteirona *f*.

old master *n* **-1.** [painter] grande mestre *m* **-2.** [painting] obra-prima *f*.

old people's home *n* lar *m* de idosos.

Old Testament *n*: **the ~** o Antigo Testamento.

old-time *adj* de antigamente.

old-timer *n* **-1.** [veteran] veterano *m*, -na *f* **-2.** *esp US* [old man] velho(lha).

old wives' tale *n* conto *m* da carochinha.

Old World *n*: **the ~** o Velho Mundo.

O level (*abbr of* **ordinary level**) *n* UK *até há pouco tempo, primeira etapa do GCE, exame prestado pelos estudantes britânicos aos 16 anos, agora substituído pelo GCSE.*

oligarchy ['ɒlɪgɑːkɪ] (*pl* **-ies**) *n* oligarquia *f*.

olive ['ɒlɪv] ◇ *adj* da cor de oliva. ◇ *n* **-1.** [fruit] azeitona *f* **-2.** [tree]: **~ (tree)** oliveira *f*.

olive green *adj* verde-oliva.

olive oil *n* (*U*) azeite *m* de oliva.

Olympic [ə'lɪmpɪk] *adj* olímpico(ca).

➡ **Olympics** *npl*: **the ~s** as Olimpíadas.

Olympic Games *npl*: **the ~** os Jogos Olímpicos.

OM (*abbr of* **Order of Merit**) *n* (*beneficiário da*) *ordem do mérito britânica.*

O & M (*abbr of* **organization and method**) *n* O & M *f*.

Oman [əʊ'mɑːn] *n* Omã; **in ~** em Omã.

OMB (*abbr of* **Office of Management and Budget**) *n órgão norte-americano que assessora o presidente em questões orçamentárias.*

ombudsman ['ɒmbʊdzmən] (*pl* **-men** [-mən]) *n* ombudsman *mf*.

omelet(te) ['ɒmlɪt] *n* omelete *f*.

omen ['əʊmen] *n* presságio *m*.

ominous ['ɒmɪnəs] *adj* **-1.** ominoso(sa) **-2.** [threatening] ameaçador(ra).

ominously ['ɒmɪnəslɪ] *adv* ominosamente.

omission [ə'mɪʃn] *n* omissão *f*.

omit [ə'mɪt] (*pt* & *pp* **-ted**, *cont* **-ting**) *vt* omitir; **to ~ to do sthg** deixar de fazer algo.

omnibus ['ɒmnɪbəs] *n* **-1.** [book] antologia *f* **-2.** UK RADIO & TV programa *f* de variedades.

omnipotence [ɒm'nɪpətəns] *n* (*U*) *fml* onipotência *f*.

omnipotent [ɒm'nɪpətnt] *adj fml* onipotente.

omnipresent [,ɒmnɪ'preznt] *adj fml* onipresente.

omniscience *n fml* onisciência *f*.

omniscient [ɒm'nɪsɪənt] *adj fml* onisciente.

omnivorous [ɒm'nɪvərəs] *adj ZOOL* onívoro(ra).

on [ɒn] ◇ *prep* **-1.** [expressing position, location] em, sobre; **it's ~ the table** está na mesa, está sobre a mesa; **put it ~ the table** ponha-o na *OR* sobre a mesa; **~ my right** à minha direita; **~ the right** à direita; **a picture ~ the wall** um quadro na parede; **the exhaust ~ the car** o cano de descarga do carro; **we stayed ~ a farm** ficamos numa fazenda. **-2.** [with forms of transportation]: **~ the plane** no avião; **to get ~ a bus** subir num ônibus. **-3.** [expressing means, method] em; **~ foot** a pé; **~ the radio** no rádio; **~ TV** na televisão; **paid ~ an hourly basis** pago por hora. **-4.** [using] a; **it runs ~ unleaded gas** funciona com gasolina sem chumbo; **to be ~ drugs** drogar-se; **to be ~ medication** estar tomando medicamentos. **-5.** [about] sobre; **a book ~ Germany** um livro sobre a Alemanha. **-6.** [expressing time]: **~ arrival** ao chegar; **~ Tuesday** na terça-feira; **~ August 25th** no dia 25 de agosto. **-7.** [with regard to] em, sobre; **a tax ~ imports** um imposto sobre as importações; **the effect ~ the country** o impacto no país. **-8.** [describing activity, state]: **~ vacation** de férias; **~ sale** à venda. **-9.** [in phrases]: **do you have any money ~ you?** *inf* você tem dinheiro?; **the drinks are ~ me** as bebidas são por minha conta. ◇ *adv* **-1.** [in place, covering]: **to put one's clothes ~** vestir-se; **to put the lid ~** tapar. **-2.** [movie, play, programme]: **the news is ~** está passando o telejornal; **what's ~ at the movies?** o que é que está passando no cinema? **-3.** [with transportation]: **to get ~** subir. **-4.** [functioning]: **to turn sthg ~** [TV, radio, light] ligar *OR* acender algo; [tap] abrir algo; [engine] pôr algo para trabalhar. **-5.** [taking place]: **how long is the festival ~?** quanto tempo dura o festival?; **the game is already ~** o jogo já começou. **-6.** [farther forward]: **to drive ~** continuar a dirigir. **-7.** [in phrases]: **I already have something ~ tonight** já tenho planos para esta noite. ◇ *adj* [TV, radio, light] ligado(da), aceso(sa); [tap] aberto(ta); [engine] funcionando.

ON *abbr of* Ontario.

ONC (*abbr of* **Ordinary National Certificate**) *n* diploma técnico em nível secundário na Grã-Bretanha.

once [wʌns] ◇ *adv* **-1.** [on one occasion] uma vez; **~ again** *OR* **more** [one more time] outra vez; [yet again] novamente; **~ and for all** de uma vez por todas; **~ in a while** de vez em quando; **~ or twice** uma vez ou duas; **for ~** ao menos uma vez **-2.** [previously, formerly] outrora; **~ upon a time** era uma vez. ◇ *conj* assim que, quando.

➡ **at once** *adv* **-1.** [immediately] imediatamente **-2.** [at the same time] ao mesmo tempo; **all at ~** de repente.

once-over *n inf*: **to give sb/sthg the ~** dar uma olhada rápida em alguém/algo.

oncoming ['ɒn,kʌmɪŋ] *adj* **-1.** [traffic, vehicle] em sentido contrário **-2.** [danger] iminente.

OND (*abbr of* **Ordinary National Diploma**) *n* diploma técnico em nível superior na Grã-Bretanha, obtido em curso de 3 anos.

one [wʌn] ◇ *num* um (uma); **thirty-~** trinta e um;

~ fifth um quinto. ◇ *adj* [only] único(ca); **~ day** um dia. ◇ *pron* [referring to a particular thing or person] um *m*, uma *f*; **the green ~** o verde; **that ~** aquele *m*, aquela *f*.

one-armed bandit *n* caça-níqueis *m*.

one-liner *n* piada *f* curta.

one-man *adj* individual, solo.

one-man band *n* **-1.** [musician] homem *m* -orquestra **-2.** [business, operation] faz-tudo *m*.

one-night stand *n* **-1.** [performance] apresentação *f* única **-2.** *inf* [sexual relationship] ficada *f* de uma noite só, transa *f* passageira.

one-off *inf* ◇ *adj* único(ca). ◇ *n* **-1.** [unique event, person] único *m*, -ca *f* **-2.** [unique product] exemplar *m* único.

one-on-one *adj US* = **one-to-one**.

one-parent family *n* família *f* que possui apenas um dos pais.

one-piece *adj* de uma peça só; **a ~ swimsuit** um maiô inteiro.

onerous ['ɒnərəs] *adj* oneroso(sa), difícil.

one's *poss adj*: **to do ~ duty** fazer o seu dever; **to be on ~ own** estar sozinho(nha).

oneself [wʌn'self] *pron fml* **-1.** (reflexive) se **-2.** (after prep) si próprio(pria), si mesmo(ma).

one-sided [-'saɪdɪd] *adj* **-1.** [unequal] desigual, unilateral **-2.** [biased] parcial.

onetime ['wʌntaɪm] *adj* [former] antigo(ga).

one-to-one *UK*, **one-on-one** *US adj* **-1.** [discussion] entre dois **-2.** [tuition] individual.

one-touch dialling *UK*, **one-touch dialing** *US n* discagem *f* automática.

one-upmanship [,wʌn'ʌpmənʃɪp] *n* (U) capacidade de parecer ser melhor que os outros.

one-way *adj* **-1.** [moving in one direction] de mão única **-2.** [for outward travel only] só de ida.

ongoing ['ɒn,gəʊɪŋ] *adj* em andamento, atual.

onion ['ʌnjən] *n* cebola *f*.

online ['ɒnlaɪn] *COMPUT adj* & *adv* on-line.

online banking *n* serviço *m* de banco on-line.

online shopping *n* compras *fpl* on-line.

onlooker ['ɒn,lʊkə'] *n* espectador *m*, -ra *f*.

only ['əʊnlɪ] ◇ *adj* único(ca); **an ~ child** um filho único. ◇ *adv* **-1.** [exclusively] só **-2.** [merely, just] apenas, só **-3.** [for emphasis] só; **I was ~ too willing to help** eu queria tanto ajudar; **it's ~ natural you should be upset** é bastante natural que você fique perturbado; **not ~ ... but also** não apenas ... mas também; **~ just** por pouco. ◇ *conj* só que.

o.n.o., ono (*abbr of* **or near (est) offer**) ou a oferta mais próxima.

onrush ['ɒnrʌʃ] *n* [of feeling] irrupção *f*.

on-screen *COMPUT adj* & *adv* na tela.

onset ['ɒnset] *n* começo *m*.

onshore ['ɒnʃɔː'] ◇ *adj* **-1.** [on land] terrestre **-2.** [moving towards land] em direção à costa. ◇ *adv* **-1.** [on land] em terra **-2.** [towards land] para a praia.

onside [ɒn'saɪd] *adj* & *adv SPORT* em posição legal.

onslaught ['ɒnslɔːt] *n* investida *f*.

Ont. *abbr of* Ontario.

Ontario [ɒn'teərɪəʊ] *n* [province] Ontário; **in ~** em Ontário.

on-the-job *adj* no trabalho, prático(ca).

on-the-spot *adj* no ato, no local.

onto [*unstressed before consonant* 'ɒntə, *unstressed before vowel* 'ɒntʊ, *stressed* 'ɒntu:] *prep* ▷ **on**.

onus ['əʊnəs] *n* ônus *m*.

onward ['ɒnwəd] ▷ *adj* [advancing - in time] para a frente; [- in space] adiante, para a frente. ▷ *adv* = **onwards**.

onwards ['ɒnwədz] *adv* [forwards - in space] para a frente; [- in time] em diante.

onyx ['ɒnɪks] *n* (U) ônix *m*.

oodles ['u:dlz] *npl inf*: ~ **of sthg** um montão de algo.

oof *excl inf* uff!

ooh [u:] *excl inf* aah!

oops [ʊps, u:ps] *excl inf* ôpa!

ooze [u:z] ▷ *vt fig* exalar. ▷ *vi* exsudar; **to** ~ **from** OR **out of sthg** transpirar por algo; **sweat** ~**d from every pore** o suor transpirava-lhe por todos os poros. ▷ *n* (U) lodo *m*.

opacity [ə'pæsətɪ] *n* -**1.** [non-transparency] opacidade *f* -**2.** *fig* [obscurity] obscuridade *f*.

opal ['əʊpl] *n* [gem] opala *m*.

opaque [əʊ'peɪk] *adj* -**1.** [not transparent] opaco(ca) -**2.** *fig* [obscure] obscuro(ra).

OPEC ['əʊpek] (*abbr of* Organization of the Petroleum Exporting Countries) *n* OPEP *f*.

open ['əʊpn] ▷ *adj* -**1.** [gen] aberto(ta); **to be** ~ **to sthg** [ready to accept] ser aberto(ta) a algo; **to be** ~ **to sb** [opportunity, choice] estar aberto(ta) a alguém; **to lay o.s.** ~ **to criticism** manter-se aberto(ta) à crítica -**2.** [frank] franco(ca) -**3.** [unfastened] descobrado(da) -**4.** [not enclosed] amplo(pla) -**5.** [uncovered] descoberto(ta) -**6.** [meeting, competition, invitation] aberto(ta) a todos -**7.** [unconcealed] manifesto(ta). ▷ *n*: **in the** ~ [in the fresh air] ao ar livre; **to bring sthg out into the** ~ pôr algo para fora. ▷ *vt* -**1.** [gen] abrir -**2.** [inaugurate] inaugurar -**3.** [unblock] desbloquear. ▷ *vi* abrir.
 ➡ **open on to** *vt fus* [subj: room, door] dar para.
 ➡ **open out** *vi* -**1.** [bud, petals] abrir-se -**2.** [road, path, river] alargar-se -**3.** [view, valley] revelar-se.
 ➡ **open up** ▷ *vt* [unlock door] destrancar a porta. ▷ *vi* -**1.** [gen] abrir-se -**2.** [shop, house] abrir.

open-air *adj* ao ar livre; ~ **swimming pool** piscina descoberta.

open-and-shut *adj* evidente.

opencast ['əʊpnkɑ:st] *adj*: ~ **mining** lavra *f* a céu aberto.

open day *n* dia em que uma escola, universidade etc. podem ser visitados pelo público em geral.

open-ended [-'endɪd] *adj* sem prazo para acabar, aberto(ta).

opener ['əʊpnə'] *n* abridor *m*.

open-handed [-'hændɪd] *adj* generoso(sa).

openhearted [,əʊpn'hɑ:tɪd] *adj* de coração aberto.

open-heart surgery *n* (U) cirurgia *f* de coração aberto.

opening ['əʊpnɪŋ] ▷ *adj* [first] primeiro(ra). ▷ *n* -**1.** [beginning] lançamento *m* -**2.** [gap] abertura *f* -**3.** [opportunity] oportunidade *f*; ~ **for sthg**

oportunidade para algo -**4.** [job vacancy] vaga *f*.

opening hours *npl* horário *m* de funcionamento.

opening night *n* (noite de) estréia *f*.

opening time *n* UK hora *f* de abrir.

open letter *n* carta *f* aberta.

openly ['əʊpnlɪ] *adv* abertamente.

open market *n* mercado *m* aberto.

open marriage *n* casamento *m* aberto.

open-minded [-'maɪndɪd] *adj* compreensivo(va), sem preconceitos.

open-mouthed [-'maʊðd] *adj* boquiaberto(ta); **in** ~ **admiration** numa admiração de deixar de boca aberta.

open-necked [-'nekt] *adj* aberto(ta) no colo.

openness ['əʊpənnɪs] *n* (U) [frankness] franqueza *f*.

open-plan *adj* sem divisórias.

open prison *n* prisão *f* de regime aberto.

open sandwich *n* sanduíche *m* aberto.

open season *n* temporada *f*.

open shop *n* local de trabalho onde não é necessário pertencer a um sindicato.

Open University *n* UK: **the** ~ universidade britânica para alunos adultos que estudam em casa, através de uma combinação de programas de rádio e televisão e ensino à distância.

open verdict *n* JUR júri *m* pendente.

opera ['ɒpərə] *n* ópera *f*.

opera glasses *npl* binóculos *mpl* de teatro.

opera house *n* teatro *m* lírico.

opera singer *n* cantor *m*, -ra *f* de ópera.

operate ['ɒpəreɪt] ▷ *vt* -**1.** [cause to work] operar -**2.** COMM [manage] dirigir. ▷ *vi* -**1.** [function] funcionar -**2.** COMM dirigir -**3.** MED operar; **to** ~ **on sb/sthg** operar alguém/algo.

operatic [,ɒpə'rætɪk] *adj* de ópera, lírico(ca).

operating room ['ɒpəreɪtɪŋ-] *n* US = **operating theatre**.

operating system ['ɒpəreɪtɪŋ-] *n* COMPUT sistema *m* operacional.

operating theatre UK, **operating room** US ['ɒpəreɪtɪŋ-] *n* sala *f* de operações.

operation [,ɒpə'reɪʃn] *n* -**1.** [gen] operação *f* -**2.** MIL manobra *f* -**3.** COMM administração *f* -**4.** (U) [functioning] funcionamento *m*; **in** ~ [machine, device] em funcionamento; [law, system] em vigor -**5.** MED operação *f*, cirurgia *f*; **to have an** ~ **on one's knee** ser operado(da) no joelho; **to perform a kidney transplant** ~ fazer uma cirurgia de transplante renal.

operational [,ɒpə'reɪʃənl] *adj* operacional.

operative ['ɒprətɪv] ▷ *adj* [law] em vigor; [system] vigente. ▷ *n* [in factory] operário *m*, -ria *f*.

operator ['ɒpəreɪtə'] *n* -**1.** TELEC telefonista *mf* -**2.** [technician] operador *m*, -ra *f* -**3.** COMM [person in charge] encarregado *m*, -da *f*.

operetta [,ɒpə'retə] *n* opereta *f*.

ophthalmic optician [ɒf'θælmɪk-] *n* oculista *mf*.

ophthalmologist [,ɒfθæl'mɒlədʒɪst] *n* oftalmologista *mf*.

opinion [ə'pɪnjən] *n* opinião *f*; **to be of the** ~ **that** ser da opinião de que; **in my** ~ na minha opinião.

opinionated [ə'pɪnjəneɪtɪd] *adj pej* teimoso(sa), cabeça-dura.

opinion poll *n* pesquisa *f* de opinião.

opium ['əʊpjəm] *n* (U) ópio *m*.

opponent [ə'pəʊnənt] *n* adversário *m*, -ria *f*.

opportune ['ɒpətjuːn] *adj* oportuno(na).

opportunism [,ɒpə'tjuːnɪzm] *n* (U) oportunismo *m*.

opportunist [,ɒpə'tjuːnɪst] *n* oportunista *mf*.

opportunity [,ɒpə'tjuːnətɪ] (*pl* -ies) *n* oportunidade *f*; **to get the ~ (to do sthg)** ter a oportunidade (de fazer algo); **to take the ~ to do** *OR* **of doing sthg** aproveitar a oportunidade para fazer algo.

oppose [ə'pəʊz] *vt* opor-se a.

opposed [ə'pəʊzd] *adj* oposto(ta); **to be ~ to sthg** opor-se a algo; **as ~ to** em oposição a, em vez de; **I like beer ~ wine** prefiro vinho e não cerveja.

opposing [ə'pəʊzɪŋ] *adj* oposto(ta), contrário(ria).

opposite ['ɒpəzɪt] <> *adj* **-1.** [facing] em frente; **the ~ side (of the street/house/door)** o outro lado (da rua/casa/porta) **-2.** [very different]: **~ (to sthg)** oposto(ta) (a algo). <> *adv* (lá) em frente. <> *prep* [facing] em frente a. <> *n* [contrary] contrário *m*.

opposite number *n* número *m* equivalente.

opposite sex *n*: **the ~** o sexo oposto.

opposition [,ɒpə'zɪʃn] *n* **-1.** (U) [gen] oposição *f* **-2.** [opposing team] adversário *m*, -ria *f*.
➔ **Opposition** *n UK POL*: **the Opposition** a Oposição.

oppress [ə'pres] *vt* **-1.** [tyrannize] oprimir **-2.** [subj: anxiety, atmosphere] deprimir.

oppressed [ə'prest] <> *adj* [people, minorities] oprimido(da). <> *npl*: **the ~** os oprimidos.

oppression [ə'preʃn] *n* (U) opressão *f*.

oppressive [ə'presɪv] *adj* **-1.** [gen] opressivo(va) **-2.** [heat, weather] sufocante.

oppressor [ə'presəʳ] *n* opressor *m*, -ra *f*.

opprobrium [ə'prəʊbrɪəm] *n* (U) *fml* opróbrio *m*.

opt [ɒpt] <> *vt*: **to ~ to do sthg** optar por *OR* preferir fazer algo. <> *vi*: **to ~ for sthg** optar por *OR* escolher algo.
➔ **opt in** *vi*: **to ~ in (to sthg)** optar por participar (de algo).
➔ **opt out** *vi*: **to ~ out (of sthg)** optar por não participar (de algo); [give up] abrir mão (de algo).

optic ['ɒptɪk] *adj* óptico(ca).
➔ **optics** *n* (U) óptica *f*.

optical ['ɒptɪkl] *adj* **-1.** [relating to light] óptico(ca) **-2.** [visual] visual.

optical character reader *n COMPUT* leitora *f* óptica de caracteres.

optical character recognition *n COMPUT* reconhecimento *m* óptico de caracteres.

optical fibre *n TELEC* fibra *f* óptica.

optical illusion *n* ilusão *f* de óptica.

optician [ɒp'tɪʃn] *n* oculista *mf*; **~'s** óptica *f*.

optimism ['ɒptɪmɪzml] *n* (U) otimismo *m*.

optimist ['ɒptɪmɪst] *n* otimista *mf*.

optimistic [,ɒptɪ'mɪstɪk] *adj* otimista; **to be ~ about sthg** ser/estar otimista sobre algo.

optimize, -ise ['ɒptɪmaɪz] *vt* otimizar.

optimum ['ɒptɪməm] *adj* ótimo(ma).

option ['ɒpʃn] *n* [choice] opção *f*; **to have the ~ to**
do *OR* of doing sthg ter a opção de fazer algo.

optional ['ɒpʃənl] *adj* opcional.

opulence ['ɒpjʊləns] *n* (U) opulência *f*.

opulent ['ɒpjʊlənt] *adj* opulento(ta).

opus ['əʊpəs] (*pl* -es *OR* opera) *n MUS* opus *m*.

or [ɔːʳ] *conj* **-1.** [gen] ou **-2.** [after negative] nem; **he can't read ~ write** ele não sabe ler nem escrever **-3.** [otherwise] senão; **I'd better go now ~ I'll miss my plane** acho melhor eu ir logo, senão vou perder o vôo.

OR *abbr of* Oregon.

oracle ['ɒrəkl] *n* [prophet] oráculo *m*.

oral ['ɔːrəl] <> *adj* **-1.** [spoken] oral **-2.** [relating to the mouth] bucal. <> *n* exame *m* oral.

orally ['ɔːrəlɪ] *adv* **-1.** [in spoken form] oralmente **-2.** [via the mouth] por via oral.

orange ['ɒrɪndʒ] <> *adj* [colour] laranja. <> *n* **-1.** [fruit] laranja *f* **-2.** (U) [colour] laranja *m inv*.

orangeade [,ɒrɪndʒ'eɪd] *n* laranjada *f*.

orange blossom *n* [flowers] flor *f* de laranjeira.

orange juice *n* suco *m* de laranja.

Orangeman ['ɒrɪndʒmən] (*pl* -men [-mən]) *n UK* orangista *mf*.

orange tree *n* laranjeira *f*.

orangutang [ɔː,ræŋu'tæŋ] *n* orangotango *m*.

oration [ɔː'reɪʃn] *n fml* discurso *m*.

orator ['ɒrətəʳ] *n* orador *m*, -ra *f*.

oratorio [,ɒrə'tɔːrɪəʊ] (*pl* -s) *n* oratório *m*.

oratory ['ɒrətrɪ] *n* **-1.** [eloquence] oratória *f* **-2.** [prayer room] oratório *m*.

orb [ɔːb] *n* **-1.** [sphere] orbe *m* **-2.** [ornamental ball] esfera *f*.

orbit ['ɔːbɪt] <> *n* órbita *f*; **to be in/go into ~ (around sthg)** estar/entrar em órbita (ao redor de algo); **to put sthg into ~ (around sthg)** pôr algo em órbita (ao redor de algo). <> *vt* orbitar.

orbital road *n UK* estrada *que circunda uma cidade.*

orchard ['ɔːtʃəd] *n* pomar *m*.

orchestra ['ɔːkɪstrə] *n* orquestra *f*.

orchestral [ɔː'kestrəl] *adj* orquestral.

orchestra pit *n* fosso *m* da orquestra.

orchestrate ['ɔːkɪstreɪt] *vt* **-1.** *MUS* orquestrar **-2.** *fig* [organize] osquestrar.

orchestration [,ɔːke'streɪʃn] *n MUS & fig* orquestração *f*.

orchid ['ɔːkɪd] *n* orquídea *f*.

ordain [ɔː'deɪn] *vt* **-1.** *fml* [decree] ordenar, decretar **-2.** *RELIG*: **to be ~ed** ser ordenado(da).

ordeal [ɔː'diːl] *n* experiência *f* traumática, provação *f*.

order ['ɔːdəʳ] <> *n* **-1.** [gen] ordem *f*; **to be under ~s to do sthg** receber ordens para fazer algo; **in ~** em ordem; **in working ~** em funcionamento; **to be out of ~** [not working] estar fora de operação, não estar funcionando; [in meeting, debate] agir de forma inaceitável; [behaviour] ser improcedente; **to keep ~** manter a ordem **-2.** *COMM* [request] pedido *m*; **to place an ~ with sb for sthg** encomendar algo com alguém; **on ~** reservado(da); **to ~** sob encomenda **-3.** *US* [portion] porção *f*. <> *vt* **-1.** [command] ordenar; **to ~ sb to do sthg** ordenar alguém a fazer algo; **to ~ that** ordenar que **-2.** [request - drink, food, shopping item] pedir; [- taxi] chamar. ⋄ *vi* pedir, fazer o pedido *(em restaurante)*.

➡ **orders** *npl RELIG:* **(holy)** ~s ordens *fpl* (sagradas).

➡ **in the order of** *UK,* **on the order of** *US prep* da ordem de.

➡ **in order that** *conj* a fim de que, para que.

➡ **in order to** *conj* para.

➡ **order about, order around** *vt sep:* **he's always** ~**ing people about** ele está sempre mandando nas pessoas.

order book *n* livro *m* de encomendas.
order form *n* formulário *m* de encomenda.
orderly ['ɔ:dəlɪ] *(pl* **-ies)** ⋄ *adj* **-1.** [person] obediente **-2.** [room, office] ordenado(da). ⋄ *n* [in hospital] assistente *mf.*
order number *n* número *m* do pedido.
ordinal ['ɔ:dɪnl] ⋄ *adj* ordinal. ⋄ *n* ordinal *m.*
ordinarily ['ɔ:dənrəlɪ] *adv* [normally] geralmente.
ordinary ['ɔ:dənrɪ] ⋄ *adj* **-1.** [normal] comum, normal **-2.** *pej* [unexceptional] medíocre. ⋄ *n:* **out of the** ~ fora do comum.
ordinary level *n UK* nível *m* fundamental *(na escola).*
ordinary seaman *n UK* marinheiro *m.*
ordinary shares *npl UK FIN* ações *fpl* ordinárias.
ordination [,ɔ:dɪ'neɪʃn] *n (U)* ordenação *f.*
ordnance ['ɔ:dnəns] *n* **-1.** [military supplies] arsenal *f* bélico **-2.** [artillery] artilharia *f.*
Ordnance Survey *n UK* & *Irish* serviço oficial de topografia e cartografia.
ore [ɔ:ʳ] *n* minério *m.*
oregano [,ɒrɪ'gɑ:nəʊ] *n (U)* orégano *m.*
Oregon ['ɒrɪgən] *n* Oregon; **in** ~ no Oregon.
organ ['ɔ:gən] *n* **-1.** [gen] órgão *m* **-2.** *fig* [mouthpiece] órgão *m.*
organic [ɔ:'gænɪk] *adj* orgânico(ca).
organically [ɔ:'gænɪklɪ] *adv AGR* organicamente.
organic chemistry *n (U)* química *f* orgânica.
organism ['ɔ:gənɪzm] *n BIOL* organismo *m.*
organist ['ɔ:gənɪst] *n* organista *mf.*
organization [,ɔ:gənaɪ'zeɪʃn] *n* organização *f.*
organization chart *n* organograma *m.*
organizational [,ɔ:gənaɪ'zeɪʃnl] *adj* organizacional.
organize, -ise ['ɔ:gənaɪz] ⋄ *vt* organizar. ⋄ *vi* organizar-se.
organized ['ɔ:gənaɪzd] *adj* organizado(da).
organized crime *n (U)* crime *m* organizado.
organized labour *n (U)* mão-de-obra *f* sindicalizada.
organizer ['ɔ:gənaɪzəʳ] *n* [person] organizador *m,* -ra *f.*
organza [ɔ:'gænzə] *n (U)* organza *f.*
orgasm ['ɔ:gæzm] *n* orgasmo *m.*
orgy ['ɔ:dʒɪ] *(pl* **-ies)** *n* orgia *f.*
orient ['ɔ:rɪənt] *vt esp US* = **orientate.**
Orient ['ɔ:rɪənt] *n:* **the** ~ o Oriente.
oriental [,ɔ:rɪ'entl] ⋄ *adj* oriental. ⋄ *n* [non-PC term for East-Asian] oriental *mf.*
orientate ['ɔ:rɪənteɪt] *vt:* **to be** ~**d towards sb/**

sthg ser orientado(da) para alguém/algo; **to** ~ **o.s.** orientar-se.
orientation [,ɔ:rɪen'teɪʃn] *n (U)* orientação *f.*
orienteering [,ɔ:rɪən'tɪərɪŋ] *n (U) esporte no qual as pessoas utilizam um mapa e uma bússola para se orientar,* corrida *f* de orientação.
orifice ['ɒrɪfɪs] *n* orifício *m.*
origami [,ɒrɪ'gɑ:mɪ] *n (U)* origami *m.*
origin ['ɒrɪdʒɪn] *n* origem *f;* **country of** ~ país *m* de origem.
➡ **origins** *npl* origens *fpl.*
original [ə'rɪdʒənl] ⋄ *adj* original. ⋄ *n* original *m.*
originality [ə,rɪdʒə'nælətɪ] *n (U)* originalidade *f.*
originally [ə'rɪdʒənəlɪ] *adv* [initially] originalmente.
original sin *n (U)* pecado *m* original.
originate [ə'rɪdʒəneɪt] ⋄ *vt* originar, produzir. ⋄ *vi:* **to** ~ **(in)** originar-se (em), surgir (de); **to** ~ **from** originar-se de.
origination *n (U)* [invention, creation] origem *f,* criação *f.*
originator [ə'rɪdʒəneɪtəʳ] *n* autor *m,* -ra *f,* inventor *m,* -ra *f.*
Orinoco [,ɒrɪ'nəʊkəʊ] *n:* **the (River)** ~ o (Rio) Orinoco.
Orkney Islands ['ɔ:knɪ-], **Orkneys** ['ɔ:knɪz] *npl:* **the** ~ as Ilhas Órcadas; **in the** ~ nas Ilhas Órcadas.
ornament ['ɔ:nəmənt] *n* ornamento *m.*
ornamental [,ɔ:nə'mentl] *adj* ornamental.
ornamentation [,ɔ:nəmen'teɪʃn] *n (U)* ornamentação *f.*
ornate [ɔ:'neɪt] *adj* ornado(da).
ornately [ɔ:'neɪtlɪ] *adv* vistosamente, de forma requintada.
ornery ['ɔ:nərɪ] *adj US inf* genioso(sa).
ornithologist [,ɔ:nɪ'θɒlədʒɪst] *n* ornitólogo *m,* -ga *f.*
ornithology [,ɔ:nɪ'θɒlədʒɪ] *n (U)* ornitologia *f.*
orphan ['ɔ:fn] ⋄ *n* órfão *m,* -fã *f.* ⋄ *vt:* **to be** ~**ed** ficar órfão(fã).
orphanage ['ɔ:fənɪdʒ] *n* orfanato *m.*
orthodontist [,ɔ:θə'dɒntɪst] *n* ortodontista *mf.*
orthodox ['ɔ:θədɒks] *adj* ortodoxo(xa).
Orthodox Church *n:* **the** ~ a Igreja Ortodoxa.
orthodoxy ['ɔ:θədɒksɪ] *n* ortodoxia *f.*
orthopaedic [,ɔ:θə'pi:dɪk] *adj* ortopédico(ca).
orthopaedics [,ɔ:θə'pi:dɪks] *n (U)* ortopedia *f.*
orthopaedist [,ɔ:θə'pi:dɪst] *n* ortopedista *mf.*
orthopedic etc [,ɔ:θə'pi:dɪk] *adj* = **orthopaedic etc.**
OS ⋄ *n* (abbr of **Ordnance Survey**) *organização oficial britânica que elabora mapas detalhados da Grã-Bretanha e da Irlanda.* ⋄ **-1.** (abbr of **outsize**) GGG **-2.** (abbr of **out of stock**) fora de estoque.
Oscar ['ɒskəʳ] *n CINEMA* Oscar *m.*
oscillate ['ɒsɪleɪt] *vi* **-1.** [from side to side] oscilar **-2.** *fig* [vacillate]: **to** ~ **between** oscilar entre.
oscilloscope [ɒ'sɪləskəʊp] *n* osciloscópio *m.*
OSD (abbr of **optical scanning device**) *n* OSD *m.*
OSHA (abbr of **Occupational Safety and Health**

Administration) *n* órgão norte-americano responsável pela saúde e pela segurança no trabalho.

Oslo ['ɒzləʊ] *n* Oslo; **in** ~ em Oslo.

osmosis [ɒz'məʊsɪs] *n (U)* osmose *f*.

osprey ['ɒsprɪ] (*pl* **-s**) *n* gavião-pescador *m*.

Ostend [ɒs'tend] *n* Ostend; **in** ~ em Ostend.

ostensible [ɒ'stensəbl] *adj* ostensivo(va).

ostensibly [ɒ'stensəblɪ] *adv* ostensivamente.

ostentation [ˌɒsten'teɪʃn] *n (U)* ostentação *f*.

ostentatious [ˌɒsten'teɪʃəs] *adj* ostentoso(sa).

osteoarthritis [ˌɒstɪəʊɑː'θraɪtɪs] *n (U)* osteoartrite *f*.

osteopath ['ɒstɪəpæθ] *n* osteopático *m*, **-ca** *f*.

osteopathy [ˌɒstɪ'ɒpəθɪ] *n* osteopatia *f*.

ostracize, -ise ['ɒstrəsaɪz] *vt* condenar ao ostracismo.

ostrich ['ɒstrɪtʃ] *n* avestruz *mf*.

OT *n* **-1.** (*abbr of* **Old Testament**) AT *m* **-2.** (*abbr of* **occupational therapy**) TO *f*.

OTC (*abbr of* **Officer Training Corps**) *n* unidade de formação de oficiais da reserva do exército britânico.

OTE (*abbr of* **on target earnings**) prêmios obtidos mediante cumprimento de objetivos.

other ['ʌðəʳ] ⟨⟩ *adj* **-1.** [gen] outro(tra); **the** ~ **one** o outro, a outra **-2.** *phr*: **the** ~ **day** no outro dia; **the** ~ **week** na outra semana. ⟨⟩ *adv* : ~ **than** a não ser; **to be none** ~ **than** ser nem mais nem menos que. ⟨⟩ *pron*: **the** ~ o outro, a outra; ~**s** outros(tras); **the** ~**s** os outros, as outras; **one after the** ~ um atrás do outro, uma atrás da outra; **one or** ~ **of you must help me** um de vocês dois deve me ajudar.

⇒ **something or other** *pron* uma coisa ou outra.

⇒ **somehow or other** *adv* de um jeito ou de outro.

otherwise ['ʌðəwaɪz] ⟨⟩ *adv* **-1.** [apart from that] de resto, tirando isso **-2.** [differently, in a different way] de outra maneira; **deliberately or** ~ intencionalmente ou não. ⟨⟩ *conj* [or else] senão, do contrário.

other world *n*: **the** ~ o outro mundo.

otherworldly [ˌʌðə'wɜːldlɪ] *adj* místico(ca), espiritual.

OTT (*abbr of* **over the top**) *adj UK inf* além dos limites; **it's a bit** ~ está um pouco além dos limites.

Ottawa ['ɒtəwə] *n* Ottawa; **in** ~ em Ottawa.

otter ['ɒtəʳ] *n* lontra *f*.

OU (*abbr of* **Open University**) *n* universidade *f* aberta.

ouch [aʊtʃ] *excl* ai!

ought [ɔːt] *aux vb* dever; **I really** ~ **to go** eu realmente deveria ir; **you** ~ **not to have done that** você não deveria ter feito isso; **she** ~ **to pass her exam** ela tem chance de passar no exame.

oughtn't [ɔːtnt] *cont* = **ought not**.

Ouija board® ['wiːdʒə-] *n* ≃ jogo *m* do copo.

ounce [aʊns] *n* **-1.** [unit of measurement] onça *f* **-2.** *fig* [small amount]: **an** ~ **of**, um pouco de.

our ['aʊəʳ] *poss adj* nosso(a); ~ **books** os nossos livros.

ours ['aʊəz] *poss pron* o nosso (a nossa); **a friend of** ~ um amigo nosso; **those shoes are** ~ estes sapatos são (os) nossos; ~ **are here - where are yours?** os nossos estão aqui - onde estão os seus?

ourselves [aʊə'selvz] *pron pl* **-1.** (*reflexive*) nos **-2.** (*after prep*) nós mesmos(mas), nós próprios(prias); **we did it** ~ nós mesmos *OR* próprios o fizemos.

oust [aʊst] *vt fml*: **to** ~ **sb (from sthg)** expulsar alguém (de algo).

ouster ['aʊstəʳ] *n US* **-1.** [from country] expulsão *f* **-2.** [from office] destituição *f*.

out [aʊt] ⟨⟩ *adj* [light, cigarette] apagado(da); [not in fashion] fora de moda; **cargo pants are so** ~ **as** calças cargo estão tão fora de moda. ⟨⟩ *adv* **-1.** [outside] fora; **to get/go** ~ **(of)** sair (de); **it's cold** ~ **today** está frio lá fora hoje; **he looked** ~ ele olhou para fora. **-2.** [not at home, work] fora; **to be** ~ não estar em casa; **to go** ~ sair. **-3.** [so as to be extinguished]: **to turn sthg** ~ apagar algo; **put your cigarette** ~ apague o cigarro. **-4.** [expressing removal]: **to pour sthg** ~ despejar algo, jogar algo fora; **to take money** ~ [from cashpoint] retirar dinheiro; **to take sthg** ~ **(of)** tirar algo (de). **-5.** [outwards]: **to stick** ~ sobressair. **-6.** [expressing distribution]: **to hand sthg** ~ distribuir algo. **-7.** [in phrases]: **to get enjoyment** ~ **of sthg** divertir-se com algo; **stay** ~ **of the sun** não se exponha ao sol; **made** ~ **of wood** (feito) de madeira; **five** ~ **of ten women** cinco em cada dez mulheres; **I'm** ~ **of cigarettes** não tenho cigarros.

out-and-out *adj* completo(ta), absoluto(ta).

outback ['aʊtbæk] *n*: **the** ~ o interior da Austrália.

outbid [ˌaʊt'bɪd] (*pt* & *pp* **outbid**, *cont* **-ding**) *vt*: **to** ~ **sb (for sthg)** sobrepujar alguém (em algo).

outboard (motor) ['aʊtbɔːd-] *n* motor *m* de popa.

outbound ['aʊtbaʊnd] *adj* **-1.** [train, flight] de ida **-2.** [traffic] de saída.

outbreak ['aʊtbreɪk] *n* **-1.** [of crime, violence] explosão *f* **-2.** [of disease] surto *m* **-3.** [of war] deflagração *f*.

outbuildings ['aʊtbɪldɪŋz] *npl* dependências *fpl*.

outburst ['aʊtbɜːst] *n* **-1.** [of emotion] manifestação *f* **-2.** [sudden occurrence] explosão *f*.

outcast ['aʊtkɑːst] *n* rejeitado *m*, **-da** *f*.

outclass [ˌaʊt'klɑːs] *vt* exceder, ultrapassar.

outcome ['aʊtkʌm] *n* resultado *m*.

outcrop ['aʊtkrɒp] *n* afloramento *m*.

outcry ['aʊtkraɪ] (*pl* **-ies**) *n* protestos *mpl*.

outdated [ˌaʊt'deɪtɪd] *adj* ultrapassado(da), fora de moda.

outdid [ˌaʊt'dɪd] *pt* ▷ **outdo**.

outdistance [ˌaʊt'dɪstəns] *vt* **-1.** [in race] deixar para trás **-2.** *fig* [in business, development] ultrapassar.

outdo [ˌaʊt'duː] (*pt* **-did**, *pp* **-done** [-dʌn]) *vt* ultrapassar, superar.

outdoor ['aʊtdɔːʳ] *adj* ao ar livre.

outdoors [aʊt'dɔːz] *adv* ao ar livre; **let's eat** ~ vamos comer fora.

outer [ˈaʊtəʳ] *adj* externo(na); **Outer London** a Grande Londres.

outermost [ˈaʊtəməʊst] *adj* mais externo(na); **~ planet of the solar system** o planeta mais afastado do sistema solar.

outer space *n* (U) espaço *m* exterior.

outerwear *n* roupa *f* de cima.

outfit [ˈaʊtfɪt] *n* **-1.** [clothes] vestimenta *f*; [fancy dress] traje *m* **-2.** *inf* [organization] agrupamento *m*, grupo *m*.

outfitters [ˈaʊtˌfɪtəz] *n* UK dated confecção *f*.

outflank [ˌaʊtˈflæŋk] *vt* **-1.** MIL surpreender pela retaguarda **-2.** *fig* [in argument, business] superar.

outgoing [ˈaʊtˌɡəʊɪŋ] *adj* **-1.** [leaving] de partida **-2.** [friendly, sociable] extrovertido(da), aberto(ta).

➤ **outgoings** *npl* UK despesas *fpl*.

outgrow [ˌaʊtˈɡrəʊ] (*pt* -grew, *pp* -grown) *vt* **-1.** [grow too big for]: **he has ~n his shirts** as camisas ficaram pequenas para ele **-2.** [grow too old for] ser muito grande para.

outhouse [ˈaʊthaʊs, *pl* -haʊzɪz] *n* dependência *f*.

outing [ˈaʊtɪŋ] *n* **-1.** [trip] excursão *f* **-2.** (U) [of homosexuals] *revelação da homossexualidade de uma pessoa famosa*.

outlandish [aʊtˈlændɪʃ] *adj* estranho(nha), extravagante.

outlast [ˌaʊtˈlɑːst] *vt* sobreviver a, durar mais tempo que.

outlaw [ˈaʊtlɔː] ◇ *n* fora-da-lei *mf*. ◇ *vt* **-1.** [make illegal] declarar ilegal **-2.** [declare an outlaw] proscrever.

outlay [ˈaʊtleɪ] *n* despesa *f*, desembolso *m*.

outlet [ˈaʊtlet] *n* **-1.** [for feelings] escape *m* **-2.** [hole, pipe] saída *f* **-3.** [shop] ponto *m* de venda **-4.** US ELEC tomada *f*.

outline [ˈaʊtlaɪn] ◇ *n* **-1.** [brief description] linhas *fpl* gerais, esboço *m*; **in ~** em linhas gerais **-2.** [silhouette] contorno *m*. ◇ *vt* **-1.** [describe briefly] resumir, esboçar **-2.** [silhouette]: **to be ~d against sthg** delinear-se contra algo.

outlive [ˌaʊtˈlɪv] *vt* **-1.** [subj: person] viver mais que **-2.** *fig* [subj: idea, object] sobreviver.

outlook [ˈaʊtlʊk] *n* **-1.** [attitude, disposition] postura *f*, atitude *f* **-2.** [prospect] perspectiva *f*.

outlying [ˈaʊtˌlaɪɪŋ] *adj* distante, remoto(ta).

outmanoeuvre *UK*, **outmaneuver** *US* [ˌaʊtməˈnuːvəʳ] *vt* passar a perna em.

outmoded [ˌaʊtˈməʊdɪd] *adj* antiquado(da), fora de moda.

outnumber [ˌaʊtˈnʌmbəʳ] *vt* exceder em número.

out-of-date *adj* **-1.** [passport, season ticket] expirado(da) **-2.** [clothes, belief] antiquado(da).

out of doors *adv* ao ar livre.

out-of-the-way *adj* [isolated] remoto(ta).

outpace [ˌaʊtˈpeɪs] *vt* **-1.** [subj: person] deixar para trás **-2.** *fig* [subj: technology] deixar para trás.

outpatient [ˈaʊtˌpeɪʃnt] *n* paciente *mf* ambulatorial.

outplacement *n* COMM recolocação *f (em outra empresa)*.

outplay [ˌaʊtˈpleɪ] *vt* SPORT superar, jogar melhor que.

outpost [ˈaʊtpəʊst] *n* *fig* [bastion] posto *m* avançado.

outpouring [ˈaʊtˌpɔːrɪŋ] *literary n* efusão *f*.

output [ˈaʊtpʊt] ◇ *n* **-1.** [production] produção *f* **-2.** [COMPUT - printing out] saída *f*; [- printout] cópia *f* impressa. ◇ *vt* COMPUT gerar como saída.

outrage [ˈaʊtreɪdʒ] ◇ *n* **-1.** (U) [anger, shock] indignidade *f* **-2.** [atrocity] atrocidade *f*, ultraje *m*. ◇ *vt* ultrajar.

outraged [ˈaʊtreɪdʒd] *adj* indignado(da).

outrageous [aʊtˈreɪdʒəs] *adj* **-1.** [offensive, shocking] ultrajante **-2.** [extravagant, wild] extravagante.

outran [ˌaʊtˈræn] *pt* ➞ **outrun**.

outrank [ˌaʊtˈræŋk] *vt* exceder em hierarquia.

outrider [ˈaʊtˌraɪdəʳ] *n* escolta *f*.

outright [*adj* ˈaʊtraɪt, *adv* ˌaʊtˈraɪt] ◇ *adj* **-1.** [categoric, direct] claro(ra), categórico(ca) **-2.** [total, complete - disaster] completo(ta); [- victory, winner] indiscutível. ◇ *adv* **-1.** [ask] abertamente, francamente **-2.** [win, fail] indiscutivelmente, completamente **-3.** [deny] categoricamente **-4.** [be killed]: **to be killed ~** morrer no ato.

outrun [ˌaʊtˈrʌn] (*pt* -ran, *pp* -run, *cont* -ning) *vt* correr mais que.

outsell [ˌaʊtˈsell] (*pt* & *pp* -sold) *vt* vender mais que.

outset [ˈaʊtset] *n*: **at the ~** no princípio; **from the ~** desde o princípio.

outshine [ˌaʊtˈʃaɪn] (*pt* & *pp* -shone [-ʃɒn]) *vt* [do better than] eclipsar.

outside [*adv* ˌaʊtˈsaɪd, *adj*, *prep* & *n* ˈaʊtsaɪd] ◇ *adj* **-1.** [gen] externo(na) **-2.** [unlikely] remoto(ta). ◇ *adv* [lá] fora; **to look ~** olhar para fora; **to run ~** correr lá fora; **to go ~** ir lá para fora. ◇ *prep* **-1.** [not inside] fora de; **we live half an hour ~ London** moramos a meia hora de Londres **-2.** [beyond] além de. ◇ *n* **-1.** [exterior] exterior *m* **-2.** [limit]: **at the ~** no máximo.

➤ **outside of** *prep* US [apart from] exceto.

outside broadcast *n* UK RADIO & TV (transmissão *f*) externa *f*.

outside lane *n* AUT **-1.** [in UK] faixa *f* da direita **-2.** [in mainland Europe, US, Brazil etc] faixa *f* da esquerda.

outside line *n* linha *f* externa.

outsider [ˌaʊtˈsaɪdəʳ] *n* **-1.** SPORT azarão *m* **-2.** [from outside social group] estranho *m*, -nha *f*, desconhecido *m*, -da *f*.

outsize [ˈaʊtsaɪz] *adj* **-1.** [book, portion] enorme **-2.** [clothes] extra-grande.

outsized [ˈaʊtsaɪzd] *adj* enorme.

outskirts [ˈaʊtskɜːts] *npl*: **the ~** os arredores.

outsmart [ˌaʊtˈsmɑːt] *vt* passar a perna em.

outsold [ˌaʊtˈsəʊld] *pt* & *pp* ➞ **outsell**.

outsource [ˈaʊtsɔːs] *vt* COMM terceirizar.

outsourcing [ˈaʊtsɔːsɪŋ] *n* COMM terceirização *f*.

outspoken [ˌaʊtˈspəʊkn] *adj* franco(ca).

outspread [ˌaʊtˈspred] *adj* estendido(da).

outstanding [ˌaʊtˈstændɪŋ] *adj* **-1.** [excellent] destacado(da), notável **-2.** [very obvious, important] notável **-3.** [pending] pendente.

outstay [ˌaʊtˈsteɪ] *vt*: **to ~ one's welcome** abusar da hospitalidade de alguém.

outstretched [ˌaʊt'stretʃt] *adj* estendido(da).

outstrip [ˌaʊt'strɪp] (*pt* & *pp* **-ped**, *cont* **-ping**) *vt* **-1.** [do better than] superar **- 2.** [run faster than] ultrapassar, deixar para trás.

out-take *n* **- 1.** CINEMA sobras *fpl* de filme **- 2.** TV sobras *fpl* de programa.

out-tray *n* bandeja *f* de saída.

outvote [ˌaʊt'vəʊt] *vt* : **to ~ sb** vencer alguém por receber mais votos; **the proposal was ~d by fifty to forty (votes)** a proposta foi derrotada por cinqüenta (votos) a quarenta.

outward ['aʊtwəd] <> *adj* **-1.** [going away] de ida **- 2.** [apparent] aparente **- 3.** [visible] visível. <> *adv* US = outwards.

outwardly ['aʊtwədlɪ] *adv* [apparently] aparentemente.

outwards UK ['aʊtwədz], **outward** US *adv* para fora.

outweigh [ˌaʊt'weɪ] *vt* pesar mais que.

outwit [ˌaʊt'wɪt] (*pt* & *pp* **-ted**, *cont* **-ting**) *vt* ser mais esperto(ta) que.

outworker ['aʊtˌwɜːkəʳ] *n* colaborador *m* externo, colaboradora *f* externa.

oval ['əʊvl] <> *adj* oval. <> *n* oval *m*.

Oval Office *n*: **the ~** o Salão Oval.

ovarian [əʊ'veərɪən] *adj* ovariano(na); **~ cancer** câncer de ovário.

ovary ['əʊvərɪ] (*pl* **-ies**) *n* ANAT ovário *m*.

ovation [əʊ'veɪʃn] *novação f*; **a standing ~** ovação com o público de pé.

oven ['ʌvn] *n* [for cooking] forno *m*.

oven glove *n* luva *f* para o forno.

ovenproof ['ʌvnpruːf] *adj* refratário(ria).

oven-ready *adj* pronto(ta) para ir ao forno.

ovenware ['ʌvnweəʳ] *n* (U) louça *f* refratária.

over ['əʊvəʳ] <> *prep* **-1.** [gen] sobre; **put your coat ~ that chair** ponha o seu casaco naquela cadeira; **to rule ~ a country** governar um país **- 2.** [directly above] sobre, em cima de **- 3.** [on the far side of] ao outro lado de **- 4.** [across the surface of] por; **she walked ~ the lawn** ela caminhou pelo gramado **- 5.** [across the top or edge of] por cima de **- 6.** [more than] mais de; **~ and above** bem acima de **- 7.** [by means of] por **- 8.** [concerning, due to] por; **it was a fight ~ a woman, I think** era uma disputa por uma mulher, acho eu **- 9.** [during] durante **-10.** [recovered from] recuperado(da) (de). <> *adv* **-1.** [distance away] lá; **~ here/there** por aqui, lá **- 2.** [across]: **to cross ~** cruzar; **they flew ~ to America** eles voaram para a América; **~ at mum's** na casa da minha mãe; **to ask sb ~** convidar alguém para ir lá em casa **- 3.** [to the ground] para baixo **- 4.** [to face a different way]: **to turn sth ~** virar algo **- 5.** [more] mais **- 6.** [remaining]: **that leaves £2 ~** isso nos sobra £2; **I ate the piece of cake left ~** comi o pedaço de bolo que sobrou **- 7.** RADIO câmbio; **~ and out!** câmbio e desligo! **- 8.** [involving repetitions]: **(all) ~ again** (tudo) novamente; **~ and ~ (again)** várias e várias vezes. <> *adj* [finished] acabado(da); **the meeting was ~ by seven** a reunião acabou às sete horas. <> *n* UK [cricket] *série de seis lançamentos de um único jogador.*

➡ all over <> *prep* por todo(da). <> *adv*

[everywhere] por todas as partes. <> *adj* [finished] acabado(da).

over- ['əʊvəʳ] *prefix* muito, sobre-.

overabundance [ˌəʊvərə'bʌndəns] *n* (U) superabundância *f*.

overact [ˌəʊvər'ækt] *vi pej* [in play] exagerar na atuação.

overactive [ˌəʊvər'æktɪv] *adj* muito ativo(va).

overall [*adj* & *n* 'əʊvərɔːl, *adv* ˌəʊvər'ɔːl] <> *adj* [total] global, total. <> *adv* **-1.** [in total] no geral **- 2.** [in general] normalmente, em geral. <> *n* **-1.** [coat] avental *m*, guarda-pó *m* **- 2.** US [with trousers] macacão *m*.

➡ overalls *npl* macacão *m*.

overambitious [ˌəʊvəræm'bɪʃəs] *adj* muito ambicioso(sa).

overanxious [ˌəʊvər'æŋkʃəs] *adj* muito nervoso(-sa).

overarm ['əʊvərɑːm] <> *adj* por cima do ombro. <> *adv* por cima do ombro.

overate [ˌəʊvər'et] *pt* ▷ **overeat**.

overawe [ˌəʊvər'ɔː] *vt* intimidar.

overbalance [ˌəʊvə'bæləns] *vi* perder o equilíbrio.

overbearing [ˌəʊvə'beərɪŋ] *adj pej* arrogante.

overblown [ˌəʊvə'bləʊn] *adj pej* exagerado(da).

overboard ['əʊvəbɔːd] *adv* **-1.** NAUT: **to fall ~** cair ao mar **- 2.** *fig*: **to go ~ (about sb/sthg)** [be overenthusiastic about] empolgar-se (com alguém/algo).

overbook [ˌəʊvə'bʊk] *vi* ter mais reservas que lugares; **the plane was ~** deu overbook no avião.

overburden [ˌəʊvə'bɜːdn] *vt*: **to be ~ed with sthg** estar sobrecarregado(da) de algo.

overcame [ˌəʊvə'keɪm] *pt* ▷ **overcome**.

overcapitalize, -ise [ˌəʊvə'kæpɪtəlaɪz] *vi* FIN sobrecapitalizar.

overcast ['əʊvəkɑːst] *adj* carregado(da), nublado(da).

overcharge [ˌəʊvə'tʃɑːdʒ] <> *vt*: **to ~ sb (for sthg)** cobrar de alguém em excesso (por algo). <> *vi*: **to ~ (for sthg)** cobrar em excesso (por algo).

overcoat ['əʊvəkəʊt] *n* sobretudo *m*.

overcome [ˌəʊvə'kʌm] (*pt* **-came**, *pp* **-come**) *vt* **-1.** [control, deal with] superar, vencer **- 2.** [overwhelm]: **to be ~ (by OR with sthg)** [emotion] estar tomado(da) (por algo); [smoke, fumes] estar asfixiado(da) (por algo).

overcompensate [ˌəʊvə'kɒmpənseɪt] *vi*: **to ~ (for sthg)** compensar em excesso (por algo).

overconfident [ˌəʊvə'kɒnfɪdənt] *adj* confiante em excesso.

overcooked *adj* cozido(da) demais.

overcrowded [ˌəʊvə'kraʊdɪd] *adj* **-1.** [room, building] superlotado(da) **- 2.** [city, country] superpovoado(da).

overcrowding [ˌəʊvə'kraʊdɪŋ] *n* **-1.** (U) [of room, building] superlotação *f* **- 2.** (U) [of city, country] superpovoamento *m*.

overdeveloped [ˌəʊvədə'veləpt] *adj* **-1.** PHOT submetido a longo tempo de revelação **- 2.** [exaggerated] exagerado(da).

overdo [ˌəʊvə'duː] (*pt* **-did** [-dɪd], *pp* **-done**) *vt* **-1.** *pej* [exaggerate] exagerar - **2.** [do too much]: **to ~ the walking** caminhar demais; **the doctor told her not to ~ it** o médico disse para ela pegar leve OR não exagerar - **3.** [overcook] cozinhar demais.

overdone [ˌəʊvəˈdʌn] <> pp ▷ **overdo.** <> adj: **it's ~** cozinhou demais.

overdose [n 'əʊvədəʊs , vb əʊvə'dəʊs] <> n overdose f. <> vi: **to ~ on sthg** tomar uma overdose de algo.

overdraft ['əʊvədrɑːft] n saldo m negativo.

overdrawn [ˌəʊvə'drɔːn] adj - **1.** [person]: **to be ~** ter saldo negativo - **2.** [account] no negativo.

overdress [ˌəʊvə'dres] vi arrumar-se demais.

overdrive ['əʊvədraɪv] n (U) fig: **to go into ~** trabalhar a todo vapor.

overdue [ˌəʊvə'djuː] adj - **1.** [gen] atrasado(da); **I'm ~ for a dental checkup** já está na hora de eu fazer a revisão no dentista - **2.** [needed, awaited]: **(long) ~** (há muito) esperado(da).

overeager [ˌəʊvər'iːgəʳ] adj ansioso(sa) demais.

over easy adj US CULIN: **eggs ~** ovos mpl fritos (dos dois lados).

overeat [ˌəʊvər'iːt] (pt -ate, pp -eaten) vi comer demais, atracar-se.

overemphasize, -ise [ˌəʊvər'emfəsaɪz] vt enfatizar demais.

overenthusiastic ['əʊvərɪnˌθjuːzɪ'æstɪk] adj entusiasta demais.

overestimate [ˌəʊvər'estɪmeɪt] vt superestimar.

overexcited [ˌəʊvərɪk'saɪtɪd] adj sobreexaltado(-da).

overexpose [ˌəʊvərɪk'spəʊz] vt PHOT superexpor.

overfeed [ˌəʊvə'fiːd] (pt & pp -fed [-fed]) vt superalimentar.

overfill [ˌəʊvə'fɪl] vt encher demais.

overflow [vb ˌəʊvə'fləʊ, n 'əʊvəfləʊ] <> vi transbordar; **to be ~ing (with sthg)** estar transbordando (de algo); **full to ~ing** entupido(da). <> vt transbordar. <> n ladrão m.

overgrown [ˌəʊvə'grəʊn] adj coberto(ta) de mato.

overhang [n 'əʊvəhæŋ, vb əʊvə'hæŋ] (pt & pp -hung) <> n saliência f. <> vt sobressair-se de, projetar-se de. <> vi sobressair, projetar.

overhaul [n 'əʊvəhɔːl, vb ˌəʊvə'hɔːl] <> n revisão f. <> vt - **1.** [service] fazer a revisão de - **2.** [revise] revisar.

overhead [adv ˌəʊvə'hed, adj & n 'əʊvəhed] <> adj aéreo(rea). <> adv por cima, pelo alto. <> n US despesas fpl gerais, gastos mpl gerais.

➡ **overheads** npl UK despesas fpl gerais, gastos mpl gerais.

overhead projector n retroprojetor m.

overhear [ˌəʊvə'hɪəʳ] (pt & pp -heard [-hɜːd]) vt entreouvir.

overheat [ˌəʊvə'hiːt] <> vt superaquecer. <> vi superaquecer-se.

overhung [ˌəʊvə'hʌŋ] pt & pp ▷ **overhang.**

overindulge [ˌəʊvərɪn'dʌldʒ] <> vt ser indulgente demais com, mimar demais. <> vi: **to ~ (in sthg)** abusar (com algo).

overjoyed [ˌəʊvə'dʒɔɪd] adj: **to be ~ (at sthg)** estar contentíssimo(ma) (com algo).

overkill ['əʊvəkɪl] n (U) exagero m.

overladen [ˌəʊvə'leɪdn] <> pp ▷ **overload.** <> adj sobrecarregado(da).

overlaid [ˌəʊvə'leɪd] pt & pp ▷ **overlay.**

overland ['əʊvəlænd] <> adj terrestre. <> adv por terra.

overlap [n 'əʊvəlæp, vb ˌəʊvə'læp] (pt & pp -ped, cont -ping) <> n - **1.** (U) [similarity] coincidência f - **2.** [overlapping part, amount] sobreposição f. <> vt sobrepor-se a. <> vi - **1.** [cover each other] sobrepor-se - **2.** [be similar] coincidir; **to ~ (with sthg)** coincidir em parte (com algo).

overlay [ˌəʊvə'leɪ] (pt & pp -laid) vt: **to be overlaid with sthg** estar revestido(da) de algo.

overleaf [ˌəʊvə'liːf] adv no verso.

overload [ˌəʊvə'ləʊd] (pp -loaded OR -laden) vt sobrecarregar; **to be ~ed (with sthg)** estar sobrecarregado(da) de algo.

overlong [ˌəʊvə'lɒŋ] <> adj muito comprido(da). <> adv tempo demais.

overlook [ˌəʊvə'lʊk] vt - **1.** [look over] dar para - **2.** [disregard, miss] fazer vista grossa para - **3.** [excuse] desculpar.

overlord ['əʊvələːd] n literary senhor m.

overly ['əʊvəlɪ] adv demais; **not ~** não muito.

overmanning [ˌəʊvə'mænɪŋ] n (U) excesso m de mão-de-obra.

overnight [adj 'əʊvənaɪt, adv ˌəʊvə'naɪt] <> adj - **1.** [stay, guest, parking] por uma noite - **2.** [clothes] para uma noite - **3.** [journey] de uma noite; **~ bag** bolsa f de viagem - **4.** [very sudden] da noite para o dia. <> adv - **1.** [for all of night] durante a noite - **2.** [very suddenly] da noite para o dia.

overpaid [ˌəʊvə'peɪd] <> pt & pp ▷ **overpay.** <> adj pago(ga) em excesso.

overpass ['əʊvəpɑːs] n US viaduto m.

overpay [ˌəʊvə'peɪ] (pt & pp -paid) vt pagar demais.

overplay [ˌəʊvə'pleɪ] vt exagerar; **to ~ one's hand** exagerar (tentando tirar mais vantagem).

overpopulated [ˌəʊvə'pɒpjʊleɪtɪd] adj superpopulado(da).

overpower [ˌəʊvə'paʊəʳ] vt - **1.** [in fight] subjugar - **2.** fig [overwhelm] vencer, sobrepujar.

overpowering [ˌəʊvə'paʊərɪŋ] adj - **1.** [desire, feeling] dominante - **2.** [smell] asfixiante - **3.** [heat, sensation] sufocante - **4.** [personality] opressor(ra).

overpriced [ˌəʊvə'praɪst] adj muito caro(ra).

overproduction [ˌəʊvəprə'dʌkʃn] n (U) superprodução f, excesso m de produção.

overprotective [ˌəʊvəprə'tektɪv] adj superprotetor(ra).

overran [ˌəʊvə'ræn] pt ▷ **overrun.**

overrated [ˌəʊvə'reɪtd] adj superestimado(da).

overreach [ˌəʊvə'riːtʃ] vt: **to ~ o.s.** ir longe demais, dar o passo maior que a perna.

overreact [ˌəʊvərɪ'ækt] vi: **to ~ (to sthg)** reagir exageradamente (a algo).

override [ˌəʊvə'raɪd] (pt -rode, pp -ridden) vt - **1.** [be more important than] passar por cima de, não fazer caso de - **2.** [overrule] desautorizar.

overriding [ˌəʊvə'raɪdɪŋ] adj predominante.

overripe [ˌəʊvəˈraɪp] *adj* **-1.** [fruit] maduro(ra) demais **-2.** [cheese] passado(da).

overrode [ˌəʊvəˈrəʊd] *pt* ⊳ **override**.

overrule [ˌəʊvəˈruːl] *vt* **-1.** [person, decision] desautorizar **-2.** [objection] negar.

overrun [ˌəʊvəˈrʌn] (*pt* **-ran**, *pp* **-run**, *cont* **-running**) ⊳ *vt* **-1.** MIL [occupy] invadir **-2.** *fig* [cover, fill]: **to be ~ with sthg** estar repleto(ta) de algo. ⊳ *vi* passar do tempo previsto.

oversaw [ˌəʊvəˈsɔː] *pt* ⊳ **oversee**.

overseas [*adj* ˈəʊvəsiːz, *adv* ˌəʊvəˈsiːz] ⊳ *adj* **-1.** [market] exterior **-2.** [network, branches] no exterior **-3.** [sales, aid] para o exterior **-4.** [from abroad] estrangeiro(ra). ⊳ *adv* **-1.** [travel, sell] para o exterior **-2.** [study, live] no exterior.

oversee [ˌəʊvəˈsiː] (*pt* **-saw**, *pp* **-seen** [-ˈsiːn]) *vt* supervisionar.

overseer [ˈəʊvəˌsiːəʳ] *n* supervisor *m*, -ra *f*.

overshadow [ˌəʊvəˈʃædəʊ] *vt* **-1.** [make darker] fazer sombra em **-2.** *fig* [outweigh, eclipse]: **to be ~ed by sb/sthg** ser eclipsado(da) por alguém/algo **-3.** *fig* [mar, cloud]: **to be ~ed by sthg** ser ofuscado(da) por algo.

overshoot [ˌəʊvəˈʃuːt] (*pt* & *pp* **-shot**) *vt* passar.

oversight [ˈəʊvəsaɪt] *n* deslize *m*, descuido *m*.

oversimplification [əʊvəˌsɪmplɪfɪˈkeɪʃn] *n* simplificação *f* excessiva.

oversimplify [ˌəʊvəˈsɪmplɪfaɪ] (*pt* & *pp* **-ied**) ⊳ *vt* simplificar demais ⊳ *vi* simplificar demais.

oversleep [ˌəʊvəˈsliːp] (*pt* & *pp* **-slept** [-ˈslept]) *vi* dormir demais, ficar dormindo.

overspend [ˌəʊvəˈspend] (*pt* & *pp* **-spent** [-ˈspent]) *vi* gastar além da conta.

overspill [ˈəʊvəspɪl] *n* (*U*) excesso *m* de população.

overstaffed [ˌəʊvəˈstɑːft] *adj* com excesso de funcionários.

overstate [ˌəʊvəˈsteɪt] *vt* exagerar.

overstay [ˌəʊvəˈsteɪ] *vt*: **to ~ one's welcome** abusar da hospitalidade de alguém.

overstep [ˌəʊvəˈstep] (*pt* & *pp* **-ped**, *cont* **-ping**) *vt* passar por cima de; **to ~ the mark** passar dos limites.

overstock [ˌəʊvəˈstɒk] *vt* abarrotar, entupir.

overstrike [ˈəʊvəstraɪk] (*pt* & *pp* **-struck**) COMPUT ⊳ *n* sobreposição *f* de caracteres. ⊳ *vt* sobrepor caracteres.

oversubscribed [ˌəʊvəsʌbˈskraɪbd] *adj* subscrito (ta) em excesso.

overt [ˈəʊvɜːt] *adj* aberto(ta), manifesto(ta).

overtake [ˌəʊvəˈteɪk] (*pt* **-took**, *pp* **-taken** [-ˈteɪkn]) ⊳ *vt* **-1.** AUT ultrapassar **-2.** [subj: disaster, misfortune] surpreender, pegar de surpresa. ⊳ *vi* AUT ultrapassar.

overtaking [ˌəʊvəˈteɪkɪŋ] *n* (*U*) ultrapassagem *f*; 'no **~**' 'proibido ultrapassar'.

overthrow [*n* ˈəʊvəθrəʊ, *vb* ˌəʊvəˈθrəʊ] (*pt* **-threw**, *pp* **-thrown**) ⊳ *n* deposição *f*, destituição *f*. ⊳ *vt* **-1.** [government, president] depor, destituir **-2.** [concept, idea, standard] derrubar.

overtime [ˈəʊvətaɪm] ⊳ *n* **-1.** [extra time worked] hora *f* extra **-2.** US SPORT prorrogação *f*.

⊳ *adv*: **to work ~** fazer hora extra.

overtly [ˈəʊvɜːtlɪ] *adv* abertamente, publicamente.

overtones [ˈəʊvətəʊnz] *npl* insinuações *fpl*.

overtook [ˌəʊvəˈtʊk] *pt* ⊳ **overtake**.

overture [ˈəʊvəˌtjʊəʳ] *n* MUS abertura *f*.

➡ **overtures** *npl*: **to make ~s to sb** fazer uma proposta a alguém.

overturn [ˌəʊvəˈtɜːn] ⊳ *vt* **-1.** [turn over] virar **-2.** [overrule] invalidar **-3.** [overthrow] depor. ⊳ *vi* **-1.** [boat] virar **-2.** [lorry, car] capotar.

overuse [ˌəʊvəˈjuːz] *vt* usar demais.

overview [ˈəʊvəvjuː] *n* visão *f* geral.

overweening [ˌəʊvəˈwiːnɪŋ] *adj* desmedido(da).

overweight [ˌəʊvəˈweɪt] *adj* obeso(sa), gordo(da).

overwhelm [ˌəʊvəˈwelm] *vt* **-1.** [make helpless] subjugar **-2.** MIL [gain control of] dominar, passar a controlar.

overwhelming [ˌəʊvəˈwelmɪŋ] *adj* **-1.** [feeling, quality] impressionante **-2.** [victory, defeat, majority] esmagador(ra).

overwhelmingly [ˌəʊvəˈwelmɪŋlɪ] *adv* em peso, em massa.

overwork [ˌəʊvəˈwɜːk] ⊳ *n* (*U*) trabalho *m* excessivo. ⊳ *vt* **-1.** [give too much work to] fazer trabalhar demais **-2.** *fig* [overuse] usar demais. ⊳ *vi* trabalhar demais.

overwrought [ˌəʊvəˈrɔːt] *adj* muito nervoso(sa).

ovulate [ˈɒvjʊleɪt] *vi* ovular.

ovulation [ˌɒvjʊˈleɪʃn] *n* (*U*) ovulação *f*.

ow [aʊ] *excl* ai!

owe [əʊ] *vt*: **to ~ sthg to sb**, **to ~ sb sthg** dever algo a alguém.

owing [ˈəʊɪŋ] *adj* que se deve.

➡ **owing to** *prep* por causa de, devido a.

owl [aʊl] *n* coruja *f*.

own [əʊn] ⊳ *adj* [indicating possession] próprio(pria); **my/your ~ car** meu/teu próprio carro; **he doesn't need a lift, he has his ~ car** ele não precisa de carona, tem seu próprio carro; **she has her ~ style** ela tem um estilo próprio. ⊳ *pron* [indicating possession]: **my ~ o(a)** meu(minha); **your ~ o(a)** seu(sua); **a house of my ~** minha própria casa; **the city has a special atmosphere of its ~ a** cidade tem uma atmosfera especial que lhe é própria; **on one's ~** [alone] sozinho(nha); **to get one's ~ back** dar o troco, vingar-se. ⊳ *vt* possuir, ter.

➡ **own up** *vi*: **to ~ up (to sthg)** confessar (algo), admitir (algo).

own brand *n* COMM marca *f* própria.

owner [ˈəʊnəʳ] *n* proprietário *m*, -ria *f*, dono *m*, -na *f*.

owner-occupier *n* esp UK morador *m* proprietário, moradora *f* proprietária.

ownership [ˈəʊnəʃɪp] *n* (*U*) posse *f*, propriedade *f*.

own goal *n* esp UK **-1.** FTBL gol *m* contra; **to score an ~** marcar um gol contra **-2.** UK *fig* [foolish mistake] gol *m* contra.

ox [ɒks] (*pl* **oxen**) *n* boi *m*.

Oxbridge [ˈɒksbrɪdʒ] *n* (*U*) as universidades de Oxford e Cambridge.

oxen ['ɒksn] *pl* ▷ **ox**.
OXFAM *n organização británica de caridade para ajuda a países subdesenvolvidos.*
oxide ['ɒksaɪd] *n* óxido *m*.
oxidize, -ise ['ɒksɪdaɪz] *vi* oxidar.
oxtail soup ['ɒksteɪl-] *n* (U) rabada *f*.
ox tongue *n* (U) língua *f* de boi.
oxyacetylene [,ɒksɪə'setɪliːn] ◇ *n* (U) oxiacetileno *m*. ◇ *comp* oxiacetilênico(ca).
oxygen ['ɒksɪdʒən] *n* (U) oxigênio *m*.
oxygenate ['ɒksɪdʒəneɪt] *vt* oxigenar.
oxygen mask *n* máscara *f* de oxigênio.
oxygen tent *n* tenda *f* de oxigênio.
oyster ['ɔɪstə'] *n* ostra *f*.
oz. *abbr of* **ounce**.
ozone ['əʊzəʊn] *n* ozônio *m*.
ozone-friendly *adj* não-prejudicial à camada de ozônio.
ozone layer *n* camada *f* de ozônio.

p¹ (*pl* **p's** *OR* **ps**), **P** (*pl* **P's** *OR* **Ps**) [piː] *n* [letter] p *m*.
▸ **P** - **1.** (*abbr of* **president**) Pres. - **2.** (*abbr of* **prince**) Pr.
p² - **1.** (*abbr of* **page**) p. - **2.** *abbr of* **penny, pence**.
P45 *n documento oficial que o empregado recebe do empregador na Grã-Bretanha ao deixar o emprego e repassa ao próximo empregador, contendo informações salariais.*
P60 *n documento oficial fornecido pelo empregador ao empregado na Grã-Bretanha com informações sobre salário recebido e impostos pagos durante aquele ano,* ≃ *declaração f de rendimentos.*
pa [pɑː] *n inf esp US* pai *m*.
p.a. (*abbr of* **per annum**) p.a.
PA ◇ *n* - **1.** *UK* (*abbr of* **personal assistant**) assessor *m*, -ra *f* pessoal - **2.** (*abbr of* **public address system**) sistema *m* de alto-falantes - **3.** (*abbr of* **Press Association**) agência de notícias britânica.

◇ *abbr of* **Pennsylvania**.
PABX (*abbr of* **private automatic branch exchange**) *n* PABX *m*.
PAC *n* - **1.** (*abbr of* **political action committee**) *comitê de levantamento de fundos para causas políticas nos Estados Unidos* - **2.** (*abbr of* **Pan Africanist Congress**) Congresso *m* Pan-Africano.
pace [peɪs] ◇ *n* - **1.** (U) [speed, rate] ritmo *m*, andamento *m*; **at one's own ~** no próprio ritmo de alguém; **to keep ~ (with sb/sthg)** acompanhar o ritmo (de alguém/algo) - **2.** [step] passo *m*. ◇ *vt* andar por. ◇ *vi* andar de um lado para o outro.
pacemaker ['peɪs,meɪkə'] *n* - **1.** *MED* marca-passo *m* - **2.** [in race] *competidor que estabelece o ritmo da corrida.*
pacesetter ['peɪs,setə'] *n US SPORT atleta que estabelece o ritmo da corrida.*
pachyderm ['pækɪdɜːml] *n* paquiderme *m*.
Pacific [pə'sɪfɪk] ◇ *adj* do Pacífico. ◇ *n*: **the ~ (Ocean)** o (Oceano) Pacífico.
pacification [,pæsɪfɪ'keɪʃn] *n* (U) *fml* - **1.** [of person] apaziguamento *m* - **2.** [of country, region] pacificação *f*.
Pacific Rim *n*: **the ~** a Região do Pacífico.
pacifier ['pæsɪfaɪə'] *n US* bico *m*.
pacifism ['pæsɪfɪzm] *n* (U) pacifismo *m*.
pacifist ['pæsɪfɪst] *n* pacifista *mf*.
pacify ['pæsɪfaɪ] (*pt & pp* **-ied**) *vt* - **1.** [person] acalmar - **2.** [country, region] pacificar.
pack [pæk] ◇ *n* - **1.** [rucksack] mochila *f* - **2.** [bundle] pacote *m*, embrulho *m* - **3.** [of cigarettes] maço *m* - **4.** *esp US* [washing powder, tissues] caixa *f* - **5.** [of cards] baralho *m* - **6.** [of animals - dogs] matilha *f*; [- wolves] alcatéia *f*; [- of thieves] quadrilha *f* - **7.** *CYCLING, RUGBY* pelotão *m* - **8.** *phr*: **that's a ~ of lies!** é um monte de mentiras! ◇ *vt* - **1.** [bag, suitcase] fazer - **2.** [clothes, etc] colocar na mala - **3.** [put in container, parcel] embalar - **4.** [crowd into] lotar; **to be ~ed into sthg** estar socado(da) em algo. ◇ *vi* - **1.** [for journey, holiday] fazer as malas - **2.** [push tightly] apertar-se, amontoar-se.
▸ **pack in** ◇ *vt sep UK inf* [job, boyfriend, smoking] deixar; **~ it in!** [stop annoying me] pare com isso!, chega!; [shut up] boca fechada! ◇ *vi* pifar.
▸ **pack off** *vt sep inf* enviar, mandar.
▸ **pack up** ◇ *vt sep* arrumar. ◇ *vi* - **1.** [pack one's suitcase] fazer as malas - **2.** *inf* [finish work] cair fora (do trabalho) - **3.** *UK inf* [break down] pifar.
package ['pækɪdʒ] ◇ *n* - **1.** [gen] pacote *m* - **2.** [box] caixa *f* - **3.** *US* [of cigarettes] maço *m*, carteira *f* *OR* *m* - **4.** [set, group] pacote *m*. ◇ *vt* embalar, empacotar.
package deal *n* pacote *m* de acordo.
package holiday *n* pacote *m* de férias.
packager ['pækɪdʒə'] *n* - **1.** [person packaging] embalador *m*, -deira *f* - **2.** *COMM* produtora *f* independente.
package tour *n* pacote *m* turístico.
packaging ['pækɪdʒɪŋ] *n* (U) embalagem *f*.
packed [pækt] *adj* - **1.** [place]: **~ (with)** lotado(da) (de) - **2.** [magazine, information pack]: **~ with** repleto(-ta) de.

packed lunch n UK **-1.** [for school] f merenda f **-2.** [for work] marmita f.

packed out adj UK inf apinhado(da).

packet ['pækɪt] n **-1.** [gen] pacote m **-2.** [box] caixa f **-3.** [of cigarettes] maço m, carteira f **-4.** UK inf [lot of money] bolada f, dinheirama f.

packhorse n cavalo m de carga.

pack ice n (U) gelo m flutuante.

packing ['pækɪŋ] n (U) **-1.** [protective material] embalagem f **-2.** [for journey, holiday]: **to do the** ~ fazer as malas.

packing case n caixote m de embalagem.

pact [pækt] n pacto m.

pad [pæd] (pt & pp **-ded**, cont **-ding**) ⬦ n **-1.** [for clothes, body]: **shoulder** ~ ombreira f; **knee** ~ joelheira f; **shin** ~ tornozeleira f **-2.** [notepad] bloco m de anotações **-3.** [for absorbing liquid - cotton wool] chumaço m; [- sanitary] absorvente m higiênico **-4.** SPACE: **(launch)** ~ plataforma f (de lançamento) **-5.** [of cat or dog] almofadinha f **-6.** inf dated [home] casa f. ⬦ vt **-1.** [clothing, furniture] revestir, forrar **-2.** [wound] cobrir **-3.** fig [speech, letter, essay] alongar de forma desnecessária. ⬦ vi andar com suavidade.

➡ **pad out** vt sep **-1.** [clothing, furniture] revestir, forrar **-2.** [speech, letter, essay] alongar de forma desnecessária.

padded ['pædɪd] adj **-1.** [jacket] revestido(da), forrado(da) **-2.** [shoulders] com ombreiras **-3.** [chair] acolchoado(da).

padded cell n cela f acolchoada.

padding ['pædɪŋ] n (U) **-1.** [in jacket] revestimento m **-2.** [in shoulders] ombreira f **-3.** [in chair] enchimento m **-4.** [in speech, essay, letter] enrolação f.

paddle ['pædl] ⬦ n **-1.** [for canoe, dinghy] remo m **-2.** [wade]: **to have a** ~ patinhar na água. ⬦ vt remar. ⬦ vi **-1.** [in canoe, dinghy] remar **-2.** [wade] patinhar.

paddle boat, paddle steamer n vapor m movido a rodas.

paddling pool ['pædlɪŋ-] n **-1.** [in park] piscina f infantil **-2.** [inflatable] piscina f inflável.

paddock ['pædək] n **-1.** [small field] manejo m **-2.** [at racecourse] paddock m.

paddy field ['pædɪ-] n arrozal m.

paddy wagon ['pædɪ-] n US inf camburão m.

padlock ['pædlɒk] ⬦ n cadeado m. ⬦ vt fechar com cadeado.

paederast ['pedəræst] n = pederast.

paediatric [,piːdɪ'ætrɪk] adj = pediatric.

paediatrician [,piːdɪə'trɪʃn] n = pediatrician.

paediatrics [,piːdɪ'ætrɪks] n = pediatrics.

paedophile UK ['piːdəfaɪl], **pedophile** US n pedófilo m, -la f.

paella [paɪ'elə] n (U) paelha f.

paeony ['piːənɪ] (pl **-ies**) n = peony.

pagan ['peɪgən] ⬦ adj pagão(gã). ⬦ n pagão m, -gã f.

paganism ['peɪgənɪzm] n (U) paganismo m.

page [peɪdʒ] ⬦ n página f. ⬦ vt chamar (pelo alto-falante).

page [peɪdʒ] vt [using pager]: **to be** ~**d** receber chamadas pelo pager; **to** ~ **sb** chamar alguém pelo pager.

pageant ['pædʒənt] n desfile m, cortejo m cívico.

pageantry ['pædʒəntrɪ] n (U) fausto m, pompa f.

page boy n **-1.** UK [at wedding] pajem m **-2.** [hairstyle] chanel m.

page break n COMPUT quebra f de página.

pager ['peɪdʒə'] n pager m.

pagination [,pædʒɪ'neɪʃn] n (U) paginação f.

pagoda [pə'gəʊdə] n pagode m.

paid [peɪd] ⬦ pt & pp ⊳ pay. ⬦ adj pago(ga); **badly/well** ~ bem/mal pago(ga).

paid-up adj UK remido(da).

pail [peɪl] n balde m.

pain [peɪn] ⬦ n **-1.** dor f; **to be in** ~ sentir dor; **a** ~ **in the neck** inf uma mala-sem-alça **-2.** (U) [mental suffering] sofrimento m, pena f **-3.** inf [annoyance]: **it's such a** ~ ! é tão chato!; **he is a real** ~ ! ele é um saco! ⬦ vt fml fazer sofrer, atormentar; **to** ~ **sb to do sthg** ser muito difícil para alguém fazer algo.

➡ **pains** npl esforços mpl; **to be at** ~**s to do sthg** empenhar-se para fazer algo; **to take** ~**s to do sthg** esforçar-se para fazer algo; **he got absolutely nothing for his** ~**s** tanto esforço e ele não conseguiu absolutamente nada.

pained [peɪnd] adj aflito(ta), consternado(da).

painful ['peɪnfʊl] adj **-1.** [sore] dolorido(da) **-2.** [causing pain] doloroso(sa) **-3.** [distressing] penoso(sa), doloroso(sa).

painfully ['peɪnfʊlɪ] adv **-1.** [distressingly] dolorosamente **-2.** [for emphasis] terrivelmente.

painkiller ['peɪn,kɪlə'] n analgésico m, calmante m.

painless ['peɪnlɪs] adj indolor, fácil.

painlessly ['peɪnlɪslɪ] adv **-1.** [without hurting] sem dor **-2.** [unproblematically] de forma fácil, de forma indolor.

painstaking ['peɪnz,teɪkɪŋ] adj meticuloso(sa), minucioso(sa).

painstakingly ['peɪnz,teɪkɪŋlɪ] adv meticulosamente, minuciosamente.

paint [peɪnt] ⬦ n tinta f. ⬦ vt **-1.** pintar; **to** ~ **the wall white** pintar o teto de branco **-2.** [with make-up] maquiar. ⬦ vi pintar.

paintbox ['peɪntbɒks] n ART estojo m de tintas.

paintbrush ['peɪntbrʌʃ] n **-1.** [of artist] pincel m **-2.** [of decorator] broxa f.

painted ['peɪntɪd] adj pintado(da).

painter ['peɪntə'] n pintor m, -ra f.

painting ['peɪntɪŋ] n **-1.** [picture] pintura f, quadro m **-2.** (U) ACTIVITY pintura f.

paint stripper n (U) removedor m (de tinta).

paintwork ['peɪntwɜːk] n (U) pintura f.

pair [peə'] n par m; **a** ~ **of idiots** uma dupla de idiotas; **a** ~ **of scissors** uma tesoura; **a** ~ **of trousers** uma calça; **a** ~ **of spectacles** um óculos.

➡ **pair off** ⬦ vt sep fazer par com. ⬦ vi: **let's** ~ **and meet back here later** vamos nos separar aos pares e nos reencontrar aqui mais tarde.

pajamas [pə'dʒɑːməz] npl US = pyjamas.

Pakistan [UK ,pɑːkɪ'stɑːn, US ,pækɪ'stæn] n Paquistão; **in** ~ no Paquistão.

Pakistani [UK ,pɑːkɪ'stɑːnɪ, US ,pækɪ'stænɪ] ⬦ adj

paquistanês(esa). <> *n* paquistanês, -esa *f*.

pal [pæl] *n inf* **-1.** [friend] camarada *mf*, companheiro *m*, -ra *f* **-2.** [as term of address]: **now wait a minute, ~, I was first!** espera um pouco, meu chapa, eu cheguei primeiro!

PAL (*abbr of* phase alternate line) *n* PAL *f*.

palace [ˈpælɪs] *n* palácio *m*.

palaeontology *UK*, **paleontology** *US* [ˌpælɪɒnˈtɒlədʒɪ] *n (U)* paleontologia *f*.

palatable [ˈpælətəbl] *adj* **-1.** [pleasant to taste] saboroso(sa) **-2.** [acceptable] aceitável, admissível.

palate [ˈpælət] *n* **-1.** ANAT palato *m* **-2.** [sense of taste] paladar *m*.

palatial [pəˈleɪʃl] *adj* palaciano(na).

palaver [pəˈlɑːvəʳ] *n inf* **-1.** [talk] palavrório *m* **-2.** [fuss] bagunça *f*, rebuliço *m*.

pale [peɪl] <> *adj* **-1.** [colour] fosco(ca) **-2.** [light] ênue **-3.** [clothes] claro(ra) **-4.** [face, complexion] pálido(da). <> *vi* **-1.** [become pale] empalidecer **-2.** [become insignificant]: **to ~ into insignificance (beside sb/sth)** perder toda importância (junto a alguém/algo).

pale ale *n UK tipo de cerveja clara*.

paleness [ˈpeɪlnɪs] *n (U)* palidez *f*.

paleontology *n US* = **palaeontology**.

Palestine [ˈpælɪˌstaɪn] *n* Palestina; **in ~** na Palestina.

Palestinian [ˌpæləˈstɪnɪən] <> *adj* palestino(na). <> *n* palestino *m*, -na *f*.

palette [ˈpælət] *n* paleta *f*.

palette knife *n* espátula *f*.

palimony [ˈpælɪmənɪ] *n (U) pensão alimentícia paga à ex-amante*.

palindrome *n* palíndromo *m*.

palings [ˈpeɪlɪŋz] *npl* cerca *f*.

pall [pɔːl] <> *n* **-1.** [of smoke] nuvem *f*, cortina *f* **-2.** *US* [coffin] caixão *m*. <> *vi* perder a graça.

pallbearer [ˈpɔːlˌbeərəʳ] *n* carregador *m*, -ra *f* de caixão.

pallet [ˈpælɪt] *n* palete *m*, plataforma *f* de carga.

palliative [ˈpælɪətɪv] *n fml* paliativo *m*.

pallid [ˈpælɪd] *adj* pálido(da).

pallor [ˈpæləʳ] *n* palor *m*.

palm [pɑːm] *n* **-1.** [tree] palmeira *f* **-2.** [of hand] palma *f*.

 ◆ **palm off** *vt sep inf*: **to ~ sth off on sb** empurrar algo para alguém; **to ~ sb off with sth** enganar alguém com algo; **to ~ sth off as sth** fazer passar algo como algo.

palmistry [ˈpɑːmɪstrɪ] *n (U)* quiromancia *f*.

palm oil *n (U)* azeite-de-dendê *m*.

Palm Sunday *n* Domingo *m* de Ramos.

palmtop [ˈpɑːmtɒp] *n* COMPUT palmtop *m*.

palm tree *n* palmeira *f*.

palomino [ˌpæləˈmiːnəʊ] (*pl* -s) *n* palomino *m*.

palpable [ˈpælpəbl] *adj* palpável.

palpably [ˈpælpəblɪ] *adv* obviamente.

palpitate [ˈpælpɪteɪt] *vi* palpitar.

palpitations [ˌpælpɪˈteɪʃənz] *npl* palpitações *fpl*.

palsy *n (U)* paralisia *f*.

paltry [ˈpɔːltrɪ] (*compar* -ier, *superl* -iest) *adj* irrisório(ria).

pampas [ˈpæmpəz] *n*: **the ~** o pampa.

pampas grass *n (U)* capim-dos-pampas *m inv*.

pamper [ˈpæmpəʳ] *vt* mimar.

pamphlet [ˈpæmflɪt] <> *n* panfleto *m*. <> *vi* panfletar.

pamphleteer [ˌpæmfləˈtɪəʳ] *n* POL panfletário *m*, -ria *f*, panfletista *mf*.

pan [pæn] (*pt & pp* -ned, *cont* -ning) <> *n* **-1.** [for frying] fridigeira **-2.** [for boiling] panela *f* **-3.** *US* [for baking] assadeira *f* **-4.** [of scales] prato *m* **-5.** [of toilet] vaso *m* sanitário. <> *vt inf* esculachar. <> *vi* **-1.** [for gold] batear **-2.** CINEMA capturar uma vista panorâmica.

panacea [ˌpænəˈsɪə] *n fig*: **a ~ (for sthg)** uma panacéia (para algo).

panache [pəˈnæʃ] *n (U)* bravata *f*, elã *m*.

panama *n*: **~ (hat)** panamá *m*.

Panama [ˈpænəmɑː] *n* Panamá *m*; **in ~** no Panamá.

Panama Canal *n*: **the ~** o Canal do Panamá.

Panama City *n* Cidade *f* do Panamá.

Panamanian [ˌpænəˈmeɪnɪən] <> *adj* panamenho(nha). <> *n* panamenho *m*, -nha *f*.

pan-American *adj* pan-americano(na).

pancake [ˈpænkeɪk] *n* panqueca *f*.

Pancake Day *n UK* ≃ Terça-feira *f* de Carnaval.

pancake roll *n* rolinho *m* primavera.

Pancake Tuesday *n* = **Pancake Day**.

pancreas [ˈpæŋkrɪəs] *n* pâncreas *m inv*.

panda [ˈpændə] (*pl inv OR* -s) *n* panda *m*.

Panda car *n UK* patrulha *f* policial.

pandemonium [ˌpændɪˈməʊnjəm] *n (U)* pandemônio *m*.

pander [ˈpændəʳ] *vi*: **to ~ to sb/sthg** fazer concessões a alguém/algo.

pane [peɪn] *n* vidraça *f*, vidro *m* de vidraça.

panel [ˈpænl] *n* **-1.** [group of people] equipe *f* **-2.** TECH painel *m*.

panel game *n UK jogo televisivo em que um grupo de pessoas deve realizar determinada tarefa*.

panelling *UK*, **paneling** *US* [ˈpænəlɪŋ] *n (U)* apainelamento *m*.

panellist *UK*, **panelist** *US* [ˈpænəlɪst] *n* painelista *mf*.

panel pin *n UK* prego *m* sem cabeça.

pang [pæŋ] *n* acesso *m* (*de fome, de culpa etc*).

panic [ˈpænɪk] (*pt & pp* -ked, *cont* -king) <> *n (U)* pânico *m*. <> *vi* entrar em pânico.

panicky [ˈpænɪkɪ] *adj* **-1.** [person] aterrorizado(da) **-2.** [feeling] aterrorizante.

panic stations *n (U) inf*: **it was ~** foi uma verdadeira loucura.

panic-stricken *adj* em pânico.

pannier [ˈpænɪəʳ] *n* **-1.** [on back, horse] alforje *m* **-2.** [bicycle] cesto *m*.

panoply [ˈpænəplɪ] *n (U) fml* panóplia *f*.

panorama [ˌpænəˈrɑːmə] *n* panorama *m*.

panoramic [ˌpænəˈræmɪk] *adj* panorâmico(ca).

pansy (*pl* -ies) *n* **-1.** [flower] amor-perfeito *m* **-2.** *inf pej* [man] veado *m*.

pant [pænt] *vi* ofegar.

 ◆ **pants** *npl* **-1.** *UK* [underpants] calcinha *f* **-2.** *US* [trousers] calças *fpl*.

panther [ˈpænθəʳ] (*pl inv OR* -s) *n* pantera *f*.

panties ['pæntɪz] *npl inf* calcinha *f.*

pantihose ['pæntɪhəʊz] *npl* = **panty hose.**

panto ['pæntəʊ] (*pl* -s) *n UK inf* = **pantomime.**

pantomime ['pæntəmaɪm] *n UK* peça de teatro para crianças realizada no Reino Unido no Natal.

pantry ['pæntrɪ] (*pl* -ies) *n* despensa *f.*

panty hose ['pæntɪ-] *npl US* meia-calça *f.*

papa [*UK* pə'pɑː, *US* 'pæpə] *n* papá *m.*

papacy (*pl* -ies) *n* -**1.** [period] papado *m* -**2.** [office, institution]: **the** ~ o papado, o pontificado.

papadum ['pæpədəm] *n* = **popadum.**

papal ['peɪpl] *adj* papal.

paparazzi [ˌpæpə'rætsɪ] *npl pej* paparazzi *mpl.*

papaya [pə'paɪə] *n* papaia *m.*

paper ['peɪpə^r] ◇ *n* -**1.** (*U*) [material] papel *m*;**a piece of** ~ uma folha de papel; **on** ~ [written down] no papel; [in theory] teoricamente -**2.** [newspaper] jornal *m* -**3.** [in exam] trabalho *m* -**4.** [essay] ensaio *m* -**5.** [at conference] apostila *f*, polígrafo *m.* ◇ *adj* -**1.** [cup, napkin, hat] de papel -**2.** [theoretical] no papel. ◇ *vt* empapelar.

➡ **papers** *npl* -**1.** [identity papers] documentos *mpl* (de identidade) -**2.** [documents] documentação *f.*

➡ **paper over** *vt fus fig* encobrir, disfarçar.

paperback ['peɪpəbæk] *n*: ~ **(book)** brochura *f*; **in** ~ em brochura.

paper bag *n* saco *m* de papel.

paperboy ['peɪpəbɔɪ] *n* jornaleiro *m.*

paper clip *n* clipe *m.*

papergirl ['peɪpəgɜːl] *n* jornaleira *f.*

paper handkerchief *n* lenço *m* de papel.

paper knife *n* abridor *m* de cartas.

paper mill *n* fábrica *f* de papel.

paper money *n* (*U*) papel-moeda *m.*

paper shop *n UK* banca *f* de jornais.

paperweight ['peɪpəweɪt] *n* peso *m* para papel.

paperwork ['peɪpəwɜːk] *n* (*U*) papelada *f.*

papier-mâché [ˌpæpjeɪ'mæʃeɪ] ◇ *n* (*U*) papel *m* machê. ◇ *comp* de papel machê.

papist ['peɪpɪst] *n pej* papista *mf.*

paprika ['pæprɪkə] *n* (*U*) páprica *f.*

Papua *n* Papua.

Papuan ['pæpjʊən] ◇ *adj* papua. ◇ *n* papua *mf.*

Papua New Guinea *n* Papua Nova Guiné; **in** ~ em Papua Nova Guiné.

par [pɑː^r] *n* -**1.** [parity]: **on a** ~ **with sb/sthg** no mesmo nível que alguém/algo -**2.** (*U*) *GOLF* par *m*; **under/over** ~ abaixo/acima do par -**3.** [good health]: **below** *OR* **under** ~ indisposto(ta) -**4.** *FIN* valor *m* (ao par).

para ['pærə] *n UK inf* paraquedista *mf (do exército).*

parable ['pærəbl] *n* parábola *f.*

parabola [pə'ræbələ] *n TECH* parábola *f.*

paracetamol [ˌpærə'siːtəmɒl] *n* paracetamol *m.*

parachute ['pærəʃuːt] ◇ *n* pára-quedas *m inv.* ◇ *vi* saltar de pára-quedas.

parade [pə'reɪd] ◇ *n* -**1.** [procession] desfile *m* -**2.** *MIL* parada *f*; **on** ~ em revista -**3.** *UK* [street of shops] via *f* comercial -**4.** [street, path] passeio *m* público. ◇ *vt* -**1.** [*MIL* - soldiers] fazer desfilar; [- prisoners] apresentar -**2.** [object] exibir -**3.** *fig* [flaunt] fazer alarde de, mostrar-se com. ◇ *vi* desfilar.

parade ground *n* praça *f* de armas.

paradigm ['pærədaɪm] *n* paradigma *m.*

paradigmatic *adj* paradigmático(ca).

paradise ['pærədaɪs] *n* paraíso *m.*

➡ **Paradise** *n* Paraíso *m.*

paradox ['pærədɒks] *n* paradoxo *m.*

paradoxical [ˌpærə'dɒksɪkl] *adj* paradoxal.

paradoxically [ˌpærə'dɒksɪklɪ] *adv* paradoxalmente.

paraffin ['pærəfɪn] *n* (*U*) querosene *m.*

paraffin wax *n* (*U*) parafina *f.*

paragliding ['pærəˌglaɪdɪŋ] *n* vôo *m* de paraglider.

paragon *n* modelo *m.*

paragraph ['pærəgrɑːf] *n* parágrafo *m.*

Paraguay ['pærəgwaɪ] *n* Paraguai; **in** ~ no Paraguai.

Paraguayan [ˌpærə'gwaɪən] ◇ *adj* paraguaio(ia). ◇ *n* paraguaio *m*, -ia *f.*

parakeet ['pærəkiːt] *n* periquito *m.*

paralegal [ˌpærə'liːgl] *n US* secretária altamente especializada que auxilia os advogados em seu trabalho.

parallel ['pærəlel] (*pt & pp* -**led**, *cont* -**ling**) ◇ *adj* [gen] paralelo(la); ~ **to** *OR* **with sthg** paralelo(la) a algo. ◇ *n* paralelo *m*; **to have no** ~ não ter precedente *OR* paralelo. ◇ *vt* igualar-se a.

parallel bars *npl* barras *fpl* paralelas.

paralyse *UK*, **paralyze** *US* ['pærəlaɪz] *vt* paralisar.

paralysed *UK*, **paralyzed** *US* ['pærəlaɪzd] *adj MED* paralisado(da).

paralysis [pə'rælɪsɪs] (*pl* -**lyses** [-lɪsɪːz]) *n* -**1.** *MED* paralisia *f* -**2.** [of industry, traffic] imobilidade *f.*

paralytic [ˌpærə'lɪtɪk] ◇ *adj* -**1.** *MED* paralítico(ca) -**2.** *UK inf* [drunk] bêbado(da) feito um gambá. ◇ *n* paralítico *m*, -ca *f.*

paralyze *vt US* = **paralyse.**

paralyzed *adj US* = **paralysed.**

paramedic [ˌpærə'medɪk] *n* paramédico *m*, -ca *f.*

paramedical [ˌpærə'medɪkl] *adj* paramédico(ca).

parameter [pə'ræmɪtə^r] *n* parâmetro *m.*

paramilitary [ˌpærə'mɪlɪtrɪ] *adj* paramilitar.

paramount ['pærəmaʊnt] *adj* vital, fundamental; **of** ~ **importance** de suma importância.

paranoia [ˌpærə'nɔɪə] *n* (*U*) paranóia *f.*

paranoiac [ˌpærə'nɔɪæk] *MED* ◇ *adj* paranóico(ca). ◇ *n* paranóico *m*, -ca *f.*

paranoid ['pærənɔɪd] *adj* -**1.** [person] paranóico(ca) -**2.** [disorder] paranóico(ca).

paranormal [ˌpærə'nɔːml] *adj* paranormal.

parapet ['pærəpɪt] *n* parapeito *m.*

paraphernalia [ˌpærəfə'neɪljə] *n* (*U*) parafernália *f.*

paraphrase ['pærəfreɪz] ◇ *n* paráfrase *f.* ◇ *vt & vi* parafrasear.

paraplegia *n* (*U*) paraplegia *f.*

paraplegic [ˌpærə'pliːdʒɪk] ◇ *adj* paraplégico (ca). ◇ *n* paraplégico *m*, -ca *f.*

parapsychology [ˌpærəsaɪ'kɒlədʒɪ] *n* (*U*) parapsicologia *f.*

paraquat® *n* (*U*) *CHEM* paraquat *m.*

parascending [ˌpærə'sendɪŋ] n vôo m de para-pente.

parasite ['pærəsaɪt] n parasita m.

parasitic [ˌpærə'sɪtɪk] adj parasita.

parasol ['pærəsɒl] n sombrinha f.

paratrooper ['pærətruː,pəʳ] n pára-quedista mf (do exército).

parboil ['pɑːbɔɪl] vt aferventar.

parcel ['pɑːsl] (UK pt & pp -led, cont -ling, US pt & pp -ed, cont -ing) n pacote m, encomenda f.

➡ **parcel up** vt sep empacotar.

parcel post n (U) serviço de encomenda f postal.

parched [pɑːtʃt] adj -1. [grass, plain] seco(ca) -2. [throat, lips] ressecado(da) -3. inf [very thirsty] seco(-ca).

parchment ['pɑːtʃmənt] n (U) pergaminho m.

pardon ['pɑːdn] <> n -1. JUR indulto m -2. (U) [forgiveness] perdão m; **I beg your ~?** [showing surprise or offence] como é?, o que foi?; [what did you say?] como?, o que você disse?; **I beg your ~!** [to apologize] perdão!, desculpe! <> vt -1. JUR indultar -2. [forgive] perdoar; **to ~ sb for sthg** perdoar alguém por algo; **~ me!** me desculpe!

pardonable ['pɑːdnəbl] adj perdoável.

pare [peəʳ] vt -1. [apple] descascar -2. [fingernail] aparar, cortar.

➡ **pare down** vt sep -1. [remove layer] aparar -2. [reduce] reduzir.

parent ['peərənt] n -1. [mother] mãe f -2. [father] pai m.

➡ **parents** npl pais mpl.

parentage ['peərəntɪdʒ] n (U) ascendência f, origem f.

parental [pə'rentl] adj dos pais.

parent company n matriz f.

parenthesis [pə'renθɪsɪs] (pl -theses [-θiːsiːz]) n parêntese m.

parenthetical adj entre parênteses.

parenthood ['peərənthʊd] n (U) paternidade f, maternidade f.

parenting ['peərəntɪŋ] n (U) cuidados mpl dos pais.

parent-teacher association n associação f de pais e mestres.

par excellence adj por excelência.

pariah [pə'raɪə] n pej pária mf.

Paris ['pærɪs] n Paris; **in ~** em Paris.

parish ['pærɪʃ] n -1. [of church] paróquia f -2. UK [area of local government] distrito m.

parish council n UK conselho m distrital.

parishioner [pə'rɪʃənəʳ] n paroquiano m, -na f.

parish priest n pároco m.

Parisian [pə'rɪzjən] <> adj parisiense. <> n parisiense mf.

parity ['pærətɪ] n (U) igualdade f; **~ with** igualdade com; **~ between** paridade f de or entre.

park [pɑːk] <> n -1. [public] parque m -2. US AUT posição da alavanca de carro hidramático usada para estacionar. <> vt & vi estacionar.

parka ['pɑːkə] n parca f.

parking ['pɑːkɪŋ] n (U) estacionamento m; **I find ~ very difficult** acho muito difícil estacionar; **'no ~'** 'proibido estacionar'.

parking garage n US edifício-garagem m.

parking light n US luz f de estacionamento.

parking lot n US área f de estacionamento.

parking meter n parquímetro m.

parking place n vaga f para estacionar.

parking ticket n multa f por estacionamento proibido.

Parkinson's (disease) ['pɑːkɪnsnz-] n (U) mal m de Parkinson.

park keeper n UK guarda mf de parque.

parkland ['pɑːklænd] n (U) parque m.

parkway ['pɑːkweɪ] n US alameda f.

parky ['pɑːkɪ] (compar -ier, superl -iest) adj UK inf frio (fria), fresco(ca).

parlance ['pɑːləns] n (U): **in common/legal ~** em linguagem coloquial/legal.

parliament ['pɑːləmənt] n -1. [gen] parlamento m -2. [session] legislatura f.

parliamentarian [ˌpɑːləmən'teərɪən] n parlamentar mf.

parliamentary [ˌpɑːlə'mentərɪ] adj parlamentar.

parlour UK, **parlor** US ['pɑːləʳ] n -1. dated [in house] sala f de visitas -2. [cafe]: **ice cream ~** sorveteria f.

parlour game n jogo m de salão.

parlous ['pɑːləs] adj fml precário(ria).

Parmesan (cheese) [ˌpɑːmɪ'zæn-] n (U) queijo m parmesão.

parochial [pə'rəʊkjəl] adj pej provinciano(na).

parochial school n US escola f particular católica.

parody ['pærədɪ] (pl -ies, pt & pp -ied) <> n paródia f. <> vt parodiar.

parole [pə'rəʊl] <> n (U) liberdade f condicional; **on ~** em liberdade condicional. <> vt pôr em liberdade condicional.

paroxysm ['pærəksɪzm] n -1. [feeling] paroxismo m -2. [movement] acesso m.

parquet ['pɑːkeɪ] n (U) parquê m.

parrot ['pærət] n papagaio m.

parrot fashion adv como um papagaio.

parry ['pærɪ] (pt & pp -ied) vt -1. [blow] desviar -2. [question] esquivar-se de.

parsimonious [ˌpɑːsɪ'məʊnjəs] adj fml & pej avarento(ta).

parsley ['pɑːslɪ] n (U) salsa f.

parsnip ['pɑːsnɪp] n chirivia f.

parson ['pɑːsn] n pároco m.

parson's nose n UK inf sambiquira f.

part [pɑːt] <> n -1. [gen] parte f; **in ~** em parte; **for the most ~** em sua maioria; **~ and parcel of** parte integrante de; **that's only ~ of the story** isso é só uma parte da história; **the best or better ~ of** a maior parte de -2. [component] peça f -3. [acting role] papel m -4. [involvement]: **~ in sthg** participação f em algo; **to take ~ in sthg** participar de algo; **to play an important ~ in sthg** ter um papel importante em algo; **to want no ~ in sthg** não querer se envolver em algo; **for my/your** etc **~** por minha/sua parte; **on my/your** etc **~** de minha/sua parte -5. US [hair parting] linha f. <> adv em parte. <> vt -1. [separate] separar -2. [move apart, open] abrir -3. [hair] repartir. <> vi

-1. [leave one another] separar-se **-2.** [move apart, open] abrir-se.
➤ **parts** *npl* terras *fpl.*
➤ **part with** *vt fus* desfazer-se de.

partake [pɑːˈteɪk] (*pt* -**took**, *pp* -**taken**) *vi fml*: to ~ of [wine] beber; [food] comer.

part exchange *n* **-1.** [deal] *negociação em que se paga parte do valor de um produto com um artigo usado* **-2.** (*U*) [system] *sistema através do qual se paga parte do valor do produto com um artigo usado*; in ~ como parte do pagamento.

partial [ˈpɑːʃl] *adj* **-1.** [gen] parcial **-2.** [fond]: ~ to sthg afeiçoado(da) a algo.

partiality [ˌpɑːʃɪˈælətɪ] *n* **-1.** (*U*) [bias] parcialidade *f* **-2.** [fondness]: ~ for sthg afeição *f* a algo, predileção *f* a algo.

partially [ˈpɑːʃəlɪ] *adv* parcialmente, em parte.

partially sighted *adj* com visão parcial.

participant [pɑːˈtɪsɪpənt] *n* participante *mf.*

participate [pɑːˈtɪsɪpeɪt] *vi* participar; to ~ in sthg participar de algo.

participation [pɑːˌtɪsɪˈpeɪʃn] *n* (*U*) participação *f.*

participle [ˈpɑːtɪsɪpl] *n* particípio *m.*

particle [ˈpɑːtɪkl] *n* partícula *f.*

parti-coloured *adj* multicor, matizado(da).

particular [pəˈtɪkjʊləʳ] *adj* **-1.** [gen] especial **-2.** [fussy] exigente.
➤ **particulars** *npl* particularidades *fpl.*
➤ **in particular** *adv* em especial, em particular.

particularity (*pl* -ies) *n fml* particularidade *f.*

particularly [pəˈtɪkjʊləlɪ] *adv* **-1.** [in particular] especialmente **-2.** [very] muito.

parting [ˈpɑːtɪŋ] *n* **-1.** (*U*) despedida *f* **-2.** *UK* [in hair] repartição *f.*

parting shot *n* tirada *f* final; to deliver a ~ fazer um último comentário antes de sair, dar uma tirada final.

partisan [ˌpɑːtɪˈzæn] <> *adj* partidário(ria). <> *n* guerrilheiro *m,* -ra *f.*

partition [pɑːˈtɪʃn] <> *n* **-1.** [wall] divisória *f* **-2.** [screen] separação *f* **-3.** [of a country] divisão *f.* <> *vt* **-1.** [room] separar com divisórias **-2.** [country] dividir.

partly [ˈpɑːtlɪ] *adv* em parte.

partner [ˈpɑːtnəʳ] <> *n* parceiro *m,* -ra *f.* <> *vt* ser parceiro de.

partnership [ˈpɑːtnəʃɪp] *n* parceria *f.*

partook [pɑːˈtʊk] *pt* ⊳ **partake.**

partridge [ˈpɑːtrɪdʒ] (*pl inv OR* -s) *n* perdiz *f.*

part-time <> *adj* de meio período. <> *adv* em meio período.

part-timer *n* funcionário *m,* -ria *f* de meio período.

party [ˈpɑːtɪ] (*pl* -ies, *pt* & *pp* -ied) <> *n* **-1.** *POL* partido *m* **-2.** [social gathering] festa *f* **-3.** [group] grupo *m* **-4.** *JUR, COMM* [individual] parte *f* **-5.** [involved person]: to be a ~ to sthg ter parte em algo. <> *vi inf* festejar.

party line *n* **-1.** *POL* linha *f* (política) do partido **-2.** *TELEC* extensão *f* de linha telefônica.

party piece *n inf* espetáculo *m* particular.

party political broadcast *n UK* propaganda *f* política em rádio e TV.

party politics *n* (*U*) política *f* partidária.

party wall *n* parede-meia *f.*

parvenu [ˈpɑːvənjuː] *n pej* novo-rico *m,* nova-rica *f.*

pass [pɑːs] <> *n* **-1.** [gen] passe *m* **-2.** *UK* [successful result] aprovação *f*; to get a ~ ser aprovado *m,* -da *f* em algo **-3.** [route between mountains] desfiladeiro *m* **-4.** *phr*: to make a ~ at sb *inf* passar-se com alguém. <> *vt* **-1.** [gen] passar; to ~ sthg to sb, to ~ sb sthg passar algo a alguém **-2.** [move past] passar por **-3.** *AUT* [overtake] ultrapassar **-4.** [exceed] passar de **-5.** [exam, test] passar em **-6.** [approve] aprovar **-7.** [express - opinion, judgment] formular; [- sentence] ditar. <> *vi* **-1.** [gen] passar **-2.** *AUT* [overtake] ultrapassar **-3.** *SPORT* fazer passes **-4.** [occur] ocorrer.
➤ **pass around** *vt sep* = **pass round.**
➤ **pass as** *vt fus* passar por.
➤ **pass away** *vi* falecer.
➤ **pass by** <> *vt sep fig* passar desapercebido (da) por. <> *vi* passar.
➤ **pass for** *vt fus* = **pass as.**
➤ **pass off** *vt sep*: to pass sb/sthg off as sthg fazer alguém/algo passar por algo.
➤ **pass on** <> *vt sep* **-1.** [object]: to pass sthg on (to sb) passar algo adiante (para alguém) **-2.** [characteristic, tradition, information] transmitir. <> *vi* **-1.** [move on]: to ~ on to the next question passar para a próxima questão **-2.** = **pass away.**
➤ **pass out** *vi* **-1.** [faint] desmaiar **-2.** *UK MIL* graduar-se.
➤ **pass over** *vt fus* passar por cima.
➤ **pass round** *vt sep* ir passando, passar.
➤ **pass to** *vt fus* passar para.
➤ **pass up** *vt sep* deixar passar.

passable [ˈpɑːsəbl] *adj* **-1.** [satisfactory] passável, aceitável **-2.** [not blocked] livre.

passably [ˈpɑːsəblɪ] *adv* aceitavelmente.

passage [ˈpæsɪdʒ] *n* **-1.** [gen] passagem *f* **-2.** *ANAT* trato *m* **-3.** [sea journey] travessia *f.*

passageway [ˈpæsɪdʒweɪ] *n* passagem *f,* corredor *m.*

passbook [ˈpɑːsbʊk] *n* caderneta *f* de conta bancária.

passé *adj pej* ultrapassado(da).

passenger [ˈpæsɪndʒəʳ] *n* passageiro *m,* -ra *f.*

passerby [ˌpɑːsəˈbaɪ] (*pl* **passersby** [ˌpɑːsəzˈbaɪ]) *n* passante *mf,* transeunte *mf.*

passing [ˈpɑːsɪŋ] <> *adj* passageiro(ra). <> *n* (*U*) passagem *f.*
➤ **in passing** *adv* de passagem.

passion [ˈpæʃn] *n* (*U*) paixão *f*; ~ for sthg paixão por algo.
➤ **Passion** *n*: the Passion a Paixão de Cristo.
➤ **passions** *npl* paixões *fpl.*

passionate [ˈpæʃənət] *adj* apaixonado(da).

passionately [ˈpæʃənətlɪ] *adv* apaixonadamente.

passionfruit [ˈpæʃənfruːt] *n* (*U*) maracujá *m.*

passive [ˈpæsɪv] <> *adj* passivo(va). <> *n*: the ~ a passiva.

passively [ˈpæsɪvlɪ] *adv* passivamente.

passive resistance *n* (*U*) resistência *f* passiva.

passive smoker *n* (*U*) fumante *mf* passivo, -va.

passivity [pæˈsɪvətɪ] *n* (*U*) passividade *f.*

passkey ['pɑ:ski:] *n* **-1.** [particular] chave *f* pessoal **-2.** [universal] chave-mestra *f*.

Passover ['pɑ:s͟ˌəʊvə͟ʳ] *n*: (the) ~ a Páscoa Judia.

passport ['pɑ:spɔ:t] *n* **-1.** [document] passaporte *m* **-2.** [means]: ~ **to sthg** passaporte para algo.

passport control *n* controle *m* de passaportes.

password ['pɑ:swɜ:d] *n* senha *f*.

past [pɑ:st] ⟨⟩ *adj* **-1.** [former] passado(da) **-2.** [last] último(ma); **over the ~ week** durante a última semana **-3.** [finished] terminado(da), passado(da); **our problems are now ~** nossos problemas terminaram. ⟨⟩ *adv* **-1.** [telling the time]: **it's ten ~ eleven** são onze e dez **-2.** [by] por; **to walk ~** passar por; **to run ~** passar correndo por; **he didn't see me as I drove ~** ele não me viu quando passei por ele de carro. ⟨⟩ *n* **-1.** [time]: **the ~** o passado; **in the ~** no passado **-2.** [personal history] passado *m*. ⟨⟩ *prep* **-1.** [telling the time]: **at five ~ nine** às nove e cinco; **it's half ~ eight** são oito e meia **-2.** [by] pela frente de **-3.** [beyond] além de; **the post office is ~ the bank** o correio é passando o banco; **to be ~ it** *inf* passar da idade disso; **I wouldn't put it ~ him** *inf* tratando-se dele eu não me surpreenderia.

pasta ['pæstə] *n* (U) massa *f*, macarrão *m*.

paste [peɪst] ⟨⟩ *n* **-1.** [smooth mixture] pasta *f* **-2.** (U) CULIN patê *m* **-3.** (U) [glue] cola *f* **-4.** (U) [jewellery] bijuteria *f*. ⟨⟩ *vt* [gen] colar.

pastel ['pæstl] ⟨⟩ *adj* pastel. ⟨⟩ *n* pastel *m*.

paste-up *n* TYPO colagem *f*.

pasteurize, -ise ['pɑ:stʃəraɪz] *vt* pasteurizar.

pastiche [pæ'sti:ʃ] *n* **-1.** [work of imitation] imitação *f* **-2.** [mixed work] pastiche *m*.

pastille ['pæstɪl] *n* pastilha *f*.

pastime ['pɑ:staɪm] *n* passatempo *m*.

pasting ['peɪstɪŋ] *n* *inf* surra *f*.

pastor ['pɑ:stə͟ʳ] *n* pastor *m*.

pastoral ['pɑ:stərəl] *adj* **-1.** RELIG pastoral **-2.** [countryside] bucólico(ca).

past participle *n* particípio *m* passado.

pastrami [pə'strɑ:mɪ] *n* (U) *carne de vaca defumada e muito condimentada.*

pastry ['peɪstrɪ] (*pl* -ies) *n* **-1.** (U) [mixture] massa *f* **-2.** [cake] torta *f*.

past tense *n* passado *m*.

pasture ['pɑ:stʃə͟ʳ] *n* pasto *m*.

pastureland ['pɑ:stʃələænd] *n* pastagem *f*.

pasty¹ ['peɪstɪ] (*compar* -ier, *superl* -iest) *adj* pálida (da).

pasty² ['pæstɪ] (*pl* -ies) *n* UK CULIN pastelão *m* de carne.

pasty-faced ['peɪstɪ-] *adj* com rosto pálido.

pat [pæt] (*compar* -ter, *superl* -test, *pt & pp* -ted, *cont* -ting) ⟨⟩ *adj* preparado(da), ensaiado(da). ⟨⟩ *adv*: **to have sthg off ~** ter algo na ponta da língua. ⟨⟩ *n* **-1.** [light stroke] palmadinha *f* **-2.** [small portion] porção *f* pequena. ⟨⟩ *vt* **-1.** [surface] bater de leve em **-2.** [dog] acariciar **-3.** [back, shoulder, hand] dar uma palmadinha em.

Patagonia [ˌpætə'gəʊnɪə] *n* Patagônia; **in ~** na Patagônia.

Patagonian ⟨⟩ *adj* patagônio(nia). ⟨⟩ *n* patagônio *m*, -nia *f*.

patch [pætʃ] ⟨⟩ *n* **-1.** [piece of material] remendo *m* **-2.** [to cover eye] venda *f* **-3.** [small area] área *f* **-4.** [of land] pedaço *m* **-5.** [period of time] período *m* **-6.** *phr*: **not to be a ~ on sb/sthg** *inf* não se comparar nem de longe com alguém/algo. ⟨⟩ *vt* remendar.

◆ **patch together** *vt sep* [assemble hastily - government] formar a duras penas; [- agreement] alcançar a duras penas.

◆ **patch up** *vt sep* **-1.** [mend] consertar, remendar **-2.** *fig* [resolve] resolver.

patchwork ['pætʃwɜ:k] ⟨⟩ *adj* de retalhos; **a ~ quilt** uma colcha de retalhos. ⟨⟩ *n* **-1.** colcha *f* de retalhos **-2.** *fig* [mixed collection - of fields] mosaico *m*; [- cultures, religions] mistura *m*; *inf* [hotchpotch] salada *m*.

patchy ['pætʃɪ] (*compar* -ier, *superl* -iest) *adj* **-1.** [gen] irregular **-2.** [incomplete] incompleto(ta).

pâté ['pæteɪ] *n* patê *m*.

patent [UK 'peɪtənt, US 'pætənt] ⟨⟩ *adj* evidente. ⟨⟩ *n* patente *f*. ⟨⟩ *vt* patentear.

patented [UK 'peɪtəntɪd, US 'pætəntɪdl *adj* patenteado(da).

patentee [UK ˌpeɪtən'ti:, US ˌpætən'ti:] *n* detentor *m*, -ra *f* de uma patente.

patent leather *n* (U) couro *m* envernizado.

patently [UK 'peɪtəntlɪ, US 'pætəntlɪ] *adv* evidentemente.

Patent Office *n*: **the ~** o Registro de Patentes.

paternal [pə'tɜ:nl] *adj* **-1.** [love, attitude] paternal **-2.** [relation] paterno(na).

paternalistic [pəˌtɜ:nə'lɪstɪk] *adj pej* paternalista.

paternity [pə'tɜ:nətɪ] *n* (U) paternidade *f*.

paternity leave *n* licença-paternidade *f*.

paternity suit *n* ação *f* de paternidade.

path [pɑ:θ, *pl* pɑ:ðz] *n* **-1.** [track] trilha *f* **-2.** [way ahead] caminho *m*; **our ~s had crossed before** nossos caminhos já se haviam cruzado antes **-3.** [trajectory] trajetória *f* **-4.** [course of action] curso *m*.

pathetic [pə'θetɪk] *adj* **-1.** [causing pity] patético(ca) **-2.** [useless] inútil, infeliz.

pathetically [pə'θetɪklɪ] *adv* **-1.** [causing pity] pateticamente **-2.** [uselessly] inutilmente.

pathological [ˌpæθə'lɒdʒɪkl] *adj* patológico(ca).

pathologist [pə'θɒlədʒɪst] *n* patologista *mf*.

pathology [pə'θɒlədʒɪ] *n* (U) patologia *f*.

pathos ['peɪθɒs] *n* (U) patos *m*.

pathway ['pɑ:θweɪ] *n* caminho *m*.

patience ['peɪʃns] *n* (U) paciência *f*; **to try sb's ~** testar a paciência de alguém.

patient ['peɪʃnt] ⟨⟩ *adj* paciente. ⟨⟩ *n* paciente *mf*.

patiently ['peɪʃntlɪ] *adv* pacientemente.

patina ['pætɪnə] *n* pátina *f*.

patio ['pætɪəʊ] (*pl* -s) *n* pátio *m*.

patio doors *npl* portas de vidros que dão para um pátio.

patisserie [pə'ti:sərɪ] *n* loja *f* de bolos e tortas.

Patna rice ['pætnə-] *n* (U) arroz *m* Patna.

patois ['pætwɑ:] (*pl inv*) *n* patoá *m*.

patriarch ['peɪtrɪɑ:k] *n* patriarca *m*.

patriarchy ['peɪtrɪɑ:kɪ] (*pl* -ies) *n* patriarcado *m*.

patrimony [*UK* 'pætrɪmənɪ, *US* 'pætrɪməʊnɪ] *n (U) fml* patrimônio *m*.

patriot [*UK* 'pætrɪət, *US* 'peɪtrɪət] *n* patriota *mf*.

patriotic [*UK* ˌpætrɪ'ɒtɪk, *US* ˌpeɪtrɪ'ɒtɪk] *adj* patriótico(ca).

patriotism [*UK* 'pætrɪətɪzm, *US* 'peɪtrɪətɪzm] *n (U)* patriotismo *m*.

patrol [pə'trəʊl] (*pt & pp* **-led**, *cont* **-ling**) ⇔ *n* patrulha *f*; **on ~ de** guarda. ⇔ *vt* patrulhar.

patrol car *n* radiopatrulha *f*.

patrolman [pə'trəʊlmən] (*pl* **-men** [-mən]) *n US* patrulheiro *m*, policial *m*.

patrol wagon *n US* camburão *m*.

patrolwoman [pə'trəʊlˌwʊmən] (*pl* **-women** [-ˌwɪmɪn]) *n US* patrulheira *f*.

patron [*'*peɪtrən] *n* **-1.** [gen] patrono *m*, -nesse *f* **-2.** *fml* [customer] cliente *mf*.

patronage [*'*pætrənɪdʒ] *n (U)* patrocínio *m*.

patronize, -ise [*'*pætrənaɪz] *vt* **-1.** *pej* [talk down to] tratar com condescendência **-2.** *fml* [be a customer of] ser cliente de **-3.** *fml* [back financially] patrocinar.

patronizing [*'*pætrənaɪzɪŋ] *adj pej* condescendente.

patron saint *n* (santo *m*) padroeiro *m*, (santa *f*) padroeira *f*.

patter [*'*pætə^r] ⇔ *n* **-1.** [sound of feet] passinhos *mpl* **-2.** *fig*: **the ~ of raindrops on the roof** o barulhinho da chuva no telhado **-3.** [talk] arenga *f*. ⇔ *vi* **-1.** [dog] dar passinhos rápidos **-2.** [rain] tamborilar.

pattern [*'*pætən] ⇔ *n* **-1.** [gen] padrão *m* **-2.** [for sewing, knitting] molde *m* **-3.** [model] modelo *m*. ⇔ *vt*: **to be ~ed on sthg** ser baseado(ada) em algo.

patterned [*'*pætənd] *adj* estampado(da).

patty [*'*pætɪ] (*pl* **-ies**) *n* **-1.** [pasty] empanada *f* **-2.** [savoury cake] tortinha *f*.

paucity [*'*pɔːsətɪ] *n fml* escassez *f*.

paunch [pɔːntʃ] *n* pança *f*, barriga *f*.

paunchy [*'*pɔːntʃɪ] (*compar* **-ier**, *superl* **-iest**) *adj* barrigudo(da).

pauper [*'*pɔːpə^r] *n* indigente *mf*.

pause [pɔːz] ⇔ *n* **-1.** [short silence] pausa *f* **-2.** [break, rest] interrupção *f*. ⇔ *vi* fazer uma pausa.

pave [peɪv] *vt* pavimentar; **to ~ the way for sb/sthg** preparar o terreno para alguém/algo.

paved [peɪvd] *adj* calçado(da), pavimentado(da).

pavement [*'*peɪvmənt] *n* **-1.** *UK* [at side of road] calçada *f* **-2.** *US* [roadway] rua *f*.

pavement artist *n UK* artista *mf* de rua.

pavilion [pə'vɪljən] *n* pavilhão *m*.

paving [*'*peɪvɪŋ] *n (U)* **-1.** [material] material *m* para pavimentação **-2.** [paved surface] pavimento *m*, calçamento *m*.

paving stone *n* paralelepípedo *m*.

paw [pɔː] ⇔ *n* pata *f*. ⇔ *vt* **-1.** [subj: animal] dar patadas em **-2.** *pej* [subj: person] apalpar.

pawn [pɔːn] ⇔ *n* **-1.** [chesspiece] peão *m* **-2.** [unimportant person] joguete *m*, marionete *f*. ⇔ *vt* empenhar.

pawnbroker [*'*pɔːnˌbrəʊkə^r] *n* penhorista *mf*.

pawnshop [*'*pɔːnʃɒp] *n* casa *f* de penhores.

pay [peɪ] (*pt & pp* **paid**) ⇔ *vt* **-1.** [gen] pagar; **to ~ sb/sth for sthg** pagar alguém/algo por algo; **to ~ one's way** pagar as despesas **-2.** *UK* [into bank account]: **to ~ sthg into sthg** depositar algo em algo **-3.** [be profitable to] ser rentável para; **it won't ~ you to sell just now** não vale a pena vender agora **-4.** [be advantageous to] ser proveitoso(sa) para; **it will ~ you not to say anything** é melhor você não dizer nada **-5.** [compliment, respects, attention] prestar; [visit, call] fazer. ⇔ *vi* **-1.** [gen] pagar; **to ~ for sthg** pagar algo; **the work ~s well** o trabalho é bem remunerado; **crime doesn't ~** o crime não compensa **-2.** *fig* [suffer] pagar; **to ~ dearly for sthg** pagar caro por algo. ⇔ *n* **-1.** [wage] paga *f* **-2.** [salary] salário *m*.

➡ pay back *vt sep* **-1.** [return loan of money to] devolver **-2.** [revenge o.s. on]: **to ~ sb back (for sthg)** pagar a alguém na mesma moeda (por algo).

➡ pay off ⇔ *vt sep* **-1.** [repay] saldar, liquidar **-2.** [dismiss] despedir com indenização **-3.** [bribe] subornar, comprar. ⇔ *vi* obter êxito.

➡ pay out ⇔ *vt sep* **-1.** [spend] desembolsar **-2.** [let out] soltar. ⇔ *vi* gastar.

➡ pay up *vi* saldar dívida.

payable [*'*peɪəbl] *adj* **-1.** [to be paid] a pagar **-2.** [on cheque]: **~ to sb** para crédito de alguém.

pay as you earn *n (U) UK* imposto *m* de renda retido na fonte.

pay-as-you-go *n* [for mobile phone, Internet, etc] *sistema de pagamento por tempo de uso*.

paybed [*'*peɪbed] *n UK* leito *m* pago *(em hospital público)*.

paycheck [*'*peɪtʃek] *n US* [cheque] contracheque *m*; [money] salário *m*.

pay cheque *n UK* contracheque *m*.

payday [*'*peɪdeɪ] *n (U)* dia *m* de pagamento.

PAYE (*abbr of* **pay as you earn**) *n (U)* imposto *m* de renda retido na fonte.

payee [peɪ'iː] *n* beneficiário *m*, -ria *f*.

pay envelope *n US* envelope *m* de pagamento.

payer [*'*peɪə^r] *n* pagador *m*, -ra *f*.

paying guest [*'*peɪɪŋ-] *n* pensionista *mf*.

paying-in book *n UK* formulário *m* para depósitos.

payload [*'*peɪləʊd] *n* **-1.** [load] carga *f* útil **-2.** *MIL, AERON* carga *f*.

paymaster [*'*peɪˌmɑːstə^r] *n aquele que detém o controle econômico sobre alguém*.

paymaster general *n UK responsável do governo britânico encarregado de pagar os funcionários do governo*.

payment [*'*peɪmənt] *n* pagamento *m*.

payoff [*'*peɪɒf] *n* **-1.** [result] resultado *m* **-2.** *UK* [redundancy payment] indenização *f (por demissão)*.

payola [peɪ'əʊlə] *n* [bribing] *(U) inf US* suborno *m*.

pay packet *n UK* **-1.** [envelope] envelope *m* de pagamento **-2.** [wages] pagamento *m*.

pay-per-view ⇔ *adj* [channel] pay-per-view. ⇔ *n* pay-per-view.

pay phone, pay station *US n* telefone *m* público.

payroll [*'*peɪrəʊl] *n* folha *f* de pagamento.

payslip *UK* ['peɪslɪp], **paystub** *US* *n* contracheque *m*.

pay station *n US* = pay phone.

paystub ['peɪstʌb] *n US* = payslip.

PBS (*abbr of* Public Broadcasting Service) *n* companhia de televisão norte-americana que produz programas de qualidade.

PBX (*abbr of* private branch exchange) *n* PBX *m*.

pc ◇ *n* (*abbr of* postcard) cartão-postal *m*. ◇ (*abbr of* per cent) por cento.

p/c (*abbr of* petty cash).

PC ◇ *n* -1. (*abbr of* personal computer) PC *m* -2. (*abbr of* police constable) policial *mf*. ◇ *adj* (*abbr of* politically correct) politicamente correto.

PCB (*abbr of* printed circuit board) *n* placa *f* de circuito impresso.

pcm (*abbr of* per calendar month) por mês (do calendário).

PCV (*abbr of* passenger-carrying vehicle) *n* veículo *m* de passageiros.

pd (*abbr of* paid) pg.

PD (*abbr of* police department) ≃ DP *f*.

PDA (*abbr of* personal digital assistant) *n* COMPUT PDA *m*.

PDF (*abbr of* portable document format) *n* COMPUT PDF *m*.

pdq (*abbr of* pretty damn quick) *adv inf* muito rápido.

PDSA (*abbr of* People's Dispensary for Sick Animals) *n* organização britânica que oferece atendimento veterinário gratuito.

PDT (*abbr of* Pacific Daylight Time) *n* horário de verão na costa oeste dos Estados Unidos.

PE (*abbr of* physical education) *n UK* ≃ Ed.Fis.

pea [piː] *n* CULIN ervilha *f*.

peace [piːs] *n (U)* -1. [gen] paz *f*; to be at ~ with sb/o.s./sthg estar em paz com alguém/consigo mesmo/com algo; to make (one's) ~ with sb/sthg fazer as pazes com alguém/algo -2. [law and order] paz *f*, ordem *f*.

peaceable ['piːsəbl] *adj* pacífico(ca).

peaceably ['piːsəbli] *adv* pacificamente.

Peace Corps *n* organização norte-americana que colabora com os projetos dos países em desenvolvimento.

peaceful ['piːsfʊl] *adj* -1. [tranquil] tranqüilo(la) -2. [non-violent] pacífico(ca).

peacefully ['piːsfʊli] *adv* -1. [tranquilly] tranqüilamente -2. [without violence] pacificamente.

peacefulness ['piːsfʊlnɪs] *n (U)* tranqüilidade *f*.

peacekeeping force ['piːsˌkiːpɪŋ-] *n* força *f* de paz.

peacemaker ['piːsˌmeɪkə'] *n* pacificador *m*, -ra *f*, conciliador *m*, -ra *f*.

peace offering *n inf* bandeira *f* branca.

peacetime ['piːstaɪm] *n (U)* tempo *m* de paz.

peach [piːtʃ] ◇ *adj* da cor de pêssego. ◇ *n* -1. [fruit] pêssego *m* -2. [colour] cor *f* de pêssego. ◇ *comp* de pêssego.

Peach Melba [-'melbə] *n* pêche *m* melba, composta de pêssego servida com sorvete de baunilha.

peacock ['piːkɒk] *n* pavão *m*.

peahen ['piːhen] *n* pavoa *f*.

peak [piːk] ◇ *adj* -1. [time] de pico -2. [productivity, condition] máximo(ma). ◇ *n* -1. [mountain top] pico *m* -2. [highest point] cume *m*, apogeu *m* -3. [of cap] viseira *f*. ◇ *vi* atingir o máximo.

peaked [piːkt] *adj* com viseira; ~ cap boné *m* (com viseira).

peak hour *n* hora *f* de pico.

peak period *n* período *m* de pico.

peak rate *n* tarifa *f* máxima.

peaky ['piːki] (*compar* -ier, *superl* -iest) *adj UK inf* acabado(da).

peal [piːl] ◇ *n* -1. [of bells] repique *m* -2. [of thunder] estrondo *m*; ~ (of laughter) gargalhada *f*. ◇ *vi* repicar.

peanut ['piːnʌt] *n* amendoim *m*.

peanut butter *n (U)* manteiga *f* de amendoim.

pear [peə'] *n* pêra *f*.

pearl [pɜːl] *n* pérola *f*.

pearly ['pɜːli] (*compar* -ier, *superl* -iest) *adj* perolado(da).

peasant ['peznt] *n* -1. [in countryside] camponês *m*, -esa *f* -2. *pej* [ignorant person] caipira *mf*.

peasantry ['pezntri] *n*: the ~ os camponeses.

peashooter ['piːˌʃuːtə'] *n* sarabatana *f*.

peat [piːt] *n (U)* turfa *f*.

peaty ['piːti] (*compar* -ier, *superl* -iest) *adj* turfoso(sa).

pebble ['pebl] *n* cascalho *m*, seixo *m*.

pebble-dash *n UK* argamassa *f* com cascalho.

pecan (nut) [pɪ'kæn-] *n* noz-pecã *f*.

pecan pie *n* torta *f* de noz-pecã.

peck [pek] ◇ *n* -1. [with beak] bicada *f* -2. [kiss] bicota *f*. ◇ *vt* -1. [with beak] bicar -2. [kiss] dar uma bicota. ◇ *vi* bicar.

pecking order ['pekɪŋ-] *n* hierarquia *f*.

peckish ['pekɪʃ] *adj UK inf* esfomeado(da).

pectin ['pektɪn] *n (U)* pectina *f*.

pectoral ['pektərəl] *adj* peitoral.

peculiar [pɪ'kjuːljə'] *adj* -1. [odd] esquisito(ta) -2. [slightly ill] estranho(nha) -3. [characteristic]: to be ~ to sb/sthg ser característico(ca) de alguém/algo.

peculiarity [pɪˌkjuːlɪ'ærətɪ] (*pl* -ies) *n* -1. [strange habit] peculiaridade *f* -2. [individual characteristic] singularidade *f* -3. [oddness] excentricidade *f*.

peculiarly [pɪ'kjuːljəlɪ] *adv* -1. [especially] particularmente -2. [oddly] estranhamente -3. [characteristically] tipicamente.

pecuniary [pɪ'kjuːnjərɪ] *adj* pecuniário(ria).

pedagogical [ˌpedə'gɒdʒɪkl] *adj* pedagógico(ca).

pedagogy [ˌpedə'gɒdʒɪ] *n (U)* pedagogia *f*.

pedal ['pedl] (*UK pt* & *pp* -led, *cont* -ling, *US pt* & *pp* -ed, *cont* -ing) ◇ *n* pedal *m*; brake ~ freio *m*. ◇ *vi* pedalar.

pedal bin *n* lixeira *f* com pedal.

pedalo ['pedələʊ] (*pl* -s OR -es) *n UK* pedalinho *m*.

pedant ['pednt] *n pej* pedante *mf*, formalista *mf*.

pedantic [pɪ'dæntɪk] *adj pej* pedante.

pedantry ['pedntrɪ] *n (U) pej* pedantismo *m*.

peddle ['pedl] *vt* -1. [sell] traficar -2. [spread] espalhar.

peddler ['pedlə'] *n* -1. [drug dealer] traficante *mf* -2. *US* = pedlar.

pederast ['pedəræst] *n* pederasta *m*.

pedestal ['pedɪstl] n pedestal m; **to put sb on a ~** colocar alguém num pedestal.

pedestrian [pɪ'destrɪən] ◇ adj pej enfadonho (nha). ◇ n pedestre mf.

pedestrian crossing n UK faixa f para pedestres.

pedestrianize, -ise [pɪ'destrɪənaɪz] vt transformar em área só para pedestres.

pedestrian precinct UK, **pedestrian zone** US n área f só para pedestres.

pediatric [ˌpiːdɪ'ætrɪk] adj pediátrico(ca).

pediatrician [ˌpiːdɪə'trɪʃn] n pediatra mf.

pediatrics [ˌpiːdɪ'ætrɪks] n (U) pediatria f.

pedicure ['pedɪˌkjʊəʳ] n pedicure mf.

pedigree ['pedɪgriː] ◇ adj com pedigree. ◇ n -1. [of animal] pedigree m -2. [of person] linhagem f.

pedlar UK, **peddler** US ['pedləʳ] n vendedor m, -ra f ambulante.

pedophile ['piːdəfaɪl] n = paedophile.

pee [piː] inf ◇ n xixi m; **to have a ~** fazer xixi. ◇ vi fazer xixi.

peek [piːk] inf ◇ n espiadela f. ◇ vi espiar.

peel [piːl] ◇ n (U) casca f. ◇ vt & vi descascar.
  ◆ **peel off** vt sep -1. [pull off] arrancar, desgrudar -2. [take off] tirar.

peeler ['piːləʳ] n descascador m.

peelings ['piːlɪŋz] npl cascas fpl.

peep [piːp] ◇ n -1. [look] espiada f -2. inf [sound] pio m. ◇ vi dar uma espiada em.
  ◆ **peep out** vi surgir.

peephole ['piːphəʊl] n vigia f (em porta).

peeping Tom [ˌpiːpɪŋ'tɒm] n voyeur m.

peep show n cineminha f, caixa que contém imagens em movimento que se pode ver através de um pequeno buraco.

peer [pɪəʳ] ◇ n -1. [noble] nobre m -2. [equal] par m. ◇ vi: **to ~ at** observar; **to ~ through the clouds** observar por entre as nuvens.

peerage ['pɪərɪdʒ] n pariato m; **the ~** o pariato.

peeress ['pɪərɪs] n -1. [woman peer] nobre f -2. [wife or widow of peer] esposa f de nobre.

peer group n grupo de mesma faixa etária ou classe social.

peer pressure n (U) pressão exercida pelo grupo da mesma faixa etária ou classe social a que se pertence.

peeved [piːvd] adj inf aborrecido(da).

peevish ['piːvɪʃ] adj irritadiço(ça), mal-humorado (da).

peg [peg] (pt & pp -ged, cont -ging) ◇ n -1. [hook] cabide m -2. [for washing line] prendedor m (de roupa) -3. [for tent] pino m. ◇ vt [price, increase] fixar.
  ◆ **peg out** ◇ vt sep estender. ◇ vi UK inf esticar as canelas.

PEI n abbr of Prince Edward Island.

pejorative [pɪ'dʒɒrətɪv] adj pejorativo(va).

pekinese (pl inv OR -s) n [dog] pequinês m.
  ◆ **Pekinese, Pekingese** ◇ adj pequinês(esa). ◇ n pequinês m, -esa f.

Peking [piː'kɪŋ] n Pequim; **in ~** em Pequim.

pekingese (pl inv OR -s) n = pekinese.

pelican ['pelɪkən] (pl inv OR -s) n pelicano m.

pelican crossing n UK faixa f de segurança (com semáforo acionado pelo pedestre).

pellet ['pelɪt] n -1. [small ball - of paper] bolinha f; [- of food, mud] bolo m -2. [for gun] chumbinho m.

pell-mell [ˌpel'mel] adv atropeladamente.

pelmet ['pelmɪt] n UK bandô m.

Peloponnese [ˌpeləpə'niːz] n: **the ~** o Peloponeso.

pelt [pelt] ◇ n -1. [animal skin] pele f -2. [speed]: **(at) full ~** a toda velocidade. ◇ vt: **to ~ sb with sthg** arremessar algo em alguém. ◇ vi -1. [rain] chover a cântaros -2. [run very fast] correr a toda.

pelvic ['pelvɪk] adj pélvico(ca).

pelvis ['pelvɪs] (pl -vises OR -ves [-viːz]) n pélvis f inv.

pen [pen] (pt & pp -ned, cont -ning) ◇ n -1. [for writing] caneta f -2. [enclosure] curral m. ◇ vt -1. literary [write] redigir, escrever -2. [enclose - livestock] cercar; [- people] encurralar.

penal ['piːnl] adj JUR penal.

penalize, -ise ['piːnəlaɪz] vt -1. [gen] penalizar -2. [put at a disadvantage] prejudicar.

penal settlement n colônia f penal.

penalty ['penltɪ] (pl -ies) n -1. [punishment] penalidade f; **to pay the ~ (for sthg)** fig pagar pena (por algo) -2. [fine] pena f -3. SPORT pênalti m; **~ (kick)** pênalti.

penalty area, penalty box n UK SPORT área f de pênalti, grande área f.

penalty clause n cláusula f penal.

penalty goal n gol m de pênalti.

penalty kick n ~ penalty.

penance ['penəns] n (U) penitência f.

pen-and-ink adj à tinta.

pence [pens] UK pl ▷ penny.

penchant [UK pɑ̃ʃɑ̃, US 'pentʃənt] n: **to have a ~ for sthg/for doing sthg** ter uma queda por algo/ por fazer algo.

pencil ['pensl] (UK pt & pp -led, cont -ling, US pt & pp -ed, cont -ing) ◇ n lápis m inv; **in ~** a lápis. ◇ vt escrever a lápis.
  ◆ **pencil in** vt sep -1. [person] inscrever provisoriamente -2. [date] marcar provisoriamente.

pencil case n estojo m (de canetas).

pencil sharpener n apontador m de lápis.

pendant ['pendənt] n pendente m.

pending ['pendɪŋ] fml ◇ adj -1. [about to happen] iminente -2. [waiting to be dealt with] pendente. ◇ prep à espera de.

pending tray n UK bandeja f de assuntos pendentes.

pendulum ['pendjʊləm] (pl -s) n pêndulo m.

penetrate ['penɪtreɪt] ◇ vt -1. [get through - subj: person, object] penetrar em, adentrar-se em; [- rain] infiltrar-se em -2. [infiltrate - party] entrar nisto; [- terrorist group, spy ring] infiltrar-se em. ◇ vi inf [be understood] cair a ficha.

penetrating ['penɪtreɪtɪŋ] adj -1. [gen] penetrante -2. [wind, cold] cortante.

penetration [ˌpenɪ'treɪʃn] n (U) -1. [gen] penetração f -2. fml [insight] perspicácia f.

penfriend ['penfrend] n amigo m, -ga f por correspondência.

penguin ['peŋgwɪn] n pingüim m.

penicillin [ˌpenɪˈsɪlɪn] *n (U)* penicilina *f.*
peninsula [pəˈnɪnsjʊlə] (*pl* **-s**) *n* península *f.*
penis [ˈpiːnɪs] (*pl* **penises** [ˈpiːnɪsɪz]) *n* pênis *m inv.*
penitent [ˈpenɪtənt] *adj fml* penitente.
penitentiary [ˌpenɪˈtenʃərɪ] (*pl* **-ies**) *n US* penitenciária *f.*
penknife [ˈpennaɪf] (*pl* **-knives** [-naɪvz]) *n* canivete *m*, navalha *f.*
pen-name *n* pseudônimo *m.*
pennant [ˈpenənt] *n* bandeirola *f.*
penniless [ˈpenɪlɪs] *adj* sem dinheiro.
Pennines [ˈpenaɪnz] *npl*: **the** ~ as Pennines.
Pennsylvania [ˌpensɪlˈveɪnɪə] *n* Pensilvânia *f.*
penny [ˈpenɪ] (*pl senses 1* & *2* **-ies**, *pl sense 3* **pence**) *n*
- **1.** *UK* [coin] pêni *m* - **2.** *US* [coin] centavo *m* - **3.** *UK* [value] centavo *m* - **4.** *phr*: **a** ~ **for your thoughts** um centavo por seus pensamentos; **the** ~ **dropped** *UK inf* caiu a ficha; **to spend a** ~ *UK inf* fazer xixi; **two** *OR* **ten a** ~ *UK inf* a preço de banana.
penny-pinching [-ˌpɪntʃɪŋ] <> *adj* avarento(ta). <> *n (U)* avareza *f.*
pen pal *n inf* amigo *m*, -ga *f* por correspondência.
pension [ˈpenʃn] *n* - **1.** *UK* [on retirement - state scheme] pensão *f*; [- private scheme] previdência *f* privada - **2.** [for disability] pensão *f* por invalidez.
➨ **pension off** *vt sep* aposentar-se.
pensionable [ˈpenʃənəbl] *adj* com direito à aposentadoria; ~ **age** idade *f* de se aposentar.
pension book *n UK* carnê dado pelo governo britânico a todos os pensionistas e cujos cupons podem ser trocados semanalmente por dinheiro nas agências dos correios.
pensioner [ˈpenʃənəʳ] *n UK*: **(old-age)** ~ pensionista *mf.*
pension fund *n* fundo *m* de pensão.
pension plan, pension scheme *n* plano *m* de aposentadoria.
pensive [ˈpensɪv] *adj* pensativo(va).
pentagon [ˈpentəgən] *n* pentágono *m.*
➨ **Pentagon** *n US*: **the Pentagon** o Pentágono.

PENTAGON

O Pentágono, imenso edifício de cinco faces situado em Washington, abriga o ministério da Defesa dos EUA. De modo geral, o termo é empregado também para designar o poder militar estadunidense.

pentathlete [penˈtæθliːt] *n* pentatleta *mf.*
pentathlon [penˈtæθlən] (*pl* **-s**) *n* pentatlo *m.*
Pentecost [ˈpentɪkɒst] *n* Pentecostes *m inv.*
penthouse [ˈpenthaʊs, *pl* -haʊzɪz] *n* cobertura *f.*
pent up [ˈpent-] *adj* contido(da), reprimido(da).
penultimate [peˈnʌltɪmət] *adj* penúltimo(ma).
penury [ˈpenjʊrɪ] *n (U) fml* penúria *f.*
peony [ˈpɪənɪ] (*pl* **-ies**) *n* peônia *f.*
people [ˈpiːpl] <> *n* [nation, race] povo *m.* <> *npl* - **1.** [gen] pessoas *fpl*; ~ **say that ...** dizem que ... - **2.** [inhabitants] habitantes *mpl* - **3.** *POL*: **the** ~ o povo. <> *vt*: **to be** ~ **d by** *OR* **with** ser povoado(da) por.
people carrier *n* monovolume *m.*
pep [pep] (*pt* & *pp* **-ped**, *cont* **-ping**) *n inf* vigor *m*, vitalidade *f.*

➨ **pep up** *vt sep* - **1.** [person] revigorar - **2.** [party, event] animar.
PEP (*abbr of* **personal equity plan**) *n plano de poupança popular na Grã-Bretanha.*
pepper [ˈpepəʳ] *n* - **1.** *(U)* [spice] pimenta *f*; **black / white** ~ pimenta preta/branca - **2.** [vegetable] pimentão *m*; **red/green** ~ pimentão vermelho/verde.
pepperbox *n US* = **pepper pot**.
peppercorn [ˈpepəkɔːn] *n* grão *m* de pimenta.
peppered [ˈpepəd] *adj* - **1.** [sprinkled]: ~ **(with sthg)** salpicado(da) (de algo) - **2.** [hit repeatedly]: ~ **(with sthg)** crivado(da) (de algo).
pepper mill *n* moedor *m* de pimenta.
peppermint [ˈpepəmɪnt] *n* - **1.** [sweet] menta *f* - **2.** *(U)* [herb] hortelã-pimenta *f.*
pepper pot *UK*, **pepperbox** *US* [ˈpepəbɒks] *n* pimenteira *f.*
peppery [ˈpepərɪ] *adj* apimentado(da).
pep talk *n inf* palavras *fpl* de ânimo *OR* incentivo.
peptic ulcer [ˈpeptɪk-] *n* úlcera *f* péptica.
per [pɜːʳ] *prep* por; ~ **hour/day/kilo/person** por hora/dia/quilo/pessoa; **as** ~ **instructions** conforme/segundo as instruções.
per annum *adv* por ano.
p/e ratio (*abbr of* **price-earnings ratio**) *n* índice *m* de benefício.
per capita [pəˈkæpɪtə] *adj, adv* per capita.
perceive [pəˈsiːv] *vt* - **1.** [see] distinguir - **2.** [notice, realize] perceber, ver - **3.** [conceive, consider]: **to** ~ **sb/sthg as** ver alguém/algo como.
per cent *adv* por cento.
percentage [pəˈsentɪdʒ] *n* porcentagem *f.*
perceptible [pəˈseptəbl] *adj* perceptível.
perception [pəˈsepʃn] *n* - **1.** *(U)* [gen] distinção *f* - **2.** *(U)* [insight, understanding] percepção *f*, perspicácia *f* - **3.** [opinion] idéia *f.*
perceptive [pəˈseptɪv] *adj* perspicaz.
perceptively [pəˈseptɪvlɪ] *adv* de modo perspicaz.
perch [pɜːtʃ] (*pl sense 3 only inv OR* **-es**) <> *n* - **1.** [for bird] poleiro *m* - **2.** [high position] posição *f* elevada - **3.** [fish] perca *f.* <> *vi*: **to** ~ **(on sthg)** [bird] pousar (em algo); [person] empoleirar-se (em algo).
percolate [ˈpɜːkəleɪt] *vi* - **1.** [brew] coar - **2.** [seep - water] infiltrar-se; [- news] vazar.
percolator [ˈpɜːkəleɪtəʳ] *n* cafeteira *f.*
percussion [pəˈkʌʃn] *n (U) MUS* percussão *f*; **the** ~ **(section)** a percussão.
percussionist [pəˈkʌʃənɪst] *n* percussionista *mf.*
peremptory [pəˈremptərɪ] *adj* peremptório(ria), categórico(ca).
perennial [pəˈrenjəl] <> *adj* perene. <> *n BOT* planta *f* perene.
perestroika [ˌperəˈstrɔɪkə] *n (U)* perestroika *f.*
perfect [*adj* & *n* ˈpɜːfɪkt, *vb* pəˈfekt] <> *adj* perfeito(ta); **it makes** ~ **sense** é perfeitamente lógico(ca). <> *n GRAMM*: ~ **(tense)** o perfeito. <> *vt* aperfeiçoar.
perfect competition *n (U) ECON* concorrência *f* perfeita.
perfection [pəˈfekʃn] *n* perfeição *f*; **to** ~ à perfeição.
perfectionist [pəˈfekʃənɪst] *n* perfeccionista *mf.*

perfectly ['pɜːfɪktlɪ] adv perfeitamente; ~ **hon-est/ridiculous** totalmente honesto/ridículo, totalmente honesta/ridícula.

perforate ['pɜːfəreɪt] vt perfurar.

perforations [,pɜːfə'reɪʃnz] npl perfurações fpl.

perform [pə'fɔːm] ⟨> vt **-1.** [carry out] realizar, levar a cabo **-2.** [in front of audience - play] representar, interpretar; [- music, dance] apresentar. ⟨> vi **-1.** [function - car, machine] funcionar; [- person, team] sair-se **-2.** [in front of audience] apresentar-se, atuar.

performance [pə'fɔːməns] n **-1.** (U) [carrying out, doing] execução f, realização f **-2.** [show] apresentação f **-3.** [rendition] performance f, desempenho m **-4.** (U) [of car, engine] desempenho m, rendimento m.

performance art n (U) expressão artística em que se combina diversas atividades como teatro, música, dança, escultura, fotografia etc.

performance car n carro m de alto desempenho.

performer [pə'fɔːmə'] n performer mf.

performing arts [pə'fɔːmɪŋ-] npl: **the** ~ as artes performáticas.

perfume ['pɜːfjuːm] n **-1.** [for woman] perfume m **-2.** [pleasant smell] aroma f.

perfumed [UK 'pɜːfjuːmd, US pər'fjuːmd] adj perfumado(da).

perfunctory [pə'fʌŋktərɪ] adj superficial, feito(ta) às pressas.

perhaps [pə'hæps] adv talvez; ~ **you're right** talvez você esteja certo; ~ **so/not** talvez sim/não; ~ **you should go and see her?** quem sabe você vai dar uma olhada nela?

peril ['perɪl] n (U) literary perigo m; **at one's** ~ por sua conta e risco.

perilous ['perələs] adj literary perigoso(sa).

perilously ['perələslɪ] adv perigosamente.

perimeter [pə'rɪmɪtə'] n perímetro m; ~ **fence/wall** alambrado m, cerca f.

period ['pɪərɪəd] ⟨> n **-1.** [gen] período m; **free** ~ período livre **-2.** HISTORY era f **-3.** [menstruation] período m menstrual **-4.** US [full stop] ponto m. ⟨> comp [dress, furniture] de época.

periodic [,pɪərɪ'ɒdɪk] adj periódico(ca).

periodical [,pɪərɪ'ɒdɪkl] ⟨> adj = periodic. ⟨> n periódico m.

periodic table n tabela f periódica.

period pains npl cólicas fpl menstruais.

period piece n obra f de época.

peripatetic [,perɪpə'tetɪk] adj itinerante.

peripheral [pə'rɪfərəl] ⟨> adj **-1.** [of little importance] secundário(ria) **-2.** [at edge] periférico(ca). ⟨> n COMPUT periférico m.

periphery [pə'rɪfərɪ] (pl-ies) n **-1.** [edge] periferia f **-2.** [unimportant area] margens fpl.

periscope ['perɪskəʊp] n periscópio m.

perish ['perɪʃ] vi **-1.** [die] perecer **-2.** [decay] deteriorar-se.

perishable ['perɪʃəbl] adj perecível.

➔ **perishables** npl produtos mpl perecíveis.

perishing ['perɪʃɪŋ] adj UK inf **-1.** [cold] frio (fria) de

rachar; **it's** ~ está fazendo um frio de rachar **-2.** [for emphasis] danado(da).

peritonitis [,perɪtə'naɪtɪs] n (U) peritonite f.

perjure ['pɜːdʒə'] vt JUR: **to** ~ **o.s.** perjurar-se.

perjury ['pɜːdʒərɪ] n (U) JUR perjúrio m.

perk [pɜːk] n inf mordomia m, regalia f.

➔ **perk up** vi animar-se.

perky ['pɜːkɪ] (compar -ier, superl -iest) adj inf animado(da), alegre.

perm [pɜːm] ⟨> n permanente m. ⟨> vt fazer permanente.

permanence ['pɜːmənəns] n (U) permanência f.

permanent ['pɜːmənənt] ⟨> adj **-1.** [not temporary - job] fixo(xa); [- damage, feature] permanente **-2.** [continuous, constant] permanente, constante. ⟨> n US permanente m.

permanently ['pɜːmənəntlɪ] adv **-1.** [forever] permanentemente **-2.** [continuously] permanentemente.

permeable ['pɜːmjəbl] adj permeável.

permeate ['pɜːmɪeɪt] vt permear.

permissible [pə'mɪsəbl] adj permissível.

permission [pə'mɪʃn] n (U) permissão f; ~ **to do sthg** permissão para fazer algo.

permissive [pə'mɪsɪv] adj permissivo(va), tolerante.

permissiveness [pə'mɪsɪvnɪs] n (U) tolerância f.

permit [vb pə'mɪt, n 'pɜːmɪt] (pt & pp -ted, cont -ting) ⟨> n autorização f. ⟨> vt permitir; **to** ~ **sb to do sthg** permitir que alguém faça algo; **my mother won't** ~ **me to go out** minha mãe não vai me deixar sair; **to** ~ **sb sthg** permitir algo a alguém. ⟨> vi permitir; **weather permitting** se o tempo deixar.

permutation [,pɜːmjuː'teɪʃn] n permutação f.

pernicious [pə'nɪʃəs] adj fml pernicioso(sa).

pernickety UK [pə'nɪkətɪ], **persnickety** US adj inf meticuloso(sa).

peroxide [pə'rɒksaɪd] n (U) peróxido m.

peroxide blonde n loura f oxigenada OR de farmácia.

perpendicular [,pɜːpən'dɪkjʊlə'] ⟨> adj **-1.** MATH perpendicular; ~ **to sthg** perpendicular a algo **-2.** [upright] vertical. ⟨> n MATH perpendicular f.

perpetrate ['pɜːpɪtreɪt] vt fml perpetrar.

perpetration [,pɜːpɪ'treɪʃn] n (U) fml perpetração f.

perpetrator ['pɜːpɪtreɪtə'] n fml perpetrador m, -ra f.

perpetual [pə'petʃʊəl] adj **-1.** pej [continuous] constante **-2.** [everlasting - darkness] perpétuo(tua); [- hunger] eterno(na).

perpetually [pə'petʃʊəlɪ] adv **-1.** pej [continuously] constantemente, continuamente **-2.** [forever] perpetuamente, eternamente.

perpetual motion n (U) moto-contínuo m.

perpetuate [pə'petʃʊeɪt] vt perpetuar.

perpetuation [pə,petʃʊ'eɪʃn] n (U) perpetuação f.

perpetuity [,pɜːpɪ'tjuːətɪ] n (U): **in** ~ fml para sempre.

perplex [pə'pleks] vt desconcertar, deixar perplexo(xa).

perplexed [pə'plekst] adj perplexo(xa).

perplexing [pə'pleksɪŋ] *adj* desconcertante.

perplexity [pə'pleksətɪ] *n (U)* perplexidade *f*.

perquisite ['pɜːkwɪzɪt] *n fml* privilégios *mpl* adicionais.

per se [pɜː'seɪ] *adv* **-1.** [as such] como tal **-2.** [in itself] em si.

persecute ['pɜːsɪkjuːt] *vt* perseguir, oprimir.

persecution [ˌpɜːsɪ'kjuːʃn] *n* **-1.** [act of cruelty] perseguição *f* **-2.** [cruel treatment] opressão *f*.

persecutor ['pɜːsɪkjuːtəʳ] *n* opressor *m*, -ra *f*, perseguidor *m*, -ra *f*.

perseverance [ˌpɜːsɪ'vɪərəns] *n (U)* perseverança *f*.

persevere [ˌpɜːsɪ'vɪəʳ] *vi* **-1.** [with difficulty] perseverar; **to** ~ **with sthg** persistir em algo **-2.** [with determination]: **to** ~ **in doing sthg** insistir em fazer algo.

Persia ['pɜːʃə] *n* Pérsia; **in** ~ na Pérsia.

Persian ['pɜːʃn] <> *adj* persa. <> *n* **-1.** [person] persa *mf* **-2.** [language] persa *m*.

Persian cat *n* gato *m*, -ta *f* persa.

Persian Gulf *n*: **the** ~ o Golfo Pérsico.

persist [pə'sɪst] *vi* **-1.** [problem, situation, rain] persistir **-2.** [person]: **to** ~ **in doing sthg** insistir em fazer algo.

persistence [pə'sɪstəns] *n (U)* **-1.** [continuation] persistência *f* **-2.** [determination] obstinação *f*, determinação *f*.

persistent [pə'sɪstənt] *adj* **-1.** [constant] constante **-2.** [determined] obstinado(da) determinado(da).

persistently [pə'sɪstəntlɪ] *adv* **-1.** [constantly] constantemente **-2.** [determinedly] obstinadamente, de forma determinada.

persnickety [pə'snɪkɪtɪ] *adj US* = pernickety.

person ['pɜːsn] (*pl* people OR persons *fml*) *n* **-1.** [man or woman] pessoa *f*; **in** ~ pessoalmente, em pessoa; **in the** ~ **of** na pessoa de **-2.** [body]: **about one's** ~ em seu corpo **-3.** GRAMM pessoa *f*.

persona [pə'səʊnə] (*pl* -s OR -ae [-iː]) *n* imagem *f*.

personable ['pɜːsnəbl] *adj* bem-apessoado(da).

personage ['pɜːsənɪdʒ] *n fml* personalidade *f*.

personal ['pɜːsənl] <> *adj* **-1.** [gen] pessoal **-2.** [letter, message] particular **-3.** *pej* [rude] ofensivo (va). <> *n US* [advert] nota *f* pessoal (em jornal).

personal account *n* conta *f* pessoal.

personal allowance *n* FIN desconto *m* simplificado (na declaração do imposto de renda).

personal assistant *n* assistente *mf* particular.

personal call *n* telefonema *m* particular, chamada *f* pessoal.

personal column *n* seção *f* de recados (em jornal).

personal computer *n* computador *m* pessoal.

personal estate *n* bens *mpl* móveis.

personal hygiene *n (U)* higiene *f* pessoal.

personality [ˌpɜːsə'nælətɪ] (*pl*-ies) *n* personalidade *f*.

personalize, -ise ['pɜːsənəlaɪz] *vt* **-1.** [mark with name, initials] personalizar **-2.** *pej* [issue, argument] levar para o lado pessoal.

personalized ['pɜːsənəlaɪzd] *adj* personalizado (da).

personally ['pɜːsnəlɪ] *adv* pessoalmente; **to take**

sthg ~ levar algo para o lado pessoal.

personal organizer *n* agenda *f* pessoal.

personal pension plan *n* plano *m* de previdência particular.

personal pronoun *n* pronome *m* pessoal.

personal property *n (U)* JUR bens *mpl* móveis.

personal stereo *n* walkman *m*.

persona non grata [-'grɑːtə] (*pl* personae non gratae [-'grɑːtiː]) *n* persona non grata *f*.

personify [pə'sɒnɪfaɪ] (*pt* & *pp* -ied) *vt* personificar.

personnel [ˌpɜːsə'nel] <> *n (U)* [in firm, organization] equipe *f*. <> *npl* [staff] funcionários *mpl*.

personnel department *n* departamento *m* de pessoal.

personnel officer *n* funcionário *m*, -ria *f* do departamento pessoal.

person-to-person *adj* TELEC de pessoa a pessoa.

perspective [pə'spektɪv] *n* perspectiva *f*; **to get sthg in** ~ *fig* pôr algo em perspectiva.

Perspex® ['pɜːspeks] *n UK* plexiglás® *m*.

perspicacious [ˌpɜːspɪ'keɪʃəs] *adj fml* perspicaz.

perspiration [ˌpɜːspə'reɪʃn] *n* transpiração *f*.

perspire [pə'spaɪəʳ] *vi* transpirar.

persuade [pə'sweɪd] *vt* persuadir; **to** ~ **sb to do sthg** persuadir alguém a fazer algo; **to** ~ **sb that** convencer alguém de que; **to** ~ **sb of sthg** convencer alguém de algo.

persuasion [pə'sweɪʒn] *n* **-1.** *(U)* [act of persuading] persuasão *f* **-2.** [belief] crença *f*.

persuasive [pə'sweɪsɪv] *adj* persuasivo(va).

persuasively [pə'sweɪsɪvlɪ] *adv* persuasivamente.

pert [pɜːt] *adj* **-1.** [person, reply] vivo(va), atrevido(da) **-2.** [nose, bottom] gracioso(sa).

pertain [pə'teɪn] *vi fml*: ~ **ing to sb/sthg** relacionado(da) a alguém/algo.

pertinence ['pɜːtɪnəns] *n (U)* pertinência *f*, relevância *f*.

pertinent ['pɜːtɪnənt] *adj* pertinente, relevante.

perturb [pə'tɜːb] *vt fml* perturbar.

perturbed [pə'tɜːbd] *adj fml* perturbado(da).

Peru [pə'ruː] *n* Peru; **in** ~ no Peru.

perusal [pə'ruːzl] *n* **-1.** [thorough reading] leitura *f* **-2.** [quick reading] leitura *f* rápida.

peruse [pə'ruːz] *vt* **-1.** [read thoroughly] ler com atenção **-2.** [read quickly] ler por cima.

Peruvian [pə'ruːvjən] <> *adj* peruano(na). <> *n* peruano *m*, -na *f*.

pervade [pə'veɪd] *vt* impregnar.

pervasive [pə'veɪsɪv] *adj* penetrante.

perverse [pə'vɜːs] *adj* perverso(sa).

perversely [pə'vɜːslɪ] *adv* perversamente.

perversion [UK pə'vɜːʃn, US pə'vɜːrʒn] *n* perversão *f*.

perversity [pə'vɜːsətɪ] *n (U)* perversidade *f*.

pervert [*n* 'pɜːvɜːt, *vb* pə'vɜːt] <> *n* pervertido *m*, -da *f*. <> *vt* **-1.** [distort] distorcer **-2.** [corrupt morally] perverter.

perverted [pə'vɜːtɪd] *adj* **-1.** [sexually deviant] pervertido(da) **-2.** [distorted] distorcido(da).

peseta [pə'seɪtə] *n* peseta *f*.

peso ['peɪsəʊl] (*pl* **-s**) *n* peso *m*.
pessary ['pesərɪ] (*pl* **-ies**) *n* pessário *m*.
pessimism ['pesɪmɪzml] *n (U)* pessimismo *m*.
pessimist ['pesɪmɪstl] *n* pessimista *mf*.
pessimistic [ˌpesɪ'mɪstɪk] *adj* pessimista.
pest [pestl] *n* [gen] praga *f*, peste *f*.
pester ['pestə'] *vt* importunar, incomodar.
pesticide ['pestɪsaɪd] *n* pesticida *f*.
pestle ['pesl] *n* pilão *m*.
pet [petl] (*pt* & *pp* **-ted**, *cont* **-ting**) <> *adj* [favourite] predileto(ta), preferido(da). <> *n* **-1.** [domestic animal] animal *m* de estimação **- 2.** [favourite person] preferido *m*, -da *f*. <> *vt* acariciar, afagar. <> *vi* acariciar-se.
petal ['petl] *n* pétala *f*.
peter ['piːtə'] ➡ **peter out** *vi* **-1.** [food, interest] esgotar-se **- 2.** [path] desaparecer.
pethidine ['peθɪdiːn] *n (U)* petidina *f*.
petit bourgeois [pəˌtiː'bʊəʒwaː] (*pl* **petits bourgeois** [pəˌtiː'bʊəʒwaː]) <> *adj* pequeno-burguês (guesa). <> *n* pequeno-burguês *m*, -guesa *f*.
petite [pə'tiːt] *adj* diminuto(ta).
petit four [ˌpeti-] (*pl* **petits fours** [ˌpeti-]) *n* bolo pequeno ou biscoito servido com café no final da refeição.
petition [pɪ'tɪʃn] <> *n* **-1.** [supporting campaign] abaixo-assinado *m* **- 2.** *JUR* petição *f*. <> *vt* peticionar. <> *vi* **-1.** [campaign]: **to** ~ **for/against sthg** fazer um abaixo-assinado a favor de/contra algo **- 2.** *JUR*: **to** ~ **for divorce** pedir o divórcio.
petitioner [pɪ'tɪʃənə'] *n* **-1.** *JUR* [in divorce] requerente *mf* **- 2.** [on petition] peticionário *m*, -ria *f*.
pet name *n* apelido *m* carinhoso.
petrified ['petrɪfaɪd] *adj* petrificado(da).
petrify ['petrɪfaɪ] (*pt* & *pp* **-ied**) *vt* petrificar.
petrochemical [ˌpetrəʊ'kemɪkl] *adj* petroquímico(ca).
petrodollar ['petrəʊˌdɒlə'] *n FIN* petrodólar *m*.
petrol ['petrəl] *n (U) UK* gasolina *f*.
petrolatum *n US* vaselina *f (líquida)*.
petrol bomb *n UK* coquetel *m* molotov.
petrol can *n UK* lata *f* de gasolina.
petrol cap *n UK* tampa *f* do tanque de combustível.
petroleum [pɪ'trəʊljəm] *n (U)* petróleo *m*.
petroleum jelly *n UK* vaselina *f*.
petrol pump *n UK* bomba *f* de gasolina.
petrol pump attendant *n UK* frentista *mf*.
petrol station *n UK* posto *m* de gasolina.
petrol tank *n UK* tanque *m* de gasolina.
pet shop *n* pet shop *f*, loja *f* de produtos para animais de estimação.
petticoat ['petɪkəʊt] *n* anágua *f*.
pettiness ['petɪnɪs] *n (U)* mesquinharia *f*.
petty ['petɪ] (*compar* **-ier**, *superl* **-iest**) *adj* **-1.** [small-minded] mesquinho(nha) **- 2.** [trivial] insignificante.
petty cash *n (U)* dinheiro *m* para pequenas despesas, trocado *m*.
petty officer *n* suboficial *mf*.
petulant ['petjʊlənt] *adj* petulante.
petunia [pɪ'tjuːnjə] *n* petúnia *f*.
pew [pjuː] *n* banco *m (de igreja)*.

pewter ['pjuːtə'] *n (U)* peltre *m*.
PG (*abbr of* **parental guidance**) *para menores acompanhados*.
PGA (*abbr of* **Professional Golfers' Association**) *n* associação de jogadores profissionais de golfe nos Estados Unidos.
p & h (*abbr of* **postage and handling**) *n US* valor *m* de postagem.
pH (*abbr of* **potential of hydrogen**) *n CHEM* ph.
PH (*abbr of* **Purple Heart**) *n (beneficiário de) honraria concedida pelo governo norte-americano a soldados feridos em ação*.
PHA (*abbr of* **Public Housing Administration**) *n órgão norte-americano encarregado de fornecer alojamento a pessoas necessitadas*.
phallic ['fælɪk] *adj* fálico(ca); ~ **symbol** símbolo *m* fálico.
phallus ['fæləs] (*pl* **-es** OR **phalli** ['fælaɪ]) *n* falo *m*.
phantom ['fæntəm] <> *adj* [imaginary] ilusório(ria). <> *n* [ghost] fantasma *m*.
phantom pregnancy *n* gravidez *f* psicológica.
pharaoh ['feərəʊ] *n* faraó *m*.
Pharisee ['færɪsiː] *n* fariseu *m*.
pharmaceutical [ˌfɑːmə'sjuːtɪkl] *adj* farmacêutico(ca).
➡ **pharmaceuticals** *npl* produtos *mpl* farmacêuticos.
pharmacist ['fɑːməsɪst] *n* farmacêutico *m*, -ca *f*.
pharmacology [ˌfɑːmə'kɒlədʒɪ] *n (U)* farmacologia *f*.
pharmacy ['fɑːməsɪ] (*pl* **-ies**) *n* farmácia *f*.
phase [feɪz] <> *n* fase *f*. <> *vt* dividir em etapas, escalonar.
➡ **phase in** *vt sep* introduzir gradualmente.
➡ **phase out** *vt sep* retirar gradualmente.
PhD (*abbr of* **Doctor of Philosophy**) *n (titular de) doutorado em ciências humanas*.
pheasant ['feznt] (*pl inv* OR **-s**) *n* faisão *m*.
phenobarbitone *UK* [ˌfiːnəʊ'bɑːbɪtəʊnl], **phenobarbitol** *US* [ˌfiːnəʊ'bɑːbɪtl] *n (U)* fenobarbital *m*.
phenomena [fɪ'nɒmɪnə] *pl* ▷ **phenomenon**.
phenomenal [fɪ'nɒmɪnl] *adj* fenomenal.
phenomenon [fɪ'nɒmɪnən] (*pl* **-mena**) *n* fenômeno *m*.
phew [fjuː] *excl* ufa!
phial ['faɪəl] *n* frasco *m*.
Philadelphia [ˌfɪlə'delfɪə] *n* Filadélfia.
philanderer [fɪ'lændərə'] *n* galanteador *m*, sedutor *m*.
philanthropic [ˌfɪlən'θrɒpɪk] *adj* filantrópico(ca).
philanthropist [fɪ'lænθrəpɪst] *n* filantropo *m*.
philately [fɪ'lætəlɪ] *n (U)* filatelia *f*.
philharmonic [ˌfɪlɑː'mɒnɪk] *adj* filarmônico(ca).
Philippine ['fɪlɪpiːn] *adj* filipino(na); **the** ~ **Islands** as (Ilhas) Filipinas.
➡ **Philippines** *npl*: **the** ~ **s** as Filipinas.
philistine [*UK* 'fɪlɪstaɪn, *US* 'fɪlɪstiːn] *n* filisteu *m*, -éia *f*.
Phillips® ['fɪlɪps] *comp*: ~ **screw** parafuso *m* Phillips; ~ **screwdriver** chave *f* Phillips.
philosopher [fɪ'lɒsəfə'] *n* filósofo *m*, -fa *f*.
philosophical [ˌfɪlə'sɒfɪkl] *adj* filosófico(ca).

philosophize, -ise [fɪ'lɒsəfaɪz] *vi* filosofar.
philosophy [fɪ'lɒsəfɪ] *(pl* -ies) *n* filosofia *f.*
phlegm [flem] *n (U)* fleuma *f.*
phlegmatic [fleg'mætɪk] *adj* fleumático(ca).
Phnom Penh [ˌnɒm'pen] *n* Phnom Penh.
phobia ['fəʊbjə] *n* fobia *f*; **to have a ~ about sthg**
ter fobia a algo.
phoenix ['fiːnɪks] *n* fênix *f.*
phone [fəʊn] <> *n* telefone *m*; **to be on the ~**
[speaking] estar no telefone; *UK* [connected to net-
work] ter telefone. <> *comp* telefônico(ca). <> *vt*
telefonar, ligar para. <> *vi* telefonar, ligar.
 ➡ **phone back** *vt sep & vi* ligar de volta.
 ➡ **phone up** *vt sep & vi* ligar.
phone book *n* lista *f* telefônica.
phone booth *n US* cabine *f* telefônica.
phone box *n UK* cabine *f* telefônica.
phone call *n* ligação *f*, chamada *f* telefônica; **to**
make a ~ fazer uma ligação.
phonecard ['fəʊnkaːd] *n* cartão *m* telefônico.
phone-in *n RADIO, TV* programa para o qual as
pessoas ligam e suas perguntas ou opiniões
vão para o ar.
phone line *n* -1. [wire] cabo *m* telefônico -2. [con-
nection] linha *f* telefônica.
phone number *n* número *m* de telefone.
phone-tapping [-ˌtæpɪŋ] *n (U)* grampo *m (no*
telefone).
phonetics [fə'netɪks] *n (U)* fonética *f.*
phoney *UK*, **phony** *US* ['fəʊnɪ] *(compar* -ier,
superl -iest, *pl* -ies) <> *adj* falso(sa). <> *n* farsante
mf.
phoney war *n* período entre o início da
segunda guerra mundial e abril de 1940 em
que houve pouca atividade militar entre a
Alemanha e a Grã-Bretanha.
phony *adj* & *n US* = phoney.
phosphate ['fɒsfeɪt] *n* fosfato *m.*
phosphorus ['fɒsfərəs] *n (U)* fósforo *m.*
photo ['fəʊtəʊ] *n* foto *f*; **to take a ~ (of sb/sthg)**
tirar *or* bater uma foto (de alguém/algo).
photo booth *n* cabine *f* de foto automática.
photocall ['fəʊtəʊkɔːl] *n* sessão *f* de fotos.
photocopier ['fəʊtəʊˌkɒpɪə'] *n* fotocopiadora *f.*
photocopy ['fəʊtəʊˌkɒpɪ] *(pl* -ies, *pt & pp* -ied) <>
n fotocópia *f.* <> *vt* fotocopiar.
photoelectric cell [ˌfəʊtəʊɪ'lektrɪk-] *n* célula *f*
fotoelétrica.
photo finish *n SPORT* photo finish *f*, decisão do
vencedor de uma corrida através de fotografia.
photofit® *n*: ~ **(picture)** retrato de alguém
procurado pela polícia montado a partir de
outras fotos ou feito com desenhos de diversas
partes do rosto.
photogenic [ˌfəʊtəʊ'dʒenɪk] *adj* fotogênico(ca).
photograph ['fəʊtəgraːf] <> *n* fotografia *f*; **to**
take a ~ (of sb/sthg) tirar *or* bater uma
fotografia (de alguém/algo). <> *vt* fotografar.
photographer [fə'tɒgrəfə'] *n* fotógrafo *m*, -fa *f.*
photographic [ˌfəʊtə'græfɪk] *adj* fotográfico(ca).
photographic memory *n* memória *f* fotográfica.
photography [fə'tɒgrəfɪ] *n (U)* fotografia *f.*

photojournalism [ˌfəʊtəʊ'dʒɜːnəlɪzm] *n (U)* foto-
jornalismo *m.*
photon ['fəʊtɒn] *n* fóton *m.*
photo opportunity *n* oportunidade, planejada ou acidental, que um político ou uma
celebridade tem de ser fotografado em um
contexto que o favorece.
photosensitive [ˌfəʊtəʊ'sensɪtɪv] *adj* fotossensí-
vel.
Photostat® ['fəʊtəstæt] *(pt & pp* -ted, *cont* -ting) *n*
cópia *f* fotostática.
 ➡ **photostat** *vt* tirar cópia fotostática.
photosynthesis [ˌfəʊtəʊ'sɪnθəsɪs] *n (U)* fotossíntese *f.*
photovoltaic cell [ˌfəʊtəʊvɒl'teɪk-] *n* célula *f*
fotovoltaica.
phrasal verb ['freɪzl-] *n* combinação de um verbo
e de uma preposição ou um advérbio, que juntos
possuem sentido único.
phrase [freɪz] <> *n* -1. [part of sentence] frase *f* -2.
[expression] expressão *f.* <> *vt* [express - letter]
redigir; [- apology, refusal] expressar; **sorry, I've**
~ d that badly desculpe, eu me expressei mal.
phrasebook ['freɪzbʊk] *n* manual *m* de conversação.
phraseology [ˌfreɪzɪ'ɒlədʒɪ] *n (U)* fraseologia *f.*
physical ['fɪzɪkl] <> *adj* físico(ca). <> *n* exame *m*
médico.
physical chemistry *n (U)* físico-química *f.*
physical education *n (U) SCH* educação *f* física.
physical examination *n* exame *m* médico.
physical geography *n (U)* geografia *f* física.
physically ['fɪzɪklɪ] *adv* fisicamente.
physically handicapped <> *adj* portador(-
ra) de deficiência física. <> *npl*: **the ~** os
portadores de deficiência física.
physical science *n (U)* ciência *f* física.
physical training *n* treinamento *m* físico.
physician [fɪ'zɪʃn] *n* médico *m*, -ca *f.*
physicist ['fɪzɪsɪst] *n* físico *m*, -ca *f.*
physics ['fɪzɪks] *n (U)* física *f.*
physio ['fɪzɪəʊ] *(pl* -s) *n inf* -1. [physiotherapist]
fisioterapeuta *mf* -2. [physiotherapy] fisioterapia *f.*
physiognomy [ˌfɪzɪ'ɒnəmɪ] *(pl* -ies) *n fml* fisionomia *f.*
physiology [ˌfɪzɪ'ɒlədʒɪ] *n* fisiologia *f.*
physiotherapist [ˌfɪzɪəʊ'θerəpɪst] *n* fisioterapeuta *mf.*
physiotherapy [ˌfɪzɪəʊ'θerəpɪ] *n (U)* fisioterapia *f.*
physique [fɪ'ziːk] *n* físico *m.*
pianist ['pɪənɪst] *n* pianista *mf.*
piano [pɪ'ænəʊ] *(pl* -s) *n* piano *m*; **to play the ~**
tocar piano.
piano accordion *n* acordeão *m.*
Picardy ['pɪkədɪ] *n* Picardia *(região da França).*
piccalilli [ˌpɪkə'lɪlɪ] *n (U)* molho quente feito com
vegetais e servido com carne fria.
piccolo ['pɪkələʊ] *(pl* -s) *n* flautim *m.*
pick [pɪk] <> *n* -1. [tool] picareta *f* -2. [selection]: **to**
take one's ~ escolher o que quiser -3. [best]: **the**
~ of o melhor de. <> *vt* -1. [select, choose]
escolher; **to ~ one's way across/through sthg**
atravessar algo com cuidado -2. [gather] colher

- 3. [remove] tirar **- 4.** [nose]: **to ~ one's nose** pôr o dedo no nariz **- 5.** [teeth]: **to ~ one's teeth** palitar os dentes **- 6.** [provoke] provocar; **to ~ a fight (with sb)** arranjar briga (com alguém) **- 7.** [lock] forçar *(com instrumento ou ferramenta).* ◇ *vi* escolher; **to ~ and choose** ser exigente *(na escolha).*

◆ **pick at** *vt fus* [food] beliscar.

◆ **pick on** *vt fus* meter-se com.

◆ **pick out** *vt sep* **- 1.** [recognize] reconhecer **- 2.** [select, choose] escolher.

◆ **pick up** ◇ *vt sep* **- 1.** [lift up] pegar, apanhar; **to ~ up the pieces** *fig* juntar os pedaços, voltar à normalidade **- 2.** [collect] pegar **- 3.** [acquire] adquirir; **to ~ up speed** pegar velocidade **- 4.** [subj: police]: **to ~ sb up for sthg** pegar alguém por algo **- 5.** *inf* [start relationship with] dar em cima de **- 6.** [detect, receive] captar **- 7.** [resume] retomar. ◇ *vi* **- 1.** [improve] melhorar **- 2.** [resume] retomar.

pickaxe *UK*, **pickax** *US* ['pɪkæks] *n* picareta *f.*

picker ['pɪkəʳ] *n* colheiteiro *m*, -ra *f.*

picket ['pɪkɪt] ◇ *n* [at place of work - person] piqueteiro *m*, -ra *f*; [- instance of picketing] piquete *m.* ◇ *vt* fazer piquete em.

picketing ['pɪkətɪŋ] *n (U)* piquetes *mpl.*

picket line *n* piquete *m* de grevistas.

pickings ['pɪkɪŋz] *npl*: **easy/rich ~** dinheiro *m* fácil.

pickle ['pɪkl] ◇ *n* **- 1.** [food] picles *m inv* **- 2.** *inf* [difficult situation]: **to be in a ~** estar numa enrascada. ◇ *vt* fazer conserva de.

pickled ['pɪkld] *adj* em conserva.

pick-me-up *n inf* estimulante *m*, tônico *m.*

pickpocket ['pɪk,pɒkɪt] *n* batedor *m*, -ra *f* de carteiras.

pick-up *n* **- 1.** [of record player] pickup *f* **- 2.** [truck] picape *f.*

pick-up truck *n* picape *f.*

picky ['pɪkɪ] *(compar* -ier, *superl* -iest) *adj* difícil de contentar, enjoado(da).

picnic ['pɪknɪk] *(pt* & *pp* -ked, *cont* -king) ◇ *n* piquenique *m.* ◇ *vi* fazer piquenique.

picnicker ['pɪknɪkəʳ] *n* excursionista *mf.*

Pict [pɪkt] *n*: **the ~s** os Pictos.

pictorial [pɪk'tɔːrɪəl] *adj* ilustrado(da).

picture ['pɪktʃəʳ] ◇ *n* **- 1.** [painting, drawing] quadro *m* **- 2.** [photograph] fotografia *f* **- 3.** [image] imagem *f* **- 4.** [movie] filme *m* **- 5.** [prospect] cenário *m* **- 6.** [epitome]: **he's the ~ of misery** ele é a personificação da miséria **- 7.** *phr*: **to get the ~** *inf* entender; **to put sb in the ~** colocar alguém a par; **to be in/out of the ~** estar por dentro/fora. ◇ *vt* **- 1.** [in mind] imaginar **- 2.** [in photo] fotografar **- 3.** [in painting, drawing] retratar.

◆ **pictures** *npl UK*: **the ~s** o cinema.

picture book *n* livro *m* ilustrado.

picture rail *n* moldura *f* para pendurar quadros.

picturesque [,pɪktʃə'resk] *adj* pitoresco(ca).

picture window *n* janela *f* panorâmica.

piddling ['pɪdlɪŋ] *adj inf pej* irrisório(ria).

pidgin ['pɪdʒɪn] ◇ *n* pídgin *m.* ◇ *comp*: **~ English** inglês *m* macarrônico.

pie [paɪ] *n* **- 1.** [sweet] torta *f* **- 2.** [savoury] pastelão

m; **~ in the sky** castelos no ar.

piece [piːs] *n* **- 1.** [gen] pedaço *m*; **to be smashed to ~s** ser esmagado(da) em pedaços; **to fall to ~s** ficar em pedaços; **to pull** OR **tear sb/sthg to ~s** [criticize] arrasar com alguém/algo; **to take sthg to ~s** desmontar algo; **in ~s** em pedaços; **in one ~** [intact] sem um arranhão, intacto(ta); [unharmed] são e salvo, sã e salva; **to go to ~s** *fig* vir abaixo **- 2.** [of food] pedaço *f* **- 3.** *(with uncountable noun)* [gen] peça *f*; **~ of paper** folha *f* de papel; **~ of luck** golpe *m* de sorte; **~ of information** informação *f* **- 4.** [of journalism] artigo *m* **- 5.** [coin] moeda *f.*

◆ **piece together** *vt sep* reunir.

pièce de résistance [,pjesdərezɪs'tãs] *(pl* **pièces de résistance** [,pjesdərezɪs'tãs]) *n* [main attraction] atração *m* principal.

piecemeal ['piːsmiːl] ◇ *adj* pouco sistemático (ca). ◇ *adv* aos poucos, gradualmente.

piecework ['piːswɜːk] *n (U)* trabalho *m* por tarefas.

pie chart *n* gráfico *m* circular.

pied-à-terre *(pl* **pieds-à-terre)** *n pequena casa ou apartamento para uso ocasional como segunda residência.*

pie-eyed *adj inf* bêbum.

pie plate *n US* prato *m* para torta.

pier [pɪəʳ] *n* píer *m.*

pierce [pɪəs] *vt* **- 1.** [subj: bullet, needle] furar; **to have one's ears ~d** furar as orelhas **- 2.** [subj: noise, light, pain] romper.

pierced [pɪəst] *adj* furado(da).

piercing ['pɪəsɪŋ] ◇ *adj* **- 1.** [sound, voice] agudo (da), estridente **- 2.** [wind] cortante **- 3.** [look, eyes] penetrante. ◇ *n* piercing *m.*

piety ['paɪətɪ] *n* piedade *f.*

piffle ['pɪfl] *n inf* asneira *f.*

piffling ['pɪflɪŋ] *adj inf* ridículo(la).

pig [pɪg] *(pt* & *pp* -ged, *cont* -ging) *n* **- 1.** [animal] porco *m*, -ca *f* **- 2.** *inf pej* [greedy eater] glutão *m*, -ona *f*; **to make a ~ of o.s.** empanturrar-se **- 3.** *inf pej* [unkind person] grosseirão *m*, -rona *f.*

◆ **pig out** *vi inf* empanturrar-se.

pigeon ['pɪdʒɪn] *(pl inv* OR -s) *n* pomba *f.*

pigeon-chested [-,tʃestɪd] *adj* de peito para frente.

pigeonhole ['pɪdʒɪnhəʊl] ◇ *n* [compartment] escaninho *m.* ◇ *vt* [classify] classificar.

pigeon-toed [-,təʊd] *adj* com pés voltados para dentro.

piggish ['pɪgɪʃ] *adj inf* porcalhão(lhona).

piggy ['pɪgɪ] *(compar* -ier, *superl* -iest, *pl* -ies) ◇ *adj* de porco. ◇ *n inf* [piglet] porquinho *m*, -nha *f.*

piggyback ['pɪgɪbæk] *n*: **to give sb a ~** levar alguém na garupa.

piggybank ['pɪgɪbæŋk] *n* porquinho *m (de moedas).*

pig-headed *adj* cabeçudo(da).

piglet ['pɪglɪt] *n* leitão *m*, -toa *f*, porquinho *m*, -nha *f.*

pigment ['pɪgmənt] *n* pigmento *m.*

pigmentation [,pɪgmən'teɪʃn] *n* pigmentação *f.*

pigmy *(pl* -ies) *n* = pygmy.

pigpen *n US* = pigsty.

pigskin ['pɪgskɪn] <> *n (U)* couro *m* de porco. <> *comp* de couro de porco.

pigsty ['pɪgstaɪ] (*pl* -ies), **pigpen** *US* ['pɪgpen] *n* chiqueiro *m*.

pigswill ['pɪgswɪl] *n (U)* lavagem *f*.

pigtail ['pɪgteɪl] *n* trança *f*.

pike [paɪk] (*pl sense 1 only inv OR* -s) *n* -1. [fish] lúcio *m* -2. [spear] pique *m*.

pikestaff ['paɪksta:f] *n*: **plain as a** ~ claro como um dia de sol.

pilaster [pɪ'læstə^r] *n* pilastra *f*.

pilchard ['pɪltʃəd] *n* sardinha *f*.

pile [paɪl] <> *n* -1. [heap] monte *m*; **a** ~ *OR* ~**s of sthg** *inf* um monte de algo -2. [neat stack] pilha *f* -3. [of carpet, fabric] felpa *f*. <> *vt* empilhar; **to be** ~**d with sthg** estar entulhado(da) de algo.
➤ **piles** *npl MED* hemorróidas *fpl*.
➤ **pile in** *vi inf* apinhar-se.
➤ **pile into** *vt fus inf* amontoar-se.
➤ **pile out** *vi inf* debandar; **to** ~ **out of sthg** debandar de algo.
➤ **pile up** <> *vt sep* amontoar, empilhar. <> *vi* acumular-se.

pile driver *n* bate-estaca *m*.

pile-up *n* engavetamento *m*.

pilfer ['pɪlfə^r] <> *vt*: **to** ~ **sthg (from)** furtar algo (de). <> *vi*: **to** ~ **(from)** furtar (de), surrupiar (de).

pilgrim ['pɪlgrɪm] *n* peregrino *m*, -na *f*.

PILGRIM FATHERS

Assim é chamado o grupo de puritanos ingleses que, perseguido por suas crenças religiosas, embarcou para a América, em 1620, a bordo do navio *Mayflower*. Os *Pilgrim Fathers* fundaram a primeira colônia inglesa, onde hoje é o estado de Massachusetts. Durante o primeiro inverno que passaram no novo mundo, muitos morreram de fome. Mas, a partir do segundo ano na América, os nativos da região os ensinaram a plantar trigo e outras lavouras. Dessa forma, no outono, quando os colonos viram que tinham comida suficiente para sobreviver ao inverno, celebraram uma refeição de Ação de Graças com os nativos. Muitos anos depois, em 1863, o presidente Lincoln transformou o dia de Ação de Graças em feriado nacional, em comemoração ao sucesso daquela primeira colheita.

---

pilgrimage ['pɪlgrɪmɪdʒ] *n* peregrinação *f*.

pill [pɪl] *n* -1. *MED* pílula *f* -2. [contraceptive]: **the** ~ a pílula anticoncepcional; **to be on the** ~ tomar pílula (anticoncepcional).

pillage ['pɪlɪdʒ] <> *n (U)* pilhagem *f*. <> *vt* pilhar.

pillar ['pɪlə^r] *n* -1. *ARCHIT* pilar *m* -2. *fig* [of community, church etc] bastião *m*; **to be a** ~ **of strength** ser uma fortaleza; **to be a** ~ **of the church** ser um bastião da igreja.

pillar box *n UK* caixa *f* coletora (*do correio*).

pillbox ['pɪlbɒks] *n* -1. [box for pills] caixa *f* de comprimidos -2. *MIL* casamata *f*.

pillion ['pɪljən] *n* assento *m* traseiro; **to ride** ~ ir na garupa.

pillock ['pɪlək] *n UK inf* imbecil.

pillory ['pɪlərɪ] (*pl* -ies, *pt & pp* -ied) <> *n* [form of punishment] pelourinho *m*. <> *vt fig* [ridicule]: **to be pilloried** ser ridicularizado(da).

pillow ['pɪləʊ] *n* -1. [for bed] travesseiro *m* -2. *US* [on sofa, chair] almofada *f*.

pillowcase ['pɪləʊkeɪs], **pillowslip** ['pɪləʊslɪp] *n* fronha *f*.

pilot ['paɪlət] <> *n* piloto *m*. <> *comp* [trial] piloto; ~ **project** projeto-piloto *m*. <> *vt* -1. [gen] pilotar -2. [bill] pôr em prática -3. [scheme] aplicar.

pilot light, pilot burner *n* [on gas appliance] piloto *m*.

pilot scheme *n* projeto-piloto *m*.

pilot study *n* estudo *m* -piloto.

pimento [pɪ'mentəʊ] (*pl inv OR* -s) *n* pimentão *m*.

pimp [pɪmp] *n inf* cafetão *m*.

pimple ['pɪmpl] *n* espinha *f*.

pimply ['pɪmplɪ] (*compar* -ier, *superl* -iest) *adj* espinhento(ta), cheio (cheia) de espinhas.

pin [pɪn] (*pt & pp* -ned, *cont* -ning) <> *n* -1. [for sewing] alfinete *m*; **to have** ~**s and needles** *fig* estar com formigamento; **to be on** ~**s and needles** *US* estar uma pilha -2. [drawing pin] percevejo *m* -3. [safety pin] alfinete *m* de segurança -4. [of plug, grenade] pino *m* -5. *TECH* pino *m*, cavilha *f* -6. *US* [brooch] broche *m*; [badge] bottom *m* -7. *GOLF*: **the** ~ a bandeira. <> *vt* -1. [attach]: **to** ~ **sthg to** *OR* **on sthg** prender *OR* colocar algo em algo -2. [immobilize]: **to** ~ **sb against** *OR* **to sthg** prender alguém contra/em algo -3. [apportion]: **to** ~ **sthg on sb** botar a culpa de algo em alguém, culpar alguém de algo.
➤ **pin down** *vt sep* -1. [identify] determinar, identificar -2. [force to make a decision] obrigar a se decidir.
➤ **pin up** *vt sep* -1. [poster, list of results] afixar -2. [hem, hair] prender.

PIN [pɪn] (*abbr of* **personal identification number**) *n* senha *f*.

pinafore ['pɪnəfɔ:^r] *n* -1. [apron] avental *m* -2. *UK* [dress] jardineira *f*.

pinball ['pɪnbɔ:l] *n (U)* fliperama *f*.

pinball machine *n* máquina *f* de fliperama.

pincers ['pɪnsəz] *npl* -1. [tool] torquês *f* -2. [front claws] pinças *fpl*.

pinch [pɪntʃ] <> *n* -1. [nip] beliscão *m*; **to feel the** ~ apertar o cinto -2. [small quantity] pitada *f*. <> *vt* -1. [nip] beliscar -2. *inf* [steal - money, clothes] passar a mão em; [- car] pegar.
➤ **at a pinch** *UK*, **in a pinch** *US adv* em último caso.

pinched [pɪntʃt] *adj* -1. [thin, pale] abatido(da); ~ **with cold/hunger** pálido(da) de frio/fome -2. [short of]: ~ **for sthg** escasso(sa) de algo.

pincushion ['pɪnˌkʊʃn] *n* alfineteira *f*.

pine [paɪn] <> *n* -1. [tree] pinheiro *m* -2. *(U)* [wood] pinho *m*. <> *comp* [furniture] de pinho. <> *vi*: **to** ~ **for sb/sthg** suspirar por alguém/algo.
➤ **pine away** *vi* consumir-se (de desgosto).

pineapple ['paɪnæpl] *n* abacaxi *m*.

pine cone *n* pinha *f*.

pine needle *n* agulha *f* de pinheiro.

pine tree *n* pinheiro *m*.

pinewood ['paɪnwʊd] n -1. [forest] pinheiral m -2. (U) [material] madeira f de pinho.

ping [pɪŋ] <> n tinido m. <> vi retinir.

Ping-Pong® [-pɒŋ] n (U) ping-pong m.

pinhole ['pɪnhəʊl] n buraquinho m.

pinion ['pɪnjən] <> n TECH pinhão m. <> vt imobilizar.

pink [pɪŋk] <> adj -1. [in colour] cor-de-rosa -2. [with embarrassment] vermelho(lha); **to turn ~** ficar vermelho(lha). <> n -1. [colour] rosa m -2. [flower] cravina f, cravo m.

pinkie ['pɪŋkɪ] n US & Scot minguinho m.

pinking scissors, pinking shears npl tesoura f de picotar.

pink pound UK, **pink dollar** n: **the ~** poder aquisitivo da comunidade gay.

pin money n (U) pequena quantia de dinheiro extra recebido (geralmente do marido) para despesas pessoais.

pinnacle ['pɪnəkl] n -1. fig [of career, success] auge m -2. [mountain peak] topo m -3. ARCHIT [spire] pináculo m.

pinny ['pɪnɪ] (pl -ies) n inf avental m.

pinpoint ['pɪnpɔɪnt] vt -1. [difficulty, cause] determinar, identificar -2. [position, target, leak] identificar.

pinprick ['pɪnprɪk] n -1. [mark, hole] pontinho m -2. fig [slight irritation] chateação f.

pin-striped [-straɪpt] adj riscado(da).

pint [paɪnt] n -1. UK [unit of measurement] quartilho m (0,568 litro) -2. US [unit of measurement] pint m (0,473 litro) -3. UK [beer] cerveja f.

pintable n UK máquina f de fliperama.

pint-size(d) adj inf minúsculo(la).

pin-up n pin-up f.

pioneer [,paɪə'nɪəʳ] <> n -1. [first settler] pioneiro m, -ra f -2. [innovator] pioneiro m, -ra f. <> vt lançar, ser pioneiro(na) de.

pioneering [,paɪə'nɪərɪŋ] adj pioneiro(ra).

pious ['paɪəs] adj -1. [religious] piedoso(sa) -2. pej [sanctimonious] devoto(ta).

piously ['paɪəslɪ] adv -1. [religiously] piedosamente -2. pej [sanctimoniously] devotadamente.

pip [pɪp] n -1. [seed] semente f -2. UK [bleep] sinal m.

pipe [paɪp] <> n -1. [for gas, water] tubo m, cano m -2. [for smoking] cachimbo m -3. MUS flauta f. <> vt canalizar.

➠ **pipes** npl MUS [bagpipes] gaita f de foles.

➠ **pipe down** vi inf fechar a matraca.

➠ **pipe up** vi inf: **there was silence and then she ~d up with a suggestion** fez-se silêncio e então ela saiu com uma sugestão.

pipe cleaner n limpador m para cachimbo.

piped music [paɪpt-] n UK música f ambiente.

pipe dream n castelo m no ar, sonho m impossível.

pipeline ['paɪplaɪn] n -1. [for oil] oleoduto m -2. [for gas] gasoduto m; **to be in the ~** fig estar a caminho.

piper ['paɪpəʳ] n MUS tocador m, -ra f de gaita de foles.

piping hot ['paɪpɪŋ-] adj extremamente quente.

pipsqueak ['pɪpskwiːk] n pej coisa f insignificante.

piquant ['piːkənt] adj -1. [spicy] picante -2. [interesting] intrigante.

pique [piːk] n (U) ressentimento m; **a fit of ~** um ataque de despeito.

piracy ['paɪrəsɪ] n pirataria f.

piranha [pɪ'rɑːnə] n piranha f.

pirate ['paɪrət] <> adj [illegally copied] pirateado(da). <> n -1. [sailor] pirata m -2. [illegal copy] cópia f pirata. <> vt piratear.

pirate radio n UK rádio f pirata.

pirouette [,pɪrʊ'et] <> n pirueta f. <> vi fazer pirueta.

Pisces ['paɪsiːz] n -1. [sign] peixes m -2. [person] pisciano(na); **I'm ~** sou de Peixes.

piss [pɪs] vulg <> n -1. [urine] mijo m; **to take the ~ out of sb/sthg** tirar um sarro de algo/alguém -2. [urination]: **to have a ~** dar uma mijada. <> vi -1. [urinate] mijar -2. [rain]: **it's ~ing with rain** está chovendo canivete.

➠ **piss down** vi UK vulg [rain]: **the rain was ~ing down** chovia a cântaros.

➠ **piss off** vulg <> vt sep encher o saco. <> vi UK ir à merda; **~ off!** vai à merda!

pissed [pɪst] adj vulg -1. UK [drunk] mamado(da) -2. US [annoyed] puto(ta) da cara.

pissed off adj vulg de saco cheio.

pistachio [pɪ'stɑːʃɪəʊ] (pl -s) n pistache m.

piste [piːst] n SKIING pista f.

pistol ['pɪstl] n pistola f.

piston ['pɪstən] n pistom m.

pit [pɪt] (pt & pp -ted, cont -ting) <> n -1. [large hole] cova f -2. [small, shallow hole] marca f -3. [for orchestra] fosso m da orquestra -4. [mine] mina f -5. [quarry] canteiro m -6. US [of fruit] caroço m -7. phr: **the ~ of one's stomach** a boca do estômago. <> vt: **to be ~ted against sb** ser incitado(da) contra alguém; **to ~ one's wits against sb/sthg** medir forças contra alguém/algo.

➠ **pits** npl -1. [in motor racing]: **the ~s** o box -2. inf [awful]: **the ~s** o fim da picada.

pit bull (terrier) n pit bull terrier m.

pitch [pɪtʃ] <> n -1. SPORT campo m -2. MUS tom m -3. (U) [level, degree] grau m -4. [street vendor's place] ponto m -5. inf [spiel]: **sales ~** papo m de vendedor -6. [of ship, aircraft] arfagem f -7. [of slope, roof] (grau m de) inclinação f -8. [throw] arremesso m -9. [tar] piche m. <> vt -1. [throw] arremessar; **to be ~ed into sthg** [person] ser posto(ta) em algo da noite para o dia -2. [set level of - price] estabelecer um preço para; [- speech] dar um tom a -3. [camp, tent] armar. <> vi -1. [fall over] despencar; **to ~ forward** precipitar-se para frente -2. [ship, plane] arfar.

➠ **pitch in** vi inf -1. [start work] botar a mão na massa -2. [lend a hand] colaborar.

pitch-black adj preto(ta) como carvão.

pitched [pɪtʃt] adj inclinado(da).

pitched battle [,pɪtʃt-] n batalha f campal.

pitcher ['pɪtʃəʳ] n US -1. [jug] jarro m -2. [in baseball] lançador m.

pitchfork ['pɪtʃfɔːk] n forcado m.

piteous ['pɪtɪəs] adj lastimável, comovente.

piteously ['pɪtɪəslɪ] adv de forma comovente.

pitfall ['pɪtfɔːl] n armadilha f, perigo m.

pith [pɪθ] n (U) parte branca da casca de uma fruta.

pithead ['pɪthɛd] *n* boca *f* da mina.
pith helmet *n* chapéu *m* de palha.
pithy ['pɪθɪ] (*compar* -ier, *superl* -iest) *adj* denso(sa), contundente.
pitiable ['pɪtɪəbll] *adj* -1. [arousing pity] lastimoso(sa) -2. [arousing contempt] lamentável.
pitiful ['pɪtɪfʊl] *adj* -1. [arousing pity] lastimável -2. [arousing contempt] lastimoso(sa).
pitifully ['pɪtɪfʊlɪ] *adv* -1. [arousing pity] comovedoramente -2. [arousing contempt]: **a ~ lame excuse** uma desculpa lamentável.
pitiless ['pɪtɪlɪs] *adj* impiedoso(sa).
pit stop *n* pit stop *m*.
pitta bread ['pɪtə-] *n* (*U*) pão *m* sírio; *tipo de pão oval sem levedura.*
pittance ['pɪtəns] *n* miséria *f*.
pitted ['pɪtɪd] *adj* -1. descaroçado(da) -2.: **~ with** sthg marcado(da) com algo.
pitter-patter ['pɪtə,pætə'] *n* ruído *m* (*de passos, de chuva*).
pituitary [pɪ'tjʊɪtrɪ] (*pl* -ies) *n*: **~ (gland)** glândula *f* pituitária.
pity ['pɪtɪ] (*pt* & *pp* -ied) <> *n* -1. [sympathy, sorrow] compaixão *f*; **to take** OR **have ~ on sb** ficar com pena de alguém -2. [shame] pena *f*; **what a ~!** que pena! <> *vt* sentir pena de.
pitying ['pɪtɪŋ] *adj* compassivo(va).
pivot ['pɪvət] <> *n* -1. TECH eixo *m* -2. *fig* [crux] centro *m*, eixo *m*. <> *vi*: **to ~ (on sthg)** girar (sobre algo).
pixel ['pɪksl] *n* COMPUT píxel *m*.
pixie, pixy ['pɪksɪ] (*pl* -ies) *n* duende *m*.
pizza ['piːtsə] *n* pizza *f*.
pizzazz [pɪ'zæz] *n* (*U*) *inf* vitalidade *f*, energia *f*.
Pk (*abbr of* **park**) parque *m*.
pl. *abbr of* **please**.
P & L (*abbr of* **profit and loss**) *n* perdas *fpl* e lucros *mpl*.
PLA (*abbr of* **People's Liberation Army**) *n* forças armadas da República Popular da China.
placard ['plækɑːd] *n* cartaz *m*.
placate [plə'keɪt] *vt* aplacar, acalmar.
placatory [plə'keɪtərɪ] *adj* apaziguante.
place [pleɪs] <> *n* -1. [gen] lugar *m*; **~ of birth** local de nascimento; **to put sb in their ~** colocar alguém em seu lugar; **to fall into ~** fazer sentido -2. [suitable occasion] momento *m* -3. [home] casa *f*; **decimal ~** MATH casa decimal -4. [post, vacancy] vaga *f* -5. [role, function] papel *m* -6. [rank] posição *f* -7. [instance]: **why didn't you say so in the first ~?** por que você não disse isso logo?; **in the first ~ ..., and in the second ~ ...** em primeiro lugar ..., e em segundo lugar ... -8. *phr*: **the market takes ~ every Sunday** a feira acontece todos os domingos; **the events that took ~ that day became infamous** os acontecimentos que tiveram lugar naquele dia tornaram-se notórios; **to take the ~ of sb/sthg** tomar o lugar de alguém/algo, substituir alguém/algo. <> *vt* -1. [position, put] colocar -2. [lay, apportion]: **to ~ blame on sb/sthg** colocar a culpa em alguém/algo; **to ~ emphasis on sb/sthg** dar ênfase a alguém/algo; **to ~ pressure on sb/sthg** exercer pressão sobre alguém/algo; **to**

~ responsibility on sb/sthg pôr a responsabilidade em alguém/algo -3. [identify] identificar -4. [make]: **to ~ an order** COMM fazer um pedido; **to ~ a bet** fazer uma aposta -5. [situate] situar; **how are we ~d for money?** como estamos de dinheiro? -6. [in race]: **to be ~d** classificar-se.
➡ **all over the place** *adv* por todo lado.
➡ **in place** *adv* -1. [in proper position] no lugar -2. [established, set up] estabelecido(da).
➡ **in place of** *prep*: **in ~ of me** em meu lugar.
➡ **out of place** *adv* -1. [in wrong position] fora do lugar -2. [unsuitable] fora de propósito.
placebo [plə'siːbəʊ] (*pl* -s OR -es) *n* placebo *m*.
place card *n* cartão *m* de reserva (*de mesa em jantar*).
place kick *n* tiro *m* livre (*com a bola colocada*).
place mat *n* toalha *f* de mesa individual.
placement ['pleɪsmənt] *n* -1. (*U*) [positioning] disposição *f* -2. [work experience] estágio *m*.
placement service *n* US serviço *m* de colocação profissional.
placenta [plə'sentə] (*pl* -s OR -tae [-tiː]) *n* placenta *f*.
place setting *n* jogo *m* de mesa para uma pessoa.
placid ['plæsɪd] *adj* -1. [even-tempered] plácido(da) -2. [peaceful] sereno(na).
placidly ['plæsɪdlɪ] *adv* calmamente.
plagiarism ['pleɪdʒərɪzm] *n* (*U*) plágio *m*.
plagiarist ['pleɪdʒərɪst] *n* plagiador *m*, -ra *f*.
plagiarize, -ise ['pleɪdʒəraɪz] *vt* plagiar.
plague [pleɪg] <> *n* praga *f*; **to avoid sb/sthg like the ~** fugir de alguém/algo como uma praga. <> *vt*: **to ~ sb with sthg** importunar alguém com algo; **to be ~d by sthg** ser/estar atormentado(da) por algo.
plaice [pleɪs] (*pl inv*) *n* linguado *m*.
plaid [plæd] *n* (*U*) tecido *m* em xadrez da Escócia.
Plaid Cymru [,plaɪd'kʌmrɪ] *n* UK POL Plaid Cymru (*partido nacionalista galês*).
plain [pleɪn] <> *adj* -1. [not patterned] liso(sa) -2. [simple, not fancy] simples; **~ yoghurt** iogurte *m* natural -3. [clear] claro(ra); **to make sthg ~ to sb** deixar algo claro para alguém -4. [blunt] direto(ta) -5. [absolute] absoluto(ta) -6. [not pretty] sem atrativos. <> *adv inf* [completely] claramente. <> *n* GEOGR planície *f*.
plain chocolate *n* UK chocolate *m* meio amargo.
plain-clothes *adj* à paisana.
plain flour *n* UK farinha *f* sem fermento.
plainly ['pleɪnlɪ] *adv* -1. [upset, angry] completamente -2. [remember, hear] claramente -3. [frankly] francamente, abertamente -4. [simply] de forma simples.
plain sailing *n* (*U*) caminho *m* livre.
plain-spoken *adj* franco(ca).
plaintiff ['pleɪntɪf] *n* querelante *mf*.
plaintive ['pleɪntɪv] *adj* triste, melancólico(ca).
plait [plæt] <> *n* trança *f*. <> *vt* trançar.
plan [plæn] (*pt* & *pp* -ned, *cont* -ning) <> *n* -1. [strategy] plano *m*; **to go according to ~** sair de acordo com o planejado -2. [outline] esboço *m* -3. [diagram, map - of garden, building] planta *f*; [- of inside of

a machine] esquema *m* de montagem. <> *vt* -**1**. [organize] planejar -**2**. [intend] pretender; **to ~ to do sthg** pensar em fazer algo -**3**. [design, devise] projetar. <> *vi* fazer planos; **to ~ for sthg** fazer planos para algo.

● **plans** *npl* planos *mpl*; **to have ~s for** ter planos para.

● **plan on** *vt fus*: **to ~ on doing sthg** pretender fazer algo.

● **plan out** *vt sep* traçar.

plane [pleɪn] <> *adj* plano(na). <> *n* -**1**. [aircraft] avião *m* -**2**. GEOM plano *m* -**3**. fig [level] patamar *m* -**4**. [tool] plaina *f* -**5**. [tree] plátano *m.* <> *vt* aplainar.

planet ['plænɪt] *n* planeta *f.*

planetarium [ˌplænɪ'teərɪəm] (*pl* -**riums** OR -**ria** [-rɪə]) *n* planetário *m.*

planetary ['plænɪtrɪ] *adj* planetário(ria).

plane tree *n* plátano *m.*

plank [plæŋk] *n* -**1**. [piece of wood] tábua *f* -**2**. POL [main policy] item *m.*

plankton ['plæŋktən] *n (U)* plâncton *m.*

planned [plænd] *adj* planejado(da).

planner ['plænə'] *n* planejador *m*, -ra *f*; **town ~** urbanista *mf.*

planning ['plænɪŋ] *n* planejamento *m.*

planning permission *n (U)* autorização *f* para construir.

plan of action *n* plano *m* de ação.

plant [plɑːnt] <> *n* -**1**. BOT planta *f.* -**2**. [factory] fábrica *f*; **nuclear ~** usina *f* nuclear -**3**. *(U)* [heavy machinery] maquinários *mpl.* <> *vt* -**1**. [seed, tree] plantar; [field, garden] semear; **to ~ sthg with sthg** semear algo com algo -**2**. [blow, kiss] dar -**3**. [place - oneself] plantar-se; [- object] fincar -**4**. [offload] despachar -**5**. [spy] infiltrar -**6**. [bomb, microphone] colocar secretamente; **to ~ sthg on sb** esconder algo em alguém -**7**. [thought, idea] incutir.

● **plant out** *vt sep* transplantar.

plantain ['plæntɪn] *n* banana-da-terra *f.*

plantation [plæn'teɪʃn] *n* plantação *f.*

planter ['plɑːntə'] *n* -**1**. [farmer] fazendeiro *m*, -ra *f* -**2**. [container] jardineira *f.*

plant pot *n* vaso *m* para plantas.

plaque [plɑːk] *n* placa *f.*

plasma ['plæzmə] *n (U)* plasma *m.*

plaster ['plɑːstə'] <> *n* -**1**. [gen] gesso *m*; **in ~** engessado(da) -**2**. UK [for cut]: **(sticking) ~** esparadrapo *m*, Band-Aid® *m.* <> *vt* -**1**. [put plaster on] revestir com gesso -**2**. [cover]: **to ~ sthg with sthg** cobrir algo com algo -**3**. [make stick] fixar.

plasterboard ['plɑːstəbɔːd] *n (U)* chapa *f* de gesso.

plaster cast *n* molde *m* de gesso.

plastered ['plɑːstəd] *adj inf* [drunk] de porre.

plasterer ['plɑːstərə'] *n* rebocador *m*, -ra *f.*

plastering ['plɑːstərɪŋ] *n (U)* ato *m* de rebocar.

plaster of paris *n* gesso *m* de Paris.

plastic ['plæstɪk] <> *adj* de plástico. <> *n* -**1**. [material] plástico *m* -**2**. *inf* [credit cards] cartão *m* (de crédito).

plastic bullet *n* bala *f* de borracha.

plastic explosive *n* explosivo *m* plástico.

Plasticine® UK ['plæstɪsiːn], **play dough** US *n (U)* plasticina *f.*

plastic money *n* cartões *mpl* de crédito.

plastic surgeon *n* cirurgião *m* plástico, cirurgiã *f* plástica.

plastic surgery *n (U)* cirurgia *f* plástica.

plastic wrap *n* US filme *m* de PVC transparente.

plate [pleɪt] <> *n* -**1**. [gen] prato *m*; **to have a lot on one's ~** ter muito com o que se preocupar; **to be handed sthg on a ~** receber algo de mão beijada -**2**. [on wall, door or surgical] placa *f* -**3**. *(U)* [gold, silver etc] baixela *f* -**4**. [photograph] chapa *f* -**5**. [in dentistry] dentadura *f* -**6**. [in baseball] base *f.* <> *vt*: **to be ~d (with sthg)** ser banhado (a algo).

Plate [pleɪt] *n*: **the River ~** o Rio da Prata.

plateau ['plætəʊ] (*pl* -**s** OR -**x** [-z]) *n* -**1**. GEOGR planalto *m* -**2**. fig [steady level] nível *m* estável.

plateful ['pleɪtfʊl] *n* pratada *f.*

plate-glass *adj* de vidro laminado.

platelet ['pleɪtlɪt] *n* plaqueta *f.*

plate rack *n* escorredor *m* de pratos.

platform ['plætfɔːm] *n* -**1**. [gen] plataforma *f* -**2**. [for speaker, performer] palanque *m* -**3**. fig [arena] veículo *m.*

platform game *n* COMPUT jogo *m* de obstáculos.

platform ticket *n* UK bilhete *m* de plataforma.

platinum ['plætɪnəm] <> *adj* platinado(da). <> *n* platina *f.* <> *comp* de platina.

platinum blonde *n* loira *f* platinada.

platitude ['plætɪtjuːd] *n* lugar-comum *m*, chavão *m.*

platonic [plə'tɒnɪk] *adj* platônico(ca).

platoon [plə'tuːn] *n* pelotão *m.*

platter ['plætə'] *n* travessa *f.*

platypus ['plætɪpəs] (*pl* -**es**) *n* ornitorrinco *m.*

plaudits ['plɔːdɪts] *npl* aclamações *fpl*, aplausos *mpl.*

plausible ['plɔːzəbl] *adj* [reason, excuse] plausível; [person] convincente.

plausibly ['plɔːzəblɪ] *adv* plausivelmente, convincentemente.

play [pleɪ] <> *n* -**1**. *(U)* [amusement] brincadeira *f*; **children at ~** crianças brincando -**2**. [piece of drama] peça *f* -**3**. SPORT **in/out of ~** em/fora de jogo -**4**. [consideration]: **to come into ~** fig entrar em jogo -**5**. [pun]: **~ on words** trocadilho -**6**. TECH folga *f.* <> *vt* -**1**. [gen] jogar; **to ~ hide-and-seek** brincar de esconde-esconde -**2**. [opposing player or team] jogar contra -**3**. [joke, trick] pregar -**4**. [perform] desempenhar, representar; **to ~ a part** OR **role in sthg** fig desempenhar um papel em algo -**5**. [MUS - instrument, CD] tocar; [- tune] executar -**6**. [pretend to be] fingir -**7**. *phr*: **to ~ it cool** agir com calma. <> *vi* -**1**. [amuse o.s.] brincar; **to ~ with sb/sthg** brincar com alguém/algo -**2**. SPORT jogar; **to ~ for sb** jogar para alguém; **to ~ against sb** jogar contra alguém -**3**. PERFORM: **to ~ in sthg** atuar em algo -**4**. [music] tocar -**5**. *literary* [breeze, sun, light] brincar com -**6**. *phr*: **to ~ safe** não se arriscar.

● **play along** *vi*: **to ~ along (with sb)** fazer o jogo (de alguém).

● **play at** *vt fus* fazer de conta que.

● **play back** *vt sep* colocar de novo.

◆ **play down** vt sep menosprezar.

◆ **play off** ⬦ vt sep: **to ~ sb/sthg off against sb/sthg** colocar alguém/algo contra alguém/algo. ⬦ vi SPORT enfrentar-se novamente *(para obter um desempate)*.

◆ **play (up)on** vt fus tirar proveito de.

◆ **play up** ⬦ vt sep enfatizar. ⬦ vi **-1.** [cause problems] dar trabalho **-2.** [misbehave] descomportar-se.

playable ['pleɪəbl] adj em condições de jogo.

play-act vi fazer fita.

playbill ['pleɪbɪl] n cartaz m de lançamento.

playboy ['pleɪbɔɪ] n playboy m.

play dough n US = Plasticine®.

player ['pleɪə'] n **-1.** [of game, sport] jogador m, -ra f **-2.** MUS músico m, -ca f; **guitar ~** guitarrista mf; **saxophone ~** saxofonista mf **-3.** dated & THEATRE ator m, atriz f.

playfellow ['pleɪ,feləʊ] n amigo m, -ga f de infância.

playful ['pleɪfʊl] adj **-1.** [good-natured] divertido(da) **-2.** [frisky] brincalhão(lhona).

playfully ['pleɪfʊlɪ] adv divertidamente.

playgoer ['pleɪ,gəʊə'] n freqüentador m, -ra f de teatro.

playground ['pleɪgraʊnd] n [at school] pátio m de recreio; [in park] parque m de diversões.

playgroup ['pleɪgruːp] n jardim-de-infância m.

playhouse ['pleɪhaʊs, pl -haʊzɪz] n **-1.** [toy house] casa f de brinquedo **-2.** dated [theatre] teatro m.

playing card ['pleɪŋ-] n carta f de baralho.

playing field ['pleɪŋ-] n quadra f de esportes.

playlist ['pleɪlɪst] n UK lista f de músicas *(para tocar num programa de rádio)*.

playmate ['pleɪmeɪt] n amigo m, -ga f de infância.

play-off n partida f de desempate.

playpen ['pleɪpen] n cercadinho m para crianças, chiqueirinho m.

playroom ['pleɪrʊm] n sala f de recreação.

playschool ['pleɪskuːl] n jardim-de-infância m.

plaything ['pleɪθɪŋ] n **-1.** [toy] brinquedo m **-2.** fig [person] joguete m.

playtime ['pleɪtaɪm] n (U) (hora f do) recreio m.

playwright ['pleɪraɪt] n dramaturgo m, -ga f.

plaza ['plɑːzə] n **-1.** [public square] praça f **-2.** [building complex] complexo m.

plc (abbr of public limited company) UK companhia f pública limitada.

plea [pliː] n **-1.** [appeal] apelo m **-2.** JUR contestação f.

plea bargaining n (U) acordo segundo o qual o réu se declara culpado por uma acusação menor e o promotor público, em troca, o inocenta de uma acusação mais grave.

plead [pliːd] (pt & pp -ed OR pled) ⬦ vt **-1.** JUR defender; **to ~ insanity** alegar insanidade mental; **to ~ guilty** declarar culpado(da) **-2.** [give as excuse] alegar. ⬦ vi **-1.** [beg] implorar; **to ~ with sb to do sthg** implorar a alguém que faça algo; **to ~ for sthg** implorar algo **-2.** JUR responder a uma acusação.

pleading ['pliːdɪŋ] ⬦ adj de súplica. ⬦ n súplica f.

pleasant ['pleznt] adj agradável.

pleasantly ['plezntlɪ] adv agradavelmente.

pleasantry ['plezntrɪ] (pl -ies) n: **to exchange pleasantries** trocar amabilidades.

please [pliːz] ⬦ adv por favor. ⬦ vt agradar; **to ~ o.s.** fazer o que se deseja; **~ yourself!** como queira! ⬦ vi **-1.** [give satisfaction] agradar **-2.** [choose]: **to do as one ~s** fazer como quiser; **if you ~** se quiser.

pleased [pliːzd] adj contente, feliz; **to be ~ about sthg** estar satisfeito(ta) com algo; **to be ~ with sb/sthg** estar satisfeito(ta) com alguém/algo; **~ to meet you!** prazer em conhecê-lo(-la)!

pleasing ['pliːzɪŋ] adj agradável.

pleasingly ['pliːzɪŋlɪ] adv agradavelmente.

pleasurable ['pleʒərəbl] adj agradável.

pleasure ['pleʒə'] n **-1.** (U) [feeling of happiness] alegria f; **with ~** com (muito) prazer **-2.** [enjoyment] prazer m; **it's a ~** OR **my ~!** é um prazer!, não tem de quê!

pleat [pliːt] ⬦ n prega f. ⬦ vt fazer prega em.

pleated ['pliːtɪd] adj pregueado(da).

plebeian [plə'biːən] adj pej plebeu(béia).

plebiscite ['plebɪsaɪt] n plebiscito m.

plectrum ['plektrəm] (pl -s) n palheta f.

pled [pled] pt & pp ⊳ **plead**.

pledge [pledʒ] ⬦ n **-1.** [promise] promessa f **-2.** [token] símbolo m **-3.** [as a security] garantia f. ⬦ vt **-1.** [promise to provide] prometer **-2.** [commit]: **to be ~d to sthg** estar comprometido(da) com algo; **to ~ o.s.** comprometer-se com algo **-3.** [pawn] penhorar.

plenary session ['pliːnərɪ-] n sessão f plenária.

plentiful ['plentɪfʊl] adj abundante.

plenty ['plentɪ] ⬦ n (U) fartura f. ⬦ pron bastante; **~ of** bastante; **~ of time** bastante tempo; **~ of reasons** inúmeras razões. ⬦ adv US [very] muito.

plethora ['pleθərə] n excesso m.

pleurisy ['plʊərəsɪ] n (U) pleurisia f.

Plexiglas® ['pleksɪglɑːs] n (U) US Plexiglas® m.

pliable ['plaɪəbl], **pliant** ['plaɪənt] adj **-1.** [supple] flexível **-2.** [adaptable] dócil.

pliers ['plaɪəz] npl alicate m.

plight [plaɪt] n péssima situação f; **in a ~** em apuros.

plimsoll ['plɪmsəl] n UK calçados mpl para prática de esportes.

Plimsoll line n linha f de flutuação.

plinth [plɪnθ] n plinto m.

PLO (abbr of Palestine Liberation Organization) n OLP f.

plod [plɒd] (pt & pp -ded, cont -ding) vi **-1.** [walk slowly] arrastar-se **-2.** [work slowly] trabalhar vagarosamente.

plodder ['plɒdə'] n pej trabalhador m lerdo e pouco criativo.

plonk [plɒŋk] n UK inf vinho m fajuto.

◆ **plonk down** vt sep inf deixar cair.

plop [plɒp] (pt & pp -ped, cont -ping) ⬦ n chape m. ⬦ vi estatelar-se.

plot [plɒt] (pt & pp -ted, cont -ting) ⬦ n **-1.** [conspiracy] compô m; **the ~ thickens** a coisa está se complicando **-2.** [story] enredo m, trama f **-3.** [of land] lote *m* **- 4.** *US* [house plan] planta *f.* ◇ *vt* **-1.** [conspire] tramar; **to ~ to do sthg** tramar para fazer algo **- 2.** [chart] traçar **- 3.** *MATH* traçar, plotar. ◇ *vi* conspirar; **to ~ against sb** conspirar contra alguém.

plotter ['plɒtə^r] *n* [schemer] conspirador *m*, -ra *f.*

plough *UK*, **plow** *US* [plaʊ] ◇ *n* arado *m.* ◇ *vt* **-1.** *AGR* arar, lavrar **- 2.** [invest]: **to ~ money into sthg** investir muito dinheiro em algo. ◇ *vi*: **to ~ into sthg** colidir contra algo.
▸ **plough on** *vi* prosseguir.
▸ **plough up** *vt sep* arar.

ploughman's ['plaʊmənz] (*pl inv*) *n UK*: **~ (lunch)** refeição que consiste em pão, queijo, cebola e picles.

ploughshare *UK*, **plowshare** *US* ['plaʊʃeə^r] *n* relha *f* de arado.

plow etc *n* & *vt US* = plough etc.

ploy [plɔɪ] *n* estratagema *f.*

PLR (*abbr of* **Public Lending Right**) *n* valor que o autor recebe na Grã-Bretanha quando um livro seu é retirado nas bibliotecas públicas.

pls (*abbr of* **please**) por favor.

pluck [plʌk] ◇ *vt* **-1.** [flower, fruit] colher **- 2.** [pull] apanhar; **the helicopter ~ed the survivors off the ship** o helicóptero resgatou os sobreviventes do navio **- 3.** [chicken] depenar **- 4.** [eyebrows] depilar **- 5.** [musical instrument] dedilhar. ◇ *n* (*U*) dated [courage] garra *f.*
▸ **pluck up** *vt fus*: **to ~ up the courage to do sthg** criar coragem para fazer algo.

plucky ['plʌkɪ] (*compar* -ier, *superl* -iest) *adj* dated valente.

plug [plʌg] (*pt* & *pp* -ged, *cont* -ging) ◇ *n* **-1.** *ELEC* tomada *f*; [socket] plugue *m* **- 2.** [for bath or sink] tampa *f*, válvula *f* **- 3.** *inf* [in advertising] lance *m* de marketing. ◇ *vt* **-1.** [block] tampar **- 2.** *inf* [advertise] fazer propaganda de.
▸ **plug in** *vt sep* ligar.

plughole ['plʌghəʊl] *n* ralo *m.*

plum [plʌm] ◇ *adj* **-1.** [colour] da cor de ameixa **- 2.** [choice]: **a ~ job** uma jóia de emprego. ◇ *n* **-1.** [fruit] ameixa *m* **- 2.** [colour] cor *m* de ameixa.

plumage ['plu:mɪdʒ] *n* (*U*) plumagem *f.*

plumb [plʌm] ◇ *adv* **-1.** *UK* [exactly] exatamente **- 2.** *US* [completely] totalmente. ◇ *vt*: **to ~ the depths of sthg** atingir o auge de algo.
▸ **plumb in** *vt sep UK* instalar.

plumber ['plʌmə^r] *n* encanador *m*, -ra *f.*

plumbing ['plʌmɪŋ] *n* (*U*) **-1.** [fittings] encanamento *m* **- 2.** [work] trabalho *m* do encanador.

plumb line *n* prumo *m.*

plume [plu:m] *n* **-1.** [on bird] pluma *f* **- 2.** [on hat, helmet] penacho *m* **- 3.** [column]: **a ~ of smoke** um penacho de fumaça.

plummet ['plʌmɪt] *vi* **-1.** [dive] mergulhar (*em direção ao solo*) **- 2.** [decrease rapidly] despencar.

plummy ['plʌmɪ] (*compar* -ier, *superl* -iest) *adj UK inf pej* afetado(da).

plump [plʌmp] ◇ *adj* roliço(ça). ◇ *vi*: **to ~ for sthg** optar por algo.
▸ **plump up** *vt sep* afofar.

plum pudding *n* pudim *m* de passas.

plum tree *n* ameixeira *f.*

plunder ['plʌndə^r] ◇ *n* **-1.** [pillaging] pilhagem *f* **- 2.** [booty] saque *m.* ◇ *vt* saquear.

plunge [plʌndʒ] ◇ *n* **-1.** [rapid decrease] caída *f* **- 2.** [dive] mergulho; **to take the ~** mergulhar de cabeça, dar um passo decisivo. ◇ *vt* **-1.** [immerse]: **to ~ sthg into sthg** mergulhar algo em algo **- 2.** *fig* [thrust]: **to ~ sthg into sthg** enfiar algo em algo; **the room was ~d into darkness** a sala mergulhou na escuridão. ◇ *vi* **-1.** [dive, throw o.s.] mergulhar **- 2.** [decrease rapidly] despencar.

plunger ['plʌndʒə^r] *n* desentupidor *m.*

plunging ['plʌndʒɪŋ] *adj* profundo(da).

pluperfect [.plu:'pɜ:fɪkt] *n*: **the ~ (tense)** o (tempo) mais-que-perfeito.

plural ['plʊərəl] ◇ *adj* plural. ◇ *n* plural *m.*

pluralistic [.plʊərə'lɪstɪk] *adj* pluralista.

plurality [plʊ'rælətɪ] *n* **-1.** [large number]: **a ~ of** uma pluralidade de **- 2.** *US* [majority] maioria *f.*

plus [plʌs] (*pl* -es *OR* -ses) ◇ *adj* mais; **thirty-five ~** trinta e cinco ou mais. ◇ *n* **-1.** *MATH* sinal *m* de adição, sinal *m* de mais **- 2.** *inf* [bonus] vantagem *f.* ◇ *prep* mais. ◇ *conj* [moreover] além disso.

plus fours *npl* calças *fpl* de golfe/de caça.

plush [plʌʃ] *adj* suntuoso(sa).

plus sign *n* sinal *m* de mais.

Pluto ['plu:təʊ] *n* Plutão.

plutonium [plu:'təʊnɪəm] *n* (*U*) plutônio *m.*

ply [plaɪ] (*pt* & *pp* plied) ◇ *n* espessura. ◇ *vt* **-1.** [work at] trabalhar em **- 2.** [supply, provide]: **to ~ sb with sthg** prover alguém com algo **- 3.** [travel] navegar em. ◇ *vi* [travel] navegar em.

-ply *adj* de espessura.

plywood ['plaɪwʊd] *n* (*U*) compensado *m.*

p.m., pm (*abbr of* **post meridiem**): **at three ~** às três da tarde.

PM (*abbr of* **prime minister**) *n* primeiro-ministro *m*, primeira-ministra *f.*

PMS (*abbr of* **premenstrual syndrome**) *n* SPM *f.*

PMT (*abbr of* **premenstrual tension**) *n* TPM *f.*

pneumatic [nju:'mætɪk] *adj* **-1.** [air-powered] pneumático(ca) **- 2.** [air-filled] de ar.

pneumatic drill *n* perfuratriz *f.*

pneumonia [nju:'məʊnjə] *n* (*U*) pneumonia *f.*

Po *n*: **the (River) ~** o (Rio) Pó.

PO *n* **-1.** (*abbr of* **Post Office**) correio *m* **- 2.** (*abbr of* **postal order**) vale *m* postal.

poach [pəʊtʃ] ◇ *vt* **-1.** [hunt illegally] caçar ilegalmente **- 2.** [copy] plagiar **- 3.** [*CULIN*- salmon] escaldar; [- egg] escalfar. ◇ *vi* caçar ilegalmente.

poacher ['pəʊtʃə^r] *n* **-1.** [person] caçador *m* furtivo, caçadora *f* furtiva **- 2.** *CULIN* panela *f* para cozinhar ovos.

poaching ['pəʊtʃɪŋ] *n* (*U*) caça *f* ilegal.

PO Box (*abbr of* **Post Office Box**) *n* caixa *f* postal.

pocket ['pɒkɪt] ◇ *n* **-1.** [in clothes] bolso *m*; **to live in each other's ~s** estar sempre juntos(tas); **the deal left us £10 out of ~** o negócio nos deu um prejuízo de £10; **to pick sb's ~** roubar do bolso de alguém **- 2.** [in car door etc] porta-mapas *m* **- 3.** [small area] foco *m* **- 4.** [of snooker, pool table] caçapa *f.* ◇ *adj* [pocket-sized] de bolso. ◇ *vt* **-1.** [place in pocket] pôr no bolso -**2.** [steal] embolsar -**3.** [in snooker, pool] encaçapar.

pocketbook ['pɒkɪtbʊk] n -**1.** [notebook] livro m de bolso -**2.** US [handbag] carteira f.

pocketbook computer n computador m de bolso.

pocket calculator n calculadora f de bolso.

pocketful ['pɒkɪtfʊl] n bolso m cheio.

pocket-handkerchief n lenço m de bolso.

pocketknife ['pɒkɪtnaɪf] (pl -**knives** [-naɪvz]) n canivete m.

pocket money n (U) mesada m.

pocket-size(d) adj de bolso.

pockmark ['pɒkmɑːk] n sinal m de varíola.

pod [pɒd] n -**1.** [of plants] vagem f -**2.** [of spacecraft] módulo m.

podgy ['pɒdʒɪ] (compar -ier, superl -iest) adj inf atarracado(da).

podiatrist [pə'daɪətrɪst] n US podiatra mf.

podium ['pəʊdɪəm] (pl -diums OR -dia [-dɪə]) n pódio m.

poem ['pəʊɪm] n poema f.

poet ['pəʊɪt] n poeta mf, poetisa f.

poetic [pəʊ'etɪk] adj poético(ca).

poetic justice n (U) justiça f poética.

poet laureate n poeta mf laureado, poetisa f laureada.

poetry ['pəʊɪtrɪ] n (U) -**1.** [poems] poesia f -**2.** fig [beauty] beleza f.

pogo stick n pula-pula m.

pogrom ['pɒgrəm] n massacre m organizado (de um grupo étnico em particular).

poignancy ['pɔɪnjənsɪ] n (U) comoção f.

poignant ['pɔɪnjənt] adj comovente.

poinsettia [pɔɪn'setɪə] n poinsétia f.

point [pɔɪnt] ⟨⟩ n -**1.** [gen] ponto m; at this ~ in time neste momento; ~ of no return ponto sem volta; to have a ~ ter razão; to make a ~ fazer uma observação; to make one's ~ dar sua opinião; a sore ~ questão dolorosa -**2.** [tip] ponta f -**3.** [essence, heart] parte f essencial; to get OR come to the ~ ir ao ponto principal; beside the ~ irrelevante; to the ~ objetivo(va) -**4.** [feature, characteristic] característica f -**5.** [purpose] propósito m, razão f -**6.** [of compass] ponto m cardeal -**7.** UK ELEC ponto m -**8.** US [full stop] ponto m final -**9.** phr: to make a ~ of doing sthg fazer questão de fazer algo. ⟨⟩ vt: to ~ sthg (at sb/sthg) apontar algo (para alguém/algo); to ~ the way (to sthg) mostrar a direção (para algo). ⟨⟩ vi apontar; to ~ at sb/sthg, to ~ to sb/sthg apontar para alguém/algo.

➡ **points** npl UK RAIL pontos mpl.

➡ **up to a point** adv até certo ponto.

➡ **on the point of** prep prestes a.

➡ **point out** vt sep -**1.** [indicate] indicar -**2.** [call attention to] salientar.

point-blank ⟨⟩ adj -**1.** [direct] categórico(ca) -**2.** [close-range] à queima-roupa. ⟨⟩ adv -**1.** [directly] categoricamente -**2.** [at close range] à queima-roupa.

point duty n (U) UK serviço m de controle de trânsito.

pointed ['pɔɪntɪd] adj -**1.** [sharp] pontiagudo(da) -**2.** [meaningful] sugestivo(va).

pointedly ['pɔɪntɪdlɪ] adv sugestivamente.

pointer ['pɔɪntəʳ] n -**1.** [tip, hint] dica f -**2.** [needle on dial] agulha f -**3.** [stick] indicador m -**4.** [dog] pointer m -**5.** COMPUT ponteiro m.

pointing ['pɔɪntɪŋ] n (U) rejuntamento m.

pointless ['pɔɪntlɪs] adj inútil.

point of order (pl points of order) n questão f de ordem.

point of sale (pl points of sale) n COMM ponto m de venda.

point of view (pl points of view) n ponto m de vista.

point-to-point n UK corrida de cavalos que atravessa uma região, sinalizada com bandeirinhas.

poise [pɔɪz] n (U) compostura f.

poised [pɔɪzd] adj -**1.** [ready] pronto(ta), preparado(da); to be ~ to do sthg estar pronto(ta) para fazer algo; to be ~ for sthg estar pronto(ta) para algo -**2.** [calm and dignified] equilibrado(da).

poison ['pɔɪzn] ⟨⟩ n veneno m. ⟨⟩ vt -**1.** [gen] envenenar -**2.** [pollute] poluir -**3.** fig [spoil, corrupt] corromper.

poisoning ['pɔɪznɪŋ] n (U) envenenamento m, intoxicação f.

poisonous ['pɔɪznəs] adj -**1.** [gas, chemical] tóxico (ca) -**2.** [snake, mushroom, plant] venenoso(sa) -**3.** fig [corrupting] pernicioso(sa).

poison-pen letter n carta f anônima.

poke [pəʊk] ⟨⟩ n remexida f. ⟨⟩ vt -**1.** [prod, jab] remexer, cutucar -**2.** [stick, thrust] enfiar em -**3.** [fire] atiçar, remexer. ⟨⟩ vi projetar-se; his head ~ d round the corner a cabeça dele apareceu na esquina.

➡ **poke about, poke around** vi inf escarafunchar.

➡ **poke at** vt fus: he ~ d at my eye with his finger ele cutucou meu olho com seu dedo.

poker ['pəʊkəʳ] n -**1.** [game] pôquer m -**2.** [for fire] atiçador m.

poker-faced adj de rosto inexpressivo.

poky ['pəʊkɪ] (compar -ier, superl -iest) adj pej apertado(da).

Poland ['pəʊlənd] n Polônia f; in ~ na Polônia.

polar ['pəʊləʳ] adj GEOGR polar.

polar bear n urso m polar.

polarity [pəʊ'lærətɪ] n polaridade f.

polarization [ˌpəʊləraɪ'zeɪʃn] n (U) polarização f.

polarize, -ise ['pəʊləraɪz] vt polarizar.

Polaroid® ['pəʊlərɔɪd] n polaróide® f.

Polaroids® ['pəʊlərɔɪdz] npl [sunglasses] óculos mpl de sol (Polaroid).

pole [pəʊl] n -**1.** [gen] pólo m; to be ~ s apart ser totalmente diferente(s) -**2.** [rod, post] poste m.

Pole [pəʊl] n polonês m, -esa f.

poleaxe ['pəʊlæks] vt nocautear.

poleaxed ['pəʊlækst] adj atordoado(da).

polecat ['pəʊlkæt] n [in Europe and Asia] furão-bravo m.

polemic [pə'lemɪk] n fml polêmica f.

pole position n SPORT (U) pole position f.

Pole Star *n*: the ~ a Estrela Polar.
pole vault *n*: the ~ o salto com vara.
➤ **pole-vault** *vi* saltar com vara.
pole-vaulter [-ˌvɔːltəᵊ] *n* saltador(ra) com vara.
police [pəˈliːs] ◇ *npl* -1. [police force]: the ~ a polícia -2. [policemen, policewomen] policial *mf.* ◇ *vt* policiar.
police car *n* rádio-patrulha *f.*
police constable *n UK* policial *mf.*
police department *n US* departamento *m* de polícia, polícia *f.*
police dog *n* cão *m* policial.
police force *n* força *f* policial.
policeman [pəˈliːsmən] (*pl* -men [-mən]) *n* policial *m.*
police officer *n* oficial *mf* de polícia.
police record *n* ficha *f* policial; **to have a** ~ ter ficha na polícia.
police state *n* estado *m* policial.
police station *n UK* delegacia *f.*
policewoman [pəˈliːsˌwʊmən] (*pl* -women [-ˌwɪmɪn]) *n* policial *f.*
policy [ˈpɒləsɪ] (*pl* -ies) *n* -1. [plan, practice] política *f* -2. [document, agreement] apólice *f.*
policy-holder *n* segurado *m*, -da *f.*
polio [ˈpəʊlɪəʊ] *n* (U) poliomelite *f*, paralisia *f* infantil.
polish [ˈpɒlɪʃ] ◇ *n* -1. [cleaning material] polidor *m* -2. [shine] polimento *m* -3. *fig* [refinement] requinte *m.* ◇ *vt* -1. polir -2. *fig* [perfect]: to ~ sthg (up) refinar algo.
➤ **polish off** *vt sep inf* -1. [meal] comer/beber rapidamente -2. [job, book] dar um fim rápido em.
Polish [ˈpəʊlɪʃ] ◇ *adj* polonês(esa). ◇ *n* [language] polonês *m.* ◇ *npl*: the ~ os poloneses.
polished [ˈpɒlɪʃt] *adj* -1. [gen] polido(da) -2. [performer, performance] elegante.
polite [pəˈlaɪt] *adj* -1. [person, remark] educado(da), cortês(tesa) -2. [society] polido(da).
politely [pəˈlaɪtlɪ] *adv* educadamente.
politeness [pəˈlaɪtnɪs] *n* (U) educação *f*, cortesia *f.*
politic [ˈpɒlətɪk] *adj fml* prudente.
political [pəˈlɪtɪkl] *adj* político(ca).
political asylum *n* (U) asilo *m* político.
political football *n* debate *m* político acirrado.
political geography *n* (U) geografia *f* política.
politically [pəˈlɪtɪklɪ] *adv* politicamente.
politically correct [pəˌlɪtɪklɪ-] *adj* politicamente correto(ta).
political prisoner *n* prisioneiro *m* político, prisioneira *f* política.
political science *n* (U) ciência *f* política.
politician [ˌpɒlɪˈtɪʃn] *n* político *m*, -ca *f.*
politicize, -ise [pəˈlɪtɪsaɪz] *vt* politizar.
politics [ˈpɒlətɪks] ◇ *n* política *f.* ◇ *npl* [of a person, group] política *f.*
polka [ˈpɒlkə] *n* polca *f*; **to do the** ~ dançar a polca.
polka dot *n* bolinhas *fpl* (em um padrão de tecido).
poll [pəʊl] ◇ *n* -1. [election] eleição *f* -2. [survey]

pesquisa *f.* ◇ *vt* -1. [people] entrevistar -2. [votes] receber, obter.
➤ **polls** *npl*: **to go to the** ~s ir às urnas.
pollen [ˈpɒlən] *n* (U) pólen *m.*
pollen count *n* contagem *f* de pólen.
pollinate [ˈpɒləneɪt] *vt* polinizar.
pollination [ˌpɒlɪˈneɪʃn] *n* (U) polinização *f.*
polling [ˈpəʊlɪŋ] *n* (U) votação *f.*
polling booth [ˈpəʊlɪŋ-] *n* cabine *f* de votação.
polling day [ˈpəʊlɪŋ-] *n UK* dia *f* de eleição.
polling station [ˈpəʊlɪŋ-] *n* zona *f* eleitoral.
pollster [ˈpəʊlstəᵊ] *n* especialista *mf* em sondagem pública.
poll tax *n* imposto *m* per capita.
➤ **Poll Tax** *n UK* *imposto sobre votantes na Grã-Bretanha.*
pollutant [pəˈluːtnt] *n* poluente *m.*
pollute [pəˈluːtl] *vt* poluir.
pollution [pəˈluːʃn] *n* poluição *f.*
polo [ˈpəʊləʊl] *n* (U) pólo *m.*
polo neck *n UK* -1. [collar] gola *f* alta -2. [jumper] blusão *m* de gola alta.
➤ **polo-neck** *adj UK* de gola alta.
polo shirt *n* camisa *f* pólo.
poltergeist [ˈpɒltəgaɪst] *n fantasma que move objetos e faz barulhos.*
polyanthus [ˌpɒlɪˈænθəs] (*pl* -thuses OR -thi [-θaɪ]) *n* primavera-dos-jardins *f.*
poly bag *n UK inf* saco *m* plástico.
polyester [ˌpɒlɪˈestəᵊ] *n* (U) poliéster *m.*
polyethylene *n US* = polythene.
polygamist [pəˈlɪgəmɪst] *n* polígamo *m*, -ma *f.*
polygamy [pəˈlɪgəmɪ] *n* (U) poligamia *f.*
polygon [ˈpɒlɪgɒn] *n* polígono *m.*
polymer [ˈpɒlɪməᵊ] *n* polímero *m.*
Polynesia [ˌpɒlɪˈniːʒə] *n* Polinésia; **in** ~ na Polinésia; **French** ~ Polinésia Francesa.
Polynesian [ˌpɒlɪˈniːʒən] ◇ *adj* polinésio(sia). ◇ *n* -1. [person] polinésio *m*, -sia *f* -2. [language] polinésio *m.*
polyp [ˈpɒlɪp] *n* pólipo *m.*
polystyrene [ˌpɒlɪˈstaɪriːn] *n* (U) poliestireno *m*, isopor *m.*
polytechnic [ˌpɒlɪˈteknɪk] *n UK* politécnica *f.*
polythene *UK* [ˈpɒlɪθiːn], **polyethylene** *US* [ˈpɒlɪˈeθɪliːn] *n* (U) polietileno *m.*
polythene bag *n UK* saco *m* de polietileno.
polyunsaturated [ˌpɒlɪʌnˈsætʃəreɪtɪd] *adj* poliinsaturado(da).
polyurethane [ˌpɒlɪˈjʊərəθeɪn] *n* (U) poliuretano *m.*
pom [pɒm] *n Austr pej* inglês(esa).
pomander [pəˈmændəᵊ] *n* sachê *m* (aromático).
pomegranate [ˈpɒmɪˌgrænɪt] *n* romã *f.*
pommel [ˈpɒml] *n* -1. [on saddle] maçaneta *f* -2. [on sword] botão *m.*
pomp [pɒmp] *n* (U) pompa *f.*
pompom [ˈpɒmpɒm] *n* pompom *m.*
pompous [ˈpɒmpəs] *adj* [pretentious - speech, style] pomposo(sa); [- person] pretensioso(sa).
ponce [pɒns] *n UK v inf pej* -1. [effeminate man] marica *m* -2. [pimp] gigolô *m.*

poncho 334

poncho ['pɒntʃəʊl] (*pl* **-s**) *n* poncho *m*.
pond [pɒnd] *n* lago *m* (*natural ou artificial*); the ~ *inf* o Atlântico.
ponder ['pɒndə'] ⇔ *vt* ponderar. ⇔ *vi* ponderar; **to** ~ **on** *OR* **over** sthg meditar sobre algo.
ponderous ['pɒndərəs] *adj* **-1.** [dull, solemn] ponderoso(sa) **-2.** [large and heavy] pesado(da) **-3.** [slow, clumsy] enfadonho(nha).
pong [pɒŋ] *UK inf* ⇔ *n* fedor *m*. ⇔ *vi* feder.
pontiff ['pɒntɪf] *n* pontífice *m*.
pontificate [pɒn'tɪfɪkeɪt] *vi pej* pontificar; **to** ~ **about** *OR* **on** sthg pontificar sobre algo.
pontoon [pɒn'tuːn] *n* **-1.** [bridge] barcaça *f* **-2.** *UK* [game] vinte-e-um *m*.
pony ['pəʊnɪ] (*pl* **-ies**) *n* pônei *m*.
ponytail ['pəʊnɪteɪl] *n* rabo-de-cavalo *m*.
pony-trekking [-ˌtrekɪŋ] *n* (*U*) excursão *f* em pôneis.
poodle ['puːdl] *n* poodle *m*.
poof [pʊf] *n UK v inf offensive* veado *m*.
pooh-pooh *vt inf* fazer pouco caso de, desdenhar.
pool [puːl] ⇔ *n* **-1.** [natural] lago *m* **-2.** [swimming pool] piscina *f* **-3.** [of liquid, light] poça *f* **-4.** [of workers, cars, talent] grupo *m* **-5.** (*U*) *SPORT* bilhar *m*. ⇔ *vt* juntar.
➡ **pools** *npl UK*: **the** ~**s** ≃ a loteria esportiva.
pooped [puːpt] *adj inf* esgotado(da).
poor [pɔː'] ⇔ *adj* pobre. ⇔ *npl*: **the** ~ os pobres.
poorhouse ['pɔːhaʊs, *pl* -haʊzɪz] *n* albergue *m* (*para pobres*).
poorly ['pɔːlɪ] ⇔ *adj UK inf* [ill] mal. ⇔ *adv* mal.
poor relation *n fig* primo *m* pobre.
pop [pɒp] (*pt* & *pp* **-ped**, *cont* **-ping**) ⇔ *n* **-1.** (*U*) [music] pop *m* **-2.** (*U*) *inf* [fizzy drink] gasosa *f* **-3.** *esp US inf* [father] pai *m* **-4.** [noise] estouro *m*. ⇔ *vt* **-1.** [burst] estourar **-2.** [put quickly] pôr rapidamente. ⇔ *vi* **-1.** [burst] estourar **-2.** [spring, fly off] soltar-se **-3.** [eyes] arregalar **-4.** [go quickly] dar uma passada; **he** ~**ped from behind the sofa** ele apareceu de atrás do sofá.
➡ **pop in** *vi* entrar por um momento.
➡ **pop up** *vi* aparecer de repente.
popadum ['pɒpədəm] *n* pão *indiano* frito em óleo.
pop art *n* (*U*) arte *f* pop.
pop concert *n* concerto *m* pop.
popcorn ['pɒpkɔːn] *n* (*U*) pipoca *f*.
pope [pəʊp] *n* papa *m*.
pop group *n* grupo *m* pop.
poplar ['pɒplə'] *n* choupo *m*.
poplin ['pɒplɪn] *n* (*U*) popeline *m*.
popper ['pɒpə'] *n UK* presilha *f*.
poppy ['pɒpɪ] (*pl* **-ies**) *n* papoula *f*.
poppycock ['pɒpɪkɒk] *n* (*U*) *inf* papo *m* furado.
Poppy Day *n UK* Dia *m* do Armistício.

POPPY DAY

O *Poppy Day* ou *Remembrance Day* é celebrado no segundo domingo de novembro. Nesse dia, os britânicos carregam uma amapola de papel na lapela, em memória de seus soldados mortos nas guerras mundiais.

Popsicle® ['pɒpsɪkl] *n US* picolé *m*.
pop singer *n* cantor *m*, -ra *f* pop.
populace ['pɒpjʊləs] *n*: **the** ~ o populacho.
popular ['pɒpjʊlə'] *adj* popular.
popularity [ˌpɒpjʊ'lærətɪ] *n* (*U*) popularidade *f*.
popularize, -ise ['pɒpjʊləraɪz] *vt* popularizar.
popularly ['pɒpjʊləlɪ] *adv* popularmente.
populate ['pɒpjʊleɪt] *vt* **-1.** [inhabit] povoar **-2.** [colonize] urbanizar.
populated ['pɒpjʊleɪtɪd] *adj* povoado(da).
population [ˌpɒpjʊ'leɪʃn] *n* população *f*.
population explosion *n* explosão *f* demográfica.
populist ['pɒpjʊlɪst] *n* populista *mf*.
pop-up *adj* **-1.** [toaster] com sistema de ejeção **-2.** [book] com ilustrações tridimensionais.
porcelain ['pɔːsəlɪn] *n* (*U*) porcelana *f*.
porch [pɔːtʃ] *n* **-1.** [entrance] átrio *m* **-2.** *US* [veranda] alpendre *m*.
porcupine ['pɔːkjʊpaɪn] *n* porco-espinho *m*.
pore [pɔː'] *n* poro *m*.
➡ **pore over** *vt fus* examinar minuciosamente.
pork [pɔːk] *n* (*U*) carne *f* de porco.
pork chop *n* costeleta *f* de porco.
pork pie *n* pastelão *m* de porco.
porn [pɔːn] *n* (*U*) *inf* pornô *m*; **hard** ~ pornografia pesada; **soft** ~ pornografia leve.
pornographic [ˌpɔːnə'græfɪk] *adj* pornográfico (ca).
pornography [pɔː'nɒgrəfɪ] *n* (*U*) pornografia *f*.
porous ['pɔːrəs] *adj* poroso(sa).
porpoise ['pɔːpəs] *n* porco-do-mar *m*.
porridge ['pɒrɪdʒ] *n* (*U*) mingau *m* com cereais.
port [pɔːt] ⇔ *n* **-1.** [gen] porto *m* **-2.** (*U*) *NAUT* bombordo *m*; **to** ~ a bombordo **-3.** (*U*) [drink] vinho *m* do Porto **-4.** *COMPUT* porta *f*. ⇔ *comp* **-1.** [relating to a harbour] porteiro(ra) **-2.** *NAUT* a bombordo.
portable ['pɔːtəbl] *adj* portável.
Portacrib® ['pɔːtəˌkrɪb] *n US* moisés *m*.
portal ['pɔːtl] *n* **-1.** *literary* portada *f* **-2.** *COMPUT* portal *m*.
Port-au-Prince [ˌpɔːtəʊ'prɪns] *n* Porto-Príncipe *m*.
portcullis [ˌpɔːt'kʌlɪs] *n* portão *m* levadiço (*em um castelo*).
portend [pɔː'tend] *vt literary* prognosticar.
portent ['pɔːtənt] *n literary* prognóstico *m*.
porter ['pɔːtə'] *n* **-1.** *UK* [doorman] porteiro *m*, -ra *f* **-2.** [for luggage] carregador *m*, -ra *f* **-3.** *US* [on train] cabineiro *m*, -ra *f*.
portfolio [ˌpɔːt'fəʊljəʊ] (*pl* **-s**) *n* **-1.** [case] pasta *f* **-2.** [sample of work] portfólio *m* **-3.** *FIN* carteira *f*.
porthole ['pɔːthəʊl] *n* vigia *mf*.
portion ['pɔːʃn] *n* **-1.** [part, share] porção *f* **-2.** [set amount of food] parte *f*.
portly ['pɔːtlɪ] (*compar* **-ier**, *superl* **-iest**) *adj* corpulento(ta).
port of call *n* **-1.** *NAUT* porto *m* de escala **-2.** *fig* [on journey] ponto *m* de parada.
Port of Spain *n* Porto *m* de Espanha.
portrait ['pɔːtrɪt] *n* retrato *m*.

portraitist [ˈpɔːtrɪtɪst] n retratista mf.

portray [pɔːˈtreɪ] vt **-1.** [in a play, film] interpretar **-2.** [describe, represent] descrever **-3.** [subj: artist] retratar.

portrayal [pɔːˈtreɪəl] n **-1.** [in a play, film] interpretação f **-2.** [description, representation] descrição f **-3.** [painting, photograph] retrato m.

Portugal [ˈpɔːtʃʊgl] n Portugal; **in** ~ em Portugal.

Portuguese [ˌpɔːtʃʊˈgiːz] (pl inv) <> adj português(guesa). <> n [language] português m. <> npl: **the** ~ os portugueses.

POS (abbr of point of sale) n UK ponto m de venda.

pose [pəʊz] <> n **-1.** [position, stance] pose f **-2.** pej [pretence, affectation] pose f. <> vt **-1.** [problem, danger, threat] constituir **-2.** [question] fazer. <> vi **-1.** [model] posar **-2.** pej [behave affectedly] fazer-se **-3.** [pretend to be]: **to** ~ **as sb/sthg** fazer-se passar por alguém/algo.

poser [ˈpəʊzəʳ] n **-1.** pej [person] fingido m, -da f **-2.** inf [hard question] quebra-cabeça f.

poseur [pəʊˈzɜːʳ] n pej fingido m, -da f.

posh [pɒʃ] adj inf **-1.** [hotel, clothes] chique **-2.** [upper-class] chique.

posit [ˈpɒzɪt] vt fml postular.

position [pəˈzɪʃn] <> n **-1.** [gen] posição f; **in** ~ em posição **-2.** [job] cargo m **-3.** [state, situation] posição f, situação f; **to be in a/no** ~ **to do sthg** estar/não estar em condições de fazer algo **-4.** [stance, opinion]: ~ **on sthg** posição sobre algo. <> vt posicionar; **to** ~ **o.s.** posicionar-se.

positive [ˈpɒzətɪv] adj **-1.** [gen] positivo(va); **to be** ~ **about sthg** ser positivo(va) sobre algo; **be** ~ **about the exam!** seja otimista em relação à prova! **-2.** [irrefutable] irrefutável **-3.** [for emphasis]: **a** ~ **joy** uma ótima brincadeira; **a** ~ **nightmare** um pesadelo terrível.

positive discrimination n (U) discriminação f positiva.

positively [ˈpɒzətɪvlɪ] adv **-1.** [gen] positivamente **-2.** [irrefutably] irrefutavelmente **-3.** [for emphasis] definitivamente.

positive vetting n (U) UK investigação completa a que é submetido um candidato a cargo público relacionado com a segurança nacional.

posse [ˈpɒsɪ] n **-1.** [of sheriff] US destacamento m **-2.** inf [gang] bando m armado.

possess [pəˈzes] vt **-1.** [gen] possuir **-2.** [subj: emotion] levar a.

possessed [pəˈzest] adj possuído(da).

possession [pəˈzeʃn] n (U) posse f; **to have sthg in one's** ~, **to be in** ~ **of sthg** estar em posse de algo.
➤ **possessions** npl posses fpl, bens mpl.

possessive [pəˈzesɪv] <> adj **-1.** pej [clinging] possessivo(va) **-2.** GRAMM possessivo(va). <> n GRAMM possessivo m.

possessively [pəˈzesɪvlɪ] adv possessivamente.

possessor [pəˈzesəʳ] n fml proprietário m, -ria f.

possibility [ˌpɒsəˈbɪlətɪ] (pl -ies) n possibilidade f.

possible [ˈpɒsəbl] <> adj possível; **as soon as** ~ o mais cedo possível; **as much as** ~ o máximo possível. <> n possível m.

possibly [ˈpɒsəblɪ] adv **-1.** [perhaps, maybe] possivelmente **-2.** [conceivably]: **I'll do all I** ~ **can** vou fazer tudo que estiver ao meu alcance; **how could he** ~ **do that?** como ele foi capaz de fazer isso?; **I can't** ~ **take the money!** simplesmente não posso aceitar o dinheiro!

possum [ˈpɒsəm] (pl inv OR -s) n US gambá m.

post [pəʊst] <> n **-1.** [mail service]: **the** ~ o correio; **by** ~ pelo correio; **in the** ~ no correio **-2.** (U) [letters etc] correio m **-3.** [delivery] mala f postal **-4.** UK [collection] coleta f **-5.** [pole] poste m **-6.** [position, job] posto m **-7.** MIL guarnição f **-8.** phr: **to pip sb at the** ~ vencer alguém na última hora. <> vt **-1.** [by mail] postar, pôr no correio **-2.** [transfer] transferir **-3.** phr: **to keep sb** ~ **ed** manter alguém informado(da).

post [pəʊst] vt COMPUT [message, query] enviar.

post- [pəʊst] prefix pós-.

postage [ˈpəʊstɪdʒ] n (U) franquia f; ~ **and packing** despesas fpl de envio.

postage stamp n fml selo m (postal).

postal [ˈpəʊstl] adj postal.

postal order n vale m postal.

postbag [ˈpəʊstbæg] n **-1.** UK [bag] sacola f de correio **-2.** inf [letters received] mala f de cartas.

postbox [ˈpəʊstbɒks] n UK caixa f de correio.

postcard [ˈpəʊstkɑːd] n cartão m postal.

postcode [ˈpəʊstkəʊd] n UK código m (de endereçamento) postal.

post-date vt pós-datar.

poster [ˈpəʊstəʳ] n cartaz m, pôster m.

poste restante [ˌpəʊstˈrestɑːnt] n (U) esp UK posta-restante f.

posterior [pɒˈstɪərɪəʳ] <> adj posterior. <> n hum traseiro m.

posterity [pɒˈsterətɪ] n (U) posteridade f.

poster paint n têmpera f.

post-free adj esp UK com porte pago.

postgraduate [ˌpəʊstˈgrædʒʊət] <> adj pós-graduado(da). <> n pós-graduado m, -da f.

post-haste adv dated de pronto.

posthumous [ˈpɒstjʊməs] adj póstumo(ma).

posthumously [ˈpɒstjʊməslɪ] adv postumamente.

post-industrial adj pós-industrial.

posting [ˈpəʊstɪŋ] n [assignment] nomeação f.

postman [ˈpəʊstmən] (pl -men [-mən]) n carteiro m.

postmark [ˈpəʊstmɑːk] <> n carimbo m (postal). <> vt carimbar.

postmaster [ˈpəʊstˌmɑːstəʳ] n agente m de correio.

Postmaster General (pl Postmasters General) n diretor m geral dos correios.

postmistress [ˈpəʊstˌmɪstrɪs] n agente f de correio.

postmortem [ˌpəʊstˈmɔːtəm] <> adj post-mortem. <> n **-1.** [autopsy] autópsia f **-2.** fig [analysis] análise f detalhada.

postnatal [ˌpəʊstˈneɪtl] adj pós-natal.

post office n **-1.** [organization]: **the Post Office** a Agência dos Correios **-2.** [building] correio m.

post office box n caixa f postal.

post-operative adj pós-operatório(ria).

post-paid adj com porte pago.
postpone [pəs'pəʊn] vt adiar.
postponement [,pəʊst'pəʊnmənt] n adiamento m.
postscript ['pəʊstskrɪpt] n -1. [to letter] pós-escrito m -2. fig [additional information] adendo m.
postulate [n 'pɒstjʊlət, vb 'pɒstjʊleɪt] vt fml postular.
posture ['pɒstʃə'] <> n postura f; ~ on sthg postura em relação a algo. <> vi: he's always posturing ele está sempre bancando pose.
posturing n (U) pose f, atitude f.
postviral syndrome [,pəʊst'vaɪrəl-] n síndrome f pós-virótica.
postwar [,pəʊst'wɔ:'] adj pós-guerra.
posy ['pəʊzɪ] (pl -ies) n ramalhete m.
pot [pɒt] (pt & pp -ted, cont -ting) <> n -1. [for cooking] panela f; **to go to ~** ir para o brejo; **the ~ calling the kettle black** rir-se o roto do esfarrapado -2. [for tea, coffee] bule m -3. [for paint, jam] frasco m -4. [flowerpot] vaso m -5. (U) drugs sl [cannabis] maconha f. <> vt -1. [plant] plantar (em vaso) -2. [billiards ball] encaçapar.
potash ['pɒtæʃ] n (U) potassa f.
potassium [pə'tæsɪəm] n (U) potássio m.
potato [pə'teɪtəʊ] (pl -es) n batata f.
potato crisps UK, **potato chips** US npl batatinhas fpl fritas.
potato peeler [-,pi:lə'] n descascador m de batatas.
pot-bellied [-,belɪd] adj barrigudo(da).
potboiler ['pɒt,bɔɪlə'] n pej livro, quadro ou outro artigo de pouco valor artístico, produzido rapidamente com fins apenas comerciais.
pot-bound adj sufocado(da) com muitas raízes.
potency ['pəʊtənsɪ] n (U) -1. [of argument] força f -2. [of drink, drug] teor m -3. [virility] potência f, virilidade f.
potent ['pəʊtənt] adj -1. [argument] forte -2. [drink, drug] de alto teor, poderoso(sa) -3. [virile] potente, viril.
potentate ['pəʊtənteɪt] n potentado m.
potential [pə'tenʃl] <> adj potencial, em potencial. <> n [of person] potencial m; **to have ~** ter potencial.
potentially [pə'tenʃəlɪ] adv potencialmente.
pothole ['pɒthəʊl] n buraco m.
potholer ['pɒt,həʊlə'] n UK espeleologista mf.
potholing ['pɒt,həʊlɪŋ] n UK espeleologia; **to go ~** explorar cavernas.
potion ['pəʊʃn] n poção f.
potluck [,pɒt'lʌk] n: **to take ~** [at meal] contentarse com o que houver para comer; [in choice] arriscar OR tentar a sorte.
pot plant n planta f de vaso.
potpourri [,pəʊ'pʊərɪ] n pot-pourri m.
pot roast n carne f assada.
potshot ['pɒt,ʃɒt] n: **to take a ~ (at sthg)** atirar a esmo (em algo).
potted ['pɒtɪd] adj -1. [grown in pot] de vaso -2. [preserved] em conserva -3. UK fig [condensed] condensado(da).
potter ['pɒtə'] n oleiro m, -ra f.
➤ **potter about, potter around** vi UK

ocupar-se em trabalhos pequenos.
Potteries ['pɒtərɪz] npl: **the ~** os Potteries (distrito na Inglaterra típico por sua cerâmica).
potter's wheel n roda f de oleiro.
pottery ['pɒtərɪ] (pl -ies) n -1. [gen] cerâmica f -2. [factory] olaria f.
potting compost ['pɒtɪŋ-] n (U) adubo m para plantas de interiores.
potty ['pɒtɪ] (compar -ier, superl -iest, pl -ies) UK inf <> adj doido(da); **to be ~ about sb/sthg** ser doido(da) por alguém/algo. <> n [for children] penico m.
potty-trained [-,treɪnd] adj: **a ~ child** uma criança que já sabe pedir para ir ao banheiro.
pouch [paʊtʃ] n bolsa f.
pouffe [pu:f] n UK [seat] pufe m.
poultice ['pəʊltɪs] n cataplasma f.
poultry ['pəʊltrɪ] <> n (U) [meat] carne f de aves (domésticas). <> npl [birds] aves fpl domésticas.
pounce [paʊns] vi -1. [subj: animal, bird]: **to ~ (on OR upon sthg)** agarrar (algo) -2. [subj: person, police]: **to ~ (on OR upon sb)** lançar-se (sobre alguém) -3. fig [on mistake, suggestion]: **to ~ (up)on sthg** precipitar-se sobre algo.
pound [paʊnd] <> n -1. UK [unit of money] libra f -2. UK [currency system]: **the ~** a libra -3. [unit of weight] libra f -4. [for dogs] canil -5. [for cars] depósito m (para automóveis apreendidos). <> vt -1. [strike loudly] esmurrar -2. [pulverize] pulverizar. <> vi -1. [strike loudly]: **to ~ on sthg** esmurrar algo -2. [beat, throb - heart] palpitar; [- head] latejar.
pound coin n moeda f de libra.
pounding ['paʊndɪŋ] n -1. [of drums, fists] surra f -2. [of heart] palpitação f -3. [of head] latejamento m -4. phr: **to get OR take a ~** [be severely damaged] ser seriamente atingido(da); [be heavily defeated] levar uma surra.
pound sterling n libra f esterlina.
pour [pɔ:'] <> vt -1. [cause to flow] despejar; **to ~ sthg into sthg** despejar algo em algo; **to ~ sb a drink, to ~ a drink for sb** servir um drinque a alguém -2. fig [invest]: **to ~ money into sthg** investir muito dinheiro em algo. <> vi -1. [flow quickly] fluir, correr -2. fig [rush] correr. <> v impers [rain hard] chover a cântaros.
➤ **pour in** vi vir em enxurrada.
➤ **pour out** vt sep -1. [empty] esvaziar -2. [serve] servir -3. fig [emotions] abrir.
pouring ['pɔ:rɪŋ] adj [rain] torrencial.
pout [paʊt] <> n beiço m. <> vi fazer beiço.
poverty ['pɒvətɪ] n (U) -1. [hardship] miséria f -2. [lack]: **~ of sthg** pobreza de algo.
poverty line n linha f da pobreza.
poverty-stricken adj carente, necessitado(da).
poverty trap n UK situação na qual uma pessoa pobre não tem vantagem em arrumar emprego por perder os benefícios do governo.
pow [paʊ] excl paf!
POW (abbr of prisoner of war) n prisioneiro m, -ra f de guerra.
powder ['paʊdə'] <> n [tiny particles] pó m; **face ~**

pó-de-arroz *m*; **gun** ~ pólvora *f*; **washing** ~ detergente *m*. <> *vt* [make-up] maquiar; **to** ~ **o.s.** maquiar-se.

powder compact *n* estojo *m (de pó-de-arroz)*.

powdered ['paʊdəd] *adj* [in powder form] em pó.

powder puff *n* esponja *f* de pó-de-arroz.

powder room *n* toalete *m*.

powdery ['paʊdərɪ] *adj* **-1.** [like powder] poeirento (ta) **-2.** [covered in powder] cheio (cheia) de pó.

power ['paʊəʳ] <> *n* **-1.** *(U)* [control, influence] poder *m*; **to be in** ~ estar no poder; **to come to** ~ chegar ao poder; **to have** ~ **over sb** ter poder sobre alguém; **to take** ~ assumir o poder **-2.** [ability, capacity] força *f*; **mental** ~ **s** poderes *mpl* mentais; **to be (with)in one's** ~ to do sthg competir a alguém fazer algo **-3.** [legal authority] autoridade *f*; **to have the** ~ **to do sthg** ter autoridade para fazer algo **-4.** [strength] força *f*; **the** ~ **s that be** os poderes constituídos **-5.** *(U)* TECH energia *f* **-6.** *(U)* [electricity] luz *f*. <> *vt* alimentar.

power base *n* reduto *m (de força)*.

powerboat ['paʊəbəʊt] *n* powerboat *m, pequeno barco de corrida muito veloz*.

power broker *n* pessoa *que exerce grande influência através do controle de votos ou de indivíduos*.

power cut *n* corte *m* de energia.

power failure *n* falha *f* no sistema elétrico.

powerful ['paʊəfʊl] *adj* **-1.** [influential] poderoso(sa) **-2.** [strong] poderoso(sa), forte **-3.** [very convincing, very moving] vigoroso(sa).

powerhouse ['paʊəhaʊs, *pl* -haʊzɪz] *n fig* fonte *f* de influência.

powerless ['paʊəlɪs] *adj* fraco(ca); **to be** ~ **to do sthg** ser impotente para fazer algo.

power line *n* linha *f* de força.

power of attorney *n* procuração *f*.

power plant *n* central *f* elétrica.

power point *n UK* ponto *m* de força, tomada *f*.

power-sharing *n* POL divisão *f* de poder *(entre partidos políticos)*.

power station *n* estação *f* de força.

power steering *n (U)* direção *f* hidráulica.

power worker *n* eletricitário *m*, -ria *f*.

Powys ['paʊɪs] *n* Powys.

pp *(abbr of* per procurationem*)* p/.

p & p *(abbr of* postage and packing*)* *n* postagem *f* e empacotamento.

PPE *(abbr of* philosophy, politics and economics*)* *n* filosofia, política e economia, famoso curso oferecido pela Universidade de Oxford.

ppm *(abbr of* parts per million*)* ppm.

PPS <> *n (abbr of* parliamentary private secretary*)* deputado britânico que assessora um ministro. <> *(abbr of* post postscriptum*)* P.P.S.

PQ *abbr of* Province of Quebec.

PR <> *n* **-1.** *(abbr of* public relations*)* RP *mf* **-2.** *(abbr of* proportional representation*)* representação *f* proporcional. <> *abbr of* Puerto Rico.

practicable ['præktɪkəbl] *adj* praticável.

practical ['præktɪkl] <> *adj* **-1.** [gen] prático(ca) **-2.** [practicable] praticável. <> *n* prática *f*.

practicality [ˌpræktɪ'kælətɪ] *n (U)* praticabilidade *f*.

    practicalities *npl* aspectos *mpl* práticos.

practical joke *n* peça *f*, trote *m*.

practically ['præktɪklɪ] *adv* praticamente.

practice ['præktɪs], **practise** *US n* **-1.** *(U)* [gen] prática *f*; **to be out of** ~ estar destreinado(da); **the athlete is out of** ~ estar fora de forma **-2.** *(U)* [implementation]: **to put sthg into** ~ pôr algo em prática; **in** ~ [in fact] na prática **-3.** [training session] sessão *f* de treino.

practiced *adj US* = practised.

practicing *adj US* = practising.

practise, practice *US* ['præktɪs] <> *vt* praticar. <> *vi* **-1.** [train] treinar **-2.** [professional] exercer.

practised, practiced *US* ['præktɪst] *adj* experiente, treinado(da); **to be** ~ **at doing sthg** ser competente ao fazer algo.

practising, practicing *US* ['præktɪsɪŋ] *adj* **-1.** [doctor, lawyer] que exerce **-2.** [Christian, Catholic] praticante **-3.** [homosexual] assumido(da).

practitioner [præk'tɪʃnəʳ] *n* MED: **a medical** ~ um profissional da área médica.

pragmatic [præg'mætɪk] *adj* pragmático(ca).

pragmatism ['prægmətɪzm] *n (U)* pragmatismo *m*.

pragmatist ['prægmətɪst] *n* pragmatista *m*.

Prague [prɑːg] *n* Praga; **in** ~ em Praga.

prairie ['preərɪ] *n* pradaria *f*.

praise [preɪz] <> *n* **-1.** *(U)* [commendation] elogio *m* **-2.** RELIG louvor *m*; ~ **be to God!** louvado seja Deus! **-3.** *phr*: **to sing sb's** ~ **s** tecer elogios a alguém. <> *vt* **-1.** [commend] elogiar **-2.** RELIG louvar.

praiseworthy ['preɪzˌwɜːðɪ] *adj* louvável.

praline ['prɑːliːn] *n* pralina *f*.

pram [præm] *n UK* carrinho *m* de bebê.

PRAM *(abbr of* programmable random access memory*)* *n* RAM *f* programável.

prance [prɑːns] *vi* empinar-se.

prang [præŋ] *UK inf dated* <> *n* desastre *m*. <> *vt* espatifar-se.

prank [præŋk] *n* peça *f*.

prat [præt] *n UK v inf* palerma *mf*.

prattle ['prætl] *pej* <> *n* tagarelice *m*. <> *vi* tagarelar; **to** ~ **on about sthg** tagarelar sobre algo.

prawn [prɔːn] *n* pitu *m*.

prawn cocktail *n* coquetel *m* de pitus.

prawn cracker *n petisco de origem chinesa parecido com batatas fritas.*

pray [preɪ] *vi* RELIG rezar; **to** ~ **to sb** rezar para alguém; **to** ~ **for sthg** rezar por algo.

prayer [preəʳ] *n* **-1.** *(U)* [act of praying] prece *f* **-2.** [set of words] oração *f*; **to say one's** ~ **s** fazer suas orações **-3.** *fig* [strong hope] pedido *m*.

    prayers *npl* [service] preces *fpl*.

prayer book *n* missal *m*.

prayer meeting *n* serviço *m* de oração.

pre- [priː] *prefix* pré-.

preach [priːtʃ] <> *vt* pregar. <> *vi* **-1.** RELIG pregar; **to** ~ **to sb** fazer sermões a alguém **-2.** *pej* [pontificate] dar sermões em; **to** ~ **at sb** dar sermões em alguém.

preacher ['pri:tʃəʳ] n pregador m, -ra f.
preamble [pri:'æmbl] n preâmbulo m.
prearranged [,pri:ə'reɪndʒd] adj já combinado(-da).
precarious [prɪ'keərɪəs] adj precário(ria).
precariously [prɪ'keərɪəslɪ] adv precariamente.
precast [,pri:'kɑːst] adj pré-moldado(da).
precaution [prɪ'kɔ:ʃn] n precaução f; **as a ~ against** sthg como precaução contra algo.
precautionary [prɪ'kɔ:ʃənərɪ] adj de precaução.
precede [prɪ'si:d] vt **-1.** [gen] preceder **-2.** [walk in front of] adiantar-se.
precedence ['presɪdəns] n: **to take ~ over** sthg ter prioridade sobre algo; **to take ~ over** sb ter precedência sobre alguém.
precedent ['presɪdənt] n precedente m.
preceding [prɪ'si:dɪŋ] adj **-1.** [previous] anterior **-2.** [written before] anterior, precedente.
precept ['pri:sept] n preceito m.
precinct ['pri:sɪŋkt] n **-1.** UK [shopping area] zona f comercial **-2.** US [district] distrito m.
➡ **precincts** npl [around building] arredores mpl.
precious ['preʃəs] adj **-1.** [friendship, moment, time] precioso(sa), querido(da) **-2.** [jewel, object, material] precioso(sa) **-3.** inf iro [damned] maldito(ta); **~ little** muito pouco **-4.** [affected] afetado(da).
precious metal n metal m precioso.
precious stone n pedra f preciosa.
precipice ['presɪpɪs] n precipício m.
precipitate [adj prɪ'sɪpɪtət , vb prɪ'sɪpɪteɪt] fml ⟨⟩ adj precipitado(da). ⟨⟩ vt precipitar.
precipitation [prɪ,sɪpɪ'teɪʃn] n precipitação f.
precipitous [prɪ'sɪpɪtəs] adj **-1.** [very steep] íngreme **-2.** [hasty] precipitado(da).
précis [UK 'preɪsi:, US 'preɪsi:] (pl inv) n resumo m.
precise [prɪ'saɪs] adj preciso(sa), exato(ta); **to be ~** [speaking exactly] para ser preciso.
precisely [prɪ'saɪslɪ] adv exatamente; **to describe/explain** sthg **~** descrever/explicar algo com precisão.
precision [prɪ'sɪʒn] ⟨⟩ n (U) precisão f; **to do sthg with ~** fazer algo com precisão. ⟨⟩ comp de precisão.
preclude [prɪ'klu:d] vt fml impedir, evitar; **to ~ sb/sthg from doing** sthg impedir alguém/algo de fazer algo.
precocious [prɪ'kəʊʃəs] adj precoce.
precocity [prɪ'kɒsətɪ] n (U) precocidade f.
preconceived [,pri:kən'si:vd] adj preconcebido(-da).
preconception [,pri:kən'sepʃn] n idéia f preconcebida.
precondition [,pri:kən'dɪʃn] n fml precondição f, condição f prévia; **to be a ~ for** OR **of** sthg ser um pré-requisito para algo.
precooked [pri:'kʊkt] adj pré-cozido(da).
precursor [,pri:'kɜ:səʳ] n fml precursor m, -ra f; **to be a ~ of** OR **to** sthg ser um precursor de algo.
predate [pri:'deɪt] vt preceder, ser anterior a.
predator ['predətəʳ] n **-1.** [animal, bird] predador m, -ra f **-2.** fig [exploitative person] explorador m, -ra f.
predatory ['predətrɪ] adj predatório(ria).
predecease [,pri:dɪ'si:s] vt fml morrer antes de.

predecessor ['pri:dɪsesəʳ] n **-1.** [person] predecessor m, -ra f, antecessor m, -ra f **-2.** [thing] antecessor m, -ra f.
predestination [pri:,destɪ'neɪʃn] n (U) RELIG predestinação f.
predestine [,pri:'destɪn] vt: **to be ~d to** sthg to do sthg estar predestinado(da) a algo/a fazer algo.
predetermine [,pri:dɪ'tɜ:mɪn] vt predeterminar.
predetermined [,pri:dɪ'tɜ:mɪnd] adj predeterminado(da).
predicament [prɪ'dɪkəmənt] n aperto m; **to be in a ~** estar num aperto.
predicate ['predɪkət] n GRAMM predicado m.
predict [prɪ'dɪkt] vt prever.
predictable [prɪ'dɪktəbl] adj previsível.
predictably [prɪ'dɪktəblɪ] adv **-1.** [in an expected way] de forma previsível **-2.** [as was expected] como era de se imaginar.
prediction [prɪ'dɪkʃn] n **-1.** [something foretold] previsão f, prognóstico m **-2.** (U) [foretelling] previsão f.
predictor [prɪ'dɪktəʳ] n indicador m.
predigest [,pri:daɪ'dʒest] vt fig simplificar; **~ed** mastigado (mastigada).
predilection [,pri:dɪ'lekʃn] n: **~ for** sthg predileção f por algo.
predispose [,pri:dɪs'pəʊz] vt: **to be ~d to** sthg to do sthg estar predisposto(ta) a algo/a fazer algo.
predisposition ['pri:,dɪspə'zɪʃn] n: **~ to(wards)** sthg predisposição f a algo; **~ to do** sthg predisposição para fazer algo.
predominance [prɪ'dɒmɪnəns] n **-1.** [preponderance] predominância f, predomínio m **-2.** [control] predomínio m.
predominant [prɪ'dɒmɪnənt] adj predominante.
predominantly [prɪ'dɒmɪnəntlɪ] adv predominantemente.
predominate [prɪ'dɒmɪneɪt] vi **-1.** [be greater in number] predominar **-2.** [prevail] predominar, prevalecer.
pre-eminent adj preeminente.
pre-empt [-'empt] vt antecipar-se a.
pre-emptive [-'emptɪv] adj preventivo(va).
pre-emptive strike n ataque m preventivo.
preen [pri:n] vt **-1.** [subj: bird] alisar com o bico **-2.** fig [subj: person]: **to ~ o.s.** arrumar-se, ajeitar-se.
pre-exist vi preexistir.
prefab ['pri:fæb] n inf casa f pré-fabricada.
prefabricate [,pri:'fæbrɪkeɪt] vt pré-fabricar.
preface ['prefɪs] ⟨⟩ n [in book] prefácio m; **~ to** sthg [to text] prefácio a algo; [to speech] preâmbulo m. ⟨⟩ vt: **to ~ sthg with** sthg/**by doing** sthg introduzir algo com algo/fazendo algo.
prefect ['pri:fekt] n UK monitor m, -ra f, prefeito m, -ta f (em escola).
prefer [prɪ'fɜ:ʳ] (pt & pp -red, cont -ring) vt preferir; **to ~ sthg to** sthg preferir algo a algo; **to ~ to do** sthg preferir fazer algo.
preferable ['prefrəbl] adj: **to be ~ (to** sthg) ser preferível(a algo).
preferably ['prefrəblɪ] adv preferivelmente.

preference ['prefərəns] *n*: ~ (for sthg) preferência *f*(por algo); **to give sb/sthg** ~, **to give** ~ **to sb/sthg** dar preferência a alguém/algo.

preference shares *UK npl*, **preferred stock** *US n* ações *fpl* preferenciais.

preferential [,prefə'renʃl] *adj* preferencial.

preferred [prɪ'fɜ:d] *adj* preferido(da).

preferred stock *n US* = preference shares.

prefigure [pri:'fɪgə'] *vt fml* prefigurar, anunciar.

prefix ['pri:fɪks] *n GRAMM* prefixo *m*.

pregnancy ['pregnənsɪ] (*pl* -ies) *n* gravidez *f*.

pregnancy test *n* teste *m* de gravidez.

pregnant ['pregnənt] *adj* -1. [carrying unborn baby - human] grávido(da); [- animal] prenho(ha) -2. *fig* [significant] significativo(va).

preheated [,pri:'hi:tɪd] *adj* preaquecido(da).

prehistoric [,pri:hɪ'stɒrɪk] *adj* pré-histórico(ca).

prehistory [,pri:'hɪstərɪ] *n* (*U*) pré-história *f*.

pre-industrial *adj* pré-industrial.

prejudge [,pri:'dʒʌdʒ] *vt* prejulgar.

prejudice ['predʒʊdɪs] <> *n* -1. [bias] preconceito *m*; ~ **in favour of sb/sthg** tendência *f* de favorecer alguém/algo; ~ **against sb/sthg** preconceito contra alguém/algo -2. [harm] prejuízo *m*. <> *vt* -1. [bias] ter preconceito em relação a; **to** ~ **sb in favour of/against sthg** predispor alguém a favor de/contra algo -2. [jeopardize] prejudicar.

prejudiced ['predʒʊdɪst] *adj* preconceituoso(sa), parcial; **to be** ~ **in favour of sb/sthg** favorecer alguém/algo; **to be** ~ **against sb/sthg** ser preconceituoso(sa) em relação a alguém/algo.

prejudicial [,predʒʊ'dɪʃl] *adj* prejudicial; **to be** ~ **to sb/sthg** ser prejudicial para alguém/algo.

prelate ['prelɪt] *n RELIG* prelado *m*.

preliminary [prɪ'lɪmɪnərɪ] (*pl* -ies) *adj* preliminar.
◆ **preliminaries** *npl* -1. [preliminary events or stages] preliminares *fpl* -2. [eliminating contests] eliminatórias *fpl* -3. *US POL* prévias *fpl*.

prelims ['pri:lɪmz] *npl UK* [exams] exames *mpl* preliminares.

prelude ['prelju:d] *n*: ~ **to sthg** prelúdio *m* de algo.

premarital [,pri:'mærɪtl] *adj* pré-marital, antes do casamento.

premature ['premə,tjʊə'] *adj* prematuro(ra).

prematurely [,premə'tjʊəlɪ] *adv* prematuramente.

premeditated [,pri:'medɪteɪtɪd] *adj* premeditado(da).

premenstrual syndrome, premenstrual tension [pri:'menstrʊəl-] *n* síndrome *f* pré-menstrual.

premier ['premjə'] <> *adj* principal, primeiro(ra). <> *n* [prime minister] primeiro-ministro *m*, primeira-ministra *f*.

premiere ['premɪeə'] *n* estréia *f*.

premiership ['premɪəʃɪp] *n* [office] cargo *m* de primeiro-ministro; [term of office] mandato *m* (*do primeiro-ministro*).
◆ **Premiership** *n UK FTBL*: **the** ~ ≃ o Clube dos 13.

premise ['premɪs] *n* premissa *f*; **on the** ~ **that** com a premissa de que.

◆ **premises** *npl* [site] local *m*; **on the** ~**s** no local.

premium ['pri:mjəm] *n* -1. [gen] prêmio *m*; **at a** ~ [above usual value] *a um valor superior ao nominal*; [in great demand] muito disputado(da) -2. *phr*: **to put** *OR* **place a high** ~ **on sthg** dar grande importância a algo.

premium bond *n UK obrigação emitida pelo governo que dá direito a prêmios mensais em dinheiro mediante sorteio.*

premonition [,premə'nɪʃn] *n* premonição *f*.

prenatal [,pri:'neɪtl] *adj US* pré-natal.

preoccupation [pri:,ɒkjʊ'peɪʃn] *n* preocupação *f*; ~ **with sthg** preocupação com algo.

preoccupied [pri:'ɒkjʊpaɪd] *adj* preocupado(da); **to be** ~ **with sthg** estar preocupado(da) com algo.

preoccupy [pri:'ɒkjʊpaɪ] (*pt* & *pp* -ied) *vt* preocupar.

preordain [,pri:ɔ:'deɪn] *vt* predeterminar; **to be** ~**ed to do sthg** estar predestinado(da) a fazer algo.

prep [prep] *n UK inf* [homework]: **to do one's** ~ fazer o dever de casa.

pre-packed *adj* pré-embalado(da).

prepaid [,pri:'peɪd] *adj* com porte pago.

preparation [,prepə'reɪʃn] *n* -1. (*U*) [act of preparing] preparação *f*; **in** ~ **for sthg** em preparação para algo -2. [prepared mixture] preparado *m*.
◆ **preparations** *npl* [plans] preparativos *mpl*; **to make** ~**s for sthg** fazer preparativos para algo.

preparatory [prɪ'pærətrɪ] *adj* preparatório(ria).

preparatory school *n* -1. [in UK] colégio pago para crianças de 7 a 13 anos -2. [in US] *escola particular que prepara alunos para entrar na universidade.*

prepare [prɪ'peə'] <> *vt* preparar; **to** ~ **to do sthg** preparar-se para fazer algo. <> *vi*: **to** ~ **for sthg** preparar-se para algo.

prepared [prɪ'peəd] *adj* [organized, done beforehand] preparado(da); **to be** ~ *OR* **for sthg** *OR* **to do sthg** estar preparado(da) para algo/para fazer algo.

preponderance [prɪ'pɒndərəns] *n* predomínio *m*.

preponderantly [prɪ'pɒndərəntlɪ] *adv* predominantemente, majoritariamente.

preposition [,prepə'zɪʃn] *n* preposição *f*.

prepossessing [,pri:pə'zesɪŋ] *adj fml* atraente, agradável.

preposterous [prɪ'pɒstərəs] *adj* absurdo(da).

preppy ['prepɪ] (*pl* -ies) *US inf* <> *adj* -1. [male] de mauricinho -2. [female] de patricinha. <> *n* -1. [male] mauricinho *m* -2. [female] patricinha *f*.

prep school (*abbr of* **preparatory school**) *n escola particular primária para crianças de 7 a 12 anos na Grã-Bretanha.*

Pre-Raphaelite [,pri:'ræfəlaɪt] <> *adj* pré-rafaelita. <> *n* pré-rafaelita *mf*.

pre-recorded *adj* pré-gravado(da).

prerequisite [,pri:'rekwɪzɪt] *n* pré-requisito *m*; ~ **of** *OR* **for sthg** pré-requisito para algo.

prerogative [prɪ'rɒgətɪv] *n* prerrogativa *f*.

presage ['presɪdʒ] *vt fml* pressagiar.

Presbyterian [ˌprezbɪˈtɪərɪən] <> adj presbiteriano(na). <> n presbiteriano m, -na f.
presbytery [ˈprezbɪtrɪ] n presbitério m.
pre-school <> adj pré-escolar. <> n US pré-escola f.
prescient [ˈpresɪənt] adj fml presciente.
prescribe [prɪˈskraɪb] vt -1. MED prescrever -2. [order] ordenar, mandar.
prescription [prɪˈskrɪpʃn] n [MED - written form] receita f (médica); [- medicine] prescrição f; on ~ com receita (médica).
prescription charge n UK no Reino Unido, quantia fixa que se paga por quaisquer remédios receitados por um médico.
prescriptive [prɪˈskrɪptɪv] adj GRAMM prescritivo (va).
presence [ˈprezns] n presença f; in the ~ of sb na presença de alguém; to have ~ ter presença.
presence of mind n presença f de espírito.
present [adj & n ˈpreznt, vb prɪˈzent] <> adj -1. [gen] presente, atual -2. [in attendance] presente; to be ~ at sthg estar presente em algo. <> n -1.: the ~ o presente; at ~ atualmente; for the ~ no momento -2. GRAMM: ~ (tense) presente m. <> vt -1. [gen] apresentar; to ~ sb to sb apresentar alguém para alguém -2. [give] presentear; to ~ sb with sthg, to ~ sthg to sb presentar alguém com algo -3. [provide, pose] deparar-se com; to ~ sb with sthg, to ~ sthg to sb representar algo para alguém -4. [arrive, go]: to ~ o.s. apresentar-se.
presentable [prɪˈzentəbl] adj apresentável.
presentation [ˌpreznˈteɪʃn] n -1. [gen] apresentação f -2. [ceremony] cerimônia f -3. [performance] representação f.
presentation copy n cópia f de apresentação, exemplar m gratuito.
present day n: the ~ o momento atual.
◆ **present-day** adj atual, de hoje em dia.
presenter [prɪˈzentəʳ] n UK apresentador m, -ra f.
presentiment [prɪˈzentɪmənt] n fml pressentimento m.
presently [ˈprezntlɪ] adv -1. [soon] em breve, daqui a pouco -2. [now] atualmente.
preservation [ˌprezəˈveɪʃn] n (U) -1. [gen] preservação f -2. [of food] conservação f.
preservation order n esp UK ordem f de tombamento.
preservative [prɪˈzɜːvətɪv] n -1. [for food] conservante m -2. [for wood] revestimento m.
preserve [prɪˈzɜːv] <> n [jam] compota f, conserva f. <> vt -1. [gen] preservar -2. [food] conservar.
preserved [prɪˈzɜːvd] adj -1. [food] em conserva -2. [building] preservado(da) -3. [furniture, wood] conservado(da).
preset [ˌpriːˈset] (pt & pp preset, cont -ting) vt programar.
pre-shrunk adj pré-encolhido(da).
preside [prɪˈzaɪd] vi presidir; to ~ over OR at sthg presidir algo.
presidency [ˈprezɪdənsɪ] (pl -ies) n presidência f.
president [ˈprezɪdənt] n presidente mf.

President-elect n presidente mf eleito, -ta.
presidential [ˌprezɪˈdenʃl] adj presidencial.
press [pres] <> n -1. [push] pressionamento m -2. [journalism]: the ~ a imprensa; to get a good ~ ser elogiado(da) na/pela imprensa; to get a bad ~ ser criticado(da) na/pela imprensa, -3. [printing machine] imprensa f -4. [pressing machine] prensa f. <> vt -1. [push firmly - switch] ligar; [- accelerator] pisar em; to ~ sthg against sthg prensar algo contra algo -2. [squeeze] espremer -3. [iron] passar -4. [press person, button] pressionar; he didn't need much ~ and readily agreed ele não precisava de muita pressão e concordou prontamente; to ~ sb for sthg pressionar alguém buscando algo; to ~ sb to do sthg OR into doing sthg pressionar alguém a fazer algo; to ~ sthg (up)on sb empurrar algo a alguém, obrigar alguém a aceitar algo -5. [pursue] insistir em -6. JUR: to ~ charges (against sb) fazer acusações (contra alguém). <> vi -1. [push hard] to ~ (on sthg) apertar (algo) com força -2. [surge] comprimir-se; to ~ forwards empurrar para frente.
◆ **press on** vi [continue] continuar; to ~ on with sthg continuar com algo.
press agency n assessoria f de imprensa.
press agent n acessor m, -ra f de imprensa.
press baron n UK magnata m da imprensa.
press box n cabine f de imprensa.
press conference n entrevista f coletiva.
press corps n US equipe f de jornalistas.
press cutting n UK recorte m de jornal.
pressed [prest] adj: to be ~ (for time/ money) estar meio apertado(da) (de tempo/dinheiro).
press fastener n UK botão m de pressão.
press gallery n tribuna f de imprensa.
pressgang [ˈpresgæl] <> n grupo de homens que recrutavam marinheiros à força. <> vt UK: to ~ sb into doing sthg forçar alguém a fazer algo.
pressing [ˈpresɪŋ] adj urgente, premente.
pressman [ˈpresmæn] (pl -men [-men]) n UK jornalista m.
press officer n acessor m, -ra f de imprensa.
press release n press-release m, comunicado m de imprensa.
press-stud n UK botão m de pressão.
press-up n UK flexão f, apoio m (como exercício).
pressure [ˈpreʃəʳ] <> n pressão f; to put ~ on sb (to do sthg) pressionar alguém (a fazer algo OR para que faça algo), exercer pressão sobre alguém (para fazer algo). <> vt: to ~ sb to do OR into doing sthg pressionar alguém a fazer algo.
pressure cooker n panela f de pressão.
pressure gauge n manômetro m.
pressure group n grupo m de pressão.
pressurize, -ise [ˈpreʃəraɪz] vt -1. TECH pressurizar -2. UK [force]: to ~ sb to do OR into doing sthg pressionar alguém a fazer algo.
Prestel® [ˈprestel] n UK serviço público de videotexto oferecido pela British Telecom.
prestige [preˈstiːʒ] <> n (U) prestígio m. <> comp de prestígio.

prestigious [pre'stɪdʒəs] *adj* prestigioso(sa).

prestressed concrete [,pri:'strest-] *n (U)* concreto *m* protendido.

presumably [prɪ'zju:məblɪ] *adv* presumivelmente; **~ you've read the book** suponho que você já tenha lido o livro.

presume [prɪ'zju:m] *vt* presumir, supor; **to be ~d dead/innocent** ser julgado(da) morto(ta)/inocente; **to ~ (that)** supor *or* imaginar que.

presumption [prɪ'zʌmpʃn] *n* **-1.** [assumption] pressuposição *f*, suposição *f* **-2.** *(U)* [audacity] presunção *f*.

presumptuous [prɪ'zʌmptʃʊəs] *adj* presunçoso (sa).

presuppose [,pri:sə'pəʊz] *vt* pressupor.

pre-tax *adj* bruto(ta).

pretence, pretense US [prɪ'tens] *n* fingimento *m*; **under false ~s** com falsos pretextos.

pretend [prɪ'tend] <> *vt* **-1.** [make believe]: **to ~ to be/to do sthg** fingir ser/fazer algo; **to ~ (that)** fingir (que), fazer de conta (que) **-2.** [claim]: **to ~ to do sthg** fingir fazer algo. <> *vi* fingir.

pretense *n* US = pretence.

pretension [prɪ'tenʃn] *n* pretensão *f*; **to have ~s to sthg/to be sthg** ter pretensões de algo/de ser algo.

pretentious [prɪ'tenʃəs] *adj* pretencioso(sa).

pretentiously [prɪ'tenʃəslɪ] *adv* pretenciosamente.

pretentiousness [prɪ'tenʃəsnɪs] *n (U)* pretensão *f*, caráter *m* pretencioso.

preterite ['pretərɪt] *n* pretérito *m*.

pretext ['pri:tekst] *n* pretexto *m*; **on** *or* **under the ~ that** com o pretexto de que; **on** *or* **under the ~ of doing sthg** com o pretexto de estar fazendo algo.

Pretoria [prɪ'tɔ:rɪə] *n* Pretória.

prettify ['prɪtɪfaɪ] *(pt & pp* -ied) *vt* embelezar.

prettily ['prɪtɪlɪ] *adv* de uma forma encantadora.

pretty ['prɪtɪ] *(compar* -ier, *superl* -iest) <> *adj* bonito(ta). <> *adv* [quite, rather] bastante; **~ much** *or* **well** mais ou menos.

pretzel ['pretsl] *n rosca salgada em forma de nó*, pretzel *m*.

prevail [prɪ'veɪl] *vi* **-1.** [be widespread] prevalecer, predominar **-2.** [triumph] prevalecer; **to ~ over sb/sthg** prevalecer sobre alguém/algo **-3.** [persuade]: **to ~ (up)on sb to do sthg** persuadir alguém a fazer algo *or* para que faça algo.

prevailing [prɪ'veɪlɪŋ] *adj* predominante.

prevalence ['prevələns] *n* predomínio *m*.

prevalent ['prevələnt] *adj* predominante, prevalecente.

prevaricate [prɪ'værɪkeɪt] *vi* prevaricar.

prevent [prɪ'vent] *vt* evitar, impedir; **to ~ sb (from) doing sthg** impedir alguém de fazer algo; **to ~ sthg (from) doing sthg** evitar que algo faça algo; **they tried to ~ any pain to the animal** eles tentaram não causar nenhuma dor ao animal.

preventable [prɪ'ventəbl] *adj* evitável.

preventative [prɪ'ventətɪv] *adj* = preventive.

prevention [prɪ'venʃn] *n (U)* prevenção *f*; **~ is**

better than cure é melhor prevenir do que remediar.

preventive [prɪ'ventɪv] *adj* preventivo(va).

preview ['pri:vju:] *n* **-1.** [early showing] pré-estréia *f* **-2.** [trailer] trailer *m*.

previous ['pri:vjəs] *adj* **-1.** [earlier, prior] anterior, prévio(via); **~ convictions** antecedentes *mpl* criminais; **it was the ~ President who did it** foi o ex-presidente que fez isso **-2.** [days and dates] anterior.

previously ['pri:vjəslɪ] *adv* **-1.** [formerly] anteriormente, antes **-2.** [with days and dates] antes.

prewar [,pri:'wɔ:] *adj* anterior à guerra.

pre-wash *n* pré-lavagem *f*.

prey [preɪ] *n (U)* presa *f*, vítima *f*; **to fall ~ to sb/sthg** ser vítima de alguém/algo.

■ **prey on** *vt fus* **-1.** [live off] caçar, alimentar-se de **-2.** [trouble]: **to ~ on sb's mind** atormentar alguém.

price [praɪs] <> *n* **-1.** preço *m*; **at a ~** a que preço; **at any ~** a qualquer preço, a todo custo **-2.** *fig* [penalty]: **to pay the ~ for sthg** pagar o preço por algo. <> *vt* pôr preço em; **it was ~d highly** seu preço era muito elevado.

price-cutting *n (U)* redução *f* de preços.

price-fixing [-,fɪksɪŋ] *n (U)* cartel *m*.

priceless ['praɪslɪs] *adj* **-1.** [very valuable] inestimável, que não tem preço **-2.** *inf* [funny] impagável.

price list *n* lista *f* de preços.

price tag *n* **-1.** [label] etiqueta *f* de preço **-2.** [sacrifice] *fig* preço *m*.

price war *n* guerra *f* de preços.

pricey ['praɪsɪ] *(compar* -ier, *superl* -iest) *adj inf* caro(ra).

prick [prɪk] <> *n* **-1.** [scratch, wound] picada *f* **-2.** *vulg* [penis] cacete *m*, caralho *m* **-3.** *vulg* [stupid person] pau-no-cu *m*. <> *vt* **-1.** [jab, pierce] espetar **-2.** [sting] arder.

■ **prick up** *vt fus*: **to ~ up one's ears** [subj: animal] levantar as orelhas; [subj: person] aguçar os ouvidos.

prickle ['prɪkl] <> *n* **-1.** [thorn] espinho *m* **-2.** [sensation] formigamento *m*, comichão *f*. <> *vi* formigar, comichar.

prickly ['prɪklɪ] *(compar* -ier, *superl* -iest) *adj* **-1.** [thorny] espinhoso(sa), espinhento(ta) **-2.** *fig* [touchy] suscetível.

prickly heat *n (U)* brotoeja *f*.

pride [praɪd] <> *n* orgulho *m*; **to swallow one's ~** engolir o orgulho; **to take ~ in sthg/in doing sthg** sentir-se orgulhoso(sa) em algo/ao fazer algo; **his new car was his ~ and joy** seu novo carro era a menina dos olhos dele; **to have ~ of place** ter lugar de honra. <> *vt*: **to ~ o.s. on sthg** orgulhar-se de algo.

priest [pri:st] *n* **-1.** [Christian] padre *m*, sacerdote *m* **-2.** [non-Christian] homem *m* religioso.

priestess ['pri:stɪs] *n* sacerdotisa *f*.

priesthood ['pri:sthʊd] *n (U)* **-1.** [position, office]: **the ~** o sacerdócio **-2.** [priests collectively]: **the ~** o clero.

prig [prɪg] *n* moralista *mf*, puritano *m*, -na *f*.

prim [prɪm] *(compar* -mer, *superl* -mest) *adj* afetado (da), empertigado(da).

primacy ['praɪməsɪl] *n (U)* primazia *f.*

prima donna [ˌpriːmə'dɒnə] (*pl* **-s**) *n* **-1.** [female singer] prima-dona *f* **-2.** *pej* [self-important person] prima-dona *f.*

primaeval [praɪ'miːvəl] *adj* = **primeval.**

prima facie [ˌpraɪmə'feɪʃiː] *adj* à primeira vista.

primal ['praɪml] *adj* **-1.** [original] primário(ria) **-2.** [most important] principal.

primarily ['praɪmərɪlɪ] *adv* primeiramente, principalmente.

primary ['praɪmərɪ] (*pl* **-ies**) ⟨⟩ *adj* primário(ria). ⟨⟩ *n US* POL prévias *fpl.*

PRIMARIES

As *Primaries* (primárias) são as eleições norte-americanas - diretas ou indiretas, dependendo do estado - mediante as quais se selecionam os candidatos dos dois partidos nacionais, o Democrata e o Republicano, que vão concorrer às eleições presidenciais.

primary colour *n* cor *f* primária.

primary election *n US* prévias *fpl.*

primary school *n* escola *f* primária.

primary teacher *n* [in UK] professor *m* primário, professora *f* primária.

primate ['praɪmeɪt] *n* **-1.** ZOOL primata *m* **-2.** RELIG primaz *m.*

prime [praɪml] ⟨⟩ *adj* **-1.** [main] primeiro(ra) principal **-2.** [excellent] excelente, de primeira. ⟨⟩ *n* [peak] auge *m*, plenitude *f*; **in one's** ~ na flor da idade. ⟨⟩ *vt* **-1.** [inform]: **to** ~ **sb about sthg** instruir alguém sobre algo **-2.** [paint] imprimar, preparar para pintura **-3.** [make ready - gun] carregar; [- machine] aprontar; [- pump] escorvar.

prime minister *n* primeiro-ministro *m*, primeira-ministra *f.*

prime mover [-'muːvəʳ] *n fig* força *f* motora.

prime number *n* número *m* primo.

primer ['praɪməʳ] *n* **-1.** [paint] imprimadura *f* **-2.** [textbook] manual *m.*

prime time *n (U)* horário *m* nobre.
➡ **prime-time** *adj* **-1.** [TV] de maior audiência **-2.** [viewing, advertising] no horário nobre.

primeval [praɪ'miːvl] *adj* primitivo(va).

primitive ['prɪmɪtɪv] *adj* **-1.** [not civilized, of an early type] primitivo(va) **-2.** [simple, basic] rudimentar.

primordial [praɪ'mɔːdjəl] *adj fml* primordial.

primrose ['prɪmrəʊz] *n* prímula *f.*

Primus stove® ['praɪməs-] *n* fogareiro *m.*

prince [prɪns] *n* príncipe *m*; **Prince of Wales** Príncipe de Gales.

Prince Charming *n hum* príncipe *m* encantado.

princely ['prɪnslɪ] (*compar* **-ier**, *superl* **-iest**) *adj* **-1.** [of a prince] principesco(ca) **-2.** [generous, lavish] generoso(sa).

princess [prɪn'ses] *n* princesa *f*; **Princess Royal** Princesa Real.

principal ['prɪnsəpl] ⟨⟩ *adj* principal. ⟨⟩ *n* **-1.** [of school] diretor *m*, -ra *f* **-2.** [of college] reitor *m*, -ra *f.*

principality [ˌprɪnsɪ'pælətɪ] (*pl* **-ies**) *n* principado *m.*

principally ['prɪnsəplɪ] *adv* especialmente, principalmente.

principle ['prɪnsəpl] *n* **-1.** princípio *m* **-2.** *(U)* [integrity] princípios *mpl*; **he lacks** ~ ele não tem princípios; **(to do sthg) on** ~ OR **as a matter of** ~ fazer algo por (uma questão de) princípios.
➡ **in principle** *adv* em princípio.

principled ['prɪnsəpld] *adj* de princípio.

print [prɪmt] ⟨⟩ *n* **-1.** *(U)* [type] caracteres *mpl (de imprensa)*; **the book is still in** ~ o livro ainda está disponível *(não esgotado)*; **he saw his name in** ~ ele viu seu nome impresso; **to be out of** ~ estar esgotado(da) **-2.** ART gravura *f* **-3.** [photograph] cópia *f* **-4.** [fabric] estampado *m* **-5.** [footprint] pegada *f*; [fingerprint] impressão *f* digital. ⟨⟩ *vt* **-1.** [produce by printing] imprimir **-2.** [publish] publicar **-3.** [on fabric] estampar **-4.** [write clearly] escrever em letra de forma. ⟨⟩ *vi* **-1.** [in handwriting] escrever em letra de forma **-2.** [printer] imprimir.
➡ **print out** *vt sep* COMPUT imprimir.

printed circuit ['prɪntɪd-] *n* circuito *m* impresso.

printed matter ['prɪntɪd-] *n (U)* impresso *m.*

printer ['prɪntəʳ] *n* **-1.** [person, firm] impressor *m*, -ra *f* **-2.** COMPUT impressora *f.*

printing ['prɪntɪŋ] *n* impressão *f.*

printing press *n* prensa *f*, máquina *f* impressora.

printout ['prɪntaʊt] *n* saída *f* de impressora, impressão *f.*

prior ['praɪəʳ] ⟨⟩ *adj* **-1.** [previous] prévio(via), anterior **-2.** [more important] mais importante. ⟨⟩ *n* [monk] prior *m.*
➡ **prior to** *prep* antes de; ~ **to doing sthg** antes de fazer algo.

prioress ['praɪəres] *n* prioresa *f.*

prioritize, -ise [praɪ'ɒrɪtaɪz] *vt* priorizar, dar prioridade a.

priority [praɪ'ɒrətɪ] (*pl* **-ies**) ⟨⟩ *adj* prioritário (ria). ⟨⟩ *n* prioridade *f*; **to have** OR **take** ~ **(over sthg)** ter prioridade (sobre algo).
➡ **priorities** *npl* prioridades *fpl.*

priory ['praɪərɪ] (*pl* **-ies**) *n* convento *m (dirigido por um prior).*

prise [praɪz] *vt*: **to** ~ **sthg open** abrir algo com força; **to** ~ **sthg away** separar algo usando força.

prism ['prɪzm] *n* prisma *m.*

prison ['prɪzn] *n* prisão *f.*

prison camp *n* campo *m* de prisioneiros.

prisoner ['prɪznəʳ] *n* prisioneiro *m*, -ra *f*; **to be taken** ~ ser levado prisioneiro, ser levada prisioneira.

prisoner of war (*pl* **prisoners of war**) *n* prisioneiro *m*, -ra *f* de guerra.

prissy ['prɪsɪ] (*compar* **-ier**, *superl* **-iest**) *adj* fresco(ca).

pristine ['prɪstiːn] *adj* imaculado(da).

privacy [UK 'prɪvəsɪ, US 'praɪvəsɪ] *n* privacidade *f.*

private ['praɪvɪt] ⟨⟩ *adj* **-1.** [confidential, not for the public] privado(da) **-2.** [not state-controlled] privado (da), particular **-3.** [personal] privado(da), pessoal **-4.** [secluded] afastado(da), retirado(da) **-5.** [reserved] reservado(da). ⟨⟩ *n* **-1.** [soldier] soldado *m* raso **-2.** [secrecy]: **(to do sthg) in** ~ fazer algo em particular.

➡ **privates** *npl inf* ANAT partes *fpl (pudendas)*.
private company *n* empresa *f* privada.
private detective *n* detetive *mf* particular.
private enterprise *n (U)* empresa *f* privada.
private eye *n* detetive *mf* particular.
private income *n UK* renda *f* pessoal.
private investigator *n* detetive *mf* particular.
private limited company *n* COMM companhia *f* privada limitada.
privately ['praɪvɪtlɪ] *adv* -**1.** [not by the state] de forma privada; ~ **owned** de propriedade privada; ~ **educated** educado(da) em escola particular -**2.** [confidentially] privadamente, em particular -**3.** [personally] no fundo.
private member's bill *n UK* projeto de lei apresentado ao parlamento britânico por um deputado sem cargo no governo.
private parts *npl inf* partes *fpl* pudendas.
private practice *n (U) UK* prática *f* privada *(de uma profissão)*.
private property *n* propriedade *f* privada.
private school *n* escola *f* particular.
private sector *n (U)*: **the** ~ o setor privado.
privation [praɪ'veɪʃn] *n* privação *f*.
privatization [ˌpraɪvɪtaɪ'zeɪʃn] *n (U)* privatização *f*.
privatize, -ise ['praɪvɪtaɪz] *vt* privatizar.
privet ['prɪvɪt] *n (U)* alfena *f*.
privilege ['prɪvɪlɪdʒ] *n* -**1.** [special advantage] privilégio *m* -**2.** [honour] privilégio *m*, honra *f*.
privileged ['prɪvɪlɪdʒd] *adj* privilegiado(da).
privy ['prɪvɪ] *adj*: **to be** ~ **to sthg** *fml* inteirar-se de algo.
Privy Council *n UK*: **the** ~ conselho privado que aconselha o monarca em questões políticas.
Privy Purse *n*: **the** ~ quantia aprovada pelo parlamento britânico e destinada a cobrir os gastos do monarca.
prize [praɪz] ◇ *adj* -**1.** [prizewinning] premiado(da) -**2.** [perfect] perfeito(ta) -**3.** [valued] de estimação. ◇ *n* prêmio *m*. ◇ *vt* apreciar, valorizar.
prize day *n UK* (dia *m* de) entrega *f* de prêmios.
prizefight ['praɪzfaɪt] *n* luta *f* de boxe profissional.
prize-giving [-ˌgɪvɪŋ] *n UK* entrega *f* de prêmios.
prize money *n* dinheiro *m* ganho em prêmio.
prizewinner ['praɪzˌwɪnə'] *n* premiado *m*, -da *f*.
pro [prəʊ] *(pl -s) n* -**1.** *inf* [professional] profissional *mf* -**2.** [advantage]: **the** ~**s and cons** os prós e os contras.
pro- [prəʊ] *prefix* pró-.
PRO *n* -**1.** *(abbr of* **public relations officer)** chefe *mf* de relações públicas -**2.** *(abbr of* **public Record Office)** arquivo público na Grã-Bretanha.
pro-am ◇ *adj* de profissionais e amadores. ◇ *n* competição mista entre profissionais e amadores.
probability [ˌprɒbə'bɪlətɪ] *(pl -ies) n* probabilidade *f*; **in all** ~ **they will win** é muito provável que eles vençam.
probable ['prɒbəbl] *adj* provável.
probably ['prɒbəblɪ] *adv* provavelmente.
probate ['prəʊbeɪt] JUR ◇ *n* legitimação *f* de

testamento. ◇ *vt US* legitimar *(um testamento)*.
probation [prə'beɪʃn] *n (U)* -**1.** [of prisoner] liberdade *f* condicional; **to put sb on** ~ colocar alguém em liberdade condicional -**2.** [trial period] período *m* de experiência; **to be on** ~ estar em período de experiência.
probationary [prə'beɪʃnrɪ] *adj* -**1.** [teacher, nurse] em período de experiência -**2.** [year] de experiência; ~ **period** período *m* de experiência.
probationer [prə'beɪʃnə'] *n* -**1.** [employee] funcionário *m*, -ria *f* em período de experiência -**2.** [offender] pessoa *f* em liberdade condicional.
probation officer *n* pessoa encarregada de vigiar detentos em liberdade condicional.
probe [prəʊb] ◇ *n* -**1.** [investigation] sindicância *f*, investigação *f*; ~ **into sthg** sindicância sobre algo -**2.** MED, TECH sonda *f*. ◇ *vt* -**1.** [investigate] investigar -**2.** [prod] explorar. ◇ *vi*: **to** ~ **for/ into sthg** investigar para encontrar algo.
probing ['prəʊbɪŋ] *adj* inquiridor(ra).
probity ['prəʊbətɪ] *n (U) fml* probidade *f*.
problem ['prɒbləm] ◇ *n* problema *f*; **no** ~! *inf* sem problema! ◇ *comp* problemático(ca).
problematic(al) [ˌprɒblə'mætɪk(l)] *adj* problemático(ca), difícil.
problem page *n* página *f* com perguntas dos leitores *(em revistas, jornais)*.
procedural [prə'siːdʒərəl] *adj* processual.
procedure [prə'siːdʒə'] *n* procedimento *m*.
proceed [*vb* prə'siːd, *npl* 'prəʊsiːdz] ◇ *vt* [do subsequently]: **to** ~ **to do sthg** passar a fazer algo. ◇ *vi* -**1.** [continue] prosseguir, continuar; **to** ~ **with sthg** prosseguir com algo -**2.** *fml* [go, advance] dirigir-se para.
➡ **proceeds** *npl* proventos *mpl*.
proceedings [prə'siːdɪŋz] *npl* -**1.** [series of events] ação *f* -**2.** [legal action] processo *m*.
process ['prəʊses] ◇ *n* processo *m*; **in the** ~ no decorrer; **to be in the** ~ **of doing sthg** estar em vias de fazer algo. ◇ *vt* processar.
processed cheese ['prəʊsest-] *n* queijo *m* processado.
processing ['prəʊsesɪŋ] *n* processamento *m*.
procession [prə'seʃn] *n* -**1.** [ceremony] cortejo *m* -**2.** [demonstration] passeata *f* -**3.** [continuous line] procissão *f*.
processor ['prəʊsesə'] *n* -**1.** COMPUT processador *m* -**2.** CULIN processador *m* de alimentos.
pro-choice *adj* favorável ao direito da mulher de optar ou não pelo aborto.
proclaim [prə'kleɪm] *vt* -**1.** [declare] proclamar, declarar -**2.** [law] promulgar.
proclamation [ˌprɒklə'meɪʃn] *n* -**1.** proclamação *f* -**2.** [of law] promulgação *f*.
proclivity [prə'klɪvɪtɪ] *(pl -ies) n fml*: ~ **(to** OR **towards sthg)** propensão *f* OR tendência *f* (a algo).
procrastinate [prə'kræstɪneɪt] *vi* procrastinar, protelar.
procrastination [prəˌkræstɪ'neɪʃn] *n (U)* procrastinação *f*, protelação *f*.
procreate ['prəʊkrɪeɪt] *vi* procriar.
procreation [ˌprəʊkrɪ'eɪʃn] *n (U)* procriação *f*.

procurator fiscal ['prɒkjʊreɪtǝ'-] n *Scot* oficial público responsável por *levar as pessoas a julgamento*.

procure [prǝ'kjʊǝ'] vt conseguir, obter.

procurement [prǝ'kjʊǝmǝnt] n (U) aquisição f.

prod [prɒd] (*pt* & *pp* -**ded**, *cont* -**ding**) <> n -**1**. [push, poke] cutucão m, empurrão m -**2**. *fig* [reminder] toque m. <> vt -**1**. [push, poke] cutucar, empurrar -**2**. [remind, prompt]: **to ~ sb (into doing sthg)** dar um toque em alguém (para fazer algo *OR* para que faça algo).

prodigal ['prɒdɪgl] adj pródigo(ga).

prodigious [prǝ'dɪdʒǝs] adj prodigioso(sa).

prodigy ['prɒdɪdʒɪ] (*pl* -**ies**) n prodígio m.

produce [n 'prɒdjuːs, vb prǝ'djuːs] <> n -**1**. [goods] produtos mpl -**2**. [fruit and vegetables] produtos mpl agrícolas. <> vt -**1**. [gen] produzir -**2**. *BIOL* gerar -**3**. [yield - raw materials, crop] produzir; [- interest, profit] gerar -**4**. [present, show] apresentar.

producer [prǝ'djuːsǝ'] n -**1**. [gen] produtor m, -ra f -**2**. [theatre] diretor m, -ra f.

product ['prɒdʌkt] n -**1**. [thing manufactured or grown] produto m -**2**. [result]: **to be a ~ of sthg** ser resultado *OR* produto de algo.

production [prǝ'dʌkʃn] n produção f; **to put sthg/go into ~** começar a produzir *OR* fabricar algo.

production line n linha f de produção.

production manager n gerente mf de produção.

productive [prǝ'dʌktɪv] adj produtivo(va).

productively [prǝ'dʌktɪvlɪ] adv de forma produtiva.

productivity [ˌprɒdʌk'tɪvǝtɪ] n (U) produtividade f.

productivity deal n acordo m de produtividade.

Prof. [prɒf] (*abbr of* **Professor**) n Prof.

profane [prǝ'feɪn] adj obsceno(na).

profanity [prǝ'fænǝtɪ] (*pl* -**ies**) n -**1**. [of language, behaviour] obscenidade f, indecência f -**2**. [word] blasfêmia f.

profess [prǝ'fes] vt -**1**. [claim] alegar; **to ~ to do/to be sthg** alegar fazer/ser algo -**2**. [declare] declarar.

professed [prǝ'fest] adj -**1**. [avowed] declarado(da) -**2**. [alleged] pretenso(sa).

profession [prǝ'feʃn] n -**1**. [career] profissão f; **by ~** por profissão -**2**. [body of people] categoria f (profissional).

professional [prǝ'feʃǝnl] <> adj profissional. <> n profissional mf.

professional foul n falta f intencional.

professionalism [prǝ'feʃnǝlɪzm] n [high quality] profissionalismo m.

professionally [prǝ'feʃnǝlɪ] adv profissionalmente; **to be ~ trained** receber orientação profissional.

professor [prǝ'fesǝ'] n -**1**. *UK* [head of department] chefe mf de departamento -**2**. *US* & *Can* [teacher, lecturer] professor m (universitário), professora f (universitária).

professorship [prǝ'fesǝʃɪp] n *UK* cátedra f; *US* cargo de professor universitário.

proffer ['prɒfǝ'] vt: **to ~ sthg (to sb)** oferecer algo (a alguém).

proficiency [prǝ'fɪʃǝnsɪ] n (U) proficiência f; **~ in** sthg proficiência em algo.

proficient [prǝ'fɪʃǝnt] adj proficiente, competente; **to be ~ in** *OR* **at sthg** ter competência em algo; **to be ~ in a foreign language** ter proficiência em uma língua estrangeira.

profile ['prǝʊfaɪl] n perfil m; **in ~** de perfil; **to keep a low profile** *fig* não chamar a atenção.

profit ['prɒfɪt] <> n -**1**. [financial gain] lucro m; **to make a ~** ter lucro; **to sell sthg at a ~** vender algo com lucro -**2**. (U) [advantage] proveito m, benefício m. <> vi: **to ~ (from** *OR* **by sthg)** tirar proveito (de algo).

profitability [ˌprɒfɪtǝ'bɪlǝtɪ] n (U) lucratividade f, rentabilidade f.

profitable ['prɒfɪtǝbl] adj -**1**. [making a profit] lucrativo(va), rentável -**2**. [beneficial] proveitoso (sa).

profitably ['prɒfɪtǝblɪ] adv -**1**. [at a profit] com lucro -**2**. [usefully] de forma proveitosa.

profiteering [ˌprɒfɪ'tɪǝrɪŋ] n (U) especulação f.

profit-making <> adj com fins lucrativos. <> n (U) obtenção f de lucros.

profit margin n margem f de lucro.

profit sharing [-ˌʃeǝrɪŋ] n (U) participação f nos lucros.

profligate ['prɒflɪgɪt] adj -**1**. [extravagant] extravagante -**2**. [immoral] libertino(na).

pro forma [-'fɔːmǝ] adj pro forma.

profound [prǝ'faʊnd] adj profundo(da).

profoundly [prǝ'faʊndlɪ] adv -**1**. [intensely] profundamente -**2**. [wisely] com profundidade.

profuse [prǝ'fjuːs] adj -**1**. [abundant] abundante -**2**. [generous, extravagant] profuso(sa).

profusely [prǝ'fjuːslɪ] adv -**1**. [abundantly] abundantemente -**2**. [generously, extravagantly] profusamente.

profusion [prǝ'fjuːʒn] n profusão f.

progeny ['prɒdʒǝnɪ] (*pl* -**ies**) n *fml* progênie f.

progesterone [prǝ'dʒestǝrǝʊn] n (U) progesterona f.

prognosis [prɒg'nǝʊsɪs] (*pl* -**noses** [-'nǝʊsiːzl) n prognóstico m.

prognostication [prɒgˌnɒstɪ'keɪʃn] n prognóstico m.

program ['prǝʊgræm] (*pt* & *pp* -**med** *OR* -**ed**, *cont* -**ming** *OR* -**ing**) <> n -**1**. *COMPUT* programa m -**2**. *US* = **programme**. <> vt -**1**. *COMPUT* programar -**2**. *US* = **programme**.

programer n *US* = **programmer**.

programmable [prǝʊ'græmǝbl] adj programável.

programme *UK*, **program** *US* ['prǝʊgræm] <> n programa m. <> vt programar; **to ~ sthg to do sthg** programar algo para fazer algo *OR* para que faça algo.

programmer *UK*, **programer** *US* ['prǝʊgræmǝ'] n *COMPUT* programador m, -ra f.

programming ['prǝʊgræmɪŋ] n *COMPUT* programação f.

programming language n linguagem f de programação.

progress [*n* 'prəʊgres, *vb* prə'gres] <> *n* **-1.** [gen] progresso *m*;**to make** ~ [improve] fazer progresso; **to make** ~ **in sthg** [get on] progredir em algo; **in** ~ em andamento **-2.** [physical movement] avanço *m*. <> *vi* **-1.** [gen] progredir **-2.** [move forward]: **to** ~ **to sthg** prosseguir para algo.

progression [prə'greʃn] *n* **-1.** [advance] progressão *f* **-2.** [series] sucessão *f*.

progressive [prə'gresɪv] *adj* **-1.** [forward-looking] progressista **-2.** [gradual] progressivo(va).

progressively [prə'gresɪvlɪ] *adv* progressivamente.

progress report *n* **-1.** [on student] relatório *m* de desempenho **-2.** [on patient] boletim *m* médico **-3.** [on work, on project] relatório *m* de acompanhamento.

prohibit [prə'hɪbɪt] *vt* proibir; **to** ~ **sb from doing sthg** proibir alguém de fazer algo.

prohibition [prəʊɪ'bɪʃn] *n* proibição *f*.

prohibitive [prə'hɪbətɪv] *adj* exorbitante.

project [*n* 'prɒdʒekt, *vb* prə'dʒekt] <> *n* **-1.** [plan, idea] projeto *m* **-2.** *SCH* projeto *m*, estudo *m*; ~ **on sthg** projeto estudo sobre algo. <> *vt* **-1.** [gen] projetar; **to** ~ **sthg on to sthg** projetar algo em algo **-2.** [estimate] projetar, estimar **-3.** [present] apresentar, dar uma imagem de. <> *vi* projetar.

projectile [prə'dʒektaɪl] *n* projétil *m*.

projection [prə'dʒekʃn] *n* **-1.** [gen] projeção *f* **-2.** [protrusion] saliência *f*.

projectionist [prə'dʒekʃənɪst] *n* operador *m*, -ra *f* de projeção *(no cinema)*.

projection room *n* sala *f* de projeção.

projector [prə'dʒektə'] *n* projetor *m*.

proletarian [prəʊlɪ'teərɪən] *adj* proletário(ria).

proletariat [prəʊlɪ'teərɪət] *n* proletariado *m*.

pro-life *adj* pró-vida.

proliferate [prə'lɪfəreɪt] *vi* proliferar.

prolific [prə'lɪfɪk] *adj* prolífico(ca).

prologue, prolog *US* ['prəʊlɒg] *n* **-1.** [introduction] prólogo *m* **-2.** *fig* [preceding event]: ~ **to sthg** preâmbulo *m* para algo.

prolong [prə'lɒŋ] *vt* prolongar.

prom [prɒm] *n* **-1.** *UK inf* (*abbr of* **promenade**) [at seaside] *caminho junto ao mar* **-2.** *US* [ball] *baile de gala estudantil* **-3.** *UK inf* (*abbr of* **promenade concert**): **the Proms** *concertos que acontecem no Albert Hall, em Londres, no verão.*

promenade [prɒmə'nɑːd] *n UK* [at seaside] calçadão *m*.

promenade concert *n UK* concerto sinfônico ao qual boa parte das pessoas assiste de pé.

prominence ['prɒmɪnəns] *n* (*U*) **-1.** [importance] importância *f* **-2.** [conspicuousness] notoriedade *f*, proeminência *f*.

prominent ['prɒmɪnənt] *adj* **-1.** [important - person, politician] destacado(da); [- ideas, issues] proeminente **-2.** [noticeable - building, landmark] em evidência; [- cheekbones] saliente.

prominently ['prɒmɪnəntlɪ] *adv* em evidência.

promiscuity [prɒmɪs'kjuːətɪ] *n* (*U*) promiscuidade *f*.

promiscuous [prɒ'mɪskjʊəs] *adj* promíscuo(cua).

promise ['prɒmɪs] <> *n* promessa *f*; **to make (sb)**

a ~ fazer uma promessa (a alguém); **to show** ~ ser promissor(ra). <> *vt* **-1.** [pledge]: **to** ~ **(sb) sthg** prometer algo (a alguém); **to** ~ **(sb) to do sthg** prometer (a alguém) fazer algo **-2.** [indicate]: **to** ~ **sthg** prometer algo; **it** ~ **s to be a wonderful day** promete ser um dia maravilhoso. <> *vi* prometer.

promising ['prɒmɪsɪŋ] *adj* promissor(ra).

promissory note ['prɒmɪsərɪ-] *n* nota *f* promissória.

promo ['prəʊməʊ] (*pl* **-s**) *n inf* filme *m* promocional.

promontory ['prɒməntrɪ] (*pl* **-ies**) *n* promontório *m*.

promote [prə'məʊt] *vt* **-1.** [foster] promover, fomentar **-2.** [push, advertise] promover **-3.** [in job]: **to** ~ **sb (to sthg)** promover alguém (a algo) **-4.** *SPORT*: **to be** ~ **d to the First Division** subir para a Primeira Divisão.

promoter [prə'məʊtə'] *n* **-1.** [organizer] patrocinador *m*, -ra *f* **-2.** [supporter] defensor *m*, -ra *f*.

promotion [prə'məʊʃn] *n* promoção *f*; **to get** *OR* **be given** ~ ser promovido(da).

prompt [prɒmpt] <> *adj* **-1.** [quick] pronto(ta), rápido(da) **-2.** [punctual] pontual. <> *adv* pontualmente. <> *n* [THEATRE - line] deixa *f*; [- person] ponto *m*. <> *vt* **-1.** [provoke, persuade]: **to** ~ **sb (to do sthg)** levar alguém (a fazer algo) **-2.** *THEATRE* dar a deixa.

prompter ['prɒmptə'] *n* ponto *m* *(no teatro)*.

promptly ['prɒmptlɪ] *adv* **-1.** [quickly] prontamente, rapidamente **-2.** [punctually] pontualmente.

promptness ['prɒmptnɪs] *n* (*U*) **-1.** [quickness] rapidez *f* **-2.** [punctuality] pontualidade *f*.

promulgate ['prɒmlgeɪt] *vt* **-1.** [law, decree] promulgar **-2.** [belief, idea] propagar.

prone [prəʊn] *adj* **-1.** [susceptible]: **to be** ~ **to sthg/ to do sthg** ser propenso(sa) a algo/a fazer algo **-2.** [lying flat] deitado(da)] de bruços.

prong [prɒŋ] *n* dente *m* *(de garfo)*.

pronoun ['prəʊnaʊn] *n* pronome *m*.

pronounce [prə'naʊns] <> *vt* **-1.** [say aloud] pronunciar **-2.** [declare, state] declarar. <> *vi*: **to** ~ **on sthg** pronunciar-se sobre algo.

pronounced [prə'naʊnst] *adj* pronunciado(da), marcado(da).

pronouncement [prə'naʊnsmənt] *n* pronunciamento *m*.

pronto ['prɒntəʊ] *adv inf* imediatamente.

pronunciation [prənʌnsɪ'eɪʃn] *n* pronúncia *f*.

proof [pruːf] *n* **-1.** [gen] prova *f* **-2.** [of alcohol] teor *m* alcoólico.

proofread ['pruːfriːd] (*pt & pp* **-read** [-red]) *vt* revisar.

proofreader ['pruːfriːdə'] *n* revisor *m*, -ra *f*.

prop [prɒp] (*pt & pp* **-ped**, *cont* **-ping**) <> *n* **-1.** [physical support] escora *f*, estaca *f* **-2.** *fig* [supporting thing, person] apoio *m* **-3.** *RUGBY* pilar *m*. <> *vt*: **to** ~ **sthg against sthg** apoiar algo em *OR* contra algo.

➡ **props** *npl* [in film, play] acessórios *mpl*.

➡ **prop up** *vt sep* **-1.** [support physically] escorar, sustentar **-2.** *fig* [sustain] apoiar.

Prop. (*abbr of* **proprietor**) proprietário *m*, -ria *f*.

propaganda [prɒpə'gændə] *n* (*U*) propaganda *f*.

propagate ['propəgeit] <> vt propagar. <> vi propagar-se.

propagation [,propə'geiʃn] n -1. BOT propagação f -2. [dissemination] propagação f, disseminação f.

propane ['prəʊpeɪn] n (U) propano m.

propel [prə'pel] (pt & pp -led, cont -ling) vt -1. [drive forward] impulsionar -2. fig [urge] impelir.

propeller [prə'pelə'] n hélice f.

propelling pencil [prə'peliŋ-] n UK lapiseira f.

propensity [prə'pensəti] (pl -ies) n fml: ~ for OR to sthg propensão f a algo; ~ to do sthg propensão para fazer algo.

proper ['propə'] adj -1. [real] verdadeiro(ra) -2. [correct] correto(ta), exato(ta) -3. [decent] decente, apropriado(da) -4. [specifically] próprio(pria) -5. UK inf [for emphasis]: a ~ idiot um perfeito idiota.

properly ['propəli] adv -1. [satisfactorily] adequadamente, bem -2. [correctly] direito -3. [decently] adequadamente.

proper noun n nome m próprio.

property ['propəti] (pl -ies) n -1. [gen] propriedade f -2. (U) [buildings] imóveis mpl -3. (U) [land] terrenos mpl.

property developer n (empresa f) construtora f.

property owner n proprietário m, -ria f de um imóvel.

property tax n imposto m predial e territorial.

prophecy ['profisi] (pl -ies) n profecia f.

prophesy ['profisai] (pt & pp -ied) vt profetizar.

prophet ['profit] n profeta mf.

prophetic [prə'fetik] adj profético(ca).

propitious [prə'piʃəs] adj fml propício(cia).

proponent [prə'pəʊnənt] n defensor m, -ra f, partidário m, -ria f.

proportion [prə'pɔ:ʃn] n -1. [part] parte f -2. [ratio, comparison] proporção f; in ~ to em proporção a; out of all ~ to totalmente fora de proporção em relação a -3. (U) ART: in ~ proporcional; out of ~ fora de proporção; a sense of ~ fig senso m de proporção; to get sthg out of ~ fig fazer uma tempestade em um copo d'água sobre algo.

proportional [prə'pɔ:ʃənl] adj proporcional, em proporção a; to be ~ to sthg ser proporcional a algo.

proportional representation n (U) representação f proporcional.

proportionate [prə'pɔ:ʃnət] adj proporcional; ~ to sthg proporcional a algo.

proposal [prə'pəʊzl] n proposta f; marriage ~ proposta f (de casamento).

propose [prə'pəʊz] <> vt -1. [suggest] propor -2. [introduce] apresentar -3. [toast] brindar a -4. [intend]: to ~ doing OR to do sthg ter a intenção de fazer algo. <> vi [make offer of marriage] pedir em casamento; to ~ to sb pedir a mão de alguém em casamento.

proposed [prə'pəʊzd] adj proposto(ta).

proposition [,propə'ziʃn] <> n -1. [statement of theory] proposição f -2. [suggestion] proposta f; to make sb a ~ fazer uma proposta a alguém. <> vt fml fazer uma propósta indecorosa a.

propound [prə'paʊnd] vt fml expor.

proprietary [prə'praiətri] adj fml COMM registrado (da).

proprietor [prə'praiətə'] n proprietário m, -ria f.

proprietorial [pra,praiə'tɔ:riəl] adj possessivo(va).

propriety [prə'praiəti] n (U) fml retidão f.

propulsion [prə'pʌlʃn] n (U) propulsão f.

pro rata [-'rɑ:tə] adj & adv pro rata.

prosaic [prəʊ'zeik] adj prosaico(ca).

proscenium (arch) [prə'si:njəm-] n proscênio m.

proscribe [prəʊ'skraib] vt fml proscrever.

prose [prəʊz] <> n (U) prosa f. <> comp em prosa.

prosecute ['prosikju:t] <> vt JUR processar; to be ~d for sthg ser processado(da) por algo. <> vi -1. [bring a charge] promover ação penal -2. [represent in court] sustentar acusação em juizo.

prosecution [,prosi'kju:ʃn] n -1. [criminal charge] acusação f -2. [lawyers]: the ~ a acusação.

prosecutor ['prosikju:tə'] n promotor m, -ra f.

prospect [n 'prospekt, vb prə'spekt] <> n -1. [hope] possibilidade f -2. [probability] perspectiva f. <> vi prospectar; to ~ for sthg prospectar algo.
➤ **prospects** npl [chances of success]: ~s (for sthg) perspectivas fpl (de algo).

prospecting [prə'spektiŋ] n (U) prospecção f.

prospective [prə'spektiv] adj provável, possível.

prospector [prə'spektə'] n prospector m, -ra f.

prospectus [prə'spektəs] (pl -es) n prospecto m, folheto m informativo.

prosper ['prospə'] vi prosperar.

prosperity [pro'sperəti] n (U) prosperidade f.

prosperous ['prosperəs] adj próspero(ra).

prostate (gland) ['prosteit-] n próstata f.

prosthesis [pros'θi:sis] (pl -theses ['θi:si:z]) n prótese f.

prostitute ['prostitju:t] n prostituta f; male ~ prostituto m.

prostitution [,prosti'tju:ʃn] n (U) prostituição f.

prostrate [adj 'prostreit, vb pro'streit] <> adj prostrado(da). <> vt: to ~ o.s. (before sb) prostrar-se (diante de alguém).

protagonist [prə'tægənist] n protagonista mf.

protect [prə'tekt] vt proteger; to ~ sb/sthg from, to ~ sb/sthg against proteger alguém/algo de/contra.

protection [prə'tekʃn] n (U) proteção f; ~ from sb/sthg, ~ against sb/sthg proteção de OR contra alguém/algo.

protectionism [prə'tekʃnizm] n (U) protecionismo m.

protectionist [prə'tekʃənist] adj protecionista.

protection money n (U) dinheiro m pago em troca de proteção.

protective [prə'tektiv] adj protetor(ra); to be/feel ~ towards sb ser/sentir-se protetor(ra) em relação a alguém.

protective custody n (U) custódia f preventiva.

protectiveness [prə'tektivnis] n (U) sentimento m de proteção.

protector [prə'tektə'] n -1. [person] protetor m, -ra f -2. [on machine] dispositivo m de proteção.

protectorate [prə'tektərət] n protetorado m.

protégé ['proteʒei] n protegido m.

protégée ['prɒteʒeɪl] *n* protegida *f*.

protein ['prəʊti:n] *n (U)* proteína *f*.

protest [*n* 'prəʊtest, *vb* prə'test] ⬥ *n* protesto *m*. ⬥ *vt* -**1.** [state] protestar, declarar -**2.** *US* [protest against] protestar contra. ⬥ *vi* [complain] protestar; **to ~ about/against sthg** protestar por/contra algo.

Protestant ['prɒtɪstənt] ⬥ *adj* protestante. ⬥ *n* protestante *mf*.

Protestantism ['prɒtɪstəntɪzm] *n (U)* protestantismo *m*.

protestation [ˌprɒte'steɪʃn] *n fml* -**1.** [declaration] declaração *f* -**2.** [protest] protesto *m*.

protester [prə'testəʳ] *n* manifestante *mf*.

protest march *n* marcha *f* de protesto, manifestação *f*.

protocol ['prəʊtəkɒl] *n (U)* protocolo *m*.

proton ['prəʊtɒn] *n* próton *m*.

prototype ['prəʊtətaɪp] *n* protótipo *m*.

protracted [prə'træktɪd] *adj* prolongado(da).

protractor [prə'træktəʳ] *n* transferidor *m*.

protrude [prə'tru:d] *vi* salientar-se, sobressair-se; **to ~ from sthg** sobressair-se em algo.

protrusion [prə'tru:ʒn] *n* saliência *f*.

protuberance [prə'tju:bərəns] *n* protuberância *f*.

proud [praʊd] *adj* -**1.** [gen] orgulhoso(sa); **to be ~ of sb/sthg** estar orgulhoso(sa) de alguém/algo; **to be ~ to do sthg** ter a honra de fazer algo -**2.** *pej* [arrogant] orgulhoso(sa), arrogante.

proudly ['praʊdlɪ] *adv* -**1.** [with satisfaction] orgulhosamente -**2.** *pej* [arrogantly] arrogantemente.

provable ['pru:vəbl] *adj* demonstrável.

prove [pru:v] (*pp* -**d** OR **proven**) *vt* -**1.** [show to be true] provar, demonstrar -**2.** [show o.s. to be]: **to ~ (to be) sthg** demonstrar ser algo; **to ~ o.s. to be sthg** mostrar-se algo.

proven ['pru:vn, 'prəʊvn] ⬥ *pp* ▷ **prove**. ⬥ *adj* comprovado(da).

Provençal [ˌprovɒn'sɑ:l] ⬥ *adj* provençal. ⬥ *n* [language] provençal *m*.

Provence [prɒ'vɒns] *n* Provença; **in ~** na Provença.

proverb ['prɒvɜ:b] *n* provérbio *m*.

proverbial [prə'vɜ:bjəl] *adj* proverbial.

provide [prə'vaɪd] *vt* fornecer, prover; **to ~ sb with sthg** proporcionar algo a alguém; **to ~ sthg for sb** oferecer algo a alguém.

⬥ **provide for** *vt fus* -**1.** [support] sustentar, manter -**2.** *fml* [make arrangements for] prever, tomar medidas para.

provided [prə'vaɪdɪd] ⬥ **provided (that)** *conj* desde que, contanto que.

providence ['prɒvɪdəns] *n (U)* providência *f*.

providential [ˌprɒvɪ'denʃl] *adj fml* providencial.

provider [prə'vaɪdəʳ] *n* provedor *m*, -ra *f*.

providing [prə'vaɪdɪŋ] ⬥ **providing (that)** *conj* desde que.

province ['prɒvɪns] *n* -**1.** [part of country] província *f* -**2.** [specialist subject] campo *m*, ramo *m* do conhecimento; [area of responsibility] alçada *f*.

⬥ **provinces** *npl*: **the ~s** o interior.

provincial [prə'vɪnʃl] *adj* -**1.** [of a province] da província -**2.** *pej* [narrow-minded] provinciano(na).

provision [prə'vɪʒn] *n* -**1.** *(U)* [act of supplying] provisão *f* -**2.** *(U)* [arrangement] providência *f*; **to make ~ for/sthg** tomar providências para algo; **to make ~ for/sb** garantir o sustento de alguém -**3.** [in agreement, law] cláusula *f*.

⬥ **provisions** *npl* [supplies] provisões *fpl*.

provisional [prə'vɪʒənl] *adj* provisório(ria).

Provisional IRA *n*: **the ~** braço armado do Sinn Féin, Irlanda do Norte.

provisional licence *n UK* carteira *f* provisória.

provisionally [prə'vɪʒnəlɪ] *adv* temporariamente.

proviso [prə'vaɪzəʊ] (*pl* -**s**) *n* condição *f*; **with the ~ that** com a condição de que.

provocation [ˌprɒvə'keɪʃn] *n* provocação *f*.

provocative [prə'vɒkətɪv] *adj* -**1.** [controversial] provocativo(va) -**2.** [sexy] provocante.

provocatively [prə'vɒkətɪvlɪ] *adv* -**1.** [controversially] provocativamente -**2.** [sexily] provocantemente.

provoke [prə'vəʊk] *vt* provocar.

provoking [prə'vəʊkɪŋ] *adj* provocador(ra).

provost *n* -**1.** *UK* [head of college] reitor *m*, -ra *f* -**2.** *Scot* [head of town council] prefeito *m*, -ta *f*.

prow [praʊ] *n* proa *f*.

prowess ['praʊɪs] *n (U)* *fml* façanha *f*.

prowl [praʊl] ⬥ *n*: **on the ~** de ronda, rondando. ⬥ *vt* rondar por. ⬥ *vi* fazer a ronda.

prowl car *n US* carro *m* patrulha.

prowler ['praʊləʳ] *n* gatuno *m*, -na *f*.

proximity [prɒk'sɪmətɪ] *n (U)* *fml* proximidade *f*; **~ to sthg** proximidade a algo; **in the ~ of sthg** nas proximidades de algo.

proxy ['prɒksɪ] (*pl* -**ies**) *n*: **by ~** por procuração.

prude [pru:d] *n* pessoa *f* pudica, puritano *m*, -na *f*.

prudence ['pru:dns] *n (U)* *fml* prudência *f*.

prudent ['pru:dnt] *adj* prudente.

prudently ['pru:dntlɪ] *adv* prudentemente.

prudish ['pru:dɪʃ] *adj* pudico(ca).

prune [pru:n] ⬥ *n* ameixa *f* seca. ⬥ *vt* podar.

prurient ['prʊərɪənt] *adj fml* lascivo(va).

Prussian ['prʌʃn] ⬥ *adj* prussiano(na). ⬥ *n* prussiano *m*, -na *f*.

pry [praɪ] (*pt & pp* **pried**) *vi* bisbilhotar; **to ~ into sthg** intrometer-se em algo.

PS (*abbr of* **postscript**) *n* PS.

psalm [sɑ:m] *n* salmo *m*.

pseud [sju:d] *n UK inf* intelectualóide *mf*.

pseudo- [ˌsju:dəʊ] *prefix* pseudo(-).

pseudonym ['sju:dənɪm] *n* pseudônimo *m*.

psi (*abbr of* **pounds per square inch**) psi *f*.

psoriasis [sɒ'raɪəsɪs] *n (U)* psoríase *f*.

psst [pst] *excl* psiu!

PST (*abbr of* **Pacific Standard Time**) *n* horário oficial da costa oeste dos Estados Unidos.

psych [saɪk] ⬥ **psych up** *vt sep inf* preparar psicologicamente; **to ~ o.s. up** preparar-se psicologicamente.

psyche ['saɪkɪ] *n* psique *f*.

psychedelic [ˌsaɪkɪ'delɪk] *adj* psicodélico(ca).

psychiatric [ˌsaɪkɪ'ætrɪk] *adj* psiquiátrico(ca).

psychiatric nurse *n* enfermeiro *m* psiquiátrico, enfermeira *f* psiquiátrica.

psychiatrist [saɪ'kaɪətrɪst] *n* psiquiatra *mf*.

psychiatry [saɪˈkaɪətrɪ] *n (U)* psiquiatria *f*.
psychic [ˈsaɪkɪk] <> *adj* -**1.** [clairvoyant] paranormal -**2.** [mental] psíquico(ca). <> *n* paranormal *mf*, médium *mf*.
psychoanalyse, -yze *US* [ˌsaɪkəʊˈænəlaɪz] *vt* psicanalisar.
psychoanalysis [ˌsaɪkəʊəˈnæləsɪs] *n (U)* psicanálise *f*.
psychoanalyst [ˌsaɪkəʊˈænəlɪst] *n* psicanalista *mf*.
psychological [ˌsaɪkəˈlɒdʒɪkl] *adj* psicológico(ca).
psychological warfare *n (U)* guerra *f* psicológica.
psychologist [saɪˈkɒlədʒɪst] *n* psicólogo *m*, -ga *f*.
psychology [saɪˈkɒlədʒɪ] *n* psicologia *f*.
psychopath [ˈsaɪkəpæθ] *n* psicopata *mf*.
psychosis [saɪˈkəʊsɪs] (*pl* -**choses** [ˈkəʊsiːz]) *n* psicose *f*.
psychosomatic [ˌsaɪkəʊsəˈmætɪk] *adj* psicossomático(ca).
psychotherapy [ˌsaɪkəʊˈθerəpɪ] *n (U)* psicoterapia *f*.
psychotic [saɪˈkɒtɪk] <> *adj* psicótico(ca). <> *n* psicótico *m*, -ca *f*.
pt -**1.** *abbr of* **pint** - **2.** (*abbr of* **point**) pt.
Pt. (*abbr of* **Point**) [on map] Pta.
PT (*abbr of* **physical training**) *n* treinamento *m* físico.
PTA (*abbr of* **parent-teacher association**) *n* ≃ APM *f*.
Pte. (*abbr of* **Private**) *soldado do exército britânico*.
PTO (*abbr of* **please turn over**) vide verso.
PTV *n* (*abbr of* **pay television**) televisão *f* por assinatura.
pub [pʌb] *n* pub *m*, bar *m*.

pub. (*abbr of* **published**) publicado.
pub-crawl *n UK*: **to go on a** ~ andar de bar em bar.
puberty [ˈpjuːbətɪ] *n (U)* puberdade *f*.
pubescent [pjuːˈbesnt] *adj* púbere.
pubic [ˈpjuːbɪk] *adj* pubiano(na).
public [ˈpʌblɪk] <> *adj* -**1.** [gen] público(ca); **to go** ~ **on sthg** *inf* levar a público; **to make sthg** ~ tornar algo público - **2.** *COMM*: **to go** ~ abrir o capital. <> *n*: **the** ~ o público; **in** ~ em público.
public-address system *n* sistema *m* de autofalantes.
publican [ˈpʌblɪkən] *n UK* dono *m*, -na *f* de um pub.
publication [ˌpʌblɪˈkeɪʃn] *n* publicação *f*.

public company *n* sociedade *f* anônima (*com ações na Bolsa*).
public convenience *n UK* sanitário *m* público.
public domain *n*: **in the** ~ em domínio público.
public holiday *n* feriado *m* nacional.
public house *n UK fml* bar *m*, pub *m*.
publicist [ˈpʌblɪsɪst] *n* publicitário *m*, -ria *f*.
publicity [pʌbˈlɪsɪtɪ] <> *n* publicidade *f*. <> *comp* publicitário(ria).
publicity stunt *n* golpe *f* publicitário, jogada *f* de marketing.
publicize, -ise [ˈpʌblɪsaɪz] *vt* divulgar.
public limited company *n* sociedade *f* anônima (*com ações na Bolsa*).
publicly [ˈpʌblɪklɪ] *adv* publicamente.
public office *n* cargo *m* público.
public opinion *n (U)* opinião *f* pública.
public ownership *n (U)* bem *m* público.
public prosecutor *n* promotor *m* público, promotora *f* pública.
public relations <> *n (U)* relações *fpl* públicas. <> *npl* relações *f* públicas.
public relations officer *n* agente *mf* de relações públicas.
public school *n* -**1.** *UK* [private school] escola *f* particular - **2.** *US* & *Scot* [state school] escola *f* pública.

public sector *n* setor *m* público.
public servant *n* servidor *m* público, servidora *f* pública.
public service vehicle *n UK* veículo *m* do serviço público.
public-spirited *adj* com espírito cívico.
public transport *n (U)* transporte *m* público.
public utility *n* utilidade *f* pública.
public works *npl* obras *fpl* públicas.
publish [ˈpʌblɪʃ] <> *vt* -**1.** [gen] publicar - **2.** [make known] divulgar, tornar público(ca). <> *vi* publicar.
publisher [ˈpʌblɪʃəʳ] *n* -**1.** [company] editora *f* - **2.** [person] editor *m*, -ra *f*.
publishing [ˈpʌblɪʃɪŋ] *n (U)* setor *m* editorial.
publishing company, publishing house *n* editora *f*.
pub lunch *n* almoço servido em um pub.
puce [pjuːs] *adj* marrom-avermelhado(da).
puck [pʌk] *n* [ice hockey] disco *m*.
pucker [ˈpʌkəʳ] <> *vt* franzir. <> *vi* enrugar.
pudding [ˈpʊdɪŋ] *n* -**1.** [food - sweet] pudim *m*; [- savoury] pastelão *m* -**2.** (U) *UK* [part of meal] sobremesa *f*.
puddle [ˈpʌdl] *n* poça *f*.
pudgy [ˈpʌdʒɪ] *adj* = **podgy**.

puerile ['pjʊəraɪl] *adj fml* pueril.

Puerto Rican [,pwɜ:təʊ'ri:kən] <> *adj* porto-riquenho(nha). <> *n* porto-riquenho *m*, -nha *f*.

Puerto Rico [,pwɜ:təʊ'ri:kəʊ] *n* Porto Rico.

puff [pʌf] <> *n* -1. [of cigarette, pipe] baforada *f* -2. [of air, smoke] golfada *f*. <> *vt* baforar. <> *vi* -1. [smoke]: **to ~ at** *or* **on sthg** dar tragadas em algo -2. [pant] ofegar.

◆ **puff out** *vt sep* -1. [chest, cheeks] inflar -2. [feathers] eriçar.

◆ **puff up** *vi* -1. [eyes, skin] inchar -2. [feathers] eriçar.

puffed [pʌft] *adj* -1. [swollen]: **~ up** inchado(da) -2. *UK inf* [out of breath]: **~ (out)** ofegante.

puffed sleeve *n* manga *f* bufante.

puffin ['pʌfɪn] *n* papagaio-do-mar *m*.

puffiness ['pʌfɪnɪs] *n* inchação *f*.

puff pastry, puff paste *US n (U)* massa *f* folhada.

puffy ['pʌfɪ] (*compar* **-ier**, *superl* **-iest**) *adj* inchado(-da).

pug [pʌg] *n* dogue *m*.

pugnacious [pʌg'neɪʃəs] *adj fml* belicoso(sa).

puke [pju:k] *vi* v *inf* vomitar.

pull [pʊl] <> *n* -1. [tug with hand] puxão *m* -2. [influence] prestígio *m*. <> *vt* -1. [gen] puxar; **to ~ sthg to pieces** despedaçar algo -2. [curtains - open] abrir; [- close] puxar -3. [take out - cork, tooth] arrancar; [- gun] sacar; **she ~ ed herself out of the water** ela se afastou da água -4. [muscle, hamstring] distender -5. [attract] atrair. <> *vi* [tug with hand] puxar.

◆ **pull ahead** *vi* ultrapassar; **to ~ ahead of sb/sthg** passar a frente de alguém/algo.

◆ **pull apart** *vt sep* desmontar.

◆ **pull at** *vt fus* puxar, dar puxões em.

◆ **pull away** *vi* -1. [from roadside]: **to ~ away (from)** afastar-se (da margem da estrada) -2. [in race]: **to ~ away (from)** disparar na frente (de).

◆ **pull back** *vi* recuar.

◆ **pull down** *vt sep* demolir.

◆ **pull in** *vi* [vehicle] encostar.

◆ **pull off** *vt sep* -1. [take off] tirar rapidamente -2. [succeed in] conseguir levar a cabo.

◆ **pull on** *vt sep* -1. [clothes] vestir rapidamente -2. [shoes] calçar rapidamente.

◆ **pull out** <> *vt sep* retirar. <> *vi* -1. [train] partir -2. [vehicle] entrar na estrada -3. [withdraw] retirar.

◆ **pull over** *vi* [vehicle, driver] encostar.

◆ **pull through** <> *vi* [patient] restabelecer-se, recuperar-se. <> *vt sep* [subj: doctor] ajudar na recuperação de.

◆ **pull together** <> *vt sep*: **to ~ o.s. together** acalmar-se. <> *vi* cooperar, unir forças.

◆ **pull up** <> *vt sep* -1. [raise] levantar -2. [move closer] aproximar -3. [stop]: **to ~ sb up short** deter alguém. <> *vi* parar, deter.

pull-down menu *n* COMPUT menu *m* suspenso.

pulley ['pʊlɪ] (*pl* **pulleys**) *n* roldana *f*.

pullout ['pʊlaʊt] *n* -1. [of troops] retirada *f* -2. [in magazine] encarte *m*.

pullover ['pʊl,əʊvəʳ] *n* pulôver *m*.

pulp [pʌlp] <> *adj* barato(ta), de má qualidade. <> *n* -1. [soft mass] pasta *f* -2. [of fruit] polpa *f* -3. [of

wood] cerne *m*. <> *vt* reduzir à pasta de papel.

pulpit ['pʊlpɪt] *n* púlpito *m*.

pulsar ['pʌlsɑ:ʳ] *n* pulsar *m*.

pulsate [pʌl'seɪt] *vi* -1. [heart] pulsar, palpitar -2. [air, sound] vibrar; **pulsating rhythm** ritmo *m* vibrante.

pulse [pʌls] <> *n* -1. [in body] pulso *m*; **to take sb's ~** tomar o pulso de alguém -2. TECH impulso *m*. <> *vi* [throb - blood] pulsar; [- music, room] vibrar.

◆ **pulses** *npl* [food] grãos *mpl*.

pulverize, -ise ['pʌlvəraɪz] *vt* pulverizar.

puma ['pju:mə] (*pl inv OR* **-s**) *n* puma *m*.

pumice (stone) ['pʌmɪs-] *n (U)* pedra-pomes *f*.

pummel ['pʌml] (*UK pt* & *pp* **-led**, *cont* **-ling**, *US pt* & *pp* **-ed**, *cont* **-ing**) *vt* esmurrar.

pump [pʌmp] <> *n* bomba *f*. <> *vt* -1. [convey by pumping] bombear -2. *inf* [invest]: **to ~ money into sthg** injetar dinheiro em algo -3. *inf* [interrogate] sondar. <> *vi* -1. [machine] bater -2. [person] arfar -3. [heart] palpitar.

◆ **pumps** *npl* [shoes] sapatilhas *fpl*.

pumpernickel ['pʌmpənɪkl] *n (U)* pão *m* de centeio.

pumpkin ['pʌmpkɪn] *n* abóbora *f*.

pumpkin pie *n* torta *f* de abóbora.

pun [pʌn] *n* jogo *m* de palavras.

punch [pʌntʃ] <> *n* -1. [blow] soco *m* -2. [tool] punção *m* -3. *(U)* [drink] ponche *m*. <> *vt* -1. [hit] esmurrar, soquear -2. [perforate - paper, ticket] picar; [- hole] perfurar.

◆ **punch in** *vi US* bater o ponto *(na entrada)*.

◆ **punch out** *vi US* bater o ponto *(na saída)*.

Punch-and-Judy show [-'dʒu:dɪ-] *n* teatro de fantoches para crianças apresentado normalmente na praia.

punch-bag, punching bag *US n* saco *m* de pancadas.

punch ball *n* saco *m* de pancadas.

punch bowl *n* poncheira *f*.

punch-drunk *adj* zonzo(za), grogue.

punch(ed) card [pʌntʃ(t)-] *n* cartão *m* perfurado.

punching bag *n US* = punch-bag.

punch line *n* frase *f* final, arremate *m* *(de uma história)*.

punch-up *n UK inf* briga *f*.

punchy ['pʌntʃɪ] (*compar* **-ier**, *superl* **-iest**) *adj inf* incisivo(va).

punctilious [pʌŋk'tɪlɪəs] *adj fml* escrupuloso(sa), meticuloso(sa).

punctual ['pʌŋktʃʊəl] *adj* pontual.

punctually ['pʌŋktʃʊəlɪ] *adv* pontualmente.

punctuate ['pʌŋktʃʊeɪt] *vt* -1. [add punctuation to] pontuar -2. [interrupt]: **to be ~d by** *or* **with sthg** ser interrompido(da) por algo.

punctuation [,pʌŋktʃʊ'eɪʃn] *n (U)* pontuação *f*.

punctuation mark *n* sinal *m* de pontuação.

puncture ['pʌŋktʃəʳ] <> *n* furo *m*. <> *vt* -1. [tyre, ball] furar -2. [lung, skin] perfurar.

pundit ['pʌndɪt] *n* especialista *mf*, autoridade *f* *(em algum assunto)*.

pungent ['pʌndʒənt] *adj* -1. [strong-smelling] forte, penetrante -2. *fig* [powerful] pujente.

punish ['pʌnɪʃ] *vt* punir; **to ~ sb for sthg/for doing**

sthg punir alguém por algo/por fazer algo.

punishable ['pʌnɪʃəbll] *adj* punível, castigável.

punishing ['pʌnɪʃɪŋ] *adj* penoso(sa).

punishment ['pʌnɪʃmənt] *n* -1. [gen] punição *f*, castigo *m* -2. [heavy use]: **to take a lot of** ~ sofrer estragos.

punitive ['pjuːnətɪv] *adj* punitivo(va).

Punjab [ˌpʌn'ʒɑːbl] *n*: **the** ~ o Punjab; **in the** ~ no Punjab.

Punjabi [ˌpʌn'ʒɑːbɪ] <> *adj* punjabi. <> *n* -1. [person] punjabi *mf* -2. [language] punjabi *m*.

punk [pʌŋk] <> *adj* punk. <> *n* -1. (U) [music]: ~ **(rock)** rock *m* punk -2. [person]: ~ **(rocker)** roqueiro *m*, -ra *f* punk -3. *US inf* [lout] rebelde *mf*.

punnet ['pʌnɪt] *n UK* cesto *m*.

punt [pʌnt] <> *n* -1. [boat] barco *m* a remo -2. [Irish currency] libra *f* irlandesa. <> *vi* [in boat] navegar em barco a remo.

punter ['pʌntə'] *n* -1. [someone who bets] apostador *m*, -ra *f* -2. *UK inf* [customer] cliente *mf*.

puny ['pjuːnɪ] *(compar*-ier, *superl*-iest) *adj* -1. [person] raquítico(ca) -2. [limbs] fraco(ca) -3. [effort] débil.

pup [pʌp] *n* -1. [young dog] cachorrinho *m*, -nha *f* -2. [young seal, otter] filhote *m*.

pupil ['pjuːpll] *n* -1. [student] aluno *m*, -na *f* -2. [follower] pupilo *m*, -la *f* -3. [of eye] pupila *f*.

puppet ['pʌpɪt] *n* -1. [string puppet] marionete *f* -2. [glove puppet] fantoche *m* -3. *pej* [person, country] fantoche *mf*.

puppet government *n* governo *m* de marionetes.

puppet show *n* teatro *m* de marionetes.

puppy ['pʌpɪ] *(pl*-ies) *n* cachorrinho *m*, -nha *f*.

puppy fat *n* (U) *inf* dobrinhas *fpl (do bebê)*.

purchase ['pɜːtʃəs] *fml* <> *n* -1. (U) [act of buying] compra *f*, aquisição *f* -2. [thing bought] aquisição *f* -3. [grip] apoio *m*. <> *vt* comprar, adquirir.

purchase order *n* ordem *f* de compra.

purchase price *n* preço *m* de compra.

purchaser ['pɜːtʃəsə'] *n* comprador *m*, -ra *f*.

purchase tax *n UK* imposto *m* de compras.

purchasing power ['pɜːtʃəsɪŋ-] *n* (U) poder *m* de compra.

purdah ['pɜːdə] *n* (U) RELIG *prática muçulmana de manter as mulheres longe do contato com os homens.*

pure [pjʊə'] *adj* -1. [gen] puro(ra) -2. [clear] cristalino(na) -3. *literary* [chaste] puro(ra) -4. [for emphasis] mero(ra), puro(ra).

purebred ['pjʊəbred] *adj* puro-sangue.

puree ['pjʊəreɪ] <> *n* purê *m*. <> *vt* amassar.

purely ['pjʊəlɪ] *adv* puramente.

pureness ['pjʊənɪs] *n* (U) pureza *f*.

purgative ['pɜːgətɪv] *n* purgante *m*.

purgatory ['pɜːgətrɪ] *n* (U) *hum* [suffering] purgatório *m*.

➤ Purgatory *n* [place] Purgatório *m*.

purge [pɜːdʒ] <> *n* POL expurgo *m*. <> *vt* -1. POL purgar -2. [rid]: **to** ~ **sthg (of sthg)** livrar algo (de algo); **to** ~ **o.s. (of sthg)** livrar-se de algo).

purification [ˌpjʊərɪfɪ'keɪʃn] *n* (U) purificação *f*.

purifier ['pjʊərɪfaɪə'] *n* purificador *m*.

purify ['pjʊərɪfaɪ] *(pt & pp*-ied) *vt* purificar.

purist ['pjʊərɪst] *n* purista *mf*.

puritan ['pjʊərɪtən] <> *adj* puritano(na). <> *n* puritano *m*, -na *f*.

puritanical [ˌpjʊərɪ'tænɪkl] *adj pej* puritano(na).

purity ['pjʊərətɪ] *n* (U) -1. pureza *f* -2. *literary* [chastity] pureza *f*.

purl [pɜːl] <> *n* laçada *f*. <> *vt* dar uma laçada.

purloin [pɜː'lɔɪn] *vt fml* surrupiar.

purple ['pɜːpl] <> *adj* purpúreo(rea). <> *n* púrpura *f*.

purport [pə'pɔːt] *vi fml*: **to** ~ **to do/be sthg** pretender fazer/ser algo.

purpose ['pɜːpəs] *n* -1. [objective, reason] objetivo *m*, propósito *m* -2. [use] propósito *m*; **to no** ~ em vão -3. [determination] determinação *f*.

➤ on purpose *adv* de propósito.

purpose-built *adj* especialmente construído (da), feito(ta) sob medida.

purposeful ['pɜːpəsfʊl] *adj* determinado(da), resoluto(ta).

purposely ['pɜːpəslɪ] *adv* deliberadamente, intencionalmente.

purr [pɜː'] <> *n* -1. [of cat] ronrom *m* -2. [of engine] ronco *m*. <> *vi* -1. [gen] roncar -2. [cat] ronronar.

purse [pɜːs] <> *n* -1. [for money] carteira *f* -2. *US* [handbag] bolsa *f*. <> *vt* franzir *(em desagrado)*.

purser ['pɜːsə'] *n* comissário *m*, -ria *f* de bordo.

purse snatcher [-ˌsnætʃə'] *n US* trombadinha *mf*.

purse strings *npl*: **to hold the** ~ controlar os gastos, administrar o dinheiro.

pursue [pə'sjuː] *vt* -1. [follow] perseguir -2. [hobby] dedicar-se a -3. [interest, aim] buscar, ir atrás de -4. [take further] aprofundar-se em.

pursuer [pə'sjuːə'] *n* perseguidor *m*, -ra *f*.

pursuit [pə'sjuːt] *n* -1. [gen] perseguição *f*; **in** ~ **of** **sb/sthg** de busca de alguém/algo; **to be in hot** ~ perseguir de perto -2. [of happiness, security etc] *fml* busca *f* -3. [occupation, activity] atividade *f*.

purveyor [pə'veɪə'] *n fml* fornecedor *m*, -ra *f*.

pus [pʌs] *n* (U) pus *m*.

push [pʊʃ] <> *n* -1. [shove] empurrão *m* -2. [on button, bell] pressionamento *m* -3. [campaign] pressão *f* -4. *phr*: **to give sb the** ~ *UK inf* [end relationship] dar o fora em alguém; [dismiss] mandar alguém embora. <> *vt* -1. [press, move - door, person] empurrar; [- button] apertar -2. [encourage] incitar; **to** ~ **sb to do sthg** incitar alguém a fazer algo -3. [force] impelir; **to** ~ **sb into doing sthg** impelir alguém a fazer algo -4. *inf* [promote] promover -5. *drugs sl* [sell illegally] traficar -6. *inf* [approach]: **we were** ~ **ing 90 miles an hour** estávamos beirando as 90 milhas por hora. <> *vi* -1. [shove] empurrar; **to** ~ **through** abrir caminho aos empurrões em -2. [on button, bell] apertar -3. [campaign]: **to** ~ **for** sthg fazer pressão por algo.

➤ push ahead *vi* prosseguir; **to** ~ **ahead with** sthg seguir em frente com algo.

➤ push around *vt sep inf fig* [bully] mandar.

➤ push in *vi* [in queue] furar.

➤ push off *vi inf* [go away] largar-se.

➤ push on *vi* [continue] seguir em frente sem parar.

➤ push over *vt sep* derrubar.

push through *vt sep* [force to be accepted] conseguir que se aprove.

pushbike ['puʃbaɪk] *n UK* bici *f.*

push-button *adj* de botão.

pushcart ['puʃkɑːt] *n* carrinho *m* de mão.

pushchair ['puʃtʃeəʳ] *n UK* carrinho *m* de bebê.

pushed [puʃt] *adj inf:* to be ~ for sthg andar meio curto(ta) de algo; **to be hard** ~ **to do sthg** estar com dificuldades para fazer algo.

pusher ['puʃəʳ] *n drugs sl* traficante *mf*, vendedor *m*, -ra *f* de drogas.

pushover ['puʃ,əuvəʳ] *n inf* otário *m*, -ria *f.*

push-start *vt* arrancar empurrando.

push-up *n US* flexão *f.*

pushy ['puʃɪ] (*compar* -ier, *superl* -iest) *adj pej* agressivo(va).

puss [pus], **pussy (cat)** ['pusɪ-] *n inf* gatinho *m*, bichano *m.*

pussy willow ['pusɪ-] *n* salgueiro *m.*

put [put] (*pt* & *pp* put, *cont* -ting) *vt* -**1.** [gen] colocar, pôr -**2.** [express] colocar, expressar; **to** ~ **it to sb that** expor a alguém que, colocar para alguém que -**3.** [ask] colocar, perguntar -**4.** [cause to be] colocar; **to** ~ **sb out of work** deixar alguém sem trabalho -**5.** [estimate]: **to** ~ **sthg at** avaliar algo em -**6.** [invest]: **to** ~ **sthg into sthg** investir algo em algo, colocar algo em algo -**7.** [apply - responsibility]: **to** ~ **responsiblity on sb/sthg** colocar responsabilidade em alguém/algo; **to** ~ **pressure on sb/sthg** pressionar alguém/algo; **to** ~ **tax on sthg** colocar impostos sobre algo -**8.** [write] escrever.

◆ **put across** *vt sep* expor.

◆ **put aside** *vt sep* -**1.** [place on one side] colocar de lado -**2.** [save] poupar -**3.** [disregard] deixar de lado.

◆ **put away** *vt sep* -**1.** [tidy away] colocar no lugar, organizar -**2.** *inf* [lock up] encerrar *(na prisão).*

◆ **put back** *vt sep* -**1.** [replace] repor no lugar -**2.** [postpone] adiar -**3.** [clock, watch] atrasar.

◆ **put by** *vt sep* [money] poupar.

◆ **put down** *vt sep* -**1.** [lay down] largar, pôr no chão -**2.** [quell] sufocar -**3.** *inf* [criticize] humilhar, rebaixar -**4.** [write down] apontar -**5.** *UK* [kill] sacrificar.

◆ **put down to** *vt sep* atribuir a.

◆ **put forward** *vt sep* -**1.** [propose] apresentar, propor -**2.** [advance] adiar -**3.** [clock, watch] adiantar.

◆ **put in** *vt sep* -**1.** [spend] dedicar -**2.** [submit] apresentar.

◆ **put off** *vt sep* -**1.** [postpone] adiar -**2.** [switch off - radio, light] desligar; [- brake] soltar -**3.** [cause to wait] fazer esperar -**4.** [discourage] desanimar, dissuadir -**5.** [disturb] distrair -**6.** [cause to dislike] desanimar, desestimular; **to** ~ **sb off sthg** desestimular alguém de algo.

◆ **put on** *vt sep* -**1.** [wear - trousers, hat] vestir; [- shoes] calçar -**2.** [arrange] montar -**3.** [gain in weight]: **to** ~ **on weight** engordar -**4.** [switch on - radio, light] ligar; [- brake] acionar -**5.** [play] tocar, pôr -**6.** [start cooking] colocar no fogo -**7.** [pretend] fingir -**8.** [bet] apostar -**9.** [add] acrescentar -**10.** *US inf* [tease] zombar de.

◆ **put onto** *vt sep* [tell about]: **to** ~ **sb onto sthg** indicar algo a alguém.

◆ **put out** *vt sep* -**1.** [place outside] colocar *OR* pôr para fora -**2.** [issue] tornar público(ca) -**3.** [extinguish] apagar -**4.** [switch off] desligar -**5.** [extend] espichar -**6.** *inf* [injure] deslocar -**7.** [annoy, upset]: **to be** ~ **out** ficar chateado(da) -**8.** [inconvenience] importunar, incomodar; **to** ~ **o.s. out** incomodar-se.

◆ **put over** *vt sep* = put across.

◆ **put through** *vt sep TELEC* transferir.

◆ **put together** *vt sep* -**1.** [assemble] montar -**2.** [combine] juntar, misturar -**3.** [organize] organizar.

◆ **put up** ◇ *vt sep* -**1.** [build] erguer -**2.** [raise and open - umbrella] abrir; [- flag] hastear -**3.** [fix to wall] afixar -**4.** [provide] pôr -**5.** [propose] indicar -**6.** [increase] aumentar -**7.** [provide accommodation for] hospedar. ◇ *vt fus* [offer, present] manifestar.

◆ **put upon** *vt fus UK*: **to be** ~ **upon** ser explorado(da).

◆ **put up to** *vt sep*: **to** ~ **sb up to sthg** induzir alguém a algo.

◆ **put up with** *vt fus* suportar, agüentar.

putative ['pju:tətɪv] *adj fml* suposto(ta).

put-down *n inf* comentário *m* maldoso.

putrefaction [,pju:trɪ'fækʃn] *n* (*U*) putrefação *f.*

putrefy ['pju:trɪfaɪ] (*pt* & *pp* -ied) *vi fml* putrefazer.

putrid ['pju:trɪd] *adj fml* putrefato(ta).

putsch [putʃ] *n* golpe *m* de estado.

putt [pʌt] ◇ *n* tacada *f* leve *(no golfe).* ◇ *vt* dar uma tacada leve em. ◇ *vi* dar uma tacada leve.

putter ['pʌtəʳ] *n* taco *m* de golfe *(para tacadas leves).*

◆ **putter about, putter around** *US vi* = potter about.

putting green ['pʌtɪŋ-] *n* minicampo *m* sem obstáculos *(para jogar golfe).*

putty ['pʌtɪ] *n* (*U*) massa *f* de vidraceiro.

put-up job *n inf* embuste *m.*

put-upon *adj inf* explorado(da); **to feel** ~ sentir-se usado (usa) da.

puzzle ['pʌzl] ◇ *n* -**1.** [toy, game] quebra-cabeça *m* -**2.** [mystery] enigma *m.* ◇ *vt* deixar perplexo(xa). ◇ *vi*: **to** ~ **over sthg** quebrar a cabeça com algo.

◆ **puzzle out** *vt sep* decifrar.

puzzled ['pʌzld] *adj* confuso(sa), perplexo(xa).

puzzling ['pʌzlɪŋ] *adj* desconcertante.

PVC (*abbr of* polyvinyl chloride) *n* PVC *m.*

Pvt. (*abbr of* Private) soldado *m* raso.

p.w. (*abbr of* per week) por semana.

PWR (*abbr of* pressurized-water reactor) *n reator de água pressurizada.*

PX (*abbr of* post exchange) *n loja em base militar norte-americana.*

Pygmy (*pl* -ies) *n* pigmeu *m*, -méia *f.*

pyjama *comp* de pijama.

pyjamas [pə'dʒɑːməz] *npl* pijama *m.*

pylon ['paɪlən] *n ELEC* torre *f (de eletricidade).*

PYO (*abbr of* pick your own) *colha você mesmo, cartaz em fazendas convidando a pessoa a colher vegetais ou frutas a preços inferiores aos cobrados em supermercados.*

pyramid ['pırəmıd] n pirâmide f.

pyramid selling n (U) vendas fpl em pirâmide.

pyre ['paɪəʳ] n pira f.

Pyrenean [ˌpɪrə'niːən] adj pirenaico(ca).

Pyrenees [ˌpɪrə'niːz] npl: **the** ~ os Pireneus.

Pyrex® ['paɪreks] <> n (U) pírex® m inv. <> comp de pírex.

pyromaniac [ˌpaɪrə'meɪnɪæk] n piromaníaco m, -ca f.

pyrotechnics [ˌpaɪrəʊ'tek.nɪks] <> n (U) [science] pirotécnica f. <> npl fig [show of brilliance] espetáculo m pirotécnico.

python ['paɪθn] (pl inv OR -s) n píton m.

q (pl **q's** OR **qs**), **Q** (pl **Q's** OR **Qs**) [kjuː] n [letter] q, Q m.

Qatar [kæ'tɑːʳ] n Qatar; **in** ~ no Qatar.

QC (abbr of **Queen's Counsel**) n advogado que representa clientes nas cortes superiores britânicas.

QED (abbr of **quod erat demonstrandum**) q.e.d., c.q.d.

QM (abbr of **quartermaster**) n quartelmestre m.

q.t., QT (abbr of **quiet**) inf: **on the** ~ em segredo.

Q-tip® n US cotonete m.

qty (abbr of **quantity**) qtd f.

quack [kwæk] <> n -**1.** [noise] grasnido m -**2.** inf pej [doctor] curandeiro m charlatão, curandeira f charlatona. <> vi grasnir.

quad [kwɒd] n -**1.** (abbr of **quadruplet**) quádruplos mpl, -plas fpl -**2.** (abbr of **quadrangle**) pátio cercado por edifícios, em geral em escola ou universidade.

quadrangle ['kwɒdrængl] n -**1.** [figure] quadrângulo m -**2.** [courtyard] pátio m.

quadrant ['kwɒdrənt] n quadrante m.

quadraphonic [ˌkwɒdrə'fɒnɪk] adj quadrafônico (ca).

quadrilateral [ˌkwɒdrɪ'lætərəl] <> adj quadrilateral. <> n quadrilátero m.

quadruped ['kwɒdruped] n quadrúpede m.

quadruple [kwɒ'druːpl] <> adj quadruplicado (da). <> vt & vi quadruplicar.

quadruplets ['kwɒdruplɪts] npl quadrigêmeos mpl, -meas fpl.

quads [kwɒdz] npl inf quadrigêmeos mpl, -meas fpl.

quaff [kwɒf] vt dated emborcar (bebida alcoólica).

quagmire ['kwægmaɪəʳ] n pântano m.

quail [kweɪl] (pl inv OR -s) <> n codorna f. <> vi literary amedrontar-se.

quaint [kweɪnt] adj pitoresco(ca), singular.

quaintness n (U) singularidade f.

quake [kweɪk] <> n (abbr of **earthquake**) inf terremoto m. <> vi tremer.

Quaker ['kweɪkəʳ] n quacre m.

qualification [ˌkwɒlɪfɪ'keɪʃn] n -**1.** [examination, certificate] qualificação f, título m -**2.** [quality, skill] qualificação f -**3.** [qualifying statement] restrição f, ressalva f.

qualified ['kwɒlɪfaɪd] adj -**1.** [trained] qualificado (da) -**2.** [able]: **to be** ~ **to do sthg** estar qualificado(da) para fazer algo -**3.** [limited] com ressalvas.

qualify ['kwɒlɪfaɪ] (pt & pp -ied) <> vt -**1.** [modify] restringir -**2.** [entitle]: **to** ~ **sb to do sthg** qualificar alguém para fazer algo. <> vi -**1.** [pass exams] habilitar-se -**2.** [be entitled]: **to** ~ **(for sthg)** qualificar-se(para algo) -**3.** SPORT classificar-se.

qualifying ['kwɒlɪfaɪɪŋ] adj -**1.** [modifying] qualificativo(va) -**2.** [entitling] qualificador(ra) -**3.** SPORT classificatório(ria); ~ **round** fase f classificatória, eliminatórias fpl.

qualitative ['kwɒlɪtətɪv] adj qualitativo(va).

quality ['kwɒlətɪ] (pl -ies) <> n qualidade f. <> comp de qualidade.

quality control n (U) controle m de qualidade.

quality press n UK: **the** ~ a imprensa não-sensacionalista OR de qualidade.

qualms [kwɑːmz] npl receio m, escrúpulos mpl.

quandary ['kwɒndərɪ] (pl -ies) n dilema m; **to be in a** ~ **about** OR **over sthg** estar num dilema sobre algo.

quango ['kwæŋɡəʊ] (abbr of **quasi-autonomous non-governmental organization**) (pl -s) n UK usu pej na Grã-Bretanha, conselho administrativo não-eleito, indicado pelo governo para administrar um serviço público.

quantifiable [kwɒntɪ'faɪəbl] adj quantificável.

quantify ['kwɒntɪfaɪ] (pt & pp -ied) vt quantificar.

quantitative ['kwɒntɪtətɪv] adj quantitativo(va).

quantity ['kwɒntətɪ] (pl -ies) n -**1.** quantidade f; **in** ~ em quantidade -**2.** phr: **an unknown** ~ uma incógnita.

quantity surveyor n calculista mf de obra.

quantum leap ['kwɒntəm-] n avanço m impressionante.

quantum theory ['kwɒntəm-] n teoria f quântica.

quarantine ['kwɒrəntiːn] <> n quarentena f; **to be in** ~ estar em OR de quarentena. <> vt pôr em quarentena.

quark [kwɑːk] n -**1.** PHYSICS quark m -**2.** CULIN queijo m tipo quark.

quarrel ['kwɒrəl] (UK pt & pp -led, cont -ling, US pt & pp -ed, cont -ing) <> n discussão f; **to have no** ~ **with sb/sthg** não ter nada contra alguém/algo. <> vi discutir; **to** ~ **with sb** discutir com alguém; **to** ~ **with sthg** não estar de acordo sobre algo.

quarrelsome ['kwɒrəlsəm] adj briguento(ta).

quarry ['kwɒrɪ] (pl -ies, pt & pp -ied) <> n -**1.** [place] pedreira f -**2.** [prey] presa f. <> vt extrair.

quarry tile n ladrilho m.

quart [kwɔːt] n -**1.** UK [unit of measurement] quarto m de galão (1,14 litro) -**2.** US [unit of measurement] quarto *m* de galão *(0,95 litro)*.

quarter ['kwɔːtə^r] *n* -**1.** [fraction] quarto *m* - **2.** [in telling time]: **it's a ~ past two** *UK*, **it's a ~ after two** *US* são duas e quinze; **it's a ~ to two** *UK*, **it's a ~ of two** *US* faltam quinze para as duas -**3.** [of year] trimestre *m* -**4.** *US* [coin] moeda *f* de 25 centavos -**5.** [four ounces] quarto *m* de libra *(113,396 gr)* - **6.** [area in town] quarteirão *m* -**7.** [direction] lugar *m*, parte *f*; **they came from all ~s of the globe** eles vieram de todos os cantos da terra.
  ◆ **quarters** *npl* [rooms] alojamentos *mpl*.
  ◆ **at close quarters** *adv* de perto.

quarterback ['kwɔːtəbæk] *n US* jogador de futebol americano que lança a bola nas jogadas ofensivas.

quarterdeck ['kwɔːtədek] *n* tombadilho *m* superior.

quarter-final *n* quarta-de-final *f*.

quarter-hour *adj* de quinze minutos.

quarter-light *n UK* janelinha *f* para ventilação *(no automóvel)*.

quarterly ['kwɔːtəlɪ] *(pl* -**ies)** <> *adj* trimestral. <> *adv* trimestralmente. <> *n* revista *f* trimestral.

quartermaster ['kwɔːtə,mɑːstə^r] *n* MIL quartelmestre *m*.

quarter note *n US* MUS semínima *f*.

quartet [kwɔːˈtet] *n* quarteto *m*.

quarto ['kwɔːtəʊ] *(pl* -**s)** *n* in quarto *m inv.*

quartz [kwɔːts] *n (U)* quartzo *m*.

quartz watch *n* relógio *m* de quartzo.

quasar ['kweɪzɑː^r] *n* quasar *m*.

quash [kwɒʃ] *vt* -**1.** [reject] revogar, anular - **2.** [quell] sufocar, reprimir.

quasi- ['kweɪzaɪ] *prefix* quase-.

quaver ['kweɪvə^r] <> *n* -**1.** MUS colcheia *f* - **2.** [in voice] tremor *m*. <> *vi* tremer.

quavering ['kweɪvərɪŋ] *adj* trêmulo(la).

quay [kiː] *n* cais *m*.

quayside ['kiːsaɪd] *n* cais *m*.

queasy ['kwiːzɪ] *(compar* -**ier**, *superl* -**iest)** *adj* enjoado(da).

Quebec [kwɪˈbek] *n* [province, city] Québec; **in ~** em Québec.

Quebecer, Quebecker [kwɪˈbekə^r] *n* quebequense *mf*.

queen [kwiːn] *n* -**1.** [gen] rainha *f* -**2.** [playing card] dama *f*.

queen bee *n* (abelha *f*) rainha *f*.

queen mother *n*: **the ~** a rainha-mãe.

Queen's Counsel *n UK* advogado inglês de alta ordem.

Queen's English *n UK*: **the ~** o inglês falado com perfeição na Grã-Bretanha.

queen's evidence *n UK*: **to turn ~** tesmunhar *(um criminoso)* frente a um tribunal contra outros criminosos em troca de diminuição da pena.

queer [kwɪə^r] <> *adj* [odd] esquisito(ta), estranho(nha). <> *n inf pej* [homosexual] veado *m*, bicha *f*.

quell [kwel] *vt* -**1.** [rebellion] sufocar, reprimir - **2.** [unease, anger] dominar, conter.

quench [kwentʃ] *vt*: **to ~ one's thirst** matar a sede.

querulous ['kwerʊləs] *adj fml* lamuriante.

query ['kwɪərɪ] *(pl* -**ies**, *pt* & *pp* -**ied)** <> *n* pergunta *f*, dúvida *f*. <> *vt* pôr em dúvida.

quest [kwest] *n literary* busca *f*; **~ for sthg** busca por algo.

question ['kwestʃn] <> *n* -**1.** [gen] questão *f* - **2.** [query] pergunta *f*; **to ask (sb) a ~** fazer uma pergunta a alguém -**3.** [doubt] dúvida *f*; **to** OR **call sthg into ~** por OR colocar algo em dúvida; **to** OR **bring sthg into ~** colocar algo em questão; **beyond ~** sem nenhuma dúvida; **open to ~** debatível; **without ~** sem dúvida -**4.** *phr*: **there's no ~ of ...** não há dúvida de (que) ... <> *vt* -**1.** [interrogate] interrogar -**2.** [express doubt about] questionar.
  ◆ **in question** *adv*: **the matter in ~** o assunto em questão.
  ◆ **out of the question** *adj* fora de questão.

questionable ['kwestʃənəbl] *adj* questionável.

questioner ['kwestʃənə^r] *n* interrogador *m*, -ra *f*.

questioning ['kwestʃənɪŋ] <> *adj* de interrogação. <> *n (U)* interrogatório *m*.

question mark *n* ponto *m* de interrogação.

question master *esp UK*, **quizmaster** ['kwɪz,mɑːstə^r] *esp US n* apresentador *m*, -ra *f (de um show de perguntas)*.

questionnaire [,kwestʃəˈneə^r] *n* questionário *m*.

question time *n UK* POL audiência no parlamento britânico na qual os ministros respondem a perguntas dos parlamentares.

queue [kjuː] *UK* <> *n* fila *f*; **to jump the ~** furar a fila. <> *vi* fazer fila; **to ~ (up) for sthg** fazer fila para algo.

queue-jump *vi UK* furar a fila.

quibble ['kwɪbl] *pej* <> *n* chorumela *f*. <> *vi* queixar-se por bobagem, lamuriar-se; **to ~ over** OR **about sthg** queixar-se por bobagem sobre algo.

quiche [kiːʃ] *n* quiche *f*.

quick [kwɪk] <> *adj* rápido(da). <> *adv* depressa, rápido.

quicken ['kwɪkn] <> *vt* [make faster] apressar, acelerar. <> *vi* [get faster] acelerar(-se).

quickly ['kwɪklɪ] *adv* -**1.** [rapidly] rapidamente - **2.** [without delay] depressa, rápido.

quickness ['kwɪknɪs] *n* rapidez *f*.

quicksand ['kwɪksænd] *n* areia *f* movediça.

quicksilver ['kwɪk,sɪlvə^r] *n (U) dated* mercúrio *m*.

quickstep ['kwɪkstep] *n*: **the ~** dança de salão de passos rápidos.

quick-tempered *adj* irritadiço(ça).

quick-witted [-ˈwɪtɪd] *adj* arguto(ta).

quid [kwɪd] *(pl inv) n UK inf* libra *f (esterlina)*.

quid pro quo [-ˈkwəʊ] *(pl* quid pro quos) *n* compensação *f*, troca *f*.

quiescent [kwaɪˈesnt] *adj fml* quiescente.

quiet ['kwaɪət] <> *adj* -**1.** [not loud - voice] numa voz baixa; **to keep ~ about sthg** guardar silêncio sobre algo; **be ~!** fique quieto (ta)! -**2.** [tranquil] tranqüilo(la) -**3.** [not busy] parado(da) -**4.** [discreet] suave, discreto(ta); **to have a ~**

word with **sb** falar discretamente com alguém
- **5.** [intimate] íntimo(ma). ◇ ~ *n (U)* tranqüilidade
f, silêncio *m*; **on the** ~ *inf* na surdina, às
escondidas. ◇ *vt US* acalmar, tranqüilizar.
➡ **quiet down** ◇ *vt sep US* acalmar, tranqüilizar. ◇ *vi* acalmar-se, tranqüilizar-se.
quieten ['kwaɪətn] *vt* acalmar, tranqüilizar.
➡ **quieten down** ◇ *vt sep* acalmar, tranqüilizar. ◇ *vi* acalmar-se, tranqüilizar-se.
quietly ['kwaɪətlɪ] *adv* - **1.** [without noise] sem fazer
barulho - **2.** [without excitement] tranqüilamente
- **3.** [without fuss] discretamente.
quietness ['kwaɪətnɪs] *n (U)* quietude *f*, tranqüilidade *f*.
quiff [kwɪf] *n UK* topete *m*.
quill (pen) [kwɪl-] *n* pena *f (de escrever)*.
quilt [kwɪlt] *n* acolchoado *m*, edredom *m*.
quilted ['kwɪltɪd] *adj* acolchoado(da).
quince [kwɪns] *n* marmelo *m*.
quinine [kwɪ'ni:n] *n (U)* quinina *f*.
quins *UK* [kwɪnz], **quints** *US* [kwɪnts] *npl inf*
quíntuplos *mpl*, -plas *fpl*.
quintessential [kwɪntə'senʃl] *adj* puro(ra); **this
passage is** ~ **Dickens** esta passagem é Dickens
puro.
quintet [kwɪn'tet] *n* quinteto *m*.
quints *npl US* = **quins**.
quintuplets [kwɪn'tju:plɪts] *npl* quíntuplos *mpl*,
-plas *fpl*.
quip [kwɪp] *(pt & pp* -**ped**, *cont* -**ping**) ◇ *n* gracejo
m. ◇ *vi* gracejar.
quire [kwaɪəʳ] *n* mão *f* de papel.
quirk [kwɜ:k] *n* - **1.** [habit] mania *f*, esquisitice *f* - **2.**
[strange event] estranha coincidência *f*; **by a** ~ **of
fate** por um capricho do destino.
quirky ['kwɜ:kɪ] *(compar* -**ier**, *superl* -**iest**) *adj* peculiar.
quit [kwɪt] *(UK pt & pp* quit *OR* -**ted**, *cont* -**ting**, *US pt
& pp* quit, *cont* -**ting**) ◇ *vt* - **1.** [resign from]
abandonar, deixar - **2.** [stop]: **to** ~ **smoking** deixar
de fumar. ◇ *vi* - **1.** [resign] demitir-se - **2.** [give up]
desistir.
quite [kwaɪt] *adv* - **1.** [completely] completamente,
totalmente - **2.** [fairly] bem; ~ **a lot of people**
bastante gente; ~ **a few times** várias vezes - **3.**
[after negative]: **I don't** ~ **understand** não entendo
muito bem; **this room is not** ~ **big enough** essa
sala não é tão grande quanto deveria ser - **4.** [for
emphasis]: **she's** ~ **a singer** ela é uma cantora e
tanto - **5.** [to express agreement]: ~ **(so)!** exatamente!
Quito ['ki:təʊ] *n* Quito.
quits [kwɪts] *adj inf*: **to be** ~ **(with sb)** estar
quite(com alguém); **to call it** ~ ficar quite.
quitter ['kwɪtəʳ] *n inf pej*: **she's not a** ~ ela não é
das que desistem fácil.
quiver ['kwɪvəʳ] ◇ *n* - **1.** [shiver] estremecimento
m - **2.** [for arrows] aljava *f*. ◇ *vi* estremecer.
quivering ['kwɪvərɪŋ] *adj* trêmulo(la).
quixotic [kwɪk'sɒtɪk] *adj literary* quixotesco(ca).
quiz [kwɪz] *(pl* -**zes**, *pt & pp* -**zed**, *cont* -**zing**) ◇ *n* - **1.**
[competitions, game] jogo *m* de perguntas e respos-
tas - **2.** *US SCH* exame *m*. ◇ *vt*: **to** ~ **sb (about**

sthg) interrogar alguém (sobre algo).
quizmaster ['kwɪzmɑ:stəʳ] *n esp US* = **question master**.
quizzical ['kwɪzɪkl] *adj* interrogativo(va).
quoits [kwɔɪts] *n (U)* jogo *m* das argolas.
Quonset hut® ['kwɒnsɪt-] *n US* barracão *m* do
exército.
quorate ['kwɔ:reɪt] *adj UK* que tem quorum.
quorum ['kwɔ:rəm] *n* quórum *m*.
quota ['kwəʊtə] *n* cota *f*.
quotation [kwəʊ'teɪʃn] *n* - **1.** [citation] citação *f* - **2.**
COMM cotação *f*.
quotation marks *npl* aspas *fpl*; **in** ~ entre
aspas.
quote [kwəʊt] ◇ *n* - **1.** [citation] citação *f* - **2.** *COMM*
cotação *f*. ◇ *vt* - **1.** [cite] citar - **2.** *COMM* cotar; **she**
~ **d £100** ela fixou um preço de £100. ◇ *vi*
- **1.** [cite] citar; **to** ~ **from sthg** citar de algo - **2.**
COMM: **to** ~ **.for sthg** estabelecer um preço para
algo.
➡ **quotes** *npl inf* aspas *fpl*; **single/double** ~ **s**
aspas simples/duplas; **in** ~ **s** entre aspas.
quoted company ['kwəʊtɪd-] *n UK* empresa *f*
registrada em bolsa.
quotient ['kwəʊʃnt] *n* quociente *m*.
q.v. *(abbr of quod vide)* veja.
qwerty keyboard ['kwɜ:tɪ-] *n UK* teclado *m*
qwerty.

R

r *(pl* r's *OR* rs), **R** *(pl* R's *OR* Rs) [ɑ:ʳ] *n* [letter] r, R *m*.
➡ **R** - **1.** *(abbr of* **right**) dir. - **2.** *(abbr of* **River**) R. - **3.**
(abbr of **restricted**) não recomendado(da) para
menores - **4.** *US (abbr of* **Republican**) republicano
m, -na *f*.
RA *(abbr of* **Royal Academy**) *n (membro da) Academia Real de Artes na Grã-Bretanha.*
RAAF *(abbr of* **Royal Australian Air Force**) *n força
aérea real australiana.*
Rabat [rə'bɑ:t] *n* Rabat.
rabbi ['ræbaɪ] *n* rabino *m*.
rabbit ['ræbɪt] *n* - **1.** [animal] coelho *m*, -lha *f* - **2.** *(U)*
[food] coelho *m*.
rabbit hole *n* toca *f* de coelho.
rabbit hutch *n* coelheira *f*.
rabbit warren *n* - **1.** [for rabbits] coelheira *f* - **2.**
[building] labirinto *m*.
rabble ['ræbl] *n* - **1.** [disorderly crowd] povaréu *m* - **2.**
[riffraff] gentalha *f*.
rabble-rousing *adj* que agita a multidão.
rabid ['ræbɪd, 'reɪbɪd] *adj* - **1.** [infected with rabies]

raivoso(sa) **-2.** *pej* [fanatical] ferrenho(nha), fanáti-co(ca).

rabies ['reɪbi:z] *n (U)* raiva *f*.

RAC (*abbr of* **Royal Automobile Club**) *n automóvel clube britânico.*

raccoon [rə'ku:n] *n* racum *m*.

race [reɪs] <> *n* **-1.** [ethnicity] raça *f* **-2.** [competition] corrida *f*; **a ~ against time** uma corrida contra o tempo. <> *vt* competir com *(em corrida).* <> *vi* **-1.** [compete]: **to ~ against sb** bater uma corrida com alguém **-2.** [rush] ir correndo **-3.** acelerar.

race car *n US* = **racing car.**

racecourse ['reɪskɔ:s] *n* hipódromo *m.*

race driver *n US* = **racing driver.**

racehorse ['reɪshɔ:s] *n* cavalo *m* de corrida.

race meeting *n* concurso *m* hípico.

race relations *npl* relações *fpl* inter-raciais.

race riot *n* conflito *m* racial.

racetrack ['reɪstræk] *n* autódromo *m.*

racial ['reɪʃl] *adj* racial.

racial discrimination *n (U)* discriminação *m* racial.

racialism ['reɪʃəlɪzml] *n* = **racism.**

racing ['reɪsɪŋ] *n (U) SPORT* corrida *f.*

racing car *UK,* **race car** *US n* carro *m* de corrida.

racing driver *UK,* **race driver** *US n* piloto *m* de corrida.

racism ['reɪsɪzml] *n (U)* racismo *m.*

racist ['reɪsɪst] <> *adj* racista. <> *n* racista *mf.*

rack [ræk] <> *n* **-1.** [frame - for plates] escorredor *m* de louça; [- for toast] prateleira *f*; [- for bottles] porta-garrafas *m inv* **-2.** [for luggage] porta-baga-gens *m inv.* <> *vt literary:* **to be ~ed by** *OR* **with sthg** estar atormentado(da) por algo.

racket ['rækɪt] *n* **-1.** [noise] algazarra *f*, zoeira *f* **-2.** [illegal activity] golpe *m*, fraude *f* **-3.** *SPORT* raquete *f.*

racketeering [,rækə'tɪərɪŋ] *n (U) pej:* **to be indicted on ~ charges** ser acusado(da) de extorquir dinheiro.

raconteur [,rækɒn'tɜ:ʳ] *n pessoa que sabe contar piadas.*

racoon *n* = **raccoon.**

racquet ['rækɪt] *n* raquete *f.*

racy ['reɪsɪ] *(compar* **-ier,** *superl* **-iest)** *adj* vivaz.

RADA ['rɑ:də] (*abbr of* **Royal Academy of Dramatic Art**) *n academia britânica de arte dramática.*

radar ['reɪdɑ:ʳ] *n (U)* radar *m.*

radar trap *n* radar *m (usado pela polícia).*

radial (tyre) ['reɪdjəl-] *n* pneu *m* radial.

radian ['reɪdjən] *n (U)* radiano *m.*

radiance ['reɪdjəns] *n* **-1.** [of face, smile] brilho *m* **-2.** *literary* [brilliance] brilho *m.*

radiant ['reɪdjənt] *adj* **-1.** [happy] radiante **-2.** *literary* [brilliant] brilhante **-3.** *TECH* por radiação.

radiate ['reɪdɪeɪt] <> *vt* irradiar. <> *vi* **-1.** [be emitted] irradiar **-2.** [spread from centre] sair, partir do centro.

radiation [,reɪdɪ'eɪʃn] *n* radiação *f.*

radiation sickness *n (U)* doença *f causada pela radiação.*

radiator ['reɪdɪeɪtəʳ] *n* **-1.** [in house] aquecedor *m* **-2.** *AUT* radiador *m.*

radiator grille *n* grade *f* do radiador.

radical ['rædɪkl] <> *adj* radical. <> *n POL* radical *mf.*

radically ['rædɪklɪ] *adv* radicalmente.

radii ['reɪdɪaɪ] *pl* ▷ **radius.**

radio ['reɪdɪəʊ] *(pl* **-s)** <> *n* **-1.** [gen] rádio *m* **-2.** [station] rádio *f.* <> *comp* de rádio. <> *vt* transmi-tir por rádio.

radioactive [,reɪdɪəʊ'æktɪv] *adj* radioativo(va).

radioactive waste *n (U)* lixo *m* radioativo.

radioactivity [,reɪdɪəʊæk'tɪvətɪ] *n (U)* radioativi-dade *f.*

radio alarm *n* rádio-relógio *m.*

radio-controlled [-kən'trəʊld] *adj* de controle remoto.

radio frequency *n* radiofreqüência *f.*

radiogram ['reɪdɪəʊˌgræm] *n* radiograma *m.*

radiographer [,reɪdɪ'ɒgrəfəʳ] *n* radiologista *mf.*

radiography [,reɪdɪ'ɒgrəfɪ] *n (U)* radiografia *f.*

radiology [,reɪdɪ'ɒlədʒɪ] *n (U)* radiologia *f.*

radiotherapist [,reɪdɪəʊ'θerəpɪst] *n* radioterapeu-ta *mf.*

radiotherapy [,reɪdɪəʊ'θerəpɪ] *n (U)* radioterapia *f.*

radish ['rædɪʃ] *n* rabanete *m.*

radium ['reɪdɪəm] *n (U)* rádio *m.*

radius ['reɪdɪəs] *(pl* **radii)** *n* **-1.** *MATH* raio *m* **-2.** *ANAT* rádio *m.*

radon ['reɪdɒn] *n (U)* radônio *m.*

RAF [ɑ:reɪ'ef, ræf] (*abbr of* **Royal Air Force**) *n força aérea real britânica.*

raffia ['ræfɪə] *n (U)* ráfia *f.*

raffish ['ræfɪʃ] *adj que é atraente e tem estilo, apesar de não ser muito respeitável ou conven-cional.*

raffle ['ræfl] <> *n* rifa *f.* <> *vt* rifar.

raffle ticket *n* bilhete *m* de rifa.

raft [rɑ:ft] *n* **-1.** [of wood] jangada *f* **-2.** [of rubber, plas-tic] bote *m* **-3.** [large number] monte *m*; **a ~ of policies** *POL* um monte de políticas.

rafter ['rɑ:ftəʳ] *n* viga *f.*

rag [ræg] *n* **-1.** [piece of cloth] trapo *m*; **it was like a red ~ to a bull** estava pedindo pra levar **-2.** *pej* [newspaper] jornaleco *m.*
  ➤ **rags** *npl* [clothes] trapos *mpl*; **from ~s to riches** da pobreza à riqueza.

ragamuffin ['rægəˌmʌfɪn] *n* maltrapilho *m*, -lha *f.*

rag-and-bone man *n pessoa que compra e vende roupas e móveis velhos na rua.*

ragbag ['rægbæg] *n fig* salada *f*, mixórdia *f.*

rag doll *n* boneca *f* de pano.

rage [reɪdʒ] <> *n* **-1.** [fury] fúria *f*; **to fly into a ~** ficar enraivecido(da) **-2.** *inf* [fashion]: **all the ~** a última moda. <> *vi* **-1.** [person] enfurecer-se **-2.** [storm, argument] recrudescer.

ragged ['rægɪd] *adj* **-1.** [wearing torn clothes] mal-trapilho(lha) **-2.** [torn] esfarrapado(da) **-3.** [wavy] irregular **-4.** [poor-quality] pobre.

raging ['reɪdʒɪŋ] *adj* terrível.

ragout ['rægu:] *n* ragu *m.*

rag trade *n inf:* **the ~** a indústria do vestuário.

rag week *n UK semana em que as universi-dades britânicas organizam atividades diver-tidas para fins beneficentes.*

raid [reɪd] <> n -1. MIL [attack] incursão f -2. [forced entry - by robbers] assalto m; [- by police] batida f. <> vt -1. MIL [attack] atacar de surpresa -2. [enter by force - robbers] assaltar; [- police] fazer uma batida em.

raider ['reɪdə'] n -1. [attacker] invasor m, -ra f -2. [thief] ladrão m, -dra f, assaltante mf.

rail [reɪl] <> n -1. [on staircase] corrimão m -2. [on walkway] ferro m de proteção -3. [on bridge] parapeito m -4. [on ship] amurada f -5. [bar] barra f -6. [of railway line] trilho m -7. (U) [form of transport] trem m. <> comp ferroviário(a).

railcard ['reɪlkɑːd] n UK cartão m de desconto (no trem).

railing ['reɪlɪŋ] n -1. [round basement] grade f -2. [on walkway] ferro m de proteção -3. [on ship] amurada f -4. [on bridge] parapeito m.

railway UK ['reɪlweɪl, **railroad** US ['reɪlrəʊd] n -1. [track] estrada f de ferro -2. [company] companhia f ferroviária -3. [system] sistema m ferroviário.

railway engine n locomotiva f.

railway line n -1. [route] linha f de trem -2. [track] via f férrea, trilhos mpl.

railwayman ['reɪlweɪmən] (pl -men [-mən]) n UK ferroviário m.

railway station n estação f de trem.

railway track n via f férrea, trilhos mpl.

rain [reɪn] <> n (U) chuva f. <> v impers METEOR chover. <> vi [fall like rain] cair como chuva.
    ◆ **rain down** vi chover.
    ◆ **rain off** UK, **rain out** US vt sep: the match was ~ed off o jogo foi cancelado devido ao mau tempo.

rainbow ['reɪnbəʊl] n arco-íris m.

rainbow trout n truta-arco-íris f.

rain check n US: to take a ~ (on sthg) deixar (algo) para outra hora OR para a próxima.

raincoat ['reɪnkəʊt] n capa f de chuva.

raindrop ['reɪndrɒp] n pingo m de chuva.

rainfall ['reɪnfɔːl] n (U) precipitação f.

rain forest n floresta f tropical.

rain gauge n pluviômetro m.

rainproof ['reɪnpruːf] adj impermeável.

rainstorm ['reɪnstɔːm] n pancada f OR temporal m de chuva.

rainwater ['reɪnˌwɔːtə'] n (U) água f da chuva.

rainy ['reɪnɪ] (compar -ier, superl -iest) adj chuvoso(-sa).

raise [reɪz] <> n US aumento m. <> vt -1. [gen] levantar - 2. [lift up] levantar, erguer; to ~ o.s. levantar-se -3. [increase] aumentar; to ~ one's voice levantar a voz -4. [improve] elevar -5. [evoke] evocar -6. [child, animals] criar -7. [crop] cultivar -8. [build] erguer.

raisin ['reɪzn] n passa f (de uva).

Raj [rɑːdʒ] n: the ~ o Império Britânico na Índia.

rajah ['rɑːdʒə] n rajá m.

rake [reɪk] <> n -1. [implement] rastelo m -2. dated & literary [immoral man] devasso m, libertino m. <> vt -1. [smooth] rastelar -2. [gather] juntar com o rastelo.
    ◆ **rake in** vt sep inf faturar.
    ◆ **rake up** vt sep [past] remexer em.

rake-off n inf propina f, lucro m ilícito.

rakish ['reɪkɪʃ] adj -1. [dissolute] libertino(na) -2. [jaunty] charmoso(sa).

rally ['rælɪ] (pl-ies, pt & pp-ied) <> n -1. [gen] rali m -2. [meeting] comício m. <> vt reunir. <> vi -1. [come together] reunir-se -2. [recover] recuperar-se.
    ◆ **rally round** <> vt fus mobilizar. <> vi mobilizar-se.

rallying ['rælɪŋ] n (U) rali m.

rallying cry n grito m de guerra.

rallying point n ponto m de encontro.

ram [ræm] (pt & pp-med, cont-ming) <> n carneiro m. <> vt -1. [crash into] bater contra OR em -2. [force] enfiar -3. phr: to ~ sthg home deixar algo bem claro.

RAM [ræm] (abbr of random-access memory) n RAM f.

Ramadan [ˌræmə'dæn] n (U) ramadã m.

ramble ['ræmbl] <> n passeio m no campo. <> vi -1. [walk] passear -2. [talk] divagar.

rambler ['ræmblə'] n excursionista mf.

rambling ['ræmblɪŋ] adj -1. [building] cheio (cheia) de voltas e curvas -2. [conversation, book] desconexo(xa).

RAMC (abbr of Royal Army Medical Corps) n corpo médico das forças armadas reais britânicas.

ramekin ['ræmɪkɪn] n recipiente f individual (para ir ao forno).

ramification [ˌræmɪfɪ'keɪʃn] n ramificação f.

ramp [ræmp] n -1. [slope] rampa f -2. AUT [in road] viaduto m.

rampage [ræm'peɪdʒ] <> n: to go on the ~ sair em debandada, debandar-se. <> vi sair em debandada, debandar-se.

rampant ['ræmpənt] adj desenfreado(da).

ramparts ['ræmpɑːts] npl muralha f.

ramshackle ['ræmˌʃækl] adj desmantelado(da).

ran [ræn] pt ▷ run.

RAN (abbr of Royal Australian Navy) n marinha real australiana.

ranch [rɑːntʃ] n fazenda m, rancho m.

rancher ['rɑːntʃə'] n fazendeiro m, -ra f.

ranch house n US -1. [house on ranch] casa f na fazenda -2. [ranch-style house] casa f de campo.

rancid ['rænsɪd] adj rançoso(sa).

rancour UK, **rancor** US ['ræŋkə'] n (U) rancor m.

random ['rændəm] <> adj aleatório(ria). <> n: at ~ aleatoriamente.

random access memory n (U) COMPUT memória f de acesso aleatório, memória f RAM.

randomly ['rændəmlɪ] adv ao acaso.

R and R (abbr of rest and recreation) n US termo militar norte-americano para licença.

randy ['rændɪ] (compar -ier, superl -iest) adj inf tarado(da).

rang [ræŋ] pt ▷ ring.

range [reɪndʒ] <> n -1. [distance covered - of telescope, gun] alcance m; [- of ship, plane] autonomia f; to be out of ~ estar fora de alcance; to be within ~ of sthg estar ao alcance de algo; at close ~ à queima-roupa -2. [variety] variedade f -3. [bracket] faixa f -4. [of mountains, hills] cadeia f -5. [shooting

area] linha f - **6.** MUS alcance m. ◇ vt [place in row]
enfileirar. ◇ vi **-1.** [vary]: **to ~ from ... to ...**
variar de ... a ...; **to ~ between ... and ...** oscilar
entre ... e ... - **2.** [deal with, include]: **to ~ over sthg**
passar por algo.
ranger ['reɪndʒəˀ] n guarda-florestal mf.
Rangoon [ræŋ'guːn] n Rangum.
rank [ræŋk] ◇ adj **-1.** [utter, absolute - disgrace, stupidity] completo(ta); [- injustice, bad luck] total **- 2.** [offensive] rançoso(sa). ◇ n **-1.** [in army, police] posto m;
the ~ and file MIL soldados rasos; [of political party,
organization] bases fpl; **to pull ~** abusar da
autoridade; **to close ~s** fig estreitar os laços **- 2.**
[social class] nível m **- 3.** [row, line] fila f. ◇ vt **-1.** [classify] classificar **- 2.** US [outrank] ocupar posição
mais alta que. ◇ vi classificar-se; **to ~ as/
among** classificar-se como/entre.
➡ ranks npl **-1.** MIL: **the ~s** os soldados rasos **- 2.**
fig [members] filas fpl.
ranking ['ræŋkɪŋ] ◇ n classificação f. ◇ adj US
[highest-ranking] do alto escalão.
rankle ['ræŋkl] vi causar dor; **it still ~s with me!**
isso ainda me dói!
ransack ['rænsæk] vt **-1.** [plunder] saquear **- 2.**
[search] revistar.
ransom ['rænsəm] n resgate m; **to hold sb to ~**
[keep prisoner] pedir resgate por alguém; fig [put in
impossible position] chantagear alguém.
rant [rænt] vi falar asneira.
ranting ['ræntɪŋ] n falatório m.
rap [ræp] (pt & pp **-ped,** cont **-ping**) ◇ n **-1.** [knock]
batidinha f **- 2.** MUS rap m **- 3.** phr: **to take the ~**
pagar o pato. ◇ vt [knock] dar batidinhas em
algo. ◇ vi **-1.** [knock]: **to ~ on sthg** dar batidinhas em
algo **- 2.** MUS cantar rap.
rapacious [rə'peɪʃəs] adj fml voraz.
rapacity [rə'pæsɪtɪ] n (U) fml voracidade f.
rape [reɪp] ◇ n **-1.** [gen] estupro m **- 2.** fig [destruction] destruição f **- 3.** (U) [plant] colza f. ◇ vt
estuprar.
rapeseed n semente f de colza.
rapid ['ræpɪd] adj rápido(da).
➡ rapids npl corredeira f.
rapid-fire adj **-1.** MIL de fogo cerrado **- 2.** fig [spoken quickly] feito um atrás do outro, feita uma
atrás da outra.
rapidity [rə'pɪdətɪ] n (U) rapidez f.
rapidly ['ræpɪdlɪ] adv rapidamente.
rapidness n = rapidity.
rapist ['reɪpɪst] n estuprador m, -ra f.
rapper ['ræpəˀ] n MUS rapper mf.
rapport [ræ'pɔːˀ] n afinidade f; **a ~ with/between**
uma afinidade com/entre.
rapprochement n reaproximação f.
rapt [ræpt] adj absorto(ta).
rapture ['ræptʃəˀ] n arrebatamento m; **to go into
~s over sb/sthg, to go into ~s about sb/sthg**
desfazer-se em elogios por alguém/algo.
rapturous ['ræptʃərəs] adj arrebatador(ra).
rare [reəˀ] adj **-1.** [gen] raro(ra) **- 2.** CULIN [underdone]
malpassado(da).
rarefied ['reərɪfaɪd] adj **-1.** [air, atmosphere] rarefeito(ta) **- 2.** [refined] exclusivo(va).

rarely ['reəlɪ] adv raramente.
rareness ['reənɪs] (U) n **-1.** [scarcity, uncommonness]
raridade f **- 2.** [infrequency] infreqüência f **- 3.** CULIN
qualidade f de malpassado.
raring ['reərɪŋ] adj: **to be ~ to go** estar ansioso(sa)
para começar.
rarity ['reərətɪ] (pl **-ies**) n raridade f.
rascal ['rɑːskl] n patife mf, malandro m, -dra f.
rash [ræʃ] ◇ adj precipitado(da). ◇ n **-1.** MED
erupção f **- 2.** [spate] onda f.
rasher ['ræʃəˀ] n fatia f fina (de bacon).
rashly ['ræʃlɪ] adv precipitadamente.
rashness ['ræʃnɪs] n (U) precipitação f.
rasp [rɑːsp] ◇ n rangido m. ◇ vi esganiçar-se.
raspberry ['rɑːzbərɪ] (pl **-ies**) n **-1.** [fruit] framboesa
f **- 2.** [rude noise]: **to blow a ~** debochar fazendo
barulho com a boca.
rasping ['rɑːspɪŋ] adj áspero(ra) e estridente.
rasta ['ræstə] n inf rasta mf.
rastafarian [ˌræstə'feərɪən] n rastafári mf.
rat [ræt] n **-1.** [animal] rato m, ratazana f; **to smell a
~** suspeitar que há algo errado **- 2.** pej [person]
tratante mf.
ratbag ['rætbæg] n UK inf pej canalha mf.
ratchet ['rætʃɪt] n catraca f.
rate [reɪt] ◇ n **-1.** [speed] velocidade f; **at this ~**
nesse ritmo **- 2.** [ratio, proportion - birth, death, inflation] taxa f; [- unemployment] índice m **- 3.** [price]
tarifa f. ◇ vt **-1.** [consider]: **to ~ sb/sthg (as)**
considerar alguém/algo; **to ~ sb/sthg (among)**
classificar alguém/algo (entre) **- 2.** [deserve] merecer.
➡ at any rate adv pelo menos.
rateable value ['reɪtəbl-] n UK valor m tributável.
rate of exchange n (taxa f de) câmbio m.
ratepayer ['reɪtˌpeɪəˀ] n UK contribuinte mf.
rather ['rɑːðəˀ] adv **-1.** [slightly, a bit] um pouco **- 2.**
[for emphasis] bem, bastante **- 3.** [expressing a preference]: **I would ~ wait** eu preferiria esperar **- 4.**
[more exactly]: **or ~ ...** ou melhor ... **- 5.** [on the contrary]: **(but) ~ ...** (senão) pelo contrário ...
➡ rather than conj em vez de.
ratification [ˌrætɪfɪ'keɪʃn] n (U) ratificação f.
ratify ['rætɪfaɪ] (pt & pp **-ied**) vt ratificar.
rating ['reɪtɪŋ] n **-1.** [standing - high, low, popularity]
índice m; [- opinion poll] posição f **- 2.** UK [sailor]
marinheiro m, -ra f.
➡ ratings npl TV índices mpl de audiência.
ratio ['reɪʃɪəʊ] (pl **-s**) n razão f, proporção f.
ration ['ræʃn] ◇ n ração f. ◇ vt [goods]
racionar.
➡ rations npl ração f.
rational ['ræʃənl] adj racional.
rationale [ˌræʃə'nɑːl] n lógica f, fundamento m
lógico.
rationalization [ˌræʃənəlaɪ'zeɪʃn] n racionalização f.
rationalize, -ise ['ræʃənəlaɪz] vt racionalizar.
rationing ['ræʃənɪŋ] n (U) racionamento m.
rat race n competição f acirrada (no mundo dos
negócios).
rattle ['rætl] ◇ n **-1.** [noise] barulho m, ruído m **- 2.**
[toy] chocalho m. ◇ vt **-1.** [make rattling noise with]

chacoalhar **-2.** [unsettle] desconcertar. <> *vi* [make rattling noise] chacoalhar.

◆ **rattle off** *vt sep* repetir de memória.

◆ **rattle on** *vi*: **to ~ on (about sthg)** tagarelar (sobre algo).

◆ **rattle through** *vt fus* tratar de encerrar.

rattlesnake ['rætlsneɪk], **rattler** *US* ['rætləʳ] *n* cascavel *f*.

ratty ['rætɪ] (*compar* -**ier**, *superl* -**iest**) *adj inf* -**1.** *UK* [in bad mood] rabugento(ta) -**2.** *US* [in bad condition] surrado(da), roto(ta).

raucous ['rɔːkəs] *adj* -**1.** [laughter, voice] rouco(ca) e estridente -**2.** [behaviour] escandaloso(sa).

raunchy ['rɔːntʃɪ] (*compar* -**ier**, *superl* -**iest**) *adj* insinuante.

ravage ['rævɪdʒ] *vt* devastar.

◆ **ravages** *npl* estragos *mpl*.

rave [reɪv] <> *adj* entusiasmado(da). <> *n UK inf* [party] rave *f*. <> *vi* -**1.** [talk angrily]: **to ~ at sb** xingar alguém; **to ~ against sthg** vociferar contra algo -**2.** [talk enthusiastically]: **to ~ about sthg** falar com entusiasmo sobre algo.

raven ['reɪvn] <> *adj* totalmente negro(gra). <> *n* corvo *m*.

ravenous ['rævənəs] *adj* -**1.** [person, animal] faminto (ta) -**2.** [appetite] voraz.

raver ['reɪvəʳ] *n UK inf* festeiro *m*, -ra *f*.

rave-up *n UK inf* rave *f*.

ravine [rə'viːn] *n* ravina *f*.

raving ['reɪvɪŋ] *adj* [for emphasis] delirante; **~ lunatic** doido *m* varrido, doida *f* varrida.

◆ **ravings** *npl* delírios *mpl*.

ravioli [ˌrævɪ'əʊlɪ] *n (U)* ravióli *m*.

ravish ['rævɪʃ] *vt* -**1.** *literary* [rape] violentar -**2.** [delight] extasiar.

ravishing ['rævɪʃɪŋ] *adj* -**1.** [sight, beauty] extasiante -**2.** [person] belíssimo(ma).

raw [rɔː] *adj* -**1.** [uncooked] cru (crua) -**2.** [untreated] bruto(ta) -**3.** [painful] em carne viva -**4.** [inexperienced] inexperiente -**5.** [cold] frio (fria).

raw deal *n*: **to get a ~** receber um tratamento injusto.

Rawlplug® ['rɔːlplʌg] *n* bucha *f*.

raw material *n* -**1.** [natural substance] matéria-prima *f* -**2.** *(U) fig* [basis] base *f*.

ray [reɪ] *n* -**1.** [beam] raio *m* -**2.** *fig* [glimmer] resquício *m*.

rayon ['reɪɒn] *n (U)* raiom *m*.

raze [reɪz] *vt* destruir completamente, arrasar.

razor ['reɪzəʳ] *n* -**1.** [electric] barbeador *m* elétrico -**2.** [disposable] barbeador *m*, aparelho *m* de barbear.

razor blade *n* lâmina *f* de barbear.

razor-sharp *adj* -**1.** [very sharp] muito afiado(da) -**2.** *fig* [very quick - person] ágil; [- mind] afiado(da), perspicaz.

razzle ['ræzl] *n UK inf*: **to go on the ~** cair na gandaia.

razzmatazz ['ræzəmətæz] *n (U) inf* auê *m*.

R & B (*abbr of* **rhythm and blues**) *n* mistura de ritmos de blues e jazz precursora do rock and roll.

RC (*abbr of* **Roman Catholic**) *adj* católico romano, católica romana.

RCA (*abbr of* **Royal College of Art**) *n* escola londrina de belas artes.

RCAF (*abbr of* **Royal Canadian Air Force**) *n* força aérea real canadense.

RCMP (*abbr of* **Royal Canadian Mounted Police**) *n* polícia montada canadense.

RCN *n* (*abbr of* **Royal Canadian Navy**) *marinha real canadense*.

Rd (*abbr of* **Road**) estrada *f*.

R & D (*abbr of* **research and development**) *n* P & D.

RDC (*abbr of* **Rural District Council**) *n* câmara de vereadores de uma comunidade rural britânica.

re [riː] *prep* referente a.

RE *n* -**1.** (*abbr of* **religious education**) educação *f* religiosa -**2.** (*abbr of* **Royal Engineers**) *unidade de engenharia do exército britânico responsável pela construção de fortes, pontes e outras obras*.

reach [riːtʃ] <> *n* [of arm, boxer] alcance *m*; **within (sb's) ~** [easily touched] ao alcance (de alguém); [easily travelled to] a pouca distância (de alguém); **out of** *OR* **beyond sb's ~** [not easily touched] fora/ além do alcance de alguém; [not easily travelled to] fora/além do alcance de alguém. <> *vt* -**1.** [arrive at] chegar a, alcançar -**2.** [be able to touch] alcançar -**3.** [contact] contatar, entrar em contato com -**4.** [extend as far as] atingir -**5.** [attain, achieve] chegar a. <> *vi* -**1.** [person]: **to ~ out/across** alcançar; **to ~ down** abaixar-se -**2.** [land] alcançar, ir até.

◆ **reaches** *npl*: **the upper/lower ~es** a parte alta/baixa.

reachable ['riːtʃəbl] *adj* -**1.** [accessible] acessível -**2.** [contactable] localizável; **he's ~ by phone** ele pode ser contatado por telefone.

react [rɪ'ækt] *vi* -**1.** [respond]: **to ~ (to sthg)** reagir (a algo) -**2.** [rebel]: **to ~ against sthg** reagir contra algo -**3.** *CHEM*: **to ~ with sthg** reagir com algo.

reaction [rɪ'ækʃn] *n* -**1.** reação *f* -**2.** [response]: **~ (to sthg)** reação *f* (a algo) -**3.** [rebellion]: **~ (against sthg)** reação *f* (contra algo).

reactionary [rɪ'ækʃənrɪ] <> *adj* reacionário(ria). <> *n* reacionário *m*, -ria *f*.

reactivate [rɪ'æktɪveɪt] *vt* reativar.

reactor [rɪ'æktəʳ] *n* [nuclear reactor] reator *m*.

read [riːd] (*pt* & *pp* **read** [red]) <> *n*: **to be a good ~** ser uma boa leitura. <> *vt* -**1.** [gen] ler; **to ~ sb's mind** ler os pensamentos de alguém; **to ~ events** ver os acontecimentos; **the man came to ~ the electricity meter** o funcionário veio tirar a leitura da luz; **to be well ~ in a subject** conhecer bem um assunto -**2.** [subj: sign, notice] dizer; [subj: gauge, meter, barometer] marcar -**3.** *UK UNIV* estudar. <> *vi* -**1.** [person] ler; **to ~ (to sb)** ler (para alguém); **to ~ between the lines** ler nas entrelinhas; **to ~ sb like a book** compreender alguém perfeitamente -**2.** [text]: **it ~s well/badly** isto está bem/mal escrito.

◆ **read into** *vt sep*: **I wouldn't ~ much into what he said** eu não levaria a sério o que ele disse; **what do you ~ into the minister's decision?** como você vê a decisão do ministro?

◆ **read out** *vt sep* ler em voz alta.

◆ **read up on** *vt fus* estudar.

readable ['riːdəbl] *adj* -**1.** [book] interessante de se ler -**2.** *COMPUT* [disk] legível.

readdress [ˌriːəˈdres] vt reendereçar.
reader [ˈriːdə^r] n leitor m, -ra f.
readership [ˈriːdəʃɪp] n público m leitor.
readily [ˈredɪlɪ] adv -1. [willingly] de boa vontade -2. [easily] facilmente.
readiness [ˈredɪnɪs] n (U) -1. [preparedness] prontidão f-2. [willingness]: ~ (to do sthg) presteza (para fazer algo).
reading [ˈriːdɪŋ] n -1. [gen] leitura f -2. [recital] recital m -3. [from gauge, meter, thermometer] marcação f-4. POL [of bill] revisão f.
reading lamp n lâmpada f de leitura.
reading room n sala f de leitura.
readjust [ˌriːəˈdʒʌst] <> vt reajustar. <> vi: to ~ (to sthg) reorganizar-se (para algo).
readmit [ˌriːədˈmɪt] vt readmitir.
readout [ˈriːdaʊt] n COMPUT exibição f de dados.
read-through [riːd-] n olhada f geral.
ready [ˈredɪ] (pt & pp -ied) <> adj -1. [prepared] pronto(ta); to be ~ to do sthg estar pronto(ta) para fazer algo; to be ~ for sthg estar pronto(ta) para algo; to get ~ preparar-se; to get sthg ~ preparar algo -2. [willing]: to be ~ to do sthg estar disposto(ta) a fazer algo -3. [in need of]: to be ~ for sthg precisar de algo -4. [likely]: to be ~ to do sthg estar prestes a fazer algo -5. [easily accessible] à mão. <> vt preparar.
ready cash n (U) dinheiro m em mão.
ready-made adj pronto(ta).
ready money n (U) dinheiro m à vista.
ready-to-wear adj prêt-à-porter.
reaffirm [ˌriːəˈfɜːm] vt reafirmar.
reafforest [ˌriːəˈfɒrɪst] vt reflorestar.
reafforestation [ˈriːəˌfɒrɪˈsteɪʃn] n (U) reflorestamento m.
real [ˈrɪəl] <> adj -1. [gen] real; in ~ terms em termos reais-2. [authentic - problem, situation] real; [- gold, jewels,] legítimo(ma); the ~ thing a verdade; a ~ job um emprego de verdade; it's for ~ é real -3. [for emphasis] verdadeiro(ra). <> adv US bem.
real ale n (U) UK cerveja f artesanal.
real estate n (U) bens mpl imobiliários.
realign [ˌriːəˈlaɪn] vt -1. POL reorganizar -2. [brakes] realinhar.
realignment [ˌriːəˈlaɪnmənt] n -1. POL reestruturação f-2. [of wheels] realinhamento m.
realism [ˈrɪəlɪzml] n (U)-1. [common sense] bom senso m-2. [artistic style] realismo m.
realist [ˈrɪəlɪst] n realista mf.
realistic [ˌrɪəˈlɪstɪk] adj realista; ~ chance chance real; to be ~ about sthg ser realista em relação a algo.
realistically [ˌrɪəˈlɪstɪklɪ] adv -1. [reasonably] realisticamente -2. [accurately] de forma realista.
reality [rɪˈælətɪ] (pl -ies) n [gen] realidade f; in ~ [in fact] na realidade; [in real life] na vida real.
reality TV n (U) reality shows mpl.
realization [ˌrɪəlaɪˈzeɪʃn] n (U) -1. [awareness, recognition] percepção f-2. [achievement] realização f.
realize, -ise [ˈrɪəlaɪz] vt -1. [become aware of, understand] perceber, dar-se conta de -2. [achieve] concretizar -3. COMM atingir.

reallocate [ˌriːˈæləkeɪt] vt realocar.
really [ˈrɪəlɪ] <> adv -1. [gen] realmente -2. [to reduce force of negative statements] na real. <> excl -1. [expressing doubt]: really? é mesmo?, não é mesmo? -2. [expressing surprise, disbelief]: really? mesmo? -3. [expressing disapproval]: really! francamente!
realm [relm] n -1. [field] domínio m -2. [kingdom] reino m.
real-time adj COMPUT de tempo real.
realtor [ˈrɔːltər] n US corretor m, -ra f de imóveis.
ream [riːm] n resma f.
➡ **reams** npl fig [a lot] páginas fpl e páginas.
reap [riːp] vt colher; you ~ what you sow você colhe o que planta.
reappear [ˌriːəˈpɪə^r] vi reaparecer.
reappearance [ˌriːəˈpɪərəns] n reaparecimento m.
reapply [ˌriːəˈplaɪ] (pt & pp -ied) vi reaplicar; to ~ for sthg recandidatar-se a algo.
reappraisal [ˌriːəˈpreɪzl] n reavaliação f.
reappraise [ˌriːəˈpreɪz] vt reavaliar.
rear [rɪə^r] <> adj -1. [door, window] dos fundos-2. [wheel] traseiro(ra). <> n -1. [back - of building] fundos mpl; [- of vehicle] traseira f; to be at the ~ estar no final; to bring up the ~ fechar a raia-2. inf [buttocks] bunda f. <> vt -1. [children, animals, plants] criar -2. fig [lift up]: it has ~ed its head again ele deu as caras novamente. <> vi: to ~ (up) empinar, empinar-se.
rear admiral n contra-almirante m.
rearguard action [ˈrɪəgɑːd-] n ação f pela retaguarda.
rear light n lanterna f traseira.
rearm [riːˈɑːm] vt & vi rearmar.
rearmament [rɪˈɑːməmənt] n (U) rearmamento m.
rearmost [ˈrɪəməʊst] adj último(ma).
rearrange [ˌriːəˈreɪndʒ] vt -1. [arrange differently] reorganizar -2. [reschedule] reajustar.
rearrangement [ˌriːəˈreɪndʒmənt] n -1. [different arrangement] reorganização f -2. [rescheduling] reajuste m.
rearview mirror [ˈrɪəvjuː-] n espelho m retrovisor.
reason [ˈriːzn] <> n -1. [cause] razão f, motivo m; ~ for sthg razão para algo; by ~ of fml em razão de; for some ~ por alguma razão -2. (U) [justification]: to have ~ to do sthg ter razões para fazer algo -3. (U) [rationality, common sense] razão f; to listen to ~ ouvir a razão; it stands to ~ é lógico. <> vt concluir. <> vi raciocinar.
➡ **reason with** vt fus argumentar com.
reasonable [ˈriːznəbl] adj -1. [sensible] sensato(ta) -2. [acceptable] razoável -3. [fairly large] aceitável.
reasonably [ˈriːznəblɪ] adv -1. [quite] razoavelmente -2. [sensibly] sensatamente.
reasoned [ˈriːznd] adj racional.
reasoning [ˈriːznɪŋ] n (U) raciocínio m.
reassemble [ˌriːəˈsembl] <> vt -1. [machinery] remontar -2. [people] reagrupar. <> vi reunir-se novamente.
reassess [ˌriːəˈses] vt reavaliar.
reassessment [ˌriːəˈsesmənt] n reavaliação f.

reassurance [ˌriːəˈʃɔːrəns] n - 1. (U) [comfort] reconforto m - 2. [promise] nova garantia f.

reassure [ˌriːəˈʃɔːʳ] vt tranqüilizar.

reassuring [ˌriːəˈʃɔːrɪŋ] adj tranqüilizador(ra).

reawaken [ˌriːəˈweɪkn] vt redespertar.

rebate ['riːbeɪt] n restituição f.

rebel [n 'rebl, vb rɪ'bel] (pt & pp -led, cont -ling) ⟨⟩ n rebelde mf. ⟨⟩ vi - 1. [revolt]: to ~ (against sb/sthg) rebelar-se (contra alguém/algo) - 2. [not conform]: to ~ (against sb/sthg) revoltar-se (contra alguém/algo).

rebellion [rɪ'beljən] n - 1. [armed revolt] rebelião f - 2. [opposition] oposição f - 3. (U) [nonconformity] revolta f.

rebellious [rɪ'beljəs] adj rebelde.

rebirth [ˌriː'bɜːθ] n (U) renascimento m.

rebound [n 'riːbaʊnd, vb ˌrɪ'baʊnd] ⟨⟩ n: on the ~ [ball] no ricochete; [person] no impulso. ⟨⟩ vi - 1. [ball] ricochetear - 2. [harm]: to ~ (up)on sb recair sobre alguém.

rebuff [rɪ'bʌf] ⟨⟩ n recusa f. ⟨⟩ vt recusar.

rebuild [ˌriː'bɪld] (pt & pp -built) vt reconstruir.

rebuke [rɪ'bjuːk] ⟨⟩ n reprimenda f. ⟨⟩ vt: to ~ sb (for sthg) repreender alguém (por algo).

rebut [rɪ'bʌt] (pt & pp -ted, cont -ting) vt refutar.

rebuttal [rɪ'bʌtl] n refutação f.

rec n inf - 1. (abbr of recreation ground) UK playground m - 2. (abbr of recreation) US recreação f.

rec. (abbr of received) recebido.

recalcitrant [rɪ'kælsɪtrənt] adj obstinado(da).

recall [rɪ'kɔːl] ⟨⟩ n - 1. (U) [memory] recordação f - 2. [on faulty goods] recall m - 3. [change]: beyond ~ impossível de ser alterado(da). ⟨⟩ vt - 1. [remember] relembrar-se de - 2. [summon back - parliament] reconvocar; [- ambassador] chamar de volta.

recant [rɪ'kænt] ⟨⟩ vt - 1. [faith, religion] renegar - 2. [statement] retirar - 3. [opinion] reconsiderar. ⟨⟩ vi retratar-se.

recap ['riːkæp] (pt & pp -ped, cont -ping) inf ⟨⟩ n recapitulação f. ⟨⟩ vt - 1. [summarize] recapitular - 2. US [tyre] recauchutar. ⟨⟩ vi [summarize] recapitular.

recapitulate [ˌriːkə'pɪtjʊleɪt] vt & vi recapitular.

recapture [ˌriː'kæptʃəʳ] ⟨⟩ n recaptura f. ⟨⟩ vt - 1. [prisoner, town] recapturar - 2. [mood, feeling] resgatar.

recd, rec'd (abbr of received) recebido.

recede [riː'siːd] vi - 1. [move away] afastar-se - 2. fig [disappear, fade] desaparecer - 3. [subj: hair] formar entradas.

receding [rɪ'siːdɪŋ] adj - 1. [hair]: ~ hairline entrada f (no cabelo) - 2. [chin]: ~ chin queixo m retraído.

receipt [rɪ'siːt] n - 1. [piece of paper] recibo m - 2. (U) [act of receiving] recebimento m.
→ **receipts** npl receita f.

receivable [rɪ'siːvəbl] adj a receber.

receive [rɪ'siːv] ⟨⟩ vt - 1. [gen] receber - 2. [welcome] recepcionar - 3. [greet]: to be well/badly ~ d ser bem/mal recebido(da). ⟨⟩ vi [in tennis etc] receber.

receiver [rɪ'siːvəʳ] n - 1. [of telephone] fone m - 2. [radio, TV set] receptor m - 3. [criminal] receptador m, -ra f - 4. FIN [official] curador m, -ra f.

receivership [rɪ'siːvəʃɪp] n (U): to go into ~ ir para curadoria.

receiving end [rɪ'siːvɪŋ-] n: to be on the ~ (of sthg) estar na linha de tiro (de algo).

recent ['riːsnt] adj recente.

recently ['riːsntlɪ] adv recentemente; until ~, no one knew of his existence até pouco tempo atrás, ninguém sabia da existência dele.

receptacle [rɪ'septəkl] n recipiente m.

reception [rɪ'sepʃn] n recepção f.

reception centre n UK (centro m de) alojamento m.

reception class n aula f de boas-vindas.

reception desk n recepção f.

receptionist [rɪ'sepʃənɪst] n recepcionista mf.

reception room n recepção f.

receptive [rɪ'septɪv] adj receptivo(va); to be ~ to sthg ser receptivo(va) a algo.

receptiveness n (U) receptividade f.

recess ['riːses, UK rɪ'ses] n - 1. [vacation] recesso m; to be in/go into ~ estar/entrar em recesso - 2. [alcove] reentrância f, vão m - 3. [of mind, memory] refluxo m - 4. US SCH recreio m, intervalo m.

recessed ['riːsest, UK rɪ'sest] adj embutido(da).

recession [rɪ'seʃn] n recessão f.

recessionary [rɪ'seʃənrɪ] adj recessivo(va).

recessive [rɪ'sesɪv] adj recessivo(va).

recharge [ˌriː'tʃɑːdʒ] vt recarregar.

rechargeable [ˌriː'tʃɑːdʒəbl] adj recarregável.

recipe ['resɪpɪ] n receita f.

recipient [rɪ'sɪpɪənt] ⟨⟩ adj recebedor(ra), receptor(ra). ⟨⟩ n - 1. [of letter] destinatário(ria) - 2. [of cheque] beneficiário(ria) - 3. [of award] ganhador(ra).

reciprocal [rɪ'sɪprəkl] adj recíproco(ca).

reciprocate [rɪ'sɪprəkeɪt] ⟨⟩ vt retribuir a. ⟨⟩ vi retribuir.

recital [rɪ'saɪtl] n recital m.

recitation [ˌresɪ'teɪʃn] n recitação f.

recite [rɪ'saɪt] vt - 1. [perform aloud] recitar - 2. [list] enumerar.

reckless ['reklɪs] adj imprudente.

recklessness ['reklɪsnɪs] n (U) imprudência f.

reckon ['rekn] vt - 1. inf [think] achar - 2. [consider, judge]: he was ~ ed to be too old for the job ele foi considerado velho demais para o trabalho - 3. [expect]: to ~ to do sthg esperar fazer algo - 4. [calculate] calcular.
→ **reckon on** vt fus contar com.
→ **reckon with** vt fus - 1. [expect] esperar - 2. [face, deal with]: a force to be ~ ed with uma força a ser considerada.
→ **reckon without** vt fus não levar em conta.

reckoning ['rekənɪŋ] n cálculo m; day of ~ dia do ajuste de contas.

reclaim [rɪ'kleɪm] vt - 1. [claim back] recuperar - 2. [make fit for use] desbravar.

reclamation [ˌreklə'meɪʃn] n (U) aproveitamento m.

recline [rɪ'klaɪn] vi reclinar-se.

reclining [rɪ'klaɪnɪŋ] adj reclinável.

recluse [rɪ'kluːs] n recluso m, -sa f.

reclusive [rɪ'kluːsɪv] adj recluso(sa).

recognition [ˌrekəg'nɪʃn] n - 1. [identification]

reconhecimento *m*; **beyond** OR **out of all** ~ irreconhecível- **2.** [acknowledgment] identificação f; **in** ~ **of** em reconhecimento a.

recognizable ['rekəgnaɪzəbl] *adj* reconhecível; **he was barely** ~ mal dava para reconhecê-lo.

recognize, -ise ['rekəgnaɪz] *vt* reconhecer.

recoil [*vb* rɪ'kɔɪl, *n* 'ri:kɔɪl] ◇ *n* coice *m*. ◇ *vi* recuar; **to** ~ **from/at sthg** recuar diante de algo; **she** ~**ed at his suggestion** ela recuou diante da sugestão dele.

recollect [,rekə'lekt] *vt* recordar-se de, lembrar-se de.

recollection [,rekə'lekʃn] *n* recordação f, lembrança f.

recommence [,ri:kə'mens] *vt* & *vi* recomeçar.

recommend [,rekə'mend] *vt* - **1.** [commend, speak in favour of]: **to** ~ **sb/sthg (to sb)** recomendar alguém/algo (para alguém) - **2.** [advise] recomendar.

recommendation [,rekəmen'deɪʃn] *n* recomendação f.

recommended retail price [,rekə'mendɪd-] *n* preço *m* sugerido ao varejo.

recompense ['rekəmpens] ◇ *n*: ~ **(for sthg)** recompensa (por algo). ◇ *vt*: **to** ~ **sb (for sthg)** recompensar alguém (por algo).

reconcile ['rekənsaɪl] *vt* - **1.** [beliefs, ideas] conciliar; **to** ~ **sthg with sthg** conciliar algo com algo - **2.** [people] reconciliar; **to be** ~**d with sb** reconciliar-se com alguém- **3.** [resign]: **to** ~ **o.s. to sthg** resignar-se a algo.

reconciliation [,rekənsɪlɪ'eɪʃn] *n* - **1.** [of beliefs, ideas] conciliação f- **2.** [of people] reconciliação f.

recondite ['rekəndaɪt] *adj fml* recôndito(ta).

reconditioned [,ri:kən'dɪʃnd] *adj* recondicionado(da).

reconnaissance [rɪ'kɒnɪsəns] *n (U)* reconhecimento *m*.

reconnect [,ri:kə'nekt] *vt* religar.

reconnoitre UK, **reconnoiter** US [,rekə'nɔɪtə^r] ◇ *vt* reconhecer. ◇ *vi* fazer um reconhecimento.

reconsider [,ri:kən'sɪdə^r] *vt* & *vi* reconsiderar.

reconstitute [,ri:'kɒnstɪtju:t] *vt* - **1.** [re-form] reconstituir - **2.** [dried food] hidratar.

reconstruct [,ri:kən'strʌkt] *vt* reconstruir.

reconstruction [,ri:kən'strʌkʃn] *n* - **1.** [gen] reconstrução f- **2.** [of event, crime] reconstituição f.

reconvene [,ri:kən'vi:n] *vt* reunir-se novamente.

record [*n* & *adj* 'rekɔ:d, *vb* rɪ'kɔ:d] ◇ *adj* recorde. ◇ *n* - **1.** [gen] registro *m*; **off the** ~ em off; **on** ~ [on file] em registro; [ever recorded] já registrado(da); **to go on** ~ [say publicly] ir a público - **2.** [vinyl disc] disco *m* - **3.** [best achievement] recorde *m* - **4.** *phr*: **to set** OR **put the** ~ **straight** corrigir um mal-entendido. ◇ *vt* - **1.** [write down] registrar - **2.** [put on tape etc] gravar.

record-breaker *n* recordista *mf*.

record-breaking *adj* que quebra recordes.

recorded delivery [rɪ'kɔ:dɪd-] *n (U)*: **to send sthg by** ~ enviar algo como carta registrada.

recorder [rɪ'kɔ:də^r] *n* - **1.** [machine] gravador *m*- **2.** [musical instrument] flauta f doce.

record holder *n* detentor *m*, -ra f do recorde.

recording [rɪ'kɔ:dɪŋ] *n* gravação f.

recording studio *n* estúdio *m* de gravação.

record library *n* discoteca f.

record player *n* toca-discos *m*.

recount [*n* 'ri:kaʊnt, *vt sense 1* rɪ'kaʊnt, *sense 2* ,ri:'kaʊnt] ◇ *n* recontagem f. ◇ *vt* - **1.** [narrate] relatar - **2.** [count again] recontar.

recoup [rɪ'ku:p] *vt* recuperar.

recourse [rɪ'kɔ:s] *n (U) fml*: **to have** ~ **to sthg** recorrer a algo.

recover [rɪ'kʌvə^r] ◇ *vt* - **1.** [stolen goods, money] recuperar; **to** ~ **sthg (from sb/somewhere)** recuperar algo (de alguém/algum lugar) - **2.** [consciousness, one's breath] recobrar; **to** ~ **o.s.** recuperar-se. ◇ *vi* - **1.** [from illness, accident] [finances]: **to** ~ **(from sthg)** recuperar-se (de algo)- **2.** [from shock, setback, sb's death]: **to** ~ **(from sthg)** refazer-se (de algo).

recoverable [rɪ'kʌvrəbl] *adj* FIN recuperável.

recovery [rɪ'kʌvərɪ] (*pl* -ies) *n* - **1.**: ~ **(from sthg)** recuperação (de algo) - **2.** recuperação f.

recovery vehicle *n* UK guincho *m*.

recreate ['ri:krɪ,eɪt] *vt* recriar.

recreation [,rekrɪ'eɪʃn] *n (U)* recreação f, divertimento *m*.

recreational [,rekrɪ'eɪʃənl] *adj* recreativo(ta); ~ **facilities** local para recreação.

recreation room *n* - **1.** [in public building] sala f de recreação - **2.** US [in house] sala f de jogos.

recrimination [rɪ,krɪmɪ'neɪʃn] *n (U)* recriminação f.

➡ **recriminations** *npl* recriminações *fpl*.

recrudescence [,ri:kru:'desns] *n fml* recrudescimento *m*.

recruit [rɪ'kru:t] ◇ *n* recruta *mf*. ◇ *vt* recrutar; **to** ~ **sb (for sthg/to do sthg)** recrutar alguém (para algo/para fazer algo). ◇ *vi* [take on new staff] recrutar gente.

recruitment [rɪ'kru:tmənt] *n (U)* recrutamento *m*.

rectangle ['rek,tæŋgl] *n* retângulo *m*.

rectangular [rek'tæŋgjolə^r] *adj* retangular.

rectification [,rektɪfɪ'keɪʃn] *n (U) fml* retificação f.

rectify ['rektɪfaɪ] (*pt* & *pp* -**ied**) *vt fml* retificar.

rectitude ['rektɪtju:d] *n (U) fml* retidão f.

rector ['rektə^r] *n* - **1.** [priest] pároco *m*- **2.** Scot [head - of school] diretor *m*, -ra f; [- of college, university] reitor *m*, -ra f.

rectory ['rektərɪ] (*pl* -ies) *n* residência f paroquial.

rectum ['rektəm] (*pl* -s) *n* reto *m*.

recuperate [rɪ'ku:pəreɪt] *vi fml*: **to** ~ **(from sthg)** restabelecer-se (de algo).

recuperation [rɪ,ku:pə'reɪʃn] *n (U)* recuperação f, restabelecimento *m*.

recur [rɪ'kɜ:^r] (*pt* & *pp* -**red**, *cont* -**ring**) *vi* repetir-se.

recurrence [rɪ'kʌrəns] *n fml* recorrência f.

recurrent [rɪ'kʌrənt] *adj* recorrente.

recurring [rɪ'kɜ:rɪŋ] *adj* - **1.** [often repeated] recorrente - **2.** MATH periódico(ca).

recyclable [,ri:'saɪkləbl] *adj* reciclável.

recycle [,ri:'saɪkl] *vt* reciclar.

recycling *n* reciclagem f.

red [red] (*compar* -**der**, *superl* -**dest**) ◇ *adj* - **1.** [gen]

vermelho(lha) **-2.** [hair] ruivo(va). ◇ *n (U)* [colour] vermelho *m*; **to be in the** ~ *inf* estar no vermelho; **to see** ~ enfurecer-se.

◆ **Red** *pej* ◇ *adj* [left-wing, communist] vermelho(lha). ◇ *n* [left-winger, communist] vermelho *m*, lha *f*.

red alert *n* **-1.** *(U)* [state of readiness]: **on** ~ em alerta vermelho **-2.** [order to be ready] alerta *f* vermelho.

red blood cell *n* glóbulo *m* vermelho.

red-blooded [-'blʌdɪd] *adj hum* com aquilo roxo.

red-brick *adj UK* [building] de tijolo à vista.

◆ **redbrick** *adj UK UNIV:* **redbrick university** *universidade construída em grandes centros fora de Londres nos séculos XIX e XX.*

red card *n FTBL:* **to be shown the** ~, **to get a** ~ receber cartão vermelho.

red carpet *n:* **to roll out the** ~ **for sb** estender o tapete vermelho para alguém.

◆ **red-carpet** *adj:* **to give sb the red-carpet treatment** dar tratamento VIP para alguém.

Red Crescent *n:* **the** ~ o Crescente Vermelho.

Red Cross *n:* **the** ~ a Cruz Vermelha.

redcurrant ['redkʌrənt] *n* **-1.** [fruit] groselha *f* **-2.** [bush] groselheira *f*.

red deer *n* veado *m*.

redden ['rednl] ◇ *vt* [make red] avermelhar. ◇ *vi* [flush] ruborizar-se, ficar ruborizado(da).

redecorate [ˌriː'dekəreɪt] ◇ *vt* redecorar. ◇ *vi* redecorar a casa.

redeem [rɪ'diːm] *vt* **-1.** [save, rescue] redimir; **to** ~ **o.s.** redimir-se **-2.** [from pawnbroker] resgatar.

redeemer *n RELIG:* **the Redeemer** o Redentor.

redeeming [rɪ'diːmɪŋ] *adj* redentor, que redime.

redefine [ˌriːdɪ'faɪnl] *vt* redefinir.

redemption [rɪ'dempʃn] *n (U) RELIG* redenção *f*, salvação *f*; **beyond** *OR* **past** ~ *fig* irrecuperável.

redeploy [ˌriːdɪ'plɔɪl] *vt* remanejar.

redeployment [ˌriːdɪ'plɔɪmənt] *n (U)* remanejamento *m*.

redesign [ˌriːdɪ'zaɪn] *vt* **-1.** [replan, redraw] remodelar **-2.** [reorganize, rethink] repensar.

redevelop [ˌriːdɪ'veləp] *vt* renovar.

redevelopment [ˌriːdɪ'veləpmənt] *n (U)* renovação *f*.

red-faced [-'feɪst] *adj* **-1.** [after exercise, with heat] vermelho(lha) **-2.** [with embarrassment] corado(da).

red-haired [-'heəd] *adj* ruivo(va).

red-handed [-'hændɪd] *adj:* **to catch sb** ~ pegar alguém com a mão na massa.

redhead ['redhed] *n* ruiva *f*.

red herring *n fig* pista *f* falsa.

red-hot *adj* **-1.** [extremely hot] em brasa **-2.** [very enthusiastic] apaixonado(da) **-3.** *inf* [very good] supimpa.

redid [ˌriː'dɪd] *pt* ⊳ **redo**.

Red Indian ◇ *adj* dos peles-vermelhas. ◇ *n* pele-vermelha *mf*.

redirect [ˌriːdɪ'rekt] *vt* **-1.** [mail] redirecionar **-2.** [traffic, aircraft] desviar **-3.** [one's energies, money, aid] direcionar.

rediscover [ˌriːdɪs'kʌvə^r] *vt* **-1.** [re-experience] redescobrir **-2.** [make popular, famous again]: **to be**

~ **ed** ser redescoberto(ta).

redistribute [ˌriːdɪs'trɪbjuːt] *vt* redistribuir.

red-letter day *n* dia *m* memorável.

red light *n* [traffic signal] luz *f* vermelha.

red-light district *n* zona *f* do baixo meretrício.

red meat *n (U)* carne *f* vermelha.

red mullet *n* salmonete *m*.

redness ['rednɪs] *n (U)* vermelhidão *f*.

redo [ˌriː'duː] *(pt* **-did***, pp* **-done***) vt* **-1.** [do again] refazer **-2.** *inf* [redecorate] redecorar.

redolent ['redələnt] *adj literary* **-1.** [reminiscent]: ~ **of** sthg rememorativo(va) de algo **-2.** [smelling]: ~ **of** sthg com aroma de algo.

redone *pp* ⊳ **redo**.

redouble [ˌriː'dʌbl] *vt:* **to** ~ **one's efforts (to do sthg)** redobrar os esforços (para fazer algo).

redoubtable [rɪ'daʊtəbl] *adj fml* formidável.

redraft [ˌriː'drɑːft] *vt* reescrever.

redraw [ˌriː'drɔː] *(pt* **-drew***, pp* **-drawn** [-'drɔːn]*) vt* redesenhar.

redress [rɪ'dres] *fml* ◇ *n (U)* retificação *f.* ◇ *vt:* **to** ~ **the balance** compensar.

redrew [ˌriː'druː] *pt* ⊳ **redraw**.

Red Sea *n:* **the** ~ o Mar Vermelho.

red setter *n* cão *m* perdigueiro.

Red Square *n* Praça *f* Vermelha.

red squirrel *n* esquilo *m* vermelho.

red tape *n (U) fig* burocracia *f*.

reduce [rɪ'djuːs] ◇ *vt* **-1.** [make smaller, less] reduzir; **to** ~ **sthg to a pulp** reduzir algo à essência **-2.** *CULIN* engrossar no fogo **-3.** [force, bring]: **to be** ~ **d to doing sthg** ser forçado(da) a fazer algo; **to be** ~ **d to sthg** estar reduzido(da) a algo. ◇ *vi US* [lose weight] emagrecer.

reduced [rɪ'djuːst] *adj* reduzido(da); **in** ~ **circumstances** em circunstâncias limitadas.

reduction [rɪ'dʌkʃn] *n* **-1.** [decrease]: ~ **(in sthg)** redução (em algo) **-2.** [amount of decrease]: ~ **(of)** redução de.

redundancy [rɪ'dʌndənsɪ] *(pl* **-ies***) n UK* **-1.** [job loss] demissão *f* **-2.** *(U)* [jobless state] desemprego *m*.

redundancy payment *n UK* indenização *f (por demissão sem justa causa).*

redundant [rɪ'dʌndənt] *adj* **-1.** *UK* [jobless]: **to be made** ~ ficar desempregado(da) **-2.** [superfluous] supérfluo(a).

redwood ['redwʊd] *n:* **a** ~ **(tree)** uma sequóia.

re-echo ◇ *vt* [repeat] repetir. ◇ *vi* [echo] repercutir, ecoar.

reed [riːd] ◇ *n* **-1.** [plant] junco *m* **-2.** [of musical instrument] palheta *f.* ◇ *comp* [made of reeds] de junco.

re-educate *vt* reabilitar.

reedy ['riːdɪ] *(compar* **-ier***, superl* **-iest***) adj* [voice] estridente.

reef [riːfl] *n* recife *m*.

reek [riːk] ◇ *n* fedor *m.* ◇ *vi:* **to** ~ **(of sthg)** feder (a algo).

reel [riːll] ◇ *n* **-1.** [roll] rolo *m* **-2.** [on fishing rod] molinete *m.* ◇ *vi* **-1.** [stagger] cambalear **-2.** [head, mind] girar; **to** ~ **from sthg** estar confuso(sa) por (causa de) algo.

◆ **reel in** *vt sep* enrolar.

➡ **reel off** *vt sep* [list] enumerar.

re-elect *vt*: **to ~ sb (as) sthg** reeleger alguém (como algo).

re-election *n (U)* reeleição *f*.

re-emphasize *vt* reenfatizar.

re-enact *vt* reviver.

re-enter *vt* **-1.** [room, country] reentrar em **-2.** COMPUT [data] reinserir em.

re-entry *n* **-1.** [into room, country] reentrada *f* **-2.** COMPUT [of data] reinserção *f*.

re-examine *vt* **-1.** [question, case] reexaminar **-2.** [witness] reinquirir **-3.** [candidate] rever.

re-export COMM ◇ *n* **-1.** *(U)* [act of exporting] reexportação *f* **-2.** [goods exported] reexportações *fpl*. ◇ *vt* reexportar.

ref [ref] *n* **-1.** *inf (abbr of* referee*)* SPORT árbitro *m* **-2.** *(abbr of* reference*)* ADMIN ref.

refectory [rɪ'fektərɪ] *(pl* -ies*)* *n* **-1.** [in school, college] cantina *f* **-2.** [in monastery] refeitório *m*.

refer [rɪ'fɜː^r] *(pt & pp* -red, *cont* -ring*)* *vt* **-1.** [person]: **to ~ sb to sthg** encaminhar alguém para algo **-2.** [report, case, decision]: **to ~ sthg to sb/sthg** encaminhar algo para alguém/algo.

➡ **refer to** *vt fus* **-1.** [mention, speak about] referir-se a **-2.** [apply to, concern] aplicar-se a **-3.** [consult] consultar.

referee [,refə'riː] ◇ *n* **-1.** SPORT árbitro *m*, -tra *f* **-2.** *UK* [for job application] referência *f*. ◇ *vt & vi* SPORT apitar.

reference ['refrəns] *n* **-1.** [gen] referência *f* **-2.** *(U)* [act of mentioning]: **to make ~ to sb/sthg** referência a alguém/algo; **with ~ to** *fml* com referência a **-3.** [mention]: **~ (to sb/sthg)** menção a alguém /algo **-4.** *(U)* [for advice, information]: **~ (to sb/sthg)** referência a alguém/algo; **for future ~** para consulta futura **-5.** COMM [in letter] referências *fpl*.

reference book *n* livro *m* de consulta.

reference library *n* biblioteca *f* de consulta.

reference number *n* número *m* de referência.

referendum [,refə'rendəm] *(pl* -s *OR* -da [-də]*)* *n* POL plebiscito *m*.

referral [rɪ'fɜːrəl] *n fml* referência *f*.

refill [*n* 'riː.fɪl, *vb* ,riː'fɪl] ◇ *n* **-1.** [for pen, lighter] carga *f* nova **-2.** *inf* [drink] dose *f* extra. ◇ *vt* [fill again - bottle, glass] encher novamente; [- petrol tank] reabastecer.

refillable [,riː'fɪləbl] *adj* recarregável.

refine [rɪ'faɪn] *vt* **-1.** [purify] refinar **-2.** [details, speech] aprimorar.

refined [rɪ'faɪnd] *adj* refinado(da).

refinement [rɪ'faɪnmənt] *n* **-1.** [improvement]: **~ (on sthg)** refinamento (de algo) **-2.** *(U)* [gentility] requinte *m*.

refinery [rɪ'faɪnərɪ] *(pl* -ies*)* *n* refinaria *f*.

refit [*n* 'riː.fɪt, *vb* ,riː'fɪt] *(pt & pp* -ted, *cont* -ting*)* ◇ *n* [of ship] reaparelhamento *m*. ◇ *vt* [ship] reaparelhar.

reflate [,riː'fleɪt] *vt* ECON reinflacionar.

reflation [,riː'fleɪʃn] *n (U)* ECON reflação *f*.

reflationary [riː'fleɪʃənrɪ] *adj* ECON reflacionário(-ria).

reflect [rɪ'flekt] ◇ *vt* refletir; **to be ~ed in sthg** estar refletido(da) em algo, refletir-se em algo; **to**

~ that ... refletir que ... ◇ *vi* [think, consider]: **to ~ (on** *OR* **upon sthg)** refletir (sobre algo).

reflection [rɪ'flekʃn] *n* **-1.** [gen] reflexo *m* **-2.** [comment, thought] reflexão *f*; **~ on sthg** reflexão sobre algo; **on ~** pensando bem.

reflective [rɪ'flektɪv] *adj* **-1.** [thoughtful] reflexivo(va) **-2.** [shiny] brilhante.

reflector [rɪ'flektə^r] *n* refletor *m*.

reflex ['riːfleks] *n*: **~ (action)** (ato) reflexo *m*.

➡ **reflexes** *npl* reflexos *mpl*.

reflex camera *n* câmera *f* reflex.

reflexive [rɪ'fleksɪv] *adj* GRAMM reflexivo(va).

reflexology [,riːflek'sɒlədʒɪ] *n* reflexoterapia *f*.

reforest [,riː'fɒrɪst] *vt esp US* = **reafforest**.

reforestation [riː,fɒrɪ'steɪʃn] *n esp US* = **reafforestation**.

reform [rɪ'fɔːm] ◇ *n* reforma *f*. ◇ *vt* **-1.** [change] reformar **-2.** [improve behaviour of] corrigir. ◇ *vi* corrigir-se.

reformat [,riː'fɔːmæt] *(pt & pp* -ted, *cont* -ting*)* *vt* COMPUT reformatar.

Reformation [,refə'meɪʃn] *n*: **the ~** a Reforma.

reformatory [rɪ'fɔːmətrɪ] *(pl* -ies*)* *n US* reformatório *m*.

reformed [rɪ'fɔːmd] *adj* regenerado(da).

reformer [rɪ'fɔːmə^r] *n* reformador *m*, -ra *f*.

reformist [rɪ'fɔːmɪst] ◇ *adj* reformista. ◇ *n* reformista *mf*.

refract [rɪ'frækt] ◇ *vt* refratar. ◇ *vi* refratar-se.

refrain [rɪ'freɪn] ◇ *n* refrão *m*. ◇ *vi fml*: **to ~ from doing sthg** abster-se de fazer algo.

refresh [rɪ'freʃ] *vt* refrescar; **to ~ sb's memory** refrescar a memória de alguém.

refreshed [rɪ'freʃt] *adj* revigorado(da).

refresher course [rɪ'freʃə^r-] *n* curso *m* de aperfeiçoamento *OR* atualização.

refreshing [rɪ'freʃɪŋ] *adj* **-1.** [pleasantly different] reconfortante **-2.** [cooling, energy-giving] refrescante.

refreshments [rɪ'freʃmənts] *npl* comes *mpl* e bebes, lanche *m*.

refrigerate [rɪ'frɪdʒəreɪt] *vt* refrigerar.

refrigeration [rɪ,frɪdʒə'reɪʃn] *n (U)* refrigeração *f*.

refrigerator [rɪ'frɪdʒəreɪtə^r] *n* geladeira *f*, refrigerador *m*.

refuel [,riː'fjʊəl] *(UK pt & pp* -led, *cont* -ling, *US pt & pp* -ed, *cont* -ing*)* ◇ *vt* reabastecer. ◇ *vi* reabastecer-se *(de combustível)*.

refuge ['refjuːdʒ] *n* **-1.** [place of safety] refúgio *m* **-2.** *(U)* [safety]: **to seek** *OR* **take ~** [hide] procurar refúgio, refugiar-se; **to seek** *OR* **take ~ in sthg** *fig* procurar *OR* buscar refúgio em algo, refugiar-se em algo.

refugee [,refjʊ'dʒiː] *n* refugiado *m*, -da *f*.

refugee camp *n* campo *m* de refugiados.

refund [*n* 'riː.fʌnd, *vb* rɪ'fʌnd] ◇ *n* reembolso *m*. ◇ *vt*: **to ~ sthg to sb, to ~ sb sthg** reembolsar algo a alguém.

refurbish [,riː'fɜːbɪʃ] *vt* **-1.** [shop, office] reformar **-2.** [building] restaurar.

refurbishment [,riː'fɜːbɪʃmənt] *n* **-1.** [of shop, office] reforma *f* **-2.** [building] restauração *f*.

refurnish [,riː'fɜːnɪʃ] *vt* mobiliar novamente.

refusal [rɪ'fju:zl] *n* recusa *f*; **her ~ to accept the conditions** o fato de ela não ter aceitado as condições; **to meet with ~** ser rechaçado(da).

refuse¹ [rɪ'fju:z] <> *vt* - **1.** [withhold, deny]: **to ~ sb sthg**, **to ~ sthg to sb** negar algo a alguém - **2.** [decline] recusar; **to ~ to do sthg** recusar-se a fazer algo, negar-se a fazer algo. <> *vi* negar-se, dizer que não.

refuse² ['refju:s] *n (U)* lixo *m*, refugo *m*.

refuse collection ['refju:s-] *n* coleta *f* de lixo.

refuse collector ['refju:s-] *n* lixeiro *m*, -ra *f*.

refuse dump ['refju:s-] *n* depósito *m* de lixo, lixeira *f*.

refute [rɪ'fju:t] *vt fml* refutar.

reg. (*abbr of* **registered**): **~ trademark** marca *f* registrada.

regain [rɪ'geɪn] *vt* recuperar.

regal ['ri:gl] *adj* régio(gia).

regale [rɪ'geɪl] *vt*: **to ~ sb with sthg** entreter alguém com algo.

regalia [rɪ'geɪljə] *n (U) fml* insígnias *fpl* reais.

regard [rɪ'gɑ:d] <> *n* - **1.** *(U) fml* [respect, esteem] respeito *m*, estima *f*; **~ (for sb/sthg)** respeito *or* estima (por alguém/algo) - **2.** [aspect]: **in this/that~** a este respeito. <> *vt* considerar; **to ~ o.s. intelligent** considerar-se inteligente; **to ~ sb/sthg as** considerar alguém/algo; **to ~ sb/sthg with** ver alguém/algo com; **to be highly ~ed** ser muito bem considerado(da).
  ◆ **regards** *npl* [in greetings] lembranças *fpl*; **with my best ~s** cordialmente.
  ◆ **as regards** *prep* em relação a, no que se refere a.
  ◆ **in regard to**, **with regard to** *prep* a respeito de, em relação a.

regarding [rɪ'gɑ:dɪŋ] *prep* a respeito de, em relação a.

regardless [rɪ'gɑ:dlɪs] *adv* apesar de tudo.
  ◆ **regardless of** *prep* independentemente de; **~ the cost** custe o que custar.

regatta [rɪ'gætə] *n* regata *f*.

regd. = **reg.**

Regency ['ri:dʒənsɪ] *adj* (com período) regencial.

regenerate [rɪ'dʒenəreɪt] <> *vt* regenerar. <> *vi* - **1.** [organs, tissue] regenerar-se - **2.** [economy] recuperar-se - **3.** [project] ser reformado(da).

regeneration [rɪˌdʒenə'reɪʃn] *n* - **1.** *(U)* [of organs, tissue] regeneração *f* - **2.** *(U)* [of economy] recuperação *f* - **3.** *(U)* [of project] reforma *f*.

regent ['ri:dʒənt] <> *adj* regente. <> *n* regente *mf*.

reggae ['regeɪ] *n (U)* reggae *m*.

regime [reɪ'ʒi:m] *n pej* regime *m*.

regiment ['redʒɪmənt] *n* MIL regimento *m*.

regimental [ˌredʒɪ'mentl] *adj* MIL do regimento, regimental.

regimented ['redʒɪmentɪd] *adj* - **1.** *pej* [workforce] estritamente controlado(da) - **2.** [in rows] ordenado(da) em fileiras.

region ['ri:dʒən] *n* - **1.** [gen] região *f* - **2.** [range]: **in the ~ of** por volta de.

regional ['ri:dʒənl] *adj* regional.

register ['redʒɪstə'] <> *n* registro *f*. <> *vt* - **1.**

registrar - **2.** [express] expressar, mostrar. <> *vi* - **1.** [enrol]: **to ~ as/for sthg** inscrever-se como/para algo - **2.** [book in] registrar-se - **3.** *inf* [be properly understood] assimilar.

registered ['redʒɪstəd] *adj* - **1.** [officially listed] oficialmente inscrito(ta) - **2.** [letter, parcel] registrado (da).

registered nurse *n* enfermeira *f* formada.

registered post *UK*, **registered mail** *US n (U)*: **to send sthg by ~** enviar algo registrado (pelo correio).

registered trademark *n* marca *f* registrada.

registrar ['redʒɪstrɑ:'] *n* - **1.** [keeper of records] escrivão *m*, -vã *f*, oficial *mf* de registro - **2.** UNIV [administrator] secretário *m*, -ria *f* geral - **3.** *UK* [doctor] médico *m*, -ca *f* em estágio de especialização.

registration [ˌredʒɪ'streɪʃn] *n* - **1.** [course enrolment] matrícula *f* - **2.** [of births, marriages and deaths] registro *m* - **3.** AUT = **registration number**.

registration document *n* certificado *m* de registro de veículo.

registration number *n* AUT número *m* de licença.

registry ['redʒɪstrɪ] (*pl* -**ies**) *n* registro *m*.

registry office *n* registro *m* civil.

regress [rɪ'gres] *vi fml*: **to ~ (to sthg)** regredir (a algo).

regression [rɪ'greʃn] *n (U) fml* regressão *f*.

regressive [rɪ'gresɪv] *adj fml* regressivo(va).

regret [rɪ'gret] (*pt* & *pp* -**ted**, *cont* -**ting**) <> *n* - **1.** *(U) fml* [sorrow] pesar *m* - **2.** [sad feeling]: **to have no ~a about sthg** não lamentar algo em absoluto. <> *vt*: **to ~ sthg/doing sthg** lamentar algo/ter feito algo; **we ~ to announce ...** lamentamos comunicar ...

regretful [rɪ'gretful] *adj* - **1.** [smile look] de arrependimento - **2.** [person] arrependido(da).

regretfully [rɪ'gretfulɪ] *adv* pesarosamente; **~ we have to announce ...** lamentamos ter que anunciar ...

regrettable [rɪ'gretəbl] *adj fml* lamentável.

regrettably [rɪ'gretəblɪ] *adv* lamentavelmente.

regroup [ˌri:'gru:p] *vi* reagrupar-se.

regt (*abbr of* **regiment**) regto.

regular ['regjulə'] <> *adj* - **1.** [gen] regular - **2.** [frequent - occurrence] frequente; [- customer] habitual; [- visitor] assíduo(dua) - **3.** [usual] habitual, normal - **4.** *US* [in size] médio(dia) - **5.** *US* [pleasant] amigável - **6.** *US* [normal] normal. <> *n* [customer, client] cliente *mf* habitual.

regular army *n* exército *m* ativo.

regularity [ˌregju'lærətɪ] *n (U)* regularidade *f*.

regularly ['regjuləlɪ] *adv* - **1.** [equally spaced] de maneira uniforme - **2.** [repeated at expected time] regularmente.

regulate ['regjuleɪt] *vt* regular.

regulation [ˌregju'leɪʃn] <> *adj* regulamentar. <> *n* - **1.** [rule] regra *f*, lei *f* - **2.** *(U)* [control] regulamento *m*, regulamentação *f*.

regurgitate [rɪ'gɜ:dʒɪteɪt] *vt* - **1.** [bring up] regurgitar - **2.** *fig* & *pej* [repeat] repetir maquinalmente.

rehabilitate [ˌri:ə'bɪlɪteɪt] *vt* - **1.** [convict, addict] reabilitar - **2.** [patient, invalid] recuperar.

rehabilitation [ˌriːəˌbɪlɪˈteɪʃn] n -1. [of convict, addict] reabilitação f - 2. [of patient, invalid] recuperação f.

rehash [ˌriːˈhæʃ] inf ⬦ vt pej retocar. ⬦ n retoque m.

rehearsal [rɪˈhɜːsl] n ensaio m.

rehearse [rɪˈhɜːs] ⬦ vt ensaiar. ⬦ vi: to ~ (for sthg) ensaiar (para algo).

reheat [ˌriːˈhiːt] vt reaquecer, esquentar de novo.

rehouse [ˌriːˈhaʊz] vt: to be ~d ser realojado (da).

reign [reɪn] ⬦ n reinado m. ⬦ vi: to ~ (over sb/sthg) reinar (sobre alguém/algo).

reigning [ˈreɪnɪŋ] adj atual.

reimburse [ˌriːɪmˈbɜːs] vt: to ~ sb (for sthg) reembolsar alguém (por algo).

reimbursement [ˌriːɪmˈbɜːsmənt] n (U) fml: ~ (for sthg) reembolso m (por algo).

rein [reɪn] n fig: to give (a) free ~ to sb, to give sb free ~ dar carta branca a alguém; to keep a tight ~ on sb/sthg controlar alguém/algo com firmeza.
➡ **reins** npl -1. [for horse] rédeas fpl - 2. [for child] andadeira f.
➡ **rein in** vt sep [horse] puxar as rédeas de.

reincarnation [ˌriːɪnkɑːˈneɪʃn] n (U) reencarnação f.

reindeer [ˈreɪnˌdɪəʳ] (pl inv) n rena f.

reinforce [ˌriːɪnˈfɔːs] vt: to ~ sthg (with sthg) reforçar algo (com algo).

reinforced concrete [ˌriːɪnˈfɔːst-] n (U) concreto m armado.

reinforcement [ˌriːɪnˈfɔːsmənt] n reforço m.
➡ **reinforcements** npl reforços mpl.

reinstate [ˌriːɪnˈsteɪt] vt - 1. [person - in job] readmitir; [- in position, office] reempossar, reintegrar - 2. [payment, idea, policy] restabelecer.

reinstatement [ˌriːɪnˈsteɪtmənt] n - 1. [of person - in job] readmissão f; [- in position, office] reintegração f - 2. [of payment, idea, policy] restabelecimento m.

reinterpret [ˌriːɪnˈtɜːprɪt] vt reinterpretar.

reintroduce [ˈriːˌɪntrəˈdjuːs] vt reintroduzir.

reintroduction [riːˌɪntrəˈdʌkʃn] n (U) reintrodução f.

reissue [riːˈɪʃuː] ⬦ n reedição f, reimpressão f. ⬦ vt reeditar, reimprimir.

reiterate [riːˈɪtəreɪt] vt fml reiterar.

reiteration [riːˌɪtəˈreɪʃn] n fml reiteração f.

reject [n ˈriːdʒekt, vb rɪˈdʒekt] ⬦ n [in factory, shop] refugo m, rejeito m. ⬦ vt - 1. [not agree to] rejeitar, não concordar com - 2. [dismiss, not accept] rejeitar - 3. [for job] recusar.

rejection [rɪˈdʒekʃn] n - 1. (U) [act of refusal] rejeição f - 2. [for job] recusa f.

rejig [ˌriːˈdʒɪg] (pt & pp -ged, cont -ging) vt UK inf modificar or alterar um pouco.

rejoice [rɪˈdʒɔɪs] vi: to ~ (at or in sthg) regozijar-se or alegrar-se (por algo).

rejoicing [rɪˈdʒɔɪsɪŋ] n (U) regozijo m, alegria f; ~ at or over sthg regozijo m por algo.

rejoin [rɪˈdʒɔɪn] vt - 1. [group, friends] reunir-se novamente com - 2. [regiment] reingressar em - 3. [motorway] pegar novamente - 4. [club, society] voltar a ser sócio(cia) de - 5. [reply] replicar, retorquir.

rejoinder [rɪˈdʒɔɪndəʳ] n réplica f.

rejuvenate [rɪˈdʒuːvəneɪt] vt rejuvenescer.

rejuvenation [rɪˌdʒuːvəˈneɪʃn] n (U) rejuvenescimento m.

rekindle [ˌriːˈkɪndl] vt fig reacender, reavivar.

relapse [rɪˈlæps] ⬦ n recaída f; to have a ~ ter uma recaída. ⬦ vi: to ~ into [coma] entrar novamente em; [drunken stupor, old ways] voltar a cair em; [crime] reincidir em.

relate [rɪˈleɪt] ⬦ vt - 1. [connect]: to ~ sthg to sthg relacionar algo a algo - 2. [tell] contar. ⬦ vi - 1. [connect]: to ~ to sthg relacionar-se a algo - 2. [concern]: to ~ to sthg referir-se a algo - 3. [empathize]: to ~ (to sb/sthg) ter muito em comum (com alguém/algo).
➡ **relating to** prep sobre, acerca de.

related [rɪˈleɪtɪd] adj - 1. [in same family] aparentado (da); to be ~ to sb ser aparentado(da) de alguém - 2. [connected] relacionado(da).

relation [rɪˈleɪʃn] n - 1. (U) [connection]: ~ (to/between) relação f (com/entre); to bear no ~ to não ter nada a ver com; in ~ to [state, size] em relação a - 2. [family member] parente mf, familiar mf.
➡ **relations** npl [relationship] relações fpl; ~ between/with relações entre/com.

relational [rɪˈleɪʃənl] adj COMPUT relacional.

relationship [rɪˈleɪʃnʃɪp] n - 1. [gen] relação f - 2. [relations] relação f, relacionamento m - 3. [connection] ligação f.

relative [ˈrelətɪv] ⬦ adj relativo(va). ⬦ n parente mf, familiar mf.
➡ **relative to** prep fml - 1. [compared to] em comparação com - 2. [connected with] relativo(va) a, com relação a.

relatively [ˈrelətɪvlɪ] adv relativamente.

relativity [ˌreləˈtɪvətɪ] n (U) relatividade f.

relax [rɪˈlæks] ⬦ vt - 1. [gen] relaxar - 2. [loosen, free up] afrouxar. ⬦ vi - 1. [person] relaxar, descontrair-se; ~! It's OK! relaxe! Está tudo bem! - 2. [grip] afrouxar-se.

relaxation [ˌriːlækˈseɪʃn] n (U) - 1. [rest] relaxamento m - 2. [of rule, discipline, regulation] afrouxamento m.

relaxed [rɪˈlækst] adj - 1. [person] relaxado(da), descontraído(da) - 2. [meeting, evening, mood] descontraído(da).

relaxing [rɪˈlæksɪŋ] adj relaxante.

relay [ˈriːleɪ] (pt & pp senses 1 & 2 -ed, pt & pp sense 3 relaid) ⬦ n - 1. SPORT: ~ (race) corrida f de revezamento; in ~s fig em turnos - 2. [broadcast] retransmissão f. ⬦ vt - 1. [broadcast] retransmitir - 2. [message, news]: to ~ sthg (to sb) transmitir algo (a alguém) - 3. [cable, carpet, tiles] repor.

release [rɪˈliːs] ⬦ n - 1. (U) [from captivity] soltura f, libertação f - 2. (U) [from pain, suffering] liberação f - 3. [statement] comunicado m - 4. (U) [of gas, fumes] escapamento m, emissão f - 5. [of film, video, CD] lançamento m; on ~ CINEMA em exibição - 6. [film, video, CD]: new ~ novo lançamento. ⬦ vt - 1. [set free] soltar, libertar; to ~ sb from prison/captivity libertar or soltar alguém da prisão/do cativeiro; to ~ sb from sthg [promise, contract] liberar alguém de algo - **2.** [make available] liberar - **3.** [control, grasp, mechanism] soltar - **4.** [let out, emit]: **heat is ~d from the liquid into the air** o calor é liberado do líquido para o ar - **5.** [film, video, CD] lançar; [statement, news story] divulgar.

relegate ['relɪgeɪt] vt - **1.** [demote]: **to ~ sb/sthg (to)** relegar alguém/algo (a) - **2.** SPORT: **to be ~d** UK ser rebaixado(da).

relegation [ˌrelɪ'geɪʃn] n (U) - **1.** [demotion]: **~ (to)** relegação f (a) - **2.** SPORT: **~ (to)** rebaixamento m (a).

relent [rɪ'lent] vi - **1.** [person] condescender - **2.** [wind, storm] abrandar-se, acalmar-se.

relentless [rɪ'lentlɪs] adj implacável.

relentlessly [rɪ'lentlɪslɪ] adv implacavelmente.

relevance ['reləvəns] n (U) - **1.** [connection]: **~ (to sb/sthg)** relevância f (a alguém/algo) - **2.** [significance]: **~ (to sb/sthg)**, **~ (for sb/sthg)** importância f (para alguém/algo).

relevant ['reləvənt] adj - **1.** [gen] relevante; **~ (to sb/sthg)** relevante (a alguém/algo) - **2.** [important]: **~ (to sb/sthg)** importante (a alguém/algo).

reliability [rɪˌlaɪə'bɪlətɪ] n (U) confiabilidade f.

reliable [rɪ'laɪəbl] adj - **1.** [dependable] confiável - **2.** [correct, true] seguro(ra).

reliably [rɪ'laɪəblɪ] adv - **1.** [dependably] de forma confiável - **2.** [correctly, truly]: **to be ~ informed that ...** saber de fonte segura que ...

reliance [rɪ'laɪəns] n (U): **~ (on sb/sthg)** dependência f (de alguém/algo).

reliant [rɪ'laɪənt] adj: **~ on sb/sthg** dependente de alguém/algo.

relic ['relɪk] n relíquia f.

relief [rɪ'li:f] n - **1.** [comfort] alívio m; **she sighed with ~** ela suspirou aliviada - **2.** (U) [for poor, refugees] auxílio m - **3.** US [social security] subsídio m.

relief map n mapa m em relevo.

relief road n UK desvio m.

relieve [rɪ'li:v] vt - **1.** [ease, lessen] aliviar; **to ~ sb of sthg** aliviar alguém de algo - **2.** [take over from] substituir - **3.** [give help to] auxiliar.

relieved [rɪ'li:vd] adj aliviado(da).

religion [rɪ'lɪdʒn] n religião f.

religious [rɪ'lɪdʒəs] adj religioso(sa).

reline [ˌri:'laɪn] vt - **1.** [gen] revestir novamente - **2.** [brakes] trocar o forro de.

relinquish [rɪ'lɪŋkwɪʃ] vt - **1.** [power, post, claim] renunciar a - **2.** [hold] soltar.

relish ['relɪʃ] <> n - **1.** (U) [enjoyment]: **with (great) ~** com(grande)satisfação - **2.** [pickle] picles mpl. <> vt desfrutar de; **to ~ the thought** OR **idea** OR **prospect of doing sthg** desfrutar de antemão da idéia OR da perspectiva de fazer algo.

relive [ˌri:'lɪv] vt reviver.

relocate [ˌri:ləʊ'keɪt] <> vt realocar, transferir. <> vi transferir-se.

relocation [ˌri:ləʊ'keɪʃn] n (U) realocação f.

relocation expenses npl gastos mpl com transferência.

reluctance [rɪ'lʌktəns] n (U) relutância f; **with ~** com relutância.

reluctant [rɪ'lʌktənt] adj relutante; **to be ~ to do sthg** estar pouco disposto(ta) a fazer algo.

reluctantly [rɪ'lʌktəntlɪ] adv relutantemente.

rely [rɪ'laɪ] (pt & pp -ied) ➤ **rely on** vt fus - **1.** [count on] contar com; **to ~ on sb/sthg to do sthg** estar certo(ta) de que alguém/algo fará algo - **2.** [be dependent on]: **to ~ on sb/sthg for sthg** depender de alguém/algo para algo.

REM (abbr of rapid eye movement) n REM m.

remain [rɪ'meɪn] vi - **1.** [stay] permanecer, ficar; **to ~ the same** continuar sendo igual - **2.** [be left] ficar; **the problem ~** o problema continua; **to ~ to be done** ficar para ser feito(ta); **it ~ s to be seen ...** isso ainda tem que ver ...
➤ **remains** npl - **1.** [of meal, fortune, body] restos mpl - **2.** [corpses] corpos mpl - **3.** [of ancient civilization, buildings] ruínas fpl.

remainder [rɪ'meɪndər] n - **1.** [rest]: **the ~** o resto - **2.** MATH resto m; **three into ten goes three ~ one** dez (dividido) por três é igual a três e sobra um.

remaining [rɪ'meɪnɪŋ] adj restante; **it's my last ~ pound!** é a última libra que eu tenho!

remake [n 'ri:meɪk, vb ˌri:'meɪk] CINEMA <> n nova versão f, remake m. <> vt fazer uma nova versão de.

remand [rɪ'mɑ:nd] JUR <> n: **on ~** sob prisão preventiva. <> vt recolocar em prisão preventiva; **to be ~ed in custody** estar sob custódia.

remand centre n UK instituição para a qual são enviadas as pessoas que aguardam julgamento.

remark [rɪ'mɑ:k] <> n comentário m. <> vt: **to ~ (that)** comentar que. <> vi: **to ~ on sthg** fazer comentários sobre algo.

remarkable [rɪ'mɑ:kəbl] adj excepcional, extraordinário(ria).

remarkably [rɪ'mɑ:kəblɪ] adv excepcionalmente, extraordinariamente.

remarry [ˌri:'mærɪ] (pt & pp -ied) vi casar-se de novo.

remedial [rɪ'mi:djəl] adj - **1.** [pupil] atrasado(da) - **2.** [teacher, class] de reforço - **3.** [corrective] corretivo (va).

remedy ['remədɪ] (pl -ies, pt & pp -ied) <> n - **1.** [for ill health]: **~ (for sthg)** remédio m (para algo) - **2.** fig [solution]: **~ (for sthg)** OR solução f (para algo). <> vt remediar.

remember [rɪ'membər] <> vt - **1.** lembrar-se de, lembrar; **to ~ doing sthg** lembrar-se de ter feito algo; **to ~ to do sthg** lembrar-se de fazer algo - **2.** [as greeting]: **~ me to your wife** dê lembranças minhas à sua esposa. <> vi lembrar(-se).

remembrance [rɪ'membrəns] n (U) fml: **in ~ of** em memória de.

Remembrance Day n na Grã-Bretanha, dia em memória das pessoas mortas nas duas guerras mundiais.

remind [rɪ'maɪnd] vt - **1.** [tell]: **to ~ sb (about sthg/ to do sthg)** lembrar alguém (de algo/de fazer algo) - **2.** [be reminiscent of]: **to ~ sb of sb/sthg** fazer alguém se lembrar de alguém/algo; **she ~ s me of my sister** ela me faz lembrar a minha irmã.

reminder [rɪ'maɪndər] n - **1.** [to jog memory]: **~ of sthg/to do sthg** lembrança f de algo/de fazer algo - **2.** [for bill, membership, licence] lembrete m.

reminisce [ˌremɪ'nɪs] vi: **to ~ (about sthg)** rememorar(algo).

reminiscences [ˌremɪ'nɪsənsɪz] npl reminiscências fpl.

reminiscent [ˌremɪ'nɪsnt] adj: **~ of sb/sthg** que faz lembrar alguém/algo.

remiss [rɪ'mɪs] adj descuidado(da), negligente.

remission [rɪ'mɪʃn] n -1. JUR redução f de pena - 2. MED remissão f.

remit [rɪ'mɪt] (pt & pp -ted, cont -ting) <> n UK alçada f; **that's outside my ~** isto está fora da minha alçada. <> vt remeter.

remittance [rɪ'mɪtns] n -1. [payment] remessa f - 2. COMM [settlement of invoice] remessa f de valores.

remnant ['remnənt] n [of cloth] sobra f; [of beauty, culture] resto m.

remodel [ˌriː'mɒdl] (UK pt & pp -led, cont -ling, US pt & pp -ed, cont -ing) vt -1. [change shape of] remodelar - 2. US [renovate] reformar.

remold n US = **remould**.

remonstrate ['remənstreɪt] vi fml: **to ~ (with sb about sthg)** protestar (com alguém sobre algo).

remorse [rɪ'mɔːs] n (U) remorso m.

remorseful [rɪ'mɔːsfʊl] adj cheio (cheia) de remorso.

remorseless [rɪ'mɔːslɪs] adj -1. [pitiless] desapiedado(da) - 2. [unstoppable] impiedoso(sa), implacável.

remorselessly [rɪ'mɔːslɪslɪ] adv -1. [pitilessly] de forma desapiedada - 2. [unstoppably] impiedosamente, implacavelmente.

remote [rɪ'məʊt] adj -1. [gen] remoto(ta) - 2. [unconnected, detached]: **~ from** distante de.

remote control n controle m remoto.

remote-controlled [-kən'trəʊld] adj operado(da) por controle remoto.

remotely [rɪ'məʊtlɪ] adv remotamente.

remoteness [rɪ'məʊtnɪs] n (U) - 1. [distance - in space] isolamento f; [- in time] distanciamento m - 2. [aloofness] indiferença m.

remould UK, **remold** US ['riː'məʊld] n pneu m recauchutado.

removable [rɪ'muːvəbl] adj desmontável.

removal [rɪ'muːvl] n -1. UK [change of house] mudança f - 2. (U) [act of removing] remoção f.

removal man n UK encarregado m da mudança.

removal van n UK caminhão m de mudança.

remove [rɪ'muːv] vt -1. [gen]: **to ~ sthg (from)** remover algo (de) - 2. [take off garment] tirar - 3. [from a job, post]: **to ~ sb (from)** demitir alguém (de) - 4. [injustice, difficulty] eliminar - 5. [problem] resolver - 6. [suspicion] dissipar.

removed [rɪ'muːvd] adj: **to be far ~ from** estar muito distante de.

remover [rɪ'muːvə'] n removedor m.

remuneration [rɪˌmjuːnə'reɪʃn] n fml (U) remuneração f.

Renaissance [rə'neɪsəns] <> n: **the ~** o Renascimento. <> comp do Renascimento.

rename [ˌriː'neɪm] vt renomear.

rend ['rend] (pt & pp rent) vt fml rasgar, despedaçar.

render ['rendə'] vt -1. [make, change] tornar; **to ~ sthg useless** tornar algo inútil; **to ~ sb speechless**

deixar alguém boquiaberto(ta) - 2. [give] dar, prestar; **to ~ good services** prestar bons serviços - 3. COMPUT exibir.

rendering ['rendərɪŋ] n -1. [performance - of play] interpretação f; [- of song, piece of music] execução f - 2. [translation] tradução f - 3. COMPUT exibição f.

rendezvous ['rɒndɪvuː] (pl inv) n -1. [meeting] encontro m - 2. [place] ponto m de encontro.

rendition [ren'dɪʃn] n -1. [of piece of music] execução f - 2. [of poem] declamação f.

renegade ['renɪgeɪd] <> adj renegado(da). <> n renegado m, -da f.

renege [rɪ'niːg] vi fml: **to ~ on sthg** deixar de cumprir algo.

renegotiate [ˌriːnɪ'gəʊʃɪeɪt] vt & vi renegociar.

renew [rɪ'njuː] vt -1. [gen] renovar - 2. [start again] reiniciar.

renewable [rɪ'njuːəbl] adj renovável.

renewal [rɪ'njuːəl] n renovação f.

rennet ['renɪt] n (U) coalheira f.

renounce [rɪ'naʊns] vt renunciar a.

renovate ['renəveɪt] vt renovar, reformar.

renovation [ˌrenə'veɪʃn] n (U) reforma f, renovação f.

   renovations npl reformas fpl.

renown [rɪ'naʊn] n (U) renome m.

renowned [rɪ'naʊnd] adj: **~ (for sthg)** renomado(da) (por algo).

rent [rent] <> pt & pp ⊢ **rend**. <> n aluguel m. <> vt alugar.

   rent out vt sep alugar.

rental ['rentl] <> adj de aluguel. <> n [money] aluguel m.

rent book n livro m de registro do aluguel.

rent boy n UK inf garoto m de programa.

rented ['rentɪd] adj alugado(da).

rent-free <> adj isento(ta) de aluguel. <> adv sem pagar aluguel.

renumber [ˌriː'nʌmbə'] vt renumerar.

renunciation [rɪˌnʌnsɪ'eɪʃn] n (U) renúncia f.

reoccurrence [ˌriːə'kʌrəns] n nova ocorrência f, repetição f.

reopen [ˌriː'əʊpn] <> vt -1. [open again] reabrir - 2. [start again] recomeçar. <> vi -1. [open again] reabrir - 2. [start again] recomeçar.

reorganization ['riːˌɔːgənər'zeɪʃn] n (U) reorganização f.

reorganize, -ise [ˌriː'ɔːgənaɪz] <> vt reorganizar. <> vi reorganizar-se.

rep [rep] n -1. (abbr of **representative**) inf representante mf - 2. (abbr of **repertory**) apresentação de uma série de peças teatrais em seqüencia por uma mesma companhia teatral em um mesmo teatro.

Rep. -1. (abbr of **Representative**) US deputado m, -da f - 2. (abbr of **Republican**) republicano m, -na f.

repaid [riː'peɪd] pt & pp ⊢ **repay**.

repaint [ˌriː'peɪnt] vt repintar.

repair [rɪ'peə'] <> n -1. (U) [act of mending] reparo m, conserto m; **it's beyond ~** não tem conserto; **ingood/bad ~** em bom/mau estado - 2. [instance of mending] reparo m. <> vt reparar.

repair kit n caixa f de ferramentas (de bicicleta).

repaper [ˌriːˈpeɪpəʳ] *vt*: **to ~ the wall** trocar o papel de parede.

reparations [ˌrepəˈreɪʃnz] *npl* indenizações *fpl*.

repartee [ˌrepɑːˈtiː] *n (U)* troca *f* de réplicas engenhosas.

repatriate [ˌriːˈpætrɪeɪt] *vt* repatriar.

repay [riːˈpeɪ] (*pt & pp* **repaid**) *vt* **-1.** [money] reembolsar, devolver; **to ~ sb sthg, to ~ sthg to sb** reembolsar *or* devolver algo a alguém **-2.** [favour] retribuir; **to ~ sb for sthg** retribuir alguém por algo.

repayment [riːˈpeɪmənt] *n* **-1.** *(U)* [act of paying back] reembolso *m*, devolução *f* **-2.** [sum] pagamento *m*.

repeal [rɪˈpiːl] ◇ *n* revogação *f*. ◇ *vt* revogar.

repeat [rɪˈpiːt] ◇ *vt* **-1.** [gen] repetir; **to ~ o.s.** repetir-se **-2.** [broadcast] reprisar. ◇ *n* [broadcast] reprise *f*.

repeated [rɪˈpiːtɪd] *adj* repetido(da).

repeatedly [rɪˈpiːtɪdlɪ] *adv* repetidamente.

repel [rɪˈpel] (*pt & pp* **-led**, *cont* **-ling**) *vt* **-1.** [disgust] repugnar **-2.** [drive away] repelir.

repellent [rɪˈpelənt] ◇ *adj* repugnante. ◇ *n* repelente *m*.

repent [rɪˈpent] ◇ *vt* arrepender-se de. ◇ *vi*: **to ~ of sthg** arrepender-se de algo.

repentance [rɪˈpentəns] *n (U)* arrependimento *m*.

repentant [rɪˈpentənt] *adj* **-1.** [person] arrependido(da) **-2.** [smile] de arrependimento.

repercussions [ˌriːpəˈkʌʃnz] *npl* repercussões *fpl*.

repertoire [ˈrepətwɑːʳ] *n* repertório *m*.

repertory [ˈrepətrɪ] *n (U)* repertório *m*.

repertory company *n* companhia *f* teatral de repertório.

repetition [ˌrepɪˈtɪʃn] *n* repetição *f*.

repetitious [ˌrepɪˈtɪʃəs], **repetitive** [rɪˈpetɪtɪv] *adj* repetitivo(va).

rephrase [ˌriːˈfreɪz] *vt* **-1.** [question] reformular **-2.** [statement] dizer com outras palavras.

replace [rɪˈpleɪs] *vt* **-1.** [take the place of] substituir; **to ~ sthg (with sthg)** substituir *or* trocar algo (por algo); **to ~ sb (with sb)** substituir alguém (por alguém); **if I lose your book, I'll ~ it** se eu perder o teu livro, eu te dou outro **-2.** [put back] recolocar no lugar.

replacement [rɪˈpleɪsmənt] *n* **-1.** *(U)* [act of replacing] reposição *f*, substituição *f* **-2.** [new person, object]: **~ (for sthg)** substituto *m*, -ta *f* (para algo); **~ (for sb)** suplente *mf* (para alguém).

replacement part *n* peça *f* de reposição.

replay [*n* ˈriːpleɪ, *vb* ˌriːˈpleɪ] ◇ *n* **-1.** [recording] replay *m* **-2.** [game] partida *f* de desempate. ◇ *vt* **-1.** [match, game] jogar de novo **-2.** [film, tape] reprisar.

replenish [rɪˈplenɪʃ] *vt fml*: **to ~ sthg (with sthg)** reabastecer *or* prover novamente algo (com algo).

replete [rɪˈpliːt] *adj* **-1.** *fml* [object] cheio(a) **-2.** *fml* [person] satisfeito(ta), saciado(da).

replica [ˈreplɪkə] *n* réplica *f*, cópia *f*.

replicate [ˈreplɪkeɪt] *vt fml* duplicar, reproduzir com exatidão.

replication [ˌreplɪˈkeɪʃn] *n fml* **-1.** *(U)* [process of copying] reprodução *f* exata **-2.** [copy] réplica *f*, cópia *f*.

reply [rɪˈplaɪ] (*pl* **-ies**, *pt & pp* **-ied**) ◇ *n* resposta *f*; **in ~ to sthg** em resposta a algo. ◇ *vt* responder; **to ~ that** responder que. ◇ *vi* responder; **to ~ to sb/sthg** responder a alguém/algo.

reply coupon *n* cupom *m* de resposta.

reply-paid *adj* pré-pago(ga), com porte pago.

report [rɪˈpɔːt] ◇ *n* **-1.** [description, account] relatório *m* **-2.** *PRESS* reportagem *f* **-3.** *UK SCH* boletim *m* de avaliação. ◇ *vt* **-1.** [news, crime] informar, comunicar **-2.** [make known]: **to ~ that** informar que; **~ sthg (to sb)** relatar algo (a alguém) **-3.** [complain about]: **to ~ sb (to sb)** denunciar alguém (a alguém); **to ~ sb for sthg** denunciar alguém por algo. ◇ *vi* **-1.** [give account] relatar; **to ~ on sthg** fazer um relatório sobre algo **-2.** *PRESS*: **to ~ on sthg** fazer uma reportagem sobre algo **-3.** [present o.s.]: **to ~ to** apresentar-se a; **to ~ for sthg** apresentar-se para algo.

➤ **report back** *vi*: **to ~ back (to sb)** dar retorno (para alguém).

reportage [ˌrepɔːˈtɑːʒ] *n* reportagem *f*.

report card *n US SCH* boletim *m*, caderneta *f* escolar.

reportedly [rɪˈpɔːtɪdlɪ] *adv* segundo se diz; **he is ~ not intending to return to this country** sabe-se que ele não pretende voltar a este país.

reported speech [rɪˈpɔːtɪd-] *n (U)* discurso *m* indireto.

reporter [rɪˈpɔːtəʳ] *n* repórter *mf*.

repose [rɪˈpəʊz] *n (U) literary* repouso *m*.

repository [rɪˈpɒzɪtrɪ] (*pl* **-ies**) *n* depósito *m*, armazém *m*.

repossess [ˌriːpəˈzes] *vt* retomar a posse de.

repossession [ˌriːpəˈzeʃn] *n (U)* reintegração *f* de posse.

repossession order *n* ordem *f* de despejo.

reprehensible [ˌreprɪˈhensəbl] *adj fml* repreensível.

represent [ˌreprɪˈzent] *vt* **-1.** [gen] representar **-2.** [describe]: **to ~ sb/sth gas** descrever *or* representar alguém/algo como **-3.** *phr*: **to be well** *or* **strongly ~ed** estar bem representado(da).

representation [ˌreprɪzenˈteɪʃn] *n (U)* representação *f*.

➤ **representations** *npl fml*: **to make ~s to sb** apresentar reclamações a alguém.

representative [ˌreprɪˈzentətɪv] ◇ *adj* representativo(va); **~ (of sb/sthg)** representativo(va) (de alguém/algo). ◇ *n* **-1.** [of company, organization, group] representante *mf* **-2.** *COMM*: **(sales) ~** representante *mf* (de vendas) **-3.** *US POL* deputado *m*, -da *f*.

repress [rɪˈpres] *vt* reprimir.

repressed [rɪˈprest] *adj* reprimido(da).

repression [rɪˈpreʃn] *n (U)* repressão *f*.

repressive [rɪˈpresɪv] *adj* repressivo(va).

reprieve [rɪˈpriːv] ◇ *n* **-1.** [of death sentence] indulto *m* **-2.** [respite] trégua *f*. ◇ *vt* indultar.

reprimand [ˈreprɪmɑːnd] ◇ *n* reprimenda *f*, repreensão *f*. ◇ *vt* repreender.

reprint [n'ri:prɪnt, vb ˌri:'prɪnt] ◇ n reimpressão f. ◇ vt reimprimir.

reprisal [rɪ'praɪzl] n retaliação f, represália f.

reproach [rɪ'prəʊtʃ] ◇ n -1. (U) [disapproval] censura f, repreensão f -2. [words of blame] acusação f. ◇ vt: to ~ sb (for OR with sthg) censurar OR repreender alguém (por algo).

reproachful [rɪ'prəʊtʃfʊl] adj de reprovação.

reprobate ['reprəbeɪt] n hum réprobo m, -ba f.

reproduce [ˌri:prə'dju:s] ◇ vt reproduzir. ◇ vi reproduzir-se.

reproduction [ˌri:prə'dʌkʃn] n reprodução f.

reproductive [ˌri:prə'dʌktɪv] adj BIOL reprodutor (ra).

reprogram [ˌri:'prəʊgræml] (pt & pp -ed OR -med, cont-ing OR -ming) vt reprogramar.

reproof [rɪ'pru:f] n -1. [words of blame] censura f -2. (U) [disapproval] reprovação f.

reprove [rɪ'pru:f] vt: to ~ sb (for sthg) reprovar alguém (por algo).

reproving [rɪ'pru:vɪŋ] adj reprovador(ra), de reprovação.

reptile ['reptaɪl] n réptil m.

Repub. (abbr of Republican) n republicano m, -na f.

republic [rɪ'pʌblɪk] n república f.

republican [rɪ'pʌblɪkən] ◇ adj republicano(na). ◇ n republicano m, -na f.
  ➡ **Republican** ◇ adj -1. [in USA] republicano (na); **the Republican Party** o Partido Republicano -2. [in Northern Ireland] independentista. ◇ n -1. [in USA] republicano m, -na f -2. [in Northern Ireland] independentista mf.

repudiate [rɪ'pju:dɪeɪt] vt fml repudiar.

repudiation [rɪˌpju:dɪ'eɪʃn] n (U) fml repúdio m.

repugnant [rɪ'pʌgnənt] adj fml repugnante.

repulse [rɪ'pʌls] vt repelir.

repulsion [rɪ'pʌlʃn] n (U) -1. [disgust] repulsa f -2. PHYSICS repulsão f.

repulsive [rɪ'pʌlsɪv] adj repulsivo(va).

reputable ['repjʊtəbl] adj de boa reputação.

reputation [ˌrepjʊ'teɪʃn] n reputação f; **to have a ~ for sthg/for being sthg** ter fama de algo/de ser algo.

repute [rɪ'pju:t] n (U) fml -1. [reputation]: **of good/ ill ~** de boa/má reputação -2. [distinction]: **of ~** de renome.

reputed [rɪ'pju:tɪd] adj de renome; **to be ~ to be/ do sthg** ter fama de ser/fazer algo.

reputedly [rɪ'pju:tɪdlɪ] adv supostamente, segundo dizem.

reqd (abbr of required) requerido.

request [rɪ'kwest] ◇ n: ~ **(for sthg)** solicitação f (de algo); **on ~** através de solicitação; **at sb's ~** por solicitação de alguém. ◇ vt solicitar, pedir; **to ~ sb to do sthg** solicitar a alguém que faça algo.

request stop n UK parada f de ônibus não-obrigatória.

requiem (mass) ['rekwɪəm-] n réquiem m.

require [rɪ'kwaɪəʳ] vt -1. [need] requerer, necessitar de -2. [demand] exigir; **to ~ sb to do sthg** exigir que alguém faça algo; **employees are ~d to wear**

a uniform exige-se que os funcionários usem uniformes.

required [rɪ'kwaɪəd] adj necessário(ria); **formal dress is ~ d** exigem-se trajes formais.

requirement [rɪ'kwaɪəmənt] n -1. [need] necessidade f -2. [condition] requisito m, condição f.

requisite ['rekwɪzɪt] adj fml necessário(ria), requerido(da).

requisition [ˌrekwɪ'zɪʃn] vt requisitar.

reran [ˌri:'ræn] pt ▷ rerun.

reread [ˌri:'ri:dl] (pt & pp reread [ˌri:'redl) vt reler.

rerecord [ˌri:rɪ'kɔ:dl] vt regravar.

reroute [ˌri:'ru:t] vt redirecionar.

rerun [n 'ri:ˌrʌn, vb ri:'rʌn] (pt reran, pp rerun, cont-ning) ◇ n -1. [film, programme] reprise f -2. [similar situation] repetição f. ◇ vt -1. [race, competition] voltar a participar de -2. [film, programme] reprisar -3. [tape] pôr novamente.

resale price maintenance ['ri:seɪl-] n (U) UK FIN manutenção f do preço de revenda.

resat [ˌri:'sæt] pt & pp ▷ resit.

reschedule [UK ˌri:'ʃedjʊl, US ˌri:'skedʒʊl] vt FIN renegociar.

rescind [rɪ'sɪnd] vt [JUR - contract] rescindir; [- law] revogar.

rescue ['reskju:] ◇ n -1. [help] auxílio f; **to go/ come to sb's ~** ir/vir em auxílio de alguém -2. [successful attempt] resgate m, salvamento m. ◇ vt resgatar, salvar; **to ~ sb from sb/sthg** resgatar OR salvar alguém de alguém/algo; **to ~ sthg from sb/sthg** salvar algo de alguém/algo.

rescue operation n operação f de resgate.

rescuer ['reskjʊəʳ] n resgatador m, -ra f.

reseal [ˌri:'si:l] vt fechar novamente.

resealable [ˌri:'si:ləbl] adj que se pode fechar novamente.

research [ˌrɪ'sɜ:tʃ] ◇ n (U): ~ **(on OR into sthg)** pesquisa f (sobre algo); ~ **and development** pesquisa e desenvolvimento. ◇ vt pesquisar, fazer uma pesquisa sobre. ◇ vi: **to ~ (into sthg)** fazer uma pesquisa (sobre algo).

researcher [rɪ'sɜ:tʃəʳ] n pesquisador m, -ra f.

research work n (U) trabalho m de pesquisa.

resell [ˌri:'sell] (pt & pp resold) vt revender.

resemblance [rɪ'zembləns] n semelhança f; ~ **to sb/sthg** semelhança com alguém/algo; ~ **between** semelhança entre.

resemble [rɪ'zembl] vt assemelhar-se a, parecer-se com.

resent [rɪ'zent] vt ofender-se com, ressentir-se de.

resentful [rɪ'zentfʊl] adj ressentido(da).

resentfully [rɪ'zentfʊlɪ] adv com ressentimento.

resentment [rɪ'zentmənt] n (U) ressentimento m.

reservation [ˌrezə'veɪʃn] n -1. [gen] reserva f; **without ~** sem reserva -2. US [for Native Americans] reserva f (indígena).
  ➡ **reservations** npl [doubts] reservas fpl, dúvidas fpl.

reserve [rɪ'zɜ:v] ◇ n reserva f; **in ~** de reserva. ◇ vt -1. [keep for particular purpose]: **to ~ sthg for sb/sthg** reservar algo para alguém/algo -2. [retain]: **to ~ the right to do sthg** reservar-se o direito de fazer algo.

reserve bank *n US* banco *m* de reserva federal.
reserve currency *n* moeda *f* de reserva.
reserved [rɪ'zɜːvd] *adj* reservado(da).
reserve price *n UK* preço *m* mínimo (de venda).
reserve team *n UK* time *m* reserva.
reservist [rɪ'zɜːvɪst] *n* reservista *mf.*
reservoir ['rezəvwɑː'] *n* -**1.** [lake] reservatório *m* natural -**2.** [large supply] reservatório *m.*
reset [ˌriː'set] (*pt* & *pp* reset, *cont* -ting) <> *vt* -**1.** [clock, meter, controls] reajustar -**2.** [bone] recolocar no lugar -**3.** *COMPUT* reinicializar. <> *vi COMPUT* reinicializar.
resettle [ˌriː'setl] <> *vt* -**1.** [land] ocupar -**2.** [people] reassentar. <> *vi* [people] reassentar-se.
resettlement [ˌriː'setlmənt] *n* (*U*) -**1.** [of land] ocupação *f* -**2.** [of people] reassentamento *m.*
reshape [ˌriː'ʃeɪp] *vt* reformar, remodelar.
reshuffle [ˌriː'ʃʌfl] <> *n POL* reorganização *f*, reforma *f*; cabinet ~ reforma *f* do gabinete. <> *vt ADMIN* & *POL* reformar.
reside [rɪ'zaɪd] *vi fml* residir; **happiness does not ~ in wealth** a felicidade não reside na riqueza.
residence ['rezɪdəns] *n* -**1.** [house] residência *f* -**2.** (*U*) [fact of residing]: **to apply for ~** *fml* estabelecer residência (em), instalar-se -**3.** (*U*) [residing at a particular time]: **to be in ~** *fml* estar presente -**4.** (*U*) *UNIV*: **writer in ~** escritor(ra) residente (*que atua temporariamente numa universidade*).
residence permit *n* visto *m* de residência.
resident ['rezɪdənt] <> *adj* residente; **she's been ~ in france for two years** faz dois anos que ela está morando na França. <> *n* residente *mf.*
residential [ˌrezɪ'denʃl] *adj* em regime de internato.
residential area *n* zona *f* residencial.
residents' association *n* associação *f* de moradores.
residual [rɪ'zɪdjʊəl] *adj* residual.
residue ['rezɪdjuː] *n CHEM* resíduo *m.*
resign [rɪ'zaɪn] <> *vt* -**1.** [give up - job] demitir-se de; [- post] renunciar a -**2.** [accept calmly]: **to ~ o.s. to sthg** resignar-se a algo. <> *vi* pedir demissão, demitir-se; **to ~ (from sthg)** pedir demissão *OR* demitir-se (de algo).
resignation [ˌrezɪg'neɪʃn] *n* -**1.** [from job] demissão *f* -**2.** [from post] renúncia *f* -**3.** (*U*) [calm acceptance] resignação *f.*
resigned [rɪ'zaɪnd] *adj*: **~ (to sthg)** resignado(da) (a algo).
resilience [rɪ'zɪlɪəns] *n* (*U*) capacidade *f* de recuperação.
resilient [rɪ'zɪlɪənt] *adj* -**1.** [rubber, metal] elástico(ca) -**2.** [person] que se recupera rapidamente, resistente.
resin ['rezɪn] *n* (*U*) resina *f.*
resist [rɪ'zɪst] *vt* -**1.** [gen] resistir a -**2.** [oppose] opor-se a.
resistance [rɪ'zɪstəns] *n* (*U*) -**1.** [to enemy, attack, infection] resistência *f*; ~ **to sthg** resistência a algo -**2.** [to change, proposal, attempt] oposição *f.*
resistant [rɪ'zɪstənt] *adj* -**1.** *MED* [immune]: ~ **(to**

sthg) resistente (a algo) -**2.** [opposed]: ~ **to sthg** que se opõe a algo.
resistor [rɪ'zɪstə'] *n ELEC* resistor *m.*
resit [*n* 'riːsɪt, *vb* ˌriː'sɪt] (*pt* & *pp* resat, *cont* -ting) *UK* <> *n* exame *m* de recuperação. <> *vt* fazer de novo (*um exame*).
resold [ˌriː'səʊld] *pt* & *pp* ⊳ resell.
resolute ['rezəluːt] *adj* resoluto(ta), determinado(da).
resolutely ['rezəluːtlɪ] *adv* resolutamente, com determinação.
resolution [ˌrezə'luːʃn] *n* -**1.** [gen] resolução *f* -**2.** [vow, promise] promessa *f.*
resolve [rɪ'zɒlv] <> *n* (*U*) resolução *f.* <> *vt* [solve] resolver; [vow, promise]: **to ~ that** prometer que; **to ~ to do sthg** resolver fazer algo.
resonance ['rezənəns] *n* (*U*) ressonância *f.*
resonant ['rezənənt] *adj* ressonante.
resonate ['rezəneɪt] *vi* ressoar.
resort [rɪ'zɔːt] *n* -**1.** [for holidays] estância *f* de férias -**2.** [solution]: **as a last ~** como último recurso; **in the last ~** em última instância.
➡ **resort to** *vt fus* apelar para.
resound [rɪ'zaʊnd] *vi* -**1.** [noise] ressoar, retumbar -**2.** [place]: **the room ~ed with laughter** as risadas ressoavam em toda a sala.
resounding [rɪ'zaʊndɪŋ] *adj* -**1.** [gen] retumbante -**2.** [extremely loud] estrondoso(sa) -**3.** [unequivocal] clamoroso(sa).
resource [rɪ'sɔːs] *n* recurso *m.*
resourceful [rɪ'sɔːsfʊl] *adj* versátil, habilidoso(sa).
resourcefulness [rɪ'sɔːsfʊlnɪs] *n* (*U*) versatilidade *f.*
respect [rɪ'spekt] <> *n* (*U*) respeito *m*; ~ **(for sb/sthg)** respeito *m OR* admiração *f* (por alguém/algo); **with ~, ...** com todo o respeito, ...; **in this ~** a este respeito; **in that ~** quanto a isso. <> *vt* respeitar; **to ~ sb for sthg** respeitar alguém por algo.
➡ **respects** *npl* saudações *fpl*, cumprimentos *mpl*; **to pay one's last ~s to sb** prestar uma última homenagem a alguém.
➡ **with respect to** *prep* com respeito a.
respectability [rɪˌspektə'bɪlətɪ] *n* (*U*) respeitabilidade *f.*
respectable [rɪ'spektəbl] *adj* respeitável.
respectably [rɪ'spektəblɪ] *adv* de forma respeitável.
respected *adj* respeitado(da).
respectful [rɪ'spektfʊl] *adj* respeitoso(sa).
respectfully [rɪ'spektfʊlɪ] *adv* respeitosamente.
respective [rɪ'spektɪv] *adj* respectivo(va).
respectively [rɪ'spektɪvlɪ] *adv* respectivamente.
respiration [ˌrespə'reɪʃn] *n* (*U*) respiração *f.*
respirator ['respəreɪtə'] *n* -**1.** [gas mask] máscara *f* antigás -**2.** [machine] respirador *m.*
respiratory [*UK* rɪ'spɪrətrɪ, *US* 'respərətɔːrɪ] *adj* respiratório(ria).
respire [rɪ'spaɪə'] *vi* respirar.
respite ['respaɪt] *n* -**1.** [pause] descanso *m* -**2.** [delay] adiamento *m*, novo prazo *m.*
resplendent [rɪ'splendənt] *adj literary* resplandescente.

respond [rɪ'spɒnd] ⟨⟩ *vt* responder. ⟨⟩ *vi*: **to ~ (to sthg)** responder (a algo); **to ~ by doing sthg** responder fazendo algo.

response [rɪ'spɒns] *n* resposta *f*; **in ~** em resposta.

responsibility [rɪ,spɒnsə'bɪlətɪ] (*pl* -ies) *n*: **~ (for sthg)** responsabilidade *f* (por algo); **~ (to sb)** responsabilidade *f* (diante de alguém).

responsible [rɪ'spɒnsəbl] *adj* **-1.** [gen]: **~ (for sthg)** responsável (por algo) **-2.** [answerable]: **~ to sb** que presta contas a alguém **-3.** [requiring sense] de responsabilidade.

responsibly [rɪ'spɒnsəblɪ] *adv* de forma responsável.

responsive [rɪ'spɒnsɪv] *adj* que responde muito bem; **~ (to sthg)** sensível OR atencioso(sa) (a algo).

respray [*n* 'ri:spreɪ, *vb* ,ri:'spreɪ] ⟨⟩ *n* nova pintura *f*. ⟨⟩ *vt* repintar.

rest [rest] ⟨⟩ *n* **-1.** [remainder]: **the ~** o resto; **the ~ of** o resto de **-2.** (U) [relaxation] descanso *m* **-3.** [break] pausa *f*, descanso *m* **-4.** [support] apoio *m* **-5.** *phr*: **to lay** OR **put sthg to ~** sepultar algo; **to come to ~** deter-se. ⟨⟩ *vt* **-1.** [relax] descansar **-2.** [support, lean]: **to ~ sthg on/against sthg** apoiar OR descansar algo em algo **-3.** *phr*: **~ assured (that)** fique descansado(da) que. ⟨⟩ *vi* **-1.** [relax, be still] descansar **-2.** [depend]: **to ~ (up)on sb/sthg** depender de alguém/algo **-3.** [duty, responsibility]: **to ~ with sb** pesar sobre alguém **-4.** [be supported]: **to ~ on/against sthg** apoiar-se em/contra algo.

rest area *n* US & Austr área *f* de descanso (numa estrada).

restart [*n* 'ri:stɑ:t, *vb* ,ri:'stɑ:t] ⟨⟩ *n* COMPUT reinício *m*. ⟨⟩ *vt* **-1.** [vehicle, engine] ligar novamente **-2.** [work] recomeçar **-3.** COMPUT reiniciar. ⟨⟩ *vi* **-1.** [play, film] recomeçar **-2.** [vehicle] dar partida, pegar **-3.** [engine] ligar novamente.

restate [,ri:'steɪt] *vt* reformular, expor novamente.

restaurant ['restərɒnt] *n* restaurante *m*.

restaurant car *n* UK vagão-restaurante *m*.

rest cure *n* cura *f* pelo descanso forçado.

rested ['restɪd] *adj* descansado(da).

restful ['restfʊl] *adj* tranqüilo(la), sossegado(da).

rest home *n* **-1.** [for the elderly] lar *m* de idosos **-2.** [for the sick] casa *f* de repouso.

resting place ['restɪŋ-] *n* última morada *f*.

restitution [,restɪ'tju:ʃn] *n* (U) *fml* restituição *f*.

restive ['restɪv] *adj* inquieto(ta).

restless ['restlɪs] *adj* **-1.** [bored, dissatisfied] impaciente **-2.** [fidgety] inquieto(ta), agitado(da) **-3.** [sleepless]: **a ~ night** uma noite em claro.

restlessly ['restlɪslɪ] *adv* **-1.** [impatiently] impacientemente **-2.** [sleeplessly] sem conseguir dormir.

restock [,ri:'stɒk] ⟨⟩ *vt* reabastecer. ⟨⟩ *vi* reabastecer-se.

restoration [,restə'reɪʃn] *n* (U) restauração *f*.

restorative [rɪ'stɒrətɪv] *adj fml* revigorante.

restore [rɪ'stɔːʳ] *vt* **-1.** [reestablish, bring back] restabelecer; **the king was ~ed to power** o rei foi reconduzido ao poder; **I feel completely ~ed to health** sinto-me totalmente recuperado(da); **to ~ sthg to sb/sthg** devolver algo a alguém/algo

-2. [renovate] restaurar **-3.** [give back] restituir.

restorer [rɪ'stɔːrəʳ] *n* **-1.** [person] restaurador *m*, -ra *f* **-2.** (U) [substance] tônico *m*.

restrain [rɪ'streɪn] *vt* **-1.** [gen] reprimir; **to ~ o.s. from doing sthg** conter-se para não fazer algo **-2.** [overpower, bring under control] controlar.

restrained [rɪ'streɪnd] *adj* comedido(da).

restraint [rɪ'streɪnt] *n* **-1.** [rule, check] restrição *f*, limitação *f* **-2.** (U) [control] controle *m*.

restrict [rɪ'strɪkt] *vt* restringir, limitar; **to ~ sb to sthg** restringir alguém a algo; **to ~ sthg to sb/ sthg** restringir algo a alguém/algo; **to ~ o.s. to sthg** limitar-se a algo.

restricted [rɪ'strɪktɪd] *adj* **-1.** [not public] restrito(ta) **-2.** [limited] limitado(da).

restriction [rɪ'strɪkʃn] *n* **-1.** [limitation, regulation] restrição *f*; **to place ~s on sthg** impor restrições a algo **-2.** (U) [impediment, hindrance] limitação *f*.

restrictive [rɪ'strɪktɪv] *adj* restritivo(va).

restrictive practices *npl* práticas *fpl* restritivas.

rest room *n* US banheiro *m*.

restructure [,ri:'strʌktʃəʳ] *vt* reestruturar.

result [rɪ'zʌlt] ⟨⟩ *n* resultado *m*; **as a ~** como resultado, por conseguinte; **as a ~ of sthg** como resultado de algo. ⟨⟩ *vi*: **to ~ in sthg** ter algo como resultado; **to ~ from sthg** ser resultado de algo.

resultant [rɪ'zʌltənt] *adj fml* resultante.

resume [rɪ'zju:m] ⟨⟩ *vt* **-1.** [activity] recomeçar **-2.** *fml* [place, position] retomar. ⟨⟩ *vi* recomeçar, continuar.

résumé ['rezjuːmeɪ] *n* **-1.** [summary] resumo *m* **-2.** US [of career, qualifications] currículo *m*.

resumption [rɪ'zʌmpʃn] *n* (U) retomada *f*.

resurface [,ri:'sɜ:fɪs] ⟨⟩ *vt* repavimentar. ⟨⟩ *vi* vir à tona.

resurgence [rɪ'sɜ:dʒəns] *n* (U) ressurgimento *m*.

resurrect [,rezə'rekt] *vt* ressuscitar.

resurrection [,rezə'rekʃn] *n* (U) ressurreição *f*.
  ◆ **Resurrection** *n* RELIG: **the Resurrection** a Ressurreição.

resuscitate [rɪ'sʌsɪteɪt] *vt* **-1.** [bring back to life] ressuscitar **-2.** [prevent from dying] reanimar.

resuscitation [rɪ,sʌsɪ'teɪʃn] *n* (U) ressuscitação *f*, reanimação *f*.

retail ['ri:teɪl] ⟨⟩ *n* (U) varejo *m*. ⟨⟩ *adv* no varejo. ⟨⟩ *vi*: **to ~ at** ser vendido(da) no varejo.

retailer ['ri:teɪləʳ] *n* varejista *mf*.

retail outlet *n* ponto *m* de venda.

retail price *n* preço *m* no varejo.

retail price index *n* UK índice *m* de preço ao consumidor.

retain [rɪ'teɪn] *vt* reter.

retainer [rɪ'teɪnəʳ] *n* **-1.** [fee] adiantamento *m* **-2.** [servant] criado *m*, -da *f* (com muitos anos de serviço numa casa).

retaining wall [rɪ'teɪnɪŋ-] *n* muro *m* de arrimo.

retaliate [rɪ'tælɪeɪt] *vi* retaliar.

retaliation [rɪ,tælɪ'eɪʃn] *n* retaliação *f*.

retarded [rɪ'tɑ:dɪd] *adj* mentalmente retardado(da).

retch [retʃ] *vi* fazer força para vomitar.

retd (*abbr of* **retired**) aposentado(da).

retention [rɪ'tenʃn] *n* **-1.** [of pride, power, independence] manutenção *f* **-2.** [of heat, water] retenção *f*.

retentive [rɪ'tentɪv] *adj* retentivo(va).

rethink [*n* 'riːθɪŋk, *vb* ˌriː'θɪŋk] (*pt* & *pp* **-thought** [-'θɔːtl]) <> *n*: **to have a ~ about sthg** ter que repensar algo; **to have a ~** dar uma repensada. <> *vt* repensar, reconsiderar. <> *vi* repensar, reconsiderar.

reticence ['retɪsəns] *n* (*U*) reticência *f*.

reticent ['retɪsənt] *adj* reticente.

retina ['retɪnə] (*pl* **-nas** OR **-nae** [-niːl]) *n* retina *f*.

retinue ['retɪnjuː] *n* séquito *m*.

retire [rɪ'taɪəʳ] *vi* **-1.** [from work] aposentar-se **-2.** *fml* [to another place] retirar-se **-3.** *fml* [to bed] recolher-se.

retired [rɪ'taɪəd] *adj* aposentado(da).

retirement [rɪ'taɪəmənt] *n* aposentadoria *f*.

retirement age *n* idade *f* de aposentadoria OR de se aposentar.

retirement pension *n* aposentadoria *f*.

retiring [rɪ'taɪərɪŋ] *adj* **-1.** [shy] retraído(da), tímido(da) **-2.** [from work] *que está a ponto de se aposentar*.

retort [rɪ'tɔːt] <> *n* réplica *f*. <> *vt*: **to ~ (that)** retrucar (que).

retouch [ˌriː'tʌtʃ] *vt* retocar.

retrace [rɪ'treɪs] *vt*: **to ~ one's steps** refazer o mesmo caminho.

retract [rɪ'trækt] <> *vt* **-1.** [take back] retratar **-2.** [draw in] recolher. <> *vi* **-1.** [recant] retratar-se **-2.** [be drawn in] recolher-se.

retractable [rɪ'træktəbl] *adj* retrátil.

retraction [rɪ'trækʃn] *n* (*U*) retratação *f*.

retrain [ˌriː'treɪn] <> *vt* reabilitar. <> *vi* reabilitar-se, reciclar-se.

retraining [ˌriː'treɪnɪŋ] *n* (*U*) reciclagem *f*.

retread ['riːtred] *n* pneu *m* recauchutado.

retreat [rɪ'triːt] <> *n* **-1.** MIL [withdrawal]: **~ (from)** retirada *f* (de) **-2.** *fig* [from principle, policy, lifestyle]: **to beat a (hasty) ~** bater em retirada **-3.** [refuge] refúgio *m*. <> *vi*: **to ~ (to/from)** retirar-se (para/de).

retrenchment [riː'trentʃmənt] *n fml* redução *f* OR corte *m* de gastos.

retrial [ˌriː'traɪəl] *n* novo julgamento *m*.

retribution [ˌretrɪ'bjuːʃn] *n* (*U*) castigo *m* merecido.

retrieval [rɪ'triːvl] *n* (*U*) COMPUT recuperação *f*.

retrieve [rɪ'triːv] *vt* **-1.** [get back] reaver **-2.** COMPUT recuperar **-3.** [rescue, rectify] reparar, remediar.

retriever [rɪ'triːvəʳ] *n* [dog] perdigueiro *m*; [of specific breed] labrador *m*.

retroactive [ˌretrəʊ'æktɪv] *adj fml* retroativo(va).

retrograde ['retrəgreɪd] *adj fml* retrógrado(da);**a ~ step** um passo para trás.

retrogressive [ˌretrə'gresɪv] *adj fml* & *pej* retrógrado(da).

retrospect ['retrəspekt] *n* (*U*): **in ~** em retrospecto.

retrospective [ˌretrə'spektɪv] <> *adj* **-1.** [mood, look] retrospectivo(va) **-2.** [law, pay rise] retroativo (va). <> *n* retrospectiva *f*.

retrospectively [ˌretrə'spektɪvlɪ] *adv* **-1.** [describe, feel] retrospectivamente **-2.** [come into force, pay] de forma retroativa.

return [rɪ'tɜːn] <> *n* **-1.** (*U*) [arrival back] volta *f*, regresso *m*; **~ (to)** regresso *m* (para); **~ to sthg** *fig* volta a algo **-2.** [giving back] devolução *f* **-3.** TENNIS rebatida *f* **-4.** UK [ticket] passagem *f* de ida e volta **-5.** [profit] retorno *m* **-6.** COMPUT [on keyboard] tecla *f* Return. <> *comp* [journey] de volta. <> *vt* **-1.** [gen] devolver **-2.** [reciprocate, give in exchange] retribuir **-3.** JUR dar **-4.** POL eleger. <> *vi*: **to ~ (from/to)** voltar (de/a).
  ◆ **returns** *npl* **-1.** COMM retorno *m*, rendimentos *mpl* **-2.** [on birthday]: **many happy ~s (of the day)!** que a data se repita por muitos e muitos anos!
  ◆ **in return** *adv* em troca.
  ◆ **in return for** *prep* em troca de.

returnable [rɪ'tɜːnəbl] *adj* retornável.

returning officer [rɪ'tɜːnɪŋ-] *n* UK oficial existente em cada distrito eleitoral da Grã-Bretanha que organiza a eleição para o Parlamento e anuncia o resultado oficial.

return key *n* COMPUT tecla *f* Return.

return match *n* partida *f* de volta.

return ticket *n* UK passagem *f* de ida e volta.

reunification [ˌriːjuːnɪfɪ'keɪʃn] *n* (*U*) reunificação *f*.

reunion [ˌriː'juːnjən] *n* reunião *f*.

Reunion [ˌriː'juːnjən] *n*: **~ (Island)** Ilha Réunion; **in ~** na Ilha Réunion.

reunite [ˌriːjuː'naɪt] *vt* reunir; **to be ~d with sb/sthg** estar reunido com alguém/algo.

reupholster [ˌriːʌp'həʊlstəʳ] *vt* estofar novamente.

reusable [riː'juːzəbl] *adj* reutilizável, reciclável.

reuse [*n* ˌriː'juːs, *vb* ˌriː'juːz] <> *n* (*U*) reutilização *f*. <> *vt* reutilizar.

rev [rev] (*pt* & *pp* **-ved**, *cont* **-ving**) *inf* <> *n* (*abbr of* **revolution**) rotação *f*. <> *vt*: **to ~ sthg (up)** acelerar algo. <> *vi*: **to ~ (up)** acelerar o motor.

Rev. (*abbr of* **Reverend**) Revdo.

revalue [ˌriː'væljuː] *vt* **-1.** [reassess] reavaliar **-2.** FIN [increase value of] valorizar.

revamp [ˌriː'væmp] *vt inf* **-1.** [reorganize] reformar **-2.** [redecorate] redecorar.

rev counter *n* tacómetro *m*.

reveal [rɪ'viːl] *vt* revelar.

revealing [rɪ'viːlɪŋ] *adj* **-1.** [clothes]: **a ~ dress** um vestido que mostra tudo **-2.** [comment] revelador(-ra), esclarecedor(ra).

reveille [UK rɪ'vælɪ, US 'revəlɪ] *n* toque *m* de alvorada.

revel ['revl] (UK *pt* & *pp* **-led**, *cont* **-ling**, US *pt* & *pp* **-ed**, *cont* **-ing**) *vi*: **to ~ in sthg** desfrutar de algo, deleitar-se com algo.

revelation [ˌrevə'leɪʃn] *n* **-1.** [surprising fact] revelação *f* **-2.** [surprising experience] surpresa *f*.

reveller UK, **reveler** US ['revələʳ] *n* farrista *mf*.

revelry ['revlrɪ] *n* (*U*) farra *f*.

revenge [rɪ'vendʒ] <> *n* (*U*) vingança *f*; **to take ~ (on sb)** vingar-se (de alguém). <> *comp* por vingança. <> *vt* vingar; **to ~ o.s. on sb/sthg** vingar-se de alguém/algo.

revenue ['revǝnju:] n -1. [income] receita f -2. [from investment] rendimento f -3. UK FIN: **the Inland Revenue** a Receita Federal.

reverberate [rɪ'vɜ:bǝreɪt] vi -1. [re-echo] ressoar, retumbar -2. [have repercussions] repercutir.

reverberations [rɪ,vɜ:bǝ'reɪʃnz] npl -1. [echoes] reverberação f -2. [repercussions] repercussões fpl.

revere [rɪ'vɪǝʳ] vt fml reverenciar, venerar.

reverence ['revǝrǝns] n (U) fml reverência f.

Reverend ['revǝrǝnd] n reverendo m.

Reverend Mother n madre f superiora.

reverent ['revǝrǝnt] adj reverente.

reverential [,revǝ'renʃl] adj fml reverencial.

reverie ['revǝrɪ] n fml devaneio m.

reversal [rɪ'vɜ:sl] n -1. [of trend, policy, decision] reviravolta f -2. [of roles, order, position] inversão f -3. [piece of ill luck] contratempo m.

reverse [rɪ'vɜ:s] <> adj reverso(sa), inverso(sa). <> n -1. AUT: ~ **(gear)** marcha f a ré; **to be in** ~ estar com a marcha a ré engatada; **to go into** ~ dar ré -2. [opposite]: **the** ~ o contrário -3. [back, other side - of paper] verso m; [- of coin] outro lado m. <> vt -1. AUT dar marcha a ré em -2. [trend, policy, decision] reverter -3. [roles, order, position] inverter -4. [turn over] virar -5. UK TELEC: **to** ~ **the charges** fazer uma ligação a cobrar. <> vi AUT dar marcha a ré.

reverse-charge call n UK chamada f a cobrar.

reversible [rɪ'vɜ:sǝbl] adj reversível.

reversing light [rɪ'vɜ:sɪŋ-] n UK luz f de ré.

reversion [rɪ'vɜ:ʃn] n (U) reversão f, volta f; ~ **to** sthg reversão OR volta a algo.

revert [rɪ'vɜ:t] vi: **to** ~ **to** sthg voltar a algo.

review [rɪ'vju:] <> n -1. [examination] revisão f, reavaliação f; **to come up for** ~ ser revisado(da), ser reavaliado(da); **the situation is under** ~ a situação está sendo avaliada -2. [critique] crítica f, resenha f. <> vt -1. [reassess] reavaliar -2. [write an article on] fazer resenha OR crítica de -3. [troops] passar em revista -4. US [study] revisar.

reviewer [rɪ'vju:ǝʳ] n crítico m, -ca f.

revile [rɪ'vaɪl] vt literary insultar, injuriar.

revise [rɪ'vaɪz] <> vt -1. [reconsider] revisar -2. [rewrite] corrigir, alterar -3. UK [study] revisar. <> vi UK: **to** ~ **(for sthg)** fazer revisão (para algo).

revised [rɪ'vaɪzd] adj revisado(da).

revision [rɪ'vɪʒn] n -1. [alteration] alteração f, correção f -2. (U) [study] revisão f.

revisionist [rɪ'vɪʒnɪst] <> adj revisionista. <> n revisionista mf.

revisit [,ri:'vɪzɪt] vt revisitar.

revitalize, -ise [,ri:'vaɪtǝlaɪz] vt revitalizar.

revival [rɪ'vaɪvl] n -1. COMM reativação f -2. [of interest, cultural activity] renovação f -3. [of play] revival m.

revive [rɪ'vaɪv] <> vt -1. [resuscitate] ressuscitar -2. [revitalize - plant, economy] revitalizar; [- interest, hopes] despertar -3. [bring back into use, being - tradition] restabelecer; [- musical, play] reviver; [- memories] trazer à baila. <> vi -1. [regain consciousness] voltar a si, recobrar os sentidos -2. [be revitalized - plant, economy] revitalizar-se; [- interest, hopes] renovar-se.

revoke [rɪ'vǝʊk] vt fml revogar.

revolt [rɪ'vǝʊlt] <> n revolta f, rebelião f. <> vt revoltar. <> vi: **to** ~ **(against sb/sthg)** revoltar-se OR rebeliar-se (contra alguém/algo).

revolting [rɪ'vǝʊltɪŋ] adj revoltante, repugnante.

revolution [,revǝ'lu:ʃn] n revolução f; ~ **in** sthg revolução em algo.

revolutionary [revǝ'lu:ʃnǝrɪ] (pl -ies) <> adj revolucionário(ria). <> n POL revolucionário m, -ria f.

revolutionize, -ise [,revǝ'lu:ʃǝnaɪz] vt revolucionar.

revolve [rɪ'vɒlv] vi girar, dar voltas; **to** ~ **(a)round** sthg girar em torno de algo; **to** ~ **(a)round** sb girar em torno de alguém.

revolver [rɪ'vɒlvǝʳ] n revólver m.

revolving [rɪ'vɒlvɪŋ] adj giratório(ria).

revolving door n porta f giratória.

revue [rɪ'vju:] n teatro m de revista.

revulsion [rɪ'vʌlʃn] n (U) repugnância f, asco m.

reward [rɪ'wɔ:d] <> n -1. [recompense] recompensa f -2. [sum of money] recompensa f, gratificação f. <> vt recompensar; **to** ~ **sb for/with sthg** recompensar alguém por/com algo.

rewarding [rɪ'wɔ:dɪŋ] adj gratificante.

rewind [,ri:'waɪnd] (pt & pp rewound) vt rebobinar.

rewire [,ri:'waɪǝʳ] vt trocar a fiação elétrica de.

reword [,ri:'wɜ:d] vt expressar com outras palavras.

rework [,ri:'wɜ:k] vt reelaborar.

rewound [,ri:'waʊnd] pt & pp ⊳ rewind.

rewrite [,ri:'raɪt] (pt rewrote [,ri:'rǝʊt], pp rewritten [,ri:'rɪtnl]) vt reescrever.

REX (abbr of real-time executive routine) n [comput] programa em tempo real.

Reykjavik ['rekjǝvɪk] n Reykjavik.

RFC (abbr of Rugby Football Club) n clube de rugby britânico.

RGN (abbr of registered general nurse) n titular de diploma em enfermagem na Grã-Bretanha.

r.h. (abbr of right hand) mão f direita.

Rh (abbr of rhesus) Rh.

rhapsody ['ræpsǝdɪ] (pl -ies) n -1. MUS rapsódia f -2. [strong approval] entusiasmo m.

Rheims n Rheims.

Rhesus ['ri:sǝs] n: ~ **positive/negative** Rh m positivo/negativo.

rhetoric ['retǝrɪk] n (U) retórica f.

rhetorical question [rɪ'tɒrɪkl-] n pergunta f retórica.

rheumatic [ru:'mætɪk] adj reumático(ca).

rheumatism ['ru:mǝtɪzm] n (U) reumatismo m.

rheumatoid arthritis ['ru:mǝtɔɪd-] n (U) artrite f reumatóide.

Rhine [raɪn] n: **the** ~ o Reno.

Rhineland ['raɪnlænd] n Renânia f.

rhinestone ['raɪnstǝʊn] n diamante m falso.

rhino ['raɪnǝʊ] (pl inv OR -s) n inf rino m.

rhinoceros [raɪ'nɒsǝrǝs] (pl inv OR -es) n rinoceronte m.

Rhode Island [rǝʊd-] n Rhode Island.

Rhodes [rǝʊdz] n Rodes.

Rhodesia [rǝʊ'di:ʃǝ] n Rodésia.

Rhodesian [rəʊˈdiːʃn] ◇ adj rodesiano(na). ◇ n rodesiano m, -na f.

rhododendron [ˌrəʊdəˈdendrən] n rododendro m.

Rhone n: **the (River)** ~ o Rio Ródano.

rhubarb [ˈruːbɑːb] n (U) ruibarbo m.

rhyme [raɪm] ◇ n -1. [word] rima f; **in** ~ em verso -2. [poem] poesia f, versos mpl. ◇ vi rimar; **to** ~ **with sthg** rimar com algo.

rhyming slang [ˈraɪmɪŋ-] n (U) UK tipo de gíria do leste londrino que consiste em contrapor duas palavras que dão significado a uma terceira, rimando a segunda com essa terceira.

rhythm [ˈrɪðm] n ritmo m.

rhythm and blues n (U) rhythm m and blues.

rhythmic(al) [ˈrɪðmɪk(l)] adj ritmado(da).

RI ◇ n (abbr of religious instruction) educação f religiosa. ◇ abbr of Rhode Island.

rib [rɪb] n -1. ANAT costela f -2. [of metal or wood] vareta f.

RIBA (abbr of Royal Institute of British Architects) n instituto real dos arquitetos britânicos.

ribald [ˈrɪbəld] adj grosseiro(ra).

ribbed [rɪbd] adj canelado(da).

ribbon [ˈrɪbən] n fita f.

rib cage n caixa f torácica.

rice [raɪs] n (U) arroz m.

rice field n arrozal m.

rice paper n (U) papel m de palha de arroz.

rice pudding n arroz-doce m, arroz-de-leite m.

rich [rɪtʃ] ◇ adj -1. [gen] rico(ca). **to be** ~ **in sthg** ser rico(ca) em algo -2. [indigestible] pesado(da) -3. [vibrant] vibrante -4. [sumptuous, expensive] suntuoso(sa). ◇ npl: **the** ~ os ricos.
 ➡ **riches** npl -1. [natural resources] riquezas fpl -2. [wealth] riqueza f.

richly [ˈrɪtʃlɪ] adv [gen] ricamente; ~ **deserved** bem merecido(da).

richness [ˈrɪtʃnɪs] n (U) -1. [gen] riqueza f -2. [of food] peso m.

Richter scale [ˈrɪktə-] n: **the** ~ a escala Richter.

rickets [ˈrɪkɪts] n (U) raquitismo m.

rickety [ˈrɪkətɪ] adj instável, sem solidez.

rickshaw [ˈrɪkʃɔː] n jinriquixá m.

ricochet [ˈrɪkəʃeɪ] (pt & pp -ed OR -ted, cont -ing OR -ting) ◇ n ricochete m. ◇ vi ricochetear; **to** ~ **off sthg** ricochetear em algo.

rid [rɪd] (pt rid OR -ded, pp rid, cont -ding) ◇ adj: **to be** ~ **of sb/sthg** estar livre de alguém/algo. ◇ vt: **to** ~ **sb/sthg of sthg** livrar alguém/algo de algo; **to** ~ **o.s. of sthg** livrar-se de algo; **to get** ~ **of sb/sthg** livrar-se de alguém/algo.

riddance [ˈrɪdəns] n inf: **good** ~ **!** já vai tarde!, que bons ventos o levem!

ridden [ˈrɪdn] pp ▷ ride.

riddle [ˈrɪdl] n -1. [verbal puzzle] adivinhação f -2. [mystery] enigma m.

riddled [ˈrɪdld] adj -1. [holes, errors] cheio (cheia) -2. [bullet holes] crivado(da) -3. [woodworm] infestado(da).

ride [raɪd] (pt rode, pp ridden) ◇ n -1. [gen] passeio m; **to go for a** OR **horse/bike** ~ dar um passeio a cavalo/de bicicleta; **to go for a car** ~ dar uma volta OR um passeio de carro -2. phr: **to take sb for a** ~ inf [trick] levar alguém no bico. ◇ vt -1. [horse] montar em -2. [bicycle, motorbike] andar de -3. [distance] percorrer -4. US [travel in] ir de. ◇ vi -1. [on horseback] montar -2. [on bicycle] andar de bicicleta -3. [on motorbike] andar de moto -4. [in car, bus]: **to** ~ **in sthg** andar de algo.
 ➡ **ride up** vi subir.

rider [ˈraɪdə] n -1. [on horseback - male] jinete m; [- female] amazona f -2. [on bicycle] ciclista mf -3. [on motorbike] motoqueiro m, -ra f.

ridge [rɪdʒ] n -1. [on mountain] crista f -2. [on flat surface - in sand, of muscles] saliência f; [- in fabric] ruga f.

ridicule [ˈrɪdɪkjuːl] ◇ n (U) zombaria f. ◇ vt ridicularizar.

ridiculous [rɪˈdɪkjʊləs] adj ridículo(la).

ridiculously [rɪˈdɪkjʊləslɪ] adv ridiculamente.

riding [ˈraɪdɪŋ] ◇ n (U) equitação f. ◇ comp de equitação.

riding crop n chicote m, rebenque m.

riding habit n traje m de montar.

riding school n escola f de equitação.

rife [raɪf] adj muito comum; **to be** ~ **with sthg** estar cheio(cheia) de algo.

riffraff [ˈrɪfræf] n (U) gentalha f, ralé f.

rifle [ˈraɪfl] ◇ n rifle m. ◇ vt roubar.
 ➡ **rifle through** vt fus vasculhar.

rifle range n estande m de tiro ao alvo.

rift [rɪft] n -1. GEOL fenda f -2. [quarrel] desavença f; ~ **between/in** desavença entre/em.

Rift Valley n: **the** ~ o Rift Valley.

rig [rɪg] (pt & pp -ged, cont -ging) ◇ n [structure - onshore] torre f de perfuração; [- offshore] plataforma f petrolífera. ◇ vt manipular.
 ➡ **rig up** vt sep armar, construir.

rigging [ˈrɪgɪŋ] n -1. [of ship] (U) cordame m -2. [of votes] fraude f em uma votação.

right [raɪt] ◇ adj -1. [gen] certo(ta), correto(ta); **to be** ~ **about sthg** estar certo(ta) sobre algo, ter razão sobre algo; **to get sthg** ~ acertar algo; **to be** ~ **to do sthg** estar certo(ta) ao fazer algo -2. [going well] bem -3. [socially desirable, appropriate] apropriado(da) -4. [not left] direito(ta) -5. UK inf [complete] perfeito(ta). ◇ adv -1. [correctly] corretamente, bem -2. [not left] para a direita -3. [emphatic use]: ~ **here** aqui mesmo; ~ **down** bem para baixo; ~ **in the middle** bem no meio -4. [immediately]: **I'll be** ~ **back** eu já volto; ~ **after** Christmas logo depois do Natal; ~ **now** [immediately] agora; [at this very moment] já; ~ **away** em seguida. ◇ n -1. (U) [moral correctness] certo m; **to be in the** ~ ter razão -2. [entitlement, claim] direito m; **by** ~**s** por direito; **in one's own** ~ por seus próprios méritos -3. [right-hand side] direita f; **on the** ~ à direita. ◇ vt -1. [correct] corrigir -2. [make upright] endireitar. ◇ excl certo!
 ➡ **Right** n POL: **the Right** a direita.

right angle n ângulo m reto; **at** ~**s to sthg** em ângulo reto com algo.

righteous [ˈraɪtʃəs] adj -1. [anger, indignation] justo(ta) -2. [person] honrado(da).

righteousness [ˈraɪtʃəsnɪs] n (U) honradez f, retidão f.

rightful [ˈraɪtfʊl] adj legítimo(ma).

rightfully ['raɪtfʊlɪ] *adv* legitimamente.
right-hand *adj* direito(ta); ~ **side** o lado direito.
right-hand drive *adj* com direção do lado direito.
right-handed [-'hændɪd] *adj* destro(tra).
right-hand man *n* braço *m* direito.
rightly ['raɪtlɪ] *adv* -1. [gen] corretamente -2. [justifiably] com razão.
right-minded [-'maɪndɪd] *adj* honrado(da).
rightness *n (U)* -1. [soundness] correção *f* -2. [appropriateness] conveniência *f*.
righto ['raɪtəʊ] *excl inf* certo!
right of way *n* -1. AUT preferência *f* -2. [access] direito *m* de passagem.
rights issue *n* emissão *f* de bônus de subscrição.
right-thinking *adj* correto(ta), sensato(ta).
right wing *n:* the ~ a direita.
➡ **right-wing** *adj* de direita.
right-winger *n* direitista *mf*.
rigid ['rɪdʒɪd] *adj* -1. [gen] rígido(da) -2. [inflexible] inflexível.
rigidity [rɪ'dʒɪdətɪ] *n (U)* rigidez *f*.
rigidly ['rɪdʒɪdlɪ] *adv* -1. [fixedly] firmemente -2. [harshly, strictly] rigidamente.
rigmarole ['rɪgmərəʊl] *n inf pej* -1. [process] ritual *m* -2. [story] ladainha *f*.
rigor *n US* = rigour.
rigor mortis [-'mɔːtɪs] *n (U)* rigidez *f* cadavérica.
rigorous ['rɪgərəs] *adj* rigoroso(sa).
rigorously ['rɪgərəslɪ] *adv* rigorosamente.
rigour UK, **rigor** US ['rɪgəʳ] *n (U)* rigor *m*.
➡ **rigours** *npl* rigores *mpl*.
rig-out *n UK inf* traje *m*, beca *f*.
rile [raɪl] *vt* irritar.
rim [rɪm] *n* -1. [top edge of container] borda *f* -2. [outer edge of round object - of spectacles, glass] moldura *f*; [- of wheel] aro *m*.
rind [raɪnd] *n* casca *f*.
ring [rɪŋ] (*pt* rang, *pp vt senses 1 & 2 & vi* rung, *pt & pp vt senses 3 & 4 only* ringed) <> *n* -1. [telephone call]: to give sb a ~ dar uma ligada para alguém -2. [sound of bell] toque *m* -3. [quality, tone] tom *m*; it has a familiar ~ soa familiar -4. [circular object - for curtains, napkin] argola *f*; napkin ~ argola *f* para guardanapo; [- hoop] aro *m* -5. [piece of jewellery] anel *m* -6. [of people, trees] círculo *m* -7. [for boxing] ringue *m* -8. [people working together] cartel *m* -9. *phr:* to run ~s round sb *fig* superar alguém facilmente. <> *vt* -1. UK [phone] telefonar para, ligar para -2. [bell, doorbell] tocar -3. [draw a circle round] fazer um círculo ao redor de -4. [surround] cercar, rodear; to be ~ed with sthg estar cercado(da) de algo. <> *vi* -1. UK [phone] telefonar, ligar -2. [bell, doorbell] tocar -3. [to attract attention]: to ~ (for sb/sthg) chamar (por alguém/algo) -4. [resound]: to ~ with sthg ressoar com algo -5. *phr:* to ~ true soar verdadeiro(ra).
➡ **ring back** UK <> *vt sep* voltar a ligar para. <> *vi* voltar a ligar.
➡ **ring off** *vi* UK desligar.
➡ **ring out** *vi* -1. [sound] soar claramente -2. UK TELEC ligar.

➡ **ring up** *vt sep* UK ligar.
ring binder *n* fichário *m* com aros de metal.
ringer ['rɪŋəʳ] *n:* to be a dead ~ for sb ser o retrato vivo de alguém.
ring finger *n* (dedo *m*) anular *m*.
ringing ['rɪŋɪŋ] <> *adj* [clear, loud] alto e claro, alta e clara. <> *n* -1. *(U)* [of bell] toque *m* -2. *(U)* [in ears] zumbido *m*.
ringing tone *n* UK TELEC tom *m* de discagem.
ringleader ['rɪŋ,liːdəʳ] *n* cabeça *m*.
ringlet ['rɪŋlɪt] *n* anel *m* de cabelo.
ringmaster ['rɪŋ,mɑːstəʳ] *n* diretor *m*, -ra *f* de circo.
ring road *n* UK anel *m* rodoviário.
ringside ['rɪŋsaɪd] <> *n:* the ~ o ringue. <> *comp* de primeira fila.
ring tone *n* [for mobile phone] toque *m* musical.
ringway ['rɪŋweɪ] *n* UK anel *m* rodoviário.
ringworm ['rɪŋwɜːm] *n (U)* tinha *f*.
rink [rɪŋk] *n* rinque *m*.
rinse [rɪns] <> *n* enxágue *m*. <> *vt* enxaguar; to ~ one's mouth out enxaguar a boca.
Rio (de Janeiro) [,riːəʊ(dədʒə'nɪərəʊ)] *n* Rio de Janeiro.
Rio Grande [,riːəʊ'grændɪ] *n:* the ~ o Rio Grande.
Rio Negro *n:* the ~ o Rio Negro.
riot ['raɪət] <> *n* desordem *f*; to run ~ descontrolar-se. <> *vi* amotinar-se.
rioter ['raɪətəʳ] *n* desordeiro *m*, -ra *f*.
rioting ['raɪətɪŋ] *n (U)* desordem *f*.
riotous ['raɪətəs] *adj* -1. [party] barulhento(ta) -2. [behaviour, mob] desordeiro(ra).
riot police *npl* tropa *f* de choque.
riot shield *n* escudo *m* antimotim.
rip [rɪp] (*pt & pp* -ped, *cont* -ping) <> *n* rasgão *m*. <> *vt* -1. [tear, shred] rasgar -2. [remove] arrancar. <> *vi* rasgar.
➡ **rip off** *vt sep inf* -1. [cheat] trapacear, passar a perna em -2. [steal] roubar.
➡ **rip up** *vt sep* rasgar, fazer em pedaços.
RIP (*abbr of* rest in peace) descanse em paz.
ripcord ['rɪpkɔːd] *n* corda *f* de abertura.
ripe [raɪp] *adj* maduro(ra); to be ~ (for sthg) *fig* estar pronto(ta) (para algo).
ripen ['raɪpn] *vt & vi* amadurecer.
ripeness ['raɪpnɪs] *n (U)* maturação *f*.
rip-off *n inf* -1. [swindle] assalto *m* -2. [imitation] imitação *f* barata.
ripple ['rɪpl] <> *n* -1. [in water] ondulação *f* -2. [of laughter, applause] onda *f*. <> *vt* ondular.
rip-roaring *adj inf* estrondoso(sa).
rise [raɪz] (*pt* rose, *pp* risen ['rɪzn]) <> *n* -1. UK [increase in amount] aumento *m*, subida *f* -2. UK [increase in salary] aumento *m* -3. [to power, fame] ascensão *f* -4. [slope] ladeira *f* -5. *phr:* to give ~ to sthg originar algo. <> *vi* -1. [gen] elevar-se -2. [sun, moon] nascer, sair -3. UK [increase] aumentar, subir -4. [stand up] levantar-se -5. *literary* [get out of bed] levantar-se -6. [to a challenge]: to ~ to sthg mostrar-se à altura de algo; to ~ to the occasion elevar-se à altura (de algo) -7. [rebel] sublevar-se -8. [in status] ascender; to ~ to sthg ascender a algo -9. [bread, soufflé] crescer.

↠ rise above vt fus superar, mostrar-se superior a.

riser ['raɪzə'] n: **an early** ~ um madrugador; **a late** ~ pessoa f que se levanta tarde.

risible ['rɪzəbl] adj fml risível.

rising ['raɪzɪŋ] ◇ adj **-1.** [gen] em ascensão **-2.** [sloping upwards] em aclive **-3.** [tide] que sobe. ◇ n [rebellion] levante m, rebelião f.

rising damp n (U) umidade f proveniente do solo.

risk [rɪsk] ◇ n risco m; **to run the** ~ **of sthg/of doing sthg** correr o risco de algo/de fazer algo; **to take a** ~ arriscar-se; **it's at your own** ~ é por sua conta e risco; **at** ~ em perigo; **at the** ~ **of** sob risco de. ◇ vt **-1.** [put in danger] arriscar **-2.** [take the chance of]: **to** ~ **doing sthg** arriscar-se a fazer algo; **go on,** ~ **it!** vamos, arrisque-se!

risk capital n (U) capital m de risco.

risk-taking n (U) aceitação f de riscos.

risky ['rɪskɪ] (compar **-ier,** superl **-iest**) adj arriscado (da).

risotto [rɪ'zɒtəʊ] (pl **-s**) n risoto m.

risqué ['riːskeɪ] adj picante.

rissole ['rɪsəʊl] n UK bolinho m de carne, rissole m.

rite [raɪt] n rito m.

ritual ['rɪtʃʊəl] ◇ adj ritual. ◇ n ritual m.

rival ['raɪvl] (UK pt & pp **-led,** cont **-ling,** US pt & pp **-ed,** cont **-ing**) ◇ adj **-1.** [gen] rival **-2.** [company] concorrente. ◇ n **-1.** [gen] rival mf **-2.** [company] concorrente mf. ◇ vt rivalizar or competir com.

rivalry ['raɪvlrɪ] n rivalidade f.

river ['rɪvə'] n rio m.

river bank n margem f do rio.

riverbed ['rɪvəbed] n leito m do rio.

riverside ['rɪvəsaɪd] n: **the** ~ a margem do rio.

rivet ['rɪvɪt] ◇ n rebite m. ◇ vt **-1.** [fasten with rivets] rebitar **-2.** fig [fascinate]: **to be** ~**ed by sthg** estar fascinado(da) por algo.

riveting ['rɪvɪtɪŋ] adj fascinante.

Riviera [ˌrɪvɪ'eərə] n: **the French** ~ a Riviera Francesa; **the Italian** ~ a Riviera Italiana.

Riyadh ['riːæd] n Riyadh.

RM (abbr of **Royal Marines**) n fuzileiros navais britânicos.

RN n **-1.** (abbr of **Royal Navy**) marinha f real britânica **-2.** (abbr of **registered nurse**) titular de diploma de enfermagem na Grã-Bretanha.

RNA (abbr of **ribonucleic acid**) n RNA m.

RNLI (abbr of **Royal National Lifeboat Institution**) n organização de voluntários na Grã-Bretanha e na Irlanda que oferece resgate marítimo.

RNZAF (abbr of **Royal New Zealand Air Force**) n força aérea real neozelandesa.

RNZN (abbr of **Royal New Zealand Navy**) n marinha real neozelandesa.

roach [rəʊtʃ] (pl sense 1 inv OR **-es,** pl senses 2 & 3 **-es**) n **-1.** [fish] peixe semelhante à carpa **-2.** drugs sl bagana f de baseado **-3.** US [cockroach] barata f.

road [rəʊd] n **-1.** [major] estrada f; **by** ~ por estrada; **on the** ~ [travelling] na estrada; **on the** ~ **to** fig a caminho de **-2.** [minor] caminho m **-3.** [street] rua f.

road atlas n guia f rodoviário.

roadblock ['rəʊdblɒk] n barreira f policial.

road-fund licence n UK ≃ imposto m sobre veículos automotores, ≃ IPVA m.

road haulage n transportes mpl rodoviários.

road hog n inf pej dono m, -na f da estrada.

roadholding ['rəʊdˌhəʊldɪŋ] n (U) estabilidade f (na estrada).

roadie ['rəʊdɪ] n inf roadie mf.

road map n mapa m rodoviário.

road rage n raiva f no trânsito.

road roller n rolo m compressor.

road safety n (U) segurança f no trânsito.

road sense n (U) senso m de direção.

roadshow ['rəʊdʃəʊ] n programa de rádio transmitido diretamente por um disc-jóquei itinerante.

roadside ['rəʊdsaɪd] ◇ n: **the** ~ a beira da estrada. ◇ comp de beira da estrada.

road sign n placa f de trânsito.

roadsweeper ['rəʊdˌswiːpə'] n [vehicle] caminhão m de limpeza das ruas.

road tax n ≃ imposto m sobre veículos automotores, ≃ IPVA m.

road test n teste m de direção.

↠ road-test vt fazer um teste de direção com.

road transport n (U) transporte m rodoviário.

roadway ['rəʊdweɪ] n pista f (da estrada).

road works npl obras fpl na pista.

roadworthy ['rəʊdˌwɜːðɪ] adj em condições de tráfego.

roam [rəʊm] ◇ vt vagar por. ◇ vi vagar.

roar [rɔː'] ◇ vi **-1.** [lion] rugir **-2.** [traffic, plane, engine] roncar **-3.** [person] urrar; **to** ~ **with laughter** rir às gargalhadas **-4.** [wind] bramir. ◇ vt bradar. ◇ n **-1.** [of lion] rugido m **-2.** [of engine] ronco m **-3.** [of traffic] barulho m **-4.** [of wind] sopro m **-5.** [of person] urro m.

roaring ['rɔːrɪŋ] ◇ adj **-1.** [traffic, wind] barulhento(ta) **-2.** [fire] crepitante **-3.** [for emphasis] estrondoso(sa); **a** ~ **success** um sucesso estrondoso; **to do a** ~ **trade** vender bem. ◇ adv [for emphasis] completamente.

roast [rəʊst] ◇ adj assado(da). ◇ n assado m. ◇ vt **-1.** [meat, potatoes] assar **-2.** [coffee beans, nuts] torrar.

roast beef n (U) rosbife m.

roasting ['rəʊstɪŋ] inf ◇ adj muito quente; **I'm** ~! estou derretendo de calor! ◇ adv: **it's a** ~ **hot day!** hoje está um inferno de quente!

roasting tin n assadeira f.

rob [rɒb] (pt & pp **-bed,** cont **-bing**) vt roubar; **to** ~ **sb of sthg** [of money, goods] roubar algo de alguém; fig [of opportunity, glory] privar alguém de algo.

robber ['rɒbə'] n ladrão m, -dra f.

robbery ['rɒbərɪ] (pl **-ies**) n roubo m.

robe [rəʊb] n **-1.** [of priest] túnica f **-2.** [judge] toga f **-3.** [monarch] manto m **-4.** US [dressing gown] robe m.

robin ['rɒbɪn] n pintarroxo m.

robot ['rəʊbɒt] n robô m.

robotics [rəʊ'bɒtɪks] n (U) robótica f.

robust [rəʊ'bʌst] adj [person] **-1.** robusto(ta) **-2.** [economy] forte **-3.** [health] de ferro **-4.** [criticism, defence] vigoroso(sa).

robustly [rəʊ'bʌstlɪ] *adv* vigorosamente.
rock [rɒk] <> *n* -1. (U) [substance] rocha *f* -2. [boulder] rochedo *m*, penhasco *m* -3. *US* [pebble] pedregulho *m* -4. (U) [music] rock *m* -5. (U) *UK* [sweet] barra *f* de caramelo. <> *comp* [music] de rock. <> *vt* -1. [cause to move] balançar -2. [shock] abalar. <> *vi* balançar-se.
   ➤ **on the rocks** *adv* -1. [drink] com gelo, on the rocks -2. [marriage, relationship] que vai mal.
rock and roll *n* (U) rock and roll *m*.
rock bottom *n* (U) nível *m* baixíssimo; **to hit ~** atingir o fundo do poço.
   ➤ **rock-bottom** *adj* baixíssimo(ma).
rock cake *n UK* bolo com frutas secas.
rock climber *n* alpinista *mf*.
rock-climbing *n* (U) alpinismo *m*.
rocker ['rɒkəʳ] *n* [chair] embaladeira *f*; **to be off one's ~** *inf* ter um parafuso a menos.
rockery ['rɒkərɪ] (*pl* -ies) *n* jardim *m* de pedras.
rocket ['rɒkɪt] <> *n* foguete *m*. <> *vi* disparar.
rocket launcher [-ˌlɔ:ntʃəʳ] *n* lança-foguetes *m inv*.
rock face *n* parede *f* de pedra.
rockfall ['rɒkfɔ:l] *n* deslizamento *m* de pedras.
rock-hard *adj* duro(ra) como pedra.
Rockies ['rɒkɪz] *npl*: **the ~** as Montanhas Rochosas.
rocking chair ['rɒkɪŋ-] *n* cadeira *f* de balanço.
rocking horse ['rɒkɪŋ-] *n* cavalinho *m* de balanço.
rock music *n* (U) rock *m*.
rock 'n' roll *n* = rock and roll.
rock pool *n* piscina formada por pedras na praia.
rock salt *n* (U) sal-gema *m*.
rock singer *n* cantor *m*, -ra *f* de rock, roqueiro *m*, -ra *f*.
rocky ['rɒkɪ] (*compar* -ier, *superl* -iest) *adj* -1. [full of rocks] rochoso(sa) -2. [unsteady] instável.
Rocky Mountains *npl*: **the ~** as Montanhas Rochosas.
rococo [rə'kəʊkəʊ] *adj* rococó.
rod [rɒd] *n* -1. [wooden] vara *f* -2. [metal] barra *f*.
rode [rəʊd] *pt* ⊳ **ride**.
rodent ['rəʊdəntl] *n* roedor *m*.
rodeo ['rəʊdɪəʊ] (*pl* -s) *n* rodeio *m*.
roe [rəʊl] *n* ova *f* (de peixe).
roe deer *n* corço *m*, -ça *f*.
rogue [rəʊg] <> *adj* -1. [animal] solitário e perigoso, solitária e perigosa -2. *fig* [person] rebelde. <> *n* -1. [likable rascal] malandro *m*, -dra *f* -2. *dated* [dishonest person] vigarista *mf*.
roguish ['rəʊgɪʃ] *adj* malandro(dra).
role [rəʊl] *n* -1. [position, function] função *f*, papel *m* -2. *CINEMA, THEATRE* papel *m*.
roll [rəʊl] <> *n* -1. [of material, paper, film] rolo *m* -2. [of banknotes] maço *m* -3. [of cloth] peça *f* -4. [of bread] pãozinho *m* -5. [list] lista *f* -6. [sound - of drum] rufar *m*; [- of thunder] estrondo *m*. <> *vt* -1. [turn over] rolar; **to ~ one's eyes** [in fear, despair] revirar os olhos -2. [make into cylinder] enrolar; **~ed into one** *fig* tudo num só. <> *vi* -1. [of a round object] rolar -2. [move] andar -3. [sway from side to side] balançar

-4. [sound - drum] rufar; [- thunder] retumbar.
   ➤ **roll about, roll around** *vi* rolar.
   ➤ **roll back** *vt sep US* [prices] reduzir.
   ➤ **roll in** *vi inf* -1. [money] chegar de balde -2. [person] pintar.
   ➤ **roll over** *vi* virar-se.
   ➤ **roll up** <> *vt sep* -1. [make into cylinder] enrolar -2. [sleeves] arregaçar. <> *vi* -1. [vehicle] chegar -2. *inf* [person] pintar.
roll bar *n* santantônio *m*.
roll call *n* toque *m* de chamada.
rolled gold [rəʊld-] *n* (U) plaquê *m*.
roller ['rəʊləʳ] *n* -1. [cylinder] cilindro *m* -2. [curler] rolo *m*.
Rollerblades® ['rəʊləˌbleɪdz] *npl* patins *mpl* em linha.
rollerblading ['rəʊləˌbleɪdɪŋ] *n* patinação *f* (com patins em linha); **to go ~** praticar patinação (com patins em linha).
roller blind *n* persiana *f* de enrolar.
roller coaster *n* montanha-russa *f*.
roller skate *n* patim *m* de rodas.
   ➤ **roller-skate** *vi* patinar.
roller towel *n* toalha *f* de rolo.
rollicking ['rɒlɪkɪŋ] *adj* divertido(da).
rolling ['rəʊlɪŋ] *adj* -1. [undulating] ondulado(da) -2. [swaying from side to side] bamboleante -3. *phr*: **to be ~ in it** *inf* estar nadando em dinheiro.
rolling mill *n* laminador *m*.
rolling pin *n* rolo *m* de massa.
rolling stock *n* (U) material *m* rodante.
roll-neck *adj* com gola rulê.
roll of honour *n* lista *f* de honra.
roll-on <> *adj* de rolo, roll-on. <> *n* desodorante *m* de rolo *OR* roll-on.
roll-on roll-off *adj UK*: **a ~ ferry** uma balsa para veículos.
roly-poly (*pl* -ies) *n UK*: **~ (pudding)** rocambole *m*.
ROM [rɒm] (*abbr of* read-only memory) *n* ROM *f*.
romaine lettuce [rəʊ'meɪn-] *n US* alface *f* (de folha larga).
Roman ['rəʊmən] <> *adj* romano(na). <> *n* romano *m*, -na *f*.
Roman candle *n* pistolão *m*.
Roman Catholic <> *adj* católico (romano), católica (romana). <> *n* católico *m* (romano), católica *f* (romana).
romance [rəʊ'mæns] *n* -1. [gen] romance *m* -2. (U) [romantic quality] romantismo *m*.
Romanesque [ˌrəʊmə'nesk] *adj* românico(ca).
Romani *adj* & *n* = **Romany**.
Romania [rə'meɪnjə] *n* Romênia; **in ~** na Romênia.
Romanian [rə'meɪnjən] <> *adj* romeno(na). <> *n* -1. [person] romeno *m*, -na *f* -2. [language] romeno *m*.
Roman numerals *npl* algarismos *mpl* romanos.
romantic [rəʊ'mæntɪk] *adj* romântico(ca).
romanticism [rəʊ'mæntɪsɪzm] *n* romantismo *m*.
romanticize, -ise [rəʊ'mæntɪsaɪz] <> *vt* romantizar. <> *vi* romantizar, fantasiar.
Romany ['rəʊmənɪ] (*pl* -ies) <> *adj* cigano(na).

◇ n -1. [person] cigano m, -na f -2. [language] romani m.

Rome [rəʊm] n Roma.

romp [rɒmp] ◇ n travessura f. ◇ vi brincar ruidosamente.

rompers ['rɒmpəz] npl, **romper suit** ['rɒmpə'-] n macacão m de criança.

roof [ru:f] n -1. [covering - of vehicle] capota f; [- of building] telhado m; **not under my ~!** não na minha casa!; **under the same ~** sob o mesmo teto; **to have a ~ over one's head** ter onde morar; **to go through** OR **hit the ~** subir pelas paredes -2. [upper part - of cave] teto m; [- of mouth] céu m da boca.

roof garden n jardim m de cobertura.

roofing ['ru:fɪŋ] n (U) material m para cobertura.

roof rack n bagageiro m (na capota do carro).

rooftop ['ru:ftɒp] n telhado m.

rook [rʊk] n -1. [bird] gralha f -2. [chess piece] torre f.

rookie ['rʊkɪ] n US inf novato m, -ta f.

room [ru:m, rʊm] n -1. [in building] sala f -2. [bedroom] quarto m -3. (U) [space] espaço m; **to make ~ for sb/sthg** abrir espaço para alguém/algo -4. (U) [opportunity, possibility] possibilidade f; ~ **to** OR **for manoeuvre** espaço para manobrar.

rooming house ['ru:mɪŋ-] n US pensão f.

roommate ['ru:mmeɪt] n companheiro m, -ra f de quarto.

room service n serviço m de quarto.

room temperature n temperatura f ambiente.

roomy ['ru:mɪ] (compar -ier, superl -iest) adj espaçoso(sa), amplo(pla).

roost [ru:st] ◇ n poleiro m; **to rule the ~** cantar de galo. ◇ vi empoleirar-se.

rooster ['ru:stə'] n galo m.

root [ru:t] ◇ adj básico(ca), fundamental. ◇ n [gen] raiz f; **to put down ~s** [person] criar raízes; **to take ~** [plant] pegar; [idea] consolidar-se. ◇ vi remexer.

➜ **roots** npl raízes fpl.

➜ **root for** vt fus esp US inf torcer por.

➜ **root out** vt sep arrancar até a raiz, extirpar.

root beer n US cerveja sem álcool feita de raízes.

root crop n tubérculos mpl.

rooted ['ru:tɪd] adj: **to be ~ to the spot** ficar paralisado(da) (de medo).

rootless ['ru:tlɪs] adj sem raízes, desarraigado(da).

root vegetable n tubérculo m.

rope [rəʊp] ◇ n corda f; **to know the ~s** estar por dentro do assunto. ◇ vt amarrar com corda.

➜ **rope in** vt sep inf arrastar para.

➜ **rope off** vt sep isolar com cordas.

rop(e)y ['rəʊpɪ] (compar -ier, superl -iest) adj UK inf -1. [poor-quality] ruim -2. [unwell] indisposto(ta), mal.

rosary ['rəʊzərɪ] (pl -ies) n rosário m.

rose [rəʊz] ◇ pt ⊳ **rise**. ◇ adj [pink] rosa, cor-de-rosa. ◇ n [flower] rosa f; **it's not a bed of ~s** não é feito de rosas.

rosé ['rəʊzeɪ] n (U) vinho m rosé.

rosebed ['rəʊzbed] n canteiro m de rosas.

rosebud ['rəʊzbʌd] n botão m de rosa.

rose bush n roseira f.

rose-coloured adj cor-de-rosa.

rose hip n rosa-mosqueta f.

rosemary ['rəʊzmərɪ] n (U) alecrim m.

rose-tinted adj: **to look through ~ glasses** ver tudo cor-de-rosa.

rosette [rəʊ'zet] n roseta f.

rosewater ['rəʊz,wɔ:tə'] n (U) água-de-rosas f.

rosewood ['rəʊzwʊd] n (U) pau-rosa m.

RoSPA (abbr of Royal Society for the Prevention of Accidents) n organização britânica para prevenção de acidentes.

roster ['rɒstə'] n lista f.

rostrum ['rɒstrəm] (pl -trums OR -tra [-trə]) n tribuna f, rostro m.

rosy ['rəʊzɪ] (compar -ier, superl -iest) adj -1. [pink] rosado(da) -2. [hopeful] promissor(ra).

rot [rɒt] (pt & pp -ted, cont -ting) ◇ n -1. [decay - of wood, food] putrefação f; [- in society, organization] decadência f -2. UK dated [nonsense] besteira f, bobagem f. ◇ vt [cause to decay] corroer, decompor. ◇ vi apodrecer.

rota ['rəʊtə] n lista f de turnos.

rotary ['rəʊtərɪ] ◇ adj rotatório(ria). ◇ n US [roundabout] rotatória f.

Rotary Club n: **the ~** o Rotary Club.

rotate [rəʊ'teɪt] ◇ vt -1. [gen] alternar -2. [turn] girar. ◇ vi -1. [turn] girar, dar voltas -2. [in sequence - jobs] alternar-se; [- crops] alternar.

rotation [rəʊ'teɪʃn] n -1. [turning movement] rotação f -2. (U) [sequence - of jobs] revezamento m, alternância f; [- of crops] rodízio m; **in ~** por turnos.

rote [rəʊt] n (U): **by ~** de cor OR memória.

rote learning n decoreba f.

rotor ['rəʊtə'] n rotor m.

rotten ['rɒtn] adj -1. [decayed] podre -2. inf [poor-quality, unskilled] péssimo(ma) -3. inf [unpleasant, nasty] perverso(sa), ruim -4. inf [unenjoyable] detestável -5. inf [unwell]: **to feel ~** sentir-se péssimo(ma) -6. [unhappy, bad]: **to feel ~ (about sthg)** sentir-se péssimo(ma) (por algo).

rotund [rəʊ'tʌnd] adj fml rotundo(da).

rouble ['ru:bl] n rublo m.

rouge [ru:ʒ] n (U) ruge m.

rough [rʌf] ◇ adj -1. [not smooth - surface] áspero(ra); [- road] acidentado(da) -2. [violent] rude, grosseiro(ra) -3. [crude, basic - people, manners] rústico(ca); [- shelter, conditions, situation] precário(ria) -4. [approximate - not detailed] rudimentar; [- not exact] aproximado(da) -5. [unpleasant, tough - life, time] duro(ra), difícil; [- area, town etc] tumultuoso(sa) -6. [stormy - weather] tormentoso(sa); [- crossing] movimentado(da); [- sea] agitado(da); [- wind] violento(ta); [- day] tempestuoso(sa) -7. [sounding harsh] áspero(ra) -8. [tasting harsh] azedo(da) -9. [tired, ill] abatido(da). ◇ adv: **to sleep ~** dormir na rua. ◇ n -1. GOLF: **the ~** o rough -2. [undetailed form]: **in ~** em rascunho. ◇ vt phr: **to ~ it** viver sem comodidades.

➡ **rough out** *vt sep* esboçar.

➡ **rough up** *vt sep* bater em, atacar.

roughage ['rʌfɪdʒ] *n* fibras *fpl*.

rough and ready *adj* rústico(ca), feito(ta) às pressas.

rough-and-tumble *n (U)* tumulto *m*.

roughcast *n (U)* reboco *m* grosso.

rough diamond *n UK fig* diamante *m* bruto.

roughen ['rʌfn] *vt* tornar áspero(ra).

rough justice *n (U)* injustiça *f*.

roughly ['rʌflɪ] *adv* -**1.** [not gently] bruscamente -**2.** [crudely] rusticamente -**3.** [approximately] aproximadamente, mais ou menos.

roughneck ['rʌfnek] *n* -**1.** [oilrig worker] *petroleiro que trabalha em campo de perfuração* -**2.** *US inf* [ruffian] casca-grossa *mf*.

roughness ['rʌfnɪs] *n (U)* -**1.** [lack of smoothness] aspereza *f* -**2.** [lack of gentleness] rudeza *f*, grosseria *f*.

roughshod ['rʌfʃɒd] *adv*: **to ride ~ over sb/sthg** tratar alguém/algo a pontapés.

roulette [ruː'let] *n (U)* roleta *f*.

round [raʊnd] ⟨⟩ *adj* -**1.** [gen] redondo(da) -**2.** [fat, curved - cheeks, hips] roliço(ça), redondo(da); [- bulge] redondo(da). ⟨⟩ *prep* -**1.** [surrounding] ao redor de -**2.** [near] em volta de; **~ here** por aqui -**3.** [all over] por todo(da) -**4.** [in circular movement, in circumference] ao redor de; **she measures 70 cm ~ the waist** ela mede *or* tem 70 cm de cintura -**5.** [to/on the other side of]: **to drive ~ the corner** dobrar a esquina; **I live just ~ the corner** eu moro logo ali -**6.** [so as to avoid - hole, obstacle]: **to go ~ an obstacle** contornar um obstáculo; [- problem]: **to find a way ~ sthg** achar um jeito de contornar algo. ⟨⟩ *adv* -**1.** [surrounding]: **all ~** por toda a volta, por todos os lados -**2.** [near]: **~ about** [in distance] por perto; [in number, amount] aproximadamente -**3.** [all over]: **to travel ~** viajar por aí -**4.** [in circular movement]: **~ (and ~)** em círculos; **to go ~** circular; **to spin ~** girar -**5.** [in circumference]: **it's at least 3 km ~** tem no mínimo 3 km de circunferência -**6.** [to the other side or direction] ao redor; **to turn ~** virar; **to go ~** dar a volta -**7.** [on a visit]: **come ~ sometime!** apareçam uma hora dessas! ⟨⟩ *n* -**1.** [gen] rodada *f*; **a ~ of applause** uma salva de palmas -**2.** [professional visit] percurso *m* -**3.** [of ammunition] cartucho *m* -**4.** *BOXING* assalto *m* -**5.** *GOLF* partida *f*. ⟨⟩ *vt* [turn] dobrar, virar.

➡ **rounds** *npl* [professional visits] percurso *m*; **to do** *or* **go the ~s** *fig* espalhar-se, propagar-se.

➡ **round off** *vt sep* encerrar, terminar.

➡ **round up** *vt sep* -**1.** [gather together] reunir -**2.** *MATH* arredondar.

roundabout ['raʊndəbaʊt] ⟨⟩ *adj* indireto(ta). ⟨⟩ *n UK* -**1.** [on road] rotatória *f* -**2.** [at fairground] carrossel *m* -**3.** [at playground] gira-gira *m*.

rounded ['raʊndɪd] *adj* redondo(da).

rounders ['raʊndəz] *n (U) UK* bete *m*.

Roundhead ['raʊndhed] *n HIST seguidor de Oliver Cromwell na guerra civil inglesa*, Cabeça *m* Redonda.

roundly ['raʊndlɪ] *adv* totalmente, terminantemente.

round-neck *adj* de gola redonda.

round-shouldered [-'ʃəʊldəd] *adj* de ombros caídos.

round-table *adj* em igualdade de condições.

round the clock *adv* durante as 24 horas do dia.

➡ **round-the-clock** *adj* contínuo(nua), 24 horas do dia.

round trip ⟨⟩ *adj US* de ida e volta. ⟨⟩ *n* viagem *f* de ida e volta.

round-up *n* resumo *m*.

rouse [raʊz] *vt* -**1.** [wake up] despertar -**2.** [impel]: **to ~ sb to do sthg** animar alguém a fazer algo; **to ~ o.s. to do sthg** animar-se a fazer algo -**3.** [excite] estimular -**4.** [give rise to] suscitar.

rousing ['raʊzɪŋ] *adj* estimulante.

rout [raʊt] ⟨⟩ *n* derrota *f* esmagadora. ⟨⟩ *vt* derrotar de forma esmagadora.

route [ruːt] ⟨⟩ *n* -**1.** [line of travel - of journey] rota *f*; [- of or person, procession] trajeto *m*, percurso *m* -**2.** [of bus, train] linha *f* -**3.** [of plane, ship] rota *f* -**4.** *fig* [to achievement] caminho *m*. ⟨⟩ *vt* -**1.** [flight, traffic] direcionar -**2.** [goods] enviar.

route map *n* mapa *m (de localização)*.

route march *n* marcha *f*.

routine [ruː'tiːn] ⟨⟩ *adj* -**1.** [normal] de rotina -**2.** *pej* [humdrum, uninteresting] rotineiro(ra). ⟨⟩ *n* -**1.** *(U)* [normal pattern of activity] rotina *f* -**2.** *pej* [boring repetition] rotina *f*.

routinely [ruː'tiːnlɪ] *adv* freqüentemente.

rove [rəʊv] *literary* ⟨⟩ *vt* errar, vagar por. ⟨⟩ *vi*: **to ~ around** vagar.

roving ['rəʊvɪŋ] *adj* itinerante; **~ eyes** olhar *m* errante.

row[1] [rəʊ] ⟨⟩ *n* -**1.** [gen] fileira *f* -**2.** [succession] seqüência *f*, série *f*; **four in a ~** quatro seguidos. ⟨⟩ *vt* -**1.** [boat] remar -**2.** [person] conduzir de barco a remo. ⟨⟩ *vi* [in boat] remar.

row[2] [raʊ] ⟨⟩ *n* -**1.** [quarrel] briga *f* -**2.** *inf* [noise] alvoroço *m*, barulho *m*. ⟨⟩ *vi* [quarrel] discutir, brigar.

rowboat ['rəʊbəʊt] *n US* barco *m* a remo.

rowdiness ['raʊdɪnɪs] *n (U)* alvoroço *m*, tumulto *m*.

rowdy ['raʊdɪ] *(compar* -**ier**, *superl* -**iest**) *adj* -**1.** [person] brigão(gona) -**2.** [party, atmosphere] barulhento(ta).

rower ['rəʊə[r]] *n* remador *m*, -ra *f*.

row house [rəʊ-] *n US* casa *f* geminada.

rowing ['rəʊɪŋ] *n (U)* remo *m*.

rowing boat *n UK* barco *m* a remo.

rowing machine *n* remo *m* seco.

royal ['rɔɪəl] ⟨⟩ *adj* real. ⟨⟩ *n inf* membro *m* da família real.

Royal Air Force *n (U)*: **the ~** a Força Aérea Británica.

royal blue *adj* azul-imperial.

royal family *n* família *f* real.

royalist ['rɔɪəlɪst] *n* monarquista *mf*.

royal jelly *n (U)* geléia *f* real.

Royal Mail *n UK*: **the ~** os Correios da Grã-Bretanha.

Royal Marines *n UK*: **the ~** os Fuzileiros Navais Británicos.

Royal Navy *n*: the ~ a Marinha Real Britânica.
royalty [ˈrɔɪəltɪ] *n (U)* realeza *f.*
◆ **royalties** *npl* direitos *mpl* autorais.
RP *(abbr of* **received pronunciation)** *n pronúncia padrão do inglês.*
RPI *(abbr of* **retail price index)** *n* ≃ IPC *m.*
rpm *(abbr of* **revolutions per minute)** *npl* rpm.
RR *(abbr of* **railroad)** *US* ferrovia *f.*
RRP *(abbr of* **recommended retail price)** *n UK* preço *m* sugerido.
RSA *n -* **1.** *(abbr of* **Republic of South Africa)** República *f* da África do Sul **- 2.** *(abbr of* **Royal Society of Arts)** *sociedade britânica para o fomento às artes, à indústria e ao comércio.*
RSC *(abbr of* **Royal Shakespeare Company)** *n importante companhia teatral britânica especializada em Shakespeare.*
RSI *(abbr of* **repetitive strain injury)** *n* LER *f.*
RSJ *(abbr of* **rolled steel joist)** *n* vigamento *m* folheado a aço.
RSPB *(abbr of* **Royal Society for the Protection of Birds)** *n organização britânica para a proteção de pássaros em seu habitat.*
RSPCA *(abbr of* **Royal Society for the Prevention of Cruelty to Animals)** *n sociedade britânica protetora de animais.*
RSVP *(abbr of* **répondez s'il vous plaît)** RSVP.
rub [rʌb] *(pt & pp* **-bed,** *cont* **-bing)** ◇ *vt* esfregar; **to ~ shoulders with** acotovelar-se com; **to ~ sthg against sthg** esfregar algo em *or* contra algo; **to ~ sthg on sthg** [polish] esfregar algo em algo; **to ~ sthg in (to) sthg** esfregar algo em algo; **to ~ it in** *inf fig* trazer à tona; **to ~ sb up the wrong way** *UK*, **to ~ sb the wrong way** *US* ofender alguém sem intenção. ◇ *vi*: **to ~ (against** *or* **on sthg)** roçar (em algo); **to ~ (together)** esfregar-se; **to ~ along** dar-se bem com.
◆ **rub off on** *vt fus* influir em.
◆ **rub out** *vt sep* apagar.
rubber [ˈrʌbəʳ] ◇ *adj* de borracha. ◇ *n -* **1.** *(U)* [substance] borracha *f* **- 2.** *UK* [eraser] borracha *f* **- 3.** [in bridge] rubber *m* **- 4.** *US inf* [condom] camisinha *f* **- 5.** *US* [overshoe] galocha *f.*
rubber band *n* atilho *m,* borrachinha *f (para papel).*
rubber boot *n US* bota *f* de borracha.
rubber dinghy *n* bote *m* de borracha.
rubberize, -ise [ˈrʌbəraɪz] *vt* revestir de borracha.
rubberneck [ˈrʌbənek] *vi US inf* [stare] olhar com curiosidade.
rubber plant *n* goma-elástica *f.*
rubber stamp *n* carimbo *m.*
◆ **rubber-stamp** *vt* aprovar sem questionar.
rubber tree *n* seringueira *f.*
rubbery [ˈrʌbərɪ] *adj* borrachento(ta).
rubbing [ˈrʌbɪŋ] *n* [of brass] calcografia *f.*
rubbish [ˈrʌbɪʃ] ◇ *n -* **1.** [refuse] lixo *m* **- 2.** *inf fig* [worthless matter] porcaria *f* **- 3.** *inf* [nonsense] besteira *f,* bobagem *f.* ◇ *vt inf* rebaixar. ◇ *excl* bobagem!
rubbish bag *n UK* saco *m* de lixo.
rubbish bin *n UK* lata *f* de lixo.

rubbish dump, rubbish tip *n UK* depósito *m* de lixo.
rubbishy [ˈrʌbɪʃɪ] *adj inf* porcaria.
rubble [ˈrʌbl] *n (U)* entulho *m.*
rubella [ruːˈbelə] *n (U)* rubéola *f.*
ruby [ˈruːbɪ] *(pl* -ies) *n* rubi *m.*
RUC *(abbr of* **Royal Ulster Constabulary)** *n força policial na Irlanda do Norte.*
ruck *n -* **1.** *inf* [fight] arruaça *f* **- 2.** *RUGBY* luta *f* pela posse da bola.
rucksack [ˈrʌksæk] *n* mochila *f.*
ructions [ˈrʌkʃnz] *npl inf* alvoroço *m,* tumulto *m.*
rudder [ˈrʌdəʳ] *n* leme *m.*
ruddy [ˈrʌdɪ] *(compar* -ier, *superl* -iest) *adj -* **1.** [reddish] corado(da) **- 2.** *UK dated* [for emphasis] maldito(ta).
rude [ruːd] *adj -* **1.** [impolite] rude, grosseiro(ra) **- 2.** [dirty, naughty - joke] sujo(ja); [- word] grosseiro(ra); [- noise] violento(ta) **- 3.** [unexpected] brusco(ca); **~ awakening** um despertar brusco **- 4.** *literary* [primitive] rústico(ca).
rudely [ˈruːdlɪ] *adv -* **1.** [gen] de forma grosseira **- 2.** [unexpectedly] bruscamente, violentamente.
rudeness [ˈruːdnɪs] *n (U)* grosseria *f.*
rudimentary [ˌruːdɪˈmentərɪ] *adj* rudimentar.
rudiments [ˈruːdɪmənts] *npl* rudimentos *mpl,* noções *fpl* básicas.
rue [ruː] *vt* lamentar, arrepender-se de.
rueful [ˈruːfʊl] *adj* arrependido(da).
ruff [rʌf] *n* gola *f* franzida.
ruffian [ˈrʌfjən] *n* rufião *m,* -ona *f.*
ruffle [ˈrʌfl] ◇ *n* rufo *m.* ◇ *vt -* **1.** [mess up - hair, fur] revolver; [- water] agitar **- 2.** [upset] enervar.
rug [rʌg] *n -* **1.** [carpet] tapete *m (pequeno)* **- 2.** [blanket] manta *f.*
rugby [ˈrʌgbɪ] *n (U)* rúgbi *m.*
Rugby League *n* rúgbi profissional disputado com equipes de 13 jogadores.
Rugby Union *n* rúgbi amador disputado com equipes de 15 jogadores.
rugged [ˈrʌgɪd] *adj -* **1.** [rocky, uneven] acidentado(da) **- 2.** [sturdy] potente **- 3.** [roughly handsome] rústico(ca) e atraente.
ruggedness [ˈrʌgɪdnɪs] *n (U)* aspereza *f.*
rugger [ˈrʌgəʳ] *n (U) UK inf* rúgbi *m.*
ruin [ˈruːɪn] ◇ *n* ruína *f.* ◇ *vt -* **1.** [spoil] arruinar, estragar **- 2.** [bankrupt] arruinar.
◆ **in ruin(s)** *adv* em ruínas.
ruination [ˌruːɪˈneɪʃn] *n (U)* arruinação *f,* ruína *f.*
ruinous [ˈruːɪnəs] *adj* dispendioso(sa).
rule [ruːl] ◇ *n -* **1.** [regulation - *SPORT*] regra *f;* **to bend the ~s** abrir uma exceção nas regras; [- *SCH*] norma *f* **- 2.** [convention, guideline] regra *f;* **as a ~ of thumb** por experiência (própria) **- 3.** [norm]: **the ~** a regra, a norma; **as a ~** via de regra **- 4.** *(U)* [control] domínio *m* **- 5.** [ruler] régua *f.* ◇ *vt -* **1.** [control, guide] comandar **- 2.** [govern] governar **- 3.** [decide]: **to ~ that** ordenar *or* decretar que. ◇ *vi -* **1.** [give decision] deliberar **- 2.** *fml* [be paramount] dominar **- 3.** [govern] governar.
◆ **rule out** *vt sep -* **1.** [reject as unsuitable] descartar **- 2.** [prevent, make impossible - possibility, circumstances] descartar; [- event, decision] impedir.
rulebook [ˈruːlbʊk] *n*: **the ~** o regulamento.

ruled [ru:ld] *adj* pautado(da).

ruler ['ru:lə^r] *n* **-1.** [for measurement] régua *f* **-2.** [leader] soberano *m*, -na *f*.

ruling ['ru:lɪŋ] <> *adj* no poder, dominante. <> *n* sentença *f*, parecer *m*.

rum [rʌm] (*compar* -**mer**, *superl* -**mest**) <> *adj UK inf dated* esquisito(ta). <> *n* (*U*) rum *m*.

Rumania [ru:'meɪnjə] *n* = **Romania**.

Rumanian [ru:'meɪnjən] *adj* & *n* = **Romanian**.

rumba ['rʌmbə] *n* rumba *f*.

rumble ['rʌmbl] <> *n* **-1.** [noise - of thunder] · estrondo *m*; [- of stomach, train] ronco *m*; [- of traffic] barulho *m* **-2.** *US inf* [fight] arruaça *f*. <> *vt UK inf dated* revelar, descobrir. <> *vi* **-1.** [thunder] trovejar **-2.** [stomach, train] roncar **-3.** [traffic] fazer barulho.

rumbustious [rʌm'bʌstʃəs] *adj UK* esfuziante, enérgico(ca).

ruminate ['ru:mɪneɪt] *vi fml*: to ~ (about OR on sthg) ruminar (algo).

rummage ['rʌmɪdʒ] *vi* escarafunchar.

rummage sale *n US* bazar *m* beneficente *(de artigos usados)*.

rummy ['rʌmɪ] *n* (*U*) jogo de cartas semelhante à canastra e ao buraco.

rumour *UK*, **rumor** *US* ['ru:mə^r] *n* rumor *m*, boato *m*.

rumoured *UK*, **rumored** *US* ['ru:məd] *adj*: to be ~ed that comenta-se que.

rump [rʌmp] *n* **-1.** [of animal] anca *f*, garupa *f* **-2.** *inf* [of person] nádegas *fpl*.

rumple ['rʌmpl] *vt* **-1.** [clothes] amarrotar **-2.** [hair] despentear.

rump steak *n* filé *m* de alcatra.

rumpus ['rʌmpəs] *n inf* bafafá *m*, rolo *m*.

rumpus room *n US* sala *f* de jogos.

run [rʌn] (*pt* ran, *pp* run, *cont* -ning) <> *n* **-1.** [on foot] corrida *f*; to go for a ~ ir dar uma corrida; to break into a ~ sair em disparada; to take the dog for a ~ levar o cão para um passeio; on the ~ em fuga **-2.** [in car] passeio *f*; it's a long ~ down to Cornwall é um longo caminho até Cornwall **-3.** [series - of luck] alternância *f*; [- of disasters, wins] série *f* **-4.** *THEATRE* temporada *f* **-5.** [great demand]: ~ on sthg procura *f* OR demanda *f* por algo **-6.** [in tights] fio *m* puxado **-7.** [in cricket, baseball] ponto *m* **-8.** [sports track] pista *f* **-9.** [term, period]: in the short/long ~ a curto/longo prazo. <> *vt* **-1.** [on foot] correr **-2.** [manage, control] dirigir, administrar **-3.** [machine] operar **-4.** [car] dirigir, fazer andar **-5.** [water, bath, tap] abrir **-6.** [publish] publicar **-7.** *inf* [drive] levar **-8.** [move, pass]: to ~ sthg along/over sthg passar algo em/sobre algo. <> *vi* **-1.** [gen] passar; to be running late estar atrasado(da) **-2.** [on foot] correr; to ~ for it fugir **-3.** *US* [in election]: to ~ (for sthg) concorrer (a algo) **-4.** [progress, develop]: to ~ smoothly ir bem **-5.** [machine, factory, engine] funcionar; to ~ on OR off sthg funcionar com algo **-6.** [liquid, river] escorrer; to ~ dry secar **-7.** [nose] escorrer **-8.** [tap] pingar **-9.** [colour] borrar **-10.** [continue] continuar; to have two months to ~ o contrato ainda é válido por dois meses; feelings are ~ning high os ânimos estão exaltados.

run about *vi* **-1.** [from place to place] correr (de um lugar para outro) **-2.** [associate] andar.

run across *vt fus* encontrar-se com.

run along *vi dated*: ~ along now! andando!

run around *vi* = **run about**.

run away *vi* **-1.** [flee]: to ~ away (from sb/sthg) fugir (de alguém/algo) **-2.** *fig* [avoid]: to ~ away from sthg fugir de algo.

run away with *vt fus*: he lets his enthusiasm ~ away with him ele se deixa levar pelo entusiasmo.

run down <> *vt sep* **-1.** [in vehicle] atropelar **-2.** [criticize] falar mal de **-3.** [allow to decline] enfraquecer. <> *vi* perder força.

run in *vt sep* [car] amaciar.

run into *vt fus* **-1.** [encounter - problem] deparar-se com; [- person] topar com **-2.** [in vehicle] chocar-se com OR contra **-3.** [amount to] chegar a, atingir.

run off <> *vt sep* [a copy] imprimir. <> *vi* [abscond, elope]: to ~ off (with sb/sthg) fugir (com alguém/algo).

run on *vi* continuar.

run out *vi* **-1.** [become used up] esgotar **-2.** [expire] vencer, caducar.

run out of *vt fus* ficar sem; we've ~ out of food acabou a nossa comida.

run over *vt sep* atropelar.

run through *vt fus* **-1.** [spread through] permear **-2.** [practise] ensaiar, praticar **-3.** [read through] passar os olhos em.

run to *vt fus* **-1.** [amount to] chegar a **-2.** [afford]: my budget doesn't ~ to a new car meu orçamento não me permite comprar um carro novo.

run up *vt fus* contrair.

run up against *vt fus* deparar-se com.

run-around *n inf*: to give sb the ~ enrolar alguém.

runaway ['rʌnəweɪ] <> *adj* [out of control - train, inflation] descontrolado(da); [- victory] fácil. <> *n* fugitivo *m*, -va *f*.

rundown ['rʌndaʊn] *n* **-1.** [report] relatório *m* detalhado **-2.** [decline] desmantelamento *m* gradual.

run-down *adj* **-1.** [dilapidated] arruinado(da), em ruínas **-2.** [tired] esgotado(da).

rung [rʌŋ] <> *pp* ⊳ **ring**. <> *n* degrau *m*.

run-in *n inf* rixa *f*.

runner ['rʌnə^r] *n* **-1.** [athlete] corredor *m*, -ra *f* **-2.** [smuggler - guns] contrabandista *mf*; [- drugs] traficante *mf* **-3.** [wood or metal strip - of sledge, skate] lâmina *f*; [- of drawer] corrediça *f*.

runner bean *n UK* feijão-trepador *m*.

runner-up (*pl* runners-up) *n* segundo colocado *m*, segunda colocada *f*.

running ['rʌnɪŋ] <> *adj* **-1.** [continuous] constante **-2.** [consecutive] consecutivo(va) **-3.** [water - not stagnant] corrente; [- in pipes] encanado(da). <> *n* **-1.** (*U*) *SPORT* corrida *f*; she loves ~ in the park ela gosta de correr no parque **-2.** [management, control] gestão *f*, direção *f* **-3.** [of machine] funcionamento *m* **-4.** *phr*: to make the ~ tomar as rédeas; to be in/out of the ~ (for sthg) ter/não ter possibilidades (de algo). <> *comp SPORT* de corrida.

running commentary *n* comentário *m* ao vivo.

running costs *npl* despesas *fpl* de manutenção.

running mate *n US* candidato *m*, -ta *f* a vice-presidente.

running repairs *npl* pequenos reparos *mpl*.

runny ['rʌnɪ] (*compar* -ier, *superl* -iest) *adj* -1. [food - eggs] mal-passado(da); [- jam, honey] mole; [- butter, chocolate] derretido(da) -2. [nose] escorrendo -3. [eyes] lacrimejante.

run-of-the-mill *adj* corriqueiro(ra).

runt [rʌnt] *n* -1. [animal] filhote *m* mais fraco -2. *pej* [person] tampinha *mf*.

run-through *n* ensaio *m*.

run-up *n* -1. [preceding time] período *m* anterior -2. *SPORT* impulso *m*.

runway ['rʌnweɪ] *n* pista *f* (de pouso/decolagem).

rupture ['rʌptʃəʳ] *n* -1. *MED* hérnia *f* -2. [of relationship] rompimento *m*.

rural ['rʊərəl] *adj* rural.

ruse [ruːz] *n* ardil *m*.

rush [rʌʃ] <> *n* -1. [hurry] pressa *f*; **there's no ~** não há pressa; **to make a ~ for** sthg disparar até algo -2. [demand]: **~ (for OR on sthg)** procura *f* excessiva (por algo); **~ to do** sthg corrida para fazer algo -3. [busiest period] corre-corre *m* -4. [surge - physical] fluxo *m*; **~ of air** corrente *m* de ar; [- mental, emotional] torrente *f*. <> *vt* -1. [hurry] apressar; **to ~ sb into** sthg apressar alguém em algo; **to ~ sb into doing** sthg apressar alguém para que faça algo -2. [send quickly] levar com urgência -3. [attack suddenly] investir repentinamente contra. <> *vi* -1. [hurry] apressar-se; **to ~ into** sthg entrar de cabeça em algo -2. [crowd] correr.

➡ **rushes** *npl* -1. *BOT* juncos *mpl* -2. *CINEMA* primeiras cópias *fpl*.

rushed [rʌʃt] *adj* -1. [person] apressado(da) -2. [work] feito(ta) às pressas.

rush hour *n* hora *f* do rush.

rush job *n* -1. [urgent job] trabalho *m* urgente -2. [bad work] trabalho *m* feito às pressas.

rusk [rʌsk] *n* biscoito *m* seco.

russet ['rʌsɪt] *adj* ferrugíneo(nea).

Russia ['rʌʃə] *n* Rússia; **in ~** na Russia.

Russian ['rʌʃn] <> *adj* russo(sa). <> *n* -1. [person] russo *m*, -sa *f* -2. [language] russo *m*.

Russian roulette *n* (*U*) roleta *f* russa.

rust [rʌst] <> *n* (*U*) ferrugem *f*. <> *vi* enferrujar.

rustic ['rʌstɪk] *adj* rústico(ca).

rustle ['rʌsl] <> *n* ruído *m*. <> *vt* -1. [paper, leaves] farfalhar -2. *US* [cattle] roubar. <> *vi* farfalhar.

rustproof ['rʌstpruːf] *adj* inoxidável.

rusty ['rʌstɪ] (*compar* -ier, *superl* -iest) *adj* enferrujado(da).

rut [rʌt] *n* -1. [furrow] sulco *m*; **to get into/be in a ~** tornar-se/ser escravo(va) da rotina -2. [animal] cio *m*.

rutabaga [,ruːtəˈbeɪgə] *n US* nabo *m* sueco.

ruthless ['ruːθlɪs] *adj* impiedoso(sa).

ruthlessly ['ruːθlɪslɪ] *adv* impiedosamente.

ruthlessness ['ruːθlɪsnɪs] *n* (*U*) crueldade *f*.

RV *n* -1. (*abbr of* **revised version**) *tradução da Bíblia para o inglês no final do século XIX* -2. (*abbr of* **recreational vehicle**) *US* motor-home *m*.

Rwanda [rʊˈændə] *n* Ruanda; **in ~** em Ruanda.

Rwandan [rʊˈændən] <> *adj* ruandês(esa). <> *n* ruandês *m*, -esa *f*.

rye [raɪ] *n* (*U*) centeio *m*.

rye bread *n* (*U*) pão *m* de centeio.

rye grass *n* (*U*) azevém *m*.

rye whiskey *n* (*U*) uísque *m* de centeio.

S

s (*pl* ss *OR* s's), **S** (*pl* Ss *OR* S's) [es] *n* [letter] s, S *m*.
➡ **S** (*abbr of* **south**) S.

SA -1. (*abbr of* **South Africa**) África *f* do Sul -2. (*abbr of* **South America**) América *f* do Sul -3. (*abbr of* **South Australia**) *região sul da Austrália*.

Saar *n*: **the ~** o Sarre.

Sabbath ['sæbəθ] *n*: **the ~** o sabá.

sabbatical [səˈbætɪkl] *n* período *m* sabático; **on ~** em período sabático.

saber ['seɪbəʳ] *n US* = **sabre**.

sable *n* zibelina *f*.

sabotage ['sæbətɑːʒ] <> *n* (*U*) sabotagem *f*. <> *vt* sabotar.

saboteur [,sæbəˈtɜːʳ] *n* sabotador *m*, -ra *f*.

sabre *UK*, **saber** *US* ['seɪbəʳ] *n* sabre *m*.

saccharin(e) ['sækərɪn] *n* (*U*) sacarina *f*.

sachet ['sæʃeɪ] *n* sachê *m*.

sack [sæk] <> *n* -1. [bag] saco *m* -2. *UK inf* [dismissal]: **to get** *OR* **be given the ~** ser despedido(da). <> *vt UK inf* [dismiss] despedir, mandar embora.

sackful ['sækfʊl] *n* saca *f*.

sacking ['sækɪŋ] *n* (*U*) linhagem *f*.

sacrament ['sækrəmənt] *n* sacramento *m*.

sacred ['seɪkrɪd] *adj* sagrado(da).

sacrifice ['sækrɪfaɪs] <> *n* sacrifício *m*. <> *vt* sacrificar.

sacrilege ['sækrɪlɪdʒ] *n* (*U*) sacrilégio *m*.

sacrilegious [,sækrɪˈlɪdʒəs] *adj* sacrílego(ga).

sacrosanct ['sækrəʊsæŋkt] *adj* sacrossanto(ta).

sad [sæd] (*compar* -der, *superl* -dest) *adj* triste.

sadden ['sædn] *vt* entristecer.

saddle ['sædl] <> *n* -1. [for horse] sela *f* -2. [of bicycle, motorcycle] selim *m*. <> *vt* -1. [put saddle on] selar -2. *fig* [burden]: **to ~ sb with** sthg encarregar alguém de algo.

➡ **saddle up** <> *vt fus* selar. <> *vi* selar.

saddlebag ['sædlbæg] *n* -1. [for horse] alforje *m* -2.

[for bicycle, motorcycle] bolsa f.
saddler ['sædlə'] n seleiro m, -ra f.
sadism ['seɪdɪzm] n (U) sadismo m.
sadist ['seɪdɪst] n sádico m, -ca f.
sadistic [sə'dɪstɪk] adj sádico(ca).
sadly ['sædlɪ] adv -1. [sorrowfully] tristemente -2. [regrettably] lamentavelmente.
sadness ['sædnɪs] n tristeza f.
sadomasochistic adj sadomasoquista.
s.a.e., sae (abbr of stamped addressed envelope) n envelope-resposta com porte pago.
safari [sə'fɑːrɪ] n safári m; **to go on** ~ fazer um safári.
safari park n parque-safári m.
safe [seɪf] ⟨⟩ adj -1. [not causing harm or danger] seguro(ra); **in** ~ **hands** em boas mãos -2. [not in danger] protegido(da); **to be** ~ **from attack** estar a salvo de ataques; ~ **and sound** são e salvo, sã e salva -3. [not causing disagreement] pacífico(ca); **it's** ~ **to say that ...** pode-se dizer com segurança que ... -4. [not involving any risk] seguro(ra); **to be on the** ~ **side** por precaução -5. [secret] bem guardado(da). ⟨⟩ n cofre m.
safe-breaker n arrombador m, -ra f de cofre.
safe-conduct n -1. [document giving protection] salvo-conduto m -2. (U) [protection] salvaguarda f.
safe-deposit box n caixa-forte f.
safeguard ['seɪfgɑːd] ⟨⟩ n salvaguarda f, proteção f; ~ **against sthg** proteção contra algo. ⟨⟩ vt: **to** ~ **sb/sthg (against sthg)** proteger OR salvaguardar alguém/algo (de algo).
safe haven n refúgio m.
safe house n esconderijo m.
safe keeping n (U) proteção f, custódia f; **in sb's** ~ aos cuidados de alguém.
safely ['seɪflɪ] adv -1. [gen] com segurança -2. [unharmed] ileso(sa), a salvo -3. [for certain]: **I can** ~ **say (that)** ... posso dizer seguramente que ...
safe sex n (U) sexo m seguro.
safety ['seɪftɪ] ⟨⟩ n segurança f. ⟨⟩ comp de segurança.
safety belt n cinto m de segurança.
safety catch n trava f de segurança.
safety curtain n cortina f corta-fogo, cortina f de amianto.
safety-deposit box n = safe-deposit box.
safety island n US ilha f (na rua).
safety match n fósforo m de segurança.
safety net n -1. [in circus] rede f de segurança -2. fig [means of protection] proteção f.
safety pin n alfinete m de segurança.
safety valve n -1. TECH válvula f de segurança -2. fig [for emotions] válvula f de escape.
saffron ['sæfrən] n (U) -1. [spice] açafrão m -2. [colour] amarelo-laranja m.
sag [sæg] (pt & pp -ged, cont -ging) vi -1. [sink downwards] afundar, ceder -2. fig [lessen] diminuir.
saga ['sɑːgə] n -1. LITERATURE saga f -2. pej [drawn-out account] novela f.
sage [seɪdʒ] ⟨⟩ adj [wise] sábio(bia). ⟨⟩ n -1. (U) [herb] sálvia f -2. [wise man] sábio m.
saggy ['sægɪ] (compar -ier, superl -iest) adj [bed] afundado(da); [breasts] caído(da).

Sagittarius [,sædʒɪ'teərɪəs] n -1. [sign] Sagitário m -2. [person] sagitariano m, -na f; **I'm** ~ **sou de** Sagitário.
Sahara [sə'hɑːrə] n: **the** ~ **(Desert)** o (Deserto do) Saara.
Saharan [sə'hɑːrən] adj saariano(na).
said [sed] pt & pp ▷ **say**.
sail [seɪl] ⟨⟩ n -1. [of boat] vela f; **to set** ~ zarpar -2. [journey by boat]: **let's go for a** ~ vamos velejar. ⟨⟩ vt -1. [boat] governar -2. [sea] cruzar. ⟨⟩ vi -1. [to depart] zarpar -2. [sport] velejar -3. [to travel, move - person] navegar; [- boat] singrar -4. fig [through air] voar.
◆ **sail through** vt fus passar fácil por.
sailboard ['seɪlbɔːd] n prancha f de windsurfe.
sailboat n US = sailing boat.
sailcloth ['seɪlklɒθ] n (U) lona f.
sailing ['seɪlɪŋ] n -1. (U) SPORT navegação f a vela, vela f; **I like to go** ~ eu gosto de (ir) velejar; **plain** ~ sem maiores dificuldades -2. [trip by ship] travessia f.
sailing boat UK, **sailboat** US ['seɪlbəʊt] n barco m a vela.
sailing dinghy n dinga f.
sailing ship n veleiro m.
sailor ['seɪlə'] n marinheiro m, -ra f; **to be a good** ~ não ficar mareado(da).
saint [seɪnt] n -1. RELIG santo m, -ta f -2. inf [very good person] santo m, -ta f.

SAINT PATRICK'S DAY

Em 17 de março, comemora-se o dia de são Patrício, o patrono da Irlanda. Lá, esse dia é feriado nacional, mas a data é celebrada também em várias partes do mundo pelos irlandeses ou seus descendentes, sobretudo nos Estados Unidos. Nesse dia, a tradição manda usar um shamrock, uma espécie de trevo, que é o emblema nacional da Irlanda; ou vestir verde, que é a cor que representa o país.

Saint Helena n Santa Helena.
Saint Lawrence n: **the** ~ **(River)** o (Rio) São Lourenço.
Saint Lucia n Santa Lúcia.
saintly ['seɪntlɪ] (compar -ier, superl -iest) adj santo(ta), santificado(da).
Saint Petersburg n São Petersburgo.
sake [seɪk] n -1. [benefit, advantage]: **for the** ~ **of** para o bem de; **for my** ~ por mim -2. [purpose]: **for the** ~ **of** pelo bem de; **let us say, for the** ~ **of argument, that ...** digamos, só para argumentar, que ... -3. phr: **to do sthg for its own** ~ fazer algo só por fazer; **for God's** OR **Heaven's** ~! pelo amor de Deus!
salad ['sæləd] n salada f.
salad bowl n saladeira f.
salad cream n (U) UK molho m para salada (à base de maionese).
salad dressing n (U) molho m para salada (à base de vinagre, óleo e ervas).
salad oil n (U) azeite m para salada.
salamander ['sælə,mændə'] n salamandra f.
salami [sə'lɑːmɪ] n (U) salame m.

salaried ['sælərɪd] *adj* **-1.** [employee] assalariado(da) **-2.** [job] remunerado(da).

salary ['sælərɪ] (*pl* **-ies**) *n* salário *m*.

salary scale *n* escala *f* salarial.

sale [seɪl] *n* **-1.** [gen] venda *f*; **on** ~ à venda; **(up) for** ~ à venda; **'for** ~' 'vende-se' **-2.** [at reduced prices] liquidação *f*, saldo *m* **-3.** [auction] leilão *m*.
➡ **sales** ⇔ *npl* **-1.** [quantity sold] vendas *fpl* **-2.** [at reduced prices]: **the** ~**s** os saldos. ⇔ *comp* de vendas.

saleroom *UK* ['seɪlrʊm], **salesroom** *US* ['seɪlzrʊm] *n* sala *f* de leilão.

sales assistant ['seɪlz-], **salesclerk** *US* ['seɪlzklɜːrk] *n* balconista *mf*, vendedor *m*, -ra *f* (*em loja*).

sales conference *n* conferência *f* de vendas.

sales drive *n* campanha *f* de vendas.

sales force *n* força *f* de vendas.

salesman ['seɪlzmən] (*pl* **-men** [-mən]) *n* [gen] vendedor *m*; [representative] representante *m* de vendas.

sales pitch *n* lábia *f* de vendedor.

sales rep *n inf* representante *mf* de vendas.

sales representative *n* representante *mf* de vendas.

salesroom *n US* = **saleroom**.

sales slip *n US* recibo *m*.

sales tax *n* (*U*) imposto pago ao governo sobre mercadorias ou bens comprados.

sales team *n* equipe *f* de vendas.

saleswoman ['seɪlz‚wʊmən] (*pl* **-women** [-‚wɪmɪn]) *n* [gen] vendedora *f*; [representative] representante *f* de vendas.

salient ['seɪljənt] *adj fml* evidente, notável.

saline ['seɪlaɪn] *adj* salino(na).

saliva [sə'laɪvə] *n* (*U*) saliva *f*.

salivate ['sælɪveɪt] *vi* salivar.

sallow ['sæləʊ] *adj* amarelado(da).

sally ['sælɪ] (*pl* **-ies**, *pt* & *pp* **-ied**) *n* gracejo *m*, chiste *m*.
➡ **sally forth** *vi hum or literary* sair com garra e ímpeto.

salmon ['sæmən] (*pl inv OR* **-s**) *n* salmão *m*.

salmonella [‚sælmə'nelə] *n* (*U*) salmonela *f*.

salmon pink ⇔ *adj* rosa-salmão. ⇔ *n* rosa-salmão *f*.

salon ['sælɒn] *n* **-1.** [hairdresser's] salão *m* **-2.** [clothes shop] butique *f*.

saloon [sə'luːn] *n* **-1.** *UK* [car] sedã *m* **-2.** *US* [bar] bar *m* **-3.** *UK* [in pub]: ~ **(bar)** em alguns pubs e hotéis, bar finamente decorado e de preços mais altos do que os do public bar **-4.** [on ship] salão *m*.

salopettes [‚sælə'pets] *npl* calças *fpl* de ski.

salt [sɔːlt, sɒlt] ⇔ *n* **-1.** sal *m* **-2.** *phr:* **the** ~ **of the earth** o sal da terra; **to rub** ~ **into sb's wounds** pôr o dedo na ferida (de alguém); **to take sthg with a pinch of** ~ ficar com o pé atrás em relação a algo, considerar algo com uma certa reserva. ⇔ *comp* salgado(da). ⇔ *vt* **-1.** [food] salgar **-2.** [roads] jogar sal em (*para derreter o gelo*).
➡ **salt away** *vt sep inf* guardar.

SALT [sɔːlt] (*abbr of* **Strategic Arms Limitation Talks/ Treaty**) *n* SALT *m*.

salt cellar *UK*, **salt shaker** *US* [-‚ʃeɪkəʳ] *n* saleiro *m*.

salted ['sɔːltɪd] *adj* salgado(da), com sal.

saltpetre *UK*, **saltpeter** *US* [‚sɔːlt'piːtəʳ] *n* (*U*) salitre *m*.

salt shaker *n US* = **salt cellar**.

saltwater ['sɔːlt‚wɔːtəʳ] ⇔ *adj* de água salgada. ⇔ *n* (*U*) água *f* salgada, água *f* do mar.

salty ['sɔːltɪ] (*compar* **-ier**, *superl* **-iest**) *adj* salgado(da).

salubrious [sə'luːbrɪəs] *adj* salubre.

salutary ['sæljʊtrɪ] *adj* salutar.

salute [sə'luːt] ⇔ *n* **-1.** MIL [with hand] continência *f* **-2.** MIL [firing of guns] salva *f* **-3.** (*U*) [act of saluting] cumprimento *m* **-4.** [formal acknowledgment] saudação *f*. ⇔ *vt* **-1.** MIL [with hand] fazer continência a **-2.** [acknowledge formally, honour] cumprimentar. ⇔ *vi* MIL [with hand] fazer continência.

Salvadorean, Salvadorian [‚sælvə'dɔːrɪən] ⇔ *adj* salvadorenho(nha). ⇔ *n* salvadorenho *m*, -nha *f*.

salvage ['sælvɪdʒ] ⇔ *n* **-1.** [rescue of ship] salvamento *m* **-2.** [property rescued] objetos *mpl* recuperados. ⇔ *vt* **-1.** [rescue]: **to** ~ **sthg (from)** salvar algo (de) **-2.** *fig* [gain from failure]: **to** ~ **sthg (from)** preservar algo (de).

salvage vessel *n* barco *m* de salvamento.

salvation [sæl'veɪʃn] *n* salvação *f*.

Salvation Army *n:* **the** ~ o Exército da Salvação.

salve [sælv] *vt:* **to do sthg to** ~ **one's conscience** fazer algo para aliviar a consciência.

salver ['sælvəʳ] *n* salva *f*, bandeja *f*.

salvo ['sælvəʊ] (*pl* **-s** *OR* **-es**) *n* salva *f*.

Samaritan [sə'mærɪtn] *n:* **good** ~ bom samaritano *m*.

samba ['sæmbə] *n* samba *m*.

same [seɪm] ⇔ *adj* [gen] mesmo(ma); **at the** ~ **time** [simultaneously] ao mesmo tempo; [yet] mesmo assim; **one and the** ~ o mesmo, a mesma. ⇔ *adv:* **the** ~ o mesmo, a mesma. ⇔ *pron* [unchanged, identical]: **the** ~ o mesmo, a mesma; **the hats they were wearing were the** ~ os chapéus que eles estavam usando eram iguais; **all** *OR* **just the** ~ [nevertheless, anyway] mesmo assim; **it's all the** ~ **to me** para mim dá no mesmo, para mim tanto faz; **it's not the** ~ não é a mesma coisa.

sameness ['seɪmnɪs] *n* **-1.** (*U*) [lack of variety] mesmice *f* **-2.** [similarity] uniformidade *f*.

Samoa [sə'məʊə] *n* Samoa; **in** ~ em Samoa; **American** ~ Samoa Americana *OR* Oriental.

Samoan [sə'məʊən] ⇔ *adj* samoano(na). ⇔ *n* samoano *m*, -na *f*.

samosa [sə'məʊsə] *n* espécie de pastel indiano feito de vegetais, temperos e carne.

sample ['sɑːmpl] ⇔ *n* amostra *f*. ⇔ *vt* **-1.** [taste] provar **-2.** [try out, test] experimentar **-3.** MUS amostrar.

sampler ['sɑːmpləʳ] *n* SEWING bordado com palavras e figuras bordadas, normalmente feito como prova da habilidade de quem o confeccionou.

sanatorium (*pl* **-riums** *OR* **-ria** [-rɪə]), **sanitorium** *US* (*pl* **-riums** *OR* **-ria** [-rɪə]) [‚sænə'tɔːrɪəm] *n* sanatório *m*.

sanctify ['sæŋktɪfaɪ] (*pt* & *pp* **-ied**) *vt* **-1.** *RELIG* santificar **- 2.** [approve] abençoar.

sanctimonious [ˌsæŋktɪ'məʊnjəs] *adj pej* santarrão(rrona).

sanction ['sæŋkʃn] <> *n* sanção *f.* <> *vt* sancionar.

   → sanctions *npl POL* sanções *fpl.*

sanctity ['sæŋktətɪ] *n (U)* santidade *f.*

sanctuary ['sæŋktʃʊərɪ] (*pl* **-ies**) *n* **-1.** [gen] santuário *m* **- 2.** [place of safety] abrigo *m* **- 3.** *(U)* [safety, refuge] refúgio *m.*

sanctum ['sæŋktəm] (*pl* **-s**) *n inf* lugar *m* sagrado, santuário *m.*

sand [sænd] <> *n (U)* areia *f.* <> *vt* lixar.

   → sands *npl* [beach] areias *fpl.*

   → sand down *vt sep* lixar.

sandal ['sændl] *n* sandália *f.*

sandalwood ['sændlwʊd] *n (U)* sândalo *m.*

sandbag ['sændbæg] *n* saco *m* de areia.

sandbank ['sændbæŋk] *n* banco *m* de areia.

sandblast ['sændblɑːst] *vt* *limpar com jato de areia.*

sandbox *n US* = **sandpit**.

sandcastle ['sændˌkɑːsl] *n* castelo *m* de areia.

sand dune *n* duna *f.*

sander ['sændər] *n* lixadeira *f.*

sandpaper ['sændˌpeɪpər] <> *n (U)* lixa *f.* <> *vt* lixar.

sandpit *UK* ['sændpɪt], **sandbox** *US* ['sændbɒks] *n* caixa *f* de areia.

sandstone ['sændstəʊn] *n (U)* arenito *m.*

sandstorm ['sændstɔːm] *n* tempestade *f* de areia.

sand trap *n US GOLF* armadilha *f* de areia.

sandwich ['sænwɪdʒ] <> *n* sanduíche *m.* <> *vt fig*: to be ~ ed between ser prensado(da) entre.

sandwich course *n UK* curso universitário que inclui um certo tempo de experiência profissional.

sandy ['sændɪ] (*compar* **-ier**, *superl* **-iest**) *adj* **-1.** [made of sand] arenoso(sa) **- 2.** [sand-coloured] cor-de-areia.

sane [seɪn] *adj* **-1.** [not mad] são(sã) **- 2.** [sensible] sensato(ta).

sang [sæŋ] *pt* ⊳ **sing**.

sanguine ['sæŋgwɪn] *adj* esperançoso(sa), otimista.

sanitary ['sænɪtrɪ] *adj* **-1.** [connected with health] sanitário(ria) **- 2.** [clean, hygienic] higiênico(ca).

sanitary towel, sanitary napkin *US n* absorvente *m* higiênico.

sanitation [ˌsænɪ'teɪʃn] *n* **-1.** [in streets] saneamento *m* **- 2.** [in houses] instalações *fpl* sanitárias.

sanitation worker *n US* lixeiro *m*, -ra *f.*

sanitize, -ise ['sænɪtaɪz] *vt* suavizar.

sanitorium *n US* = **sanatorium**.

sanity ['sænɪtɪ] *n* **-1.** [saneness] sanidade *f* **- 2.** [good sense] sensatez *f.*

sank [sæŋk] *pt* ⊳ **sink**.

San Marino [ˌsænmə'riːnəʊ] *n* San Marino; **in** ~ em San Marino.

San Salvador [ˌsæn'sælvədɔːr] *n* São Salvador.

Sanskrit ['sænskrɪt] *n* sânscrito *m.*

Santa (Claus) ['sæntə(ˌklɔːz)] *n* Papai *m* Noel.

São Paulo [ˌsaʊ'paʊləʊ] *n* São Paulo.

sap [sæp] (*pt* & *pp* **-ped**, *cont* **-ping**) <> *n* **-1.** [of plant] seiva *m* **- 2.** *US inf* [gullible person] bobo(ba). <> *vt* enfraquecer, consumir.

sapling ['sæplɪŋ] *n* árvore *m* nova, arvorezinha *f.*

sapphire ['sæfaɪər] *n* safira *f.*

Sarajevo [ˌsærə'jevəʊ] *n* Sarajevo.

sarcasm ['sɑːkæzm] *n (U)* sarcasmo *m.*

sarcastic [sɑː'kæstɪk] *adj* sarcástico(ca).

sarcophagus [sɑː'kɒfəgəs] (*pl* **-gi** [-gaɪ], **-es**) *n* sarcófago *m.*

sardine [sɑː'diːn] *n* sardinha *f.*

Sardinia [sɑː'dɪnjə] *n* Sardenha; **in** ~ na Sardenha.

sardonic [sɑː'dɒnɪk] *adj* mordaz.

Sargasso Sea [sɑː'gæsəʊ-] *n*: **the** ~ o Mar de Sargaço.

sari ['sɑːrɪ] *n* sári *m.*

sarong [sə'rɒŋ] *n* sarongue *m.*

sarsaparilla [ˌsɑːspə'rɪlə] *n* salsaparrilha *f.*

sartorial [sɑː'tɔːrɪəl] *adj fml* no vestir.

SAS (*abbr of* **Special Air Service**) *n* unidade especial do exército britânico encarregada de operações de antiterrorismo e sabotagem.

SASE (*abbr of* **self-addressed stamped envelope**) *n US* envelope auto-endereçado e já selado.

sash [sæʃ] *n* faixa *f.*

sash window *n* janela *f* de guilhotina.

Saskatchewan [ˌsæs'kætʃɪwən] *n* Saskatchewan.

sassy ['sæsɪ] *adj US inf* descarado(da), atrevido(da).

sat [sæt] *pt* & *pp* ⊳ **sit**.

Sat. (*abbr of* **Saturday**) sáb.

SAT [sæt] *n* **-1.** (*abbr of* **Standard Assessment Test**) exames de aptidão que os estudantes da Inglaterra e do País de Gales prestam aos 7, 11 e 14 anos de idade **- 2.** (*abbr of* **Scholastic Aptitude Test**) exame prestado por estudantes no último ano da escola secundária nos Estados Unidos, importante ao se ingressar na universidade.

Satan ['seɪtn] *n* Satã *m*, Satanás *m.*

satanic [sə'tænɪk] *adj* satânico(ca).

satchel ['sætʃəl] *n* pasta *f*, mochila *f* escolar.

sated ['seɪtɪd] *adj fml* saciado(da); ~ **with sthg** saciado(da) com algo.

satellite ['sætəlaɪt] <> *n* satélite *m.* <> *comp* **-1.** *TELEC* por satélite **- 2.** [dependent]: ~ **city** cidadesatélite *f.*

satellite dish *n* [for TV] antena *f* parabólica.

satellite TV *n* tevê *f* via satélite.

satiate ['seɪʃɪeɪt] *vt fml* saciar.

satin ['sætɪn] <> *n (U)* cetim *m.* <> *comp* **-1.** [made of satin] de cetim **- 2.** [smooth] acetinado(da).

satire ['sætaɪəʳ] *n* sátira *f.*

satirical [sə'tɪrɪkl] *adj* satírico(ca).

satirist ['sætərɪst] *n* satirista *mf.*

satirize, -ise ['sætəraɪz] *vt* satirizar.

satisfaction [ˌsætɪs'fækʃn] *n* **- 1.** [gen] satisfação *f*; **to do sthg to sb's** ~ fazer algo ao gosto de alguém **- 2.** *(U)* [fulfilment of need] atendimento *m*, cumprimento *m*; ~ **guaranteed** satisfação garantida.

satisfactory [ˌsætɪs'fæktərɪ] *adj* satisfatório(ria).

satisfied ['sætɪsfaɪd] *adj* **- 1.** [happy] satisfeito(ta); **to be** ~ **with sthg** estar satisfeito(ta) com algo **- 2.** [convinced] convencido(da); **to be** ~ **(that)** estar convencido(da) de que.

satisfy ['sætɪsfaɪ] *(pt & pp -ied) vt* **- 1.** [make happy] satisfazer **- 2.** [convince] convencer; **to** ~ **sb that** convencer alguém de que; **to** ~ **o.s. that** convencer-se de que **- 3.** [fulfil] satisfazer, atender a.

satisfying ['sætɪsfaɪŋ] *adj* satisfatório(ria), agradável.

satsuma [ˌsæt'suːmə] *n* tipo de tangerina proveniente do Japão.

saturate ['sætʃəreɪt] *vt* **- 1.** [drench] ensopar, empapar; **to** ~ **sthg with sthg** ensopar OR empapar algo com algo **- 2.** [fill completely, swamp] inundar; **to** ~ **sthg with sthg** saturar algo com algo.

saturated *adj* **- 1.** [drenched] ensopado(da), empapado(da) **- 2.** [fat] saturado(da).

saturation [ˌsætʃə'reɪʃn] *n* **- 1.** [drenching] ensopamento *m* **- 2.** [complete filling] saturamento *m.* <> *comp* [bombing] por saturação; [TV] ~ **coverage** cobertura *f* exaustiva.

saturation point *n*: **to reach** ~ alcançar o ponto de saturação.

Saturday ['sætədɪ] <> *n* sábado *m*; **what day is it? - it's** ~ que dia é hoje? - é sábado; **are you going** ~**?** *inf* você vai sábado?; **see you** ~**!** *inf* até sábado!; **on** ~ no sábado; **on** ~**s** aos sábados; **to work** ~**s** trabalhar aos sábados; **last** ~ sábado passado; **this** ~ este sábado; **next** ~ sábado da semana que vem; **every** ~ todos os sábados; **every other** ~ um sábado sim, outro não; **the** ~ **before** no sábado anterior; **the** ~ **before last** há dois sábados; **the** ~ **after next**, ~ **week, a week on** ~ não no próximo sábado, no outro. <> *comp* aos sábados; ~ **morning/afternoon/night** sábado de manhã/tarde/noite; ~ **evening** no fim da tarde de sábado; **a** ~ **job** um trabalho aos sábados.

Saturn ['sætɜːn] *n* Saturno.

sauce [sɔːs] *n* **- 1.** CULIN molho *m* **- 2.** UK *inf* [cheek] atrevimento *m.*

sauce boat *n* molheira *f.*

saucepan ['sɔːspən] *n* panela *f* com um cabo.

saucer ['sɔːsəʳ] *n* pires *m inv.*

saucy ['sɔːsɪ] *(compar -ier, superl -iest) adj inf* atrevido(da).

Saudi Arabia [ˌsaʊdɪə'reɪbjə] *n* Arábia Saudita; **in** ~ na Arábia Saudita.

Saudi (Arabian) ['saʊdɪ-] <> *adj* árabe-saudita. <> *n* árabe-saudita *mf.*

sauna ['sɔːnə] *n* sauna *f.*

saunter ['sɔːntəʳ] *vi* passear *(tranqüilamente).*

sausage ['sɒsɪdʒ] *n* **- 1.** *(U)* [meat] lingüiça *f* **- 2.** [shaped piece of meat] salsicha *f.*

sausage roll *n UK* enroladinho *m* de salsicha.

sauté [UK 'səʊteɪ, US səʊ'teɪ] *(pt & pp sautéed OR sautéd)* <> *adj* sauté. <> *vt* fritar levemente.

savage ['sævɪdʒ] <> *adj* selvagem. <> *n* selvagem *mf.* <> *vt* **- 1.** [attack physically] atacar ferozmente **- 2.** [criticize] atacar.

savageness ['sævɪdʒnɪs], **savagery** ['sævɪdʒrɪ] *n (U)* selvageria *f.*

savanna(h) [sə'vænə] *n* savana *f.*

save [seɪv] <> *n* SPORT defesa *f.* <> *prep fml:* ~ **(for)** exceto. <> *vt* **- 1.** [gen] salvar; **to** ~ **sb from sthg/from doing sthg** salvar alguém de algo/de fazer algo; **to** ~ **sb's life** salvar a vida de alguém **- 2.** [prevent waste of] economizar **- 3.** [set aside] guardar **- 4.** [make unnecessary] poupar; **to** ~ **sb/sthg from doing sthg** poupar alguém/algo de fazer algo **- 5.** SPORT defender. <> *vi* economizar.
➡ **save up** *vi* economizar.

save as you earn *n UK* forma de poupança em que a contribuição mensal gera renda livre de impostos.

saveloy ['sævəlɔɪ] *n UK* salsichão *m* de porco.

saver ['seɪvəʳ] *n* **- 1.** [object]: **a time/money** ~ algo que economiza tempo/dinheiro **- 2.** FIN [at bank, building society] poupador *m*, -ra *f.*

saving grace ['seɪvɪŋ-] *n* mérito *m.*

savings ['seɪvɪŋz] *npl* economias *fpl.*

savings account *n US* (caderneta *f* de) poupança *f.*

savings and loan association *n US* sociedade *f* de empréstimos imobiliários.

savings bank *n* caixa *f* econômica, banco *m* só de cadernetas de poupança.

saviour UK, **savior** US ['seɪvjəʳ] *n* salvador *m*, -ra *f.*
➡ **Saviour** *n*: **the Saviour** o Salvador.

savoir-faire [ˌsævwɑː'feəʳ] *n (U)* savoir-faire *m.*

savour UK, **savor** US ['seɪvəʳ] *vt* **- 1.** [enjoy taste of] saborear **- 2.** *fig* [enjoy greatly] saborear, aproveitar.

savoury UK *(pl -ies)*, **savory** *(pl -ies)* US ['seɪvərɪ] <> *adj* **- 1.** [not sweet] condimentado(da) **- 2.** [respectable, pleasant] agradável. <> *n* tira-gosto *m.*

Savoy *n* Savoy.

savoy (cabbage) *n* repolho *m* crespo.

saw [sɔː] *(UK pt -ed, pp sawn, US pt & pp -ed)* <> *pt* ➡ **see.** <> *n* serra *f.* <> *vt* serrar.
➡ **saw up** *vt sep* serrar.

sawdust ['sɔːdʌst] *n (U)* serragem *f.*

sawed-off shotgun *n US* = **sawn-off shotgun.**

sawmill ['sɔːmɪl] *n* serraria *f.*

sawn [sɔːn] *pp UK* ➡ **saw.**

sawn-off shotgun UK, **sawed-off shotgun** US ['sɔːd-] *n* arma *f* de cano serrado.

sax [sæks] *n inf* sax *m.*

Saxon ['sæksn] <> *adj* saxão(xã). <> *n* saxão *m*, -xã *f.*

saxophone ['sæksəfəʊn] *n* saxofone *m.*

saxophonist [UK ˌsæks'ɒfənɪst, US 'sæksəfəʊnɪst] *n* saxofonista *mf.*

say [seɪ] *(pt & pp said)* <> *vt* **- 1.** [gen] dizer; **to** ~

sthg again repetir algo; **to ~ yes** dizer que sim; **to ~ to o.s.** dizer para si mesmo(ma); **to ~ nothing of** sem mencionar; **to ~ (that)** dizer que; **he's said to be the best footballer in the world** dizem que ele é o melhor jogador do mundo - **2.** [giving information] mostrar; **the clock ~s two thirty** o relógio está marcando duas e meia - **3.** [assume, suppose] supor; **let's ~ you win** digamos que você vença - **4.** phr: **that goes without ~ing** nem precisa dizer isso; **I'll ~ this for him/her ...** há que se admitir OR dizer que ele/ela ...; **it has a lot to be said for it** tem muitos pontos em seu favor; **she didn't have much to ~ for herself** inf ela era uma pessoa muito reservada; **what have you got to ~ for yourself?** o que você tem a dizer para se defender?; **you don't ~!** não diga!, não é verdade! <> n [power of decision]: **to have a/no ~ (in sthg)** ter/não ter voz nem vez (em algo); **let me have my ~** deixe-me dizer o que eu penso.

➡ **that is to say** adv quer dizer.

SAYE (abbr of **save as you earn**) n tipo de poupança na Grã-Bretanha com vantagens em relação a impostos.

saying ['seɪɪŋ] n ditado m popular, dito m.

say-so n inf [permission] permissão f.

SBA (abbr of **Small Business Administration**) n órgão do governo norte-americano de ajuda à pequena empresa.

s/c (abbr of **self-contained**) UK acomodação, normalmente um apartamento, que contém cozinha, banheiro e geralmente porta externa próprios.

SC <> n (abbr of **supreme court**) ≃ STF m. <> abbr of **South Carolina**.

scab [skæb] n - **1.** [of wound] casca f, crosta f - **2.** pej [non-striker] fura-greve mf.

scabby ['skæbɪ] (compar -ier, superl -iest) adj coberto(ta) de feridas.

scabies ['skeɪbɪːz] n (U) sarna f.

scaffold ['skæfəʊld] n - **1.** [frame] andaime m - **2.** [for executions] cadafalso m, patíbulo m.

scaffolding ['skæfəldɪŋ] n (U) andaime m.

scalawag n US = **scallywag**.

scald [skɔːld] <> n escaldadura f. <> vt escaldar.

scalding ['skɔːldɪŋ] adj escaldante.

scale [skeɪl] <> n - **1.** [gen] escala f; **to ~ em escala - 2.** [size, extent] tamanho m; **on a large ~** de grande escala - **3.** [of fish, snake] escama f - **4.** US = **scales**. <> vt - **1.** [climb] escalar - **2.** [remove scales from] escamar.

➡ **scales** npl balança f.

➡ **scale down** vt fus reduzir.

scale diagram n diagrama m em escala.

scale model n maquete f.

scallion ['skæljən] n US & Irish [spring onion] cebolinha f verde.

scallop ['skɒləp] <> n [shellfish] vieira f. <> vt [decorate edge of] guarnecer.

scallywag ['skælɪwæg], **scalawag** US ['skæləwæg] n - **1.** inf [child] pestinha mf - **2.** [adult] safado(da).

scalp [skælp] <> n - **1.** ANAT couro m cabeludo - **2.** [removed from head] escalpo m. <> vt escalpelar.

scalpel ['skælpəl] n bisturi m.

scalper ['skælpəʳ] n US [tout] cambista mf.

scam [skæm] n inf esquema f, estratagema m.

scamp [skæmp] n inf pestinha mf, moleque mf.

scamper ['skæmpəʳ] vi fugir rapidamente.

scampi ['skæmpɪ] n (U) camarão-castanho m.

scan [skæn] (pt & pp -ned, cont -ning) <> n MED & TECH exame m, escaneamento m. <> vt - **1.** [gen] escanear - **2.** [examine carefully] examinar cuidadosamente - **3.** [glance at] correr os olhos por. <> vi - **1.** LITERATURE estar bem escandido(da) - **2.** COMPUT escanear.

scandal ['skændl] n escândalo m.

scandalize, ise ['skændəlaɪz] vt escandalizar.

scandalous ['skændələs] adj - **1.** [shocking] escandaloso(sa) - **2.** [infuriating] exasperador(ra).

Scandinavia [ˌskændɪ'neɪvjə] n Escandinávia; **in ~** na Escandinávia.

Scandinavian [ˌskændɪ'neɪvjən] <> adj escandinavo(va). <> n escandinavo m, -va f.

scanner ['skænəʳ] n escaneador m, scanner m.

scant [skænt] adj insuficiente, escasso(sa).

scanty ['skæntɪ] (compar -ier, superl -iest) adj - **1.** [dress] mínimo(ma) - **2.** [amount, resources] escasso(sa) - **3.** [meal] insuficiente.

scapegoat ['skeɪpgəʊt] n bode m expiatório.

scar [skɑːʳ] (pt & pp -red, cont -ring) <> n - **1.** [physical] cicatriz f - **2.** fig [mental] seqüela f. <> vt - **1.** [physically] deixar cicatriz em - **2.** fig [mentally] deixar seqüelas em.

scarce ['skeəs] adj escasso(sa); **to make o.s. ~** manter-se afastado(da).

scarcely ['skeəslɪ] adv apenas; **~ anyone/ever** quase ninguém/nunca.

scarcity ['skeəsətɪ] n (U) escassez f.

scare [skeəʳ] <> n - **1.** [sudden fright] susto m - **2.** [public panic] ameaça f; **bomb ~** ameaça de bomba. <> vt assustar.

➡ **scare away, scare off** vt sep afugentar.

scarecrow ['skeəkrəʊ] n espantalho m.

scared ['skeəd] adj - **1.** [very frightened] apavorado(da); **to be ~ stiff** OR **to death** estar morrendo de medo - **2.** [nervous, worried]: **to be ~ that ...** estar com medo de que ...

scaremonger n alarmista mf.

scarey ['skeərɪ] adj = **scary**.

scarf [skɑːf] (pl -s OR **scarves**) n - **1.** [long - to keep warm] cachecol m; [- as accessory] echarpe f - **2.** [square] lenço m.

scarlet ['skɑːlət] <> adj escarlate. <> n escarlate m.

scarlet fever n (U) escarlatina f.

scarper ['skɑːpə] vi UK inf fugir.

scarves [skɑːvz] pl ⇒ **scarf**.

scary ['skeərɪ] (compar -ier, superl -iest) adj inf apavorante.

scathing ['skeɪðɪŋ] adj mordaz; **to be ~ about sb/sthg** fazer uma crítica mordaz a alguém/algo.

scatter ['skætəʳ] <> vt espalhar. <> vi dispersar-se.

➡ **scatter about, scatter around** vt sep espalhar.

scatterbrained ['skætəbreɪnd] adj inf desmiolado(da), avoado(da).

scattered ['skætəd] *adj* disperso(sa).

scattering ['skætərɪŋ] *n*: **a ~ of snow** uma fina camada de neve.

scatty ['skætɪ] (*compar* -ier, *superl* -iest) *adj UK inf* desmiolado(da), avoado(da).

scavenge ['skævɪndʒ] <> *vt* [subj: animal, bird]: **to ~ sthg** cavucar algo; *fig* [subj: person] cavucar algo. <> *vi* [animal, bird]: **to ~ for sthg** cavucar por algo; *fig* [person] cavucar por algo.

scavenger ['skævɪndʒəʳ] *n* -**1.** [animal] *animal que se alimenta de carniça* -**2.** *fig* [person] catador *m*, -ra *f* de lixo.

SCE (*abbr of* Scottish Certificate of Education) *n exame de conhecimentos em três níveis prestado pelos estudantes na Escócia.*

scenario [sɪ'nɑːrɪəʊ] (*pl* -s) *n* cenário *m*.

scene [siːn] *n* -**1.** [gen] cena *f*; **on the ~** no local; **a change of ~** uma mudança de ares *OR* ambiente; **behind the ~s** nos bastidores -**2.** [picture of place] paisagem *f*, cenário *m* -**3.** [sight, impression] vista *f* -**4.** [area of activity] área *f* -**5.** [embarrassing fuss] cena *f*, escândalo *m* -**6.** *phr*: **to set the ~** [for person] descrever a cena; [for event] preparar o cenário.

scenery ['siːnərɪ] *n (U)* -**1.** [of countryside] paisagem *f* -**2.** THEATRE cenário *m*.

scenic ['siːnɪk] *adj* -**1.** [view] pitoresco(ca) -**2.** [tour] turístico(ca).

scenic route *n* rota *f* turística.

scent [sent] <> *n* -**1.** [smell - of flowers] perfume *m*, fragrância *f*; [- of animal] cheiro *m*, odor *m* -**2.** *fig* [track] rastro *m*, pista *f* -**3.** *(U)* [perfume] perfume *m*. <> *vt* -**1.** [subj: animal] farejar -**2.** *fig* [subj: person] sentir cheiro de.

scented ['sentɪd] *adj* perfumado(da).

scepter *n US* = **sceptre**.

sceptic *UK*, **skeptic** *US* ['skeptɪk] *n* céptico(ca).

sceptical *UK*, **skeptical** *US* ['skeptɪkl] *adj* céptico (ca); **to be ~ about sthg** ser céptico(ca) em relação a algo.

scepticism *UK*, **skepticism** *US* ['skeptɪsɪzm] *n (U)* ceticismo *m*.

sceptre *UK*, **scepter** *US* ['septəʳ] *n* cetro *m*.

SCF (*abbr of* Save the Children Fund) *n organização internacional de caridade pelo bem-estar das crianças.*

schedule [*UK* 'ʃedjuːl, *US* 'skedʒʊl] <> *n* -**1.** [plan] plano *m*; **(according) to ~** de acordo com o planejado; **to be ahead of ~** estar adiantado(da); **to be behind ~** estar atrasado(da); **on ~** sem atraso -**2.** [written list - of prices, contents] lista *f*; [- of times] horários *mpl*. <> *vt*: **to ~ sthg (for)** marcar algo(para).

scheduled flight [*UK* 'ʃedjuːld-, *US* 'skedʒʊld-] *n* vôo *m* regular.

schematic [skɪ'mætɪk] *adj* esquemático(ca).

scheme [skiːm] <> *n* -**1.** [plan] projeto *m* -**2.** *pej* [dishonest plan] esquema *f* -**3.** [arrangement, decoration] disposição *f*; **colour ~** combinação *f* de cores -**4.** *phr*: **in the ~ of things** na ordem das coisas. <> *vt pej*: **to ~ to do sthg** conspirar para fazer algo. <> *vi pej* tramar.

scheming ['skiːmɪŋ] *adj* que faz intriga.

schism ['sɪzm, 'skɪzml] *n* cisma *m*.

schizophrenia [ˌskɪtsə'friːnjə] *n (U)* esquizofrenia *f*.

schizophrenic [ˌskɪtsə'frenɪk] <> *adj* esquizofrênico(ca). <> *n* esquizofrênico *m*, -ca *f*.

schlepp *US inf* <> *vt* arrastar. <> *vi*: **to ~ (around)** ficar de papo pro ar.

schmal(t)z [ʃmɔːlts] *n (U) inf* sentimentalismo *m*.

schmuck [ʃmʌk] *n US inf* idiota *mf*.

scholar ['skɒləʳ] *n* -**1.** [expert]: **he's a Greek ~** ele é perito em grego -**2.** *dated* [student] aluno *m*, -na *f* -**3.** [holder of scholarship] bolsista *mf*.

scholarship ['skɒləʃɪp] *n* -**1.** [grant] bolsa *f* -**2.** *(U)* [learning] erudição *f*.

scholastic [skə'læstɪk] *adj fml* educacional.

school [skuːl] *n* -**1.** [place of education] escola *f*, colégio *m* -**2.** [hours spent in school] escola *f* -**3.** UNIV [department] faculdade *f* -**4.** *US* [university] universidade *f* -**5.** [group of fish] cardume *m* -**6.** [of whales, dolphins] grupo *m*.

school age *n (U)* idade *f* escolar.

schoolbook ['skuːlbʊk] *n* livro *m* escolar.

schoolboy ['skuːlbɔɪ] *n* aluno *m*.

schoolchild ['skuːltʃaɪld] (*pl* -children [-tʃɪldrən]) *n* aluno *m*, -na *f*.

schooldays ['skuːldeɪz] *npl* tempos *mpl* de colégio *OR* escola.

school dinner *n* refeição *f* escolar.

school district *n US autoridade local nos Estados Unidos com competência em termos de educação primária e secundária.*

school friend *n* colega *mf* (de escola).

schoolgirl ['skuːlɡɜːl] *n* aluna *f*.

schooling ['skuːlɪŋ] *n (U)* educação *f*, ensino *m*.

schoolkid ['skuːlkɪd] *n inf* aluno *m*, -na *f*.

school-leaver [-ˌliːvəʳ] *n UK jovem que concluiu o ensino obrigatório.*

school-leaving age [-ˈliːvɪŋ-] *n (U) UK idade de conclusão do ensino obrigatório.*

schoolmarm *n US* professora *f* antiquada.

schoolmaster ['skuːlˌmɑːstəʳ] *n dated* mestre *m*.

schoolmistress ['skuːlˌmɪstrɪs] *n dated* mestra *f*.

school of thought *n* escola *f* de pensamento.

school report *n* boletim *m* escolar.

schoolroom ['skuːlruːm] *n dated* classe *f*.

schoolteacher ['skuːlˌtiːtʃəʳ] *n* professor *m*, -ra *f*.

school uniform *n* uniforme *m* escolar.

schoolwork ['skuːlwɜːk] *n (U)* trabalho *m* escolar.

school year *n* ano *m* letivo.

schooner ['skuːnəʳ] *n* -**1.** [ship] escuna *f* -**2.** *UK* [sherry glass] caneca *f* (*para xerez*).

sciatica [saɪ'ætɪkə] *en (U)* ciática *f*.

science ['saɪəns] <> *n* ciência *f*. <> *comp* -**1.** [student] de ciências -**2.** [degree] em ciências.

science fiction *n (U)* ficção *f* científica.

science park *n* complexo *m* científico (*em empresas*).

scientific [ˌsaɪən'tɪfɪk] *adj* científico(ca).

scientist ['saɪəntɪst] *n* cientista *mf*.

sci-fi ['saɪ'faɪ] (*abbr of* science fiction) *n inf* ficção *f* científica.

Scilly Isles ['sɪlɪ-], **Scillies** ['sɪlɪz] *npl*: **the ~** as Ilhas Scilly; **in the ~** nas Ilhas Scilly.

scintillating ['sɪntɪleɪtɪŋ] *adj* brilhante.

scissors ['sɪzəz] *npl* tesoura *f*; **a pair of** ~ uma tesoura.

sclerosis *n* ▷ **multiple sclerosis**.

scoff [skɒf] ◇ *vt UK inf* devorar, engolir. ◇ *vi* zombar; **to** ~ **at sb/sthg** zombar de alguém/algo.

scold [skəʊld] *vt* repreender, xingar.

scone [skɒn] *n* bolinho geralmente tomado à hora do chá com manteiga ou geléia.

scoop [sku:p] ◇ *n* **-1.** [kitchen implement - for sugar] colher *f*; [- for ice cream] pá *f* **-2.** [scoopful] concha *f*, colher *f* grande; **two** ~**s of ice cream** duas bolas de sorvete **-3.** [news report] furo *m*. ◇ *vt* **-1.** [with hands] tirar com as mãos **-2.** [with implement] tirar com colher.

◆ **scoop out** *vt sep* tirar com colher.

scoot [sku:t] *vi inf* correr com muita pressa.

scooter ['sku:tə'] *n* **-1.** [toy] patinete *f* **-2.** [motorcycle] lambreta *f*.

scope [skəʊp] *n (U)* **-1.** [opportunity] possibilidades *fpl* **-2.** [range] escopo *m*.

scorch [skɔ:tʃ] ◇ *vt* **-1.** [clothes, food, skin] chamuscar **-2.** [grass, fields] queimar. ◇ *vi* **-1.** [clothes, food] chamuscar **-2.** [face, skin] queimar.

scorched earth policy [skɔ:tʃt-] *n* política *f* de terra queimada.

scorcher ['skɔ:tʃə'] *n inf* dia *m* escaldante.

scorching ['skɔ:tʃɪŋ] *adj inf* escaldante.

score [skɔ:'] ◇ *n* **-1.** SPORT placar *m* **-2.** [in test, competition] nota *f* **-3.** *dated* [twenty] vintena *f* **-4.** MUS partitura *f* **-5.** [subject]: **on that** ~ a esse respeito. ◇ *vt* **-1.** SPORT marcar **-2.** [achieve] conseguir, obter **-3.** [win in an argument] ganhar **-4.** [cut] gravar, entalhar. ◇ *vi* **-1.** SPORT marcar **-2.** [in an argument]: **to** ~ **over sb** levar vantagem sobre alguém.

◆ **scores** *npl* [lots]: ~**s (of sthg)** um monte (de algo).

◆ **score out** *vt sep UK* riscar.

scoreboard ['skɔ:bɔ:d] *n* placar *m*.

scorecard ['skɔ:kɑ:d] *n* cartão *m* para marcação de pontos.

score-draw *n* FTBL empate *m* com gols.

scorer ['skɔ:rə'] *n* **-1.** [official] anotador *m*, -ra *f* de pontos **-2.** [player - football] goleador *m*, -ra *f*; [- basketball] cestinha *mf*; [- sports in general] jogador(ra) que marca mais pontos.

scorn [skɔ:n] ◇ *n (U)* desdém *m*, menosprezo *m*; **to pour** ~ **on sb/sthg** menosprezar alguém/algo, desdenhar de alguém/algo. ◇ *vt* **-1.** [despise] desprezar **-2.** *fml* [refuse to accept] desdenhar.

scornful ['skɔ:nfʊl] *adj* desdenhoso(osa); **to be** ~ **of sthg** desdenhar de algo.

Scorpio ['skɔ:pɪəʊ] (*pl* -s) *n* **-1.** [sign] Escorpião *m* **-2.** [person] escorpiano *m*, -na *f*; **I'm** ~ sou de Escorpião.

scorpion ['skɔ:pjən] *n* escorpião *m*.

Scot [skɒt] *n* escocês *m*, -esa *f*.

scotch [skɒtʃ] *vt* **-1.** [idea] acabar com **-2.** [rumour] desmentir.

Scotch [skɒtʃ] ◇ *adj* escocês(esa). ◇ *n* [whisky] uísque *m* escocês.

Scotch egg *n UK* ovo cozido coberto com lingüiça e farinha de rosca e depois frito em óleo quente.

Scotch (tape)® *n US* fita *f* adesiva, durex® *m*.

scot-free *adj inf*: **to get off** ~ sair impune.

Scotland ['skɒtlənd] *n* Escócia *f*; **in** ~ na Escócia.

Scotland Yard *n* Scotland Yard *f*.

Scots [skɒts] ◇ *adj* escocês(esa). ◇ *n (U)* [dialect] escocês *m*.

Scotsman ['skɒtsmən] (*pl* -men [-mən]) *n* escocês *m*.

Scotswoman ['skɒtswʊmən] (*pl* -women [-ˌwɪmɪn]) *n* escocesa *f*.

Scottish ['skɒtɪʃ] *adj* escocês(esa).

Scottish National Party *n*: **the** ~ o Partido Nacionalista Escocês.

scoundrel ['skaʊndrəl] *n dated* canalha *mf*.

scour [skaʊə'] *vt* **-1.** [clean] esfregar **-2.** [search] esquadrinhar.

scourer ['skaʊrə'] *n* esponja *f* de aço, bombril® *m*.

scourge [skɜ:dʒ] *n* **-1.** [cause of suffering] flagelo *m* **-2.** [critic] tormento *m*.

Scouse *n inf* **-1.** [person] pessoa proveniente de Liverpool **-2.** [accent] dialeto falado pelas pessoas provenientes de Liverpool.

scout [skaʊt] *n* MIL batedor *m*, explorador *m*.

◆ **Scout** *n* escoteiro *m*.

◆ **scout around** *vi*: **to** ~ **around (for sthg)** explorar a área (em busca de algo).

scoutmaster *n* chefe *m* dos escoteiros.

scowl [skaʊl] ◇ *n* carranca *f*, cara *f* feia. ◇ *vi* franzir o cenho; **to** ~ **at sb** fazer cara feia para alguém.

scrabble ['skræbl] *vi* **-1.** [scramble] escalar com dificuldade; **to** ~ **up/down** subir/descer escalando **-2.** [scrape]: **to** ~ **at sthg** arranhar algo **-3.** [feel around] escarafunchar; **to** ~ **around for sthg** escarafunchar à procura de algo.

Scrabble® ['skræbl] *n (U)* Palavras *fpl* Cruzadas *(jogo)*.

scraggy ['skrægɪ] (*compar* -ier, *superl* -iest) *adj inf* magricela.

scram [skræm] (*pt & pp* -med, *cont* -ming) *vi inf* chispar.

scramble ['skræmbl] ◇ *n* briga *f*. ◇ *vi* **-1.** [climb] trepar em **-2.** [move clumsily] caminhar cambaleando; **she** ~**d for her handbag in the crush** ela teve que brigar pela bolsa no meio do tumulto.

scrambled eggs ['skræmbld-] *npl* ovos *mpl* mexidos.

scrambler ['skræmblə'] *n* COMPUT misturador *m*.

scrap [skræp] (*pt & pp* -ped, *cont* -ping) ◇ *n* **-1.** [small piece] pedaço *m*; ~ **of conversation** trecho *m*; ~ **of information** uma informação; **there isn't a** ~ **of evidence** não há prova alguma; **it won't make a** ~ **of difference** não fará a mínima diferença **-2.** [metal] sucata *f* **-3.** *inf* [fight, quarrel] briga *f*. ◇ *vt* abandonar.

◆ **scraps** *npl* sobras *fpl*.

scrapbook ['skræpbʊk] *n* album *m* de recortes.

scrap dealer *n* ferro-velho *m*, sucateiro *m*, -ra *f*.

scrape [skreɪp] ◇ *n* **-1.** [scraping noise] rangido *m*, arranhão *m* **-2.** *dated* [difficult situation] enrascada *f*. ◇ *vt* **-1.** [remove]: **to** ~ **sthg off sthg** raspar algo de algo **-2.** [peel] raspar **-3.** [rub against - car, bumper, glass] riscar; [- knee, elbow, skin] arranhar. ◇ *vi* **-1.**

[rub]: **to ~ against/on sthg** raspar contra/em algo **-2.** [save money] economizar.

➡ **scrape through** vt fus passar com as calças na mão.

➡ **scrape together, scrape up** vt sep juntar a duras penas.

scraper ['skreɪpə'] n raspador m.

scrap heap n **-1.** [of waste metal] monte m de sucata **-2.** fig: **to end up on the** [of people] ~ acabar rejeitado(da); [of ideas] acabar na lata de lixo.

scrapings ['skreɪpɪŋz] npl raspas fpl.

scrap merchant n UK sucateiro m, -ra f.

scrap metal n (U) sucata f, ferro-velho m.

scrap paper UK, **scratch paper** US n (U) papel m rascunho.

scrappy ['skræpɪ] (compar -ier, superl -iest) adj pej desconexo(xa).

scrapyard ['skræpjɑːd] n ferro-velho m.

scratch [skrætʃ] <> n **-1.** [gen] arranhão m **-2.** phr: **to do sthg from ~** fazer algo começando do nada; **to be up to ~** estar à altura. <> vt **-1.** [wound] arranhar **-2.** [surface] riscar **-3.** [rub] coçar; **to ~ o.s.** coçar-se. <> vi **-1.** [branch, knife, thorn]: **to ~ at/against sthg** roçar em algo **-2.** [person, animal] coçar-se.

scratchpad ['skrætʃpæd] n US bloco m de anotações.

scratch paper n US = scrap paper.

scratchy ['skrætʃɪ] (compar -ier, superl -iest) adj **-1.** [sound] arranhado(da) **-2.** [material] que pinica.

scrawl [skrɔːl] <> n rabisco m. <> vt rabiscar.

scrawny ['skrɔːnɪ] (compar -ier, superl -iest) adj esquelético(ca).

scream [skriːm] <> n **-1.** [of person] grito m; ~ **s of laughter** gargalhadas fpl **-2.** [of tyres, machine] guincho m **-3.** inf [funny person] pessoa f divertida. <> vt gritar. <> vi **-1.** [person] gritar, vociferar **-2.** [tyres, machine] guinchar.

scree [skriː] n (U) acúmulo de pedras soltas na encosta de uma montanha.

screech [skriːtʃ] <> n **-1.** [gen] guincho m **-2.** [of person] grito m; **a ~ of laughter** gargalhadas fpl. <> vt berrar, gritar. <> vi **-1.** [gen] guinchar **-2.** [person] gritar, berrar.

screen [skriːn] <> n **-1.** [viewing surface] tela f **-2.** CINEMA: **the (big) ~** a tela de cinema **-3.** [protective or dividing panel] biombo m. <> vt **-1.** [gen] exibir **-2.** [hide, shield] proteger; **to ~ sb/sthg (from sb/sthg)** proteger alguém/algo (de alguém/algo) **-3.** [question, examine] examinar; **to ~ sb for sthg** fazer exames em alguém em busca de algo.

➡ **screen off** vt sep separar com biombo.

screen door n porta f com tela.

screen dump n COMPUT despejo m de tela.

screening ['skriːnɪŋ] n **-1.** [in cinema] exibição f, projeção f **-2.** [on TV] exibição f **-3.** (U) [for security] triagem f **-4.** (U) MED [examination] exame m médico.

screenplay ['skriːnpleɪ] n roteiro m.

screen print n serigrafia f.

screen saver n COMPUT protetor m de tela.

screen test n teste m de filmagem.

screenwriter ['skriːnˌraɪtə'] n roteirista mf.

screw [skruː] <> n parafuso m. <> vt **-1.** [fix with screws]: **to ~ sthg to sthg** aparafusar algo em algo **-2.** [twist] enroscar **-3.** vulg [have sex with] trepar com, foder. <> vi **-1.** [fix together] enroscar **-2.** vulg [have sex] trepar, foder.

➡ **screw up** vt sep **-1.** [crumple up] amassar **-2.** [contort, twist] contrair **-3.** inf [ruin] ferrar.

screwball ['skruːbɔːl] n US inf cabeça mf oca.

screwdriver ['skruːˌdraɪvə'] n chave f de fenda.

screwtop jar ['skruːtɒp-] n pote m com tampa de rosca.

screwy ['skruːɪ] adj US inf maluco(ca).

scribble ['skrɪbl] <> n rabisco m, garrancho m. <> vt & vi rabiscar.

scribe [skraɪb] n fml escriba m.

scrimp [skrɪmp] vi: **to ~ and save (to do sthg)** apertar o cinto (para fazer algo).

script [skrɪpt] n **-1.** [of play, film] script m, roteiro m **-2.** [system of writing] escrita f **-3.** [handwriting] letra f.

scripted ['skrɪptɪd] adj com roteiro.

Scriptures ['skrɪptʃəz] npl: **the ~** as Escrituras.

scriptwriter ['skrɪptˌraɪtə'] n roteirista mf.

scroll [skrəʊl] <> n rolo m de papel OR pergaminho. <> vt COMPUT rolar.

➡ **scroll down** vi COMPUT mover para baixo, baixar.

➡ **scroll up** vi COMPUT mover para cima, subir.

scroll bar n COMPUT barra f de rolagem.

scrooge [skruːdʒ] n inf pej avarento m, -ta f, miserável.

scrotum ['skrəʊtəm] (pl -ta [-tə], -tums) n escroto m.

scrounge [skraʊndʒ] inf <> vt: **to ~ sthg (off sb)** filar algo (de alguém). <> vi filar; **to ~ off sb** UK viver às custas de alguém.

scrounger ['skraʊndʒə'] n inf parasita mf.

scrub [skrʌb] (pt & pp -bed, cont -bing) <> n **-1.** [rub] esfregação f; **give it a good ~** dá uma boa esfregada (nisso) **-2.** (U) [undergrowth] moita f. <> vt esfregar.

scrubbing brush UK ['skrʌbɪŋ-], **scrub brush** US n escovão m.

scruff [skrʌf] n ANAT: **by the ~ of the neck** pelo cangote.

scruffy ['skrʌfɪ] (compar -ier, superl -iest) adj **-1.** [gen] sujo(ja) **-2.** [room, part of town] bagunçado(da).

scrum(mage) ['skrʌm(ɪdʒ)] n RUGBY disputa f de bola.

scrumptious ['skrʌmpʃəs] adj inf delicioso(sa).

scrumpy ['skrʌmpɪ] n UK cidra f (de alto teor alcoólico).

scrunch [skrʌntʃ] inf <> vt amassar. <> vi ranger, estalar.

scrunchy ['skrʌntʃɪ] (pl -ies) n rabicó m.

scruples ['skruːplz] npl escrúpulos mpl.

scrupulous ['skruːpjʊləs] adj **-1.** [fair] escrupuloso (sa) **-2.** [thorough] completo(ta).

scrupulously ['skruːpjʊləslɪ] adv **-1.** [fairly] com escrúpulos **-2.** [thoroughly] totalmente.

scrutinize, -ise ['skruːtɪnaɪz] vt escrutinar.

scrutiny ['skruːtɪnɪ] n (U) escrutínio m.

scuba diving ['skuːbɑː-] n (U): **to go ~** mergulhar com tubo de oxigênio.

scud [skʌd] (*pt* & *pp* **-ded**, *cont* **-ding**) *vi literary* deslizar rapidamente.

scuff [skʌf] *vt* - **1.** [drag] arrastar - **2.** [damage - shoes] gastar; [- surface] riscar.

scuffle ['skʌfl] <> *n* briga *f.* <> *vi* brigar; **to ~ with sb** brigar com alguém.

scull [skʌl] <> *n* ginga *f.* <> *vi* remar.

scullery ['skʌlərɪ] (*pl* **-ies**) *n* copa *f (para lavar e guardar louça).*

sculpt [skʌlpt] *vt* esculpir.

sculptor ['skʌlptəʳ] *n* escultor *m*, -ra *f.*

sculpture ['skʌlptʃəʳ] <> *n* escultura *f.* <> *vt* esculpir.

scum [skʌm] *n* - **1.** [froth] espuma *f* - **2.** *v inf pej* [worthless people] escória *f.*

scupper ['skʌpəʳ] *vt* - **1.** *NAUT* [sink] afundar - **2.** *UK fig* [ruin] arruinar.

scurf [skɜːf] *n* (*U*) caspa *f.*

scurrilous ['skʌrələs] *adj fml* difamatório(ria).

scurry ['skʌrɪ] (*pt* & *pp* **-ied**) *vi*: **to ~ off** escapulir-se.

scurvy ['skɜːvɪ] *n* (*U*) escorbuto *m.*

scuttle ['skʌtl] <> *n* balde *m* para carvão. <> *vi* correr.

scuzzy (*compar* **-ier**, *superl* **-iest**) *adj inf* chulo(la).

scythe [saɪð] <> *n* foice *f.* <> *vt* ceifar.

SD *abbr of* South Dakota.

SDI (*abbr of* **Strategic Defense Initiative**) *n plano estratégico norte-americano de defesa antimíssil, conhecido também como Star Wars.*

SDLP (*abbr of* **Social Democratic and Labour Party**) *n partido político da Irlanda do Norte que defende a integração pacífica com a República da Irlanda.*

SE (*abbr of* southeast) SE.

sea [siː] <> *n* mar *m*; **to be at ~** [ship, sailor] estar no mar; **to be all at ~** *fig* [person] estar totalmente perdido(da); **by ~** pelo mar; **by the ~** junto ao mar; **out to ~** [away from land] para alto mar. <> *comp* - **1.** [travel, voyage] marítimo(ma) - **2.** [animal] marinho(nha).
  ◆ **seas** *npl*: **the ~s** os mares.

sea air *n* (*U*) ar *m* do mar.

sea anemone *n* anêmona *f* do mar.

seabed ['siːbed] *n*: **the ~** o fundo do mar.

seabird ['siːbɜːd] *n* ave *f* marinha.

seaboard ['siːbɔːd] *n fml* litoral *m.*

sea breeze *n* brisa *f* do mar.

seafaring ['siːˌfeərɪŋ] *adj* - **1.** [man] do mar - **2.** [nation] de navegantes.

seafood ['siːfuːd] *n* (*U*) frutos *mpl* do mar.

seafront ['siːfrʌnt] *n* orla *f* marítima.

seagoing ['siːˌgəʊɪŋ] *adj* de alto-mar.

seagull ['siːgʌl] *n* gaivota *f.*

seahorse ['siːhɔːs] *n* cavalo *m* marinho.

seal [siːl] (*pl sense 1 only inv OR* **-s**) <> *n* - **1.** [gen] selo *m*; **~ of approval** carimbo *m* de aprovação; **to put** *OR* **set the ~ on sthg** selar algo - **2.** [animal] foca *f* - **3.** *TECH* vedação *f.* <> *vt* - **1.** [stick down] selar - **2.** [block up] vedar.
  ◆ **seal off** *vt sep* interditar.

sealable ['siːləbl] *adj* vedável.

sea lane *n* rota *f* marítima.

sealant ['siːlənt] *n* selador *m.*

sea level *n* (*U*) nível *m* do mar.

sealing wax ['siːlɪŋ-] *n* (*U*) lacre *m.*

sea lion (*pl inv OR* **-s**) *n* leão-marinho *m.*

sealskin ['siːlskɪn] *n* (*U*) pele *f* de foca.

seam [siːm] *n* - **1.** *SEWING* costura *f*; **the room was bursting at the ~s** a sala estava entupida de gente - **2.** [of coal] veio *m.*

seaman ['siːmən] (*pl* **-men** [-mən]) *n* marinheiro *m.*

seamanship ['siːmənʃɪp] *n* (*U*) náutica *f.*

sea mist *n* (*U*) nevoeiro *m* do mar.

seamless ['siːmlɪs] *adj* - **1.** [gen] sem costuras - **2.** *fig* [faultless] perfeito(ta).

seamstress ['semstrɪs] *n* costureira *f.*

seamy ['siːmɪ] (*compar* **-ier**, *superl* **-iest**) *adj* sórdido(-da).

séance ['seɪɒns] *n* sessão *f* espírita.

seaplane ['siːpleɪn] *n* hidroavião *m.*

seaport ['siːpɔːt] *n* porto *m* de mar.

search [sɜːtʃ] <> *n* - **1.** [for lost person, object] procura *f*, busca *f*; **~ for sthg** busca *OR* procura por algo; **in ~ of** a procura de, em busca de - **2.** [of person, luggage, house] procura *f.* <> *vt* - **1.** [gen] procurar; **to ~ sthg for sthg** procurar algo em algo - **2.** [mind, memory] vascular - **3.** [frisk] revistar. <> *vi* - **1.** [look for] procurar; **to ~ for sb/sthg** procurar (por) alguém/algo - **2.** [try to recall]: **to ~ for sthg** tentar lembrar algo.
  ◆ **search out** *vt sep* descobrir, encontrar.

search engine *n* *COMPUT* mecanismo *m* de busca.

searcher ['sɜːtʃəʳ] *n* investigador *m*, -ra *f.*

searching ['sɜːtʃɪŋ] *adj* - **1.** [question] perspicaz - **2.** [examination, review] minucioso(sa) - **3.** [look] penetrante.

searchlight ['sɜːtʃlaɪt] *n* holofote *m.*

search party *n* equipe *f* de busca.

search warrant *n* mandado *m* de busca.

searing ['sɪərɪŋ] *adj* - **1.** [intense] intenso(sa) - **2.** [highly critical] contundente.

sea salt *n* (*U*) sal *m* marinho.

seashell ['siːʃel] *n* concha *f* (marinha).

seashore ['siːʃɔːʳ] *n*: **the ~** o litoral.

seasick ['siːsɪk] *adj* mareado(da).

seaside ['siːsaɪd] *n*: **the ~** a praia.

seaside resort *n* local *m* de veraneio *(na praia).*

season ['siːzn] <> *n* - **1.** [time of year] estação *f* - **2.** [for particular activity] período *m*, época *f* - **3.** [of holiday] temporada *f*; **out of ~** fora de temporada - **4.** [of food]: **in ~** da estação; **out of ~** fora da estação - **5.** [series - of films] festival *m*; [- of lectures] série *f.* <> *vt* temperar.

seasonal ['siːzənl] *adj* sazonal.

seasoned ['siːznd] *adj* experiente.

seasoning ['siːznɪŋ] *n* tempero *m.*

season ticket *n* bilhete *m* para a temporada.

season-ticket holder *n* pessoa *que comprou um bilhete que lhe dá direito de assistir a todos os jogos da temporada.*

seat [siːt] <> *n* - **1.** [gen] assento *m* - **2.** [place to sit] banco *m* - **3.** [of clothing] fundilho *m* - **4.** *POL* [in parliament] cadeira *f.* <> *vt* - **1.** [sit down] sentar; **to ~ o.s.** sentar-se - **2.** [subj: building, vehicle] acomodar.

seat belt *n* cinto *m* de segurança.

seated ['si:tɪd] *adj* sentado(da).

-seater ['si:tə^r] *suffix*: **a two** ~ **car** um carro com dois lugares.

seating ['si:tɪŋ] <> *n (U)* acomodação *f.* <> *comp* de acomodação; ~ **plan** distribuição *f* dos lugares *(na mesa).*

SEATO ['si:təʊ] *(abbr of* **South-East Asia Treaty Organization)** *n* OTSEA *f.*

sea urchin *n* ouriço-do-mar *m.*

seawall ['si:'wɔ:l] *n* quebra-mar *m,* dique *m.*

seawater ['si:,wɔ:tə^r] *n (U)* água *f* do mar.

seaweed ['si:wi:d] *n (U)* alga *f* marinha.

seaworthy ['si:,wɜ:ðɪ] *adj* em condições de navegar.

sebaceous [sɪ'beɪʃəs] *adj* sebáceo(cea).

sec. *(abbr of* **second)** *n* seg.

Sec. *(abbr of* **secretary)** secretário *m,* -ria *f.*

SEC *(abbr of* **Securities and Exchange Commission)** *n organismo do governo norte-americano que supervisiona as transações da bolsa.*

secateurs [,sekə'tɜ:z] *npl UK* tesoura *f* para podar.

secede [sɪ'si:d] *vi fml* separar-se; **to** ~ **from sthg** separar-se de algo.

secession [sɪ'seʃn] *n (U) fml* secessão *f.*

secluded [sɪ'klu:dɪd] *adj* isolado(da), afastado(da).

seclusion [sɪ'klu:ʒn] *n (U)* isolamento *m.*

second¹ ['sekənd] <> *n* **- 1.** [gen] segundo *m* **- 2.** *UK UNIV* diploma *m* com louvor **- 3.** *AUT*: ~ **(gear)** segunda *f.* <> *num* segundo(da); **what are you doing on the** ~**?** o que você vai fazer no dia dois (deste mês)?; **the** ~ **of March** dia 2 de Março; **...** ~ **only to Boris** ... perdendo apenas para Boris; **he is** ~ **to none** ele não perde para ninguém; *see also* **sixth.** <> *vt* secundar.

➡ **seconds** *npl* **- 1.** *COMM* artigos *mpl* de segunda-linha **- 2.** [of food] repetição *f.*

second² [sɪ'kɒnd] *vt UK* transferir provisoriamente.

secondary ['sekəndrɪ] *adj* secundário(ria); **to be** ~ **to sthg** ser secundário para algo.

secondary picketing *n (U)* piquete feito por *pessoas não envolvidas na categoria reivindicante.*

secondary school *n* escola *f* secundária.

second best ['sekənd-] *adj* segundo(da) melhor; **to settle for** ~ contentar-se com a segunda opção.

second-class ['sekənd-] *adj* **- 1.** [gen] de segunda classe **- 2.** *pej* [less important] de segunda classe **- 3.** *UK UNIV tipo de grau universitário com louvor concedido por universidades britânicas.*

second cousin ['sekənd-] *n* primo *m,* -ma *f* em segundo grau.

second-degree burn ['sekənd-] *n* queimadura *f* de segundo grau.

seconder ['sekəndə^r] *n* pessoa *f* que secunda.

second floor ['sekənd-] *n* **- 1.** *UK* [third storey] terceiro andar *m* **- 2.** *US* [second storey] segundo andar *m.*

second-guess ['sekənd-] *vt* **- 1.** *US* [with hindsight] julgar a posteriori **- 2.** [predict] prever.

second-hand ['sekənd-] <> *adj* **- 1.** [gen] de

segunda mão **- 2.** [shop] de objetos usados. <> *adv* **- 1.** [not new] de segunda mão **- 2.** *fig* [indirectly]: **to hear sthg** ~ ouvir algo de terceiros.

second hand ['sekənd-] *n* ponteiro *m* dos segundos.

second-in-command ['sekənd-] *n* suplente *mf.*

secondly ['sekəndlɪ] *adv* em segundo lugar.

secondment [sɪ'kɒndmənt] *n UK* transferência *f* temporária.

second nature ['sekənd-] *n (U)* segunda natureza *f.*

second-rate ['sekənd-] *adj pej* de segunda categoria.

second thought ['sekənd-] *n*: **to have** ~**s about sthg** estar em dúvida sobre algo; **on** ~**s** *UK,* **on** ~ *US* pensando bem.

secrecy ['si:krəsɪ] *n (U)* sigilo *m.*

secret ['si:krɪt] <> *adj* secreto(ta); **to keep sthg** ~ manter algo em segredo. <> *n* segredo *m;* **in** ~ em segredo.

secret agent *n* agente *mf* secreto.

secretarial [,sekrə'teərɪəl] *adj* **- 1.** [course] de secretário **- 2.** [staff] de secretários **- 3.** [training] para secretariado.

secretariat [,sekrə'teərɪət] *n* secretariado *m.*

secretary [*UK* 'sekrətrɪ, *US* 'sekrə,terɪ] *(pl* **-ies)** *n* **- 1.** [gen] secretário *m,* -ria *f* **- 2.** *POL* [minister] ministro *m,* -tra *f.*

secretary-general *(pl* **secretaries-general)** *n* secretário *m,* -ria *f* geral.

Secretary of State *n* **- 1.** *UK* [minister]: ~ **(for sthg)** ministro *m* (de algo) **- 2.** *US* [in charge of foreign affairs] secretário *m,* -ria *f* das relações exteriores.

secrete [sɪ'kri:t] *vt* **- 1.** [produce] secretar **- 2.** *fml* [hide] ocultar.

secretion [sɪ'kri:ʃn] *n* secreção *f.*

secretive ['si:krətɪv] *adj* **- 1.** [person] reservado(da) **- 2.** [organization] secreto(ta).

secretly ['si:krɪtlɪ] *adv* secretamente, em segredo.

secret police *n (U)* polícia *f* secreta.

secret service *n* serviço *m* secreto.

sect [sekt] *n* seita *f.*

sectarian [sek'teərɪən] *adj* sectário(ria).

section ['sekʃn] <> *n* seção *f.* <> *vt* **- 1.** *GEOM* seccionar **- 2.** *fml* [cut] seccionar.

sector ['sektə^r] *n* setor *m.*

secular ['sekjʊlə^r] *adj* secular.

secure [sɪ'kjʊə^r] <> *adj* **- 1.** [tightly locked up] seguro(ra), protegido(da) **- 2.** [fixed in place] seguro(ra), firme **- 3.** [safe, not likely to change] garantido(da) **- 4.** [strong, solid] firme **- 5.** [free of anxiety, confident] confiante. <> *vt* **- 1.** [obtain] conseguir, obter **- 2.** [make safe] proteger **- 3.** [fasten] fechar bem.

securely [sɪ'kjʊəlɪ] *adv* firmemente.

security [sɪ'kjʊərətɪ] *(pl* **-ies)** <> *n* **- 1.** [gen] segurança *f* **- 2.** *(U)* [legal protection] segurança *f,* garantia *f;* ~ **of tenure** cargo *m* vitalício. <> *comp* de segurança.

➡ **securities** *npl FIN* papéis *mpl* negociáveis.

security blanket *n* cobertor ou outro obejeto de *estimação com o qual a pessoa se sente protegida.*

Security Council *n*: the ~ o Conselho de Segurança.
security forces *npl* forças *fpl* de segurança.
security guard *n* (guarda *mf* de) segurança *mf*.
security risk *n* ameaça *f* à segurança.
sedan [sɪ'dæn] *n US* sedã *m*.
sedan chair *n* liteira *f*.
sedate [sɪ'deɪt] <> *adj* calmo(ma), sossegado(da). <> *vt* sedar.
sedation [sɪ'deɪʃn] *n (U)* sedação *f*.
sedative ['sedətɪv] <> *adj* sedativo(va). <> *n* sedativo *m*.
sedentary ['sedntrɪ] *adj* sedentário(ria).
sediment ['sedɪmənt] *n* sedimento *m*.
sedition [sɪ'dɪʃn] *n (U)* sedição *f*.
seditious [sɪ'dɪʃəs] *adj* sedicioso(sa).
seduce [sɪ'dju:s] *vt* seduzir; **to ~ sb into doing sthg** persuadir alguém a fazer algo.
seduction [sɪ'dʌkʃn] *n* sedução *f*.
seductive [sɪ'dʌktɪv] *adj* sedutor(ra).
see [si:] (*pt* saw, *pp* seen) <> *vt* **-1.** [gen] ver; **we're going to ~ each other tonight** vamos nos ver hoje à noite; **~ you!** até mais!; **~ you soon/later/tomorrow!** até breve/mais tarde/amanhã! **-2.** [friend, doctor] visitar **-3.** [realize]: **to ~ (that)** perceber que **-4.** [understand] entender **-5.** [accompany] levar, acompanhar **-6.** [find out, ascertain] descobrir; **I'll ~ what I can do** verei o que posso fazer **-7.** [make sure]: **I'll ~ (that the work gets done)** vou providenciar (para que o trabalho fique pronto) **-8.** [judge, consider] ver, considerar **-9.** [subj: day, date]: **today saw ...** hoje aconteceu ... <> *vi* **-1.** [perceive with eyes] enxergar **-2.** [understand] entender; **I ~** entendo; **you ~, ...** veja bem, ... **-3.** [find out] ver; **to ~ if one can do sthg** ver se se pode fazer algo; **let's ~, let me ~** vamos ver, vejamos.
 ➡ **seeing as, seeing that** *conj inf* já que, como.
 ➡ **see about** *vt fus* **-1.** [organize]: **I'll ~ about getting you some work** vou dar um jeito de te arrumar algum trabalho **-2.** [think about] ver.
 ➡ **see off** *vt sep* **-1.** [say goodbye to] despedir-se de **-2.** *UK* [chase away] afugentar.
 ➡ **see through** <> *vt fus* [not be deceived by] não se deixar enganar por. <> *vt sep* [to conclusion] levar a termo.
 ➡ **see to** *vt fus* cuidar de.
seed [si:d] <> *n* **-1.** [of plant] semente *f* **-2.** *SPORT* pré-selecionado *m*, -da *f*. <> *vt*: **she's ~ed first in the world** ela é a número um do mundo.
 ➡ **seeds** *npl fig* [beginnings] semente *f*.
seedless ['si:dlɪs] *adj* sem semente/caroço.
seedling ['si:dlɪŋ] *n* muda *f*.
seedy ['si:dɪ] (*compar* -ier, *superl* -iest) *adj* **-1.** [person] maltrapilho(lha) **-2.** [room, area] usado(da).
seek [si:k] (*pt & pp* sought) *fml* <> *vt* procurar; **to ~ to do sthg** procurar fazer algo. <> *vi* **-1.** [search]: **to ~ for sthg** procurar (por) algo **-2.** [request]: **to ~ for sthg** pedir algo.
 ➡ **seek out** *vt sep* perseguir.
seem [si:m] <> *vi* parecer; **it ~s too good to be true** parece bom demais para ser verdade; **I ~ to remember that ...** parece que eu me lembro de

que ...; **I can't ~ to do that** por mais que eu tente, não consigo fazer isso. <> *v impers*: **it ~s (that)** parece que.
seeming ['si:mɪŋ] *adj fml* aparente.
seemingly ['si:mɪŋlɪ] *adv* aparentemente.
seemly (*compar* -ier, *superl* -iest) *adj literary* decoroso(sa).
seen [si:n] *pp* ➤ see.
seep [si:p] *vi* infiltrar-se, penetrar.
seersucker ['sɪə,sʌkəʳ] *n (U)* tecido leve de algodão listado.
seesaw ['si:sɔ:] *n* gangorra *f*.
seethe [si:ð] *vi* fervilhar; **to be seething with sthg** estar fervilhando com algo.
seething ['si:ðɪŋ] *adj* **-1.** [furious] furioso(sa) **-2.** [teeming] fervilhante.
see-through *adj* transparente.
segment ['segmənt] *n* **-1.** [of market, report, audience] segmento *m* **-2.** [of fruit] gomo *m*.
segregate ['segrɪgeɪt] *vt* segregar.
segregation [,segrɪ'geɪʃn] *n (U)* segregação *f*.
Seine [seɪn] *n*: the (River) ~ o (Rio) Sena.
seismic ['saɪzmɪk] *adj* sísmico(ca).
seize [si:z] *vt* **-1.** [grab] agarrar, pegar **-2.** [win, capture] tomar **-3.** [arrest] prender, deter **-4.** [take advantage of] aproveitar.
 ➡ **seize (up)on** *vt fus* valer-se de.
 ➡ **seize up** *vi* **-1.** [body] enrijecer **-2.** [engine] emperrar.
seizure ['si:ʒəʳ] *n* **-1.** *MED* ataque *m* **-2.** *(U)* [taking, capturing] tomada *f*.
seldom ['seldəm] *adv* raramente.
select [sɪ'lekt] <> *adj* **-1.** [carefully chosen] selecionado(da) **-2.** [exclusive] seleto(ta). <> *vt* selecionar.
select committee *n* comissão *f* parlamentar de inquérito.
selected [sɪ'lektɪd] *adj* escolhido(da).
selection [sɪ'lekʃn] *n* **-1.** [gen] seleção *f* **-2.** [range of goods] coleção *f*.
selective [sɪ'lektɪv] *adj* seletivo(va).
selector [sɪ'lektəʳ] *n SPORT* selecionador *m*, -ra *f*.
self [self] (*pl* selves) *n*: **she's her old ~** ela volta a ser ela mesma; **the ~** o eu.
self- [self] *prefix* auto-; ~**defence** *UK*, ~**defense** *US* autodefesa *f*; ~**accusation** auto-acusação *f*.
self-addressed envelope [-ə'drest-] *n* envelope *m* de resposta.
self-addressed stamped envelope [-ə,drest'stæmpt-] *n US* envelope *m* de resposta pré-pago.
self-adhesive *adj* auto-adesivo(va).
self-appointed [-ə'pɔɪntɪd] *adj pej* autodesignado(da).
self-assembly *adj UK* desmontável.
self-assertive *adj* seguro(ra) de si.
self-assurance *n (U)* autoconfiança *f*.
self-assured *adj* confiante em si mesmo(ma), seguro(ra) de si.
self-catering *adj* sem refeições incluídas.
self-centred [-'sentəd] *adj* egocêntrico(ca).
self-cleaning *adj* autolimpante.
self-coloured *adj UK* unicolor.
self-confessed [-kən'fest] *adj* assumido(da).

self-confidence n autoconfiança f.
self-confident adj **-1.** [person] seguro(ra) de si **-2.** [remark, attitude] que passa segurança.
self-conscious adj inibido(da).
self-contained [-kən'teɪnd] adj **-1.** [person] reservado(da) **-2.** [flat] independente.
self-control n (U) autocontrole m.
self-controlled adj controlado(da), sereno(na).
self-defence n (U) legítima defesa f; **in ~** em legítima defesa.
self-denial n (U) abnegação f.
self-destruct [-dɪs'trʌkt] <> adj autodestrutivo (va). <> vi autodestruir-se.
self-determination n (U) autodeterminação f.
self-discipline n (U) autodisciplina f.
self-doubt n (U) insegurança f.
self-drive adj UK alugado(da) sem motorista.
self-educated adj autodidata.
self-effacing [-ɪ'feɪsɪŋ] adj modesto(ta), humilde.
self-employed [-ɪm'plɔɪd] adj autônomo(ma), que trabalha por conta própria.
self-esteem n (U) amor-próprio m.
self-evident adj óbvio(via).
self-explanatory adj claro(ra), manifesto(ta).
self-expression n (U) expressão f própria.
self-focusing [-'fəʊkəsɪŋ] adj com foco automático.
self-government n (U) governo m autônomo.
self-help n (U) auto-ajuda f.
self-important adj pej presunçoso(sa), convencido(da).
self-imposed [-ɪm'pəʊzd] adj imposto a si mesmo, imposta a si mesma.
self-indulgent adj pej comodista, que se permite excessos.
self-inflicted [-ɪn'flɪktɪd] adj auto-infligido(da).
self-interest n (U) pej interesse m pessoal OR próprio.
selfish ['selfɪʃ] adj egoísta.
selfishness ['selfɪʃnɪs] n (U) egoísmo m.
selfless ['selflɪs] adj desinteressado(da).
self-locking [-'lɒkɪŋ] adj de fechamento automático.
self-made adj que se fez por si mesmo(ma).
self-opinionated adj pej presunçoso(sa).
self-perpetuating [-pə'petʃʊeɪtɪŋ] adj que se perpetua a si mesmo(ma).
self-pity n (U) pej autocomiseração f.
self-portrait n auto-retrato m.
self-possessed [-pə'zest] adj dono de si mesmo, dona de si mesma.
self-preservation n autopreservação f.
self-proclaimed [-prə'kleɪmd] adj pej autodenominado(da).
self-raising flour UK [-ˌreɪzɪŋ-], **self-rising flour** US n (U) farinha f com fermento.
self-regard n (U) **-1.** [self-esteem] amor-próprio m **-2.** pej [conceit] narcisismo m.
self-regulating [-'regjʊleɪtɪŋ] adj auto-regulador (ra).
self-reliant adj independente.
self-respect n (U) amor m próprio.

self-respecting [-rɪs'pektɪŋ] adj que se presta, digno(na).
self-restraint n (U) autocontrole m.
self-righteous adj pej hipócrita.
self-rising flour n US = **self-raising flour**.
self-rule n (U) autonomia f (de um governo).
self-sacrifice n (U) abnegação f.
selfsame ['selfseɪm] adj mesmíssimo(míssima).
self-satisfied adj pej convencido(da).
self-sealing [-'siːlɪŋ] adj auto-adesivo(va).
self-seeking [-'siːkɪŋ] pej adj interesseiro(ra).
self-service <> n (U) auto-serviço m, self-service m. <> comp de auto-serviço, self-service; **a ~ shop** uma loja self-service.
self-starter n **-1.** AUT arranque m automático **-2.** [person] empreendedor m, -ra f.
self-styled [-'staɪld] adj pej pretenso(sa).
self-sufficient adj: **~ (in sthg)** auto-suficiente (em algo).
self-supporting [-sə'pɔːtɪŋ] adj economicamente independente.
self-tanning adj autobronzeador(ra).
self-taught adj autodidata.
self-test vi COMPUT autotestar.
self-willed adj pej obstinado(da).
sell [sell (pt & pp sold)] <> vt **-1.** vender; **to ~ sthg to sb, to ~ sb sthg** vender algo para alguém; **to ~ sthg for** vender algo por; **to ~ o.s.** vender-se; **~ o.s. short** desmerecer-se **-2.** fig [make enthusiastic about]: **to ~ sthg to sb, to ~ sb sthg** vender algo para alguém; **to ~ sb an idea** vender uma idéia a alguém; **I'm not really sold on the idea** não consigo comprar essa idéia. <> vi vender; **to ~ for** OR **at** ser vendido(da) por OR a.
▸ **sell off** vt sep liquidar.
▸ **sell out** <> vt sep: **to be sold out** estar esgotado(da). <> vi **-1.** [shop, ticket office]: **to ~ out (of sthg)** vender todo o estoque (de algo) **-2.** [betray one's principles] vender-se.
▸ **sell up** vi vender tudo.
sell-by date n UK prazo m de validade.
seller ['selə'] n vendedor m, -ra f.
seller's market n mercado m de demanda OR favorável ao vendedor.
selling ['selɪŋ] n (U) venda f.
selling price ['selɪŋ-] n preço m de venda.
Sellotape® ['seləteɪp] n UK fita f adesiva, durex® m.
▸ **sellotape** vt segurar com fita adesiva.
sell-out n **-1.** [performance, match] sucesso m de bilheteria **-2.** [of principles] traição f.
sell-through n US COMM venda f direta (ao consumidor).
seltzer n US água f de soda.
selves [selvz] pl ⊳ **self**.
semantic [sɪ'mæntɪk] adj semântico(ca).
▸ **semantics** n (U) semântica f.
semaphore ['seməfɔː'] n (U) semáforo m.
semblance ['sembləns] n fml aparência f.
semen ['siːmən] n (U) sêmen m.
semester [sɪ'mestə'] n semestre m.
semi ['semɪ] n **-1.** UK inf [house] casa f geminada **-2.** US [lorry] caminhão m articulado.

semi- ['semɪ] *prefix* semi-.

semi-automatic *adj* semi-automático(ca).

semicircle ['semɪ,sɜ:kl] *n* semicírculo *m*.

semicircular [,semɪ'sɜ:kjʊlə^r] *adj* semicircular.

semicolon [,semɪ'kəʊlən] *n* ponto-e-vírgula *m*.

semi-conscious *adj* semiconsciente.

semi-detached ◇ *adj UK* geminado(do). ◇ *n UK* casa *f* geminada.

semi-final *n* semifinal *f*.

semi-finalist *n* semifinalista *mf*.

seminal *adj* **- 1.** [important] muito influente **- 2.** [of semen] seminal.

seminar ['semmɑ:^r] *n* seminário *m*.

seminary ['semmərɪ] (*pl* -ies) *n* RELIG seminário *m*.

semiotics *n* (*U*) semiótica *f*. •

semi-precious *adj* semiprecioso(sa).

semi-skilled *adj* semi-especializado(da).

semi-skimmed [-'skɪmd] *adj* semidesnatado(-da).

semi-trailer *n* **- 1.** [trailer] reboque *m* **- 2.** *US* [lorry] caminhão *m* articulado.

semolina [,semə'li:nə] *n* (*U*) semolina *f*.

Sen. - 1. (*abbr of* **senator**) Sen. **- 2.** (*abbr of* **Senior**) sênior.

Senate ['senɪt] *n* POL: **the** ~ o Senado; **the United States** ~ o Senado dos Estados Unidos.

SENATE

Senado e Câmara de Representantes (*House of Representatives*) formam o poder legislativo nos EUA. Composto de 100 membros, dois senadores por estado, o Senado norte-americano tem entre suas prerrogativas a solicitação do *impeachment* do presidente da república.

---

senator ['senətə^r] *n* senador *m*, -ra *f*.

send [send] (*pt* & *pp* **sent**) *vt* **- 1.** [letter, message, money] enviar, mandar; **to** ~ **sb sthg**, **to** ~ **sthg to sb** enviar *OR* mandar algo para alguém **- 2.** [tell to go]: **to** ~ **sb (to)** mandar alguém (para); **to** ~ **sb for sthg** mandar alguém buscar algo **- 3.** [propel] lançar **- 4.** [into a specific state] deixar; **to** ~ **sb mad** deixar alguém louco(ca); **to** ~ **sb to sleep** dar sono em alguém; **to** ~ **sb flying** arremessar alguém longe.

◆ **send back** *vt sep* devolver; **to** ~ **sb back** fazer alguém voltar.

◆ **send down** *vt sep inf* encarcerar.

◆ **send for** *vt fus* **- 1.** [person] mandar chamar **- 2.** [by post] encomendar.

◆ **send in** *vt sep* **- 1.** [visitor] fazer entrar **- 2.** [troops, police] enviar, mandar **- 3.** [submit] enviar.

◆ **send off** *vt sep* **- 1.** [by post] enviar (*pelo correio*) **- 2.** *SPORT* expulsar.

◆ **send off for** *vt fus* encomendar (*pelo correio*).

◆ **send up** *vt sep inf* **- 1.** *UK* [imitate] arremedar, imitar **- 2.** *US* [send to prison] mandar para a prisão.

sender ['sendə^r] *n* remetente *mf*.

send-off *n* despedida *f*.

send-up *n* *UK inf* paródia *f*, sátira *f*.

Senegal [,senɪ'gɔ:l] *n* Senegal; **in** ~ no Senegal.

Senegalese [,senɪgə'li:z] ◇ *adj* senegalês(esa). ◇ *npl*: **the** ~ os senegaleses.

senile ['si:naɪl] *adj* senil.

senile dementia *n* (*U*) demência *f* senil.

senility [sɪ'nɪlətɪ] *n* (*U*) senilidade *f*.

senior ['si:njə^r] ◇ *adj* **- 1.** [highest-ranking] superior(ra) **- 2.** [higher-ranking]: ~ **to sb** superior a alguém **- 3.** *SCH* [pupils, classes] veterano(na); ~ **year** *US* último ano do ensino secundário e das universidades nos Estados Unidos. ◇ *n* **- 1.** [older person] mais velho(lha); **I'm five years his** ~ sou cinco anos mais velho do que ele **- 2.** *SCH* & *UNIV* veterano *m*, -na *f*.

senior citizen *n* idoso *m*, -sa *f*.

senior high school *n* *US* escola *f* de ensino médio (*dos 16 aos 18 anos*).

seniority [,si:nɪ'ɒrətɪ] *n* (*U*) grau *m* de poder ou competência.

sensation [sen'seɪʃn] *n* sensação *f*.

sensational [sen'seɪʃənl] *adj* **- 1.** [causing a stir] sensacional **- 2.** *inf* [wonderful] sensacional **- 3.** [sensationalist] sensacionalista.

sensationalist [sen'seɪʃnəlɪst] *adj pej* sensacionalista.

sense [sens] ◇ *n* **- 1.** [gen] sentido *m*; **to make** ~ [have clear meaning] fazer sentido; [be logical] ser lógico(ca); **to make** ~ **of sthg** entender algo **- 2.** [feeling, sensation - of guilt, terror, honour] sentimento *m*; [- of justice, duty, urgency] senso *m* **- 3.** [natural ability]: ~ **of direction** senso *m* de direção; ~ **of style** idéia *f* de estilo **- 4.** (*U*) [wisdom, reason] bom senso *m*, sabedoria *f*; **to talk** ~ falar seriamente; **there's no** ~ **in arguing/fighting** não faz sentido brigar/lutar **- 5.** *phr*: **to come to one's** ~**s** [be sensible again] recobrar o juízo; [regain consciousness] recobrar os sentidos; **to be out of one's** ~**s** perder o juízo. ◇ *vt* sentir; **to** ~ **that** sentir que.

◆ **in a sense** *adv* de certo modo, em certo sentido.

senseless ['senslɪs] *adj* **- 1.** [stupid] sem sentido, estúpido(da) **- 2.** [unconscious] inconsciente; **to knock sb** ~ bater em alguém até ficar inconsciente.

sensibilities [,sensɪ'bɪlətɪz] *npl* sensibilidade *f*.

sensible ['sensəbl] *adj* **- 1.** [reasonable, practical] prático(ca) **- 2.** [person] sensato(ta).

sensibly ['sensəblɪ] *adv* sensatamente.

sensitive ['sensɪtɪv] *adj* **- 1.** [eyes, skin]: ~ **(to sthg)** sensível (a algo) **- 2.** [understanding, aware]: ~ **(to sthg)** compreensivo(va) (com algo) **- 3.** [easily hurt, touchy]: ~ **(to/about sthg)** sensível *OR* suscetível (a algo) **- 4.** [controversial] delicado(da) **- 5.** [instrument] sensível.

sensitivity [,sensɪ'tɪvətɪ] *n* sensibilidade *f*.

sensor ['sensə^r] *n* sensor *m*.

sensual ['sensjʊəl] *adj* sensual.

sensuous ['sensjʊəs] *adj* sensual.

sent [sent] *pt* & *pp* ▷ **send**.

sentence ['sentəns] ◇ *n* **- 1.** [group of words] frase *f*, oração *f* **- 2.** *JUR* sentença *f*. ◇ *vt*: **to** ~ **sb (to sthg)** condenar alguém (a algo).

sententious [sen'tenʃəs] *adj pej* sentencioso(sa).

sentiment ['sentɪmənt] *n* **- 1.** [feeling] sentimento *m* **- 2.** [opinion] opinião *f* **- 3.** (*U*) *pej* [sentimentality] sentimentalismo *m*.

sentimental [ˌsentɪ'mentl] *adj* -**1.** *pej* [over-emotional] sentimental -**2.** [emotional] sentimental.

sentimentality [ˌsentɪmen'tælətɪ] *n (U) pej* sentimentalismo *m*.

sentinel ['sentɪnl] *n* sentinela *mf*.

sentry ['sentrɪ] (*pl* -**ies**) *n* sentinela *mf*.

Seoul [səʊl] *n* Seul.

separable ['seprəbl] *adj*: ~ **(from sthg)** separável (de algo).

separate [*adj* & *n* 'seprət, *vb* 'sepəreɪt] <> *adj* -**1.** [not joined, apart] separado(da); ~ **from sthg** separado(da) de algo -**2.** [individual] separado(da), diferente -**3.** [distinct] distinto(ta). <> *vt* separar; **to** ~ **sb/sthg from** separar alguém/algo de; **to** ~ **sb/sthg into** separar alguém/algo em; **to** ~ **sb/sthg from** separar alguém/algo de. <> *vi* -**1.** [gen] separar-se; **to** ~ **into sthg** separar-se em algo -**2.** [go different ways]: **to** ~ **(from sb/sthg)** separar-se (de alguém/algo).

➡ **separates** *npl UK* peças *fpl* avulsas *(de roupa)*.

separated ['sepəreɪtɪd] *adj* separado(da).

separately ['seprətlɪ] *adv* separadamente.

separation [ˌsepə'reɪʃn] *n* separação *f*; ~ **(from sb/sthg)** separação (de alguém/algo).

separatism *n* separatismo *m*.

separatist ['seprətɪst] *n* separatista *mf*.

sepia ['siːpjə] *adj* sépia.

Sept. (*abbr of* **September**) set.

September [sep'tembə^r] <> *n* setembro; **when are you going? -** ~ quando você vai? - em setembro; **one of the hottest** ~**s on record** um dos setembros mais quentes que já se registrou; **in** ~ em setembro; **last/this/next** ~ em setembro do ano passado/deste ano/do ano que vem; **by** ~ até setembro; **every** ~ todos os anos em setembro; **during** ~ em setembro, durante o mês de setembro; **at the beginning/end of** ~ no início/fim de setembro; **in the middle of** ~ em meados de setembro, no meio do mês de setembro. <> *comp* de setembro; ~ **birthday** aniversário *m* em setembro.

septet *n* septeto *m*.

septic ['septɪk] *adj* séptico(ca); **to go** ~ infeccionar.

septicaemia *UK*, **septicemia** *US* [ˌseptɪ'siːmɪə] *n (U)* septicemia *f*.

septic tank *n* fossa *f* séptica.

sepulchre *UK*, **sepulcher** *US* ['sepʌlkər] *n literary* sepulcro *m*.

sequel ['siːkwəl] *n* -**1.** [book, film]: ~ **to sthg** continuação *f* de algo -**2.** [consequence]: ~ **to sthg** seqüela *f* de algo.

sequence ['siːkwəns] *n* -**1.** [gen] seqüência *f*; **in** ~ em seqüência -**2.** [series] seqüência *f*, sucessão *f*.

sequester, sequestrate *vt JUR* confiscar, colocar sob custódia.

sequin ['siːkwɪn] *n* lantejoula *f*.

sera ['sɪərəl] *pl* ▷ **serum**.

Serb *adj* & *n* = **Serbian**.

Serbia ['sɜːbjə] *n* Sérvia; **in** ~ na Sérvia.

Serbian ['sɜːbjən], **Serb** [sɜːb] <> *adj* sérvio(via). <> *n* -**1.** [person] sérvio *m*, -via *f* -**2.** [language] sérvio *m*.

Serbo-Croat [ˌsɜːbəʊ'krəʊæt], **Serbo-Croatian** [ˌsɜːbəʊkrəʊ'eɪʃn] <> *adj* servo-croata. <> *n* [language] servo-croata *m*.

serenade [ˌserə'neɪd] <> *n* serenata *f*. <> *vt* fazer uma serenata para.

serene [sɪ'riːn] *adj* sereno(na).

serenely [sɪ'riːnlɪ] *adv* serenamente.

serenity [sɪ'renətɪ] *n (U)* serenidade *f*.

serf [sɜːf] *n HIST* servo *m*, -va *f*.

serge [sɜːdʒ] *n (U)* sarja *f*.

sergeant ['sɑːdʒəntl] *n* -**1.** *MIL* sargento *m* -**2.** *POLICE* tenente *m*.

sergeant major *n* primeiro-sargento *m*.

serial ['sɪərɪəl] *n* série *f*, seriado *m*.

serialize, -ise ['sɪərɪəlaɪz] *vt* publicar em folhetim.

serial killer *n* assassino *m*, -na *f* em série, serial killer *m*.

serial number *n* número *m* de série.

series ['sɪəriːz] (*pl inv*) *n* -**1.** [sequence] série *f* -**2.** *RADIO* & *TV* série *f*, seriado *m*.

serious ['sɪərɪəs] *adj* -**1.** [gen] sério(ria); **are you** ~? fala sério? -**2.** [problem, illness] grave.

serious crime *n* crime *m* grave.

seriously ['sɪərɪəslɪ] *adv* -**1.** [earnestly] seriamente; **to take sb/sthg** ~ levar alguém/algo a sério -**2.** [very badly] gravemente.

seriousness ['sɪərɪəsnɪs] *n (U)* -**1.** [of person, expression, voice] seriedade *f*; **in all** ~ seriamente -**2.** [of illness, situation, loss] gravidade *f*.

sermon ['sɜːmən] *n* -**1.** *RELIG* sermão *m* -**2.** *fig* & *pej* [lecture] sermão *m*.

serpent ['sɜːpənt] *n literary* serpente *f*.

serrated [sɪ'reɪtɪd] *adj* serrilhado(da), dentado(da).

serum ['sɪərəm] (*pl* serums *OR* sera) *n* soro *m*.

servant ['sɜːvənt] *n* criado *m*, -da *f*, empregado *m*, -da *f*.

serve [sɜːv] <> *n SPORT* serviço *m*, saque. *m*. <> *vt* -**1.** [gen] servir; **to** ~ **sthg to sb, to** ~ **sb sthg** servir algo a alguém -**2.** [have effect]: **to** ~ **to do sthg** servir para fazer algo; **to** ~ **a purpose** cumprir o propósito -**3.** [provide] abastecer; **which motorway** ~**s** Birmingham que rodovia atende à região de Birmingham? -**4.** *JUR*: **to** ~ **sb with sthg, to** ~ **sthg on sb** entregar algo a alguém -**5.** [complete, carry out] cumprir; **he's serving time** ele está cumprindo pena -**6.** *SPORT* servir, sacar -**7.** *phr*: **it** ~**s you right** bem feito! <> *vi* -**1.** [be employed - as soldier] servir o exército; [- in profession, on committee] prestar serviços -**2.** [function]: **to** ~ **as sthg** servir como algo -**3.** [in shop, bar etc] servir -**4.** *SPORT* sacar.

➡ **serve out, serve up** *vt sep* servir.

server ['sɜːvə^r] *n COMPUT* servidor *m*.

service ['sɜːvɪs] <> *n* -**1.** [gen] serviço *m*; **in** ~ em funcionamento; **out of** ~ fora de serviço -**2.** *(U)* [in shop, bar etc] atendimento *m* -**3.** [mechanical check] revisão *f* -**4.** *RELIG* serviço *m*, culto *m* -**5.** [set of tableware] jogo *m*; **dinner** ~ aparelho *m* de jantar -**6.** *SPORT* serviço *m*, saque *m* -**7.** [use, help]: **to be of** ~ **(to sb)** servir (a alguém). <> *vt* -**1.** [car, machine] fazer a revisão de -**2.** *FIN* [debt, loan] pagar os juros de.

➡ **services** *npl* -**1.** [on motorway] estação *f* de serviços -**2.** [armed forces]: **the** ~**s** as forças armadas **- 3.** [help] serviços *mpl.*

serviceable [ˈsɜːvɪsəbl] *adj* resistente, prático(ca).

service area *n* estação *f* de serviços.

service charge *n* taxa *f* de serviço.

service industries *npl* setor *m* de prestação de serviços.

serviceman [ˈsɜːvɪsmən] (*pl* **-men** [-mən]) *n* MIL militar *m*.

service provider *n* COMPUT provedor *m*.

service station *n* posto *m* de gasolina, posto *m* de serviços.

servicewoman [ˈsɜːvɪsˌwʊmən] (*pl* **-women**) *n* MIL militar *f*.

serviette [ˌsɜːvɪˈet] *n* guardanapo *m*.

servile [ˈsɜːvaɪl] *adj* servil.

servility [sɜːˈvɪlətɪ] *n (U)* servilismo *m*.

serving [ˈsɜːvɪŋ] ⇔ *adj* **-1.** [spoon, dish, fork] de servir **- 2.** [member, chairman] que presta serviços. ⇔ *n* [portion] porção *f*.

sesame [ˈsesəmɪ] *n (U)* gergelim *m*, sésamo *m*; **open ~!** abre-te, sésamo!

session [ˈseʃn] *n* **-1.** [gen] sessão *f*; **in ~** em sessão **- 2.** *US* [school term] período *m* letivo.

set [set] (*pt* & *pp* **set**, *cont* **-ting**) ⇔ *adj* **-1.** [specified, prescribed] estabelecido(da) **- 2.** [fixed, rigid] fixo(xa); **~ phrase** frase *f* feita; **to be ~ in one's ways** ter costumes arraigados **- 3.** [ready] pronto(ta); **~ for sthg/to do sthg** pronto(ta) para algo/para fazer algo **- 4.** [determined]: **to be ~ on sthg/on doing sthg** estar empenhado(da) em algo/em fazer algo; **to be dead ~ against sthg** ser completamente contra algo. ⇔ *n* **-1.** [collection, group - stamps] série *f*; [- chess, tea] jogo *m* (de); [- keys, tyres, saucepans] conjunto *m*; [- books] coleção *f* (de) **- 2.** [apparatus] aparelhagem *f* **- 3.** [of film, play] cenário *m* **- 4.** TENNIS set *m*. ⇔ *vt* **-1.** [put in specified position, place] pôr, colocar **- 2.** [fix, insert]: **to ~ sthg in(to) sthg** fixar algo em algo **- 3.** [indicating change of state or activity] pôr; **to ~ sb free** pôr alguém em liberdade; **to ~ sb's mind at rest** tranqüilizar alguém; **to ~ sthg in motion** pôr algo em movimento; **to ~ sthg right** emendar algo; **to ~ sb thinking** fazer alguém pensar; **to ~ sthg on fire** pôr fogo em algo **- 4.** [lay, prepare in advance] pôr, colocar **- 5.** [adjust] ajustar, botar; **she ~ the meter at zero** ela ajustou o medidor para zero **- 6.** [decide on] estabelecer, fixar **- 7.** [establish, create - example] dar; [- precedent] abrir; [- trend] impor; [- record] estabelecer **- 8.** [assign - target, problem] determinar; [- school work] passar; [- exam, test work] aplicar **- 9.** MED [mend] recompor **- 10.** MUS [arrange]: **to ~ sthg to music** musicar algo **- 11.** [story] passar-se; **the film is ~ in Scotland** o filme se passa na Escócia **- 12.** [hair] fazer mise-en-plis. ⇔ *vi* **-1.** [sun] pôr-se **- 2.** [solidify - jelly] endurecer; [- glue, cement] secar.

◆ **set about** *vt fus*: **to ~ about sthg** começar algo; **to ~ about doing sthg** pôr-se a fazer algo.

◆ **set against** *vt sep* **-1.** [compare] comparar **- 2.** [put in opposition] pôr contra; **the war ~ brother against brother** a guerra colocou irmão contra irmão **- 3.** FIN compensar com; **we can ~ our expenses against tax** podemos deduzir nossos gastos do imposto de renda.

◆ **set ahead** *vt sep US* [clock] adiantar.

◆ **set apart** *vt sep* distinguir; **to ~ sb/sthg apart from** distinguir alguém/algo de.

◆ **set aside** *vt sep* **-1.** [keep, save] guardar **- 2.** [not consider] deixar de lado.

◆ **set back** *vt sep* **-1.** [delay] atrasar **- 2.** *inf* [cost]: **this book ~ me back £20** este livro me custou £20.

◆ **set down** *vt sep* **-1.** [write down] pôr por escrito **- 2.** [put down] deixar.

◆ **set in** *vi* manifestar-se.

◆ **set off** ⇔ *vt sep* **-1.** [initiate, cause] provocar **- 2.** [ignite] fazer explodir. ⇔ *vi* pôr-se a caminho.

◆ **set on** *vt sep* atiçar em; **he ~ the dogs on her** ele atiçou os cachorros nela.

◆ **set out** ⇔ *vt sep* **-1.** [arrange, spread out] dispor **- 2.** [clarify, explain] expor. ⇔ *vt fus*: **to ~ out to do sthg** propor-se a fazer algo. ⇔ *vi* pôr-se a caminho.

◆ **set up** ⇔ *vt sep* **-1.** [gen] montar **- 2.** [establish, arrange - company] montar, fundar; [- committee, organization] criar; [- interview, meeting] organizar; **to ~ o.s. up** estabelecer-se; **to ~ up house** OR **home** instalar-se **- 3.** *inf* [make appear guilty] convencer; **to ~ sb up** armar contra alguém; **I was ~ up!** me armaram uma! ⇔ *vi* estabelecer-se.

setback [ˈsetbæk] *n* contratempo *m*.

set menu *n* cardápio *m* a preço fixo.

set piece *n* ART & LITERATURE *parte de um filme, romance ou música de grande efeito dramático e que normalmente não é parte essencial da história principal.*

set square *n* UK esquadro *m*.

settee [seˈtiː] *n* sofá *m*.

setter [ˈsetər] *n* cão *m* de caça.

setting [ˈsetɪŋ] *n* **-1.** [surroundings] cenário *m* **- 2.** [of dial, control] posição *f*.

settle [ˈsetl] ⇔ *vt* **-1.** [conclude, decide] resolver **- 2.** [pay] saldar **- 3.** [make comfortable] acomodar; **to ~ o.s. somewhere** acomodar-se em algum lugar **- 4.** [calm] acalmar, tranqüilizar. ⇔ *vi* **-1.** [go to live] instalar-se **- 2.** [make o.s. comfortable] acomodar-se **- 3.** [come to rest] depositar-se; **to ~ on sthg** pousar em algo.

◆ **settle down** *vi* **-1.** [give one's attention]: **to ~ down (to sthg/to doing sthg)** dedicar-se (a algo/ a fazer algo) **- 2.** [become stable] estabelecer-se **- 3.** [make o.s. comfortable] acomodar-se; **to ~ down (for sthg)** preparar-se (para algo) **- 4.** [become calm] acalmar-se.

◆ **settle for** *vt fus* conformar-se com.

◆ **settle in** *vi* **-1.** [new house] instalar-se **- 2.** [in new job] adaptar-se.

◆ **settle on** *vt fus* decidir-se por.

◆ **settle up** *vi*: **to ~ up (with sb)** ajustar as contas (com alguém).

settled [ˈsetld] *adj* estável.

settlement [ˈsetlmənt] *n* **-1.** [agreement] acordo *m* **- 2.** [village] povoado *m* **- 3.** [payment] pagamento *m*.

settler [ˈsetlər] *n* colonizador *m*, -ra *f*.

set-to *n* *inf* briga *f*.

set-up *n* *inf* **- 1.** [system, organization] estrutura *f* **- 2.** [deception to incriminate] armação *f*.

seven [ˈsevn] *num* sete; *see also* **six**.

seventeen [ˌsevnˈtiːn] *num* dezessete; *see also* **six**.

seventeenth [ˌsevnˈtiːnθ] *num* décimo sétimo, décima sétima; *see also* **sixth**.

seventh [ˈsevnθ] *num* sétimo(ma); *see also* **sixth**.

seventh heaven *n (U)*: **to be in ~** estar no sétimo céu.

seventieth [ˈsevntjəθ] *num* septuagésimo(ma); *see also* **sixth**.

seventy [ˈsevntɪ] *num* setenta; *see also* **sixty**.

sever [ˈsevəʳ] *vt* **-1.** [rope, limb] cortar **- 2.** [relationship] romper.

several [ˈsevrəl] <> *adj* vários(rias). <> *pron* vários *mpl*, -rias *fpl*.

severance [ˈsevrəns] *n (U) fml* rompimento *m*.

severance pay *n (U)* indenização *m* por demissão.

severe [sɪˈvɪəʳ] *adj* **-1.** [extreme, bad - shock] forte; [- weather] ruim; [- pain] agudo(da); [- injury, illness] grave **- 2.** [stern] severo(ra).

severely [sɪˈvɪəlɪ] *adv* **-1.** [extremely, badly] gravemente **- 2.** [sternly] severamente.

severity [sɪˈverətɪ] *n (U)* **-1.** [seriousness] gravidade *f* **- 2.** [strength] força *f* **- 3.** [sternness] severidade *f*.

sew [səʊ] *(UK pp* sewn, *US pp* sewed *OR* sewn) *vt & vi* costurar.

➔ **sew up** *vt sep* **-1.** [join] costurar **- 2.** *inf* [arrange, fix] costurar; **it's all sewn up!** está tudo muito bem costurado!

sewage [ˈsuːɪdʒ] *n (U)* águas *fpl* residuais.

sewage farm *n* estação *f* de tratamento de esgoto.

sewage works *n* estação *f* de tratamento de esgoto.

sewer [ˈsʊəʳ] *n* esgoto *m*; **the city's ~ system** o sistema de esgotos da cidade.

sewerage [ˈsʊərɪdʒ] *n (U)* rede *f* de esgotos.

sewing [ˈsəʊɪŋ] *n (U)* **-1.** [activity] trabalho *m* de costura **- 2.** [items] costura *f*.

sewing machine *n* máquina *f* de costura.

sewn [səʊn] *pp* ⊳ **sew**.

sex [seks] *n* sexo *m*; **to have ~ (with sb)** fazer sexo (com alguém).

sex appeal *n (U)* sex appeal *m*, atração *f* sexual.

sex education *n (U)* educação *f* sexual.

sexism [ˈseksɪzm] *n (U)* sexismo *m*.

sexist [ˈseksɪst] <> *adj* sexista. <> *n* sexista *mf*.

sex life *n* vida *f* sexual.

sex object *n* objeto *m* sexual.

sex shop *n* sex shop *m*.

sextet [seksˈtet] *n* sexteto *m*.

sextuplet [seksˈtjuː plɪt] *n* sêxtuplo *m*.

sexual [ˈsekʃʊəl] *adj* sexual.

sexual assault *n* ataque *m* sexual.

sexual discrimination *n* discriminação *f* sexual.

sexual harassment *n (U)* assédio *m* sexual.

sexual intercourse *n (U)* relações *fpl* sexuais.

sexuality [ˌsekʃʊˈælɪtɪ] *n (U)* sexualidade *f*.

sexually transmitted disease *n* doença *f* sexualmente transmissível.

sexy [ˈseksɪ] *(compar* -ier, *superl* -iest) *adj inf* sexy, sexualmente atraente.

Seychelles [seɪˈʃelz] *npl*: **the ~** as Ilhas Seychelles; **in the ~** nas Ilhas Seychelles.

sf, SF *(abbr of* science fiction) *n* ficção *f* científica.

SFO *(abbr of* Serious Fraud Office) *n* departamento de polícia britânico que investiga questões econômicas.

SG *(abbr of* Surgeon General) *n* autoridade responsável pela saúde pública nos Estados Unidos.

Sgt *(abbr of* sergeant) Sgt.

sh [ʃ] *excl* psiu!

shabby [ˈʃæbɪ] *(compar* -ier, *superl* -iest) *adj* **-1.** [in bad condition - clothes, briefcase] em mau estado; [- street] abandonado(da) **- 2.** [wearing old clothes] esfarrapado(da) **- 3.** [mean] mesquinho(nha).

shack [ʃæk] *n* cabana *f*.

shackle [ˈʃækl] *vt* **-1.** [chain] algemar **- 2.** *literary* [restrict] impedir.

➔ **shackles** *npl* **-1.** [metal restraints] algemas *pl* **- 2.** *literary* [restrictions] impedimentos *mpl*.

shade [ʃeɪd] <> *n* **-1.** *(U)* [shadow] sombra *f* **- 2.** [lampshade] abajur *m*, quebra-luz *m* **- 3.** [colour] tonalidade *f* **- 4.** [nuance] tom *m*. <> *vt* **-1.** [from light] fazer sombra em, proteger do sol; **to ~ one's eyes** proteger os olhos do sol *(usando a mão)* **- 2.** [by drawing lines] sombrear. <> *vi*: **to ~ into sthg** fundir-se em algo.

➔ **shades** *npl inf* óculos *mpl* escuros.

shading [ˈʃeɪdɪŋ] *n* sombreado *m*.

shadow [ˈʃædəʊ] *n* **-1.** [dark area] sombra *f* **- 2.** [under eyes] olheiras *fpl* **- 3.** *phr*: **to be a ~ of one's former self** ser uma sombra do que se era; **there's not a OR the ~ of a doubt** não há sombra de dúvida. <> *adj UK POL* na sombra.

shadow cabinet *n* gabinete-sombra *m*, gabinete do principal partido de oposição na Grã-Bretanha.

shadowy [ˈʃædəʊɪ] *adj* **-1.** [dark] escuro(ra) **- 2.** [hard to see] vago(ga) **- 3.** [unknown, sinister] obscuro (ra).

shady [ˈʃeɪdɪ] *(compar* -ier, *superl* -iest) *adj* **-1.** [sheltered from sun] sombreado(da) **- 2.** [providing shade] que dá sombra **- 3.** *inf* [dishonest, sinister] suspeito(ta).

shaft [ʃɑːft] <> *n* **-1.** [vertical passage] poço *m* **- 2.** [rod] haste *f* **- 3.** [of light] feixe *m*. <> *vt v inf* ludibriar.

shaggy [ˈʃægɪ] *(compar* -ier, *superl* -iest) *adj* **-1.** [hair, beard] desgrenhado(da) **- 2.** [dog] peludo(da) **- 3.** [carpet, rug] felpudo(da).

shaggy-dog story *n* piada *f* longa e boba.

shake [ʃeɪk] *(pt* shook, *pp* shaken) [ˈʃeɪkən]) <> *vt* **-1.** [gen] abalar **- 2.** [move vigorously] sacudir; **to ~ sb's hand** apertar a mão de alguém; **to ~ hands** apertar as mãos; **to ~ one's head** [to say no] negar com a cabeça. <> *vi* tremer. <> *n* sacudida *f*.

➔ **shake down** *vt sep US inf* **-1.** [rob] chantagear **- 2.** [search] revistar.

➔ **shake off** *vt sep* livrar-se de.

➔ **shake up** *vt sep* abalar.

shakedown *n US inf* **-1.** [extortion] extorsão *f* **- 2.** [search] revista *f*.

shaken [ˈʃeɪkn] *pp* ⊳ **shake**.

shake-out *n* **-1.** *FIN* [slight recession] ligeira recessão *f* **- 2.** [shake-up] reestruturação *f*.

Shakespearean [ʃeɪk'spɪərɪən] *adj* shakespeariano(na).

shake-up *n inf* reestruturação *f*.

shaky ['ʃeɪkɪ] (*compar* -**ier**, *superl* -**iest**) *adj* - **1.** [unsteady - chair, table] frágil, instável; [- hand, writing, voice] trêmulo(la); [- person] abalado(da) - **2.** [weak, uncertain] débil.

shale [ʃeɪl] *n (U)* xisto *m*.

shall [*weak form* ʃəl, *strong form* ʃæl] *aux vb* - **1.** [to express future tense]: **we ~ be in Scotland in June** estaremos na Escócia em junho; **I ~ ring next week** vou ligar semana que vem - **2.** [in questions]: **~ we have our tea now?** vamos tomar nosso chá agora?; **where ~ I put this?** onde eu coloco isto?; **~ I give her a ring, then?** ligo para ela, então?; **I'll do that, ~ I?** eu faço isso, pode ser? - **3.** [will definitely]: **we ~ overcome!** venceremos!; **you ~ go to the ball, Cinderella!** você irá ao baile, Cinderela! - **4.** [in orders]: **you ~ tell me what happened!** você deve me contar o que aconteceu!

shallot [ʃə'lɒt] *n* cebolinha *f*.

shallow ['ʃæləʊ] *adj* - **1.** [in size] raso(sa) - **2.** *pej* [superficial] superficial - **3.** [breathing] não-profundo(da).

➡ **shallows** *npl* baixio *m*.

sham [ʃæm] (*pt & pp* -**med**, *cont* -**ming**) ◇ *adj* falso(sa), fingido(da). ◇ *n* farsa *f*. ◇ *vi* fingir.

shambles ['ʃæmblz] *n* - **1.** [disorder] confusão *f* - **2.** [fiasco] fiasco *m*.

shame [ʃeɪm] ◇ *n* - **1.** *(U)* [remorse] vergonha *f* - **2.** *(U)* [dishonour]: **to bring ~ (up)on sb** trazer desonra *or* vergonha a alguém - **3.** [pity]: **it's a ~ (that)** é uma pena *or* lástima que; **what a ~!** que pena! ◇ *vt* - **1.** [fill with shame] envergonhar - **2.** [force by making ashamed]: **I ~d him into telling the truth** eu o forcei a dizer a verdade ao fazê-lo sentir-se envergonhado por não dizer.

shamefaced [ˌʃeɪm'feɪst] *adj* envergonhado(da).

shameful ['ʃeɪmfʊl] *adj* vergonhoso(sa).

shameless ['ʃeɪmlɪs] *adj* desavergonhado(da).

shammy ['ʃæmɪ] (*pl* -**ies**) *n inf*: **~ (leather)** camurça *f*.

shampoo [ʃæm'pu:] (*pl* -**s**, *pt & pp* -**ed**, *cont* -**ing**) ◇ *n* - **1.** [liquid - for hair] xampu *m*; [- for carpet] detergente *m* - **2.** [act of shampooing] lavada *f* com xampu. ◇ *vt* lavar.

shamrock ['ʃæmrɒk] *n (U)* trevo *m*.

shandy ['ʃændɪ] (*pl* -**ies**) *n* shandy *m*, *bebida preparada com limonada e cerveja*.

shan't [ʃɑ:nt] *cont* = shall not.

shanty town *n* ≃ favela *f*.

shape [ʃeɪp] ◇ *n* - **1.** [form] forma *f*; **to take ~** tomar forma - **2.** [figure, silhouette] silhueta *f* - **3.** [guise]: **in the ~ of** na forma de; **not in any ~ or form** de maneira nenhuma - **4.** [form, health]: **to be in good/bad ~** estar em boa/má forma; **to lick** *or* **knock sb/sthg into ~** deixar alguém no ponto. ◇ *vt* - **1.** [mould physically]: **to ~ sthg (into)** dar a algo forma (de); **a birthmark ~d like a strawberry** uma marca de nascença com a forma de morango - **2.** [influence] influenciar.

➡ **shape up** *vi* desenvolver-se.

SHAPE [ʃeɪp] (*abbr of* **Supreme Headquarters Allied Powers Europe**) *n quartel-general das potências aliadas na Europa*.

-shaped ['ʃeɪpt] *suffix com forma de*; **star~** em forma de estrela.

shapeless ['ʃeɪplɪs] *adj* sem forma.

shapely ['ʃeɪplɪ] (*compar* -**ier**, *superl* -**iest**) *adj* bem formado(da); **~ legs** pernas *fpl* bem torneadas.

shard [ʃɑ:d] *n* caco *m*.

share [ʃeə^r] ◇ *n*: **~ (of/in sthg)** parte *f* (em/de algo); **to have/do one's ~ of sthg** ter/fazer a parte que toca a alguém de algo; **everyone must do his ~ of the work** todo mundo deve fazer a parte que lhe toca do trabalho; **to have a ~ in the profits** ter participação nos lucros. ◇ *vt* - **1.** [gen] compartilhar; **to ~ sthg (with sb)** compartilhar algo (com alguém) - **2.** [reveal] revelar; **to ~ sthg (with sb)** revelar algo (a alguém). ◇ *vi* dividir, compartilhar; **to ~ in sthg** compartilhar algo.

➡ **shares** *npl FIN* ações *fpl*.

➡ **share out** *vt sep* dividir, compartilhar.

share capital *n (U)* capital *m* acionário.

share certificate *n* cautela *f* de ações.

shareholder ['ʃeəˌhəʊldə^r] *n* acionista *mf*.

share index *n* índice *m* de cotações.

share-out *n* compartilhamento *m*, divisão *f*.

shareware ['ʃeəˌweə^r] *n* shareware *m*.

shark [ʃɑ:k] (*pl inv OR* -**s**) *n* - **1.** [fish] tubarão *m* - **2.** *fig* [dishonest person] trapaceiro *m*, -ra *f*.

sharp [ʃɑ:p] ◇ *adj* - **1.** [not blunt - teeth, pencil] apontado(da); [- needle] pontudo(da); [- knife, razor] afiado(da) - **2.** [well-defined] claro(ra), bem-definido(da) - **3.** [intelligent, keen - person, mind] inteligente, esperto(ta); [- eyesight] penetrante; [- hearing] atento(ta) - **4.** [abrupt, sudden] abrupto(ta), brusco(ca) - **5.** [angry, severe] seco(ca) - **6.** [sound, pain] agudo(da) - **7.** [cold, wind] cortante - **8.** [bitter] acre - **9.** *MUS* sustenido(da); **C ~** dó sustenido. ◇ *adv* - **1.** [punctually] pontualmente; **at eight o'clock ~** pontualmente às oito horas - **2.** [quickly, suddenly] de repente. ◇ *n MUS* sustenido *m*.

sharpen ['ʃɑ:pn] ◇ *vt* - **1.** [make sharp - knife, tool] afiar; [- pencil] apontar - **2.** [heighten - sense, abilities] apurar; [- disagreements, differences] aumentar. ◇ *vi* - **1.** [become keener, quicker - senses, abilities] apurar; [- appetite, disagreements] aumentar - **2.** [become more piercing, louder] esganiçar-se.

sharp end *n UK fig*: **to be at the ~ of sthg** levar todo o peso de algo nas costas.

sharpener ['ʃɑ:pnə^r] *n* - **1.** [for pencil] apontador *m* - **2.** [for knife] amolador *m*.

sharp-eyed [-'aɪd] *adj* perspicaz.

sharply ['ʃɑ:plɪ] *adv* - **1.** [distinctly] claramente - **2.** [suddenly] de repente, repentinamente - **3.** [harshly] duramente.

sharpness ['ʃɑ:pnɪs] *n (U)* - **1.** [of point, edge - of pencil] ponta *f*; [- of knife, razor] fio *m* - **2.** [of outline, image] nitidez *f* - **3.** [of mind, senses, sound] agudeza *f* - **4.** [of pain] intensidade *f* - **5.** [of remarks, criticism, tone] dureza *f*, aspereza *f* - **6.** [of taste, smell] acridez *f*.

sharpshooter *n* atirador *m*, -ra *f* de primeira.

sharp-tongued *adj* de língua afiada, mordaz.

sharp-witted [-'wɪtɪd] *adj* perspicaz, sagaz.

shat [ʃæt] *pt & pp* ⊳ shit.

shatter ['ʃætə^r] ◇ *vt* - **1.** [glass, window] estilhaçar - **2.** *fig* [beliefs, hopes, dreams] destruir, arrasar; **to**

be ~ed (by sthg) ficar arrasado(da) (com algo). ◇ vi estilhaçar-se.

shattered ['ʃætəd] adj -1. [shocked, upset] arrasado(da) -2. UK inf [very tired] podre.

shattering ['ʃætərɪŋ] adj -1. [gen] arrasador(ra) -2. UK [very tiring] extenuante.

shatterproof ['ʃætəpruːf] adj que não estilhaça.

shave [ʃeɪv] ◇ n: to have a ~ fazer a barba; to be a close ~ fig ser por pouco OR por um triz. ◇ vt -1. [with razor - face] barbear, fazer a barba de; [- body] depilar, raspar -2. [cut pieces off] cortar. ◇ vi barbear-se, fazer a barba.
➡ **shave off** vt sep raspar.

shaven ['ʃeɪvn] adj raspado(da).

shaver ['ʃeɪvəʳ] n barbeador m, aparelho m de barbear.

shaving brush ['ʃeɪvɪŋ-] n pincel m de barba.

shaving cream ['ʃeɪvɪŋ-] n (U) creme m de barbear.

shaving foam ['ʃeɪvɪŋ-] n (U) espuma f de barbear.

shavings ['ʃeɪvɪŋz] npl -1. [of wood] cavacos mpl, lascas fpl -2. [of metal] cisalha f.

shaving soap ['ʃeɪvɪŋ-] n (U) sabão m de barbear.

shawl [ʃɔːl] n xale m.

she [ʃiː] ◇ pers pron ela; ~'s tall ela é alta.

sheaf [ʃiːf] (pl sheaves) n -1. [of papers, letters] maço m -2. [of corn, grain] feixe m.

shear [ʃɪəʳ] (pt -ed, pp -ed OR shorn) vt tosquiar.
➡ **shears** npl -1. [for garden] tesoura f de podar -2. [for dressmaking] tesoura f.
➡ **shear off** ◇ vt sep romper. ◇ vi romper-se.

sheath [ʃiːθ] (pl -s) n -1. [for sword, dagger] bainha f -2. UK [condom] camisinha f.

sheathe [ʃiːð] vt -1. [sword, dagger] embainhar -2. [cable, pipe]: ~d in sthg revestido(da) de algo.

sheath knife n faca f com bainha.

sheaves [ʃiːvz] pl ▷ sheaf.

shed [ʃed] (pt & pp shed, cont -ding) ◇ n galpão m. ◇ vt -1. [lose naturally] perder -2. [discard, get rid of] desfazer-se de; **the company decided to** ~ **100 employees** a empresa decidiu despedir 100 funcionários; **after a drink she** ~s **any inhibition** depois de um drinque, ela deixa de lado qualquer inibição -3. [accidentally lose] perder -4. [tears, blood] derramar.

she'd [weak form ʃɪd, strong form ʃiːd] = she had, she would.

sheen [ʃiːn] n brilho m.

sheep [ʃiːp] (pl inv) n -1. [animal] ovelha f, -2. fig [person] cordeiro m.

sheepdog ['ʃiːpdɒg] n cão m pastor.

sheepfold n aprisco m, redil m.

sheepish ['ʃiːpɪʃ] adj encabulado(da).

sheepishly ['ʃiːpɪʃlɪ] adv encabuladamente.

sheepskin ['ʃiːpskɪn] n (U) pele f de carneiro.

sheepskin jacket n jaqueta f de couro (de carneiro).

sheepskin rug n tapete m de pele de carneiro.

sheer [ʃɪəʳ] adj -1. [absolute] puro(ra) -2. [very steep - cliff] escarpado(da); [- drop] vertical -3. [delicate] diáfano(na).

sheet [ʃiːt] n -1. [for bed] lençol m; **as white as a** ~ branco(ca) como uma folha de papel -2. [of paper] folha f -3. [of glass, metal, wood] lâmina f.

sheet feed n alimentador m de papel.

sheet ice n (U) capa f de gelo.

sheeting ['ʃiːtɪŋ] n (U) chapa f.

sheet lightning n (U) relâmpago m irradiado entre nuvens.

sheet metal n (U) metal m em chapas.

sheet music n (U) partituras fpl soltas.

sheik(h) [ʃeɪk] n xeque m.

shelf [ʃelf] (pl shelves) n prateleira f.

shelf life n validade f (de um produto).

shell [ʃel] ◇ n -1. [gen] casca f -2. [of tortoise] carapaça f -3. [on beach] concha f -4. [of building] estrutura f -5. [of boat] casco m -6. [of car] chassi m -7. MIL granada f. ◇ vt -1. [remove covering] descascar -2. MIL [fire shells at] bombardear.
➡ **shell out** inf ◇ vt sep desembolsar. ◇ vi: to ~ out for sthg desembolsar para algo.

she'll [ʃiːl] cont = she will, she shall.

shellfish ['ʃelfɪʃ] (pl inv) n -1. [creature] molusco m, crustáceo m -2. (U) [food] marisco m.

shelling ['ʃelɪŋ] n (U) bombardeio m.

shell shock n (U) trauma f de guerra.

shell suit n UK conjunto de calça e jaqueta de náilon à prova d'água.

shelter ['ʃeltəʳ] ◇ n -1. [building, structure] abrigo m, refúgio m -2. (U) [cover, protection] abrigo m, proteção f -3. (U) [accommodation] abrigo m. ◇ vt -1. [from rain, sun, bombs]: to be ~ed by/from sthg estar protegido(da) por/de algo -2. [give asylum to] abrigar. ◇ vi: to ~ from/in sthg abrigar-se de/em algo.

sheltered ['ʃeltəd] adj -1. [protected] protegido(da) -2. [supervised] assistencial.

shelve [ʃelv] ◇ vt engavetar. ◇ vi inclinar-se.

shelves [ʃelvz] pl ▷ shelf.

shelving ['ʃelvɪŋ] n (U) prateleiras fpl.

shenanigans npl inf -1. [trickery] trapaça f -2. [mischief] travessura f.

shepherd ['ʃepəd] ◇ n pastor m. ◇ vt fig acompanhar.

shepherd's pie ['ʃepədz-] n (U) gratinado de carne moída temperada com ervas e coberto com purê de batatas.

sherbet ['ʃɜːbət] n -1. (U) UK [sweet powder] pó efervescente ingerido como doce -2. US [sorbet] sorvete m de frutas.

sheriff ['ʃerɪf] n -1. US [law officer] xerife m -2. Scot [judge] juiz m, -íza f.

sherry ['ʃerɪ] (pl -ies) n xerez m.

she's [ʃiːz] = she is, she has.

Shetland ['ʃetlənd] n: ~, the ~ Islands as Ilhas Shetland; in ~, in the ~ Islands nas Ilhas Shetland.

shh [ʃ] excl = sh.

shield [ʃiːld] ◇ n -1. [armour] escudo m -2. UK [sports trophy] troféu m (na forma de escudo) -3. [protection]: ~ against sthg proteção f contra algo. ◇ vt: to ~ sb (from sthg) proteger alguém (de algo); to ~ o.s. (from sthg) proteger-se (de algo).

shift [ʃɪft] ◇ n -1. [gen] turno m -2. [slight change]

mudança f. <> vt -1. [move, put elsewhere] mover, mudar de lugar - 2. [change slightly] mudar de - 3. *fig* [blame, responsibility]: **to ~ sthg (onto sb)** transferir algo (a alguém) - 4. *US AUT* [gear] trocar - 5. [stain] remover, limpar. <> vi -1. [move] mover-se - 2. [change slightly] mudar - 3. *US AUT* trocar de marcha - 4. [stain] sair.

shift key n tecla f shift.

shiftless ['ʃɪftlɪs] adj folgado(da).

shift stick n *US* alavanca f de mudanças, alavanca f de marcha.

shifty ['ʃɪftɪ] (compar -ier, superl -iest) adj inf matreiro(ra).

Shiite ['ʃiːaɪt] <> adj xiita. <> n xiita mf.

shilling ['ʃɪlɪŋ] n *UK* xelim m.

shilly-shally ['ʃɪlɪˌʃælɪ] (pt & pp -ied) vi vacilar, titubear.

shimmer ['ʃɪməʳ] <> n reflexo m trêmulo, cintilação f. <> vi cintilar, tremeluzir.

shin [ʃɪn] (pt & pp -ned, cont -ning) n canela f (na perna).
⇒ **shin up** *UK*, **shinny up** *US* vt fus trepar em.

shin bone n tíbia f.

shine [ʃaɪn] (pt & pp shone) <> n brilho m. <> vt -1. [focus] direcionar - 2. [polish] lustrar. <> vi -1. [give out light] brilhar - 2. [excel]: **to ~ at sthg** sobressair-se em algo.

shingle ['ʃɪŋgl] n (U) cascalhos m, pedrinhas fpl.
⇒ **shingles** n *MED* herpes-zoster m.

shining ['ʃaɪnɪŋ] adj brilhante.

shinny ⇒ **shinny up** vt fus *US* = shin up.

shin pads npl caneleira f.

shiny ['ʃaɪnɪ] (compar -ier, superl -iest) adj brilhante.

ship [ʃɪp] (pt & pp -ped, cont -ping) <> n navio m, barco m. <> vt enviar por via marítima.

shipbuilder ['ʃɪpˌbɪldəʳ] n empresa f de construção naval.

shipbuilding ['ʃɪpˌbɪldɪŋ] n (U) construção f naval.

ship canal n canal m de navegação.

shipment ['ʃɪpmənt] n carregamento m.

shipper ['ʃɪpəʳ] n - 1. [person] exportador(ra) - 2. [company] empresa f exportadora.

shipping ['ʃɪpɪŋ] n (U) - 1. [transport] envio m, transporte m - 2. [ships] navegação f.

shipping agent n - 1. [person] agente m marítimo - 2. [company] agência f marítima.

shipping company n companhia f de navegação.

shipping forecast n previsão f das condições marítimas.

shipping lane n rota f marítima.

shipshape ['ʃɪpʃeɪp] adj em ordem.

shipwreck ['ʃɪprek] <> n - 1. [destruction of ship] naufrágio m - 2. [wrecked ship] navio m naufragado. <> vt: **to be ~ed** naufragar.

shipwrecked ['ʃɪprekt] adj naufragado(da).

shipyard ['ʃɪpjɑːd] n estaleiro m.

shire [ʃaɪəʳ] n condado m.
⇒ **Shire** n: **the Shires** the Shires, os condados centrais da Inglaterra.

shire horse n cavalo m de tiro.

shirk [ʃɜːk] vt escapar a.

shirker ['ʃɜːkəʳ] n vadio m, -dia f.

shirt [ʃɜːt] n camisa f.

shirtsleeves ['ʃɜːtsliːvz] npl: **to be in (one's) ~** estar em mangas de camisa.

shirt tail n fralda f (da camisa).

shirty ['ʃɜːtɪ] (compar -ier, superl -iest) adj *UK* inf estúpido(da).

shit [ʃɪt] (pt & pp shit OR -ted OR shat, cont -ting) vulg <> n merda f. <> vi cagar. <> excl merda!

shiver ['ʃɪvəʳ] <> n tremer; **to give sb the ~s** dar arrepios a alguém. <> vi: **to ~ (with sthg)** tremer (de algo).

shoal [ʃəʊl] n cardume m.

shock [ʃɒk] <> n - 1. [gen] choque m - 2. (U) *MED*: **to be suffering from ~, to be in (a state of) ~** estar em estado de choque - 3. [thick mass] mecha f. <> vt -1. [upset] chocar - 2. [offend] ofender. <> vi chocar.

shock absorber [-əbˌzɔːbəʳ] n amortecedor m.

shocked [ʃɒkt] adj - 1. [upset] chocado(da) - 2. [offended] chocado(da), ofendido(da).

shocking ['ʃɒkɪŋ] adj - 1. [very bad] péssimo(ma) - 2. [scandalous] escandaloso(sa) - 3. [horrifying] chocante.

shockproof ['ʃɒkpruːf] adj à prova de choque.

shock tactics npl - 1. *MIL* tática f de choque - 2. *fig* [surprising manoeuvre] tratamento m de choque.

shock therapy, shock treatment n (U) *MED* terapia f à base de eletrochoques.

shock troops npl tropas fpl de choque.

shock wave n onda f de choque.

shod [ʃɒd] <> pt & pp ▷ shoe. <> adj calçado(da).

shoddy ['ʃɒdɪ] (compar -ier, superl -iest) adj - 1. [badly done or made] de segunda qualidade - 2. *fig* [poor, unworthy] inferior.

shoe [ʃuː] (pt & pp -ed OR shod, cont -ing) <> n - 1. [for person] sapato m - 2. [for horse] ferradura f - 3. [for brake] sapata f. <> vt ferrar.

shoebrush ['ʃuːbrʌʃ] n escova f para sapato.

shoe cleaner n [liquid] líquido m para limpar sapatos.

shoehorn ['ʃuːhɔːn] n calçadeira f.

shoelace ['ʃuːleɪs] n cadarço m.

shoemaker ['ʃuːˌmeɪkəʳ] n sapateiro m, -ra f.

shoe polish n (U) graxa f de sapato.

shoe repairer n sapateiro m, -ra f.

shoe shop n sapataria f.

shoestring ['ʃuːstrɪŋ] <> adj restrito(ta). <> n *fig*: **on a ~** com orçamento mínimo.

shoetree ['ʃuːtriː] n fôrma f para sapato.

shone [ʃɒn] pt & pp ▷ shine.

shoo [ʃuː] <> vt enxotar. <> excl xô!

shook [ʃʊk] pt ▷ shake.

shoot [ʃuːt] (pt & pp shot) <> vt -1. [fire gun at - killing] matar a tiros, balear; [- wounding] ferir a tiros, balear; **to ~ o.s.** [kill o.s.] dar-se um tiro, atirar em si mesmo(ma) - 2. *UK* [hunt] caçar - 3. [arrow, question] disparar - 4. [glance, look] relancear - 5. *CINEMA* filmar, rodar - 6. *US* [pool] jogar. <> vi -1. [fire gun]: **to ~ (at sb/sthg)** atirar (em alguém/algo) - 2. *UK* [hunt] caçar - 3. [move quickly]: **to ~ in/**

out/past entrar/sair/passar rapidamente; **to ~ ahead** sair na frente; **to ~ off** partir rapidamente - **4.** *CINEMA* filmar, rodar - **5.** [*SPORT*- football] chutar; [- basketball, netball etc] arremessar. <> *n* - **1.** *UK* [hunting expedition] caçada *f* - **2.** [new growth] brote *m*. <> **excl US inf** - **1.** [go ahead] manda! - **2.** [damn] droga!

➡ **shoot down** *vt sep* - **1.** [person] matar a tiros - **2.** [plane] derrubar - **3.** *fig* [reject] derrubar por terra.

➡ **shoot up** *vi* - **1.** [grow quickly] dar um pulo - **2.** [increase quickly] disparar - **3.** *drugs sl* [take drugs] drogar-se.

shooting [ˈʃuːtɪŋ] *n* - **1.** [firing of gun] tiroteio *m* - **2.** *(U)* [hunting] caça *f.*

shooting range *n* área *f* de tiro.

shooting star *n* estrela *f* cadente.

shooting stick *n* bastão *que serve como assento*.

shoot-out *n* tiroteio *m.*

shop [ʃɒp] (*pt* & *pp*-ped, *cont* -ping) <> *n* - **1.** [store] loja *f*; **to talk ~** falar sobre trabalho - **2.** [workshop] oficina *f*, seminário *m.* <> *vi* comprar; **to go shopping** fazer compras.

➡ **shop around** *vi* comparar preços.

shop assistant *n UK* vendedor *m*, -ra *f* (de loja).

shop floor *n*: **the ~** o chão de fábrica, os operários.

shopkeeper [ˈʃɒpˌkiːpəʳ] *n* lojista *mf.*

shoplifter [ˈʃɒpˌlɪftəʳ] *n* ladrão *m*, -dra *f* de lojas.

shoplifting [ˈʃɒpˌlɪftɪŋ] *n (U)* roubo *m* numa loja.

shopper [ˈʃɒpəʳ] *n* comprador *m*, -ra *f.*

shopping [ˈʃɒpɪŋ] *n* compras *fpl*; **to go ~** fazer compras.

shopping bag *n* sacola *f* de compras.

shopping basket *n UK* - **1.** [in supermarket] cesta *f* - **2.** [for online shopping] cesta *f* de compras.

shopping cart *n US* - **1.** [in supermarket] carrinho *m* - **2.** [for online shopping] carrinho *m* de compras.

shopping centre *UK*, **shopping mall** *US*, **shopping plaza** *US* [-ˌplɑːzə] *n* shopping (center) *m*, centro *m* comercial.

shopping list *n* lista *f* de compras.

shopping mall, shopping plaza *n US* = **shopping centre.**

shopsoiled *UK* [ˈʃɒpsɔɪld], **shopworn** *US* [ˈʃɒpwɔːn] *adj* deteriorado(da) por ficar exposto numa loja.

shop steward *n* representante *mf* sindical.

shopwalker *n UK* supervisor *m*, -ra *f* (de loja).

shopwindow [ˌʃɒpˈwɪndəʊ] *n* vitrina *f.*

shopworn *adj US* = **shopsoiled.**

shore [ʃɔːʳ] *n* - **1.** [land by water] beira *f*, margem *f*; **sea ~** litoral *m* - **2.** *(U)* [not at sea]: **on ~** em terra.

➡ **shore up** *vt sep* - **1.** [prop up] reforçar, sustentar - **2.** *fig* [sustain] sustentar.

shore leave *n (U)* licença *f* para desembarcar.

shoreline [ˈʃɔːlaɪn] *n* linha *f* costeira.

shorn [ʃɔːn] <> *pp* ⊳ **shear.** <> *adj* - **1.** [grass] cortado(da) - **2.** [hair] raspado(da); **~ of** *fig* desprovido(da) de, despojado(da) de; **she was shorn of her responsibility** retiraram todo o poder dela.

short [ʃɔːt] <> *adj* - **1.** [in length, distance] curto(ta) - **2.** [in height] baixo(xa) - **3.** [in time] curto(ta), breve; **in two ~ days we'll be in Spain!** em apenas dois dias, estaremos na Espanha! - **4.** [curt]: **to be ~ (with sb)** ser seco(ca) (com alguém) - **5.** [lacking]: **money is always ~ around Christmas** o dinheiro anda sempre curto no Natal; **we're a pound ~** falta (-nos) uma libra; **she's a bit ~ on brain power** falta a ela um pouco de agilidade mental; **to be ~ of sthg** andar mal de algo; **to be ~ of breath** estar com falta de ar - **6.** [abbreviated]: **to be ~ for sthg** ser o diminutivo de algo. <> *adv* - **1.** [lacking]: **we're running ~ of food** está acabando a comida - **2.** [suddenly, abruptly]: **to cut sthg ~** interromper algo antes do fim; **to stop ~** parar de repente; **to bring** *OR* **pull sb up ~** fazer alguém parar de repente. <> *n* - **1.** *UK* [alcoholic drink] drinque *m* (*bebida forte*) - **2.** *CINEMA* [film] curta *f.*

➡ **shorts** *npl* - **1.** [short trousers] shorts *mpl* - **2.** *US* [underwear] cuecas *fpl.*

➡ **for short** *adv* para abreviar, para simplificar.

➡ **in short** *adv* enfim.

➡ **nothing short of** *prep*: **it was nothing ~ of madness** foi uma verdadeira loucura.

➡ **short of** *prep*: **~ of doing sthg** a não ser fazendo algo.

shortage [ˈʃɔːtɪdʒ] *n* falta *f*, escassez *f.*

short back and sides *n UK* corte *m* de cabelo do exército.

shortbread [ˈʃɔːtbred] *n (U)* biscoito *m* amanteigado.

short-change *vt* - **1.** [in shop, restaurant] dar mal o troco - **2.** *fig* [reward unfairly] passar para trás.

short circuit *n* curto-circuito *m*, curto *m.*

➡ **short-circuit** <> *vt* provocar curto-circuito em. <> *vi* dar curto-circuito.

shortcomings [ˈʃɔːtˌkʌmɪŋz] *npl* defeitos *mpl.*

shortcrust pastry [ˈʃɔːtkrʌst-] *n (U)* massa *f* podre.

short cut *n* - **1.** [quick route] atalho *m* - **2.** [quick method] método *m* rápido.

shorten [ˈʃɔːtn] <> *vt* encurtar; **'Robert' can be ~ed to 'Bob'** Bob é a forma reduzida de Robert. <> *vi* encurtar.

shortening [ˈʃɔːtnɪŋ] *n (U)* *CULIN* gordura *f* vegetal.

shortfall [ˈʃɔːtfɔːl] *n* déficit *m*; **~ in** *OR* **of sthg** déficit em *OR* de algo.

shorthand [ˈʃɔːthænd] *n (U)* - **1.** [writing system] taquigrafia *f*, estenografia *f* - **2.** [short form]: **~ (for sthg)** maneira *f* suave (de dizer algo).

shorthanded [ˌʃɔːtˈhændɪd] *adj*: **to be ~** estar com falta de pessoal.

shorthand typist *n UK* taquígrafo *m*, -fa *f*, estenógrafo *m*, -fa *f.*

short-haul *adj* de curta distância.

short list *n UK* - **1.** [for job] lista *f* de candidatos selecionados - **2.** [for prize] relação *f* dos finalistas.

➡ **short-list** *vt UK*: **to be short-listed (for sthg)** [for job] estar entre os candidatos selecionados (para algo); [for prize] estar entre os finalistas (de algo).

short-lived [-ˈlɪvd] *adj* fugaz, efêmero(ra).

shortly [ˈʃɔːtlɪ] *adv* - **1.** [soon] em breve, logo; **~ ~**

before/after pouco antes/depois de **-2.** [curtly, abruptly] bruscamente, secamente.

shortness [ˈʃɔːtnɪs] n (U) **-1.** [in time] brevidade f **-2.** [in length] curteza f **-3.** [in height] baixa estatura f **-4.** [in distance] proximidade f.

short-range adj **-1.** [missile, weapon] de curto alcance **-2.** [forecast] a curto prazo.

short shrift [-ˈʃrɪft] n: **to give sb** ~ prestar pouca atenção a alguém.

shortsighted [ˌʃɔːtˈsaɪtɪd] adj **-1.** [myopic] míope **-2.** fig [lacking foresight] de visão curta.

short-staffed [-ˈstɑːft] adj: **to be** ~ estar com falta de pessoal.

short-stay adj: **a** ~ **car park** estacionamento para curtos períodos de tempo, geralmente 2-3 horas; ~ **accommodation** acomodação para poucos dias; **a** ~ **patient** paciente hospitalizado por três dias ou menos.

short story n conto m.

short-tempered [-ˈtempəd] adj irritadiço(ça).

short-term adj **-1.** [happening soon] a curto prazo **-2.** [of short duration] de curto prazo.

short time n UK: **to be on** ~ trabalhar com jornada reduzida.

short wave n onda f curta.

shot [ʃɒt] <> pt & pp ⊳ **shoot.** <> n **-1.** [gunshot] tiro m; **like a** ~ [quickly] como um raio **-2.** [marksman] atirador m, -ra f **-3.** SPORT chute m **-4.** [photograph] foto f **-5.** CINEMA tomada f **-6.** inf [try, go] tentativa f **-7.** [injection] injeção f **-8.** [of alcohol] dose f.

shotgun [ˈʃɒtɡʌn] n espingarda f.

shot put n: **the** ~ o lançamento de peso.

should [ʃʊd] aux vb **-1.** [indicating duty, necessity]: **we** ~ **leave now** deveríamos ir agora **-2.** [seeking advice, permission]: ~ **I go too?** eu vou também? **-3.** [as suggestion]: **I** ~ **deny everything** eu negaria tudo **-4.** [indicating probability]: **she** ~ **be home soon** ela deve chegar em casa logo **-5.** [was or were expected to]: **they** ~ **have won the match** eles deveriam ter ganhado o jogo **-6.** (as conditional): **I** ~ **like to come with you** eu gostaria de ir com você; **how** ~ **I know?** como é que eu poderia saber?; ~ **you be interested,** ... caso você esteja interessado, ... **-7.** (in subordinate clauses): **we decided that you** ~ **meet him** decidimos que você deveria encontrá-lo **-8.** [expressing uncertain opinion]: **I** ~ **think he's about 50 years old** eu diria que ele tem uns 50 anos **-9.** (after who or what) [expressing surprise]: **and who** ~ **I see but Ann!** e então quem é que eu vejo? A Ann!

shoulder [ˈʃəʊldəʳ] <> n **-1.** [part of body] ombro m; **to look over one's** ~ olhar para trás; **a** ~ **to cry on** um ombro no qual chorar; **to rub** ~**s with sb** conviver com alguém (rico e famoso) **-2.** [part of clothing] ombreira f **-3.** CULIN [joint] quarto m dianteiro. <> vt **-1.** [load] carregar nos ombros **-2.** [responsibility] arcar com.

shoulder bag n mochila f.

shoulder blade n omoplata f.

shoulder-length adj na altura dos ombros.

shoulder pad n ombreira f.

shoulder strap n alça f.

shouldn't [ˈʃʊdnt] = **should not**.

should've [ˈʃʊdəv] = **should have**.

shout [ʃaʊt] <> n grito m. <> vt gritar. <> vi gritar; **to** ~ **at sb** [tell off] gritar com alguém.
  ◆ **shout down** vt sep calar com gritos.
  ◆ **shout out** vt sep gritar.

shouting [ˈʃaʊtɪŋ] n (U) gritos mpl; **a lot of** ~ uma gritaria.

shove [ʃʌv] inf <> n: **to give sb/sthg a** ~ dar um empurrão em alguém/algo. <> vt empurrar; **to** ~ **sb in** colocar alguém para dentro aos empurrões; **to** ~ **sb out** tirar alguém aos empurrões.
  ◆ **shove off** vi **-1.** [in boat] afastar-se da costa **-2.** inf [go away] cair fora.

shovel [ˈʃʌvl] (UK pt & pp -**led**, cont -**ling**, US pt & pp -**ed**, cont -**ing**) <> n pá f. <> vt **-1.** [with a shovel] tirar com pá **-2.** fig [food, meal] devorar; **they** ~**led down their food and left** eles engoliram a janta e saíram.

show [ʃəʊ] (pt -**ed**, pp **shown** OR -**ed**) <> n **-1.** [piece of entertainment - theatre] espetáculo m; [- TV, radio] show m, programa m **-2.** CINEMA sessão f **-3.** [exhibition] exposição f; **on** ~ à mostra **-4.** [display] demonstração f; **for** ~ para bonito **-5.** [pretence] demonstração f falsa. <> vt **-1.** [gen] mostrar; **to** ~ **sb sthg, to** ~ **sthg to sb** mostrar algo para alguém; **to** ~ **sb how to do sthg** mostrar a alguém como fazer algo; **to have something to** ~ **for sthg** ganhar alguma coisa por algo; **to have nothing to** ~ **for sthg** não ter ganhado nada por algo; **to** ~ **o.s.** apresentar-se; **it just goes to** ~ **(that)** ... isso só prova que ... **-2.** [reveal] mostrar, revelar; **to** ~ **sb sthg** demostrar algo por alguém **-3.** [escort]: **to** ~ **sb to sthg** levar OR acompanhar alguém até algo **-4.** [broadcast] apresentar, passar **-5.** [profit, loss] registrar **-6.** [work of art, produce] mostrar, exibir. <> vi **-1.** [indicate, make clear] mostrar, indicar **-2.** [be visible] aparecer; **inside he was very angry but it didn't** ~ por dentro ele estava muito bravo mas não aparentava **-3.** CINEMA passar.
  ◆ **show around** vt sep = **show round.**
  ◆ **show in** vt sep mandar entrar.
  ◆ **show off** <> vt sep exibir. <> vi exibir-se.
  ◆ **show out** vt sep levar até a porta.
  ◆ **show round** vt sep mostrar (uma cidade, um apartamento); **to** ~ **sb round town** mostrar a cidade a alguém.
  ◆ **show up** <> vt sep: **to** ~ **sb up in public** fazer alguém passar vergonha em público. <> vi **-1.** [stand out] destacar-se **-2.** [arrive] aparecer.

showbiz [ˈʃəʊbɪz] n (U) inf showbiz m.

show business n (U) showbusiness m, mundo m dos espetáculos.

showcase [ˈʃəʊkeɪs] n **-1.** [glass case] vitrina f **-2.** fig [advantageous setting] prato m cheio.

showdown [ˈʃəʊdaʊn] n: **to have a** ~ **with sb** ter um acerto final de contas com alguém.

shower [ˈʃaʊəʳ] <> n **-1.** [gen] chuva f **-2.** [device] chuveiro m **-3.** [wash]: **to have** OR **take a** ~ tomar uma ducha **-4.** US [for wedding] chá m de panela **-5.** [for a baby] chá m de fralda. <> vt **-1.** [sprinkle] jogar; **the newlyweds were** ~**ed with confetti** os recém-casados ganharam uma chuva de confetes **-2.** [bestow]: **to** ~ **sb with sthg, to** ~ **sthg**

(up)on sb encher alguém de algo. <> *vi* tomar banho.

shower cap *n* touca *f* de banho.

showerproof ['ʃaʊəpru:f] *adj* resistente à chuva, impermeável.

showery ['ʃaʊərɪ] *adj* chuvoso(sa).

showing ['ʃəʊɪŋ] *n* sessão *f*.

show jumping [-ˌdʒʌmpɪŋ] *n (U)* concurso *m* hípico de saltos.

showman ['ʃəʊmən] (*pl* **-men** [-mən]) *n* **-1.** [at fair, circus] apresentador *m* **-2.** *fig* [publicity-seeker] astro *m*, showman *m*.

showmanship ['ʃəʊmənʃɪp] *n (U)* encenação *f*; **to be pure ~** ser um verdadeiro show OR espetáculo.

shown [ʃəʊn] *pp* ⊳ **show**.

show-off *n inf* exibido(da).

show of hands *n*: they voted by a **~** eles votaram levantando as mãos.

showpiece ['ʃəʊpi:s] *n* atração *f* principal.

showroom ['ʃəʊrʊm] *n* salão *m* de exposição.

showy ['ʃəʊɪ] (*compar* **-ier**, *superl* **-iest**) *adj* chamativo(va).

shrank [ʃræŋk] *pt* ⊳ **shrink**.

shrapnel ['ʃræpnl] *n (U)* metralha *f*.

shred [ʃred] (*pt* & *pp* **-ded**, *cont* **-ding**) <> *n* **-1.** [small piece] pedaço *m* **-2.** *fig* [scrap]: **there was not a ~ of evidence that ...** não havia a mais remota evidência de que ...; **a ~ of truth** um pingo de verdade. <> *vt* **-1.** CULIN picar **-2.** [paper] picar, rasgar.

shredder ['ʃredə'] *n* **-1.** CULIN [in food processor] triturador *m* **-2.** [for documents] picadora *f* de papel.

shrew [ʃru:] *n* musaranho *m*.

shrewd [ʃru:d] *adj* perspicaz, astuto(ta).

shrewdness ['ʃru:dnɪs] *n (U)* perspicácia *f*, astúcia *f*.

shriek [ʃri:k] <> *n* grito *m*; **a ~ of laughter** uma gargalhada. <> *vt* gritar. <> *vi*: **to ~ (with/in)** gritar (de); **to ~ with laughter** gargalhar.

shrill [ʃrɪl] *adj* agudo(da).

shrimp [ʃrɪmp] *n* camarão *m*.

shrine [ʃraɪn] *n* santuário *m*.

shrink [ʃrɪŋk] (*pt* **shrank**, *pp* **shrunk**) <> *vt* encolher. <> *vi* **-1.** [become smaller] encolher **-2.** *fig* [contract, diminish] diminuir **-3.** [recoil]: **to ~ away from sthg** recuar frente a algo **-4.** [be reluctant]: **to ~ from doing sthg** fugir de algo/de fazer algo. <> *n inf* [psychoanalyst] psicanalista *mf*.

shrinkage ['ʃrɪŋkɪdʒ] *n (U)* **-1.** [loss in size] encolhimento *m* **-2.** *fig* [contraction] redução *f*.

shrink-wrap *vt* embalar com plástico termorretrátil.

shrivel ['ʃrɪvl] (*UK pt* & *pp* **-led**, *cont* **-ling**, *US pt* & *pp* **-ed**, *cont* **-ing**) <> *vt*: **to ~ (up)** secar, murchar. <> *vi*: **to ~ (up)** secar, murchar.

shroud [ʃraʊd] <> *n* mortalha *f*. <> *vt*: **to be ~ed in sthg** [darkness, fog] estar encoberto(ta) em algo; [mystery] estar envolto(ta) em algo.

Shrove Tuesday ['ʃrəʊv-] *n* terça-feira *f* de Carnaval.

shrub [ʃrʌb] *n* arbusto *m*.

shrubbery ['ʃrʌbərɪ] (*pl* **-ies**) *n* arbustos *mpl*.

shrug [ʃrʌg] (*pt* & *pp* **-ged**, *cont* **-ging**) <> *n* encolhimento *m* dos ombros. <> *vt* encolher. <> *vi* dar de ombros, encolher os ombros.

➤ **shrug off** *vt sep* não dar bola para.

shrunk [ʃrʌŋk] *pp* ⊳ **shrink**.

shrunken ['ʃrʌŋkn] *adj* **-1.** [person] enrugado(da) **-2.** [business] reduzido(da) **-3.** [fruit] seco(ca).

shucks [ʃʌks] *excl US inf* **-1.** [it was nothing] ora bolas! **-2.** [damn] droga!

shudder ['ʃʌdə'] <> *n* calafrio *m*. <> *vi* **-1.** [person]: **to ~ (with sthg)** estremecer-se (de algo); **I ~ to think** me dá calafrios só de pensar **-2.** [machine, vehicle] tremer, balançar.

shuffle ['ʃʌfl] <> *n* **-1.** [of feet] arrasto *m* **-2.** [of cards] baralhamento *m*; **to give the cards a ~** embaralhar as cartas. <> *vt* **-1.** [feet] arrastar **-2.** [cards] embaralhar **-3.** [papers] mudar de lugar. <> *vi* **-1.** [walk]: **to ~ (in/out/along)** entrar/sair/andar arrastando os pés **-2.** [fidget] remexer-se nervosamente.

shun [ʃʌn] (*pt* & *pp* **-ned**, *cont* **-ning**) *vt* evitar.

shunt [ʃʌnt] *vt* **-1.** RAIL manobrar, trocar de via férrea **-2.** *fig* [move]: **we were ~ed from one room to another** ficaram nos mandando de uma sala para outra.

shunter *n* **-1.** [engine] locomotiva *f* de manobras **-2.** [person] guarda-chaves *mf inv*.

shush [ʃʊʃ] *excl* psit!

shut [ʃʌt] (*pt* & *pp* **shut**, *cont* **-ting**) <> *adj* fechado(da). <> *vt* & *vi* fechar; **~ your mouth** OR **face!** *v inf* fecha o bico OR a matraca.

➤ **shut away** *vt sep* **-1.** [criminal] trancafiar; **to ~ o.s. away** encerrar-se **-2.** [valuables] guardar.

➤ **shut down** <> *vt sep* & *vi* fechar.

➤ **shut in** *vt sep* trancar; **to ~ o.s. in** trancar-se em.

➤ **shut out** *vt sep* **-1.** [of building, room] não deixar entrar **-2.** [block out of mind] bloquear.

➤ **shut up** <> *vt sep* **-1.** [shop, factory] fechar **-2.** [silence] calar, fazer calar. <> *vi* **-1.** *inf* [be quiet] calar a boca **-2.** [close] fechar.

shutter ['ʃʌtə'] *n* **-1.** [on window] veneziana *f* **-2.** [in camera] obturador *m*.

shuttle ['ʃʌtl] <> *adj*: **~ service** [of planes] ponte *f* aérea; [of buses, train] linha *f* regular. <> *n* **-1.** [train, bus] linha *f* regular **-2.** [plane] avião *m* da ponte aérea. <> *vi* ir e vir. <> *vt* transportar.

shuttlecock ['ʃʌtlkɒk] *n* peteca *f*.

shy [ʃaɪ] (*pt* & *pp* **shied**) <> *adj* tímido(da); **to be ~ of doing sthg** não se atrever a fazer algo. <> *vi* espantar-se.

➤ **shy away from** *vt fus*: **to ~ away from sthg** fugir de algo; **to ~ away from doing sthg** negar-se a fazer algo.

shyly ['ʃaɪlɪ] *adv* timidamente.

shyness ['ʃaɪnɪs] *n (U)* timidez *f*.

Siam *n* Sião; **in ~** no Sião.

Siamese [ˌsaɪə'mi:z] (*pl inv*) <> *adj* siamês(esa). <> *n* **-1.** [person] siamês *m*, -esa *f* **-2.** [cat] gato *m* siamês.

Siamese twins *npl* irmãos *mpl* siameses, irmãs *fpl* siamesas.

SIB (*abbr of* **Securities and Investment Board**) *n* *organismo britânico regulador de investimentos na bolsa.*

Siberia [saɪ'bɪərɪəl] *n* Sibéria; **in ~** na Sibéria.

Siberian [saɪ'bɪərɪən] <> *adj* siberiano(na). <> *n* siberiano *m*, -na *f*.

sibling ['sɪblɪŋ] *n* irmão *m*, -mã *f*.

Sicilian [sɪ'sɪljən] <> *adj* siciliano(na). <> *n* siciliano *m*, -na *f*.

Sicily ['sɪsɪlɪ] *n* Sicília; **in ~** na Sicília.

sick [sɪk] *adj* **- 1.** [unwell] doente **- 2.** [nauseous]: **to feel ~** sentir-se mal **- 3.** [vomiting]: **to be ~** *UK* vomitar **- 4.** [fed up]: **to be ~ of sthg/of doing sthg** estar farto(ta) de algo/de fazer algo **- 5.** [angry, disgusted]: **to make sb ~** *fig* deixar alguém doente **- 6.** [offensive] de mau gosto.

sickbay ['sɪkbeɪ] *n* enfermaria *f*.

sickbed ['sɪkbed] *n* leito *m* de doente.

sicken ['sɪkn] <> *vt* deixar doente. <> *vi UK*: **to be ~ing for sthg** estar ficando doente de algo.

sickening ['sɪknɪŋ] *adj* **- 1.** [disgusting] repugnante **- 2.** *hum* [infuriating] irritante, exasperante.

sickle ['sɪkl] *n* foice *f*.

sick leave *n* (*U*) licença *f* de saúde.

sickly ['sɪklɪ] (*compar* -ier, *superl* -iest) *adj* **- 1.** [unhealthy] doentio(tia) **- 2.** [nauseating] nauseante.

sickness ['sɪknɪs] *n* **- 1.** (*U*) [general illness] doença *f*, enfermidade *f* **- 2.** *UK* (*U*) [nausea, vomiting] náusea *f*, enjôo *m* **- 3.** [specific illness] doença *f*.

sickness benefit *n* (*U*) ≃ auxílio-doença *m*.

sick pay *n* (*U*) *espécie de auxílio-doença pago pelo empregador.*

sickroom ['sɪkrʊm] *n* enfermaria *f*.

side [saɪd] <> *n* **- 1.** [gen] lado *m*; **on every ~**, **on all ~s** por todos os lados; **from ~ to ~** de um lado a outro; **to put sthg to** *OR* **on one ~** pôr *OR* colocar algo de lado; **at** *OR* **by sb's ~** ao lado de alguém; **~ by ~** lado a lado; **on my mother's ~** por parte da minha mãe **- 2.** [surface] lateral *f* **- 3.** [of table, river] borda *f*, beira *f* **- 4.** [slope] ladeira *f*, encosta *f* **- 5.** [in sport] equipe *f* **- 6.** [viewpoint] ponto *m* de vista; **to take sb's ~** ficar do lado de alguém; **to be on sb's ~** estar do lado de alguém **- 7.** [aspect] aspecto *m*; **to be on the safe ~** por via das dúvidas **- 8.** *phr*: **on the large/small ~** um pouco grande/pequeno demais; **to do sthg on the ~** [in addition] fazer algo para ganhar um dinheiro extra; [dishonestly] fazer algo por fora (*sem que a Receita saiba*); **to keep** *OR* **stay on the right ~ of sb** ficar quieto(ta) ao lado de alguém. <> *adj* lateral.
<> **side with** *vt fus* pôr-se ao lado de.

sideboard ['saɪdbɔːd] *n* armário *m*, guarda-louça *m*.

sideboards *UK* ['saɪdbɔːdz], **sideburns** *US* ['saɪdbɜːnz] *npl* suíças *fpl*, costeletas *fpl*.

sidecar ['saɪdkɑːʳ] *n* side-car *m*.

side dish *n* acompanhamento *m*, guarnição *f*.

side effect *n* efeito *m* colateral.

sidekick ['saɪdkɪk] *n inf* cupincha *mf*, comparsa *mf*.

sidelight ['saɪdlaɪt] *n* luz *f* lateral.

sideline ['saɪdlaɪn] *n* **- 1.** [extra business] ocupação *f* secundária **- 2.** *SPORT* [painted line] linha *f* lateral **- 3.** [periphery]: **on the ~s** nas margens.

sidelong ['saɪdlɒŋ] <> *adj* de lado. <> *adv*: **to look ~ atsb/sthg** olhar de lado para alguém/algo.

side-on <> *adj* lateral. <> *adv* de lado.

side plate *n* prato *m* para pão.

side road *n* estrada *f* secundária.

sidesaddle ['saɪdˌsædl] *adv*: **to ride ~** montar de silhão.

sideshow ['saɪdʃəʊ] *n* *área de jogos ou de espetáculos paralelos numa feira ou num circo.*

sidestep ['saɪdstep] (*pt* & *pp* -ped, *cont* -ping) *vt* **- 1.** [step to one side to avoid] desviar, evitar **- 2.** *fig* [problem, question] esquivar-se de.

side street *n* rua *f* secundária.

sidetrack ['saɪdtræk] *vt*: **to be ~ed** desviar (dos objetivos).

sidewalk ['saɪdwɔːk] *n US* calçada *f*.

sideways ['saɪdweɪz] <> *adj* **- 1.** [movement] lateral **- 2.** [look] de soslaio. <> *adv* **- 1.** [move] de lado **- 2.** [look] de soslaio.

siding ['saɪdɪŋ] *n* **- 1.** *UK* [for shunting] via *f* morta **- 2.** *US* [loop line] tapume *m*.

sidle ['saɪdl] <> **sidle up** *vi*: **to ~ up to sb** aprochegar-se furtivamente de alguém.

SIDS (*abbr of* **sudden infant death syndrome**) *n* morte súbita de recém-nascido.

siege [siːdʒ] *n* cerco *m*.

Sierra Leone [siːˌɛərəlɪ'əʊn] *n* Serra Leoa; **in ~** em Serra Leoa.

Sierra Leonean [siːˌɛərəlɪ'əʊnɪən] <> *adj* serra-leonês(esa). <> *n* serra-leonês *m*, -esa *f*.

siesta [siː'estə] *n* sesta *f*.

sieve [sɪv] <> *n* peneira *f*; **to have a head** *OR* **memory like a ~** ter uma memória terrível. <> *vt* peneirar.

sift [sɪft] <> *vt* **- 1.** [sieve] peneirar **- 2.** *fig* [examine carefully] examinar cuidadosamente. <> *vi*: **to ~ through sthg** analisar algo minuciosamente.

sigh [saɪ] <> *n* suspiro *m*; **to heave a ~ of relief** suspirar aliviado(da). <> *vi* suspirar.

sight [saɪt] <> *n* **- 1.** visão *f*; **his first ~ of the sea** a primeira vez que ele viu o mar; **in ~** à vista; **out of ~** longe de vista; **to catch ~ of sb/sthg** avistar alguém/algo; **to know sb by ~** conhecer alguém de vista; **to lose ~ of sb/sthg** perder algo/alguém de vista; **to shoot on ~** atirar sem aviso; **at first ~** à primeira vista **- 2.** [spectacle] espetáculo *m* **- 3.** [on gun] mira *f*; **to set one's ~s on doing sthg** propor-se a fazer algo; **to set one's ~ on sthg** botar algo na cabeça **- 4.** [a lot]: **a ~ better/worse** muito melhor/pior. <> *vt* avistar, divisar.
<> **sights** *npl* pontos *mpl* turísticos.

sighting ['saɪtɪŋ] *n*: **there have been two ~s of the prisoner** o prisioneiro foi visto duas vezes.

sightseeing ['saɪtˌsiːɪŋ] *n* (*U*) turismo *m*; **to do some ~** fazer turismo.

sightseer ['saɪtˌsiːəʳ] *n* turista *mf*.

sign [saɪn] <> *n* **- 1.** [gen] sinal *m* **- 2.** [in music] símbolo *m* **- 3.** [notice] placa *f*. <> *vt* **- 1.** [document] assinar **- 2.** *SPORT* [player] contratar.
<> **sign away** *vt sep* ceder (*assinando um documento*).

sign for vt fus -**1.** [sign receipt for] assinar o recibo de -**2.** [sign contract for] assinar um contrato com.

sign in vi dar entrada.

sign on vi -**1.** [enrol]**: to ~ on (for sthg)** [for course] inscrever-se (em algo); MIL alistar-se (em algo) -**2.** [register as unemployed] cadastrar-se para receber o seguro desemprego.

sign out vi dar saída.

sign up <> vt sep -**1.** [employee] contratar -**2.** [soldier] recrutar. <> vi [enrol]**: to ~ up (for sthg)** [for course] inscrever-se (em algo); MIL alistar-se (em algo).

signal ['sɪgnl] (UK pt & pp -**led**, cont -**ling**, US pt & pp -**ed**, cont -**ing**) <> n sinal m. <> vt -**1.** [send signals to] enviar sinais a -**2.** [indicate - a turn] sinalizar; [- a warning] indicar; **to ~ sb (to do sthg)** fazer sinal para alguém (fazer algo) -**3.** fig marcar, anunciar. <> adj fml marcante. <> vi -**1.** AUT sinalizar -**2.** [indicate]**: to ~ to sb (to do sthg)** fazer sinal para alguém (fazer algo); **he ~led to the waiter for the bill** ele fez um sinal para o garçom pedindo a conta.

signal box UK, **signal tower** US n cabina f de sinaleiro.

signalman ['sɪgnlmən] (pl -**men** [-mən]) n sinaleiro m.

signal tower n US = **signal box**.

signatory ['sɪgnətrɪ] (pl -**ies**) n signatário m, -ria f.

signature ['sɪgnətʃəʳ] n assinatura f.

signature tune n tema m.

signet ring ['sɪgnɪt-] n anel m com sinete.

significance [sɪg'nɪfɪkəns] n (U) -**1.** [importance] importância f -**2.** [meaning] significado m.

significant [sɪg'nɪfɪkənt] adj significativo(va).

significantly [sɪg'nɪfɪkəntlɪ] adv -**1.** [improve, increase, change] significativamente -**2.** [smile, nod, wink] sugestivamente.

signify ['sɪgnɪfaɪ] (pt & pp -**ied**) vt significar.

signing ['saɪnɪŋ] n UK contratação f.

sign language n (U) linguagem f de sinais.

signpost ['saɪnpəʊst] n placa f de sinalização.

Sikh [siːk] <> adj sique. <> n sique mf.

Sikhism ['siːkɪzm] n siquismo m.

silage ['saɪlɪdʒ] n (U) silagem f.

silence ['saɪləns] <> n silêncio m; **in ~** em silêncio. <> vt silenciar, calar.

silencer ['saɪlənsəʳ] n -**1.** [on gun] silenciador m -**2.** AUT silenciador m, silencioso m.

silent ['saɪlənt] adj -**1.** [gen] silencioso(sa) -**2.** [taciturn] silencioso(sa), taciturno(na) -**3.** [not revealing anything]**: to be ~ about sthg** ser discreto(ta) sobre algo -**4.** CINEMA & LING mudo(da).

silently ['saɪləntlɪ] adv -**1.** [without speaking] em silêncio -**2.** [noiselessly] silenciosamente.

silent partner n US sócio m comanditário, sócia f comanditária.

silhouette [ˌsɪluːˈet] <> n silhueta f. <> vt**: to be ~d against sthg** destacar-se (contra algo).

silicon ['sɪlɪkən] n (U) silício m.

silicon chip [ˌsɪlɪkən-] n chip m de silício.

silicone ['sɪlɪkəʊn] n (U) silicone m.

Silicon Valley n Vale do Silício.

silk [sɪlk] <> n (U) seda f. <> comp de seda.

silk screen printing n (U) serigrafia f.

silkworm ['sɪlkwɜːm] n bicho-da-seda m.

silky ['sɪlkɪ] (compar -**ier**, superl -**iest**) adj sedoso(sa).

sill [sɪl] n peitoril m.

silliness ['sɪlɪnɪs] n (U) imbecilidade f, estupidez f.

silly ['sɪlɪ] (compar -**ier**, superl -**iest**) adj -**1.** [foolish] bobo(ba) -**2.** [comical] bobo(ba), ridículo(la).

silo ['saɪləʊ] (pl -**s**) n silo m.

silt [sɪlt] n (U) sedimento m, lodo m.

silt up vi assorear.

silver ['sɪlvəʳ] <> adj prateado(da). <> n (U) -**1.** [metal] prata f -**2.** [coins] moedas fpl -**3.** [silverware] prataria f. <> comp [made of silver] de prata.

silver-plated [-'pleɪtɪd] adj prateado(da).

silver screen n inf**: the ~** o cinema.

silversmith ['sɪlvəsmɪθ] n prateiro m, -ra f.

silverware ['sɪlvəweəʳ] n -**1.** [objects made of silver] prataria f -**2.** US [cutlery] prataria f.

silver wedding n bodas fpl de prata.

silvery ['sɪlvərɪ] adj prateado(da).

similar ['sɪmɪləʳ] adj parecido(da), semelhante; **~ to sthg** parecido(da) or similar a algo.

similarity [ˌsɪmɪˈlærətɪ] (pl -**ies**) n**: ~ (between)** semelhança f (entre), similaridade f (entre); **~ to sthg** semelhança f com algo.

similarly ['sɪmɪləlɪ] adv igualmente, da mesma forma.

simile ['sɪmɪlɪ] n símile m.

simmer ['sɪməʳ] vt & vi cozinhar em fogo baixo.

simmer down vi inf sossegar o facho.

simper ['sɪmpəʳ] <> n sorriso m bobo. <> vi sorrir de forma boba.

simpering ['sɪmpərɪŋ] adj -**1.** [person] que sorri com cara de bobo(ba) -**2.** [smile] bobo(ba).

simple ['sɪmpl] adj -**1.** [gen] simples -**2.** inf [mentally retarded] simplório(ria).

simple-minded [-'maɪndɪd] adj simplório(ria).

simpleton ['sɪmpltən] n dated basbaque mf.

simplicity [sɪm'plɪsətɪ] n simplicidade f.

simplification [ˌsɪmplɪfɪ'keɪʃn] n simplificação f.

simplify ['sɪmplɪfaɪ] (pt & pp -**ied**) vt simplificar.

simplistic [sɪm'plɪstɪk] adj simplista.

simply ['sɪmplɪ] adv -**1.** [gen] simplesmente; **you ~ must go and see the film** você só tem que ir ver o filme -**2.** [in an uncomplicated way] de forma simples.

simulate ['sɪmjʊleɪt] vt -**1.** [feign] simular, fingir -**2.** [produce effect, appearance of] simular.

simulation [ˌsɪmjʊ'leɪʃn] n -**1.** [feigning] simulação f, fingimento m -**2.** [simulated appearance, effect] simulacro m -**3.** COMPUT simulação f.

simulator ['sɪmjʊleɪtəʳ] n simulador m.

simultaneous [UK ˌsɪmʊl'teɪnjəs, US ˌsaɪməl'teɪnjəs] adj simultâneo(nea).

simultaneously [UK ˌsɪmʊl'teɪnjəslɪ, US ˌsaɪməl'-teɪnjəslɪ] adv simultaneamente.

sin [sɪn] (pt & pp -**ned**, cont -**ning**) <> n pecado m; **to live in ~** viver em pecado. <> vi**: to ~ (against sb/sthg)** pecar (contra alguém/algo).

sin bin n inf ICE HOCKEY banco m para os suspensos do jogo.

since [sɪns] <> adv**: ~ (then)** desde então; **long ~**

há muito tempo. <> *prep* desde. <> *conj* **-1.** [in time]: **it's ages ~ I saw him** faz séculos que eu não o vejo **-2.** [because] já que, como.

sincere [sɪn'sɪə'] *adj* sincero(ra).

sincerely [sɪn'sɪəlɪ] *adv* sinceramente; **Yours ~** [at end of letter] atenciosamente.

sincerity [sɪn'serətɪ] *n* (U) sinceridade *f*.

sine [saɪn] *n* MATH seno *m*.

sinecure ['saɪnɪ.kjʊə'] *n* sinecura *f*.

sinew ['sɪnjuː] *n* tendão *m*.

sinewy ['sɪnjuːɪ] *adj* musculoso(sa).

sinful ['sɪnfʊl] *adj* **-1.** [guilty of sin] pecador(ra) **-2.** [wicked, immoral] pecaminoso(sa).

sing [sɪŋ] (*pt* sang, *pp* sung) <> *vt* cantar; **to ~ sb a song, to ~ a song to sb** cantar uma música para alguém. <> *vi* cantar.

Singapore [.sɪŋə'pɔː'] *n* Cingapura.

Singaporean [.sɪŋəpə'rɪən] <> *adj* cingapuriano(-na). <> *n* cingapuriano *m*, -na *f*.

singe [sɪndʒ] (*cont* singeing) *vt* chamuscar.

singer ['sɪŋə'] *n* cantor *m*, -ra *f*.

Singhalese [.sɪŋə'liːz] <> *adj* cingalês(esa). <> *n* **-1.** [person] cingalês *m*, -esa *f* **-2.** [language] cingalês *m*.

singing ['sɪŋɪŋ] <> *adj* de canto. <> *n* canto *m*.

singing telegram *n* telegrama *m* cantado.

single ['sɪŋgl] <> *adj* **-1.** [sole] único(ca); **to sweep up every ~ leaf** varrer todas as folhas, sem deixar nenhuma; **every ~ day** todo santo dia **-2.** [unmarried] solteiro(ra) **-3.** UK [one-way] de ida. <> *n* **-1.** UK [one-way ticket] passagem *f* de ida **-2.** MUS single *m*.
  singles *npl* TENNIS simples *f inv*.
  single out *vt sep*: **to ~ sb out (for sthg)** escolher alguém (para algo).

single bed *n* cama *f* de solteiro.

single-breasted [-'brestɪd] *adj* não-trespassado (da).

single cream *n* (U) UK creme *m* leve.

single-decker (bus) *n* UK ônibus *m inv* de um andar.

Single European Market *n*: **the ~** o Mercado Comum Europeu.

single file *n*: **in ~** em fila indiana.

single-handed [-'hændɪd] *adv* sem ajuda.

single-minded [-'maɪndɪd] *adj* determinado(da), resoluto(ta); **to be ~ about sthg** ter um objetivo muito claro em relação a algo.

single parent *n* pai *m* solteiro, mãe *f* solteira.

single-parent family *n* família *f* em que falta um dos pais.

single room *n* quarto *m* simples.

singles bar *n* bar *m* para solteiros.

singlet ['sɪŋglɪt] *n* camiseta *f* (sem mangas).

single ticket *n* UK passagem *f* de ida.

singsong ['sɪŋsɒŋ] *inf* <> *adj* monótono(na). <> *n* UK reunião *f* para cantar.

singular ['sɪŋgjʊlə'] <> *adj* **-1.** GRAMM no singular **-2.** [unusual, remarkable] singular. <> *n* singular *m*.

singularly ['sɪŋgjʊləlɪ] *adv* notavelmente.

Sinhalese ['sɪnhəliːz] *adj* & *n* = **Singhalese**.

sinister ['sɪnɪstə'] *adj* sinistro(tra).

sink [sɪŋk] (*pt* sank, *pp* sunk) <> *n* pia *f*. <> *vt* **-1.**

[cause to go underwater] afundar **-2.** [cause to penetrate]: **to ~ sthg into sthg** cravar algo em algo. <> *vi* **-1.** [gen] afundar; **to ~ without trace** sumir sem deixar vestígio **-2.** [below ground - person] afundar-se; [- sun] pôr-se **-3.** [slump]: **he sank back into his chair** ele se afundou na cadeira; **she sank to her knees** ela caiu sobre os joelhos **-4.** *fig* [heart, spirits] congelar **-5.** [fall] baixar; **her voice sank to a whisper** sua voz foi baixando até ficar um sussurro **-6.** *fig* [slip]: **to ~ into sthg** [despair, poverty] cair em algo; [depression, coma] entrar em algo.
  sink in *vi*: **it hasn't sunk in yet** ainda não caiu a ficha.

sinking ['sɪŋkɪŋ] *n* afundamento *m*.

sinking fund *n* fundo *m* de amortização.

sink unit *n* pia *f*.

sinner ['sɪnə'] *n* pecador *m*, -ra *f*.

Sinn Fein [.ʃɪn'feɪn] *n* Sinn Fein *m*, *braço político do IRA*.

sinuous ['sɪnjʊəs] *adj* sinuoso(sa).

sinus ['saɪnəs] (*pl* -es) *n* seio *m* (*paranasal*).

sinusitis [.saɪnə'saɪtɪs] *n* sinusite *f*.

sip [sɪp] (*pt* & *pp* -ped, *cont* -ping) <> *n* gole *m*. <> *vt* bebericar.

siphon ['saɪfn] <> *n* sifão *m*. <> *vt* **-1.** [draw off] tirar com sifão **-2.** *fig* [transfer] desviar.
  siphon off *vt sep* **-1.** [draw off] tirar com sifão **-2.** *fig* [transfer] desviar.

sir [sɜː'] *n* **-1.** [form of address] senhor *m* **-2.** [in titles] sir *m*.

siren ['saɪərən] *n* sirene *f*.

sirloin (steak) ['sɜːlɔɪn] *n* bife *m* de lombo de vaca.

sissy ['sɪsɪ] (*pl* -ies) *n inf* fresco *m*.

sister ['sɪstə'] <> *adj* **-1.** [organization] congênere **-2.** [ship] gêmeo(mea). <> *n* **-1.** [gen] irmã *f* **-2.** [nun] irmã *f*, freira *f* **-3.** UK [senior nurse] (enfermeira *f*) supervisora *f*.

sisterhood ['sɪstəhʊd] *n* (U) irmandade *f*.

sister-in-law (*pl* sisters-in-law OR sister-in-laws) *n* cunhada *f*.

sisterly ['sɪstəlɪ] *adj* de irmã.

sit [sɪt] (*pt* & *pp* sat, *cont* -ting) <> *vt* **-1.** [place] sentar **-2.** UK [examination] fazer. <> *vi* **-1.** [gen] sentar-se **-2.** [be member]: **to ~ on sthg** integrar algo, fazer parte de algo **-3.** [be in session] reunir-se **-4.** [be situated] ficar **-5.** *phr*: **to ~ tight** ficar onde se está.
  sit about, sit around *vi* ver o tempo passar.
  sit back *vi* **-1.** [relax] recostar-se, relaxar **-2.** [not act] ficar sentado(da).
  sit down <> *vt sep* sentar. <> *vi* sentar-se.
  sit in on *vt fus* estar presente (sem tomar parte).
  sit out *vt sep* **-1.** [tolerate] agüentar (*até o final*) **-2.** [not participate in] não participar de.
  sit through *vt fus* agüentar até o final.
  sit up *vi* **-1.** [be sitting upright] sentar-se reto(ta); [move into upright position] endireitar-se **-2.** [stay up] ficar acordado(da).

sitcom ['sɪtkɒm] *n inf* comédia *f* de situação, sitcom *f*.

sit-down ◇ *adj* [gen] com os participantes sentados à mesa; **a ~ strike** uma greve de braços cruzados. ◇ *n UK*: **to have a ~** sentar-se um pouco.

site [saɪt] ◇ *n* **-1.** [piece of land - archaeology] sítio *m*; [- building] lote *m*; [- missile] campo *m*; [- camp] área *f* **-2.** [location, place] local *m* **-3.** COMPUT site *m*. ◇ *vt* localizar-se, situar-se.

sit-in *n* greve *f* branca.

sitter [ˈsɪtəʳ] *n* **-1.** ART modelo *mf* vivo, -va **-2.** [babysitter] babá *f*.

sitting [ˈsɪtɪŋ] *n* **-1.** [serving of meal] turno *m* para as refeições **-2.** [session] sessão *f*.

sitting duck *n inf* alvo *m* fácil, presa *f* fácil.

sitting room *n* sala *f* de estar.

sitting tenant *n UK* inquilino que tem o direito de permanecer numa casa mesmo após sua venda.

situate [ˈsɪtjʊeɪt] *vt* **-1.** [locate] situar **-2.** [put in context] contextualizar.

situated [ˈsɪtjʊeɪtɪd] *adj*: **to be ~** estar localizado (da), localizar-se.

situation [ˌsɪtjʊˈeɪʃn] *n* **-1.** [gen] situação *f* **-2.** [location] localização *f* **-3.** [job] emprego *m*, colocação *f*; **'Situations Vacant'** *UK* 'Empregos'.

situation comedy *n* comédia *f* de situação.

sit-up *n* abdominal *m*.

SI unit (*abbr of* Système international d'unités unit) *n* unidade do sistema internacional de medidas, como o metro, o litro etc.

six [sɪks] ◇ *num adj* **-1.** [numbering six] seis **-2.** [referring to age]: **she's ~ (years old)** ela tem seis anos (de idade). ◇ *num pron* seis; **I want ~** quero seis; **~ of us went** seis do nosso grupo foram; **there were ~ of us** éramos seis **-1.** [gen] seis; **groups of ~** grupos *mpl* de seis. ◇ *num* **-1.** [gen] seis; **two hundred and ~** duzentos e seis **-2.** [six o'clock] seis *(horas)*; **we arrived at ~** chegamos às seis **-3.** [six degrees]: **it's ~ below** faz seis graus abaixo de zero **-4.** [in addresses]: **~ Peyton Place** Praça Peyton, casa OR número 6; **we sell them in ~es** são vendidos(das) de seis em seis; **to form into ~es** formar grupos de seis; **~-nil** seis a zero.

six-shooter [-ˈʃuːtəʳ] *n US* revólver *m* (de seis tiros).

sixteen [sɪksˈtiːn] *num* dezesseis; *see also* **six**.

sixteenth [sɪksˈtiːnθ] *num* décimo sexto, décima sexta; *see also* **sixth**.

sixth [sɪksθ] ◇ *num adj* sexto(ta). ◇ *num adv* sexto. ◇ *num pron* sexto(ta). ◇ *n* **-1.** [fraction] sexto *m* **-2.** [in dates]: **the ~** o dia seis; **the ~ of September** o dia seis de setembro.

sixth form *n UK* SCH curso opcional de dois anos no ensino secundário britânico oferecido aos alunos de 16 anos a fim de ingressarem na universidade.

sixth form college *n UK* escola pública na Inglaterra para adolescentes de 16 a 18 anos na qual se preparam para ingressar na universidade ou para fazer testes de formação profissional.

sixth sense *n* sexto sentido *m*.

sixtieth [ˈsɪkstɪəθ] *num* sexagésimo(ma); *see also* **sixth**.

sixty [ˈsɪkstɪ] (*pl* **-ies**) *num* sessenta; *see also* **six**.

sixties *npl* **-1.** [decade]: **the sixties** os anos sessenta **-2.** [in ages]: **to be in one's sixties** estar na casa dos sessenta.

size [saɪz] *n* **-1.** tamanho *m*; **an organization of that ~** uma organização daquele porte **-2.** *phr*: **to cut sb down to ~** colocar alguém em seu devido lugar.

➤ **size up** *vt sep* **-1.** [situation] avaliar **-2.** [person] julgar.

sizeable [ˈsaɪzəbl] *adj* considerável.

-sized [saɪzd] *suffix*: **life ~ models** modelos *mpl* em tamanho natural; **medium ~ companies** empresas *fpl* de médio porte.

sizzle [ˈsɪzl] *vi* chiar.

SK *abbr of* Saskatchewan.

skate [skeɪt] (*pl sense 3 only inv* OR **-s**) ◇ *n* **-1.** [gen] patim *m* **-2.** [fish] raia *f*. ◇ *vi* **-1.** [on ice skates] patinar no gelo **-2.** [on roller skates] patinar, andar de patins.

➤ **skate over, skate round** *vt fus* evitar, fugir de.

skateboard [ˈskeɪtbɔːd] *n* skate *m*.

skateboarder [ˈskeɪtbɔːdəʳ] *n* skatista *mf*.

skater [ˈskeɪtəʳ] *n* patinador *m*, -ra *f*.

skating [ˈskeɪtɪŋ] *n (U)* **-1.** [on ice] patinação *f* no gelo; **to go ~** patinar no gelo **-2.** [on roller skates] patinação *f*; **to go ~** andar de patins.

skating rink *n* [for ice skating] pista *f* de patinação no gelo; [for roller skating] rinque *m*, pista *f* de patinação.

skein [skeɪn] *n* madeixa *f*.

skeletal [ˈskelɪtl] *adj* esquelético(ca).

skeleton [ˈskelɪtn] ◇ *adj* básico(ca), mínimo (ma). ◇ *n* esqueleto *m*; **to have a ~ in the cupboard** *fig* ter o rabo preso.

skeleton key *n* chave-mestra *f*.

skeleton staff *n* contingente *m* mínimo de pessoal.

skeptic etc *n US* = **sceptic etc.**

sketch [sketʃ] ◇ *n* **-1.** [drawing] esboço *m*, croqui *m* **-2.** [brief description] resumo *m* **-3.** [onTV, radio, stage] esquete *m*. ◇ *vt* **-1.** [draw] fazer um esboço de **-2.** [describe] resumir. ◇ *vi* fazer croquis.

➤ **sketch in, sketch out** *vt sep* dar uma rápida idéia de.

sketchbook [ˈsketʃbʊk] *n* caderno *m* de desenhos.

sketchpad [ˈsketʃpæd] *n* bloco *m* de desenhos.

sketchy [ˈsketʃɪ] (*compar* **-ier**, *superl* **-iest**) *adj* incompleto(ta), pouco detalhado(da).

skew [skjuː] ◇ *n UK*: **on the ~** torcido(da). ◇ *vt* distorcer. ◇ *vi* atravessar-se.

skewer [ˈskjʊəʳ] ◇ *n* espeto *m*. ◇ *vt* espetar.

skew-whiff [ˌskjuːˈwɪf] *adj UK inf* torto(ta).

ski [skiː] (*pt & pp* **skied**, *cont* **skiing**) ◇ *n* esqui *m*. ◇ *comp* de esqui. ◇ *vi* esquiar.

ski boots *npl* botas *fpl* de esqui.

skid [skɪd] (*pt & pp* **-ded**, *cont* **-ding**) ◇ *n* AUT derrapagem *f*; **to go into a ~** derrapar. ◇ *vi* derrapar.

skid mark *n* marca *f* de derrapagem.

skid row [-rəʊ] *n (U) US inf*: **to be on ~** estar na rua da amargura.

skier ['ski:əᶜ] *n* esquiador *m*, -ra *f*.

skiing ['ski:ɪŋ] ◇ *n (U)* esqui *m*; **to go ~** ir esquiar. ◇ *comp* **-1.** [holiday, accident] de esqui **-2.** [enthusiast] do esqui.

ski instructor *n* instrutor *m*, -ra *f* de esqui.

ski jump *n* **-1.** [slope] rampa *f* para saltos de esqui **-2.** [sporting event] salto *m* de esqui.

skilful, skillful *US* ['skɪlfʊl] *adj* hábil.

skilfully, skillfully *US* ['skɪlfʊlɪ] *adv* habilmente.

ski lift *n* teleférico *m*.

skill [skɪl] *n* **-1.** *(U)* [expertise] experiência *f*, destreza *f* **-2.** [craft, technique] habilidade *f*.

skilled [skɪld] *adj* **-1.** [skilful] habilidoso(sa); **to be ~ in** *OR* **at doing sthg** ter muito jeito para fazer algo **-2.** [trained] especializado(da), qualificado(da).

skillet ['skɪlɪt] *n US* frigideira *f*.

skillful *etc adj US* = **skilful** *etc*.

skim [skɪm] (*pt* & *pp* **-med**, *cont* **-ming**) ◇ *vt* **-1.** [remove - cream] tirar a nata de; [- fat] tirar a gordura de; [- sap] extrair **-2.** [glide over] roçar **-3.** [glance through] passar os olhos em. ◇ *vi* **-1.** : **to ~ over sthg** [bird] dar uma rasante em algo; [stone] ricochetear em algo **-2.** [read]: **to ~ through sthg** ler algo por cima.

skim(med) milk [skɪm(d)mɪlk] *n (U)* leite *m* desnatado.

skimp [skɪmp] *vi*: **to ~ on sthg** [food, material, time] restringir algo; [money] economizar em algo; [work] fazer algo correndo.

skimpy ['skɪmpɪ] (*compar* **-ier**, *superl* **-iest**) *adj* **-1.** [meal] parco(ca) **-2.** [clothes] justo(ta) **-3.** [facts] insuficiente.

skin [skɪn] (*pt* & *pp* **-ned**, *cont* **-ning**) ◇ *n* **-1.** *(U)* [gen] pele *f*; **to save sthg by the ~ of one's teeth** fazer algo por um triz; **to jump out of one's ~** *UK* perder o chão; **it makes my ~ crawl** me dá calafrios; **to save one's own ~** salvar a própria pele **-2.** [of fruit, vegetable, on paint, pudding] casca *f* **-3.** [on milk] nata *f*. ◇ *vt* **-1.** [remove skin from - fruit] descascar; [- dead animal] pelar **-2.** [graze] esfolar.

skin-deep *adj* superficial.

skin diver *n* mergulhador *m*, -ra que pratica mergulho livre *f*.

skin diving *n (U)*: **to go ~** praticar mergulho *m* livre.

skinflint ['skɪnflɪnt] *n* pão-duro *m*.

skin graft *n* enxerto *m* de pele.

skinhead ['skɪnhed] *n UK* skinhead *m*.

skinny ['skɪnɪ] (*compar* **-ier**, *superl* **-iest**) *adj inf* magricela.

skint [skɪnt] *adj UK v inf* pelado(da), sem um tostão.

skin test *n* teste *m* de pele.

skin-tight *adj* muito justo(ta).

skip [skɪp] (*pt* & *pp* **-ped**, *cont* **-ping**) ◇ *n* **-1.** [little jump] pulinho *m* **-2.** *UK* [large container] caçamba *f* (*para entulho*). ◇ *vt* **-1.** [page] pular **-2.** [class] perder **-3.** [meal] faltar a. ◇ *vi* **-1.** [move in little jumps] ir pulando **-2.** *UK* [using rope] pular.

ski pants *npl* calças *fpl* de esqui.

ski pole *n* bastão *m* de esqui.

skipper ['skɪpəᶜ] *n* capitão *m*, -tã *f*.

skipping ['skɪpɪŋ] *n UK*: **to do some ~** pular corda.

skipping rope ['skɪpɪŋ-] *n UK* corda *f* de pular.

ski resort *n* estação *f* de esqui.

skirmish ['skɜːmɪʃ] ◇ *n* **-1.** *MIL* escaramuça *f* **-2.** *fig* [disagreement] desavença *f*. ◇ *vi MIL* & *fig* ter uma escaramuça.

skirt [skɜːt] ◇ *n* [garment] saia *f*. ◇ *vt* **-1.** [go round] contornar **-2.** [avoid dealing with] evitar.

➤ **skirt round** *vt fus* **-1.** [go round]: **to ~ round sb/sthg** desviar de alguém/algo **-2.** [avoid dealing with]: **to ~ round sthg** evitar algo.

skirting board ['skɜːtɪŋ-] *n UK* rodapé *m*.

ski stick *n* bastão *m* de esqui.

skit [skɪt] *n*: **~ on sthg** sátira *f OR* paródia *f* sobre algo.

ski tow *n* ski lift *m*.

skittish ['skɪtɪʃ] *adj* **-1.** [person] esquivo(va) **-2.** [animal] arisco(ca).

skittle ['skɪtl] *n UK* pino *m* de boliche.

➤ **skittles** *n (U) UK* boliche *m*.

skive [skaɪv] *vi UK inf*: **to ~ (off)** [at school] matar aula; [at work] matar o serviço.

skivvy ['skɪvɪ] (*pl* **-ies**, *pt* & *pp* **-ied**) *UK inf* ◇ *n* serviçal *mf*. ◇ *vi*: **to ~ (for sb)** servir de empregada(da) (*para alguém*).

skulduggery [skʌl'dʌɡərɪ] *n (U)* trapaça *f*.

skulk [skʌlk] *vi* esconder-se.

skull [skʌl] *n* **-1.** *ANAT* crânio *m* **-2.** [on skeleton] caveira *f*.

skullcap ['skʌlkæp] *n* solidéu *m*.

skunk [skʌŋk] *n* gambá *m*.

sky [skaɪ] (*pl* **skies**) *n* céu *m*.

skycap *n US* carregador *m*, -ra *f* de bagagem (*no aeroporto*).

skydiver ['skaɪˌdaɪvəᶜ] *n* pára-quedista *mf*.

skydiving ['skaɪˌdaɪvɪŋ] *n (U)* pára-quedismo *m*.

sky-high *inf* ◇ *adj* nas alturas. ◇ *adv*: **to blow sthg ~** [bridge, building] mandar algo para os ares; *fig* [argument, theory] mandar algo para o espaço; **to go ~** ir para as alturas.

skylark ['skaɪlɑːk] *n* calandra *f*.

skylight ['skaɪlaɪt] *n* clarabóia *f*.

skyline ['skaɪlaɪn] *n* linha *f* do horizonte.

skyscraper ['skaɪˌskreɪpəᶜ] *n* arranha-céu *m*.

slab [slæb] *n* **-1.** [of concrete, stone] laje *f* **-2.** [of meat, cake] fatia *f* **-3.** [of chocolate] barra *f*.

slack [slæk] ◇ *adj* **-1.** [not tight] frouxo(xa) **-2.** [not busy] parado(da) **-3.** [not efficient] desleixado(da), negligente. ◇ *n (U)* ponta *f* solta.

➤ **slacks** *npl dated* slack *m*.

slacken ['slækn] ◇ *vt* **-1.** [make slower] reduzir **-2.** [make looser] afrouxar. ◇ *vi* **-1.** [become slower] reduzir **-2.** [become looser] afrouxar.

➤ **slacken off** *vi* **-1.** [rain, storm] abrandar **-2.** [work, trade] desacelerar.

slag [slæg] *n* **-1.** *(U)* [waste material] escombros *mpl* **-2.** *inf pej* [promiscuous woman] vagabunda *f*.

slagheap ['slæɡhiːp] *n* monte *m* de entulho.

slain [sleɪn] *pp* ▷ **slay**.

slalom ['slɑːləm] *n* corrida *f* com obstáculos (*de esqui e canoagem*).

slam [slæm] (*pt* & *pp* **-med**, *cont* **-ming**) ◇ *vt* **-1.** [shut] bater **-2.** [place roughly]: **to ~ sthg on (to)** sthg jogar algo com violência sobre algo **-3.** *fig* [criticize] criticar. ◇ *vi* [shut] bater.

slander ['slɑ:ndə'] ⬦ n (U) calúnia f. ⬦ vt caluniar.

slanderous ['slɑ:ndrəs] adj calunioso(sa).

slang [slæŋ] ⬦ adj popular. ⬦ n (U) gíria f.

slant [slɑ:ntl] ⬦ n -1. [diagonal angle - of table, shelf] inclinação f; [- of land] declive m; **on** or **ata ~** inclinado(da) -2. [point of view] perspectiva f, enfoque m. ⬦ vt [bias] distorcer. ⬦ vi [slope] inclinar-se.

slanting ['slɑ:ntɪŋ] adj inclinado(da).

slap [slæp] (pt & pp -ped, cont -ping) ⬦ n -1. [on face] bofetada f; a **~ in the face** [fig] uma bofetada -2. [on back] tapa m. ⬦ vt -1. [smack - on face] esbofetear; [- on back] dar um tapa em -2. [put]: **to ~ sthg on** dar uma retocada em. ⬦ adv inf [exactly] em cheio; **~ in the middle of the city** bem no meio da cidade.

slapdash ['slæpdæʃ], **slaphappy** ['slæp,hæpɪ] adj relaxado(da).

slapstick ['slæpstɪk] n (U) pastelão m; **the film is pure ~** este filme é um pastelão só.

slap-up adj UK inf farto(ta); a **~ dinner** um jantar formidável.

slash [slæʃ] ⬦ n -1. [long cut] rasgão m, corte m -2. [oblique stroke] barra f oblíqua; **forward ~** barra f (inclinada) -3. UK inf [pee]: **to have a ~** fazer xixi. ⬦ vt -1. [cut - material, tyres] rasgar; [- wrists] cortar -2. inf [reduce drastically] cortar.

slat [slæt] n ripa f, sarrafo m.

slate [sleɪt] ⬦ n -1. (U) [material] ardósia f -2. [on roof] telha f de ardósia; **to wipe the ~ clean** sacudir a poeira; **put it on the ~** põe na conta. ⬦ vt [criticize] malhar.

slatted adj com ripas.

slaughter ['slɔ:tə'] ⬦ n -1. [of animals] matança f -2. [of people] chacina f. ⬦ vt -1. [animals] matar, carnear -2. [people] chacinar.

slaughterhouse ['slɔ:təhaʊs, pl -haʊzɪz] n matadouro m.

Slav [slɑ:v] ⬦ adj eslavo(va). ⬦ n eslavo m, -va f.

slave [sleɪv] ⬦ n escravo m, -va f; **to be a ~ to sthg** ser escravo(va) de algo. ⬦ vi [work hard]: **to ~ (over sthg)** trabalhar como um escravo em algo, trabalhar como uma escrava em algo.

slaver ['sleɪvə'] vi babar.

slavery ['sleɪvərɪ] n (U) escravidão f.

slave trade n: **the ~** o tráfico or comércio de escravos.

Slavic ⬦ adj eslavo(va). ⬦ n -1. [language] eslavo m -2. HIST eslavo m, -va f.

slavish ['sleɪvɪʃ] adj pej [unoriginal, servile] servil.

Slavonic [slə'vɒnɪk] adj & n = **Slavic**.

slay [sleɪ] (pt slew, pp slain) vt literary assassinar.

sleaze n sujeira f.

sleazy ['sli:zɪ] (compar -ier, superl -iest) adj sujo(ja).

sledge [sledʒ], **sled** US [sledl] n trenó m.

sledgehammer ['sledʒ,hæmə'] n marreta f.

sleek [sli:k] adj -1. [hair] sedoso(sa) -2. [fur] brilhoso(sa) -3. [animal, bird] lustroso(sa) -4. [car, plane] vistoso(sa) -5. [person] polido(da).

sleep [sli:p] (pt & pp slept) ⬦ n -1. (U) [rest] sono m; **to go to ~** [doze off] adormecer; [go numb] ficar dormente; **to put to ~** [patient] anestesiar; [animal

sacrificar -2. [period of sleeping] sono m. ⬦ vi dormir.

⬥ **sleep around** vi inf pej dormir com qualquer um(ma).

⬥ **sleep in** vi dormir até mais tarde.

⬥ **sleep off** vt sep: **to ~ sthg off** curar algo dormindo.

⬥ **sleep through** vt fus: **to ~ through sthg** não despertar com algo.

⬥ **sleep together** vi euphemism dormir juntos(tas).

⬥ **sleep with** vt fus euphemism dormir com.

sleeper ['sli:pə'] n -1. [person]: **to be a heavy/light ~** ter sono pesado/leve -2. [sleeping compartment] leito m -3. [train] trem-leito m -4. UK [on railway line] dormente m.

sleepily ['sli:pɪlɪ] adv sonolentamente, quase dormindo.

sleeping bag ['sli:pɪŋ-] n saco m de dormir.

sleeping car ['sli:pɪŋ-] n vagão-leito m.

sleeping partner ['sli:pɪŋ-] n UK sócio m comanditário, sócia f comanditária.

sleeping pill ['sli:pɪŋ-] n pílula f para dormir.

sleeping policeman ['sli:pɪŋ-] n UK inf quebra-molas m inv.

sleeping tablet ['sli:pɪŋ-] n comprimido m para dormir.

sleepless ['sli:plɪs] adj em claro, sem dormir.

sleeplessness ['sli:plɪsnɪs] n (U) falta f de sono, insônia f.

sleepwalk ['sli:pwɔ:k] vi sonambular.

sleepy ['sli:pɪ] (compar -ier, superl -iest) adj -1. [person] sonolento(ta) -2. [place] pacato(ta).

sleet [sli:t] ⬦ n (U) granizo m. ⬦ v impers chover granizo.

sleeve [sli:v] n -1. [of garment] manga f; **to have sthg up one's ~** ter uma carta escondida na manga -2. [for record] capa f.

sleeveless ['sli:vlɪs] adj sem mangas.

sleigh [sleɪ] n trenó m.

sleight of hand [,slaɪt-] n (U) -1. [skill with hands] prestidigitação f -2. fig [deception] artimanha f.

slender ['slendə'] adj -1. [thin - person, figure] esbelto(ta); [- legs] delgado(da) -2. [scarce] escasso(sa).

slept [slept] pt & pp ⊳ **sleep**.

sleuth [slu:θ] n inf hum detetive mf.

slew [slu:] ⬦ pt ⊳ **slay**. ⬦ vi: **the car ~ed off the road** o carro rodopiou para fora da estrada.

slice [slaɪs] ⬦ n -1. [gen] fatia f -2. [of lemon] rodela f -3. [proportion] parte f -4. SPORT cortada f. ⬦ vt -1. [cut into slices] fatiar -2. SPORT cortar. ⬦ vi: **to ~ through/into sthg** cortar algo com facilidade.

⬥ **slice off** vt sep [sever] arrancar fora.

⬥ **slice up** vt sep [food] fatiar, cortar em fatias.

sliced bread [slaɪst-] n (U) pão m fatiado.

slick [slɪk] ⬦ adj -1. [smoothly efficient - performance, teamwork] talentoso(sa); [- technique, crime] engenhoso(sa) -2. pej [glib] ardiloso(sa). ⬦ n local m escorregadio.

slicker n US capa f de chuva.

slide [slaɪd] (pt & pp slid [slɪd]) ⬦ n -1. PHOT eslaide m -2. [in playground] escorregador m -3. [for microscope] lâmina f -4. UK [for hair] passador m -5.

[decline] declínio *m*. <> *vt* [move smoothly] deslizar. <> *vi* **-1.** [on ice, slippery surface] escorregar **-2.** [move quietly] deslizar **-3.** [decline gradually] sucumbir a; **to let things** ~ deixar que as coisas piorem.

slide projector *n* projetor *m* de eslaides.

slide rule *n* régua *f* de cálculo.

sliding door [ˌslaɪdɪŋ-] *n* porta *f* de correr.

sliding scale [ˌslaɪdɪŋ-] *n* escala *f* móvel.

slight [slaɪt] <> *adj* **-1.** [minor] ligeiro(ra); **not in the** ~ **est** nem de leve; **I haven't got the** ~ **est interest in his car** eu não tenho o menor interesse no carro dele **-2.** [slender] de aspecto frágil. <> *n* menosprezo *m*. <> *vt* [offend] menosprezar.

slightly [ˈslaɪtlɪ] *adv* **-1.** [to small extent] ligeiramente, levemente **-2.** [slenderly]: ~ **built** magrinho(nha).

slim [slɪm] (*compar* **-mer**, *superl* **-mest**, *pt* & *pp* **-med**, *cont* **-ming**) <> *adj* **-1.** [person] esbelto(ta) **-2.** [object] fino(na) **-3.** [chance, possibility] remoto(ta). <> *vi* [lose weight] emagrecer; **I'm** ~ **ming** estou de dieta; [diet] emagrecer.

slime [slaɪm] *n (U)* muco *m*.

slimline *adj* mais fino(na) *(que o normal)*.

slimmer [ˈslɪmə^r] *n* pessoa *f* de dieta.

slimming [ˈslɪmɪŋ] <> *n (U)* emagrecimento *m*. <> *adj* **-1.** [magazine] de dieta **-2.** [product] para emagrecer.

slimness [ˈslɪmnɪs] *n (U)* esbelteza *f*, elegância *f*.

slimy [ˈslaɪmɪ] (*compar* **-ier**, *superl* **-iest**) *adj* **-1.** [covered in slime] coberto(ta) com lodo *or* muco **-2.** *pej* [servile] fingido(da).

sling [slɪŋ] (*pt* & *pp* **slung**) <> *n* **-1.** [for injured arm] tipóia *f* **-2.** [for carrying things] linga *f*. <> *vt* **-1.** [hang roughly] pendurar **-2.** [throw] atirar, jogar **-3.** [hang by both ends] pendurar.

slingback [ˈslɪŋbæk] *n* sandália *f*.

slingshot [ˈslɪŋʃɒt] *n US* catapulta *f*.

slink [slɪŋk] (*pt* & *pp* **slunk**) *vi*: **to** ~ **(away** *or* **off)** escapulir-se.

slip [slɪp] (*pt* & *pp* **-ped**, *cont* **-ping**) <> *n* **-1.** [mistake] deslize *m*, descuido *m*; **a** ~ **of the pen** um erro de ortografia; **a** ~ **of the tongue** um lapso verbal **-2.** [form] formulário *m* **-3.** [of paper] folha *f* **-4.** [underwear] combinação *f*, anágua *f* **-5.** *phr*: **to give sb the** ~ *inf* safar-se de alguém. <> *vt* **-1.** [slide] enfiar, meter **-2.** [clothes]: **to** ~ **sthg on** vestir algo rapidamente; ~ **your clothes off** tira fora essas tuas roupas **-3.** [escape] fugir; **it** ~ **ped my mind** me esqueci. <> *vi* **-1.** [lose balance] escorregar **-2.** [move unexpectedly] escapulir **-3.** [move gradually] entrar em **-4.** [decline] baixar; **to let things** ~ deixar escapar algo *(falando)* **-5.** [move discreetly] escapulir-se; **to** ~ **into/out of sthg** [clothes] vestir/tirar algo **-6.** *AUT* [clutch] patinar **-7.** *phr*: **to let sthg** ~ dizer algo sem querer.

➡ **slip away** *vi* [leave] ir embora.

➡ **slip on** *vt sep* [clothes, shoes] enfiar.

➡ **slip up** *vi* [make a mistake] cometer um deslize.

slip-on *adj* [shoes] sem cadarço.

➡ **slip-ons** *npl* [shoes] mocassim *m*.

slippage *n (U)* deslizamento *m*.

slipped disc [ˌslɪpt-] *n* hérnia *f* de disco.

slipper [ˈslɪpə^r] *n* pantufa *f*.

slippery [ˈslɪpərɪ] *adj* **-1.** [surface, soap] escorregadio(dia) **-2.** *pej* [person] evasivo(va).

slip road *n UK* acesso *m (na estrada)*.

slipshod [ˈslɪpʃɒd] *adj* desleixado(da).

slipstream [ˈslɪpstriːm] *n* rastro *m*.

slip-up *n inf* mancada *f*.

slipway [ˈslɪpweɪl] *n* carreira *f (para navios)*.

slit [slɪt] (*pt* & *pp* **slit**, *cont* **-ting**) <> *n* **-1.** [opening] fenda *f* **-2.** [cut] corte *m*. <> *vt* **-1.** [cut open] cortar **-2.** [cut through] fender.

slither [ˈslɪðə^r] *vi* **-1.** [car, person] arrastar-se **-2.** [snake] rastejar.

sliver [ˈslɪvə^r] *n* **-1.** [gen] caco *f* **-2.** [of ice, wood] lasca *f*.

slob [slɒb] *n inf* [disgusting person - in habits] porcalhão *m*, -lhona *f*; [- in appearance] porco *m*, -ca *f*.

slobber [ˈslɒbə^r] *vi* babar.

slog [slɒg] (*pt* & *pp* **-ged**, *cont* **-ging**) *inf* <> *n* **-1.** [tiring work] chatice *f* **-2.** [tiring journey] maçada *f*. <> *vi* **-1.** [work]: **to** ~ **(away) at sthg** trabalhar sem descanso em algo **-2.** [walk, move] andar a custo.

slogan [ˈsləʊgən] *n* slogan *m*.

slop [slɒp] (*pt* & *pp* **-ped**, *cont* **-ping**) <> *vt* derramar. <> *vi* transbordar.

slope [sləʊp] <> *n* **-1.** [of roof, ground] inclinação *f* **-2.** [hill] encosta *f* **-3.** *phr*: **he's on the slippery** ~ **to** alcoholism ele está indo direto para o alcoolismo. <> *vi* inclinar-se.

sloping [ˈsləʊpɪŋ] *adj* inclinado(da).

sloppy [ˈslɒpɪ] (*compar* **-ier**, *superl* **-iest**) *adj* **-1.** [careless] desleixado(da), relaxado(da) **-2.** *inf* [sentimental] meloso(sa), piegas.

slosh [slɒʃ] <> *vt* **-1.** [spill] chapinhar **-2.** [pour] despejar **-3.** [apply] espalhar. <> *vi* **-1.** [liquid] chapinhar **-2.** [through liquid, mud] patinhar.

sloshed [slɒʃt] *adj UK inf* com a cara cheia.

slot [slɒt] (*pt* & *pp* **-ted**, *cont* **-ting**) *n* **-1.** [opening] abertura *f* **-2.** [groove] ranhura *f* **-3.** [place in schedule] espaço *m* **-4.** *COMPUT* slot *m*.

➡ **slot in** <> *vt sep* [insert] encaixar. <> *vi* [fit neatly] encaixar.

sloth [sləʊθ] *n* **-1.** [animal] bicho-preguiça *m* **-2.** *(U) literary* [laziness] preguiça *f*.

slot machine *n* **-1.** [vending machine] máquina *f* automática *(de bebidas, cigarros etc)* **-2.** [arcade machine] caça-níqueis *m inv*.

slot meter *n UK* medidor *m (de luz ou gás)* que funciona com moedas.

slouch [slaʊtʃ] <> *n* [person] incompetente *mf*. <> *vi* [in posture] ter má postura.

slough *vt sep* **-1.** [shed] trocar *or* mudar *(de pele)* **-2.** *fig* [get rid of] livrar-se de.

Slovak [ˈsləʊvæk] <> *adj* eslavo(va). <> *n* **-1.** [person] eslavo *m*, -va *f* **-2.** [language] eslavo *m*.

Slovakia [sləˈvækɪə] *n* Eslováquia; **in** ~ na Eslováquia.

Slovakian [sləˈvækɪən] <> *adj* eslovaco(ca). <> *n* eslovaco *m*, -ca *f*.

Slovenia [sləˈviːnjə] *n* Eslovênia; **in** ~ na Eslovênia.

Slovenian [sləˈviːnjən] <> *adj* esloveno(na). <> *n* esloveno *m*, -na *f*.

slovenly [ˈslʌvnlɪ] *adj* **-1.** [person, work] desmazelado(da) **-2.** [appearance] desleixado(da) **-3.** [dress] desalinhado(da).

slow [sləʊ] <> *adj* -**1.** [not fast] lento(ta) -**2.** [clock, watch] atrasado(da) -**3.** [not busy] parado(da) -**4.** [not intelligent] lerdo(da). <> *adv* : **to go ~** [driver] ir devagar; [workers] fazer operação-tartaruga. <> *vt* retardar. <> *vi* ir mais devagar, desacelerar.

➥ **slow down, slow up** <> *vt sep* -**1.** [growth] retardar -**2.** [car] reduzir a velocidade de. <> *vi* -**1.** [car] reduzir a velocidade de -**2.** [walker] diminuir a marcha.

slow-acting *adj* de ação lenta.

slowcoach ['sləʊkəʊtʃ], **slowpoke** *US n inf* molenga *mf*.

slowdown ['sləʊdaʊn] *n* desaceleração *f*.

slow handclap *n* aplauso lento e ritmado em sinal de protesto.

slowly ['sləʊlɪ] *adv* devagar; **~ but surely** devagar e sempre.

slow motion *n* (U) câmera *f* lenta.

➥ **slow-motion** *adj* em câmera lenta.

slowpoke *n US* = **slowcoach**.

SLR (*abbr of* **single-lens reflex**) *n* tipo de câmera fotográfica que usa uma lente única.

sludge [slʌdʒ] *n* -**1.** [mud] lama *f* -**2.** [sediment] lodo *m*.

slug [slʌg] (*pt & pp* -**ged**, *cont* -**ging**) <> *n* -**1.** *ZOOL* lesma *f* -**2.** [of alcohol] trago *m* -**3.** *US inf* [bullet] bala *f* (*de revólver*). <> *vt inf* [hit] esmurrar.

sluggish ['slʌgɪʃ] *adj* -**1.** [lethargic] vagaroso(sa) -**2.** [reaction, business] moroso(sa).

sluice [slu:s] <> *n* [lock] comporta *f*. <> *vt* [rinse]: **to ~ sthg down/out** lavar algo com muita água.

slum [slʌm] (*pt & pp* -**med**, *cont* -**ming**) <> *n* [area of poor housing] favela *f*, cortiço *m*. <> *vt* : **to ~ it** *inf* baixar o padrão de vida.

slumber ['slʌmbəʳ] *literary* <> *n* (U) sono *m*. <> *vi* adormecer.

slump [slʌmp] <> *n* -**1.** [decline]: **~ (in sthg)** queda *f* (em algo) -**2.** *ECON* crise *f* econômica. <> *vi* -**1.** [business, prices, market] cair -**2.** [person] afundar-se.

slung [slʌŋ] *pt & pp* ▷ **sling**.

slunk [slʌŋk] *pt & pp* ▷ **slink**.

slur [slɜ:ʳ] (*pt & pp* -**red**, *cont* -**ring**) <> *n* -**1.** [in voice] balbuceio *m* -**2.** [insult]: **~ (on sb/sthg)** ultraje *m or* afronta *f* (a alguém/algo). <> *vt* [speech] balbuciar; **to ~ one's words** engolir as palavras.

slurp [slɜ:p] *vt* sorver fazendo barulho.

slurred [slɜ:d] *adj* ininteligível.

slurry *n* (U) purina *f*.

slush [slʌʃ] *n* (U) neve *f* meio derretida.

slush fund, slush money *US n* caixa *m* dois.

slut [slʌt] *n* -**1.** *inf* [dirty or untidy woman] mulher *f* relaxada -**2.** *v inf* [sexually immoral woman] rameira *f*.

sly [slaɪ] (*compar* **slyer** *OR* **slier**, *superl* **slyest** *OR* **sliest**) <> *adj* -**1.** [look, smile, grin] dissimulado(da) -**2.** [cunning] astuto(ta) -**3.** [secretive] fingido(da). <> *n*: **on the ~** às escondidas.

slyness ['slaɪnɪs] *n* (U) dissimulação *f*.

S & M (*abbr of* **sadism and masochism**) *n* SM *m*.

smack [smæk] <> *n* -**1.** [slap] palmada *f* -**2.** [impact] batida *f*. <> *vt* -**1.** [slap] dar uma palmada em -**2.** [put] colocar bruscamente -**3.** [make sound]: **to ~**

one's lips estalar os lábios. <> *vi*: **to ~ of sthg** cheirar a algo. <> *adv inf* [exactly]: **~ in the middle** bem no meio.

small [smɔ:l] <> *adj* -**1.** [gen] pequeno(na); **in a ~ way** em pequena escala -**2.** [person] baixo(xa) -**3.** [importance] pouco(ca) -**4.** [matter, alteration] de pouca importância. <> *n*: **the ~ of the back** a região lombar.

➥ **smalls** *npl UK inf dated* roupa *f* de baixo.

small ads [-ædz] *npl UK* classificados *mpl*.

small arms *npl* armas *fpl* portáteis *OR* de mão.

small change *n* (U) trocado *m*.

small fry *n* (U) peixe *m* pequeno, fichinha *f*.

smallholder ['smɔ:l,həʊldəʳ] *n UK* minifundiário *m*, -ria *f*.

smallholding ['smɔ:l,həʊldɪŋ] *n UK* minifúndio *m*.

small hours *npl* primeiras horas *fpl* da manhã.

small letters *npl*: **in ~** em minúscula.

smallness ['smɔ:lnɪs] *n* -**1.** (U) [of building, person] pequenez *f* -**2.** [rise, amount] escassez *f*.

smallpox ['smɔ:lpɒks] *n* (U) varíola *f*.

small print *n*: **the ~** as letras miúdas (*de um contrato*).

small-scale *adj* em pequena escala.

small talk *n* (U): **to make ~** conversar amenidades.

small-time *adj* de segunda; **a ~ criminal** um ladrão de galinha.

smarmy ['smɑ:mɪ] (*compar* -**ier**, *superl* -**iest**) *adj inf* adulador(ra).

smart [smɑ:t] <> *adj* -**1.** [elegant] elegante -**2.** [clever] inteligente -**3.** [fashionable, exclusive] chique, elegante -**4.** [rapid] rápido(da) -**5.** [impertinent] insolente. <> *vi* -**1.** [sting] pungir, arder -**2.** [feel anger, humiliation] ofender-se.

smart card *n* cartão *m* inteligente.

smarten ['smɑ:tn] ➥ **smarten up** *vt sep* arrumar; **to ~ o.s. up** arrumar-se.

smash [smæʃ] <> *n* -**1.** [sound] estilhaço *m* -**2.** *inf* [car crash] acidente *m* -**3.** *inf* [success] estouro *m* -**4.** *TENNIS* cortada *f*. <> *vt* -**1.** [break into pieces] quebrar -**2.** [hit, crash] bater em; **to ~ one's fist into sthg** dar um soco em algo -**3.** *fig* [defeat] derrotar. <> *vi* -**1.** [break into pieces] quebrar-se -**2.** [crash, collide]: **to ~ through/into sthg** espatifar-se contra/em algo.

➥ **smash up** *vt sep* destruir completamente.

smash-and-grab (raid) *n UK* saque *m* após arrombamento (*numa loja*).

smashed [smæʃt] *adj inf* mamado(da) (*de bêbado*).

smash hit *n* sucesso *m* absoluto.

smashing ['smæʃɪŋ] *adj inf* fabuloso(sa), fenomenal.

smash-up *n* choque *m* violento, desastre *m*.

smattering ['smætərɪŋ] *n* noções *fpl*; **to have a ~ of Welsh** falar meia dúzia de palavras de galês.

SME (*abbr of* **small and medium-sized enterprise**) *n* pequena e média empresa *f*.

smear [smɪəʳ] <> *n* -**1.** [dirty mark] mancha *f* (*de gordura*) -**2.** *MED* esfregaço *m* -**3.** [slander] calúnia *f*. <> *vt* -**1.** [smudge - page] manchar; [- painting] borrar -**2.** [spread]: **to ~ sthg onto sthg** espalhar algo sobre algo; **to ~ sthg with sthg** untar algo com algo **- 3.** [slander] caluniar.

smear campaign n campanha f de difamação.

smear test n esfregaço m.

smell [smel] (pt & pp **-ed** OR **smelt**) ◇ n **-1.** [odour] cheiro m, odor m **- 2.** (U) [sense of smell] olfato m. ◇ vt **-1.** [notice an odour of] sentir cheiro de **- 2.** [sniff at] cheirar **- 3.** fig [sense] pressentir. ◇ vi **-1.** [have sense of smell] sentir cheiro **- 2.** [have particular smell]: **to ~ of sthg** cheirar a algo; **to ~ like sthg** cheirar como algo; **to ~ good/bad** cheirar bem/mal **- 3.** [smell unpleasantly] feder.

smelling salts npl sais mpl aromáticos.

smelly ['smelɪ] (compar **-ier**, superl **-iest**) adj fedorento(ta).

smelt [smelt] ◇ pt & pp ⊳ **smell**. ◇ vt TECH fundir.

smile [smaɪl] ◇ n sorriso m. ◇ vi sorrir. ◇ vt sorrir; **to ~ one's thanks** sorrir em agradecimento.

smiley ['smaɪlɪ] n COMPUT smiley m.

smiling ['smaɪlɪŋ] adj sorridente, risonho(nha).

smirk [smɜːk] ◇ n sorriso m afetado. ◇ vi sorrir de forma afetada.

smith [smɪθ] n ferreiro m, -ra f.

smithereens [ˌsmɪðəˈriːnz] npl inf: **to be smashed to ~** ser quebrado(da) em pedacinhos OR em mil pedaços.

smithy ['smɪðɪ] (pl **-ies**) n ferraria f.

smitten ['smɪtn] adj inf hum: **to be ~ (with sb/ sthg)** estar apaixonado(da) (por alguém/algo).

smock [smɒk] n avental m, guarda-pó m.

smog [smɒg] n (U) bruma f.

smoke [sməʊk] ◇ n **-1.** (U) [from burning] fumaça f **- 2.** [act of smoking]: **to have a ~** fumar. ◇ vt **-1.** [cigarette, cigar] fumar **- 2.** [fish, meat, cheese] defumar. ◇ vi **-1.** [chimney, engine, lamp] fumegar **- 2.** [person] fumar.

smoked [sməʊkt] adj [food] defumado(da).

smokeless fuel ['sməʊklɪs-] n (U) combustível m limpo.

smokeless zone ['sməʊklɪs-] n área na qual se proíbe o uso de combustíveis que produzam fumaça.

smoker ['sməʊkəʳ] n **-1.** [person who smokes] fumante mf **- 2.** inf RAIL [compartment] vagão m para fumantes.

smokescreen ['sməʊkskriːn] n fig cortina f de fumaça.

smoke shop n US tabacaria f.

smokestack n chaminé f.

smokestack industry n US indústria f pesada OR de base.

smoking ['sməʊkɪŋ] n (U): **~ is bad for you** fumar não te faz bem; **'no ~ '** 'é proibido fumar'.

smoking compartment UK, **smoking car** US n vagão m para fumantes.

smoky ['sməʊkɪ] (compar **-ier**, superl **-iest**) adj **-1.** [full of smoke] enfumaçado(da) **- 2.** [resembling smoke - taste] com gosto de fumaça; [- colour] cinzento(ta).

smolder vi US = smoulder.

smooch [smuːtʃ] vi inf dar amassos.

smooth [smuːð] ◇ adj **-1.** [surface - skin, fabric] macio(cia); [- stone] liso(sa); [- water, sea] calmo(ma) **- 2.** CULIN [texture] uniforme **- 3.** [flow, supply] fluido(da)

- 4. [pace] tranqüilo(la) **- 5.** [taste, ride] suave **- 6.** [engine] macio(cia) **- 7.** pej [person, manner] lisonjeiro(ra) **- 8.** [trouble-free] tranqüilo(la), sem problemas. ◇ vt **-1.** [gen] alisar; **to ~ the way** preparar o terreno **- 2.** [rub] passar.

◆ **smooth out** vt sep **-1.** [gen] alisar **- 2.** fig [difficulties] resolver-se.

◆ **smooth over** vt fus resolver.

smoothly ['smuːðlɪ] adv **-1.** [gen] suavemente **- 2.** [talk] calmamente, sem se alterar **- 3.** [without problems] tranqüilamente, sem problemas.

smoothness ['smuːðnɪs] n (U) **-1.** [gen - skin, fabric, engine] maciez f; [- road, stone] lisura f; [- sea, water, flight] tranqüilidade f; [- finish] perfeição f **- 2.** CULIN [of texture] uniformidade f **- 3.** [of flow, supply] fluidez f **- 4.** [of pace] tranqüilidade f, calma f.

smooth-talking adj de lábia fácil.

smother ['smʌðəʳ] vt **-1.** [cover thickly]: **to ~ sthg in** OR **with sthg** cobrir algo de algo **- 2.** [suffocate] sufocar **- 3.** [extinguish] abafar **- 4.** fig [repress] reprimir **- 5.** [suffocate with love] mimar demais.

smoulder UK, **smolder** US ['sməʊldəʳ] vi **-1.** [fire] fumegar **- 2.** fig [feelings] arder.

SMS (abbr of short message service) n COMPUT SMS m, mensagens fpl curtas de texto.

smudge [smʌdʒ] ◇ n [dirty mark] borrão m. ◇ vt [spoil - by blurring] borrar; [- by dirtying] manchar.

smug [smʌg] (compar **-ger**, superl **-gest**) adj pej presunçoso(sa).

smuggle ['smʌgl] vt **-1.** [across frontiers] contrabandear **- 2.** [against rules]: **to ~ sthg in/out** trazer algo escondido.

smuggler ['smʌgləʳ] n contrabandista mf.

smuggling ['smʌglɪŋ] n (U) contrabando m.

smugness ['smʌgnɪs] n (U) pej presunção f.

smut [smʌt] n **-1.** [of soot, dirt] sujeira f, fuligem f **- 2.** (U) inf pej [lewd matter] obscenidade f.

smutty ['smʌtɪ] (compar **-ier**, superl **-iest**) adj inf pej obsceno(na), indecente.

snack [snæk] ◇ n lanche m. ◇ vi US lanchar.

snack bar n lancheria f.

snag [snæg] (pt & pp **-ged**, cont **-ging**) ◇ n **-1.** [small problem] dificuldade f **- 2.** [in nail, tights, fabric] ponta f saliente. ◇ vt enganchar. ◇ vi: **to ~ (on sthg)** enganchar-se (em algo).

snail [sneɪl] n caracol m.

snail mail n correio m tradicional.

snake [sneɪk] ◇ n cobra f, serpente f. ◇ vi serpentear.

snap [snæp] (pt & pp **-ped**, cont **-ping**) ◇ adj atropelado(da), repentino(na). ◇ n **-1.** [act or sound of snapping] estalo m **- 2.** inf [photograph] foto f **- 3.** [card game] jogo de cartas semelhante ao burro mecânico. ◇ vt **-1.** [break] partir (em dois) **- 2.** [make cracking sound with]: **to ~ sthg open/shut** abrir/fechar algo com um golpe; **to ~ one's fingers** estalar os dedos **- 3.** [speak sharply] falar bruscamente **- 4.** inf [photograph] bater foto. ◇ vi **-1.** [break] partir (em dois) **- 2.** [make cracking sound] estalar; **to ~ into place** ir para o lugar com uma pancada **- 3.** [attempt to bite]: **to ~ (at sb/sthg)** tentar morder (alguém/algo) **- 4.** [speak sharply]: **to ~ (at sb)** ficar brabo(ba) (com alguém) **- 5.** phr: **to ~ out of it** animar-se de repente.

snap up *vt sep* não deixar escapar.

snap fastener *n esp US* botão *m* de pressão.

snappy ['snæpɪ] (*compar* -ier, *superl* -iest) *adj inf* - **1.** [stylish] chique - **2.** [quick] rápido(da); **make it ~!** anda logo!

snapshot ['snæpʃɒt] *n* instantânea *f.*

snare [sneə^r] <> *n* armadilha *f.* <> *vt* pegar numa armadilha.

snarl [snɑːl] <> *n* rosnado *m.* <> *vi* - **1.** [animal] rosnar - **2.** [person] resmungar.

snarl-up *n* rolo *m*, confusão *f.*

snatch [snætʃ] <> *n* [fragment] trecho *m.* <> *vt* - **1.** [grab] agarrar - **2.** *fig* [sleep, opportunity, look] aproveitar; **to ~ some sleep** tirar um tempo para dormir. <> *vi* [grab]: **to ~ (at sthg)** tentar agarrar (algo).

snazzy ['snæzɪ] (*compar* -ier, *superl* -iest) *adj inf* chamativo(va).

sneak [sniːk] (*US pt* **snuck**) <> *n UK inf* mexeriqueiro *m*, -ra *f.* <> *vt* levar escondido(da); **to ~ a look at sb/sthg** espiar alguém/algo. <> *vi* [move quietly] esgueirar-se.

sneakers ['sniːkəz] *npl US* tênis *m inv.*

sneaking ['sniːkɪŋ] *adj* [feeling, suspicion] secreto(ta).

sneak preview *n* pré-estréia *f.*

sneaky ['sniːkɪ] (*compar* -ier, *superl* -iest) *adj inf* sorrateiro(ra).

sneer [snɪə^r] <> *n* escárnio *m.* <> *vi* - **1.** [smile unpleasantly] sorrir com escárnio - **2.** [ridicule]: **to ~ (at sthg)** zombar (de algo).

sneeze [sniːz] <> *n* espirro *m.* <> *vi* espirrar; **it's not to be ~d at** *inf* não é de se jogar fora.

snicker ['snɪkə^r] *vi* rir por dentro.

snide [snaɪd] *adj* sarcástico(ca).

sniff [snɪf] <> *n* fungada *f.* <> *vt* - **1.** [smell] fungar - **2.** [drug] cheirar. <> *vi* - **1.** [to clear nose] assoar - **2.** [to show disapproval] torcer o nariz.

sniff out *vt sep* - **1.** [detect by sniffing] farejar - **2.** *inf* [seek out] descobrir.

sniffer dog ['snɪfə^r-] *n* cão *m* farejador.

sniffle ['snɪfl] *vi* fungar.

snigger ['snɪgə^r] <> *n* escárnio *m.* <> *vi* rir por dentro.

snip [snɪp] (*pt & pp* -ped, *cont* -ping) <> *n inf* [bargain] pechincha *f.* <> *vt* [cut] cortar (em pedaços).

snipe [snaɪp] *vi* - **1.** [shoot]: **to ~ (at sb/sthg)** disparar (em alguém/algo) - **2.** [criticize]: **to ~ at sb** criticar alguém.

sniper ['snaɪpə^r] *n* franco-atirador *m*, -ra *f.*

snippet ['snɪpɪt] *n* fragmento *m.*

snivel ['snɪvl] (*UK pt & pp* -led, *cont* -ling, *US pt & pp* -ed, *cont* -ing) *vi* choramingar.

snob [snɒb] *n* esnobe *mf.*

snobbery ['snɒbərɪ] *n (U)* esnobismo *m.*

snobbish ['snɒbɪʃ], **snobby** ['snɒbɪ] (*compar* -ier, *superl* -iest) *adj* esnobe.

snog (*pt & pp* -ged, *cont* -ging) *vi UK inf* agarrar-se.

snooker ['snuːkə^r] <> *n (U)* snooker *m.* <> *vt UK inf* [thwart]: **to be ~ed** estar com as mãos atadas.

snoop [snuːp] *vi inf* bisbilhotar.

snooper ['snuːpə^r] *n inf* bisbilhoteiro *m*, -ra *f.*

snooty ['snuːtɪ] (*compar* -ier, *superl* -iest) *adj* presunçoso(sa).

snooze [snuːz] <> *n* cochilo *m*, soneca *f*; **to have a ~** tirar uma soneca *OR* um cochilo. <> *vi* cochilar.

snore [snɔː^r] <> *n* ronco *m.* <> *vi* roncar.

snoring ['snɔːrɪŋ] *n (U)* roncos *mpl.*

snorkel ['snɔːkl] *n* (tubo *m*) snorkel *m.*

snorkelling *UK*, **snorkeling** *US* ['snɔːklɪŋ] *n (U)* mergulho *m* com (tubo) snorkel.

snort [snɔːt] <> *n* bufo *m.* <> *vi* bufar. <> *vt drugs sl* cheirar.

snotty ['snɒtɪ] (*compar* -ier, *superl* -iest) *adj inf* [snooty] presunçoso(sa).

snout [snaʊt] *n* focinho *m.*

snow [snəʊ] <> *n (U)* neve *f.* <> *v impers* nevar.

snow in *vt sep*: **to be ~ed in** estar preso(sa) por causa da neve.

snow under *vt sep*: **to be ~ed under (with sthg)** estar atolado(da) (de algo).

snowball ['snəʊbɔːl] <> *n* bola *f* de neve. <> *vi fig* [increase rapidly] crescer como bola de neve.

snow blindness *n* ofuscação *f (da neve).*

snowboard ['snəʊbɔːd] *n* snowboard *m.*

snowboarding ['snəʊbɔːdɪŋ] *n* snowboard *m*; **to go ~** praticar snowboard.

snowbound ['snəʊbaʊnd] *adj* bloqueado(da) pela neve.

snow-capped [-ˌkæpt] *adj* com o pico coberto de neve.

snowdrift ['snəʊdrɪft] *n* monte *m* de neve.

snowdrop ['snəʊdrɒp] *n* campainha *f* branca.

snowfall ['snəʊfɔːl] *n* - **1.** [fall of snow] nevada *f* - **2.** [amount of snow over time] quantidade *f* de neve.

snowflake ['snəʊfleɪk] *n* floco *m* de neve.

snowman ['snəʊmæn] (*pl* -men [-men]) *n* boneco *m* de neve.

snow pea *n US* ervilha *f* torta.

snowplough *UK*, **snowplow** *US* ['snəʊplaʊ] *n* [vehicle] limpa-neve *m.*

snowshoe ['snəʊʃuː] *n* raquete *f* de neve.

snowstorm ['snəʊstɔːm] *n* nevasca *f.*

snowy ['snəʊɪ] (*compar* -ier, *superl* -iest) *adj* - **1.** [weather, day] de muita neve - **2.** [road, landscape] com muita neve.

SNP (*abbr of* **Scottish National Party**) *n partido nacional escocês que prega a independência da Grã-Bretanha.*

Snr, snr (*abbr of* **senior**) sênior.

snub [snʌb] (*pt & pp* -bed, *cont* -bing) <> *n* repulsa *f.* <> *vt* desprezar.

snuck [snʌk] *pt US* ⊳ **sneak**.

snuff [snʌf] <> *n (U)* [tobacco] rapé *m.* <> *vt*: **to ~ it** *inf* morrer.

snuffle ['snʌfl] *vi* fungar.

snuff movie *n filme pornográfico com um assassinato como desenlace.*

snug [snʌg] (*compar* -ger, *superl* -gest) *adj* - **1.** [person, feeling] agradável - **2.** [place] confortável - **3.** [close-fitting] cômodo(da).

snuggle ['snʌgl] *vi* aconchegar-se; **to ~ down** cobrir-se (*com coberta*).

so [səʊ] <> *adv* - **1.** [emphasizing degree] tão; **don't be ~ stupid!** não seja tão idiota!; **it's ~ difficult (that ...)** é tão difícil (que ...); **~ much** tanto(ta); **~ many**

tantos(tas). **- 2.** [referring back]: **I don't think** ~ acho que não; **I'm afraid** ~ receio que sim; ~ **you knew already** então você já sabia; **if** ~ nesse caso. **- 3.** [also] também; ~ **do I** eu também. **- 4.** [in this way] deste modo, assim. **- 5.** [expressing agreement]: ~ **there is** pois é, é verdade. **- 6.** [in phrases]: **or** ~ mais ou menos; ~ **as** para; ~ **that** para. <> *conj* **-1.** [therefore] por isso; **I'm away next week** ~ **I won't be there** viajo na semana que vem, portanto não estarei lá. **- 2.** [summarizing] então; ~ **what have you been up to?** então, o que é que você tem feito? **- 3.** [in phrases]: ~ **what?** *inf* e daí?; ~ **there!** *inf* pronto!, nada a fazer!

SO (*abbr of* **standing order**) débito *m* em conta.

soak [səʊk] <> *vt* **-1.** [leave immersed] pôr de molho **- 2.** [wet thoroughly] ensopar; **to be** ~**ed with sthg** estar ensopado(da) de algo. <> *vi* **-1.** [become thoroughly wet]: **to leave sthg to** ~, **to let sthg** ~ deixar de molho **- 2.** [spread]: **to** ~ **into sthg** espalhar-se por algo; **to** ~ **through (sthg)** infiltrar-se em algo.

➡ **soak up** *vt sep* [liquid] absorver.

soaked [səʊkt] *adj* ensopado(da); **to be** ~ **through** ficar ensopado(da) dos pés à cabeça.

soaking ['səʊkɪŋ] *adj* ensopado(da).

so-and-so *n inf* **-1.** [to replace a name] fulano *m*, -na *f* **- 2.** [annoying person] filho *m*, -lha *f* da mãe.

soap [səʊp] <> *n* **-1.** (*U*) [for washing] sabão *m* **- 2.** *TV* novela *f*. <> *vt* ensaboar.

soap bubble *n* bolha *f* de sabão.

soap dish *n* saboneteira *f*.

soap flakes *npl* sabão *m* em flocos.

soap opera *n* novela *f*.

soap powder *n* (*U*) sabão *m* em pó.

soapsuds ['səʊpsʌdz] *npl* espuma *f* de sabão.

soapy ['səʊpɪ] (*compar* -**ier**, *superl* -**iest**) *adj* **-1.** [full of soap] ensaboado(da) **- 2.** [resembling soap] de sabão.

soar [sɔːr] *vi* **-1.** [bird] levantar vôo **- 2.** [rise into the sky] subir **- 3.** [increase rapidly] aumentar rapidamente **- 4.** *literary* [be impressively high] elevar-se **- 5.** [rise in volume or pitch] aumentar de intensidade.

soaring ['sɔːrɪŋ] *adj* **-1.** [rapidly increasing] cada vez mais alto(ta) **- 2.** [spire, tower] altíssimo(ma) **- 3.** [rising in volume or pitch] cada vez mais intenso(sa).

sob [sɒb] (*pt* & *pp* -**bed**, *cont* -**bing**) <> *n* soluço *m*. <> *vt* soluçar. <> *vi* [cry] soluçar.

sobbing ['sɒbɪŋ] *n* (*U*) soluços *mpl*.

sober ['səʊbər] *adj* **-1.** [not drunk] sóbrio(bria) **- 2.** [serious] sério(ria) **- 3.** [plain] simples.

➡ **sober up** *vi* ficar sóbrio(bria).

sobering ['səʊbərɪŋ] *adj* que faz refletir.

sobriety [səʊ'braɪətɪ] *n* (*U*) *fml* sobriedade *f*.

Soc. (*abbr of* **Society**) Soc.

so-called [-kɔːld] *adj* **-1.** [misleadingly named] suposto(ta) **- 2.** [widely known as] chamado(da).

soccer ['sɒkər] *n* (*U*) futebol *m*.

sociable ['səʊʃəbl] *adj* sociável.

social ['səʊʃl] *adj* social.

social climber *n pej* arrivista *mf*.

social club *n* clube *m* social.

social conscience *n* consciência *f* social.

social democracy *n* (*U*) social-democracia *f*.

social event *n* evento *m* social.

social fund *n* *na Grã-Bretanha, fundo de auxílio em casos de extrema necessidade*.

socialism ['səʊʃəlɪzm] *n* (*U*) socialismo *m*.

socialist ['səʊʃəlɪst] <> *adj* socialista. <> *n* socialista *mf*.

socialite ['səʊʃəlaɪt] *n* socialite *m*.

socialize, -ise ['səʊʃəlaɪz] *vi*: **to** ~ **(with sb)** socializar-se (com alguém).

socialized medicine *n* *US* saúde *f* pública.

social life *n* **-1.** [of individual] vida *f* social **- 2.** (*U*) [in general] vida *f* em sociedade.

socially ['səʊʃəlɪ] *adv* **-1.** [towards society] socialmente **- 2.** [outside business] fora do trabalho.

social order *n* ordem *f* social.

social science *n* ciência *f* social; **the** ~**s** as ciências sociais.

social security *n* (*U*) previdência *f* social.

social services *npl* assistência *f* social.

social studies *n* estudos *mpl* sociais.

social work *n* (*U*) trabalho *m* social.

social worker *n* assistente *mf* social.

society [sə'saɪətɪ] (*pl* -**ies**) *n* sociedade *f*.

socioeconomic ['səʊsɪəʊˌiːkə'nɒmɪk] *adj* *POL* socioeconômico(ca).

sociological [ˌsəʊsjə'lɒdʒɪkl] *adj* sociológico(ca).

sociologist [ˌsəʊsɪ'ɒlədʒɪst] *n* sociólogo *m*, -ga *f*.

sociology [ˌsəʊsɪ'ɒlədʒɪ] *n* (*U*) sociologia *f*.

sock [sɒk] *n* meia *f*; **to pull one's** ~**s up** *inf fig* empenhar-se.

socket ['sɒkɪt] *n* **-1.** *ELEC* tomada *f* **- 2.** [de lâmpada] soquete *m* **- 3.** [*ANAT* - of arm, hipbone] concavidade *f*; [- of eye] órbita *f*.

sod [sɒd] *n* **-1.** [of turf] torrão *m* **- 2.** **vinf** [person] sujeito *m*.

soda ['səʊdə] *n* **-1.** [gen] soda *f* **- 2.** *US* [fizzy drink] refrigerante *m*.

soda syphon *n* garrafa d'água com sifão para servir soda.

soda water *n* (*U*) soda *f*, água *f* com gás.

sodden ['sɒdn] *adj* encharcado(da).

sodium ['səʊdɪəm] *n* (*U*) sódio *m*.

sofa ['səʊfə] *n* sofá *m*.

sofabed *n* sofá-cama *m*.

Sofia ['səʊfjə] *n* Sofia.

soft [sɒft] *adj* **-1.** [gen] mole **- 2.** [to touch] macio(cia) **- 3.** [gentle] suave **- 4.** [kind, caring] meigo(ga), bondoso(sa) **- 5.** [not strict] flexível.

softball *n* *SPORT* espécie de beisebol que se joga com uma bola mais macia e maior.

soft-boiled *adj*: ~ **eggs** ovos *mpl* quentes.

soft drink *n* **-1.** [fruit juice] refresco *m* **- 2.** [fizzy drink] refrigerante *m*.

soft drugs *npl* drogas *fpl* leves.

soften ['sɒfn] <> *vt* **-1.** [substance] suavizar **- 2.** [blow, impact, effect] amortecer **- 3.** [attitude] enternecer. <> *vi* **-1.** [substance] amaciar **- 2.** [attitude] amolecer **- 3.** [eyes, voice, expression] suavizar.

➡ **soften up** *vt sep inf* [make amenable] amaciar.

softener ['sɒfnər] *n* [for washing] amaciante *m*.

soft focus *n* (*U*) foco *m* enevoado; **in** ~ em foco enevoado.

soft furnishings *npl UK* complementos *mpl* para decoração.

softhearted [ˌsɒft'hɑːtɪd] *adj* de bom coração.

softly ['sɒftlɪ] *adv* -**1.** [gently, without violence] com delicadeza -**2.** [quietly] suavemente -**3.** [dimly] tenuamente -**4.** [fondly] carinhosamente.

softness ['sɒftnɪs] *n (U)* -**1.** [malleability] maleabilidade *f* -**2.** [to touch] maciez *f* -**3.** [gentleness] suavidade *f* -**4.** [kindness] bondade *f*.

soft-pedal *vi inf*: **to ~ on sthg** maneirar em algo.

soft return *n COMPUT* quebra *f* de linha condicional.

soft sell *n inf* sistema de venda em que não se pressiona o comprador.

soft-spoken *adj* de voz suave.

soft toy *n* bichinho *m* de pelúcia.

software ['sɒftweəʳ] *n (U) COMPUT* software *m*.

software package *n COMPUT* pacote *m* de software.

softwood *n* [timber] madeira *f* branca.

softy ['sɒftɪ] (*pl* -ies) *n inf* -**1.** *pej* [weak person] fracote *mf* -**2.** [sensitive person] manteiga-derretida *mf*.

soggy ['sɒgɪ] (*compar* -ier, *superl* -iest) *adj* empapado(da), encharcado(da).

soil [sɔɪl] <> *n* -**1.** [earth] terra *f*, solo *m* -**2.** *fig* [territory] solo *m*. <> *vt* [dirty] sujar.

soiled [sɔɪld] *adj* sujo(ja).

solace ['sɒləs] *n literary* consolo *m*.

solar ['səʊləʳ] *adj* solar.

solar energy *n* energia *f* solar.

solarium [sə'leərɪəm] (*pl* -riums *OR* -ria [-rɪə]) *n* solário *m*.

solar panel *n* painel *m* solar.

solar plexus [-'pleksəs] *n* plexo *m* solar.

solar power *n* energia *f* solar.

solar system *n* sistema *f* solar.

sold [səʊld] *pt & pp* >> **sell.**

solder ['səʊldəʳ] <> *n (U)* solda *f*. <> *vt* soldar.

soldering iron ['səʊldərɪŋ-] *n* ferro *m* de soldar.

soldier ['səʊldʒəʳ] *n* soldado(da).

➡ **soldier on** *vi UK* agüentar firme.

sold out *adj* esgotado(da).

sole [səʊl] (*pl sense 2 only inv OR* -s) <> *adj* -**1.** [only] único(ca) -**2.** [exclusive] exclusivo(va). <> *n* -**1.** [of foot] sola *f* -**2.** [fish] linguado *m*.

solely ['səʊlɪ] *adv* [entirely] unicamente.

solemn ['sɒləm] *adj* solene.

solemnly ['sɒləmlɪ] *adv* solenemente.

sole trader *n UK COMM* comerciante *mf* individual.

solicit [sə'lɪsɪt] <> *vt fml* [request] solicitar. <> *vi* [prostitute] oferecer seus serviços.

solicitor [sə'lɪsɪtəʳ] *n UK* solicitador *m*, -ra *f*.

solicitous [sə'lɪsɪtəs] *adj* -**1.** [caring] solícito(ta) -**2.** [anxious]: **~ of OR for sthg** desejoso(sa) de algo.

solid ['sɒlɪd] <> *adj* -**1.** [gen] sólido(da) -**2.** [of a single substance] maciço(ça) -**3.** [reliable, respectable] coerente -**4.** [unbroken, continuous] ininterrupto(ta). <> *adv*: **to be packed ~** estar superlotado(da). <> *n* [not liquid or gas] sólido *m*.

➡ **solids** *npl* [food] sólidos *mpl*; **she can't eat ~s** ela não pode comer nada sólido.

solidarity [ˌsɒlɪ'dærətɪ] *n (U)* solidariedade *f*.

solid fuel *n* combustível *m* sólido.

solidify [sə'lɪdɪfaɪ] (*pt & pp* -ied) *vi* solidificar-se.

solidly ['sɒlɪdlɪ] *adv* -**1.** [sturdily] solidamente -**2.** [completely, definitely] inteiramente -**3.** [without interruption] ininterruptamente.

soliloquy [sə'lɪləkwɪ] (*pl* -ies) *n LITER* solilóquio *m*.

solitaire [ˌsɒlɪ'teəʳ] *n* -**1.** [jewel] solitário *m* -**2.** [card game] paciência *f*.

solitary ['sɒlɪtrɪ] *adj* -**1.** [gen] solitário(ria) -**2.** [single] isolado(da).

solitary confinement *n (U)* solitária *f*.

solitude ['sɒlɪtjuːd] *n (U)* solidão *f*.

solo ['səʊləʊ] (*pl* -s) <> *adj* -**1.** *MUS* solo *inv* -**2.** [attempt, flight] único(ca). <> *n MUS* solo *m*. <> *adv* -**1.** *MUS* em solo -**2.** [fly, climb] sozinho(nha).

soloist ['səʊləʊɪst] *n* solista *mf*.

Solomon Islands ['sɒləmən-] *npl*: **the ~** as Ilhas Salomão; **in the ~** nas Ilhas Salomão.

solstice ['sɒlstɪs] *n* solstício *m*.

soluble ['sɒljʊbl] *adj* -**1.** [substance] solúvel -**2.** [problem] solucionável.

solution [sə'luːʃn] *n* -**1.** [to problem, puzzle]: **~ (to sthg)** solução *f* (para algo) -**2.** [liquid] solução *f*.

solve [sɒlv] *vt* resolver.

solvency ['sɒlvənsɪ] *n (U) FIN* solvência *f*.

solvent ['sɒlvənt] <> *adj FIN* solvente. <> *n* [substance] solvente *m*.

solvent abuse [-ə'bjuːs] *n (U)* inalação *f* de cola e solventes.

Somali [sə'mɑːlɪ] <> *adj* somali. <> *n* -**1.** [person] somali *mf* -**2.** [language] somali *m*.

Somalia [sə'mɑːlɪə] *n* Somália; **in ~** na Somália.

sombre *UK*, **somber** *US* ['sɒmbəʳ] *adj* -**1.** [person, mood] lúgubre -**2.** [colour, place] sombrio(bria).

some [sʌm] <> *adj* -**1.** [certain, large amount of] algum (alguma); **~ meat** um pouco de carne; **~ money** um pouco de dinheiro; **I had ~ difficulty getting here** tive algumas dificuldades para chegar aqui. -**2.** [certain, large number of] alguns (algumas); **~ sweets** alguns doces; **~ people** algumas pessoas; **I've known him for ~ years** já o conheço há alguns anos. -**3.** [not all] alguns (algumas); **~ jobs are better paid than others** alguns empregos são mais bem pagos que outros. -**4.** [in imprecise statements] um (uma) ... qualquer; **~ woman phoned** telefonou uma mulher. <> *pron* -**1.** [certain amount] algum *m*, alguma *f*, parte *f*; **can I have ~?** posso ficar com uma parte?; **~ of the money** algum dinheiro, parte do dinheiro. -**2.** [certain number] alguns *mpl*, algumas *fpl*; **can I have ~?** posso ficar com alguns?; **~ (of them) left early** alguns (deles) foram embora cedo. <> *adv* [approximately] aproximadamente; **there were ~ 7,000 people there** havia umas 7.000 pessoas.

somebody ['sʌmbədɪ] *pron* alguém.

someday ['sʌmdeɪ] *adv* algum dia.

somehow ['sʌmhaʊ], **someway** *US* ['sʌmweɪ] *adv* -**1.** [by some action] de alguma maneira -**2.** [for some reason] por alguma razão; **~ I don't think he'll come** tenho a impressão de que ele não virá.

someone ['sʌmwʌn] *pron* = **somebody.**

someplace adv US = somewhere.

somersault ['sʌmǝsɔːlt] <> n salto m mortal. <> vi dar um salto mortal.

Somerset n Somerset.

something ['sʌmθɪŋ] <> pron -1. algo, alguma coisa; or ~ inf ou (qualquer) coisa parecida -2. phr: it's really ~! é demais! <> adv [in approximations]: ~ like uns(umas), qualquer coisa como.

sometime ['sʌmtaɪm] adv: ~ in June em junho.

sometimes ['sʌmtaɪmz] adv às OR por vezes.

someway adv US = somehow.

somewhat ['sʌmwɒt] adv um tanto.

somewhere UK ['sʌmweǝ'], **someplace** US ['sʌmpleɪs] adv -1. [unknown place] em algum lugar, em alguma parte -2. [specific place] a alguma parte -3. [in approximations]: ~ around OR between aproximadamente.

son [sʌn] n filho m.

sonar ['sǝʊnɑː'] n (U) sonar m.

sonata [sǝ'nɑːtǝ] n sonata f.

song [sɒŋ] n -1. [piece of music] música f; for a ~ [cheaply] por uma bagatela; to make a ~ and dance about sthg inf fazer uma tempestade num copo d'água em relação a algo -2. (U) [act of singing]: they burst into ~ desataram a cantar -3. [of bird] canto m.

songbook ['sɒŋbʊk] n cancioneiro m.

sonic ['sɒnɪk] adj sônico(ca).

sonic boom n ruído m sônico.

son-in-law (pl sons-in-law OR son-in-laws) n genro m.

sonnet ['sɒnɪt] n soneto m.

sonny ['sʌnɪ] n inf filhinho m.

soon [suːn] adv -1. [in a short time] logo -2. [early] cedo; how ~ can you finish it? para quando você consegue terminar?; as ~ as assim que; as ~ as possible o quanto antes -3. phr: I'd just as ~ ... eu preferiria (que) ...

sooner ['suːnǝ'] adv -1. [earlier] mais cedo; no ~ did he arrive than ... ele tinha acabado de chegar quando ...; ~ or later mais cedo ou mais tarde; the ~ the better quanto mais cedo, melhor -2. [expressing preference]: I'd ~ ... preferiria ...

soot [sʊt] n (U) fuligem f.

soothe [suːð] vt -1. [relieve] aliviar -2. [calm] acalmar.

soothing ['suːðɪŋ] adj -1. [pain-relieving] analgésico(ca), calmante -2. [calming] tranqüilizante.

sooty ['sʊtɪ] (compar -ier, superl -iest) adj fuliginoso(-sa).

sop n pej compensação f de pouco valor; ~ to sb/sthg compensação de pouco valor para alguém/algo.

SOP (abbr of standard operating procedure) n procedimento m habitual.

sophisticated [sǝ'fɪstɪkeɪtɪd] adj -1. [stylish] sofisticado(da) -2. [intelligent] inteligente -3. [complicated] complicado(da).

sophistication [sǝ,fɪstɪ'keɪʃn] n (U) -1. [stylishness] sofisticação f -2. [intelligence] inteligência f -3. [complexity] complexidade f.

sophomore ['sɒfǝmɔː'] n US estudante do segundo ano de faculdade.

soporific [,sɒpǝ'rɪfɪk] adj soporífero(ra).

sopping ['sɒpɪŋ] adj: ~ (wet) encharcado(da).

soppy ['sɒpɪ] (compar -ier, superl -iest) adj inf pej sentimentalóide.

soprano [sǝ'prɑːnǝʊ] (pl -s) n -1. [person] soprano mf -2. [voice] soprano f.

sorbet ['sɔːbeɪ] n sorbet m.

sorcerer ['sɔːsǝrǝ'] n feiticeiro m.

sorceress n feiticeira f.

sordid ['sɔːdɪd] adj sórdido(da).

sore [sɔː'] <> adj -1. [painful] dolorido(da); a ~ throat uma dor de garganta -2. US inf [angry] zangado(da) -3. literary [dire, great] imenso(sa). <> n MED inflamação f.

sorely ['sɔːlɪ] adv literary imensamente.

sorority [sǝ'rɒrǝtɪ] (pl -ies) n US irmandade feminina numa universidade.

sorrel ['sɒrǝl] n (U) azeda-miúda f.

sorrow ['sɒrǝʊ] n -1. (U) [feeling of sadness] mágoa f -2. [cause of sadness] desgosto m.

sorrowful ['sɒrǝfʊl] adj magoado(da), triste.

sorry ['sɒrɪ] (compar -ier, superl -iest) <> adj -1. [expressing apology]: I'm ~ desculpe; to be ~ about sthg lamentar algo; to be ~ for sthg estar arrependido(da) por algo; to be ~ to do sthg desculpar-se por fazer algo -2. [expressing disappointment]: to be ~ (that) lamentar que; to be ~ about sthg ficar sentido(da) por algo -3. [expressing regret]: I'm ~ to have to say that ... lamento ter que dizer que ...; to be ~ to do sthg estar triste por fazer algo -4. [expressing sympathy]: to be OR feel ~ for sb estar com/sentir pena de alguém; to be OR feel ~ for o.s. estar com/sentir pena de si mesmo -5. [expressing polite disagreement]: I'm ~, but I think that ... me desculpa, mas eu acho que ... -6. [poor, pitiable] lamentável. <> excl -1. [expressing apology] desculpe! -2. [asking for repetition] como! -3. [to correct o.s.]: a boy, ~, a man um garoto, quer dizer, um homem.

sort [sɔːt] <> n -1. [gen] tipo m; a ~ of um tipo de, uma espécie de -2. [act of sorting out] escolha f. <> vt [classify, separate] classificar.

  ➡ **sorts** npl: a lawyer of ~s um advogado medíocre, um advogadozinho; to be out of ~s não se sentir bem.

  ➡ **sort of** adv [rather] mais ou menos.

  ➡ **sort out** vt sep -1. [into groups] classificar -2. [tidy up] pôr em ordem -3. [solve] resolver -4. [work out] concluir.

sortie ['sɔːtiː] n [MIL - by troops] surtida f; [- by aircraft] ação f de reconhecimento.

sorting office ['sɔːtɪŋ-] n centro f de triagem.

sort-out n UK inf: to have a ~ dar uma geral.

SOS (abbr of save our souls) n SOS f.

so-so inf adj, adv mais ou menos.

soufflé ['suːfleɪ] n suflê m.

sought [sɔːt] pt & pp ▷ seek.

sought-after adj solicitado(da).

soul [sǝʊl] n -1. [gen] alma f -2. [emotional depth] sentimento m -3. [perfect example] exemplo m perfeito -4. (U) [music] (música f) soul m.

soul-destroying [-dɪ,strɔɪɪŋ] adj [boring] massante; [discouraging] desmoralizador(ra).

soul food n US comida tradicional dos negros do sul dos Estados Unidos.

soulful ['səʊlfʊl] adj cheio (cheia) de sentimentos.

soulless ['səʊllɪs] adj desalmado(da).

soul mate n alma f gêmea.

soul music n (U) música f soul.

soul-searching n (U) exame m de consciência.

sound [saʊnd] <> adj -1. [healthy] sadio(dia) -2. [sturdy] sólido(da) -3. [reliable] confiável, seguro(ra) -4. [thorough] completo(ta). <> adv: **to be ~ asleep** estar num sono profundo. <> n -1. [particular noise] barulho m -2. (U) [in general] som m -3. (U) [volume] volume m -4. [impression, idea] tom m. <> vt [alarm, bell, horn] tocar. <> vi -1. [make a noise] fazer barulho; **to ~ like sthg** soar como algo -2. [seem] parecer; **to ~ like sthg** parecer algo.
➡ **sound out** vt sep: **to ~ sb out (on** OR **aboutsthg)** sondar alguém(sobre algo).

sound barrier n barreira f do som.

sound bite n declaração f mordaz (feita por políticos no rádio ou na tevê).

sound card n COMPUT placa f de som.

sound effects npl efeitos mpl sonoros.

sounding board n -1. caixa f de ressonância -2. fig [person]: **he needs a ~, rather than thinking alone** ele precisa de alguém com quem possa trocar idéias, em vez de pensar sozinho.

sounding ['saʊndɪŋ] n -1. NAUT [measurement] prumada f -2. fig [investigation] sondagem f.

soundly ['saʊndlɪ] adv -1. [thoroughly] completamente -2. [deeply] profundamente.

soundness ['saʊndnɪs] n (U) [reliability] solidez f.

soundproof ['saʊndpruːf] adj à prova de som.

soundtrack ['saʊndtræk] n trilha f sonora.

sound wave n onda f sonora.

soup [suːp] n sopa f, caldo m.
➡ **soup up** vt sep inf [car] envenenar.

soup kitchen n bandejão m público.

soup plate n prato m fundo.

soup spoon n colher f de sopa.

sour [saʊəʳ] <> adj -1. [acidic] ácido(da) -2. [milk] azedo(da); **to go** OR **turn sour** [milk] azedar; fig [be spoiled] degringolar -3. [ill-tempered] mal-humorado(da). <> vt & vi [person, relationship] azedar.

source [sɔːs] n -1. [gen] fonte f -2. [cause] origem f -3. [of river] nascente f.

soured cream n (U) nata f azeda.

sour grapes n (U) inf inveja f pura.

sourness ['saʊənɪs] n (U) -1. [gen] azedume m -2. [acidity] acidez f.

south [saʊθ] <> adj sul. <> adv para o sul; **~ of** ao sul de. <> n -1. [direction] sul m -2. [region]: **the ~ o** sul.

South Africa n África f do Sul; **in ~** na África do Sul; **the Republic of ~** a República da África do Sul.

South African <> adj sul-africano(na). <> n [person] sul-africano m, -na f.

South America n América f do Sul; **in ~** na América do Sul.

South American <> adj sul-americano(na). <> n [person] sul-americano m, -na f.

southbound ['saʊθbaʊnd] adj para o sul.

South Carolina n Carolina f do Sul.

South Dakota n Dakota f do Sul.

south-east <> adj sudeste. <> adv para o sudeste; **~ of** a sudeste de. <> n -1. [direction] sudeste m -2. [region]: **the ~ o** sudeste.

South-East Asia n Sudeste m Asiático; **in ~** no Sudeste Asiático.

south-easterly adj -1. [in the south-east] sudeste -2. [towards the south-east] para o sudeste -3. [from the south-east] do sudeste.

south-eastern adj do sudeste.

southerly ['sʌðəlɪ] adj -1. [in the south] ao sul -2. [towards the south] para o sul -3. [from the south] do sul.

southern ['sʌðən] adj sulista.

Southern Africa n África Meridional; **in ~** na África Meridional.

Southerner ['sʌðənəʳ] n sulista mf.

South Korea n Coréia f do Sul; **in ~** na Coréia do Sul.

South Korean <> adj sul-coreano(na). <> n sul-coreano m, -na f.

South Pole n: **the ~ o** Pólo Sul.

South Vietnam n Vietnã m do Sul; **in ~** no Vietnã do Sul.

South Vietnamese <> adj sul-vietnamita. <> n sul-vietnamita mf.

southward ['saʊθwəd] <> adj sul. <> adv = southwards.

southwards ['saʊθwədz] adv para o sul.

south-west <> adj sudoeste. <> adv para o sudoeste; **~ of** a sudoeste de. <> n -1. [direction] sudoeste m -2. [region]: **the ~ o** sudoeste.

south-westerly adj -1. [in the south-west] ao sudoeste -2. [towards the south-west] para o sudoeste -3. [from the south-west] do sudoeste.

south-western adj do sudoeste.

South Yemen n Iêmen m do Sul; **in ~** no Iêmen do Sul.

South Yorkshire n South Yorkshire.

souvenir [,suːvəˈnɪəʳ] n suvenir m, lembrança f.

sou'wester [saʊˈwestəʳ] n [hat] sueste m.

sovereign ['sɒvrɪn] <> adj -1. [state, territory] soberano(na) -2. [excellent] magnífico(ca). <> n -1. [ruler] soberano m, -na f -2. [coin] soberano m.

sovereignty ['sɒvrɪntɪ] n [supreme power] soberania f.

soviet n soviético(ca).
➡ **Soviet** <> adj soviético m, -ca f. <> n [person] soviético m, -ca f.

Soviet Union n: **the (former) ~** a (antiga) União Soviética; **in the ~** na União Soviética.

sow¹ [saʊ] (pt -ed, pp sown OR -ed) vt semear.

sow² [saʊ] n [pig] porca f.

sown [saʊn] pp ⊳ sow.

sox npl US ⊳ bobby sox.

soya ['sɔɪə] n (U) soja f.

soy(a) bean ['sɔɪ(ə)-] n grão m de soja.

soy sauce [sɔɪ-] n (U) molho m de soja.

sozzled ['sɒzld] adj UK inf pinguço(ça).

spa [spɑː] n -1. [mineral spring] termas fpl -2. [for health care] spa m.

space [speɪs] <> n -1. [gen] espaço m; **to stare into**

~ olhar para o nada -**2.** [gap] lugar *m*, espaço *m* -**3.** [period of time] intervalo *m* -**4.** [seat, place] lugar *m*. ◇ *comp* espacial. ◇ *vt* espaçar.

◆ **space out** *vt sep* [arrange] espaçar.

space age *n*: **the** ~ a era espacial.

◆ **space-age** *adj inf* da era espacial.

space bar *n* barra *f* de espaço.

space capsule *n* cápsula *f* espacial.

spacecraft ['speɪskrɑːft] (*pl inv*) *n* espaçonave *f*.

spaceman ['speɪsmæn] (*pl* -**men** [-men]) *n inf* [astronaut] astronauta *m*.

space probe *n* sonda *f* espacial.

spaceship ['speɪsʃɪp] *n* nave *f* espacial, astronave *f*.

space shuttle *n* ônibus *m inv* espacial.

space station *n* estação *f* espacial.

spacesuit ['speɪsuːt] *n* roupa *f* espacial.

spacewoman ['speɪs,wʊmən] (*pl* -**women** [-,wɪmɪn]) *n inf* [astronaut] astronauta *f*.

spacing ['speɪsɪŋ] *n (U)* TYPO espaçamento *m*.

spacious ['speɪʃəs] *adj* espaçoso(sa).

spade [speɪd] *n* -**1.** [tool] pá *f* -**2.** [playing card] espada *f*.

◆ **spades** *npl* espadas *fpl*; **the six of** ~ **s** o seis de espadas.

spadework ['speɪdwɜːk] *n (U) inf* trabalho *m* preliminar.

spaghetti [spə'getɪ] *n (U)* espaguete *m*.

Spain [speɪn] *n* Espanha *f*; **in** ~ na Espanha.

spam [spæm] (*pt & pp* -**med**, *cont* -**ming**) COMPUT ◇ *n* spam *m*. ◇ *vt* enviar spam para.

span [spæn] (*pt & pp* -**ned**, *cont* -**ning**) ◇ *pt* ▷ **spin**. ◇ *n* -**1.** [in time] período *m*; **concentration** ~ tempo *m* de concentração -**2.** [range] gama *f* -**3.** [of hand] palmo *m* -**4.** [of arms] braçada *f* -**5.** [of wings] envergadura *f* -**6.** [of bridge, arch] extensão *f*. ◇ *vt* -**1.** [encompass] cobrir um período de -**2.** [cross] atravessar, cruzar.

spandex *n* spandex *m*.

spangled ['spæŋɡld] *adj literary*: ~ **(with sthg)** adornado(da) (de algo).

Spaniard ['spænjəd] *n* espanhol *m*, -la *f*.

spaniel ['spænjəl] *n* cocker *m* spaniel.

Spanish ['spænɪʃ] ◇ *adj* espanhol(la). ◇ *n* [language] espanhol *m*. ◇ *npl*: **the** ~ os espanhóis.

Spanish America *n* América Espanhola.

Spanish American ◇ *adj* -**1.** [in US] hispano(-na) -**2.** [in Latin America] hispano-americano(na). ◇ *n* -**1.** [in US] hispano *m*, -na *f* -**2.** [in Latin America] hispano-americano *m*, -na *f*.

spank [spæŋk] ◇ *n* palmada *f*. ◇ *vt* dar palmadas em.

spanner ['spænə'] *n* chave *f* inglesa.

spar [spɑː'] (*pt & pp* -**red**, *cont* -**ring**) *vi* -**1.** BOXING treinar boxe -**2.** [verbally]: **to** ~ **(with sb)** discutir amigavelmente (com alguém).

spare [speə'] ◇ *adj* -**1.** [surplus] sobressalente, de sobra; **have you got a** ~ **pencil?** você tem um lápis sobrando? -**2.** [free] livre. ◇ *n* [surplus object] sobressalente *mf*. ◇ *vt* -**1.** [put aside, make available] dispor de; **to have sthg to** ~ [extra] ter algo de sobra -**2.** [not harm] preservar -**3.** [economize]

poupar; **to** ~ **no expense** não poupar despesas -**4.** [save, protect from]: **to** ~ **sb sthg** poupar alguém de algo.

spare part *n* peça *f* sobressalente.

spare tyre *n* estepe *m*.

spare wheel *n* roda *f* sobressalente.

spare room *n* quarto *m* de hóspedes.

spare time *n (U)* tempo *m* livre.

sparing ['speərɪŋ] *adj*: **to be** ~ **with** OR **of sthg** ser econômico(ca) em algo.

sparingly ['speərɪŋlɪ] *adv* com moderação.

spark [spɑːk] ◇ *n* -**1.** [from fire] fagulha *f* -**2.** [from electricity] faísca *f* -**3.** *fig* [of interest, humour *etc*] lampejo *m*. ◇ *vt* [trigger] provocar.

sparking plug ['spɑːkɪŋ-] *n UK* = spark plug.

sparkle ['spɑːkl] ◇ *n* -**1.** [gen] brilho *m* -**2.** [of person, conversation, wit] estilo *m*, brilho *m*. ◇ *vi* -**1.** [gen] brilhar -**2.** [person, conversation, wit] ser brilhante, brilhar.

sparkler ['spɑːklə'] *n* [firework] estrelinha *f*.

sparkling *adj* -**1.** [mineral water] com gás, gaseificado(da) -**2.** [wit] brilhante.

sparkling wine ['spɑːklɪŋ-] *n* vinho *m* espumante.

spark plug *n* vela *f* (*de ignição*).

sparrow ['spærəʊ] *n* pardal *m*.

sparse [spɑːs] *adj* esparso(sa).

spartan ['spɑːtn] *adj* espartano(na).

spasm ['spæzm] *n* -**1.** MED [muscular contraction] espasmo *m* -**2.** [fit] acesso *m*.

spasmodic [spæz'mɒdɪk] *adj* [intermittent] espasmódico(ca).

spastic ['spæstɪk] MED ◇ *adj* espástico(ca). ◇ *n* espasmofílico *m*, -ca *f*.

spat [spæt] *pt & pp* ▷ **spit**.

spate [speɪt] *n* série *f*, sucessão *f*.

spatial ['speɪʃl] *adj* espacial; ~ **awareness** noção *f* de espaço.

spatter ['spætə'] *vt & vi* respingar.

spatula ['spætjʊlə] *n* CULIN, MED espátula *f*.

spawn [spɔːn] ◇ *n (U)* [of frogs, fish] ovas *fpl*. ◇ *vt fig* [produce] gerar. ◇ *vi* ZOOL desovar.

spay [speɪ] *vt* castrar (*fêmea*).

speak [spiːk] (*pt* spoke, *pp* spoken) ◇ *vt* -**1.** [say] dizer -**2.** [express opinion]: **to** ~ **ill of sb** falar mal de alguém -**3.** [language] falar. ◇ *vi* -**1.** [say words] falar; **to** ~ **to** OR **with sb** falar com alguém; **to** ~ **sb about sthg** falar com alguém sobre algo; **to** ~ **about sb/sthg** falar sobre alguém/algo; **to** ~ **well** OR **highly of sb** falar bem de alguém; **nobody/ nothing to** ~ **of** ninguém/nada em especial -**2.** [make a speech] discursar; **to** ~ **to sb** discursar para alguém; **to** ~ **on sthg** falar OR discursar sobre algo -**3.** [in giving an opinion]: **generally** ~**ing** falando em termos gerais; **personally** ~**ing** pessoalmente falando; ~**ing as** [in the position of] falando como; ~**ing of** [on the subject of] falando sobre.

◆ **so to speak** *adv* por assim dizer.

◆ **speak for** *vt fus* [represent] falar em nome de; **it** ~**s for itself** isso fala por si mesmo; ~ **for yourself!** fala isso por ti!

◆ **speak out** *vi* falar publicamente; **to** ~ **out**

against sb/sthg fazer declarações contra alguém/algo.
◆ **speak up** vi **-1.** [say something] falar claro; **to ~ up for sb/sthg** sair em defesa de alguém/algo **-2.** [speak louder] falar mais alto.
speaker ['spiːkə^r] n **-1.** [person talking, of a language] falante mf **-2.** [in lecture] orador m, -ra f, conferencista mf **-3.** [loudspeaker] alto-falante m **-4.** [in stereo system] caixa f de som.
◆ **Speaker** n UK [in House of Commons] Presidente mf da Câmara dos Comuns.
speaking ['spiːkɪŋ] n discurso m.
speaking clock n UK serviço m de hora certa.
spear [spɪə^r] <> n [weapon] lança f. <> vt lancear.
spearhead ['spɪəhed] <> n ponta-de-lança f. <> vt encabeçar.
spec [spek] n UK inf: **to buy sthg on ~** comprar algo sem garantia; **to go on ~** ir sem ter feito reserva.
special ['speʃl] <> adj especial. <> n **-1.** [on menu]: **today's ~** prato m do dia **-2.** [onTV] especial m **-3.** [train] trem m especial.
special agent n agente mf especial.
special constable n UK policial mf voluntário, -ria.
special correspondent n correspondente mf especial.
special delivery n (U) [service] entrega f especial.
special effects npl efeitos mpl especiais.
specialist ['speʃəlɪst] <> adj especializado(da). <> n [expert] especialista mf.
speciality [,speʃɪ'ælətɪ] (pl -ies), **specialty** US ['speʃltɪ] (pl -ies) n especialidade f.
specialize, -ise ['speʃəlaɪz] vi especializar-se; **to ~ in sthg** especializar-se em algo.
specially ['speʃəlɪ] adv **-1.** [on purpose, specifically] especialmente **-2.** [really] realmente; **do you want to go? - not ~** quer ir? - na verdade não.
special offer n oferta f especial, promoção f.
special school n escola f especial.
specialty n US = speciality.
species ['spiːʃiːz] (pl inv) n espécie f.
specific [spə'sɪfɪk] adj [particular, precise] específico(ca); **~ to sb/sthg** específico(ca) de alguém/algo.
◆ **specifics** npl [details] detalhes mpl específicos.
specifically [spə'sɪfɪklɪ] adv especificamente.
specification [,spesɪfɪ'keɪʃn] n [plan] especificação f.
◆ **specifications** npl TECH especificações fpl técnicas.
specify ['spesɪfaɪ] (pt & pp -ied) vt especificar.
specimen ['spesɪmən] n **-1.** [example] espécime m, exemplar m **-2.** [sample] amostra f.
specimen copy n cópia f de amostra.
specimen signature n assinatura f reconhecida em cartório.
speck [spek] n **-1.** [small stain] mancha f pequena **-2.** [small particle] partícula f.
speckled ['spekld] adj manchado(da); **~ with sthg** pintado(da) de algo.
specs [speks] npl inf [glasses] óculos m inv.

spectacle ['spektəkl] n **-1.** [sight] visão f **-2.** [event] espetáculo m.
◆ **spectacles** npl UK [glasses] óculos m inv.
spectacular [spek'tækjʊlə^r] <> adj espetacular. <> n espetáculo m.
spectate [spek'teɪt] vi assistir como espectador(-ra).
spectator [spek'teɪtə^r] n espectador m, -ra f.
spectator sport n esporte m de multidões.
spectre UK, **specter** US ['spektə^r] n **-1.** fml [ghost] espectro m **-2.** fig [frightening prospect]: **the ~ of famine** o fantasma da fome.
spectrum ['spektrəm] (pl -tra [-trə]) n **-1.** PHYS espectro m **-2.** fig [range] gama f.
speculate ['spekjʊleɪt] <> vt: **to ~ that** especular que. <> vi especular.
speculation [,spekjʊ'leɪʃn] n especulação f.
speculative ['spekjʊlətɪv] adj especulativo(va).
speculator ['spekjʊleɪtə^r] n FIN especulador m, -ra f.
sped [sped] pt & pp ⊳ speed.
speech [spiːtʃ] n **-1.** [gen] fala f **-2.** [formal talk]: **to give** OR **make a ~ (on sthg)** dar OR fazer um discurso (sobre algo); **to give** OR **make a ~ (to sb)** dar OR fazer um discurso (para alguém) **-3.** [manner of speaking] maneira f de falar **-4.** (U) [dialect] dialeto m, maneira f de falar **-5.** GRAMM discurso m.
speech day n UK dia de encerramento do ano letivo quando são proferidos discursos e os estudantes recebem prêmios.
speech impediment n defeito m na fala.
speechless ['spiːtʃlɪs] adj: **to be ~ (with sthg)** ficar emudecido(da) (de algo).
speech processing n COMPUT processamento m da fala.
speech therapist n fonoaudiólogo m.
speech therapy n (U) fonoaudiologia f.
speed [spiːd] (pt & pp -ed OR sped) <> n **-1.** [rate, pace] velocidade f; **at ~** a grande velocidade **-2.** (U) [rapid rate] rapidez f **-3.** [gear] marcha f. <> vi **-1.** [move fast]: **to ~ (along/away/by)** ir/acelerar/passar a toda velocidade **-2.** AUT [go too fast] exceder a velocidade.
◆ **speed up** <> vt sep acelerar. <> vi acelerar.
speedboat ['spiːdbəʊt] n lancha f.
speed-dial button n [on phone, fax] tecla m de discagem rápida.
speeding ['spiːdɪŋ] n (U) excesso m de velocidade.
speed limit n limite m de velocidade.
speedo (pl -s) n UK inf velocímetro m.
speedometer [spɪ'dɒmɪtə^r] n velocímetro m.
speed trap n **-1.** [radar] radar m **-2.** [camera] pardal m.
speedway ['spiːdweɪ] n **-1.** SPORT corrida f de motos **-2.** US [road] pista f de corrida.
speedy ['spiːdɪ] (compar -ier, superl -iest) adj rápido(da).
speleology [,spiːlɪ'ɒlədʒɪ] n (U) fml espeleologia f.
spell [spel] (UK pt & pp spelt OR -ed, US pt & pp -ed) <> n **-1.** [period of time] período m **-2.** [enchantment] feitiço m, encanto m **-3.** [magic words] palavras fpl mágicas. <> vt **-1.** [write] soletrar **-2.** fig [signify] significar. <> vi escrever corretamente.

➡ **spell out** *vt sep* -**1.** [read aloud] soletrar -**2.** [explain]: **to ~ sthg out (for** *OR* **to sb)** explicar algo em detalhes (para alguém).

spellbound ['spelbaʊnd] *adj* encantado(da).

spellcheck ['speltʃek] *vt COMPUT* passar o corretor ortográfico em.

spellchecker ['speltʃekəᵣ] *n COMPUT* corretor *m* ortográfico.

spelling ['spelɪŋ] *n* ortografia *f*.

spelt [spelt] *pt & pp UK* ▭ **spell**.

spend [spend] (*pt & pp* **spent**) *vt* -**1.** [pay out] gastar; **to ~ sthg on sb/sthg** gastar algo em alguém/algo -**2.** [time, life] passar -**3.** [energy] gastar.

spender ['spendəᵣ] *n* [person] esbanjador *m*, -ra *f*, gastador *m*, -ra *f*.

spending ['spendɪŋ] *n* (*U*) gastos *mpl*.

spending money *n* (*U*) dinheiro *m* para pequenos gastos pessoais.

spending power *n* (*U*) poder *m* aquisitivo.

spendthrift ['spendθrɪft] *n* perdulário *m*, -ria *f*.

spent [spent] ◇ *pt & pp* ▭ **spend**. ◇ *adj* [consumed, burned out - matches, ammunition] usado(da); [- force, patience, energy] esgotado(da).

sperm [spɜːm] (*pl inv OR* -**s**) *n* esperma *m*.

spermicidal cream [ˌspɜːmɪˈsaɪdl-] *n* creme *m* espermicida.

sperm whale *n* baleia *f* cachalote.

spew [spjuː] ◇ *vt* [cause to flow, spread] expelir, cuspir. ◇ *vi* [flow, spread]: **to ~ (out) from sthg** lançar-se (para fora) de algo; **flames ~ed out of the volcano** o vulcão cuspia chamas.

sphere [sfɪəᵣ] *n* esfera *f*.

spherical ['sferɪkl] *adj* esférico(ca).

sphincter ['sfɪŋktəᵣ] *n* esfíncter *m*.

sphinx [sfɪŋks] (*pl* -**es**) *n* esfinge *f*.

spice [spaɪs] ◇ *n* tempero *m*. ◇ *vt* -**1.** *CULIN*: **to ~ sthg (with sthg)** temperar algo (com algo) -**2.** *fig* [add excitement to]: **to ~ sthg (up)** dar sabor a algo.

spick-and-span [ˌspɪkənˈspæn] *adj* asseado(da).

spicy ['spaɪsɪ] (*compar* -**ier**, *superl* -**iest**) *adj* picante.

spider ['spaɪdəᵣ] *n* aranha *f*.

spider's web, spiderweb *US* ['spaɪdəweb] *n* teia *f* de aranha.

spidery ['spaɪdərɪ] *adj* aranhoso(sa).

spiel [ʃpiːl] *n* lábia *f*.

spike [spaɪk] ◇ *n* -**1.** [on railings] prego *m* -**2.** [on shoe] cravo *m* -**3.** [on plant] espigão *m* -**4.** [of hair] corte *m* escovinha. ◇ *vt* reforçar com mais álcool.

➡ **spikes** *npl UK* tênis *m inv* com travas.

spiky ['spaɪkɪ] (*compar* -**ier**, *superl* -**iest**) *adj* -**1.** [branch] pontudo(da) -**2.** [plant] espinhento(ta) -**3.** [hair] eriçado(da).

spill [spɪl] (*UK pt & pp* spilt *OR* -**ed**, *US pt & pp* -**ed**) ◇ *vt* derramar. ◇ *vi* -**1.** [liquid] derramar; **the wine ~ed all over the carpet** o vinho esparramou por todo o carpete -**2.** [salt, sugar, etc] esparramar -**3.** [crowd]: **the fans ~ed out of stadium** os torcedores saíram em massa do estádio; **the crowd ~ed into the main square** a multidão espalhou-se pela praça principal.

spillage ['spɪlɪdʒ] *n* derramamento *m*.

spilt [spɪlt] *pt & pp UK* ▭ **spill**.

spin [spɪn] (*pt* span *OR* spun, *pp* spun, *cont* -**ning**) ◇ *n* -**1.** [turn] giro *m*, volta *f* -**2.** *AERON* parafuso *m* -**3.** *inf* [in car] volta *f* -**4.** *SPORT* [on ball] efeito *m*. ◇ *vt* -**1.** [cause to rotate] rodar, girar -**2.** [in spin-dryer] centrifugar -**3.** [thread, cloth, wool] fiar -**4.** *SPORT* [ball] fazer girar. ◇ *vi* -**1.** [rotate] girar, dar voltas -**2.** [feel dizzy]: **to be spinning** estar rodando -**3.** [spinner] fiar -**4.** [in spin-dryer] centrifugar.

➡ **spin out** *vt sep* -**1.** [story, explanation] prorrogar -**2.** [food, money] esticar.

spina bifida [ˌspaɪnəˈbɪfɪdə] *n* (*U*) espinha *f* bífida.

spinach ['spɪnɪdʒ] *n* (*U*) espinafre *m*.

spinal column ['spaɪnl-] *n* coluna *f* vertebral.

spinal cord *n* medula *f* espinhal.

spindle ['spɪndl] *n* -**1.** [machine rod] eixo *m* -**2.** [for spinning] fuso *m*.

spindly ['spɪndlɪ] (*compar* -**ier**, *superl* -**iest**) *adj* longo e fino, longa e fina.

spin doctor *n pej* pessoa encarregada das relações com a imprensa, geralmente para um político ou partido, e que manipula as informações a serem dadas.

spin-dry *vt UK* centrifugar.

spin-dryer *n UK* centrifugadora *f* (de roupas).

spine [spaɪn] *n* -**1.** *ANAT* espinha *f* dorsal -**2.** [of book] lombada *f* -**3.** [spike, prickle] espinho *m*.

spine-chilling *adj* de arrepiar, horripilante.

spineless ['spaɪnlɪs] *adj* [feeble] pobre de espírito.

spinner ['spɪnəᵣ] *n* [of thread] fiandeiro *m*, -ra *f*.

spinning ['spɪnɪŋ] *n* (*U*) fiação *f*.

spinning top *n* pião *m*.

spin-off *n* [by-product] subproduto *m*.

spinster ['spɪnstəᵣ] *n* solteirona *f*.

spiral ['spaɪərəl] (*UK pt & pp* -**led**, *cont* -**ling**, *US pt & pp* -**ed**, *cont* -**ing**) ◇ *adj* espiral. ◇ *n* -**1.** [curve] espiral *f* -**3.** [decrease] queda *f*. ◇ *vi* -**1.** [move in spiral curve] mover-se em espiral -**2.** [increase rapidly] subir vertiginosamente -**3.** [decrease rapidly]: **to ~ downwards** despencar.

spiral staircase *n* escada *f* caracol.

spire [spaɪəᵣ] *n* pináculo *m*.

spirit ['spɪrɪt] ◇ *n* espírito *m*; **to enter into the ~ of sthg** entrar no espírito de algo. ◇ *vt* : **to ~ sb into/out of sthg** colocar/tirar alguém às escondidas de algo.

➡ **spirits** *npl* -**1.** [mood] astral *m*; **to be in high/low ~ s** estar de alto/baixo astral -**2.** [alcohol] bebidas *fpl* destiladas.

spirited ['spɪrɪtɪd] *adj* animado(da).

spirit level *n* nível *m* de pedreiro *OR* bolha.

spiritual ['spɪrɪtʃʊəl] *adj* espiritual.

spiritualism ['spɪrɪtʃʊəlɪzml] *n* (*U*) espiritualismo *m*.

spiritualist ['spɪrɪtʃʊəlɪst] *n* espiritualista *mf*.

spit [spɪt] (*UK pt & pp* spat, *cont* -**ting**, *US pt & pp* spit, *cont* -**ting**) ◇ *n* -**1.** (*U*) [saliva] cuspe *m* -**2.** [skewer] espeto *m*. ◇ *vi* [from mouth] cuspir. ◇ *v impers UK* [rain lightly] chuviscar.

➡ **spit out** *vt sep* cuspir; **come on, ~ it out!** vamos, desembucha!

spite [spaɪt] ◇ *n* (*U*) rancor *m*; **to do sthg out of** *OR* **from ~** fazer algo por maldade. ◇ *vt* magoar.

➡ **in spite of** *prep* apesar de; **to do sthg in ~ of**

o.s. [unintentionally] fazer algo a contragosto.
spiteful ['spaɪtfʊl] *adj* maldoso(sa), mal-intencionado(da).
spitting image ['spɪtɪŋ-] *n*: **to be the ~ of sb** ser o retrato cuspido e escarrado de alguém.
spittle ['spɪtl] *n (U)* cuspe *m*.
splash [splæʃ] ◇ *n* -**1.** [sound] chape *m*, pancada *f* na água -**2.** [small quantity] respingo *m*; **a ~ of lemonade** uma esguichada de limonada -**3.** [patch] mancha *f*. ◇ *vt* -**1.** [subj: person] respingar -**2.** [subj: water] molhar -**3.** [apply haphazardly] espalhar. ◇ *vi* -**1.** [person]: **to ~ about** OR **around** patinhar -**2.** [water, liquid]: **to ~ on/against sthg** espirrar em/contra algo.
➡ **splash down** *vi* amerissar.
➡ **splash out** *inf* ◇ *vt sep*: **to ~ sthg out on sthg** gastar algo em algo. ◇ *vi*: **to ~ out (on sthg)** gastar um dinheirão (em algo).
splashdown ['splæʃdaʊn] *n* amerissagem *f*.
splash guard *n US* pára-lama *m*.
splay [spleɪ] ◇ *vt* esticar. ◇ *vi*: **to ~ (out)** esticar.
spleen [spli:n] *n* -**1.** ANAT baço *m* -**2.** *(U) fig* [anger] cólera *f*.
splendid ['splendɪd] *adj* -**1.** [very good] esplêndido(da) -**2.** [magnificent, beautiful] esplendoroso(sa).
splendidly ['splendɪdlɪ] *adv* -**1.** [perform, write, behave] maravilhosamente -**2.** [design, dress, entertain] magnificamente, esplendidamente.
splendour *UK*, **splendor** *US* ['splendə'] *n* -**1.** *(U)* [beauty, magnificence] esplendor *m* -**2.** [magnificent feature] maravilha *f*.
splice [splaɪs] *vt* [join - rope] juntar, unir; [- film, tape] montar.
splint [splɪnt] *n* tala *f*.
splinter ['splɪntə'] ◇ *n* lasca *f*. ◇ *vt*: **to be ~ed** estar lascado(da). ◇ *vi* [glass, bone, wood] lascar.
splinter group *n* grupo *m* dissidente.
split [splɪt] *(pt & pp* **split**, *cont* -**ting**) ◇ *n* -**1.** [crack] racha *f*, fenda *f*; **~ (in sthg)** fenda (em algo) -**2.** [tear] rasgão *m*; **~ in sthg** rasgão em algo -**3.** [division, schism] separação *f*; **~ in sthg** racha *m* em algo; **~ between** divisão *f* entre. ◇ *vt* -**1.** [crack] rachar, partir -**2.** [tear] rasgar -**3.** [divide - group, organization] rachar; [- road] dividir-se -**4.** [share] dividir; **to ~ the difference** rachar a diferença. ◇ *vi* -**1.** [crack] rachar-se -**2.** [tear] rasgar-se -**3.** *inf* [leave] sair.
➡ **splits** *npl*: **to do the ~s** fazer espacato OR grande écart.
➡ **split off** ◇ *vt sep* [snap off]: **to ~ sthg off (from sthg)** separar algo (de algo). ◇ *vi* -**1.** [snap off]: **to ~ off (from sthg)** desprender-se (de algo) -**2.** [separate]: **to ~ off (from sb)** separar-se (de alguém).
➡ **split up** ◇ *vt sep*: **to ~ sthg up (into sthg)** dividir algo (em algo). ◇ *vi* separar-se; **to ~ up with sb** romper com alguém.
split end *n* ponta *f* dupla *(no cabelo)*.
split-level *adj* -**1.** [building, house, room] dúplex *inv* -**2.** [grill] duplo.
split peas *npl* ervilhas *fpl* secas.
split personality *n* dupla personalidade *f*.

split screen *n* -**1.** CINEMA & TV tela *f* múltipla -**2.** COMPUT divisão *f* de tela.
split second *n* fração *f* de segundo.
splitting ['splɪtɪŋ] *adj*: **~ headache** enxaqueca *f*.
splutter ['splʌtə'] ◇ *n* [of person] balbucio *m*. ◇ *vi* -**1.** [person] balbuciar -**2.** [car, engine] estalar -**3.** [spit] crepitar.
spoil [spɔɪl] *(pt & pp* -**ed** OR **spoilt)** *vt* -**1.** [ruin] estragar -**2.** [pamper] mimar; **to ~ sb** fazer um agrado a alguém; **to ~ o.s.** dar-se um capricho.
➡ **spoils** *npl* butim *m*; **~ of war** despojos *mpl* de guerra.
spoiled [spɔɪld] *adj* = **spoilt**.
spoiler ['spɔɪlə'] *n* spoiler *m*.
spoilsport ['spɔɪlspɔ:t] *n* desmancha-prazeres *mf inv*.
spoilt [spɔɪlt] ◇ *pt & pp* ⊳ **spoil**. ◇ *adj* -**1.** [child] mimado(da) -**2.** [food, dinner] estragado(da).
spoke [spəʊk] ◇ *pt* ⊳ **speak**. ◇ *n* raio *m (da roda)*.
spoken ['spəʊkn] *pp* ⊳ **speak**.
spokesman ['spəʊksmən] *(pl* -**men** [-mən]) *n* porta-voz *m*.
spokesperson ['spəʊks,pɜ:sn] *(pl* **spokespeople)** *n* porta-voz *mf*.
spokeswoman ['spəʊks,wʊmən] *(pl* -**women** [-,wɪmɪn]) *n* porta-voz *f*.
sponge [spʌndʒ] *(UK cont* **spongeing**, *US cont* **sponging)** ◇ *n* -**1.** [for cleaning, washing] esponja *f* -**2.** [cake] pão-de-ló *m*. ◇ *vt* limpar com esponja. ◇ *vi inf*: **to ~ off sb** viver às custas de alguém.
sponge bag *n UK* nécessaire *m*.
sponge cake *n* pão-de-ló *m*.
sponge pudding *n UK* pudim *de bolacha feito ao banho-maria.*
sponger ['spʌndʒə'] *n inf pej* parasita *mf*.
spongy ['spʌndʒɪ] *(compar* -**ier**, *superl* -**iest)** *adj* esponjoso(sa).
sponsor ['spɒnsə'] ◇ *n* patrocinador *m*, -ra *f*. ◇ *vt* -**1.** patrocinar -**2.** [bill, appeal, proposal] dar o respaldo a.
sponsored walk [,spɒnsəd-] *n* marcha *f* beneficente.
sponsorship ['spɒnsəʃɪp] *n (U)* patrocínio *m*.
spontaneity [,spɒntə'neɪətɪ] *n (U)* espontaneidade *f*.
spontaneous [spɒn'teɪnjəs] *adj* espontâneo(nea).
spontaneously [spɒn'teɪnjəslɪ] *adv* espontaneamente.
spoof [spu:f] *n*: **~ (of** OR **on sthg)** sátira *f* (de OR sobre algo).
spook [spu:k] *vt US* assustar.
spooky ['spu:kɪ] *(compar* -**ier**, *superl* -**iest)** *adj* -**1.** *inf* [place, house] assombrado(da) -**2.** *inf* [film] aterrorizante.
spool [spu:l] ◇ *n* -**1.** [of thread, tape, film] carretel *m* -**2.** COMPUT spool *m*. ◇ *vi* COMPUT direcionar trabalho de impressão para o spool.
spoon [spu:n] ◇ *n* -**1.** [piece of cutlery] colher *f* -**2.** [spoonful] colherada *f*. ◇ *vt*: **to ~ sthg onto/into sthg** pôr OR colocar uma colherada de algo em algo.
spoon-feed *vt* -**1.** [feed with spoon] dar de comer

com colher a **-2. fig** [give too much help to] dar mastigado *OR* de mão beijada a.

spoonful ['spu:nfʊl] (*pl* **-s** *OR* **spoonsful** ['spu:nzfʊl]) *n* colherada *f*.

sporadic [spə'rædɪk] *adj* esporádico(ca).

sport [spɔ:t] ◇ *n* **-1.** [gen] esporte *m* **-2. dated** [cheerful person] pessoa *f* amável. ◇ *vt* [wear] exibir, ostentar.
➡ **sports** ◇ *npl UK* ▷ **sports day**. ◇ *comp* esportivo(va).

sporting ['spɔ:tɪŋ] *adj* **-1.** [relating to sport] esportivo(va) **-2.** [generous, fair] nobre; **that's very** ~ **of you** é muita bondade sua.

sports car ['spɔ:ts-] *n* carro *m* esporte.

sports day *n UK dia dedicado a competições esportivas na escola.*

sports jacket ['spɔ:ts-] *n* jaqueta *f* esportiva.

sportsman ['spɔ:tsmən] (*pl* **-men** [-mən]) *n* esportista *m*.

sportsmanship ['spɔ:tsmənʃɪp] *n* (*U*) espírito *m* esportivo.

sports pages *npl* página *f OR* seção *f* de esportes.

sportswear ['spɔ:tsweə'] *n* (*U*) roupas *fpl* esportivas.

sportswoman ['spɔ:ts‚wʊmən] (*pl* **-women** [-‚wɪmɪn]) *n* esportista *f*.

sporty ['spɔ:tɪ] (*compar* **-ier**, *superl* **-iest**) *adj inf* **-1.** [person] aficcionado(da) por esportes **-2.** [car, clothes] esportivo(va).

spot [spɒtl] (*pt* & *pp* **-ted**, *cont* **-ting**) ◇ *n* **-1.** [mark, dot] mancha *f* **-2.** [pimple] sinal *m* **-3. inf: a** ~ **of sleep** uma dormida; **a** ~ **of work** um pouco de trabalho; [- of milk, liquid] gole *m*; [- of rain] pingo *m*, gota *f* **-4.** [place] local *m*; **on the** ~ no local; **to do sthg on the** ~ fazer algo no ato **-5.** *RADIO* & *TV* espaço *m* **-6. phr: to have a soft** ~ **for sb** ter uma leve caída por alguém; **to put sb on the** ~ colocar alguém em maus lençóis. ◇ *vt* [notice] enxergar.

spot check *n* controle *m* aleatório.

spotless ['spɒtlɪs] *adj* [clean] impecável.

spotlight ['spɒtlaɪt] *n* [bright light] refletor *m*; **to be in the** ~ **fig** ser o centro das atenções.

spot-on *adj UK inf* certeiro(ra).

spot price *n* preço *m* para entrega imediata.

spotted ['spɒtɪd] *adj* de bolinhas.

spotty ['spɒtɪ] (*compar* **-ier**, *superl* **-iest**) *adj* **-1.** *UK* [skin] sardento(ta) **-2.** *US* [patchy] de remendos, irregular.

spouse [spaʊs] *n* esposo *m*, -sa *f*.

spout [spaʊt] ◇ *n* **-1.** [of container] bico *m* **-2.** [of water - from fountain, geyser] jorro *m*; [- from whale] esguicho *m*. ◇ *vt pej* [churn out] jorrar. ◇ *vi:* **to** ~ **from** *OR* **out of sthg** jorrar de algo.

sprain [spreɪn] ◇ *n* torção *f*, distensão *f*. ◇ *vt* torcer, distender.

sprang [spræŋ] *pt* ▷ **spring**.

sprat [spræt] *n* espadilha *f*.

sprawl [sprɔ:l] ◇ *n* (*U*) expansão *f*; **urban** ~ expansão *f* urbana descontrolada. ◇ *vi* **-1.** [person] estirar-se **-2.** [city, suburbs] expandir-se.

sprawling ['sprɔ:lɪŋ] *adj* [city, suburbs] de expansão descontrolada.

spray [spreɪ] ◇ *n* **-1.** (*U*) [droplets] borrifo *m* **-2.** [pressurized liquid] spray *m* **-3.** [insect] pulverizador *m* **-4.** [can, container] vaporizador *m* **-5.** [of flowers] ramo *m*. ◇ *vt* & *vi* **-1.** [treat] pulverizar **-2.** [apply] borrifar.

spray can *n* spray *m*, aerosol *m*.

spray paint *n* tinta *f* spray.

spread [spred] (*pt* & *pp* **spread**) ◇ *n* **-1.** (*U*) *CULIN* [paste] pasta *f* **-2.** [diffusion, growth] propagação *f* **-3.** [range] extensão *f* **-4.** *PRESS* chapado *m* **-5.** [buffet] banquete *m* **-6.** *US* [bedspread] colcha *f*. ◇ *vt* **-1.** [open out, unfold - map, tablecloth, rug] estender; [- arms, legs, fingers] abrir **-2.** [apply - butter, jam] untar; **to** ~ **sthg over sthg** untar algo com algo; [- glue] passar; **to** ~ **sthg over sthg** passar algo em algo **-3.** [diffuse, disseminate] espalhar **-4.** [over a period of time]: **to be** ~ **over ...** ter uma duração de ... **-5.** [over an area] espalhar; **the floor was** ~ **with straw** o chão estava coberto de palha **-6.** [distribute evenly] expandir. ◇ *vi* [gen] espalhar-se; [disease, infection] alastrar-se.
➡ **spread out** ◇ *vt sep* **-1.** [distribute]: **to be** ~ **out** [far apart] estar espalhado(da); [sprawling] estender-se **-2.** [open out, unfold - fingers, arms] abrir; [- map, tablecloth, rug] estender. ◇ *vi* [disperse] dispersar-se.

spread-eagled [-‚i:gld] *adj* de braços e pernas abertos.

spreadsheet ['spredʃi:t] *n COMPUT* panilha *f* eletrônica.

spree [spri:] *n* farra *f*.

sprig [sprɪg] *n* broto *m*, ramo *m*.

sprightly ['spraɪtlɪ] (*compar* **-ier**, *superl* **-iest**) *adj* ativo(va).

spring [sprɪŋ] (*pt* **sprang**, *pp* **sprung**) ◇ *n* **-1.** [season] primavera *f*; **in** ~ na primavera **-2.** [coil] mola *f* **-3.** [leap] pulo *m* **-4.** [water source] fonte *f*. ◇ *comp* **-1.** [rain, weather, colours] de primavera **-2.** [mattress] de mola **-3.** [water] de nascente. ◇ *vt* **-1.** [make known suddenly]: **to** ~ **sthg on sb** revelar subitamente algo a alguém **-2.** [develop]: **to** ~ **a leak** começar a fazer água. ◇ *vi* **-1.** [leap] saltar; **to** ~ **into action/to life** pôr-se em marcha/ funcionamento **-2.** [be released] soltar-se; **to** ~ **shut/open** fechar/abrir rapidamente **-3.** [originate]: **to** ~ **from sthg** originar-se de algo.
➡ **spring up** *vi* **-1.** [get up] levantar-se **-2.** [grow in size, height] elevar-se **-3.** [appear] surgir de repente.

springboard ['sprɪŋbɔ:d] *n fig* [launch pad]: ~ **for/ to sthg** trampolim *m* para algo.

spring-clean ◇ *vt* fazer uma faxina geral em. ◇ *vi* fazer uma faxina geral.

spring-loaded *adj* de mola.

spring onion *n UK* cebolinha *f* verde.

spring roll *n UK* rolinho *m* primavera.

spring tide *n* maré *f* viva.

springtime ['sprɪŋtaɪm] *n* (*U*): **in (the)** ~ na primavera.

springy ['sprɪŋɪ] (*compar* **-ier**, *superl* **-iest**) *adj* **-1.** [carpet, mattress, ground] flexível **-2.** [rubber] elástico(ca).

sprinkle ['sprɪŋkl] *vt* **-1.** salpicar; **to** ~ **sthg over** *OR* **on sthg** salpicar algo sobre *OR* em algo; **to** ~ **sthg with sthg** regar algo com algo **-2.** [powder]

polvilhar -**3.** [liquid] borrifar.
sprinkler ['sprɪŋklə'] n -**1.** [for gardens] regador m -**2.** [for extinguishing fires] extintor m.
sprinkling ['sprɪŋklɪŋ] n -**1.** [of water] borrifo m -**2.** [of sand] punhado m -**3.** [of people] grupo m pequeno -**4.** [of salt] pitada f.
sprint [sprɪnt] ◇ n SPORT [race] corrida f de velocidade. ◇ vi correr a toda (velocidade).
sprinter ['sprɪntə'] n [runner] corredor m, -ra f de velocidade.
sprite n fada f.
spritzer ['sprɪtsə'] n vinho com água mineral.
sprocket ['sprɒkɪt] n [wheel] roda f dentada.
sprout [spraʊt] ◇ n -**1.** CULIN: (brussels) ~s couve-de-bruxelas f -**2.** [shoot] broto m. ◇ vt -**1.** [germinate] germinar -**2.** [bud] brotar -**3.** [grow] crescer. ◇ vi -**1.** [germinate] germinar -**2.** [bud] brotar -**3.** [grow] crescer -**4.** [appear]: **to ~ (up)** surgir rapidamente.
spruce [spruːs] ◇ adj alinhado(da). ◇ n [tree] abeto m.
➡ **spruce up** vt sep arrumar; **to ~ o.s. up** arrumar-se.
sprung [sprʌŋ] pp ⊳ **spring.**
spry [spraɪ] (compar -ier, superl -iest) adj ativo(va).
SPUC (abbr of Society for the Protection of the Unborn Child) n organização antiaborto.
spud [spʌd] n inf batata f.
spun [spʌn] pt & pp ⊳ **spin.**
spunk [spʌŋk] n (U) inf [courage] coragem f.
spur [spɜː'] (pt & pp -red, cont -ring) ◇ n -**1.** [incentive]: ~ **(to sthg)** estímulo m (a algo) -**2.** [on rider's boot] espora f. ◇ vt -**1.** [encourage]: **to ~ sb to do sthg** incentivar alguém a fazer algo -**2.** [horse] esporear.
➡ **on the spur of the moment** adv sem pensar duas vezes.
➡ **spur on** vt sep [encourage] estimular.
spurious ['spʊərɪəs] adj -**1.** [not genuine] espúrio(ria) -**2.** [based on false reasoning] falso(sa).
spurn [spɜːn] vt rejeitar, desprezar.
spurt [spɜːt] ◇ n -**1.** [of steam] jato m -**2.** [of water] jorro m -**3.** [of flame] labareda f -**4.** [of activity, energy] acesso m -**5.** [burst of speed] acelerada f; **to put on a ~** [while running, cycling] dar uma acelerada; [while working] dar um esforço. ◇ vi -**1.** [water]: **to ~ (out of OR from sthg)** jorrar (de algo); [steam] sair um jato de vapor (de algo); [flame] sair uma labareda (de algo) -**2.** [run] acelerar.
sputter ['spʌtə'] vi -**1.** [engine] estalar -**2.** [stutter] gaguejar -**3.** [fire] crepitar -**4.** [oil in pan] espirrar.
spy [spaɪ] (pl spies, pt & pp spied) ◇ n espião m, -â f. ◇ vt inf espionar. ◇ vi -**1.** [work as spy] espionar -**2.** [watch secretly]: **to ~ on sb** espionar alguém.
spying ['spaɪɪŋ] n (U) espionagem f.
spy satellite n satélite m espião.
Sq., sq. (abbr of square) pça.
squabble ['skwɒbl] ◇ n rinha f, discussão f. ◇ vi: **to ~ (about OR over sthg)** discutir (sobre algo).
squad [skwɒd] n -**1.** [of police] esquadrão m -**2.** MIL pelotão m -**3.** [SPORT, group of players - of club] time m; [- of national team] seleção f.

squad car n radiopatrulha f.
squadron ['skwɒdrən] n esquadrão m.
squadron leader n UK comandante m de aviação.
squalid ['skwɒlɪd] adj -**1.** [filthy] esquálido(da), sórdido(da) -**2.** [base, dishonest] depreciável.
squall [skwɔːl] n [storm] tempestade f.
squalor ['skwɒlə'] n (U) sordidez f, miséria f.
squander ['skwɒndə'] vt desperdiçar.
square [skweə'] ◇ adj -**1.** quadrado(da) -**2.** [not owing money]: **we're ~ now** estamos quites agora. ◇ n -**1.** [shape] quadrado m -**2.** [in town, city] praça f -**3.** inf [unfashionable person] quadrado m, -da f -**4.** phr: **to be back to ~ one** voltar ao ponto de partida. ◇ vt -**1.** MATH [multiply by itself] elevar ao quadrado -**2.** [balance, reconcile]: **to ~ sthg with sthg** conciliar algo com algo.
➡ **square up** vi -**1.** [settle up]: **to ~ up with sb** acertar-se com alguém, acertar as contas com alguém -**2.** [confront]: **to ~ up to sb/sthg** fazer frente a alguém/algo.
squared [skweəd] adj quadriculado(da).
square dance n quadrilha f (de dança).
square deal n negócio m limpo.
squarely ['skweəlɪ] adv -**1.** [directly] exatamente -**2.** [honestly] honestamente, abertamente.
square meal n boa refeição f.
square root n raiz f quadrada.
squash [skwɒʃ] ◇ n -**1.** (U) SPORT squash m -**2.** UK [drink]: **lemon/orange ~** refresco m de limão/laranja -**3.** US [vegetable] abóbora f. ◇ vt [squeeze, flatten] esmagar.
squat [skwɒt] (compar -ter, superl -test, pt & pp -ted, cont -ting) ◇ adj atarracado(da). ◇ n UK [building] moradia f ilegal. ◇ vi -**1.** [crouch]: **to ~ (down)** agachar-se -**2.** UK [be a squatter] viver num lugar ilegalmente.
squatter ['skwɒtə'] n UK [in empty building] posseiro m, -ra f.
squawk [skwɔːk] ◇ n [of bird] grasnado m. ◇ vi [bird] grasnar.
squeak [skwiːk] ◇ n -**1.** [of animal] guincho m -**2.** [of door, hinge] rangido m. ◇ vi -**1.** [animal] guinchar -**2.** [floorboard, bed, hinge] ranger.
squeaky ['skwiːkɪ] (compar -ier, superl -iest) adj -**1.** [floorboard, bed, hinge] que range -**2.** [voice] estridente.
squeal [skwiːl] ◇ n -**1.** [of person, animal] grito m agudo -**2.** [of brakes, tyres] guincho m. ◇ vi -**1.** [person, animal] gritar -**2.** [brakes, tyres] guinchar.
squeamish ['skwiːmɪʃ] adj apreensivo(va).
squeeze [skwiːz] ◇ n -**1.** [pressure] aperto m -**2.** inf [crush of people] aperto m. ◇ vt -**1.** [press firmly] apertar -**2.** [extract, press out] espremer -**3.** [cram]: **to ~ sthg into sthg** [into place] espremer algo dentro de algo; [into time] virar-se para fazer algo em algo -**4.** fig [information]: **to ~ sthg out of sb** arrancar algo de alguém. ◇ vi: **to ~ into/through sthg** conseguir se enfiar em algo.
squeezebox n UK acordeão m.
squeezer ['skwiːzə'] n espremedor m.
squelch [skweltʃ] vi chapinhar.
squib [skwɪb] n: **damp ~** decepção f.

squid [skwɪd] (*pl inv* OR **-s**) *n* lula *f.*

squiffy (*compar* **-ier**, *superl* **-iest**) *adj UK inf dated* embriagado(da).

squiggle [ˈskwɪgl] *n* rabisco *m.*

squint [skwɪntl] ◇ *n* MED estrabismo *m.* ◇ *vi* **-1.** MED ser estrábico(ca) **-2.** [half-close one's eyes]: **to ~ at sthg** olhar com os olhos semicerrados para algo.

squire [ˈskwaɪəʳ] *n* [landowner] proprietário *m,* -ria *f* rural.

squirm [skwɜːm] *vi* **-1.** [wriggle] contorcer-se **-2.** [wince]: **to ~ (with sthg)** demonstrar mal-estar (com algo).

squirrel [*UK* ˈskwɪrəl, *US* ˈskwɜːrəl] *n* esquilo *m.*

squirt [skwɜːt] ◇ *vt* **-1.** [force out] esguichar **-2.** [cover with liquid]: **to ~ sb/sthg with sthg** esguichar algo em alguém/algo. ◇ *vi*: **to ~ (out of sthg)** esguichar (para fora de algo).

Sr -1. (*abbr of* **senior**) *forma utilizada após o nome de um homem para indicar que ele é pai de alguém com o mesmo nome* **-2.** (*abbr of* **sister**) *irmã f (de caridade).*

SRC *n* **-1.** (*abbr of* **Science Research Council**) *conselho britânico de pesquisa científica* **-2.** (*abbr of* **Students' Representative Council**) *diretório acadêmico britânico.*

Sri Lanka [ˌsriːˈlæŋkə] *n* Sri Lanka; **in ~** em Sri Lanka.

Sri Lankan ◇ *adj* de Sri Lanka. ◇ *n* [person] *habitante de Sri Lanka.*

SS (*abbr of* **steamship**) SS.

SSA (*abbr of* **Social Security Administration**) *n organismo norte-americano de previdência social.*

SSSI (*abbr of* **Site of Special Scientific Interest**) *n área de especial interesse científico na Grã-Bretanha.*

St (*abbr of* **saint**) Sto.

ST (*abbr of* **Standard Time**) *n* hora *f* oficial.

stab [stæb] (*pt & pp* **-bed,** *cont* **-bing**) ◇ *n* **-1.** [with knife] punhalada *f* **-2.** *inf* [attempt]: **to have a ~ (at sthg)** ter uma experiência (em algo) **-3.** [twinge] pontada *f.* ◇ *vt* **-1.** apunhalar, esfaquear **-2.** [jab] fincar. ◇ *vi* [jab]: **to ~ at sthg** fincar em algo.

stabbing [ˈstæbɪŋ] ◇ *adj* lancinante. ◇ *n* punhalada *f.*

stability [stəˈbɪlətɪ] *n (U)* estabilidade *f.*

stabilize, -ise [ˈsteɪbəlaɪz] ◇ *vt* estabilizar. ◇ *vi* estabilizar-se.

stabilizer [ˈsteɪbəlaɪzəʳ] *n* [on ship, aircraft, bicycle] estabilizador *m.*

stable [ˈsteɪbl] ◇ *adj* **-1.** [gen] estável **-2.** [solid, anchored] firme. ◇ *n* [building] estábulo *m*; [horses] cavalariça *f.*

stable lad *n* cavalariço *m.*

staccato [stəˈkɑːtəʊ] ◇ *adj* staccato. ◇ *adv* em staccato.

stack [stæk] ◇ *n* **-1.** [pile] pilha *f* **-2.** *inf* [a lot, lots]: **~s** OR **a ~ of sthg** um monte de algo. ◇ *vt* **-1.** [pile up] empilhar **-2.** [fill]: **to be ~ed with sthg** estar empilhado(da) de algo.

➡ **stack up** *vi* **-1.** *inf* [add up, work out] encaixar-se **-2.** *inf* [compare]: **to ~ up against** OR **to sb/sthg** comparar-se com relação a alguém/algo.

stadium [ˈsteɪdjəm] (*pl* **-diums** OR **-dia** [-djə]) *n* estádio *m.*

staff [stɑːf] ◇ *n* [employees] pessoal *m,* quadro *m.* ◇ *vt*: **the shop was ~ ed by women** a equipe da loja era composta de mulheres.

staffing [ˈstɑːfɪŋ] *n (U)* contratação *f* de pessoal.

staff nurse *n UK* enfermeiro *m,* -ra *f* assistente.

staff room *n* sala *f* dos professores.

stag [stæg] (*pl inv* OR **-s**) *n* ZOOL veado *m.*

stage [steɪdʒ] ◇ *n* **-1.** [period, phase] etapa *f,* estágio *m* **-2.** [platform] palco *m*; **on ~** em cena; **to set the ~ for sthg** preparar o terreno para algo **-3.** [acting profession]: **the ~** o teatro. ◇ *vt* **-1.** THEATRE representar **-2.** [organize] organizar.

stagecoach [ˈsteɪdʒkəʊtʃ] *n* diligência *f.*

stage door *n* entrada *f* de artistas.

stage fright *n (U)* medo *m* do palco.

stagehand [ˈsteɪdʒhænd] *n* assistente *mf* de palco.

stage-manage *vt* **-1.** THEATRE dirigir **-2.** *fig* [orchestrate] orquestrar.

stage manager *n* contra-regra *mf,* diretor *m,* -ra *f* de cena.

stage name *n* nome *m* artístico.

stagflation *n* POL estagflação *f.*

stagger [ˈstægəʳ] ◇ *vt* **-1.** [astound] abalar, chocar **-2.** [arrange at different times] escalonar. ◇ *vi* [totter] cambalear.

staggering [ˈstægərɪŋ] *adj* assombroso(sa).

staging [ˈsteɪdʒɪŋ] *n* **-1.** THEATRE encenação *f* **-2.** [performing, organizing] organização *f.*

stagnant [ˈstægnənt] *adj* **-1.** [water, air] estancado(da) **-2.** [business, career, economy] estagnado(da).

stagnate [stægˈneɪt] *vi* **-1.** [water, air] estancar **-2.** [business, career, economy] estagnar-se.

stagnation [stægˈneɪʃn] *n* **-1.** [of water, air] estancamento *m* **-2.** [of business, career, economy] estagnação *f.*

stag night OR **party** *n* despedida *f* de solteiro.

staid [steɪd] *adj* sério(ria), recatado(da).

stain [steɪn] ◇ *n* [mark] mancha *f.* ◇ *vt* [discolour] manchar.

stained [steɪnd] *adj* **-1.** [soiled, marked] manchado(da) **-2.** [wood] tingido(da).

stained glass [ˌsteɪnd-] *n (U)* vitral *m.*

stained-glass window *n* janela *f* de vitral.

stainless steel [ˌsteɪnlɪs-] *n (U)* aço *m* inoxidável.

stain remover [-rɪˌmuːvəʳ] *n* removedor *m* de manchas.

stair [steəʳ] *n* [step] degrau *m.*

➡ **stairs** *npl* [flight] escada *f.*

staircase [ˈsteəkeɪs] *n* escadas *fpl.*

stairway [ˈsteəweɪ] *n* escadas *fpl,* escadaria *f.*

stairwell [ˈsteəwel] *n* vão *m* OR poço *m* das escadas.

stake [steɪk] ◇ *n* **-1.** [share]: **to have a ~ in sthg** ter interesses em algo **-2.** [wooden post] estaca *f* **-3.** [in gambling] aposta *f.* ◇ *vt* **-1.** [risk]: **to ~ sthg (on** OR **upon sthg)** arriscar algo (com algo) **-2.** [in gambling] apostar **-3.** [state]: **to ~ a claim to sthg** reivindicar algo.

➡ **stakes** *npl* **-1.** [prize] prêmio *m* **-2.** [contest] disputa *f.*

➡ **at stake** *adv*: **to be at ~** estar em jogo.

stakeout ['steɪkaʊt] *n esp US* [police surveillance] vigilância *f*.

stalactite ['stæləktaɪt] *n* estalactite *f*.

stalagmite ['stæləgmaɪt] *n* estalagmite *f*.

stale [steɪl] *adj* -1. [food] passado(da) -2. [air] viciado(da) -3. [bread] amanhecido(da) -4. [breath] velho(lha) -5. [athlete] esgotado(da) -6. [artist] sem inspiração -7. [idea] batido(da).

stalemate ['steɪlmeɪt] *n* -1. [deadlock] impasse *m* -2. *CHESS* empate *m*.

staleness ['steɪlnɪs] *n* -1. [person, news, idea, air] envelhecimento *m* -2. [of bread] dureza *f* -3. [of food] rancidez *f*.

stalk [stɔ:k] ⬥ *n* -1. [of flower, plant] caule *m* -2. [of leaf] talo *m* -3. [of fruit] cabo *m*. ⬥ *vt* [hunt] tocaiar. ⬥ *vi* [walk] andar de forma irritada.

stall [stɔ:l] ⬥ *n* -1. [table] estande *m*, banca *f* -2. [in stable] baia *f*. ⬥ *vt* -1. *AUT* fazer morrer -2. [delay] ganhar tempo. ⬥ *vi* -1. *AUT* morrer -2. [delay] ganhar tempo.
⬥ **stalls** *npl UK* platéia *f*.

stallholder ['stɔ:l,həʊldəʳ] *n UK* dono *m*, -na *f* de banca *(no mercado)*.

stallion ['stæljən] *n* garanhão *m*.

stalwart ['stɔ:lwət] ⬥ *adj* [loyal] leal, fiel. ⬥ *n* leal partidário *m*, -ia *f*.

stamen ['steɪmən] *n* estame *m*.

stamina ['stæmɪnə] *n (U)* resistência *f*.

stammer ['stæməʳ] ⬥ *n* gagueira *f*. ⬥ *vi* gaguejar.

stamp [stæmp] ⬥ *n* -1. [postage stamp] selo *m* -2. [rubber stamp] carimbo *m* -3. *fig* [hallmark] selo *m*. ⬥ *vt* -1. [mark, word, sign] carimbar -2. [pattern] timbrar -3. [stomp]: **to ~ one's foot** bater com o pé no chão -4. [stick stamp on] selar -5. *fig* [with characteristic quality] estampar. ⬥ *vi* -1. [walk] andar com passos pesados -2. [with one foot]: **to ~ on sthg** pisar em algo.
⬥ **stamp out** *vt sep* -1. [fire] abafar -2. [opposition] sufocar -3. [crime, disease] erradicar.

stamp album *n* álbum *m* de selos.

stamp-collecting *n (U)* filatelia *f*.

stamp collector *n* filatelista *mf*.

stamp duty *n (U) UK* imposto *m* de selo.

stamped addressed envelope ['stæmptə,dr-est-] *n UK* envelope selado e endereçado ao remetente, que o usa para enviar algo a si próprio através de outra pessoa.

stampede [stæm'pi:d] ⬥ *n* -1. [of animals] debandada *f* -2. [of people] fuga *f* em pânico. ⬥ *vi* [animals] debandar.

stamp machine *n* máquina *f* de selos.

stance [stæns] *n* -1. [posture] atitude *f*, postura *f* -2. [attitude]: **~ (on sthg)** postura (sobre algo) -3. *Scot* [for bus] ponto *m*.

stand [stænd] (*pt & pp* **stood**) ⬥ *n* -1. [stall] banca *f*, barraca *f* -2. [for umbrella, hat] cabide *m* -3. [for bicycle, lamp] suporte *m* -4. *SPORT* arquibancada *f* -5. *MIL* posição *f*; **to make a ~** resistir ao inimigo -6. [position] posição *f*; **to take a ~ on sthg** tomar uma posição em algo -7. *US JUR* depoimento *m*; **to take the ~** tomar o depoimento. ⬥ *vt* -1. [place] colocar -2. [withstand] agüentar -3. [put up with] suportar -4. [treat]: **to ~ sb sthg** convidar algo

para alguém -5. *JUR*: **to ~ trial** ser processado(-da). ⬥ *vi* -1. [be on one's feet] ficar em pé -2. [rise to one's feet] levantar-se -3. [be located] estar -4. [be left undisturbed] repousar -5. [be valid] seguir de pé -6. [indicating current situation]: **as things ~** ... do jeito que as coisas andam; **unemployment ~s at three million** o desemprego já atinge três milhões de pessoas -7. [on issue]: **where do you ~ on ...?** qual é a sua opinião sobre ...? -8. *UK POL* [be a candidate], candidatar-se (a) -9. [be likely]: **I ~ to win** é provável que eu ganhe -10. *US* [stop]: **'no ~ing'** proibido parar e estacionar.
⬥ **stand aside** *vi* [move aside] ficar de lado.
⬥ **stand back** *vi* [get out of way] afastar-se.
⬥ **stand by** ⬥ *vt fus* -1. [person] estar ao lado de -2. [promise, decision, offer] manter. ⬥ *vi* -1. [in readiness]: **to ~ by (for sthg/to do sthg)** estar preparado (da) (a algo/a fazer algo) -2. [not intervene] ficar de lado.
⬥ **stand down** *vi* [resign] retirar-se.
⬥ **stand for** *vt fus* -1. [signify] significar, representar -2. [tolerate] agüentar.
⬥ **stand in** *vi*: **to ~ in (for sb)** substituir (alguém).
⬥ **stand out** *vi* -1. [be clearly visible] sobressair -2. [be distinctive] destacar-se.
⬥ **stand up** ⬥ *vt sep inf* [miss appointment with] deixar plantado(da). ⬥ *vi* -1. [be on one's feet, upright] ficar de pé -2. [rise to one's feet] levantar-se -3. [be accepted as true] ser convincente.
⬥ **stand up for** *vt fus* sair em defesa de.
⬥ **stand up to** *vt fus* -1. [weather, heat, bad treatment] resistir a -2. [person, boss] peitar.

standard ['stændəd] ⬥ *adj* -1. [gen] normal -2. [type, feature] comum -3. [size] padronizado -4. [text, work] -padrão; **~ practice** prática-padrão *f*. ⬥ *n* -1. [level] nível *m* -2. [point of reference] padrão *m*, critério *m* -3. [flag] estandarte *m*.
⬥ **standards** *npl* [principles] valores *mpl* morais.

standard-bearer *n fig* porta-estandarte *mf*.

standardize, -ise ['stændədaɪz] *vt* padronizar.

standard lamp *n UK* abajur *m* de pé.

standard of living (*pl* **standards of living**) *n* padrão *m* de vida.

standard time *n (U)* hora *f* oficial.

standby ['stændbaɪ] (*pl* **standbys**) ⬥ *n* [substitute] reserva *f*; **to be on ~** estar a postos. ⬥ *comp* stand-by.

stand-in *n* -1. [replacement] suplente *mf*, -2. [stunt person] dublê *mf*.

standing ['stændɪŋ] ⬥ *adj* [permanent] permanente; **a ~ joke** uma piada manjada; **a ~ invitation** um convite em aberto. ⬥ *n* -1. [reputation] reputação *f* -2. [duration] duração *f*; **friends of 20 years' ~** amigos há mais de 20 anos.

standing charge *n* taxa *f* fixa.

standing committee *n* comissão *f* permanente.

standing order *n* débito *m* automático em conta.

standing ovation *n* ovação *f* em pé.

standing room *n (U)* lugar *m* em pé.

standoffish [,stænd'ɒfɪʃ] *adj* reservado(da).

standpipe *n* tubo *m* ascendente.

standpoint ['stændpɔɪnt] *n* ponto *m* de vista.

standstill ['stændstɪl] *n*: **at a ~** [not moving] parado(da); *fig* [not active] paralisado(da); **to come to a ~** [stop moving] parar; *fig* [cease] estancar.

stand-up *adj*: **~ comedian** comediante *mf* de platéia; **~ fight** briga *f* violenta.

stank [stæŋk] *pt* ▷ **stink**.

Stanley knife® *n* estilete *m*.

stanza ['stænzə] *n* estrofe *f*.

staple ['steɪpl] ⬦ *adj* [principal] básico(ca), de primeira necessidade. ⬦ *n* **-1.** [for paper] grampo *m* **-2.** [principal commodity] produto *m* de primeira necessidade. ⬦ *vt* grampear.

staple diet *n* dieta *f* básica.

staple gun *n* grampeador *m* industrial.

stapler ['steɪplə'] *n* grampeador *m*.

star [stɑː'] (*pt* & *pp* **-red**, *cont* **-ring**) ⬦ *n* **-1.** [gen] estrela *f* **-2.** [asterisk] asterisco *m*. ⬦ *comp* de estrela. ⬦ *vt* [include as celebrity]: **the film ~ s Mel Gibson** o filme é estrelado por Mel Gibson. ⬦ *vi* [actor]: **to ~ (in sthg)** ser protagonista(de algo).
➤ **stars** *npl* [horoscope] horóscopo *m*.

star attraction *n* atração *f* principal.

starboard ['stɑːbəd] ⬦ *adj* de estibordo. ⬦ *n* (*U*) estibordo *m*; **to ~** a estibordo.

starch [stɑːtʃ] *n* **-1.** [stiffening substance] goma *f* **-2.** [in food] amido *m*.

starched [stɑːtʃt] *adj* engomado(da).

starchy ['stɑːtʃɪ] (*compar* **-ier**, *superl* **-iest**) *adj* [foods] amiláceo(cea).

stardom ['stɑːdəm] *n* (*U*) estrelato *m*.

stare [steə'] ⬦ *n* olhar *m* fixo. ⬦ *vi*: **to ~ (at sb/ sthg)** olhar fixamente (para alguém/algo).

starfish ['stɑːfɪʃ] (*pl inv OR* **-es**) *n* estrela-do-mar *f*.

stark [stɑːk] ⬦ *adj* **-1.** [bare, bleak] desolado(da) **-2.** [rock] áspero(ra) **-3.** [decoration] desguarnecido(da) **-4.** [room] sem mobília **-5.** [contrast] duro(ra) **-6.** [reality] nu(a) e cru(a) **-7.** [fact] às claras. ⬦ *adv*: **~ naked** em pêlo.

starlet *n pej* estrelinha *f*.

starlight ['stɑːlaɪt] *n* (*U*) luz *f* das estrelas.

starling ['stɑːlɪŋ] *n* estorninho *m*.

starlit ['stɑːlɪt] *adj* iluminado(da) pelas estrelas.

starry ['stɑːrɪ] (*compar* **-ier**, *superl* **-iest**) *adj* estrela-do(da).

starry-eyed [-'aɪd] *adj* [naive] iludido(da).

Stars and Stripes *n*: **the ~** *a bandeira dos Estados Unidos*.

star sign *n* signo *m* (do horóscopo).

star-studded *adj*: **a ~ cast** um elenco de estrelas.

start [stɑːt] ⬦ *n* **-1.** [beginning] início *m*, começo *m*; **for a ~** para começar **-2.** [jump] sobressalto *m*, susto *m* **-3.** *SPORT* saída *f* **-4.** [lead] vantagem *f*. ⬦ *vt* **-1.** [begin] começar; **to ~ doing** *OR* **to do sthg** começar a fazer algo **-2.** [turn on] ligar **-3.** [set up - ger] criar, formar; [- business] montar **-4.** [initiate, instigate] iniciar. ⬦ *vi* **-1.** [begin] começar; **to ~ with sb/sthg** começar com alguém/algo; **to ~ with, ...** [at first] para começar, ... **-2.** [car] pegar **-3.** [engine] pôr-se em funcionamento **-4.** [tape] ligar **-5.** [set out] sair **-6.** [jump] sobressair-se, assustar-se **-7.** *inf* [be annoying]: **don't you ~!** não começa!

➤ **start off** ⬦ *vt sep* [cause to start - person] pôr -se a caminho; **this should be enough work to ~ you off** com isso já tem trabalho suficiente para começar; [- meeting] começar; [- rumour, discussion] desencadear. ⬦ *vi* **-1.** [begin] começar **-2.** [set out] sair.

➤ **start on** *vt fus* [begin] começar; **she finished off the biscuits and ~ ed on the cake** ela terminou com os biscoitos e partiu para o bolo.

➤ **start out** *vi* **-1.** [in life, career] começar **-2.** [set out] partir.

➤ **start up** ⬦ *vt sep* **-1.** [set up - business] montar; [- shop] botar; [- women's group] criar, formar **-2.** [car, engine, machine] ligar. ⬦ *vi* **-1.** [guns, music, noise] começar **-2.** [car, engine, machine] ligar **-3.** [set up business] estabelecer-se.

starter ['stɑːtə'] *n* **-1.** *UK* [hors d'oeuvre] entrada *f*, primeiro prato *m* **-2.** *AUT* (motor *m* de) arranque *m* **-3.** [SPORT- official] juiz *m*, -íza *f*; [- competitor] corredor *m*, -ra *f*.

starter motor *n* (motor *m* de) arranque *m*.

starter pack *n* pacote *m* inicial.

starting block ['stɑːtɪŋ-] *n* bloco *m* de partida (*numa corrida*).

starting point ['stɑːtɪŋ-] *n* ponto *m* de partida.

starting price *n* preço *m* de inauguração.

startle ['stɑːtl] *vt* assustar.

startling ['stɑːtlɪŋ] *adj* assustador(ra), surpreendente.

starvation [stɑː'veɪʃn] *n* (*U*) fome *f*, inanição *f*.

starve [stɑːv] ⬦ *vt* **-1.** [deprive of food] não dar comida para **-2.** [deprive]: **to ~ sb of sthg** privar alguém de algo. ⬦ *vi* **-1.** [have no food] passar fome **-2.** *inf* [be hungry]: **I'm starving to death!** estou morrendo de fome!

starving *adj* **-1.** [without food] esfomeado(da) **-2.** *inf* [hungry] faminto(ta).

star wars *n* guerra *f* nas estrelas, *programa espacial militar norte-americano*.

state [steɪt] ⬦ *n* **-1.** [condition] estado *m*; **not to be in a fit ~ to do sthg** não estar em condições de fazer algo; **to be in a ~** estar com os nervos à flor da pele **-2.** [authorities]: **the ~** o Estado. ⬦ *comp* de estado. ⬦ *vt* [declare] afirmar, declarar; **to ~ that** afirmar que; [specify] estabelecer.
➤ **State** *n* [government]: **the State** o Estado.
➤ **States** *npl* [USA]: **the States** os Estados Unidos.

state-controlled *adj* controlado(da) pelo estado.

State Department *n US* ≃ Ministério *m* das Relações Exteriores.

state education *n UK* ensino *m* público.

stateless *adj* sem pátria.

stately ['steɪtlɪ] (*compar* **-ier**, *superl* **-iest**) *adj* [dignified] majestoso(sa).

stately home *n UK* casa *grande de campo aberta à visitação*.

statement ['steɪtmənt] *n* **-1.** [declaration] afirmação *f*, declaração *f* **-2.** *JUR* declaração *f* **-3.** [from bank] extrato *m*.

state of affairs *n* situação *f* em geral.

state of emergency *n* estado *m* de emergência.

state of mind (*pl* states of mind) *n* estado *m* de espírito.

state-of-the-art *adj* de vanguarda, moderno(-na).

state-owned [-'əʊnd] *adj* estatal.

state school *n* escola *f* pública.

state secret *n* segredo *m* de estado.

state's evidence *n US*: to turn ~ testemunhar a favor de um delinqüente num tribunal contra outros em troca de uma redução na pena.

stateside ['steɪtsaɪd] <> *adj* dos Estados Unidos. <> *adv* -1. [travel] para os Estados Unidos -2. [live] nos Estados Unidos.

statesman ['steɪtsmən] (*pl* -men [-mən]) *n* estadista *m*, homem *m* de estado.

statesmanship ['steɪtsmənʃɪp] *n* (*U*) competência *f* para governar.

static ['stætɪk] <> *adj* [unchanging] estável. <> *n* (*U*) *ELEC* estática *f*.

static electricity *n* (*U*) eletricidade *f* estática.

station ['steɪʃn] <> *n* -1. [gen] estação *f*; **police** ~ delegacia *f*; **fire** ~ corpo *m* de bombeiros -2. [position] posto *m* -3. *fml* [rank] posição *f*. <> *vt* -1. [position] situar, colocar -2. MIL estacionar.

stationary ['steɪʃnərɪ] *adj* estacionário(ria).

stationer *n* dono *m*, -na *f* de papelaria; ~ 's (shop) papelaria *f*.

stationery ['steɪʃnərɪ] *n* (*U*) artigos *mpl* de escritório.

station house *n US* distrito *m* policial.

stationmaster ['steɪʃn,mɑːstə'] *n* chefe *mf* da estação.

station wagon *n US* perua *f* (*camioneta*).

statistic [stə'tɪstɪk] *n* [number] estatística *f*.
➡ **statistics** *n* (*U*) [science] estatística *f*.

statistical [stə'tɪstɪkl] *adj* estatístico(ca).

statistician [,stætɪ'stɪʃn] *n* estatístico *m*, -ca *f*.

statue ['stætʃuː] *n* estátua *f*.

statuesque [,stætjʊ'esk] *adj* escultural.

statuette [,stætjʊ'et] *n* estatueta *f*.

stature ['stætʃə'] *n* (*U*) -1. [height, size] estatura *f* -2. [importance] categoria *f*.

status ['steɪtəs] *n* (*U*) -1. [legal or social position] condição *f*, estado *m* -2. [prestige] status *m inv*.

status bar *n COMPUT* barra *f* de status.

status quo [-'kwəʊ] *n*: the ~ o status quo.

status symbol *n* símbolo *m* de status.

statute ['stætjuːt] *n* estatuto *m*.

statute book *n*: the ~ o código de leis.

statutory ['stætjʊtrɪ] *adj* estatutário(ria).

staunch [stɔːntʃ] <> *adj* leal, fiel. <> *vt* estancar.

stave [steɪv] (*pt* & *pp* -d *OR* stove) *n MUS* pauta *f*.
➡ **stave off** *vt sep* afastar temporariamente.

stay [steɪ] <> *n* [visit] estada *f*, estadia *f*. <> *vi* -1. [remain] ficar; **to** ~ **put** ficar no lugar -2. [reside temporarily] ficar, permanecer -3. [continue to be] permanecer; **I don't want to** ~ **a teacher all my life** não quero ser professor toda a minha vida; **she** ~ed **awake till midnight** ficou acordada até a meia-noite -4. *Scot* [reside permanently] hospedar-se.
➡ **stay away** *vi*: **to** ~ **away from sb/somewhere** ficar longe de alguém/algum lugar.

➡ **stay in** *vi* [stay at home] ficar em casa.
➡ **stay on** *vi* ficar, permanecer.
➡ **stay out** *vi* -1. [not come home] ficar fora -2. [strikers] permanecer em greve -3. [not get involved]: **to** ~ **out of sthg** ficar fora de algo.
➡ **stay up** *vi* -1. [not go to bed] ficar acordado(da) -2. [not fall] ficar de pé.

stayer *n UK* -1. [horse] cavalo *m* resistente -2. [person] pessoa *f* resistente.

staying power ['steɪɪŋ-] *n* (*U*) resistência *f*.

St Bernard [*UK* -'bɜːnəd, *US* -bər'nɑːrd] *n* [dog] são-bernardo *m*.

STD *n* -1. (*abbr of* subscriber trunk dialling) *sistema de chamadas telefônicas diretas de longa distância na Grã-Bretanha* -2. (*abbr of* sexually transmitted disease) DST *f*.

stead [sted] *n*: **to stand sb in good** ~ servir muito a alguém.

steadfast ['stedfɑːst] *adj* -1. [supporter] fiel -2. [resolve] resoluto(ta) -3. [gaze] fixo(xa).

steadily ['stedɪlɪ] *adv* -1. [gradually] gradualmente -2. [regularly] normalmente -3. [calmly - look, stare] fixamente; [- say] calmamente.

steady ['stedɪ] (*compar* -ier, *superl* -iest, *pt* & *pp* -ied) <> *adj* -1. [gradual] gradual -2. [regular, constant] constante -3. [not shaking] firme -4. [calm - voice] calmo(ma); [- stare] fixo(xa) -5. [stable - boyfriend, girlfriend] firme; [- relationship] sério(ria); [- job] estável -6. [sensible] sensato(ta). <> *vt* -1. [stabilize] estabilizar; **to** ~ **o.s.** equilibrar-se -2. [calm] controlar; **to** ~ **o.s.** acalmar-se, controlar os nervos.

steak [steɪk] *n* -1. (*U*) [meat] bife *m* -2. [piece of meat or fish] filé *m*.

steakhouse ['steɪkhaʊs, *pl* -haʊzɪz] *n* churrascaria *f*.

steal [stiːl] (*pt* stole, *pp* stolen) <> *vt* roubar; **to** ~ **a glance at sb** lançar um olhar furtivo em alguém. <> *vi* -1. [take illegally] roubar -2. [move stealthily] mover-se furtivamente.

stealing ['stiːlɪŋ] *n* (*U*) roubo *m*.

stealth [stelθ] *n* (*U*): **by** ~ furtivamente, às escondidas.

stealthy ['stelθɪ] (*compar* -ier, *superl* -iest) *adj* furtivo(va).

steam [stiːm] <> *n* (*U*) vapor *m*; **to let off** ~ desabafar; **to run out of** ~ ficar sem forças. <> *comp* a vapor. <> *vt CULIN* cozinhar no vapor. <> *vi* -1. [gen] largar vapor -2. [train, ship] partir largando fumaça.
➡ **steam up** <> *vt sep* -1. [mist up] embaçar -2. *fig* [get angry]: **to get** ~ed **up about sthg** soltar fumaça pelas ventas por causa de algo. <> *vi* [window, glasses] embaçar.

steamboat ['stiːmbəʊt] *n* barco *m* a vapor.

steam engine *n* máquina *f* a vapor.

steamer ['stiːmə'] *n* -1. [ship] navio *m* a vapor -2. *CULIN* panela *f* que cozinha no vapor.

steam iron *n* ferro *m* a vapor.

steamroller ['stiːm,rəʊlə'] *n* rolo *m* compressor.

steam shovel *n US* escavadeira *f* a vapor.

steamy ['stiːmɪ] (*compar* -ier, *superl* -iest) *adj* -1. [full of steam] cheio (cheia) de vapor -2. *inf* [erotic] quente.

steel [sti:l] ⟨> *n (U)* aço *m*. ⟨> *comp* de aço. ⟨> *vt* : **to ~ o.s. (for sthg)** encher-se de forças (para algo).

steel industry *n* indústria *f* do aço.

steel wool *n (U)* palha *f* de aço.

steelworker ['sti:l,wɜ:kəʳ] *n* operário *m* siderúrgico, operária *f* siderúrgica.

steelworks ['sti:lwɜ:ks] *(pl inv) n* (usina *f*) siderúrgica *f*.

steely ['sti:lɪ] *(compar* -**ier**, *superl* -**iest**) *adj* - **1.** [steel-coloured] azerado(da) - **2.** [strong, determined] inflexível, inabalável.

steep [sti:p] ⟨> *adj* - **1.** [hill, road] íngreme - **2.** [increase, fall] acentuado(da) - **3.** *inf* [expensive] abusivo(va) - **4.** *inf* [unreasonable] exagerado(da). ⟨> *vt* - **1.** [soak] embeber, molhar - **2.** [fruit] macerar.

steeped [sti:pt] *adj fig:* **~ in sthg** imerso(sa) em algo.

steeple ['sti:pl] *n* agulha *f (do campanário)*.

steeplechase ['sti:pltʃeɪs] *n* corrida *f* de obstáculos.

steeplejack *n* consertador *m*, -ra *f* de chaminés e campanários.

steeply ['sti:plɪ] *adv* - **1.** [at steep angle] vertiginosamente - **2.** [considerably] consideravelmente.

steer ['stɪəʳ] ⟨> *n* [bullock] boi *m*. ⟨> *vt* conduzir, guiar. ⟨> *vi* conduzir; **the car ~ s well** é um carro bom de dirigir; **the bus ~ed into the hedge** o ônibus foi direto para a cerca viva; **to ~ clear (of sb/sthg)** *fig* ficar longe (de alguém/algo).

steering ['stɪərɪŋ] *n (U)* AUT direção *f*.

steering column *n* coluna *f* de direção.

steering committee *n* comitê *m* de direção.

steering lock *n* capacidade *f* de giro.

steering wheel *n* volante *m*, direção *f*.

stellar ['steləʳ] *adj* estelar.

stem [stem] *(pt & pp* -**med**, *cont* -**ming**) ⟨> *n* - **1.** [of plant] caule *m* - **2.** [of glass] pé *m*, base *f* - **3.** [of pipe] tubo *m* - **4.** GRAMM raiz *f*. ⟨> *vt* [stop - flow] conter; [- blood] estancar.

➡ **stem from** *vt fus* derivar-se de, ser o resultado de.

stench [stentʃ] *n* fedor *m*.

stencil ['stensl] *(UK pt & pp* -**led**, *cont* -**ling**, *US pt & pp* -**ed**, *cont* -**ing**) ⟨> *n* [template] matriz *f*. ⟨> *vt* reproduzir com matriz.

stenographer [stə'nɒgrəfəʳ] *n* estenógrafo *m*, -fa *f*.

stenography [stə'nɒgrəfɪ] *n (U)* estenografia *f*.

step [step] *(pt & pp* -**ped**, *cont* -**ping**) ⟨> *n* - **1.** [pace] passo *m*; **in ~ with** *fig* [in touch with] em acordo com; **out of ~ with** *fig* [out of touch with] em desacordo com; **to watch one's ~** [when walking] olhar onde se pisa; *fig* [be cautious] tomar cuidado - **2.** [action] medida *f* - **3.** [stage, degree] grau *m*; **~ by ~** passo a passo - **4.** [stair, ladder] degrau *m* - **5.** US MUS tom *m*. ⟨> *vi* - **1.** [take a single step] dar um passo; **to ~ forward** dar um passo à frente; **watch where you ~** olhe onde você pisa; **to ~ off sthg** descer de algo; **to ~ over sthg** pisar em algo - **2.** [put one's foot down]: **to ~ on sthg** pisar em algo; **~ on it!** [drive fast, hurry up] acelera!; **to ~ in sthg** meter o pé em algo.

➡ **steps** *npl* - **1.** [stairs] escadas *fpl* - **2.** UK [stepladder] escada *f* de mão.

➡ **step aside** *vi* - **1.** [move to one side] afastar-se, ficar de lado - **2.** [resign] renunciar.

➡ **step back** *vi* [pause to reflect] parar para pensar.

➡ **step down** *vi* [resign] renunciar.

➡ **step in** *vi* [intervene] intervir.

➡ **step up** *vt sep* [increase] aumentar.

step aerobics *n* step *m*.

stepbrother ['step,brʌðəʳ] *n* meio-irmão *m*.

stepchild ['steptʃaɪld] *(pl* -**children** [-,tʃɪldrən]) *n* enteado *m*, -da *f*.

stepdaughter ['step,dɔ:təʳ] *n* enteada *f*.

stepfather ['step,fɑ:ðəʳ] *n* padrasto *m*.

stepladder ['step,lædəʳ] *n* escada *f* de mão.

stepmother ['step,mʌðəʳ] *n* madrasta *f*.

stepping-stone ['stepɪŋ-] *n* - **1.** [in river] passadeira *f* - **2.** *fig* [way to success] trampolim *m*.

stepsister ['step,sɪstəʳ] *n* meia-irmã *f*.

stepson ['stepsʌn] *n* enteado *m*.

stereo ['sterɪəʊ] *(pl* -**s**) ⟨> *adj* estéreo(rea). ⟨> *n* - **1.** [stereo system] (aparelho *m* de) som *m* - **2.** *(U)* [stereo sound] estéreo *m*.

stereophonic *adj* estereofônico(ca).

stereotype ['sterɪətaɪp] ⟨> *n* estereótipo *m*. ⟨> *vt* estereotipar.

sterile ['steraɪl] *adj* - **1.** [germ-free] esterilizado(da) - **2.** [unable to produce offspring] estéril - **3.** *pej* [unimaginative] improdutivo(va).

sterility [ste'rɪlətɪ] *n (U)* - **1.** [gen] esterilidade *f* - **2.** *pej* [lack of imagination] improdutividade *f*.

sterilization [,sterəlaɪ'zeɪʃn] *n (U)* [gen] esterilização *f*.

sterilize, -ise ['sterəlaɪz] *vt* esterilizar.

sterilized milk ['sterəlaɪzd-] *n (U)* leite *m* esterilizado.

sterling ['stɜ:lɪŋ] ⟨> *adj* - **1.** [of British money] esterlino(na) - **2.** [excellent] excelente. ⟨> *n (U)* libra *f* esterlina. ⟨> *comp* em libras esterlinas.

sterling silver *n (U)* prata *f* de lei.

stern [stɜ:n] ⟨> *adj* severo(ra). ⟨> *n* popa *f*.

sternly ['stɜ:nlɪ] *adv* [disapprovingly] em desaprovação.

steroid ['stɪərɔɪd] *n* esteróide *m*.

stethoscope ['steθəskəʊp] *n* estetoscópio *m*.

stetson ['stetsn] *n* chapéu *m* de vaqueiro.

stevedore ['sti:vədɔ:ʳ] *n* US estivador *m*, -ra *f*.

stew [stju:] ⟨> *n* ensopado *m*, refogado *m*. ⟨> *vt* ensopar, refogar. ⟨> *vi*: **to let sb ~** *fig* deixar alguém cozinhando.

steward ['stjʊəd] *n* - **1.** UK [on plane] comissário *m* de bordo - **2.** UK [ship, train] camareiro *m* - **3.** UK [marshal] coordenador *m*, -ra *f (de uma corrida, um desfile etc)*.

stewardess ['stjʊədɪs] *n* comissária *f* de bordo.

stewing steak UK ['stju:ɪŋ-], **stewbeef** US ['stju:bi:f] *n (U)* carne *f* para refogado.

St. Ex. *(abbr of* **stock exchange**) bolsa *f* de valores.

stg *(abbr of* **sterling**) libra *f* esterlina.

stick [stɪk] *(pt & pp* **stuck**) ⟨> *n* - **1.** [piece of wood] graveto *m* - **2.** [of chalk] (pedaço *m* de) giz *m* - **3.** [of dynamite] (banana *f*) de dinamite - **4.** [of celery] talho *m* de aipo **- 5.** [walking stick] bastão *m* **- 6.** *SPORT* taco *m* **- 7.** *phr*: **to get the wrong end of the** ~ entender justamente o contrário. <> *vt* **- 1.** [jab]: **to** ~ **sthg in(to) sthg** fincar *OR* espetar algo em algo; **to** ~ **sthg through sthg** atravessar algo com algo **- 2.** [with adhesive] colar; **to** ~ **sthg on** *OR* **to sthg** colar algo em algo **- 3.** *inf* [put] socar **- 4.** *UK inf* [tolerate] agüentar; **to** ~ **it** conseguir agüentar. <> *vi* **- 1.** [arrow, dart, spear]: **I've got a splinter stuck in my finger** há uma felpa enfiada no meu dedo **- 2.** [adhere]: **to** ~ **(to sthg)** colar (em algo) **- 3.** [become jammed] emperrar **- 4.** [remain]: **to** ~ **in one's mind** ficar na cabeça de alguém.

➡ **sticks** *npl pej* [country]: **(out) in the** ~**s** lá nos cafundós, no fim do mundo.

➡ **stick around** *vi inf* ficar.

➡ **stick at** *vt fus* continuar firme em; **to** ~ **at it** continuar firme.

➡ **stick by** *vt fus* **- 1.** [person] ficar ao lado de **- 2.** [decision] manter.

➡ **stick out** <> *vt sep* **- 1.** [extend] colocar para fora; **to** ~ **one's tongue out at sb** botar a língua (para alguém) **- 2.** *inf* [endure]: **to** ~ **it out** agüentar. <> *vi* **- 1.** [protrude] sobressair **- 2.** *inf* [be noticeable] destacar-se, chamar a atenção.

➡ **stick out for** *vt fus UK* insistir até conseguir.

➡ **stick to** *vt fus* **- 1.** [person, path] não abandonar **- 2.** [principles, decision] ser fiel a; **if I were you, I'd** ~ **to French** se eu fosse tu, ficaria apenas com o francês **- 3.** [promise] cumprir.

➡ **stick together** *vi* [people] manter-se unidos(-das).

➡ **stick up** <> *vt sep* **- 1.** [sign, notice, postcard] fixar na parede **- 2.** [with gun]: ~ **'em up!** mãos ao alto! <> *vi* sobressair; **to be** ~**ing up** estar espetado(da).

➡ **stick up for** *vt fus* defender.

➡ **stick with** *vt fus* **- 1.** [activity, decision] manter **- 2.** [person] ficar perto de.

sticker ['stɪkə^r] *n* [piece of paper] adesivo *m*.

sticking plaster ['stɪkɪŋ-] *n* **- 1.** *(U)* [bandaging material] esparadrapo *m* **- 2.** [bandage] curativo *m*.

stick insect *n* bicho-pau *m*.

stick-in-the-mud *n inf* retrógrado *m*, -da *f*.

stickleback ['stɪklbæk] *n* esgana-gata *m*.

stickler ['stɪklə^r] *n*: ~ **for sthg** obsessivo(va) por algo.

stick-on *adj* adesivo(va).

stickpin *n US* alfinete *m* de gravata.

stick shift *n US* [gear lever] alavanca *f* da marcha *OR* mudança; [car] carro *m* com câmbio manual.

stick-up *n inf* assalto *m* à mão armada.

sticky ['stɪkɪ] (*compar* **-ier,** *superl* **-iest**) *adj* **- 1.** [tacky] grudento(ta) **- 2.** [adhesive] adesivo(va) **- 3.** *inf* [awkward] chato(ta) **- 4.** [humid] abafado(da).

stiff [stɪf] <> *adj* **- 1.** [inflexible] duro(ra) **- 2.** [difficult to move] emperrado(da) **- 3.** [difficult to stir] consistente **- 4.** [aching] dolorido(da); ~ **neck** torcicolo *m* **- 5.** [formal] formal **- 6.** [severe] severo(ra) **- 7.** [difficult] duro(ra) **- 8.** *inf* [drink] forte **- 9.** [breeze] forte. <> *adv inf* [for emphasis] muito; **to be bored** ~ estar completamente entediado(da); **to be scared/frozen** ~ estar morrendo de medo/de frio.

stiffen ['stɪfn] <> *vt* **- 1.** [paper, fabric] endurecer **- 2.**

[resistance, resolve] reforçar. <> *vi* **- 1.** [tense up - people] ficar tenso(sa); [- joints, muscles, back] enrijecer **- 2.** [become difficult to move] emperrar **- 3.** [become more severe, intense - competition] ficar mais acirrado(da); [- resistance, resolve] fortalecer-se **- 4.** [breeze] ficar mais forte.

stiffener ['stɪfnə^r] *n* [in collar] *tira fina de plástico ou cartão inserida num colar para manter os pontos compactados.*

stiffness ['stɪfnɪs] *n (U)* **- 1.** [of paper, fabric] rigidez *f* **- 2.** [of hinge, handle, door] emperramento *m* **- 3.** [of joints, limbs, back] enrijecimento *m*, tensão *f* **- 4.** [of manner, smile, welcome] formalidade *f*, frieza *f* **- 5.** [of sentence, punishment] rigorosidade *f* **- 6.** [of resistance, resolve] firmeza *f* **- 7.** [of exam] dificuldade *f*.

stifle ['staɪfl] <> *vt* **- 1.** [suffocate] sufocar **- 2.** [suppress] sufocar, reprimir. <> *vi* [suffocate] sufocar.

stifling ['staɪflɪŋ] *adj* sufocante.

stigma ['stɪgmə] *n* estigma *m*.

stigmatize, -ise ['stɪgmətaɪz] *vt* estigmatizar.

stile [staɪl] *n escada para passar sobre uma cerca.*

stiletto (heel) [stɪ'letəʊ-] *n UK* salto *m* alto.

still [stɪl] <> *adv* **- 1.** [in time] ainda; **do you** ~ **live in ...?** você ainda mora em ...? **- 2.** [all the same] ainda assim **- 3.** *(with comparatives)* ainda; **more interesting** ~**, ...** ainda mais interessante que isso, ... **- 4.** [motionless] sem se mover; **sit** ~**!** te senta e fica quieto! <> *adj* **- 1.** [not moving] parado(da) **- 2.** [calm, quiet] calmo(ma), tranqüilo(la) **- 3.** [not windy] sem vento **- 4.** [not fizzy] sem gás. <> *n* **- 1.** *PHOT* foto *f* fixa **- 2.** [for making alcohol] alambique *m*.

stillborn ['stɪlbɔ:n] *adj* nado-morto(ta).

still life *(pl* **-s)** *n* natureza-morta *f*.

stillness ['stɪlnɪs] *n (U)* quietude *f*.

stilted ['stɪltɪd] *adj* forçado(da).

stilts [stɪlts] *npl* **- 1.** [for person] pernas *fpl* de pau **- 2.** [for building] estacas *fpl*.

stimulant ['stɪmjʊlənt] *n* estimulante *m*.

stimulate ['stɪmjʊleɪt] *vt* **- 1.** [gen] estimular **- 2.** [physically] excitar.

stimulating ['stɪmjʊleɪtɪŋ] *adj* estimulante.

stimulation [,stɪmjʊ'leɪʃn] *n (U)* estímulo *m*.

stimulus ['stɪmjʊləs] *(pl* **-li** [-laɪ]) *n* estímulo *m*.

sting [stɪŋ] *(pt & pp* **stung)** <> *n* **- 1.** [from bee] ferroada *f*; **to take the** ~ **out of sthg** *fig* atenuar algo **- 2.** [from insect] picada *f* **- 3.** [from nettle] urticária *f* **- 4.** [part of bee, wasp, scorpion] ferrão *m*. <> *vt* **- 1.** [subj: bee, wasp, scorpion] picar; [subj: nettle] queimar; [subj: smoke, acid] irritar **- 2.** *fig* [subj: remark, criticism] ferir. <> *vi* **- 1.** [bee, wasp, scorpion] picar; [nettle] queimar; [smoke, acid] irritar **- 2.** [eyes, skin] arder.

stinging nettle ['stɪŋɪŋ-] *n UK* urtiga *f*.

stingy ['stɪndʒɪ] *(compar* **-ier,** *superl* **-iest**) *adj* **- 1.** *inf* [person] sovina **- 2.** *inf* [amount] escasso(sa).

stink [stɪŋk] *(pt* **stank** *OR* **stunk,** *pp* **stunk**) <> *n* fedor *m*. <> *vi* **- 1.** [smell] feder **- 2.** *inf fig* [be worthless] ser uma porcaria, não valer nada.

stink-bomb *n* bomba *f* de cheiro.

stinking ['stɪŋkɪŋ] *inf* <> *adj* **- 1.** [smelly] fedorento(ta) **- 2.** *fig* [for emphasis] maldito(ta). <> *adv* extremamente; **he's** ~ **rich** está podre de rico.

stint [stɪnt] ⬦ *n* [period of time] período *m.* ⬦ *vi*: **to ~ on sthg** pechinchar algo.

stipend ['staɪpend] *n* estipêndio *m.*

stipulate ['stɪpjʊleɪt] *vt* estipular.

stipulation [ˌstɪpjʊ'leɪʃn] *n* **- 1.** *(U)* [stating of conditions] estipulação *f* **- 2.** [condition] condição *f.*

stir [stɜːʳ] *(pt & pp* -red, *cont* -ring) ⬦ *n* **- 1.** [act of mixing] mexida *f* **- 2.** [public excitement] agitação *f,* alvoroço *m.* ⬦ *vt* **- 1.** [mix] mexer, misturar **- 2.** [move physically] mexer; **to ~ o.s.** mexer-se *(para fazer algo)* **- 3.** [rouse, excite] instigar. ⬦ *vi* **-1.** [move gently] mover-se, mexer-se **- 2.** [awaken] despertar.
➡ **stir up** *vt sep* **- 1.** [dust, mud] levantar **- 2.** [trouble, dissent, feelings, memories] provocar.

stir-fry *vt* refogar.

stirring ['stɜːrɪŋ] ⬦ *adj* instigante. ⬦ *n* [feeling] indício *m.*

stirrup ['stɪrəp] *n* estribo *m.*

stitch [stɪtʃ] ⬦ *n* **- 1.** GEN ponto *m* **- 2.** [pain]: **to have a ~** sentir pontadas de dor **- 3.** *phr*: **to be in ~es** chorar de tanto rir. ⬦ *vt* costurar.

stitching ['stɪtʃɪŋ] *n* *(U)* costura *f.*

stoat [stəʊt] *n* arminho *m.*

stock [stɒk] ⬦ *n* **-1.** [gen] estoque *m*; **in ~** em estoque; **out of ~** esgotado(da) **- 2.** [FIN - of company] capital *m*; [- of government] títulos *mpl* do governo; **~s and shares** títulos *mpl* mobiliários, ações *fpl* **- 3.** *(U)* [ancestry] estirpe *f,* linhagem *f* **- 4.** CULIN caldo *m* **- 5.** *(U)* [livestock] rebanho *m* **- 6.** [of gun] coronha *f* **- 7.** *phr*: **to take ~ (of sthg)** refletir (sobre algo). ⬦ *adj* [typical] típico(ca). ⬦ *vt* **- 1.** COMM ter em estoque **- 2.** [fill] encher (de); **to be ~ed with** estar cheio (cheia) de.
➡ **stock up** *vi*: **to ~ up (on** OR **with sthg)** fazer estoque (de algo).

stockade [stɒ'keɪd] *n* paliçada *f.*

stockbroker ['stɒkˌbrəʊkəʳ] *n* corretor *m,* -ra *f* da bolsa.

stockbroking ['stɒkˌbrəʊkɪŋ] *n* *(U)* corretagem *f* na bolsa.

stockcar *n* stockcar *m.*

stock company *n* US sociedade *f* anônima de capital acionário.

stock control *n* controle *m* de estoque.

stock cube *n* UK caldo *m* em cubo.

stock exchange *n* bolsa *f* de valores.

stockholder ['stɒkˌhəʊldəʳ] *n* US acionista *mf.*

Stockholm ['stɒkhəʊm] *n* Estocolmo; **in ~** em Estocolmo.

stocking ['stɒkɪŋ] *n* meia *f.*

stock-in-trade *n* **- 1.** *(U)* [usual behaviour] mote *m* **- 2.** *(U)* [work] ferramenta *f* de trabalho.

stockist ['stɒkɪst] *n* UK varejista *mf.*

stock market *n* mercado *m* de ações.

stock phrase *n* frase *f* feita.

stockpile ['stɒkpaɪl] ⬦ *n* estoque *m.* ⬦ *vt* estocar, armazenar.

stockroom ['stɒkrʊm] *n* depósito *m.*

stock-still *adv* imóvel.

stocktaking ['stɒkˌteɪkɪŋ] *n* *(U)* inventário *m.*

stocky ['stɒkɪ] *(compar* -ier, *superl* -iest) *adj* reforça-do(da), corpulento(ta).

stodgy ['stɒdʒɪ] *(compar* -ier, *superl* -iest) *adj* **- 1.** [indigestible] pesado(da) **- 2.** *pej* [uninteresting] enfadonho(-nha).

stoic ['stəʊɪk] ⬦ *adj* estóico(ca). ⬦ *n* estóico *m,* -ca *f.*

stoical ['stəʊɪkl] *adj* estóico(ca).

stoicism ['stəʊɪsɪzm] *n* estoicismo *m.*

stoke [stəʊk] *vt* [keep burning] alimentar.

stole [stəʊl] ⬦ *pt* ⊳ **steal.** ⬦ *n* [shawl] estola *f.*

stolen ['stəʊln] *pp* ⊳ **steal.**

stolid ['stɒlɪd] *adj* impassível.

stomach ['stʌmək] ⬦ *n* **- 1.** [organ] estômago *m*; **on a full/an empty stomach** com o estômago cheio/vazio **- 2.** [abdomen] ventre *m.* ⬦ *vt* [tolerate] tolerar.

stomach ache *n* dor *f* de estômago.

stomach pump *n* bomba *f* para lavagem estomacal.

stomach ulcer *n* úlcera *f* de estômago.

stomach upset [-'ʌpset] *n* indigestão *f.*

stomp [stɒmp] *vi* pisar forte.

stone [stəʊn] *(pl sense 5 only inv* OR *-s)* ⬦ *n* **- 1.** [gen] pedra *f*; **a ~'s throw from** bem perto de **- 2.** [jewel] pedra *f* preciosa **- 3.** [in fruit] caroço *m* **- 4.** [unit of measurement] *equivalent to 6,35kg.* ⬦ *comp* de pedra. ⬦ *vt* apedrejar.

Stone Age *n*: **the ~** a Idade da Pedra.

stone-cold *adj* gelado(da) como pedra.

stoned [stəʊnd] *adj vinf* **-1.** [drunk] mamado(da) **- 2.** [drugged] chapado(da).

stonemason ['stəʊnˌmeɪsn] *n* canteiro *m,* -ra *f.*

stonewall [ˌstəʊn'wɔːl] *vi* [avoid questions] andar com evasivas.

stoneware *n* *(U)* faiança *f.*

stonewashed ['stəʊnwɒʃt] *adj* estonado(da).

stonework ['stəʊnwɜːk] *n* *(U)* cantaria *f.*

stony ['stəʊnɪ] *(compar* -ier, *superl* -iest) *adj* **- 1.** [covered with stones] pedregoso(sa) **- 2.** [unfriendly] impassível, frio (fria).

stood [stʊd] *pt & pp* ⊳ **stand.**

stooge [stuːdʒ] *n* **-1.** *inf* [manipulated person] fantoche *m* **- 2.** [in comedy act] comparsa *mf.*

stool [stuːl] *n* [seat] mocho *m,* banquinho *m.*

stoop [stuːp] ⬦ *n* **- 1.** [bent back]: **to walk with a ~** caminhar encurvado(da) **- 2.** US [of house] varanda *f.* ⬦ *vi* **- 1.** [bend forwards and down] abaixar-se **- 2.** [hunch shoulders] encurvar-se **- 3.** *fig* [debase o.s.]: **to ~ to sthg** rebaixar-se a algo.

stop [stɒp] *(pt & pp* -ped, *cont* -ping) ⬦ *n* **- 1.** [gen] parada *f* **- 2.** [standstill]: **to come to a ~** dar uma parada **- 3.** [end]: **to put a ~ to sthg** dar um basta em algo **- 4.** [in punctuation] ponto *m* **- 5.** *phr*: **to pull out all the ~s** *fig* remover todos os empecilhos **- 6.** TECH trava *f,* ferrolho *m.* ⬦ *vt* **- 1.** [gen] parar; **to ~ doing sthg** parar de fazer algo **- 2.** [prevent] impedir; **to ~ sb/sthg from doing sthg** impedir alguém/algo de fazer algo **- 3.** [interrupt - wages] suspender; [- cheque] sustar; [- match] interromper; [- newspaper] parar **- 4.** [hole, gap] tapar. ⬦ *vi* **- 1.** [gen] parar; **to ~ at nothing (to do sthg)** não parar por nada (para conseguir algo) **- 2.** [stay] ficar.
➡ **stop off** *vi* dar uma parada.

stop over *vi* passar a noite.

stop up ⇔ *vt sep* [block] entupir. ⇔ *vi UK* ficar acordado(da).

stopcock ['stɒpkɒk] *n* torneira *f* de passagem.

stopgap ['stɒpgæp] *n* quebra-galho *m*.

stopover ['stɒpˌəʊvə'] *n* parada *f*.

stoppage ['stɒpɪdʒ] *n* -**1.** [strike] paralização *f* -**2.** *UK* [deduction] dedução *f*.

stopper ['stɒpə'] *n* rolha *f*.

stopping *adj UK*: ~ **train** trem com parada em todas as estações.

stop press *n* notícias *fpl* de última hora.

stop sign *n* AUT sinal *m* de parada.

stopwatch ['stɒpwɒtʃ] *n* cronômetro *m*.

storage ['stɔ:rɪdʒ] *n (U)* armazenamento *m*.

storage heater *n UK* aquecedor que acumula calor à noite, quando a eletricidade é mais barata, e libera calor durante o dia.

store [stɔ:'] ⇔ *n* -**1.** *esp US* [shop] loja *f* -**2.** [supply] reserva *f*, provisão *f* -**3.** [storage place] depósito *m* -**4.** *phr*: **to set great** ~ **by** OR **on sthg** dar muita importância a algo. ⇔ *vt* -**1.** [gen] armazenar -**2.** [details, address, ideas] guardar.

in store *adv* [imminent]: **who knows what the future has in** ~ **for us?** quem sabe o que o futuro nos reserva?

store up *vt sep* -**1.** [objects] armazenar -**2.** [facts, information] guardar.

store card *n* cartão *m* de crédito *(de lojas)*.

store detective *n* segurança *mf* de loja.

storehouse ['stɔ:haʊs, *pl* -haʊzɪz] *n* -**1.** *esp US* [warehouse] depósito *m* -**2.** *fig* [treasury] mina *f*.

storekeeper ['stɔ:ˌki:pə'] *n US* lojista *mf*.

storeroom ['stɔ:rʊm] *n* -**1.** [gen] almoxarifado *m* -**2.** [for food] despensa *f*.

storey *UK* (*pl* storeys), **story** *US* (*pl* -ies) ['stɔ:rɪ] *n* andar *m*.

stork [stɔ:k] *n* cegonha *f*.

storm [stɔ:m] ⇔ *n* -**1.** [bad weather] temporal *m*, tempestade *f*; **a** ~ **in a teacup** uma tempestade num copo d'água -**2.** [violent reaction] torrente *f*. ⇔ *vt* -**1.** MIL tomar de assalto -**2.** [say angrily] esbravejar. ⇔ *vi* [go angrily]: **to** ~ **into/out of** entrar/sair intempestivamente.

storm cloud *n* [bringing rain] nuvem *f* de chuva.

storming *n* -**1.** [assault] assalto *m*, investida *f* -**2.** [capture] tomada *f*.

stormy ['stɔ:mɪ] (*compar* -ier, *superl* -iest) *adj* -**1.** [weather, sea] tempestuoso(sa) -**2.** *fig* [relationship, meeting] turbulento(ta).

story ['stɔ:rɪ] (*pl* -ies) *n* -**1.** [tale] história *f*, conto *m*; **it's the (same) old** ~ é a velha história de sempre; **to cut a long** ~ **short, ...** para encurtar a história ... -**2.** HIST & *euphemism* história *f* -**3.** [article - newspaper] artigo *m*; [- TV, radio] reportagem *f* -**4.** *US* = storey.

storybook ['stɔ:rɪbʊk] *adj* de novela.

storyteller ['stɔ:rɪˌtelə'] *n* -**1.** [teller of story] contador *m*, -ra *f* de histórias -**2.** *euphemism* [liar] mentiroso *m*, -sa *f*.

stout [staʊt] ⇔ *adj* -**1.** [corpulent] corpulento(ta) -**2.** [strong] forte, resistente -**3.** [brave] firme, forte. ⇔ *n (U)* cerveja *f* escura, stout *f*.

stoutness ['staʊtnɪs] *n (U)* [corpulence] corpulência *f*.

stove [stəʊv] ⇔ *pt & pp* ⊳ **stave**. ⇔ *n* -**1.** [for cooking] forno *m* -**2.** [for heating] estufa *f*.

stow [stəʊ] *vt*: **to** ~ **sthg (away)** guardar algo.

stow away *vi* [on ship, plane] embarcar como clandestino(na).

stowaway ['stəʊəweɪ] *n* clandestino *m*, -na *f*.

straddle ['strædl] *vt* -**1.** [subj: person] escarranchar -se em -**2.** [subj: bridge, town] atravessar, cruzar.

strafe *vt* MIL metralhar.

straggle ['strægl] *vi* -**1.** [buildings, hair, plant] espalhar -se -**2.** [person, group] ficar para trás.

straggler ['stræglə'] *n* retardatário *m*, -ria *f*.

straggly ['stræglɪ] (*compar* -ier, *superl* -iest) *adj* emaranhado(da).

straight [streɪt] ⇔ *adj* -**1.** [gen] reto(ta) -**2.** [not curly] liso(sa) -**3.** [honest, frank] direto(ta), franco(ca) -**4.** [tidy] arrumado(da) -**5.** [simple] fácil, simples -**6.** [undiluted] puro(ra) -**7.** *inf* [conventional] convencional -**8.** *gay sl* [heterosexual] heterossexual -**9.** [quits] quite -**10.** *phr*: **to get something** ~ deixar uma coisa clara. ⇔ *adv* -**1.** [in a straight line]: ~ **ahead** bem na frente; **I couldn't see** ~ não podia ver direito -**2.** [upright] reto(ta); **why won't that painting hang** ~ por que aquele quadro não fica reto? -**3.** [directly, immediately] imediatamente; **I'll go** ~ **to bed** vou direto para a cama -**4.** [honestly, frankly] com toda a franqueza -**5.** [undiluted]: **I drink my whisky** ~ tomo meu uísque puro -**6.** *phr*: **to go** ~ corrigir-se. ⇔ *n* SPORT: **the** ~ a reta final.

straight off *adv* no ato.

straight out *adv* sem rodeios.

straightaway *adv* em seguida.

straighten ['streɪtn] ⇔ *vt* -**1.** [tidy] arrumar, organizar -**2.** [make straight] endireitar -**3.** [make level] pôr reto(ta), endireitar. ⇔ *vi* [stand or sit up]: **to** ~ **(up)** endireitar-se.

straighten out *vt sep* [sort out - mess] arrumar; [- problem] resolver.

straight face *n*: **to keep a** ~ ficar sério(ria).

straightforward [ˌstreɪt'fɔ:wəd] *adj* -**1.** [easy] simples -**2.** [honest, frank - answer] direto(ta); [- person] aberto(ta), franco(ca).

strain [streɪn] ⇔ *n* -**1.** [mental] tensão *f* -**2.** MED [of muscle, back] distenção *f* -**3.** [TECH - weight] peso *m*; [- pressure] pressão *f*; [- force] força *f* -**4.** [type, variety] variedade *f*. ⇔ *vt* -**1.** [work hard] forçar -**2.** MED [injure] distender -**3.** [overtax - resources, budget] esticar; [- enthusiasm] acabar; [- patience] esgotar -**4.** [drain - vegetables] escorrer; [- tea] coar -**5.** TECH [rope, girder, ceiling] estirar. ⇔ *vi* [try very hard]: **to** ~ **to do sthg** esforçar-se para fazer algo.

strains *npl literary* [of music] acordes *mpl*.

strained [streɪnd] *adj* -**1.** [forced] forçado(da) -**2.** [tense] tenso(sa) -**3.** MED [sprained] distendido(da) -**4.** [culin - liquid] coado(da); [- vegetables] escorrido (da).

strainer ['streɪnə'] *n* coador *m*.

strait [streɪt] *n* GEOGR estreito *m*.

straits *npl*: **in dire** OR **desperate** ~ **s** em sérios apuros.

straitened ['streɪtnd] *adj fml*: ~ **circumstances** dificuldades financeiras.

straitjacket [ˈstreɪtˌdʒækɪt] *n* [garment] camisa *f* de força.

straitlaced [ˌstreɪtˈleɪst] *adj pej* puritano(na).

Strait of Gibraltar *n*: the ~ o Estreito de Gibraltar.

Strait of Hormuz *n*: the ~ o Estreito de Hormuz.

strand [strænd] *n* **-1.** [of hair, cotton, wool] mecha *f*; **a** ~ **of hair** um fio de cabelo **-2.** [of story, argument, plot] linha *f*.

stranded [ˈstrændɪd] *adj* **-1.** [person] preso(sa) **-2.** [car] atolado(da) **-3.** [boat] encalhado(da).

strange [streɪndʒ] *adj* **-1.** [unusual, unexpected] estranho(nha) **-2.** [unfamiliar] desconhecido(da), estranho(nha).

strangely [ˈstreɪndʒlɪ] *adv* **-1.** [in an odd manner] de forma estranha **-2.** [unexpectedly, mysteriously] inesperadamente **-3.** [surprisingly]: ~ **(enough)** por mais estranho que pareça.

stranger [ˈstreɪndʒəʳ] *n* **-1.** [unknown person] estranho *m*, -nha *f*; **to be a/no ~ to sthg** estar/não estar familiarizado com algo **-2.** [person from elsewhere] forasteiro *m*, -ra *f*.

strangle [ˈstræŋgl] *vt* **-1.** [kill - person] estrangular; [- chicken] torcer o pescoço de **-2.** *fig* [stifle] sufocar.

stranglehold [ˈstræŋglhəʊld] *n* **-1.** [round neck] gravata *f* **-2.** *fig* [strong influence]: ~ **(on sb/sthg)** controle *m* total (sobre alguém/algo).

strangulation [ˌstræŋgjʊˈleɪʃn] *n* (U) [act of killing] estrangulamento *m*.

strap [stræp] (*pt* & *pp* -**ped**, *cont*-**ping**) ⬥ *n* **-1.** [for carrying] correia *f*, tira *f* **-2.** [for fastening] alça *f* **-3.** [of watch] pulseira *f*. ⬥ *vt* [fasten] prender *(com correia)*.

strapless [ˈstræplɪs] *adj* [garment] sem alça.

strapping [ˈstræpɪŋ] *adj* robusto(ta).

Strasbourg [ˈstræzbɜːg] *n* Estrasburgo; **in** ~ em Estrasburgo.

strata [ˈstrɑːtə] *pl* ⊳ **stratum**.

stratagem [ˈstrætədʒəm] *n* estratagema *m*.

strategic [strəˈtiːdʒɪk] *adj* estratégico(ca).

strategist [ˈstrætɪdʒɪst] *n* MIL estrategista *mf*.

strategy [ˈstrætɪdʒɪ] (*pl*-**ies**) *n* estratégia *f*.

stratified [ˈstrætɪfaɪd] *adj* estratificado(da).

stratosphere [ˈstrætəˌsfɪəʳ] *n*: the ~ a estratosfera.

stratum [ˈstrɑːtəm] (*pl*-**ta**) *n* **-1.** GEOL estrato *m* **-2.** *fig* [of society] estrato *m* social.

straw [strɔː] ⬥ *n* **-1.** (U) [dried corn] palha *f* **-2.** [for drinking] canudinho *m* **-3.** *phr*: **to clutch at** ~**s** agarrar-se a qualquer coisa em desespero; **the last** ~ a gota d'água. ⬥ *comp* de palha.

strawberry [ˈstrɔːbərɪ] (*pl*-**ies**) ⬥ *n* [fruit] morango *m*. ⬥ *comp* de morango.

straw poll *n* sondagem *f* de opinião.

stray [streɪ] ⬥ *adj* perdido(da). ⬥ *n* [animal] animal *m* perdido. ⬥ *vi* **-1.** [from group] perder-se **-2.** [from path] desviar-se **-3.** [thoughts, mind]: **to** ~ **from the point** desviar-se do tema.

streak [striːk] *n* **-1.** [of grease] faixa *f* **-2.** [of lightning] raio *m* **-3.** [in hair] listra *f* **-4.** [in character] traço *m* **-5.** [period]: **a winning/losing** ~ período *m* em que só se ganha/perde. ⬥ *vi* [move

quickly] passar como um raio.

streaked [striːkt] *adj* [marked]: ~ **with sthg** manchado(da) de algo.

streaky [ˈstriːkɪ] (*compar*-**ier**, *superl*-**iest**) *adj* [colour, surface] riscado(da), listrado(da).

streaky bacon *n* UK bacon *m*.

stream [striːm] ⬥ *n* **-1.** [brook] riacho *m* **-2.** [of liquid] curso *m* **-3.** [of air] corrente *f* **-4.** [of light] raio *m*, faixa *f* **-5.** [of liquid, air, light] rio *m* **-6.** [of people, traffic] torrente *f* **-7.** [of abuse, queries, complaints, books] série *f* **-8.** UK SCH grupo *m*. ⬥ *vt* UK SCH agrupar de acordo com o rendimento escolar. ⬥ *vi* **-1.** [gen] jorrar **-2.** [air] fluir **-3.** [people]: **to** ~ **in/out** entrar/sair em massa **-4.** [traffic] mover-se rapidamente.

streamer [ˈstriːməʳ] *n* [for party] serpentina *f*, flâmula *f*.

streamline [ˈstriːmlaɪn] *vt* **-1.** [make aerodynamic] dar forma aerodinâmica a **-2.** [make efficient] racionalizar.

streamlined [ˈstriːmlaɪnd] *adj* **-1.** [aerodynamic] aerodinâmico(ca) **-2.** [efficient] racional.

street [striːt] *n* rua *f*; **to be right up sb's** ~ UK *inf* ser exatamente o que se precisa; **to be** ~**s ahead of sb/sthg** UK estar muito além de alguém/algo.

streetcar [ˈstriːtkɑːʳ] *n* US bonde *m*.

street-cred(ibility) *n* (U) *inf* imagem *f*, aceitação *f* (*entre as pessoas jovens*).

street lamp, street light *n* lâmpada *f* de rua.

street lighting *n* (U) iluminação *f* pública.

street map *n* mapa *m* (*da cidade*).

street market *n* feira *f* ao ar livre.

street plan *n* mapa *m* viário.

street value *n* preço *m* de venda (de uma droga).

streetwise [ˈstriːtwaɪz] *adj* esperto(ta); **she's very** ~ ela se vira muito bem na rua.

strength [streŋθ] *n* **-1.** (U) [gen] força *f* **-2.** (U) [power, influence] poder *m*; **on the** ~ **of** com base em; **to go from** ~ **to** ~ ir de vento em popa **-3.** [quality, ability] ponto *m* forte **-4.** (U) [solidity] solidez *f* **-5.** [intensity - gen] intensidade *f*; [- of alcohol] teor *m* alcoólico; [- of drug] potência *f* **-6.** FIN [of currency] solidez *f* **-7.** (U) [number] número *m*; **to be at full** ~ estar com força total; **to be below** ~ não estar com força total; **in** ~ em grande número.

strengthen [ˈstreŋθn] ⬥ *vt* **-1.** [gen] fortalecer **-2.** [reinforce] reforçar **-3.** [intensify] intensificar **-4.** [make braver, more confident] encorajar. ⬥ *vi* **-1.** [physically - body, muscle] fortalecer-se; [- voice] tornar-se mais forte **-2.** [intensify] intensificar-se **-3.** FIN [currency] fortalecer-se.

strenuous [ˈstrenjʊəs] *adj* extenuante.

stress [stres] ⬥ *n* **-1.** [emphasis]: ~ **(on sthg)** ênfase *f* (em algo) **-2.** [tension, anxiety] estresse *m*; **to be under** ~ estar estressado(da) **-3.** TECH [physical pressure]: ~ **(on sthg)** pressão *f* (sobre algo) **-4.** LING [on word, syllable] acento *m* tônico. ⬥ *vt* **-1.** [emphasize] enfatizar, realçar **-2.** LING [word, syllable] acentuar (*na pronúncia*).

stressed [strest] *adj* estressado(da).

stressful [ˈstresfʊl] *adj* estressante.

stretch [stretʃ] ⬥ *n* **-1.** [area] extensão *f* **-2.** [period of time] período *m* -**3.** [effort]: **by no ~ of the imagi-nation** por mais que se queira. ⬦ *vt* -**1.** [gen] esticar - **2.** [pull taut] estirar - **3.** [rules, meaning, truth] distorcer - **4.** [challenge] fazer render ao máximo. ⬦ *vi* -**1.** [gen] esticar-se - **2.** [area]: **to ~ over** estender-se por; **to ~ from ... to** estender-se de ... até - **3.** [person] espreguiçar-se. ⬦ *adj* elásti-co(ca).

➡ **at a stretch** *adv* sem parar.

➡ **stretch out** ⬦ *vt sep* estender, esticar. ⬦ *vi* esticar-se *(deitando)*.

stretcher ['stretʃə˞] *n* maca *f*.

stretcher party *n* (equipe *f* de) padioleiros *mpl*.

stretchmarks ['stretʃmɑːks] *npl* estrias *fpl*.

stretchy ['stretʃi] *(compar* -**ier***, superl* -**iest***) adj* elástico(ca).

strew [struː] *(pt* -**ed***, pp* **strewn** [struːn], -**ed***) vt*: **to be strewn on** *OR* **over sthg** estar esparramado(da) em/sobre algo; **to be strewn with sthg** estar coberto(ta) de algo.

stricken ['strɪkn] *adj*: **to be ~ by** *OR* **with sthg** [grief] estar abalado(da) por algo; [doubt, horror, panic] ser tomado(da) por algo; [illness, complaint] estar atacado(da) por algo.

strict [strɪkt] *adj* -**1.** [severe] rígido(da) - **2.** [inflexible] rigoroso(sa) - **3.** [exact, precise] exato(ta), preciso(-sa).

strictly ['strɪktli] *adv* -**1.** [severely] rigidamente - **2.** [rigidly, absolutely] estritamente - **3.** [precisely, exactly] exatamente, precisamente; **~ speaking** a rigor - **4.** [exclusively] exclusivamente.

strictness ['strɪktnɪs] *n (U)* -**1.** [severity] rigidez *f* - **2.** [rigidity] rigor *m*.

stride [straɪd] *(pt* **strode***, pp* **stridden** ['strɪdn]*)* ⬦ *n* passada *f*; **to take sthg in one's ~** *fig* encarar algo com tranqüilidade. ⬦ *vi* caminhar a passos largos.

➡ **strides** *npl*: **to make (great) ~s** fazer (grandes) progressos.

strident ['straɪdnt] *adj* -**1.** [voice, sound] estridente - **2.** [demand] rigoroso(sa).

strife [straɪf] *n (U) fml* conflitos *mpl*.

strike [straɪk] *(pt & pp* **struck***)* ⬦ *n* -**1.** [gen] greve *f*; **to be (out) on ~** estar em greve; **to go on ~** entrar em greve - **2.** *MIL* [attack] ataque *m* - **3.** [find] descoberta *f*. ⬦ *comp* de greve. ⬦ *vt* -**1.** [hit - deliberately] bater, golpear; [- accidentally] atingir, pegar em - **2.** [subj: hurricane, disaster, lightning] atingir - **3.** [subj: thought] ocorrer; **to ~ sb as sthg** parecer algo a alguém - **4.** [impress]: **to be struck by** *OR* **with sthg** ficar impressionado(da) com algo - **5.** [reach, arrive at] fechar - **6.** [ignite] acender - **7.** [find] descobrir; **to ~ a balance (between)** encontrar um ponto de equilíbrio (entre); **to ~ a serious/happy note** passar uma idéia séria/alegre - **8.** [chime] bater - **9.** *phr*: **to be struck blind/dumb** ficar cego/mudo, ficar cega/muda; **to ~ fear** *OR* **terror into sb** infundir medo/terror em alguém; **to ~ (it) lucky** ter sorte; **to ~ it rich** ficar rico(ca). ⬦ *vi* -**1.** [stop working] entrar em greve - **2.** [hit accidentally]: **to ~ against sthg** bater em algo - **3.** [happen suddenly - hurricane, disaster] ocorrer; [- lightning] cair - **4.** [attack] atacar - **5.** [chime]: **the clock struck seven** o relógio bateu sete horas.

➡ **strike back** *vi* revidar.

➡ **strike down** *vt sep* derrubar.

➡ **strike off** *vt sep*: **to be struck off** perder a licença profissional.

➡ **strike out** ⬦ *vt sep* rasurar. ⬦ *vi* -**1.** [head out] partir, pôr-se a caminho - **2.** [do sthg different] partir para outra.

➡ **strike up** ⬦ *vt fus* -**1.** [friendship, conversation] travar - **2.** [music] começar a tocar. ⬦ *vi* começar a tocar.

strikebound ['straɪkbaʊnd] *adj* paralisado(da) pela greve.

strikebreaker ['straɪkˌbreɪkə˞] *n* fura-greve *mf*.

strike pay *n (U)* fundo *m* de greve.

striker ['straɪkə˞] *n* -**1.** [person on strike] grevista *mf* - **2.** *FTBL* atacante *mf*.

striking ['straɪkɪŋ] *adj* -**1.** [noticeable, unusual] impressionante, chocante - **2.** [attractive] que chama a atenção.

striking distance *n (U)*: **within ~ (of sthg)** muito perto (de algo).

string [strɪŋ] *(pt & pp* **strung***)* ⬦ *n* -**1.** *(U)* [thin rope] cordão *m*, barbante *m* - **2.** [piece of thin rope] cordel *m*; **(with) no ~s attached** sem restrições; **to pull ~s** mexer os pauzinhos - **3.** [row, chain - of beads, pearls] colar *m*; [- of onions] réstia *f* - **4.** [series] série *f*, sucessão *f* - **5.** [for bow, tennis racket] corda *f*; **to be highly strung** *fig* ter o pavio curto - **6.** *COMPUT* string *m*. ⬦ *comp* [vest, bag] de cordão.

➡ **strings** *npl MUS*: **the ~s** as cordas.

➡ **string along** *vt sep inf* dar falsas esperanças a.

➡ **string out** *vt sep*: **to be strung out** estar disperso(sa).

➡ **string together** *vt sep fig* juntar.

➡ **string up** *vt sep inf* enforcar.

string bean *n* vagem *f*.

stringed instrument ['strɪŋd-] *n* instrumento *m* de corda.

stringent ['strɪndʒənt] *adj* rigoroso(sa).

string quartet *n* quarteto *m* de cordas.

stringy *(compar* -**ier***, superl* -**iest***) adj* fibroso(sa).

strip [strɪp] *(pt & pp* -**ped***, cont* -**ping***)* ⬦ *n* -**1.** [of fabric, paper, carpet] tira *f*; **to tear a ~ off sb**, **to tear sb off a ~** *UK* dar uma bronca em alguém - **2.** [of land, water, forest] faixa *f* - **3.** *UK SPORT* camiseta *f (de time)*. ⬦ *vt* -**1.** [undress] despir; **~ped to the waist** nu (nua) até o peito - **2.** [remove layer of] descascar - **3.** [take away from]: **to ~ sb of sthg** despojar alguém de algo. ⬦ *vi* -**1.** [undress] despir-se - **2.** [do a striptease] fazer um striptease.

➡ **strip off** ⬦ *vt sep* tirar. ⬦ *vi* despir-se.

strip cartoon *n UK* tira *f* em quadrinhos.

stripe [straɪp] *n* -**1.** [band of colour] lista *f*, faixa *f* - **2.** [sign of rank] galão *m*.

striped [straɪpt] *adj* listado(da).

strip lighting *n (U)* iluminação *f* fluorescente.

stripper ['strɪpə˞] *n* -**1.** [performer of striptease] stripper *mf* - **2.** [tool, liquid] removedor *m*.

strip-search ⬦ *n* revista *f* policial *(fazendo tirar a roupa)*. ⬦ *vt* revistar *(fazendo tirar a roupa)*.

strip show *n* show *m* de striptease.

striptease ['striptiːz] *n* striptease *m*.

stripy ['straɪpɪ] (*compar* -ier, *superl* -iest) *adj* listado(-da).

strive [straɪv] (*pt* strove, *pp* striven ['strɪvn]) *vi fml*: to ~ for sthg/to do sthg lutar por algo/para fazer algo.

strobe (light) ['strəʊb-] *n* luz *f* estroboscópica.

strode [strəʊd] *pt* ⊳ stride.

stroke [strəʊk] ⟨⟩ *n* -1. *MED* derrame *m* cerebral - 2. [of brush] pincelada *f* - 3. [of pen] traço *m* - 4. [in swimming - movement] braçada *f*; [- style] nado *m* - 5. [movement in rowing] remada *f* - 6. [in tennis] raquetada *f* - 7. [in golf] tacada *f* - 8. [of clock] batida *f* - 9. [of bell] dobre *m* - 10. *UK TYPO* [slash] barra *f* - 11. [piece]: a ~ of genius um lance de gênio; a ~ of luck um golpe de sorte; not to do a ~ of work não levantar um dedo; at a ~ de um golpe só. ⟨⟩ *vt* acariciar.

stroll [strəʊl] ⟨⟩ *n* passeio *m*. ⟨⟩ *vi* passear.

stroller ['strəʊlə'] *n US* [for baby] carrinho *m* de bebê.

strong [strɒŋ] ⟨⟩ *adj* -1. [gen] forte; I've never been ~ in mathematics matemática nunca foi o meu forte; ~ point ponto forte; ~ nerves nervos *mpl* de aço - 2. [solid, sturdy] reforçado(da) - 3. [in number] de ... pessoas; the crowd was 2000 ~ a multidão tinha 2000 pessoas. ⟨⟩ *adv*: to be still going ~ [person, group] ser forte ainda; [machine] funcionar bem ainda.

strongarm ['strɒŋɑ:m] *adj*: to use ~ tactics ter pulso firme.

strongbox ['strɒŋbɒks] *n* caixa-forte *f*.

stronghold ['strɒŋhəʊld] *n fig* baluarte *m*.

strong language *n* (U) *euphemism* linguagem *f* pesada.

strongly ['strɒŋlɪ] *adv* -1. [sturdily, solidly - built] solidamente; [- protected] fortemente - 2. [in degree or intensity] intensamente; the kitchen smells ~ of onions tem um cheiro forte de cebola na cozinha - 3. [very definitely] totalmente; to feel ~ about sthg ter uma opinião firme sobre algo.

strong man *n* homem *m* forte.

strong-minded [-'maɪndɪd] *adj* de caráter.

strong room *n* casa-forte *f*.

strong-willed [-'wɪld] *adj* obstinado(da).

stroppy ['strɒpɪ] (*compar* -ier, *superl* -iest) *adj UK inf* emburrado(da).

strove [strəʊv] *pt* ⊳ strive.

struck [strʌk] *pt & pp* ⊳ strike.

structural ['strʌktʃərəl] *adj* estrutural.

structurally ['strʌktʃərəlɪ] *adv* estruturalmente.

structure ['strʌktʃə'] ⟨⟩ *n* -1. [organization, arrangement] estrutura *f* - 2. [building, construction] construção *f*. ⟨⟩ *vt* estruturar.

struggle ['strʌgl] ⟨⟩ *n* -1. [gen]: ~ (for sthg/to do sthg) luta *f* (por algo/por fazer algo) - 2. [fight] briga *f*. ⟨⟩ *vi* -1. [try hard, strive] esforçar-se; to ~ free lutar para ser solto(ta); to ~ (for sthg/to do sthg) lutar (por algo/por fazer algo) - 2. [fight]: to ~ (with sb) brigar (com alguém) - 3. [move with difficulty] mover-se com dificuldade; he ~d to his feet ele conseguiu se levantar a duras penas.
➡ **struggle on** *vi*: to ~ on (with sthg) continuar (algo)a duras penas.

struggling ['strʌglɪŋ] *adj* esforçado(da).

strum [strʌm] (*pt & pp* -med, *cont* -ming) ⟨⟩ *vt*

dedilhar. ⟨⟩ *vi*: to ~ (on sthg) dedilhar (algo).

strung [strʌŋ] *pt & pp* ⊳ string.

strut [strʌt] ⟨⟩ *n* -1. *CONSTR* escora *f* - 2. *AERON* montante *m*. ⟨⟩ *vi* andar empertigado(da).

strychnine ['strɪkni:n] *n* (U) estricnina *f*.

stub [stʌb] (*pt & pp* -bed, *cont* -bing) ⟨⟩ *n* -1. [of cigarette, pencil] toco *m* - 2. [of ticket, cheque] canhoto *m*. ⟨⟩ *vt*: to ~ one's toe (on) dar uma topada com o dedo do pé (em).
➡ **stub out** *vt sep* apagar.

stubble ['stʌbl] *n* (U) -1. [in field] restolho *m* - 2. [on chin] barba *f* curta.

stubborn ['stʌbən] *adj* -1. [person] teimoso(sa), cabeçudo(da) - 2. [stain] persistente, difícil.

stubbornly ['stʌbənlɪ] *adv* -1. [wait] teimosamente - 2. [refuse] resistentemente - 3. [declare] resolutamente.

stubby ['stʌbɪ] (*compar* -ier, *superl* -iest) *adj* atarracado(da).

stucco ['stʌkəʊ] *n* (U) estuque *m*.

stuck [stʌk] ⟨⟩ *pt & pp* ⊳ stick. ⟨⟩ *adj* -1. [gen] preso(sa) - 2. [window] emperrado(da) - 3. [stumped]: can you help with this problem? I'm ~ pode me ajudar com esse problema? (eu) empaquei.

stuck-up *adj inf pej* convencido(da), metido(da).

stud [stʌd] *n* -1. [metal decoration] tachão *m* - 2. [earring] pingente *m* - 3. *UK* [on boot, shoe] taco *m* - 4. (U) [of horses] plantel *m*; to be put out to ~ ser usado(da) para reprodução.

studded ['stʌdɪd] *adj*: ~ (with sthg) adornado(da) (com algo); a ~ jacket uma jaqueta adornada; ~ with precious stones cravejado(da) de pedras preciosas.

student ['stju:dnt] ⟨⟩ *n* -1. [at college, university] estudante *mf* - 2. [scholar] estudioso *m*, -sa *f*. ⟨⟩ *comp* -1. [nurse, teacher] em estágio - 2. [politics] estudantil - 3. [lifestyle] de estudante - 4. [disco] para estudantes.

student loan *n UK* crédito *m* educativo.

students' union *n* grêmio *m* estudantil.

stud farm *n* haras *m inv*.

studied ['stʌdɪd] *adj* -1. [answer] pensado(da) - 2. [smile] estudado(da).

studio ['stju:dɪəʊ] (*pl* -s) *n* estúdio *m*.

studio apartment *n US* = studio flat.

studio audience *n* público *m* no auditório.

studio flat *UK*, **studio apartment** *US* *n* (apartamento *m*) JK *m*.

studious ['stju:djəs] *adj* estudioso(sa).

studiously ['stju:djəslɪ] *adv* cuidadosamente.

study ['stʌdɪ] (*pl* -ies, *pt & pp* -ied) ⟨⟩ *n* -1. (U) [gen] estudo *m* - 2. [room] sala *f* de estudos. ⟨⟩ *vt* -1. [learn] estudar - 2. [examine] examinar, estudar. ⟨⟩ *vi* estudar.
➡ **studies** *npl* estudos *mpl*.

stuff [stʌf] ⟨⟩ *n* (U) *inf* -1. [matter, things] coisa *f*; to know one's ~ entender do riscado; and all that ~ e tudo isso - 2. [substance]: what's that ~ in your pocket? o que é isso aí no seu bolso? - 3. [belongings] coisas *fpl*. ⟨⟩ *vt* -1. [push, put] enfiar - 2. [fill, cram]: to ~ sthg (with sthg) encher algo (com algo) - 3. [with food]: to ~ o.s. (with OR on sthg) *inf* empanturrar-se (de algo) - **4.** *CULIN* rechear.

stuffed [stʌftl] *adj* -**1.** [filled, crammed]: ~ **with sthg** atulhado(da) de algo - **2.** *inf* [with food] empanturrado(da) - **3.** *CULIN* recheado(da) - **4.** [animal] empalhado(da) - **5.** *phr*: **get** ~! *UK v inf* vai te catar!

stuffing [ˈstʌfɪŋ] *n* (*U*) -**1.** [filling - for furniture] estofamento *m*; [- for toys] enchimento *m* - **2.** *CULIN* recheio *m*.

stuffy [ˈstʌfɪ] (*compar* -**ier**, *superl* -**iest**) *adj* -**1.** [room] abafado(da) - **2.** [formal, old-fashioned] retrógrado(da).

stumble [ˈstʌmbl] *vi* -**1.** [trip] tropeçar - **2.** [hesitate, make mistake] equivocar-se.

➡ **stumble across, stumble on** *vt fus* -**1.** [person] topar com - **2.** [objects] encontrar por acaso.

stumbling block [ˈstʌmblɪŋ-] *n* pedra *f* no caminho, obstáculo *m*.

stump [stʌmp] ◇ *n* -**1.** [of tree] toco *m* - **2.** [of limb] coto *m*. ◇ *vt* deixar perplexo(xa). ◇ *vi* caminhar com passo firme; **he** ~**ed up the steps** ele subiu a escada com passo firme.

➡ **stumps** *npl CRICKET* varetas *fpl* verticais.
➡ **stump up** *vt fus inf UK* desembolsar.

stun [stʌn] (*pt & pp* -**ned**, *cont* -**ning**) *vt* -**1.** [knock unconscious] deixar sem sentidos - **2.** [shock, surprise] atordoar.

stung [stʌŋ] *pt & pp* ⟶ **sting**.

stun grenade *n* granada *f* de efeito moral.

stunk [stʌŋk] *pt & pp* ⟶ **stink**.

stunned *adj* -**1.** [unconscious] inconsciente - **2.** [shocked, surprised] atordoado(da).

stunning [ˈstʌnɪŋ] *adj* -**1.** [very beautiful] imponente - **2.** [very shocking, surprising] espantoso(sa).

stunt [stʌnt] ◇ *n* -**1.** [for publicity] golpe *m* publicitário - **2.** *CINEMA* cena *f* arriscada, cena *f* perigosa. ◇ *vt* inibir.

stunted [ˈstʌntɪd] *adj* mirrado(da).

stunt man *n* dublê *m*.

stunt woman *n* dublê *f*.

stupefy [ˈstjuːpɪfaɪ] (*pt & pp* -**ied**) *vt* -**1.** [tire, bore] entorpecer - **2.** [surprise] deixar estupefato(ta).

stupendous [stjuːˈpendəs] *adj inf* -**1.** [wonderful] estupendo(da) - **2.** [very large] enorme.

stupid [ˈstjuːpɪd] *adj* -**1.** [foolish] estúpido(da) - **2.** *inf* [wretched, damned] idiota.

stupidity [stjuːˈpɪdətɪ] *n* (*U*) estupidez *f*.

stupidly [ˈstjuːpɪdlɪ] *adv* estupidamente.

stupor [ˈstjuːpəʳ] *n* estupor *m*.

sturdy [ˈstɜːdɪ] (*compar* -**ier**, *superl* -**iest**) *adj* -**1.** [person] forte, robusto(ta) - **2.** [furniture, platform] sólido(da), firme.

sturgeon [ˈstɜːdʒən] (*pl inv*) *n* esturjão *m*.

stutter [ˈstʌtəʳ] ◇ *n* gagueira *f*. ◇ *vi* gaguejar.

sty [staɪ] (*pl* **sties**) *n* chiqueiro *m*.

stye [staɪ] *n* terçol *m*.

style [staɪl] ◇ *n* -**1.** [manner] estilo *m*; **in the** ~ **of** ao estilo de - **2.** (*U*) [smartness, elegance] classe *f* - **3.** [fashion, design] modelo *m*. ◇ *vt* pentear de acordo com a moda.

styling mousse *n* (*U*) mousse *f* modeladora.

stylish [ˈstaɪlɪʃ] *adj* de estilo.

stylist [ˈstaɪlɪst] *n* estilista *mf*.

stylized, -ised [ˈstaɪlaɪzd] *adj* estilizado(da).

stylus [ˈstaɪləs] (*pl* -**es**) *n* -**1.** [on record player] agulha *f* - **2.** *COMPUT* caneta *f* gráfica.

stymie [ˈstaɪmɪ] *vt inf*: **to be** ~**d** estar entravado(da).

suave [swɑːv] *adj* afável.

sub [sʌb] *n inf* -**1.** *SPORT* (*abbr of* **substitute**) reserva *mf* - **2.** (*abbr of* **submarine**) submarino *m* - **3.** *UK* (*abbr of* **subscription**) assinatura *f* - **4.** *UK* (*abbr of* **advance payment**) adiantamento *m* - **5.** *US* [sandwich] *tipo de sanduíche*.

sub- [sʌb] *prefix* sub(-).

subcommittee [ˈsʌbkəˌmɪtɪ] *n* subcomissão *f*.

subconscious [ˌsʌbˈkɒnʃəs] ◇ *adj* subconsciente. ◇ *n*: **the** ~ o subconsciente.

subconsciously [ˌsʌbˈkɒnʃəslɪ] *adj* de forma subconsciente.

subcontinent [ˌsʌbˈkɒntɪnənt] *n* subcontinente *m*.

subcontract [ˌsʌbkənˈtrækt] *vt* subcontratar.

subculture [ˈsʌbˌkʌltʃəʳ] *n* subcultura *f*.

subdivide [ˌsʌbdɪˈvaɪd] *vt* subdividir.

subdue [səbˈdjuː] *vt* -**1.** [enemy, rioters, crowds] subjugar - **2.** [feelings, passions] conter, dominar.

subdued [səbˈdjuːd] *adj* -**1.** [person] desanimado(da) - **2.** [feelings] reprimido(da) - **3.** [light, sound, colour] fraco(ca).

subeditor [ˌsʌbˈedɪtəʳ] *n* copidesque *mf*.

subgroup [ˈsʌbgruːp] *n* subgrupo *m*.

subheading [ˈsʌbˌhedɪŋ] *n* subtítulo *m*.

subhuman [ˌsʌbˈhjuːmən] *adj pej* subumano(na).

subject [*adj, n & prep* ˈsʌbdʒekt, *vt* səbˈdʒekt] ◇ *adj*: ~ **(to sthg)** sujeito(ta) (a algo). ◇ *n* -**1.** [topic, person under consideration] assunto *m*, tema *m* - **2.** *GRAMM* sujeito *m* - **3.** *SCH & UNIV* cadeira *f* - **4.** [citizen] súdito *m*, -ta *f*. ◇ *vt* -**1.** [bring under strict control] sujeitar, dominar - **2.** [force to experience]: **to** ~ **sb to sthg** sujeitar alguém a algo.

➡ **subject to** *prep* sujeito(ta) a; ~ **to the budget** dependendo do orçamento.

subjection [səbˈdʒekʃn] *n* sujeição *f*, subordinação *f*.

subjective [səbˈdʒektɪv] *adj* subjetivo(va).

subjectively [səbˈdʒektɪvlɪ] *adv* subjetivamente.

subject matter [ˈsʌbdʒekt-] *n* (*U*) temática *f*, tema *m*.

sub judice *adj JUR* sub judice.

subjugate [ˈsʌbdʒʊgeɪt] *vt fml* -**1.** [gen] subjugar - **2.** [feelings, desires] dominar.

subjunctive [səbˈdʒʌŋktɪv] *n GRAMM*: ~ **(mood)** (modo *m*) subjuntivo *m*.

sublet [ˌsʌbˈlet] (*pt & pp* **sublet**, *cont* -**ting**) *vt* sublocar.

sublime [səˈblaɪm] *adj* sublime; **from the** ~ **to the ridiculous** do sublime ao ridículo.

sublimely [səˈblaɪmlɪ] *adv* totalmente, completamente.

subliminal [ˌsʌbˈlɪmɪnl] *adj* subliminar.

submachine gun [ˌsʌbməˈʃiːn-] *n* metralhadora *f*.

submarine [ˌsʌbməˈriːn] *n* submarino *m*.

submerge [səbˈmɜːdʒ] ◇ *vt* -**1.** [flood] inundar - **2.** [plunge into liquid] submergir - **3.** *fig* [in activity]: **to** ~ **o.s. in sthg** mergulhar em algo. ◇ *vi* mergulhar.

submission [səb'mɪʃn] *n (U)* -**1.** [obedience, capitulation] submissão *f* -**2.** [presentation] apresentação *f*.

submissive [səb'mɪsɪv] *adj* submisso(sa).

submit [səb'mɪt] (*pt* & *pp* -**ted**, *cont* -**ting**) ◇ *vt* submeter. ◇ *vi*: **to ~ (to sb)** render-se (a alguém); **to ~ (to sthg)** submeter-se (a algo).

subnormal [ˌsʌb'nɔːml] *adj* subnormal.

subordinate [*adj* & *n* sə'bɔːdɪnət, *vt* sə'bɔːdɪneɪt] ◇ *adj fml*: **~ (to sthg)** subordinado(da) (a algo). ◇ *n* subordinado *m*, -da *f*. ◇ *vt fml* subordinar.

subordinate clause [sə'bɔːdɪnət-] *n* oração *f* subordinada.

subordination [sə,bɔːdɪ'neɪʃn] *n (U)*: **~ (of/to sthg)** subordinação *f* (de/a algo).

subpoena [sə'piːnə] (*pt* & *pp* -**ed**) *JUR* ◇ *n* intimação *f* (*para comparecimento em juízo*). ◇ *vt* intimar (*para comparecimento em juízo*).

sub-post office *n UK* pequena agência de correios local que oferece menos serviços que uma agência central.

subroutine [ˈsʌbruːˌtiːn] *n COMPUT* sub-rotina *f*.

subscribe [səb'skraɪb] ◇ *vi* -**1.** [to magazine, newspaper]: **to ~ (to sthg)** fazer assinatura (de algo) -**2.** [to view, belief]: **to ~ to sthg** concordar com algo. ◇ *vt* contribuir com, doar.

subscriber [səb'skraɪbəʳ] *n* -**1.** [to magazine, newspaper] assinante *mf* -**2.** [to service] usuário *m*, -ria *f* -**3.** [to charity, campaign] doador *m*, -ra *f*.

subscription [səb'skrɪpʃn] *n* -**1.** [to newspaper, magazine] assinatura *f* -**2.** [to club, organization - monthly] mensalidade *f*; [- yearly] anuidade *f*.

subsection [ˈsʌbˌsekʃn] *n* subseção *f*.

subsequent [ˈsʌbsɪkwənt] *adj* subseqüente.

subsequently [ˈsʌbsɪkwəntlɪ] *adv* subseqüentemente, por conseguinte.

subservient [səb'sɜːvjənt] *adj* -**1.** [servile]: **~ (to sb)** subserviente (a alguém) -**2.** [less important]: **~ (to sthg)** subordinado(da) (a algo).

subset *n MATH* subconjunto *m*.

subside [səb'saɪd] *vi* -**1.** [storm, anger] acalmar; [pain, grief] passar -**2.** [floods] baixar; [swelling] diminuir -**3.** *CONSTR* ceder.

subsidence [səb'saɪdns, 'sʌbsɪdns] *n (U) CONSTR*: **the problems were caused by ~** os problemas foram causados pelo fato de o terreno ter cedido.

subsidiarity [səbsɪdɪ'ærɪtɪ] *n política de permitir que as próprias pessoas numa organização tomem decisões sobre questões que as afetam, em vez de deixá-las para o grupo todo*.

subsidiary [səb'sɪdjərɪ] (*pl* -**ies**) ◇ *adj* subsidiário(ria). ◇ *n*: **~ (company)** (empresa *f*) subsidiária *f*.

subsidize, -ise [ˈsʌbsɪdaɪz] *vt* subsidiar.

subsidy [ˈsʌbsɪdɪ] (*pl* -**ies**) *n* subsídio *m*.

subsist [səb'sɪst] *vi*: **to ~ (on sthg)** sobreviver (à base de algo).

subsistence [səb'sɪstəns] *n (U)* subsistência *f*.

subsistence allowance *n UK* diária *f*.

subsistence farming *n (U)* agricultura *f* de subsistência.

subsistence level *n* nível *m* mínimo de subsistência.

substance [ˈsʌbstəns] *n* -**1.** [gen] substância *f* -**2.** [essence, gist] essência *f* -**3.** *(U)* [importance] importância *f*.

substandard [ˌsʌb'stændəd] *adj* inferior.

substantial [səb'stænʃl] *adj* -**1.** [large, considerable] substancial -**2.** [solid, well-built] sólido(da).

substantially [səb'stænʃəlɪ] *adv* -**1.** [quite a lot] substancialmente, consideravelmente -**2.** [mainly] basicamente.

substantiate [səb'stænʃɪeɪt] *vt fml* fundamentar.

substantive *adj fml* pertinente, substancioso(sa).

substitute [ˈsʌbstɪtjuːt] ◇ *n* -**1.** [replacement]: **~ (for sb/sthg)** substituto *m*, -ta *f* (de alguém/algo); **to be no ~ (for sthg)** não estar à altura (de algo) -**2.** *SPORT* reserva *mf*, suplente *mf*. ◇ *vt*: **to ~ sb for sb** substituir alguém por alguém; **to ~ sthg for sthg** substituir algo por algo. ◇ *vi*: **to ~ for sb/sthg** substituir alguém/algo.

substitute teacher *n US* professor *m*, -ra *f* suplente.

substitution [ˌsʌbstɪ'tjuːʃn] *n* substituição *f*.

subterfuge [ˈsʌbtəfjuːdʒ] *n* subterfúgio *m*.

subterranean [ˌsʌbtə'reɪnjən] *adj* subterrâneo(nea).

subtitle [ˈsʌbˌtaɪtl] *n* subtítulo *m*.
  ◆ **subtitles** *npl CINEMA* legenda *f*.

subtle [ˈsʌtl] *adj* sutil.

subtlety [ˈsʌtltɪ] *n* -**1.** [gen] sutileza *f* -**2.** [delicacy, understatement] delicadeza *f*.

subtly [ˈsʌtlɪ] *adv* sutilmente.

subtotal [ˈsʌbtəʊtl] *n* subtotal *m*.

subtract [səb'trækt] *vt*: **to ~ sthg (from sthg)** subtrair algo (de algo).

subtraction [səb'trækʃn] *n* subtração *f*.

subtropical [ˌsʌb'trɒpɪkl] *adj* subtropical.

suburb [ˈsʌbɜːb] *n* periferia *f*.
  ◆ **suburbs** *npl*: **the ~s** a periferia.

suburban [sə'bɜːbn] *adj* -**1.** [of suburbs] da periferia -**2.** *pej* [boring] suburbano(na).

suburbia [sə'bɜːbɪə] *n (U)* bairros *mpl* residenciais.

subversion [səb'vɜːʃn] *n (U)* subversão *f*.

subversive [səb'vɜːsɪv] ◇ *adj* subversivo(va). ◇ *n* subversivo *m*, -va *f*.

subvert [səb'vɜːt] *vt* subverter.

subway [ˈsʌbweɪ] *n* -**1.** *UK* [underground walkway] passagem *f* subterrânea -**2.** *US* [underground railway] metrô *m*.

sub-zero *adj* abaixo de zero.

succeed [sək'siːd] ◇ *vt* -**1.** [person] suceder a -**2.** [event, emotion]: **to be ~ed by sthg** ser sucedido(da) por algo. ◇ *vi* -**1.** [achieve desired result]: **to ~ in sthg/in doing sthg** conseguir algo/fazer algo -**2.** [work well, come off] dar bons resultados, sair-se bem -**3.** [go far in life] triunfar.

succeeding [sək'siːdɪŋ] *adj* seguinte.

success [sək'ses] *n* sucesso *m*.

successful [sək'sesful] *adj* -**1.** [attempt] bem-sucedido(da) -**2.** [film, book *etc*] de sucesso -**3.** [person] bem-sucedido(da), de sucesso.

successfully [sək'sesfulɪ] *adv* com sucesso.

succession [sək'seʃn] *n* -**1.** [series] sucessão *f*; **to**

follow in (quick OR **close)** ~ ocorrer numa (rápida) seqüência - **2.** (U) fml [to high position] sucessão f.

successive [sək'sesɪv] adj sucessivo(va).

successor [sək'sesəˈ] n sucessor m, -ra f.

success story n história f de sucesso.

succinct [sək'sɪŋkt] adj sucinto(ta).

succinctly [sək'sɪŋktlɪ] adv sucintamente.

succulent [ˈsʌkjʊləntl] adj suculento(ta).

succumb [sə'kʌm] vi: **to** ~ **(to sthg)** sucumbir (a algo).

such [sʌtʃ] <> adj - **1.** [referring back] tal, semelhante; **I never heard** ~ **nonsense!** nunca ouvi tal absurdo! - **2.** [referring forward] assim; **have you got** ~ **a thing as a tin opener?** você teria algo como um abridor de latas?; ~ **words as 'duty' and 'honour'** palavras como dever e honra - **3.** [whatever]: **I've spent** ~ **as I had** gastei o pouco dinheiro que eu tinha - **4.** [so great, so extreme]: ~ **... that** tal ... que; **the state of the economy is** ~ **that ...** tal é o estado da economia que ... <> adv tão; ~ **nice people** essas pessoas tão gentis; ~ **a lot of books** tantos livros; ~ **a long time** tanto tempo. <> pron [referring back]: **and** ~ **(like)** e coisas do gênero; **this is my car,** ~ **as it is** este é o meu carro, embora não seja grande coisa; **help yourself to wine,** ~ **as there is** sirva-se de vinho, ainda que não tenha muito.

➤ **as such** adv propriamente dito(ta).

➤ **such and such** adj: **at** ~ **and** ~ **a time** de tal em tal hora.

suchlike [ˈsʌtʃlaɪk] <> adj deste tipo, do estilo. <> pron - **1.** [things] coisas do estilo - **2.** [people] gente desse tipo.

suck [sʌk] vt - **1.** [by mouth] chupar - **2.** [draw in] aspirar, sugar - **3.** fig [involve]: **to be** ~**ed into sthg** estar absorvido(da) em algo.

➤ **suck up** vi inf: **to** ~ **up (to sb)** puxar o saco (de alguém).

sucker [ˈsʌkəˈ] n - **1.** [suction pad] ventosa f - **2.** inf [gullible person] trouxa mf.

suckle [ˈsʌkl] <> vt amamentar. <> vi amamentar.

sucrose [ˈsuːkrəʊz] n (U) sacarose f.

suction [ˈsʌkʃn] n (U) - **1.** [drawing in] sucção f - **2.** [adhesion] adesão f.

suction pump n bomba f de sucção.

Sudan [suːˈdɑːn] n Sudão m; **in (the)** ~ no Sudão.

Sudanese [ˌsuːdəˈniːz] <> adj sudanês(esa). <> n sudanês m, -esa f. <> npl: **the** ~ os sudaneses.

sudden [ˈsʌdn] adj - **1.** [quick] repentino(na); **all of a** ~ de repente - **2.** [unforeseen] inesperado(da).

sudden death n FTBL morte f súbita.

suddenly [ˈsʌdnlɪ] adv de repente.

suddenness [ˈsʌdnnɪs] n (U) rapidez f repentina OR inesperada.

suds [sʌdz] npl espuma f de sabão.

sue [suː] vt: **to** ~ **sb (for sthg)** processar alguém (por algo).

suede [sweɪd] <> n (U) camurça f. <> comp de camurça.

suet [ˈsʊɪt] n (U) sebo m.

Suez [ˈsuːɪz] n Suez.

Suez Canal n: **the** ~ o Canal de Suez.

suffer [ˈsʌfəˈ] <> vt sofrer. <> vi - **1.** [feel physical pain] sofrer de; **to** ~ **from sthg** MED sofrer de algo - **2.** [experience difficulties or loss] sair prejudicado(-da).

sufferance [ˈsʌfrəns] n (U): **on** ~ por condescendência OR tolerância.

sufferer [ˈsʌfrəˈ] n paciente mf.

suffering [ˈsʌfrɪŋ] n sofrimento m.

suffice [səˈfaɪs] vi fml ser suficiente, bastar.

sufficient [səˈfɪʃnt] adj suficiente.

sufficiently [səˈfɪʃntlɪ] adv suficientemente.

suffix [ˈsʌfɪks] n sufixo m.

suffocate [ˈsʌfəkeɪt] <> vt sufocar, asfixiar. <> vi sufocar-se, asfixiar-se.

suffocation [ˌsʌfəˈkeɪʃn] n (U) asfixia f.

suffrage [ˈsʌfrɪdʒ] n (U) sufrágio m.

suffuse [səˈfjuːz] vt: ~ **d with sthg** banhado(da) de algo.

sugar [ˈʃʊgəˈ] <> n (U) açúcar m. <> vt adoçar.

sugar beet n (U) beterraba f (açucareira).

sugar bowl n açucareiro m.

sugarcane [ˈʃʊgəkeɪn] n (U) cana-de-açúcar f.

sugar-coated [-ˈkəʊtɪd] adj cristalizado(da).

sugared [ˈʃʊgəd] adj adoçado(da).

sugar lump n torrão m de açúcar.

sugar refinery n refinaria f de açúcar.

sugary [ˈʃʊgərɪ] adj - **1.** [high in sugar] açucarado(da), muito doce - **2.** fig & pej [sentimental] meloso(sa).

suggest [səˈdʒest] vt - **1.** [propose] sugerir, propor; **to** ~ **that sb do sthg** sugerir que alguém faça algo - **2.** [imply] insinuar.

suggestion [səˈdʒestʃn] n - **1.** [gen] sugestão f - **2.** (U) [implication] insinuação f.

suggestive [səˈdʒestɪv] adj - **1.** [implying sexual connotation] insinuante, provocante - **2.** [implying a certain conclusion]: ~ **(of sthg)** indicativo(va) (de algo) - **3.** [reminiscent]: ~ **of sthg** evocativo(va) de algo.

suicidal [ˌsʊɪˈsaɪdl] adj suicida.

suicide [ˈsuːɪsaɪd] n (U) suicídio m; **to commit** ~ cometer suicídio, suicidar-se.

suicide attempt n tentativa f de suicídio.

suit [suːt] n - **1.** [of matching clothes - for man] terno m; [- for woman] conjunto m - **2.** SPORT [outfit] traje m - **3.** [in cards] naipe m; **to follow** ~ seguir no mesmo naipe; fig seguir o exemplo - **4.** JUR processo m. <> vt - **1.** [look attractive on] cair bem - **2.** [be convenient or agreeable to] convir; ~ **yourself!** como quiser! - **3.** [be appropriate to]: **that job** ~**s you perfectly!** este trabalho é a sua cara! <> vi [be convenient or agreeable]: **does that** ~? está bom para ti?

suitability [ˌsuːtəˈbɪlətɪ] n (U) adequação f, conveniência f.

suitable [ˈsuːtəbl] adj adequado(da), apropriado (da); **the most** ~ **person** a pessoa mais indicada.

suitably [ˈsuːtəblɪ] adv adequadamente, apropriadamente.

suitcase [ˈsuːtkeɪs] n mala f.

suite [swiːt] n - **1.** [of rooms] suíte f - **2.** [of furniture] conjunto m.

suited [ˈsuːtɪd] adj - **1.** [suitable]: ~ **to/for sthg** adequado(da) para algo - **2.** [compatible]: **they are well** ~ eles combinam muito bem.

suitor [ˈsuːtəˈ] n dated pretendente m.

sulfate n US = sulphate.

sulfur n US = sulphur.

sulfuric acid n US = sulphuric acid.

sulk [sʌlk] n: to go into a ~ ficar emburrado(da). <> vi emburrar-se.

sulky ['sʌlkı] (compar -ier, superl -iest) adj emburrado(da).

sullen ['sʌlən] adj mal-humorado(da), atacado(da).

sulphate UK, **sulfate** US ['sʌlfeıt] n (U) sulfato m.

sulphur UK, **sulfur** US ['sʌlfə'] n (U) enxofre m.

sulphuric acid UK, **sulfuric acid** US [sʌl'fjuərık-] n (U) ácido m sulfúrico.

sultan ['sʌltən] n sultão m.

sultana [səl'tɑ:nə] n UK [dried grape] passa f branca.

sultry ['sʌltrı] (compar -ier, superl -iest) adj -1. [hot] abafado(da), mormacento(ta) -2. [sexy] quente.

sum [sʌm] (pt & pp -med, cont -ming) n soma f.
  ➡ **sum up** vt sep [summarize] resumir. <> vi recapitular.

Sumatra n Sumatra. **in** ~ em Sumatra.

Sumatran adj de ou relativo a Sumatra. <> n habitante ou natural de Sumatra.

summarily ['sʌmərəlı] adv sumariamente.

summarize, -ise ['sʌməraız] vt resumir. <> vi resumir.

summary ['sʌmərı] (pl -ies) adj fml sumário(ria). <> n resumo m.

summation [sʌ'meıʃn] n -1. [summing-up] recapitulação f -2. [total] soma f.

summer ['sʌmə'] n verão m; **in** ~ no verão. <> comp de verão.

summer camp n US colônia f de férias.

summer house n -1. [in garden] quiosque m (em jardim) -2. [for holidays] casa f de veraneio.

summer school n escola f de verão.

summertime ['sʌmətaım] adj de verão. <> n: (the) ~ o verão.

Summer Time n UK horário m de verão.

summery ['sʌmərı] adj de verão.

summing-up [,sʌmıŋ-] (pl summings-up) n JUR recapitulação f.

summit ['sʌmıt] n -1. [mountaintop] topo m, cume m -2. [meeting] reunião f de cúpula.

summon ['sʌmən] vt convocar.
  ➡ **summon up** vt sep armar-se de.

summons ['sʌmənz] (pl summonses) JUR n intimação f. <> vt intimar.

sumo (wrestling) ['su:məu-] n sumô m.

sump [sʌmp] n AUT cárter m.

sumptuous ['sʌmptʃuəs] adj suntuoso(sa).

sum total n soma f total.

sun [sʌn] (pt & pp -ned, cont -ning) n: the ~ o sol. <> vt: to ~ o.s. tomar sol.

Sun. (abbr of Sunday) dom.

sunbathe ['sʌnbeıð] vi tomar (banho de) sol.

sunbather ['sʌnbeıðə'] n banhista mf.

sunbeam ['sʌnbi:m] n raio m de sol.

sunbed ['sʌnbed] n câmara f de bronzeamento artificial.

sunburn ['sʌnbɜ:n] n (U) queimadura f de sol.

sunburned ['sʌnbɜ:nd], **sunburnt** ['sʌnbɜ:nt] adj queimado(da) de sol.

sun cream n (U) protetor m solar.

sundae ['sʌndeı] n sundae m.

Sunday ['sʌndı] n domingo m; see also Saturday.

Sunday paper n UK edição f dominical (de um jornal).

Sunday school n catequese f.

sundial ['sʌndaıəl] n relógio m de sol.

sundown ['sʌndaun] n (U) crepúsculo m.

sun-dried adj seco(ca), desidratado(da).

sundry ['sʌndrı] adj fml diversos(sas); **all and** ~ todos(das) sem exceção.
  ➡ **sundries** npl fml artigos mpl diversos.

sunflower ['sʌn,flauə'] n girassol m.

sung [sʌŋ] pp ⊳ sing.

sunglasses ['sʌn,glɑ:sız] npl óculos mpl escuros OR de sol.

sunhat ['sʌnhæt] n chapéu m de praia.

sunk [sʌŋk] pp ⊳ sink.

sunken ['sʌŋkən] adj -1. [in water] submerso(sa) -2. [low-level - garden] rebaixado(f da); [- bath] embutido(da) -3. [cheeks] encovado(da) -4. [eyes] fundo(da).

sunlamp ['sʌnlæmp] n lâmpada f ultravioleta.

sunlight ['sʌnlaıt] n (U) luz f do sol OR solar.

sunlit ['sʌnlıt] adj ensolarado(da).

Sunni ['sunı] (pl -s) adj sunita. <> n sunita mf.

sunny ['sʌnı] (compar -ier, superl -iest) adj -1. [full of sun] ensolarado(da) -2. fig [cheerful] luminoso(sa) -3. phr: ~ side up US [fried egg] com a gema para cima.

sunray lamp n lâmpada f ultravioleta.

sunrise ['sʌnraız] n -1. [time of day] amanhecer m -2. [event] nascer m do sol.

sunroof ['sʌnru:f] n teto m solar.

sunset ['sʌnset] n -1. (U) [time of day] anoitecer m -2. [event] pôr-do-sol m, crepúsculo m.

sunshade ['sʌnʃeıd] n guarda-sol m.

sunshine ['sʌnʃaın] n (U) luz f do sol m.

sunspot ['sʌnspɒt] n -1. ASTRON mancha f solar -2. [holiday resort] local ensolarado para se passar as férias.

sunstroke ['sʌnstrəuk] n (U) insolação f.

suntan ['sʌntæn] n bronzeado m. <> comp bronzeador(ra).

suntanned ['sʌntænd] adj bronzeado(da).

suntrap ['sʌntræp] n local m muito ensolarado.

sun-up n US inf nascer m do sol.

super ['su:pə'] adj inf excelente. <> n [petrol] gasolina f premium.

superabundance [,su:pərə'bʌndəns] n superabundância f.

superannuation ['su:pə,rænju'eıʃn] n -1. (U) [pension] aposentadoria f, pensão f -2. [contribution] contribuição f para a previdência.

superb [su:'pɜ:b] adj soberbo(ba).

superbly [su:'pɜ:blı] adv soberbamente.

Super Bowl n US: the ~ a final do campeonato de futebol americano.

supercilious [,su:pə'sılıəs] adj convencido(da), arrogante.

superficial [,su:pə'fıʃl] adj superficial.

superfluous [su:'pɜ:fluəs] adj supérfluo(flua).

superglue ['su:pəglu:] n (U) superbonder® f.

superhuman [ˌsu:pə'hju:mən] adj sobre-humano (na).

superimpose [ˌsu:pərɪm'pəʊz] vt: **to ~ sthg on sthg** sobrepor algo a algo.

superintend [ˌsu:pərɪn'tend] vt superintender.

superintendent [ˌsu:pərɪn'tendənt] n **-1.** UK [of police] chefe mf de polícia **-2.** fml [of department] superintendente mf.

superior [su:'pɪərɪəʳ] adj **-1.** [gen] superior; **~ to sthg/sb** superior a algo/alguém **-2.** pej [arrogant] arrogante. <> n superior m, -ra f.

superiority [su:ˌpɪərɪ'ɒrətɪ] n (U) **-1.** [gen] superioridade f **-2.** pej [arrogance] arrogância f.

superlative [su:'pɜ:lətɪv] adj [of the highest quality] excelente. <> n GRAMM superlativo m.

superloo n toalete público com dispositivos especiais e muitas vezes automatizado.

superman n super-homem m.

supermarket ['su:pəˌmɑ:kɪt] n supermercado m.

supernatural [ˌsu:pə'nætʃrəl] adj sobrenatural. <> n: **the ~** o sobrenatural.

superpower ['su:pəˌpaʊəʳ] n superpotência f.

superscript adj sobrescrito(ta).

supersede [ˌsu:pə'si:d] vt suplantar.

supersonic [ˌsu:pə'sɒnɪk] adj supersônico(ca).

superstar ['su:pəstɑːʳ] n superstar mf.

superstition [ˌsu:pə'stɪʃn] n **-1.** (U) [superstitious beliefs] superstição f **-2.** [particular belief] crendice f.

superstitious [ˌsu:pə'stɪʃəs] adj supersticioso(sa).

superstore ['su:pəstɔːʳ] n hipermercado m.

superstructure ['su:pəˌstrʌktʃəʳ] n superestrutura f.

supertanker ['su:pəˌtæŋkəʳ] n superpetroleiro m.

supertax ['su:pətæks] n sobretaxa f.

supervise ['su:pəvaɪz] vt supervisionar.

supervision [ˌsu:pə'vɪʒn] n (U) supervisão f.

supervisor ['su:pəvaɪzəʳ] n supervisor m, -ra f.

supper ['sʌpəʳ] n **-1.** [main evening meal] jantar m **-2.** [snack before bedtime] lanche m antes de dormir.

supplant [sə'plɑ:nt] vt fml suplantar.

supple ['sʌpl] adj flexível.

supplement [n 'sʌplɪmənt, vb 'sʌplɪment] n **-1.** [addition] acréscimo m **-2.** [in book] suplemento m; [of newspaper] suplemento m, encarte m. <> vt complementar.

supplementary [ˌsʌplɪ'mentərɪ] adj suplementar.

supplier [sə'plaɪəʳ] n fornecedor m, -ra f.

supply [sə'plaɪ] (pl -ies, pt & pp -ied) n **-1.** [store, reserve] estoque m; **to be in short ~** estar escasso(sa) **-2.** [network] abastecimento m **-3.** (U) ECON oferta f. <> vt: **to ~ sthg (to sb)** fornecer algo (a alguém); **if you ~ the food, I'll bring the drink** se você entrar com a comida, eu trago a bebida; **to ~ sb (with sthg)** prover alguém (com algo); **to ~ sthg with sthg** abastecer algo com algo.
➝ **supplies** npl **-1.** [food] provisões fpl **-2.** [office equipment] material m **-3.** MIL apetrechos mpl.

supply teacher n UK professor m substituto, professora f substituta.

support [sə'pɔ:t] n **-1.** [gen] apoio m **-2.** (U) [financial] ajuda f **-3.** (U) [substantiation] embasamento m **-4.** [object, person] suporte m. <> vt **-1.** [physically] sustentar, apoiar **-2.** [back, back up] apoiar **-3.** [financially] ajudar **-4.** [theory] fundamentar **-5.** SPORT torcer para.

supporter [sə'pɔ:təʳ] n **-1.** [of person, plan] partidário m, -ria f **-2.** SPORT torcedor m, -ra f.

supportive [sə'pɔ:tɪv] adj incentivador(ra).

suppose [sə'pəʊz] vt **-1.** [assume] supor; **I don't ~ ...?** [in polite requests] eu não sei se você poderia ...?; **you don't ~ ...?** [asking opinion] você não acha que ...? **-2.** [concede reluctantly] supor, achar. <> vi **-1.** [assume] crer; **I ~ (so)** suponho que sim; **I ~ not** suponho que não **-2.** [admit] admitir; **I ~ so/not** admito que sim/que não. <> conj [what if]: **~ we went out?** que tal OR e se a gente saísse?

supposed [sə'pəʊzd] adj **-1.** [doubtful] suposto(posta) **-2.** [intended]: **you weren't ~ to be outside** não era para você estar na rua **-3.** [reputed]: **he was ~ to be here at eight** era para ele estar aqui às oito horas; **it's ~ to be very good** dizem que é muito bom.

supposedly [sə'pəʊzɪdlɪ] adv supostamente.

supposing [sə'pəʊzɪŋ] conj: **~ we went out?** que tal OR e se a gente saísse?

supposition [ˌsʌpə'zɪʃn] n suposição f.

suppository [sə'pɒzɪtrɪ] (pl -ies) n supositório m.

suppress [sə'pres] vt **-1.** [uprising, revolt] reprimir **-2.** [information, report] ocultar **-3.** [emotions] conter.

suppression [sə'preʃn] n (U) **-1.** [of uprising, revolt] repressão f **-2.** [of information, report] ocultação f **-3.** [of emotions] dissimulação f.

suppressor n ELEC supressor m.

supranational adj supranacional.

supremacy [sʊ'preməsɪ] n (U) supremacia f.

supreme [sʊ'pri:m] adj **-1.** [highest in rank] supremo(ma) **-2.** [great] extraordinário(ria).

Supreme Court n [in US]: **the ~** a Suprema Corte.

SUPREME COURT

A Corte Suprema é a mais alta instância judiciária federal dos Estados Unidos. Seus nove membros, chamados justices (juízes), são nomeados pelo presidente da República em caráter vitalício. Eles cumprem o papel de aprovar ou vetar as leis estaduais e federais, e também de interpretar a Constituição.

supremely [sʊ'pri:mlɪ] adv: **~ important** de suma importância.

supremo [sʊ'pri:məʊ] (pl -s) n UK inf manda-chuva mf.

Supt (abbr of superintendent) superintendente mf.

surcharge ['sɜ:tʃɑ:dʒ] n: **~ (on sthg)** sobretaxa f (a algo). <> vt: **to ~ sb (on sthg)** sobretaxar alguém (em algo).

sure [ʃʊəʳ] adj **-1.** [reliable] confiável, seguro(ra) **-2.** [certain] certo(ta); **to be ~ about sthg** ter certeza sobre algo; **to be ~ of sthg** estar certo de algo; **to be ~ of doing sthg** ter certeza de que vai fazer algo; **the dollar is ~ to fall soon** [be certain] com (toda) certeza o dólar vai cair em breve; [remember] certificar-se de; **to make ~ (that) ...** certificar-se de que ...; **I'm ~ (that) ...** tenho certeza de que

... **- 3.** [confident]: **to be ~ of o.s.** estar seguro(ra) de si mesmo(ma). <> *adv* **-1.** *inf* [yes] com certeza, claro **- 2.** *US* [really] realmente.

➡ **for sure** *adv* com (toda) certeza.

➡ **sure enough** *adv* de fato.

surefire [ˈʃʊəfaɪəˈ] *adj inf* certeiro(ra).

surefooted [ˌʃʊəˈfʊtɪd] *adj* com os pés firmes.

surely [ˈʃʊəlɪ] *adv* com certeza; **~ you can't be serious!** você não pode estar falando a verdade!

sure thing *excl US inf* [expressing assent] claro!

surety [ˈʃʊərətɪ] *n* garantia *f*, fiança *f*.

surf [sɜːf] *n (U)* espuma *f (das ondas do mar)*. <> *vi* surfar. <> *vt:* **to ~ the Internet** navegar na Internet.

surface [ˈsɜːfɪs] *n* **-1.** superfície *f*; **on the ~** à primeira vista; **below** *OR* **beneath the ~** abaixo *OR* acima da superfície **- 2.** *phr:* **to scratch the ~** encher lingüiça. <> *vi* **-1.** [from water] emergir, vir à tona **- 2.** [become generally known] vir à tona **- 3.** *inf hum* [appear, reappear - after sleep] acordar; [- after prolonged absence] dar o ar da graça.

surface mail *n* correio *m* terrestre *OR* marítimo.

surface-to-air *adj* terra-ar.

surfboard [ˈsɜːfbɔːd] *n* prancha *f* de surfe.

surfeit [ˈsɜːfɪt] *n fml* excesso *m*.

surfer [ˈsɜːfəˈ] *n* surfista *mf*.

surfing [ˈsɜːfɪŋ] *n (U)* surfe *m*; **to go ~** ir surfar.

surge [sɜːdʒ] *n* **-1.** [gen] onda *f*; [of electricity] sobretensão *f* **- 2.** [of water] torrente *f* **- 3.** [of sales, applications] onda *f*, aumento *m*. <> *vi* **-1.** [gen] aumentar **- 2.** [people, vehicles] avançar em massa **- 3.** [water] subir **- 4.** [emotion] intensificar-se **- 5.** [interest, support] crescer.

surgeon [ˈsɜːdʒən] *n* cirurgião *m*, -giã *f*.

surgery [ˈsɜːdʒərɪ] *(pl* -ies*) n* **-1.** *(U)* MED [activity, operation] cirurgia *f* **- 2.** *UK* MED [place] consultório *m* **- 3.** *UK* MED [consulting period] consulta *f* **- 4.** *UK* POL audiência *f*.

surgical [ˈsɜːdʒɪkl] *adj* **-1.** [connected with surgery] cirúrgico(ca) **- 2.** [worn as treatment] ortopédico(ca).

surgical spirit *n (U) UK* anti-séptico *m*.

Surinam *n* Suriname; **in ~** no Suriname.

surly [ˈsɜːlɪ] *(compar* -ier*, superl* -iest*) adj* ríspido(da).

surmise [sɜːˈmaɪz] *vt fml* presumir.

surmount [sɜːˈmaʊnt] *vt* superar, vencer.

surname [ˈsɜːneɪm] *n* sobrenome *m*.

surpass [səˈpɑːs] *vt fml* ultrapassar, superar.

surplus [ˈsɜːpləs] *adj* excedente; **he was ~ to requirements** ele estava além do que se precisava. <> *n* **-1.** [gen] excedente *m* **- 2.** [in budget] superávit *m*.

surprise [səˈpraɪz] *n* surpresa *f*; **to take sb by ~** pegar alguém de surpresa. <> *vt* surpreender.

surprised [səˈpraɪzd] *adj* surpreso(f sa); **I wouldn't be ~ (if ...)** não me surpreenderia (se ...).

surprising [səˈpraɪzɪŋ] *adj* surpreendente.

surprisingly [səˈpraɪzɪŋlɪ] *adv* surpreendentemente.

surreal [səˈrɪəl] *adj* surreal.

surrealism [səˈrɪəlɪzm] *n (U)* surrealismo *m*.

surrealist [səˈrɪəlɪst] *adj* surrealista. <> *n* surrealista *mf*.

surrender [səˈrendəˈ] *n* rendição *f*. <> *vt* **-1.**

[weapons, passport] entregar **- 2.** [liberty, right, claims] renunciar a. <> *vi* **-1.** [stop fighting]: **to ~ (to sb)** render-se (a alguém) **- 2.** *fig* [give in]: **to ~ (to sthg)** sucumbir *OR* ceder (a algo).

surreptitious [ˌsʌrəpˈtɪʃəs] *adj* clandestino(na), furtivo(va).

surrogate [ˈsʌrəgeɪt] *adj* suplente. <> *n* substituto *m*, -ta *f*.

surrogate mother *n* mãe *f* de aluguel.

surround [səˈraʊnd] *n* borda *f*. <> *vt* **-1.** [encircle] circundar, rodear **- 2.** [trap] cercar **- 3.** *fig* [be associated with] rondar.

surrounding [səˈraʊndɪŋ] *adj* **-1.** [all around] circundante **- 2.** [associated] relacionado(da).

➡ **surroundings** *npl* **-1.** [physical] arredores *mpl* **- 2.** [social] ambiente *m*.

surtax [ˈsɜːtæks] *n (U)* sobretaxa *f*.

surveillance [sɜːˈveɪləns] *n (U)* vigilância *f*.

survey [*n* ˈsɜːveɪ, *vb* səˈveɪ] *n* **-1.** [statistical investigation] pesquisa *f*, levantamento *m* **- 2.** [physical examination - of land] medição *f*; [- of building] vistoria *f*, inspeção *f*. <> *vt* **-1.** [contemplate] contemplar **- 2.** [investigate statistically] fazer um levantamento de **- 3.** [examine, assess - land] medir; [- building] vistoriar, inspecionar.

surveyor [səˈveɪəˈ] *n* [of land] agrimensor *m*, -ra *f*; [of building] vistoriador *m*, -ra *f*.

survival [səˈvaɪvl] *n* **-1.** *(U)* [continuing to live] sobrevivência *f* **- 2.** [relic] relíquia *f*.

survive [səˈvaɪv] *vt* **-1.** [live through] sobreviver a **- 2.** [live longer than] sobreviver. <> *vi* **-1.** [gen] sobreviver **- 2.** *inf* [cope successfully] sobreviver.

➡ **survive on** *vt fus* sustentar-se *OR* manter-se com.

survivor [səˈvaɪvəˈ] *n* **-1.** [gen] sobrevivente *mf* **- 2.** *fig* [fighter] lutador *m*, -ra *f*.

susceptible [səˈseptəbl] *adj* **-1.** [likely to be influenced]: **~ (to sthg)** suscetível (a algo) **- 2.** MED: **~ (to sthg)** propenso(sa) (a algo).

suspect [*adj* & *n* ˈsʌspekt, *vb* səˈspekt] *adj* suspeito(ta). <> *n* suspeito *m*, -ta *f*. <> *vt* **-1.** suspeitar; **I ~ corruption in the system** imagino que haja corrupção no sistema **- 2.** [consider guilty]: **to ~ sb (of sthg)** suspeitar de alguém (em algo).

suspend [səˈspend] *vt* **-1.** [gen] suspender **- 2.** [temporarily discontinue] suspender, interromper.

suspended animation [səˈspendɪd-] *n (U)* morte *f* aparente.

suspended sentence [səˈspendɪd-] *n* condenação *f* condicional.

suspender belt [səˈspendəˈ-] *n UK* cinta-liga *f*.

suspenders [səˈspendəz] *npl* **-1.** *UK* [for stockings] cintas-ligas *fpl* **- 2.** *US* [for trousers] suspensórios *mpl*.

suspense [səˈspens] *n (U)* suspense *m*; **to keep sb in ~** deixar alguém em suspense.

suspension [səˈspenʃn] *n* suspensão *f*.

suspension bridge *n* ponte *f* suspensa.

suspicion [səˈspɪʃn] *n* suspeita *f*; **under ~** sob suspeita.

suspicious [səˈspɪʃəs] *adj* **-1.** [having suspicions] desconfiado(da) **- 2.** [causing suspicion] suspeito(ta).

suspiciously [səˈspɪʃəslɪ] *adv* **-1.** [showing a suspicious attitude] desconfiadamente; **he asked me ~ if ...** ele me perguntou desconfiado se ... **- 2.** [causing suspicion] de forma suspeita.

suss ← **suss out** *UK inf vt sep* sacar; **I can't suss him out at all** ainda não saquei qual é a dele.

sustain [sə'steɪn] *vt* **- 1.** [gen] manter **- 2.** [nourish spiritually] sustentar **- 3.** [suffer] sofrer **- 4.** [withstand] suportar.

sustenance ['sʌstɪnəns] *n (U) fml* subsistência *f.*

suture ['su:tʃə^r] *n* sutura *f.*

svelte [svelt] *adj* esbelto(ta).

SW - 1. (*abbr of* **short wave**) OC *f* **- 2.** (*abbr of* **south-west**) SO.

swab [swɒb] *n* (bucha *f* de) algodão *m.*

swagger ['swægə^r] *n* andar *m* garboso. ◇ *vi* andar com ar garboso.

Swahili [swɑː'hiːlɪ] *adj* suaíli. ◇ *n* [language] suaíli *m.*

swallow ['swɒləʊ] *n* **- 1.** [bird] andorinha *f* **- 2.** [of food] bocado *m* **- 3.** [of drink] gole *m.* ◇ *vt* **- 1.** [gen] engolir **- 2.** *fig* [hold back] engolir em seco. ◇ *vi* engolir.

swam [swæm] *pt* ⊳ **swim.**

swamp [swɒmp] *n* pântano *m,* brejo *m.* ◇ *vt* **- 1.** [flood] inundar **- 2.** [overwhelm]: **to ~ sb/sthg (with sthg)** sobrecarregar alguém/algo (de algo).

swan [swɒn] *n* cisne *m.*

swap [swɒp] (*pt & pp* **-ped,** *cont* **-ping**) *n* troca *f.* ◇ *vt*: **to ~ sthg (with sb)** trocar algo com alguém; **to ~ sthg (over OR round)** trocar algo; **to ~ sthg for sthg** trocar algo por algo. ◇ *vi* trocar.

swap meet *n US* mercado *m* de trocas.

swarm [swɔːm] *n* **- 1.** [of bees] enxame *m* **- 2.** *fig* [of people] mundaréu *m.* ◇ *vi* **- 1.** [bees] enxamear **- 2.** *fig* [people] apinhar-se **- 3.** *fig* [place]: **to be ~ ing (with)** estar fervilhando de.

swarthy ['swɔːðɪ] (*compar* **-ier,** *superl* **-iest**) *adj* moreno(f na).

swashbuckling ['swɒʃˌbʌklɪŋ] *adj* de aventura.

swastika ['swɒstɪkə] *n* suástica *f.*

swat [swɒt] (*pt & pp* **-ted,** *cont* **-ting**) *vt* golpear.

swatch [swɒtʃ] *n* amostra *f.*

swathe [sweɪð] *n* vastidão *f.*

swathed [sweɪðd] *adj literary*: **~ in sthg** enrolado(da) em algo.

swatter ['swɒtə^r] *n* mata-moscas *m inv.*

sway [sweɪ] *vt* **- 1.** [cause to swing] balançar **- 2.** [influence] persuadir, convencer. ◇ *vi* oscilar. ◇ *n (U) fml*: **to come under the ~ of sb/sthg** ficar sob influência de alguém/algo; **to hold ~ (over sb/sthg)** exercer influência (sobre alguém/algo).

Swazi *n* suazi *mf.*

Swaziland ['swɑːzɪlænd] *n* Suazilândia; **in ~ na** Suazilândia.

swear [sweə^r] (*pt* **swore,** *pp* **sworn**) *vt* **- 1.** [gen] jurar; **to ~ to do sthg** jurar fazer algo **- 2.** [pronounce]: **to ~ an oath** prestar juramento **- 3.** *inf* [state emphatically] jurar. ◇ *vi* **- 1.** [state emphatically] jurar **- 2.** [use swearwords] praguejar.

← **swear by** *vt fus inf* confiar totalmente em.

← **swear in** *vt sep JUR* prestar juramento a.

swearword ['sweəwɜːd] *n* blasfêmia *f,* palavrão *m.*

sweat [swet] *n* **- 1.** *(U)* [perspiration] suor *m* **- 2.** *(U) inf* [hard work] trabalheira *f* **- 3.** *inf* [state of anxiety] suador *m*; **to be in a cold ~** suar frio. ◇ *vi* **-1.** [perspire] suar **- 2.** *inf* [worry] preocupar-se com.

sweatband ['swetbænd] *n* **- 1.** [for wrist] munhequeira *f* **- 2.** [for head] faixa *f* para cabeça.

sweater ['swetə^r] *n* suéter *m.*

sweatshirt ['swetʃɜːt] *n* moletom *m.*

sweatshop ['swetʃɒp] *n estabelecimento que oferece más condições de trabalho e baixos salários aos empregados.*

sweaty ['swetɪ] (*compar* **-ier,** *superl* **-iest**) *adj* **- 1.** [skin, clothes] suado(f da) **- 2.** [place] abafado(f da) **- 3.** [activity] exaustivo(f va).

swede [swiːd] *n UK* rutabaga *f.*

Swede [swiːd] *n* sueco *m,* -ca *f.*

Sweden ['swiːdn] *n* Suécia; **in ~ na** Suécia.

Swedish ['swiːdɪʃ] *adj* sueco(ca). ◇ *n* [language] sueco *m.* ◇ *npl*: **the ~** os suecos.

sweep [swiːp] (*pt & pp* **swept**) *n* **- 1.** [sweeping movement] movimento *m* (circular) **- 2.** [with brush] varrida *f* **- 3.** [electronic examination] varredura *f* **- 4.** [chimneysweep] limpador *m,* -ra f de chaminé. ◇ *vt* **-1.** [gen] varrer **- 2.** [with eyes] examinar **- 3.** [spread through] disseminar **- 4.** [for bugs or bombs] vasculhar, examinar **- 5.** [force] arrastar; **to ~ sb off his/her feet** abarrotar o coração dele/dela **- 6.** [push with hand] afastar; **she swept the papers off her desk** ela tirou os papéis do escritório. ◇ *vi* **-1.** [wind, rain] precipitar-se **- 2.** [vehicle] ir a toda velocidade **- 3.** [emotion, laughter, rumour] espalhar-se; **fear swept through the crowd** o medo se espalhou pela multidão **- 4.** [walk quickly] passar como um raio.

← **sweep aside** *vt sep* afastar.

← **sweep away** *vt sep* varrer do mapa.

← **sweep up** ◇ *vt sep &* vi escovar.

sweeper ['swiːpə^r] *n FTBL* líbero *m.*

sweeping ['swiːpɪŋ] *adj* **- 1.** [effect] radical **- 2.** [statement] muito genérico(ca) **- 3.** [curve] amplo(pla).

sweepstake ['swiːpsteɪk] *n loteria que se baseia nas corridas de cavalo.*

sweet [swiːt] *adj* **- 1.** [gen] doce **- 2.** [smell] doce, perfumado(da) **- 3.** [sound] doce, melodioso(sa) **- 4.** [gentle, kind] amável; **that's very ~ of you** é muita gentileza de sua parte **- 5.** [attractive] meigo(ga). ◇ *n UK* **- 1.** [candy] doce *m* **- 2.** [dessert] sobremesa *f.*

sweet-and-sour *adj* agridoce.

sweet corn *n (U)* milho *m* verde.

sweeten ['swiːtn] *vt* adoçar.

sweetener ['swiːtnə^r] *n* **- 1.** [substance] adoçante *m* **- 2.** *inf fig* [bribe] suborno *m.*

sweetheart ['swiːthɑːt] *n* **- 1.** [term of endearment] querido *m,* -da *f* **- 2.** [boyfriend or girlfriend] namorado *m,* -da *f.*

sweetness ['swiːtnɪs] *n (U)* **- 1.** [gen] doçura *f* **- 2.** [of feelings] prazer *f* **- 3.** [of smell] aroma *f* **- 4.** [of sound] melodia *f.*

sweet pea *n* ervilha-de-cheiro *f.*

sweet potato *n* batata-doce *f.*

sweet shop *n UK* confeitaria *f.*

sweet-talk *vt*: **to ~ sb (into doing sthg)** levar alguém na conversa (para fazer algo).

sweet tooth *n inf*: **to have a ~** ser louco(ca) por doce.

swell [swel] (*pt* -ed, *pp* swollen OR -ed) *vi* -**1.** [become larger]: **to ~ (up)** inchar - **2.** [fill with air] inflar - **3.** [increase in number] aumentar - **4.** [become louder] intensificar-se - **5.** [with pride] encher-se. <> *vt* aumentar. <> *n* elevação *f*; **sea ~** vaivém *m* do mar. <> *adj US inf* genial, excelente.

swelling ['swelɪŋ] *n* -**1.** *(U)* [swollenness] inchamento *m* - **2.** [swollen area] inchaço *m*.

sweltering ['sweltərɪŋ] *adj* -**1.** [weather] abafado(da) - **2.** [person] sufocado(da).

swept [swept] *pt & pp* ▷ **sweep**.

swerve [swɜːv] *vi* -**1.** [car, lorry] dar uma guinada - **2.** [person] desviar repentinamente.

swift [swɪft] *adj* -**1.** [fast] veloz - **2.** [prompt, ready] rápido(da). <> *n* [bird] andorinhão *m* preto.

swiftly ['swɪftlɪ] *adj* -**1.** [rapidly] velozmente - **2.** [without delay] rapidamente.

swiftness ['swɪftnɪs] *n (U)* rapidez *f*.

swig [swɪg] (*pt & pp* -ged, *cont* -ging) *inf vt* beber a grandes goles. <> *n* trago *m*.

swill [swɪl] *n (U)* lavagem *f*. <> *vt UK* enxaguar.

swim [swɪm] (*pt* swam, *pp* swum, *cont* -ming) *n* banho *m (de mar, de piscina)*; **to have a ~** nadar; **to go for a ~** ir nadar OR tomar banho *(de mar, de piscina)*. <> *vi* -**1.** [move through water] nadar; **can you ~?** você sabe nadar? - **2.** [feel dizzy] dar voltas; **my head was ~ming** minha cabeça estava girando.

swimmer ['swɪmə'] *n* nadador *m*, -ra *f*.

swimming ['swɪmɪŋ] *n* [bathing] natação *f*; **to go ~** ir nadar.

swimming baths *npl UK* piscina *f* pública coberta.

swimming cap *n* touca *f* de natação.

swimming costume *n UK* traje *m* de banho.

swimming pool *n* piscina *f*.

swimming trunks *npl* sunga *m*.

swimsuit ['swɪmsuːt] *n* traje *m* de banho.

swindle ['swɪndl] *n* logro *m*, fraude *f*. <> *vt* lograr; **to ~ sb out of sthg** lograr alguém em algo.

swine [swaɪn] *n inf pej* [person] porco *m*, -ca *f*.

swing [swɪŋ] (*pt & pp* swung) *n* -**1.** [child's toy] balanço *m* - **2.** [change] virada *f*, mudança *f* - **3.** [swaying movement] rebolado *m* - **4.** *inf* [blow]: **to take a ~ at sb** dar um golpe em alguém - **5.** *phr*: **to be in full ~** estar a todo vapor; **to get into the ~ of sthg** entrar no ritmo de algo. <> *vt* -**1.** [move back and forth] balançar - **2.** [turn] virar bruscamente. <> *vi* -**1.** [move back and forth] balançar - **2.** [turn] girar; **to ~ open** abrir-se - **3.** [hit out]: **to ~ at sb** dar um golpe em alguém - **4.** [change] virar, mudar.

swing bridge *n* ponte *f* giratória.

swing door *n* porta *f* corrediça.

swingeing ['swɪndʒɪŋ] *adj* severo(ra).

swinging ['swɪŋɪŋ] *adj inf* -**1.** [party] divertido(da), alegre - **2.** [era, lifestyle] descontraído(da).

swipe [swaɪp] <> *n*: **to take a ~ at sb/sthg** tentar bater em algo/alguém. <> *vt* -**1.** *inf* [steal] roubar - **2.** [plastic card] passar. <> *vi*: **to ~ at sthg** tentar golpear algo.

swirl [swɜːl] <> *n* -**1.** [swirling movement] rodopio *m* - **2.** [eddy] redemoinho *m*. <> *vt* girar como um redemoinho. <> *vi* girar.

swish [swɪʃ] <> *adj inf* [posh] bacana. <> *n* [movement - of dress] ruge-ruge *m*; [- of tail] meneio *m*. <> *vt* [tail] balançar, agitar. <> *vi* [move] menear.

Swiss [swɪs] <> *adj* suíço(ça). <> *n* [person] suíço *m*, -ça *f*. <> *npl*: **the ~** os suíços.

Swiss chard *n* acelga *f*.

swiss roll *n UK* rocambole *m*.

switch [swɪtʃ] <> *n* -**1.** [control device] chave *f*, interruptor *m* - **2.** [change] mudança *f*, virada *f* - **3.** *US* RAIL desvio *m*. <> *vt* -**1.** [transfer] trocar; **to ~ one's attention to sthg** dirigir a atenção a algo - **2.** [swap, exchange] trocar de; **to ~ sthg round** trocar algo de lugar. <> *vi* [transfer] trocar; **to ~ to/from sthg** transferir para/de algo.

◆ **switch off** <> *vt sep* desligar. <> *vi inf* [person] desconcentrar-se.

◆ **switch on** *vt sep* ligar.

Switch® [swɪtʃ] *n UK* cartão de débito automático Switch.

switchblade ['swɪtʃbleɪd] *n US* canivete *m*.

switchboard ['swɪtʃbɔːd] *n* mesa *f* telefônica.

switchboard operator *n* telefonista *mf*.

switched-on *adj inf* [person] antenado(da).

Switzerland ['swɪtsələnd] *n* Suíça; **in ~** na Suíça.

swivel ['swɪvl] (*UK pt & pp* -led, *cont* -ling, *US pt & pp* -ed, *cont* -ing) *vt & vi* girar.

swivel chair *n* cadeira *f* giratória.

swollen ['swəʊln] <> *pp* ▷ **swell**. <> *adj* -**1.** [ankle, arm] inchado(dá) - **2.** [river] cheio (cheia).

swoon [swuːn] *vi literary or hum* desmaiar.

swoop [swuːp] <> *n* -**1.** [downward flight] arremetida *f*; **in one fell ~** de uma só vez - **2.** [raid] ataque -surpresa *m*. <> *vi* -**1.** [fly downwards] precipitar-se, mergulhar - **2.** [pounce] atacar de surpresa.

swop [swɒp] *n*, *vt & vi* = **swap**.

sword [sɔːd] *n* espada *f*; **to cross ~s (with sb)** discutir (com alguém).

swordfish ['sɔːdfɪʃ] (*pl inv* OR -es) *n* peixe-espada *m*.

swordsman ['sɔːdzmən] (*pl* -men [-mən]) *n* esgrimista *m*, espadachim *m*.

swore [swɔː'] *pt* ▷ **swear**.

sworn [swɔːn] <> *pp* ▷ **swear**. <> *adj* -**1.** [committed]: **to be ~ enemies** ser inimigos declarados - **2.** *JUR* sob juramento.

swot [swɒt] (*pt & pp* -ted, *cont* -ting) *UK inf* <> *n pej* cê-dê-efe *mf*. <> *vi*: **to ~ (for sthg)** matar-se de estudar (para algo).

◆ **swot up** *inf* <> *vt sep* matar-se de estudar. <> *vi*: **to ~ up (on sthg)** matar-se de estudar (algo).

swum [swʌm] *pp* ▷ **swim**.

swung [swʌŋ] *pt & pp* ▷ **swing**.

sycamore ['sɪkəmɔː'] *n* falso-plátano *m*.

sycophant ['sɪkəfænt] *n* bajulador *m*, -ra *f*.

Sydney ['sɪdnɪ] *n* Sydney.

syllable ['sɪləbl] *n* sílaba *f*.

syllabub ['sɪləbʌb] *n* doce feito de creme, claras de ovos e vinho ou suco de frutas.

syllabus ['sɪləbəs] (*pl* **-buses** OR **-bi** [-baɪ]) *n* programa *m* da disciplina.

symbol ['sɪmbl] *n* símbolo *m*.

symbolic [sɪm'bɒlɪk] *adj* simbólico(ca); **to be ~ of** sthg ser símbolo de algo.

symbolism ['sɪmbəlɪzm] *n (U)* simbolismo *m*.

symbolize, -ise ['sɪmbəlaɪz] *vt* simbolizar.

symmetrical [sɪ'metrɪkl] *adj* simétrico(ca).

symmetry ['sɪmətrɪ] *n (U)* simetria *f*.

sympathetic [ˌsɪmpə'θetɪk] *adj* **-1.** [understanding] compreensivo(va) **-2.** [willing to support] favorável; **~ to** sthg favorável a algo **-3.** [likable] simpático(ca), agradável.

sympathize, -ise ['sɪmpəθaɪz] *vi* **-1.** [feel sorry] compadecer-se; **to ~ with** sb solidarizar-se com alguém, compadecer-se de alguém **-2.** [understand] compreender; **to ~ with** sthg compreender algo **-3.** [support]: **to ~ with** sthg apoiar algo.

sympathizer, -iser ['sɪmpəθaɪzə'] *n* simpatizante *mf*.

sympathy ['sɪmpəθɪ] *n* **-1.** [understanding] empatia *f*; **~ for** sb empatia por alguém **-2.** [agreement] simpatia *f*, **in ~ (with** sthg**)** de acordo (com algo) **-3.** [support]: **in ~** em solidariedade; **in ~ with** sb em solidariedade a alguém.

➡ **sympathies** *npl* **-1.** [approval] simpatias *fpl* **-2.** [condolences] pêsames *mpl*.

symphonic [sɪm'fɒnɪk] *adj* sinfônico(ca).

symphony ['sɪmfənɪ] (*pl* **-ies**) *n* sinfonia *f*.

symphony orchestra *n* orquestra *f* sinfônica.

symposium [sɪm'pəʊzjəm] (*pl* **-siums** OR **-sia** [-zjə]) *n fml* simpósio *m*.

symptom ['sɪmptəm] *n* sintoma *m*.

symptomatic [ˌsɪmptə'mætɪk] *adj* sintomático(ca); **to be ~ of** sthg ser um sintoma de algo.

synagogue ['sɪnəgɒg] *n* sinagoga *f*.

sync [sɪŋk] *n (U) inf*: **out of ~** fora de sincronia; **in ~** sincronizado(da).

synchronize, -ise ['sɪŋkrənaɪz] *vt, vi* sincronizar.

synchronized swimming ['sɪŋkrənaɪzd-] *n (U)* nado *m* sincronizado.

syncopated ['sɪŋkəpeɪtɪd] *adj* sincopado(da).

syncopation [ˌsɪŋkə'peɪʃn] *n (U)* síncope *f*.

syndicate [*n* 'sɪndɪkət, *vb* 'sɪndɪkeɪt] <> *n* sindicato *m*. <> *vt* PRESS distribuir em cadeia.

syndrome ['sɪndrəʊm] *n* síndrome *f*.

synergy (*pl* **-ies**) *n* sinergia *f*.

synod *n* sínodo *m*.

synonym ['sɪnənɪm] *n* sinônimo *m*; **~ for** OR **of** sthg sinônimo para OR de algo.

synonymous [sɪ'nɒnɪməs] *adj* **-1.** [having the same meaning] sinônimo(ma) **-2.** [associated]: **~ with** sthg sinônimo de algo.

synopsis [sɪ'nɒpsɪs] (*pl* **-ses** [-si:z]) *n* sinopse *f*.

syntax ['sɪntæks] *n* LING sintaxe *f*.

synthesis ['sɪnθəsɪs] (*pl* **-ses** [-si:z]) *n* síntese *f*.

synthesize, -ise ['sɪnθəsaɪz] *vt* sintetizar.

synthesizer ['sɪnθəsaɪzə'] *n* MUS sintetizador *m*.

synthetic [sɪn'θetɪk] *adj* **-1.** [man-made] sintético(ca) **-2.** *pej* [insincere] artificial.

syphilis ['sɪfɪlɪs] *n (U)* sífilis *f inv*.

syphon ['saɪfn] *n & vt* = **siphon**.

Syria ['sɪrɪə] *n* Síria; **in ~** na Síria.

Syrian ['sɪrɪən] <> *adj* sírio(ria). <> *n* sírio *m*, -ria *f*.

syringe [sɪ'rɪndʒ] (*cont* **syringeing** OR **syringing**) <> *n* seringa *f*. <> *vt* lavar, limpar.

syrup ['sɪrəp] *n (U)* **-1.** [sugar and water] calda *f* **-2.** *UK* [golden syrup] melado *m* **-3.** [medicine] xarope *m*.

system ['sɪstəm] *n* **-1.** [gen] sistema *m* **-2.** [network, structure - road] rede *f*; [- railway] malha *f* **-3.** *inf* [government]: **the ~** o sistema **-4.** *(U)* [methodical approach] sistemática *f* **-5.** *phr*: **to get** sthg **out of one's ~** *inf* parar de se preocupar com algo.

systematic [ˌsɪstə'mætɪk] *adj* sistemático(ca).

systematize, -ise ['sɪstəmətaɪz] *vt UK* sistematizar.

system disk *n* COMPUT disco *m* de sistema.

systems analyst ['sɪstəmz-] *n* COMPUT analista *mf* de sistemas.

systems engineer ['sɪstəmz-] *n* COMPUT engenheiro *m*, -ra *f* de sistemas.

system software *n* COMPUT software *m* de sistema.

t (*pl* **t's** OR **ts**), **T** (*pl* **T's** OR **Ts**) [ti:] *n* t, T *m*.

ta [tɑ:] *excl UK inf* brigado(da!); **~ very much** brigado(da)!

TA (*abbr of* **Territorial Army**) *n* organização militar britânica de pessoas que não são membros regulares do exército.

tab [tæb] *n* **-1.** [of cloth] etiqueta *f* **-2.** [of metal] lingüeta *f* **-3.** *US* [bill] conta *f*; **to pick up the ~** pagar a conta **-4.** (*abbr of* **tabulator**) [on keyboard] (tecla *f*) tab *m* **-5.** *phr*: **to keep ~s on** sb ficar de olho em alguém.

tabby ['tæbɪ] (*pl* **-ies**) *n*: **~ (cat)** gato *m* tigrado.

tabernacle ['tæbənækl] *n* tabernáculo *m*.

tab key *n* tecla *f* tab.

table ['teɪbl] <> *n* **-1.** [piece of furniture] mesa *f* **-2.** [diagram] tabela *f* **-3.** *phr*: **to turn the ~s on** sb inverter as posições com alguém. <> *vt* **-1.** *UK* [propose] apresentar **-2.** *US* [postpone] adiar.

tableau ['tæbləʊ] (*pl* **-x** ['tæbləʊz], **-s**) *n* quadro *m* vivo.

tablecloth ['teɪblklɒθ] *n* toalha *f* de mesa.

table d'hôte ['tɑ:bl,dəʊt] *n*: **the ~** o cardápio do dia.

table football *n* pebolim *m*.

table lamp *n* luminária *f*.

table licence *n* licença para venda de bebidas alcoólicas apenas com a refeição.

table linen *n (U)* roupa *f* de mesa.

table manners *npl* modos *mpl* à mesa.

table mat *n* descanço *m* para panelas.

table of contents *n* sumário *m*.

table salt *n (U)* sal *m* de mesa.

tablespoon ['teɪblspuːn] *n* **-1.** [spoon] colher *f (de sopa)* **-2.** [spoonful] colherada *f* de sopa.

tablet ['tæblɪt] *n* **-1.** [pill] comprimido *m*, pastilha *f* **-2.** [piece of stone] pedra *f* lascada **-3.** [piece of soap] barra *f*.

table tennis *n (U)* tênis *m inv* de mesa.

tableware *n (U)* utensílios *mpl* de mesa.

table wine *n (U)* vinho *m* de mesa.

tabloid ['tæblɔɪd] *n*: ~ **(newspaper)** tablóide *m*; **the ~ press** a imprensa sensacionalista.

TABLOID

Nos países anglo-saxões, o formato pequeno, ou tablóide, é característico dos jornais sensacionalistas. No Reino Unido, são publicações diárias desse tipo o *Daily Express*, o *Daily Mail*, *Daily Mirror*, *The Star* e *The Sun*. Nos Estados Unidos, esse tipo de jornal também existe, embora sua publicação seja, em geral, semanal. Os mais conhecidos são *The National Enquirer*, *The Star* e *The Globe*.

---

taboo [tə'buː] (*pl* **-s**) ⬦ *adj* tabu. ⬦ *n* tabu *m*.

tabulate ['tæbjʊleɪt] *vt* dispor em formato de tabela.

tachograph ['tækəgrɑːf] *n* tacógrafo *m*.

tachometer [tæ'kɒmɪtə'] *n* tacômetro *m*.

tacit ['tæsɪt] *adj fml* tácito(ta).

taciturn ['tæsɪtɜːn] *adj fml* taciturno(na).

tack [tæk] ⬦ *n* **-1.** [nail] tacha *f* **-2.** *NAUT* rumo *m* **-3.** *fig* [course of action] tática *f*; **to change** ~ mudar de tática. ⬦ *vt* **-1.** [fasten with nail] afixar (com tachas) **-2.** [in sewing] alinhavar. ⬦ *vi NAUT* virar.

➨ **tack on** *vt sep inf* [add as afterthought] anexar.

tackle ['tækl] ⬦ *n* **-1.** *FTBL* entrada *f* **-2.** *RUGBY* obstrução *f* **-3.** [equipment, gear] apetrechos *mpl* **-4.** [for lifting] guincho *m*. ⬦ *vt* **-1.** [job] lidar com **-2.** [problem] atacar **-3.** *FTBL* roubar a bola de **-4.** *RUGBY* derrubar **-5.** [attack] enfrentar **-6.** [talk to]: **to** ~ **sb about** *OR* **on sthg** pegar alguém para falar sobre algo.

tacky ['tækɪ] (*compar* **-ier**, *superl* **-iest**) *adj* **-1.** *inf* [cheap and nasty] barato(ta) **-2.** [sticky] grudento(ta), pegajoso(sa).

taco ['tækəʊ] (*pl* **-s**) *n* taco *m*.

tact [tækt] *n (U)* tato *m*.

tactful ['tæktfʊl] *adj* discreto(ta); **that wasn't very** ~ **of you** você não agiu com muito tato.

tactfully ['tæktfʊlɪ] *adv* discretamente.

tactic ['tæktɪk] *n* tática *f*.

➨ **tactics** *n (U)* *MIL* tática *f*.

tactical ['tæktɪkl] *adj* **-1.** [gen] estratégico(ca) **-2.** *MIL* tático(ca).

tactical voting *n (U)* *UK* votação *f* tática.

tactile ['tæktaɪl] *adj* tátil.

tactless ['tæktlɪs] *adj* indiscreto(ta); **he's so** ~ falta tato nele.

tactlessly ['tæktlɪslɪ] *adv* indiscretamente.

tadpole ['tædpəʊl] *n* girino *m*.

Tadzhikistan [tɑː,dʒɪkɪ'stɑːn] *n* Tadjiquistão; **in** ~ no Tadjiquistão.

taffeta ['tæfɪtə] *n (U)* tafetá *m*.

taffy ['tæfɪ] (*pl* **-ies**) *n US* puxa-puxa *m*.

tag [tæg] ⬦ *n* [pt & pp **-ged**, *cont* **-ging**] ⬦ *n* **-1.** [gen] etiqueta *f* **-2.** *(U)* [game] pega-pega *f* **-3.** *COMPUT* tag *f*, marca *f*. ⬦ *vt* etiquetar.

➨ **tag along** *vi inf*: **she always has to** ~ **along** ela sempre tem de vir junto.

Tagus *n*: **the** ~ o Tejo.

Tahiti [tɑː'hiːtɪ] *n* Taiti; **in** ~ no Taiti.

Tahitian ⬦ *adj* taitiano(na). ⬦ *n* taitiano *m*, -na *f*.

tail [teɪl] ⬦ *n* **-1.** [gen] rabo *m*; **with one's** ~ **between one's legs** [person] com o rabo entre as pernas **-2.** [of coat, shirt] fralda *f* **-3.** [of comet, plane] cauda *f* **-4.** [of car] parte *f* traseira. ⬦ *comp* [rear] traseiro(ra). ⬦ *vt inf* ir atrás de.

➨ **tails** ⬦ *adv* [when tossing a coin] coroa *f*. ⬦ *npl* [coat] fraque *m*.

➨ **tail off** *vi* diminuir.

tailback ['teɪlbæk] *n UK* fila *f (de carros)*.

tailcoat ['teɪl,kəʊt] *n* fraque *m*.

tail end *n* final *m*, parte *f* final.

tailgate ['teɪlgeɪt] *n* tampa *f* traseira.

taillight ['teɪllaɪt] *n* luz *f* traseira.

tailor ['teɪlə'] ⬦ *n* alfaiate *m*. ⬦ *vt* adaptar.

tailored ['teɪləd] *adj* [well-fitting] feito(ta) sob medida.

tailor-made *adj fig* [role, job] sob medida.

tail pipe *n US* cano *m* de descarga.

tailplane ['teɪlpleɪn] *n* leme *m (do avião)*.

tailwind ['teɪlwɪnd] *n* vento *m* de cauda.

taint [teɪnt] ⬦ *n* mancha *f*. ⬦ *vt* manchar.

tainted ['teɪntɪd] *adj* **-1.** [reputation] manchado(da) **-2.** *US* [food] estragado(da).

Taiwan [,taɪ'wɑːn] *n* Taiwan; **in** ~ em Taiwan.

Taiwanese [,taɪwə'niːz] ⬦ *adj* taiwanês(esa). ⬦ *n* taiwanês *m*, -esa *f*.

take [teɪk] (*pt* **took**, *pp* **taken**) ⬦ *vt* **-1.** [gen] levar **-2.** [accompany] levar, acompanhar **-3.** [capture, undergo, swallow, measure] tomar **-4.** [receive] receber; **to** ~ **a seat** sentar-se; **to** ~ **control/command** tomar o controle/comando **-5.** [rent] alugar **-6.** [object, hand, road, means of transport] pegar **-7.** [accept, take on] aceitar; ~ **my word for it** acredita em mim; **what batteries does it** ~? que pilha vai aí? **-8.** [contain] suportar **-9.** [bear] agüentar **-10.** [require] precisar; **it could** ~ **years** pode levar anos **-11.** [holiday] tirar; **to** ~ **a walk** dar uma caminhada; **to** ~ **a bath** tomar um banho; **to** ~ **a photo** tirar *OR* bater uma foto **-12.** [pity, interest] ter; **to** ~ **offence** ofender-se; **I** ~ **the view that ...** sou da opinião de que ...; **to** ~ **sthg seriously/badly** levar algo a sério/a mal **-13.** [wear as a particular size - shoe] calçar; [- dress] vestir **-14.** [consider] pensar em, considerar **-15.** [assume]: **I** ~ **it (that) ...** presumo que ... ⬦ *vi* [have intended effect - dye] tingir; [- fire] prender. ⬦ *n* tomada *f*.

➨ **take aback** *vt sep* surpreender; **to be taken aback** ficar espantado(da).

➨ **take after** *vt fus* parecer-se com.

➨ **take apart** *vt sep* desmontar.

➨ **take away** *vt sep* **-1.** [remove] levar embora

- 2. [deduct] subtrair, tirar.

◆ **take back** vt sep **-1.** [return] devolver **- 2.** [accept] aceitar de volta **- 3.** [statement, accusation] retirar.

◆ **take down** vt sep **-1.** [dismantle] desmontar **- 2.** [write down] escrever, tomar nota de **- 3.** [lower] baixar.

◆ **take in** vt sep **-1.** [deceive] enganar **- 2.** [understand] compreender **- 3.** [include] incluir **- 4.** [provide accommodation for] acolher.

◆ **take off** ⟨⟩ vt sep **-1.** [remove] tirar **- 2.** [have as holiday] tirar de folga; **she took the afternoon off** ela tirou a tarde de folga; **to ~ time off** tirar uma folga **- 3.** UK inf [imitate] imitar **- 4.** inf [go away suddenly]: **to ~ o.s. off** mandar-se (embora). ⟨⟩ vi **- 1.** [gen] decolar **- 2.** [go away suddenly] mandar-se (embora), ir-se embora.

◆ **take on** ⟨⟩ vt sep **-1.** [accept - work, job] aceitar; [- responsibility] assumir **- 2.** [employ] admitir **- 3.** [confront] desafiar. ⟨⟩ vt fus [assume, develop] adquirir.

◆ **take out** vt sep **-1.** [from container] tirar **- 2.** [delete] suprimir, tirar **- 3.** [go out with] convidar para sair **- 4.** phr: **to ~ it** or **a lot out of one** inf esgotar alguém.

◆ **take out on** vt sep descarregar em, descontar em.

◆ **take over** ⟨⟩ vt sep **-1.** [take control of] tomar o controle de, assumir **- 2.** [job, role] assumir. ⟨⟩ vi **- 1.** [take control] tomar o poder **- 2.** [in job] assumir.

◆ **take to** vt fus **-1.** [feel a liking for - person] ter afeição especial por; [- activity] gostar de **- 2.** [begin]: **to ~ to doing sthg** começar a fazer algo.

◆ **take up** vt fus **-1.** [begin - acting, singing] começar a se dedicar a; [- post, job] assumir **- 2.** [continue] prosseguir **- 3.** [discuss further] voltar a discutir **- 4.** [use up - time] tomar; [- space] ocupar; [- effort] exigir.

◆ **take up on** vt sep **-1.** [an offer] aceitar **- 2.** [ask to explain]: **I'd like to ~ you up on that point** gostaria que você explicasse melhor esse ponto.

◆ **take upon** vt sep: **to ~ it upon o.s. to do sthg** permitir-se fazer algo.

takeaway UK ['teɪkə,weɪl], **takeout** US ['teɪkaʊt] ⟨⟩ n **-1.** [shop] estabelecimento que vende comida para levar **- 2.** [food] comida f para levar. ⟨⟩ comp [food] para levar.

take-home pay n (U) salário m líquido.

taken ['teɪknl] ⟨⟩ pp ⊳ take. ⟨⟩ adj [pleased]: **~ with sb/sthg** contente com alguém/algo.

takeoff ['teɪkɒfl] n decolagem f.

takeout US = takeaway.

takeover ['teɪk,əʊvəʳ] n **-1.** [of company] aquisição f **- 2.** [of government] tomada f do poder.

takeover bid n oferta f pública de compra de ações.

taker ['teɪkəʳ] n interessado m, -da f.

takeup ['teɪkʌpl] n [of shares] resposta f.

taking adj dated gracioso(sa).

takings npl féria f, arrecadação f.

talc [tælk], **talcum (powder)** ['tælkəm-] n (U) talco m.

tale [teɪl] n **-1.** [fictional story] conto m **- 2.** [anecdote] história f.

talent ['tælntl] n: **~ (for sthg)** talento m (para algo).

talented ['tæləntɪdl] adj talentoso(sa).

talent scout n caçador m, -ra f de talentos.

talisman ['tælɪzmən] (pl -s) n talismã m.

talk [tɔːk] ⟨⟩ n **-1.** [conversation] conversa f **- 2.** (U) [gossip] boatos mpl, falatório m **- 3.** [lecture] palestra f. ⟨⟩ vi **- 1.** [gen] falar; **to ~ to sb** falar or conversar com alguém; **to ~ about sb/sthg** falar sobre alguém/algo; **~ing of sb/sthg, ...** falando de alguém/algo, ..., por falar em alguém/algo, ...; **to ~ big** contar vantagem **- 2.** [gossip] fofocar **- 3.** [make a speech] dar palestra; **to ~ on** or **about sthg** falar sobre algo. ⟨⟩ vt **-1.** [discuss] tratar de **- 2.** [spout] falar.

◆ **talks** npl negociações fpl.

◆ **talk down to** vt fus desmerecer.

◆ **talk into** vt sep: **to ~ sb into sthg/into doing sthg** convencer alguém de algo/a fazer algo.

◆ **talk out of** vt sep: **to ~ sb out of sthg/out of doing sthg** dissuadir alguém de algo/de fazer algo.

◆ **talk over** vt sep discutir.

talkative ['tɔːkətɪv] adj loquaz.

talker ['tɔːkəʳ] n orador m, -ra f.

talking point ['tɔːkɪŋ-] n tema m da conversa.

talking-to ['tɔːkɪŋ-] n inf bronca f.

talk show US ⟨⟩ n programa m de entrevistas, talk-show m. ⟨⟩ comp de programa de entrevistas.

talk time n (U) [on mobile phone] tempo m de conversação.

tall [tɔːl] adj [in height] alto(ta); **she's two metres ~** ela mede dois metros (de altura); **how ~ are you?** qual é a sua altura?

tallboy ['tɔːlbɔɪ] n cômoda f.

tall order n tarefa f impossível.

tall story n história f fantasiosa.

tally ['tælɪ] (pl -ies, pt & pp -ied) ⟨⟩ n [record] conta f; **to keep ~ of sthg** manter registro de algo. ⟨⟩ vi [correspond] fechar.

talon ['tælən] n garra f.

tambourine [,tæmbə'riːn] n pandeiro m.

tame [teɪm] ⟨⟩ adj **-1.** [animal, bird] domesticado(da) **- 2.** pej [person] parado(da) **- 3.** pej [unexciting] monótono(na). ⟨⟩ vt **-1.** [animal, bird] domesticar **- 2.** [person] dominar.

tamely ['teɪmlɪ] adv docilmente.

tamer ['teɪməʳ] n domador m, -ra f.

Tamil ['tæmɪl] ⟨⟩ adj tâmil. ⟨⟩ n **-1.** [person] tâmil mf **- 2.** [language] tâmil m.

tamper ['tæmpəʳ] ◆ **tamper with** vt fus **-1.** [gen] mexer em **- 2.** [lock] forçar.

tampon ['tæmpɒn] n absorvente m interno.

tan [tæn] (pt & pp -ned, cont -ning) ⟨⟩ adj castanho(nha). ⟨⟩ n bronzeado m; **to get a ~** bronzear-se. ⟨⟩ vi bronzear-se.

tandem ['tændəm] n **-1.** [bicycle] bicicleta f de dois lugares; **in ~** em colaboração com.

tandoori [tæn'dʊərl] ⟨⟩ n (U) método indiano de assar a carne em forno de barro. ⟨⟩ comp cozido(da) em forno de barro.

tang [tæŋ] n [smell] cheiro m forte; [taste] gosto m forte.

tangent ['tændʒənt] n GEOM tangente f; **to go off at a ~** fig sair pela tangente.

tangerine [,tændʒə'ri:n] n tangerina f.

tangible ['tændʒəbl] adj tangível.

Tangier [tæn'dʒɪə'] n Tânger.

tangle ['tæŋgl] ◇ n -1. [mass] emaranhado m -2. fig [mess] rolo m; **they got into a ~** eles se meteram num rolo. ◇ vt: **to get ~d (up)** emaranhar-se. ◇ vi emaranhar-se.
◆ **tangle with** vt fus inf meter-se com.

tangled ['tæŋgld] adj -1. [gen] emaranhado(da) -2. fig [life, relationship] enrolado(da).

tango ['tæŋgəʊ] (pl -s, pt & pp -ed, cont -ing) ◇ n tango m. ◇ vi dançar tango.

tangy ['tæŋɪ] (compar -ier, superl -iest) adj forte.

tank [tæŋk] n tanque m.

tankard ['tæŋkəd] n caneção m (para cerveja).

tanker ['tæŋkə'] n -1. [ship] navio-tanque m; **oil ~** petroleiro m -2. [truck] caminhão-tanque m -3. [train] vagão-tanque m.

tankful ['tæŋkfʊl] n tanque m.

tanned [tænd] adj bronzeado(da).

tannin ['tænɪn] n (U) tanino m.

Tannoy® ['tænɔɪ] n alto-falante m.

tantalize, -ise ['tæntəlaɪz] vt tentar, provocar.

tantalizing ['tæntəlaɪzɪŋ] adj tentador(ra).

tantamount ['tæntəmaʊnt] adj: **~ to sthg** equivalente a algo.

tantrum ['tæntrəm] (pl -s) n acesso m de fúria.

Tanzania [,tænzə'nɪə] n Tanzânia; **in ~** na Tanzânia.

Tanzanian [,tænzə'nɪən] ◇ adj tanzaniano(na). ◇ n tanzaniano m, -na f.

Taoiseach n primeiro ministro da República da Irlanda.

tap [tæp] (pt & pp -ped, cont -ping) ◇ n -1. [device] torneira f -2. [light blow] batida f leve, palmadinha f. ◇ vt -1. [knock] bater de leve; **to ~ one's fingers on sthg** tamborilar em algo -2. [make use of] utilizar -3. [listen secretly to] grampear. ◇ vi bater.

tap dance n sapateado m.

tap dancer n sapateador m, -ra f.

tape [teɪp] ◇ n -1. [gen] fita f -2. SPORT [at finishing line] fita f de chegada -3. [adhesive material] fita f adesiva. ◇ vt -1. [record] gravar -2. [fasten with adhesive tape] juntar com fita adesiva -3. US [bandage] enfaixar.

tape deck n deck m.

tape measure n fita f métrica.

taper ['teɪpə'] ◇ n vela f fina. ◇ vi estreitar-se, afilar-se.
◆ **taper off** vi ir diminuindo.

tape-record [-rɪ,kɔ:d] vt gravar.

tape recorder n gravador m.

tape recording n gravação f.

tapered ['teɪpəd] adj afilado(da).

tapestry ['tæpɪstrɪ] (pl -ies) n -1. [gen] tapeçaria f -2. fig [of life] trama f.

tapeworm ['teɪpwɜ:m] n solitária f.

tapioca [,tæpɪ'əʊkə] n (U) tapioca f.

tapir ['teɪpə'] (pl inv OR -s) n anta f, tapir m.

tappet n tucho m.

tar [tɑ:'] n (U) alcatrão m.

tarantula [tə'ræntjʊlə] n tarântula f.

target ['tɑ:gɪt] ◇ n -1. [gen] alvo m -2. fig [goal] meta f; **to be on ~ to do sthg** fazer algo de acordo com o previsto. ◇ vt -1. [as object of attack] mirar -2. [as customer] visar.

tariff ['tærɪf] n -1. [tax] tarifa f -2. UK [price list] tabela f de preços.

Tarmac® ['tɑ:mæk] n alcatrão m.
◆ **tarmac** n AERON: **the tarmac** a pista.

tarnish ['tɑ:nɪʃ] ◇ vt -1. [make dull] embaciar -2. fig [damage] manchar. ◇ vi [become dull] embaciar.

tarnished ['tɑ:nɪʃt] adj -1. [dull] embaciado(da) -2. fig [damaged] manchado(da).

tarot ['tærəʊ] n: **the ~** o tarô.

tarot card n carta f de tarô.

tarpaulin [tɑ:'pɔ:lɪn] n -1. (U) [material] encerado m -2. [sheet] lona f alcatroada.

tarragon ['tærəgən] n (U) estragão m.

tart [tɑ:t] ◇ adj -1. [bitter-tasting] azedo(da) -2. [sarcastic] mordaz. ◇ n -1. [sweet pastry] torta f -2. UK vinf [prostitute] piranha f.
◆ **tart up** vt sep UK inf pej [smarten up]: **to ~ o.s. up** emperiquitar-se.

tartan ['tɑ:tn] ◇ n -1. [pattern] xadrez m -2. (U) [cloth] tartan m. ◇ comp de tartan.

tartar n tártaro m.

tartar(e) sauce ['tɑ:tə'-] n (U) molho m tártaro.

tartness ['tɑ:tnɪs] n (U) -1. [of taste] acidez f -2. [of comment] mordacidade f.

task [tɑ:sk] n tarefa f.

task force n força-tarefa f.

taskmaster ['tɑ:sk,mɑ:stə'] n capataz m; **a hard ~** um tirano.

Tasmania [tæz'meɪnjəl] n Tasmânia.

Tasmanian [tæz'meɪnjən] ◇ adj tasmaniano(na). ◇ n tasmaniano m, -na f.

tassel ['tæsl] n borla f.

taste [teɪst] ◇ n -1. [gen] gosto m; **in bad/good ~** de mau/bom gosto -2. fig [liking, preference]: **~ (for sthg)** gosto (por algo) -3. fig [experience]: **I've had a ~ of success** eu senti o gostinho do sucesso -4. (U) [sense of taste] paladar m -5. [try]: **have a ~** dá uma provada. ◇ vt -1. [gen] sentir o gosto de -2. [test, try] provar. ◇ vi: **it ~s horrible** tem um gosto horrível; **to ~ of/like sthg** ter gosto de algo.

taste bud n papila f gustativa.

tasteful ['teɪstfʊl] adj de bom gosto.

tastefully ['teɪstfʊlɪ] adv com bom gosto.

tasteless ['teɪstlɪs] adj -1. [cheap and unattractive] sem graça -2. [offensive] de mau gosto -3. [without flavour] sem gosto.

taster ['teɪstə'] n degustador m, -ra f.

tasty ['teɪstɪ] (compar -ier, superl -iest) adj saboroso(-sa).

tat [tæt] n (U) UK inf pej bugigangas fpl.

tattered ['tætəd] adj -1. [clothes] esfarrapado(da) -2. [paper] gasto(ta).

tatters ['tætəz] npl: **in ~** [clothes] em farrapos; fig [confidence, reputation] em frangalhos.

tattle-tale n US = telltale.

tattoo [tə'tu:] (pl -s) <> n - **1.** [design] tatuagem f - **2.** [rhythmic beating] rufar m de tambores - **3.** UK [military display] parada f OR desfile m militar. <> vt tatuar.

tattooist [tə'tu:ɪst] n tatuador m, -ra f.

tatty ['tætɪ] (compar -ier, superl -iest) adj UK inf pej - **1.** [clothes] surrado(da) - **2.** [area] enxovalhado(da).

taught [tɔ:t] pt & pp ⊳ teach.

taunt [tɔ:nt] <> n insulto m. <> vt insultar.

Taurus ['tɔ:rəs] n - **1.** [sign] Touro m - **2.** [person] taurino(na); **I'm** ~ sou de Touro.

taut [tɔ:t] adj retesado(da).

tauten ['tɔ:tn] <> vt retesar. <> vi retesar.

tautology [tɔ:'tɒlədʒɪ] n tautologia f.

tavern ['tævn] n dated taberna f.

tawdry ['tɔ:drɪ] (compar -ier, superl -iest) adj pej de mau gosto.

tawny ['tɔ:nɪ] adj fulvo(va).

tax [tæks] <> n imposto m. <> vt - **1.** [gen] tributar - **2.** [strain, test] esgotar.

taxable ['tæksəbl] adj tributável.

tax allowance n limite m de isenção fiscal.

taxation [tæk'seɪʃn] n (U) - **1.** [system] sistema m tributário - **2.** [amount] tributação f.

tax avoidance [-ə'vɔɪdəns] n (U) dedução f fiscal.

tax collector n cobrador m, -ra f de impostos.

tax cut n redução f tributária.

tax-deductible [-dɪ'dʌktəbl] adj dedutível.

tax disc n UK disco fixado no pára-brisa do veículo para mostrar que o imposto já foi pago.

tax evasion n sonegação f de impostos.

tax-exempt adj US = tax-free.

tax exemption n (U) isenção f de impostos.

tax exile n UK pessoa que vive no exterior para evitar o pagamento de impostos.

tax-free UK, **tax-exempt** US adj isento(ta) de imposto.

tax haven n paraíso m fiscal.

taxi ['tæksɪ] <> n táxi m. <> vi taxiar.

taxicab ['tæksɪkæb] n táxi m.

taxidermist ['tæksɪdɜ:mɪst] n empalhador m, -ra f.

taxi driver n motorista mf de táxi, taxista mf.

taximeter n taxímetro m.

taxing ['tæksɪŋ] adj árduo(a).

tax inspector n inspetor m, -ra f da Receita.

taxi rank UK, **taxi stand** n ponto m de táxi.

taxman ['tæksmæn] (pl -men [-men]) n - **1.** [tax collector] coletor m de impostos - **2.** inf [tax office]: **the** ~ ≃ o Leão, ≃ o Fisco.

taxpayer ['tæks,peɪə'] n contribuinte mf.

tax relief n (U) dedução f tributária.

tax return n declaração f de renda.

tax year n ano m fiscal.

TB (abbr of tuberculosis) n tuberculose f.

T-bone steak n bisteca f de boi.

tbs., tbsp. (abbr of tablespoon(ful)) colher f de sopa.

TD n - **1.** (abbr of Treasury Department) departamento do tesouro norte-americano - **2.** (abbr of touchdown) jogada do futebol norte-americano e do rugby.

tea [ti:] n - **1.** [gen] chá m - **2.** UK [afternoon meal] lanche m - **3.** UK [evening meal] chá m.

teabag ['ti:bæg] n saquinho m de chá.

tea ball n US esfera metálica perfurada na qual são colocadas as folhas de chá para infusão.

tea break n UK pausa f para o chá.

tea caddy [-,kædɪ] n caixa f para chá.

teacake ['ti:keɪk] n UK bolinho m (que acompanha o chá).

teach [ti:tʃ] (pt & pp taught) <> vt - **1.** [instruct] ensinar; **to** ~ **sb sthg, to** ~ **sthg to sb** ensinar algo a alguém; **to** ~ **sb to do sthg** ensinar alguém a fazer algo; **to** ~ **(sb) that** ensinar (a alguém) que - **2.** [give lessons in] dar aulas de - **3.** [advocate] preconizar. <> vi lecionar.

teacher ['ti:tʃə'] n professor m, -ra f.

teachers college n US = teacher training college.

teacher's pet n pej queridinho m, -nha f da classe.

teacher training college UK, **teachers college** US n curso f de licenciatura.

teaching ['ti:tʃɪŋ] n - **1.** (U) [profession, work] magistério m - **2.** [thing taught] ensinamento m.

teaching aid n material m pedagógico.

teaching hospital n UK hospital-escola m.

teaching practice n (U) prática f de ensino.

teaching staff n corpo m docente.

tea cloth n - **1.** [tablecloth] toalha f de mesa - **2.** [tea towel] pano m de prato.

tea cosy UK, **tea cozy** US n abafador m (de chá).

teacup ['ti:kʌp] n xícara f de chá.

teak [ti:k] <> n (U) teca f. <> comp de teca.

tealeaves npl borra f de chá.

team [ti:m] n - **1.** SPORT time m - **2.** [group] equipe f.
➡ **team up** vi montar uma equipe; **to** ~ **up with sb** associar-se a alguém.

team game n esporte m de equipe.

teammate ['ti:mmeɪt] n companheiro m, -ra f de equipe.

team spirit n (U) espírito m de equipe.

teamster ['ti:mstə'] n US caminhoneiro m, -ra f.

teamwork ['ti:mwɜ:k] n (U) trabalho m em equipe.

tea party n chá m da tarde.

teapot ['ti:pɒt] n bule m de chá.

tear¹ [tɪə'] n lágrima f; **in** ~ **s** aos prantos; **to burst into** ~ **s** debulhar-se em lágrimas.

tear² [teə'] (pt tore, pp torn) <> vt - **1.** [rip] rasgar; **to** ~ **sthg open** abrir algo rasgando; **to** ~ **sb/sthg to pieces** fig [criticize] demolir alguém/algo; **to be torn between** fig estar dividido(da) entre - **2.** [remove roughly] arrancar. <> vi - **1.** [rip] rasgar - **2.** inf [move quickly] ir a toda - **3.** phr: **to** ~ **loose** [get free] soltar-se. <> n [rip] rasgão m.
➡ **tear apart** vt sep - **1.** [rip up] destroçar - **2.** fig [disrupt greatly] desmantelar - **3.** [upset greatly] magoar.
➡ **tear at** vt fus avançar contra.
➡ **tear away** vt sep: **to** ~ **o.s. away (from sthg)** desvencilhar-se (de algo).
➡ **tear down** vt sep - **1.** [demolish] demolir - **2.** [remove] remover.
➡ **tear off** vt sep [clothes] arrancar.
➡ **tear out** vt sep [coupon, page] arrancar.

tear up *vt sep* despedaçar, fazer em pedaços.

tearaway ['teərə͵weɪ] *n UK inf* arruaceiro *m*, -ra *f*.

teardrop ['tɪədrɒp] *n* lágrima *f*.

tearful ['tɪəfʊl] *adj* -**1.** [person] choroso(rosa) -**2.** [event] triste.

tear gas [tɪə˚-] *n (U)* gás *m* lacrimogêneo.

tearing ['teərɪŋ] *adj inf* apressado(da).

tear jerker *n hum* dramalhão *m*.

tearoom ['ti:rʊm] *n* salão *f* de chá.

tease [ti:z] <> *n inf* -**1.** [joker] gozador *m*, -ra *f* -**2.** [sexually] provocador *m*, -ra *f*. <> *vt*: **to ~ sb (about sthg)** gozar de alguém (sobre algo).

tea shop *n* casa *f* de chá.

teasing ['ti:zɪŋ] *adj* importuno(na).

teaspoon ['ti:spu:n] *n* colher *f* de chá.

tea strainer *n* coador *m* de chá.

teat [ti:t] *n* -**1.** [of animal] teta *f* -**2.** [of bottle] bico *m*.

teatime ['ti:taɪm] *n (U) UK* hora *f* do chá.

tea towel *n* pano *m* de prato.

tea urn *n* cilindro dotado de torneira usado para preparar grandes quantidades de chá.

technical ['teknɪkl] *adj* técnico(ca).

technical college *n UK* escola *f* técnica.

technical drawing *n (U)* desenho *m* técnico.

technicality [͵teknɪ'kælətɪ] *(pl* -**ies)** *n* detalhe *m* técnico.

technically ['teknɪklɪ] *adv* tecnicamente.

technician [tek'nɪʃn] *n* -**1.** [worker] técnico *m*, -ca *f* -**2.** [artist] especialista *mf*.

Technicolor® ['teknɪ͵kʌlə˚] *n (U)* tecnicolor® *m*.

technique [tek'ni:k] *n* técnica *f*.

techno ['teknəʊ] *n MUS* tecno *m*.

technocrat ['teknəʊkræt] *n* tecnocrata *mf*.

technological [͵teknə'lɒdʒɪkl] *adj* tecnológico(ca).

technologist [tek'nɒlədʒɪst] *n* tecnologista *mf*, tecnólogo *m*, -ga *f*.

technology [tek'nɒlədʒɪ] *(pl* -**ies)** *n* tecnologia *f*.

teddy ['tedɪ] *(pl* -**ies)** *n*: **~ (bear)** ursinho *m* de pelúcia.

tedious ['ti:djəs] *adj* tedioso(sa).

tedium ['ti:djəm] *n fml* tédio *m*.

tee [ti:] *n GOLF* -**1.** [area] tee *m*, ponto *m* de partida -**2.** [for ball] tee *m*.

tee off *vi GOLF* dar a tacada inicial.

teem [ti:m] *vi* -**1.** [rain] chover torrencialmente; **the rain ~ed down** caiu uma chuva torrencial -**2.** [be busy]: **to be ~ing with** estar inundado(da) de.

teen [ti:n] *adj inf* adolescente.

teenage ['ti:neɪdʒ] *adj* adolescente.

teenager ['ti:n͵eɪdʒə˚] *n* adolescente *mf*.

teens [ti:nz] *npl* adolescência *f*.

teeny (weeny) [͵ti:nɪ('wi:nɪ)], **teensy (weensy)** [͵ti:nzɪ('wi:nzɪ)] *adj inf* pequenininho(-nha).

tee shirt *n* camiseta *f*.

teeter ['ti:tə˚] *vi* -**1.** [wobble] balançar, oscilar -**2.** *fig* [be in danger]: **to ~ on the brink of bankruptcy** estar à beira da falência.

teeter-totter *n US* gangorra *f*.

teeth [ti:θ] *pl* ⊳ **tooth**.

teethe [ti:ð] *vi* começar a ter dentes.

teething ring ['ti:ðɪŋ-] *n* mordedor *m*.

teething troubles ['ti:ðɪŋ-] *npl fig* dificuldades *fpl* iniciais.

teetotal [ti:'təʊtl] *adj* abstêmio(mia).

teetotaller *UK*, **teetotaler** *US* [ti:'təʊtlə˚] *n* abstêmio *m*, -mia *f*.

TEFL ['tefl] *(abbr of* teaching of English as a foreign language) *n* ensino *de inglês para estrangeiros*.

Teflon® ['teflɒn] <> *n (U)* teflon® *m*. <> *comp* de teflon®.

Teh(e)ran *n* Teerã.

tel. *(abbr of* telephone) tel. *m*.

Tel-Aviv [͵telə'vi:v] *n*: **~ (-Jaffa)** Tel-Aviv(-Jafa).

tele- ['telɪ] *prefix* [over a distance] tele-.

telecast ['telɪkɑ:st] *n* programa *m* de televisão.

telecom ['telɪkɒm] *n UK*, **telecoms** ['telɪkɒmz] *npl inf* telecom.

telecommunications ['telɪkə͵mju:nɪ'keɪʃnz] *npl* telecomunicações *fpl*.

telecon *(abbr of* telephone conversation) *n*.

telegram ['telɪgræm] *n* telegrama *m*.

telegraph ['telɪgrɑ:f] <> *n* telégrafo *m*. <> *vt* telegrafar.

telegraph pole, telegraph post *UK n* poste *m* de telégrafo.

telepathic [͵telɪ'pæθɪk] *adj* telepático(ca).

telepathy [tɪ'lepəθɪ] *n (U)* telepatia *f*.

telephone ['telɪfəʊn] <> *n (U)* telefone *m*; **to be on the ~** *UK* [have a telephone line] ter telefone; [be talking on the telephone] estar no telefone. <> *vt* telefonar. <> *vi* telefonar.

telephone banking *n* serviço *m* de banco por telefone.

telephone book *n* lista *f* telefônica.

telephone booth *n UK* telefone *m* público.

telephone box *n UK* cabine *f* telefônica.

telephone call *n* telefonema *m*.

telephone directory *n* lista *f* telefônica.

telephone exchange *n* central *f* telefônica.

telephone kiosk *n UK* cabine *f* telefônica.

telephone line *n* linha *f* de telefone.

telephone number *n* número *m* de telefone.

telephone operator *n* telefonista *mf*.

telephone tapping *n (U)* escuta *f* telefônica.

telephonist [tɪ'lefənɪst] *n UK* telefonista *mf*.

telephoto lens [͵telɪ'fəʊtəʊ-] *n* (lente *f*) tele-objetiva *f*.

teleprinter ['telɪ͵prɪntə˚], **teletypewriter** *US* [͵telɪ'taɪp͵raɪtə˚] *n* teleimpressor *m*, teletipo *m*.

Teleprompter® [͵telɪ'prɒmptə˚] *n* teleprompter *m*.

telesales ['telɪseɪlz] *npl* televendas *fpl*.

telescope ['telɪskəʊp] *n* telescópio *m*.

telescopic [͵telɪ'skɒpɪk] *adj* telescópico(ca).

teleshopping *n* telecompras *fpl*.

teletext ['telɪtekst] *n (U)* teletexto *m*.

telethon ['telɪθɒn] *n* teleton *m*.

teletypewriter *n US* = teleprinter.

televideo [telɪ'vɪdɪəʊ] *n* televisor *m* com videocassete.

televise ['telɪvaɪz] *vt* televisionar.

television ['telɪ͵vɪʒn] *n* televisão *f*; **on ~** na televisão.

television licence n UK taxa paga ao governo para ter acesso à televisão.

television programme n programa f de televisão.

television set n (aparelho m de) televisão f.

teleworker ['telɪwɜːkə^r] n teletrabalhador m, -ra f.

teleworking n teletrabalho m.

telex ['teleks] <> n telex m. <> vt transmitir por telex.

tell [tell] (pt & pp told) <> vt - 1. [gen] contar; **to ~ sb (that)** contar a alguém que; **to ~ sb sthg; to ~ sthg to sb** contar algo a alguém; **I told you so!** eu te falei! - 2. [instruct, judge, reveal] dizer; **do as you're told!** faça como lhe disseram!; **to ~ sb to do sthg** dizer para alguém fazer algo; **to ~ sb (that)** dizer a alguém que; **to ~ what sb is thinking** saber o que alguém está pensando; **there's no ~ing ...** nunca se sabe ... <> vi - 1. [speak] falar - 2. [judge] dizer - 3. [have effect] surtir efeito.

◆ **tell apart** vt sep distinguir, diferenciar.

◆ **tell off** vt sep repreender.

teller ['telə^r] n - 1. [of votes] escrutinador m, -ra f - 2. [in bank] caixa mf.

telling ['telɪŋ] adj - 1. [relevant] contundente - 2. [revealing] revelador(ra).

telling-off (pl tellings-off) n bronca f.

telltale ['telteɪl] <> adj revelador(ra). <> n mexeriqueiro m, -ra f.

telly ['telɪ] (pl -ies) n UK inf televisão f; **on ~** na televisão.

temerity [tɪ'merətɪ] n (U) fml temeridade f.

temp UK [temp] inf <> n (abbr of **temporary (employee)**) funcionário m temporário, funcionária f temporária. <> vi trabalhar em emprego temporário.

temp. (abbr of **temperature**) temp. f.

temper ['tempə^r] <> n - 1. [state of mind, mood] humor m; **to be in a good/bad ~** estar de bom/mau humor; **to lose one's ~** perder a cabeça; **to have a short ~** ter pavio curto - 2. [temperament] temperamento m. <> vt fml controlar, conter.

temperament ['temprəmənt] n temperamento m.

temperamental [,temprə'mentl] adj temperamental.

temperance ['temprəns] n (U) - 1. fml [moderation] temperança f - 2. [not drinking alcohol] abstinência f.

temperate ['temprət] adj temperado(da).

temperature ['temprətʃə^r] n temperatura f; **to have a ~** ter febre; **to take sb's ~** tirar a temperatura de alguém.

tempered ['tempəd] adj contido(da), comedido(da).

tempest ['tempɪst] n literary tempestade f.

tempestuous [tem'pestjuəs] adj - 1. literary [stormy] turbulento(ta) - 2. fig [emotional] tempestuoso(sa).

tempi ['tempiː] pl <> **tempo**.

template ['templɪt] n - 1. [of shape, pattern] molde m, modelo m - 2. COMPUT gabarito m.

temple ['templ] n - 1. RELIG templo m - 2. ANAT têmpora f.

templet n = template.

tempo ['tempəʊ] (pl -pos OR -pi) n - 1. MUS ritmo m,

velocidade f - 2. [of an event] tempo m.

temporarily [,tempə'rerəlɪ] adv temporariamente.

temporary ['tempərərɪ] adj temporário(ria).

tempt [tempt] vt tentar; **to ~ sb to do sthg** tentar alguém a fazer algo; **to be OR feel ~ed to do sthg** estar/sentir-se tentado(da) a fazer algo.

temptation [temp'teɪʃn] n tentação f.

tempting ['temptɪŋ] adj tentador(ra).

ten [ten] num dez; see also **six**.

tenable ['tenəbl] adj - 1. [reasonable, credible] sustentável - 2. [job, post] seguro(ra), estável; **the post is ~ for one year** o cargo terá duração de um ano.

tenacious [tɪ'neɪʃəs] adj tenaz.

tenacity [tɪ'næsətɪ] n (U) tenacidade f.

tenancy ['tenənsɪ] (pl -ies) n - 1. [period] aluguel m - 2. (U) [possession] locação f.

tenant ['tenənt] n - 1. [of a house] inquilino m, -na f - 2. [of a pub] locatário m, -ria f.

Ten Commandments npl: **the ~** os Dez Mandamentos.

tend [tend] vt - 1. [have tendency]: **to ~ to do sthg** ter a tendência a fazer algo; **I ~ to think (that) ...** sou levado(da) a crer que ... - 2. [look after] cuidar.

tendency ['tendənsɪ] (pl -ies) n - 1. [gen]: **~ towards sthg/to do sthg** tendência f a algo/a fazer algo; **~ towards sthg** tendência f a algo - 2. [leaning, habit] tendência f.

tender ['tendə^r] <> adj - 1. [caring, gentle] terno(na), meigo(ga) - 2. [meat] macio(cia) - 3. [sore] dolorido(da) - 4. [young, innocent]: **at a ~ age** em tenra idade. <> n COMM proposta f, oferta f. <> vt fml oferecer.

tenderize, -ise ['tendəraɪz] vt amaciar.

tenderly ['tendəlɪ] adv carinhosamente.

tenderness ['tendənɪs] n (U) - 1. [care, compassion] ternura f, meiguice f - 2. [soreness] sensibilidade f.

tendon ['tendən] n tendão m.

tendril ['tendrəl] n gavinha f.

tenement ['tenəmənt] n cortiço m.

Tenerife n Tenerife; **in ~** em Tenerife.

tenet ['tenɪt] n fml dogma m.

tenner ['tenə^r] n UK inf - 1. [amount]: **it cost a ~** custou dez libras - 2. [note] nota f de dez libras.

Tennessee n Tennessee.

tennis ['tenɪs] <> n (U) tênis m. <> comp de tênis.

tennis ball n bola f de tênis.

tennis court n quadra f de tênis.

tennis player n jogador m, -ra f de tênis.

tennis racket n raquete f de tênis.

tenor ['tenə^r] <> adj de tenor. <> n - 1. [singer] tenor m - 2. fml [meaning, mood] teor m.

tenpin bowling UK ['tenpɪn-], **tenpins** US ['tenpɪnz] n (U) boliche m (com dez pinos).

tense [tens] <> adj tenso(sa). <> n GRAMM tempo m (verbal). <> vt tencionar, retesar. <> vi endurecer-se.

tensed up [tenst-] adj tenso(sa).

tension ['tenʃn] n tensão f.

◆ **tensions** npl conflitos mpl.

ten-spot n US nota f de dez dólares.

tent [tent] n tenda f, barraca f.

tentacle ['tentəkl] n tentáculo m.

tentative ['tentətɪv] adj -1. [unconfident, hesitant - person] indeciso(sa); [- handshake] vacilante -2. [temporary, not final] provisório(ria).

tentatively ['tentətɪvlɪ] adv -1. [hesitantly] hesitantemente -2. [not finally] provisoriamente.

tenterhooks ['tentəhʊks] npl: to be on ~ estar com os nervos à flor da pele.

tenth [tenθ] num décimo(ma); see also sixth.

tent peg n estaca f de barraca.

tent pole n mastro m de barraca.

tenuous ['tenjʊəs] adj -1. [argument] pouco convincente -2. [connection] de pouca importância -3. [hold] tênue.

tenuously ['tenjʊəslɪ] adv sutilmente.

tenure ['tenjəʳ] n (U) fml -1. [of property] posse f- 2. [of job] estabilidade f.

tepee ['ti:pi:] n tenda f indígena.

tepid ['tepɪd] adj -1. [liquid] tépido(da), morno(na) -2. pej [lacking gusto] morno(na).

tequila [tɪ'ki:lə] n tequila f.

Ter. abbr of terrace.

term [tɜ:m] ⟨⟩ n -1. [word, expression] termo m -2. SCH & UNIV [third of school year] semestre m -3. POL [period in political office]: ~ (of office) mandato m - 4. [stretch of time] período m; in the long/short ~ a longo/curto prazo. ⟨⟩ vt designar.
➡ **terms** npl -1. [of contract, agreement] termos mpl -2. [conditions]: in international/real ~ s em termos internacionais/reais -3. [of relationship]: on equal or the same ~ s de igual para igual, em condições de igualdade; to be on good ~ s (with sb) dar-se bem (com alguém); are you on speaking ~ s? vocês estão se falando? - 4. phr: to come to ~ s with sthg aceitar algo.
➡ **in terms of** prep no que diz respeito a; to think in ~ s of doing sthg pensar em fazer algo.

terminal ['tɜ:mɪnl] ⟨⟩ adj terminal. ⟨⟩ n terminal m.

terminally ['tɜ:mɪnəlɪ] adv: to be ~ ill ser um doente (em fase) terminal.

terminate ['tɜ:mɪneɪt] ⟨⟩ vt -1. [agreement, discussion] fml pôr fim a, encerrar -2. [pregnancy] interromper -3. [contract] rescindir. ⟨⟩ vi -1. [bus, train]: this bus ~ s in the city centre este ônibus pára no centro na cidade -2. [contract] terminar.

termination [,tɜ:mɪ'neɪʃn] n -1. (U) fml [ending] término m - 2. [abortion] interrupção f da gravidez.

termini ['tɜ:mɪnaɪ] pl ➤ terminus.

terminology [,tɜ:mɪ'nɒlədʒɪ] n terminologia f.

terminus ['tɜ:mɪnəs] (pl -ni or -nuses) n terminal m.

termite ['tɜ:maɪt] n cupim m.

terrace ['terəs] n -1. UK [of houses] fileira f de casas geminadas -2. [patio] terraço m -3. [on hillside] terraço m, socalco m.
➡ **terraces** npl FTBL: the ~ s as arquibancadas.

terraced ['terəst] adj escalonado(da).

terraced house n UK casa f geminada.

terracotta [,terə'kɒtə] n (U) terracota f.

terrain [te'reɪn] n (U) terreno m.

terrapin ['terəpɪn] (pl inv or -s) n tartaruga f aquática.

terrestrial [tə'restrɪəl] adj fml terrestre.

terrible ['terəbl] adj terrível.

terribly ['terəblɪ] adv -1. [very badly] terrivelmente -2. [extremely] imensamente.

terrier ['terɪəʳ] n terrier m.

terrific [tə'rɪfɪk] adj -1. [wonderful] fabuloso(sa), maravilhoso(so) -2. [enormous] enorme.

terrified ['terɪfaɪd] adj: ~ (of sb/sthg) aterrorizado(da) (com alguém/algo); to be ~ of sthg ter horror a algo.

terrify ['terɪfaɪ] (pt & pp -ied) vt aterrorizar.

terrifying ['terɪfaɪɪŋ] adj aterrorizante.

terrine [te'ri:n] n terrina f.

territorial [,terɪ'tɔ:rɪəl] adj territorial.

Territorial Army n UK: the ~ o exército voluntário da Grã-Bretanha.

territorial waters npl águas fpl territoriais.

territory ['terətrɪ] (pl -ies) n -1. [political area] território m - 2. [terrain] terreno m -3. [area of knowledge] campo m, área f.

terror ['terəʳ] n -1. (U) [fear] terror m -2. [something feared] horror m -3. inf [rascal] pestinha mf.

terrorism ['terərɪzm] n (U) terrorismo m.

terrorist ['terərɪst] n terrorista mf.

terrorize, -ise ['terəraɪz] vt aterrorizar.

terror-stricken adj em pânico, aterrorizado(da).

terry (cloth) n (U) tecido m atoalhado.

terse [tɜ:s] adj seco(ca).

tersely ['tɜ:slɪ] adv secamente.

tertiary ['tɜ:ʃərɪ] adj fml terciário(ria).

tertiary education n (U) educação f de terceiro grau.

Terylene® ['terəli:n] n (U) tergal® m.

TES (abbr of Times Education Supplement) n suplemento semanal do Times britânico direcionado à educação.

TESL ['tesl] (abbr of teaching of English as a second language) n ensino de inglês como segunda língua.

TESOL (abbr of teaching of English to speakers of other languages) n ensino de inglês para falantes de outras línguas.

TESSA ['tesə] (abbr of tax-exempt special savings account) n sistema de poupança britânica que tem isenção de impostos sobre o juro do capital depositado a prazo fixo.

test [test] ⟨⟩ n -1. [trial] teste m; to put sb/sthg to the ~ colocar alguém/algo à prova - 2. [MED, examination of knowledge, skill] exame m; SCH prova f, teste m. ⟨⟩ vt -1. [try out] testar -2. [examine, check] examinar; to ~ sb on sthg examinar algo de alguém.

testament ['testəmənt] n -1. [gen] testamento m -2. [proof]: ~ to sthg testemunho m de algo.

test ban n suspensão f de testes nucleares.

test card n UK mira f.

test case n JUR caso m precedente.

test-drive vt test-drive m.

tester ['testəʳ] n -1. [person testing] provador m, -ra f -2. [sample] amostra f.

test flight n vôo m de prova.

testicles ['testɪklz] npl testículos mpl.

testify ['testɪfaɪ] (pt & pp -ied) ⟨⟩ vt declarar; to ~

that testemunhar que. ⟨⟩ *vi* **-1.** *JUR* declarar sob juramento **-2.** [be proof]: **to ~ to sthg** evidenciar algo.

testimonial [ˌtestɪ'məʊnjəll *n* **-1.** [reference] carta *f* de recomendação **-2.** [tribute] homenagem *f.*

testimony [*UK* 'testɪmənɪ, *US* 'testəməʊnɪ] *n (U)* **-1.** *JUR* depoimento *m*, testemunho *m*; **to bear ~** testemunhar **-2.** [proof, demonstration]: **~ to sthg** testemunho de algo.

testing ['testɪŋ] *adj* [trying, difficult] duro(ra).

testing ground *n* área *f* de testes.

test match *n UK* partida *f* internacional.

testosterone *n* testosterona *f.*

test paper *n* **-1.** *SCH* teste *m* escrito **-2.** *CHEM* papel *m* reativo.

test pattern *n US* padrão *m* de teste.

test pilot *n* piloto *m* de prova.

test tube *n* tubo *m* de ensaio, proveta *f.*

test-tube baby *n* bebê *m* de proveta.

testy ['testɪ] (*compar* **-ier**, *superl* **-iest**) *adj* **-1.** [person] irritadiço(ça) **-2.** [remark, comment] agressivo(va).

tetanus ['tetənəs] *n (U)* tétano *m.*

tetchy ['tetʃɪ] (*compar* **-ier**, *superl* **-iest**) *adj* irritável, rabugento(ta).

tête-à-tête [ˌteɪtɑː'teɪt] *n* tête-à-tête *m.*

tether ['teðəʳ] ⟨⟩ *vt* **-1.** [horse] apear **-2.** [dog] amarrar. ⟨⟩ *n*: **to be at the end of one's ~** estar no limite.

Texan ['teksn] *n* texano *m*, -na *f.*

Texas ['teksəs] *n* Texas.

Tex-Mex *adj* mexicano(na) do Texas.

text [tekst] *n* texto *m.*

textbook ['tekstbʊk] *n* livro-texto *m.*

textile ['tekstaɪl] ⟨⟩ *n* tecido *m.* ⟨⟩ *comp* **-1.** [industry] têxtil **-2.** [worker] da indústria têxtil.

texting ['tekstɪŋ] *n inf* mensagens *fpl* de texto.

text message *n* [on mobile phone] mensagem *m* de texto.

text messaging [-'mesɪdʒɪŋ] *n* [on mobile phone] mensagem *f* de texto.

texture ['tekstʃəʳ] *n* textura *f.*

Thai [taɪ] ⟨⟩ *adj* tailandês(esa). ⟨⟩ *n* **-1.** [person] tailandês *m*, -esa *f* **-2.** [language] tailandês *m.*

Thailand ['taɪlænd] *n* Tailândia; **in ~** na Tailândia.

thalidomide [θə'lɪdəmaɪd] *n (U)* talidomida *f.*

Thames [temz] *n*: **the ~** o Tâmisa.

than [weak form ðən, strong form ðæn] ⟨⟩ *conj* que; **more ~ ten** mais de dez; **I'd rather stay in ~ go out** prefiro ficar em casa a sair.

thank [θæŋk] *vt*: **to ~ sb (for sthg)** agradecer alguém (por algo); **~ God** *OR* **goodness** *OR* **heavens! graças a Deus/aos céus!**
◆ **thanks** ⟨⟩ *npl* agradecimento *m.* ⟨⟩ *excl* obrigado(da)!
◆ **thanks to** *prep* graças a.

thankful ['θæŋkfʊl] *adj* agradecido(da); **~ for sthg** agradecido(da) por algo.

thankfully ['θæŋkfʊlɪ] *adv* **-1.** [with gratitude] agradecidamente **-2.** [thank goodness] graças a Deus.

thankless ['θæŋklɪs] *adj* ingrato(ta).

thanksgiving *n* ação *f* de graças.
◆ **Thanksgiving (Day)** *n* Dia *m* de Ação de Graças.

THANKSGIVING ■

Nos Estados Unidos, o dia de Ação de Graças, a quarta quinta-feira de novembro, comemora o estabelecimento dos primeiros colonos no país. O almoço em família, que geralmente marca essa data, consiste em peru com mirtilos, acompanhado de batatas, e, para terminar, torta de abóbora. No Canadá, comemoração similar acontece em 1° de outubro.

---

thank you *excl* obrigado(da); **~ for** obrigado(da) por.
◆ **thankyou** *n* agradecimento *m.*

that [ðæt, weak form of pron & conj ðət] (*pl* **those**) ⟨⟩ *adj* **-1.** [referring to thing, person mentioned] esse (essa); **I prefer ~ book** prefiro esse livro. **-2.** [referring to thing, person farther away] aquele (aquela); **~ book at the back** aquele livro lá atrás; **I'll have ~ one** quero aquele (ali) *OR* esse. ⟨⟩ *pron* **-1.** [referring to thing, person mentioned] esse *m*, essa *f*; [indefinite] isso; **what's ~?** o que é isso?; **who's ~?** [on the phone] quem fala?; [pointing] e esse, quem é?; **~'s interesting** que interessante. **-2.** [referring to thing, person farther away] aquele *m*, aquela *f*; [indefinite] aquilo; [pointing] aquela é a Lucy?; **I want those at the back** quero aqueles lá atrás; **what's ~ on the roof?** o que é aquilo no telhado? **-3.** [introducing relative clause] que; **a shop ~ sells antiques** uma loja que vende antiguidades; **the movie ~ I saw** o filme que eu vi; **the room ~ I slept in** o quarto onde *OR* em que dormi. ⟨⟩ *adv* assim tão; **it wasn't ~ bad/good** não foi assim tão mau/bom; **it didn't cost ~ much** não custou tanto assim. ⟨⟩ *conj* que; **tell him ~ I'm going to be late** diga-lhe que vou chegar atrasado.

thatched [θætʃt] *adj* com telhado de palha.

Thatcherism ['θætʃərɪzm] *n (U)* thatcherismo *m.*

that's [ðæts] = that is.

thaw [θɔː] ⟨⟩ *vt* **-1.** [ice] derreter **-2.** [frozen food] descongelar. ⟨⟩ *vi* **-1.** [ice] derreter **-2.** [food] descongelar **-3.** *fig* [people, relations] tornar-se um pouco mais amistoso. ⟨⟩ *n* [warm spell] degelo *m.*

the [weak form ðə, before vowel ðɪ, strong form ðiː] *definite article* **-1.** [gen] o (a), os (as) *(pl)*; **~ book** o livro; **~ apple** a maçã; **~ girls** as meninas; **~ Wilsons** os Wilson; **to play ~ piano** tocar piano. **-2.** [with an adjective to form a noun] o (a), os (as) *(pl)*; **~ British** os britânicos; **~ young** os jovens; **~ impossible** impossível. **-3.** [in dates]: **~ twelfth** o dia doze; **~ forties** os anos quarenta. **-4.** [in titles]: **Elizabeth ~ Second** Elizabeth Segunda.

theatre, theater *US* ['θɪətəʳ] *n* **-1.** [building] teatro *m* **-2.** [art, industry]: **the ~** o teatro **-3.** [in hospital] sala *f* de cirurgia **-4.** *US* [cinema] cinema *m.*

theatregoer, theatergoer *US* ['θɪətəˌgəʊəʳ] *n* aficionado *m*, -da *f* por teatro.

theatrical [θɪ'ætrɪkl] *adj* teatral.

theft [θeft] *n* roubo *m.*

their [ðeəʳ] *adj* seu (sua), deles (delas); **~ house** a sua casa, a casa deles.

theirs [ðeəz] *pron* o/a deles (o/a delas); **a friend of** ~ um amigo deles; **these books are** ~ estes livros são (os) deles; **these are ours - where are** ~? estes são os nossos - onde estão os deles?

them [*weak form* ðəm, *strong form* ðeml *pron* **-1.** (*direct*) os *mpl*, as *fpl*; **I know** ~ eu os conheço **-2.** (*indirect*)lhes; **send this to** ~ mande-lhes isso; **tell** ~ diga-lhes **-3.** (*after prep*) eles *mpl*, elas *fpl*; **Anna and Sam brought it with** ~ a Anna e o Sam trouxeram-no com eles.

thematic [θɪ'mætɪk] *adj* temático(ca).

theme [θi:m] *n* **-1.** [gen] tema *m* **-2.** [signature tune] sintonia *f.*

theme park *n* parque *m* temático.

theme song *n* música-tema *f,* tema *m* musical.

theme tune *n* música-tema *f,* tema *f* musical.

themselves [ðem'selvz] *pron* **-1.** (*reflexive*) se; **they hurt** ~ eles machucaram-se **-2.** (*after prep*) eles *mpl* próprios, elas *fpl* próprias, si *mpl* próprios, si *fpl* próprias; **they blame** ~ eles culpam-se a si próprios; **they did it** ~ fizeram-no eles mesmos *OR* próprios.

then [ðen] <> *adv* **-1.** [later, as a result] então; **if you help me out now,** ~ **I'll return the favour** se você me ajudar agora, eu te devolvo o favor; **it starts at eight - I'll see you** ~ começa às oito - te vejo a essa hora **-2.** [next, afterwards] depois **-3.** [in that case] então, neste caso; **all right** ~ então, tudo certo **-4.** [therefore] então, portanto **-5.** [furthermore, also] além disso. <> *adj* então.

thence [ðens] *adv fml & literary* de lá.

theologian [θɪə'ləʊdʒən] *n* teólogo *m*, -ga *f.*

theology [θɪ'ɒlədʒi] *n* teologia *f.*

theorem ['θɪərəm] *n* teorema *f.*

theoretical [θɪə'retɪkl] *adj* teórico(ca).

theoretically [θɪə'retɪklɪ] *adv* teoricamente, em teoria.

theorist ['θɪərɪst] *n* teórico *m*, -ca *f.*

theorize, -ise ['θɪəraɪz] *vi*: **to** ~ **(about sthg)** teorizar (sobre algo).

theory ['θɪərɪ] (*pl* -ies) *n* teoria *f*; **in** ~ em teoria.

therapeutic [θerə'pju:tɪk] *adj* terapêutico(ca).

therapist ['θerəpɪst] *n* terapeuta *mf.*

therapy ['θerəpɪ] *n (U)* terapia *f.*

there [ðeə^r] <> *pron* [indicating existence of sthg]: ~ **is/are someone at the door** tem alguém na porta <> *adv* **-1.** [in existence, available] lá, alí; **is Sam** ~, **please?** [when telephoning] o Sam está? **-2.** [referring to place] lá; **I'm going** ~ **next week** vou lá para a semana; **over** ~ ali; **it's right** ~ **by the phone** está aí bem ao lado do telefone.

➡ **there you are** *adv* handing sthg to sb] aqui está.

thereabouts [ðeərə'baʊts], **thereabout** *US* [ðeərə'baʊt] *adv*: **or** ~ ou por ali; **by 1998 or** ~ mais ou menos em 1998.

thereafter [ðeər'ɑ:ftə^r] *adv fml* conseqüentemente, depois disso.

thereby [ðeər'baɪ] *adv fml* desse modo.

therefore ['ðeəfɔ:^r] *adv* portanto, por isso.

therein [ðeər'ɪn] *adv fml* **-1.** [inside] lá dentro **-2.** [in that matter]: ~ **lies the problem** aí é que está o problema.

there's [ðeəz] *cont* = there is.

thereupon [ðeərə'pɒn] *adv fml* **-1.** [as a result] em razão disso **-2.** [then] por isso.

thermal ['θɜ:ml] *adj* térmico(ca); ~ **waters** águas *fpl* termais.

thermal reactor *n* reator *m* térmico.

thermal underwear *n (U)* roupa *f* térmica.

thermodynamics [θɜ:məʊdaɪ'næmɪks] *n (U)* termodinâmica *f.*

thermoelectric *adj* termoelétrico(ca).

thermometer [θə'mɒmɪtə^r] *n* termômetro *m.*

thermonuclear [θɜ:məʊ'nju:klɪə^r] *adj* termonuclear.

thermoplastic [θɜ:məʊ'plæstɪk] <> *adj* termoplástico(ca). <> *n* (polímero *m*) termoplástico *m.*

Thermos (flask)® ['θɜ:məs-] *n* garrafa *f* térmica.

thermostat ['θɜ:məstæt] *n* termostato *m.*

thesaurus [θɪ'sɔ:rəs] (*pl* -es) *n* tesauro *m.*

these [ði:z] *pl* ➡ this.

thesis ['θi:sɪs] (*pl* theses ['θi:si:z]) *n* tese *f.*

they [ðeɪ] *pers pron pl* eles *mpl*, elas *fpl.*

they'd [ðeɪd] = they had, they would.

they'll [ðeɪl] = they shall, they will.

they're [ðeə^r] = they are.

they've [ðeɪv] = they have.

thick [θɪk] <> *adj* **-1.** [bulky] grosso(sa); **it's 6 cm** ~ tem 6 cm de grossura; **how** ~ **is that wall?** qual é a espessura da parede? **-2.** [dense] denso(sa) **-3.** *inf* [stupid] estúpido(da) **-4.** [viscous] espesso(sa) **-5.** [voice - with anger] enraivecido(da); [- with emotion] embargado(da); [- with drink] enrolado(da) **-6.** [full, covered]: **to be** ~ **with sthg** estar cheio (cheia) de algo. <> *n*: **to be in the** ~ **of sthg** estar no centro de algo.

➡ **thick and fast** *adv*: **questions came** ~ **and fast** choviam perguntas de todos os lados.

➡ **through thick and thin** *adv*: **I'll do it through** ~ **and thin!** vou fazer isso de qualquer maneira!

thicken ['θɪkn] <> *vt* engrossar. <> *vi* **-1.** [become denser] ficar mais denso(sa) **-2.** [become more solid] engrossar.

thicket ['θɪkɪt] *n* moita *f.*

thickly ['θɪklɪ] *adv* **-1.** [not thinly - spread] em camadas grossas; [- cut] em fatias grossas **-2.** [voice - with anger] com voz enraivecida; [- with emotion] com voz embargada; [- with drink] com voz enrolada **-3.** [densely] densamente.

thickness ['θɪknɪs] *n* **-1.** [width, depth] espessura *f* **-2.** [density - of forest, hedge] densidade *f*; [- of hair] grossura *f* **-3.** [of soup, sauce] consistência *f.*

thickset [θɪk'set] *adj* robusto(ta).

thick-skinned [-'skɪnd] *adj* insensível.

thief [θi:f] (*pl* thieves) *n* ladrão *m*, -dra *f.*

thieve [θi:v] <> *vt* roubar. <> *vi* roubar.

thieves [θi:vz] *pl* ➡ thief.

thieving ['θi:vɪŋ] <> adj ladrão(dra). <> n (U) roubo m, furto m.

thigh [θaɪl n coxa f.

thighbone ['θaɪbəʊn] n fêmur m.

thimble ['θɪmbl] n dedal m.

thin [θɪn] (compar -ner, superl -nest, pt & pp -ned, cont -ning) <> adj -1. [in width, depth] fino(na) -2. [skinny] magro(gra) -3. [watery] ralo(la), aguado(da) -4. [sparse - crowd, vegetation] disperso(sa); [- hair] ralo(la); to be ~ on top estar ficando calvo(va) -5. [excuse] fraco(ca). <> adv: to be wearing ~ [becoming boring] estar perdendo o interesse; [beginning to fail] my patience is wearing ~ está acabando a minha paciência. <> vi: my hair is ~ning meu cabelo está começando a cair.
 • **thin down** vt sep diluir.

thin air n (U): to appear out of ~ aparecer do nada; to disappear into ~ desaparecer sem deixar vestígio.

thing [θɪŋ] n -1. [gen] coisa f; you poor ~! coitadinho(nha); the next ~ on the list o próximo item da lista; the (best) ~ to do would be ... o melhor a fazer seria ...; for one ~ em primeiro lugar; (what) with one ~ and another entre uma coisa e outra; the ~ is ... a questão é ..., acontece que ...; it's just one of those ~s inf é apenas uma dessas coisas que acontecem; to have a ~ about sb/sthg inf [like] gostar muito de alguém/algo; [dislike] não suportar alguém/algo; to make a ~ (out) of sthg inf fazer um alarde de algo -2. [anything]: not a ~ nada; I don't know a ~ (about) não sei nada (sobre or de) -3. inf [fashion]: the ~ a última moda.
 • **things** npl -1. [clothes, possessions] coisas fpl -2. inf [life] coisas fpl.

thingamabob ['θɪŋəmə,bɒb], **thingamajig** ['θɪŋəmədʒɪg], **thingummy(jig)** UK ['θɪŋəmɪ-], **thingy** UK ['θɪŋɪ] n -1. [thing] coisa f -2. [person] fulano(na).

think [θɪŋk] (pt & pp thought) <> vt -1. [believe]: to ~ (that) achar or acreditar que; I ~ so acho que sim; I don't ~ so acho que não -2. [have in mind] pensar -3. [imagine] entender, imaginar -4. [remember] pensar, lembrar -5. [in polite requests]: do you ~ you could help me? você acha que pode me ajudar? <> vi -1. [use mind] pensar -2. [have stated opinion]: what do you ~ of or about his new film? o que você acha do novo filme dele?; I don't ~ much of them/it não tenho uma opinião muito boa sobre eles/ele; to ~ a lot of sb/sthg ter alguém/algo em grande estima -3. phr: to ~ better of sthg/of doing sthg pensar melhor sobre algo/sobre fazer algo; he ~s nothing of doing it ele tira isso de letra; to ~ twice pensar duas vezes. <> n inf: to have a ~ (about sthg) pensar (sobre algo).
 • **think about** vt fus [consider] pensar em; I'll have to ~ about it vou ter que pensar sobre isso.
 • **think back** vi: to ~ back (to sthg) recordar-se (de algo).
 • **think of** vt fus -1. [gen] pensar em; to ~ of doing sthg pensar em fazer algo -2. [remember] lembrar-se de -3. [show consideration for]: it was

kind of you to ~ of me foi muito gentil de tua parte se lembrar de mim.
 • **think out, think through** vt sep -1. [plan] elaborar -2. [problem] examinar.
 • **think over** vt sep refletir sobre.
 • **think up** vt sep imaginar, bolar.

thinker ['θɪŋkəʳ] n pensador m, -ra f.

thinking ['θɪŋkɪŋ] <> adj: the ~ man o homem que pensa. <> n (U) -1. [opinion] opinião f; to my way of ~ na minha opinião -2. [reflection] reflexão f; I'll have to do a lot of hard ~ about your proposal vou ter que pensar bastante sobre a tua proposta -3. [theory] teoria f.

think tank n assessoria f técnica.

thinly ['θɪnlɪ] adv -1. [in width, depth - slice] em fatias finas; [- spread] numa camada fina -2. [forested] escassamente -3. [barely] pouco.

thinner ['θɪnəʳ] n (U) tíner m, solvente m.

thinness ['θɪnnɪs] n -1. [in width, depth] finura f -2. [slim build] magreza f.

thin-skinned [-'skɪnd] adj suscetível.

third [θɜːd] <> num terceiro(ra). <> n -1. [fraction] terço m -2. UK UNIV ≃ nota f C (num título universitário); see also sixth.

third-class adj UK UNIV ≃ nota f C (num título universitário).

third-degree burns npl queimaduras fpl de terceiro grau.

thirdly ['θɜːdlɪ] adv em terceiro lugar.

third party n terceiros mpl.

third party insurance n seguro m contra terceiros.

third-rate adj pej de terceira categoria.

Third World n: the ~ o Terceiro Mundo.

thirst [θɜːst] n sede f; ~ for sthg fig sede de algo.

thirsty ['θɜːstɪ] (compar -ier, superl -iest) adj -1. [parched]: to be or feel ~ estar com or sentir sede -2. [causing thirst] que dá sede.

thirteen [,θɜː'tiːn] num treze; see also six.

thirteenth [,θɜː'tiːnθ] num décimo terceiro, décima terceira; see also sixth.

thirtieth ['θɜːtɪəθ] num trigésimo(ma); see also sixth.

thirty ['θɜːtɪ] (pl -ies) num trinta; see also sixty.

thirty-something adj típico das pessoas que já passaram dos trinta anos e vivem confortavelmente.

this [ðɪs] (pl these) <> adj -1. [referring to thing, person] este (esta); these chocolates are delicious estes chocolates são deliciosos; ~ morning/week esta manhã/semana; I prefer ~ book prefiro este livro; I'll take ~ one quero este. -2. inf [used when telling a story]: there was ~ man ... havia um homem ... <> pron -1. [referring to thing, person] este m, esta f; [indefinite] isto ~; ~ is for you isto é para você; what are these? o que é isto?, o que é que são estas coisas?; ~ is David Gregory [introducing someone] este é o David Gregory; [on telephone] aqui fala David Gregory. <> adv: it was ~ big era deste tamanho; I don't remember it being ~ tiring não me lembro de ser tão cansativo assim.

thistle ['θɪsl] n cardo m.

thither ['ðɪðə'] adv ⊳ hither.
tho' [ðəʊ] conj & adv =.though.
thong [θɒŋ] n -1. [piece of leather] correia f, tira f de couro -2. [bikini] tanga f -3. US [sandal] sandália f.
thorn [θɔ:n] n -1. [prickle] espinho m; **to be a ~ in sb's flesh** OR **side** ser um tormento na vida de alguém -2. [bush, tree] espinheiro m.
thorny ['θɔ:nɪ] (compar -ier, superl -iest) adj -1. [prickly] espinhoso(sa), cheio (cheia) de espinhos -2. fig [tricky, complicated] espinhoso(sa).
thorough ['θʌrə] adj -1. [gen] completo(ta) -2. [meticulous] minucioso(sa).
thoroughbred ['θʌrəbred] n puro-sangue m.
thoroughfare ['θʌrəfeə'] n fml via f pública.
thoroughly ['θʌrəlɪ] adv -1. [fully, in detail] a fundo, exaustivamente -2. [completely, utterly] completamente, totalmente.
thoroughness ['θʌrənɪs] n (U) -1. [exhaustiveness] profundidade f, meticulosidade f -2. [meticulousness] minúcia f.
those [ðəʊz] pl ⊳ that.
though [ðəʊ] ◇ conj -1. [in spite of the fact that] embora -2. [even if] ainda que; **even ~** embora. ◇ adv no entanto.
thought [θɔ:t] ◇ pt & pp ⊳ think. ◇ n -1. [notion] idéia f -2. (U) [act of thinking] reflexão f -3. (U) [philosophy] pensamento m -4. [gesture] intenção f.
➡ **thoughts** npl -1. [reflections] opiniões fpl; **she keeps her ~ to herself** ela não expressa o que pensa; **to collect one's ~s** concentrar-se -2. [views] opiniões fpl, idéias fpl.
thoughtful ['θɔ:tfʊl] adj -1. [pensive] pensativo(va) -2. [considerate] atencioso(sa).
thoughtfulness ['θɔ:tfʊlnɪs] n (U) -1. [pensiveness] ar m pensativo -2. [considerateness] atenção f, consideração f.
thoughtless ['θɔ:tlɪs] adj indelicado(da).
thoughtlessness ['θɔ:tlɪsnɪs] n (U) indelicadeza f.
thousand ['θaʊznd] num: **a ~** mil; **two ~** dois mil; **~s of** milhares de.
thousandth ['θaʊzntθ] num -1. milésimo(ma) -2. [fraction] milésimo(ma); see also **sixth**.
thrash [θræʃ] vt -1. [beat, hit] surrar, dar uma surra em -2. inf [trounce] dar uma surra em.
➡ **thrash about, thrash around** vi debater -se; **to be ~ing about in one's sleep** ter um sono agitado.
➡ **thrash out** vt sep esgotar (um assunto).
thrashing ['θræʃɪŋ] n -1. [beating, hitting] surra f -2. inf [trouncing] surra f.
thread [θred] ◇ n -1. [of cotton, wool] fio m -2. [of screw] rosca f -3. fig [theme] fio m da meada. ◇ vt -1. [pass thread through] enfiar -2. [move]: **to ~ one's way through** abrir caminho.
threadbare ['θredbeə'] adj -1. [clothes, carpet] surrado(da) -2. [argument, joke] manjado(da).
threat [θret] n -1. [warning] ameaça f -2. [menace]: **~ (to sb/sthg)** ameaça (a alguém/algo) -3. [risk]: **~ (of sthg)** ameaça (de algo).
threaten ['θretn] ◇ vt -1. [issue threat]: **to ~ sb (with sthg)** ameaçar alguém (com algo); **to ~ to do sthg** ameaçar fazer algo -2. [endanger]

ameaçar. ◇ vi ameaçar.
threatening ['θretnɪŋ] adj ameaçador(ra).
three [θri:] num três; see also **six**.
three-D adj tridimensional.
three-day event n concurso hípico de três dias.
three-dimensional [-dɪ'menʃənl] adj tridimensional.
threefold ['θri:fəʊld] ◇ adj triplo(pla). ◇ adv três vezes; **to increase ~** triplicar.
three-legged race [-'legɪd-] n corrida f de três pernas.
three-piece adj de três peças.
three-ply adj -1. [wood] com três espessuras -2. [wool] com três fios.
three-point turn n UK volta f de três pontos.
three-quarters npl três quartos mpl.
threesome ['θri:səm] n trio m.
three-star adj de três estrelas.
three-wheeler [-'wi:lə'] n triciclo m.
thresh [θreʃ] vt debulhar.
threshing machine ['θreʃɪŋ-] n debulhadora f.
threshold ['θreʃhəʊld] n -1. [doorway] soleira f -2. [level] limiar m -3. fig [verge]: **to be on the ~ of sthg** estar no limiar de algo.
threshold agreement n acordo m para indexação salarial.
threw [θru:] pt ⊳ throw.
thrift [θrɪft] n -1. [prudent expenditure] economia f, poupança f -2. US [savings bank] = **thrift institution**.
thrift institution n US ≃ banco m de poupança.
thrift shop n US loja f beneficente.
thrifty ['θrɪftɪ] (compar -ier, superl -iest) adj econômico(ca).
thrill [θrɪl] ◇ n -1. [sudden feeling - of joy] vibração f; [- of horror] estremecimento m -2. [exciting experience] emoção f. ◇ vt emocionar, entusiasmar. ◇ vi: **to ~ to sthg** emocionar-se OR entusiasmar-se com algo.
thrilled [θrɪld] adj: **~ (with sthg/to do sthg)** encantado(da) (com algo/por fazer algo).
thriller ['θrɪlə'] n suspense m (enquanto obra).
thrilling ['θrɪlɪŋ] adj emocionante.
thrive [θraɪv] (pt -d OR throve, pp -d) vi -1. [person, plant] desenvolver-se -2. [business] prosperar.
thriving ['θraɪvɪŋ] adj -1. próspero(ra) -2. [plant] que se desenvolve.
throat [θrəʊt] n -1. [inside mouth] garganta f; **to ram** OR **force sthg down sb's ~** fig empurrar algo goela abaixo (em alguém); **to stick in sb's ~** fig ficar preso(sa) na garganta de alguém -2. [front of neck] pescoço m; **to be at each other's ~s** estar batendo boca; **to cut sb's ~** [kill] cortar a garganta de alguém.
throaty ['θrəʊtɪ] (compar -ier, superl -iest) adj rouco(ca).
throb [θrɒb] (pt & pp -bed, cont -bing) ◇ n -1. [of pulse] pulsação f -2. [of head] latejamento m -3. [of heart] palpitação f; [of engine, machine, drums] vibração f. ◇ vi -1. [beat - pulse, blood] pulsar; [- heart] palpitar; [- engine, machine] vibrar; [- music, drums] vibrar, ressoar -2. [be painful] latejar.
throes [θrəʊz] npl: **death ~** agonia f da morte; **to**

be in the ~ of sthg estar no meio de algo.

thrombosis [θrɒmˈbəʊsɪs] (*pl* -boses [-siːzl]) *n* trombose *f*.

throne [θrəʊn] *n* -**1.** [chair] trono *m* -**2.** [position, authority]: **the** ~ o trono.

throng [θrɒŋ] <> *n* aglomeração *f*. <> *vt* aglomerar. <> *vi* aglomerar-se.

throttle [ˈθrɒtl] <> *n* -**1.** [valve] válvula *f* de estrangulamento -**2.** [lever] alavanca *f (da válvula de estrangulamento)*; [pedal] afogador *m*. <> *vt* estrangular.

through [θruː] <> *adj* [finished] terminado(da); **to be ~ with sthg** ter terminado algo; **to be ~ with sb** terminar com alguém. <> *adv* -**1.** [from one end to another] até o fim; **they let us ~** nos deixaram passar -**2.** [until] até; **I slept ~ till ten** dormi até as dez. <> *prep* -**1.** [from one side to another] através de; **to cut ~** cortar algo; **to get ~ sthg** passar por algo -**2.** [during, throughout] durante; **to go ~ an experience** passar por uma experiência -**3.** [because of] por; **to happen ~ sthg** acontecer devido a algo -**4.** [by means of] graças a -**5.** *US* [up till and including]: **Monday ~ Friday** de segunda a sexta.
 ➧ **through and through** *adv* -**1.** [completely] dos pés à cabeça -**2.** [thoroughly]: **to know sthg ~ and ~** conhecer algo de cima a baixo.

throughout [θruːˈaʊt] <> *prep* -**1.** [during] durante todo(da) -**2.** [everywhere in] por todo(da). <> *adv* -**1.** [all the time] o tempo todo -**2.** [everywhere] por todo o lado.

throughput [ˈθruːˌpʊt] *n UK* -**1.** rendimento *m* -**2.** *COMPUT* throughput *m*.

throve [θrəʊv] *pt* ⊳ **thrive**.

throw [θrəʊ] (*pt* threw, *pp* thrown) <> *vt* -**1.** [gen] atirar; **to ~ one's arms around sb/sthg** abraçar alguém/algo -**2.** [move suddenly]: **to ~ o.s.** jogar-se, atirar-se; **to ~ o.s. into sthg** *fig* atirar-se em algo -**3.** [rider] derrubar, desmontar -**4.** *fig* [force into]: **we were all thrown into confusion** ficamos todos muito confusos; **he was thrown into the job at short notice** largaram o trabalho nas costas dele sem avisar -**5.** [shadow, light]: **to ~ sthg on sthg** projetar algo em algo -**6.** [tantrum, fit]: **to ~ a tantrum/fit** ter um acesso de fúria/um ataque -**7.** *fig* [confuse] deixar confuso(sa). <> *n* [toss, pitch] arremesso *m*, lançamento *m*.
 ➧ **throw away** *vt sep* jogar fora.
 ➧ **throw in** *vt sep* incluir (*como brinde*).
 ➧ **throw out** *vt sep* -**1.** [discard] jogar fora -**2.** *fig* [reject] rejeitar -**3.** [force to leave] expulsar.
 ➧ **throw up** <> *vt sep* [cause to rise] jogar. <> *vi inf* [vomit] vomitar, botar para fora.

throwaway [ˈθrəʊəˌweɪ] *adj* -**1.** [disposable] descartável -**2.** [casual] fortuito(ta), casual.

throwback [ˈθrəʊbæk] *n*: ~ **(to sthg)** retrocesso *m* (a algo).

throw-in *n UK FTBL* arremesso *m* lateral.

thrown [θrəʊn] *pp* ⊳ **throw**.

thru [θruː] *adj, adv & prep US inf* = **through**.

thrush [θrʌʃ] *n* -**1.** [bird] tordo *m* -**2.** *MED* cândida *f*.

thrust [θrʌst] (*pt & pp* thrust) <> *n* -**1.** [forward movement - of knife, sword] golpe *m*; [- of army] investida *f*; [- of body] impulso *m* -**2.** *(U)* [forward force] (força *f* de) propulsão *f* -**3.** [main aspect]

essência *f*. <> *vt* -**1.** [shove, jab] empurrar -**2.** [jostle]: **to ~ one's way through** abrir caminho à força.
 ➧ **thrust upon** *vt sep*: **to ~ sthg upon sb** impor algo a alguém.

thrusting [ˈθrʌstɪŋ] *adj* agressivo(va).

thruway [ˈθruːweɪ] *n US* rodovia *f*.

thud [θʌd] (*pt & pp* -ded, *cont* -ding) <> *n* baque *m*. <> *vi* dar um baque seco.

thug [θʌg] *n* marginal *mf*.

thumb [θʌm] <> *n* [of hand] polegar *m*; **to twiddle one's ~s** ficar à toa. <> *vt inf* [hitch]: **to ~ a lift** pedir carona (*com o dedo*).
 ➧ **thumb through** *vt fus* folhear.

thumb index *n* índice *m* alfabético.

thumbnail [ˈθʌmneɪl] <> *adj* breve. <> *n* unha *f* do polegar.

thumbnail sketch *n* descrição *f* breve.

thumbs down [ˌθʌmz-] *n*: **to get OR be given the ~** ser recebido(da) com desaprovação, não ser bem recebido(da).

thumbs up [ˌθʌmz-] *n* [go-ahead]: **to give sb/sthg the ~** dar luz verde a alguém/algo.

thumbtack [ˈθʌmtæk] *n US* percevejo *m* (*para fixar*).

thump [θʌmp] <> *n* -**1.** [blow] soco *m* -**2.** [thud] baque *m*. <> *vt* -**1.** [punch] dar um soco em -**2.** [place heavily]: **he ~ed the books down on the table** ele bateu os livros na mesa com força. <> *vi* -**1.** [move heavily] caminhar pesadamente; **to ~ in/out** entrar/sair com passos pesados -**2.** [pound - heart] palpitar; [- head] latejar.

thunder [ˈθʌndəʳ] <> *n (U)* -**1.** *METEOR* trovão *m* -**2.** *fig* [loud sound] estrondo *m*. <> *vt* [say angrily] vociferar, esbravejar. <> *vi* [make loud sound] fazer um estrondo. <> *v impers METEOR* trovejar.

thunderbolt [ˈθʌndəbəʊlt] *n* -**1.** *METEOR* raio *m* -**2.** *fig* [shock] choque *m*.

thunderclap [ˈθʌndəklæp] *n* trovão *m*.

thundercloud [ˈθʌndəklaʊd] *n* nuvem *f* de temporal.

thundering *adj* enorme, descomunal.

thunderous [ˈθʌndərəs] *adj* ensurdecedor(ra).

thunderstorm [ˈθʌndəstɔːm] *n* temporal *m*.

thunderstruck [ˈθʌndəstrʌk] *adj* fig atônito(ta).

thundery [ˈθʌndərɪ] *adj* carregado(da).

Thur, Thurs (*abbr of* Thursday) qui.

Thursday [ˈθɜːzdɪ] *n* quinta-feira *f*; *see also* **Saturday**.

thus [ðʌs] *adv fml* -**1.** [as a consequence] assim, por isso -**2.** [in this way] desse modo -**3.** [as follows] assim.

thwart [θwɔːt] *vt* frustrar, impedir.

thyme [taɪm] *n (U)* tomilho *m*.

thyroid [ˈθaɪrɔɪd] *n* tireóide *f*.

tiara [tɪˈɑːrə] *n* tiara *f*.

Tiber [ˈtaɪbəʳ] *n*: **the (River) ~** o (Rio) Tibre.

Tibet [tɪˈbet] *n* Tibete; **in ~** no Tíbete.

Tibetan [tɪˈbetn] <> *adj* tibetano(na). <> *n* -**1.** [person] tibetano *m*, -na *f* -**2.** [language] tibetano *m*.

tibia [ˈtɪbɪə] (*pl* -biae [-biːl], -s) *n* tíbia *f*.

tic [tɪk] *n* tique *m*.

tick [tɪk] <> *n* -**1.** [written mark] (sinal *m* de) visto *m* -**2.** [sound] tiquetaque *m*; **I shan't be a ~** não vou demorar **-3.** [insect] carrapato *m.* ◇ *vt* marcar *(com sinal de visto).* ◇ *vi* **-1.** [make ticking sound] fazer tiquetaque **-2.** *fig* [behave in a certain way]: **what makes him ~?** o que o motiva? **►tick away, tick by** *vi* passar.

►tick off *vt sep* **-1.** [mark off] marcar *(com sinal de visto)* **-2.** [tell off]: **to ~ sb off (for sthg)** dar uma bronca em alguém (por algo).

►tick over *vi* funcionar em marcha lenta.

ticked [tɪkd] *adj US inf* [annoyed] incomodado(da).

ticker tape *n (U)* fita *f* de teleimpressor; **~ parade** desfile *m* com confete e serpentinas.

ticket ['tɪkɪt] *n* **-1.** [for entry, access - plane] bilhete *m*; [- bus, train] passagem *f*; [- for footbal match, concert] entrada *f*, ingresso *m* **-2.** [label on product] etiqueta *f* **-3.** [notice of traffic offence] multa *f* **-4.** POL chapa *f*.

ticket agency *n agência que vende entradas de teatro ou passagens de trem, avião etc.*

ticket collector *n UK* revisor *m*, -ra *f (no trem).*

ticket holder *n* portador *m*, -ra *f* do ingresso.

ticket inspector *n UK* revisor *m*, -ra *f (no trem).*

ticket machine *n* máquina *f* automática que vende ingressos.

ticket office *n* **-1.** [in theatre] bilheteria *f* **-2.** [in station] guichê *m* de venda.

ticking off ['tɪkɪŋ-] *(pl* **tickings off)** *n*: **to get a ~** levar uma bronca; **to give sb a ~** dar uma bronca em alguém.

tickle ['tɪkl] ◇ *vt* **-1.** [touch lightly] fazer cócegas em **-2.** *fig* [amuse] divertir. ◇ *vi*: **my feet are tickling** sinto cócegas nos pés.

ticklish ['tɪklɪʃ] *adj* **-1.** [sensitive to touch]: **to be ~** sentir cócegas **-2.** *fig* [delicate] delicado(da).

tick-tack-toe *n US* [game] jogo-da-velha *m.*

tidal ['taɪdl] *adj* da maré.

tidal wave *n* maremoto *m.*

tidbit *n US* = titbit.

tiddler ['tɪdlə^r] *n UK* [fish] peixinho *m.*

tiddly ['tɪdlɪ] *(compar* **-ier,** *superl* **-iest)** *adj inf* **-1.** [tipsy] grogue **-2.** [tiny] pequenininho(nha).

tiddlywinks ['tɪdlɪwɪŋks], **tiddledywinks** *US* ['tɪdldɪwɪŋks] *n (U)* [game] jogo *m* da pulga.

tide [taɪd] *n* **-1.** [of sea] maré *f* **-2.** *fig* [trend] tendência *f*; **the ~ of history** o curso da história **-3.** *fig* [large quantity] corrente *f.*

►tide over *vt sep* dar uma força *(por um certo tempo).*

tidemark *n* **-1.** [of sea] linha *f* da maré alta **-2.** *UK* [round bath] marca *f* do nível da água escoada.

tidily ['taɪdɪlɪ] *adv* [nearly] ordenadamente.

tidiness ['taɪdɪnɪs] *n* **-1.** [or room, desk] *(U)* ordem *f* **-2.** [of appearance] asseio *m.*

tidings ['taɪdɪŋz] *npl literary* novas *fpl.*

tidy ['taɪdɪ] *(compar* **-ier,** *superl* **-iest,** *pt &* *pp* **-ied)** ◇ *adj* **-1.** [gen] arrumado(da) **-2.** [in habits] asseado(da) **-3.** *inf* [sizeable] razoável. ◇ *vt* arrumar.

►tidy away *vt sep* pôr em ordem.

►tidy up ◇ *vt sep* arrumar. ◇ *vi*: **I'll have to ~ up before going out** [objects] vou ter que arrumar tudo antes de sair.; [hair, appearance] vou ter que me arrumar antes de sair.

tie [taɪ] *(pt &* *pp* **tied,** *cont* **tying)** ◇ *n* **-1.** [necktie] gravata *f* **-2.** [string, cord] nó *m*, laçada *f* **-3.** [bond, link]

laço *m*, vínculo *m* **-4.** [in game, competition] empate *m* **-5.** *US RAIL* dormente *m.* ◇ *vt* **-1.** [attach]: **to ~ sthg (on)** to sthg amarrar algo (em algo); **to ~ sthg round sthg** amarrar algo em volta de algo; **to ~ sthg with sthg** amarrar algo com algo **-2.** [do up, fasten - shoelaces] atar, amarrar; [- knot] dar **-3.** *fig* [link]: **to be ~d to sb/sthg** estar ligado(da) a alguém/algo **-4.** *fig* [restricted]: **to be ~d to sthg** estar limitado(da) a algo. ◇ *vi* [draw]: **to ~ (with sb)** empatar (com alguém).

►tie down *vt sep fig* [restrict] prender; **to feel tied down by sthg** sentir-se preso(sa) a algo.

►tie in with *vt fus* concordar com, ajustar-se com.

►tie up *vt sep* **-1.** [secure with string, rope] amarrar **-2.** *fig* [restrict use of] limitar o uso de **-3.** *fig* [link]: **to be ~d up with sthg** estar ligado(da) a algo.

tiebreak(er) ['taɪbreɪk(ə^r)] *n* **-1.** TENNIS tie-break *m* **-2.** [extra question] desempate *m.*

tied [taɪd] *adj SPORT* empatado(da).

tied cottage *n UK casa que o agricultor aluga a um de seus trabalhadores enquanto durar o serviço.*

tied up *adj* [busy] ocupado(da).

tie-dye *vt* tie-dye.

tie-in *n* **-1.** [link]: **~ between/with sthg** ligação *f* entre/com algo **-2.** [promotional product] produto *m* promocional *(de um filme, programa de televisão).*

tiepin ['taɪpɪn] *n* alfinete *m* de gravata.

tier [tɪə^r] *n* **-1.** [of seats, shelves] fileira *f* **-2.** [cake] camada *f.*

Tierra del Fuego *n* Terra do Fogo; **in ~** na Terra do Fogo.

tie-up *n* **-1.** [link]: **~ between/with sthg** relação *f* próxima entre/com algo **-2.** *US* [interruption - in work] suspensão *f*; [- in traffic] engarrafamento *m* rápido.

tiff [tɪf] *n* desavença *f*, briguinha *f.*

tiger ['taɪgə^r] *n* tigre *m.*

tiger cub *n* filhote *m* de tigre.

tight [taɪt] ◇ *adj* **-1.** [gen] apertado(da); **a ~ fit** justo(ta) **-2.** [taut] esticado(da), teso(sa) **-3.** [close together] comprimido(da) **-4.** [painful]: **my chest feels ~** sinto uma dor forte no peito **-5.** [strict] rigoroso(sa) **-6.** [at sharp angle] cerrado(da) **-7.** *inf* [drunk] bêbado(da) **-8.** *inf* [miserly] sovina. ◇ *adv* **-1.** [firmly, securely] com força; **to hold ~** segurar bem; **to shut** *or* **close sthg ~** fechar bem algo **-2.** [tautly] bem esticado(da).

►tights *npl* meia-calça *f.*

tighten ['taɪtn] ◇ *vt* **-1.** [knot, belt, rules] apertar **-2.** [make tauter] esticar **-3.** [strengthen]: **to ~ one's hold** *or* **grip on sthg** agarrar *or* segurar algo com força **-4.** [security] intensificar. ◇ *vi* [make tighter] apertar.

►tighten up *vt sep* **-1.** [belt, screw, rule] apertar **-2.** [control, security] intensificar.

tightfisted [,taɪt'fɪstɪd] *adj inf pej* pão-duro.

tightknit [,taɪt'nɪt] *adj* muito unido(da).

tight-lipped [-'lɪpt] *adj* **-1.** [with lips pressed together] de lábios cerrados **-2.** [silent] calado(da).

tightly ['taɪtlɪ] *adv* **-1.** [closely]: **the dress fitted her**

~ o vestido entrava bem apertado nela **- 2.** [firmly, securely] com força; [fasten, tie] bem **- 3.** [tautly] bem esticado(da).

tightness ['taɪtnɪs] *n (U)* **- 1.** [gen] aperto *m* **- 2.** [strictness] rigor *m* **- 3.** [of schedule] pressão *f* de tempo.

tightrope ['taɪtrəʊp] *n* corda *f* bamba; **to be on** OR **walking a** ~ estar OR andar na corda bamba.

tightrope walker *n* funâmbulo *m*, -la *f*.

Tigré *n* Tigre; **in** ~ em Tigre.

tigress ['taɪgrɪs] *n* tigresa *f*.

Tigris *n*: **the (River)** ~ o (Rio) Tigre.

tilde ['tɪldə] *n* til *m*.

tile [taɪl] *n* **- 1.** [on roof] telha *f* **- 2.** [on floor] piso *m* **- 3.** [on wall] azulejo *m*.

tiled [taɪld] *adj* **- 1.** [roof] telhado(da) **- 2.** [floor] ladrilhado(da) **- 3.** [wall] azulejado(da).

tiling ['taɪlɪŋ] *n (U)* **- 1.** [act of tiling - roof, floor, wall] colocação *f* **- 2.** [tiled surface - roof] telhas *fpl*; [- floor] piso *m*; [- wall] azulejos *mpl*.

till [tɪl] <> *prep* até; ~ **now** até agora. <> *conj* até; **wait** ~ **I come back** espere até eu voltar OR que eu volte. <> *n* caixa *f* (registradora).

tiller ['tɪlə'] *n* cana *f* do leme.

tilt [tɪlt] <> *n* inclinação *f*. <> *vt* inclinar. <> *vi* inclinar-se.

timber ['tɪmbə'] *n* **- 1.** *(U)* [wood] madeira *f* (*para a construção*) **- 2.** [beam - of ship] viga *f* mestra; [- of house] madeiramento *m*.

timbered ['tɪmbəd] *adj* revestido(da) com madeira.

time [taɪm] <> *n* **- 1.** *(U)* [general measurement, spell] tempo *m*; **to get the** ~ **to do sthg** ter tempo para fazer algo; **to take** ~ levar tempo; **to take** ~ **out to do sthg** tirar tempo para fazer algo; **it's high** ~ **...** já é hora de ...; **to get** ~ **and a half** receber o pagamento combinado mais a metade; **to have no** ~ **for sb/sthg** não ter tempo a perder com alguém/algo; **to make good** ~ fazer uma boa média (de tempo); **to pass the** ~ passar o tempo; **to play for** ~ tentar ganhar tempo; **to take one's** ~ **(doing sthg)** dar-se seu tempo(para fazer algo); **it was a long** ~ **before he came** passou muito tempo antes que ele viesse; **for a** ~ por um tempo **- 2.** [as measured by clock, moment] hora *f*; **the** ~ **is three o'clock** são três horas; **what** ~ **is it?**, **what's the** ~? que horas são?, tem horas?; **in a week's/year's** ~ daqui a uma semana/um mês; **to keep** ~ manter a hora certa; **to lose** ~ atrasar; **to tell the** ~ dizer as horas; **now would be a good** ~ **to ask** agora seria uma boa hora para perguntar **- 3.** [point in time in past] época *f*; **at that** ~ naquela época **- 4.** [era] era *f*; **in ancient** ~**s** na antiguidade; **to be ahead of one's** ~ estar à frente de seu tempo; **before my** ~ [before I was born] antes de eu nascer; [before I worked here] antes de eu trabalhar ali; **to be behind the** ~**s** estar parado(da) no tempo **- 5.** [occasion] vez *f*; **at the best of** ~**s** até nos melhores momentos; **from** ~ **to** ~ de vez em quando; ~ **after** ~, ~ **and again** uma e outra vez **- 6.** [experience]: **we had a good** ~ nos divertimos muito; **we had a terrible** ~ foi uma situação horrível; **to have a hard** ~ **trying to do sthg** ter dificuldade tentando fazer algo **- 7.** [degree of lateness]: **in good** ~ na hora certa;

ahead of ~ cedo; **on** ~ na hora **- 8.** MUS compasso *m*. <> *vt* **- 1.** [schedule] marcar **- 2.** [measure duration, speed of] cronometrar **- 3.** [choose appropriate moment for] escolher o momento certo para.

◆ **times** <> *npl*: **four** ~ **s as much as me** quatro vezes mais do que eu. <> *prep* MATH: **four** ~ **s five is twenty** quatro vezes cinco é vinte.

◆ **about time** *adv*: **it's about** ~ já era hora.

◆ **at a time** *adv*: **for months at a** ~ por meses seguidos; **one at a** ~ um (uma) por vez; **I always read several maganizes at a** ~ sempre leio várias revistas ao mesmo tempo.

◆ **at (any) one time** *adv* em qualquer momento.

◆ **at times** *adv* às vezes.

◆ **at the same time** *adv* ao mesmo tempo.

◆ **for the time being** *adv* por enquanto.

◆ **in time** *adv* **- 1.** [not late]: **in** ~ **(for sthg)** a tempo (para algo) **- 2.** [eventually] com o tempo.

time-and-motion study *n* estudo de métodos e técnicas para melhorar o rendimento no trabalho.

time bomb *n* bomba-relógio *f*.

time-consuming [-kən,sjuː'mɪŋ] *adj* que exige muito tempo.

timed [taɪmd] *adj* **- 1.** [race, test] cronometrado(da) **- 2.** [opportune]: **well** ~ oportuno(na); **badly** ~ pouco oportuno(na).

time difference *n* diferença *f* de fuso horário.

time-honoured *adj* consagrado(da).

timekeeping ['taɪm,kiːpɪŋ] *n (U)* pontualidade *f*; **he was sacked for bad** ~ foi demitido por chegar atrasado.

time lag *n* intervalo *m*.

time-lapse *adj* PHOT time-lapse.

timeless ['taɪmlɪs] *adj* eterno(na).

time limit *n* prazo *m*, limite *m* de tempo.

timely ['taɪmlɪ] (*compar* -ier, *superl* -iest) *adj* oportuno(na).

time machine *n* máquina *f* do tempo.

time off *n (U)* (tempo *m* de) folga *f*; ~ **(from) sthg** folga (de algo); **I'm owed** ~ me devem alguns dias de folga.

time-out (*pl* **time-outs** OR **times-out**) *n* US SPORT intervalo *m*.

timepiece ['taɪmpiːs] *n dated* relógio *m*.

timer ['taɪmə'] *n* temporizador *m*.

timesaving ['taɪm,seɪvɪŋ] *adj* que economiza tempo.

time scale *n* escala *f* de tempo.

time-share *n* UK propriedade *f* comprada em sociedade.

time sheet *n* folha *f* de ponto.

time signal *n* sinal *m* horário (*emitido nas rádios*).

time switch *n* temporizador *m* (*numa máquina*).

timetable ['taɪm,teɪbl] *n* **- 1.** [gen] horário *m* **- 2.** [schedule] programação *f*, programa *m*.

time zone *n* fuso *m* horário.

timid ['tɪmɪd] *adj* tímido(da).

timidly ['tɪmɪdlɪ] *adv* timidamente.

timing ['taɪmɪŋ] *n (U)* **- 1.** [of actor, musician, tennis player] timing *m* -**2.** [chosen moment]: **she made her comment with perfect** ~ ela fez seu comentário no momento certo -**3.** SPORT [measuring] cronometragem *f.*

timing device *n* dispositivo *m* de retardamento *(numa bomba).*

timpani ['tɪmpənɪ] *npl* timbales *mpl*, tímpanos *mpl.*

tin [tɪn] ⬦ *n* -**1.** *(U)* [metal] estanho *m*; ~ **plate** folha-de-fandres *f*-**2.** UK [for food, storage] lata *f*-**3.** [for cooking] assadeira *f.* ⬦ *comp* -**1.** [tin] de estanho -**2.** [tinplate] de folha-de-flandres.

tin can *n* lata *f.*

tinder *n (U)* isca *f (para acender o fogo).*

tinfoil ['tɪnfɔɪl] *n (U)* papel *m* OR folha *f* de estanho.

tinge [tɪndʒ] *n* -**1.** [of colour] tom *m*, matiz *m* -**2.** [of feeling] rápida sensação *f*; **a** ~ **of guilt** uma ponta de culpa.

tinged [tɪndʒd] *adj* -**1.** [colour]: ~ **with sthg** com um toque de algo -**2.** [feeling]: ~ **with sthg** com uma pontinha de algo.

tingle ['tɪŋgl] *vi* formigar; **to** ~ **with sthg** agitar-se com algo.

tingling ['tɪŋglɪŋ] *n* formigamento *m.*

tinker ['tɪŋkə ͬ] ⬦ *n* -**1.** *pej* [gipsy] cigano *m*, -na *f*-**2.** [rascal] diabinho *m*, -nha *f.* ⬦ *vi* atamancar; **to** ~ **with sthg** fuçar em algo.

tinkle ['tɪŋkl] ⬦ *n* -**1.** [of bell] tilintar *m* -**2.** UK *inf* [phone call]: **to give sb a** ~ bater um fio para alguém. ⬦ *vi* -**1.** [bell] tilintar -**2.** [phone] tocar.

tin mine *n* mina *f* de estanho.

tinned [tɪnd] *adj* UK enlatado(da), em conserva.

tinny ['tɪnɪ] *(compar* -**ier***, superl* -**iest***) adj* -**1.** [sound] metálico(ca) -**2.** *inf pej* [badly made] malfeito(ta).

tin opener *n* UK abridor *m* de lata.

tinpot *adj* UK *pej* de araque.

tinsel ['tɪnsl] *n (U)* lantejoula *f*, ouropel *m.*

tint [tɪnt] ⬦ *n* matiz *m.* ⬦ *vt* -**1.** [gen] matizar -**2.** [window, glass] colorir -**3.** [hair] tingir.

tinted ['tɪntɪd] *adj* -**1.** [window, glass] colorido(da) -**2.** [hair] tingido(da).

tiny ['taɪnɪ] *(compar* -**ier***, superl* -**iest***) adj* minúsculo(-la), diminuto(ta).

tip [tɪp] *(pt & pp* -**ped***, cont* -**ping***)* ⬦ *n* -**1.** [end] ponta *f*; **it's on the** ~ **of my tongue** está na ponta da língua -**2.** UK [dump]: **rubbish** ~ lixão *m*, depósito *m* de lixo -**3.** [gratuity] gorjeta *f*-**4.** [piece of advice] dica *f.* ⬦ *vt* -**1.** [tilt] inclinar -**2.** [spill] derramar -**3.** [give a gratuity to] dar gorjeta a. ⬦ *vi* -**1.** [tilt] inclinar-se -**2.** [spill] derramar -**3.** [give a gratuity] dar gorjeta.

 ➡ **tip off** *vt sep* avisar, alertar.

 ➡ **tip over** *vt sep & vi* virar.

 ➡ **tip up** *vi* virar.

tip-off *n* informação *f (secreta).*

tipped [tɪpt] *adj* -**1.** [spear] com ponta de aço -**2.** [cigarette] com filtro -**3.** [pen]: **felt-**~ **pen** caneta *f* hidrográfica.

Tipp-Ex® ['tɪpeks] *n* UK ≃ errorex® corretivo *m.*

 ➡ **tipp-ex** *vt* UK corrigir com corretivo.

tipple ['tɪpl] *n inf* bebida *f.*

tipsy ['tɪpsɪ] *(compar* -**ier***, superl* -**iest***) adj inf* alto(ta) *(por ingerir bebida alcoólica),* tocado(da).

tiptoe ['tɪptəʊ] ⬦ *n*: **on** ~ nas pontas dos pés.

⬦ *vi* andar nas pontas dos pés.

tip-top *adj inf dated* ótimo(ma).

tirade [taɪˈreɪd] *n* descascadela *f.*

Tirana, Tiranë *n* Tirana.

tire ['taɪə ͬ] ⬦ *n* US = tyre. ⬦ *vt* cansar. ⬦ *vi* -**1.** [get tired] cansar-se, ficar cansado(da) -**2.** [get fed up]: **to** ~ **of sb/sthg** cansar-se de alguém/algo.

 ➡ **tire out** *vt sep* esgotar.

tired ['taɪəd] *adj* -**1.** [sleepy] cansado(da) -**2.** [fed up]: ~ **of sthg/of doing sthg** cansado(da) de algo/de fazer algo.

tiredness ['taɪədnɪs] *n (U)* cansaço *m.*

tireless ['taɪəlɪs] *adj* incansável.

tiresome ['taɪəsəm] *adj* cansativo(va), enfadonho(-nha).

tiring ['taɪərɪŋ] *adj* cansativo(va).

Tirol *n* = Tyrol.

tissue ['tɪʃuː] *n* -**1.** [paper handkerchief] lenço *m* de papel -**2.** *(U)* BIOL tecido *m* -**3.** *phr*: **a** ~ **of lies** um emaranhado de mentiras.

tissue paper *n (U)* papel *m* de seda.

tit [tɪt] *n* -**1.** [bird] chapim *m* -**2.** *vulg* [breast] teta *f.*

titbit UK ['tɪtbɪt], **tidbit** US ['tɪdbɪt] *n* -**1.** [of food] petisco *m* -**2.** *fig* [of news]: **a** ~ **of gossip** uma pequena fofoca.

tit for tat [-ˈtæt] *n*: **it's** ~ é olho por olho.

titillate ['tɪtɪleɪt] ⬦ *vt* excitar. ⬦ *vi* excitar-se.

titivate ['tɪtɪveɪt] *vt* arrumar, enfeitar.

title ['taɪtl] *n* título *m.*

titled ['taɪtld] *adj* com título de nobreza.

title deed *n* título *m* de propriedade.

titleholder ['taɪtl,həʊldə ͬ] *n* SPORT campeão *m*, -peã *f.*

title page *n* página *f* de rosto.

title role *n* papel *m* principal.

titter ['tɪtə ͬ] *vi* rir baixinho.

tittle-tattle ['tɪtl,tætl] *n (U) inf pej* mexerico *m.*

titular ['tɪtjʊlə ͬ] *adj* honorário(ria), nominal.

T-junction *n* junção-tê *f.*

TLS *(abbr of* **Times Literary Supplement***) n* suplemento semanal do *Times* britânico direcionado à literatura.

TM ⬦ *n* -**1.** *(abbr of* **transcendental meditation***)* meditação *f* transcendental -**2.** *(abbr of* **translation memory***)* MT *f.* ⬦ *abbr of* **trademark**.

TN *abbr of* **Tennessee**.

TNT *(abbr of* **trinitrotoluene***) n* TNT *m.*

to [unstressed before consonant tə, unstressed before vowel tʊ, stressed tuː] ⬦ *prep* -**1.** [indicating direction] para; **to go** ~ **Brazil** ir ao Brasil; **to go** ~ **school** ir para a escola. -**2.** [indicating position] a; ~ **the left/right** à esquerda/direita. -**3.** [expressing indirect object] a; **to give sthg** ~ **sb** dar algo a alguém; **give it** ~ **me** dê-me isso; **to listen** ~ **the radio** ouvir rádio. -**4.** [indicating reaction, effect]: ~ **my surprise** para surpresa minha; **it's** ~ **your advantage** é em seu benefício. -**5.** [until] até; **to count** ~ **ten** contar até dez; **we work from nine** ~ **five** trabalhamos das nove (até) às cinco. -**6.** [in stating opinion] para; ~ **me, he's lying** para mim, ele está mentindo. -**7.** [indicating change of state]: **to turn** ~ **sthg** transformar-se em algo; **it could lead** ~ **trouble** pode vir a dar problemas. -**8.** UK [in expressions of time] para; **it's ten ~ three** são dez para as três; **at quarter ~ seven** às quinze para as sete. **- 9.** [in ratios, rates]: **40 miles ~ the gallon** 40 milhas por galão. **-10.** [of, for]: **the answer ~ the question** a resposta à pergunta; **the key ~ the car** a chave do carro; **a letter ~ my daughter** uma carta para a minha filha. **-11.** [indicating attitude] (para) com; **to be rude ~ sb** ser grosseiro com alguém. <> **with** *infinitive* **-1.** [forming simple infinitive]: **~ walk** andar; **~ laugh** rir. **-2.** [following another verb]: **to begin ~ do sthg** começar a fazer algo; **to try ~ do sthg** tentar fazer algo. **-3.** [following an adjective]: **difficult ~ do** difícil de fazer; **pleased ~ meet you** prazer em conhecê-lo; **ready ~ go** pronto para partir. **-4.** [indicating purpose] para; **we came here ~ look at the castle** viemos para ver o castelo.

toad [təʊd] *n* sapo *m*.

toadstool ['təʊdstu:l] *n* cogumelo *m* venenoso.

toady ['təʊdɪ] (*pl* **-ies**, *pt* & *pp* **-ied**) *pej* <> *n* bajulador *m*, -ra *f.* <> *vi*: **to ~ (to sb)** puxar o saco (de alguém).

toast [təʊst] <> *n* **-1.** *(U)* [bread] torrada *f*, pão *m* torrado **-2.** [drink] brinde *m*; **to drink a ~ to sb/sthg** fazer um brinde a alguém/algo **-3.** [person]: **the ~ of the town** o herói da cidade. <> *vt* **-1.** [bread] tostar, torrar **-2.** [person] brindar a.

toasted sandwich [ˌtəʊstɪd-] *n* misto-quente *m.*

toaster ['təʊstə^r] *n* torradeira *f.*

toast rack *n* porta-torradas *m inv.*

tobacco [tə'bækəʊ] *n* tabaco *m.*

tobacconist *n* charuteiro *m*, -ra *f*, vendedor *m*, -ra *f* de fumo *OR* tabaco; **~'s (shop)** tabacaria *f.*

Tobago [tə'beɪgəʊ] *n* ▷ **Trinidad and Tobago.**

toboggan [tə'bɒgən] <> *n* tobogã *m.* <> *vi* deslizar-se em tobogã.

today [tə'deɪ] <> *adv (U)* **-1.** [this day] hoje **-2.** [nowadays] de hoje, atual; **~'s technology** a tecnologia hoje em dia. <> *adv* **-1.** [this day] hoje **-2.** [nowadays] hoje (em dia).

toddle ['tɒdl] *vi* **-1.** [walk unsteadily] dar os primeiros passos **-2.** *inf* [go]: **to ~ off** *OR* **along** cair fora.

toddler ['tɒdlə^r] *n* criança *f* pequena *(que começa a andar).*

toddy ['tɒdɪ] (*pl* **-ies**) *n* ponche *m.*

to-do (*pl* **-s**) *n inf dated* tumulto *m*, alvoroço *m.*

toe [təʊ] <> *n* **-1.** [of foot] dedo *m (do pé)* **-2.** [of sock] ponta *f* **-3.** [of shoe] biqueira *f.* <> *vt*: **to ~ the line** cumprir as normas.

toehold ['təʊhəʊld] *n* **-1.** [in rock] ponto *m* de apoio **-2.** *fig* [in market]: **to gain a ~ in** conseguir uma brecha em.

toenail ['təʊneɪl] *n* unha *f* do pé.

toffee ['tɒfɪ] *n* **-1.** [sweet] tofe *m*, caramelo *m* **-2.** *(U)* [substance] tofe *m.*

toffee apple *n UK* maçã *f* do amor.

tofu ['təʊfu:] *n (U)* tofu *m.*

toga ['təʊgə] *n* toga *f.*

together [tə'geðə^r] <> *adj inf* sensato(ta). <> *adv* juntos(tas); **to go ~** combinar.

➡ **together with** *prep* junto com.

togetherness [tə'geðənɪs] *n (U)* união *f*, camaradagem *f.*

toggle switch ['tɒgl-] *n* **-1.** *ELECTRON* chave *f* articulada **-2.** *COMPUT* comutador *m* (alternado).

Togo ['təʊgəʊ] *n* Togo; **in ~** no Togo.

Togolese <> *adj* togolês(esa). <> *n* togolês *m*, -esa *f.*

togs [tɒgz] *npl inf* traje *m*, roupa *f.*

toil [tɔɪl] *fml* <> *n* trabalho *m* duro. <> *vi* trabalhar duro.

➡ **toil away** *vi*: **to ~ away (at sthg)** trabalhar duro (em algo).

toilet ['tɔɪlɪt] *n* vaso *m* sanitário; **to go to the ~** ir ao banheiro.

toilet bag *n* nécessaire *m.*

toilet paper *n (U)* papel *m* higiênico.

toiletries ['tɔɪlɪtrɪz] *npl* artigos *mpl* de toalete.

toilet roll *n* **-1.** *(U)* [paper] papel *m* higiênico **-2.** [roll] rolo *m* de papel higiênico.

toilet soap *n (U)* sabonete *f.*

toilet tissue *n (U)* papel *m* higiênico.

toilet-trained [-ˌtreɪnd] *adj* que já sabe ir ao banheiro.

toilet water *n (U)* água-de-colônia *f*, colônia *f.*

to-ing and fro-ing [ˌtu:ɪŋən'frəʊɪŋ] *n (U)* idas *fpl* e vindas.

token ['təʊkn] <> *adj* simbólico(ca). <> *n* **-1.** [voucher, disc - for machines] ficha *f*; [- for books, records] vale *m*; **-2.** [symbol] símbolo *m*, mostra *f.*

➡ **by the same token** *adv* da mesma forma.

Tokyo ['təʊkjəʊ] *n* Tóquio; **in ~** em Tóquio.

told [təʊld] *pt* & *pp* ▷ **tell.**

tolerable ['tɒlərəbl] *adj* tolerável, passável.

tolerably ['tɒlərəblɪ] *adv* razoavelmente.

tolerance ['tɒlərəns] *n* tolerância *f.*

tolerant ['tɒlərənt] *adj* **-1.** [not bigoted]: **~ of sb/sthg** tolerante com alguém/algo **-2.** [resistant]: **~ to sthg** resistente a algo.

tolerate ['tɒləreɪt] *vt* **-1.** [put up with] suportar, tolerar **-2.** [permit] tolerar.

toleration [ˌtɒlə'reɪʃn] *n (U)* tolerância *f.*

toll [təʊl] <> *n* **-1.** [number]: **death ~** número *m* de vítimas fatais **-2.** [fee] pedágio *m* **-3.** *phr*: **to take its ~** ter suas implicações. <> *vt* [bell] tocar, badalar. <> *vi* [bell] tocar, dobrar.

tollbooth ['təʊlbu:θ] *n* cabine *f* de pedágio.

toll bridge *n* ponte *f* com pedágio.

toll-free *US* <> *adj* gratuito(ta). <> *adv*: **to call ~** telefonar *OR* ligar gratuitamente.

tomato [*UK* tə'mɑ:təʊ, *US* tə'meɪtəʊ] (*pl* **-es**) *n* tomate *m.*

tomb [tu:m] *n* túmulo *m*, tumba *f.*

tombola [tɒm'bəʊlə] *n esp UK* tômbola *f.*

tomboy ['tɒmbɔɪ] *n* menina que gosta de jogos e brincadeiras de meninos.

tombstone ['tu:mstəʊn] *n* lápide *f.*

tomcat ['tɒmkæt] *n* gato *m (macho).*

tomfoolery [tɒm'fu:lərɪ] *n (U)* tolice *f.*

tomorrow [tə'mɒrəʊ] <> *n* **-1.** [day after today] amanhã *m* **-2.** *fig* [future] futuro *m.* <> *adv* **-1.** [the day after today] amanhã; **~ week** uma semana a contar de amanhã **-2.** [in future] no futuro.

ton [tʌn] (*pl inv or* **-s**) *n* **-1.** *UK* [imperial unit of measurement] tonelada *f* inglesa *or* longa *(1016,05 kg)* **-2.** *US* [unit of measurement] tonelada *f (907,19 kg)* **-3.** [metric unit of measurement] tonelada *f* métrica **-4.** *phr*: **to weigh a ~** *inf* pesar uma tonelada; **to come down on sb like a ~ of bricks** soltar os cachorros em cima de alguém.
  ◆ **tons** *npl UK inf*: **~s (of)** um monte de.

tonal ['təʊnl] *adj* tonal.

tone [təʊn] *n* **-1.** [gen] tom *m* **-2.** *TELEC* sinal *m*; **dialling ~** linha *f* de discagem **-3.** *phr*: **to lower the ~ of** sthg baixar o nível de algo.
  ◆ **tone down** *vt sep* suavizar, moderar.
  ◆ **tone in** *vi* combinar; **to ~ in with** sthg combinar com algo.
  ◆ **tone up** *vt sep* pôr em forma.

tone-deaf *adj* que não tem ouvido musical.

toner ['təʊnəʳ] *n* **-1.** [for photocopier, printer] toner *m* **-2.** [cosmetic] tônico *m*, tonificante *m*.

tongs [tɒŋz] *npl* **-1.** [for sugar] pinça *f* para açúcar **-2.** [for hair] pinças *fpl*.

tongue [tʌŋ] *n* **-1.** [gen] língua *f*; **to have one's ~ in one's cheek** *inf* falar brincando; **to hold one's ~** *fig* fechar o bico; **~s will wag** as pessoas vão falar a respeito **-2.** *fml* [language] língua *f* **-3.** [of shoe] lingüeta *f*.

tongue-in-cheek *adj* em tom de brincadeira.

tongue-tied [-ˌtaɪd] *adj* mudo(da) *(por timidez ou nervosismo)*.

tongue twister [-ˌtwɪstəʳ] *n* trava-língua *m*.

tonic ['tɒnɪk] *n* **-1.** [gen] tônico *m* **-2.** *(U)* [tonic water] (água *f*) tônica *f* **-3.** *fig* [beneficial thing] bálsamo *m*.

tonic water *n (U)* (água *f*) tônica *f*.

tonight [təˈnaɪt] ◇ *n (U)* esta noite *f*. ◇ *adv* hoje à noite, esta noite.

tonnage ['tʌnɪdʒ] *n (U)* *NAUT* **-1.** [weight] tonelagem *f* **-2.** [amount of cargo] tonelagem *f* (de arqueação).

tonne [tʌn] (*pl inv or* **-s**) *n* tonelada *f* métrica.

tonsil ['tɒnsl] *n* amígdala *f*.

tonsil(l)itis [ˌtɒnsɪˈlaɪtɪs] *n (U)* amigdalite *f*.

too [tu:] *adv* **-1.** [also] também **-2.** [excessively]: **~ much** demais; **~ old** velho demais; **~ many things** muitas e muitas coisas; **~ long a book** um livro longo demais; **all ~ soon** cedo demais; **only ~ ...** muito ...; **I'd be only ~ happy to help** eu adoraria ajudar **-3.** *(with negatives)*: **not ~ bad** nada mal; **I wasn't ~ impressed** não fiquei muito impressionado.

took [tʊk] *pt* ⊳ **take.**

tool [tu:l] *n* **-1.** [implement] ferramenta *f*; **to down ~s** *UK* parar de trabalhar em protesto **-2.** *fig* [means] ferramenta *f*, instrumento *m*; **the ~s of one's trade** as ferramentas de trabalho de alguém.
  ◆ **tool around** *vi US inf* passear.

tool box *n* caixa *f* de ferramentas.

tool kit *n* jogo *m* de ferramentas.

toot [tu:t] ◇ *n* buzinada *f*. ◇ *vt* buzinar. ◇ *vi* buzinar.

tooth [tu:θ] (*pl* teeth) *n* dente *m*; **to be long in the ~** *UK pej* estar um pouco passado(da); **to be fed up to the back teeth with** sthg *UK inf* estar até aqui com algo; **to grit one's teeth** cerrar os dentes; **to have no teeth** *fig* [be powerless] não ter poder

algum; **to lie through one's teeth** mentir até não poder mais.

toothache ['tu:θeɪk] *n (U)* dor *f* de dente.

toothbrush ['tu:θbrʌʃ] *n* escova *f* de dentes.

toothless ['tu:θlɪs] *adj* desdentado(da).

toothpaste ['tu:θpeɪst] *n (U)* pasta *f* de dentes.

toothpick ['tu:θpɪk] *n* palito *m*.

tooth powder *n (U)* pó *m* dentifrício.

tootle ['tu:tl] *vi inf* [move unhurriedly] passear.

top [tɒp] (*pt* & *pp* **-ped**, *cont* **-ping**) ◇ *adj* **-1.** [highest] de cima, superior **-2.** [most important, successful] importante; **she got the ~ mark** ela tirou a melhor nota **-3.** [maximum] máximo(ma). ◇ *n* **-1.** [gen] topo *m*, parte *f* de cima; **from ~ to bottom** de cima a baixo; **on ~** em cima; **to go over the ~** *UK* passar um pouco dos limites; **at the ~ of one's voice** a toda voz **-2.** [highest point - of list, class] primeiro(ra); [- of tree] copa *f*; [- of hill] cume *m*; [- of page] topo *m* **-3.** [lid, cap] tampa *f* **-4.** [upper side] superfície *f* **-5.** [clothing - bikini, pyjama] parte *f* de cima; [- blouse] blusa *f* **-6.** [toy] pião *m* **-7.** [highest rank - of an organization] topo *m*; [- of a league, class] primeiro(ra). ◇ *vt* **-1.** [to be first in - league, poll] liderar, estar em primeiro lugar em; [- table, chart] liderar, encabeçar **-2.** [better] superar **-3.** [exceed] passar de **-4.** [put on top of] cobrir.
  ◆ **on top of** *prep* **-1.** [in space] em cima de **-2.** [in addition to] além de; **on ~ of that** como se não bastasse **-3.** [in control of]: **to be ~ of** sthg ter algo sob controle **-4.** *phr*: **to get on ~ of sb** deixar alguém preocupado(da).
  ◆ **top up** *UK*, **top off** *US vt sep* encher novamente.

topaz ['təʊpæz] *n* topázio *m*.

top brass *n (U) inf*: **the ~** os altos cargos, os figurões.

topcoat ['tɒpkəʊt] *n* **-1.** [item of clothing] sobretudo *m* **-2.** [paint] última demão *f*.

top dog *n inf* manda-chuva *mf*.

top-flight *adj* de primeira qualidade.

top floor *n* último andar *m*.

top gear *n* marcha *f* mais rápida *(de um veículo)*.

top hat *n* cartola *f*.

top-heavy *adj* muito pesado(da) na parte de cima.

topic ['tɒpɪk] *n* tópico *m*.

topical ['tɒpɪkl] *adj* atual, da atualidade.

topknot ['tɒpnɒt] *n* coque *m*.

topless ['tɒplɪs] *adj* [barebreasted] topless; **to go ~** fazer topless.

top-level *adj* do mais alto nível.

topmost ['tɒpməʊst] *adj* mais alto(ta).

top-notch *adj inf* de primeira.

topographer *n* topógrafo *m*, -fa *f*.

topography [təˈpɒgrəfɪ] *n (U)* topografia *f*.

topped [tɒpt] *adj*: **~ by** *or* **with** sthg com algo em cima.

topping ['tɒpɪŋ] *n* cobertura *f*.

topple ['tɒpl] ◇ *vt* derrubar. ◇ *vi* vir abaixo.
  ◆ **topple over** *vi* vir abaixo.

top-ranking [-ˈræŋkɪŋ] *adj* do mais alto nível.

TOPS [tɒps] (*abbr of* Training Opportunities Scheme)

n programa de formação vocacional do governo britânico.

top-secret *adj* ultra-secreto(ta).

top-security *adj* de segurança máxima.

topsoil ['tɒpsɔɪl] *n* (U) solo *m* arável, camada *f* superficial do solo.

topspin *n* (U) topspin *m*.

topsy-turvy [,tɒpsɪ'tɜːvɪ] ⬦ *adj* -**1.** [messy] de pernas para o ar -**2.** [haywire] louco(ca). ⬦ *adv* [upside down] de ponta-cabeça.

top-up card *n* [for mobile phone] cartão *m* de recarga.

tor *n esp UK* [hill] colina *f* rochosa *(típica da Inglaterra).*

torch [tɔːtʃ] *n* -**1.** *UK* [electric] lanterna *f* -**2.** [flaming stick] tocha *f.*

tore [tɔːʳ] *pt* ⊢ **tear** ².

torment [*n* 'tɔːment, *vb* tɔː'ment] ⬦ *n* tormento *m.* ⬦ *vt* atormentar.

tormentor [tɔː'mentəʳ] *n* atormentador *m*, -ra *f.*

torn [tɔːn] *pp* ⊢ **tear** ².

tornado [tɔː'neɪdəʊ] *(pl* -es *OR* -s) *n* tornado *m.*

Toronto *n* Toronto; **in** ~ em Toronto.

torpedo [tɔː'piːdəʊ] *(pl* -es) ⬦ *n* torpedo *m.* ⬦ *vt* torpedear.

torpedo boat *n* torpedeiro *m.*

torpor ['tɔːpəʳ] *n* (U) torpor *m.*

torque [tɔːk] *n* TECH torque *m.*

torrent ['tɒrənt] *n* torrente *f.*

torrential [tɒ'renʃl] *adj* torrencial.

torrid ['tɒrɪd] *adj* tórrido(da).

torso ['tɔːsəʊ] *(pl* -s) *n* torso *m.*

tortoise ['tɔːtəs] *n* tartaruga *f* terrestre.

tortoiseshell ['tɔːtəʃel] ⬦ *adj* [cat] escama-de -tartaruga. ⬦ *n* (U) [material] tartaruga *f.* ⬦ *comp* de tartaruga.

tortuous ['tɔːtʃʊəs] *adj* -**1.** [twisty] sinuoso(sa) -**2.** [over-complicated] tortuoso(sa).

torture ['tɔːtʃəʳ] ⬦ *n* tortura *f.* ⬦ *vt* torturar.

torturer ['tɔːtʃərəʳ] *n* torturador *m*, -ra *f.*

Tory ['tɔːrɪ] *(pl* -ies) ⬦ *adj* tóri, do partido conservador britânico. ⬦ *n* tóri *mf*, membro *m* do partido conservador britânico.

toss [tɒs] ⬦ *vt* -**1.** [throw carelessly] atirar, jogar -**2.** [head] sacudir -**3.** [food] misturar -**4.** [coin] jogar *(ao ar);* **to** ~ **a coin** tirar no cara ou coroa -**5.** [throw about] jogar, arremessar. ⬦ *vi* -**1.** [with coin] tirar no cara ou coroa -**2.** [move about]: **to** ~ **and turn** rolar na cama. ⬦ *n* -**1.** [of coin] arremesso *m (de moeda)* -**2.** [of head] sacudida *f*, meneio *m.*

➥ **toss up** *vi* disputar no cara ou coroa.

toss-up *n inf:* **it's a** ~ **whether they win or lose** impossível dizer *OR* saber se eles ganham ou perdem.

tot [tɒt] *(pt & pp* -**ted**, *cont* -**ting**) *n* -**1.** *inf* [small child] nenezinho *f*, -nha -**2.** [of drink] golinho *m.*

➥ **tot up** *vt sep inf* somar.

total ['təʊtl] *(UK pt & pp* -**led**, *cont* -**ling**, *US pt & pp* -**ed**, *cont* -**ing**) ⬦ *adj* total. ⬦ *n* total *m*; **in** ~ no total. ⬦ *vt* -**1.** [add up] somar -**2.** [amount to] totalizar -**3.** *US inf* [wreck] arruinar.

totalitarian [,təʊtælɪ'teərɪən] *adj* totalitário(ria).

totality [təʊ'tælətɪ] *n* totalidade *f.*

totally ['təʊtəlɪ] *adv* totalmente.

tote bag [təʊt-] *n US* sacola *f* de compras.

totem pole ['təʊtəm-] *n* totem *m.*

totter ['tɒtəʳ] *vi* cambalear.

toucan ['tuːkən] *n* tucano *m.*

touch [tʌtʃ] ⬦ *n* -**1.** [gen] toque *m*; **to put the finishing** ~**es to sthg** dar os últimos retoques a algo -**2.** [contact]: **to get in** ~ **(with sb)** entrar em contato (com alguém); **to keep in** ~ **(with sb)** manter contato (com alguém); **to lose** ~ **(with sb)** perder o contato (com alguém); **to be out of** ~ **with sthg** estar por fora de algo -**3.** [small amount]: **a** ~ **(of sthg)** um pouco (de algo) -**4.** *SPORT:* **in** ~ na lateral -**5.** *phr:* **it was** ~ **and go whether we left or stayed** a gente não sabia se saía ou ficava; **to be a soft** ~ [for money] não saber dizer que não *(empresta dinheiro)* -**6.** (U) [sense] tato *m*; **soft to the** ~ suave ao toque; **the** ~ **of her lips** o toque de seus lábios. ⬦ *vt* -**1.** [make contact with] tocar -**2.** [move emotionally] tocar, comover -**3.** [eat] comer -**4.** [drink] beber. ⬦ *vi* -**1.** [make contact] tocar -**2.** [be in contact] tocar-se.

➥ **a touch** *adv* um pouco.

➥ **touch down** *vi* [plane] aterrissar.

➥ **touch on** *vt fus* tocar por cima.

➥ **touch up** *vt sep* [paintwork] retocar.

touch-and-go *adj* incerto(ta), duvidoso(sa).

touchdown ['tʌtʃdaʊn] *n* -**1.** [on land, sea] aterrissagem *f* -**2.** [in American football] touchdown *m.*

touched [tʌtʃt] *adj* -**1.** [grateful] comovido(da), emocionado(da) -**2.** *inf* [slightly mad] tantã.

touching ['tʌtʃɪŋ] *adj* tocante, comovente.

touch judge *n* RUGBY bandeirinha *m*, juiz *m*, -íza *f* de linha.

touchline ['tʌtʃlaɪn] *n* SPORT linha *f* lateral.

touchpaper ['tʌtʃ,peɪpəʳ] *n* estopim *m.*

touch screen *n* tela *f* tátil.

touch-type *vi* -**1.** [typewriter] datilografar sem olhar para o teclado -**2.** [computer] digitar sem olhar para o teclado.

touchy ['tʌtʃɪ] *(compar* -**ier**, *superl* -**iest**) *adj* -**1.** [person] suscetível; **to be** ~ **about sthg** ser sensível em relação a algo -**2.** [subject, question] delicado(-da).

tough [tʌf] *adj* -**1.** [gen] duro(ra) -**2.** [person, character] forte -**3.** [material] resistente -**4.** [decision, life] difícil -**5.** [criminal, neighbourhood] da pesada -**6.** *inf* [unfortunate] difícil; ~ **luck** má sorte; [as exclamation] que azar!

toughen ['tʌfn] *vt* endurecer.

toughened ['tʌfnd] *adj* temperado(da).

toughness ['tʌfnɪs] *n* (U) -**1.** [of character - strength] força *f*; [- hardness] firmeza *f* -**2.** [of material] resistência *f* -**3.** [of meat] dureza *f.*

toupee ['tuːpeɪ] *n* peruca *f.*

tour [tʊəʳ] ⬦ *n* -**1.** [trip] excursão *f*, viagem *f* -**2.** [of building, town, museum] visita *f*; **guided** ~ visita *f* guiada -**3.** [official journey] turnê *f.* ⬦ *vt* -**1.** [visit] visitar -**2.** *SPORT & THEATRE* fazer uma turnê por. ⬦ *vi* [go on trip] fazer uma excursão, viajar; **to** ~ **round somewhere** fazer uma excursão em algum lugar, viajar por algum lugar.

tourer ['tʊərəʳ] *n* [car] carro *m* de turismo.

touring ['tʊərɪŋ] ⬦ adj - **1.** [exhibition] itinerante - **2.** [show, theatre group] em turnê. ⬦ n (U) viagens fpl turísticas; **to go** ~ fazer turismo.

tourism ['tʊərɪzm] n (U) turismo m.

tourist ['tʊərɪst] n turista mf.

tourist class n (U) classe f econômica OR turística.

tourist (information) office n (serviço m de) informações fpl turísticas.

touristy ['tʊərɪstɪ] adj pej muito turístico(ca).

tournament ['tɔːnəmənt] n CHESS & SPORT torneio m.

tourniquet ['tʊənɪkeɪ] n torniquete m.

tour operator n agência f de viagens.

tousle vt - **1.** [hair] despentear - **2.** [fur, feathers] desarrumar.

tout [taʊt] ⬦ n cambista mf. ⬦ vt [tickets, goods] revender (como cambista). ⬦ vi: **to** ~ **for sthg** angariar algo; **to** ~ **for trade** tentar obter algo; **to** ~ **for clients** aliciar algo; **to** ~ **for investment** buscar algo.

tow [taʊ] ⬦ n reboque m; **on** ~ UK a reboque; **with sb in** ~ com alguém a reboque. ⬦ vt rebocar.

towards UK [tə'wɔːdz], **toward** US [tə'wɔːd] prep - **1.** [in the direction of] para, em direção a - **2.** [indicating attitude] em relação a - **3.** [near in time, space] perto de - **4.** [as contribution to] para.

towaway zone ['taʊəweɪ-] n US zona f de estacionamento proibido.

towbar ['taʊbɑːl] n engate m para reboque.

towel ['taʊəl] n toalha f.

towelling UK, **toweling** US ['taʊəlɪŋ] ⬦ n (U) tecido m atoalhado. ⬦ comp atoalhado(da).

towel rail n toalheiro m.

tower ['taʊə'] ⬦ n torre f; **a** ~ **of strength** UK um forte apoio. ⬦ vi destacar-se; **to** ~ **over sb** ser muito mais alto(ta) do que alguém; **to** ~ **over/sthg** destacar-se por cima de algo.

tower block n UK prédio m alto de escritórios.

towering ['taʊərɪŋ] adj [very tall] altíssimo(ma).

town [taʊn] n - **1.** [population centre] cidade f - **2.** (U) [centre of town, city] centro m (da cidade); **to go out on the** ~ ir divertir-se; **to go to** ~ fig botar para quebrar.

town centre n centro m (da cidade).

town clerk n secretário m, -ria f da câmara municipal.

town council n câmara f municipal.

town hall n - **1.** [building] prefeitura f - **2.** (U) fig [council] prefeitura f.

town house n [fashionable house] mansão f.

town plan n - **1.** [map] mapa m da cidade - **2.** [project, plan] projeto m de urbanização.

town planner n urbanista mf.

town planning n (U) - **1.** [study] urbanismo m - **2.** [practice] urbanização f.

townsfolk ['taʊnzfəʊk], **townspeople** ['taʊnz-ˌpiːpl] npl: **the** ~ os habitantes (de uma cidade), os cidadãos.

township ['taʊnʃɪp] n - **1.** [in South Africa] zona urbana atribuída antigamente pelo governo à população negra - **2.** [in US] ≃ município m.

towpath ['taʊpɑːθ, pl -pɑːðz] n caminho m de sirga.

towrope ['taʊrəʊp] n cabo m para reboque.

tow truck n US guincho m, reboque m.

toxic ['tɒksɪk] adj tóxico(ca).

toxin ['tɒksɪn] n toxina f.

toy [tɔɪ] n brinquedo m.
➡ **toy with** vt fus - **1.** [idea]: **to** ~ **with sthg** pensar em algo - **2.** [play]: **to** ~ **with sthg** brincar com algo.

toyboy n inf amante m de uma coroa.

toy shop n loja f de brinquedos.

trace [treɪs] ⬦ n - **1.** [evidence, remains] vestígio m; **without** ~ sem deixar vestígio - **2.** [small amount] vestígio m. ⬦ vt - **1.** [find] localizar - **2.** [follow progress of] traçar - **3.** [mark outline of] traçar ; [with tracing paper] decalcar.

trace element n CHEM elemento-traço m.

tracer bullet ['treɪsə'-] n projétil m luminoso.

tracing ['treɪsɪŋ] n [on paper] decalque m.

tracing paper ['treɪsɪŋ-] n (U) papel m de decalque.

track [træk] ⬦ n - **1.** [path] trilha f; **off the beaten** ~ isolado(da) - **2.** SPORT pista f - **3.** RAIL trilho m - **4.** [mark, trace] pegada f; **to hide** OR **cover one's** ~s não deixar rasto; **to stop dead in one's** ~s parar atônito(ta) - **5.** [on record, tape, CD] faixa f - **6.** phr: **to keep** ~ **of sb/sthg** não perder alguém/algo de vista; **to lose** ~ **of sb/sthg** perder alguém/algo de vista; **to be on the right/wrong** ~ estar no caminho certo/errado. ⬦ vt [follow] seguir a pista de.
➡ **track down** vt sep localizar.

tracker dog ['trækə'-] n cão m de caça OR policial.

track event n prova f de atletismo (na pista).

tracking station ['trækɪŋ-] n estação f de rastreamento.

track record n histórico m (de reputação).

track shoes npl calçados mpl de corrida.

tracksuit ['træksuːt] n abrigo m esportivo.

tract [trækt] n - **1.** [pamphlet] panfleto m - **2.** [of land, forest] extensão f - **3.** MED trato m; **digestive** ~ aparelho m digestivo.

traction ['trækʃn] n (U) - **1.** PHYSICS tração f - **2.** MED tração f; **to have one's leg in** ~ fazer tração na perna.

traction engine n veículo m de carga pesada.

tractor ['træktə'] n trator m.

tractor-trailer n US veículo m articulado.

trade [treɪd] ⬦ n - **1.** (U) [commerce] comércio m - **2.** [job] profissão f, ofício m; **by** ~ por formação. ⬦ vt [exchange] negociar; **to** ~ **sthg for sthg** trocar algo por algo. ⬦ vi - **1.** COMM [do business] negociar; **to** ~ **with sb** negociar com alguém - **2.** US [shop]: **to** ~ **at** OR **with** comprar em.
➡ **trade in** vt sep [exchange] dar como entrada.

trade barrier n barreira f comercial.

trade deficit n déficit m comercial.

trade discount n (U) desconto m para revendedor.

trade fair n feira f industrial.

trade gap n déficit m na balança comercial.

trade-in n objeto ou artigo que se entrega como entrada ao se comprar um novo, base f de troca.

trademark ['treɪdmɑːk] *n* **-1.** *COMM* marca *f* registrada **- 2.** *fig* [characteristic] marca *f* registrada.
trade name *n COMM* razão *f* social.
trade-off *n* equilíbrio *m.*
trade price *n* preço *m* de atacado.
trader ['treɪdə'] *n* comerciante *mf.*
trade route *n* rota *f* de comércio.
trade secret *n* segredo *m* comercial.
tradesman ['treɪdzmən] (*pl* **-men** [-mən]) *n* [shopkeeper, trader] comerciante *m.*
tradespeople ['treɪdz,piːpl] *npl* comerciantes *mfpl.*
trades union *n UK* = trade union.
Trades Union Congress *n UK*: **the** ~ *a associação britânica dos sindicatos.*
trades unionist *n UK* = trade unionist.
trade union *n* sindicato *m.*
trade unionist *n* sindicalista *mf.*
trading ['treɪdɪŋ] *n (U)* comércio *m.*
trading estate *n UK* distrito *m* industrial.
trading stamp *n* cupom *m* promocional.
tradition [trə'dɪʃn] *n* **-1.** *(U)* [system of customs] tradição *f* **- 2.** [established practice] costume *m.*
traditional [trə'dɪʃənl] *adj* tradicional.
traditionally [trə'dɪʃnəlɪ] *adv* tradicionalmente.
traffic ['træfɪk] (*pt* & *pp*-**ked**, *cont*-**king**) <> *n (U)*-**1.** [vehicles] tráfego *m* **- 2.** [illegal trade] tráfico *m*; ~ **in sthg** tráfico de algo. <> *vi*: **to** ~ **in sthg** traficar algo.
traffic circle *n US* rotatória *f.*
traffic island *n* canteiro *m* central.
traffic jam *n* congestionamento *m.*
trafficker ['træfɪkə'] *n* traficante *mf*; ~ **in sthg** traficante de algo.
traffic lights *npl* semáforo *m.*
traffic offence *UK*, **traffic violation** *US n* infração *f* de trânsito.
traffic sign *n* sinal *m* de trânsito.
traffic violation *n US* = traffic offence.
traffic warden *n UK* guarda *mf* de trânsito.
tragedy ['trædʒədɪ] (*pl* -**ies**) *n* **-1.** *(U)* [ill fate, dramatic form] tragédia *f* **- 2.** [terrible event, play] tragédia *f.*
tragic ['trædʒɪk] *adj* trágico(ca).
tragically ['trædʒɪklɪ] *adv* tragicamente.
trail [treɪl] <> *n* **-1.** [path] trilha *f*; **to blaze a** ~ *fig* abrir caminho **- 2.** [traces] rastro *m*; **on the** ~ **of sb/sthg** na pista de alguém/algo. <> *vt*-**1.** [drag behind, tow] arrastar **- 2.** [lag behind] estar atrás de. <> *vi*-**1.** [drag behind] arrastar **- 2.** [move slowly] andar lentamente **- 3.** *SPORT* [lose] perder.
➡ **trail away, trail off** *vi* apagar-se.
trailblazing ['treɪl,bleɪzɪŋ] *adj* pioneiro(ra).
trailer ['treɪlə'] *n* **-1.** [vehicle for luggage] reboque *m* **- 2.** *esp US* [for living in] trailer *m* **- 3.** *CINEMA* trailer *m.*
trailer court, trailer park *n US* camping *m (para trailers).*
train [treɪn] <> *n* **-1.** *RAIL* trem *m* **- 2.** [of dress] cauda *f* **- 3.** [connected sequence]: ~ **of thought** linha *f* de raciocínio. <> *vt*-**1.** [teach] treinar; **to** ~ **sb to do sthg** treinar alguém para fazer algo; **to** ~ **sb in sthg** treinar alguém em algo **- 2.** [for job]: **to** ~ **sb as sthg** preparar *OR* formar alguém para ser algo **- 3.** *SPORT* treinar; **to** ~ **sb for sthg** treinar alguém

para algo **- 4.** [plant] dirigir **- 5.** [gun, camera] apontar. <> *vi* -**1.** [for job] preparar-se; **to** ~ **as sthg** estudar para algo **- 2.** *SPORT* treinar; **to** ~ **for sthg** treinar para algo.
train driver *n* maquinista *mf.*
trained [treɪnd] *adj* -**1.** [psychologist] formado(da) - **2.** [singer] profissional **- 3.** [cartographer] qualificado(da) **- 4.** [doctor] especializado(da).
trainee [treɪ'niː] <> *adj* estagiário(ria). <> *n* estagiário *m*, -ria *f*, trainee *mf.*
trainer ['treɪnə'] *n* -**1.** [of animals] amestrador *m*, -ra *f* **- 2.** *SPORT* treinador *m*, -ra *f.*
➡ **trainers** *npl UK* [shoes] tênis *m inv* para a prática desportiva.
training ['treɪnɪŋ] *n (U)* -**1.** [for job]: ~ **in sthg** formação *f* em algo, treinamento *m* para algo **- 2.** *SPORT* treinamento *m.*
training college *n UK* escola *f* profissionalizante.
training course *n* curso *m* de formação profissional.
training shoes *npl UK* tênis *m inv* para a prática desportiva.
train set *n* trenzinho *m.*
train spotter [-,spɒtə'] *n* aficionado por trens que vai até as estações para contar o número que trens que passam.
train station *n US* & *Scot* estação *f* ferroviária.
traipse [treɪps] *vi* vaguear.
trait [treɪt] *n* traço *m.*
traitor ['treɪtə'] *n* traidor *m*, -ra *f*; ~ **to sthg** traidor(ra) de algo.
trajectory [trə'dʒektərɪ] (*pl* -**ies**) *n TECH* trajetória *f.*
tram [træm], **tramcar** ['træmkɑː'] *n UK* bonde *m.*
tramcar *n UK fml* bonde *m.*
tramlines ['træmlaɪnz] *npl* -**1.** [for trams] trilhos *mpl* do bonde **- 2.** *TENNIS* linha *f* lateral de duplas.
tramp [træmp] <> *n* vagabundo *m*, -da *f.* <> *vt* caminhar a pé por. <> *vi* andar com passos pesados.
trample ['træmpl] <> *vt* esmagar com os pés, pisar em. <> *vi* -**1.** [tread]: **to** ~ **on sthg** pisar em algo **- 2.** *fig* [act cruelly]: **to** ~ **on sb** espezinhar alguém.
trampoline ['træmpəliːn] *n* trampolim *m.*
trance [trɑːns] *n* [hypnotic state] transe *m*; **in a** ~ em transe.
tranquil ['træŋkwɪl] *adj literary* plácido(da).
tranquility *n US* = tranquillity.
tranquilize *vt US* = tranquillize.
tranquilizer *n US* = tranquillizer.
tranquillity *UK*, **tranquility** *US* [træŋ'kwɪlətɪ] *n (U)* tranqüilidade *f.*
tranquillize, -ise *UK*, **tranquilize** *US* ['træŋkwɪlaɪz] *vt* tranqüilizar.
tranquillizer *UK*, **tranquilizer** *US* ['træŋkwɪdlaɪzə'] *n* tranqüilizante *m.*
transact [træn'zækt] *vt fml* fazer, levar a cabo.
transaction [træn'zækʃn] *n* transação *f.*
transatlantic [,trænzət'læntɪk] *adj* -**1.** [crossing the Atlantic] transatlântico(ca) **- 2.** [on the other side of the Atlantic] de além-mar.

transceiver [træn'si:vəʳ] n rádio m transmissor-receptor.

transcend [træn'send] vt fml [go beyond] transcender.

transcendental meditation [ˌtrænsen'dentl-] n (U) meditação f transcedental.

transcribe [træn'skraɪb] vt transcrever.

transcript ['trænskrɪpt] n [of speech, conversation] transcrição f.

transept ['trænsept] n transepto m.

transfer [n 'trænsfɜ:ʳ, vb træns'fɜ:r] (pt & pp -red, cont -ring) ⬦ n -1. [gen] transferência f -2. [design] decalcomania f -3. US [ticket] passagem f válida para conexão. ⬦ vt transferir. ⬦ vi transferir-se.

transferable [træns'fɜ:rəbl] adj transferível.

transference ['trænsfərəns] n (U) fml [act of transferring] transferência f.

transfer fee n UK SPORT (valor m do) passe m.

transfigure [træns'fɪgəʳ] vt literary transfigurar.

transfix [træns'fɪks] vt [immobilize] paralisar.

transform [træns'fɔ:m] vt transformar; **to ~ sb/sthg into sthg** transformar alguém/algo em algo.

transformation [ˌtrænsfə'meɪʃn] n transformação f.

transformer [træns'fɔ:məʳ] n ELEC transformador m.

transfusion [træns'fju:ʒn] n transfusão f.

transgress [træns'gres] fml ⬦ vt transgredir. ⬦ vi cometer uma transgressão.

transgression [træns'greʃn] n fml transgressão f.

transient ['trænzɪənt] ⬦ adj fml [fleeting] transitório(ria). ⬦ n US [person] pessoa f em trânsito.

transistor [træn'zɪstəʳ] n ELECTRON transistor m.

transistor radio n dated (rádio m) transistor m.

transit ['trænsɪt] n: **in ~** de passagem.

transit camp n acampamento m provisório.

transition [træn'zɪʃn] n -1. [change] transição f -2. (U) [act of changing] transição f. **~ from sthg to sthg** transição de algo para algo; **in ~** em transição.

transitional [træn'zɪʃənl] adj de transição.

transitive ['trænzɪtɪv] adj GRAMM transitivo(va).

transit lounge n sala f de trânsito.

transitory ['trænzɪtrɪ] adj transitório(ria).

translate [træns'leɪt] ⬦ vt -1. [languages] traduzir -2. fig [transform]: **to ~ sthg into sthg** transformar algo em algo. ⬦ vi -1. [words] traduzir-se; **to ~ from sthg into sthg** traduzir de algo para algo -2. [person] traduzir.

translation [træns'leɪʃn] n tradução f.

translator [træns'leɪtəʳ] n tradutor m, -ra f.

translucent [trænz'lu:snt] adj translúcido(da).

transmission [trænz'mɪʃn] n transmissão f.

transmit [trænz'mɪt] (pt & pp -ted, cont -ting) vt transmitir.

transmitter [trænz'mɪtəʳ] n ELECTRON transmissor m.

transparency [trans'pærənsɪ] (pl -ies) n transparência f.

transparent [træns'pærənt] adj -1. [gen] transparente -2. [obvious] óbvio(via).

transpire [træn'spaɪəʳ] fml ⬦ vt: **it ~s that ...** descobre-se que ... ⬦ vi [happen] acontecer, ocorrer.

transplant [n 'trænspla:nt, vb træns'pla:ntl] ⬦ n transplante m. ⬦ vt -1. [gen] transplantar -2. [population] transferir.

transport [n 'trænspɔ:t, vb træn'spɔ:t] ⬦ n transporte m. ⬦ vt [goods, people] transportar.

transportable [træn'spɔ:təbl] adj transportável.

transportation [ˌtrænspɔ:'teɪʃn] n (U) esp US = transport.

transport cafe ['trænspɔ:t-] n UK lanchonete m deestrada.

transporter [træn'spɔ:təʳ] n caminhão m para transporte de automóveis.

transpose [træns'pəʊz] vt [change round] inverter.

transsexual [træns'sekʃʊəl] n transexual mf.

transvestite [trænz'vestaɪt] n travesti mf.

trap [træp] (pt & pp -ped, cont -ping) ⬦ n -1. [for animal, bird] armadilha f -2. fig [trick] cilada f. ⬦ vt -1. [animal, bird] apanhar em armadilha -2. fig [trick] armar uma cilada -3. [immobilize, catch]: **to be ~ ped in sthg** ficar preso(sa) em algo -4. [retain] guardar.

trapdoor [ˌtræp'dɔ:ʳ] n alçapão m.

trapeze [trə'pi:z] n trapézio m.

trapper ['træpəʳ] n caçador m, -ra f que põe armadilhas.

trappings ['træpɪŋz] npl pompas fpl.

trash [træʃ] ⬦ n (U) -1. US [refuse] lixo m -2. inf pej [sthg of poor quality] lixo m, porcaria f. ⬦ vt US -1. [criticize] acabar com, demolir -2. [damage] arrasar.

trashcan ['træʃkæn] n US lata f de lixo.

trashy ['træʃɪ] (compar -ier, superl -iest) adj inf imprestável.

trauma ['trɔ:mə] n -1. [distressing experience] trauma m -2. (U) [distress] trauma m.

traumatic [trɔ:'mætɪk] adj traumático(ca).

traumatize, -ise ['trɔ:mətaɪz] vt [shock] traumatizar.

travel ['trævl] (UK pt & pp -led, cont -ling, US pt & pp -ed, cont -ing) ⬦ n (U) viagem f; **I'm keen on ~** eu adoro viajar. ⬦ vt -1. [place] viajar por -2. [distance] viajar. ⬦ vi -1. [gen] viajar -2. [news] voar. ➡ **travels** npl viagens fpl.

travel agency n agência f de viagens.

travel agent n agente mf de viagens; **~'s** agência f de viagens.

travel brochure n catálogo m de viagens.

travel card n passe m.

traveler etc n US = traveller etc.

travelled UK, **traveled** US ['trævld] adj -1. [person] viajado(da) -2. [road, route] movimentado(da).

traveller UK, **traveler** US ['trævləʳ] n -1. [gen] viajante mf -2. [sales representative] representante mf comercial.

traveller's cheque n cheque m de viagem, traveler's cheque m.

travelling UK, **traveling** US ['trævlɪŋ] adj -1. [itinerant] itinerante, ambulante -2. [portable, of travel] de viagem.

travelling expenses npl despesas fpl de viagem.

travelling salesman n caixeiro-viajante m.

travelogue, travelog US ['trævəlɒg] n -1. [talk]

conferência f sobre uma viagem -**2.** [film] documentário m sobre viagem.

travelsick ['trævəlsɪk] adj enjoado(da) (pela viagem).

traverse ['trævəs, ˌtrəˈvɜːs] vt fml atravessar.

travesty ['trævəstɪ] (pl -ies) n paródia f.

trawl [trɔːl] ⬦ n -**1.** [fishing net] rede f de arrasto -**2.** [search] busca f. ⬦ vt -**1.** [fish]: **to ~ sthg (for sthg)** vasculhar algo (à procura de algo) -**2.** [search]: **to ~ sthg for sthg** conferir algo à procura de algo. ⬦ vi -**1.** [fish]: **to ~ for sthg** pescar com rede de arrasto à procura de algo -**2.** [search]: **to ~ for sthg** procurar (por) algo.

trawler ['trɔːləʳ] n traineira f.

tray [treɪ] n bandeja f.

treacherous ['tretʃərəs] adj -**1.** [person] traidor(ra) -**2.** [plan, behaviour] traiçoeiro(ra) -**3.** [dangerous] perigoso(sa).

treachery ['tretʃərɪ] n (U) traição f.

treacle ['triːkl] n (U) UK melado m.

tread [tred] (pt trod, pp trodden) ⬦ n -**1.** [on tyre] banda f de rodagem -**2.** [shoe] sola f -**3.** [sound or way of walking] passos mpl. ⬦ vt [crush] esmagar com os pés; **to ~ sthg into sthg** esmagar algo em algo. ⬦ vi -**1.** [place foot]: **to ~ on sthg** pisar em algo -**2.** [walk, progress] andar; **to ~ carefully** fig andar com cuidado.

treadle ['tredl] n pedal m.

treadmill ['tredmɪl] n -**1.** [wheel] roda f de moinho -**2.** fig [dull routine] rotina f.

treas. (abbr of **treasurer**) tesoureiro m, -ra f.

treason ['triːzn] n (U) traição f.

treasure ['treʒəʳ] ⬦ n lit & fig tesouro m. ⬦ vt dar valor a.

treasure hunt n caça f ao tesouro.

treasurer ['treʒərəʳ] n tesoureiro m, -ra f.

treasure trove n (U) JUR tesouro m escondido.

treasury ['treʒərɪ] (pl -ies) n [room] sala f do tesouro.

➡ **Treasury** n: **the Treasury** ≃ o Ministério da Fazenda.

treasury bill n letra f do Tesouro.

treat [triːt] ⬦ vt -**1.** [handle, deal with] tratar; **to ~ sb/sthg as sthg**, **to ~ sb/sthg like sthg** tratar alguém/algo como algo -**2.** [give sthg special]: **to ~ sb (to sthg)** invitar alguém (para algo); **to ~ o.s. to sthg** presentear-se com algo -**3.** [MED, process] tratar. ⬦ n -**1.** [food] delícia f -**2.** [gift] prazer m.

treatise ['triːtɪs] n fml: **~ (on sthg)** tratado m (sobre algo).

treatment ['triːtmənt] n tratamento m.

treaty ['triːtɪ] (pl -ies) n [written agreement] tratado m.

treble ['trebl] ⬦ adj -**1.** MUS de soprano -**2.** [with numbers]: **my phone extension is ~ 4** meu ramal é 444. ⬦ n MUS soprano m. ⬦ vt & vi triplicar.

treble clef n clave f de sol.

tree [triː] n árvore f; **to be barking up the wrong ~** acusar erroneamente.

tree-lined adj arborizado(da).

tree surgeon n especialista no cuidado de árvores.

treetop ['triːtɒp] n copa f (de árvore).

tree-trunk n tronco m (de árvore).

trek [trek] (pt & pp -ked, cont -king) ⬦ n expedição f. ⬦ vi -**1.** [go on long journey] fazer uma expedição -**2.** inf [walk laboriously] caminhar com dificuldade.

trellis ['trelɪs] n treliça f.

tremble ['trembl] vi tremer.

tremendous [trɪˈmendəs] adj -**1.** [impressive, large] tremendo(da), enorme -**2.** inf [really good] fabuloso(sa).

tremendously [trɪˈmendəslɪ] adv [impressively, hugely] enormemente.

tremor ['treməʳ] n tremor m.

tremulous ['tremjʊləs] adj literary trêmulo(la).

trench [trentʃ] n -**1.** [narrow channel] vala f -**2.** MIL trincheira f.

trenchant ['trentʃənt] adj fml mordaz.

trench coat n capa f de chuva.

trench warfare n (U) guerra f de trincheiras.

trend [trend] n [tendency] tendência f.

trendsetter ['trendˌsetəʳ] n iniciador m, -ra f de modas.

trendy ['trendɪ] (compar -ier, superl -iest, pl -ies) inf ⬦ adj -**1.** [person] moderno(na) -**2.** [clothes, music] da moda. ⬦ n pessoa f moderna.

trepidation [ˌtrepɪˈdeɪʃn] n (U) fml: **in** OR **with ~** com ansiedade.

trespass ['trespəs] vi [on sb's land] invadir; **'no ~ing'** 'entrada proibida'.

trespasser ['trespəsəʳ] n invasor m, -ra f; **'~s will be prosecuted'** 'os invasores serão punidos por lei'.

trestle ['tresl] n cavalete m.

trestle table n mesa f de cavalete.

trial ['traɪəl] n -**1.** JUR julgamento m; **to be on ~ (for sthg)** ser processado(da) (por algo) -**2.** [test, experiment] teste m; **on ~** em testes; **by ~ and error** por tentativa e erro -**3.** [unpleasant experience] suplício m; **~s and tribulations** dificuldades fpl e problemas.

trial basis n: **on a ~** como experiência.

trial period n período m de experiência.

trial run n ensaio m.

trial-size(d) adj em tamanho de amostra.

triangle ['traɪæŋgl] n -**1.** [gen] triângulo m -**2.** US [set square] esquadro m.

triangular [traɪˈæŋgjʊləʳ] adj [in triangle shape] triangular.

triathlon [traɪˈæθlɒn] (pl -s) n triatlo m.

tribal ['traɪbl] adj tribal.

tribe [traɪb] n [social group] tribo f.

tribulation [ˌtrɪbjʊˈleɪʃn] n ▷ **trial**.

tribunal [traɪˈbjuːnl] n tribunal m.

tribune ['trɪbjuːn] n HIST tribuno m.

tributary ['trɪbjʊtrɪ] (pl -ies) n GEOGR afluente m.

tribute ['trɪbjuːt] n -**1.** [act of respect, admiration] tributo m; **to be a ~ to sb/sthg** ser um tributo para alguém/algo; **to pay ~ (to sb/sthg)** prestar homenagem (a alguém/algo) -**2.** [evidence] prova f -**3.** (U) [respect, admiration] homenagem f; **to pay ~ (to sb/sthg)** prestar homenagem (a alguém/algo).

trice [traɪs] n: **in a ~** num abrir e fechar de olhos.

triceps ['traɪseps] (pl inv OR -cepses) n tríceps m inv.

trick [trɪk] <> n -**1.** [to deceive] trapaça f; **to play a ~ on sb** pregar uma peça em alguém - **2.** [to entertain] truque m - **3.** [ability, knack] hábito m; **to do the ~** dar resultado. <> adj -**1.** [knife] de brincadeira - **2.** [moustache] postiço(ça). <> vt enganar; **to ~ sb into sthg** enrolar alguém sobre algo; **to ~ sb into doing sthg** enrolar alguém para que faça algo.

trickery ['trɪkərɪ] n (U) trapaça f.

trickle ['trɪkl] <> n -**1.** [of liquid] fio m - **2.** [of people or things] pingo m. <> vi -**1.** [liquid] gotejar, pingar - **2.** [people, things]: **to trickle in/out** entrar/sair aos poucos.

trick or treat n (U) gostosuras fpl ou travessuras.

trick question n pega-ratão m.

tricky ['trɪkɪ] (compar -ier, superl -iest) adj [difficult] enrolado(da), complicado(da).

tricycle ['traɪsɪkl] n triciclo m.

trident ['traɪdnt] n tridente f.

tried [traɪd] <> pt & pp ⊳ try. <> adj: **~ and tested** testado e aprovado, testada e aprovada.

trier ['traɪə[r]] n batalhador m, -ra f.

trifle ['traɪfl] n - **1.** CULIN sobremesa de biscoito feito com gelatina, creme, frutas e nata - **2.** [unimportant thing] ninharia f.
 ◆ **a trifle** adv fml ligeiramente, um pouco.
 ◆ **trifle with** vt fus: **he's not a person to be ~ d with** não é uma pessoa com a qual se possa brincar.

trifling ['traɪflɪŋ] adj pej insignificante.

trigger ['trɪgə[r]] <> n [on gun] gatilho m. <> vt -**1.** [mechanism] acionar - **2.** [explosion, reaction] desencadear - **3.** [revolution, protest] provocar.
 ◆ **trigger off** vt sep = trigger.

trigger-happy adj provocador(ra).

trigonometry [ˌtrɪgə'nɒmətrɪ] n (U) trigonometria f.

trilby ['trɪlbɪ] (pl -ies) n UK chapéu m de feltro.

trill [trɪl] <> n - **1.** MUS tremolo m - **2.** [of birds] trinado m. <> vi trinar.

trillions ['trɪljənz] npl inf milhares mpl; **~ of** um monte de.

trilogy ['trɪlədʒɪ] (pl -ies) n trilogia f.

trim [trɪm] (compar -mer, superl -mest, pt & pp -med, cont -ming) <> adj - **1.** [neat and tidy] bem cuidado(-da) - **2.** [slim] esbelto(ta). <> n - **1.** [cut - hair] corte m; [- hedge] poda f - **2.** [decoration] enfeite m. <> vt - **1.** [cut - hair, nails, lawn] cortar; [- hedge] podar; [- moustache] aparar - **2.** [decorate] enfeitar; **to ~ sthg with sthg** enfeitar algo com algo.
 ◆ **trim away, trim off** vt sep cortar.

trimmed [trɪmd] adj: **~ with sthg** enfeitado(da) com algo.

trimming n [on clothing] enfeite m.
 ◆ **trimmings** npl - **1.** CULIN guarnição f - **2.** [scraps] aparas fpl.

Trinidad and Tobago ['trɪnɪdæd-] n Trinidad e Tobago; **in ~** em Trinidad e Tobago.

Trinidadian <> adj trinitário(ria). <> n trinitário m, -ria f.

Trinity ['trɪnətɪ] n RELIG: **the ~** a Trindade.

trinket ['trɪŋkɪt] n adorno m.

trio ['tri:əʊ] (pl -s) n trio m.

trip [trɪp] (pt & pp -ped, cont -ping) <> n -**1.** [journey] viagem f - **2.** drugs sl [experience] viagem f. <> vt [make stumble] fazer tropeçar, passar uma rasteira em. <> vi [stumble]: **to ~ (over)** tropeçar (em); **to ~ over sthg** tropeçar em algo.
 ◆ **trip up** vt sep - **1.** [make stumble] fazer tropeçar - **2.** [catch out] passar uma rasteira em.

tripartite [ˌtraɪ'pɑːtaɪt] adj fml [agreement, talks] tripartite.

tripe [traɪp] n (U) - **1.** CULIN dobradinha f - **2.** inf [nonsense] bobajada f.

triple ['trɪpl] <> adj triplo(pla). <> vt & vi triplicar.

triple jump n: **the ~** o salto triplo.

triplets ['trɪplɪts] npl trigêmeos mpl, -meas fpl.

triplicate ['trɪplɪkət] <> adj fml em triplicata. <> n: **in ~** em três vias.

tripod ['traɪpɒd] n tripé m.

Tripoli ['trɪpəlɪ] n Tripoli.

tripper ['trɪpə[r]] n esp UK excursionista mf, turista mf.

tripwire ['trɪpwaɪə[r]] n fio m de armadilha.

trite [traɪt] adj pej banal.

triumph ['traɪəmf] <> n - **1.** [success] triunfo m - **2.** (U) [satisfaction] triunfo m. <> vi triunfar; **to ~ over sb/sthg** triunfar sobre alguém/algo.

triumphal [traɪ'ʌmfl] adj fml triunfal.

triumphant [traɪ'ʌmfənt] adj [exultant] triunfante.

triumphantly [trɪ'ʌmfəntlɪ] adv triunfalmente.

triumvirate n HIST triunvirato m.

trivet n - **1.** [over fire] trempe f - **2.** [to protect table] suporte m para pratos.

trivia ['trɪvɪə] n (U) trivialidades fpl.

trivial ['trɪvɪəl] adj pej trivial.

triviality [ˌtrɪvɪ'ælətɪ] (pl -ies) n - **1.** [sthg unimportant] trivialidade f - **2.** (U) [lack of importance] trivialidade f.

trivialize, -ise ['trɪvɪəlaɪz] vt banalizar.

trod [trɒd] pt ⊳ tread.

trodden ['trɒdn] <> pp ⊳ tread. <> adj pisoteado(da).

Trojan ['trəʊdʒən] <> adj HIST troiano(na). <> n - **1.** HIST troiano m, -na f - **2.** fig [hard worker]: **to work like a ~** trabalhar como um escravo.

troll [trəʊl] n [goblin] troll m, trasgo m.

trolley ['trɒlɪ] (pl trolleys) n - **1.** UK [gen] carrinho m - **2.** US [vehicle] bonde m.

trolleybus ['trɒlɪbʌs] n ônibus m inv elétrico.

trolley case n mala f com rodinhas.

trombone [trɒm'bəʊn] n trombone m.

troop [tru:p] <> n [band] bando m, grupo m. <> vi [march] andar em bando; **to ~ in/out** entrar/sair em bando.
 ◆ **troops** npl MIL tropas fpl.

trooper ['tru:pə[r]] n - **1.** MIL soldado m de cavalaria - **2.** US [policeman] policial mf militar.

troopship ['tru:pʃɪp] n navio-transporte m.

trophy ['trəʊfɪ] (pl -ies) n SPORT troféu m.

tropical ['trɒpɪkl] adj tropical.

Tropic of Cancer ['trɒpɪk-] n: **the ~** o Trópico de Cancer.

Tropic of Capricorn ['trɒpɪk-] n: **the ~** o Trópico de Capricórnio.

tropics ['trɒpɪks] npl: **the ~** os trópicos.

trot [trɒt] (*pt* & *pp* -**ted**, *cont* -**ting**) ⬦ *n* -**1.** [of horse] trote *m* -**2.** [of person] passo *m* apressado. ⬦ *vi* -**1.** [horse] trotar -**2.** [person] andar apressadamente.
➥ **on the trot** *adv inf:* **four times on the** ~ quatro vezes seguidas.
➥ **trot out** *vt sep pej:* **to** ~ **out the same old excuses** ficar repetindo as mesmas desculpas manjadas.

Trotskyism ['trɒtskɪɪzm] *n (U)* trotskismo *m*.

trotter ['trɒtə^r] *n* [pig's foot] pé *m* de porco.

trouble ['trʌbl] ⬦ *n* -**1.** *(U)* [difficulty] problema *m*; **to be in** ~ [having problems] estar com problemas; **to get into** ~ [with sb in authority] ter conflitos; **the** ~ **with sb/sthg is ...** o problema com alguém/algo é ... -**2.** [bother] incômodo *m*; **to take the** ~ **to do sthg** dar-se ao trabalho de fazer algo; **to be asking for** ~ procurar problema -**3.** *(U)* [pain, illness] problema *m* -**4.** *(U)* [fighting] confusão *f* -**5.** POL [unrest] agitação *f*. ⬦ *vt* -**1.** [worry, upset] preocupar -**2.** [interrupt, disturb] importunar -**3.** [cause pain to] incomodar.
➥ **troubles** *npl* -**1.** [worries] problemas *mpl*, preocupações *fpl* -**2.** POL [unrest] conflitos *mpl*.

troubled ['trʌbld] *adj* -**1.** [worried, upset] preocupado(da) -**2.** [disturbed - sleep] agitado(da); [- life, place, time] tumultuado(da).

trouble-free *adj* sem problemas.

troublemaker ['trʌblˌmeɪkə^r] *n* agitador *m*, -ra *f*.

troubleshooter ['trʌblˌʃu:tə^r] *n* solucionador *m*, -ra *f* de problemas; **he's the** ~ **here** é ele quem resolve os problemas aqui.

troublesome ['trʌblsəm] *adj* problemático(ca).

trouble spot *n* área *f* de conflito.

trough [trɒf] *n* -**1.** [for animals] cocho *m* -**2.** [low point] baixa *f*.

trounce [traʊns] *vt inf* [team, rivals] dar uma surra em, derrubar.

troupe [tru:p] *n* trupe *f*.

trouser press ['traʊzə^r-] *n* máquina *f* de passar calças.

trousers ['traʊzəz] *npl* calças *fpl*.

trouser suit ['traʊzə^r-] *n UK* terninho *m*.

trousseau ['tru:səʊ] (*pl* -**x** [-z], -**s**) *n* enxoval *m*.

trout [traʊt] (*pl inv OR* -**s**) *n* truta *f*.

trove [trəʊv] ⬦ **treasure trove**.

trowel ['traʊəl] *n* -**1.** [for the garden] pá *f* de jardim -**2.** [for cement, plaster] colher *f* de pedreiro.

truancy ['tru:ənsɪ] *n (U)* gazeio *m*, falta *f* às aulas.

truant ['tru:ənt] *n* [child] criança *f* que mata às aulas; **to play** ~ gazear *OR* matar aula.

truce [tru:s] *n* trégua *f*; ~ **between** trégua entre.

truck [trʌk] ⬦ *n* -**1.** *esp US* [lorry] caminhão *m* -**2.** RAIL vagão *m*. ⬦ *vt US* transportar de caminhão.

truck driver *n esp US* motorista *mf* de caminhão.

trucker ['trʌkə^r] *n US* caminhoneiro *m*, -ra *f*.

truck farm *n US* chácara *f*.

trucking ['trʌkɪŋ] *n (U) US* transporte *m* por caminhão.

truck stop *n US* restaurante *m* para caminhoneiros.

truculent ['trʌkjʊlənt] *adj* truculento(ta).

trudge [trʌdʒ] ⬦ *n* caminhada *f* difícil. ⬦ *vi* arrastar-se.

true [tru:] *adj* -**1.** [factual] verdadeiro(ra); **I can't believe it's** ~ não acredito que seja verdade; **to come** ~ tornar-se realidade -**2.** [faithful, genuine] verdadeiro(ra); [- friend] de verdade -**3.** [precise, exact] exato(ta).

true-life *adj* baseado(da) na vida real.

truffle ['trʌfl] *n* trufa *f*.

truism ['tru:ɪzm] *n* truísmo *m*.

truly ['tru:lɪ] *adv* -**1.** [in fact] verdadeiramente -**2.** [sincerely] realmente; ~, **I didn't do it** com toda sinceridade eu não fiz isso -**3.** [for emphasis] realmente -**4.** *phr:* **yours** ~ [at end of letter] cordialmente; **and who do you think did that? - yours** ~, **of course!** e quem você acha que fez isso? - euzinho em pessoa, obviamente!

trump [trʌmp] ⬦ *n* [card] trunfo *m*. ⬦ *vt* trunfar.

trump card *n fig* trunfo *m*.

trumped-up ['trʌmpt-] *adj pej* forjado(da).

trumpet ['trʌmpɪt] ⬦ *n* MUS trompete *m*. ⬦ *vi* [elephant] barrir.

trumpeter ['trʌmpɪtə^r] *n* trompetista *mf*.

truncate *vt fml* truncado(da).

truncheon ['trʌntʃən] *n* cassetete *m*.

trundle ['trʌndl] ⬦ *vt* empurrar lentamente. ⬦ *vi* rodar lentamente.

trunk [trʌŋk] *n* -**1.** [gen] tronco *m* -**2.** [of elephant] tromba *f* -**3.** [box] baú *m* (de viagem) -**4.** *US* [of car] porta-malas *m inv*.
➥ **trunks** *npl* [for swimming] calção *m* de banho, sunga *f*.

trunk road *n UK* ≃ rodovia *f* nacional.

truss [trʌs] *n* -**1.** MED funda *f OR* cinta *f* para hérnia -**2.** CONSTR viga *f*.

trust [trʌst] ⬦ *vt* -**1.** [have confidence in] confiar em; **to** ~ **sb to do sthg** confiar em alguém para fazer algo; ~ **you!** *iro* conto com você! -**2.** [entrust]: **to** ~ **sb with sthg** confiar algo a alguém -**3.** *fml* [hope]: **to** ~ **(that)** esperar que. ⬦ *n* -**1.** *(U)* [faith] confiança *f*; ~ **in sb/sthg** confiança em alguém/algo; **to put** *OR* **place one's** ~ **in sb/sthg** depositar sua confiança em alguém/algo; **to take sthg on** ~ tomar algo como verdade -**2.** *(U)* [responsibility] confiança *f* -**3.** FIN fideicomisso *m*; **in** ~ em fideicomisso -**4.** COMM truste *m*.

trust company *n* sociedade *f* fiduciária.

trusted ['trʌstɪd] *adj* de confiança.

trustee [trʌs'ti:] *n* -**1.** FIN & JUR fideicomissário *m*, -ria *f* -**2.** [of institution] curador *m*, -ra *f*.

trusteeship [ˌtrʌs'ti:ʃɪp] *n (U)* fideicomisso *m*.

trust fund *n* fundo *m* fiduciário.

trusting ['trʌstɪŋ] *adj* crédulo(la).

trustworthy ['trʌstˌwɜ:ðɪ] *adj* digno(na) de confiança.

trusty ['trʌstɪ] (*compar* -**ier**, *superl* -**iest**) *adj hum* fiel.

truth [tru:θ] *n* -**1.** [gen]: **the** ~ a verdade; **to tell the** ~ dizer a verdade; **to tell the** ~, ... para dizer a verdade, ... -**2.** *(U)* [veracity] veracidade *f*; **in (all)** ~ em verdade, na realidade.

truth drug *n* droga *f* da verdade.

truthful ['tru:θfʊl] *n* -**1.** [person] sincero(ra), verdadeiro(ra) -**2.** [story] verídico(ca).

try [traɪ] (*pt* & *pp* -**ied**, *pl* -**ies**) ⬦ *vt* -**1.** [attempt]

tentar; **to ~ to do sthg** tentar fazer algo **-2.** [sample, test] experimentar **-3.** *JUR* levar a juízo **-4.** [tax, strain] cansar; **to ~ sb's patience** esgotar a paciência de alguém. ⬦ *vi* tentar; **to ~ for sthg** tratar de conseguir algo. ⬦ *n* **-1.** [attempt] tentativa *f*; **to give sthg a ~** provar algo; **to have a ~ at sthg** tentar fazer algo **-2.** *RUGBY* ato de levar a bola até a linha de fundo do adversário e posicioná-la no solo para se marcar pontos.

➡ **try on** *vt sep* [clothes] experimentar.
➡ **try out** *vt sep* **-1.** [car, machine] testar **-2.** [plan] pôr à prova.

trying ['traɪɪŋ] *adj* difícil, árduo(dua).

try-out *n inf*: **can I have a ~ of the car?** posso experimentar o carro?

tsar [zɑː'] *n* czar *m*.

T-shirt *n* camiseta *f*.

tsp. (*abbr of* **teaspoon**) colher *f* de chá.

T-square *n* régua-tê *f*.

TT (*abbr of* **teetotal**) *adj* abstêmio(mia).

Tuareg *npl* [people] tuaregue *mf*.

tub [tʌb] *n* **-1.** [container - for ice cream, margarine] pote *m*; [- for water] tina *f* **-2.** *inf* [bath] banheira *f*.

tuba ['tjuːbə] *n* tuba *f*.

tubby ['tʌbɪ] (*compar* -**ier**, *superl* -**iest**) *adj inf* rolha-de-poço, gorducho(cha).

tube [tjuːb] *n* **-1.** [gen] tubo *m* **-2.** *UK* [underground train] metrô *m*; [underground system]: **the ~** o metrô; **by ~** de metrô.

tubeless ['tjuːblɪs] *adj* [tyre] sem câmara (de ar).

tuber ['tjuːbə'] *n* tubérculo *m*.

tuberculosis [tjuːˌbɜːkjʊ'ləʊsɪs] *n (U)* tuberculose *f*.

tube station *n UK* estação *f* de metrô.

tubing ['tjuːbɪŋ] *n (U)* tubulação *f*.

tubular ['tjuːbjʊlə'] *adj* tubular.

TUC (*abbr of* **Trades Union Congress**) *n federação dos sindicatos na Grã-Bretanha*, ≃ *CUT f*.

tuck [tʌk] ⬦ *n SEWING* prega *f*. ⬦ *vt* [place neatly] enfiar, meter.

➡ **tuck away** *vt sep* [store] guardar; **to be ~ed away** [hidden] estar escondido(da).
➡ **tuck in** ⬦ *vt sep* **-1.** [child, patient in bed] ajeitar na cama **-2.** [clothes] meter para dentro. ⬦ *vi inf* comer com apetite.
➡ **tuck up** *vt sep* enfiar, meter.

tuck shop *n UK* confeitaria *f* (*perto de um colégio*).

Tudor ['tjuːdə'] ⬦ *adj* **-1.** *HIST* da dinastia Tudor **-2.** *ARCHIT* da era Tudor. ⬦ *n*: **the ~s** os Tudors.

Tue., Tues. (*abbr of* **Tuesday**) ter.

Tuesday ['tjuːzdɪ] *n* terça-feira *f*; *see also* **Saturday**.

tuft [tʌft] *n* tufo *m*.

tug [tʌg] (*pt & pp* -**ged**, *cont* -**ging**) ⬦ *n* **-1.** [pull] puxão *m* **-2.** [boat] rebocador *m*. ⬦ *vt* dar um puxão em. ⬦ *vi* dar um puxão; **to ~ at sthg** dar um puxão em algo.

tugboat ['tʌgbəʊt] *n* (barco *m*) rebocador *m*.

tug-of-love *n UK inf* conflito pela custódia de uma criança.

tug-of-war *n* cabo-de-guerra *m*.

tuition [tjuː'ɪʃn] *n (U)* ensino *m*; **private ~** aulas *fpl* particulares.

tulip ['tjuːlɪp] *n* tulipa *f*.

tulle *n (U)* tule *m*.

tumble ['tʌmbl] ⬦ *vi* **-1.** [person] tombar **-2.** [water] jorrar **-3.** *fig* [prices] despencar. ⬦ *n* tombo *m*.

➡ **tumble down** *vi* [building] vir abaixo.
➡ **tumble to** *vt fus UK inf* sacar, tocar-se de.

tumbledown ['tʌmbldaʊn] *adj* em ruínas.

tumble-dry *vt* secar em secadora.

tumble-dryer [-ˌdraɪə'] *n* secadora *f* (de roupa).

tumbler ['tʌmblə'] *n* [glass] copo *m*.

tummy ['tʌmɪ] (*pl* -**ies**) *n inf* **-1.** [outside of stomach] barriga *f* **-2.** [inside of stomach] barriga *f*.

tumour *UK*, **tumor** *US* ['tjuːmə'] *n* tumor *m*.

tumult ['tjuːmʌlt] *n fml* tumulto *m*.

tumultuous ['tjuːmʌltjʊəs] *adj fml* [applause] efusivo(va).

tuna [*UK* 'tjuːnə, *US* 'tuːnə] (*pl inv OR* -**s**), **tuna fish** (*pl* **tuna fish**) *n* **-1.** [fish] atum *m* **-2.** *(U)* [food] atum *m*.

tundra ['tʌndrə] *n* tundra *f*.

tune [tjuːn] ⬦ *n* [song, melody] melodia *f*; **to the ~ of** *fig* no montante de; **to change one's ~** *inf* virar a casaca. ⬦ *vt* **-1.** *MUS* afinar **-2.** *RADIO & TV* sintonizar; **to ~ sthg to sthg** sintonizar algo em algo **-3.** [engine] ajustar, regular. ⬦ *vi RADIO & TV*: **to ~ to sthg** sintonizar em algo.

➡ **tune in** *vi RADIO & TV* sintonizar-se; **to ~ in to sthg** sintonizar-se em algo.
➡ **tune up** *vi MUS* afinar *OR* consertar os instrumentos.

➡ **in tune** ⬦ *adj MUS* afinado(da). ⬦ *adv* **-1.** *MUS* harmonicamente **-2.** [in agreement]: **in ~ with sb/sthg** em sintonia com alguém/algo.
➡ **out of tune** ⬦ *adj MUS* desafinado(da). ⬦ *adv* **-1.** *MUS* desarmonicamente **-2.** [not in agreement]: **out of ~ with sb/sthg** fora de sintonia com alguém /algo.

tuneful ['tjuːnfʊl] *adj* melodioso(sa).

tuneless ['tjuːnlɪs] *adj* desarmônico(ca).

tuner ['tjuːnə'] *n* **-1.** *RADIO & TV* sintonizador *m* **-2.** *MUS* afinador *m*.

tuner amplifier *n* amplificador *m* sintonizador.

tungsten ['tʌŋstən] ⬦ *n (U)* tungstênio *m*. ⬦ *comp* de tungstênio.

tunic ['tjuːnɪk] *n* [clothing] túnica *f*.

tuning fork ['tjuːnɪŋ-] *n* diapasão *m*.

Tunis ['tjuːnɪs] *n* Túnis.

Tunisia [tjuː'nɪzɪə] *n* Tunísia *f*; **in ~** na Tunísia.

Tunisian [tjuː'nɪzɪən] ⬦ *adj* tunisiano(na). ⬦ *n* [person] tunisiano *m*, -na *f*.

tunnel ['tʌnl] (*UK pt & pp* -**led**, *cont* -**ling**, *US pt & pp* -**ed**, *cont* -**ing**) ⬦ *n* túnel *m*. ⬦ *vi*: **to ~ through sthg** atravessar um túnel por algo.

tunnel vision *n (U)* **-1.** *MED* visão *f* em túnel **-2.** *fig & pej* [narrow-mindedness] visão *f* estreita.

tunny ['tʌnɪ] (*pl inv OR* -**ies**) *n* [fish] tuna *f*.

tuppence *n UK dated* (moeda *f* de) dois pennies *mpl*.

turban ['tɜːbən] *n* [man's headdress] turbante *m*.

turbid ['tɜːbɪd] *adj* túrbido(da).

turbine ['tɜːbaɪn] *n* turbina *f*.

turbo ['tɜːbəʊ] (*pl* -**s**) *n* turbo *m*.

turbocharged ['tɜːbəʊtʃɑːdʒd] *adj* com turbo; ~ car carro-turbo *m*.

turbojet [,tɜːbəʊ'dʒet] *n* -1. [engine] turborreator *m* -2. [plane] turbojacto *m*.

turboprop *n* -1. [engine] turbopropulsor *m* -2. [plane] avião *m* com turbopropulsor.

turbot ['tɜːbət] (*pl inv OR* -s) *n* linguado *m*.

turbulence ['tɜːbjʊləns] *n* (U) turbulência *f*.

turbulent ['tɜːbjʊlənt] *adj* turbulento(ta).

tureen [tə'riːn] *n* sopeira *f*.

turf [tɜːf] (*pl* -s *OR* **turves**) ◇ *n* -1. (U) [grass surface] gramado *m* -2. [clod] turfa *f*. ◇ *vt* [with grass] gramar.
   ◆ **turf out** *vt sep UK inf* -1. [evict] chutar, dar patadas em -2. [throw away] jogar fora.

turf accountant *n UK fml* agenciador *m*, -ra *f* de apostas.

turgid ['tɜːdʒɪd] *adj fml* [style, prose] empolado(da).

Turk [tɜːk] *n* turco *m*, -ca *f*.

Turkestan, Turkistan [,tɜːkɪ'stɑːn] *n* Turquistão; **in** ~ no Turquistão.

turkey ['tɜːkɪ] (*pl* **turkeys**) *n* -1. [bird] peru *m* -2. (U) [meat] peru *m*.

Turkey ['tɜːkɪ] *n* Turquia; **in** ~ na Turquia.

Turkish ['tɜːkɪʃ] ◇ *adj* turco(ca). ◇ *n* [language] turco *m*. ◇ *npl*: **the** ~ os turcos.

Turkish bath *n* banho *m* turco.

Turkish delight *n* (U) doce *feito de substância gelatinosa em cubos com cobertura de açúcar ou chocolate*.

Turkistan *n* = Turkestan.

Turkmenian *adj* turcomano(na).

Turkmenistan [,tɜːkmenɪ'stɑːn] *n* Turcomênia.

turmeric ['tɜːmərɪk] *n* (U) [spice] açafrão-da-terra *m*.

turmoil ['tɜːmɔɪl] *n* (U) desordem *f*.

turn [tɜːn] ◇ *n* -1. [in road, river] curva *f* -2. [revolution, twist] volta *f* -3. [change] reviravolta *f*; **to take a** ~ **for the better/worse** mudar para melhor/pior -4. [in game]: **it's my** ~ é a minha vez -5. [in order] vez *f*; **in** ~ por vez; **to take (it in)** ~**s to do sthg** revezar-se para fazer algo -6. [end] virada *f*; **the** ~ **of the century** a virada do século -7. [performance] número *m*, apresentação *f* -8. MED ataque *m*, crise *f* -9. *phr*: **to do sb a good** ~ fazer uma boa ação a alguém. ◇ *vt* -1. [cause to rotate] girar -2. [move round, turn over] virar -3. [go round] dobrar -4. [direct]: **to** ~ **sthg to sb/sthg** voltar algo para alguém/algo -5. [change]: **to** ~ **sthg into sthg** transformar algo em algo -6. [make, cause to become] deixar; **to** ~ **sthg inside out** virar algo pelo avesso. ◇ *vi* -1. [change direction] virar, dobrar; **to** ~ **to sb/sthg** voltar-se para alguém/algo -2. [rotate] girar -3. [move round] voltar-se -4. [in book]: ~ **to page 102** vão até a página 102 -5. [for consolation]: **to** ~ **to sb/sthg** buscar consolo em alguém/algo -6. [become] tornar-se; **my hair's** ~**ing grey** meu cabelo está ficando branco; **to** ~ **into sthg** transformar-se em algo.
   ◆ **turn against** *vt fus* voltar-se contra.
   ◆ **turn around** *vt sep & vi* = turn round.
   ◆ **turn away** ◇ *vt sep* [refuse entry to] não deixar entrar. ◇ *vi* distanciar-se.
   ◆ **turn back** ◇ *vt sep* -1. [force to return] fazer voltar -2. [fold back] dobrar. ◇ *vi* [return] voltar atrás.
   ◆ **turn down** *vt sep* -1. [reject] recusar -2. [heating, lighting] diminuir -3. [sound] abaixar.
   ◆ **turn in** *vi inf* [go to bed] ir dormir.
   ◆ **turn off** ◇ *vt fus* [road, path] sair de. ◇ *vt sep* [switch off - appliance, engine] desligar; [- gas, tap] fechar. ◇ *vi* [leave road, path] dobrar.
   ◆ **turn on** ◇ *vt sep* -1. [make work - appliance, engine] ligar; [- gas, tap] abrir; [- light] acender -2. *inf* [excite sexually] acender. ◇ *vt fus* [attack] avançar em.
   ◆ **turn out** ◇ *vt sep* -1. [switch off] apagar -2. *inf* [produce] fazer; **the factory** ~**s out cars** a fábrica produz carros -3. [eject] expulsar -4. [empty] esvaziar. ◇ *vt fus*: **to** ~ **out to be** acabar sendo, vir a ser; **it** ~**s out that ...** acontece que ... ◇ *vi* -1. [end up] acabar, terminar -2. [attend]: **to** ~ **out (for sthg)** comparecer (em algo).
   ◆ **turn over** ◇ *vt sep* -1. [playing card, stone, page] virar -2. [consider]: **I** ~ **ed his ideas over in my mind** fiquei com as idéias dele dando voltas na minha cabeça -3. [hand over] entregar; **to** ~ **sb/sthg over to sb** entregar alguém/algo para alguém. ◇ *vi* -1. [roll over] revirar-se -2. *UK TV* mudar de canal.
   ◆ **turn round** ◇ *vt sep* -1. [chair, picture] virar -2. [wheel] girar -3. [words, sentence] expressar de outra maneira -4. [quantity of work] aliviar -5. [company] reerguer. ◇ *vi* [person] virar-se.
   ◆ **turn up** ◇ *vt sep* [heat, lighting, radio, TV] aumentar. ◇ *vi inf* -1. [gen] aparecer -2. [opportunity, solution] surgir.

turnabout ['tɜːnəbaʊt] *n* mudança *f* radical.

turnaround *n US* = turnround.

turncoat ['tɜːnkəʊt] *n pej* vira-casaca *mf*.

turning ['tɜːnɪŋ] *n* [side road]: **the first** ~ **to the left** a primeira (rua) à esquerda.

turning circle *n* raio *m* de viragem.

turning point *n* momento *m* decisivo.

turnip ['tɜːnɪp] *n* nabo *m*.

turnout ['tɜːnaʊt] *n* [attendance] comparecimento *m*, número *m* de participantes.

turnover ['tɜːn,əʊvəʳ] *n* (U) -1. [of personnel] rotatividade *f* -2. *FIN* volume *m* de vendas.

turnpike ['tɜːnpaɪk] *n US* rodovia *f* com pedágio.

turnround *UK* ['tɜːnraʊnd], **turnaround** *US* ['tɜːnəraʊnd] *n* -1. *COMM* tempo *m* de carga e descarga *(de um barco, avião)* -2. [change] reviravolta *f*.

turn signal lever *n US* pisca-pisca *m*.

turnstile ['tɜːnstaɪl] *n* borboleta *f* (em ônibus).

turntable ['tɜːn,teɪbl] *n* [on record player] prato *m* (giratório).

turn-up *n UK* -1. [on trousers] bainha *f* -2. *inf* [surprise]: **a** ~ **for the books** *inf* uma surpresa total.

turpentine ['tɜːpəntaɪn] *n* (U) terebintina *f*.

turps [tɜːps] *n UK inf* aguarrás *f inv*.

turquoise ['tɜːkwɔɪz] ◇ *adj* turquesa. ◇ *n* -1. (U) [mineral, gem] turquesa *f* -2. [colour] turquesa *m*.

turret ['tʌrɪt] *n* [on castle] torre *f* pequena.

turtle ['tɜːtl] (*pl inv OR* -s) *n* tartaruga *f*.

turtledove ['tɜːtldʌv] *n* pomba-rola *f*.

turtleneck ['tɜːtlnek] n **-1.** [garment]blusa f de gola olímpica **- 2.** [neck] gola f olímpica.

turves [tɜːvz] UK pl ⊏> **turf.**

tusk [tʌsk] n [of animal] presa f.

tussle ['tʌsl] <> n briga f. <> vi brigar; **to ~ over** sthg brigar por algo.

tut [tʌt] excl tsc!

tutor ['tjuːtə^r] <> n **-1.** [private] professor m, -ra f particular **- 2.** UNIV professor m universitário, professora f universitária. <> vt: **to ~ sb in sthg** dar aulas particulares de algo para alguém. <> vi dar aulas particulares.

tutorial [tjuːˈtɔːrɪəl] <> adj: **~ group** grupo reduzido de estudantes que assiste a uma aula. <> n aula f para grupos pequenos.

tutu ['tuːtuː] n tutu f.

tux [tʌks] n inf smoking m.

tuxedo [tʌkˈsiːdəʊ] (pl -s) n US smoking m.

TV (abbr of **television**) <> n **-1.** [medium, industry, apparatus] TV f; **on ~** na TV. <> comp de TV.

TV dinner n refeição completa em porção individual pronta para esquentar.

TVP (abbr of **textured vegetable protein**) n proteína f vegetal.

twaddle ['twɒdl] n inf pej lorota f.

twang [twæŋ] <> n **-1.** [sound - of guitar] som m metálico; [- of string, elastic] som m vibrante **- 2.** [accent] som m nasalado. <> vt **-1.** [guitar] vibrar **- 2.** [wire, string] fazer vibrar. <> vi produzir um som vibrante.

tweak [twiːk] vt inf [pull] beliscar.

twee [twiː] adj UK pej piegas inv.

tweed [twiːd] <> n (U) tweed m. <> comp de tweed.

tweet [twiːt] vi inf piar.

tweezers ['twiːzəz] npl pinças fpl.

twelfth [twelfθ] num décimo segundo, décima segunda; see also **sixth.**

Twelfth Night n Noite f de Reis.

twelve [twelv] num doze; see also **six.**

twentieth ['twentɪəθ] num vigésimo(ma); see also sixth.

twenty ['twentɪ] (pl -ies) num vinte; see also **sixty.**

twenty-twenty vision n (U) visão f perfeita.

twerp [twɜːp] n UK inf imbecil mf.

twice [twaɪs] adv duas vezes; **~ a week** duas vezes por semana; **he earns ~ as much as me** ele ganha o dobro que eu.

twiddle ['twɪdl] <> vt girar (entre os dedos). <> vi: **to ~ with sthg** brincar com algo entre os dedos.

twig [twɪg] n graveto m.

twilight ['twaɪlaɪt] n **-1.** [in evening] crepúsculo m vespertino **- 2.** fig [last stages, end] ocaso m.

twill [twɪl] n (U) sarja f.

twin [twɪn] <> adj **-1.** [child, sibling] gêmeo(mea) **- 2.** [beds] duplo(pla) **- 3.** [towns, towers] gêmeos(meas). <> n [sibling] gêmeos mpl, -meas fpl.

twin-bedded [-'bedɪd] adj com duas camas.

twin carburettor n carburador m duplo.

twine [twaɪn] <> n (U) barbante m. <> vt: **to ~ sthg round sthg** enrolar algo em algo.

twin-engined [-'endʒɪnd] adj bimotor.

twinge [twɪndʒ] n **-1.** [of pain] pontada f **- 2.** [of guilt] remorso m.

twinkle ['twɪŋkl] <> n brilho m. <> vi **-1.** [star, light] cintilar **- 2.** [eyes] brilhar.

twin room n quarto m com duas camas.

twinset n UK conjunto de blusa e casaquinho.

twin town n cidade-irmã f.

twin tub n máquina f de lavar e secar.

twirl [twɜːl] <> vt **-1.** [spin] girar **- 2.** [twist] torcer. <> vi rodopiar.

twist [twɪst] <> n **-1.** [gen] volta f **- 2.** [turn, twirl] giro m; **to give sthg a ~** girar algo **- 3.** fig [in plot] reviravolta f. <> vt **-1.** [gen] retorcer **- 2.** [face, frame] torcer **- 3.** [head] voltar **- 4.** [lid, knob, dial] girar **- 5.** [words, meaning] distorcer. <> vi **-1.** [road, river] dar voltas **- 2.** [body, part of body] torcer.

twisted ['twɪstɪd] adj pej [bizarre] deturpado(da).

twister ['twɪstə^r] n US tornado m.

twisty ['twɪstɪ] (compar -ier, superl -iest) adj inf cheio (cheia) de curvas.

twit [twɪt] n UK inf idiota mf, imbecil mf.

twitch [twɪtʃ] <> n espasmo m; **nervous ~** tique m nervoso. <> vt [ears, nose] tremer. <> vi contrair-se.

twitter ['twɪtə^r] vi **-1.** [bird] cantar, pipilar **- 2.** pej [person] cantar vantagem.

two [tuː] num dois (duas); **in ~** em dois; see also **six.**

two-bit adj US pej barato(ta); **a ~ little dictator** um ditadorzinho de meia-tigela OR araque.

two-dimensional adj **-1.** [picture] em duas dimensões, bidimensional **- 2.** pej [report, description] simples, sem profundidade.

two-door adj [car] de duas portas.

twofaced [ˌtuːˈfeɪst] adj pej de duas caras.

twofold ['tuːfəʊld] <> adj duplo(pla). <> adv: **to increase ~** duplicar-se.

two-handed [-'hændɪd] adj **-1.** [sword] que se usa com as duas mãos **- 2.** [backhand] que se dá com as duas mãos.

two-piece adj [suit, swimsuit] de duas peças.

two-ply adj de duas camadas.

two-seater [-'siːtə^r] n carro m esporte (com apenas dois lugares).

twosome ['tuːsəm] n inf dupla f.

two-stroke <> adj **-1.** [engine] de dois tempos **- 2.** [oil] para motor de dois tempos. <> n motor m de dois tempos.

two-time vt inf botar chifre em.

two-tone adj bicolor.

two-way adj **-1.** [traffic] de mão dupla **- 2.** [discussion, debate] de duas vias **- 3.** [cooperation] mútuo(tua) **- 4.** TELEC: **~ radio** aparelho m emissor e receptor.

TX abbr of **Texas.**

tycoon [taɪˈkuːn] n magnata mf.

type [taɪp] <> n **-1.** [gen] tipo m **- 2.** (U) TYPO: **in bold/ italic ~** em negrito/itálico. <> vt & vi **-1.** [on typewriter] datilografar **- 2.** [on computer] digitar; **to ~ sthg into sthg** inserir algo em algo.

➡ **type up** vt sep **-1.** [on typewriter] datilografar **- 2.** [on computer] digitar.

typecast ['taɪpkɑːst] (pt & pp typecast) vt escalar sempre para o mesmo tipo de papel; **to be ~ as**

sthg ser sempre escalado(da) (para atuar) como algo.

typeface ['taɪpfeɪs] *n* TYPO tipo *m*, letra *f*.

typescript ['taɪpskrɪpt] *n* cópia *f* datilografada.

typeset ['taɪpset] (*pt* & *pp* typeset, *cont*-ting) *vt* TYPO compor.

typesetter *n* [company] tipografia *f*.

typesetting *n* composição *f* (para impressão).

typewriter ['taɪpˌraɪtə'] *n* máquina *f* de escrever.

typhoid (fever) ['taɪfɔɪd-] *n* (*U*) febre *f* tifóide.

typhoon [taɪ'fuːn] *n* tufão *m*.

typhus ['taɪfəs] *n* (*U*) tifo *m*.

typical ['tɪpɪkl] *adj* típico(ca); ~ **of sb/sthg** típico(ca) de alguém/algo.

typically ['tɪpɪklɪ] *adv* -**1.** [usually] geralmente, normalmente -**2.** [characteristically] tipicamente.

typify ['tɪpɪfaɪ] (*pt* & *pp* -ied) *vt* -**1.** [be characteristic of] tipificar -**2.** [embody, symbolize] simbolizar.

typing ['taɪpɪŋ] *n* -**1.** (*U*) [on typewriter] datilografia *f* -**2.** (*U*) [on computer] digitação *f*.

typing error *n* -**1.** [on typewriter] erro *m* de datilografia -**2.** [on computer] erro *m* de digitação.

typing pool *n* -**1.** [typewriter] serviço *m* de datilografia -**2.** [computer] serviço *m* de digitação.

typist ['taɪpɪst] *n* -**1.** [on typewriter] datilógrafo *m*, -fa *f* -**2.** [on computer] digitador *m*, -ra *f*.

typo ['taɪpəʊ] *n inf* erro *m* tipográfico.

typographic(al) error [ˌtaɪpə' græfɪk(l)-] *n* erro *m* tipográfico.

typography [taɪ'pɒɡrəfɪ] *n* -**1.** (*U*) [process, job] tipografia *f* -**2.** [format] composição *f* tipográfica.

tyrannical [tɪ'rænɪkl] *adj* tirânico(ca).

tyranny ['tɪrənɪ] *n* (*U*) [of person, government] tirania *f*.

tyrant ['taɪrənt] *n* tirano *m*, -na *f*.

tyre *UK*, **tire** *US* ['taɪə'] *n* pneu *m*.

tyre pressure *n* (*U*) pressão *f* do pneu.

Tyrol, Tirol [tɪ'rəʊl] *n*: the ~ o Tirol.

Tyrolean [tɪrə'liːən], **Tyrolese** [ˌtɪrə'liːz] <> *adj* tirolês(esa). <> *n* tirolês *m*, -esa *f*.

Tyrrhenian Sea [tɪ'riːnɪən-] *n*: the ~ o Mar Tirreno.

tzar [zɑː'] *n* = tsar.

u (*pl* u's *OR* us), **U** (*pl* U's *OR* Us) [juː] *n* [letter] u, U *m*.
➤ **U** (*abbr of* universal) livre.

U (*abbr of* universal) *filme de censura livre.*

UAE (*abbr of* United Arab Emirates) *n* EAU *mpl*.

UB40 (*abbr of* unemployment benefit form 40) *n* certificado de recebimento do seguro-desemprego na Grã-Bretanha.

U-bend *n* sifão *m*.

ubiquitous [juː'bɪkwɪtəs] *adj fml* ubíquo(qua).

u.c. (*abbr of* upper case) *n* caixa-alta *f*.

UCAS (*abbr of* Universities and Colleges Admissions Service) *n* organização britânica que trata da admissão às faculdades e universidades.

UCL (*abbr of* University College, London) *n* uma das faculdades da Universidade de Londres.

UDA (*abbr of* Ulster Defence Association) *n* organização paramilitar protestante da Irlanda do Norte, favorável à permanência da Irlanda do Norte no Reino Unido.

UDC (*abbr of* Urban District Council) *n* câmara de vereadores britânica de comunidade urbana.

udder ['ʌdə'] *n* úbere *m*.

UDI (*abbr of* unilateral declaration of independence) *n* -**1.** HIST declaração unilateral de independência (na Rodésia) -**2.** hum: to declare ~ on sb passar alguém para trás.

UDR (*abbr of* Ulster Defence Regiment) *n* antigo regimento de reservistas na Irlanda do Norte, agora parte do Regimento Real Irlandês.

UEFA [juː'eɪfə] (*abbr of* Union of European Football Associations) *n* UEFA *f*.

UFC (*abbr of* Universities Funding Council) *n* órgão britânico responsável por gerir as doações universitárias.

UFO (*abbr of* unidentified flying object) *n* OVNI *m*.

Uganda [juː'ɡændə] *n* Uganda; **in** ~ em Uganda.

Ugandan [juː'ɡændən] <> *adj* ugandense. <> *n* [person] ugandense *mf*.

ugh [ʌɡ] *excl* puf!

ugliness ['ʌɡlɪnɪs] *n* (*U*) -**1.** [unattractiveness] feiúra *f* -**2.** fig [unpleasantness] repulsa *f*.

ugly ['ʌɡlɪ] (*compar* -ier, *superl* -iest) *adj* -**1.** [unattractive] feio (feia) -**2.** fig [unpleasant] desagradável.

UHF (*abbr of* ultra-high frequency) *n* UHF *m*.

UHT (*abbr of* ultra-heat treated) *adj* UHT; ~ **milk** leite *m* longa-vida.

UK (*abbr of* United Kingdom) *n* RU *m*.

UKAEA (*abbr of* United Kingdom Atomic Energy Authority) *n* órgão responsável pelo controle da energia atômica no Reino Unido.

Ukraine [juː'kreɪn] *n*: the ~ a Ucrânia; **in the** ~ na Ucrânia.

Ukrainian [juː'kreɪnjən] <> *adj* ucraniano(na). <> *n* -**1.** [person] ucraniano *m*, -na *f* -**2.** [language] ucraniano *m*.

ulcer ['ʌlsə'] *n* -**1.** [in stomach] úlcera *f* -**2.** [in mouth] afta *f*.

ulcerated ['ʌlsəreɪtɪd] *adj* ulcerado(da).

Ulster ['ʌlstə'] *n* Irlanda *f* do Norte; **in** ~ na Irlanda do Norte.

Ulster Unionist Party *n* partido político norte-irlandês que defende a permanência da Irlanda do Norte como parte do Grã-Bretanha.

ulterior [ʌl'tɪərɪə'] *adj*: ~ **motive** motivo *m* ulterior.

ultimata [ˌʌltɪ'meɪtə] *pl* ⊳ ultimatum.

ultimate ['ʌltɪmət] <> *adj* -**1.** [success, objetive] final, definitivo(va) **-2.** [failure] último(ma) **-3.** [most powerful] máximo(ma). <> *n*: the ~ in sthg a última palavra em algo.

ultimately [ˈʌltɪmətlɪ] *adv* **-1.** [finally, in the long term] finalmente, por fim **-2.** [fundamentally] no fundo.

ultimatum [ˌʌltɪˈmeɪtəm] (*pl* **-tums** OR **-ta**) *n* ultimato *m.*

ultra- [ˈʌltrə] *prefix* ultra-.

ultramarine [ˌʌltrəməˈriːn] *adj* ultramarino(na).

ultrasonic [ˌʌltrəˈsɒnɪk] *adj* ultra-sônico(ca).

ultrasound [ˈʌltrəsaʊnd] *n (U)* ultra-som *m.*

ultraviolet [ˌʌltrəˈvaɪələt] *adj* ultravioleta.

um [ʌm] *excl* hum!

umbilical cord [ʌmˈbɪlɪkl-] *n* cordão *m* umbilical.

umbrage [ˈʌmbrɪdʒ] *n*: to take ~ (at sthg) ofender-se (com algo).

umbrella [ʌmˈbrelə] <> *n* **-1.** [gen] guarda-chuva *m*; **-2.** [fixed] guarda-sol *m.* <> *adj* guarda-chuva; ~ **word** palavra guarda-chuva.

UMIST (*abbr of* University of Manchester Institute of Science and Technology) *n instituto de ciência e tecnologia da Universidade de Manchester*, UMIST *m.*

umpire [ˈʌmpaɪəʳ] <> *n* árbitro *m.* <> *vt* & *vi* arbitrar, apitar.

umpteen [ˌʌmpˈtiːn] *num adj inf*: ~ times um milhão de vezes.

umpteenth [ˌʌmpˈtiːnθ] *num adj inf* enésimo(ma).

UN (*abbr of* United Nations) *n*: the ~ a ONU.

unabashed [ˌʌnəˈbæʃt] *adj* imperturbável.

unabated [ˌʌnəˈbeɪtɪd] *adj* incessante.

unable [ʌnˈeɪbl] *adj* incapaz; to be ~ to do sthg não poder fazer algo.

unabridged [ˌʌnəˈbrɪdʒd] *adj* integral.

unacceptable [ˌʌnəkˈseptəbl] *adj* inaceitável.

unaccompanied [ˌʌnəˈkʌmpənɪd] *adj* **-1.** [child] sozinho(nha) **-2.** [luggage] desacompanhado(da) **-3.** [song] sem acompanhamento.

unaccountable [ˌʌnəˈkaʊntəbl] *adj* **-1.** [inexplicable] incompreensível **-2.** [not responsible] que não é responsável; to be ~ for sthg não ser responsável por algo; to be ~ to sb não ter de dar satisfações para alguém.

unaccountably [ˌʌnəˈkaʊntəblɪ] *adv* [inexplicably] inexplicavelmente.

unaccounted [ˌʌnəˈkaʊntɪd] *adj*: ~ for desaparecido(da).

unaccustomed [ˌʌnəˈkʌstəmd] *adj* **-1.** [unused]: to be ~ to sthg/to doing sthg estar desacostumado(da) a algo/a fazer algo **-2.** *fml* [not usual] inusual.

unacquainted [ˌʌnəˈkweɪntɪd] *adj*: to be ~ with sb/sthg não conhecer alguém/algo.

unadulterated [ˌʌnəˈdʌltəreɪtɪd] *adj* **-1.** [unspoiled] não-adulterado(da) **-2.** [absolute] puro(ra).

unadventurous [ˌʌnədˈventʃərəs] *adj* pouco aventureiro(ra).

unaffected [ˌʌnəˈfektɪd] *adj* **-1.** [unchanged] intacto(ta); to be ~ by sthg não ser atingido(da) por algo **-2.** [natural] natural.

unafraid [ˌʌnəˈfreɪd] *adj* destemido(da).

unaided [ʌnˈeɪdɪd] <> *adj* feito(ta) sem ajuda. <> *adv* sem ajuda.

unambiguous [ˌʌnæmˈbɪgjʊəs] *adj* inequívoco(ca).

un-American [ˈʌn-] *adj* antiamericano(na).

unanimity [ˌjuːnəˈnɪmətɪ] *n (U) fml* unanimidade *f.*

unanimous [juːˈnænɪməs] *adj* unânime.

unanimously [juːˈnænɪməslɪ] *adv* unanimemente.

unannounced [ˌʌnəˈnaʊnst] <> *adj* não-anunciado(da). <> *adv* sem anunciar.

unanswered [ˌʌnˈɑːnsəd] *adj* não-respondido(da).

unappealing [ˌʌnəˈpiːlɪŋ] *adj* desagradável.

unappetizing, -ising [ˌʌnˈæpɪtaɪzɪŋ] *adj* **-1.** [food] pouco apetitoso(sa) **-2.** [sight, thought] pouco apetecível.

unappreciated [ˌʌnəˈpriːʃɪeɪtɪd] *adj* não-reconhecido(da).

unappreciative [ˌʌnəˈpriːʃɪətɪv] *adj* ingrato(ta); to be ~ of sthg ser incapaz de apreciar algo.

unapproachable [ˌʌnəˈprəʊtʃəbl] *adj* [person] inacessível.

unarmed [ˌʌnˈɑːmd] *adj* desarmado(da).

unarmed combat *n (U)* combate *m* sem armas.

unashamed [ˌʌnəˈʃeɪmd] *adj* descarado(da).

unassisted [ˌʌnəˈsɪstɪd] *adj* sem ajuda.

unassuming [ˌʌnəˈsjuːmɪŋ] *adj* despretensioso(sa).

unattached [ˌʌnəˈtætʃt] *adj* **-1.** [not fastened, linked] independente; ~ to sthg separado(da) de algo **-2.** [without partner] sem compromisso.

unattainable [ˌʌnəˈteɪnəbl] *adj* inatingível.

unattended [ˌʌnəˈtendɪd] *adj* **-1.** [luggage, children] desacompanhado(da) **-2.** [fire, shop] sem vigilância.

unattractive [ˌʌnəˈtræktɪv] *adj* **-1.** [person, building, place] sem atrativos **-2.** [idea, prospect] sem brilho.

unauthorized, -ised [ˌʌnˈɔːθəraɪzd] *adj* não-autorizado(da).

unavailable [ˌʌnəˈveɪləbl] *adj* que não está disponível.

unavoidable [ˌʌnəˈvɔɪdəbl] *adj* inevitável.

unavoidably [ˌʌnəˈvɔɪdəblɪ] *adv* inevitavelmente.

unaware [ˌʌnəˈweəʳ] *adj* desconhecedor(ra); to be ~ of sb/sthg não estar consciente de alguém/algo.

unawares [ˌʌnəˈweəz] *adv*: to catch OR take sb ~ pegar alguém desprevenido(da).

unbalanced [ˌʌnˈbælənst] *adj* **-1.** [biased] parcial **-2.** [deranged] desequilibrado(da).

unbearable [ʌnˈbeərəbl] *adj* insuportável, insustentável.

unbearably [ʌnˈbeərəblɪ] *adv* insuportavelmente, insustentavelmente.

unbeatable [ˌʌnˈbiːtəbl] *adj* imbatível.

unbecoming [ˌʌnbɪˈkʌmɪŋ] *adj fml* [dress, colour] pouco favorecedor(ra).

unbeknown(st) [ˌʌnbɪˈnəʊn(st)] *adv*: ~ to sem o conhecimento de.

unbelievable [ˌʌnbɪˈliːvəbl] *adj* **-1.** [amazing] incrível **-2.** [not believable] inacreditável.

unbelievably [ˌʌnbɪˈliːvəblɪ] *adv* [extremely] extremamente.

unbend [ˌʌnˈbend] (*pt* & *pp* unbent) *vi* [relax] relaxar.

unbending [ˌʌnˈbendɪŋ] *adj* [intransigent] resoluto(ta).

unbent [ˌʌnˈbent] *pt* & *pp* ▷ **unbend**.

unbia(s)sed [ˌʌnˈbaɪəst] *adj* imparcial.

unblemished [ˌʌnˈblemɪʃt] *adj fig* irretocável.

unblock [ˌʌnˈblɒk] *vt* - **1.** [drain, tunnel] desbloquear - **2.** [pipe] desentupir.

unbolt [ˌʌnˈbəʊlt] *vt* [door] destrancar.

unborn [ˌʌnˈbɔːn] *adj* [child] nascituro(ra).

unbreakable [ˌʌnˈbreɪkəbl] *adj* inquebrável.

unbridled [ˌʌnˈbraɪdld] *adj* desenfreado(da).

unbuckle [ˌʌnˈbʌkl] *vt* desafivelar.

unbutton [ˌʌnˈbʌtn] *vt* desabotoar.

uncalled-for [ˌʌnˈkɔːld-] *adj* injusto(ta), desnecessário(ria).

uncanny [ʌnˈkænɪ] (*compar* -**ier**, *superl* -**iest**) *adj* sinistro(tra).

uncared-for [ˌʌnˈkeəd-] *adj* abandonado(da).

uncaring [ˌʌnˈkeərɪŋ] *adj* insensível.

unceasing [ˌʌnˈsiːsɪŋ] *adj fml* incessante.

unceremonious [ˈʌnˌserɪˈməʊnjəs] *adj* [abrupt] abrupto(ta).

unceremoniously [ˈʌnˌserɪˈməʊnjəslɪ] *adj* [abruptly] abruptamente.

uncertain [ʌnˈsɜːtn] *adj* - **1.** [gen] incerto(ta) - **2.** [person] indeciso(sa); **in no** ~ **terms** sem meias palavras.

unchain [ˌʌnˈtʃeɪn] *vt* desacorrentar.

unchallenged [ˌʌnˈtʃælɪndʒd] *adj* [authority, leadership, version] inquestionável.

unchanged [ˌʌnˈtʃeɪndʒd] *adj* sem alterar.

unchanging [ˌʌnˈtʃeɪndʒɪŋ] *adj* imutável.

uncharacteristic [ˈʌnˌkærəktəˈrɪstɪk] *adj* não-característico(ca).

uncharitable [ˌʌnˈtʃærɪtəbl] *adj* mesquinho(nha).

uncharted [ˌʌnˈtʃɑːtɪd] *adj* - **1.** [not recorded on maps] não-cartografado(da) - **2.** *fig* [unfamiliar] desconhecido(da).

unchecked [ˌʌnˈtʃekt] ◇ *adj* [unrestrained] desenfreado(da). ◇ *adv* [unrestrained] sem restrições.

uncivilized, -ised [ˌʌnˈsɪvɪlaɪzd] *adj* [barbaric] não-civilizado(da).

unclassified [ˌʌnˈklæsɪfaɪd] *adj* - **1.** [not confidential] não-confidencial - **2.** [not categorised] não-classificado.

uncle [ˈʌŋkl] *n* tio *m*.

unclean [ˌʌnˈkliːn] *adj* - **1.** [dirty] sujo(ja) - **2.** *RELIG* impuro(ra).

unclear [ˌʌnˈklɪəʳ] *adj* - **1.** [meaning, instructions] confuso(sa), pouco claro(ra) - **2.** [future] obscuro(ra) - **3.** [motives, details] confuso(sa) - **4.** [person]: **to be** ~ **about sthg** não ter algo claro.

unclothed [ˌʌnˈkləʊðd] *adj fml* despido(da).

uncomfortable [ˌʌnˈkʌmftəbl] *adj* - **1.** [giving discomfort] desconfortável - **2.** *fig* [awkward] desagradável - **3.** [person - in physical discomfort] desconfortável; [- ill at ease] incomodado(da).

uncomfortably [ˌʌnˈkʌmftəblɪ] *adv* - **1.** [in physical discomfort] desconfortavelmente - **2.** *fig* [uneasily] de forma incômoda - **3.** [unpleasantly] desagradavelmente.

uncommitted [ˌʌnkəˈmɪtɪd] *adj* não-comprometido(da).

uncommon [ʌnˈkɒmən] *adj* - **1.** [rare] raro(ra) - **2.** *fml* [extreme] fora do comum.

uncommonly [ʌnˈkɒmənlɪ] *adv fml* extraordinariamente.

uncommunicative [ˌʌnkəˈmjuːnɪkətɪv] *adj* reservado(da).

uncomplicated [ˌʌnˈkɒmplɪkeɪtɪd] *adj* descomplicado(da).

uncomprehending [ˈʌnˌkɒmprɪˈhendɪŋ] *adj* atônito(ta).

uncompromising [ˌʌnˈkɒmprəmaɪzɪŋ] *adj* resoluto(ta), inflexível.

unconcerned [ˌʌnkənˈsɜːnd] *adj* [not anxious] indiferente.

unconditional [ˌʌnkənˈdɪʃənl] *adj* incondicional.

uncongenial [ˌʌnkənˈdʒiːnjəl] *adj fml* desagradável.

unconnected [ˌʌnkəˈnektɪd] *adj* desconexo(xa).

unconquered [ˌʌnˈkɒŋkəd] *adj* não-conquistado(da).

unconscious [ʌnˈkɒnʃəs] ◇ *adj* - **1.** [gen] inconsciente - **2.** *fig* [unaware]: **to be** ~ **of sthg** não estar ciente de algo. ◇ *n PSYCH*: **the** ~ o inconsciente.

unconsciously [ʌnˈkɒnʃəslɪ] *adv* inconscientemente.

unconstitutional [ˈʌnˌkɒnstɪˈtjuːʃənl] *adj* inconstitucional.

uncontested [ˌʌnkənˈtestɪd] *adj* - **1.** [gen] incontestado(da) - **2.** [election] sem oponente.

uncontrollable [ˌʌnkənˈtrəʊləbl] *adj* incontrolável.

uncontrolled [ˌʌnkənˈtrəʊld] *adj* descontrolado(da).

unconventional [ˌʌnkənˈvenʃənl] *adj* não-convencional.

unconvinced [ˌʌnkənˈvɪnst] *adj* não-convencido(da).

unconvincing [ˌʌnkənˈvɪnsɪŋ] *adj* não-convincente.

uncooked [ˌʌnˈkʊkt] *adj* cru (crua).

uncooperative [ˌʌnkəʊˈɒpərətɪv] *adj* não-disposto(ta) a ajudar.

uncork [ˌʌnˈkɔːk] *vt* desarrolhar.

uncorroborated [ˌʌnkəˈrɒbəreɪtɪd] *adj* não-confirmado(da).

uncouth [ʌnˈkuːθ] *adj* grosseiro(ra).

uncover [ʌnˈkʌvəʳ] *vt* - **1.** [saucepan] destampar - **2.** [corruption, truth] revelar, expor.

uncurl [ˌʌnˈkɜːl] *vi* - **1.** [hair] alisar - **2.** [wire] esticar - **3.** [animal] desenroscar-se.

uncut [ˌʌnˈkʌt] *adj* - **1.** [film] sem cortes - **2.** [jewel] bruto(ta).

undamaged [ˌʌnˈdæmɪdʒd] *adj* intacto(ta).

undaunted [ˌʌnˈdɔːntɪd] *adj* inabalável, destemido(da).

undecided [ˌʌndɪˈsaɪdɪd] *adj* - **1.** [person] indeciso(sa) - **2.** [issue] pendente.

undemanding [ˌʌndɪˈmɑːndɪŋ] *adj* - **1.** [task] que exige pouco esforço - **2.** [person] pouco exigente.

undemonstrative [ˌʌndɪˈmɒnstrətɪv] *adj* [person] reservado(da).

undeniable [ˌʌndɪˈnaɪəbl] *adj* inegável.

under [ˈʌndəʳ] ◇ *prep* - **1.** [beneath, below] embaixo de; **they walked** ~ **the bridge** passaram por baixo da ponte - **2.** [less than] menos de - **3.** [indicating conditions or circumstances]: ~ **the circumstances** dadas as circunstâncias; **I'm ~ the impression that ...** tenho a impressão de que ... **- 4.** [undergoing]: ~ **discussion** em discussão **- 5.** [directed, governed by]: **he has ten people ~ him** tem dez pessoas trabalhando sob seu comando **- 6.** [according to] de acordo com **- 7.** [in classification, name, title]: **he filed it ~ 'D'** arquivou na letra D; ~ **an alias** sob outro nome. <> *adv* **-1.** [beneath] embaixo; **to go ~** fracassar **- 2.** [less]: **children of five years and ~** crianças de cinco anos ou menos.

under- [ˈʌndəʳ] *prefix* sub-.

underachiever [ˌʌndərəˈtʃiːvəʳ] *n* pessoa que não rende tudo o que pode.

underage [ˌʌndərˈeɪdʒ] *adj* **-1.** [person] menor de idade **- 2.** [drinking, sex] para menor de idade.

underarm [ˈʌndərɑːm] <> *adj* **-1.** [deodorant, hair] para as axilas **- 2.** SPORT [bowling] com a mão por baixo do ombro. <> *adv* [throw, bowl] por baixo do ombro.

underbrush [ˈʌndəbrʌʃ] *n* US vegetação *f* rasteira *(numa floresta)*.

undercarriage [ˈʌndəˌkærɪdʒ] *n* trem *m* de aterrissagem.

undercharge [ˌʌndəˈtʃɑːdʒ] *vt* cobrar menos que o estipulado.

underclothes [ˈʌndəkləʊðz] *npl* roupas *fpl* íntimas OR de baixo.

undercoat [ˈʌndəkəʊt] *n* [of paint] primeira demão *f*.

undercook [ˌʌndəˈkʊk] *vt* não cozinhar suficientemente.

undercover [ˈʌndəˌkʌvəʳ] <> *adj* secreto(ta). <> *adv* na clandestinidade.

undercurrent [ˈʌndəˌkʌrənt] *n* fig [tendency] sentimento *m* oculto.

undercut [ˌʌndəˈkʌt] *(pt & pp* **undercut,** *cont* **-ting)** *vt* [in price] vender mais barato que.

underdeveloped [ˌʌndədɪˈveləpt] *adj* subdesenvolvido(da), em desenvolvimento.

underdog [ˈʌndədɒg] *n*: **the ~** os menos favorecidos.

underdone [ˌʌndəˈdʌn] *adj* [food] meio cru (crua).

underemployment [ˌʌndərɪmˈplɔɪmənt] *n (U)* subemprego *m*.

underestimate [*n* ˌʌndərˈestɪmət, *vb* ˌʌndərˈestɪmeɪt] <> *n* subestimação *f*. <> *vt* subestimar.

underexposed [ˌʌndərɪkˈspəʊzd] *adj* PHOT subexposto(ta).

underfinanced [ˌʌndəˈfaɪnænst] *adj* insuficientemente financiado(da).

underfoot [ˌʌndəˈfʊt] *adv* debaixo dos pés; **the ground is wet ~** o chão está molhado.

undergo [ˌʌndəˈgəʊ] *(pt* **-went,** *pp* **-gone)** *vt* **-1.** [change, difficulties] passar por **- 2.** [operation, examination] submeter-se a.

undergraduate [ˌʌndəˈgrædʒʊət] <> *adj* de graduação. <> *n* universitário *m*, -ria *f (que ainda não colou grau)*.

underground [*adj & n* ˈʌndəgraʊnd, *adv* ˌʌndəˈgraʊnd] <> *adj* **-1.** [below the ground] subterrâneo(nea) **- 2.** fig [secret, illegal] clandestino(na). <> *adv*: **to go ~** passar à clandestinidade; **to be**

forced ~ ter de passar à clandestinidade. <> *n* **-1.** UK [transport system] metrô *m* **- 2.** [activist movement] resistência *f*.

undergrowth [ˈʌndəgrəʊθ] *n (U)* vegetação *f* rasteira *(numa floresta)*.

underhand [ˌʌndəˈhænd] *adj* clandestino(na).

underinsured [ˌʌndərɪnˈʃʊəd] *adj* segurado(da) abaixo do valor corrente.

underlay [ˈʌndəleɪ] *n* [for carpet] forração *f*.

underline [ˌʌndəˈlaɪn] *vt* **-1.** [draw line under] sublinhar **- 2.** fig [stress] salientar.

underling *n* subalterno *m*, -na *f*.

underlying [ˌʌndəˈlaɪɪŋ] *adj* subjacente.

undermanned [ˌʌndəˈmænd] *adj* com falta de mão-de-obra.

undermentioned [ˌʌndəˈmenʃnd] *adj* fml abaixo mencionado(da).

undermine [ˌʌndəˈmaɪn] *vt* fig [weaken] minar.

underneath [ˌʌndəˈniːθ] <> *prep* debaixo de. <> *adv* **-1.** [beneath] por baixo **- 2.** fig [within oneself] por dentro, no fundo. <> *adj* inf de baixo. <> *n* [underside]: **the ~** a parte de baixo; **on the ~** no fundo; **on the ~ of the box** na parte de baixo da caixa.

undernourished [ˌʌndəˈnʌrɪʃt] *adj* subnutrido(da).

underpaid [*pt & pp* ˌʌndəˈpeɪd, *adj* ˈʌndəpeɪd] <> *pt & pp* ⊳ **underpay.** <> *adj* mal pago(ga).

underpants [ˈʌndəpænts] *npl* cueca *f*.

underpass [ˈʌndəpɑːs] *n* passagem *f* subterrânea.

underpay [ˌʌndəˈpeɪ] *(pt & pp* **-paid)** *vt* pagar mal.

underpin [ˌʌndəˈpɪn] *(pt & pp* **-ned,** *cont* **-ning)** *vt* fig [back up] embasar.

underplay [ˌʌndəˈpleɪ] *vt* [minimize the importance of] minimizar.

underprice [ˌʌndəˈpraɪs] *vt* cotar algo abaixo de seu valor real.

underprivileged [ˌʌndəˈprɪvɪlɪdʒd] *adj* [children] desamparado(da).

underproduction [ˌʌndəprəˈdʌkʃn] *n (U)* produção *f* insuficiente.

underrated [ˌʌndəˈreɪtɪd] *adj* subestimado(da).

underscore [ˌʌndəˈskɔːʳ] *vt* **-1.** [underline] sublinhar **- 2.** fig [emphasize] salientar.

undersea [ˈʌndəsiː] *adj* submarino(na).

undersecretary [ˌʌndəˈsekrətərɪ] *(pl* **-ies)** *n* subsecretário *m*, -ria *f*.

undersell [ˌʌndəˈsel] *(pt & pp* **-sold)** *vt* **-1.** COMM [sell at lower prices than] vender mais barato que **- 2.** fig [undervalue]: **to ~ o.s.** vender-se barato.

undershirt [ˈʌndəʃɜːt] *n* US camiseta *f*.

underside [ˈʌndəsaɪd] *n*: **the ~** a parte de baixo.

undersigned [ˈʌndəsaɪnd] *n* fml: **the ~** o abaixo-assinado.

undersize(d) [ˌʌndəˈsaɪz(d)] *adj* menor que o normal.

underskirt [ˈʌndəskɜːt] *n* anágua *f*.

undersold [ˌʌndəˈsəʊld] *pt & pp* ⊳ **undersell.**

understaffed [ˌʌndəˈstɑːft] *adj* com falta de pessoal.

understand [ˌʌndəˈstænd] *(pt & pp* **-stood)** <> *vt* **-1.** entender, compreender; **to make o.s. understood** fazer-se entender **- 2.** fml [believe]: **to ~ that**

acreditar que. <> *vi* entender, compreender.

understandable [ˌʌndəˈstændəbl] *adj* compreensível.

understandably [ˌʌndəˈstændəblɪ] *adv* naturalmente; **he was ~ upset** é compreensível que ele estivesse chateado.

understanding [ˌʌndəˈstændɪŋ] <> *n* -1. [knowledge, insight] compreensão *f*, entendimento *m* -2. *(U)* [sympathy] compreensão *f* mútua -3. [interpretation, conception]: **it is my ~ that ...** tenho a impressão de que ... -4. [informal agreement] entendimento *m*; **on the ~ that ...** à condição de que ... <> *adj* [sympathetic] compreensivo(va).

understate [ˌʌndəˈsteɪt] *vt* [minimize] atenuar.

understated *adj* [elegance, clothes] sóbrio(bria).

understatement [ˌʌndəˈsteɪtmənt] *n* -1. [inadequate statement] atenuação *f* -2. *(U)* [quality of understating] atenuação *f*; **he is a master of ~** ele é o rei dos eufemismos.

understood [ˌʌndəˈstʊd] *pt & pp* ⊳ **understand**.

understudy [ˈʌndəˌstʌdɪ] *(pl -ies, pt & pp -ied)* <> *n* ator *m* substituto, atriz *f* substituta. <> *vt*: **to ~ the role of Macbeth** substituit alguém no papel de Macbeth.

undertake [ˌʌndəˈteɪk] *(pt -took, pp -taken)* *vt* -1. [take on - responsibility, control] assumir; [- task] incumbir-se de -2. [promise]: **to ~ to do sthg** comprometer-se a fazer algo.

undertaker [ˈʌndəˌteɪkəʳ] *n* agente *mf* funerário, -ria; **~'s** [place] funerária *f*.

undertaking [ˌʌndəˈteɪkɪŋ] *n* -1. [task] incumbência *f* -2. [promise] promessa *f*.

undertone [ˈʌndətəʊn] *n* -1. [quiet voice] voz *f* baixa -2. [vague feeling] traço *m*; **an ~ of sadness** um traço de tristeza.

undertook [ˌʌndəˈtʊk] *pt* ⊳ **undertake**.

undertow [ˈʌndətəʊ] *n* ressaca *f (no mar)*.

undervalue [ˌʌndəˈvæljuː] *vt* -1. [person] subestimar -2. [house, object] avaliar algo abaixo de seu real valor.

underwater [ˌʌndəˈwɔːtəʳ] <> *adj* submarino(na). <> *adv* debaixo d'água.

underwear [ˈʌndəweəʳ] *n (U)* roupa *f* íntima *oʀ* de baixo.

underweight [ˌʌndəˈweɪt] *adj* abaixo do peso.

underwent [ˌʌndəˈwent] *pt* ⊳ **undergo**.

underwired *adj* [bra] com suporte.

underworld [ˈʌndəˌwɜːld] *n* [criminal society]: **the ~** o submundo.

underwrite [ˈʌndəraɪt] *(pt -wrote, pp -written)* *vt* -1. *fml* [guarantee] comprometer-se com -2. [in insurance business] subscrever.

underwriter [ˈʌndəˌraɪtəʳ] *n* segurador *m*, -ra *f*.

underwritten [ˈʌndəˌrɪtn] *pp* ⊳ **underwrite**.

underwrote [ˈʌndərəʊt] *pt* ⊳ **underwrite**.

undeserved [ˌʌndɪˈzɜːvd] *adj* não-merecido(da).

undesirable [ˌʌndɪˈzaɪərəbl] *adj* indesejável.

undeveloped [ˌʌndɪˈveləpt] *adj* -1. [country] subdesenvolvido(da), em desenvolvimento -2. [land, resource] não explorado(da).

undid [ˌʌnˈdɪd] *pt* ⊳ **undo**.

undies [ˈʌndɪz] *npl inf* roupas *fpl* íntimas *oʀ* de baixo.

undignified [ʌnˈdɪgnɪfaɪd] *adj* indecoroso(sa), impróprio(pria).

undiluted [ˌʌndaɪˈljuːtɪd] *adj* -1. [quality, emotion] puro(ra) -2. [liquid] não-diluído(da).

undiplomatic [ˌʌndɪpləˈmætɪk] *adj* pouco diplomático(ca), indelicado(da).

undischarged [ˌʌndɪsˈtʃɑːdʒd] *adj* -1. [debt] pendente -2. [person]: **~ bankrupt** pessoa *f* falida não-reabilitada.

undisciplined [ʌnˈdɪsɪplɪnd] *adj* indisciplinado(da).

undiscovered [ˌʌndɪsˈkʌvəd] *adj* [unknown] não-descoberto(ta).

undisputed [ˌʌndɪˈspjuːtɪd] *adj* indiscutível.

undistinguished [ˌʌndɪˈstɪŋgwɪʃt] *adj* sem graça.

undivided [ˌʌndɪˈvaɪdɪd] *adj* [whole] inteiro(ra); **my ~ attention** toda a minha atenção.

undo [ˌʌnˈduː] *(pt -did, pp -done)* *vt* -1. [knot] desfazer, desatar -2. [buttons] desabotoar -3. [garment] desamarrar -4. [good work, efforts] anular.

undoing [ˌʌnˈduːɪŋ] *n (U) fml* ruína *f*, perdição *f*.

undone [ˌʌnˈdʌn] <> *pp* ⊳ **undo**. <> *adj* -1. [coat] desabotoado(da) -2. [shoe] desamarrado(da) -3. *fml* [not done] por fazer.

undoubted [ʌnˈdaʊtɪd] *adj* indubitável.

undoubtedly [ʌnˈdaʊtɪdlɪ] *adv* indubitavelmente.

undreamed-of [ʌnˈdriːmdɒv], **undreamt-of** [ʌnˈdremtɒv] *adj* [unimaginable] jamais imaginado(da).

undress [ˌʌnˈdres] <> *vt* despir. <> *vi* despir-se.

undressed [ˌʌnˈdrest] *adj* [person] despido(da); **to get ~** tirar a roupa, despir-se.

undue [ˌʌnˈdjuː] *adj fml* desmedido(da).

undulate [ˈʌndjʊleɪt] *vi fml* ondular.

unduly [ˌʌnˈdjuːlɪ] *adv fml* demasiadamente.

undying [ʌnˈdaɪɪŋ] *adj literary* imperecível.

unearned income [ˌʌnˈɜːnd-] *n (U)* renda *f* diferida.

unearth [ʌnˈɜːθ] *vt* -1. [dig up] desenterrar -2. *fig* [discover] descubrir.

unearthly [ʌnˈɜːθlɪ] *adj* -1. [ghostly] sobrenatural -2. *inf* [time of day]: **at an ~ hour in the morning** num horário absurdo da manhã.

unease [ʌnˈiːz] *n (U)* inquietação *f*, apreensão *f*.

uneasy [ʌnˈiːzɪ] *(compar -ier, superl -iest)* *adj* -1. [troubled] apreensivo(va) -2. [embarrassed] constrangido(da); **an ~ silence** um silêncio constrangedor -3. [peace, truce] duvidoso(sa).

uneatable [ˌʌnˈiːtəbl] *adj* -1. [dangerous to eat] que não se pode comer -2. [bad-tasting] indigesto(ta).

uneaten [ˌʌnˈiːtn] *adj*: **lots of ~ food** muita comida que sobrou.

uneconomic [ˈʌnˌiːkəˈnɒmɪk] *adj* pouco rentável.

uneducated [ˌʌnˈedjʊkeɪtɪd] *adj* -1. [person] inculto(ta), sem instrução -2. [behaviour, manners, speech] em que se percebe falta de instrução.

unemotional [ˌʌnɪˈməʊʃənl] *adj* -1. [person] impassível -2. [voice, tone] frio (fria) -3. [statement] objetivo(va).

unemployable [ˌʌnɪmˈplɔɪəbl] *adj* que dificilmente encontrará trabalho.

unemployed [ˌʌnɪmˈplɔɪd] ⟨⟩ *adj* [out-of-work] desempregado(da). ⟨⟩ *npl*: **the ~** os desempregados.

unemployment [ˌʌnɪmˈplɔɪməntl] *n* desemprego *m*.

unemployment benefit *UK*, **unemployment compensation** *US n (U)* ≃ seguro-desemprego *m*.

unenviable [ˌʌnˈenvɪəbl] *adj* nada invejável.

unequal [ˌʌnˈiːkwəl] *adj* desigual.

unequalled *UK*, **unequaled** *US* [ˌʌnˈiːkwəld] *adj* inigualável.

unequivocal [ˌʌnɪˈkwɪvəkl] *adj fml* inequívoco(ca).

unerring [ˌʌnˈɜːrɪŋ] *adj* infalível.

UNESCO [juːˈneskəʊ] (*abbr of* United Nations Educational, Scientific and Cultural Organization) *n* UNESCO *f*.

unethical [ʌnˈeθɪkl] *adj* antiético(ca).

uneven [ˌʌnˈiːvn] *adj* - **1.** [surface] irregular - **2.** [road] acidentado(da) - **3.** [performance, coverage *etc*] desigual, desparelho(lha) - **4.** [competition] injusto(ta).

uneventful [ˌʌnɪˈventfʊl] *adj* sem maiores incidentes.

unexceptional [ˌʌnɪkˈsepʃənl] *adj* sem nada de mais, normal.

unexpected [ˌʌnɪkˈspektɪd] *adj* inesperado(da).

unexpectedly [ˌʌnɪkˈspektɪdlɪ] *adv* inesperadamente.

unexplained [ˌʌnɪkˈspleɪnd] *adj* inexplicado(da).

unexploded [ˌʌnɪkˈspləʊdɪd] *adj* [bomb] que não detonou.

unexpurgated [ˌʌnˈekspɜːgeɪtɪd] *adj* sem cortes, na íntegra.

unfailing [ʌnˈfeɪlɪŋ] *adj* [loyalty, support, good humour] infalível.

unfair [ˌʌnˈfeəʳ] *adj* injusto(ta).

unfair dismissal *n (U)* demissão *f* sem justa causa.

unfairly *adv* injustamente.

unfairness [ˌʌnˈfeənɪs] *n* injustiça *f*.

unfaithful [ˌʌnˈfeɪθfʊl] *adj* [sexually] infiel.

unfamiliar [ˌʌnfəˈmɪljəʳ] *adj* - **1.** [not well-known] desconhecido(da) - **2.** [not acquainted]: **to be ~ with sb/sthg** desconhecer alguém/algo.

unfashionable [ˌʌnˈfæʃnəbl] *adj* ultrapassado(da).

unfasten [ˌʌnˈfɑːsn] *vt* - **1.** [garment, buttons] desabotoar - **2.** [rope] desamarrar.

unfavourable *UK*, **unfavorable** *US* [ˌʌnˈfeɪvrəbl] *adj* desfavorável.

unfeeling [ʌnˈfiːlɪŋ] *adj* insensível.

unfinished [ˌʌnˈfɪnɪʃt] *adj* inacabado(da).

unfit [ˌʌnˈfɪt] *adj* - **1.** [not in good shape] fora de forma - **2.** [not suitable]: **~ (for sthg)** inadequado(da) (para algo).

unflagging [ˌʌnˈflægɪŋ] *adj* - **1.** [support, enthusiasm] inesgotável - **2.** [supporter] incansável.

unflappable [ˌʌnˈflæpəbl] *adj esp UK* inabalável.

unflattering [ˌʌnˈflætərɪŋ] *adj* pouco favorecedor(ra).

unflinching [ʌnˈflɪntʃɪŋ] *adj* impávido(da).

unfold [ʌnˈfəʊld] ⟨⟩ *vt* - **1.** [open out] desdobrar - **2.** [explain] expor. ⟨⟩ *vi* [become clear] esclarecer-se.

unforeseeable [ˌʌnfɔːˈsiːəbl] *adj* imprevisível.

unforeseen [ˌʌnfɔːˈsiːn] *adj* imprevisto(ta).

unforgettable [ˌʌnfəˈgetəbl] *adj* inesquecível.

unforgivable [ˌʌnfəˈgɪvəbl] *adj* imperdoável.

unformatted [ˌʌnˈfɔːmætɪd] *adj COMPUT* não-formatado(da).

unfortunate [ʌnˈfɔːtʃnət] *adj* - **1.** [unlucky] azarento(ta) - **2.** [regrettable] lamentável.

unfortunately [ʌnˈfɔːtʃnətlɪ] *adv* infelizmente.

unfounded [ˌʌnˈfaʊndɪd] *adj* infundado(da).

unfriendly [ˌʌnˈfrendlɪ] (*compar* -ier, *superl* -iest) *adj* hostil.

unfulfilled [ˌʌnfʊlˈfɪld] *adj* - **1.** [ambition, promise, prophecy] que não se realizou - **2.** [person] insatisfeito(ta).

unfurl [ˌʌnˈfɜːl] *vt* - **1.** [flag, sail] desfraldar - **2.** [umbrella] abrir.

unfurnished [ˌʌnˈfɜːnɪʃt] *adj* desmobiliado(da), sem móveis.

ungainly [ʌnˈgeɪnlɪ] *adj* desajeitado(da).

ungenerous [ˌʌnˈdʒenərəs] *adj* - **1.** [mean] miserável; **a not ~ gift** um presente bastante generoso - **2.** [uncharitable] pouco generoso(sa).

ungodly [ˌʌnˈgɒdlɪ] *adj* - **1.** [irreligious] ímpio(pia) - **2.** *inf* [unreasonable]: **why are you phoning me at this ~ hour?** por que você está me ligando nesta hora da madrugada?

ungrateful [ʌnˈgreɪtfʊl] *adj* mal-agradecido(da).

ungratefulness [ʌnˈgreɪtfʊlnɪs] *n (U)* ingratidão *f*.

unguarded [ˌʌnˈgɑːdɪd] *adj* - **1.** [not guarded] desprotegido(da) - **2.** [careless]: **in an ~ moment** num momento de descuido.

unhappily [ʌnˈhæpɪlɪ] *adv* - **1.** [sadly] tristemente - **2.** *fml* [unfortunately] lamentavelmente.

unhappiness [ʌnˈhæpɪnɪs] *n (U)* infelicidade *f*.

unhappy [ʌnˈhæpɪ] (*compar* -ier, *superl* -iest) *adj* - **1.** [sad] triste - **2.** [uneasy]: **to be ~ (with OR about sthg)** estar descontente(com algo) - **3.** *fml* [unfortunate] lamentável, infeliz.

unharmed [ˌʌnˈhɑːmd] *adj* ileso(sa).

UNHCR (*abbr of* United Nations High Commission for Refugees) *n organização internacional que faz parte da ONU responsável pela ajuda a refugiados.*

unhealthy [ʌnˈhelθɪ] (*compar* -ier, *superl* -iest) *adj* - **1.** [in bad health] doentio(tia) - **2.** [causing bad health] insalubre - **3.** *fig* [undesirable] prejudicial.

unheard [ˌʌnˈhɜːd] *adj*: **to be OR go ~** passar sem ser ouvido(da).

unheard-of [ʌnˈhɜːd-] *adj* - **1.** [unknown, completely absent] inaudito(ta) - **2.** [unprecedented] sem precedente.

unheeded [ˌʌnˈhiːdɪd] *adj*: **to go ~** passar desapercebido(da).

unhelpful [ˌʌnˈhelpfʊl] *adj* - **1.** [unwilling to help - person] pouco prestativo(va); [- attitude] com má vontade - **2.** [not useful] inútil.

unhindered [ʌnˈhɪndəd] *adj* sem impedimentos.

unhook [ˌʌnˈhʊk] *vt* - **1.** [unfasten hooks of] desenganchar - **2.** [remove from hook] desprender.

unhurt [ˌʌnˈhɜːt] *adj* ileso(sa).

unhygienic [ˌʌnhaɪˈdʒiːnɪk] *adj* anti-higiênico(ca).

uni (*abbr of* university) *n UK inf* universidade *f*.

UNICEF [ˈjuːnɪˌsef] (*abbr of* United Nations Children's Fund) *n* UNICEF *f*.

unicorn [ˈjuːnɪkɔːn] *n* unicórnio *m*.

unicycle [ˈjuːnɪsaɪkl] *n* monociclo *m*.

unidentified [ˌʌnaɪˈdentɪfaɪd] *adj* não-identificado(da).

unidentified flying object *n* objeto *m* voador não-identificado.

unification [ˌjuːnɪfɪˈkeɪʃn] *n (U)* unificação *f*.

uniform [ˈjuːnɪfɔːm] <> *adj* uniforme. <> *n* uniforme *m*.

uniformity [ˌjuːnɪˈfɔːmətɪ] *n (U)* uniformidade *f*.

uniformly [ˈjuːnɪfɔːmlɪ] *adv* uniformemente.

unify [ˈjuːnɪfaɪ] (*pt* & *pp* -ied) *vt* unificar.

unifying [ˈjuːnɪfaɪɪŋ] *adj* unificador(ra).

unilateral [ˌjuːnɪˈlætərəl] *adj* unilateral.

unimaginable [ˌʌnɪˈmædʒɪnəbl] *adj* inimaginável.

unimaginative [ˌʌnɪˈmædʒɪnətɪv] *adj* sem imaginação.

unimpaired [ˌʌnɪmˈpeəd] *adj* -1. [gen] intacto(ta) -2. [health] inalterado(da).

unimpeded [ˌʌnɪmˈpiːdɪd] *adj* desimpedido(da), sem obstáculos.

unimportant [ˌʌnɪmˈpɔːtənt] *adj* insignificante, sem importância.

unimpressed [ˌʌnɪmˈprest] *adj* pouco impressionado(da).

uninhabited [ˌʌnɪnˈhæbɪtɪd] *adj* desabitado(da).

uninhibited [ˌʌnɪnˈhɪbɪtɪd] *adj* desinibido(da).

uninitiated [ˌʌnɪˈnɪʃɪeɪtɪd] *npl*: the ~ os inexperientes.

uninjured [ˌʌnˈɪndʒəd] *adj* ileso(sa).

uninspiring [ˌʌnɪnˈspaɪrɪŋ] *adj* nada inspirador(ra).

unintelligent [ˌʌnɪnˈtelɪdʒent] *adj* pouco inteligente.

unintentional [ˌʌnɪnˈtenʃənl] *adj* involuntário(ria).

uninterested [ˌʌnˈɪntrəstɪd] *adj* desinteressado(da).

uninterrupted [ˈʌnˌɪntəˈrʌptɪd] *adj* ininterrupto(ta).

uninvited [ˌʌnɪnˈvaɪtɪd] *adj* não-convidado(da).

union [ˈjuːnjən] <> *n* -1. [trade union] sindicato *m* -2. [alliance] união *f*. <> *comp* sindical.

Unionist [ˈjuːnjənɪst] *n UK* POL membro de partido político que deseja que a Irlanda do Norte continue fazendo parte do Reino Unido, unionista *mf*.

unionize, -ise [ˈjuːnjənaɪz] *vt* sindicalizar.

unionized, -ised *adj* sindicalizado(da).

Union Jack *n*: the ~ a bandeira do Reino Unido.

union shop *n US* empresa na qual todos os empregados devem pertencer a um sindicato.

unique [juːˈniːk] *adj* -1. [unparalleled] incomparável, único(ca) -2. *fml* [peculiar, exclusive]: ~ to sb/sthg peculiar a alguém/algo.

uniquely [juːˈniːklɪ] *adv* -1. [exclusively] unicamente -2. [exceptionally] excepcionalmente.

unisex [ˈjuːnɪseks] *adj* unissex *inv*.

unison [ˈjuːnɪzn] *n (U)* [agreement] harmonia *f*; in ~ [simultaneously] em uníssono.

UNISON [ˈjuːnɪzn] *n sindicato gigante que reúne a maioria dos funcionários britânicos*, ≃ CUT *f*.

unit [ˈjuːnɪt] *n* -1. [gen] unidade *f* -2. [piece of furniture] módulo *m*.

unit cost *n* custo *m* unitário.

unite [juːˈnaɪt] <> *vt* unificar. <> *vi* unir-se, juntar-se.

united [juːˈnaɪtɪd] *adj* -1. [in harmony] unido(da); they are ~ on this point eles estão todos de acordo neste ponto -2. [unified] unificado(da).

United Arab Emirates *npl*: the ~ os Emirados Árabes Unidos.

united front *n*: to present a ~ fazer frente única.

United Kingdom *n*: the ~ o Reino Unido.

United Nations *n*: the ~ as Nações Unidas.

United States *n*: the ~ (of America) os Estados Unidos (da América); in the ~ nos Estados Unidos.

unit price *n* preço *m* unitário.

unit trust *n UK* fundo *m* de investimento.

unity [ˈjuːnətɪ] *n* -1. [union] união *f*, unidade *f* -2. [harmony] união *f*.

Univ. (*abbr of* University) univ.

universal [ˌjuːnɪˈvɜːsl] *adj* [belief, truth] universal.

universal joint *n* junta *f* universal.

universe [ˈjuːnɪvɜːs] *n* ASTRON universo *m*.

university [ˌjuːnɪˈvɜːsətɪ] (*pl* -ies) <> *n* universidade *f*. <> *comp* universitário(ria); ~ student estudante *m* universitário, -ria *f*.

unjust [ˌʌnˈdʒʌst] *adj* injusto(ta).

unjustifiable [ʌnˈdʒʌstɪˌfaɪəbl] *adj* injustificável.

unjustified [ʌnˈdʒʌstɪfaɪd] *adj* injustificado(da).

unkempt [ˌʌnˈkempt] *adj* [hair, beard, appearance] desajeitado(da).

unkind [ʌnˈkaɪnd] *adj* -1. [gen] indelicado(da) -2. *fig* [climate] rigoroso(sa).

unkindly [ʌnˈkaɪndlɪ] *adv* de forma indelicada.

unknown [ˌʌnˈnəʊn] <> *adj* desconhecido(da). <> *n* -1. [unknown thing]: the ~ o desconhecido -2. [unknown person] desconhecido *m*, -da *f*, estranho *m*, -nha *f*.

unlace [ˌʌnˈleɪs] *vt* desamarrar.

unladen [ˌʌnˈleɪdn] *adj* sem carga.

unlawful [ˌʌnˈlɔːful] *adj* ilegal.

unleaded [ˌʌnˈledɪd] *adj* sem chumbo.

unleash [ˌʌnˈliːʃ] *vt literary* desencadear.

unleavened [ˌʌnˈlevnd] *adj* [bread] sem fermento.

unless [ənˈles] *conj* a menos que; ~ I'm mistaken, ... a não ser que eu esteja enganado, ...

unlicensed, unlicenced *US* [ˌʌnˈlaɪsənst] *adj* -1. [fishing, hunting] proibido(da) -2. [car] não-licenciado(da) -3. [premises, restaurant] sem licença.

unlike [ˌʌnˈlaɪk] *prep* -1. [different from] diferente de -2. [in contrast to] ao contrário de -3. [not typical of] atípico(ca); it's very ~ you to complain você não é de reclamar.

unlikely [ʌnˈlaɪklɪ] *adj* -1. [not probable] improvável -2. [bizarre] estranho(nha).

unlimited [ʌnˈlɪmɪtɪd] *adj* ilimitado(da).

unlisted [ʌn'lɪstɪd] adj US [phone number] fora da lista.

unlit [ˌʌn'lɪt] adj -**1.** [not burning] apagado(da) -**2.** [dark] sem luz.

unload [ˌʌn'ləʊd] vt -**1.** [gen] descarregar -**2.** fig [unburden]: **to ~ sthg on(to) sb** descarregar algo em alguém.

unlock [ˌʌn'lɒk] vt destrancar, abrir (com chave).

unloved [ˌʌn'lʌvd] adj: **to be/feel ~** não ser/se sentir amado(da).

unluckily [ʌn'lʌkɪlɪ] adv infelizmente; **~ for us, ...** para nosso azar, ...

unlucky [ʌn'lʌkɪ] (compar -ier, superl -iest) adj -**1.** [unfortunate] infeliz -**2.** [bringing bad luck] de mau agouro.

unmanageable [ʌn'mænɪdʒəbl] adj -**1.** [vehicle, situation] fora de controle -**2.** [size, parcel] de difícil manuseio.

unmanly [ˌʌn'mænlɪ] (compar -ier, superl -iest) adj [behaviour, attitude] indigno(na) de um homem.

unmanned [ˌʌn'mænd] adj não-tripulado(da).

unmarked [ˌʌn'mɑːkt] adj -**1.** [uninjured] sem marca -**2.** [unidentified] não-identificado(da).

unmarried [ˌʌn'mærɪd] adj solteiro(ra).

unmask [ˌʌn'mɑːsk] vt desmascarar.

unmatched [ˌʌn'mætʃt] adj inigualável.

unmentionable [ʌn'menʃnəbl] adj indizível.

unmistakable [ˌʌnmɪ'steɪkəbl] adj inconfundível.

unmitigated [ʌn'mɪtɪgeɪtɪd] adj completo(ta), absoluto(ta); **he's talking ~ nonsense!** ele não está dizendo coisa com coisa!

unmoved [ˌʌn'muːvd] adj: **to be ~ by sthg** ser indiferente a algo.

unnamed [ˌʌn'neɪmd] adj [anonymous] anônimo(ma).

unnatural [ʌn'nætʃrəl] adj -**1.** [unusual, strange] estranho(nha) -**2.** [affected] pouco natural.

unnecessary [ʌn'nesəsərɪ] adj desnecessário(ria).

unnerving [ˌʌn'nɜːvɪŋ] adj enervante.

unnoticed [ˌʌn'nəʊtɪst] adj despercebido(da).

UNO (abbr of United Nations Organization) n ONU f.

unobserved [ˌʌnəb'zɜːvd] adj desapercebido(da).

unobtainable [ˌʌnəb'teɪnəbl] adj inacessível.

unobtrusive [ˌʌnəb'truːsɪv] adj discreto(ta).

unoccupied [ˌʌn'ɒkjʊpaɪd] adj desocupado(da).

unofficial [ˌʌnə'fɪʃl] adj não-oficial.

unopened [ˌʌn'əʊpənd] adj fechado(da).

unorthodox [ˌʌn'ɔːθədɒks] adj não-ortodoxo(xa).

unpack [ˌʌn'pæk] <> vt -**1.** [bag, suitcase] desfazer -**2.** [clothes, books, shopping] desembrulhar. <> vi desfazer as malas.

unpaid [ˌʌn'peɪd] adj não-remunerado(da).

unpalatable [ʌn'pælətəbl] adj -**1.** [unpleasant to taste] intragável -**2.** fig [difficult to accept] desagradável.

unparalleled [ʌn'pærəleld] adj sem paralelo.

unpatriotic [ˈʌnˌpætrɪ'ɒtɪk] adj antipatriótico(ca).

unpick [ˌʌn'pɪk] vt descosturar.

unpin [ˌʌn'pɪn] (pt & pp -ned, cont -ning) vt [remove pin from] desprender.

unplanned [ˌʌn'plænd] adj não-planejado(da).

unpleasant [ʌn'pleznt] adj desagradável.

unpleasantness [ʌn'plezntnɪs] n (U) -**1.** [of person, experience, weather] dissabor m -**2.** [discord] desentendimento m.

unplug [ʌn'plʌg] (pt & pp -ged, cont -ging) vt ELEC desligar.

unpolished [ˌʌn'pɒlɪʃt] adj -**1.** [furniture, brass, shoes] não-polido(da) -**2.** [person, manner] grosseiro(ra).

unpolluted [ˌʌnpə'luːtɪd] adj despoluído(da).

unpopular [ˌʌn'pɒpjʊlə'] adj impopular.

unprecedented [ʌn'presɪdəntɪd] adj sem precedente.

unpredictable [ˌʌnprɪ'dɪktəbl] adj imprevisível.

unprejudiced [ˌʌn'predʒʊdɪst] adj imparcial.

unprepared [ˌʌnprɪ'peəd] adj: **to be ~ (for sthg)** não estar preparado(da) (para algo).

unprepossessing [ˈʌnˌpriːpə'zesɪŋ] adj pouco atraente.

unpretentious [ˌʌnprɪ'tenʃəs] adj despretencioso(sa).

unprincipled [ʌn'prɪnsəpld] adj inescrupuloso(sa).

unprintable [ˌʌn'prɪntəbl] adj impublicável.

unproductive [ˌʌnprə'dʌktɪv] adj improdutivo(va).

unprofessional [ˌʌnprə'feʃənl] adj não-profissional.

unprofitable [ˌʌn'prɒfɪtəbl] adj [not making a profit] não-lucrativo(va).

unprompted [ˌʌn'prɒmptɪd] adj espontâneo(nea).

unpronounceable [ˌʌnprə'naʊnsəbl] adj impronunciável.

unprotected [ˌʌnprə'tektɪd] adj [person, skin] desprotegido(da); **~ sex** relação f sexual desprotegida.

unprovoked [ˌʌnprə'vəʊkt] adj não-provocado(da), espontâneo(nea).

unpublished [ˌʌn'pʌblɪʃt] adj inédito(ta).

unpunished [ˌʌn'pʌnɪʃt] adj: **to go ~** ficar impune.

unqualified [ˌʌn'kwɒlɪfaɪd] adj -**1.** [not qualified] desqualificado(da) -**2.** [total, complete] absoluto(ta).

unquestionable [ʌn'kwestʃənəbl] adj inquestionável.

unquestioning [ʌn'kwestʃənɪŋ] adj incondicional.

unravel [ʌn'rævl] (UK pt & pp -led, cont -ling, US pt & pp -ed, cont -ing) <> vt -**1.** [undo] desembaraçar -**2.** fig [solve] elucidar. <> vi [become undone] desembaraçar-se.

unreadable [ˌʌn'riːdəbl] adj -**1.** [gen] ilegível -**2.** [difficult, tedious to read] difícil de ler.

unreal [ˌʌn'rɪəl] adj [strange] irreal.

unrealistic [ˌʌnrɪə'lɪstɪk] adj pouco realista.

unreasonable [ʌn'riːznəbl] adj -**1.** [unfair, not sensible] injusto(ta) -**2.** [not justifiable] absurdo(da), irracional.

unrecognizable [ˌʌn'rekəgnaɪzəbl] adj irreconhecível.

unrecognized [ˌʌn'rekəgnaɪzd] adj -**1.** [not known, noticed] não-reconhecido(da); **to be ~** não ser reconhecido(da) -**2.** [unacknowledged] inconfesso(sa).

unrecorded [ˌʌnrɪˈkɔːdɪd] adj -1. [remark, fact, event] não-registrado(da) -2. [music, voice] desconhecido(-da).

unrefined [ˌʌnrɪˈfaɪnd] adj -1. [petrol, sugar, flour] não-refinado(da) -2. [person, manners] impolido(da).

unrehearsed [ˌʌnrɪˈhɜːst] adj improvisado(da).

unrelated [ˌʌnrɪˈleɪtɪd] adj: to be ~ (to sthg) não estar relacionado(da) (a algo).

unrelenting [ˌʌnrɪˈlentɪŋ] adj -1. [pressure] contínuo(nua) -2. [questions] implacável.

unreliable [ˌʌnrɪˈlaɪəbl] adj inconfiável.

unrelieved [ˌʌnrɪˈliːvd] adj -1. [pain] que não alivia -2. [gloom, boredom]: a period of ~ boredom um período de tédio sem fim.

unremarkable [ˌʌnrɪˈmɑːkəbl] adj comum.

unremitting [ˌʌnrɪˈmɪtɪŋ] adj incessante.

unrepeatable [ˌʌnrɪˈpiːtəbl] adj -1. [not fit to be repeated] irrepetível -2. [exceptional] excepcional.

unrepentant [ˌʌnrɪˈpentənt] adj não-arrependido(da).

unrepresentative [ˌʌnreprɪˈzentətɪv] adj pouco representativo(va); ~ of sthg pouco representativo de algo.

unrequited [ˌʌnrɪˈkwaɪtɪd] adj não-correspondido(da).

unreserved [ˌʌnrɪˈzɜːvd] adj -1. [admiration, support, approval] integral -2. [seat, place] não-reservado(da).

unresolved [ˌʌnrɪˈzɒlvd] adj sem solução.

unresponsive [ˌʌnrɪˈspɒnsɪv] adj: to be ~ to sthg ser indiferente a algo.

unrest [ʌnˈrest] n (U) agitação f.

unrestrained [ˌʌnrɪˈstreɪnd] adj desenfreado(da).

unrestricted [ˌʌnrɪˈstrɪktɪd] adj irrestrito(ta).

unrewarding [ˌʌnrɪˈwɔːdɪŋ] adj pouco compensador(ra).

unripe [ʌnˈraɪp] adj verde.

unrivalled UK, **unrivaled** US [ʌnˈraɪvld] adj incomparável.

unroll [ʌnˈrəʊl] vt [unfold] desenrolar.

unruffled [ʌnˈrʌfld] adj [calm] sereno(na).

unruly [ʌnˈruːlɪ] (compar -ier, superl -iest) adj -1. [wayward] indisciplinado(da) -2. [untidy] desarrumado(da).

unsafe [ʌnˈseɪf] adj -1. [dangerous] perigoso(sa) -2. [in danger] inseguro(ra).

unsaid [ʌnˈsed] adj: to leave sthg ~ não falar algo.

unsaleable, unsalable US [ʌnˈseɪləbl] adj invendável.

unsatisfactory [ˈʌnˌsætɪsˈfæktərɪ] adj insatisfatório(ria).

unsavoury, unsavory US [ʌnˈseɪvərɪ] adj -1. [behaviour, person, habits] (moralmente) ofensivo(va) -2. [smell] repugnante.

unscathed [ʌnˈskeɪðd] adj ileso(sa), são e salvo, sã e salva.

unscheduled [UK ˌʌnˈʃedjʊld, US ˌʌnˈskedʒʊld] adj imprevisto(ta).

unscientific [ˈʌnˌsaɪənˈtɪfɪk] adj não-científico(ca).

unscrew [ʌnˈskruː] vt -1. [lid, bottle top] desenroscar -2. [sign, mirror] desparafusar.

unscripted [ʌnˈskrɪptɪd] adj de improviso.

unscrupulous [ʌnˈskruːpjʊləs] adj inescrupuloso(sa).

unseat [ʌnˈsiːt] vt -1. [rider] derrubar (da sela) -2. fig [politician] depor.

unseeded [ʌnˈsiːdɪd] adj [player, team] que não é cabeça de chave.

unseemly [ʌnˈsiːmlɪ] (compar -ier, superl -iest) adj inconveniente.

unseen [ʌnˈsiːn] <> adj [not observed] despercebido(da); [not visible] escondido(da). <> adv despercebido(da).

unselfish [ʌnˈselfɪʃ] adj desinteressado(da).

unselfishly [ʌnˈselfɪʃlɪ] adv desinteressadamente.

unsettle [ʌnˈsetl] vt inquietar.

unsettled [ʌnˈsetld] adj -1. [unstable - person] inquieto(ta); [- weather] instável -2. [unfinished, unresolved - argument] incerto(ta); [- issue] vago(ga) -3. [account, bill] duvidoso(sa) -4. [area, region] despovoado(da).

unsettling [ʌnˈsetlɪŋ] adj inquietante.

unshak(e)able [ʌnˈʃeɪkəbl] adj inabalável.

unshaven [ʌnˈʃeɪvn] adj [face, chin] com a barba por fazer.

unsheathe [ʌnˈʃiːð] vt desembainhar.

unsightly [ʌnˈsaɪtlɪ] adj de péssima aparência.

unskilled [ʌnˈskɪld] adj [worker] não-especializado(da), incapaz; [work] não-especializado(da).

unsociable [ʌnˈsəʊʃəbl] adj [person, place] anti-social.

unsocial [ʌnˈsəʊʃl] adj: to work ~ hours trabalhar fora de hora.

unsold [ʌnˈsəʊld] adj não-vendido(da).

unsolicited [ʌnsəˈlɪsɪtɪd] adj que não foi pedido(da).

unsolved [ʌnˈsɒlvd] adj não-solucionado(da).

unsophisticated [ˌʌnsəˈfɪstɪkeɪtɪd] adj -1. [gen] simples -2. [person - in dress, style] pouco sofisticado(da); [- in attitudes] simples, natural.

unsound [ʌnˈsaʊnd] adj -1. [based on false ideas] equivocado(da) -2. [in poor condition] inseguro(ra); to be of ~ mind estar fora de si.

unspeakable [ʌnˈspiːkəbl] adj terrível.

unspeakably [ʌnˈspiːkəblɪ] adv terrivelmente.

unspecified [ʌnˈspesɪfaɪd] adj indefinido(da).

unspoiled [ʌnˈspɔɪld], **unspoilt** [ʌnˈspɔɪlt] adj -1. [person] incólume -2. [place] intocado(da).

unspoken [ʌnˈspəʊkən] adj -1. [not expressed openly] subentendido(da) -2. [tacit] tácito(ta).

unsporting [ʌnˈspɔːtɪŋ] adj pouco esportivo(va).

unstable [ʌnˈsteɪbl] adj instável.

unstated [ʌnˈsteɪtɪd] adj não-afirmado(da).

unsteady [ʌnˈstedɪ] (compar -ier, superl -iest) adj -1. [person, step, voice] inseguro(ra) -2. [chair, ladder] pouco seguro(ra).

unstinting [ʌnˈstɪntɪŋ] adj irrestrito(ta).

unstoppable [ʌnˈstɒpəbl] adj inevitável.

unstrap [ʌnˈstræp] (pt & pp -ped, cont -ping) vt desapertar.

unstructured [ʌnˈstrʌktʃəd] adj desorganizado(da).

unstuck [ʌnˈstʌk] adj: to come ~ [notice, stamp,

label] descolar-se; *fig* [plan, system] degringolar; *fig* [person] dar-se mal.

unsubstantiated [ˌʌnsəb'stænʃɪeɪtɪd] *adj* **-1.** [statement, story, report] que não foi confirmado(da) **-2.** [accusation] sem provas.

unsuccessful [ˌʌnsək'sesfʊl] *adj* malsucedido(da).

unsuccessfully [ˌʌnsək'sesfʊlɪ] *adv* em vão.

unsuitable [ˌʌn'su:təbl] *adj* inconveniente; **to be ~ for sthg** ser inapropriado(da) para algo.

unsuited [ˌʌn'su:tɪd] *adj* **-1.** [not appropriate]: **to be ~ to** OR **for sthg** ser inadequado(da) para algo. **-2.** [not compatible]: **to be ~ (to each other)** ser totalmente incompatível (um em relação ao outro).

unsung [ˌʌn'sʌŋ] *adj* [deed, hero] não-aclamado(da).

unsure [ˌʌn'ʃɔ:'] *adj* **-1.** [not confident]: **to be ~ (of o.s.)** não ser seguro(ra) (de si) **-2.** [not certain]: **to be ~ (about/of sthg)** não ter certeza (sobre/de algo).

unsurpassed [ˌʌnsə'pɑ:st] *adj* incomparável.

unsuspecting [ˌʌnsə'spektɪŋ] *adj* insuspeitável.

unsweetened [ˌʌn'swi:tnd] *adj* sem açúcar.

unswerving [ʌn'swɜ:vɪŋ] *adj* resoluto(ta).

unsympathetic ['ʌnˌsɪmpə'θetɪk] *adj* [unfeeling] insensível.

untamed [ˌʌn'teɪmd] *adj* **-1.** [not domesticated] não-domesticado(da) **-2.** [not cultivated] não-cultivado(da) **-3.** [not subjugated] indômito(ta).

untangle [ˌʌn'tæŋgl] *vt* [disentangle] desemaranhar.

untapped [ˌʌn'tæpt] *adj* [unexploited] inexplorado(da).

untaxed [ˌʌn'tækst] *adj* isento(ta) de imposto.

untenable [ˌʌn'tenəbl] *adj* insustentável.

unthinkable [ʌn'θɪŋkəbl] *adj* [inconceivable] inconcebível.

unthinkingly [ʌn'θɪŋkɪŋlɪ] *adv* sem pensar.

untidy [ʌn'taɪdɪ] (*compar* **-ier**, *superl* **-iest**) *adj* **-1.** [gen] desarrumado(da) **-2.** [person, work] desleixado(da).

untie [ˌʌn'taɪ] (*cont* **untying**) *vt* [string, knot, bonds] desatar; [prisoner] soltar.

until [ən'tɪl] <> *prep* **-1.** [up to, till] até **-2.** (*after negative*) antes de; **I can't come ~ tomorrow** eu não posso vir antes de amanhã. <> *conj* **-1.** [up to, till] até; **we were told to wait ~ he arrived** pediram-nos para esperar até que ele chegasse OR até ele chegar **-2.** (*after negative*) antes de, até; **they never help ~ I tell them to** eles só ajudam quando eu peço; **don't sign ~ you've checked everything** não assine nada antes de ter verificado tudo.

untimely [ʌn'taɪmlɪ] *adj* **-1.** [premature] prematuro(ra) **-2.** [inopportune] inoportuno(na).

untiring [ʌn'taɪərɪŋ] *adj* incansável.

untold [ˌʌn'təʊld] *adj* [incalculable, vast] inimaginável.

untouched [ˌʌn'tʌtʃt] *adj* intocado(da).

untoward [ˌʌntə'wɔ:d] *adj* [unfortunate] inconveniente.

untrained [ˌʌn'treɪnd] *adj* destreinado(da).

untrammelled UK, **untrammeled** US [ʌn'træməld] *adj fml* irrestrito(ta); **~ by** não restrito(ta) a, livre de.

untranslatable [ˌʌntræns'leɪtəbl] *adj* intraduzível.

untreated [ˌʌn'tri:tɪd] *adj* **-1.** MED não-tratado(da) **-2.** [unprocessed] sem tratamento.

untried [ˌʌn'traɪd] *adj* [not tested] não-testado(da).

untroubled [ˌʌn'trʌbld] *adj* [undisturbed]: **to be ~ by sthg** ficar calmo(ma) diante de algo.

untrue [ˌʌn'tru:] *adj* **-1.** [inaccurate] falso(sa) **-2.** [unfaithful, disloyal]: **to be ~ to sb** ser infiel a alguém.

untrustworthy [ˌʌn'trʌstˌwɜ:ðɪ] *adj* indigno(na) de confiança.

untruth [ʌn'tru:θ] *n* inverdade *f*.

untruthful [ˌʌn'tru:θfʊl] *adj* mentiroso(sa).

untutored [ˌʌn'tju:təd] *adj* [untrained] destreinado(da).

unusable [ˌʌn'ju:zəbl] *adj* inutilizável, imprestável.

unused [*sense 1* ˌʌn'ju:zd, *sense 2* ʌn'ju:st] *adj* **-1.** [new] novo(va) **-2.** [unaccustomed]: **to be ~ to sthg/to doing sthg** não estar acostumado(da) a algo/a fazer algo.

unusual [ʌn'ju:ʒl] *adj* [rare] raro(ra).

unusually [ʌn'ju:ʒəlɪ] *adv* [exceptionally] excepcionalmente.

unvarnished [ʌn'vɑ:nɪʃt] *adj fig* [plain, straightforward] cru.

unveil [ˌʌn'veɪl] *vt* **-1.** [remove covering from] desvelar **-2.** *fig* [reveal, divulge] expor.

unwaged [ˌʌn'weɪdʒd] *adj* UK desassalariado(da).

unwanted [ˌʌn'wɒntɪd] *adj* indesejado(da).

unwarranted [ʌn'wɒrəntɪd] *adj* injustificado(da).

unwavering [ʌn'weɪvərɪŋ] *adj* firme.

unwelcome [ʌn'welkəm] *adj* **-1.** [news, experience] desagradável **-2.** [visitor] desconfortável.

unwell [ˌʌn'wel] *adj*: **to be/feel ~** estar/sentir-se indisposto(ta).

unwholesome [ˌʌn'həʊlsəm] *adj* **-1.** [food, drink] insalubre **-2.** [behaviour, thought] doentio(tia) **-3.** [appearance] doente.

unwieldy [ʌn'wi:ldɪ] (*compar* **-ier**, *superl* **-iest**) *adj* **-1.** [cumbersome] pesado(da) **-2.** *fig* [inefficient] ineficiente.

unwilling [ˌʌn'wɪlɪŋ] *adj* [reluctant] relutante; **to be ~ to do sthg** estar relutante para/em fazer algo.

unwind [ˌʌn'waɪnd] (*pt & pp* **-wound**) <> *vt* desenrolar. <> *vi fig* [person] relaxar.

unwise [ˌʌn'waɪz] *adj* imprudente.

unwitting [ʌn'wɪtɪŋ] *adj fml* inadvertido(da), impremeditado(da).

unwittingly [ʌn'wɪtɪŋlɪ] *adv fml* inadvertidamente.

unworkable [ˌʌn'wɜ:kəbl] *adj* impraticável.

unworldly [ˌʌn'wɜ:ldlɪ] *adj* [spiritual, ascetic] espiritual.

unworthy [ʌn'wɜ:ðɪ] (*compar* **-ier**, *superl* **-iest**) *adj* [undeserving]: **to be ~ of sb/sthg** ser indigno(na) de alguém/algo.

unwound [ˌʌn'waʊnd] *pt & pp* ▷ **unwind**.

unwrap [ˌʌn'ræp] (*pt & pp* **-ped**, *cont* **-ping**) *vt* desembrulhar.

unwritten law [ˌʌn'rɪtn-] *n* lei *f* não-escrita.

unyielding [ʌn'ji:ldɪŋ] *adj* inflexível.

unzip [ˌʌn'zɪp] (*pt & pp* **-ped**, *cont* **-ping**) *vt* abrir o zíper de.

unzip [ˌʌn'zɪp] *vt* descompactar.

up [ʌp] <> *adv* **-1.** [toward higher position, level] para cima; **to go ~** subir; **prices are going ~** os preços

estão subindo; **we walked ~ to the top** subimos
até o topo; **to pick sthg ~** apanhar algo. **-2.** [in
higher position]: **she's ~ in her bedroom** está lá
em cima no seu quarto; **~ there** ali OR lá em cima.
-3. [into upright position]: **to stand ~** pôr-se em OR
de pé; **to sit ~** [from lying position] sentar-se; [sit
straight] sentar-se direito. **-4.** [northward]: **~ in Canada** no Canadá. **-5.** [in phrases]: **to walk ~ and
down** andar de um lado para o outro; **to jump ~
and down** dar pulos; **~ to six weeks** até seis
semanas; **~ to ten people** até dez pessoas; **are
you ~ to travelling?** você está em condições de
viajar?; **what are you ~ to?** o que você está
tramando?; **it's ~ to you** depende de você; **~ until ten o'clock** até às dez horas. ⬦ *prep* **-1.** [to-
ward higher position]: **to walk ~ a hill** subir um
monte; **I went ~ the stairs** subi as escadas. **-2.** [in
higher position] no topo de; **~ a hill** no topo de um
monte; **~ a ladder** no topo de uma escada. **-3.** [at
end of]: **they live ~ the block from us** eles vivem
no final da nossa rua. ⬦ *adj* **-1.** [out of bed]
levantado(da); **I got ~ at six today** levantei-me
às seis hoje. **-2.** [at an end]: **time's ~** acabou-se o
tempo. **-3.** [rising]: **the ~ escalator** a escada
rolante ascendente. ⬦ *n:* **~s and downs** altos e
baixos *mpl*.

up-and-coming *adj* promissor(ra).

up-and-up *n:* **to be on the ~** *UK* [improving] estar
para cima; *US* [honest] ser confiável.

upbeat [ˈʌpbiːt] *adj* otimista.

upbraid [ʌpˈbreɪd] *vt fml:* **to ~ sb (for sthg/for
doing sthg)** repreender alguém por algo/por
fazer algo.

upbringing [ˈʌpˌbrɪŋɪŋ] *n (U)* educação *f*.

update [ˌʌpˈdeɪt] *vt* [bring up-to-date] atualizar.

upend [ʌpˈend] *vt* [stand on end] pôr de pé; [turn upside down] virar de ponta-cabeça.

upfront [ˌʌpˈfrʌnt] ⬦ *adj:* **to be ~ (about sthg)**
ser franco(ca) sobre algo. ⬦ *adv* adiantado(da).

upgrade [ˌʌpˈgreɪd] *vt* **-1.** [improve - facilities] melhorar; [- computer system] fazer um upgrade em
-2. [promote] promover.

upheaval [ʌpˈhiːvl] *n* convulsão *f*.

upheld [ʌpˈheld] *pt & pp* **⊳ uphold**.

uphill [ˌʌpˈhɪl] ⬦ *adj* **-1.** [rising] íngreme **-2.** *fig*
[difficult] árduo(dua). ⬦ *adv* para cima.

uphold [ʌpˈhəʊld] *(pt & pp* **-held)** *vt* [support] apoiar.

upholster [ʌpˈhəʊlstə^r] *vt* estofar.

upholstery [ʌpˈhəʊlstərɪ] *n (U)* estofamento *m*.

upkeep [ˈʌpkiːp] *n (U)* manutenção *f*.

upland [ˈʌplənd] *adj* no planalto.
⬦ **uplands** *npl* planaltos *mpl*.

uplift [ʌpˈlɪft] *vt* [cheer] extasiar.

uplifting [ʌpˈlɪftɪŋ] *adj* [cheering] extasiante, edificante.

uplighter *n* ELEC *luminária que projeta a luz
para cima.*

up-market *adj* de alta categoria.

upon [əˈpɒn] *prep fml* **-1.** [gen] sobre; **the weekend is
~ us** o final de semana já está em cima da gente;
summer is ~ us o verão está chegando **-2.** [when]
após.

upper [ˈʌpə^r] ⬦ *adj* **-1.** [gen] superior **-2.** GEOGR [in-
land] alto(ta). ⬦ *n* [of shoe] gáspea *f*.

upper class *n:* **the ~** a alta classe.
⬦ **upper-class** *adj* de alta classe.

upper-crust *adj* da alta roda.

uppercut [ˈʌpəkʌt] *n* direto *m* no queixo.

upper hand *n:* **to have the ~** ter a palavra final;
to gain OR **get the ~** obter o controle.

Upper House *n UK* POL Câmara *f* dos Lordes.

uppermost [ˈʌpəməʊst] *adj* **-1.** [highest] mais
alto(ta) **-2.** [most important]: **to be ~ in one's mind**
ser o mais importante na cabeça de alguém.

Upper Volta [-ˈvɒltə] *n* Alto Volta; **in ~** em Alto
Volta.

uppity [ˈʌpɪtɪ] *adj inf* arrogante.

upright [*adj senses 1 & 2 & adv* ˌʌpˈraɪt, *n* ˈʌpraɪt] ⬦
adj **-1.** [erect] vertical **-2.** *fig* [honest] honesto(ta).
⬦ *adv* verticalmente. ⬦ *n* **-1.** [of door] marco *m*
-2. [of bookshelf] pilar *m* **-3.** [of goal] poste *m*.

upright piano *n* piano *m* de armário.

uprising [ˈʌpˌraɪzɪŋ] *n* revolta *f* rebelião *f*.

uproar [ˈʌprɔː^r] *n* **-1.** [commotion] algazarra *f* **-2.**
[protest] protesto *m*.

uproarious [ʌpˈrɔːrɪəs] *adj* [noisy] barulhento(ta).

uproot [ʌpˈruːt] *vt* **-1.** [force to leave] arrancar; **to ~
o.s.** desarraigar-se **-2.** BOT [tear out of ground]
arrancar.

upset [ʌpˈset] *(pt & pp* upset, *cont* -ting) ⬦ *adj* **-1.**
[distressed] descontrolado(da); [offended] chatea-
do(da) **-2.** MED: **to have an ~ stomach** ter um
estômago fraco. ⬦ *n* **-1.** MED: **to have a stomach
~** ficar com dor de estômago **-2.** [surprise result]
surpresa *f*. ⬦ *vt* **-1.** [distress] deixar nervoso(sa),
irritar **-2.** [mess up] atrapalhar **-3.** [overturn, knock
over] virar.

upsetting [ʌpˈsetɪŋ] *adj* [distressing] desconcertante.

upshot [ˈʌpʃɒt] *n* desfecho *m*.

upside down [ˌʌpsaɪd-] ⬦ *adj* [inverted] inverti-
do(da), ao contrário. ⬦ *adv* de cabeça para
baixo; **to turn sthg ~** *fig* [disorder] virar algo de
pernas para o ar.

upstage [ˌʌpˈsteɪdʒ] *vt fig* roubar a cena de.

upstairs [ˌʌpˈsteəz] ⬦ *adj* de cima. ⬦ *adv* **-1.**
[not downstairs] em cima **-2.** [on one of the floors
above] de cima. ⬦ *n* andar *m* de cima.

upstanding [ˌʌpˈstændɪŋ] *adj* [honest] honrado
(da).

upstart [ˈʌpstaːt] *n* novo-rico *m*, nova-rica *f*.

upstate [ˌʌpˈsteɪt] *US* ⬦ *adj:* **~ New York** do
interior de Nova Iorque. ⬦ *adv* no interior.

upstream [ˌʌpˈstriːm] ⬦ *adj:* **the bridge is a few
miles ~ (from here)** a ponte fica poucas milhas
rio acima (a partir daqui). ⬦ *adv* correnteza
acima.

upsurge [ˈʌpsɜːdʒ] *n:* **~ of/in sthg** aumento *m* de/
em algo.

upswing [ˈʌpswɪŋ] *n:* **~ (in sthg)** impulso *m* (em
algo).

uptake [ˈʌpteɪk] *n:* **to be quick/slow on the ~** ter
um raciocínio rápido/lento.

uptight [ʌpˈtaɪt] *adj inf* nervoso(sa).

up-to-date *adj* **-1.** [machinery, methods] moder-
no(na) **-2.** [news, information] atualizado(da); **to keep
~ with sthg** manter-se a par de algo.

up-to-the-minute *adj* mais recente.

uptown [ˌʌpˈtaʊn] *US* ◇ *adj* da parte alta da cidade. ◇ *adv* na parte alta da cidade.

upturn [ˈʌptɜːn] *n*: ~ **(in sthg)** melhoria *f* (em algo).

upturned [ˌʌpˈtɜːnd] *adj* -**1.** [pointing upwards] virado(da) para cima; ~ **nose** nariz *m* arrebitado -**2.** [upside down] virado(da) de cabeça para baixo.

upward [ˈʌpwəd] ◇ *adj* [movement, trend] para cima. ◇ *adv US* = **upwards.**

upwardly-mobile *adj* de franca ascensão.

upwards [ˈʌpwədz] *adv* para cima.
  ➡ **upwards of** *prep* mais de.

upwind [ˌʌpˈwɪnd] *adj*: **to be** ~ **of sb/sthg** estar fora do raio de ação de alguém/algo.

URA (*abbr of* **Urban Renewal Administration**) *n* órgão norte-americano responsável pelo desenvolvimento das áreas urbanas menos favorecidas.

Urals [ˈjʊərəlz] *npl*: **the** ~ os Urais; **in the** ~ nos Urais.

uranium [jʊˈreɪnjəm] *n* (*U*) urânio *m*.

Uranus [ˈjʊərənəs] *n* [planet] Urano *m*.

urban [ˈɜːbən] *adj* urbano(na).

urbane [ɜːˈbeɪn] *adj* gentil.

urbanize, -ise [ˈɜːbənaɪz] *vt* urbanizar.

urban renewal *n* reurbanização *f*.

Urdu [ˈʊəduː] *n* (*U*) urdu *m*.

urge [ɜːdʒ] ◇ *n* impulso *m*; **to have an** ~ **to do sthg** ter um impulso de fazer algo. ◇ *vt* -**1.** [try to persuade]: **to** ~ **sb to do sthg** incitar alguém a fazer algo -**2.** [advocate] defender.

urgency [ˈɜːdʒənsɪ] *n* (*U*) urgência *f*.

urgent [ˈɜːdʒənt] *adj* -**1.** [pressing] urgente -**2.** [desperate] insistente.

urgently [ˈɜːdʒəntlɪ] *adv* [as soon as possible] urgentemente.

urinal [ˌjʊəˈraɪnl] *n* [receptacle] urinol *m*; [room] mictório *m*.

urinary [ˈjʊərɪnərɪ] *adj* urinário(ria).

urinate [ˈjʊərɪneɪt] *vi* urinar.

urine [ˈjʊərɪn] *n* (*U*) urina *f*.

URL (*abbr of* **uniform resource locator**) *n* COMPUT URL *f*.

urn [ɜːn] *n* -**1.** [for ashes] urna *f* funerária -**2.** [for tea, coffee] chaleira *f*.

Uruguay [ˈjʊərəgwaɪ] *n* Uruguai *m*; **in** ~ no Uruguai.

Uruguayan [ˌjʊərəˈgwaɪən] ◇ *adj* uruguaio(-guaia). ◇ *n* uruguaio *m*, -guaia *f*.

us [ʌs] *pers pron* (*direct*) nos; (*indirect, after prep*) nós; **they know** ~ conhecem-nos; **it's** ~ somos nós; **send it to** ~ envie-nos isso; **tell** ~ diga-nos; **we brought it with** ~ trouxemo-lo conosco.

US (*abbr of* **United States**) *n*: **the** ~ os EUA; **in the** ~ nos EUA.

USA *n* -**1.** (*abbr of* **United States of America**): **the** ~ os EUA, **in the** ~ nos EUA -**2.** (*abbr of* **United States Army**) forças armadas norte-americanas.

usable [ˈjuːzəbl] *adj* utilizável, usável.

USAF (*abbr of* **United States Air Force**) *n* força aérea norte-americana.

usage [ˈjuːzɪdʒ] *n* -**1.** (*U*) [use of language] uso *m* -**2.**

[meaning] sentido *m* -**3.** (*U*) [handling, treatment] uso *m*.

USB (*abbr of* **Universal Serial Bus**) *n* COMPUT USB *m*.

USB port *n* COMPUT porta *f* USB.

USCG (*abbr of* **United States Coast Guard**) *n* guarda-costeira norte-americana.

USDA (*abbr of* **United States Department of Agriculture**) *n* ministério da agricultura norte-americano.

USDI (*abbr of* **United States Department of the Interior**) *n* ministério do interior norte-americano.

use [*n* & *aux vb* juːs, *vt* juːz] ◇ *n* -**1.** [gen] uso *m*; **to be in** ~ estar em uso; **to be out of** ~ estar fora de uso; **to make** ~ **of sthg** fazer uso de algo; **to let sb have the** ~ **of sthg** deixar que alguém utilize algo -**2.** [purpose, usefulness] utilidade *f*; **to be of** ~ ser útil; **to be no** ~ ser inútil; **what's the** ~ **(of doing sthg)?** qual é a utilidade (de se fazer algo)? ◇ *aux vb* costumar; **I** ~ **d to live in London** eu morava em Londres; **there** ~ **d to be a tree here** havia uma árvore aqui. ◇ *vt* -**1.** [utilize] usar, utilizar -**2.** *pej* [exploit] usar.
  ➡ **use up** *vt sep* esgotar.

used [*sense 1* juːzd, *sense 2* juːst] *adj* -**1.** [object, car *etc*] usado(da) -**2.** [accustomed]: **to be** ~ **to sthg/to doing sthg** estar acostumado(da) a algo/a fazer algo; **to get** ~ **to sthg** acostumar-se a algo.

useful [ˈjuːsfʊl] *adj* útil; **to come in** ~ mostrar-se útil.

usefulness [ˈjuːsfʊlnɪs] *n* (*U*) utilidade *f*.

useless [ˈjuːslɪs] *adj* -**1.** [gen] inútil -**2.** *inf* [hopeless] incorrigível.

uselessness [ˈjuːslɪsnɪs] *n* (*U*) inutilidade *f*.

user [ˈjuːzəʳ] *n* usuário *m*, -ria *f*.

user-friendly *adj* de fácil utilização.

USES (*abbr of* **United States Employment Service**) *n* ministério do trabalho norte-americano.

usher [ˈʌʃəʳ] ◇ *n* -**1.** [at wedding] recepcionista *m* -**2.** [at theatre, concert] lanterninha *m*. ◇ *vt* conduzir.

usherette [ˌʌʃəˈret] *n* -**1.** [at wedding] recepcionista *f* -**2.** [at theatre, concert] lanterninha *f*.

USIA (*abbr of* **United States Information Agency**) *n* agência de informações norte-americana.

USM *n* -**1.** (*abbr of* **United States Mail**) serviço de correio norte-americano -**2.** (*abbr of* **United States Mint**) casa da moeda norte-americana -**3.** (*abbr of* **unlisted securities market**) parte da bolsa de valores de Londres que negocia os papéis das empresas menores.

USN (*abbr of* **United States Navy**) *n* marinha norte-americana.

USPHS (*abbr of* **United States Public Health Service**) *n* ministério norte-americano de saúde e previdência social.

USS (*abbr of* **United States Ship**) navio de guerra norte-americano.

USSR (*abbr of* **Union of Soviet Socialist Republics**) *n*: **the (former)** ~ a (ex-)URSS.

usu. (*abbr of* **usually**) usualmente.

usual [ˈjuːʒəl] *adj* usual, habitual; **as** ~ [as normal] como de costume; [as often happens] como sempre.

usually [ˈjuːʒəlɪ] *adv* geralmente, normalmente; **more than** ~ mais do que normalmente.

usurp [juːˈzɜːp] *vt fml* usurpar.
usury [ˈjuːʒərɪ] *n (U) fml* usura *f.*
UT *abbr of* Utah.
Utah [ˈjuːtɑː] *n* Utah.
utensil [juːˈtensl] *n* utensílio *m.*
uterus [ˈjuːtərəs] (*pl* -**ri** [-raɪ], -**ruses**) *n* útero *m.*
utilitarian [ˌjuːtɪlɪˈteərɪən] *adj* [functional] utilitário (ria), funcional.
utility [juːˈtɪlətɪ] (*pl*-**ies**) *n* -**1.** (U)[usefulness] utilidade *f* -**2.** [public service] serviço *m* público -**3.** COMPUT utilitário *m.*
utility room *n* área *f* de serviços.
utilize, -ise [ˈjuːtəlaɪz] *vt* utilizar.
utmost [ˈʌtməʊst] <> *adj* máximo(ma), supremo(ma). <> *n* -**1.** [best effort]: **to do one's ∼** fazer o impossível -**2.** [maximum] máximo *m*; **to the ∼** ao máximo, até não poder mais.
utopia [juːˈtəʊpjə] *n* utopia *f.*
utter [ˈʌtəʳ] <> *adj* total, completo(ta). <> *vt* -**1.** [sound, cry] emitir -**2.** [word] proferir.
utterly [ˈʌtəlɪ] *adv* totalmente, completamente.
U-turn *n* -**1.** [turning movement] retorno *m* -**2.** *fig* [complete change] guinada *f* de 180 graus.
UV (*abbr of* ultraviolet) U.V.
Uzbek <> *adj* usbeque. <> *n* -**1.** [person] usbeque *mf*-**2.** [language] usbeque *m.*
Uzbekistan [ʊzˌbekɪˈstɑːn] *n* Usbequistão; **in ∼** no Usbequistão.

v¹ (*pl* v's OR vs), **V** (*pl* V's OR Vs) [viː] *n* [letter] v, V *m.*
v² -**1.** (*abbr of* verse) v -**2.** (*abbr of* vide) [cross-reference] vide -**3.** (*abbr of* versus) versus -**4.** (*abbr of* volt) v.
VA *abbr of* Virginia.
vacancy [ˈveɪkənsɪ] (*pl* -**ies**) *n* -**1.** [job, position] vaga *f* -**2.** [room available] quarto *m* livre; **'vacancies'** 'há vagas'; **'no vacancies'** 'lotação esgotada'.
vacant [ˈveɪkənt] *adj* -**1.** [gen] vago(ga) -**2.** [look, expression] distraído(da).
vacant lot *n* lote *m* disponível.
vacantly [ˈveɪkəntlɪ] *adv* distraidamente.
vacate [vəˈkeɪt] *vt* -**1.** [give up, resign] deixar vago(ga) -**2.** [leave empty, stop using] desocupar.
vacation [vəˈkeɪʃn] *n* -**1.** UNIV [period when closed] férias *fpl* -**2.** US [holiday] férias *fpl.*
vacationer [vəˈkeɪʃənəʳ] *n* US veranista *mf.*
vacation resort *n* US colônia *f* de férias.
vaccinate [ˈvæksɪneɪt] *vt*: **to ∼ sb (against sthg)** vacinar alguém (contra algo).

vaccination [ˌvæksɪˈneɪʃn] *n* vacinação *f*; **have you had your ∼?** já tomou sua vacina?
vaccine [UK ˈvæksiːn, US vækˈsiːn] *n* vacina *f.*
vacillate [ˈvæsɪleɪt] *vi*: **to ∼ (between)** oscilar (entre); **she ∼d for a long time before making up her mind** ela hesitou por muito tempo antes de se decidir.
vacuum [ˈvækjʊəm] <> *n* -**1.** [gen] vácuo *m* -**2.** [machine]: **∼ (cleaner)** aspirador *m* (de pó). <> *vt* aspirar, passar o aspirador em.
vacuum cleaner *n* aspirador *m* de pó.
vacuum-packed *adj* embalado(da) a vácuo.
vacuum pump *n* bomba *f* de vácuo.
vagabond [ˈvægəbɒnd] *n literary* vagabundo *m*, -da *f.*
vagaries [ˈveɪgərɪz] *npl fml* caprichos *mpl.*
vagina [vəˈdʒaɪnə] *n* vagina *f.*
vaginal *adj* vaginal.
vagrancy [ˈveɪgrənsɪ] *n* (U) vagabundagem *f.*
vagrant [ˈveɪgrənt] *n* vagabundo *m*, -da *f.*
vague [veɪg] *adj* -**1.** [imprecise] vago(ga), impreciso(-sa) -**2.** [feeling] leve -**3.** [evasive] evasivo(va) -**4.** [absent-minded] distraído(da) -**5.** [indistinct] vago(ga).
vaguely [ˈveɪglɪ] *adv* -**1.** [imprecisely] vagamente -**2.** [slightly, not very] levemente -**3.** [absent-mindedly] distraidamente -**4.** [indistinctly]: **I could ∼ make out a ship on the horizon** mal dava para distinguir um navio no horizonte.
vain [veɪn] *adj* -**1.** *pej* [conceited] vaidoso(sa) -**2.** [futile, worthless] vão (vã).
➤ **in vain** *adv* em vão.
vainly [ˈveɪnlɪ] *adv* -**1.** [in vain] em vão -**2.** [conceitedly] vaidosamente.
valance [ˈvæləns] *n* -**1.** [on bed] dossel *m* -**2.** US [on curtains] sanefa *f.*
vale [veɪl] *n literary* vale *m.*
valedictory [ˌvælɪˈdɪktərɪ] *adj fml* de adeus.
valentine card [ˈvæləntam-] *n* cartão *m* de dia dos namorados.
Valentine's Day [ˈvæləntamz-] *n*: **(St) ∼** Dia *m* dos Namorados.
valet [ˈvæleɪ, ˈvælɪt] *n* [manservant] camareiro *m.*
valet parking *n*: **'∼'** serviço *m* de manobrista.
valet service *n* serviço *m* de lavanderia.
valiant [ˈvæljənt] *adj* valente.
valid [ˈvælɪd] *adj* válido(da).
validate [ˈvælɪdeɪt] *vt* -**1.** [argument, claim] validar, corroborar -**2.** [document] validar, legitimar.
validity [vəˈlɪdətɪ] *n* validade *f.*
Valium® [ˈvælɪəm] *n (U)* valium® *m.*
valley [ˈvælɪ] (*pl* valleys) *n* vale *m.*
valour UK, **valor** US [ˈvæləʳ] *n (U) fml & literary* valor *m.*
valuable [ˈvæljʊəbl] *adj* valioso(sa).
➤ **valuables** *npl* objetos *mpl* de valor.
valuation [ˌvæljʊˈeɪʃn] *n* avaliação *f.*
value [ˈvæljuː] <> *n* -**1.** (U) [gen] valor *m*; **to place a high ∼ on sthg** dar muita importância a algo -**2.** [financial] valor *m*; **to be good ∼** estar com o preço muito bom; **to be ∼ for money** estar bem em conta; **to take sb/sthg at face ∼** levar alguém/algo ao pé da letra. <> *vt* -**1.** [estimate price of] avaliar -**2.** [cherish] valorizar.

→ **values** *npl* [morals] valores *mpl* morais, princípios *mpl*.

value added tax *n* ≃ imposto *m* sobre circulação de mercadorias e serviços.

valued ['vælju:d] *adj* estimado(da).

value judg(e)ment *n* juízo *m* de valor.

valuer ['væljuə'] *n* avaliador *mf*, -ra de preços.

valve [vælv] *n* válvula *f*.

vamoose [və'mu:s] *vi inf* dar o fora.

vamp *n* vampe *f*.

vampire ['væmpaɪə'] *n* vampiro *m*.

van [væn] *n* -**1.** *AUT* caminhonete *f*, van *f* -**2.** *UK RAIL* vagão *m* de carga.

vandal ['vændl] *n* vândalo *m*, -la *f*.

vandalism ['vændəlɪzm] *n (U)* vandalismo *m*.

vandalize, -ise ['vændəlaɪz] *vt* destruir.

vanguard ['vænga:d] *n* vanguarda *f*; **in the ~ of** sthg na vanguarda de algo.

vanilla [və'nɪlə] ◇ *n (U)* baunilha *f*. ◇ *comp* de baunilha.

vanish ['vænɪʃ] *vi* desaparecer.

vanishing point ['vænɪʃɪŋ-] *n* ponto *m* de fuga.

vanity ['vænətɪ] *n (U) pej* vaidade *f*.

vanity unit *n* armário *m* de banheiro.

vanquish ['væŋkwɪʃ] *vt literary* vencer.

vantage point ['vɑ:ntɪdʒ,pɔɪnt] *n* -**1.** [for view] ponto *m* de observação -**2.** *fig* [advantageous position] posição *f* vantajosa.

vapour *UK*, **vapor** *US* ['veɪpə'] *n (U)* vapor *m*.

vapour trail *n* risco *m* de fumaça *(de avião no céu)*.

variable ['veərɪəbl] ◇ *adj* variável. ◇ *n* -**1.** [indefinite thing] variáveis *fpl* -**2.** *MATH* variável *f*.

variance ['veərɪəns] *n fml*: **at ~ with** sthg em desacordo com algo.

variant ['veərɪənt] ◇ *adj* [different] variante. ◇ *n* [different form, spelling] variante *f*.

variation [,veərɪ'eɪʃn] *n* -**1.** *(U)* [fact of difference] variação *f*; **~ in** sthg variação em algo -**2.** [degree of difference] variação *f*; **~ in** sthg variação em algo -**3.** [different version & *MUS*] variação *f*; **~ on** sthg variação em algo.

varicose veins ['værɪkəʊs-] *npl* varizes *fpl*.

varied ['veərɪd] *adj* variado(da).

variety [və'raɪətɪ] *(pl -ies)* *n* -**1.** *(U)* [difference in type] variedade *f* -**2.** [selection] variedade *f* -**3.** [type] tipo *m* -**4.** *(U) THEATRE* (teatro *m* de) variedades *fpl*.

variety show *n* programa *m* de variedades.

various ['veərɪəs] *adj* -**1.** [several] vários(rias) -**2.** [different] variados(das).

varnish ['vɑ:nɪʃ] ◇ *n* -**1.** [for wood] verniz *m* -**2.** [for nails] esmalte *m*. ◇ *vt* -**1.** [wood] envernizar -**2.** [nails] pintar.

varnished ['vɑ:nɪʃt] *adj* -**1.** [wood, pottery] envernizado(da) -**2.** [nails] pintado(da).

vary ['veərɪ] *(pt & pp -ied)* ◇ *vt* variar. ◇ *vi*; **to ~ in** sthg variar em algo; **to ~ with** sthg variar de acordo com algo.

varying ['veərɪŋ] *adj* [different] variado(da); [fluctuating] diverso(sa).

vascular ['væskjʊlə'] *adj* vascular.

vase [*UK* vɑ:z, *US* veɪz] *n* vaso *m*.

vasectomy [və'sektəmɪ] *(pl -ies)* *n* -**1.** *(U)* [process] vasectomia *f* -**2.** [operation] vasectomia *f*.

Vaseline® ['væsəli:n] *n (U)* vaselina® *f*.

vast [vɑ:st] *adj* enorme, imenso(sa).

vastly ['vɑ:stlɪ] *adv* enormemente, muito.

vastness ['vɑ:stnɪs] *n (U)* [hugeness] imensidão *f*.

vat [væt] *n* tina *f*.

Vatican ['vætɪkən] *n*: **the ~** o Vaticano.

Vatican City *n* Cidade *f* do Vaticano; **in ~** na Cidade do Vaticano.

vault [vɔ:lt] ◇ *n* -**1.** [in bank] caixa-forte *f* -**2.** [in church] cripta *f* -**3.** [roof] abóbada *f* -**4.** [jump] salto *m*. ◇ *vt* saltar. ◇ *vi*: **to ~ over** sthg pular por cima de algo.

vaulted ['vɔ:ltɪd] *adj ARCHIT* abobadado(da).

vaulting horse ['vɔ:ltɪŋ-] *n SPORT* cavalo-de-pau *m (na ginástica)*.

vaunted ['vɔ:ntɪd] *adj fml* alardeado(da).

veal [vi:l] *n (U)* vitela *f*.

veer [vɪə'] *vi* -**1.** [vehicle, road, wind] virar -**2.** *fig* [conversation, mood] alternar-se.

veg [vedʒ] *n UK inf* -**1.** *(abbr of* **vegetable)** verduras *fpl* -**2.** *(U) (abbr of* **vegetables)** verduras *fpl*.

vegan ['vi:gən] ◇ *adj* vegan. ◇ *n* vegan *mf*.

vegetable ['vedʒtəbl] ◇ *n* -**1.** *BOT* vegetal *m* -**2.** [food] hortaliças *fpl*, legume *m*. ◇ *adj* -**1.** [protein] vegetal -**2.** [soup] de legumes.

vegetable garden *n* horta *f*.

vegetable oil *n (U)* óleo *m* vegetal.

vegetarian [,vedʒɪ'teərɪən] ◇ *adj* vegetariano(na). ◇ *n* vegetariano *m*, -na *f*.

vegetarianism [,vedʒɪ'teərɪənɪzm] *n (U)* vegetarianismo *m*.

vegetate ['vedʒɪteɪt] *vi pej* vegetar.

vegetation [,vedʒɪ'teɪʃn] *n (U)* vegetação *f*.

veggie ['vedʒɪ] *UK inf* ◇ *adj* vegetariano(na). ◇ *n* vegetariano *m*, -na *f*.

vehement ['vi:əmənt] *adj* -**1.** [gesture, attack] violento(ta) -**2.** [person, denial] veemente.

vehemently ['vi:əməntlɪ] *adv* -**1.** [attack] violentamente -**2.** [deny, refuse] veementemente.

vehicle ['vi:əkl] *n* -**1.** [for transport] veículo *m* -**2.** *fig* [medium]: **a ~ for** sthg um meio para algo.

vehicular [vɪ'hɪkjʊlə'] *adj fml* de veículos automotores.

veil [veɪl] *n* -**1.** [for face] véu *m* -**2.** *fig* [obscuring thing] manto *m*.

veiled [veɪld] *adj* [hidden] velado(da).

vein [veɪn] *n* -**1.** *ANAT* veia *f* -**2.** [of leaf] nervura *f* -**3.** [of mineral] veio *m* -**4.** [style, mood] estilo *m*; **in the same ~** no mesmo estilo.

Velcro® ['velkrəʊ] *n (U)* velcro® *m*.

vellum ['veləm] *n (U)* papel *m* velino.

velocity [vɪ'lɒsətɪ] *(pl -ies)* *n PHYSICS* velocidade *f*.

velour [və'lʊə'] *n (U)* tecido *m* aveludado.

velvet ['velvɪt] ◇ *n (U)* veludo *m*. ◇ *comp* de veludo.

vend *vt* -**1.** *fml* [sell] vender -**2.** *JUR* vender.

vendetta [ven'detə] *n* vendeta *f*.

vending machine ['vendɪŋ-] *n* máquina *f* de venda automática.

vendor ['vendɔ:'] *n* vendedor *m*, -ra *f*.

veneer [vəˈnɪə^r] n -1. (U) [of wood] compensado m -2. fig [appearance] aparência f.

venerable [ˈvenərəbl] adj fml venerável.

venerate [ˈvenəreɪt] vt fml & RELIG venerar.

venereal disease [vɪˈnɪərɪəl-] n (U) doença f venérea.

Venetian [vɪˈniːʃn] <> adj veneziano(na). <> n veneziano m, -na f.

venetian blind n persiana f.

Venezuela [ˌvenɪzˈweɪlə] n Venezuela; in ~ na Venezuela.

Venezuelan [ˌvenɪzˈweɪlən] <> adj venezuelano(-na). <> n venezuelano m, -na f.

vengeance [ˈvendʒəns] n (U) vingança f; it started raining with a ~ começou a chover para valer.

vengeful [ˈvendʒfʊl] adj literary vingativo(va).

Venice [ˈvenɪs] n Veneza; in ~ em Veneza.

venison [ˈvenɪzn] n (U) carne f de veado.

venom [ˈvenəm] n (U) -1. [poison] veneno m -2. fig [spite, bitterness] veneno m.

venomous [ˈvenəməs] adj venenoso(sa).

vent [vent] <> n saída f de ar, abertura f de ar; to give ~ to sthg dar vazão a algo. <> vt [express] descarregar; to ~ sthg on sb/sthg descarregar algo em alguém/algo.

ventilate [ˈventɪleɪt] vt ventilar.

ventilation [ˌventɪˈleɪʃn] n (U) ventilação f.

ventilator [ˈventɪleɪtə^r] n ventilador m.

ventriloquist [venˈtrɪləkwɪst] n ventríloquo m, -qua f.

venture [ˈventʃə^r] <> n empreendimento m. <> vt [proffer] arriscar; to ~ to do sthg arriscar-se a fazer algo. <> vi -1. [go somewhere dangerous] aventurar-se -2. [embark]: to ~ into sthg lançar-se em algo.

venture capital n (U) capital m de risco.

venturesome adj -1. [person] aventureiro(ra) -2. [action] arriscado(da).

venue [ˈvenjuː] n local m (em que se realiza algo).

Venus [ˈviːnəs] n [planet] Vênus.

veracity [vəˈræsɪtɪ] n (U) fml veracidade f.

veranda(h) [vəˈrændə] n varanda f.

verb [vɜːb] n verbo m.

verbal [ˈvɜːbl] adj verbal.

verbally [ˈvɜːbəlɪ] adv [in spoken words] verbalmente.

verbatim [vɜːˈbeɪtɪm] <> adj literal. <> adv literalmente, palavra por palavra.

verbose [vɜːˈbəʊs] adj fml prolixo(xa).

verdict [ˈvɜːdɪkt] n -1. JUR veredito m -2. [opinion] parecer m; ~ on sthg parecer sobre algo.

verge [vɜːdʒ] n -1. [edge, side] acostamento m -2. [brink]: on the ~ of sthg à beira de algo; on the ~ of doing sthg a ponto de fazer algo.

➡ **verge (up)on** vt fus beirar.

verger [ˈvɜːdʒə^r] n sacristão m.

verification [ˌverɪfɪˈkeɪʃn] n -1. [check] (U) verificação f -2. [confirmation] confirmação f.

verify [ˈverɪfaɪ] (pt & pp -ied) vt -1. [check] verificar -2. [confirm] confirmar.

veritable [ˈverɪtəbl] adj fml or hum legítimo(ma).

vermilion [vəˈmɪljən] <> adj vermelho-alaranjado(da). <> n vermelhão m.

vermin [ˈvɜːmɪn] npl -1. [ZOOL - rodents] bichos mpl; [- insects] insetos mpl nocivos -2. pej [people] parasita mf.

Vermont n Vermonte.

vermouth [ˈvɜːməθ] n (U) vermute m.

vernacular [vəˈnækjʊlə^r] <> adj LING vernacular. <> n: the ~ o vernáculo.

verruca [vəˈruːkə] (pl -cas OR -cae [-kaɪ]) n verruga f.

versa ▷ vice versa.

versatile [ˈvɜːsətaɪl] adj -1. [multitalented] versátil -2. [multipurpose] multifuncional.

versatility [ˌvɜːsəˈtɪlətɪ] n (U) -1. [multitalented nature] versatilidade f -2. [multipurpose nature] multifuncionalidade f.

verse [vɜːs] n -1. (U) [poetry] versos mpl, poesia f -2. [stanza] estrofe m -3. [in Bible] versículo m.

versed [vɜːst] adj: to be well ~ in sthg ser bem versado(da) em algo.

version [ˈvɜːʃn] n -1. [gen] versão f -2. [translation] tradução f.

versus [ˈvɜːsəs] prep -1. SPORT contra -2. [as opposed to] em oposição a.

vertebra [ˈvɜːtɪbrə] (pl -brae [-briː]) n vértebra f.

vertebrate [ˈvɜːtɪbreɪt] n vertebrado m.

vertical [ˈvɜːtɪkl] adj vertical.

vertical integration n (U) FIN integração f vertical.

vertically [ˈvɜːtɪklɪ] adv verticalmente.

vertigo [ˈvɜːtɪgəʊ] n (U) vertigem f.

verve [vɜːv] n (U) vivacidade f, entusiasmo m.

very [ˈverɪ] <> adv -1. [for emphasis] muito; to like sthg ~ much gostar muito de algo -2. [as euphemism]: he's not ~ intelligent ele não é muito inteligente. <> adj mesmíssimo(ma); the ~ book I've been looking for justo o livro que eu estava procurando; the ~ thought make me bad só de pensar eu já fico mal; fighting for his ~ life lutando por sua própria vida; the ~ best o melhor de todos; a house of my ~ own minha própria casa.

➡ **very well** adv muito bem; you can't ~ well stop him now é um pouco tarde para impedi-lo.

vespers [ˈvespəz] n (U) vésperas fpl.

vessel [ˈvesl] n fml -1. [boat] embarcação f -2. [container] recipiente m, vasilha f.

vest [vest] n -1. UK [undershirt] camiseta f -2. US [waistcoat] colete m.

vested interest [ˈvestɪd-] n capital m investido; ~ in sthg capital investido em algo.

vestibule [ˈvestɪbjuːl] n -1. fml [entrance hall] vestíbulo m -2. US [on train] vestíbulo m.

vestige [ˈvestɪdʒ] n fml vestígio m.

vestry [ˈvestrɪ] (pl -ies) n sacristia f.

Vesuvius [vɪˈsuːvjəs] n Vesúvio m.

vet [vet] (pt & pp -ted, cont -ting) <> n -1. UK (abbr of veterinary surgeon) veterinário m, -ria f -2. US (abbr of veteran) veterano m, -na f de guerra. <> vt UK [check] submeter a uma investigação.

veteran [ˈvetrən] <> adj [experienced] veterano(na). <> n veterano m, -na f.

veteran car n UK carro m de época (feito antes de 1905).

Veterans Day n US Dia m dos Veteranos, 11 de

novembro, dia em que os Estados Unidos comemoram o fim das duas guerras mundiais e homenageiam seus veteranos.

veterinarian [ˌvetərɪˈneərɪən] *n US* veterinário *m*, -ria *f.*

veterinary science [ˈvetərɪnrɪ-] *n (U)* veterinária *f.*

veterinary surgeon [ˈvetərɪnrɪ-] *n UK fml* veterinário *m*, -ria *f.*

veto [ˈviːtəʊ] *(pl -es, pt & pp -ed, cont -ing)* ⬦ *n -1. (U)* [power to forbid] veto *m* -2. [act of forbidding] veto *m.* ⬦ *vt* vetar.

vetting [ˈvetɪŋ] *n (U)* investigação *f (sobre o passado de uma pessoa).*

vex [veks] *vt fml* [annoy] importunar.

vexed question [ˌvekst-] *n* pomo *m* de discórdia.

VI *abbr of* Virgin Islands.

via [ˈvaɪə] *prep -1.* [travelling through] via; **they flew to China ~ Karachi** eles viajaram para a China (passando) por Karachi -2. [by means of] através de; **~ satellite** via satélite.

viability [ˌvaɪəˈbɪlətɪ] *n* viabilidade *f.*

viable [ˈvaɪəbl] *adj* viável.

viaduct [ˈvaɪədʌkt] *n* viaduto *m.*

vibrant [ˈvaɪbrənt] *adj -1.* [colour, light] forte -2. [person] dinâmico(ca) -3. [city, atmosphere] animado(da) -4. [sound] vibrante.

vibrate [vaɪˈbreɪt] *vi* vibrar.

vibration [vaɪˈbreɪʃn] *n* vibração *f.*

vicar [ˈvɪkəʳ] *n* vigário *m*, pároco *m.*

vicarage [ˈvɪkərɪdʒ] *n* casa *f* paroquial.

vicarious [vɪˈkeərɪəs] *adj* indireto(ta).

vice [vaɪs] *n -1. (U)* [immorality] vício *m* -2. [moral fault] vício *m* -3. [tool] torno *m* de mesa.

vice- [vaɪs] *prefix* vice-.

vice-admiral *n* vice-almirante *m.*

vice-chairman *n* vice-presidente *m.*

vice-chancellor *n UK UNIV* reitor *m*, -ra *f.*

vice-president *n* vice-presidente *mf.*

vice squad *n* delegacia *f* de costumes.

vice versa [ˌvaɪsˈvɜːsə] *adv* vice-versa.

vicinity [vɪˈsɪnətɪ] *n -1.* [neighbourhood] proximidades *fpl*, redondezas *fpl*; **in the ~ (of)** nas proximidades *or* redondezas(de) -2. [approximate figures]: **in the ~ of** cerca de.

vicious [ˈvɪʃəs] *adj -1.* [attack, blow] violento(ta) -2. [person, gossip] cruel -3. [dog] feroz, brabo(ba).

vicious circle *n* círculo *m* vicioso.

viciousness [ˈvɪʃəsnɪs] *n -1.* [of attack] violência *f* -2. [of person, gossip] crueldade *f* -3. [of dog] ferocidade *f.*

vicissitudes [vɪˈsɪsɪtjuːdz] *npl fml* vicissitudes *fpl.*

victim [ˈvɪktɪm] *n* vítima *f.*

victimize, -ise [ˈvɪktɪmaɪz] *vt* vitimar.

victor [ˈvɪktəʳ] *n* vencedor *m*, -ra *f.*

Victoria Cross [vɪkˈtɔːrɪə-] *n* condecoração militar britânica.

Victoria Falls [vɪkˈtɔːrɪə-] *npl*: **the ~** as Cataratas de Vitória.

Victorian [vɪkˈtɔːrɪən] *adj -1.* [from Victorian era] vitoriano(na) -2. *usu pej* [overstrict] vitoriano(na).

Victoriana [ˌvɪktɔːrɪˈɑːnə] *n (U)* antiguidades *fpl* da era vitoriana.

victorious [vɪkˈtɔːrɪəs] *adj* [winning] vitorioso(sa).

victory [ˈvɪktərɪ] *(pl -ies) n -1. (U)* [act of winning] vitória *f* -2. [win] vitória *f*; **~ over sb/sthg** vitória sobre alguém/algo.

video [ˈvɪdɪəʊ] *(pl -s, pt & pp -ed, cont -ing)* ⬦ *n -1. (U)* [medium] vídeo *m* -2. [recording, machine] vídeo *m* -3. [cassette] videocassete *m.* ⬦ *comp* de vídeo. ⬦ *vt -1.* [using videorecorder] gravar em vídeo -2. [using camera] gravar um vídeo de.

video camera *n* câmera *f* de vídeo.

video cassette *n* videocassete *m*, vídeo *m.*

videodisc *UK*, **videodisk** *US* [ˈvɪdɪəʊdɪsk] *n* videodisco *m.*

video game *n* video game *m.*

video machine *n* vídeo *m.*

videophone [ˈvɪdɪəʊfəʊn] *n* videofone *m.*

videorecorder [ˈvɪdɪəʊrɪˌkɔːdəʳ] *n* videocassete *m*, vídeo *m.*

video recording *n -1.* [copy on video] cópia *f* em vídeo -2. *(U) TV* gravação *f* em vídeo.

video shop *n* videolocadora *f.*

videotape [ˈvɪdɪəʊteɪp] *n -1.* [cassette] videoteipe *m* -2. *(U)* [ribbon] fita *f.*

vie [vaɪ] *(pt & pp vied, cont vying) vi*: **to ~ for sthg** competir por algo; **to ~ with sb (for sthg/to do sthg)** competir com alguém (por algo/para fazer algo].

Vienna [vɪˈenə] *n* Viena.

Viennese [ˌvɪəˈniːz] ⬦ *adj* vienense. ⬦ *n* vienense *mf.*

Vietnam [*UK* ˌvjetˈnæm, *US* ˌvjetˈnɑːm] *n* Vietnã; **in ~** no Vietnã.

Vietnamese [ˌvjetnəˈmiːz] ⬦ *adj* vietnamita. ⬦ *n -1.* [person] vietnamita *mf* -2. [language] vietnamita *m.* ⬦ *npl*: **the ~** os vietnamitas.

view [vjuː] ⬦ *n -1.* [opinion] visão *f*, opinião *f*; **~ of sthg** visão de algo; **~ on sb/sthg** opinião sobre alguém/algo; **in my ~** na minha opinião; **to take the ~ that** ser da opinião de que -2. [vista] vista *f* -3. [ability to see] visão *f*; **to come into ~** aparecer. ⬦ *vt -1.* [consider] ver -2. *fml* [house] visitar -3. [solar system] observar.

⬥ **in view of** *prep* em vista de.

⬥ **with a view to** *conj* com o intuito de.

viewer [ˈvjuːəʳ] *n -1.* [person] telespectador *m*, -ra *f* -2. [apparatus] visor *m.*

viewfinder [ˈvjuːˌfaɪndəʳ] *n* visor *m.*

viewpoint [ˈvjuːpɔɪnt] *n -1.* [opinion] ponto *m* de vista -2. [place] mirante *m.*

vigil [ˈvɪdʒɪl] *n* vigília *f.*

vigilance [ˈvɪdʒɪləns] *n (U)* vigilância *f.*

vigilant [ˈvɪdʒɪlənt] *adj* vigilante.

vigilante [ˌvɪdʒɪˈlæntɪ] *n* vigilante *mf.*

vigor *n US* = vigour.

vigorous [ˈvɪgərəs] *adj -1.* [gen] vigoroso(sa) -2. [attempt] enérgico(ca) -3. [person, animal] vivaz -4. [plant] viçoso(sa).

vigour *UK*, **vigor** *US* [ˈvɪgəʳ] *n (U)* vigor *m.*

Viking [ˈvaɪkɪŋ] ⬦ *adj* viking, viquingue. ⬦ *n* viking *mf*, viquingue *mf.*

vile [vaɪl] *adj -1.* [person] vil -2. [mood] muito ruim -3. [act] desprezível -4. [food] repugnante.

vilify [ˈvɪlɪfaɪ] *(pt & pp -ied) vt fml* difamar.

villa ['vɪlə] *n* casa *f* de campo, chalé *m*.

village ['vɪlɪdʒ] *n* vilarejo *m* povoado *m*.

villager ['vɪlɪdʒə'] *n* população *f* de um vilarejo.

villain ['vɪlən] *n* **-1.** [of film, book, play] vilão *m*, -lã *f* **-2.** dated [criminal] criminoso *m*, -sa *f*.

vinaigrette [‚vɪnɪ'gret] *n (U)* molho *m* vinagrete.

vindicate ['vɪndɪkeɪt] *vt* [confirm] vindicar; [justify] justificar.

vindication [‚vɪndɪ'keɪʃn] *n* [confirmation] vindicação *f*; [justification] justificação *f*.

vindictive [vɪn'dɪktɪv] *adj* vingativo(va).

vine [vaɪn] *n* [grapevine] videira *f*, parreira *f*.

vinegar ['vɪnɪgə'] *n (U)* vinagre *m*.

vine leaf *n* folha *f* de parreira.

vineyard ['vɪnjəd] *n* vinhedo *m*.

vintage ['vɪntɪdʒ] ◇ *adj* **-1.** [wine] de boa safra **-2.** *fig* [classic] clássico(ca). ◇ *n* [wine] safra *f*.

vintage car *n UK* carro *m* de época *(feito entre 1919 e 1930)*.

vintage wine *n* vinho *m* de uma boa safra.

vintner *n* comerciante *mf* de vinhos.

vinyl ['vaɪnɪl] ◇ *n (U)* vinil *m*. ◇ *comp* de vinil.

viola [vɪ'əʊlə] *n* **-1.** *MUS* viola *f* **-2.** *BOT* violeta *f*.

violate ['vaɪəleɪt] *vt* **-1.** [disregard] violar **-2.** [disrupt] invadir **-3.** [break into] profanar.

violation [‚vaɪə'leɪʃn] *n* **-1.** *(U)* [disregarding] violação *f* **-2.** [disruption] invasão *f* **-3.** [breaking into] profanação *f*.

violence ['vaɪələns] *n (U)* **-1.** [physical force] violência *f* **-2.** [of words, reaction] violência *f*.

violent ['vaɪələnt] *adj* **-1.** [gen] violento(ta) **-2.** [emotion, colour] intenso(sa).

violently ['vaɪələntlɪ] *adv* violentamente.

violet ['vaɪələt] ◇ *adj* violeta. ◇ *n* **-1.** [flower] violeta *f* **-2.** *(U)* [colour] violeta *f*.

violin [‚vaɪə'lɪn] *n* violino *m*.

violinist [‚vaɪə'lɪnɪst] *n* violinista *mf*.

viper ['vaɪpə'] *n* víbora *f*.

viral ['vaɪrəl] *adj* viral, virótico(ca).

virgin ['vɜːdʒɪn] ◇ *adj literary* **-1.** [sexually] virgem **-2.** [forest, snow, soil] virgem. ◇ *n* virgem *mf*.

Virginia [və'dʒɪnjə] *n* Virgínia.

Virginia creeper *n* videira *f* virgem.

Virgin Islands *n*: the ~ as Ilhas Virgens; in the ~ nas Ilhas Virgens.

virginity [və'dʒɪnətɪ] *n (U)* virgindade *f*.

Virgo ['vɜːgəʊ] *(pl -s) n* **-1.** [sign] Virgem *m* **-2.** [person] virginiano *m*, -na *f*; I'm ~ sou de Virgem.

virile ['vɪraɪl] *adj* viril.

virility [vɪ'rɪlətɪ] *n (U)* virilidade *f*.

virtual ['vɜːtʃʊəl] *adj* [certainty, necessity] virtual.

virtually ['vɜːtʃʊəlɪ] *adv* [almost] praticamente.

virtual memory *n COMPUT* memória *f* virtual.

virtual reality *n* realidade *f* virtual.

virtue ['vɜːtjuː] *n* **-1.** *(U)* [goodness] virtude *f* **-2.** [merit, quality] virtude *f* **-3.** [benefit] vantagem *f*; ~ in sthg vantagem em algo.

➤ **by virtue of** *prep fml* em virtude de.

virtuoso [‚vɜːtjʊ'əʊzəʊ] *(pl* **-sos** *OR* **-si** [-siː]) *n* virtuoso *m*, -sa *f*.

virtuous ['vɜːtʃʊəs] *adj* virtuoso(sa).

virulent ['vɪrʊlənt] *adj* **-1.** *fml* [bitter and hostile]

virulento(ta) **-2.** *MED* [very powerful] virulento(ta).

virus ['vaɪrəs] *n* vírus *m inv*.

visa ['viːzə] *n* visto *m*.

vis-à-vis [‚viːzɑː'viː] *prep fml* em relação a.

viscose ['vɪskəʊs] *n (U)* **-1.** [solution] viscose *f* **-2.** [material] viscose *f*.

viscosity [vɪ'skɒsətɪ] *n CHEM* viscosidade *f*.

viscount ['vaɪkaʊnt] *n* visconde *m*.

viscous ['vɪskəs] *adj CHEM* viscoso(sa).

vise [vaɪs] *n US* torno *m* de mesa.

visibility [‚vɪzɪ'bɪlətɪ] *n* visibilidade *f*.

visible ['vɪzəbl] *adj* visível.

visibly ['vɪzəblɪ] *adv* [clearly] visivelmente.

vision ['vɪʒn] *n* **-1.** *(U)* [ability to see] visão *f*, vista *f* **-2.** *(U) fig* [foresight] visão *f* **-3.** [impression, dream] visão *f* **-4.** *(U) TV* imagem *f*.

visionary ['vɪʒənrɪ] *(pl* **-ies)** ◇ *adj* [full of foresight] visionário(ria). ◇ *n* [person] visionário *m*, -ria *f*.

visit ['vɪzɪt] ◇ *n* visita *f*; on a ~ to numa visita a. ◇ *vt* visitar.

➤ **visit with** *vt fus US* **-1.** [talk with] conversar com **-2.** [go and see] visitar, ir ver.

visiting card ['vɪzɪtɪŋ-] *n* cartão *m* de visita.

visiting hours ['vɪzɪtɪŋ-] *npl* hora *f* de visita.

visitor ['vɪzɪtə'] *n* **-1.** [to person] visita *mf* **-2.** [to place] visitante *mf*.

visitors' book *n* livro *m* de visitantes.

visitor's passport *n UK* passaporte *m* temporário.

visor ['vaɪzə'] *n* [on helmet] viseira *f*.

vista ['vɪstə] *n* **-1.** [view] vista *f*, perspectiva *f* **-2.** *fig* [perspective] perspectiva *f*.

visual ['vɪʒʊəl] *adj* **-1.** [gen] visual **-2.** [examination] de vista.

visual aids *npl* recursos *mpl* visuais.

visual display unit *n* monitor *m*.

visualize, -ise ['vɪʒʊəlaɪz] *vt* visualizar; to ~ (sb) doing sthg imaginar (alguém) fazendo algo.

visually ['vɪʒʊəlɪ] *adv* visualmente; ~ handicapped person pessoa *f* com problemas visuais.

vital ['vaɪtl] *adj* **-1.** [essential] vital, essencial **-2.** [full of life] cheio (cheia) de vida.

vitality [vaɪ'tælətɪ] *n (U)* vitalidade *f*.

vitally ['vaɪtlɪ] *adv* extremamente.

vital statistics *npl inf* [of figure] medidas *fpl (do corpo de uma mulher)*.

vitamin [*UK* 'vɪtəmɪn, *US* 'vaɪtəmɪn] *n* vitamina *f*.

vitreous *adj* vítreo(trea).

vitriolic [‚vɪtrɪ'ɒlɪk] *adj fml* acrimonioso(osa), virulento(ta).

viva ['vaɪvə] *n UNIV* = viva voce.

vivacious [vɪ'veɪʃəs] *adj* vivaz, animado(da).

vivacity [vɪ'væsətɪ] *n (U)* vivacidade *f*.

viva voce [‚vaɪvə'vəʊsɪ] *n UNIV* exame *m* oral.

vivid ['vɪvɪd] *adj* **-1.** [bright] vivo(va) **-2.** [clear] vívido(da).

vividly ['vɪvɪdlɪ] *adv* **-1.** [brightly] com cores muito vivas **-2.** [clearly] vividamente.

vivisection [‚vɪvɪ'sekʃn] *n (U)* vivissecção *f*.

vixen ['vɪksn] *n* raposa *f* (fêmea).

viz [vɪz] *(abbr of* videlicet*)* a saber.

VLF *(abbr of* very low frequency*) n* VLF *f*.

V-neck n **-1.** [sweater, dress] decote m em V **-2.** [neck] gola f em V.

VOA (abbr of **Voice of America**) n emissora oficial de rádio norte-americana com transmissões para todo o mundo em inglês e outras línguas.

vocabulary [vəˈkæbjʊlərɪ] (pl **-ies**) n vocabulário m.

vocal [ˈvəʊkl] adj **-1.** [outspoken] sincero(ra) **-2.** [of the voice] vocal.

  ➡ **vocals** npl vocais mpl; **on ~s** no vocal.

vocal cords npl cordas fpl vocais.

vocalist [ˈvəʊkəlɪst] n vocalista mf.

vocation [vəʊˈkeɪʃn] n [calling] vocação f.

vocational [vəʊˈkeɪʃənl] adj vocacional.

vociferous [vəˈsɪfərəs] adj fml vociferante.

vodka [ˈvɒdkə] n vodca f.

vogue [vəʊg] ◇ adj em voga. ◇ n moda f; **~ for** sthg moda de algo; **in ~** na moda, em voga.

voice [vɔɪs] ◇ n **-1.** [gen] voz f; **to raise/lower one's ~** levantar/baixar a voz; **to keep one's ~ down** manter a voz baixa **-2.** [influence] influência f. ◇ vt [opinion, emotion] manifestar.

voice box n laringe f.

Voice of America n Voz f da América (emissora de rádio dos Estados Unidos).

voice-over n narração f (num comercial para tevê).

void [vɔɪd] ◇ adj **-1.** [invalid] inválido(da) ▷ **null -2.** fml [empty]: **~ of sthg** desprovido(da) de algo. ◇ n literary vazio m.

voile [vɔɪl] n (U) voile m.

vol. (abbr of **volume**) vol.

volatile [UK ˈvɒlətaɪl, US ˈvɒlətl] adj [unpredictable - situation] imprevisível; [- person] volúvel; [- market] volátil.

vol-au-vent [ˈvɒləʊvɒ̃:] n petisco de massa folhada com recheio.

volcanic [vɒlˈkænɪk] adj [of volcanoes] vulcânico(ca).

volcano [vɒlˈkeɪnəʊ] (pl **-es** OR **-s**) n vulcão m.

vole [vəʊl] n rato-calunga m.

Volga [ˈvɒlgə] n: **the (River) ~** o (Rio) Volga.

volition [vəˈlɪʃn] n fml: **of one's own ~** por vontade própria.

volley [ˈvɒlɪ] (pl **volleys**) ◇ n **-1.** [of gunfire] rajada f, saraivada f **-2.** fig [rapid succession] torrente f **-3.** SPORT voleio m. ◇ vt dar de voleio em.

volleyball [ˈvɒlɪbɔːl] n (U) voleibol m, vôlei m.

volt [vəʊlt] n volt m.

Volta [ˈvɒltə] n **-1.** [river]: **the (River) ~** o (Rio) Volta **-2.** [lake]: **Lake ~** Lago m Volta.

voltage [ˈvəʊltɪdʒ] n voltagem f.

voluble [ˈvɒljʊbl] adj fml loquaz.

volume [ˈvɒljuːm] n (U) volume m.

volume control n controle m de volume.

voluminous [vəˈluːmɪnəs] adj fml **-1.** [garment] volumoso(sa) **-2.** [container] espaçoso(sa).

voluntarily [UK ˈvɒləntrɪlɪ, US ˌvɒlənˈterəlɪ] adv voluntariamente.

voluntary [ˈvɒləntrɪ] adj voluntário(ria); **~ organization** organização f beneficente.

voluntary liquidation n (U) liquidação f voluntária.

voluntary redundancy n UK demissão f voluntária.

voluntary work n trabalho m voluntário.

volunteer [ˌvɒlənˈtɪəʳ] ◇ n voluntário m, -ria f. ◇ vt **-1.** [offer of one's free will]: **to ~ to do sthg** oferecer-se (de livre e espontânea vontade) para fazer algo **-2.** [information, advice] oferecer. ◇ vi **-1.** [freely offer one's services]: **to ~ (for sthg)** oferecer-se (para algo) **-2.** MIL alistar-se como voluntário(ria).

voluptuous [vəˈlʌptjʊəs] adj voluptuoso(sa).

vomit [ˈvɒmɪt] ◇ n (U) vômito m. ◇ vi vomitar.

voodoo n vodu m.

voracious [vəˈreɪʃəs] adj voraz.

vortex [ˈvɔːteks] (pl **-texes** OR **-tices** [-tɪsiːz]) n **-1.** TECH vórtice m **-2.** fig [of events] turbilhão m.

vote [vəʊt] ◇ n **-1.** [individual decision] voto m; **~ for sb/sthg** voto em alguém/algo; **~ against sb/sthg** voto contra alguém/algo **-2.** [session, ballot] votação f; **to put sthg to the ~** levar algo à votação **-3.** [result of ballot]: **the ~** a votação **-4.** [section of voters] eleitorado m **-5.** [suffrage] voto m. ◇ vt **-1.** [declare, elect] eleger **-2.** [choose in ballot] votar em; **they ~ed to return to work** eles votaram pela volta ao trabalho **-3.** [suggest] votar. ◇ vi [express one's choice] votar; **to ~ for/against sb** votar em/contra alguém; **to ~ for/against sthg** votar a favor de/contra algo.

  ➡ **vote in** vt sep eleger.

  ➡ **vote out** vt sep derrotar (nas urnas).

vote of confidence (pl **votes of confidence**) n voto m de confiança.

vote of no confidence (pl **votes of no confidence**) n voto m de censura.

vote of thanks (pl **votes of thanks**) n: **to give a ~** fazer um discurso de agradecimento.

voter [ˈvəʊtəʳ] n votante mf.

voting [ˈvəʊtɪŋ] n votação f.

vouch [vaʊtʃ] ➡ **vouch for** vt fus **-1.** [take responsibility for] responsabilizar-se por **-2.** [declare belief in] dar testemunho de.

voucher [ˈvaʊtʃəʳ] n [for restaurant, purchase, petrol] vale m.

vow [vaʊ] ◇ n **-1.** juramento m, promessa f solene **-2.** RELIG voto m. ◇ vt: **to ~ to do sthg** jurar fazer algo; **to ~ (that)** jurar que.

vowel [ˈvaʊəl] n vogal f.

voyage [ˈvɔɪdʒ] n viagem f.

voyeur [vwaˈjɜːʳ] n voyeur m, -euse f.

voyeurism [vwaˈjɜːrɪzm] n (U) voyeurismo m.

VP n (abbr of **vice-president**) vice-presidente mf.

vs (abbr of **versus**) vs.

VSO (abbr of **Voluntary Service Overseas**) n organização britânica de voluntários para ajuda a países em desenvolvimento.

VSOP (abbr of **very special old pale**) expressão que indica que uma bebida tem de 20 a 25 anos.

VT abbr of Vermont.

VTOL (abbr of **vertical takeoff and landing**) n decolagem e aterrissagem na vertical.

VTR (abbr of **videotape recorder**) n vídeo m.

vulgar [ˈvʌlgəʳ] adj **-1.** [common] comum **-2.** [rude] vulgar, baixo(xa).

vulgarity [vʌlˈgærətɪ] n (U) **-1.** [commonness] vulgaridade f **-2.** [rudeness] grosseria f, vulgaridade f.

vulnerability [ˌvʌlnərəˈbɪlətɪ] *n* vulnerabilidade *f*.
vulnerable [ˈvʌlnərəbl] *adj* **-1.** [easily hurt] vulnerável; ~ **to** sthg [to being hurt] vulnerável a algo **-2.** [easily influenced]: ~ **(to** sthg**)** facilmente influenciável (por algo).
vulture [ˈvʌltʃəʳ] *n* **-1.** [bird] abutre *m*, urubu *m* **-2.** *fig* [exploitative person] abutre *m*.

W

w (*pl* **w's** OR **ws**), **W** (*pl* **W's** OR **Ws**) [ˈdʌbljuː] *n* w, W *m*.
W -1. (*abbr of* west) O. **-2.** (*abbr of* watt) W *m*.
WA *abbr of* Washington.
wacky [ˈwækɪ] (*compar* **-ier**, *superl* **-iest**) *adj inf* excêntrico(ca), extravagante.
wad [wɒd] *n* **-1.** [of cotton wool] chumaço *m*; [of paper, bank notes, documents] pilha *f*; [of tobacco] masca *f* **-2.** [of chewing gum] pedaço *f*.
wadding [ˈwɒdɪŋ] *n* [stuffing] enchimento *m*.
waddle [ˈwɒdll] *vi* caminhar se balançando.
wade [weɪd] *vi* patinhar.
➤ **wade through** *vt fus fig*: he was wading through the documents ele penava muito para ler os documentos.
wadge [wɒdʒ] *n* **-1.** *UK inf* [gen] pilha *f*, porção *f* **-2.** [of cotton wool] chumaço *m*; [of papers] feixe *m*; [of pie] fatia *f*.
wading pool [ˈweɪdɪŋ-] *n* US piscina *f* para crianças.
wafer [ˈweɪfəʳ] *n* [thin biscuit] wafer *m*.
wafer-thin *adj* finíssimo(ma).
waffle [ˈwɒfl] ◇ *n* **-1.** CULIN waffle *m* **-2.** (U) UK inf [vague talk] lengalenga *f*, ladainha *f*. ◇ *vi inf* enrolar.
waft [wɑːft, wɒft] *vi* flutuar.
wag [wæg] (*pt* & *pp* **-ged**, *cont* **-ging**) ◇ *vt* sacudir. ◇ *vi* [tail] abanar.
wage [weɪdʒ] ◇ *n* salário *m*. ◇ *vt*: to ~ war against sb/sthg guerrear com alguém/algo.
➤ **wages** *npl* [of worker] pagamento *m*, salário *m*; I always get my ~s at the end of the week eu recebo sempre nos finais de semana.
wage claim *n* reivindicação *f* salarial.
wage differential *n* diferença *f* salarial.
wage earner [-ˌɜːnəʳ] *n* assalariado *m*, -da *f*.
wage freeze *n* congelamento *m* de salário.
wage packet *n* **-1.** [envelope] envelope *m* de pagamento **-2.** [pay] pagamento *m*.
wager [ˈweɪdʒəʳ] *n* aposta *f*.
wage rise *n* UK aumento *m* de salário.
waggish *adj* **-1.** *inf* [remark, mood, behaviour] jocoso(sa) **-2.** *inf* [person] divertido(da).

waggle [ˈwægl] *inf* *vt* & *vi* balançar.
wagon [ˈwægən], **waggon** *UK* *n* **-1.** [horse-drawn vehicle] carroça *f* **-2.** *UK RAIL* vagão *m*.
wagtail *n* lavandisca *f*.
waif [weɪf] *n literary* criança *f* abandonada.
wail [weɪl] ◇ *n* lamento *m*, gemido *m*. ◇ *vi* **-1.** [baby] choramingar **-2.** [person] gemer **-3.** [wind, siren] soar.
wailing [ˈweɪlɪŋ] *n* **-1.** [of baby] choramingo *m* **-2.** [of person] gemido *m* **-3.** [of wind, siren] som *m*.
waist [weɪst] *n* cintura *f*.
waistband [ˈweɪstbænd] *n* cintura *f*, cós *m*.
waistcoat [ˈweɪskəʊt] *n* colete *m*.
waistline [ˈweɪstlaɪn] *n* cintura *f*.
wait [weɪt] ◇ *n* espera *f*; to lie in ~ for sb esperar alguém numa emboscada. ◇ *vi* esperar; to ~ and see esperar para ver; ~ a minute OR second OR moment [interrupting sb] espere um minuto/segundo/momento; [interrupting o.s.] espera (aí) um pouquinho; **(just) you** ~! espere que você vai ver! ◇ *vt* **-1.**: I/he etc couldn't ~ to do sthg eu/ele mal podia esperar para fazer algo **-2.** US [delay]: don't ~ dinner for me não precisa me esperar para jantar.
➤ **wait about, wait around** *vi* esperar, aguardar.
➤ **wait for** *vt fus* esperar; to ~ for sb to do sthg esperar que alguém faça algo.
➤ **wait on** *vt fus* [serve food to] servir; **she ~s on her family hand and foot** ela responde a todas as necessidades da família.
➤ **wait up** *vi* ficar acordado(da) esperando.
waiter [ˈweɪtəʳ] *n* garçom *m*.
waiting game [ˈweɪtɪŋ-] *n*: to play a ~ esperar o momento certo.
waiting list [ˈweɪtɪŋ-] *n* lista *f* de espera.
waiting room [ˈweɪtɪŋ-] *n* sala *f* de espera.
waitress [ˈweɪtrɪs] *n* garçonete *f*.
waive [weɪv] *vt* **-1.** *fml* [rule] não aplicar **-2.** *fml* [entrance fee] abrir mão de.
waiver [ˈweɪvəʳ] *n* JUR renúncia *f*.
wake [weɪk] (*pt* **woke** OR **-d**, *pp* **woken** OR **-d**) ◇ *n* **-1.** [of ship, boat] esteira *f*; **in one's** ~ *fig* pelo caminho; **in the** ~ **of** *fig* nas águas de **-2.** [for dead person] velório *m*. ◇ *vt* acordar. ◇ *vi* acordar-se.
➤ **wake up** ◇ *vt sep* acordar. ◇ *vi* **-1.** [wake] acordar-se **-2.** *fig* [become aware]: **to** ~ **up (to** sthg**)** conscientizar-se (de algo).
waken [ˈweɪkən] *fml* ◇ *vt* despertar. ◇ *vi* despertar-se.
waking hours [ˈweɪkɪŋ-] *npl* horas *fpl* de vigília.
Wales [weɪlz] *n* País de Gales; **in** ~ no País de Gales.
walk [wɔːk] ◇ *n* **-1.** [stroll] passeio *m*, caminhada *f*; to go for a ~ dar um passeio **-2.** [path] caminho *m* **-3.** [gait] jeito *m* de andar. ◇ *vt* **-1.** [escort] acompanhar **-2.** [take out for exercise] levar para passear **-3.** [cover on foot] caminhar; **to ~ the streets** [be homeless] vagar pela rua; [in search of sthg] percorrer as ruas; [prostitute] prostituir-se. ◇ *vi* caminhar, andar.
➤ **walk away with** *vt fus inf fig* [carry off] levar.
➤ **walk in on** *vt fus* [interrupt] interromper.

➡ **walk off** vt sep [headache, cramp, meal] dar uma volta para aliviar.

➡ **walk off with** vt fus inf -**1.** [steal] levar -**2.** [win easily] levar de barbada.

➡ **walk out** vi -**1.** [leave suddenly] sair -**2.** [go on strike] entrar em greve branca.

➡ **walk out on** vt fus deixar, abandonar.

walkabout ['wɔːkə,baʊt] n UK [by politician] caminhada f pelas ruas; **to go on a ~** caminhar entre as pessoas (nas ruas).

walker ['wɔːkə'] n [for pleasure, sport] caminhante mf.

walkie-talkie [,wɔːkɪ'tɔːkɪ] n walkie-talkie m.

walk-in adj -**1.** [cupboard] espaçoso(sa) -**2.** US [easy] fácil.

walking ['wɔːkɪŋ] n [for pleasure, sport] caminhada f; **to go ~** dar uma caminhada.

walking shoes npl sapatos mpl de caminhada.

walking stick n bengala f.

Walkman® ['wɔːkmən] n walkman® m.

walk of life (pl walks of life) n -**1.** [job] profissão f -**2.** [social position] posição f social.

walk-on adj de figurante.

walkout ['wɔːkaʊt] n [of members, spectators, workers] greve f branca.

walkover ['wɔːk,əʊvə'] n UK inf [victory] barbada f, vitória f fácil.

walkway ['wɔːkweɪ] n passadiço m, passagem f.

wall [wɔːl] n -**1.** [interior] parede f -**2.** [exterior] muro m; **to come up against a brick ~** chegar a um beco sem saída; **to drive sb up the ~** deixar alguém louco -**3.** ANAT parede f.

wallaby ['wɒləbɪ] (pl -ies) n marsupial australiano parecido com um pequeno canguru.

wallchart ['wɔːltʃɑːt] n mural m.

wall cupboard n armário m embutido.

walled [wɔːld] adj cercado(da) (com muros).

wallet ['wɒlɪt] n carteira f.

wallflower ['wɔːl,flaʊə'] n -**1.** [plant] aleli m -**2.** inf fig [person] azeite m.

Walloon ◇ adj valão(ona). ◇ n -**1.** [person] valão m, -ona f -**2.** [language] valão m.

wallop ['wɒləp] inf ◇ n surra f. ◇ vt [hit] surrar.

wallow ['wɒləʊ] vi -**1.** [in water] mergulhar -**2.** [in mud] chafurdar -**3.** [in emotion]: **to ~ in sthg** afundar-se em algo.

wall painting n afresco m, mural m.

wallpaper ['wɔːl,peɪpə'] ◇ n (U) papel m de parede. ◇ vt forrar com papel de parede.

Wall Street n Wall Street; **on ~** em Wall Street.

WALL STREET

A Wall Street, em Nova York, é o centro financeiro mais importante dos Estados Unidos. É nessa rua que se situa o edifício da Bolsa de Valores. Por extensão, o termo é utilizado para designar o mundo financeiro estadunidense.

wall-to-wall adj: **~ carpet** carpete m.

wally ['wɒlɪ] (pl -ies) n UK inf pateta mf.

walnut ['wɔːlnʌt] n -**1.** [nut] noz m -**2.** [tree, material] nogueira f.

walrus ['wɔːlrəs] (pl inv OR -es) n morsa f.

waltz [wɔːls] ◇ n valsa f. ◇ vi -**1.** [dance] dançar uma valsa -**2.** inf [walk confidently]: **to ~ in/out** entrar/sair de fininho.

wan [wɒn] (compar -ner, superl -nest) adj abatido(da).

wand [wɒnd] n varinha f mágica.

wander ['wɒndə'] vi -**1.** [person] perambular -**2.** [mind, thoughts] divagar.

wanderer ['wɒndərə'] n andarilho m, -lha f.

wandering ['wɒndərɪŋ] adj [itinerant] ambulante.

wanderlust ['wɒndəlʌst] n (U) paixão f por viajar.

wane [weɪn] ◇ n: **on the ~** em declínio. ◇ vi -**1.** [influence, interest] declinar -**2.** [moon] minguar.

wangle ['wæŋgl] vt inf arranjar, conseguir.

wanna ['wɒnə] cont esp US = want a, want to.

wannabe adj inf que gostaria de ser igual a outra pessoa ou grupo de pessoas.

want [wɒnt] ◇ n -**1.** [need] necessidade f -**2.** [lack] falta f; **for ~ of** por falta de -**3.** (U) [deprivation] penúria f; **to be in ~** passar necessidades. ◇ vt -**1.** [desire] querer; **to ~ to do sthg** querer fazer algo; **to ~ sb to do sthg** querer que alguém faça algo -**2.** inf [need] precisar.

want ad n US inf anúncio m (classificado).

wanted ['wɒntɪd] adj: **to be ~ (by the police)** ser procurado(da) (pela polícia).

wanting ['wɒntɪŋ] adj fml [inadequate]: **to be ~ (in sthg)** carecer (de algo); **the play is ~ in humour** está faltando humor na peça; **to be found ~** deixar a desejar.

wanton ['wɒntən] adj -**1.** fml [malicious] gratuito(ta), sem motivo -**2.** [immoral] libertino(na).

WAP [wæp] (abbr of wireless application protocol) n WAP m.

WAP phone n telefone m WAP.

war [wɔː'] (pt & pp -red, cont -ring) n guerra f; **at ~** em guerra; **to go to ~** entrar em guerra; **to have been in the ~s** UK estar num estado deplorável.

warble ['wɔːbl] vi literary [bird] trinar, chilrear.

war crime n crime m de guerra.

war criminal n criminoso m, -sa f de guerra.

war cry n [in battle] grito m de guerra.

ward [wɔːd] n -**1.** [in hospital] ala f -**2.** UK POL distrito m eleitoral -**3.** JUR tutelado m, -da f.

➡ **ward off** vt fus proteger-se de.

war dance n dança f de guerra.

warden ['wɔːdn] n -**1.** [of park] guarda mf -**2.** UK [of youth hostel, hall of residence] diretor m, -ra f -**3.** US [prison governor] diretor m, -ra f.

warder ['wɔːdə'] n [in prison] carcereiro m, -ra f.

ward of court n menor mf sob tutela judicial.

wardrobe ['wɔːdrəʊb] n -**1.** [piece of furniture] guarda-roupa m, armário m -**2.** [collection of clothes] guarda-roupa m.

wardrobe mistress n UK figurinista f.

warehouse ['weəhaʊs, pl -haʊzɪz] n armazém m, depósito m.

wares [weəz] npl literary mercadorias fpl.

warfare ['wɔːfeə'] n combate m; **gang ~** disputa f entre gangues.

war game n -**1.** [military exercise] manobra f OR exercício m militar -**2.** [game of strategy] jogo m de estratégia militar.

warhead ['wɔːhed] n MIL ogiva f.

warily [ˈweərəlɪ] *adv* com desconfiança.

warlike [ˈwɔːlaɪk] *adj* guerreiro(ra), belicoso(sa).

warm [wɔːm] ⟨⟩ *adj* **-1.** [gen] quente; **I'm ~ estou com calor; are you ~ enough?** não está com frio, certo? **- 2.** [clothing, blanket] que protege do frio **- 3.** [sound] cálido(da) **- 4.** [person] afetuoso(sa), caloroso(sa) **- 5.** [friendly - congratulations] efusivo(va); [- attitude, smile, handshake] caloroso(sa). ⟨⟩ *vt* [heat gently] aquecer.

➡ **warm over** *vt sep US* **-1.** [food] requentar **- 2.** [ideas] insistir em.

➡ **warm to** *vt fus* tomar simpatia por.

➡ **warm up** ⟨⟩ *vt sep* **-1.** [heat] esquentar **- 2.** [audience] esquentar. ⟨⟩ *vi* **-1.** [get warmer - gen] esquentar; [- person] esquentar-se **- 2.** [prepare - for exercise] aquecer, aquecer-se; [- for performance] preparar-se.

warm-blooded [-ˈblʌdɪd] *adj* de sangue quente.

war memorial *n* memorial *m* de guerra.

warm front *n* frente *f* quente.

warm-hearted [-ˈhɑːtɪd] *adj* afetuoso(sa).

warmly [ˈwɔːmlɪ] *adv* **-1.** [in warm clothes]: **to dress ~** agasalhar-se bem **- 2.** [in a friendly way] calorosamente, efusivamente.

warmness [ˈwɔːmnɪs] *n (U)* [friendliness] cordialidade *f*.

warmonger [ˈwɔːˌmʌŋɡəʳ] *n* belicista *mf*.

warmth [wɔːmθ] *n (U)* **-1.** [of temperature] calor *m* **- 2.** [of welcome, smile, support] cordialidade *f*.

warm-up *n* [preparation] aquecimento *m*.

warn [wɔːn] ⟨⟩ *vt* **-1.** [advise] advertir, prevenir; **to ~ sb of** OR **about sthg** advertir alguém de/sobre algo; **to ~ sb against doing sthg** advertir alguém sobre (os riscos de) fazer algo; **to ~ sb not to do sthg** avisar a alguém para que não faça algo **- 2.** [inform] avisar. ⟨⟩ *vi* [forecast]: **to ~ of sthg** alertar para a possbilidade de algo.

warning [ˈwɔːnɪŋ] ⟨⟩ *adj* de advertência. ⟨⟩ *n* **-1.** [official caution] advertência *f* **- 2.** [prior notice] aviso *m*.

warning light *n* luz *f* de advertência.

warning triangle *n UK* triângulo *m* luminoso *(do carro)*.

warp [wɔːp] ⟨⟩ *n* [of cloth] urdidura *f*. ⟨⟩ *vt* **-1.** [wood] empenar **- 2.** [personality, mind] desvirtuar; [judgement] distorcer. ⟨⟩ *vi* [wood] empenar.

warpath [ˈwɔːpɑːθ] *n*: **to be/go on the ~** *fig* estar procurando briga.

warped [wɔːpt] *adj* **-1.** [wood] empenado(da) **- 2.** [person] corrompido(da).

warrant [ˈwɒrənt] ⟨⟩ *n* JUR [written order] mandado *m* (judicial). ⟨⟩ *vt fml* [justify] merecer.

warrant officer *n* **-1.** MIL suboficial *mf* **- 2.** NAUT subtenente *mf*.

warranty [ˈwɒrəntɪ] *(pl* **-ies)** *n* garantia *f*.

warren [ˈwɒrən] *n* [of rabbit] toca *f*.

warring [ˈwɔːrɪŋ] *adj* rival.

warrior [ˈwɒrɪəʳ] *n literary* guerreiro *m*, -ra *f*.

Warsaw [ˈwɔːsɔː] *n* Varsóvia; **in ~** em Varsóvia; **the ~ Pact** o Pacto de Varsóvia.

warship [ˈwɔːʃɪp] *n* navio *m* de guerra.

wart [wɔːt] *n* verruga *f*.

wartime [ˈwɔːtaɪm] ⟨⟩ *adj* de guerra. ⟨⟩ *n (U)*

tempos *mpl* de guerra; **in ~** em tempos de guerra.

war widow *n* viúva *f* de guerra.

wary [ˈweərɪ] *(compar* **-ier,** *superl* **-iest)** *adj* receoso (sa); **~ of sthg/of doing sthg** receoso(sa) de algo/ de fazer algo.

was [*weak form* wəz, *strong form* wɒz] *pt* ⊳ **be**.

wash [wɒʃ] ⟨⟩ *n* **-1.** [act of washing] lavada *f*; **to have a ~** lavar-se; **to give sthg a ~** dar uma lavada em algo **- 2.** [clothes to be washed] roupa *f* para lavar OR suja **- 3.** [from boat] esteira *f*. ⟨⟩ *vt* **-1.** [clean] lavar **- 2.** [subj: current, sea, rain] levar, arrastar. ⟨⟩ *vi* [clean o.s.] lavar-se.

➡ **wash away** *vt sep* levar, arrastar.

➡ **wash down** *vt sep* **-1.** [food] regar **- 2.** [clean] lavar.

➡ **wash out** *vt sep* **-1.** [stain, dye] tirar lavando **- 2.** [container] enxaguar.

➡ **wash up** ⟨⟩ *vt sep* **-1.** UK [dishes] lavar **- 2.** [subj: sea, river] trazer, arrastar. ⟨⟩ *vi* **-1.** UK [wash the dishes] lavar os pratos **- 2.** US [wash o.s.] lavar-se.

washable [ˈwɒʃəbl] *adj* lavável.

wash-and-wear *adj que não precisa ser passado.*

washbasin UK [ˈwɒʃˌbeɪsn], **washbowl** US [ˈwɒʃbəʊl] *n* lavatório *m*.

washcloth [ˈwɒʃˌklɒθ] *n US* toalha *f* de rosto.

washed-out [wɒʃt-] *adj* **-1.** [pale] desbotado(da) **- 2.** [exhausted] exausto(ta).

washed-up [wɒʃt-] *adj inf* acabado(da).

washer [ˈwɒʃəʳ] *n* **-1.** TECH arruela *f* **- 2.** [washing machine] lavadora *f* (de roupa).

washer-dryer *n* lavadora *f* e secadora.

washing [ˈwɒʃɪŋ] *n (U)* **-1.** [act] lavagem *f* **- 2.** [clothes] roupa *f* para lavar OR suja.

washing line *n* varal *m*.

washing machine *n* lavadora *f* (de roupa).

washing powder *n (U) UK* sabão *m* em pó.

Washington [ˈwɒʃɪŋtən] *n* **-1.** [state]: **~ State** Estado de Washington **- 2.** [city]: **~ D.C.** Washington D.C.

washing-up *n* **-1.** UK [crockery, pans etc] louça *f* para lavar OR suja **- 2.** [act]: **to do the ~** lavar a louça.

washing-up liquid *n UK* detergente *m*.

washout [ˈwɒʃaʊt] *n inf* fracasso *m*, desastre *m*.

washroom [ˈwɒʃrʊm] *n US* lavabo *m*.

wasn't [wɒznt] = **was not**.

wasp [wɒsp] *n* [insect] vespa *f*.

Wasp, WASP [wɒsp] *(abbr of* White Anglo-Saxon Protestant) *n inf nos Estados Unidos e no Canadá, pessoa branca de origem anglo-saxônica e protestante.*

waspish [ˈwɒspɪʃ] *adj* mordaz.

wastage [ˈweɪstɪdʒ] *n* desperdício *m*.

waste [weɪst] ⟨⟩ *adj* **-1.** [material, fuel] de sobra **- 2.** [area of land] improdutivo(va). ⟨⟩ *n* **-1.** [misuse] desperdício *m*; **to go to ~** perder-se; **a ~ of time** uma perda de tempo **- 2.** [refuse] resíduos *mpl*. ⟨⟩ *vt* [misuse] desperdiçar; **it would be ~d on me** eu não saberia aproveitar isso.

➡ **wastes** *npl literary* [wastelands] desertos *mpl*.

➡ **waste away** *vi* definhar.

wastebasket n US cesto m de lixo.

wasted adj [misused] perdido(da).

waste disposal unit n triturador m de lixo.

wasteful ['weɪstfʊl] adj: **to be very ~ to do sthg** ser muito desperdício fazer algo.

waste ground n (U) terra f improdutiva, descampados mpl.

wasteland ['weɪst͵lænd] n terreno m deserto.

waste paper n (U) papel m usado.

wastepaper basket [͵weɪst'peɪpəʳ-], **wastepaper bin** [͵weɪst'peɪpəʳ-], **wastebasket** US ['weɪst͵bɑːskɪt] n cesto m para papel.

watch [wɒtʃ] <> n -1. [timepiece] relógio m -2. [act of guarding]: **to keep ~ ficar de guarda**; **to keep ~ on sb/sthg** vigiar alguém/algo -3. [guard] guarda mf. <> vt -1. [look at - television, programme, match] ver; [- scene, activity] contemplar -2. [spy on] vigiar -3. [be careful about] cuidar; **~ what you're doing** presta atenção no que você está fazendo; **~ it!** inf cuidado! <> vi [observe] observar.
◆ **watch for** vt fus esperar.
◆ **watch out** vi -1. [be careful]: **to ~ out (for sthg)** ter cuidado (com algo); **~ out!** cuidado! -2. [keep a lookout]: **to ~ out for sthg** prestar atenção em algo.
◆ **watch over** vt fus [look after] cuidar de.

watchdog ['wɒtʃdɒg] n -1. [dog] cão m de guarda -2. fig [organization] comissão que fiscaliza as empresas e impede que realizem ações ilegais ou irresponsáveis.

watchful ['wɒtʃfʊl] adj [vigilant] atento(ta); **to keep a ~ eye on sb/sthg** estar atento(ta) a alguém/algo.

watchmaker ['wɒtʃ͵meɪkəʳ] n relojoeiro m, -ra f.

watchman ['wɒtʃmən] (pl -men [-mən]) n segurança m, vigia m.

watchword ['wɒtʃwɜːd] n palavra f de ordem, lema m.

water ['wɔːtəʳ] <> n -1. [gen] água f; **to pour** OR **throw OR ~ on sthg** fig dar um banho de água fria em algo; **to tread ~** [in sea, pool] boiar mexendo as pernas; fig [do same thing] marcar passo; **that's ~ under the bridge** são águas passadas -2. [urine]: **to pass ~** tirar água do joelho. <> vt [plants, soil] regar. <> vi -1. [eyes] lacrimejar -2. [mouth]: **it makes my mouth ~** fico com água na boca.
◆ **waters** npl águas fpl.
◆ **water down** vt sep -1. [dilute] diluir -2. usu pej [moderate] suavizar, moderar.

water bed n colchão m d'água.

water bird n ave f aquática.

water biscuit n bolacha f de água e sal.

waterborne ['wɔːtəbɔːn] adj transmitido(da) pela água.

water bottle n garrafa f d'água, cantil m.

water buffalo n búfalo-da-índia m.

water cannon n canhão m de água.

water chestnut n castanha-d'água f.

water closet n dated w.c. m.

watercolour ['wɔːtə͵kʌləʳ] n aquarela f.

water-cooled [-͵kuːld] adj refrigerado(da) a água.

watercourse ['wɔːtəkɔːs] n [river, stream] córrego m.

watercress ['wɔːtəkres] n (U) agrião m.

watered-down [͵wɔːtəd-] adj usu pej suavizado(da).

waterfall ['wɔːtəfɔːl] n queda-d'água f, cachoeira f.

waterfront ['wɔːtəfrʌntl] n orla f marítima.

water heater n aquecedor m de água.

waterhole ['wɔːtəhəʊl] n cacimba f.

watering can ['wɔːtərɪŋ-] n regador m.

water jump n valado m de água (nas corridas de cavalo).

water level n nível m de água.

water lily n nenúfar m.

waterline ['wɔːtəlaɪn] n NAUT linha-d'água f.

waterlogged ['wɔːtəlɒgd] adj -1. [land] alagado(da) -2. [vessel] inundado(da).

water main n adutora f.

watermark ['wɔːtəmɑːk] n -1. [in paper] marca f d'água -2. [showing water level] linha-d'água f.

watermelon ['wɔːtə͵melən] n melancia f.

water pipe n [in building] cano m de água.

water pistol n pistola f d'água.

water polo n (U) pólo m aquático.

waterproof ['wɔːtəpruːf] <> adj à prova d'água. <> n capa f impermeável; **~s** roupa f à prova d'água. <> vt impermeabilizar.

water rates npl UK tarifa f de água.

water-resistant adj resistente à água.

watershed ['wɔːtəʃedl] n -1. GEOGR linha f divisória das águas -2. fig [turning point] divisor m de águas.

waterside ['wɔːtəsaɪd] <> adj ribeirinho(nha). <> n: **the ~** a orla.

water skiing n (U) esqui m aquático.

water softener n abrandador m de água.

water-soluble adj solúvel em água.

watersports npl esportes mpl aquáticos.

waterspout n tromba f d'água.

water supply n fornecimento m de água.

water table n (nível m do) lençol m freático.

water tank n caixa f d'água.

watertight ['wɔːtətaɪt] adj -1. [waterproof] hermético(ca) -2. fig [faultless] infalível.

water tower n torre f d'água.

waterway ['wɔːtəweɪ] n via f navegável, canal m.

waterworks ['wɔːtəwɜːks] (pl inv) n [building] instalações fpl para a distribuição de água.

watery ['wɔːtərɪ] adj -1. [food, drink] aguado(da) -2. [light, sun, moon] pálido(da).

watt [wɒt] n watt m.

wattage ['wɒtɪdʒ] n potência f em watts.

wave [weɪv] <> n -1. GEN onda f -2. [of people] leva f -3. [in hair] ondulação f -4. [gesture] aceno m. <> vt -1. [brandish - hand, flag] agitar; [- baton] manejar; [- stick, pistol, gun] empunhar -2. [gesture to] fazer sinal para -3. [hair] ondular. <> vi -1. [with hand] abanar; **to ~ at** OR **to sb** abanar para alguém -2. [flag] tremular -3. [tree] balançar -4. [hair] ondular.
◆ **wave aside** vt sep fig [dismiss] rejeitar.
◆ **wave down** vt sep fazer sinal para parar.

wave band n faixa f de onda.

wavelength ['weɪvleŋθ] n comprimento m de onda; **to be on the same ~** fig estar em sintonia.

waver ['weɪvə^r] *vi* -**1.** [gen] vacilar; **to ~ in sthg** hesitar em algo -**2.** [light, temperature] oscilar -**3.** [flame] tremer.

wavy ['weɪvɪ] (*compar* -**ier**, *superl* -**iest**) *adj* -**1.** [hair] ondulado(da) -**2.** [line] sinuoso(sa).

wax [wæks] ◇ *n* [gen] cera *f.* ◇ *vt* -**1.** [floor, table] encerar ; [skis] passar cera em -**2.** [legs] depilar com cera. ◇ *vi* -**1.** *dated or hum* [become] tornar -se; **to ~ and wane** aumentar e diminuir -**2.** [moon] crescer.

waxen ['wæksən] *adj* [face, complexion] pálido(da).

wax paper *n US* papel *m* encerado.

waxworks ['wækswɜːks] (*pl inv*) *n* [museum] museu *m* de cera.

way [weɪ] ◇ *n* -**1.** [means, method] maneira *f,* modo *m;* **~s and means** meios *mpl;* **to get** OR **have one's ~** conseguir o que se quer; **to have everything one's own ~** ter o que se quer -**2.** [manner, style] jeito *m,* maneira *f;* **in the same ~** da mesma forma; **this/that ~** dessa/daquela forma; **in a ~** de certa forma OR maneira; **in a big/small ~** em grande/pequena escala; **to fall for sb in a big ~** apaixonar-se loucamente por alguém; **to be in a bad ~** ficar mal; **in no ~** de maneira alguma -**3.** [skill]: **to have a ~ with sb/sthg** ter jeito para lidar com alguém/algo; **to have a ~ of doing sthg** ter o costume de fazer algo -**4.** [thoroughfare, path] caminho *m;* **across** OR **over the ~** do outro lado da rua; **'give ~'** *UK* AUT dê passagem -**5.** [route leading to a specified place] caminho *m;* **do you know the ~ to the cathedral?** sabe como se faz para chegar na catedral?; **to lose one's ~** perder-se; **out of one's ~** [place] fora do caminho de alguém; **can you post this letter on the** OR **one's ~ (to the shops)** quando você for (fazer compras), pode colocar esta carta no correio?; **to be under ~** [ship] estar navegando; [project, meeting] estar em andamento; **to get under ~** [ship] zarpar; [project, meeting] estar em andamento; **to be in the ~** estar na passagem OR frente; **to be out of the ~** [finished] estar pronto(ta); [not blocking] **if you put your suitcase over there, it will be out of the ~** se colocar sua mala lá, ela não vai ficar atrapalhando; **to go out of one's ~** to do sthg não poupar esforços para fazer algo; **to keep out of sb's ~** não cruzar o caminho de alguém; **keep out of the ~!** saia do caminho!; **to make one's ~** dirigir-se; **to make ~ for sb/sthg** abrir espaço para alguém/algo; **to stand in sb's ~** *fig* ficar no caminho de alguém; **to work one's ~ to** abrir caminho para chegar a -**6.** [route leading in a specified direction]: **come this ~** vem por aqui; **~ in** entrada; **~ out** saída -**7.** [side] lado *m;* **the right/wrong ~ round** do jeito certo/ errado; **the right/wrong ~ up** com o lado certo/ errado para cima -**8.** [distance]: **all the ~** todo o caminho; **most of the ~** quase todo o caminho; **a long ~** um longo caminho; **to go a long ~ to-wards doing sthg** *fig* contribuir muito no sentido de se fazer algo -**9.** *phr:* **to give ~** [under weight, pressure] ceder; **no ~!** de maneira alguma! ◇ *adv inf* [by far] muito; **it's ~ too big!** é enorme de grande!

➤ **ways** *npl* [customs, habits] costumes *mpl,* hábitos *mpl.*

➤ **by the way** *adv* a propósito, aliás.

➤ **by way of** *prep* -**1.** [via] passando por -**2.** [as a sort of] como forma de.

➤ **in the way of** *prep* [in the form of]: **what do you have in the of ~ red wine?** o que tem de vinho branco?

waylay [ˌweɪ'leɪ] (*pt* & *pp* -**laid**) *vt* abordar.

way of life *n* estilo *m* OR modo *m* de vida.

way-out *adj inf* arrojado(da).

wayside ['weɪsaɪd] *n* [roadside] beira *f* da estrada; **to fall by the ~** *fig* ir por água abaixo.

wayward ['weɪwəd] *adj* incorrigível.

WC (*abbr of* **water closet**) *n* WC *m.*

WCC (*abbr of* **World Council of Churches**) *n conselho mundial de igrejas.*

we [wiː] *pers pron pl* nós **~'re young** (nós) somos jovens.

weak [wiːk] *adj* -**1.** [gen] fraco(ca) -**2.** [lacking knowledge, skill]: **to be ~ on sthg** ser fraco(ca) em algo).

weaken ['wiːkn] ◇ *vt* -**1.** [gen] enfraquecer; FIN [devalue] desvalorizar -**2.** [debilitate] debilitar. ◇ *vi* -**1.** [person - physically] debilitar-se; [- morally] desgastar-se; **no signs of ~ing** nenhum sinal de desgaste -**2.** [influence, power] diminuir -**3.** [structure] enfraquecer-se -**4.** FIN [dollar, mark] desvalorizar-se.

weak-kneed [-'niːd] *adj inf pej* sem iniciativa.

weakling ['wiːklɪŋ] *n pej* fraco *m,* -ca *f (de corpo e mente).*

weakly ['wiːklɪ] *adv* fracamente.

weak-minded [-'maɪndɪd] *adj* fraco(ca) de caráter.

weakness ['wiːknɪs] *n* -**1.** (U) [of person - physical] fraqueza *f;* [- moral] ponto *m* fraco; **to have a ~ for sthg** ter um fraco por algo -**2.** [of government, structure, plan] debilidade *f* -**3.** FIN [of currency] fragilidade *f.*

weal [wiːl] *n* vergão *m.*

wealth [welθ] *n* -**1.** (U) [riches] riqueza *f* -**2.** [abundance]: **a ~ of sthg** uma profusão de algo.

wealth tax *n UK* imposto *m* sobre bens.

wealthy ['welθɪ] (*compar* -**ier**, *superl* -**iest**) *adj* rico(-ca).

wean [wiːn] *vt* -**1.** [from mother's milk] desmamar -**2.** [from habit]: **to ~ sb from** OR **off sthg** afastar alguém gradualmente de algo.

weapon ['wepən] *n* arma *f.*

weaponry ['wepənrɪ] *n* (U) armamento *m.*

wear [weə^r] (*pt* **wore**, *pp* **worn**) ◇ *n* -**1.** [type of clothes] roupa *f* -**2.** [damage] desgaste *m;* **~ and tear** desgaste -**3.** [use] uso *m;* **to be the worse for ~** [tired] estar um trapo; [drunk] estar num estado deplorável. ◇ *vt* -**1.** [gen] usar -**2.** [clothes] vestir -**3.** [shoes] calçar -**4.** [damage - gen] danificar; [-holes] abrir. ◇ *vi* -**1.** [deteriorate] gastar -**2.** [last]: **to ~ well/badly** durar bastante/pouco -**3.** *phr:* **to ~ thin** ficar gasto(ta).

➤ **wear away** ◇ *vt sep* desgastar. ◇ *vi* desgastar-se.

➤ **wear down** ◇ *vt sep* -**1.** [reduce size of] gastar -**2.** [weaken] esgotar. ◇ *vi* gastar, desgastar.

➤ **wear off** *vi* passar.

➤ **wear on** *vi* transcorrer.

➤ **wear out** ◇ *vt sep* -**1.** [clothing, machinery]

usar até estragar **- 2.** [patience, strength, reserves] esgotar **- 3.** [person] ficar esgotado(da). ◇ *vi* [clothing, shoes] gastar.

wearable ['weərəbl] *adj* que se pode usar.

wearily ['wɪərɪlɪ] *adv* com cansaço.

weariness ['wɪərɪnɪs] *n (U)* exaustão *f*, cansaço *m*.

wearing ['weərɪŋ] *adj* [exhausting] fatigante.

weary ['wɪərɪ] (*compar* **-ier**, *superl* **-iest**) *adj* **- 1.** [exhausted] exausto(ta) **- 2.** [fed up]: **to be ~ of sthg/of doing sthg** estar farto(ta) de algo/de fazer algo.

weasel ['wi:zl] *n* doninha *f*.

weather ['weðəʳ] ◇ *n* tempo *m*; **to make heavy ~ of sthg** complicar algo desnecessariamente; **to be under the ~** estar se sentindo um pouco indisposto(ta). ◇ *vt* [survive] superar. ◇ *vi* ser resistente.

weather-beaten [-ˌbi:tn] *adj* **- 1.** [stone, rocks] desgastado(da) **- 2.** [face, skin] desgastado(da) pelo tempo.

weathercock ['weðəkɒk] *n* cata-vento *m (em forma de galo)*.

weathered ['weðəd] *adj* **- 1.** [face] marcado(da) **- 2.** [wood, building, stone] deteriorado(da).

weather forecast *n* previsão *f* do tempo.

weatherman ['weðəmæn] (*pl* **-men** [-men]) *n* meteorologista *m*.

weather map *n* mapa *m* do tempo.

weatherproof ['weðəpru:f] *adj* **- 1.** [clothing] impermeável **- 2.** [building] resistente às intempéries.

weather report *n* previsão *f* do tempo.

weather ship *n* navio *m* meteorológico.

weather vane [-veɪn] *n* cata-vento *m*.

weave [wi:v] (*pt* **wove**, *pp* **woven**) ◇ *n* trama *f (do tecido)*. ◇ *vt* **- 1.** [using loom] tecer **- 2.** [move along]: **to ~ one's way** costurar *(no trânsito)*. ◇ *vi* [move]: **to ~ in and out** ziguezaguear.

weaver ['wi:vəʳ] *n* tecelão *m*, -lã *f*.

web [web] *n* **- 1.** [cobweb] teia *f* **- 2.** *fig* [of lies, intrigue] rede *f* **- 3.** *COMPUT* Web *f*, Rede *f*.

webbed [webd] *adj* palmado(da).

webbing ['webɪŋ] *n (U)* [material] tira *f* de tecido resistente.

web browser *n COMPUT* navegador *m*.

webcam ['webkæm] *n* câmera *f* web, webcam *f*.

webcast ['webkɑ:st] *n* transmissão *f* ao vivo pela Internet.

web designer *n* web designer *mf*.

web-footed [-'fʊtɪd] *adj* palmípede.

web page *n* página *f* da Web.

webphone ['webfəʊn] *n* webphone *m*.

website ['websaɪt] *n* site *m* da Web.

wed [wed] (*pt & pp* **wed** OR **-ded**) *literary* ◇ *vt* [marry] desposar. ◇ *vi* casar.

we'd [wi:d] = **we had**, **we would**.

Wed. (*abbr of* **Wednesday**) qua.

wedded ['wedɪd] *adj* [committed]: **~ to sthg** dedicado(da) a algo.

wedding ['wedɪŋ] *n* casamento *m (cerimônia)*.

wedding anniversary *n* aniversário *m* de casamento.

wedding cake *n* bolo *m* de casamento.

wedding dress *n* vestido *m* de noiva.

wedding night *n* noite *f* de núpcias.

wedding reception *n* recepção *f* de casamento.

wedding ring *n* aliança *f*.

wedge [wedʒ] ◇ *n* **- 1.** [gen] cunha *f*; **to drive a ~ between** piorar o relacionamento entre; **the thin end of the ~** a ponta do iceberg **- 2.** [of cheese, cake, pie] fatia *f*, porção *f*. ◇ *vt* **- 1.** [make fixed or steady] calçar com cunha **- 2.** [squeeze, push] enfiar; **she sat ~d between us** ela se sentou enfiada entre nós.

wedlock ['wedlɒk] *n (U) literary* matrimônio *m*.

Wednesday ['wenzdɪ] *n* quarta-feira *f*; *see also* **Saturday**.

wee [wi:] ◇ *adj Scot* pequenino(na). ◇ *n inf* xixi *m*. ◇ *vi inf* fazer xixi.

weed [wi:d] ◇ *n* **- 1.** [wild plant] erva *f* daninha **- 2.** *UK inf* [feeble person] fracote *m*, -ta *f*. ◇ *vt* capinar.
  ➡ **weed out** *vt sep* eliminar.

weeding ['wi:dɪŋ] *n (U)* capina *f*.

weedkiller ['wi:dˌkɪləʳ] *n* herbicida *m*.

weedy ['wi:dɪ] (*compar* **-ier**, *superl* **-iest**) *adj* **- 1.** [overgrown with weeds] com muito inço **- 2.** *UK inf* [feeble] fracote(ta).

week [wi:k] *n* [gen] semana *f*; **during the ~** durante a semana; **in three ~s' time** dentro de três semanas; **a ~ on Saturday** OR **Saturday ~** sem ser este sábado, no outro; **a ~ last Saturday** uma semana antes de sábado.

weekday ['wi:kdeɪ] *n* dia *m* da semana.

weekend [ˌwi:k'end] *n* fim *m* de semana; **at the ~** no fim de semana.

weekend bag *n* bolsa *f* pequena *(para sair no fim de semana)*.

weekly ['wi:klɪ] (*pl* **-ies**) ◇ *adj* semanal. ◇ *adv* semanalmente. ◇ *n* semanário *m*.

weeny *adj UK inf* pouquinho(nha); **a ~ bit** um pouquinho.

weep [wi:p] (*pt & pp* **wept**) ◇ *n*: **to have a ~** chorar. ◇ *vt* derramar. ◇ *vi* chorar.

weeping willow [ˌwi:pɪŋ-] *n* salgueiro-chorão *m*.

weepy [wi:pɪ] (*compar* **-ier**, *superl* **-iest**) ◇ *adj* choroso(sa), triste. ◇ *n* [sentimental film] dramalhão *m*.

weft *n* trama *f*.

weigh [weɪ] ◇ *vt* **- 1.** [gen] pesar **- 2.** [raise]: **to ~ anchor** levantar âncora. ◇ *vi* [have specific weight] pesar.
  ➡ **weigh down** *vt sep* **- 1.** [physically] sobrecarregar **- 2.** [mentally]: **to be ~ed down by** OR **with sthg** estar prostrado(da) por algo.
  ➡ **weigh (up)on** *vt fus* oprimir.
  ➡ **weigh out** *vt sep* pesar.
  ➡ **weigh up** *vt sep* [situation, pros and cons] pesar; [person, opposition] fazer uma idéia de.

weighbridge ['weɪbrɪdʒ] *n UK* balança *f* para veículos.

weighing machine ['weɪŋ-] *n* balança *f*.

weight [weɪt] ◇ *n* **- 1.** [gen] peso *m*; **to put on** OR **gain ~** engordar; **to lose ~** perder peso; **to take the ~ off one's feet** descansar **- 2.** *fig* [power, influence]: **the ~ of public opinion** a opinião pública em peso; **to carry** ~ ter peso; **to pull one's** ~ fazer sua parte; **to throw one's** ~ **about** ficar dando ordens. ◇ *vt*: **to** ~ **sthg (down)** colocar lastro em algo.

weighted ['weɪtɪd] *adj*: **to be** ~ **in favour of/ against sb** pesar a favor de/contra alguém; **to be** ~ **in favour of/against sthg** pesar a favor de/contra algo.

weighting ['weɪtɪŋ] *n* (U) pagamento adicional *por se viver numa cidade com alto custo de vida*.

weightlessness ['weɪtlɪsnɪs] *n* (U) imponderabilidade *f*, ausência *f* de peso.

weight lifter *n* levantador *m*, -ra *f* de peso, halterofilista *mf*.

weight lifting *n* (U) levantamento *m* de peso.

weight training *n* (U) levantamento *m* de peso.

weighty ['weɪtɪ] (*compar* **-ier**, *superl* **-iest**) *adj* [serious, important] de peso.

weir [wɪəʳ] *n* represa *f*.

weird [wɪəd] *adj* estranho(nha), esquisito(ta).

weirdo ['wɪədəʊl] (*pl* **-s**) *n inf* excêntrico *m*, -ca *f*.

welcome ['welkəm] ◇ *adj* **-1.** [gen] bem-vindo(da); **to make sb** ~ receber alguém muito bem **-2.** [free]: **to be** ~ **to do sthg** ter toda a liberdade para fazer algo **-3.** [in reply to thanks]: **you're** ~ de nada. ◇ *n* acolhida *f*. ◇ *vt* [gen] acolher. ◇ *excl* bem-vindo(da)!

welcoming ['welkəmɪŋ] *adj* cordial.

weld [weld] ◇ *n* solda *f*. ◇ *vt* soldar.

welder ['weldəʳ] *n* soldador *m*, -ra *f*.

welfare ['welfeəʳ] ◇ *adj* de assistência social. ◇ *n* **-1.** [state of wellbeing] bem-estar *m* **-2.** *US* [income support] assistência *f* social (do governo).

welfare state *n* estado *m* de bem-estar social.

well [wel] (*compar* **better**, *superl* **best**) ◇ *adj* bem; **to get** ~ ficar bem; **all is** ~ está tudo bem; **(all)** ~ **and good** tudo bem; **just as** ~ ainda bem que. ◇ *adv* **-1.** [gen] bem; **to go** ~ ir bem; ~ **done!** muito bem!; ~ **and truly** completamente; **to be** ~ **in with sb** *inf* ser muito amiguinho(nha) de alguém; **you're** ~ **out of it** *inf* ainda bem que você caiu fora **-2.** [definitely, certainly] certamente, definitivamente; **it was** ~ **worth it** ficou claro que valeu a pena; **she's** ~ **over 40** ela tem muito mais de 40 **-3.** [easily, possibly] (muito) bem. ◇ *n* [water, oil] poço *m*. ◇ *excl* **-1.** [in hesitation] bem!, bom! **-2.** [to correct o.s.] bem **-3.** [to express resignation]: **oh** ~! enfim! **-4.** [in surprise] quem diria!, olha só!

➤ **as well** *adv* [in addition] também; **you may/ might as** ~ **tell the truth** e por que você não conta a verdade?

➤ **as well as** *conj* além de.

➤ **well up** *vi* brotar.

we'll [wi:l] = **we shall**, **we will**.

well-adjusted *adj* [psychologically] sensato(ta).

well-advised [-əd'vaɪzd] *adj* prudente; **he/you would be** ~ **to do sthg** seria prudente que ele/você fizesse algo.

well-appointed [-ə'pɔɪntɪd] *adj* bem equipado(da).

well-balanced *adj* **-1.** [mentally healthy] equilibrado(da) **-2.** [nutritious] balanceado(da).

well-behaved [-bɪ'heɪvd] *adj* bem-comportado(-da).

wellbeing [ˌwel'bi:ɪŋ] *n* (U) bem-estar *m*.

well-bred [-'bred] *adj* bem-educado(da).

well-built *adj* [person] robusto(ta), fornido(da).

well-chosen *adj* bem escolhido(da).

well-disposed *adj*: **to be** ~ **to(wards) sb/sthg** ser favorável a alguém/algo.

well-done *adj* [thoroughly cooked] bem passado(-da).

well-dressed [-'drest] *adj* bem vestido(da).

well-earned [-'ɜ:nd] *adj* merecido(da).

well-established *adj* **-1.** [custom, tradition] antigo(ga) **-2.** [company] de sólida reputação.

well-fed *adj* bem alimentado(da).

well-groomed [-'gru:md] *adj* bem-apresentado(da).

wellhead *n* nascente *f*.

well-heeled [-hi:ld] *adj inf* rico(ca).

wellies ['welɪz] *npl UK inf* botas *fpl* impermeáveis.

well-informed *adj*: **to be** ~ **(about/on sthg)** estar bem informado(da) (sobre algo).

wellington (boot) *n* bota *f* impermeável.

well-intentioned [-ɪn'tenʃnd] *adj* bem-intencionado(da).

well-kept *adj* **-1.** [garden, village] bem cuidado(da) **-2.** [secret] bem guardado(da).

well-known *adj* conhecido(da).

well-mannered [-'mænəd] *adj*: **to be** ~ ter boas maneiras.

well-meaning *adj* bem-intencionado(da).

well-nigh [-naɪ] *adv* quase.

well-off *adj* **-1.** [financially] rico(ca), próspero(ra) **-2.** [in a good position]: **to be** ~ **for sthg** estar bem de algo; **not to know when one is** ~ *inf* não se dar conta da própria sorte.

well-paid *adj* bem pago(ga).

well-preserved *adj fig* [person] bem conservado(da).

well-proportioned [-prə'pɔ:ʃnd] *adj* bem-proporcionado(da).

well-read [-'red] *adj* instruído(da), culto(ta).

well-rounded [-'raʊndɪd] *adj* [varied] variado(da).

well-spoken *adj*: **to be** ~ falar bem.

well-thought-of *adj* de boa reputação.

well-thought-out *adj* bem elaborado(da).

well-timed *adj* oportuno(na).

well-to-do *adj* abastado(da), de dinheiro.

well-wisher *n* simpatizante *mf*.

well-woman clinic *n UK* clínica *para o bem-estar da mulher*.

welly (*pl* **-ies**) (*abbr of* **wellington**) *n UK inf* botas *fpl* de borracha.

Welsh [welʃ] ◇ *adj* galês(esa). ◇ *n* (U) [language] galês *m*. ◇ *npl*: **the** ~ os galeses.

Welshman ['welʃmən] (*pl* **-men** [-mən]) *n* galês *m*.

Welsh rarebit [-'reəbɪt] *n* torrada coberta com queijo derretido.

Welshwoman ['welʃˌwʊmən] (*pl* **-women** [-ˌwɪmɪn]) *n* galesa *f*.

welter ['weltəʳ] *n* confusão *f*, rebuliço *m*.

welterweight ['weltəweɪt] *n* peso *m* meio-médio.

wend [wend] *vt literary*: **to ~ one's way** dirigir-se vagarosamente.

wendy house ['wendı-] *n UK* casa *f* de bonecas.

went [went] *pt* ▷ **go**.

wept [wept] *pt & pp* ▷ **weep**.

were [wɜ:ʳ] *vb* ▷ **be**.

we're [wɪəʳ] = **we are**.

weren't [wɜ:nt] = **were not**.

werewolf ['wɪəwʊlf] (*pl* **-wolves** [-wʊlvz]) *n* lobisomem *m*.

west [west] ◇ *n* **-1.** [direction] oeste *m*; **the ~** o oeste **-2.** [region]: **the ~** o Oeste. ◇ *adj* oeste. ◇ *adv* para o oeste; **~ of** ao oeste de.
➡ **West** *n POL*: **the West** o Ocidente.

West Bank *n*: **the ~** a Cisjordânia; **on the ~** na Cisjordânia.

westbound ['westbaʊnd] *adj* em direção ao oeste.

West Country *n*: **the ~** o sudoeste da Inglaterra.

westerly ['westəlı] *adj* **-1.** [towards the west]: **in a ~ direction** para o oeste **-2.** [in the west] ocidental **-3.** [from the west] oeste.

western ['westən] ◇ *adj* **-1.** [part of country, continent] ocidental **-2.** *POL* [relating to the West] do Ocidente. ◇ *n* [book, film] western *m*.

Westerner ['westənəʳ] *n* **-1.** *POL* [inhabitant of the West] ocidental *mf* **-2.** [inhabitant of west of country] habitante *mf* do oeste.

westernize, -ise ['westənaız] *vt* ocidentalizar.

Western Isles *npl* Western Isles.

Western Samoa *n* Samoa Ocidental; **in ~** em Samoa Ocidental.

West German ◇ *adj* da Alemanha Ocidental. ◇ *n* [person] alemão *m*, -mã *f* ocidental *f*.

West Germany *n*: (former) **~** a (antiga)Alemanha Ocidental; **in ~** na Alemanha Ocidental.

West Indian ◇ *adj* antilhano(na). ◇ *n* [person] antilhano *m*, -na *f*.

West Indies [-'ındi:z] *npl*: **the ~** as Antilhas; **in the ~** nas Antilhas.

Westminster ['westmınstəʳ] *n* **-1.** [area] Westminster **-2.** *fig* [British parliament] parlamento *m* britânico.

West Virginia *n* Virgínia Ocidental.

westward ['westwəd] ◇ *adj* para o oeste. ◇ *adv* = **westwards**.

westwards ['westwədz] *adv* para o oeste.

wet [wet] (*compar* **-ter**, *superl* **-test**, *pt & pp* **wet** *OR* **-ted**, *cont* **-ting**) ◇ *adj* **-1.** [damp] úmido(da) **-2.** [soaked] molhado(da) **-3.** [rainy] chuvoso(sa) **-4.** [ink, concrete] fresco(ca); **'~ paint'** tinta fresca **-5.** *UK inf pej* [weak, feeble] fraco(ca). ◇ *n inf UK POL* político conservador moderado. ◇ *vt* **-1.** [soak] molhar

-2. [dampen] umedecer **-3.** [bed]: **to ~ the bed** fazer xixi na cama; **to ~ o.s.** mijar-se.

wet blanket *n inf pej* desmancha-prazeres *mf inv*.

wet-look *adj* brilhante.

wetness ['wetnıs] *n* **-1.** [dampness] umidade *f* **-2.** *UK inf pej* [feebleness] fraqueza *f*.

wet nurse *n* ama-de-leite *f*.

wet rot *n* [decay] apodrecimento *f* (*devido à umidade*).

wet suit *n* roupa *f* de mergulho.

WEU (*abbr of* **Western European Union**) *n* união de países da Europa Ocidental formada em 1955 para elaboração de políticas de defesa.

we've [wi:v] = **we have**.

whack [wæk] *inf* ◇ *n* **-1.** [hit] pancada *f* **-2.** *inf* [share]: **one's ~ of the profits** a sua parte nos lucros. ◇ *vt* dar pancadas em.

whacked [wækt] *adj UK inf* [exhausted] demolido(da).

whacky *adj* = **wacky**.

whale [weıl] *n* [animal] baleia *f*; **to have a ~ of a time** *inf* divertir-se para valer.

whaling ['weılıŋ] *n (U)* caça *f* às baleias.

wham [wæm] *excl inf* bum!

wharf [wɔ:f] (*pl* **-s** *OR* **wharves** [wɔ:vz]) *n* cais *m inv*.

what [wɒt] ◇ *adj* **-1.** [in questions] que; **~ colour is it?** de que cor é?; **he asked me ~ colour it was** ele perguntou-me de que cor era. **-2.** [in exclamations] que; **~ a surprise!** mas que surpresa!; **~ a beautiful day!** mas que dia lindo! ◇ *pron* **-1.** [in questions] o que; **~ is going on?** o que é que está acontecendo?; **~ is that?** o que é isso?; **~ is that thing called?** como é que se chama aquilo?; **~ is the problem?** qual é o problema?; **she asked me ~ had happened** ela perguntou-me o que é que tinha acontecido; **she asked me ~ I had seen** ela perguntou-me o que é que eu tinha visto. **-2.** (in questions: after prep) que; **~ are they talking about?** de que é que eles estão falando?; **~ is it for?** para que é isso?; **she asked me ~ I was thinking about** ela me perguntou em que eu estava pensando. **-3.** [introducing relative clause] o que; **I didn't see ~ happened** não vi o que aconteceu; **you can't have ~ you want** você não pode ter o que quer. **-4.** [in phrases]: **~ for?** para quê?; **~ about going out for a meal?** que tal irmos comer fora? ◇ *excl* o quê!

whatever [wɒt'evəʳ] ◇ *adj* qualquer; **eat ~ food you find** come o que encontrar; **no chance ~** nem a mais remota chance; **nothing ~** absolutamente nada. ◇ *pron* **-1.** [no matter what] o que quer que; **~ they may offer** ofereçam o que oferecerem **-2.** [indicating surprise]: **~ did you say?** o que foi que você disse? **-3.** [indicating lack of precision]: **~ that is** seja lá o que for; **or ~** ou o que seja.

whatnot ['wɒtnɒt] *n inf* [something, anything]: **and ~** e coisas assim.

what's-her-name *n inf* a tal fulana.

what's-his-name *n inf* o tal fulano.

whatsit *n inf* treco *m*.

whatsoever [‚wɒtsəʊ'evəʳ] *adj* absolutamente.

wheat [wi:t] *n* trigo *m*.

wheat germ *n (U)* germe *m* de trigo.

wheatmeal ['wi:tmi:l] *n* (*U*) farinha *f* de trigo integral.

wheedle ['wi:dl] *vt*: **to ~ sb into doing sthg** bajular alguém para que faça algo; **to ~ sthg out of sb** conseguir algo de alguém por bajulação.

wheel [wi:l] ◇ *n* -**1.** [of bicycle, car, train] roda *f* -**2.** *AUT* [steering wheel] direção *f* (do carro). ◇ *vt* empurrar *(algo com rodas).* ◇ *vi* -**1.** [move in circle] dar voltas -**2.** [turn round]: **to ~ round** dar a volta.

wheelbarrow ['wi:l,bærəʊ] *n* carrinho *m* de mão.

wheelbase *n* distância *f* entre eixos.

wheelchair ['wi:l,tʃeəʳ] *n* cadeira *f* de rodas.

wheel clamp *n grampo posto nas rodas de veículo estacionado em lugar proibido.*
➤ **wheel-clamp** *vt* grampear a roda *(de veículo mal estacionado).*

wheeler-dealer ['wi:lə'-] *n pej* negociante *mf* astuto, -ta.

wheelie bin *n UK* lixeira *f* com rodas.

wheeling and dealing ['wi:lɪŋ-] *n* (*U*) *pej* negócios *m* escusos.

wheeze [wi:z] ◇ *n* [sound of wheezing] respiração *f* ofegante. ◇ *vi* resfolegar.

wheezy ['wi:zɪ] (*compar* -**ier**, *superl* -**iest**) *adj* resfolegante.

whelk [welk] *n* caramujo *m*.

when *adv* & *conj* quando.

whenever [wen'evəʳ] ◇ *conj* sempre que. ◇ *adv* -**1.** [indicating surprise] quando é que -**2.** [indicating lack of precision]: **or ~** ou quando quiser.

where [weəʳ] *adv* & *conj* onde.

whereabouts [*adv* ,weərə'baʊts, *n* 'weərəbaʊts] ◇ *adv* por onde. ◇ *npl* paradeiro *m*.

whereas [weər'æz] *conj* enquanto que, ao passo que.

whereby [weə'baɪ] *conj fml* através do (da) qual, pelo(la) qual.

wheresoever *conj* & *adv* = **wherever**.

whereupon [,weərə'pɒn] *conj fml* depois do que.

wherever [weər'evəʳ] ◇ *conj* -**1.** [no matter where, everywhere] em todo o lugar que -**2.** [anywhere, in whatever place] onde quer que; **sit ~ you like** senta onde quiser -**3.** [in any situation] sempre que -**4.** [indicating ignorance]: **~ that is** seja lá onde for. ◇ *adv* -**1.** [indicating surprise] onde é que -**2.** [indicating lack of precision] em qualquer lugar.

wherewithal ['weəwɪðɔ:l] *n fml*: **to have the ~ to do sthg** dispor dos meios necessários para fazer algo.

whet [wet] (*pt* & *pp* -**ted**, *cont* -**ting**) *vt*: **to ~ sb's appetite (for sthg)** despertar o interesse de alguém (por algo).

whether ['weðəʳ] *conj* -**1.** [indicating choice, doubt] se -**2.** [no matter if]: **~ I want to or not** queira ou não queira.

whew [hwju:] *excl* uau!

whey *n* (*U*) soro *m* do leite.

which [wɪtʃ] ◇ *adj* [in questions] qual, que; **~ room do you want?** qual é o quarto que você quer?, que quarto você quer?; **~ one?** qual (deles)?; **she**

asked me **~ room I wanted** ela perguntou-me qual *OR* que quarto eu queria ◇ *pron* -**1.** [in questions] qual; **~ one is the cheapest?** qual é o mais barato?; **~ one do you prefer?** qual (é o que) você prefere?; **he asked me ~ one I preferred** ele perguntou-me qual é que eu preferia -**2.** [introducing relative clause: subject]: **I can't remember ~ was better** não me lembro qual era o melhor -**3.** [introducing relative clause: object, after prep] que; **the sofa on ~ I'm sitting** o sofá em que estou sentado -**4.** [to refer back to a clause] o que; **he's late, ~ annoys me** ele está atrasado, o que me aborrece; **he's always late, ~ I don't like** ele está sempre atrasado, coisa que eu detesto

whichever [wɪtʃ'evəʳ] ◇ *adj* -**1.** [no matter which]: **~ route you take** por qualquer dos caminhos que você for -**2.** [the one which]: **~ colour you prefer** a cor que preferir. ◇ *pron* -**1.** [the one which] o (a) que, os (as) que -**2.** [no matter which one] qualquer um(ma).

whiff [wɪf] *n* -**1.** [smell] cheirinho *m* -**2.** *fig* [sign] cheiro *m*.

while [waɪl] ◇ *n* algum tempo *m*; **it's a long ~ since I did that** faz muito tempo que não faço isso; **for a ~** por algum tempo; **after a ~** depois de algum tempo; **to be worth one's ~** valer a pena para alguém. ◇ *conj* -**1.** [as long as, during the time that] enquanto -**2.** [whereas] enquanto (que), ao passo que.
➤ **while away** *vt sep* passar o tempo *(de forma agradável).*

whilst [waɪlst] *conj* = **while**.

whim [wɪm] *n* capricho *m*.

whimper ['wɪmpəʳ] ◇ *n* choradeira *f*. ◇ *vt* lamuriar-se. ◇ *vi* choramingar.

whimsical ['wɪmzɪkl] *adj* -**1.** [idea, story] fantasioso(sa) -**2.** [look] estranho(nha) -**3.** [remark] esquisito(ta).

whine [waɪn] ◇ *n* -**1.** [child] gemido *m* -**2.** [dog] ganido *m* -**3.** [siren] grito *m* -**4.** [engine] zunido *m*. ◇ *vi* -**1.** [child] gemer -**2.** [dog] ganir -**3.** [siren] gritar -**4.** [engine] zunir -**5.** [complain]: **to ~ (about sb/sthg)** queixar-se (de alguém/algo).

whinge [wɪndʒ] (*cont* whingeing) *vi UK*: **to ~ (about sb/sthg)** queixar-se (de alguém/algo).

whip [wɪp] (*pt* & *pp* -**ped**, *cont* -**ping**) ◇ *n* -**1.** [for hitting] chicote *m* -**2.** *UK POL* membro do partido político responsável por fazer com que seus correligionários compareçam a votações importantes no parlamento. ◇ *vt* -**1.** [beat with whip] chicotear -**2.** *fig* [subj: rain, wind] açoitar -**3.** [take quickly]: **to ~ sthg out/off** arrancar algo de -**4.** *CULIN* bater.
➤ **whip up** *vt sep* [provoke] incitar.

whiplash injury ['wɪplæʃ-] *n* lesão *f* por efeito chicote.

whipped cream [wɪpt-] *n* creme *m* batido.

whippet ['wɪpɪt] *n* galgo *m*.

whip-round *n UK inf*: **to have a ~** fazer uma vaquinha.

whirl [wɜ:l] ◇ *n* -**1.** [rotating movement] redemoinho *m*; **to be in a ~** estar totalmente confuso(sa) -**2.** *fig* [flurry, round] turbilhão *m*, agitação *f* -**3.** *phr*: **let's give it a ~** *inf* vamos tentar. ◇ *vt*: **to ~**

wholesale

sb/sthg round rodopiar alguém/algo. <> *vi* -1.
[move around] rodopiar -2. *fig* [be confused, excited]
dar voltas.
whirlpool ['wɜːlpuːl] *n* redemoinho *m.*
whirlwind ['wɜːlwɪnd] <> *adj fig* vertiginoso(sa).
<> *n* furacão *m.*
whirr [wɜːʳ] <> *n* zumbido *m.* <> *vi* zumbir.
whisk [wɪsk] <> *n* CULIN batedeira *f.* <> *vt* -1. [put or
take quickly - away]: **to ~ sb/sthg away** levar
alguém/algo rapidamente; [- out]: **to ~ sthg out**
tirar algo rapidamente -2. CULIN bater.
whisker ['wɪskəʳ] *n* [of animal] bigode *m.*
  ➡ **whiskers** *npl* [of man] suíças *fpl.*
whiskey (*pl* **whiskeys**) *n* uísque *m* (de cevada).
whisky *UK* (*pl* -ies), **whiskey** *US* & *Irish* (*pl* -s)
['wɪskɪ] *n* uísque *m.*
whisper ['wɪspəʳ] <> *n* sussurro *m,* cochicho *m.*
<> *vt* sussurrar, cochichar. <> *vi* sussurrar,
cochichar.
whispering ['wɪspərɪŋ] *n* (U) cochichos *mpl,* sus-
surros *mpl.*
whist [wɪst] *n* (U) uíste *m.*
whistle ['wɪsl] <> *n* -1. [gen] apito *m* -2. [through
lips]·assobio *m* -3. [of bird] piado *m,* pio *m* -4. [of kettle]
chiar *m.* <> *vt* assobiar. <> *vi* -1. [gen] assobiar;
to ~ at sb assobiar para alguém -2. [using whistle]
apitar -3. [bird] piar -4. [kettle] chiar.
whistle-stop tour *n percurso rápido com
várias paradas no caminho.*
whit *n*: not a **~** nem um pouco.
Whit [wɪt] *n UK* Pentecostes *m.*
white [waɪt] <> *adj* -1. [gen] branco(ca); **to go** OR
turn ~ [hair] ficar branco(ca); [face] empalidecer
-2. [milky] com leite. <> *n* -1. [gen] branco *m* -2.
[person] branco *m,* -ca *f* -3. [of egg] clara *f.*
  ➡ **whites** *npl* roupas *fpl* brancas.
white blood cell *n* glóbulo *m* branco.
whiteboard ['waɪtbɔːd] *n* quadro *m* branco.
white Christmas *n* Natal *m* com neve.
white-collar *adj* de colarinho branco.
white elephant *n fig* elefante *m* branco.
white goods *npl* [household machines] eletrodomésticos *mpl.*
white-haired [-'heəd] *adj* de cabelos brancos.
Whitehall ['waɪthɔːl] *n* Whitehall.

white horses *npl UK* [on sea] crista *f* da onda.
white-hot *adj* incandescente.
White House *n*: the **~** a Casa Branca.

white knight *n pessoa ou organização que
auxilia uma empresa em dificuldades.*
white lie *n* mentira *f* branca.
white light *n* luz *f* branca.
white magic *n* (U) magia *f* branca.
white meat *n* (U) carne *f* branca.
whiten ['waɪtn] <> *vt* -1. [clothes] branquear -2.
[shoes] clarear -3. [wall] caiar. <> *vi* branquear.
whitener ['waɪtnəʳ] *n* -1. [for clothes] alvejante *m* -2.
[for shoes] branqueador *m.*
whiteness ['waɪtnɪs] *n* (U) brancura *f.*
white noise *n* ruído *m* branco.
whiteout ['waɪtaʊt] *n* perda total de visibilidade
devido à neve, whiteout *m.*
white paper *n* POL relatório *m* oficial do governo.
white sauce *n* (U) molho *m* branco.
White Sea *n*: the **~** o Mar Branco.
white spirit *n* (U) *UK* aguarrás *f inv.*
white-tie *adj* de gala.
white trash *n US pej* [people] branquelo *m,* -la *f.*
whitewash ['waɪtwɒʃ] <> *n* -1. (U) [paint] (água
f de) cal *f* -2. *pej* [cover-up] disfarce *m.* <> *vt* -1.
[paint] caiar, pintar com cal -2. *pej* [cover up]
disfarçar.
whitewater rafting ['waɪt,wɔːtəʳ-] *n* rafting *m.*
white wedding *n* casamento *m* tradicional.
whiting ['waɪtɪŋ] (*pl inv* OR -s) *n* merlúcio *m.*
Whit Monday *n* segunda-feira *f* de Pentecostes.
Whitsun ['wɪtsn] *n* [day] Pentecostes *m inv.*
whittle ['wɪtl] *vt*: **to ~ sthg away** OR **down** reduzir
algo gradualmente.
whiz, whizz (*pt* & *pp* -zed, *cont* -zing), **whizz** [wɪz] <> *n*
inf: **to be a ~ at sthg** ser uma fera em algo. <> *vi*
passar zunindo.
whiz(z) kid *n inf* (menino *m*) prodígio *m,* (menina
f) prodígia *f.*
who [huː] *pron* -1. (in direct, indirect questions) quem
-2. (in relative clauses) que.
WHO (*abbr of* World Health Organization) *n* OMS *f.*
who'd [huːd] = who had, who would.
whodu(n)nit [,huː'dʌnɪt] *n inf* romance *m* policial.
whoever [huː'evəʳ] *pron* -1. [gen] quem quer que; **I
don't like him, ~** he is não gosto dele, quem quer
que ele seja -2. [indicating surprise] quem será que;
~ can that be? quem poderá ser?
whole [həʊl] <> *adj* -1. [entire, complete] inteiro(ra)
-2. [for emphasis]: **a ~ lot of** muitos e muitos,
muitas e muitas, ; **a ~ lot bigger** muitíssimo
maior. <> *adv* [for emphasis] totalmente. <> *n* -1.
[all, entirety]: **the ~ of the summer** o verão todo
-2. [unit, complete thing] todo *m.*
  ➡ **as a whole** *adv* como um todo.
  ➡ **on the whole** *adv* em geral.
wholefood ['həʊlfuːd] *n UK* comida *f* integral.
whole-hearted [-'hɑːtɪd] *adj* sincero(ra).
wholemeal *UK* ['həʊlmiːl], **whole wheat** *US adj*
integral.
wholemeal bread *n UK* pão *m* integral.
whole note *n US* semibreve *f.*
wholesale ['həʊlseɪl] <> *adj* -1. [bulk] por atacado
-2. *pej* [excessive - slaughter] exagerado(da); [- de-
struction] em massa, em grande escala; [- theft]

indiscriminado(da). <> *adv* -**1.** [in bulk] por atacado -**2.** *pej* [excessively] indiscriminadamente.

wholesaler [ˈhəʊlˌseɪləʳ] *n* atacadista *mf*.

wholesome [ˈhəʊlsəm] *adj* saudável.

whole wheat *adj US* = wholemeal.

who'll [hu:l] = who will.

wholly [ˈhəʊlɪ] *adv* totalmente, completamente.

whom [hu:m] *pron fml* -**1.** (in direct, indirect questions) quem -**2.** (in relative clauses) que; **to ~** a quem.

whoop [wu:p] <> *n* grito *m*; **a ~ of glee** um grito de alegria. <> *vi* gritar.

whoopee [wʊˈpi:] *excl* hip hurra!

whooping cough [ˈhu:pɪŋ-] *n* (U) coqueluche *f*.

whoops [wʊps] *excl* opa!

whoosh [wʊʃ] *inf* <> *n* [sudden rush - of air] rajada *f*; [- of water] esguicho *m*. <> *vi* -**1.** [air] soprar forte -**2.** [water] esguichar.

whop (pt & pp -**ped**, cont -**ping**) *vt inf* [defeat] derrubar, derrotar.

whopper [ˈwɒpəʳ] *n inf* -**1.** [something big] exagero *m* -**2.** [lie] mentira *f* deslavada.

whopping [ˈwɒpɪŋ] *inf* <> *adj* tremendo(da), enorme. <> *adv*: **a ~ great lie** uma mentira enorme.

whore [hɔ:ʳ] *n pej* puta *f*, vagabunda *f*.

who're [ˈhu:əʳ] = who are.

whose [hu:z] <> *pron* de quem <> *adj* -**1.** (in direct, indirect questions) de quem; **~ book is this?** de quem é este livro? -**2.** (in relative clauses) cujo(ja).

whosoever [ˌhu:səʊˈevəʳ] *pron literary*: **~ it is** quem quer que seja, seja quem for.

who's who [hu:z-] *n* [book] quem é quem *m*, *livro contendo informações sobre as pessoas mais ricas e famosas do mundo*.

who've [hu:v] = who have.

why [waɪ] <> *adv* & *conj* porque; **~ not?** porque não?; **I know ~ Tom isn't here** eu sei porque é que o Tom não está; **tell me ~** (diga-me) porquê.

WI <> *n* (abbr of **Women's Institute**) *associação britânica de mulheres que se reúnem para atividades sociais e culturais, principalmente em áreas rurais.* <> -**1.** *abbr of* **West Indies** -**2.** *abbr of* **Wisconsin**.

wick [wɪk] *n* -**1.** pavio *m* -**2.** *phr*: **to get on sb's ~** *UK inf* dar nos nervos de alguém.

wicked [ˈwɪkɪd] *adj* -**1.** [evil] malvado(da) -**2.** [mischievous, devilish] perverso(sa) -**3.** *inf* [very good] bárbaro(ra).

wickedness *n* -**1.** [evil] maldade *f* -**2.** [mischievousness] perversidade *f*.

wicker [ˈwɪkəʳ] *adj* de vime.

wickerwork [ˈwɪkəwə:k] <> *n* (U) trabalho *m* em vime. <> *comp* de vime.

wicket [ˈwɪkɪt] *n CRICKET* -**1.** [stumps] meta *f* -**2.** [pitch] wicket *m* -**3.** [dismissal] demissão *f* do batedor.

wicket keeper *n* guarda-meta *mf*.

wide [waɪd] <> *adj* -**1.** [gen] largo(ga); **it's 6 metres ~** tem 6 metros de largura; **how ~ is the room?** qual é a largura da sala? -**2.** [eyes] arregalado(da) -**3.** [coverage, selection] amplo(pla) -**4.** [implications, issues] maior -**5.** [shot, punch, ball] desviado(da). <> *adv* -**1.** [as far as possible] amplamente; **open ~!** abra bem! -**2.** [off-target]: **to go ~** desviar-se.

wide-angle lens *n PHOT* (objetiva *f*) grande-angular *f*.

wide-awake *adj* desperto(ta), bem acordado(da).

wide boy *n UK inf pej* pilantra *m*.

wide-eyed [-ˈaɪd] *adj* -**1.** [surprised, frightened] de olhos arregalados -**2.** [innocent, gullible] ingênuo(nua).

widely [ˈwaɪdlɪ] *adv* -**1.** [gen] muito; **~ known** amplamente conhecido(da) -**2.** [considerably] bastante.

widen [ˈwaɪdn] <> *vt* -**1.** [make broader] alargar -**2.** [increase scope or variety of] ampliar -**3.** [gap, difference] aumentar. <> *vi* -**1.** [become broader] alargar -**2.** [increase in scope or variety] estender -**3.** [eyes] arregalar -**4.** [gap, difference] aumentar.

wide open *adj* -**1.** [window, door] escancarado(da) -**2.** [eyes] arregalado(da) -**3.** [spaces] extenso(sa).

wide-ranging [-ˈreɪndʒɪŋ] *adj* de amplo alcance.

widescreen TV [ˈwaɪdskri:n-] *n* tv *f* widescreen.

widespread [ˈwaɪdspred] *adj* disseminado(da), geral.

widow [ˈwɪdəʊ] *n* viúva *f*.

widowed [ˈwɪdəʊd] *adj* viúvo(va).

widower [ˈwɪdəʊəʳ] *n* viúvo *m*.

width [wɪdθ] *n* -**1.** [breadth] largura *f*; **in ~** de largura -**2.** [in swimming pool] largura *f*; **she swam 20 ~s** ela nadou 20 piscinas.

widthways [ˈwɪdθweɪz] *adv* na transversal, transversalmente.

wield [wi:ld] *vt* -**1.** [weapon] manejar -**2.** [power] controlar, exercer.

wife [waɪf] (*pl* **wives**) *n* esposa *f*.

wig [wɪg] *n* peruca *f*.

wiggle [ˈwɪgl] *inf* <> *n* -**1.** [movement] balanço *m* -**2.** [wavy line] linha *f* ondulada. <> *vt* balançar, agitar. <> *vi* balançar.

wiggly [ˈwɪglɪ] (*compar* -**ier**, *superl* -**iest**) *adj inf* -**1.** [wavy] ondulado(da) -**2.** [movable] solto(ta).

wigwam [ˈwɪgwæm] *n* tenda *f* indígena (em forma de cone).

wild [waɪld] <> *adj* -**1.** [animal, land] selvagem -**2.** [person, dog, attack] violento(ta) -**3.** [plant] silvestre -**4.** [scenery, landscape] agreste -**5.** [sea] revolto(ta) -**6.** [weather] turbulento(ta) -**7.** [laughter, crowd, applause] frenético(ca); **the crowd went ~** a multidão foi à loucura; **to run ~** descontrolar-se -**8.** [hair] desarrumado(da) -**9.** [eyes, features] inquieto(ta) agitado(ta) -**10.** [dream, scheme] maluco(ca) -**11.** [estimate]: **a ~ guess** uma vaga idéia -**12.** *inf* [very enthusiastic]: **to be ~ about sthg** ser louco(ca) por algo. <> *n*: **in the ~** na natureza, em seu habitat natural.

➤ **wilds** *npl*: **the ~s** as regiões selvagens.

wild card *n COMPUT* -**1.** curinga *m* -**2.** [person]: **to be a ~** ser completamente imprevisível.

wildcat [ˈwaɪldkæt] *n* gato-mourisco *m*.

wildcat strike *n* greve-relâmpago *f*.

wildebeest [ˈwɪldɪbi:st] (*pl inv OR* -**s**) *n* gnu *m*.

wilderness [ˈwɪldənɪs] *n* -**1.** [barren land] sertão *m* -**2.** [overgrown land] matagal *m* -**3.** *fig* [unimportant place]: **in the political ~** no ostracismo político.

wildfire [ˈwaɪldˌfaɪəʳ] *n*: **to spread like ~**

espalhar-se como fogo na mata.

wild flower n flor f silvestre.

wildfowl n aves fpl silvestres.

wild-goose chase n inf busca m infrutífera.

wildlife ['waıldlaıf] n (U) fauna f.

wildly ['waıldlı] adv -1. [enthusiastically, fanatically] freneticamente -2. [without reason or control] inadvertidamente -3. [very] extremamente -4. [menacingly] ameaçadoramente.

wild rice n (U) arroz m silvestre.

wild west n inf: the ~ o oeste selvagem.

wiles [waılz] npl artimanhas fpl.

wilful UK, **willful** US ['wılfʊl] adj -1. [determined] que sempre apronta das suas -2. [deliberate] proposital, intencional.

will¹ [wıl] <> n -1. [wish, desire] vontade f; **against my** ~ contra a minha vontade -2. [document] testamento m.

will² [wıl] aux vb -1. [expressing future tense]: **it** ~ **be difficult to repair** vai ser difícil de consertar; ~ **you be here next Friday?** você vai estar aqui na próxima sexta?; **I** ~ **see you next week** vejo-lhe para a semana; **yes I** ~ sim; **no I won't** não. -2. [expressing willingness]: **I won't do it** recuso-me a fazê-lo. -3. [expressing polite question]: ~ **you have some more tea?** você quer mais um chá? -4. [in commands, requests]: ~ **you please be quiet!** pode ficar calado, por favor!; **close that window,** ~ **you?** feche a janela, por favor.

willful adj US = wilful.

willing ['wılıŋ] adj -1. [prepared] disposto(ta); **to be** ~ **to do sthg** estar disposto(ta) a fazer algo -2. [eager] prestativo(va).

willingly ['wılıŋlı] adv de bom grado.

willingness ['wılıŋnıs] n -1. [preparedness] disposição f, boa vontade f; ~ **to do sthg** disposição para fazer algo -2. [keenness] determinação f, ânsia f.

willow (tree) ['wıləʊ-] n salgueiro m.

willowy ['wıləʊı] adj longilíneo(nea).

willpower ['wıl‚paʊəʳ] n (U) força f de vontade.

willy ['wılı] (pl -ies) n UK inf piu-piu m.

willy-nilly [‚wılı'nılı] adv -1. [at random] ao acaso -2. [wanting to or not] quer queria quer não.

wilt [wılt] vi -1. [plant] murchar -2. fig [person] definhar.

wily ['waılı] (compar -ier, superl -iest) adj ardiloso(sa).

wimp [wımp] n inf pej bunda-mole mf.

win [wın] (pt & pp won, cont -ning) <> n vitória f. <> vt -1. [gen] ganhar -2. [game, fight, competition] vencer. <> vi ganhar; **you/I etc can't** ~ não tem jeito.

  ◆ **win over, win round** vt sep convencer.

wince [wıns] <> vi contrair-se; **to** ~ **at sthg** perturbar-se com algo; **to** ~ **with sthg** retrair-se de algo. <> n contração f de dor.

winch [wıntʃ] <> n guindaste m. <> vt levantar OR suspender com guindaste.

Winchester disk n COMPUT winchester m, disco m rígido.

wind¹ [wınd] <> n -1. METEOR vento m -2. (U) [breath] fôlego m; **to get one's second** ~ fig recobrar o

fôlego -3. (U) [in stomach] gases mpl; **to break** ~ euphemism soltar gases -4. [in orchestra] instrumento m de sopro -5. phr: **to get** ~ **of sthg** inf tomar conhecimento de algo; **to sail close to the** ~ andar na corda bamba; **to put the** ~ **up sb** inf fazer alguém tremer nas bases; **it really put the** ~ **up me** inf realmente tremi nas bases. <> vt -1. [knock breath out of] ficar sem fôlego -2. UK [baby] arrotar.

wind² [waınd] (pt & pp wound) <> vt -1. [string, thread] enrolar -2. [clock] dar corda em -3. phr: **to** ~ **one's way** serpentear. <> vi [river, road] serpentear.

  ◆ **wind back** vt sep [tape] rebobinar.

  ◆ **wind down** <> vt sep -1. [car window] baixar -2. [business] fechar aos poucos. <> vi -1. [clock] parar -2. [relax] espairecer.

  ◆ **wind forward** vt sep [tape] avançar.

  ◆ **wind on** vt sep rebobinar.

  ◆ **wind up** <> vt sep -1. [finish - meeting] encerrar; [- business] fechar, liquidar -2. [clock] dar corda em -3. [car window] levantar -4. UK inf [deliberately annoy] azucrinar -5. inf [end up]: **to** ~ **up doing sthg** acabar fazendo algo. <> vi inf [end up] acabar em.

windbreak ['wındbreık] n quebra-vento m.

windcheater UK ['wınd‚tʃi:təʳ], **windbreaker** US ['wınd‚breıkəʳ] n dated japona f.

windchill ['wındtʃıl] n (U) sensação m térmica.

winded ['wındıd] adj sem fôlego.

windfall ['wındfɔ:l] n -1. [fruit] fruto m caído (da árvore) -2. [unexpected gift] dinheiro m que caiu do céu.

wind farm [wınd-] n parque m eólico.

winding ['waındıŋ] adj sinuoso(sa).

wind instrument [wınd-] n instrumento m de sopro.

windmill ['wındmıl] n moinho m de vento.

window ['wındəʊ] n -1. [gen] janela f -2. [of shop] vitrina f -3. [free time] tempo m livre.

window box n floreira f de janela.

window cleaner n limpador m de vidros.

window display n vitrina f.

window dressing n -1. [in shop] decoração m de vitrina -2. fig [non-essentials] fachada f.

window envelope n envelope m de janela.

window frame n caixilho m de janela.

window ledge n parapeito m.

windowpane n vidraça f.

window shade n US persiana f.

window-shopping n (U): **to go** ~ ir olhar vitrinas.

window sill n parapeito m.

windpipe ['wındpaıp] n traquéia f.

windscreen UK ['wındskri:n], **windshield** US ['wındʃi:ld] n pára-brisa m.

windscreen washer n lavador m de pára-brisa.

windscreen wiper n limpador m de pára-brisa.

windshield n US = windscreen.

windsock ['wındsɒk] n biruta f.

windsurfer ['wınd‚sɜ:fəʳ] n -1. [person] windsurfista

mf-**2.** [board] prancha *f* de windsurfe.

windsurfing ['wɪnd,sɜːfɪŋ] *n* (U) windsurfe *m*; **to go** ~ praticar windsurfe.

windswept ['wɪndsweptl] *adj* -**1.** [scenery] varrido(-da) ao vento -**2.** [person, hair] em desalinho.

wind tunnel [wɪnd-] *n* tunel *m* aerodinâmico.

wind turbine [wɪnd-] *n* turbina *f* eólica.

windy ['wɪndɪ] (*compar* -**ier**, *superl* -**iest**) *adj* -**1.** [weather, day] de muito vento; **it's** ~ está ventando -**2.** [place] exposto(ta) ao vento.

wine [waɪn] *n* vinho *m*; **red/rosé/white** ~ vinho tinto/rosé/branco.

wine bar *n UK* cantina *f*.

wine bottle *n* garrafa *f* de vinho.

wine box *n* garrafão *m* de vinho.

wine cellar *n* adega *f*.

wineglass ['waɪnglɑːs] *n* copo *m* de vinho.

wine list *n* carta *f* de vinhos.

wine merchant *n UK* mercador *m*, -ra *f* de vinhos.

winepress ['waɪnpres] *n* lagar *m*.

wine rack *n* suporte *m* para vinhos.

wine tasting [-,teɪstɪŋ] *n* (U) degustação *f* de vinhos.

wine waiter *n* sommelier *m*.

wing [wɪŋ] *n* -**1.** [gen] asa *f* -**2.** [of car] flanco *m* -**3.** [of building, organization] ala *f*.

◆ **wings** *npl* THEATRE: **the** ~**s** os bastidores.

wing commander *n UK* tenente-coronel *m* (*de aviação*).

winger ['wɪŋəʳ] *n* SPORT ala *f*; **left-**~ ponta-esquerda *mf*; **right-**~ ponta-direita *mf*.

wing nut *n* porca *f* borboleta.

wingspan ['wɪŋspæn] *n* envergadura *f*.

wink [wɪŋk] ◇ *n* [of eye] piscada *f*; **to have forty** ~**s** *inf* tirar uma soneca; **not to sleep a** ~, **not to get a** ~ **of sleep** *inf* não pregar o olho. ◇ *vi* -**1.** [eye] piscar, pestanejar; **to** ~ **at sb** piscar para alguém -**2.** *literary* [lights] cintilar.

winkle ['wɪŋkl] *n* caramujo *m*.

◆ **winkle out** *vt sep* -**1.** [remove] arrancar -**2.** *fig* [extract]: **to** ~ **sthg out of sb** arrancar algo de alguém.

winner ['wɪnəʳ] *n* -**1.** [person] vencedor *m*, -ra *f*, ganhador *m*, -ra *f* -**2.** *inf* [success] vencedor *m*, -ra *f*; **to be onto a** ~ ser bem-sucedido(da).

winning ['wɪnɪŋ] *adj* -**1.** [victorious, successful] vencedor(ra), vitorioso(sa) -**2.** [pleasing] encantador(ra).

◆ **winnings** *npl* ganhos *mpl* (*de aposta*).

winning post *n* meta *f*.

Winnipeg *n* Winnipeg.

winsome ['wɪnsəm] *adj literary* encantador(ra).

winter ['wɪntəʳ] ◇ *n* inverno *m*; **in** ~ no inverno. ◇ *comp* de inverno.

winter sports *npl* esportes *mpl* de inverno.

wintertime ['wɪntətaɪm] *n* (U) inverno *m*; **in** ~ no inverno.

wint(e)ry ['wɪntrɪ] *adj* invernal, de inverno.

wipe [waɪp] ◇ *n* [clean]: **to give sthg a** ~ dar uma limpada em algo. ◇ *vt* -**1.** [rub to clean] limpar, passar um pano em -**2.** [rub to dry] secar.

◆ **wipe away** *vt sep* [tears] enxugar.

◆ **wipe out** *vt sep* -**1.** [erase] limpar -**2.** [kill] aniquilar -**3.** [eradicate] erradicar.

◆ **wipe up** ◇ *vt sep* -**1.** [dirt, mess] limpar -**2.** [water] secar. ◇ *vi* limpar.

wiper ['waɪpəʳ] *n* [windscreen wiper] limpador *m* de pára-brisa.

wire [waɪəʳ] ◇ *n* -**1.** (U) [metal] cabo *m*, fio *m* -**2.** [length of wire] fio *m* -**3.** *US* [telegram] telegrama *m*. ◇ *comp* de arame. ◇ *vt* -**1.** [fasten, connect]: **to** ~ **sthg to sthg** ligar algo em algo -**2.** ELEC ligar à rede elétrica; **he** ~**d the whole house himself** ele mesmo fez a instalação elétrica da casa -**3.** *US* [send telegram to] passar um telegrama para.

◆ **wire up** *vt sep* [house] fazer a instalação elétrica.

wire brush *n* escova *f* de aço.

wire cutters *npl* alicate *m* de arame.

wireless ['waɪəlɪs] *n dated* radiofone *m*.

wire netting *n* (U) tela *f* de arame.

wire-tapping [-,tæpɪŋ] *n* (U) escuta *f* telefônica.

wire wool *n UK* esponja *f* de aço.

wiring ['waɪərɪŋ] *n* (U) instalação *f* elétrica.

wiry ['waɪərɪ] (*compar* -**ier**, *superl* -**iest**) *adj* -**1.** [hair] eriçado(da) -**2.** [body, man] esguio(guia).

Wisconsin *n* Wisconsin.

wisdom ['wɪzdəm] *n* (U) sabedoria *f*.

wisdom tooth *n* dente *m* do juízo.

wise [waɪz] *adj* sábio(bia); **to get** ~ **to sthg** *inf* manjar algo; **to be no** ~**r** OR **none the** ~**r** continuar sem entender.

◆ **wise up** *vi US* compreender.

wisecrack ['waɪzkræk] *n pej* gafe *f*, mancada *f*.

wisely *adv* sabiamente.

wish [wɪʃ] ◇ *n* -**1.** [desire] desejo *m*; ~ **to do sthg** desejo de fazer algo; ~ **for sthg** desejo por algo -**2.** [magic request] pedido *m*. ◇ *vt* -**1.** [want]: **to** ~ **to do sthg** *fml* desejar fazer algo; **to** ~ **(that)** esperar que -**2.** [desire, request by magic]: **to** ~ **(that)** desejar que; **I** ~ **I were rich** ah, se eu fosse rico -**3.** [in greeting]: **to** ~ **sb sthg** desejar algo a alguém. ◇ *vi* [by magic]: **to** ~ **for sthg** pedir algo.

◆ **wishes** *npl*: **best** ~**es** cumprimentos *mpl*, parabéns *mpl*; **(with) best** ~**es** [at end of letter] com os cumprimentos.

◆ **wish on** *vt sep*: **to** ~ **sthg on sb** desejar algo para alguém.

wishbone ['wɪʃbəʊn] *n* osso *m* da sorte.

wishful thinking [,wɪʃfʊl-] *n* (U) fantasia *f*, ilusão *f*.

wishy-washy ['wɪʃɪ,wɒʃɪ] *adj inf pej* [vague] sem graça.

wisp [wɪsp] *n* -**1.** [tuft - of hair] mecha *f*, tufo *m*; [- of grass] bola *f* -**2.** [small cloud] nuvem *f*.

wispy ['wɪspɪ] (*compar* -**ier**, *superl* -**iest**) *adj* ralo(la).

wisteria *n* glicínia *f*.

wistful ['wɪstfʊl] *adj* melancólico(ca), triste.

wit [wɪt] *n* -**1.** (U) [humour] presença *f* de espírito, gracejo *m* -**2.** [funny person] brincalhão *m*, -na *f* -**3.** [intelligence]: **to have the** ~ **to do sthg** ter astúcia para fazer algo.

◆ **wits** *npl* [intelligence, mind]: **to have** OR **keep one's** ~**s about one** manter-se alerta; **to be scared out of one's** ~**s** *inf* estar morto(ta) de medo;

to be at one's ~s end estar à beira da loucura.
witch [wɪtʃ] *n* bruxa *f*.
witchcraft [ˈwɪtʃkrɑːft] *n (U)* bruxaria *f*.
witchdoctor [ˈwɪtʃˌdɒktəʳ] *n* curandeiro *m*, -ra *f*.
witch-hazel *n* - **1.** *(U)* [liquid] água *f* de hamamélis - **2.** [tree] hamamélis *f inv*.
witch-hunt *n pej* caça *f* às bruxas.
with [wɪð] *prep* - **1.** [in company of] com; **come ~ me/ us** venha comigo/conosco; **can I go ~ you?** posso ir com você?; **we stayed ~ friends** ficamos em casa de amigos. - **2.** [in descriptions] com; **a man ~ a beard** um homem de barba; **a room ~ a bathroom** um quarto com banheiro. - **3.** [indicating means, manner] com; **I washed it ~ detergent** lavei-o com detergente; **they won ~ ease** ganharam com facilidade. - **4.** [indicating emotion] de; **to tremble ~ fear** tremer de medo. - **5.** [regarding] com; **be careful ~ that!** tenha cuidado com isso! - **6.** [indicating opposition] com; **to argue ~ sb** discutir com alguém. - **7.** [indicating covering, contents]: **to fill sthg ~ sthg** encher algo com *OR* de algo; **packed ~ people** cheio de gente; **topped ~ cream** coberto com creme.
withdraw [wɪðˈdrɔː] *(pt* -**drew**, *pp* -**drawn**) <> *vt* - **1.** [remove] afastar; **to ~ sthg from sthg** remover algo de algo - **2.** FIN sacar - **3.** [troops, statement, offer] retirar. <> *vi* - **1.** [gen] retirar-se; **to ~ from** retirar-se de; **to ~ to** retirar-se para - **2.** [quit, give up] afastar-se; **to ~ from sthg** afastar-se de algo.
withdrawal [wɪðˈdrɔːəl] *n* - **1.** *(U)* [gen] retirada *f*; **~ from sthg** afastamento *m* de algo - **2.** *(U)* [removal] remoção *f* - **3.** *(U)* [retraction] retratação *f* - **4.** *(U)* MED [síndrome *f* da] abstinência *f* - **5.** FIN saque *m*.
withdrawal symptoms *npl* síndrome *f* de abstinência.
withdrawn [wɪðˈdrɔːn] <> *pp* ▷ **withdraw**. <> *adj* [shy, quiet] retraído(da).
withdrew [wɪðˈdruː] *pt* ▷ **withdraw**.
wither [ˈwɪðəʳ] <> *vt* secar. <> *vi* - **1.** [dry up] murchar - **2.** [become weak] debilitar-se.
withered [ˈwɪðəd] *adj* - **1.** [plant] murcho(cha) - **2.** [skin] seco(ca).
withering [ˈwɪðərɪŋ] *adj* - **1.** [look] fulminante - **2.** [remark] mordaz.
withhold [wɪðˈhəʊld] *(pt & pp* -**held** [-ˈheld]) *vt* reter.
within [wɪˈðɪn] <> *prep* - **1.** [gen] dentro de - **2.** [less than - distance]: **~ 5 quilometers of London** a menos de 5 quilômetros de Londres; [- time] em menos de. <> *adv* dentro.
without [wɪðˈaʊt] <> *prep* sem; **~ doing sthg** sem fazer algo. <> *adv*: **to go** *OR* **do ~ (sthg)** ficar sem (algo).
withstand [wɪðˈstænd] *(pt & pp* -**stood** [-ˈstʊd]) *vt* resistir a, agüentar.
witness [ˈwɪtnɪs] <> *n* - **1.** testemunha *f*; **to be ~ to sthg** ser testemunha de algo - **2.** *(U)* [testimony]: **to bear ~ to sthg** [give testimony of] dar testemunho de algo; [be proof of] testemunhar algo. <> *vt* - **1.** [see] testemunhar - **2.** [countersign] assinar como testemunha.
witness box *UK*, **witness stand** *US n* banco *m* das testemunhas.

witter [ˈwɪtəʳ] *vi UK inf pej* dizer abobrinhas.
witticism [ˈwɪtɪsɪzm] *n* sagacidade *f*.
witty [ˈwɪtɪ] *(compar* -**ier**, *superl* -**iest**) *adj* espirituoso(sa).
wives [waɪvz] *pl* ▷ **wife**.
wizard [ˈwɪzəd] *n* - **1.** [man with magic powers] feiticeiro *m*, mago *m* - **2.** *fig* [skilled person] gênio *m*.
wizened [ˈwɪznd] *adj* envelhecido(da).
wk *(abbr of* **week**) semana *f*.
WO *(abbr of* **warrant officer**) *n* posto militar.
wobble [ˈwɒbl] *vi* - **1.** [chair] cambalear - **2.** [hands] tremer - **3.** [aeroplane] balançar.
wobbly [ˈwɒblɪ] *(compar* -**ier**, *superl* -**iest**) *adj* - **1.** [table, chair] *inf* bambo(ba) - **2.** [jelly] molenga.
woe [wəʊ] *n literary* lamúria *f*, infortúnio *m*.
wok [wɒk] *n* panela *f* wok.
woke [wəʊk] *pt* ▷ **wake**.
woken [ˈwəʊkn] *pp* ▷ **wake**.
wolf [wʊlf] *(pl* **wolves**) <> *n* - **1.** [animal] lobo *m* - **2.** [man] gavião *m*, paquerador *m*. <> *vt inf*: **to ~ sthg (down)** devorar algo.
wolf whistle *n* fiu-fiu *m (para as mulheres)*, assobio *m (para as mulheres)*.
wolves [wʊlvz] *pl* ▷ **wolf**.
woman [ˈwʊmən] *(pl* **women**) <> *n* mulher *f*. <> *comp*: **a ~ doctor** uma doutora; **a ~ governor** uma governadora; **a ~ teacher** uma professora; **a ~ footballer** uma jogadora de futebol; **a ~ prime minister** uma primeira-ministra.
womanhood [ˈwʊmənhʊd] *n* - **1.** [adult life] maioridade *f* feminina - **2.** [all women] mulheres *fpl*.
womanizer, -iser *n pej* paquerador *m*.
womanly [ˈwʊmənlɪ] *adj* feminino(na).
womb [wuːm] *n* ventre *m*.
wombat [ˈwɒmbæt] *n* vombatídeo *m*.
women [ˈwɪmɪn] *pl* ▷ **woman**.
women's group *n* grupo *m* feminista.
Women's Institute *n UK*: **the ~** organização de mulheres, especialmente da área rural, que se encontram regularmente e participam de atividades culturais e trabalho social.
women's lib [-ˈlɪb] *n inf* libertação *f* da mulher.
women's liberation *n* - **1.** [aim] libertação *f* da mulher - **2.** [movement] movimento *m* pela libertação da mulher.
won [wʌn] *pt & pp* ▷ **win**.
wonder [ˈwʌndəʳ] <> *n* - **1.** *(U)* [amazement] espanto *m* - **2.** [cause for surprise]: **it's a ~ (that) ...** é de se admirar que ...; **no** *OR* **little** *OR* **small ~** não é de se admirar - **3.** [amazing thing, person] maravilha *f*; **to work** *OR* **do ~s** realizar milagres. <> *vt* - **1.** [speculate] perguntar-se; **to ~ if** *OR* **whether** perguntar-se a si próprio(pria) se - **2.** [in polite requests]: **I ~ whether you would mind shutting the window?** será que você se importaria de fechara janela? <> *vi* - **1.** [speculate] perguntar; **why did you ask?** - **oh, I just ~ed** por que você perguntou isso? - ah, foi só por perguntar; **to ~ about sthg** pensar sobre algo - **2.** *literary* [be amazed]: **to ~ at sthg** admirar-se com algo.
wonderful [ˈwʌndəfʊl] *adj* maravilhoso(sa).

wonderfully ['wʌndəfʊlɪ] *adv* maravilhosamente.

wonderland ['wʌndəlænd] *n* [fairyland] paraíso *m*.

wonky ['wɒŋkɪ] (*compar* **-ier**, *superl* **-iest**) *adj UK inf* [wobbly] cambaleante; [crooked] torto(ta).

wont [wəʊnt] ◇ *adj*: **to be ~ to do sthg** estar acostumado(da) a fazer algo. ◇ *n dated or literary*: **as is one's ~** como é do feitio de alguém.

won't [wəʊnt] = **will not**.

woo [wu:] *vt* **-1.** *literary* [court] cortejar **-2.** *fig* [try to win over] persuadir.

wood [wʊd] ◇ *n* **-1.** *(U)* [timber] madeira *f* **-2.** [group of trees] bosque *m*, floresta *f* **-3.** *GOLF* bastão *m (de madeira)* **-4.** *phr*: **not to see the ~ for the trees** *UK* prender-se às partes e não ver o todo; **touch ~!** bata na madeira! ◇ *comp* de madeira.

→ **woods** *npl* floresta *f*.

wooded ['wʊdɪd] *adj* arborizado(da).

wooden ['wʊdn] *adj* **-1.** [of wood] de madeira **-2.** *pej* [actor] sem expressão.

wooden spoon *n* colher *f* de pau; **to win OR get the ~** *UK fig* vir na rabeira.

woodland ['wʊdlənd] *n* floresta *f*.

woodlouse (*pl* **-lice**) *n* bicho-de-conta *m*.

woodpecker ['wʊdˌpekəʳ] *n* pica-pau *m*.

wood pigeon *n* pombo *m* torcaz.

woodshed ['wʊdʃed] *n* depósito *m* para madeira.

woodwind ['wʊdwɪnd] ◇ *adj* instrumento *m* doce *(de madeira)*. ◇ *n*: **the ~** os instrumentos doces.

woodwork ['wʊdwɜːk] *n* **-1.** [wooden objects] obra *f* de madeira **-2.** [craft] carpintaria *f*.

woodworm ['wʊdwɜːm] *n* caruncho *m*.

woof [wu:f] ◇ *n* uivo *m*. ◇ *excl* auu!

wool [wʊl] *n* **-1.** [gen] lã *f* **-2.** *phr*: **he is pulling the ~ over your eyes** *inf* ele está te vendendo gato por lebre.

woollen *UK*, **woolen** *US* ['wʊlən] *adj* [garment] de lã.

→ **woollens** *npl* produtos *mpl* de lã.

woolly ['wʊlɪ] (*compar* **-ier**, *superl* **-iest**, *pl* **-ies**) ◇ *adj* **-1.** [woollen] de lã, lanoso(sa) **-2.** *inf* [fuzzy, unclear] desatinado(da). ◇ *n inf* roupas *fpl* de lã.

woolly-headed [-'hedɪd] *adj inf pej* desatinado (desatina) da.

woozy ['wu:zɪ] (*compar* **-ier**, *superl* **-iest**) *adj inf* atordoado(da).

Worcester sauce ['wʊstəʳ-] *n (U)* molho *m* inglês.

word [wɜːd] ◇ *n* **-1.** [gen] palavra *f*; **~ for ~** ao pé da letra; **in other ~s** em outras palavras; **in your own ~s** em suas próprias palavras; **not in so many ~s** não com todas as palavras; **in a ~** em uma palavra; **too ... for ~s** ser extremamente ...; **by ~ of mouth** oralmente; **to put in a (good) ~ for sb** recomendar alguém; **just say the ~** é só avisar; **to have a ~ (with sb)** ter uma palavra (com alguém), falar (com alguém); **to have ~s with sb** *inf* bater boca com alguém; **to have the last ~** ter a última palavra; **she doesn't mince her ~s** ela não tem papas na língua; **to weigh one's ~s** medir as palavras; **I couldn't get a ~ in edgeways** eu não pude entrar na conversa; **to give sb one's ~** dar a palavra a alguém; **to be as good as one's ~**, **to be true to one's ~** cumprir bem a palavra **-2.** *(U)* [news] notícias *fpl*. ◇ *vt* redigir.

word game *n* qualquer jogo que envolva a construção ou a seleção de palavras.

wording ['wɜːdɪŋ] *n (U)* palavreado *m*.

word-perfect *adj* de cor e salteado.

wordplay ['wɜːdpleɪ] *n (U)* jogo *m* de palavras.

word processing *n (U)* processamento *m* de texto.

word processor [-'prəʊsesəʳ] *n* processador *m* de texto.

wordwrap ['wɜːdræp] *n COMPUT* marginação *f* automática.

wordy ['wɜːdɪ] (*compar* **-ier**, *superl* **-iest**) *adj pej* floreado(da).

wore [wɔːʳ] *pt* ► **wear**.

work [wɜːk] ◇ *n* **-1.** *(U)* [employment] emprego *m*; **temporary/casual ~** trabalho temporário; **in/out of ~** empregado/desempregado; **at ~** no trabalho **-2.** *(U)* [activity, tasks] trabalho *m*; **at ~** em atividade; **to have one's ~ cut out doing sthg** OR **to do sthg** ser extremamente difícil para alguém fazer algo **-3.** [something made, created, composed] obra *f* **-4.** *phr*: **he's a nasty piece of ~** *inf* ele é uma pessoa detestável. ◇ *vt* **-1.** [person, staff] fazer trabalhar **-2.** [machine] operar **-3.** [shape, manipulate] trabalhar em **-4.** [cultivate] cultivar **-5.** [cause to become]: **to ~ o.s. into sthg** contrair-se em algo **-6.** [make]: **to ~ one's way** [progress physically] avançar; [in career] progredir. ◇ *vi* **-1.** [do a job] trabalhar **-2.** [function, succeed] funcionar **-3.** [have effect]: **to ~ against sb/sthg** ir contra alguém/algo **-4.** [gradually become] tornar-se; **to ~ loose** soltar-se; **to ~ into a tangle** entrelaçar-se.

→ **works** ◇ *n* [factory] usina *f*. ◇ *npl* **-1.** [mechanism] mecanismo *m* **-2.** [digging, building] obras *fpl* **-3.** *inf* [everything]: **the ~s** os aparatos.

→ **work at** *vt fus* tentar melhorar.

→ **work off** *vt sep* libertar-se de.

→ **work on** *vt fus* **-1.** [concentrate on] dedicar-se a **-2.** [take as basis] basear-se em **-3.** [try to persuade] tentar persuadir.

→ **work out** ◇ *vt sep* **-1.** [formulate] elaborar **-2.** [calculate] calcular. ◇ *vi* **-1.** [figure, total]: **to ~ out at** totalizar; **the bill ~s out at £5 a head** a conta dá 5 libras para cada um **-2.** [turn out] surtir efeito **-3.** [be successful] dar certo **-4.** [train, exercise] treinar.

→ **work up** *vt sep* **-1.** [excite]: **to ~ o.s. up into a frenzy** excitar-se de tal forma **-2.** [generate] gerar.

workable ['wɜːkəbl] *adj* viável.

workaday ['wɜːkədeɪ] *adj pej* prosaico(ca).

workaholic [ˌwɜːkə'hɒlɪk] *n* burro *m* de carga, workaholic *mf*.

workbasket *n* cesta *f* de costura.

workbench ['wɜːkbentʃ] *n* bancada *f*.

workbook ['wɜːkbʊk] *n* livro-texto *m*.

workday ['wɜːkdeɪ] *n* **-1.** [day's work] dia *m* de trabalho **-2.** [not weekend] dia *m* útil.

worked up [ˌwɜːkt-] *adj* exaltado(da).

worker ['wɜːkə'] n trabalhador m, -ra f, operário m, -ria f; **an office ~** um empregado de escritório; **a hard/good ~** um ótimo/bom trabalhador.

workforce ['wɜːkfɔːs] n força f de trabalho.

workhouse ['wɜːkhaʊs] n -1. UK [poorhouse] albergue m -2. US [prison] casa f de correção.

working ['wɜːkɪŋ] adj -1. [in operation] em operação; **to be ~** estar funcionando -2. [having employment - mothers, children] que trabalha; [- population] ativo(va) -3. [relating to work] de trabalho.
  ➤ **workings** npl -1. [of system, machine] operação f -2. fig [of mind] funcionamento m.

working capital n -1. [assets minus liabilities] capital m de giro -2. [assets] ativo m circulante -3. [available money] dinheiro m em caixa.

working class n: **the ~** a classe operária.
  ➤ **working-class** adj da classe operária.

working day n = workday.

working group n grupo m de trabalho.

working knowledge n conhecimento m de causa.

working man n trabalhador m.

working model n maquete m.

working order n (U): **in ~** em funcionamento.

working party n grupo m de trabalho.

working week n semana f de trabalho.

work-in-progress n trabalho m em andamento.

workload ['wɜːkləʊd] n carga f de trabalho.

workman ['wɜːkmən] (pl -men [-mən]) n trabalhador m, operário m.

workmanship ['wɜːkmənʃɪp] n (U) acabamento m.

workmate ['wɜːkmeɪt] n colega mf de trabalho.

work of art n obra f de arte.

workout ['wɜːkaʊt] n treinamento m.

work permit [-ˌpɜːmɪt] n visto m de trabalho.

workplace ['wɜːkpleɪs] n local m de trabalho.

work placement n colocação f no mercado de trabalho.

workroom ['wɜːkrʊm] n sala f de trabalho.

works council n comissão f de trabalhadores.

workshop ['wɜːkʃɒp] n -1. [room] oficina f -2. [building] fábrica f -3. [discussion] oficina f, workshop f.

workshy ['wɜːkʃaɪ] adj UK avesso(sa) ao trabalho.

workstation ['wɜːkˌsteɪʃn] n COMPUT estação f de trabalho.

work surface n superfície f de trabalho.

worktable ['wɜːkˌteɪbl] n mesa f de trabalho.

worktop ['wɜːktɒp] n UK superfície f de trabalho.

work-to-rule n UK paralisação f de trabalho extra.

world [wɜːld] ◇ n -1. [gen] mundo m; **to be dead to the ~** estar ferrado(da) no sono; **the best of both ~s** o melhor de dois mundos; **the ~** o mundo; **how/what/in the ~ ...?** como/o que é que ..., pelo amor de Deus?; **where/why in the ~ ...?** onde/por que diabos ...?; **the ~ over** no mundo inteiro -2. [great deal]: **to think the ~ of sb** ter grande afeição por alguém; **to do one the ~ of good** fazer alguém se sentir extremamente feliz;

a ~ of difference toda uma diferença. ◇ comp mundial.

World Bank n: **the ~** o Banco Mundial.

world-class adj muito superior(ra).

World Cup FTBL ◇ n: **the ~** a Copa do Mundo. ◇ comp da Copa do Mundo.

world-famous adj famoso(sa) no mundo todo.

worldly ['wɜːldlɪ] adj mundano(na); **~ goods** coisas mundanas.

world music n (U) música f mundial.

world power n força f OR potência f mundial.

World Series n US: **the ~** o Campeonato Nacional de Beisebol.

WORLD SERIES

A *World Series* é a grande final do campeonato norte-americano de beisebol. Ela é disputada em até sete partidas, nas quais, ao final da temporada, se enfrentam os campeões das duas mais importantes ligas do país: a *National League* e a *American League*. O campeão será o time que primeiro obtiver quatro vitórias. Trata-se de um dos mais importantes acontecimentos esportivos anuais do país. Conforme a tradição, a primeira bola do jogo é lançada pelo presidente da República.

World Service n serviço da BBC que transmite programas de rádio e TV em inglês e em vários idiomas para o mundo todo.

world-weary adj entediado(da).

worldwide ['wɜːldwaɪd] ◇ adj mundial. ◇ adv no mundo inteiro.

worm [wɜːm] ◇ n [animal - in stomach] lombriga f, verme m; [- earthwork] minhoca f. ◇ vt: **to ~ one's way** mover-se; **to ~ one's way into sb's confidence** engambelar alguém.
  ➤ **worms** npl vermes mpl.
  ➤ **worm out** vt sep: **to ~ sthg out of sb** arrancar algo de alguém.

worn [wɔːn] ◇ pp ▷ wear. ◇ adj -1. [threadbare] surrado(da) -2. [tired] exausto(ta).

worn-out adj -1. [old, threadbare] usado(da), gasto(ta) -2. [tired] exausto(ta).

worried ['wʌrɪd] adj preocupado(da); **to be ~ about sb/sthg** estar preocupado(da) com alguém/algo; **to be ~ sick** estar profundamente preocupado(da).

worrier ['wʌrɪəʳ] n: **he's a terrible ~** ele se preocupa com tudo.

worry ['wʌrɪ] (pl -ies, pt & pp -ied) ◇ n -1. (U) [feeling] preocupação f -2. [problem] problema m. ◇ vt [cause to be troubled] preocupar. ◇ vi preocupar-se; **to ~ about sb/sthg** preocupar-se com alguém/algo; **not to ~!** nada com o que se preocupar!

worrying ['wʌrɪŋ] adj preocupante.

worse [wɜːs] ◇ adj pior; **to get ~** piorar. ◇ adv pior; **~ off** em pior situação. ◇ n pior m; **for the ~** para o pior.

worsen ['wɜːsn] vt & vi agravar, piorar.

worsening ['wɜːsnɪŋ] adj agravante, que piora.

worship ['wɜːʃɪp] (UK pt & pp -ped, cont -ping, US pt

& *pp* -**ed**, *cont* -**ing**) ◇ *vt* -**1.** *RELIG* adorar - **2.** [admire, adore] admirar, adorar. ◇ *n* (*U*) adoração *f*.
→ **Worship** *n:* **Your/Her/His Worship** Vossa Excelência.

worshipper *UK*, **worshiper** *US* ['wɜːʃɪpəʳ] *n* -**1.** *RELIG* devoto *m*, -ta *f* - **2.** [admirer] admirador *m*, -ra *f*.

worst [wɜːst] ◇ *adj* & *adv* pior. ◇ *n*: **the ~** o pior; **if the ~ comes to the ~** se o pior acontecer; **to get the ~ of it** ficar com o pior.
→ **at (the) worst** *adv* na pior das hipóteses.

worsted ['wʊstɪd] *n* (*U*) lã *f* penteada.

worth [wɜːθ] ◇ *prep* -**1.** [having the value of] valor *m*; **it's ~ £50** vale £50 - **2.** [deserving of]: **it's ~ going to Brazil** vale a pena ir para a Brasil; **it's ~ a visit** vale a visita; **to be ~ doing sthg** valer a pena fazer algo. ◇ *n* -**1.** [value] valor *m* - **2.** [supply] provisão *f*.

worthless ['wɜːθlɪs] *adj* -**1.** [object] sem valor - **2.** [person] inútil.

worthwhile [ˌwɜːθ'waɪl] *adj* que vale a pena.

worthy ['wɜːðɪ] (*compar* -**ier**, *superl* -**iest**) *adj* -**1.** [deserving of respect] respeitável - **2.** [deserving]: **to be ~ of sthg** ser merecedor(ra) de algo - **3.** *pej* [good but unexciting] adequado(da).

would [wʊd] *modal vb* -**1.** [in reported speech]: **she said she ~ come** ela disse que viria; **he promised he ~ help me** ele prometeu que me ajudaria - **2.** [indicating likely result]: **what ~ you do if he phoned?** o que você faria se ele ligasse?; **I doubt she ~ have noticed** duvido que ela percebesse; **if he had lost, he ~ have resigned** ele teria renunciado - **3.** [indicating willingness]: **she ~n't go** ela não queria ir embora; **he ~ do anything for her** ele faria qualquer coisa por ela; **she ~n't give an answer even if ...** ela não teria respondido mesmo que ... - **4.** [in polite questions]: **~ you like a drink?** você gostaria de tomar um drinque?; **~ you mind closing the window?** você poderia fechar a janela, por favor?; **help me shut the door, ~ you?** me ajuda a fechar a porta, por favor? - **5.** [indicating inevitability]: **he ~ say that** não me surpreende que ele tenha dito isso; **I said yes - well, you ~** eu disse sim - bem, era o esperado - **6.** [expressing opinions]: **I ~ have thought that she'd be pleased** eu pensava que ela tivesse gostado; **I ~ prefer a blue one** eu preferia um azul - **7.** [in giving advice]: **I'd report it if I were you** no teu lugar, eu denunciaria - **8.** [describing habitual past actions]: **I ~ go for a walk every evening** eu costumava dar uma caminhada todas as tardes; **we ~ meet and he ~ say...** a gente se encontrava e ele dizia ...

would-be *adj* aspirante.

wouldn't ['wʊdnt] = **would not.**

would've ['wʊdəv] = **would have.**

wound¹ [wauːnd] *n* ferida *f*, ferimento *m*; **to lick one's ~s** recuperar-se. ◇ *vt* ferir.

wound² [waʊnd] *pt* & *pp* ⊳ **wind** ².

wounded ['wuːndɪd] ◇ *adj* ferido(da). ◇ *npl*: **the ~** os feridos.

wounding ['wuːndɪŋ] *adj* prejudicial.

wove [wəʊv] *pt* ⊳ **weave.**

woven ['wəʊvn] *pp* ⊳ **weave.**

wow [waʊ] *inf* ◇ *n* estouro *m*. ◇ *vt* empolgar. ◇ *excl* uau!

WP ◇ *n* - **1.** (*abbr of* **word processing**) processamento *m* de textos - **2.** (*abbr of* **word processor**) processador *m* de textos. ◇ (*abbr of* **weather permitting**) se o tempo permitir.

WPC (*abbr of* **woman police constable**) *n policial feminina britânica de posto inferior.*

wpm (*abbr of* **words per minute**) ppm.

WRAC [ræk] (*abbr of* **Women's Royal Army Corps**) *n corporação feminina do exército britânico.*

WRAF [ræf] (*abbr of* **Women's Royal Air Force**) *n corporação feminina da força aérea real britânica.*

wrangle ['ræŋgl] ◇ *n* disputa *f*, briga *f*. ◇ *vi* brigar; **to ~ with sb (over sthg)** discutir com alguém (sobre algo).

wrap [ræp] (*pt* & *pp* -**ped**, *cont* -**ping**) ◇ *vt* -**1.** [cover in paper or cloth] embrulhar; **to ~ sthg in sthg** enrolar algo em algo; **to ~ sthg (a)round sthg** enrolar algo ao redor de algo - **2.** [encircle]: **to ~ sthg (a)round sthg** enrolar algo em algo. ◇ *n* [garment] xale *m*.
→ **wrap up** ◇ *vt sep* -**1.** [cover in paper or cloth] embrulhar - **2.** *inf* [complete] terminar. ◇ *vi* [put warm clothes on]: **~ up well** *OR* **warmly!** agasalhe-se bem!

wrapped up [ræpt-] *adj inf*: **to be ~ in sb/sthg** estar afundado(da) em alguém/algo.

wrapper ['ræpəʳ] *n* embalagem *f*.

wrapping ['ræpɪŋ] *n* embrulho *m*, invólucro *m*.

wrapping paper *n* (*U*) papel *m* de embrulho.

wrath [rɒθ] *n* (*U*) *literary* ira *f*.

wreak [riːk] *vt* causar.

wreath [riːθ] *n* coroa *f* (*de flores*).

wreathe [riːð] *vt literary* envolver.

wreck [rek] ◇ *n* -**1.** [car, plane] destroços *mpl* - **2.** [ship] restos *mpl* - **3.** *inf* [person] caco *m*. ◇ *vt* -**1.** [break, destroy] destruir - **2.** *NAUT* [cause to run aground] naufragar - **3.** [spoil, ruin] arruinar.

wreckage ['rekɪdʒ] *n* -**1.** [of plane, car] restos *mpl* - **2.** [of building] escombros *mpl*.

wrecker ['rekəʳ] *n US* reboque *m*.

wren [ren] *n* garriça *f*.

wrench [rentʃ] ◇ *n* -**1.** [tool] chave *f* inglesa - **2.** [injury, twist] torcedura *f*, distensão *f* - **3.** [cause of sadness] tristeza *f*. ◇ *vt* -**1.** [pull violently] arrancar - **2.** [twist and injure] torcer, distender - **3.** [force away] arrebatar; **to ~ sthg away from sthg** varrer algo para longe de algo.

wrest [rest] *vt literary*: **to ~ sthg from sb** extorquir algo de alguém.

wrestle ['resl] ◇ *vt* derrubar. ◇ *vi* -**1.** [fight] lutar; **to ~ with sb** lutar com alguém - **2.** *fig* [struggle]: **to ~ with sthg** lutar contra algo.

wrestler ['resləʳ] *n* lutador *m*, -ra *f* de luta livre.

wrestling ['reslɪŋ] *n* (*U*) luta *f* livre.

wretch [retʃ] *n* [unhappy person] desgraçado *m*, -da *f*.

wretched ['retʃɪd] *adj* -**1.** [miserable] infeliz - **2.** *inf* [damned] maldito(ta).

wriggle ['rɪgl] ◇ *vt* mexer. ◇ *vi* -**1.** [move about] mexer-se - **2.** [twist] retorcer-se.

wriggle out of *vt fus*: to ~ out of sthg/of doing sthg safar-se de algo/de fazer algo.

wring [rɪŋ] (*pt & pp* wrung) *vt* -**1.** [squeeze out water from] torcer -**2.** *literary* [hands] esfregar -**3.** [neck] virar.

↪ **wring out** *vt sep* arrancar.

wringing ['rɪŋɪŋ] *adj*: ~ (wet) encharcado(da), ensopado(da).

wrinkle ['rɪŋkl] ⟨⟩ *n* -**1.** [on skin] ruga *f*-**2.** [in cloth] prega *f*. ⟨⟩ *vt* [screw up] enrugar. ⟨⟩ *vi* [crease] dobrar-se.

wrinkled ['rɪŋkld], **wrinkly** ['rɪŋklɪ] *adj* -**1.** [skin] enrugado(da) -**2.** [cloth] com prega.

wrist [rɪst] *n* pulso *m*.

wristband ['rɪstbænd] *n* [of watch] pulseira *f*.

wristwatch ['rɪstwɒtʃ] *n* relógio *m* de pulso.

writ [rɪt] *n* mandado *m* judicial.

write [raɪt] (*pt* wrote, *pp* written) ⟨⟩ *vt* -**1.** [gen] escrever; to ~ sb a letter escrever uma carta para alguém -**2.** *US* [person] escrever para -**3.** [cheque, prescription] preencher -**4.** *COMPUT* gravar. ⟨⟩ *vi* -**1.** [gen] escrever; to ~ to sb escrever para alguém -**2.** *COMPUT* gravar.

↪ **write back** ⟨⟩ *vt sep* escrever de volta. ⟨⟩ *vi* responder.

↪ **write down** *vt sep* anotar.

↪ **write in** *vi* [to radio or TV station, shop] responder.

↪ **write into** *vt sep* [contract] acrescentar.

↪ **write off** ⟨⟩ *vt sep* -**1.** [project] cancelar -**2.** [debt, investment] cancelar, reduzir -**3.** [person] descartar -**4.** *UK inf* [vehicle] destroçar. ⟨⟩ *vi* [for information] solicitar (*informações*); to ~ off to sb/sthg solicitar informações a alguém; to ~ off for sthg solicitar algo.

↪ **write out** *vt sep* [list, names] escrever por extenso.

↪ **write up** *vt sep* [notes] redigir.

write-off *n* [car] perda *f* total.

write-protect *vt COMPUT* proteger contra gravação.

writer ['raɪtə'] *n* escritor *m*, -ra *f*.

write-up *n inf* crítica *f*.

writhe [raɪð] *vi* contorcer-se.

writing ['raɪtɪŋ] *n* -**1.** [gen] escrita *f*; I couldn't see the ~ não conseguia ler o que estava escrito; in ~ por escrito -**2.** [handwriting] caligrafia *f*; I can't read your ~ não consigo ler o que você escreveu.

↪ **writings** *npl* escritos *mpl*.

writing case *n UK* estojo *m* para escrever.

writing desk *n* escrivaninha *f*.

writing paper *n (U)* papel *m* de carta.

written ['rɪtn] ⟨⟩ *pp* ⊳ write. ⟨⟩ *adj* -**1.** [not oral] escrito(ta) -**2.** [official] por escrito.

WRNS (*abbr of* Women's Royal Naval Service) *n* corporação feminina da marinha real britânica.

wrong [rɒŋ] ⟨⟩ *adj* -**1.** [gen] errado(da); to be ~ to do sthg enganar-se ao fazer algo -**2.** [morally bad] feio (feia). ⟨⟩ *adv* [incorrectly] errado; to get sthg ~ enganar-se sobre algo; to go ~ [make a mistake] errar; [stop functioning] funcionar mal; don't get me ~ *inf* não me interprete mal. ⟨⟩ *n* erro *m*; to be in the ~ estar equivocado(da). ⟨⟩ *vt literary* ofender.

wrong-foot *vt UK* -**1.** *SPORT* fintar -**2.** *fig* [surprise] surpreender.

wrongful ['rɒŋfʊl] *adj* injusto(ta).

wrongly ['rɒŋlɪ] *adv* -**1.** [unsuitably] inadequadamente -**2.** [mistakenly] erroneamente.

wrong number *n* número *m* errado.

wrote [rəʊt] *pt* ⊳ write.

wrought iron [rɔːt-] *n (U)* ferro *m* forjado.

wrung [rʌŋ] *pt & pp* ⊳ wring.

WRVS (*abbr of* Women's Royal Voluntary Service) *n* associação de voluntárias britânicas para ajuda a necessitados em emergências.

wry [raɪ] *adj* -**1.** [amused] entretido(da) -**2.** [displeased] desgostoso(sa).

wt. (*abbr of* weight) peso *m*.

WV *abbr of* West Virginia.

WW (*abbr of* world war) GM *f*.

WWF (*abbr of* World Wildlife Fund) *n* organização internacional de proteção a plantas, animais selvagens e áreas naturais, WWF *m*.

WY *abbr of* Wyoming.

Wyoming *n* Wyoming.

WYSIWYG ['wɪzɪwɪg] (*abbr of* what you see is what you get) *adj* WYSIWYG.

x (*pl* x's *OR* xs), **X** (*pl* X's *OR* Xs) [eks] *n* -**1.** [letter] x, X *m* -**2.** [unknown name] X *m* -**3.** [unknown quantity] x *m* -**4.** [in algebra] x *m* -**5.** [at end of letter] beijos *mpl*.

xenophobia [ˌzenəˈfəʊbjə] *n (U)* xenofobia *f*.

Xerox® *n* Xerox® *f*.

↪ **xerox** *vt* xerocar.

Xmas ['eksməs] ⟨⟩ *n (U)* Natal *m*. ⟨⟩ *comp* de Natal.

X-ray ⟨⟩ *n* -**1.** [ray] raio *m* X -**2.** [picture] raio-X *m*. ⟨⟩ *vt* tirar um raio-X de, tirar uma radiografia de.

xylophone ['zaɪləfəʊn] *n* xilofone *m*.

y (pl y's OR ys), **Y** (pl Y's OR Ys) [waɪ] n [letter] y, Y m.

yacht [jɒt] n iate m.

yachting ['jɒtɪŋ] n (U) iatismo m.

yachtsman ['jɒtsmən] (pl -men [-mən]) n iatista m.

yachtswoman ['jɒts,wʊmən] (pl -women [-,wɪmɪn]) n iatista f.

yahoo [ˌjæ'huː] n brutamontes mf inv.

yak [jæk] n iaque m.

Yale lock® [jeɪl-] n fechadura f cilíndrica.

yam [jæm] n inhame m.

Yangon n = Rangoon.

yank [jæŋk] vt arrancar.

Yank [jæŋk] n UK inf pej ianque mf.

Yankee ['jæŋkɪ] n **-1.** UK inf pej [American] ianque mf **-2.** US [northerner] pessoa oriunda dos Estados do norte.

YANKEE

Em sua origem, o termo *yankee* referia-se aos imigrantes holandeses que se estabeleceram sobretudo no noroeste dos Estados Unidos. Mais tarde, passou a designar qualquer pessoa proveniente dessa região. Assim, 'ianques' eram chamados os soldados nortistas, durante a Guerra de Secessão nos Estados Unidos. Nos dias atuais, sulistas ainda empregam a palavra em tom pejorativo, para referir-se aos americanos do norte do país.

---

yap [jæp] (pt & pp -ped, cont -ping) vi **-1.** [dog] ganir, latir **-2.** pej [person] tagarelar.

yard [jɑːd] n **-1.** [unit of measurement] jarda f **-2.** [walled area] pátio m **-3.** [place of work] oficina f **-4.** US [attached to house] jardim m.

yardstick ['jɑːdstɪk] n padrão m de medida.

yarn [jɑːn] n **-1.** (U) [thread] fio m **-2.** inf [story] lorota f; **to spin sb a** ~ contar lorotas para alguém.

yashmak ['jæʃmæk] n burca f.

yawn [jɔːn] <> n **-1.** [when tired] bocejo m **-2.** UK inf [boring event] chateação f. <> vi **-1.** [when tired] bocejar **-2.** [gape] abrir-se.

yd abbr of yard.

yeah [jeə] adv inf sim; **bring us something to drink -** ~, ~! traz algo para a gente beber - tá, já trago!

year [jɪəʳ] n ano m; **all (the)** ~ **round** durante todo o ano; ~ **in** ~ **out** entra ano, sai ano.

→ **years** npl [ages] séculos mpl.

yearbook ['jɪəbʊk] n anuário m.

yearling ['jɪəlɪŋ] n **-1.** [horse] potro m **-2.** [sheep, calves] filhote m.

yearly ['jɪəlɪ] <> adj anual. <> adv anualmente.

yearn [jɜːn] vi: **to** ~ **for sthg/to do sthg** ansiar por algo/para fazer algo.

yearning ['jɜːnɪŋ] n ânsia f; ~ **for sb/sthg** ânsia por alguém/algo.

yeast [jiːst] n (U) levedura f.

yell [jel] <> n grito m. <> vi gritar. <> vt gritar.

yellow ['jeləʊ] <> adj **-1.** [in colour] amarelo(la) **-2.** inf [cowardly] covarde. <> n amarelo m. <> vi amarelar.

yellow card n FTBL cartão m amarelo.

yellow fever n (U) febre f amarela.

yellow lines n faixa f amarela.

yellowness n (U) amarelidão m.

Yellow Pages® n UK: **the** ~ as Páginas Amarelas.

Yellow River n: **the** ~ o Rio Amarelo.

Yellow Sea n: **the** ~ o Mar Amarelo.

yelp [jelp] <> n latido m. <> vi latir.

Yemen ['jemən] n: **(the)** ~ o Iêmen; **in (the)** ~ no Iêmen.

Yemeni ['jemənɪ] <> adj iemenita. <> n iemenita mf.

yen [jen] (pl sense 1 inv) n **-1.** [Japanese currency] iene m **-2.** [longing]: **to have a** ~ **for sthg/to do sthg** desejar muito algo/fazer algo.

yeoman of the guard (pl -men of the guard) n membro m da guarda real.

yep adv inf sim.

yes [jes] <> adv sim; ~, **please** sim, por favor; **to say** ~ **to sthg** dizer sim para algo. <> n [vote in favour] sim m.

yes-man n pej capacho m.

yesterday ['jestədɪ] <> n ontem m; **the day before yesterday** anteontem. <> adv **-1.** [day before today] ontem **-2.** [the past] passado.

yet [jet] <> adv **-1.** [gen] ainda; **not** ~ ainda não **-2.** [up until now] já; **as** ~ até agora **-3.** [in the future] até **-4.** [to emphasize number, frequency] mais; ~ **again** mais uma vez. <> conj porém.

yeti n ieti m.

yew [juː] n teixo m.

Y-fronts npl UK cueca f com abertura na frente.

YHA (abbr of Youth Hostels Association) n associação britânica de albergues da juventude.

Yiddish ['jɪdɪʃ] <> adj relativo(va) ao iídiche. <> n (U) iídiche m.

yield [jiːld] <> n lucro m, rendimento m. <> vt **-1.** [produce - fruit, answer, clue] produzir; [- profits, result] gerar **-2.** [give up] ceder. <> vi **-1.** [open, give way, break] ceder **-2.** fml [give up, surrender] render-se; **to** ~ **to sb/sthg** ceder a alguém/algo.

yippee [UK jɪ'piː, US 'jɪpɪ] excl iupi!

Y2K (abbr of year two thousand) n ano m 2000.

YMCA (abbr of Young Men's Christian Association) n ≃ ACM f.

yo excl inf oi!

yob(bo) ['jɒb(əʊ)] n UK inf bagunceiro m, -ra f.

yodel ['jəʊdll] (*UK pt* & *pp* **-led**, *cont* **-ling**, *US pt* & *pp* **-ed**, *cont* **-ing**) *vi* cantar à moda dos tiroleses.

yoga ['jəʊgəl] *n* (*U*) ioga *f*.

yoghourt, yoghurt, yogurt [*UK* 'jɒgət, *US* 'jəʊgərtl] *n* iogurte *m*.

yoke [jəʊk] *n* **-1.** [for oxen] junta *f* **-2.** *literary* [burden, suffering] jugo *m*.

yokel ['jəʊkll] *n pej* caipira *mf*.

yolk [jəʊk] *n* gema *f*.

yonder ['jɒndə'] *adv literary* acolá.

Yorkshire pudding ['jɔːkʃə'-] *n* comida preparada com farinha, ovos e leite, e servida com carne.

you [ju:] *pron* **-1.** [subject: singular] você, tu; [subject: singular polite form] o senhor (a senhora); [subject: plural] vocês; [subject: plural polite form] os senhores (as senhoras); **do ~ speak Portuguese?** [singular] você fala português?; [polite form] (o senhor) fala português?; **~ Brazilians** vocês brasileiros. **-2.** [direct object: singular] o (a), te; [direct object: singular polite form] o senhor (a senhora); [direct object: plural] os (as), vos; [direct object: plural polite form] os (as), os senhores (as senhoras); **I saw ~** [singular] eu o vi; **can I help ~?** [polite form: singular] em que posso ajudá-lo?; [polite form: plural] em que posso ajudá-los?; **I'll see ~ later** [plural] vejo-os mais tarde. **-3.** [indirect object: singular] lhe, te; [indirect object: singular polite form] lhe; [indirect object: plural] lhes, vos; **I would like to ask ~ something** [polite form: singular] gostaria de perguntar algo a você; **didn't I tell ~ what happened?** [polite form: plural] não lhes contei o que aconteceu? **-4.** [after prep: singular] você, ti; [after prep: singular polite form] o senhor (a senhora), si; [after prep: plural] vocês; [after prep: plural polite form] os senhores (as senhoras), vós; **this is for ~** isto é para você/o senhor, etc; **with ~** [singular] com você, contigo; [singular: polite form] com o senhor (a senhora); [plural] com vocês; [plural: polite form] com os senhores (as senhoras). **-5.** [indefinite use: subject]: **the coffee ~ get in Brazil is very strong** o café que se bebe no Brasil é muito forte; **~ never know** nunca se sabe. **-6.** [indefinite use: object]: **exercise is good for ~** exercício faz bem (para a saúde).

you'd [ju:d] = **you had, you would.**

you'll [ju:l] = **you will.**

young [jʌŋ] *adj* **-1.** [person] jovem **-2.** [plant, wine, animal] novo(va). *npl* **-1.** [young people]: **the ~** a juventude **-2.** [baby animals] filhotes *mpl*.

younger *adj* mais novo(va); **Pitt the Younger** Pitt Júnior.

youngish ['jʌŋɪʃ] *adj* bem novo(va).

young man *n* moço *m*, rapaz *m*.

youngster ['jʌŋstə'] *n* **-1.** [child] filho *m*, -lha *f* **-2.** [young person] jovem *mf*.

young woman *n* moça *f*, rapariga *f*.

your [jɔː'l] *adj* **-1.** [singular subject] o seu (a sua), o teu (a tua); [singular subject: polite form] o/a do senhor (da senhora); [plural subject] o vosso (a vossa); [plural subject: polite form] o/a dos senhores (das senhoras); **~ dog** o seu/teu/vosso cão, o cão do senhor

(da senhora), o cão dos senhores (das senhoras); **~ house** a sua/tua/vossa casa, etc; **~ children** os seus/teus/vossos filhos, etc. **-2.** [indefinite subject]: **it's good for ~ health** é bom para a saúde.

you're [jɔː'] = **you are.**

yours [jɔːz] *pron* [singular subject] o seu (a sua), o teu (a tua); [plural subject] o vosso (a vossa); [formal - singular subject] o/a do senhor (da senhora); [- plural subject] o/a dos senhores (das senhoras); **a friend of ~** um amigo seu/teu/vosso/do senhor/da senhora/dos senhores/das senhoras; **these shoes are ~** estes sapatos são (os) teus/seus/vossos, etc; **these are mine – where are ~?** estes são os meus – onde estão os seus/teus/vossos, etc?

yourself [jɔː'selfl] *pron* **-1.** [reflexive: singular] se, te; [reflexive: plural] se; **did you hurt ~?** [singular] você se machucou? **-2.** [after prep: singular] você mesmo(ma), tu mesmo(ma); [after prep: plural] vocês mesmos(mas); [after prep: plural polite form] os senhores mesmos (as senhoras mesmas), vós mesmos(mas); **did you do it ~?** [singular] você fez isso sozinho?; [polite form] foi o senhor mesmo que o fez?; **did you do it yourselves?** vocês fizeram isso sozinhos?; [polite form] foram os senhores mesmos que o fizeram?

youth [ju:θ] *n* **-1.** [gen] juventude *f* **-2.** [boy, young man] mocidade *f* **-3.** (*U*) [young people] mocidade *f*, juventude *f*.

youth club *n* clube *m* da juventude.

youthful ['ju:θful] *adj* juvenil.

youthfulness ['ju:θfulnɪs] *n* (*U*) juventude *f*.

youth hostel *n* albergue *m* da juventude.

youth hostelling [-'hɒstəlɪŋ] *n UK*: **to go youth hostelling** ir para albergues da juventude.

you've [ju:v] *cont* = **you have.**

yowl [jaʊl] *n* **-1.** [dog] uivo *m* **-2.** [cat] miado *m*. *vi* **-1.** [dog] uivar **-2.** [cat] miar.

yo-yo ['jəʊjəʊ] *n* ioiô *m*.

yr (*abbr of* **year**) ano *m*.

YT *n abbr of* **Yukon Territory.**

Yucatan [ˌjʌkə'tɑːn] *n* Yucatan.

yucca *n* iúca *f*.

yuck [jʌk] *excl inf* argh!

Yugoslav *adj* & *n* = **Yugoslavian.**

Yugoslavia [ˌjuːgə'slɑːvɪə] *n* Iugoslávia *f*; **in ~** na Iugoslávia.

Yugoslavian [ˌjuːgə'slɑːvɪən], **Yugoslav** [ˌjuːgə'slɑːv] *adj* iugoslavo(va). *n* iugoslavo *m*, -va *f*.

Yukon Territory *n* território *m* Yukon.

yule log *n* **-1.** [piece of wood] acha *f* de Natal **-2.** [cake] torta *f* de Natal.

yuletide ['ju:ltaɪd] *n* (*U*) *literary* época *f* de Natal.

yummy ['jʌmɪ] (*compar* **-ier**, *superl* **-iest**) *adj inf* delicioso(sa).

yuppie, yuppy ['jʌpɪ] (*pl* **-ies**) (*abbr of* **young urban professional**) *n* yuppie *mf*.

YWCA (*abbr of* **Young Women's Christian Association**) *n* ≃ ACM *f*.

Z

z (pl z's OR **zs**), **Z** (pl Z's OR **Zs**) [UK zed, US zi:] n [letter] z, Z m.

Zagreb n Zagreb.

Zaïre [za:'ɪəʳ] n Zaire; **in ~** no Zaire.

Zaïrese ◇ adj zairense. ◇ n zairense mf.

Zambesi, Zambezi n: the **~** o Zambesi.

Zambia ['zæmbɪə] n Zâmbia; **in ~** no Zâmbia.

Zambian ['zæmbɪən] ◇ adj zambiano(na). ◇ n zambiano m, -na f.

zany ['zeɪnɪ] (compar -ier, superl -iest) adj inf bobo(ba).

Zanzibar n Zanzibar.

zap [zæp] (pt & pp -ped, cont -ping) inf ◇ vt -**1.** [kill] despachar -**2.** [in video games] destruir. ◇ vi -**1.** [rush] correr; **to ~ off to** correr para; **to ~ through** sthg passar os olhos por algo -**2.** TV zapear; **to ~ from channel to channel** ficar trocando de um canal para o outro.

zeal [zi:l] n (U) fml zelo m.

zealot ['zelət] n fml fanático m, -ca f.

zealous ['zeləs] adj fml zeloso(sa).

zebra [UK 'zebrə, US 'zi:brə] (pl inv OR -s) n zebra f.

zebra crossing n UK faixa f de segurança.

zenith [UK 'zenɪθ, US 'zi:nəθ] n -**1.** ASTRON zênite m -**2.** fig [highest point] apogeu m.

zeppelin ['zepəlɪn] n zepelim m.

zero [UK 'zɪərəʊ, US 'zi:rəʊ] (pl -s OR -es, pt & pp -ed, cont -ing) ◇ adj zero. ◇ n zero m.

◆ **zero in on** vt fus -**1.** [subj: weapon] fazer mira em -**2.** [subj: person] concentrar-se em.

zero-rated [-ˌreɪtɪd] adj UK ≃ isento(ta) de IVA.

zest [zest] n -**1.** [excitement] entusiasmo m -**2.** (U) [eagerness] vivacidade f -**3.** (U) [of orange, lemon] sabor m.

zigzag ['zɪgzæg] (pt & pp -ged, cont -ging) ◇ n ziguezague m. ◇ vi ziguezaguear.

zilch [zɪltʃ] n US inf: **I know she'll do ~ while I'm away** nada de nada, sei que ela não vai fazer nada de nada enquanto eu estiver fora.

Zimbabwe [zɪm'bɑ:bwɪ] n Zimbábue; **in ~** no Zimbábue.

Zimbabwean [zɪm'bɑ:bwɪən] ◇ adj zimbabuano(na). ◇ n zimbabuano m, -na f.

Zimmer frame® ['zɪməʳ-] n andador m.

zinc [zɪŋk] n (U) zinco m.

Zionism ['zaɪənɪzm] n sionismo m.

Zionist ['zaɪənɪst] ◇ adj sionista. ◇ n sionista mf.

zip [zɪp] (pt & pp -ped, cont -ping) ◇ n UK [fastener] fecho m ecler, zíper m. ◇ vt -**1.** [clothing] fechar com zíper -**2.** COMPUT zipar, compactar.

◆ **zip up** vt sep fechar o zíper de.

zip [zɪp]

zip code n US ≃ CEP m.

Zip disk® n COMPUT disco m Zip®.

Zip drive® n COMPUT unidade f Zip®.

zip fastener n UK = zip.

zipper ['zɪpəʳ] n US = zip.

zippy (compar -ier, superl -iest) adj inf [car] possante.

zit [zɪt] n esp US inf mancha f (na pele).

zither ['zɪðəʳ] n citara f.

zodiac ['zəʊdɪæk] n: the **~** o zodíaco; **sign of the ~** signo m do zodíaco.

zombie ['zɒmbɪ] n [automaton] zumbi m.

zone [zəʊn] n [district] zona f.

zoo [zu:] n zoológico m.

zoological [ˌzəʊə'lɒdʒɪkl] adj zoológico(ca).

zoologist [zəʊ'ɒlədʒɪst] n zoólogo m, -ga f, zoologista mf.

zoology [zəʊ'ɒlədʒɪ] n (U) zoologia f.

zoom [zu:m] vi inf -**1.** [move quickly] arrancar-se -**2.** [rise rapidly] disparar.

◆ **zoom in** vi: **to ~ in (on sb/sthg)** dar um close em alguém/algo.

◆ **zoom off** vi inf arrancar-se.

zoom lens n (lentes fpl de) zum m.

zucchini [zu:'ki:nɪ] (pl inv OR -s) n US abobrinha f italiana.

Zulu ['zu:lu:] ◇ adj zulu. ◇ n zulu mf.

Zürich ['zjʊərɪk] n Zurique; **in ~** em Zurique.

PORTUGUESE VERBS
ENGLISH IRREGULAR VERBS

CONJUGAÇÃO DOS VERBOS PORTUGUESES
VERBOS IRREGULARES INGLESES

	1 ter	2 haver	3 ser
ind. presente	eu tenho, tu tens, ele tem, nós temos, vós tendes, eles têm	eu hei, tu hás, ele há, nós havemos/hemos, vós haveis/heis, eles hão	eu sou, tu és, ele é, nós somos, vós sois, eles são
ind. imperfeito	eu tinha	eu havia	eu era
ind. perfeito	eu tive	eu houve	eu fui
ind. m.-q.-p. simpl.	eu tivera	eu houvera	eu fora
ind. m.-q.-p. comp.	eu tinha tido	eu tinha havido	eu tinha sido
ind fut. do pres.	eu terei	eu haverei	eu serei
ind fut. do pret.	eu teria	eu haveria	eu seria
subj. presente	que eu tenha	que eu haja	que eu seja
subj. imperfeito	que eu tivesse	que eu houvesse	que eu fosse
subj. perfeito	que eu tenha tido	que eu tenha havido	que eu tenha sido
subj. m.-q.-perf.	que eu tivesse tido	que eu tivesse havido	que eu tivesse sido
subj. futuro	quando eu tiver	quando eu houver	quando eu for
inf. pessoal	eu ter, tu teres, ele ter, nós termos, vós terdes, eles terem	eu haver, tu haveres, ele haver, nós havermos, vós haverdes, eles haverem	eu ser, tu seres, ele ser, nós sermos, vós serdes, eles serem
imper. afirm.	tem (tu)	há (tu)	sê (tu)
imper. neg.	não tenhas	não hajas	não sejas
gerúndio	tendo	havendo	sendo
particípio	tido	havido	sido

	4 falar	5 comer	6 partir
ind. presente	eu falo, tu falas, ele fala, nós falamos, vós falais, eles falam	eu como, tu comes, ele come, nós comemos, vós comeis, eles comem	eu parto, tu partes, ele parte, nós partimos, vós partis, eles partem
ind. imperfeito	eu falava	eu comia	eu partia
ind. perfeito	eu falei	eu comi	eu parti
ind. m.-q.-p. simpl.	eu falara	eu comera	eu partira
ind. m.-q.-p. comp.	eu tinha falado	eu tinha comido	eu tinha partido
ind fut. do pres.	eu falarei	eu comerei	eu partirei
ind fut. do pret.	eu falaria	eu comeria	eu partiria
subj. presente	que eu fale	que eu coma	que eu parta
subj. imperfeito	que eu falasse	que eu comesse	que eu partisse
subj. perfeito	que eu tenha falado	que eu tenha comido	que eu tenha partido
subj. m.-q.-perf.	que eu tivesse falado	que eu tivesse comido	que eu tivesse partido
subj. futuro	quando eu falar	quando eu comer	quando eu partir
inf. pessoal	eu falar, tu falares, ele falar, nós falarmos, vós falardes, eles falarem	eu comer, tu comeres, ele comer, nós comermos, vós comerdes, eles comerem	eu partir, tu partires, ele partir, nós partirmos, vós partirdes, eles partirem
imper. afirm.	fala (tu)	come (tu)	parte (tu)
imper. neg.	não fales	não comas	não partas
gerúndio	falando	comendo	partindo
particípio	falado	comido	partido

	7 cortar-se	8 chamá-lo	9 ser amado
ind. presente	eu me corto, tu te cortas, ele se corta, nós nos cortamos, vós vos cortais, eles se cortam	eu o chamo, tu o chamas, ele o chama, nós o chamamos, vós o chamais, eles o chamam	eu sou amado, tu és amado, ele é amado, nós somos amados, vós sois amados, eles são amados
ind. imperfeito	eu me cortava	eu o chamava	eu era amado
ind. perfeito	eu me cortei	eu o chamei	eu fui amado
ind. m.-q.-p. simpl.	eu me cortara	eu o chamara	eu fora amado
ind. m.-q.-p. comp.	eu me tinha cortado	eu o tinha chamado	eu tinha sido amado
ind fut. do pres.	eu me cortarei	eu o chamarei	eu serei amado
ind fut. do pret.	eu me cortaria	eu o chamaria	eu seria amado
subj. presente	que eu me corte	que eu o chame	que eu seja amado
subj. imperfeito	que eu me cortasse	que eu o chamasse	que eu fosse amado
subj. perfeito	que eu me tenha cortado	que eu o tenha chamado	que eu tenha sido amado
subj. m.-q.-perf.	que eu me tivesse cortado	que eu o tivesse chamado	que eu tivesse sido amado
subj. futuro	quando eu me cortar	quando eu o chamar	quando eu for amado
inf. pessoal	eu me cortar, tu te cortares, ele se cortar, nós nos cortarmos, vós vos cortardes, eles se cortarem	eu o chamar, tu o chamares, ele o chamar, nós o chamarmos, vós o chamardes, eles o chamarem	eu ser amado, tu seres amado, ele ser amado, nós sermos amados, vós serdes amados, eles serem amados
imper. afirm.	corta-te (tu)	chama-o (tu)	sê amado (tu)
imper. neg.	não te cortes	não o chames	não sejas amado
gerúndio	cortando	chamando	amando
particípio	cortado	chamado	amado

	10 estar	11 dar	12 ficar
ind. presente	eu estou, tu estás, ele está, nós estamos, vós estais, eles estão	eu dou, tu dás, ele dá, nós damos, vós dais, eles dão	eu fico, tu ficas, ele fica, nós ficamos, vós ficais, eles ficam
ind. imperfeito	eu estava	eu dava	eu ficava
ind. perfeito	eu estive	eu dei	eu fiquei
ind. m.-q.-p. simpl.	eu estivera	eu dera	eu ficara
ind. m.-q.-p. comp.	eu tinha estado	eu tinha dado	eu tinha ficado
ind fut. do pres.	eu estarei	eu darei	eu ficarei
ind fut. do pret.	eu estaria	eu daria	eu ficaria
subj. presente	que eu esteja	que eu dê	que eu fique
subj. imperfeito	que eu estivesse	que eu desse	que eu ficasse
subj. perfeito	que eu tenha estado	que eu tenha dado	que eu tenha ficado
subj. m.-q.-perf.	que eu tivesse estado	que eu tivesse dado	que eu tivesse ficado
subj. futuro	quando eu estiver	quando eu der	quando eu ficar
inf. pessoal	eu estar, tu estares, ele estar, nós estarmos, vós estardes, eles estarem	eu dar, tu dares, ele dar, nós darmos, vós dardes, eles darem	eu ficar, tu ficares, ele ficar, nós ficarmos, vós ficardes, eles ficarem
imper. afirm.	está (tu)	dá (tu)	fica (tu)
imper. neg.	não estejas	não dês	não fiques
gerúndio	estando	dando	ficando
particípio	estado	dado	ficado

	13 dançar	14 pagar	15 passear
ind. presente	eu danço, tu danças, ele dança, nós dançamos, vós dançais, eles dançam	eu pago, tu pagas, ele paga, nós pagamos, vós pagais, eles pagam	eu passeio, tu passeias, ele passeia, nós passeamos, vós passeais, eles passeiam
ind. imperfeito	eu dançava	eu pagava	eu passeava
ind. perfeito	eu dancei	eu paguei	eu passeei
ind. m.-q.-p. simpl.	eu dançara	eu pagara	eu passeara
ind. m.-q.-p. comp.	eu tinha dançado	eu tinha pagado	eu tinha passeado
ind fut. do pres.	eu dançarei	eu pagarei	eu passearei
ind fut. do pret.	eu dançaria	eu pagaria	eu passearia
subj. presente	que eu dance	que eu pague	que eu passeie
subj. imperfeito	que eu dançasse	que eu pagasse	que eu passeasse
subj. perfeito	que eu tenha dançado	que eu tenha pagado	que eu tenha passeado
subj. m.-q.-perf.	que eu tivesse dançado	que eu tivesse pagado	que eu tivesse passeado
subj. futuro	quando eu dançar	quando eu pagar	quando eu passear
inf. pessoal	eu dançar, tu dançares, ele dançar, nós dançarmos, vós dançardes, eles dançarem	eu pagar, tu pagares, ele pagar, nós pagarmos, vós pagardes, eles pagarem	eu passear, tu passeares, ele passear, nós passearmos, vós passeardes, eles passearem
imper. afirm.	dança (tu)	paga (tu)	passeia (tu)
imper. neg.	não dances	não pagues	não passeies
gerúndio	dançando	pagando	passeando
particípio	dançado	pagado/pago	passeado

	16 enviar	17 odiar	18 comerciar
ind. presente	eu envio, tu envias, ele envia, nós enviamos, vós enviais, eles enviam	eu odeio, tu odeias, ele odeia, nós odiamos, vós odiais, eles odeiam	eu comerc(e)io, tu comerc(e)ias, ele comerc(e)ia, nós comerciamos, vós comerciais, eles comerc(e)iam
ind. imperfeito	eu enviava	eu odiava	eu comerciava
ind. perfeito	eu enviei	eu odiei	eu comerciei
ind. m.-q.-p. simpl.	eu enviara	eu odiara	eu comerciara
ind. m.-q.-p. comp.	eu tinha enviado	eu tinha odiado	eu tinha comerciado
ind fut. do pres.	eu enviarei	eu odiarei	eu comerciarei
ind fut. do pret.	eu enviaria	eu odiaria	eu comerciaria
subj. presente	que eu envie	que eu odeie	que eu comerc(e)ie
subj. imperfeito	que eu enviasse	que eu odiasse	que eu comerciasse
subj. perfeito	que eu tenha enviado	que eu tenha odiado	que eu tenha comerciado
subj. m.-q.-perf.	que eu tivesse enviado	que eu tivesse odiado	que eu tivesse comerciado
subj. futuro	quando eu enviar	quando eu odiar	quando eu comerciar
inf. pessoal	eu enviar, tu enviares, ele enviar, nós enviarmos, vós enviardes, eles enviarem	eu odiar, tu odiares, ele odiar, nós odiarmos, vós odiardes, eles odiarem	eu comerciar, tu comerciares, ele comerciar, nós comerciarmos, vós comerciardes, eles comerciarem
imper. afirm.	envia (tu)	odeia (tu)	comerc(e)ia (tu)
imper. neg.	não envies	não odeies	não comerc(e)ies
gerúndio	enviando	odiando	comerciando
particípio	enviado	odiado	comerciado

	19 saudar	20 doar	21 averiguar
ind. presente	eu saúdo, tu saúdas, ele saúda, nós saudamos, vós saudais, eles saúdam	eu dôo, tu doas, ele doa, nós doamos, vós doais, eles doam	eu averiguo, tu averiguas, ele averigua, nós averiguamos, vós averiguais, eles averiguam
ind. imperfeito	eu saudava	eu doava	eu averiguava
ind. perfeito	eu saudei	eu doei	eu averigüei
ind. m.-q.-p. simpl.	eu saudara	eu doara	eu averiguara
ind. m.-q.-p. comp.	eu tinha saudado	eu tinha doado	eu tinha averiguado
ind fut. do pres.	eu saudarei	eu doarei	eu averiguarei
ind fut. do pret.	eu saudaria	eu doaria	eu averiguaria
subj. presente	que eu saúde	que eu doe	que eu averigúe
subj. imperfeito	que eu saudasse	que eu doasse	que eu averiguasse
subj. perfeito	que eu tenha saudado	que eu tenha doado	que eu tenha averiguado
subj. m.-q.-perf.	que eu tivesse saudado	que eu tivesse doado	que eu tivesse averiguado
subj. futuro	quando eu saudar	quando eu doar	quando eu averiguar
inf. pessoal	eu saudar, tu saudares, ele saudar, nós saudarmos, vós saudardes, eles saudarem	eu doar, tu doares, ele doar, nós doarmos, vós doardes, eles doarem	eu averiguar, tu averiguares, ele averiguar, nós averiguarmos, vós averiguardes, eles averiguarem
imper. afirm.	saúda (tu)	doa (tu)	averigua (tu)
imper. neg.	não saúdes	não does	não averigúes
gerúndio	saudando	doando	averiguando
particípio	saudado	doado	averiguado

	22 enxaguar	23 adequar	24 relampaguear
ind. presente	eu enxáguo, tu enxáguas, ele enxágua, nós enxaguamos, vós enxaguais, eles enxáguam	nós adequamos, vós adequais	relampagueia, relampagueiam
ind. imperfeito	eu enxaguava	eu adequava	
ind. perfeito	eu enxagüei	eu adeqüei	
ind. m.-q.-p. simpl.	eu enxaguara	eu adequara	
ind. m.-q.-p. comp.	eu tinha enxaguado	eu tinha adequado	
ind fut. do pres.	eu enxaguarei	eu adequarei	
ind fut. do pret.	eu enxaguaria	eu adequaria	
subj. presente	que eu enxágüe		
subj. imperfeito	que eu enxaguasse	que eu adequasse	
subj. perfeito	que eu tenha enxaguado	que eu tenha adequado	
subj. m.-q.-perf.	que eu tivesse enxaguado	que eu tivesse adequado	
subj. futuro	quando eu enxaguar	quando eu adequar	
inf. pessoal	eu enxaguar, tu enxaguares, ele enxaguar, nós enxaguarmos, vós enxaguardes, eles enxaguarem	eu adequar, tu adequares, ele adequar, nós adequarmos, vós adequardes, eles adequarem	relampaguear
imper. afirm.	enxágua (tu)	adequai (vós)	
imper. neg.	não enxágües		
gerúndio	enxaguando	adequando	relampagueando
particípio	enxaguado	adequado	relampagueado

	25 agradecer	26 eleger	27 erguer
ind. presente	eu agradeço, tu agradeces, ele agradece, nós agradecemos, vós agradeceis, eles agradecem	eu elejo, tu eleges, ele elege, nós elegemos, vós elegeis, eles elegem	eu ergo, tu ergues, ele ergue, nós erguemos, vós ergueis, eles erguem
ind. imperfeito	eu agradecia	eu elegia	eu erguia
ind. perfeito	eu agradeci	eu elegi	eu ergui
ind. m.-q.-p. simpl.	eu agradecera	eu elegera	eu erguera
ind. m.-q.-p. comp.	en tinha agradecido	en tinha elegido	eu tinha erguido
ind fut. do pres.	eu agradecerei	eu elegerei	eu erguerei
ind fut. do pret.	eu agradeceria	eu elegeria	eu ergueria
subj. presente	que eu agradeça	que eu eleja	que eu erga
subj. imperfeito	que eu agradecesse	que eu elegesse	que eu erguesse
subj. perfeito	que eu tenha agradecido	que eu tenha elegido	que eu tenha erguido
subj. m.-q.-perf.	que eu tivesse agradecido	que eu tivesse elegido	que eu tivesse erguido
subj. futuro	quando eu agradecer	quando eu eleger	quando eu erguer
inf. pessoal	eu agradecer, tu agradeceres, ele agradecer, nós agradecermos, vós agradecerdes, eles agradecerem	eu eleger, tu elegeres, ele eleger, nós elegermos, vós elegerdes, eles elegerem	eu erguer, tu ergueres, ele erguer, nós erguermos, vós erguerdes, eles erguerem
imper. afirm.	agradece (tu)	elege (tu)	ergue (tu)
imper. neg.	não agradeças	não elejas	não ergas
gerúndio	agradecendo	elegendo	erguendo
particípio	agradecido	elegido, eleito	erguido

	28 roer	29 dizer	30 trazer
ind. presente	eu rôo, tu róis, ele rói, nós roemos, vós roeis, eles roem	eu digo, tu dizes, ele diz, nós dizemos, vós dizeis, eles dizem	eu trago, tu trazes, ele traz, nós trazemos, vós trazeis, eles trazem
ind. imperfeito	eu roía	eu dizia	eu trazia
ind. perfeito	eu roí	eu disse	eu trouxe
ind. m.-q.-p. simpl.	eu roera	eu dissera	eu trouxera
ind. m.-q.-p. comp.	eu tinha roído	eu tinha dito	eu tinha trazido
ind fut. do pres.	eu roerei	eu direi	eu trarei
ind fut. do pret.	eu roeria	eu diria	eu traria
subj. presente	que eu roa	que eu diga	que eu traga
subj. imperfeito	que eu roesse	que eu dissesse	que eu trouxesse
subj. perfeito	que eu tenha roído	que eu tenha dito	que eu tenha trazido
subj. m.-q.-perf.	que eu tivesse roído	que eu tivesse dito	que eu tivesse trazido
subj. futuro	quando eu roer	quando eu disser	quando eu trouxer
inf. pessoal	eu roer, tu roeres, ele roer, nós roermos, vós roerdes, eles roerem	eu dizer, tu dizeres, ele dizer, nós dizermos, vós dizerdes, eles dizerem	eu trazer, tu trazeres, ele trazer, nós trazermos, vós trazerdes, eles trazerem
imper. afirm.	rói (tu)	diz, dize (tu)	traz, traze (tu)
imper. neg.	não roas	não digas	não tragas
gerúndio	roendo	dizendo	trazendo
particípio	roído	dito	trazido

	31 fazer	32 aprazer	33 jazer
ind. presente	eu faço, tu fazes, ele faz, nós fazemos, vós fazeis, eles fazem	eu aprazo, tu aprazes, ele apraz, nós aprazemos, vós aprazeis, eles aprazem	eu jazo, tu jazes, ele jaz, nós jazemos, vós jazeis, eles jazem
ind. imperfeito	eu fazia	eu aprazia	eu jazia
ind. perfeito	eu fiz	eu aprouve	eu jazi
ind. m.-q.-p. simpl.	eu fizera	eu aprouvera	eu jazera
ind. m.-q.-p. comp.	eu tinha feito	eu tinha aprazido	eu tinha jazido
ind fut. do pres.	eu farei	eu aprazerei	eu jazerei
ind fut. do pret.	eu faria	eu aprazeria	eu jazeria
subj. presente	que eu faça	que eu apraza	que eu jaza
subj. imperfeito	que eu fizesse	que eu aprouvesse	que eu jazesse
subj. perfeito	que eu tenha feito	que eu tenha aprazido	que eu tenha jazido
subj. m.-q.-perf.	que eu tivesse feito	que eu tivesse aprazido	que eu tivesse jazido
subj. futuro	quando eu fizer	quando eu aprouver	quando eu jazer
inf. pessoal	eu fazer, tu fazeres, ele fazer, nós fazermos, vós fazerdes, eles fazerem	eu aprazer, tu aprazeres, ele aprazer, nós aprazermos, vós aprazerdes, eles aprazerem	eu jazer, tu jazeres, ele jazer, nós jazermos, vós jazerdes, eles jazerem
imper. afirm.	faz, faze (tu)	apraz, apraze (tu)	jaz, jaze (tu)
imper. neg.	não faças	não aprazas	não jazas
gerúndio	fazendo	aprazendo	jazendo
particípio	feito	aprazido	jazido

	34 caber	35 saber	36 poder
ind. presente	eu caibo, tu cabes, ele cabe, nós cabemos, vós cabeis, eles cabem	eu sei, tu sabes, ele sabe, nós sabemos, vós sabeis, eles sabem	eu posso, tu podes, ele pode, nós podemos, vós podeis, eles podem
ind. imperfeito	eu cabia	eu sabia	eu podia
ind. perfeito	eu coube	eu soube	eu pude
ind. m.-q.-p. simpl.	eu coubera	eu soubera	eu pudera
ind. m.-q.-p. comp.	eu tinha cabido	eu tinha sabido	eu tinha podido
ind fut. do pres.	eu caberei	eu saberei	eu poderei
ind fut. do pret.	eu caberia	eu saberia	eu poderia
subj. presente	que eu caiba	que eu saiba	que eu possa
subj. imperfeito	que eu coubesse	que eu soubesse	que eu pudesse
subj. perfeito	que eu tenha cabido	que eu tenha sabido	que eu tenha podido
subj. m.-q.-perf.	que eu tivesse cabido	que eu tivesse sabido	que eu tivesse podido
subj. futuro	quando eu couber	quando eu souber	quando eu puder
inf. pessoal	eu caber, tu caberes, ele caber, nós cabermos, vós caberdes, eles caberem	eu saber, tu saberes, ele saber, nós sabermos, vós saberdes, eles saberem	eu poder, tu poderes, ele poder, nós podermos, vós poderdes, eles poderem
imper. afirm.		sabe (tu)	
imper. neg.		não saibas	
gerúndio	cabendo	sabendo	podendo
particípio	cabido	sabido	podido

	37 crer	38 querer	39 requerer
ind. presente	eu creio, tu crês, ele crê, nós cremos, vós credes, eles crêem	eu quero, tu queres, ele quer, nós queremos, vós quereis, eles querem	eu requeiro, tu requeres, ele requer, nós requeremos, vós requereis, eles requerem
ind. imperfeito	eu cria	eu queria	eu requeria
ind. perfeito	eu cri	eu quis	eu requeri
ind. m.-q.-p. simpl.	eu crera	eu quisera	eu requerera
ind. m.-q.-p. comp.	eu tinha crido	eu tinha querido	eu tinha requerido
ind fut. do pres.	eu crerei	eu quererei	eu requererei
ind fut. do pret.	eu creria	eu quereria	eu requereria
subj. presente	que eu creia	que eu queira	que eu requeira
subj. imperfeito	que eu cresse	que eu quisesse	que eu requeresse
subj. perfeito	que eu tenha crido	que eu tenha querido	que eu tenha requerido
subj. m.-q.-perf.	que eu tivesse crido	que eu tivesse querido	que eu tivesse requerido
subj. futuro	quando eu crer	quando eu quiser	quando eu requerer
inf. pessoal	eu crer, tu creres, ele crer, nós crermos, vós crerdes, eles crerem	eu querer, tu quereres, ele querer, nós querermos, vós quererdes, eles quererem	eu requerer, tu requereres, ele requerer, nós requerermos, vós requererdes, eles requererem
imper. afirm.	crê (tu)	quer (tu)	requer (tu)
imper. neg.	não creias	não queiras	não requeiras
gerúndio	crendo	querendo	requerendo
particípio	crido	querido	requerido

	40 ver	41 prover	42 ler
ind. presente	eu vejo, tu vês, ele vê, nós vemos, vós vedes, eles vêem	eu provejo, tu provês, ele provê, nós provemos, vós provedes, eles provêem	eu leio, tu lês, ele lê, nós lemos, vós ledes, eles lêem
ind. imperfeito	eu via	eu provia	eu lia
ind. perfeito	eu vi	eu provi	eu li
ind. m.-q.-p. simpl.	eu vira	eu provera	eu lera
ind. m.-q.-p. comp.	eu tinha visto	eu tinha provido	eu tinha lido
ind fut. do pres.	eu verei	eu proverei	eu lerei
ind fut. do pret.	eu veria	eu proveria	eu leria
subj. presente	que eu veja	que eu proveja	que eu leia
subj. imperfeito	que eu visse	que eu provesse	que eu lesse
subj. perfeito	que eu tenha visto	que eu tenha provido	que eu tenha lido
subj. m.-q.-perf.	que eu tivesse visto	que eu tivesse provido	que eu tivesse lido
subj. futuro	quando eu vir	quando eu prover	quando eu ler
inf. pessoal	eu ver, tu veres, ele ver, nós vermos, vós verdes, eles verem	eu prover, tu proveres, ele prover, nós provermos, vós proverdes, eles proverem	eu ler, tu leres, ele ler, nós lermos, vós lerdes, eles lerem
imper. afirm.	vê (tu)	provê (tu)	lê (tu)
imper. neg.	não vejas	não provejas	não leias
gerúndio	vendo	provendo	lendo
particípio	visto	provido	lido

	43 valer	44 perder	45 pôr
ind. presente	eu valho, tu vales, ele vale, nós valemos, vós valeis, eles valem	eu perco, tu perdes, ele perde, nós perdemos, vós perdeis, eles perdem	eu ponho, tu pões, ele põe, nós pomos, vós pondes, eles põem
ind. imperfeito	eu valia	eu perdia	eu punha
ind. perfeito	eu vali	eu perdi	eu pus
ind. m.-q.-p. simpl.	eu valera	eu perdera	eu pusera
ind. m.-q.-p. comp.	eu tinha valido	eu tinha perdido	eu tinha posto
ind fut. do pres.	eu valerei	eu perderei	eu porei
ind fut. do pret.	eu valeria	eu perderia	eu poria
subj. presente	que eu valha	que eu perca	que eu ponha
subj. imperfeito	que eu valesse	que eu perdesse	que eu pusesse
subj. perfeito	que eu tenha valido	que eu tenha perdido	que eu tenha posto
subj. m.-q.-perf.	que eu tivesse valido	que eu tivesse perdido	que eu tivesse posto
subj. futuro	quando eu valer	quando eu perder	quando eu puser
inf. pessoal	eu valer, tu valeres, ele valer, nós valermos, vós valerdes, eles valerem	eu perder, tu perderes, ele perder, nós perdermos, vós perderdes, eles perderem	eu pôr, tu pores, ele pôr, nós pormos, vós pordes, eles porem
imper. afirm.	vale (tu)	perde (tu)	põe (tu)
imper. neg.	não valhas	não percas	não ponhas
gerúndio	valendo	perdendo	pondo
particípio	valido	perdido	posto

	46 acontecer	47 chover	48 doer
ind. presente	acontece, acontecem	chove	dói, doem
ind. imperfeito	acontecia, aconteciam	chovia	doía, doíam
ind. perfeito	aconteceu, aconteceram	choveu	doeu, doeram
ind. m.-q.-p. simpl.	acontecera, aconteceram	chovera	doera, doeram
ind. m.-q.-p. comp.	tinha acontecido	tinha chovido	tinha doído
ind. fut. do pres.	acontecerá, acontecerão	choverá	doerá, doerão
ind. fut. do pret.	aconteceria, aconteceriam	choveria	doeria, doeriam
subj. presente	que ele aconteça	chova	doa, doam
subj. imperfeito	que ele acontecesse	chovesse	doesse, doessem
subj. perfeito	que ele tenha acontecido	tenha chovido	tenha doído
subj. m.-q.-perf.	que ele tivesse acontecido	tivesse chovido	tivesse doído
subj. futuro	quando ele acontecer	quando chover	quando doer
inf. pessoal	ele acontecer, eles acontecerem	chover	doer, doerem
imper. afirm.			
imper. neg.			
gerúndio	acontecendo	chovendo	doendo
particípio	acontecido	chovido	doído

	49 prazer	50 precaver	51 reaver
ind. presente	praz, prazem	nós precavemos, vós precaveis	nós reavemos, vós reaveis
ind. imperfeito	prazia, praziam	eu precavia	eu reavia
ind. perfeito	prouve, prouveram	eu precavi	eu reouve
ind. m.-q.-p. simpl.	prouvera, prouveram	eu precavera	eu reouvera
ind. m.-q.-p. comp.	tinha prazido	eu tinha precavido	eu tinha reavido
ind fut. do pres.	prazerá, prazerão	eu precaverei	eu reaverei
ind fut. do pret.	prazeria, prazeriam	eu precaveria	eu reaveria
subj. presente	praza, prazam		
subj. imperfeito	prouvesse, prouvessem	que eu precavesse	que eu reouvesse
subj. perfeito	que ele tenha prazido	que eu tenha precavido	que eu tenha reavido
subj. m.-q.-perf.	que ele tivesse prazido	que eu tivesse precavido	que eu tivesse reavido
subj. futuro	quando ele prouver	quando eu precaver	quando eu reouver
inf. pessoal	prazer, prazerem	eu precaver, tu precaveres, ele precaver, nós precavermos, vós precaverdes, eles precaverem	eu reaver, tu reaveres, ele reaver, nós reavermos, vós reaverdes, eles reaverem
imper. afirm.	praza (você)	precavei (vós)	reavei (vós)
imper. neg.	não praza (você)		
gerúndio	prazendo	precavendo	reavendo
particípio	prazido	precavido	reavido

	52 fingir	53 distinguir	54 servir
ind. presente	eu finjo, tu finges, ele finge, nós fingimos, vós fingis, eles fingem	eu distingo, tu distingues, ele distingue, nós distinguimos, vós distinguis, eles distinguem	eu sirvo, tu serves, ele serve, nós servimos, vós servis, eles servem
ind. imperfeito	eu fingia	eu distinguia	eu servia
ind. perfeito	eu fingi	eu distingui	eu servi
ind. m.-q.-p. simpl.	eu fingira	eu distinguira	eu servira
ind. m.-q.-p. comp.	eu tinha fingido	eu tinha distinguido	eu tinha servido
ind fut. do pres.	eu fingirei	eu distinguirei	eu servirei
ind fut. do pret.	eu fingiria	eu distinguiria	eu serviria
subj. presente	que eu finja	que eu distinga	que eu sirva
subj. imperfeito	que eu fingisse	que eu distinguisse	que eu servisse
subj. perfeito	que eu tenha fingido	que eu tenha distinguido	que eu tenha servido
subj. m.-q.-perf.	que eu tivesse fingido	que eu tivesse distinguido	que eu tivesse servido
subj. futuro	quando eu fingir	quando eu distinguir	quando eu servir
inf. pessoal	eu fingir, tu fingires, ele fingir, nós fingirmos, vós fingirdes, eles fingirem	eu distinguir, tu distinguires, ele distinguir, nós distinguirmos, vós distinguirdes, eles distinguirem	eu servir, tu servires, ele servir, nós servirmos, vós servirdes, eles servirem
imper. afirm.	finge (tu)	distingue (tu)	serve (tu)
imper. neg.	não finjas	não distingas	não sirvas
gerúndio	fingindo	distinguindo	servindo
particípio	fingido	distinguido	servido

	55 seguir	56 sentir	57 ferir
ind. presente	eu sigo, tu segues, ele segue, nós seguimos, vós seguis, eles seguem	eu sinto, tu sentes, ele sente, nós sentimos, vós sentis, eles sentem	eu firo, tu feres, ele fere, nós ferimos, vós feris, eles ferem
ind. imperfeito	eu seguia	eu sentia	eu feria
ind. perfeito	eu segui	eu senti	eu feri
ind. m.-q.-p. simpl.	eu seguira	eu sentira	eu ferira
ind. m.-q.-p. comp.	eu tinha seguido	eu tinha sentido	eu tinha ferido
ind fut. do pres.	eu seguirei	eu sentirei	eu ferirei
ind fut. do pret.	eu seguiria	eu sentiria	eu feriria
subj. presente	que eu siga	que eu sinta	que eu fira
subj. imperfeito	que eu seguisse	que eu sentisse	que eu ferisse
subj. perfeito	que eu tenha seguido	que eu tenha sentido	que eu tenha ferido
subj. m.-q.-perf.	que eu tivesse seguido	que eu tivesse sentido	que eu tivesse ferido
subj. futuro	quando eu seguir	quando eu sentir	quando eu ferir
inf. pessoal	eu seguir, tu seguires, ele seguir, nós seguirmos, vós seguirdes, eles seguirem	eu sentir, tu sentires, ele sentir, nós sentirmos, vós sentirdes, eles sentirem	eu ferir, tu ferires, ele ferir, nós ferirmos, vós ferirdes, eles ferirem
imper. afirm.	segue (tu)	sente (tu)	fere (tu)
imper. neg.	não sigas	não sintas	não firas
gerúndio	seguindo	sentindo	ferindo
particípio	seguido	sentido	ferido

	58 prevenir	59 dormir	60 polir
ind. presente	eu previno, tu prevines, ele previne, nós prevenimos, vós prevenis, eles previnem	eu durmo, tu dormes, ele dorme, nós dormimos, vós dormis, eles dormem	eu pulo, tu pules, ele pule, nós polimos, vós polis, eles pulem
ind. imperfeito	eu prevenia	eu dormia	eu polia
ind. perfeito	eu preveni	eu dormi	eu poli
ind. m.-q.-p. simpl.	eu prevenira	eu dormira	eu polira
ind. m.-q.-p. comp.	eu tinha prevenido	eu tinha dormido	eu tinha polido
ind fut. do pres.	eu prevenirei	eu dormirei	eu polirei
ind fut. do pret.	eu preveniria	eu dormiria	eu poliria
subj. presente	que eu previna	que eu durma	que eu pula
subj. imperfeito	que eu prevenisse	que eu dormisse	que eu polisse
subj. perfeito	que eu tenha prevenido	que eu tenha dormido	que eu tenha polido
subj. m.-q.-perf.	que eu tivesse prevenido	que eu tivesse dormido	que eu tivesse polido
subj. futuro	quando eu prevenir	quando eu dormir	quando eu polir
inf. pessoal	eu prevenir, tu prevenires, ele prevenir, nós prevenirmos, vós prevenirdes, eles prevenirem	eu dormir, tu dormires, ele dormir, nós dormirmos, vós dormirdes, eles dormirem	eu polir, tu polires, ele polir, nós polirmos, vós polirdes, eles polirem
imper. afirm.	previne (tu)	dorme (tu)	pule (tu)
imper. neg.	não previnas	não durmas	não pulas
gerúndio	prevenindo	dormindo	polindo
particípio	prevenido	dormido	polido

	61 subir	62 fugir	63 frigir
ind. presente	eu subo, tu sobes, ele sobe, nós subimos, vós subis, eles sobem	eu fujo, tu foges, ele foge, nós fugimos, vós fugis, eles fogem	eu frijo, tu friges, ele frige, nós frigimos, vós frigis, eles frigem
ind. imperfeito	eu subia	eu fugia	eu frigia
ind. perfeito	eu subi	eu fugi	eu frigi
ind. m.-q.-p. simpl.	eu subira	eu fugira	eu frigi
ind. m.-q.-p. comp.	eu tinha subido	eu tinha fugido	eu tinha frigido
ind fut. do pres.	eu subirei	eu fugirei	eu frigirei
ind fut. do pret.	eu subiria	eu fugiria	eu frigiria
subj. presente	que eu suba	que eu fuja	que eu frija
subj. imperfeito	que eu subisse	que eu fugisse	que eu frigisse
subj. perfeito	que eu tenha subido	que eu tenha fugido	que eu tenha frigido
subj. m.-q.-perf.	que eu tivesse subido	que eu tivesse fugido	que eu tivesse frigido
subj. futuro	quando eu subir	quando eu fugir	quando eu frigir
inf. pessoal	eu subir, tu subires, ele subir, nós subirmos, vós subirdes, eles subirem	eu fugir, tu fugires, ele fugir, nós fugirmos, vós fugirdes, eles fugirem	eu frigir, tu frigires, ele frigir, nós frigirmos, vós frigirdes, eles frigirem
imper. afirm.	sobe (tu)	foge (tu)	frige (tu)
imper. neg.	não subas	não fujas	não frijas
gerúndio	subindo	fugindo	frigindo
particípio	subido	fugido	frigido, frito

	64 convergir	65 refletir	66 ir
ind. presente	eu convirjo, tu converges, ele converge, nós convergimos, vós convergis, eles convergem	eu reflito, tu refletes, ele reflete, nós refletimos, vós refletis, eles refletem	eu vou, tu vais, ele vai, nós vamos, vós ides, eles vão
ind. imperfeito	eu convergia	eu refletia	eu ia
ind. perfeito	eu convergi	eu refleti	eu fui
ind. m.-q.-p. simpl.	eu convergira	eu refletira	eu fora
ind. m.-q.-p. comp.	eu tinha convergido	eu tinha refletido	eu tinha ido
ind fut. do pres.	eu convergirei	eu refletirei	eu irei
ind fut. do pret.	eu convergiria	eu refletiria	eu iria
subj. presente	que eu convirja	que eu reflita	que eu vá
subj. imperfeito	que eu convergisse	que eu refletisse	que eu fosse
subj. perfeito	que eu tenha convergido	que eu tenha refletido	que eu tenha ido
subj. m.-q.-perf.	que eu tivesse convergido	que eu tivesse refletido	que eu tivesse ido
subj. futuro	quando eu convergir	quando eu refletir	quando eu for
inf. pessoal	eu convergir, tu convergires, ele convergir, nós convergirmos, vós convergirdes, eles convergirem	eu refletir, tu refletires, ele refletir, nós refletirmos, vós refletirdes, eles refletirem	eu ir, tu ires, ele ir, nós irmos, vós irdes, eles irem
imper. afirm.	converge (tu)	reflete (tu)	vai (tu)
imper. neg.	não convirjas	não reflitas	não vás
gerúndio	convergindo	refletindo	indo
particípio	convergido	refletido	ido

	67 vir	68 sair	69 rir
ind. presente	eu venho, tu vens, ele vem, nós vimos, vós vindes, eles vêm	eu saio, tu sais, ele sai, nós saímos, vós saís, eles saem	eu rio, tu ris, ele ri, nós rimos, vós rides, eles riem
ind. imperfeito	eu vinha	eu saía	eu ria
ind. perfeito	eu vim	eu saí	eu ri
ind. m.-q.-p. simpl.	eu viera	eu saíra	eu rira
ind. m.-q.-p. comp.	eu tinha vindo	eu tinha saído	eu tinha rido
ind fut. do pres.	eu virei	eu sairei	eu rirei
ind fut. do pret.	eu viria	eu sairia	eu riria
subj. presente	que eu venha	que eu saia	que eu ria
subj. imperfeito	que eu viesse	que eu saísse	que eu risse
subj. perfeito	que eu tenha vindo	que eu tenha saído	que eu tenha rido
subj. m.-q.-perf.	que eu tivesse vindo	que eu tivesse saído	que eu tivesse rido
subj. futuro	quando eu vier	quando eu sair	quando eu rir
inf. pessoal	eu vir, tu vires, ele vir, nós virmos, vós virdes, eles virem	eu sair, tu saires, ele sair, nós sairmos, vós sairdes, eles saírem	eu rir, tu rires, ele rir, nós rirmos, vós rirdes, eles rirem
imper. afirm.	vem (tu)	sai (tu)	ri (tu)
imper. neg.	não venhas	não saias	não rias
gerúndio	vindo	saindo	rindo
particípio	vindo	saído	rido

	70 pedir	71 ouvir	72 produzir
ind. presente	eu peço, tu pedes, ele pede, nós pedimos, vós pedis, eles pedem	eu ouço/oiço, tu ouves, ele ouve, nós ouvimos, vós ouvis, eles ouvem	eu produzo, tu produzes, ele produz, nós produzimos, vós produzis, eles produzem
ind. imperfeito	eu pedia	eu ouvia	eu produzia
ind. perfeito	eu pedi	eu ouvi	eu produzi
ind. m.-q.-p. simpl.	eu pedira	eu ouvira	eu produzira
ind. m.-q.-p. comp.	eu tinha pedido	eu tinha ouvido	eu tinha produzido
ind fut. do pres.	eu pedirei	eu ouvirei	eu produzirei
ind fut. do pret.	eu pediria	eu ouviria	eu produziria
subj. presente	que eu peça	que eu ouça	que eu produza
subj. imperfeito	que eu pedisse	que eu ouvisse	que eu produzisse
subj. perfeito	que eu tenha pedido	que eu tenha ouvido	que eu tenha produzido
subj. m.-q.-perf.	que eu tivesse pedido	que eu tivesse ouvido	que eu tivesse produzido
subj. futuro	quando eu pedir	quando eu ouvir	quando eu produzir
inf. pessoal	eu pedir, tu pedires, ele pedir, nós pedirmos, vós pedirdes, eles pedirem	eu ouvir, tu ouvires, ele ouvir, nós ouvirmos, vós ouvirdes, eles ouvirem	eu produzir, tu produzires, ele produzir, nós produzirmos, vós produzirdes, eles produzirem
imper. afirm.	pede (tu)	ouve (tu)	produz, produze (tu)
imper. neg.	não peças	não ouças	não produzas
gerúndio	pedindo	ouvindo	produzindo
particípio	pedido	ouvido	produzido

	73 construir	74 atribuir	75 argüir
ind. presente	eu construo, tu constróis, ele constrói, nós construímos, vós construís, eles constroem	eu atribuo, tu atribuis, ele atribui, nós atribuímos, vós atribuís, eles atribuem	eu arguo, tu argúis, ele argúi, nós argüimos, vós argüis, eles argúem
ind. imperfeito	eu construía	eu atribuía	eu argüia
ind. perfeito	eu construí	eu atribuí	eu argüi
ind. m.-q.-p. simpl.	eu construíra	eu atribuíra	eu argüira
ind. m.-q.-p. comp.	eu tinha construído	eu tinha atribuído	eu tinha argüido
ind fut. do pres.	eu construirei	eu atribuirei	eu argüirei
ind fut. do pret.	eu construiria	eu atribuiria	eu argüiria
subj. presente	que eu construa	que eu atribua	que eu argua
subj. imperfeito	que eu construísse	que eu atribuísse	que eu argüisse
subj. perfeito	que eu tenha construído	que eu tenha atribuído	que eu tenha argüido
subj. m.-q.-perf.	que eu tivesse construído	que eu tivesse atribuído	que eu tivesse argüido
subj. futuro	quando eu construir	quando eu atribuir	quando eu argüir
inf. pessoal	eu construir, tu construíres, ele construir, nós construirmos, vós construirdes, eles construírem	eu atribuir, tu atribuíres, ele atribuir, nós atribuirmos, vós atribuirdes, eles atribuírem	eu argüir, tu argüires, ele argüir, nós argüirmos, vós argüirdes, eles argüirem
imper. afirm.	constrói (tu)	atribui (tu)	argúi (tu)
imper. neg.	não construas	não atribuas	não arguas (tu)
gerúndio	construindo	atribuindo	argüindo
particípio	construído	atribuído	argüido

	76 reunir	77 proibir	78 emergir
ind. presente	eu reúno, tu reúnes, ele reúne, nós reunimos, vós reunis, eles reúnem	eu proíbo, tu proíbes, ele proíbe, nós proibimos, vós proibis, eles proíbem	eu emerjo, tu emerges, ele emerge, nós emergimos, vós emergis, eles emergem
ind. imperfeito	eu reunia	eu proibia	eu emergia
ind. perfeito	eu reuni	eu proibi	eu emergi
ind. m.-q.-p. simpl.	eu reunira	eu proibira	eu emergira
ind. m.-q.-p. comp.	eu tinha reunido	eu tinha proibido	eu tinha emergido
ind fut. do pres.	eu reunirei	eu proibirei	eu emergirei
ind fut. do pret.	eu reuniria	eu proibiria	eu emergiria
subj. presente	que eu reúna	que eu proíba	que eu emerja
subj. imperfeito	que eu reunisse	que eu proibisse	que eu emergisse
subj. perfeito	que eu tenha reunido	que eu tenha proibido	que eu tenha emergido
subj. m.-q.-perf.	que eu tivesse reunido	que eu tivesse proibido	que eu tivesse emergido
subj. futuro	quando eu reunir	quando eu proibir	quando eu emergir
inf. pessoal	eu reunir, tu reunires, ele reunir, nós reunirmos, vós reunirdes, eles reunirem	eu proibir, tu proibires, ele proibir, nós proibirmos, vós proibirdes, eles proibirem	eu emergir, tu emergires, ele emergir, nós emergirmos, vós emergirdes, eles emergirem
imper. afirm.	reúne (tu)	proíbe (tu)	emerge (tu)
imper. neg.	não reúnas	não proíbas	não emerjas
gerúndio	reunindo	proibindo	emergindo
particípio	reunido	proibido	emergido, emerso

	79 falir	80 remir
ind. presente	nós falimos, vós falis	nós remimos, vós remis
ind. imperfeito	eu falia	eu remia
ind. perfeito	eu fali	eu remi
ind. m.-q.-p. simpl.	eu falira	eu remira
ind. m.-q.-p. comp.	eu tinha falido	eu tinha remido
ind fut. do pres.	eu falirei	eu remirei
ind fut. do pret.	eu faliria	eu remiria
subj. presente		
subj. imperfeito	que eu falisse	que eu remisse
subj. perfeito	que eu tenha falido	que eu tenha remido
subj. m.-q.-perf.	que eu tivesse falido	que eu tivesse remido
subj. futuro	quando eu falir	quando eu remir
inf. pessoal	eu falir, tu falires, ele falir, nós falirmos, vós falirdes, eles falirem	eu remir, tu remires, ele remir, nós remirmos, vós remirdes, eles remirem
imper. afirm.	fali (vós)	remi (vos)
imper. neg.		
gerúndio	falindo	remindo
particípio	falido	remido

Infinitive	Past Tense	Past Participle
arise	arose	arisen
awake	awoke	awoken
be	was, were	been
bear	bore	born(e)
beat	beat	beaten
become	became	become
begin	began	begun
bend	bent	bent
beseech	besought	besought
bet	bet (*also* betted)	bet (*also* betted)
bid	bid (*also* bade)	bid (*also* bidden)
bind	bound	bound
bite	bit	bitten
bleed	bled	bled
blow	blew	blown
break	broke	broken
breed	bred	bred
bring	brought	brought
build	built	built
burn	burnt (*also* burned)	burnt (*also* burned)
burst	burst	burst
buy	bought	bought
can	could	- -
cast	cast	cast
catch	caught	caught
choose	chose	chosen
cling	clung	clung
come	came	come
cost	cost	cost
creep	crept	crept
cut	cut	cut
deal	dealt	dealt
dig	dug	dug
do	did	done
draw	drew	drawn
dream	dreamed (*also* dreamt)	dreamed (*also* dreamt)
drink	drank	drunk
drive	drove	driven
dwell	dwelt	dwelt
eat	ate	eaten
fall	fell	fallen
feed	fed	fed
feel	felt	felt
fight	fought	fought
find	found	found
flee	fled	fled
fling	flung	flung
fly	flew	flown
forbid	forbade	forbidden
forget	forgot	forgotten
forsake	forsook	forsaken
freeze	froze	frozen
get	got	got (*US* gotten)

Infinitive	Past Tense	Past Participle
give	gave	given
go	went	gone
grind	ground	ground
grow	grew	grown
hang	hung (*also* hanged)	hung (*also* hanged)
have	had	had
hear	heard	heard
hide	hid	hidden
hit	hit	hit
hold	held	held
hurt	hurt	hurt
keep	kept	kept
kneel	knelt (*also* kneeled)	knelt (*also* kneeled)
know	knew	known
lay	laid	laid
lead	led	led
lean	leant (*also* leaned)	leant (*also* leaned)
leap	leapt (*also* leaped)	leapt (*also* leaped)
learn	learnt (*also* learned)	learnt (*also* learned)
leave	left	left
lend	lent	lent
let	let	let
lie	lay	lain
light	lit (*also* lighted)	lit (*also* lighted)
lose	lost	lost
make	made	made
may	might	-
mean	meant	meant
meet	met	met
mistake	mistook	mistaken
mow	mowed	mown (*also* mowed)
pay	paid	paid
put	put	put
quit	quit (*also* quitted)	quit (*also* quitted)
read	read	read
rend	rent	rent
rid	rid	rid
ride	rode	ridden
ring	rang	rung
rise	rose	risen
run	ran	run
saw	sawed	sawn
say	said	said
see	saw	seen
seek	sought	sought
sell	sold	sold
send	sent	sent
set	set	set
shake	shook	shaken
shall	should	-
shear	sheared	shorn (*also* sheared)
shed	shed	shed
shine	shone	shone

Infinitive	Past Tense	Past Participle
shoot	shot	shot
show	showed	shown
shrink	shrank	shrunk
shut	shut	shut
sing	sang	sung
sink	sank	sunk
sit	sat	sat
slay	slew	slain
sleep	slept	slept
slide	slid	slid
sling	slung	slung
slit	slit	slit
smell	smelt (*also* smelled)	smelt (*also* smelled)
sow	sowed	sown (*also* sowed)
speak	spoke	spoken
speed	sped (*also* speeded)	sped (*also* speeded)
spell	spelt (*also* spelled)	spelt (*also* spelled)
spend	spent	spent
spill	spilt (*also* spilled)	spilt (*also* spilled)
spin	spun	spun
spit	spat	spat
split	split	split
spoil	spoiled (*also* spoilt)	spoiled (*also* spoilt)
spread	spread	spread
spring	sprang	sprung
stand	stood	stood
steal	stole	stolen
stick	stuck	stuck
sting	stung	stung
stink	stank	stunk
stride	strode	stridden
strike	struck	struck (*also* stricken)
strive	strove	striven
swear	swore	sworn
sweep	swept	swept
swell	swelled	swollen (*also* swelled)
swim	swam	swum
swing	swung	swung
take	took	taken
teach	taught	taught
tear	tore	torn
tell	told	told
think	thought	thought
throw	threw	thrown
thrust	thrust	thrust
tread	trod	trodden
wake	woke (*also* waked)	woken (*also* waked)
wear	wore	worn
weave	wove (*also* weaved)	woven (*also* weaved)
wed	wedded	wedded
weep	wept	wept
win	won	won
wind	wound	wound
wring	wrung	wrung
write	wrote	written

Achevé d'imprimer par l'Imprimerie
Maury-Eurolivres à Manchecourt en septembre 2003
N° de projet 10108289
Dépôt légal : février 2003 - N° d'imprimeur : 20976

Imprimé en France - (Printed in France)